Collins

Collins

Collins
English
Dictionary

William Collins' dream of knowledge for all began with the publication of his first book in 1819. A self-educated mill worker, he not only enriched millions of lives, but also founded a flourishing publishing house. Today, staying true to this spirit, Collins books are packed with inspiration, innovation, and practical expertise. They place you at the centre of a world of possibility and give you exactly what you need to explore it.

Language is the key to this exploration, and at the heart of Collins Dictionaries is language as it is really used. New words, phrases, and meanings spring up every day, and all of them are captured and analysed by the Collins Word Web. Constantly updated, and with over 2.5 billion entries, this living language resource is unique to our dictionaries.

Words are tools for life. And a Collins Dictionary makes them work for you.

Collins. Do more.

Collins

Collins
English
Dictionary

HarperCollins Publishers
Westerhill Road
Bishopbriggs
Glasgow
G64 2QT

Eighth Edition 2006

© William Collins Sons & Co. Ltd. 1979, 1986

© HarperCollins Publishers 1991, 1994, 1998, 2000, 2003, 2005, 2006

ISBN-10 0–00–723230-6
ISBN-13 978-0–00–723230-7

Collins® is a registered trademark
of HarperCollins Publishers Limited

www.collins.co.uk

A catalogue record for this book is
available from the British Library.

Designed by Mark Thomson

This edition typeset by
Interactive Sciences Limited,
Gloucester, England
Printed and bound in Italy by Legoprint

Collins

Acknowledgments

We would like to thank those authors and publishers who kindly gave permission for copyright material to be used in the Collins Word Web. We would also like to thank Times Newspapers Ltd for providing valuable data.

About the type

This dictionary is typeset in CollinsFedra, a special version of the Fedra family of types designed by Peter Bil'ak. CollinsFedra has been customized especially for Collins dictionaries; it includes both sans serif (for headwords) and serif (entries) versions, in several different weights. Its large x-height, its open 'eye', and its basis in the tradition of humanist letterforms make CollinsFedra both familiar and easy to read at small sizes. It has been designed to use the minimum space without sacrificing legibility, as well as including a number of characters and signs that are specific to dictionary typography. Its companion phonetic type is the first of its kind to be drawn according to the same principles as the regular typeface, rather than assembled from rotated and reflected characters from other types.

Peter Bil'ak (born 1973, Slovakia) is a graphic and type designer living in the Netherlands. He is the author of two books, *Illegibility* and *Transparency*. As well as the Fedra family, he has designed several other typefaces including Eureka. His typotheque.com website has become a focal point for research and debate around contemporary type design.

THE PUBLISHERS WOULD LIKE TO THANK CONTRIBUTORS TO COLLINS WORD EXCHANGE, ESPECIALLY:

Fred Bauder, Ian Billings, David Boocock, Adam Booth, June Bright, MC (Bermuda), Jim Chamberlain, Tim Chapman, Benn Edward Coley, Roisin Cooper, Collette Eales, Eric Evans, Peter Finlinson, Paul Gendle, Dave Gittins, Tim Grey, Michael Heaney, Richard F Hedges, Mark Hornsby, John Jay, Luke Keen, Nuala McKeown, Martin McMahon, Gary Morris, Anantha Narayan, Cormac Ó Murchú, Sam O'Regan, Mark Oswin, Mick Roberts, Timothy Robinson, Keith Shotton, Michael Spence, Eamonn Walsh, C J Young

Contents

Foreword

Since its inception, the Collins Dictionary has provided English speakers around the globe with the most accurate and up-to-the-minute representation of their language as it is really used. This new Seventh Edition is no exception. Drawing on vast and ever-growing linguistic data resources, we have put together a dictionary we believe to be the sharpest possible 'snapshot' of today's English. Thousands of new words have been added, including both recent coinages and a broader range of world, regional, and dialect English than ever before. As users of our dictionaries have come to expect, a comprehensive range of general lexical items and language notes is complemented by a strong emphasis on scientific, technical, and geographical entries, giving you access to a staggering amount of reliable information within one volume.

The principal strength of this dictionary – and what makes it the reference of choice for many newspapers and broadcasters – lies in its unstinting concentration on living English. Language never sits still, and English is evolving more rapidly than ever, thanks largely to the acceleration of communications technology. Ever-faster internet connections and the ubiquity of the mobile phone are working together to erode the boundaries between the various branches of World English. The internet has also had a marked democratizing effect, as traditional media outlets find themselves competing with bloggers and podcasters, so that there are now thousands of individual voices reaching mass audiences. To keep up to speed with it all, Collins lexicographers have had to advance the frontiers of linguistic monitoring. In addition to an extensive reading, listening, and viewing programme, two unique tools have been developed: Collins Word Web and Collins Word Exchange

Collins Word Web is an unparalleled 2.5-billion-word 'corpus' of lexical data. A constant flow of text is fed into it from sources around the globe – books, newspapers, websites, and even transcripts of radio and TV shows. Every month, Collins Word Web grows by more than 35 million words, making it the biggest such resource in the world. All the definitions, usage notes, and examples in this dictionary are informed by it. So when, for example, we suggest that an expression previously considered to be incorrect is becoming more widely accepted, we can back up theory with hard evidence. When a word appears to be shifting in meaning we can call up reams of examples from the real world. And it's in the discovery of new words and phrases that this way of working really comes into its own – our 'monitor corpus' automatically alerts us to new coinages

and collocations at the moment they take their place in the common vocabulary.

Our most recent innovation, the Collins Word Exchange website (www.collins.co.uk/wordexchange, www.harpercollins.com.au/wordexchange), is a revolutionary concept in dictionary publishing – and this edition is the first to have benefited from it. The site gives English speakers from New Brunswick to New Delhi a greater say than ever before in the way their language is represented. Anyone who visits the website can influence the content of our online Living Dictionary as well as that of our printed titles (indeed, this book contains many words suggested through the Word Exchange, some of which are listed in a dedicated supplement, while others are incorporated as entries within the main text). Visitors are invited to submit neologisms they have just heard, dialect words they grew up with but have never seen in a dictionary, or new definitions for existing terms that have taken on novel meanings. Various discussion forums are available and have already proved extremely useful in allowing our lexicographers to ascertain the precise meaning of dialect words or technical jargon.

The material gathered through these invaluable systems is scrutinized by Collins lexicographers and consultants based in Australia, Canada, Africa, Southeast Asia, and the UK, ensuring that our coverage reflects the truly global nature of the English language. In addition, specialist advisers have continued to cull new terms from their own fields of expertise, particularly from the front line of science and technology, further enhancing our traditional strength in this area.

Almost as important as the information in the dictionary is the ease with which it can be accessed. This latest edition of the Collins Dictionary has an entirely new typeface and design. Developed to be both easy to use and easy on the eye, the new layout is refreshingly clutter-free – taking you to the information you need with the minimum of fuss. The understated design belies the depth of detail in the myriad definitions, usage notes, examples, etymologies, and cross-references.

This dictionary is the child of a formidable marriage: the most advanced methods in linguistic monitoring coupled with the knowhow of Britain's oldest dictionary publisher. Whether you have a passion for English in all its vigour, subtlety, and glorious irregularity, or simply need hard facts at your fingertips, we are confident that this Collins Dictionary is the ideal resource.

Guide to the Use of the Dictionary

This dictionary is designed to be easy to use so that you can go straight to the word you want. The Guide that follows sets out the main principles on which the dictionary is arranged and enables you to make full use of the dictionary by showing the range of information that it contains.

HEADWORD

All main entries, including place names, abbreviations, prefixes, and suffixes, are printed in large bold type and are listed in strict alphabetical order. This applies even if the headword consists of more than one word.

Order of entries
Words that have the same spelling but are derived from different sources (homographs) are entered separately with superscript numbers after the headwords.

> **saw¹** (sɔ:) *n* **1** any of various hand tools ...
> **saw²** (sɔ:) *vb* the past tense of **see¹**
> **saw³** (sɔ:) *n* a wise saying, maxim, or proverb ...

A word with a capital initial letter, if entered separately, follows the lower-case form. For example, **Arras** follows **arras**.

Place names
If a place has more than one name, its main entry is given at the name most often used in modern English, with a cross-reference at other names. Thus, the main entry for the capital of Bavaria is at **Munich**, with a cross-reference at **München**. If a place name has no current anglicized form, its main entry is at the form of the name used in the official language of the area. Thus, the main entry is at **Brno**, with a cross-reference at **Brünn**. Historical names of importance are also given, with dates where these can be ascertained.

> **Paris¹** ('pæris; *French* pari) *n* ... Ancient name:
> Lutetia
> **Volgograd** (*Russian* vəlga'grat; *English* 'vɒlgəʊ,græd) *n*
> ... Former names: **Tsaritsyn** (until 1925), **Stalingrad**
> (1925–61)

Statistical information about places has been obtained from the most up-to-date and reliable sources available. Population figures are derived from the most recent census available, the date of which is always given.

Abbreviations, acronyms, and symbols
Abbreviations, acronyms, and symbols are entered as headwords in the main alphabetical list. In line with modern practice, full stops are generally not used but it can be assumed that nearly all abbreviations are equally acceptable with or without stops.

Alphanumeric representations of words such as those now commonly used in electronic communication – **GR8** (great), **B4** (before), etc – are ordered such that the numeral is not regarded as representing a letter or a word. Instead, such entries are ordered like other alphanumeric abbreviations, for example **G8** (Group of Eight) and **K2** (the mountain).

> **gr**
> **GR**
> **Gr.**
> **GR8**
> **Graafian follicle**

This rule, however, does not apply to the small number of alphanumeric representations of words that start with a numeral. In such cases the numeral is spelled out as the letter or series of letters that it represents.

> **foretriangle**
> **4EVA**
> **forever**

Prefixes, suffixes, and combining forms
Prefixes (eg **in-**, **pre-**, **sub-**), suffixes (eg **-able**, **-ation**, **-ity**), and combining forms (eg **psycho-**, **-iatry**) have been entered as headwords if they are still used freely to produce new words in English.

Plural headwords
Words that have a standard use or uses in the plural may be entered as separate headwords at both singular and plural forms, with a cross-reference to the plural form at the singular entry if other headwords intervene.

> **affair** (ə'fɛə) *n* **1** a thing to be done or attended to ...
> ▷ See also **affairs**
> **affairs** (ə'fɛəz) *pl n* **1** personal or business interests ...

Variant spellings
Common acceptable variant spellings of English words are given as alternative forms of the headword.

> **capitalize** *or* **capitalise** ('kæpɪtə,laɪz) *vb* ...

US spellings
Where different, US spellings are also recorded in the headword.

> **centre** *or* US **center** ('sɛntə) *n* ...

PRONUNCIATIONS

Pronunciations of words in this dictionary represent those that are common in educated British English speech. They are transcribed in the International Phonetic Alphabet (IPA). A *Pronunciation Key* is printed at the end of this Guide. The pronunciation is normally given in brackets immediately after the headword.

> **abase** (ə'beɪs) *vb* (*tr*) **1** to humble ...

The stress pattern is marked by the symbols ' for primary stress and ˌ for secondary stress. The stress mark precedes the syllable to which it applies.

Variant pronunciations
When a headword has an acceptable variant pronunciation or stress pattern, the variant is given by repeating only the syllable or syllables that change.

> **economic** (ˌi:kə'nɒmɪk, ˌɛkə-) *adj* **1** of or relating
> to ...

Pronunciations with different parts of speech
When two or more parts of speech of a word have different pronunciations, the pronunciations are shown in brackets before the relevant group of senses.

> **record** *n* ('rɛkɔːd) **1** an account in permanent
> form ...
> ▷ *vb* (rɪ'kɔːd) (*mainly tr*) **19** to set down in some
> permanent form ...

Pronunciation of individual senses
If one sense of a headword is pronounced differently from the other senses, the pronunciation is given in brackets after the sense number.

> **conjure** ('kʌndʒə) *vb* **1** (*intr*) to practise conjuring
> or be a conjuror **2** (*intr*) to call upon supposed
> supernatural forces by spells and incantations
> **3** (kən'dʒʊə) (*tr*) to appeal earnestly or strongly to:
> *I conjure you to help me*

Foreign words and phrases
Foreign words or phrases are printed in bold italic type and are given foreign-language pronunciations only, unless they are regarded as having become accepted into English.

> *Zeitgeist* German ('tsaɪtgaɪst) *n* ...

INFLECTED FORMS

Where inflections are not shown, it may be assumed that they are formed as follows:

nouns regular plurals are formed by the addition of -s (eg pencils, monkeys) or, in the case of nouns ending in -s, -x, -z, -ch, or -sh, by the addition of -es (eg losses).

verbs in regular inflected verbs: the third person singular of the present tense is formed by the addition of -s to the infinitve (eg plays) or, for verbs ending in -s, -x, -z, -ch, or -sh, by the addition of -es (eg passes, reaches); the past tense and past participle are formed by the addition of -ed to the infinitive (eg played); the present participle is formed by the addition of -ing to the infinitive (eg playing). Verbs that end in a consonant plus -e (eg locate, snare) regularly lose the final -e before the addition of -ed and -ing.

adjectives regular comparatives and superlatives of adjectives are formed by adding -er and -est to the base (eg short, shorter, shortest). Adjectives that end in a consonant plus -e regularly lose the -e before -er and -est (eg fine, finer, finest).

PARTS OF SPEECH

A part-of-speech label in italics precedes the sense or senses relating to that part of speech.

Standard parts of speech
The standard parts of speech, with the abbreviations used, are as follows: adjective (*adj*), adverb (*adv*), conjunction (*conj*), interjection (*interj*), noun (*n*), preposition (*prep*), pronoun (*pron*), verb (*vb*).

Less traditional parts of speech
Some less traditional parts of speech have been used in this dictionary: *determiner* this denotes such words as *the, a, some, any, that, this,* as well as the numerals, and possessives such as *my* and *your*. Many determiners can have a pronoun function without a change of meaning:

> **some** (sʌm) *determiner* ... **2 a** an unknown or unspecified quantity or amount of: *there's some rice on the table; he owns some horses* **b** (*as pronoun; functioning as sing or plural*): *we'll buy some* ...

sentence connector this description replaces the traditional classification of certain words, such as *therefore* and *however*, as adverbs or conjunctions. These words link sentences together rather in the manner of conjunctions; however, they are not confined to the first position in a clause as conjunctions are.

sentence substitute these are words such as *yes, no, perhaps, definitely,* and *maybe*. They can stand alone as meaningful utterances.

Words used as more than one part of speech
If a word can be used as more than one part of speech, the senses of one part of speech are separated from the others by an empty arrow (▷)

> **lure** (lʊə) *vb* (*tr*) ... **2** *falconry* to entice (a hawk or falcon) from the air to the falconer by a lure
> ▷ **3** a person or thing that lures ...

GRAMMATICAL INFORMATION

Grammatical information is provided in brackets and typically in italics to distinguish it from other types of information.

Adjectives and determiners
Some adjectives and determiners are restricted by usage to a particular position relative to the nouns they qualify. This is indicated by the following labels:

postpositive (used predicatively or after the noun, but not before it):

> **ablaze** (ə'bleɪz) *adj* (*postpositive*), *adv* **1** on fire; burning ...

immediately postpositive (always used immediately following the noun qualified and never used predicatively):

> **galore** (gə'lɔː) *determiner* (*immediately postpositive*) in great numbers or quantity: *there were daffodils galore in the park* ...

prenominal (used before the noun, and never used predicatively):

> **chief** (tʃiːf) ... *adj* **5** (*prenominal*) **a** most important; principal ...

Intensifiers
Adjectives and adverbs that perform an exclusively intensifying function, with no addition of meaning, are described as (intensifier) without further explanation.

> **blooming** ('bluːmɪŋ) *adv, adj Brit informal* (*intensifier*): *a blooming genius; blooming painful*

Conjunctions
Conjunctions are divided into two classes, marked by the following labels:

coordinating coordinating conjunctions connect words, phrases, or clauses that perform an identical function and are not dependent on each other. They include *and, but,* and *or.*

subordinating subordinating conjunctions introduce clauses that are dependent on a main clause in a complex sentence. They include *where, until,* and *if.*

Some conjunctions, such as *while* and *whereas,* can function as either coordinating or subordinating conjunctions.

Singular and plural labelling of nouns
Headwords and senses that are apparently plural in form but that take a singular verb, etc, are marked (*functioning as sing*):

> **physics** ('fɪzɪks) *n* (*functioning as sing*) **1** the branch of science ...

Headwords and senses that appear to be singular, such as collective nouns, but that take a plural verb, etc, are marked (*functioning as plural*):

> **cattle** ('kætəl) *n* (*functioning as plural*) **1** bovid mammals of the tribe *Bovini* ...

Headwords and senses that may take either a singular or a plural verb, etc, are marked (*functioning as sing or plural*):

> **bellows** ('bɛləʊz) *n* (*functioning as sing or plural*) **1** Also called: **pair of bellows** an instrument consisting of an air chamber ...

Modifiers
A noun that is commonly used as if it were an adjective is labelled *modifier*. If the sense of the modifier can be understood from the sense of the noun, the modifier is shown without further explanation, with an example to illustrate its use. Otherwise its meaning and/or usage is explained separately.

> **key**[1] (kiː) *n* ... **24** (*modifier*) of great importance: *a key issue*

Verbs
The principal parts given are: 3rd person singular of the present tense; present participle; past tense; past participle (if different from the past tense).

Intransitive and transitive verbs
When a sense of a verb (*vb*) is restricted to transitive use, it is labelled (*tr*); if it is intransitive only, it is labelled (*intr*). If all the senses of a verb are transitive or all are intransitive, the appropriate label appears before the first numbered sense and is not repeated.
Absence of a label is significant: it indicates that the sense may be used both transitively and intransitively.

If nearly all the senses of a verb are transitive, the label (*mainly tr*) appears immediately before the first numbered sense. This indicates that, unless otherwise labelled, any given sense of the verb is transitive. Similarly, all the senses of a verb may be labelled (*mainly intr*).

Copulas

A verb that takes a complement is labelled (*copula*).

> **seem** (siːm) *vb* (*may take an infinitive*) **1** (*copula*) to appear to the mind or eye; look: *this seems nice; the car seems to be running well* ...

Phrasal verbs

Verbal constructions consisting of a verb and a prepositional or an adverbial particle are given headword status if the meaning of the phrasal verb cannot be deduced from the separate meanings of the verb and the particle.

Phrasal verbs are labelled to show four possible distinctions: a transitive verb with an adverbial particle (*tr, adverb*); a transitive verb with a prepositional particle (*tr, preposition*); an intransitive verb with an adverbial particle (*intr, adverb*); an intransitive verb with a prepositional particle (*intr, preposition*):

> **turn on** ... **4** (*tr, adverb*) *informal* to produce (charm, tears, etc) suddenly or automatically
> **take for** *vb* (*tr, preposition*) *informal* to consider or suppose to be, esp mistakenly: *the fake coins were taken for genuine; who do you take me for?*
> **break off** ... **3** (*intr, adverb*) to stop abruptly: *he broke off in the middle of his speech*
> **turn on** ... **2** (*intr, preposition*) to depend or hinge on: *the success of the party turns on you*

The absence of a label is significant. If there is no label (*tr*) or (*intr*), the verb may be used either transitively or intransitively. If there is no label (*adverb*) or (*preposition*), the particle may be either adverbial or prepositional.

Any noun, adjective, or modifier formed from a phrasal verb is entered under the phrasal-verb headword. In some cases, where the noun or adjective is more common than the verb, the phrasal verb is entered after the noun or adjective form:

> **breakaway** ('breɪkəˌweɪ) *n* **1 a** loss or withdrawal of a group of members from an association, club, etc **b** (*as modifier*): *a breakaway faction* ... *vb* **break away** (*intr, adverb*) **4** (*often foll by from*) to leave hastily or escape

RESTRICTIVE LABELS

If a particular sense is restricted as to appropriateness, connotation, subject field, etc, an italic label is placed immediately before the relevant definition:

> **hang on** *vb* (*intr*) ... **5** (*adverb*) *informal* to wait or remain: *hang on for a few minutes*

If a label applies to all senses of one part of speech, it is placed immediately after the part-of-speech label.

> **assured** (əˈʃʊəd) *adj* ... *n* **4** *chiefly Brit* **a** the beneficiary under a life assurance policy **b** the person whose life is insured ...

If a label applies to all senses of a headword, it is placed immediately after the pronunciation (or inflections).

> **con¹** (kɒn) *informal* ▷ *n* **1 a** short for confidence trick **b** (*as modifier*): *con man* ▷ *vb* **cons, conning, conned 2** (*tr*) to swindle or defraud

Usage labels

slang refers to words or senses that are informal and restricted in context, for example, to members of a particular social or cultural group. Slang words are inappropriate in formal speech or writing.

informal applies to words or senses that may be widely used, especially in conversation, letter-writing, etc, but that are not common in formal writing. Such words are subject to fewer contextual restrictions than slang words.

taboo indicates words that are not acceptable in polite use.

offensive indicates that a word might be regarded as offensive by the person described or referred to, even if the speaker uses the word without any malicious intention.

derogatory implies that the connotations of a word are unpleasant with intent on the part of the speaker or writer.

not standard indicates words or senses that are frequently encountered but widely regarded as incorrect.

archaic denotes a word or sense that is no longer in common use but that may be found in literary works or used to impart a historical colour to contemporary writing.

obsolete denotes a word or sense that is no longer in use. In specialist or technical fields the label often implies that the term has been superseded.

The word 'formerly' is placed in brackets before a sense when the practice, concept, etc, being described, rather than the word itself, is obsolete or out of date.

A number of other usage labels, such as *ironic*, *facetious*, and *euphemistic*, are used where appropriate.

Further help on usage is provided in usage notes after certain entries.

Subject-field labels

A number of italic labels are used to indicate that a word or sense is used in a particular specialist or technical field.

National and regional labels

Words or senses restricted to or associated with a particular country or region are labelled accordingly. The following labels are the ones most frequently used: *Austral* (Australian), *Brit* (British), *Canadian*, *Caribbean*, *Irish*, *NZ* (New Zealand), *Scot* (Scottish), *South African* (South African), *US* (United States).

The label *Brit* is used mainly to distinguish a particular word or sense from its North American equivalent or to identify a term or concept that does not exist in North American English. The North American equivalent may be given in bold type after the appropriate numbered sense.

Regional dialects (*Scot and Northern English dialect, Midland dialect,* etc) have been specified as precisely as possible, even at the risk of overrestriction, in order to give the reader an indication of the appropriate regional flavour.

MEANING

The meaning of each headword in this dictionary is explained in one or more definitions, together with information about context and typical use.

Order of senses

As a general rule, where a headword has more than one sense, the first sense given is the one most common in current usage.

> **complexion** (kəmˈplɛkʃən) *n* **1** the colour and general appearance of a person's skin, esp of the face **2** aspect, character, or nature: *the general complexion of a nation's finances* **3** *obsolete* **a** the temperament of a person ...

Where the lexicographers consider that a current sense is the 'core meaning', in that it illuminates the meaning of other senses, the core meaning may be placed first.

> **competition** (ˌkɒmpɪˈtɪʃən) *n* **1** the act of competing; rivalry **2** a contest in which a winner is selected from among two or more entrants **3** a series of games, sports events, etc **4** the opposition offered by a competitor or competitors

Subsequent senses are arranged so as to give a coherent account of the meaning of a headword. If a word is used as more than one part of speech, all the senses of each part of speech are grouped together in a single block. Within a part-of-speech block, closely related senses are grouped together; technical senses usually follow general senses; archaic and obsolete senses follow technical senses; idioms and fixed phrases are generally placed last.

Scientific and technical definitions

Units, physical quantities, formulas, etc In accordance with the recommendations of the International Standards Organization, all scientific measurements are expressed in SI units (*Système International d'Unités*). Measurements and quantities in more traditional units are often given as well as SI units. The entries for chemical compounds give the systematic names as well as the more familiar popular names.

Plants and animals When the scientific (Latin) names of phyla, divisions, classes, orders, families, genera, and species are used in definitions, they are printed in italic type and all except the specific name have an initial capital letter. Taxonomic information is always given.

> **moss** (mɒs) *n* **1** any bryophyte of the phylum *Bryophyta*, typically growing in dense mats on trees ...

CROSS-REFERENCES

The main entry is always given at the most common spelling or form of the word. Cross-reference entries refer to this main entry. Thus the entry for **deoxyribonucleic acid** cross-refers to **DNA,** where the full explanantion is given.

Comparisons

Cross-references introduced by the words 'See also' or 'Compare' refer the reader to additional information elsewhere in the Dictionary. If the cross-reference is preceded by an empty arrow ▷, it applies to all senses of the headword that have gone before it, unless otherwise stated. If there is no empty arrow, the cross-reference applies only to the sense immediately preceding it.

Variant spellings

Variant spellings (eg **foetus** ... a variant spelling of **fetus**) are generally entered as cross-references if their place in the alphabetical lists is more than ten entries distant from the main entry.

Alternative names

Alternative names or terms are printed in bold type and introduced by the words 'Also' or 'Also called'. If the alternative name or term is preceded by an empty arrow, it applies to the entire entry.

RELATED ADJECTIVES

Certain nouns, especially of Germanic origin, have related adjectives that are derived from Latin or French. For example, **mural** (from Latin) is an adjective related in meaning to **wall**. Such adjectives are shown in a number of cases after the sense (or part-of-speech block) to which they are related.

> **wall** (wɔːl) *n* **1a** a vertical construction made of stone, brick, wood, etc ... Related adj: **mural** ...

IDIOMS

Fixed noun phrases, such as **dark horse**, and certain other idioms are given full headword status. Other idioms are placed under the key word of the idiom, as a separate sense, generally at the end of the appropriate part-of-speech block.

> **ground**[1] (graʊnd) *n* ... **21 break new ground** to do something that has not been done before ...

ETYMOLOGIES

Etymologies are within square brackets and appear after the definition. They are given for most headwords except those that are derivative forms (consisting of a base word and a suffix or prefix), compound words, inflected forms, and proper names.

Many headwords, such as **enlighten** and **prepossess**, consist of a prefix and a base word and are not accompanied by etymologies since the essential etymological information is shown for the component parts, all of which are entered in the dictionary as headwords in their own right.

The purpose of the etymologies is to trace briefly the history of the word back from the present day, through its first recorded appearance in English, to its origin, often in some source language other than English. The etymologies show the history of the word both in English (wherever there has been significant change in form or sense) and in its pre-English source languages. Words printed in SMALL CAPITALS refer to other headwords where relevant or additional information, either in the definition or in the etymology, may be found.

Dating

The etymology records the first known occurrence (a written citation) of a word in English. Words first appearing in the language during the Middle English period or later are dated by century, abbreviated C.

> **mantis** ... [C17 New Latin, from Greek: prophet, alluding to its praying posture]

This indicates that there is a written citation for **mantis** in the seventeenth century. The absence of a New Latin or Greek form in the etymology means that the form of the word was the same in those languages as in English.

Old English

Native words from Old English are not dated, written records of Old English being scarce, but are simply identified as being of Old English origin.

DERIVED WORDS

Words derived from a base word by the addition of suffixes such as *-ly*, *-ness*, etc, are entered in bold type immediately after the etymology or after the last definition if there is no etymology.
They are preceded by the icon >. The meanings of such words may be deduced from the meanings of the suffix and the headword.

USAGE NOTES

A brief note introduced by the label USAGE has been added after entries in order to comment on matters of usage.

Pronunciation Key

The symbols used in the pronunciation transcriptions are those of the International Phonetic Alphabet. The following consonant symbols have their usual English values: *b, d, f, h, k, l, m, n, p, r, s, t, v, w, z*. The remaining symbols and their interpretations are listed below.

Length
The symbol : denotes length and is shown together with certain vowel symbols when the vowels are typically long.

Stress
Three grades of stress are shown in the transcriptions by the presence or absence of marks placed immediately *before* the affected syllable. Primary or strong stress is shown by ' , while secondary or weak stress is shown by ˌ . Unstressed syllables are not marked. In *photographic* (ˌfəʊtəˈɡræfɪk), for example, the first syllable carries secondary stress and the third primary stress, while the second and fourth are unstressed.

Notes
(i) Though words like *castle*, *path*, and *fast* are shown as pronounced with an /ɑː / sound, many speakers use an /æ/. Such variations are acceptable and are to be assumed by the reader.
(ii) The letter 'r' in some positions is not sounded in the speech of Southern England and elsewhere. However, many speakers in other areas do sound the 'r' in such positions with varying degrees of distinctness. Again such variations are to be assumed, and in such words as *fern*, *fear*, and *arm* the reader will sound or not sound the 'r' according to his or her speech habits.
(iii) Though the widely received pronunciation of words like *which* and *why* is with a simple /w/ sound and is so shown in the dictionary, many speakers in Scotland and elsewhere preserve an aspirated sound: /hw/. Once again this variation is to be assumed.

English Sounds

ɑː	as in *father* ('fɑːðə), *alms* (ɑːmz), *clerk* (klɑːk), *heart* (hɑːt), *sergeant* ('sɑːdʒənt)
æ	as in *act* (ækt), *Caedmon* ('kædmən), *plait* (plæt)
aɪ	as in *dive* (daɪv), *aisle* (aɪl), *guy* (ɡaɪ), *might* (maɪt), *rye* (raɪ)
aɪə	as in *fire* ('faɪə), *buyer* ('baɪə), *liar* ('laɪə), *tyre* ('taɪə)
aʊ	as in *out* (aʊt), *bough* (baʊ), *crowd* (kraʊd), *slouch* (slaʊtʃ)
aʊə	as in *flour* ('flaʊə), *cower* ('kaʊə), *flower* ('flaʊə), *sour* ('saʊə)
ɛ	as in *bet* (bɛt), *bury* ('bɛrɪ), *heifer* ('hɛfə), *said* (sɛd), *says* (sɛz)
eɪ	as in *paid* (peɪd), *day* (deɪ), *deign* (deɪn), *gauge* (ɡeɪdʒ), *grey* (ɡreɪ), *neigh* (neɪ)
ɛə	as in *bear* (bɛə), *dare* (dɛə), *prayer* (prɛə), *stairs* (stɛəz), *where* (wɛə)
ɡ	as in *get* (ɡɛt), *give* (ɡɪv), *ghoul* (ɡuːl), *guard* (ɡɑːd), *examine* (ɪɡ'zæmɪn)
ɪ	as in *pretty* ('prɪtɪ), *build* (bɪld), *busy* ('bɪzɪ), *nymph* (nɪmf), *pocket* ('pɒkɪt), *sieve* (sɪv), *women* ('wɪmɪn)
iː	as in *see* (siː), *aesthete* ('iːsθiːt), *evil* ('iːvəl), *magazine* (ˌmæɡə'ziːn), *receive* (rɪ'siːv), *siege* (siːdʒ)
ɪə	as in *fear* (fɪə), *beer* (bɪə), *mere* (mɪə), *tier* (tɪə)
j	as in *yes* (jɛs), *onion* ('ʌnjən), *vignette* (vɪ'njɛt)
ɒ	as in *pot* (pɒt), *botch* (bɒtʃ), *sorry* ('sɒrɪ)
əʊ	as in *note* (nəʊt), *beau* (bəʊ), *dough* (dəʊ), *hoe* (həʊ), *slow* (sləʊ), *yeoman* ('jəʊmən)
ɔː	as in *thaw* (θɔː), *broad* (brɔːd), *drawer* ('drɔːə), *fault* (fɔːlt), *halt* (hɔːlt), *organ* ('ɔːɡən)
ɔɪ	as in *void* (vɔɪd), *boy* (bɔɪ), *destroy* (dɪ'strɔɪ)
ʊ	as in *pull* (pʊl), *good* (ɡʊd), *should* (ʃʊd), *woman* ('wʊmən)
uː	as in *zoo* (zuː), *do* (duː), *queue* (kjuː), *shoe* (ʃuː), *spew* (spjuː), *true* (truː), *you* (juː)
ʊə	as in *poor* (pʊə), *skewer* (skjʊə), *sure* (ʃʊə)
ə	as in *potter* ('pɒtə), *alone* (ə'ləʊn), *furious* ('fjʊərɪəs), *nation* ('neɪʃən), *the* (ðə)
ɜː	as in *fern* (fɜːn), *burn* (bɜːn), *fir* (fɜː), *learn* (lɜːn), *term* (tɜːm)
ʌ	as in *cut* (kʌt), *flood* (flʌd), *rough* (rʌf), *son* (sʌn)
ʃ	as in *ship* (ʃɪp), *election* (ɪ'lɛkʃən), *machine* (mə'ʃiːn), *mission* ('mɪʃən), *pressure* ('prɛʃə), *schedule* ('ʃɛdjuːl), *sugar* ('ʃʊɡə)
ʒ	as in *treasure* ('trɛʒə), *azure* ('æʒə), *closure* ('kləʊʒə), *evasion* (ɪ'veɪʒən)
tʃ	as in *chew* (tʃuː), *nature* ('neɪtʃə)
dʒ	as in *jaw* (dʒɔː), *adjective* ('ædʒɪktɪv), *lodge* (lɒdʒ), *soldier* ('səʊldʒə), *usage* ('juːsɪdʒ)
θ	as in *thin* (θɪn), *strength* (strɛŋθ), *three* (θriː)
ð	as in *these* (ðiːz), *bathe* (beɪð), *lather* ('lɑːðə)
ŋ	as in *sing* (sɪŋ), *finger* ('fɪŋɡə), *sling* (slɪŋ)
ᵊ	indicates that the following consonant (*l* or *n*) is syllabic, as in *bundle* ('bʌndᵊl), *button* ('bʌtᵊn)
x	as in Scottish *loch* (lɒx)
əɪ	as in Scottish *aye* (əɪ), *bile* (bəɪl), *byke* (bəɪk)

Foreign Sounds

The symbols above are also used to represent foreign sounds where these are similar to English sounds. However, certain common foreign sounds require symbols with markedly different values, as follows:

a   *a* in French *ami*, German *Mann*, Italian *pasta*: a sound between English (æ) and (ɑː), similar to the vowel in Northern English *cat* or London *cut*

ɑ   *a* in French *bas*: a sound made with a tongue position similar to that of English (ɑː), but shorter

e   *é* in French *été*, *eh* in German *sehr*, *e* in Italian *che*: a sound similar to the first part of the English diphthong (eɪ) in *day* or to the Scottish vowel in *day*

i   *i* in French *il*, German *Idee*, Spanish *filo*, Italian *signore*: a sound made with a tongue position similar to that of English (iː), but shorter

ɔ   *o* in Italian *no*, French *bonne*, German *Sonne*: a vowel resembling English (ɒ), but with a higher tongue position and more rounding of the lips

o   *o* in French *rose*, German *so*, Italian *voce*: a sound between English (ɔː) and (uː) with closely rounded lips, similar to the Scottish vowel in *so*

u   *ou* in French *genou*, *u* in German *kulant*, Spanish *puna*: a sound made with a tongue position similar to that of English (uː), but shorter

y   *u* in French *tu*, *ü* in German *über* or *fünf*: a sound made with a tongue position similar to that of English (iː), but with closely rounded lips

ø   *eu* in French *deux*, *ö* in German *schön*: a sound made with the tongue position of (e), but with closely rounded lips

œ   *œu* in French *œuf*, *ö* in German *zwölf*: a sound made with a tongue position similar to that of English (ɛ), but with open rounded lips

~   above a vowel indicates nasalization, as in French *un* (œ̃), *bon* (bɔ̃), *vin* (vɛ̃), *blanc* (blɑ̃)

x   *ch* in Scottish *loch*, German *Buch*, *j* in Spanish *Juan*

ç   *ch* in German *ich*: a (j) sound as in *yes*, said without voice; similar to the first sound in *huge*

β   *b* in Spanish *Habana*: a voiced fricative sound similar to (v), but made by the two lips

ʎ   *ll* in Spanish *llamar*, *gl* in Italian *consiglio*: similar to the (lj) sequence in *million*, but with the tongue tip lowered and the sounds said simultaneously

ɥ   *u* in French *lui*: a short (y)

ɲ   *gn* in French *vigne*, Italian *gnocchi*, *ñ* in Spanish *España*: similar to the (nj) sequence in *onion*, but with the tongue tip lowered and the two sounds said simultaneously

ɣ   *g* in Spanish *luego*: a weak (g) made with voiced friction

Abbreviations

adj	adjective
adv	adverb(ial)
Amerind	American Indian
anthropol	anthropology
archaeol	archaeology
archit	architecture
Austral	Australian
bibliog	bibliography
biochem	biochemistry
Brit	Britain; British
c	century (eg c14 = 14th century)
°C	degrees Celsius
conj	conjunction
crystallog	crystallography
E	east(ern)
embryol	embryology
eg	for example
entomol	entomology
esp	especially
est	estimate
foll	followed
ft	foot *or* feet
ie	that is
in	inch(es)
interj	interjection
intr	intransitive
km	kilometre(s)
m	metre(s)
maths	mathematics
myth	mythology
n	noun
N	north(ern)
NE	northeast(ern)
no	number
NW	northwest(ern)
NZ	New Zealand
ornithol	ornithology
pathol	pathology
pharmacol	pharmacology
photog	photography
physiol	physiology
pop	population
prep	preposition(al)
pron	pronoun
psychol	psychology
pt	point
RC	Roman Catholic
S	south(ern)
Scot	Scottish; Scots
SE	southeast(ern)
sing	singular
sq	square
SW	southwest(ern)
telecom	telecommunications
theol	theology
tr	transitive
US	United States
vb	verb
W	west(ern)
wt	weight

Aa

a or **A** (eɪ) *n, pl* **a's, A's** or **As 1** the first letter and first vowel of the modern English alphabet **2** any of several speech sounds represented by this letter, in English as in *take, bag, calm, shortage,* or *cobra* **3** Also called: **alpha** the first in a series, esp the highest grade or mark, as in an examination **4 from A to Z** from start to finish, thoroughly and in detail

a¹ (ə; *stressed or emphatic* eɪ) *determiner (indefinite article;* used before an initial consonant. Compare **an¹**) **1** used preceding a singular countable noun, if the noun is not previously specified or known: *a dog; a terrible disappointment* **2** used preceding a proper noun to indicate that a person or thing has some of the qualities of the one named: *a Romeo; a Shylock* **3** used preceding a noun or determiner of quantity: *a cupful; a dozen eggs; a great many; to read a lot* **4** used preceding a noun indicating a concrete or abstract thing capable of being divided: *half a loaf; a quarter of a minute* **5** (preceded by *once, twice, several times,* etc) each or every; per: *once a day; fifty pence a pound* **6** a certain; one: *to change policy at a stroke; a Mr Jones called* **7** (preceded by *not*) any at all: *not a hope* ▷ Compare **the¹**

a² (ə) *vb* an informal or dialect word for **have** *they'd a said if they'd known*

a³ (ə) *prep* (usually linked to the preceding noun) an informal form of **of** *sorta sad; a kinda waste*

a⁴ *symbol for* **1** acceleration **2** are(s) (metric measure of land) **3** atto- **4** *chess* See **algebraic notation**

A *symbol for* **1** *music* **a** a note having a frequency of 440 hertz (**A above middle C**) or this value multiplied or divided by any power of 2; the sixth note of the scale of C major **b** a key, string, or pipe producing this note **c** the major or minor key having this note as its tonic **2** a human blood type of the ABO group, containing the A antigen **3** (in Britain) a major arterial road: *the A3 runs from London to Portsmouth* **4** (formerly, in Britain) **a** a film certified for viewing by anyone, but which contains material that some parents may not wish their children to see **b** (*as modifier*): *an A film* **5** mass number **6** the number 10 in hexadecimal notation **7** *cards* ace **8** argon (now superseded by Ar) **9** ampere(s) **10** Also: **a** ampere-turn **11** absolute (temperature) **12** (in circuit diagrams) ammeter **13** area **14** (*in combination*) atomic: *an A-bomb; an A-plant* **15** *chem* affinity **16** *biochem* adenine **17** *logic* a universal affirmative categorical proposition, such as *all men are mortal: often symbolized as* SaP Compare **E, I², O¹** [from Latin *a(ffirmo)* I affirm] **18 a** a person whose job is in top management, or who holds a senior administrative or professional position **b** (*as modifier*): *an A worker* ▷ See also **occupation groupings 19** ▷ *international car registration for* Austria

Å *symbol for* angstrom unit

A. *abbreviation for* **1** acre(s) or acreage **2** America(n) **3** answer

a', aa or **aw** (ɔ:) *determiner Scot* variants of **all**

a-¹ or before a vowel **an-** *prefix* not; without; opposite to: *atonal; asocial* [from Greek *a-, an-* not, without]

a-² *prefix* **1** on; in; towards: *afoot; abed; aground; aback* **2** literary or archaic (used before a present participle) in the act or process of: *come a-running; go a-hunting* **3** in the condition or state of: *afloat; alive; asleep*

A1, A-1 or **A-one** ('eɪ'wʌn) *adj* **1** in good health; physically fit **2** *informal* first class; excellent **3** (of a vessel) with hull and equipment in first-class condition

A2 *n Brit* an advanced level of a subject taken for the General Certificate of Education, forming the second part of an A level course, after the AS level

A3¹ *n* **a** a standard paper size, 297 × 420 mm **b** (*as adjective*): *an A3 book* ▷ See also **A sizes**

A3² *text messaging abbreviation for* anytime, anywhere, anyplace

A4 *n* **a** a standard paper size, 210 × 297 mm **b** (*as adjective*): *an A4 book* ▷ See also **A sizes**

A5 *n* **a** a standard paper size (half A4), 148 × 210 mm **b** (*as adjective*): *A5 notepaper* ▷ See also **A sizes**

aa¹ ('ɑːɑ:) *n* a volcanic rock consisting of angular blocks of lava with a very rough surface [Hawaiian]

aa² *abbreviation for* ana¹

AA *abbreviation for* **1 Alcoholics Anonymous 2** anti-aircraft **3** Architectural Association **4** (in Britain) Automobile Association **5** (in Britain) Advertising Association ▷ *symbol for* **6** (in Britain, formerly) a film that may not be shown publicly to a child under fourteen

AAA *abbreviation for* **1** *Brit* Amateur Athletic Association **2** anti-aircraft artillery. See also **triple A 3** *US* Automobile Association of America **4** Automobile Association of Australia

Aachen ('ɑ:kən; *German* 'a:xən) *n* a city and spa in W Germany, in North Rhine-Westphalia: the northern capital of Charlemagne's empire. Pop: 256 605 (2003 est). French name: **Aix-la-Chapelle**

Aalborg or **Ålborg** (*Danish* 'ɔlbɔr) *n* a city and port in Denmark, in N Jutland. Pop: 121 549 (2004 est)

Aalesund (*Norwegian* 'ɔ:ləsun) *n* a variant spelling of **Ålesund**

aalii (ɑ:'li:i:) *n* a bushy sapindaceous shrub, *Dodonaea viscosa,* of Australia, Hawaii, Africa, and tropical America, having small greenish flowers and sticky foliage [Hawaiian]

Aalst (a:lst) *n* the Flemish name for **Alost**

AAM *text messaging abbreviation for* **1** air-to-air missile **2** as a matter of fact

A & E *abbreviation for* Accident and Emergency (department in hospitals)

A & M *abbreviation for* **1** Agricultural and Mechanical **2** Ancient and Modern (hymn book)

A & P (in New Zealand) *abbreviation for* Agricultural and Pastoral (Association, Show, etc)

A & R *abbreviation for* artists and repertoire

AAP *abbreviation for* **1** Australian Associated Press **2** (in the US) affirmative action program

Aarau (*German* 'a:rau) *n* a town in N Switzerland, capital of Aargau canton: capital of the Helvetic Republic from 1798 to 1803. Pop: 15 470 (2000)

aardvark ('ɑːd̩vɑːk) *n* a nocturnal mammal, *Orycteropus afer,* the sole member of its family (*Orycteropodidae*) and order (*Tubulidentata*). It inhabits the grasslands of Africa, has long ears and snout, and feeds on termites. Also called: **ant bear** [c19 from obsolete Afrikaans, from *aarde* earth + *varken* pig]

aardwolf ('ɑːd̩wʊlf) *n, pl* **-wolves** a nocturnal mammal, *Proteles cristatus,* that inhabits the plains of southern Africa and feeds on termites and insect larvae: family *Hyaenidae* (hyenas), order *Carnivora* (carnivores) [c19 from Afrikaans, from *aarde* earth + *wolf* wolf]

Aargau (*German* 'a:rgau) *n* a canton in N Switzerland. Capital: Aarau. Pop: 556 200 (2002 est). Area: 1404 sq km (542 sq miles). French name: Argovie

Aarhus or **Århus** (*Danish* 'ʌhuːs) *n* a city and port in Denmark, in E Jutland. Pop: 228 547 (2004 est)

AARNet *abbreviation for* Australian Academic Research Network

Aaron ('ɛərən) *n Old Testament* the first high priest of the Israelites, brother of Moses (Exodus 4:14)

Aaronic (ɛə'rɒnɪk) *adj* **1** of or relating to Aaron, his family, or the priestly dynasty initiated by him **2** of or relating to the Israelite high priesthood **3** of or relating to the priesthood in general **4** *Mormon Church* denoting or relating to the second order of the Mormon priesthood

Aaron's beard *n* another name for **rose of Sharon** (sense 1)

Aaron's rod *n* **1** the rod used by Aaron in performing a variety of miracles in Egypt. It later blossomed and produced almonds (Numbers 17) **2** a widespread Eurasian scrophulariaceous plant, *Verbascum thapsus,* having woolly leaves and tall erect spikes of yellow flowers

aarti ('ɑːtɪ) *n* a Hindu ceremony in which lights with wicks soaked in ghee are lit and offered up to one or more deities [c21 Hindi]

A'asia *abbreviation for* Australasia

AAVE *abbreviation for* African-American Vernacular English

Ab (æb) *n* a variant of **Av**

AB *abbreviation for* **1** Also: **a.b.** able-bodied seaman **2** (in the US) Bachelor of Arts **3** (esp in postal addresses) Alberta (Canada) ▷ *symbol for* **4** a human blood type of the ABO group, containing both the A antigen and the B antigen

ab-¹ *prefix* away from; off; outside of; opposite to: *abnormal; abaxial; aboral* [from Latin *ab* away from]

ab-² *prefix* denoting a cgs unit of measurement in the electromagnetic system: *abvolt* [abstracted from ABSOLUTE]

aba ('ɑːbə) *n* **1** a type of cloth from Syria, made of goat hair or camel hair **2** a sleeveless outer garment of such cloth [from Arabic]

ABA *abbreviation for* **1** (in Britain) Amateur Boxing Association **2** American Booksellers Association

abac ('eɪbæk) *n* another name for **nomogram** [c20 from French, from Latin ABACUS]

abaca ('æbəkə) *n* **1** a Philippine plant, *Musa textilis*, related to the banana: family *Musaceae*. Its leafstalks are the source of Manila hemp **2** another name for **Manila hemp** [via Spanish from Tagalog *abaká*]

aback (ə'bæk) *adv* **1** taken aback **a** startled or disconcerted **b** *nautical* (of a vessel or sail) having the wind against the forward side so as to prevent forward motion **2** *rare* towards the back; backwards [Old English *on bæc* to the back]

abactinal (æb'æktɪnəl) *adj zoology* (of organisms showing radial symmetry) situated away from or opposite to the mouth; aboral > ab'actinally *adv*

abacus ('æbəkəs) *n*, *pl* -ci (-,saɪ) *or* -cuses **1** a counting device that consists of a frame holding rods on which a specific number of beads are free to move. Each rod designates a given denomination, such as units, tens, hundreds, etc, in the decimal system, and each bead represents a digit or a specific number of digits **2** *architect* the flat upper part of the capital of a column [c16 from Latin, from Greek *abax* board covered with sand for tracing calculations, from Hebrew *ābhāq* dust]

Abadan (,æbə'dɑːn) *n* a port in SW Iran, on an island in the Shatt-al-Arab delta. Pop: 307 000 (2005 est)

Abaddon (ə'bædᵊn) *n* **1** the Devil (Revelation 9:11) **2** (in rabbinical literature) a part of Gehenna; Hell [Hebrew: literally, destruction]

abaft (ə'bɑːft) *nautical* ⊳ *adv* ⊳ *adj* (postpositive) **1** closer to the stern than to another place on a vessel: *with the wind abaft* ⊳ *prep* **2** behind; aft of: *abaft the mast* [c13 *on baft; baft* from Old English *beæftan*, from *be* by + *æftan* behind]

Abakan (*Russian* aba'kan) *n* a city in S central Russia, capital of the Khakass Republic, at the confluence of the Yenisei and Abakan Rivers. Pop: 167 000 (2005 est)

abalone (,æbə'ləʊnɪ) *n* any of various edible marine gastropod molluscs of the genus *Haliotis*, having an ear-shaped shell that is perforated with a row of respiratory holes. The shells are used for ornament or decoration. Also called: **ear shell** See also **ormer** [c19 from American Spanish *abulón*; origin unknown]

abampere (æb'æmpɛə) *n* the cgs unit of current in the electromagnetic system; the constant current that, when flowing through two parallel straight infinitely long conductors 1 centimetre apart, will produce a force between them of 2 dynes per centimetre: equivalent to 10 amperes. Abbreviation: abamp

abandon (ə'bændən) *vb* (*tr*) **1** to forsake completely; desert; leave behind: *to abandon a baby; drivers had to abandon their cars* **2** abandon ship the order given to the crew of a ship that is about to sink to take to the lifeboats **3** to give up completely: *to abandon a habit; to abandon hope* **4** to yield control of or concern in; relinquish: *to abandon office* **5** to give up (something begun) before completion: *to abandon a job; the game was abandoned* **6** to surrender (oneself) to emotion without restraint **7** to give (insured property that has suffered partial loss or damage) up to the insurers in order that a claim for a total loss may be made ⊳ *n* **8** freedom from inhibitions, restraint, concern, or worry: *she danced with abandon* [c14 *abandounen* (vb), from Old French, from *a bandon* under one's control, in one's power, from *a* at, to + *bandon* control, power] > a'bandonment *n*

abandoned (ə'bændənd) *adj* **1** deserted: *an abandoned windmill* **2** forsaken: *an abandoned child* **3** unrestrained; uninhibited: *wild, abandoned dancing* **4** depraved; profligate

abandonee (ə,bændə'niː) *n law* a person to whom something is formally relinquished, esp an insurer having the right to salvage a wreck

abandonware (ə'bændən,wɛə) *n* computer software which is no longer sold or supported by its publisher [c20 from ABANDON + (SOFT(WARE)]

abapical (æb'eɪpɪkᵊl) *adj biology* away from or opposite the apex

à bas *French* (a ba) *interj* down with!

abase (ə'beɪs) *vb* (*tr*) **1** to humble or belittle (oneself, etc) **2** to lower or reduce, as in rank or estimation [c15 *abessen*, from Old French *abaissier* to make low. See BASE²] > a'basement *n*

abash (ə'bæʃ) *vb* (*tr; usually passive*) to cause to feel ill at ease, embarrassed, or confused; make ashamed [c14 via Norman French from Old French *esbair* to be astonished, from *es*- out + *bair* to gape, yawn] > a'bashment *n*

abashed (ə'bæʃt) *adj* ill at ease, embarrassed, or confused; ashamed

abate (ə'beɪt) *vb* **1** to make or become less in amount, intensity, degree, etc: *the storm has abated* **2** (*tr*) *law* **a** to remove, suppress, or terminate (a nuisance) **b** to suspend or extinguish (a claim or action) **c** to annul (a writ) **3** (*intr*) *law* (of a writ, legal action, etc) to become null and void **4** (*tr*) to subtract or deduct, as part of a price [c14 from Old French *abatre* to beat down, fell]

abatement (ə'beɪtmənt) *n* **1** diminution or alleviation; decrease **2** suppression or termination: *the abatement of a nuisance* **3** the amount by which something is reduced, such as the cost of an article **4** *property law* a decrease in the payment to creditors or legatees when the assets of the debtor or estate are insufficient to meet all payments in full **5** *property law* (formerly) a wrongful entry on land by a stranger who takes possession after the death of the owner and before the heir has entered into possession

abatis *or* **abattis** ('æbətɪs, 'æbəti:) *n fortifications* **1** a rampart of felled trees bound together placed with their branches outwards **2** a barbed-wire entanglement before a position [c18 from French, from *abattre* to fell]

abator (ə'beɪtə) *n law* a person who effects an abatement

abattoir ('æbə,twɑ:) *n* another name for **slaughterhouse** [c19 French, from *abattre* to fell]

abaxial (æb'æksɪəl) *adj* facing away from the axis, as the surface of a leaf. Compare **adaxial**

abaya (ə'baɪə) *n* a long black long-sleeved robe worn by Muslim women in Arabic-speaking countries, often with a headscarf or veil [Arabic]

Abba ('æbə) *n* **1** *New Testament* father (used of God) **2** a title given to bishops and patriarchs in the Syrian, Coptic, and Ethiopian Churches [from Aramaic]

abbacy ('æbəsɪ) *n*, *pl* -cies the office, term of office, or jurisdiction of an abbot or abbess [c15 from Church Latin *abbātia*, from *abbāt*- ABBOT]

abbatial (ə'beɪʃəl) *adj* of or relating to an abbot, abbess, or abbey [c17 from Church Latin *abbātiālis*, from *abbāt*- ABBOT; see -AL¹]

abbé ('æbeɪ; *French* abe) *n* **1** a French abbot **2** a title used in addressing any other French cleric, such as a priest

Abbe condenser ('æbɪ; *German* 'a:bə) *n* a microscope condenser invented by Ernst Abbe (1840-1905), German physicist

abbed (æbd) *adj informal* displaying well-developed abdominal muscles

abbess ('æbɪs) *n* the female superior of a convent [c13 from Old French, from Church Latin *abbātissa*]

Abbeville (*French* abəvil) *n* a town in N France: brewing, sugar-refining, and carpet industries. Pop: 24 567 (1999)

Abbevillian (æb'vɪlɪən, -jən) *archaeol* ⊳ *n* **1** the period represented by Lower Palaeolithic European sites containing the earliest hand axes, dating from the Mindel glaciation. See also **Acheulian** ⊳ *adj* **2** of or relating to this period [c20 after ABBEVILLE, where the stone tools were discovered]

abbey ('æbɪ) *n* **1** a building inhabited by a community of monks or nuns governed by an abbot or abbess **2** a church built in conjunction with such a building **3** such a community of monks or nuns [c13 via Old French *abeie* from Church Latin *abbātia* ABBACY]

Abbey Theatre *n* an influential theatre in Dublin (opened 1904): associated with it were Synge, Yeats, Lady Gregory, and O'Casey. It was destroyed by fire in 1951 but was rebuilt; it reopened in 1966

abbot ('æbət) *n* the superior of an abbey of monks. Related adj: **abbatial** [Old English *abbod*, from Church Latin *abbāt*- (stem of *abbas*), ultimately from Aramaic *abbā* ABBA] > 'abbot,ship *or* 'abbotcy *n*

abbrev *or* **abbr.** *abbreviation for* abbreviation

abbreviate (ə'bri:vɪ,eɪt) *vb* (*tr*) **1** to shorten (a word or phrase) by contraction or omission of some letters or words **2** to shorten (a speech or piece of writing) by omitting sections, paraphrasing, etc **3** to cut short [c15 from the past participle of Late Latin *abbreviāre*, from Latin *brevis* brief] > ab'brevi,ator *n*

abbreviation (ə,bri:vɪ'eɪʃən) *n* **1** a shortened or contracted form of a word or phrase used in place of the whole **2** the process or result of abbreviating

ABC¹ *n* **1** (*plural in US*) the rudiments of a subject **2** an alphabetical guide to a subject **3** (*often plural in US*) the alphabet

ABC² *abbreviation for* **1** (formerly, of weapons or warfare) atomic, biological, and chemical **2** Australian Broadcasting Corporation **3** American Broadcasting Company **4** Audit Bureau of Circulation **5** *Austral* Australian-born Chinese: a person with Chinese parents, born and raised in Australia **6** *US* American-born Chinese: a person with Chinese parents, born and raised in the US **7** *Brit* acceptable behaviour contract: a voluntary written agreement between someone who has been involved in anti-social behaviour and a local agency such as a housing association, council, or police

abcoulomb (æb'ku:lɒm) *n* the cgs unit of electric charge in the electromagnetic system; the charge per second passing any cross section of a conductor through which a steady current of 1 abampere is flowing: equivalent to 10 coulombs

Abdias (æb'daɪəs) *n Bible* the Douay form of **Obadiah**

abdicate ('æbdɪ,keɪt) *vb* to renounce (a throne, power, responsibility, rights, etc), esp formally [c16 from the past participle of Latin *abdicāre* to proclaim away, disclaim] > abdicable ('æbdɪkəbᵊl) *adj* > ,abdi'cation *n* > abdicative (æb'dɪkətɪv) *adj* > 'abdi,cator *n*

abdomen ('æbdəmən, æb'dəʊ-) *n* **1** the region of the body of a vertebrate that contains the viscera other than the heart and lungs. In mammals it is separated from the thorax by the diaphragm **2** the front or surface of this region; belly. Related adj: **coeliac 3** (in arthropods) the posterior part of the body behind the thorax, consisting of up to ten similar segments [c16 from Latin; origin obscure] > abdominal (æb'dɒmɪnᵊl) *adj* > ab'dominally *adv*

abdominal crunch *n* another term for **sit-up**

abdominal thrust *n* another name for **Heimlich manoeuvre**

abdominoplasty (æb'dɒmɪnəʊ,plæstɪ) *n*, *pl* -ies the surgical removal of excess skin and fat from the abdomen

abducens nerve (æb'dju:sənz) *n* either of the sixth pair of cranial nerves, which supply the lateral rectus muscle of the eye [scc ABDUCENT]

abducent (æb'dju:sᵊnt) *adj* (of a muscle) abducting [c18 from Latin *abdūcent-, abdūcens* leading away, from *abdūcere*, from *ab*- away + *dūcere* to lead, carry]

abduct (æb'dʌkt) *vb* (*tr*) **1** to remove (a person) by force or cunning; kidnap **2** (of certain muscles) to pull (a leg, arm, etc) away from the median axis of the body. Compare **adduct** [c19 from the past participle of Latin *abdūcere* to lead away] > ab'ductor *n*

abduction (æb'dʌkʃən) *n* **1** the act of taking someone away by force or cunning; kidnapping **2** the action of certain muscles in pulling a leg, arm, etc away from the median axis of the body

abeam (ə'bi:m) *adv, adj* (*postpositive*) at right angles to the length and directly opposite the centre of a vessel or aircraft [C19 A-² + BEAM]

abecedarian (ˌeɪbiːsiː'dɛərɪən) *n* **1** a person who is learning the alphabet or the rudiments of a subject ▷ *adj* **2** alphabetically arranged [C17 from Late Latin *abecedarius*, from the letters *a, b, c, d*]

abed (ə'bɛd) *adv archaic* in bed

Abednego (ə'bɛdnɪˌgəʊ) *n Old Testament* one of Daniel's three companions who, together with Shadrach and Meshach, was miraculously saved from destruction in Nebuchadnezzar's fiery furnace (Daniel 3:12–30)

Abel ('eɪbəl) *n Old Testament* the second son of Adam and Eve, a shepherd, murdered by his brother Cain (Genesis 4:1–8)

abele (ə'bi:l, 'eɪbəl) *n* another name for **white poplar** [C16 from Dutch *abeel*, ultimately related to Latin *albus* white]

Abelian group (ə'bi:lɪən) *n* a group the defined binary operation of which is commutative: if *a* and *b* are members of an Abelian group then *ab* = *ba* [C19 named after Niels Henrik *Abel* (1802–29), Norwegian mathematician]

abelmosk ('eɪbəlˌmɒsk) *n* a tropical bushy malvaceous plant, *Hibiscus abelmoschus*, cultivated for its yellow-and-crimson flowers and for its musk-scented seeds, which yield an oil used in perfumery. Also called: **musk mallow** [New Latin, from Arabic *abu'l misk* father of musk]

Abeokuta (ˌæbɪəʊ'ku:tə) *n* a town in W Nigeria, capital of Ogun state. Pop: 487 000 (2005 est)

Aberdare (ˌæbə'dɛə) *n* a town in South Wales, in Rhondda, Cynon, Taff county borough. Pop: 31 705 (2001)

Aberdeen (ˌæbə'di:n) *n* **1** a city in NE Scotland, on the North Sea: centre for processing North Sea oil and gas; university (1494). Pop: 184 788 (2001) **2 City of** a council area in NE Scotland, established in 1996. Pop: 206 600 (2003 est). Area: 186 sq km (72 sq miles)

Aberdeen Angus *n* a black hornless breed of beef cattle originating in Scotland

Aberdeenshire (ˌæbə'di:nʃɪə, -ʃə) *n* a council area and historical county of N Scotland, on the North Sea: became part of Grampian Region in 1975 but reinstated as an independent unitary authority (with adjusted borders) in 1996: rises to the Grampian and Cairngorm Mountains in the SW: chiefly agricultural (esp sheep and stock raising). Administrative centre: Aberdeen. Pop: 229 330 (2003 est). Area 6319 sq km (2439 sq miles)

Aberdeen terrier *n* a former name for **Scottish terrier**

aberdevine (ˌæbədɪ'vi:n) *n* a former name for the **siskin** (sense 1), as a cagebird [C18 of unknown origin]

Aberdonian (ˌæbə'dəʊnɪən) *n* **1** a native or inhabitant of Aberdeen ▷ *adj* **2** of or relating to Aberdeen or its inhabitants

Aberfan (ˌæbə'væn) *n* a former coal-mining village in S Wales, in Merthyr Tydfil county borough: scene of a disaster in 1966 when a slag heap collapsed onto part of the village killing 144 people (including 116 children)

abernethy (ˌæbə'nɛθɪ) *n* a crisp unleavened biscuit [C19 perhaps named after Dr John *Abernethy* (1764–1831), English surgeon interested in diet]

aberrant (æ'bɛrənt) *adj* **1** deviating from the normal or usual type, as certain animals from the group in which they are classified **2** behaving in an abnormal or untypical way **3** deviating from truth, morality, etc [rare before C19 from the present participle of Latin *aberrāre* to wander away] > ab'**errance** or ab'**errancy** *n*

aberration (ˌæbə'reɪʃən) *n* **1** deviation from what is normal, expected, or usual **2** departure from truth, morality, etc **3** a lapse in control of one's mental faculties **4** *optics* a defect in a lens or mirror that causes the formation of either a distorted image (see **spherical aberration**) or one with coloured fringes (see **chromatic aberration**) **5** *astronomy* the apparent displacement of a celestial body due to the finite speed of light and the motion of the observer with the earth

Aberystwyth (ˌæbə'rɪstwɪθ) *n* a resort and university town in Wales, in Ceredigion on Cardigan Bay. Pop: 15 935 (2001)

abet (ə'bɛt) *vb* **abets, abetting, abetted** (*tr*) to assist or encourage, esp in crime or wrongdoing [C14 from Old French *abeter* to lure on, entice, from *beter* to bait] > a'**betment** or a'**bettal** *n* > a'**better** or *esp law* a'**bettor** *n*

abeyance (ə'beɪəns) *n* **1** (usually preceded by *in* or *into*) a state of being suspended or put aside temporarily **2** (usually preceded by *in*) *law* an indeterminate state of ownership, as when the person entitled to an estate has not been ascertained [C16-17 from Anglo-French, from Old French *abeance* expectation, literally a gaping after, a reaching towards] > a'**beyant** *adj*

abfarad (æb'færæd, -əd) *n* the cgs unit of capacitance in the electromagnetic system; the capacitance of a capacitor having a charge of 1 abcoulomb and a potential difference of 1 abvolt between its conductors: equivalent to 10⁹ farads

ABH *abbreviation for* **actual bodily harm**

abhenry (æb'hɛnrɪ) *n, pl* **-ries** the cgs unit of inductance in the electromagnetic system; the inductance that results when a rate of change of current of 1 abampere per second generates an induced emf of 1 abvolt: equivalent to 10⁻⁹ henry

abhor (əb'hɔ:) *vb* **-hors, -horring, -horred** (*tr*) to detest vehemently; find repugnant; reject [C15 from Latin *abhorrēre* to shudder at, shrink from, from *ab-* away from + *horrēre* to bristle, shudder] > ab'**horrer** *n*

abhorrence (əb'hɒrəns) *n* **1** a feeling of extreme loathing or aversion **2** a person or thing that is loathsome

abhorrent (əb'hɒrənt) *adj* **1** repugnant; loathsome **2** (when *postpositive*, foll by *of*) feeling extreme aversion or loathing (for): *abhorrent of vulgarity* **3** (usually *postpositive* and foll by *to*) conflicting (with): *abhorrent to common sense* > ab'**horrently** *adv*

Abia (æb'i:a) *n* a state of SE Nigeria. Capital: Umuahia. Pop: 2 569 362 (1995 est). Area (including Imo state): 11 850 sq km (4575 sq miles)

Abib (*Hebrew* a'bi:b) *n Judaism* an older name for the month of **Nisan** (Exodus 13:4) [Hebrew *ābhībh* ear of grain, hence the month when grain was fresh]

abide (ə'baɪd) *vb* **abides, abiding, abode** or **abided** **1** (*tr*) to tolerate; put up with **2** (*tr*) to accept or submit to; suffer: *to abide the court's decision* **3** (*intr*; foll by *by*) **a** to comply (with): *to abide by the decision* **b** to remain faithful (to): *to abide by your promise* **4** (*intr*) to remain or continue **5** (*intr*) *archaic* to dwell **6** (*tr*) *archaic* to await in expectation **7** (*tr*) *archaic* to withstand or sustain; endure: *to abide the onslaught* [Old English *ābīdan*, from *a-* (intensive) + *bīdan* to wait, bide] > a'**bidance** *n* > a'**bider** *n*

abiding (ə'baɪdɪŋ) *adj* permanent; enduring: *an abiding belief* > a'**bidingly** *adv*

Abidjan (æb'dʒɑ:n; *French* abidʒɑ̃) *n* a port in Côte d'Ivoire, on the Gulf of Guinea: the legislative capital (Yamoussoukro became the administrative capital in 1983). Pop: 3 516 000 (2005 est)

abietic acid (ˌæbɪ'ɛtɪk) *n* a yellowish powder occurring naturally as a constituent of rosin and used in lacquers, varnishes, and soap. Formula: $C_{19}H_{29}COOH$; melting pt: 173°C [C19 *abietic*, from Latin *abiēt-*, from *abiēs* silver fir (the acid originally being extracted from the resin)]

Abigail ('æbɪˌgeɪl) *n Old Testament* the woman who brought provisions to David and his followers and subsequently became his wife (I Samuel 25:1–42)

Abilene ('æbɪˌli:n) *n* a city in central Texas. Pop: 114 889 (2003 est)

ability (ə'bɪlɪtɪ) *n, pl* **-ties** **1** possession of the qualities required to do something; necessary skill, competence, or power: *the ability to cope with a problem* **2** considerable proficiency; natural capability: *a man of ability* **3** (*plural*) special talents [C14 from Old French from Latin *habilitās* aptitude, handiness, from *habilis* ABLE]

Abingdon ('æbɪŋdən) *n* a market town in S England, in Oxfordshire. Pop: 36 010 (2001)

ab initio *Latin* (æb ɪ'nɪʃɪˌəʊ) from the start; from scratch: *ab initio courses*

abiogenesis (ˌeɪbaɪəʊ'dʒɛnɪsɪs) *n* **1** Also called: **autogenesis** the hypothetical process by which living organisms first arose on earth from nonliving matter **2** another name for **spontaneous generation** Compare **biogenesis** [C19 New Latin, from A-¹ + BIO- + GENESIS] > ˌabioge'**netic** *adj* > ˌabiogenist (ˌeɪbaɪ'ɒdʒɪnɪst) *n*

abiosis (ˌeɪbaɪ'əʊsɪs) *n* absence of life [C20 from A-¹ + Greek *biōsis* a way of living] > **abiotic** (ˌeɪbaɪ'ɒtɪk) *adj*

abiotrophy (ˌeɪbaɪəʊ'trɒfɪ) *n* the progressive degeneration of tissues, cells, etc [C20 from Greek A-¹ + BIO- + TROPHY] > ˌabio'**trophic** *adj*

abirritant (æb'ɪrɪtənt) *adj* **1** relieving irritation ▷ *n* **2** any drug or agent that relieves irritation

abirritate (æb'ɪrɪˌteɪt) *vb* (*tr*) *med obsolete* to soothe or make less irritable

abject ('æbdʒɛkt) *adj* **1** utterly wretched or hopeless **2** miserable; forlorn; dejected **3** indicating humiliation; submissive: *an abject apology* **4** contemptible; despicable; servile: *an abject liar* [C14 (in the sense: rejected, cast out): from Latin *abjectus* thrown or cast away, from *abjicere*, from *ab-* away + *jacere* to throw] > ab'**jection** *n* > '**abjectly** *adv* > '**abjectness** *n*

abjure (əb'dʒʊə) *vb* (*tr*) **1** to renounce or retract, esp formally, solemnly, or under oath **2** to abstain from or reject [C15 from Old French *abjurer* or Latin *abjurāre* to deny on oath] > ˌabju'**ration** *n* > ab'**jurer** *n*

a

Abkhaz (æb'kɑ:z) *n* **1** *pl* **-khaz** Also called: **Abkhazi, Abkhazian** a member of a Georgian people living east of the Black Sea **2** the language of this people, belonging to the North-West Caucasian family

Abkhazia (æb'kɑ:zɪə) *n* an administrative division of NW Georgia, between the Black Sea and the Caucasus Mountains: a subtropical region, with mountains rising over 3900 m (13 000 ft); Abkhazian separatists seized control of the region in 1993. Capital: Sukhumi. Pop: 516 600 (1993 est). Area: 8600 sq km (3320 sq miles). Also called: **Abkhaz Autonomous Republic**

abl. *abbreviation for* **ablative**

ablactation (ˌæblæk'teɪʃən) *n* **1** the weaning of an infant **2** the cessation of milk secretion in the breasts

ablate (æb'leɪt) *vb* (*tr*) to remove by ablation [C20 back formation from ABLATION]

ablation (æb'leɪʃən) *n* **1** the surgical removal of an organ, structure, or part **2** the melting or wearing away of an expendable part, such as the heat shield of a space re-entry vehicle on passing through the earth's atmosphere **3** the wearing away of a rock or glacier [C15 from Late Latin *ablatiōn-*, from Latin *auferre* to carry away, remove]

ablative ('æblətɪv) *grammar* ▷ *adj* **1** (in certain inflected languages such as Latin) denoting a case of nouns, pronouns, and adjectives indicating the agent in passive sentences or the instrument, manner, or place of the action described by the verb ▷ *n* **2 a** the ablative case **b** a word or speech element in the ablative case **3** taking away or removing: *ablative surgery* **4** able to disintegrate or be worn away at a very high temperature: *a thick layer of ablative material*

ablative absolute *n* an absolute construction in Latin grammar in which a governor noun and a modifier in the ablative case function as a sentence modifier; for example, *hostibus victis*, "the enemy having been beaten"

ablator (æb'leɪtə) *n* the heat shield of a space vehicle, which melts or wears away during re-entry into the earth's atmosphere [C20 from ABLATION]

ablaut ('æblaʊt; *German* 'aplaut) *n linguistics* vowel gradation, esp in Indo-European languages. See **gradation** (sense 5) [German, coined 1819 by Jakob Grimm from *ab* off + *Laut* sound]

ablaze (ə'bleɪz) *adj* (*postpositive*) ▷ *adv* **1** on fire; burning **2** brightly illuminated **3** emotionally aroused

able ('eɪbʰl) *adj* **1** (*postpositive*) having the necessary power, resources, skill, time, opportunity, etc, to do something: *able to swim* **2** capable; competent; talented: *an able teacher* **3** *law* qualified, competent, or authorized to do some specific act [C14 ultimately from Latin *habilis* easy to hold, manageable, apt, from *habēre* to have, hold + *-ilis* -ILE]

-able *suffix forming adjectives* **1** capable of, suitable for, or deserving of (being acted upon as indicated): *enjoyable; pitiable; readable; separable; washable* **2** inclined to; given to; able to; causing: *comfortable; reasonable; variable* [via Old French from Latin *-ābilis, -ībilis,* forms of *-bilis,* adjectival suffix] ▷ **-ably** *suffix forming adverbs* ▷ **-ability** *suffix forming nouns*

able-bodied *adj* physically strong and healthy; robust

able-bodied seaman *n* an ordinary seaman, esp one in the merchant navy, who has been trained in certain skills. Also: **able seaman** Abbreviations: **AB, a.b.**

abled ('eɪbʰld) *adj* having a range of physical powers as specified (esp in the phrases **less abled, differently abled**)

ableism ('eɪbʰl,ɪzəm) *n* discrimination against disabled or handicapped people

able rating *n* (esp in the Royal Navy) a rating who is qualified to perform certain duties of seamanship

abloom (ə'bluːm) *adj* (*postpositive*) in flower; blooming

ablution (ə'bluːʃən) *n* **1** the ritual washing of a priest's hands or of sacred vessels **2** (*often plural*) the act of washing (esp in the phrase **perform one's ablutions**) **3** (*plural*) *military informal* a washing place [C14 ultimately from Latin *ablūere* to wash away] ▷ **ab'lutionary** *adj*

ably ('eɪblɪ) *adv* in a competent or skilful manner

ABM *abbreviation for* **antiballistic missile**

Abnaki (æb'nɑːkɪ) *n* **1** (*pl* **-ki** *or* **-kis**) a member of a North American Indian people formerly living in Maine and Quebec **2** the language of this people, belonging to the Algonquian family

abnegate ('æbnɪ,geɪt) *vb* (*tr*) to deny to oneself; renounce (privileges, pleasure, etc) [C17 from Latin *abnegāre* to deny] ▷ **,abne'gation** *n* ▷ **'abne,gator** *n*

Abney level ('æbnɪ) *n* a surveying instrument consisting of a spirit level and a sighting tube, used to measure the angle of inclination of a line from the observer to another point [C20 named after Sir William *Abney* (1843–1920), British chemist and physicist]

abnormal (æb'nɔːməl) *adj* **1** not normal; deviating from the usual or typical; extraordinary **2** *informal* odd in behaviour or appearance; strange [C19 AB-¹ + NORMAL, replacing earlier *anormal* from Medieval Latin *anormalus,* a blend of Late Latin *anōmalus* ANOMALOUS + Latin *abnormis* departing from a rule] ▷ **ab'normally** *adv*

abnormality (,æbnɔː'mælɪtɪ) *n, pl* **-ties 1** an abnormal feature, event, etc **2** a physical malformation; deformity **3** deviation from the typical or usual; irregularity

abnormal psychology *n* the study of behaviour patterns that diverge widely from generally accepted norms, esp those of a pathological nature

Abo ('æbəʊ) *n, pl* **Abos** (*sometimes not capital*) *Austral informal, offensive* **a** short for **Aborigine b** (*as modifier*): *an Abo reserve*

Åbo ('oːbuː) *n* the Swedish name for **Turku**

aboard (ə'bɔːd) *adv, adj* (*postpositive*) ▷ *prep* **1** on, in, onto, or into (a ship, train, aircraft, etc) **2** *nautical* alongside (a vessel) **3** **all aboard!** a warning to passengers to board a vehicle, ship, etc

abode¹ (ə'bəʊd) *n* a place in which one lives; one's home [C17 n formed from ABIDE]

abode² (ə'bəʊd) *vb* a past tense and past participle of **abide**

abohm (æb'əʊm, 'æb,əʊm) *n* the cgs unit of resistance in the electromagnetic system: equivalent to 10⁻⁹ ohm

aboideau ('æbə,dəʊ) *or* **aboiteau** ('æbə,təʊ) *n, pl* **-deaus, -deaux** (-,dəʊz) *or* **-teaus, -teaux** (-,təʊz) (in the Canadian Maritimes) **1** a dyke with a sluicegate that allows flood water to drain but keeps the sea water out **2** a sluicegate in a dyke [Canadian French]

abolish (ə'bɒlɪʃ) *vb* (*tr*) to do away with (laws, regulations, customs, etc); put an end to [C15 from Old French *aboliss-* (lengthened stem of *abolir*), ultimately from Latin *abolēre* to destroy] ▷ **a'bolishable** *adj* ▷ **a'bolisher** *n* ▷ **a'bolishment** *n*

abolition (,æbə'lɪʃən) *n* **1** the act of abolishing or the state of being abolished; annulment **2** (*often capital*) (in British territories) the ending of the slave trade (1807) or the ending of slavery (1833): accomplished after a long campaign led by William Wilberforce **3** (*often capital*) (in the US) the emancipation of the slaves, accomplished by the Emancipation Proclamation issued in 1863 and ratified in 1865 [C16 from Latin *abolitio,* from *abolēre* to destroy] ▷ **,abo'litionary** *adj* ▷ **,abo'litionism** *n* ▷ **,abo'litionist** *n, adj*

abomasum (,æbə'meɪsəm) *n* the fourth and last compartment of the stomach of ruminants, which receives and digests food from the psalterium and passes it on to the small intestine [C18 New Latin, from AB-¹ + *omāsum* bullock's tripe]

A-bomb *n* short for **atomic bomb**

abominable (ə'bɒmɪnəbʰl) *adj* **1** offensive; loathsome; detestable **2** *informal* very bad, unpleasant, or inferior: *abominable weather; abominable workmanship* [C14 from Latin *abōminābilis,* from *abōminārī* to ABOMINATE] ▷ **a'bominably** *adv*

abominable snowman *n* a large legendary manlike or apelike creature, alleged to inhabit the Himalayan Mountains. Also called: **yeti** [a translation of Tibetan *metohkangmi,* from *metoh* foul + *kangmi* snowman]

abominate (ə'bɒmɪ,neɪt) *vb* (*tr*) to dislike intensely; loathe; detest [C17 from the past participle of Latin *abōminārī* to regard as an ill omen, from *ab-* away from + *ōmin-,* from OMEN] ▷ **a'bomi,nator** *n*

abomination (ə,bɒmɪ'neɪʃən) *n* **1** a person or thing that is disgusting **2** an action that is vicious, vile, etc **3** intense loathing

abondance (French abɔ̃dɑ̃s) *n cards* a variant spelling of **abundance** (sense 6)

à bon marché French (a bɔ̃ marʃe) *adv* at a bargain price

aboral (æb'ɔːrəl) *adj zoology* away from or opposite the mouth

aboriginal (,æbə'rɪdʒɪnʰl) *adj* existing in a place from the earliest known period; indigenous; autochthonous ▷ **,abo'riginally** *adv*

Aboriginal (,æbə'rɪdʒɪnʰl) *adj* **1** of, relating to, or characteristic of the native peoples of Australia ▷ *n* **2** another word for an Australian **Aborigine**

Aboriginality (,æbə,rɪdʒɪ'nælɪtɪ) *n* the state of being Aboriginal, esp with regard to having a common Aboriginal culture

aborigine (,æbə'rɪdʒɪnɪ) *n* an original inhabitant of a country or region who has been there from the earliest known times [C16 back formation from *aborigines,* from Latin: inhabitants of Latium in pre-Roman times, probably representing some tribal name but associated in folk etymology with *ab origine* from the beginning]

Aborigine (,æbə'rɪdʒɪnɪ) *n* **1** Also called: **native Australian, Aboriginal,** (*Austral*) **native,** (*Austral*)

Black a member of a dark-skinned hunting and gathering people who were living in Australia when European settlers arrived **2** any of the languages of this people. See also **Australian** (sense 3)

aborning (ə'bɔːnɪŋ) *adv US* while being born, developed, or realized (esp in the phrase **die aborning**) [C20 from A-² + *borning,* from BORN]

abort (ə'bɔːt) *vb* **1** to undergo or cause (a woman) to undergo the termination of pregnancy before the fetus is viable **2** (*tr*) to cause (a fetus) to be expelled from the womb before it is viable **3** (*intr*) to fail to come to completion; go wrong **4** (*tr*) to stop the development of; cause to be abandoned **5** (*intr*) to give birth to a dead or nonviable fetus **6** (of a space flight, military operation, etc) to fail or terminate prematurely **7** (*intr*) (of an organism or part of an organism) to fail to develop into the mature form ▷ *n* **8** the premature termination or failure of (a space flight, military operation, etc) [C16 from Latin *abortāre,* from the past participle of *aborīrī* to miscarry, from *ab-* wrongly, badly + *orīrī* to appear, arise, be born]

abortifacient (ə,bɔːtɪ'feɪʃənt) *adj* **1** causing abortion ▷ *n* **2** a drug or agent that causes abortion

abortion (ə'bɔːʃən) *n* **1** an operation or other procedure to terminate pregnancy before the fetus is viable **2** the premature termination of pregnancy by spontaneous or induced expulsion of a nonviable fetus from the uterus **3** the products of abortion; an aborted fetus **4** the arrest of development of an organ **5** a failure to develop to completion or maturity: *the project proved an abortion* **6** a person or thing that is deformed ▷ **a'bortional** *adj*

abortionist (ə'bɔːʃənɪst) *n* **1** a person who performs abortions, esp illegally **2** a person who is in favour of abortion on demand

abortion pill *n* a drug, such as mifepristone, used to terminate a pregnancy in its earliest stage

abortive (ə'bɔːtɪv) *adj* **1** failing to achieve a purpose; fruitless **2** (of organisms) imperfectly developed; rudimentary **3** causing abortion; abortifacient

ABO system *n* a system for classifying human blood on the basis of the presence or absence of two antigens on the red cell membrane: there are four such blood types (A, B, AB, and O)

Aboukir Bay *or* **Abukir Bay** (,æbuː'kɪə) *n* a bay on the N coast of Egypt, where the Nile enters the Mediterranean: site of the Battle of the Nile (1798), in which Nelson defeated the French fleet. Arabic name: Abu Qîr (abu'kiːr)

aboulia (ə'buːlɪə, -'bjuː-) *n* a variant spelling of **abulia**

abound (ə'baʊnd) *vb* (*intr*) **1** to exist or occur in abundance; be plentiful: *a swamp in which snakes abound* **2** (foll by *with* or *in*) to be plentifully supplied (with); teem (with): *the gardens abound with flowers; the fields abound in corn* [C14 via Old French from Latin *abundāre* to overflow, from *undāre* to flow, from *unda* wave]

about (ə'baʊt) *prep* **1** relating to; concerning; on the subject of **2** near or close to (in space or time) **3** carried on: *I haven't any money about me* **4** on every side of; all the way around **5** active in or engaged in: *she is about her business* **6** about to **a** on the point of; intending to: *she was about to jump* **b** (with a negative) determined not to: *nobody is about to miss it* ▷ *adv* **7** approximately; near in number, time, degree, etc: *about 50 years old* **8** nearby **9** here and there; from place to place; in no particular direction: *walk about to keep warm* **10** all around; on every side **11** in or to the opposite direction: *he turned about and came back* **12** in rotation or revolution: *turn and turn about* **13** used in informal phrases to indicate understatement: *I've had just about enough of your insults; it's about time you stopped* **14** *archaic* in circumference; around ▷ *adj* **15** (*predicative*) active; astir after sleep: *up and about* **16** (*predicative*) in existence, current, or in circulation:

there aren't many about nowadays [Old English *abūtan*, *onbūtan* on the outside of, around, from ON + *būtan* outside]

about-ship *vb* -ships, -shipping, -shipped (*intr*) *nautical* to manoeuvre a vessel onto a new tack

about turn or *US* **about face** *interj* **1** a military command to a formation of men to reverse the direction in which they are facing ▷ *n* about-turn or *US* about-face **2** a complete change or reversal, as of opinion, attitude, direction, etc ▷ *vb* about-turn or *US* about-face **3** (*intr*) to perform an about-turn

above (ə'bʌv) *prep* **1** on top of or higher than; over: *the sky above the earth* **2** greater than in quantity or degree: *above average in weight* **3** superior to or prior to: *to place honour above wealth* **4** too honourable or high-minded for: *above petty gossiping* **5** too respected for; beyond: *above suspicion; above reproach* **6** too difficult to be understood by: *the talk was above me* **7** louder or higher than (other noise): *I heard her call above the radio* **8** in preference to: *I love you above all others* **9** north of: *which town lies just above London?* **10** upstream from **11** above all most of all; especially **12** above and beyond in addition to **13** above oneself presumptuous or conceited ▷ *adv* **14** in or to a higher place: *the sky above* **15 a** in a previous place (in something written) **b** (in combination): *the above-mentioned clause* **16** higher in rank or position **17** in or concerned with heaven: *seek the things that are above* ▷ *n* **18** the above something that is above or previously mentioned ▷ *adj* **19** mentioned or appearing in a previous place (in something written) [Old English *abufan*, from *a-* on + *bufan* above]

above board *adj* (**aboveboard** when prenominal) ▷ *adv* in the open; without dishonesty, concealment, or fraud

above-the-line *adj* **1** denoting entries printed above the horizontal line on a company's profit-and-loss account separating the entries that show how the profit (or loss) was made from the entries showing how the profit is to be distributed **2** (of an advertising campaign) employing an advertising agency to use the press, television, radio, cinema, and posters **3** (in national accounts) denoting transactions concerned with revenue shown above a horizontal line that separates them from capital transactions. Compare **below-the-line**

ab ovo *Latin* (æb 'əʊvəʊ) from the beginning [literally: from the egg]

Abp or **abp** *abbreviation for* archbishop

abracadabra (ˌæbrəkə'dæbrə) *interj* **1** a spoken formula, used esp by conjurors ▷ *n* **2** a word used in incantations, etc, considered to possess magic powers **3** gibberish; nonsense [c17 from Latin: magical word used in certain Gnostic writings, perhaps related to Greek *Abraxas; see* ABRAXAS]

abrade (ə'breɪd) *vb* (*tr*) to scrape away or wear down by friction; erode [c17 from Latin *abrādere* to scrape away, from AB-¹ + *rādere* to scrape] > a'bradant *n* > a'brader *n*

Abraham ('eɪbrə,hæm, -həm) *n* **1** *Old Testament* the first of the patriarchs, the father of Isaac and the founder of the Hebrew people (Genesis 11–25) **2** Abraham's bosom the place where the just repose after death (Luke 16:22)

abranchiate (ə'bræŋkɪɪt, -,eɪt) or **abranchial** *adj zoology* having no gills [c19 A-¹ + BRANCHIATE]

abrasion (ə'breɪʒən) *n* **1** the process of scraping or wearing down by friction **2** a scraped area or spot; graze **3** *geography* the effect of mechanical erosion of rock, esp a river bed, by rock fragments scratching and scraping it; wearing down. Compare **attrition** (sense 4f), **corrasion** [c17 from Medieval Latin *abrāsiōn-*, from the past participle of Latin *abrādere* to ABRADE]

abrasive (ə'breɪsɪv) *n* **1** a substance or material such as sandpaper, pumice, or emery, used for cleaning, grinding, smoothing, or polishing ▷ *adj* **2** causing abrasion; grating; rough **3** irritating in manner or personality; causing tension or

annoyance > a'brasiveness *n*

abraxas (ə'bræksəs) or **abrasax** (ə'bræsəks) *n* an ancient charm composed of Greek letters: originally believed to have magical powers and inscribed on amulets, etc, but from the second century AD personified by Gnostics as a deity, the source of divine emanations [from Greek: invented word]

abreact (ˌæbrɪ'ækt) *vb* (*tr*) *psychoanal* to alleviate (emotional tension) through abreaction

abreaction (ˌæbrɪ'ækʃən) *n psychoanal* the release and expression of emotional tension associated with repressed ideas by bringing those ideas into consciousness

abreast (ə'brest) *adj* (*postpositive*) **1** alongside each other and facing in the same direction **2** (foll by *of* or *with*) up to date (with); fully conversant (with)

abri (æ'bri:) *n* a shelter or place of refuge, esp in wartime [French, from Latin *apricum* an open place]

abridge (ə'brɪdʒ) *vb* (*tr*) **1** to reduce the length of (a written work) by condensing or rewriting **2** to curtail; diminish **3** *archaic* to deprive of (privileges, rights, etc) [c14 via Old French *abregier* from Late Latin *abbreviāre* to shorten] > a'bridgable or a'bridgeable *adj* > a'bridger *n*

abridgment or **abridgement** (ə'brɪdʒmənt) *n* **1** a shortened version of a written work **2** the act of abridging or state of being abridged

abroach (ə'brəʊtʃ) *adj* (*postpositive*) (of a cask, barrel, etc) tapped; broached [c14 from Old French *abrochier* from *a-* to + *brochier* to BROACH¹]

abroad (ə'brɔ:d) *adv* **1** to or in a foreign country or countries ▷ *adj* (*postpositive*) **2** (of news, rumours, etc) in general circulation; current **3** out in the open **4** over a wide area **5** *archaic* in error [c13 from A-² + BROAD]

abrogate ('æbrəʊ,geɪt) *vb* (*tr*) to cancel or revoke formally or officially; repeal; annul [c16 from Latin *abrogātus* repealed, from AB-¹ + *rogāre* to propose (a law)] > ,abro'gation *n* > 'abro,gator *n*

abrupt (ə'brʌpt) *adj* **1** sudden; unexpected **2** brusque or brief in speech, manner, etc; curt **3** (of a style of writing or speaking) making sharp transitions from one subject to another; disconnected **4** precipitous; steep **5** *botany* shaped as though a part has been cut off; truncate **6** *geology* (of strata) cropping out suddenly [c16 from Latin *abruptus* broken off, from AB-¹ + *rumpere* to break] > ab'ruptly *adv* > ab'ruptness *n*

abruption (ə'brʌpʃən) *n* a breaking off of a part or parts from a mass [c17 from Latin *abruptio; see* ABRUPT]

Abruzzi (*Italian* a'bruttsi) or **Abruzzo** (*Italian* a'bruttso) *n* a region of S central Italy, between the Apennines and the Adriatic: separated from the former administrative region **Abruzzi e Molise** in 1965. Capital: Aquila. Pop: 1 273 284 (2003 est.). Area: 10 794 sq km (4210 sq miles)

abs (æbz) *pl n informal* abdominal muscles

ABS *abbreviation for* acrylonitrile-butadiene-styrene: any of a range of tough copolymers used esp for making moulded articles

Absalom ('æbsələm) *n Old Testament* the third son of David, who rebelled against his father and was eventually killed by Joab (II Samuel 15–18)

ABS brake *n* another name for **antilock brake** [from German *Antiblockiersystem*]

abscess ('æbses, -sɪs) *n* **1** a localized collection of pus formed as the product of inflammation and usually caused by bacteria ▷ *vb* **2** (*intr*) to form such a collection of pus [c16 from Latin *abscessus* a going away, a throwing off of bad humours, hence an abscess, from *abscēdere* to go away] > 'abscessed *adj*

abscise (æb'saɪz) *vb* to separate or be separated by abscission [c17 from Latin *abscisus*, from *abscīdere* to cut off]

abscissa (æb'sɪsə) *n, pl* -scissas or -scissae (-'sɪsi:) the horizontal or x-coordinate of a point in a two-dimensional system of Cartesian coordinates. It is

the distance from the y-axis measured parallel to the x-axis. Compare **ordinate** [c17 New Latin, originally *linea abscissa* a cut-off line]

abscission (æb'sɪʒən, -'sɪʃ-) *n* **1** the separation of leaves, branches, flowers, and bark from plants by the formation of an abscission layer **2** the act of cutting off [c17 from Latin *abscissiōn-*, from AB-¹ + *scissiō* a cleaving]

abscission layer *n* a layer of parenchyma cells that is formed at the bases of fruits, flowers, and leaves before abscission. As the parenchyma disintegrates, the organ becomes separated from the plant

abscond (əb'skɒnd) *vb* (*intr*) to run away secretly, esp from an open institution or to avoid prosecution or punishment [c16 from Latin *abscondere* to hide, put away, from *abs-* AB-¹ + *condere* to stow] > ab'sconder *n*

abseil ('æbseɪl) *vb* (*intr*) **1** *mountaineering* to descend a steep slope or vertical drop by a rope secured from above and coiled around one's body or through karabiners attached to one's body in order to control the speed of descent **2** to descend by rope from a helicopter ▷ *n* **3** an instance or the technique of abseiling ▷ Also called: **rappel** [c20 from German *abseilen* to descend by a rope, from *ab-* down + *Seil* rope]

absence ('æbsəns) *n* **1** the state of being away **2** the time during which a person or thing is away **3** the fact of being without something; lack [c14 via Old French from Latin *absentia*, from *absēns* a being away]

absent *adj* ('æbsənt) **1** away or not present **2** lacking; missing **3** inattentive; absent-minded ▷ *vb* (æb'sent) **4** (*tr*) to remove (oneself) or keep away [c14 from Latin *absent-*, stem of *absēns*, present participle of *abesse* to be away] > ab'senter *n*

absentee (ˌæbsən'ti:) *n* **a** a person who is absent **b** (as modifier): *an absentee voter*

absenteeism (ˌæbsən'ti:ɪzəm) *n* persistent absence from work, school, etc

absentee landlord *n* a landlord who does not live in or near a property from which he draws an income

absente reo (æb'sentɪ 'ri:əʊ) *law* in the absence of the defendant [Latin, literally: the defendant being absent]

absently ('æbsəntlɪ) *adv* in an absent-minded or preoccupied manner; inattentively

absent-minded *adj* preoccupied; forgetful; inattentive > ,absent-'mindedly *adv* > ,absent-'mindedness *n*

absent without leave *adj military* the full form of AWOL

absinthe or **absinth** ('æbsɪnθ) *n* **1** a potent green alcoholic drink, technically a gin, originally having high wormwood content **2** another name for **wormwood** (the plant) [c15 via French and Latin from Greek *apsinthion* wormwood]

absinthism ('æbsɪn,θɪzəm) *n pathol* a diseased condition resulting from excessive drinking of absinthe

absit omen *Latin* ('æbsɪt 'əʊmen) may the presentiment not become real or take place [literally: may the (evil) omen be absent]

absolute ('æbsə,lu:t) *adj* **1** complete; perfect **2** free from limitations, restrictions, or exceptions; unqualified: *an absolute choice* **3** having unlimited authority; despotic: *an absolute ruler* **4** undoubted; certain: *the absolute truth* **5** not dependent on, conditioned by, or relative to anything else; independent: *an absolute term in logic; the absolute value of a quantity in physics* **6** pure; unmixed: *absolute alcohol* **7** (of a grammatical construction) syntactically independent of the main clause, as for example the construction *Joking apart* in the sentence *Joking apart, we'd better leave now* **8** *grammar* (of a transitive verb) used without a direct object, as the verb *intimidate* in the sentence *His intentions are good, but his rough manner tends to intimidate* **9** *grammar* (of an adjective) used as a noun, as for

a

instance *young* and *aged* in the sentence *The young care little for the aged* **10** *physics* **a** (*postpositive*) (of a pressure measurement) not relative to atmospheric pressure: *the pressure was 5 bar absolute.* Compare **gauge** (sense 18) **b** denoting absolute or thermodynamic temperature **11** *maths* **a** (of a constant) never changing in value **b** Also: **numerical** (of an inequality) unconditional **c** (of a term) not containing a variable **12** *law* (of a court order or decree) coming into effect immediately and not liable to be modified; final. See **decree absolute 13** *law* (of a title to property, etc) not subject to any encumbrance or condition ▷ *n* **14** something that is absolute [C14 from Latin *absolūtus* unconditional, freed from, from *absolvere*. See ABSOLVE]

Absolute ('æbsə,luːt) *n* (*sometimes not capital*) **1** *philosophy* **a** the ultimate basis of reality **b** that which is totally unconditioned, unrestricted, pure, perfect, or complete **2** (in the philosophy of Hegel) that towards which all things evolve dialectically

absolute alcohol *n* a liquid containing at least 99 per cent of pure ethanol by weight

absolute ceiling *n* the maximum height above sea level, usually measured in feet or metres, at which an aircraft can maintain horizontal flight. Compare **service ceiling**

absolute configuration *n* *chem* the spatial arrangement of atoms or groups in a chemical compound about an asymmetric atom. Also called: **absolute stereochemistry**. See **chirality**

absolute humidity *n* the humidity of the atmosphere, usually expressed as the number of grams of water contained in 1 cubic metre of air. Compare **relative humidity**

absolute judgment *n* *psychol* any judgment about a single stimulus, eg about the value of one of its properties or about whether it is present or absent. Compare **comparative judgment**

absolutely (,æbsə'luːtlɪ) *adv* **1** in an absolute manner, esp completely or perfectly ▷ *sentence substitute* **2** yes; certainly; unquestionably

absolute magnitude *n* the apparent magnitude a given star would have if it were situated at a distance of 10 parsecs (32.6 light years) from the earth

absolute majority *n* a number of votes totalling over 50 per cent, such as the total number of votes or seats obtained by a party that beats the combined opposition. Compare **relative majority**

absolute monarchy *n* a monarchy without constitutional limits. Compare **constitutional monarchy**

absolute music *n* music that is not designed to depict or evoke any scene or event. Compare **programme music**

absolute pitch *n* **1** Also called (not in technical usage): **perfect pitch** the ability to identify exactly the pitch of a note without comparing it to another **2** the exact pitch of a note determined by its number of vibrations per second

absolute temperature *n* another name for **thermodynamic temperature**

absolute threshold *n* *psychol* the minimum intensity of a stimulus at which it can just be perceived. Compare **difference threshold**

absolute unit *n* **1** a unit of measurement forming part of the electromagnetic cgs system, such as an abampere or abcoulomb **2** a unit of measurement forming part of a system of units that includes a unit of force defined so that it is independent of the acceleration of free fall

absolute value *n* *maths* **1** the positive real number equal to a given real but disregarding its sign. Written $|x|$. Where *r* is positive, $|r| = r = |−r|$ **2** Also called: **modulus** a measure of the magnitude of a complex number, represented by the length of a line in the Argand diagram: $|x + iy| = \sqrt{(x^2+y^2)}$, so $|4 + 3i| = 5$

absolute viscosity *n* a full name for **viscosity**, used to distinguish it from kinematic viscosity

and specific viscosity

absolute zero *n* the lowest temperature theoretically attainable, at which the particles constituting matter would be in the lowest energy states available; the zero of thermodynamic temperature; zero on the International Practical Scale of Temperature: equivalent to −273.15°C or −459.67°F

absolution (,æbsə'luːʃən) *n* **1** the act of absolving or the state of being absolved; release from guilt, obligation, or punishment **2** *Christianity* **a** a formal remission of sin pronounced by a priest in the sacrament of penance **b** the prescribed form of words granting such a remission [C12 from Latin *absolūtiōn-* acquittal, forgiveness of sins, from *absolvere* to ABSOLVE] > **absolutory** (æb'sɒljutərɪ, -trɪ) *adj*

absolutism ('æbsəlu:,tɪzəm) *n* **1** the principle or practice of a political system in which unrestricted power is vested in a monarch, dictator, etc; despotism **2** *philosophy* **a** any theory which holds that truth or moral or aesthetic value is absolute and universal and not relative to individual or social differences. Compare **relativism b** the doctrine that reality is unitary and unchanging and that change and diversity are mere illusion. See also **monism** (sense 2), **pluralism** (sense 5b) **3** *Christianity* an uncompromising form of the doctrine of predestination > '**abso,lutist** *n, adj*

absolve (əb'zɒlv) *vb* (*tr*) **1** (usually foll by *from*) to release from blame, sin, punishment, obligation, or responsibility **2** to pronounce not guilty; acquit; pardon [C15 from Latin *absolvere* to free from, from AB-¹ + *solvere* to make loose] > ab'**solvable** *adj* > ab'**solver** *n*

absorb (əb'sɔːb, -'zɔːb) *vb* (*tr*) **1** to soak or suck up (liquids) **2** to engage or occupy (the interest, attention, or time) of (someone); engross **3** to receive or take in (the energy of an impact) **4** *physics* to take in (all or part of incident radiated energy) and retain the part that is not reflected or transmitted **5** to take in or assimilate; incorporate **6** to accept and find a market for (goods, etc) **7** to pay for as part of a commercial transaction: *the distributor absorbed the cost of transport* **8** *chem* to cause to undergo a process in which one substance, usually a liquid or gas, permeates into or is dissolved by a liquid or solid: *porous solids absorb water; hydrochloric acid absorbs carbon dioxide* Compare **adsorb** [C15 via Old French from Latin *absorbēre* to suck, swallow, from AB-¹ + *sorbēre* to suck] > ab,sorba'**bility** *n* > ab'**sorbable** *adj*

absorbance (əb'sɔːbəns, -'zɔː-) *n* *physics* a measure of the light-absorbing ability of an object, expressed as the logarithm to base 10 of the reciprocal of the internal transmittance. See **transmittance**

absorbed (əb'sɔːbd, -'zɔːbd) *adj* engrossed; deeply interested > absorbedly (əb'sɔːbɪdlɪ, -'zɔː-) *adv*

absorbed dose *n* the amount of energy transferred by nuclear or ionizing radiation to a unit mass of absorbing material

absorbefacient (əb,sɔːbɪ'feɪʃənt, -,zɔː-) *med* ▷ *n* **1** a medicine or other agent that promotes absorption ▷ *adj* **2** causing or promoting absorption

absorbent (əb'sɔːbənt, -'zɔː-) *adj* **1** able to absorb ▷ *n* **2** a substance that absorbs > ab'**sorbency** *n*

absorbent cotton *n* a US term for **cotton wool** (sense 1)

absorber (əb'sɔːbə, -'zɔː-) *n* **1** a person or thing that absorbs **2** *physics* a material that absorbs radiation or causes it to lose energy

absorbing (əb'sɔːbɪŋ, -'zɔː-) *adj* occupying one's interest or attention; engrossing; gripping > ab'**sorbingly** *adv*

absorptance (əb'sɔːptəns, -'zɔː-) *or* **absorption factor** *n* *physics* a measure of the ability of an object to absorb radiation, equal to the ratio of the absorbed radiant flux to the incident flux. For a layer of material the ratio of the flux absorbed between the entry and exit surfaces of the layer to

the flux leaving the entry surface is the **internal absorptance**. Symbol: α Compare **reflectance, transmittance** [C20 ABSORPTION + -ANCE]

absorption (əb'sɔːpʃən, -'zɔːp-) *n* **1** the process of absorbing or the state of being absorbed **2** *physiol* **a** normal assimilation by the tissues of the products of digestion **b** the passage of a gas, fluid, drug, etc, through the mucous membranes or skin **3** *physics* a reduction of the intensity of any form of radiated energy as a result of energy conversion in a medium, such as the conversion of sound energy into heat **4** *immunol* the process of removing superfluous antibodies or antigens from a mixture using a reagent [C16 from Latin *absorptiōn-*, from *absorbēre* to ABSORB] > ab'**sorptive** *adj*

absorption costing *n* a method of cost accounting in which overheads are apportioned to cost centres, where they are absorbed using predetermined rates. Compare **marginal costing**

absorption spectrum *n* the characteristic pattern of dark lines or bands that occurs when electromagnetic radiation is passed through an absorbing medium into a spectroscope. An equivalent pattern occurs as coloured lines or bands in the emission spectrum of that medium

absorptivity (,æbsɔːp'tɪvɪtɪ, -zɔːp-) *n* *physics* a measure of the ability of a material to absorb radiation, equal to the internal absorptance of a homogeneous layer of the material under conditions in which the path of the radiation has unit length and the boundaries of the layer have no influence

absquatulate (æb'skwɒtjʊ,leɪt) *vb* (*intr*) to leave; decamp [C19 humorous formation as if from Latin]

abstain (əb'steɪn) *vb* (*intr*; usually foll by *from*) **1** to choose to refrain: *he abstained from alcohol* **2** to refrain from voting, esp in a committee, legislature, etc [C14 via Old French from Latin *abstinēre*, from *abs-* AB-¹ + *tenēre* to hold, keep] > ab'**stainer** *n*

abstemious (əb'stiːmɪəs) *adj* moderate or sparing, esp in the consumption of alcohol or food; temperate [C17 from Latin *abstēmius*, from *abs-* AB-¹ + *tēm-*, from *tēmētum* intoxicating drink] > ab'**stemiously** *adv* > ab'**stemiousness** *n*

abstention (əb'stenʃən) *n* **1** a voluntary decision not to act; the act of refraining or abstaining **2** the act of withholding one's vote [C16 from Late Latin *abstentiōn-*, from *abstinēre*. See ABSTAIN] > ab'**stentious** *adj*

abstergent (əb'stɜːdʒənt) *adj* cleansing or scouring [C17 from Latin *abstergent-*, *abstērgens* wiping off, from *abs-* away, off + *tergēre* to wipe]

abstinence ('æbstɪnəns) *n* **1** the act or practice of refraining from some action or from the use of something, esp alcohol **2** *chiefly RC Church* the practice of refraining from specific kinds of food or drink, esp from meat, as an act of penance [C13 via Old French from Latin *abstinentia*, from *abstinēre* to ABSTAIN] > '**abstinent** *adj*

abstract *adj* ('æbstrækt) **1** having no reference to material objects or specific examples; not concrete **2** not applied or practical; theoretical **3** hard to understand; recondite; abstruse **4** denoting art characterized by geometric, formalized, or otherwise nonrepresentational qualities **5** defined in terms of its formal properties: *an abstract machine* **6** *philosophy* (of an idea) functioning for some empiricists as the meaning of a general term: *the word "man" does not name all men but the abstract idea of manhood* ▷ *n* ('æbstrækt) **7** a condensed version of a piece of writing, speech, etc; summary **8** an abstract term or idea **9** an abstract painting, sculpture, etc **10** in the abstract without reference to specific circumstances or practical experience ▷ *vb* (æb'strækt) (*tr*) **11** to think of (a quality or concept) generally without reference to a specific example; regard theoretically **12** to form (a general idea) by abstraction **13** ('æbstrækt) (*also intr*) to summarize or epitomize **14** to remove or extract **15** *euphemistic* to steal [c14 (in the sense: extracted): from Latin *abstractus* drawn off, removed from (something specific), from abs- AB-¹ + *trahere* to draw]

abstracted (æb'stræktɪd) *adj* **1** lost in thought; preoccupied **2** taken out or separated; extracted > ab'stractedly *adv* > ab'stractedness *n*

abstract expressionism *n* a school of painting in New York in the 1940s that combined the spontaneity of expressionism with abstract forms in unpremeditated, apparently random, compositions. See also **action painting, tachisme**

abstraction (æb'strækʃən) *n* **1** absence of mind; preoccupation **2** the process of formulating generalized ideas or concepts by extracting common qualities from specific examples **3** an idea or concept formulated in this way: *good and evil are abstractions* **4** *logic* an operator that forms a class name or predicate from any given expression. See also **lambda calculus 5** an abstract painting, sculpture, etc **6** the act of withdrawing or removing > ab'stractive *adj* > ab'stractively *adv*

abstractionism (æb'strækʃə,nɪzəm) *n* the theory and practice of the abstract, esp of abstract art > ab'stractionist *n*

abstract noun *n* a noun that refers to an abstract concept, as for example *kindness*. Compare **concrete noun**

abstract of title *n* *property law* a summary of the ownership of land, showing the original grant, conveyances, and any incumbrances

abstriction (æb'strɪkʃən) *n* the separation and release of a mature spore from a sporophore by the formation of a septum. This process occurs in some fungi [c17 from Latin AB-¹ + *strictio* a binding, from *stringere* to bind]

abstruse (əb'struːs) *adj* not easy to understand; recondite; esoteric [c16 from Latin *abstrūsus* thrust away, concealed, from abs- AB-¹ + *trūdere* to thrust] > ab'strusely *adv* > ab'struseness *n*

absurd (əb'sɜːd) *adj* **1** at variance with reason; manifestly false **2** ludicrous; ridiculous ▷ *n* **3** *philosophy* (*sometimes capital; often preceded by the*) the conception of the world, esp in Existentialist thought, as neither designed nor predictable but irrational and meaningless ▷ See also **theatre of the absurd** [c16 via French from Latin *absurdus* dissonant, senseless, from AB-¹ (intensive) + *surdus* dull-sounding, indistinct] > ab'surdity *or* ab'surdness *n* > ab'surdly *adv*

ABTA ('æbtə) *n acronym for* Association of British Travel Agents

Abu Dhabi ('æbuː 'dɑːbɪ) *n* a sheikhdom (emirate) of SE Arabia, on the S coast of the Persian Gulf: the chief sheikhdom and capital of the United Arab Emirates, consisting principally of the port of Abu Dhabi and a desert hinterland; contains major oilfields. Pop: 476 000 (2005 est). Area: 67 350 sq km (25 998 sq miles)

Abuja (ə'buːdʒə) *n* the federal capital of Nigeria, in the centre of the country. Pop: 467 000 (2005 est)

Abukir Bay (,æbuː'kɪə) *n* a variant spelling of Aboukir Bay

abulia *or* **aboulia** (ə'buːlɪə, -'bjuː-) *n psychiatry* a pathological inability to take decisions [c19 New Latin, from Greek *aboulia* lack of resolution, from A-¹ + *boulē* will] > a'bulic *adj*

abundance (ə'bʌndəns) *n* **1** a copious supply; great amount **2** fullness or benevolence: *from the abundance of my heart* **3** degree of plentifulness **4** *chem* the extent to which an element or ion occurs in the earth's crust or some other specified environment: often expressed in parts per million or as a percentage **5** *physics* the ratio of the number of atoms of a specific isotope in a mixture of isotopes of an element to the total number of atoms present: often expressed as a percentage: *the abundance of neon-22 in natural neon is 8.82 per cent* **6** Also called: **abondance** a call in solo whist undertaking to make nine tricks **7** affluence [c14

via Old French from Latin *abundantia,* from *abundāre* to ABOUND]

abundant (ə'bʌndənt) *adj* **1** existing in plentiful supply **2** (*postpositive;* foll by *in*) having a plentiful supply (of) **3** (of a chemical element or mineral) occurring to an extent specified in relation to other elements or minerals in the earth's crust or some other specified environment **4** (of an isotope) occurring to an extent specified in relation to other isotopes in a mixture of isotopes [c14 from Latin *abundant-,* present participle of *abundāre* to ABOUND]

abundantly (ə'bʌndəntlɪ) *adv* **1** very: *he made his disagreement with her abundantly clear* **2** plentifully; in abundance

ab urbe condita *Latin* (æb 'ɜːbɪ 'kɒndɪtə) the full form of **AUC** (sense a) [literally: from the founding of the city]

A bursary *n NZ* the higher of two bursaries available for students entering university, polytechnic, etc. Compare **B bursary**

abuse *vb* (ə'bjuːz) (*tr*) **1** to use incorrectly or improperly; misuse **2** to maltreat, esp physically or sexually **3** to speak insultingly or cruelly to; revile **4** (*reflexive*) to masturbate ▷ *n* (ə'bjuːs) **5** improper, incorrect, or excessive use; misuse **6** maltreatment of a person; injury **7** insulting, contemptuous, or coarse speech **8** an evil, unjust, or corrupt practice **9** See **child abuse 10** *archaic* a deception [C14 (vb): via Old French from Latin *abūsus,* past participle of *abūtī* to misuse, from AB-¹ + *ūtī* to USE] > a'buser *n*

Abu Simbel (,æbuː 'sɪmbəl) *n* a former village in S Egypt: site of two temples of Rameses II, which were moved to higher ground (1966–67) before the area behind the Aswan High Dam was flooded. Also called: Ipsambul

abusive (ə'bjuːsɪv) *adj* **1** characterized by insulting or coarse language **2** characterized by maltreatment **3** incorrectly used; corrupt > a'busively *adv* > a'busiveness *n*

abut (ə'bʌt) *vb* abuts, abutting, abutted (usually foll by *on, upon,* or *against*) to adjoin, touch, or border on (something) at one end [c15 from Old French *abouter* to join at the ends, border on; influenced by *abuter* to touch at an end, buttress]

abutilon (ə'bjuːtɪlən) *n* any shrub or herbaceous plant of the malvaceous genus *Abutilon,* such as the flowering maple, that have showy white, yellow, or red flowers [c18 New Latin from Arabic]

abutment (ə'bʌtmənt) *or* **abuttal** *n* **1** the state or process of abutting **2 a** something that abuts **b** the thing on which something abuts **c** the point of junction between them **3** *architect, civil engineering* a construction that takes the thrust of an arch or vault or supports the end of a bridge

abuttals (ə'bʌtəlz) *pl n property law* the boundaries of a plot of land where it abuts against other property

abutter (ə'bʌtə) *n property law* the owner of adjoining property

abuzz (ə'bʌz) *adj* (*postpositive*) humming, as with conversation, activity, etc; buzzing

ABV *abbreviation for* alcohol by volume: the number of ml of ethyl alcohol present in each 100 ml of an alcoholic beverage when measured at 20°C; displayed on the packaging of alcoholic drinks in EU countries and used to calculate the amount of tax payable

abvolt ('æb,vəʊlt) *n* the cgs unit of potential difference in the electromagnetic system; the potential difference between two points when work of 1 erg must be done to transfer 1 abcoulomb of charge from one point to the other: equivalent to 10⁻⁸ volt

abwatt ('æb,wɒt) *n* the cgs unit of power in the electromagnetic system, equal to the power dissipated when a current of 1 abampere flows across a potential difference of 1 abvolt: equivalent to 10⁻⁷ watt

aby *or* **abye** (ə'baɪ) *vb* abys *or* abyes, abying, abought (*tr*) *archaic* to pay the penalty for; redeem

[Old English *ābycgan* to pay for, atone for, from *bycgan* to buy]

Abydos (ə'baɪdəs) *n* **1** an ancient town in central Egypt: site of many temples and tombs **2** an ancient Greek colony on the Asiatic side of the Dardanelles (Hellespont): scene of the legend of Hero and Leander

abysm (ə'bɪzəm) *n* an archaic word for **abyss** [c13 via Old French from Medieval Latin *abysmus* ABYSS]

abysmal (ə'bɪzməl) *adj* **1** immeasurable; very great: *abysmal stupidity* **2** *informal* extremely bad: *an abysmal film* > a'bysmally *adv*

abyss (ə'bɪs) *n* **1** a very deep or unfathomable gorge or chasm **2** anything that appears to be endless or immeasurably deep, such as time, despair, or shame **3** hell or the infernal regions conceived of as a bottomless pit [c16 via Late Latin from Greek *abussos* bottomless (as in the phrase *abussos limnē* bottomless lake), from A-¹ + *bussos* depth]

abyssal (ə'bɪsəl) *adj* **1** of or belonging to the ocean depths, esp below 2000 metres (6500 feet): *abyssal zone* **2** *geology* another word for **plutonic**

Abyssinia (,æbɪ'sɪnɪə) *n* a former name for Ethiopia

Abyssinian (,æbɪ'sɪnɪən) *n* **1** a native or inhabitant of Abyssinia ▷ *adj* **2** of or relating to Abyssinia or its inhabitants

Abyssinian cat *n* a variety of cat with a long body and a short brown coat with black or dark brown markings

Abyssinian guinea pig *n* a breed of short-haired guinea pig with rosettes all over its body

abyssopelagic (ə,bɪsəʊpə'lædʒɪk) *adj* referring to or occurring in the region of deep water above the floor of the ocean

ac the internet domain name for Ascension Island

Ac the chemical symbol for actinium

AC *abbreviation for* **1 alternating current.** Compare **DC 2** ante Christum [Latin: before Christ] **3** Air Corps **4** athletic club **5** Companion of the Order of Australia **6** appellation d'origine contrôlée: the highest French wine classification; indicates that the wine meets strict requirements concerning area of production, strength, etc. Compare *VDQS vin de pays vin de table* **7** Aelodau'r Cynulliad: Member of the Assembly (that is, the National Assembly of Wales)

a.c. *obsolete abbreviation for* (in prescriptions) ante cibum [Latin: before meals]

a/c *book-keeping abbreviation for* **1** account **2** account current

A/C (in Canada) *abbreviation for* Air Commodore

ACA *abbreviation for* Associate of the Institute of Chartered Accountants

acacia (ə'keɪʃə) *n* **1** any shrub or tree of the tropical and subtropical leguminous genus *Acacia,* having compound or reduced leaves and small yellow or white flowers in dense inflorescences. See also **wattle** (sense 4) **2** false acacia another name for **locust** (senses 2, 3) **3** gum acacia another name for **gum arabic** [c16 from Latin, from Greek *akakia,* perhaps related to *akē* point]

academe ('ækə,diːm) *n literary* **1** any place of learning, such as a college or university **2** the grove(s) of Academe the academic world [c16 first used by Shakespeare in *Love's Labour's Lost* (1594); see ACADEMUS]

academia (,ækə'diːmɪə) *n* the academic world

academic (,ækə'dɛmɪk) *adj* **1** belonging or relating to a place of learning, esp a college, university, or academy **2** of purely theoretical or speculative interest: *an academic argument* **3** excessively concerned with intellectual matters and lacking experience of practical affairs **4** (esp of a schoolchild) having an aptitude for study **5** conforming to set rules and traditions; conventional: *an academic painter* **6** relating to studies such as languages, philosophy, and pure science, rather than applied, technical, or professional studies ▷ *n* **7** a member of a college or university > ,aca'demically *adv*

a

academicals (ˌækəˈdɛmɪkᵊlz) *pl n* another term for **academic dress**

academic dress *n* formal dress, usually comprising cap, gown, and hood, worn by university staff and students

academician (əˌkædəˈmɪʃən, ˌækədə-) *n* a member of an academy (sense 1)

academicism (ˌækəˈdɛmɪˌsɪzəm) *or* **academism** (əˈkædəˌmɪzəm) *n* adherence to rules and traditions in art, literature, etc; conventionalism

academy (əˈkædəmɪ) *n, pl* **-mies** **1** an institution or society for the advancement of literature, art, or science **2** a school for training in a particular skill or profession: *a military academy* **3** a secondary school: now used only as part of a name, and often denoting a private school [c16 via Latin from Greek *akadēmeia* name of the grove where Plato taught, named after the legendary hero *Akadēmos*]

Academy (əˈkædəmɪ) *n* **the** **1 a** the grove or garden near Athens where Plato taught in the late 4th century BC **b** the school of philosophy founded by Plato **c** the members of this school and their successors **2** short for the **French Academy**, **Royal Academy**, etc

Academy Award *n* the official name for an **Oscar**

Acadia (əˈkeɪdɪə) *n* **1 a** the Atlantic Provinces of Canada **b** the French-speaking areas of these provinces **2** (formerly) a French colony in the present-day Atlantic Provinces: ceded to Britain in 1713 ▷ French name: **Acadie** (akadi)

Acadian (əˈkeɪdɪən) *adj* **1** denoting or relating to Acadia or its inhabitants ▷ *n* **2** any of the early French settlers in Nova Scotia, many of whom were deported to Louisiana in the 18th century. See also **Cajun**

açaí (*Portuguese* asai) *n* a berry that grows on palm trees in the Brazilian rainforests. Because it is rich in nutrients, it is used to make energy drinks. Also called: **palm berry** [c21 Portuguese]

acajou (ˈækəˌʒuː) *n* **1** a type of mahogany used by cabinet-makers in France **2** a less common name for **cashew** [c18 via French from Portuguese *acajú*, from Tupi]

acalculia (ˌækælˈkjuːlɪə) *n psychol* an inability to make simple mathematical calculations [c20 from A-¹ + Latin *calculāre* to calculate]

acaleph (ˈækəˌlɛf) *n obsolete* any of the coelenterates of the former taxonomic group *Acalephae*, which included the jellyfishes [c18 from New Latin, from Greek *akalēphē* a sting]

acanthaceous (ˌækænˈθeɪʃəs) *adj* **1** of or relating to the *Acanthaceae*, a mainly tropical and subtropical family of flowering plants that includes the acanthus **2** having spiny or prickly outgrowths

acanthine (əˈkænθaɪn, -θiːn) *adj* **1** of or resembling an acanthus **2** decorated with acanthus leaves

acantho- *or before a vowel* **acanth-** *combining form* indicating a spine or thorn: *acanthocephalan* [New Latin from Greek *akanthos* thorn plant, from *akantha* thorn]

acanthocephalan (əˌkænθəʊˈsɛfələn) *n* **1** any of the parasitic wormlike invertebrates of the phylum *Acanthocephala*, the adults of which have a spiny proboscis and live in the intestines of vertebrates ▷ *adj* **2** of, relating to, or belonging to the *Acanthocephala*

acanthoid (əˈkænθɔɪd) *adj* resembling a spine; spiny

acanthopterygian (ˌækənˌθɒptəˈrɪdʒɪən) *adj* **1** of, relating to, or belonging to the *Acanthopterygii*, a large group of teleost fishes having spiny fin rays. The group includes most saltwater bony fishes ▷ *n* **2** any fish belonging to the *Acanthopterygii* ▷ Compare **malacopterygian** [c19 from New Latin *Acanthopterygii*, from ACANTHO- + Greek *pterúgion* fin]

acanthous (əˈkænθəs) *adj* another term for **spinous**

acanthus (əˈkænθəs) *n, pl* **-thuses** *or* **-thi** (-θaɪ) **1** any shrub or herbaceous plant of the genus

Acanthus, native to the Mediterranean region but widely cultivated as ornamental plants, having large spiny leaves and spikes of white or purplish flowers: family *Acanthaceae*. See also **bear's-breech** **2** a carved ornament based on the leaves of the acanthus plant, esp as used on the capital of a Corinthian column [c17 New Latin, from Greek *akanthos*, from *akantha* thorn, spine]

a cappella (ɑː kəˈpɛlə) *adj, adv music* without instrumental accompaniment [Italian: literally, according to (the style of the) chapel]

Acapulco (ˌækəˈpʊlkəʊ; *Spanish* akaˈpulko) *n* a port and resort in SW Mexico, in Guerrero state. Pop: 761 000 (2005 est). Official name: **Acapulco de Juárez** (*Spanish* de ˈxwares)

acariasis (ˌækəˈraɪəsɪs) *n* infestation of the hair follicles and skin with acarids, esp mites [c19 New Latin. See ACARUS, -IASIS]

acaricide (əˈkærɪˌsaɪd) *n* any drug or formulation for killing acarids

acarid (ˈækərɪd) *or* **acaridan** (əˈkærɪdᵊn) *n* **1** any of the small arachnids of the order *Acarina* (or *Acari*), which includes the ticks and mites ▷ *adj* **2** of or relating to the order *Acarina* [c19 from ACARUS]

acaroid (ˈækəˌrɔɪd) *adj* resembling a mite or tick [c19 see ACARUS, -OID]

acaroid gum *or* **resin** *n* a red alcohol-soluble resin that exudes from various species of grass tree, esp *Xanthorrhoea hastilis*, and is used in varnishes, for coating paper, etc. Also called: **gum acaroides, acaroid resin** [c19 *acaroid*, of uncertain origin (apparently not related to ACARUS)]

acarology (ˌækəˈrɒlədʒɪ) *n* the study of mites and ticks

acarpellous *or US* **acarpelous** (eɪˈkɑːpələs) *adj* (of flowers) having no carpels

acarpous (eɪˈkɑːpəs) *adj* (of plants) producing no fruit [from Greek *akarpos*, from A-¹ + *karpos* fruit]

acarus (ˈækərəs) *n, pl* **-ri** (-ˌraɪ) any of the free-living mites of the widely distributed genus *Acarus*, several of which, esp *A. siro*, are serious pests of stored flour, grain, etc [c17 New Latin, from Greek *akari* a small thing, a mite]

ACAS *or* **Acas** (ˈeɪkæs) *n* (in Britain) ▷ *acronym for* Advisory Conciliation and Arbitration Service

acatalectic (æˌkætəˈlɛktɪk) *prosody* ▷ *adj* **1** having the necessary number of feet or syllables, esp having a complete final foot ▷ *n* **2** a verse having the full number of syllables [c16 via Late Latin from Greek *akatalēktikos*. See A-¹, CATALECTIC]

acaudal (eɪˈkɔːdᵊl) *or* **acaudate** *adj zoology* having no tail

acaulescent (ˌækɔːˈlɛsᵊnt) *adj* having no visible stem or a very short one

acauline (ˈækɔːˌlaɪn) *or* **acaulose** *adj biology* having no stem

ACC (in New Zealand) *abbreviation for* Accident Compensation Corporation

acc. *abbreviation for* **1** book-keeping account **2** *grammar* accusative

acca *or* **acker** (ˈækə) *n Austral informal* an academic [c20 shortened form of ACADEMIC]

ACCA *abbreviation for* Associate of the Chartered Association of Certified Accountants

Accad (ˈækæd) *n* a variant spelling of **Akkad**

Accademia (Italian akkaˈdɛmja) *n* an art gallery in Venice housing a collection of paintings by Venetian masters from the 13th to 18th centuries. Full name: **Galleria dell' Accademia** (Italian galleˈria dell akkaˈdɛmja)

ACCC *abbreviation for* Australian Competition and Consumer Commission

accede (ækˈsiːd) *vb* (*intr*; usually foll by *to*) **1** to assent or give one's consent; agree **2** to enter upon or attain (to an office, right, etc): *the prince acceded to the throne* **3** *international law* to become a party (to an agreement between nations, etc), as by signing a treaty [c15 from Latin *accēdere* to approach, agree, from *ad-* to + *cēdere* to go, yield] ▷ **ac'cedence** *n* ▷ **ac'ceder** *n*

accel. *abbreviation for* accelerando

accelerando (ækˌsɛləˈrændəʊ) *music* ▷ *adj, adv* **1** (to be performed) with increasing speed ▷ *n, pl* **-dos** **2** an increase in speed [Italian]

accelerant (ækˈsɛlərənt) *n chem* another name for **accelerator** (sense 3) [c20 from Latin from *accelerāns*, present participle of *accelerāre* to go faster]

accelerate (ækˈsɛləˌreɪt) *vb* **1** to go, occur, or cause to go or occur more quickly; speed up **2** (*tr*) to cause to happen sooner than expected **3** (*tr*) to increase the velocity of (a body, reaction, etc); cause acceleration [c16 from Latin *accelerātus*, from *accelerāre* to go faster, from *ad-* (intensive) + *celerāre* to hasten, from *celer* swift] ▷ **ac'celerable** *adj* ▷ **ac'celerative** *or* **ac'celeratory** *adj*

acceleration (ækˌsɛləˈreɪʃən) *n* **1** the act of accelerating or the state of being accelerated **2** the rate of increase of speed or the rate of change of velocity. Symbol: *a*

acceleration of free fall *n* the acceleration of a body falling freely in a vacuum near the surface of the earth in the earth's gravitational field: the standard value is 9.806 65 metres per second per second or 32.174 feet per second per second. Symbol: *g* Also called: **acceleration due to gravity, acceleration of gravity**

accelerator (ækˈsɛləˌreɪtə) *n* **1** a device for increasing speed, esp a pedal for controlling the fuel intake in a motor vehicle; throttle **2** Also called (not in technical usage): **atom smasher** *physics* a machine for increasing the kinetic energy of subatomic particles or atomic nuclei and focusing them on a target **3** *chem* a substance that increases the speed of a chemical reaction, esp one that increases the rate of vulcanization of rubber, the rate of development in photography, the rate of setting of synthetic resins, or the rate of setting of concrete; catalyst **4** *economics* (in an economy) the relationship between the rate of change in output or sales and the consequent change in the level of investment **5** *anatomy* a muscle or nerve that increases the rate of a function

accelerometer (ækˌsɛləˈrɒmɪtə) *n* an instrument for measuring acceleration, esp of an aircraft or rocket

accent *n* (ˈæksənt) **1** the characteristic mode of pronunciation of a person or group, esp one that betrays social or geographical origin **2** the relative prominence of a spoken or sung syllable, esp with regard to stress or pitch. Compare **pitch¹** (sense 28), **stress** (sense 3) **3** a mark (such as ˈ, ˌ, ´ or `) used in writing to indicate the stress or prominence of a syllable. Such a mark may also be used to indicate that a written syllable is to be pronounced, esp when such pronunciation is not usual, as in *turnèd* **4** any of various marks or symbols conventionally used in writing certain languages to indicate the quality of a vowel, or for some other purpose, such as differentiation of homographs. See **acute** (sense 10), **grave²** (sense 5), **circumflex** **5** (in some languages, such as Chinese) any of the tones that have phonemic value in distinguishing one word from another. Compare **tone** (sense 7) **6** rhythmic stress in verse or prose **7** *music* **a** stress placed on certain notes in a piece of music, indicated by a symbol printed over the note concerned **b** the rhythmic pulse of a piece or passage, usually represented as the stress on the first beat of each bar. See also **syncopation** **8** *maths* either of two superscript symbols indicating a specific unit, such as feet ('), inches ("), minutes of arc ('), or seconds of arc (") **9** a distinctive characteristic of anything, such as taste, pattern, style, etc **10** particular attention or emphasis: *an accent on learning* **11** a strongly contrasting detail: *a blue rug with red accents* ▷ *vb* (ækˈsɛnt) **12** to mark with an accent in writing, speech, music, etc **13** to lay particular emphasis or stress on [c14 via Old French from Latin *accentus*, from *ad-* to + *cantus* chant, song. The Latin is a rendering of Greek *prosōidia* a song sung to music, the tone of a syllable]

accentor (æk'sɛntə) *n* any small sparrow-like songbird of the genus *Prunella*, family *Prunellidae*, which inhabit mainly mountainous regions of Europe and Asia. See also **hedge sparrow**

accentual (æk'sɛntʃʊəl) *adj* **1** of, relating to, or having accents; rhythmic **2** *prosody* of or relating to verse based on the number of stresses in a line rather than on the number of syllables. Compare **quantitative**. > ac'centually *adv*

accentuate (æk'sɛntʃʊˌeɪt) *vb* (*tr*) to stress or emphasize > ac,centu'ation *n*

accept (ək'sɛpt) *vb* (*mainly tr*) **1** to take or receive (something offered) **2** to give an affirmative reply to: *to accept an invitation* **3** to take on the responsibilities, duties, etc, of: *he accepted office* **4** to tolerate or accommodate oneself to **5** to consider as true or believe in (a philosophy, theory, etc): *I cannot accept your argument* **6** (*may take a clause as object*) to be willing to grant or believe: *you must accept that he lied* **7** to receive with approval or admit, as into a community, group, etc **8** *commerce* to agree to pay (a bill, draft, shipping document, etc), esp by signing **9** to receive as adequate, satisfactory, or valid **10** to receive, take, or hold (something applied, inserted, etc) **11** (*intr; sometimes foll by of*) *archaic* to take or receive an offer, invitation, etc [c14 from Latin *acceptāre*, from *ad-* to + *capere* to take] > ac'cepter *n*

acceptable (ək'sɛptəb°l) *adj* **1** satisfactory; adequate **2** pleasing; welcome **3** tolerable > ac,cepta'bility *or* ac'ceptableness *n* > ac'ceptably *adv*

acceptance (ək'sɛptəns) *n* **1** the act of accepting or the state of being accepted or acceptable **2** favourable reception; approval **3** (*often foll by of*) belief (in) or assent (to) **4** *commerce* **a** a formal agreement by a debtor to pay a draft, bill, etc **b** the document so accepted. Compare **bank acceptance 5** (*plural*) *Austral and NZ* a list of horses accepted as starters in a race **6** *contract law* words or conduct by which a person signifies his assent to the terms and conditions of an offer or agreement

acceptant (ək'sɛptənt) *adj* receiving willingly; receptive

acceptation (ˌæksɛp'teɪʃən) *n* the accepted meaning, as of a word, phrase, etc

accepted (ək'sɛptɪd) *adj* commonly approved or recognized; customary; established > ac'ceptedly *adv*

accepting house *n* a financial institution that guarantees a bill of exchange, as a result of which it can be discounted on more favourable terms

acceptor (ək'sɛptə) *n* **1** *commerce* the person or organization on which a draft or bill of exchange is drawn after liability has been accepted, usually by signature **2** Also called: **acceptor impurity** *electronics* an impurity, such as gallium, added to a semiconductor material to increase its p-type conductivity by increasing the number of holes in the semiconductor. Compare **donor** (sense 5) **3** *electronics* a circuit tuned to accept a particular frequency **4** *chem* the atom or group that accepts electrons in a coordinate bond

access ('æksɛs) *n* **1** the act of approaching or entering **2** the condition of allowing entry, esp (of a building or room) allowing entry by wheelchairs, prams, etc **3** the right or privilege to approach, reach, enter, or make use of something **4** a way or means of approach or entry **5** the opportunity or right to see or approach someone: *she fights for divorce and free access to her children* **6** (*modifier*) designating programmes made by the general public as distinguished from those made by professional broadcasters: *access television* **7** a sudden outburst or attack, as of rage or disease ▷ *vb* **8** to gain access to; make accessible or available **9** (*tr*) *computing* **a** to obtain or retrieve (information) from a storage device **b** to place (information) in a storage device. See also **direct**

access, sequential access [c14 from Old French or from Latin *accessus* an approach, from *accēdere* to ACCEDE]

accessary (ək'sɛsərɪ) *n, pl* -ries, *adj law* a less common spelling of **accessory**. > ac'cessarily *adv* > ac'cessariness *n*

access course *n* (in Britain) an intensive course of study for people without academic qualifications that enables them to apply for higher education

accessible (ək'sɛsəb°l) *adj* **1** easy to approach, enter, or use **2 accessible to** likely to be affected by; open to; susceptible to **3** obtainable; available **4** easy for disabled people to enter or use **5** *logic* (of a possible world) surveyable from some other world so that the truth value of statements about it can be known. A statement *possibly p* is true in a world W if and only if *p* is true in some worlds accessible to W > ac,cessi'bility *n* > ac'cessibly *adv*

accession (ək'sɛʃən) *n* **1** the act of entering upon or attaining to an office, right, condition, etc **2** an increase due to an addition **3** an addition, as to a collection **4** *property law* **a** an addition to land or property by natural increase or improvement **b** the owner's right to the increased value of such land **5** *international law* the formal acceptance of a convention or treaty **6** agreement; consent **7** a less common word for **access** (sense 1) ▷ *vb* **8** (*tr*) to make a record of (additions to a collection) > ac'cessional *adj*

accession number *n library science* the number given to record a new addition to a collection

accessorius (ˌæksɛs'ɔːrɪəs) *n anatomy* a muscle or nerve that has an augmenting action

accessorize *or* **accessorise** (ək'sɛsəˌraɪz) *vb* (*tr*) to add accessories to: *accessorize a plain jacket with feminine jewellery*

accessory (ək'sɛsərɪ) *n, pl* -ries **1** a supplementary part or object, as of a car, appliance, etc **2** (*often plural*) a small accompanying item of dress, esp women's dress **3** a person who incites someone to commit a crime or assists the perpetrator of a crime, either before or during its commission ▷ *adj* **4** supplementary; additional; subordinate **5** assisting in or having knowledge of an act, esp a crime [c17 from Late Latin *accessōrius*: see ACCESS] > accessorial (ˌæksɛ'sɔːrɪəl) *adj* > ac'cessorily *adv* > ac'cessoriness *n*

accessory fruit *n* another name for **pseudocarp**

accessory nerve *n* either one of the eleventh pair of cranial nerves, which supply the muscles of the head, shoulders, larynx, and pharynx and the viscera of the abdomen and thorax

accessory shoe *n photog* a bracket on top of a camera to which a flash unit or other accessory may be fitted

access road *n* a road providing a means of entry into a region or of approach to another road, esp a motorway

access time *n computing* the time required to retrieve a piece of stored information

acciaccatura (ɑːˌtʃɑːkɑː'tʊərə) *n, pl* -ras *or* -re (-reɪ, -riː) **1** a small grace note melodically adjacent to a principal note and played simultaneously with or immediately before it **2** (in modern music) a very short appoggiatura [c18 Italian: literally, a crushing sound]

accidence ('æksɪdəns) *n* inflectional morphology; the part of grammar concerned with changes in the form of words by internal modification or by affixation, for the expression of tense, person, case, number, etc [c15 from Latin *accidentia* accidental matters, hence inflections of words, from *accidere* to happen. See ACCIDENT]

accident ('æksɪdənt) *n* **1** an unforeseen event or one without an apparent cause **2** anything that occurs unintentionally or by chance; chance; fortune: *I met him by accident* **3** a misfortune or mishap, esp one causing injury or death **4** Also called: **adjunct** *logic, philosophy* a nonessential attribute or characteristic of something (as

opposed to substance) **5** *metaphysics* a property as contrasted with the substance in which it inheres **6** *geology* a surface irregularity in a natural formation, esp in a rock formation or a river system [c14 via Old French from Latin *accident-*chance, happening, from the present participle of *accidere* to befall, happen, from *ad-* to + *cadere* to fall]

accidental (ˌæksɪ'dɛnt°l) *adj* **1** occurring by chance, unexpectedly, or unintentionally **2** nonessential; incidental **3** *music* denoting sharps, flats, or naturals that are not in the key signature of a piece **4** *logic* (of a property) not essential; contingent ▷ *n* **5** an incidental, nonessential, or supplementary circumstance, factor, or attribute **6** *music* a symbol denoting a sharp, flat, or natural that is not a part of the key signature > ,acci'dentally *adv*

accident insurance *n* insurance providing compensation for accidental injury or death

accidentology (ˌæksɪdən'tɒlədʒɪ) *n* the study of the prevention of accidents

accident-prone *adj* more liable than most people to be involved in accidents

accident proneness *n* the unconscious tendency, thought to exist in some people, to involve themselves in a large number of accidents

accidie ('æksɪdɪ) *or* **acedia** *n* spiritual sloth; apathy; indifference [in use c13 to c16 and revived c19 via Late Latin from Greek *akēdia*, from A-¹ + *kēdos* care]

accipiter (æk'sɪpɪtə) *n* any hawk of the genus *Accipiter*, typically having short rounded wings and a long tail [c19 New Latin, from Latin: hawk]

accipitrine (æk'sɪpɪˌtraɪn, -trɪn) *adj* **1** Also: **accipitral** (æk'sɪpɪtrəl) of, relating to, or resembling a hawk; rapacious **2** of, relating to, or belonging to the subfamily *Accipitrinae*, which includes the hawks

acclaim (ə'kleɪm) *vb* **1** (*tr*) to acknowledge publicly the excellence of (a person, act, etc) **2** to salute with cheering, clapping, etc; applaud **3** (*tr*) to acknowledge publicly that (a person) has (some position, quality, etc): *they acclaimed him king* ▷ *n* **4** an enthusiastic approval, expression of enthusiasm, etc [c17 from Latin *acclāmāre* to shout at, shout applause, from *ad-* to + *clamāre* to shout] > ac'claimer *n*

acclamation (ˌæklə'meɪʃən) *n* **1** an enthusiastic reception or exhibition of welcome, approval, etc **2** an expression of approval by a meeting or gathering through shouts or applause **3** *Canadian* an instance of electing or being elected without opposition: *there were two acclamations in the 1985 election* **4 by acclamation a** by an overwhelming majority without a ballot **b** *Canadian* (of an election or electoral victory) without opposition: *he won by acclamation* > **acclamatory** (ə'klæmətərɪ, -trɪ) *adj*

acclimatize, acclimatise (ə'klaɪməˌtaɪz) *or* **acclimate** (ə'klaɪmeɪt, 'æklɪˌmeɪt) *vb* to adapt or become accustomed to a new climate or environment > ac'clima,tizable, ac'clima,tisable *or* ac'climatable *adj* > ac,climati'zation, ac,climati'sation *or* ,accli'mation > ac'clima,tizer *or* ac'clima,tiser *n*

acclivity (ə'klɪvɪtɪ) *n, pl* -ties an upward slope, esp of the ground. Compare **declivity** [c17 from Latin *acclīvitās*, from *acclīvis* sloping up, steep] > ac'clivitous *or* acclivous (ə'klaɪvəs) *adj*

accolade ('ækəˌleɪd, ˌækə'leɪd) *n* **1** strong praise or approval; acclaim **2** an award or honour **3** the ceremonial gesture used to confer knighthood, originally an embrace, now a touch on the shoulder with a sword **4** a rare word for **brace** (sense 7) **5** *architect* a curved ornamental moulding, esp one having the shape of an ogee arch [c17 via French and Italian from Vulgar Latin *accollāre* (unattested) to hug; related to Latin *collum* neck]

accommodate (ə'kɒməˌdeɪt) *vb* **1** (*tr*) to supply or provide, esp with lodging or board and lodging **2**

(tr) to oblige or do a favour for **3** to adjust or become adjusted; adapt **4** *(tr)* to bring into harmony; reconcile **5** *(tr)* to allow room for; contain **6** *(tr)* to lend money to, esp on a temporary basis until a formal loan has been arranged [c16 from Latin *accommodāre* to make fit, from *ad-* to + *commodus* having the proper measure] > ac'commo,dative *adj*

accommodating (ə'kɒmə,deɪtɪŋ) *adj* willing to help; kind; obliging > ac'commo,datingly *adv*

accommodation (ə,kɒmə'deɪʃən) *n* **1** lodging or board and lodging **2** adjustment, as of differences or to new circumstances; adaptation, settlement, or reconciliation **3** something fulfilling a need, want, etc; convenience or facility **4** *physiol* the automatic or voluntary adjustment of the shape of the lens of the eye for far or near vision **5** willingness to help or oblige **6** *commerce* a loan, usually made as an act of favour by a bank before formal credit arrangements are agreed

accommodation address *n* an address on letters, etc, to a person or business that does not wish or is not able to receive post at a permanent or actual address

accommodation bill *n commerce* a bill of exchange cosigned by a guarantor: designed to strengthen the acceptor's credit. Also called: windbill, windmill

accommodation ladder *n nautical* a flight of stairs or a ladder for lowering over the side of a ship for access to and from a small boat, pier, etc

accommodation platform or **rig** *n* a platform or semisubmersible rig specially built or adapted to act as living accommodation for offshore personnel in the oil industry

accompaniment (ə'kʌmpənɪmənt, ə'kʌmpnɪ-) *n* **1** something that accompanies or is served or used with something else **2** something inessential or subsidiary that is added, as for ornament or symmetry **3** *music* a subordinate part for an instrument, voices, or an orchestra

accompanist (ə'kʌmpənɪst, ə'kʌmpnɪst) *or sometimes US* **accompanyist** (ə'kʌmpəni:ɪst) *n* a person who plays a musical accompaniment for another performer, esp a pianist accompanying a singer

accompany (ə'kʌmpəni, ə'kʌmpnɪ) *vb* -nies, -nying, -nied **1** *(tr)* to go along with, so as to be in company with or escort **2** *(tr; foll by with)* to supplement: *the food is accompanied with a very hot mango pickle* **3** *(tr)* to occur, coexist, or be associated with **4** to provide a musical accompaniment for (a performer) [c15 from Old French *accompaignier*, from *compaing* COMPANION¹] > ac'companier *n*

accomplice (ə'kɒmplɪs, ə'kʌm-) *n* a person who helps another in committing a crime [c15 from *a complice*, interpreted as one word. See COMPLICE]

accomplish (ə'kɒmplɪʃ, ə'kʌm-) *vb (tr)* **1** to manage to do; achieve **2** to conclude successfully; complete [c14 from Old French *acomplir* to complete, ultimately from Latin *complēre* to fill up. See COMPLETE] > ac'complishable *adj* > ac'complisher *n*

accomplished (ə'kɒmplɪʃt, ə'kʌm-) *adj* **1** successfully completed; achieved **2** expert; proficient

accomplishment (ə'kɒmplɪʃmənt, ə'kʌm-) *n* **1** the act of carrying out or achieving **2** something achieved or successfully completed **3** *(often plural)* skill or talent **4** *(often plural)* social grace, style, and poise

accord (ə'kɔ:d) *n* **1** agreement; conformity; accordance (esp in the phrase **in accord with**) **2** consent or concurrence of opinion **3** **with one accord** unanimously **4** pleasing relationship between sounds, colours, etc; harmony **5** a settlement of differences, as between nations; compromise **6** **of one's own accord** voluntarily ▷ *vb* **7** to be or cause to be in harmony or agreement **8** *(tr)* to grant; bestow [c12 via Old French from Latin *ad-* to + *cord-*, stem of *cor* heart]

> ac'cordable *adj* > ac'corder *n*

accordance (ə'kɔ:dəns) *n* **1** conformity; agreement; accord (esp in the phrase **in accordance with**) **2** the act of granting; bestowal: *accordance of rights*

accordant (ə'kɔ:dʰnt) *adj (usually postpositive and foll by with)* in conformity or harmony > ac'cordantly *adv*

according (ə'kɔ:dɪŋ) *adj* **1** *(foll by to)* in proportion; in relation: *salary will be according to age and experience* **2** *(foll by to)* on the report (of); as stated (by) **3** *(foll by to)* in conformity (with); in accordance (with): *everything went according to plan* **4** *(foll by as)* depending (on whether) **5** *not standard* dependent on: *it's all according where you want to go*

accordingly (ə'kɔ:dɪŋlɪ) *adv* **1** in an appropriate manner; suitably ▷ *sentence connector* **2** consequently

accordion (ə'kɔ:dɪən) *n* **1** a portable box-shaped instrument of the reed organ family, consisting of metallic reeds that are made to vibrate by air from a set of bellows controlled by the player's hands. Notes are produced by means of studlike keys **2** short for **piano accordion** [c19 from German *Akkordion*, from *Akkord* harmony, chord] > ac'cordionist *n*

accordion pleats *pl n* tiny knife pleats

accost (ə'kɒst) *vb* **1** *(tr)* to approach, stop, and speak to (a person), as to ask a question, accuse of a crime, solicit sexually, etc ▷ *n* **2** *rare* a greeting [c16 from Late Latin *accostāre* to place side by side, from Latin *costa* side, rib] > ac'costable *adj*

accouchement French (akuʃmā; English ə'ku:ʃmənt) *n* childbirth or the period of confinement [c19 from *accoucher* to put to bed, to give birth. See COUCH]

accoucheur French (akuʃœr) *n* a male obstetrician or midwife [literally: one who is present at the bedside]

accoucheuse French (akuʃøz) *n* a female obstetrician or midwife [literally: one who is present at the bedside]

account (ə'kaʊnt) *n* **1** a verbal or written report, description, or narration of some occurrence, event, etc **2** an explanation of conduct, esp one made to someone in authority **3** ground; basis; consideration (often in the phrases **on this** (**that, every, no**, etc) **account, on account of**) **4** importance, consequence, or value: *of little account* **5** assessment; judgment **6** profit or advantage: *to turn an idea to account* **7** part or behalf (only in the phrase **on one's** or **someone's account**) **8** *finance* **a** a business relationship between a bank, department store, stockbroker, etc, and a depositor, customer, or client permitting the latter certain banking or credit services **b** the sum of money deposited at a bank **c** the amount of credit available to the holder of an account **d** a record of these **9** a statement of monetary transactions with the resulting balance **10** (on the London Stock Exchange) the period, ordinarily of a fortnight's duration, in which transactions formerly took place and at the end of which settlements were made **11** *book-keeping* a chronological list of debits and credits relating to a specified asset, liability, expense, or income of a business and forming part of the ledger **12 a** a regular client or customer, esp a firm that purchases commodities on credit **b** an area of business assigned to another: *they transferred their publicity account to a new agent* **13 call** (or **bring**) **to account a** to insist on explanation **b** to rebuke; reprimand **c** to hold responsible **14 give a good** (**bad**, etc) **account of oneself** to perform well (badly, etc): *he gave a poor account of himself in the examination* **15 on account a** on credit **b** Also: **to account** as partial payment **16 on account of** *(preposition)* because of; by reason of **17 take account of** or **take into account** to take into consideration; allow for **18 settle** or **square accounts with a** to pay or receive a balance due **b** to get revenge on (someone) **19** See **bank account** or **credit account** ▷ *vb* **20** *(tr)* to consider or

reckon: *he accounts himself poor* [c13 from Old French *acont*, from *conter, compter* to COUNT¹]

accountable (ə'kaʊntəbʰl) *adj* **1** responsible to someone or for some action; answerable **2** able to be explained > ac,counta'bility *n* > ac'countably *adv*

accountancy (ə'kaʊntənsɪ) *n* the profession or business of an accountant

accountant (ə'kaʊntənt) *n* a person concerned with the maintenance and audit of business accounts and the preparation of consultant reports in tax and finance

account day *n* (on the London Stock Exchange) the day on which deliveries and payments relating to transactions made during the preceding account are made

account executive *n* an executive in an advertising agency or public relations firm who manages a client's account

account for *vb (intr, preposition)* **1** to give reasons for (an event, act, etc) **2** to make or provide a reckoning of (expenditure, payments, etc) **3** to be responsible for destroying, killing, or putting (people, aircraft, etc) out of action

accounting (ə'kaʊntɪŋ) *n* **a** the skill or practice of maintaining and auditing accounts and preparing reports on the assets, liabilities, etc, of a business **b** *(as modifier): an accounting period; accounting entity*

account payable *n accounting, US* a current liability account showing amounts payable by a firm to suppliers for purchases of materials, stocks, or services on credit

account receivable *n accounting, US* a current asset account showing amounts payable to a firm by customers who have made purchases of goods and services on credit

accouplement (ə'kʌpʰlmənt) *n* a timber joist or beam that serves as a tie or support [c15 French, from *accoupler*, from Latin *copulāre* to COUPLE]

accoutre or US **accouter** (ə'ku:tə) *vb (tr; usually passive)* to provide with equipment or dress, esp military [c16 from Old French *accoustrer* to equip with clothing, ultimately related to Latin *consuere* to sew together]

accoutrement (ə'ku:trəmənt, ə'ku:tə-) *or US* **accouterment** (ə'ku:tərmənt) *n* **1** equipment worn by soldiers in addition to their clothing and weapons **2** *(usually plural)* clothing, equipment, etc; trappings: *the correct accoutrements for any form of sport*

Accra (ə'krɑ:) *n* the capital of Ghana, a port on the Gulf of Guinea: built on the site of three 17th-century trading fortresses founded by the English, Dutch, and Danish. Pop: 1 970 000 (2005 est)

accredit (ə'krɛdɪt) *vb (tr)* **1** to ascribe or attribute **2** to give official recognition to; sanction; authorize **3** to certify or guarantee as meeting required standards **4** *(often foll by at or to)* **a** to furnish or send (an envoy, etc) with official credentials **b** to appoint (someone) as an envoy, etc **5** NZ to pass (a candidate) for university entrance on school recommendation without external examination: *there are six accrediting schools in the area* [c17 from French *accréditer*, from the phrase *mettre à crédit* to put to CREDIT] > ac,credi'tation *n*

accrescent (æ'krɛsʰnt) *adj botany* (of a calyx or other part) continuing to grow after flowering [c18 from Latin *accrēscere* to continue to grow, from *crēscere* to grow]

accrete (ə'kri:t) *vb* **1** to grow or cause to grow together, be or become fused **2** to make or become bigger, as by addition [c18 back formation from ACCRETION]

accretion (ə'kri:ʃən) *n* **1** any gradual increase in size, as through growth or external addition **2** something added, esp extraneously, to cause growth or an increase in size **3** the growing together of normally separate plant or animal parts **4** *pathol* **a** abnormal union or growing together of parts; adhesion **b** a mass of foreign matter collected in a cavity **5** *law* an increase in the share of a beneficiary in an estate, as when a co-beneficiary fails to take his share **6** *astronomy* the process in which matter under the influence of gravity is attracted to and increases the mass of a celestial body. The matter usually forms an **accretion disc** around the accreting object **7** *geology* the process in which a continent is enlarged by the tectonic movement and deformation of the earth's crust [c17 from Latin *accretiō* increase, from *accrēscere*. See ACCRUE] > ac'cretive or ac'cretionary *adj*

accretionary wedge or **prism** *n geology* a body of deformed sediments, wedge-shaped in two dimensions or prism-shaped in three dimensions, that has been scraped off the surface of the oceanic lithosphere as it moves downwards beneath a continent or island arc. The sediments are added to the continental edge

Accrington ('ækrɪŋtən) *n* a town in NW England, in SE Lancashire. Pop: 35 203 (2001)

accrual (ə'kruː əl) *n* **1** the act of accruing **2** something that has accrued **3** *accounting* a charge incurred in one accounting period that has not been paid by the end of it

accrue (ə'kruː) *vb* -crues, -cruing, -crued (*intr*) **1** to increase by growth or addition, esp (of capital) to increase by periodic addition of interest **2** (often foll by *to*) to fall naturally (to); come into the possession (of); result (for) **3** *law* (of a right or demand) to become capable of being enforced [c15 from Old French *accreue* growth, ultimately from Latin *accrēscere* to increase, from *ad-* to, in addition + *crēscere* to grow]

acculturate (ə'kʌltʃəˌreɪt) *vb* (of a cultural or social group) to assimilate the cultural traits of another group [c20 from AD- + CULTURE + -ATE¹] > ac,cultur'ation *n*

accumbent (ə'kʌmbənt) *adj* **1** *botany* (of plant parts and plants) lying against some other part or thing **2** a rare word for **recumbent** [c18 from Latin *accumbere* to recline] > ac'cumbency *n*

accumulate (ə'kjuːmjʊˌleɪt) *vb* to gather or become gathered together in an increasing quantity; amass; collect [c16 from Latin *accumulātus*, past participle of *accumulāre* to heap up, from *cumulus* a heap] > ac'cumulable *adj* > ac'cumulative *adj* > ac'cumulatively *adv* > ac'cumulativeness *n*

accumulation (əˌkjuːmjʊ'leɪʃən) *n* **1** the act or process of collecting together or becoming collected **2** something that has been collected, gathered, heaped, etc **3** *finance* **a** the continuous growth of capital by retention of interest or earnings **b** (in computing the yield on a bond purchased at a discount) the amount that is added to each yield to bring the cost of the bond into equality with its par value over its life. Compare **amortization** (sense 2) **4** the taking of a first and an advanced university degree simultaneously

accumulation point *n maths* another name for **limit point**

accumulator (ə'kjuːmjʊˌleɪtə) *n* **1** Also called: **battery, storage battery** a rechargeable device for storing electrical energy in the form of chemical energy, consisting of one or more separate secondary cells **2** *horse racing, Brit* a collective bet, esp on four or more races, in which the stake and winnings on each successive race are carried forward to become the stake on the next, so that both stakes and winnings accumulate progressively so long as the bet continues to be a winning one **3 a** a register in a computer or calculator used for holding the results of a computation or data transfer **b** a location in a computer store in which arithmetical results are produced

accuracy ('ækjʊrəsɪ) *n, pl* -cies **1** faithful measurement or representation of the truth; correctness; precision **2** *physics, chem* the degree of agreement between a measured or computed value of a physical quantity and the standard or accepted value for that quantity

accurate ('ækjərɪt) *adj* **1** faithfully representing or describing the truth **2** showing a negligible or permissible deviation from a standard: *an accurate ruler* **3** without error; precise; meticulous **4** *maths* **a** (to *n* significant digits) representing the first *n* digits of the given number starting with the first nonzero digit, but approximating to the nearest digit in the final position: *since π = 3.14159..., the approximation 3.1416 is accurate to 5 significant digits.* **b** (to *n* decimal places) giving the first *n* digits after the decimal point without further approximation: *π = 3.1415 is in this sense accurate to 4 decimal places* [c16 from Latin *accūrātus*, past participle of *accūrāre* to perform with care, from *cūra* care] > 'accurately *adv* > 'accurateness *n*

accursed (ə'kɜːsɪd, ə'kɜːst) or **accurst** (ə'kɜːst) *adj* **1** under or subject to a curse; doomed **2** (*prenominal*) hateful; detestable; execrable [Old English *ācursod*, past participle of *ācursian* to put under a CURSE] > accursedly (ə'kɜːsɪdlɪ) *adv* > ac'cursedness *n*

accusal (ə'kjuːzəl) *n* another word for **accusation**

accusation (ˌækjʊ'zeɪʃən) *n* **1** an allegation that a person is guilty of some fault, offence, or crime; imputation **2** a formal charge brought against a person stating the crime that he is alleged to have committed

accusative (ə'kjuːzətɪv) *adj* **1** *grammar* denoting a case of nouns, pronouns, and adjectives in inflected languages that is used to identify the direct object of a finite verb, of certain prepositions, and for certain other purposes. See also **objective** (sense 5) **2** another word for **accusatorial** ▷ *n* **3** *grammar* **a** the accusative case **b** a word or speech element in the accusative case [c15 from Latin; in grammar, from the phrase *cāsus accūsātivus* accusative case, a mistaken translation of Greek *ptōsis aitiatikē* the case indicating causation. See ACCUSE] > accusatival (əˌkjuːzə'taɪvəl) *adj* > ac'cusatively *adv*

accusatorial (əˌkjuːzə'tɔːrɪəl) or **accusatory** (ə'kjuːzətərɪ, -trɪ, ˌækjʊ'zeɪtərɪ) *adj* **1** containing or implying blame or strong criticism **2** *law* denoting criminal procedure in which the prosecutor is distinct from the judge and the trial is conducted in public. Compare **inquisitorial** (sense 3)

accuse (ə'kjuːz) *vb* to charge (a person or persons) with some fault, offence, crime, etc; impute guilt or blame [c13 via Old French from Latin *accūsāre* to call to account, from *ad-* to + *causa* lawsuit] > ac'cuser *n* > ac'cusing *adj* > ac'cusingly *adv*

accused (ə'kjuːzd) *n* (preceded by *the*) *law* the defendant or defendants appearing on a criminal charge

accustom (ə'kʌstəm) *vb* (*tr*; usually foll by *to*) to make (oneself) familiar (with) or used (to), as by practice, habit, or experience [c15 from Old French *acostumer*, from *costume* CUSTOM]

accustomed (ə'kʌstəmd) *adj* **1** usual; customary **2** (*postpositive*; foll by *to*) used or inured (to) **3** (*postpositive*; foll by *to*) in the habit (of): *accustomed to walking after meals*

Accutron ('ækjuːˌtrɒn) *n trademark* a type of watch in which the balance wheel and hairspring are replaced by a tuning fork kept in vibration by a tiny internal battery

AC/DC *adj informal* (of a person) bisexual [c20 humorous reference to electrical apparatus that is adaptable for ALTERNATING CURRENT and DIRECT CURRENT]

ace (eɪs) *n* **1** any die, domino, or any of four playing cards with one spot **2** a single spot or pip on a playing card, die, etc **3** *tennis* a winning serve that the opponent fails to reach **4** *golf, chiefly US* a hole in one **5** a fighter pilot accredited with destroying several enemy aircraft **6** *informal* an expert or highly skilled person: *an ace at driving* **7 an ace up one's sleeve** or **an ace in the hole** a hidden and powerful advantage **8 hold all the**

aces to have all the advantages or power **9 play one's ace** to use one's best weapon or resource **10 within an ace of** almost to the point of: *he came within an ace of winning* ▷ *adj* **11** *informal* superb; excellent ▷ *vb* (*tr*) **12** *tennis* to serve an ace against **13** *golf, chiefly US* to play (a hole) in one stroke **14** *US and Canadian* to perform extremely well or score very highly in (an examination, etc) [c13 via Old French from Latin *as* a unit, perhaps from a Greek variant of *heis* one]

ACE (eɪs) *n acronym for* **1** (in Britain) Advisory Centre for Education; a private organization offering advice on schools to parents **2** Allied Command Europe **3** angiotensin-converting enzyme. See **ACE inhibitor**

-acea *suffix forming plural proper nouns* denoting animals belonging to a class or order: *Crustacea* (class); *Cetacea* (order) [New Latin, from Latin, neuter plural of *-āceus* -ACEOUS]

-aceae *suffix forming plural proper nouns* denoting plants belonging to a family: *Liliaceae; Ranunculaceae* [New Latin, from Latin, feminine plural of *-āceus* -ACEOUS]

acedia (ə'siːdɪə) *n* another word for **accidie**

Aceh ('aːtʃeɪ) *n* an autonomous region of N Indonesia, in N Sumatra; mountainous with rain forests; scene of separatist conflict since the later 1990s; coastal areas suffered badly in the Indian Ocean tsunami of December 2004. Capital: Banda Aceh. Pop: 3 930 905 (2000). Area: 55 392 sq km (21 381 sq miles)

ACE inhibitor *n* any one of a class of drugs, including captopril, enalapril, and ramipril, that cause the arteries to widen by preventing the synthesis of angiotensin: used to treat high blood pressure and heart failure [c20 from *a(ngiotensin-) c(onverting) e(nzyme) inhibitor*]

Aceldama (ə'seldəmə) *n New Testament* the place near Jerusalem that was bought with the 30 pieces of silver paid to Judas for betraying Jesus (Matthew 27:8; Acts 1:19) [c14 from Aramaic *haqēl demā* field of blood]

acellular (eɪ'seljʊlə) *adj biology* not made up of or containing cells

acentric (eɪ'sentrɪk) *adj* **1** without a centre **2** not on centre; eccentric **3** *genetics* (of a chromosome or chromosome fragment) lacking a centromere ▷ *n* **4** an acentric chromosome or fragment

-aceous *suffix forming adjectives* relating to, belonging to, having the nature of, or resembling: *herbaceous; larvaceous* [New Latin, from Latin *-āceus* of a certain kind; related to *-āc, -āx*, adjectival suffix]

acephalous (ə'sefələs) *adj* **1** having no head or one that is reduced and indistinct, as certain insect larvae **2** having or recognizing no ruler or leader [c18 via Medieval Latin from Greek *akephalos*. See A-¹, -CEPHALIC]

acer ('eɪsə) *n* any tree or shrub of the genus *Acer*, often cultivated for their brightly coloured foliage. See also **maple**

ACER *abbreviation for* Australian Council for Educational Research

acerate ('æsəˌreɪt, -rɪt) *adj* another word for **acerose** [c19 from Latin *ācer* sharp + -ATE¹]

acerbate ('æsəˌbeɪt) *vb* (*tr*) **1** to embitter or exasperate **2** to make sour or bitter [c18 from Latin *acerbātus*, past participle of *acerbāre* to make sour]

acerbic (ə'sɜːbɪk) *adj* harsh, bitter, or astringent; sour [c17 from Latin *acerbus* sour, bitter]

acerbity (ə'sɜːbɪtɪ) *n, pl* -ties **1** vitriolic or embittered speech, temper, etc **2** sourness or bitterness of taste

acerola (ˌæsə'rəʊlə) *n* **1** a small tree or shrub, *Malpighia glabra*, that grows in the rainforests of N South America, Central America, and Jamaica **2** the small, soft, bright red fruit of this tree, which looks like a cherry but has a sharp flavour ▷ Also called: **Amazon cherry** [c21 from Portuguese]

acerose ('æsəˌrəʊs, -ˌrəʊz) or **acerous** *adj* shaped like a needle, as pine leaves [c18 from Latin

a

acerōsus full of chaff (erroneously used by Linnaeus as if derived from *ācer* sharp)]

acervate (ə'sɜ:vɪt, -ˌveɪt) *adj* growing in heaps or clusters [C19 from Latin *acervātus*, from *acervāre* to heap up, from *acervus* a heap] > a'**cervately** *adv*

acescent (ə'sesᵊnt) *adj* slightly sour or turning sour [C18 from Latin *acēscent-*, from *acēscere* to become sour, from *ācer* sharp] > a'**cescence** or a'**cescency** *n*

acetabulum (ˌæsɪ'tæbjʊləm) *n, pl* -**la** (-lə) **1** the deep cuplike cavity on the side of the hipbone that receives the head of the thighbone **2** a round muscular sucker in flatworms, leeches, and cephalopod molluscs **3** the aperture in the thorax of an insect that holds the leg [Latin: vinegar cup, hence a cuplike cavity, from *acētum* vinegar + -*abulum*, suffix denoting a container]

acetal ('æsɪˌtæl) *n* **1** 1,1-diethoxyethane; a colourless volatile liquid used as a solvent and in perfumes. Formula: $CH_3CH(OC_2H_5)_2$ **2** any organic compound containing the group -CH(OR₁)OR₂, where R₁ and R₂ are other organic groups [C19 from German *Azetal*, from ACETO- + ALCOHOL]

acetaldehyde (ˌæsɪ'tældɪˌhaɪd) *n* a colourless volatile pungent liquid, miscible with water, used in the manufacture of organic compounds and as a solvent and reducing agent. Formula: CH_3CHO. Systematic name: ethanal

acetamide (ˌæsɪ'tæmaɪd, ə'setɪˌmaɪd) or **acetamid** (ˌæsɪ'tæmɪd, ə'setɪmɪd) *n* a white or colourless soluble deliquescent crystalline compound, used in the manufacture of organic chemicals. Formula: CH_3CONH_2 [C19 from German *Azetamid*, from ACETO- + AMIDE]

acetanilide (ˌæsɪ'tænɪˌlaɪd) or **acetanilid** (ˌæsɪ'tænɪlɪd) *n* a white crystalline powder used in the manufacture of dyes and rubber, as an analgesic in medicine, and as a precursor in penicillin manufacture. Formula: $C_6H_5NHCOCH_3$ [C19 from ACETO- + ANILINE + -IDE]

acetate ('æsɪˌteɪt) *n* **1** any salt or ester of acetic acid, containing the monovalent ion CH_3COO^- or the group CH_3COO-. Systematic name: ethanoate **2** (*modifier*) consisting of, containing, or concerned with the group CH_3COO-: *acetate group* or *radical* **3** short for **acetate rayon** or **cellulose acetate** **4** a sound recording disc composed of an acetate lacquer coating on an aluminium or plastic base: used for demonstration or other short-term purposes [C19 from ACETIC + -ATE¹] > 'ace,tated *adj*

acetate rayon *n* a synthetic textile fibre made from cellulose acetate. Also called: **acetate**

acetic (ə'si:tɪk, ə'set-) *adj* of, containing, producing, or derived from acetic acid or vinegar [C19 from Latin *acētum* vinegar]

acetic acid *n* a colourless pungent liquid, miscible with water, widely used in the manufacture of acetic anhydride, vinyl acetate, plastics, pharmaceuticals, dyes etc Formula: CH_3COOH. Systematic name: ethanoic acid See also **glacial acetic acid, vinegar**

acetic anhydride *n* a colourless pungent liquid used in the manufacture of cellulose and vinyl acetates for synthetic fabrics. Formula: $(CH_3CO)_2O$

acetify (ə'setɪˌfaɪ) *vb* -**fies**, -**fying**, -**fied** to become or cause to become acetic acid or vinegar > a,cetifi'cation *n* > a'ceti,fier *n*

aceto- or before a vowel **acet-** *combining form* containing an acetyl group or derived from acetic acid: *acetone* [from Latin *acētum* vinegar]

acetometer (ˌæsɪ'tɒmɪtə) *n* a device for measuring the concentration of acetic acid in a solution, esp in vinegar

acetonaemia or US **acetonemia** (ˌæsɪtəʊ'ni:mɪə, əˌsi:tə-) *n* another name for **ketosis**

acetone ('æsɪˌtəʊn) *n* a colourless volatile flammable pungent liquid, miscible with water, used in the manufacture of chemicals and as a solvent and thinner for paints, varnishes, and lacquers. Formula: CH_3COCH_3. Systematic name: propanone [C19 from German *Azeton*, from ACETO- + -ONE] > acetonic (ˌæsɪ'tɒnɪk) *adj*

acetone body *n* another name for **ketone body**

acetonuria (ˌæsɪtəʊ'njʊərɪə, əˌsi:tə-) *n* another name for **ketonuria**

acetophenetidin (əˌsi:təʊfə'netɪdɪn) *n* another name for **phenacetin**

acetous ('æsɪtəs, ə'si:-) or **acetose** ('æsɪˌtəʊs, -ˌtəʊz) *adj* **1** containing, producing, or resembling acetic acid or vinegar **2** tasting like vinegar [C18 from Late Latin *acētōsus* vinegary, from *acētum* vinegar]

acetum (ə'si:təm) *n* **1** another name for **vinegar 2** a solution that has dilute acetic acid as solvent [Latin]

acetyl ('æsɪˌtaɪl, ə'si:taɪl) *n* (*modifier*) of, consisting of, or containing the monovalent group CH_3CO-: *acetyl group* or *radical* [C19 from ACET(IC) + -YL] > acetylic (ˌæsɪ'tɪlɪk) *adj*

acetylate (ə'setɪˌleɪt) *vb* **1** (*tr*) to introduce an acetyl group into (a chemical compound) **2** (*intr*) (of a chemical compound) to gain or suffer substitution of an acetyl group > a,cety'lation *n*

acetyl chloride *n* a colourless pungent liquid used as an acetylating agent. Formula: CH_3COCl. Also called: ethanoyl chloride

acetylcholine (ˌæsɪtaɪl'kəʊli:n, -lɪn) *n* a chemical substance secreted at the ends of many nerve fibres, esp in the autonomic nervous system, and responsible for the transmission of nervous impulses. Formula: $CH_3CO_2(CH_2)_2N (CH_3)_3^+$

acetylcholinesterase (əˌsi:taɪlˌkəʊli:n'estərˌeɪz, ˌæsɪtaɪl-) *n* an enzyme in nerve cells that is responsible for the destruction of acetylcholine and thus for switching off excitation of the nerve

acetylene (ə'setɪˌli:n) *n* **1** a colourless flammable gas used in the manufacture of organic chemicals and in cutting and welding metals. Formula: C_2H_2. Systematic name: ethyne **2 a** another name for **alkyne b** (*as modifier*): *acetylene series* > acetylenic (əˌsetɪ'lenɪk) *adj*

acetylide (ə'setɪˌlaɪd) *n* any of a class of carbides in which the carbon is present as a diatomic divalent ion (C_2^{2-}). They are formally derivatives of acetylene

acetylsalicylic acid (ˌæsɪtaɪlˌsælɪ'sɪlɪk, ə'si:taɪl-) *n* the chemical name for **aspirin**

acey-deucy ('eɪsɪ'dju:sɪ) *n* a form of backgammon

ACGI *abbreviation for* Associate of the City and Guilds Institute

ach (ɑ:x) *interj Scot* an expression of surprise, impatience, disgust, etc. Also: **och**

Achaea (ə'ki:ə) or **Achaia** (ə'kaɪə) *n* **1** a department of Greece, in the N Peloponnese. Capital: Patras. Pop: 318 928 (2001). Area: 3209 sq km (1239 sq miles). Modern Greek name: Akhaïa **2** a province of ancient Greece, in the N Peloponnese on the Gulf of Corinth: enlarged as a Roman province in 27 BC

Achaean (ə'ki:ən) or **Achaian** (ə'kaɪən) *n* **1** a member of a principal Greek tribe in the Mycenaean era **2** a native or inhabitant of the later Greek province of Achaea ▷ *adj* **3** of or relating to Achaea or the Achaeans

Achaean League *n* a confederation of Achaean cities formed in the early third century BC, which became a political and military force in Greece, directed particularly against Macedonian domination of the Peloponnesus

Achaemenid (ə'ki:mənɪd, ə'kem-) *n, pl* **Achaemenids, Achaemenidae** (ˌækɪ'menɪˌdi:) or **Achaemenides** (ˌækɪ'menɪˌdi:z) any member of a Persian dynasty of kings, including Cyrus the Great, that ruled from about 550 to 331 BC, when Darius III was overthrown by Alexander the Great [from Greek, after *Akhaimenēs*, name of the founder]

achalasia (ˌækə'leɪzɪə) *n pathol* failure of the cardiac sphincter of the oesophagus to relax, resulting in difficulty in swallowing [New Latin, from A-¹ + Greek *chalasis* relaxation]

acharya (a'tʃærɪə) *n Hinduism* a prominent religious teacher and spiritual guide [from Sanskrit, literally: teacher]

Achates (ə'keɪti:z) *n* **1** *classical myth* Aeneas' faithful companion in Virgil's *Aeneid* **2** a loyal friend

ache (eɪk) *vb* (*intr*) **1** to feel, suffer, or be the source of a continuous dull pain **2** to suffer mental anguish ▷ *n* **3** a continuous dull pain [Old English *ācan* (vb), *æce* (n), Middle English *aken* (vb), *ache* (n). Compare BAKE, BATCH] > 'aching *adj* > 'achingly *adv*

Achelous (ˌækɪ'ləʊəs) *n classical myth* a river god who changed into a snake and a bull while fighting Hercules but was defeated when Hercules broke off one of his horns

achene or **akene** (ə'ki:n) *n* a dry one-seeded indehiscent fruit with the seed distinct from the fruit wall. It may be smooth, as in the buttercup, or feathery, as in clematis [C19 from New Latin *achaenium* that which does not yawn or open, from A-¹ + Greek *khainein* to yawn] > a'chenial or a'kenial *adj*

Achernar ('eɪkəˌnɑ:) *n* the brightest star in the constellation Eridanus, visible only in the S hemisphere. Visual magnitude: 0.5; spectral type: B3V; distance: 144 light years [from Arabic *ākhīr al-nahr*, literally: end of the river, alluding to the star's location in the constellation]

Acheron ('ækəˌrɒn) *n Greek myth* **1** one of the rivers in Hades over which the souls of the dead were ferried by Charon. Compare **Styx 2** the underworld or Hades

Acheulian or **Acheulean** (ə'ʃu:lɪən, -jən) *archaeol* ▷ *n* **1** (in Europe) the period in the Lower Palaeolithic following the Abbevillian, represented by the use of soft hammerstones in hand axe production made of chipped stone, bone, antler, or wood. The Acheulian dates from the Riss glaciation **2** (in Africa) the period represented by every stage of hand axe development ▷ *adj* **3** of or relating to this period [C20 after *St Acheul*, town in northern France]

à cheval *French* (a ʃəval) *adv* (of a bet, esp in roulette) made on two adjacent numbers, cards, etc [literally: on horseback]

achieve (ə'tʃi:v) *vb* (*tr*) **1** to bring to a successful conclusion; accomplish; attain **2** to gain as by hard work or effort: *to achieve success* [C14 from Old French *achever* to bring to an end, from the phrase *a chef* to a head, to a conclusion] > a'chievable *adj* > a'chiever *n*

achievement (ə'tʃi:vmənt) *n* **1** something that has been accomplished, esp by hard work, ability, or heroism **2** successful completion; accomplishment **3** *heraldry* a less common word for **hatchment**

achievement age *n psychol* the age at which a child should be able to perform a standardized test successfully. Compare **mental age**

achievement quotient *n psychol* a measure of ability derived by dividing an individual's achievement age by his actual age. Abbreviation: AQ

achievement test *n psychol* a test designed to measure the effects that learning and teaching have on individuals

achillea (ˌækɪ'li:ə) *n* any plant of the N temperate genus *Achillea*, with white, yellow, or purple flowers, some species of which are widely grown as garden plants: family Asteraceae (composites). See also **sneezewort, yarrow** [from ACHILLES, who was credited with discovering medicinal properties in the plant]

Achilles (ə'kɪli:z) *n Greek myth* Greek hero, the son of Peleus and the sea goddess Thetis: in the *Iliad* the foremost of the Greek warriors at the siege of Troy. While he was a baby his mother plunged him into the river Styx making his body invulnerable except for the heel by which she held him. After slaying Hector, he was killed by Paris who wounded him in the heel > Achillean (ˌækɪ'li:ən) *adj*

Achilles heel *n* a small but fatal weakness

Achilles tendon *n* the fibrous cord that connects the muscles of the calf to the heelbone

Achill Island ('ækɪl) *n* an island in the Republic of Ireland, off the W coast of Co Mayo. Area: 148 sq km (57 sq miles). Pop: 2620 (2002)

achimenes (,ækɪ'miːniːz) *n* any plant of the tropical S American tuberous-rooted perennial genus *Achimenes*, with showy red, blue, or white tubular flowers, some of which are grown as greenhouse plants: family *Gesneriaceae* [from Latin *achaemenis*, from Greek *achaimenis*, a species of euphorbia]

Achitophel (ə'kɪtə,fɛl) *n Bible* the Douay spelling of **Ahithophel**

achlamydeous (,æklə'mɪdɪəs) *adj* (of flowers such as the willow) having neither petals nor sepals [c19 from Greek *a-* not, without + *chlamys* cloak]

ach-laut ('æklaʊt, 'æx-) *n* (*sometimes capital*) *phonetics* the voiceless velar fricative sound that is written as *ch* in Scottish *loch* or in German *ach*, often allophonic with the ich-laut. See also **ich-laut** [from German, from *ach* ah + *Laut* sound]

achlorhydria (,eɪklɔː'haɪdrɪə) *n* the absence of free hydrochloric acid in the gastric juice [c20 New Latin; see A-¹, CHLORO-, HYDRO-]

achondrite (eɪ'kɒndraɪt) *n* a rare stony meteorite that consists mainly of silicate minerals and has the texture of igneous rock but contains no chondrules. Compare **chondrite**. > achondritic (,eɪkɒn'drɪtɪk) *adj*

achondroplasia (eɪ,kɒndrəʊ'pleɪzɪə) *n* a skeletal disorder, characterized by failure of normal conversion of cartilage into bone, that begins during fetal life and results in dwarfism [c20 New Latin; see A-¹, CHONDRO-, -PLASIA] > achondroplastic (eɪ,kɒndrəʊ'plæstɪk) *adj*

achromat ('ækrə,mæt) *n* **1** Also called: **achromatic lens** a lens designed to bring light of two chosen wavelengths to the same focal point, thus reducing chromatic aberration. Compare **apochromat 2** a person who has no colour vision at all and can distinguish only black, white, and grey. The condition is very rare

achromatic (,ækrə'mætɪk) *adj* **1** without colour **2** capable of reflecting or refracting light without chromatic aberration **3** *cytology* **a** not staining with standard dyes **b** of or relating to achromatin **4** *music* **a** involving no sharps or flats **b** another word for **diatonic 5** denoting a person who is an achromat > ,achro'matically *adv* > achromatism (ə'krəʊmə,tɪzəm) *or* achromaticity (ə,krəʊmə'tɪsɪtɪ) *n*

achromatic colour *n physics* colour, such as white, black, and grey, that is devoid of hue. See **colour** (sense 2)

achromatin (ə'krəʊmətɪn) *n* the material of the nucleus of a cell that does not stain with basic dyes. Compare **chromatin**

achromatize *or* **achromatise** (ə'krəʊmətaɪz) *vb* (*tr*) to make achromatic; to remove colour from > a,chromati'zation *or* a,chromati'sation *n*

achromatous (ə'krəʊmətəs) *adj* having little or no colour or less than is normal

achromic (ə'krəʊmɪk) *or* **achromous** *adj* colourless

achy ('eɪkɪ) *adj* achier, achiest affected by a continuous dull ache

ach-y-fi (,axə'viː, ,ʌx-) *interj Welsh dialect* an expression of disgust or abhorrence [Welsh, probably from *ach, achy* general exclamation of disgust + *fi* I, me]

acicula (ə'sɪkjʊlə) *n, pl* -lae (-,liː) a needle-shaped part, such as a spine, prickle, or crystal [c19 New Latin, diminutive of *acus* needle] > a'cicular *adj*

aciculate (ə'sɪkjʊlɪt, -,leɪt) *or* **aciculated** *adj* **1** having aciculae **2** marked with or as if with needle scratches

aciculum (ə'sɪkjʊləm) *n, pl* -lums *or* -la (-lə) a needle-like bristle that provides internal support for the appendages (chaetae) of some polychaete worms [c19 New Latin; see ACICULA]

acid ('æsɪd) *n* **1** any substance that dissociates in water to yield a sour corrosive solution containing hydrogen ions, having a pH of less than 7, and turning litmus red. See also **Lewis acid 2** a sour-tasting substance **3** a slang name for LSD ⊳ *adj* **4** *chem* **a** of, derived from, or containing acid: *an acid radical* **b** being or having the properties of an acid: *sodium bicarbonate is an acid salt* **5** sharp or sour in taste **6** cutting, sharp, or hurtful in speech, manner, etc; vitriolic; caustic **7** (of rain, snow, etc) containing pollutant acids in solution **8** (of igneous rocks) having a silica content of more than 60% of the total and containing at least one tenth quartz **9** *metallurgy* of or made by a process in which the furnace or converter is lined with an acid material: *acid steel* [c17 (first used by Francis Bacon): from French *acide* or Latin *acidus*, from *acēre* to be sour or sharp] > 'acidly *adv* > 'acidness *n* > 'acidy *adj*

acid anhydride *n* another name for **anhydride** (sense 3)

acidanthera (,æsɪ'dænθərə) *n* any plant of the African cormous genus *Acidanthera*, cultivated for its graceful tubular white and red or white and purple flowers, often scented: family *Iridaceae* [from Greek *akis* point + New Latin *anthera* anther, from the shape of the anthers]

acid drop *n* a boiled sweet with a sharp taste

acid dye *n* a dye in which the chromophore is part of a negative ion usually applied from an acidic solution

acid-fast *adj* (of bacteria and tissues) resistant to decolorize by mineral acids after staining

acid-forming *adj* **1** (of an oxide or element) yielding an acid when dissolved in water or having an oxide that forms an acid in water; acidic **2** (of foods) producing an acid residue following digestion

acid halide *n* another name for **acyl halide**

acidhead ('æsɪd,hɛd) *n slang* a person who uses LSD

Acid House *or* **Acid** *n* a type of funk-based electronically edited disco music of the late 1980s, which has hypnotic sound effects and is associated with hippy culture and the use of the drug ecstasy [c20 perhaps from ACID (LSD) + HOUSE (MUSIC)]

acidic (ə'sɪdɪk) *adj* **1** another word for **acid 2** (of an oxide) yielding an acid in aqueous solution

acidify (ə'sɪdɪ,faɪ) *vb* -fies, -fying, -fied to convert into or become acid > a'cidi,fiable *adj* > a,cidifi'cation *n* > a'cidi,fier *n*

acidimeter (,æsɪ'dɪmɪtə) *n* **1** any instrument or standard solution for determining the amount of acid in a sample solution **2** another name for **acidometer**

acidimetry (,æsɪ'dɪmɪtrɪ) *n* the determination of the amount of acid present in a solution, measured by an acidimeter or by volumetric analysis > acidimetric (,æsɪdɪ'mɛtrɪk) *or* ,acidi'metrical *adj* > ,acidi'metrically *adv*

acidity (ə'sɪdɪtɪ) *n, pl* -ties **1** the quality or state of being acid **2** the amount of acid present in a solution, often expressed in terms of pH **3** another name for **hyperacidity**

acidometer (,æsɪ'dɒmɪtə) *n* a type of hydrometer for measuring the relative density of an acid solution, esp the acid in a battery. Also called: acidimeter

acidophil ('æsɪdəʊ,fɪl, ə'sɪdə-) *or* **acidophile** ('æsɪdəʊ,faɪl, ə'sɪdə-) *adj also* acidophilic (,æsɪdəʊ'fɪlɪk, ə,sɪdə-) *or* acidophilous (,æsɪ'dɒfɪləs) **1** (of cells or cell contents) easily stained by acid dyes **2** (of microorganisms) growing well in an acid environment ⊳ *n* **3** an acidophil organism [c20 see ACID, -PHILE]

acidophilus milk (,æsɪ'dɒfɪləs) *n med* milk fermented by bacteria of the species *Lactobacillus acidophilus*, used in treating disorders of the gastrointestinal tract

acidosis (,æsɪ'dəʊsɪs) *n* a condition characterized by an abnormal increase in the acidity of the blood and extracellular fluids > acidotic (,æsɪ'dɒtɪk) *adj*

acid rain *n* rain that contains a high concentration of pollutants, chiefly sulphur dioxide and nitrogen oxide, released into the atmosphere by the burning of fossil fuels such as coal or oil

acid reflux *n* the regurgitation of stomach acid into the oesophagus, causing heartburn

acid rock *n* a type of rock music characterized by electronically amplified bizarre instrumental effects [c20 from ACID (sense 3), alluding to its supposed inspiration by drug-induced states of consciousness]

acid salt *n chem* a salt formed by partial replacement of the acidic hydrogen atoms of the parent acid

acid soil *n* a soil that gives a pH reaction of below about 6, found especially in cool moist areas where soluble bases are leached away

acid test *n* a rigorous and conclusive test to establish worth or value: *the play passed the critic's acid test* [c19 from the testing of gold with nitric acid]

acidulate (ə'sɪdjʊ,leɪt) *vb* (*tr*) to make slightly acid or sour [c18 ACIDULOUS + -ATE¹] > a,cidu'lation *n*

acidulous (ə'sɪdjʊləs) *or* **acidulent** *adj* **1** rather sour **2** sharp or sour in speech, manner, etc; acid [c18 from Latin *acidulus* sourish, diminutive of *acidus* sour]

acid value *n* the number of milligrams of potassium hydroxide required to neutralize the free fatty acid in one gram of a fat, oil, resin, etc

acierate ('æsɪə,reɪt) *vb* (*tr*) to change (iron) into steel [c19 from French *acier* steel, from Latin *aciēs* sharpness] > ,acier'ation *n*

ACII *abbreviation for* Associate of the Chartered Insurance Institute

acinaciform (,æsɪ'næsɪ,fɔːm) *adj* (of leaves) shaped like a scimitar; curved [c19 via Latin *acīnacēs*, from Greek *akinakēs* short sword, ultimately from Iranian + -FORM]

aciniform (ə'sɪnɪ,fɔːm) *adj* shaped like a bunch of grapes [c19 from New Latin *aciniformis*; see ACINUS]

acinus ('æsɪnəs) *n, pl* -ni (-,naɪ) **1** *anatomy* any of the terminal saclike portions of a compound gland **2** *botany* any of the small drupes that make up the fruit of the blackberry, raspberry, etc **3** *botany obsolete* a collection of berries, such as a bunch of grapes [c18 New Latin, from Latin: grape, berry] > acinic (ə'sɪnɪk), 'acinous *or* 'acinose *adj*

Acis ('eɪsɪs) *n Greek myth* a Sicilian shepherd and the lover of the nymph Galatea. In jealousy, Polyphemus crushed him with a huge rock, and his blood was turned by Galatea into a river

ack-ack ('æk,æk) *n military* **1 a** anti-aircraft fire **b** (*as modifier*): *ack-ack guns* **2** anti-aircraft arms [c20 British army World War I phonetic alphabet for AA, abbreviation of *anti-aircraft*]

ackee *or* **akee** ('ækiː) *n* **1 a** a sapindaceous tree, *Blighia sapida*, native to tropical Africa and cultivated in the Caribbean for its fruit, edible when cooked **b** the red pear-shaped fruit of this tree **2** a sapindaceous tree, *Melicoccus bijugatus*, that grows on some Caribbean islands and is valued for its timber and edible fruit **3** the green tough-skinned berry of this tree [c18 of African origin]

ack-emma ('æk'ɛmə) *adv old-fashioned* in the morning; a.m [World War I phonetic alphabet for A, M]

acker ('ækə) *n* **1** *Austral informal* a variant spelling of **acca 2** *Austral slang* a pimple [for sense 2, a shortened form of ACNE]

acknowledge (ək'nɒlɪdʒ) *vb* (*tr*) **1** (may take a clause as object) to recognize or admit the existence, truth, or reality of **2** to indicate recognition or awareness of, as by a greeting, glance, etc **3** to express appreciation or thanks for: *to acknowledge a gift* **4** to make the receipt of known to the sender: *to acknowledge a letter* **5** to recognize, esp in legal

a

form, the authority, rights, or claims of [c15 probably from earlier *knowledge,* on the model of Old English *oncnāwan,* Middle English *aknowen* to confess, recognize] > ac'knowledgeable *adj* > ac'knowledger *n*

acknowledgment *or* **acknowledgement** (ək'nɒlɪdʒmənt) *n* **1** the act of acknowledging or state of being acknowledged **2** something done or given as an expression of thanks, as a reply to a message, etc **3** (*plural*) an author's statement acknowledging his use of the works of other authors, usually printed at the front of a book

ACL *abbreviation for* anterior cruciate ligament

aclinic line (ə'klɪnɪk) *n* another name for **magnetic equator** [c19 *aclinic,* from Greek *aklinēs* not bending, from A-¹ + *klinein* to bend, lean]

ACLU *abbreviation for* American Civil Liberties Union

ACM *abbreviation for* Air Chief Marshal

acme ('ækmɪ) *n* the culminating point, as of achievement or excellence; summit; peak [c16 from Greek *akmē*]

acme screw thread *n* a type of screw thread having inclined flat flanks and a flat top and bottom: used in machine tools

acne ('æknɪ) *n* a chronic skin disease common in adolescence, involving inflammation of the sebaceous glands and characterized by pustules on the face, neck, and upper trunk. Also called: acne vulgaris ▷ See also **rosacea** [c19 New Latin, from a misreading of Greek *akmē* eruption on the face. See ACME]

acnode ('æk,nəʊd) *n* a point whose coordinates satisfy the equation of a curve although it does not lie on the curve; an isolated point. The origin is an acnode of the curve $y^2 + x^2 = x^3$ [c19 from Latin *acus* a needle + NODE] > ac'nodal *adj*

Acol ('æk²l) *n bridge* a popular British bidding system favouring light opening bids and a flexible approach [c20 named after a club in Acol Road, London]

acolyte ('ækə,laɪt) *n* **1** a follower or attendant **2** *Christianity* an officer who attends or assists a priest [c16 via Old French and Medieval Latin from Greek *akolouthos* a follower]

Aconcagua (*Spanish* akon'kaɣwa) *n* a mountain in W Argentina: the highest peak in the Andes and in the W Hemisphere. Height: 6960 m (22 835 ft)

aconite ('ækə,naɪt) *or* **aconitum** (,ækə'naɪtəm) *n* **1** any of various N temperate plants of the ranunculaceous genus *Aconitum,* such as monkshood and wolfsbane, many of which are poisonous. Compare **winter aconite 2** the dried poisonous root of many of these plants, sometimes used as an antipyretic [c16 via Old French or Latin from Greek *akoniton* aconite, monkshood] > aconitic (,ækə'nɪtɪk) *adj*

Açôres (ə'soraʃ) *n* the Portuguese name for (the) **Azores**

acorn ('eɪkɔːn) *n* the fruit of an oak tree, consisting of a smooth thick-walled nut in a woody scaly cuplike base [c16 a variant (through influence of *corn*) of Old English *æcern* the fruit of a tree, acorn; related to Gothic *akran* fruit, yield]

acorn barnacle *or* **shell** *n* any of various barnacles, such as *Balanus balanoides,* that live attached to rocks and have a volcano-shaped shell from the top of which protrude feathery food-catching appendages (cirri)

acorn valve *or US* **tube** *n* a small electronic valve, approximately acorn-shaped with small closely-spaced electrodes, used in ultrahigh-frequency applications

acorn worm *n* any of various small burrowing marine animals of the genus *Balanoglossus* and related genera, having an elongated wormlike body with an acorn-shaped eversible proboscis at the head end: subphylum *Hemichordata* (hemichordates)

A Coruña (*Spanish* a ko'ruɲa) *n* the Galician name for **La Coruña**

---

acotyledon (ə,kɒtɪ'liːd³n) *n* any plant, such as a fern or moss, that does not possess cotyledons > a,coty'ledonous *adj*

acouchi *or* **acouchy** (ə'kuːʃɪ) *n, pl* -chis *or* -chies any of several South American rodents of the genus *Myoprocta,* closely related to the agoutis but much smaller, with a white-tipped tail: family *Dasyproctidae* [c19 via French from a native name in Guiana]

acoustic (ə'kuːstɪk) *or* **acoustical** *adj* **1** of or related to sound, the sense of hearing, or acoustics **2** designed to respond to, absorb, or control sound: *an acoustic tile* **3** (of a musical instrument or recording) without electronic amplification: *an acoustic bass;* [c17 from Greek *akoustikos,* from *akouein* to hear] > a'coustically *adv*

acoustic coupler *n computing* a device converting computer-data signals into acoustic form for transmission down a telephone line, through the handset microphone. See also **modem**

acoustic feature *n phonetics* any of the acoustic components or elements present in a speech sound and capable of being experimentally observed, recorded, and reproduced

acoustic guitar *n* an ordinary guitar, which produces its normal sound through the sounding board and is not amplified in any way. Compare **electric guitar**

acoustician (,ækuː'stɪʃən) *n* an expert in acoustics

acoustic nerve *n* the former name for **vestibulocochlear nerve**

acoustic phonetics *n* (*functioning as singular*) the branch of phonetics concerned with the acoustic properties of human speech. Compare **auditory phonetics, articulatory phonetics**

acoustics (ə'kuːstɪks) *n* **1** (*functioning as singular*) the scientific study of sound and sound waves **2** (*functioning as plural*) the characteristics of a room, auditorium, etc, that determine the fidelity with which sound can be heard within it

acoustic shock *n* a condition characterized by dizziness and partial hearing loss suffered by some people exposed to sudden loud noises over telephone or radio headsets; associated esp with workers in call centres

acoustoelectronic (ə,kuːstəʊ,ɪlɛk'trɒnɪk) *adj* denoting a device in which electronic signals are converted into acoustic waves, esp in delay lines, etc. Also: electroacoustic > a,cousto,elec'tronics *n*

acquaint (ə'kweɪnt) *vb* (*tr*) **1** (foll by *with* or *of*) to make (a person) familiar or conversant (with); inform (of) **2** (foll by *with*) *chiefly US* to introduce (to); bring into contact (with) [c13 via Old French and Medieval Latin from Latin *accognitus,* from *accognōscere* to know perfectly, from *ad-* (intensive) + *cognōscere* to know]

acquaintance (ə'kweɪntəns) *n* **1** a person with whom one has been in contact but who is not a close friend **2** knowledge of a person or thing, esp when slight **3** **make the acquaintance of** to come into social contact with **4** those persons collectively whom one knows **5** *philosophy* the relation between a knower and the object of his knowledge, as contrasted with knowledge by description (esp in the phrase **knowledge by acquaintance**) > ac'quaintance,ship *n*

acquaintance violence *n* impulsive aggressive behaviour towards someone with whom the attacker has been in contact

acquainted (ə'kweɪntɪd) *adj* (*postpositive*) **1** (sometimes foll by *with*) on terms of familiarity but not intimacy **2** (foll by *with*) having knowledge or experience (of); familiar (with)

acquiesce (,ækwɪ'ɛs) *vb* (*intr;* often foll by *in* or *to*) to comply (with); assent (to) without protest [c17 from Latin *acquiēscere* to remain at rest, agree without protest, from *ad-* at + *quiēscere* to rest, from *quiēs* QUIET] > ,acqui'escence *n* > ,acqui'escent *adj* > ,acqui'escently *adv*

▌ **USAGE** The use of *to* after *acquiesce* was formerly regarded as incorrect, but is now acceptable

---

acquire (ə'kwaɪə) *vb* (*tr*) to get or gain (something, such as an object, trait, or ability), esp more or less permanently [c15 via Old French from Latin *acquīrere,* from *ad-* in addition + *quaerere* to get, seek] > ac'quirable *adj* > ac'quirement *n* > ac'quirer *n*

acquired behaviour *n psychol* the behaviour of an organism resulting from the effects of the environment

acquired characteristic *n* a characteristic of an organism that results from increased use or disuse of an organ or the effects of the environment and cannot be inherited. See also Lamarckism

acquired drive *n psychol* a drive, like the desire for money, that has not been inherited but is learned, presumably because it leads to the satisfaction of innate drives

acquired immune deficiency syndrome *or* **acquired immunodeficiency syndrome** *n* the full name for AIDS

acquired immunity *n* the immunity produced by exposure to antigens, which stimulates the production of antibodies

acquired taste *n* **1** a liking for something that is at first considered unpleasant **2** the thing so liked

acquisition (,ækwɪ'zɪʃən) *n* **1** the act of acquiring or gaining possession **2** something acquired **3** a person or thing of special merit added to a group **4** *astronautics* the process of locating a spacecraft, satellite, etc, esp by radar, in order to gather tracking and telemetry information [c14 from Latin *acquīsītiōn-,* from *acquīrere* to ACQUIRE]

acquisition accounting *n* an accounting procedure in which the assets of a company that has recently been taken over are changed from the book value to the fair market value

acquisitive (ə'kwɪzɪtɪv) *adj* inclined or eager to acquire things, esp material possessions: *we currently live in an acquisitive society* > ac'quisitively *adv* > ac'quisitiveness *n*

acquit (ə'kwɪt) *vb* -quits, -quitting, -quitted (*tr*) **1** (foll by *of*) **a** to free or release (from a charge of crime) **b** to pronounce not guilty **2** (foll by *of*) to free or relieve (from an obligation, duty, responsibility, etc) **3** to repay or settle (something, such as a debt or obligation) **4** to perform (one's part); conduct (oneself) [c13 from Old French *aquiter,* from *quiter* to release, free from, QUIT] > ac'quitter *n*

acquittal (ə'kwɪt²l) *n* **1** *criminal law* the deliverance and release of a person appearing before a court on a charge of crime, as by a finding of not guilty **2** a discharge or release from an obligation, duty, debt, etc

acquittance (ə'kwɪtəns) *n* **1** a release from or settlement of a debt, etc **2** a record of this, such as a receipt

acre ('eɪkə) *n* **1** a unit of area used in certain English-speaking countries, equal to 4840 square yards or 4046.86 square metres **2** (*plural*) **a** land, esp a large area **b** *informal* a large amount: *he has acres of space in his room* **3** **farm the long acre** NZ to graze cows on the verge of a road [Old English *æcer* field, acre; related to Old Norse *akr,* German *Acker,* Latin *ager* field, Sanskrit *ajra* field]

Acre *n* **1** ('aːkrə) a state of W Brazil: mostly unexplored tropical forests; acquired from Bolivia in 1903. Capital: Rio Branco. Pop: 586 942 (2002). Area: 152 589 sq km (58 899 sq miles) **2** ('eɪkə, 'aːkə) a city and port in N Israel, strategically situated on the **Bay of Acre** in the E Mediterranean: taken and retaken during the Crusades (1104, 1187, 1191, 1291), taken by the Turks (1517), by Egypt (1832), and by the Turks again (1839). Pop: 45 600 (2001). Old Testament name: Accho (ə'kəʊ) Arabic name: 'Akka (aː'kaː) Hebrew name: 'Akko (aː'kəʊ)

acreage ('eɪkərɪdʒ) *n* **1** land area in acres ▷ *adj* **2** *Austral* of or relating to a large allotment of land, esp in a rural area

acred ('eɪkəd) *adj* (*usually in combination*) having

---

acres of land: *a many-acred farm; a well-acred nobleman*

acre-foot *n, pl* **-feet** the volume of water that would cover an area of 1 acre to a depth of 1 foot: equivalent to 43 560 cubic feet or 1233.5 cubic metres

acre-inch *n* the volume of water that would cover an area of 1 acre to a depth of 1 inch; one twelfth of an acre-foot: equivalent to 3630 cubic feet or 102.8 cubic metres

acrid ('ækrɪd) *adj* **1** unpleasantly pungent or sharp to the smell or taste **2** sharp or caustic, esp in speech or nature [C18 from Latin *ācer* sharp, sour; probably formed on the model of ACID] > **acridity** (ə'krɪdɪtɪ) *or* '**acridness** *n* > '**acridly** *adv*

acridine ('ækrɪˌdiːn) *n* a colourless crystalline solid used in the manufacture of dyes. Formula: $C_{13}H_9N$

acriflavine (ˌækrɪ'fleɪvɪn, -viːn) *n* a brownish or orange-red powder used in medicine as an antiseptic and disinfectant. Formula: $C_{14}H_{14}N_3Cl$ [C20 from ACRIDINE + FLAVIN]

acriflavine hydrochloride *n* a red crystalline water-soluble solid substance obtained from acriflavine and used as an antiseptic. Also called: flavine

Acrilan ('ækrɪˌlæn) *n* *trademark* an acrylic fibre or fabric, characterized by strength, softness, and crease-resistance and used for carpets, etc

acrimonious (ˌækrɪ'məʊnɪəs) *adj* characterized by bitterness or sharpness of manner, speech, temper, etc > ˌacri'moniously *adv* > ˌacri'moniousness *n*

acrimony ('ækrɪmənɪ) *n, pl* **-nies** bitterness or sharpness of manner, speech, temper, etc [C16 from Latin *ācrimōnia*, from *ācer* sharp, sour]

acro- *combining form* **1** denoting something at a height, summit, top, tip, beginning, or end: *acropolis; acrogen* **2** denoting an extremity of the human body: *acromegaly* [from Greek *akros* extreme, topmost]

acrobat ('ækrəˌbæt) *n* **1** an entertainer who performs acts that require skill, agility, and coordination, such as tumbling, swinging from a trapeze, or walking a tightrope **2** a person noted for his frequent and rapid changes of position or allegiances: *a political acrobat* [C19 via French from Greek *akrobatēs* acrobat, one who walks on tiptoe, from ACRO- + *bat-*, from *bainein* to walk] > ˌacro'batic *adj* > ˌacro'batically *adv*

acrobatics (ˌækrə'bætɪks) *n* **1** (*functioning as plural*) the skills or feats of an acrobat **2** (*functioning as singular*) the art of an acrobat **3** (*functioning as plural*) any activity requiring agility and skill: *mental acrobatics*

acrocarpous (ˌækrəʊ'kɑːpəs) *adj* (of mosses) having clustered upright stems and the reproductive parts borne at the tip of a stem. Compare **pleurocarpous** [C19 from New Latin, from Greek *akrokarpos*]

acrocentric (ˌækrəʊ'sentrɪk) *adj* **1** (of a chromosome) having the centromere at one end > *n* **2** an acrocentric chromosome

acrocyanosis (ˌækrəʊˌsaɪə'nəʊsɪs) *n* cyanosis of the hands and feet due to poor circulation of the blood

acrodont ('ækrəˌdɒnt) *adj* **1** (of the teeth of some reptiles) having no roots and being fused at the base to the margin of the jawbones. See also **pleurodont** (sense 1) **2** having acrodont teeth [C19 from ACRO- + -ODONT]

acrodrome ('ækrəˌdrəʊm) *adj* (of the veins of a leaf) running parallel to the edges of the leaf and fusing at the tip. Also: **acrodromous** (ə'krɒdrəməs) [from ACRO- + -DROMOUS]

acrogen ('ækrədʒən) *n* any flowerless plant, such as a fern or moss, in which growth occurs from the tip of the main stem [C19 from ACRO- + Greek *genēs* born; see -GEN] > **acrogenic** (ˌækrə'dʒenɪk) *or* **acrogenous** (ə'krɒdʒɪnɪs) *adj* > a'crogenously *adv*

acrolein (ə'krəʊlɪɪn) *n* a colourless or yellowish flammable poisonous pungent liquid used in the manufacture of resins and pharmaceuticals.

Formula: CH₂:CHCHO [C19 from Latin *ācer* sharp + *olēre* to smell + -IN]

acrolith ('ækrəlɪθ) *n* (esp in ancient Greek sculpture) a wooden, often draped figure with only the head, hands, and feet in stone [C19 via Latin *acrolithus* from Greek *akrolithos* having stone extremities] > ˌacro'lithic *adj*

acromegaly (ˌækrəʊ'megəlɪ) *n* a chronic disease characterized by enlargement of the bones of the head, hands, and feet, and swelling and enlargement of soft tissue, esp the tongue. It is caused by excessive secretion of growth hormone by the pituitary gland. Compare **gigantism** [C19 from French *acromégalie*, from ACRO- + Greek *megal-*, stem of *megas* big] > **acromegalic** (ˌækrəʊmɪ'gælɪk) *adj, n*

acromion (ə'krəʊmɪən) *n, pl* **-mia** (-mɪə) the outermost edge of the spine of the shoulder blade [C17 New Latin, from Greek *akrōmion* the point of the shoulder, from ACRO- + *ōmion*, diminutive of *ōmos* shoulder]

acronychal, acronycal *or US* **acronical** (ə'krɒnɪk^əl) *adj* occurring at sunset: *the star has an acronychal rising* [C16 from Greek *akronychos* at sunset, from ACRO- + *nykh-*, *nyx* night] > a'cronychally, a'cronycally *or US* a'cronically *adv*

acronym ('ækrənɪm) *n* a pronounceable name made up of a series of initial letters or parts of words; for example, UNESCO for the *United Nations Educational, Scientific, and Cultural Organization* [C20 from ACRO- + -ONYM] > ˌacro'nymic *or* **acronymous** (ə'krɒnɪməs) *adj*

acroparaesthesia (ˌækrəʊˌpærɛs'θiːzɪə) *or US* **acroparesthesia** *n pathol* a persistent sensation of numbness and tingling in the hands and feet

acropetal (ə'krɒpɪt^əl) *adj* (of leaves and flowers) produced in order from the base upwards so that the youngest are at the apex. Compare **basipetal**

acrophobia (ˌækrə'fəʊbɪə) *n* abnormal fear or dread of being at a great height [C19 from ACRO- + -PHOBIA] > acro'phobic *adj*

acropolis (ə'krɒpəlɪs) *n* the citadel of an ancient Greek city [C17 from Greek, from ACRO- + *polis* city]

Acropolis (ə'krɒpəlɪs) *n* the citadel of Athens on which the Parthenon and the Erechtheum stand

acrospire ('ækrəˌspaɪə) *n* the first shoot developing from the plumule of a germinating grain seed [C17 from obsolete *akerspire*, from *aker* EAR² + *spire* sprout, SPIRE¹; the modern form is influenced by ACRO-]

across (ə'krɒs) *prep* **1** from one side to the other side of **2** on or at the other side of **3** so as to transcend boundaries or barriers: *people united across borders by religion and history; the study of linguistics across cultures* > *adv* **4** from one side to the other **5** on or to the other side [C13 *on croice, acros*, from Old French *a croix* crosswise]

across-the-board *adj* **1** (of salary increases, taxation cuts, etc) affecting all levels or classes equally **2** *horse racing* the US term for **each way**

acrostic (ə'krɒstɪk) *n* **a** a number of lines of writing, such as a poem, certain letters of which form a word, proverb, etc. A **single acrostic** is formed by the initial letters of the lines, a **double acrostic** by the initial and final letters, and a **triple acrostic** by the initial, middle, and final letters **b** the word, proverb, etc, so formed **c** (*as modifier*): *an acrostic sonnet* [C16 via French from Greek *akrostikhis*, from ACRO- + *stikhos* line of verse, STICH] > a'crostically *adv*

acroter (ə'krəʊtə, 'ækrətə) *n architect* a plinth bearing a statue, etc, at either end or at the apex of a pediment [C18 from French, from Latin *acroterium*, from Greek *akrōtērion* summit, from *akros* extreme]

acrylic (ə'krɪlɪk) *adj* **1** of, derived from, or concerned with acrylic acid > *n* **2** short for **acrylic fibre, acrylic resin 3** a paint or colour containing acrylic resin [C20 from ACROLEIN + -YL + -IC]

acrylic acid *n* a colourless corrosive pungent liquid, miscible with water, used in the manufacture of acrylic resins. Formula:

CH₂:CHCOOH. Systematic name: **propenoic acid**

acrylic fibre *n* a textile fibre, such as Orlon or Acrilan, produced from acrylonitrile

acrylic resin *n* any of a group of polymers or copolymers of acrylic acid, its esters, or amides, used as synthetic rubbers, textiles, paints, adhesives, and as plastics such as Perspex

acrylonitrile (ˌækrɪləʊ'naɪtraɪl) *n* a colourless liquid that is miscible with water and has toxic fumes: used in the manufacture of acrylic fibres and resins, rubber, and thermoplastics. Formula: CH₂:CHCN. Also called: **vinylcyanide** [C20 from ACRYLIC + NITRILE]

acrylyl ('ækrɪlɪl) *n* (*modifier*) of, consisting of, or containing the monovalent group CH₂:CHCO-: *acrylyl group or radical*

act (ækt) *n* **1** something done or performed; a deed **2** the performance of some physical or mental process; action **3** (*capital when part of a name*) the formally codified result of deliberation by a legislative body; a law, edict, decree, statute, etc **4** (*often plural*) a formal written record of transactions, proceedings, etc, as of a society, committee, or legislative body **5** a major division of a dramatic work **6 a** a short performance of skill, a comic sketch, dance, etc, esp one that is part of a programme of light entertainment **b** those giving such a performance **7** an assumed attitude or pose, esp one intended to impress **8** *philosophy* an occurrence effected by the volition of a human agent, usually opposed at least as regards its explanation to one which is causally determined. Compare **event** (sense 4) > *vb* **9** (*intr*) to do something; carry out an action **10** (*intr*) to function in a specified way; operate; react: *his mind acted quickly* **11** to perform (a part or role) in a play, etc **12** (*tr*) to present (a play, etc) on stage **13** (*intr; usually foll by for or as*) to be a substitute (for); function in place (of) **14** (*intr; foll by as*) to serve the function or purpose (of): *the glass acted as protection* **15** (*intr*) to conduct oneself or behave (as if one were): *she usually acts like a lady* **16** (*intr*) to behave in an unnatural or affected way **17** (*copula*) to pose as; play the part of: *to act the fool* **18** (*copula*) to behave in a manner appropriate to (esp in the phrase **act one's age**) **19** (*copula*) *not standard* to seem or pretend to be: *to act tired* **20** clean up one's **act** to start to behave in a responsible manner **21** get in on the **act** *informal* to become involved in a profitable undertaking or advantageous situation in order to share in the benefits **22** get one's **act together** *informal* to become organized or prepared ▷ See also **act on, act out, act up** [C14 from Latin *actus* a doing, performance, and *actum* a thing done, from the past participle of *agere* to do] > 'actable *adj* > ˌacta'bility *n*

ACT¹ *abbreviation for* **1** Australian Capital Territory **2** (formerly in Britain) advance corporation tax

ACT² (ækt) *n* (in New Zealand) *acronym for* Association of Consumers and Taxpayers: a small political party of the right

Actaeon (æk'tiːən, ˌæktɪən) *n Greek myth* a hunter of Boeotia who, having accidentally seen Artemis bathing, was turned into a stag and torn apart by his own hounds

actant ('æktənt) *n linguistics* (in valency grammar) a noun phrase functioning as the agent of the main verb of a sentence

actg *abbreviation for* acting

ACTH *n* adrenocorticotrophic hormone; a polypeptide hormone, secreted by the anterior lobe of the pituitary gland, that stimulates growth of the adrenal gland and the synthesis and secretion of corticosteroids. It is used in treating rheumatoid arthritis, allergic and skin diseases, and many other disorders. Also called: corticotrophin

actin ('æktɪn) *n* a protein that participates in many kinds of cell movement, including muscle contraction, during which it interacts with filaments of a second protein, myosin [C20 from ACT + -IN]

a

actinal ('æktɪnəl, æk'taɪnəl) *adj* **1** of or denoting the oral part of a radiate animal, such as a jellyfish, sea anemone, or sponge, from which the rays, tentacles, or arms grow **2** possessing rays or tentacles, as a jellyfish [C19 see ACTINO-, -AL¹] > **'actinally** *adv*

acting ('æktɪŋ) *adj* (prenominal) **1** taking on duties temporarily, esp as a substitute for another: *the acting president* **2** operating or functioning: *an acting order* **3** intended for stage performance; provided with directions for actors: *an acting version of "Hedda Gabler"* ▷ *n* **4** the art or profession of an actor

actinia (æk'tɪnɪə) *n, pl* **-tiniae** (-'tɪnɪ,i:) or **-tinias** any sea anemone of the genus *Actinia*, which are common in rock pools [C18 New Latin, literally: things having a radial structure. See ACTINO-, -IA]

actinic (æk'tɪnɪk) *adj* (of radiation) producing a photochemical effect [C19 from ACTINO- + -IC] > **ac'tinically** *adv* > **actin,ism** *n*

actinide ('æktɪ,naɪd) *n* a member of the actinide series. Also called: **actinon** [C19 from ACTINO- + -IDE]

actinide series *n* a series of 15 radioactive elements with increasing atomic numbers from actinium to lawrencium

actiniform (æk'tɪnɪ,fɔ:m) *adj* another word for **actinoid** [C20 from ACTINO- + -FORM]

actinium (æk'tɪnɪəm) *n* a radioactive element of the actinide series, occurring as a decay product of uranium. It is used as an alpha-particle source and in neutron production. Symbol: Ac; atomic no: 89; half-life of most stable isotope,²²⁷Ac: 21.6 years; relative density: 10.07; melting pt: 1051°C; boiling pt: 3200 ± 300°C [C19 New Latin, from ACTINO- + -IUM]

actinium series *n* a radioactive decay series that starts with uranium-235 and ends with lead-207

actino- or before a vowel **actin-** *combining form* **1** indicating a radial structure: *actinomorphic* **2** indicating radioactivity or radiation: *actinometer* [from Greek *aktino-*, from *aktis* beam, ray]

actinobacillosis (ækti:nəʊ,bæsɪl'əʊsɪs) *n vet science* a disease of cattle and sheep, caused by infection with an *Actinobacillus lignieresii* and characterized by soft tissue lesions, esp of the tongue. Also called: **wooden tongue, woody tongue, cruels**

actinobiology (,æktɪnəʊbaɪ'ɒlədʒɪ) *n* the branch of biology concerned with the effects of radiation on living organisms

actinochemistry (æk,tɪnəʊ'kɛmɪstrɪ) *n* another name for **photochemistry**

actinodermatitis (,æktɪnəʊ,dɜ:mə'taɪtɪs) *n* dermatitis from exposure to radiation, esp ultraviolet light or X-rays

actinoid ('æktɪ,nɔɪd) *adj* having a radiate form, as a sea anemone or starfish

actinolite (æk'tɪnə,laɪt) *n* a green mineral of the amphibole group consisting of calcium magnesium iron silicate. Formula: $Ca_2(Mg,Fe)_5Si_8O_{22}(OH)_2$ [C19 from ACTINO- (from the radiating crystals in some forms) + -LITE]

actinomere ('æktɪnəʊ,mɪə) *n* another name for **antimere**

actinometer (,æktɪ'nɒmɪtə) *n* an instrument for measuring the intensity of radiation, esp of the sun's rays > **actinometric** (,æktɪnəʊ'mɛtrɪk) or ,**actino'metrical** *adj* > ,**acti'nometry** *n*

actinomorphic (,æktɪnəʊ'mɔ:fɪk) or **actinomorphous** *adj botany* (esp of a flower) having radial symmetry, as buttercups. See also **zygomorphic.** > **'actino,morphy** *n*

actinomycete (,æktɪnəʊmaɪ'si:t) *n* any bacterium of the group *Actinomycetes*, usually filamentous in form [C20 from ACTINO- + -MYCETE]

actinomycin (,æktɪnəʊ'maɪsɪn) *n* any of several toxic antibiotics obtained from bacteria of the genus *Streptomyces*, used in treating some cancers; the most commonly used is dactinomycin (actinomycin D)

actinomycosis (,æktɪnəʊmaɪ'kəʊsɪs) *n* a fungal disease of cattle and of cats and dogs, sometimes transmitted to humans esp by bites, characterized by a swelling of the affected part, most often the jaw or lungs. Nontechnical name: **lumpy jaw** > **actinomycotic** (,æktɪnəʊmaɪ'kɒtɪk) *adj*

actinon ('æktɪ,nɒn) *n* **1** a radioisotope of radon that is a decay product of radium. Symbol: An or ²¹⁹Rn; atomic no: 86; half-life: 3.92s **2** another name for **actinide** [C20 New Latin, from ACTINIUM + -ON]

actinopod (æk'tɪnə,pɒd) *n* any protozoan of the phylum *Actinopoda*, such as a radiolarian or a heliozoan, having stiff radiating cytoplasmic projections

actinotherapy (,æktɪnəʊ'θɛrəpɪ) *n* a former name for **radiotherapy**

actinouranium (,æktɪnəʊjʊ'reɪnɪəm) *n* the isotope of uranium that has a mass number of 235

actinozoan (,æktɪnəʊ'zəʊən) *n, adj* another word for **anthozoan**

action ('ækʃən) *n* **1** the state or process of doing something or being active; operation **2** something done, such as an act or deed **3** movement or posture during some physical activity **4** activity, force, or energy: *a man of action* **5** (usually plural) conduct or behaviour **6** *law* **a** a legal proceeding brought by one party against another, seeking redress of a wrong or recovery of what is due; lawsuit **b** the right to bring such a proceeding **7** the operating mechanism, esp in a piano, gun, watch, etc **8** (of a guitar) the distance between the strings and the fingerboard **9** (of keyboard instruments) the sensitivity of the keys to touch **10** the force applied to a body: *the reaction is equal and opposite to the action* **11** the way in which something operates or works **12** *physics* **a** a property of a system expressed as twice the mean kinetic energy of the system over a given time interval multiplied by the time interval **b** the product of work or energy and time, usually expressed in joule seconds: *Planck's constant of action* **13** the events that form the plot of a story, film, play, or other composition **14** *military* **a** a minor engagement **b** fighting at sea or on land: *he saw action in the war* **15** *philosophy* behaviour which is voluntary and explicable in terms of the agent's reasons, as contrasted with that which is coerced or determined causally **16** *Brit* short for **industrial action** **17** *informal* the profits of an enterprise or transaction (esp in the phrase **a piece of the action**) **18** *slang* the main activity, esp social activity ▷ *vb (tr)* **19** to put into effect; take action concerning: *matters decided at the meeting cannot be actioned until the following week* ▷ *interj* **20** a command given by a film director to indicate that filming is to begin. See also **cue¹** (senses 1, 8) [C14 *accioun*, ultimately from Latin *āctiōn-*, stem of *āctiō*, from *agere* to do, act]

actionable ('ækʃənəbəl) *adj law* affording grounds for legal action > **'actionably** *adv*

action at a distance *n physics* the supposed interaction of two separated bodies without any intervening medium. In modern theories all interactions are assumed to require a field of force

actioner ('ækʃənə) *n informal* a film with a fast-moving plot, usually containing scenes of violence

action figure *n* a small figure of a character from a film, television programme, comic book etc, designed as a toy and often collected by enthusiasts

action painting *n* a development of abstract expressionism evolved in the 1940s, characterized by broad vigorous brush strokes and accidental effects of thrown, smeared, dripped, or spattered paint. Also called: **tachisme** See also **abstract expressionism**

action potential *n* a localized change in electrical potential, from about -70 mV to +30 mV and back again, that occurs across a nerve fibre during transmission of a nerve impulse

action replay *n* the rerunning of a small section of a television film or tape of a match or other sporting contest, often in slow motion. US and Canadian name: **instant replay**

action stations *pl n* **1** *military* the positions taken up by individuals in preparation for or during a battle ▷ *interj* **2** *military* a command to take up such positions **3** *informal* a warning to get ready for something

Actium ('æktɪəm) *n* a town of ancient Greece that overlooked the naval battle in 31 BC at which Octavian's fleet under Agrippa defeated that of Mark Antony and Cleopatra

activate ('æktɪ,veɪt) *vb (tr)* **1** to make active or capable of action **2** *physics* to make radioactive **3** *chem* **a** to increase the rate of (a reaction) **b** to treat (a substance, such as carbon or alumina) so as to increase powers of adsorption **4** *physiol* to prepare by arousal (the body or one of its organs (eg the brain)) for action **5** to purify (sewage) by aeration **6** *US military* to create, mobilize, or organize (a unit) > ,**acti'vation** *n* > **'acti,vator** *n*

activated alumina *n* a granular highly porous and adsorptive form of aluminium oxide, used for drying gases and as an oil-filtering material and catalyst

activated carbon *n* a porous highly adsorptive form of carbon used to remove colour or impurities from liquids and gases, in the separation and extraction of chemical compounds, and in the recovery of solvents. Also called: **activated charcoal, active carbon**

activated sludge *n* a mass of aerated precipitated sewage added to untreated sewage to bring about purification by hastening decomposition by microorganisms

active ('æktɪv) *adj* **1** in a state of action; moving, working, or doing something **2** busy or involved: *an active life* **3** physically energetic **4** exerting influence; effective: *an active ingredient* **5** *grammar* **a** denoting a voice of verbs used to indicate that the subject of a sentence is performing the action or causing the event or process described by the verb, as *kicked* in *The boy kicked the football*. Compare **passive** (sense 5) **b** another word for **nonstative 6** being fully engaged in military service (esp in the phrase **on active service**) **7** (of a volcano) erupting periodically; not extinct. Compare **dormant** (sense 3), **extinct** (sense 3) **8** *astronomy* (of the sun) exhibiting a large number of sunspots, solar flares, etc, and a marked variation in intensity and frequency of radio emission. Compare **quiet** (sense 8) **9** *commerce* **a** producing or being used to produce profit, esp in the form of interest: *active balances* **b** of or denoting stocks or shares that have been actively bought and sold as recorded in the Official List of the London Stock Exchange **10** *electronics* **a** containing a source of power: *an active network* **b** capable of amplifying a signal or controlling some function: *an active component; an active communication satellite* ▷ *n* **11** *grammar* **a** the active voice **b** an active verb **12** *chiefly US* a member of an organization who participates in its activities [C14 from Latin *āctīvus*. See ACT, -IVE] > **'actively** *adv* > **'activeness** *n*

active centre *n biochem* the region in an enzyme molecule in which the reactive groups that participate in its action are juxtaposed. Also called: **active site**

active galaxy *n* a galaxy that emits usually large amounts of energy from a very compact central source, such as Seyfert galaxies, radio galaxies, and quasars. Also called: **active galactic nucleus**

active list *n military* a list of officers available for full duty

active matrix *n computing* **a** a liquid crystal display in which each pixel is individually controlled to provide a sharp image at a wide viewing angle; it is used in laptop and notebook computers **b** (as modifier): *an active-matrix screen*

active optics *n* (functioning as singular) a system to compensate for any deformation caused by gravity in the surface accuracy and alignment of the mirrors of an astronomical telescope by means of actuators that control the movable mirror supports

active safety *n* the practice of taking measures to avoid accidents, as opposed to merely reducing their consequences. Compare **passive safety**

active service *or esp US* **active duty** *n* military duty in an operational area

active transport *n biochem, physiol* a process by which molecules are enabled to pass across a membrane from a region in which they are in a low concentration to one of high concentration; this requires the expenditure of energy in metabolism and is assisted by carrier proteins, commonly referred to as pumps

active vocabulary *n* the total number of words a person uses in his own speech and writing. Compare **passive vocabulary**

activism ('ækti,vizəm) *n* a policy of taking direct and often militant action to achieve an end, esp a political or social one > 'activist *n*

activity (æk'tiviti) *n, pl* -ties 1 the state or quality of being active 2 lively action or movement 3 any specific deed, action, pursuit, etc: *recreational activities* 4 the number of disintegrations of a radioactive substance in a given unit of time, usually expressed in curies or disintegrations per second 5 a the capacity of a substance to undergo chemical change b the effective concentration of a substance in a chemical system. The **absolute activity** of a substance B, λ_B, is defined as exp $(\mu_B RT)$ where μ_B is the chemical potential

act of contrition *n Christianity* a short prayer of penitence

act of faith *n Christianity* an act that demonstrates or tests a person's religious beliefs

act of God *n law* a sudden and inevitable occurrence caused by natural forces and not by the agency of man, such as a flood, earthquake, or a similar catastrophe

act of war *n* an aggressive act, usually employing military force, which constitutes an immediate threat to peace

actomyosin (,æktəu'maiəsin) *n* a complex protein in skeletal muscle that is formed by actin and myosin and which, when stimulated, shortens to cause muscle contraction

acton ('æktən) *n* (in medieval Europe) 1 a jacket or jerkin, originally of quilted cotton, worn under a coat of mail 2 a leather jacket padded with mail [c14 from Old French *auqueton*, probably ultimately from Arabic *alqutun* the cotton]

Acton ('æktən) *n* a district of the London borough of Ealing

act on *or* **upon** *vb (intr, preposition)* 1 to regulate one's behaviour in accordance with (advice, information, etc) 2 to have an effect on (illness, a part of the body, etc)

actor ('æktə) *n* 1 a person who acts in a play, film, broadcast, etc 2 *informal* a person who puts on a false manner in order to deceive others (often in the phrase **bad actor**)

> **USAGE** To avoid referring to people by their gender, *actor* is often used as a general term for women and men who act

act out *vb (adverb)* 1 (*tr*) to reproduce (an idea, former event, etc) in actions, often by mime 2 *psychiatry* to express unconsciously (a repressed impulse or experience) in overt behaviour

ACTRA ('æktrə) *n acronym for* Alliance of Canadian Cinema, Television, and Radio Artists

actress ('æktris) *n* 1 a woman who acts in a play, film, broadcast, etc 2 *informal* a woman who puts on a false manner in order to deceive others

actressy ('æktrisi) *adj* exaggerated and affected in manner; theatrical

Acts of the Apostles *n* the fifth book of the New Testament, describing the development of the early Church from Christ's ascension into heaven to Paul's sojourn at Rome. Often shortened to: Acts

ACTT *abbreviation for* Association of Cinematograph and Television Technicians

ACTU *abbreviation for* Australian Council of Trade Unions

actual ('æktʃʊəl) *adj* 1 existing in reality or as a matter of fact 2 real or genuine 3 existing at the present time; current 4 (usually preceded by *your*) *Brit informal, often facetious* (intensifier): *that music's by your actual Mozart, isn't it?* ▷ See also **actuals** [c14 *actuel* existing, from Late Latin *āctuālis* relating to acts, practical, from Latin *āctus* ACT]

> **USAGE** The excessive use of *actual* and *actually* should be avoided. They are unnecessary in sentences such as *in actual fact, he is forty-two*, and *he did actually go to the play but did not enjoy it*

actual bodily harm *n criminal law* injury caused by one person to another that interferes with the health or comfort of the victim. Abbreviation: **ABH**

actualité (,æktʃʊ'æltei; *French* aktɥalite) *n humorous* the truth: *economic with the actualité* [c20 French: literally, truth]

actuality (,æktʃʊ'æliti) *n, pl* -ties 1 true existence; reality 2 (*sometimes plural*) a fact or condition that is real

actualize *or* **actualise** ('æktʃʊə,laiz) *vb (tr)* 1 to make actual or real 2 to represent realistically > ,actuali'zation *or* ,actuali'sation *n*

actually ('æktʃʊəli) *adv* 1 a as an actual fact; really b (*as sentence modifier*): *actually, I haven't seen him* 2 at present 3 *informal* a parenthetic filler used to add slight emphasis: *I don't know, actually*

actuals ('æktʃʊəlz) *pl n* See **physicals**

actual sin *n Christianity* any sin that a person commits of his own free will and for which he is personally responsible. Compare **original sin**

actuary ('æktʃʊəri) *n, pl* -aries a person qualified to calculate commercial risks and probabilities involving uncertain future events, esp in such contexts as life assurance [c16 (meaning: registrar): from Latin *āctuārius* one who keeps accounts, from *actum* public business, and *acta* documents, deeds. See ACT, -ARY] > actuarial (,æktʃʊ'ɛəriəl) *adj*

actuate ('æktʃʊ,eit) *vb (tr)* 1 to put into action or mechanical motion 2 to motivate or incite into action: *actuated by unworthy desires* [c16 from Medieval Latin *actuātus*, from *actuāre* to incite to action, from Latin *āctus* ACT] > ,actu'ation *n* > 'actu,ator *n*

act up *vb (intr, adverb) informal* to behave in a troublesome way: *the engine began to act up when we were miles from anywhere*

actus reus ('æktəs 'reiəs) *n law* a criminal action regarded as a constituent element of a crime, as compared with the state of mind of the perpetrator. Compare **mens rea** [Latin, literally: guilty act]

acuity (ə'kju:iti) *n* 1 keenness or acuteness, esp in vision or thought 2 the capacity of the eye to see fine detail, measured by determining the finest detail that can just be detected [c15 from Old French, from Latin *acūtus* ACUTE]

aculeate (ə'kju:liit, -,eit) *or* **aculeated** *adj* 1 cutting; pointed 2 having prickles or spines, as a rose 3 having a sting, as bees, wasps, and ants [c17 from Latin *acūleātus*; see ACULEUS]

aculeus (ə'kju:liəs) *n* 1 a prickle or spine, such as the thorn of a rose 2 a sting or ovipositor [c19 from Latin, diminutive of *acus* needle]

acumen ('ækjʊ,mɛn, ə'kju:mən) *n* the ability to judge well; keen discernment; insight [c16 from Latin: sharpness, from *acuere* to sharpen, from *acus* needle] > a'cuminous *adj*

acuminate *adj* (ə'kju:minit, -,neit) 1 narrowing to a sharp point, as some types of leaf ▷ *vb* (ə'kju:mi,neit) 2 (*tr*) to make pointed or sharp [c17 from Latin *acūmināre* to sharpen; see ACUMEN] > a,cumi'nation *n*

acupoint ('ækjʊ,point) *n* any of the specific points on the body where a needle is inserted in

acupuncture or pressure is applied in acupressure [c19 from ACU(PUNCTURE) + POINT]

acupressure ('ækjʊ,prɛʃə) *n* another name for **shiatsu** [c19 from ACU(PUNCTURE) + PRESSURE]

acupuncture ('ækjʊ,pʌŋktʃə) *n* the insertion of the tips of needles into the skin at specific points for the purpose of treating various disorders by stimulating nerve impulses. Originally Chinese, this method of treatment is practised in many parts of the world. Also called: **stylostixis** [c17 from Latin *acus* needle + PUNCTURE] > 'acu,punctural *adj* > 'acu,puncturist *n*

acutance (ə'kju:tⁿns) *n* a physical rather than subjective measure of the sharpness of a photographic image

acute (ə'kju:t) *adj* 1 penetrating in perception or insight 2 sensitive to details; keen 3 of extreme importance; crucial 4 sharp or severe; intense: *acute pain; an acute drought* 5 having a sharp end or point 6 *maths* a (of an angle) less than 90° b (of a triangle) having all its interior angles less than 90° 7 (of a disease) a arising suddenly and manifesting intense severity b of relatively short duration. Compare **chronic** (sense 2) 8 *phonetics* a (of a vowel or syllable in some languages with a pitch accent, such as ancient Greek) spoken or sung on a higher musical pitch relative to neighbouring syllables or vowels b of or relating to an accent (´) placed over vowels, denoting that the vowel is pronounced with higher musical pitch (as in ancient Greek), with a certain special quality (as in French), etc. Compare (for senses 8a, 8b) **grave²** (sense 5), **circumflex** 9 (of a hospital, hospital bed, or ward) intended to accommodate short-term patients with acute illnesses ▷ *n* 10 an acute accent [c14 from Latin *acūtus*, past participle of *acuere* to sharpen, from *acus* needle] > a'cutely *adv* > a'cuteness *n*

acute accent *n* the diacritical mark (´), used in the writing system of some languages to indicate that the vowel over which it is placed has a special quality (as in French *été*) or that it receives the strongest stress in the word (as in Spanish *hablé*)

acute arch *n* another name for **lancet arch**

acute dose *n* a total dose of radiation administered over such a short period that biological recovery is impossible

ACW *abbreviation for* aircraftwoman

acyclic (ei'saiklik, ei'siklik) *adj* 1 *chem* not cyclic; having an open chain structure 2 *botany* having flower parts arranged in a spiral rather than a whorl

acyl ('eisail) *n* 1 (*modifier*) of, denoting, or containing the monovalent group of atoms RCO-, where R is an organic group: *acyl group or radical; acyl substitution* 2 an organometallic compound in which a metal atom is directly bound to an acyl group [c20 from ACID + -YL]

acyl anhydride *n* another name for **anhydride** (sense 3)

acylation (,eisai'leiʃən) *n* the introduction into a chemical compound of an acyl group

acyl halide *n* any derivative of carboxylic acid in which the hydroxyl group has been replaced by a halogen atom. Also called: **acid halide**

ad¹ (æd) *n* short for **advertisement**

ad² (æd) *n* tennis, US and Canadian short for **advantage** Brit equivalent: **van**

ad³ *the internet domain name for* Andorra

AD *abbreviation for* 1 (indicating years numbered from the supposed year of the birth of Christ) anno Domini: *70 AD*. Compare **BC** 2 *military* active duty 3 *military* air defence 4 Dame of the Order of Australia [(sense 4) Latin: in the year of the Lord]

> **USAGE** In strict usage, AD is only employed with specific years: *he died in 1621 AD*, but *he died in the 17th century* (and not *the 17th century AD*). Formerly the practice was to write AD preceding the date (AD 1621), and it is

a

also strictly correct to omit *in* when AD is used, since this is already contained in the meaning of the Latin *anno Domini* (in the year of Our Lord), but this is no longer general practice. BC is used with both specific dates and indications of the period: *Heraclitus was born about 540* BC; *the battle took place in the 4th century* BC

ad- *prefix* **1** to; towards: *adsorb*; *adverb* **2** near; next to: *adrenal* [from Latin: to, towards. As a prefix in words of Latin origin, *ad-* became *ac-*, *af-*, *ag-*, *al-*, *an-*, *acq-*, *ar-*, *as-*, and *at-* before *c, f, g, l, n, q, r, s*, and *t*, and became *a-* before *gn, sc, sp, st*]

-ad¹ *suffix forming nouns* **1** a group or unit (having so many parts or members): *triad* **2** an epic poem concerning (the subject indicated by the stem): *Dunciad* [via Latin from Greek *-ad-* (plural *-ades*), originally forming adjectives; names of epic poems are all formed on the model of the *Iliad*]

-ad² *suffix forming adverbs* denoting direction towards a specified part in anatomical descriptions: *cephalad* [from Latin *ad* to, towards]

Ada ('eɪdə) *n* a high-level computer programming language designed for dealing with real-time processing problems: used for military and other systems [C20 named after *Ada*, Lady Lovelace, the English mathematician, daughter of Lord Byron (1815–52), who worked with Charles Babbage (1792–1871) and whose description of his computing machines preserved them for posterity]

adactylous (eɪ'dæktɪləs) *adj* possessing no fingers or toes [C19 from A-¹ + DACTYL + -OUS]

adage ('ædɪdʒ) *n* a traditional saying that is accepted by many as true or partially true; proverb [C16 via Old French from Latin *adagium*; related to *āio* I say]

adagio (ə'dɑːdʒɪˌəʊ; *Italian* a'dadʒo) *music* ▷ *adj, adv* **1** (to be performed) slowly ▷ *n, pl* **-gios** **2** a movement or piece to be performed slowly **3** *ballet* a slow section of a pas de deux [C18 Italian, from *ad* at + *agio* ease]

Adam¹ ('ædəm) *n* **1** *Old Testament* the first man, created by God: the progenitor of the human race (Genesis 2–3) **2** **not know (someone) from Adam** to have no knowledge of or acquaintance with (someone) **3** **the old Adam** the evil supposedly inherent in human nature

Adam² *n modifier* in the neoclassical style made popular by Robert Adam (1728–92), Scottish architect and furniture designer

adamant ('ædəmənt) *adj* **1** unshakable in purpose, determination, or opinion; unyielding **2** a less common word for **adamantine** (sense 1) ▷ *n* **3** any extremely hard or apparently unbreakable substance **4** a legendary stone said to be impenetrable, often identified with the diamond or loadstone [Old English: from Latin *adamant-*, stem of *adamas*, from Greek; literal meaning perhaps: unconquerable, from A-¹ + *daman* to tame, conquer] ▷ '**adamantly** *adv*

adamantine (ˌædə'mæntaɪn) *adj* **1** very hard; unbreakable or unyielding **2** having the lustre of a diamond

Adamawa (ˌædə'mɑːwə) *n* a small group of languages of W Africa, spoken chiefly in E Nigeria, N Cameroon, the Central African Republic, and N Democratic Republic of Congo (formerly Zaïre), forming a branch of the Niger-Congo family

Adamite ('ædəˌmaɪt) *n* **1** a human being **2** a nudist, esp a member of an early Christian sect who sought to imitate Adam > **Adamitic** (ˌædə'mɪtɪk) *adj*

Adams ('ædəmz) *n* a mountain in SW Washington, in the Cascade Range. Height: 3751 m (12 307 ft)

Adam's ale or **wine** *n Old-fashioned jocular* water [C17 from the name of the first man to appear in the Old Testament]

Adam's apple *n* the visible projection of the thyroid cartilage of the larynx at the front of the neck

adamsite ('ædəmˌzaɪt) *n* a yellow poisonous crystalline solid that readily sublimes; diphenylaminechlorarsine. It is used in chemical warfare as a vomiting agent. Formula: $C_6H_4AsClNHC_6H_4$; relative density: 1.65; melting pt: 195°C; boiling pt: 410°C. Also called: **phenarsazine chloride** [C20 named after Roger *Adams* (1899–1971), American chemist]

Adam's-needle *n* a North American liliaceous plant, *Yucca filamentosa*, that has a tall woody stem, stiff pointed leaves, and large clusters of white flowers arranged in spikes. It is cultivated as an ornamental plant. See also **Spanish bayonet**

Adams-Stokes syndrome (-'stəʊks) *n* another term for **heart block** [C19 named after R. *Adams* (1791–1875) and W. *Stokes* (1804–78), Irish physicians]

Adana ('ædənə) *n* a city in S Turkey, capital of Adana province. Pop: 1 248 000 (2005 est). Also called: **Seyhan**

adapt (ə'dæpt) *vb* **1** (often foll by *to*) to adjust (someone or something, esp oneself) to different conditions, a new environment, etc **2** (*tr*) to fit, change, or modify to suit a new or different purpose: *to adapt a play for use in schools* [C17 from Latin *adaptāre*, from *ad-* + *aptāre* to fit, from *aptus* APT] > **a'daptable** *adj* > **aˌdapta'bility** *or* **a'daptableness** *n* > **a'daptive** *adj*

adaptation (ˌædəp'teɪʃən, ˌædæp-) *n* **1** the act or process of adapting or the state of being adapted; adjustment **2** something that is produced by adapting something else **3** something that is changed or modified to suit new conditions or needs **4** *biology* an inherited or acquired modification in organisms that makes them better suited to survive and reproduce in a particular environment **5** *physiol* the decreased response of a sense organ to a repeated or sustained stimulus **6** *psychol* (in learning theory) the weakening of a response to a stimulus with repeated presentation of the stimulus without reinforcement; applied mainly to innate responses **7** *social welfare* alteration to a dwelling to make it suitable for a disabled person, as by replacing steps with ramps

adaption (ə'dæpʃən) *n* another word for **adaptation**

adaptive optics *n* (*functioning as singular*) a technique used to increase the resolution of a ground-based astronomical telescope by counteracting the effects of the atmosphere on the image. A deforming mirror in the light path of the telescope maintains a pointlike image of the celestial body using either a real star or a laser beam as a reference

adaptive radiation *n* evolution of a number of divergent species from a common ancestor, each species becoming adapted to occupy a different environment. This type of evolution occurred in the Tertiary manuals and the Mesozoic reptiles

adaptogen (ə'dæptədʒən) *n* any of various natural substances used in herbal medicine to normalize and regulate the systems of the body [C20 from ADAPT + -GEN]

adaptogenic (əˌdæptə'dʒɛnɪk) *adj* acting to normalize and regulate the systems of the body: *adaptogenic herbs*

adaptor or **adapter** (ə'dæptə) *n* **1** a person or thing that adapts **2** any device for connecting two parts, esp ones that are of different sizes or have different mating fitments **3 a** a plug used to connect an electrical device to a mains supply when they have different types of terminals **b** a device used to connect several electrical appliances to a single mains socket

Adar (a'dar) *n* (in the Jewish calendar) the twelfth month of the year according to biblical reckoning and the sixth month of the civil year, usually falling within February and March. In a leap year, an additional month **Adar Rishon** (first Adar) is intercalated between Shevat and Adar, and the latter is known as **Adar Sheni** (second Adar) [from Hebrew]

adaxial (æd'æksɪəl) *adj* facing towards the axis, as the surface of a leaf that faces the stem. Compare **abaxial**

ADC *abbreviation for* **1** aide-de-camp **2** analogue-digital converter

add (æd) *vb* **1** to combine (two or more numbers or quantities) by addition **2** (*tr*; foll by *to*) to increase (a number or quantity) by another number or quantity using addition **3** (*tr*; often foll by *to*) to join (something) to something else in order to increase the size, quantity, effect, or scope; unite (with): *to add insult to injury* **4** (*intr*; foll by *to*) to have an extra and increased effect (on): *her illness added to his worries* **5** (*tr*) to say or write further **6** (*tr*; foll by *in*) to include ▷ See also **add up** [C14 from Latin *addere*, literally: to put to, from *ad-* to + *-dere* to put]

ADD *abbreviation for* **attention deficit disorder**

addax ('ædæks) *n* a large light-coloured antelope, *Addax nasomaculatus*, having ribbed loosely spiralled horns and inhabiting desert regions in N Africa: family *Bovidae*, order *Artiodactyla* [C17 Latin, from an unidentified ancient N African language]

added sixth *n* a chord much used esp in jazz, consisting of a triad with an added sixth above the root. Also called: **added sixth chord**. Compare **sixth chord**

addend ('ædɛnd, ə'dɛnd) *n* any of a set of numbers that is to be added. Compare **sum** (sense 1) [C20 short for ADDENDUM]

addendum (ə'dɛndəm) *n, pl* **-da** (-də) **1** something added; an addition **2** a supplement or appendix to a book, magazine, etc **3** the radial distance between the major and pitch cylinders of an external screw thread **4** the radial distance between the pitch circle and tip of a gear tooth [C18 from Latin, literally: a thing to be added, neuter gerundive of *addere* to ADD]

adder¹ ('ædə) *n* **1** Also called: **viper** a common viper, *Vipera berus*, that is widely distributed in Europe, including Britain, and Asia and is typically dark greyish in colour with a black zigzag pattern along the back **2** any of various similar venomous or nonvenomous snakes ▷ See also **death adder, puff adder** [Old English *nǣdre* snake; in Middle English a *naddre* was mistaken for an *addre*; related to Old Norse *nathr*, Gothic *nadrs*]

adder² ('ædə) *n* a person or thing that adds, esp a single element of an electronic computer, the function of which is to add a single digit of each of two inputs

adder's-meat *n* another name for the **greater stitchwort** (see **stitchwort**)

adder's-mouth *n* any of various orchids of the genus *Malaxis* that occur in all parts of the world except Australia and New Zealand and have small usually greenish flowers. See also **bog orchid**

adder's-tongue *n* **1** any of several terrestrial ferns of the genus *Ophioglossum*, esp *O. vulgatum*, that grow in the N hemisphere and have a spore-bearing body that sticks out like a spike from the leaf: family *Ophioglossaceae* **2** another name for **dogtooth violet**

addict *vb* (ə'dɪkt) **1** (*tr*; usually passive; often foll by *to*) to cause (someone or oneself) to become dependent (on something, esp a narcotic drug) ▷ *n* ('ædɪkt) **2** a person who is addicted, esp to narcotic drugs **3** *informal* a person who is devoted to something: *a jazz addict* [C16 (as adj and as vb; n use C20): from Latin *addictus* given over, from *addīcere* to give one's assent to, from *ad-* to + *dīcere* to say]

addiction (ə'dɪkʃən) *n* the condition of being abnormally dependent on some habit, esp compulsive dependency on narcotic drugs

addictive (ə'dɪktɪv) *adj* of, relating to, or causing addiction

adding ('ædɪŋ) *n* **1** an act or instance of addition ▷ *adj* **2** of, for, or relating to addition **3** (in systemic grammar) denoting a bound clause that qualifies the meaning of an antecedent noun rather than of the sentence as a whole. Compare **contingency** (sense 4)

adding machine *n* a mechanical device, operated manually or electrically, for adding and often subtracting, multiplying, and dividing

Addis Ababa ('ædɪs 'æbəbə) *n* the capital of Ethiopia, on a central plateau 2400 m (8000 ft) above sea level: founded in 1887; became capital in 1896. Pop: 2 899 000 (2005 est)

Addison's disease ('ædɪs²nz) *n* a disease characterized by deep bronzing of the skin, anaemia, and extreme weakness, caused by underactivity of the adrenal glands. Also called: **adrenal insufficiency** [C19 named after Thomas *Addison* (1793–1860), British physician who identified it]

addition (ə'dɪʃən) *n* **1** the act, process, or result of adding **2** a person or thing that is added or acquired **3** a mathematical operation in which the sum of two numbers or quantities is calculated. Usually indicated by the symbol + **4** *chiefly US and Canadian* a part added to a building or piece of land; annexe **5** *obsolete* a title following a person's name **6** **in addition** (*adverb*) also; as well; besides **7** **in addition to** (*preposition*) besides; as well as [C15 from Latin *additiōn-*, from *addere* to ADD]

additional (ə'dɪʃən²l) *adj* added or supplementary > ad'ditionally *adv*

additionality (ə,dɪʃə'nælɪtɪ) *n* **1** (in Britain) the principle that money raised by the National Lottery should only be spent on projects that would not otherwise be funded by government spending **2** (in the European Union) the principle that the EU contributes to the funding of a project in a member country provided that the member country also contributes

Additional Member System *n* a system of voting in which people vote separately for the candidate and the party of their choice. Parties are allocated extra seats if the number of constituencies they win does not reflect their overall share of the vote. See also **proportional representation**

additive ('ædɪtɪv) *adj* **1** characterized or produced by addition; cumulative ▷ *n* **2** any substance added to something to improve it, prevent deterioration, etc **3** short for **food additive** [C17 from Late Latin *additīvus*, from *addere* to ADD]

additive process *n* a photographic process in which the desired colours are produced by adding together appropriate proportions of three primary colours. Compare **subtractive process**

addle[1] ('æd²l) *vb* **1** to make or become confused or muddled **2** to make or become rotten ▷ *adj* **3** (*in combination*) indicating a confused or muddled state: *addle-brained*; *addle-pated* **1** (*vb*), back formation from *addled*, from C13 *addle* rotten, from Old English *adela* filth; related to dialect German *Addel* liquid manure]

addle[2] ('æd²l) *vb Northern English dialect* to earn (money or one's living) [C13 *addlen*, from Old Norse *öthlask* to gain possession of property, from *öthal* property]

add-on *n* a feature that can be added to a standard model or package to give increased benefits

address (ə'drɛs) *n* **1** the conventional form by which the location of a building is described **2** the written form of this, as on a letter or parcel, preceded by the name of the person or organization for whom it is intended **3** the place at which someone lives **4** a speech or written communication, esp one of a formal nature **5** skilfulness or tact **6** *archaic* manner or style of speaking or conversation **7** *computing* a number giving the location of a piece of stored information. See also **direct access 8** *Brit government* a statement of the opinions or wishes of either or both Houses of Parliament that is sent to the sovereign **9** the alignment or position of a

part, component, etc, that permits correct assembly or fitting **10** (*usually plural*) expressions of affection made by a man in courting a woman ▷ *vb* -**dresses**, -**dressing**; -**dressed** *or obsolete or poetic* -**drest 11** to mark (a letter, parcel, etc) with an address **12** to speak to, refer to in speaking, or deliver a speech to **13** (*used reflexively, foll by to*) **a** to speak or write to: *he addressed himself to the chairman* **b** to apply oneself to: *he addressed himself to the task* **14** to direct (a message, warning, etc) to the attention of **15** to consign or entrust (a ship or a ship's cargo) to a factor, merchant, etc **16** to adopt a position facing (the ball in golf, a partner in a dance, the target in archery, etc) **17** to treat of; deal with: *chapter 10 addresses the problem of transitivity* **18** an archaic word for **woo** [C14 (in the sense: to make right, adorn) and C15 (in the modern sense: to direct words): via Old French from Vulgar Latin *addrictiāre* (unattested) to make straight, direct oneself towards, from Latin *ad-* to + *dīrectus* DIRECT] > ad'dresser *or* ad'dressor *n*

addressable (ə'drɛsəb²l) *adj computing* possessing or capable of being reached by an address > ad,dressa'bility *n*

address bar *n computing* the space provided (on a browser) for showing the addresses of websites

addressee (,ædrɛ'si:) *n* **1** a person or organization to whom a letter, parcel, etc, is addressed **2** a person who is addressed in conversation, a speech, a poem, etc

Addressograph (ə'drɛsəu,grɑ:f, -,græf) *n trademark* a machine for addressing envelopes, etc

adduce (ə'dju:s) *vb* (*tr*) to cite (reasons, examples, etc) as evidence or proof [C15 from Latin *addūcere* to lead or bring to] > ad'ducent *adj* > ad'ducible *or* ad'duceable *adj* > adduction (ə'dʌkʃən) *n*

adduct (ə'dʌkt) *vb* (*tr*) **1** (of a muscle) to draw or pull (a leg, arm, etc) towards the median axis of the body. Compare **abduct** (sense 2) ▷ *n* **2** *chem* a compound formed by direct combination of two or more different compounds or elements [C19 from Latin *addūcere*; see ADDUCE] > ad'duction *n*

adductor (ə'dʌktə) *n* a muscle that adducts

add up *vb* (*adverb*) **1** to find the sum (of) **2** (*intr*) to result in a correct total **3** (*intr*) *informal* to make sense **4** (*intr*; foll by *to*) to amount to

addy ('ædɪ) *n*, *pl* **addies** *informal* an e-mail address

-**ade** *suffix forming nouns* a sweetened drink made of various fruits: *lemonade*; *limeade* [from French, from Latin *-āta* made of, feminine past participle of verbs ending in *-āre*]

Adelaide ('ædɪ,leɪd) *n* the capital of South Australia: **Port Adelaide,** 11 km (7 miles) away on St Vincent Gulf, handles the bulk of exports. Pop: 1 002 127 (2001)

Adélie Land ('ædɪlɪ; *French* adeli) *n* a part of Antarctica, between Wilkes Land and George V Land: the mainland section of the French Southern and Antarctic Territories (claim suspended under the Antarctic Treaty). Also called: **Adélie Coast** French name: **Terre Adélie**

ademption (ə'dɛmpʃən) *n property law* the failure of a specific legacy, as by a testator disposing of the subject matter in his lifetime [C16 from Latin *ademptiōn-* a taking away, from *adimere* to take away, take to (oneself), from *ad-* to + *emere* to buy, take]

Aden ('eɪd²n) *n* **1** the main port and commercial capital of Yemen, on the N coast of the **Gulf of Aden,** an arm of the Indian Ocean at the entrance to the Red Sea: capital of South Yemen until 1990: formerly an important port of call on shipping routes to the East. Pop: 584 000 (2005 est) **2** a former British colony and protectorate on the S coast of the Arabian Peninsula: became part of South Yemen in 1967, now part of Yemen. Area: 195 sq km (75 sq miles)

adenectomy (,ædə'nɛktəmɪ) *n*, *pl* -**mies 1** surgical removal of a gland **2** another name for **adenoidectomy** [C19 from ADENO- + -ECTOMY]

adenine ('ædənɪn, -,ni:n, -,naɪn) *n* a purine base present in tissues of all living organisms as a

constituent of the nucleic acids DNA and RNA and of certain coenzymes; 6-aminopurine. Formula: $C_5H_5N_5$; melting pt: 360–365°C

adenitis (,ædə'naɪtɪs) *n* inflammation of a gland or lymph node [C19 New Latin, from ADENO- + -ITIS]

adeno- *or before a vowel* **aden-** *combining form* gland or glandular: *adenoid; adenology* [New Latin, from Greek *adēn* gland]

adenocarcinoma (,ædɪnəu,kɑ:sɪ'nəumə) *n*, *pl* -**mas** *or* -**mata** (-mətə) **1** a malignant tumour originating in glandular tissue **2** a malignant tumour with a glandlike structure

adenohypophysis (,ædɪnəuhaɪ'pɒfɪsɪs) *n* the anterior lobe of the pituitary gland. Compare **neurohypophysis**

adenoid ('ædɪ,nɔɪd) *adj* **1** of or resembling a gland **2** of or relating to lymphoid tissue, as that found in the lymph nodes, spleen, tonsils, etc **3** of or relating to the adenoids [C19 from Greek *adenoeidēs*. See ADENO-, -OID]

adenoidal (,ædɪ'nɔɪd²l) *adj* **1** having the nasal tones or impaired breathing of one with enlarged adenoids **2** another word for **adenoid** (for all senses)

adenoidectomy (,ædɪnɔɪ'dɛktəmɪ) *n*, *pl* -**mies** surgical removal of the adenoids

adenoids ('ædɪ,nɔɪdz) *pl n* a mass of lymphoid tissue at the back of the throat behind the uvula: when enlarged it often restricts nasal breathing, esp in young children. Technical name: **pharyngeal tonsil**

adenoma (,ædɪ'nəumə) *n*, *pl* -**mas** *or* -**mata** (-mətə) **1** a tumour, usually benign, occurring in glandular tissue **2** a tumour having a glandlike structure

adenopathy (,ædɪ'nɒpəθɪ) *n pathol* **1** enlargement of the lymph nodes **2** enlargement of a gland

adenosine (æ'dɛnə,si:n, ,ædɪ'nəusi:n) *n biochem* a nucleoside formed by the condensation of adenine and ribose. It is present in all living cells in a combined form, as in ribonucleic acids. Formula: $C_{10}H_{13}N_5O_4$ [C20 a blend of ADENINE + RIBOSE]

adenosine diphosphate *n* the full name of ADP

adenosine monophosphate (,mɒnəu'fɒsfeɪt) *n* another term for **adenylic acid** Abbreviation: AMP

adenosine triphosphate *n* the full name of ATP

adenovirus (,ædɪnəu'vaɪrəs) *n* any of a group of viruses that can cause upper respiratory diseases in man. Compare **enterovirus, myxovirus**

adenylic acid (,ædə'nɪlɪk) *n* a nucleotide consisting of adenine, ribose or deoxyribose, and a phosphate group. It is a constituent of DNA or RNA. Also called: **adenosine monophosphate**

adept *adj* (ə'dɛpt) **1** very proficient in something requiring skill or manual dexterity **2** skilful; expert ▷ *n* ('ædɛpt) **3** a person who is skilled or proficient in something [C17 from Medieval Latin *adeptus*, from Latin *adipiscī* to attain, from *ad-* to + *apiscī* to attain] > a'deptly *adv* > a'deptness *n*

adequate ('ædɪkwɪt) *adj* able to fulfil a need or requirement without being abundant, outstanding, etc [C17 from Latin *adaequāre* to equalize, from *ad-* to + *aequus* EQUAL] > adequacy ('ædɪkwəsɪ) *n* > 'adequately *adv*

à deux *French* (a dø) *adj*, *adv* of or for two persons

ADFA *abbreviation for* Australian Defence Force Academy

ADH *abbreviation for* antidiuretic hormone. See **vasopressin**

adhan (,a'ða:n) *n Islam* a call to prayer [changed from Arabic *adhān*, literally: announcement]

ADHD *abbreviation for* attention deficit hyperactivity disorder

adhere (əd'hɪə) *vb* (*intr*) **1** (usually foll by *to*) to stick or hold fast **2** (foll by *to*) to be devoted (to a political party, cause, religion, etc); be a follower (of) **3** (foll by *to*) to follow closely or exactly: *adhere to the rules* [C16 via Medieval Latin *adhērēre* from Latin *adhaerēre* to stick to] > ad'herence *n*

a

■ USAGE See at **adhesion**

adherent (əd'hɪərənt) *n* **1** (usually foll by *of*) a supporter or follower ▷ *adj* **2** sticking, holding fast, or attached

adhesion (əd'hi:ʒən) *n* **1** the quality or condition of sticking together or holding fast **2** ability to make firm contact without skidding or slipping **3** attachment or fidelity, as to a political party, cause, etc **4** an attraction or repulsion between the molecules of unlike substances in contact: distinguished from *cohesion* **5** *pathol* abnormal union of structures or parts [c17 from Latin *adhaesiōn-* a sticking. See ADHERE]

■ USAGE *Adhesion* is the preferred term when talking about sticking or holding fast in a physical sense. *Adherence* is preferred when talking about attachment to a political party, cause, etc

adhesive (əd'hi:sɪv) *adj* **1** able or designed to adhere; sticky: *adhesive tape* **2** tenacious or clinging ▷ *n* **3** a substance used for sticking objects together, such as glue, cement, or paste > ad'hesively *adv* > ad'hesiveness *n*

adhesive binding *n bookbinding* a style of binding used mainly for paperback books, where the backs of the gathered sections are trimmed and inserted into a cover along with adhesive to hold the pages and cover together. Also called: **perfect binding**

adhibit (əd'hɪbɪt) *vb* (*tr*) *rare* **1** to administer or apply **2** to affix; attach [c16 from Latin *adhibēre* to bring on, from AD- to + *habēre* to have, hold] > adhibition (,ædhɪ'bɪʃən) *n*

ad hoc (æd 'hɒk) *adj, adv* for a particular purpose only; lacking generality or justification: *an ad hoc decision; an ad hoc committee* [Latin, literally: to this]

adhocracy (æd'hɒkrəsɪ) *n* management that responds to urgent problems rather than planning to avoid them

ad hominem *Latin* (æd 'hɒmɪˌnɛm) *adj, adv* **1** directed against a person rather than against his arguments **2** based on or appealing to emotion rather than reason ▷ Compare **ad rem**. See also **argumentum ad hominem** [literally: to the man]

adiabatic (,ædɪə'bætɪk, ,eɪ-) *adj* **1** (of a thermodynamic process) taking place without loss or gain of heat ▷ *n* **2** a curve or surface on a graph representing the changes in two or more characteristics (such as pressure and volume) of a system undergoing an adiabatic process [c19 from Greek *adiabatos* not to be crossed, impassable (to heat), from A-[1] + *diabatos* passable, from *dia-* across + *bainein* to go]

adiactinic (,ædɪæk'tɪnɪk) *adj physics* denoting a substance that does not transmit radiation affecting photochemically sensitive materials, such as a safelight in a photographic darkroom

adiaphorism (,ædɪ'æfəˌrɪzəm) *n* a Christian Protestant theological theory that certain rites and actions are matters of indifference in religion since not forbidden by the Scriptures [c19 see ADIAPHOROUS] > ,adi'aphorist *n* > ,adi,apho'ristic *adj*

adiaphorous (,ædɪ'æfərəs) *adj med* having no effect for good or ill, as a drug or placebo [c17 from Greek *adiaphoros* indifferent, from A-[1] + *diaphoros* different]

adiathermancy (,ædɪə'θɜ:mənsɪ) *n* another name for **athermancy**. > adia'thermanous *adj*

adieu (ə'dju:; *French* adjø) *sentence substitute, n, pl* **adieus** *or* **adieux** (ə'dju:z; *French* adjø) goodbye; farewell [c14 from Old French, from *a* to + *dieu* God]

Adige (*Italian* 'a:didʒe) *n* a river in N Italy, flowing southeast to the Adriatic. Length: 354 km (220 miles)

Adi Granth (,a:dɪ 'grʌnt) *n* another name for **Guru Granth** [from Punjabi: first book]

ad infinitum (æd ,ɪnfɪ'naɪtəm) *adv* without end; endlessly; to infinity. Abbreviation: **ad inf** [Latin]

ad interim (æd 'ɪntərɪm) *adj, adv* for the meantime; for the present: *ad interim measures* Abbreviation: **ad int** [Latin]

adios (,ædɪ'ɒs; *Spanish* a'ðjos) *sentence substitute* goodbye; farewell [literally: to God]

adipic acid (ə'dɪpɪk) *n* a colourless crystalline solid used in the preparation of nylon. Formula: $HOOC(CH_2)_4COOH$ [c19 from New Latin *adiposus* fat + -IC]

adipocere (,ædɪpəʊ'sɪə, ,ædɪpəʊ,sɪə) *n* a waxlike fatty substance formed during the decomposition of corpses. Nontechnical name: **grave-wax** [c19 via French from New Latin *adiposus* fat (see ADIPOSE) + French *cire* wax] > adipocerous (,ædɪ'pɒsərəs) *adj*

adipocyte ('ædɪpəʊ,saɪt) *n* a fat cell that accumulates and stores fats

adipose ('ædɪ,pəʊs, -,pəʊz) *adj* **1** of, resembling, or containing fat; fatty ▷ *n* **2** animal fat [c18 from New Latin *adiposus*, from Latin *adeps* fat]

adipose fin *n* a posterior dorsal fin occurring in some fish, such as those of the salmon and catfish families

Adiprene ('ædɪpri:n) *n trademark* a polyurethane elastomer with exceptional abrasion resistance and strength

adipsia (eɪ'dɪpsɪə) *n* **1** complete lack of thirst **2** abnormal abstinence from drinking [c20 from A-[1] + Greek *dipsa* thirst]

Adirondack Mountains (,ædɪ'rɒndæk) *or* **Adirondacks** *pl n* a mountain range in NE New York State. Highest peak: Mount Marcy, 1629 m (5344 ft)

adit ('ædɪt) *n* an almost horizontal shaft into a mine, for access or drainage [c17 from Latin *aditus* an approach, from *adīre*, from *ad-* towards + *īre* to go]

Adivasi ('a:dɪ,va:sɪ) *n* a member of any of the aboriginal peoples of India [Sanskrit, from *adi* beginning + *vasi* dweller]

adj. *abbreviation for* **1** adjective **2** Also: **adjt** adjutant

adjacent (ə'dʒeɪsənt) *adj* **1** being near or close, esp having a common boundary; adjoining; contiguous **2** *maths* **a** (of a pair of vertices in a graph) joined by a common edge **b** (of a pair of edges in a graph) meeting at a common vertex ▷ *n* **3** *geometry* the side lying between a specified angle and a right angle in a right-angled triangle [c15 from Latin *adjacēre* to lie next to, from *ad-* near + *jacēre* to lie] > ad'jacency *n* > ad'jacently *adv*

adjacent angles *pl n* two angles that have the same vertex and a side in common

adjective ('ædʒɪktɪv) *n* **1 a** a word imputing a characteristic to a noun or pronoun **b** (*as modifier*): *an adjective phrase* Abbreviation: **adj** ▷ *adj* **2** additional or dependent **3** (of law) relating to court practice and procedure, as opposed to the principles of law dealt with by the courts. Compare **substantive** (sense 7) [c14 from Late Latin *adjectivus* attributive, from *adicere* to throw to, add, from *ad-* to + *jacere* to throw; in grammatical sense, from the Latin phrase *nōmen adjectīvum* attributive noun] > **adjectival** (,ædʒɪk'taɪvəl) *adj*

adjigo ('ædʒɪ,gəʊ) *n* a yam plant, *Dioscorea hastifolia*, native to SW Australia that has edible tubers [c19 from a native Australian language]

adjoin (ə'dʒɔɪn) *vb* **1** to be next to (an area of land, etc) **2** (*tr; foll by to*) to join; affix or attach [c14 via Old French from Latin *adjungere*, from *ad-* to + *jungere* to join]

adjoining (ə'dʒɔɪnɪŋ) *adj* being in contact; connected or neighbouring

adjoint ('ædʒɔɪnt) *n* **1** *maths* **a** another name for **Hermitian conjugate b** a generalization in category theory of this notion

adjourn (ə'dʒɜːn) *vb* **1** (*intr*) (of a court, etc) to close at the end of a session **2** to postpone or be postponed, esp temporarily or to another place **3** (*tr*) to put off (a problem, discussion, etc) for later consideration; defer **4** (*intr*) *informal* **a** to move elsewhere: *let's adjourn to the kitchen* **b** to stop work [c14 from Old French *ajourner* to defer to an arranged day, from *a-* to + *jour* day, from Late Latin *diurnum*, from Latin *diurnus* daily, from *diēs* day] > ad'journment *n*

adjudge (ə'dʒʌdʒ) *vb* (*tr; usually passive*) **1** to pronounce formally; declare: *he was adjudged the winner* **2 a** to determine judicially; judge **b** to order or pronounce by law; decree: *he was adjudged bankrupt* **c** to award (costs, damages, etc) **3** *archaic* to sentence or condemn [c14 via Old French from Latin *adjūdicāre*. See ADJUDICATE]

adjudicate (ə'dʒuːdɪ,keɪt) *vb* **1** (when *intr*, usually foll by *upon*) to give a decision (on), esp a formal or binding one **2** (*intr*) to act as an adjudicator **3** (*tr*) *chess* to determine the likely result of (a game) by counting relative value of pieces, positional strength, etc **4** (*intr*) to serve as a judge or arbiter, as in a competition [c18 from Latin *adjūdicāre* to award something to someone, from *ad-* to + *jūdicāre* to act as a judge, from *jūdex* judge] > adjudi'cation *n* > adjudicative (ə'dʒuːdɪkətɪv) *adj*

adjudicator (ə'dʒuːdɪ,keɪtə) *n* **1** a judge, esp in a competition **2** an arbitrator, esp in a dispute

adjunct ('ædʒʌŋkt) *n* **1** something incidental or not essential that is added to something else **2** a person who is subordinate to another **3** *grammar* **a** part of a sentence other than the subject or the predicate **b** (in systemic grammar) part of a sentence other than the subject, predicator, object, or complement; usually a prepositional or adverbial group **c** part of a sentence that may be omitted without making the sentence ungrammatical; a modifier **4** *logic* another name for **accident** (sense 4) ▷ *adj* **5** added or connected in a secondary or subordinate position; auxiliary [c16 from Latin *adjunctus*, past participle of *adjungere* to ADJOIN] > adjunctive (ə'dʒʌŋktɪv) *adj* > 'adjunctly *adv*

adjunction (ə'dʒʌŋkʃən) *n* (in phrase-structure grammar) the relationship between a branch of a tree representing a sentence to other branches to its left or right that descend from the same node immediately above

adjure (ə'dʒʊə) *vb* (*tr*) **1** to command, often by exacting an oath; charge **2** to appeal earnestly to [c14 from Latin *adjūrāre* to swear to, from *ad-* + *jūrāre* to swear, from *jūs* oath] > adjuration (,ædʒʊə'reɪʃən) *n* > ad'juratory *adj* > ad'jurer *or* ad'juror *n*

adjust (ə'dʒʌst) *vb* **1** (*tr*) to alter slightly, esp to achieve accuracy; regulate: *to adjust the television* **2** to adapt, as to a new environment, etc **3** (*tr*) to put into order **4** (*tr*) *insurance* to determine the amount payable in settlement of (a claim) [c17 from Old French *adjuster*, from *ad-* to + *juste* right, JUST] > ad'justable *adj* > ad'justably *adv* > ad'juster *n*

adjustment (ə'dʒʌstmənt) *n* **1** the act of adjusting or state of being adjusted **2** a control for regulating: *the adjustment for volume is beside the speaker*

adjutant ('ædʒətənt) *n* **1** an officer who acts as administrative assistant to a superior officer. Abbreviations: **adjt, adj 2** short for **adjutant bird** [c17 from Latin *adjūtāre* to AID] > 'adjutancy *n*

adjutant bird *or* **stork** *n* either of two large carrion-eating storks, *Leptoptilos dubius* or *L. javanicus*, which are closely related and similar to the marabou and occur in S and SE Asia [so called for its supposedly military gait]

adjutant general *n, pl* **adjutants general 1** *Brit army* **a** a member of the Army Board responsible for personnel and administrative functions **b** a general's executive officer **2** *US army* the adjutant of a military unit with general staff

adjuvant ('ædʒəvənt) *adj* **1** aiding or assisting ▷ *n* **2** something that aids or assists; auxiliary **3** *med* a drug or other substance that enhances the activity of another **4** *immunol* a substance that enhances the immune response stimulated by an antigen when injected with the antigen [c17 from Latin *adjuvāns*, present participle of *adjuvāre*, from *juvāre* to help]

adland ('æd,lænd) *n informal* the advertising

industry and the people who work in it [c20 from AD(VERTISING) + LAND]

Adlerian (æd'lɪərɪən) *adj* of or relating to the Austrian psychiatrist Alfred Adler (1870–1937) or his ideas

ad-lib (æd'lɪb) *vb* **-libs, -libbing, -libbed 1** to improvise and deliver without preparation (a speech, musical performance, etc) ▷ *adj* (**ad lib** *when predicative*) **2** improvised; impromptu ▷ *adv* **ad lib 3** without restraint; freely *4 music* short for **ad libitum** ▷ *n* **5** an improvised performance, often humorous [c18 short for Latin *ad libitum,* literally: according to pleasure] > **ad-'libber** *n*

ad libitum ('lɪbɪtʊm, -təm) *adj music* (to be performed) at the performer's discretion. Often shortened to: **ad lib** [see AD-LIB]

ad litem *Latin* (æd 'laɪtɛm) *adj* (formerly, esp of a guardian) appointed for a lawsuit

Adm. *abbreviation for* Admiral

adman ('æd,mæn, -mən) *n, pl* **-men** *informal* a person who works in advertising

admeasure (æd'mɛʒə) *vb* **1** to measure out (land, etc) as a share; apportion **2** (*tr*) to determine the dimensions, capacity, weight, and other details of (a vessel), as for an official registration, documentation, or yacht handicap rating [c14 *amesuren,* from Old French *amesurer,* from *mesurer* to MEASURE; the modern form derives from AD- + MEASURE] > **ad'measurement** *n*

Admetus (æd'miːtəs) *n Greek myth* a king of Thessaly, one of the Argonauts, who was married to Alcestis

admin ('ædmɪn) *n informal* short for **administration**

adminicle (æd'mɪnɪkəl) *n law* something contributing to prove a point without itself being complete proof [c16 from Latin *adminiculum* support]

administer (əd'mɪnɪstə) *vb* (*mainly tr*) **1** (*also intr*) to direct or control (the affairs of a business, government, etc) **2** to put into execution; dispense: *administer justice* **3** (when *intr*, foll by *to*) to give or apply (medicine, assistance, etc) as a remedy or relief **4** to apply formally; perform: *to administer extreme unction* **5** to supervise or impose the taking of (an oath, etc) **6** to manage or distribute (an estate, property, etc) [c14 *amynistre,* via Old French from Latin *administrare,* from *ad-* to + *ministrāre* to MINISTER]

administrate (əd'mɪnɪ,streɪt) *vb* to manage or direct (the affairs of a business, institution, etc)

administration (əd,mɪnɪ'streɪʃən) *n* **1** management of the affairs of an organization, such as a business or institution **2** the duties of an administrator **3** the body of people who administer an organization **4** the conduct of the affairs of government **5** term of office: often used of presidents, governments, etc **6** the executive branch of government along with the public service; the government as a whole **7** (*often capital*) *chiefly US* the political executive, esp of the US; the government **8** *chiefly US* a government board, agency, authority, etc **9** *property law* **a** the conduct or disposal of the estate of a deceased person **b** the management by a trustee of an estate subject to a trust **10 a** the administering of something, such as a sacrament, oath, or medical treatment **b** the thing that is administered > **ad'ministrative** *adj* > **ad'ministratively** *adv*

administration order *n law* **1** an order by a court appointing a person to manage a company that is in financial difficulty, in an attempt to ensure the survival of the company or achieve the best realization of its assets **2** an order by a court for the administration of the estate of a debtor who has been ordered by the court to pay money that he owes

administrator (əd'mɪnɪ,streɪtə) *n* **1** a person who administers the affairs of an organization, official body, etc **2** *property law* a person authorized to manage an estate, esp when the owner has died intestate or without having appointed executors

3 a person who manages a computer system > **ad,minis'tratrix** *fem n*

admirable ('ædmərəbəl) *adj* deserving or inspiring admiration; excellent > **'admirably** *adv*

admiral ('ædmərəl) *n* **1** the supreme commander of a fleet or navy **2** *Also called:* **admiral of the fleet, fleet admiral** a naval officer of the highest rank, equivalent to general of the army or field marshal **3** a senior naval officer entitled to fly his own flag. *See also* **rear admiral, vice admiral 4** *chiefly Brit* the master of a fishing fleet **5** any of various nymphalid butterflies, esp the red admiral or white admiral [c13 *amyral,* from Old French *amiral* emir, and from Medieval Latin *admirālis* (the spelling with *d* probably influenced by *admirābilis* admirable); both from Arabic *amīr* emir, commander, esp in the phrase *amīr-al* commander of, as in *amīr-al-bahr* commander of the sea] > **'admiral,ship** *n*

admiralty ('ædmərəltɪ) *n, pl* **-ties 1** the office or jurisdiction of an admiral **2 a** jurisdiction over naval affairs **b** (*as modifier*): *admiralty law*

Admiralty Board *n* **the** (formerly) a department of the British Ministry of Defence, responsible for the administration and planning of the Royal Navy

Admiralty House *n* the official residence of the Governor General of Australia, in Sydney

Admiralty Islands *pl n* a group of about 40 volcanic and coral islands in the SW Pacific, part of Papua New Guinea, in the Bismarck Archipelago: main island: Manus. Pop: 35 200 (1995). Area: about 2000 sq km (800 sq miles). *Also called:* **Admiralties**

Admiralty mile *n* another name for **nautical mile**

Admiralty Range *n* a mountain range in Antarctica, on the coast of Victoria Land, northwest of the Ross Sea

admiration (,ædmə'reɪʃən) *n* **1** pleasurable contemplation or surprise **2** a person or thing that is admired: *she was the admiration of the court* **3** *archaic* wonder

admire (əd'maɪə) *vb* (*tr*) **1** to regard with esteem, respect, approval, or pleased surprise **2** *archaic* to wonder at [c16 from Latin *admīrārī* to wonder at, from *ad-* to, at + *mīrārī* to wonder, from *mīrus* wonderful] > **ad'mirer** *n* > **ad'miring** *adj* > **ad'miringly** *adv*

admissible (əd'mɪsəbəl) *adj* **1** able or deserving to be considered or allowed **2** deserving to be admitted or allowed to enter **3** *law* (esp of evidence) capable of being or bound to be admitted in a court of law > **ad,missi'bility** or **ad'missibleness** *n*

admission (əd'mɪʃən) *n* **1** permission to enter or the right, authority, etc, to enter **2** the price charged for entrance **3** acceptance for a position, office, etc **4** a confession, as of a crime, mistake, etc **5** an acknowledgment of the truth or validity of something [c15 from Latin *admissiōn-,* from *admittere* to ADMIT] > **ad'missive** *adj*

admit (əd'mɪt) *vb* **-mits, -mitting, -mitted** (*mainly tr*) **1** (may take a clause as object) to confess or acknowledge (a crime, mistake, etc) **2** (may take a clause as object) to concede (the truth or validity of something) **3** to allow to enter; let in **4** (foll by *to*) to allow participation (in) or the right to be part (of): *to admit to the profession* **5** (when *intr,* foll by *of*) to allow (of); leave room (for) **6** (*intr*) to give access: *the door admits onto the lawn* [c14 from Latin *admittere* to let come or go to, from *ad-* to + *mittere* to send]

admittance (əd'mɪtəns) *n* **1** the right or authority to enter **2** the act of giving entrance **3** *electrical engineering* the reciprocal of impedance, usually measured in siemens. It can be expressed as a complex quantity, the real part of which is the conductance and the imaginary part the susceptance. *Symbol:* y

admittedly (əd'mɪtɪdlɪ) *adv* (*sentence modifier*) willingly conceded: *admittedly I am afraid*

admix (əd'mɪks) *vb* (*tr*) *rare* to mix or blend [c16

back formation from obsolete *admixt,* from Latin *admīscēre* to mix with]

admixture (əd'mɪkstʃə) *n* **1** a less common word for **mixture 2** anything added in mixing; ingredient

admonish (əd'mɒnɪʃ) *vb* (*tr*) **1** to reprove firmly but not harshly **2** to advise to do or against doing something; warn; caution [c14 via Old French from Vulgar Latin *admonestāre* (unattested), from Latin *admonēre* to put one in mind of, from *monēre* to advise] > **ad'monisher** or **ad'monitor** *n* > **admonition** (,ædmə'nɪʃən) *n* > **ad'monitory** *adj*

ADN *international car registration for* Yemen (from Aden)

adnate ('ædneɪt) *adj botany* growing closely attached to an adjacent part or organ [c17 from Latin *adnātus,* a variant form of *agnātus* AGNATE]

ad nauseam (æd 'nɔːzɪˌæm, -sɪ-) *adv* to a disgusting extent [Latin: to (the point of) nausea]

adnexa (æd'nɛksə) *pl n anatomy* adjoining organs, esp of the uterus [c19 New Latin: appendages] > **ad'nexal** *adj*

adnominal (əd'nɒmɪnəl) *grammar* ▷ *n* **1** a word modifying a noun ▷ *adj* **2** of or relating to an adnoun

adnoun ('ædnaʊn) *n* an adjective used as a noun; absolute adjective [c18 from Latin *ad* to + NOUN, formed on the model of ADVERB]

ado (ə'duː) *n* bustling activity; fuss; bother; delay (esp in the phrases **without more ado, with much ado**) [c14 from the phrase *at do* a to-do, from Old Norse *at* to (marking the infinitive) + DO[1]]

ADO *Austral* ▷ *abbreviation for* accumulated day off

adobe (ə'dəʊbɪ) *n* **1 a** a sun-dried brick used for building **b** (*as modifier*): *an adobe house* **2** a building constructed of such bricks **3** the clayey material from which such bricks are made [c19 from Spanish]

adobe flat *n chiefly US* a gently sloping clayey plain formed by a short-lived stream or flood water

adobo (ə'dəʊbəʊ) *n, pl* **-bos** the national dish of the Philippines, which consists of chunks of meat, fish, or vegetables, marinated in vinegar, soy sauce, garlic, and spices and then stewed in the marinade [c20 from Spanish]

adolescence (,ædə'lɛsəns) *n* the period in human development that occurs between the beginning of puberty and adulthood [c15 via Old French from Latin *adolēscentia,* from *adolēscere* to grow up, from *alēscere* to grow, from *alēre* to feed, nourish]

adolescent (,ædə'lɛsənt) *adj* **1** of or relating to adolescence **2** *informal* behaving in an immature way; puerile ▷ *n* **3** an adolescent person

Adonai (,ædəʊ'naɪ, -'neɪaɪ) *n Judaism* a name for God [c15 from Hebrew: lord; compare ADONIS]

Adonic (ə'dɒnɪk) *adj* **1** (in classical prosody) of or relating to a verse line consisting of a dactyl (---) followed by a spondee (--) or by a trochee (--), thought to have been first used in laments for Adonis **2** of or relating to Adonis ▷ *n* **3** an Adonic line or verse

Adonis (ə'dəʊnɪs) *n* **1** *Greek myth* a handsome youth loved by Aphrodite. Killed by a wild boar, he was believed to spend part of the year in the underworld and part on earth, symbolizing the vegetative cycle **2** a handsome young man [c16 from Latin, via Greek *Adōnis* from Phoenician *adōni* my lord, a title of the god Tammuz; related to Hebrew ADONAI]

adopt (ə'dɒpt) *vb* (*tr*) **1** *law* to bring (a person) into a specific relationship, esp to take (another's child) as one's own child **2** to choose and follow (a plan, technique, etc) **3** to take over (an idea, etc) as if it were one's own **4** to take on; assume: *to adopt a title* **5** to accept (a report, etc) [c16 from Latin *adoptāre* to choose for oneself, from *optāre* to choose] > **a'doptee** *n* > **a'doption** *n*

adopted (ə'dɒptɪd) *adj* having been adopted: *an adopted child*. *Compare* **adoptive**

adoption panel *n social welfare* (in Britain) a committee appointed by an adoption agency, such

a

as a local authority, to make recommendations concerning the suitability of prospective adoption cases

adoptive (ə'dɒptɪv) *adj* **1** acquired or related by adoption: *an adoptive father* **2** of or relating to adoption. Compare **adopted**

adorable (ə'dɔːrəbəl) *adj* **1** very attractive; charming; lovable **2** *becoming rare* deserving or eliciting adoration > a'dorably *adv*

adoration (ˌædə'reɪʃən) *n* **1** deep love or esteem **2** the act of worshipping

adore (ə'dɔː) *vb* **1** (*tr*) to love intensely or deeply **2** to worship (a god) with religious rites **3** (*tr*) *informal* to like very much: *I adore chocolate* [c15 via French from Latin *adōrāre*, from *ad-* to + *ōrāre* to pray] > a'dorer *n* > a'doring *adj* > a'doringly *adv*

adorn (ə'dɔːn) *vb* (*tr*) **1** to decorate: *she adorned her hair with flowers* **2** to increase the beauty, distinction, etc, of [c14 via Old French from Latin *adōrnāre*, from *ōrnāre* to furnish, prepare] > a'dornment *n*

Adowa ('ɑːdʊˌwɑː) *n* a variant spelling of **Aduwa**

ADP *n biochem* adenosine diphosphate; a nucleotide derived from ATP with the liberation of energy that is then used in the performance of muscular work

ADR *abbreviation for* adverse drug reaction

Adrastea (ə'dræstɪə) *n* a small satellite of Jupiter, discovered in 1979

Adrastus (ə'dræstəs) *n Greek myth* a king of Argos and leader of the Seven against Thebes of whom he was the sole survivor

ad referendum *adv, adj* subject to agreement by others and finalization of details: *an ad referendum contract* [Latin]

ad rem *Latin* (æd 'rɛm) *adj, adv* to the point; without digression: *to reply ad rem; an ad rem discussion*. Compare **ad hominem**

adrenal (ə'driːnəl) *adj* **1** on or near the kidneys **2** of or relating to the adrenal glands or their secretions ⊳ *n* **3** an adrenal gland [c19 from AD- (near) + RENAL]

adrenal gland *n* an endocrine gland at the anterior end of each kidney. Its medulla secretes adrenaline and noradrenaline and its cortex secretes several steroid hormones. Also called: suprarenal gland

Adrenalin (ə'drɛnəlɪn) *n trademark* a brand of **adrenaline**

adrenaline *or* **adrenalin** (ə'drɛnəlɪn) *n* a hormone that is secreted by the adrenal medulla in response to stress and increases heart rate, pulse rate, and blood pressure, and raises the blood levels of glucose and lipids. It is extracted from animals or synthesized for such medical uses as the treatment of asthma. Chemical name: aminohydroxyphenylpropionic acid; formula: $C_9H_{13}NO_3$. US name: epinephrine

adrenal insufficiency *n* another name for Addison's disease

adrenalized *or* **adrenalised** (ə'driːnəlaɪzd) *adj* tense or highly charged: *adrenalized with excitement*

adrenergic (ˌædrə'nɜːdʒɪk) *adj* releasing or activated by adrenaline or an adrenaline-like substance [c20 ADRENALINE + Greek *ergon* work]

adrenocorticotrophic (əˌdriːnəʊˌkɔːtəkəʊ'trɒfɪk) *or* **adrenocorticotropic** (əˌdriːnəʊˌkɔːtəkəʊ'trɒpɪk) *adj* stimulating the adrenal cortex

adrenocorticotrophic hormone *n* the full name of **ACTH**

Adrianople (ˌeɪdrɪə'nəʊpəl) *or* **Adrianopolis** (ˌeɪdrɪə'nɒpəlɪs) *n* former names of **Edirne**

Adrian Quist [ˌeɪdrɪən 'kwɪst] *adj Austral slang* intoxicated; drunk [rhyming slang for PISSED]

Adriatic (ˌeɪdrɪ'ætɪk) *adj* **1** of or relating to the Adriatic Sea, or to the inhabitants of its coast or islands ⊳ *n* **2** the short for the **Adriatic Sea**

Adriatic Sea *n* an arm of the Mediterranean between Italy and the Balkan Peninsula

adrift (ə'drɪft) *adj* (*postpositive*) ⊳ *adv* **1** floating without steering or mooring; drifting **2** without

purpose; aimless **3** *informal* off course or amiss: *the project went adrift*

adroit (ə'drɔɪt) *adj* **1** skilful or dexterous **2** quick in thought or reaction [c17 from French *à droit* according to right, rightly] > a'droitly *adv* > a'droitness *n*

adscititious (ˌædsɪ'tɪʃəs) *adj* added or supplemental; additional [c17 from Latin *adscītus* admitted (from outside), from *adscīscere* to admit, from *scīscere* to seek to know, from *scīre* to know] > ˌadsci'titiously *adv*

adscription (əd'skrɪpʃən) *n* a less common word for **ascription**

adsorb (əd'sɔːb, -'zɔːb) *vb* to undergo or cause to undergo a process in which a substance, usually a gas, accumulates on the surface of a solid forming a thin film, often only one molecule thick: *to adsorb hydrogen on nickel; oxygen adsorbs on tungsten*. Compare **absorb** (sense 8) [c19 AD- + -*sorb* as in ABSORB] > ad'sorbable *adj* > adˌsorba'bility *n* > ad'sorption *n*

adsorbate (əd'sɔːbeɪt, -bɪt, -'zɔː-) *n* a substance that has been or is to be adsorbed on a surface

adsorbent (əd'sɔːbənt, -'zɔː-) *adj* **1** capable of adsorption ⊳ *n* **2** a material, such as activated charcoal, on which adsorption can occur

adsuki bean (əd'zuːkɪ) *n* a variant spelling of **adzuki bean**

adsum ('ædˌsʊm) *sentence substitute* I am present [Latin]

aduki (æ'duːkɪ) *n* a variant of **adzuki**

adularescent (əˌdjʊlə'rɛsənt) *adj* (of minerals, such as moonstone) having or emitting a milky or bluish iridescence [c19 from ADULAR(IA) + -ESCENT] > aˌdula'rescence *n*

adularia (ˌædjʊ'lɛərɪə) *n* a white or colourless glassy variety of orthoclase in the form of prismatic crystals. It occurs in metamorphic rocks and is a minor gemstone. Formula: $KAlSi_3O_8$ [c18 via Italian from French *adulaire*, after *Adula*, a group of mountains in Switzerland]

adulate ('ædjʊˌleɪt) *vb* (*tr*) to flatter or praise obsequiously [c17 back formation from C15 *adulation*, from Latin *adūlāri* to flatter] > 'aduˌlator *n*

adulation (ˌædjʊ'leɪʃən) *n* obsequious flattery or praise; extreme admiration

adulatory (ˌædjʊ'leɪtərɪ, 'ædjʊˌleɪtərɪ) *adj* expressing praise, esp obsequiously; flattering

Adullamite (ə'dʌləˌmaɪt) *n* a person who has withdrawn from a political group and joined with a few others to form a dissident group [c19 originally applied to members of the British House of Commons who withdrew from the Liberal party (1866); alluding to the cave of *Adullam* in the Bible, to which David and others fled (1 Samuel 22: 1–2)]

adult ('ædʌlt, ə'dʌlt) *adj* **1** having reached maturity; fully developed **2** of or intended for mature people: *adult education* **3** regarded as suitable only for adults, esp of being pornographic: *adult films and magazines* ⊳ *n* **4** a person who has attained maturity; a grownup **5** a mature fully grown animal or plant **6** *law* a person who has attained the age of legal majority (18 years for most purposes). Compare **infant** [c16 from Latin *adultus*, from *adolēscere* to grow up, from *alēscere* to grow, from *alēre* to feed, nourish] > 'adulthood *n*

adulterant (ə'dʌltərənt) *n* **1** a substance or ingredient that adulterates ⊳ *adj* **2** adulterating

adulterate *vb* (ə'dʌltəˌreɪt) **1** (*tr*) to debase by adding inferior material: *to adulterate milk with water* ⊳ *adj* (ə'dʌltərɪt, -ˌreɪt) **2** adulterated; debased or impure **3** a less common word for **adulterous** [c16 from Latin *adulterāre* to corrupt, commit adultery, probably from *alter* another, hence to approach another, commit adultery] > aˌdulter'ation *n* > a'dulterˌator *n*

adulterer (ə'dʌltərə) *n* a person who has committed adultery [c16 originally also *adulter*, from Latin *adulter*, back formation from *adulterāre* to ADULTERATE]

adulteress (ə'dʌltərəs) *n* a woman who has committed adultery

adulterine (ə'dʌltəraɪn, -ˌriːn, -ˌraɪn) *adj* **1** of or made by adulteration; fake **2** conceived in adultery: *an adulterine child*

adulterous (ə'dʌltərəs) *adj* **1** of, characterized by, or inclined to adultery **2** an obsolete word for **adulterate** (sense 2) > a'dulterously *adv*

adultery (ə'dʌltərɪ) *n, pl* -teries voluntary sexual intercourse between a married man or woman and a partner other than the legal spouse [c15 *adulterie*, altered (as if directly from Latin *adulterium*) from C14 *avoutrie*, via Old French from Latin *adulterium*, from *adulter*, back formation from *adulterāre*. See ADULTERATE]

adultescent (ˌædəl'tɛsənt) *informal* ⊳ *n* **1** an adult who is still actively interested in youth culture ⊳ *adj* **2** aimed at or suitable for adultescents

Adult Training Centre *n social welfare* a day centre, run by a local authority, for people with learning difficulties to gain work experience

adumbral (æd'ʌmbrəl) *adj usually poetic* shadowy [c19 from AD- (in the sense: in) + Latin *umbra* shadow]

adumbrate ('ædʌmˌbreɪt) *vb* (*tr*) **1** to outline; give a faint indication of **2** to foreshadow **3** to overshadow; obscure [c16 from Latin *adumbrātus* represented only in outline, from *adumbrāre* to cast a shadow on, from *umbra* shadow] > ˌadum'bration *n* > adumbrative (æd'ʌmbrətɪv) *adj* > ad'umbratively *adv*

adust (ə'dʌst) *adj* *archaic* **1** dried up or darkened by heat; burnt or scorched **2** gloomy or melancholy [c14 (in the sense: gloomy): from Latin *adūstus*, from *adūrere* to set fire to, from *ūrere* to burn]

Aduwa *or* **Adowa** ('ɑːdʊˌwɑː) *n* a town in N Ethiopia: Emperor Menelik II defeated the Italians here in 1896. Pop: 17 476 (1989 est). Italian name: Adua (a'dua)

adv. *abbreviation for* **1** adverb **2** adverbial [Latin: against]

ad val. *abbreviation for* ad valorem

ad valorem (æd və'lɔːrəm) *adj, adv* (of taxes) in proportion to the estimated value of the goods taxed. Abbreviations: ad val, a.v., A/V [from Latin]

advance (əd'vɑːns) *vb* **1** to go or bring forward in position **2** (foll by *on*) to move (towards) in a threatening manner **3** (*tr*) to present for consideration; suggest **4** to bring or be brought to a further stage of development; improve; further **5** (*tr*) to cause (an event) to occur earlier **6** (*tr*) to supply (money, goods, etc) beforehand, either for a loan or as an initial payment **7** to increase (a price, value, rate of occurrence, etc) or (of a price, etc) to be increased **8** (*intr*) to improve one's position; be promoted: *he advanced rapidly in his job* **9** (*tr*) *archaic* to promote in rank, status, or position ⊳ *n* **10** forward movement; progress in time or space **11** improvement; progress in development **12** *commerce* **a** the supplying of commodities or funds before receipt of an agreed consideration **b** the commodities or funds supplied in this manner **c** (*as modifier*): *an advance supply* **13** Also called: advance payment a money payment made before it is legally due: *this is an advance on your salary* **14** a loan of money **15** an increase in price, value, rate of occurrence, etc **16** a less common word for **advancement** (sense 1) **17** in advance **a** beforehand: *payment in advance* **b** (foll by *of*) ahead in time or development: *ideas in advance of the time* **18** (*modifier*) forward in position or time: *advance booking* ⊳ See also **advances** [c15 *advauncen*, altered (on the model of words beginning with Latin *ad-*) from C13 *avauncen*, via Old French from Latin *abante* from before, from *ab-* away from + *ante* before] > ad'vancer *n* > ad'vancingly *adv*

advance corporation tax *n* a former UK tax in which a company paying a dividend had to deduct the basic rate of income tax from the grossed-up value of the dividend and pay it to the Inland Revenue. Abbreviation: ACT

advanced (əd'vɑːnst) *adj* **1** being ahead in development, knowledge, progress, etc: *advanced studies* **2** having reached a comparatively late stage: *a man of advanced age* **3** ahead of the times: *advanced views on religion*

advanced gas-cooled reactor *n* a nuclear reactor using carbon dioxide as the coolant, graphite as the moderator, and ceramic uranium dioxide cased in stainless steel as the fuel. Abbreviation: AGR

Advanced Higher *n* (in Scotland) **1 a** the highest level of qualification offered within the school system, replacing the former Certificate of Sixth Year Studies **b** (*as modifier*): *Advanced Higher Maths* **2** a pass in a particular subject at Advanced Higher level

advance directive *n* another name for **living will**

Advanced level *n* (in Britain) the formal name for **A level**

advanced skills teacher *n Brit education* a teacher who has achieved high standards of classroom practice and success and who, after passing a national assessment, is paid to share his or her skills and experience with other teachers. Abbreviation: AST

advance guard *n* **1** a military unit sent ahead of a main body to find gaps in enemy defences, clear away minor opposition, and prevent unexpected contact **2** a temporary military detachment sent ahead of a force to prepare for a landing or other operation, esp by making reconnaissance

advance man *n US* an agent of a political candidate or other public figure who travels in advance of the candidate to organize publicity, arrange meetings, and make security checks

advancement (əd'vɑːnsmənt) *n* **1** promotion in rank, status, etc; preferment **2** a less common word for **advance** (senses 10, 11) **3** *property law* the use during a testator's lifetime of money or property for the benefit of a child or other person who is a prospective beneficiary in the testator's will

advance notice *n* See **notice** (sense 6)

advance poll *n Canadian* (in an election) a poll held prior to election day to permit voters who expect to be absent then to cast their ballots

advance ratio *n aeronautics* **1** the ratio of wind speed along the axis of a rotor or propeller to the speed of the blade tip **2** the ratio of forward flight speed to the speed of the rotor tip of a helicopter

advances (əd'vɑːnsɪz) *pl n* (*sometimes singular; often foll by to or towards*) personal overtures made in an attempt to become friendly, gain a favour, etc

advantage (əd'vɑːntɪdʒ) *n* **1** (*often foll by over or of*) superior or more favourable position or power: *he had an advantage over me because of his experience* **2** benefit or profit (esp in the phrase **to one's advantage**) **3** *tennis* **a** the point scored after deuce **b** the resulting state of the score **4** take advantage of **a** to make good use of **b** to impose upon the weakness, good nature, etc, of; abuse **c** to seduce **5 to advantage** to good effect: *he used his height to advantage at the game* **6 you have the advantage of me** you know me but I do not know you [c14 *avantage* (later altered to *advantage* on the model of words beginning with Latin *ad-*), from Old French *avant* before, from Latin *abante* from before, away. See ADVANCE]

advantaged (əd'vɑːntɪdʒd) *adj* in a superior social or economic position

advantageous (ˌædvən'teɪdʒəs) *adj* producing advantage > ˌadvan'tageously *adv* > ˌadvan'tageousness *n*

advection (əd'vɛkʃən) *n* the transference of heat energy in a horizontal stream of gas, esp of air [c20 from Latin *advectiō* conveyance, from *advehere*, from *ad-* to + *vehere* to carry]

advent (ˈædvɛnt, -vənt) *n* an arrival or coming, esp one which is awaited [c12 from Latin *adventus*, from *advenīre*, from *ad-* to + *venīre* to come]

Advent (ˈædvɛnt, -vənt) *n Christianity* the season including the four Sundays preceding Christmas

or (in Eastern Orthodox churches) the forty days preceding Christmas

Advent calendar *n Brit* a large card with a brightly coloured sometimes tinselled design on it that contains small numbered doors for children to open on each of the days of Advent, revealing pictures beneath them

Adventist (ˈædvɛntɪst, ˈædvən-) *n* a member of any of the Christian groups, such as the **Seventh-Day Adventists** that hold that the Second Coming of Christ is imminent

adventitia (ˌædvɛn'tɪʃɪə, -'tɪʃə) *n* the outermost covering of an organ or part, esp the outer coat of a blood vessel [c19 New Latin, from the neuter plural of Latin *adventīcius*; see ADVENTITIOUS]

adventitious (ˌædvɛn'tɪʃəs) *adj* **1** added or appearing accidentally or unexpectedly **2** (of a plant or animal part) developing in an abnormal position, as a root that grows from a stem [c17 from Latin *adventīcius* coming from outside, from *adventus* a coming] > ˌadven'titiously *adv*

adventive (əd'vɛntɪv) *biology* ▷ *adj* **1** (of a species) introduced to a new area and not yet established there; exotic ▷ *n* **2** such a plant or animal ▷ Also called: **casual**

Advent Sunday *n* the first of the four Sundays of Advent, and the one that falls nearest to November 30

adventure (əd'vɛntʃə) *n* **1** a risky undertaking of unknown outcome **2** an exciting or unexpected event or course of events **3** a hazardous financial operation; commercial speculation **4** *obsolete* **a** danger or misadventure **b** chance ▷ *vb* **5** to take a risk or put at risk **6** (*intr; foll by into, on, upon*) to dare to go or enter (into a place, dangerous activity, etc) **7** to dare to say (something): *he adventured his opinion* (later altered to *adventure* after the Latin spelling), via Old French ultimately from Latin *advenīre* to happen to (someone), arrive] > ad'ventureful *adj*

adventure playground *n Brit* a playground for children that contains building materials, discarded industrial parts, etc, used by the children to build with, hide in, climb on, etc

adventurer (əd'vɛntʃərə) *n* **1** a person who seeks adventure, esp one who seeks success or money through daring exploits **2** a person who seeks money or power by unscrupulous means **3** a speculator

adventuress (əd'vɛntʃərɪs) *n* **1** a woman who seeks adventure, esp one who seeks success or money through daring exploits **2** a woman who seeks money or power by unscrupulous means **3** a speculator

adventure tourism *n Austral and NZ* tourism involving activities that are physically challenging

adventurism (əd'vɛntʃəˌrɪzəm) *n* recklessness, esp in politics and finance > ad'venturist *n*

adventurous (əd'vɛntʃərəs) *adj* **1** Also: **adventuresome** daring or enterprising **2** dangerous; involving risk > ad'venturously *adv*

adverb (ˈædˌvɜːb) *n* **a** a word or group of words that serves to modify a whole sentence, a verb, another adverb, or an adjective; for example, *probably, easily, very,* and *happily* respectively in the sentence *They could probably easily envy the very happily married couple* **b** (*as modifier*): *an adverb marker.* Abbreviation: adv [c15–c16 from Latin *adverbium* adverb, literally: added word, a translation of Greek *epirrhēma* a word spoken afterwards]

adverbial (æd'vɜːbɪəl) *n* **1** a word or group of words playing the grammatical role of an adverb, such as *in the rain* in the sentence *I'm singing in the rain* ▷ *adj* **2** of or relating to an adverb or adverbial > ad'verbially *adv*

adversarial (ˌædvɜː'sɛərɪəl) *adj* **1** pertaining to or characterized by antagonism and conflict **2** *Brit* having or involving opposing parties or interests in a legal contest. US term: **adversary**

adversary (ˈædvəsərɪ) *n, pl* -saries **1** a person or group that is hostile to someone; enemy **2** an

opposing contestant in a game or sport ▷ *adj* **3** the US term for **adversarial** (sense 2) [c14 from Latin *adversārius,* from *adversus* against. See ADVERSE]

adversative (əd'vɜːsətɪv) *grammar* ▷ *adj* **1** (of a word, phrase, or clause) implying opposition or contrast. *But* and *although* are adversative conjunctions introducing adversative clauses ▷ *n* **2** an adversative word or speech element

adverse (ˈædvɜːs, æd'vɜːs) *adj* **1** antagonistic or inimical; hostile: *adverse criticism* **2** unfavourable to one's interests: *adverse circumstances* **3** contrary or opposite in direction or position: *adverse winds* **4** (of leaves, flowers, etc) facing the main stem. Compare **averse** (sense 2) [c14 from Latin *adversus* opposed to, hostile, from *advertere* to turn towards, from *ad-* to, towards + *vertere* to turn] > ad'versely *adv* > ad'verseness *n*

adverse possession *n property law* the occupation or possession of land by a person not legally entitled to it. If continued unopposed for a period specifed by law, such occupation extinguishes the title of the rightful owner

adverse pressure gradient *n aerodynamics* an increase of pressure in the direction of flow

adversity (əd'vɜːsɪtɪ) *n, pl* -ties **1** distress; affliction; hardship **2** an unfortunate event or incident

advert¹ (əd'vɜːt) *vb* (*intr; foll by to*) to draw attention (to); refer (to) [c15 from Latin *advertere* to turn one's attention to. See ADVERSE]

advert² (ˈædvɜːt) *n Brit informal* short for **advertisement**

advertence (əd'vɜːtəns) or **advertency** *n* heedfulness or attentiveness > ad'vertent *adj* > ad'vertently *adv*

advertise or *sometimes US* **advertize** (ˈædvəˌtaɪz) *vb* **1** to present or praise (goods, a service, etc) to the public, esp in order to encourage sales **2** to make (something, such as a vacancy, article for sale, etc) publicly known, as to possible applicants, buyers, etc: *to advertise a job* **3** (*intr; foll by for*) to make a public request (for), esp in a newspaper, etc: *she advertised for a cook* **4** *obsolete* to warn; caution [c15 from a lengthened stem of Old French *avertir*, ultimately from Latin *advertere* to turn one's attention to. See ADVERSE] > ad'verˌtiser or *sometimes US* 'adverˌtizer *n*

advertisement or *sometimes US* **advertizement** (əd'vɜːtɪsmənt, -tɪz-) *n* any public notice, as a printed display in a newspaper, short film on television, announcement on radio, etc, designed to sell goods, publicize an event, etc. Shortened forms: ad, advert

advertising or *sometimes US* **advertizing** (ˈædvəˌtaɪzɪŋ) *n* **1** the promotion of goods or services for sale through impersonal media, such as radio or television **2** the business that specializes in creating such publicity **3** advertisements collectively; publicity

advertising agency *n* an organization that creates advertising material, contracts for publication space, and sometimes undertakes market research on behalf of its clients

Advertising Standards Authority *n* an independent UK body set up by the advertising industry to ensure that all advertisements comply with the British Code of Advertising Practice. Abbreviation: ASA

advertorial (ˌædvɜː'tɔːrɪəl) *n* advertising material presented under the guise of editorial material [c20 from ADVERT² + (EDIT)ORIAL]

advice (əd'vaɪs) *n* **1** recommendation as to appropriate choice of action; counsel **2** (*sometimes plural*) formal notification of facts, esp when communicated from a distance [c13 *avis* (later *advise*), via Old French from a Vulgar Latin phrase based on Latin *ad* to, according to + *vīsum* view (hence: according to one's view, opinion)]

advice note *n* a document sent by a supplier to a customer to inform him that goods he ordered have been dispatched. It usually gives details such

a

as the quantity of goods and how they have been sent

advisable (əd'vaɪzəbəl) *adj* worthy of recommendation; prudent; sensible ▷ **ad'visably** *adv* ▷ **ad,visa'bility** *or* **ad'visableness** *n*

advise (əd'vaɪz) *vb* (*when tr, may take a clause as object or an infinitive*) **1** to offer advice (to a person or persons); counsel: *he advised the king; to advise caution; he advised her to leave* **2** (*tr; sometimes foll by of*) *formal* to inform or notify **3** (*intr; foll by with*) *chiefly US, obsolete in Brit* to consult or discuss [c14 via Old French from Vulgar Latin *advisāre* (unattested) to consider, from Latin *ad-* to + *visāre* (unattested) to view, from *vidēre* to see]

advised (əd'vaɪzd) *adj* resulting from deliberation. See also **ill-advised, well-advised.** ▷ **advisedly** (əd'vaɪzɪdlɪ) *adv*

advisement (əd'vaɪzmənt) *n chiefly US, archaic in Britain* consultation; deliberation

adviser *or* **advisor** (əd'vaɪzə) *n* **1** a person who advises **2** *education* a person responsible for advising students on academic matters, career guidance, etc **3** *Brit education* a subject specialist who advises heads of schools on current teaching methods and facilities

advisory (əd'vaɪzərɪ) *adj* **1** giving advice; empowered to make recommendations: *an advisory body* ▷ *n, pl* **-ries** **2** a statement issued to give advice, recommendations, or a warning: *a travel advisory* **3** a person or organization with an advisory function: *the Prime Minister's media advisory*

advisory teacher *n Brit* a teacher who visits schools to advise teachers on curriculum developments within a particular subject area

advocaat ('ædvəʊˌkɑː, -ˌkɑːt, ˌædvə-) *n* a liqueur having a raw egg base [c20 Dutch, from *advocatenborrel*, from *advocaat* ADVOCATE (n) + *borrel* drink]

advocacy ('ædvəkəsɪ) *n, pl* **-cies** active support, esp of a cause

advocate *vb* ('ædvəˌkeɪt) **1** (*tr; may take a clause as object*) to support or recommend publicly; plead for or speak in favour of ▷ *n* ('ædvəkɪt, -ˌkeɪt) **2** a person who upholds or defends a cause; supporter **3** a person who intercedes on behalf of another **4** a person who pleads his client's cause in a court of law. See also **barrister, solicitor, counsellor 5** *Scots law* the usual word for **barrister** [c14 via Old French from Latin *advocātus* legal witness, advocate, from *advocāre* to call as witness, from *vocāre* to call] ▷ **advo'catory** *adj*

Advocate Depute *n* a Scottish law officer with the functions of public prosecutor

advocation (ˌædvə'keɪʃən) *n Scots law, papal law* the transfer to itself by a superior court of an action pending in a lower court

advocatus diaboli *Latin* (ˌædvə'kɑːtəs daɪ'æbəˌlaɪ) *n* another name for the **devil's advocate**

advowson (əd'vaʊzən) *n English ecclesiastical law* the right of presentation to a vacant benefice [c13 via Anglo-French and Old French from Latin *advocātiōn-* the act of summoning, from *advocāre* to summon]

advt *abbreviation for* advertisement

adware ('ædˌwɛə) *n* **1** a type of computer software that collects information about a user's browsing patterns in order to display relevant advertisements in his or her Web browser **2** computer software that is given to a user with advertisements already embedded

Adygei *or* **Adyghe** ('ɑːdɪˌgeɪ, ˌɑːdɪ'geɪ, ˌɑːdɪ'gɛ) *n* **1** (*pl* **-gei, -geis** *or* **-ghe, -ghes**) a member of a Circassian people of the Northwest Caucasus **2** the Circassian language, esp its Western dialect. Compare **Kabardian**

Adygei Republic *or* **Adygea** (ˌɑːdɪ'geɪə; *Russian* adɪ'gʲeɪa) *n* a constituent republic of SW Russia, bordering on the Caucasus Mountains: chiefly agricultural but with some mineral resources. Capital: Maikop. Pop: 447 000 (2002). Area: 7600 sq km (2934 sq miles)

adynamia (ˌædɪ'neɪmɪə) *n obsolete* loss of vital power or strength, esp as the result of illness; weakness or debility [c19 New Latin, from A-¹ + -*dynamia*, from Greek *dunamis* strength, force] ▷ **adynamic** (ˌædɪ'næmɪk) *adj*

adytum ('ædɪtəm) *n, pl* **-ta** (-tə) the most sacred place of worship in an ancient temple from which the laity was prohibited [c17 Latin, from Greek *aduton* a place not to be entered, from A-¹ + *duein* to enter]

adze *or US* **adz** (ædz) *n* a heavy hand tool with a steel cutting blade attached at right angles to a wooden handle, used for dressing timber [Old English *adesa*]

Adzhar Autonomous Republic (ə'dʒɑː) *or* **Adzharia** (ə'dʒɑːrɪə) *n* an administrative division of SW Georgia, on the Black Sea: part of Turkey from the 17th century until 1878; mostly mountainous, reaching 2805 m (9350 ft) with a subtropical coastal strip. Capital: Batumi. Pop: 386 700 (1993 est). Area: 3000 sq km (1160 sq miles)

adzuki (æd'zuːkɪ), **aduki** (ə'duːkɪ) *or* **adsuki** *n* **1** a leguminous plant, *Phaseolus angularis*, that has yellow flowers and pods containing edible brown seeds and is widely cultivated as a food crop in China and Japan **2** the seed of this plant. Also: **adzuki bean, adsuki bean** [*adzuki*, from Japanese: red bean]

ae¹ (e) *or* **yae** *determiner Scot* one; a single [from Old English *ān*]

æ *or* **Æ 1** a digraph in Latin representing either a native diphthong, as in *æquus*, or a Greek αɪ (*ai*) in Latinized spellings, as in *æschylus*: now usually written *ae*, or *e* in some words, such as *demon* **2** a ligature used in Old and early Middle English to represent the vowel sound of *a* in *cat* **3** a ligature used in modern phonetic transcription also representing the vowel sound *a* in *cat*

ae² *the internet domain name for* United Arab Emirates

ae. *abbreviation for* aetatis [Latin: at the age of; aged]

AEA (*in Britain*) *abbreviation for* **Atomic Energy Authority**

AE & P *abbreviation for* Ambassador Extraordinary and Plenipotentiary

AEC (*in the US*) *abbreviation for* **Atomic Energy Commission**

aeciospore ('iːsɪəˌspɔː) *n* any of the spores produced in an aecium of the rust fungi, which spread to and infect the primary host. Also called: **aecidospore** [c20 from AECIUM + SPORE]

aecium ('iːsɪəm) *or* **aecidium** (iː'sɪdɪəm) *n, pl* **-cia** (-sɪə) *or* **-cidia** (-'sɪdɪə) a globular or cup-shaped structure in some rust fungi in which aeciospores are produced [c19 New Latin, from Greek *aikia* injury (so called because of the damage the fungi cause)]

AECL *abbreviation for* Atomic Energy of Canada Limited

aedes (eɪ'iːdiːz) *n* any mosquito of the genus *Aedes* (formerly *Stegomyia*) of tropical and subtropical regions, esp *A. aegypti*, which transmits yellow fever and dengue [c20 New Latin, from Greek *aēdēs* unpleasant, from A-¹ + *ēdos* pleasant]

aedicule ('ɛdɪˌkjuːl) *n* an opening such as a door or a window, framed by columns on either side, and a pediment above [c19 from Latin *aediculum* small house, from *aedēs* building]

aedile *or sometimes US* **edile** ('iːdaɪl) *n* a magistrate of ancient Rome in charge of public works, games, buildings, and roads [c16 from Latin *aedīlis* concerned with buildings, from *aedēs* a building]

Aeëtes (iː'iːtiːz) *n Greek myth* a king of Colchis, father of Medea and keeper of the Golden Fleece

Aegean (iː'dʒiːən) *adj* **1** of or relating to the Aegean Sea or Islands **2** of or relating to the Bronze Age civilization of Greece, Asia Minor, and the Aegean Islands

Aegean Islands *pl n* the islands of the Aegean Sea, including the Cyclades, Dodecanese, Euboea, and Sporades. The majority are under Greek administration

Aegean Sea *n* an arm of the Mediterranean between Greece and Turkey

Aegeus (iː'dʒiːuːs, iː'dʒiːəs) *n Greek myth* an Athenian king and father of Theseus

Aegina (iː'dʒaɪnə) *n* **1** an island in the Aegean Sea, in the Saronic Gulf. Area: 85 sq km (33 sq miles) **2** a town on the coast of this island: a city-state of ancient Greece **3** **Gulf of** another name for the **Saronic Gulf**. Greek name: Aiyina

Aegir ('iːdʒɪə) *n Norse myth* the god of the sea

aegis *or sometimes US* **egis** ('iːdʒɪs) *n* **1** sponsorship or protection; auspices (esp in the phrase **under the aegis of**) **2** *Greek myth* the shield of Zeus, often represented in art as a goatskin [c18 from Latin, from Greek *aigis* shield of Zeus, perhaps related to *aig-*, stem of *aix* goat]

Aegisthus (iː'dʒɪsθəs) *n Greek myth* a cousin to and the murderer of Agamemnon, whose wife Clytemnestra he had seduced. He usurped the kingship of Mycenae until Orestes, Agamemnon's son, returned home and killed him

Aegospotami (ˌiːgəs'pɒtəˌmaɪ) *n* a river of ancient Thrace that flowed into the Hellespont. At its mouth the Spartan fleet under Lysander defeated the Athenians in 405 BC, ending the Peloponnesian War

aegrotat (ˈaɪgrəʊˌtæt, 'iː-, iː'grəʊtæt) *n* **1** (in British and certain other universities, and, sometimes, schools) a certificate allowing a candidate to pass an examination although he has missed all or part of it through illness **2** a degree or other qualification obtained in such circumstances [c19 Latin, literally: he is ill]

Aegyptus (iː'dʒɪptəs) *n Greek myth* a king of Egypt and twin brother of Danaüs

-aemia, -haemia *or US* **-emia, -hemia** *n combining form* denoting blood, esp a specified condition of the blood in names of diseases: *leukaemia* [New Latin, from Greek -*aimia*, from *haima* blood]

Aeneas (iː'niːəs) *n classical myth* a Trojan prince, the son of Anchises and Aphrodite, who escaped the sack of Troy and sailed to Italy via Carthage and Sicily. After seven years, he and his followers established themselves near the site of the future Rome

Aeneid (ɪ'niːɪd) *n* an epic poem in Latin by Virgil relating the experiences of Aeneas after the fall of Troy, written chiefly to provide an illustrious historical background for Rome

aeolian (iː'əʊlɪən) *adj* of or relating to the wind; produced or carried by the wind [c18 from AEOLUS, god of the winds]

Aeolian *or* **Eolian** (iː'əʊlɪən) *n* **1** a member of a Hellenic people who settled in Thessaly and Boeotia and colonized Lesbos and parts of the Aegean coast of Asia Minor ▷ *adj* **2** of or relating to this people or their dialect of Ancient Greek; Aeolic **3** of or relating to Aeolus **4** denoting or relating to an authentic mode represented by the ascending natural diatonic scale from A to A: the basis of the modern minor key. See also **Hypo-**

aeolian deposits *pl n geology* sediments, such as loess, made up of windblown grains of sand or dust

aeolian harp *n* a stringed instrument that produces a musical sound when a current of air passes over the strings. Also called: **wind harp**

Aeolian Islands *pl n* another name for the **Lipari Islands**

aeolian tone *n* the musical tone produced by the passage of a current of air over a stretched string, etc, as in an aeolian harp

Aeolic *or* **Eolic** (iː'ɒlɪk, iː'əʊlɪk) *adj* **1** of or relating to the Aeolians or their dialect ▷ *n* **2** one of four chief dialects of Ancient Greek, spoken chiefly in Thessaly, Boeotia, and Aeolis ▷ Compare **Arcadic, Doric, Ionic** See also **Attic** (sense 3)

aeolipile (iː'ɒlɪˌpaɪl) *n* a device illustrating the reactive forces of a gas jet: usually a spherical vessel mounted so as to rotate and equipped with angled exit pipes from which steam within it escapes [C17 from Latin *aeolīpilae* balls of AEOLUS or *aeolīpylae* gates of AEOLUS]

Aeolis ('iːəlɪs) or **Aeolia** (iːˈəʊlɪə) *n* the ancient name for the coastal region of NW Asia Minor, including the island of Lesbos, settled by the Aeolian Greeks (about 1000 BC)

aeolotropic (ˌiːələʊˈtrɒpɪk) *adj* a lɛss common word for **anisotropic** [C19 from Greek *aiolos* fickle + -TROPIC]

Aeolus ('iːələs, iːˈəʊləs) *n Greek myth* **1** the god of the winds **2** the founding king of the Aeolians in Thessaly

aeon or *esp US* **eon** ('iːən, 'iːɒn) *n* **1** an immeasurably long period of time; age **2** a period of one thousand million years **3** (*often capital*) *gnosticism* one of the powers emanating from the supreme being and culminating in the demiurge [C17 from Greek *aiōn* an infinitely long time]

aeonian or **eonian** (iːˈəʊnɪən) *adj literary* everlasting

aepyornis (ˌiːpɪˈɔːnɪs) *n* any of the large extinct flightless birds of the genus *Aepyornis*, remains of which have been found in Madagascar [C19 New Latin, from Greek *aipus* high + *ornis* bird]

aer- *combining form* a variant of **aero-** before a vowel

aerate ('ɛəreɪt) *vb* (*tr*) **1** to charge (a liquid) with a gas, esp carbon dioxide, as in the manufacture of effervescent drink **2** to expose to the action or circulation of the air, so as to purify > aer'ation *n* > 'aerator *n*

aerenchyma (ɛəˈrɛŋkɪmə) *n* plant tissue with large air-filled spaces, which is typical of aquatic plants and allows air to reach waterlogged parts [C19 from AER(O)- + Greek *enkhuma* infusion]

aeri- *combining form* a variant of **aero-**

aerial ('ɛərɪəl) *adj* **1** of, relating to, or resembling air **2** existing, occurring, moving, or operating in the air: *aerial cable car; aerial roots of a plant* **3** ethereal; light and delicate **4** imaginary; visionary **5** extending high into the air; lofty **6** of or relating to aircraft: *aerial combat* ▷ *n* **7** Also called: antenna the part of a radio or television system having any of various shapes, such as a dipole, Yagi, long-wire, or vertical aerial, by means of which radio waves are transmitted or received [C17 via Latin from Greek *aērios*, from *aēr* air]

aerialist ('ɛərɪəlɪst) *n chiefly US* a trapeze artist or tightrope walker

aerial ladder *n US and Canadian* a power-operated extending ladder mounted on a fire engine. Also called: turntable ladder

aerial perspective *n* a means of indicating relative distance in terms of a gradation of clarity, tone, and colour, esp blue. Also called: atmospheric perspective

aerial pingpong *n Austral slang* Australian Rules football

aerial top dressing *n* the process of spreading lime, fertilizer, etc over farmland from an aeroplane

aerie ('ɛərɪ, 'ɪərɪ) *n* a variant spelling (esp US) of **eyrie**

aeriform ('ɛərɪˌfɔːm) *adj* **1** having the form of air; gaseous **2** unsubstantial

aerify ('ɛərɪˌfaɪ) *vb* -fies, -fying, -fied **1** to change or cause to change into a gas **2** to mix or combine with air > aerifi'cation *n*

aero¹ ('ɛərəʊ) *n* (*modifier*) of or relating to aircraft or aeronautics: *an aero engine*

aero² *an internet domain name for* an organization in the air-transport industry

aero-, aeri- or before a vowel **aer-** *combining form* **1** denoting air, atmosphere, or gas: *aerodynamics* **2** denoting aircraft: *aeronautics* [ultimately from Greek *aēr* air]

aeroacoustics (ˌɛərəʊəˈkuːstɪks) *n* (*functioning as singular*) the study of the generation and transmittance of sound by fluid flow

aeroballistics (ˌɛərəʊbəˈlɪstɪks) *n* (*functioning as singular*) the ballistics of projectiles dropped, launched, or fired from aircraft

aerobatics (ˌɛərəʊˈbætɪks) *n* (*functioning as singular or plural*) spectacular or dangerous manoeuvres, such as loops or rolls, performed in an aircraft or glider; stunt flying [C20 from AERO- + (ACRO)BATICS] > ˌaero'batic *adj*

aerobe ('ɛərəʊb) or **aerobium** (ɛəˈrəʊbɪəm) *n, pl* -obes or -obia (-'əʊbɪə) an organism that requires oxygen for respiration. Compare **anaerobe** [C19 from AERO- + Greek *bios* life. Compare MICROBE]

aerobic (ɛəˈrəʊbɪk) *adj* **1** (of an organism or process) depending on oxygen **2** of or relating to aerobes **3** designed for or relating to aerobics: *aerobic shoes; aerobic dances* ▷ Compare **anaerobic**

aerobics (ɛəˈrəʊbɪks) *n* (*functioning as singular*) any system of sustained exercises designed to increase the amount of oxygen in the blood and strengthen the heart and lungs > aer'obicist *n*

aerobiology (ˌɛərəʊbaɪˈɒlədʒɪ) *n* the study of airborne organisms, spores, etc > aerobiological (ˌɛərəʊˌbaɪəˈlɒdʒɪkᵊl) *adj* > ˌaerobi'ologist *n*

aerobiosis (ˌɛərəʊbaɪˈəʊsɪs) *n* life in the presence of oxygen > aerobiotic (ˌɛərəʊbaɪˈɒtɪk) *adj*

aerobraking (ˈɛərəʊˌbreɪkɪŋ) *n* the use of aerodynamic braking in extremely low-density atmospheres in space at hypersonic Mach numbers

aerodonetics (ˌɛərəʊdəˈnɛtɪks) *n* (*functioning as singular*) the study of soaring or gliding flight, esp the study of gliders [C20 from Greek *aerodonetos* tossed in the air, from AERO- + *donetos*, past participle of *donein* to toss]

aerodrome ('ɛərəˌdrəʊm) or *US* **airdrome** ('ɛəˌdrəʊm) *n obsolete* a landing area, esp for private aircraft, that is usually smaller than an airport

aerodynamic braking *n* **1** the use of aerodynamic drag to slow spacecraft re-entering the atmosphere **2** the use of airbrakes to retard flying vehicles or objects **3** the use of a parachute or reversed thrust to decelerate an aircraft during landing

aerodynamics (ˌɛərəʊdaɪˈnæmɪks) *n* (*functioning as singular*) the study of the dynamics of gases, esp of the forces acting on a body passing through air. Compare **aerostatics** (sense 1) > ˌaerody'namic *adj* > ˌaerody'namically *adv* > ˌaerody'namicist *n*

aerodyne ('ɛərəʊˌdaɪn) *n* any heavier-than-air machine, such as an aircraft, that derives the greater part of its lift from aerodynamic forces [C20 back formation from AERODYNAMIC; see DYNE]

aeroembolism (ˌɛərəʊˈɛmbəˌlɪzəm) *n* a former name for **air embolism**

aero engine *n* an engine for powering an aircraft

aerofoil ('ɛərəʊˌfɔɪl) or *US and Canadian* **airfoil** ('ɛəˌfɔɪl) *n* a cross section of an aileron, wing, tailplane, or rotor blade

aerogel ('ɛərəˌdʒɛl) *n* a colloid that has a continuous solid phase containing dispersed gas

aerogram or **aerogramme** ('ɛərəˌɡræm) *n* **1** Also called: air letter an airmail letter written on a single sheet of lightweight paper that folds and is sealed to form an envelope **2** another name for **radiotelegram**

aerography (ɛəˈrɒɡrəfɪ) *n archaic* the description of the character of the upper atmosphere

aerolite ('ɛərəˌlaɪt) *n* a stony meteorite consisting of silicate minerals > aerolitic (ˌɛərəˈlɪtɪk) *adj*

aerology (ɛəˈrɒlədʒɪ) *n* the study of the atmosphere, particularly its upper layers > aerologic (ˌɛərəˈlɒdʒɪk) or ˌaero'logical *adj* > aer'ologist *n*

aeromechanic (ˌɛərəʊmɪˈkænɪk) *n* **1** an aircraft mechanic ▷ *adj* **2** of or relating to aeromechanics

aeromechanics (ˌɛərəʊmɪˈkænɪks) *n* (*functioning as singular*) the mechanics of gases, esp air > ˌaerome'chanical *adj*

aerometeorograph (ˌɛərəʊˌmiːtɪərəˌɡrɑːf, -ˌɡræf) *n chiefly US* an aircraft instrument that records temperature, humidity, and atmospheric pressure

aerometer (ɛəˈrɒmɪtə) *n* an instrument for determining the mass or density of a gas, esp air

> aerometric (ˌɛərəˈmɛtrɪk) *adj*

aerometry (ɛəˈrɒmɪtrɪ) *n* another name for **pneumatics**

aeron. *abbreviation for* **1** aeronautics **2** aeronautical

aeronaut ('ɛərəˌnɔːt) *n* a person who flies in a lighter-than-air craft, esp the pilot or navigator

aeronautical (ˌɛərəˈnɔːtɪkᵊl) *adj* of or relating to aeronauts or aeronautics > ˌaero'nautically *adv*

aeronautical engineering *n* the branch of engineering concerned with the design, production, and maintenance of aircraft > aeronautical engineer *n*

aeronautics (ˌɛərəˈnɔːtɪks) *n* (*functioning as singular*) the study or practice of all aspects of flight through the air

aeroneurosis (ˌɛərəʊnjʊˈrəʊsɪs) *n* a functional disorder of aeroplane pilots characterized by anxiety and various psychosomatic disturbances, caused by insufficient oxygen at high altitudes and the emotional tension of flying

aeronomy (ɛəˈrɒnəmɪ) *n* the science of the earth's upper atmosphere

aero-optics (ˌɛərəʊˈɒptɪks) *n* (*functioning as singular*) the study of the effect of aircraft-induced and atmospheric disturbances on the efficiency of laser weapons

aeropause ('ɛərəˌpɔːz) *n* the region of the upper atmosphere above which aircraft cannot fly

aerophagia (ˌɛərəˈfeɪdʒɪə, -dʒə) or **aerophagy** (ɛəˈrɒfədʒɪ) *n* spasmodic swallowing of air, a habit that can lead to belching and stomach pain

aerophobia (ˌɛərəˈfəʊbɪə) *n* a pathological fear of draughts of air > ˌaero'phobic *adj*

aerophyte ('ɛərəˌfaɪt) *n* another name for **epiphyte**

aeroplane ('ɛərəˌpleɪn) or *US and Canadian* **airplane** ('ɛəˌpleɪn) *n* a heavier-than-air powered flying vehicle with fixed wings [C19 from French *aéroplane*, from AERO- + Greek *-planos* wandering, related to PLANET]

aeroplane cloth or **fabric** *n* **1** a strong fabric made from cotton, linen, and nylon yarns, used for some light aircraft fuselages and wings **2** a similar lightweight fabric used for clothing ▷ Also called: aircraft fabric

aeroplane spin *n* a wrestling attack in which a wrestler lifts his opponent onto his shoulders and spins around, leaving the opponent dizzy

aerosol ('ɛərəˌsɒl) *n* **1** a colloidal dispersion of solid or liquid particles in a gas; smoke or fog **2** a substance, such as a paint, polish, or insecticide, dispensed from a small metal container by a propellant under pressure **3** Also called: air spray such a substance together with its container [C20 from AERO- + SOL(UTION)]

aerospace ('ɛərəˌspeɪs) *n* **1** the atmosphere and space beyond **2** (*modifier*) of or relating to rockets, missiles, space vehicles, etc, that fly or operate in aerospace: *the aerospace industry*

aerosphere ('ɛərəˌsfɪə) *n archaic* the entire atmosphere surrounding the earth

aerostat ('ɛərəˌstæt) *n* a lighter-than-air craft, such as a balloon [C18 from French *aérostat*, from AERO- + Greek *-statos* standing] > ˌaero'static or ˌaero'statical *adj*

aerostatics (ˌɛərəˈstætɪks) *n* (*functioning as singular*) **1** the study of gases in equilibrium and bodies held in equilibrium in gases. Compare **aerodynamics 2** the study of lighter-than-air craft, such as balloons

aerostation (ˌɛərəˈsteɪʃən) *n* the science of operating lighter-than-air craft

aerostructure ('ɛərəʊˌstrʌktʃə) *n* any separately manufactured unit, component, or section of an aircraft or other vehicle capable of flight

aerothermodynamics (ˌɛərəʊˌθɜːməʊdaɪˈnæmɪks) *n* (*functioning as singular*) the study of the exchange of heat between solids and gases, esp of the heating effect on aircraft flying through the air at very high speeds > ˌaeroˌthermody'namic *adj*

a

aerugo (ɪˈruːɡəʊ) *n* (esp of old bronze) another name for **verdigris** [c18 from Latin, from *aes* copper, bronze] > **aeruginous** (ɪˈruːdʒɪnəs) *adj*

aery[1] (ˈɛərɪ, ˈeɪərɪ) *adj poetic* **1** a variant spelling of **airy** **2** lofty, insubstantial, or visionary [c16 via Latin from Greek *aērios*, from *aēr* AIR]

aery[2] (ˈɛərɪ, ˈɪərɪ) *n, pl* **aeries** a variant spelling of **eyrie**

Aesculapian (ˌiːskjʊˈleɪpɪən) *adj* of or relating to Aesculapius or to the art of medicine

Aesculapius (ˌiːskjʊˈleɪpɪəs) *n* the Roman god of medicine or healing. Greek counterpart: **Asclepius**

Aesir (ˈeɪsɪə) *pl n* the chief gods of Norse mythology dwelling in Asgard [Old Norse, literally: gods]

aesthesia *or US* **esthesia** (iːsˈθiːzɪə) *n* the normal ability to experience sensation, perception, or sensitivity [c20 back formation from ANAESTHESIA]

aesthete *or US* **esthete** (ˈiːsθiːt) *n* a person who has or who affects a highly developed appreciation of beauty, esp in poetry and the visual arts [c19 back formation from AESTHETICS]

aesthetic (iːsˈθɛtɪk, ɪs-) *or sometimes US* **esthetic** *adj also* **aesthetical** *or sometimes US* **esthetical** **1** connected with aesthetics or its principles **2** **a** relating to pure beauty rather than to other considerations **b** artistic or relating to good taste: *an aesthetic consideration* ▷ *n* **3** a principle of taste or style adopted by a particular person, group, or culture: *the Bauhaus aesthetic of functional modernity* > **aesˈthetically** *or sometimes US* **esˈthetically** *adv*

aesthetician *or sometimes US* **esthetician** (ˌiːsθɪˈtɪʃən, ˌɛs-) *n* **1** a student of aesthetics **2** another name for **beauty therapist**

aestheticism *or sometimes US* **estheticism** (iːsˈθɛtɪˌsɪzəm, ɪs-) *n* **1** the doctrine that aesthetic principles are of supreme importance and that works of art should be judged accordingly **2** sensitivity to beauty, esp in art, music, literature, etc

aesthetic labour *n* workers employed by a company for their appearance or accent, with the aim of promoting the company's image

aesthetics *or sometimes US* **esthetics** (iːsˈθɛtɪks, ɪs-) *n (functioning as singular)* **1** the branch of philosophy concerned with the study of such concepts as beauty, taste, etc **2** the study of the rules and principles of art [c18 from Greek *aisthētikos* perceptible by the senses, from *aisthesthai* to perceive]

aestival *or US* **estival** (iːˈstaɪvəl, ˈɛstɪ-) *adj rare* of or occurring in summer [c14 from French, from Late Latin *aestīvālis*, from Latin *aestās* summer]

aestivate *or US* **estivate** (ˈiːstɪˌveɪt, ˈɛs-) *vb (intr)* **1** to pass the summer **2** (of animals such as the lungfish) to pass the summer or dry season in a dormant condition. Compare **hibernate** [c17 from Latin *aestīvātus*, from *aestīvāre* to stay during the summer, from *aestās* summer] > **ˈaestiˌvator** *or US* **ˈestiˌvator** *n*

aestivation *or US* **estivation** (ˌiːstɪˈveɪʃən, ˌɛs-) *n* **1** the act or condition of aestivating **2** the arrangement of the parts of a flower bud, esp the sepals and petals

aet. *or* **aetat.** *abbreviation for* aetatis [Latin: at the age of]

aether (ˈiːθə) *n* a variant spelling of **ether** (senses 3–5)

aethereal (ɪˈθɪərɪəl) *adj* a variant spelling of **ethereal** (senses 1, 2, 3) > **aethereality** (ɪˌθɪərɪˈælɪtɪ) *n* > **aeˈthereally** *adv*

aetiological *or* **etiological** (ˌiːtɪəˈlɒdʒɪkəl) *adj* **1** of or relating to aetiology **2** *philosophy* (of an explanation) in terms of causal precedents, as opposed, for instance, to the intentions of an agent > **ˌaetioˈlogically** *or* **ˌetioˈlogically** *adv*

aetiology *or* **etiology** (ˌiːtɪˈɒlədʒɪ) *n, pl* **-gies** **1** the philosophy or study of causation **2** the study of the causes of diseases **3** the cause of a disease [c16 from Late Latin *aetologia*, from Greek *aitiologia*, from *aitia* cause] > **ˌaetiˈologist** *or* **ˌetiˈologist** *n*

Aetna (ˈɛtnə) *n* the Latin name for Mount **Etna**

Aetolia (iːˈtəʊlɪə) *n* a mountainous region forming (with the region of Acarnania) a department of W central Greece, north of the Gulf of Patras: a powerful federal state in the 3rd century BC Chief city: Missolonghi. Pop (with Acarnania): 219 092 (2001). Area: 5461 sq km (2108 sq miles)

AEW *abbreviation for* airborne early warning (aircraft)

af *the internet domain name for* Afghanistan

AF *abbreviation for* **1** Anglo-French **2** **automatic focus** **3** **audio frequency** **4** (in Canada) Air Force

a.f. *abbreviation for* audio frequency

A/F (in auction catalogues, etc) *abbreviation for* as found

AFAIK *text messaging abbreviation for* as far as I know

afar (əˈfɑː) *adv* **1** at, from, or to a great distance ▷ *n* **2** a great distance (esp in the phrase **from afar**) [c14 *a fer*, altered from earlier *on fer* and *of fer*; see A-[2], FAR]

Afars and the Issas (ˈɑːfɑːz, ˈiːsɑːs) *n* **Territory of the** a former name (1967–77) of **Djibouti**

AFB *abbreviation for* (US) Air Force Base

AFC *abbreviation for* **1** Air Force Cross **2** Association Football Club **3** automatic flight control **4** **automatic frequency control**

afeard *or* **afeared** (əˈfɪəd) *adj (postpositive)* an archaic or dialect word for **afraid** [Old English *āfǣred*, from *afǣran* to frighten, from *fǣran* to FEAR]

afebrile (æˈfiːbraɪl, eɪ-) *adj* without fever

aff (æf) *Scot* ▷ *adv* **1** off ▷ *prep* **2** off **3** from; out of [Old English *of*; Old Norse *af*]

affable (ˈæfəbəl) *adj* **1** showing warmth and friendliness; kindly; mild; benign **2** easy to converse with; approachable; amicable [c16 from Latin *affābilis* easy to talk to, from *affārī* to talk to, from *ad-* to + *fārī* to speak; compare FABLE, FATE] > **ˌaffaˈbility** *n* > **ˈaffably** *adv*

affair (əˈfɛə) *n* **1** a thing to be done or attended to; matter; business: *this affair must be cleared up* **2** an event or happening: *a strange affair* **3** *(qualified by an adjective or descriptive phrase)* something previously specified, esp a man-made object; thing: *our house is a tumbledown affair* **4** a sexual relationship between two people who are not married to each other ▷ See also **affairs** [c13 from Old French, from *à faire* to do]

affaire *French* (afɛr) *n* a love affair

affaire d'amour *French* (afɛr damur) *n, pl* ***affaires d'amour*** (afɛr damur) a love affair

affaire de coeur *French* (afɛr də kœr) *n, pl* ***affaires de coeur*** (afɛr də kœr) an affair of the heart; love affair

affaire d'honneur *French* (afɛr dɔnœr) *n, pl* ***affaires d'honneur*** (afɛr dɔnœr) a duel

affairs (əˈfɛəz) *pl n* **1** personal or business interests: *his affairs were in disorder* **2** matters of public interest: *current affairs*

affect[1] *vb* (əˈfɛkt) *(tr)* **1** to act upon or influence, esp in an adverse way: *damp affected the sparking plugs* **2** to move or disturb emotionally or mentally: *her death affected him greatly* **3** (of pain, disease, etc) to attack ▷ *n* (ˈæfɛkt, əˈfɛkt) **4** *psychol* the emotion associated with an idea or set of ideas. See also **affection** [c17 from Latin *affectus*, past participle of *afficere* to act upon, from *ad-* to + *facere* to do]

affect[2] (əˈfɛkt) *vb (mainly tr)* **1** to put on an appearance or show of; make a pretence of: *to affect ignorance* **2** to imitate or assume, esp pretentiously: *to affect an accent* **3** to have or use by preference: *she always affects funereal clothing* **4** to adopt the character, manner, etc, of: *he was always affecting the politician* **5** (of plants or animals) to live or grow in: *penguins affect an arctic climate* **6** to incline naturally or habitually towards: *falling drops of liquid affect roundness* [c15 from Latin *affectāre* to strive after, pretend to have; related to *afficere* to AFFECT[1]]

affectation (ˌæfɛkˈteɪʃən) *n* **1** an assumed manner of speech, dress, or behaviour, esp one that is intended to impress others **2** (often foll by *of*) deliberate pretence or false display: *affectation of nobility* [c16 from Latin *affectātiōn-* an aiming at, striving after, from *affectāre*; see AFFECT[2]]

affected[1] (əˈfɛktɪd) *adj (usually postpositive)* **1** deeply moved, esp by sorrow or grief: *he was greatly affected by her departure* **2** changed, esp detrimentally [c17 from AFFECT[1] + -ED[2]]

affected[2] (əˈfɛktɪd) *adj* **1** behaving, speaking, etc, in an artificial or assumed way, esp in order to impress others **2** feigned: *affected indifference* **3** *archaic* inclined; disposed [c16 from AFFECT[2] + -ED[2]] > **affectedly** *adv* > **affectedness** *n*

affecting (əˈfɛktɪŋ) *adj* evoking feelings of pity, sympathy, or pathos; moving > **affectingly** *adv*

affection (əˈfɛkʃən) *n* **1** a feeling of fondness or tenderness for a person or thing; attachment **2** *(often plural)* emotion, feeling, or sentiment: *to play on a person's affections* **3** *pathol* any disease or pathological condition **4** *psychol* any form of mental functioning that involves emotion. See also **affect** (sense 1) **5** the act of affecting or the state of being affected **6** *archaic* inclination or disposition [c13 from Latin *affectiōn-* disposition, from *afficere* to AFFECT[1]] > **affectional** *adj*

affectionate (əˈfɛkʃənɪt) *adj* having or displaying tender feelings, affection, or warmth: *an affectionate mother; an affectionate letter* > **affectionately** *adv*

affective (əˈfɛktɪv) *adj* **1** *psychol* relating to affects **2** concerned with or arousing the emotions or affection > **affectivity** (ˌæfɛkˈtɪvɪtɪ) *or* **affectiveness** *n*

affective disorder *n* any mental disorder, such as depression or mania, that is characterized by abnormal disturbances of mood

affective psychosis *n* a severe mental disorder characterized by extreme moods of either depression or mania

affectless (əˈfɛktlɪs) *adj* **a** showing no emotion or concern for others **b** not giving rise to any emotion or feeling: *an affectless novel* [c20 from AFFECT[1] (sense 4) + -LESS]

affenpinscher (ˈæfənˌpɪnʃə) *n* a small wire-haired breed of dog of European origin, having tufts of hair on the muzzle [German, literally: monkey-terrier, so called because its face resembles a monkey's]

afferent (ˈæfərənt) *adj* bringing or directing inwards to a part or an organ of the body, esp towards the brain or spinal cord. Compare **efferent** [c19 from Latin *afferre* to carry to, from *ad-* to + *ferre* to carry]

affettuoso (æˌfɛtʃuːˈəʊsəʊ) *adj, adv music* with feeling [c18 from Italian]

affiance (əˈfaɪəns) *vb* **1** *(tr)* to bind (a person or oneself) in a promise of marriage; betroth ▷ *n* **2** *archaic* a solemn pledge, esp a marriage contract [c14 via Old French from Medieval Latin *affīdāre* to trust (oneself) to, from *fīdāre* to trust, from *fīdus* faithful]

affiant (əˈfaɪənt) *n US law* a person who makes an affidavit [c19 Old French, from *affier* to trust to, from Medieval Latin *affīdāre*; see AFFIANCE]

affiche *French* (afiʃ) *n* a poster or advertisement, esp one drawn by an artist, as for the opening of an exhibition [c18 from *afficher* to post]

affidavit (ˌæfɪˈdeɪvɪt) *n law* a declaration in writing made upon oath before a person authorized to administer oaths, esp for use as evidence in court [c17 from Medieval Latin, literally: he declares on oath, from *affīdare* to trust (oneself) to; see AFFIANCE]

affiliate *vb* (əˈfɪlɪˌeɪt) **1** *(tr; foll by* to *or* with*)* to receive into close connection or association (with a larger body, group, organization, etc); adopt as a member, branch, etc **2** (foll by *with*) to associate (oneself) or be associated, esp as a subordinate or subsidiary; bring or come into close connection: *he affiliated himself with the Union* ▷ *n* (əˈfɪlɪɪt, -ˌeɪt) **3** **a** a person or organization that is affiliated with another **b** *(as modifier)*: *an affiliate member* [c18 from Medieval Latin *affīliātus* adopted as a son, from

affiliāre, from Latin *filius* son] > af,fili'ation *n*
affiliation order *n law* (formerly) an order made by a magistrates' court that a man adjudged to be the father of an illegitimate child shall contribute a specified periodic sum towards the child's maintenance
affiliation proceedings *pl n* (formerly) legal proceedings, usually initiated by an unmarried mother, claiming legal recognition that a particular man is the father of her child, often associated with a claim for financial support
affine ('æfaɪn) *adj maths* of, characterizing, or involving transformations which preserve collinearity, esp in classical geometry, those of translation, rotation and reflection in an axis [C16 via French from Latin *affinis* bordering on, related]
affined (ə'faɪnd) *adj* closely related; connected
affinity (ə'fɪnɪtɪ) *n, pl* **-ties** **1** (foll by *with* or *for*) a natural liking, taste, or inclination towards a person or thing **2** the person or thing so liked **3** a close similarity in appearance or quality; inherent likeness **4** relationship by marriage or by ties other than of blood, as by adoption. Compare **consanguinity** **5** similarity in structure, form, etc, between different animals, plants, or languages **6** *chem* **a** the tendency for two substances to combine; chemical attraction **b** a measure of the tendency of a chemical reaction to take place expressed in terms of the free energy change. Symbol: *A* **7** *biology* a measure of the degree of interaction between two molecules, such as an antigen and antibody or a hormone and its receptor [C14 via Old French from Latin *affinitāt-* connected by marriage, from *affinis* bordering on, related] > af'finitive *adj*
affinity card *n* **1** *Brit* a credit card issued by a bank or credit-card company, which donates a small percentage of the money spent using the card to a specified charity **2** *US* a card entitling members of an affinity group (eg club, college) to a discount when used for purchases
affirm (ə'fɜːm) *vb (mainly tr)* **1** (*may take a clause as object*) to declare to be true; assert positively **2** to uphold, confirm, or ratify **3** (*intr*) *law* to make an affirmation [C14 via Old French from Latin *affirmāre* to present (something) as firm or fixed, assert, from *ad-* to + *firmāre* to make FIRM[1]] > af'firmer *or* af'firmant *n*
affirmation (,æfə'meɪʃən) *n* **1** the act of affirming or the state of being affirmed **2** a statement of the existence or truth of something; assertion **3** *law* a solemn declaration permitted on grounds of conscientious objection to taking an oath
affirmative (ə'fɜːmətɪv) *adj* **1** confirming or asserting something as true or valid: *an affirmative statement* **2** indicating agreement or assent: *an affirmative answer* **3** *logic* **a** (of a categorial proposition) affirming the satisfaction by the subject of the predicate, as in *all birds have feathers; some men are married* **b** not containing negation. Compare **negative** (sense 12) ▷ *n* **4** a positive assertion **5** a word or phrase stating agreement or assent, such as *yes* (esp in the phrase **answer in the affirmative**) **6** *logic* an affirmative proposition **7** **the affirmative** *chiefly US and Canadian* the side in a debate that supports the proposition ▷ *sentence substitute* **8** *military* a signal codeword used to express assent or confirmation > af'firmatively *adv*
affirmative action *n US* a policy or programme designed to counter discrimination against minority groups and women in areas such as employment and education. Brit equivalent: positive discrimination
affix *vb* (ə'fɪks) (*tr; usually foll by to or on*) **1** to attach, fasten, join, or stick: *to affix a poster to the wall* **2** to add or append: *to affix a signature to a document* **3** to attach or attribute (guilt, blame, etc) ▷ *n* ('æfɪks) **4** a linguistic element added to a word or root to produce a derived or inflected form: *-ment* in *establishment* is a derivational affix; *-s* in *drowns* is an inflectional affix. See also **prefix, suffix, infix** **5** something fastened or attached; appendage [C15 from Medieval Latin *affixāre*, from *ad-* to + *fixāre* to FIX] > **affixation** (,æfɪk'seɪʃən) *or* **affixture** (ə'fɪkstʃə) *n*
afflatus (ə'fleɪtəs) *n* an impulse of creative power or inspiration, esp in poetry, considered to be of divine origin (esp in the phrase **divine afflatus**) [C17 Latin, from *afflātus*, from *afflāre* to breathe or blow on, from *flāre* to blow]
afflict (ə'flɪkt) *vb (tr)* to cause suffering or unhappiness to; distress greatly [C14 from Latin *afflictus*, past participle of *affligere* to knock against, from *fligere* to knock, to strike] > af'flictive *adj*
afflicting (ə'flɪktɪŋ) *adj* deeply distressing; painful
affliction (ə'flɪkʃən) *n* **1** a condition of great distress, pain, or suffering **2** something responsible for physical or mental suffering, such as a disease, grief, etc
affluence ('æflʊəns) *n* **1** an abundant supply of money, goods, or property; wealth **2** *rare* abundance or profusion
affluent ('æflʊənt) *adj* **1** rich; wealthy **2** abundant; copious **3** flowing freely ▷ *n* **4** *archaic* a tributary stream [C15 from Latin *affluent-*, present participle of *affluere* to flow towards, from *fluere* to flow]
affluential (,æflʊ'ɛnʃəl) *n* an affluent person who does not display his or her wealth in the form of material possessions
affluent society *n* a society in which the material benefits of prosperity are widely available
affluenza (,æflʊ'ɛnzə) *n* the guilt or lack of motivation experienced by people who have made or inherited large amounts of money. Also called: **sudden-wealth syndrome** [C20 from AFF(LUENT) + (IN)FLUENZA]
afflux ('æflʌks) *n* a flowing towards a point: *an afflux of blood to the head* [C17 from Latin *affluxus*, from *fluxus* FLUX]
afford (ə'fɔːd) *vb* **1** (preceded by *can, could*, etc) to be able to do or spare something, esp without incurring financial difficulties or without risk of undesirable consequences: *we can afford to buy a small house; I can afford to give you one of my chess sets; we can't afford to miss this play* **2** to give, yield, or supply: *the meeting afforded much useful information* [Old English *geforthian* to further, promote, from *forth* FORTH; the Old English prefix *ge-* was later reduced to *a-*, and the modern spelling (C16) is influenced by words beginning *aff-*] > af'fordable *adj* > af,forda'bility *n*
afforest (ə'fɒrɪst) *vb (tr)* to plant trees on; convert into forested land [C15 from Medieval Latin *afforestāre*, from *forestis* FOREST] > af,forest'ation *n*
affranchise (ə'fræntʃaɪz) *vb (tr)* to release from servitude or an obligation [C15 from Old French *afranchiss-*, a stem of *afranchir*, from *franchir* to free; see FRANK] > af'franchisement *n*
affray (ə'freɪ) *n* **1** *law* a fight, noisy quarrel, or disturbance between two or more persons in a public place ▷ *vb* **2** (*tr*) *archaic* to frighten [C14 via Old French from Vulgar Latin *exfridāre* (unattested) to break the peace; compare German *Friede* peace]
affreightment (ə'freɪtmənt) *n* a contract hiring a ship to carry goods [C19 from French *affréter* to charter a ship, from *fret* FREIGHT]
affricate ('æfrɪkɪt) *n* a composite speech sound consisting of a stop and a fricative articulated at the same point, such as the sound written *ch*, as in *chair* [C19 from Latin *affricāre* to rub against, from *fricāre* to rub; compare FRICTION]
affricative (ə'frɪkətɪv, 'æfrə,keɪ-) *n* **1** another word for **affricate** ▷ *adj* **2** of, relating to, or denoting an affricate
affright (ə'fraɪt) *archaic or poetic* ▷ *vb* **1** (*tr*) to frighten ▷ *n* **2** a sudden terror [Old English *āfyrhtan*, from *a-*, a prefix indicating the beginning or end of an action + *fyrhtan* to FRIGHT]
affront (ə'frʌnt) *n* **1** a deliberate insult ▷ *vb* (*tr*) **2** to insult, esp openly **3** to offend the pride or dignity of **4** *obsolete* to confront defiantly [C14 from Old French *afronter* to strike in the face, from Vulgar Latin *affrontāre* (unattested), from the Latin phrase *ad frontem* to the face]
affusion (ə'fjuːʒən) *n* the baptizing of a person by pouring water onto his head. Compare **aspersion** (sense 3), **immersion** [C17 from Late Latin *affūsiōn-* a pouring upon, from *affundere*, from *fundere* to pour]
AFG *international car registration for* Afghanistan
Afg. *or* **Afgh.** *abbreviation for* Afghanistan
afghan ('æfgæn, -gən) *n* **1** a knitted or crocheted wool blanket or shawl, esp one with a geometric pattern **2** a sheepskin coat, often embroidered and having long fur trimming around the edges
Afghan ('æfgæn, -gən) *or* **Afghani** (æf'gænɪ, -'gɑː-) *n* **1** a native, citizen, or inhabitant of Afghanistan **2** another name for **Pashto** (the language) **3** *history* an Indian camel driver employed in the outback of Australia ▷ *adj* **4** denoting or relating to Afghanistan, its people, or their language
Afghan hound *n* a tall graceful breed of hound with a long silky coat
afghani (æf'gɑːnɪ) *n* the standard monetary unit of Afghanistan, divided into 100 puli
Afghanistan (æf'gænɪ,stɑːn, -,stæn) *n* a republic in central Asia: became independent in 1919; occupied by Soviet troops, 1979–89; controlled by mujaheddin forces from 1992 until 1996 when Taliban forces seized power; in the US-led 'war against terrorism' (2001) the Taliban were overthrown and replaced by an interim administration; generally arid and mountainous, with the Hindu Kush range rising over 7500 m (25 000 ft) and fertile valleys of the Amu Darya, Helmand, and Kabul Rivers. Official languages: Pashto and Dari (Persian), Tajik also widely spoken. Religion: Muslim. Currency: afghani. Capital: Kabul. Pop: 24 926 000 (2004 est). Area: 657 500 sq km (250 000 sq miles)
aficionado (ə,fɪʃjə'nɑːdəʊ; *Spanish* afiθjo'naðo) *n, pl* **-dos** (-dəʊz; *Spanish* -ðos) **1** an ardent supporter or devotee: *a jazz aficionado* **2** a devotee of bullfighting [Spanish, from *aficionar* to arouse affection, from *aficion* AFFECTION] a
afield (ə'fiːld) *adv, adj (postpositive)* **1** away from one's usual surroundings or home (esp in the phrase **far afield**) **2** off the subject; away from the point (esp in the phrase **far afield**) **3** in or to the field, esp the battlefield
afire (ə'faɪə) *adv, adj (postpositive)* **1** on fire; ablaze **2** intensely interested or passionate: *he was afire with enthusiasm for the new plan*
AFIS *n* Automated Fingerprint Identification System: a computer system that scans fingerprints from crime scenes and compares them with millions of others around the world
AFK *text messaging abbreviation for* away from keyboard
AFL *abbreviation for* Australian Football League: the national body for Australian Rules football
aflame (ə'fleɪm) *adv, adj (postpositive)* **1** in flames; ablaze **2** deeply aroused, as with passion: *he was aflame with desire* **3** (of the face) red or inflamed
aflatoxin (,æflə'tɒksɪn) *n* a toxin produced by the fungus *Aspergillus flavus* growing on peanuts, maize, etc, causing liver disease (esp cancer) in man [C20 from *A(spergillus) fla(vus)* + TOXIN]
AFL-CIO *abbreviation for* American Federation of Labor and Congress of Industrial Organizations: a federation of independent American trade unions formed by the union of these two groups in 1955
afloat (ə'fləʊt) *adj (postpositive)* ▷ *adv* **1** floating **2** aboard ship; at sea **3** covered with water; flooded **4** aimlessly drifting: *afloat in a sea of indecision* **5** in circulation; afoot: *nasty rumours were afloat* **6** free of debt; solvent
aflutter (ə'flʌtə) *adj (postpositive)* ▷ *adv* in or into a nervous or excited state
AFM *abbreviation for* Air Force Medal
AFN (in Canada) *abbreviation for* Assembly of First Nations
AFNOR *abbreviation for* Association Française de

Normalisation: the standards organization of France

afoot (əˈfʊt) *adj* (*postpositive*) ▷ *adv* **1** in circulation or operation; astir: *mischief was afoot* **2** on or by foot

afore (əˈfɔː) *adv, prep, conj* an archaic or dialect word for **before**

aforementioned (əˈfɔːˌmɛnʃənd) *adj* (*usually prenominal*) (chiefly in legal documents) stated or mentioned before or already

aforesaid (əˈfɔːˌsɛd) *adj* (*usually prenominal*) (chiefly in legal documents) spoken of or referred to previously

aforethought (əˈfɔːˌθɔːt) *adj* (*immediately postpositive*) premeditated (esp in the phrase **malice aforethought**)

aforetime (əˈfɔːˌtaɪm) *adv archaic* formerly

a fortiori (eɪ ˌfɔːtɪˈɔːraɪ, -rɪ, ɑː) *adv* for similar but more convincing reasons: *if Britain cannot afford a space programme, then, a fortiori, neither can India* [Latin]

afoul (əˈfaʊl) *adv, adj* (*postpositive*) **1** (usually foll by *of*) in or into a state of difficulty, confusion, or conflict (with) **2** (often foll by *of*) in or into an entanglement or collision (with) (often in the phrase **run afoul of**): *a yacht with its sails afoul; the boat ran afoul of a steamer*

afp *abbreviation for* alpha-fetoprotein

AFRAeS (in Britain) *abbreviation for* Associate Fellow of the Royal Aeronautical Society

afraid (əˈfreɪd) *adj* (*postpositive*) **1** (often foll by *of*) feeling fear or apprehension; frightened: *he was afraid of cats* **2** reluctant (to do something), as through fear or timidity: *he was afraid to let himself go* **3** (often foll by *that*; used to lessen the effect of an unpleasant statement) regretful: *I'm afraid that I shall have to tell you to go* [C14 *affraied*, past participle of AFFRAY (to frighten)]

A-frame *adj* (of a house) constructed with an A-shaped elevation

afreet *or* **afrit** (ˈæfriːt, əˈfriːt) *n Arabian myth* a powerful evil demon or giant monster [C19 from Arabic *'ifrīt*]

afresh (əˈfrɛʃ) *adv* once more; once again; anew

Africa (ˈæfrɪkə) *n* the second largest of the continents, on the Mediterranean in the north, the Atlantic in the west, and the Red Sea, Gulf of Aden, and Indian Ocean in the east. The Sahara desert divides the continent unequally into North Africa (an early centre of civilization, in close contact with Europe and W Asia, now inhabited chiefly by Arabs) and Africa south of the Sahara (relatively isolated from the rest of the world until the 19th century and inhabited chiefly by Negroid peoples). It was colonized mainly in the 18th and 19th centuries by Europeans and now comprises independent nations. The largest lake is Lake Victoria and the chief rivers are the Nile, Niger, Congo, and Zambezi. Pop: 887 964 000 (2005 est). Area: about 30 300 000 sq km (11 700 000 sq miles)

African (ˈæfrɪkən) *adj* **1** denoting or relating to Africa or any of its peoples, languages, nations, etc ▷ *n* **2** a native, inhabitant, or citizen of any of the countries of Africa **3** a member or descendant of any of the peoples of Africa, esp a Black person

Africana (ˌæfrɪˈkɑːnə) *pl n* objects of cultural or historical interest of African origin

African-American *n* **1** an American of African descent ▷ *adj* **2** of or relating to Americans of African descent

African-American Vernacular English *n* a dialect of English typically spoken by working-class African-Americans. Abbreviation: **AAVE** Also called: **ebonics**

African-Canadian *n* **1** a Canadian of African descent ▷ *adj* **2** of or relating to Canadians of African descent

African horse sickness *n vet science* a fatal infectious disease of horses, mules, and donkeys, which is transmitted by insect vectors. It is caused by an arbovirus and is characterized by pulmonary or cardiac signs

Africanism (ˈæfrɪkəˌnɪzəm) *n* something characteristic of Africa or Africans, esp a

characteristic feature of an African language when introduced into a non-African language

Africanist (ˈæfrɪkənɪst) *n* a person specializing in the study of African affairs or culture

Africanize *or* **Africanise** (ˈæfrɪkəˌnaɪz) *vb* (*tr*) to make African, esp to give control of (policy, government, etc) to Africans ▷ **Africaniˈzation** *or* **Africaniˈsation** *n*

African lily *n* another name for **agapanthus**

African mahogany *n* **1** any of several African trees of the meliaceous genus *Khaya*, esp *K. ivorensis*, that have wood similar to that of true mahogany **2** the wood of any of these trees, used for furniture, etc **3** any of various other African woods that resemble true mahogany

African National Congress *n* (in South Africa) a political party, founded in 1912 as an African nationalist movement and banned there from 1960 to 1990 because of its active opposition to apartheid: in 1994 won South Africa's first multiracial elections. Abbreviation: **ANC**

African potato *n* the corm of a southern African plant, *Hypoxis hemerocallidea*, believed to possess medicinal properties

African swine fever *n vet science* a highly contagious fatal disease of pigs caused by a myxovirus. The disease is characterized by fever, blotches on the skin, depression, and lack of coordination

African time *n South African slang* unpunctuality

African Union *n* an organization of African states established in 2002 as successor to the OAU; it aims to encourage economic development and political stability through increased cooperation between its members. Abbreviation: **AU**

African violet *n* any of several tropical African plants of the genus *Saintpaulia*, esp *S. ionantha*, cultivated as house plants, with violet, white, or pink flowers and hairy leaves: family *Gesneriaceae*

Afrikaans (ˌæfrɪˈkɑːns, -ˈkɑːnz) *n* one of the official languages of the Republic of South Africa, closely related to Dutch. Sometimes called: **South African Dutch** [C20 from Dutch: African]

Afrikander *or* **Africander** (afriˈkandə, ˌæfrɪˈkændə) *n* **1** a breed of humpbacked beef cattle originally raised in southern Africa **2** a southern African breed of fat-tailed sheep **3** a former name for an **Afrikaner** [C19 from South African Dutch, formed on the model of *Hollander*]

Afrikaner (afriˈkɑːnə, ˌæfrɪˈkɑːnə) *n* a White native of the Republic of South Africa whose mother tongue is Afrikaans. See also **Boer**

Afrikanerdom (afriˈkɑːnədəm, ˌæfrɪˈkɑːnədəm) *n* (in South Africa) Afrikaner nationalism based on pride in the Afrikaans language and culture, conservative Calvinism, and a sense of heritage as pioneers

afrit (ˈæfriːt, əˈfriːt) *n* a variant spelling of **afreet**

Afro (ˈæfrəʊ) *n, pl* **-ros** a hairstyle in which the hair is shaped into a wide frizzy bush [C20 independent use of AFRO-]

Afro- *combining form* indicating Africa or African: *Afro-Asiatic*

Afro-American *n, adj* another word for **African-American**

Afro-Asian *adj* of or relating to both Africa and Asia, esp as part of the Third World

Afro-Asiatic *n* **1** Also called: **Semito-Hamitic** a family of languages of SW Asia and N Africa, consisting of the Semitic, ancient Egyptian, Berber, Cushitic, and Chadic subfamilies ▷ *adj* **2** denoting, belonging to, or relating to this family of languages

Afro-British *adj* of or relating to British people of African descent

Afro-Caribbean *adj* **1** denoting or relating to Caribbean people of African descent or their culture ▷ *n* **2** a Caribbean of African descent

Afro-chain *n* (in the Caribbean) a large chain necklace with a central pendant: usually worn with a dashiki by men

Afro-comb *n* a comb with a handle and long

teeth used esp on curly hair

Afro-Cuban *adj* of or relating to a type of jazz influenced by Cuban variants of African rhythms. Compare **Cu-bop**

Afro-pessimism *n* the belief that the provision of aid to African countries is futile

afrormosia (ˌæfrɔːˈməʊzɪə) *n* a hard teaklike wood obtained from tropical African trees of the leguminous genus *Pericopsis* [C20 from AFRO- + *Ormosia* (genus name)]

AFSLAET *abbreviation for* Associate Fellow of the Society of Licensed Aircraft Engineers and Technologists

aft (ɑːft) *adv, adj chiefly nautical* towards or at the stern or rear: *the aft deck; aft of the engines* [C17 perhaps a shortened form of earlier ABAFT]

after (ˈɑːftə) *prep* **1** following in time; in succession to: *after dinner; time after time* **2** following; behind: *they entered one after another* **3** in pursuit or search of: *chasing after a thief; he's only after money* **4** concerning: *to inquire after his health* **5** considering: *after what you have done, you shouldn't complain* **6** next in excellence or importance to: *he ranked Jonson after Shakespeare* **7** in imitation of; in the manner of: *a statue after classical models* **8** in accordance with or in conformity to: *a man after her own heart* **9** with a name derived from: *Mary was named after her grandmother* **10** US past (the hour of): *twenty after three* **11** **after all a** in spite of everything: *it's only a game, after all* **b** in spite of expectations, efforts, etc: *he won the race after all!* **12** **after you** please go, enter, etc, before me ▷ *adv* **13** at a later time; afterwards **14** coming afterwards; in pursuit **15** *nautical* further aft; sternwards ▷ *conj* **16** (*subordinating*) at a time later than that at which: *he came after I had left* ▷ *adj* **17** *nautical* further aft: *the after cabin* [Old English *æfter*; related to Old Norse *aptr* back, *eptir* after, Old High German *aftar*]

afterbirth (ˈɑːftəˌbɜːθ) *n* the placenta and fetal membranes expelled from the uterus after the birth of the offspring

afterbody (ˈɑːftəˌbɒdɪ) *n, pl* **-bodies** any discarded part that continues to trail a satellite, rocket, etc, in orbit

afterbrain (ˈɑːftəˌbreɪn) *n* a nontechnical name for **myelencephalon**

afterburner (ˈɑːftəˌbɜːnə) *n* **1** a device in the exhaust system of an internal-combustion engine for removing or rendering harmless potentially dangerous components in the exhaust gases **2** a system of fuel injection and combustion located behind the turbine of an aircraft jet engine to produce additional thrust

afterburning (ˈɑːftəˌbɜːnɪŋ) *n* **1** Also called: **reheat** a process in which additional fuel is ignited in the exhaust gases of a jet engine to produce additional thrust **2** irregular burning of fuel in a rocket motor after the main burning has ceased **3** persistence of combustion in an internal-combustion engine, either in an incorrect part of the cycle or after the ignition has been switched off

aftercare (ˈɑːftəˌkɛə) *n* **1** support services by a welfare agency for a person discharged from an institution, such as hospital, hostel, or prison **2** *med* the care before and after discharge from hospital of a patient recovering from an illness or operation **3** any system of maintenance or upkeep of an appliance or product: *contact lens aftercare*

afterdamp (ˈɑːftəˌdæmp) *n* a poisonous mixture of gases containing carbon dioxide, carbon monoxide, and nitrogen formed after the explosion of firedamp in coal mines. See also **whitedamp**

afterdeck (ˈɑːftəˌdɛk) *n nautical* the unprotected deck behind the bridge of a ship

aftereffect (ˈɑːftərɪˌfɛkt) *n* **1** any result occurring some time after its cause **2** *med* any delayed response to a stimulus or agent. Compare **side effect 3** *psychol* any illusory sensation caused by a stimulus that has ceased

afterglow ('ɑːftəˌgləʊ) n **1** the glow left after a light has disappeared, such as that sometimes seen after sunset **2** the glow of an incandescent metal after the source of heat has been removed **3** *physics* luminescence persisting on the screen of a cathode-ray tube or in a gas discharge tube after the power supply has been disconnected **4** a trace, impression, etc, of past emotion, brilliance, etc

afterheat ('ɑːftəˌhiːt) n the heat generated in a nuclear reactor after it has been shut down, produced by residual radioactivity in the fuel elements

afterimage ('ɑːftərˌɪmɪdʒ) n a sustained or renewed sensation, esp visual, after the original stimulus has ceased. Also called: **aftersensation**, **photogene**

afterlife ('ɑːftəˌlaɪf) n life after death or at a later time in a person's lifetime

aftermath ('ɑːftəˌmɑːθ, -ˌmæθ) n **1** signs or results of an event or occurrence considered collectively, esp of a catastrophe or disaster: *the aftermath of war* **2** *agriculture* a second mowing or crop of grass from land that has already yielded one crop earlier in the same year [c16 AFTER + *math* a mowing, from Old English *mæth*]

aftermost ('ɑːftəˌməʊst) adj closer or closest to the rear or (in a vessel) the stern; last

afternoon (ˌɑːftə'nuːn) n **1 a** the period of the day between noon and evening **b** (*as modifier*): *afternoon tea* **2** a middle or later part: *the afternoon of life*

afternoons (ˌɑːftə'nuːnz) adv informal during the afternoon, esp regularly

afterpains ('ɑːftəˌpeɪnz) pl n cramplike pains caused by contraction of the uterus after childbirth

afterpeak ('ɑːftəˌpiːk) n *nautical* the space behind the aftermost bulkhead, often used for storage

afterpiece ('ɑːftəˌpiːs) n a brief usually comic dramatic piece presented after a play

after-ripening n *botany* the period of internal change that is necessary in some apparently mature seeds before germination can occur

afters ('ɑːftəz) n (*functioning as singular or plural*) *Brit* **1** *informal* dessert; sweet **2** *slang* a confrontation or physical violence between football players immediately after they have been involved in a challenge for the ball

aftersensation ('ɑːftəsɛnˌseɪʃən) n another word for **afterimage**

aftershaft ('ɑːftəˌʃɑːft) n *ornithol* a secondary feather arising near the base of a contour feather

aftershave lotion ('ɑːftəˌʃeɪv) n a lotion, usually styptic and perfumed, for application to the face after shaving. Often shortened to: **aftershave**

aftershock ('ɑːftəˌʃɒk) n one of a series of minor tremors occurring after the main shock of an earthquake. Compare **foreshock**

aftershow ('ɑːftəˌʃəʊ) n **a** a party held after a public performance of a play or film **b** (*as modifier*): *an aftershow bash*

aftersun ('ɑːftəˌsʌn) n **a** a moisturizing lotion applied to the skin to soothe sunburn and avoid peeling **b** (*as modifier*): *aftersun lotion*

aftertaste ('ɑːftəˌteɪst) n **1** a taste that lingers on after eating or drinking **2** a lingering impression or sensation

afterthought ('ɑːftəˌθɔːt) n **1** a comment, reply, etc, that occurs to one after the opportunity to deliver it has passed **2** an addition to something already completed

afterwards ('ɑːftəwədz) or **afterward** adv after an earlier event or time; subsequently [Old English *æftewerd, æftewerd*, from AFT + WARD]

afterword ('ɑːftəˌwɜːd) n an epilogue or postscript in a book, etc

afterworld ('ɑːftəˌwɜːld) n a world inhabited after death

AFTN abbreviation for Aeronautical Fixed Telecommunications Network: a worldwide system of radio and cable links for transmitting and recording messages

AFV abbreviation for armoured fighting vehicle

ag¹ (æx) interj South African **1** an expression of surprise, annoyance, pleasure, etc ▷ *sentence connector* **2** an expression used to preface a remark, gain time, etc

ag² the internet domain name for Antigua and Barbuda

Ag the chemical symbol for silver [from Latin *argentum*]

AG abbreviation for **1** Adjutant General **2** Attorney General **3** Aktiengesellschaft [(for sense 3) German: joint-stock company]

aga or **agha** ('ɑːgə) n (in the Ottoman Empire) **1** a title of respect, often used with the title of a senior position **2** a military commander [c17 Turkish, literally: lord]

Aga ('ɑːgə) n trademark Brit a cooking range and heating system powered by solid fuel, electricity, or gas [c20 from (Svenskaa) A(ktiebolaget) Ga(sackumulator), the original Swedish manufacturer]

Agadir (ˌægə'dɪə) n a port in SW Morocco, which became the centre of an international crisis (1911), when a gunboat arrived to protect German interests. Britain issued a strong warning to Germany but the French negotiated and war was averted. In 1960 the town was virtually destroyed by an earthquake, about 10 000 people being killed. Pop: 385 000 (2003)

again (ə'gɛn, ə'geɪn) adv **1** another or second time; once more; anew: *he had to start again* **2** once more in a previously experienced or encountered place, state, or condition: *he is ill again; he came back again* **3** in addition to the original amount, quantity, etc (esp in the phrases **as much again; half as much again**) **4** (*sentence modifier*) on the other hand: *he might come and then again he might not* **5** besides; also: *she is beautiful and, again, intelligent* **6** archaic in reply; back: *he answered again to the questioning voice* **7** **again and again** continuously; repeatedly **8** (*used with a negative*) Caribbean any more; any longer: *I don't eat pumpkin again* ▷ *sentence connector* **9** moreover; furthermore: *again, it could be said that he is not dead* [Old English *ongegn* opposite to, from A-² + *gegn* straight]

against (ə'gɛnst, ə'geɪnst) prep **1** opposed to; in conflict or disagreement with: *they fought against the legislation* **2** standing or leaning beside or in front of: *a ladder against the wall* **3** coming in contact with: *the branches of a tree brushed against the bus* **4** in contrast to: *silhouettes are outlines against a light background* **5** having an adverse or unfavourable effect on: *the economic system works against small independent companies* **6** as a protection from or means of defence from the adverse effects of: *a safeguard against contaminated water* **7** in exchange for or in return for **8** now rare in preparation for: *he gave them warm clothing against their journey through the night* **9** as against as opposed to or as compared with: *he had two shots at him this time as against only one last time* [c12 *ageines*, from *again, ageyn*, etc, AGAIN + -*es* genitive ending; the spelling with -*t* (c16) was probably due to confusion with superlatives ending in -*st*]

Aga Khan ('ɑːgə 'kɑːn) n the hereditary title of the head of the Ismaili sect of Muslims

agalactia (ˌægə'læktɪə) n *pathol obsolete* absence or failure of secretion of milk [c19 New Latin, from A-¹ + Greek *galaktos* milk]

agalloch (ə'gæ[ə]k) n another name for **eaglewood** [c17 from Greek *agallokhon*]

agama ('ægəmə, ə'gæmə) n **1** any small terrestrial lizard of the genus *Agama*, which inhabit warm regions of the Old World: family *Agamidae* **2** Also called: agamid ('ægəmɪd, ə'gæmɪd) any other lizard of the family *Agamidae*, which occur in the Old World and Australia and show a wide range of habits and diversity of structure [c19 Carib]

Agamemnon (ˌægə'mɛmnɒn) n *Greek myth* a king of Mycenae who led the Greeks at the siege of Troy. On his return home he was murdered by his wife Clytemnestra and her lover Aegisthus. See also **Menelaus**

agamete (ə'gæmiːt) n a reproductive cell, such as the merozoite of some protozoans, that develops into a new form without fertilization [c19 from Greek *agametos* unmarried; see A-¹, GAMETE]

agamic (ə'gæmɪk) adj asexual; occurring or reproducing without fertilization [c19 from Greek *agamos* unmarried, from A-¹ + *gamos* marriage] > a'gamically adv

agamogenesis (ˌægəməʊ'dʒɛnɪsɪs) n asexual reproduction, such as fission or parthenogenesis [c19 AGAMIC + GENESIS] > agamogenetic (ˌægəməʊdʒə'nɛtɪk) adj > ˌagamoge'netically adv

agamogony (ˌægə'mɒgənɪ) n another name for **schizogony**

agamont ('ægəmɒnt) n another name for **schizont**

agamospermy ('ægəməʊˌspɜːmɪ) n *botany* formation of seeds in the absence of fertilization; a form of apomixis [c19 AGAMIC + Greek *sperma* seed]

Agaña (ə'gɑːnjə) n the capital of the Pacific island of Guam, on its W coast. Pop: 1100 (2000)

agapanthus (ˌægə'pænθəs) n a liliaceous plant, *Agapanthus africanus*, of southern Africa, having rounded clusters of blue or white funnel-shaped flowers. Also called: **African lily** [c19 New Latin, from Greek *agapē* love + *anthos* flower]

agape (ə'geɪp) adj (*postpositive*) **1** (esp of the mouth) wide open **2** very surprised, expectant, or eager, esp as indicated by a wide open mouth [c17 A-² + GAPE]

Agape ('ægəpɪ) n *Christianity* **1** Christian love, esp as contrasted with erotic love; charity **2** a communal meal in the early Church taken in commemoration of the Last Supper; love feast [c17 Greek *agapē* love]

agar ('eɪgə) n a complex gelatinous carbohydrate obtained from seaweeds, esp those of the genus *Gelidium*, used as a culture medium for bacteria, a laxative, in food such as ice cream as a thickening agent (E406), etc. Also called: **agar-agar** [c19 Malay]

agaric ('ægərɪk, ə'gærɪk) n **1** any saprotrophic basidiomycetous fungus of the family *Agaricaceae*, having gills on the underside of the cap. The group includes the edible mushrooms and poisonous forms such as the fly agaric **2** the dried spore-producing bodies of certain fungi, esp *Polyphorus officinalis* (or *Boletus laricis*), formerly used in medicine [c16 via Latin *agaricum*, from Greek *agarikon*, perhaps named after *Agaria*, a town in Sarmatia] > agaricaceous (ˌægærɪ'keɪʃəs) adj

Agartala ('ʌgətə,lɑː) n a city in NE India, capital of the state of Tripura. Pop: 189 327 (2001)

Aga saga n Brit a novel or drama depicting the lives and concerns of the English middle classes [c20 allusion to the popularity of AGA cookers among the English middle classes]

agate¹ ('ægɪt) n **1** an impure microcrystalline form of quartz consisting of a variegated, usually banded chalcedony, used as a gemstone and in making pestles and mortars, burnishers, and polishers. Formula: SiO_2 **2** a playing marble of this quartz or resembling it **3** *printing, US and Canadian* (formerly) a size of printer's type approximately equal to 5½ point. Also called: **ruby** [c16 via French from Latin *achātēs*, from Greek *akhatēs*]

agate² (ə'geɪt) adv Northern English dialect on the way [c16 A-² + GATE³]

agateware ('ægɪtˌwɛə) n ceramic ware made to resemble agate or marble

agave (ə'geɪvɪ, 'ægeɪv) n any plant of the genus *Agave*, native to tropical America, with tall flower stalks rising from a massive, often armed, rosette of thick fleshy leaves: family *Agavaceae*. Some species are the source of fibres such as sisal or of alcoholic beverages such as pulque and tequila. See also **century plant** [c18 New Latin, from Greek

a

agauē, feminine of *agauos* illustrious, probably alluding to the height of the plant]

AGC *abbreviation for* **automatic gain control**

age (eɪdʒ) *n* **1** the period of time that a person, animal, or plant has lived or is expected to live: *the age of a tree; what age was he when he died?; the age of a horse is up to thirty years* **2** the period of existence of an object, material, group, etc: *the age of this table is 200 years* **3 a** a period or state of human life: *he should know better at his age; she had got beyond the giggly age* **b** (*as modifier*): *age group* **4** the latter part of life **5 a** a period of history marked by some feature or characteristic; era **b** (*capital when part of a name*): *the Middle Ages; the Space Age* **6** generation: *the Edwardian age* **7** *geology, palaeontol* **a** a period of the earth's history distinguished by special characteristics: *the age of reptiles* **b** the period during which a stage of rock strata is formed; a subdivision of an epoch **8** *myth* any of the successive periods in the legendary history of man, which were, according to Hesiod, the golden, silver, bronze, heroic, and iron ages **9** (*often plural*) *informal* a relatively long time: *she was an age washing her hair; I've been waiting ages* **10** *psychol* the level in years that a person has reached in any area of development, such as mental or emotional, compared with the normal level for his chronological age. See also **achievement age, mental age** **11** **age before beauty** (often said humorously when yielding precedence) older people take precedence over younger people **12** **of age** adult and legally responsible for one's actions (usually at 18 or, formerly, 21 years) ▷ *vb* **ages, ageing** *or* **aging, aged** **13** to grow or make old or apparently old; become or cause to become old or aged **14** to begin to seem older: *to have aged a lot in the past year* **15** *brewing* to mature or cause to mature [C13 via Old French from Vulgar Latin *aetatīcum* (unattested), from Latin *aetās*, ultimately from *aevum* lifetime; compare AEON]

-age *suffix forming nouns* **1** indicating a collection, set, or group: *acreage; baggage* **2** indicating a process or action or the result of an action: *haulage; passage; breakage* **3** indicating a state, condition, or relationship: *bondage; parentage* **4** indicating a house or place: *orphanage* **5** indicating a charge or fee: *postage* **6** indicating a rate: *dosage; mileage* [from Old French, from Late Latin *-āticum*, noun suffix, neuter of *-āticus*, adjectival suffix, from *-ātus* -ATE[1] + *-icus* -IC]

age allowance *n* an income tax allowance given to taxpayers aged 65 or over

aged (ˈeɪdʒɪd) *adj* **1 a** advanced in years; old **b** (*as collective noun; preceded by the*): *the aged* **2** of, connected with, or characteristic of old age **3** (eɪdʒd) (*postpositive*) having the age of: *a woman aged twenty* **4** *geography* (*not in technical use*) having reached an advanced stage of erosion

agee *or* **ajee** (əˈdʒiː) *Scot and English dialect* ▷ *adj* **1** awry, crooked, or ajar ▷ *adv* **2** awry; at an angle [C19 A-[2] + GEE[1]]

age hardening *n* the hardening of metals by spontaneous structural changes over a period of time. See also **precipitation hardening**

ageing *or* **aging** (ˈeɪdʒɪŋ) *n* **1** the process of growing old or developing the appearance and characteristics of old age **2** the change of properties that occurs in some metals after heat treatment or cold working ▷ *adj* **3** becoming or appearing older or elderly: *an ageing car* **4** giving or creating the appearance of age or elderliness: *that dress is really ageing on her*

ageism *or* **agism** (ˈeɪdʒɪzəm) *n* discrimination against people on the grounds of age; specifically, discrimination against the elderly > **ˈageist** *or* **ˈagist** *adj*

ageless (ˈeɪdʒlɪs) *adj* **1** apparently never growing old **2** timeless; eternal: *an ageless quality* > **ˈagelessness** *n*

Agen (*French* aʒɑ̃) *n* a market town in SW France, on the Garonne river. Pop: 30 170 (1999)

agency (ˈeɪdʒənsɪ) *n, pl* **-cies** **1** a business or other organization providing a specific service: *an employment agency* **2** the place where an agent conducts business **3** the business, duties, or functions of an agent **4** action, power, or operation: *the agency of fate* **5** intercession or mediation **6** one of the administrative organizations of a government [C17 from Medieval Latin *agentia*, from Latin *agere* to do]

agenda (əˈdʒɛndə) *n* **1** (*functioning as singular*) Also called: **agendum** a schedule or list of items to be attended to **2** (*functioning as plural*) Also called: **agendas, agendums** matters to be attended to, as at a meeting of a committee [C17 Latin, literally: things to be done, from *agere* to do]

agenesis (eɪˈdʒɛnɪsɪs) *n* **1** (of an animal or plant) imperfect development **2** impotence or sterility > **agenetic** (ˌeɪdʒəˈnɛtɪk) *adj*

agent (ˈeɪdʒənt) *n* **1** a person who acts on behalf of another person, group, business, government, etc; representative **2** a person or thing that acts or has the power to act **3** a phenomenon, substance, or organism that exerts some force or effect: *a chemical agent* **4** the means by which something occurs or is achieved; instrument: *wind is an agent of plant pollination* **5** a person representing a business concern, esp a travelling salesman **6** *Brit* short for **estate agent** **7** short for **secret agent** [C15 from Latin *agent-*, noun use of the present participle of *agere* to do] > **agential** (eɪˈdʒɛnʃəl) *adj*

agent-general *n, pl* **agents-general** a representative in London of a Canadian province or an Australian state

agentive (ˈeɪdʒəntɪv) *or* **agential** (eɪˈdʒɛnʃəl) *grammar* ▷ *adj* **1** (in some inflected languages) denoting a case of nouns, etc, indicating the agent described by the verb **2** (of a speech element) indicating agency: *"-er" in "worker" is an agentive suffix* ▷ *n* **3 a** the agentive case **b** a word or element in the agentive case

agent of production *n* another name for **factor of production**

Agent Orange *n* a highly poisonous herbicide used as a spray for defoliation and crop destruction, esp by US forces during the Vietnam War [C20 named after the identifying colour stripe on its container]

agent provocateur *French* (aʒɑ̃ prɔvɔkatœr) *n, pl* ***agents provocateurs*** (aʒɑ̃ prɔvɔkatœr) a secret agent employed to provoke suspected persons to commit illegal acts and so be discredited or liable to punishment

age of consent *n* **1** the age at which a person is considered legally competent to consent to sexual intercourse **2** the age at which a person can enter into a legally binding contract

Age of Reason *n* (usually preceded by *the*) the 18th century in W Europe. See also **Enlightenment**

age-old *or* **age-long** *adj* very old or of long duration; ancient

age-proof *adj* **1** not adversely affected by a person's age: *an age-proof career* ▷ *vb* **2** (*tr*) to make (something) age-proof

ageratum (ˌædʒəˈreɪtəm) *n* any tropical American plant of the genus *Ageratum*, such as *A. houstonianum* and *A. conyzoides*, which have thick clusters of purplish-blue flowers [C16 New Latin, via Latin from Greek *agēraton* that which does not age, from A-[1] + *gērat-*, stem of *gēras* old age; the flowers of the plant remain vivid for a long time]

ageusia (eɪˈgjuːsɪə) *n* *pathol* lack of the sense of taste [C20 from A-[1] + Greek *geusis* taste]

Aggadah (ɑgɔˈdɑ) *n, pl* **Aggadoth** (-ˈdɔːt, -ˈdaʊt) *Judaism* **1 a** a homiletic passage of the Talmud **b** collectively, the homiletic part of traditional Jewish literature, as contrasted with Halacha, consisting of elaborations on the biblical narratives or tales from the lives of the ancient Rabbis **2** any traditional homiletic interpretation of scripture ▷ Also called: **Aggadatah** (əˈgadəta), **Haggadah** [from Hebrew]

agger (ˈædʒə) *n* an earthwork or mound forming a rampart, esp in a Roman military camp [C14 from Latin *agger* a heap, from *ad-* to + *gerere* to carry, bring]

aggers (ˈægəz) *adj* *Austral slang* aggressive

aggiornamento *Italian* (addʒornaˈmento) *n, pl* ***-ti*** (-ti) *RC Church* the process of bringing up to date methods, ideas, etc

agglomerate *vb* (əˈglɒməˌreɪt) **1** to form or be formed into a mass or cluster; collect ▷ *n* (əˈglɒmərɪt, -ˌreɪt) **2** a confused mass **3** a rock consisting of angular fragments of volcanic lava. Compare **conglomerate** (sense 2) ▷ *adj* (əˈglɒmərɪt, -ˌreɪt) **4** formed into a mass [C17 from Latin *agglomerāre*, from *glomerāre* to wind into a ball, from *glomus* ball, mass] > **agˌglomerˈation** *n* > **agˈglomerative** *adj*

agglutinate *vb* (əˈgluːtɪˌneɪt) **1** to adhere or cause to adhere, as with glue **2** *linguistics* to combine or be combined by agglutination **3** (*tr*) to cause (bacteria, red blood cells, etc) to clump together ▷ *adj* (əˈgluːtɪnɪt, -ˌneɪt) **4** united or stuck, as by glue [C16 from Latin *agglūtināre* to glue to, from *gluten* glue] > **agˌglutinaˈbility** *n* > **agˈglutinable** *adj* > **agˈglutinant** *adj*

agglutination (əˌgluːtɪˈneɪʃən) *n* **1** the act or process of agglutinating **2** the condition of being agglutinated; adhesion **3** a united mass or group of parts **4** *chem* the formation of clumps of particles in a suspension **5** *biochem* proteinaceous particles, such as blood cells and bacteria, that form clumps in antibody–antigen reactions **6** *immunol* the formation of a mass of particles, such as erythrocytes, by the action of antibodies **7** *linguistics* the building up of words from component morphemes in such a way that these undergo little or no change of form or meaning in the process of combination

agglutinative (əˈgluːtɪnətɪv) *adj* **1** tending to join or capable of joining **2** Also: **agglomerative** *linguistics* denoting languages, such as Hungarian, whose morphology is characterized by agglutination. Compare **analytic** (sense 3), **synthetic** (sense 3), **polysynthetic**

agglutinin (əˈgluːtɪnɪn) *n* a substance, such as an antibody or a lectin, that causes agglutination of cells or bacteria [C19 AGGLUTINATE + -IN]

agglutinogen (ˌægluˈtɪnədʒən) *n* an antigen that reacts with or stimulates the formation of a specific agglutinin [C20 from AGGLUTINATE + -GEN]

aggrade (əˈgreɪd) *vb* (*tr*) to build up the level of (any land surface) by the deposition of sediment. Compare **degrade** (sense 4) > **aggradation** (ˌægrəˈdeɪʃən) *n*

aggrandize *or* **aggrandise** (ˈægrənˌdaɪz, əˈgrænˌdaɪz) *vb* (*tr*) **1** to increase the power, wealth, prestige, scope, etc, of **2** to cause (something) to seem greater; magnify; exaggerate [C17 from Old French *aggrandiss-*, long stem of *aggrandir* to make bigger, from Latin *grandis* GRAND; the ending *-ize* is due to the influence of verbs ending in *-ise, -ize*] > **aggrandizement** *or* **aggrandisement** (əˈgrændɪzmənt) *n* > **ˈaggranˌdizer** *or* **ˈaggranˌdiser** *n*

aggravate (ˈægrəˌveɪt) *vb* (*tr*) **1** to make (a disease, situation, problem, etc) worse or more severe **2** *informal* to annoy; exasperate, esp by deliberate and persistent goading [C16 from Latin *aggravāre* to make heavier, from *gravis* heavy] > **ˈaggraˌvating** *adj* > **ˌaggraˈvation** *n*

aggravated (ˈægrəˌveɪtɪd) *adj* *law* (of a criminal offence) made more serious by its circumstances

aggravated trespass *n* *law* an offence in which a trespasser in the open air attempts to interfere with a lawful activity, such as hunting

aggregate *adj* (ˈægrɪgɪt, -ˌgeɪt) **1** formed of separate units collected into a whole; collective; corporate **2** (of fruits and flowers) composed of a dense cluster of carpels or florets ▷ *n* (ˈægrɪgɪt, -ˌgeɪt) **3** a sum or assemblage of many separate units; sum total **4** *geology* a rock, such as granite, consisting of a mixture of minerals **5** the sand and stone mixed with cement and water to make concrete **6** a group of closely related biotypes produced by apomixis, such as brambles, which are the *Rubus fruticosus* aggregate **7** in the aggregate taken as a whole ▷ *vb* ('ægrɪ,ɡeɪt) **8** to combine or be combined into a body, etc **9** (*tr*) to amount to (a number) [c16 from Latin *aggregāre* to add to a flock or herd, attach (oneself) to, from *grex* flock] > 'aggregately *adv* > aggregative ('ægrɪ,ɡeɪtɪv) *adj*

aggregation (,ægrɪ'ɡeɪʃən) *n* **1** the act or process of aggregating **2** *ecology* dispersion in which the individuals of a species are closer together than if they were randomly dispersed

aggregator ('ægrɪ,ɡeɪtə) *n* **1** a business organization that collates the details of an individual's financial affairs so that the information can be presented on a single website **2** a firm that brings together a large group of consumers on whose behalf it negotiates reduced rates for good or services, esp in the energy sector

aggress (ə'ɡrɛs) *vb* (*intr*) to attack first or begin a quarrel [c16 from Medieval Latin *aggressāre* to attack, from Latin *aggredī* to attack, approach]

aggression (ə'ɡrɛʃən) *n* **1** an attack or harmful action, esp an unprovoked attack by one country against another **2** any offensive activity, practice, etc: *an aggression against personal liberty* **3** *psychol* a hostile or destructive mental attitude or behaviour [c17 from Latin *aggression-*, from *aggredī* to attack] > aggressor (ə'ɡrɛsə) *n*

aggressive (ə'ɡrɛsɪv) *adj* **1** quarrelsome or belligerent: *an aggressive remark* **2** assertive; vigorous: *an aggressive business executive* > ag'gressively *adv* > ag'gressiveness *n*

aggrieve (ə'ɡriːv) *vb* (*tr*) **1** (*often impersonal or passive*) to grieve; distress; afflict: *it aggrieved her much that she could not go* **2** to injure unjustly, esp by infringing a person's legal rights [c14 *agreven*, via Old French from Latin *aggravāre* to AGGRAVATE]

aggrieved (ə'ɡriːvd) *adj* feeling resentment at having been treated unjustly > aggrievedly (ə'ɡriːvɪdlɪ) *adv*

aggro ('ægrəʊ) *n* *Brit slang* aggressive behaviour, esp by youths in a gang [c20 from AGGRAVATION]

agha ('ɑːɡə) *n* a variant spelling of **aga**

aghast (ə'ɡɑːst) *adj* (*postpositive*) overcome with amazement or horror [c13 *agast*, from Old English *gæstan* to frighten. The spelling with *gh* is on the model of GHASTLY]

agile ('ædʒaɪl) *adj* **1** quick in movement; nimble **2** mentally quick or acute [c15 from Latin *agilis*, from *agere* to do, act] > 'agilely *adv* > agility (ə'dʒɪlɪtɪ) *n*

agin (ə'ɡɪn) *prep* an informal, facetious, or dialect word for **against** [c19 from obsolete *again* AGAINST]

Agincourt ('ædʒɪn,kɔːt; French aʒɛ̃kur) *n* a battle fought in 1415 near the village of Azincourt, N France: a decisive victory for English longbowmen under Henry V over French forces vastly superior in number

agio ('ædʒɪəʊ) *n*, *pl* -ios **1 a** the difference between the nominal and actual values of a currency **b** the charge payable for conversion of the less valuable currency **2** a percentage payable for the exchange of one currency into another **3** an allowance granted to compensate for differences in currency values, as on foreign bills of exchange **4** an informal word for **agiotage** [c17 from Italian, literally: ease]

agiotage ('ædʒətɪdʒ) *n* **1** the business of exchanging currencies **2** speculative dealing in stock exchange securities or foreign exchange [c19 French, from AGIO]

agist (ə'dʒɪst) *vb* (*tr*) *law* **1** to care for and feed (cattle or horses) for payment **2** to assess and charge (land or its owner) with a public burden, such as a tax [c14 from Old French *agister*, from *gister* to lodge, ultimately from Latin *jacēre* to lie down]

agitate ('ædʒɪ,teɪt) *vb* **1** (*tr*) to excite, disturb, or trouble (a person, the mind, or feelings); worry **2** (*tr*) to cause to move vigorously; shake, stir, or disturb **3** (*intr*; often foll by *for* or *against*) to

attempt to stir up public opinion for or against something **4** (*tr*) to discuss or debate in order to draw attention to or gain support for (a cause, etc): *to agitate a political cause* [c16 from Latin *agitātus*, from *agitāre* to move to and fro, set in motion, from *agere* to act, do] > 'agi,tated *adj* > 'agi,tatedly *adv*

agitated depression *n* severe depression accompanied by extreme anxiety and agitation. Also called: **agitated melancholia**

agitation (,ædʒɪ'teɪʃən) *n* **1** a state of excitement, disturbance, or worry **2** the act of moving something vigorously; the shaking or stirring of something **3** the act of attempting to stir up public opinion for or against something > ,agi'tational *adj*

agitato (,ædʒɪ'tɑːtəʊ) *adj*, *adv music* (to be performed) in an agitated manner

agitator (ə'dʒɪ,teɪtə) *n* **1** a person who agitates for or against a cause, etc **2** a device, machine, or part used for mixing, shaking, or vibrating a material, usually a fluid

agitpop ('ædʒɪt,pɒp) *n* the use of pop music to promote political propaganda

agitprop ('ædʒɪt,prɒp) *n* **1** (*often capital*) (formerly) a bureau of the Central Committee of the Communist Party of the Soviet Union, in charge of agitation and propaganda on behalf of Communism **2 a** any promotion, as in the arts, of political propaganda, esp of a Communist nature **b** (*as modifier*): *agitprop theatre* [c20 short for Russian *Agitpropbyuro*, from *agit(atsiya)* agitation + *prop(aganda)* propaganda]

Aglaia (ə'ɡlaɪə) *n Greek myth* one of the three Graces [Greek: splendour, from *aglaos* splendid]

agleam (ə'ɡliːm) *adj* (*postpositive*) glowing; gleaming

aglet ('æɡlɪt) or **aiglet** *n* **1** a metal sheath or tag at the end of a shoelace, ribbon, etc **2** a variant spelling of **aiguillette 3** any ornamental pendant [c15 from Old French *aiguillette* a small needle]

agley (ə'ɡleɪ, ə'ɡlaɪ, ə'ɡliː) or **aglee** (ə'ɡliː) *adv*, *adj Scot* awry; askew [from *gley* squint]

aglimmer (ə'ɡlɪmə) *adj* (*postpositive*) glimmering

aglitter (ə'ɡlɪtə) *adj* (*postpositive*) sparkling; glittering

aglossia (ə'ɡlɒsɪə) *n pathol* congenital absence of the tongue [c19 from A-¹ + GLOSSA + -IA] > a'glossal *adj* > a'glossate *adj*

aglow (ə'ɡləʊ) *adj* (*postpositive*) glowing

aglu (ə'ɡluː) or **agloo** ('æɡluː) *n Canadian* a breathing hole made in ice by a seal [c19 from Inuktitut]

AGM *abbreviation for* **annual general meeting**

agma ('æɡmə) *n phonetics* the symbol (ŋ), used to represent a velar nasal consonant, as in *long* (lɒŋ) or *tank* (tæŋk)

AGN *abbreviation for* active galactic nucleus. See **active galaxy**

agnail ('æɡ,neɪl) *n* another name for **hangnail**

agnate ('æɡneɪt) *adj* **1** related by descent from a common male ancestor **2** related in any way; cognate ▷ *n* **3** a male or female descendant by male links from a common male ancestor [c16 from Latin *agnātus* born in addition, added by birth, from *agnāsci*, from *ad-* in addition + *gnāsci* to be born] > agnatic (æɡ'nætɪk) *adj* > ag'nation *n*

agnathan (æɡ'neɪθən) *n* **1** any jawless eel-like aquatic vertebrate of the superclass *Agnatha*, which includes the lampreys and hagfishes ▷ *adj* **2** of, relating to, or belonging to the superclass *Agnatha*. See also **cyclostome** [c19 from New Latin *agnatha*, from A-¹ + Greek *gnathos* jaw]

agnathous (æɡ'neɪθəs) *adj zoology* (esp of lampreys and hagfishes) lacking jaws

Agni ('ʌɡnɪ) *n Hinduism* the god of fire, one of the three chief deities of the Vedas [Sanskrit: fire]

agnoiology (,æɡnɔɪ'ɒlədʒɪ) *n philosophy* the theory of ignorance [c19 from Greek *a-* without + *gnōsis* knowledge]

agnomen (æɡ'nəʊmɛn) *n*, *pl* -nomina (-'nɒmɪnə) **1** the fourth name or second cognomen occasionally acquired by an ancient Roman. See also **cognomen, nomen, praenomen 2** another word for **nickname** [c18 from Late Latin, from *ad-* in addition to + *nōmen* name] > agnominal (æɡ'nɒmɪn°l) *adj*

agnosia (æɡ'nəʊzɪə) *n psychol* loss or diminution of the power to recognize familiar objects or people, usually as a result of brain damage [c20 New Latin, from Greek *agnōsia*, from *a-* without + *gnōsis* knowledge] > ag'nosic *adj*

agnostic (æɡ'nɒstɪk) *n* **1** a person who holds that knowledge of a Supreme Being, ultimate cause, etc, is impossible. Compare **atheist, theist 2** a person who claims, with respect to any particular question, that the answer cannot be known with certainty ▷ *adj* **3** of or relating to agnostics [c19 coined 1869 by T. H. Huxley from A-¹ + GNOSTIC] > ag'nosticism *n*

Agnus Dei ('æɡnʊs 'deɪɪ) *n Christianity* **1** the figure of a lamb bearing a cross or banner, emblematic of Christ **2** a chant beginning with these words or a translation of them, forming part of the Roman Catholic Mass or sung as an anthem in the Anglican liturgy **3** a wax medallion stamped with a lamb as emblem of Christ and blessed by the pope [Latin: Lamb of God]

ago (ə'ɡəʊ) *adv* in the past: *five years ago; long ago* [c14 *ago*, from Old English *āgān* to pass away]

> **USAGE** The use of *ago* with *since* (*it's ten years ago since he wrote the novel*) is redundant and should be avoided: *it is ten years since he wrote the novel*

agog (ə'ɡɒɡ) *adj* (*postpositive*) highly impatient, eager, or curious [c15 perhaps from Old French *en gogues* in merriments, origin unknown]

à gogo (ə 'ɡəʊ,ɡəʊ) *adj*, *adv informal* as much as one likes; galore: *wine à gogo* [c20 from French]

-agogue or esp US **-agog** *n combining form* **1** indicating a person or thing that leads or incites to action: *pedagogue; demagogue* **2** denoting a substance that stimulates the secretion of something: *galactagogue* [via Late Latin from Greek *agōgos* leading, from *agein* to lead] > -agogic *adj combining form* > -agogy *n combining form*

agon ('æɡəʊn, -ɡɒn) *n*, *pl* agones (ə'ɡəʊniːz) (in ancient Greece) a festival at which competitors contended for prizes. Among the best known were the Olympic, Pythian, Nemean, and Isthmian Games [c17 Greek: contest, from *agein* to lead]

agone (ə'ɡɒn) *adv* an archaic word for **ago**

agonic (ə'ɡɒnɪk, eɪ'ɡɒnɪk) *adj* forming no angle [c19 from Greek *agōnos*, from A-¹ + *gōnia* angle]

agonic line *n* an imaginary line on the surface of the earth connecting points of zero magnetic declination

agonist ('æɡənɪst) *n* **1** any muscle that is opposed in action by another muscle. Compare **antagonist** (sense 2) **2** a competitor, as in an agon [c17 from Greek *agōn* AGON]

agonistic (,æɡə'nɪstɪk) *adj* **1** striving for effect; strained **2** eager to win in discussion or argument; competitive [c17 via Late Latin from Greek *agōnistikos*, from *agōn* contest]

agonize or **agonise** ('æɡə,naɪz) *vb* **1** to suffer or cause to suffer agony **2** (*intr*) to make a desperate effort; struggle; strive [c16 via Medieval Latin from Greek *agōnizesthai* to contend for a prize, from *agōn* AGON] > 'ago,nizingly or 'ago,nisingly *adv*

agony ('æɡənɪ) *n*, *pl* -nies **1** acute physical or mental pain; anguish **2** the suffering or struggle preceding death **3** pile, put, *or* turn on the agony *Brit informal* to exaggerate one's distress for sympathy or greater effect **4** (*modifier*) relating to or advising on personal problems about which people have written to the media: *agony column; agony writer* [c14 via Late Latin from Greek *agōnia* struggle, from *agōn* contest]

agony aunt *n* (*sometimes capital*) a person who writes the replies to readers' letters in an **agony column** (sense 1)

agony column *n* **1** a magazine or newspaper feature in which advice is offered to readers who have sent in letters about their personal problems **2** a part of a newspaper containing advertisements for lost relatives, personal messages, etc

agora¹ (ˈægərə) *n, pl* **-rae** (-riː, -raɪ) *(often capital)* **a** the marketplace in Athens, used for popular meetings, or any similar place of assembly in ancient Greece **b** the meeting itself [from Greek, from *agorein* to gather]

agora² (ˌæɡəˈrɑː) *n, pl* **-rot** (-ˈrɒt) an Israeli monetary unit worth one hundredth of a shekel [Hebrew, from *āgōr* to collect]

agoraphobia (ˌæɡərəˈfəʊbɪə) *n* a pathological fear of being in public places, often resulting in the sufferer becoming housebound > **ˌagoraˈphobic** *adj*

agouti (əˈɡuːtɪ) *n, pl* **-tis** *or* **-ties 1** any hystricomorph rodent of the genus *Dasyprocta*, of Central and South America and the Caribbean: family *Dasyproctidae*. Agoutis are agile and long-legged, with hooflike claws, and are valued for their meat **2** a pattern of fur in certain rodents, characterized by irregular stripes [c18 via French and Spanish from Guarani]

AGR *abbreviation for* **advanced gas-cooled reactor**

agr. *or* **agric.** *abbreviation for* **1** agricultural **2** agriculture

Agra (ˈɑːɡrə) *n* a city in N India, in W Uttar Pradesh on the Jumna River: a capital of the Mogul empire until 1658; famous for its Mogul architecture, esp the Taj Mahal. Pop: 1 259 979 (2001)

agraffe *or sometimes US* **agrafe** (əˈɡræf) *n* **1** a fastening consisting of a loop and hook, formerly used in armour and clothing **2** a metal cramp used to connect stones [c18 from French, from *grafe* a hook]

Agram (ˈɑːɡram) *n* the German name for **Zagreb**

agranulocytosis (əˌɡrænjʊləʊsaɪˈtəʊsɪs) *n* a serious and sometimes fatal illness characterized by a marked reduction of leucocytes, usually caused by hypersensitivity to certain drugs [c20 New Latin; see A-¹, GRANULE, -CYTE, -OSIS]

agrapha (ˈæɡrəfə) *pl n* Christianity sayings of Jesus not recorded in the canonical Gospels [Greek: things not written, from A-¹ + *graphein* to write]

agraphia (əˈɡræfɪə) *n* loss of the ability to write, resulting from a brain lesion [c19 New Latin, from A-¹ + Greek *graphein* to write]

agrarian (əˈɡreərɪən) *adj* **1** of or relating to land or its cultivation or to systems of dividing landed property **2** of or relating to rural or agricultural matters ▷ *n* **3** a person who favours the redistribution of landed property [c16 from Latin *agrārius*, from *ager* field, land] > **aˈgrarianism** *n*

agree (əˈɡriː) *vb* **agrees, agreeing, agreed** *(mainly intr)* **1** (often foll by *with*) to be of the same opinion; concur **2** *(also tr; when intr, often foll by to; when tr, takes a clause as object or an infinitive)* to give assent; consent: *she agreed to go home; I'll agree to that* **3** *(also tr; when intr, foll by on or about; when tr, may take a clause as object)* to come to terms (about); arrive at a settlement (on): *they agreed a price; they agreed on the main points* **4** (foll by *with*) to be similar or consistent; harmonize; correspond **5** (foll by *with*) to be agreeable or suitable (to one's health, temperament, etc) **6** *(tr; takes a clause as object)* to concede or grant; admit: *they agreed that the price they were asking was too high* **7** *(tr)* to make consistent with: *to agree the balance sheet with the records by making adjustments, writing off, etc* **8** *grammar* to undergo agreement [c14 from Old French *agreer*, from the phrase *a gre* at will or pleasure]

agreeable (əˈɡriːəbəl) *adj* **1** pleasing; pleasant **2** prepared to consent **3** (foll by *to* or *with*) in keeping; consistent: *salaries agreeable with current trends* **4** (foll by *to*) to one's liking: *he said the terms were not agreeable to him* > **aˈgreeableness** *n* > **aˈgreeably** *adv*

agreed (əˈɡriːd) *adj* **1** determined by common

consent: *the agreed price* ▷ *interj* **2** an expression of agreement or consent

agreement (əˈɡriːmənt) *n* **1** the act of agreeing **2** a settlement, esp one that is legally enforceable; covenant; treaty **3** a contract or document containing such a settlement **4** the state of being of the same opinion; concord; harmony **5** the state of being similar or consistent; correspondence; conformity **6** *grammar* the determination of the inflectional form of one word by some grammatical feature, such as number or gender, of another word, esp one in the same sentence. Also called: **concord 7** See **collective agreement, national agreement** [c14 from Old French]

agrestal (əˈɡrestəl) *adj* (of uncultivated plants such as weeds) growing on cultivated land

agrestic (əˈɡrestɪk) *adj* **1** rural; rustic **2** unpolished; uncouth [c17 from Latin *agrestis*, from *ager* field]

agribusiness (ˈæɡrɪˌbɪznɪs) *n* the various businesses collectively that process, distribute, and support farm products [c20 from AGRI(CULTURE) + BUSINESS]

agriculture (ˈæɡrɪˌkʌltʃə) *n* the science or occupation of cultivating land and rearing crops and livestock; farming; husbandry. Related adj: **geoponic** [c17 from Latin *agricultūra*, from *ager* field, land + *cultūra* CULTURE] > **ˌagriˈcultural** *adj* > **ˌagriˈculturally** *adv* > **ˌagriˈculturist** *or* **ˌagriˈculturalist** *n*

agri-environmental *or* **agro-environmental** *adj* of or relating to the impact of agricultural practices on the environment

Agrigento (Italian agriˈdʒɛnto) *n* a town in Italy, in SW Sicily: site of six Greek temples. Pop: 54 619 (2001). Former name (until 1927): **Girgenti** (dʒɜːˈɡɛnti)

agrimony (ˈæɡrɪmənɪ) *n* **1** any of various N temperate rosaceous plants of the genus *Agrimonia*, which have compound leaves, long spikes of small yellow flowers, and bristly burlike fruits **2** any of several other plants, such as hemp agrimony [c15 altered from *egrimonie* (c14), via Old French from Latin *agrimōnia*, variant of *argemōnia* from Greek *argemōnē* poppy]

agritourism (ˈæɡrɪˌtʊərɪzəm) *or* **agrotourism** (ˈæɡrəʊˌtʊərɪzəm) *n* tourism in which customers stay in accommodation on working farms and may have the opportunity to help with farm work > **ˈagriˌtourist** *n*

agro- *combining form* denoting fields, soil, or agriculture: *agronomy* [from Greek *agros* field]

agrobiology (ˌæɡrəʊbaɪˈɒlədʒɪ) *n* the science of plant growth and nutrition in relation to agriculture > **agrobiological** (ˌæɡrəʊˌbaɪəˈlɒdʒɪkəl) *adj* > **ˌagrobiˈologist** *n*

agrochemical (ˌæɡrəʊˈkɛmɪkəl) *n* a chemical, such as a pesticide, used for agricultural purposes

agrodolce (ˌæɡrəʊˈdɒltʃɪ) *n* an Italian sweet-and-sour sauce, made with onions, garlic, red wine vinegar, sugar, and raisins [c21 from Italian]

agro-environmental *adj* a variant spelling of **agri-environmental**

agroforestry (ˌæɡrəʊˈfɒrɪstrɪ) *n* a method of farming integrating herbaceous and tree crops

agrology (əˈɡrɒlədʒɪ) *n* the scientific study of soils and their potential productivity > **agrological** (ˌæɡrəˈlɒdʒɪkəl) *adj*

agronomics (ˌæɡrəˈnɒmɪks) *n (functioning as singular)* the branch of economics dealing with the distribution, management, and productivity of land > **ˌagroˈnomic** *or* **ˌagroˈnomical** *adj*

agronomy (əˈɡrɒnəmɪ) *n* the science of cultivation of land, soil management, and crop production > **aˈgronomist** *n*

agrostemma (ˌæɡrəʊˈstɛmə) *n* **1** See **corncockle 2** See **silene** [New Latin, from Greek *agros* a field + *stemma* a garland]

agrostology (ˌæɡrəˈstɒlədʒɪ) *n* the branch of botany concerned with the study of grasses [c19 from Greek *agrōstis* a type of grass + -LOGY]

agroterrorism (ˌæɡrəʊˈtɛrərɪzəm) *n* the use of biological agents as weapons against agricultural and food-supply industries [c20 from AGRO- + TERRORISM]

agrotourism (ˈæɡrəʊˌtʊərɪzəm) *n* a variant spelling of **agritourism**. > **ˈagroˌtourist** *n*

aground (əˈɡraʊnd) *adv, adj (postpositive)* on or onto the ground or bottom, as in shallow water

agrypnotic (ˌæɡrɪpˈnɒtɪk) *adj* **1** obsolete inducing, relating to, or characterized by insomnia ▷ *n* **2** obsolete a drug or agent that induces insomnia [c20 from Greek *agrupnos* wakeful, from *agrein* to pursue + *hupnos* sleep]

agt *abbreviation for* **1** agent **2** agreement

agterskot (ˈaxtəˌskɒt) *n* South African the final payment to a farmer for crops. Compare **voorskot** [c20 Afrikaans *agter* after + *skot* shot, payment]

aguardiente *Spanish* (aɣwarˈðjente) *n* any inferior brandy or similar spirit, esp from Spain, Portugal, or South America [c19 Spanish: burning water]

Aguascalientes (Spanish aɣwaskaˈljentes) *n* **1** a state in central Mexico. Pop: 943 506 (2000). Area: 5471 sq km (2112 sq miles) **2** a city in central Mexico, capital of Aguascalientes state, about 1900 m (6200 ft) above sea level, with hot springs. Pop: 830 000 (2005 est)

ague (ˈeɪɡjuː) *n* **1** a fever with successive stages of fever and chills esp when caused by malaria **2** a fit of shivering [c14 from Old French *(fievre)* ague acute fever; see ACUTE] > **ˈaguish** *adj*

agueweed (ˈeɪɡjuːˌwiːd) *n* **1** a North American gentianaceous plant, *Gentiana quinquefolia*, that has clusters of pale blue-violet or white flowers **2** another name for **boneset**

Agulhas (əˈɡʌləs) *n* **Cape** a headland in South Africa, the southernmost point of the African continent

ah (ɑː) *interj* an exclamation expressing pleasure, pain, sympathy, etc, according to the intonation of the speaker

AH (indicating years in the Muslim system of dating, numbered from the Hegira (622 AD)) *abbreviation for* anno Hegirae [Latin]

aha (ɑːˈhɑː) *interj* an exclamation expressing triumph, surprise, etc, according to the intonation of the speaker

Ahab (ˈeɪhæb) *n* Old Testament the king of Israel from approximately 869 to 850 BC and husband of Jezebel: rebuked by Elijah (I Kings 16:29–22:40)

aha moment *n* an instant at which the solution to a problem becomes clear

Ahasuerus (əˌhæzjuːˈɪərəs) *n* Old Testament a king of ancient Persia and husband of Esther, generally identified with Xerxes

ahead (əˈhɛd) *adj* **1** *(postpositive)* in front; in advance ▷ *adv* **2** at or in the front; in advance; before **3** onwards; forwards: *go straight ahead* **4** **ahead of a** in front of; at a further advanced position than **b** *stock exchange* in anticipation of: *the share price rose ahead of the annual figures* **5** be ahead *informal* to have an advantage; be winning: *to be ahead on points* **6** get ahead to advance or attain success

ahem (əˈhɛm) *interj* a clearing of the throat, used to attract attention, express doubt, etc

ahemeral (æˈhɛmərəl, eɪ-) *adj* not constituting a full 24-hour day [c20 from Greek *a-* not + *hēmera* a day]

AHHA (ˈɑːhɑː) *n acronym for* after hours home avoider: a young person who prefers to spend time after work socializing, rather than return to an empty home

ahi (ˈɑːhiː) *n* another name for **yellowfin tuna** [Hawaiian]

ahimsa (ɑːˈhɪmsɑː) *n* (in Hindu, Buddhist, and Jainist philosophy) the law of reverence for, and nonviolence to, every form of life [Sanskrit, from A-¹ + *himsā* injury]

ahistorical (ˌeɪhɪsˈtɒrɪkəl) *or* **ahistoric** *adj* not related to history; not historical

Ahithophel (əˈhɪθəˌfɛl) *or* **Achitophel** *n* Old Testament a member of David's council, who became one of Absalom's advisers in his rebellion and hanged himself when his advice was overruled (II Samuel 15:12–17:23)

Ahmadiyyah (ˌɑːməˈdiːjə) or **Ahmadiyah** n 1 a messianic Islamic sect founded in Qadian, India, in 1889 by Mirza Ghulam Ahmad; it split into two branches in 1914 2 any of various Sufi sects

Ahmedabad or **Ahmadabad** (ˈɑːmədəˌbɑːd) n a city in W India, in Gujarat: famous for its mosque. Pop: 3 515 361 (2001)

Ahmednagar or **Ahmadnagar** (ˌɑːmədˈnʌɡə) n a city in W India, in Maharashtra: formerly one of the kingdoms of Deccan. Pop: 307 455 (2001)

A horizon n the top layer of a soil profile, usually dark-coloured and containing humus and from which soluble salts may have been leached. See **B horizon, C horizon**

ahoy (əˈhɔɪ) interj nautical a hail used to call a ship or to attract attention

AHQ abbreviation for Army Headquarters

Ahriman (ˈɑːrɪmən) n Zoroastrianism the supreme evil spirit and diabolical opponent of Ormazd

Ahura Mazda (əˈhuərə ˈmæzdə) n Zoroastrianism another name for **Ormazd**

ahuru (ˈɑːhuːruː) n, pl ahuru a small pink cod, Auchenoceros punctatus, of SW Pacific waters. Also called: ahuruhuru [Māori]

Ahvenanmaa (ˈɑhvənɑmmɑː) n the Finnish name for the **Åland Islands**

Ahwaz (ɑːˈwɑːz) or **Ahvaz** (ɑːˈvɑːz) n a town in SW Iran, on the Karun River. Pop: 967 000 (2005 est)

ai¹ (ˈɑːɪ) n, pl ais another name for **three-toed sloth** (see **sloth** (sense 1)) [c17 from Portuguese, from Tupi]

ai² the internet domain name for Anguilla

AI abbreviation for 1 **artificial insemination** 2 **artificial intelligence**

AIA abbreviation for Associate of the Institute of Actuaries

AICC abbreviation for All India Congress Committee: the national assembly of the Indian National Congress

aid (eɪd) vb 1 to give support to (someone to do something); help or assist 2 (tr) to assist financially ▷ n 3 assistance; help; support 4 a person, device, etc, that helps or assists: a teaching aid 5 Also: artificial aid mountaineering any of various devices such as piton or nut when used as a direct help in the ascent 6 (in medieval Europe; in England after 1066) a feudal payment made to the king or any lord by his vassals, usually on certain occasions such as the marriage of a daughter or the knighting of an eldest son 7 in aid of Brit informal in support of; for the purpose of [c15 via Old French aidier from Latin adjūtāre to help, from juvāre to help] > 'aider n

Aid or **-aid** n combining form denoting a charitable organization or function that raises money for a cause: Band Aid; Ferryaid

AID abbreviation for 1 acute infectious disease 2 artificial insemination (by) donor: former name for Donor Insemination (DI)

aid climbing n mountaineering climbing that employs mechanical devices (aids) to accomplish difficult manoeuvres (artificial moves). Also called: peg climbing, pegging, artificial climbing

aide (eɪd) n 1 an assistant 2 social welfare an unqualified assistant to a professional welfare worker 3 short for **aide-de-camp**

aide-de-camp or **aid-de-camp** (ˈeɪd də ˈkɒŋ) n, pl aides-de-camp or aids-de-camp a military officer serving as personal assistant to a senior. Abbreviation: ADC [c17 from French: camp assistant]

aide-mémoire French (ɛdmemwaːr; English ˈeɪd mɛmˈwaː) n, pl aides-mémoire (ɛdmemwaːr; English ˈeɪdz mɛmˈwaː) a memorandum or summary of the items of an agreement, etc [from aider to help + mémoire memory]

Aidin (ˈaɪdɪn) n a variant spelling of **Aydin**

AIDS or **Aids** (eɪdz) n acronym for acquired immune (or immuno-)deficiency syndrome: a condition, caused by a virus, in which certain white blood cells (lymphocytes) are destroyed, resulting in loss of the body's ability to protect itself against disease. AIDS is transmitted by sexual intercourse, through infected blood and blood products, and through the placenta

AIDS-related complex n See **ARC**

AIF history abbreviation for Australian Imperial Force

aiga (ˈɑːɪɡə) n a variant of **ainga**

aiglet (ˈeɪɡlɪt) n a variant of **aglet**

aigrette or **aigret** (ˈeɪɡrɛt, eɪˈɡrɛt) n 1 a long plume worn on hats or as a headdress, esp one of long egret feathers 2 an ornament or piece of jewellery in imitation of a plume of feathers [c19 French]

aiguille (eɪˈɡwiːl, ˈeɪɡwiːl) n 1 a rock mass or mountain peak shaped like a needle 2 an instrument for boring holes in rocks or masonry [c19 French, literally: needle]

aiguillette (ˌeɪɡwɪˈlɛt) n 1 an ornamentation worn by certain military officers, consisting of cords with metal tips 2 a variant of **aglet**

AIH abbreviation for artificial insemination (by) husband

aikido (ˈaɪkɪdəʊ) n a Japanese system of self-defence employing similar principles to judo, but including blows from the hands and feet [from Japanese, from ai to join, receive + ki spirit, force + do way]

aikona (ˈaɪkɔːnə) interj South African an informal word expressing strong negation [from Nguni]

ail (eɪl) vb 1 (tr) to trouble; afflict 2 (intr) to feel unwell [Old English eglan to trouble, from egle troublesome, painful, related to Gothic agls shameful]

ailanthus (eɪˈlænθəs) n, pl -thuses an E Asian simaroubaceous deciduous tree, Ailanthus altissima, planted in Europe and North America, having pinnate leaves, small greenish flowers, and winged fruits. Also called: tree of heaven [c19 New Latin, from native name (in Amboina) ai lanto tree (of) the gods]

aileron (ˈeɪlərɒn) n a flap hinged to the trailing edge of an aircraft wing to provide lateral control, as in a bank or roll [c20 from French, diminutive of aile wing]

ailing (ˈeɪlɪŋ) adj unwell or unsuccessful

ailment (ˈeɪlmənt) n a slight but often persistent illness

ailurophile (aɪˈluərəˌfaɪl) n a person who likes cats [c20 facetious coinage from Greek ailuros cat + -PHILE] > ailurophilia (aɪˌluərəˈfɪlɪə) n

ailurophobe (aɪˈluərəˌfəʊb) n a person who dislikes or is afraid of cats [c20 from Greek ailuros cat + -PHOBE]

aim (eɪm) vb 1 to point (a weapon, missile, etc) or direct (a blow) at a particular person or object; level 2 (tr) to direct (satire, criticism, etc) at a person, object, etc 3 (intr; foll by at or an infinitive) to propose or intend: we aim to leave early 4 (intr; often foll by at or for) to direct one's efforts or strive (towards): to aim at better communications; to aim high ▷ n 5 the action of directing something at an object 6 the direction in which something is pointed; line of sighting (esp in the phrase to take aim) 7 the object at which something is aimed; target 8 intention; purpose [c14 via Old French aesmer from Latin aestimāre to ESTIMATE]

AIM abbreviation for **Alternative Investment Market**

aimless (ˈeɪmlɪs) adj having no goal, purpose, or direction: several hours of aimless searching > 'aimlessly adv > 'aimlessness n

ain¹ (eɪn) determiner a Scot word for **own**

ain² (ˈɑːɪn) n a variant of **ayin**

Ain (French ɛ̃) n 1 a department in E central France, in Rhône-Alpes region. Capital: Bourg. Pop: 539 006 (2003 est). Area: 5785 sq km (2256 sq miles) 2 a river in E France, rising in the Jura Mountains and flowing south to the Rhône. Length: 190 km (118 miles)

ainga (ˌɑːˈɪŋə) n (in Samoa) a large family, often spanning several generations. Also called: aiga [Samoan]

ain't (eɪnt) not standard ▷ contraction of am not, is not, are not, have not, or has not: I ain't seen it

Aintab (aɪnˈtɑːb) n the former name (until 1921) of **Gaziantep**

A into G NZ slang abbreviation for arse into gear (esp in the phrase **get your A into G**)

Aintree (ˈeɪntrɪ) n a suburb of Liverpool, in Merseyside: site of the racecourse over which the Grand National steeplechase has been run since 1839

Ainu (ˈaɪnuː) n 1 (pl -nus, -nu) a member of the aboriginal people of Japan, now mostly intermixed with Mongoloid immigrants whose skin colour is more yellowish 2 the language of this people, sometimes tentatively associated with Altaic, still spoken in parts of Hokkaido and elsewhere [Ainu: man]

aïoli (aɪˈəʊlɪ, eɪ-) n garlic mayonnaise [from French ail garlic]

air (ɛə) n 1 the mixture of gases that forms the earth's atmosphere. At sea level dry air has a density of 1.226 kilograms per cubic metre and consists of 78.08 per cent nitrogen, 20.95 per cent oxygen, 0.93 per cent argon, 0.03 per cent carbon dioxide, with smaller quantities of ozone and inert gases; water vapour varies between 0 and 4 per cent and in industrial areas sulphur gases may be present as pollutants 2 the space above and around the earth; sky. Related adj: **aerial** 3 breeze; slight wind 4 public expression; utterance: to give air to one's complaints 5 a distinctive quality: an air of mystery 6 a person's distinctive appearance, manner, or bearing 7 music a a simple tune for either vocal or instrumental performance b another word for **aria** 8 transportation in aircraft (esp in the phrase **by air**) 9 an archaic word for **breath** (senses 1–3) 10 Austral informal the height gained when getting airborne in surfing, snowboarding, etc 11 clear the air to rid a situation of tension or discord by settling misunderstandings, etc 12 give (someone) the air slang to reject or dismiss (someone) 13 in the air a in circulation; current b in the process of being decided; unsettled 14 into thin air leaving no trace behind 15 on (or off) the air (not) in the act of broadcasting or (not) being broadcast on radio or television 16 out of or from thin air suddenly and unexpectedly 17 take the air to go out of doors, as for a short walk or ride 18 up in the air a uncertain b informal agitated or excited 19 walk on air to feel elated or exhilarated 20 (modifier) astrology of or relating to a group of three signs of the zodiac, Gemini, Libra, and Aquarius. Compare **earth** (sense 10), **fire** (sense 24), **water** (sense 12) ▷ vb 21 to expose or be exposed to the air so as to cool or freshen; ventilate: to air a room 22 to expose or be exposed to warm or heated air so as to dry: to air linen 23 (tr) to make known publicly; display; publicize: to air one's opinions 24 (intr) (of a television or radio programme) to be broadcast ▷ See also **airs** [c13 via Old French and Latin from Greek aēr the lower atmosphere]

Aïr (ˈɑːɪə) n a mountainous region of N central Niger, in the Sahara, rising to 1500 m (5000 ft): a former native kingdom. Area: about 77 700 sq km (30 000 sq miles). Also called: Asben, Azbine

AIR abbreviation for All India Radio

air alert n military 1 the condition in which combat aircraft are airborne and ready for an operation 2 a signal to prepare for this

air bag n 1 a safety device in a car, consisting of a bag that inflates automatically in an accident and prevents the passengers from being thrown forwards 2 one of a number of large inflatable bags comprising part of a spacecraft's landing system, enabling the craft to come to rest through a series of bounces

air base n a centre from which military aircraft operate. Also called: air station

air bed *n* an inflatable mattress

air bladder *n* **1** *ichthyol* an air-filled sac, lying above the alimentary canal in bony fishes, that regulates buoyancy at different depths by a variation in the pressure of the air. Also called: swim bladder **2** any air-filled sac, such as one of the bladders of seaweeds

airboat ('ɛə,bəʊt) *n* another name for **swamp boat**

airborne ('ɛə,bɔ:n) *adj* **1** conveyed by or through the air **2** (of aircraft) flying; in the air

air brake *n* **1** a brake operated by compressed air, esp in heavy vehicles and trains **2** Also called: dive brake an articulated flap or small parachute for reducing the speed of an aircraft **3** a rotary fan or propeller connected to a shaft to reduce its speed

airbrick ('ɛə,brɪk) *n chiefly Brit* a brick with holes in it, put into the wall of a building for ventilation

air bridge *n Brit* a link by air transport between two places, esp two places separated by a stretch of sea

airbrush ('ɛə,brʌʃ) *n* **1** an atomizer for spraying paint or varnish by means of compressed air ▷ *vb* (*tr*) **2** to paint or varnish (something) by using an airbrush **3** to improve the image of (a person or thing) by concealing defects beneath a bland exterior: *an airbrushed version of the government's record*

airbrush out *vb* (*tr, adverb*) to remove evidence of (someone or something from photographs, books, or history)

airburst ('ɛə,bɜ:st) *n* the explosion of a bomb, shell, etc, in the air

Airbus ('ɛə,bʌs) *n trademark* a commercial aircraft manufactured and marketed by an international consortium of aerospace companies

air chief marshal *n* a senior officer of the Royal Air Force and certain other air forces, of equivalent rank to admiral in the Royal Navy. Abbreviation: **ACM**

air cleaner *n* a filter that prevents dust and other particles from entering the air-intake of an internal-combustion engine. Also called: air filter

Air Command *n Canadian* the Canadian air force

air commodore *n* a senior officer of the Royal Air Force and certain other air forces, of equivalent rank to brigadier in the Army

air-con ('ɛə,kɒn) *n informal* air conditioning

air-condition *vb* (*tr*) to apply air conditioning to

air conditioning *n* a system or process for controlling the temperature and sometimes the humidity and purity of the air in a house, etc ▷ air conditioner *n*

air-cool *vb* (*tr*) to cool (an engine) by a flow of air. Compare **water-cool**

air corridor *n* an air route along which aircraft are allowed to fly

air cover *n* **a** the use of aircraft to provide aerial protection for ground forces against enemy air attack **b** the aircraft used in this ▷ Also called: air support

aircraft ('ɛə,krɑːft) *n, pl* -craft any machine capable of flying by means of buoyancy or aerodynamic forces, such as a glider, helicopter, or aeroplane

aircraft carrier *n* a warship built with an extensive flat deck space for the launch and recovery of aircraft

aircraft cloth *or* **fabric** *n* variants of **aeroplane cloth**

aircraftman ('ɛə,krɑːftmən) *n, pl* -men a serviceman of the most junior rank in the RAF. Also (not in official use): **aircraftsman** ▷ 'aircraft,woman *or not in official use* 'aircrafts,woman *fem n*

aircrew ('ɛə,kruː) *n* (*sometimes functioning as plural*) the crew of an aircraft

air curtain *n* an air stream across a doorway to exclude draughts, etc

air cushion *n* **1** an inflatable cushion, usually made of rubber or plastic **2** the pocket of air that supports a hovercraft **3** a form of pneumatic

suspension consisting of a constricted volume of air. See also **air spring**

air cylinder *n* a cylinder containing air, esp one fitted with a piston and used for damping purposes

air dam *n* any device, such as a spoiler, that reduces air resistance and increases the stability of a car, aircraft, etc

Airdrie ('ɛədrɪ; *Scot* 'ɛrdrɪ) *n* a town in W central Scotland, in North Lanarkshire, E of Glasgow: manufacturing and pharmaceutical industries. Pop: 36 326 (2001)

airdrome ('ɛə,drəʊm) *n* the US name for aerodrome

airdrop ('ɛə,drɒp) *n* **1** a delivery of supplies, troops, etc, from an aircraft by parachute ▷ *vb* -drops, -dropping, -dropped **2** (*tr*) to deliver (supplies, etc) by an airdrop

air-dry *vb* -dries, -drying, -dried (*tr*) to dry by exposure to the air

Aire (ɛə) *n* a river in N England rising in the Pennines and flowing southeast to the Ouse. Length: 112 km (70 miles)

Airedale ('ɛə,deɪl) *n* a large rough-haired tan-coloured breed of terrier characterized by a black saddle-shaped patch covering most of the back. Also called: Airedale terrier [C19 name of a district in Yorkshire]

air embolism *or* **aeroembolism** *n* the presence in the tissues and blood of a gas, such as air or nitrogen bubbles, caused by an injection of air or, in the case of nitrogen, by an abrupt and substantial reduction in the ambient pressure. See **decompression sickness**

air engine *n* **1** an engine that uses the expansion of heated air to drive a piston **2** a small engine that uses compressed air to drive a piston

air-entrained concrete *n* a low-density type of concrete throughout which small air bubbles are dispersed in order to increase its frost resistance: used for making roads. With 1 per cent of air, the loss of strength is approximately 5 per cent

airfield ('ɛə,fiːld) *n* a landing and taking-off area for aircraft, usually with permanent buildings

air filter *n* another name for **air cleaner**

airflow ('ɛə,fləʊ) *n* the flow of air in a wind tunnel or past a moving aircraft, car, train, etc; airstream

airfoil ('ɛə,fɔɪl) *n US and Canadian* a cross section of an aileron, wing, tailplane, or rotor blade. Also called: aerofoil

air force *n* **1 a** the branch of a nation's armed services primarily responsible for air warfare **b** (*as modifier*): *an air-force base* **2** a formation in the US and certain other air forces larger than an air division but smaller than an air command

airframe ('ɛə,freɪm) *n* the body of an aircraft, excluding its engines

air freight *n* **1** freight transported by aircraft ▷ *vb* air-freight **2** (*tr*) to send (goods) to their destination by aircraft

air frost *n* the deposition of ice condensed from water vapour in the atmosphere on the surface when the air temperature is below 0°C

air gas *n* another name for **producer gas**

airglow ('ɛə,gləʊ) *n* the faint light from the upper atmosphere in the night sky, esp in low latitudes

air guitar *n* an imaginary guitar played while miming to rock music

air gun *n* a gun discharged by means of compressed air

air hardening *n* a process of hardening high-alloy steels by heating and cooling in a current of air. Compare **oil hardening**

airhead¹ ('ɛə,hɛd) *n military* an area secured in hostile territory, used as a base for the supply and evacuation of troops and equipment by air [C20 modelled on BEACHHEAD]

airhead² ('ɛə,hɛd) *n slang* a stupid or simple-minded person; idiot [C20 from AIR + HEAD]

air hole *n* **1** a hole that allows the passage of air, esp for ventilation **2** a section of open water in a

frozen surface **3** a less common name for **air pocket** (sense 1)

air hostess *n* a stewardess on an airliner

airily ('ɛərɪlɪ) *adv* **1** in a jaunty or high-spirited manner **2** in a light or delicate manner

airiness ('ɛərɪnɪs) *n* **1** the quality or condition of being fresh, light, or breezy **2** lightness of heart; gaiety

airing ('ɛərɪŋ) *n* **1 a** exposure to air or warmth, as for drying or ventilation **b** (*as modifier*): *airing cupboard* **2** an excursion in the open air **3** exposure to public debate

air-intake *n* **1 a** an opening in an aircraft through which air is drawn, esp for the engines **b** the amount of air drawn in **2** the part of a carburettor or similar device through which air enters an internal-combustion engine **3** any opening, etc, through which air enters, esp for combustion or cooling purposes

air jacket *n* **1** an air-filled envelope or compartment surrounding a machine or part to reduce the rate at which heat is transferred to or from it. Compare **water jacket 2** a less common name for **life jacket**

air kiss *n* **1** a kissing gesture, esp one directed towards a person's cheeck, made without making physical contact ▷ *vb* air-kiss **2** to make such a gesture towards a person

airless ('ɛəlɪs) *adj* **1** lacking fresh air; stuffy or sultry **2** devoid of air > 'airlessness *n*

air letter *n* another name for **aerogram** (sense 1)

airlift ('ɛə,lɪft) *n* **1** the transportation by air of troops, cargo, etc, esp when other routes are blocked ▷ *vb* **2** (*tr*) to transport by an airlift

air-lift pump *n* a pump that pumps liquid by injecting air into the lower end of an open pipe immersed in the liquid: often used in boreholes

airline ('ɛə,laɪn) *n* **1 a** a system or organization that provides scheduled flights for passengers or cargo **b** (*as modifier*): *an airline pilot* **2** a hose or tube carrying air under pressure **3** *chiefly US* a beeline

airliner ('ɛə,laɪnə) *n* a large passenger aircraft

airlock ('ɛə,lɒk) *n* **1** a bubble in a pipe causing an obstruction or stoppage to the flow **2** an airtight chamber with regulated air pressure used to gain access to a space that has air under pressure

airmail ('ɛə,meɪl) *n* **1** the system of conveying mail by aircraft **2** mail conveyed by aircraft ▷ *adj* **3** of, used for, or concerned with airmail ▷ *vb* **4** (*tr*) to send by airmail

airman ('ɛəmən) *n, pl* -men an aviator, esp a man who serves in his country's air force > 'air,woman *fem n*

air marshal *n* **1** a senior Royal Air Force officer of equivalent rank to a vice admiral in the Royal Navy **2** a Royal Australian Air Force officer of the highest rank **3** a Royal New Zealand Air Force officer of the highest rank when chief of defence forces **4** a person employed to travel as an armed guard on commercial flights to protect against hijacking

air mass *n* a large body of air having characteristics of temperature, moisture, and pressure that are approximately uniform horizontally

air mile *n* another name for **nautical mile** (sense 1)

Air Miles *pl n* points awarded by certain companies to purchasers of flight tickets and some other products that may be used to pay for other flights

air-minded *adj* interested in or promoting aviation or aircraft > 'air-,mindedness *n*

air miss *n* a situation in which two aircraft pass very close to one another in the air; near miss

Air Officer *n* a term used to denote the appointment of any officer in the Royal Air Force above the rank of Air Commodore to a position of command

airplane ('ɛə,pleɪn) *n US and Canadian* a heavier-than-air powered flying vehicle with fixed wings. Also called: aeroplane

air plant *n* an epiphyte, esp an orchid of the large Old World tropical genus *Aerides,* grown for its white scented flowers spotted with red, purple, or rose, or a bromeliad, esp of the genus *Tillandsia*

airplay ('ɛəˌpleɪ) *n* (of recorded music) radio exposure

air pocket *n* **1** a localized region of low air density or a descending air current, causing an aircraft to suffer an abrupt decrease in height **2** any pocket of air that prevents the flow of a liquid or gas, as in a pipe

airport ('ɛəˌpɔːt) *n* a landing and taking-off area for civil aircraft, usually with surfaced runways and aircraft maintenance and passenger facilities

air power *n* the strength of a nation's air force

air pump *n* a device for pumping air in or out of something

air rage *n* aggressive behaviour by an airline passenger that endangers the safety of the crew or other passengers

air raid *n* **a** an attack by hostile aircraft **b** (*as modifier*): *an air-raid shelter*

air-raid warden *n* a member of a civil defence organization responsible for enforcing regulations, etc, during an air attack

air rifle *n* a rifle discharged by compressed air

airs (ɛəz) *pl n* affected manners intended to impress others (esp in the phrases **give oneself airs, put on airs**)

air sac *n* **1** any of the membranous air-filled extensions of the lungs of birds, which increase the efficiency of gaseous exchange in the lungs **2** any of the thin-walled extensions of the tracheae of insects having a similar function

air scoop *n* a device fitted to the surface of an aircraft to provide air pressure or ventilation from the airflow

Air Scout *n* a scout belonging to a scout troop that specializes in flying, gliding, etc. See **Scout**

airscrew ('ɛəˌskruː) *n Brit* an aircraft propeller

air-sea rescue *n* an air rescue at sea

air shaft *n* a shaft for ventilation, esp in a mine or tunnel

airship ('ɛəˌʃɪp) *n* a lighter-than-air self-propelled craft. Also called: **dirigible, zeppelin**

air shot *n golf* a shot that misses the ball completely but counts as a stroke

airshow ('ɛəˌʃəʊ) *n* an occasion when an air base is open to the public and a flying display and, usually, static exhibitions are held

airsick ('ɛəˌsɪk) *adj* sick or nauseated from travelling in an aircraft > **'air,sickness** *n*

airside ('ɛəˌsaɪd) *n* the part of an airport nearest the aircraft, the boundary of which is the security check, customs, passport control, etc. Compare **landside** (sense 1)

air sock *n* another name for **windsock**

airspace ('ɛəˌspeɪs) *n* the atmosphere above the earth or part of the earth, esp the atmosphere above a country deemed to be under its jurisdiction

airspeed ('ɛəˌspiːd) *n* the speed of an aircraft relative to the air in which it moves. Compare **groundspeed**

air spray *n* another name for **aerosol** (sense 3)

air spring *n mechanical engineering* an enclosed pocket of air used to absorb shock or sudden fluctuations of load

air station *n* an airfield, usually smaller than an airport but having facilities for the maintenance of aircraft

airstream ('ɛəˌstriːm) *n* **1** a wind, esp at a high altitude **2** a current of moving air

airstrip ('ɛəˌstrɪp) *n* a cleared area for the landing and taking off of aircraft; runway. Also called: landing strip

airt (ɛət; *Scot* ert) or **airth** (ɛəθ; *Scot* erθ) *n Scot* a direction or point of the compass, esp the direction of the wind; quarter; region [c14 from Scots Gaelic *aird* point of the compass, height]

air terminal *n* **1** *Brit* a building in a city from which air passengers are taken by road or rail to an airport or the terminal building of an airport **2** a building at an airport from which air passengers depart or at which they arrive

airtight ('ɛəˌtaɪt) *adj* **1** not permitting the passage of air either in or out **2** having no weak points; rigid or unassailable: *this categorization is hardly airtight*

airtime ('ɛəˌtaɪm) *n* **1** the time allocated to a particular programme, item, topic, or type of material on radio or television **2** the time of the start of a radio or television broadcast

air-to-air *adj* operating between aircraft in flight

air traffic *n* **1** the organized movement of aircraft within a given space **2** the passengers, cargo, or mail carried by aircraft

air-traffic control *n* an organization that determines the altitude, speed, and direction at which planes fly in a given area, giving instructions to pilots by radio > **air-traffic controller** *n*

airtsy-mairtsy ('ɛətsɪ'mɛətsɪ) *adj Midlands English dialect* affected; effeminate

air turbine *n* a small turbine driven by compressed air, esp one used as a starter for engines

air valve *n* **1** a device for controlling the flow of air in a pipe **2** a valve for exhausting air from a fluid system, esp from a central-heating installation. See also **bleed valve**

air vesicle or **cavity** *n* **1** a large air-filled intercellular space in some aquatic plants **2** a large intercellular space in a leaf into which a stoma opens

air vice-marshal *n* **1** a senior Royal Air Force officer of equivalent rank to a rear admiral in the Royal Navy **2** a Royal Australian Air Force officer of the second highest rank **3** a Royal New Zealand Air Force officer of the highest rank. Abbreviation: AVM

airwaves ('ɛəˌweɪvz) *pl n informal* radio waves used in radio and television broadcasting

airway ('ɛəˌweɪ) *n* **1** an air route, esp one that is fully equipped with emergency landing fields, navigational aids, etc **2** a passage for ventilation, esp in a mine **3** a passage down which air travels from the nose or mouth to the lungs **4** *med* a tubelike device inserted via the throat to keep open the airway of an unconscious patient

air waybill *n* a document made out by the consignor of goods by air freight giving details of the goods and the name of the consignee

airworthy ('ɛəˌwɜːðɪ) *adj* (of an aircraft) safe to fly > **'air,worthiness** *n*

airy ('ɛərɪ) *adj* **airier, airiest 1** abounding in fresh air **2** spacious or uncluttered **3** nonchalant; superficial **4** visionary; fanciful: *airy promises; airy plans* **5** of or relating to air **6** weightless and insubstantial: *an airy gossamer* **7** light and graceful in movement **8** having no material substance: *airy spirits* **9** high up in the air; lofty **10** performed in the air; aerial

airy-fairy ('ɛərɪ'fɛərɪ) *adj* **1** *informal* fanciful and unrealistic: *an airy-fairy scheme* **2** delicate to the point of being insubstantial; light [c19 from Tennyson's poem *Lillian* (1830), where the central figure is described as "Airy, fairy Lillian"]

AIS *abbreviation for* Australian Institute of Sport

aisle (aɪl) *n* **1** a passageway separating seating areas in a theatre, church, etc; gangway **2** a lateral division in a church flanking the nave or chancel **3** (rolling) **in the aisles** *informal* (of an audience) overcome with laughter [c14 *ele* (later *aile, aisle,* through confusion with *isle* (island)), via Old French from Latin *āla* wing] > **aisled** *adj* > **'aisleless** *adj*

Aisne (eɪn; *French* ɛn) *n* **1** a department of NE France, in Picardy region. Capital: Laon. Pop: 535 326 (2003 est). Area: 7428 sq km (2897 sq miles) **2** a river in N France, rising in the Argonne Forest and flowing northwest and west to the River Oise: scene of a major Allied offensive in 1918 which turned the tide finally against Germany in World War I. Length: 282 km (175 miles)

ait (eɪt) or **eyot** *n dialect* an islet, esp in a river [Old English *ȳgett* small island, from *ieg* ISLAND]

aitch (eɪtʃ) *n* the letter h or the sound represented by it: *he drops his aitches* [c16 phonetic spelling]

aitchbone ('eɪtʃˌbəʊn) *n* **1** the rump bone or floor of the pelvis in cattle **2** a cut of beef from or including the rump bone [c15 hach-boon, altered from earlier *nache-bone, nage-bone* (a *nache* mistaken for an *ache,* an *aitch;* compare ADDER[1]; *nache* buttock, via Old French from Late Latin *natica,* from Latin *natis* buttock]

Aix-en-Provence (*French* ɛksɑ̃prɔvɑ̃s) *n* a city and spa in SE France: the medieval capital of Provence. Pop: 134 222 (1999). Also called: **Aix**

Aix-la-Chapelle (*French* ɛkslaʃapɛl) *n* the French name for **Aachen**

Aix-les-Bains (*French* ɛkslebɛ̃) *n* a town in E France: a resort with sulphurous springs. Pop: 25 732 (1999)

Aíyina ('ɛjina) *n* transliteration of the Modern Greek name for **Aegina**

AJA *abbreviation for* Australian Journalists' Association

Ajaccio (əˈdʒætsɪˌəʊ, -ˈdʒeɪ-) *n* the capital of Corsica, a port on the W coast. Pop: 52 880 (1999)

ajar[1] (əˈdʒɑː) *adj* (*postpositive*) ▷ *adv* (esp of a door or window) slightly open [c18 altered form of obsolete *on char,* literally: on the turn; *char,* from Old English *cierran* to turn]

ajar[2] (əˈdʒɑː) *adj* (*postpositive*) not in harmony [c19 altered form of *at jar* at discord. See JAR[2]]

Ajax ('eɪdʒæks) *n Greek myth* **1** the son of Telamon; a Greek hero of the Trojan War who killed himself in vexation when Achilles' armour was given to Odysseus **2** called *Ajax the Lesser,* a Locrian king, a swift-footed Greek hero of the Trojan War

AJC *abbreviation for* Australian Jockey Club

Ajmer (ʌdʒˈmɪə) *n* a city in NW India, in Rajasthan: textile centre. Pop: 485 197 (2001)

AK *abbreviation for* **1** Alaska **2** Knight of the Order of Australia

AK-47 *n* a type of Kalashnikov assault rifle [c20 from *A(utomat) K(alashnikov)*]

aka ('ɑːkə) *n, pl* **aka** a vine, *Metrosideros scandens,* found in New Zealand [Māori]

a.k.a. or **AKA** *abbreviation for* also known as

Akademi (əˈkɑːdəmɪ) *n* (in India) a learned society

Akan ('ɑːkɑːn) *n* **1** (*pl* -kan or -kans) a member of a people of Ghana and the E Ivory Coast **2** the language of this people, having two chief dialects, Fanti and Twi, and belonging to the Kwa branch of the Niger-Congo family

akaryote (eɪˈkærɪəʊt) *n biology* a cell without a nucleus [from A-[1] + KARYO- + -ote as in *zygote*] > **a,kary'otic** *adj*

akatea (ˌɑːkəˈteɪə) *n, pl* **akatea** a vine with white flowers, *Metrosideros diffusa,* found in New Zealand [Māori]

akathisia (ˌækəˈθiːzɪə) *n* the inability to sit still because of uncontrolled movement caused by reaction to drugs [c20 from A- + -kithisia, ultimately from Greek *cathedra* seat]

akeake (ɑːkiːˈɑːkiː) *n* a small hardwood New Zealand tree, *Dodonea viscosa,* with silver leaves and reddish bark. Also called: **ake** [Māori]

Akela (ɑːˈkeɪlə) *n Brit* the adult leader of a pack of Cub Scouts. US equivalent: **Den Mother** [c20 after a character in Kipling's *The Jungle Book* (1894–95), who is the leader of a wolfpack]

akene (əˈkiːn) *n* a variant spelling of **achene**

Akhaïa (aˈxaːja) *n* transliteration of the Modern Greek name for **Achaea**

akhara (əˈkɑːrɑː) *n* (in India) a gymnasium

akimbo (əˈkɪmbəʊ) *adj, adv* (with) arms akimbo with hands on hips and elbows projecting outwards [c15 *in kenebowe,* literally: in keen bow, that is, in a sharp curve]

akin (əˈkɪn) *adj* (*postpositive*) **1** related by blood; of the same kin **2** (often foll by *to*) having similar characteristics, properties, etc

a

akiraho ('ɑ:ˌki:rɑ:həʊ) *n, pl* akiraho a small New Zealand shrub, *Olearia paniculata*, with white flowers [Māori]

akita (ə'ki:tə) *n* a large powerfully-built dog of a Japanese breed with erect ears, a typically white coat, and a large full tail carried curled over its back [C20 named after a district in N Japan]

Akkad *or* **Accad** ('ækæd) *n* **1** a city on the Euphrates in N Babylonia, the centre of a major empire and civilization (2360–2180 BC). Ancient name: **Agade** (ə'gɑ:dɪ, ə'geɪdɪ) **2** an ancient region lying north of Babylon, from which the Akkadian language and culture is named

Akkadian *or* **Accadian** (ə'kædɪən, ə'keɪ-) *n* **1** a member of an ancient Semitic people who lived in central Mesopotamia in the third millennium BC **2** the extinct language of this people, belonging to the E Semitic subfamily of the Afro-Asiatic family ⊳ *adj* **3** of or relating to this people or their language

Akkerman (*Russian* akɪr'man) *n* the former name (until 1946) of **Belgorod-Dnestrovski**

Akmola *or* **Aqmola** (æk'məʊlə; *Kazakh* ɑkmɔ'lɑ) *n* a former name (1994–98) of **Astana**

Akmolinsk (*Russian* ak'mɔlinsk) *n* a former name (until 1961) of **Akmola**

akrasia (ə'kreɪzɪə) *n philosophy* weakness of will; acting in a way contrary to one's sincerely held moral values [C20 from A-² + Greek *kratos* power] > a'kratic *adj*

Akron ('ækrɒn) *n* a city in NE Ohio. Pop: 212 215 (2003 est.)

Aksum *or* **Axum** ('ɑ:ksʊm) *n* an ancient town in N Ethiopia, in the Tigré region: capital of the Aksumite Empire (1st to 6th centuries AD). According to tradition, the Ark of the Covenant was brought here from Jerusalem

Aktobe (aktə'be) *n* an industrial city in W Kazakhstan. Pop: 291 000 (2005 est). Kazakh name: **Aqtöbe** Former name (until 1991): **Aktyubinsk**

Aktyubinsk (*Russian* ak'tjubinsk) *n* the former name (until 1991) of **Aktobe**

Akubra (ə'ku:brə) *n trademark* a brand of Australian hat

Akure (ə'ku:re) *n* a city in SW Nigeria, capital of Ondo state: agricultural trade centre. Pop: 434 000 (2005 est)

akvavit ('ɑːkvəˌviːt) *n* a variant spelling of **aquavit**

al *the internet domain name for* Albania

Al *the chemical symbol for* aluminium

AL *abbreviation for* **1** Alabama **2** Anglo-Latin **3** (in the US and Canada) American League (of baseball teams) **4** *international car registration for* Albania

-al¹ *suffix forming adjectives* of; related to; connected with: *functional; sectional; tonal* [from Latin *-ālis*]

-al² *suffix forming nouns* the act or process of doing what is indicated by the verb stem: *rebuttal; recital; renewal* [via Old French *-aille, -ail*, from Latin *-ālia*, neuter plural used as substantive, from *-ālis* -AL¹]

-al³ *suffix forming nouns* **1** indicating an aldehyde: *ethanal* **2** indicating a pharmaceutical product: *phenobarbital* [shortened from ALDEHYDE]

ala ('eɪlə) *n, pl* alae ('eɪli:) **1** *zoology* a wing or flat winglike process or structure, such as a part of some bones and cartilages **2** *botany* a winglike part, such as one of the wings of a sycamore seed or one of the flat petals of a sweet pea flower [C18 from Latin *āla* a wing]

à la (ɑ: lɑ:, æ lə; *French* a la) *prep* **1** in the manner or style of **2** as prepared in (a particular place) or by or for (a particular person) [C17 from French, short for *à la mode de* in the style of]

Ala. *abbreviation for* Alabama

Alabama (ˌælə'bæmə) *n* **1** a state in the southeastern US, on the Gulf of Mexico: consists of coastal and W lowlands crossed by the Tombigbee, Black Warrior, and Alabama Rivers, with parts of the Tennessee Valley and Cumberland Plateau in the north: noted for producing cotton and white marble. Capital:

Montgomery. Pop: 4 500 752 (2003 est). Area: 131 333 sq km (50 708 sq miles). Abbreviations: **Ala,** (with zip code) **AL 2** a river in Alabama, flowing southwest to the Mobile and Tensaw Rivers. Length: 507 km (315 miles)

Alabamian (ˌælə'bæmɪən) *adj* **1** of or relating to Alabama or its inhabitants ⊳ *n* **2** a native or inhabitant of Alabama

alabaster ('ælə,bɑːstə, -,bæstə) *n* **1** a fine-grained usually white, opaque, or translucent variety of gypsum used for statues, vases, etc **2** a variety of hard semitranslucent calcite, often banded like marble ⊳ *adj* **3** of or resembling alabaster [C14 from Old French *alabastre*, from Latin *alabaster*, from Greek *alabastros*] > ˌala'bastrine *adj*

Alacant (*Spanish* alakant) *n* the Catalan name for **Alicante**

à la carte (ɑ: lɑ: 'kɑ:t, æ lə; *French* a la kart) *adj, adv* **1** (of a menu or a section of a menu) having dishes listed separately and individually priced. Compare **table d'hôte 2** (of a dish) offered on such a menu; not part of a set meal [C19 from French, literally: according to the card]

alack (ə'læk) *or* **alackaday** (ə'lækə,deɪ) *interj* an archaic or poetic word for **alas** [C15 from *a* ah! + *lack* loss, LACK]

alacrity (ə'lækrɪtɪ) *n* liveliness or briskness [C15 from Latin *alacritās*, from *alacer* lively] > a'lacritous *adj*

Ala Dağ *or* **Ala Dagh** (*Turkish* ɑ'lɑ dɑː) *n* **1** the E part of the Taurus Mountains, in SE Turkey, rising over 3600 m (12 000 ft) **2** a mountain range in E Turkey, rising over 3300 m (11 000 ft) **3** a mountain range in NE Turkey, rising over 3000 m (10 000 ft)

Aladdin (ə'lædɪn) *n* (in *The Arabian Nights' Entertainments*) a poor youth who obtains a magic lamp and ring, with which he summons genies who grant his wishes

Aladdin's cave *n* **1** a place containing fabulous riches **2** a place where something is abundant: *an Aladdin's cave of presents for children*

Alagez *or* **Alagöz** (ɑlɑ'gœz) *n* the Turkish name for (Mount) **Aragats**

Alagoas (*Portuguese* ala'goːaʃ) *n* a state in NE Brazil, on the Atlantic coast. Capital: Maceió. Pop: 2 887 535 (2002). Area: 30 776 sq km (11 031 sq miles)

Alai (ɑ:'laɪ) *n* a mountain range in central Asia, in SW Kyrgyzstan, running from the Tian Shan range in China into Tajikistan. Average height: 4800 m (16 000 ft), rising over 5850 m (19 500 ft)

à la king (ɑ: lɑ: 'kɪŋ, æ lə) *adj* (usually postpositive) cooked in a cream sauce with mushrooms and green peppers

alalia (æ'leɪlɪə) *n* a complete inability to speak; mutism [A-¹ + -LALIA]

alameda (ˌælə'meɪdə) *n chiefly Southwestern US* a public walk or promenade lined with trees, often poplars

Alamein ('ælə,meɪn) *n* See **El Alamein**

Alamo ('ælə,məʊ) *n* the a mission in San Antonio, Texas, the site of a siege and massacre in 1836 by Mexican forces under Santa Anna of a handful of American rebels fighting for Texan independence from Mexico

à la mode (ɑ: lɑ: 'məʊd, æ lə; *French* a la mɔd) *adj* **1** fashionable in style, design, etc **2** (of meats) braised with vegetables in wine **3** *chiefly US and Canadian* (of desserts) served with ice cream [C17 from French: according to the fashion]

alamode ('ælə,məʊd) *n* a soft light silk used for shawls and dresses, esp in the 19th century. See also **surah** [C17 from À LA MODE]

Åland Islands ('ɑ:lənd, 'ɔ:lənd; *Swedish* 'ɔːland) *pl n* a group of over 6000 islands under Finnish administration, in the Gulf of Bothnia. Capital: Mariehamn. Pop: 26 347 (2003 est). Finnish name: **Ahvenanmaa**

Alania (ə'lænɪə) *n* another name for **North Ossetian Republic**

alanine (ˈælə,niːn, -,naɪn) *n* a nonessential aliphatic amino acid that occurs in many proteins

[C19 from German *Alanin*, from AL(DEHYDE) + *-an-* (euphonic infix) + *-in* -INE²]

alannah (ə'lænə) *interj Irish* my child: used as a term of address or endearment [from Irish Gaelic *a leanbh*]

Al-Anon ('ælə,nɒn) *n* an association for the families and friends of alcoholics to give mutual support

Alaouite *or* **Alawite** ('ælə,wiːt) *n* **1** a member of a Shiite sect of Syrian Muslims ⊳ *adj* **2** of or relating to this sect [via French from Arabic, from *'alaoui* upper, celestial, from *'ala* (vb) to excel, surpass]

alap (ə'lɑːp) *n* Indian vocal music without words

al-Aqsa (æl 'æksə) *n* See **Dome of the Rock**

alar ('eɪlə) *adj* **1** relating to, resembling, or having wings or alae **2** denoting the cells at the base of a moss leaf, to the sides, that sometimes differ in structure from cells in the rest of the leaf [C19 from Latin *āla* a wing]

Alar ('eɪlɑː) *n* a chemical sprayed on cultivated apple trees in certain countries, to increase fruit set. Also called: **daminozide**

alarm (ə'lɑːm) *vb (tr)* **1** to fill with apprehension, anxiety, or fear **2** to warn about danger; alert **3** to fit or activate a burglar alarm on a house, car, etc ⊳ *n* **4** fear or terror aroused by awareness of danger; fright **5** apprehension or uneasiness: *the idea of failing filled him with alarm* **6** a noise, signal, etc, warning of danger **7** any device that transmits such a warning: *a burglar alarm* **8 a** the device in an alarm clock that triggers off the bell or buzzer **b** short for **alarm clock 9** *archaic* a call to arms **10** *fencing* a warning or challenge made by stamping the front foot [C14 from Old French *alarme*, from Old Italian *all'arme* to arms; see ARM²] > a'larming *adj* > a'larmingly *adv*

alarm clock *n* a clock with a mechanism that sounds at a set time: used esp for waking a person up

alarmist (ə'lɑːmɪst) *n* **1** a person who alarms or attempts to alarm others needlessly or without due grounds **2** a person who is easily alarmed ⊳ *adj* **3** characteristic of an alarmist > a'larmism *n*

alarum (ə'lærəm, -'lɑːr-, -'lɛər-) *n* **1** *archaic* an alarm, esp a call to arms **2** (used as a stage direction, esp in Elizabethan drama) a loud disturbance or conflict (esp in the phrase **alarums and excursions**) [C15 variant of ALARM]

alary ('eɪlərɪ, 'æ-) *adj* of, relating to, or shaped like wings [C17 from Latin *ālārius*, from *āla* wing]

alas (ə'læs) *interj* an exclamation of grief, compassion, or alarm [C13 from Old French *ha las!* oh wretched!; *las* from Latin *lassus* weary]

Alas. *abbreviation for* Alaska

Alaska (ə'læskə) *n* **1** the largest state of the US, in the extreme northwest of North America: the aboriginal inhabitants are Inuit and Yupik; the earliest White settlements were made by the Russians; it was purchased by the US from Russia in 1867. It is mostly mountainous and volcanic, rising over 6000 m (20 000 ft), with the Yukon basin in the central region; large areas are covered by tundra; it has important mineral resources (chiefly coal, oil, and natural gas). Capital: Juneau. Pop: 648 818 (2003 est). Area: 1 530 694 sq km (591 004 sq miles). Abbreviations: **Alas,** (with zip code) **AK 2 Gulf of** the N part of the Pacific, between the Alaska Peninsula and the Alexander Archipelago

Alaska Highway *n* a road extending from Dawson Creek, British Columbia, to Fairbanks, Alaska: built by the US Army (1942). Length: 2452 km (1523 miles). Originally called: **Alcan Highway**

Alaskan (ə'læskən) *adj* **1** of or relating to Alaska or its inhabitants ⊳ *n* **2** a native or inhabitant of Alaska

Alaska Peninsula *n* an extension of the mainland of SW Alaska between the Pacific and the Bering Sea, ending in the Aleutian Islands. Length: about 644 km (400 miles)

Alaska Range *n* a mountain range in S central

Alaska. Highest peak: Mount McKinley, 6194 m (20 320 ft)

alate ('eɪleɪt) *adj* having wings or winglike extensions [c17 from Latin *ālātus,* from *āla* wing]

alb (ælb) *n Christianity* a long white linen vestment with sleeves worn by priests and others [Old English *albe,* from Medieval Latin *alba (vestis)* white (clothing)]

Alb. *abbreviation for* Albania(n)

Albacete (*Spanish* alβa'θete) *n* a city in SE Spain: metal goods manufacturing. Pop: 155 142 (2003 est)

albacore ('ælbə,kɔ:) *n* a tunny, *Thunnus alalunga,* occurring mainly in warm regions of the Atlantic and Pacific. It has very long pectoral fins and is a valued food fish. Also called: **long-fin tunny** [c16 from Portuguese *albacor,* from Arabic *al-bakrah,* from *al* the + *bakr* young camel]

Alba Longa ('ælbə 'lɒŋgə) *n* a city of ancient Latium, southeast of modern Rome: the legendary birthplace of Romulus and Remus

Albania (æl'beɪnɪə) *n* a republic in SE Europe, on the Balkan Peninsula: became independent in 1912 after more than four centuries of Turkish rule; established as a republic (1946) under Communist rule; multiparty constitution adopted in 1991. It is generally mountainous, rising over 2700 m (9000 ft), with extensive forests. Language: Albanian. Religion: Muslim majority. Currency: lek. Capital: Tirana. Pop: 3 193 000 (2004 est). Area: 28 749 sq km (11 100 sq miles)

Albanian (æl'beɪnɪən) *n* **1** the official language of Albania: of uncertain relationship within the Indo-European family, but thought to be related to ancient Illyrian **2 a** a native, citizen, or inhabitant of Albania **b** a native speaker of Albanian ▷ *adj* **3** of or relating to Albania, its people, or their language

Albany ('ɔ:lbənɪ) *n* **1** a city in E New York State, on the Hudson River: the state capital. Pop: 93 919 (2003 est) **2** a river in central Canada, flowing east and northeast to James Bay. Length: 982 km (610 miles) **3** a port in southwest Western Australia: founded as a penal colony. Pop: 22 415 (2001)

albata (æl'beɪtə) *n* a variety of German silver consisting of nickel, copper, and zinc [c19 from Latin, literally: clothed in white, from *albus* white]

albatross ('ælbə,trɒs) *n* **1** any large oceanic bird of the genera *Diomedea* and *Phoebetria,* family *Diomedeidae,* of cool southern oceans: order *Procellariiformes* (petrels). They have long narrow wings and are noted for a powerful gliding flight. See also **wandering albatross 2** a constant and inescapable burden or handicap: *an albatross of debt* **3** *golf* a score of three strokes under par for a hole [c17 from Portuguese *alcatraz* pelican, from Arabic *al-ghattās,* from *al* the + *ghattās* white-tailed sea eagle; influenced by Latin *albus* white: C20 in sense 2, from *The Rime of the Ancient Mariner* (1798) by English poet Samuel Taylor Coleridge (1772–1834)]

albedo (æl'bi:dəʊ) *n* **1** the ratio of the intensity of light reflected from an object, such as a planet, to that of the light it receives from the sun **2** *physics* the probability that a neutron passing through a surface will return through that surface [c19 from Church Latin: whiteness, from Latin *albus* white]

albeit (ɔ:l'bi:ɪt) *conj* even though [C14 *al be it,* that is, although it be (that)]

Albemarle Sound ('ælbə,ma:l) *n* an inlet of the Atlantic in NE North Carolina. Length: about 96 km (60 miles)

Alberich (*German* 'albərɪç) *n* (in medieval German legend) the king of the dwarfs and guardian of the treasures of the Nibelungs

albert ('ælbət) *n* **1** a kind of watch chain usually attached to a waistcoat **2** *Brit* a standard size of notepaper, 6 × 3⅞ inches [c19 named after Prince Albert (1819–61), Prince Consort of Queen Victoria of Great Britain and Ireland]

Albert ('ælbət) *n* **Lake** a lake in E Africa, between the Democratic Republic of Congo (formerly Zaïre) and Uganda in the great Rift Valley, 660 m (2200

ft) above sea level: a source of the Nile, fed by the Victoria Nile, which leaves as the Albert Nile. Area: 5345 sqkm (2064 sq miles). Former name: Lake Mobutu

Alberta (æl'bɜ:tə) *n* a province of W Canada: mostly prairie, with the Rocky Mountains in the southwest. Capital: Edmonton. Pop: 3 201 895 (2004 est). Area: 661 188 sq km (255 285 sq miles). Abbreviations: Alta, AB

Alberta clipper *n meteorol* (in Canada) an area of low pressure that forms in winter near the Rocky Mountains

Albertan (æl'bɜ:tən) *adj* **1** of or relating to Alberta or its inhabitants ▷ *n* **2** a native or inhabitant of Alberta

Albert Edward *n* a mountain in SE New Guinea, in the Owen Stanley Range. Height: 3993 m (13 100 ft)

albertite ('ælbə,taɪt) *n* a black solid variety of bitumen that has a conchoidal fracture and occurs in veins in oil-bearing strata [c19 named after *Albert* county, New Brunswick, Canada, where it is mined]

albescent (æl'bɛsᵊnt) *adj* shading into, growing, or becoming white [c19 from Latin *albēscere* to grow white, from *albus* white] > al'bescence *n*

Albi (*French* albi) *n* a town in S France: connected with the Albigensian heresy and the crusade against it. Pop: 46 274 (1999)

Albigenses (,ælbɪ'dʒɛnsi:z) *pl n* members of a Manichean sect that flourished in S France from the 11th to the 13th century [from Medieval Latin: inhabitants of Albi, from *Albiga* ALBI] > Albi'gensian *adj* > Albi'gensianism *n*

albino (æl'bi:nəʊ) *n, pl* -nos **1** a person with congenital absence of pigmentation in the skin, eyes, and hair **2** any animal or plant that is deficient in pigment [c18 via Portuguese from Spanish, from *albo* white, from Latin *albus*] > albinic (æl'bɪnɪk) *or* ,albin'istic *adj* > albinism ('ælbɪ,nɪzəm) *n* > albinotic (,ælbɪ'nɒtɪk) *adj*

Albion ('ælbɪən) *n archaic or poetic* Britain or England [c13 from Latin, of Celtic origin]

albite ('ælbaɪt) *n* a colourless, milky-white, yellow, pink, green, or black mineral of the feldspar group and plagioclase series, found in igneous sedimentary and metamorphic rocks. It is used in the manufacture of glass and ceramics. Composition: sodium aluminium silicate. Formula: NaAlSi₃O₈. Crystal structure: triclinic [c19 from Latin *albus* white] > albitic (æl'bɪtɪk) *adj*

Ålborg (*Danish* 'ɔlbɔr) *n* a variant spelling of **Aalborg**

album ('ælbəm) *n* **1** a book or binder consisting of blank pages, pockets, or envelopes for keeping photographs, stamps, autographs, drawings, poems, etc **2** one or more CDs, cassettes, or long-playing records released as a single item **3** a booklike holder containing sleeves for gramophone records **4** *chiefly Brit* an anthology, usually large and illustrated [c17 from Latin: blank tablet, from *albus* white]

albumblatt ('ælbəm,blat) *n music* a short occasional instrumental composition, usually light in character [c19 German: album-leaf]

albumen ('ælbjʊmɪn, -mɛn) *n* **1** the white of an egg; the nutritive and protective gelatinous substance, mostly an albumin, that surrounds the yolk **2** a rare name for **endosperm 3** a variant spelling of **albumin** [c16 from Latin: white of an egg, from *albus* white]

albumenize *or* **albumenise** (æl'bju:mɪ,naɪz) *vb* (*tr*) to coat with a solution containing albumen or albumin

albumin *or* **albumen** ('ælbjʊmɪn) *n* any of a group of simple water-soluble proteins that are coagulated by heat and are found in blood plasma, egg white, etc [c19 from ALBUMEN + -IN]

albuminate (æl'bju:mɪ,neɪt) *n now rare* any of several substances formed from albumin by the action of acid or alkali

albuminoid (æl'bju:mɪ,nɔɪd) *adj* **1** resembling

albumin ▷ *n* **2** another name for **scleroprotein**

albuminous (æl'bju:mɪnəs) *adj* of or containing albumin

albuminuria (æl,bju:mɪ'njʊərɪə) *n pathol* the presence of albumin in the urine. Also called: proteinuria

albumose ('ælbjʊ,məʊs, -,məʊz) *n* the US name for **proteose** [c19 from ALBUMIN + -OSE²]

Albuquerque ('ælbə,kɜ:kɪ) *n* a city in central New Mexico, on the Rio Grande. Pop: 471 856 (2003 est)

alburnum (æl'bɜ:nəm) *n* a former name for **sapwood** [c17 from Latin: sapwood, from *albus* white]

Albury-Wodonga ('ɔ:bərɪ, -brɪ wə'dɒŋgə) *n* a town in SE Australia, in S central New South Wales, on the Murray River: commercial centre of an agricultural region. Pop: 69 880 (2001)

alcahest ('ælkə,hɛst) *n* a variant spelling of **alkahest**

Alcaic (æl'keɪɪk) *adj* **1** of or relating to a metre used by the 7th-century BC Greek lyric poet Alcaeus, consisting of a strophe of four lines each with four feet ▷ *n* **2** (*usually plural*) verse written in the Alcaic form [c17 from Late Latin *Alcaicus* of Alcaeus]

alcaide (æl'keɪd; *Spanish* al'kaɪðe) *n* (in Spain and Spanish America) **1** the commander of a fortress or castle **2** the governor of a prison [c16 from Spanish, from Arabic *al-qā'id* the captain, commander, from *qād* to give orders]

alcalde (æl'kældɪ; *Spanish* al'kalde) *or* **alcade** (æl'keɪd) *n* (in Spain and Spanish America) the mayor or chief magistrate in a town [c17 from Spanish, from Arabic *al-qādī* the judge, from *qadā* to judge]

Alcan Highway ('ælkæn) *n* original name of the **Alaska Highway**

Alcántara (æl'kæntə,rə) *n* a town in W Spain: a Roman bridge spans the River Tagus. Pop: 1739 (2003 est)

Alcatraz ('ælkə,træz) *n* an island in W California, in San Francisco Bay: a federal prison until 1963

alcazar (,ælkə'za:; *Spanish* al'kaθar) *n* any of various palaces or fortresses built in Spain by the Moors [c17 from Spanish, from Arabic *al-qasr* the castle]

Alcazar de San Juan ('ælkə,za:; *Spanish* al'kaθar) *n* a town in S central Spain: associated with Cervantes and Don Quixote. Pop: 27 229 (2003 est)

Alcestis (æl'sɛstɪs) *n Greek myth* the wife of king Admetus of Thessaly. To save his life, she died in his place, but was rescued from Hades by Hercules

alchemist ('ælkəmɪst) *n* a person who practises alchemy

alchemize *or* **alchemise** ('ælkə,maɪz) *vb* (*tr*) to alter (an element, metal, etc) by alchemy; transmute

alchemy ('ælkəmɪ) *n, pl* -mies **1** the pseudoscientific predecessor of chemistry that sought a method of transmuting base metals into gold, an elixir to prolong life indefinitely, a panacea or universal remedy, and an alkahest or universal solvent **2** a power like that of alchemy: *her beauty had a potent alchemy* [C14 *alkamye,* via Old French from Medieval Latin *alchimia,* from Arabic *al-kīmiyā',* from *al* the + *kīmiyā'* transmutation, from Late Greek *khēmeia* the art of transmutation] > alchemic (æl'kɛmɪk), al'chemical *or* ,alchem'istic *adj*

alcheringa (,æltʃə'rɪŋgə) *n* another name for **Dreamtime** [from a native Australian language, literally: dream time]

Alchevsk (æl'tʃevsk) *n* a city in E Ukraine. Pop: 117 000 (2005 est). Former name (until 1992): Kommunarsk

Alcides (æl'saɪdi:z) *n* another name for **Hercules'** (sense 1)

alcidine ('ælsɪ,daɪn) *adj* of, relating to, or belonging to the *Alcidae,* a family of sea birds including the auks, guillemots, puffins, and related forms [c20 from New Latin *Alcidae,* from *Alca* type genus]

Alcinoüs (ælˈsɪnəʊəs) *n* (in Homer's *Odyssey*) a Phaeacian king at whose court the shipwrecked Odysseus told of his wanderings. See also **Nausicaä**

ALCM *abbreviation for* air-launched cruise missile: a type of cruise missile that can be launched from an aircraft

Alcmene (ælkˈmiːnɪ) *n Greek myth* the mother of Hercules by Zeus who visited her in the guise of her husband, Amphitryon

alcohol (ˈælkəˌhɒl) *n* **1** a colourless flammable liquid, the active principle of intoxicating drinks, produced by the fermentation of sugars, esp glucose, and used as a solvent and in the manufacture of organic chemicals. Formula: C_2H_5OH. Also called: **ethanol, ethyl alcohol 2** a drink or drinks containing this substance **3** *chem* any one of a class of organic compounds that contain one or more hydroxyl groups bound to carbon atoms. The simplest alcohols have the formula ROH, where R is an alkyl group. Compare **phenol** (sense 2) See also **diol, triol** [c16 via New Latin from Medieval Latin, from Arabic *al-kuhl* powdered antimony; see KOHL]

alcohol-free *adj* **1** (of beer or wine) containing only a trace of alcohol. Compare **low-alcohol 2** (of a period of time) during which no alcoholic drink is consumed: *there should be one or two alcohol-free days a week*

alcoholic (ˌælkəˈhɒlɪk) *n* **1** a person affected by alcoholism ▷ *adj* **2** of, relating to, containing, or resulting from alcohol

alcoholicity (ˌælkəhɒˈlɪsɪtɪ) *n* the strength of an alcoholic liquor

Alcoholics Anonymous *n* an association of alcoholics who try, esp by mutual assistance, to overcome alcoholism

alcoholism (ˈælkəhɒˌlɪzəm) *n* a condition in which dependence on alcohol harms a person's health, social functioning, or family life

alcoholize *or* **alcoholise** (ˈælkəhɒˌlaɪz) *vb* (*tr*) to turn into alcoholic drink, as by fermenting or mixing with alcohol > ˌalcoˌholiˈzation *or* ˌalcoˌholiˈsation *n*

alcoholometer (ˌælkəhɒˈlɒmɪtə) *n* an instrument, such as a specially calibrated hydrometer, for determining the percentage of alcohol in a liquid

alcolock (ˈælkəʊˌlɒk) *n informal* a breath-alcohol ignition-interlock device, which is fitted to the ignition in certain motor vehicles. The driver must blow into a tube and, if his or her breath contains too much alcohol, a lock is activated to prevent the vehicle starting [c21 from ALCO(HOL) + LOCK¹ (sense 2)]

alcool (ˈælkuːl) *n* a form of pure grain spirit distilled in Quebec [from French: alcohol]

alcopop (ˈælkəʊˌpɒp) *n informal* an alcoholic drink that tastes like a soft drink [c20 from ALCO(HOL) + POP¹ (sense 12)]

Alcoran *or* **Alkoran** (ˌælkɒˈrɑːn) *n* another name for the **Koran**. > ˌAlcoˈranic *or* ˌAlkoˈranic *adj*

alcove (ˈælkəʊv) *n* **1** a recess or niche in the wall of a room, as for a bed, books, etc **2** any recessed usually vaulted area, as in a garden wall **3** any covered or secluded spot, such as a summerhouse [c17 from French *alcôve*, from Spanish *alcoba*, from Arabic *al-qubbah* the vault, arch]

Alcyone¹ (ælˈsaɪənɪ) *n Greek myth* Also called: Halcyone the daughter of Aeolus and wife of Ceyx, who drowned herself in grief for her husband's death. She was transformed into a kingfisher. See also **Ceyx**

Alcyone² (ælˈsaɪənɪ) *n* the brightest star system in the Pleiades, located in the constellation Taurus

Ald. *or* **Aldm.** *abbreviation for* Alderman

Aldabra (ælˈdæbrə) *n* an island group in the Indian Ocean: part of the British Indian Ocean Territory (1965–76); now administratively part of the Seychelles

Aldan (*Russian* alˈdan) *n* a river in E Russia in the SE Sakha Republic, rising in the **Aldan Mountains** and flowing north and west to the Lena River. Length: about 2700 km (1700 miles)

Aldebaran (ælˈdɛbərən) *n* a binary star, one component of which is a red giant, the brightest star in the constellation Taurus. It appears in the sky close to the star cluster Hyades. Visual magnitude: 0.85; spectral type: K5III; distance: 65 light years [c14 via Medieval Latin from Arabic *al-dabarān* the follower (of the Pleiades)]

Aldeburgh (ˈɔːlbərə) *n* a small resort in SE England, in Suffolk: site of an annual music festival established in 1948 by Benjamin Britten. Pop: 2654 (2001)

aldehyde (ˈældɪˌhaɪd) *n* **1** any organic compound containing the group -CHO. Aldehydes are oxidized to carboxylic acids and take part in many addition reactions **2** (*modifier*) consisting of, containing, or concerned with the group -CHO: *aldehyde group or radical* [c19 from New Latin *al(cohol) dehyd(rogenátum)* dehydrogenated alcohol] > aldehydic (ˌældəˈhɪdɪk) *adj*

al dente *Italian* (al ˈdɛnte) *adj* (of a pasta dish) cooked so as to be firm when eaten [literally: to the tooth]

alder (ˈɔːldə) *n* **1** any N temperate betulaceous shrub or tree of the genus *Alnus*, having toothed leaves and conelike fruits. The bark is used in dyeing and tanning and the wood for bridges, etc because it resists underwater rot **2** any of several similar trees or shrubs [Old English *alor*; related to Old High German *elira*, Latin *alnus*]

alder buckthorn *n* a Eurasian rhamnaceous shrub, *Frangula alnus*, with small greenish flowers and black berry-like fruits

alder fly *n* any of various neuropterous insects of the widely distributed group *Sialoidea*, such as *Sialis lutaria*, that have large broad-based hind wings, produce aquatic larvae, and occur near water

alderman (ˈɔːldəmən) *n*, *pl* -men **1** (in England and Wales until 1974) one of the senior members of a local council, elected by other councillors **2** (in the US, Canada, Australia, etc) a member of the governing body of a municipality **3** *history* a variant spelling of **ealdorman** ▷ Abbreviations (for senses 1, 2): Ald, Aldm [Old English *aldormann*, from *ealdor* chief (comparative of *eald* OLD) + *mann* MAN] > aldermanic (ˌɔːldəˈmænɪk) *adj* > ˈaldermanry *n* > ˈaldermanˌship *n*

Aldermaston (ˈɔːldəˌmɑːstən) *n* a village in S England, in West Berkshire unitary authority, Berkshire, SW of Reading: site of the Atomic Weapons Research Establishment and starting point of the Aldermaston marches (1958–63), organized by the Campaign for Nuclear Disarmament. Pop: 2157 (1987 est)

Alderney (ˈɔːldənɪ) *n* **1** one of the Channel Islands, in the English Channel: separated from the French coast by a dangerous tidal channel (the **Race of Alderney**). Pop: 2294 (2001). Area: 8 sq km (3 sq miles). French name: Aurigny **2** an early, but now extinct, breed of dairy cattle originating from the island of Alderney

Aldershot (ˈɔːldəˌʃɒt) *n* a town in S England, in Hampshire: site of a large military camp. Pop: 58170 (2001)

Aldine (ˈɔːldaɪn, -diːn) *adj* **1** relating to Aldus Manutius (1450–1515), Italian printer, or to his editions of the classics ▷ *n* **2** a book printed by the Aldine press **3** any of the several typefaces designed by Aldus Manutius

Aldis lamp (ˈɔːldɪs) *n* a portable lamp used to transmit Morse code [c20 originally a trademark, after A. C. W. *Aldis*, its inventor]

aldohexose (ˌældəʊˈhɛksəʊs, -əʊz) *n* any aldose containing six carbon atoms, such as glucose or mannose

aldol (ˈældɒl) *n* **1** a colourless or yellowish oily liquid, miscible with water, used in the manufacture of rubber accelerators, as an organic solvent, in perfume, and as a hypnotic and sedative. Formula: $CH_3CHOHCH_2CHO$. Systematic name: 3-hydroxybutanal **2** any organic compound containing the functional group -CHOHCH₂CHO **3** (*modifier*) consisting of, containing, or concerned with the group -CHOHCH₂CHO: *aldol group or radical; aldol reaction* [c19 from ALD(EHYDE) + -OL¹]

aldose (ˈældəʊs, -dəʊz) *n* a sugar that contains the aldehyde group or is a hemiacetal [c20 from ALD(EHYDE) + -OSE²]

aldosterone (ælˈdɒstəˌrəʊn) *n* the principal mineralocorticoid secreted by the adrenal cortex. A synthesized form is used in the treatment of Addison's disease. Formula: $C_{21}H_{27}O_5$ [c20 from ALD(EHYDE) + -O- + STER(OL) + -ONE]

aldoxime (ælˈdɒksiːm) *n* an oxime formed by reaction between hydroxylamine and an aldehyde

Aldridge-Brownhills (ˈɔːldrɪdʒˈbraʊnˌhɪlz) *n* a town in central England, in Walsall unitary authority, West Midlands: formed by the amalgamation of neighbouring towns in 1966. Pop: 35 525 (2001)

aldrin (ˈɔːldrɪn) *n* a brown to white poisonous crystalline solid, more than 95 per cent of which consists of the compound $C_{12}H_8Cl_6$, which is used as an insecticide. Melting pt: 105°C [c20 named after K. *Aldrin* (1902–58) German chemist]

ale (eɪl) *n* **1** a beer fermented in an open vessel using yeasts that rise to the top of the brew. Compare **beer, lager¹ 2** (formerly) an alcoholic drink made by fermenting a cereal, esp barley, but differing from beer by being unflavoured by hops **3** *chiefly Brit* another word for **beer** [Old English *alu, ealu*; related to Old Norse *öl*, Old Saxon *alofat*]

aleatory (ˈeɪlɪətərɪ, -trɪ) *or* **aleatoric** (ˌeɪlɪəˈtɒrɪk) *adj* **1** dependent on chance **2** (esp of a musical composition) involving elements chosen at random by the performer [c17 from Latin *āleātōrius*, from *āleātor* gambler, from *ālea* game of chance, dice, of uncertain origin]

alecithal (eɪˈlɛsɪθəl) *adj zoology* (of an ovum) having little or no yolk [from A-¹ + Greek *lekithos* egg yolk]

ale conner *n English history* a local official appointed to examine the measure and quality of ale, beer, and bread [c14 from ALE + *conner*, from Old English *cunnere* one who tests]

alecost (ˈeɪlˌkɒst) *n* another name for **costmary**

Alecto (əˈlɛktəʊ) *n Greek myth* one of the three Furies; the others are Megaera and Tisiphone

alee (əˈliː) *adv, adj* (*postpositive*) *nautical* on or towards the lee: *with the helm alee*. Compare **aweather**

alegar (ˈeɪlɪgə, ˈæ-) *n* malt vinegar [c14 from ALE + VINEGAR]

alehouse (ˈeɪlˌhaʊs) *n* **1** *archaic* a place where ale was sold; tavern **2** *informal* another name for **pub**

Aleksandropol (*Russian* alɪksanˈdrɔpəlj) *n* the former name (from 1837 until after the Revolution) of **Kumayri**

Aleksandrovsk (*Russian* alɪkˈsandrəfsk) *n* the former name (until 1921) of **Zaporozhye**

Alemanni (ˌæləˈmɑːnɪ) *n* a West Germanic people who settled in the 4th century AD between the Rhine, the Main, and the Danube [c18 from Latin, of Germanic origin; related to Gothic *alamans* a totality of people]

Alemannic (ˌæləˈmænɪk) *n* **1 a** the group of High German dialects spoken in Alsace, Switzerland, and SW Germany **b** the language of the ancient Alemanni, from which these modern dialects have developed. See also **Old High German** ▷ *adj* **2** of or relating to the Alemanni, their speech, or the High German dialects descended from it [c18 from Late Latin *Alamannicus*, of Germanic origin]

alembic (əˈlɛmbɪk) *n* **1** an obsolete type of retort used for distillation **2** anything that distils or purifies [c14 from Medieval Latin *alembicum*, from Arabic *al-anbīq* the still, from Greek *ambix* cup]

alembicated (əˈlɛmbɪˌkeɪtɪd) *adj* (of a literary style) excessively refined; precious > aˈlembiˈcation *n*

Alençon (*French* alɑ̃sɔ̃) *n* a town in NW France:

early lace-manufacturing centre. Pop: 28 935 (1999)

Alençon lace *n* an elaborate lace worked on a hexagonal mesh and used as a border, or a machine-made copy of this

aleph ('ɑːlɪf; *Hebrew* 'aːlɛf) *n* the first letter in the Hebrew alphabet (ℵ) articulated as a glottal stop and transliterated with a superior comma (') [Hebrew: ox]

aleph-bet ('alef'bet) *or* **aleph-beis** ('alef'beis) *n* the Hebrew alphabet [from the first two letters]

aleph-null *or* **aleph-zero** *n* the smallest infinite cardinal number; the cardinal number of the set of positive integers. Symbol: $\aleph_0$

Aleppo (əˈlɛpəʊ) *n* an ancient city in NW Syria: industrial and commercial centre. Pop: 2 505 000 (2005 est). French name: Alep (alɛp) Arabic name: Haleb ('halɛp)

Aleppo gall *n* a type of nutgall occurring in oaks in W Asia and E Europe

alerce (əˈlɜːs, æˈlɜːsɪ) *n* **1** the wood of the sandarac tree **2** a cupressus-like Chilean pine, *Fitzroya cupressoides*, cut for timber [Spanish: larch, from Latin *larix*, influenced by Arabic *al-arz*]

alert (əˈlɜːt) *adj* (*usually postpositive*) **1** vigilantly attentive: *alert to the problems* **2** brisk, nimble, or lively ▷ *n* **3** an alarm or warning, esp a siren warning of an air raid **4** the period during which such a warning remains in effect **5** **on the alert a** on guard against danger, attack, etc **b** watchful; ready: *on the alert for any errors* ▷ *vb* (*tr*) **6** to warn or signal (troops, police, etc) to prepare for action **7** to warn of danger, an attack, etc [C17 from Italian *all'erta* on the watch, from *erta* lookout post, from *ergere* to build up, from Latin *ērigere*; see ERECT] > a'**lertly** *adv* > a'**lertness** *n*

-ales *suffix forming plural proper nouns* denoting plants belonging to an order: *Rosales; Filicales* [New Latin, from Latin, plural of *-ālis* -AL¹]

Alessandria (*Italian* alesˈsandrja) *n* a town in NW Italy, in Piedmont. Pop: 85 438 (2001)

Ålesund *or* **Aalesund** (*Norwegian* 'oːləsun) *n* a port and market town in W Norway, on an island between Bergen and Trondheim: fishing and sealing fleets. Pop: 40 001 (2004 est)

alethic (əˈliːθɪk) *adj logic* **a** of or relating to such philosophical concepts as truth, necessity, possibility, contingency, etc **b** designating the branch of modal logic that deals with the formalization of these concepts [C20 from Greek *alētheia* truth]

aleurone layer (əˈlʊərən, -rəʊn) *or* **aleuron** (əˈlʊərɒn, -rən) *n* the outer protein-rich layer of certain seeds, esp of cereal grains [C19 from Greek *aleuron* flour]

Aleut (æˈluːt, ˈæliːʊt) *n* **1** a member of a people inhabiting the Aleutian Islands and SW Alaska, related to the Inuit **2** the language of this people, related to Inuktitut [from Russian *aleút*, probably of Chukchi origin]

Aleutian (əˈluːʃən) *adj* **1** of, denoting, or relating to the Aleutian Islands, the Aleuts, or their language ▷ *n* **2** another word for **Aleut**

Aleutian Islands *pl n* a chain of over 150 volcanic islands, extending southwestwards from the Alaska Peninsula between the N Pacific and the Bering Sea

A level *n* (in Britain) **1 a** a public examination in a subject taken for the General Certificate of Education (GCE), usually at the age of 17–18 **b** the course leading to this examination **c** (*as modifier*):: *A-level maths* **2** a pass in a particular subject at A level: *she has three A levels*

A2 level *n* (British Education) **a** the second part of an A-level course, taken after the AS level examination **b** the examination at the end of this

alevin ('ælɪvɪn) *n* a young fish, esp a young salmon or trout [C19 from French, from Old French *alever* to rear (young), from Latin *levāre* to raise]

alewife ('eɪlˌwaɪf) *n, pl* **-wives** a North American fish, *Pomolobus pseudoharengus*, similar to the herring *Clupea harengus*: family *Clupeidae* (herrings) [C19 perhaps an alteration (through influence of *alewife*, that is, a large rotund woman, alluding to the fish's shape) of French *alose* shad]

Alexander Archipelago (ˌælɪgˈzaːndə) *n* a group of over 1000 islands along the coast of SE Alaska

Alexander I Island *n* an island of Antarctica, west of Palmer Land, in the Bellingshausen Sea. Length: about 378 km (235 miles)

alexanders (ˌælɪgˈzaːndəz) *n* **1** a biennial umbelliferous plant, *Smyrnium olusatrum*, native to S Europe, with dense umbels of yellow-green flowers and black fruits **2** **golden alexanders** an umbelliferous plant, *Zizia aurea*, of North America, having yellow flowers in compound umbels [Old English, from Medieval Latin *alexandrum*, probably (through association in folk etymology with *Alexander* the Great) changed from Latin *holus atrum* black vegetable]

Alexander technique *n* a technique for developing awareness of one's posture and movement in order to improve it [C20 named after Frederick Matthias *Alexander* (died 1955), Australian actor who originated it]

Alexandretta (ˌælɪgzaːnˈdrɛtə) *n* the former name of **Iskenderun**

Alexandria (ˌælɪgˈzændrɪə, -ˈzaːn-) *n* the chief port of Egypt, on the Nile Delta: cultural centre of ancient times, founded by Alexander the Great (332 BC). Pop: 3 760 000 (2005 est). Arabic name: El Iskandariyah

Alexandrian (ˌælɪgˈzændrɪən, -ˈzaːn-) *adj* **1** of or relating to Alexander the Great (356–323 BC), king of Macedon, who conquered Greece (336), Egypt (331), and the Persian Empire (328) **2** of or relating to Alexandria in Egypt **3** relating to the Hellenistic philosophical, literary, and scientific ideas that flourished in Alexandria in the last three centuries BC **4** (of writers, literary works, etc) erudite and imitative rather than original or creative ▷ *n* **5** a native or inhabitant of Alexandria

Alexandrine (ˌælɪgˈzændraɪn, -drɪn, -ˈzaːn-) *prosody* ▷ *n* **1** a line of verse having six iambic feet, usually with a caesura after the third foot ▷ *adj* **2** of, characterized by, or written in Alexandrines [C16 from French *alexandrin*, from *Alexandre*, title of 15th-century poem written in this metre]

alexandrite (ˌælɪgˈzændraɪt) *n* a green variety of chrysoberyl used as a gemstone [C19 named after *Alexander* I (1777–1825), tsar of Russia (1801–25); see -ITE¹]

Alexandroúpolis (*Greek* alɛksanˈðrupolis) *n* a port in NE Greece, in W Thrace. Pop: 39 283 (1991 est). Former name (until the end of World War I): Dedéagach

alexia (əˈlɛksɪə) *n* a disorder of the central nervous system characterized by impaired ability to read. Nontechnical name: **word blindness** Compare **aphasia** [C19 from New Latin, from A-¹ + Greek *lexis* speech; influenced in meaning by Latin *legere* to read]

alexin (əˈlɛksɪn) *n* *immunol* a former word for **complement** (sense 9) [C19 from German, from Greek *alexein* to ward off] > alexinic (ˌælɪkˈsɪnɪk) *adj*

alexipharmic (əˌlɛksɪˈfaːmɪk) *med* ▷ *adj* **1** acting as an antidote ▷ *n* **2** an antidote [C17 from Greek *alexipharmakon* antidote, from *alexein* to avert + *pharmakon* drug]

alf (ælf) *n* *Austral slang* an uncultivated Australian [from shortening of the name *Alfred*]

ALF (in Britain) *abbreviation for* **Animal Liberation Front**

Alfa ('ælfə) *n* a variant spelling of **Alpha** (sense 2)

alfalfa (ælˈfælfə) *n* a leguminous plant, *Medicago sativa*, of Europe and Asia, having compound leaves with three leaflets and clusters of small purplish flowers. It is widely cultivated for forage and as a nitrogen fixer and used as a commercial source of chlorophyll. Also called: **lucerne** [C19 from Spanish, from Arabic *al-fasfasah*, from *al* the + *fasfasah* the best sort of fodder]

Al Fatah (æl ˈfætə) *n* See **Fatah**

alfilaria *or* **alfileria** (ˌælfɪˈlɛarɪə) *n* a geraniaceous plant, *Erodium cicutarium*, native to Europe, with finely divided leaves and small pink or purplish flowers. It is widely naturalized in North America and is used as fodder. Also called: **pin clover** [via American Spanish from Spanish *alfilerillo*, from *alfiler* pin, from Arabic *al-khilāl* the thorn]

alforja (ælˈfɔːdʒə) *n* *Southwestern US* a saddlebag made of leather or canvas [C17 from Spanish, from Arabic *al-khurj* the saddlebag]

alfresco (ælˈfrɛskəʊ) *adj, adv* in the open air [C18 from Italian: in the cool]

Alfvén wave (ælˈvɛn) *n* a generally transverse magnetohydrodynamic wave that is propagated in a plasma [C20 after Hannes Olaf Gösta *Alfvén* (1908–95), Swedish physicist]

Alg. *abbreviation for* Algeria(n)

algae ('ældʒiː) *pl n, sing* **alga** ('ælgə) unicellular or multicellular organisms formerly classified as plants, occurring in fresh or salt water or moist ground, that have chlorophyll and other pigments but lack true stems, roots, and leaves. Algae, which are now regarded as protoctists, include the seaweeds, diatoms, and spirogyra [C16 from Latin, plural of *alga* seaweed, of uncertain origin] > **algal** ('ælgəl) *adj*

algarroba *or* **algaroba** (ˌælgəˈrəʊbə) *n* **1** another name for **mesquite** *or* **carob 2** the edible pod of these trees [C19 from Spanish, from Arabic *al* the + *kharrūbah* CAROB]

Algarve (ælˈgaːv) *n* **the** an area in the south of Portugal, on the Atlantic; it approximately corresponds to the administrative district of Faro: fishing and tourism important

algebra ('ældʒɪbrə) *n* **1** a branch of mathematics in which arithmetical operations and relationships are generalized by using alphabetic symbols to represent unknown numbers or members of specified sets of numbers **2** the branch of mathematics dealing with more abstract formal structures, such as sets, groups, etc [C14 from Medieval Latin, from Arabic *al-jabr* the bone-setting, reunification, mathematical reduction] > algebraist (ˌældʒɪˈbreɪɪst) *n*

algebraic (ˌældʒɪˈbreɪɪk) *or* **algebraical** *adj* **1** of or relating to algebra: *an algebraic expression* **2** using or relating to finite numbers, operations, or relationships > ˌalge'**braically** *adv*

algebraic function *n* *maths* any function which can be constructed in a finite number of steps from the elementary operations and the inverses of any function already constructed. Compare **transcendental function**

algebraic notation *n* *chess* the standard method of denoting the squares on the chessboard, by allotting a letter, a, b, c, up to h, to each of the files running up the board from White's side, starting from the left, and a number to each of the ranks across the board, starting with White's first rank

algebraic number *n* any number that is a root of a polynomial equation having rational coefficients such as $\sqrt{2}$ but not π. Compare **transcendental number**

Algeciras (ˌældʒɪˈsɪrəs; *Spanish* alxeˈθiras) *n* a port and resort in SW Spain, on the Strait of Gibraltar: scene of a conference of the Great Powers in 1906. Pop: 108 779 (2003 est)

Algeria (ælˈdʒɪərɪə) *n* a republic in NW Africa, on the Mediterranean: became independent in 1962, after more than a century of French rule; one-party constitution adopted in 1976; religious extremists led a campaign of violence from 1988 until 2000; consists chiefly of the N Sahara, with the Atlas Mountains in the north, and contains rich deposits of oil and natural gas. Official languages: Arabic and Berber; French also widely spoken. Religion: Muslim. Currency: dinar. Capital: Algiers. Pop: 32 339 000 (2004 est). Area: about 2 382 800 sq km (920 000 sq miles). French

a

name: Algérie (alʒeri)

Algerian (ælˈdʒɪərɪən) *adj* **1** of or relating to Algeria or its inhabitants ▷ *n* **2** a native or inhabitant of Algeria

algerine (ˌældʒəˈriːn) *n* a soft striped woollen cloth [c19 from French, from *algérien* Algerian: because the cloth was originally made in Algeria]

Algerine (ˌældʒəˈriːn) *adj* **1** of or relating to Algeria or its inhabitants ▷ *n* **2** a native or inhabitant of Algeria

algesia (ælˈdʒiːzɪə, -sɪə) *n physiol* the capacity to feel pain [New Latin from Greek *algēsis* sense of pain] > al'gesic *or* al'getic *adj*

-algia *n combining form* denoting pain or a painful condition of the part specified: *neuralgia; odontalgia* [from Greek *algos* pain] > **-algic** *adj combining form*

algicide (ˈældʒɪˌsaɪd) *n* any substance that kills algae

algid (ˈældʒɪd) *adj med* chilly or cold [c17 from Latin *algidus*, from *algēre* to be cold] > al'gidity *n*

Algiers (ælˈdʒɪəz) *n* the capital of Algeria, an ancient port on the Mediterranean; until 1830 a centre of piracy. Pop: 3 260 000 (2005 est). Arabic name: Al-Jezair (ˌældʒɛˈzɑːɪə) French name: Alger (alʒe)

algin (ˈældʒɪn) *n* alginic acid or one of its esters or salts, esp the gelatinous solution obtained as a by-product in the extraction of iodine from seaweed, used in mucilages and for thickening jellies

alginate (ˈældʒɪˌneɪt) *n* a salt or ester of alginic acid

alginic acid (ælˈdʒɪnɪk) *n* a white or yellowish powdery polysaccharide having marked hydrophilic properties. Extracted from kelp, it is used mainly in the food and textile industries and in cosmetics and pharmaceuticals. Formula: $(C_6H_8O_6)_n$; molecular wt: 32 000–250 000

algo- *combining form* denoting pain: *algometer; algophobia* [from Greek *algos* pain]

algoid (ˈælgɔɪd) *adj* resembling or relating to algae

Algol[1] (ˈælgɒl) *n* the second brightest star in Perseus, the first known eclipsing binary. Visual magnitude: 2.2–3.5; period: 68.8 hours; spectral type (brighter component): B8V [c14 from Arabic *al ghūl* the GHOUL]

Algol[2] (ˈælgɒl) *n* a computer programming language designed for mathematical and scientific purposes; a high-level language [c20 *alg(orithmic) o(riented) l(anguage)*]

algolagnia (ˌælgəˈlægnɪə) *n* a perversion in which sexual pleasure is gained from the experience or infliction of pain. See also **sadism, masochism.** > ˌalgoˈlagnic *adj* > ˌalgoˈlagnist *n*

algology[1] (ælˈgɒlədʒɪ) *n* the branch of biology concerned with the study of algae > algological (ˌælgəˈlɒdʒɪkᵊl) *adj* > ˌalgoˈlogically *adv* > al'gologist *n*

algology[2] (ælˈgɒlədʒɪ) *n* the branch of medicine concerned with the study of pain [from Greek *algos* pain]

algometer (ælˈgɒmɪtə) *n* an instrument for measuring sensitivity to pressure (**pressure algometer**) or to pain > al'gometry *n*

Algonkian (ælˈgɒŋkɪən) *n, adj* **1** an obsolete term for **Proterozoic** **2** a variant of **Algonquian**

Algonquian (ælˈgɒŋkɪən, -kwɪ-) *or* **Algonkian** *n* **1** a family of North American Indian languages whose speakers ranged over an area stretching from the Atlantic between Newfoundland and Delaware to the Rocky Mountains, including Micmac, Mahican, Ojibwa, Fox, Blackfoot, Cheyenne, and Shawnee. Some linguists relate it to Muskogean in a Macro-Algonquian phylum **2** (*pl* **-ans** *or* **-an**) a member of any of the North American Indian peoples that speak one of these languages ▷ *adj* **3** denoting, belonging to, or relating to this linguistic family or its speakers

Algonquin (ælˈgɒŋkɪn, -kwɪn) *or* **Algonkin** (ælˈgɒŋkɪn) *n* **1** (*pl* **-quins, -quin** *or* **-kins, -kin**) a member of a North American Indian people

formerly living along the St Lawrence and Ottawa Rivers in Canada **2** the language of this people, a dialect of Ojibwa ▷ *n, adj* **3** a variant of **Algonquian** [c17 from Canadian French, earlier written as *Algoumequin;* perhaps related to Micmac *algoomaking* at the fish-spearing place]

Algonquin Park *n* a provincial park in S Canada, in E Ontario, containing over 1200 lakes. Area: 7100 sq km (2741 sq miles)

algophobia (ˌælgəˈfəʊbɪə) *n psychiatry* an acute fear of experiencing or witnessing bodily pain

algor (ˈælgɔː) *n med obsolete* chill [c15 from Latin]

algorism (ˈælgəˌrɪzəm) *n* **1** the Arabic or decimal system of counting **2** the skill of computation using any system of numerals **3** another name for **algorithm** [c13 from Old French *algorisme*, from Medieval Latin *algorismus*, from Arabic *al-khuwārizmi*, from the name of abu-Jaʿfar Mohammed ibn-Mūsa al-Khuwārizmi, ninth-century Persian mathematician] > ˌalgoˈrismic *adj*

algorithm (ˈælgəˌrɪðəm) *n* **1** a logical arithmetical or computational procedure that if correctly applied ensures the solution of a problem. Compare **heuristic 2** *logic, maths* a recursive procedure whereby an infinite sequence of terms can be generated ▷ Also called: **algorism** [c17 changed from ALGORISM, through influence of Greek *arithmos* number] > ˌalgoˈrithmic *adj* > ˌalgoˈrithmically *adv*

Alhambra (ælˈhæmbrə) *n* a citadel and palace in Granada, Spain, built for the Moorish kings during the 13th and 14th centuries: noted for its rich ornamentation > **Alhambresque** (ˌælhæmˈbrɛsk) *adj*

Al Hijrah *or* **Al Hijra** (æl ˈhɪdʒrə) *n* an annual Muslim festival marking the beginning of the Muslim year. It commemorates Mohammed's move from Mecca to Medina and involves the exchange of gifts and the telling of stories about Mohammed. See also **Hegira** [from Arabic, *hijrah* emigration or flight]

Al Hufuf *or* **Al Hofuf** (æl hʊˈfuːf) *n* a town in E Saudi Arabia: a trading centre with nearby oilfields and oases. Pop: 331 000 (2005 est)

alias (ˈeɪlɪəs) *adv* **1** at another time or place known as or named: *Dylan, alias Zimmerman* ▷ *n, pl* **-ases 2** an assumed name [c16 from Latin *aliās* (adv) otherwise, at another time, from *alius* other]

aliasing (ˈeɪlɪəsɪŋ) *n radio, television* the error in a vision or sound signal arising from limitations in the system that generates or processes the signal

Ali Baba (ˈælɪ ˈbɑːbə) *n* (in *The Arabian Nights' Entertainments*) a poor woodcutter who discovers that the magic words "open sesame" will open the doors of the cave containing the treasure of the Forty Thieves

alibi (ˈælɪˌbaɪ) *n, pl* **-bis 1** *law* **a** a defence by an accused person that he was elsewhere at the time the crime in question was committed **b** the evidence given to prove this **2** *informal* an excuse ▷ *vb* **3** (*tr*) to provide with an alibi [c18 from Latin *alibī* elsewhere, from *alius* other + *-bī* as in *ubī* where]

Alicante (ˌælɪˈkæntɪ) *n* a port in SE Spain: commercial centre. Pop: 305 911 (2003 est). Catalan name: Alacant

Alice (ˈælɪs) *or* **the Alice** *n Austral slang* short for **Alice Springs**

Alice band *n* an ornamental band worn across the front of the hair to hold it back from the face

Alice-in-Wonderland *adj* fantastic; irrational [c20 alluding to the absurdities of Wonderland in Lewis Carroll's book]

Alice Springs *n* a town in central Australia, in the Northern Territory, in the Macdonnell Ranges. Pop: 23 640 (2001). Former name (until 1931): Stuart

alicyclic (ˌælɪˈsaɪklɪk, -ˈsɪk-) *adj* (of an organic compound) having aliphatic properties, in spite of the presence of a ring of carbon atoms [c19 from German *alicyclisch*, from ALI(PHATIC) + CYCLIC]

alidade (ˈælɪˌdeɪd) *or* **alidad** (ˈælɪˌdæd) *n* **1** a

surveying instrument used in plane-tabling for drawing lines of sight on a distant object and taking angular measurements **2** the upper rotatable part of a theodolite, including the telescope and its attachments [c15 from French, from Medieval Latin *allidada*, from Arabic *al-ʿidāda* the revolving radius of a circle]

alien (ˈeɪljən, ˈeɪlɪən) *n* **1** a person owing allegiance to a country other than that in which he lives; foreigner **2** any being or thing foreign to the environment in which it now exists **3** (in science fiction) a being from another world, sometimes specifically an extraterrestrial ▷ *adj* **4** unnaturalized; foreign **5** having foreign allegiance: *alien territory* **6** unfamiliar; strange: *an alien quality in a work of art* **7** (*postpositive* and foll by *to*) repugnant or opposed (to): *war is alien to his philosophy* **8** (in science fiction) of or from another world ▷ *vb* **9** (*tr*) *rare* to transfer (property, etc) to another [c14 from Latin *aliēnus* foreign, from *alius* other] > **alienage** (ˈeɪljənɪdʒ, ˈeɪlɪə-) *n*

alienable (ˈeɪljənəbᵊl, ˈeɪlɪə-) *adj law* (of property) transferable to another owner > ˌaliena'bility *n*

alienate (ˈeɪljəˌneɪt, ˈeɪlɪə-) *vb* (*tr*) **1** to cause (a friend, sympathizer, etc) to become indifferent, unfriendly, or hostile; estrange **2** to turn away; divert: *to alienate the affections of a person* **3** *law* to transfer the ownership of (property, title, etc) to another person > 'alienˌator *n*

alienation (ˌeɪljəˈneɪʃən, ˌeɪlɪə-) *n* **1** a turning away; estrangement **2** the state of being an outsider or the feeling of being isolated, as from society **3** *psychiatry* a state in which a person's feelings are inhibited so that eventually both the self and the external world seem unreal **4** *law* **a** the transfer of property, as by conveyance or will, into the ownership of another **b** the right of an owner to dispose of his property

alienee (ˌeɪljəˈniː, ˌeɪlɪə-) *n law* a person to whom a transfer of property is made

alienism (ˈeɪljəˌnɪzəm, ˈeɪlɪə-) *n obsolete* the study and treatment of mental illness

alienist (ˈeɪljənɪst, ˈeɪlɪə-) *n* **1** *US* a psychiatrist who specializes in the legal aspects of mental illness **2** *obsolete* a person who practises alienism

alienor (ˈeɪljənə, ˈeɪlɪə-) *n law* a person who transfers property to another

aliform (ˈælɪˌfɔːm, ˈeɪlɪ-) *adj* wing-shaped; alar [c19 from New Latin *āliformis*, from Latin *āla* a wing]

Aligarh (ˌɑːlɪˈgɜː, ˌælɪ-) *n* a city in N India, in W Uttar Pradesh, with a famous Muslim university (1920). Pop: 667 732 (2001)

alight[1] (əˈlaɪt) *vb* **alights, alighting, alighted** *or* **alit** (*intr*) **1** (usually foll by *from*) to step out (of) or get down (from): *to alight from a taxi* **2** to come to rest; settle; land: *a thrush alighted on the wall* [Old English *ālīhtan*, from A-[2] + *līhtan* to make less heavy, from *līht* LIGHT[2]]

alight[2] (əˈlaɪt) *adj* (*postpositive*) ▷ *adv* **1** burning; on fire **2** illuminated; lit up [Old English *ālīht* lit up, from *ālīhtan* to light up; see LIGHT[1]]

alighting gear *n* another name for **undercarriage** (sense 1)

align (əˈlaɪn) *vb* **1** to place or become placed in a line **2** to bring (components or parts, such as the wheels of a car) into proper or desirable coordination or relation **3** (*tr;* usually foll by *with*) to bring (a person, country, etc) into agreement or cooperation with the policy, etc of another person or group **4** (*tr*) *psychol* to integrate or harmonize the aims, practices, etc of a group **5** (usually foll by *with*) *psychol* to identify with or match the behaviour, thoughts, etc of another person [c17 from Old French *aligner*, from *à ligne* into line]

alignment (əˈlaɪnmənt) *n* **1** arrangement in a straight line **2** the line or lines formed in this manner **3** alliance or union with a party, cause, etc **4** proper or desirable coordination or relation of components **5** a ground plan of a railway, motor road, etc **6** *archaeol* an arrangement of one or more ancient rows of standing stones, of uncertain significance **7** *psychol* integration or harmonization of aims, practices, etc within a group **8** *psychol* identification with or matching of the behaviour, thoughts, etc of another person

alike (əˈlaɪk) *adj* (*postpositive*) **1** possessing the same or similar characteristics: *they all look alike to me* ▷ *adv* **2** in the same or a similar manner, way, or degree: *they walk alike* [Old English *gelīc*; see LIKE¹]

aliment *n* (ˈælɪmənt) **1** something that nourishes or sustains the body or mind **2** *Scots law* another term for **alimony** ▷ *vb* (ˈælɪˌmɛnt) **3** (*tr*) *obsolete* to support or sustain [c15 from Latin *alimentum* food, from *alere* to nourish] > ˌaliˈmental *adj*

alimentary (ˌælɪˈmɛntərɪ, -trɪ) *adj* **1** of or relating to nutrition **2** providing sustenance or nourishment **3** *Scots law* free from the claims of creditors: *an alimentary trust*

alimentary canal *or* **tract** *n* the tubular passage extending from the mouth to the anus, through which food is passed and digested

alimentation (ˌælɪmɛnˈteɪʃən) *n* **1** nourishment **2** sustenance; support > ˌaliˈmentative *adj*

alimony (ˈælɪmənɪ) *n* *law* (formerly) an allowance paid under a court order by one spouse to another when they are separated but not divorced. See also **maintenance** [c17 from Latin *alimōnia* sustenance, from *alere* to nourish]

aline (əˈlaɪn) *vb* a rare spelling of **align** > aˈlinement *n* > aˈliner *n*

A-line *adj* (of a garment, esp a skirt or dress) flaring slightly from the waist or shoulders

aliped (ˈælɪˌpɛd) *adj* **1** (of bats and similar animals) having the digits connected by a winglike membrane ▷ *n* **2** an aliped animal [c19 from Latin *ālipēs* having winged feet, from *āla* wing + -PED]

aliphatic (ˌælɪˈfætɪk) *adj* (of an organic compound) not aromatic, esp having an open chain structure, such as alkanes, alkenes, and alkynes [c19 from Greek *aleiphat-*, *aleiphar* oil]

aliquant (ˈælɪkwənt) *adj* *maths* of, signifying, or relating to a quantity or number that is not an exact divisor of a given quantity or number: *5 is an aliquant part of 12*. Compare **aliquot** (sense 1) [c17 from New Latin, from Latin *aliquantus* somewhat, a certain quantity of]

aliquot (ˈælɪˌkwɒt) *adj* **1** *maths* of, signifying, or relating to an exact divisor of a quantity or number: *3 is an aliquot part of 12*. Compare **aliquant** **2** consisting of equal quantities: *the sample was divided into five aliquot parts* ▷ *n* **3** an aliquot part [c16 from Latin: several, a few]

alison (ˈælɪsᵊn) *n* **1** **sweet alison** another name for **sweet alyssum** **2** **small alison** a rare compact annual, *Alyssum alyssoides*, having small yellow flowers: family *Brassicaceae* (crucifers) [altered from ALYSSUM]

A list *n* **a** the most socially desirable category **b** (*as modifier*): *an A-list event* ▷ Compare **B list**

alit (əˈlɪt) *vb* a rare past tense and past participle of **alight¹**

aliterate (eɪˈlɪtərɪt) *n* **1** a person who is able to read but disinclined to do so ▷ *adj* **2** of or relating to aliterates

aliunde (ˌeɪlɪˈʌndɪ) *adv, adj* from a source extrinsic to the matter, document, or instrument under consideration: *evidence aliunde* [Latin: from elsewhere]

alive (əˈlaɪv) *adj* (*postpositive*) **1** (of people, animals, plants, etc) living; having life **2** in existence; active: *they kept hope alive; the tradition was still alive* **3** (*immediately postpositive and usually used with a superlative*) of those living; now living: *the happiest woman alive* **4** full of life; lively: *she was wonderfully alive for her age* **5** (usually foll by *with*) animated: *a face alive with emotion* **6** (foll by *to*) aware (of); sensitive (to) **7** (foll by *with*) teeming (with): *the mattress was alive with fleas* **8** *electronics* another word for **live²** (sense 11) **9** **alive and kicking** (of a person) active and in good health **10** **look alive!** hurry up! get busy! [Old English *on līfe* in LIFE] > aˈliveness *n*

aliyah *n* *Judaism* **1** (aliˈja) *pl* -yoth (-ˈjɒt) immigration to the Holy Land **2** (əˈliːə) the honour of being called to read from the Torah [from Hebrew, literally: act of going up, ascent]

alizarin (əˈlɪzərɪn) *n* a brownish-yellow powder or orange-red crystalline solid used as a dye and in the manufacture of other dyes. Formula: $C_6H_4(CO)_2C_6H_2(OH)_2$ [c19 probably from French *alizarine*, probably from Arabic *al-ʿaṣārah* the juice, from *ʿaṣara* to squeeze]

alk. *abbreviation for* alkali

alkahest *or* **alcahest** (ˈælkəˌhɛst) *n* the hypothetical universal solvent sought by alchemists [c17 apparently coined by Paracelsus on the model of Arabic words]

alkali (ˈælkəˌlaɪ) *n, pl* -lis *or* -lies **1** *chem* a soluble base or a solution of a base **2** a soluble mineral salt that occurs in arid soils and some natural waters [c14 from Medieval Latin, from Arabic *al-qili* the ashes (of the plant saltwort)]

alkalic (ælˈkælɪk) *adj* **1** (of igneous rocks) containing large amounts of alkalis, esp sodium and potassium **2** another word for **alkaline**

alkali flat *n* an arid plain encrusted with alkaline salts derived from the streams draining into it

alkalify (ˈælkəlɪˌfaɪ, ælˈkæl-) *vb* -fies, -fying, -fied to make or become alkaline

alkali metal *n* any of the monovalent metals lithium, sodium, potassium, rubidium, caesium, and francium, belonging to group 1A of the periodic table. They are all very reactive and electropositive

alkalimeter (ˌælkəˈlɪmɪtə) *n* **1** an apparatus for determining the concentration of alkalis in solution **2** an apparatus for determining the quantity of carbon dioxide in carbonates > alkalimetric (ˌælkəlɪˈmɛtrɪk) *adj*

alkalimetry (ˌælkəˈlɪmɪtrɪ) *n* determination of the amount of alkali or base in a solution, measured by an alkalimeter or by volumetric analysis

alkaline (ˈælkəˌlaɪn) *adj* having the properties of or containing an alkali

alkaline earth *n* **1** Also called: **alkaline earth metal** *or* **alkaline earth element** any of the divalent electropositive metals beryllium, magnesium, calcium, strontium, barium, and radium, belonging to group 2A of the periodic table **2** an oxide of one of the alkaline earth metals

alkaline soil *n* a soil that gives a pH reaction of 8.5 or above, found esp in dry areas where the soluble salts, esp of sodium, have not been leached away but have accumulated in the B horizon of the soil profile

alkalinity (ˌælkəˈlɪnɪtɪ) *n* **1** the quality or state of being alkaline **2** the amount of alkali or base in a solution, often expressed in terms of pH

alkali soil *n* a soil that gives a pH reaction of 8.5 or above, found esp in dry areas where the soluble salts, esp of sodium, have not been leached away but have accumulated in the B horizon of the soil profile

alkalize *or* **alkalise** (ˈælkəˌlaɪz) *vb* (*tr*) to make alkaline > ˈalkaˌlizable *or* ˈalkaˌlisable *adj*

alkaloid (ˈælkəˌlɔɪd) *n* any of a group of nitrogenous basic compounds found in plants, typically insoluble in water and physiologically active. Common examples are morphine, strychnine, quinine, nicotine, and caffeine

alkalosis (ˌælkəˈləʊsɪs) *n* an abnormal increase in the alkalinity of the blood and extracellular fluids

alkane (ˈælkeɪn) *n* **a** any saturated aliphatic hydrocarbon with the general formula C_nH_{2n+2} **b** (*as modifier*): *alkane series* ▷ Also called: **paraffin**

alkanet (ˈælkəˌnɛt) *n* **1** a European boraginaceous plant, *Alkanna tinctoria*, the roots of which yield a red dye **2** Also called: **anchusin, alkannin** the dye obtained from this plant **3** any of certain hairy blue-flowered Old World plants of the boraginaceous genus *Anchusa* (or *Pentaglottis*), such as *A. sempervirens* of Europe. See also **bugloss** **4** another name for **puccoon** (sense 1) [c14 from Spanish *alcaneta*, diminutive of *alcana* henna, from Medieval Latin *alchanna*, from Arabic *al* the + *hinnā'* henna]

alkene (ˈælkiːn) *n* **a** any unsaturated aliphatic hydrocarbon with the general formula C_nH_{2n}. Also called: **olefine, olefin** **b** (*as modifier*): *alkene series* ▷ Also called: **olefine**

Alkmaar (*Dutch* ˈɑlkmaːr) *n* a city in the W Netherlands, in North Holland. Pop: 93 000 (2003 est)

alko *or* **alco** (ˈælkəʊ) *n, pl* **alkos, alcos** *Austral slang* a heavy drinker or alcoholic

Alkoran *or* **Alcoran** (ˌælkɒˈrɑːn) *n* a less common name for the **Koran**

alky *or* **alkie** (ˈælkɪ) *n, pl* -kies *slang* a heavy drinker or alcoholic

alkyd resin (ˈælkɪd) *n* any synthetic resin made from a dicarboxylic acid, such as phthalic acid, and diols or triols: used in paints and adhesives

alkyl (ˈælkɪl) *n* **1** (*modifier*) of, consisting of, or containing the monovalent group C_nH_{2n+1}: *alkyl group or radical* **2** an organometallic compound, such as tetraethyl lead, containing an alkyl group bound to a metal atom [c19 from German, from *Alk(ohol)* ALCOHOL + -YL]

alkylating agent (ˈælkɪˌleɪtɪŋ) *n* any cytotoxic drug containing alkyl groups, such as chlorambucil, that acts by damaging DNA; widely used in chemotherapy

alkylation (ˌælkɪˈleɪʃən) *n* **1** the attachment of an alkyl group to an organic compound, usually by the addition or substitution of a hydrogen atom or halide group **2** the addition of an alkane hydrocarbon to an alkene in producing high-octane fuels

alkyne (ˈælkaɪn) *n* **a** any unsaturated aliphatic hydrocarbon that has a formula of the type C_nH_{2n-2} **b** (*as modifier*): *alkyne series* ▷ Also called: **acetylene**

all (ɔːl) *determiner* **1** **a** the whole quantity or amount of; totality of; every one of a class: *all the rice; all men are mortal* **b** (*as pronoun; functioning as sing or plural*): *all of it is nice; all are welcome* **c** (*in combination with a noun used as a modifier*): *an all-ticket match; an all-amateur tournament; an all-night sitting* **2** the greatest possible: *in all earnestness* **3** any whatever: *to lose all hope of recovery; beyond all doubt* **4** **above all** most of all; especially **5** **after all** See **after** (sense 11) **6** **all along** all the time **7** **all but** almost; nearly: *all but dead* **8** **all of** no less or smaller than: *she's all of thirteen years* **9** **all over** **a** finished; at an end: *the affair is all over between us* **b** over the whole area (of something); everywhere (in, on, etc): *all over England* **c** Also (Irish): **all out** typically; representatively (in the phrase **that's me (you, him, us, them, *etc*) all over**) **d** unduly effusive towards **e** *sport* in a dominant position over **10** See **all in** **11** **all in all** **a** everything considered: *all in all, it was a great success* **b** the object of one's attention or interest: *you are my all in all* **12** **all that** Also: **that** (*usually used with a negative*) *informal* (intensifier): *she's not all that intelligent* **13** **all the** (foll by a comparative adjective or adverb) so much (more or less) than otherwise: *we must work all the faster now* **14** **all too** definitely but regrettably: *it's all too true* **15** **and all** **a** *Brit informal* as well; too: *and you can take that smile off your face and all* **b** *South African* a parenthetical filler phrase used at the end of a statement to make a slight pause in speaking **16** **and all that** *informal* **a** and similar or associated things; et cetera: *coffee, tea, and all that will be served in the garden* **b** used as a filler or to make what precedes more vague: in this sense, it often occurs with concessive force: *she was sweet and pretty and all that, but I still didn't like her* **c** See **that** (sense 4) **17** **as all that** as one might expect or hope: *she's not as pretty as all that, but she has personality* **18** **at all** **a** (*used with a negative or in a question*) in any way whatsoever or to any extent or degree: *I didn't know that at all* **b** even so; anyway: *I'm surprised you came at all* **19** **be all for** *informal* to be strongly in favour of **20** **be all that**

informal, chiefly US to be exceptionally good, talented, or attractive **21 for all a** in so far as; to the extent that: *for all anyone knows, he was a baron* **b** notwithstanding: *for all my pushing, I still couldn't move it* **22 for all that** in spite of that: *he was a nice man for all that* **23 in all** altogether: *there were five of them in all* ▷ *adv* **24** (in scores of games) apiece; each: *the score at half time was three all* **25** completely: *all alone* ▷ *n* **26** (preceded by *my, your, his,* etc) (one's) complete effort or interest: *to give your all; you are my all* **27** totality or whole ▷ Related prefixes: **pan-, panto-** [Old English *eall*; related to Old High German *al*, Old Norse *allr*, Gothic *alls* all]

all- *combining form* a variant of **allo-** before a vowel

alla breve ('ælə 'breɪvɪ; *Italian* 'alla 'brɛːve) *n* **1** a musical time signature indicating two or four minims to a bar ▷ *adj* ▷ *adv* **2** twice as fast as normal. Musical symbol: ¢ [C19 Italian, literally: (according) to the breve]

Allah ('ælə) *n Islam* the Muslim name for God; the one Supreme Being [C16 from Arabic, from *al* the + *Ilāh* god; compare Hebrew *elōah*]

Allahabad (,æləhə'bæd, -'baːd) *n* a city in N India, in SE Uttar Pradesh at the confluence of the Ganges and Jumna Rivers: Hindu pilgrimage centre. Pop: 990 298 (2001)

Allahu Akbar ('ælə,hu 'ak,baː) *interj Islam* an exclamation used in the call to prayer and also used as a call to the defence of Muslims, an expression of approval, and a funeral litany [from Arabic, literally: God is most great]

all-American *adj US* **1** representative of the whole of the United States **2** composed exclusively of American members **3** (of a person) typically American: *the company looks for all-American clean-cut college students*

Allan-a-Dale (,ælənə'deɪl) *n* (in English balladry) a member of Robin Hood's band who saved his sweetheart from an enforced marriage and married her himself

allanite ('ælə,naɪt) *n* a rare black or brown mineral consisting of the hydrated silicate of calcium, aluminium, iron, cerium, lanthanum, and other rare earth minerals. It occurs in granites and other igneous rocks. Formula: $(Ca,Ce,La,Y)_2(Al,Fe,Be,Mn,Mg)_3(SiO_4)_3(OH)$ [C19 named after T. *Allan* (1777–1833), English mineralogist]

allantoid (ə'læntɔɪd) *adj* **1** relating to or resembling the allantois **2** *botany* shaped like a sausage ▷ *n* **3** another name for **allantois** [C17 from Greek *allantoeidēs* sausage-shaped, from *allas* sausage + -OID] > **allantoidal** (,ælən'tɔɪdəl) *adj*

allantoin (,ælən'təʊɪn) *n* a substance derived from the secretions of snails and contained in some plants, used in skin care products and valued for its soothing properties [C19 from ALLANTOIS]

allantois (,ælən'təʊɪs, ə'læntɔɪs) *n* a membranous sac growing out of the ventral surface of the hind gut of embryonic reptiles, birds, and mammals. It combines with the chorion to form the mammalian placenta [C17 New Latin, irregularly from Greek *allantoeidēs* sausage-shaped, ALLANTOID] > **allantoic** (,ælən'təʊɪk) *adj*

alla prima ('aːla 'priːmə) *adj* (of a painting) painted with a single layer of paint, in contrast to paintings built up layer by layer [C19 from Italian: at once]

allargando (,aːlaː'gændəʊ) *adj, adv music* (to be performed) with increasing slowness [Italian, from *allargare* to make slow or broad]

all-around *adj* (*prenominal*) the US equivalent of **all-round**

allay (ə'leɪ) *vb* **1** to relieve (pain, grief, etc) or be relieved **2** (*tr*) to reduce (fear, anger, etc) [Old English *alecgan* to put down, from *lecgan* to LAY¹]

All Blacks *pl n* **the** the international Rugby Union football team of New Zealand [so named because of the players' black playing strip]

all clear *n* **1** a signal, usually a siren, indicating that some danger, such as an air raid, is over **2** an

indication that obstacles are no longer present; permission to proceed: *he received the all clear on the plan*

all-dayer (,ɔː'ldeɪə) *n* an entertainment, such as a pop concert or film screening, that lasts all day

all-dressed *adj Canadian* (of a hot dog, hamburger, etc) served with all available garnishes

allegation (,ælɪ'geɪʃən) *n* **1** the act of alleging **2** an unproved statement or assertion, esp one in an accusation

allege (ə'lɛdʒ) *vb* (*tr; may take a clause as object*) **1** to declare in or as if in a court of law; state without or before proof: *he alleged malpractice* **2** to put forward (an argument or plea) for or against an accusation, claim, etc **3** *archaic* to cite or quote, as to confirm [C14 *aleggen*, ultimately from Latin *allēgāre* to dispatch on a mission, from *lēx* law]

alleged (ə'lɛdʒd) *adj* (*prenominal*) **1** stated or described to be such; presumed: *the alleged murderer* **2** dubious: *an alleged miracle*

allegedly (ə'lɛdʒɪdlɪ) *adv* **1** reportedly; supposedly: *payments allegedly made to a former colleague* **2** (*sentence modifier*) it is alleged that ▷ *interj* **3** an exclamation expressing disbelief or scepticism

▐ **USAGE** In recent years it has become common for speakers to include *allegedly* in statements that are controversial or possibly even defamatory. The implication is that, by saying *allegedly*, the speaker is distancing himself or herself from the controversy and even protecting himself or herself from possible prosecution. However, the effect created may be deliberate. The use of *allegedly* can be a signal that, although the statement may seem outrageous, it is in fact true: *He was drunk at work. Allegedly.* Conversely, it is also possible to use *allegedly* as an expression of ironic scepticism: *He's a hard worker. Allegedly*

Allegheny Mountains (,ælɪ'geɪnɪ) *or* **Alleghenies** *pl n* a mountain range in Pennsylvania, Maryland, Virginia, and West Virginia: part of the Appalachian system; rising from 600 m (2000 ft) to over 1440 m (4800 ft)

allegiance (ə'liːdʒəns) *n* **1** loyalty, as of a subject to his sovereign or of a citizen to his country **2** (in feudal society) the obligations of a vassal to his liege lord. See also **fealty, homage** (sense 2) [C14 from Old French *ligeance*, from *lige* LIEGE]

allegorical (,ælɪ'gɒrɪkəl) *or* **allegoric** *adj* used in, containing, or characteristic of allegory > **alle'gorically** *adv*

allegorize *or* **allegorise** ('ælɪgə,raɪz) *vb* **1** to transform (a story, narrative, fable, etc) into or compose in the form of allegory **2** (*tr*) to interpret allegorically > **allegori'zation** *or* **allegori'sation** *n*

allegory ('ælɪgərɪ) *n, pl* -**ries 1** a poem, play, picture, etc, in which the apparent meaning of the characters and events is used to symbolize a deeper moral or spiritual meaning **2** the technique or genre that this represents **3** use of such symbolism to illustrate truth or a moral **4** anything used as a symbol or emblem [C14 from Old French *allegorie*, from Latin *allēgoria*, from Greek, from *allēgorein* to speak figuratively, from *allos* other + *agoreuein* to make a speech in public, from *agora* a public gathering] > **'allegorist** *n*

allegretto (,ælɪ'grɛtəʊ) *music* ▷ *adj, adv* **1** (to be performed) fairly quickly or briskly ▷ *n, pl* -**tos 2** a piece or passage to be performed in this manner [C19 diminutive of ALLEGRO]

allegro (ə'leɪgrəʊ, -'lɛg-) *music* ▷ *adj* ▷ *adv* **1** (to be performed) quickly, in a brisk lively manner ▷ *n, pl* -**gros 2** a piece or passage to be performed in this manner [C17 from Italian: cheerful, from Latin *alacer* brisk, lively]

allele (ə'liːl) *n* any of two or more variants of a gene that have the same relative position on

homologous chromosomes and are responsible for alternative characteristics, such as smooth or wrinkled seeds in peas. Also called: **allelomorph** (ə'liːlə,mɔːf) See also **multiple alleles** [C20 from German *Allel*, shortened from *allelomorph*, from Greek *allēl-* one another + *morphē* form] > **al'lelic** *adj* > **al'lelism** *n*

allelopathy (,ælɪ'lɒpəθɪ) *n* the inhibitory effect of one living plant upon another by the release of toxic substances [from French *allélopathie*, from Greek *allēl-* one another + *pathos* suffering]

alleluia (,ælɪ'luːjə) *interj* **1** praise the Lord! Used more commonly in liturgical contexts in place of *hallelujah* ▷ *n* **2** a song of praise to God [C14 via Medieval Latin from Hebrew *hallelūyāh*]

allemande ('ælɪmænd; *French* almãd) *n* **1** the first movement of the classical suite, composed in a moderate tempo in a time signature of four-four **2** any of several German dances **3** a figure in country dancing or square dancing by means of which couples change position in the set [C17 from French *danse allemande* German dance]

Allen ('ælən) *n* **1 Bog of** a region of peat bogs in central Ireland, west of Dublin. Area: over 10 sq km (3.75 sq miles) **2 Lough** a lake in Ireland, in county Leitrim

Allen key *n* an L-shaped tool consisting of a rod having a hexagonal cross section, used to turn a screw (**Allen screw**) with a hexagonal recess in the head. A different size of key is required for each size of screw

Allentown ('ælən,taʊn) *n* a city in E Pennsylvania, on the Lehigh River. Pop: 105 958 (2003 est)

Alleppey ('ʌləpɪ) *n* a port in S India, in Kerala on the Malabar Coast. Pop: 177 079 (2001)

allergen ('ælə,dʒɛn) *n* any substance capable of inducing an allergy > **,aller'genic** *adj* > **,allerge'nicity** *n*

allergic (ə'lɜːdʒɪk) *adj* **1** of, relating to, having, or caused by an allergy **2** (*postpositive; foll by to*) *informal* having an aversion (to): *he's allergic to work*

allergic rhinitis *n pathol* a technical name for **hay fever**

allergist ('ælədʒɪst) *n* a physician skilled in the diagnosis and treatment of diseases or conditions caused by allergy

allergy ('ælədʒɪ) *n, pl* -**gies 1** a hypersensitivity to a substance that causes the body to react to any contact with that substance. Hay fever is an allergic reaction to pollen **2** *informal* aversion: *he has an allergy to studying* [C20 from German *Allergie* (indicating a changed reaction), from Greek *allos* other + *ergon* activity]

allethrin (æ'lɛθrɪn) *n* a clear viscous amber-coloured liquid used as an insecticide and synergist. Formula: $C_{19}H_{26}O_3$; relative density: 1.005 [C20 from ALL(YL) + (PYR)ETHRIN]

alleviate (ə'liːvɪ,eɪt) *vb* (*tr*) to make (pain, sorrow, etc) easier to bear; lessen; relieve [C15 from Late Latin *alleviāre* to mitigate, from Latin *levis* light] > **al,levi'ation** *n* > **al'leviative** *adj* > **al'levi,ator** *n*

▐ **USAGE** See at **ameliorate**

alley¹ ('ælɪ) *n* **1** a narrow lane or passage, esp one between or behind buildings **2** See **bowling alley 3** *tennis, chiefly US* the space between the singles and doubles sidelines **4** a walk in a park or garden, esp one lined with trees or bushes **5 up** (*or down*) **one's alley** a variant of **up one's street** (see **street** (sense 8)) [C14 from Old French *alee*, from *aler* to go, ultimately from Latin *ambulāre* to walk]

alley² ('ælɪ) *n* a large playing marble [C18 shortened and changed from ALABASTER]

alley cat *n* a homeless cat that roams in back streets

alley gate *n* a metal spiked gate erected behind a terrace of houses to deter burglars

alleyway ('ælɪ,weɪ) *n* a narrow passage; alley

all-fired *slang, chiefly US* ▷ *adj* **1** (*prenominal*) excessive; extreme ▷ *adv* **2** (intensifier): *don't be so all-fired sure of yourself!* [altered from *hell-fired*]

all-flying tail *n* a type of aircraft tailplane in which the whole of the tailplane is moved for control purposes

All Fools' Day *n* another name for **April Fools' Day** (see **April fool**)

all fours *n* **1** both the arms and legs of a person or all the legs of a quadruped (esp in the phrase **on all fours**) **2** another name for **seven-up**

all hail *interj* an archaic greeting or salutation [C14, literally: all health (to someone)]

Allhallows (ˌɔːlˈhæləʊz) *n* **1** a less common term for **All Saints' Day 2 Allhallows Eve** a less common name for **Halloween**

Allhallowtide (ˌɔːlˈhæləʊˌtaɪd) *n* the season of All Saints' Day (Allhallows)

allheal (ˈɔːlˌhiːl) *n* any of several plants reputed to have healing powers, such as selfheal and valerian

alliaceous (ˌælɪˈeɪʃəs) *adj* **1** of or relating to *Allium*, a genus of plants that have a strong onion or garlic smell and often have bulbs: family *Alliaceae.* The genus occurs in the N hemisphere and includes onion, garlic, leek, chive, and shallot **2** tasting or smelling like garlic or onions **3** of, relating to, or belonging to the *Alliaceae*, a family of flowering plants that includes the genus *Allium* [C18 from Latin *allium* garlic; see -ACEOUS]

alliance (əˈlaɪəns) *n* **1** the act of allying or state of being allied; union; confederation **2** a formal agreement or pact, esp a military one, between two or more countries to achieve a particular aim **3** the countries involved in such an agreement **4** a union between families through marriage **5** affinity or correspondence in qualities or characteristics **6** *botany* a taxonomic category consisting of a group of related families; subclass [C13 from Old French *aliance,* from *alier* to ALLY]

Alliance (əˈlaɪəns) *n* (in Britain) **a the** the Social Democratic Party and the Liberal Party acting or regarded as a political entity from 1981 to 1988 **b** (as modifier): *an Alliance candidate*

allied (əˈlaɪd, ˈælaɪd) *adj* **1** joined, as by treaty, agreement, or marriage; united **2** of the same type or class; related

Allied (ˈælaɪd) *adj* of or relating to the Allies

Allier (French alje) *n* **1** a department of central France, in Auvergne region. Capital: Moulins. Pop: 342 307 (2003 est). Area: 7382 sq km (2879 sq miles) **2** a river in S central France, rising in the Cévennes and flowing north to the Loire. Length: over 403 km (250 miles)

allies (ˈælaɪz) *n* the plural of **ally**

Allies (ˈælaɪz) *pl n* **1** (in World War I) the powers of the Triple Entente (France, Russia, and Britain) together with the nations allied with them **2** (in World War II) the countries that fought against the Axis. The main Allied powers were Britain and the Commonwealth countries, the US, the Soviet Union, France, China, and Poland. See also **Axis**

alligator (ˈælɪˌgeɪtə) *n* **1** a large crocodilian, *Alligator mississipiensis,* of the southern US, having powerful jaws and sharp teeth and differing from the crocodiles in having a shorter and broader snout: family *Alligatoridae* (alligators and caymans) **2** a similar but smaller species, *A. sinensis,* occurring in China near the Yangtse River **3** any crocodilian belonging to the family *Alligatoridae* **4** any of various tools or machines having adjustable toothed jaws, used for gripping, crushing, or compacting [C17 from Spanish *el lagarto* the lizard, from Latin *lacerta*]

alligator pear *n* another name for **avocado**

alligator pepper *n* chiefly W African **1** a tropical African zingiberaceous plant, *Amomum melegueta,* having red or orange spicy seed capsules **2** the capsules or seeds of this plant, used as a spice

all-important *adj* crucial; vital

all in *adj* **1** (postpositive) informal completely exhausted; tired out ▷ *adv, adj* (**all-in** when prenominal) **2 a** with all expenses or costs included in the price: *the flat is one hundred pounds a week all in* **b** (prenominal): *the all-in price is thirty pounds*

all-inclusive *adj* including everything; comprehensive

all-in wrestling *n* another name for **freestyle** (sense 2b)

alliterate (əˈlɪtəˌreɪt) *vb* **1** to contain or cause to contain alliteration **2** (*intr*) to speak or write using alliteration

alliteration (əˌlɪtəˈreɪʃən) *n* the use of the same consonant (**consonantal alliteration**) or of a vowel, not necessarily the same vowel (**vocalic alliteration**), at the beginning of each word or each stressed syllable in a line of verse, as in *around the rock the ragged rascal ran* [C17 from Medieval Latin *alliterātiō* (from Latin *al*– (see AD-) + *litera* letter), on the model of *obliterātiō* OBLITERATION] > al'literative *adj*

allium (ˈælɪəm) *n* any plant of the genus *Allium,* such as the onion, garlic, shallot, leek, or chive: family *Alliaceae* [C19 from Latin: garlic]

all-nighter (ˌɔːlˈnaɪtə) *n* an entertainment, such as a pop concert or film screening, that lasts all night

allo- *or before a vowel* **all-** *combining form* indicating difference, variation, or opposition: *allopathy; allomorph; allophone; allonym* [from Greek *allos* other, different]

Alloa (ˈæləʊə) *n* a town in E central Scotland, the administrative centre of Clackmannanshire. Pop: 18 989 (2001)

allocate (ˈæləˌkeɪt) *vb* (*tr*) **1** to assign or allot for a particular purpose **2** a less common word for **locate** (sense 2) [C17 from Medieval Latin *allocāre,* from Latin *locāre* to place, from *locus* a place] > 'allo,catable *adj*

allocation (ˌæləˈkeɪʃən) *n* **1** the act of allocating or the state of being allocated **2** a part that is allocated; share **3** *accounting, Brit* a system of dividing overhead expenses between the various departments of a business **4** *social welfare* (in a Social Services Department) the process of assigning **referrals** to individual workers, thus changing their status to **cases**

allochthonous (əˈlɒkθənəs) *adj* (of rocks, deposits, etc) found in a place other than where they or their constituents were formed. Compare **autochthonous** (sense 1) [C20 from Greek *allokhthon,* from ALLO- + *khthōn* (genitive *khthonos*) earth]

allocution (ˌæləˈkjuːʃən) *n* *rhetoric* a formal or authoritative speech or address, esp one that advises, informs, or exhorts [C17 from Late Latin *allocūtiō,* from Latin *alloquī* to address, from *loquī* to speak]

allodial (əˈləʊdɪəl) *adj* **1** (of land) held as an allodium **2** (of tenure) characterized by or relating to the system of holding land in absolute ownership: *the allodial system* **3** (of people) holding an allodium

allodium (əˈləʊdɪəm) *or* **allod** (ˈælɒd) *n, pl* -**lodia** (-ˈləʊdɪə) *or* -**lods** *history* lands held in absolute ownership, free from such obligations as rent or services due to an overlord. Also: **alodium** [C17 from Medieval Latin, from Old German *allōd* (unattested) entire property, from *al*– ALL + *-ōd* property; compare Old High German *ōt,* Old English *ēad* property]

allogamy (əˈlɒgəmɪ) *n* cross-fertilization in flowering plants > al'logamous *adj*

allograft (ˈæləʊˌgrɑːft) *n* a tissue graft from a donor genetically unrelated to the recipient

allograph (ˈæləˌgrɑːf) *n* **1** a document written by a person who is not a party to it **2** a signature made by one person on behalf of another. Compare **autograph 3** *linguistics* any of the written symbols that constitute a single grapheme: m *and* M *are allographs in the Roman alphabet* > allographic (ˌæləˈgræfɪk) *adj*

allomerism (əˈlɒməˌrɪzəm) *n* similarity of crystalline structure in substances of different chemical composition > allomeric (ˌæləˈmɛrɪk) *or* al'lomerous *adj*

allometry (əˈlɒmɪtrɪ) *n* **1** the study of the growth

of part of an organism in relation to the growth of the entire organism **2** a change in proportion of any of the parts of an organism that occurs during growth > allometric (ˌæləˈmɛtrɪk) *adj*

allomone (ˈæləˌməʊn) *n* a chemical substance secreted externally by certain animals, such as insects, affecting the behaviour or physiology of another species detrimentally. Compare **pheromone**

allomorph (ˈæləˌmɔːf) *n* **1** *linguistics* any of the phonological representations of a single morpheme. For example, the final (s) and (z) sounds of *bets* and *beds* are allomorphs of the English noun-plural morpheme **2** any of two or more different crystalline forms of a chemical compound, such as a mineral > ˌallo'morphic *adj*

allomorphism (ˌæləˈmɔːfɪzəm) *n* variation in the crystalline form of a chemical compound

allonym (ˈælənɪm) *n* a name, often one of historical significance or that of another person, assumed by a person, esp an author

allopath (ˈæləˌpæθ) *or* **allopathist** (əˈlɒpəθɪst) *n* a person who practises or is skilled in allopathy

allopathic (ˌæləˈpæθɪk) *adj* of, relating to, or used in allopathy > ˌallo'pathically *adv*

allopathy (əˈlɒpəθɪ) *n* the orthodox medical method of treating disease, by inducing a condition different from or opposed to the cause of the disease. Compare **homeopathy.** > allopathic (ˌæləˈpæθɪk) *adj* > ˌallo'pathically *adv*

allopatric (ˌæləˈpætrɪk) *adj* (of biological speciation or species) taking place or existing in areas that are geographically separated from one another. Compare **sympatric** [C20 from ALLO- + -*patric,* from Greek *patris* native land] > ˌallo'patrically *adv*

allophane (ˈæləˌfeɪn) *n* a variously coloured amorphous mineral consisting of hydrated aluminium silicate and occurring in cracks in some sedimentary rocks [C19 from Greek *allophanēs* appearing differently, from ALLO- + *phainesthai* to appear]

allophone (ˈæləˌfəʊn) *n* **1** any of several speech sounds that are regarded as contextual or environmental variants of the same phoneme. In English the aspirated initial (p) in *pot* and the unaspirated (p) in *spot* are allophones of the phoneme /p/ **2** *Canadian* a Canadian whose native language is neither French nor English > allophonic (ˌæləˈfɒnɪk) *adj*

alloplasm (ˈæləˌplæzəm) *n* *biology* part of the cytoplasm that is specialized to form cilia, flagella, and similar structures > ˌallo'plasmic *adj*

allopolyploid (ˌæləˈpɒlɪˌplɔɪd) *adj* **1** (of cells, organisms, etc) having more than two sets of haploid chromosomes inherited from different species ▷ *n* **2** an interspecific hybrid of this type that is therefore fertile ▷ See also **autopolyploid, polyploid.** > ˌallo'poly,ploidy *n*

allopurinol (ˌæləʊˈpjʊərɪˌnɒl) *n* a synthetic drug that reduces blood concentrations of uric acid and is administered orally in the treatment of gout. Formula: $C_5H_4N_4O$ [C20 from ALLO- + PURINE + -OL[1]]

All-Ordinaries Index *n* an index of share prices on the Australian Stock Exchange giving a weighted arithmetic average of 245 ordinary shares

allosaur (ˈæləˌsɔː) *or* **allosaurus** (ˌæləˈsɔːrəs) *n* any large carnivorous bipedal dinosaur of the genus *Antrodemus* (formerly *Allosaurus*), common in North America in late Jurassic times: suborder *Theropoda* (theropods) [C19 from ALLO- + -SAUR]

allosteric (ˌæləʊˈstɪərɪk) *adj* *biochem* of, relating to, or designating a function of an enzyme in which the structure and activity of the enzyme are modified by the binding of a metabolic molecule

allot (əˈlɒt) *vb* -**lots**, -**lotting**, -**lotted** (*tr*) **1** to assign or distribute (shares, etc) **2** to designate for a particular purpose: **3** (foll by *to*) apportion: *we allotted two hours to the case* [C16 from Old French *aloter,* from *lot* portion, LOT]

a

allotment (ə'lɒtmənt) *n* **1** the act of allotting; apportionment **2** a portion or amount allotted **3** *Brit* a small piece of usually public land rented by an individual for cultivation

allotrope ('ælə,trəʊp) *n* any of two or more physical forms in which an element can exist: *diamond and graphite are allotropes of carbon*

allotropous (ə'lɒtrəpəs) *adj* (of flowers) having the nectar accessible to any species of insect

allotropy (ə'lɒtrəpɪ) *or* **allotropism** *n* the existence of an element in two or more physical forms. The most common elements having this property are carbon, sulphur, and phosphorus ▷ allotropic (,ælə'trɒpɪk) *adj* ▷ ,allo'tropically *adv*

all'ottava (ælə'tɑːvə) *adj, adv music* to be played an octave higher or lower than written. Symbol: 8va [Italian: at the octave]

allottee (əlɒt'iː) *n* a person to whom something is allotted

allotype ('ælə,taɪp) *n* **1** *biology* an additional type specimen selected because of differences from the original type specimen, such as opposite sex or morphological details **2** *immunol* any of the variant forms of a particular immunoglobulin found among members of the same species

all-out *informal* ▷ *adj* **1** using one's maximum powers: *an all-out effort* ▷ *adv* **all out 2** to one's maximum effort or capacity: *he went all out on the home stretch*

all-over *adj* covering the entire surface

allow (ə'laʊ) *vb* **1** (*tr*) to permit (to do something); let **2** (*tr*) to set aside: *five hours were allowed to do the job* **3** (*tr*) to let enter or stay: *they don't allow dogs* **4** (*tr*) to acknowledge or concede (a point, claim, etc) **5** (*tr*) to let have; grant: *he was allowed few visitors* **6** (*intr*; foll by *for*) to take into account: *allow for delays* **7** (*intr*; often foll by *of*) to permit; admit: *a question that allows of only one reply* **8** (*tr*; may take a clause as object) *US dialect* to assert; maintain **9** (*tr*) *archaic* to approve; accept [C14 from Old French *alouer*, from Late Latin *allaudāre* to extol, influenced by Medieval Latin *allocāre* to assign, ALLOCATE]

allowable (ə'laʊəbᵊl) *adj* permissible; admissible ▷ al'lowably *adv*

allowance (ə'laʊəns) *n* **1** an amount of something, esp money or food, given or allotted usually at regular intervals **2** a discount, as in consideration for something given in part exchange or to increase business; rebate **3** (in Britain) an amount of a person's income that is not subject to a particular tax and is therefore deducted before his or her liability to taxation is assessed **4** a portion set aside to compensate for something or to cover special expenses **5** *Brit education* a salary supplement given to a teacher who is appointed to undertake extra duties and responsibilities **6** admission; concession **7** the act of allowing; sanction; toleration **8** something allowed **9** **make allowances** (*or* allowance) (usually foll by *for*) **a** to take mitigating circumstances into account in consideration (of) **b** to allow (for) ▷ *vb* **10** (*tr*) to supply (something) in limited amounts

Alloway ('æIə,weɪ) *n* a village in Scotland, in South Ayrshire, S of Ayr: birthplace of Robert Burns

allowedly (ə'laʊɪdlɪ) *adv* (*sentence modifier*) by general admission or agreement; admittedly

alloy *n* ('ælɔɪ, ə'lɔɪ) **1** a metallic material, such as steel, brass, or bronze, consisting of a mixture of two or more metals or of metallic elements with nonmetallic elements. Alloys often have physical properties markedly different from those of the pure metals **2** something that impairs the quality or reduces the value of the thing to which it is added ▷ *vb* (ə'lɔɪ) (*tr*) **3** to add (one metal or element to another metal or element) to obtain a substance with a desired property **4** to debase (a pure substance) by mixing with an inferior element **5** to diminish or impair [C16 from Old French *aloi* a mixture, from *aloier* to combine, from Latin *alligāre*, from *ligāre* to bind]

alloyed junction *n* a semiconductor junction used in some junction transistors and formed by alloying metal contacts, functioning as emitter and collector regions, to a wafer of semiconductor that acts as the base region. Compare **diffused junction**

allozyme ('æləʊ,zaɪm) *n* any one of a number of different structural forms of the same enzyme coded for by a different allele [C20 from ALLO- + (EN)ZYME]

all-points bulletin *n* (in the US) an alert broadcast to all police officers within an area, instructing the arrest of a suspect

all-powerful *adj* possessing supreme power; omnipotent

all right *adj* (*postpositive except in slang use*) **1** adequate; satisfactory **2** unharmed; safe **3** all-right *US slang* **a** acceptable: *an all-right book* **b** reliable: *an all-right guy* ▷ *sentence substitute* **4** very well: used to express assent ▷ *adv* **5** satisfactorily; adequately: *the car goes all right* **6** without doubt: *he's a bad one, all right* ▷ Also: **alright**

■ USAGE See at **alright**

all-round *adj* **1** efficient in all respects, esp in sport; versatile: *an all-round player* **2** comprehensive; many-sided; not narrow: *an all-round education*

all-rounder *n* a versatile person, esp in a sport

All Saints' Day *n* a Christian festival celebrated on Nov 1 to honour all the saints

allseed ('ɔːl,siːd) *n* any of several plants that produce many seeds, such as knotgrass

all-sorts *pl n* a mixture, esp a mixture of liquorice sweets

All Souls' Day *n* *RC Church* a day of prayer (Nov 2) for the dead in purgatory

allspice ('ɔːl,spaɪs) *n* **1** a tropical American myrtaceous tree, *Pimenta officinalis*, having small white flowers and aromatic berries **2** the whole or powdered seeds of this berry used as a spice, having a flavour said to resemble a mixture of cinnamon, cloves, and nutmeg ▷ Also called: pimento, Jamaica pepper

all square *adj* (*postpositive*) **1** mutually clear of all debts or obligations **2** (of contestants or teams in sports) having equal scores

all-star *adj* (*prenominal*) consisting of star performers

all-time *adj* (*prenominal*) *informal* unsurpassed in some respect at a particular time: *an all-time record at the Olympics*

all told *adv* (*sentence modifier*) taking every one into account; in all: *we were seven all told*

allude (ə'luːd) *vb* (*intr*; foll by *to*) **1** to refer indirectly, briefly, or implicitly **2** (loosely) to mention [C16 from Latin *allūdere*, from *lūdere* to sport, from *lūdus* a game]

■ USAGE Avoid confusion with **elude**

allure (ə'ljʊə, ə'lʊə) *vb* **1** (*tr*) to entice or tempt (someone) to a person or place or to a course of action; attract ▷ *n* **2** attractiveness; appeal: *the cottage's allure was its isolation* [C15 from Old French *alurer*, from *lure* bait, LURE] ▷ al'lurement *n* ▷ al'lurer *n*

alluring (ə'ljʊərɪŋ, ə'lʊə-) *adj* enticing; fascinating; attractive ▷ al'luringly *adv*

allusion (ə'luːʒən) *n* **1** the act of alluding **2** a passing reference; oblique or obscure mention [C16 from Late Latin *allūsiō*, from Latin *allūdere* to sport with, ALLUDE]

allusive (ə'luːsɪv) *adj* containing or full of allusions ▷ al'lusively *adv* ▷ al'lusiveness *n*

alluvial (ə'luːvɪəl) *adj* **1** of or relating to alluvium ▷ *n* **2** another name for **alluvium 3** *Austral and NZ* alluvium containing any heavy mineral, esp gold

alluvial fan *or* **cone** *n* a fan-shaped accumulation of silt, sand, gravel, and boulders deposited by fast-flowing mountain rivers when they reach flatter land

alluvial mining *n* a method of extracting minerals by dredging alluvial deposits

alluvion (ə'luːvɪən) *n* **1 a** the wash of the sea or of a river **b** an overflow or flood **c** matter deposited as sediment; alluvium **2** *law* the gradual formation of new land, as by the recession of the sea or deposit of sediment on a riverbed [C16 from Latin *alluviō* an overflowing, from *luere* to wash]

alluvium (ə'luːvɪəm) *n, pl* -viums *or* -via (-vɪə) a fine-grained fertile soil consisting of mud, silt, and sand deposited by flowing water on flood plains, in river beds, and in estuaries [C17 from Latin; see ALLUVION]

All Whites *pl n* **the** the former name for the international soccer team of New Zealand [so named because of the players' white strip and also an allusion to ALL BLACKS]

ally *vb* (ə'laɪ) -lies, -lying, -lied (usually foll by *to* or *with*) **1** to unite or be united, esp formally, as by treaty, confederation, or marriage **2** (*tr; usually passive*) to connect or be related, as through being similar or compatible ▷ *n* ('ælaɪ, ə'laɪ) *pl* -lies **3** a country, person, or group allied with another **4** a plant, animal, substance, etc, closely related to another in characteristics or form [C14 from Old French *alier* to join, from Latin *alligāre* to bind to, from *ligāre* to bind]

allyl ('ælaɪl, 'ælɪl) *n* (*modifier*) of, consisting of, or containing the monovalent group $CH_2:CHCH_2$: *allyl group or radical; allyl resin* [C19 from Latin *allium* garlic + -YL; first distinguished in a compound isolated from garlic]

allyl alcohol *n* a colourless pungent poisonous liquid used in the manufacture of resins, plasticizers, and other organic chemicals. Formula: $CH_2:CHCH_2OH$; relative density: 0.85; melting pt: −129°C; boiling pt: 96.9°C

allyl resin *n* any of several thermosetting synthetic resins made by polymerizing esters of allyl alcohol with a dibasic acid. They are used as adhesives

allyl sulphide *n* a colourless liquid that smells like garlic and is used as a flavouring. Formula: $(CH_2:CHCH_2)_2S$; relative density: 0.888; boiling pt.: 139°C

allyou ('ɔːl,juː, 'ɔː,jʊ) *pron* (*used in addressing more than one person*) *Caribbean informal* all of you

Alma-Ata (*Russian* al'maa'ta) *n* the former name of **Almaty**

Almada (*Portuguese* al'mɑːdə) *n* a town in S central Portugal, on the S bank of the Tagus estuary opposite Lisbon: statue of Christ 110 m (360 ft) high, erected 1959. Pop: 160 826 (2001)

Almadén (*Spanish* alma'ðen) *n* a town in S Spain: rich cinnabar mines, worked since Roman times. Pop: 6659 (2003 est)

Al Madinah (,æl mæ'diːnə) *n* the Arabic name for **Medina**

Almagest ('ælmə,dʒɛst) *n* **1** a work on astronomy compiled by Ptolemy in the 2nd century AD containing a description of the geocentric system of the universe and a star catalogue **2** (*sometimes not capital*) any of various similar medieval treatises on astrology, astronomy, or alchemy [C14 from Old French, from Arabic *al-majisti*, from *al* the + *majisti*, from Greek *megistē* greatest (treatise)]

alma mater ('ælmə 'mɑːtə, 'meɪtə) *n* (*often capitals*) one's school, college, or university [C17 from Latin: bountiful mother]

almanac ('ɔːlmə,næk) *n* a yearly calendar giving statistical information on events and phenomena, such as the phases of the moon, times of sunrise and sunset, tides, anniversaries, etc. Also (archaic): almanack [C14 from Medieval Latin *almanachus*, perhaps from Late Greek *almenikhiaka*]

almandine ('ælməndɪn, -,daɪn) *n* a deep violet-red garnet that consists of iron aluminium silicate and is used as a gemstone. Formula: $Fe_3Al_2(SiO_4)_3$ [C17 from French, from Medieval Latin *alabandīna*, from *Alabanda*, ancient city of Asia Minor where these stones were cut]

Al Mansûrah (,æl mæn'sʊərə) *n* a variant of **El Mansûra**

Al Marj (æl 'mɑːdʒ) *n* an ancient town in N Libya:

founded in about 550 BC Pop: 25 166 (latest est). Italian name: **Barce**

Almaty (æl'mɑːtɪ) *n* a city in SE Kazakhstan; capital of Kazakhstan (1991–97): an important trading centre. Pop: 1 103 000 (2005 est). Former name (until 1927): **Verny** Also called: **Alma-Ata**

Almelo (Dutch 'ɒlməloː) *n* a city in the E Netherlands, in Overijssel province. Pop: 72 000 (2003 est)

almemar (æl'miːmɑː) *n Judaism* (in Ashkenazic usage) the raised platform in a synagogue on which the reading desk stands. Also called: **bema**, **bimah**, **bima** [from Hebrew, from Arabic *al-minbar* the pulpit, platform]

Almería (*Spanish* alme'ria) *n* a port in S Spain. Pop: 176 727 (2003 est)

almighty (ɔːl'maɪtɪ) *adj* **1** all-powerful; omnipotent **2** *informal* (intensifier): *an almighty row* ▷ *adv* **3** *informal* (intensifier): *an almighty loud bang* > al'mightily *adv* > al'mightiness *n*

Almighty (ɔːl'maɪtɪ) *n* **the** another name for **God**

Almohade (ˈælmə,heɪd, -ˌheɪdɪ) *or* **Almohad** (ˈælmə,hæd) *n, pl* -**hades** *or* -**hads** a member of a group of puritanical Muslims, originally Berbers, who arose in S Morocco in the 12th century as a reaction against the corrupt Almoravides and who ruled Spain and all Maghrib from about 1147 to after 1213 [from Arabic *al-muwahhid*]

almond ('ɑːmənd) *n* **1** a small widely cultivated rosaceous tree, *Prunus amygdalus*, that is native to W Asia and has pink flowers and a green fruit containing an edible nutlike seed **2** the oval-shaped nutlike edible seed of this plant, which has a yellowish-brown shell **3** (*modifier*) made of or containing almonds: *almond cake*. Related adjs: **amygdaline**, **amygdaloid 4 a** a pale yellowish-brown colour **b** (*as adjective*): *almond wallpaper* **5** Also called: **almond green a** yellowish-green colour **b** (*as adjective*): *an almond skirt* **6** anything shaped like an almond nut [C13 from Old French *almande*, from Medieval Latin *amandula*, from Latin *amygdala*, from Greek *amugdalē*]

almond-eyed *adj* having narrow oval eyes

almoner ('ɑːmənə) *n* **1** *Brit obsolete* a trained hospital social worker responsible for the welfare of patients **2** (*formerly*) a person who distributes alms or charity on behalf of a household or institution [C13 from Old French *almosnier*, from *almosne* alms, from Vulgar Latin *alemosina* (unattested), from Late Latin *eleēmosyna*; see ALMS]

almonry ('ɑːmənrɪ) *n, pl* -**ries** *history* the house of an almoner, usually the place where alms were given [C15 from Old French *almosnerie*; see ALMONER, ALMS]

Almoravide (æl'mɔːrə,vaɪd) *or* **Almoravid** (æl'mɔːrəvɪd) *n* a member of a fanatical people of Berber origin and Islamic faith, who founded an empire in N Africa that spread over much of Spain in the 11th century AD [from Arabic *al-murābitūn* the holy ones]

almost ('ɔːlməʊst) *adv* little short of being; very nearly

alms (ɑːmz) *pl n* charitable donations of money or goods to the poor or needy [Old English *ælmysse*, from Late Latin *eleēmosyna*, from Greek *eleēmosunē* pity; see ELEEMOSYNARY]

almshouse ('ɑːmz,haʊs) *n* **1** *Brit history* a privately supported house offering accommodation to the aged or needy **2** *chiefly Brit* another name for **poorhouse**

almsman ('ɑːmzmən) *n, pl* -**men** *archaic* a person who gives or receives alms

almswoman ('ɑːmzwʊmən) *n, pl* -**women** *archaic* a woman who gives or receives alms

almucantar *or* **almacantar** (ˌælmə'kæntə) *n* **1** a circle on the celestial sphere parallel to the horizontal plane **2** an instrument for measuring altitudes [C14 from French, from Arabic *almukantarāt* sundial]

almuce ('ælmjuːs) *n* a fur-lined hood or cape formerly worn by members of certain religious orders, more recently by canons of France [C15

from Old French *aumusse*, from Medieval Latin *almucia*, of unknown origin]

Alnico ('ælnɪ,kəʊ) *n trademark* an alloy of aluminium, nickel, cobalt, iron, and copper, used to make permanent magnets

alocasia (ˌælə'keɪʃə) *n* any of various tropical plants of the genus *Alocasia*. See **aroid** [New Latin from Greek *kolokāsiā* lotus root]

alodium (ə'ləʊdɪəm) *n, pl* -**dia** (-dɪə) a variant spelling of **allodium**. > a'lodial *adj*

aloe ('æləʊ) *n, pl* -**oes 1** any plant of the liliaceous genus *Aloe*, chiefly native to southern Africa, with fleshy spiny-toothed leaves and red or yellow flowers **2** American aloe another name for **century plant** [C14 from Latin *aloē*, from Greek] > aloetic (ˌæləʊ'ɛtɪk) *adj*

aloes ('æləʊz) *n* (*functioning as singular*) **1** Also called: **aloes wood** another name for **eaglewood 2** bitter aloes a bitter purgative drug made from the leaves of several species of aloe

aloe vera ('æləʊ 'vɪərə) *n* **1** a juice obtained from the leaves of a liliaceous plant, *Aloe vera*, used as an emollient in skin and hair preparations **2** the juice of this plant, used in skin and hair preparations

aloft (ə'lɒft) *adv, adj* (*postpositive*) **1** in or into a high or higher place; up above **2** *nautical* in or into the rigging of a vessel [C12 from Old Norse *ā lopt* in the air; see LIFT[1], LOFT]

aloha (ə'ləʊə, ɑː'ləʊhɑː) *n, sentence substitute* a Hawaiian word for **hello** *or* **goodbye**

aloin ('æləʊɪn) *n* a bitter crystalline compound derived from various species of aloe: used as a laxative and flavouring agent [C19 from ALOE + -IN]

alone (ə'ləʊn) *adj* (*postpositive*) ▷ *adv* **1** apart from another or others; solitary **2** without anyone or anything else: *one man alone could lift it* **3** without equal; unique: *he stands alone in the field of microbiology* **4** to the exclusion of others; only: *she alone believed him* **5** leave *or* let alone *or* be to refrain from annoying or interfering with **6** leave *or* let well (enough) alone to refrain from interfering with something that is satisfactory **7** let alone much less; not to mention: *he can't afford beer, let alone whisky* [Old English *al one*, literally: all (entirely) one]

along (ə'lɒŋ) *prep* **1** over or for the length of, esp in a more or less horizontal plane: *along the road* ▷ *adv* **2** continuing over the length of some specified thing **3** in accompaniment; together with some specified person or people: *he says he'd like to come along* **4** forward: *the horse trotted along at a steady pace* **5** to a more advanced state: *he got the work moving along* **6** along with accompanying; together with: *consider the advantages along with the disadvantages* [Old English *andlang*, from *and-* against + *lang* LONG[1]; compare Old Frisian *andlinga*, Old Saxon *antlang*]

▪ USAGE See at **plus**

alongshore (ə,lɒŋ'ʃɔː) *adv, adj* (*postpositive*) close to, by, or along a shore

alongside (ə'lɒŋ,saɪd) *prep* **1** (*often foll by of*) along the side of; along beside: *alongside the quay* ▷ *adv* **2** along the side of some specified thing: *come alongside*

aloof (ə'luːf) *adj* distant, unsympathetic, or supercilious in manner, attitude, or feeling [C16 from A-[1] + *loof*, a variant of LUFF] > a'loofly *adv* > a'loofness *n*

alopecia (ˌælə'piːʃɪə) *n* loss of hair, esp on the head; baldness [C14 from Latin, from Greek *alōpekia*, originally: mange in foxes, from *alōpēx* fox]

Alost (*French* alɔst) *n* a town in central Belgium, in East Flanders province. Pop: 76 852 (2004 est). Flemish name: **Aalst**

aloud (ə'laʊd) *adv, adj* (*postpositive*) **1** in a normal voice; not in a whisper **2** in a spoken voice; not silently **3** *archaic* in a loud voice

alow (ə'ləʊ) *adv, adj* (*postpositive*) *nautical* in or into the lower rigging of a vessel, near the deck

alp (ælp) *n* **1** (in the European Alps) an area of

pasture above the valley bottom but below the mountain peaks **2** a high mountain ▷ See also **Alps, Australian Alps** [C14 back formation from *Alps*, from French *Alpes* (pl), from Latin *Alpēs*, from Greek *Alpeis*]

ALP *abbreviation for* Australian Labor Party

alpaca[1] (æl'pækə) *n* **1** a domesticated cud-chewing artiodactyl mammal, *Lama pacos*, closely related to the llama and native to South America: family *Camelidae*. Its dark shaggy hair is a source of wool **2** the cloth made from the wool of this animal **3** a glossy fabric simulating this, used for linings, etc [C18 via Spanish from Aymara *allpaca*]

alpaca[2] *or sometimes* **alpacca** (æl'pækə) *n* a type of nickel silver used in jewellery [of uncertain origin]

alpenglow ('ælpən,gləʊ) *n* a reddish light on the summits of snow-covered mountain peaks at sunset or sunrise [partial translation of German *Alpenglühen*, from *Alpen* ALPS + *glühen* to GLOW]

alpenhorn ('ælpən,hɔːn) *n* another name for **alphorn**

alpenstock ('ælpən,stɒk) *n* an early form of ice axe, consisting of a stout stick with an iron tip and sometimes having a pick and adze at the head, formerly used by mountain climbers [C19 from German, from *Alpen* ALPS + *Stock* STICK[1]]

Alpes-de-Haute-Provence (*French* alpdəotprovɑ̃s) *n* a department of SE France in Provence-Alpes-Côte-d'Azur region. Capital: Digne. Pop: 144 508 (2003 est). Area: 6988 sq km (2725 sq miles). Former name: **Basses-Alpes**

Alpes-Maritimes (*French* alp maritim) *n* a department of the SE corner of France in Provence-Alpes-Côte-d'Azur region. Capital: Nice. Pop: 1 045 973 (2003 est). Area: 4298 sq km (1676 sq miles)

alpestrine (æl'pɛstrɪn) *adj* (of plants) growing at high altitudes; subalpine [C19 from Medieval Latin *alpestris*, from Latin *Alpēs* the Alps]

alpha ('ælfə) *n* **1** the first letter in the Greek alphabet (Α, α), a vowel transliterated as *a* **2** *Brit* the highest grade or mark, as in an examination **3** (*modifier*) **a** involving or relating to helium-4 nuclei: *an alpha particle* **b** relating to one of two or more allotropes or crystal structures of a solid: *alpha iron* **c** relating to one of two or more isomeric forms of a chemical compound, esp one in which a group is attached to the carbon atom to which the principal group is attached **4** (*modifier*) denoting the dominant person or animal in a group: *the alpha male* [via Latin from Greek, of Phoenician origin; related to Hebrew *āleph*, literally: ox]

Alpha ('ælfə) *n* **1** (*foll by the genitive case of a specified constellation*) usually the brightest star in a constellation: *Alpha Centauri* **2** *communications* a code word for the letter *a*

alpha and omega *n* **1** the first and last, a phrase used in Revelation 1:8 to signify God's eternity **2** the basic reason or meaning; most important part

alphabet ('ælfə,bɛt) *n* **1** a set of letters or other signs used in a writing system, usually arranged in a fixed order, each letter or sign being used to represent one or sometimes more than one phoneme in the language being transcribed **2** any set of symbols or characters, esp one representing sounds of speech **3** basic principles or rudiments, as of a subject [C15 from Late Latin *alphabētum*, from Greek *alphabētos*, from the first two letters of the Greek alphabet; see ALPHA, BETA]

alphabetical (ˌælfə'bɛtɪkəl) *or* **alphabetic** *adj* **1** in the conventional order of the letters or symbols of an alphabet **2** of, characterized by, or expressed by an alphabet > ˌalpha'betically *adv*

alphabetize *or* **alphabetise** ('ælfəbə,taɪz) *vb (tr)* **1** to arrange in conventional alphabetical order **2** to express by an alphabet > ˌalphabeti'zation *or* ˌalphabeti'sation *n* > 'alphabet,izer *or* 'alphabet,iser *n*

alpha-blocker *n* any of a class of drugs that prevent the stimulation of alpha adrenoceptors, a type of receptor in the sympathetic nervous system, by adrenaline and noradrenaline and that therefore cause widening of blood vessels: used in the treatment of high blood pressure and prostatic hyperplasia

Alpha Centauri system (sɛnˈtɔːrɪ) *n* a star system comprising the binary star **Alpha Centauri A** and **B** and Proxima Centauri (also called **Alpha Centauri C**), which is 0.1 light years closer to the sun. Visual magnitude: 0.01 (A), 1.33 (B); spectral type: G2V (A); distance from earth: 4.3 light years. Also called: Rigil Kent See also **Proxima**

alpha decay *n* the radioactive decay process resulting in emission of alpha particles

alpha emitter *n* a radioactive isotope that emits alpha particles

alpha-fetoprotein (ˌælfəˌfiːtəʊˈprəʊtiːn) *n* a protein that forms in the liver of the human fetus. Excessive quantities in the amniotic fluid and maternal blood may indicate spina bifida in the fetus; low levels may point to Down's syndrome. Abbreviation: **afp**

alpha geek *n slang* the person in a group or office who has the most knowledge about computer technology

alpha helix *n biochem* a helical conformation of a polypeptide chain, found abundantly in the structure of proteins

alpha-hydroxy acid *n* a type of organic acid, commonly used in skin-care preparations, that has a hydroxyl group attached to the carbon atom next to the carbon atom carrying the carboxyl group

alpha iron *n* a magnetic allotrope of iron that is stable below 910°C; ferrite

alpha-linolenic acid *n* another name for **lenolenic acid**

alpha male *n* the dominant male animal or person in a group

alphanumeric (ˌælfənjuːˈmɛrɪk) *or* **alphameric** (ˌælfəˈmɛrɪk) *adj* (of a character set, code, or file of data) consisting of alphabetical and numerical symbols > ˌalphanuˈmerically *or* ˌalphaˈmerically *adv*

alpha particle *n* a helium-4 nucleus, containing two neutrons and two protons, emitted during some radioactive transformations

alpha privative *n* (in Greek grammar) the letter alpha (or *an-* before vowels) used as a negative or privative prefix. It appears in English words derived from Greek, as in *atheist, anaesthetic*

alpha radiation *n* alpha particles emitted from a radioactive isotope

alpha ray *n* ionizing radiation consisting of a stream of alpha particles

alpha rhythm *or* **wave** *n physiol* the normal bursts of electrical activity from the cerebral cortex of a drowsy or inactive person, occurring at a frequency of 8 to 12 hertz and detectable with an electroencephalograph. See also **brain wave**

alpha stock *n* any of the most active securities on the Stock Exchange of which there are between 100 and 200; at least ten market makers must continuously display the prices of an alpha stock and all transactions in them must be published immediately

alpha-test *n* **1** an in-house test of a new or modified piece of computer software > *vb* (*tr*) **2** to test (software) in this way. Compare **beta-test**

Alpheus (ælˈfiːəs) *n Greek myth* a river god, lover of the nymph Arethusa. She changed into a spring to evade him, but he changed into a river and mingled with her

Alphonsus (ælˈfɒnsəs) *n* a crater in the SE quadrant of the moon, about 112 km in diameter, in which volcanic activity may have occurred

alphorn (ˈælpˌhɔːn) *or* **alpenhorn** *n music* a wind instrument used in the Swiss Alps, consisting of a very long tube of wood or bark with a cornet-like mouthpiece [c19 from German *Alpenhorn* Alps horn]

alphosis (ælˈfəʊsɪs) *n pathol* absence of skin

pigmentation, as in albinism [c19 from New Latin, from Greek *alphos* leprosy]

alpine (ˈælpaɪn) *adj* **1** of or relating to high mountains **2** (of plants) growing on mountains, esp above the limit for tree growth **3** connected with or used in mountaineering in medium-sized glaciated mountain areas such as the Alps **4** *skiing* of or relating to racing events on steep prepared slopes, such as the slalom and downhill. Compare **nordic** ▷ *n* **5** a plant that is native or suited to alpine conditions

Alpine (ˈælpaɪn) *adj* **1** of or relating to the Alps or their inhabitants **2** *geology* **a** of or relating to an episode of mountain building in the Tertiary period during which the Alps were formed **b** of or relating to a high mountainous environment heavily modified by glacial erosion

alpine-style *adj, adv mountaineering* of or in an ascent (esp in high mountains like the Himalayas) in which the climbers carry all their equipment with them in a single ascent from base to summit

alpinist (ˈælpɪnɪst) *n* a mountaineer who climbs in medium-sized glaciated mountain areas such as the Alps > ˈalpinism *n*

Alps (ælps) *pl n* **1** a mountain range in S central Europe, extending over 1000 km (650 miles) from the Mediterranean coast of France and NW Italy through Switzerland, N Italy, and Austria to Slovenia. Highest peak: Mont Blanc, 4807 m (15 771 ft) **2** a range of mountains in the NW quadrant of the moon, which is cut in two by a straight fracture, the **Alpine Valley**

al-Qaeda *or* **al-Qaida** (ælˈkaɪdə, ælkɑːˈiːdə) *n* a loosely-knit militant Islamic organization led and funded by Osama bin Laden, and whom it was established in the late 1980s from Arab volunteers who had fought the Soviet troops previously based in Afghanistan; known or believed to be behind a number of operations against Western, especially US, interests, including bomb attacks on two US embassies in Africa in 1998 and the destruction of the World Trade Center in New York in 2001 [c20 from Arabic *al-qa'ida* the base]

already (ɔːlˈrɛdɪ) *adv* **1** by or before a stated or implied time: *he is already here* **2** at a time earlier than expected: *is it ten o'clock already?*

alright (ɔːlˈraɪt) *adv, sentence substitute, adj* a variant spelling of **all right**

> **USAGE** The form *alright*, though very common, is still considered by many people to be wrong or less acceptable than *all right*

ALS *abbreviation for* autograph letter signed

Alsace (ælˈsæs; *French* alzas) *n* a region and former province of NE France, between the Vosges mountains and the Rhine: famous for its wines. Area: 8280 sq km (3196 sq miles). Ancient name: Alsatia German name: Elsass

Alsace-Lorraine *n* an area of NE France, comprising the modern regions of Alsace and Lorraine: under German rule 1871–1919 and 1940–44. Area: 14 522 sq km (5607 sq miles). German name: Elsass-Lothringen

Alsatia (ælˈseɪʃə) *n* **1** the ancient name for **Alsace** **2** an area around Whitefriars, London, in the 17th century, which was a sanctuary for criminals and debtors

Alsatian (ælˈseɪʃən) *n* **1** a large wolflike breed of dog often used as a guard or guide dog and by the police. Also called: German shepherd, German shepherd dog **2** a native or inhabitant of Alsace **3** (in the 17th century) a criminal or debtor who took refuge in the Whitefriars area of London ▷ *adj* **4** of or relating to Alsace or its inhabitants

alsike (ˈælsaɪk, -sɪk, ˈɔːl-) *n* a clover, *Trifolium hybridum*, native to Europe and Asia but widely cultivated as a forage crop. It has trifoliate leaves and pink or whitish flowers. Also called: alsike clover [c19 named after *Alsike*, Sweden]

Al Sirat (ˌæl sɪˈræt) *n Islam* **1** the correct path of religion **2** the razor-edged bridge by which all

who enter paradise must pass [from Arabic: the road, from Latin *via strāta* paved way]

also (ˈɔːlsəʊ) *adv* **1** (*sentence modifier*) in addition; as well; too ▷ *sentence connector* **2** besides; moreover [Old English *alswā*; related to Old High German *alsō*, Old Frisian *alsa*; see ALL, SO[1]]

also-ran *n* **1** a contestant, horse, etc, failing to finish among the first three in a race **2** an unsuccessful person; loser or nonentity

alstroemeria (ˌælstrəˈmiːrɪə) *n* any plant of the tuberous perennial liliaceous genus *Alstroemeria*, originally S American, grown for their brightly coloured orchid-like flowers. Also called: Peruvian lily [named by Linnaeus for his friend Baron Klas von *Alstroemer*]

alt (ælt) *music* ▷ *adj* **1** (esp of vocal music) high in pitch **2** of or relating to the octave commencing with the G above the top line of the treble staff ▷ *n* **3** in alt in the octave directly above the treble staff [c16 from Provençal, from Latin *altus* high, deep]

Alta. *abbreviation for* Alberta

Altaic (ælˈteɪɪk) *n* **1** a postulated family of languages of Asia and SE Europe, consisting of the Turkic, Mongolic, and Tungusic branches, and perhaps also Japanese, Korean, and Ainu. See also **Ural-Altaic** ▷ *adj* **2** denoting, belonging to, or relating to this linguistic family or its speakers

Altai Mountains (ɑːlˈtaɪ) *pl n* a mountain system of central Asia, in W Mongolia, W China, and S Russia. Highest peak: Belukha, 4506 m (14 783 ft)

Altair (ælˈteə) *n* the brightest star in the constellation Aquila. Visual magnitude: 0.77; spectral type: A7V; distance: 16.8 light years [Arabic, from *al* the + *tā'ir* bird]

Altai Republic *n* another name for **Gorno-Altai Republic**

Altamira (*Spanish* altaˈmira) *n* a cave in N Spain, SW of Santander, noted for Old Stone Age wall drawings

altar (ˈɔːltə) *n* **1** a raised place or structure where sacrifices are offered and religious rites performed **2** (in Christian churches) the communion table **3** a step in the wall of a dry dock upon which structures supporting a vessel can stand **4** lead to the altar *informal* to marry [Old English, from Latin *altāria* (plural) altar, from *altus* high]

altar boy *n RC Church, Church of England* a boy serving as an acolyte

altar cloth *n Christianity* the cloth used for covering an altar: often applied also to the frontal

altarpiece (ˈɔːltəˌpiːs) *n* a work of art set above and behind an altar; a reredos

altazimuth (ælˈtæzɪməθ) *n* an instrument for measuring the altitude and azimuth of a celestial body by the horizontal and vertical rotation of a telescope [c19 from ALT(ITUDE) + AZIMUTH]

altazimuth mounting *n* a telescope mounting that allows motion of the telescope about a vertical axis (in azimuth) and a horizontal axis (in altitude)

alt.country (ˈɔːlt) *n* a genre of country music originating in the 1990s and influenced by both early country music and contemporary rock music [c20 from ALT(ERNATIVE) + COUNTRY]

Altdorf (*German* ˈaltdɔrf) *n* a town in central Switzerland, capital of Uri canton: setting of the William Tell legend. Pop: 8541 (2000)

Alte Pinakothek (*German* ˈaltə pinakoˈteːk) *n* a museum in Munich housing a collection of paintings dating from the Middle Ages to the late 18th century

alter (ˈɔːltə) *vb* **1** to make or become different in some respect; change **2** (*tr*) *informal, chiefly US* a euphemistic word for **castrate** *or* **spay** [c14 from Old French *alterer*, from Medieval Latin *alterāre* to change, from Latin *alter* other] > ˈalterable *adj* > ˈaltera'bility *n*

alteration (ˌɔːltəˈreɪʃən) *n* **1** an adjustment, change, or modification **2** the act of altering or state of being altered

alterative (ˈɔːltərətɪv) *adj* **1** likely or able to

produce alteration **2** *obsolete* (of a drug) able to restore normal health ▷ *n* **3** *obsolete* a drug that restores normal health

altercate (ˈɔːltəˌkeɪt) *vb* (*intr*) to argue, esp heatedly; dispute [c16 from Latin *altercārī* to quarrel with another, from *alter* other]

altercation (ˌɔːltəˈkeɪʃən) *n* an angry or heated discussion or quarrel; argument

altered chord *n music* a chord in which one or more notes are chromatically changed by the introduction of accidentals

alter ego (ˈæltər ˈiːɡəʊ, ˈɛɡəʊ) *n* **1** a second self **2** a very close and intimate friend [Latin: other self]

alternant (ɔːˈltɜːnənt) *adj* alternating [c17 from French, from Latin *alternāre* to ALTERNATE]

alternate *vb* (ˈɔːltəˌneɪt) **1** (often foll by *with*) to occur or cause to occur successively or by turns: *day and night alternate* **2** (*intr*; often foll by *between*) to swing repeatedly from one condition, action, etc, to another: *he alternates between success and failure* **3** (*tr*) to interchange regularly or in succession **4** (*intr*) (of an electric current, voltage, etc) to reverse direction or sign at regular intervals, usually sinusoidally, the instantaneous value varying continuously **5** (*intr*; often foll by *for*) *theatre* to understudy another actor or actress ▷ *adj* (ɔːˈltɜːnɪt) **6** occurring by turns: *alternate feelings of love and hate* **7** every other or second one of a series: *he came to work on alternate days* **8** being a second or further choice; alternative: *alternate director* **9** *botany* **a** (of leaves, flowers, etc) arranged singly at different heights on either side of the stem **b** (of parts of a flower) arranged opposite the spaces between other parts. Compare **opposite** (sense 4) ▷ *n* (ˈɔːltənɪt, ɔːˈlˈtɜːnɪt) **10** *US and Canadian* a person who substitutes for another in his absence; stand-in [c16 from Latin *alternāre* to do one thing and then another, from *alternus* one after the other, from *alter* other]

alternate angles *pl n* two angles at opposite ends and on opposite sides of a transversal cutting two lines

alternately (ɔːˈlˈtɜːnɪtlɪ) *adv* in an alternating sequence or position

alternating current *n* a continuous electric current that periodically reverses direction, usually sinusoidally. Abbreviation: AC Compare **direct current**

alternating-gradient focusing *n physics* a method of focusing beams of charged particles in high-energy accelerators, in which a series of magnetic or electrostatic lenses alternately converge and diverge the beam, producing a net focusing effect and thus preventing the beam from spreading

alternation (ˌɔːltəˈneɪʃən) *n* **1** successive change from one condition or action to another and back again repeatedly **2** *logic* another name for **disjunction** (sense 3)

alternation of generations *n* the production within the life cycle of an organism of alternating asexual and sexual reproductive forms. It occurs in many plants and lower animals. Also called: **metagenesis, heterogenesis, digenesis, xenogenesis**

alternative (ɔːˈlˈtɜːnətɪv) *n* **1** a possibility of choice, esp between two things, courses of action, etc **2** either of such choices: *we took the alternative of walking* ▷ *adj* **3** presenting a choice, esp between two possibilities only **4** (of two things) mutually exclusive **5** denoting a lifestyle, culture, art form, etc, regarded by its adherents as preferable to that of contemporary society because it is less conventional, materialistic, or institutionalized, and, often, more in harmony with nature **6** *logic* another word for **disjunctive** (sense 3) ▷ alˈternatively *adv* ▷ alˈternativeness *n*

alternative curriculum *n Brit education* any course of study offered as an alternative to the National Curriculum

alternative energy *n* a form of energy derived from a natural source, such as the sun, wind, tides, or waves. Also called: renewable energy

alternative history *or esp US* **alternate history** *n* a genre of fiction in which the author speculates on how the course of history might have been altered if a particular historical event had had a different outcome

alternative hypothesis *n statistics* the hypothesis that given data do not conform with a given null hypothesis: the null hypothesis is accepted only if its probability exceeds a predetermined significance level. See **hypothesis testing** Compare **null hypothesis**

Alternative Investment Market *n* a market on the London Stock Exchange enabling small companies to raise capital and have their shares traded in a market without the expenses of a main-market listing. Abbreviation: AIM

alternative medicine *n* another name for **complementary medicine** See also **holism** (sense 2)

Alternative Vote *n* (*modifier*) of or relating to a system of voting in which voters list the candidates in order of preference. If no candidate obtains more than 50% of first-preference votes, the votes for the bottom candidate are redistributed according to the voters' next preference. See **proportional representation**

alternator (ˈɔːltəˌneɪtə) *n* an electrical machine that generates an alternating current

althaea *or US* **althea** (ælˈθiːə) *n* **1** any Eurasian plant of the malvaceous genus *Althaea*, such as the hollyhock, having tall spikes of showy white, yellow, or red flowers **2** another name for **rose of Sharon** (sense 2) [c17 from Latin *althaea*, from Greek *althaia* marsh mallow (literally: healing plant), from Greek *althein* to heal]

Althing (ˈælθɪŋ) *n* the bicameral parliament of Iceland

althorn (ˈæltˌhɔːn) *n* a valved brass musical instrument belonging to the saxhorn or flügelhorn families

Althorp House (ˈɔːlθɔːp, -θrəp) *n* a mansion in Northamptonshire: seat of the Earls Spencer since 1508; originally a medieval house; altered (1787) to its present neoclassical style by Henry Holland. Diana, Princess of Wales is buried on Round Oval Island in the centre of the ornamental lake in Althorp Park

although (ɔːlˈðəʊ) *conj* (*subordinating*) despite the fact that; even though: *although she was ill, she worked hard*

alti- *combining form* indicating height or altitude: *altimeter* [from Latin *altus* high]

altimeter (ælˈtɪmɪtə, ˈæltɪˌmiːtə) *n* an instrument that indicates height above sea level, esp one based on an aneroid barometer and fitted to an aircraft

altimetry (ælˈtɪmɪtrɪ) *n* the science of measuring altitudes, as with an altimeter ▷ altimetrical (ˌæltɪˈmɛtrɪkəl) *adj* ▷ altiˈmetrically *adv*

Altiplano (*Spanish* altiˈplano) *n* a plateau of the Andes, covering two thirds of Bolivia and extending into S Peru: contains Lake Titicaca. Height: 3000 m (10 000 ft) to 3900 m (13 000 ft)

altissimo (ælˈtɪsɪˌməʊ) *adj* **1** (of music) very high in pitch **2** of or relating to the octave commencing on the G lying an octave above the treble clef ▷ *n* **3** in altissimo in the octave commencing an octave above the treble clef [Italian, literally: highest]

altitude (ˈæltɪˌtjuːd) *n* **1** the vertical height of an object above some chosen level, esp above sea level; elevation **2** *geometry* the perpendicular distance from the vertex to the base of a geometrical figure or solid **3** Also called: elevation *astronomy, navigation* the angular distance of a celestial body from the horizon measured along the vertical circle passing through the body. Compare **azimuth** (sense 1) **4** *surveying* the angle of elevation of a point above the horizontal plane of the observer **5** (*often plural*) a high place or region [c14 from Latin *altitūdō*, from *altus* high, deep] > ˌaltiˈtudinal *adj*

altitude sickness *n* another name for **mountain sickness**

alto (ˈæltəʊ) *n, pl* -tos **1** the highest adult male voice; countertenor **2** (in choral singing) a shortened form of **contralto 3** a singer with such a voice **4** another name for **viola**[1] (sense 1) **5** a flute, saxophone, etc, that is the third or fourth highest instrument in its group ▷ *adj* **6** denoting a flute, saxophone, etc, that is the third or fourth highest instrument in its group [c18 from Italian: high, from Latin *altus*]

alto- *combining form* high: *altocumulus; altostratus* [from Latin *altus* high]

alto clef *n* the clef that establishes middle C as being on the third line of the staff. Also called: viola clef See also **C clef**

altocumulus (ˌæltəʊˈkjuːmjʊləs) *n, pl* -li (-laɪ) a globular cloud at an intermediate height of about 2400 to 6000 metres (8000 to 20 000 feet)

altogether (ˌɔːltəˈɡɛðə, ˈɔːltəˌɡɛðə) *adv* **1** with everything included: *altogether he owed me sixty pounds* **2** completely; utterly; totally: *he was altogether mad* **3** on the whole: *altogether it was a very good party* ▷ *n* **4** in the altogether *informal* naked

alto horn *n* another term for **althorn**

altoist (ˈæltəʊɪst) *n* a person who plays the alto saxophone

Alton Towers (ˈɒltən) *n* a 19th-century Gothic Revival mansion with extensive gardens in NW central England, in Staffordshire: site of a large amusement park

alto-relievo *or* **alto-rilievo** (ˌæltəʊrɪˈliːvəʊ) *n, pl* -vos another name for **high relief** [c18 from Italian]

altostratus (ˌæltəʊˈstreɪtəs, -ˈstrɑː-) *n, pl* -ti (-taɪ) a layer cloud at an intermediate height of about 2400 to 6000 metres (8000 to 20 000 feet)

altrices (ælˈtraɪsiːz) *pl n* altricial birds

altricial (ælˈtrɪʃəl) *adj* **1** (of the young of some species of birds after hatching) naked, blind, and dependent on the parents for food ▷ *n* **2** an altricial bird, such as a pigeon ▷ Compare **precocial** [c19 from New Latin *altriciālis*, from Latin *altrix* a nurse, from *alere* to nourish]

Altrincham (ˈɔːltrɪŋəm) *n* a residential town in NW England, in Trafford unitary authority, Greater Manchester. Pop: 40 695 (2001)

alt.rock (ɔːlt) *n* a genre of rock music regarded by its practitioners and fans as being outside the mainstream [c20 from ALT(ERNATIVE) + ROCK]

altruism (ˈæltruːˌɪzəm) *n* **1** the principle or practice of unselfish concern for the welfare of others **2** the philosophical doctrine that right action is that which produces the greatest benefit to others ▷ Compare **egoism** See also **utilitarianism** [c19 from French *altruisme*, from Italian *altrui* others, from Latin *alterī*, plural of *alter* other] > ˈaltruist *n* > ˌaltruˈistic *adj* > ˌaltruˈistically *adv*

ALU *computing* abbreviation for arithmetic and logic unit

aludel (ˈæljʊˌdɛl) *n chem* a pear-shaped vessel, open at both ends, formerly used with similar vessels for collecting condensates, esp for subliming mercury [c16 via Old French from Spanish, from Arabic *al-uthāl* the vessel]

alula (ˈæljʊlə) *n, pl* -lae (-liː) another name for **bastard wing** [c18 New Latin: a little wing, from Latin *āla* a wing] > ˈalular *adj*

alum (ˈæləm) *n* **1** Also called: potash alum a colourless soluble hydrated double sulphate of aluminium and potassium used in the manufacture of mordants and pigments, in dressing leather and sizing paper, and in medicine as a styptic and astringent. Formula: $K_2SO_4.Al_2(SO_4)_3.24H_2O$ **2** any of a group of isomorphic double sulphates of a monovalent metal or group and a trivalent metal. Formula: $X_2SO_4.Y_2(SO_4)_3.24H_2O$, where X is monovalent and Y is trivalent [c14 from Old French, from Latin *alūmen*]

a

alumina (ə'lu:mɪnə) *n* another name for **aluminium oxide** [c18 from New Latin, plural of Latin *alūmen* ALUM]

aluminate (ə'lu:mɪneɪt) *n* a salt of the ortho or meta acid forms of aluminium hydroxide containing the ions AlO$_2^-$ or AlO$_3^{3-}$

aluminiferous (ˌəˌlu:mɪ'nɪfərəs) *adj* containing or yielding aluminium or alumina

aluminium (ˌæljʊ'mɪnɪəm) *or US and Canadian* **aluminum** (ə'lu:mɪnəm) *n* a light malleable ductile silvery-white metallic element that resists corrosion; the third most abundant element in the earth's crust (8.1 per cent), occurring only as a compound, principally as bauxite. It is used, esp in the form of its alloys, in aircraft parts, kitchen utensils, etc. Symbol: Al; atomic no: 13; atomic wt: 26.9815; valency: 3; relative density: 2.699; melting pt: 660.45°C; boiling pt: 2520°C

aluminium bronze *n* any of a range of copper alloys that contain between 5 and 10 per cent aluminium

aluminium hydroxide *n* a white crystalline powder derived from bauxite and used in the manufacture of glass and ceramics, aluminium and its salts, and in dyeing. Formula: Al(OH)$_3$ or Al$_2$O$_3$.3H$_2$O

aluminium oxide *n* a white or colourless insoluble powder occurring naturally as corundum and used in the production of aluminium and its compounds, abrasives, glass, and ceramics. Formula: Al$_2$O$_3$. Also called: **alumina** See also **activated alumina**

aluminium sulphate *n* a white crystalline salt used in the paper, textile, and dyeing industries and in the purification of water. Formula: Al$_2$(SO$_4$)$_3$

aluminize *or* **aluminise** (ə'lu:mɪˌnaɪz) *vb* (*tr*) to cover with aluminium or aluminium paint

aluminosilicate (əˌlu:mɪnəʊ'sɪlɪkɪt) *n* a silicate in which some of the silicon in the tetrahedral unit SiO$_4$ has been replaced by aluminium

aluminothermy (ə'lu:mɪnəʊˌθɜ:mɪ) *n* a process for reducing metallic oxides using finely divided aluminium powder. The mixture of aluminium and the oxide is ignited, causing the aluminium to be oxidized and the metal oxide to be reduced to the metal. Also called: **thermite process**

aluminous (ə'lu:mɪnəs) *adj* 1 resembling aluminium 2 another word for **aluminiferous**. ▷ **aluminosity** (əˌlu:mɪ'nɒsɪtɪ) *n*

aluminous cement *n* another term for **Ciment Fondu**

alumna (ə'lʌmnə) *n, pl* -**nae** (-ni:) *chiefly US and Canadian* a female graduate of a school, college, etc [c19 feminine of ALUMNUS]

alumnus (ə'lʌmnəs) *n, pl* -**ni** (-naɪ) *chiefly US and Canadian* a graduate of a school, college, etc [c17 from Latin: nursling, pupil, foster son, from *alere* to nourish]

alumroot ('æləmˌru:t) *n* 1 any of several North American plants of the saxifragaceous genus *Heuchera*, having small white, reddish, or green bell-shaped flowers and astringent roots 2 the root of such a plant

Alundum (ə'lʌndəm) *n trademark* a hard material composed of fused alumina, used as an abrasive and a refractory

alunite ('æljʊˌnaɪt) *n* a white, grey, or reddish mineral consisting of hydrated aluminium sulphate. It occurs in volcanic igneous rocks and is a source of potassium and aluminium compounds. Formula: KAl$_3$(SO$_4$)$_2$(OH)$_6$ [c19 from French *alun* alum (from Latin *alūmen*) + -ITE^1]

alveolar (æl'vɪələ, ˌælvɪ'əʊlə) *adj* 1 *anatomy* of, relating to, or resembling an alveolus 2 denoting the part of the jawbone containing the roots of the teeth 3 (of a consonant) articulated with the tongue in contact with the projecting part of the jawbone immediately behind the upper teeth ▷ *n* 4 an alveolar consonant, such as the speech sounds written *t*, *d*, and *s* in English

alveolate (æl'vɪəlɪt, -ˌleɪt) *adj* 1 having many

alveoli 2 resembling the deep pits of a honeycomb [c19 from Late Latin *alveolātus* forming a channel, hollowed, from Latin: ALVEOLUS] ▷ ˌalveo'lation *n*

alveolus (æl'vɪələs) *n, pl* -li (-ˌlaɪ) 1 any small pit, cavity, or saclike dilation, such as a honeycomb cell 2 any of the sockets in which the roots of the teeth are embedded 3 any of the tiny air sacs in the lungs at the end of the bronchioles, through which oxygen is taken into the blood [c18 from Latin: a little hollow, diminutive of *alveus*]

alvine ('ælvɪn, -vaɪn) *adj obsolete* of or relating to the intestines or belly [c18 from Latin *alvus* belly]

always ('ɔ:lweɪz, -wɪz) *adv* 1 without exception; on every occasion; every time: *he always arrives on time* 2 continually; repeatedly 3 in any case: *you could always take a day off work* 4 *informal* for ever; without end: *our marriage is for always* ▷ Also (archaic): **alway** [c13 *alles weiss*, from Old English *ealne weg*, literally: all the way; see ALL, WAY]

alyssum ('ælɪsəm) *n* any widely cultivated herbaceous garden plant of the genus *Alyssum*, having clusters of small yellow or white flowers: family *Brassicaceae* (crucifers). See also **sweet alyssum, alison** [c16 from New Latin, from Greek *alusson*, from *alussos* (adj) curing rabies, referring to the ancient belief in the plant's healing properties]

Alzheimer's disease ('ælts,haɪməz) *n* a disorder of the brain resulting in a progressive decline in intellectual and physical abilities and eventual dementia. Often shortened to: **Alzheimer's** [c20 named after A. *Alzheimer* (1864–1915), German physician who first identified it]

am[1] (æm; *unstressed* əm) *vb* (used with I) a form of the present tense (indicative mood) of **be** [Old English *eam*; related to Old Norse *em*, Gothic *im*, Old High German *bim*, Latin *sum*, Greek *eimi*, Sanskrit *asmi*]

am[2] 1 *abbrev* See AM (sense 5) 2 See **a.m.**

am[3] *the internet domain name for* Armenia

Am *the chemical symbol for* americium

AM *abbreviation for* 1 associate member 2 Assembly Member (of the National Assembly of Wales) 3 Albert Medal 4 *US* Master of Arts 5 Also: **am** amplitude modulation 6 See **a.m.** 7 Member of the Order of Australia

Am. *abbreviation for* America(n)

A/M (in Canada) *abbreviation for* Air Marshal

a.m., A.M., am *or* **AM** (indicating the time period from midnight to midday) *abbreviation for* ante meridiem. Compare **p.m.** [Latin: before noon]

AMA *abbreviation for* 1 American Medical Association 2 Australian Medical Association

amabokoboko (ama'bɒkɒbɒkɒ) *pl n South African* the official name for the **Springbok** rugby team [c20 from Nguni *ama*, a plural prefix + *bokoboko*, from *bok* a diminutive of SPRINGBOK]

amadavat (ˌæmədə'væt) *n* another name for **avadavat**

amadoda (ama'dəʊda) *pl n South African* grown men [from Nguni *ama*, a plural prefix + *doda* men]

amadou ('æməˌdu:) *n* a spongy substance made from certain fungi, such as *Polyporus* (or *Fomes*) *fomentarius* and related species, used as tinder to light fires, in medicine to stop bleeding, and, esp formerly, by anglers to dry off dry flies between casts [c18 from French, from Provençal: lover, from Latin *amātor*, from *amāre* to love; so called because it readily ignites]

Amagasaki (əˌmɑ:gə'sɑ:kɪ) *n* an industrial city in Japan, in W Honshu, on Osaka Bay. Pop: 463 256 (2002 est)

amah ('ɑ:mə, 'æmə) *n* (in the East, esp formerly) a nurse or maidservant, esp one of Chinese origin. Compare **ayah** [c19 from Portuguese *ama* nurse, wet nurse]

amain (ə'meɪn) *adv archaic or poetic* with great strength, speed, or haste [c16 from A-^{2} + MAIN^1]

amakrokokroko (ama'krɒkɒkrɒkɒ) *pl n South African* a nickname for the South African Paralympic team [c20 modelled on AMABOKOBOKO,

with a play on CROCK^2]

amakwerekwere (ˌamaˈkwerɪ'kwerɪ) *pl n South African informal derogatory* a term used by Blacks to refer to foreign Africans [c20 from Xhosa *ama*, a plural prefix, + *kwerekwere* imitatitive of unintelligible sound]

Amalekite (ə'mælə,kaɪt) *n Old Testament* a member of a nomadic tribe descended from Esau (Genesis 36:12), dwelling in the desert between Sinai and Canaan and hostile to the Israelites: they were defeated by Saul and destroyed by David (I Samuel 15–30)

Amalfi (ə'mælfɪ) *n* a town in Italy: a major Mediterranean port from the 10th to the 18th century, now a resort

amalgam (ə'mælgəm) *n* 1 an alloy of mercury with another metal, esp with silver: *dental amalgam* 2 a rare white metallic mineral that consists of silver and mercury and occurs in deposits of silver and cinnabar 3 a blend or combination [c15 from Medieval Latin *amalgama*, of obscure origin]

amalgamate (ə'mælgəˌmeɪt) *vb* 1 to combine or cause to combine; unite 2 to alloy (a metal) with mercury

amalgamation (əˌmælgə'meɪʃən) *n* 1 the action or process of amalgamating 2 the state of being amalgamated 3 a method of extracting precious metals from their ores by treatment with mercury to form an amalgam 4 *commerce* another word for **merger** (sense 1)

Amalthea[1] (ˌæmæl'θi:ə) *n Greek myth* **a** a nymph who brought up the infant Zeus on goat's milk **b** the goat itself ▷ Also: **Amaltheia**

Amalthea[2] (ˌæmæl'θi:ə) *n* an inner satellite of Jupiter

amandla (a'mɑ:ndla) *n South African* a political slogan calling for power to the Black population [c20 Nguni, literally: power]

amanita (ˌæmə'naɪtə) *n* any of various saprotrophic agaricaceous fungi constituting the genus *Amanita*, having white gills and a broken membranous ring (volva) around the stalk. The genus includes several highly poisonous species, such as death cap, destroying angel, and fly agaric [c19 from Greek *amanitai* (plural) a variety of fungus]

amanuensis (əˌmænjʊ'ɛnsɪs) *n, pl* -**ses** (-si:z) a person employed to take dictation or to copy manuscripts [c17 from Latin *āmanuensis*, from the phrase *servus ā manū* slave at hand (that is, handwriting)]

Amapá (*Portuguese* əmə'pɑ:) *n* a state of N Brazil, on the Amazon delta. Capital: Macapá. Pop: 516 511 (2002). Area: 143 716 sq km (55 489 sq miles)

amaranth ('æməˌrænθ) *n* 1 an imaginary flower that never fades 2 any of numerous tropical and temperate plants of the genus *Amaranthus*, having tassel-like heads of small green, red, or purple flowers: family *Amaranthaceae*. See also **love-lies-bleeding, tumbleweed, pigweed** (sense 1) 3 a synthetic red food colouring (**E123**), used in packet soups, cake mixes, etc [c17 from Latin *amarantus*, from Greek *amarantos* unfading, from A-^{1} + *marainein* to fade]

amaranthaceous (ˌæməræn'θeɪʃəs) *adj* of, relating to, or belonging to the *Amaranthaceae* (or *Amarantaceae*), a family of tropical and temperate herbaceous or shrubby flowering plants that includes the amaranths and cockscomb

amaranthine (ˌæmə'rænθaɪn) *adj* 1 of a dark reddish-purple colour 2 of or resembling the amaranth

amarelle ('æmɪəˌrɛl) *n* a variety of sour cherry that has pale red fruit and colourless juice. Compare **morello** [c20 from German, from Medieval Latin *amārellum*, from Latin *amārus* bitter; compare MORELLO]

amaretti (æmə'rɛtɪ) *pl n* Italian almond biscuits [c20 from Italian *amaro* bitter]

amaretto (æmə'rɛtəʊ) *n* an Italian liqueur with a flavour of almonds [c20 from Italian *amaro* bitter]

Amarillo (ˌæməˈrɪləʊ) *n* an industrial city in NW Texas. Pop: 178 612 (2003 est)

amaryllidaceous (ˌæməˌrɪlɪˈdeɪʃəs) *adj* of, relating to, or belonging to the *Amaryllidaceae,* a family of widely cultivated flowering plants having bulbs and including the amaryllis, snowdrop, narcissus, and daffodil

amaryllis (ˌæməˈrɪlɪs) *n* **1** Also called: belladonna lily an amaryllidaceous plant, *Amaryllis belladonna,* native to southern Africa and having large lily-like reddish or white flowers **2** any of several related plants, esp hippeastrum [c18 from New Latin: named after AMARYLLIS]

Amaryllis (ˌæməˈrɪlɪs) *n* (in pastoral poetry) a name for a shepherdess or country girl

amass (əˈmæs) *vb* **1** (*tr*) to accumulate or collect (esp riches, etc) **2** to gather in a heap; bring together [c15 from Old French *amasser,* from *masse* MASS] > a'masser *n*

amateur (ˈæmətə, -tʃə, -ˌtjʊə, ˌæməˈtɜː) *n* **1** a person who engages in an activity, esp a sport, as a pastime rather than professionally or for gain **2** an athlete or sportsman **3** a person unskilled in or having only a superficial knowledge of a subject or activity **4** a person who is fond of or admires something **5** (*modifier*) consisting of or for amateurs: *an amateur event* ▷ *adj* **6** amateurish; not professional or expert: *an amateur approach* [c18 from French, from Latin *amātor* lover, from *amāre* to love] > 'amateurism *n*

amateurish (ˈæmətərɪʃ, -tʃər-, -ˌtjʊər-, ˌæməˈtɜːrɪʃ) *adj* lacking professional skill or expertise > 'amateurishly *adv* > 'amateurishness *n*

Amati (əˈmɑːtɪ) *n, pl* Amatis a violin or other stringed instrument made by any member of the Amati family of Italian violin makers (active in Cremona in the 16th and 17th centuries)

amative (ˈæmətɪv) *adj* a rare word for **amorous** [c17 from Medieval Latin *amātīvus,* from Latin *amāre* to love] > 'amatively *adv* > 'amativeness *n*

amatol (ˈæməˌtɒl) *n* an explosive mixture of ammonium nitrate and TNT, used in shells and bombs [c20 from AM(MONIUM) + (TRINITRO)TOL(UENE)]

amatory (ˈæmətərɪ) *or* **amatorial** (ˌæməˈtɔːrɪəl) *adj* of, relating to, or inciting sexual love or desire [c16 from Latin *amātōrius,* from *amāre* to love]

amaurosis (ˌæmɔːˈrəʊsɪs) *n pathol* blindness, esp when occurring without observable damage to the eye [c17 via New Latin from Greek: darkening, from *amaurouon* to dim, darken] > amaurotic (ˌæmɔːˈrɒtɪk) *adj*

amaut *or* **amowt** (əˈmaʊt) *n Canadian* a hood on an Inuit woman's parka for carrying a child [from Inuktitut]

amaze (əˈmeɪz) *vb* (*tr*) **1** to fill with incredulity or surprise; astonish **2** an obsolete word for **bewilder** ▷ *n* **3** an archaic word for **amazement** [Old English *amasian*]

amazement (əˈmeɪzmənt) *n* **1** incredulity or great astonishment; complete wonder or surprise **2** *obsolete* bewilderment or consternation

amazing (əˈmeɪzɪŋ) *adj* causing wonder or astonishment: *amazing feats* > a'mazingly *adv*

amazon (ˈæməzˀn) *n* any of various tropical American parrots of the genus *Amazona,* such as *A. farinosa* (green amazon), having a short tail and mainly green plumage

Amazon[1] (ˈæməzˀn) *n* **1** *Greek myth* one of a race of women warriors of Scythia near the Black Sea **2** one of a legendary tribe of female warriors of South America **3** (*often not capital*) any tall, strong, or aggressive woman [c14 via Latin from Greek *Amazōn,* of uncertain origin] > Amazonian (ˌæməˈzəʊnɪən) *adj*

Amazon[2] (ˈæməzˀn) *n* a river in South America, rising in the Peruvian Andes and flowing east through N Brazil to the Atlantic: in volume, the largest river in the world; navigable for 3700 km (2300 miles). Length: over 6440 km (4000 miles). Area of basin: over 5 827 500 sq km (2 250 000 sq miles)

amazon ant *n* any of several small reddish ants of the genus *Polyergus,* esp *P. rufescens,* that enslave the young of other ant species

Amazonas (ˌæməˈzəʊnəs) *n* a state of W Brazil, consisting of the central Amazon basin: vast areas of unexplored tropical rainforest. Capital: Manaus. Pop: 2 961 801 (2002). Area: 1 542 777 sq km (595 474 sq miles)

Amazon cherry *n* another name for **acerola**

Amazonia (ˌæməˈzəʊnɪə) *n* the land around the Amazon river

Amazonian (ˌæməˈzəʊnɪən) *adj* of or relating to the Amazon river, the land around it, or the inhabitants of this land

amazonite (ˈæməzəˌnaɪt) *n* a green variety of microcline used as a gemstone. Formula: $KAlSi_3O_8$. Also called: Amazon stone

Ambala (əmˈbɑːlə) *n* a city in N India, in Haryana: site of archaeological remains of a prehistoric Indian civilization: grain, cotton, food processing. Pop: 139 222 (2001)

ambary *or* **ambari** (æmˈbɑːrɪ) *n, pl* -ries *or* -ris **1** a tropical Asian malvaceous plant, *Hibiscus cannabinus,* that yields a fibre similar to jute **2** the fibre derived from this plant ▷ Also called: kenaf [c20 from Hindi *ambārī*]

ambassador (æmˈbæsədə) *n* **1** short for **ambassador extraordinary and plenipotentiary**; a diplomatic minister of the highest rank, accredited as permanent representative to another country or sovereign **2** ambassador extraordinary a diplomatic minister of the highest rank sent on a special mission **3** ambassador plenipotentiary a diplomatic minister of the first rank with treaty-signing powers **4** ambassador-at-large *US* an ambassador with special duties who may be sent to more than one government **5** an authorized representative or messenger [c14 from Old French *ambassadeur,* from Italian *ambasciator,* from Old Provençal *ambaisador,* from *ambaisa* (unattested) mission, errand; see EMBASSY] > am'bassadress *fem n* > ambassadorial (æmˌbæsəˈdɔːrɪəl) *adj* > am'bassadorˌship *n*

ambatch *or* **ambach** (ˈæmˌbætʃ) *n* a tree or shrub of the Nile Valley, *Aeschynomene elaphroxylon,* valued for its light-coloured pithlike wood [c19 probably from the Ethiopian name]

amber (ˈæmbə) *n* **1 a** a yellow or yellowish-brown hard translucent fossil resin derived from extinct coniferous trees that occurs in Tertiary deposits and often contains trapped insects. It is used for jewellery, ornaments, etc **b** (*as modifier*): *an amber necklace.* Related adj: **succinic** **2** fly in amber a strange relic or reminder of the past **3 a** a medium to dark brownish-yellow colour, often somewhat orange, similar to that of the resin **b** (*as adjective*): *an amber dress* **4** an amber traffic light used as a warning between red and green [c14 from Medieval Latin *ambar,* from Arabic *'anbar* ambergris]

Amber alert *n US and Canadian* a notification to the general public, such as by commercial radio or electronic traffic-condition signs, regarding an abduction of a child [c20 named after Amber *Hagerman,* a child who was abducted and murdered in 1996 in Arlington, Texas]

amber fluid *n Austral slang* beer

amber gambler *n Brit informal* a driver who races through traffic lights when they are at amber

ambergris (ˈæmbəˌgriːs, -ˌgrɪs) *n* a waxy substance consisting mainly of cholesterol secreted by the intestinal tract of the sperm whale and often found floating in the sea: used in the manufacture of perfumes [c15 from Old French *ambre gris* grey amber]

amberjack (ˈæmbəˌdʒæk) *n* any of several large carangid fishes of the genus *Seriola,* esp *S. dumerili,* with golden markings when young, occurring in tropical and subtropical Atlantic waters [c19 from AMBER + JACK[1]]

amberoid (ˈæmbəˌrɔɪd) *or* **ambroid** *n* a synthetic amber made by compressing pieces of amber and other resins together at a high temperature

ambi- *combining form* indicating both: *ambidextrous; ambivalence; ambiversion* [from Latin: round, on both sides, both, from *ambo* both; compare AMPHI-]

ambidentate (ˌæmbɪˈdɛnteɪt) *adj chem* another word for **amphidentate**

ambidextrous (ˌæmbɪˈdɛkstrəs) *adj* **1** equally expert with each hand **2** *informal* highly skilled or adept **3** underhanded; deceitful > ambidexterity (ˌæmbɪdɛkˈstɛrɪtɪ) *or* ˌambiˈdextrousness *n* > ˌambiˈdextrously *adv*

ambience *or* **ambiance** (ˈæmbɪəns; *French* ãbjãs) *n* the atmosphere of a place [c19 from French *ambiance,* from *ambiant* surrounding; see AMBIENT]

ambient (ˈæmbɪənt) *adj* **1** of or relating to the immediate surroundings: *the ambient temperature was 15°C* **2** creating a relaxing atmosphere: *ambient music* ▷ *n* **3** *informal* ambient music [c16 from Latin *ambiēns* going round, from *ambīre,* from AMBI- + *īre* to go]

ambient noise *n* the level of the total noise in an area

ambiguity (ˌæmbɪˈgjuːɪtɪ) *n, pl* -ties **1** the possibility of interpreting an expression in two or more distinct ways **2** an instance of this, as in the sentence *they are cooking apples* **3** vagueness or uncertainty of meaning: *there are several ambiguities in the situation*

ambiguous (æmˈbɪgjʊəs) *adj* **1** having more than one possible interpretation or meaning **2** difficult to understand or classify; obscure [c16 from Latin *ambiguus* going here and there, uncertain, from *ambigere* to go around, from AMBI- + *agere* to lead, act] > am'biguously *adv* > am'biguousness *n*

ambiophony (ˌæmbɪˈɒfənɪ) *n* the reproduction of sound to create an illusion to a listener of being in a spacious room, such as a concert hall

ambipolar (ˌæmbɪˈpəʊlə) *adj electronics* (of plasmas and semiconductors) involving both positive and negative charge carriers

ambisexual (ˌæmbɪˈsɛksjʊəl) *adj* **1** *biology* relating to or affecting both the male and female sexes **2** Also: ambosexual bisexual

ambisonics (ˌæmbɪˈsɒnɪks) *n* (*functioning as singular*) the technique of reproducing and transmitting surround sound. See **surround sound**

ambit (ˈæmbɪt) *n* **1** scope or extent **2** limits, boundary, or circumference [c16 from Latin *ambitus* a going round, from *ambīre* to go round, from AMBI- + *īre* to go]

ambition (æmˈbɪʃən) *n* **1** strong desire for success, achievement, or distinction **2** something so desired; goal; aim [c14 from Old French, from Latin *ambitiō* a going round (of candidates), a striving to please, from *ambīre* to go round; see AMBIT]

ambitious (æmˈbɪʃəs) *adj* **1** having a strong desire for success or achievement; wanting power, money, etc **2** necessitating extraordinary effort or ability: *an ambitious project* **3** (*often foll by of*) having a great desire (for something or to do something) > am'bitiously *adv* > am'bitiousness *n*

ambivalence (æmˈbɪvələns) *or* **ambivalency** *n* the simultaneous existence of two opposed and conflicting attitudes, emotions, etc > am'bivalent *adj*

ambivert (ˈæmbɪˌvɜːt) *n psychol* a person who is intermediate between an extrovert and an introvert > ambiversion (ˌæmbɪˈvɜːʃən) *n*

amble (ˈæmbˀl) *vb* (*intr*) **1** to walk at a leisurely relaxed pace **2** (of a horse) to move slowly, lifting both legs on one side together **3** to ride a horse at an amble or leisurely pace ▷ *n* **4** a leisurely motion in walking **5** a leisurely walk **6** the ambling gait of a horse [c14 from Old French *ambler,* from Latin *ambulāre* to walk] > 'ambler *n*

Ambleside (ˈæmbˀlˌsaɪd) *n* a town in NW England, in Cumbria: a tourist centre for the Lake District. Pop: 3064 (2001)

a

amblygonite (æm'blɪɡə,naɪt) *n* a white or greyish mineral consisting of lithium aluminium fluorophosphate in triclinic crystalline form. It is a source of lithium. Formula: (Li,Na)Al(PO₄)(F,OH) [c16 from Greek *amblugōnios,* from *amblus* blunt + *gōnia* angle; referring to the obtuse angles in its crystals]

amblyopia (,æmblɪ'əʊpɪə) *n* impaired vision with no discernible damage to the eye or optic nerve [c18 New Latin, from Greek *ambluōpia,* from *amblus* dull, dim + *ōps* eye] > **amblyopic** (,æmblɪ'ɒpɪk) *adj*

ambo¹ ('æmbəʊ) *n, pl* **ambos** or **ambones** (æm'bəʊni:z) either of two raised pulpits from which the gospels and epistles were read in early Christian churches [c17 from Medieval Latin, from Greek *ambōn* raised rim, pulpit]

ambo² ('æmbəʊ) *n, pl* **ambos** *Austral informal* **1** an ambulance driver **2** an ambulance

amboceptor ('æmbəʊ,septə) *n* an immune body formed in the blood during infection or immunization that serves to link the complement to the antigen [c20 from Latin *ambō* both (see AMBI-) + (RE)CEPTOR]

Amboina (æm'bɔɪnə) *n* **1** an island in Indonesia, in the Moluccas. Capital: Amboina. Area: 1000 sq km (386 sq miles) **2** Also called: **Ambon** ('a:mbɒn) a port in the Moluccas, the capital of Amboina island

Amboise (*French* ābwaz) *n* a town in NW central France, on the River Loire: famous castle, a former royal residence. Pop: 11 457 (1999)

ambosexual (,æmbəʊ'sɛksjʊəl) *adj* a variant of **ambisexual**

amboyna or **amboina** (æm'bɔɪnə) *n* the mottled curly-grained wood of an Indonesian leguminous tree, *Pterocarpus indicus,* used in making furniture [c19 from the island of AMBOINA]

ambroid ('æmbrɔɪd) *n* a variant of **amberoid**

ambrosia (æm'brəʊzɪə) *n* **1** *classical myth* the food of the gods, said to bestow immortality. Compare **nectar** (sense 2) **2** anything particularly delightful to taste or smell **3** another name for **beebread 4** any of various herbaceous plants constituting the genus *Ambrosia,* mostly native to America but widely naturalized: family *Asteraceae* (composites). The genus includes the ragweeds [c16 via Latin from Greek: immortality, from *ambrotos,* from A-¹ + *brotos* mortal] > **am'brosial** or **am'brosian** *adj* > **am'brosially** *adv*

ambrosia beetle *n* any of various small beetles of the genera *Anisandrus, Xyleborus,* etc, that bore tunnels into solid wood, feeding on fungi growing in the tunnels: family *Scolytidae* (bark beetles)

Ambrosian (æm'brəʊzɪən) *adj* of or relating to Saint Ambrose, the bishop of Milan and church music composer (?340–397 AD)

ambrotype ('æmbrəʊ,taɪp) *n photog* an early type of glass negative that could be made to appear as a positive by backing it with black varnish or paper [c19 from Greek *ambrotos* immortal + -TYPE; see AMBROSIA]

ambry ('æmbrɪ) or **aumbry** ('ɔ:mbrɪ) *n, pl* -**bries 1** a recessed cupboard in the wall of a church near the altar, used to store sacred vessels, etc **2** *obsolete* a small cupboard or other storage space [c14 from Old French *almarie,* from Medieval Latin *almārium,* from Latin *armārium* chest for storage, from *arma* arms]

ambsace or **amesace** ('eɪmz,eɪs, 'æmz-) *n* **1** double ace, the lowest throw at dice **2** bad luck [c13 from Old French *ambes as,* both aces; *as* from Latin: unit]

ambulacrum (,æmbjʊ'leɪkrəm) *n, pl* -**ra** (-rə) any of five radial bands on the ventral surface of echinoderms, such as the starfish and sea urchin, on which the tube feet are situated [c19 from Latin: avenue, from *ambulāre* to walk] > ,ambu'lacral *adj*

ambulance ('æmbjʊləns) *n* a motor vehicle designed to carry sick or injured people [c19 from French, based on (*hôpital*) *ambulant* mobile or field

(hospital), from Latin *ambulāre* to walk]

ambulance chaser *n US slang* a lawyer who seeks to encourage and profit from the lawsuits of accident victims > **ambulance chasing** *n*

ambulance stocks *pl n* high performance stocks and shares recommended by a broker to a dissatisfied client to improve their relationship

ambulant ('æmbjʊlənt) *adj* **1** moving about from place to place **2** *med* another word for **ambulatory** (sense 3)

ambulate ('æmbjʊ,leɪt) *vb* (*intr*) to wander about or move from one place to another [c17 from Latin *ambulāre* to walk, AMBLE] > ,ambu'lation *n*

ambulatory ('æmbjʊlətərɪ) *adj* **1** of, relating to, or designed for walking **2** changing position; not fixed **3** Also: **ambulant** able to walk **4** *law* (esp of a will) capable of being altered or revoked ▷ *n, pl* -**ries 5** *architect* **a** an aisle running around the east end of a church, esp one that passes behind the sanctuary **b** a place for walking, such as an aisle or a cloister

ambulatory care *n* care given at a hospital to non-resident patients, including minor surgery and outpatient treatment

ambuscade (,æmbə'skeɪd) *n* **1** an ambush ▷ *vb* **2** to ambush or lie in ambush [c16 from French *embuscade,* from Old Italian *imboscata,* probably of Germanic origin; compare AMBUSH]

ambush ('æmbʊʃ) *n* **1** the act of waiting in a concealed position in order to launch a surprise attack **2** a surprise attack from such a position **3** the concealed position from which such an attack is launched **4** the person or persons waiting to launch such an attack ▷ *vb* **5** to lie in wait (for) **6** (*tr*) to attack suddenly from a concealed position [c14 from Old French *embuschier* to position in ambush, from *em-* IM- + -*buschier,* from *busche* piece of firewood, probably of Germanic origin; see BUSH¹]

AMDG *abbreviation for* ad majorem Dei gloriam (the Jesuit motto) [Latin: to the greater glory of God]

am-dram *Brit informal abbreviation for* amateur dramatics

ameba (ə'mi:bə) *n, pl* -**bae** (-bi:) or -**bas** the usual US spelling of **amoeba.** > a'mebic *adj*

ameer (ə'mɪə) *n* **1** a variant spelling of **emir 2** (formerly) the ruler of Afghanistan; amir

ameiosis (,eɪmaɪ'əʊsɪs) *n biology* the absence of pairing of chromosomes during meiosis

amelia (ə'mi:lɪə) *n* the congenital absence of arms or legs [from A-¹ + Greek *melos* limb + -IA]

ameliorate (ə'mi:ljə,reɪt) *vb* to make or become better; improve [c18 from MELIORATE, influenced by French *améliorer,* from Old French *ameillorer* to make better, from *meillor* better, from Latin *melior*] > ameliorable (ə'mi:ljərəb³l) *adj* > a'meliorant *n* > a'meliorative *adj* > a'melio,rator *n*

> USAGE *Ameliorate* is often wrongly used where *alleviate* is meant. *Ameliorate* is properly used to mean 'improve', not 'make easier to bear', so one should talk about *alleviating* pain or hardship, not *ameliorating* it

amelioration (ə,mi:ljə'reɪʃən) *n* **1** the act or an instance of ameliorating or the state of being ameliorated **2** something that ameliorates; an improvement **3** Also called: **elevation** *linguistics* (of the meaning of a word) a change from pejorative to neutral or positively pleasant. The word *nice* has achieved its modern meaning by amelioration from the earlier sense *foolish, silly*

ameloblast (ə'mi:ləʊblæst, -blɑ:st) *n* a type of cell involved in forming dental enamel [c19 from (EN)AMEL + -O- + -BLAST]

amelogenesis (ə,mi:ləʊ'dʒɛnɪsɪs) *n* the production of enamel by ameloblasts

amen (,eɪ'mɛn, ,ɑ:'mɛn) *interj* **1** so be it!: a term used at the end of a prayer or religious statement ▷ *n* **2** the use of the word *amen,* as at the end of a prayer **3 say amen to** to express strong approval of or support for (an assertion, hope, etc) [c13 via

Late Latin via Greek from Hebrew *āmēn* certainly]

Amen, Amon or **Amūn** ('ɑ:mən) *n Egyptian myth* a local Theban god, having a ram's head and symbolizing life and fertility, identified by the Egyptians with the national deity Amen-Ra

amenable (ə'mi:nəb³l) *adj* **1** open or susceptible to suggestion; likely to listen, cooperate, etc **2** accountable for behaviour to some authority; answerable **3** capable of being or liable to be tested, judged, etc [c16 from Anglo-French, from Old French *amener* to lead up, from Latin *mināre* to drive (cattle), from *minārī* to threaten] > a,mena'bility or a'menableness *n* > a'menably *adv*

amen corner *n* the *US* the part of a church, usually to one side of the pulpit, occupied by people who lead the responsive amens during the service

amend (ə'mɛnd) *vb* (*tr*) **1** to improve; change for the better **2** to remove faults from; correct **3** to alter or revise (legislation, a constitution, etc) by formal procedure [c13 from Old French *amender,* from Latin *ēmendāre* to EMEND] > a'mendable *adj* > a'mender *n*

amendatory (ə'mɛndətərɪ, -trɪ) *adj US* serving to amend; corrective

amende honorable *French* (amād ɔnɔrablə) *n, pl* **amendes honorables** (amāds ɔnɔrablə) a public apology and reparation made to satisfy the honour of the person wronged. Sometimes shortened to: **amende** [c18 literally: honourable compensation]

amendment (ə'mɛndmənt) *n* **1** the act of amending; correction **2** an addition, alteration, or improvement to a motion, document, etc

amends (ə'mɛndz) *n* (*functioning as singular*) recompense or compensation given or gained for some injury, insult, etc: *to make amends* [c13 from Old French *amendes* fines, from *amende* compensation, from *amender* to EMEND]

amenity (ə'mi:nɪtɪ) *n, pl* -**ties 1** (*often plural*) a useful or pleasant facility or service: *a swimming pool was just one of the amenities* **2** the fact or condition of being pleasant or agreeable **3** (*usually plural*) a social courtesy or pleasantry [c14 from Latin *amoenitās* pleasantness, from *amoenus* agreeable]

amenity bed *n* (in Britain) a hospital bed whose occupant receives free treatment but pays for nonmedical advantages, such as privacy. Also called (*informal*): **pay bed**

amenorrhoea or *esp US* **amenorrhea** (æ,mɛnə'rɪə, eɪ-) *n* abnormal absence of menstruation [c19 from A-¹ + MENO- + -RRHOEA]

Amen-Ra (,ɑ:mən'rɑ:) *n Egyptian myth* the sun-god; the principal deity during the period of Theban hegemony

a mensa et thoro (eɪ 'mɛnsə ɛt 'θɔ:rəʊ) *adj law* denoting or relating to a form of divorce in which the parties remain married but do not cohabit: abolished in England in 1857 [Latin: from table and bed]

ament¹ ('æmənt, 'eɪmənt) *n* another name for **catkin** Also called: **amentum** (ə'mɛntəm) [c18 from Latin *āmentum* strap, thong] > ,amen'taceous *adj* > ,amen'tiferous *adj*

ament² (æ'mɛnt, 'eɪmənt) *n psychiatry* a mentally deficient person [c19 from Latin *āment-, āmens* without mind; see AMENTIA]

amentia (ə'mɛnʃə) *n* severe mental deficiency, usually congenital. Compare **dementia** [c14 from Latin: insanity, from *āmēns* mad, from *mēns* mind]

Amer. *abbreviation for* America(n)

Amerasian (ə,mɛr'eɪʃən, ə,mɛr'eɪʒən) *n* **1** a person of mixed American and Asian parentage; used especially to refer to someone with an American father and an Asian mother ▷ *adj* **2** of or relating to Amerasians

amerce (ə'mɜ:s) *vb* (*tr*) *obsolete* **1** *law* to punish by a fine **2** to punish with any arbitrary penalty [c14 from Anglo-French *amercier,* from Old French *à merci* at the mercy (because the fine was arbitrarily fixed); see MERCY] > a'merceable *adj*

> a'mercement *n* > a'mercer *n*

America (ə'mɛrɪkə) *n* **1** short for the **United States of America 2** Also called: the Americas the American continent, including North, South, and Central America [c16 from *Americus*, Latin form of *Amerigo*; after Amerigo Vespucci (?1454–1512), Florentine navigator in the New World]

American (ə'mɛrɪkən) *adj* **1** of or relating to the United States of America, its inhabitants, or their form of English **2** of or relating to the American continent ▷ *n* **3** a native or citizen of the US **4** a native or inhabitant of any country of North, Central, or South America **5** the English language as spoken or written in the United States

Americana (ə,mɛrɪ'kɑːnə) *pl n* objects, such as books, documents, relics, etc, relating to America, esp in the form of a collection

American aloe *n* another name for **century plant**

American chameleon *n* another name for **anole**

American cheese *n* a type of smooth hard white or yellow cheese similar to a mild Cheddar

American cloth *n* a glazed or waterproofed cotton cloth

American Curl *n* a breed of slender cat with curled-back ears and a plumed tail

American Dream *n* **the** the notion that the American social, economic, and political system makes success possible for every individual

American eagle *n* another name for **bald eagle**, esp when depicted as the national emblem of the US

American Expeditionary Forces *pl n* the troops sent to Europe by the US during World War I

American Federation of Labor *n* the first permanent national labour movement in America, founded in 1886. It amalgamated with the Congress of Industrial Organizations in 1955. See also **AFL-CIO**

American football *n* **1** a team game similar to rugby, with 11 players on each side. Forward passing is allowed and planned strategies and formations for play are decided during the course of the game **2** the oval-shaped inflated ball used in this game

American Indian *n* **1** Also called: **Indian, Red Indian, Amerindian, Native American** a member of any of the indigenous peoples of North, Central, or South America, having Mongoloid affinities, notably straight black hair and a yellow to brown skin ▷ *adj* **2** Also: **Amerindian** of or relating to any of these peoples, their languages, or their cultures

American Indian Movement *n* a militant movement or grouping of American Indians, organized in 1968 to combat discrimination, injustice, etc

Americanism (ə'mɛrɪkə,nɪzəm) *n* **1** a custom, linguistic usage, or other feature peculiar to or characteristic of the United States, its people, or their culture **2** loyalty to the United States, its people, customs, etc

Americanist (ə'mɛrɪkənɪst) *n* a person who studies some aspect of America, such as its history or languages

Americanize or **Americanise** (ə'mɛrɪkə,naɪz) *vb* to make or become American in outlook, attitudes, etc > A,merican'zation or A,mericani'sation *n* > A'merican,izer or A'merican,iser *n*

American pit bull terrier *n* another name for **pit bull terrier**

American plan *n* US a hotel rate in which the charge includes meals. Compare **European plan**

American Revolution *n* the usual US term for **War of American Independence**

American Samoa *n* the part of Samoa administered by the US Capital: Pago Pago. Pop: 67 000 (2003 est). Area: 197 sq km (76 sq miles)

American sign language *n* See **Ameslan**

American Standard Version *n* a revised version of the Authorized (King James) Version of the Bible, published by a committee of American scholars in 1901

American trypanosomiasis *n pathol* another name for **Chagas' disease**

American Wake *n Irish* an all-night farewell party for a person about to emigrate to America

American wirehair ('waɪə,hɛə) *n* a breed of medium-large cat with a coarse wiry coat

America's Cup *n* an international yachting trophy, first won by the schooner *America* in 1851 and held as a challenge trophy by the New York Yacht Club until 1983

americium (,æmə'rɪsɪəm) *n* a white metallic transuranic element artificially produced from plutonium. It is used as an alpha-particle source. Symbol: Am; atomic no: 95; half-life of most stable isotope, ^{243}Am: 7.4×10^3 years; valency: 2,3,4,5, or 6; relative density: 13.67; melting pt: 1176°C; boiling pt: 2607°C (est) [c20 from AMERICA (because it was discovered at Berkeley, California) + -IUM]

Amerindian (,æmə'rɪndɪən) *n also* **Amerind** ('æmərɪnd) ▷ *adj* another word for **American Indian**. > **Amer'indic** *adj*

Amersfoort (*Dutch* 'aːmərsfoːrt) *n* a town in the central Netherlands, in E Utrecht province. Pop: 131 000 (2003 est)

amesace ('eɪmz,eɪs, 'æmz-) *n* a variant spelling of **ambsace**

Ameslan ('æməs,læn) *n* American sign language: a language in which meaning is conveyed by hand gestures and their position in relation to the upper part of the body. Abbreviation: ASL [c20 from *Ame(rican) s(ign) lan(guage)*]

Ames test (eɪmz) *n* a method of preliminary screening for carcinogens, based on their ability to cause mutations in bacteria [named after Bruce Ames (born 1928), US biochemist who invented the test]

ametabolic (ə,mɛtə'bɒlɪk) *adj* (of certain insects) having no obvious metamorphosis

amethyst ('æmɪθɪst) *n* **1** a purple or violet transparent variety of quartz used as a gemstone. Formula: SiO_2 **2** a purple variety of sapphire; oriental amethyst **3** the purple colour of amethyst [c13 from Old French *amatiste*, from Latin *amethystus*, from Greek *amethustos*, literally: not drunken, from A-¹ + *methuein* to make drunk; referring to the belief that the stone could prevent intoxication] > **amethystine** (,æmɪ'θɪstaɪn) *adj*

ametropia (,æmɪ'trəʊpɪə) *n* loss of ability to focus images on the retina, caused by an imperfection in the refractive function of the eye [c19 New Latin, from Greek *ametros* unmeasured (from A-¹ + *metron* measure) + *ōps* eye]

Amex ('æmɛks) *n acronym for* **1** *trademark* American Express **2** American Stock Exchange

AMF *abbreviation for* Australian Military Forces

Amfortas (æm'fɔːtəs) *n* (in medieval legend) the leader of the knights of the Holy Grail

Amhara (æm'hɑːrə) *n* **1** a region of NW Ethiopia: formerly a kingdom **2** an inhabitant of the former kingdom of Amhara

Amharic (æm'hærɪk) *n* **1** the official language of Ethiopia, belonging to the SE Semitic subfamily of the Afro-Asiatic family ▷ *adj* **2** denoting or relating to this language

ami French (ami) *n* a male friend

amiable ('eɪmɪəbəl) *adj* having or displaying a pleasant or agreeable nature; friendly [c14 from Old French, from Late Latin *amīcābilis* AMICABLE] > ,amia'bility or 'amiableness *n* > 'amiably *adv*

amianthus (,æmɪ'ænθəs) *n* any of the fine silky varieties of asbestos [c17 from Latin *amiantus*, from Greek *amiantos* unsullied, from A-¹ + *miainein* to pollute] > ,ami'anthine, ,ami'anthoid or ,amian'thoidal *adj*

amicable ('æmɪkəbəl) *adj* characterized by friendliness: *an amicable agreement* [c15 from Late Latin *amīcābilis*, from Latin *amīcus* friend; related to *amāre* to love] > ,amica'bility or 'amicableness *n* > 'amicably *adv*

amice¹ ('æmɪs) *n Christianity* a rectangular piece of white linen worn by priests around the neck and shoulders under the alb or, formerly, on the head [c15 from Old French *amis*, plural of *amit*, or from Medieval Latin *amicia*, both from Latin *amictus* cloak, from *amicīre* to clothe, from *am-* AMBI- + *iacere* to throw]

amice² ('æmɪs) *n* another word for **almuce**

AMICE *abbreviation for* Associate Member of the Institution of Civil Engineers

AMIChemE *abbreviation for* Associate Member of the Institution of Chemical Engineers

amicus curiae (æ'miːkʊs 'kjʊərɪ,iː) *n, pl* amici curiae (æ'miːkaɪ) *law* a person not directly engaged in a case who advises the court [Latin, literally: friend of the court]

amid (ə'mɪd) *or* **amidst** *prep* in the middle of; among [Old English *on middan* in the middle; see MID¹]

Amida (amidə) *n* the Japanese name for **Amitabha**

Amidah (ami'daː, a'midə) *n Judaism* the central prayer in each of the daily services, recited silently and standing. Also called: **Shemona Esrei**

amide ('æmaɪd) *n* **1** any organic compound containing the functional group $-CONH_2$ **2** (*modifier*) consisting of, containing, or concerned with the group $-CONH_2$: *amide group or radical* **3** an inorganic compound having the general formula $M(NH_2)_x$, where M is a metal atom [c19 from AM(MONIA) + -IDE] > **amidic** (ə'mɪdɪk) *adj*

amido- *combining form* (in chemistry) indicating the presence of an amide group [from AMIDE]

Amidol ('æmɪdɒl) *n trademark* a grey to colourless soluble crystalline solid that is used as a photographic developer; 2,4-diaminophenol dihydrochloride. Formula: $C_6H_3(NH_2)_2(OH).2HCl$

amidships (ə'mɪdʃɪps) *adv, adj* (*postpositive*) *nautical* at, near, or towards the centre of a vessel

amie French (ami) *n* a female friend

AMIEE (in Britain) *abbreviation for* Associate Member of the Institution of Electrical Engineers

Amiens ('æmɪənz; *French* amjɛ̃) *n* a city in N France: its Gothic cathedral is the largest church in France. Pop: 135 501 (1999)

amigo (æ'miːgəʊ, ə-) *n, pl* -gos a friend; comrade [Spanish, from Latin *amicus*]

AMIMechE (in Britain) *abbreviation for* Associate Member of the Institution of Mechanical Engineers

Amin (æ'miːn, ɑː-) *n* **Lake** a former official name for (Lake) **Edward**

amine (ə'miːn, 'æmɪn) *n* an organic base formed by replacing one or more of the hydrogen atoms of ammonia by organic groups [c19 from AM(MONIUM) + -INE²]

-amine *n combining form* indicating an amine: *histamine; methylamine*

amino (ə'maɪnəʊ, -'miː-) *n* (*modifier*) of, consisting of, or containing the group of atoms $-NH_2$: *amino group or radical; amino acid*

amino- *combining form* indicating the presence of an amino group: *aminobenzoic acid* [from AMINE]

amino acid *n* any of a group of organic compounds containing one or more amino groups, $-NH_2$, and one or more carboxyl groups, $-COOH$. The alpha-amino acids $RCH(NH_2)COOH$ (where R is either hydrogen or an organic group) are the component molecules of proteins; some can be synthesized in the body (**nonessential amino acids**) and others cannot and are thus essential components of the diet (**essential amino acids**)

amino acid sequence *n* the unique sequence of amino acids that characterizes a given protein

aminobenzoic acid (ə,maɪnəʊbɛn'zəʊɪk, -,miː-) *n* a derivative of benzoic acid existing in three isomeric forms, the *para-* form being used in the manufacture of dyes and sunburn preventatives. Formula: $NH_2C_6H_4COOH$

aminophenazone (ə,maɪnəʊ'fiːnə,zəʊn, -,miː-) *n* a crystalline compound used to reduce pain and

a

fever. Formula: $C_{13}H_{17}N_3O$. Also called: aminopyrine

aminophenol (ə,mainəʊ'fi:nɒl, -,mi:-) *n chem* any of three isomeric forms that are soluble crystalline solids, used as a dye intermediate (meta- and ortho-), in dyeing hair, fur, and textiles (ortho- and para-), and as a photographic developer (para-). Formula: $C_6H_4NH_2OH$

aminophylline (æmɪ'nɒfɪli:n) *n* a derivative of theophylline that relaxes smooth muscle and is used mainly to dilate the airways in the treatment of asthma and emphysema [c20 from AMINO- + PHYLLO- + -INE²]

aminopyrine (ə,mainəʊ'pairi:n, -,mi:-) *n* another name for **aminophenazone**

amino resin *n* any thermosetting synthetic resin formed by copolymerization of amines or amides with aldehydes. Amino resins are used as adhesives and as coatings for paper and textiles. See also **urea-formaldehyde resin, melamine**

amir (ə'mɪə) *n* **1** a variant spelling of **emir 2** (formerly) the ruler of Afghanistan; ameer [c19 from Arabic, variant of EMIR]

Amish ('ɑ:mɪʃ, 'æ-) *adj* **1** of or relating to a US and Canadian Mennonite sect that traces its origin to Jakob Amman ▷ *n* **2 the** the Amish people [c19 from German *Amisch*, after Jakob *Amman*, 17th-century Swiss Mennonite bishop]

amiss (ə'mɪs) *adv* **1** in an incorrect, inappropriate, or defective manner **2** take (something) amiss to be annoyed or offended by (something) ▷ *adj* **3** (*postpositive*) wrong, incorrect, or faulty [c13 *a mis*, from *mis* wrong; see MISS¹]

Amitabha (,ami'tɑbə) *n Buddhism* (in Pure Land sects) a Bodhisattva who presides over a Pure Land in the west of the universe. Japanese name: Amida [Sanskrit, literally: immeasurable light, from *amita* infinite + *ābhā* light]

amitosis (,æmɪ'təʊsɪs) *n* an unusual form of cell division in which the nucleus and cytoplasm divide by constriction without the formation of chromosomes; direct cell division [c19 A-¹ + MITOSIS] > amitotic (,æmɪ'tɒtɪk) *adj* > ,ami'totically *adv*

amitriptyline (,æmɪ'trɪptɪ,li:n, -lɪn) *n* a tricyclic antidepressant drug. Formula: $C_{20}H_{23}N$ [c20 from AMINO + TRYPTAMINE + METHYL + -INE²]

amity ('æmɪtɪ) *n, pl* -ties friendship; cordiality [c15 from Old French *amité*, from Medieval Latin *amīcitās* friendship, from Latin *amīcus* friend]

AMM *abbreviation for* antimissile (missile)

Amman (ə'mɑ:n) *n* the capital of Jordan, northeast of the Dead Sea: ancient capital of the Ammonites, rebuilt by Ptolemy in the 3rd century BC Pop: 1 292 000 (2005 est). Ancient names: Rabbath Ammon, Philadelphia

ammeter ('æm,mi:tə) *n* an instrument for measuring an electric current in amperes [c19 AM(PERE) + -METER]

amine ('æmi:n, ə'mi:n) *n* a compound that has molecules containing one or more ammonia molecules bound to another molecule, group, or atom by coordinate bonds. Also called: ammoniate, ammonate [c19 from AMM(ONIA) + -INE²]

ammo ('æməʊ) *n informal* short for **ammunition**

ammocoete ('æmə,si:t) *n* the larva of primitive jawless vertebrates, such as the lamprey, that lives buried in mud and feeds on microorganisms [c19 from New Latin *ammocoeteēs*, literally: that lie in sand, from Greek *ammos* sand + *koitē* bed, from *keisthai* to lie]

Ammon¹ ('æmən) *n Old Testament* the ancestor of the Ammonites

Ammon² ('æmən) *n myth* the classical name of the Egyptian god Amen, identified by the Greeks with Zeus and by the Romans with Jupiter

ammonal ('æmən³l) *n* an explosive made by mixing TNT, ammonium nitrate, and aluminium powder [c20 from AMMON(IUM) + AL(UMINIUM)]

ammonate ('æmə,neɪt) *n* another name for **amine**

ammonia (ə'məʊnɪə, -njə) *n* **1** a colourless pungent highly soluble gas mainly used in the manufacture of fertilizers, nitric acid, and other nitrogenous compounds, and as a refrigerant and solvent. Formula: NH_3 **2** a solution of ammonia in water, containing the compound ammonium hydroxide [c18 from New Latin, from Latin (*sal*) *ammōniacus* (sal) AMMONIAC¹]

ammoniac¹ (ə'məʊnɪ,æk) *adj* a variant of **ammoniacal**

ammoniac² (ə'məʊnɪ,æk) *n* a strong-smelling gum resin obtained from the stems of the N Asian umbelliferous plant *Dorema ammoniacum* and formerly used as an expectorant, stimulant, perfume, and in porcelain cement. Also called: gum ammoniac [c14 from Latin *ammōniacum*, from Greek *ammōniakos* belonging to Ammon (apparently the gum resin was extracted from plants found in Libya near the temple of Ammon)]

ammoniacal (,æmə'naɪəkªl) *adj* of, containing, using, or resembling ammonia. Also: ammoniac

ammonia clock *n* an atomic clock based on the frequency of inversion of the ammonia molecule

ammoniate (ə'məʊnɪ,eɪt) *vb* **1** to unite or treat with ammonia ▷ *n* **2** another name for **ammine**. > am,moni'ation *n*

ammonic (ə'mɒnɪk, ə'məʊnɪk) *adj* of or concerned with ammonia or ammonium compounds > am'monical *adj*

ammonify (ə'mɒnɪ,faɪ, ə'məʊnɪ-) *vb* -fies, -fying, -fied to treat or impregnate with ammonia or a compound of ammonia > am,monifi'cation *n*

ammonite¹ ('æmə,naɪt) *n* **1** any extinct marine cephalopod mollusc of the order *Ammonoidea*, which were common in Mesozoic times and generally had a coiled partitioned shell. Their closest modern relative is the pearly nautilus **2** the shell of any of these animals, commonly occurring as a fossil [c18 from New Latin *Ammonītēs*, from Medieval Latin *cornū Ammōnis*, literally: horn of Ammon] > ammonitic (,æmə'nɪtɪk) *adj*

ammonite² ('æmə,naɪt) *n* **1** an explosive consisting mainly of ammonium nitrate with smaller amounts of other substances, such as TNT **2** a nitrogenous fertilizer made from animal wastes [c20 from AMMO(NIUM) + NI(TRA)TE]

Ammonites ('æmə,naɪts) *pl n Old Testament* a nomadic tribe living east of the Jordan: a persistent enemy of the Israelites

ammonium (ə'məʊnɪəm, -njəm) *n* (*modifier*) of, consisting of, or containing the monovalent group NH_4– or the ion NH_4^+: *ammonium compounds*

ammonium carbamate *n* a white soluble crystalline compound produced by reaction between dry ammonia and carbon dioxide and used as a nitrogen fertilizer. Formula: $(NH_4)CO_2NH_2$

ammonium carbonate *n* **1** an unstable pungent soluble white powder that is a double salt of ammonium bicarbonate and ammonium carbamate: used in the manufacture of baking powder, smelling salts, and ammonium compounds. Formula: $(NH_4)HCO_3.(NH_4)CO_2NH_2$ **2** an unstable substance that is produced by treating this compound with ammonia. Formula: $(NH_4)_2CO_3$

ammonium chloride *n* a white soluble crystalline solid used chiefly as an electrolyte in dry batteries and as a mordant and soldering flux. Formula: NH_4Cl. Also called: sal ammoniac

ammonium hydroxide *n* a compound existing only in aqueous solution, formed when ammonia dissolves in water to form ammonium ions and hydroxide ions. Formula: NH_4OH

ammonium ion *n* the ion NH_4^+, formed from ammonia and present in aqueous solutions of ammonia and in many salts

ammonium nitrate *n* a colourless highly soluble crystalline solid used mainly as a fertilizer and in explosives and pyrotechnics. Formula: NH_4NO_3

ammonium sulphate *n* a white soluble crystalline solid used mainly as a fertilizer and in water purification. Formula: $(NH_4)_2SO_4$

ammonolysis (,æmə'nɒlɪsɪs) *n chem* solvolysis in liquid ammonia

ammunition (,æmjʊ'nɪʃən) *n* **1** any projectiles, such as bullets, rockets, etc, that can be discharged from a weapon **2** bombs, missiles, chemicals, biological agents, nuclear materials, etc, capable of use as weapons **3** any means of defence or attack, as in an argument [c17 from obsolete French *amunition*, by mistaken division from earlier *la munition*; see MUNITION]

amnesia (æm'ni:zjə, -ʒjə, -zɪə) *n* a defect in memory, esp one resulting from pathological cause, such as brain damage or hysteria [c19 via New Latin from Greek: forgetfulness, probably from *amnēstia* oblivion; see AMNESTY] > amnesiac (æm'ni:zɪ,æk) or amnesic (æm'ni:sɪk, -zɪk) *adj, n*

amnesty ('æmnɪstɪ) *n, pl* -ties **1** a general pardon, esp for offences against a government **2** a period during which a law is suspended to allow offenders to admit their crime without fear of prosecution **3** *law* a pardon granted by the Crown or Executive and effected by statute ▷ *vb* -ties, -tying, -tied **4** (*tr*) to overlook or forget (an offence) [c16 from Latin *amnēstia*, from Greek: oblivion, from *amnēstos* forgetting, from A-¹ + -*mnēstos*, from *mnasthai* to remember]

Amnesty International *n* an international organization founded in Britain in 1961 that works to secure the release of people imprisoned for their beliefs, to ban the use of torture, and to abolish the death penalty. Abbreviation: AI

amnio ('æmnɪəʊ) *n* short for **amniocentesis**

amniocentesis (,æmnɪəʊsen'ti:sɪs) *n, pl* -ses (-si:z) removal of some amniotic fluid by the insertion into the womb of a hollow needle, for therapeutic or diagnostic purposes [c20 from AMNION + *centesis*, from Greek *kentēsis* a puncture, from *kentein* to prick]

amnion ('æmnɪən) *n, pl* -nions or -nia (-nɪə) the innermost of two membranes (see also **chorion**) enclosing an embryonic reptile, bird, or mammal [c17 via New Latin from Greek: a little lamb, from *amnos* a lamb]

amniote ('æmnɪəʊt) *n* any vertebrate animal, such as a reptile, bird, or mammal, that possesses an amnion, chorion, and allantois during embryonic development. Compare **anamniote**

amniotic (,æmnɪ'ɒtɪk) *adj* of or relating to the amnion

amniotic fluid *n* the fluid surrounding the fetus in the womb

amoeba or US **ameba** (ə'mi:bə) *n, pl* -bae (-bi:) or -bas any protozoan of the phylum *Rhizopoda*, esp any of the genus *Amoeba*, able to change shape because of the movements of cell processes (pseudopodia). They live in fresh water or soil or as parasites in man and animals [c19 from New Latin, from Greek *amoibē* change, from *ameibein* to change, exchange] > a'moebic or US a'mebic *adj*

amoebaean or **amoebean** (,æmɪ'bi:ən) *adj prosody* of or relating to lines of verse dialogue that answer each other alternately

amoebiasis (,æmɪ'baɪəsɪs) *n, pl* -ses (-,si:z) infection, esp of the intestines, caused by the parasitic amoeba *Endamoeba histolytica*

amoebic dysentery *n* inflammation of the intestines caused by the parasitic amoeba *Endamoeba histolytica*

amoebocyte or US **amebocyte** (ə'mi:bə,saɪt) *n* any cell having properties similar to an amoeba, such as shape, mobility, and ability to engulf particles

amoeboid or US **ameboid** (ə'mi:bɔɪd) *adj* of, related to, or resembling amoebae

amok (ə'mʌk, ə'mɒk) or **amuck** (ə'mʌk) *n* **1** a state of murderous frenzy, originally observed among Malays ▷ *adv* **2 run amok** to run about with or as if with a frenzied desire to kill [c17 from Malay *amoq* furious assault]

amokura (ˈɑːˌməʊkuːrə) *n, pl* amokura a white pelagian bird, *Paethon rubricauda,* of tropical latitudes in the Indian and Pacific oceans, with a red beak and long red tail feathers [Māori]

Amon (ˈɑːmən) *n Egyptian myth* a variant spelling of **Amen**

among (əˈmʌŋ) *or* **amongst** *prep* **1** in the midst of: *he lived among the Indians* **2** to each of: *divide the reward among yourselves* **3** in the group, class, or number of: *ranked among the greatest writers* **4** taken out of (a group): *he is only one among many* **5** with one another within a group; by the joint action of: *a lot of gossip among the women employees; decide it among yourselves* [Old English *amang,* contracted from *on gemang* in the group of, from ON + *gemang* crowd; see MINGLE, MONGREL]

> ▋ USAGE See at **between**

amontillado (əˌmɒntɪˈlɑːdəʊ) *n* a medium dry Spanish sherry, not as pale in colour as a fino [c19 from Spanish *vino amontillado* wine of *Montilla,* town in Spain]

amoral (eɪˈmɒrəl) *adj* **1** having no moral quality; nonmoral **2** without moral standards or principles > amorality (ˌeɪmɒˈrælɪtɪ) *n* > a'morally *adv*

> ▋ USAGE *Amoral* is often wrongly used where *immoral* is meant. *Immoral* is properly used to talk about the breaking of moral rules, *amoral* about people who have no moral code or about places or situations where moral considerations do not apply

amoretto (ˌæməˈrɛtəʊ) *or* **amorino** (ˌæmɔːˈriːnəʊ) *n, pl* -retti (-ˈrɛtɪ) *or* -rini (-ˈriːnɪ) (esp in painting) a small chubby naked boy representing a cupid. Also called: putto [c16 from Italian, diminutive of *Amore* Cupid, from Latin *Amor* Love]

amorist (ˈæmərɪst) *n* a lover or a writer about love

amoroso (ˌæməˈrəʊsəʊ) *adj, adv* **1** *music* (to be played) lovingly ▷ *n* **2** a rich sweetened sherry of a dark colour [from Italian and Spanish: AMOROUS]

amorous (ˈæmərəs) *adj* **1** inclined towards or displaying love or desire **2** in love **3** of or relating to love [c14 from Old French, from Medieval Latin *amōrōsus,* from Latin *amor* love] > 'amorously *adv* > 'amorousness *n*

amor patriae Latin (ˈæmɔː ˈpætrɪˌiː) *n* love of one's country; patriotism

amorphous (əˈmɔːfəs) *adj* **1** lacking a definite shape; formless **2** of no recognizable character or type **3** (of chemicals, rocks, etc) not having a crystalline structure [c18 from New Latin, from Greek *amorphos* shapeless, from A-¹ + *morphē* shape] > a'morphism *n* > a'morphously *adv* > a'morphousness *n*

amortization *or* **amortisation** (əˌmɔːtaɪˈzeɪʃən) *n* **1 a** the process of amortizing a debt **b** the money devoted to amortizing a debt **2** (in computing the redemption yield on a bond purchased at a premium) the amount that is subtracted from the annual yield. Compare **accumulation** (sense 3b) > amortizement *or* amortisement (əˈmɔːtɪzmənt) *n*

amortize *or* **amortise** (əˈmɔːtaɪz) *vb* (tr) **1** *finance* to liquidate (a debt, mortgage, etc) by instalment payments or by periodic transfers to a sinking fund **2** to write off (a wasting asset) by annual transfers to a sinking fund **3** *property law* (formerly) to transfer (lands, etc) in mortmain [c14 from Medieval Latin *admortizāre,* from Old French *amortir* to reduce to the point of death, ultimately from Latin *ad* to + *mors* death] > a'mortizable *or* a'mortisable *adj*

Amos (ˈeɪmɒs) *n Old Testament* **1** a Hebrew prophet of the 8th century BC **2** the book containing his oracles

amount (əˈmaʊnt) *n* **1** extent; quantity; supply **2** the total of two or more quantities; sum **3** the full value, effect, or significance of something **4** a principal sum plus the interest on it, as in a loan ▷ *vb* **5** (intr; usually foll by *to*) to be equal or add up in effect, meaning, or quantity [c13 from Old French *amonter* to go up, from *amont* upwards, from *a* to + *mont* mountain (from Latin *mōns*)]

> ▋ USAGE The use of a plural noun after *amount of (an amount of bananas; the amount of refugees)* should be avoided: *a quantity of bananas; the number of refugees*

amount of substance *n* a measure of the number of entities (atoms, molecules, ions, electrons, etc) present in a substance, expressed in moles

amour French (amur) *n* a love affair, esp a secret or illicit one [c13 from Old French, from Latin *amor* love]

amour-propre French (amurprɔprə) *n* self-respect

amowt (əˈmaʊt) *n* a variant spelling of **amaut**

Amoy (əˈmɔɪ) *n* **1** a port in SE China, in Fujian province on Amoy Island, at the mouth of the Jiulong River opposite Taiwan: one of the first treaty ports opened to European trade (1842). Pop: 746 000 (2005 est). Modern Chinese name: Xiamen **2** the dialect of Chinese spoken in Amoy, Taiwan, and elsewhere: a Min dialect

amp (æmp) *n* **1** an ampere **2** *informal* an amplifier ▷ *vb* **3** *Austral informal* to excite or become excited ▷ See also **amp up**

AMP *abbreviation for* **1** adenosine monophosphate **2** Australian Mutual Provident Society

amp. *abbreviation for* ampere

ampelopsis (ˌæmpɪˈlɒpsɪs) *n* any woody vine of the vitaceous genus *Ampelopsis,* of tropical and subtropical Asia and America [c19 from New Latin, from Greek *ampelos* grapevine]

amperage (ˈæmpərɪdʒ) *n* the magnitude of an electric current measured in amperes, esp the rated current of an electrical component or device

ampere (ˈæmpɛə) *n* **1** the basic SI unit of electric current; the constant current that, when maintained in two parallel conductors of infinite length and negligible cross section placed 1 metre apart in free space, produces a force of 2×10^{-7} newton per metre between them. 1 ampere is equivalent to 1 coulomb per second **2** a former unit of electric current (**international ampere**); the current that, when passed through a solution of silver nitrate, deposits silver at the rate of 0.001118 gram per second. 1 international ampere equals 0.999835 ampere ▷ Abbreviation: amp Symbol: A [c19 named after André Marie *Ampère* (1775–1836), French physicist and mathematician]

ampere-hour *n* a practical unit of quantity of electricity; the quantity that flows in one hour through a conductor carrying a current of 1 ampere. 1 ampere-hour is equivalent to 3600 coulombs. Abbreviation: a.h.

ampere-turn *n* a unit of magnetomotive force; the magnetomotive force produced by a current of 1 ampere passing through one complete turn of a coil. 1 ampere-turn is equivalent to 4π/10 or 1.257 gilberts. Abbreviations: At, A

ampersand (ˈæmpəˌsænd) *n* the character (&), meaning *and*: *John Brown & Co* [c19 shortened from *and per se and,* that is, the symbol & by itself (represents) *and*]

amphetamine (æmˈfɛtəˌmiːn, -mɪn) *n* a synthetic colourless volatile liquid used medicinally as the white crystalline sulphate, mainly for its stimulant action on the central nervous system, although it also stimulates the sympathetic nervous system. It can have unpleasant or dangerous side effects and drug dependence can occur; 1-phenyl-2-aminopropane. Formula: $C_6H_5CH_2CH(NH_2)CH_3$ [c20 from A(LPHA) + M(ETHYL) + PH(ENYL) + ET(HYL) + -AMINE]

amphi- *prefix* **1** on both sides; at both ends; of both kinds: *amphipod; amphitrichous; amphibious* **2** around: *amphibole* [from Greek]

amphiarthrosis (ˌæmfɪɑːˈθrəʊsɪs) *n, pl* -ses (-siːz) *anatomy* a type of articulation permitting only slight movement, as between the vertebrae of the backbone [c19 from AMPHI- + Greek *arthrōsis* articulation, from *arthron* a joint]

amphiaster (ˈæmfɪˌæstə) *n cytology* the structure that occurs in a cell undergoing mitosis, consisting of a spindle with an aster at each end [c19 from AMPHI- + New Latin *aster;* see ASTER]

amphibian (æmˈfɪbɪən) *n* **1** any cold-blooded vertebrate of the class *Amphibia,* typically living on land but breeding in water. Their aquatic larvae (tadpoles) undergo metamorphosis into the adult form. The class includes the newts and salamanders, frogs and toads, and caecilians **2** a type of aircraft able to land and take off from both water and land **3** any vehicle able to travel on both water and land ▷ *adj* **4** another word for **amphibious 5** of, relating to, or belonging to the class *Amphibia*

amphibiotic (ˌæmfɪbaɪˈɒtɪk) *adj* having an aquatic larval form and a terrestrial adult form, as amphibians

amphibious (æmˈfɪbɪəs) *adj* **1** able to live both on land and in the water, as frogs, toads, etc **2** designed for operation on or from both water and land **3** relating to military forces and equipment organized for operations launched from the sea against an enemy shore **4** having a dual or mixed nature [c17 from Greek *amphibios,* literally: having a double life, from AMPHI- + *bios* life] > am'phibiously *adv* > am'phibiousness *n*

amphiblastic (ˌæmfɪˈblæstɪk) *adj* (of animal ova) showing complete but unequal cleavage after fertilization

amphiblastula (ˌæmfɪˈblæstjʊlə) *n* the free-swimming larva of certain sponges, which consists of a hollow spherical mass of cells some of which have flagella

amphibole (ˈæmfɪˌbəʊl) *n* any of a large group of minerals consisting of the silicates of calcium, iron, magnesium, sodium, and aluminium, usually in the form of long slender dark-coloured crystals. Members of the group, including hornblende, actinolite, and tremolite, are common constituents of igneous rocks [c17 from French, from Greek *amphibolos* uncertain; so called from the large number of varieties in the group]

amphibolite (æmˈfɪbəˌlaɪt) *n* a metamorphic rock consisting mainly of amphibole and plagioclase

amphibology (ˌæmfɪˈbɒlədʒɪ) *or* **amphiboly** (æmˈfɪbəlɪ) *n, pl* -gies *or* -lies ambiguity of expression, esp when due to a grammatical construction, as in *save rags and waste paper* [c14 from Late Latin *amphibologia,* ultimately from Greek *amphibolos* ambiguous; see AMPHIBOLE, -LOGY] > ˌamphi'bolic *or* amphibolous (æmˈfɪbələs) *adj* > amphibological (æmˌfɪbəˈlɒdʒɪk⁹l) *adj* > amˌphibo'logically *adv*

amphibrach (ˈæmfɪˌbræk) *n prosody* a metrical foot consisting of a long syllable between two short syllables (˘—˘). Compare **cretic** [c16 from Latin, from Greek *amphibrakhus,* literally: both ends being short, from AMPHI- + *brakhus* short] > ˌamphi'brachic *adj*

amphichroic (ˌæmfɪˈkrəʊɪk) *or* **amphichromatic** (ˌæmfɪkrəʊˈmætɪk) *adj* producing two colours, one on reacting with an acid, the other on reacting with a base

amphicoelous (ˌæmfɪˈsiːləs) *adj* (of the vertebrae of most fishes and some amphibians) concave at the anterior and posterior ends [c19 from AMPHI- + Greek *koilos* hollow]

amphictyon (æmˈfɪktɪən) *n* a delegate to an amphictyonic council [c16 back formation from *amphictyons,* from Greek *amphiktiones* neighbours, from AMPHI- + *ktizein* to found]

amphictyony (æmˈfɪktɪənɪ) *n, pl* -nies (in ancient Greece) a religious association of states for the maintenance of temples and the cults connected with them > amphictyonic (æmˌfɪktɪˈɒnɪk) *adj*

amphidentate (ˌæmfɪˈdɛnteɪt) *adj* (of a ligand) able to coordinate through either of two different atoms, as in CN⁻. Also: ambidentate

amphidiploid (ˌæmfɪˈdɪplɔɪd) *n* a plant originating from hybridization between two species in which the chromosome number is the

a

sum of the chromosome numbers of both parental species. It behaves as an independent species

amphigory ('æmfɪgərɪ) or **amphigouri** ('æmfɪˌgʊərɪ) n, pl -ries or -ris a piece of nonsensical writing in verse or, less commonly, prose [c19 from French amphigouri, of unknown origin] > amphigoric (ˌæmfɪ'gɒrɪk) adj

amphimacer (æm'fɪməsə) n prosody another word for **cretic** [c16 from Latin amphimacrus, from Greek amphimakros both ends being long, from AMPHI- + makros long]

amphimixis (ˌæmfɪ'mɪksɪs) n, pl -mixes (-'mɪksiːz) true sexual reproduction by the fusion of gametes from two organisms. Compare **apomixis** [c19 from AMPHI- + Greek mixis a blending, from mignunai to mingle] > ˌamphi'mictic adj

amphioxus (ˌæmfɪ'ɒksəs) n, pl -oxi (-'ɒksaɪ) or -oxuses another name for the **lancelet** [c19 from New Latin: both ends being sharp, from AMPHI- + Greek oxus sharp]

amphipathic (ˌæmfɪ'pæθɪk) or **amphipath** ('æmfɪˌpæθ) adj chem, biochem of or relating to a molecule that possesses both hydrophobic and hydrophilic elements, such as are found in detergents, or phospholipids of biological membranes

amphipod ('æmfɪˌpɒd) n 1 any marine or freshwater crustacean of the order Amphipoda, such as the sand hoppers, in which the body is laterally compressed: subclass Malacostraca ▷ adj 2 of, relating to, or belonging to the Amphipoda

amphipodous (æm'fɪpədəs) adj (of certain invertebrates, such as sand hoppers) having both swimming and jumping appendages

amphiprostyle (æm'fɪprəˌstaɪl, ˌæmfɪ'prəʊstaɪl) adj 1 (esp of a classical temple) having a set of columns at both ends but not at the sides ▷ n 2 a temple of this kind > amˌphipro'stylar adj

amphiprotic (ˌæmfɪ'prəʊtɪk) adj another word for amphoteric

amphisbaena (ˌæmfɪs'biːnə) n, pl -nae (-niː) or -nas 1 any worm lizard of the genus Amphisbaena 2 classical myth a poisonous serpent having a head at each end and able to move forwards or backwards [c16 via Latin from Greek amphisbaina, from amphis both ways + bainein to go] > ˌamphis'baenic adj

amphistomatal (ˌæmfɪ'stəʊmətᵊl) or **amphistomatic** (ˌæmfɪstə'mætɪk) adj (of a leaf) having stomata on both surfaces

amphistomous (æm'fɪstəʊməs) adj (of certain animals, such as leeches) having a sucker at either end of the body

amphistylar (ˌæmfɪ'staɪlə) adj 1 (esp of a classical temple) having a set of columns at both ends or at both sides ▷ n 2 a temple of this kind

amphitheatre or US **amphitheater** ('æmfɪˌθɪətə) n 1 a building, usually circular or oval, in which tiers of seats rise from a central open arena, as in those of ancient Rome 2 a place where contests are held; arena 3 any level circular area of ground surrounded by higher ground 4 a the first tier of seats in the gallery of a theatre b any similarly designated seating area in a theatre 5 a lecture room in which seats are tiered away from a central area > amphitheatric (ˌæmfɪθɪ'ætrɪk) or ˌamphithe'atrical adj > ˌamphithe'atrically adv

amphithecium (ˌæmfɪ'θiːsɪəm) n, pl -cia (-sɪə) the outer layer of cells of the sporophyte of mosses and liverworts that develops into the outer parts of the spore-bearing capsule [c19 from New Latin, from AMPHI- + Greek thēkion a little case, from thēkē case]

amphitricha (æm'fɪtrɪkə) pl n bacteria that have flagella at both ends [c20 from AMPHI- + -tricha, from Greek thrix hair] > am'phitrichous adj

Amphitrite (ˌæmfɪ'traɪtɪ) n Greek myth a sea goddess, wife of Poseidon and mother of Triton

amphitropous (æm'fɪtrəpəs) adj (of a plant ovule) partially inverted so that the base and the micropyle at the apex are the same distance from the funicle

Amphitryon (æm'fɪtrɪən) n Greek myth the grandson of Perseus and husband of Alcmene

amphora ('æmfərə) n, pl -phorae (-fəˌriː) or -phoras an ancient Greek or Roman two-handled narrow-necked jar for oil, wine, etc [c17 from Latin, from Greek amphoreus, from AMPHI- + phoreus bearer, from pherein to bear]

amphoric (æm'fɒrɪk) adj resembling the sound produced by blowing into a bottle. Amphoric breath sounds are heard through a stethoscope placed over a cavity in the lung

amphoteric (ˌæmfə'tɛrɪk) adj chem able to function as either a base or an acid. Also: amphiprotic [c19 from Greek amphoteros each of two (from amphō both) + -ic]

ampicillin (ˌæmpɪ'sɪlɪn) n a semisynthetic penicillin used to treat various infections

ample ('æmpᵊl) adj 1 more than sufficient; abundant: an ample helping 2 large in size, extent, or amount: of ample proportions [c15 from Old French, from Latin amplus spacious] > 'ampleness n

amplexicaul (æm'plɛksɪˌkɔːl) adj (of some sessile leaves, stipules, etc) having an enlarged base that encircles the stem [c18 from New Latin amplexicaulis, from Latin amplectī to embrace + caulis stalk]

amplification (ˌæmplɪfɪ'keɪʃən) n 1 the act or result of amplifying 2 material added to a statement, story, etc, in order to expand or clarify it 3 a statement, story, etc, with such additional material 4 electronics a the increase in strength of an electrical signal by means of an amplifier b another word for **gain**¹ (sense 13) 5 genetics Also called: gene amplification the production of multiple copies of a particular gene or DNA sequence. It can occur naturally or artificially, by genetic engineering techniques

amplifier ('æmplɪˌfaɪə) n 1 an electronic device used to increase the strength of the signal fed into it 2 such a device used for the amplification of audio frequency signals in a radio, etc 3 photog an additional lens for altering the focal length of a camera lens 4 a person or thing that amplifies

amplify ('æmplɪˌfaɪ) vb -fies, -fying, -fied 1 (tr) to increase in size, extent, effect, etc, as by the addition of extra material; augment; enlarge; expand 2 electronics to produce amplification of (electrical signals); increase the amplitude of (signals) 3 (tr) US to exaggerate 4 (intr) to expand or enlarge a speech, narrative, etc [c15 from Old French amplifier, ultimately from Latin amplificāre to enlarge, from amplus spacious + facere to make] > 'ampliˌfiable adj

amplitude ('æmplɪˌtjuːd) n 1 greatness of extent; magnitude 2 abundance or copiousness 3 breadth or scope, as of the mind 4 astronomy the angular distance along the horizon measured from true east or west to the point of intersection of the vertical circle passing through a celestial body 5 Also called: argument maths (of a complex number) the angle that the vector representing the complex number makes with the positive real axis. If the point (x, y) has polar coordinates (r, θ), the amplitude of x + iy is θ, that is, arctan y/x. Compare **modulus** (sense 2) See also **Argand diagram** 6 physics the maximum variation from the zero or mean value of a periodically varying quantity [c16 from Latin amplitūdō breadth, from amplus spacious]

amplitude modulation n 1 one of the principal methods of transmitting audio, visual, or other types of information using radio waves, the relevant signal being superimposed onto a radio-frequency carrier wave. The frequency of the carrier wave remains unchanged but its amplitude is varied in accordance with the amplitude of the input signal. Abbreviations: AM, am Compare **frequency modulation** 2 a wave that has undergone this process

amply ('æmplɪ) adv more than sufficiently; fully; generously: he was amply rewarded

ampoule ('æmpuːl, -pjuːl) or esp US **ampule** n med

a small glass vessel in which liquids for injection are hermetically sealed

ampulla (æm'pʊlə) n, pl -pullae (-'pʊliː) 1 anatomy the dilated end part of certain ducts or canals, such as the end of a uterine tube 2 Christianity a a vessel for containing the wine and water used at the Eucharist b a small flask for containing consecrated oil 3 a Roman two-handled bottle for oil, wine, or perfume [c16 from Latin, diminutive of AMPHORA] > ampullaceous (ˌæmpʊ'leɪʃəs) or ˌampul'laceal adj > ampullar (æm'pʊlə) or ampullary (æm'pʊlərɪ) adj

amp up vb (tr, adverb) informal 1 to increase 2 to increase the power or force of (something) 3 to excite, arouse, or work up (a person, emotions, etc)

amputate ('æmpjʊˌteɪt) vb surgery to remove (all or part of a limb, esp an arm or leg) [c17 from Latin amputāre, from am- around + putāre to trim, prune] > ˌampu'tation n > 'ampuˌtator n

amputee (ˌæmpjʊ'tiː) n a person who has had a limb amputated

Amravati (æm'rɑːvətɪ) n a town in central India, in NE Maharashtra: cotton centre. Pop: 549 370 (2001). Former name: Amraoti (ˌæm'rɑːətɪ, 'æm-)

amrit ('æmrit) n Sikhism a sanctified solution of sugar and water used in the Amrit Ceremony [from Punjabi: nectar]

amrita or **amreeta** (æm'riːtə) n Hindu myth 1 the ambrosia of the gods that bestows immortality 2 the immortality it confers [from Sanskrit amrta immortal, from a- without + mrta death]

Amrit Ceremony n Sikhism the ceremony of initiation into the Khalsa, at which amrit is drunk by and sprinkled on the heads of candidates for initiation

Amritsar (æm'rɪtsə) n a city in India, in NW Punjab: centre of the Sikh religion; site of a massacre in 1919 of unarmed supporters of Indian self-government by British troops; in 1984 the Golden Temple, fortified by Sikhs, was attacked by Indian troops with the loss of many Sikh lives. Pop: 975 695 (2001)

Amsterdam (ˌæmstə'dæm; Dutch amstər'dɑm) n the commercial capital of the Netherlands, a major industrial centre and port on the IJsselmeer, connected with the North Sea by canal: built on about 100 islands within a network of canals. Pop: 737 000 (2003 est)

amt abbreviation for amount

amu abbreviation for atomic mass unit

AMU (in Britain) abbreviation for Associated Metalworkers Union

amuck (ə'mʌk) n, adv a variant of amok

Amu Darya (Russian a'mu dar'ja) n a river in central Asia, rising in the Pamirs and flowing northwest through the Hindu Kush and across Turkmenistan and Uzbekistan to its delta in the Aral Sea: forms much of the N border of Afghanistan and is important for irrigation. Length: 2400 km (1500 miles). Ancient name: Oxus

amulet ('æmjʊlɪt) n a trinket or piece of jewellery worn as a protection against evil; charm [c17 from Latin amulētum, of unknown origin]

Amūn ('ɑːmən) n Egyptian myth a variant spelling of Amen

Amundsen Sea ('ɑːmʊndsən) n a part of the South Pacific Ocean, in Antarctica off Byrd Land

Amur (ə'mʊə) n a river in NE Asia, rising in N Mongolia as the Argun and flowing southeast, then northeast to the Sea of Okhotsk: forms the boundary between Manchuria and Russia. Length: about 4350 km (2700 miles). Modern Chinese name: Heilong Jiang

amusable or **amuseable** (ə'mjuːzəbᵊl) adj capable of being amused

amuse (ə'mjuːz) vb (tr) 1 to keep pleasantly occupied; entertain; divert 2 to cause to laugh or smile [c15 from Old French amuser to cause to be idle, from muser to MUSE¹]

amuse-bouche French (amyzbuʃ) n an appetizer

before a meal [from French *amuser* amuse, gratify + *bouche* mouth]

amusement (əˈmjuːzmənt) *n* **1** something that amuses, such as a game or other pastime **2** a mechanical device used for entertainment, as at a fair **3** the act of amusing or the state or quality of being amused

amusement arcade *n Brit* a covered area having coin-operated game machines

amusement park *n* an open-air entertainment area consisting of stalls, side shows, etc

amusing (əˈmjuːzɪŋ) *adj* mildly entertaining; pleasantly diverting; causing a smile or laugh > a'musingly *adv*

amygdala (əˈmɪɡdələ) *n, pl* -lae (-ˌliː) *anatomy* an almond-shaped part, such as a tonsil or a lobe of the cerebellum [c16 from Medieval Latin: ALMOND]

amygdalate (əˈmɪɡdəlɪt, -ˌleɪt) *adj* relating to, having, or bearing almonds

amygdale (əˈmɪɡdeɪl) *n* a vesicle in a volcanic rock, formed from a bubble of escaping gas, that has become filled with light-coloured minerals, such as quartz and calcite. Also called: amygdule (əˈmɪɡdjuːl) [c19 from Greek: ALMOND]

amygdalin (əˈmɪɡdəlɪn) *n* a white soluble bitter-tasting crystalline glycoside extracted from bitter almonds and stone fruits such as peaches and apricots. Formula: $C_6H_5CHCNOC_{12}H_{21}O_{10}$

amygdaline (əˈmɪɡdəlɪn, -ˌlaɪn) *adj* **1** *anatomy* of or relating to a tonsil **2** of or resembling almonds

amygdaloid (əˈmɪɡdəˌlɔɪd) *n* **1** a volcanic igneous rock containing amygdales ▷ *adj* **2** having the shape of an almond **3** a less common form of **amygdaloidal** (sense 1)

amygdaloidal (əˌmɪɡdəˈlɔɪdᵊl) *adj* **1** (of a volcanic rock) containing amygdales **2** a less common form of **amygdaloid** (sense 2)

amyl (ˈæmɪl) *n* (*modifier, no longer in technical usage*) of, consisting of, or containing any of eight isomeric forms of the monovalent group C_5H_{11}-: *amyl group or radical*. See also **pentyl** [c19 from Latin: AMYLUM]

amylaceous (ˌæmɪˈleɪʃəs) *adj* of or resembling starch

amyl acetate *n* another name (no longer in technical usage) for **pentyl acetate**

amyl alcohol *n* a colourless flammable liquid existing in eight isomeric forms that is used as a solvent and in the manufacture of organic compounds and pharmaceuticals. Formula: $C_5H_{11}OH$

amylase (ˈæmɪˌleɪz) *n* any of several enzymes that hydrolyse starch and glycogen to simple sugars, such as glucose. They are present in saliva

amylene (ˈæmɪˌliːn) *n* another name (no longer in technical usage) for **pentene**

amyl nitrite *n* a yellowish unstable volatile fragrant liquid used in medicine as a vasodilator and in perfumes. Formula: $(CH_3)_2CHCH_2CH_2NO_2$

amylo- *or before a vowel* **amyl-** *combining form* indicating starch: *amylolysis; amylase* [from Latin: AMYLUM]

amyloid (ˈæmɪˌlɔɪd) *n* **1** *pathol* a complex protein resembling starch, deposited in tissues in some degenerative diseases **2** any substance resembling starch ▷ *adj* **3** starchlike

amyloidosis (ˌæmɪlɔɪˈdəʊsɪs) *n pathol* the deposition of amyloid in various tissues of the body, as occurs in certain chronic infections

amylolysis (ˌæmɪˈlɒlɪsɪs) *n* the conversion of starch into sugar > amylolytic (əˌmaɪləʊˈlɪtɪk) *adj*

amylopectin (ˌæmɪləʊˈpɛktɪn) *n* the major component of starch (about 80 per cent), consisting of branched chains of glucose units. It is insoluble and gives a red-brown colour with iodine. Compare **amylose**

amylopsin (ˌæmɪˈlɒpsɪn) *n* an enzyme of the pancreatic juice that converts starch into sugar; pancreatic amylase [c19 from AMYLO(LYSIS) + (PE)PSIN]

amylose (ˈæmɪˌləʊz, -ləʊs) *n* the minor component (about 20 per cent) of starch,

consisting of long unbranched chains of glucose units. It is soluble in water and gives an intense blue colour with iodine. Compare **amylopectin**

amylum (ˈæmɪləm) *n* another name for **starch** (sense 2) [Latin, from Greek *amulon* fine meal, starch, from *amulos* not ground at the mill, from A-¹ + *mulē* mill]

amyotonia (ˌeɪmaɪəˈtəʊnɪə) *n* another name for **myotonia**

amyotrophic lateral sclerosis (ˌæmɪəˈtrəʊfɪk) *n* a form of motor neurone disease in which degeneration of motor tracts in the spinal cord causes progressive muscular paralysis starting in the limbs. Also called: Lou Gehrig's disease

amyotrophy (ˌæmɪˈɒtrəfɪ) *n pathol* wasting of muscles, caused by disease of the nerves supplying them

Amytal (ˈæmɪˌtæl) *n trademark* a barbiturate, a brand of amobarbital, used as a sedative and hypnotic

an¹ (æn; *unstressed* ən) *determiner* (*indefinite article*) a form of **a¹** used before an initial vowel sound: *an old car; an elf; an honour* [Old English *ān* ONE]

> **USAGE** *An* was formerly often used before words that begin with *h* and are unstressed on the first syllable: *an hotel; an historic meeting*. Sometimes the initial *h* was not pronounced. This usage is now becoming obsolete

an² *or* **an'** (æn; *unstressed* ən) *conj* (*subordinating*) an obsolete or dialect word for **if** See **and** (sense 9)

an³ *the internet domain name for* Netherlands Antilles

An¹ (ɑːn) *n myth* the Sumerian sky god. Babylonian counterpart: Anu

An² *the chemical symbol for* actinon

AN *abbreviation for* Anglo-Norman

an- *or before a consonant* **a-** *prefix* not; without: *anaphrodisiac* [from Greek]

-an, -ean *or* **-ian** *suffix* **1** (*forming adjectives and nouns*) belonging to or relating to; a person belonging to or coming from: *European* **2** (*forming adjectives and nouns*) typical of or resembling; a person typical of: *Elizabethan* **3** (*forming adjectives and nouns*) adhering to or following; an adherent of: *Christian* **4** (*forming nouns*) a person who specializes or is expert in: *dietitian; phonetician* [from Latin *-ānus*, suffix of adjectives]

ana¹ (ˈeɪnə, ˈɑːnə) *adv pharmacol obsolete* (of ingredients in a prescription) in equal quantities. Abbreviation: aa [c16 via Medieval Latin from Greek: of every one similarly]

ana² (ˈɑːnə) *n* **1** a collection of reminiscences, sketches, etc, of or about a person or place **2** an item of or for such a collection [c18 independent use of -ANA]

ANA *commerce abbreviation for* Article Number Association: (in Britain) an organization of manufacturers, retailers, and wholesalers that provides a system (**article numbering**) by which a product is identified by a unique machine-readable number (see **bar code**) compatible with article-numbering systems used in other countries

ana- *or before a vowel* **an-** *prefix* **1** up; upwards: *anadromous* **2** again: *anagram* **3** back; backwards: *anatropous* [from Greek *ana*]

-ana *or* **-iana** *suffix forming nouns* denoting a collection of objects or information relating to a particular individual, subject, or place: *Shakespeareana; Victoriana; Americana* [New Latin, from Latin *-āna*, literally: matters relating to, neuter plural of *-ānus*; see -AN]

anabaena (ˌænəˈbiːnə) *n, pl* -nas any freshwater alga of the genus *Anabaena*. sometimes occurring in drinking water, giving it a fishy taste and smell [New Latin, from Greek *anabainein* to shoot up, go up, from ANA- + *bainein* to go; so called because they rise to the surface at intervals]

anabantid (ˌænəˈbæntɪd) *n* **1** any of various spiny-finned fishes constituting the family *Anabantidae* and including the fighting fish, climbing perch, and gourami. See also **labyrinth**

fish ▷ *adj* **2** of, relating to, or belonging to the family *Anabantidae*

Anabaptist (ˌænəˈbæptɪst) *n* **1** a member of any of various 16th-century Protestant movements that rejected infant baptism, insisted that adults be rebaptized, and sought to establish Christian communism **2** a member of a later Protestant sect holding the same doctrines, esp with regard to baptism ▷ *adj* **3** of or relating to these movements or sects or their doctrines [c16 from Ecclesiastical Latin *anabaptista*, from *anabaptizāre* to baptize again, from Late Greek *anabaptizein;* see ANA-, BAPTIZE] > ˌAna'baptism *n*

anabas (ˈænəˌbæs) *n* any of several labyrinth fishes of the genus Anabas, esp the **climbing fish** [c19 from New Latin, from Greek *anabainein* to go up; see ANABAENA]

anabasis (əˈnæbəsɪs) *n, pl* -ses (-ˌsiːz) **1** the march of Cyrus the Younger and his Greek mercenaries from Sardis to Cunaxa in Babylonia in 401 BC, described by Xenophon in his *Anabasis* Compare **katabasis 2** any military expedition, esp one from the coast to the interior [c18 from Greek: a going up, ascent, from *anabainein* to go up; see ANABAENA]

anabatic (ˌænəˈbætɪk) *adj meteorol* (of air currents) rising upwards, esp up slopes. Compare **katabatic** [c19 from Greek *anabatikos* relating to ascents, from *anabainein* to go up; see ANABASIS]

anabiosis (ˌænəbaɪˈəʊsɪs) *n* the ability to return to life after apparent death; suspended animation [c19 via New Latin from Greek, from *anabioein* to come back to life, from ANA- + *bios* life] > anabiotic (ˌænəbaɪˈɒtɪk) *adj*

anableps (ˈænəˌblɛps) *n, pl* -bleps any of various cyprinodont fishes constituting the genus *Anableps*, which includes the four-eyed fishes [New Latin, literally: one who looks up, from Greek, from *anablepein* to look up]

anabolic (ˌænəˈbɒlɪk) *adj* of or relating to anabolism

anabolic steroid *n* any of a group of synthetic steroid hormones (androgens) used to stimulate muscle and bone growth for therapeutic or athletic purposes

anabolism (əˈnæbəˌlɪzəm) *n* a metabolic process in which complex molecules are synthesized from simpler ones with the storage of energy; constructive metabolism. Compare **catabolism** [c19 from ANA- + (META)BOLISM]

anabolite (əˈnæbəˌlaɪt) *n* a product of anabolism > anabolitic (əˌnæbəˈlɪtɪk) *adj*

anabranch (ˈɑːnəˌbrɑːntʃ) *n* a stream that leaves a river and enters it again further downstream [c19 from *ana(stomosing) branch*]

anacardiaceous (ˌænəˌkɑːdɪˈeɪʃəs) *adj* of, relating to, or belonging to the *Anacardiaceae*, a chiefly tropical family of trees and shrubs many of which have edible drupes. The family includes the cashew, mango, pistachio, and sumach [c19 from New Latin *Anacardiāceae*, from ANA- + Greek *kardia* heart; so called from the shape of the top of the fruit stem]

anachorism (əˈnækəˌrɪzəm) *n* a geographical misplacement; something located in an incongruous position. Compare **anachronism** [c19 from ANA- + *khōros* place]

anachronic (ˌænəˈkrɒnɪk) *or* **anachronical** *adj* out of chronological order or out of date [c19 see ANACHRONISM] > ˌana'chronically *adv*

anachronism (əˈnækrəˌnɪzəm) *n* **1** the representation of an event, person, or thing in a historical context in which it could not have occurred or existed **2** a person or thing that belongs or seems to belong to another time: *she regards the Church as an anachronism* [c17 from Latin *anachronismus*, from Greek *anakhronismos* a mistake in chronology, from *anakhronizein* to err in a time reference, from ANA- + *khronos* time] > aˌnachro'nistic *adj* > aˌnachro'nistically *adv*

anaclinal (ˌænəˈklaɪnᵊl) *adj* (of valleys and similar formations) progressing in a direction opposite to

a

the dip of the surrounding rock strata [C19 see ANA-, -CLINE]

anaclitic (ˌænəˈklɪtɪk) *adj psychoanal* of or relating to relationships that are characterized by the strong dependence of one person on others or another [C20 from Greek *anaklitos* for leaning upon; see ANA-, -CLINE] > **anaclisis** (ˌænəˈklaɪsɪs) *n*

anacoluthia (ˌænəkəˈluːθɪə) *n rhetoric* lack of grammatical sequence, esp within a single sentence > ˌanacoˈluthic *adj*

anacoluthon (ˌænəkəˈluːθɒn) *n*, *pl* **-tha** (-θə) *rhetoric* a construction that involves the change from one grammatical sequence to another within a single sentence; an example of anacoluthia [C18 from Late Latin, from Greek *anakolouthon*, from *anakolouthos* not consistent, from AN- + *akolouthos* following]

anaconda (ˌænəˈkɒndə) *n* a very large nonvenomous arboreal and semiaquatic snake, *Eunectes murinus*, of tropical South America, which kills its prey by constriction: family *Boidae* (boas) [C18 probably changed from Sinhalese *henakandayā* whip snake, from *hena* lightning + *kanda* stem; originally referring to a snake of Sri Lanka]

anacoustic (ˌænəˈkuːstɪk) *adj* unable to support the propagation of sound; soundless

Anacreontic (əˌnækrɪˈɒntɪk) (*sometimes not capital*) *adj* **1** in the manner of the Greek lyric poet Anacreon (?572–?488 BC), noted for his short songs celebrating love and wine **2** ▷ *n* (of verse) in praise of love or wine; amatory or convivial **3** an Anacreontic poem > Aˌnacreˈontically *adv*

anacrusis (ˌænəˈkruːsɪs) *n*, *pl* **-ses** (-siːz) **1** *prosody* one or more unstressed syllables at the beginning of a line of verse **2** *music* **a** an unstressed note or group of notes immediately preceding the strong first beat of the first bar **b** another word for **upbeat** [C19 from Greek *anakrousis* prelude, from *anakrouein* to strike up, from ANA- + *krouein* to strike] > **anacrustic** (ˌænəˈkrʌstɪk) *adj*

anadem (ˈænəˌdɛm) *n poetic* a garland for the head [C17 from Latin *anadēma* wreath, from Greek *anadēma*, from *anadein* to wreathe, from ANA- + *dein* to bind]

anadiplosis (ˌænədɪˈpləʊsɪs) *n rhetoric* repetition of the words or phrase at the end of one sentence, line, or clause at the beginning of the next [C16 via Latin from Greek: repetition, from *anadiploun* to double back, from ANA- + *diploun* to double]

anadromous (əˈnædrəməs) *adj* (of fishes such as the salmon) migrating up rivers from the sea in order to breed. Compare **catadromous** [C18 from Greek *anadromos* running upwards, from ANA- + *dromos* a running]

Anadyr (*Russian* aˈnadir) *n* **1** a town in Russia, in NE Siberia at the mouth of the Anadyr River. Pop: 6586 (1993 est) **2** a mountain range in Russia, in NE Siberia, rising over 1500 m (5000 ft) **3** a river in Russia, rising in mountains on the Arctic Circle, south of the Anadyr Range, and flowing east to the Gulf of Anadyr. Length: 725 km (450 miles) **4** **Gulf of** an inlet of the Bering Sea, off the coast of NE Russia

anaemia *or US* **anemia** (əˈniːmɪə) *n* **1** a deficiency in the number of red blood cells or in their haemoglobin content, resulting in pallor, shortness of breath, and lack of energy **2** lack of vitality or vigour **3** pallid complexion [C19 from New Latin, from Greek *anaimia* lack of blood, from AN- + *haima* blood]

anaemic *or US* **anemic** (əˈniːmɪk) *adj* **1** relating to or suffering from anaemia **2** pale and sickly looking; lacking vitality

anaerobe (æˈnɛərəʊb, ˈænərəʊb) *or* **anaerobium** (ˌænɛəˈrəʊbɪəm) *n*, *pl* **-obes** *or* **-obia** (-ˈəʊbɪə) an organism that does not require oxygen for respiration. Compare **aerobe**

anaerobic (ˌænəˈrəʊbɪk) *adj* **1** (of an organism or process) requiring the absence of or not dependent on the presence of oxygen **2** of or relating to anaerobes ▷ Compare **aerobic** > ˌanaerˈobically *adv*

anaerobiosis (ˌænɛərəʊbaɪˈəʊsɪs) *n* life in the absence of oxygen

anaesthesia *or US* **anesthesia** (ˌænɪsˈθiːzɪə) *n* **1** local or general loss of bodily sensation, esp of touch, as the result of nerve damage or other abnormality **2** loss of sensation, esp of pain, induced by drugs: called **general anaesthesia** when consciousness is lost and **local anaesthesia** when only a specific area of the body is involved **3** a general dullness or lack of feeling [C19 from New Latin, from Greek *anaisthēsia* absence of sensation, from AN- + *aisthēsis* feeling]

anaesthesiology *or US* **anesthesiology** (ˌænɪsˌθiːzɪˈɒlədʒɪ) *n* the US name for **anaesthetics**

anaesthetic *or US* **anesthetic** (ˌænɪsˈθɛtɪk) *n* **1** a substance that causes anaesthesia ▷ *adj* **2** causing or characterized by anaesthesia

anaesthetics (ˌænɪsˈθɛtɪks) *n* (*functioning as singular*) the science, study, and practice of anaesthesia and its application. US name: **anesthesiology**

anaesthetist (əˈniːsθətɪst) *n* **1** *Brit* a qualified doctor specializing in the administration of anaesthetics. US name: **anesthesiologist 2** *US* a person qualified to administer anaesthesia, often a nurse or someone other than a physician. Compare **anesthesiologist**

anaesthetize, anaesthetise *or US* **anesthetize** (əˈniːsθəˌtaɪz) *vb* (*tr*) to render insensible to pain by administering an anaesthetic > aˌnaestheˈtization, aˌnaestheˈtisation *or US* aˌnestheˈtization *n*

anaglyph (ˈænəˌglɪf) *n* **1** *photog* a stereoscopic picture consisting of two images of the same object, taken from slightly different angles, in two complementary colours, usually red and cyan (green-blue). When viewed through spectacles having one red and one cyan lens, the images merge to produce a stereoscopic sensation **2** anything cut to stand in low relief, such as a cameo [C17 from Greek *anagluphē* carved in low relief, from ANA- + *gluphē* carving, from *gluphein* to carve] > ˌanaˈglyphic, ˌanaˈglyphical *or* anaglyptic (ˌænəˈglɪptɪk) *or* ˌanaˈglyptical *adj* > anaglyphy (əˈnægləfɪ, ˈænəˌglɪfɪ) *n*

Anaglypta (ˌænəˈglɪptə) *n trademark* a type of thick embossed wallpaper [C19 from Greek *anagluptos*; see ANAGLYPH]

anagnorisis (ˌænəgˈnɒrɪsɪs) *n*, *pl* **-ses** (-ˌsiːz) (in Greek tragedy) the recognition or discovery by the protagonist of the identity of some character or the nature of his own predicament, which leads to the resolution of the plot; denouement [from Greek: recognition]

anagoge *or* **anagogy** (ˈænəˌgɒdʒɪ) *n* **1** allegorical or spiritual interpretation, esp of sacred works such as the Bible **2** *Christianity* allegorical interpretation of the Old Testament as typifying or foreshadowing subjects in the New Testament [C18 via Late Latin from Greek *anagōgē* a lifting up, from *anagein*, from ANA- + *agein* to lead] > anagogic (ˌænəˈgɒdʒɪk) *or* ˌanaˈgogical *adj* > ˌanaˈgogically *adv*

anagram (ˈænəˌgræm) *n* a word or phrase the letters of which can be rearranged into another word or phrase [C16 from New Latin *anagramma*, shortened from Greek *anagrammatismos*, from *anagrammatizein* to transpose letters, from ANA- + *gramma* a letter] > anagrammatic (ˌænəgrəˈmætɪk) *or* ˌanagramˈmatical *adj* > ˌanagramˈmatically *adv*

anagrammatize *or* **anagrammatise** (ˌænəˈgræməˌtaɪz) *vb* to arrange into an anagram > ˌanaˈgrammaˌtism *n* > ˌanaˈgrammatist *n*

anagrammer (ˌænəˈgræmə) *n* a person who enjoys solving anagrams

Anaheim (ˈænəˌhaɪm) *n* a city in SW California: site of Disneyland. Pop: 332 361 (2003 est)

anal (ˈeɪnəl) *adj* **1** of, relating to, or near the anus **2** *psychoanal* **a** relating to a stage of psychosexual development during which the child's interest is concentrated on the anal region and excremental functions **b** designating personality traits in the adult, such as orderliness, meanness,

stubbornness, etc, due to fixation at the anal stage of development. Compare **genital** (sense 2), **oral** (sense 7), **phallic** (sense 2) [C18 from New Latin *ānālis*; see ANUS] > ˈanally *adv*

anal canal *n* the terminal part of the rectum forming the passage to the anus

analcite (əˈnælsaɪt, ˈænəlˌsaɪt, -sɪt) *or* **analcime** (æˈnælsɪm, -saɪm, -siːm) *n* a white, grey, or colourless zeolite mineral consisting of hydrated sodium aluminium silicate in cubic crystalline form. Formula: $NaAlSi_2O_6.H_2O$ [C19 from Greek *analkimos* weak (from AN- + *alkimos* strong, from *alkē* strength) + -ITE[1]]

analects (ˈænəˌlɛkts) *or* **analecta** (ˌænəˈlɛktə) *pl n* selected literary passages from one or more works [C17 via Latin from Greek *analekta*, from *analegein* to collect up, from *legein* to gather] > ˌanaˈlectic *adj*

analemma (ˌænəˈlɛmə) *n*, *pl* **-mas** *or* **-mata** (-mətə) a graduated scale shaped like a figure eight that indicates the daily declination of the sun [C17 from Latin: sundial, pedestal of sundial, from Greek *analēmma* pedestal, from *analambanein* to support] > analemmatic (ˌænəlɛˈmætɪk) *adj*

analeptic (ˌænəˈlɛptɪk) *adj* **1** (of a drug, etc) stimulating the central nervous system ▷ *n* **2** any drug, such as doxapram, that stimulates the central nervous system **3** (formerly) a restorative remedy or drug [C17 from New Latin *analēpticus*, from Greek *analēptikos* stimulating, from *analambanein* to take up; see ANALEMMA]

anal erotic *n* a person with anal personality traits

anal fin *n* a median ventral unpaired fin, situated between the anus and the tail fin in fishes, that helps to maintain stable equilibrium

analgesia (ˌænəlˈdʒiːzɪə, -sɪə) *or* **analgia** (ænˈældʒɪə) *n* **1** inability to feel pain **2** the relief of pain [C18 via New Latin from Greek: insensibility, from AN- + *algēsis* sense of pain]

analgesic (ˌænəlˈdʒiːzɪk, -sɪk) *adj* **1** of or causing analgesia ▷ *n* **2** a substance that produces analgesia

anal intercourse *n* a form of sexual intercourse in which the penis is inserted into the anus

analog (ˈænəˌlɒg) *n* a variant spelling of **analogue**

> USAGE The spelling *analog* is a US variant of *analogue* in all its senses, and is also the generally preferred spelling in the computer industry

analog computer *n* a mechanical, electrical, or electronic computer that performs arithmetical operations by using some variable physical quantity, such as mechanical movement or voltage, to represent numbers

analogize *or* **analogise** (əˈnæləˌdʒaɪz) *vb* **1** (*intr*) to make use of analogy, as in argument; draw comparisons **2** (*tr*) to make analogous or reveal analogy in

analogous (əˈnæləgəs) *adj* **1** similar or corresponding in some respect **2** *biology* (of organs and parts) having the same function but different evolutionary origin: *the paddle of a whale and the fin of a fish are analogous*. Compare **homologous** (sense 4) **3** *linguistics* formed by analogy: *an analogous plural* [C17 from Latin *analogus*, from Greek *analogos* proportionate, from ANA- + *logos* speech, ratio] > aˈnalogously *adv* > aˈnalogousness *n*

> USAGE The use of *with* after *analogous* should be avoided: *swimming has no event that is analogous to* (not *with*) *the 100 metres in athletics*

analogue *or sometimes US* **analog** (ˈænəˌlɒg) *n* **1 a** a physical object or quantity, such as a pointer on a dial or a voltage, used to measure or represent another quantity **b** (*as modifier*): *analogue watch; analogue recording* **2** something analogous to something else **3** *biology* an analogous part or organ **4** *chem* **a** an organic chemical compound related to another by substitution of hydrogen atoms with alkyl groups: *toluene is an analogue of benzene* **b** an organic compound that is similar in structure to another organic compound: *thiols are sulphur analogues of alcohols* **5** *informal* a person who is afraid of using new technological devices. Compare **digital native, digital immigrant**

▥ USAGE See at **analog**

analogue clock *or* **watch** *n* a clock or watch in which the hours, minutes, and sometimes seconds are indicated by hands on a dial. Compare **digital clock**

analogue-digital converter *n* a device converting an analogue electrical signal into a digital representation so that it can be processed by a digital system. Abbreviation: **ADC**

analogue recording *n* a sound recording process in which an audio input is converted into an analogous electrical waveform

analogy (əˈnælədʒɪ) *n, pl* **-gies 1** agreement or similarity, esp in a certain limited number of features or details **2** a comparison made to show such a similarity: *to draw an analogy between an atom and the solar system* **3** *biology* the relationship between analogous organs or parts **4** *logic, maths* a form of reasoning in which a similarity between two or more things is inferred from a known similarity between them in other respects **5** *linguistics* imitation of existing models or regular patterns in the formation of words, inflections, etc: *a child may use "sheeps" as the plural of "sheep" by analogy with "dog", "dogs", "cat", "cats", etc* [c16 from Greek *analogia* ratio, correspondence, from *analogos* ANALOGOUS] > **analogical** (ˌænəˈlɒdʒɪkˀl) *or* ˌanaˈlogic *adj* > ˌanaˈlogically *adv* > aˈnalogist *n*

analphabetic (ˌænælfəˈbɛtɪk, æn,æl-) *adj* **1** not in alphabetical order ▷ *n, adj* **2** a less common word for **illiterate** [c20 from Greek *analphabētos;* see AN-, ALPHABET] > ˌanalphaˈbetically *adv*

anal retentive *psychoanal* ▷ *n* **1** a person who exhibits anal personality traits ▷ *adj* anal-retentive **2** exhibiting anal personality traits

analysand (əˈnælɪˌsænd) *n* any person who is undergoing psychoanalysis [c20 from ANALYSE + -*and*, on the model of *multiplicand*]

analyse *or US* **analyze** (ˈænəˌlaɪz) *vb* (*tr*) **1** to examine in detail in order to discover meaning, essential features, etc **2** to break down into components or essential features: *to analyse a financial structure* **3** to make a mathematical, chemical, grammatical, etc, analysis of **4** another word for **psychoanalyse** [c17 back formation from ANALYSIS] > ˌanaˈlysable *or US* ˌanaˈlyzable *adj* > ˌanalyˈsation *or US* ˌanalyˈzation *n* > ˈanaˌlyser *or US* ˈanaˌlyzer *n*

analysis (əˈnælɪsɪs) *n, pl* **-ses** (-ˌsiːz) **1** the division of a physical or abstract whole into its constituent parts to examine or determine their relationship or value. Compare **synthesis** (sense 1) **2** a statement of the results of this **3** short for **psychoanalysis 4** *chem* **a** the decomposition of a substance into its elements, radicals, or other constituents in order to determine the kinds of constituents present (**qualitative analysis**) or the amount of each constituent (**quantitative analysis**) **b** the result obtained by such a determination **5** *linguistics* the use of word order together with word function to express syntactic relations in a language, as opposed to the use of inflections. Compare **synthesis** (sense 4) **6** *maths* the branch of mathematics principally concerned with the properties of functions, largely arising out of calculus **7** *philosophy* (in the writings of Kant) the separation of a concept from another that contains it. Compare **synthesis** (sense 6a) **8** **in the last, final,** *or* **ultimate analysis** after everything has been given due consideration [c18 from New Latin, from Greek *analusis,* literally: a dissolving, from *analuein,* from ANA- + *luein* to loosen]

analysis of variance *n* *statistics* any of a number of techniques for resolving the observed variance between sets of data into components, esp to determine whether the difference between two

samples is explicable as random sampling variation with the same underlying population. Abbreviation: ANOVA

analysis situs *n* a former name for **topology** (sense 2)

analyst (ˈænəlɪst) *n* **1** a person who analyses or is skilled in analysis **2** short for **psychoanalyst**

analytic (ˌænəˈlɪtɪk) *or* **analytical** (ˌænəˈlɪtɪkˀl) *adj* **1** relating to analysis **2** capable of or given to analysing: *an analytic mind* **3** Also: isolating *linguistics* denoting languages, such as Chinese, whose morphology is characterized by analysis. Compare **synthetic** (sense 3), **agglutinative** (sense 2), **polysynthetic 4** *logic* (of a proposition) **a** true by virtue of the meanings of the words alone without reference to the facts, as *all spinsters are unmarried* **b** true or false by virtue of meaning alone; so *all spinsters are married* is analytically false ▷ Compare **synthetic** (sense 4), **a priori 5** Also: regular, holomorphic *maths* (of a function of a complex variable) having a derivative at each point of its domain [c16 via Late Latin from Greek *analutikos* from *analuein* to dissolve, break down; see ANALYSIS] > ˌanaˈlytically *adv*

analytical geometry *n* the branch of geometry that uses algebraic notation and analysis to locate a geometric point in terms of a coordinate system; coordinate geometry

analytical philosophy *n* a school of philosophy which flourished in the first half of the 20th century and which sought to resolve philosophical problems by analysing the language in which they are expressed, esp in terms of formal logic as in Russell's theory of descriptions. Compare **linguistic philosophy**

analytical psychology *n* a school of psychoanalysis founded by Jung as a result of disagreements with Freud. See also **archetype, collective unconscious**

analytical reagent *n* a chemical compound of a known standard of purity

Anam (æˈnæm, ˈænæm) *n* a variant spelling of **Annam**

Anambra (əˈnæmbrə) *n* a state of S Nigeria, formed in 1976 from part of East-Central State. Capital: Enugu. Pop: 3 094 783 (1995 est). Area: 4844 sq km (1870 sq miles)

anamnesis (ˌænæmˈniːsɪs) *n, pl* **-ses** (-siːz) **1** the ability to recall past events; recollection **2** the case history of a patient [c17 via New Latin from Greek, from *anamimnēskein* to recall, from *mimnēskein* to call to mind]

anamnestic (ˌænæmˈnɛstɪk) *adj* **1** of or relating to anamnesis **2** *immunol* denoting a response to antigenic stimulation characterized by the production of large amounts of antibody specific to a different antigen from that which elicited the response > ˌanamˈnestically *adv*

anamniote (ænˈæmnɪəʊt) *n* any vertebrate animal, such as a fish or amphibian, that lacks an amnion, chorion, and allantois during embryonic development. Compare **amniote**. > anamniotic (ænˌæmnɪˈɒtɪk) *adj*

anamorphic (ˌænəˈmɔːfɪk) *adj* of, relating to, or caused by anamorphosis or anamorphism

anamorphic lens *n* a component in the optical system of a film projector for converting standard 35mm film images into wide-screen format

anamorphism (ˌænəˈmɔːˌfɪzəm) *n* intense metamorphism of a rock in which high-density complex minerals are formed from simpler minerals of lower density

anamorphoscope (ˌænəˈmɔːfəˌskəʊp) *n* an optical device, such as a cylindrical lens, for correcting an image that has been distorted by anamorphosis

anamorphosis (ˌænəˈmɔːfəsɪs, -mɔːˈfəʊsɪs) *n, pl* **-ses** (-ˌsiːz) **1** *optics* **a** an image or drawing distorted in such a way that it becomes recognizable only when viewed in a specified manner or through a special device **b** the process by which such images or drawings are produced **2**

the evolution of one type of organism from another by a series of gradual changes [c18 from Greek, from *anamorphoun* to transform, from *morphē* form, shape]

ananas (əˈnænəs) *n* another name for the **pineapple,** or for a related tropical American bromeliaceous plant, the pinguin, that has an edible plum-shaped fruit [c17 from the native name in Peru]

Anancy *or* **Anansi** (əˈnænsɪ) *n* a character in Caribbean folklore, a cunning trickster generally depicted as a spider with a human head; the subject of many **Anancy stories,** the character has its origins among the Ashanti of W Africa

anandamide (əˈnændəˌmaɪd) *n* a naturally occurring endogenous cannabinoid neurotransmitter found in the brains of mammals and in small quantities in the cocoa bean [c20 from Sanskrit *ananda* bliss]

anandrous (ænˈændrəs) *adj* (of flowers) having no stamens [c19 from Greek *anandros* lacking males, from AN- + *anēr* man]

Ananias (ˌænəˈnaɪəs) *n* **1** *New Testament* a Jewish Christian of Jerusalem who was struck dead for lying (Acts 5) **2** a liar

Ananke (əˈnænkɪ) *n* a small outer satellite of Jupiter

ananthous (ænˈænθəs) *adj* (of higher plants) having no flowers [c19 from Greek *ananthēs,* from AN- + *anthos* flower]

anapaest *or* **anapest** (ˈænəpɛst, -piːst) *n* *prosody* a metrical foot of three syllables, the first two short, the last long (--‑) [c17 via Latin from Greek *anapaistos* reversed (that is, a dactyl reversed), from *anapaiein,* from *ana-* back + *paiein* to strike] > ˌanaˈpaestic *or* ˌanaˈpestic *adj*

anaphase (ˈænəˌfeɪz) *n* **1** the third stage of mitosis, during which the chromatids separate and migrate towards opposite ends of the spindle. See also **prophase, metaphase, telophase 2** the corresponding stage of the first division of meiosis [c19 from ANA- + PHASE]

anaphora (əˈnæfərə) *n* **1** *grammar* the use of a word such as a pronoun that has the same reference as a word previously used in the same discourse. In the sentence *John wrote the essay in the library but Peter did it at home,* both *did* and *it* are examples of anaphora. Compare **cataphora, exophoric 2** *rhetoric* the repetition of a word or phrase at the beginning of successive clauses [c16 via Latin from Greek: repetition, from *anapherein,* from ANA- + *pherein* to bear]

anaphoresis (ˌænəfəˈriːsɪs) *n* *chem* the movement of suspended charged particles towards the anode in an electric field

anaphoric (ˌænəˈfɒrɪk) *adj* of or relating to anaphorism > ˌanaˈphorically *adv*

anaphrodisiac (ˌænæfrəˈdɪzɪˌæk) *adj* **1** tending to lessen sexual desire ▷ *n* **2** an anaphrodisiac drug > ˌanaphroˈdisia *n*

anaphylactic shock *n* a severe, sometimes fatal, reaction to a substance to which a person has an extreme sensitivity, often involving respiratory difficulty and circulation failure

anaphylaxis (ˌænəfɪˈlæksɪs) *n* extreme sensitivity to an injected antigen, esp a protein, following a previous injection [c20 from ANA- + (PRO)PHYLAXIS] > ˌanaphyˈlactic *or* ˌanaphyˈlactoid *adj* > ˌanaphyˈlactically *adv*

anaplasia (ˌænəˈpleɪsɪə) *n* reversion of plant or animal cells to a simpler less differentiated form

anaplasmosis (ˌænəplæzˈməʊsɪs) *n* another name for **gallsickness**

anaplastic (ˌænəˈplæstɪk) *adj* **1** of or relating to anaplasia **2** relating to plastic surgery

anaplasty (ˈænəˌplæstɪ) *n* *surgery* another name for **plastic surgery**

anaptyxis (ˌænæpˈtɪksɪs) *n, pl* **-tyxes** (-ˈtɪksiːz) the insertion of a short vowel between consonants in order to make a word more easily pronounceable [c19 via New Latin from Greek *anaptuxis,* from *anaptussein* to unfold, from ANA- + *ptussein* to fold]

a

> **anaptyctic** (ˌænæpˈtɪktɪk) or **anapˈtyctical** adj

Anapurna (ˌænəˈpʊənə) n a variant spelling of **Annapurna**

anarch (ˈænɑːk) n archaic an instigator or personification of anarchy

anarchism (ˈænəˌkɪzəm) n **1** political theory a doctrine advocating the abolition of government **2** the principles or practice of anarchists

anarchist (ˈænəkɪst) n **1** a person who advocates the abolition of government and a social system based on voluntary cooperation **2** a person who causes disorder or upheaval > ˌanarˈchistic adj

anarchy (ˈænəkɪ) n **1** general lawlessness and disorder, esp when thought to result from an absence or failure of government **2** the absence or lack of government **3** the absence of any guiding or uniting principle; disorder; chaos **4** the theory or practice of political anarchism [c16 from Medieval Latin anarchia, from Greek anarkhia, from anarkhos without a ruler, from AN- + arkh- leader, from arkhein to rule] > **anarchic** (ænˈɑːkɪk) or **anˈarchical** adj > **anˈarchically** adv

anarthria (ænˈɑːθrɪə) n pathol loss of the ability to speak coherently [c19 New Latin, from Greek anarthros lacking vigour, from AN- + arthros joint]

anarthrous (ænˈɑːθrəs) adj **1** (of a noun) used without an article **2** having no joints or articulated limbs [c19 from Greek anarthros, from AN- + arthros joint, definite article] > **anˈarthrously** adv > **anˈarthrousness** n

anasarca (ˌænəˈsɑːkə) n pathol a generalized accumulation of serous fluid within the subcutaneous connective tissue, resulting in oedema [c14 from New Latin, from ANA- (puffed up) + Greek sarx flesh] > **anaˈsarcous** adj

anastigmat (æˈnæstɪɡˌmæt, ˌænəˈstɪɡmæt) n a lens or system of lenses designed to be free of astigmatism

anastigmatic (ˌænəstɪɡˈmætɪk) adj (of a lens or optical device) not astigmatic. Also: **stigmatic**

anastomose (əˈnæstəˌməʊz) vb to join (two parts of a blood vessel, etc) by anastomosis

anastomosis (əˌnæstəˈməʊsɪs) n, pl -ses (-siːz) **1** a natural connection between two tubular structures, such as blood vessels **2** the surgical union of two hollow organs or parts that are normally separate **3** the separation and rejoining in a reticulate pattern of the veins of a leaf or of branches [c16 via New Latin from Greek: opening, from anastomoun to equip with a mouth, from stoma mouth] > **anastomotic** (əˌnæstəˈmɒtɪk) adj

anastrophe (əˈnæstrəfɪ) n rhetoric another term for **inversion** (sense 3) [c16 from Greek, from anastrephein to invert]

anastrozole (əˈnæstrəˌzəʊl) n an anti-oestrogen drug used in the treatment of breast cancer in post-menopausal women. Also called: **Arimidex**

anat. abbreviation for **1** anatomical **2** anatomy

anata (ˈænətə) n (in Theravada Buddhism) the belief that since all things are constantly changing, there can be no such thing as a permanent, unchanging self: one of the three basic characteristics of existence. Sanskrit word: anatman Compare **anicca**, **dukkha** [Pali, literally: no self]

anatase (ˈænəˌteɪz) n a rare blue or black mineral that consists of titanium oxide in tetragonal crystalline form and occurs in veins in igneous rocks. Formula: TiO_2. Also called: **octahedrite** [c19 from French, from Greek anatasis an extending (referring to the length of the crystals), from anateinein to stretch out]

anathema (əˈnæθəmə) n, pl -mas **1** a detested person or thing: he is anathema to me **2** a formal ecclesiastical curse of excommunication or a formal denunciation of a doctrine **3** the person or thing so cursed **4** a strong curse; imprecation [c16 via Church Latin from Greek: something accursed, dedicated (to evil), from anatithenai to dedicate, from ANA- + tithenai to set]

anathematize or **anathematise** (əˈnæθɪməˌtaɪz) vb to pronounce an anathema (upon a person, etc); curse > aˌnathematiˈzation or aˌnathematiˈsation n

Anatolia (ˌænəˈtəʊlɪə) n the Asian part of Turkey, occupying the peninsula between the Black Sea, the Mediterranean, and the Aegean: consists of a plateau, largely mountainous, with salt lakes in the interior. Historical name: **Asia Minor**

Anatolian (ˌænəˈtəʊlɪən) adj **1** of or relating to Anatolia or its inhabitants **2** denoting, belonging to, or relating to an ancient family of languages related to the Indo-European family and including Hittite ▷ n **3** this family of languages, sometimes regarded as a branch of Indo-European **4** a native or inhabitant of Anatolia

Anatolian shepherd dog n a large powerfully-built dog of a breed with a large head and a short dense cream or fawn coat, originally used for guarding sheep

anatomical (ˌænəˈtɒmɪkᵊl) adj of or relating to anatomy > ˌanaˈtomically adv

anatomical snuffbox n the triangular depression on the back of the hand between the thumb and the index finger

anatomist (əˈnætəmɪst) n an expert in anatomy

anatomize or **anatomise** (əˈnætəˌmaɪz) vb (tr) **1** to dissect (an animal or plant) **2** to examine in minute detail > aˌnatomiˈzation or aˌnatomiˈsation n > aˈnatoˌmizer or aˈnatoˌmiser n

anatomy (əˈnætəmɪ) n, pl -mies **1** the science concerned with the physical structure of animals and plants **2** the physical structure of an animal or plant or any of its parts **3** a book or treatise on this subject **4** dissection of an animal or plant **5** any detailed analysis: the anatomy of a crime **6** informal the human body [c14 from Latin anatomia, from Greek anatomē, from anatemnein to cut up, from ANA- + temnein to cut]

anatropous (əˈnætrəpəs) adj (of a plant ovule) inverted during development by a bending of the stalk (funicle) attaching it to the carpel wall. Compare **orthotropous** [c19 from ANA- (inverted) + -TROPOUS]

anatto (əˈnætəʊ) n, pl -tos a variant spelling of **annatto**

anaxial (ænˈæksɪəl) adj biology asymmetrical

anbury (ˈænbərɪ) n, pl -buries **1** a soft spongy tumour occurring in horses and oxen **2** Brit dialect another name for **club root** [c16 of uncertain origin]

ANC abbreviation for **African National Congress**

-ance or **-ancy** suffix forming nouns indicating an action, state or condition, or quality: hindrance; tenancy; resemblance. Compare **-ence** [via Old French from Latin -antia; see -ANCY]

ancestor (ˈænsɛstə) n **1** (often plural) a person from whom another is directly descended, esp someone more distant than a grandparent; forefather **2** an early type of animal or plant from which a later, usually dissimilar, type has evolved **3** a person or thing regarded as a forerunner of a later person or thing: the ancestor of the modern camera [c13 from Old French ancestre, from Late Latin antecēssor one who goes before, from Latin antecēdere; see ANTECEDE] > ˈancestress fem n

ancestral (ænˈsɛstrəl) adj **1** of, inherited from, or derived from ancestors: his ancestral home ▷ n **2** logic a relation that holds between x and y if there is a chain of instances of a given relation leading from x to y. Thus the ancestral of parent of is ancestor of, since x is the ancestor of y if and only if x is a parent of...a parent of...a parent of y > anˈcestrally adv

ancestry (ˈænsɛstrɪ) n, pl -tries **1** lineage or descent, esp when ancient, noble, or distinguished **2** ancestors collectively

Anchises (ænˈkaɪsiːz) n classical myth a Trojan prince and father of Aeneas. In the Aeneid, he is rescued by his son at the fall of Troy and dies in Sicily

anchor (ˈæŋkə) n **1** any of several devices, usually of steel, attached to a vessel by a cable and dropped overboard so as to grip the bottom and restrict the vessel's movement **2** an object used to hold something else firmly in place: the rock provided an anchor for the rope **3** a source of stability or security: religion was his anchor **4 a** a metal cramp, bolt, or similar fitting, esp one used to make a connection to masonry **b** (as modifier): anchor bolt **5 a** the rear person in a tug-of-war team **b** short for **anchorman** or **anchorwoman 6 at anchor** (of a vessel) anchored **7 cast, come to, or drop anchor** to anchor a vessel **8 drag anchor** See **drag** (sense 13) **9 ride at anchor** to be anchored **10 weigh anchor** to raise a vessel's anchor or (of a vessel) to have its anchor raised in preparation for departure ▷ vb **11** to use an anchor to hold (a vessel) in one place **12** to fasten or be fastened securely; fix or become fixed firmly **13** (tr) radio, television to act as an anchorman on ▷ See also **anchors** [Old English ancor, from Latin ancora, from Greek ankura; related to Greek ankos bend; compare Latin uncus bent, hooked]

anchorage¹ (ˈæŋkərɪdʒ) n **1** the act of anchoring **2** any place where a vessel is anchored **3** a place designated for vessels to anchor **4** a fee imposed for anchoring **5** anything used as an anchor **6** a source of security or strength **7** something that supplies a secure hold for something else

anchorage² (ˈæŋkərɪdʒ) n the cell or retreat of an anchorite

Anchorage (ˈæŋkərɪdʒ) n the largest city in Alaska, a port in the south, at the head of Cook Inlet. Pop: 270 951 (2003 est)

anchorette (ˌæŋkəˈrɛt) n informal (in broadcasting) a young and inexperienced anchorwoman [c20 from ANCHOR (sense 5b) + -ETTE (sense 2)]

anchor ice n Canadian ice that forms at the bottom of a lake or river

anchorite (ˈæŋkəˌraɪt) n a person who lives in seclusion, esp a religious recluse; hermit [c15 from Medieval Latin anchorīta, from Late Latin anachōrēta, from Greek anakhōrētēs, from anakhōrein to retire, withdraw, from khōra a space] > ˈanchoress fem n

anchorman (ˈæŋkəmæn) n, pl -men **1** sport the last person in a team to compete, esp in a relay race **2** (in broadcasting) a person in a central studio who links up and maintains contact with various outside camera units, reporters, etc

anchor ring n a ring made from an iron bar of circular cross-section

anchors (ˈæŋkəz) pl n slang the brakes of a motor vehicle: he rammed on the anchors

anchorwoman (ˈæŋkəˌwʊmən) n, pl -women **1** sport the last woman in a team to compete, esp in a relay race **2** (in broadcasting) a woman in a central studio who links up and maintains contact with various outside camera units, reporters, etc

anchoveta (ˌæntʃəˈvɛtə) n a small anchovy, Cetengraulis mysticetus, of the American Pacific, used as bait by tuna fishermen [c20 Spanish, diminutive of anchova ANCHOVY]

anchovy (ˈæntʃəvɪ) n, pl -vies any of various small marine food fishes of the genus Engraulis and related genera, esp E. encrasicolus of S Europe: family Clupeidae (herrings). They have a salty taste and are often tinned or made into a paste or essence [c16 from Spanish anchova, perhaps ultimately from Greek aphuē small fish]

anchovy pear n a Jamaican tree, Grias cauliflora, bearing edible fruits that taste like the mango: family Lecythidaceae [c18 so called from the use of the fruit as an hors d'oeuvre]

anchusa (æŋˈkjuːsə) n any Eurasian plant of the boraginaceous genus Anchusa, having rough hairy stems and leaves and blue flowers. See also **alkanet** (sense 3), **bugloss** [c18 from Latin]

anchusin (æŋˈkjuːsɪn) n another name for **alkanet** (sense 2)

anchylose (ˈæŋkɪˌləʊz) vb a former spelling of **ankylose**. > ˌanchyˈlosis n > anchylotic (ˌæŋkɪˈlɒtɪk) adj

anchylostomiasis (ˌæŋkɪˌlɒstəˈmaɪəsɪs) *n* a variant of **ancylostomiasis**

ancien régime *French* (ɑ̃sjɛ̃ reʒim) *n, pl anciens régimes* (ɑ̃sjɛ̃ reʒim) **1** the political and social system of France before the Revolution of 1789 **2** a former or outdated regime [literally: old regime]

ancient[1] (ˈeɪnʃənt) *adj* **1** dating from very long ago: *ancient ruins* **2** very old; aged **3** of the far past, esp before the collapse of the Western Roman Empire (476 AD). Compare **medieval, modern** **4** *law* having existed since before the time of legal memory ▷ *n* **5** (*often plural*) a member of a civilized nation in the ancient world, esp a Greek, Roman, or Hebrew **6** (*often plural*) one of the classical authors of Greek or Roman antiquity **7** *archaic* an old man [c14 from Old French *ancien*, from Vulgar Latin *anteanus* (unattested), from Latin *ante* before] > ˈancientness *n*

ancient[2] (ˈeɪnʃənt) *n archaic* **1** a flag or other banner; standard **2** a standard-bearer; ensign [c16 changed from ENSIGN through the influence of ANCIENT[1]]

Ancient Greek *n* the Greek language from the earliest records to about 300 BC, the chief dialect areas of which were Aeolic, Arcadic, Doric, and Ionic (including Attic). Compare **Koine, Late Greek, Medieval Greek**

ancient history *n* **1** the history of the **ancient world** from the earliest known civilizations to the collapse of the Western Roman Empire in 476 AD **2** *informal* a recent event or fact sufficiently familiar to have lost its pertinence

ancient lights *n* (*usually functioning as singular*) the legal right to receive, by a particular window or windows, adequate and unobstructed daylight

anciently (ˈeɪnʃəntlɪ) *adv* in ancient times

ancient monument *n Brit* a historical building or the remains of one, usually dating from no later than the medieval period, that has been designated as worthy of preservation and is often in the care of a government department

Ancient of Days *n* a name for God, originating in the Authorized Version of the Old Testament (Daniel 7:9)

ancient wisdom *n* pre-Christian knowledge, philosophy, and beliefs

ancillary (ænˈsɪlərɪ) *adj* **1** subsidiary **2** auxiliary; supplementary: *ancillary services* ▷ *n, pl* -laries **3** a subsidiary or auxiliary thing or person: *the company has an ancillary abroad* [c17 from Latin *ancillāris* concerning maidservants, from *ancilla*, diminutive of *ancŭla* female servant]

ancipital (ænˈsɪpɪtᵊl) or **ancipitous** (ænˈsɪpɪtəs) *adj biology* flattened and having two edges: *ancipital stems* [c18 from Latin *anceps* two-headed]

Ancohuma (ˌæŋkəʊˈuːmə) *n* one of the two peaks of Mount **Sorata**

ancon (ˈæŋkɒn) or **ancone** (ˈæŋkəʊn) *n, pl* ancones (ˈæŋkəʊniːz) **1** *architect* a projecting bracket or console supporting a cornice **2** a former technical name for **elbow** [c18 from Greek *ankōn* a bend] > anconal (ænˈkəʊnᵊl) or anconeal (ænˈkəʊnɪəl) *adj*

Ancona (*Italian* aŋˈkoːna) *n* a port in central Italy, on the Adriatic, capital of the Marches: founded by Greeks from Syracuse in about 390 BC Pop: 100 507 (2001)

-ancy *suffix forming nouns* a variant of **-ance**, indicating condition or quality: *expectancy; poignancy; malignancy*

ancylostomiasis (ˌænsɪˌlɒstəˈmaɪəsɪs), **ankylostomiasis** or **anchylostomiasis** *n* infestation of the human intestine with blood-sucking hookworms, causing progressive anaemia. Also called: hookworm disease [from New Latin, from *Ancylostoma* genus of hookworms, from Greek *ankulos* hooked, crooked + *stoma* mouth]

and (ænd; *unstressed* ənd, ən) *conj* (*coordinating*) **1** along with; in addition to: *boys and girls* **2** as a consequence: *he fell down and cut his knee* **3** afterwards: *we pay the man and go through that door* **4** (preceded by *good* or *nice*) (*intensifier*): *the sauce is good and thick* **5** plus: *two and two equals four* **6** used to join identical words or phrases to give emphasis or indicate repetition or continuity: *better and better; we ran and ran; it rained and rained* **7** used to join two identical words or phrases to express a contrast between instances of what is named: *there are jobs and jobs* **8** *informal* used in place of *to* in infinitives after verbs such as *try, go,* and *come: try and see it my way* **9** an obsolete word for *if and it please you.* Informal spellings: an, an', 'n ▷ *n* **10** (*usually plural*) an additional matter or problem: *ifs, ands, or buts* [Old English *and*; related to Old Frisian *anda*, Old Saxon *ande*, Old High German *anti*, Sanskrit *atha*]

USAGE See at **to**

AND *international car registration for* Andorra

-and or **-end** *suffix forming nouns* indicating a person or thing that is to be dealt with in a specified way: *analysand; dividend; multiplicand* [from Latin gerundives ending in *-andus, -endus*]

Andalusia (ˌændəˈluːzɪə) *n* a region of S Spain, on the Mediterranean and the Atlantic, with the Sierra Morena in the north, the Sierra Nevada in the southeast, and the Guadalquivir River flowing over fertile lands between them; a centre of Moorish culture; it became an autonomous region in 1981. Area: about 87 280 sq km (33 700 sq miles). Spanish name: Andalucía (andaluˈθia)

andalusite (ˌændəˈluːsaɪt) *n* a grey, pink, or brown hard mineral consisting of aluminium silicate in orthorhombic crystalline form. It occurs in metamorphic rocks and is used as a refractory and as a gemstone. Formula: Al_2SiO_5

Andaman and Nicobar Islands (ˈændəmən, ˈnɪkəʊˌbɑː) *pl n* a territory of India, in the E Bay of Bengal, consisting of two groups of over 200 islands; suffered badly in the Indian Ocean tsunami of December 2004. Capital: Port Blair. Pop: 356 265 (2001). Area: 8140 sq km (3143 sq miles)

Andaman Islands *pl n* a group of islands in the E Bay of Bengal, part of the Indian territory of the Andaman and Nicobar Islands. Area: 6408 sq km (2474 sq miles). Pop: 240 089 (1991 est)

Andaman Sea *n* part of the Bay of Bengal, between the Andaman and Nicobar Islands and the Malay Peninsula

andante (ænˈdæntɪ) *music* ▷ *adj, adv* **1** (to be performed) at a moderately slow tempo ▷ *n* **2** a passage or piece to be performed in this manner [c18 Italian: going, from *andare* to go, from Latin *ambulāre* to walk]

andantino (ˌændænˈtiːnəʊ) *music* ▷ *adj, adv* **1** (to be performed) slightly faster, or slightly more slowly, than andante ▷ *n, pl* -nos **2** a passage or piece to be performed in this manner [c19 diminutive of ANDANTE]

AND circuit or **gate** (ænd) *n computing* a logic circuit having two or more input wires and one output wire that has a high-voltage output signal if and only if all input signals are at a high voltage simultaneously: used extensively as a basic circuit in computers. Compare **NAND circuit, NOR circuit, OR circuit** [c20 so named because the action performed on electrical signals is similar to the operation of the conjunction *and* in logical constructions]

Andean (ænˈdiːən, ˈændɪən) *adj* of, relating to, or resembling the Andes

Anderlecht (*Flemish* ˈɑndərlɛxt) *n* a town in central Belgium, a suburb of Brussels. Pop: 92 755 (2004 est)

Anderson (ˈændəsᵊn) *n* a river in N Canada, in the Northwest Territories, rising in lakes north of Great Bear Lake and flowing west and north to the Beaufort Sea. Length: about 580 km (360 miles)

Anderson shelter *n Brit* a small prefabricated air-raid shelter of World War II consisting of an arch of corrugated metal and designed to be partly buried in people's gardens and covered with earth for protection [c20 so named because its use was adopted while Sir John *Anderson* was Home Secretary (1939–40)]

Andes (ˈændiːz) *pl n* a major mountain system of South America, extending for about 7250 km (4500 miles) along the entire W coast, with several parallel ranges or cordilleras and many volcanic peaks: rich in minerals, including gold, silver, copper, iron ore, and nitrates. Average height: 3900 m (13 000 ft). Highest peak: Aconcagua, 6960 m (22 835 ft)

andesine (ˈændɪˌziːn, -zɪn) *n* a feldspar mineral of the plagioclase series consisting of an aluminium silicate of sodium and calcium. Formula: $NaAlSi_3O_8.CaAl_2Si_2O_8$ [c19 from the ANDES (where it is found) + -INE[1]]

andesite (ˈændɪˌzaɪt) *n* a fine-grained tan or grey volcanic rock consisting of plagioclase feldspar, esp andesine, amphibole, and pyroxene [c19 from ANDES + -ITE[1]]

Andhra Pradesh (ˈændrə prɑːˈdɛʃ) *n* a state of SE India, on the Bay of Bengal: formed in 1953 from parts of Madras and Hyderabad states. Capital: Hyderabad. Pop: 75 727 541 (2001). Area: about 275 068 sq km (106 204 sq miles)

andiron (ˈændˌaɪən) *n* another name for **firedog** [c14 from Old French *andier*, of unknown origin; influenced by IRON]

Andizhan (*Russian* andiˈʒan) *n* a city in E Uzbekistan. Pop: 413 000 (2005 est)

Andong (ˈænˈdʊŋ) *n* a port in E China, in Liaoning province at the mouth of the Yalu River. Pop: 730 000 (2005 est). Also called: Dandong, Tantung

and/or *conj* (*coordinating*) used to join terms when either one or the other or both is indicated: *passports and/or other means of identification*

USAGE Many people think that *and/or* is only acceptable in legal and commercial contexts. In other contexts, it is better to use *or both: some alcoholics lose their jobs or their driving licences or both* (not *their jobs and/or their driving licences*)

Andorra (ænˈdɔːrə) *n* a mountainous principality in SW Europe, between France and Spain: according to tradition, given independence by Charlemagne in the 9th century for helping to fight the Moors; placed under the joint sovereignty of the Comte de Foix and the Spanish bishop of Urgel in 1278; under the joint overlordship of the French head of state and the bishop of Urgel from the 16th century; adopted a constitution reducing the powers of the overlords in 1993. Languages: Catalan (official), French, and Spanish. Religion: Roman Catholic. Currency: euro. Capital: Andorra la Vella. Pop: 71 000 (2003 est). Area: 464 sq km (179 sq miles). Official name: Principat d'Andorra

Andorra la Vella (*Spanish* anˈdɔrra la ˈbeʎa) *n* the capital of Andorra, situated in the west of the principality. Pop: 22 035 (2003 est). French name: Andorre la Vieille (ɑ̃dɔr la vjɛj)

Andorran (ænˈdɔːrən) *adj* **1** of or relating to Andorra or its inhabitants ▷ *n* **2** a native or inhabitant of Andorra

andouille (*French* ɑ̃duj) *n* a spicy smoked pork sausage with a blackish skin

andradite (ˈændrəˌdaɪt) *n* a yellow, green, or brownish-black garnet that consists of calcium iron silicate and is used as a gemstone. Formula: $Ca_3Fe_2(SiO_4)_3$ [c19 named after J. B. d'*Andrada* e Silva (1763–1838), Brazilian mineralogist; see -ITE[1]]

Andreanof Islands (ˌændrɪˈɑːnɒf) *pl n* a group of islands in the central Aleutian Islands, Alaska. Area: 3710 sq km (1432 sq miles)

andro- or before a vowel **andr-** *combining form* **1** male; masculine: *androsterone* **2** (in botany) stamen or anther: *androecium* [from Greek *anēr* (genitive *andros*) man]

androcentric (ˌændrəʊˈsɛntrɪk) *adj* having or regarding man or the male sex as central or primary > ˌandroˈcentrism *n*

a

Androcles ('ændrə,kli:z) or **Androclus** ('ændrəkləs) *n* (in Roman legend) a slave whose life was spared in the arena by a lion from whose paw he had once extracted a thorn

androclinium (,ændrə'klınıəm) *n, pl* -clinia (-'klınıə) another name for **clinandrium** [C19 New Latin, from ANDRO- + -*clinium,* from Greek *klinē* slope; see CLINO-]

androdioecious (,ændrəʊdaı'i:ʃəs) *adj* (of a plant species) having hermaphrodite and male flowers on separate plants

androecium (æn'dri:sıəm) *n, pl* -cia (-sıə) the stamens of a flowering plant collectively [C19 from New Latin, from ANDRO- + Greek *oikion* a little house] > an'droecial *adj*

androgen ('ændrədʒən) *n* any of several steroids, produced as hormones by the testes or made synthetically, that promote development of male sexual organs and male secondary sexual characteristics > androgenic (,ændrə'dʒɛnık) *adj*

androgenous (æn'drɒdʒınəs) *adj* biology producing only male offspring

androgyne ('ændrə,dʒaın) *n* another word for **hermaphrodite** [C17 from Old French, via Latin from Greek *androgunos,* from *anēr* man + *gunē* woman]

androgynophore (,ændrəʊ'gaınəʊfɔ:) *n* another name for **androphore**

androgynous (æn'drɒdʒınəs) *adj* **1** botany having male and female flowers in the same inflorescence, as cuckoo pint **2** having male and female characteristics; hermaphrodite > an'drogyny *n*

android ('ændrɔıd) *n* **1** (in science fiction) a robot resembling a human being ▷ *adj* **2** resembling a human being [C18 from Late Greek *androeidēs* manlike; see ANDRO-, -OID]

andrology (æn'drɒlədʒı) *n* the branch of medicine concerned with diseases in men, esp of the reproductive organs [C20 from ANDRO- + -LOGY] > an'drologist *n*

Andromache (æn'drɒməkı) *n* Greek myth the wife of Hector

Andromeda[1] (æn'drɒmıdə) *n* Greek myth the daughter of Cassiopeia and wife of Perseus, who saved her from a sea monster

Andromeda[2] (æn'drɒmıdə) *n, Latin genitive* Andromedae (æn'drɒmı,di:) a constellation in the N hemisphere lying between Cassiopeia and Pegasus, the three brightest stars being of the second magnitude. It contains the **Andromeda Galaxy** a spiral galaxy 2.2 million light years away

andromonoecious (,ændrəʊmɒ'ni:ʃəs) *adj* (of a plant species) having hermaphrodite and male flowers on the same plant

andropause ('ændrəʊ,pɔ:z) *n* the period, usually occurring between the ages of 45 and 55, during which a man's testosterone levels may fall, leading to a reduction in vigour and sexual drive. Also called: **male menopause** [C20 from ANDRO- + (MENO)PAUSE]

androphore ('ændrəʊfɔ:) *n* botany an extension of the receptacle carrying the androecium and the gynoecium, typical of the caper family (*Capparidaceae*). Also called: androgynophore

Andropov (æn'drɒpɒv; *Russian* ɑn'drɔ:pəf) *n* a former name (1984–91) for **Rybinsk**

Andros ('ændrəs) *n* **1** an island in the Aegean Sea, the northernmost of the Cyclades: long famous for wine. Capital: Andros. Pop: 10 009 (2001). Area: about 311 sq km (120 sq miles) **2** an island in the N Caribbean, the largest of the Bahamas. Pop: 7686 (2000). Area: 4144 sq km (1600 sq miles)

androsphinx ('ændrə,sfıŋks) *n, pl* -sphinxes or -sphinges (-,sfındʒi:z) a sphinx having the head of a man

androsterone (æn'drɒstə,rəʊn) *n* an androgenic steroid hormone produced in the testes. Formula: $C_{19}H_{30}O_2$

-androus *adj combining form* (in botany) indicating number or type of stamens: *diandrous* [from New Latin -*andrus,* from Greek -*andros,* from *anēr* man]

-andry *n combining form* indicating number of husbands: *polyandry* [from Greek -*andria,* from *anēr* man]

Andvari (æn'dwa:rı) *n* Norse myth a dwarf who possessed a treasure hoard, which was robbed by Loki

ane (eın) *determiner, pron, n* a Scot word for **one**

-ane *suffix forming nouns* indicating an alkane hydrocarbon: *hexane* [coined to replace -*ene,* -*ine,* and -*one*]

anear (ə'nıə) *archaic* ▷ *prep* **1** near ▷ *adv* **2** nearly

anecdotage ('ænık,dəʊtıdʒ) *n* **1** anecdotes collectively **2** humorous talkative or garrulous old age

anecdotal (,ænɛk'dəʊt³l) *adj* containing or consisting exclusively of anecdotes rather than connected discourse or research conducted under controlled conditions

anecdote ('ænık,dəʊt) *n* a short usually amusing account of an incident, esp a personal or biographical one [C17 from Medieval Latin *anecdota* unpublished items, from Greek *anekdotos* unpublished, from AN- + *ekdotos* published, from *ekdidonai,* from *ek-* out + *didonai* to give] > ,anec'dotic *adj* > ,anec'dotalist or 'anec,dotist *n*

anecdysis (,ænɛk'daısıs) *n* the period between moults in arthropods [C20 New Latin, from Greek; see AN-, ECDYSIS]

anechoic (,ænı'kəʊık) *adj* having a low degree of reverberation of sound: *an anechoic recording studio*

anelace ('ænə,leıs) *n* a variant spelling of **anlace**

anele (ə'ni:l) *vb* (*tr*) archaic to anoint, esp to give extreme unction to [C14 *anelen,* from *an-* (from Old English *an-* ON) + *elen* to anoint (from *ele* oil, from Latin *oleum*)]

anemia (ə'ni:mıə) *n* the usual US spelling of **anaemia** [C19 from New Latin, from Greek *anaimia* lack of blood]

anemic (ə'ni:mık) *adj* the usual US spelling of **anaemic**

anemo- *combining form* indicating wind: *anemometer; anemophilous* [from Greek *anemos* wind]

anemochore (ə'ni:məʊ,kɔ:) *n* a plant in which the fruits or seeds are dispersed by wind > a,nemo'chorous *adj*

anemograph (ə'nɛməʊ,grɑ:f) *n* a self-recording anemometer > anemographic (ə,nɛməʊ'græfık) *adj* > a,nemo'graphically *adv*

anemography (,ænı'mɒgrəfı) *n* meteorol the technique of recording wind measurements

anemology (,ænı'mɒlədʒı) *n* archaic the study of winds

anemometer (,ænı'mɒmıtə) *n* **1** Also called: wind gauge an instrument for recording the speed and often the direction of winds **2** any instrument that measures the rate of movement of a fluid > anemometric (,ænıməʊ'mɛtrık) or ,anemo'metrical *adj*

anemometry (,ænı'mɒmıtrı) *n* meteorol the technique of measuring wind speed and direction

anemone (ə'nɛmənı) *n* any ranunculaceous woodland plant of the genus *Anemone* of N temperate regions, such as the white-flowered *A. nemorosa* (**wood anemone** or **windflower**). Some cultivated anemones have lilac, pale blue, pink, purple, or red flowers. See also **pasqueflower**. Compare **sea anemone** (an animal) [C16 via Latin from Greek: windflower, from *anemos* wind]

anemone fish *n* any of various damselfishes of the genus *Amphiprion,* such as *A. percula* (clown anemone fish), that usually live closely associated with sea anemones

anemophilous (,ænı'mɒfıləs) *adj* (of flowering plants such as grasses) pollinated by the wind. Compare **entomophilous.** > ,ane'mophily *n*

anemoscope (ə'nɛmə,skəʊp) *n* meteorol any device that shows the presence and direction of a wind

anencephalic (,ænɛnsə'fælık) *adj* born with no or only a partial brain [AN- + ENCEPHALIC] > anencephaly (,ænɛn'sɛfəlı) *n*

anent (ə'nɛnt) *prep* Scot **1** lying against; alongside **2** concerning; about [Old English *on efen,* literally: on even (ground)]

anergy ('ænədʒı) *n* **1** lack of energy **2** immunol diminution or lack of immunity to an antigen [from New Latin *anergia,* from AN- + Greek *ergon* work] > anergic (æ'nɜ:dʒık) *adj*

aneroid ('ænə,rɔıd) *adj* not containing a liquid [C19 from French, from AN- + Greek *nēros* wet + -OID]

aneroid barometer *n* a device for measuring atmospheric pressure without the use of fluids. It consists of a partially evacuated metal chamber, the thin corrugated lid of which is displaced by variations in the external air pressure. This displacement is magnified by levers and made to operate a pointer

anesthesia (,ænıs'θi:zıə) *n* the usual US spelling of **anaesthesia**

anesthesiologist or **anaesthesiologist** (,ænıs,θi:zı'ɒlədʒıst) *n* the US name for an **anaesthetist**; in the US, a qualified doctor specializing in the administration of anaesthesia. Compare **anesthetist**

anesthetic (,ænıs'θɛtık) *n, adj* the usual US spelling of **anaesthetic**

anesthetist (ə'nɛsθətıst) *n* (in the US) a person qualified to administer anaesthesia, often a nurse or someone other than a physician. Compare **anesthesiologist**

anestrus (æn'i:strəs) *n* a variant spelling (esp US) of **anoestrus.** > an'estrous *adj*

anethole ('ænı,θəʊl) *n* a white water-soluble crystalline substance with a liquorice-like odour, used as a flavouring and a sensitizer in the processing of colour photographs. Formula: $CH_3CH:CHC_6H_4OCH_3$ [C19 from Latin *anēthum* dill, anise, from Greek *anēthon*]

Aneto (*Spanish* a'neto) *n* **Pico de** ('piko de). a mountain in N Spain, near the French border: the highest in the Pyrenees. Height: 3404 m (11 168 ft)

aneuploid ('ænjʊ,plɔıd) *adj* **1** (of polyploid cells or organisms) having a chromosome number that is not an exact multiple of the haploid number, caused by one chromosome set being incomplete ▷ *n* **2** a cell or individual of this type ▷ Compare **euploid.** > 'aneu,ploidy *n*

aneurin (ə'njʊərın) *n* a less common name for **thiamine** [C20 from A(NTI-) + (POLY)NEUR(ITIS) + (VITAM)IN]

aneurysm or **aneurism** ('ænjə,rızəm) *n* a sac formed by abnormal dilation of the weakened wall of a blood vessel [C15 from Greek *aneurusma,* from *aneurunein* to dilate, from *eurunein* to widen] > ,aneu'rysmal, ,aneu'rismal, ,aneurys'matic or ,aneuris'matic *adj* > ,aneu'rysmally, ,aneu'rismally, ,aneurys'matically or ,aneuris'matically *adv*

anew (ə'nju:) *adv* **1** over again; once more **2** in a different way [Old English *of nīwe;* see OF, NEW]

anfractuosity (,ænfræktʃʊ'ɒsıtı) *n* **1** the condition or quality of being anfractuous **2** a winding, circuitous, or intricate passage, surface, process, etc

anfractuous (æn'fræktʃʊəs) *adj* characterized by twists and turns; convoluted [C17 from Late Latin *anfractuōsus,* from Latin *anfractus* a digression, literally: a bending]

Angara (*Russian* anga'ra) *n* a river in S Russia, in Siberia, flowing from Lake Baikal north and west to the Yenisei River: important for hydroelectric power. Length: 1840 km (1150 miles)

Angarsk (*Russian* an'garsk) *n* an industrial city in SE central Russia, northwest of Irkutsk. Pop: 244 000 (2005 est)

angary ('æŋgərı) *n* international law the right of a belligerent state to use the property of a neutral state or to destroy it if necessary, subject to payment of full compensation to the owners [C19 from French *angarie,* from Late Latin *angaria* enforced service, from Greek *angareia* office of a courier, from *angaros* courier, of Persian origin]

angashore ('æŋɪʃɔ:r) *n* Irish a miserable person given to complaining [from Irish Gaelic *ainniseoir*]

angel ('eɪndʒəl) *n* **1** *theol* one of a class of spiritual beings attendant upon God. In medieval angelology they are divided by rank into nine orders: seraphim, cherubim, thrones, dominations (or dominions), virtues, powers, principalities (or princedoms), archangels, and angels **2** a divine messenger from God **3** a guardian spirit **4** a conventional representation of any of these beings, depicted in human form with wings **5** *informal* a person, esp a woman, who is kind, pure, or beautiful **6** *informal* an investor in a venture, esp a backer of a theatrical production **7** Also called: **angel-noble** a former English gold coin with a representation of the archangel Michael on it, first minted in Edward IV's reign **8** *informal* an unexplained signal on a radar screen [Old English, from Late Latin *angelus*, from Greek *angelos* messenger]

angel cake *or esp US* **angel food cake** *n* a very light sponge cake made without egg yolks

angel dust *n* a slang name for **PCP**

Angeleno (,ændʒə'liːnəʊ) *n, pl* **-nos** a native or inhabitant of Los Angeles

Angel Falls *n* a waterfall in SE Venezuela, on the Caroní River. Height (probably the highest in the world): 979 m (3211 ft)

angelfish ('eɪndʒəl,fɪʃ) *n, pl* **-fish** *or* **-fishes 1** any of various small tropical marine percoid fishes of the genus *Pomacanthus* and related genera, which have a deep flattened brightly coloured body and brushlike teeth: family *Chaetodontidae*. See also **butterfly fish 2** Also called: **scalare** a South American cichlid, *Pterophyllum scalare*, of the Amazon region, having a compressed body and large dorsal and anal fins: a popular aquarium fish **3** another name for **angel shark**

angel gear *n Austral informal* the neutral gear in a motor vehicle, esp when used to coast downhill

angel hair *or* **angel's hair** *n* a kind of pasta in the shape of very fine long strands

angelic (æn'dʒɛlɪk) *adj* **1** of or relating to angels **2** Also: **angelical** resembling an angel in beauty, purity, etc ⊳ an'**gelically** *adv*

angelica (æn'dʒɛlɪkə) *n* **1** Also called: **archangel** any tall umbelliferous plant of the genus *Angelica*, having compound leaves and clusters of small white or greenish flowers, esp *A. archangelica*, the aromatic seeds, leaves, and stems of which are used in medicine and cookery **2** the candied stems of this plant, used for decorating and flavouring sweet dishes [c16 from Medieval Latin (*herba*) *angelica* angelic (herb)]

angel investor *n* same as **business angel**

Angel of the North *n* a steel sculpture of an angel with wide-open arms, created in 1998 by British sculptor Antony Gormley, which stands on a hilltop outside Gateshead, NE England. It stands 20 m (85 ft) high and has a wingspan of 54 m (175 ft)

angelology (,eɪndʒə'lɒlədʒɪ) *n* a doctrine or theory treating of angels

angel shark *or* **angelfish** *n* any of several sharks constituting the family *Squatinidae*, such as *Squatina squatina*, that have very large flattened pectoral fins and occur in the Atlantic and Pacific Oceans. Also called: **monkfish**

angels-on-horseback *n Brit* a savoury of oysters wrapped in bacon slices and served on toast

angel's tears *n* (*functioning as singular*) another name for **moonflower** (sense 2)

Angelus ('ændʒɪləs) *n RC Church* **1** a series of prayers recited in the morning, at midday, and in the evening, commemorating the Annunciation and Incarnation **2** the bell (**Angelus bell**) signalling these prayers [c17 Latin, from the phrase *Angelus domini nuntiavit Mariae* the angel of the Lord brought tidings to Mary]

anger ('æŋgə) *n* **1** a feeling of great annoyance or antagonism as the result of some real or supposed grievance; rage; wrath ⊳ *vb* **2** (*tr*) to make angry; enrage [c12 from Old Norse *angr* grief; related to Old English *enge*, Old High German *engi* narrow,

Latin *angere* to strangle]

Angers (*French* ãʒe) *n* a city in W France, on the River Maine. Pop: 151 279 (1999)

Angevin ('ændʒɪvɪn) *n* **1** a native or inhabitant of Anjou **2** *history* a member of the Plantagenet royal line descended from Geoffrey, Count of Anjou, esp one of the kings of England from Henry II to John (1154–1216) ⊳ *adj* **3** of or relating to Anjou or its inhabitants **4** of or relating to the Plantagenet kings of England between 1154 and 1216 [from French, from medieval Latin *Andegavinus*, from *Andegavum*, ANGERS capital of ANJOU]

angina (æn'dʒaɪnə) *n* **1** any disease marked by painful attacks of spasmodic choking, such as Vincent's angina and quinsy **2** Also called: **angina pectoris** ('pɛktərɪs) a sudden intense pain in the chest, often accompanied by feelings of suffocation, caused by momentary lack of adequate blood supply to the heart muscle [c16 from Latin: quinsy, from Greek *ankhonē* a strangling] ⊳ an'**ginal** *adj* ⊳ **anginose** (æn'dʒaɪnəʊs, -nəʊz) *or* an'**ginous** *adj*

angio- *or before a vowel* **angi-** *combining form* indicating a blood or lymph vessel; seed vessel: *angiology; angiosperm; angioma* [from Greek *angeion* vessel]

angiogenesis (,ændʒɪə'dʒɛnɪsɪs) *n* the induction of blood-vessel growth, often in association with a particular organ or tissue, or with a tumour

angiogram ('ændʒɪəʊ,græm) *n* an X-ray picture obtained by angiography

angiography (,ændʒɪ'ɒgrəfɪ) *n* a method of obtaining an X-ray of blood vessels by injecting into them a substance, such as one containing iodine, that shows up as opaque on an X-ray picture

angiology (,ændʒɪ'ɒlədʒɪ) *n* the branch of medical science concerned with the blood vessels and the lymphatic system

angioma (,ændʒɪ'əʊmə) *n, pl* **-mas** *or* **-mata** (-mətə) a tumour consisting of a mass of blood vessels (**haemangioma**) or a mass of lymphatic vessels (**lymphangioma**) ⊳ ,angi'**omatous** *adj*

angioplasty ('ændʒɪə,plæstɪ) *n* a surgical technique for restoring normal blood flow through an artery narrowed or blocked by atherosclerosis, either by inserting a balloon into the narrowed section and inflating it or by using a laser beam

angiosperm ('ændʒɪə,spɜːm) *n* any seed-bearing plant of the phylum *Angiospermophyta* (division *Angiospermae* in traditional systems), in which the ovules are enclosed in an ovary, which develops into the fruit after fertilization; any flowering plant. Compare **gymnosperm** ⊳ ,angio'**spermous** *adj*

angiotensin (,ændʒɪə'tɛnsɪn) *n* a peptide of physiological importance that is capable of causing constriction of blood vessels, which raises blood pressure [from ANGIO- + TENSE[1] + -IN]

Angkor ('æŋkɔː) *n* a large area of ruins in NW Cambodia, containing **Angkor Thom** (tɔːm), the capital of the former Khmer Empire, and **Angkor Wat** (wɒt), a three-storey temple, which were overgrown with dense jungle from the 14th to 19th centuries

angle[1] ('æŋgl) *n* **1** the space between two straight lines that diverge from a common point or between two planes that extend from a common line **2** the shape formed by two such lines or planes **3** the extent to which one such line or plane diverges from another, measured in degrees or radians **4** an angular projection or recess; corner **5** standpoint; point of view: *look at the question from another angle; the angle of a newspaper article* **6** *informal* a selfish or devious motive or purpose **7** See **angle iron** ⊳ *vb* **8** to move in or bend into angles or an angle **9** (*tr*) to produce (an article, statement, etc) with a particular point of view **10** (*tr*) to present, direct, or place at an angle **11** (*intr*) to turn or bend in a different direction: *the*

path angled sharply to the left [c14 from French, from Old Latin *angulus* corner]

angle[2] ('æŋgl) *vb* (*intr*) **1** to fish with a hook and line **2** (*often foll by for*) to attempt to get: *he angled for a compliment* ⊳ *n* **3** *obsolete* any piece of fishing tackle, esp a hook [Old English *angul* fish-hook; related to Old High German *ango*, Latin *uncus*, Greek *onkos*]

Angle ('æŋgl) *n* a member of a West Germanic people from N Germany who invaded and settled large parts of E and N England in the 5th and 6th centuries AD [from Latin *Anglus*, from Germanic (compare ENGLISH), an inhabitant of *Angul*, a district in Schleswig (now *Angeln*), a name identical with Old English *angul* hook, ANGLE[2], referring to its shape]

angle bracket *n* either of a pair of brackets having the shapes < and >

angledug ('æŋgl,dʌg) *n Southwestern English dialect* an earthworm. Also: **angletwitch**

angle iron *n* **1** Also called: **angle, angle bar** an iron or a steel structural bar that has an L-shaped cross section **2** any piece of iron or steel forming an angle, esp a right angle

angle of advance *n engineering* **1** the angle in excess of 90° that a steam-engine valve gear is in advance of the crank **2** the angle between the point of ignition and bottom dead-centre in a spark-ignition engine

angle of attack *n* the acute angle between the chord line of an aerofoil and the undisturbed relative airflow. Also called: **angle of incidence**

angle of bank *n* the angle between the lateral axis of an aircraft in flight and the horizontal

angle of deviation *n* the angle between the direction of the refracted ray and the direction of the incident ray when a ray of light passes from one medium to another

angle of dip *n* the full name for **dip** (sense 27)

angle of friction *n physics* the angle of a plane to the horizontal when a body placed on the plane will just start to slide. The tangent of the angle of friction is the **coefficient of static friction**

angle of incidence *n* **1** the angle that a line or beam of radiation makes with the normal to the surface at the point of incidence **2** another name for **angle of attack 3** Also called: **rigging angle of incidence** the angle between the chord line of an aircraft wing or tailplane and the aircraft's longitudinal axis

angle of reflection *n* the angle that a beam of reflected radiation makes with the normal to a surface at the point of reflection

angle of refraction *n* the angle that a refracted beam of radiation makes with the normal to the surface between two media at the point of refraction

angle of repose *n* the maximum angle to the horizontal at which rocks, soil, etc, will remain without sliding

angle plate *n* a steel structural plate, esp one in the shape of a right-angled triangle, used to connect structural members and stiffen frameworks

angler ('æŋglə) *n* **1** a person who fishes with a rod and line **2** *informal* a person who schemes or uses devious methods to secure an advantage **3** Also called: **angler fish** any spiny-finned fish of the order *Pediculati* (or *Lophiiformes*). They live at the bottom of the sea and typically have a long spiny movable dorsal fin with which they lure their prey

Anglesey ('æŋglsɪ) *n* an island and county of N Wales, formerly part of Gwynedd (1974–96), separated from the mainland by the Menai Strait. Administrative centre: Llangefni. Pop: 59 500 (2003 est). Area: 720 sq km (278 sq miles). Welsh name: Ynys Môn

anglesite ('æŋgl,saɪt) *n* a white or grey secondary mineral consisting of lead sulphate in orthorhombic crystalline form. It occurs in lead-ore deposits and is a source of lead. Formula:

a

PbSO₄ [C19 from ANGLESEY, where it was first found]

angletwitch ('æŋgᵊl,twɪtʃ) *n* another word for **angledug**

angleworm ('æŋgᵊl,wɜːm) *n* an earthworm used as bait by anglers

Anglia ('æŋglɪə) *n* a Latin name for **England**

Anglian ('æŋglɪən) *adj* **1** of or relating to the Angles or to the Anglian dialects of Old English ▷ *n* **2** the group of Old and Middle English dialects spoken in the Midlands and the north of England, divided into Mercian and Northumbrian. See also **Kentish, West Saxon** ▷ See also **East Anglia**

Anglican ('æŋglɪkən) *adj* **1** denoting or relating to the Anglican communion ▷ *n* **2** a member of the Church of England or one of the Churches in full communion with it [C17 from Medieval Latin *Anglicānus*, from *Anglicus* English, from Latin *Anglī* the Angles]

Anglican Church *n* any Church of the Anglican Communion or the Anglican Communion itself

Anglican Communion *n* a group of Christian Churches including the Church of England, the Church of Ireland, the Episcopal Church in Scotland, the Church in Wales, and the Episcopal Church in the US, all of which are in full communion with each other

Anglicanism ('æŋglɪkə,nɪzəm) *n* the doctrine and practice of the Church of England and other Anglican Churches

Anglice ('æŋglɪsɪ) *adv* in English: *Roma, Anglice Rome* [from Medieval Latin]

Anglicism ('æŋglɪ,sɪzəm) *n* **1** a word, phrase, or idiom peculiar to the English language, esp as spoken in England **2** an English attitude, custom, etc **3** the fact or quality of being English

Anglicist ('æŋglɪsɪst) *or* **Anglist** *n rare* an expert in or student of English literature or language

anglicize, anglicise ('æŋglɪ,saɪz) *or* **anglify** ('æŋglɪ,faɪ) *vb* -cizes, -cizing, -cized, -cises, -cising, -cised *or* -fies, -fying, -fied (*sometimes capital*) to make or become English in outlook, attitude, form, etc > ,anglici'zation *or* ,anglici'sation *n*

angling ('æŋglɪŋ) *n* **a** the art or sport of catching fish with a rod and line and a baited hook or other lure, such as a fly; fishing **b** (*as modifier*): *an angling contest*

Anglo ('æŋgləʊ) *n, pl* -glos **1** *US* a White inhabitant of the United States who is not of Latin extraction **2** *Austral derogatory* an Australian of Anglo-Celtic descent

Anglo- ('æŋgləʊ-) *combining form* denoting English or England: *Anglo-Saxon* [from Medieval Latin *Anglī*]

Anglo-American *adj* **1** of or relating to relations between England and the United States or their peoples ▷ *n* **2** *chiefly US* an inhabitant or citizen of the United States who was or whose ancestors were born in England

Anglo-Catholic *adj* **1** of or relating to a group within the Church of England or the Anglican Communion that emphasizes the Catholic elements in its teaching and practice ▷ *n* **2** a member of this group > ,Anglo-Ca'tholi,cism *n*

Anglo-Celtic *n, adj Austral* of or relating to an inhabitant of Australia who was or whose ancestors were born in the British Isles

Anglo-Egyptian Sudan *n* the former name (1899–1956) of the **Sudan**

Anglo-French *adj* **1** of or relating to England and France **2** of or relating to Anglo-French ▷ *n* **3** the Norman-French language of medieval England

Anglo-Indian *adj* **1** of or relating to England and India **2** denoting or relating to Anglo-Indians **3** (of a word) introduced into English from an Indian language ▷ *n* **4** a person of mixed English and Indian descent **5** an English person who lives or has lived for a long time in India

Anglo-Irish *n* **1** (preceded by *the; functioning as plural*) the inhabitants of Ireland of English birth or descent **2** the English language as spoken in Ireland ▷ *adj* **3** of or relating to the Anglo-Irish **4** of or relating to English and Irish **5** of or relating to the English language as spoken in Ireland

Anglomania (,æŋgləʊ'meɪnɪə) *n* excessive respect for English customs, etc > Anglo'mani,ac *n*

Anglo-Norman *history* ▷ *adj* **1** relating to the Norman conquerors of England, their society, or their language ▷ *n* **2** a Norman inhabitant of England after 1066 **3** the Anglo-French language

Anglophile ('æŋgləʊfɪl, -,faɪl) *or* **Anglophil** *n* **1** a person having admiration for England or the English ▷ *adj* **2** marked by or possessing such admiration > Anglophilia (,æŋgləʊ'fɪlɪə) *n* > Anglophiliac (,æŋgləʊ'fɪlɪ,æk) *or* Anglophilic (,æŋgləʊ'fɪlɪk) *adj*

Anglophobe ('æŋgləʊ,fəʊb) *n* **1** a person who hates or fears England or its people **2** *Canadian* a person who hates or fears Canadian Anglophones > Anglo'phobia *n*

Anglophone ('æŋglə,fəʊn) (*often not capital*) *n* **1** a person who speaks English, esp a native speaker ▷ *adj* **2** speaking English

Anglo-Saxon *n* **1** a member of any of the West Germanic tribes (Angles, Saxons, and Jutes) that settled in Britain from the 5th century AD and were dominant until the Norman conquest **2** the language of these tribes. See **Old English** **3** any White person whose native language is English and whose cultural affiliations are those common to Britain and the US **4** *informal* plain blunt English, esp English containing taboo words ▷ *adj* **5** forming part of the Germanic element in Modern English: *"forget" is an Anglo-Saxon word* **6** of or relating to the Anglo-Saxons or the Old English language **7** of or relating to the White Protestant culture of Britain, Australia, and the US **8** *informal* (of English speech or writing) plain and blunt **9** of or relating to Britain and the US, esp their common legal, political, and commercial cultures, as compared to continental Europe

Angola (æŋ'gəʊlə) *n* a republic in SW Africa, on the Atlantic: includes the enclave of Cabinda, north of the River Congo; a Portuguese possession from 1575 until its independence in 1975; multiparty constitution adopted in 1991; factional violence. It consists of a narrow coastal plain with a large fertile plateau in the east. Currency: kwanza. Religion: Christian majority. Capital: Luanda. Pop: 14 078 000 (2004 est). Area: 1 246 693 sq km (481 351 sq miles)

Angolan (æŋ'gəʊlən) *adj* **1** of or relating to Angola or its inhabitants ▷ *n* **2** a native or inhabitant of Angola

angophora (æŋ'gɒfərə) *n* any tree of the genus *Angophora*, related to the eucalyptus and native to E Australia [New Latin, from Greek *angeion* vessel + *phoreus* bearer]

angora (æŋ'gɔːrə) *n* (*sometimes capital*) **a** the long soft hair of the outer coat of the Angora goat or the fur of the Angora rabbit **b** yarn, cloth, or clothing made from this hair **c** a material made to resemble this yarn or cloth **d** (*as modifier*): *an angora sweater* See also **mohair**

Angora *n* **1** (æŋ'gɔːrə, 'æŋgərə) the former name (until 1930) of **Ankara** **2** (æŋ'gɔːrə) short for **Angora cat, Angora goat** *or* **Angora rabbit**

Angora cat *n* **1** a long-haired variety of cat, originating in Britain from crosses between Abyssinian and Siamese breeds in the 1960s **2** a former Turkish breed of cats popular in the 19th century

Angora goat *n* a breed of domestic goat with long soft hair

Angora rabbit *n* a breed of rabbit with long usually white silky hair

Angostura (*Spanish* aŋgɔs'tura) *n* the former name (1764–1846) for **Ciudad Bolívar**

angostura bark (,æŋgə'stjʊərə) *n* the bitter aromatic bark of certain South American rutaceous trees of the genus *Cusparia* or *Galipea*, formerly used medicinally to reduce fever

Angostura bitters *pl n trademark* a bitter aromatic tonic made from gentian and various spices and vegetable colourings, used as a flavouring in alcoholic drinks

Angra do Heroísmo (*Portuguese* 'ɐ̃ɡrɐ du: iru'iʒmu) *n* a port in the Azores, on Terceira Island. Pop: 35 581 (2001)

angry ('æŋgrɪ) *adj* -grier, -griest **1** feeling or expressing annoyance, animosity, or resentment; enraged **2** suggestive of anger: *angry clouds* **3** severely inflamed: *an angry sore* > 'angrily *adv*

⬛ **USAGE** It was formerly considered incorrect to talk about being *angry at* a person, but this use is now acceptable

angry young man *n* **1** (*often capitals*) one of several British novelists and playwrights of the 1950s who shared a hostility towards the established traditions and ruling elements of their country **2** any similarly rebellious person

angst (æŋst; *German* aŋst) *n* **1** an acute but nonspecific sense of anxiety or remorse **2** (in Existentialist philosophy) the dread caused by man's awareness that his future is not determined but must be freely chosen [German]

angstrom ('æŋstrʌm, -strəm) *n* a unit of length equal to 10^{-10} metre, used principally to express the wavelengths of electromagnetic radiations. It is equivalent to 0.1 nanometre. Symbol: Å or A Also called: **angstrom unit** [C20 named after Anders J. Ångström (1814–74), Swedish physicist]

angsty ('æŋstɪ) *adj* angstier, angstiest *informal* displaying or feeling angst, esp in a self-conscious manner: *two angsty teenagers*

Anguilla (æŋ'gwɪlə) *n* an island in the Caribbean, in the Leeward Islands: part of the British associated state of St Kitts-Nevis-Anguilla from 1967 until 1980, when it reverted to the status of a British dependency and is now a UK Overseas Territory. Pop: 12 000 (2003 est). Area: 90 sq km (35 sq miles)

anguilliform (æŋ'gwɪlɪ,fɔːm) *adj* having the shape or form of an eel [C17 from Latin *anguilla* eel, diminutive of *anguis* snake]

anguine ('æŋgwɪn) *adj* of, relating to, or similar to a snake [C17 from Latin *anguīnus*, from *anguis* snake]

anguish ('æŋgwɪʃ) *n* **1** extreme pain or misery; mental or physical torture; agony ▷ *vb* **2** to afflict or be afflicted with anguish [C13 from Old French *angoisse* a strangling, from Latin *angustia* narrowness, from *angustus* narrow]

anguished ('æŋgwɪʃt) *adj* feeling or expressing anguish

angular ('æŋgjʊlə) *adj* **1** lean or bony **2** awkward or stiff in manner or movement **3** having an angle or angles **4** placed at an angle **5** measured by an angle or by the rate at which an angle changes [C15 from Latin *angulāris*, from *angulus* ANGLE¹] > 'angularly *adv* > 'angularness *n*

angular acceleration *n* **1** the rate of change of angular velocity **2** *astronautics* the acceleration of a space vehicle around an axis

angular displacement *n physics* the angle through which a point, line, or body is rotated about a specific axis in a given direction

angular frequency *n physics* the frequency of a periodic process, wave system, etc, expressed in radians per second

angularity (,æŋgjʊ'lærɪtɪ) *n, pl* -ties **1** the condition of being angular **2** an angular form or shape

angular magnification *n physics* the ratio of the angle subtended at the eye by an image formed by an optical instrument to the angle subtended at the unaided eye by the object

angular momentum *n* a property of a mass or system of masses turning about some fixed point; it is conserved in the absence of the action of external forces

angular velocity *n* the velocity of a body rotating about a specified axis measured as the rate of change of the angle subtended at that axis by the path of the body. Symbol: ω

angulate *adj* ('æŋgjʊlɪt, -ˌleɪt) **1** having angles or an angular shape ▷ *vb* ('æŋgjʊˌleɪt) **2** to make or become angular [c18 from Late Latin *angulāre* to make angled, from Latin *angulus* ANGLE¹] > 'angu,lated *adj*

angulation (ˌæŋgjʊ'leɪʃən) *n* **1** an angular formation **2** the precise measurement of angles

Angus ('æŋgəs) *n* **a** council area of E Scotland on the North Sea: the historical county of Angus became part of Tayside region in 1975; reinstated as a unitary authority (excluding City of Dundee) in 1996. Administrative centre: Forfar. Pop: 107 520 (2003 est). Area: 2181 sq km (842 sq miles)

Angus Og (əʊg) *n Irish myth* the god of love and beauty

angwantibo (æŋ'gwæntɪˌbəʊ) *n, pl* -bos a rare gold-coloured prosimian primate of tropical Africa, *Arctocebus calabarensis*, having digits that are specialized as a pair of pincers for climbing: family *Lorisidae* (lorises). Also called: golden potto [c19 from Efik]

Anhalt (*German* 'anhalt) *n* a former duchy and state of central E Germany, now part of the state of Saxony-Anhalt: part of East Germany until 1990

anharmonic (ˌænhɑː'mɒnɪk) *adj physics* of or concerned with an oscillation whose frequency is not an integral factor or multiple of the base frequency

anhedral (æn'hiːdrəl) *n* the downward inclination of an aircraft wing in relation to the lateral axis. Compare **dihedral** (sense 4)

anhidrosis (ˌænhɪ'drəʊsɪs) *or* **anidrosis** *n pathol* the absence of sweating [from AN- + Greek *hidrōs* sweat + -OSIS]

anhidrotic (ˌænhɪ'drɒtɪk) *med* ▷ *adj* **1** curbing the secretion of sweat ▷ *n* **2** a substance that suppresses sweating

anhinga (æn'hɪŋgə) *n* another name for **darter** (the bird) [c18 via Portuguese from Tupi]

Anhui *or* **Anhwei** (æn'weɪ) *n* a province of E China, crossed by the Yangtze River. Capital: Hefei. Pop: 64 100 000 (2003 est). Area: 139 860 sq km (54 000 sq miles)

anhydride (æn'haɪdraɪd, -drɪd) *n* **1** a compound that has been formed from another compound by dehydration **2** a compound that forms an acid or base when added to water **3** Also called: acid anhydride *or* acyl anhydride any organic compound containing the group -CO.O.CO- formed by removal of one water molecule from two carboxyl groups [c19 from ANHYDR(OUS) + -IDE]

anhydrite (æn'haɪdraɪt) *n* a colourless or greyish-white mineral, found in sedimentary rocks. It is used in the manufacture of cement, fertilizers, and chemicals. Composition: anhydrous calcium sulphate. Formula: CaSO₄. Crystal structure: orthorhombic [c19 from ANHYDR(OUS) + -ITE¹]

anhydrous (æn'haɪdrəs) *adj* containing no water, esp no water of crystallization [c19 from Greek *anudros*; see AN-, HYDRO-]

ani ('ɑːnɪ) *n, pl* anis any of several gregarious tropical American birds of the genus *Crotophaga*: family *Cuculidae* (cuckoos). They have a black plumage, long square-tipped tail, and heavily hooked bill [Spanish *aní*, from Tupi]

Aniakchak (ˌænɪ'æktʃæk) *n* an active volcanic crater in SW Alaska, on the Alaska Peninsula: the largest explosion crater in the world. Height: 1347 m (4420 ft). Diameter: 9 km (6 miles)

anicca ('ænɪkə) *n* (in Theravada Buddhism) the belief that all things, including the self, are impermanent and constantly changing: the first of the three basic characteristics of existence. Compare **anatta, dukkha** [Pali, literally: impermanence]

aniconic (ˌænaɪ'kɒnɪk) *adj* (of images of deities, symbols, etc) not portrayed in a human or animal form [c19 from AN- + ICONIC]

anil ('ænɪl) *n* a leguminous West Indian shrub, *Indigofera suffruticosa*: a source of indigo. Also called: indigo [c16 from Portuguese, from Arabic *an-nīl*,

the indigo, from Sanskrit *nīla* dark blue]

anile ('ænaɪl, 'eɪnaɪl) *adj* of or like a feeble old woman [c17 from Latin *anīlis*, from *anus* old woman] > anility (ə'nɪlɪtɪ) *n*

aniline ('ænɪlɪn, -ˌliːn) *n* a colourless oily pungent poisonous liquid used in the manufacture of dyes, plastics, pharmaceuticals, and explosives. Formula: C₆H₅NH₂. Also called: phenylamine

aniline dye *n* any synthetic dye originally made from raw materials, such as aniline, obtained from coal tar

anilingus (ˌeɪnɪ'lɪŋgəs) *n* sexual stimulation involving oral contact with the anus [c20 from *ani-* ANUS + *-lingus*, as in CUNNILINGUS]

anim. abbreviation for animato

anima ('ænɪmə) *n* (in Jungian psychology) **a** the feminine principle as present in the male unconscious **b** the inner personality, which is in communication with the unconscious. See also **animus** [Latin: air, breath, spirit, feminine of ANIMUS]

animadversion (ˌænɪmæd'vɜːʃən) *n* **1** criticism or censure **2** a carefully considered observation

animadvert (ˌænɪmæd'vɜːt) *vb* (*intr*) **1** (usually foll by *on* or *upon*) to comment with strong criticism (upon); make censorious remarks (about) **2** to make an observation or comment [c16 from Latin *animadvertere* to notice, pay attention, from *animus* mind + *advertere* to turn to, from *vertere* to turn]

animal ('ænɪməl) *n* **1** *zoology* any living organism characterized by voluntary movement, the possession of cells with noncellulose cell walls and specialized sense organs enabling rapid response to stimuli, and the ingestion of complex organic substances such as plants and other animals. Related prefix: **zoo-** **2** any mammal, esp any mammal except man **3** a brutish person **4** *facetious* a person or thing (esp in the phrase **no such animal**) **5** *Austral informal* a very dirty car ▷ *adj* **6** of, relating to, or derived from animals: *animal products; an animal characteristic* **7** of or relating to the physical needs or desires; carnal; sensual [c14 from Latin *animal* (n), from *animālis* (adj) living, breathing; see ANIMA]

animalcule (ˌænɪ'mælkjuːl) *or* **animalculum** (ˌænɪ'mælkjʊləm) *n, pl* -cules *or* -cula (-kjʊlə) a microscopic animal such as an amoeba or rotifer [c16 from New Latin *animalculum* a small ANIMAL] > ani'malcular *adj*

animal husbandry *n* the science of breeding, rearing, and caring for farm animals

animalier ('ænɪməˌlɪə, ˌænɪ'mælɪeɪ) *n* **a** a painter or sculptor of animal subjects, esp a member of a group of early 19th-century French sculptors who specialized in realistic figures of animals, usually in bronze **b** (*as modifier*): *an animalier bronze* [from French]

animalism ('ænɪməˌlɪzəm) *n* **1** satisfaction of or preoccupation with physical matters; sensuality **2** the doctrine or belief that man lacks a spiritual nature **3** a trait or mode of behaviour typical of animals > 'animalist *n*

animality (ˌænɪ'mælɪtɪ) *n* **1** the animal side of man, as opposed to the intellectual or spiritual **2** the fact of being or having the characteristics of an animal

animalize *or* **animalise** ('ænɪməˌlaɪz) *vb* (*tr*) to rouse to brutality or sensuality or make brutal or sensual > ˌanimali'zation *or* ˌanimali'sation *n*

animal kingdom *n* a category of living organisms comprising all animals. Compare **plant kingdom, mineral kingdom**

Animal Liberation Front *n* (in Britain) an animal-rights movement often using direct action. Abbreviation: ALF

animal magnetism *n* **1** *sometimes facetious* the quality of being attractive, esp to members of the opposite sex **2** *obsolete* hypnotism

animal rights *pl n* **a** the rights of animals to be protected from exploitation and abuse by humans **b** (*as modifier*): *the animal-rights lobby*

animal spirits *pl n* cheerful and exuberant boisterousness [originally, referring to a vital force believed to be dispatched throughout the body by the brain]

animal starch *n* a less common name for **glycogen**

animate *vb* ('ænɪˌmeɪt) (*tr*) **1** to give life to or cause to come alive **2** to make lively; enliven **3** to encourage or inspire **4** to impart motion to; move to action or work **5** to record on film or video tape so as to give movement to: *an animated cartoon* ▷ *adj* ('ænɪmɪt) **6** being alive or having life **7** gay, spirited, or lively [c16 from Latin *animāre* to fill with breath, make alive, from *anima* breath, spirit]

animated ('ænɪˌmeɪtɪd) *adj* **1** full of vivacity and spirit; lively **2** characterized by movement and activity: *an animated scene met her eye* **3** possessing life; animate **4** moving or appearing to move as if alive: *an animated display* **5** pertaining to cinematographic animation > 'ani,matedly *adv*

animated cartoon *n* a film produced by photographing a series of gradually changing drawings, etc, which give the illusion of movement when the series is projected rapidly

animation (ˌænɪ'meɪʃən) *n* **1** liveliness; vivacity **2** the condition of being alive **3 a** the techniques used in the production of animated cartoons **b** a variant of **animated cartoon**

animatism ('ænɪməˌtɪzəm) *n* the belief that inanimate objects have consciousness

animato (ˌænɪ'mɑːtəʊ) *adj, adv music* (to be performed) in a lively manner [Italian]

animator *or* **animater** ('ænɪˌmeɪtə) *n* **1** an artist who produces animated cartoons **2** *Canadian* a person who coordinates or facilitates something, esp a television or radio presenter

animatronic (ˌænɪmə'trɒnɪk) *adj* of, concerned with, or operated by animatronics: *animatronic dinosaurs*

animatronics (ˌænɪmə'trɒnɪks) *n* (*functioning as singular*) a branch of film and theatre technology that combines traditional puppetry techniques with electronics to create lifelike animated effects [c20 from ANIMA(TION) + (ELEC)TRONICS]

anime ('ænɪˌmeɪ) *n* a type of Japanese animated film with themes and styles similar to manga comics [c20 from Japanese]

animé¹ ('ænɪˌmeɪ, -mɪ) *n* any of various resins, esp that obtained from the tropical American leguminous tree *Hymenaea courbaril* [French: of uncertain origin]

animé² ('ænɪˌmeɪ) *adj, adv music* the French word for **animato**

animism ('ænɪˌmɪzəm) *n* **1** the belief that natural objects, phenomena, and the universe itself have desires and intentions **2** (in the philosophies of the Greek philosophers Plato (?427–?347 BC) and Pythagoras (?580–?500 BC)) the hypothesis that there is an immaterial force that animates the universe [c19 from Latin *anima* vital breath, spirit] > 'animist *n* > animistic (ˌænɪ'mɪstɪk) *adj*

animosity (ˌænɪ'mɒsɪtɪ) *n, pl* -ties a powerful and active dislike or hostility; enmity [c15 from Late Latin *animōsitās*, from Latin *animōsus* spirited, from ANIMUS]

animus ('ænɪməs) *n* **1** intense dislike; hatred; animosity **2** motive, intention, or purpose **3** (in Jungian psychology) the masculine principle present in the female unconscious. See also **anima** [c19 from Latin: mind, spirit]

anion ('ænˌaɪən) *n* a negatively charged ion; an ion that is attracted to the anode during electrolysis. Compare **cation** [c19 from ANA- + ION] > anionic (ˌænaɪ'ɒnɪk) *adj*

anise ('ænɪs) *n* a Mediterranean umbelliferous plant, *Pimpinella anisum*, having clusters of small yellowish-white flowers and liquorice-flavoured seeds (see **aniseed**) [c13 from Old French *anis*, via Latin from Greek *anison*]

aniseed ('ænɪˌsiːd) *n* the liquorice-flavoured aromatic seeds of the anise plant, used medicinally for expelling intestinal gas and in

a

cookery as a flavouring, esp in cakes and confections. Also called: **anise**

aniseikonia (ˌænaɪsaɪˈkəʊnɪə) *n* a condition caused by a defect in the lens of the eye in which the images produced in the two eyes differ in size or shape [c20 New Latin, from ANISO- + Greek *eikon* image] ▷ ˌaniseiˈkonic *adj*

anisette (ˌænɪˈzɛt, -ˈsɛt) *n* a liquorice-flavoured liqueur made from aniseed [c19 from French; see ANISE, -ETTE]

aniso- *or before a vowel* **anis-** *combining form* not equal: *anisogamy* [New Latin, from Greek *anisos*; see AN-, ISO-]

anisocercal (ænˌaɪsəʊˈsɜːkəl) *adj* (of fish) having unequal tail-fin lobes [c19 from ANISO- + Greek *kerkos* tail]

anisodactyl (ænˌaɪsəʊˈdæktɪl, ænaɪ-) *adj also* **anisodactylous 1** (of the feet of passerine birds) having the first toe directed backwards and the other three toes directed forwards ▷ *n* **2** a bird having this type of feet

anisogamy (ˌænaɪˈsɒɡəmɪ) *n* a type of sexual reproduction in which the gametes are dissimilar, either in size alone or in size and form ▷ ˌaniˈsogamous *adj*

anisole (ˈænɪˌsəʊl) *n* a colourless pleasant-smelling liquid used as a solvent and vermicide and in perfume and flavouring. Formula: $C_6H_5OCH_3$; relative density: 0.996; melting pt: −37.5°C; boiling pt: 155°C. Also called: methoxybenzene [c19 from ANISE + -OLE¹]

anisomeric (ænˌaɪsəʊˈmɛrɪk) *adj* (of a chemical compound) lacking isomers

anisomerous (ˌænɪˈsɒmərəs) *adj* (of flowers) having floral whorls that differ in the number of their parts. Compare **isomerous** (sense 2)

anisometric (ænˌaɪsəʊˈmɛtrɪk) *adj* **1** not isometric; having unsymmetrical parts or unequal measurements **2** (of a crystal) having unequal axes

anisometropia (ænˌaɪsəʊməˈtrəʊpɪə, ænaɪ-) *n* an imbalance in the power of the two eyes to refract light

anisomorphic (ænˌaɪsəʊˈmɔːfɪk) *adj linguistics* differing in the semantic scope of terms referring to the real world: for instance, English and Russian are anisomorphic with regard to colour terms, English treating light blue and navy blue as shades of one colour but Russian treating these two shades as unrelated

anisophyllous (ænˌaɪsəʊˈfɪləs) *adj* another word for **heterophyllous**. ▷ anˈisoˌphylly *n*

anisotropic (ænˌaɪsəʊˈtrɒpɪk, ænaɪ-) *adj* **1** not isotropic; having different physical properties in different directions: *anisotropic crystals* **2** (of a plant) responding unequally to an external stimulus in different parts of the plant ▷ anˌisoˈtropically *adv* ▷ anisotropy (ˌænaɪˈsɒtrəpɪ)

Anjou (*French* ãʒu) *n* a former province of W France, in the Loire valley: a medieval countship from the 10th century, belonging to the English crown from 1154 until 1204; annexed by France in 1480. Related adj: **Angevin**

Ankara (ˈæŋkərə) *n* the capital of Turkey: an ancient city in the Anatolian highlands: first a capital in the 3rd century BC, in the Celtic kingdom of Galatia. Pop: 3 593 000 (2005 est). Ancient name: **Ancyra** Former name (until 1930): **Angora**

ankerite (ˈæŋkəˌraɪt) *n* a greyish to brown mineral that resembles dolomite and consists of a carbonate of calcium, magnesium, and iron. Formula: $(Ca,Mg,Fe)CO_3$ [c19 named after M. J. *Anker* (died 1843), Austrian mineralogist]

ankh (æŋk) *n* a tau cross with a loop on the top, symbolizing eternal life: often appearing in Egyptian personal names, such as Tutankhamen. Also called: **ansate cross, crux ansata** [from Egyptian *'nh* life, soul]

Anking (ˈɑːnˈkɪŋ) *n* a variant transliteration of the Chinese name for **Anqing**

ankle (ˈæŋkəl) *n* **1** the joint connecting the leg and the foot. See **talus¹ 2** the part of the leg just above the foot [c14 from Old Norse; related to German, Dutch *enkel*, Latin *angulus* ANGLE¹]

ankle biter *n Austral slang* a child

anklebone (ˈæŋkəlˌbəʊn) *n* the nontechnical name for **talus¹**

ankle sock *n* (*often plural*) *Brit* a short sock coming up to the ankle. US term: **anklet**

anklet (ˈæŋklɪt) *n* **1** an ornamental chain worn around the ankle **2** the US word for **ankle sock**

ankus (ˈæŋkəs) *n, pl* **-kus** *or* **-kuses** a stick used, esp in India, for goading elephants [from Hindi]

ankylosaur (ˈæŋkɪləʊˌsɔː) *n* any of various quadrupedal herbivorous ornithischian dinosaurs constituting the suborder *Ankylosauria*, which were most abundant in upper Cretaceous times and had a very heavily armoured tanklike body [c20 from New Latin, from Greek *ankulos* crooked + -SAUR]

ankylose *or* **anchylose** (ˈæŋkɪˌləʊs, -ˌləʊz) *vb* (of bones in a joint, etc) to fuse or stiffen by ankylosis

ankylosis *or* **anchylosis** (ˌæŋkɪˈləʊsɪs) *n* abnormal adhesion or immobility of the bones in a joint, as by a direct joining of the bones, a fibrous growth of tissues within the joint, or surgery [c18 from New Latin, from Greek *ankuloun* to crook] ▷ ankylotic *or* anchylotic (ˌæŋkɪˈlɒtɪk) *adj*

ankylostomiasis (ˌæŋkɪˌlɒstəˈmaɪəsɪs) *n* a variant of **ancylostomiasis**

anlace (ˈænlɪs) *or* **anelace** *n* a medieval short dagger with a broad tapering blade [c13 of unknown origin]

anlage (ˈænˌlɑːɡə) *n, pl* **-gen** (-ɡən) *or* **-ges** another word for **primordium** [German: predisposition, layout]

anna (ˈænə) *n* a former Indian copper coin, worth one sixteenth of a rupee [c18 from Hindi *ānā*]

Annaba (ˈænəbə) *n* a port in NE Algeria: site of the Roman city of Hippo Regius. Pop: 382 000 (2005 est). Former name: **Bône**

annabergite (ˈænəˌbɜːɡaɪt) *n* a rare green secondary mineral consisting of hydrated nickel arsenate in monoclinic crystalline form. Formula: $Ni_3(AsO_4)_2.8H_2O$. Also called: **nickel bloom** [c19 named after *Annaberg* in Saxony, where it was discovered; see -ITE¹]

annal (ˈænəl) *n* the recorded events of one year. See also **annals**

annals (ˈænəlz) *pl n* **1** yearly records of events, generally in chronological order **2** history or records of history in general **3** regular reports of the work of a society, learned body, etc [c16 from Latin (*librī*) *annālēs* yearly (books), from *annus* year] ▷ 'annalist *n* ▷ ˌannaˈlistic *adj*

Annam *or* **Anam** (æˈnæm, ˈænæm) *n* a former kingdom (3rd century–1428), empire (1428–1884), and French protectorate (1884–1945) of E Indochina: now part of Vietnam

Annamese (ˌænəˈmiːz) *adj* **1** of or relating to Annam ▷ *adj* ▷ *n* **2** a former word for **Vietnamese**

Annapolis (əˈnæpəlɪs) *n* the capital of Maryland, near the mouth of the Severn River on Chesapeake Bay: site of the US Naval Academy. Pop: 36 178 (2003 est)

Annapolis Royal *n* a town in SE Canada in W Nova Scotia on an arm of the Bay of Fundy: the first settlement in Canada (1605). Pop: 550 (2001). Former name (until 1710): **Port Royal**

Annapurna *or* **Anapurna** (ˌænəˈpʊənə) *n* a massif of the Himalayas, in Nepal. Highest peak: 8078 m (26 502 ft)

Ann Arbor (æn ˈɑːbə) *n* a city in SE Michigan: seat of the University of Michigan. Pop: 114 498 (2003 est)

annates (ˈæneɪts, -əts) *pl n RC Church* the first year's revenue of a see, an abbacy, or a minor benefice, paid to the pope [c16 plural of French *annate*, from Medieval Latin *annāta*, from Latin *annus* year]

annatto *or* **anatto** (əˈnætəʊ) *n, pl* **-tos 1** a small tropical American tree, *Bixa orellana*, having red or pinkish flowers and pulpy seeds that yield a dye: family *Bixaceae* **2** the yellowish-red dye obtained from the pulpy outer layer of the coat of the seeds of this tree, used for colouring fabrics, butter, varnish, etc [from Carib]

anneal (əˈniːl) *vb* **1** to temper or toughen (something) by heat treatment **2** to subject to or undergo some physical treatment, esp heating, that removes internal stress, crystal defects, and dislocations **3** (*tr*) to toughen or strengthen (the will, determination, etc) **4** (*often foll by out*) *physics* to disappear or cause to disappear by a rearrangement of atoms: *defects anneal out at different temperatures* ▷ *n* **5** an act of annealing [Old English *onǣlan*, from ON + *ǣlan* to burn, from *āl* fire] ▷ an'nealer *n*

Annecy (*French* ansi) *n* **1** a city and resort in E France, on Lake Annecy. Pop: 50 348 (1999) **2 Lake** a lake in E France, in the Alps

annelid (ˈænɪlɪd) *n* **1** any worms of the phylum *Annelida*, in which the body is divided into segments both externally and internally. The group includes the earthworms, lugworm, ragworm, and leeches ▷ *adj* **2** of, relating to, or belonging to the *Annelida* [c19 from New Latin *Annelida*, from French *annelés*, literally: the ringed ones, from Old French *annel* ring, from Latin *ānellus*, from *ānulus* ring] ▷ annelidan (əˈnɛlɪdən) *n, adj*

annex *vb* (æˈnɛks) (*tr*) **1** to join or add, esp to something larger; attach **2** to add (territory) by conquest or occupation **3** to add or append as a condition, warranty, etc **4** to appropriate without permission ▷ *n* (ˈænɛks) **5** a variant spelling (esp US) of **annexe** [c14 from Medieval Latin *annexāre*, from Latin *annectere* to attach to, from *nectere* to join] ▷ an'nexable *adj*

annexation (ˌænɪkˈseɪʃən, -ɛk-) *n* **1** the act of annexing, esp territory, or the condition of being annexed **2** something annexed ▷ ˌannexˈational *adj* ▷ ˌannexˈationism *n* ▷ ˌannexˈationist *n*

annexe *or esp US* **annex** (ˈænɛks) *n* **1 a** an extension to a main building **b** a building used as an addition to a main building nearby **2** something added or annexed, esp a supplement to a document

annihilate (əˈnaɪəˌleɪt) *vb* **1** (*tr*) to destroy completely; extinguish **2** (*tr*) *informal* to defeat totally, as in debate or argument **3** (*intr*) *physics* to undergo annihilation [c16 from Late Latin *annihilāre* to bring to nothing, from Latin *nihil* nothing] ▷ annihilable (əˈnaɪələbəl) *adj* ▷ an'nihilative *adj* ▷ an'nihiˌlator *n*

annihilation (əˌnaɪəˈleɪʃən) *n* **1** total destruction **2** the act of annihilating **3** *physics* the destruction of a particle and its antiparticle when they collide. The annihilation of an electron with a positron generates two or, very rarely, three photons of **annihilation radiation**. The annihilation of a nucleon with its antiparticle generates several pions

anniversary (ˌænɪˈvɜːsərɪ) *n, pl* **-ries 1** the date on which an event occurred in some previous year: *a wedding anniversary* **2** the celebration of this ▷ *adj* **3** of or relating to an anniversary **4** recurring every year, esp on the same date [c13 from Latin *anniversārius* returning every year, from *annus* year + *vertere* to turn]

anniversary day *n NZ* a day for celebrating the foundation date of one of the former Provinces

anno Domini (ˈænəʊ ˈdɒmɪˌnaɪ, -ˌniː) *adv* **1** the full form of **AD** ▷ *n* **2** *informal* advancing old age [Latin: in the year of our Lord]

anno regni *Latin* (ˈænəʊ ˈrɛɡnaɪ) in the year of the reign

annotate (ˈænəʊˌteɪt, ˈænə-) *vb* to supply (a written work, such as an ancient text) with critical or explanatory notes [c18 from Latin *annotāre*, from *nota* mark] ▷ 'annoˌtatable *adj* ▷ 'annoˌtative *adj* ▷ 'annoˌtator *n*

annotation (ˌænəʊˈteɪʃən, ˌænə-) *n* **1** the act of

annotating 2 a note added in explanation, etc, esp of some literary work

announce (əˈnaʊns) vb **1** (tr; may take a clause as object) to make known publicly; proclaim **2** (tr) to declare the arrival of: *to announce a guest* **3** (tr; may take a clause as object) to reveal to the mind or senses; presage: *the dark clouds announced rain* **4** (intr) to work as an announcer, as on radio or television **5** US to make known (one's intention to run as a candidate): *to announce for the presidency* [C15 from Old French *anoncer*, from Latin *annuntiāre*, from *nuntius* messenger]

announcement (əˈnaʊnsmənt) n **1** a public statement **2** a brief item or advertisement, as in a newspaper **3** a formal printed or written invitation **4** the act of announcing

announcer (əˈnaʊnsə) n a person who announces, esp one who introduces programmes, etc, on radio or television

anno urbis conditae Latin (ˈænəʊ ˈɜːbɪs ˈkɒndɪˌtiː) the full form of **AUC** (sense b) [literally: in the year of the founding of the city]

annoy (əˈnɔɪ) vb **1** to irritate or displease **2** to harass with repeated attacks [C13 from Old French *anoier*, from Late Latin *inodiāre* to make hateful, from Latin *in odiō (esse)* (to be) hated, from *odium* hatred] > an'noyer n

annoyance (əˈnɔɪəns) n **1** the feeling of being annoyed **2** the act of annoying **3** a person or thing that annoys

annoying (əˈnɔɪɪŋ) adj causing irritation or displeasure > an'noyingly adv

annual (ˈænjʊəl) adj **1** occurring, done, etc, once a year or every year; yearly: *an annual income* **2** lasting for a year: *an annual subscription* ⊳ n **3** a plant that completes its life cycle in less than one year. Compare **perennial** (sense 3), **biennial** (sense 3) **4** a book, magazine, etc, published once every year [C14 from Late Latin *annuālis*, from Latin *annuus* yearly, from *annus* year] > 'annually adv

annual general meeting n Brit the statutory meeting of the directors and shareholders of a company or of the members of a society, held once every financial year, at which the annual report is presented. Abbreviation: AGM

annualize or **annualise** (ˈænjʊəˌlaɪz) vb (tr) to convert (a rate of interest) to an annual rate when it is quoted for a period of less than a year: *credit card companies are obliged to quote an annualized percentage rate to borrowers*

annual parallax n See **parallax** (sense 2)

annual percentage rate n the annual equivalent of a rate of interest when the rate is quoted more frequently than annually, usually monthly. Abbreviation: APR

annual report n a report presented by the directors of a company to its shareholders each year, containing the profit-and-loss account, the balance sheet, and details of the past year's activity

annual ring n a ring of wood indicating one year's growth, seen in the transverse section of stems and roots of woody plants growing in temperate climates. Also called: **tree ring**

annuitant (əˈnjuːɪtənt) n a person in receipt of or entitled to an annuity

annuity (əˈnjuːɪtɪ) n, pl -ties **1** a fixed sum payable at specified intervals, esp annually, over a period, such as the recipient's life, or in perpetuity, in return for a premium paid either in instalments or in a single payment **2** the right to receive or the duty to pay such a sum [C15 from French *annuité*, from Medieval Latin *annuitās*, from Latin *annuus* ANNUAL]

annul (əˈnʌl) vb -nuls, -nulling, -nulled (tr) to make (something, esp a law or marriage) void; cancel the validity of; abolish [C14 from Old French *annuler*, from Late Latin *annullāre* to bring to nothing, from Latin *nullus* not any; see NULL] > an'nullable adj

annular (ˈænjʊlə) adj ring-shaped; of or forming a ring [C16 from Latin *annulāris*, from *annulus, ānulus*

ring] > annularity (ˌænjʊˈlærɪtɪ) n > 'annularly adv

annular eclipse n an eclipse of the sun in which the moon does not cover the entire disc of the sun, so that a ring of sunlight surrounds the shadow of the moon. Compare **total eclipse, partial eclipse**

annular ligament n anatomy any of various ligaments that encircle a part, such as the wrist, ankle, or trachea

annulate (ˈænjʊlɪt, -ˌleɪt) adj having, composed of, or marked with rings [C19 from Latin *ānulātus*, from *ānulus* a ring] > 'annuˌlated adj

annulation (ˌænjʊˈleɪʃən) n **1** the formation of rings **2** a ringlike formation or part

annulet (ˈænjʊlɪt) n **1** architect a moulding in the form of a ring, as at the top of a column adjoining the capital **2** heraldry a ring-shaped device on a shield; hollow roundel **3** a little ring [C16 from Latin *ānulus* ring + -ET]

annulment (əˈnʌlmənt) n **1** a formal invalidation, as of a marriage, judicial proceeding, etc **2** the act of annulling

annulose (ˈænjʊˌləʊs, -ˌləʊz) adj (of earthworms, crustaceans, and similar animals) having a body formed of a series of rings; segmented [C19 from New Latin *annulōsus*; see ANNULUS]

annulus (ˈænjʊləs) n, pl -li (-ˌlaɪ) or -luses **1** the area between two concentric circles **2** a ring-shaped part, figure, or space [C16 from Latin, variant of *ānulus* ring]

annunciate (əˈnʌnsɪˌeɪt, -ʃɪ-) vb (tr) a less common word for **announce** [C16 from Latin *annunciātus*, Medieval Latin misspelling of *annuntiātus*, past participle of Latin *annuntiāre*; see ANNOUNCE] > anˌnunci'ation n > annunciative (əˈnʌnsɪətɪv, -ʃətɪv) or annunciatory (əˈnʌnsɪətərɪ, -ʃə-) adj

Annunciation (əˌnʌnsɪˈeɪʃən) n **1** the New Testament the announcement of the Incarnation by the angel Gabriel to the Virgin Mary (Luke 1:26–38) **2** Also called: Annunciation Day the festival commemorating this, held on March 25 (Lady Day)

annunciator (əˈnʌnsɪˌeɪtə) n **1** a device that gives a visual indication as to which of a number of electric circuits has operated, such as an indicator in a hotel showing in which room a bell has been rung **2** a device giving an audible signal indicating the position of a train **3** a less common word for **announcer**

annus horribilis (ˈænʊs hɒˈriːbɪlɪs) n a terrible year [C20 from Latin, modelled on ANNUS MIRABILIS, first used by Elizabeth II of the year 1992]

annus mirabilis Latin (ˈænʊs mɪˈræbɪlɪs) n, pl anni mirabiles (ˈænaɪ mɪˈræbɪlɪs) a year of wonders, catastrophes, or other notable events

anoa (əˈnəʊə) n the smallest of the cattle tribe *Anoa depressicornis*, having small straight horns and inhabiting the island of Celebes in Indonesia. Compare **tamarau** [from a native name in Celebes]

anobiid (əˈnəʊbɪɪd) n any coleopterous beetle of the family *Anobiidae*, in which the pronotum characteristically forms a hood that more or less covers the head. The family includes such notorious pests as the **furniture beetle** (*Anobium punctatum*) and the **deathwatch beetle**, the larvae of which attack furniture and beams. See also **deathwatch**

anode (ˈænəʊd) n **1** the positive electrode in an electrolytic cell **2** Also called (esp US): plate the positively charged electrode in an electronic valve **3** the negative terminal of a primary cell. Compare **cathode** [C19 from Greek *anodos* a way up, from *hodos* a way; alluding to the movement of the current to or from the positive pole] > anodal (eɪˈnəʊdəl) or anodic (əˈnɒdɪk) adj

anodize or **anodise** (ˈænəˌdaɪz) vb to coat (a metal, such as aluminium or magnesium) with a protective oxide film by electrolysis

anodontia (ˌænəʊˈdɒnʃɪə) n the congenital absence of teeth [from AN- + Greek *odōn* tooth + -IA]

anodyne (ˈænəˌdaɪn) n **1** a drug that relieves pain; analgesic **2** anything that alleviates mental distress ⊳ adj **3** capable of relieving pain or distress [C16 from Latin *anōdynus*, from Greek *anōdunos* painless, from AN- + *odunē* pain]

anoestrus or US **anestrus** (ænˈiːstrəs) n a period of sexual inactivity between two periods of oestrus in many mammals [C20 New Latin; see AN-, OESTRUS] > an'oestrous or US an'estrous adj

anoint (əˈnɔɪnt) vb (tr) **1** to smear or rub over with oil or an oily liquid **2** to apply oil to as a sign of consecration or sanctification in a sacred rite [C14 from Old French *enoint*, from *enoindre*, from Latin *inunguere*, from IN-² + *unguere* to smear with oil] > a'nointer n > a'nointment n

anointing of the sick n RC Church a sacrament in which a person who is seriously ill or dying is anointed by a priest with consecrated oil. Former name: extreme unction

anole (əˈnəʊl) n any small arboreal tropical American insectivorous lizards of the genus *Anolis*, such as *A. carolinensis* (**green anole**): family Iguanidae (iguanas). They are able to change the colour of their skin. Also called: American chameleon [C18 *annolis*, from French *anolis*, from Carib *anoli*]

anomalistic month n the interval between two successive passages of the moon through perigee; 27.55455 days

anomalistic year n the interval between two successive passages of the earth through perihelion; 365.25964 mean solar days

anomalous (əˈnɒmələs) adj deviating from the normal or usual order, type, etc; irregular, abnormal, or incongruous [C17 from Late Latin *anōmalus*, from Greek *anōmalos* uneven, inconsistent, from AN- + *homalos* even, from *homos* one and the same] > a'nomalously adv > a'nomalousness n

anomalous monism n the philosophical doctrine that although all mental states consist merely in states of the brain, there exist no regular correspondences between classes of mental and physical states, and so no psychophysical laws. See also **identity theory**

anomaly (əˈnɒməlɪ) n, pl -lies **1** something anomalous **2** deviation from the normal or usual order, type, etc; irregularity **3** astronomy **a** Also called: true anomaly the angle between a planet, the sun, and the previous perihelion of the planet **b** Also called: eccentric anomaly the angle between the periapsis of a particular point on a circle round the orbit as seen from the centre of the orbit. This point is obtained by producing a perpendicular to the major axis of the ellipse through the orbiting body until it reaches the circumference of the circle **c** Also called: mean anomaly the angle between the periapsis of an orbit and the position of an imaginary body orbiting at a constant angular speed and in the same period as the real orbiting body **4** geology **a** Also called: gravity anomaly a deviation from the normal value of gravity at the earth's surface, caused by density differences at depth, for example those caused by a buried mineral body **b** Also called: magnetic anomaly a magnetic field, for example one produced by a buried mineral body, that deviates from an expected or standard value, usually that of the earth's magnetic field > a,noma'listic adj > a,noma'listically adv

anomie or **anomy** (ˈænəʊmɪ) n sociol lack of social or moral standards in an individual or society [from Greek *anomia* lawlessness, from A-¹ + *nomos* law] > anomic (əˈnɒmɪk) adj

anon (əˈnɒn) adv archaic or literary **1** in a short time; soon **2** ever and anon now and then [Old English *on āne*, literally: in one, that is, immediately]

anon. abbreviation for anonymous

anonym (ˈænənɪm) n **1** a less common word for **pseudonym 2** an anonymous person or publication

anonymize or **anonymise** (əˈnɒnɪˌmaɪz) vb (tr)

to carry out or organize in such a way as to preserve anonymity: *anonymized AIDS screening*

anonymous (ə'nɒnɪməs) *adj* **1** from or by a person, author, etc, whose name is unknown or withheld: *an anonymous letter* **2** having no known name **3** lacking individual characteristics; unexceptional **4** (*often capital*) denoting an organization which provides help to applicants who remain anonymous: *Alcoholics Anonymous* [C17 via Late Latin from Greek *anōnumos*, from AN- + *onoma* name] > **anonymity** (ˌænə'nɪmɪtɪ) *n* > a'**nonymously** *adv* > a'**nonymousness** *n*

anopheles (ə'nɒfɪˌliːz) *n, pl* **-les** any of various mosquitoes constituting the genus *Anopheles*, some species of which transmit the malaria parasite to man [C19 via New Latin from Greek *anōphelēs* useless, from AN- + *ōphelein* to help, from *ophelos* help]

anorak ('ænəˌræk) *n* **1** a warm waterproof hip-length jacket usually with a hood, originally worn in polar regions, but now worn for any outdoor activity **2** *informal* a socially inept person with a hobby considered by most people to be boring [from Inuktitut *ánorâq*]

anorexia (ˌænɒ'rɛksɪə) *n* **1** loss of appetite **2** Also called: **anorexia nervosa** (nɜː'vəʊsə) a disorder characterized by fear of becoming fat and refusal of food, leading to debility and even death [C17 via New Latin from Greek, from AN- + *orexis* appetite] > ˌano'**rectic** or ˌano'**rexic** *adj, n*

anorthic (æn'ɔːθɪk) *adj* another word for **triclinic** [C19 from AN- + ORTHO- + -IC]

anorthite (æn'ɔːθaɪt) *n* a white to greyish-white or reddish-white mineral of the feldspar group and plagioclase series, found chiefly in igneous rocks and more rarely in metamorphic rocks. It is used in the manufacture of glass and ceramics. Composition: calcium aluminium silicate. Formula: $CaAl_2Si_2O_8$. Crystal structure: triclinic [C19 from AN- + ORTHO- + -ITE¹] > **anorthitic** (ˌænɔː'θɪtɪk) *adj*

anorthosite (æn'ɔːθəˌsaɪt) *n* a coarse-grained plutonic igneous rock consisting almost entirely of plagioclase feldspar [C19 from French *anorthose* (see AN-, ORTHO-) + -ITE¹]

anosmia (æn'ɒzmɪə, -'ɒs-) *n pathol* loss of the sense of smell, usually as the result of a lesion of the olfactory nerve, disease in another organ or part, or obstruction of the nasal passages [C19 from New Latin, from AN- + Greek *osmē* smell, from *ozein* to smell] > **anosmatic** (ˌænɒz'mætɪk) or **an'osmic** *adj*

another (ə'nʌðə) *determiner* **1 a** one more; an added: *another chance* **b** (*as pronoun*): *help yourself to another* **2 a** a different; another era from ours **b** (*as pronoun*): *to try one path, then another* **3 a** a different example of the same sort: *another Beethoven* **b** (*as pronoun*): *we got rid of one loafer, but I think this new man's another* **4 another place** the other House of Parliament (used in the House of Commons to refer to the House of Lords and vice versa) [C14 originally *an other*]

A.N. Other *n Brit* an unnamed person: used in team lists, etc, to indicate a place that remains to be filled

ANOVA ('ænəʊvə) *n acronym for* analysis of variance

anoxaemia or US **anoxemia** (ˌænɒk'siːmɪə) *n* a deficiency in the amount of oxygen in the arterial blood [C19 from New Latin, from AN- + OX(YGEN) + -AEMIA] > ˌanox'**aemic** or US ˌanox'**emic** *adj*

anoxia (æn'ɒksɪə) *n* **1** lack or absence of oxygen **2** a deficiency of oxygen in tissues and organs. Compare **hypoxia** [C20 from AN- + OX(YGEN) + -IA] > **an'oxic** *adj*

Anqing ('ɑːn'tʃɪŋ) or **Anking** *n* a city in E China, in SW Anhui province on the Yangtze River: famous seven-storeyed pagoda. Pop: 686 000 (2005 est)

ansate ('ænseɪt) *adj* having a handle or handle-like part [C19 from Latin *ansātus*, from *ansa* handle]

Anschluss ('ænʃlʊs) *n* a political or economic union, esp the annexation of Austria by Nazi

Germany (1938) [German: from *anschliessen* to join]

anserine ('ænsəˌraɪn, -rɪn) or **anserous** ('ænsərəs) *adj* **1** of or resembling a goose **2** of, relating to, or belonging to the subfamily *Anserinae*, which includes geese, swans, and certain ducks: family *Anatidae*, order *Anseriformes* **3** silly; foolish [C19 from Latin *anserīnus*, from *anser* goose]

Anshan (ˌæn'ʃæn) *n* **1** a city in NE China, in Liaoning province. Pop: 1 459 000 (2005 est) **2** an ancient city and region in Persia, associated with Elam

ANSI *abbreviation for* American National Standards Institution

answer ('ɑːnsə) *n* **1** a reply, either spoken or written, as to a question, request, letter, or article **2** a reaction or response in the form of an action: *drunkenness was his answer to disappointment* **3** a solution, esp of a mathematical problem **4** *law* **a** a party's written reply to his opponent's interrogatories **b** (in divorce law) the respondent's written reply to the petition **5** a musical phrase that follows the subject of a fugue, reproducing it a fifth higher or a fourth lower ▷ *vb* **6** (when *tr, may take a clause as object*) to reply or respond (to) by word or act: *to answer a question; he answered; to answer the door; he answered that he would come* **7** (*tr*) to reply correctly to; solve or attempt to solve: *I could answer only three questions* **8** (*intr*; usually foll by *to*) to respond or react (to a stimulus, command, etc): *the steering answers to the slightest touch* **9** (*tr*) to pay off (a debt, obligation, etc); discharge **10** (when *intr*, often foll by *for*) to meet the requirements (of); be satisfactory (for); serve the purpose (of): *this will answer his needs; this will answer for a chisel* **11** (when *intr*, foll by *to*) to match or correspond (esp in the phrase **answer** (or **answer to**) **the description**) **12** (*tr*) to give a defence or refutation of (a charge) or in (an argument) [Old English *andswaru* an answer; related to Old Frisian *ondser*, Old Norse *andsvar*; see SWEAR]

answerable ('ɑːnsərəb°l) *adj* **1** (*postpositive*; foll by *for* or *to*) responsible or accountable: *answerable for someone's safety; answerable to one's boss* **2** able to be answered > ˌanswera'**bility** or '**answerableness** *n* > '**answerably** *adv*

answer back *vb* (*adverb*) to reply rudely to (a person, esp someone in authority) when one is expected to remain silent

answer for *vb* (*intr, preposition*) **1** to be liable or responsible for (a person's actions, behaviour, etc) **2** to vouch for or speak on behalf of (a person) **3** to suffer or atone for (one's wrongdoing)

answering machine *n* a device by means of which a telephone call is answered automatically and the caller enabled to leave a recorded message. In full: **telephone answering machine** Also called: **answerphone**

ant (ænt) *n* **1** any small social insect of the widely distributed hymenopterous family *Formicidae*, typically living in highly organized colonies of winged males, wingless sterile females (workers), and fertile females (queens), which are winged until after mating. See also **army ant, fire ant, slave ant, wood ant** Related adj: **formic 2 white ant** another name for a **termite 3 have ants in one's pants** *slang* to be restless or impatient [Old English *æmette*; related to Old High German *āmeiza*, Old Norse *meita*; see EMMET]

an't *chiefly Brit contraction* **1** (ɑːnt) a rare variant spelling of **aren't 2** (eɪnt) *dialect* a variant spelling of **ain't**

ant- *prefix* a variant of **anti-** *antacid*

-ant *suffix forming adjectives and nouns* causing or performing an action or existing in a certain condition; the agent that performs an action: *pleasant; claimant; deodorant; protestant; servant* [from Latin *-ant-*, ending of present participles of the first conjugation]

anta ('æntə) *n, pl* **antae** ('æntiː) *architect* a pilaster attached to the end of a side wall or sometimes to the side of a doorway

Antabuse ('æntəˌbjuːs) *n trademark* a drug, a brand of disulfiram, used in the treatment of alcoholism, that acts by inducing nausea and other unpleasant symptoms following ingestion of alcohol; tetraethylthiuram disulphide

antacid (ænt'æsɪd) *n* **1** a substance used to neutralize acidity, esp in the stomach ▷ *adj* **2** having the properties of this substance: *antacid tablets*

Antaeus (æn'tiːəs) *n Greek myth* an African giant who was invincible as long as he touched the ground, but was lifted into the air by Hercules and crushed to death

antagonism (æn'tægəˌnɪzəm) *n* **1** openly expressed and usually mutual opposition **2** the inhibiting or nullifying action of one substance or organism on another **3** *physiol* the normal opposition between certain muscles **4** *biology* the inhibition or interference of growth of one kind of organism by another

antagonist (æn'tægənɪst) *n* **1** an opponent or adversary, as in a contest, drama, sporting event, etc **2** any muscle that opposes the action of another. Compare **agonist** (sense 1) **3** a drug that counteracts the effects of another drug. Compare **synergist** (sense 1)

antagonistic (ænˌtægə'nɪstɪk) *adj* **1** in active opposition **2** mutually opposed > anˌtago'**nistically** *adv*

antagonize or **antagonise** (æn'tægəˌnaɪz) *vb* (*tr*) **1** to make hostile; annoy or irritate **2** to act in opposition to or counteract [C17 from Greek *antagōnizesthai*, from ANTI- + *agōnizesthai* to strive, from *agōn* contest] > an'**tago**ˌ**nizable** or an'**tago**ˌ**nisable** *adj* > anˌtagoni'**zation** or anˌtagoni'**sation** *n*

Antakiya (ˌæntə'kiːjə) *n* the Arabic name for **Antioch**

Antakya (ɑn'tɑkjə) *n* the Turkish name for **Antioch**

antalkali (ænt'ælkəˌlaɪ) *n, pl* **-lis** or **-lies** a substance that neutralizes alkalis, esp one used to treat alkalosis > **antalkaline** (ænt'ælkəˌlaɪn, -lɪn) *adj, n*

Antalya (Turkish ɑn'tɑljə) *n* a port in SW Turkey, on the **Gulf of Antalya**. Pop: 751 000 (2005 est)

Antananarivo (ˌæntəˌnænə'riːvəʊ) *n* the capital of Madagascar, on the central plateau: founded in the 17th century by a Hova chief; university (1961). Pop: 1 808 000 (2005 est). Former name: **Tananarive**

Antarctic (ænt'ɑːktɪk) *n* **1 the** Also called: **Antarctic Zone**. Antarctica and the surrounding waters ▷ *adj* **2** of or relating to the south polar regions [C14 via Latin from Greek *antarktikos*; see ANTI-, ARCTIC]

Antarctica (ænt'ɑːktɪkə) *n* a continent around the South Pole: consists of an ice-covered plateau, 1800–3000 m (6000 ft to 10 000 ft) above sea level, and mountain ranges rising to 4500 m (15 000 ft) with some volcanic peaks; average temperatures all below freezing and human settlement is confined to research stations. All political claims to the mainland are suspended under the Antarctic Treaty of 1959

Antarctic Archipelago *n* the former name of the **Palmer Archipelago**

Antarctic beech *n* any tree of the genus *Nothofagus*, related to the beech and native to temperate Australasia and South America, esp *Nothofagus cunninghamii* of SE Australia or *Nothofagus moorei* of NE Australia

Antarctic Circle *n* the imaginary circle around the earth, parallel to the equator, at latitude 66° 32′ S; it marks the southernmost point at which the sun appears above the level of the horizon at the winter solstice

Antarctic Ocean *n* the sea surrounding Antarctica, consisting of the most southerly parts of the Pacific, Atlantic, and Indian Oceans. Also called: **Southern Ocean**

Antarctic Peninsula *n* the largest peninsula of

Antarctica, between the Weddell Sea and the Pacific: consists of Graham Land in the north and the Palmer Peninsula in the south. Former name (until 1964): **Palmer Peninsula**

Antarctic prion *n* another name for **dove prion**

Antares (æn'tɛəriːz) *n* the brightest star in the constellation Scorpius. It is a variable binary star whose main component, a red supergiant, is associated with a fainter green component. Visual magnitude: 1.2 (red), 6.8 (green); spectral type: M1.5Ib (red); distance: 600 light years [from Greek *Antarēs*, literally: simulating Mars (in colour), from ANTI- + *Arēs* Mars]

ant bear *n* another name for **aardvark**

ant bird *n* any of various dull-coloured South American passerine birds of the family *Formicariidae*, such as *Hylophylax naevioides* (spotted ant bird), that typically feed on ants. Also called: **bush shrike, ant thrush**

ant cow *n* an insect, esp an aphid, that excretes a sweet honey-like substance that is collected and eaten by ants

ante ('ænti) *n* **1** the gaming stake put up before the deal in poker by the players **2** *informal* a sum of money representing a person's share, as in a syndicate **3 up the ante** *informal* to increase the costs, risks, or considerations involved in taking an action or reaching a conclusion: *whenever they reached their goal, they upped the ante by setting more complex challenges for themselves* ▷ *vb* **-tes, -teing; -ted** *or* **-teed** **4** to place (one's stake) in poker **5** (usually foll by *up*) *informal, chiefly US* to pay

ante- *prefix* before in time or position; previous to; in front of: *antedate; antechamber* [from Latin]

anteater ('ænt,iːtə) *n* **1** any toothless edentate mammal of the family *Myrmecophagidae* of Central and South America, esp *Myrmecophaga tridactyla* (or *jubata*) (**giant anteater**), having a long tubular snout used for eating termites. See also **tamandua 2 scaly anteater** another name for **pangolin 3 spiny anteater** another name for **echidna 4 banded anteater** another name for **numbat**

antebellum (,ænti'beləm) *adj* of or during the period before a war, esp the American Civil War: *the antebellum South* [Latin *ante bellum*, literally: before the war]

antecede (,ænti'siːd) *vb* (*tr*) to go before, as in time, order, etc; precede [C17 from Latin *antecēdere*, from *cēdere* to go]

antecedence (,ænti'siːdəns) *n* **1** precedence; priority **2** *astronomy* retrograde motion

antecedent (,ænti'siːdənt) *n* **1** an event, circumstance, etc, that happens before another **2** *grammar* a word or phrase to which a pronoun refers. In the sentence "People who live in glass houses shouldn't throw stones," *people* is the antecedent of *who* **3** *logic* the hypothetical clause, usually introduced by "if", in a conditional statement: that which implies the other **4** *maths* an obsolescent name for **numerator** (sense 1) **5 denying the antecedent** *logic* the fallacy of inferring the falsehood of the consequent of a conditional statement, given the truth of the conditional and the falsehood of its antecedent, as *if there are five of them, there are more than four: there are not five, so there are not more than four* ▷ *adj* **6** preceding in time or order; prior ▷ See also **antecedents**

antecedents (,ænti'siːdənts) *pl n* **1** ancestry **2** a person's past history

antechamber ('ænti,tʃeimbə) *n* another name for **anteroom** [C17 from Old French, from Italian *anticamera*; see ANTE-, CHAMBER]

antechoir ('ænti,kwaiə) *n* the part of a church in front of the choir, usually enclosed by screens, tombs, etc

antedate *vb* ('ænti,deit, ,ænti'deit) (*tr*) **1** to be or occur at an earlier date than **2** to affix a date to (a document, etc) that is earlier than the actual date **3** to assign a date to (an event, etc) that is earlier than its previously assigned date **4** to cause to occur sooner ▷ *n* ('ænti,deit) **5** an earlier date

antediluvian (,ændidi'luːviən, -dai-) *adj* **1** belonging to the ages before the biblical Flood (Genesis 7, 8) **2** old-fashioned or antiquated ▷ *n* **3** an antediluvian person or thing [C17 from ANTE- + Latin *dīluvium* flood]

antefix ('ænti,fiks) *n, pl* **-fixes** *or* **-fixa** (-,fiksə) a carved ornament at the eaves of a roof to hide the joint between the tiles [C19 from Latin *antefixa* (things) fastened in front, from *figere* to FIX] > **antefixal** (,ænti'fiksəl) *adj*

antelope ('ænti,ləup) *n, pl* **-lopes** *or* **-lope 1** any bovid mammal of the subfamily *Antilopinae*, of Africa and Asia. They are typically graceful, having long legs and horns, and include the gazelles, springbok, impala, gerenuk, blackbuck, and dik-diks **2** any of various similar bovids of Africa and Asia **3** American antelope another name for **pronghorn** [C15 from Old French *antelop*, from Medieval Latin *antalopus*, from Late Greek *antholops* a legendary beast]

antemeridian (,æntimə'ridiən) *adj* before noon; in the morning [C17 from Latin *antemerīdiānus*; see ANTE-, MERIDIAN]

ante meridiem ('ænti mə'ridiəm) the full form of **a.m.** [Latin, from ANTE- + *merīdiēs* midday]

ante-mortem *adj* ▷ *adv* (esp in legal or medical contexts) before death [Latin]

antenatal (,ænti'neit*ə*l) *adj* **1** occurring or present before birth; during pregnancy ▷ *n* **2** Also called: **prenatal** *informal* an examination during pregnancy > **ante'natally** *adv*

antenna (æn'tɛnə) *n* **1** *pl* **-nae** (-niː) one of a pair of mobile appendages on the heads of insects, crustaceans, etc, that are often whiplike and respond to touch and taste but may be specialized for swimming or attachment **2** *pl* **-nas** another name for **aerial** (sense 7) [C17 from Latin: sail yard, of obscure origin] > **an'tennal** *or* **an'tennary** *adj*

antennule (æn'tɛnjuːl) *n* one of a pair of small mobile appendages on the heads of crustaceans in front of the antennae, usually having a sensory function [C19 from French, diminutive of ANTENNA]

antenuptial marriage contract (,ænti'nʌpʃəl, -tʃəl) *n* a contract made between a man and a woman before they marry, agreeing on the distribution of their assets in the event of divorce. Sometimes shortened to: **antenuptial**

antependium (,ænti'pɛndiəm) *n, pl* **-dia** (-diə) a covering hung over the front of an altar [C17 from Medieval Latin, from Latin ANTE- + *pendēre* to hang]

antepenult (,æntipi'nʌlt) *n* the third last syllable in a word [C16 shortened from Latin (*syllaba*) *antepenultima*; see ANTE-, PENULT]

antepenultimate (,æntipi'nʌltimit) *adj* **1** third from last ▷ *n* **2** anything that is third from last

anteposition ('æntipə,ziʃən) *n botany* the position opposite a given part of a plant

ante-post *adj Brit* (of a bet) placed before the runners in a race are confirmed

anterior (æn'tiəriə) *adj* **1** situated at or towards the front **2** earlier in time **3** *zoology* of or near the head end **4** *botany* (of part of a flower or leaf) situated farthest away from the main stem ▷ Compare **posterior** [C17 from Latin, comparative of *ante* before] > **anteriority** (æn,tiəri'ɒriti) *n*

anterograde amnesia ('æntərəu,greid) *n* amnesia caused by brain damage in which the memory loss relates to events occurring after the damage. Compare **retrograde amnesia** [from Latin *anterior* previous and -GRADE]

anteroom ('ænti,ruːm, -,rum) *n* a room giving entrance to a larger room, often used as a waiting room

antetype ('ænti,taip) *n* an earlier form; prototype

anteversion (,ænti'vɜːʃən) *n* abnormal forward tilting of a bodily organ, esp the uterus

antevert (,ænti'vɜːt) *vb* (*tr*) to displace (an organ or part) by tilting it forward [C17 from Latin *antevertere* to go in front, from *vertere* to turn]

anthelion (ænt'hiːliən, æn'θiː-) *n, pl* **-lia** (-liə) **1** a faint halo sometimes seen in polar or high altitude regions around the shadow of an object cast onto a thick cloud bank or fog **2** a white spot occasionally appearing on the parhelic circle at the same height as and opposite to the sun [C17 from Late Greek, from *anthēlios* opposite the sun, from ANTE- + *hēlios* SUN]

anthelix (ænt'hiːliks, æn'θiː-) *or* **antihelix** *n, pl* **-helices** (-'hiːlisiːz) *or* **-helixes** *anatomy* a prominent curved fold of cartilage just inside the outer rim of the external ear

anthelmintic (,ænθɛl'mintik), **anthelminthic** (,ænθɛl'minθik) *or* **antihelmintic** (,ænθɛl'mintik), **antihelminthic** (,ænθɛl'minθik) *n med* another name for **vermifuge**

anthem ('ænθəm) *n* **1** a song of loyalty or devotion, as to a nation or college: *a national anthem* **2** a musical composition for a choir, usually set to words from the Bible, sung as part of a church service **3** a religious chant sung antiphonally **4** a popular rock or pop song [Old English *antemne*, from Late Latin *antiphōna* ANTIPHON] > **anthemic** (æn'θɛmik) *adj*

anthemion (æn'θiːmiən) *n, pl* **-mia** (-miə) a floral design, used esp in ancient Greek and Roman architecture and decoration, usually consisting of honeysuckle, lotus, or palmette leaf motifs [from Greek: a little flower, from *anthos* flower]

anther ('ænθə) *n* the terminal part of a stamen consisting usually of two lobes each containing two sacs in which the pollen matures [C18 from New Latin *anthēra*, from Latin: a remedy prepared from flowers, from Greek: from *anthēros* flowery, from *anthos* flower] > **'antheral** *adj*

antheridium (,ænθə'ridiəm) *n, pl* **-ia** (-iə) the male sex organ of algae, fungi, bryophytes, and spore-bearing vascular plants, such as ferns, which produces antherozoids [C19 from New Latin, diminutive of *anthēra* ANTHER] > **,anther'idial** *adj*

antherozoid (,ænθərə'zəuid, -'zɔid) *n* one of many small male gametes produced in an antheridium [C19 see ANTHER, ZO(O)ID]

anthesis (æn'θiːsis) *n* the time when a flower becomes sexually functional [C19 via New Latin from Greek: full bloom, from *anthein* to bloom, from *anthos* flower]

ant hill *n* **1** a mound of soil, leaves, etc, near the entrance of an ants' nest, carried and deposited there by the ants while constructing the nest **2** a mound of earth, usually about 2 metres high, built up by termites in forming a nest

antho- *combining form* denoting a flower: *anthophore; anthotaxy; anthozoan* [from Greek *anthos*]

anthocyanin (,ænθəu'saiənin) *or* **anthocyan** (,ænθəu'saiən) *n* any of a class of water-soluble glycosidic pigments, esp those responsible for the red and blue colours in flowers. They are closely related to vitamins E and P [C19 from ANTHO- + -*cyanin*, from Greek *kuanos* dark blue]

anthodium (æn'θəudiəm) *n, pl* **-dia** (-diə) *botany* another name for **capitulum** (sense 1) [C19 from New Latin, from Greek *anthōdēs* flower-like, from *anthos* flower + -ōdēs -OID]

anthologize *or* **anthologise** (æn'θɒlə,dʒaiz) *vb* to compile or put into an anthology

anthology (æn'θɒlədʒi) *n, pl* **-gies 1** a collection of literary passages or works, esp poems, by various authors **2** any printed collection of literary pieces, songs, works of art, etc [C17 from Medieval Latin *anthologia*, from Greek, literally: a flower gathering, from *anthos* flower + *legein* to collect] > **anthological** (,ænθə'lɒdʒik*ə*l) *adj* > **an'thologist** *n*

anthophilous (æn'θɒfiləs) *adj* **1** (esp of insects) frequenting flowers **2** feeding on flowers

anthophore ('ænθəu,fɔː, -θə-) *n* an elongation of the receptacle of a flower between the calyx and corolla

anthotaxy ('ænθə,tæksi) *n* the arrangement of flowers on a stem or parts on a flower

anthozoan (,ænθə'zəuən) *n* **1** any of the solitary

or colonial sessile marine coelenterates of the class *Anthozoa,* including the corals, sea anemones, and sea pens, in which the body is in the form of a polyp ▷ *adj* **2** Also: **actinozoan** of or relating to the class *Anthozoa*

anthracene (ˈænθrəˌsiːn) *n* a colourless tricyclic crystalline solid having a slight blue fluorescence, used in the manufacture of chemicals, esp diphenylamine and alizarin, and as crystals in scintillation counters. Formula: $C_6H_4(CH)_2C_6H_4$ [C19 from ANTHRAX + -ENE]

anthracite (ˈænθrəˌsaɪt) *n* a hard jet-black coal that burns slowly with a nonluminous flame giving out intense heat. Fixed carbon content: 86–98 per cent; calorific value: 3.14×10^7–3.63×10^7 J/kg. Also called: **hard coal** [C19 from Latin *anthracītes* type of bloodstone, from Greek *anthrakitēs* coal-like, from *anthrax* coal, ANTHRAX] ▷ **anthracitic** (ˌænθrəˈsɪtɪk) *adj*

anthracnose (ænˈθræknəʊs) *n* any of several fungus diseases of plants and trees, such as vines and beans, characterized by oval dark depressed spots on the fruit and elsewhere [C19 from French, from Greek *anthrax* coal, carbuncle + *nosos* disease]

anthracoid (ˈænθrəˌkɔɪd) *adj* **1** resembling anthrax **2** resembling carbon, coal, or charcoal

anthracosis (ˌænθrəˈkəʊsɪs) *n* a lung disease due to inhalation of coal dust. Informal name: **coal miner's lung**

anthraquinone (ˌænθrəkwɪˈnəʊn, -ˈkwɪnəʊn) *n* a yellow crystalline solid used in the manufacture of dyes, esp **anthraquinone dyes,** which have excellent colour properties. Formula: $C_6H_4(CO)_2C_6H_4$ [C19 ANTHRA(CENE) + QUINONE]

anthrax (ˈænθræks) *n, pl* -thraces (-θrəˌsiːz) **1** a highly infectious and often fatal disease of herbivores, esp cattle and sheep, characterized by fever, enlarged spleen, and swelling of the throat. Carnivores are relatively resistant. It is caused by the spore-forming bacterium *Bacillus anthracis* and can be transmitted to man **2** a pustule or other lesion caused by this disease [C19 from Late Latin, from Greek: carbuncle]

anthrop. *abbreviation for* **1** anthropological **2** anthropology

anthropic (ænˈθrɒpɪk) *adj* of or relating to human beings

anthropic principle *n astronomy* the cosmological theory that the presence of life in the universe limits the ways in which the very early universe could have evolved

anthropo- *combining form* indicating man or human: *anthropology; anthropomorphism* [from Greek *anthrōpos*]

anthropocentric (ˌænθrəpəʊˈsɛntrɪk) *adj* regarding man as the most important and central factor in the universe ▷ ˌanthropoˈcentrism *n*

anthropogenesis (ˌænθrəpəʊˈdʒɛnɪsɪs) *or* **anthropogeny** (ˌænθrəˈpɒdʒɪnɪ) *n* the study of the origins of man ▷ **anthropogenetic** (ˌænθrəpəʊdʒɪˈnɛtɪk) *adj*

anthropogenic (ˌænθrəpəʊˈdʒɛnɪk) *adj* **1** relating to anthropogenesis **2** created by people or caused by human activity: *anthropogenic pollution*

anthropoid (ˈænθrəˌpɔɪd) *adj* **1** resembling man **2** resembling an ape; apelike **3** of or relating to the suborder *Anthropoidea* ▷ *n* **4** any primate of the suborder *Anthropoidea,* including monkeys, apes, and man. Compare **prosimian.** ▷ ˌanthroˈpoidal *adj*

anthropoid ape *n* any primate of the family *Pongidae,* having no tail, elongated arms, and a highly developed brain. The group includes gibbons, orang-utans, chimpanzees, and gorillas

anthropology (ˌænθrəˈpɒlədʒɪ) *n* the study of humans, their origins, physical characteristics, institutions, religious beliefs, social relationships, etc. See also **cultural anthropology, ethnology, physical anthropology, social anthropology.** ▷ anthropological (ˌænθrəpəˈlɒdʒɪkᵊl) *adj* ▷ ˌanthropoˈlogically *adv* ▷ ˌanthroˈpologist *n*

anthropometry (ˌænθrəˈpɒmɪtrɪ) *n* the comparative study of sizes and proportions of the human body ▷ **anthropometric** (ˌænθrəpəˈmɛtrɪk) *or* ˌanthropoˈmetrical *adj* ▷ ˌanthropoˈmetrically *adv* ▷ ˌanthroˈpometrist *n*

anthropomorphic (ˌænθrəpəˈmɔːfɪk) *adj* **1** of or relating to anthropomorphism **2** resembling the human form ▷ ˈanthropoˌmorph *n* ▷ ˌanthropoˈmorphically *adv*

anthropomorphism (ˌænθrəpəˈmɔːfɪzəm) *n* the attribution of human form or behaviour to a deity, animal, etc ▷ ˌanthropoˈmorphist *n*

anthropomorphize *or* **anthropomorphise** (ˌænθrəpəˈmɔːfaɪz) *vb* to attribute or ascribe human form or behaviour to (a god, animal, object, etc)

anthropomorphosis (ˌænθrəpəˈmɔːfəsɪs) *n* transformation into human form

anthropomorphous (ˌænθrəpəˈmɔːfəs) *adj* **1** shaped like a human being **2** another word for **anthropomorphic.** ▷ ˌanthropoˈmorphously *adv*

anthropopathy (ˌænθrəˈpɒpəθɪ) *or* **anthropopathism** *n* the attribution of human passions, etc, to a deity, object, etc ▷ anthropopathic (ˌænθrəpəˈpæθɪk) *adj*

anthropophagi (ˌænθrəˈpɒfəˌgaɪ) *pl n, sing* -gus (-gəs) cannibals [C16 from Latin, from Greek *anthrōpophagos*; see ANTHROPO-, -PHAGY]

anthropophagite (ˌænθrəˈpɒfəˌgaɪt) *n* a rare word for **cannibal.** ▷ anthropophagy (ˌænθrəˈpɒfədʒɪ) *n* ▷ anthropophagic (ˌænθrəpəˈfædʒɪk) *adj* ▷ ˌanthroˈpophagous *adj*

anthropophyte (ænˈθrɒpəˌfaɪt) *n* a plant species accidentally introduced during the cultivation of another

anthroposophy (ˌænθrəˈpɒsəfɪ) *n* the spiritual and mystical teachings of Rudolph Steiner, based on the belief that creative activities such as myth making, which formed a part of life in earlier times, are psychologically valuable, esp for educational and therapeutic purposes ▷ anthroposophic (ˌænθrəpəʊˈsɒfɪk) *adj* ▷ ˌanthroˈposophist *n*

anthurium (ænˈθjʊərɪəm) *n* any of various tropical American aroid plants constituting the genus *Anthurium,* many of which are cultivated as house plants for their showy foliage and their flowers, which are borne in a long-stalked spike surrounded by a flaring heart-shaped white or red bract [C19 New Latin, from ANTHO- + Greek *oura* a tail]

anti (ˈæntɪ) *informal* ▷ *adj* **1** opposed to a party, policy, attitude, etc: *he won't join because he is rather anti* ▷ *n* **2** an opponent of a party, policy, etc

anti- *prefix* **1** against; opposing: *anticlerical; antisocial* **2** opposite to: *anticlimax; antimere* **3** rival; false: *antipope* **4** counteracting, inhibiting, or neutralizing: *antifreeze; antihistamine* [from Greek *anti*]

anti-abortion *adj* opposed to abortion: *anti-abortion activists* ▷ ˌanti-aˈbortionist *n, adj*

anti-ageing *adj* of or relating to any product or procedure claiming to reverse or slow down the effects of ageing

anti-aircraft (ˌæntɪˈɛəkrɑːft) *n* (modifier) of or relating to defence against aircraft attack: *anti-aircraft batteries*

anti-alias *vb* (tr) to process (a digital graphic image) so that it has a smooth, rather than a jagged, edge

anti-American *adj* opposed to anything of or relating to the United States of America

anti-androgen (ˌæntɪˈændrədʒən) *n* any of a class of drugs that oppose the action of androgens; used in the treatment of prostate cancer and various male sexual disorders

anti-apartheid *adj* opposed to apartheid: *the anti-apartheid movement*

antiar (ˈæntɪˌɑː) *n* another name for **upas** (senses 1, 2) [from Javanese]

anti-atom *n* an atom composed of antiparticles, in which the nucleus contains antiprotons with orbiting positrons

antibacterial (ˌæntɪbækˈtɪərɪəl) *adj* effective against bacteria

antiballistic (ˌæntɪbəˈlɪstɪk) *adj* of or relating to defence against ballistic weapons

antiballistic missile *n* a missile designed to destroy an incoming ballistic missile before it reaches its target. Abbreviation: **ABM**

antibaryon (ˌæntɪˈbærɪən) *n physics* the antiparticle of any of the baryons

Antibes (*French* ɑ̃tib) *n* a port and resort in SE France, on the Mediterranean: an important Roman town. Pop: 72 412 (1999)

antibiosis (ˌæntɪbaɪˈəʊsɪs) *n* an association between two organisms, esp microorganisms, that is harmful to one of them

antibiotic (ˌæntɪbaɪˈɒtɪk) *n* **1** any of various chemical substances, such as penicillin, streptomycin, chloramphenicol, and tetracycline, produced by various microorganisms, esp fungi, or made synthetically and capable of destroying or inhibiting the growth of microorganisms, esp bacteria ▷ *adj* **2** of or relating to antibiotics

antibody (ˈæntɪˌbɒdɪ) *n, pl* -bodies any of various proteins produced in the blood in response to the presence of an antigen. By becoming attached to antigens on infectious organisms antibodies can render them harmless or cause them to be destroyed. See also **immunoglobulin**

anti-Bolshevik *n* **1** a person who is opposed to Bolshevism ▷ *adj* **2** opposed to Bolshevism: *anti-Bolshevik propaganda*

anti-British *adj* opposed to anything characteristic of or relating to Britain

antic (ˈæntɪk) *n* **1** *archaic* an actor in a ludicrous or grotesque part; clown; buffoon ▷ *adj* **2** *archaic* fantastic; grotesque ▷ See also **antics** [C16 from Italian *antico* something ancient, or grotesque (from its application to fantastic carvings found in ruins of ancient Rome); see ANTIQUE]

antical (ˈæntɪkᵊl) *adj* (of the position of plant parts) in front of or above another part; anterior [from ANTE- + -ICAL]

anticapitalist (ˌæntɪˈkæpɪtəlɪst) *adj* **1** opposed to or against the principles or practice of capitalism: *anticapitalist riots* ▷ *n* **2** someone opposed to or against capitalism: *a group of anticapitalists*

anticatalyst (ˌæntɪˈkætəlɪst) *n* **1** a substance that destroys or diminishes the activity of a catalyst **2** another name for **inhibitor** (sense 2)

anticathode (ˌæntɪˈkæθəʊd) *n* the target electrode for the stream of electrons in a vacuum tube, esp an X-ray tube

anti-Catholic *adj* **1** opposed to the beliefs, practices, and adherents of the Roman Catholic Church ▷ *n* **2** someone opposed to the Roman Catholic Church and its adherents: *he called him an anti-Catholic* ▷ ˌanti-Caˈtholiˌcism *n*

anticensorship (ˌæntɪˈsɛnsəʃɪp) *adj* opposed to a policy or programme of censoring

antichlor (ˈæntɪˌklɔː) *n* a substance used to remove chlorine from a material after bleaching or to neutralize the chlorine present [C19 from ANTI- + CHLOR(INE)] ▷ antichloˈristic *adj*

anticholinergic (ˌæntɪˌkɒlɪˈnɜːdʒɪk) *adj* **1** *physiol* blocking nerve impulses through the parasympathetic nerves ▷ *n* **2** *med* a drug or agent that blocks these nerve impulses, used to control intestinal spasm, increase the heart rate, dilate the pupils for examination of the eyes, dry secretions in anaesthesia, and in some forms to treat Alzheimer's disease

anticholinesterase (ˌæntɪˌkɒlɪˈnɛstəˌreɪz) *n* any of a group of substances that inhibit the action of cholinesterase

Antichrist (ˈæntɪˌkraɪst) *n* **1** *New Testament* the antagonist of Christ, expected by early Christians to appear and reign over the world until overthrown at Christ's Second Coming **2** (sometimes *not capital*) an enemy of Christ or Christianity ▷ Antiˈchristian *adj*

anticipant (ænˈtɪsɪpənt) *adj* **1** operating in advance; expectant; anticipating ▷ *n* **2** a person who anticipates; anticipator

anticipate (ænˈtɪsɪˌpeɪt) *vb* (*mainly tr*) **1** (*may take a clause as object*) to foresee and act in advance of: *he anticipated the fall in value by selling early* **2** to thwart by acting in advance of; forestall: *I anticipated his punch by moving out of reach* **3** (*also intr*) to mention (something) before its proper time: *don't anticipate the climax of the story* **4** (*may take a clause as object*) to regard as likely; expect; foresee: *he anticipated that it would happen* **5** to make use of in advance of possession: *he anticipated his salary in buying a house* **6** to pay (a bill, etc) before it falls due **7** to cause to happen sooner: *the spread of nationalism anticipated the decline of the Empire* [C16 from Latin *anticipāre* to take before, realize beforehand, from *anti-* ANTE- + *capere* to take] ⊳ anˈticiˌpator *n* ⊳ anˈticipatory or anˈticipative *adj* ⊳ anˈticipatorily or anˈticipatively *adv*

USAGE The use of *anticipate* to mean *expect* should be avoided

anticipation (ænˌtɪsɪˈpeɪʃən) *n* **1** the act of anticipating; expectation, premonition, or foresight **2** the act of taking or dealing with funds before they are legally available or due **3** *music* an unstressed, usually short note introduced before a downbeat and harmonically related to the chord immediately following it. Compare **suspension** (sense 11)

anticlastic (ˌæntɪˈklæstɪk) *adj maths* (of a surface) having a curvature, at a given point and in a particular direction, that is of the opposite sign to the curvature at that point in a perpendicular direction. Compare **synclastic**

anticlerical (ˌæntɪˈklɛrɪkəl) *adj* **1** opposed to the power and influence of the clergy, esp in politics ⊳ *n* **2** a supporter of an anticlerical party ⊳ ˌantiˈclericalism *n*

anticlimax (ˌæntɪˈklaɪmæks) *n* **1** a disappointing or ineffective conclusion to a series of events, etc **2** a sudden change from a serious subject to one that is disappointing or ludicrous **3** *rhetoric* a descent in discourse from the significant or important to the trivial, inconsequential, etc > anticlimactic (ˌæntɪklaɪˈmæktɪk) *adj* > ˌanticliˈmactically *adv*

anticlinal (ˌæntɪˈklaɪnəl) *adj* **1** of, relating to, or resembling an anticline **2** *botany* of or relating to the plane at right angles to the surface of an organ

anticline (ˈæntɪˌklaɪn) *n* a formation of stratified rock raised up, by folding, into a broad arch so that the strata slope down on both sides from a common crest. Compare **syncline**

anticlinorium (ˌæntɪklaɪˈnɔːrɪəm) *n, pl* -noria (-ˈnɔːrɪə) a vast elongated anticline with its strata further folded into anticlines and synclines

anticlockwise (ˌæntɪˈklɒkˌwaɪz) *adv, adj* in the opposite direction to the rotation of the hands of a clock. US equivalent: **counterclockwise**

anticoagulant (ˌæntɪkəʊˈæɡjʊlənt) *adj* **1** acting to prevent or impair coagulation, esp of blood ⊳ *n* **2** an agent that prevents or impairs coagulation

anticoincidence (ˌæntɪkəʊˈɪnsɪdəns) *n* (*modifier*) of or relating to an electronic circuit that produces an output pulse if one but not both of its input terminals receives a pulse within a specified interval of time. Compare **coincidence** (sense 3)

anti-Communist *n* **1** a person who is opposed to Communism: *a staunch anti-Communist* ⊳ *adj* **2** opposed to Communism: *a big anti-Communist demonstration*

anticonvulsant (ˌæntɪkənˈvʌlsənt) *n* **1** any of a class of drugs used to prevent or abolish convulsions ⊳ *adj* **2** of or relating to this class of drugs

Anti-Corn Law League *n* an organization founded in 1839 by Richard Cobden and John Bright to oppose the Corn Laws, which were repealed in 1846

Anticosti (ˌæntɪˈkɒstɪ) *n* an island of E Canada, in the Gulf of St Lawrence; part of Quebec. Area: 7881 sq km (3043 sq miles)

antics (ˈæntɪks) *pl n* absurd or grotesque acts or postures

anticyclone (ˌæntɪˈsaɪkləʊn) *n meteorol* a body of moving air of higher pressure than the surrounding air, in which the pressure decreases away from the centre. Winds circulate around the centre in a clockwise direction in the N hemisphere and anticlockwise in the S hemisphere. Also called: high > **anticyclonic** (ˌæntɪsaɪˈklɒnɪk) *adj*

antidazzle mirror (ˈæntɪˌdæzəl) *n* a rear-view mirror for road vehicles that only partially reflects headlights behind

antidemocratic (ˌæntɪˌdɛməˈkrætɪk) *adj* opposed to the principles or practice of democracy: *anti-democratic forces*

antidepressant (ˌæntɪdɪˈprɛsənt) *n* **1** any of a class of drugs used to alleviate depression ⊳ *adj* **2** of or relating to this class of drugs

antidiuretic (ˌæntɪˌdaɪjʊˈrɛtɪk) *adj* (of a hormone, treatment, etc) acting on the kidneys to control water excretion

antidiuretic hormone *n* another name for **vasopressin** Abbreviation: ADH

antidote (ˈæntɪˌdəʊt) *n* **1** *med* a drug or agent that counteracts or neutralizes the effects of a poison **2** anything that counteracts or relieves a harmful or unwanted condition; remedy [C15 from Latin *antidotum*, from Greek *antidoton* something given as a countermeasure, from ANTI- + *didonai* to give] > ˌantiˈdotal *adj*

antidromic (ˌæntɪˈdrɒmɪk) *adj* (of nerve fibres) conducting nerve impulses in a direction opposite to normal [from ANTI- + Greek *dromos* course]

antidune (ˈæntɪˌdjuːn) *n* a sand hill or inclined bedding plane that forms a steep slope against the direction of a fast-flowing current

antiemetic (ˌæntɪˈmɛtɪk) *adj* **1** preventing vomiting ⊳ *n* **2** any antiemetic drug, such as promethazine or metoclopramide

anti-Establishment *adj* opposed to established authority

Antietam (ænˈtiːtəm) *n* a creek in NW Maryland, flowing into the Potomac: scene of a Civil War battle (1862), in which the Confederate forces of General Robert E. Lee were defeated

anti-European *adj* **1** opposed to the European Union or to political union of the countries of Europe ⊳ *n* **2** a person who is opposed to the European Union or to political union of the countries of Europe > **anti-Europeanism** *n*

antifascist (ˌæntɪˈfæʃɪst) *adj* opposed to fascism: *an antifascist demonstration*

antifebrile (ˌæntɪˈfiːbraɪl) *adj* **1** reducing fever; antipyretic ⊳ *n* **2** *obsolete* an antifebrile agent or drug

Antifederalist (ˌæntɪˈfɛdərəlɪst, -ˈfɛdrə-) *n* **1** *US history* a person who opposed the ratification of the Constitution in 1789 and thereafter allied with Thomas Jefferson's Antifederal Party, which opposed extension of the powers of the federal Government **2** (*often not capital*) any person who opposes federalism

antiferromagnetism (ˌæntɪˌfɛrəʊˈmæɡnɪˌtɪzəm) *n physics* the phenomenon exhibited by substances that resemble paramagnetic substances in the value of their relative permeability but that behave like ferromagnetic substances when their temperature is varied. See also **ferrimagnetism**

antifouling (ˌæntɪˈfaʊlɪŋ) *adj* **1** (of a paint or other coating) inhibiting the growth of barnacles and other marine organisms on a ship's bottom ⊳ *n* **2** an antifouling paint or other coating

antifreeze (ˈæntɪˌfriːz) *n* a liquid, usually ethylene glycol (ethanediol), added to cooling water to lower its freezing point, esp for use in an internal-combustion engine

antifriction metal (ˌæntɪˈfrɪkʃən) *n* another name for **white metal**

antifungal (ˌæntɪˈfʌŋɡəl) *adj* **1** inhibiting the growth of fungi **2** (of a drug) possessing

antifungal properties and therefore used to treat fungal infections. Also: antimycotic

antigen (ˈæntɪdʒən, -ˌdʒɛn) *n* a substance that stimulates the production of antibodies [C20 from ANTI(BODY) + -GEN] > ˌantiˈgenic *adj* > ˌantiˈgenically *adv*

antigenic determinant *n* the specific part of an antigen molecule to which an antibody becomes attached

anti-globalization or **anti-globalisation** *n* a political belief opposed to the emergence of a single world market dominated by multinational companies

anti-globalizer or **anti-globaliser** *n* a political activist who challenges the concept of globalization and promotes practices that do not cause environmental damage

antiglobulin (ˌæntɪˈɡlɒbjʊlɪn) *n* a serum containing an antibody specific to an immunoglobulin

Antigone (ænˈtɪɡənɪ) *n Greek myth* daughter of Oedipus and Jocasta, who was condemned to death for cremating the body of her brother Polynices in defiance of an edict of her uncle, King Creon of Thebes

anti-G suit *n* another name for **G-suit**

Antigua (ænˈtiːɡə) *n* an island in the Caribbean, one of the Leeward Islands: a British colony, with its dependency Barbuda, until 1967, when it became a British associated state; it became independent in 1981 as part of the state of Antigua and Barbuda. Area: 279 sq km (108 sq miles)

Antigua and Barbuda *n* a state in the Caribbean, comprising the islands of Antigua, Barbuda, and Redonda: gained independence in 1981: a member of the Commonwealth. Official language: English. Religion: Christian majority. Currency: East Caribbean dollar. Capital: St John's. Pop: 73 000 (2003 est). Area: 442 sq km (171 sq miles)

Antiguan (ænˈtiːɡən) *adj* **1** of or relating to Antigua or its inhabitants ⊳ *n* **2** a native or inhabitant of Antigua

antihalation (ˌæntɪhəˈleɪʃən) *n photog* **a** a process by which light, passing through the emulsion on a film or plate, is not reflected back into it but is absorbed by a layer of dye or pigment, usually on the back of the film, thus preventing halation **b** (*as modifier*): *antihalation backing*

antihelix (ˌæntɪˈhiːlɪks) *n, pl* -helices (-ˈhiːlɪsiːz) or -helixes a variant spelling of **anthelix**

antihero (ˈæntɪˌhɪərəʊ) *n, pl* -roes a central character in a novel, play, etc, who lacks the traditional heroic virtues

antihistamine (ˌæntɪˈhɪstəˌmiːn, -mɪn) *n* any drug that neutralizes the effects of histamine, used esp in the treatment of allergies

antihydrogen (ˈæntɪˌhaɪdrədʒən) *n* hydrogen in which the nucleus is an antiproton with an orbiting positron

anti-icer *n* a device fitted to an aircraft to prevent the formation of ice. Compare **de-icer**

anti-imperialist *adj* **1** opposed to imperialism: *anti-imperialist movements* ⊳ *n* **2** a person who is opposed to imperialism > ˌanti-imˈperialism *n*

anti-inflammatory *adj* **1** reducing inflammation ⊳ *n* **2** any anti-inflammatory drug, such as cortisone, aspirin, or ibuprofen

anti-inflationary *adj* of or relating to measures to counteract or combat inflation

antiknock (ˌæntɪˈnɒk) *n* a compound, such as lead tetraethyl, added to petrol to reduce knocking in the engine

Anti-Lebanon *n* a mountain range running north and south between Syria and Lebanon, east of the Lebanon Mountains. Highest peak: Mount Hermon, 2814 m (9232 ft)

antilepton (ˌæntɪˈlɛptən) *n physics* the antiparticle of any of the leptons

Antilles (ænˈtɪliːz) *pl n* **the** a group of islands in the Caribbean consisting of the **Greater Antilles** and the **Lesser Antilles**

antilock brake (ˈæntɪˌlɒk) *n* a brake fitted to some road vehicles that prevents skidding and improves control by sensing and compensating for overbraking. Also called: ABS brake

antilog (ˈæntɪˌlɒg) *n* short for **antilogarithm**

antilogarithm (ˌæntɪˈlɒgəˌrɪðəm) *n* a number whose logarithm to a given base is a given number: *100 is the antilogarithm of 2 to base 10*. Often shortened to: antilog > ˌantiˌlogaˈrithmic *adj*

antilogy (ænˈtɪlədʒɪ) *n, pl* -gies a contradiction in terms [C17 from Greek *antilogia*]

antimacassar (ˌæntɪməˈkæsə) *n* a cloth covering the back and arms of chairs, etc, to prevent soiling or as decoration [C19 from ANTI- + MACASSAR (OIL)]

antimagnetic (ˌæntɪmægˈnɛtɪk) *adj* of or constructed of a material that does not acquire permanent magnetism when exposed to a magnetic field: *an antimagnetic watch*

antimalarial (ˌæntɪməˈlɛərɪəl) *adj* 1 effective in the treatment of malaria ▷ *n* 2 an antimalarial drug or agent

antimasque (ˈæntɪˌmɑːsk) *n* a comic or grotesque dance, presented between the acts of a masque

antimatter (ˈæntɪˌmætə) *n* a form of matter composed of antiparticles, such as antihydrogen, consisting of antiprotons and positrons

antimere (ˈæntɪˌmɪə) *n* a part or organ of a bilaterally or radially symmetrical organism that corresponds to a similar structure on the other side of the axis, such as the right or left limb of a four-legged animal. Also called: actinomere > antimeric (ˌæntɪˈmɛrɪk) *adj* > antimerism (ænˈtɪməˌrɪzəm) *n*

antimetabolite (ˌæntɪmɪˈtæbəˌlaɪt) *n* any drug that acts by disrupting the normal growth of a cell. Sulfonamide drugs are antimetabolites and some antimetabolites are used in cancer treatment

antimicrobial (ˌæntɪmaɪˈkrəʊbɪˀl) *adj* capable of destroying or inhibiting the growth of disease-causing microbes

antimissile (ˌæntɪˈmɪsaɪl) *adj* 1 relating to defensive measures against missile attack: *an antimissile system* ▷ *n* 2 Also called: antimissile missile a defensive missile used to intercept and destroy attacking missiles. Abbreviation: AMM

antimonarchist (ˌæntɪˈmɒnəkɪst) *adj* 1 opposed to a monarchy ▷ *n* 2 a person who is opposed to a monarchy

antimonial (ˌæntɪˈməʊnɪəl) *adj* 1 of or containing antimony ▷ *n* 2 a drug or agent containing antimony

antimonic (ˌæntɪˈmɒnɪk) *adj* of or containing antimony in the pentavalent state

antimonous (ˈæntɪmənəs) *adj* of or containing antimony in the trivalent state

antimony (ˈæntɪmənɪ) *n* a toxic metallic element that exists in two allotropic forms and occurs principally in stibnite. The stable form is a brittle silvery-white crystalline metal that is added to alloys to increase their strength and hardness and is used in semiconductors. Symbol: Sb; atomic no: 51; atomic wt: 121.757; valency: 0, −3, +3, or +5; relative density: 6.691; melting pt: 630.76°C; boiling pt: 1587°C [C15 from Medieval Latin *antimōnium*, of uncertain origin]

antimonyl (ˈæntɪmənɪl, ænˈtɪm-) *n* (*modifier*) of, consisting of, or containing the monovalent group SbO-: *an antimonyl group or radical*

antimony potassium tartrate *n* a colourless odourless poisonous crystalline salt used as a mordant for textiles and leather, as an insecticide, and as an anthelmintic. Formula: $K(SbO)C_4H_4O_6$. Also called: tartar emetic

antimuon (ˌæntɪˈmjuːɒn) *n* the antiparticle of a muon

antimutagen (ˌæntɪˈmjuːtədʒən) *n* any substance that acts against a mutagen

antimycotic (ˌæntɪmaɪˈkɒtɪk) *adj* another word for **antifungal**

antinationalist (ˌæntɪˈnæʃənəlɪst) *n* 1 a person who is opposed to nationalism ▷ *adj* 2 opposed to nationalism

anti-Nazi *adj* 1 opposing any individual or group that espouses Nazi ideologies ▷ *n* 2 a person who is opposed to Nazism

antineutrino (ˌæntɪnjuːˈtriːnəʊ) *n, pl* -nos the antiparticle of a neutrino; a particle having oppositely directed spin to a neutrino, that is, spin in the direction of its momentum

antineutron (ˌæntɪˈnjuːtrɒn) *n* the antiparticle of a neutron; a particle having the same mass as the neutron but a magnetic moment of opposite sign

anting (ˈæntɪŋ) *n* the placing or rubbing of ants by birds on their feathers. The body fluids of the ants are thought to repel parasites

antinode (ˈæntɪˌnəʊd) *n physics* a point at which the amplitude of one of the two kinds of displacement in a standing wave has maximum value. Generally the other kind of displacement has its minimum value at this point. See also standing wave Compare node. > ˌantiˈnodal *adj*

antinoise (ˈæntɪˌnɔɪz) *n* sound generated so that it is out of phase with a noise, such as that made by an engine, in order to reduce the noise level by interference

antinomian (ˌæntɪˈnəʊmɪən) *adj* 1 relating to the doctrine that by faith and the dispensation of grace a Christian is released from the obligation of adhering to any moral law ▷ *n* 2 a member of a Christian sect holding such a doctrine > ˌantiˈnomianism *n*

antinomy (ænˈtɪnəmɪ) *n, pl* -mies 1 opposition of one law, principle, or rule to another; contradiction within a law 2 *philosophy* contradiction existing between two apparently indubitable propositions; paradox [C16 from Latin *antinomia*, from Greek: conflict between laws, from ANTI- + *nomos* law] > antinomic (ˌæntɪˈnɒmɪk) *adj* > ˌantiˈnomically *adv*

antinovel (ˈæntɪˌnɒvˀl) *n* a type of prose fiction in which conventional or traditional novelistic elements are rejected. Also called: *anti-roman, nouveau roman*

antinuclear (ˌæntɪˈnjuːklɪə) *adj* opposed to nuclear weapons > ˌantiˈnuclearist *n*

antinucleon (ˌæntɪˈnjuːklɪˌɒn) *n* an antiproton or an antineutron

Antioch (ˈæntɪˌɒk) *n* a city in S Turkey, on the Orantes River: ancient commercial centre and capital of Syria (300–64 BC); early centre of Christianity. Pop: 155 000 (2005 est). Arabic name: Antakiya Turkish name: Antakya

antioxidant (ˌæntɪˈɒksɪdənt) *n* 1 any substance that retards deterioration by oxidation, esp of fats, oils, foods, petroleum products, or rubber 2 *biology* a substance, such as vitamin C, vitamin E, or beta carotene, that counteracts the damaging effects of oxidation in a living organism

antiparallel (ˌæntɪˈpærəˌlɛl) *adj* 1 *physics* parallel but pointing in the opposite direction 2 *maths* (of vectors) parallel but having opposite directions

antiparticle (ˈæntɪˌpɑːtɪkˀl) *n* any of a group of elementary particles that have the same mass and spin as their corresponding particle but have opposite values for all other nonzero quantum numbers. When a particle collides with its antiparticle, mutual annihilation occurs

antipasto (ˌæntɪˈpɑːstəʊ, -ˈpæs-) *n, pl* -tos a course of hors d'oeuvres in an Italian meal [Italian: before food]

antipathetic (ænˌtɪpəˈθɛtɪk, ˌæntɪpə-) or **antipathetical** *adj* (often foll by *to*) having or arousing a strong aversion > ˌantipaˈthetically *adv*

antipathy (ænˈtɪpəθɪ) *n, pl* -thies 1 a feeling of intense aversion, dislike, or hostility 2 the object of such a feeling [C17 from Latin *antipathia*, from Greek *antipatheia*, from ANTI- + *patheia* feeling]

antiperiodic (ˌæntɪˌpɪərɪˈɒdɪk) *med* ▷ *adj* 1 *obsolete* efficacious against recurring attacks of a disease ▷ *n* 2 *obsolete* an antiperiodic drug or agent

antiperistalsis (ˌæntɪˌpɛrɪˈstælsɪs) *n physiol* contractions of the intestine that force the contents in the opposite direction to the normal > ˌantiˌperiˈstaltic *adj*

antipersonnel (ˌæntɪˌpɜːsəˈnɛl) *adj* (of weapons, etc) designed to cause casualties to personnel rather than to destroy equipment or defences. Abbreviation: AP

antiperspirant (ˌæntɪˈpɜːspərənt) *n* 1 an astringent substance applied to the skin to reduce or prevent perspiration ▷ *adj* 2 reducing or preventing perspiration

antiphlogistic (ˌæntɪfləˈdʒɪstɪk) *adj* 1 *obsolete* of or relating to the prevention or alleviation of inflammation ▷ *n* 2 an antiphlogistic agent or drug

antiphon (ˈæntɪfən) *n* 1 a short passage, usually from the Bible, recited or sung as a response after certain parts of a liturgical service 2 a psalm, hymn, etc, chanted or sung in alternate parts 3 any response or answer [C15 from Late Latin *antiphōna* sung responses, from Late Greek, plural of *antiphōnon* (something) responsive, from *antiphōnos*, from ANTI- + *phōnē* sound]

antiphonal (ænˈtɪfənəl) *adj* 1 sung or recited in alternation ▷ *n* 2 another word for **antiphonary** > anˈtiphonally *adv*

antiphonary (ænˈtɪfənərɪ) *n, pl* -naries 1 a bound collection of antiphons, esp for use in the divine office 2 *adj* of or relating to such a book

antiphony (ænˈtɪfənɪ) *n, pl* -nies 1 the antiphonal singing of a musical composition by two choirs 2 any musical or other sound effect that answers or echoes another

antiphrasis (ænˈtɪfrəsɪs) *n rhetoric* the use of a word in a sense opposite to its normal one, esp for ironic effect [C16 via Late Latin from Greek, from ANTI- + *phrasis*, from *phrazein* to speak]

anti-pill *adj* denoting a material that does not form pills or that resists pilling

antipodal (ænˈtɪpədˀl) *adj* 1 of or relating to diametrically opposite points on the earth's surface 2 exactly or diametrically opposite

antipode (ˈæntɪpəʊd) *n* the exact or direct opposite

antipodes (ænˈtɪpəˌdiːz) *pl n* 1 either or both of two points, places, or regions that are situated diametrically opposite to one another on the earth's surface, esp the country or region opposite one's own 2 the people who live there 3 (*often capital*) the Australia and New Zealand 4 (*sometimes functioning as singular*) the exact or direct opposite [C16 via Late Latin from Greek, plural of *antipous* having the feet opposite, from ANTI- + *pous* foot] > antipodean (ænˌtɪpəˈdiːən) *adj*

Antipodes Islands *pl n* the a group of small uninhabited islands in the South Pacific, southeast of and belonging to New Zealand. Area: 62 sq km (24 sq miles)

antipollution (ˌæntɪpəˈluːʃən) *adj* 1 (of measures, policies, etc) designed to combat pollution and its causes 2 opposed to pollution and its causes: *antipollution banners*

antipope (ˈæntɪˌpəʊp) *n* a rival pope elected in opposition to one who has been canonically chosen

antiproton (ˈæntɪˌprəʊtɒn) *n* the antiparticle of the proton; a particle having the same mass as the proton but an equal and opposite charge

antipsychiatry (ˌæntɪsaɪˈkaɪətrɪ) *n* an approach to mental disorders that makes use of concepts derived from existentialism, psychoanalysis, and sociological theory

antipsychotic (ˌæntɪsaɪˈkɒtɪk) *adj* 1 preventing or treating psychosis ▷ *n* 2 any antipsychotic drug, such as chlorpromazine: used to treat such conditions as schizophrenia

antipyretic (ˌæntɪpaɪˈrɛtɪk) *adj* 1 preventing or alleviating fever ▷ *n* 2 an antipyretic remedy or drug > antipyresis (ˌæntɪpaɪˈriːsɪs) *n*

antipyrine (ˌæntɪˈpaɪriːn, -rɪn) *n* a drug formerly used to reduce pain and fever. Formula: $C_{11}H_{12}N_2O$. Also called: phenazine

antiquarian (ˌæntɪˈkwɛərɪən) *adj* 1 concerned

with the study of antiquities or antiques ▷ *n* **2** the largest size of handmade drawing paper, 53 × 31 inches **3** a less common name for **antiquary**. > ˌanti'quarianism *n*

antiquark (ˈæntɪkwɑːk) *n* the antiparticle of a quark

antiquary (ˈæntɪkwərɪ) *n, pl* -quaries a person who collects, deals in, or studies antiques, ancient works of art, or ancient times. Also called: antiquarian

antiquate (ˈæntɪˌkweɪt) *vb* (*tr*) **1** to make obsolete or old-fashioned **2** to give an old or antique appearance to [c15 from Latin *antīquāre* to make old, from *antīquus* ancient]

antiquated (ˈæntɪˌkweɪtɪd) *adj* **1** outmoded; obsolete **2** aged; ancient > ˈanti,quatedness *n*

antique (ænˈtiːk) *n* **1 a** a decorative object, piece of furniture, or other work of art created in an earlier period, that is collected and valued for its beauty, workmanship, and age **b** (*as modifier*): *an antique shop* **2** any object made in an earlier period **3 the** the style of ancient art, esp Greek or Roman art, or an example of it ▷ *adj* **4** made in or in the style of an earlier period **5** of or belonging to the distant past, esp of or in the style of ancient Greece or Rome **6** *informal* old-fashioned; out-of-date **7** *archaic* aged or venerable **8** (of paper) not calendered or coated; having a rough surface ▷ *vb* **9** (*tr*) to give an antique appearance to [c16 from Latin *antīquus* ancient, from *ante* before]

antiquey (ænˈtiːkɪ) *adj informal* having the appearance of an antique

antiquities (ænˈtɪkwɪtɪz) *pl n* remains or relics, such as statues, buildings, or coins, that date from ancient times

antiquity (ænˈtɪkwɪtɪ) *n, pl* -ties **1** the quality of being ancient or very old: *a vase of great antiquity* **2** the far distant past, esp the time preceding the Middle Ages in Europe **3** the people of ancient times collectively; the ancients

antirachitic (ˌæntɪrəˈkɪtɪk) *adj* **1** preventing or curing rickets ▷ *n* **2** an antirachitic remedy or agent

antiracism (ˌæntɪˈreɪsɪzəm) *n* the policy of challenging racism and promoting racial tolerance > ˌanti'racist *n, adj*

antireligious (ˌæntɪrɪˈlɪdʒəs) *adj* opposed to religious ideas, beliefs, and organizations: *antireligious propaganda*

Antiremonstrant (ˌæntɪrɪˈmɒnstrənt) *n Dutch Reformed Church* the party that opposed the Remonstrants

antirepublican (ˌæntɪrɪˈpʌblɪkən) *adj* **1** opposed to the principles or practice of republicanism ▷ *n* **2** a person who is opposed to the principles or practice of republicanism

antiriot (ˌæntɪˈraɪət) *adj* (of police officers, equipment, measures, etc) designed for or engaged in the control of crowds

anti-roll bar *n* a crosswise rubber-mounted bar in the suspension of a motor vehicle, which counteracts the movement downward on one side when cornering

anti-roman *French* (ātirɔmā) *n, pl* anti-romans (ātirɔmā) another term for **antinovel** [literally: anti-novel]

antirrhinum (ˌæntɪˈraɪnəm) *n* any scrophulariaceous plant of the genus *Antirrhinum*, esp the snapdragon, which have two-lipped flowers of various colours [c16 via Latin from Greek *antirrhinon*, from ANTI- (imitating) + *rhis* nose; so called from a fancied likeness to an animal's snout]

antirust (ˌæntɪˈrʌst) *adj* (of a product or procedure) effective against rust

Antisana (*Spanish* antiˈsana) *n* a volcano in N central Ecuador, in the Andes. Height: 5756 m (18 885 ft)

antiscientific (ˌæntɪˌsaɪənˈtɪfɪk) *adj* opposed to the principles, methods, or aims of science

antiscorbutic (ˌæntɪskɔːˈbjuːtɪk) *adj* **1** preventing or curing scurvy: *antiscorbutic foods* ▷ *n* **2** an

antiscorbutic remedy or agent

anti-Semite *n* a person who persecutes or discriminates against Jews > ˌanti-'Semitism *n*

anti-Semitic *adj* prejudiced against or hostile to Jews > ˌanti-Se'mitically *adv*

antisense RNA (ˈæntɪsɛns) *n* molecules transcribed, not from DNA in the usual way, but from DNA strands complementary to those that produce normal messenger RNA. Antisense RNA occurs in nature and is inhibitory on gene action. It can be produced synthetically and offers such therapeutic possibilities as turning off viral genes

antisepsis (ˌæntɪˈsɛpsɪs) *n* **1** destruction of undesirable microorganisms, such as those that cause disease or putrefaction. Compare **asepsis 2** the state or condition of being free from such microorganisms

antiseptic (ˌæntɪˈsɛptɪk) *adj* **1** of, relating to, or effecting antisepsis **2** entirely free from contamination **3** *informal* lacking spirit or excitement; clinical ▷ *n* **4** an antiseptic agent or substance > ˌanti'septically *adv*

antiserum (ˌæntɪˈsɪərəm) *n, pl* -rums *or* -ra (-rə) blood serum containing antibodies against a specific antigen, used to treat or provide immunity to a disease

anti-site *n* a website through which people can express their contempt for a particular person, organization, pop group, etc

antislavery (ˌæntɪˈsleɪvərɪ) *adj* opposed to slavery, esp slavery of Blacks

antisocial (ˌæntɪˈsəʊʃəl) *adj* **1** avoiding the company of other people; unsociable **2** contrary or injurious to the interests of society in general > ˌanti'socially *adv*

anti-Soviet *adj* **1** opposed to anything characteristic of or relating to the former Soviet Union and its government: *anti-Soviet propaganda* **2** opposed to the government and policies of the former Soviet Union: *they are not pro-Nazi but anti-Soviet*

antispasmodic (ˌæntɪspæzˈmɒdɪk) *adj* **1** preventing or arresting spasms, esp in smooth muscle ▷ *n* **2** an antispasmodic drug

antistatic (ˌæntɪˈstætɪk) *adj* (of a substance, textile, etc) retaining sufficient moisture to provide a conducting path, thus avoiding the effects of static electricity

antistrophe (ænˈtɪstrəfɪ) *n* **1** (in ancient Greek drama) **a** the second of two movements made by a chorus during the performance of a choral ode **b** the second part of a choral ode sung during this movement **2** (in classical prosody) the second of two metrical systems used alternately within a poem > See also **strophe** [c17 via Late Latin from Greek *antistrophē* an answering turn, from ANTI- + *strophē* a turning] > antistrophic (ˌæntɪˈstrɒfɪk) *adj* > ˌanti'strophically *adv*

antisubmarine (ˌæntɪˌsʌbməˈriːn) *adj* **1** (of weapons, missiles, etc) designed to combat or destroy submarines **2** (of warfare, tactics, etc) against submarines

antisymmetric (ˌæntɪsɪˈmɛtrɪk) *adj* **1** *logic* (of a relation) never holding between a pair of arguments *x* and *y* when it holds between *y* and *x* except when *x = y*, as *"...is no younger than..."*. Compare **nonsymmetric 2** *maths* symmetric except for a change of sign. Compare **asymmetric, symmetric** (sense 1)

antitank (ˌæntɪˈtæŋk) *adj* designed to immobilize or destroy armoured vehicles: *antitank weapons*. Abbreviation: ATK

antiterrorist (ˌæntɪˈtɛrərɪst) *adj* relating to measures, policies, or organizations designed to combat terrorist activity

antitheft (ˌæntɪˈθɛft) *adj* (of a device, campaign, system, etc) designed to prevent theft

antithesis (ænˈtɪθɪsɪs) *n, pl* -ses (-ˌsiːz) **1** the exact opposite **2** contrast or opposition **3** *rhetoric* the juxtaposition of contrasting ideas, phrases, or words so as to produce an effect of balance, such as *my words fly up, my thoughts remain below* **4**

philosophy the second stage in the **Hegelian dialectic** contradicting the **thesis** before resolution by the **synthesis** [c15 via Latin from Greek: a setting against, from ANTI- + *tithenai* to place]

antithetical (ˌæntɪˈθɛtɪkᵊl) *or* **antithetic** *adj* **1** of the nature of antithesis **2** directly contrasted

antithrombotic (ˌæntɪθrɒmˈbɒtɪk) *adj* **1** preventing the formation of blood clots ▷ *n* **2** an antithrombotic drug

antitoxin (ˌæntɪˈtɒksɪn) *n* **1** an antibody that neutralizes a toxin **2** blood serum that contains a specific antibody > ˌanti'toxic *adj*

antitrades (ˌæntɪˈtreɪdz) *pl n* winds in the upper atmosphere blowing in the opposite direction from and above the trade winds

antitragus (ænˈtɪtrəgəs) *n, pl* -gi (-ˌdʒaɪ) a cartilaginous projection of the external ear opposite the tragus [c19 from New Latin, from Greek *antitragos; see* ANTI-, TRAGUS]

antitranspirant (ˌæntɪˈtrænspɪrənt) *n* any substance that decreases transpiration and, usually, photosynthesis

antitrust (ˌæntɪˈtrʌst) *n* (*modifier*) *chiefly US* regulating or opposing trusts, monopolies, cartels, or similar organizations, esp in order to prevent unfair competition

antitussive (ˌæntɪˈtʌsɪv) *adj* **1** alleviating or suppressing coughing ▷ *n* **2** an antitussive drug [from ANTI- + Latin *tussis* a cough]

antitype (ˈæntɪˌtaɪp) *n* **1** a person or thing that is foreshadowed or represented by a type or symbol, esp a character or event in the New Testament prefigured in the Old Testament **2** an opposite type > antitypic (ˌæntɪˈtɪpɪk) *or* ˌanti'typical *adj* > ˌanti'typically *adv*

antivenin (ˌæntɪˈvɛnɪn) *or* **antivenene** (ˌæntɪvɪˈniːn) *n* an antitoxin that counteracts a specific venom, esp snake venom [c19 from ANTI- + VEN(OM) + -IN]

antiviral (ˌæntɪˈvaɪrəl) *adj* **1** inhibiting the growth of viruses ▷ *n* **2** any antiviral drug: used to treat diseases caused by viruses, such as herpes infections and AIDS

antivirus (ˈæntɪˌvaɪrəs) *n* **1** (*modifier*) of or relating to software designed to prevent viruses entering a computer system or network: *antivirus software* **2** (*n*) such a piece of software

antivivisection (ˌæntɪˌvɪvɪˈsɛkʃən) *adj* opposed to the act or practice or performing experiments on living animals, involving cutting into or dissecting the body

antiwar (ˌæntɪˈwɔː) *adj* opposed to war: *the antiwar movement*

antiworld (ˈæntɪˌwɜːld) *n* a hypothetical or supposed world or universe composed of antimatter

anti-Zionist *n* **1** a person who is opposed to Zionism ▷ *adj* **2** opposed to Zionism: *he was anti-Zionist and not anti-Semitic*

antler (ˈæntlə) *n* one of a pair of bony outgrowths on the heads of male deer and some related species of either sex. The antlers are shed each year and those of some species grow more branches as the animal ages [c14 from Old French *antoillier,* from Vulgar Latin *anteoculare* (unattested) (something) in front of the eye]

antler moth *n* a European noctuid moth, *Cerapteryx* (or *Charaeas*) *graminis,* that has white antler-like markings on the forewings and produces larvae that periodically cause great damage to pastures and grasslands

Antlia (ˈæntlɪə) *n, Latin genitive* Antliae (ˈæntlɪˌiː) a faint constellation in the S hemisphere close to Hydra and Vela [c19 from Latin, from Greek: bucket]

antlike (ˈæntˌlaɪk) *adj* **1** of or like an ant or ants **2** characterized by scurrying activity or teeming restlessness

antlion (ˈæntˌlaɪən) *n* **1** Also called: antlion fly any of various neuropterous insects of the family *Myrmeleontidae,* which typically resemble

a

dragonflies and are most common in tropical regions **2** Also called (US): **doodlebug** the larva of this insect, which has very large jaws and buries itself in the sand to await its prey

Antofagasta (ˌæntəfəˈɡæstə; *Spanish* antofaˈɣasta) *n* a port in N Chile. Pop: 323 000 (2005 est)

Antonine Wall (ˈæntənaɪn) *n* a Roman frontier defence work across S Scotland, extending between the River Clyde and the Firth of Forth. It was built in 142 AD on the orders of Antoninus Pius (86–161 AD), emperor of Rome (138–161)

antonomasia (ˌæntənəˈmeɪzɪə) *n rhetoric* **1** the substitution of a title or epithet for a proper name, such as *his highness* **2** the use of a proper name for an idea: *he is a Daniel come to judgment* [c16 via Latin from Greek, from *antonomazein* to name differently, from *onoma* name] > **antonomastic** (ˌæntənəˈmæstɪk) *adj* > ˌantonoˈmastically *adv*

Anton Piller order (ˈæntɒn ˈpɪlə) *n law* the former name for: **search order** [c20 named after the plaintiff in a case (1976) in which such an order was made]

antonym (ˈæntənɪm) *n* a word that means the opposite of another word: *"empty" is an antonym of "full"* [c19 from Greek *antōnumia*, from ANTI- + *onoma* name] > **antonymous** (ænˈtɒnɪməs) *adj*

antre (ˈæntə) *n archaic* a cavern or cave [c17 from French, from Latin *antrum*, from Greek *antron*]

Antrim (ˈæntrɪm) *n* **1** a historical county of NE Northern Ireland, famous for the Giant's Causeway on the N coast: in 1973 it was replaced for administrative purposes by the districts of Antrim, Ballymena, Ballymoney, Carrickfergus, Larne, Moyle, Newtownabbey, and parts of Belfast and Lisburn. Area: 3100 sq km (1200 sq miles) **2** a district of Northern Ireland, in Co Antrim. Pop: 49 260 (2003 est). Area: 415 sq km (160 sq miles)

antrorse (ænˈtrɔːs) *adj biology* directed or pointing upwards or forwards [c19 from New Latin *antrorsus*, from *antero-* front + *-orsus*, as in Latin *introrsus*; see INTRORSE] > anˈtrorsely *adv*

antrum (ˈæntrəm) *n, pl* -**tra** (-trə) *anatomy* a natural cavity, hollow, or sinus, esp in a bone [c14 from Latin: cave, from Greek *antron*] > ˈantral *adj*

Antseranana (ˌæntsɪˈrænənə) *n* a port in N Madagascar: former French naval base. Pop: 54 418 (1990). Former name: **Diégo-Suarez**

antsy (ˈæntsɪ) *adj* **antsier, antsiest** *informal* restless, nervous, and impatient

Antung (ˈænˈtʊŋ) *n* a variant transliteration of the Chinese name for **Andong**

antwackie (ˈæntwækɪ) *adj Northern English dialect* old-fashioned

Antwerp (ˈæntwɜːp) *n* **1** a province of N Belgium. Pop: 1 668 812 (2004 est). Area: 2859 sq km (1104 sq miles) **2** a port in N Belgium, capital of Antwerp province, on the River Scheldt: a major European port. Pop: 455 148 (2004 est). Flemish name: Antwerpen (ˈɑntwɛrpə) French name: **Anvers**

Anu (ˈɑːnuː) *n Babylonian myth* the sky god

ANU *abbreviation for* Australian National University

Anubis (əˈnjuːbɪs) *n Egyptian myth* a deity, a son of Osiris, who conducted the dead to judgment. He is represented as having a jackal's head and was identified by the Greeks with Hermes

Anuradhapura (əˈnʊərədəˌpʊərə, ˌʌnuˈrɑːdə-) *n* a town in Sri Lanka: ancient capital of Ceylon; site of the sacred bo tree and place of pilgrimage for Buddhists. Pop: 42 600 (1995 est)

anuran (əˈnjʊərən) *n* **1** any of the vertebrates of the order *Anura* (or *Salientia*), characterized by absence of a tail and very long hind legs specialized for hopping: class *Amphibia* (amphibians). The group includes the frogs and toads ▷ *adj* **2** of, relating to, or belonging to the order *Anura* ▷ Also: **salientian** [c20 from New Latin *Anura*, from AN- + Greek *oura* tail]

anuresis (ˌænjʊˈriːsɪs) *n pathol* inability to urinate even though urine is formed by the kidneys and retained in the urinary bladder. Compare **anuria** [c20 New Latin, from AN- + Greek *ouresis* urination, from *ouron* urine]

anuria (əˈnjʊərɪə) *n pathol* complete suppression of urine formation, often as the result of a kidney disorder. Compare **anuresis, oliguria** [c19 from New Latin, from AN- + Greek *ouron* urine]

anurous (æˈnjʊərəs) *adj zoology* lacking a tail; tailless; acaudate [c19 from AN- + Greek *oura* tail]

anus (ˈeɪnəs) *n* the excretory opening at the end of the alimentary canal. Related adj: **anal** [c16 from Latin]

Anvers (ɑ̃vɛr) *n* the French name for **Antwerp**

anvil (ˈænvɪl) *n* **1** a heavy iron or steel block on which metals are hammered during forging **2** any part having a similar shape or function, such as the lower part of a telegraph key **3** the fixed jaw of a measurement device against which the piece to be measured is held **4** *anatomy* the nontechnical name for **incus** [Old English *anfealt*; related to Old High German *anafalz*, Middle Dutch *anvilte*; see ON, FELT²]

anxiety (æŋˈzaɪɪtɪ) *n, pl* -**ties** **1** a state of uneasiness or tension caused by apprehension of possible future misfortune, danger, etc; worry **2** intense desire; eagerness **3** *psychol* a state of intense apprehension or worry often accompanied by physical symptoms such as shaking, intense feelings in the gut, etc, common in mental illness or after a very distressing experience. See also **angst** [c16 from Latin *anxietas*; see ANXIOUS]

anxiety disorder *n* any of various mental disorders characterized by extreme anxiety and including panic disorder, post-traumatic stress disorder, and **generalized anxiety disorder**

anxiety neurosis *n* a relatively mild form of mental illness characterized by extreme distress and agitation, often occurring without any obvious cause

anxiolytic (ˌæŋksɪəʊˈlɪtɪk) *n* **1** any of a class of drugs that reduce anxiety ▷ *adj* **2** of or relating to this class of drugs

anxious (ˈæŋkʃəs, ˈæŋʃəs) *adj* **1** worried and tense because of possible misfortune, danger, etc; uneasy **2** fraught with or causing anxiety; worrying; distressing: *an anxious time* **3** intensely desirous; eager: *anxious for promotion* [c17 from Latin *anxius*; related to Latin *angere* to torment; see ANGER, ANGUISH] > ˈanxiously *adv* > ˈanxiousness *n*

any (ˈɛnɪ) *determiner* **1 a** one, some, or several, as specified, no matter how much or many, what kind or quality, etc: *any cheese in the cupboard is yours; you may take any clothes you like* **b** (*as pronoun; functioning as sing or plural*): *take any you like* **2** (*usually used with a negative*) **a** even the smallest amount or even one: *I can't stand any noise* **b** (*as pronoun; functioning as sing or plural*): *don't give her any* **3** whatever or whichever; no matter what or which: *any dictionary will do; any time of day* **4** an indefinite or unlimited amount or number (esp in the phrases **any amount** or **number**): *any number of friends* ▷ *adv* **5** (*usually used with a negative*) **a** (foll by a comparative adjective) to even the smallest extent: *it isn't any worse now* **b** *not standard* at all: *he doesn't care any* [Old English *ǣnig*; related to Old Frisian *ēnig*, Old High German *einag*, Old Norse *einigr* anyone, Latin *ūnicus* unique; see AN¹, ONE]

Anyang (ˈɑːnˈjɑːŋ) *n* a town in E China, in Henan province: archaeological site and capital of the Shang dynasty. Pop: 808 000 (2005 est)

anybody (ˈɛnɪˌbɒdɪ, -bədɪ) *pron* **1** any person; anyone **2** (*usually used with a negative or a question*) a person of any importance: *he isn't anybody in this town* ▷ *n, pl* -**bodies** **3** (often preceded by *just*) any person at random; no matter who

anyhow (ˈɛnɪˌhaʊ) *adv* **1** in any case; at any rate **2** in any manner or by any means whatever **3** in a haphazard manner; carelessly

any more *or esp US* **anymore** (ˌɛnɪˈmɔː) *adv* any longer; still; now or from now on; nowadays: *he does not work here any more*

anyone (ˈɛnɪˌwʌn, -wən) *pron* **1** any person; anybody **2** (*used with a negative or a question*) a person of any importance: *is he anyone in this town?* **3** (often

preceded by *just*) any person at random; no matter who

anyplace (ˈɛnɪˌpleɪs) *adv US and Canadian informal* in, at, or to any unspecified place

anyroad (ˈɛnɪˌrəʊd) *adv* a northern English dialect word for **anyway**

anything (ˈɛnɪˌθɪŋ) *pron* **1** any object, event, action, etc, whatever: *anything might happen* ▷ **2** a thing of any kind: *have you anything to declare?* ▷ *adv* **3** in any way: *he wasn't anything like his father* **4 anything but** by no means; not in the least: *she was anything but happy* **5 like anything** (intensifier; usually euphemistic): *he ran like anything*

anyway (ˈɛnɪˌweɪ) *adv* **1** in any case; at any rate; nevertheless; anyhow **2** in a careless or haphazard manner **3** Usually **any way**. in any manner; by any means

anyways (ˈɛnɪˌweɪz) *adv US and Canadian* a nonstandard word for **anyway**

anywhere (ˈɛnɪˌwɛə) *adv* **1** in, at, or to any place **2 get anywhere** to be successful: *it took three years before he got anywhere* **3 anywhere from** any quantity, time, degree, etc, above a specified limit: *he could be anywhere from 40 to 50 years old*

anywheres (ˈɛnɪˌwɛəz) *adv US* a nonstandard word for **anywhere**

anywise (ˈɛnɪˌwaɪz) *adv chiefly US* in any way or manner; at all

ANZ *abbreviation for* Australian and New Zealand Banking Group

ANZAAS (ˈænzəs, -zæs) *n acronym for* Australian and New Zealand Association for the Advancement of Science

Anzac (ˈænzæk) *n* **1** (in World War I) a soldier serving with the Australian and New Zealand Army Corps **2** (now) any Australian or New Zealand soldier **3** the Anzac landing at Gallipoli in 1915

Anzac Day *n* 25 April, a public holiday in Australia and New Zealand commemorating the Anzac landing at Gallipoli in 1915

Anzio (ˈænzɪˌəʊ; *Italian* ˈantsjo) *n* a port and resort on the W coast of Italy: site of Allied landings in World War II. Pop: 36 952 (2001)

ANZUS (ˈænzəs) *n acronym for* Australia, New Zealand, and the United States, with reference to the security alliance between them

ao *the internet domain name for* Angola

AO *abbreviation for* Officer of the Order of Australia

A/O *or* **a/o** *accounting, banking abbreviation for* account of

AOB *or* **a.o.b.** *abbreviation for* any other business

AOC *abbreviation for* appellation d'origine contrôlée. See AC (sense 6)

AOCB *abbreviation for* any other competent business

AOH *abbreviation for* Ancient Order of Hibernians: an Irish Catholic nationalist association founded in the 19th century; an important political force up to the founding of the Irish Free State (1922)

A-OK *or* **A-okay** *adj informal, chiefly US* in perfect working order; excellent [c20 from *a(ll systems) OK*]

AONB (in England, Wales, and Northern Ireland) *abbreviation for* Area of Outstanding Natural Beauty: an area designated by the appropriate government bodies as requiring protection to conserve and enhance its natural beauty

AOR *music abbreviation for* **1** album-oriented rock **2** adult-oriented rock **3** *US* album-oriented radio

Aorangi-Mount Cook (ˌeɪəʊˈræŋɡɪ) *n* the official name for Mount **Cook**

aorist (ˈeɪərɪst, ˈɛərɪst) *n grammar* a tense of the verb in classical Greek and in certain other inflected languages, indicating past action without reference to whether the action involved was momentary or continuous. Compare **perfect** (sense 8), **imperfect** (sense 4) [c16 from Greek *aoristos* not limited, from A-¹ + *horistos* restricted, from *horizein* to define] > ˌaoˈristic *adj* > ˌaoˈristically *adv*

aorta (eɪˈɔːtə) *n, pl* -**tas** *or* -**tae** (-tiː) the main vessel in the arterial network, which conveys oxygen-rich blood from the heart to all parts of the body except the lungs [c16 from New Latin, from Greek *aortē*, literally: something lifted, from *aeirein* to raise] > a'ortic or a'ortal *adj*

aortitis (,eio:'taitis) *n* inflammation of the aorta

Aosta (*Italian* a'ɔsta) *n* a town in NW Italy, capital of Valle d'Aosta region: Roman remains. Pop: 34 062 (2001)

Aotearoa ('æɒ,tiə,ro:ə) *n* the Māori name for **New Zealand** [from Māori *ao tea roa* Land of the Long White Cloud]

aoudad ('ɑ:ʊ,dæd) *n* a wild mountain sheep, *Ammotragus lervia*, of N Africa, having horns curved in a semicircle and long hair covering the neck and forelegs. Also called: **Barbary sheep** [from French, from Berber *audad*]

ap (æp) *prefix* son of: occurring as part of some surnames of Welsh origin: *ap Thomas* [from Welsh *mab* son]

AP *abbreviation for* **1** Air Police **2** Associated Press

a.p. *abbreviation for obsolete* (in prescriptions, etc) *ante prandium* [Latin: before a meal]

ap- *prefix* a variant of **apo-** *aphelion*

apace (ə'peɪs) *adv* quickly; rapidly [c14 probably from Old French *à pas*, at a (good) pace]

apache (ə'pɑ:ʃ, -'pæʃ; *French* apaʃ) *n* a Parisian gangster or ruffian [from French: APACHE]

Apache (ə'pætʃi) *n* **1** (*pl* **Apaches** or **Apache**) a member of a North American Indian people, formerly nomadic and warlike, inhabiting the southwestern US and N Mexico **2** the language of this people, belonging to the Athapascan group of the Na-Dene phylum [from Mexican Spanish, probably from Zuñi *Apachu*, literally: enemy]

apache dance *n* a fast violent dance in French vaudeville, supposedly between a Parisian gangster and his girl

apanage ('æpənɪdʒ) *n* a variant spelling of **appanage**

aparejo *Spanish* (apa'rexo) *n, pl* **-jos** (-xos) *Southwestern US* a kind of packsaddle made of stuffed leather cushions [American Spanish: equipment, from *aparejar* to make ready; see APPAREL]

apart (ə'pɑːt) *adj* (*postpositive*) ▷ *adv* **1** to pieces or in pieces: *he had the television apart* **2** placed or kept separately or to one side for a particular purpose, reason, etc; aside (esp in the phrases **set** or **put apart**) **3** separate in time, place, or position; at a distance: *he stood apart from the group; two points three feet apart* **4** not being taken into account; aside: *these difficulties apart, the project ran smoothly* **5** individual; distinct; separate: *a race apart* **6** separately or independently in use, thought, or function: *considered apart, his reasoning was faulty* **7** apart from (*preposition*) besides; other than ▷ See also **take apart, tell apart** [c14 from Old French *a part* at (the) side]

apartheid (ə'pɑ:thaɪt, -heɪt) *n* (in South Africa) the official government policy of racial segregation; officially renounced in 1992 [c20 Afrikaans, from *apart* APART + *-heid* -HOOD]

aparthotel (ə'pɑ:thəʊ,tɛl) *n* a hotel in which self-catering service apartments are available for rent [c20 from APART(MENT) + HOTEL]

apartment (ə'pɑ:tmənt) *n* **1** (*often plural*) any room in a building, usually one of several forming a suite, esp one that is spacious and well furnished and used as living accommodation, offices, etc **2 a** another name (esp US and Canadian) for **flat²** (sense 1) **b** (*as modifier*): *apartment building; apartment house* [c17 from French *appartement*, from Italian *appartamento*, from *appartare* to set on one side, from *apart* to set on one side, apart]

apatetic (,æpə'tɛtɪk) *adj* of or relating to coloration that disguises and protects an animal [c19 from Greek *apatētikos* deceitful, from *apateuein* to deceive]

apathetic (,æpə'θɛtɪk) *adj* having or showing little or no emotion; indifferent [c18 from APATHY + PATHETIC] > ,apa'thetically *adv*

apathy ('æpəθɪ) *n* **1** absence of interest in or

enthusiasm for things generally considered interesting or moving **2** absence of emotion [c17 from Latin, from Greek *apatheia*, from *apathēs* without feeling, from A-¹ + *pathos* feeling]

apatite ('æpə,taɪt) *n* a pale green to purple mineral, found in igneous rocks and metamorphosed limestones. It is used in the manufacture of phosphorus, phosphates, and fertilizers. Composition: calcium fluorophosphate or calcium chlorophosphate. General formula: $Ca_5(PO_4,CO_3)_3(F,OH,Cl)$. Crystal structure: hexagonal [c19 from German *Apatit*, from Greek *apatē* deceit; from its misleading similarity to other minerals]

APB (in the US) *abbreviation for* all-points bulletin

APC *n* **1** acetylsalicylic acid, phenacetin, and caffeine; the mixture formerly used in headache and cold tablets **2** *Austral slang* a quick wash [for sense 2: abbreviation for *armpits and crotch*]

ape (eɪp) *n* **1** any of various primates, esp those of the family *Pongidae* (see **anthropoid ape**), in which the tail is very short or absent ▷ See also **great ape 2** (*not in technical use*) any monkey **3** an imitator; mimic **4** *US informal* a coarse, clumsy, or rude person ▷ *vb* **5** (*tr*) to imitate [Old English *apa*; related to Old Saxon *ape*, Old Norse *api*, Old High German *affo*] > 'ape,like *adj*

apeak (ə'pi:k) *adv, adj nautical* in a vertical or almost vertical position: *with the oars apeak*

APEC ('eɪpɛk) *n acronym for* Asia-Pacific Economic Cooperation

Apeldoorn ('æpºl,dɔːn; *Dutch* 'a:pəldo:rn) *n* a town in the Netherlands, in central Gelderland province: nearby is the summer residence of the Dutch royal family. Pop: 156 000 (2003 est)

apeman ('eɪp,mæn) *n, pl* **-men** any of various extinct apelike primates thought to have been the forerunners, or closely related to the forerunners, of modern man

Apennines ('æpə,naɪnz) *pl n* **1** a mountain range in Italy, extending over 1250 km (800 miles) from the northwest to the southernmost tip of the peninsula. Highest peak: Monte Corno, 2912 m (9554 ft) **2** a mountain range lying in the N quadrants of the moon, extending over 950 km along the SE border of the Mare Imbrium and rising to 6200 m

aperçu *French* (apɛrsy) *n* **1** an outline; summary **2** an insight [from *apercevoir* to PERCEIVE]

aperient (ə'pɪərɪənt) *med* ▷ *adj* **1** laxative ▷ *n* **2** a mild laxative [c17 from Latin *aperīre* to open]

aperiodic (,eɪpɪərɪ'ɒdɪk) *adj* **1** not periodic; not occurring at regular intervals **2** *physics* **a** (of a system or instrument) being damped sufficiently to reach equilibrium without oscillation **b** (of an oscillation or vibration) not having a regular period **c** (of an electrical circuit) not having a measurable resonant frequency > ,aperi'odically *adv* > aperiodicity (,eɪpɪərɪə'dɪsɪtɪ) *n*

apéritif (ə,pɛrɪ'ti:f, ə,per-) *n* an alcoholic drink, esp a wine, drunk before a meal to whet the appetite [c19 from French, from Medieval Latin *aperitīvus*, from Latin *aperīre* to open]

aperture ('æpətʃə) *n* **1** a hole, gap, crack, slit, or other opening **2** *physics* **a** a usually circular and often variable opening in an optical instrument or device that controls the quantity of radiation entering or leaving it **b** the diameter of such an opening. See also **relative aperture** [c15 from Late Latin *apertūra* opening, from Latin *aperīre* to open]

aperture priority *n photog* an automatic exposure system in which the photographer selects the aperture and the camera then automatically sets the correct shutter speed. Compare **shutter priority**

aperture synthesis *n* an array of radio telescopes used in radio astronomy to simulate a single large-aperture telescope. Some such instruments use movable dishes while others use fixed dishes

apery ('eɪpərɪ) *n, pl* **-eries** imitative behaviour; mimicry

apetalous (eɪ'pɛtələs) *adj* (of flowering plants) having no petals [c18 from New Latin *apetalus*, see A-¹, PETAL] > a'petaly *n*

apex ('eɪpɛks) *n, pl* **apexes** or **apices** ('æpɪ,si:z, 'eɪ-) **1** the highest point; vertex **2** the pointed end or tip of something **3** a pinnacle or high point, as of a career, etc **4** Also called: **solar apex** *astronomy* the point on the celestial sphere, lying in the constellation Hercules, towards which the sun appears to move at a velocity of 20 kilometres per second relative to the nearest stars [c17 from Latin: point]

APEX ('eɪpɛks) *n acronym for* **1** Advance Purchase Excursion: a reduced airline or long-distance rail fare that must be paid a specified number of days in advance **2** (in Britain) Association of Professional, Executive, Clerical, and Computer Staff

Apex Club *n* (in Australia) an association of business and professional men founded to promote community welfare > Apexian (eɪ'pɛksɪən) *adj, n*

apgar score or **rating** ('æpgɑ:) *n* a system for determining the condition of an infant at birth by allotting a maximum of 2 points to each of the following: heart rate, breathing effort, muscle tone, response to stimulation, and colour [c20 named after V. Apgar (1909–74), US anaesthetist]

aphaeresis (ə'fɪərɪsɪs) *n* a variant spelling of **apheresis**. > aphaeretic (,æfə'rɛtɪk) *adj*

aphagia (ə'feɪdʒɪə) *n pathol* refusal or inability to swallow [c20 from A-¹ + Greek *aphagein* to consume]

aphakia (ə'feɪkɪə) *n* absence of the lens of an eye, congenital or otherwise [from A-¹ + Greek *phakos* lentil + -IA]

aphanite ('æfə,naɪt) *n* any fine-grained rock, such as a basalt, containing minerals that cannot be distinguished with the naked eye [c19 from Greek *aphanēs* invisible]

aphasia (ə'feɪzɪə) *n* a disorder of the central nervous system characterized by partial or total loss of the ability to communicate, esp in speech or writing. Compare **alexia** [c19 via New Latin from Greek, from A-¹ + *-phasia*, from *phanai* to speak] > a'phasi,ac or a'phasic *adj, n*

aphelandra (,æfə'lændrə) *n* any shrub of the evergreen genus *Aphelandra*, originally from tropical America, widely grown as a house plant for its variegated shiny leaves and brightly coloured flowers: family *Acanthaceae* [from Greek *aphelēs* simple + *andros*, genitive of *anēr* man, male, because the anthers are single celled]

aphelion (æp'hi:lɪən, ə'fi:-) *n, pl* **-lia** (-lɪə) the point in its orbit when a planet or comet is at its greatest distance from the sun. Compare **perihelion** [c17 from New Latin *aphēlium* (with pseudo-Greek ending *-ion*) from AP- + Greek *hēlios* sun] > ap'helian *adj*

apheliotropic (æp,hi:lɪə'trɒpɪk, ə,fi:-) *adj biology* growing in a direction away from the sunlight [c19 see APO-, HELIOTROPIC] > apheliotropism (,æp,hi:lɪ'ɒtrə,pɪzəm, ə,fi:-) *n*

apheresis or **aphaeresis** (ə'fɪərɪsɪs) *n* **1** the omission of a letter or syllable at the beginning of a word **2** a method of collecting blood from donors that enables its different components, such as the platelets or plasma, to be separated out [c17 via Late Latin from Greek, from *aphairein* to remove] > apheretic or aphaeretic (,æfə'rɛtɪk) *adj*

aphesis ('æfɪsɪs) *n* the gradual disappearance of an unstressed vowel at the beginning of a word, as in *squire* from *esquire* [c19 from Greek, from *aphienai* to set free, send away] > aphetic (ə'fɛtɪk) *adj* > a'phetically *adv*

aphid ('eɪfɪd) *n* any of the small homopterous insects of the family *Aphididae*, which feed by sucking the juices from plants. Also called: plant louse See also **greenfly, blackfly** [c19 back formation from *aphides*, plural of APHIS] > aphidian (ə'fɪdɪən) *adj, n* > a'phidious *adj*

aphis ('eɪfɪs) *n, pl* **aphides** ('eɪfɪ,di:z) any of

73

a

various aphids constituting the genus *Aphis*, such as the blackfly **2** any other aphid [C18 from New Latin (coined by Linnaeus for obscure reasons)]

aphonia (ə'fəʊnɪə) *or* **aphony** ('æfənɪ) *n* loss of the voice caused by damage to the vocal tract [C18 via New Latin from Greek, from A-¹ + *phōnē* sound, voice]

aphonic (ə'fɒnɪk) *adj* **1** affected with aphonia **2** *phonetics* **a** not representing a spoken sound, as *k* in *know* **b** voiceless or devoiced

aphorism ('æfə,rɪzəm) *n* a short pithy saying expressing a general truth; maxim [C16 from Late Latin *aphorismus*, from Greek *aphorismos* definition, from *aphorizein* to define, set limits to, from *horos* boundary] > **aphorist** *n*

aphoristic (,æfə'rɪstɪk) *adj* **1** of, relating to, or resembling an aphorism **2** tending to write or speak in aphorisms

aphorize *or* **aphorise** ('æfə,raɪz) *vb* (*intr*) to write or speak in aphorisms

aphotic (ə'fɒtɪk) *adj* **1** characterized by or growing in the absence of light: *an aphotic plant* **2** of or relating to the zone of an ocean below that to which sunlight can penetrate, usually about 90m (300 ft). This is the lowest level at which photosynthesis can take place [C20 from A-¹ + *-photic*, from Greek *phōs* light]

aphrodisiac (,æfrə'dɪzɪæk) *n* **1** a drug, food, etc, that excites sexual desire ▷ *adj* **2** exciting or heightening sexual desire [C18 from Greek *aphrodisiakos*, from *aphrodisios* belonging to APHRODITE]

Aphrodite (,æfrə'daɪtɪ) *n Greek myth* the goddess of love and beauty, daughter of Zeus. Roman counterpart: **Venus** Also called: **Cytherea**

aphtha ('æfθə) *n, pl* **-thae** (-θi:) **1** a small ulceration on a mucous membrane, as in thrush, caused by a fungal infection **2** *vet science* another name for **foot and mouth disease** [C17 via Latin from Greek: mouth-sore, thrush] > **aphthous** *adj*

aphyllous (ə'fɪləs) *adj* (of plants) having no leaves [C19 from New Latin *aphyllus*, from Greek *aphullos*, from A-¹ + *phullon* leaf] > **a'phylly** *n*

Apia (æ'pɪə, 'æpɪə) *n* the capital of (Western) Samoa: a port on the N coast of Upolu. Pop: 41 000 (2005 est)

apian ('eɪpɪən) *adj* of, relating to, or resembling bees [C19 from Latin *apiānus*, from *apis* bee]

apiarian (,eɪpɪ'ɛərɪən) *adj* of or relating to the breeding and care of bees

apiarist ('eɪpɪərɪst) *n* a person who studies or keeps bees

apiary ('eɪpɪərɪ) *n, pl* **-aries** a place where bees are kept, usually in beehives [C17 from Latin *apiārium* from *apis* bee]

apical ('æpɪk²l, 'eɪ-) *adj* **1** of, at, or being the apex **2** of or denoting a consonant articulated with the tip of the tongue, such as (t) or (d) [C19 from New Latin *apicālis*, from Latin: APEX] > **'apically** *adv*

apices ('æpɪ,si:z, 'eɪ-) *n* a plural of **apex**

apiculate (ə'pɪkjʊlɪt, -,leɪt) *adj* (of leaves) ending in a short sharp point [C19 from New Latin *apiculātus*, from *apiculus* a short point, from APEX]

apiculture ('eɪpɪ,kʌltʃə) *n* the breeding and care of bees [C19 from Latin *apis* bee + CULTURE] > ,api'cultural *adj* > ,api'culturist *n*

apiece (ə'pi:s) *adv* (*postpositive*) for, to, or from each one: *they were given two apples apiece*

à pied French (a pje) *adv, adj* (*postpositive*) on foot

Apiezon (,æpɪ'eɪzɒn) *adj trademark* designating any of a number of hydrocarbon oils, greases, or waxes, characterized by a low vapour pressure and used in vacuum equipment

API gravity scale *n* the American Petroleum Institute gravity scale: a universally accepted scale of the relative density of fluids that is used in fuel technology and is measured in degrees API. One degree API is equal to (141.5/*d*)−131.5, where *d* = relative density at 288.7K. See also **Baumé scale**

Apis ('ɑ:pɪs) *n* (in ancient Egypt) a sacred bull worshipped at Memphis

apish ('eɪpɪʃ) *adj* **1** stupid; foolish **2** resembling an ape **3** slavishly imitative > **'apishly** *adv* > **'apishness** *n*

apivorous (eɪ'pɪvərəs) *adj* eating bees: *apivorous birds* [C19 from Latin *apis* bee + -VOROUS]

aplacental (,eɪplə'sɛnt²l, ,æplə-) *adj* (of monotremes and marsupials) having no placenta

aplanatic (,æplə'nætɪk) *adj* (of a lens or mirror) free from spherical aberration [C18 from Greek *aplanētos* prevented from wandering, from A-¹ + *planētos*, from *planaein* to wander] > ,apla'natically *adv*

aplanetic (,æplə'nɛtɪk) *adj* (esp of some algal and fungal spores) nonmotile or lacking a motile stage (variant of APLANATIC)

aplanospore (ə'pleɪnə,spɔ:) *n* a nonmotile asexual spore produced by certain algae and fungi [C20 from A-¹ + Greek *planos* wandering + SPORE]

aplasia (ə'pleɪzɪə) *n pathol* congenital absence or abnormal development of an organ or part [C19 New Latin, from A-¹ + -*plasia*, from Greek *plassein* to form]

aplastic (eɪ'plæstɪk) *adj* **1** relating to or characterized by aplasia **2** failing to develop into new tissue; defective in the regeneration of tissue, as of blood cells: *aplastic anaemia*

aplenty (ə'plɛntɪ) *adj* (*postpositive*) ▷ *adv* in plenty

aplite ('æplaɪt) *or* **haplite** ('hæplaɪt) *n* a light-coloured fine-grained acid igneous rock with a sugary texture, consisting of quartz and feldspars [C19 from German *Aplit*, from Greek *haploos* simple + -ITE¹] > **aplitic** (æp'lɪtɪk) *or* **hap'litic** *adj*

aplomb (ə'plɒm) *n* equanimity, self-confidence, or self-possession [C18 from French: rectitude, uprightness, from *à plomb* according to the plumb line, vertically]

apneusis (æp'nu:sɪs) *n pathol* protracted gasping inhalation followed by short inefficient exhalation, which can cause asphyxia [from A-¹ + Greek *pnein* to breathe]

apneustic (æp'nu:stɪk) *adj* **1** of or relating to apneusis **2** (of certain animals) having no specialized organs for respiration

apnoea *or US* **apnea** (æp'nɪə) *n* a temporary inability to breathe [C18 from New Latin, from Greek *apnoia*, from A-¹ + *pnein* to breathe]

Apo ('ɑ:pəʊ) *n* the highest mountain in the Philippines, on SE Mindanao: active volcano with three peaks. Height: 2954 m (9690 ft)

apo- *or* **ap-** *prefix* **1** away from; off: *apogee* **2** indicating separation of: *apocarpous* **3** indicating a lack or absence of: *apogamy* **4** indicating derivation from or relationship to: *apomorphine* [from Greek *apo* away, off]

Apoc. *abbreviation for* **1** Apocalypse **2** Apocrypha *or* Apocryphal

apocalypse (ə'pɒkəlɪps) *n* **1** a prophetic disclosure or revelation **2** an event of great importance, violence, etc, like the events described in the Apocalypse [C13 from Late Latin *apocalypsis*, from Greek *apokalupsis*, from *apokaluptein* to disclose, from APO- + *kaluptein* to hide]

Apocalypse (ə'pɒkəlɪps) *n Bible* (in the Vulgate and Douay versions of the Bible) the Book of Revelation

apocalyptic (ə,pɒkə'lɪptɪk) *adj* **1** outstanding in revelation, prophecy, or significance **2** of or like an apocalypse > a,poca'lyptically *adv*

apocarp ('æpə,kɑ:p) *n* an apocarpous gynoecium or fruit

apocarpous (,æpə'kɑ:pəs) *adj* (of the ovaries of flowering plants such as the buttercup) consisting of separate carpels. Compare **syncarpous**

apochromat (,æpə'krəʊmæt) *or* **apochromatic lens** *n* a lens, consisting of three or more elements of different types of glass, that is designed to bring light of three colours to the same focal point, thus reducing its chromatic aberration. Compare **achromat**

apochromatic (,æpəkrə'mætɪk) *adj* (of a lens) almost free from spherical and chromatic

aberration > apochromatism (,æpə'krəʊmə,tɪzəm) *n*

apocopate (ə'pɒkə,peɪt) *vb* (*tr*) to omit the final sound or sounds of (a word) > a,poco'pation *n*

apocope (ə'pɒkəpɪ) *n* omission of the final sound or sounds of a word [C16 via Late Latin from Greek *apokopē*, from *apokoptein* to cut off]

apocrine ('æpəkraɪn, -krɪn) *adj* denoting a type of glandular secretion in which part of the secreting cell is lost with the secretion, as in mammary glands. Compare **merocrine, holocrine** [C20 from APO- + -*crine*, from Greek *krinein* to separate]

Apocrypha (ə'pɒkrɪfə) *n* the (*functioning as singular or plural*) the 14 books included as an appendix to the Old Testament in the Septuagint and the Vulgate but not included in the Hebrew canon. They are not printed in Protestant versions of the Bible **2** *RC Church* another name for the **Pseudepigrapha** [C14 via Late Latin *apocrypha* (*scripta*) hidden (writings), from Greek, from *apokruptein* to hide away]

apocryphal (ə'pɒkrɪfəl) *adj* **1** of questionable authenticity **2** (*sometimes capital*) of or like the Apocrypha **3** untrue; counterfeit > a'pocryphally *adv*

Apocryphal Gospels *pl n* accounts of Christ's life that are not recognized as part of the New Testament

apocynaceous (ə,pɒsɪ'neɪʃəs) *adj* of, relating to, or belonging to the *Apocynaceae*, a family of mostly tropical flowering plants with latex in their stems, including the dogbane, periwinkle, oleander, and some lianas [C19 from New Latin *Apocynum* type genus, from Latin: dogbane, from Greek *apokunon*, from *kuōn* dog]

apocynthion (,æpə'sɪnθɪən) *n* the point at which a spacecraft in lunar orbit is farthest from the moon. Compare **apolune, pericynthion** [C20 from APO- (away) + *cynthion*, from Latin *Cynthia* goddess of the moon]

apodal ('æpəd²l) *or* **apodous** *adj* (of snakes, eels, etc) without feet; having no obvious hind limbs or pelvic fins [C18 from Greek *apous* from A-¹ + *pous* foot]

apodeictic (,æpə'daɪktɪk) *or* **apodictic** (,æpə'dɪktɪk) *adj* **1** unquestionably true by virtue of demonstration **2** *logic archaic* **a** necessarily true **b** asserting that a property holds necessarily ▷ Compare **problematic** (sense 2), **assertoric** [C17 from Latin *apodīcticus*, from Greek *apodeiktikos* clearly demonstrating, from *apodeiknunai* to demonstrate] > ,apo'deictically *or* ,apo'dictically *adv*

apodosis (ə'pɒdəsɪs) *n, pl* **-ses** (-,si:z) *logic, grammar* the consequent of a conditional statement, as *the game will be cancelled* in *if it rains the game will be cancelled*. Compare **protasis** [C17 via Late Latin from Greek: a returning or answering (clause), from *apodidonai* to give back]

apoenzyme (,æpəʊ'ɛnzaɪm) *n* a protein component that together with a coenzyme forms an enzyme

apogamy (ə'pɒgəmɪ) *n* **1** a type of reproduction, occurring in some ferns, in which the sporophyte develops from the gametophyte without fusion of gametes **2** the development of a diploid cell in the embryo sac of flowering plants into an embryo without being fertilized > **apogamic** (,æpə'gæmɪk) *adj* > a'pogamous *adj*

apogee ('æpə,dʒi:) *n* **1** the point in its orbit around the earth when the moon or an artificial satellite is at its greatest distance from the earth. Compare **perigee 2** the highest point [C17 from New Latin *apogaeum* (influenced by French *apogée*), from Greek *apogaion*, from *apogaios* away from the earth, from APO- + *gaia* earth] > ,apo'gean *adj*

apogeotropism (,æpədʒɪ'ɒtrə,pɪzəm) *n* negative geotropism, as shown by plant stems [C19 from Greek *apogaios* away from the earth + *tropos* a turn] > apogeotropic (,æpə,dʒɪə'trɒpɪk) *adj*

apolipoprotein (,æpə,lɪpəʊ'prəʊti:n, -,laɪ-) *n* any of a group of glycoproteins that form part of the structure of lipoproteins, some of which have been associated with Alzheimer's disease

apolitical (ˌeɪpə'lɪtɪkəl) *adj* politically neutral; without political attitudes, content, or bias

Apollinaris (əˌpɒlɪ'nɛərɪs) *n* an effervescent mineral water [C19 named after *Apollinarisburg,* near Bonn, Germany]

apollo[1] (ə'pɒləʊ) *n, pl* **-los** a strikingly handsome youth

apollo[2] (ə'pɒləʊ) *n, pl* **-los** a handsome Eurasian mountain butterfly, *Parnassius apollo,* with palish wings and prominent red ocelli

Apollo[1] (ə'pɒləʊ) *n classical myth* the god of light, poetry, music, healing, and prophecy: son of Zeus and Leto

Apollo[2] (ə'pɒləʊ) *n* any of a series of manned US spacecraft designed to explore the moon and surrounding space. **Apollo 11** made the first moon landing in July 1969

Apollonian (ˌæpə'ləʊnɪən) *adj* **1** of or relating to Apollo or the cult of Apollo **2** (*sometimes not capital*) (in the philosophy of Nietzsche) denoting or relating to the set of static qualities that encompass form, reason, harmony, sobriety, etc **3** (*often not capital*) harmonious; serene; ordered ▷ Compare **Dionysian**

Apollyon (ə'pɒljən) *n New Testament* the destroyer, a name given to the Devil (Revelation 9:11) [C14 via Late Latin from Greek, from *apollunai* to destroy totally]

apologetic (əˌpɒlə'dʒɛtɪk) *adj* **1** expressing or anxious to make apology; contrite **2** protecting or defending in speech or writing > a,polo'getically *adv*

apologetics (əˌpɒlə'dʒɛtɪks) *n (functioning as singular)* **1** the branch of theology concerned with the defence and rational justification of Christianity **2** a defensive method of argument

apologia (ˌæpə'ləʊdʒɪə) *n* a formal written defence of a cause or one's beliefs or conduct

apologist (ə'pɒlədʒɪst) *n* a person who offers a defence by argument

apologize *or* **apologise** (ə'pɒləˌdʒaɪz) *vb (intr)* **1** to express or make an apology; acknowledge failings or faults **2** to make a formal defence in speech or writing > a'polo,gizer *or* a'polo,giser *n*

apologue (ˈæpəˌlɒg) *n* an allegory or moral fable [C17 from Latin, from Greek *apologos*]

apology (ə'pɒlədʒɪ) *n, pl* **-gies 1** an oral or written expression of regret or contrition for a fault or failing **2** a poor substitute or offering **3** another word for **apologia** [C16 from Old French *apologie,* from Late Latin *apologia,* from Greek: a verbal defence, from APO- + *logos* speech]

apolune ('æpəˌluːn) *n* the point in a lunar orbit when a spacecraft is at its greatest distance from the moon. Compare **apocynthion, perilune** [C20 from APO- + *-lune,* from Latin *lūna* moon]

apomict ('æpəˌmɪkt) *n* an organism, esp a plant, produced by apomixis

apomixis (ˌæpə'mɪksɪs) *n, pl* **-mixes** (-'mɪksiːz) (esp in plants) any of several types of asexual reproduction, such as parthenogenesis and apogamy, in which fertilization does not take place. Compare **amphimixis** [C20 New Latin, from Greek APO- + *mixis* a mixing] > ,apo'mictic *adj*

apomorphine (ˌæpə'mɔːfiːn, -fɪn) *n* a white crystalline alkaloid, derived from morphine, that is used medicinally as an emetic, as an expectorant, and in Parkinson's disease. Formula: $C_{17}H_{17}NO_2$

aponeurosis (ˌæpənjʊə'rəʊsɪs) *n, pl* **-ses** (-siːz) *anatomy* a white fibrous sheet of tissue by which certain muscles are attached to bones [C17 via New Latin from Greek, from *aponeurousthai* to change into a tendon, from *neuron* tendon] > aponeurotic (ˌæpənjʊə'rɒtɪk) *adj*

apophasis (ə'pɒfəsɪs) *n rhetoric* the device of mentioning a subject by stating that it will not be mentioned: *I shall not discuss his cowardice or his treachery* [C17 via Latin from Greek: denial, from APO- + *phanai* to say]

apophthegm *or* **apothegm** ('æpəˌθɛm) *n* a short

cryptic remark containing some general or generally accepted truth; maxim [C16 from Greek *apophthegma,* from *apophthengesthai* to speak one's opinion frankly, from *phthengesthai* to speak] > apophthegmatic *or* apothegmatic (ˌæpəθɛg'mætɪk) *adj*

apophyge (ə'pɒfɪdʒɪ) *n architect* the outward curve at each end of the shaft of a column, adjoining the base or capital. Also called: hypophyge [C16 from Greek *apophugē,* literally: escape, from *apopheugein* to escape from]

apophyllite (ə'pɒfɪˌlaɪt, ˌæpə'fɪlaɪt) *n* a white, colourless, pink, or green mineral consisting of a hydrated silicate of calcium, potassium, and fluorine in tetragonal crystalline form. It occurs in cracks in volcanic rocks. Formula: $KCa_4(Si_4O_{10})_2(OH_1F).8H_2O$ [C19 from French, from APO- + Greek *phullon* leaf + -ITE[1]; referring to its tendency to exfoliate]

apophysis (ə'pɒfɪsɪs) *n, pl* **-ses** (-ˌsiːz) **1** a process, outgrowth, or swelling from part of an animal or plant **2** *geology* a tapering offshoot from a larger igneous intrusive mass [C17 via New Latin from Greek *apophusis* a sideshoot, from APO- + *phusis* growth] > apophysate (ə'pɒfɪsɪt, -ˌseɪt) *adj* > apophysial (ˌæpə'fɪzɪəl) *adj*

apoplast ('æpəˌplæst) *n botany* the nonprotoplasmic component of a plant, including the cell walls and intercellular material

apoplectic (ˌæpə'plɛktɪk) *adj* **1** of or relating to apoplexy **2** *informal* furious ▷ *n* **3** a person having apoplexy > ,apo'plectically *adv*

apoplexy ('æpəˌplɛksɪ) *n* sudden loss of consciousness, often followed by paralysis, caused by rupture or occlusion of a blood vessel in the brain [C14 from Old French *apoplexie,* from Late Latin *apoplēxia,* from Greek: from *apoplēssein* to cripple by a stroke, from *plēssein* to strike]

apoprotein ('æpəˌprəʊtiːn) *n biochem* any conjugated protein from which the prosthetic group has been removed, such as apohaemoglobin (the protein of haemoglobin without its haem group)

apoptosis (ˌæpəp'təʊsɪs) *n biology* the programmed death of some of an organism's cells as part of its natural growth and development. Also called: programmed cell death [C20 from Greek: a falling away, from APO- + *ptōsis* a falling]

aporia (ə'pɔːrɪə) *n* **1** *rhetoric* a doubt, real or professed, about what to do or say **2** *philosophy* puzzlement occasioned by the raising of philosophical objections without any proffered solutions, esp in the works of Socrates [C16 from Greek, literally: a state of being at a loss] > aporetic (ˌæpə'rɛtɪk) *adj*

aport (ə'pɔːt) *adv, adj (postpositive) nautical* on or towards the port side: *with the helm aport*

aposematic (ˌæpəsɪ'mætɪk) *adj* (of the coloration of certain distasteful or poisonous animals) characterized by bright conspicuous markings, which predators recognize and learn to avoid; warning [C19 from APO- + Greek *sēma* sign]

aposiopesis (ˌæpəʊˌsaɪə'piːsɪs) *n, pl* **-ses** (-siːz) *rhetoric* the device of suddenly breaking off in the middle of a sentence as if unwilling to continue [C16 via Late Latin from Greek, from *aposiōpaein* to be totally silent, from *siōpaein* to be silent] > aposiopetic (ˌæpəʊˌsaɪə'pɛtɪk) *adj*

apospory ('æpəˌspɔːrɪ) *n* **1** *botany* development of the gametophyte from the sporophyte without the formation of spores **2** the development of an embryo of a flowering plant outside the embryo sac, from a cell of the nucellus or chalaza [C19 from APO- + SPORE + -Y[1]]

apostasy (ə'pɒstəsɪ) *n, pl* **-sies** abandonment of one's religious faith, party, a cause, etc [C14 from Church Latin *apostasia,* from Greek *apostasis* desertion, from *apostanai* to stand apart from, desert]

apostate (ə'pɒsteɪt, -tɪt) *n* **1** a person who abandons his religion, party, cause, etc ▷ *adj* **2** guilty of apostasy > apostatical (ˌæpə'stætɪkəl) *adj*

apostatize *or* **apostatise** (ə'pɒstəˌtaɪz) *vb (intr)* to forsake or abandon one's belief, faith, or allegiance

a posteriori (eɪ pɒsˌtɛrɪ'ɔːraɪ, -rɪ, ɑː) *adj logic* **1** relating to or involving inductive reasoning from particular facts or effects to a general principle **2** derived from or requiring evidence for its validation or support; empirical; open to revision **3** *statistics* See **posterior probability** ▷ Compare **a priori, synthetic** (sense 4) [C18 from Latin, literally: from the latter (that is, from effect to cause)]

apostil (ə'pɒstɪl) *n* a marginal note [C16 from French *apostille,* from Old French *apostiller* to make marginal notes, from Medieval Latin *postilla,* probably from Latin *post illa* (*verba*) after those (words)]

apostle (ə'pɒsəl) *n* **1** (*often capital*) one of the 12 disciples chosen by Christ to preach his gospel **2** any prominent Christian missionary, esp one who first converts a nation or people **3** an ardent early supporter of a cause, reform movement, etc **4** *Mormon Church* a member of a council of twelve officials appointed to administer and preside over the Church [Old English *apostol,* from Church Latin *apostolus,* from Greek *apostolos* a messenger, from *apostellein* to send forth]

apostle bird *n* a gregarious grey-and-brown Australian nest-building bird, *Struthidea cinerea* [C20 so called for its apparent habit of congregating in groups of twelve]

Apostles' Creed *n* a concise statement of Christian beliefs dating from about 500 AD, traditionally ascribed to the Apostles

apostle spoon *n* a silver spoon with a figure of one of the Apostles on the handle

apostolate (ə'pɒstəlɪt, -ˌleɪt) *n* the office, authority, or mission of an apostle

apostolic (ˌæpə'stɒlɪk) *adj* **1** of, relating to, deriving from, or contemporary with the Apostles **2** of or relating to the teachings or practice of the Apostles **3** of or relating to the pope regarded as chief successor of the Apostles > ,apos'tolical *adj* > ,apos'tolically *adv*

apostolic delegate *n RC Church* a representative of the pope sent to countries that do not have full or regular diplomatic relations with the Holy See

Apostolic Fathers *pl n* the Fathers of the early Church who immediately followed the Apostles

Apostolic See *n* **1** *RC Church* the see of the pope regarded as the successor to Saint Peter **2** (*often not capitals*) a see established by one of the Apostles

Apostolic succession *n* the doctrine that the authority of Christian bishops derives from the Apostles through an unbroken line of consecration

apostrophe[1] (ə'pɒstrəfɪ) *n* the punctuation mark ' used to indicate the omission of a letter or number, such as *he's* for *he has* or *he is,* also used in English to form the possessive, as in *John's father* and *twenty pounds' worth* [C17 from Late Latin, from Greek *apostrophos* mark of elision, from *apostrephein* to turn away]

apostrophe[2] (ə'pɒstrəfɪ) *n rhetoric* a digression from a discourse, esp an address to an imaginary or absent person or a personification [C16 from Latin *apostrophē,* from Greek: a turning away, digression] > apostrophic (ˌæpə'strɒfɪk) *adj*

apostrophize *or* **apostrophise** (ə'pɒstrəˌfaɪz) *vb (tr) rhetoric* to address an apostrophe to

apothecaries' measure *n* a system of liquid volume measure used in pharmacy in which 60 minims equal 1 fluid drachm, 8 fluid drachms equal 1 fluid ounce, and 20 fluid ounces equal 1 pint

apothecaries' weight *n* a system of weights, formerly used in pharmacy, based on the Troy ounce, which contains 480 grains. 1 grain is equal to 0.065 gram

apothecary (ə'pɒθɪkərɪ) *n, pl* **-caries 1** an archaic word for **pharmacist 2** *law* a chemist licensed by the Society of Apothecaries of London to prescribe,

a

prepare, and sell drugs [C14 from Old French *apotecaire*, from Late Latin *apothēcārius* warehouseman, from *apothēca*, from Greek *apothēkē* storehouse]

apothecium (ˌæpəˈθiːsɪəm) *n, pl* **-cia** (-sɪə) *botany* a cup-shaped structure that contains the asci, esp in lichens; a type of ascocarp [C19 from New Latin, from APO- + Greek *thēkion* a little case] > **apothecial** (ˌæpəˈθiːsɪəl) *adj*

apothegm (ˈæpəˌθɛm) *n* a variant spelling of **apophthegm**

apothem (ˈæpəˌθɛm) *n* the perpendicular line or distance from the centre of a regular polygon to any of its sides [C20 from APO- + Greek *thema*, from *tithenai* to place]

apotheosis (əˌpɒθɪˈəʊsɪs) *n, pl* **-ses** (-siːz) **1** the elevation of a person to the rank of a god; deification **2** glorification of a person or thing **3** a glorified ideal **4** the best or greatest time or event: *the apotheosis of De Niro's career* [C17 via Late Latin from Greek: deification, from *theos* god]

apotheosize *or* **apotheosise** (əˈpɒθɪəˌsaɪz) *vb (tr)* **1** to deify **2** to glorify or idealize

apotropaic (ˌæpəʊtrəˈpeɪɪk) *adj* preventing or intended to prevent evil [C19 from Greek *apotropaios* turning away (evil), from *apotrepein*; see APO-, TROPE]

app (æp) *n computing informal* short for **application program**

appal *or US* **appall** (əˈpɔːl) *vb* **-pals, -palling, -palled** *or US* **-palls, -palling, -palled** *(tr)* to fill with horror; shock or dismay [C14 from Old French *appalir* to turn pale]

Appalachia (ˌæpəˈleɪtʃɪə) *n* a highland region of the eastern US, containing the Appalachian Mountains, extending from Pennsylvania to Alabama

Appalachian (ˌæpəˈleɪtʃɪən) *adj* **1** of, from, or relating to the Appalachian Mountains **2** *geology* of or relating to an episode of mountain building in the late Palaeozoic era during which the Appalachian Mountains were formed

Appalachian Mountains *or* **Appalachians** *pl n* a mountain system of E North America, extending from Quebec province in Canada to central Alabama in the US: contains rich deposits of anthracite, bitumen, and iron ore. Highest peak: Mount Mitchell, 2038 m (6684 ft)

appalling (əˈpɔːlɪŋ) *adj* causing extreme dismay, horror, or revulsion > **apˈpallingly** *adv*

Appaloosa (ˌæpəˈluːsə) *n* a breed of horse, originally from America, typically having a spotted rump [C19 perhaps from *Palouse*, river in Idaho]

appanage *or* **apanage** (ˈæpənɪdʒ) *n* **1** land or other provision granted by a king for the support of a member of the royal family, esp a younger son **2** a natural or customary accompaniment or perquisite, as to a job or position [C17 from Old French, from Medieval Latin *appānāgium*, from *appānāre* to provide for, from Latin *pānis* bread]

apparat (ˌæpəˈrɑːt) *n* the Communist Party organization in the former Soviet Union and other states [Russian, literally: APPARATUS]

apparatchik (ˌæpəˈrɑːtʃɪk) *n* **1** a member of a Communist apparat **2** an official or bureaucrat in any organization

apparatus (ˌæpəˈreɪtəs, -ˈrɑːtəs, ˈæpəˌreɪtəs) *n, pl* **-ratus** *or* **-ratuses 1** a collection of instruments, machines, tools, parts, or other equipment used for a particular purpose **2** a machine having a specific function: *breathing apparatus* **3** the means by which something operates; organization: *the apparatus of government* **4** *anatomy* any group of organs having a specific function [C17 from Latin, from *apparāre* to make ready]

apparatus criticus (ˈkrɪtɪkəs) *n* textual notes, list of variant readings, etc, relating to a document, esp in a scholarly edition of a text [Latin: critical apparatus]

apparel (əˈpærəl) *n* **1** something that covers or adorns, esp outer garments or clothing **2** *nautical* a vessel's gear and equipment ▷ *vb* **-els, -elling, -elled** *or US* **-els, -eling, -eled 3** *archaic (tr)* to clothe, adorn, etc [C13 from Old French *apareillier* to make ready, from Vulgar Latin *appariculāre* (unattested), from Latin *apparāre*, from *parāre* to prepare]

apparent (əˈpærənt, əˈpɛər-) *adj* **1** readily seen or understood; evident; obvious **2** *(usually prenominal)* seeming, as opposed to real: *his apparent innocence belied his complicity in the crime* **3** *physics* as observed but ignoring such factors as the motion of the observer, changes in the environment, etc. Compare **true** (sense 9) [C14 from Latin *appārēns*, from *appārēre* to APPEAR] > **apˈparentness** *n*

apparently (əˈpærəntlɪ, əˈpɛər-) *adv (sentence modifier)* it appears that; as far as one knows; seemingly

apparent magnitude *n* another name for **magnitude** (sense 4)

apparent movement *n psychol* the sensation of seeing movement when nothing actually moves in the environment, as when two neighbouring lights are switched on and off in rapid succession

apparition (ˌæpəˈrɪʃən) *n* **1** an appearance, esp of a ghost or ghostlike figure **2** the figure so appearing; phantom; spectre **3** the act of appearing or being visible [C15 from Late Latin *appāritiō*, from Latin: attendance, from *appārēre* to APPEAR]

apparitor (əˈpærɪtə) *n* an officer who summons witnesses and executes the orders of an ecclesiastical and (formerly) a civil court [C15 from Latin: public servant, from *appārēre* to APPEAR]

appassionato (əˌpæsjəˈnɑːtəʊ) *adj, adv music* (to be performed) in an impassioned manner

appeal (əˈpiːl) *n* **1** a request for relief, aid, etc **2** the power to attract, please, stimulate, or interest: *a dress with appeal* **3** an application or resort to another person or authority, esp a higher one, as for a decision or confirmation of a decision **4** *law* **a** the judicial review by a superior court of the decision of a lower tribunal **b** a request for such review **c** the right to such review **5** *cricket* a verbal request to the umpire from one or more members of the fielding side to declare a batsman out **6** *English law* (formerly) a formal charge or accusation: *appeal of felony* ▷ *vb* **7** *(intr)* to make an earnest request for relief, support, etc **8** *(intr)* to attract, please, stimulate, or interest **9** *law* to apply to a superior court to review (a case or particular issue decided by a lower tribunal) **10** *(intr)* to resort (to), as for a decision or confirmation of a decision **11** *(intr) cricket* to ask the umpire to declare a batsman out **12** *(intr)* to challenge the umpire's or referee's decision [C14 from Old French *appeler*, from Latin *appellāre* to entreat (literally: to approach), from *pellere* to push, drive] > **apˈpealable** *adj* > **apˈpealer** *n*

appealing (əˈpiːlɪŋ) *adj* attractive or pleasing > **apˈpealingly** *adv*

appear (əˈpɪə) *vb (intr)* **1** to come into sight or view **2** *(copula; may take an infinitive)* to seem or look: *the evidence appears to support you* **3** to be plain or clear, as after further evidence, etc: *it appears you were correct after all* **4** to develop or come into being; occur: *faults appeared during testing* **5** to become publicly available; be published: *his biography appeared last month* **6** to perform or act: *he has appeared in many London productions* **7** to be present in court before a magistrate or judge: *he appeared on two charges of theft* [C13 from Old French *aparoir*, from Latin *appārēre* to become visible, attend upon, from *pārēre* to appear]

appearance (əˈpɪərəns) *n* **1** the act or an instance of appearing, as to the eye, before the public, etc **2** the outward or visible aspect of a person or thing: *her appearance was stunning; it has the appearance of powdered graphite* **3** an outward show; pretence: *he gave an appearance of working hard* **4** *(often plural)* one of the outward signs or indications by which a person or thing is assessed: *first appearances are deceptive* **5** *law* **a** the formal attendance in court of a party in an action **b** formal notice that a party or his legal representative intends to maintain or contest the issue: *to enter an appearance* **6** *philosophy* **a** the outward or phenomenal manifestation of things **b** the world as revealed by the senses, as opposed to its real nature. Compare **reality** (sense 4) **7 keep up appearances** to maintain the public impression of wellbeing or normality **8 put in** *or* **make an appearance** to come or attend briefly, as out of politeness **9 to all appearances** to the extent that can easily be judged; apparently

appearance money *n* money paid by a promoter of an event to a particular celebrity in order to ensure that the celebrity takes part in the event

appease (əˈpiːz) *vb (tr)* **1** to calm, pacify, or soothe, esp by acceding to the demands of **2** to satisfy or quell (an appetite or thirst, etc) [C16 from Old French *apaisier*, from *pais* peace, from Latin *pax*] > **apˈpeasable** *adj* > **apˈpeaser** *n*

appeasement (əˈpiːzmənt) *n* **1** the policy of acceding to the demands of a potentially hostile nation in the hope of maintaining peace **2** the act of appeasing

appel (əˈpɛl; *French* apɛl) *n fencing* **1** a stamp of the foot, used to warn of one's intent to attack **2** a sharp blow with the blade made to procure an opening [from French: challenge]

appellant (əˈpɛlənt) *n* **1** a person who appeals **2** *law* the party who appeals to a higher court from the decision of a lower tribunal ▷ *adj* **3** *law* another word for **appellate** [C14 from Old French; see APPEAL]

appellate (əˈpɛlɪt) *adj law* **1** of or relating to appeals **2** (of a tribunal) having jurisdiction to review cases on appeal and to reverse decisions of inferior courts [C18 from Latin *appellātus* summoned, from *appellāre* to APPEAL]

appellation (ˌæpɪˈleɪʃən) *n* **1** an identifying name or title **2** the act of naming or giving a title to

appellative (əˈpɛlətɪv) *n* **1** an identifying name or title; appellation **2** *grammar* another word for **common noun** ▷ *adj* **3** of or relating to a name or title **4** (of a proper noun) used as a common noun > **apˈpellatively** *adv*

appellee (ˌæpɛˈliː) *n law* a person who is accused or appealed against [C16 from Old French *apele* summoned; see APPEAL]

'appen (ˈæpᵊn) *adv, sentence substitute N English dialect* see **happen** (sense 5)

append (əˈpɛnd) *vb (tr)* **1** to add as a supplement: *to append a footnote* **2** to attach; hang on [C15 from Late Latin *appendere* to hang (something) from, from Latin *pendere* to hang]

appendage (əˈpɛndɪdʒ) *n* **1** an ancillary or secondary part attached to a main part; adjunct **2** *zoology* any organ that projects from the trunk of animals such as arthropods **3** *botany* any subsidiary part of a plant, such as a branch or leaf

appendant (əˈpɛndənt) *adj* **1** attached, affixed, or added **2** attendant or associated as an accompaniment or result **3** a less common word for **pendent 4** *law* relating to another right ▷ *n* **5** a person or thing attached or added **6** *property law* a subordinate right or interest, esp in or over land, attached to a greater interest and automatically passing with the sale of the latter

appendicectomy (əˌpɛndɪˈsɛktəmɪ) *or esp US and Canadian* **appendectomy** (ˌæpənˈdɛktəmɪ) *n, pl* **-mies** surgical removal of any appendage, esp the vermiform appendix

appendicitis (əˌpɛndɪˈsaɪtɪs) *n* inflammation of the vermiform appendix

appendicle (əˈpɛndɪkᵊl) *n* a small appendage [C17 from Latin *appendicula*; see APPENDIX]

appendicular (ˌæpənˈdɪkjʊlə) *adj* **1** relating to an appendage or appendicle **2** *anatomy* of or relating to the vermiform appendix

appendix (əˈpɛndɪks) *n, pl* **-dices** (-dɪˌsiːz) *or* **-dixes 1** a body of separate additional material at the end of a book, magazine, etc, esp one that is documentary or explanatory **2** any part that is dependent or supplementary in nature or function; appendage **3** *anatomy* See **vermiform appendix** [c16 from Latin: an appendage, from *appendere* to APPEND]

Appenzell (*German* apən'tsɛl, 'apəntsɛl) *n* **1** a canton in NE Switzerland, divided in 1597 into the Protestant demicanton of **Appenzell Outer Rhodes** and the Catholic demicanton of **Appenzell Inner Rhodes**. Capitals: Herisau and Appenzell. Pop: 53 200 and Pop: 15 000 (2002 est) respectively. Areas: 243 sq km (94 sq miles) and 171 sq km (66 sq miles) respectively **2** a town in NE Switzerland, capital of Appenzell Inner Rhodes demicanton. Pop: 5447 (2000)

apperceive (,æpə'siːv) *vb* (*tr*) **1** to be aware of perceiving **2** *psychol* to comprehend by assimilating (a perception) to ideas already in the mind [c19 from Old French *aperceveir*, from Latin *percipere* to PERCEIVE]

apperception (,æpə'sɛpʃən) *n psychol* **1** the attainment of full awareness of a sensation or idea **2** the act or process of apperceiving > ,apper'ceptive *adj*

appertain (,æpə'teɪn) *vb* (*intr*; usually foll by *to*) to belong (to) as a part, function, right, etc; relate (to) or be connected (with) [c14 from Old French *apertenir* to belong, from Late Latin *appertinēre*, from Latin AD- + *pertinēre* to PERTAIN]

appestat ('æpɪstæt) *n* a neural control centre within the hypothalamus of the brain that regulates the sense of hunger and satiety [c20 from APPE(TITE) + -STAT]

appetence ('æpɪtəns) or **appetency** *n*, *pl* -tences or -tencies **1** a natural craving or desire **2** a natural or instinctive inclination **3** an attraction or affinity [c17 from Latin *appetentia*, from *appetere* to crave]

appetite ('æpɪ,taɪt) *n* **1** a desire for food or drink **2** a desire to satisfy a bodily craving, as for sexual pleasure **3** (usually foll by *for*) a desire, liking, or willingness: *a great appetite for work* [c14 from Old French *apetit*, from Latin *appetītus* a craving, from *appetere* to desire ardently] > **appetitive** (ə'pɛtɪtɪv, 'æpɪ,taɪtɪv) *adj*

appetizer or **appetiser** ('æpɪ,taɪzə) *n* **1** a small amount of food or drink taken to stimulate the appetite **2** any stimulating foretaste

appetizing or **appetising** ('æpɪ,taɪzɪŋ) *adj* pleasing or stimulating to the appetite; delicious; tasty

Appian Way ('æpɪən) *n* a Roman road in Italy, extending from Rome to Brindisi: begun in 312 BC by Appius Claudius Caecus. Length: about 560 km (350 miles)

applaud (ə'plɔːd) *vb* **1** to indicate approval of (a person, performance, etc) by clapping the hands **2** (usually *tr*) to offer or express approval or praise of (an action, person, or thing): *I applaud your decision* [c15 from Latin *applaudere* to clap, from *plaudere* to beat, applaud] > **ap'plauder** *n* > **ap'plauding** *adj* > **ap'plaudingly** *adv*

applause (ə'plɔːz) *n* appreciation or praise, esp as shown by clapping the hands

apple ('æpᵊl) *n* **1** a rosaceous tree, *Malus sieversii*, native to Central Asia but widely cultivated in temperate regions in many varieties, having pink or white fragrant flowers and firm rounded edible fruits ▷ See also **crab apple 2** the fruit of this tree, having red, yellow, or green skin and crisp whitish flesh **3** the wood of this tree **4** any of several unrelated trees that have fruits similar to the apple, such as the custard apple, sugar apple, and May apple. See also **love apple, oak apple, thorn apple 5** apple of one's eye a person or thing that is very precious or much loved **6** bad or rotten apple a person with a corrupting influence ▷ See also **apples** [Old English *æppel*; related to Old Saxon *appel*, Old Norse *apall*, Old High German *apful*]

apple blight *n* an aphid, *Eriosoma lanigera*, that is covered with a powdery waxy secretion and infests apple trees. Also called: **American blight**

apple box *n* an ornamental Australian tree, *Eucalyptus bridgesiana*, having heart-shaped juvenile leaves, large lanceolate adult leaves, and conical fruits. Also called: **apple gum**

apple butter *n* a jam made from stewed spiced apples

Appleby ('æpᵊlbɪ) *n* a town in NW England, in Cumbria: famous for its annual horse fair. Pop: 2862 (2001)

applecart ('æpᵊl,kɑːt) *n* **1** a cart or barrow from which apples and other fruit are sold in the street **2** upset the applecart to spoil plans or arrangements

appledrain ('æpᵊl,dreɪn) *n Southwestern English dialect* a wasp

apple green *n* **a** a bright light green or moderate yellowish-green **b** (*as adjective*): *an apple-green carpet*

Apple Islander *n Austral informal* a native or inhabitant of Tasmania

Apple Isle *n* the *Austral informal* Tasmania

applejack ('æpᵊl,dʒæk) *n* a brandy made from apples; distilled cider. Also called: **applejack brandy, apple brandy**

apple maggot *n* a fruit fly, *Rhagoletis pomonella*, the larvae of which bore into and feed on the fruit of apple trees: family *Trypetidae*

apple of discord *n Greek myth* a golden apple inscribed "For the fairest." It was claimed by Hera, Athena, and Aphrodite, to whom Paris awarded it, thus beginning a chain of events that led to the Trojan War

apple-pie bed *n Brit* a way of making a bed so as to prevent the person from entering it

apple-pie order *n informal* perfect order or condition

apple polisher *n informal* a sycophant; toady

apples ('æpᵊlz) *pl n* **1** See **apples and pears 2** she's apples *Austral and NZ informal* all is going well

apples and pears *pl n Cockney rhyming slang* stairs. Often shortened to: **apples**

apple sauce *n* **1** a purée of stewed apples often served with pork **2** *US and Canadian slang* nonsense; rubbish

applet ('æplɪt) *n computing* a computer program that runs within a page on the World Wide Web [c20 from APP(LICATION PROGRAM) + -LET]

Appleton layer *n* another name for **F region** (of the ionosphere) [c20 named after Sir Edward Appleton (1892–1965), English physicist]

appley ('æplɪ) *adj* resembling or tasting like an apple: *an excellent, appley wine*

appliance (ə'plaɪəns) *n* **1** a machine or device, esp an electrical one used domestically **2** any piece of equipment having a specific function **3** a device fitted to a machine or tool to adapt it for a specific purpose **4** another name for a **fire engine**

applicable ('æplɪkəbᵊl, ə'plɪkə-) *adj* being appropriate or relevant; able to be applied; fitting > ,applica'bility or 'applicableness *n* > 'applicably *adv*

applicant ('æplɪkənt) *n* a person who applies, as for a job, grant, support, etc; candidate [c15 from Latin *applicāns*, from *applicāre* to APPLY]

application (,æplɪ'keɪʃən) *n* **1** the act of applying to a particular purpose or use **2** relevance or value: *the practical applications of space technology* **3** the act of asking for something: *an application for leave* **4** a verbal or written request, as for a job, etc: *he filed his application* **5** diligent effort or concentration: *a job requiring application* **6** something, such as a healing agent or lotion, that is applied, esp to the skin **7** *logic, maths* the process of determining the value of a function for a given argument **8** short for **application program** or **applications package**

application program *n* a computer program that is written and designed for a specific need or purpose

applications package *n computing* a specialized program or set of specialized programs and associated documentation designed to carry out a particular task

applicative (ə'plɪkətɪv) *adj* relevant or applicable > ap'plicatively *adv*

applicator ('æplɪ,keɪtə) *n* a device, such as a spatula or rod, for applying a medicine, glue, etc

applicatory ('æplɪkətərɪ) *adj* suitable for application

applied (ə'plaɪd) *adj* related to or put to practical use: *applied mathematics*. Compare **pure** (sense 5)

appliqué (æ'pliːkeɪ) *n* **1** a decoration or trimming of one material sewn or otherwise fixed onto another **2** the practice of decorating in this way ▷ *vb* -qués, -quéing, -quéd **3** (*tr*) to sew or fix (a decoration) on as an appliqué [c18 from French, literally: applied]

apply (ə'plaɪ) *vb* -plies, -plying, -plied **1** (*tr*) to put to practical use; utilize; employ **2** (*intr*) to be relevant, useful, or appropriate **3** (*tr*) to cause to come into contact with; put onto **4** (*intr; often foll by for*) to put in an application or request **5** (*tr; often foll by to*) to devote (oneself, one's efforts) with diligence **6** (*tr*) to bring into operation or use: *the police only applied the law to aliens* **7** (*tr*) to refer (a word, epithet, etc) to a person or thing [c14 from Old French *aplier*, from Latin *applicāre* to attach to] > ap'plier *n*

appoggiatura (ə,pɒdʒə'tʊərə) *n*, *pl* -ras or -re (-rɛ) *music* an ornament consisting of a nonharmonic note (short or long) preceding a harmonic one either before or on the stress. See also **acciaccatura** (sense 2) [c18 from Italian, literally: a propping, from *appoggiare* to prop, support]

appoint (ə'pɔɪnt) *vb* (*mainly tr*) **1** (*also intr*) to assign officially, as for a position, responsibility, etc: *he was appointed manager* **2** to establish by agreement or decree; fix: *a time was appointed for the duel* **3** to prescribe or ordain: *laws appointed by tribunal* **4** *property law* to nominate (a person), under a power granted in a deed or will, to take an interest in property **5** to equip with necessary or usual features; furnish: *a well-appointed hotel* [c14 from Old French *apointer* to put into a good state, from *a point* in good condition, literally: to a POINT] > ap'pointer *n*

appointee (əpɔɪn'tiː, æp-) *n* **1** a person who is appointed **2** *property law* a person to whom property is granted under a power of appointment

appointive (ə'pɔɪntɪv) *adj chiefly US* relating to or filled by appointment: *an appointive position*

appointment (ə'pɔɪntmənt) *n* **1** an arrangement to meet a person or be at a place at a certain time **2** the act of placing in a job or position **3** the person who receives such a job or position **4** the job or position to which such a person is appointed **5** (*usually plural*) a fixture or fitting **6** *property law* nomination to an interest in property under a deed or will

appointment television *n* television programmes that people set aside time to watch

appointment viewing *n* the practice of setting time aside to watch particular television programmes

appointor (ə'pɔɪntə, əpɔɪn'tɔː) *n property law* a person to whom a power to nominate persons to take property is given by deed or will. See also **power of appointment**

Appomattox (,æpə'mætəks) *n* a village in central Virginia where the Confederate army under Robert E. Lee surrendered to Ulysses S. Grant's Union forces on April 9, 1865, effectively ending the American Civil War

aport (ə'pɔːt) *n* **1 a** the production of objects by apparently supernatural means at a spiritualists' seance **b** the objects produced **2** *obsolete* bearing; demeanour **3** (*plural*) *obsolete* things brought as offerings; revenues [c15 from Old French *aport*, from *aporter* (vb), from Latin AD- + *portāre* to carry]

apportion (ə'pɔːʃən) *vb* (*tr*) to divide, distribute, or assign appropriate shares of; allot proportionally: *to apportion the blame* > ap'portionable *adj* > ap'portioner *n*

apportionment (ə'pɔːʃənmənt) *n* **1** the act of apportioning **2** *US government* the proportional distribution of the seats in a legislative body, esp the House of Representatives, on the basis of population

apposable (ə'pəʊzəb³l) *adj* **1** capable of being apposed or brought into apposition **2** *anatomy* another word for **opposable** (sense 2)

appose (ə'pəʊz) *vb* (*tr*) **1** to place side by side or near to each other **2** (usually foll by *to*) to place (something) near or against another thing [c16 from Old French *apposer*, from *poser* to put, from Latin *pōnere*]

apposite ('æpəzɪt) *adj* well suited for the purpose; appropriate; apt [c17 from Latin *appositus* placed near, from *appōnere*, from *pōnere* to put, place]
> 'appositely *adv* > 'appositeness *n*

apposition (,æpə'zɪʃən) *n* **1** a putting into juxtaposition **2** a grammatical construction in which a word, esp a noun phrase, is placed after another to modify its meaning **3** *biology* growth in the thickness of a cell wall by the deposition of successive layers of material. Compare **intussusception** (sense 2) > ,appo'sitional *adj*

appositive (ə'pɒzɪtɪv) *adj* **1** *grammar* **a** standing in apposition **b** another word for **nonrestrictive 2** of or relating to apposition ▷ *n* **3** an appositive word or phrase > ap'positively *adv*

appraisal (ə'preɪz³l) or **appraisement** *n* **1** an assessment or estimation of the worth, value, or quality of a person or thing. See also **performance appraisal 2** a valuation of property or goods

appraisal drilling *n* (in the oil industry) drilling carried out once oil or gas has been discovered in order to assess the extent of the field, the reserves, the possible rate of production, and the properties of the oil or gas

appraise (ə'preɪz) *vb* (*tr*) **1** to assess the worth, value, or quality of **2** to make a valuation of, as for taxation purposes [c15 from Old French *aprisier*, from *prisier* to PRIZE²] > ap'praisable *adj* > ap'praiser *n* > ap'praisingly *adv* > ap'praisive *adj* > ap'praisively *adv*

> USAGE *Appraise* is sometimes wrongly used where *apprise* is meant: *they had been apprised (not appraised) of my arrival*

appreciable (ə'priːʃɪəb³l, -ʃəb³l) *adj* sufficient to be easily seen, measured, or noticed
> ap'preciably *adv*

appreciate (ə'priːʃɪ,eɪt, -sɪ-) *vb* (mainly *tr*) **1** to feel thankful or grateful for: *to appreciate a favour* **2** (may take a clause as object) to take full or sufficient account of: *to appreciate a problem* **3** to value highly: *to appreciate Shakespeare* **4** (usually *intr*) to raise or increase in value [c17 from Medieval Latin *appretiāre* to value, prize, from Latin *pretium* PRICE] > ap'preci,ator *n*

appreciation (ə,priːʃɪ'eɪʃən, -sɪ-) *n* **1** thanks or gratitude **2** assessment of the true worth or value of persons or things **3** perceptive recognition of qualities, as in art **4** an increase in value, as of goods or property **5** a written review of a book, etc, esp when favourable

appreciative (ə'priːʃɪətɪv, -ʃə-) or **appreciatory** *adj* feeling, expressing, or capable of appreciation
> ap'preciatively *or* ap'preciatorily *adv*
> ap'preciativeness *n*

apprehend (,æprɪ'hɛnd) *vb* **1** (*tr*) to arrest and escort into custody; seize **2** to perceive or grasp mentally; understand **3** (*tr*) to await with fear or anxiety; dread [c14 from Latin *apprehendere* to lay hold of]

apprehensible (,æprɪ'hɛnsɪb³l) *adj* capable of being comprehended or grasped mentally
> ,appre,hensi'bility *n* > ,appre'hensibly *adv*

apprehension (,æprɪ'hɛnʃən) *n* **1** fear or anxiety over what may happen **2** the act of capturing or arresting **3** the faculty of comprehending; understanding **4** a notion or conception

apprehensive (,æprɪ'hɛnsɪv) *adj* fearful or anxious > ,appre'hensively *adv*
> ,appre'hensiveness *n*

apprentice (ə'prɛntɪs) *n* **1** someone who works for a skilled or qualified person in order to learn a

trade or profession, esp for a recognized period **2** any beginner or novice ▷ *vb* **3** (*tr*) to take, place, or bind as an apprentice [c14 from Old French *aprentis*, from Old French *aprendre* to learn, from Latin *apprehendere* to APPREHEND]
> ap'prentice,ship *n*

appressed (ə'prɛst) *adj* pressed closely against, but not joined to, a surface: *leaves appressed to a stem* [c18 from Latin *appressus*, from *apprimere*, from *premere* to press]

appressorium (,æprɛ'sɔːrɪəm) *n*, *pl* **-ria** (**-rɪə**) *botany* a flattened hypha of a parasitic fungus that penetrates the host tissues [from New Latin, from Latin *appressus*; see APPRESSED]

apprise or **apprize** (ə'praɪz) *vb* (*tr*; often foll by *of*) to make aware; inform [c17 from French *appris*, from *apprendre* to teach; learn; see APPREHEND]

> USAGE See at **appraise**

appro ('æprəʊ) *n* an informal shortening of **approval** on appro

approach (ə'prəʊtʃ) *vb* **1** to come nearer in position, time, quality, character, etc, to (someone or something) **2** (*tr*) to make advances to, as with a proposal, suggestion, etc **3** (*tr*) to begin to deal with: *to approach a problem* **4** (*tr*) *rare* to cause to come near ▷ *n* **5** the act of coming towards or drawing close or closer **6** a close approximation **7** the way or means of entering or leaving; access **8** (*often plural*) an advance or overture to a person **9** a means adopted in tackling a problem, job of work, etc **10** Also called: **approach path** the course followed by an aircraft preparing for landing [c14 from Old French *aprochier*, from Late Latin *appropiāre* to draw near, from Latin *prope* near]

approachable (ə'prəʊtʃəb³l) *adj* **1** capable of being approached; accessible **2** (of a person) friendly > ap,proacha'bility *or* ap'proachableness *n*

approach shot *n* **1** *golf* Also called: **approach** a shot made to or towards the green after a tee shot **2** *tennis* a deep drive, usually hit with slice to keep the ball low, designed to enable the player to make an approach to the net

approbate ('æprə,beɪt) *vb* (*tr*) **1** *Scots law* to accept as valid **2** **approbate and reprobate** *Scots law* to accept part of a document and reject those parts unfavourable to one's interests **3** *chiefly US* to sanction officially [c15 from Latin *approbāre* to approve, from *probāre* to test]

approbation (,æprə'beɪʃən) *n* **1** commendation; praise **2** official recognition or approval **3** an obsolete word for **proof**. > 'approbative *or* 'appro,batory *adj*

appropriacy (ə'prəʊprɪəsɪ) *n* the condition of delicate and precise fittingness of a word or expression to its context, even when it is chosen from a number of close synonyms

appropriate *adj* (ə'prəʊprɪɪt) **1** right or suitable; fitting **2** *rare* particular; own: *they had their appropriate methods* ▷ *vb* (ə'prəʊprɪ,eɪt) (*tr*) **3** to take for one's own use, esp illegally or without permission **4** to put aside (funds, etc) for a particular purpose or person [c15 from Late Latin *appropriāre* to make one's own, from Latin *proprius* one's own; see PROPER] > ap'propriable *adj*
> ap'propriately *adv* > ap'propriateness *n*
> ap'propriative *adj* > ap'propri,ator *n*

appropriation (ə,prəʊprɪ'eɪʃən) *n* **1** the act of setting apart or taking for one's own use **2** a sum of money set apart for a specific purpose, esp by a legislature

approval (ə'pruːv³l) *n* **1** the act of approving **2** formal agreement; sanction **3** a favourable opinion; commendation **4** **on approval** (of articles for sale) for examination with an option to buy or return

approve¹ (ə'pruːv) *vb* **1** (when *intr*, often foll by *of*) to consider fair, good, or right; commend (a person or thing) **2** (*tr*) to authorize or sanction **3** (*tr*) *obsolete* to demonstrate or prove by trial [c14 from Old French *aprover*, from Latin *approbāre* to approve, from *probāre* to test, PROVE]
> ap'provingly *adv*

approve² (ə'pruːv) *vb* (*tr*) *law* to improve or increase the value of (waste or common land), as by enclosure [c15 from Old French *approuer* to turn to advantage, from *prou* advantage]

approved school *n* (in Britain) a former name for **community home**

approved social worker *n* *social welfare* (in England) a qualified social worker specially trained in mental-health work, who is approved by his employing local authority to apply for a mentally disordered person to be admitted to hospital and detained there, or to apply for the person to be received into the guardianship of the local authority

approx. *abbreviation for* approximate(ly)

approximal (ə'prɒksɪməl) *adj* *anatomy* situated side by side; close together: *approximal teeth or fillings*

approximate *adj* (ə'prɒksɪmɪt) **1** almost accurate or exact **2** inexact; rough; loose: *only an approximate fit* **3** much alike; almost the same **4** near; close together ▷ *vb* (ə'prɒksɪ,meɪt) **5** (usually foll by *to*) to come or bring near or close; be almost the same (as) **6** *maths* to find an expression for (some quantity) accurate to a specified degree. See **accurate** (sense 4) [c15 from Late Latin *approximāre*, from Latin *proximus* nearest, from *prope* near]
> ap'proximative *adj*

approximately (ə'prɒksɪmɪtlɪ) *adv* close to; around; roughly or in the region of

approximation (ə,prɒksɪ'meɪʃən) *n* **1** the process or result of making a rough calculation, estimate, or guess: *he based his conclusion on his own approximation of the fuel consumption* **2** an imprecise or unreliable record or version: *an approximation of what really happened* **3** *maths* an inexact number, relationship, or theory that is sufficiently accurate for a specific purpose **4** *maths* **a** an estimate of the value of some quantity to a desired degree of accuracy **b** an expression in simpler terms than a given expression which approximates to it

appulse (ə'pʌls) *n* a very close approach of two celestial bodies so that they are in conjunction but no eclipse or occultation occurs [c17 from Latin *appulsus* brought near, from *appellere* to drive towards, from *pellere* to drive] > ap'pulsive *adj*
> ap'pulsively *adv*

appurtenance (ə'pɜːtɪnəns) *n* **1** a secondary or less significant thing or part **2** (*plural*) accessories or equipment **3** *property law* a minor right, interest, or privilege which passes when the title to the principal property is transferred [c14 from Anglo-French *apurtenance*, from Old French *apartenance*, from *apartenir* to APPERTAIN]

appurtenant (ə'pɜːtɪnənt) *adj* **1** relating, belonging, or accessory ▷ *n* **2** another word for **appurtenance**

Apr *abbreviation for* April

APR *abbreviation for* **annual percentage rate**

APRA ('æprə) *acronym for* **1** Australian Prudential Regulatory Authority **2** Australasian Performing Right Association

apraxia (ə'præksɪə) *n* a disorder of the central nervous system caused by brain damage and characterized by impaired ability to carry out purposeful muscular movements [c19 via New Latin from Greek: inactivity, from A-¹ + *praxis* action] > a'praxic *or* a'practic *adj*

après-ski (,æpreɪ'skiː) *n* **a** social activity following a day's skiing **b** (*as modifier*): *an après-ski outfit* [French, literally: after ski]

apricot ('eɪprɪ,kɒt) *n* **1** a rosaceous tree, *Prunus armeniaca*, native to Africa and W Asia, but widely cultivated for its edible fruit **2** the downy yellow juicy edible fruit of this tree, which resembles a small peach [c16 earlier *apricock*, from Portuguese (*albricoque*) or Spanish, from Arabic *al-birqūq* the apricot, from Late Greek *praikokion*, from Latin *praecox* early-ripening; see PRECOCIOUS]

April ('eɪprəl) *n* the fourth month of the year, consisting of 30 days [c14 from Latin *Aprīlis*, probably of Etruscan origin]

April fool *n* an unsuspecting victim of a practical joke or trick traditionally performed on the first of April (**April Fools' Day** *or* **All Fools' Day**)

a priori (eɪ praɪˈɔːraɪ, ɑː prɪˈɔːriː) *adj* 1 *logic* relating to or involving deductive reasoning from a general principle to the expected facts or effects 2 *logic* known to be true independently of or in advance of experience of the subject matter; requiring no evidence for its validation or support 3 *statistics* See **prior probability**, **mathematical probability** ▷ Compare **a posteriori**, **analytic** (sense 4) [c18 from Latin, literally: from the previous (that is, from cause to effect)] > **apriority** (ˌeɪpraɪˈɒrɪtɪ) *n*

apriorism (eɪˈpraɪəˌrɪzəm) *n* the philosophical doctrine that there may be genuine knowledge independent of experience. Compare **rationalism** (sense 2), **sensationalism** (sense 3)

apron (ˈeɪprən) *n* 1 a protective or sometimes decorative or ceremonial garment worn over the front of the body and tied around the waist 2 the part of a stage extending in front of the curtain line; forestage 3 a hard-surfaced area in front of or around an aircraft hangar, terminal building, etc, upon which aircraft can stand 4 a continuous conveyor belt composed usually of slats linked together 5 a protective plate screening the operator of a machine, artillery piece, etc 6 a ground covering of concrete or other material used to protect the underlying earth from water erosion 7 a panel or board between a window and a skirting in a room 8 *geology* a sheet of sand, gravel, etc, deposited at the front of a moraine 9 *golf* the part of the fairway leading onto the green 10 *machinery* the housing for the lead screw gears of a lathe 11 another name for **skirt** (sense 3) 12 **tied to someone's apron strings** dependent on or dominated by someone, esp a mother or wife ▷ *vb* 13 (*tr*) to protect or provide with an apron [c16 mistaken division (as if *an apron*) of earlier *a napron*, from Old French *naperon* a little cloth, from *nape* cloth, from Latin *mappa* napkin]

apron stage *n* a stage that projects into the auditorium so that the audience sit on three sides of it

apropos (ˌæprəˈpəʊ) *adj* 1 appropriate; pertinent ▷ *adv* 2 appropriately or pertinently 3 by the way; incidentally 4 **apropos of** (*preposition*) with regard to; in respect of [c17 from French *à propos* to the purpose]

aprotic (eɪˈprəʊtɪk) *adj chem* (of solvents) neither accepting nor donating hydrogen ions

apse (æps) *n* 1 Also called: **apsis** a domed or vaulted semicircular or polygonal recess, esp at the east end of a church 2 *astronomy* another name for **apsis** (sense 1) [c19 from Latin *apsis*, from Greek: a fitting together, arch, from *haptein* to fasten] > **apsidal** (æpˈsaɪdᵊl, ˈæpsɪdᵊl) *adj*

apsis (ˈæpsɪs) *n, pl* **apsides** (æpˈsaɪdiːz, ˈæpsɪˌdiːz) 1 Also called: **apse** either of two points lying at the extremities of an eccentric orbit of a planet, satellite, etc, such as the aphelion and perihelion of a planet or the apogee and perigee of the moon. The **line of apsides** connects two such points and is the principal axis of the orbit 2 another name for **apse** (sense 1) [c17 via Latin from Greek; see APSE] > **apsidal** (æpˈsaɪdᵊl, ˈæpsɪdᵊl) *adj*

apt (æpt) *adj* 1 suitable for the circumstance or purpose; appropriate 2 (*postpositive*; foll by an infinitive) having a tendency (to behave as specified) 3 having the ability to learn and understand easily; clever (esp in the phrase **an apt pupil**) [c14 from Latin *aptus* fitting, suitable, from *apere* to fasten] > ˈ**aptly** *adv* > ˈ**aptness** *n*

apt. *pl* **apts.** *abbreviation for* apartment

apteral (ˈæptərəl) *adj* 1 (esp of a classical temple) not having columns at the sides 2 (of a church) having no aisles [c19 from Greek *apteros* wingless; see APTEROUS]

apterous (ˈæptərəs) *adj* 1 (of insects) without wings, as silverfish and springtails 2 without

winglike expansions, as some plant stems, seeds, and fruits [c18 from Greek *apteros* wingless, from A-¹ + *pteron* wing] > ˈ**apterˌism** *n*

apterygial (ˌæptəˈrɪdʒɪəl) *adj* (of eels, certain insects, etc) lacking such paired limbs as wings or fins [c20 from New Latin *apteryx* wingless creature; see APTEROUS]

apteryx (ˈæptərɪks) *n* another name for **kiwi** (the bird) [c19 from New Latin: wingless creature; see APTEROUS]

aptitude (ˈæptɪˌtjuːd) *n* 1 inherent or acquired ability 2 ease in learning or understanding; intelligence 3 the condition or quality of being apt [c15 via Old French from Late Latin *aptitūdō*, from Latin *aptus* APT]

aptitude test *n* a test designed to assess a person's ability to do a particular type of work

Apulia (əˈpjuːljə) *n* a region of SE Italy, on the Adriatic. Capital: Bari. Pop: 4 023 957 (2003 est). Area: 19 223 sq km (7422 sq miles). Italian name: Puglia

Apure (*Spanish* aˈpure) *n* a river in W Venezuela, rising in the Andes and flowing east to the Orinoco. Length: about 676 km (420 miles)

Apurimac (ˌæpuːˈriːmæk) *n* a river in S Peru, rising in the Andes and flowing northwest into the Urubamba River. Length: about 885 km (550 miles)

Apus (ˈeɪpəs) *n, Latin genitive* **Apodis** (ˈæpədɪs) a constellation in the S hemisphere situated near Musca and Octans [New Latin, from Greek *apous*,literally: footless, from A-¹ + *pous* foot]

apyrexia (ˌæpaɪˈrɛksɪə) *n* absence of fever [c19 from A-¹ + Greek *puretos* fever] > ˌ**apyˈretic** *adj*

aq *the internet domain name for* Antarctica

AQ *abbreviation for* 1 achievement quotient 2 al-Qaeda

aq. *or* **Aq.** *abbreviation for* 1 aqua [Latin: water] 2 aqueous

Aqaba *or* **Akaba** (ˈækəbə) *n* the only port in Jordan, in the southwest, on the **Gulf of Aqaba**. Pop: 46 090 (1990 est)

Aqmola (ækˈməʊlə; *Kazakh* akmɔˈla) *n* a variant spelling of **Akmola**

aqua (ˈækwə) *n, pl* **aquae** (ˈækwiː) *or* **aquas** 1 water: used in compound names of certain liquid substances (as in **aqua regia**) or solutions of substances in water (as in **aqua ammoniae**), esp in the names of pharmacological solutions ▷ *adj* 2 short for **aquamarine** (sense 2) [Latin: water]

aquaceutical (ˌækwəˈsjuːtɪkᵊl) *n* another name for **functional water**

aquaculture (ˈækwəˌkʌltʃə) *or* **aquiculture** *n* the cultivation of freshwater and marine resources, both plant and animal, for human consumption or use

aquaerobics *or* **aquarobics** (ˌækwəˈrəʊbɪks) *n* (*functioning as singular*) same as **aquafitness** [c20 from Latin *aqua* water + AEROBICS]

aquafitness (ˈækwəˌfɪtnɪs) *n* a keep-fit regime in which exercises are performed standing up in a swimming pool

aqua fortis (ˈfɔːtɪs) *n* an obsolete name for **nitric acid** [c17 from Latin, literally: strong water]

aqualung (ˈækwəˌlʌŋ) *n* breathing apparatus used by divers, etc, consisting of a mouthpiece attached to air cylinders strapped to the back

aquamarine (ˌækwəməˈriːn) *n* 1 a pale greenish-blue transparent variety of beryl used as a gemstone 2 a a pale blue to greenish-blue colour b (*as adjective*): *an aquamarine dress* [c19 from New Latin *aqua marīna*, from Latin: sea water (referring to the gem's colour)]

aquanaut (ˈækwənɔːt) *n* 1 a person who lives and works underwater 2 a person who swims or dives underwater [c20 from AQUA + -*naut*, as in ASTRONAUT]

aquaphobia (ˌækwəˈfəʊbɪə) *n* an abnormal fear of water, esp because of the possibility of drowning. Compare **hydrophobia** (sense 2)

aquaplane (ˈækwəˌpleɪn) *n* 1 a single board on which a person stands and is towed by a

motorboat at high speed, as in water skiing ▷ *vb* (*intr*) 2 to ride on an aquaplane 3 (of a motor vehicle travelling at high speeds in wet road conditions) to rise up onto a thin film of water between the tyres and road surface so that actual contact with the road is lost

aquaporin (ˌækwəˈpɔːrɪn) *n* any one of a group of proteins in cell membranes that allow the passage of water across the membrane

aqua regia (ˈriːdʒɪə) *n* a yellow fuming corrosive mixture of one part nitric acid and three to four parts hydrochloric acid, used in metallurgy for dissolving metals, including gold. Also called: nitrohydrochloric acid [c17 from New Latin: royal water; referring to its use in dissolving gold, the royal metal]

aquarelle (ˌækwəˈrɛl) *n* 1 a method of watercolour painting in transparent washes 2 a painting done in this way [c19 from French] > ˌ**aquaˈrellist** *n*

aquarist (ˈækwərɪst) *n* 1 the curator of an aquarium 2 a person who studies aquatic life

aquarium (əˈkwɛərɪəm) *n, pl* -**riums** *or* -**ria** (-rɪə) 1 a tank, bowl, or pool in which aquatic animals and plants are kept for pleasure, study, or exhibition 2 a building housing a collection of aquatic life, as for exhibition [c19 from Latin *aquārius* relating to water, on the model of VIVARIUM]

Aquarius (əˈkwɛərɪəs) *n, Latin genitive* **Aquarii** (əˈkwɛərɪˌaɪ) 1 *astronomy* a zodiacal constellation in the S hemisphere lying between Pisces and Capricorn on the ecliptic 2 *astrology* a Also called: the Water Carrier the eleventh sign of the zodiac, symbol ♒, having a fixed air classification and ruled by the planets Saturn and Uranus. The sun is in this sign between about Jan 20 and Feb 18 b a person born during a period when the sun is in this sign ▷ *adj* 3 *astrology* born under or characteristic of Aquarius ▷ Also (for senses 2b, 3): Aquarian (əˈkwɛərɪən) [Latin]

aquashow (ˈækwəˌʃəʊ) *or US* **aquacade** (ˈækwəˌkeɪd) *n* an exhibition of swimming and diving, often accompanied by music

aquatic (əˈkwætɪk, əˈkwɒt-) *adj* 1 growing, living, or found in water 2 *sport* performed in or on water ▷ *n* 3 a marine or freshwater animal or plant [c15 from Latin *aquāticus*, from *aqua* water]

aquatics (əˈkwætɪks, əˈkwɒt-) *pl n* sports or pastimes performed in or on the water

aquatint (ˈækwəˌtɪnt) *n* 1 a technique of etching copper with acid to produce an effect resembling the flat tones of wash or watercolour. The tone or tint is obtained by acid (aqua) biting through the pores of a ground that only partially protects the copper 2 an etching made in this way ▷ *vb* 3 (*tr*) to etch (a block, etc) in aquatint [c18 from Italian *acqua tinta*: dyed water]

aquavit (ˈækwəˌvɪt) *n* a grain- or potato-based spirit from the Scandinavian countries, flavoured with aromatic seeds and spices, esp caraway. Also called: akvavit [from Scandinavian; see AQUA VITAE]

aqua vitae (ˈviːtaɪ, ˈvaɪtiː) *n* an archaic name for **brandy** [Medieval Latin: water of life]

aqueduct (ˈækwɪˌdʌkt) *n* 1 a conduit used to convey water over a long distance, either by a tunnel or more usually by a bridge 2 a structure, usually a bridge, that carries such a conduit or a canal across a valley or river 3 a channel in an organ or part of the body, esp one that conveys a natural body fluid [c16 from Latin *aquaeductus*, from *aqua* water + *dūcere* to convey]

aqueous (ˈeɪkwɪəs, ˈækwɪ-) *adj* 1 of, like, or containing water 2 dissolved in water: *aqueous ammonia* 3 (of rocks, deposits, etc) formed from material laid down in water [c17 from Medieval Latin *aqueus*, from Latin *aqua* water]

aqueous humour *n physiol* the watery fluid within the eyeball between the cornea and the lens

aquiculture (ˈeɪkwɪˌkʌltʃə, ˈækwɪ-) *n* 1 another

name for **hydroponics** **2** a variant of **aquaculture** > ˈaquiˌcultural *adj* > ˈaquiˌculturist *n*

aquifer (ˈækwɪfə) *n* a porous deposit of rock, such as a sandstone, containing water that can be used to supply wells

Aquila¹ (ˈækwɪlə, əˈkwɪlə) *n, Latin genitive* Aquilae (ˈækwɪˌliː) a constellation lying in the Milky Way close to Cygnus and situated on the celestial equator. The brightest star is Altair [from Latin: eagle]

Aquila² (ˈækwɪlə; *Italian* ˈaːkwila) *or* **l'Aquila** *n* a city in central Italy, capital of Abruzzi region. Pop: 68 503 (2001). Official name: Aquila degli Abruzzi (deˈʎʎi aˈbruttsi)

aquilegia (ˌækwɪˈliːdʒɪə) *n* another name for **columbine¹** [c19 from Medieval Latin, of uncertain origin]

Aquileia (ˌækwɪˈliːə) *n* a town in NE Italy, at the head of the Adriatic: important Roman centre, founded in 181 BC Pop: 3329 (2001)

aquiline (ˈækwɪˌlaɪn) *adj* **1** (of a nose) having the curved or hooked shape of an eagle's beak **2** of or resembling an eagle [c17 from Latin *aquilīnus,* from *aquila* eagle]

Aquitaine (ˌækwɪˈteɪn; *French* akitɛn) *n* a region of SW France, on the Bay of Biscay: a former Roman province and medieval duchy. It is generally flat in the west, rising to the slopes of the Massif Central in the northeast and the Pyrenees in the south; mainly agricultural. Ancient name: Aquitania (ˌækwɪˈteɪnɪə)

ar *the internet domain name for* Argentina

Ar *the chemical symbol for* argon

AR *abbreviation for* **1** Arkansas **2** Autonomous Region **3** Also: A/R (in the US and Canada) accounts receivable

Ar. *abbreviation for* **1** Arabia(n) **2** Also: Ar Arabic

a.r. *abbreviation for* anno regni [Latin: in the year of the reign]

-ar *suffix forming adjectives* of; belonging to; like: *linear; polar; minuscular* [via Old French *-er* from Latin *-āris,* replacing *-ālis* (-AL¹) after stems ending in *l*]

Ara (ˈɑːrə) *n, Latin genitive* **Arae** (ˈɑːriː) a constellation in the S hemisphere near Scorpius [from Latin: altar]

ARA *abbreviation for* (in Britain) Associate of the Royal Academy

araara (ˈɑːrɑːrə) *n* NZ another name for **trevally** [Māori]

Arab *n* **1** a member of a Semitic people originally inhabiting Arabia, who spread throughout the Middle East, N Africa, and Spain during the seventh and eighth centuries AD **2** a lively intelligent breed of horse, mainly used for riding **3** (*modifier*) of or relating to the Arabs: *the Arab nations* [c14 from Latin *Arabs,* from Greek *Araps,* from Arabic *'Arab*]

arabesque (ˌærəˈbɛsk) *n* **1** *ballet* a classical position in which the dancer has one leg raised behind and both arms stretched out in one of several conventional poses **2** *music* a piece or movement with a highly ornamented or decorated melody **3** *arts* **a** a type of curvilinear decoration in painting, metalwork, etc, with intricate intertwining leaf, flower, animal, or geometrical designs **b** a design of flowing lines ▷ *adj* **4** designating, of, or decorated in this style [c18 from French, from Italian *arabesco* in the Arabic style]

Arabia (əˈreɪbɪə) *n* a great peninsula of SW Asia, between the Red Sea and the Persian Gulf: consists chiefly of a desert plateau, with mountains rising over 3000 m (10 000 ft) in the west and scattered oases; includes the present-day countries of Saudi Arabia, Yemen, Oman, Bahrain, Qatar, Kuwait, and the United Arab Emirates. Area: about 2 600 000 sq km (1 000 000 sq miles)

Arabian (əˈreɪbɪən) *adj* **1** of or relating to Arabia or the Arabs ▷ *n* **2** another word for **Arab**

Arabian camel *n* a domesticated camel, *Camelus dromedarius,* having one hump on its back and used

as a beast of burden in the hot deserts of N Africa and SW Asia. See also **dromedary** Compare **Bactrian camel**

Arabian Desert *n* **1** a desert in E Egypt, between the Nile, the Gulf of Suez, and the Red Sea: mountainous parts rise over 1800 m (6000 ft). Area: about 220 000 sq km (85 000 sq miles) **2** a desert, mainly in Saudi Arabia, forming the desert area of the Arabian Peninsula, esp in the north. Area: about 2 330 000 sq km (900 000 sq miles)

Arabian Nights' Entertainments *n* The a collection of oriental folk tales dating from the tenth century. Often shortened to: the Arabian Nights Also called: **the Thousand and One Nights**

Arabian Sea *n* the NW part of the Indian Ocean, between Arabia and India

Arabic (ˈærəbɪk) *n* **1** the language of the Arabs, spoken in a variety of dialects; the official language of Algeria, Egypt, Iraq, Jordan, the Lebanon, Libya, Morocco, Saudi Arabia, the Sudan, Syria, Tunisia, and Yemen. It is estimated to be the native language of some 75 million people throughout the world. It belongs to the Semitic subfamily of the Afro-Asiatic family of languages and has its own alphabet, which has been borrowed by certain other languages such as Urdu ▷ *adj* **2** denoting or relating to this language, any of the peoples that speak it, or the countries in which it is spoken

arabica bean (əˈræbɪkə) *n* a high-quality coffee bean, obtained from the tree *Coffea arabica*

Arabic numeral *n* one of the symbols 0,1,2,3,4,5,6,7,8,9 (opposed to *Roman numerals*)

arabinose (əˈræbɪˌnəʊz, -ˌnəʊs) *n* a pentose sugar in plant gums, esp of cedars and pines. It is used as a culture medium in bacteriology. Formula: $C_5H_{10}O_5$ [c19 from *arabin* (from (GUM) ARAB(IC) + -IN) + -OSE²]

arabis (ˈærəbɪs) *n* any plant of the annual or perennial genus *Arabis,* some of which form low-growing mats with downy grey foliage and white flowers: family *Brassicaceae* (crucifers). Also called: **rock cress** [New Latin, from Greek *arabis* (fem) of Arabia]

Arabist (ˈærəbɪst) *n* a student or expert in Arabic culture, language, history, etc

arable (ˈærəbəl) *adj* **1** (of land) being or capable of being tilled for the production of crops **2** of, relating to, or using such land: *arable farming* ▷ *n* **3** arable land or farming [c15 from Latin *arābilis* that can be ploughed, from *arāre* to plough]

Arab League *n* the league of independent Arab states formed in 1945 to further cultural, economic, military, political, and social cooperation

Arab street *n* the *informal* public opinion in the Arab world

Araby (ˈærəbɪ) *n* an archaic or poetic name for **Arabia**

Aracajú (*Portuguese* ərəkəˈʒu) *n* a port in E Brazil, capital of Sergipe state. Pop: 701 000 (2005 est)

araceous (əˈreɪfəs) *adj* another word for **aroid** (sense 1) [c19 from New Latin *Arāceae;* see ARUM]

arachidonic acid (ˌærəkəˈdɒnɪk) *n* a fatty acid occurring in animal cells: the metabolic precursor of several groups of biologically active substances, including prostaglandins

Arachne (əˈræknɪ) *n Greek myth* a maiden changed into a spider for having presumptuously challenged Athena to a weaving contest [from Greek *arakhnē* spider]

arachnid (əˈræknɪd) *n* any terrestrial chelicerate arthropod of the class *Arachnida,* characterized by simple eyes and four pairs of legs. The group includes the spiders, scorpions, ticks, mites, and harvestmen [c19 from New Latin *Arachnida,* from Greek *arakhnē* spider] > aˈrachnidan *adj, n*

arachnoid (əˈræknɔɪd) *n* **1** the middle of the three membranes (see **meninges**) that cover the brain and spinal cord **2** another name for **arachnid** ▷ *adj* **3** of or relating to the middle of the three meninges **4** *botany* consisting of or

covered with soft fine hairs or fibres **5** of or relating to the arachnids

arachnology (ˌærækˈnɒlədʒɪ) *n* the study of arachnids > ˌarachˈnologist *n*

arachnophobia (əˌræknəˈfəʊbɪə) *n* an abnormal fear of spiders [c20 from Greek *arakhnē* spider + -PHOBIA]

Arad (ˈæræd) *n* a city in W Romania, on the Mureş River: became part of Romania after World War I, after belonging successively to Turkey, Austria, and Hungary. Pop: 155 000 (2005 est)

Arafat (ˈærəfæt) *n* a hill in W Saudi Arabia, near Mecca: a sacred site of Islam, visited by pilgrims performing the **hajj**. Also called: Jabal ar Rahm

Arafura Sea (ˌærəˈfʊərə) *n* a part of the W Pacific Ocean, between N Australia and SW New Guinea

Aragats (*Russian* ˌaraˈgats) *n* **Mount** a volcanic mountain in NW Armenia. Height: 4090 m (13 419 ft). Turkish name: Alagez

Aragon (ˈærəgən) *n* an autonomous region of NE Spain: independent kingdom from the 11th century until 1479, when it was united with Castile to form modern Spain. Pop: 1 059 600 (2003 est). Area: 47 609 sq km (18 382 sq miles)

Aragonese (ˌærəgəˈniːz) *n, pl* **-nese 1** a native or inhabitant of Aragon ▷ *adj* **2** of or relating to Aragon or its inhabitants

aragonite (əˈrægəˌnaɪt) *n* a generally white or grey mineral, found in sedimentary rocks and as deposits from hot springs. Composition: calcium carbonate. Formula: $CaCO_3$. Crystal structure: orthorhombic [c19 from ARAGON + -ITE¹]

Araguaia *or* **Araguaya** (ˌɑːrəˈgwaɪə) *n* a river in central Brazil, rising in S central Mato Grosso state and flowing north to the Tocantins River. Length: over 1771 km (1100 miles)

Arakan Yoma (ˌɑːrɑːˈkɑːn ˈjəʊmɑː) *n* a mountain range in Myanmar, between the Irrawaddy River and the W coast: forms a barrier between Myanmar and India; teak forests

Araks (aˈraks) *n* the Russian name for the **Aras**

Araldite (ˈærəlˌdaɪt) *n trademark* a strong epoxy resin best known as a glue

aralia (əˈreɪlɪə) *n* any plant of the genus *Aralia* of trees, shrubs, and herbaceous plants. The greenhouse and house plant generally known as aralia is *Schefflera elegantissima* of a related genus, grown for its decorative evergreen foliage: family *Araliaceae* [New Latin, of uncertain origin]

araliaceous (əˌreɪlɪˈeɪfəs) *adj* of, relating to, or belonging to the *Araliaceae,* a chiefly tropical family of trees, shrubs, or woody climbers having small clusters of whitish or greenish flowers. The family includes the ivy and ginseng

Aral Sea (ˈærəl) *n* a lake in Kazakhstan and Uzbekistan, east of the Caspian Sea, formerly the fourth largest lake in the world: shallow and saline, now badly polluted; use of its source waters for irrigation led to a loss of over 50% of its area between 1967 and 1997, after which the reduction began to be slowed. Area originally (to 1960) about 68 000 sq km (26 400 sq miles); water area reduced by 2003 to 26 687 sq km (11 076 sq miles) and the lake divided into two sections. Also called: Lake Aral

Aram (ˈɛəræm, -rəm) *n* the biblical name for ancient Syria

Aramaean *or* **Aramean** (ˌærəˈmiːən) *adj* **1** of or relating to Aram (the biblical name for ancient Syria) ▷ *n* **2** a native or inhabitant of Aram

Aramaic (ˌærəˈmeɪɪk) *n* **1** an ancient language of the Middle East, still spoken in parts of Syria and the Lebanon, belonging to the NW Semitic subfamily of the Afro-Asiatic family. Originally the speech of Aram, in the 5th century BC it spread to become the lingua franca of the Persian empire. See also **Biblical Aramaic** ▷ *adj* **2** of, relating to, or using this language

Aran (ˈærən) *adj* **1** of or relating to the Aran Islands **2** made of thick undyed wool with its natural oils retained: *an Aran sweater*

Aranda (ˈærəndə) *n* **1** an Aboriginal people of S

central Australia **2** the language of this people

araneid (əˈreɪnɪɪd) n any of numerous arachnids constituting the order *Araneae* (or *Araneida*), which comprises the spiders [c19 from New Latin *Araneida*, from Latin *arānea* spider]

Aran Islands *pl n* a group of three islands in the Atlantic, off the W coast of the Republic of Ireland: Aranmore or Inishmore (the largest), Inishmaan, and Inisheer. Pop: 1280 (2002). Area: 46 sq km (18 sq miles)

Arapaho (əˈræpəˌhəʊ) n **1** (pl -hos or -ho) a member of a North American Indian people of the Plains, now living chiefly in Oklahoma and Wyoming **2** the language of this people, belonging to the Algonquian family

arapaima (ˌærəˈpaɪmə) n a very large primitive freshwater teleost fish, *Arapaima gigas*, that occurs in tropical South America and can attain a length of 4.5 m (15 ft) and a weight of 200 kg (440 lbs): family *Osteoglossidae* [via Portuguese from Tupi]

Ararat (ˈærəˌræt) n an extinct volcanic mountain massif in E Turkey: two main peaks; **Great Ararat** 5155 m (16 916 ft), said to be the resting place of Noah's Ark after the Flood (Genesis 8:4), and **Little Ararat** 3914 m (12 843 ft)

araroba (ˌærəˈrəʊbə) n **1** a Brazilian leguminous tree, *Andira araroba* **2** Also called: Goa powder a bitter yellow powder obtained from cavities in the wood of this tree, formerly used in medicine to treat skin ailments. See also **chrysarobin** [from Portuguese, probably from Tupi, from *arara* parrot + *yba* tree]

Aras (æˈræs) n a river rising in mountains in E Turkey and flowing east to the Caspian Sea: forms part of the E border of Turkey and the N border of Iran. Length: about 1100 km (660 miles). Ancient name: Araxes Russian name: Araks

Araucania (ˌærɔːˈkeɪnɪə; *Spanish* arauˈkanja) n a region of central Chile, inhabited by Araucanian Indians

Araucanian (ˌærɔːˈkeɪnɪən) n **1** a South American Indian language; thought to be an isolated branch of the Penutian phylum, spoken in Chile and W Argentina **2** a member of the people who speak this language ▷ *adj* **3** of or relating to this people or their language

araucaria (ˌærɔːˈkɛərɪə) n any tree of the coniferous genus *Araucaria* of South America, Australia, and Polynesia, such as the monkey puzzle and bunya-bunya [c19 from New Latin (*arbor*) *Araucaria* (tree) from *Arauco*, a province in Chile]

Arawakan (ˌærəˈwækən) n **1** a family of American Indian languages found throughout NE South America ▷ *adj* **2** of or relating to the peoples speaking these languages

Araxes (əˈræksiːz) n the ancient name for the Aras

arbalest or **arbalist** (ˈɑːbəlɪst) n a large medieval crossbow, usually cocked by mechanical means [c11 from Old French *arbaleste*, from Late Latin *arcuballista*, from Latin *arcus* bow + BALLISTA]

Arbela (ɑːˈbiːlə) n an ancient city in Assyria, near which the **Battle of Arbela** took place (331 BC), in which Alexander the Great defeated the Persians. Modern name: Erbil

Arbil (ˈɑːbɪl) n a variant spelling of **Erbil**

arbiter (ˈɑːbɪtə) n **1** a person empowered to judge in a dispute; referee; arbitrator **2** a person having complete control of something [c15 from Latin, of obscure origin]

arbitrage (ˈɑːbɪˌtrɑːʒ, ˈɑːbɪtrɪdʒ) n *finance* **a** the purchase of currencies, securities, or commodities in one market for immediate resale in others in order to profit from unequal prices **b** (*as modifier*): *arbitrage operations* [c15 from French, from *arbitrer* to ARBITRATE] > arbitrageur (ˌɑːbɪtræˈʒɜː) n

arbitral (ˈɑːbɪtrəl) *adj* of or relating to arbitration

arbitrament (ɑːˈbɪtrəmənt) n **1** the decision or award made by an arbitrator upon a disputed matter **2** the power or authority to pronounce such a decision **3** another word for **arbitration**

arbitrary (ˈɑːbɪtrərɪ) *adj* **1** founded on or subject to personal whims, prejudices, etc; capricious **2** having only relative application or relevance; not absolute **3** (of a government, ruler, etc) despotic or dictatorial **4** *maths* not representing any specific value: *an arbitrary constant* **5** *law* (esp of a penalty or punishment) not laid down by statute: *within the court's discretion* [c15 from Latin *arbitrārius* arranged through arbitration, uncertain] > ˈarbitrarily *adv* > ˈarbitrariness n

arbitrate (ˈɑːbɪˌtreɪt) vb **1** to settle or decide (a dispute); achieve a settlement between parties **2** to submit to or settle by arbitration [c16 from Latin *arbitrāri* to give judgment; see ARBITER] > ˈarbitrable *adj* > ˈarbiˌtrator n

arbitration (ˌɑːbɪˈtreɪʃən) n **1** *law* the hearing and determination of a dispute, esp an industrial dispute, by an impartial referee selected or agreed upon by the parties concerned **2** *international law* the procedure laid down for the settlement of international disputes

arbitress (ˈɑːbɪtrɪs) n a female arbitrator

arbor¹ (ˈɑːbə) n the US spelling of **arbour**

arbor² (ˈɑːbə) n **1** a rotating shaft in a machine or power tool on which a milling cutter or grinding wheel is fitted **2** a rotating shaft or mandrel on which a workpiece is fitted for machining **3** *metallurgy* a part, piece, or structure used to reinforce the core of a mould [c17 from Latin: tree, mast]

arboraceous (ˌɑːbəˈreɪʃəs) *adj literary* **1** resembling a tree **2** wooded

arboreal (ɑːˈbɔːrɪəl) *adj* **1** of, relating to, or resembling a tree **2** living in or among trees: *arboreal monkeys*

arboreous (ɑːˈbɔːrɪəs) *adj* **1** thickly wooded; having many trees **2** another word for **arborescent**

arborescent (ˌɑːbəˈrɛsᵊnt) *adj* having the shape or characteristics of a tree > ˌarboˈrescence n

arboretum (ˌɑːbəˈriːtəm) n, pl -ta (-tə) or -tums a place where trees or shrubs are cultivated for their scientific or educational interest [c19 from Latin, from *arbor* tree]

arboriculture (ˈɑːbərɪˌkʌltʃə) n the cultivation of trees or shrubs, esp for the production of timber > ˌarboriˈcultural *adj* > ˌarboriˈculturist n

arborio rice (ɑːˈbɔːrɪəʊ) n a variety of round-grain rice used for making risotto [c20 after *Arborio*, a town in N Italy]

arborist (ˈɑːbərɪst) n a specialist in the cultivation of trees

arborization or **arborisation** (ˌɑːbəraɪˈzeɪʃən) n a branching treelike appearance in certain fossils and minerals

arbor vitae (ˈɑːbɔː ˈviːtaɪ, ˈvaɪtiː) n any of several Asian and North American evergreen coniferous trees of the genera *Thuja* and *Thujopsis*, esp *Thuja occidentalis*, having tiny scalelike leaves and egglike cones. See also **red cedar** [c17 from New Latin, literally: tree of life]

arbour (ˈɑːbə) n **1** a leafy glade or bower shaded by trees, vines, shrubs, etc, esp when trained about a trellis **2** *obsolete* an orchard, garden, or lawn [c14 *erber*, from Old French *herbier*, from Latin *herba* grass]

arbovirus (ˈɑːbəʊˌvaɪrəs) n any one of a group of viruses that cause such diseases as encephalitis and dengue and are transmitted to humans by arthropods, esp insects and ticks [c20 from *ar(thropod-)bo(rne) virus*]

Arbroath (ɑːˈbrəʊθ) n a port and resort in E Scotland, in Angus: scene of the barons of Scotland's declaration of independence to Pope John XXII in 1320. Pop: 22 785 (2001)

arbuscular mycorrhiza (ɑːˈbʌskjʊlə) n another name for endotrophic mycorrhiza

arbutus (ɑːˈbjuːtəs) n, pl -tuses **1** any of several temperate ericaceous shrubs of the genus *Arbutus*, esp the strawberry tree of S Europe. They have clusters of white or pinkish flowers, broad evergreen leaves, and strawberry-like berries **2**

See **trailing arbutus** [c16 from Latin; related to *arbor* tree]

arc (ɑːk) n **1** something curved in shape **2** part of an unbroken curved line **3** a luminous discharge that occurs when an electric current flows between two electrodes or any other two surfaces separated by a small gap and a high potential difference **4** *astronomy* a circular section of the apparent path of a celestial body **5** *maths* a section of a curve, graph, or geometric figure ▷ *vb* arcs, arcing, arced or arcs, arcking, arcked **6** (*intr*) to form an arc ▷ *prefix* **7** *maths* specifying an inverse trigonometric function: usually written arcsin, arctan, arcsec, etc, or sometimes sin⁻¹, tan⁻¹, sec⁻¹, etc [c14 from Old French, from Latin *arcus* bow, arch]

ARC *abbreviation for* AIDS-related complex: an early condition in which a person infected with the AIDS virus may suffer from such mild symptoms as loss of weight, fever, etc

arcade (ɑːˈkeɪd) n **1** a set of arches and their supporting columns **2** a covered and sometimes arched passageway, usually with shops on one or both sides **3** a building, or part of a building, with an arched roof [c18 from French, from Italian *arcata*, from *arco*, from Latin *arcus* bow, arch]

Arcadia (ɑːˈkeɪdɪə) n **1** a department of Greece, in the central Peloponnese. Capital: Tripolis. Pop: 91 326 (2001). Area: 4367 sq km (1686 sq miles) **2** Also called (poetic): Arcady (ˈɑːkədɪ) the traditional idealized rural setting of Greek and Roman bucolic poetry and later in the literature of the Renaissance

Arcadian (ɑːˈkeɪdɪən) *adj* **1** of or relating to Arcadia or its inhabitants, esp the idealized Arcadia of pastoral poetry **2** rustic or bucolic: *a life of Arcadian simplicity* ▷ n **3** an inhabitant of Arcadia **4** a person who leads or prefers a quiet simple rural life > Arˈcadianism n

Arcadic (ɑːˈkeɪdɪk) *adj* **1** of or relating to the Arcadians or to their dialect of Ancient Greek ▷ n **2** one of four chief dialects of Ancient Greek; the dialect spoken by the Arcadians. See also **Attic** (sense 3) ▷ Compare **Aeolic, Doric, Ionic**

arcana (ɑːˈkeɪnə, -ˈkɑː-) n either of the two divisions (the **minor arcana** and the **major arcana**) of a pack of tarot cards

arcane (ɑːˈkeɪn) *adj* requiring secret knowledge to be understood; mysterious; esoteric [c16 from Latin *arcānus* secret, hidden, from *arcēre* to shut up, keep safe] > arˈcanely *adv* > arˈcaneness n

arcanum (ɑːˈkeɪnəm) n, pl -na (-nə) **1** (*sometimes plural*) a profound secret or mystery known only to initiates **2** a secret of nature sought by alchemists [c16 from Latin; see ARCANE]

arcature (ˈɑːkətʃə) n **1** a small-scale arcade **2** a set of blind arches attached to the wall of a building as decoration

arc-boutant *French* (arkbutɑ̃) n, pl arcs-boutants (arkbutɑ̃) another name for flying buttress

arccos (ˈɑːkˌkɒs) *maths abbreviation for* arc-cosine: the function the value of which for a given argument between –1 and 1 is the angle in radians (between 0 and π), the cosine of which is that argument: the inverse of the cosine function

Arc de Triomphe (ˈɑːk də ˈtriːɒmf; *French* ark də trijɔ̃f) n the triumphal arch in Paris begun by Napoleon I to commemorate his victories of 1805–6 and completed in 1836

arc furnace n a furnace in which the charge is heated by an electric arc

arch¹ (ɑːtʃ) n **1** a curved structure, normally in the vertical plane, that spans an opening **2** Also called: archway a structure in the form of an arch that serves as a gateway **3** something curved like an arch **4 a** any of various parts or structures of the body having a curved or archlike outline, such as the transverse portion of the aorta (**arch of the aorta**) or the raised bony vault formed by the tarsal and metatarsal bones (**arch of the foot**) **b** one of the basic patterns of the human fingerprint, formed by several curved ridges one above the other. Compare **loop¹** (sense 10a), **whorl** (sense 3) ▷ *vb* **5** (*tr*) to span (an opening) with an arch **6** to form or cause to form an arch or a curve resembling that of an arch: *the cat arched its back* **7** (*tr*) to span or extend over: *the bridge arched the flooded stream* [c14 from Old French *arche*, from Vulgar Latin *arca* (unattested), from Latin *arcus* bow, ARC]

arch² (ɑːtʃ) *adj* **1** (*prenominal*) chief; principal; leading: *his arch rival* **2** (*prenominal*) very experienced; expert: *an arch criminal* **3** knowing or superior **4** playfully or affectedly roguish or mischievous [c16 independent use of ARCH-] > 'archly *adv* > 'archness *n*

arch. *abbreviation for* **1** archaic **2** archaism

arch- *or* **archi-** *combining form* **1** chief; principal; of highest rank: *archangel; archbishop; archduke* **2** eminent above all others of the same kind; extreme: *archenemy; archfiend; archfool* [ultimately from Greek *arkhi-*, from *arkhein* to rule]

-arch *n combining form* leader; ruler; chief: *patriarch; monarch; heresiarch* [from Greek *-arkhēs*, from *arkhein* to rule; compare ARCH-]

archaean (ɑːˈkiən) *n* any member of the *Archaea*, a domain of prokaryotic microorganisms, distinguished from bacteria on molecular phylogenetic grounds and often found in hostile environments, such as volcanic vents and hot springs

Archaean *or esp US* **Archean** (ɑːˈkiːən) *adj* **1** of or relating to the highly metamorphosed rocks formed in the early Precambrian era **2** the earlier of two divisions of the Precambrian era, during which the earliest forms of life are assumed to have appeared ▷ Compare **Proterozoic**

archaebacteria (ˌɑːkɪbækˈtɪərɪə) *pl n* (formerly) a group of microorganisms now regarded as members of the *Archaea* ▷ See **archaean** [from ARCHAEO- + BACTERIA]

archaeo- *or* **archeo-** *combining form* **1** indicating ancient or primitive time or condition: *archaeology; archaeopteryx* **2** of, involving, or denoting the study of remains from archaeological sites: *archaeozoology* [from Greek *arkhaio-*, from *arkhaios*, from *arkhein* to begin]

archaeoastronomy *or* **archeoastronomy** (ˌɑːkɪəʊəˈstrɒnəmɪ) *n* the scientific study of the beliefs and practices concerning astronomy that existed in ancient and prehistoric civilizations > ˌarchaeoasˈtronomer *or* ˌarcheoasˈtronomer *n*

archaeobotany *or* **archeobotany** (ˌkɪəʊˈbɒtənɪ) *n* the analysis and interpretation of plant remains found at archaeological sites > ˌarchaeoˈbotanist *or* ˌarcheoˈbotanist *n*

archaeol. *abbreviation for* archaeology

archaeology *or* **archeology** (ˌɑːkɪˈɒlədʒɪ) *n* the study of man's past by scientific analysis of the material remains of his cultures. See also **prehistory, protohistory** [c17 from Late Latin *archaeologia*, from Greek *arkhaiologia* study of what is ancient, from *arkhaios* ancient (from *arkhē* beginning)] > **archaeological** *or* **archeological** (ˌɑːkɪəˈlɒdʒɪk⁽ə⁾l) *adj* > ˌarchaeoˈlogically *or* ˌarcheoˈlogically *adv* > ˌarchaeˈologist *or* ˌarcheˈologist *n*

archaeomagnetism *or* **archeomagnetism** (ˌɑːkɪəʊˈmægnɪˌtɪzəm) *n* an archaeological technique for dating certain clay objects by measuring the extent to which they have been magnetized by the earth's magnetic field

archaeopteryx (ˌɑːkɪˈɒptərɪks) *n* any of several extinct primitive birds constituting the genus *Archaeopteryx*, esp *A. lithographica*, which occurred in Jurassic times and had teeth, a long tail, well-developed wings, and a body covering of feathers [c19 from ARCHAEO- + Greek *pterux* winged creature]

archaeornis (ˌɑːkɪˈɔːnɪs) *n* an extinct primitive Jurassic bird, formerly placed in the genus *Archaeornis* but now thought to be a species of archaeopteryx [c19 New Latin, from ARCHAEO- + Greek *ornis* bird]

Archaeozoic *or esp US* **Archeozoic** (ˌɑːkɪəˈzəʊɪk) *adj* a former word for **Archaean**

archaeozoology *or* **archeozoology** (ˌɑːkɪəʊzəʊˈblədʒɪ, -zuː-) *n* the analysis and interpretation of animal remains found in archaeological sites > ˌarchaeozoˈologist *or* ˌarcheozoˈologist *n*

archaic (ɑːˈkeɪɪk) *adj* **1** belonging to or characteristic of a much earlier period; ancient **2** out of date; antiquated: *an archaic prison system* **3** (of idiom, vocabulary, etc) characteristic of an earlier period of a language and not in ordinary use [c19 from French *archaïque*, from Greek *arkhaïkos*, from *arkhaios* ancient, from *arkhē* beginning, from *arkhein* to begin] > arˈchaically *adv*

archaism (ˈɑːkɪˌɪzəm, -keɪ-) *n* **1** the adoption or imitation of something archaic, such as a word or an artistic or literary style **2** an archaic word, expression, style, etc [c17 from New Latin *archaismus*, from Greek *arkhaïsmos*, from *arkhaizein* to model one's style upon that of ancient writers; see ARCHAIC] > ˈarchaist *n* > ˌarchaˈistic *adj*

archaize *or* **archaise** (ˈɑːkɪˌaɪz, -keɪ-) *vb* (*tr*) to give an archaic appearance or character to, as by the use of archaisms > ˈarchaˌizer *or* ˈarchaˌiser *n*

archangel (ˈɑːkˌeɪndʒəl) *n* **1** a principal angel, a member of the order ranking immediately above the angels in medieval angelology **2** another name for **angelica** (sense 1) **3 yellow archangel** a Eurasian herbaceous plant (*Lamiastrum luteum*) that has yellow helmet-shaped flowers: family *Lamiaceae* (labiates) **4** a bronze-coloured breed of domestic pigeon with black markings > **archangelic** (ˌɑːkænˈdʒɛlɪk) *adj*

Archangel (ˈɑːkˌeɪndʒəl) *n* a port in NW Russia, on the Dvina River: major centre for the timber trade and White Sea fisheries. Pop: 345 000 (2005 est). Russian name: Arkhangelsk

archbishop (ɑːtʃˈbɪʃəp) *n* a bishop of the highest rank. Abbreviations: abp, Abp, Arch, Archbp

archbishopric (ɑːtʃˈbɪʃəprɪk) *n* **1** the rank, office, or jurisdiction of an archbishop **2** the area governed by an archbishop

Archbp *abbreviation for* archbishop

Archd. *abbreviation for* **1** archdeacon **2** archduke

arch dam *n* a dam that is curved in the horizontal plane and usually built of concrete, in which the horizontal thrust is taken by abutments in the sides of a valley. Arch dams must be built on solid rock, as a yielding material would cause a failure

archdeacon (ɑːtʃˈdiːkən) *n* **1** an Anglican clergyman ranking just below a bishop and having supervisory duties under the bishop **2** a clergyman of similar rank in other Churches

archdeaconry (ɑːtʃˈdiːkənrɪ) *n, pl* -ries **1** the office, rank, or duties of an archdeacon **2** the residence of an archdeacon

archdiocese (ɑːtʃˈdaɪəˌsiːs, -sɪs) *n* the diocese of an archbishop > **archdiocesan** (ɑːtʃdaɪˈɒsɪs⁽ə⁾n) *adj*

archducal (ɑːtʃˈdjuːk⁽ə⁾l) *adj* of or relating to an archduke, archduchess, or archduchy

archduchess (ɑːtʃˈdʌtʃɪs) *n* **1** the wife or widow of an archduke **2** (since 1453) a princess of the Austrian imperial family, esp a daughter of the Austrian emperor

archduchy (ɑːtʃˈdʌtʃɪ) *n, pl* -duchies the territory ruled by an archduke or archduchess

archduke (ɑːtʃˈdjuːk) *n* a chief duke, esp (since 1453) a prince of the Austrian imperial dynasty

Archean (ɑːˈkiːən) *adj* a variant spelling (esp US) of **Archaean**

arched (ɑːtʃt) *adj* **1** provided with or spanned by an arch or arches **2** shaped like an arch; curved

archegonium (ˌɑːkɪˈɡəʊnɪəm) *n, pl* -nia (-nɪə) a female sex organ, occurring in mosses, spore-bearing vascular plants, and gymnosperms, that produces a single egg cell in its swollen base [c19 from New Latin, from Greek *arkhegonos* original parent, from *arkhe-* chief, first + *gonos* seed, race] > ˌarcheˈgoniate *adj*

archenemy (ɑːtʃˈɛnɪmɪ) *n, pl* -mies **1** a chief enemy **2** (*often capital*; preceded by *the*) the devil

archenteron (ɑːˈkɛntəˌrɒn) *n* the cavity within an embryo at the gastrula stage of development that eventually becomes the digestive cavity [c19 from Greek *arkhē* beginning + *enteron* intestine] > **archenteric** (ˌɑːkənˈtɛrɪk) *adj*

archeology (ˌɑːkɪˈɒlədʒɪ) *n* a variant spelling of **archaeology**

Archeozoic (ˌɑːkɪəˈzəʊɪk) *adj* a variant spelling (esp US) of **Archaeozoic**

archer (ˈɑːtʃə) *n* a person skilled in the use of a bow and arrow [c13 from Old French *archier*, from Late Latin *arcārius*, from Latin *arcus* bow]

Archer (ˈɑːtʃə) *n* **the** the constellation Sagittarius, the ninth sign of the zodiac

archerfish (ˈɑːtʃəˌfɪʃ) *n, pl* -fish *or* -fishes any freshwater percoid fish of the family *Toxotidae* of S and SE Asia and Australia, esp *Toxotes jaculatrix*, that catch insects by spitting water at them

archery (ˈɑːtʃərɪ) *n* **1** the art or sport of shooting with bows and arrows **2** archers or their weapons collectively

Arches (ˈɑːtʃɪz) *pl n* **Court of Arches** *Church of England* the court of appeal of the Province of Canterbury, formerly held under the arches of Bow Church

archespore (ˈɑːkɪˌspɔː) *or* **archesporium** (ˌɑːkɪˈspɔːrɪəm) *n, pl* -spores *or* -sporia (-ˈspɔːrɪə) *botany* the cell or group of cells in a sporangium that gives rise to spores > ˌarcheˈsporial *adj*

archetypal (ˌɑːkɪˈtaɪpəl) *or* **archetypical** (ˌɑːkɪˈtɪpɪk⁽ə⁾l) *adj* **1** perfect or typical as a specimen of something **2** being an original model or pattern or a prototype **3** *psychoanal* of or relating to Jungian archetypes **4** constantly recurring as a symbol or motif in literature, painting, etc > ˌarcheˈtypally *or* ˌarcheˈtypically *adv*

archetype (ˈɑːkɪˌtaɪp) *n* **1** a perfect or typical specimen **2** an original model or pattern; prototype **3** *psychoanal* one of the inherited mental images postulated by Jung as the content of the collective unconscious **4** a constantly recurring symbol or motif in literature, painting, etc [c17 from Latin *archetypum* an original, from Greek *arkhetupon*, from *arkhetupos* first-moulded; see ARCH-, TYPE]

archfiend (ˌɑːtʃˈfiːnd) *n* (*often capital*) **the** the chief of fiends or devils; Satan

archi- *combining form* a variant of **arch-**

Archibald prize (ˈɑːtʃɪˌbɔːld) *n Austral* an annual prize awarded by the Trustees of the Art Gallery of New South Wales since 1921, for outstanding contributions to art, letters, science, and politics [named after Jules François *Archibald* (1856–1919), Australian journalist]

archicarp (ˈɑːkɪˌkɑːp) *n* a female reproductive structure in ascomycetous fungi that consists of a cell or hypha and develops into the ascogonium

archidiaconal (ˌɑːkɪdaɪˈækən⁽ə⁾l) *adj* of or relating to an archdeacon or his office

archidiaconate (ˌɑːkɪdaɪˈækənɪt) *n* the office, term of office, or area of jurisdiction of an archdeacon

archiepiscopal (ˌɑːkɪɪˈpɪskəp⁽ə⁾l) *adj* of or associated with an archbishop

archiepiscopate (ˌɑːkɪɪˈpɪskəpɪt, -ˌpeɪt) *or* **archiepiscopacy** (ˌɑːkɪɪˈpɪskəpəsɪ) *n* the rank, office, or term of office of an archbishop

archil (ˈɑːtʃɪl) *n* a variant spelling of **orchil**

Archilochian (ˌɑːkɪˈləʊkɪən) *adj* denoting or relating to the 7th century BC Greek poet Archilochus or his verse, esp the iambic trimeters or trochaic tetrameters used by him

archimage (ˈɑːkɪˌmeɪdʒ) *n* a great magician or wizard [c16 from ARCHI- + *mage*, from Latin *magus* magician]

archimandrite (ˌɑːkɪˈmændraɪt) *n Greek Orthodox Church* the head of a monastery or a group of monasteries [c16 from Late Latin *archimandrīta*, from Late Greek *arkhimandrītēs*, from ARCHI- + *mandra* monastery]

Archimedean (ˌɑːkɪˈmiːdɪən, -mɪˈdiːən) *adj* of or

relating to Archimedes, the Greek mathematician and physicist (?287–212 BC)

Archimedes (ˌɑːkɪˈmiːdiːz) *n* a walled plain in the NE quadrant of the moon, about 80 km in diameter

Archimedes' principle *n* a law of physics stating that the apparent upward force (buoyancy) of a body immersed in a fluid is equal to the weight of the displaced fluid

Archimedes' screw *or* **Archimedean screw** (ˌɑːkɪˈmiːdɪən, -mɪˈdiːən) *n* an ancient type of water-lifting device making use of a spiral passage in an inclined cylinder. The water is raised when the spiral is rotated

archine (ɑːˈʃiːn) *n* a Russian unit of length equal to about 71 cm [from Russian *arshin*, of Turkic origin]

archipelago (ˌɑːkɪˈpɛlɪˌɡəʊ) *n, pl* **-gos** *or* **-goes 1** a group of islands **2** a sea studded with islands [C16 (meaning: the Aegean Sea): from Italian *arcipelago*, literally: the chief sea (perhaps originally a mistranslation of Greek *Aigaion pelagos* the Aegean Sea), from ARCHI- + *pelago* sea, from Latin *pelagus*, from Greek *pelagos*] > **archipelagic** (ˌɑːkɪpəˈlædʒɪk) *or* **archipelagian** (ˌɑːkɪpəˈleɪdʒɪən) *adj*

archiphoneme (ˈɑːkɪˌfəʊniːm, ˌɑːkɪˈfəʊniːm) *n phonetics* an abstract linguistic unit representing two or more phonemes when the distinction between these has been neutralized: conventionally shown by a capital letter within slashes, as /T/ for /t/ and /d/ in German *Rat* and *Rad*

archiplasm (ˈɑːkɪˌplæzəm) *n* a variant spelling of **archoplasm**. > ˌarchiˈplasmic *adj*

archit. *abbreviation for* architecture

architect (ˈɑːkɪˌtɛkt) *n* **1** a person qualified to design buildings and to superintend their erection **2** a person similarly qualified in another form of construction: *a naval architect* **3** any planner or creator: *the architect of the expedition* [C16 from French *architecte*, from Latin *architectus*, from Greek *arkhitektōn* director of works, from ARCHI- + *tektōn* workman; related to *tekhnē* art, skill]

architectonic (ˌɑːkɪtɛkˈtɒnɪk) *adj* **1** denoting, relating to, or having architectural qualities **2** *metaphysics* of or relating to the systematic classification of knowledge [C16 from Late Latin *architectonicus* concerning architecture; see ARCHITECT] > ˌarchitecˈtonically *adv*

architectonics (ˌɑːkɪtɛkˈtɒnɪks) *n (functioning as singular)* **1** the science of architecture **2** *metaphysics* the scientific classification of knowledge

architecture (ˈɑːkɪˌtɛktʃə) *n* **1** the art and science of designing and superintending the erection of buildings and similar structures **2** a style of building or structure: *Gothic architecture* **3** buildings or structures collectively **4** the structure or design of anything: *the architecture of the universe* **5** the internal organization of a computer's components with particular reference to the way in which data is transmitted **6** the arrangement of the various devices in a complete computer system or network > ˌarchiˈtectural *adj* > ˌarchiˈtecturally *adv*

architrave (ˈɑːkɪˌtreɪv) *n architect* **1** the lowest part of an entablature that bears on the columns **2** a moulding around a doorway, window opening, etc [C16 via French from Italian, from ARCHI- + *trave* beam, from Latin *trabs*]

archival storage *n* a method of retaining information outside of the internal memory of a computer

archive (ˈɑːkaɪv) *n (often plural)* **1** a collection of records of or about an institution, family, etc **2** a place where such records are kept **3** *computing* data transferred to a tape or disk for long-term storage rather than frequent use ▷ *vb (tr)* **4** to store (documents, data, etc) in an archive or other repository [C17 from Late Latin *archīvum*, from Greek *arkheion* repository of official records, from *arkhē* government] > *ar'chival adj*

archivist (ˈɑːkɪvɪst) *n* a person in charge of

archives, their collection, and cataloguing

archivolt (ˈɑːkɪˌvəʊlt) *n architect* **1** a moulding around an arch, sometimes decorated **2** the under surface of an arch [C18 from Italian *archivolto*; see ARC, VAULT¹]

archon (ˈɑːkɒn, -kən) *n* (in ancient Athens) one of the nine chief magistrates [C17 from Greek *arkhōn* ruler, from *arkhein* to rule] > *'archon,ship n*

archoplasm (ˈɑːkəˌplæzəm) *or* **archiplasm** *n* the protoplasmic material surrounding the centrosome, formerly thought to be involved in the formation of the asters and spindle during mitosis > ˌarcho'plasmic *adj*

archpriest (ˈɑːtʃˈpriːst) *n Christianity* **1** (formerly) a chief assistant to a bishop, performing many of his sacerdotal functions during his absence **2** a senior priest > ˈarch'priest,hood *or* ˈarch'priest,ship *n*

archway (ˈɑːtʃˌweɪ) *n* a passageway or entrance under an arch or arches

-archy *n combining form* government; rule: *anarchy; monarchy* [from Greek *-arkhia*; see ARCH] > **-archic** *adj combining form* > **-archist** *n combining form*

arc light *n* a light source in which an arc between two electrodes, usually carbon, produces intense white illumination. Also called: **arc lamp**

ARCM *abbreviation for* Associate of the Royal College of Music

arcmin (ˈɑːkmɪn) *or* **arc minute** *n* 1/60 of a degree of an angle

arcograph (ˈɑːkəˌɡrɑːf, -ˌɡræf) *n geometry* an instrument used for drawing arcs without using a central point. Also called: **cyclograph**

ARCS *abbreviation for* Associate of the Royal College of Science

arcsec (ˈɑːksɛk) *or* **arc second** *n* 1/3600 of a degree of an angle

arcsin (ˈɑːkˌsaɪn) *maths abbreviation for* arcsine: the function the value of which for a given argument between −1 and 1 is the angle in radians (between −π/2 and π/2), the sine of which is that argument: the inverse of the sine function

arctan (ˈɑːkˌtæn) *maths abbreviation for* arctangent: the function the value of which for a given argument is the angle in radians (between −π/2 and π/2) the tangent of which is that argument: the inverse of the tangent function

arctic (ˈɑːktɪk) *adj* **1** of or relating to the Arctic: *arctic temperatures* **2** *informal* cold; freezing: *the weather at Christmas was arctic* ▷ *n* **3** *US* a high waterproof overshoe with buckles **4** *(modifier)* designed or suitable for conditions of extreme cold: *arctic clothing* [C14 from Latin *arcticus*, from Greek *arktikos* northern, literally: pertaining to (the constellation of) the Bear, from *arktos* bear]

Arctic (ˈɑːktɪk) *n* **1** the Also called: **Arctic Zone**. the regions north of the Arctic Circle ▷ *adj* **2** of or relating to the regions north of the Arctic Circle

arctic char *n* a char, *Salvelinus alpinus*, that occurs in northern and arctic seas

Arctic Circle *n* the imaginary circle round the earth, parallel to the equator, at latitude 66° 32′ N; it marks the northernmost point at which the sun appears above the level of the horizon on the winter solstice

arctic fox *n* a fox, *Alopex lagopus*, of arctic regions, whose fur is dark grey in the summer and white in the winter. See also **blue fox**

arctic hare *n* a large hare, *Lepus arcticus*, of the Canadian Arctic whose fur is white in winter

Arctic Ocean *n* the ocean surrounding the North Pole, north of the Arctic Circle. Area: about 14 100 000 sq km (5 440 000 sq miles)

arctic tern *n* a black-capped tern, *Sterna paradisea*, that breeds in the Arctic and then migrates as far south as the Antarctic

arctic willow *n* a low-growing shrub, *Salix arctica*, of the tundra

arctiid (ˈɑːktɪɪd) *n* any moth of the family *Arctiidae*, which includes the footman, ermine, and tiger moths

Arctogaea (ˌɑːktəˈdʒiːə) *n* a zoogeographical area

comprising the Palaearctic, Nearctic, Oriental, and Ethiopian regions. Compare **Neogaea**, **Notogaea**

Arctogaean (ˌɑːktəˈdʒiːən) *adj* of or relating to Arctogaea

arctophile (ˈɑːktəʊˌfaɪl) *n* a person who collects teddy bears or is fond of them [C20 from Greek *arktos* bear + -PHILE]

Arcturus (ɑːkˈtjʊərəs) *n* the brightest star in the constellation Boötes: a red giant. Visual magnitude: −0.4; spectral type: K2III; distance: 37 light years [C14 from Latin, from Greek *Arktouros*, from *arktos* bear + *ouros* guard, keeper] > *Arc'turian adj*

arcuate (ˈɑːkjuːɪt, -ˌeɪt) *adj* shaped or bent like an arc or bow: *arcuate leaves; arcuate fibres of the cerebrum*. Also: **arcuated** [C17 from Latin *arcuāre*, from *arcus* ARC] > *'arcuately adv*

arcuation (ˌɑːkjʊˈeɪʃən) *n* **1** the use of arches or vaults in buildings **2** an arrangement of arches [C17 from Late Latin *arcuātiō* arch, from Latin *arcuāre* to curve]

arcus senilis (ˈɑːkəs sɪˈnaɪlɪs) *n* an opaque circle around the cornea of the eye, often seen in elderly people [Latin: senile bow]

arc welding *n* a technique in which metal is welded by heat generated by an electric arc struck between two electrodes or between one electrode and the metal workpiece > **arc welder** *n*

-ard *or* **-art** *suffix forming nouns* indicating a person who does something, esp to excess, or is characterized by a certain quality: *braggart; drunkard; dullard* [via Old French from Germanic *-hard* (literally: hardy, bold), the final element in many Germanic masculine names, such as *Bernhard* Bernard, *Gerhart* Gerard, etc]

ardeb (ˈɑːdɛb) *n* a unit of dry measure used in Egypt and other Middle Eastern countries. In Egypt it is approximately equal to 0.195 cubic metres [C19 from Arabic *ardabb*, from Greek *artabē* a Persian measure]

Ardèche (French ardɛʃ) *n* a department of S France, in Rhône-Alpes region. Capital: Privas. Pop: 294 933 (2003 est). Area: 5556 sq km (2167 sq miles)

Arden (ˈɑːdᵊn) *n* **Forest of** a region of N Warwickshire, part of a former forest: scene of Shakespeare's *As You Like It*

Ardennes (ɑːˈdɛn; French ardɛn) *n* **1** a department of NE France, in Champagne-Ardenne region. Capital: Mézières. Pop: 288 806 (2003 est). Area: 5253 sq km (2049 sq miles) **2** **the** a wooded plateau in SE Belgium, Luxembourg, and NE France: scene of heavy fighting in both World Wars

ardent (ˈɑːdᵊnt) *adj* **1** expressive of or characterized by intense desire or emotion; passionate: *ardent love* **2** intensely enthusiastic; eager: *an ardent longing* **3** glowing, flashing, or shining: *ardent eyes* **4** *rare* burning: *an ardent fever* [C14 from Latin *ārdēre* to burn] > *'ardency n* > *'ardently adv*

ardent spirits *pl n* spirits, such as rum, whisky, etc

ardour *or US* **ardor** (ˈɑːdə) *n* **1** feelings of great intensity and warmth; fervour **2** eagerness; zeal [C14 from Old French *ardour*, from Latin *ārdor*, from *ārdēre* to burn]

Ards (ɑːdz) *n* a district of Northern Ireland, in Co Down. Pop: 74 369 (2003 est). Area: 368 sq km (142 sq miles)

arduous (ˈɑːdjʊəs) *adj* **1** requiring great physical or mental effort; difficult to accomplish; strenuous **2** hard to endure; harsh: *arduous conditions* **3** hard to overcome or surmount; steep or difficult: *an arduous track* [C16 from Latin *arduus* steep, difficult] > *'arduously adv* > *'arduousness n*

are¹ (ɑː; *unstressed* ə) *vb* the plural form of the present tense (indicative mood) of **be** and the singular form used with *you* [Old English *aron*, second person plural of *bēon* to be]

are² (ɑː) *n* a unit of area equal to 100 sq metres or 119.599 sq yards; one hundredth of a hectare. Symbol: a [C19 from French, from Latin *ārea* piece

a

of level ground; see AREA]

area ('ɛərɪə) n **1** any flat, curved, or irregular expanse of a surface **2 a** the extent of a two-dimensional surface enclosed within a specified boundary or geometric figure: *the area of Ireland; the area of a triangle* **b** the two-dimensional extent of the surface of a solid, or of some part thereof, esp one bounded by a closed curve: *the area of a sphere* **3** a section, portion, or part: *an area of the body; an area of the sky* **4** region; district; locality: *a mountainous area* **5 a** a geographical division of administrative responsibility **b** (*as modifier*): *area manager* **6** a part or section, as of a building, town, etc, having some specified function or characteristic: *reception area; commercial area; slum area* **7** Also called: **areaway** a sunken area, usually enclosed, giving light, air, and sometimes access to a cellar or basement **8** the range, extent, or scope of anything **9** a subject field or field of study **10** any unoccupied or unused flat open piece of ground **11** the ground on which a building stands, or the ground surrounding a building **12** *anatomy* any of the various regions of the cerebral cortex **13** *computing* any part of a computer memory assigned to store data of a specified type [C16 from Latin: level ground, open space, threshing-floor; related to *ārēre* to be dry] > 'areal *adj*

area code n a number prefixed to an individual telephone number: used in making long-distance calls

Area of Outstanding Natural Beauty n See **AONB**

areaway ('ɛərɪə,weɪ) n **1** a passageway between parts of a building or between different buildings **2** See **area** (sense 7)

areca ('ærɪkə, ə'riːkə) n any of various tall palms of the genus *Areca*, which are native to SE Asia and have white flowers and orange or red egg-shaped nuts [C16 from Portuguese, from Malayalam *adekka*]

Arecibo Observatory (*Spanish* arɛ'θiβo) n an observatory in Puerto Rico at which the world's largest dish radio telescope (diameter 305 m) is situated. It is operated by the National Astronomy and Ionosphere Center

areg (ə'reg) n a plural of **erg²**

arena (ə'riːnə) n **1 a** an enclosure or platform, usually surrounded by seats on all sides, in which sports events, contests, entertainments, etc, take place: *a boxing arena* **b** (*as modifier*): *arena stage* **2** the central area of an ancient Roman amphitheatre, in which gladiatorial contests and other spectacles were held **3** a sphere or scene of conflict or intense activity: *the political arena* [C17 from Latin *harēna* sand, place where sand was strewn for the combats]

arenaceous (,ærɪ'neɪʃəs) *adj* **1** (of sedimentary rocks and deposits) composed of sand or sandstone. Compare **argillaceous** and **rudaceous** **2** (of plants) growing best in a sandy soil [C17 from Latin *harēnāceus* sandy, from *harēna* sand]

arena theatre n another term for **theatre-in-the-round**

arene ('æriːn) n an aromatic hydrocarbon [C20 from AR(OMATIC) + -ENE]

arenicolous (,ærɪ'nɪkələs) *adj* growing or living in sand or sandy places: *arenicolous plants* [C19 from Latin *harēna* sand + *colere* to inhabit]

arenite ('ærə,naɪt, ə'riː-) n any arenaceous rock; a sandstone [C20 from Latin *harēna* sand + -ITE¹] > arenitic (,ærə'nɪtɪk) *adj*

aren't (ɑːnt) **1** contraction of are not **2** informal, chiefly Brit (used in interrogative sentences) > contraction of am not

areography (,ɛərɪ'ɒgrəfɪ) n the description of the physical features, such as the surface, atmosphere, etc, of the planet Mars [C19 from Greek *Areos* Mars + -GRAPHY]

areola (ə'rɪələ) n, pl -lae (-,liː) or -las *anatomy* any small circular area, such as the pigmented ring around the human nipple or the inflamed area

surrounding a pimple [C17 from Latin: diminutive of AREA] > a'reolar or areolate (ə'rɪəlɪt, -,leɪt) *adj* > areolation (ə,rɪə'leɪʃən) n

areole ('ærɪəʊl) n **1** *biology* a space outlined on a surface, such as an area between veins on a leaf or on an insect's wing **2** a sunken area on a cactus from which spines, hairs, etc, arise > 'areo,late *adj*

Areopagite (,ærɪ'ɒpədʒaɪt) n a member of the Areopagus, a judicial council of ancient Athens that met on the hill of that name

Areopagus (,ærɪ'ɒpəgəs) n **1 a** the hill to the northwest of the Acropolis in Athens **b** (in ancient Athens) the judicial council whose members (Areopagites) met on this hill **2** *literary* any high court [via Latin from Greek *Areiopagus*, contracted from *Areios pagos*, hill of Ares]

Arequipa (,ærɪ'kiːpə; *Spanish* are'kipa) n a city in S Peru, at an altitude of 2250 m (7500 ft): founded in 1540 on the site of an Inca city. Pop: 791 000 (2005 est)

Ares ('ɛəriːz) n *Greek myth* the god of war, born of Zeus and Hera. Roman counterpart: **Mars**

arête (ə'reɪt, ə'rɛt) n a sharp ridge separating two cirques or glacial valleys in mountainous regions [C19 from French: fishbone, backbone (of a fish), ridge, sharp edge, from Latin *arista* ear of corn, fishbone]

arethusa (,ærɪ'θjuːzə) n a North American orchid, *Arethusa bulbosa*, having one long narrow leaf and one rose-purple flower fringed with yellow

Arethusa (,ærɪ'θjuːzə) n *Greek myth* a nymph who was changed into a spring on the island of Ortygia to escape the amorous advances of the river god Alpheus

Arezzo (ə'rɛtsəʊ; *Italian* a'rettso) n a city in central Italy, in E Tuscany. Pop: 91 589 (2001). Ancient Latin name: Arretium

Arg. *abbreviation for* Argentina

argal ('ɑːgəl) n another name for **argol**

argali ('ɑːgəlɪ) or **argal** n, pl -gali or -gals a wild sheep, *Ovis ammon*, inhabiting semidesert regions in central Asia: family *Bovidae*, order *Artiodactyla*. It is the largest of the sheep, having massive horns in the male, which may almost form a circle [C18 from Mongolian]

argan ('ɑːgæn) n a thorny evergreen tree, *Argania spinosa*, native to SW Morocco, the plum-sized fruit of which contains a nut that yields an oil valued for cooking

Argand diagram ('ɑːgænd) n *maths* a diagram in which complex numbers are represented by the points in the plane the coordinates of which are respectively the real and imaginary parts of the number, so that the number $x + iy$ is represented by the point (x, y), or by the corresponding vector $<x, y>$. If the polar coordinates of (x, y) are $(r, θ)$, r is the modulus and $θ$ the argument of $x + iy$ See also **amplitude** (sense 5) [C19 named after Jean-Robert *Argand* (1768–1822), French mathematician]

argan oil ('ɑːgən) n a yellow nutty-flavoured oil extracted from the ripe green olive-like fruits of the argan tree, *Argania spinosa* of SW Morocco, and used in cooking, medicines, and cosmetics [C21 probably from *Argana*, a village northeast of Agadir, Morocco, where it is believed to have originated]

argent ('ɑːdʒənt) n **a** an archaic or poetic word for **silver** **b** (*as adjective; often postpositive, esp in heraldry*): *a bend argent* [C15 from Old French, from Latin]

Argenteuil (*French* arʒɑ̃tœj) n a suburb of Paris, France, with a convent (656) that became famous when Héloïse was abbess (12th century). Pop: 93 961 (1999)

argentic (ɑː'dʒɛntɪk) *adj* *chem* of or containing silver in the divalent or trivalent state

argentiferous (,ɑːdʒən'tɪfərəs) *adj* containing or bearing silver

Argentina (,ɑːdʒən'tiːnə) n a republic in southern South America: colonized by the Spanish from 1516 onwards; gained independence in 1816 and became a republic in 1852; ruled by military

dictatorships for much of the 20th century; civilian rule restored in 1983; consists chiefly of subtropical plains and forests (the Chaco) in the north, temperate plains (the pampas) in the central parts, the Andes in the west, and an infertile plain extending to Tierra del Fuego in the south (Patagonia); an important meat producer. Language: Spanish. Religion: Roman Catholic. Currency: peso. Capital: Buenos Aires. Pop: 38 871 000 (2004 est). Area: 2 776 653 sq km (1 072 067 sq miles). Also called: **the Argentine**

argentine ('ɑːdʒən,taɪn) *adj* **1** of, relating to, or resembling silver ▷ n **2** any of various small marine salmonoid fishes, such as *Argentina sphyraena*, that constitute the family *Argentinidae* and are characterized by a long silvery body

Argentine ('ɑːdʒən,tiːn, -,taɪn) n **1 the** another name for **Argentina 2** a native or inhabitant of Argentina ▷ *adj* **3** of or relating to Argentina ▷ Also (for senses 2, 3): Argentinian (,ɑːdʒən'tɪnɪən)

argentite ('ɑːdʒən,taɪt) n a dark grey mineral that consists of silver sulphide, usually in cubic crystalline forms, and occurs in veins, often with native silver. It is found esp in Mexico, Nevada, and Saxony and is an important source of silver. Formula: Ag_2S

argentous (ɑː'dʒɛntəs) *adj* *chem* of or containing silver in the monovalent state

argentum (ɑː'dʒɛntəm) n an obsolete name for **silver** [Latin]

argie-bargie ('ɑːdʒɪ'bɑːdʒɪ) n a variant spelling of **argy-bargy**

argil ('ɑːdʒɪl) n clay, esp potters' clay [C16 from Latin *argilla* white clay, from Greek *argillos*]

argillaceous (,ɑːdʒɪ'leɪʃəs) *adj* (of sedimentary rocks and deposits) composed of very fine-grained material, such as clay, shale, etc Compare **arenaceous** (sense 1) and **rudaceous**

argilliferous (,ɑːdʒɪ'lɪfərəs) *adj* containing or yielding clay: *argilliferous rocks*

argillite ('ɑːdʒɪ,laɪt) n any argillaceous rock, esp a hardened mudstone [C18 from Latin *argilla* clay (from Greek *argillos*) + -ITE¹] > argillitic (,ɑːdʒɪ'lɪtɪk) *adj*

arginine ('ɑːdʒɪ,naɪn) n an essential amino acid of plant and animal proteins, necessary for nutrition and for the production of excretory urea [C19 from German *Arginin*, of uncertain origin]

Argive ('ɑːdʒaɪv, -gaɪv) *adj* **1** (in Homer, Virgil, etc) of or relating to the Greeks besieging Troy, esp those from Argos **2** of or relating to Argos or Argolis **3** a literary word for **Greek** ▷ n **4** an ancient Greek, esp one from Argos or Argolis

argle-bargle (,ɑːgᵊl'bɑːgᵊl) n another word for **argy-bargy**

Argo¹ ('ɑːgəʊ) n *Greek myth* the ship in which Jason sailed in search of the Golden Fleece

Argo² ('ɑːgəʊ) n, *Latin genitive* Argus ('ɑːgəs) an extensive constellation in the S hemisphere now subdivided into the smaller constellations of **Puppis**, **Vela**, **Carina**, and **Pyxis**. Also called: Argo Navis ('neɪvɪs)

argol ('ɑːgɒl) or **argal** n crude potassium hydrogentartrate, deposited as a crust on the sides of wine vats [C14 from Anglo-French *argoil*, of unknown origin]

Argolis ('ɑːgəlɪs) n **1** a department and ancient region of Greece, in the NE Peloponnese. Capital: Nauplion. Pop: 102 392 (2001). Area: 2261 sq km (873 sq miles) **2 Gulf of** an inlet of the Aegean Sea, in the E Peloponnese

argon ('ɑːgɒn) n an extremely unreactive colourless odourless element of the rare gas series that forms almost 1 per cent (by volume) of the atmosphere. It is used in electric lights. Symbol: Ar; atomic no: 18; atomic wt: 39.948; density: 1.7837 kg/m³; freezing pt: –189.3°C; boiling pt: –185.9°C [C19 from Greek, from *argos* idle, inactive, from A-¹ + *ergon* work]

Argonaut ('ɑːgə,nɔːt) n **1** *Greek myth* one of the heroes who sailed with Jason in quest of the Golden Fleece **2** a person who took part in the

Californian gold rush of 1849 **3** another name for the **paper nautilus** [C16 from Greek *Argonautēs*, from *Argō* the name of Jason's ship + *nautēs* sailor] > Argo'nautic *adj*

Argonne ('ɑːgɒn; *French* argɔn) *n* **the** a wooded region of NE France: scene of major battles in both World Wars

argonon ('ɑːgə,nɒn) *n* another name for **inert gas** (sense 1) [C20 from ARGON + -ON (indicating an inert gas)]

Argos ('ɑːgɒs, -gəs) *n* an ancient city in SE Greece, in the NE Peloponnese: one of the oldest Greek cities, it dominated the Peloponnese in the 7th century BC Pop: 22 000 (1995 est)

argosy ('ɑːgəsɪ) *n*, *pl* -sies *archaic or poetic* a large abundantly laden merchant ship, or a fleet of such ships [C16 from Italian *Ragusea (nave)* (ship) of Ragusa]

argot ('ɑːgəʊ) *n* slang or jargon peculiar to a particular group, esp (formerly) a group of thieves [C19 from French, of unknown origin] > argotic (ɑːˈgɒtɪk) *adj*

Argovie (argɔvi) *n* the French name for **Aargau**

arguable ('ɑːgjʊəbəl) *adj* **1** capable of being disputed; doubtful **2** capable of being supported by argument; plausible

arguably ('ɑːgjʊəblɪ) *adv* (*sentence modifier*) it can be argued that

argue ('ɑːgjuː) *vb* -gues, -guing, -gued **1** (*intr*) to quarrel; wrangle: *they were always arguing until I arrived* **2** (*intr*; often foll by *for* or *against*) to present supporting or opposing reasons or cases in a dispute; reason **3** (*tr*; *may take a clause as object*) to try to prove by presenting reasons; maintain **4** (*tr*; *often passive*) to debate or discuss: *the case was fully argued before agreement was reached* **5** (*tr*) to persuade: *he argued me into going* **6** (*tr*) to give evidence of; suggest: *her looks argue despair* [C14 from Old French *arguer* to assert, charge with, from Latin *arguere* to make clear, accuse; related to Latin *argūtus* clear, *argentum* silver] > 'arguer *n*

argufy ('ɑːgjʊˌfaɪ) *vb* -fies, -fying, -fied *facetious or dialect* to quarrel, esp over something trivial

argument ('ɑːgjʊmənt) *n* **1** a quarrel; altercation **2** a discussion in which reasons are put forward in support of and against a proposition, proposal, or case; debate: *the argument on birth control will never be concluded* **3** (*sometimes plural*) a point or series of reasons presented to support or oppose a proposition **4** a summary of the plot or subject of a book, etc **5** *logic* **a** a process of deductive or inductive reasoning that purports to show its conclusion to be true **b** formally, a sequence of statements one of which is the conclusion and the remainder the premises **6** *logic* an obsolete name for the middle term of a syllogism **7** *maths* **a** an element to which an operation, function, predicate, etc, applies, esp the independent variable of a function **b** another name for **amplitude** (sense 5) of a complex number

argumentation (,ɑːgjʊmənˈteɪʃən) *n* **1** the process of reasoning methodically **2** a less common word for **argument** (senses 2, 3)

argumentative (,ɑːgjʊˈmɛntətɪv) *adj* **1** given to arguing; contentious **2** characterized by argument; controversial > ,argu'mentatively *adv* > ,argu'mentativeness *n*

argument from design *n* another name for **teleological argument**

argumentum ad hominem *Latin* (,ɑːgjʊˈmɛntʊm æd ˈhɒmɪˌnɛm) *n logic* **1** fallacious argument that attacks not an opponent's beliefs but his motives or character **2** argument that shows an opponent's statement to be inconsistent with his other beliefs **3** an instance of either of these [literally: argument to the person]

argus ('ɑːgəs) *n* any of various brown butterflies, esp the **Scotch argus** (*Erebia aethiops*) found on moorland and in forests up to a height of 2000 m

Argus ('ɑːgəs) *n* **1** *Greek myth* a giant with a hundred eyes who was made guardian of the heifer Io. After he was killed by Hermes his eyes

were transferred to the peacock's tail **2** a vigilant person; guardian

Argus-eyed *adj* keen-sighted; observant; vigilant

argus pheasant *n* either of two pheasants, *Argusianus argus* (great argus) or *Rheinardia ocellata* (crested argus), occurring in SE Asia and Indonesia. The males have very long tails marked with eyelike spots

argy-bargy or **argie-bargie** ('ɑːdʒɪˈbɑːdʒɪ) *n*, *pl* -bargies *Brit informal* a wrangling argument or verbal dispute. Also called: **argle-bargle** [C19 from Scottish, compound based on dialect *argle*, probably from ARGUE]

argyle (ɑːˈgaɪl) *adj* **1** made of knitted or woven material with a diamond-shaped pattern of two or more colours > *n* **2** (*often plural*) a sock made of this [C20 after Campbell of *Argyle* (Argyll), the pattern being an adaptation of the tartan of this clan]

Argyll and Bute (ɑːˈgaɪl) *n* a council area in W Scotland on the Atlantic Ocean: in 1975 the historical counties of Argyllshire and Bute became part of Strathclyde region; in 1996 they were reinstated as a single unitary authority. Argyll and Bute is mountainous and includes the islands of Bute, Mull, Islay, and Jura. Administrative centre: Lochgilphead. Pop: 91 300 (2003 est). Area: 6930 sq km (2676 sq miles)

Argyllshire (ɑːˈgaɪlˌʃɪə, -ʃə) *n* (until 1975) a county of W Scotland, part of Strathclyde region (1975–96), now part of Argyll and Bute

Argyrol ('ɑːdʒɪˌrɒl, ɑːˈdʒɪərɒl) *n trademark* a dark brown compound of silver and a protein, used medicinally as a local antiseptic

arhat ('ɑːhət) *n* a Buddhist, esp a monk who has achieved enlightenment and at death passes to nirvana. Compare **Bodhisattva** [from Sanskrit: worthy of respect, from *arhati* he deserves]

Århus (*Danish* 'ʌhuːs) *n* a variant spelling of **Aarhus**

aria ('ɑːrɪə) *n* an elaborate accompanied song for solo voice from a cantata, opera, or oratorio. See also **da capo** [C18 from Italian: tune, AIR]

Ariadne (,ærɪˈædnɪ) *n Greek myth* daughter of Minos and Pasiphaë: she gave Theseus the thread with which he found his way out of the Minotaur's labyrinth

Arian ('ɛərɪən) *adj* **1** of, relating to, or characterizing Arius (?250–336 AD), the Greek Christian theologian, or Arianism > *n* **2** an adherent of Arianism > *adj* > *n* **3** a variant spelling of **Aryan**

-arian *suffix forming nouns* indicating a person or thing that advocates, believes, or is associated with something: *vegetarian; millenarian; librarian* [from Latin *-ārius* -ARY + -AN]

Arianism ('ɛərɪəˌnɪzəm) *n* the doctrine of the Greek Christian theologian Arius (?250–336 AD), pronounced heretical at the Council of Nicaea, which asserted that Christ was not of one substance with the Father, but a creature raised by the Father to the dignity of Son of God

Arica (əˈriːkə; *Spanish* aˈrika) *n* a port in extreme N Chile: awarded to Chile in 1929 after the lengthy Tacna-Arica dispute with Peru; outlet for Bolivian and Peruvian trade. Pop: 180 000 (2005 est). See also **Tacna-Arica**

arid ('ærɪd) *adj* **1** having little or no rain; dry; parched with heat **2** devoid of interest [C17 from Latin *āridus*, from *ārēre* to be dry] > aridity (əˈrɪdɪtɪ) or 'aridness *n* > 'aridly *adv*

arid zone *n* either of the zones of latitude 15–30° N and S characterized by very low rainfall and desert or semidesert terrain

Ariège (*French* arjɛʒ) *n* a department of SW France, in Midi-Pyrénées region. Capital: Foix. Pop: 139 612 (2003 est). Area: 4903 sq km (1912 sq miles)

ariel ('ɛərɪəl) *n* an Arabian gazelle, *Gazella arabica* (or *dama*) [C19 from Arabic *aryal*]

Ariel ('ɛərɪəl) *n* the smallest of the four large satellites of Uranus

Aries ('ɛəriːz) *n*, *Latin genitive* Arietis (əˈraɪɪtɪs) **1** *astronomy* a small zodiacal constellation in the N hemisphere lying between Taurus and Pisces on the ecliptic and having a second-magnitude star **2** *astrology* **a** Also called: **the Ram** the first sign of the zodiac, symbol ♈, having a cardinal fire classification, ruled by the planet Mars. The sun is in this sign between about March 21 and April 19 **b** a person born during the period when the sun is in this sign > *adj* **3** *astrology* born under or characteristic of Aries > Also (for senses 2b, 3): **Arien** ('ɛərɪən) [C14 from Latin: ram]

arietta (,ærɪˈɛtə; *Italian* ariˈetta) or **ariette** (,ærɪˈɛt) *n*, *pl* -ettas, -ette (-ˈette) or -ettes a short relatively uncomplicated aria [C18 from Italian, diminutive of ARIA]

aright (əˈraɪt) *adv* correctly; rightly; properly

ariki ('ɑːrɪkɪ) *n*, *pl* ariki NZ the first-born male or female in a notable family; chief [Māori]

aril ('ærɪl) *n* an appendage on certain seeds, such as those of the yew and nutmeg, developed from or near the funicle of the ovule and often brightly coloured and fleshy [C18 from New Latin *arillus*, from Medieval Latin *arilli* raisins, pips of grapes] > 'aril,late *adj*

arillode ('ærɪˌləʊd) *n* a structure in certain seeds that resembles an aril but is developed from the micropyle of the ovule [C19 from ARIL + -ODE[1]]

Arimathea or **Arimathaea** (,ærɪməˈθiːə) *n* a town in ancient Palestine: location unknown

Arimidex (,ærɪmɪˈdɛks) *n* a trade name for **anastrozole**

Ariminum (əˈrɪmɪnəm) *n* the ancient name of **Rimini**

arioso (,ɑːrɪˈəʊzəʊ, ,æ-) *n*, *pl* -sos or -si (-siː) *music* a recitative with the lyrical quality of an aria [C18 from Italian, from ARIA]

arise (əˈraɪz) *vb* arises, arising, arose, arisen (*intr*) **1** to come into being; originate **2** (foll by *from*) to spring or proceed as a consequence; result: *guilt arising from my actions* **3** to get or stand up, as from a sitting, kneeling, or lying position **4** to come into notice **5** to move upwards; ascend [Old English *ārīsan*; related to Old Saxon *arīsan*, Old High German *irrīsan*; see RISE]

arista (əˈrɪstə) *n*, *pl* -tae (-tiː) **1** a stiff bristle such as the awn of some grasses and cereals **2** a bristle-like appendage on the antennae of some insects [C17 from Latin: ear of corn, fishbone] > aˈristate *adj*

Aristaeus (,ærɪˈstiːəs) *n Greek myth* a son of Apollo and Cyrene: protector of herds and fields

Aristarchus (,ærɪˈstɑːkəs) *n* a crater in the NE quadrant of the moon, having a diameter of about 37 kilometres, which is the brightest formation on the moon

aristo ('ærɪstəʊ, əˈrɪstəʊ) *n*, *pl* -tos *informal* short for **aristocrat**

aristocracy (,ærɪˈstɒkrəsɪ) *n*, *pl* -cies **1** a privileged class of people usually of high birth; the nobility **2** such a class as the ruling body of a state **3** government by such a class **4** a state governed by such a class **5** a class of people considered to be outstanding in a sphere of activity [C16 from Late Latin *aristocratia*, from Greek *aristokratia* rule by the best-born, from *aristos* best; see -CRACY]

aristocrat ('ærɪstəˌkræt) *n* **1** a member of the aristocracy; a noble **2** a person who has the manners or qualities of a member of a privileged or superior class **3** a person who advocates aristocracy as a form of government

aristocratic (,ærɪstəˈkrætɪk) *adj* **1** relating to or characteristic of aristocracy or an aristocrat **2** elegant or stylish in appearance and behaviour > ,aristo'cratically *adv*

Aristotelian (,ærɪstəˈtiːlɪən) *adj* **1** of or relating to Aristotle (384–322 BC), the Greek philosopher or his philosophy **2** (of a philosophical position) derived from that of Aristotle, or incorporating such of his major doctrines as the distinctions between matter and form, and substance and accident, or

a

the primacy of individuals over universals ▷ *n* **3** a follower of Aristotle

Aristotelian logic (ˌærɪstəˈtiːlɪən) *n* the logical theories of Aristotle as developed in the Middle Ages, concerned mainly with syllogistic reasoning: traditional as opposed to modern or symbolic logic

aristotle (ˈærɪˌstɒtᵊl) *n* *Austral slang* **1** a bottle **2** the buttocks or anus [rhyming slang; in sense 2, shortened from *bottle and glass* arse]

Aristotle (ˈærɪˌstɒtᵊl) *n* a prominent crater in the NW quadrant of the moon about 83 kilometres in diameter

arithmetic (əˈrɪθmətɪk) *n* **1** the branch of mathematics concerned with numerical calculations, such as addition, subtraction, multiplication, and division **2** one or more calculations involving numerical operations **3** knowledge of or skill in using arithmetic: *his arithmetic is good* ▷ *adj* (ˌærɪθˈmɛtɪk) *also* **arithmetical 4** of, relating to, or using arithmetic [c13 from Latin *arithmētica*, from Greek *arithmētikē*, from *arithmein* to count, from *arithmos* number] > ˌarithˈmetically *adv* > aˌrithmeˈtician *n*

arithmetic mean *n* an average value of a set of integers, terms, or quantities, expressed as their sum divided by their number: *the arithmetic mean of 3, 4, and 8 is 5*. Often shortened to: **mean** Also called: **average** Compare **geometric mean**

arithmetic progression *n* a sequence of numbers or quantities, each term of which differs from the succeeding term by a constant amount, such as 3,6,9,12. Compare **geometric progression**

-arium *suffix forming nouns* indicating a place for or associated with something: *aquarium; planetarium; solarium* [from Latin *-ārium*, neuter of *-ārius* -ARY]

Ariz. *abbreviation for* Arizona

Arizona (ˌærɪˈzəʊnə) *n* a state of the southwestern US: consists of the Colorado plateau in the northeast, including the Grand Canyon, divided from desert in the southwest by mountains rising over 3750 m (12 500 ft). Capital: Phoenix. Pop: 5 580 811 (2003 est). Area: 293 750 sq km (113 417 sq miles). Abbreviations: **Ariz,** (with zip code) **AZ**

Arjuna (ˈɑːdʒʊnə) *n* *Hindu myth* the most important of the five princes in the *Mahabharata*. Krishna served as his charioteer in the battle with the Kauravas

ark (ɑːk) *n* **1** the vessel that Noah built and in which he saved himself, his family, and a number of animals and birds during the Flood (Genesis 6–9) **2** *out of the ark* *informal* very old; out of date **3** a place or thing offering shelter or protection **4** *dialect* a chest, box, or coffer [Old English *arc*, from Latin *arca* box, chest]

Ark (ɑːk) *n* *Judaism* **1** Also called: **Holy Ark** the cupboard at the front of a synagogue, usually in the eastern wall, in which the Torah scrolls are kept **2** Also called: **Ark of the Covenant** the most sacred symbol of God's presence among the Hebrew people, carried in their journey from Sinai to the Promised Land (Canaan) and eventually enshrined in the holy of holies of the Temple in Jerusalem

Ark. *abbreviation for* Arkansas

Arkansan (ɑːˈkænzən) *n* **1** a native or inhabitant of Arkansas ▷ *adj* **2** of or relating to Arkansas

Arkansas *n* **1** (ˈɑːkənˌsɔː) a state of the southern US: mountainous in the north and west, with the alluvial plain of the Mississippi in the east; has the only diamond mine in the US; the chief US producer of bauxite. Capital: Little Rock. Pop: 2 725 714 (2003 est). Area: 134 537 sq km (51 945 sq miles). Abbreviations: **Ark,** (with zip code) **AR 2** (ɑːˈkænzəs) a river in the S central US, rising in central Colorado and flowing east and southeast to join the Mississippi in Arkansas. Length: 2335 km (1450 miles)

Arkhangelsk (ɑrˈxangɪljsk) *n* the Russian name for **Archangel**

arkose (ˈɑːkəʊs) *n* a sandstone consisting of grains of feldspar and quartz cemented by a mixture of quartz and clay minerals [c19 from French]

Arlberg (*German* ˈarlˌbɛrk) *n* a mountain pass in W Austria: a winter sports region. Height: 1802 m (5910 ft)

Arles (ɑːlz; *French* arl) *n* **1** a city in SE France, on the Rhône: Roman amphitheatre. Pop: 50 513 (1999) **2 Kingdom of** a kingdom in SE France which had dissolved by 1378: known as the Kingdom of Burgundy until about 1200

Arlington (ˈɑːlɪŋtən) *n* a county of N Virginia: site of **Arlington National Cemetery**

Arlon (*French* arlɔ̃) *n* a town in SE Belgium, capital of Luxembourg province. Pop: 25 766 (2004 est)

arm¹ (ɑːm) *n* **1** (in man) either of the upper limbs from the shoulder to the wrist. Related adj: **brachial 2** the part of either of the upper limbs from the elbow to the wrist; forearm **3 a** the corresponding limb of any other vertebrate **b** an armlike appendage of some invertebrates **4** an object that covers or supports the human arm, esp the sleeve of a garment or the side of a chair, sofa, etc **5** anything considered to resemble an arm in appearance, position, or function, esp something that branches out from a central support or larger mass: *an arm of the sea; the arm of a record player* **6** an administrative subdivision of an organization: *an arm of the government* **7** power; authority: *the arm of the law* **8** any of the specialist combatant sections of a military force, such as cavalry, infantry, etc **9** *nautical* See **yardarm 10** *sport, esp ball games* ability to throw or pitch: *he has a good arm* **11** an arm and a leg *informal* a large amount of money **12** arm in arm with arms linked **13** at arm's length at a distance; away from familiarity with or subjection to another **14 give one's right arm** *informal* to be prepared to make any sacrifice **15 in the arms of Morpheus** sleeping **16 with open arms** with great warmth and hospitality: *to welcome someone with open arms* ▷ *vb* **17** (*tr*) *archaic* to walk arm in arm with [Old English; related to German *Arm*, Old Norse *armr* arm, Latin *armus* shoulder, Greek *harmos* joint] > ˈarmˌlike *adj*

arm² (ɑːm) *vb* (*tr*) **1** to equip with weapons as a preparation for war **2** to provide (a person or thing) with something that strengthens, protects, or increases efficiency: *he armed himself against the cold* **3 a** to activate (a fuse) so that it will explode at the required time **b** to prepare (an explosive device) for use by introducing a fuse or detonator **4** *nautical* to pack arming into (a sounding lead) ▷ *n* **5** (*usually plural*) a weapon, esp a firearm ▷ See also **arms** [c14 (n) back formation from *arms*, from Old French *armes*, from Latin *arma*; (vb) from Old French *armer* to equip with arms, from Latin *armāre*, from *arma* arms, equipment]

Arm. *abbreviation for* Armenia(n)

ARM *abbreviation for* **1 adjustable rate mortgage 2** *international car registration for* Armenia

armada (ɑːˈmɑːdə) *n* a large number of ships or aircraft [c16 from Spanish, from Medieval Latin *armāta* fleet, armed forces, from Latin *armāre* to provide with arms]

Armada (ɑːˈmɑːdə) *n* (*usually preceded by the*) See **Spanish Armada**

armadillo (ˌɑːməˈdɪləʊ) *n, pl* **-los 1** any edentate mammal of the family *Dasypodidae* of Central and South America and S North America, such as *Priodontes giganteus* (**giant armadillo**). They are burrowing animals, with peglike rootless teeth and a covering of strong horny plates over most of the body **2 fairy armadillo** another name for **pichiciego** [c16 from Spanish, diminutive of *armado* armed (man), from Latin *armātus* armed; compare ARMADA]

Armageddon (ˌɑːməˈgɛdᵊn) *n* **1** *New Testament* the final battle at the end of the world between the forces of good and evil, God against the kings of the earth (Revelation 16:16) **2** a catastrophic and extremely destructive conflict, esp World War I viewed as this [c19 from Late Latin *Armagedōn*,

from Greek, from Hebrew *har megiddōn*, mountain district of *Megiddo*, in N Palestine, site of various battles in the Old Testament]

Armagh (ɑːˈmɑː) *n* **1** a historical county of S Northern Ireland: in 1973 it was replaced for administrative purposes by the districts of Armagh and Craigavon. Area: 1326 sq km (512 sq miles) **2** a district in Northern Ireland, in Co Armagh. Pop: 55 449 (2003 est). Area: 667 sq km (258 sq miles) **3** a town in S Northern Ireland, in Armagh district, Co Armagh: seat of Roman Catholic and Protestant archbishops. Pop: 14 590 (2001)

Armagnac (ˈɑːmənˌjæk) *n* a dry brown brandy distilled in the French district of Gers [from *Armagnac*, the former name of this region]

Armalite (ˈɑːməlaɪt) *n* *trademark* a lightweight high-velocity rifle of various calibres, capable of automatic and semiautomatic operation [c20 from *Armalite Division*, Fairchild Engine and Airplane Company, manufacturers]

armament (ˈɑːməmənt) *n* **1** (*often plural*) the weapon equipment of a military vehicle, ship, or aircraft **2** a military force raised and armed ready for war **3** preparation for war involving the production of equipment and arms [c17 from Latin *armāmenta* utensils, from *armāre* to equip]

armamentarium (ˌɑːməmɛnˈtɛərɪəm) *n, pl* **-iums** or **-ia** (-ɪə) the items that comprise the material and equipment used by a physician in his professional practice

armature (ˈɑːmətjʊə) *n* **1** a revolving structure in an electric motor or generator, wound with the coils that carry the current **2** any part of an electric machine or device that moves under the influence of a magnetic field or within which an electromotive force is induced **3** Also called: **keeper** a soft iron or steel bar placed across the poles of a permanent magnet to close the magnetic circuit **4** such a bar placed across the poles of an electromagnet to transmit mechanical force **5** *sculpture* a framework to support the clay or other material used in modelling **6** the protective outer covering of an animal or plant **7** *archaic* armour [c15 from Latin *armātūra* armour, equipment, from *armāre* to furnish with equipment; see ARM²]

armband (ˈɑːmˌbænd) *n* **1** a band of material worn round the arm, such as one bearing an identifying mark, etc, or a black one indicating mourning **2** an inflatable buoyancy aid, worn on the upper arm of a person learning to swim **3** an elasticated band worn round the upper arm to keep the shirtsleeve in place

armchair (ˈɑːmˌtʃɛə) *n* **1** a chair, esp an upholstered one, that has side supports for the arms or elbows **2** (*modifier*) taking no active part; lacking practical experience; theoretical: *an armchair strategist* **3** (*modifier*) participated in away from the place of action or in the home: *armchair theatre*

Armco (ˈɑːmkəʊ) *n* *trademark* a metal safety barrier erected at the side of motor-racing circuits, esp on corners

armed¹ (ɑːmd) *adj* **1** equipped with or supported by arms, armour, etc **2** prepared for conflict or any difficulty **3** (of an explosive device) prepared for use; having a fuse or detonator installed **4** (of plants) having the protection of thorns, spines, etc

armed² (ɑːmd) *adj* **a** having an arm or arms **b** (*in combination*): *long-armed; one-armed*

armed forces *pl n* the military forces of a nation or nations, including the army, navy, air force, marines, etc

armed response unit *n* (in Britain) a unit of police officers who are trained to use firearms in situations where unarmed police officers would be in danger

armed response vehicle *n* (in Britain) a police vehicle carrying armed officers who are trained to respond to incidents involving firearms

Armenia (ɑːˈmiːnɪə) *n* **1** a republic in NW Asia: originally part of the historic Armenian kingdom; acquired by Russia in 1828; became the Armenian Soviet Socialist Republic in 1936; gained independence in 1991. It is mountainous, rising over 4000 m (13 000 ft). Language: Armenian. Religion: Christian (Armenian Apostolic) majority. Currency: dram. Capital: Yerevan. Pop: Pop: 3 052 000 (2004 est). Area: 29 800 sq km (11 490 sq miles) **2** a former kingdom in W Asia, between the Black Sea and the Caspian Sea, south of Georgia **3** a town in central Colombia: centre of a coffee-growing district. Pop: 349 000 (2005 est)

Armenian (ɑːˈmiːnɪən) *n* **1** a native or inhabitant of Armenia or an Armenian-speaking person elsewhere **2** the language of the Armenians: an Indo-European language probably belonging to the Thraco-Phrygian branch, but containing many non-Indo-European elements **3** an adherent of the Armenian Church or its doctrines ▷ *adj* **4** of or relating to Armenia, its inhabitants, their language, or the Armenian Church

Armenian Church *n* the national Church of Armenia, founded in the early fourth century AD, the dogmas and liturgy of which are similar to those of the Orthodox Church

Armentières (ˈɑːmənˌtɪəz; *French* armɑ̃tjɛr) *n* a town in N France: site of battles in both World Wars. Pop: 25 273 (1999)

armeria (ɑːˈmiːrɪə) *n* the generic name for **thrift** (sense 2) [New Latin, from *flos armeriae*, a species of dianthus]

armes parlantes (*French* arm parlɑ̃t) *pl n heraldry* arms using devices to illustrate the name of the bearers, such as a rose and a wall to illustrate the name *Rosewall* [literally: speaking arms]

armet (ˈɑːmɛt) *n* a close-fitting medieval visored helmet with a neck guard [c16 from Old French, from Old Spanish *almete*, from Old French HELMET]

armful (ˈɑːmfʊl) *n, pl* **-fuls** the amount that can be held by one or both arms

armhole (ˈɑːmˌhəʊl) *n* the opening in an article of clothing through which the arm passes and to which a sleeve is often fitted

Armidale (ˈɑːmɪˌdeɪl) *n* a town in Australia, in NE New South Wales: a centre for tourism. Pop: 20 271 (2001)

armiger (ˈɑːmɪdʒə) *n* **1** a person entitled to bear heraldic arms, such as a sovereign or nobleman **2** a squire carrying the armour of a medieval knight [c16 from Medieval Latin: squire, from Latin: armour-bearer, from *arma* arms + *gerere* to carry, bear] ▷ **armigerous** (ɑːˈmɪdʒərəs) *adj*

armillary (ˈɑːmɪlərɪ, ɑːˈmɪlərɪ) *adj* of or relating to bracelets [c17 from New Latin *armillaris*, from Latin *armilla* bracelet]

armillary sphere *n* a model of the celestial sphere consisting of rings representing the relative positions of the celestial equator, ecliptic, etc, used by early astronomers for determining the positions of stars

arming (ˈɑːmɪŋ) *n* **1** the act of taking arms or providing with arms **2** *nautical* a greasy substance, such as tallow, packed into the recess at the bottom of a sounding lead to pick up samples of sand, gravel, etc, from the bottom

Arminian (ɑːˈmɪnɪən) *adj* **1** denoting, relating to, or believing in the Christian Protestant doctrines of Jacobus Arminius (real name *Jacob Harmensen*.; 1560–1609), the Dutch theologian, published in 1610, which rejected absolute predestination and insisted that the sovereignty of God is compatible with free will in man. These doctrines deeply influenced Wesleyan and Methodist theology ▷ *n* **2** a follower of such doctrines ▷ **Ar'minian,ism** *n*

armipotent (ɑːˈmɪpətənt) *adj literary* strong in arms or war [c14 from Latin *armipotēns*, from *arma* arms + *potēns* powerful, from *posse* to be able] ▷ **ar'mipotence** *n*

armistice (ˈɑːmɪstɪs) *n* an agreement between opposing armies to suspend hostilities in order to discuss peace terms; truce [c18 from New Latin *armistitium*, from Latin *arma* arms + *sistere* to stop, stand still]

Armistice Day *n* the anniversary of the signing of the armistice that ended World War I, on Nov 11, 1918, now kept on Remembrance Sunday. See also Remembrance Sunday US name: Veterans Day

armlet (ˈɑːmlɪt) *n* **1** a small arm, as of a lake, the sea, etc **2** a band or bracelet worn round the arm for ornament, identification, etc **3** a very short sleeve on a garment

armoire (ɑːmˈwɑː) *n* a large cabinet, originally used for storing weapons [c16 from French, from Old French *armaire*, from Latin *armārium* chest, closet; see AMBRY]

armor (ˈɑːmə) *n* the US spelling of **armour**

armorial (ɑːˈmɔːrɪəl) *adj* **1** of or relating to heraldry or heraldic arms ▷ *n* **2** a book of coats of arms

Armorica (ɑːˈmɒrɪkə) *n* an ancient name for Brittany

Armorican (ɑːˈmɒrɪkən) *n* **1** a native or inhabitant of Armorica (an ancient name for Brittany) ▷ *adj* **2** of or relating to Armorica

armory (ˈɑːmərɪ) *n, pl* **-mories** the usual US spelling of **armoury**

armour *or US* **armor** (ˈɑːmə) *n* **1** any defensive covering, esp that of metal, chain mail, etc, worn by medieval warriors to prevent injury to the body in battle **2** the protective metal plates on a tank, warship, etc **3** *military* armoured fighting vehicles in general; military units equipped with these **4** any protective covering, such as the shell of certain animals **5** *nautical* the watertight suit of a diver **6** *engineering* permanent protection for an underwater structure **7** heraldic insignia; arms ▷ *vb* **8** (*tr*) to equip or cover with armour [c13 from Old French *armure*, from Latin *armātūra* armour, equipment]

armour-bearer *n history* a retainer who carried the arms or armour of a warrior

armoured *or US* **armored** (ˈɑːməd) *adj* **1** having a protective covering, such as armour or bone **2** comprising units making use of armoured vehicles: *an armoured brigade* **3** (of glass) toughened

armoured car *n* **1** *military* a fast lightly armed and armoured vehicle, mainly used for reconnaissance **2** any vehicle strengthened by armoured plate, esp a security van for transporting cash and valuables

armourer *or US* **armorer** (ˈɑːmərə) *n* **1** a person who makes or mends arms and armour **2** a person employed in the maintenance of small arms and weapons in a military unit

armour plate *n* a tough heavy steel, usually containing chromium, nickel, and molybdenum and often hardened on the surface, used for protecting warships, tanks, etc

armoury *or US* **armory** (ˈɑːmərɪ) *n, pl* **-mouries** *or* **-mories 1** a secure place for the storage of weapons **2** armour generally **3 a** *US* a National Guard base **b** *US* a building in which training in the use of arms and drill takes place; drill hall **c** (*plural*) *Canadian* a building used for training and as headquarters by a reserve unit of the armed forces **4** resources, as of arguments or objections, on which to draw: *they thought they had proved him wrong, but he still had a few weapons in his armoury* **5** *US* a place where arms are made

armpit (ˈɑːmˌpɪt) *n* **1** the small depression beneath the arm where it joins the shoulder. Technical name: **axilla** Related adj: **axillary 2** *slang* an extremely unpleasant place: *the armpit of the Mediterranean*

armrest (ˈɑːmˌrɛst) *n* the part of a chair, sofa, etc, that supports the arm. Sometimes shortened to: **arm**

arms (ɑːmz) *pl n* **1** weapons collectively. See also **small arms 2** military exploits: *prowess in arms* **3** the official heraldic symbols of a family, state, etc, including a shield with distinctive devices, and often supports, a crest, or other insignia **4** bear arms **a** to carry weapons **b** to serve in the armed forces **c** to have a coat of arms **5** in *or* under arms armed and prepared for war **6** lay down one's arms to stop fighting; surrender **7** present arms *military* **a** a position of salute in which the rifle is brought up to a position vertically in line with the body, muzzle uppermost and trigger guard to the fore **b** the command for this drill **8** take (up) arms to prepare to fight **9** to arms! arm yourselves! **10** up in arms indignant; prepared to protest strongly [c13 from Old French *armes*, from Latin *arma*; see ARM²]

arm's-length *adj* **1** lacking intimacy or friendliness, esp when possessing some special connection, such as previous closeness: *we now have an arm's-length relationship* **2** (of commercial transactions) in accordance with market values, disregarding any connection such as common ownership of the companies involved

arms race *n* the continuing competitive attempt by two or more nations each to have available to it more and more powerful weapons than the other(s)

armure (ˈɑːmjʊə) *n* a silk or wool fabric with a small cobbled pattern [c19 from French: ARMOUR]

arm wrestling *n* a contest in which two people sit facing each other each with one elbow resting on a table, clasp hands, and each tries to force the other's arm flat onto the table while keeping his own elbow touching the table

army (ˈɑːmɪ) *n, pl* **-mies 1** the military land forces of a nation **2** a military unit usually consisting of two or more corps with supporting arms and services **3** (*modifier*) of, relating to, or characteristic of an army: *army rations* **4** any large body of people united for some specific purpose **5** a large number of people, animals, etc; multitude [c14 from Old French *armee*, from Medieval Latin *armāta* armed forces; see ARMADA]

army ant *n* any of various mainly tropical American predatory ants of the subfamily *Dorylinae*, which live in temporary nests and travel in vast hordes preying on other animals. Also called: **legionary ant** See also **driver ant**

Army List *n Brit* an official list of all serving commissioned officers of the army and reserve officers liable for recall

army worm *n* **1** the caterpillar of a widely distributed noctuid moth, *Leucania unipuncta*, which travels in vast hordes and is a serious pest of cereal crops in North America **2** any of various similar caterpillars

Arnhem (ˈɑːnəm) *n* a city in the E Netherlands, capital of Gelderland province, on the Rhine: site of a World War II battle. Pop: 142 000 (2003 est)

Arnhem Land *n* a region of N Australia in the N Northern Territory, large areas of which are reserved for native Australians

arnica (ˈɑːnɪkə) *n* **1** any N temperate or arctic plant of the genus *Arnica*, typically having yellow flowers: family *Asteraceae* (composites) **2** the tincture of the dried flower heads of any of these plants, esp *A. montana*, used in treating bruises [c18 from New Latin, of unknown origin]

Arno (ˈɑːnəʊ) *n* a river in central Italy, rising in the Apennines and flowing through Florence to the Ligurian Sea. Length: about 240 km (150 miles)

Arnold (ˈɑːnʰld) *n* a town in N central England, in S Nottinghamshire. Pop: 37 402 (2001)

aroha (ˈɑːrɒhə) *n NZ* love, compassion, or affectionate regard [Māori]

aroid (ˈɛərɔɪd, ˈɛər-) *adj* **1** Also: **araceous** of, relating to, or belonging to the *Araceae*, a family of plants having small flowers massed on a spadix surrounded by a large petaloid spathe. The family includes arum, calla, and anthurium ▷ *n* **2** any plant of the *Araceae* [c19 from New Latin *Arum* type genus + -OID; see ARUM]

aroint thee *or* **ye** (əˈrɔɪnt) *sentence substitute archaic* away! begone! [c17 of unknown origin]

aroma (ə'rəʊmə) *n* **1** a distinctive usually pleasant smell, esp of spices, wines, and plants **2** a subtle pervasive quality or atmosphere [c18 via Latin from Greek: spice]

aromatherapy (ə,rəʊmə'θɛrəpɪ) *n* the use of fragrant essential oils extracted from plants as a treatment in complementary medicine to relieve tension and cure certain minor ailments > a,roma'therapist *n*

aromatic (,ærə'mætɪk) *adj* **1** having a distinctive, usually fragrant smell **2** (of an organic compound) having an unsaturated ring containing alternating double and single bonds, esp containing a benzene ring; exhibiting aromaticity. Compare **aliphatic** ▷ *n* **3** something, such as a plant or drug, giving off a fragrant smell > ,aro'matically *adv*

aromaticity (ə,rəʊmə'tɪsɪtɪ) *n* **1** the property of certain planar cyclic conjugated molecules, esp benzene, of behaving like unsaturated molecules and undergoing substitution reactions rather than addition as a result of delocalization of electrons in the ring **2** the quality or state of having an aroma

aromatize *or* **aromatise** (ə'rəʊmə,taɪz) *vb* **1** (*tr*) to make aromatic **2** to convert (an aliphatic compound) to an aromatic compound > a,romati'zation *or* a,romati'sation *n*

arose (ə'rəʊz) *vb* the past tense of **arise**

around (ə'raʊnd) *prep* **1** situated at various points in: *a lot of shelves around the house* **2** from place to place in: *driving around Ireland* **3** somewhere in or near: *to stay around the house* **4** approximately in: *it happened around 1957, I think* ▷ *adv* **5** surrounding, encircling, or enclosing: *a band around her head* **6** in all directions from a point of reference: *he owns the land for ten miles around* **7** in the vicinity, esp restlessly but idly: *to wait around; stand around* **8** here and there; in no particular area or direction: *dotted around* **9** *informal* (of people) active and prominent in a particular area or profession: *some pop stars are around for only a few years* **10** *informal* present in some place (the exact location being inexact): *he's around here somewhere* **11** *informal* in circulation; available: *that type of phone has been around for some years now* **12** *informal* to many places, so as to have gained considerable experience, often of a worldly or social nature: *he gets around; I've been around* [c17 (rare earlier): from A-² + ROUND]

USAGE In American English, *around* is usually used instead of *round* in adverbial and prepositional senses, except in a few fixed phrases such as *all year round*. The use of *around* in adverbial senses is less common in British English

arouse (ə'raʊz) *vb* **1** (*tr*) to evoke or elicit (a reaction, emotion, or response); stimulate **2** to awaken from sleep > a'rousal *n* > a'rouser *n*

arpa ('ɑːpə) *an internet domain name for* a site concerned with internet infrastructure [c20 acronym of *A(ddress and) R(outing) P(arameter) A(rea)*]

arpeggio (ɑː'pɛdʒɪəʊ) *n, pl* **-gios 1** a chord whose notes are played in rapid succession rather than simultaneously **2** an ascending and descending figuration used in practising the piano, voice, etc [c18 from Italian, from *arpeggiare* to perform on the harp, from *arpa* HARP]

arpent ('ɑːpənt; *French* arpɑ̃) *n* **1** a former French unit of length equal to 190 feet (approximately 58 metres) **2** an old French unit of land area equal to about one acre: still used in Quebec and Louisiana [c16 from Old French, probably from Late Latin *arepennis* half an acre, of Gaulish origin; related to Middle Irish *airchenn* unit of land measure]

arquebus ('ɑːkwɪbəs) *or* **harquebus** *n* a portable long-barrelled gun dating from the 15th century: fired by a wheel-lock or matchlock. Also called: **hackbut, hagbut** [c16 via Old French *harquebuse* from Middle Dutch *hakebusse*, literally: hook gun, from the shape of the butt, from *hake* hook + *busse* box, gun, from Late Latin *busis* box]

arr. *abbreviation for* **1** arranged (by) **2** arrival

arrack *or* **arak** ('ærək) *n* a coarse spirit distilled in various Eastern countries from grain, rice, sugar cane, etc [c17 from Arabic '*araq* sweat, sweet juice, liquor]

arraign (ə'reɪn) *vb* (*tr*) **1** to bring (a prisoner) before a court to answer an indictment **2** to call to account; complain about; accuse [c14 from Old French *araisnier* to speak, accuse, from A-² + *raisnier*, from Vulgar Latin *ratiōnāre* (unattested) to talk, argue, from Latin *ratiō* a reasoning] > ar'raigner *n* > ar'raignment *n*

Arran ('ærən) *n* an island off the SW coast of Scotland, in the Firth of Clyde. Pop: 5045 (2001). Area: 427 sq km (165 sq miles)

arrange (ə'reɪndʒ) *vb* **1** (*tr*) to put into a proper, systematic, or decorative order **2** (*tr; may take a clause as object or an infinitive*) to arrive at an agreement or understanding about; settle **3** (when *intr*, often foll by *for*; when *tr*, may take a clause as object or an infinitive) to make plans or preparations in advance (for something): *we arranged for her to be met* **4** (*tr*) to adapt (a musical composition) for performance in a different way, esp on different instruments **5** (*tr*) to adapt (a play, etc) for broadcasting **6** (*intr*; often foll by *with*) to come to an agreement [c14 from Old French *arangier*, from A-² + *rangier* to put in a row, RANGE] > ar'rangeable *adj* > ar'ranger *n*

arrangement (ə'reɪndʒmənt) *n* **1** the act of arranging or being arranged **2** the form in which things are arranged: *he altered the arrangement of furniture in the room* **3** a thing composed of various ordered parts; the result of arranging: *a flower arrangement* **4** (*often plural*) a preparatory measure taken or plan made; preparation **5** an agreement or settlement; understanding **6** an adaptation of a piece of music for performance in a different way, esp on different instruments from those for which it was originally composed **7** an adaptation (of a play, etc) for broadcasting

arrant ('ærənt) *adj* utter; out-and-out: *an arrant fool* [c14 a variant of ERRANT (wandering, vagabond); sense developed from its frequent use in phrases like *arrant thief* (hence: notorious)] > 'arrantly *adv*

arras ('ærəs) *n* a wall hanging, esp of tapestry

Arras ('ærəs; *French* aras) *n* a town in N France: formerly famous for tapestry; severely damaged in both World Wars. Pop: 40 590 (1999)

array (ə'reɪ) *n* **1** an impressive display or collection **2** an orderly or regular arrangement, esp of troops in battle order **3** *poetic* rich clothing; apparel **4** *maths* a sequence of numbers or symbols in a specified order **5** *maths* a set of numbers or symbols arranged in rows and columns, as in a determinant or matrix **6** *electronics* an arrangement of aerials spaced to give desired directional characteristics, used esp in radar **7** *law* a panel of jurors **8** the arming of military forces **9** *computing* a regular data structure in which individual elements may be located by reference to one or more integer index variables, the number of such indices being the number of dimensions in the array ▷ *vb* (*tr*) **10** to dress in rich attire; adorn **11** to arrange in order (esp troops for battle); marshal **12** *law* to draw up (a panel of jurors) [c13 from Old French *aroi* arrangement, from *arayer* to arrange, of Germanic origin; compare Old English *arǣdan* to make ready] > ar'rayal *n*

arrears (ə'rɪəz) *n* **1** (*sometimes singular*) Also called: **arrearage** (ə'rɪərɪdʒ) something outstanding or owed **2 in arrears** *or* **arrear** late in paying a debt or meeting an obligation [c18 from obsolete *arrear* (adv) behindhand, from Old French *arere*, from Medieval Latin *adretrō*, from Latin *ad* to + *retrō* backwards]

arrest (ə'rɛst) *vb* (*tr*) **1** to deprive (a person) of liberty by taking him into custody, esp under lawful authority **2** to seize (a ship) under lawful authority **3** to slow or stop the development or

progress of (a disease, growth, etc) **4** to catch and hold (one's attention, sight, etc) **5** **arrest judgment** *law* to stay proceedings after a verdict, on the grounds of error or possible error **6** **can't get arrested** *informal* (of a performer) is unrecognized and unsuccessful: *he can't get arrested here but is a megastar in the States* ▷ *n* **7** the act of taking a person into custody, esp under lawful authority **8** the act of seizing and holding a ship under lawful authority **9** the state of being held, esp under lawful authority: *under arrest* **10** Also called: **arrestation** (,ærɛs'teɪʃən) the slowing or stopping of the development or progress of something **11** the stopping or sudden cessation of motion of something: *a cardiac arrest* [c14 from Old French *arester*, from Vulgar Latin *arrestāre* (unattested), from Latin *ad* at, to + *restāre* to stop]

arrestable (ə'rɛstəbəl) *adj* **1** liable to be arrested **2** (of an offence) such that an offender may be arrested without a warrant

arrester (ə'rɛstə) *n* **1** a person who arrests **2** a thing that stops or checks motion, esp a mechanism of wires for slowing aeroplanes as they land on an aircraft carrier

arresting (ə'rɛstɪŋ) *adj* attracting attention; striking > ar'restingly *adv*

arrestment (ə'rɛstmənt) *n Scots law* the seizure of money or property to prevent a debtor paying one creditor in advance of another

arrest of judgment *n law* a stay of proceedings after a verdict, on the grounds of error or possible error

Arretine ('ærɪ,taɪn) *adj* of or relating to Arretium (the ancient Latin name of Arezzo, a city in central Italy)

Arretine ware *n* another term for **Samian ware** (sense 2)

Arretium (æ'riːtɪəm, -'rɛt-) *n* the ancient Latin name of **Arezzo**. > Arretine ('ærɪ,taɪn) *adj*

arrhythmia (ə'rɪðmɪə) *n* any variation from the normal rhythm in the heartbeat [c19 New Latin, from Greek *arrhuthmia*, from A-¹ + *rhuthmos* RHYTHM]

arrière-ban *French* (arjɛrbɑ̃) *n* **1** (in medieval France) a summons to the king's vassals to do military service **2** the vassals so assembled for military service [c16 changed from Old French *herban* call to arms, of Germanic origin; compare Old High German *heriban*, from *heri* army + *ban* summons, BAN²]

arrière-pensée *French* (arjɛrpɑ̃se) *n* an unrevealed thought or intention [c19 literally: behind thought]

Ar Rimal (ɑːr rɪ'mɑːl) *n* another name for **Rub' al Khali**

arris ('ærɪs) *n, pl* **-ris** *or* **-rises** a sharp edge at the meeting of two surfaces at an angle with one another, as at two adjacent sides of a stone block [c17 apparently from Old French *areste* beard of grain, sharp ridge; see ARÊTE]

arrish ('ærɪʃ) *n Southwest English dialect* corn stubble [Old English *ersc*]

arrival (ə'raɪvəl) *n* **1** the act or time of arriving **2** a person or thing that arrives or has arrived **3** the reaching of a condition or objective

arrive (ə'raɪv) *vb* (*intr*) **1** to come to a certain place during or after a journey; reach a destination **2** (foll by *at*) to agree upon; reach: *to arrive at a decision* **3** to occur eventually: *the moment arrived when pretence was useless* **4** *informal* (of a baby) to be born **5** *informal* to attain success or gain recognition [c13 from Old French *ariver*, from Vulgar Latin *arrīpāre* (unattested) to land, reach the bank, from Latin *ad* to + *rīpa* river bank] > ar'river *n*

arrivederci *Italian* (arrive'dertʃi) *sentence substitute* goodbye

arrivisme (,ærɪ'viːzmə; *French* arivism) *n* unscrupulous ambition

arriviste (,ærɪ'viːst; *French* arivist) *n* a person who is unscrupulously ambitious [French: see ARRIVE, -IST]

arroba (ə'rəʊbə) *n, pl* **-bas 1** a unit of weight, approximately equal to 11 kilograms, used in some

Spanish-speaking countries **2** a unit of weight, approximately equal to 15 kilograms, used in some Portuguese-speaking countries **3** a liquid measure used in some Spanish-speaking countries with different values, but in Spain used as a wine-measure, approximately equal to 16 litres [c16 from Spanish, from Arabic *ar-ruḥ'* the quarter (of a quintal)]

arrogant ('ærəgənt) *adj* having or showing an exaggerated opinion of one's own importance, merit, ability, etc; conceited; overbearingly proud: *an arrogant teacher; an arrogant assumption* [c14 from Latin *arrogāre* to claim as one's own; see ARROGATE] > **'arrogance** *n* > **'arrogantly** *adv*

arrogate ('ærə,geɪt) *vb* **1** (*tr*) to claim or appropriate for oneself presumptuously or without justification **2** (*tr*) to attribute or assign to another without justification [c16 from Latin *arrogāre*, from *rogāre* to ask] > **,arro'gation** *n* > **arrogative** (ə'rɒgətɪv) *adj* > **'arro,gator** *n*

arrondissement (*French* arɔ̃dismā) *n* (in France) **1** the largest administrative subdivision of a department **2** a municipal district of certain cities, esp Paris [c19 from *arrondir* to make round, from AB-[1] + -*rondir* from *rond* ROUND]

arrow ('ærəʊ) *n* **1** a long slender pointed weapon, usually having feathers fastened at the end as a balance, that is shot from a bow. Related adj: **sagittal 2** any of various things that resemble an arrow in shape, function, or speed, such as a sign indicating direction or position ▷ See also **arrows** [Old English *arwe*; related to Old Norse *ör*, Gothic *arhvazna*, Latin *arcus* bow, ARCH[1]]

arrowgrass ('ærəʊ,grɑːs) *n* either of two species, **sea arrowgrass** (*Triglochin maritima*) or **marsh arrowgrass** (*T. palustris*), of monocotyledonous perennials having long thin fleshy leaves and spikes of inconspicuous flowers [c18 named from the shape of the fruits when open]

arrowhead ('ærəʊ,hɛd) *n* **1** the pointed tip of an arrow, often removable from the shaft **2** something that resembles the head of an arrow in shape, such as a triangular decoration on garments used to reinforce joins **3** any aquatic herbaceous plant of the genus *Sagittaria*, esp *S. sagittifolia*, having arrow-shaped aerial leaves and linear submerged leaves: family *Alismataceae*

arrowroot ('ærəʊ,ruːt) *n* **1** a white-flowered West Indian plant, *Maranta arundinacea*, whose rhizomes yield an easily digestible starch: family *Marantaceae* **2** the starch obtained from this plant **3** any of several other plants whose rhizomes or roots yield starch

arrows ('ærəʊz) *n* (*functioning as singular*) *Brit* an informal name for **darts**

arrowwood ('ærəʊ,wʊd) *n* any of various trees or shrubs, esp certain viburnums, having long straight tough stems formerly used by North American Indians to make arrows

arrowworm ('ærəʊ,wɜːm) *n* any small marine invertebrate of the genus *Sagitta*, having an elongated transparent body with fins and prehensile oral bristles: phylum *Chaetognatha* (chaetognaths)

arroyo (ə'rɔɪəʊ) *n, pl* -os *chiefly Southwestern US* a steep-sided stream bed that is usually dry except after heavy rain [c19 from Spanish]

Arru Islands ('ɑːruː) *pl n* a variant spelling of **Aru Islands**

arse (ɑːs) *or US and Canadian* **ass** *n slang* **1** the buttocks **2** the anus **3** a stupid person; fool **4** sexual intercourse **5** *Austral* effrontery; cheek **6** **get one's arse into gear** to start to do something seriously and quickly ▷ Also called (for senses 2, 3): **arsehole** ('ɑːs,həʊl) (*US and Canadian*) **asshole**

▎ **USAGE** Dating back at least a thousand years, and taboo till around the middle of the 20th century, this venerable "Anglo-Saxon" word now seems unlikely to cause offence in all but the most formal contexts. Its acceptability has possibly been

▎ helped by such useful verb formations as "to arse about" and "I can't be arsed"

arse *or US and Canadian* **ass about, around** *vb* (*intr, adverb*) *slang* to play the fool; act stupidly, esp in an irritating manner

arse *or US and Canadian* **ass licker** *n slang* a person who curries favour > **'arse-,licking** *or US and Canadian* **'ass-,licking** *adj, n*

arsed (ɑːst) *adj* **be arsed** *slang* to be willing, inclined, or prepared (esp in the phrase **can't be arsed**)

arsenal ('ɑːsənᵊl) *n* **1** a store for arms, ammunition, and other military items **2** a workshop or factory that produces munitions **3** a store of anything regarded as weapons: *an arsenal of destructive arguments* [c16 from Italian *arsenale* dockyard, from the original Venetian *arsenal* dockyard and naval store, from Arabic *dār sin'ah*, from *dār* house + *sin'ah* manufacture]

arsenate ('ɑːsə,neɪt, -nɪt) *n* a salt or ester of arsenic acid, esp a salt containing the ion AsO_4^{3-}

arsenic *n* ('ɑːsnɪk) **1** a toxic metalloid element, existing in several allotropic forms, that occurs principally in realgar and orpiment and as the free element. It is used in transistors, lead-based alloys, and high-temperature brasses. Symbol: As; atomic no: 33; atomic wt: 74.92159; valency: −3, 0, +3, or +5; relative density: 5.73 (grey); melting pt: 817°C at a pressure of $3MN/m^2$ (grey); sublimes at 613°C (grey) **2** a nontechnical name for **arsenic trioxide** ▷ *adj* ('ɑːsɛnɪk) **3** of or containing arsenic, esp in the pentavalent state [c14 from Latin *arsenicum*, from Greek *arsenikon* yellow orpiment, from Syriac *zarnīg* (influenced in form by Greek *arsenikos* virile)]

arsenic acid *n* a white poisonous soluble crystalline solid used in the manufacture of arsenates and insecticides. Formula: H_3AsO_4

arsenical (ɑː'sɛnɪkᵊl) *adj* **1** of or containing arsenic ▷ *n* **2** a drug or insecticide containing arsenic

arsenic trioxide *n* a white poisonous powder used in the manufacture of glass and as an insecticide, rat poison, and weedkiller. Formula: As_2O_3. Also called: **arsenic**

arsenide ('ɑːsə,naɪd) *n* a compound in which arsenic is the most electronegative element

arsenious (ɑː'siːnɪəs) *or* **arsenous** ('ɑːsɪnəs) *adj* of or containing arsenic in the trivalent state

arsenite ('ɑːsɪ,naɪt) *n* a salt or ester of arsenous acid, esp a salt containing the ion AsO_3^{3-}

arsenopyrite (,ɑːsɪnəʊ'paɪraɪt, ɑː,sɛnə-) *n* a white or grey metallic mineral consisting of a sulphide of iron and arsenic that forms monoclinic crystals with an orthorhombic shape: an ore of arsenic. Formula: FeAsS. Also called: **mispickel**

arsey *or* **arsy** ('ɑːsɪ) *adj* arsier, arsiest *Brit slang* aggressive, irritable, or argumentative

arsine ('ɑːsiːn) *n* a colourless poisonous gas used in the manufacture of organic compounds, to dope transistors, and as a military poisonous gas. Formula: AsH_3

arsis ('ɑːsɪs) *n, pl* -ses (-siːz) (in classical prosody) the long syllable or part on which the ictus falls in a metrical foot. Compare **thesis** (sense 6) [c18 via Late Latin from Greek, from *airein* to raise]

ARSM (in Britain) *abbreviation for* Associate of the Royal School of Mines

ars nova ('ɑːz 'nəʊvə) *n* a style of music of the 14th century, characterized by great freedom and variety of rhythm and melody contrasted with the strictness of the music of the 13th century [Latin, literally: new art]

arson ('ɑːsᵊn) *n criminal law* the act of intentionally or recklessly setting fire to another's property or to one's own property for some improper reason [c17 from Old French, from Medieval Latin *ārsiō*, from Latin *ārdēre* to burn; see ARDENT] > **'arsonist** *n*

arsphenamine (ɑːs'fɛnəmɪn, -,miːn) *n* a drug containing arsenic, formerly used in the

treatment of syphilis and related infections

ars poetica ('ɑːz pəʊ'ɛtɪkə) *n* the art of poetry

arsy ('ɑːsɪ) *adj Brit slang* a variant spelling of **arsey**

arsy-versy ('ɑːsɪ'vɜːsɪ) *adv slang* **1** backwards or upside down **2** in reverse [c16 from ARSE + Latin *versus* turned, modelled on compounds like *hurly-burly*]

art[1] (ɑːt) *n* **1 a** the creation of works of beauty or other special significance **b** (*as modifier*): *an art movement* **2** the exercise of human skill (as distinguished from *nature*) **3** imaginative skill as applied to representations of the natural world or figments of the imagination **4 a** the products of man's creative activities; works of art collectively, esp of the visual arts, sometimes also music, drama, dance, and literature **b** (*as modifier*): *an art gallery*. See also **arts, fine art 5** excellence or aesthetic merit of conception or execution as exemplified by such works **6** any branch of the visual arts, esp painting **7** (*modifier*) intended to be artistic or decorative: *art needlework* **8 a** any field using the techniques of art to display artistic qualities: *advertising art* **b** (*as modifier*): *an art film* **9** *journalism* photographs or other illustrations in a newspaper, etc **10** method, facility, or knack: *the art of threading a needle; the art of writing letters* **11** the system of rules or principles governing a particular human activity: *the art of government* **12** artfulness; cunning **13 get something down to a fine art** to become highly proficient at something through practice ▷ See also **arts** [c13 from Old French, from Latin *ars* craftsmanship]

art[2] (ɑːt) *vb archaic* (used with the pronoun *thou*) a singular form of the present tense (indicative mood) of **be** [Old English *eart*, part of *bēon* to BE]

ART *abbreviation for* assisted reproductive technology

-art *suffix forming nouns* a variant of **-ard**

artal ('ɑːtᵊl) *n* a plural of **rotl**

Art Deco ('dɛkəʊ) *n* **a** a style of interior decoration, jewellery, architecture, etc, at its height in the 1930s and characterized by geometrical shapes, stylized natural forms, and symmetrical utilitarian designs adapted to mass production **b** (*as modifier*): *an Art-Deco carpet* [c20 shortened from *art décoratif*, after the *Exposition des arts décoratifs* held in Paris in 1925]

art director *n* a person responsible for the sets and costumes in a film

artefact *or* **artifact** ('ɑːtɪ,fækt) *n* **1** something made or given shape by man, such as a tool or a work of art, esp an object of archaeological interest **2** anything man-made, such as a spurious experimental result **3** *cytology* a structure seen in tissue after death, fixation, staining, etc, that is not normally present in the living tissue [c19 from Latin phrase *arte factum*, from *ars* skill + *facere* to make]

artel (ɑː'tɛl) *n* **1** (in the former Soviet Union) a cooperative union or organization, esp of producers, such as peasants **2** (in prerevolutionary Russia) a quasi-cooperative association of people engaged in the same activity [from Russian *artel'*, from Italian *artieri* artisans, from *arte* work, from Latin *ars* ART[1]]

Artemis ('ɑːtɪmɪs) *n Greek myth* the virgin goddess of the hunt and the moon: the twin sister of Apollo. Roman counterpart: Diana Also called: Cynthia

artemisia (,ɑːtɪ'miːzɪə) *n* any herbaceous perennial plant of the genus *Artemisia*, of the N hemisphere, such as mugwort, sagebrush, and wormwood: family *Asteraceae* (composites) [c14 via Latin from Greek, probably from ARTEMIS]

Arte Povera (*Italian* ,arte po'vera) *n* a style of minimal art originating in Italy in the late 1960s, making use of cheap and commonly available materials such as stones, newspapers etc [c20 Italian, literally: poor art]

arterial (ɑː'tɪərɪəl) *adj* **1** of, relating to, or affecting an artery or arteries: *arterial disease* **2** denoting or relating to the usually bright red

a

reoxygenated blood returning from the lungs or gills that circulates in the arteries **3** being a major route, esp one with many minor branches: *an arterial road* > ar'**terially** *adv*

arterialize *or* **arterialise** (ɑːˈtɪərɪəˌlaɪz) *vb* (*tr*) **1** to change (venous blood) into arterial blood by replenishing the depleted oxygen **2** to vascularize (tissues) **3** to provide with arteries > arˌterialiˈzation *or* arˌterialiˈsation *n*

arterio- *combining form* artery or arteries: *arteriosclerosis* [from Greek; see ARTERY]

arteriography (ɑːˌtɪərɪˈɒɡrəfɪ) *n* the X-ray examination of an artery or arterial system after injection of a contrast medium into the bloodstream

arteriole (ɑːˈtɪərɪˌəʊl) *n anatomy* any of the small subdivisions of an artery that form thin-walled vessels ending in capillaries [c19 from New Latin *arteriola*, from Latin *artēria* ARTERY]

arteriosclerosis (ɑːˌtɪərɪəʊsklɪəˈrəʊsɪs) *n, pl* -**ses** (-siːz) a pathological condition of the circulatory system characterized by thickening and loss of elasticity of the arterial walls. Nontechnical name: **hardening of the arteries** > **arteriosclerotic** (ɑːˌtɪərɪəʊsklɪəˈrɒtɪk) *adj*

arteriovenous (ɑːˌtɪərɪəʊˈviːnəs) *adj* of, relating to, or affecting an artery and a vein

arteritis (ˌɑːtəˈraɪtɪs) *n pathol* inflammation of an artery

artery (ˈɑːtərɪ) *n, pl* -**teries 1** any of the tubular thick-walled muscular vessels that convey oxygenated blood from the heart to various parts of the body. Compare **pulmonary artery, vein 2** a major road or means of communication in any complex system [c14 from Latin *artēria*, related to Greek *aortē* the great artery, AORTA]

artesian well (ɑːˈtiːzɪən, -ʒən) *n* a well sunk through impermeable strata into strata receiving water from an area at a higher altitude than that of the well, so that there is sufficient pressure to force water to flow upwards [c19 from French *artésien*, from Old French *Arteis* Artois, old province, where such wells were common]

Artex (ˈɑːtɛks) *n trademark* a brand of coating for walls and ceilings that gives a textured finish

art form *n* **1** a conventionally established form of artistic composition, such as the symphony or the sonnet **2** a genre or activity viewed or treated as an art form

artful (ˈɑːtfʊl) *adj* **1** cunning or tricky **2** skilful in achieving a desired end **3** *archaic* characterized by skill or art **4** *archaic* artificial > '**artfully** *adv* > '**artfulness** *n*

art house *n* **1** a cinema which specializes in showing films which are not part of the commercial mainstream ▷ *adj* **2 a** of or relating to such films or a cinema which specializes in showing them **b** (*as modifier*): *the surprise art-house hit of the season*

arthralgia (ɑːˈθrældʒə) *n pathol* pain in a joint > ar'**thralgic** *adj*

arthrectomy (ɑːˈθrɛktəmɪ) *n, pl* -**mies** surgical excision of a joint

arthritis (ɑːˈθraɪtɪs) *n* inflammation of a joint or joints characterized by pain and stiffness of the affected parts, caused by gout, rheumatic fever, etc. See also **rheumatoid arthritis** [c16 via Latin from Greek: see ARTHRO-, -ITIS] > **arthritic** (ɑːˈθrɪtɪk) *adj, n*

arthro- *or before a vowel* **arthr-** *combining form* indicating a joint: *arthritis; arthropod* [from Greek *arthron*]

arthrodia (ɑːˈθrəʊdɪə) *n anatomy, zoology* a joint > ar'**throdial** *adj*

arthrography (ɑːˈθrɒɡrəfɪ) *n* the X-ray examination of a joint after injection of a contrast medium into the joint space

arthromere (ˈɑːθrəˌmɪə) *n* any of the segments of the body of an arthropod > ˌarthro'**meric** *adj*

arthroplasty (ˈɑːθrəˌplæstɪ) *n* surgical repair of a diseased joint

arthropod (ˈɑːθrəˌpɒd) *n* any invertebrate of the phylum *Arthropoda*, having jointed limbs, a segmented body, and an exoskeleton made of chitin. The group includes the crustaceans, insects, arachnids, and centipedes > **arthropodous** (ɑːˈθrɒpədəs) *or* ar'**thropodal** *adj*

arthroscope (ˈɑːθrəˌskəʊp) *n* a tubular instrument that is inserted into the capsule of a joint to examine the joint, extract tissue, etc > ˌarthro'**scopic** *adj* > **arthroscopy** (ɑːˈθrɒskəpɪ) *n*

arthrospore (ˈɑːθrəˌspɔː) *n* **1** a sporelike cell of ascomycetous fungi and some algae produced by a breaking of the hyphae **2** a resting sporelike cell produced by some bacteria > ˌarthro'**sporic** *or* ˌarthro'**sporous** *adj*

Arthur (ˈɑːθə) *n* **1** a legendary king of the Britons in the sixth century AD, who led Celtic resistance against the Saxons: possibly based on a historical figure; represented as leader of the Knights of the Round Table at Camelot **2** **not know whether one is Arthur or Martha** *Austral and NZ informal* to be in a state of confusion

Arthurian (ɑːˈθjʊərɪən) *adj* of or relating to King Arthur and his Knights of the Round Table

arti (ˈʌrtɪ) *n Hinduism* a ritual performed in homes and temples in which incense and light is offered to a deity [Hindi]

artic (ɑːˈtɪk) *n informal* short for **articulated lorry**

artichoke (ˈɑːtɪˌtʃəʊk) *n* **1** *Also called:* **globe artichoke** a thistle-like Eurasian plant, *Cynara scolymus*, cultivated for its large edible flower head containing many fleshy scalelike bracts: family *Asteraceae* (composites) **2** the unopened flower head of this plant, which can be cooked and eaten **3** See **Jerusalem artichoke** [c16 from Italian *articiocco*, from Old Spanish *alcarchofa*, from Arabic *al-kharshūf*]

article (ˈɑːtɪkəl) *n* **1** one of a class of objects; item: *an article of clothing* **2** an unspecified or previously named thing, esp a small object: *he put the article on the table* **3** a distinct part of a subject or action **4** a written composition on a subject, often being one of several found in a magazine, newspaper, etc **5** *grammar* a kind of determiner, occurring in many languages including English, that lacks independent meaning but may serve to indicate the specificity of reference of the noun phrase with which it occurs. See also **definite article, indefinite article 6** a clause or section in a written document such as a treaty, contract, statute, etc **7 in articles** formerly, undergoing training, according to the terms of a written contract, in the legal profession **8** (*often capital*) *Christianity* See **article of faith, Thirty-nine Articles 9** *archaic* a topic or subject ▷ *vb* (*tr*) **10** *archaic* to accuse [c13 from Old French, from Latin *articulus* small joint, from *artus* joint]

articled (ˈɑːtɪkəld) *adj* bound by a written contract, such as one that governs a period of training: *an articled clerk*

article numbering *n commerce* See ANA

article of faith *n* **1** *Christianity* any of the clauses or propositions into which a creed or other statement of doctrine is divided **2** a deeply held belief

articles of association *pl n* **1** the constitution and regulations of a registered company as required by the British Companies Acts **2** the document containing these

Articles of Confederation *pl n* the agreement made by the original 13 states in 1777 establishing a confederacy to be known as the United States of America; replaced by the Constitution of 1788

Articles of War *pl n* **1** the disciplinary and legal procedures by which the naval and military forces of Great Britain were bound before the 19th century **2** the regulations of the US army, navy, and air force until the Uniform Code of Military Justice replaced them in 1951

articular (ɑːˈtɪkjʊlə) *adj* of or relating to joints or to the structural components in a joint [c15 from Latin *articulāris* concerning the joints, from *articulus* small joint; see ARTICLE]

articulate *adj* (ɑːˈtɪkjʊlɪt) **1** able to express oneself fluently and coherently: *an articulate lecturer* **2** having the power of speech **3** distinct, clear, or definite; well-constructed: *an articulate voice; an articulate document* **4** *zoology* (of arthropods and higher vertebrates) possessing joints or jointed segments ▷ *vb* (ɑːˈtɪkjʊˌleɪt) **5** to speak or enunciate (words, syllables, etc) clearly and distinctly **6** (*tr*) to express coherently in words **7** (*intr*) *zoology* to be jointed or form a joint **8** (*tr*) to separate into jointed segments [c16 from Latin *articulāre* to divide into joints; see ARTICLE] > ar'**ticulately** *adv* > ar'**ticulateness** *or* ar'**ticulacy** *n*

articulated vehicle *n* a large vehicle (esp a lorry) made in two separate sections, a tractor and a trailer, connected by a pivoted bar

articulation (ɑːˌtɪkjʊˈleɪʃən) *n* **1** the act or process of speaking or expressing in words **2 a** the process of articulating a speech sound **b** the sound so produced, esp a consonant **3** the act or the state of being jointed together **4** the form or manner in which something is jointed **5** *zoology* **a** a joint such as that between bones or arthropod segments **b** the way in which jointed parts are connected **6** *botany* the part of a plant at which natural separation occurs, such as the joint between leaf and stem **7** a joint or jointing > ar'**ticulatory** *adj*

articulator (ɑːˈtɪkjʊˌleɪtə) *n* **1** a person or thing that articulates **2** *phonetics* any vocal organ that takes part in the production of a speech sound. Such organs are of two types: those that can move, such as the tongue, lips, etc (**active articulators**), and those that remain fixed, such as the teeth, the hard palate, etc (**passive articulators**)

articulatory loop *n psychol* a short-term memory system that enables a person to remember short strings of words by rehearsing them repeatedly in his head

articulatory phonetics *n* (*functioning as singular*) the branch of phonetics concerned with the production of speech sounds. Compare **acoustic phonetics, auditory phonetics**

artifact (ˈɑːtɪˌfækt) *n* a variant spelling of **artefact**

artifice (ˈɑːtɪfɪs) *n* **1** a clever expedient; ingenious stratagem **2** crafty or subtle deception **3** skill; cleverness **4** a skilfully contrived device **5** *obsolete* craftsmanship [c16 from Old French, from Latin *artificium* skill, from *artifex* one possessed of a specific skill, from *ars* skill + -*fex*, from *facere* to make]

artificer (ɑːˈtɪfɪsə) *n* **1** a skilled craftsman **2** a clever or inventive designer **3** a serviceman trained in mechanics

artificial (ˌɑːtɪˈfɪʃəl) *adj* **1** produced by man; not occurring naturally: *artificial materials of great strength* **2** made in imitation of a natural product, esp as a substitute; not genuine: *artificial cream* **3** pretended; assumed; insincere: *an artificial manner* **4** lacking in spontaneity; affected: *an artificial laugh* **5** *biology* relating to superficial characteristics not based on the interrelationships of organisms: *an artificial classification* [c14 from Latin *artificiālis* belonging to art, from *artificium* skill, ARTIFICE] > **artificiality** (ˌɑːtɪˌfɪʃɪˈælɪtɪ) *n* > ˌarti'**ficially** *adv*

artificial aid *n mountaineering* another name for **aid** (sense 5)

artificial climbing *n* another name for **aid climbing**

artificial daylight *n physics* artificial light having approximately the same spectral characteristics as natural daylight

artificial disintegration *n physics* radioactive transformation of a substance by bombardment with high-energy particles, such as alpha particles or neutrons

artificial feel *n* a system, used in aircraft that have fully powered control surfaces, providing the pilot with simulated aerodynamic forces on the controls

artificial horizon *n* **1** Also called: **gyro horizon** an aircraft instrument, using a gyroscope, that indicates the aircraft's attitude in relation to the horizontal **2** *astronomy* a level reflecting surface, such as one of mercury, that measures the altitude of a celestial body as half the angle between the body and its reflection

artificial insemination *n* introduction of spermatozoa into the vagina or uterus by means other than sexual union. See **AI, AIH, DI**

artificial intelligence *n* the study of the modelling of human mental functions by computer programs. Abbreviation: **AI**

artificialize *or* **artificialise** (ˌɑːtɪˈfɪʃəˌlaɪz) *vb (tr)* to render artificial

artificial kidney *n med* a mechanical apparatus for performing haemodialysis

artificial language *n* an invented language, esp one intended as an international medium of communication or for use with computers. Compare **natural language**

artificial respiration *n* **1** any of various methods of restarting breathing after it has stopped, by manual rhythmic pressure on the chest, mouth-to-mouth breathing, etc **2** any method of maintaining respiration artificially, as by use of an iron lung

artillery (ɑːˈtɪlərɪ) *n* **1** guns, cannon, howitzers, mortars, etc, of calibre greater than 20 mm **2** troops or military units specializing in using such guns **3** the science dealing with the use of guns **4** devices for discharging heavy missiles, such as catapults or slings [C14 from Old French *artillerie*, from *artillier* to equip with weapons, of uncertain origin]

artilleryman (ɑːˈtɪlərɪmən) *n, pl* **-men** a serviceman who serves in an artillery unit

artillery plant *n* any of various tropical urticaceous plants of the genus *Pilea*, such as *P. microphylla*, all having stamens that discharge their pollen explosively

artiodactyl (ˌɑːtɪəʊˈdæktɪl) *n* **1** any placental mammal of the order *Artiodactyla*, having hooves with an even number of toes; an even-toed ungulate. The order includes pigs, hippopotamuses, camels, deer, cattle, and antelopes ▷ *adj* **2** of, relating to, or belonging to the order *Artiodactyla* [C19 from New Latin *artiodactylus*, from Greek *ártios* even + *daktulos* digit] > ˌ**artioˈdactylous** *adj*

artisan (ˈɑːtɪˌzæn, ˌɑːtɪˈzæn) *n* **1** a skilled workman; craftsman **2** *obsolete* an artist [C16 from French, from Old Italian *artigiano*, from *arte* ART[1]] > **artisanal** (ɑːˈtɪzənᵊl, ˈɑːtɪzənᵊl) *adj*

artist (ˈɑːtɪst) *n* **1** a person who practises or is skilled in an art, esp painting, drawing, or sculpture **2** a person who displays in his work qualities required in art, such as sensibility and imagination **3** a person whose profession requires artistic expertise, esp a designer: *a commercial artist* **4** a person skilled in some task or occupation: *an artist at bricklaying* **5** *obsolete* an artisan **6** *slang* a person devoted to or proficient in something: *a booze artist; a con artist*

artiste (ɑːˈtiːst; *French* artist) *n* **1** an entertainer, such as a singer or dancer **2** a person who is highly skilled in some occupation: *a hair artiste*

artistic (ɑːˈtɪstɪk) *adj* **1** of or characteristic of art or artists **2** performed, made, or arranged decoratively and tastefully; aesthetically pleasing **3** appreciative of and sensitive to beauty in art **4** naturally gifted with creative skill > **arˈtistically** *adv*

artistry (ˈɑːtɪstrɪ) *n* **1** artistic workmanship, ability, or quality **2** artistic pursuits **3** great skill

artless (ˈɑːtlɪs) *adj* **1** free from deceit, guile, or artfulness; ingenuous: *an artless remark* **2** natural, without artifice; unpretentious: *artless elegance* **3** without art or skill > ˈ**artlessly** *adv* > ˈ**artlessness** *n*

art music *n* music written by a composer rather than passed on by oral tradition. Compare **folk music**

Art Nouveau (ɑː nuːˈvəʊ; *French* ar nuvo) *n* **a** a style of art and architecture of the 1890s, characterized by swelling sinuous outlines and stylized natural forms, such as flowers and leaves **b** (*as modifier*): *an Art-Nouveau mirror* [French, literally: new art]

Artois (*French* artwa) *n* a former province of N France

art paper *n* a high-quality type of paper having a smooth coating of china clay or similar substance on it

arts (ɑːts) *pl n* **1 a the** imaginative, creative, and nonscientific branches of knowledge considered collectively, esp as studied academically **b** (*as modifier*): *an arts degree* **2** See **fine art 3** cunning or crafty actions or plots; schemes

Arts and Crafts *pl n* decorative handicraft and design, esp that of the **Arts and Crafts movement**, in late nineteenth-century Britain, which sought to revive medieval craftsmanship

art union *n Austral and NZ* a lottery, often with prizes other than cash

artwork (ˈɑːtˌwɜːk) *n* all the original nontextual matter in a publication, esp the illustrations

arty (ˈɑːtɪ) *adj* **artier, artiest** *informal* having an ostentatious or affected interest in or desire to imitate artists or artistic standards > ˈ**artiness** *n*

arty-crafty *adj informal* affectedly artistic, esp in a homespun or rural style

arty-farty *adj informal* artistic in a pretentious way

Aruba (əˈruːbə; *Dutch* ɑˈryːbaː) *n* an island in the Caribbean, off the NW coast of Venezuela, a dependency of the Netherlands with special status; part of the Netherlands Antilles until 1986. Chief town: Oranjestad. Pop: 100 000 (2003 est). Area: about 181 sq km (70 sq miles)

arugula (əˈruːgjʊlə) *n* another name for **rocket²** (sense 1) [C20 from N Italian dialect]

aruhe (ˈɑːˌruːheɪ) *n, pl* **aruhe** *NZ* the edible root of a fern. Also called: **fern root** [Māori]

Aru Islands *or* **Arru Islands** (ˈɑːruː) *pl n* a group of islands in Indonesia, in the SW Moluccas. Area: about 8500 sq km (3300 sq miles)

arum (ˈɛərəm) *n* **1** any plant of the aroid genus *Arum*, of Europe and the Mediterranean region, having arrow-shaped leaves and a typically white spathe. See also **cuckoopint 2 arum lily** another name for **calla** (sense 1) [C16 from Latin, a variant of *aros* wake-robin, from Greek *aron*]

Arunachal Pradesh (ˌɑːrəˈnɑːkᵊl prəˈdɛʃ) *n* a state in NE India, formed in 1986 from the former Union Territory. Capital: Itanagar. Pop: 1 091 117 (2001). Area: 83 743 sq km (32 648 sq miles). Former name (until 1972): **North East Frontier Agency**

Arundel (ˈærəndəl) *n* a town in S England, in West Sussex: 11th-century castle. Pop: 3297 (2001)

arundinaceous (əˌrʌndɪˈneɪʃəs) *adj botany* resembling a reed [C17 from Latin *harundināceus*, from *harundō* a reed]

aruspex (əˈrʌspɛks) *n, pl* **-pices** (-pɪˌsiːz) a variant spelling of **haruspex**

Aruwimi (ˌɑːruːˈwiːmɪ) *n* a river in NE Democratic Republic of Congo (formerly Zaïre), rising near Lake Albert as the Ituri and flowing west into the River Congo. Length: about 1288 km (800 miles)

ARV *abbreviation for* armed response vehicle

arvo (ˈɑːvəʊ) *n Austral informal* afternoon

-ary *suffix* **1** (*forming adjectives*) of; related to; belonging to: *cautionary; rudimentary* **2** (*forming nouns*) **a** a person connected with or engaged in: *missionary* **b** a thing relating to; a place for: *commentary; aviary* [from Latin *-ārius, -āria, -ārium*]

Aryan *or* **Arian** (ˈɛərɪən) *n* **1** (in Nazi ideology) a Caucasian of non-Jewish descent, esp of the Nordic type **2** a member of any of the peoples supposedly descended from the Indo-Europeans, esp a speaker of an Iranian or Indic language in ancient times ▷ *adj* **3** of, relating to, or characteristic of an Aryan or Aryans ▷ *adj, n* **4** *archaic* Indo-European [C19 from Sanskrit *ārya* of noble birth]

Aryanize *or* **Aryanise** (ˈɛərɪəˌnaɪz) *vb (tr)* (in Nazi ideology) to purge (politics and society) of all non-Aryan elements or people; make characteristically Aryan

aryl (ˈærɪl) *n* **1** (*modifier*) *chem* of, consisting of, or containing an aromatic group: *aryl group or radical* **2** an organometallic compound in which a metal atom is bound to an aryl group [C20 from AR(OMATIC) + -YL]

arytenoid *or* **arytaenoid** (ˌærɪˈtiːnɔɪd) *adj also* **arytenoidal 1** denoting either of two small cartilages of the larynx that are attached to the vocal cords **2** denoting any of three small muscles of the larynx that narrow the space between the vocal cords ▷ *n* **3** an arytenoid cartilage or muscle [C18 from New Latin *arytaenoīdes*, from Greek *arutainoeidēs* shaped like a ladle, from *arutaina* ladle]

as¹ (æz; *unstressed* əz) *conj (subordinating)* **1** (*often preceded by just*) while; when; at the time that: *he caught me as I was leaving* **2** in the way that: *dancing as only she can* **3** that which; what: *I did as I was told* **4** (of) which fact, event, etc (referring to the previous statement): *to become wise, as we all know, is not easy* **5 as it were** in a way; so to speak; as if it were really so **6 as you were a** a military command to withdraw an order, return to the previous position, etc **b** a statement to withdraw something just said **7** since; seeing that: *as you're in charge here, you'd better tell me where to wait* **8** in the same way that: *he died of cancer, as his father had done* **9** in spite of the extent to which: *intelligent as you are, I suspect you will fail* **10** for instance: *capital cities, as London* ▷ *adv, conj* **11 a** used correlatively before an adjective or adverb and before a noun phrase or a clause to indicate identity of extent, amount, etc: *she is as heavy as her sister; she is as heavy now as she used to be* **b** used with this sense after a noun phrase introduced by *the same*: *she is the same height as her sister* ▷ *prep* **12** in the role of; being: *as his friend, I am probably biased* **13 as for** *or* **to** with reference to: *as for my past, I'm not telling you anything* **14 as from** *or* **of** *formal* (in expressions of time) from: *fares on all routes will rise as from January 11* **15 as if** *or* **though** as it would be if: *he talked as if he knew all about it* **16 as (it) is** in the existing state of affairs: *as it is, I shall have difficulty finishing all this work, without any more* **17 as per** See **per** (sense 3) **18 as regards** See **regard** (sense 6) **19 as such** See **such** (sense 3) **20 such as** See **such** (sense 5) **21 as was** in a previous state **22 as well** See **well¹** (sense 13) **23 as yet** up to now; so far: *I have received no compensation as yet* [Old English *alswā* likewise; see ALSO]

USAGE See at **like**

as² (æs) *n* **1** an ancient Roman unit of weight approximately equal to 1 pound troy (373 grams) **2** the standard monetary unit and copper coin of ancient Rome [C17 from Latin *ās* unity, probably of Etruscan origin]

as³ *the internet domain name for* American Samoa

As *symbol for* **1** *chem* arsenic **2** altostratus

AS *abbreviation for* **1** Also: A.S. Anglo-Saxon **2** antisubmarine **3** Australian Standards

ASA *abbreviation for* **1** (in Britain) Amateur Swimming Association **2** (in Britain) **Advertising Standards Authority 3** (in the US) American Standards Association

ASA/BS *abbrev* an obsolete expression of the speed of a photographic film, replaced by the ISO rating [C20 from *American Standards Association/British Standard*]

asafoetida *or* **asafetida** (ˌæsəˈfɛtɪdə) *n* a bitter resin with an unpleasant onion-like smell, obtained from the roots of some umbelliferous plants of the genus *Ferula*: formerly used as a carminative, antispasmodic, and expectorant [C14 from Medieval Latin, from *asa* gum (compare Persian *azā* mastic) + Latin *foetidus* evil-smelling, FETID]

asalam-wa-leikum (ˈʌsəˈlɑːmwɑːˈleɪkəm) *interj* a salutation used in India [Urdu]

a

asana ('ɑːsənə) *n* any of various postures in yoga. See also **hatha yoga** [Sanskrit]

a.s.a.p. *abbreviation for* as soon as possible

asarabacca (ˌæsərə'bækə) *n* a perennial evergreen Eurasian plant, *Asarum europaeum*, having kidney-shaped leaves and a single brownish flower: family *Aristolochiaceae*

asarum ('æsərəm) *n* the dried strong-scented root of the wild ginger plant: a flavouring agent and source of an aromatic oil used in perfumery, formerly in medicine [c19 via New Latin from Latin: hazelwort, from Greek *asaron*]

ASB *abbreviation for* **1** (in Britain) Accounting Standards Board **2** Alternative Service Book (of the Church of England)

Asben ('æs'bɛn) *n* another name for **Aïr** (region of the Sahara)

asbestos (æs'bɛstɒs, -təs) *n* **a** any of the fibrous amphibole and serpentine minerals, esp chrysotile and tremolite, that are incombustible and resistant to chemicals. It was formerly widely used in the form of fabric or board as a heat-resistant structural material **b** (*as modifier*): *asbestos matting* [c14 (originally applied to a mythical stone the heat of which could not be extinguished): via Latin from Greek: from *asbestos* inextinguishable, from A-¹ + *sbennunai* to extinguish] > as'bestine *adj*

asbestosis (ˌæsbɛs'təʊsɪs) *n* inflammation of the lungs resulting from chronic inhalation of asbestos particles

ASBO ('æzˌbəʊ) *n acronym for Brit* anti-social behaviour order: a civil order made against a persistently anti-social individual which restricts his or her activities or movements, a breach of which results in criminal charges

Ascanius (æ'skeɪnɪəs) *n Roman myth* the son of Aeneas and Creusa; founder of Alba Longa, mother city of Rome. Also called: **Iulus**

ASCAP ('æskæp) *n acronym for* American Society of Composers, Authors, and Publishers

ascariasis (ˌæskə'raɪəsɪs) *n* infestation of the intestines with the roundworm *Ascaris lumbricoides*, causing abdominal pain, nausea and vomiting, weight loss, etc

ascarid ('æskərɪd) *n* any parasitic nematode worm of the family *Ascaridae*, such as the common roundworm of man and pigs [c14 from New Latin *ascaridae*, from Greek *askarides*, plural of *askaris*]

ascend (ə'sɛnd) *vb* **1** to go or move up (a ladder, hill, slope, etc); mount; climb **2** (*intr*) to slope or incline upwards **3** (*intr*) to rise to a higher point, level, degree, etc **4** to follow (a river) upstream towards its source **5** to trace (a genealogy, etc) back in time **6** to sing or play (a scale, arpeggio, etc) from the lower to higher notes **7 ascend the throne** to become king or queen [c14 from Latin *ascendere*, from *scandere*]

ascendancy, ascendency (ə'sɛndənsɪ) *or* **ascendance, ascendence** *n* the condition of being dominant, esp through superior economic or political power

ascendant *or* **ascendent** (ə'sɛndənt) *adj* **1** proceeding upwards; rising **2** dominant, superior, or influential **3** *botany* another term for **ascending** ▷ *n* **4** *rare* an ancestor **5** a position or condition of dominance, superiority or control **6** *astrology* (*sometimes capital*) **a** a point on the ecliptic that rises on the eastern horizon at a particular moment and changes as the earth rotates on its axis **b** the sign of the zodiac containing this point **7 in the ascendant** increasing in influence, prosperity, etc

ascender (ə'sɛndə) *n* **1** *printing* **a** the part of certain lower-case letters, such as *b* or *h*, that extends above the body of the letter **b** any letter having such a part **2** a person or thing that ascends **3** another word for **ascendeur**

ascendeur (*French* asɑ̃dœr) *n mountaineering* a metal grip that is threaded on a rope and can be alternately tightened and slackened as an aid to climbing the rope: used attached to slings for the feet and waist. Also called: **ascender** [c20]

ascending (ə'sɛndɪŋ) *adj* **1** moving upwards; rising **2** *botany* sloping or curving upwards: *the ascending stem of a vine*

ascension (ə'sɛnʃən) *n* **1** the act of ascending **2** *astronomy* the rising of a star above the horizon > as'censional *adj*

Ascension¹ (ə'sɛnʃən) *n New Testament* the passing of Jesus Christ from earth into heaven (Acts 1:9)

Ascension² (ə'sɛnʃən) *n* an island in the S Atlantic, northwest of St Helena: uninhabited until claimed by Britain in 1815. Pop: 1122 (2003 est). Area: 88 sq km (34 sq miles)

Ascension Day *n Christianity* the 40th day after Easter, when the Ascension of Christ into heaven is celebrated

ascensionist (ə'sɛnʃənɪst) *n mountaineering* a person who has completed a mountain ascent, esp a notable one

Ascensiontide (ə'sɛnʃənˌtaɪd) *n* the ten days from Ascension Day to the day before Whit Sunday

ascent (ə'sɛnt) *n* **1** the act of ascending; climb or upward movement: *the ascent of hot gases* **2** an upward slope; incline or gradient **3** movement back through time, as in tracing of earlier generations (esp in the phrase **line of ascent**)

ascertain (ˌæsə'teɪn) *vb* (*tr*) **1** to determine or discover definitely **2** *archaic* to make certain [c15 from Old French *acertener* to make certain] > ˌascer'tainable *adj* > ˌascer'tainably *adv* > ˌascer'tainment *n*

ascesis (ə'siːsɪs) *n, pl* -ses (-siːz) the exercise of self-discipline [c19 from Greek, from *askein* to exercise]

ascetic (ə'sɛtɪk) *n* **1** a person who practises great self-denial and austerities and abstains from worldly comforts and pleasures, esp for religious reasons **2** (in the early Christian Church) a monk ▷ *adj also* as'cetical **3** rigidly abstinent or abstemious; austere **4** of or relating to ascetics or asceticism **5** intensely rigorous in religious austerities [c17 from Greek *askētikos*, from *askētēs*, from *askein* to exercise] > as'cetically *adv*

asceticism (ə'sɛtɪˌsɪzəm) *n* **1** the behaviour, discipline, or outlook of an ascetic, esp of a religious ascetic **2** the principles of ascetic practices, esp in the early Christian Church **3** the theory and system of ascetic practices

Aschaffenburg (*German* a'ʃafənbʊrk) *n* a city in Germany, on the River Main in Bavaria: seat of the Imperial Diet (1447); ceded to Bavaria in 1814. Pop: 68 607 (2003 est)

asci ('æsaɪ, 'æskaɪ) *n* the plural of **ascus**

ascidian (ə'sɪdɪən) *n* **1** any minute marine invertebrate animal of the class *Ascidiacea*, such as the sea squirt, the adults of which are degenerate and sedentary: subphylum *Tunicata* (tunicates) **2 ascidian tadpole** the free-swimming larva of an ascidian, having a tadpole-like tail containing the notochord and nerve cord ▷ *adj* **3** of, relating to, or belonging to the *Ascidiacea*

ascidium (ə'sɪdɪəm) *n, pl* -cidia (-'sɪdɪə) part of a plant that is shaped like a pitcher, such as the modified leaf of the pitcher plant [c18 from New Latin, from Greek *askidion* a little bag, from *askos* bag]

ASCII ('æskiː) *n acronym for* American standard code for information interchange: a computer code for representing alphanumeric characters

ascites (ə'saɪtiːz) *n, pl* **ascites** accumulation of serous fluid in the peritoneal cavity [c14 from Latin: a kind of dropsy, from Greek *askitēs*, from *askos* wineskin] > **ascitic** (ə'sɪtɪk) *adj*

asclepiadaceous (æˌskliːpɪə'deɪʃəs) *adj* of, relating to, or belonging to the *Asclepiadaceae*, a family of mostly tropical and subtropical flowering plants, including the milkweed and swallowwort, having pollen in the form of a waxy mass (pollinium): now usually regarded as a subfamily of the *Apocynaceae* [c19 from New Latin *Asclēpias* genus name, from Latin, from Greek *asklēpias*, named after **Asclepius**]

Asclepiadean (æˌskliːpɪə'diːən) *prosody* ▷ *adj* **1** of or relating to a type of classical verse line consisting of a spondee, two or three choriambs, and an iamb ▷ *n* **2** Also called: **Asclepiad** an Asclepiadean verse [c17 via Latin from Greek *Asklēpiadēs* (about 270 BC), who invented the verse form]

asclepias (ə'skliːpɪəs) *n* any plant of the perennial mostly tuberous genus *Asclepias*; some are grown as garden or greenhouse plants for their showy orange-scarlet or purple flowers: family *Asclepiadaceae*. Sometimes called: **milkweed** [Greek *asklēpias* swallowwort]

Asclepius (ə'skliːpɪəs) *n Greek myth* a god of healing; son of Apollo. Roman counterpart: Aesculapius (ˌiːskjʊ'leɪpɪəs)

asco- *combining form* indicating a bladder or ascus: *ascomycete* [from Greek *askos* bladder]

ascocarp ('æskəˌkɑːp) *n* (in some ascomycetous fungi) a globular structure containing the asci. See **apothecium, perithecium**

ascogonium (ˌæskə'gəʊnɪəm) *n, pl* -nia (-nɪə) a female reproductive body in some ascomycetous fungi in which, after fertilization, the asci develop

Ascoli Piceno (*Italian* 'askoli pi'tʃɛːno) *n* a town in E central Italy, in the Marches: capital of the Roman province of Picenum; site of the massacre of all its Roman citizens in the Social War in 90 BC. Pop: 51 375 (2001). Latin name: Asculum Picenum ('æskjʊləm paɪ'siːnəm)

ascomycete (ˌæskəmaɪ'siːt) *n* any fungus of the phylum *Ascomycota* (formerly class *Ascomycetes*) in which the spores (ascospores) are formed inside a club-shaped cell (ascus). The group includes yeast, penicillium, aspergillus, truffles, and certain mildews > ˌascomy'cetous *adj*

ascorbic acid (ə'skɔːbɪk) *n* a white crystalline vitamin present in plants, esp citrus fruits, tomatoes, and green vegetables. A deficiency in the diet of man leads to scurvy. Formula: $C_6H_8O_6$. Also called: **vitamin C** [c20 *ascorbic* from A-¹ + SCORB(UT)IC]

ascospore ('æskəˌspɔː) *n* one of the spores (usually eight in number) that are produced in an ascus

ascot ('æskət) *n* a cravat with wide square ends, usually secured with an ornamental stud [c20 named after **Ascot**, where it was probably first worn]

Ascot ('æskət) *n* a town in S England, in Bracknell Forest unitary authority, Berkshire: noted for its horse-race meetings, esp **Royal Ascot**, a four-day meeting held in June. Pop: 8755 (2001)

ascribe (ə'skraɪb) *vb* (*tr*) **1** to credit or assign, as to a particular origin or period: *to ascribe parts of a play to Shakespeare* **2** to attribute as a quality; consider as belonging to: *to ascribe beauty to youth* [c15 from Latin *ascrībere* to enrol, from *ad* in addition + *scrībere* to write] > as'cribable *adj*

▍ USAGE *Ascribe* is sometimes wrongly used where *subscribe* is meant: *I do not subscribe* (not *ascribe*) *to this view*

ascription (ə'skrɪpʃən) *or* **adscription** (əd'skrɪpʃən) *n* **1** the act of ascribing **2** a statement ascribing something to someone, esp praise to God [c16 from Latin *ascrīptiō*, from *ascrībere* to ASCRIBE]

ascus ('æskəs) *n, pl* **asci** ('æsaɪ, 'æskaɪ) a saclike structure that produces (usually) eight ascospores during sexual reproduction in ascomycetous fungi such as yeasts and mildews [c19 from New Latin, from Greek *askos* bag]

ASDE *abbreviation for* Airport Surface Detection Equipment: a radar system that is used by aircraft controllers to assist in the safe manoeuvring of aircraft on the ground

asdic ('æzdɪk) *n* an early form of **sonar** [c20 from A(nti-)S(ubmarine) D(etection) I(nvestigation) C(ommittee)]

-ase *suffix forming nouns* indicating an enzyme: *oxidase* [abstracted from DIASTASE]

ASEAN ('æsɪ,æn) *n acronym for* Association of Southeast Asian Nations

aseismic (eɪ'saɪzmɪk) *adj* **1** denoting a region free of earthquakes **2** (*not in technical use*) denoting a region free of all but a few small earthquakes **3** (of buildings, etc) designed to withstand earthquakes

aseity (eɪ'siːɪtɪ) *n philosophy* existence derived from itself, having no other source [c17 from Medieval Latin *aseitas*, from Latin *ā* from + *sē* oneself]

asepalous (æ'sɛpələs) *adj* (of a plant or flower) having no sepals

asepsis (ə'sɛpsɪs, eɪ-) *n* **1** the state of being free from living pathogenic organisms **2** the methods of achieving a germ-free condition

aseptate (eɪ'sɛpteɪt) *adj biology* not divided into cells or sections by septa

aseptic (ə'sɛptɪk, eɪ-) *adj* **1** free from living pathogenic organisms; sterile **2** aiming to achieve a germ-free condition

asexual (eɪ'sɛksjʊəl, æ-) *adj* **1** having no apparent sex or sex organs **2** (of reproduction) not involving the fusion of male and female gametes, as in vegetative reproduction, fission, or budding ▷ **asexuality** (eɪ,sɛksjʊ'ælɪtɪ, æ-) *n* ▷ **a'sexually** *adv*

Asgard ('æsgɑːd) *or* **Asgarth** ('æsgɑːθ) *n Norse myth* the dwelling place of the principal gods, the Aesir

ash¹ (æʃ) *n* **1** the nonvolatile products and residue formed when matter is burnt **2** any of certain compounds formed by burning. See **soda ash 3** fine particles of lava thrown out by an erupting volcano **4** a light silvery grey colour, often with a brownish tinge ▷ See also **ashes** Related adj: **cinereous** [Old English *æsce*; related to Old Norse, Old High German *aska*, Gothic *azgō*, Latin *aridus* dry]

ash² (æʃ) *n* **1** any oleaceous tree of the genus *Fraxinus*, esp *F. excelsior* of Europe and Asia, having compound leaves, clusters of small greenish flowers, and winged seeds **2** the close-grained durable wood of any of these trees, used for tool handles, etc **3** any of several trees resembling the ash, such as the mountain ash **4** *Austral* any of several Australian trees resembling the ash, esp of the eucalyptus genus [Old English *æsc*; related to Old Norse *askr*, Old Saxon, Old High German *ask*, Lithuanian *uosis*]

ash³ (æʃ) *n* the digraph æ, as in Old English, representing a front vowel approximately like that of the *a* in Modern English *hat*. The character is also used to represent this sound in the International Phonetic Alphabet

ASH (æʃ) *n* (in Britain) ▷ *acronym for* Action on Smoking and Health

ashamed (ə'ʃeɪmd) *adj* (*usually postpositive*) **1** overcome with shame, guilt, or remorse **2** (foll by *of*) suffering from feelings of inferiority or shame in relation to (a person, thing, or deed) **3** (foll by *to*) unwilling through fear of humiliation, shame, etc [Old English *āscamod*, past participle of *āscamian* to shame, from *scamu* SHAME] ▷ **ashamedly** (ə'ʃeɪmɪdlɪ) *adv*

Ashanti (ə'ʃæntɪ) *n* **1** an administrative region of central Ghana: former native kingdom, suppressed by the British in 1900 after four wars. Capital: Kumasi. Pop: 3 187 607 (2000). Area: 24 390 sq km (9417 sq miles) **2** (*pl* -ti *or* -tis) a native or inhabitant of Ashanti

A shares *pl n Brit* those ordinary shares in a company which carry restricted voting rights or other restrictions

ash blond *n* **1 a** a very light blond colour **b** (as *adjective*): *ash-blond hair* **2** a person whose hair is this colour ▷ Also: **ash blonde** ▷ *fem*

Ashby-de-la-Zouch (,æʃbɪ,dələ'zuːʃ) *n* a town in central England, in Leicestershire: Mary, Queen of Scots, was imprisoned (1569) in the castle. Pop: 11 409 (2001)

ash can *n* a US word for **dustbin** Also called: garbage can, ash bin, trash can

Ash Can School *n* a group of US painters including Robert Henri and later George Bellows, founded in 1907, noted for their depiction of the sordid aspects of city life

Ashdod ('æʃdɒd) *n* a town in central Israel, on the Mediterranean coast: an important city in the Philistine Empire, with its artificial harbour (1961) it is now a major port. Pop: 192 000 (2003 est)

ashen¹ ('æʃən) *adj* **1** drained of colour; pallid **2** consisting of or resembling ashes **3** of a pale greyish colour

ashen² ('æʃən) *adj* of, relating to, or made from the ash tree or its timber

Asher ('æʃə) *n* the son of Jacob and ancestor of one of the 12 tribes of Israel

ashes ('æʃɪz) *pl n* **1** ruins or remains, as after destruction or burning: *the city was left in ashes* **2** the remains of a human body after cremation

Ashes ('æʃɪz) *pl n* **the** a cremated cricket stump in a pottery urn now preserved at Lord's. Victory or defeat in test matches between England and Australia is referred to as winning, losing, or retaining the Ashes [from the mock obituary of English cricket in *The Times* in 1882 after a great Australian victory at the Oval, in which it was said that the body would be cremated and the ashes taken to Australia]

ashet ('æʃɪt) *n Scot and northern English dialect* a shallow oval dish or large plate [c16 from French *assiette*]

Ashford ('æʃfəd) *n* a market town in SE England, in central Kent. Pop: 58 936 (2001)

Ashkenazi (,æʃkə'nɑːzɪ) *n, pl* -zim (-zɪm) **1** (*modifier*) of or relating to the Jews of Germany and E Europe **2** a Jew of German or E European descent **3** the pronunciation of Hebrew used by these Jews ▷ Compare **Sephardi** [c19 Late Hebrew, from Hebrew *Ashkenaz*, the son of Gomer (Genesis 10:3; I Chronicles 1:6), a descendant of Noah through Japheth, and hence taken to be identified with the ancient Ascanians of Phrygia and, in the medieval period, the Germans]

ashkey ('æʃkiː) *n* the winged fruit of the ash

Ashkhabad (*Russian* aʃxa'bat) *or* **Ashgabat** ('ɑːʃgəbæt; *Turkmen* aʃga'bat) *n* the capital of Turkmenistan. Pop: 598 000 (2005 est)

ashlar *or* **ashler** ('æʃlə) *n* **1** a block of hewn stone with straight edges for use in building **2** Also called: **ashlar veneer** a thin dressed stone with straight edges, used to face a wall **3** masonry made of ashlar [c14 from Old French *aisselier* crossbeam, from *ais* board, from Latin *axis* axletree; see AXIS¹]

ashlaring ('æʃlərɪŋ) *n* **1** ashlars collectively **2** a number of short upright boards forming the wall of a garret, cutting off the acute angle between the rafters and the floor

Ashmolean Museum (æʃ'məʊlɪən, ,æʃmə'lɪən) *n* a museum, attached to Oxford University and founded in 1683, noted for its paintings and archaeological collections [c19 named after Elias Ashmole (1617–92), English antiquary who donated the first collection]

ashore (ə'ʃɔː) *adv* **1** towards or onto land from the water: *we swam ashore* ▷ *adj* (*postpositive*) ▷ *adv* **2** on land, having come from the water: *a day ashore*

ashplant ('æʃ,plɑːnt) *n* a walking stick made from an ash sapling

ashram ('æʃrəm, 'ɑːʃ-) *n* **1** a religious retreat or community where a Hindu holy man lives **2** a house that provides accommodation for destitute people [from Sanskrit *āśrama*, from *ā-* near + *śrama* religious exertion]

Ashton-under-Lyne (laɪn) *n* a town in NW England, in Tameside unitary authority, Greater Manchester. Pop: 43 236 (2001)

Ashtoreth ('æʃtə,rɛθ) *n Old Testament* an ancient Semitic fertility goddess, identified with Astarte and Ishtar

ashtray ('æʃ,treɪ) *n* a receptacle for tobacco ash, cigarette butts, etc

Ashur ('æʃʊə) *n* a variant spelling of **Assur**

Ashura ('æʃʊ,rɑː) *n Islam* a Shiah festival observed on the tenth day of Muharram in the Islamic calendar to commemorate the death of the martyr Imam Hussein bin Ali at the Battle of Karbala in 61 AH (680 AD) [c21 from Arabic *'Āshūrā*]

Ash Wednesday *n* the first day of Lent, named from the practice of Christians of placing ashes on their heads as a sign of penitence

ashy ('æʃɪ) *adj* ashier, ashiest **1** of a pale greyish colour; ashen **2** consisting of, covered with, or resembling ash

'Asi ('æsɪ) *n* the Arabic name for the **Orontes**

Asia ('eɪʃə, 'eɪʒə) *n* the largest of the continents, bordering on the Arctic Ocean, the Pacific Ocean, the Indian Ocean, and the Mediterranean and Red Seas in the west. It includes the large peninsulas of Asia Minor, India, Arabia, and Indochina and the island groups of Japan, Indonesia, the Philippines, and Ceylon (Sri Lanka); contains the mountain ranges of the Hindu Kush, Himalayas, Pamirs, Tian Shan, Urals, and Caucasus, the great plateaus of India, Iran, and Tibet, vast plains and deserts, and the valleys of many large rivers including the Mekong, Irrawaddy, Indus, Ganges, Tigris, and Euphrates. Pop: 3 917 508 000 (2005 est). Area: 44 391 162 sq km (17 139 445 sq miles)

asiago (,æzɪ'ɑːgəʊ) *n* either of two varieties (ripened or fresh) of a cow's-milk cheese produced in NE Italy [Italian]

Asia Minor *n* the historical name for **Anatolia**

Asian ('eɪʃən, 'eɪʒən) *adj* **1** of or relating to Asia or to any of its peoples or languages ▷ *n* **2** a native or inhabitant of Asia or a descendant of one

▌ **USAGE** The use of *Asian* or *Asiatic* as a noun can be offensive and should be avoided

Asian flu *n* a type of influenza recurring in worldwide epidemics, caused by a virus (A2 strain or subsequent antigenic variants), which apparently originated in China in 1957

Asian pear *n* **1** a tropical pear tree, esp any of several varieties of Japanese pear *Pyrus serotina* **2** Also called: nashi the fruit of the Japanese pear, which resembles a large yellow apple, has crisp juicy flesh, and is cultivated in Japan, Korea, the US, and New Zealand

Asian semi-longhair (-'lɒŋ,heə) *n* another name for **Tiffanie**

Asian shorthair ('ʃɔːt,heə) *n* a generic term for a group of breeds of short-haired cat of Burmese type, including the Bombay

Asiatic (,eɪʃɪ'ætɪk, -zɪ-) *n, adj* another word for **Asian**

▌ **USAGE** See at **Asian**

Asiatic beetle *n* a Japanese scarabaeid beetle, *Anomala orientalis*, introduced to Hawaii and the northeastern US: a serious pest of sugar cane and cereal crops because it destroys the roots

Asiatic cholera *n* another name for **cholera**

aside (ə'saɪd) *adv* **1** on or to one side: *they stood aside to let him pass* **2** out of hearing; in or into seclusion: *he took her aside to tell her of his plan* **3** away from oneself: *he threw the book aside* **4** out of mind or consideration: *he put aside all fears* **5** in or into reserve: *to put aside money for old age* **6** aside from (*preposition*) chiefly US and Canadian **a** besides: *he has money aside from his possessions* **b** except for: *he has nothing aside from the clothes he stands in*. Compare **apart** (sense 7) ▷ *n* **7** something spoken by an actor, intended to be heard by the audience, but not by the others on stage **8** any confidential statement spoken in undertones **9** a digression

A-side *n* the side of a gramophone record regarded as the more important one

Asimovian (,æzɪ'məʊvɪən) *adj* referring to or reminiscent of the work of the prolific US science fiction writer Isaac Asimov (1920–1992)

asinine ('æsɪ,naɪn) *adj* **1** obstinate or stupid **2**

a

resembling an ass [c16 from Latin *asinīnus*, from *asinus* ASS[1]] > 'asi,ninely *adv* > asininity (,æsɪ'nɪnɪtɪ) *n*

ASIO *abbreviation for* Australian Security Intelligence Organization

Asir (æ'sɪə) *n* a region of SW Saudi Arabia, in the Southern Province on the Red Sea: under Turkish rule until 1933. Area: 81 000 sq km (31 000 sq miles)

-asis *suffix forming nouns* a variant of **-iasis**

A sizes or **A series** *n* a series of paper sizes approved by the International Standards Organization, running from 2AO to A7, each size (defined in mm) being half as large as the one preceding it, as follows: **2AO**,1189 × 1682; **AO**, 841 × 1189; **A1**, 594 × 841; **A2**, 420 × 594; **A3**, 297 × 420; **A4**, 210 × 297; **A5**, 148 × 210; **A6**, 105 × 148; **A7**, 74 × 105

ask (ɑːsk) *vb* **1** (often foll by *about*) to put a question (to); request an answer (from): *she asked (him) about God* **2** (tr) to inquire about: *she asked him the time of the train; she asked the way* **3** (tr) to direct or put (a question) **4** (*may take a clause as object or an infinitive;* often foll by *for*) to make a request or demand: *she asked (him) for information; they asked for a deposit* **5** (tr) to demand or expect (esp in the phrases **ask a lot of, ask too much of**) **6** (tr) Also: **ask out, ask over** to request (a person) politely to come or go to a place; invite: *he asked her to the party* **7** (tr) to need; require: *the job asks both time and patience* **8** (tr) *archaic* to proclaim (marriage banns) ▷ *n* **9** a **big** or **tough ask** *Austral and NZ informal* a task which is difficult to fulfil ▷ See also **ask after, ask for** [Old English *āscian*; related to Old Frisian *āskia*, Old Saxon *ēscon*, Old High German *eiscōn*] > 'asker *n*

Ask (ɑːsk) *n* *Norse myth* the first man, created by the gods from an ash tree

ask after or *Scot* **ask for** *vb* (*preposition*) to make inquiries about the health of (someone): *he asked after her mother*

askance (ə'skæns) or **askant** (ə'skænt) *adv* **1** with an oblique glance **2** with doubt or mistrust [c16 of unknown origin]

askari (as'kɑːrɪ) *n* (in East Africa) a soldier or policeman [c19 from Arabic: soldier]

askew (ə'skjuː) *adv, adj* at an oblique angle; towards one side; awry

ask for *vb* (*preposition*) **1** to try to obtain by requesting: *he asked for help* **2** (*intr*) *informal* to behave in a provocative manner that is regarded as inviting (trouble): *she's asking for trouble; you're asking for it* **3** *Scot* to ask after: *tell your parents I'm asking for them*

asking price *n* the price suggested by a seller but usually considered to be subject to bargaining

Askja ('ɑːskjə) *n* a volcano in E central Iceland: active in 1961; largest crater in Iceland. Height: 1510 m (4954 ft). Area of crater: 88 sq km (34 sq miles)

asl *abbreviation for* **1** above sea level **2** age, sex, and location

ASL *abbreviation for* American Sign Language. See **Ameslan**

aslant (ə'slɑːnt) *adv* **1** at a slant ▷ *prep* **2** at a slant across or athwart

asleep (ə'sliːp) *adj* (*postpositive*) **1** in or into a state of sleep **2** in or into a dormant or inactive state **3** (of limbs, esp when the blood supply to them has been restricted) numb; lacking sensation **4** *euphemistic* dead

ASLEF ('æzlɛf) *n* (in Britain) ▷ *acronym for* Associated Society of Locomotive Engineers and Firemen

AS level *n Brit* **1 a** a public examination taken for the General Certificate of Education, with a smaller course content than an A level: since 2000 taken either as the first part of a full A level or as a qualification in its own right **b** the course leading to this examination **c** (*as modifier*): *AS-level English* **2** a pass in a subject at AS level: *I've got three AS levels*

ASLIB ('æzlɪb) *n acronym for* Association for Information Management

aslope (ə'sləʊp) *adv, adj* (*postpositive*) sloping

ASM *abbreviation for* **1** air-to-surface missile **2** *theatre* assistant stage manager

Asmara (æs'mɑːrə) *n* the capital of Eritrea; cathedral (1922); Grand Mosque (1937); university (1958). Pop: 615 000 (2005 est)

Asmodeus (æs'məʊdɪəs, ,æsməʊ'diːəs) *n* (in Jewish demonology) prince of the demons [via Latin *Asmodaeus*, from Avestan *Aēsma-daēva*, spirit of anger]

Asnières (French anjɛr) *n* a suburb of Paris, France, on the Seine. Pop: 75 837 (1999)

Aso ('ɑːsəʊ) *n* a group of five volcanic cones in Japan on central Kyushu, one of which, Naka-dake, has the largest crater in the world, between 16 km (10 miles) and 24 km (15 miles) in diameter. Highest cone: 1592 m (5223 ft). Also called: **Asosan** (,ɑːsəʊ'sɑːn)

asocial (eɪ'səʊfəl) *adj* **1** avoiding contact; not gregarious **2** unconcerned about the welfare of others **3** hostile to society or social practices

asp[1] (æsp) *n* **1** the venomous snake, probably *Naja haje* (Egyptian cobra), that caused the death of Cleopatra and was formerly used by the Pharaohs as a symbol of their power over life and death. See also **uraeus 2** Also called: **asp viper** a viper, *Vipera aspis*, that occurs in S Europe and is very similar to but smaller than the adder **3 horned asp** another name for **horned viper** [c15 from Latin *aspis*, from Greek]

asp[2] (æsp) *n* an archaic name for the **aspen** [Old English *æspe*; related to Old Norse *ösp*, Old High German *aspa*]

asparagine (ə'spærə,dʒiːn, -dʒɪn) *n* a nonessential amino acid, a component of proteins [c19 from French, from Latin *asparagus* ASPARAGUS + -INE[2]]

asparagus (ə'spærəgəs) *n* **1** any Eurasian liliaceous plant of the genus *Asparagus*, esp the widely cultivated *A. officinalis*, having small scaly or needle-like leaves **2** the succulent young shoots of *A. officinalis*, which may be cooked and eaten **3 asparagus fern** a fernlike species of asparagus, *A. plumosus*, native to southern Africa [c15 from Latin, from Greek *asparagos*, of obscure origin]

aspartame (ə'spɑː,teɪm) *n* an artificial sweetener produced from aspartic acid. Formula: $C_{14}H_{18}N_2O_5$ [c20 from ASPART(IC ACID) + (*phenyl*)*a*(*lanine*) *m*(*ethyl*) *e*(*ster*)]

aspartic acid (ə'spɑːtɪk) *n* a nonessential amino acid that is a component of proteins and acts as a neurotransmitter [c19 from ASPAR(AGUS) + -IC]

aspect ('æspɛkt) *n* **1** appearance to the eye; visual effect: *the physical aspect of the landscape* **2** a distinct feature or element in a problem, situation, etc; facet: *to consider every aspect of a problem* **3** the way in which a problem, idea, etc, may be considered **4** a facial expression; manner of appearing: *a severe aspect* **5** a position facing a particular direction; outlook: *the southern aspect of a house* **6** a view in a certain direction: *a good aspect of the village* **7** a surface that faces a given direction: *the ventral aspect of a fish* **8** *astrology* any of several specific angular distances between two planets or a planet and the Ascendant or Midheaven measured, from the earth, in degrees along the ecliptic **9** *grammar* a category of verbs or verbal inflections that expresses such features as the continuity, repetition, or completeness of the action described. Compare **perfective** (sense 2), **progressive** (senses 8, 10) **10** *botany* **a** the compass direction to which a plant habitat is exposed, or the degree of exposure **b** the effect of the seasons on the appearance of plants **11** *archaic* glance or gaze [c14 from Latin *aspectus* a sight, from *aspicere*, from *ad-* to, at + *specere* to look]

aspect ratio *n* **1** the ratio of width to height of the picture on a television or cinema screen **2** *aeronautics* the ratio of the span of a wing to its mean chord

aspectual (æ'spɛktjʊəl) *adj* of or relating to grammatical aspect

aspen ('æspən) *n* **1** any of several trees of the salicaceous genus *Populus*, such as *P. tremula* of Europe, in which the leaves are attached to the stem by long flattened stalks so that they quiver in the wind. Archaic name: **asp** ▷ *adj* **2** *archaic, chiefly literary* trembling [Old English *æspe*; see ASP[2]]

asper ('æspə) *n* a former Turkish monetary unit, a silver coin, worth 1/120 of a piastre [from Turkish, ultimately from Latin: rough, harsh]

asperate ('æspə,reɪt) or **asperous** ('æspərəs) *adj* (of plant parts) having a rough surface due to a covering of short stiff hairs

Asperger's syndrome ('æspɜ:gəz) *n* a form of autism in which the sufferer has limited but obsessive interests, and has difficulty relating to other people [c20 after Hans *Asperger* (20th century), Austrian physician who first described it]

Asperges (æ'spɜ:dʒiːz) *n* *RC Church* **1** a short rite preceding Mass, in which the celebrant sprinkles those present with holy water to the accompaniment of the chant *Asperges me, Domine* **2** the chant opening with these words [c16 from Latin *Asperges (me hyssopo)* Thou shalt purge (me with hyssop)]

aspergillosis (æ,spɜ:dʒɪ'ləʊsɪs) *n, pl* **-ses** (-siːz) a rare fungal infection, esp of the mucous membranes or lungs, caused by various species of *Aspergillus* [c19 from New Latin, from ASPERGILLUS]

aspergillum (,æspə'dʒɪləm) or **aspergill** ('æspədʒɪl) *n, pl* **-gilla** (-'dʒɪlə) **-gillums** or **-gills** another term for **aspersorium** (sense 2) [c17 from New Latin *aspergillum*, from Latin *aspergere*, from *spargere* to sprinkle]

aspergillus (,æspə'dʒɪləs) *n, pl* **-gilli** (-'dʒɪlaɪ) any ascomycetous fungus of the genus *Aspergillus*, having chains of conidia attached like bristles to a club-shaped stalk: family *Aspergillaceae* [c19 from New Latin *aspergillum* (from its similar appearance)]

asperity (æ'spɛrɪtɪ) *n, pl* **-ties 1** roughness or sharpness of temper **2** roughness or harshness of a surface, sound, taste, etc **3** a condition hard to endure; affliction **4** *physics* the elastically compressed region of contact between two surfaces caused by the normal force [c16 from Latin *asperitās*, from *asper* rough]

aspermia (ə'spɜːmɪə) *n* *pathol* the failure to form or emit semen

asperse (ə'spɜːs) *vb* (tr) **1** to spread false rumours about; defame **2** *rare* to sprinkle, as with water in baptism [c15 from Latin *aspersus*, from *aspergere* to sprinkle] > as'perser *n* > as'persive *adj* > as'persively *adv*

aspersion (ə'spɜːʃən) *n* **1** a disparaging or malicious remark; slanderous accusation (esp in the phrase **cast aspersions** (on)) **2** the act of defaming **3** *rare* the act of sprinkling, esp of water in baptism

aspersorium (,æspə'sɔːrɪəm) *n, pl* **-ria** (-rɪə) or **-riums** *RC Church* **1** a basin containing holy water with which worshippers sprinkle themselves **2** Also called: **aspergillum** a perforated instrument used to sprinkle holy water

asphalt ('æsfælt, 'æf-, -fɒlt) *n* **1** any of several black semisolid substances composed of bitumen and inert mineral matter. They occur naturally in parts of America and as a residue from petroleum distillation: used as a waterproofing material and in paints, dielectrics, and fungicides **2** a mixture of this substance with gravel, used in road-surfacing and roofing materials **3** (*modifier*) containing or surfaced with asphalt ▷ *vb* **4** (tr) to cover with asphalt [c14 from Late Latin *aspaltus*, from Greek *asphaltos*, probably from A-[1] + *sphallein* to cause to fall; referring to its use as a binding agent] > as'phaltic *adj*

asphaltite (æs'fæltaɪt) *n* any of various naturally occurring hydrocarbons that resemble asphalt but have a higher melting point

aspherical surface *n photog* a lens or mirror surface that does not form part of a sphere and is used to reduce aberrations

asphodel ('æsfəˌdɛl) *n* **1** any of various S European liliaceous plants of the genera *Asphodelus* and *Asphodeline,* having clusters of white or yellow flowers. Compare **bog asphodel** **2** any of various other plants, such as the daffodil **3** an unidentified flower of Greek legend, probably a narcissus, said to cover the Elysian fields [C16 from Latin *asphodelus,* from Greek *asphodelos,* of obscure origin]

asphyxia (æs'fɪksɪə) *n* lack of oxygen in the blood due to restricted respiration; suffocation. If severe enough and prolonged, it causes death [C18 from New Latin, from Greek *asphuxia* a stopping of the pulse, from A-[1] + *sphuxis* pulse, from *sphuzein* to throb] > **as'phyxial** *adj*

asphyxiant (æs'fɪksɪənt) *adj* **1** causing asphyxia ▷ *n* **2** anything that causes asphyxia: *carbon monoxide is an asphyxiant*

asphyxiate (æs'fɪksɪˌeɪt) *vb* to cause asphyxia in or undergo asphyxia; smother; suffocate > **asˌphyxi'ation** *n* > **as'phyxiˌator** *n*

aspic[1] ('æspɪk) *n* a savoury jelly based on meat or fish stock, used as a relish or as a mould for meat, vegetables, etc [C18 from French: aspic (jelly), ASP[1]; variously explained as referring to its colour or coldness as compared to that of the snake]

aspic[2] ('æspɪk) *n* an archaic word for **asp**[1] [C17 from French, from Old Provençal *espic* spike, from Latin *spīca,* head (of flower); compare SPIKENARD]

aspic[3] ('æspɪk) *n* either of two species of lavender, *Lavandula spica* or *L. latifolia,* that yield an oil used in perfumery: family *Lamiaceae* (labiates) [C16 from Old French, a variant of *aspe* ASP[2]]

aspidistra (ˌæspɪ'dɪstrə) *n* any Asian plant of the liliaceous genus *Aspidistra,* esp *A. lurida,* a popular house plant with long tough evergreen leaves and purplish flowers borne on the ground [C19 from New Latin, from Greek *aspis* shield, on the model of *Tupistra* genus of liliaceous plants]

Aspinwall ('æspɪnˌwɔːl) *n* the former name of **Colón**

aspirant ('æspɪrənt, ə'spaɪərənt) *n* **1** a person who aspires, as to a high position ▷ *adj* **2** aspiring or striving

aspirate *vb* ('æspɪˌreɪt) *(tr)* **1** *phonetics* **a** to articulate (a stop) with some force, so that breath escapes with audible friction as the stop is released **b** to pronounce (a word or syllable) with an initial *h* **2** to draw in or remove by inhalation or suction, esp to suck (air or fluid) from a body cavity or to inhale (fluid) into the lungs after vomiting **3** to supply air to (an internal-combustion engine) ▷ *n* ('æspɪrɪt) **4** *phonetics* **a** a stop pronounced with an audible release of breath **b** the glottal fricative represented in English and several other languages as *h* ▷ *adj* ('æspɪrɪt) **5** *phonetics* (of a stop) pronounced with a forceful and audible expulsion of breath

aspiration (ˌæspɪ'reɪʃən) *n* **1** strong desire to achieve something, such as success **2** the aim of such desire **3** **a** the act of breathing **b** a breath **4** *phonetics* **a** the pronunciation of a stop with an audible and forceful release of breath **b** the friction of the released breath **c** an aspirated consonant **5** removal of air or fluid from a body cavity by suction **6** *med* **a** the sucking of fluid or foreign matter into the air passages of the body **b** the removal of air or fluid from the body by suction > **aspiratory** (ə'spaɪrətərɪ, -trɪ, 'æspɪrətərɪ, -trɪ) *adj*

aspirator ('æspɪˌreɪtə) *n* a device employing suction, such as a jet pump or one for removing fluids from a body cavity

aspire (ə'spaɪə) *vb (intr)* **1** (usually foll by *to* or *after*) to yearn (for) or have a powerful or ambitious plan, desire, or hope (to do or be something): *to aspire to be a great leader* **2** to rise to a great height [C15 from Latin *aspīrāre* to breathe upon, from *spīrāre* to breathe] > **as'pirer** *n* > **as'piring** *adj*

aspirin ('æsprɪn) *n, pl* **-rin** *or* **-rins** **1** a white crystalline compound widely used in the form of tablets to relieve pain and fever, to reduce inflammation, and to prevent strokes. Formula: $CH_3COOC_6H_4COOH$. Chemical name: **acetylsalicylic acid** **2** a tablet of aspirin [C19 from German, from *A(cetyl)* + *Spir(säure)* spiraeic acid (modern salicylic acid) + -IN; see also SPIRAEA]

asplanchnic (eɪ'splæŋknɪk) *adj zoology* having no gut

asplenium (æ'spliːnɪəm) *n* any fern of the very large genus *Asplenium,* of worldwide distribution. Some, esp the bird's nest fern (*A. nidus*), are grown as greenhouse or house plants for their decorative evergreen fronds: family *Polypodiaceae.* See also **spleenwort** [New Latin, from Latin *asplēnum,* from Greek *asplēnon* spleenwort, from *a-* not + *splēn* spleen (from its reputed medicinal properties)]

aspro ('æsprəʊ) *n, pl* **-pros** *Austral informal* an associate professor at an academic institution [C20 from AS(SOCIATE) + PRO(FESSOR)]

asquint (ə'skwɪnt) *adv, adj (postpositive)* with a glance from the corner of the eye, esp a furtive one [C13 perhaps from Dutch *schuinte* slant, of obscure origin]

ass[1] (æs) *n* **1** either of two perissodactyl mammals of the horse family (*Equidae*), *Equus asinus* (**African wild ass**) or *E. hemionus* (**Asiatic wild ass**). They are hardy and sure-footed, having longer ears than the horse. Related adj: **asinine** **2** *(not in technical use)* the domesticated variety of the African wild ass; donkey **3** a foolish or ridiculously pompous person **4** **not within an ass's roar of** *Irish informal* not close to obtaining, winning, etc: *she wasn't within an ass's roar of it* [Old English *assa,* probably from Old Irish *asan,* from Latin *asinus;* related to Greek *onos* ass]

ass[2] (æs) *n* **1** *chiefly US and Canadian slang* the buttocks **2** *chiefly US and Canadian slang* the anus **3** *chiefly US and Canadian offensive slang* sexual intercourse or a woman considered sexually (esp in the phrase **piece of ass**) **4** **cover one's ass** *slang, chiefly US and Canadian* to take such action as one considers necessary to avoid censure, ridicule, etc at a later time [Old English *ærs;* see ARSE]

assagai ('æsəˌgaɪ) *n, pl* **-gais** a variant spelling of **assegai**

assai[1] (æ'saɪ) *adv music* (usually preceded by a musical direction) very: *allegro assai* [Italian: enough]

assai[2] (æ'saɪ) *n* **1** any of several Brazilian palm trees of the genus *Euterpe,* esp *E. edulis,* that have small dark purple fleshy edible fruit **2** a beverage made from the fruit of this tree [via Brazilian Portuguese from Tupi]

assail (ə'seɪl) *vb (tr)* **1** to attack violently; assault **2** to criticize or ridicule vehemently, as in argument **3** to beset or disturb: *his mind was assailed by doubts* **4** to encounter with the intention of mastering: *to assail a problem; to assail a difficult mountain ridge* [C13 from Old French *asalir,* from Vulgar Latin *assalīre* (unattested) to leap upon, from Latin *assilīre,* from *salīre* to leap] > **as'sailable** *adj* > **as'sailer** *n* > **as'sailment** *n*

assailant (ə'seɪlənt) *n* a person who attacks another, either physically or verbally: *he was unable to recognize his assailants*

assam ('æsæm; *Malay* 'asam) *n* (in Malaysia) tamarind as used in cooking. **Assam ikan** is a dish of fish cooked with tamarind [from Malay *asam* sour]

Assam (æ'sæm) *n* **1** a state of NE India, situated in the central Brahmaputra valley: tropical forest, with the heaviest rainfall in the world; produces large quantities of tea. Capital: Dispur. Pop: 26 638 407 (2001 est). Area: 78 438 sq km (30 673 sq miles) **2** a high-quality black tea grown in the state of Assam

Assamese (ˌæsə'miːz) *n* **1** the state language of Assam, belonging to the Indic branch of the Indo-European family and closely related to Bengali **2** *(pl* **-mese***)* a native or inhabitant of Assam ▷ *adj* **3** of or relating to Assam, its people, or their language

assassin (ə'sæsɪn) *n* a murderer, esp one who kills a prominent political figure [C16 from Medieval Latin *assassīnus,* from Arabic *hashshāshīn,* plural of *hashshāsh* one who eats HASHISH]

Assassin (ə'sæsɪn) *n* a member of a secret sect of Muslim fanatics operating in Persia and Syria from about 1090 to 1256, murdering their victims, usually Crusaders

assassinate (ə'sæsɪˌneɪt) *vb (tr)* **1** to murder (a person, esp a public or political figure), usually by a surprise attack **2** to ruin or harm (a person's reputation, etc) by slander > **asˌsassi'nation** *n*

assassin bug *n* any long-legged predatory, often blood-sucking, insect of the heteropterous family *Reduviidae*

assassin fly *n* another name for **robber fly**

assault (ə'sɔːlt) *n* **1** a violent attack, either physical or verbal **2** *law* an intentional or reckless act that causes another person to expect to be subjected to immediate and unlawful violence. Compare **battery** (sense 4), **assault and battery** **3** **a** the culmination of a military attack, in which fighting takes place at close quarters **b** *(as modifier): assault troops* **4** rape or attempted rape ▷ *vb (tr)* **5** to make an assault upon **6** to rape or attempt to rape [C13 from Old French *asaut,* from Vulgar Latin *assaltus* (unattested), from *assalīre* (unattested) to leap upon; see ASSAIL] > **as'saulter** *n* > **as'saultive** *adj*

assault and battery *n criminal law* a threat of attack to another person followed by actual attack, which need amount only to touching with hostile intent

assault course *n* an obstacle course designed to give soldiers practice in negotiating hazards in making an assault

assault rifle *or* **assault weapon** *n chiefly US* a semiautomatic firearm with additional features such as a large magazine, a bayonet fitting, etc

assay *vb* (ə'seɪ) **1** to subject (a substance, such as silver or gold) to chemical analysis, as in the determination of the amount of impurity **2** *(tr)* to attempt (something or to do something) **3** *(tr; may take a clause as object)* to test, analyse, or evaluate: *to assay the significance of early childhood experience* ▷ *n* (ə'seɪ, 'æseɪ) **4** **a** an analysis, esp a determination of the amount of metal in an ore or the amounts of impurities in a precious metal **b** *(as modifier): an assay office* **5** a substance undergoing an analysis **6** a written report on the results of an analysis **7** a test **8** *archaic* an attempt [C14 from Old Northern French *assai;* see ESSAY] > **as'sayable** *adj* > **as'sayer** *n*

assegai *or* **assagai** ('æsəˌgaɪ) *n, pl* **-gais** **1** a southern African cornaceous tree, *Curtisia faginea,* the wood of which is used for making spears **2** a sharp light spear, esp one made of this wood [C17 from Portuguese *azagaia,* from Arabic *az zaghāyah,* from *al* the + *zaghāyah* assegai, from Berber]

assemblage (ə'sɛmblɪdʒ) *n* **1** a number of things or persons assembled together; collection **2** a list of dishes served at a meal or the dishes themselves **3** the act or process of assembling or the state of being assembled **4** (ˌæsəm'blɑːʒ) a three-dimensional work of art that combines various objects into an integrated whole

assemble (ə'sɛmbᵊl) *vb* **1** to come or bring together; collect or congregate **2** to fit or join together (the parts of something, such as a machine): *to assemble the parts of a kit* **3** to run (a computer program) that converts a set of symbolic data, usually in the form of specific single-step instructions, into machine language [C13 from Old French *assembler,* from Vulgar Latin *assimulāre* (unattested) to bring together, from Latin *simul* together]

assemblé *French* (asɑ̃ble) *n ballet* a sideways leap in which the feet come together in the air in preparation for landing [literally: brought together]

a

assembler (əˈsɛmblə) n **1** a type of computer program that converts a program written in assembly language into machine code. Compare **compiler** (sense 2) **2** another name for **assembly language**

assembly (əˈsɛmblɪ) n, pl -blies **1** a number of people gathered together, esp for a formal meeting held at regular intervals **2** the act of assembling or the state of being assembled **3** the process of putting together a number of parts to make a machine or other product **4** machinery a group of mating components before or after fitting together **5** military **a** a signal for personnel to assemble, as by drum, bugle, etc **b** (as modifier): an assembly area

Assembly (əˈsɛmblɪ) n, pl -blies **1** the lower chamber in various American state legislatures. See also **House of Assembly, legislative assembly, National Assembly 2** NZ short for **General Assembly**

assembly language n computing a low-level programming language that allows a programmer complete control of the machine code to be generated

assembly line n a sequence of machines, tools, operations, workers, etc, in a factory, arranged so that at each stage a further process is carried out

assemblyman (əˈsɛmblɪmən) n, pl -men (sometimes capital) a member of an assembly, esp a legislature

Assembly of First Nations n the national organization which represents the First Nations in Canada. Abbreviation: **AFN**

Assen (Dutch ˈɑsə) n a city in the N Netherlands, capital of Drenthe province. Pop: 62 000 (2003 est)

assent (əˈsɛnt) n **1** agreement, as to a statement, proposal, etc; acceptance **2** hesitant agreement; compliance ▷ vb **4** (intr; usually foll by to) to agree or express agreement [c13 from Old French assenter, from Latin assentīrī, from sentīre to think]

assentation (ˌæsɛnˈteɪʃən) n servile or hypocritical agreement

assentient (əˈsɛnʃɪənt) adj **1** approving or agreeing ▷ n **2** a person who assents

assentor (əˈsɛntə) n Brit government any of the eight voters legally required to endorse the nomination of a candidate in a parliamentary or local election in addition to the nominator and seconder

assert (əˈsɜːt) vb (tr) **1** to insist upon (rights, claims, etc) **2** (may take a clause as object) to state to be true; declare categorically **3** to put (oneself) forward in an insistent manner [c17 from Latin asserere to join to oneself, from serere to join] > as'serter or as'sertor n > as'sertible adj

assertion (əˈsɜːʃən) n **1** a positive statement, usually made without an attempt at furnishing evidence **2** the act of asserting

assertive (əˈsɜːtɪv) adj **1** confident and direct in claiming one's rights or putting forward one's views **2** given to making assertions or bold demands; dogmatic or aggressive > as'sertively adv > as'sertiveness n

assertoric (ˌæsəˈtɒrɪk) adj logic **1** (of a statement) stating a fact, as opposed to expressing an evaluative judgment **2** obsolete judging what is rather than what may or must be ▷ Compare **apodeictic** (sense 2), **problematic** (sense 2)

assess (əˈsɛs) vb (tr) **1** to judge the worth, importance, etc, of; evaluate **2** (foll by at) to estimate the value of (income, property, etc) for taxation purposes: the estate was assessed at three thousand pounds **3** to determine the amount of (a fine, tax, damages, etc) **4** to impose a tax, fine, etc, on (a person or property) [c15 from Old French assesser, from Latin assidēre to sit beside, from sedēre to sit] > as'sessable adj

assessment (əˈsɛsmənt) n **1** the act of assessing, esp (in Britain) the evaluation of a student's achievement on a course **2** an amount determined as payable **3** a valuation set on taxable property, income, etc **4** evaluation; estimation

assessment arrangements pl n Brit education nationally standardized plans for pupil assessment in different subjects based on attainment targets at the end of each key stage in the National Curriculum

assessor (əˈsɛsə) n **1** a person who evaluates the merits, importance, etc, of something, esp (in Britain) work prepared as part of a course of study **2** a person who values property for taxation **3** a person who estimates the value of damage to property for insurance purposes **4** a person with technical expertise called in to advise a court on specialist matters **5** a person who shares another's position or rank, esp in an advisory capacity > assessorial (ˌæsɛˈsɔːrɪəl) adj

asset (ˈæsɛt) n anything valuable or useful: experience is their main asset. See also **assets** [c19 back formation from ASSETS]

asset-backed fund n a fund in which the money is invested in property, shares, etc, rather than being deposited with a bank or building society

assets (ˈæsɛts) pl n **1** accounting the property and claims against debtors that a business enterprise may apply to discharge its liabilities. Assets may be fixed, current, liquid, or intangible and are shown balanced against liabilities. Compare **liabilities 2** law the property available to an executor or administrator for settlement of the debts and payment of legacies of the estate of a deceased or insolvent person **3** any property owned by a person or firm [C16 (in the sense: enough to discharge one's liabilities): via Anglo-French from Old French asez enough, from Vulgar Latin ad satis (unattested), from Latin ad up to + satis enough]

asset-stripping n commerce the practice of taking over a failing company at a low price and then selling the assets piecemeal before closing the company down > 'asset-ˌstripper n

asset value n the value of a share in a company calculated by dividing the difference between the total of its assets and its liabilities by the number of ordinary shares issued

asseverate (əˈsɛvəˌreɪt) vb (tr) to assert or declare emphatically or solemnly [c18 from Latin assevērāre to do (something) earnestly, from sevērus SEVERE] > as.sever'ation n

assez (ˈæseɪ) adv music (as part of a musical direction) fairly; rather [c19 French: enough]

asshole (ˈæsˌhəʊl) n slang, derogatory the usual US and Canadian word for **arsehole** (see **arse**)

Asshur (ˈæʃʊə) n a variant spelling of **Assur**

assibilate (əˈsɪbɪˌleɪt) vb phonetics **1** (intr) (of a speech sound) to be changed into a sibilant **2** (tr) to pronounce (a speech sound) with or as a sibilant [c19 from Late Latin assībilāre to hiss at, from sībilāre to hiss; see SIBILANT] > as.sibi'lation n

assiduity (ˌæsɪˈdjuːɪtɪ) n, pl -ties **1** constant and close application **2** (often plural) devoted attention

assiduous (əˈsɪdjʊəs) adj **1** hard-working; persevering: an assiduous researcher **2** undertaken with perseverance and care: assiduous editing [c16 from Latin assiduus sitting down to (something), from assidēre to sit beside, from sedēre to sit] > as'siduously adv > as'siduousness n

assign (əˈsaɪn) vb (mainly tr) **1** to select for and appoint to a post, etc: to assign an expert to the job **2** to give out or allot (a task, problem, etc): to assign advertising to an expert **3** to set apart (a place, person, time, etc) for a particular function or event: to assign a day for the meeting **4** to attribute to a specified cause, origin, or source; ascribe: to assign a stone cross to the Vikings **5** to transfer (one's right, interest, or title to property) to someone else **6** (also intr) law (formerly) to transfer (property) to trustees so that it may be used for the benefit of creditors **7** military to allocate (men or materials) on a permanent basis. Compare **attach** (sense 6) **8** computing to place (a value corresponding to a variable) in a memory location ▷ n **9** law a person to whom property is assigned; assignee [c14 from Old French assigner, from Latin assignāre, from signāre to mark out] > as'signable adj > as.signa'bility n > as'signably adv > as'signer n

assignat (ˈæsɪɡˌnæt, ˌæsɪˈnjɑː; French asiɲa) n French history the paper money issued by the Constituent Assembly in 1789, backed by the confiscated land of the Church and the émigrés [c18 from French, from Latin assignātum something appointed; see ASSIGN]

assignation (ˌæsɪɡˈneɪʃən) n **1** a secret or forbidden arrangement to meet, esp one between lovers **2** the act of assigning; assignment **3** law, chiefly Scot another word for **assignment** [c14 from Old French, from Latin assignātiō a marking out; see ASSIGN]

assignee (ˌæsaɪˈniː) n **1** law a person to whom some right, interest, or property is transferred **2** Austral history a convict who had undergone assignment

assignment (əˈsaɪnmənt) n **1** something that has been assigned, such as a mission or task **2** a position or post to which a person is assigned **3** the act of assigning or state of being assigned **4** law **a** the transfer to another of a right, interest, or title to property, esp personal property: assignment of a lease **b** the document effecting such a transfer **c** the right, interest, or property transferred **5** law (formerly) the transfer, esp by an insolvent debtor, of property in trust for the benefit of his creditors **6** logic a function that associates specific values with each variable in a formal expression **7** Austral history a system (1789–1841) whereby a convict could become the unpaid servant of a freeman

assignor (ˌæsɪˈnɔː) n law a person who transfers or assigns property

assimilate (əˈsɪmɪˌleɪt) vb **1** (tr) to learn (information, a procedure, etc) and understand it thoroughly **2** (tr) to absorb (food) and incorporate it into the body tissues **3** (intr) to become absorbed, incorporated, or learned and understood **4** (usually foll by into or with) to bring or come into harmony; adjust or become adjusted: the new immigrants assimilated easily **5** (usually foll by to or with) to become or cause to become similar **6** (usually foll by to) phonetics to change (a consonant) or (of a consonant) to be changed into another under the influence of one adjacent to it: (n) often assimilates to (ŋ) before (k), as in "include" [c15 from Latin assimilāre to make one thing like another, from similis like, SIMILAR] > as'similable adj > as'similably adv > as.simi'lation n > as'similative or as'similatory adj > as'simi.lator n > as'similatively adv

Assiniboine¹ (əˈsɪnɪˌbɔɪn) n a river in W Canada, rising in E Saskatchewan and flowing southeast and east to the Red River at Winnipeg. Length: over 860 km (500 miles)

Assiniboine² (əˈsɪnəˌbɔɪn) n **1** (pl -boine or -boines) a member of a North American Indian people living in Alberta, Saskatchewan, and Montana; one of the Sioux peoples **2** the language of this people, belonging to the Siouan family

Assisi (Italian asˈsiːzi) n a town in central Italy, in Umbria: birthplace of St Francis, who founded the Franciscan religious order here in 1208. Pop: 25 304 (2001)

assist (əˈsɪst) vb **1** to give help or support to (a person, cause, etc); aid **2** to work or act as an assistant or subordinate to (another) **3** ice hockey to help (a team-mate) to score, as by passing the puck **4** (intr; foll by at) archaic to be present; attend ▷ n **5** US and Canadian the act of helping; aid; assistance **6** baseball the act of a player who throws or deflects a batted ball in such a way that a team is enabled to put out an opponent **7** sport **a** a pass or other action by a player which enables another player to score a goal **b** a credit given for such an action [c15 from French assister to be present, from Latin assistere to stand by, from sistere to cause to stand, from stāre to stand] > as'sister n

assistance (əˈsɪstəns) *n* 1 help; support 2 the act of assisting 3 *Brit informal* See **national assistance**
assistance dog *n* a dog that has been specially trained to live with and accompany a disabled person, carrying out such tasks as prompting them to take medication or assisting them to cross a road
assistant (əˈsɪstənt) *n* 1 a a person who assists, esp in a subordinate position b (*as modifier*): *assistant manager* 2 See **shop assistant** ▷ *adj* 3 *archaic* helpful or useful as an aid
assistant professor *n* *US and Canadian* a university teacher lower in rank than an associate professor
assistant referee *n* *soccer* the official name for **linesman** (sense 1)
assisted dying *n* the suicide of a person afflicted by an incurable disease, using a lethal dose of drugs provided by a physician for this purpose
assisted living (əˈsɪstɪd) *n* a a living environment for elderly people, in which personal and medical care are supplied b (*as modifier*): *private assisted-living apartments*
assistive (əˈsɪstɪv) *adj* providing a means of reducing a physical impairment: *an assistive device such as a hearing aid*
Assiut (æˈsjuːt) *n* a variant spelling of **Asyut**
assize (əˈsaɪz) *n* 1 (in the US) a a sitting of a legislative assembly or administrative body b an enactment or order of such an assembly 2 *English history* a trial or judicial inquest, the writ instituting such inquest, or the verdict 3 *Scots law* a trial by jury b another name for **jury**[1] [C13 from Old French *assise* session, from *asseoir* to seat, from Latin *assidēre* to sit beside; see ASSESS]
assizes (əˈsaɪzɪz) *pl n* (formerly in England and Wales) the sessions, usually held four times a year, of the principal court in each county, exercising civil and criminal jurisdiction, attended by itinerant judges: replaced in 1971 by crown courts
assn *abbreviation for* association
assoc. *abbreviation for* 1 associate(d) 2 association
associate *vb* (əˈsəʊʃɪˌeɪt, -sɪ-) (usually foll by *with*) 1 (*tr*) to link or connect in the mind or imagination: *to associate Christmas with fun* 2 (*intr*) to keep company; mix socially: *to associate with writers* 3 (*intr*) to form or join an association, group, etc 4 (*tr; usually passive*) to consider in conjunction; connect: *rainfall is associated with humidity* 5 (*tr*) to bring (a person, esp oneself) into friendship, partnership, etc 6 (*tr; often passive*) to express agreement or allow oneself to be connected (with): *Bertrand Russell was associated with the peace movement* ▷ *n* (əˈsəʊʃɪɪt, -ˌeɪt, -sɪ-) 7 a person joined with another or others in an enterprise, business, etc; partner; colleague 8 a companion or friend 9 something that usually accompanies another thing; concomitant: *hope is an associate to happiness* 10 a person having a subordinate position in or admitted to only partial membership of an institution, association, etc ▷ *adj* (əˈsəʊʃɪɪt, -ˌeɪt, -sɪ-) (*prenominal*) 11 joined with another or others in an enterprise, business, etc; having equal or nearly equal status: *an associate director* 12 having partial rights and privileges or subordinate status: *an associate member* 13 accompanying; concomitant [C14 from Latin *associāre* to ally with, from *sociāre* to join, from *socius* an ally] > **asˈsociable** *adj* > **asˈsociˌator** *n* > **asˈsociatory** *adj* > **asˈsociateˌship** *n*
associated statehood *n* the semi-independent political status of various former British colonies in the Caribbean from 1967 until each became an independent state in the British Commonwealth, by which Britain retained responsibility for defence and some aspects of foreign affairs. The **associated states** were Anguilla, Antigua, Dominica, Grenada, St Kitts-Nevis, St Lucia, and St Vincent and the Grenadines
associate professor *n* 1 (in the US and Canada) a university teacher lower in rank than a full professor but higher than an assistant professor 2 (in New Zealand) a senior lecturer holding the rank below professor
association (əˌsəʊsɪˈeɪʃən, -ʃɪ-) *n* 1 a group of people having a common purpose or interest; a society or club 2 the act of associating or the state of being associated 3 friendship or companionship: *their association will not last* 4 a mental connection of ideas, feelings, or sensations: *association of revolution with bloodshed* 5 *psychol* the mental process of linking ideas so that the recurrence of one idea automatically recalls the other. See also **free association** 6 *chem* the formation of groups of molecules and ions, esp in liquids, held together by weak chemical bonds 7 *ecology* a group of similar plants that grow in a uniform environment and contain one or more dominant species
association football *n* a more formal name for **soccer**
associationism (əˌsəʊsɪˈeɪʃəˌnɪzəm) *n* *psychol* a theory that all mental activity is based on connections between basic mental events, such as sensations and feelings
association law *n* *psychol* any law governing the association of ideas
associative (əˈsəʊʃɪətɪv) *adj* 1 of, relating to, or causing association or union 2 *maths, logic* a being independent of the grouping of numbers, symbols, or terms within a given set, as in conjunction or in an expression such as $(2 \times 3) \times 4 = 2 \times (3 \times 4)$ b referring to this property: *the associative laws of arithmetic*
associative cortex *n* *anatomy* the part of the cortex that does not have direct connections to the senses or motor system and is thought to be involved in higher mental processes
associative storage *n* *computing* a storage device in which the information is identified by content rather than by an address. Also called: **content-addressable storage**
assoil (əˈsɔɪl) *vb* (*tr*) *archaic* 1 to absolve; set free 2 to atone for [C13 from Old French *assoldre*, from Latin *absolvere* to ABSOLVE]
assonance (ˈæsənəns) *n* 1 the use of the same vowel sound with different consonants or the same consonant with different vowels in successive words or stressed syllables, as in a line of verse. Examples are *time* and *light* or *mystery* and *mastery* 2 partial correspondence; rough similarity [C18 from French, from Latin *assonāre* to sound, from *sonāre* to sound] > **ˈassonant** *adj, n* > **assonantal** (ˌæsəˈnæntᵊl) *adj*
assort (əˈsɔːt) *vb* 1 (*tr*) to arrange or distribute into groups of the same type; classify 2 (*intr; usually foll by with*) to fit or fall into a class or group; match 3 (*tr*) to supply with an assortment of merchandise 4 (*tr*) to put in the same category as others; group 5 (*intr; usually foll by with*) *rare* to keep company; consort [C15 from Old French *assorter*, from *sorte* SORT] > **asˈsortative** *or* **asˈsortive** *adj* > **asˈsortatively** *adv* > **asˈsorter** *n*
assorted (əˈsɔːtɪd) *adj* 1 consisting of various kinds mixed together; miscellaneous: *assorted sweets* 2 arranged in sorts; classified: *assorted categories* 3 matched; suited (esp in the combinations **well-assorted, ill-assorted**)
assortment (əˈsɔːtmənt) *n* 1 a collection or group of various things or sorts 2 the act of assorting
ASSR *abbreviation for* (formerly) Autonomous Soviet Socialist Republic
asst *abbreviation for* assistant
assuage (əˈsweɪdʒ) *vb* (*tr*) 1 to soothe, moderate, or relieve (grief, pain, etc) 2 to give relief to (thirst, appetite, etc); satisfy 3 to pacify; calm [C14 from Old French *assouagier*, from Vulgar Latin *assuāviāre* (unattested) to sweeten, from Latin *suāvis* pleasant; see SUAVE] > **asˈsuagement** *n* > **asˈsuager** *n* > **assuasive** (əˈsweɪsɪv) *adj*
Assuan *or* **Assouan** (ɑːsˈwɑːn) *n* variant spellings of **Aswan**
assume (əˈsjuːm) *vb* (*tr*) 1 (*may take a clause as object*) to take for granted; accept without proof; suppose: *to assume that someone is sane* 2 to take upon oneself; undertake or take on or over (a position, responsibility, etc): *to assume office* 3 to pretend to; feign: *he assumed indifference, although the news affected him deeply* 4 to take or put on; adopt: *the problem assumed gigantic proportions* 5 to appropriate or usurp (power, control, etc); arrogate: *the revolutionaries assumed control of the city* 6 *Christianity* (of God) to take up (the soul of a believer) into heaven [C15 from Latin *assūmere* to take up, from *sūmere* to take up, from SUB- + *emere* to take] > **asˈsumable** *adj* > **asˈsumer** *n*
assumed (əˈsjuːmd) *adj* 1 false; fictitious: *an assumed name* 2 taken for granted: *an assumed result* 3 usurped; arrogated: *an assumed authority*
assuming (əˈsjuːmɪŋ) *adj* 1 expecting too much; presumptuous; arrogant ▷ *conj* 2 (often foll by *that*) if it is assumed or taken for granted (that): *even assuming he understands the problem, he will never take any action*
assumpsit (əˈsʌmpsɪt) *n* *law* (before 1875) an action to recover damages for breach of an express or implied contract or agreement that was not under seal [C17 from Latin, literally: he has undertaken, from *assūmere* to ASSUME]
assumption (əˈsʌmpʃən) *n* 1 the act of taking something for granted or something that is taken for granted 2 an assuming of power or possession of something 3 arrogance; presumption 4 *logic* a statement that is used as the premise of a particular argument but may not be otherwise accepted. Compare **axiom** (sense 4) [C13 from Latin *assūmptiō* a taking up, from *assūmere* to ASSUME] > **asˈsumptive** *adj* > **asˈsumptively** *adv*
Assumption (əˈsʌmpʃən) *n* *Christianity* 1 the taking up of the Virgin Mary (body and soul) into heaven when her earthly life was ended 2 the feast commemorating this, celebrated by Roman Catholics on Aug 15
Assur, Asur (ˈæsə) *or* **Asshur, Ashur** (ˈæʃʊə) *n* 1 the supreme national god of the ancient Assyrians, chiefly a war god, whose symbol was an archer within a winged disc 2 one of the chief cities of ancient Assyria, on the River Tigris about 100 km (60 miles) downstream from the present-day city of Mosul
assurance (əˈʃʊərəns) *n* 1 a statement, assertion, etc, intended to inspire confidence or give encouragement: *she was helped by his assurance that she would cope* 2 a promise or pledge of support: *he gave an assurance of help when needed* 3 freedom from doubt; certainty: *his assurance about his own superiority infuriated her* 4 forwardness; impudence 5 *chiefly Brit* insurance providing for certainties such as death as contrasted with fire or theft
assure (əˈʃʊə) *vb* (*tr; may take a clause as object*) 1 to cause to feel sure or certain; convince: *to assure a person of one's love* 2 to promise; guarantee: *he assured us that he would come* 3 to state positively or with assurance 4 to make (an event) certain; ensure 5 *chiefly Brit* to insure against loss, esp of life 6 *property law* another word for **convey** [C14 from Old French *aseürer* to assure, from Medieval Latin *assēcūrāre* to secure or make sure, from *sēcūrus* SECURE] > **asˈsurable** *adj* > **asˈsurer** *n*
assured (əˈʃʊəd) *adj* 1 made certain; sure; guaranteed 2 self-assured 3 *chiefly Brit* insured, esp by a life assurance policy ▷ *n* 4 *chiefly Brit* a the beneficiary under a life assurance policy b the person whose life is insured > **assuredly** (əˈʃʊərɪdlɪ) *adv* > **asˈsuredness** *n*
assured tenancy *n* *Brit* an agreement between a government-approved body such as a housing association and a tenant for occupation of a newly-built house or flat at an agreed market rent, under which the tenant has security of tenure. Compare **regulated tenancy**
assurgent (əˈsɜːdʒənt) *adj* (of leaves, stems, etc) curving or growing upwards; rising [C16 from Latin *assurgere* to rise up, from *surgere* to rise] > **asˈsurgency** *n*

Assyria (ə'sɪrɪə) *n* an ancient kingdom of N Mesopotamia: it established an empire that stretched from Egypt to the Persian Gulf, reaching its greatest extent between 721 and 633 BC Its chief cities were Assur and Nineveh

Assyrian (ə'sɪrɪən) *n* **1** an inhabitant of ancient Assyria **2** a modern-day descendant of the ancient Assyrians **3 a** the language of the ancient Assyrians, belonging to the E Semitic subfamily of the Afro-Asiatic family and regarded as a dialect of Akkadian **b** a dialect of Aramaic, spoken by modern Assyrians ▷ *adj* **3** of, relating to, or characteristic of the ancient or modern Assyrians, their language, or culture

Assyriology (ə,sɪrɪ'ɒlədʒɪ) *n* the study of the culture, history, and archaeological remains of ancient Assyria > As,syri'ologist *n*

AST *abbreviation for* **1** Atlantic Standard Time **2** automated screen trading (in securities) **3** *Brit education* advanced skills teacher

astable (eɪ'steɪbəl) *adj* **1** not stable **2** *electronics* capable of oscillating between two states

Astana (æ'stænə) *n* the capital of Kazakhstan, in the N of the country; replaced Almaty as capital in 1997; an important railway junction. Pop: 335 000 (2005 est). Former names: Akmolinsk (until 1961), Tselinograd (1961–94), Akmola (1994–98)

Astanga yoga *or* **Ashtanga** (æ'ʃtæŋgə) *n* a revived ancient form of yoga that involves a fast and powerful series of movements

Astarte (æ'stɑːtɪ) *n* a fertility goddess worshipped by the Phoenicians: identified with Ashtoreth of the Hebrews and Ishtar of the Babylonians and Assyrians

astatic (æ'stætɪk, eɪ-) *adj* **1** not static; unstable **2** *physics* **a** having no tendency to assume any particular position or orientation **b** (of a galvanometer) having two mutually compensating magnets arranged so that the instrument is independent of the earth's magnetic field [c19 from Greek *astatos* unsteady; see A-¹, STATIC] > a'statically *adv* > a'stati,cism *n*

astatide (æstə,taɪd) *n chem* a binary compound of astatine with a more electropositive element

astatine ('æstə,tiːn, -tɪn) *n* a radioactive element of the halogen series: a decay product of uranium and thorium that occurs naturally in minute amounts and is artificially produced by bombarding bismuth with alpha particles. Symbol: At; atomic no: 85; half-life of most stable isotope, ²¹⁰At: 8.1 hours; probable valency: 1,3,5, or 7; melting pt: 302°C; boiling pt: 337°C (est) [c20 from Greek *astatos* unstable (see ASTATIC) + -INE²]

aster ('æstə) *n* **1** any plant of the genus *Aster*, having white, blue, purple, or pink daisy-like flowers: family Asteraceae (composites). Compare **golden aster 2 China aster** a related Chinese plant, *Callistephus chinensis*, widely cultivated for its showy brightly coloured flowers **3** *cytology* a group of radiating microtubules that surrounds the centrosome before and during mitosis [c18 from New Latin, from Latin *aster* star, from Greek]

-aster *suffix forming nouns* a person or thing that is inferior or bears only a poor resemblance to what is specified: *poetaster* [from Latin: suffix indicating imperfect resemblance]

astereognosis (ə,stɛrɪəʊ'gnəʊsɪs) *n* inability to recognize objects by touch [A-¹ + STEREO- + -GNOSIS]

asteriated (æ'stɪərɪ,eɪtɪd) *adj* (of a crystal, esp a gemstone) exhibiting a star-shaped figure in transmitted or reflected light

asterisk ('æstərɪsk) *n* **1** a star-shaped character (*) used in printing or writing to indicate a cross-reference to a footnote, an omission, etc **2 a** (in historical linguistics) this sign used to indicate an unattested reconstructed form **b** (in descriptive linguistics) this sign used to indicate that an expression is ungrammatical or in some other way unacceptable ▷ *vb* **3** (*tr*) to mark with an asterisk [c17 from Late Latin *asteriscus* a small star, from Greek *asteriskos*, from *astēr* star]

asterism ('æstə,rɪzəm) *n* **1** three asterisks arranged in a triangle (⁂ or ⸪), to draw attention to the text that follows **2** a starlike effect seen in some minerals and gemstones when viewed by reflected or transmitted light **3** a cluster of stars, which may be a subset or a superset of a constellation [c16 from Greek *asterismos* arrangement of constellations, from *astēr* star]

astern (ə'stɜːn) *adv* ▷ *adj (postpositive) nautical* **1** at or towards the stern **2** with the stern first: *full speed astern!* **3** aft of the stern of a vessel

asternal (æ'stɜːnəl, eɪ-) *adj anatomy* **1** not connected or joined to the sternum **2** lacking a sternum

asteroid ('æstə,rɔɪd) *n* **1** Also called: minor planet, planetoid any of numerous small celestial bodies that move around the sun mainly between the orbits of Mars and Jupiter. Their diameters range from 930 kilometres (Ceres) to less than one kilometre **2** Also called: asteroidean (,æstə'rɔɪdɪən) any echinoderm of the class *Asteroidea*; a starfish ▷ *adj also* asteroidal (,æstə'rɔɪdəl) **3** of, relating to, or belonging to the class *Asteroidea* **4** shaped like a star [c19 from Greek *asteroeidēs* starlike, from *astēr* a star]

asthenia (æs'θiːnɪə) *or* **astheny** ('æsθənɪ) *n pathol* an abnormal loss of strength; debility [c19 via New Latin from Greek *astheneia* weakness, from A-¹ + *sthenos* strength]

asthenic (æs'θɛnɪk) *adj* **1** of, relating to, or having asthenia; weak **2** (in constitutional psychology) referring to a physique characterized by long limbs and a small trunk: claimed to be associated with a schizoid personality. See also **somatotype** ▷ *n* **3** a person having long limbs and a small trunk

asthenopia (,æsθɪ'nəʊpɪə) *n* a technical name for eyestrain [c19 from New Latin, from Greek *asthenēs* weak (from A-¹ + *sthenos* strength) + *ōps* eye] > asthenopic (,æsθɪ'nɒpɪk) *adj*

asthenosphere (əs'θiːnə,sfɪə, -'θɛn-) *n* a thin semifluid layer of the earth (100–200 km thick), below the outer rigid lithosphere, forming part of the mantle and thought to be able to flow vertically and horizontally, enabling sections of lithosphere to subside, rise, and undergo lateral movement. See also **isostasy** [c20 from astheno-, from Greek *asthenēs* weak + SPHERE]

asthma ('æsmə) *n* a respiratory disorder, often of allergic origin, characterized by difficulty in breathing, wheezing, and a sense of constriction in the chest [c14 from Greek: laborious breathing, from *azein* to breathe hard]

asthmatic (æs'mætɪk) *adj* **1** of, relating to, or having asthma ▷ *n* **2** a person who has asthma > asth'matically *adv*

Asti ('æstɪ) *n* a town in NW Italy: famous for its sparkling wine (**Asti spumante** (spuː'mæntɪ)). Pop: 71 276 (2001)

astigmatic (,æstɪg'mætɪk) *adj* **1** relating to or affected with astigmatism ▷ *n* **2** a person who has astigmatism [c19 from A-¹ + Greek *stigmat-*, *stigma* spot, focus; see STIGMA] > ,astig'matically *adv*

astigmatism (ə'stɪgmə,tɪzəm) *or* **astigmia** (ə'stɪgmɪə) *n* **1** a defect of a lens resulting in the formation of distorted images; caused by the curvature of the lens being different in different planes **2** faulty vision resulting from defective curvature of the cornea or lens of the eye

astilbe (ə'stɪlbɪ) *n* any perennial saxifragaceous plant of the genus *Astilbe* of E Asia and North America: cultivated for their ornamental spikes or panicles of pink or white flowers [c19 New Latin, from Greek: not glittering, from A-¹ + *stilbē*, from *stilbein* to glitter; referring to its inconspicuous individual flowers]

astir (ə'stɜː) *adj (postpositive)* **1** awake and out of bed **2** in motion; on the move

ASTM *abbreviation for* American Society for Testing and Materials

Astolat ('æstəʊ,læt) *n* a town in Arthurian legend: location unknown

astomatous (æ'stɒmətəs, -'stəʊ-) *adj* **1** (of animals) having no mouth **2** (of plants) having no stomata

astonied (ə'stɒnɪd) *adj archaic* stunned; dazed [c14 from *astonyen* to ASTONISH]

astonish (ə'stɒnɪʃ) *vb (tr)* to fill with amazement; surprise greatly [c15 from earlier *astonyen* (see ASTONIED), from Old French *estoner*, from Vulgar Latin *extonāre* (unattested) to strike with thunder, from Latin *tonāre* to thunder]

astonishing (ə'stɒnɪʃɪŋ) *adj* causing great surprise or amazement; astounding > a'stonishingly *adv*

astonishment (ə'stɒnɪʃmənt) *n* **1** extreme surprise; amazement **2** a cause of amazement

Astoria (ə'stɔːrɪə) *n* a port in NW Oregon, near the mouth of the Columbia River: founded as a fur-trading post in 1811 by John Jacob Astor. Pop: 9660 (2003 est)

astound (ə'staʊnd) *vb (tr)* to overwhelm with amazement and wonder; bewilder [c17 from *astoned* amazed, from Old French *estoné*, from *estoner* to ASTONISH]

astounding (ə'staʊndɪŋ) *adj* causing amazement and wonder; bewildering > a'stoundingly *adv*

astr. *or* **astron.** *abbreviation for* **1** astronomical **2** astronomy

astraddle (ə'strædəl) *adj* **1** *(postpositive)* with a leg on either side of something ▷ *prep* **2** astride

astragal ('æstrəgəl) *n* **1** *architect* **a** Also called: bead a small convex moulding, usually with a semicircular cross section **b** a moulding having the form of a string of beads **2** *furniture* a glazing bar, esp in a bookcase **3** *anatomy* the ankle or anklebone [c17 from Latin *astragalus*, from Greek *astragalos* anklebone, hence, small round moulding]

astragalus (æ'strægələs) *n, pl* -li (-,laɪ) *anatomy* another name for **talus¹** [c16 via New Latin from Latin: ASTRAGAL]

astrakhan (,æstrə'kæn, -'kɑːn) *n* **1** a fur, usually black or grey, made of the closely curled wool of lambs from Astrakhan **2** a cloth with curled pile resembling this **3** *(modifier)* made of such fur or cloth: *an astrakhan collar*

Astrakhan (,æstrə'kæn, -'kɑːn; *Russian* 'astrəxənj) *n* a city in SE Russia, on the delta of the Volga River, 21 m (70 ft) below sea level. Pop: 507 000 (2005 est)

astral ('æstrəl) *adj* **1** relating to, proceeding from, consisting of, or resembling the stars: *an astral body* **2** *biology* of or relating to the aster occurring in dividing cells **3** *theosophy* denoting or relating to a supposed supersensible substance believed to form the material of a second body for each person, taking the form of an aura discernible to certain gifted individuals [c17 from Late Latin *astrālis*, from Latin *astrum* star, from Greek *astron*] > 'astrally *adv*

astraphobia *or* **astrophobia** (,æstrə'fəʊbɪə) *n* a fear of thunder and lightning [c20 see ASTRO-, -PHOBIA] > ,astra'phobic *or* ,astro'phobic *adj*

astray (ə'streɪ) *adj (postpositive)* ▷ *adv* **1** out of the correct path or direction **2** out of the right, good, or expected way; into error [c13 from Old French *estraie* roaming, from *estraier* to STRAY]

astrict (ə'strɪkt) *vb (tr) archaic* to bind, confine, or constrict [c16 from Latin *astrictus* drawn closely together, from *astringere* to tighten, from *stringere* to bind] > as'triction *n* > as'trictive *adj* > as'trictively *adv*

astride (ə'straɪd) *adj (postpositive)* **1** with a leg on either side **2** with the legs far apart ▷ *prep* **3** with a leg on either side of **4** with a part on both sides of

astringent (ə'strɪndʒənt) *adj* **1** severe; harsh **2** sharp or invigorating **3** causing contraction of body tissues, checking blood flow, or restricting secretions of fluids; styptic ▷ *n* **4** an astringent drug or lotion [c16 from Latin *astringēns* drawing together; see ASTRICT] > as'tringency *or* as'tringence *n* > as'tringently *adv*

astro- *combining form* **1** indicating a heavenly body, star, or star-shaped structure: *astrology; astrocyte* **2** indicating outer space: *astronautics* [from Greek, from *astron* star]

astrobiology (ˌæstrəʊbaɪˈɒlədʒɪ) *n* the branch of biology that investigates the possibility of life elsewhere in the universe

astrobleme (ˈæstrəˌbliːm) *n* a mark on the earth's surface, usually circular, formed by a large ancient meteorite impact [C20 from ASTRO- + Greek *blēma* shot, wound]

astrobotany (ˌæstrəʊˈbɒtənɪ) *n* the branch of botany that investigates the possibility that plants grow on other planets

astrochemistry (ˌæstrəʊˈkɛmɪstrɪ) *n* the study of the chemistry of celestial bodies and space, esp by means of spectroscopy

astrocompass (ˌæstrəʊˈkʌmpəs) *n* a navigational instrument for giving directional bearings from the centre of the earth to a particular star. It is carried in long-range aircraft, ships, spacecraft, etc

astrocyte (ˈæstrəʊˌsaɪt) *n* any of the star-shaped cells in the tissue supporting the brain and spinal cord (neuroglia)

astrodome (ˈæstrəˌdəʊm) *n* **1** Also called: **astrohatch** a transparent dome on the top of an aircraft, through which observations can be made, esp of the stars **2** a large domed sports stadium

astrodynamics (ˌæstrəʊdaɪˈnæmɪks) *n* (*functioning as singular*) the study of the motion of natural and artificial bodies in space

astrogeology (ˌæstrəʊdʒɪˈɒlədʒɪ) *n* the study of the structure, composition, and history of other planets and other bodies in the solar system

astroid (ˈæstrɔɪd) *n maths* a hypocycloid having four cusps [C19 from ASTRO- + -OID]

astrol. *abbreviation for* **1** astrological **2** astrology

astrolabe (ˈæstrəˌleɪb) *n* an instrument used by early astronomers to measure the altitude of stars and planets and also as a navigational aid. It consists of a graduated circular disc with a movable sighting device. Compare **sextant** [C13 via Old French and Medieval Latin from Greek, from *astrolabos* (adj), literally: star-taking, from *astron* star + *lambanein* to take]

astrology (əˈstrɒlədʒɪ) *n* **1** the study of the motions and relative positions of the planets, sun, and moon, interpreted in terms of human characteristics and activities **2** the primitive study of celestial bodies, which formed the basis of astronomy [C14 from Old French *astrologie*, from Latin *astrologia*, from Greek, from *astrologos* (originally: astronomer; see ASTRO-, -LOGY] > **asˈtrologer** or **asˈtrologist** *n* > **astrological** (ˌæstrəˈlɒdʒɪkəl) *adj* > ˌastroˈlogically *adv*

astrometry (əˈstrɒmɪtrɪ) *n* the branch of astronomy concerned with the measurement of the position and motion of celestial bodies > **astrometric** (ˌæstrəˈmɛtrɪk) or ˌastroˈmetrical *adj*

astronaut (ˈæstrəˌnɔːt) *n* a person trained for travelling in space. See also **cosmonaut** [C20 from ASTRO- + -naut from Greek *nautēs* sailor, on the model of *aeronaut*]

astronautics (ˌæstrəˈnɔːtɪks) *n* (*functioning as singular*) the science and technology of space flight > ˌastroˈnautic or ˌastroˈnautical *adj* > ˌastroˈnautically *adv*

astronavigation (ˌæstrəʊˌnævɪˈɡeɪʃən) *n* another term for **celestial navigation**. > ˌastroˈnaviˌgator *n*

astronomer (əˈstrɒnəmə) *n* a scientist who studies astronomy

Astronomer Royal *n* an honorary title awarded to an eminent British astronomer: until 1971, the Astronomer Royal was also director of the Royal Greenwich Observatory

astronomical (ˌæstrəˈnɒmɪkəl) or **astronomic** *adj* **1** enormously large; immense **2** of or relating to astronomy > ˌastroˈnomically *adv*

astronomical clock *n* **1** a complex clock showing astronomical phenomena, such as the phases of the moon **2** any clock showing sidereal time used in observatories

astronomical telescope *n* any telescope designed and mounted for use in astronomy. Such telescopes usually form inverted images. See **Cassegrain telescope, Newtonian telescope, equatorial mounting**

astronomical unit *n* a unit of distance used in astronomy equal to the mean distance between the earth and the sun. 1 astronomical unit is equivalent to 1.495×10^{11} metres or about 9.3×10^7 miles

astronomical year *n* another name for **year** See **year** (sense 4)

astronomy (əˈstrɒnəmɪ) *n* the scientific study of the individual celestial bodies (excluding the earth) and of the universe as a whole. Its various branches include astrometry, astrodynamics, cosmology, and astrophysics [C13 from Old French *astronomie*, from Latin *astronomia*, from Greek; see ASTRO-, -NOMY]

astrophotography (ˌæstrəʊfəˈtɒɡrəfɪ) *n* the photography of celestial bodies used in astronomy > **astrophotographic** (ˌæstrəʊˌfəʊtəˈɡræfɪk) *adj*

astrophysics (ˌæstrəʊˈfɪzɪks) *n* (*functioning as singular*) the branch of physics concerned with the physical and chemical properties, origin, and evolution of the celestial bodies > ˌastroˈphysical *adj* > ˌastroˈphysicist *n*

astrosphere (ˈæstrəˌsfɪə) *n cytology* **1** another name for **centrosome** **2** Also called: **attraction sphere** the part of the aster excluding the centrosome

astrotourist (ˈæstrəʊˌtʊərɪst) *n* a person who pays to travels into space as a form of recreation > ˌastroˈtourism *n*

Asturias (æˈstʊərɪˌæs) *n* a region and former kingdom of NW Spain, consisting of a coastal plain and the Cantabrian Mountains: a Christian stronghold against the Moors (8th to 13th centuries); rich mineral resources

astute (əˈstjuːt) *adj* having insight or acumen; perceptive; shrewd [C17 from Latin *astūtus* cunning, from *astus* (n) cleverness] > **asˈtutely** *adv* > **asˈtuteness** *n*

Astyanax (æˈstaɪəˌnæks) *n Greek myth* the young son of Hector and Andromache, who was hurled from the walls of Troy by the Greeks

astylar (æˈstaɪlə, eɪ-) *adj architect* without columns or pilasters [C19 from A-¹ + Greek *stulos* pillar]

Asunción (*Spanish* asunˈsjon) *n* the capital and chief port of Paraguay, on the Paraguay River, 1530 km (950 miles) from the Atlantic. Pop: 1 750 000 (2005 est)

asunder (əˈsʌndə) *adv, adj* (*postpositive*) in or into parts or pieces; apart: *to tear asunder* [Old English *on sundran* apart; see SUNDER]

Asur (ˈæsə) *n* a variant spelling of **Assur**

ASW *abbreviation for* antisubmarine warfare

Aswan, Assuan or **Assouan** (ɑːˈswɑːn) *n* an ancient town in SE Egypt, on the Nile, just below the First Cataract. Pop: 249 000 (2005 est). Ancient name: **Syene**

Aswan High Dam *n* a dam on the Nile forming a reservoir (Lake Nasser) extending 480 km (300 miles) from the First to the Third Cataracts: opened in 1971, it was built 6 km (4 miles) upstream from the old **Aswan Dam** (built in 1902 and twice raised). Height of dam: 109 m (365 ft)

aswarm (əˈswɔːm) *adj* (*postpositive*) filled, esp with moving things; swarming: *flower beds aswarm with bees*

asyllabic (ˌeɪsɪˈlæbɪk, ˌæsɪ-) *adj* not functioning in the manner of a syllable

asylum (əˈsaɪləm) *n* **1** a safe or inviolable place of refuge, esp as formerly offered by the Christian Church to criminals, outlaws, etc; sanctuary (often in the phrase **give asylum to**) **2** shelter; refuge **3** *international law* refuge afforded to a person whose extradition is sought by a foreign government: *political asylum* **4** *obsolescent* an institution for the shelter, treatment, or confinement of individuals, esp a mental hospital (formerly termed **lunatic asylum**) [C15 via Latin from Greek *asulon* refuge, from *asulos* that may not be seized, from A-¹ + *sulon* right of seizure]

asylum seeker *n* a person who, from fear of persecution for reasons of race, religion, social group, or political opinion, has crossed an international frontier into a country in which he or she hopes to be granted refugee status

asymmetric (ˌæsɪˈmɛtrɪk, ˌeɪ-) or **asymmetrical** *adj* **1** not symmetrical; lacking symmetry; misproportioned **2** *chem* **a** (of a molecule) having its atoms and radicals arranged unsymmetrically **b** (of a carbon atom) attached to four different atoms or radicals so that stereoisomerism results **c** involving chiral molecules: *asymmetric synthesis* **3** *electrical engineering* (of conductors) having different conductivities depending on the direction of current flow, as of diodes **4** *aeronautics* having unequal thrust, as caused by an inoperative engine in a twin-engined aircraft **5** *logic, maths* (of a relation) never holding between a pair of values *x* and *y* when it holds between *y* and *x*, as "...is the father of...". Compare **symmetric** (sense 1), **antisymmetric, nonsymmetric** > ˌasymˈmetrically *adv*

asymmetrical warfare *n* warfare between a powerful military force and a weak guerilla force

asymmetric bars *adv, pl n gymnastics* **a** (*functioning as plural*) a pair of wooden or fibreglass bars placed parallel to each other but set at different heights, for various exercises **b** (*functioning as singular*) an event in a gymnastic competition in which competitors exercise on such bars

asymmetric time *n* musical time consisting of an odd number of beats in each bar divided into uneven combinations, such as 3 + 2, 4 + 3, 2 + 3 + 2, etc

asymmetry (æˈsɪmɪtrɪ, eɪ-) *n* lack or absence of symmetry in spatial arrangements or in mathematical or logical relations

asymptomatic (æˌsɪmptəˈmætɪk, eɪ-) *adj* (of a disease or suspected disease) without symptoms; providing no subjective evidence of existence > ˌsymptoˈmatically *adv*

asymptote (ˈæsɪmˌtəʊt) *n* a straight line that is closely approached by a plane curve so that the perpendicular distance between them decreases to zero as the distance from the origin increases to infinity [C17 from Greek *asumptōtos* not falling together, from A-¹ + SYN- + *ptōtos* inclined to fall, from *piptein* to fall]

asymptotic (ˌæsɪmˈtɒtɪk) or **asymptotical** *adj* **1** of or referring to an asymptote **2** (of a function, series, formula, etc) approaching a given value or condition, as a variable or an expression containing a variable approaches a limit, usually infinity > ˌasympˈtotically *adv*

asynapsis (ˌeɪsɪnˈæpsɪs) *n biology* failure of pairing of chromosomes at meiosis

asynchronism (æˈsɪŋkrəˌnɪzəm, eɪ-) *n* a lack of synchronism; occurrence at different times > **aˈsynchronous** *adj* > **aˈsynchronously** *adv*

asyndetic (ˌæsɪnˈdɛtɪk) *adj* **1** (of a catalogue or index) without cross references **2** (of a linguistic construction) having no conjunction, as in *I came, I saw, I conquered* > ˌasynˈdetically *adv*

asyndeton (æˈsɪndɪtən) *n, pl* -deta (-dɪtə) **1** the omission of a conjunction between the parts of a sentence **2** an asyndetic construction. Compare **syndeton** [C16 from New Latin, from Greek *asundeton*, from *asundetos* unconnected, from A-¹ + *sundein* to bind together]

asynergia (ˌæsɪˈnɜːdʒɪə) or **asynergy** (əˈsɪnədʒɪ) *n pathol* lack of coordination between muscles or parts, as occurs in cerebellar disease

asystole (əˈsɪstəlɪ) *n pathol* the absence of heartbeat; cardiac arrest > **asystolic** (ˌæsɪˈstɒlɪk) *adj*

Asyut or **Assiut** (æˈsjuːt) *n* an ancient city in central Egypt, on the Nile. Pop: 417 000 (2005 est). Ancient Greek name: **Lycopolis**

at¹ (æt) *prep* **1** used to indicate location or position: *are they at the table?; staying at a small hotel* **2** towards; in the direction of: *looking at television; throwing stones at windows* **3** used to indicate position in time: *come at three o'clock* **4** engaged in; in a state of (being): *children at play; stand at ease; he is at his most charming today* **5** (in expressions concerned with habitual activity) during the passing of (esp in the phrase **at night**): *he used to work at night* **6** for; in exchange for: *it's selling at four pounds* **7** used to indicate the object of an emotion: *angry at the driver; shocked at his behaviour* **8** where it's at *slang* the real place of action [Old English æt; related to Old Norse *at*, Latin *ad* to]

at² (ɑːt, æt) *n, pl* **at** a Laotian monetary unit worth one hundredth of a kip [from Thai]

at³ *the internet domain name for* Austria

At **1** *the chemical symbol for* astatine **2** Also: **A** ▷ *symbol for* ampere-turn

AT *abbreviation for* **attainment target**

at. *abbreviation for* **1** Also: **atm** atmosphere (unit of pressure) **2** atomic

ataata (ˈɑːˌtɑːtə) *n NZ* another name for **cat's-eye** (sense 2) [Māori]

Atacama Desert (*Spanish* ataˈkama) *n* a desert region along the W coast of South America, mainly in N Chile: a major source of nitrates. Area: about 80 000 sq km (31 000 sq miles)

atactic (eɪˈtæktɪk) *adj* **1** *chem* (of a polymer) having random sequence of the stereochemical arrangement of groups on carbon atoms in the chain; not stereospecific **2** *pathol* relating to or displaying ataxia

ataghan (ˈætəˌɡæn) *n* a variant of **yataghan**

Atalanta (ˌætəˈlæntə) *n Greek myth* a maiden who agreed to marry any man who could defeat her in a running race. She lost to Hippomenes when she paused to pick up three golden apples that he had deliberately dropped

ataman (ˈætəmən) *n, pl* **-mans** an elected leader of the Cossacks; hetman [from Russian, from Polish *hetman*, from German *Hauptmann* (literally: head man)]

ataractic (ˌætəˈræktɪk) *or* **ataraxic** (ˌætəˈræksɪk) *adj* **1** able to calm or tranquillize ▷ *n* **2** *obsolete* an ataractic drug

ataraxia (ˌætəˈræksɪə) *or* **ataraxy** (ˈætəˌræksɪ) *n* calmness or peace of mind; emotional tranquillity [C17 from Greek: serenity, from *ataraktos* undisturbed, from A-¹ + *tarassein* to trouble]

atavism (ˈætəˌvɪzəm) *n* **1** the recurrence in a plant or animal of certain primitive characteristics that were present in an ancestor but have not occurred in intermediate generations **2** reversion to a former or more primitive type [C19 from French *atavisme*, from Latin *atavus* strictly: great-grandfather's grandfather, probably from *atta* daddy + *avus* grandfather] > **ˈatavist** *n* > **atavic** (əˈtævɪk) *adj*

atavistic (ˌætəˈvɪstɪk) *adj* of or relating to reversion to a former or more primitive type > ˌataˈvistically *adv*

ataxia (əˈtæksɪə) *or* **ataxy** (əˈtæksɪ) *n pathol* lack of muscular coordination [C17 via New Latin from Greek: lack of coordination, from A-¹ + *-taxia*, from *tassein* to put in order] > aˈtaxic *or* aˈtactic *adj*

ATB *text messaging abbreviation for* all the best

Atbara (ˈætbərə, æt'bɑː-) *n* **1** a town in NE Sudan. Pop: 110 000 (2005 est) **2** a river in NE Africa, rising in N Ethiopia and flowing through E Sudan to the Nile at Atbara. Length: over 800 km (500 miles)

ATC *abbreviation for* **1** air-traffic control **2** (in Britain) Air Training Corps

at-desk *adj* carried out at a person's desk at his or her place of work: *an at-desk massage*

ate (ɛt, eɪt) *vb* the past tense of **eat**

Ate (ˈeɪtɪ, ˈɑːtɪ) *n Greek myth* a goddess who makes men blind so that they will blunder into guilty acts [C16 via Latin from Greek *atē* a rash impulse]

-ate¹ *suffix* **1** (*forming adjectives*) possessing; having the appearance or characteristics of: *fortunate;*

palmate; Latinate **2** (*forming nouns*) a chemical compound, esp a salt or ester of an acid: *carbonate; stearate* **3** (*forming nouns*) the product of a process: *condensate* **4** forming verbs from nouns and adjectives: *hyphenate; rusticate* [from Latin *-ātus*, past participial ending of verbs ending in *-āre*]

-ate² *suffix forming nouns* denoting office, rank, or a group having a certain function: *episcopate; electorate* [from Latin *-ātus*, suffix (fourth declension) of collective nouns]

Atebrin (ˈætəbrɪn) *or US* **Atabrine** (ˈætəˌbriːn, -brɪn) *n trademark* proprietary names for **mepacrine**

atelectasis (ˌætəˈlɛktəsɪs) *n* **1** failure of the lungs to expand fully at birth **2** collapse of the lung or a part of the lung, usually caused by bronchial obstruction [C19 New Latin, from Greek *atelēs* imperfect + *ektasis* extension]

atelier (əˈtɛljeɪ; *French* atəlje) *n* an artist's studio or workshop [C17 from Old French *astelier* workshop, from *astele* chip of wood, from Latin *astula* splinter, from *assis* board]

a tempo (ɑ ˈtɛmpəʊ) *music* ▷ *adj* ▷ *adv* **1** to the original tempo ▷ *n* **2** a passage thus marked ▷ Also: **tempo primo** [Italian: in (the original) time]

Aten *or* **Aton** (ˈɑːtʰən) *n* (in ancient Egypt) the solar disc worshipped as the sole god in the reign of Akhenaten

Athabaska *or* **Athabasca** (ˌæθəˈbæskə) *n* **1 Lake** a lake in W Canada, in NW Saskatchewan and NE Alberta. Area: about 7770 sq km (3000 sq miles) **2** a river in W Canada, rising in the Rocky Mountains and flowing northeast to Lake Athabaska. Length: 1230 km (765 miles)

Athamas (ˈæθəˌmæs) *n Greek myth* a king of Orchomenus in Boeotia; the father of Phrixus and Helle by his first wife Nephele, whom he deserted for Ino

athame (ˈɑːθəmeɪ) *n* (in Wicca) a witch's ceremonial knife, usually with a black handle, used in rituals rather than for cutting or carving

Athanasian (ˌæθəˈneɪʃən) *adj* of or relating to Saint Athanasius, the patriarch of Alexandria (?296–373 AD)

Athanasian Creed (ˌæθəˈneɪʃən) *n Christianity* a profession of faith widely used in the Western Church which, though formerly attributed to Athanasius, probably originated in Gaul between 381 and 428 AD

Athapascan, Athapaskan (ˌæθəˈpæskən) *or* **Athabascan, Athabaskan** (ˌæθəˈbæskən) *n* **1** a group of North American Indian languages belonging to the Na-Dene phylum, including Apache and Navaho **2** a speaker of one of these languages [from Cree *athapaskaaw* scattered grass or reeds]

Atharva-Veda (əˈtɑːvəˈveɪdə) *n Hinduism* the fourth and latest Veda, largely consisting of priestly spells and incantations

atheism (ˈeɪθɪˌɪzəm) *n* rejection of belief in God or gods [C16 from French *athéisme*, from Greek *atheos* godless, from A-¹ + *theos* god] > ˈatheist *n, adj* > ˌatheˈistic *or* ˌatheˈistical *adj* > ˌatheˈistically *adv*

atheling (ˈæθɪlɪŋ) *n* (in Anglo-Saxon England) a prince of any of the royal dynasties [Old English *ætheling*, from *æthelu* noble family + -ING³; related to Old High German *adaling*, Old Norse *öthlingr*]

athematic (ˌæθɪˈmætɪk) *adj* **1** *music* not based on themes **2** *linguistics* (of verbs) having a suffix attached immediately to the stem, without an intervening vowel

Athena (əˈθiːnə) *or* **Athene** (əˈθiːnɪ) *n Greek myth* a virgin goddess of wisdom, practical skills, and prudent warfare. She was born, fully armed, from the head of Zeus. Also called: **Pallas Athena, Pallas** Roman counterpart: **Minerva**

athenaeum *or US* **atheneum** (ˌæθɪˈniːəm) *n* **1** an institution for the promotion of learning **2** a building containing a reading room or library, esp one used by such an institution [C18 from Late Latin, from Greek *Athēnaion* temple of Athene,

frequented by poets and teachers]

Athenaeum *or sometimes US* **Atheneum** (ˌæθɪˈniːəm) *n* **1** (in ancient Greece) a building sacred to the goddess Athena, esp the Athenian temple that served as a gathering place for the learned **2** (in imperial Rome) the academy of learning established near the Forum in about 135 AD by Hadrian

Athenian (əˈθiːnɪən) *n* **1** a native or inhabitant of Athens ▷ *adj* **2** of or relating to Athens

Athens (ˈæθɪnz) *n* the capital of Greece, in the southeast near the Saronic Gulf: became capital after independence in 1834; ancient city-state, most powerful in the 5th century BC; contains the hill citadel of the Acropolis. Pop: 3 238 000 (2005 est). Greek name: Athinai (aˈθinɛ)

athermancy (æˈθɜːmənsɪ) *n* an inability to transmit radiant heat or infrared radiation. Also called: adiathermancy [C19 from Greek *athermantos* not heated, from A-¹ + *thermainein* to heat, from *thermē* heat; compare DIATHERMANCY]

athermanous (æˈθɜːmənəs) *adj* capable of stopping radiant heat or infrared radiation

atherogenic (ˌæθərəʊˈdʒɛnɪk) *adj* causing atheroma > ˌatheroˈgenesis *n*

atheroma (ˌæθəˈrəʊmə) *n, pl* **-mas** *or* **-mata** (-mətə) *pathol* a fatty deposit on or within the inner lining of an artery, often causing an obstruction to the blood flow [C18 via Latin from Greek *athērōma* tumour full of matter resembling gruel, from *athēra* gruel] > atheromatous (ˌæθəˈrɒmətəs, -ˈrəʊ-) *adj*

atherosclerosis (ˌæθərəʊskliˈrəʊsɪs) *n, pl* **-ses** (-siːz) a degenerative disease of the arteries characterized by patchy thickening of the inner lining of the arterial walls, caused by deposits of fatty material; a form of arteriosclerosis. See **atheroma** [C20 from New Latin, from Greek *athēra* gruel (see ATHEROMA) + SCLEROSIS] > atherosclerotic (ˌæθərəʊskliəˈrɒtɪk) *adj*

athetosis (ˌæθɪˈtəʊsɪs) *n pathol* a condition characterized by uncontrolled rhythmic writhing movement, esp of fingers, hands, head, and tongue, caused by cerebral lesion [C19 from Greek *athetos* not in place, from A-¹ + *tithenai* to place] > ˈatheˌtoid *adj*

athirst (əˈθɜːst) *adj* (*postpositive*) **1** (often foll by *for*) having an eager desire; longing **2** *archaic* thirsty

athlete (ˈæθliːt) *n* **1** a person trained to compete in sports or exercises involving physical strength, speed, or endurance **2** a person who has a natural aptitude for physical activities **3** *chiefly Brit* a competitor in track and field events [C18 from Latin via Greek *athlētēs*, from *athlein* to compete for a prize, from *athlos* a contest]

athlete's foot *n* a fungal infection of the skin of the foot, esp between the toes and on the soles. Technical name: **tinea pedis**

athletic (æθˈlɛtɪk) *adj* **1** physically fit or strong; muscular or active **2** of, relating to, or suitable for an athlete or for athletics **3** of or relating to a person with a muscular and well-proportioned body. See also **somatotype**. > athˈletically *adv* > athˈleticism *n*

athletics (æθˈlɛtɪks) *n* (*functioning as plural or singular*) **1 a** track and field events **b** (*as modifier*): *an athletics meeting* **2** sports or exercises engaged in by athletes **3** the theory or practice of athletic activities and training

athletic support *n* a more formal term for **jockstrap**

athodyd (ˈæθəʊˌdaɪd) *n* another name for **ramjet** [C20 from a(ero)-th(erm)ody(namic) d(uct)]

Atholl brose (ˈæθəl) *n Scot* a mixture of whisky and honey left to ferment before consumption [C19 after *Atholl*, a district of central Scotland]

at-home *n* **1** another name for **open day 2** a social gathering in a person's home

Athos (ˈæθɒs, ˈeɪ-) *n* **Mount** a mountain in NE Greece, in Macedonia Central region: site of the Monastic Republic of Mount Athos, autonomous since 1927 and inhabited by Greek Orthodox

Basilian monks in 20 monasteries founded in the 10th century. Pop: 1942 (2001)

athwart (ə'θwɔːt) *adv* **1** transversely; from one side to another ▷ *prep* **2** across the path or line of (esp a ship) **3** in opposition to; against [c15 from A-² + THWART]

athwartships (ə'θwɔːtˌʃɪps) *adv nautical* from one side to the other of a vessel at right angles to the keel

-atic *suffix forming adjectives* of the nature of the thing specified: *problematic* [from French *-atique*, from Greek *-atikos*]

atigi (ˈætɪɡɪ, əˈtiːɡɪ) *n* a type of parka worn by the Inuit in Canada

atilt (ə'tɪlt) *adv, adj (postpositive)* **1** in a tilted or inclined position **2** *archaic* in or as if in a joust

-ation *suffix forming nouns* indicating an action, process, state, condition, or result: *arbitration; cogitation; hibernation; moderation.* Compare **-ion, -tion** [from Latin *-ātiōn-*, suffix of abstract nouns, from *-ātus* -ATE¹ + *-iōn* -ION]

atishoo (ə'tɪʃuː) *interj* a representation of the sound of a sneeze [c19 of imitative origin]

-ative *suffix forming adjectives* of, relating to, or tending to: *authoritative; decorative; informative* [from Latin *-ātivus*, from *ātus* -ATE¹ + *ivus* -IVE]

ATK *text messaging, email, etc abbreviation for* **1** antitank **2** at the keyboard

Atlanta (æt'læntə) *n* a city in N Georgia: the state capital. Pop: 423 019 (2003 est)

Atlantean (ˌætlæn'tiːən, æt'læntɪən) *adj* **1** *literary* of, relating to, or like Atlas; extremely strong **2** of or connected with Atlantis

atlantes (ət'læntiːz) *n* the plural of **atlas** (sense 4)

Atlantic (ət'læntɪk) *n* **1** **the** short for the **Atlantic Ocean** ▷ *adj* **2** of or relating to or bordering the Atlantic Ocean **3** of or relating to Atlas or the Atlas Mountains [c15 from Latin *Atlanticus*, from Greek (*pelagos*) *Atlantikos* (the sea) of Atlas (so called because it lay beyond the Atlas Mountains)]

Atlantic Charter *n* the joint declaration issued by F. D. Roosevelt and Winston Churchill on Aug 14, 1941, consisting of eight principles to guide a postwar settlement

Atlantic City *n* a resort in SE New Jersey on Absecon Beach, an island on the Atlantic coast. Pop: 40 385 (2003 est)

Atlantic Intracoastal Waterway *n* a system of inland and coastal waterways along the Atlantic coast of the US from Cape Cod to Florida Bay. Length: 2495 km (1550 miles)

Atlanticism (ət'læntɪˌsɪzəm) *n* advocacy of close cooperation in military, political, and economic matters between Western Europe, esp the UK, and the US > At'lanticist *n*

Atlantic Ocean *n* the world's second largest ocean, bounded in the north by the Arctic, in the south by the Antarctic, in the west by North and South America, and in the east by Europe and Africa. Greatest depth: 9220 m (30 246 ft). Area: about 81 585 000 sq km (31 500 000 sq miles)

Atlantic Provinces *pl n* **the** certain of the Canadian provinces with coasts facing the Gulf of St Lawrence or the Atlantic: New Brunswick, Nova Scotia, Prince Edward Island, and Newfoundland and Labrador

Atlantic Standard Time *n* the local time used in eastern Canada, four hours behind Greenwich Mean Time. Abbreviation: AST

Atlantis (ət'læntɪs) *n* (in ancient legend) a continent said to have sunk beneath the Atlantic Ocean west of the Straits of Gibraltar

atlas (ˈætləs) *n* **1** a collection of maps, usually in book form **2** a book of charts, graphs, etc, illustrating aspects of a subject: *an anatomical atlas* **3** *anatomy* the first cervical vertebra, attached to and supporting the skull in man. Compare **axis¹** (sense 3) **4** *pl* **atlantes** *architect* another name for **telamon 5** a standard size of drawing paper, 26 × 17 inches [c16 via Latin from Greek; first applied to maps, from depictions of Atlas supporting the heavens in 16th-century collections of maps]

Atlas (ˈætləs) *n* **1** *Greek myth* a Titan compelled to support the sky on his shoulders as punishment for rebelling against Zeus **2** a US intercontinental ballistic missile, also used in launching spacecraft **3** *astronomy* a small satellite of Saturn, discovered in 1980

Atlas Mountains *pl n* a mountain system of N Africa, between the Mediterranean and the Sahara. Highest peak: Mount Toubkal, 4165 m (13 664 ft)

Atli (ˈɑːtlɪ) *n Norse myth* a king of the Huns who married Gudrun for her inheritance and was slain by her after he killed her brothers

ATM *text messaging abbreviation for* **1** **automated teller machine 2** asynchronous transfer mode: used in digital communications, etc **3** at the moment

atm. *abbreviation for* atmosphere (unit of pressure). Also: **at.**

atman (ˈɑːtmən) *n Hinduism* **1** the personal soul or self; the thinking principle as manifested in consciousness **2** Brahman considered as the Universal Soul, the great Self or Person that dwells in the entire created order [from Sanskrit *ātman* breath; compare Old High German *ātum* breath]

atmo- *combining form* air or vapour: *atmometer; atmosphere* [via New Latin from Greek *atmos* vapour]

atmolysis (æt'mɒlɪsɪs) *n*, *pl* **-ses** (-ˌsiːz) a method of separating gases that depends on their differential rates of diffusion through a porous substance

atmometer (æt'mɒmɪtə) *n* an instrument for measuring the rate of evaporation of water into the atmosphere. Also called: evaporimeter, evaporometer > at'mometry *n*

atmosphere (ˈætməsˌfɪə) *n* **1** the gaseous envelope surrounding the earth or any other celestial body. See also **troposphere, stratosphere, mesosphere, ionosphere 2** the air or climate in a particular place: *the atmosphere was thick with smoke* **3** a general pervasive feeling or mood: *an atmosphere of elation* **4** the prevailing tone or mood of a novel, symphony, painting, or other work of art **5** a special mood or character associated with a place **6** any local gaseous environment or medium: *an inert atmosphere* **7** Abbreviations: **at, atm** a unit of pressure; the pressure that will support a column of mercury 760 mm high at 0°C at sea level. 1 atmosphere is equivalent to 101 325 newtons per square metre or 14.72 pounds per square inch > ˌatmos'pheric *or* ˌatmos'pherical *adj* > ˌatmos'pherically *adv*

atmospheric perspective *n* another term for **aerial perspective**

atmospheric pressure *n* the pressure exerted by the atmosphere at the earth's surface. It has an average value of 1 atmosphere

atmospherics (ˌætməs'fɛrɪks) *pl n* **1** electrical disturbances produced in the atmosphere by natural causes such as lightning **2** radio interference, heard as crackling or hissing in receivers, caused by electrical disturbance

atmospheric window *n* wavelengths of the electromagnetic spectrum that can be transmitted through the earth's atmosphere. Atmospheric windows occur in the visible, infrared, and radio regions of the spectrum

ATN *abbreviation for* **1** arc tangent **2** augmented transition network

at. no. *abbreviation for* atomic number

ATO *abbreviation for* Australian Tax Office

A to J (in New Zealand) *abbreviation for* Appendices to Journals (of the House of Representatives or Parliament)

atoll (ˈætɒl, ə'tɒl) *n* a circular coral reef or string of coral islands surrounding a lagoon [c17 from *atollon*, native name in the Maldive Islands]

atom (ˈætəm) *n* **1 a** the smallest quantity of an element that can take part in a chemical reaction **b** this entity as a source of nuclear energy: *the power of the atom.* See also **atomic structure 2** any

entity regarded as the indivisible building block of a theory **3** the hypothetical indivisible particle of matter postulated by certain ancient philosophers as the fundamental constituent of matter. See also **atomism 4** a very small amount or quantity; minute fragment: *to smash something to atoms; there is not an atom of truth in his allegations* [c16 via Old French and Latin, from Greek *atomos* (n), from *atomos* (adj) that cannot be divided, from A-¹ + *temnein* to cut]

atomic (ə'tɒmɪk) *adj* **1** of, using, or characterized by atomic bombs or atomic energy: *atomic warfare* **2** of, related to, or comprising atoms: *atomic hydrogen* **3** extremely small; minute **4** *logic* (of a sentence, formula, etc) having no internal structure at the appropriate level of analysis. In predicate calculus, *Fa* is an **atomic sentence** and *Fx* an **atomic predicate** > a'tomically *adv*

atomic age *n* **the** the current historical period, initiated by the development of the first atomic bomb towards the end of World War II and now marked by a balance of power between nations possessing the hydrogen bomb and the use of nuclear power as a source of energy

atomic bomb *or* **atom bomb** *n* a type of bomb in which the energy is provided by nuclear fission. Uranium-235 and plutonium-239 are the isotopes most commonly used in atomic bombs. Also called: A-bomb, fission bomb Compare **fusion bomb**

atomic clock *n* an extremely accurate clock in which an electrical oscillator is controlled by the natural vibrations of an atomic or molecular system such as caesium or ammonia

atomic cocktail *n* an aqueous solution of radioactive substance administered orally as part of the treatment for cancer

atomic energy *n* another name for **nuclear energy**

Atomic Energy Authority *n* (in Britain) a government body established in 1954 to control research and development in atomic energy. Abbreviation: AEA

Atomic Energy Commission *n* (in the US) a federal board established in 1946 to administer and develop domestic atomic energy programmes. Abbreviation: AEC

atomic heat *n* the product of an element's atomic weight and its specific heat (capacity)

atomicity (ˌætə'mɪsɪtɪ) *n* **1** the state of being made up of atoms **2** the number of atoms in the molecules of an element **3** a less common name for **valency**

atomic mass *n chem* **1** the mass of an isotope of an element in atomic mass units **2** short for **relative atomic mass**; see **atomic weight**

atomic mass unit *n* a unit of mass used to express atomic and molecular weights that is equal to one twelfth of the mass of an atom of carbon-12. It is equivalent to 1.66×10^{-27} kg. Abbreviation: amu Also called: unified atomic mass unit, dalton

atomic number *n* the number of protons in the nucleus of an atom of an element. Abbreviation: at. no. Symbol: *Z* Also called: proton number

atomic pile *n* the original name for a **nuclear reactor**

atomic power *n* another name for **nuclear power**

atomic structure *n* the concept of an atom as a central positively charged nucleus consisting of protons and neutrons surrounded by a number of electrons. The number of electrons is equal to the number of protons: the whole entity is thus electrically neutral

atomic theory *n* **1** any theory in which matter is regarded as consisting of atoms, esp that proposed by John Dalton postulating that elements are composed of atoms that can combine in definite proportions to form compounds **2** the current concept of the atom as an entity with a definite structure. See **atomic structure**

atomic volume *n* the atomic weight (relative

atomic mass) of an element divided by its density
atomic weight *n* the former name for **relative atomic mass** Abbreviation: **at wt**
atomism ('ætəˌmɪzəm) *n* **1** an ancient philosophical theory, developed by Democritus, the Greek philosopher (?460–?370 BC) and Lucretius, the Roman poet and philosopher (?96–55 BC), that the ultimate constituents of the universe are atoms: see **atom** (sense 3) **2 a** any of a number of theories that hold that some objects or phenomena can be explained as constructed out of a small number of distinct types of simple indivisible entities **b** any theory that holds that an understanding of the parts is logically prior to an understanding of the whole. Compare **holism** (sense 3) **3** *psychol* the theory that experiences and mental states are composed of elementary units > **'atomist** *n, adj* > **ˌatom'istic** *or* **ˌatom'istical** *adj* > **ˌatom'istically** *adv*
atomize *or* **atomise** ('ætəˌmaɪz) *vb* **1** to separate or be separated into free atoms **2** to reduce (a liquid or solid) to fine particles or spray or (of a liquid or solid) to be reduced in this way **3** (*tr*) to destroy by weapons, esp nuclear weapons > **ˌatomi'zation** *or* **ˌatomi'sation** *n*
atomizer *or* **atomiser** ('ætəˌmaɪzə) *n* a device for reducing a liquid to a fine spray, such as the nozzle used to feed oil into a furnace or an enclosed bottle with a fine outlet used to spray perfumes or medicines
atom smasher *n* *physics* the nontechnical name for **accelerator** (sense 2)
atomy[1] ('ætəmɪ) *n, pl* **-mies** *archaic* **1** an atom or minute particle **2** a minute creature [C16 from Latin *atomī* atoms, but used as if singular; see ATOM]
atomy[2] ('ætəmɪ) *n, pl* **-mies** an obsolete word for **skeleton** [C16 from mistaken division of ANATOMY (as if *an atomy*)]
Aton ('ɑːtᵊn) *n* a variant spelling of **Aten**
atonal (eɪ'təʊnᵊl, æ-) *adj* *music* having no established key. Compare **tonal** (sense 2) > **a'tonalism** *n* > **a'tonally** *adv*
atonality (ˌeɪtəʊ'nælɪtɪ, ˌæ-) *n* **1** absence of or disregard for an established musical key in a composition **2** the principles of composition embodying this and providing a radical alternative to the diatonic system ▷ Compare **tonality**
atone (ə'təʊn) *vb* **1** (*intr*; foll by *for*) to make amends or reparation (for a crime, sin, etc) **2** (*tr*) to expiate: *to atone a guilt with repentance* **3** *obsolete* to be in or bring into agreement [C16 back formation from ATONEMENT] > **a'tonable** *or* **a'toneable** *adj* > **a'toner** *n*
atonement (ə'təʊnmənt) *n* **1** satisfaction, reparation, or expiation given for an injury or wrong **2** (*often capital*) *christian theol* **a** the reconciliation of man with God through the life, sufferings, and sacrificial death of Christ **b** the sufferings and death of Christ **3** *Christian Science* the state in which the attributes of God are exemplified in man **4** *obsolete* reconciliation or agreement [C16 from Middle English phrase *at onement* in harmony]
atonic (eɪ'tɒnɪk, æ-) *adj* **1** (of a syllable, word, etc) carrying no stress; unaccented **2** *pathol* relating to or characterized by atony ▷ *n* **3** an unaccented or unstressed syllable, word, etc, such as *for* in *food for thought* [C18 from Latin *atonicus*, from Greek *atonos* lacking tone; see ATONY] > **atonicity** (ˌætə'nɪsɪtɪ, ˌeɪtəʊ-) *n*
atony ('ætənɪ) *n* **1** *pathol* lack of normal tone or tension, as in muscles; abnormal relaxation of a muscle **2** *phonetics* lack of stress or accent on a syllable or word [C17 from Latin *atonia*, from Greek: tonelessness, from *atonos* slack, from A-[1] + *tonos* TONE]
atop (ə'tɒp) *adv* **1** on top; at the top ▷ *prep* **2** on top of; at the top of
atopic (ə'tɒpɪk) *adj* *immunol* of or relating to hereditary hypersensitivity to certain allergens
atopy ('ætəʊpɪ) *n* *immunol* a hereditary tendency to be hypersensitive to certain allergens
-ator *suffix forming nouns* a person or thing that performs a certain action: *agitator; escalator; radiator* [from Latin *-ātor*; see -ATE[1] -OR[1]]
-atory *suffix forming adjectives* of, relating to, characterized by, or serving to: *circulatory; exploratory; migratory; explanatory* [from Latin *-ātōrius*; see -ATE[1], -ORY[2]]
ATP[1] *n* adenosine triphosphate; a nucleotide found in the mitochondria of all plant and animal cells. It is the major source of energy for cellular reactions, this energy being released during its conversion to ADP. Formula: $C_{10}H_{16}N_5O_{13}P_3$
ATP[2] *abbreviation for* **1** advanced turboprop **2** Association of Tennis Professionals **3** automatic train protection: a safety system which automatically prevents a train from passing through a stop signal
ATPase (ˌeɪtiː'piːˌeɪz) *n* adenosine triphosphatase; an enzyme that converts ATP to ADP
atrabilious (ˌætrə'bɪljəs) *or* **atrabiliar** *adj* *rare* irritable [C17 from Latin *ātra bīlis* black bile, from *āter* black + *bīlis* BILE[1]] > **ˌatra'biliousness** *n*
atrazine ('ætrəziːn) *n* a white crystalline compound widely used as a weedkiller. Formula: $C_8H_{14}N_5Cl$ [C20 from A(MINO) TR(I)AZINE]
atresia (ə'triːʒɪə, -ʒə) *n* absence of or unnatural narrowing of a body channel [C19 New Latin, from Greek *atrētos* not perforated]
Atreus ('eɪtrɪˌuːs, 'eɪtrɪəs) *n* *Greek myth* a king of Mycenae, son of Pelops, father of Agamemnon and Menelaus, and member of the family known as the **Atreids** ('eɪtrɪɪdz)
atrioventricular (ˌeɪtrɪəʊvɛn'trɪkjʊlə) *adj* *anatomy* of, relating to, or affecting both the atria and the ventricles of the heart: *atrioventricular disease* [C19 from *atrio-*, from New Latin *atrium* heart chamber (see ATRIUM) + VENTRICULAR]
atrip (ə'trɪp) *adj* (*postpositive*) *nautical* (of an anchor) no longer caught on the bottom; tripped; aweigh
atrium ('eɪtrɪəm, 'ɑː-) *n, pl* **atria** ('eɪtrɪə, 'ɑː-) **1** the open main court of a Roman house **2** a central often glass-roofed hall that extends through several storeys in a building, such as a shopping centre or hotel **3** a court in front of an early Christian or medieval church, esp one flanked by colonnades **4** *anatomy* a cavity or chamber in the body, esp the upper chamber of each half of the heart [C17 from Latin; related to *āter* black, perhaps originally referring to the part of the house that was blackened by smoke from the hearth] > **'atrial** *adj*
atrocious (ə'trəʊʃəs) *adj* **1** extremely cruel or wicked; ruthless: *atrocious deeds* **2** horrifying or shocking: *an atrocious road accident* **3** *informal* very bad; detestable: *atrocious writing* [C17 from Latin *ātrōx* dreadful, from *āter* black] > **a'trociously** *adv* > **a'trociousness** *n*
atrocity (ə'trɒsɪtɪ) *n, pl* **-ties** **1** behaviour or an action that is wicked or ruthless **2** the fact or quality of being atrocious **3** (*usually plural*) acts of extreme cruelty, esp against prisoners or civilians in wartime
atrophic rhinitis *n* another name for **bull nose**
atrophy ('ætrəfɪ) *n, pl* **-phies** **1** a wasting away of an organ or part, or a failure to grow to normal size as the result of disease, faulty nutrition, etc **2** any degeneration or diminution, esp through lack of use ▷ *vb* **-phies, -phying, -phied** **3** to waste away or cause to waste away [C17 from Late Latin *atrophia*, from Greek, from *atrophos* ill-fed, from A-[1] + *-trophos* from *trephein* to feed] > **atrophic** (ə'trɒfɪk) *adj*
atropine ('ætrəˌpiːn, -pɪn) *or* **atropin** ('ætrəpɪn) *n* a poisonous alkaloid obtained from deadly nightshade, having an inhibitory action on the autonomic nervous system. It is used medicinally in pre-anaesthetic medication, to speed a slow heart rate, and as an emergency first-aid counter to exposure to chemical warfare nerve agents. Formula: $C_{17}H_{23}NO_3$ [C19 from New Latin *atropa* deadly nightshade, from Greek *atropos* unchangeable, inflexible; see ATROPOS]
Atropos ('ætrəˌpɒs) *n* *Greek myth* the one of the three Fates who severs the thread of life [Greek, from *atropos* that may not be turned, from A-[1] + *-tropos* from *trepein* to turn]
attaboy ('ætəˌbɔɪ) *sentence substitute* *slang, chiefly US* an expression of approval or exhortation
attach (ə'tætʃ) *vb* (*mainly tr*) **1** to join, fasten, or connect **2** (*reflexive or passive*) to become associated with or join, as in a business or other venture: *he attached himself to the expedition* **3** (*intr*; foll by *to*) to be inherent (in) or connected (with): *responsibility attaches to the job* **4** to attribute or ascribe: *to attach importance to an event* **5** to include or append, esp as a condition: *a proviso is attached to the contract* **6** (*usually passive*) *military* to place on temporary duty with another unit **7** (*usually passive*) to put (a member of an organization) to work in a different unit or agency, either with an expectation of reverting to, or while retaining some part of, the original working arrangement **8** to appoint officially **9** *law* to arrest or take (a person, property, etc) with lawful authority **10** *obsolete* to seize [C14 from Old French *atachier* to fasten, changed from *estachier* to fasten with a stake, from *estache* STAKE[1]] > **at'tachable** *adj* > **at'tacher** *n*
attaché (ə'tæʃeɪ; *French* ataʃe) *n* **1** a specialist attached to a diplomatic mission: *military attaché* **2** *Brit* a junior member of the staff of an embassy or legation [C19 from French: someone attached (to a mission), from *attacher* to ATTACH]
attaché case *n* a small flat rectangular briefcase used for carrying documents, papers, etc
attached (ə'tætʃt) *adj* **1** (foll by *to*) fond (of); full of regard (for): *he was very attached to the old lady* **2** married, engaged, or associated in an exclusive sexual relationship: *it's no good dancing with her, she's already attached*
attachment (ə'tætʃmənt) *n* **1** a means of securing; a fastening **2** (often foll by *to*) affection or regard (for); devotion (to): *attachment to a person or to a cause* **3** an object to be attached, esp a supplementary part: *an attachment for an electric drill* **4** the act of attaching or the state of being attached **5 a** the arrest of a person for disobedience to a court order **b** the lawful seizure of property and placing of it under control of a court **c** a writ authorizing such arrest or seizure **6** *law* the binding of a debt in the hands of a garnishee until its disposition has been decided by the court
attachment of earnings *n* (in Britain) a court order requiring an employer to deduct amounts from an employee's wages to pay debts or honour financial obligations
attack (ə'tæk) *vb* **1** to launch a physical assault (against) with or without weapons; begin hostilities (with) **2** (*intr*) to take the initiative in a game, sport, etc: *after a few minutes, the team began to attack* **3** (*tr*) to direct hostile words or writings at; criticize or abuse vehemently **4** (*tr*) to turn one's mind or energies vigorously to (a job, problem, etc) **5** (*tr*) to begin to injure or affect adversely; corrode, corrupt, or infect: *rust attacked the metal* **6** (*tr*) to attempt to rape ▷ *n* **7** the act or an instance of attacking **8** strong criticism or abuse: *an unjustified attack on someone's reputation* **9** an offensive move in a game, sport, etc **10** commencement of a task, etc **11** any sudden and usually severe manifestation of a disease or disorder: *a heart attack; an attack of indigestion* **12** **the attack** *ball games* the players in a team whose main role is to attack the opponents' goal or territory **13** *music* decisiveness in beginning a passage, movement, or piece **14** *music* the speed with which a note reaches its maximum volume **15** an attempted rape [C16 from French *attaquer*, from Old Italian *attaccare* to attack, attach, from *estaccare* to attach, from *stacca* STAKE[1]; compare ATTACH] > **at'tackable** *adj* > **at'tacker** *n*

attack ad *n* a public notice, such as a printed display or a short film on television, in which a political party criticizes or abuses an opponent

attain (əˈteɪn) *vb* **1** (*tr*) to achieve or accomplish (a task, goal, aim, etc) **2** (*tr*) to reach or arrive at in space or time: *to attain old age* **3** (*intr; often foll by to*) to arrive (at) with effort or exertion: *to attain to glory* [c14 from Old French *ateindre*, from Latin *attingere* to reach, from *tangere* to touch] > **atˈtainable** *adj* > **at͵tainaˈbility** *or* **atˈtainableness** *n*

attainder (əˈteɪndə) *n* **1** (formerly) the extinction of a person's civil rights resulting from a sentence of death or outlawry on conviction for treason or felony. See also **bill of attainder** **2** *obsolete* dishonour ▷ Archaic equivalent: **attainture** (əˈteɪntʃə) [c15 from Anglo-French *attaindre* to convict, from Old French *ateindre* to ATTAIN]

attainment (əˈteɪnmənt) *n* an achievement or the act of achieving; accomplishment

attainment target *n Brit education* a general defined level of ability that a pupil is expected to achieve in every subject at each key stage in the National Curriculum. Abbreviation: **AT**

attaint (əˈteɪnt) *vb* (*tr*) *archaic* **1** to pass judgment of death or outlawry upon (a person); condemn by bill of attainder **2** to dishonour or disgrace **3** to accuse or prove to be guilty **4** (of sickness) to affect or strike (somebody) ▷ *n* **5** a less common word for **attainder** **6** a dishonour; taint [c14 from Old French *ateint* convicted, from *ateindre* to ATTAIN]

attar (ˈætə), **otto** (ˈɒtəʊ) *or* **ottar** (ˈɒtə) *n* an essential oil from flowers, esp the damask rose, used pure or as a base for perfume: *attar of roses* [c18 from Persian *ʻatir* perfumed, from *ʻitr* perfume, from Arabic]

attemper (əˈtɛmpə) *vb* (*tr*) *archaic* **1** to modify by blending; temper **2** to moderate or soothe **3** to accommodate or bring into harmony > **atˈtemperment** *n*

attempt (əˈtɛmpt) *vb* (*tr*) **1** to make an effort (to do something) or to achieve (something); try **2** to try to surmount (an obstacle) **3** to try to climb: *they will attempt the north wall of the Eiger* **4** *archaic* to attack **5** *archaic* to tempt ▷ *n* **6** an endeavour to achieve something; effort **7** a result of an attempt or endeavour **8** an attack, esp with the intention to kill: *an attempt on his life* [c14 from Old French *attempter*, from Latin *attemptāre* to strive after, from *tentāre* to try] > **atˈtemptable** *adj* > **atˈtempter** *n*

> **USAGE** *Attempt* should not be used in the passive when followed by an infinitive: *attempts were made to find a solution* (not *a solution was attempted to be found*)

attend (əˈtɛnd) *vb* **1** to be present at (an event, meeting, etc) **2** (when *intr*, foll by *to*) to give care; minister **3** (when *intr*, foll by *to*) to pay attention; listen **4** (*tr; often passive*) to accompany or follow: *a high temperature attended by a severe cough* **5** (*intr;* foll by *on* or *upon*) to follow as a consequence (of) **6** (*intr;* foll by *to*) to devote one's time; apply oneself: *to attend to the garden* **7** (*tr*) to escort or accompany **8** (*intr;* foll by *on* or *upon*) to wait (on); serve; provide for the needs (of): *to attend on a guest* **9** (*tr*) *archaic* to wait for; expect **10** (*intr*) *obsolete* to delay [c13 from Old French *atendre*, from Latin *attendere* to stretch towards, from *tendere* to extend] > **atˈtender** *n*

attendance (əˈtɛndəns) *n* **1** the act or state of attending **2** the number of persons present: *an attendance of 5000 at the festival* **3** *obsolete* attendants collectively; retinue

attendance allowance *n* (in Britain) a tax-free noncontributory welfare benefit for people over 65 years old who are so severely disabled that they need frequent attention or continual supervision for a period of six months or more

attendance centre *n* (in Britain) a place at which young offenders are required to attend regularly instead of going to prison

attendant (əˈtɛndənt) *n* **1** a person who accompanies or waits upon another **2** a person employed to assist, guide, or provide a service for others, esp for the general public: *a lavatory attendant* **3** a person who is present **4** a logical consequence or natural accompaniment: *hatred is often an attendant of jealousy* ▷ *adj* **5** being in attendance **6** associated; accompanying; related: *attendant problems*

attendee (ə͵tɛnˈdiː) *n* a person who is present at a specified event

attention (əˈtɛnʃən) *n* **1** concentrated direction of the mind, esp to a problem or task **2** consideration, notice, or observation: *a new matter has come to our attention* **3** detailed care or special treatment: *to pay attention to one's appearance* **4** (*usually plural*) an act of consideration, courtesy, or gallantry indicating affection or love: *attentions given to a lover* **5** the motionless position of formal military alertness, esp in drill when an upright position is assumed with legs and heels together, arms to the sides, head and eyes facing to the front **6** *psychol* the act of concentrating on any one of a set of objects or thoughts. See also **selective attention** ▷ *sentence substitute* **7** the order to be alert or to adopt a position of formal military alertness [c14 from Latin *attentiō*, from *attendere* to apply the mind to; see ATTEND]

attention deficit disorder *n* a disorder, particularly of children, characterized by excessive activity and inability to concentrate on one task for any length of time. Abbreviation: **ADD**

attention deficit hyperactivity disorder *n* a form of attention deficit disorder in which hyperactivity is a prominent symptom. Abbreviation: **ADHD**

attentive (əˈtɛntɪv) *adj* **1** paying attention; listening carefully; observant **2** (*postpositive; often* foll by *to*) careful to fulfil the needs or wants (of); considerate (about): *she was always attentive to his needs* > **atˈtentively** *adv* > **atˈtentiveness** *n*

attenuant (əˈtɛnjʊənt) *adj* **1** causing dilution or thinness, esp of the blood ▷ *n* **2** *obsolete* an attenuant drug or agent

attenuate *vb* (əˈtɛnjʊ͵eɪt) **1** to weaken or become weak; reduce in size, strength, density, or value **2** to make or become thin or fine; extend **3** (*tr*) to make (a pathogenic bacterium, virus, etc) less virulent, as by culture in special media or exposure to heat ▷ *adj* (əˈtɛnjʊɪt, -͵eɪt) **4** diluted, weakened, slender, or reduced **5** *botany* tapering gradually to a point [c16 from Latin *attenuāre* to weaken, from *tenuis* thin]

attenuation (ə͵tɛnjʊˈeɪʃən) *n* **1** the act of attenuating or the state of being attenuated **2** the loss of energy suffered by radiation as it passes through matter, esp as a result of absorption or scattering

attenuator (əˈtɛnjʊ͵eɪtə) *n* **1** *physics* any device designed to reduce the power of a wave or electrical signal without distorting it **2** a person or thing that attenuates

attercop (ˈætəkɒp) *n archaic or dialect* **1** a spider **2** an ill-natured person [Old English *attorcoppa*, from *ātor* poison and possibly *cop* head]

attest (əˈtɛst) *vb* **1** (*tr*) to affirm the correctness or truth of **2** (when *intr*, usually foll by *to*) to witness (an act, event, etc) or bear witness to (an act, event, etc) as by signature or oath **3** (*tr*) to make evident; demonstrate: *his life of luxury attests his wealth* **4** (*tr*) to provide evidence for: *the marks in the ground attested the presence of a fossil* [c16 from Latin *attestārī* to prove, from *testārī* to bear witness, from *testis* a witness] > **atˈtestable** *adj* > **atˈtestant**, **atˈtester** *or esp in legal usage* **atˈtestor**, **atˈtestator** *n* > **attestation** (͵ætɛˈsteɪʃən) *n*

attested (əˈtɛstɪd) *adj Brit* (of cattle, etc) certified to be free from a disease, esp from tuberculosis

Att. Gen. *or* **Atty. Gen.** *abbreviation for* Attorney General

attic (ˈætɪk) *n* **1** a space or room within the roof of a house **2** *architect* a storey or low wall above the cornice of a classical façade [c18 special use of ATTIC from the use of Attic-style pilasters to adorn the façade of the top storey]

Attic (ˈætɪk) *adj* **1** of or relating to Attica, its inhabitants, or the dialect of Greek spoken there, esp in classical times **2** (*often not capital*) classically elegant, simple, or pure: *an Attic style* ▷ *n* **3** the dialect of Ancient Greek spoken and written in Athens: the chief literary dialect of classical Greek. See also **Aeolic, Arcadic, Doric, Ionic**

Attica (ˈætɪkə) *n* a region and department of E central Greece: in ancient times the territory of Athens. Capital: Athens. Pop: 3 336 700 (2001). Area: 14 157 sq km (5466 sq miles)

Atticism (ˈætɪ͵sɪzəm) *n* **1** the idiom or character of the Attic dialect of Ancient Greek, esp in the Hellenistic period **2** an elegant, simple, and clear expression > **ˈAtticist** *n*

Attic order *n* a low pilaster of any order set into the cornice of a building

Attic salt *or* **wit** *n* refined incisive wit

attire (əˈtaɪə) *vb* **1** (*tr*) to dress, esp in fine elegant clothes; array ▷ *n* **2** clothes or garments, esp if fine or decorative **3** the antlers of a mature male deer [c13 from Old French *atirier* to put in order, from *tire* row; see TIER[1]]

Attis (ˈætɪs) *n classical myth* a youth of Phrygia, loved by the goddess Cybele. In a jealous passion she caused him to go mad, whereupon he castrated himself and died

attitude (ˈætɪ͵tjuːd) *n* **1** the way a person views something or tends to behave towards it, often in an evaluative way **2** a theatrical pose created for effect (esp in the phrase **strike an attitude**) **3** a position of the body indicating mood or emotion **4** *informal* a hostile manner: *don't give me attitude, my girl* **5** the orientation of an aircraft's axes in relation to some plane, esp the horizontal. See also **axis[1]** (sense 1) **6** the orientation of a spacecraft in relation to its direction of motion **7** *ballet* a classical position in which the body is upright and one leg raised and bent behind [c17 from French, from Italian *attitudine* disposition, from Late Latin *aptitūdō* fitness, from Latin *aptus* APT] > **͵attiˈtudinal** *adj*

attitudinize *or* **attitudinise** (͵ætɪˈtjuːdɪ͵naɪz) *vb* (*intr*) to adopt a pose or opinion for effect; strike an attitude > **͵attiˈtudi͵nizer** *or* **͵attiˈtudi͵niser** *n*

attn *abbreviation for* attention

atto- *prefix* denoting 10^{-18}: *attotesla*. Symbol: a [from Norwegian, Danish *atten* eighteen]

attolaser (ˈæəʊ͵leɪzə) *n* a high-power laser capable of producing pulses with a duration measured in attoseconds

attophysics (ˈætəʊ͵fɪzɪks) *n* the physics of structures and artefacts with dimensions in the attometre range or of devices, such as lasers, capable of producing pulses with a duration measured in attoseconds

attorn (əˈtɜːn) *vb* (*intr*) **1** *law* to acknowledge a new owner of land as one's landlord **2** *feudal history* to transfer allegiance or do homage to a new lord [c15 from Old French *atourner* to direct to, from *tourner* to TURN] > **atˈtornment** *n*

attorney (əˈtɜːnɪ) *n* **1** a person legally appointed or empowered to act for another **2** *US* a lawyer qualified to represent clients in legal proceedings **3** *South African* a solicitor [c14 from Old French *atourné*, from *atourner* to direct to; see ATTORN] > **atˈtorney͵ship** *n*

attorney-at-law *n, pl* **attorneys-at-law** *law* **1** *Now chiefly US* a lawyer qualified to represent in court a party to a legal action **2** *Brit obsolete* a solicitor

attorney general *n, pl* **attorneys general** *or* **attorney generals** **1** a country's chief law officer and senior legal adviser to its government **2** (in the US) the chief law officer and legal adviser of a state government **3** (in some states of the US) a public prosecutor

Attorney General *n* **1** (in the United Kingdom

a

except Scotland) the senior law officer and chief legal counsel of the Crown: a member of the government and of the House of Commons **2** (in the US) the chief law officer and legal adviser to the Administration: head of the Department of Justice and member of the cabinet **3** (in Australia and New Zealand) the chief government law officer: a member of Parliament and usually a cabinet minister

attract (əˈtrækt) vb (mainly tr) **1** to draw (notice, a crowd of observers, etc) to oneself by conspicuous behaviour or appearance (esp in the phrase **attract attention**) **2** (also intr) to exert a force on (a body) that tends to cause an approach or oppose a separation: *the gravitational pull of the earth attracts objects to it* **3** to possess some property that pulls or draws (something) towards itself: *jam attracts wasps* **4** (also intr) to exert a pleasing, alluring, or fascinating influence (upon); be attractive (to) [c15 from Latin *attrahere* to draw towards, from *trahere* to pull] > atˈtractable adj > atˈtractor or atˈtracter n

attractant (əˈtræktənt) n a substance that attracts, esp a chemical (**sex attractant**) produced by an insect and attracting insects of the same species. See also **pheromone**

attraction (əˈtrækʃən) n **1** the act, power, or quality of attracting **2** a person or thing that attracts or is intended to attract **3** a force by which one object attracts another, such as the gravitational or electrostatic force **4** a change in the form of one linguistic element caused by the proximity of another element

attraction sphere n another name for **astrosphere** (sense 2)

attractive (əˈtræktɪv) adj **1** appealing to the senses or mind through beauty, form, character, etc **2** arousing interest: *an attractive opportunity* **3** possessing the ability to draw or pull: *an attractive force* > atˈtractively adv > atˈtractiveness n

attrib. abbreviation for **1** attribute **2** attributive

attribute vb (əˈtrɪbjuːt) **1** (tr; usually foll by to) to regard as belonging (to), produced (by), or resulting (from); ascribe (to): *to attribute a painting to Picasso* ▷ n (ˈætrɪˌbjuːt) **2** a property, quality, or feature belonging to or representative of a person or thing **3** an object accepted as belonging to a particular office or position **4** grammar **a** an adjective or adjectival phrase **b** an attributive adjective **5** logic the property, quality, or feature that is affirmed or denied concerning the subject of a proposition [c15 from Latin *attribuere* to associate with, from *tribuere* to give] > atˈtributable adj > atˈtributer or atˈtributor n > attribution (ˌætrɪˈbjuːʃən) n

attribution theory n psychol the theory that tries to explain how people link actions and emotions to particular causes, both internal and external

attributive (əˈtrɪbjutɪv) adj **1** relating to an attribute **2** grammar (of an adjective or adjectival phrase) modifying a noun and constituting part of the same noun phrase, in English normally preceding the noun, as *black* in *Fido is a black dog* (as opposed to *Fido is black*). Compare **predicative 3** philosophy relative to an understood domain, as *small* in *that elephant is small* ▷ n **4** an attributive adjective > atˈtributively adv > atˈtributiveness n

attrit (əˈtrɪt) vb -trits, -tritting, -tritted US slang (tr) **1** to wear down or dispose of gradually **2** to kill [c18 back formation from ATTRITION]

attrition (əˈtrɪʃən) n **1** the act of wearing away or the state of being worn away, as by friction **2** constant wearing down to weaken or destroy (often in the phrase **war of attrition**) **3** Also called: **natural wastage** a decrease in the size of the workforce of an organization achieved by not replacing employees who retire or resign **4** geography the grinding down of rock particles by friction during transportation by water, wind, or ice. Compare **abrasion** (sense 3), **corrasion 5** theol sorrow for sin arising from fear of damnation, esp as contrasted with contrition, which arises purely from love of God [c14 from Late Latin *attrītiō* a

rubbing against something, from Latin *atterere* to weaken, from *terere* to rub] > atˈtritional adj > attritive (əˈtraɪtɪv) adj

Attu (ˈætuː) n the westernmost of the Aleutian Islands, off the coast of SW Alaska: largest of the Near Islands

attune (əˈtjuːn) vb (tr) **1** to adjust or accustom (a person or thing); acclimatize **2** to tune (a musical instrument)

atty abbreviation for attorney

atua (ˈɑːtuːə) n NZ a spirit or demon [Māori]

ATV abbreviation for all-terrain vehicle: a vehicle with wheels designed to travel on rough ground

atween (əˈtwiːn) prep an archaic or Scot word for **between**

at wt abbreviation for atomic weight

atypical (eɪˈtɪpɪkˀl) adj not typical; deviating from or not conforming to type > aˈtypically adv

au the internet domain name for Australia

Au the chemical symbol for gold [from New Latin *aurum*]

AU abbreviation for **1 African Union 2** Also: **a.u.** angstrom unit **3** Also: **a.u. astronomical unit**

aua (ˈɑːuːɑː) n, pl aua NZ another name for **yellow-eye mullet** [Māori]

aubade (French obad) n **1** a song or poem appropriate to or greeting the dawn **2** a romantic or idyllic prelude or overture ▷ Compare **serenade** [c19 from French, from Old Provençal *aubada* (unattested), from *auba* dawn, ultimately from Latin *albus* white]

Aube (French ob) n **1** a department of N central France, in Champagne-Ardenne region. Capital: Troyes. Pop: 293 925 (2003 est). Area: 6026 sq km (2350 sq miles) **2** a river in N central France, flowing northwest to the Seine. Length: about 225 km (140 miles)

auberge (French ɔbɛrʒ) n an inn or tavern [c17 from French, from Old Provençal *alberga*, of Germanic origin; compare Old Saxon *heriberga* army shelter]

aubergine (ˈəʊbəˌʒiːn) n **1** a tropical Old World solanaceous plant, *Solanum melongena*, widely cultivated for its egg-shaped typically dark purple fruit. US, Canadian, and Australian name: **eggplant 2** the fruit of this plant, which is cooked and eaten as a vegetable **3 a** a dark purple colour **b** (as adjective): *an aubergine dress* [c18 from French, from Catalan *alberginia*, from Arabic *al-bādindjān*, ultimately from Sanskrit *vatin-ganah*, of obscure origin]

Aubervilliers (French obɛrvilje) n an industrial suburb of Paris, on the Seine. Pop: 63 136 (1999). Former name: **Notre-Dame-des-Vertus** (French nɔtrədamdəverty)

aubrietia, aubrieta or **aubretia** (ɔːˈbriːʃə) n any trailing purple-flowered plant of the genus *Aubrieta*, native to European mountains but widely planted in rock gardens: family Brassicaceae (crucifers) [c19 from New Latin, named after Claude *Aubriet*, 18th-century French painter of flowers and animals]

auburn (ˈɔːbᵊn) n **a** a moderate reddish-brown colour **b** (as adjective): *auburn hair* [c15 (originally meaning: blond): from Old French *alborne* blond, from Medieval Latin *alburnus* whitish, from Latin *albus* white]

Aubusson (French obysɔ̃) n **1** a town in central France, in the Creuse department: a centre for flat-woven carpets and for tapestries since the 16th century. Pop: 4662 (1999) ▷ adj **2** denoting or relating to these carpets or tapestries

AUC abbreviation for (indicating years numbered from the founding of Rome, taken as 753 BC) **a** ab urbe condita **b** anno urbis conditae

Auckland (ˈɔːklənd) n the chief port of New Zealand, in the northern part of North Island: former capital of New Zealand (1840–65). Pop: 420 700 (2004 est)

Auckland Islands pl n a group of six uninhabited islands, south of New Zealand. Area: 611 sq km (234 sq miles)

au contraire French (o kɔ̃trɛr) adv on the contrary

au courant French (o kurɑ̃) adj up-to-date, esp in knowledge of current affairs [literally: in the current]

auction (ˈɔːkʃən) n **1** a public sale of goods or property, esp one in which prospective purchasers bid against each other until the highest price is reached. Compare **Dutch auction 2** the competitive calls made in bridge and other games before play begins, undertaking to win a given number of tricks if a certain suit is trumps **3** See **auction bridge** ▷ vb **4** (tr; often foll by off) to sell by auction [c16 from Latin *auctiō* an increasing, from *augēre* to increase]

auction bridge n a variety of bridge, now generally superseded by contract bridge, in which all the tricks made score towards game

auctioneer (ˌɔːkʃəˈnɪə) n **1** a person who conducts an auction by announcing the lots and controlling the bidding ▷ vb **2** (tr) to sell by auction

auctorial (ɔːkˈtɔːrɪəl) adj of or relating to an author [c19 from Latin *auctor* AUTHOR]

audacious (ɔːˈdeɪʃəs) adj **1** recklessly bold or daring; fearless **2** impudent or presumptuous [c16 from Latin *audāx* bold, from *audēre* to dare] > auˈdaciously adv > auˈdaciousness or audacity (ɔːˈdæsɪtɪ) n

Aude (French od) n a department of S France on the Gulf of Lions, in Languedoc-Roussillon region. Capital: Carcassonne. Pop: 321 734 (2003 est). Area: 6342 sq km (2473 sq miles)

audible (ˈɔːdɪbˀl) adj **1** perceptible to the hearing; loud enough to be heard ▷ n **2** American football a change of playing tactics called by the quarterback when the offense is lined up at the line of scrimmage [c16 from Late Latin *audibilis*, from Latin *audīre* to hear] > ˌaudiˈbility or ˈaudibleness n > ˈaudibly adv

audience (ˈɔːdɪəns) n **1** a group of spectators or listeners, esp at a public event such as a concert or play **2** the people reached by a book, film, or radio or television programme **3** the devotees or followers of a public entertainer, lecturer, etc; regular public **4** an opportunity to put one's point of view, such as a formal interview with a monarch or head of state [c14 from Old French, from Latin *audientia* a hearing, from *audīre* to hear]

audile (ˈɔːdɪl, ˈɔːdaɪl) psychol ▷ n **1** a person who possesses a faculty for auditory imagery that is more distinct than his visual or other imagery ▷ adj **2** of or relating to such a person [c19 from AUD(ITORY) + -ILE]

audio (ˈɔːdɪˌəʊ) n (modifier) **1** of or relating to sound or hearing: *audio frequency* **2** relating to or employed in the transmission, reception, and reproduction of sound **3** of, concerned with, or operating at audio frequencies ▷ Compare **video** [c20 independent use of AUDIO-]

audio- combining form indicating hearing or sound: *audiometer; audiovisual* [from Latin *audīre* to hear]

audio book n a reading of a book recorded on tape

audio conference n a meeting that is conducted by the use of audio telecommunications

audio description n a facility provided for visually impaired people in which a film, television programme, or play is described through audio technology

audio frequency n a frequency in the range 20 hertz to 20 000 hertz. A sound wave of this frequency would be audible to the human ear

audiogenic (ˌɔːdɪəʊˈdʒɛnɪk) adj caused or produced by sound or an audio frequency: *an audiogenic epileptic fit*

audiogram (ˈɔːdɪəʊˌgræm) n a graphic record of the acuity of hearing of a person obtained by means of an audiometer

audiology (ˌɔːdɪˈɒlədʒɪ) n the scientific study of hearing, often including the treatment of persons with hearing defects > **audiological** (ˌɔːdɪəˈlɒdʒɪkˀl) adj > ˌaudioˈlogically adv > ˌaudiˈologist n

audiometer (ˌɔːdɪˈɒmɪtə) *n* an instrument for testing the intensity and frequency range of sound that is capable of detection by the human ear > audiometric (ˌɔːdɪəʊˈmetrɪk) *adj* > ˌaudioˈmetrically *adv* > ˌaudiˈometrist *n* > ˌaudiˈometry *n*

audiophile (ˈɔːdɪəʊˌfaɪl) *n* a person who has a great interest in high-fidelity sound reproduction

audio response *n* a computer response that is audible rather than textual or graphical

audiotypist (ˈɔːdɪəʊˌtaɪpɪst) *n* a typist trained to type from a dictating machine > ˈaudioˌtyping *n*

audiovisual (ˌɔːdɪəʊˈvɪzjʊəl, -ʒʊəl) *adj* (esp of teaching aids) involving or directed at both hearing and sight: *the language class had new audiovisual equipment* > ˌaudioˈvisually *adv*

audiphone (ˈɔːdɪˌfəʊn) *n* a type of hearing aid consisting of a diaphragm that, when placed against the upper teeth, conveys sound vibrations to the inner ear

audit (ˈɔːdɪt) *n* **1 a** an inspection, correction, and verification of business accounts, conducted by an independent qualified accountant **b** (*as modifier*): *audit report* **2** *US* an audited account **3** any thoroughgoing check or examination **4** *archaic* a hearing ▷ *vb* **5** to inspect, correct, and certify (accounts, etc) **6** *US and Canadian* to attend (classes, etc) as an auditor [c15 from Latin *audītus* a hearing, from *audīre* to hear]

Audit Bureau of Circulation *n* an organization that collects, audits, and publishes monthly circulation figures for newspapers and magazines. Abbreviation: ABC

audition (ɔːˈdɪʃən) *n* **1** a test at which a performer or musician is asked to demonstrate his ability for a particular role, etc **2** the act, sense, or power of hearing ▷ *vb* **3** to judge by means of or be tested in an audition [c16 from Latin *audītiō* a hearing, from *audīre* to hear]

auditioner (ɔːˈdɪʃənə) *n* a person who attends an audition

auditor (ˈɔːdɪtə) *n* **1** a person qualified to audit accounts **2** a person who hears or listens **3** *Austral, US and Canadian* a registered student who attends a class that is not an official part of his course of study, without actively participating in it [c14 from Old French *auditeur*, from Latin *audītor* a hearer] > ˌaudiˈtorial *adj*

Auditor General *n* (in Canada) a federal official responsible for auditing government departments and making an annual report

auditorium (ˌɔːdɪˈtɔːrɪəm) *n, pl* -toriums *or* -toria (-ˈtɔːrɪə) **1** the area of a concert hall, theatre, school, etc, in which the audience sits **2** *US and Canadian* a building for public meetings [c17 from Latin: a judicial examination, from *audītōrius* concerning a hearing; see AUDITORY]

auditory (ˈɔːdɪtərɪ, -trɪ) *adj also* auditive (ˈɔːdɪtɪv) **1** of or relating to hearing, the sense of hearing, or the organs of hearing ▷ *n* **2** an archaic word for **audience** *or* **auditorium** [c14 from Latin *audītōrius* relating to hearing, from *audīre* to hear]

auditory phonetics *n* (*functioning as singular*) the branch of phonetics concerned with the perception of speech sounds by humans. Compare **acoustic phonetics, articulatory phonetics**

audit trail *n* a record of all the transactions or data entries that a person or firm has carried out over a specific period

aue (ˈɑːuːə) *interj* NZ an exclamation of pain, distress, or astonishment [Māori]

AUEW (in Britain) *abbreviation for* Amalgamated Union of Engineering Workers

au fait French (o fɛ; English əʊ ˈfeɪ) *adj* fully informed; in touch [c18 literally: to the point]

Aufklärung German (ˈaufklɛːrʊŋ) *n* the Enlightenment, esp in Germany

au fond French (o fɔ̃) *adv* fundamentally; essentially [literally: at the bottom]

auf Wiedersehen German (auf ˈviːdərzeːən) *sentence substitute* goodbye, until we see each other again

Aug *abbreviation for* August

Augean (ɔːˈdʒiːən) *adj* extremely dirty or corrupt [c16 after *Augeas*; see AUGEAN STABLES]

Augean stables *pl n* *Greek myth* the stables, not cleaned for 30 years, where King Augeas kept 3000 oxen. Hercules diverted the River Alpheus through them and cleaned them in a day

augend (ˈɔːdʒend, ɔːˈdʒend) *n* a number to which another number, the addend, is added [from Latin *augendum* that is to be increased, from *augēre* to increase]

auger (ˈɔːgə) *n* **1** a hand tool with a bit shaped like a corkscrew, for boring holes in wood **2** a larger tool of the same kind for boring holes in the ground [c15 *an augur*, resulting from mistaken division of earlier *a nauger*, from Old English *nafugār* nave (of a wheel) spear (that is, tool for boring hubs of wheels), from *nafu* NAVE² + *gār* spear; see GORE²]

Auger effect (ˈəʊʒeɪ) *n* the spontaneous emission of an electron instead of a photon by an excited ion as a result of a vacancy being filled in an inner electron shell [c20 named after Pierre *Auger* (1899–1993), French physicist]

aught¹ *or* **ought** (ɔːt) (*used with a negative or in conditional or interrogative sentences or clauses*) *archaic or literary* ▷ *pron* **1** anything at all; anything whatever (esp in the phrase **for aught I know**) ▷ *adv* **2** *dialect* in any least part; to any degree [Old English *āwiht*, from *ā* ever, AY¹ + *wiht* thing; see WIGHT¹]

aught² *or* **ought** (ɔːt) *n* a less common word for **nought** (zero)

augite (ˈɔːgaɪt) *n* a black or greenish-black mineral of the pyroxene group, found in igneous rocks. Composition: calcium magnesium iron aluminium silicate. General formula: $(Ca,Mg,Fe,Al)(Si,Al)_2O_6$. Crystal structure: monoclinic [c19 from Latin *augītēs*, from Greek, from *augē* brightness] > augitic (ɔːˈgɪtɪk) *adj*

augment *vb* (ɔːgˈment) **1** to make or become greater in number, amount, strength, etc; increase **2** (*tr*) *music* to increase (a major or perfect interval) by a semitone. Compare **diminish** (sense 3) **3** (*tr*) (in Greek and Sanskrit grammar) to prefix a vowel or diphthong to (a verb) to form a past tense ▷ *n* (ˈɔːgment) **4** (in Greek and Sanskrit grammar) a vowel or diphthong prefixed to a verb to form a past tense [c15 from Late Latin *augmentāre* to increase, from *augmentum* growth, from *augēre* to increase] > augˈmentable *adj* > augˈmentor *or* augˈmenter *n*

augmentation (ˌɔːgmenˈteɪʃən) *n* **1** the act of augmenting or the state of being augmented **2** the amount by which something is increased **3** *music* the presentation of a subject of a fugue, in which the note values are uniformly increased. Compare **diminution** (sense 2)

augmentative (ɔːgˈmentətɪv) *adj* **1** tending or able to augment **2** *grammar* **a** denoting an affix that may be added to a word to convey the meaning *large* or *great*; for example, the suffix *-ote* in Spanish, where *hombre* means man and *hombrote* big man **b** denoting a word formed by the addition of an augmentative affix ▷ *n* **3** *grammar* an augmentative word or affix ▷ Compare (for senses 2, 3) **diminutive**. > augˈmentatively *adv*

augmented (ɔːgˈmentɪd) *adj* **1** *music* (of an interval) increased or expanded from the state of being perfect or major by the raising of the higher note or the dropping of the lower note by one semitone: *C to G is a perfect fifth, but C to G sharp is an augmented fifth*. Compare **diminished** (sense 2) **2** *music* **a** denoting a chord based upon an augmented triad: *an augmented seventh chord* **b** denoting a triad consisting of the root plus a major third and an augmented fifth **c** (*postpositive*) (esp in jazz) denoting a chord having as its root the note not specified: *D augmented* **3** having been increased, esp in number: *an augmented orchestra*

augmented reality *n* an artificial environment created through the combination of real-world

and computer-generated data [c20 based on VIRTUAL REALITY]

augmented transition network *n* (in certain schools of linguistics) a formalism, usually expressed as a diagram, having the power of a Turing machine, used as the basis of processes transforming sentences into their syntactic representations. Abbreviation: ATN

au gratin (French o gratɛ̃) *adj* covered and cooked with browned breadcrumbs and sometimes cheese Also: gratinated [French, literally: with the grating]

Augsburg (German ˈauksbʊrk) *n* a city in S Germany, in Bavaria: founded by the Romans in 14 BC; site of the diet that produced the **Peace of Augsburg** (1555), which ended the struggles between Lutherans and Catholics in the Holy Roman Empire and established the principle that each ruler should determine the form of worship in his lands. Pop: 259 217 (2003 est). Roman name: Augusta Vindelicorum (aʊˈguːstə vɪnˈdɛlɪˌkəʊrəm)

augur (ˈɔːgə) *n* **1** Also called: auspex (in ancient Rome) a religious official who observed and interpreted omens and signs to help guide the making of public decisions **2** any prophet or soothsayer ▷ *vb* **3** to predict (some future event), as from signs or omens **4** (*tr; may take a clause as object*) to be an omen (of); presage **5** (*intr*) to foreshadow future events to be as specified; bode: *this augurs well for us* [c14 from Latin: a diviner, perhaps from *augēre* to increase] > augural (ˈɔːgjʊrəl) *adj* > ˈaugurship *n*

augury (ˈɔːgjʊrɪ) *n, pl* -ries **1** the art of or a rite conducted by an augur **2** a sign or portent; omen

august (ɔːˈgʌst) *adj* **1** dignified or imposing: *an august presence* **2** of noble birth or high rank: *an august lineage* [c17 from Latin *augustus*; related to *augēre* to increase] > auˈgustly *adv* > auˈgustness *n*

August (ˈɔːgəst) *n* the eighth month of the year, consisting of 31 days [Old English, from Latin, named after Augustus (63 BC–14 AD), Roman emperor]

Augusta (ɔːˈgʌstə) *n* **1** a town in the US, in Georgia. Pop: 193 316 (2003 est) (including Richmond) **2** a port in S Italy, in E Sicily. Pop: 33 820 (2001) **3** a city in the US, in Maine: the state capital; founded (1628) as a trading post; timber industry. Pop: 18 618 (2003 est)

Augustan (ɔːˈgʌstən) *adj* **1** characteristic of, denoting, or relating to the Roman emperor Augustus Caesar (63 BC–14 AD), his period, or the poets, notably Virgil, Horace, and Ovid, writing during his reign **2** of, relating to, or characteristic of any literary period noted for refinement and classicism, esp the late 17th century in France (the period of the dramatists Corneille, Racine, and Molière) or the 18th century in England (the period of Swift, Pope, and Johnson, much influenced by Dryden) ▷ *n* **3** an author in an Augustan Age **4** a student of or specialist in Augustan literature

auguste *or* **august** (aʊˈguːst, ˈaʊˌgʊst) *n* (*often capital*) a type of circus clown who usually wears battered ordinary clothes and is habitually maladroit or unlucky [c20 French, from German]

Augustine (ɔːˈgʌstɪn) *n* a member of an Augustinian order

Augustinian (ˌɔːgəˈstɪnɪən) *adj* **1** of or relating to Saint Augustine of Hippo (354–430 AD), one of the Fathers of the Christian Church, or to his doctrines, or any of the Christian religious orders that were founded on his doctrines ▷ *n* **2** a member of any of several religious orders, such as the Augustinian Canons, Augustinian Hermits, and Austin Friars which are governed by the rule of Saint Augustine **3** a person who follows the doctrines of Saint Augustine

au jus French (o ʒy) *adj* (of meat) served in its own gravy [literally: with the juice]

auk (ɔːk) *n* **1** any of various diving birds of the family *Alcidae* of northern oceans having a heavy body, short tail, narrow wings, and a black-and-white plumage: order *Charadriiformes*. See also **great auk, razorbill 2** little auk Also called: **dovekie** a small short-billed auk, *Plautus alle*, abundant in Arctic regions [C17 from Old Norse *ālka*; related to Swedish *alka*, Danish *alke*]

auklet ('ɔ:klɪt) *n* any of various small auks of the genera *Aethia* and *Ptychoramphus*

au lait (əʊ 'leɪ; *French* o lɛ) *adj* prepared or served with milk [French, literally: with milk]

auld (ɔ:ld) *adj* a Scot word for **old** [Old English *āld*]

auld lang syne ('ɔ:ld læŋ 'səɪn, 'saɪn, 'zaɪn) *n* old times; times past, esp those remembered with affection or nostalgia [Scottish, literally: old long since]

Auld Reekie ('ri:kɪ) *n Scot* a nickname for **Edinburgh** [literally: Old Smoky]

aulic ('ɔ:lɪk) *adj rare* relating to a royal court [C18 from Latin *aulicus*, from Greek *aulikos* belonging to a prince's court, from *aulē* court]

Aulic Council *n* a council, founded in 1498, of the Holy Roman Emperor. It functioned mainly as a judicial body

Aulis ('ɔ:lɪs) *n* an ancient town in E central Greece, in Boeotia: traditionally the harbour from which the Greeks sailed at the beginning of the Trojan war

Auliye-Ata *n* a former name of **Taraz**

aumbry ('ɔ:mbrɪ) *n, pl* -bries a variant of **ambry**

Aum Shinrikyo ('əʊm ˌʃɪnrɪ'kjəʊ) *n* a syncretistic Japanese cult combining elements of Buddhism, Hinduism, and Christianity, founded by Shoko Asahara in 1986; responsible for a number of murders and in particular a nerve-gas attack on the Tokyo underground in 1995. Also called: Supreme Truth Cult [C20 from Sanskrit *aum* OM + Japanese *shinri kyo* supreme truth]

au naturel *French* (o natyrɛl) *adj, adv* 1 naked; nude 2 uncooked or plainly cooked [literally: in (a) natural (condition)]

aunt (ɑ:nt) *n* (*often capital, esp as a term of address*) 1 a sister of one's father or mother 2 the wife of one's uncle 3 a term of address used by children for any woman, esp for a friend of the parents 4 my (sainted) aunt! an exclamation of surprise or amazement [C13 from Old French *ante*, from Latin *amita* a father's sister]

auntie or **aunty** ('ɑ:ntɪ) *n, pl* -ies 1 a familiar or diminutive word for **aunt** 2 *Austral slang* a male homosexual

Auntie ('ɑ:ntɪ) *n Brit* an informal name for the **BBC**

auntie-ji *n Hinglish informal* a name given to a woman from the generation older than oneself [C20 from *auntie* + -JI]

auntie man *n Caribbean informal* an effeminate or homosexual male

Aunt Sally ('sælɪ) *n, pl* -lies *Brit* 1 a figure of an old woman's head, typically with a clay pipe, used in fairgrounds and fêtes as a target for balls or other objects 2 any person who is a target for insults or criticism 3 something set up as a target for disagreement or attack

Aunty ('ɑ:ntɪ) *n Austral* an informal name for the **Australian Broadcasting Association**

au pair (əʊ 'pɛə; *French* o pɛr) *n* 1 a a young foreigner, usually a girl, who undertakes housework in exchange for board and lodging, esp in order to learn the language b (*as modifier*): *an au pair girl* a young person who lives temporarily with a family abroad in exchange for a reciprocal arrangement with his or her own family ▷ *vb* 3 (*intr*) to work as an au pair ▷ *adv* 4 as an au pair: *she worked au pair in Greece* [C20 from French: on an equal footing]

aura ('ɔ:rə) *n, pl* auras or aurae ('ɔ:ri:) 1 a distinctive air or quality considered to be characteristic of a person or thing 2 any invisible emanation, such as a scent or odour 3 *pathol* strange sensations, such as noises in the ears or flashes of light, that immediately precede an attack, esp of epilepsy 4 (in parapsychology) an invisible emanation produced by and surrounding

a person or object: alleged to be discernible by individuals of supernormal sensibility [C18 via Latin from Greek: breeze]

aural¹ ('ɔ:rəl) *adj* of or relating to the sense or organs of hearing; auricular [C19 from Latin *auris* ear] > 'aurally *adv*

aural² ('ɔ:rəl) *adj* of or relating to an aura

aurar ('ɔ:rɑ:) *n* the plural of **eyrir**

aureate ('ɔ:rɪɪt, -ˌeɪt) *adj* 1 covered with gold; gilded 2 of a golden colour 3 (of a style of writing or speaking) excessively elaborate or ornate; florid [C15 from Late Latin *aureātus* gilded, from Latin *aureus* golden, from *aurum* gold] > 'aureately *adv* > 'aureateness *n*

aureole ('ɔ:rɪˌəʊl) or **aureola** (ɔ:'ri:ələ) *n* 1 (esp in paintings of Christian saints and the deity) a border of light or radiance enveloping the head or sometimes the whole of a figure represented as holy 2 a less common word for **halo** 3 another name for **corona** (sense 2) [C13 from Old French *auréole*, from Medieval Latin (*corōna*) *aureola* golden (crown), from *aureolus* golden, from *aurum* gold]

Aureomycin (ˌɔ:rɪəʊ'maɪsɪn) *n trademark* a brand of **chlortetracycline**

aureus ('ɔ:rɪəs) *n, pl* aurei ('ɔ:rɪˌaɪ) a gold coin of the Roman Empire [Latin: see AUREATE]

au revoir *French* (o rəvwar) *sentence substitute* goodbye [literally: to the seeing again]

auric ('ɔ:rɪk) *adj* of or containing gold in the trivalent state [C19 from Latin *aurum* gold]

auricle ('ɔ:rɪkəl) *n* 1 a the upper chamber of the heart; atrium b a small sac in the atrium of the heart 2 Also called: pinna *anatomy* the external part of the ear 3 Also called: auricula *biology* an ear-shaped part or appendage, such as that occurring at the join of the leaf blade and the leaf sheath in some grasses [C17 from Latin *auricula* the external ear, from *auris* ear] > 'auricled *adj*

auricula (ɔ:'rɪkjʊlə) *n, pl* -lae (-ˌli:) or -las 1 Also called: bear's-ear a widely cultivated alpine primrose, *Primula auricula*, with leaves shaped like a bear's ear 2 another word for **auricle** (sense 3) [C17 from New Latin, from Latin: external ear; see AURICLE]

auricular (ɔ:'rɪkjʊlə) *adj* 1 of, relating to, or received by the ear or organs of hearing; aural 2 shaped like an ear 3 of or relating to an auricle of the heart 4 (of feathers) occurring in tufts surrounding the ears of owls and similar birds ▷ *n* 5 (*usually plural*) an auricular feather > au'ricularly *adv*

auriculate (ɔ:'rɪkjʊlɪt, -ˌleɪt) or **auriculated** *adj* 1 having ears 2 *botany* having ear-shaped parts or appendages 3 Also called: auriform (ɔ:'rɪˌfɔ:m) shaped like an ear; auricular > au'riculately *adv*

auriferous (ɔ:'rɪfərəs) *adj* (of rock) containing gold; gold-bearing [C18 from Latin *aurifer* gold-bearing, from *aurum* gold + *ferre* to bear]

Auriga (ɔ:'raɪgə) *n, Latin genitive* Aurigae (ɔ:'raɪdʒi:) a conspicuous constellation in the N hemisphere between the Great Bear and Orion, at the edge of the Milky Way. It contains the first magnitude star Capella and the supergiant eclipsing binary star Epsilon Aurigae [Latin: charioteer]

Aurignacian (ˌɔ:rɪg'neɪʃən) *adj* of, relating to, or produced during a flint culture of the Upper Palaeolithic type characterized by the use of bone and antler tools, pins, awls, etc, and also by cave art and evidence of the beginnings of religion [C20 from French *Aurignacien*, after *Aurignac*, France, in the Pyrenees, near where is the cave where remains were discovered]

auriscope ('ɔ:rɪˌskəʊp) *n* a medical instrument for examining the external ear. Also called: otoscope > auriscopic (ˌɔ:rɪ'skɒpɪk) *adj*

aurist ('ɔ:rɪst) *n* a former name for **audiologist**

aurochs ('ɔ:rɒks) *n, pl* -rochs a recently extinct member of the cattle tribe, *Bos primigenius*, that inhabited forests in N Africa, Europe, and SW Asia. It had long horns and is thought to be one of the ancestors of modern cattle. Also called: urus

[C18 from German, from Old High German *ūrohso*, from *ūro* bison + *ohso* ox]

aurora (ɔ:'rɔ:rə) *n, pl* -ras or -rae (-ri:) 1 an atmospheric phenomenon consisting of bands, curtains, or streamers of light, usually green, red, or yellow, that move across the sky in polar regions. It is caused by collisions between air molecules and charged particles from the sun that are trapped in the earth's magnetic field 2 *poetic* the dawn [C14 from Latin: dawn; see EAST] > au'roral *adj* > au'rorally *adv*

Aurora¹ (ɔ:'rɔ:rə) *n* 1 the Roman goddess of the dawn. Greek counterpart: Eos 2 the dawn or rise of something

Aurora² (ɔ:'rɔ:rə) *n* another name for **Maewo**

aurora australis (ɒ'streɪlɪs) *n* (*sometimes capital*) the aurora seen around the South Pole. Also called: southern lights [New Latin: southern aurora]

aurora borealis (ˌbɔ:rɪ'eɪlɪs) *n* (*sometimes capital*) the aurora seen around the North Pole. Also called: northern lights [C17 New Latin: northern aurora]

aurous ('ɔ:rəs) *adj* of or containing gold, esp in the monovalent state [C19 apparently from French *aureux*, from Late Latin *aurōsus* gold-coloured, from Latin *aurum* gold]

aurum ('ɔ:rəm) *n obsolete* gold [C16 Latin]

AUS 1 *international car registration for* Australia 2 ▷ *abbreviation for* Australian Union of Students

Aus. *abbreviation for* 1 Australia(n) 2 Austria(n)

Auschwitz (*German* 'aʊʃvɪts) *n* an industrial town in S Poland; site of a Nazi concentration camp during World War II. Pop: 45 400 (latest est). Polish name: Oświęcim

auscultate (ɔ:'skʌlˌteɪt) *vb* to examine (a patient) by means of auscultation > 'auscultator *n*

auscultation (ˌɔ:skəl'teɪʃən) *n* 1 the diagnostic technique in medicine of listening to the various internal sounds made by the body, usually with the aid of a stethoscope 2 the act of listening [C19 from Latin *auscultātiō* a listening, from *auscultāre* to listen attentively; related to Latin *auris* ear] > auscultatory (ɔ:'skʌltətərɪ) or auscultative (ˌɔ:skʌltətɪv, ˌɔ:skəlˌteɪtɪv) *adj*

ausforming ('aʊsˌfɔ:mɪŋ) *n* a treatment to strengthen hard steels, prior to quenching, in which the specimen is plastically deformed while it is in the austenite temperature range [C20 from AUS(TENITIC) + (DE)FORM]

Ausgleich *German* ('ausglaɪç) *n* the agreement (1867) that established the Dual Monarchy of Austria-Hungary [German: levelling out, from *aus* OUT + *gleichen* to be similar]

Auslese ('aus,leɪsə) *n* a white wine, usually sweet, produced in Germany from individually selected bunches of very ripe grapes [C20 from German, literally: selection]

auspex ('ɔ:spɛks) *n, pl* auspices ('ɔ:spɪ,si:z) *Roman history* another word for **augur** (sense 1) [C16 from Latin: observer of birds, from *avis* bird + *specere* to look]

auspice ('ɔ:spɪs) *n, pl* -pices (-pɪsɪz) 1 (*usually plural*) patronage or guidance given in the phrase **under the auspices of**) 2 (*often plural*) a sign or omen, esp one that is favourable [C16 from Latin *auspicium* augury from birds; see AUSPEX]

auspicious (ɔ:'spɪʃəs) *adj* 1 favourable or propitious 2 *archaic* prosperous or fortunate > aus'piciously *adv* > aus'piciousness *n*

USAGE The use of *auspicious* to mean 'very special' (as in *this auspicious occasion*) should be avoided

Aussat ('ɒsæt, 'ɒzæt) *n* the Australian-owned communications satellite launched in 1985

Aussie ('ɒzɪ) *adj, n* an informal word for **Australian** or (*rare*) **Australia**

Aussie battler *n Austral slang* an Australian working-class person. Also called: little Aussie battler

Aust. *abbreviation for* 1 Australia(n) 2 Austria(n)

austenite ('ɒstə,naɪt) *n* 1 a solid solution of

carbon in face-centred-cubic gamma iron, usually existing above 723°C **2** the gamma phase of iron, stabilized at low temperatures by the addition of such elements as nickel [c20 named after Sir William C. Roberts-*Austen* (1843–1902), English metallurgist] > austenitic (ˌɔːstəˈnɪtɪk) *adj*

austenitic stainless steel *n* an alloy of iron, usually containing at least 8 per cent of nickel and 18 per cent of chromium, used where corrosion resistance, heat resistance, creep resistance, or nonmagnetic properties are required

Auster (ˈɔːstə) *n poetic* the south wind [c14 Latin]

austere (ɒˈstɪə) *adj* **1** stern or severe in attitude or manner: *an austere schoolmaster* **2** grave, sober, or serious: *an austere expression* **3** self-disciplined, abstemious, or ascetic: *an austere life* **4** severely simple or plain: *an austere design* [c14 from Old French *austère,* from Latin *austērus* sour, from Greek *austēros* astringent; related to Greek *hauein* to dry] > aus'terely *adv* > aus'tereness *n*

austerity (ɒˈstɛrɪtɪ) *n, pl* -ties **1** the state or quality of being austere **2** (*often plural*) an austere habit, practice, or act **3 a** reduced availability of luxuries and consumer goods, esp when brought about by government policy **b** (*as modifier*): *an austerity budget*

Austerlitz (ˈɔːstəlɪts) *n* a town in the Czech Republic, in Moravia: site of Napoleon's victory over the Russian and Austrian armies in 1805. Pop: 4747 (latest est.) Czech name: Slavkov

Austin¹ (ˈɒstɪn) *n* a city in central Texas, on the Colorado River: state capital since 1845. Pop: 672 011 (2003 est)

Austin² (ˈɒstɪn) *adj, n* another word for **Augustinian** [c14 shortened form of Augustine (354–430 AD), saint and one of the Fathers of the Christian Church]

austral¹ (ˈɔːstrəl) *adj* of or coming from the south: *austral winds* [c14 from Latin *austrālis,* from *auster* the south wind]

austral² (auˈstrɑːl) *n, pl* -trales a former monetary unit of Argentina equal to 100 centavos, replaced by the peso [from Spanish; see AUSTRAL¹]

Austral *abbreviation for* **1** Australasia **2** Australia(n)

Australasia (ˌɒstrəˈleɪzɪə) *n* **1** Australia, New Zealand, and neighbouring islands in the S Pacific Ocean **2** (loosely) the whole of Oceania

Australasian (ˌɒstrəˈleɪzɪən) *n* **1** a native or inhabitant of Australasia ▷ *adj* **2** of or relating to Australia, New Zealand, and the neighbouring islands **3** (of organizations) having members in Australia and New Zealand

Australia (ɒˈstreɪlɪə) *n* a country and the smallest continent, situated between the Indian Ocean and the Pacific: a former British colony, now an independent member of the Commonwealth, constitutional links with Britain formally abolished in 1986; consists chiefly of a low plateau, mostly arid in the west, with the basin of the Murray River and the Great Dividing Range in the east and the Great Barrier Reef off the NE coast. Official language: English. Religion: Christian majority. Currency: dollar. Capital: Canberra. Pop: 19 913 000 (2004 est). Area: 7 682 300 sq km (2 966 150 sq miles)

Australia Day *n* a public holiday in Australia, commemorating the landing of the British in 1788: observed on the first Monday after Jan 26

Australian (ɒˈstreɪlɪən) *n* **1** a native or inhabitant of Australia **2** the form of English spoken in Australia **3** a linguistic phylum consisting of the languages spoken by the native Australians ▷ *adj* **4** of, relating to, or characteristic of Australia, the Australians, or their form of English **5** of, relating to, or belonging to the phylum of languages spoken by the native Australians **6** of or denoting a zoogeographical region consisting of Australia, New Zealand, Polynesia, New Guinea, and the Moluccas

Australiana (ɒˌstreɪlɪˈɑːnə) *pl n* objects or documents relating to Australia and its history or culture esp in the form of a collection

Australian Alps *pl n* a mountain range in SE Australia, in E Victoria and SE New South Wales. Highest peak: Mount Kosciuszko, 2195 m (7316 ft)

Australian Antarctic Territory *n* the area of Antarctica, other than Adélie Land, that is administered by Australia (claims are suspended under the Antarctic Treaty), lying south of latitude 60°S and between longitudes 45°E and 160°E

Australian Capital Territory *n* a territory of SE Australia, within New South Wales: consists of two exclaves, one containing Canberra, the capital of Australia, and one at Jervis Bay (the latter sometimes regarded as a separate entity). Pop: 322 579 (2003 est). Former name: Federal Capital Territory

Australian cattle dog *n* a compact dog of a breed with pricked ears and a smooth bluish-grey coat, often used for controlling cattle

Australianism (ɒˈstreɪlɪəˌnɪzəm) *n* **1** the Australian national character or spirit **2** loyalty to Australia, its political independence, culture, etc **3** a linguistic usage, custom, or other feature peculiar to or characteristic of Australia, its people, or their culture

Australianize or **Australianise** (ɒˈstreɪlɪəˌnaɪz) *vb* (esp of a new immigrant) to adopt or cause to adopt Australian habits and attitudes; integrate into Australian society

Australian Mist *n* a breed of medium-sized cat with a short spotted or marbled coat. Former name **Spotted Mist**

Australian Rules *n* (*functioning as singular*) a game resembling rugby football, played in Australia between teams of 18 men each on an oval pitch, with a ball resembling a large rugby ball. Players attempt to kick the ball between posts (without crossbars) at either end of the pitch, scoring six points for a goal (between the two main posts) and one point for a behind (between either of two outer posts and the main posts). They may punch or kick the ball and run with it provided that they bounce it every ten yards. Also called: national code

Australian salmon *n* another name for **kahawai**

Australian salute *n Austral informal* a movement of the hand and arm made to brush flies away from one's face

Australian silky terrier *n* a small compact variety of terrier with pricked ears and a long straight silky coat

Australian terrier *n* a small wire-haired breed of terrier similar to the cairn

Australian Tiffanie *n* another name for **Tiffanie**

Austral Islands (ˈɔːstrəl) *pl n* another name for the **Tubuai Islands**

Australoid (ˈɒstrəˌlɔɪd) *adj* **1** denoting, relating to, or belonging to a racial group that includes the native Australians and certain other peoples of southern Asia and the Pacific islands, characterized by dark skin, flat retreating forehead, and medium stature ▷ *n* **2** any member of this racial group

australopithecine (ˌɒstrələʊˈpɪθɪˌsiːn) *n* **1** any of various extinct apelike primates of the genus *Australopithecus* and related genera, remains of which have been discovered in southern and E Africa. Some species are estimated to be over 4.5 million years old. See also **zinjanthropus** ▷ *adj* **2** of or relating to any of these primates [c20 from New Latin *Australopithecus,* from Latin *austrālis* southern, AUSTRAL¹ + Greek *pithēkos* ape]

Australorp (ˈɒstrəˌlɔːp) *n* a heavy black breed of domestic fowl [shortened from *Austral(ian Black) Orp(ington)*]

Austrasia (ɒˈstreɪʒə, -ʃə) *n* the eastern region of the kingdom of the Merovingian Franks that had its capital at Metz and lasted from 511 AD until 814 AD. It covered the area now comprising NE France, Belgium, and western Germany

Austria (ˈɒstrɪə) *n* a republic in central Europe: ruled by the Hapsburgs from 1282 to 1918; formed a dual monarchy with Hungary in 1867 and became a republic in 1919; a member of the European Union; contains part of the Alps, the Danube basin in the east, and extensive forests. Official language: German. Religion: Roman Catholic majority. Currency: euro. Capital: Vienna. Pop: 8 120 000 (2004 est). Area: 83 849 sq km (32 374 sq miles). German name: Österreich

Austria-Hungary *n* the Dual Monarchy established in 1867, consisting of what are now Austria, Hungary, the Czech Republic, Slovakia, Slovenia, Croatia, and Bosnia-Herzegovina, and parts of Poland, Romania, Ukraine, and Italy. The empire was broken up after World War I

Austrian (ˈɒstrɪən) *adj* **1** of or relating to Austria or its inhabitants ▷ *n* **2** a native or inhabitant of Austria

Austrian blind *n* a window blind consisting of rows of vertically gathered fabric that may be drawn up to form a series of ruches

Austro-¹ (ˈɒstrəʊ-) *combining form* southern: *Austro-Asiatic* [from Latin *auster* the south wind]

Austro-² (ˈɒstrəʊ-) *combining form* Austrian: *Austro-Hungarian*

Austro-Asiatic *n* a hypothetical phylum or superfamily of languages consisting of Mon-Khmer and certain other languages of India and South-East Asia. Links with Malayo-Polynesian have also been suggested

Austro-Hungarian *adj* of or relating to the Dual Monarchy of Austria-Hungary (1867-1918)

Austronesia (ˌɒstrəʊˈniːʒə, -ʃə) *n* the islands of the central and S Pacific, including Indonesia, Melanesia, Micronesia, and Polynesia

Austronesian (ˌɒstrəʊˈniːʒən, -ʃən) *adj* **1** of or relating to Austronesia, its peoples, or their languages ▷ *n* **2** another name for **Malayo-Polynesian**

AUT *abbreviation for* Association of University Teachers

aut- *combining form* a variant of **auto-** before a vowel

autacoid (ˈɔːtəˌkɔɪd) *n physiol* any natural internal secretion, esp one that exerts an effect similar to a drug [c20 from AUTO- + Greek *akos* cure + -OID]

autarchy¹ (ˈɔːtɑːkɪ) *n, pl* -chies **1** unlimited rule; autocracy **2** self-government; self-rule [c17 from Greek *autarkhia,* from *autarkhos* autocratic; see AUTO-, -ARCHY] > au'tarchic or au'tarchical *adj*

autarchy² (ˈɔːtɑːkɪ) *n, pl* -chies a variant spelling (now rare) of **autarky**

autarky (ˈɔːtɑːkɪ) *n, pl* -kies **1** (esp of a political unit) a system or policy of economic self-sufficiency aimed at removing the need for imports **2** an economically self-sufficient country [c17 from Greek *autarkeia,* from *autarkēs* self-sufficient, from AUTO- + *arkein* to suffice] > au'tarkic *adj* > 'autarkist *n*

autecious (ɔːˈtiːʃəs) *adj* a variant spelling of **autoecious**

autecology (ˌɔːtɪˈkɒlədʒɪ) *n* the ecological study of an individual organism or species. Compare **synecology.** > ˌauteco'logical *adj*

auteur (ɔːˈtɜː) *n* a director whose creative influence on a film is so great as to be considered its author [French: author] > au'teurism *n* > au'teurist *adj*

authentic (ɔːˈθɛntɪk) *adj* **1** of undisputed origin or authorship; genuine: *an authentic signature* **2** accurate in representation of the facts; trustworthy; reliable: *an authentic account* **3** (of a deed or other document) duly executed, any necessary legal formalities having been complied with **4** *music* **a** using period instruments and historically researched scores and playing techniques in an attempt to perform a piece as it would have been played at the time it was written **b** (in combination): *an authentic-instrument performance* **5** *music* **a** (of a mode as used in Gregorian chant) commencing on the final and ending an octave

a

higher **b** (of a cadence) progressing from a dominant to a tonic chord. Compare **plagal** [C14 from Late Latin *authenticus* coming from the author, from Greek *authentikos*, from *authentēs* one who acts independently, from AUTO- + *hentēs* a doer] > au'thentically *adv* > authenticity (ˌɔːθɛnˈtɪsɪtɪ) *n*

authenticate (ɔːˈθɛntɪˌkeɪt) *vb* (*tr*) **1** to establish as genuine or valid **2** to give authority or legal validity to > au,thenti'cation *n* > au'thenti,cator *n*

authigenic (ˌɔːθɪˈdʒɛnɪk) *adj* (of minerals) having crystallized in a sediment during or after deposition [C19 from German *authigene* from Greek *authigenēs* native + -IC]

author (ˈɔːθə) *n* **1** a person who composes a book, article, or other written work. Related adj: **auctorial 2** a person who writes books as a profession; writer **3** the writings of such a person: *reviewing a postwar author* **4** an originator or creator: *the author of this plan* ▷ *vb* (*tr*) **5** to write or originate [C14 from Old French *autor*, from Latin *auctor* author, from *augēre* to increase] > **authorial** (ɔːˈθɔːrɪəl) *adj*

authoress (ˈɔːθəˌrɛs) *n* now usually disparaging a female author

authoring (ˈɔːθərɪŋ) *n* computing **a** the creation of documents, esp multimedia documents **b** (*as modifier*): *an authoring tool*

authoritarian (ɔːˌθɒrɪˈtɛərɪən) *adj* **1** favouring, denoting, or characterized by strict obedience to authority **2** favouring, denoting, or relating to government by a small elite with wide powers **3** despotic; dictatorial; domineering ▷ *n* **4** a person who favours or practises authoritarian policies > au,thori'tarianism *n*

authoritative (ɔːˈθɒrɪtətɪv) *adj* **1** recognized or accepted as being true or reliable: *an authoritative article on drugs* **2** exercising or asserting authority; commanding: *an authoritative manner* **3** possessing or supported by authority; official: *an authoritative communiqué* > au'thoritatively *adv* > au'thoritativeness *n*

authority (ɔːˈθɒrɪtɪ) *n, pl* -ties **1** the power or right to control, judge, or prohibit the actions of others **2** (*often plural*) a person or group of people having this power, such as a government, police force, etc **3** a position that commands such a power or right (often in the phrase **in authority**) **4** such a power or right delegated, esp from one person to another; authorization: *she has his authority* **5** the ability to influence or control others: *a man of authority* **6** an expert or an authoritative written work in a particular field: *he is an authority on Ming china* **7** evidence or testimony: *we have it on his authority that she is dead* **8** confidence resulting from great expertise: *the violinist lacked authority in his cadenza* **9** (*capital when part of a name*) a public board or corporation exercising governmental authority in administering some enterprise: *Independent Broadcasting Authority* **10** law **a** a judicial decision, statute, or rule of law that establishes a principle; precedent **b** legal permission granted to a person to perform a specified act [C14 from French *autorité*, from Latin *auctōritas*, from *auctor* AUTHOR]

authorize or **authorise** (ˈɔːθəˌraɪz) *vb* (*tr*) **1** to confer authority upon (someone to do something); empower **2** to permit (someone to do or be something) with official sanction: *a dealer authorized by a manufacturer to retail his products* > ˌauthori'zation or ˌauthori'sation > 'authorˌizer or 'authorˌiser *n*

Authorized Version *n* the an English translation of the Bible published in 1611 under James I. Also called: King James Version, King James Bible

authorship (ˈɔːθəˌʃɪp) *n* **1** the origin or originator of a written work, plan, etc: *a book of unknown authorship* **2** the profession of writing books

Auth. Ver. *abbreviation for* Authorized Version (of the Bible)

autism (ˈɔːtɪzəm) *n* psychiatry abnormal self-absorption, usually affecting children, characterized by lack of response to people and actions and limited ability to communicate [C20 from Greek *autos* self + -ISM] > au'tistic *adj*, *n*

auto (ˈɔːtəʊ) *n, pl* -tos US and Canadian informal **1 a** short for **automobile b** (*as modifier*): *auto parts* **2** Asian English informal short for **autorickshaw**

auto- or sometimes before a vowel **aut-** combining form **1** self; same; of or by the same one: *autobiography* **2** acting from or occurring within; self-caused: *autohypnosis* **3** self-propelling; automatic: *automobile* [from Greek *autos* self]

autoallogamy (ˌɔːtəʊəˈlɒɡəmɪ) *n* the ability of some plants of a species to cross-pollinate and others to self-pollinate

autoantibody (ˌɔːtəʊˈæntɪˌbɒdɪ) *n, pl* -bodies an antibody reacting with an antigen that is a part of the organism in which the antibody is formed

autobahn (ˈɔːtəˌbɑːn) *n* a motorway in German-speaking countries [from German, from *Auto* car + *Bahn* road]

autobiographical (ˌɔːtəˌbaɪəˈɡræfɪkəl) *adj* **1** of or concerned with one's own life **2** of or relating to an autobiography > ˌauto,bio'graphically *adv*

autobiography (ˌɔːtəʊbaɪˈɒɡrəfɪ, ˌɔːtəbaɪ-) *n, pl* -phies an account of a person's life written or otherwise recorded by that person > ˌautobi'ographer *n*

autocade (ˈɔːtəʊˌkeɪd) *n* US another name for **motorcade**

autocatalysis (ˌɔːtəʊkəˈtælɪsɪs) *n, pl* -ses (-ˌsiːz) the catalysis of a reaction in which the catalyst is one of the products of the reaction

autocephalous (ˌɔːtəʊˈsɛfələs) *adj* **1** (of an Eastern Christian Church) governed by its own national synods and appointing its own patriarchs or prelates **2** (of a bishop) independent of any higher governing body > autocephalic (ˌɔːtəʊsɪˈfælɪk) *adj* > ˌauto'cephaly *n*

autochanger (ˈɔːtəʊˌtʃeɪndʒə) *n* **1** a device in a record player that enables a small stack of records to be dropped automatically onto the turntable one at a time and played separately **2** a record player with such a device

autochthon (ɔːˈtɒkθən, -θɒn) *n, pl* -thons or -thones (-θəˌniːz) **1** (*often plural*) one of the earliest known inhabitants of any country; aboriginal **2** an animal or plant that is native to a particular region [C17 from Greek *autokhthōn* from the earth itself, from AUTO- + *khthōn* the earth]

autochthonous (ɔːˈtɒkθənəs), **autochthonic** (ˌɔːtɒkˈθɒnɪk) or **autochthonal** *adj* **1** (of rocks, deposits, etc) found where they and their constituents were formed. Compare **allochthonous 2** inhabiting a place or region from earliest known times; aboriginal **3** physiol (of some functions, such as heartbeat) originating within an organ rather than from external stimulation > au'tochthonism or au'tochthony *n* > au'tochthonously *adv*

autocidal (ˌɔːtəʊˈsaɪdəl) *adj* (of insect pest control) effected by the introduction of sterile or genetically altered individuals into the wild population

autoclave (ˈɔːtəˌkleɪv) *n* **1** a strong sealed vessel used for chemical reactions at high pressure **2** an apparatus for sterilizing objects (esp surgical instruments) or for cooking by means of steam under pressure **3** civil engineering a vessel in which freshly cast concrete or sand-lime bricks are cured very rapidly in high-pressure steam ▷ *vb* **4** (*tr*) to put in or subject to the action of an autoclave [C19 from French AUTO- + -*clave*, from Latin *clāvis* key]

autocorrelation (ˌɔːtəʊˌkɒrɪˈleɪʃən) *n* statistics the condition occurring when successive items in a series are correlated so that their covariance is not zero and they are not independent. Also called: serial correlation

autocracy (ɔːˈtɒkrəsɪ) *n, pl* -cies **1** government by an individual with unrestricted authority **2** the unrestricted authority of such an individual **3** a country, society, etc, ruled by an autocrat

autocrat (ˈɔːtəˌkræt) *n* **1** a ruler who possesses absolute and unrestricted authority **2** a domineering or dictatorial person

autocratic (ˌɔːtəˈkrætɪk) *adj* **1** of or relating to an absolute and unrestricted ruler **2** domineering or dictatorial > ˌauto'cratically *adv*

autocross (ˈɔːtəʊˌkrɒs) *n* a form of motor sport in which cars race over a half-mile circuit of rough grass. See also **motocross, rallycross**

Autocue (ˈɔːtəʊˌkjuː) *n* trademark an electronic television prompting device whereby a prepared script, unseen by the audience, is enlarged line by line for the speaker. US and Canadian name (trademark): Teleprompter

autocutie (ˈɔːtəʊˌkjuːtɪ) *n* informal a young and attractive but inexperienced female television presenter [C20 from AUTOCUE + CUTIE]

autocycle (ˈɔːtəʊˌsaɪkəl) *n* obsolete a bicycle powered or assisted by a small engine

auto-da-fé (ˌɔːtəʊdəˈfeɪ) *n, pl* autos-da-fé **1** history a ceremony of the Spanish Inquisition including the pronouncement and execution of sentences passed on sinners or heretics **2** the burning to death of people condemned as heretics by the Inquisition [C18 from Portuguese, literally: act of the faith]

autodestruct (ˌɔːtəʊdɪˈstrʌkt) *adj* also **autodestructive 1** likely to or possessing the power to destroy or obliterate itself or its possessor: *autodestruct mechanism* ▷ *vb* (*intr*) **2** (of a missile, machine, etc) to destroy itself

autodidact (ˌɔːtəʊˈdaɪdækt) *n* a person who is self-taught [C16 from Greek *autodidaktos* self-taught, from *autos* self + *didaskein* to teach] > ˌautodi'dactic *adj*

autodyne (ˈɔːtəʊˌdaɪn) *adj* electronics denoting or relating to an electrical circuit in which the same elements and valves are used as oscillator and detector

autoecious or sometimes US **autecious** (ɔːˈtiːʃəs) *adj* **1** (of parasites, esp the rust fungi) completing the entire life cycle on a single species of host. Compare **heteroecious 2** (of plants, esp mosses) having male and female reproductive organs on the same plant [C19 from AUTO- + -*oecious*, from Greek *oikia* house] > au'toecism or sometimes US au'tecism *n*

autoeroticism (ˌɔːtəʊɪˈrɒtɪˌsɪzəm) or **autoerotism** (ˌɔːtəʊˈɛrəˌtɪzəm) *n* psychol the arousal and use of one's own body as a sexual object, as through masturbation > ˌautoe'rotic *adj*

autoexposure (ˌɔːtəɪkˈspəʊʒə) *n* another name for **automatic exposure**

autofocus (ˈɔːtəʊˌfəʊkəs) *n* another name for **automatic focus**

autogamy (ɔːˈtɒɡəmɪ) *n* **1** self-fertilization in flowering plants **2** a type of sexual reproduction, occurring in some protozoans, in which the uniting gametes are derived from the same cell > au'togamous or autogamic (ˌɔːtəˈɡæmɪk) *adj*

autogenesis (ˌɔːtəʊˈdʒɛnɪsɪs) or **autogeny** (ɔːˈtɒdʒɪnɪ) *n* another word for **abiogenesis** (sense 1) > autogenetic (ˌɔːtəʊdʒɪˈnɛtɪk) *adj*

autogenic training (ˌɔːtəʊˈdʒɛnɪk) *n* a technique for reducing stress through mental exercises to produce physical relaxation. Also called: autogenics

autogenous (ɔːˈtɒdʒɪnəs) *adj* **1 a** originating within the body. Compare **heterogenous b** denoting a vaccine made from bacteria obtained from the patient's own body **2** self-generated; self-produced **3** denoting a weld in which the filler metal and the parent metal are of similar composition > au'togenously *adv*

autogiro or **autogyro** (ˌɔːtəʊˈdʒaɪrəʊ) *n, pl* -ros a self-propelled aircraft supported in flight mainly by unpowered rotating horizontal blades. Also called: gyroplane Compare **helicopter** [C20 originally a trademark]

autograft (ˈɔːtəˌɡrɑːft) *n* surgery a tissue graft obtained from one part of a patient's body for use on another part

autograph (ˈɔːtəˌɡrɑːf, -ˌɡræf) *n* **1 a** a

handwritten signature, esp that of a famous person **b** (*as modifier*): *an autograph album* **2** a person's handwriting **3 a** a book, document, etc, handwritten by its author; original manuscript; holograph **b** (*as modifier*): *an autograph letter* ▷ *vb* (*tr*) **4** to write one's signature on or in; sign **5** to write with one's own hand [c17 from Late Latin, from Greek *autographos*, from *autos* self + *graphein* to write] > **autographic** (ˌɔːtəˈɡræfɪk) *or* ˌauto'graphical *adj* > ˌauto'graphically *adv*

autography (ɔːˈtɒɡrəfɪ) *n* **1** the writing of something in one's own handwriting; something handwritten **2** the precise reproduction of an illustration or of writing

Autoharp (ˈɔːtəʊˌhɑːp) *n trademark* a zither-like musical instrument used in country-and-western music, equipped with button-controlled dampers that can prevent selected strings from sounding, thus allowing chords to be played. It is plucked with the fingers or a plectrum

autohypnosis (ˌɔːtəʊhɪpˈnəʊsɪs) *n psychol* the process or result of self-induced hypnosis > **autohypnotic** (ˌɔːtəʊhɪpˈnɒtɪk) *adj* > ˌautohyp'notically *adv*

autoicous (ɔːˈtɔɪkəs) *adj* (of plants, esp mosses) having male and female reproductive organs on the same plant [c19 from AUTO- + Greek *oikos* dwelling]

autoimmune (ˌɔːtəʊɪˈmjuːn) *adj* (of a disease) caused by the action of antibodies produced against substances normally present in the body > ˌautoim'munity *n*

autoinfection (ˌɔːtəʊɪnˈfɛkʃən) *n* infection by a pathogenic agent already within the body or infection transferred from one part of the body to another

autoinoculation (ˌɔːtəʊɪˌnɒkjʊˈleɪʃən) *n* the inoculation of microorganisms (esp viruses) from one part of the body into another, usually in the form of a vaccine

autointoxication (ˌɔːtəʊɪnˌtɒksɪˈkeɪʃən) *n* self-poisoning caused by absorption of toxic products originating within the body. Also called: autotoxaemia

autoionization *or* **autoionisation** (ˌɔːtəʊˌaɪənaɪˈzeɪʃən) *n physics* the process in which spontaneous decay of excited atoms or molecules results in emission of electrons, rather than photons

autojumble (ˈɔːtəʊˌdʒʌmbəl) *n* a sale of second-hand car parts, esp for car enthusiasts

autokinetic (ˌɔːtəʊkɪˈnɛtɪk, -kaɪ-) *adj* automatically self-moving

autokinetic phenomenon *n psychol* the apparent movement of a fixed point of light when observed in a darkened room. The effect is produced by small eye movements for which the brain is unable to compensate, having no other reference points

autoloading (ˈɔːtəʊˌləʊdɪŋ) *adj* self-loading

autologous (ɔːˈtɒləɡəs) *adj* (of a tissue graft, blood transfusion, etc) originating from the recipient rather than from a donor

Autolycus¹ (ɔːˈtɒlɪkəs) *n* a crater in the NW quadrant of the moon about 38 km in diameter and 3000 m deep

Autolycus² (ɔːˈtɒlɪkəs) *n Greek myth* a thief who stole cattle from his neighbour Sisyphus and prevented him from recognizing them by making them invisible

autolyse *or US* **autolyze** (ˈɔːtəˌlaɪz) *vb biochem* to undergo or cause to undergo autolysis

autolysin (ɔːˈtəˈlaɪsɪn, ɔːˈtɒlɪ-) *n* any agent that produces autolysis

autolysis (ɔːˈtɒlɪsɪs) *n* the destruction of cells and tissues of an organism by enzymes produced by the cells themselves [c20 via German from Greek *autos* self + *lusis* loosening, release] > **autolytic** (ˌɔːtəˈlɪtɪk) *adj*

automat (ˈɔːtəˌmæt) *n* **1** Also called: vending machine a machine that automatically dispenses goods, such as cigarettes, when money is inserted

2 *chiefly US* an area or room, sometimes having restaurant facilities, where food and other goods are supplied from vending machines

automata (ɔːˈtɒmətə) *n* a plural of **automaton**

automata theory *n* the formal study of the power of computation of abstract machines

automate (ˈɔːtəˌmeɪt) *vb* to make (a process, etc) automatic, or (of a process, etc) to be made automatic

automated teller machine *n* a computerized cash dispenser. Abbreviation: ATM

automatic (ˌɔːtəˈmætɪk) *adj* **1** performed from force of habit or without conscious thought; lacking spontaneity; mechanical: *an automatic smile* **2 a** (of a device, mechanism, etc) able to activate, move, or regulate itself **b** (of an act or process) performed by such automatic equipment **3** (of the action of a muscle, gland, etc) involuntary or reflex **4** occurring as a necessary consequence **5** (of a firearm) **a** utilizing some of the force of or gas from each explosion to eject the empty shell case, replace it with a new one, and fire continuously until release of the trigger. Compare semiautomatic (sense 2) **b** short for semiautomatic (sense 2) ▷ See also **machine** (sense 5) ▷ *n* **6** an automatic firearm **7** a motor vehicle having automatic transmission **8** a machine that operates automatically [c18 from Greek *automatos* acting independently] > ˌauto'matically *adv* > **automaticity** (ˌɔːtəʊməˈtɪsɪtɪ) *n*

automatic camera *n* a camera in which the lens aperture or the shutter speed or both are automatically adjusted to the prevailing conditions

automatic door *n* a self-opening door

automatic exposure *n* the automatic adjustment of the lens aperture and shutter speed of a camera by a control mechanism. Also called: autoexposure

automatic focus *n* **a** a system in a camera which automatically adjusts the lens so that the object being photographed is in focus, often one using infrared light to estimate the distance of the object from the camera **b** (*as modifier*): *automatic-focus lens*. Abbreviation: AF Also called: autofocus

automatic frequency control *n* a system in a radio or television receiver by which the tuning of an incoming signal is accurately maintained. Abbreviation: AFC

automatic gain control *n* control of a radio receiver in which the gain varies inversely with the magnitude of the input, thus maintaining the output at an approximately constant level. Abbreviation: AGC

automatic pilot *n* **1** Also called: autopilot a device that automatically maintains an aircraft on a preset course **2** on automatic pilot *informal* acting without conscious thought because of tiredness, shock, or familiarity with the task being performed

automatic repeat *n* a key on the keyboard of a typewriter, computer, etc, which, when depressed continuously, produces the character repeatedly until the key is released

automatic transmission *n* a transmission system in a motor vehicle, usually incorporating a fluid clutch, in which the gears change automatically

automatic vending *n* selling goods by vending machines

automation (ˌɔːtəˈmeɪʃən) *n* **1** the use of methods for controlling industrial processes automatically, esp by electronically controlled systems, often reducing manpower **2** the extent to which a process is so controlled

automatism (ɔːˈtɒməˌtɪzəm) *n* **1** the state or quality of being automatic; mechanical or involuntary action **2** *law, philosophy* the explanation of an action, or of action in general, as determined by the physiological states of the individual, admissible in law as a defence when

the physiological state is involuntary, as in sleepwalking **3** *psychol* the performance of actions, such as sleepwalking, without conscious knowledge or control **4** the suspension of consciousness sought or achieved by certain artists and writers to allow free flow of uncensored thoughts > **au'tomatist** *n*

automatize *or* **automatise** (ɔːˈtɒməˌtaɪz) *vb* to make (a process, etc) automatic or (of a process, etc) to be made automatic > au,tomati'zation *or* au,tomati'sation *n*

automaton (ɔːˈtɒməˌtɒn, -tən) *n, pl* **-tons** *or* **-ta** (-tə) **1** a mechanical device operating under its own hidden power; robot **2** a person who acts mechanically or leads a routine monotonous life [c17 from Latin, from Greek, from *automatos* spontaneous, self-moving] > **au'tomatous** *adj*

autometer (ˈɔːtəʊˌmiːtə) *n* a small device inserted in a photocopier to enable the process of copying to begin and to record the number of copies made

automobile (ˈɔːtəməˌbiːl) *n* another word (esp US) for **car** (sense 1) > **automobilist** (ˌɔːtəməˈbiːlɪst, -ˈməʊbɪlɪst) *n*

automobilia (ˌɔːtəməˈbiːliə) *pl n* items connected with cars and motoring of interest to the collector

automotive (ˌɔːtəˈməʊtɪv) *adj* **1** relating to motor vehicles **2** self-propelling

autonomic (ˌɔːtəˈnɒmɪk) *adj* **1** occurring involuntarily or spontaneously **2** of or relating to the autonomic nervous system **3** Also: autonomous (of plant movements) occurring as a result of internal stimuli > ˌauto'nomically *adv*

autonomic nervous system *n* the section of the nervous system of vertebrates that controls the involuntary actions of the smooth muscles, heart, and glands. It has two divisions: the sympathetic and the parasympathetic. Compare **somatic nervous system**

autonomics (ˌɔːtəˈnɒmɪks) *n* (*functioning as singular*) *electronics* the study of self-regulating systems for process control

autonomous (ɔːˈtɒnəməs) *adj* **1** (of a community, country, etc) possessing a large degree of self-government **2** of or relating to an autonomous community **3** independent of others **4** *philosophy* **a** acting or able to act in accordance with rules and principles of one's own choosing **b** (in the moral philosophy of Kant, of an individual's will) directed to duty rather than to some other end. Compare **heteronomous** (sense 3) See also **categorical imperative 5** *biology* existing as an organism independent of other organisms or parts **6** a variant spelling of **autonomic** (sense 3) [c19 from Greek *autonomos* living under one's own laws, from AUTO- + *nomos* law] > au'tonomously *adv*

autonomy (ɔːˈtɒnəmɪ) *n, pl* **-mies 1** the right or state of self-government, esp when limited **2** a state, community, or individual possessing autonomy **3** freedom to determine one's own actions, behaviour, etc **4** *philosophy* **a** the doctrine that the individual human will is or ought to be governed only by its own principles and laws. See also **categorical imperative b** the state in which one's actions are autonomous [c17 from Greek *autonomia* freedom to live by one's own laws; see AUTONOMOUS] > au'tonomist *n*

autophyte (ˈɔːtəˌfaɪt) *n* an autotrophic plant, such as any green plant > **autophytic** (ˌɔːtəˈfɪtɪk) *adj* > ˌauto'phytically *adv*

autopilot (ˌɔːtəˈpaɪlət, -təʊ-) *n* short for **automatic pilot**

autopista (ˌɔːtəˈpiːstə) *n* a Spanish motorway [from Spanish: auto(mobile) track]

autoplasty (ˈɔːtəˌplæstɪ) *n* surgical repair of defects by grafting or transplanting tissue from the patient's own body > ˌauto'plastic *adj*

autopolyploid (ˌɔːtəʊˈpɒlɪˌplɔɪd) *adj* **1** (of cells, organisms, etc) having more than two sets of haploid chromosomes inherited from a single species ▷ *n* **2** an organism or cell of this type ▷ See also **allopolyploid, polyploid** > ˌauto'poly,ploidy *n*

a

autopsy (ˈɔːtəpsɪ, ɔːˈtɒp-) *n, pl* -sies **1** Also called: necropsy, postmortem examination dissection and examination of a dead body to determine the cause of death **2** an eyewitness observation **3** any critical analysis [c17 from New Latin *autopsia*, from Greek: seeing with one's own eyes, from AUTO- + *opsis* sight]

autoput (ˈɔːtəʊˌpʊt) *n* a motorway in the former Yugoslavia [from Serbo-Croat: auto(mobile) road]

autoradiograph (ˌɔːtəʊˈreɪdɪəˌɡrɑːf, -ˌɡræf) *n* a photograph showing the distribution of a radioactive substance in a specimen. The photographic plate is exposed by radiation from the specimen. Also called: radioautograph
> autoradiographic (ˌɔːtəʊˌreɪdɪəˈɡræfɪk) *adj*
> autoradiography (ˌɔːtəʊˌreɪdɪˈɒɡrəfɪ) *n*

auto-repeat *n* **1** *computing* a feature of computer keys whereby a character is generated repeatedly as long as the user holds down the key in question ▷ *vb (intr)* **2** *computing* (of a computer key) to go on automatically regenerating a character

autorickshaw (ˈɔːtəʊˈrɪkʃɔː) *n* (in India) a light three-wheeled vehicle driven by a motorcycle engine

autorotation (ˌɔːtəʊrəʊˈteɪʃən) *n* the continuous rotation of a body in an airflow, such as that of the rotor blades of a helicopter in an unpowered descent

autoroute (ˈɔːtəʊˌruːt) *n* a French motorway [from French, from *auto* car + *route* road]

autosome (ˈɔːtəˌsəʊm) *n* any chromosome that is not a sex chromosome > ˌautoˈsomal *adj*

autospore (ˈɔːtəʊˌspɔː) *n* a nonmotile algal spore that develops adult characteristics before being released

autostability (ˌɔːtəʊstəˈbɪlɪtɪ) *n* the property of being stable either as a result of inherent characteristics or of built-in devices

autostrada (ˈɔːtəʊˌstrɑːdə) *n* an Italian motorway [from Italian, from *auto* car + *strada* road]

autosuggestion (ˌɔːtəʊsəˈdʒɛstʃən) *n* a process of suggestion in which the person unconsciously supplies or consciously attempts to supply the means of influencing his own behaviour or beliefs > ˌautosugˈgestive *adj*

autotimer (ˈɔːtəʊˌtaɪmə) *n* a device for turning a system on and off automatically at times predetermined by advance setting

autotomize *or* **autotomise** (ɔːˈtɒtəˌmaɪz) *vb* to cause (a part of the body) to undergo autotomy

autotomy (ɔːˈtɒtəmɪ) *n, pl* -mies the casting off by an animal of a part of its body, to facilitate escape when attacked > **autotomic** (ˌɔːtəˈtɒmɪk) *adj*

autotoxaemia *or US* **autotoxemia** (ˌɔːtəʊtɒkˈsiːmɪə) *n* another name for **autointoxication**

autotoxin (ˌɔːtəʊˈtɒksɪn) *n* any poison or toxin formed in the organism upon which it acts. See **autointoxication.** > ˌautoˈtoxic *adj*

autotransformer (ˌɔːtəʊtrænsˈfɔːmə) *n* a transformer in which part of the winding is common to both primary and secondary circuits

autotrophic (ˌɔːtəˈtrɒfɪk) *adj* (of organisms such as green plants) capable of manufacturing complex organic nutritive compounds from simple inorganic sources such as carbon dioxide, water, and nitrates, using energy from the sun. Compare **heterotrophic.** > autotroph (ˈɔːtətrəʊf) *n*

autotune (ˈɔːtəʊˌtjuːn) *n* a software package that automatically manipulates a recording of a vocal track until it is in tune regardless of whether or not the original performance was in tune

autotype (ˈɔːtəˌtaɪp) *n* **1** a photographic process for producing prints in black and white, using a carbon pigment **2** an exact copy of a manuscript, etc; facsimile > **autotypic** (ˌɔːtəˈtɪpɪk) *adj* > ˈautoˌtypy *n*

autowinder (ˈɔːtəʊˌwaɪndə) *n* *photog* a battery-operated device for advancing the film in a camera automatically after each exposure. Compare **motor drive**

autoxidation (ɔːˌtɒksɪˈdeɪʃən) *n* *chem* **a** oxidation by exposure to atmospheric oxygen **b** oxidation that will only occur when another oxidation reaction is taking place in the same system

autumn (ˈɔːtəm) *n* **1** (*sometimes capital*) **a** Also called (esp US): fall the season of the year between summer and winter, astronomically from the September equinox to the December solstice in the N hemisphere and from the March equinox to the June solstice in the S hemisphere **b** (*as modifier*): autumn leaves **2** a period of late maturity, esp one followed by a decline [c14 from Latin *autumnus,* perhaps of Etruscan origin]

autumnal (ɔːˈtʌmnəl) *adj* of, occurring in, or characteristic of autumn > auˈtumnally *adv*

autumnal equinox *n* **1** the time at which the sun crosses the plane of the equator away from the relevant hemisphere, making day and night of equal length. It occurs about Sept 23 in the N hemisphere (March 21 in the S hemisphere) **2** *astronomy* **a** the point, lying in the constellation Virgo, at which the sun's ecliptic intersects the celestial equator **b** the time at which this occurs as the sun travels north to south (23 September)

autumn crocus *n* a liliaceous plant, *Colchicum autumnale,* of Europe and N Africa having pink or purplish autumn flowers. Also called: **meadow saffron** Compare **saffron**

autunite (ˈɔːtəˌnaɪt) *n* a yellowish fluorescent radioactive mineral consisting of a hydrated calcium uranium phosphate in tetragonal crystalline form. It is found in uranium ores. Formula: $Ca(UO_2)_2(PO_4)_2.10–12H_2O$ [c19 named after *Autun* in France, one of the places where it was found, + -ITE¹]

Auvergne (əʊˈveən, əʊˈvɜːn; *French* ovɛrɲ) *n* a region of S central France: largely mountainous, rising over 1800 m (6000 ft)

auxanometer (ˌɔːksəˈnɒmɪtə) *n* an instrument that measures the linear growth of plant shoots [c19 from Greek *auxanein* to increase + -METER]

Aux Cayes (əʊ ˈkeɪ; *French* o kaj) *n* the former name of **Les Cayes**

Auxerre (*French* ozɛr) *n* a town in central France, capital of Yonne department; Gothic cathedral. Pop: 37 790 (1999)

auxesis (ɔːɡˈsiːsɪs, ɔːkˈsiː-) *n* growth in animal or plant tissues resulting from an increase in cell size without cell division [c16 via Latin from Greek: increase, from *auxein* to increase, grow]

auxiliaries (ɔːɡˈzɪljərɪz, -ˈzɪlə-) *pl n* foreign or allied troops serving another nation; mercenaries

auxiliary (ɔːɡˈzɪljərɪ, -ˈzɪlə-) *adj* **1** secondary or supplementary **2** supporting **3** *nautical* (of a sailing vessel) having an engine: *an auxiliary sloop* ▷ *n, pl* -ries **4** a person or thing that supports or supplements; subordinate or assistant **5** *nautical* **a** a sailing vessel with an engine **b** the engine of such a vessel **6** *navy* a vessel such as a tug, hospital ship, etc, not used for combat [c17 from Latin *auxiliārius* bringing aid, from *auxilium* help, from *augēre* to increase, enlarge, strengthen]

auxiliary note *n* *music* a nonharmonic note occurring between two harmonic notes

auxiliary power unit *n* an additional engine fitted to an aircraft to operate when the main engines are not in use

auxiliary rotor *n* the tail rotor of a helicopter, used for directional and rotary control

auxiliary verb *n* a verb used to indicate the tense, voice, mood, etc, of another verb where this is not indicated by inflection, such as English *will* in *he will go, was* in *he was eating* and *he was eaten, do* in *I do like you,* etc

auxin (ˈɔːksɪn) *n* any of various plant hormones, such as indoleacetic acid, that promote growth and control fruit and flower development. Synthetic auxins are widely used in agriculture and horticulture [c20 from Greek *auxein* to grow]

auxochrome (ˈɔːksəˌkrəʊm) *n* a group of atoms that can be attached to a chromogen to convert it into a dye

auxocyte (ˈɔːksəˌsaɪt) *n* any cell undergoing meiosis, esp an oocyte or spermatocyte

auxospore (ˈɔːksəˌspɔː) *n* a diatom cell before its silicaceous cell wall is formed

auxotonic (ˌɔːksəˈtɒnɪk) *adj* (of muscle contraction) occurring against increasing force

auxotroph (ˈɔːksətrəʊf) *n* a mutant strain of microorganism having nutritional requirements additional to those of the normal organism > ˌauxoˈtrophic *adj*

Av (æv) *or* **Ab** *n* (in the Jewish calendar) the fifth month of the year according to biblical reckoning and the eleventh month in the civil year, usually falling within July and August [from Hebrew]

AV *abbreviation for* Authorized Version (of the Bible)

av. *abbreviation for* average

Av. *or* **av.** *abbreviation for* avenue

a.v. *or* **A/V** *abbreviation for* ad valorem

a-v, A-V *or* **AV** *abbreviation for* audiovisual

ava (əˈvɔː) *adv Scot* at all [Scot form of *of all*]

avadavat (ˌævədəˈvæt) *or* **amadavat** (ˌæmədəˈvæt) *n* either of two Asian weaverbirds of the genus *Estrilda,* esp *E. amandava,* having a red plumage: often kept as cagebirds [c18 from *Ahmadabad,* Indian city from which these birds were brought to Europe]

avail (əˈveɪl) *vb* **1** to be of use, advantage, profit, or assistance (to) **2 avail oneself of** to make use of to one's advantage ▷ *n* use or advantage (esp in the phrases **of no avail, to little avail**) [c13 *availen,* from *vailen,* from Old French *valoir,* from Latin *valēre* to be strong, prevail] > aˈvailingly *adv*

available (əˈveɪləbəl) *adj* **1** obtainable or accessible; capable of being made use of; at hand **2** *US politics derogatory* suitable for public office, usually as a result of having an inoffensive character: *Smith was a particularly available candidate* > aˌvailaˈbility *or* aˈvailableness *n* > aˈvailably *adv*

avalanche (ˈævəˌlɑːntʃ) *n* **1 a** a fall of large masses of snow and ice down a mountain **b** a fall of rocks, sand, etc **2** a sudden or overwhelming appearance of a large quantity of things **3** *physics* a group of ions or electrons produced by a single ion or electron as a result of a collision with some other form of matter ▷ *vb* **4** to come down overwhelmingly (upon) [c18 from French, by mistaken division from *la valanche,* from *valanche,* from (northwestern Alps) dialect *lavantse;* related to Old Provençal *lavanca,* of obscure origin]

Avalon (ˈævəˌlɒn) *n* *celtic myth* an island paradise in the western seas: in Arthurian legend it is where King Arthur was taken after he was mortally wounded [from Medieval Latin *insula avallonis* island of Avalon, from Old Welsh *aballon* apple]

Avalon Peninsula *n* a large peninsula of Newfoundland, between Trinity and Placentia Bays. Area: about 10 000 sq km (4000 sq miles)

avant- *prefix* of or belonging to the avant-garde of a specified field

avant-garde (ˌævɒɲˈɡɑːd; *French* avɑ̃ɡard) *n* **1** those artists, writers, musicians, etc, whose techniques and ideas are markedly experimental or in advance of those generally accepted ▷ *adj* **2** of such artists, etc, their ideas, or techniques **3** radical; daring [from French: VANGUARD] > ˌavant-ˈgardism *n* > ˌavant-ˈgardist *n*

avantist (æˈvɒntɪst) *n* short for **avant-gardist**

Avar (ˈeɪvɑː, ˈævɑː) *n* **1** a member of a people of unknown origin in E Europe from the 6th to the early 9th century AD: crushed by Charlemagne around 800 **2** a member of a people of the Caucasus **3** the language of this people, belonging to the North-East Caucasian family

avarice (ˈævərɪs) *n* extreme greed for riches; cupidity [c13 from Old French, from Latin *avaritia,* from *avārus* covetous, from *avēre* to crave] > ˌavaˈricious *adj* > ˌavaˈriciously *adv* > ˌavaˈriciousness *n*

avascular (əˈvæskjʊlə) *adj* (of certain tissues, such as cartilage) lacking blood vessels

avast (əˈvɑːst) *sentence substitute nautical* stop! cease! [c17 perhaps from Dutch *hou'vast* hold fast]

avatar ('ævəˌtɑː) *n* **1** *Hinduism* the manifestation of a deity, notably Vishnu, in human, superhuman, or animal form **2** a visible manifestation or embodiment of an abstract concept; archetype **3** a movable image that represents a person in a virtual reality environment or in cyberspace [C18 from Sanskrit *avatāra* a going down, from *avatarati* he descends, from *ava* down + *tarati* he passes over]

avaunt (ə'vɔːnt) *sentence substitute archaic* go away! depart! [C15 from Old French *avant!* forward!, from Late Latin *ab ante* forward, from Latin *ab* from + *ante* before]

AVC *abbreviation for* additional voluntary contribution: one of a series of supplementary payments made to a pension fund

avdp. *abbreviation for* avoirdupois

ave ('ɑːvɪ, 'ɑːveɪ) *sentence substitute* welcome or farewell [Latin]

Ave¹ ('ɑːvɪ) *n RC Church* **1** short for **Ave Maria**: see **Hail Mary** **2** the time for the Angelus to be recited, so called because of the threefold repetition of the Ave Maria in this devotion **3** the beads of the rosary used to count the number of Ave Marias said [C13 from Latin: hail!]

Ave² or **ave** *abbreviation for* avenue

Avebury ('eɪvbərɪ) *n* a village in Wiltshire, site of an extensive Neolithic stone circle

Aveiro (*Portuguese* ə'veɪru) *n* a port in N central Portugal, on the **Aveiro lagoon**: ancient Roman town; linked by canal with the Atlantic Ocean. Pop: 73 335 (2001). Ancient name: Talabriga (ˌtælə'briːɡə)

avel ('avɛl) *n Judaism* a variant of **ovel**

Avellaneda (*Spanish* aβeʎa'neða) *n* a city in E Argentina, an industrial suburb of Buenos Aires. Pop: 342 193 (1999 est)

Ave Maria (ma'riːə) *n* another name for **Hail Mary** [C14 from Medieval Latin: hail, Mary!]

avenge (ə'vɛndʒ) *vb* (*usually tr*) to inflict a punishment in retaliation for (harm, injury, etc) done to (a person or persons); take revenge for or on behalf of: *to avenge a crime* [C14 from Old French *avengier*, from *vengier*, from Latin *vindicāre*; see VENGEANCE, VINDICATE] > **a'venger** *n*

> USAGE The use of *avenge* with a reflexive pronoun was formerly considered incorrect, but is now acceptable: *she avenged herself on the man who killed her daughter*

avens ('ævɪnz) *n, pl* -ens (*functioning as singular*) **1** any of several temperate or arctic rosaceous plants of the genus *Geum*, such as *G. rivale* (**water avens**), which has a purple calyx and orange-pink flowers. See also **herb bennet** **2** mountain avens either of two trailing evergreen white-flowered rosaceous shrubs of the genus *Dryas* that grow on mountains in N temperate regions and in the Arctic [C15 from Old French *avence*, from Medieval Latin *avencia* variety of clover]

Aventine ('ævɪnˌtaɪn, -tɪn) *n* one of the seven hills on which Rome was built

aventurine, aventurin (ə'vɛntjʊrɪn) or **avanturine** (ə'væntjʊrɪn) *n* **1** a dark-coloured glass, usually green or brown, spangled with fine particles of gold, copper, or some other metal **2** Also called: sunstone a light-coloured translucent variety of orthoclase feldspar containing reddish-gold particles of iron compounds **3** a variety of quartz containing red or greenish particles of iron oxide or mica: a gemstone [C19 from French, from Italian *avventurina*, from *avventura* chance; so named because usually found by accident; see ADVENTURE]

avenue ('ævɪˌnjuː) *n* **1 a** a broad street, often lined with trees **b** (*capital as part of a street name*) a road, esp in a built-up area: *Shaftesbury Avenue* **2** a main approach road, as to a country house **3** a way bordered by two rows of trees: *an avenue of oaks* **4** a line of approach: *explore every avenue* [C17 from French, from *avenir* to come to, from Latin *advenīre*, from *venīre* to come]

aver (ə'vɜː) *vb* avers, averring, averred (*tr*) **1** to state positively; assert **2** *law* to allege as a fact or prove to be true [C14 from Old French *averer*, from Medieval Latin *advērāre*, from Latin *vērus* true] > **a'verment** *n*

average ('ævərɪdʒ, 'ævrɪdʒ) *n* **1** the typical or normal amount, quality, degree, etc: *above average in intelligence* **2** Also called: arithmetic mean the result obtained by adding the numbers or quantities in a set and dividing the total by the number of members in the set: *the average of 3, 4, and 8 is 5* **3** (of a continuously variable ratio, such as speed) the quotient of the differences between the initial and final values of the two quantities that make up the ratio: *his average over the journey was 30 miles per hour* **4** *maritime law* **a** a loss incurred or damage suffered by a ship or its cargo at sea **b** the equitable apportionment of such loss among the interested parties **5** (*often plural*) *stock exchange* a simple or weighted average of the prices of a selected group of securities computed in order to facilitate market comparisons **6** on (the *or* an) average usually; typically: *on average, he goes twice a week* ⊳ *adj* **7** usual or typical **8** mediocre or inferior: *his performance was only average* **9** constituting a numerical average: *the average age; an average speed* **10** approximately typical of a range of values: *the average contents of a matchbox* ⊳ *vb* **11** (*tr*) to obtain or estimate a numerical average of **12** (*tr*) to assess the general quality of **13** (*tr*) to perform or receive a typical number of: *to average eight hours' work a day* **14** (*tr*) to divide up proportionately: *they averaged the profits among the staff* **15** (*tr*) to amount to or be on average: *the children averaged 15 years of age* **16** (*intr*) *stock exchange* to purchase additional securities in a holding whose price has fallen (**average down**) or risen (**average up**) in anticipation of a speculative profit after further increases in price [C15 *averay* loss arising from damage to ships or cargoes (shared equitably among all concerned, hence the modern sense), from Old Italian *avaria*, ultimately from Arabic *awār* damage, blemish] > **'averagely** *adv*

average adjuster *n* a person who calculates average claims, esp for marine insurance. See **average** (sense 4)

average deviation *n statistics* another name for **mean deviation**

Averno (*Italian* a'vɛrno) *n* a crater lake in Italy, near Naples: in ancient times regarded as an entrance to hell. Latin name: Avernus (ə'vɜːnəs) [from Latin, from Greek *aornos* without birds, from A-¹ + *ornis* bird; referring to the legend that the lake's sulphurous exhalations killed birds]

Averroism (ˌævə'rəʊɪzəm, ə'vɛrəʊ-) *n* the teachings of Averroës (Arabic name *ibn-Rushd*; 1126–88), the Arab philosopher and physician in Spain > **Aver'roist** *n* > **Averro'istic** *adj*

averse (ə'vɜːs) *adj* **1** (*postpositive; usually foll by to*) opposed, disinclined, or loath **2** (of leaves, flowers, etc) turned away from the main stem. Compare **adverse** (sense 4) [C16 from Latin *āversus*, from *āvertere* to turn from, from *vertere* to turn] > **a'versely** *adv* > **a'verseness** *n*

aversion (ə'vɜːʃən) *n* **1** (*usually foll by to or for*) extreme dislike or disinclination; repugnance **2** a person or thing that arouses this: *he is my pet aversion*

aversion therapy *n psychiatry* a method of suppressing an undesirable habit, such as excessive smoking, by causing the subject to associate an unpleasant effect, such as an electric shock or nausea, with the habit

aversive (ə'vɜːsɪv) *adj* tending to dissuade or repel > **a'versively** *adv*

avert (ə'vɜːt) *vb* (*tr*) **1** to turn away or aside: *to avert one's gaze* **2** to ward off; prevent from occurring: *to avert danger* [C15 from Old French *avertir*, from Latin *āvertere*; see AVERSE] > **a'vertible** or **a'vertable** *adj*

Aves ('eɪviːz) *pl n* the class of vertebrates comprising the birds. See **bird** (sense 1) [pl of Latin *avis* bird]

Avesta (ə'vɛstə) *n* a collection of sacred writings of Zoroastrianism, including the Songs of Zoroaster

Avestan (ə'vɛstən) or **Avestic** (ə'vɛstɪk) *n* **1** the oldest recorded language of the Iranian branch of the Indo-European family; the language of the Avesta. Formerly called: Zend ⊳ *adj* **2** of or relating to the Avesta or its language

Aveyron (*French* avɛrɔ̃) *n* a department of S France in Midi-Pyrénées region. Capital: Rodez. Pop: 266 940 (2003 est). Area: 8771 sq km (3421 sq miles)

avgolemono (ˌævɡə'lɛmənəʊ) *n* a Greek soup made with eggs, lemon juice, and rice [C20 from Modern Greek]

avian ('eɪvɪən) *adj* of, relating to, or resembling a bird [C19 from Latin *avis* bird]

avian flu ('eɪvɪən) *n* another name for **bird flu**

aviarist ('eɪvjərɪst) *n* a person who keeps an aviary

aviary ('eɪvjərɪ) *n, pl* aviaries a large enclosure in which birds are kept [C16 from Latin *aviārium*, from *aviārius* concerning birds, from *avis* bird]

aviate ('eɪvɪˌeɪt) *vb* to pilot or fly in an aircraft

aviation (ˌeɪvɪ'eɪʃən) *n* **1 a** the art or science of flying aircraft **b** the design, production, and maintenance of aircraft **2** *US* military aircraft collectively [C19 from French, from Latin *avis* bird]

aviation medicine *n* the branch of medicine concerned with the effects on man of flight in the earth's atmosphere. Compare **space medicine**

aviator ('eɪvɪˌeɪtə) *n old-fashioned* the pilot of an aeroplane or airship; flyer > **'avi,atrix** or **'avi,atress** *fem n*

aviculture ('eɪvɪˌkʌltʃə) *n* the keeping and rearing of birds > **'avi'culturist** *n*

avid ('ævɪd) *adj* **1** very keen; enthusiastic: *an avid reader* **2** (*postpositive; often foll by for or of*) eager (for); desirous (of); greedy (for) [C18 from Latin *avidus*, from *avēre* to long for] > **'avidly** *adv*

avidin ('ævɪdɪn, ə'vɪdɪn) *n* a protein, found in egg-white, that combines with biotin to form a stable compound that cannot be absorbed, leading to a biotin deficiency in the consumer [C20 from AVID + (BIO)IN; from its characteristic avidity for biotin]

avidity (ə'vɪdɪtɪ) *n* **1** the quality or state of being avid **2 a** eagerness **b** greed; avarice **3** *chem* **a** the strength of an acid or base in proportion to its degree of dissociation **b** another term for **affinity** (sense 6b) **4** *immunol* a measure of antigen-to-antibody binding, based on the rate of formation of the complex

Aviemore (ˌævɪ'mɔː) *n* a winter sports resort in Scotland, in Moray between the Monadhliath and Cairngorm Mountains. Pop: 2397 (2001)

avifauna (ˌeɪvɪ'fɔːnə) *n* all the birds in a particular region > ˌavi'faunal *adj*

Avignon (*French* aviɲɔ̃) *n* a city in SE France, on the Rhône: seat of the papacy (1309–77); famous 12th-century bridge, now partly destroyed. Pop: 85 935 (1999)

Ávila (*Spanish* 'aβila) *n* a city in central Spain: 11th-century granite walls and Romanesque cathedral. Pop: 52 078 (2003 est)

avionics (ˌeɪvɪ'ɒnɪks) *n* **1** (*functioning as singular*) the science and technology of electronics applied to aeronautics and astronautics **2** (*functioning as plural*) the electronic circuits and devices of an aerospace vehicle [C20 from avi(ation electr)onics] > ˌavi'onic *adj*

avirulent (æ'vɪrʊlənt) *adj* (esp of bacteria) not virulent

avitaminosis (æˌvɪtəmɪn'əʊsɪs, æˌvɪˌtæmɪ'nəʊsɪs) *n, pl* -ses (-siːz) any disease caused by a vitamin deficiency in the diet

avizandum (ˌævɪ'zændəm) *n Scots law* **a** a judge's or court's decision to consider a case privately before giving judgment **b** a judge's or court's private consideration of a case before giving judgment **c** the period during which judgment is delayed in these circumstances. A judge or court makes avizandum when time is needed to consider arguments or submissions made

▷ Compare CAV [from Medieval Latin, from *avizare* to consider; see ADVISE]

Avlona (æv'ləunə) *n* the ancient name for **Vlorë**

AVM (in Britain) *abbreviation for* Air Vice-Marshal

avn *abbreviation for* aviation

avocado (,ævə'kɑ:dəu) *n, pl* **-dos** 1 a pear-shaped fruit having a leathery green or blackish skin, a large stony seed, and a greenish-yellow edible pulp 2 the tropical American lauraceous tree, *Persea americana*, that bears this fruit 3 a dull greenish colour resembling that of the fruit ▷ Also called (for senses 1, 2): **avocado pear**, **alligator pear** [c17 from Spanish *aguacate*, from Nahuatl *ahuacatl* testicle, alluding to the shape of the fruit]

avocation (,ævə'keɪʃən) *n* 1 *formal* a minor occupation undertaken as a diversion 2 *not standard* a person's regular job or vocation [c17 from Latin *āvocātiō* a calling away, diversion from, from *āvocāre* to distract, from *vocāre* to call]

avocet ('ævə,sɛt) *n* any of several long-legged shore birds of the genus *Recurvirostra*, such as the European *R. avosetta*, having black-and-white plumage and a long upward-curving bill: family *Recurvirostridae*, order *Charadriiformes* [c18 from French *avocette*, from Italian *avocetta*, of uncertain origin]

Avogadro's constant or **number** *n* the number of atoms or molecules in a mole of a substance, equal to 6.022 52 × 10²³. Symbol: L or N_A [named after Amedeo *Avogadro* (1776–1856), Italian physicist]

Avogadro's law or **hypothesis** *n* the principle that equal volumes of all gases contain the same number of molecules at the same temperature and pressure

avoid (ə'vɔɪd) *vb* (*tr*) 1 to keep out of the way of 2 to refrain from doing 3 to prevent from happening: *to avoid damage to machinery* 4 *law* to make (a plea, contract, etc) void; invalidate; quash 5 *obsolete* to expel 6 *obsolete* to depart from [c14 from Anglo-French *avoider*, from Old French *esvuidier*, from *vuidier* to empty, VOID] > a'**voidable** *adj* > a'**voidably** *adv* > a'**voider** *n*

avoidance (ə'vɔɪdəns) *n* 1 the act of keeping away from or preventing from happening 2 *law* **a** the act of annulling or making void **b** the countering of an opponent's plea with fresh evidence 3 *ecclesiastical law* the state of a benefice having no incumbent

avoidant (ə'vɔɪdənt) *adj* (of behaviour) demonstrating a tendency to avoid intimacy or interaction with others

avoirdupois or **avoirdupois weight** (,ævədə'pɔɪz, ,ævwɑ:djuː'pwɑː) *n* a system of weights used in many English-speaking countries. It is based on the pound, which contains 16 ounces or 7000 grains. 100 pounds (US) or 112 pounds (Brit) is equal to 1 hundredweight and 20 hundredweights equals 1 ton. Abbreviations: **avdp**, **avoir** [c14 from Old French *aver de peis* goods of weight]

Avon ('eɪv³n) *n* 1 a former county of SW England, created in 1974 from areas of N Somerset and S Gloucestershire: replaced in 1996 by the unitary authorities of Bath and North East Somerset (Somerset), North Somerset (Somerset), South Gloucestershire (Gloucestershire), and Bristol 2 a river in central England, rising in Northamptonshire and flowing southwest through Stratford-on-Avon to the River Severn at Tewkesbury. Length: 154 km (96 miles) 3 a river in SW England, rising in Gloucestershire and flowing south and west through Bristol to the Severn estuary at **Avonmouth**. Length: 120 km (75 miles) 4 a river in S England, rising in Wiltshire and flowing south to the English Channel. Length: about 96 km (60 miles)

avouch (ə'vautʃ) *vb* (*tr*) *archaic* 1 to vouch for; guarantee 2 to acknowledge 3 to assert [c16 from Old French *avochier* to summon, call on, from Latin *advocāre*; see ADVOCATE] > a'**vouchment** *n*

avow (ə'vau) *vb* (*tr*) 1 to state or affirm 2 to admit openly 3 *law rare* to justify or maintain (some action taken) [c13 from Old French *avouer* to confess, from Latin *advocāre* to appeal to, call upon; see AVOUCH, ADVOCATE] > a'**vowable** *adj* > a'**vowal** *n* > **avowed** (ə'vaud) *adj* > **avowedly** (ə'vauɪdlɪ) *adv* > a'**vower** *n*

avruga (ə'vruːgə) *n* herring roe with a smoky flavour, sometimes used as a less expensive alternative to caviar [Spanish]

avulsion (ə'vʌlʃən) *n* 1 a forcible tearing away or separation of a bodily structure or part, either as the result of injury or as an intentional surgical procedure 2 *law* the sudden removal of soil from one person's land to that of another, as by flooding [c17 from Latin *āvulsiō*, from *āvellere* to pluck away, from *vellere* to pull, pluck]

avuncular (ə'vʌŋkjulə) *adj* 1 of or concerned with an uncle 2 resembling an uncle; friendly; helpful [c19 from Latin *avunculus* (maternal) uncle, diminutive of *avus* grandfather]

avunculate (ə'vʌŋkjulɪt) *n* 1 the custom in some societies of assigning rights and duties to a maternal uncle concerning his sister's son ▷ *adj* 2 of, relating to, or governed by this custom

aw¹ (ɔː) *determiner Scot* a variant spelling of **a'** (all)

aw² (ɔː) *interj informal, chiefly US* an expression of disapproval, commiseration, or appeal

aw³ *the internet domain name for* Aruba

AWA *abbreviation for* Amalgamated Wireless (Australasia) Ltd

awa' (ə'wɔː) *adv Scot* away; departed; onward

AWACS or **Awacs** ('eɪwæks) *n acronym for* airborne warning and control system

await (ə'weɪt) *vb* 1 (*tr*) to wait for; expect 2 (*tr*) to be in store for 3 (*intr*) to wait with expectation 4 (*tr*) *obsolete* to wait for in order to ambush

awake (ə'weɪk) *vb* **awakes**, **awaking**; **awoke** or **awaked**; **awoken** or **awaked** 1 to emerge or rouse from sleep; wake 2 to become or cause to become alert 3 (usually foll by *to*) to become or make aware (of): *to awake to reality* 4 Also: **awaken** (*tr*) to arouse (feelings, etc) or cause to remember (memories, etc) ▷ *adj* (*postpositive*) 5 not sleeping 6 (sometimes foll by *to*) lively or alert [Old English *awacian, awacan*; see WAKE¹]

■ USAGE See at **wake**¹

awakening (ə'weɪkənɪŋ, ə'weɪknɪŋ) *n* the start of a feeling or awareness in a person: *a picture of an emotional awakening*

award (ə'wɔːd) *vb* (*tr*) 1 to give (something due), esp as a reward for merit: *to award prizes* 2 *law* to declare to be entitled, as by decision of a court of law or an arbitrator ▷ *n* 3 something awarded, such as a prize or medal: *an award for bravery* 4 (in Australia and New Zealand) the amount of an award wage (esp in the phrase **above award**) 5 *law* **a** the decision of an arbitrator **b** a grant made by a court of law, esp of damages in a civil action [c14 from Anglo-Norman *awarder*, from Old Northern French *eswarder* to decide after investigation, from *es-* EX-¹ + *warder* to observe; see WARD] > a'**wardable** *adj* > a,**ward'ee** *n* > a'**warder** *n*

award wage *n* (in Australia and New Zealand) statutory minimum pay for a particular group of workers. Sometimes shortened to: **award**

aware (ə'wɛə) *adj* 1 (*postpositive*; foll by *of*) having knowledge; cognizant: *aware of his error* 2 informed of current developments: *politically aware* [Old English *gewær*; related to Old Saxon, Old High German *giwar* Latin *verērī* to be fearful; see BEWARE, WARY] > a'**wareness** *n*

awash (ə'wɒʃ) *adv, adj* (*postpositive*) *nautical* 1 at a level even with the surface of the sea 2 washed over by the waves

awato (ɑː'faːtɔː) *n* a variant spelling of **awhato**

away (ə'weɪ) *adv* 1 from a particular place; off: *to swim away* 2 in or to another, usual, or proper place: *to put toys away* 3 apart; at a distance: *to keep away from strangers* 4 out of existence: *the music faded away* 5 indicating motion, displacement, transfer, etc, from a normal or proper place, from a person's own possession, etc: *to turn one's head away; to give away money* 6 indicating activity that is wasteful or designed to get rid of something: *to sleep away the hours* 7 continuously: *laughing away; fire away* 8 **away** with a command for a person to go or be removed: *away with you; away with him to prison!* 9 **far and away** by a very great margin: *far and away the biggest meal he'd ever eaten* 10 **from away** *Canadian* from a part of Canada other than Newfoundland ▷ *adj* (*usually postpositive*) 11 not present: *away from school* 12 distant: *he is a good way away* 13 having started; released: *he was away before sunrise; bombs away!* 14 (*also prenominal*) *sport* played on an opponent's ground: *an away game* 15 *golf* (of a ball or player) farthest from the hole 16 *baseball* (of a player) having been put out 17 *horse racing* relating to the outward portion or first half of a race ▷ *n* 18 *sport* a game played or won at an opponent's ground ▷ *interj* 19 an expression of dismissal [Old English *on weg* on way]

awayday (ə'weɪ,deɪ) *n* a trip taken for pleasure, relaxation, etc; day excursion [c20 from *awayday ticket*, name applied to some special-rate railway day returns]

away goal *n* a goal scored by a team playing away from its home ground. Away goals count for more than home goals in certain competitions

awe (ɔː) *n* 1 overwhelming wonder, admiration, respect, or dread 2 *archaic* power to inspire fear or reverence ▷ *vb* 3 (*tr*) to inspire with reverence or dread [c13 from Old Norse *agi*; related to Gothic *agis* fear, Greek *akhesthai* to be grieved] > '**aweless** or US '**awless** *adj*

aweather (ə'wɛðə) *adv, adj* (*postpositive*) *nautical* towards the weather: *with the helm aweather*. Compare **alee**

aweigh (ə'weɪ) *adj* (*postpositive*) *nautical* (of an anchor) no longer hooked into the bottom; hanging by its rode

awe-inspiring *adj* causing or worthy of admiration or respect; amazing or magnificent

awesome ('ɔːsəm) *adj* 1 inspiring or displaying awe 2 *slang* excellent or outstanding > '**awesomely** *adv* > '**awesomeness** *n*

awestruck ('ɔː,strʌk) or **awe-stricken** *adj* overcome or filled with awe

aweto ('aː,faːtɔː) *n* a variant spelling of **awhato**

awful ('ɔːful) *adj* 1 nasty or ugly 2 *archaic* inspiring reverence or dread 3 *archaic* overcome with awe; reverential ▷ *adv* 4 *not standard* (intensifier): *an awful cold day* [c13 see AWE, -FUL] > '**awfulness** *n*

awfully ('ɔːfəlɪ, 'ɔːflɪ) *adv* 1 in an unpleasant, bad, or reprehensible manner 2 *informal* (intensifier): *I'm awfully keen to come* 3 *archaic* so as to express or inspire awe

awhato, awato, aweto or **awheto** ('aː,faːtɔː) *n, pl* **awhato** *NZ* the mummified body of a caterpillar killed by the fungus *Cordyceps robertsii*, sometimes used as a dye [Māori]

awheel (ə'wiːl) *adv* on wheels

awhile (ə'waɪl) *adv* for a brief period

awkward ('ɔːkwəd) *adj* 1 lacking dexterity, proficiency, or skill; clumsy; inept: *the new recruits were awkward in their exercises* 2 ungainly or inelegant in movements or posture: *despite a great deal of practice she remained an awkward dancer* 3 unwieldy; difficult to use: *an awkward implement* 4 embarrassing: *an awkward moment* 5 embarrassed: *he felt awkward about leaving* 6 difficult to deal with; requiring tact: *an awkward situation; an awkward customer* 7 deliberately uncooperative or unhelpful: *he could help but he is being awkward* 8 dangerous or difficult: *an awkward ascent of the ridge* 9 *obsolete* perverse [c14 *awk*, from Old Norse *öfugr* turned the wrong way round + -WARD] > '**awkwardly** *adv* > '**awkwardness** *n*

awl (ɔːl) *n* a pointed hand tool with a fluted blade used for piercing wood, leather, etc. See also **bradawl** [Old English *æl*; related to Old Norse *alr*, Old High German *āla*, Dutch *aal*, Sanskrit *ārā*]

awlwort ('ɔːl,wɜːt) *n* a small stemless aquatic

plant, *Subularia aquatica,* of the N hemisphere, having slender sharp-pointed leaves and minute, often submerged, white flowers: family *Brassicaceae* (crucifers)

awn ('ɔːn) *n* any of the bristles growing from the spikelets of certain grasses, including cereals [Old English *agen* ear of grain; related to Old Norse *ögn* chaff, Gothic *ahana,* Old High German *agana,* Greek *akōn* javelin] > awned *adj* > 'awnless *adj*

awning ('ɔːnɪŋ) *n* a roof of canvas or other material supported by a frame to provide protection from the weather, esp one placed over a doorway or part of a deck of a ship [c17 of uncertain origin]

awoke (ə'wəʊk) *vb* a past tense or (now rare or dialectal) past participle of **awake**

AWOL ('eɪwɒl) or **A.W.O.L.** *adj military* absent without leave; absent from one's post or duty without official permission but without intending to desert

AWRE *abbreviation for* Atomic Weapons Research Establishment

awry (ə'raɪ) *adv, adj (postpositive)* **1** with a slant or twist to one side; askew **2** away from the appropriate or right course; amiss [c14 *on wry;* see A-², WRY]

AWS *abbreviation for* automatic warning system: a train safety system which gives audible warnings about the signals being passed, and can apply the brakes automatically if necessary

aw-shucks (ˌɔː'ʃʌks) *adj (prenominal)* seeming to be modest, self-deprecating, or shy: *don't be fooled by his aw-shucks attitude* [c20 from the US interjection *aw shucks,* an expression of modesty or diffidence]

AWU *abbreviation for* Australian Workers' Union

axe or US **ax** (æks) *n, pl* **axes 1** a hand tool with one side of its head forged and sharpened to a cutting edge, used for felling trees, splitting timber, etc. See also **hatchet 2** an axe to grind **a** an ulterior motive **b** a grievance **c** a pet subject **3** the axe *informal* **a** dismissal, esp from employment; the sack (esp in the phrase **get the axe**) **b** *Brit* severe cutting down of expenditure, esp the removal of unprofitable sections of a public service **4** *US slang* any musical instrument, esp a guitar or horn ▷ *vb (tr)* **5** to chop or trim with an axe **6** *informal* to dismiss (employees), restrict (expenditure or services), or terminate (a project) [Old English *æx;* related to Old Frisian *axa,* Old High German *acchus,* Old Norse *öx,* Latin *ascia,* Greek *axinē*]

axebird ('æksbɜːd) *n Austral* a nightjar of northern Queensland and New Guinea with a cry that sounds like a chopping axe

axe-breaker *n Austral* an Australian oleaceous tree, *Notelaea longifolia,* yielding very hard timber

axel ('æksəl) *n skating* a jump in which the skater takes off from the forward outside edge of one skate, makes one and a half, two and a half, or three and a half turns in the air, and lands on the backward outside edge of the other skate [c20 named after *Axel* Paulsen (died 1938), Norwegian skater]

axeman or US **axman** ('æksmən) *n, pl* **-men 1** a man who wields an axe, esp to cut down trees **2** a person who makes cuts in expenditure or services, esp on behalf of another: *the chancellor's axeman* **3** *US slang* a man who plays a guitar

axenic (eɪ'ziːnɪk) *adj* (of a biological culture or culture medium) free from other microorganisms; uncontaminated [c20 see A-¹, XENO-, -IC]

axes¹ ('æksiːz) *n* the plural of **axis¹**

axes² ('æksɪz) *n* the plural of **axe**

axial ('æksɪəl) *adj* **1** relating to, forming, or characteristic of an axis **2** situated in, on, or along an axis > ˌaxi'ality *n* > 'axially *adv*

axial-flow compressor *n* a device for compressing a gas by accelerating it tangentially by means of bladed rotors, to increase its kinetic energy, and then diffusing it through static vanes (stators), to increase its pressure

axial skeleton *n* the bones that together comprise the skull and the vertebral column

axial vector *n* another name for **pseudovector**

axil ('æksɪl) *n* the angle between the upper surface of a branch or leafstalk and the stem from which it grows [c18 from Latin *axilla* armpit]

axile ('æksɪl, -saɪl) *adj botany* of, relating to, or attached to the axis

axilemma (ˌæksɪ'lɛmə) *n* a variant spelling of **axolemma**

axilla (æk'sɪlə) *n, pl* **-lae (-liː) 1** the technical name for the **armpit 2** the area on the undersurface of a bird's wing corresponding to the armpit [c17 from Latin: armpit]

axillary (æk'sɪlərɪ) *adj* **1** of, relating to, or near the armpit **2** *botany* growing in or related to the axil: *an axillary bud* ▷ *n, pl* **-laries 3** *(usually plural)* Also called: axillar (æk'sɪlə, 'æksɪlə) one of the feathers growing from the axilla of a bird's wing

axiology (ˌæksɪ'ɒlədʒɪ) *n philosophy* the theory of values, moral or aesthetic [c20 from Greek *axios* worthy] > axiological (ˌæksɪə'lɒdʒɪkˀl) *adj* > ˌaxio'logically *adv* > ˌaxi'ologist *n*

axiom ('æksɪəm) *n* **1** a generally accepted proposition or principle, sanctioned by experience; maxim **2** a universally established principle or law that is not a necessary truth: *the axioms of politics* **3** a self-evident statement **4** *logic, maths* a statement or formula that is stipulated to be true for the purpose of a chain of reasoning: the foundation of a formal deductive system. Compare **assumption** (sense 4) [c15 from Latin *axiōma* a principle, from Greek, from *axioun* to consider worthy, from *axios* worthy]

axiomatic (ˌæksɪə'mætɪk) or **axiomatical** *adj* **1** relating to or resembling an axiom; self-evident **2** containing maxims; aphoristic **3** (of a logical system) consisting of a set of axioms from which theorems are derived by **transformation rules.** Compare **natural deduction.** > ˌaxio'matically *adv*

axion ('æksɪˌon) *n physics* a hypothetical neutral elementary particle postulated to account for certain conservation laws in the strong interaction [c20 from AXI(OM) + -ON]

axis¹ ('æksɪs) *n, pl* **axes** ('æksiːz) **1** a real or imaginary line about which a body, such as an aircraft, can rotate or about which an object, form, composition, or geometrical construction is symmetrical **2** one of two or three reference lines used in coordinate geometry to locate a point in a plane or in a space **3** *anatomy* the second cervical vertebra. Compare **atlas** (sense 3) **4** *botany* the main central part of a plant, typically consisting of the stem and root, from which secondary branches and other parts develop **5** an alliance between a number of states to coordinate their foreign policy **6** Also called: principal axis *optics* the line of symmetry of an optical system, such as the line passing through the centre of a lens **7** *geology* an imaginary line along the crest of an anticline or the trough of a syncline **8** *crystallog* one of three lines passing through the centre of a crystal and used to characterize its symmetry [c14 from Latin: axletree, earth's axis; related to Greek *axōn* axis]

axis² ('æksɪs) *n, pl* **axises** any of several S Asian deer of the genus *Axis,* esp *A. axis.* They typically have a reddish-brown white-spotted coat and slender antlers [c18 from Latin: Indian wild animal, of uncertain identity]

Axis ('æksɪs) *n* **a the** the alliance of Nazi Germany, Fascist Italy, and Japan, established in 1936 and lasting until their defeat in World War II **b** *(as modifier): the Axis powers*

axis of evil *n* North Korea, Iraq, and Iran when considered together as a perceived threat to world stability [c21 coined by George W Bush, 43rd US President]

axle ('æksəl) *n* a bar or shaft on which a wheel, pair of wheels, or other rotating member revolves [c17 from Old Norse *öxull;* related to German *Achse;* see AXIS¹]

axletree ('æksəl,triː) *n* a bar fixed across the underpart of a wagon or carriage that has rounded ends on which the wheels revolve

Axminster carpet ('æks,mɪnstə) *n* a type of patterned carpet with a cut pile. Often shortened to: Axminster [after *Axminster,* in Devon, where such carpets are made]

axolemma (ˌæksə'lɛmə) or **axilemma** *n* the membrane that encloses the axon of a nerve cell

axolotl ('æksə,lɒtˀl) *n* **1** any of several aquatic salamanders of the North American genus *Ambystoma,* esp *A. mexicanum* (**Mexican axolotl**), in which the larval form (including external gills) is retained throughout life under natural conditions (see **neoteny**): family *Ambystomidae* **2** any of various other North American salamanders in which neoteny occurs or is induced [c18 from Nahuatl, from *atl* water + *xolotl* servant, doll]

axon ('æksɒn) or **axone** ('æksəʊn) *n* the long threadlike extension of a nerve cell that conducts nerve impulses from the cell body. Compare **dendrite** [c19 via New Latin from Greek: axis, axle, vertebra] > 'axonal *adj*

axonometric projection (ˌæksənə'mɛtrɪk) *n* a geometric drawing of an object, such as a building, in three dimensions showing the verticals and horizontals projected to scale but with diagonals and curves distorted, so that the whole appears inclined

axonometry (ˌæksə'nɒmɪtrɪ) *n* the branch of crystallography concerned with measurement of the axes of crystals

axseed ('æks,siːd) *n* another name for **crown vetch**

Axum ('ɑːksʊm) *n* a variant spelling of **Aksum**

ay¹ (eɪ) *adv archaic, poetic* ever; always [c12 *ai,* from Old Norse *ei;* related to Old English *ā* always, Latin *aevum* an age, Greek *aiōn*]

ay² or **aye** (eɪ) *interj archaic, poetic* an expression of misery or surprise [c14 *ey:* from an involuntary cry of surprise]

ay³ (aɪ) *sentence substitute, n* a variant spelling of **aye¹**

Ayacucho (Spanish aja'kutʃo) *n* a city in SE Peru: nearby is the site of the battle (1824) that won independence for Peru. Pop: 150 000 (2005 est)

ayah ('aɪə) *n* (in the East, Africa, and other parts of the former British Empire) a maidservant, nursemaid, or governess, esp one of Indian or Malay origin. Compare **amah** [c18 from Hindi *āyā,* from Portuguese *aia,* from Latin *avia* grandmother]

ayahuasca (ˌaɪə'wɑːskə) *n* a Brazilian plant, *Banisteriopsis caapi,* that has winged fruits and yields a powerful hallucinogenic alkaloid sometimes used to treat certain disorders of the central nervous system: family *Malpighiaceae* [c20 from Quechua]

ayatollah (ˌaɪə'tɒlə) *n* one of a class of Iranian Shiite religious leaders [via Persian from Arabic, from *aya* sign + *Allah* god]

Aycliffe ('eɪklɪf) *n* a town in Co Durham: founded as a new town in 1947. Pop (including Newton Aycliffe): 25 655 (2001)

Aydin or **Aidin** ('aɪdɪn) *n* a town in SW Turkey: an ancient city of Lydia. Pop: 160 000 (2005 est). Ancient name: Tralles

aye¹ or **ay** (aɪ) *sentence substitute* **1** yes: archaic or dialectal except in voting by voice **2** aye aye **a** an expression of compliance, esp used by seamen **b** *Brit* an expression of amused surprise, esp at encountering something that confirms one's suspicions, expectations, etc ▷ *n* **3 a** a person who votes in the affirmative **b** an affirmative vote ▷ Compare **nay** [c16 probably from pronoun *I,* expressing assent]

aye² (aɪ) *adv Scot* always; still [Old Norse *ei* ever; Old English *ā;* compare Latin *aevum* an age, Greek *aion* aeon, *aiei* ever, always]

aye-aye ('aɪ,aɪ) *n* a rare nocturnal arboreal prosimian primate of Madagascar, *Daubentonia madagascariensis,* related to the lemurs: family *Daubentoniidae.* It has long bony fingers and rodent-

a

like incisor teeth adapted for feeding on insect larvae and bamboo pith [c18 from French, from Malagasy *aiay*, probably of imitative origin]

Ayers Rock (ɛəz) *n* the former name of **Uluru**

Ayia Napa (ˌaɪjə ˈnæpə) *n* a coastal resort in SE Cyprus. Pop: 9500 (2004 est)

ayin (ˈɑːjɪn; *Hebrew* ˈajiːn) *n* the 16th letter in the Hebrew alphabet (𝕪), originally a pharyngeal fricative, that is now silent and transliterated by a raised inverted comma (ʻ) [Hebrew]

aykhona wena (aɪˈkɔːnə ˈwɛnə) *interj South African* an exclamation expressive of surprise, pain, pleasure, etc [from Zulu]

Aylesbury (ˈeɪlzbərɪ, -brɪ) *n* a town in SE central England, administrative centre of Buckinghamshire. Pop: 69 021 (2001)

Aymara (ˌaɪməˈrɑː) *n* 1 (*pl* **-ras** *or* **-ra**) a member of a South American Indian people of Bolivia and Peru 2 the language of this people, probably related to Quechua [from Spanish *aimará*, of American Indian origin] > **Ayma'ran** *adj*

Ayodhya (ɑːˈjəʊdjɑː) *n* an ancient town in N India, in Uttar Pradesh state: as the birthplace of Rama it is sacred to Hindus; also a Buddhist centre. Also called: **Ayodha**, **Awadh** (əˈwɒd), **Oudh** (aʊd)

ayont (əˈjɒnt) *adv, prep Scot* beyond [*a*, from Old English *an* on + *yont* YON]

Ayr (ɛə) *n* a port in SW Scotland, in South Ayrshire. Pop: 46 431 (2001)

Ayrshire (ˈɛəʃɪə, -ʃə) *n* 1 a historical county of SW Scotland, formerly part of Strathclyde region (1975–96), now divided into the council areas of North Ayrshire, South Ayrshire, and East Ayrshire 2 any one of a hardy breed of brown-and-white dairy cattle

Ayurveda (ˈɑːjʊˌveɪdə, -ˌviːdə) *n Hinduism* an ancient medical treatise on the art of healing and prolonging life, sometimes regarded as a fifth Veda [from Sanskrit, from *āyur* life + *veda* knowledge] > **Ayur'vedic** *adj*

Ayutthaya (ɑːˈjuːtəjə) *n* a city in S Thailand, on the Chao Phraya River: capital of the country until 1767; noted for its canals and ruins. Pop: 61 185 (1990). Also called: **Ayudhya** (ɑːˈjuːdjə), **Ayuthia** (ɑːˈjuːθɪə)

az *the internet domain name for* Azerbaijan

AZ 1 *abbreviation for* Arizona 2 ▷ *international car registration for* Azerbaijan

az. *abbreviation for* azimuth

aza- *or before a vowel* **az-** *combining form* denoting the presence of nitrogen, esp a nitrogen atom in place of a -CH group or an -NH group in place of a -CH₂ group: *azathioprine* [c20 from AZ(O)- + -*a*-]

azalea (əˈzeɪljə) *n* any ericaceous plant of the group *Azalea*, formerly a separate genus but now included in the genus *Rhododendron*: cultivated for their showy pink or purple flowers [c18 via New Latin from Greek, from *azaleos* dry; from its supposed preference for a dry situation]

azan (ɑːˈzɑːn) *n Islam* the call to prayer five times a day, usually by a muezzin from a minaret [from Arabic *adhān*, from *adhina* to proclaim, invite; see MUEZZIN]

Azania (əˈzɑːnɪə, əˈzɑːnjə) *n* another name (used esp by many Black political activists) for **South Africa** [perhaps from Arabic *Adzan* East Africa]

Azanian (əˈzɑːnɪən, əˈzɑːnjən) *n* 1 a native or inhabitant of Azania (another name used esp by many Black political activists for South Africa) ▷ *adj* 2 of or relating to Azania

AZAPO (əˈzɑːpəʊ) *n acronym for* Azanian People's Organization

azathioprine (ˌæzəˈθaɪəˌpriːn) *n* a synthetic drug that suppresses the normal immune responses of the body and is administered orally during and after organ transplantation and also in certain types of autoimmune disease. Formula: C₉H₇N₇O₂S [c20 from AZA- + THIO- + P(U)RINE]

Azazel (əˈzeɪzˀl, ˈæzəˌzɛl) *n* 1 *Old Testament* a desert demon to whom the scapegoat bearing the sins of Israel was sent out once a year on the Day of

Atonement (Leviticus 16:1–28) 2 (in later Jewish and Gnostic writings and in Muslim tradition) a prince of demons

Azbine (æzˈbiːn) *n* another name for **Aïr**

azedarach (əˈzɛdəˌræk) *n* 1 the astringent bark of the chinaberry tree, formerly used as an emetic and cathartic 2 another name for **chinaberry** (sense 1) [c18 from French *azédarac*, from Persian *āzād dirakht*, from *āzād* free, noble + *dirakht* tree]

azeotrope (əˈziːəˌtrəʊp) *n* a mixture of liquids that boils at a constant temperature, at a given pressure, without change of composition [c20 from A-¹ + *zeo*-, from Greek *zein* to boil + -TROPE] > **azeotropic** (ˌeɪzɪəˈtrɒpɪk) *adj*

Azerbaijan (ˌæzəbaɪˈdʒɑːn) *n* 1 a republic in NW Asia: the region was acquired by Russia from Persia in the early 19th century; became the Azerbaijan Soviet Socialist Republic in 1936 and gained independence in 1991; consists of dry subtropical steppes around the Aras and Kura rivers, surrounded by the Caucasus; contains the extensive Baku oilfields. Language: Azerbaijani (or Azeri). Religion: Shiite Muslim. Currency: manat. Capital: Baku. Pop: Pop: 8 447 000 (2004 est). Area: 86 600 sq km (33 430 sq miles) 2 a mountainous region of NW Iran, separated from the republic of Azerbaijan by the Aras River: divided administratively into **Eastern Azerbaijan** and **Western Azerbaijan**. Capitals: Tabriz and Orumiyeh. Pop: 2 119 524 (2002 est)

Azerbaijani (ˌæzəbaɪˈdʒɑːnɪ) *n* 1 (*pl* **-ni** *or* **-nis**) a native or inhabitant of Azerbaijan. Sometimes shortened to: **Azeri** 2 the language of this people, belonging to the Turkic branch of the Altaic family

Azeri (əˈzɛərɪ) *n* short for **Azerbaijani** (sense 1)

azerty *or* **AZERTY keyboard** (əˈzɜːtɪ) *n* a common European version of typewriter keyboard layout with the characters a, z, e, r, t, and y positioned on the top row of alphabetic characters at the left side of the keyboard

azide (ˈeɪzaɪd) *n* 1 any compound containing the monovalent group –N₃ or the monovalent ion N₃⁻ 2 (*modifier*) consisting of, containing, or concerned with the group –N₃ or the ion N₃⁻: *azide group or radical*

Azilian (əˈzɪlɪən) *n* 1 a Palaeolithic culture of Spain and SW France that can be dated to the 10th millennium BC, characterized by flat bone harpoons and schematically painted pebbles ▷ *adj* 2 of or relating to this culture [c19 named after Mas d'*Azil*, France, where artefacts were found]

azimuth (ˈæzɪməθ) *n* 1 *astronomy, navigation* the angular distance usually measured clockwise from the north point of the horizon to the intersection with the horizon of the vertical circle passing through a celestial body. Compare **altitude** (sense 3) 2 *surveying* the horizontal angle of a bearing clockwise from a standard direction, such as north [c14 from Old French *azimut*, from Arabic *as-sumūt*, plural of *as-samt* the path, from Latin *semita* path] > **azimuthal** (ˌæzɪˈmʌθəl) *adj* > **ˌazi'muthally** *adv*

azimuthal projection *n* another term for **zenithal projection**

azine (ˈeɪziːn, -zɪn) *n* any organic compound having a six-membered ring containing at least one nitrogen atom. See also **diazine, triazine**

azo (ˈeɪzəʊ, ˈæ-) *adj* of, consisting of, or containing the divalent group -N:N-: *an azo group or radical*. See also **diazo** [independent use of AZO-]

azo- *or before a vowel* **az-** *combining form* indicating the presence of an azo group: *azobenzene* [from French *azote* nitrogen, from Greek *azōos* lifeless, from A-¹ + *zōē* life]

azobenzene (ˌeɪzəʊˈbɛnziːn, -bɛnˈziːn) *n* 1 a yellow or orange crystalline solid used mainly in the manufacture of dyes. Formula: C₆H₅N:NC₆H₅ 2 any organic compound that is a substituted derivative of azobenzene

azo dye *n* any of a class of artificial dyes that contain the azo group. They are usually red,

brown, or yellow and are obtained from aromatic amines

azoic (əˈzəʊɪk, eɪ-) *adj* without life; characteristic of the ages that have left no evidence of life in the form of organic remains [c19 from Greek *azōos* lifeless; see AZO-]

azole (ˈeɪzəʊl, əˈzəʊl) *n* 1 an organic five-membered ring compound containing one or more atoms in the ring, the number usually being specified by a prefix: *diazole; triazole* 2 a less common name for **pyrrole** [from AZO- + -OLE¹, on the model of *diazole*]

azonal soil (eɪˈzəʊnˀl) *n* soil that has a profile determined predominantly by factors other than local climate and vegetation. Azonal soils include some mountain, alluvial, marine, glacial, windblown, and volcanic soils. Compare **intrazonal soil, zonal soil**

azoospermia (eɪˌzəʊəˈspɜːmɪə) *n pathol* absence of spermatozoa in the semen > **aˌzooˈspermic** *adj*

Azores (əˈzɔːz) *pl n* **the** three groups of volcanic islands in the N Atlantic, since 1976 an autonomous region of Portugal. Capital: Ponta Delgada (on São Miguel). Pop: 241 762 (2001). Area: 2335 sq km (901 sq miles). Portuguese name: Açores

azotaemia *or esp US* **azotemia** (ˌæzəˈtiːmɪə) *n pathol* a less common name for **uraemia** [c20 see AZOTE, -AEMIA] > **azotaemic** *or esp US* **azotemic** (ˌæzəˈtiːmɪk) *adj*

azote (ˈeɪzəʊt, əˈzəʊt) *n* an obsolete name for **nitrogen** [c18 from French, from Greek *azōos* ungirded, intended for Greek *azōos* lifeless]

azoth (ˈæzɒθ) *n* 1 the alchemical name for **mercury**, regarded as the first principle of all metals 2 the panacea postulated by Paracelsus [from Arabic *az-zā'ūq* the mercury]

azotic (eɪˈzɒtɪk) *adj* containing nitrogen

azotize *or* **azotise** (ˈeɪzəˌtaɪz) *vb* a less common word for **nitrogenize**

azotobacter (əˈzəʊtəʊˌbæktə) *n* any bacterium of the family *Azotobacteriaceae*, important in nitrogen fixation in the soil [New Latin; see AZOTE, BACTERIA]

Azov (ˈɑːzɒv) *n* **Sea of** a shallow arm of the Black Sea, to which it is connected by the Kerch Strait: almost entirely landlocked; fed chiefly by the River Don. Area: about 37 500 sq km (14 500 sq miles)

Azrael (ˈæzreɪl, -rɪəl) *n* (in Jewish and Islamic angelology) the angel who separates the soul from the body at death

AZT *abbreviation for* azidothymidine. Also called: zidovudine

Aztec (ˈæztɛk) *n* 1 a member of a Mexican Indian people who established a great empire, centred on the valley of Mexico, that was overthrown by Cortés and his followers in the early 16th century 2 the language of the Aztecs. See also **Nahuatl** ▷ *adj also* **Aztecan** 3 of, relating to, or characteristic of the Aztecs, their civilization, or their language [c18 from Spanish *Azteca*, from Nahuatl *Aztecatl*, from *Aztlan*, their traditional place of origin, literally: near the cranes, from *azta* cranes + *tlan* near]

azure (ˈæʒə, -ʒʊə, ˈeɪ-) *n* 1 a deep blue, occasionally somewhat purple, similar to the colour of a clear blue sky 2 *poetic* a clear blue sky ▷ *adj* 3 of the colour azure; serene 4 (*usually postpositive*) *heraldry* of the colour blue [c14 from Old French *azur*, from Old Spanish, from Arabic *lāzaward* lapis lazuli, from Persian *lāzhuward*]

azurite (ˈæʒʊˌraɪt) *n* an azure-blue mineral associated with copper deposits. It is a source of copper. Composition: copper carbonate. Formula: Cu₃(CO₃)₂(OH)₂. Crystal structure: monoclinic

azygospore (əˈzaɪɡəʊˌspɔː) *n* a thick-walled spore produced by parthenogenesis in certain algae and fungi. Also called: **parthenospore**

azygous (ˈæzɪɡəs) *adj biology* developing or occurring singly [c17 via New Latin from Greek *azugos*, from A-¹ + *zugon* YOKE]

B b

b or **B** (biː) *n, pl* **b's, B's** or **Bs 1** the second letter and first consonant of the modern English alphabet **2** a speech sound represented by this letter, usually a voiced bilabial stop, as in *bell* **3** *Also:* beta the second in a series, esp the second highest grade in an examination

b *symbol for chess* See **algebraic notation**

B *symbol for* **1** *music* **a** a note having a frequency of 493.88 hertz (**B above middle C**) or this value multiplied or divided by any power of 2; the seventh note of the scale of C major **b** a key, string, or pipe producing this note **c** the major or minor key having this note as its tonic **2** the supporting or less important of two things: *the B side of a record* **3** a human blood type of the ABO group, containing the B antigen **4** (in Britain) a secondary road **5** the number 11 in hexadecimal notation **6** *chem* boron **7** magnetic flux density **8** *chess* bishop **9** (on Brit pencils, signifying degree of softness of lead) black: *B; 2B; 3B.* Compare **H** (sense 5) **10** *Also:* b *physics* baryon number **12** balboa **13** belga **14** bolivar **15** *photog* B-setting **16 a** a person whose job is in middle management, or who holds an intermediate administrative or professional position **b** (*as modifier*): *a B worker* ▷ See also **occupation groupings 17** *international car registration for* Belgium

B4 *text messaging abbreviation for* before

b. *abbreviation for* **1** born **2** *cricket* bowled

B. *abbreviation for* **1** (on maps, etc) bay **2** British

B- (of US military aircraft) *abbreviation for* bomber: *B-52*

ba *the internet domain name for* Bosnia and Herzegovina

Ba¹ (bɑː) *n Egyptian myth* the soul, represented as a bird with a human head

Ba² *the chemical symbol for* barium

BA *abbreviation for* **1** Bachelor of Arts **2** British Academy **3** British Airways **4** British Association (for the Advancement of Science) **5 British Association screw thread**

ba' or **Ba'** (bɔː, bɑː) *n Scot* **1** (usually preceded by *the*) a game somewhat like rugby played in Orkney at Christmas and New Year between two very large teams of players **2** (usually preceded by *the*) *Also called:* handba' a similar game played at Jedburgh in the Scottish Borders in mid February **3** the stuffed leather ball used in these games [Scots form of BALL]

baa (bɑː) *vb* baas, baaing, baaed **1** (*intr*) to make the cry of a sheep; bleat ▷ *n* **2** the cry made by sheep

BAA *n* the main airports operator in the United Kingdom; until privatization in 1987, an abbreviation for British Airports Authority

Baader-Meinhof Gang (*German* 'baːdər 'mainhoːf) *n* **the.** a group of left-wing West German terrorists, active in the 1970s, who were dedicated to the violent overthrow of capitalist society. *Also called:* Red Army Faction [c20 named after its leading members, Andreas *Baader* (1943–77) and Ulrike *Meinhof* (1934-76)]

Baal (bɑːl) *n* **1** any of several ancient Semitic fertility gods **2** *Phoenician myth* the sun god and supreme national deity **3** (*sometimes not capital*) any false god or idol [from Hebrew *bá'al* lord, master]

Baalbek ('bɑːlbɛk) *n* a town in E Lebanon: an important city in Phoenician and Roman times; extensive ruins. Pop: 150 000 (1998 est). Ancient name: Heliopolis

baalebos (*Yiddish* 'baləbɔs) *n, pl* baalebatim (baləˈbatəm) **1** the master of the house **2** the proprietor of a business, etc **3** *slang* an officious person [from Hebrew *ba'al La-bayis* master of the house]

baas (bɑːs) *n* a South African word for **boss¹**: often used by black or coloured people addressing a white manager or overseer [c17 from Afrikaans, from Middle Dutch *baes* master; see BOSS¹]

baaskap or **baasskap** ('bɑːsˌkap) *n* (*sometimes capital*) (formerly in South Africa) control by Whites of non-Whites [from Afrikaans, from BAAS + -skap -SHIP]

Ba'ath (bɑːˈɑːθ) *n* a variant of **Ba'th**

baba ('bɑːbɑː; *French* baba) *n* a small cake of leavened dough, sometimes mixed with currants and usually soaked in rum (**rum baba**) [c19 from French, from Polish, literally: old woman]

babaco ('bæbəˌkəʊ, bəˈbɑːkəʊ) *n, pl* -cos **1** a subtropical parthenocarpic tree, *Carica pentagona*, originating in South America, cultivated for its fruit: family *Caricaceae* **2** the greenish-yellow egg-shaped fruit of this tree, having a delicate fragrance and no pips

baba ghanoush or **baba gannoujh** (baba gaˈnuːʃ) *n* a thick purée of aubergines, tahini, olive oil, lemon juice and garlic, originating in North Africa and the Mediterranean [from Arabic]

babalas ('babalas) or **babbelas** *adj South African* drunk; hungover [c20 Afrikaans, from Zulu *I-babalazi* drunk]

babassu (ˌbabəˈsuː) *n* a Brazilian palm tree, *Orbignya martiana* (or *O. speciosa*), having hard edible nuts that yield an oil used in making soap, margarine, etc [from Portuguese *babaçú*, from a native Amerindian word]

babbitt ('bæbɪt) *vb* (*tr*) to line (a bearing) or face (a surface) with Babbitt metal or a similar soft alloy

Babbitt ('bæbɪt) *n US derogatory* a narrow-minded and complacent member of the middle class [c20 after George *Babbitt*, central character in the novel *Babbitt* (1922) by Sinclair Lewis] > '**Babbittry** *n*

Babbitt metal *n* any of a number of alloys originally based on tin, antimony, and copper but now often including lead: used esp in bearings. *Sometimes shortened to:* Babbitt [c19 named after Isaac *Babbitt* (1799–1862), American inventor]

babble ('bæbəl) *vb* **1** to utter (words, sounds, etc) in an incoherent or indistinct jumble **2** (*intr*) to talk foolishly, incessantly, or irrelevantly **3** (*tr*) to disclose (secrets, confidences, etc) carelessly or impulsively **4** (*intr*) (of streams, birds, etc) to make a low murmuring or bubbling sound ▷ *n* **5** incoherent or foolish speech; chatter **6** a murmuring or bubbling sound [c13 compare Dutch *babbelen*, Swedish *babbla*, French *babiller* to prattle, Latin *babulus* fool; probably all of imitative origin] > '**babblement** *n* > '**babbling** *n, adj*

babbler ('bæblə) *n* **1** a person who babbles **2** any of various insect-eating birds of the Old World tropics and subtropics that have a loud incessant song: family *Muscicapidae* (warblers, thrushes, etc)

babbling brook *n Austral slang* a cook [rhyming slang]

babe (beɪb) *n* **1** a baby **2** *informal* a naive, gullible, or unsuspecting person (often in the phrase **a babe in arms**) **3** *slang* a girl or young woman, esp an attractive one

babe-in-a-cradle *n* a tall orchid, *Epiblema grandiflorum*, of SW Australia with lilac to mauve flowers [named from a fancied resemblance of its column to a baby in a cradle]

Babel ('beɪbəl) *n* **1** *Old Testament* **a** *Also called:* Tower of Babel a tower presumptuously intended to reach from earth to heaven, the building of which was frustrated when Jehovah confused the language of the builders (Genesis 11:1–10) **b** the city, probably Babylon, in which this tower was supposedly built **2** (*often not capital*) **a** a confusion of noises or voices **b** a scene of noise and confusion [from Hebrew *Bābhél*, from Akkadian *Bāb-ilu*, literally: gate of God]

Bab el Mandeb ('bæb ɛl 'mændɛb) *n* a strait between SW Arabia and E Africa, connecting the Red Sea with the Gulf of Aden

babesiosis (bəˌbiːzɪˈəʊsɪs) *n vet science* a tick-borne disease of domesticated and wild mammals as well as humans, caused by a protozoan of the genera *Babesia* and characterized by fever, anaemia, jaundice, and in severe cases death

Babi ('bɑːbɪ) *n* **1** a disciple of the Bab, a Persian religious leader (1819–50), who was executed as a heretic of Islam **2** another word for **Babism**

babiche (baˈbiːʃ) *n Canadian* thongs or lacings of rawhide [c19 from Canadian French, of Algonquian origin]

babies'-breath *n* a variant of **baby's-breath**

Babinski effect or **reflex** (bəˈbɪnskɪ) *n physiol* the reflex curling upwards of the toes (instead of inwards) when the sole of the foot is stroked, normal in infants below the age of two but a pathological condition in adults [after Joseph *Babinski* (1857–1932), French neuropathologist]

babirusa (ˌbabɪˈruːsə) *n* a wild pig, *Babyrousa babyrussa*, inhabiting marshy forests in Indonesia. It has an almost hairless wrinkled skin and enormous curved canine teeth [c17 from Malay, from *bābī* hog + *rūsa* deer]

Babism ('bɑːbɪzəm) *n* a pantheistic Persian religious sect, founded in 1844 by the Bab, a Persian religious leader (1819–50), who was executed as a heretic of Islam. It forbids polygamy, concubinage, begging, trading in slaves, and indulgence in alcohol and drugs. Compare **Baha'í Faith**

baboon (bə'buːn) *n* any of several medium-sized omnivorous Old World monkeys of the genus *Papio* (or *Chaeropithecus*) and related genera, inhabiting open rocky ground or wooded regions of Africa. They have an elongated muzzle, large teeth, and a fairly long tail. See also **hamadryas, gelada** [C14 *babewyn* gargoyle, later, baboon, from Old French *babouin*, from *baboue* grimace; related to Old French *babine* a thick lip]

Babo's law ('bæbəʊz) *n chem* the law stating that the vapour pressure of a solution is reduced in proportion to the amount of solute added [C19 named after Lambert von *Babo* (1818–99), German chemist who formulated it]

babu ('baːbuː) *n* (in India) a title or form of address more or less equivalent to *Mr*, placed before a person's full name or after his first name [Hindi, literally: father]

babul (baː'buːl, 'baːbuːl) *n* any of several leguminous trees of the genus *Acacia*, esp *A. arabica* of N Africa and India, which bear small yellow flowers and are a source of gum arabic, tannin, and hardwood [from Persian *babūl*; related to Sanskrit *babbūla*]

babushka (bə'buːʃkə) *n* **1** a headscarf tied under the chin, worn by Russian peasant women **2** (in Russia) an old woman [Russian: grandmother, from *baba* old woman]

baby ('beɪbɪ) *n, pl* -**bies 1 a** a newborn or recently born child; infant **b** (*as modifier*): *baby food* **2** the youngest or smallest of a family or group **3 a** a newborn or recently born animal **b** (*as modifier*): *baby rabbits* **4** *usually derogatory* an immature person **5** *slang* a young woman or sweetheart: often used as a term of address expressing affection **6** a project of personal concern **7 be left holding the baby** to be left with the responsibility **8 throw the baby out with the bath water** to lose the essential element by indiscriminate rejection ▷ *adj* **9** (*prenominal*) comparatively small of its type: *a baby car* ▷ *vb* -**bies, -bying, -bied** (*tr*) **10** to treat with love and attention **11** to treat (someone) like a baby; pamper or overprotect [C14 probably childish reduplication; compare MAMA, PAPA] > 'babyhood *n* > 'babyish *adj*

baby bond *n Brit* a sum of money invested shortly after the birth of a child, the returns of which may not be collected until the child reaches adulthood

baby bonus *n Canadian informal* family allowance

baby boom *n* a sharp increase in the birth rate of a population, esp the one that occurred after World War II. Also called (*esp Brit*): **the bulge**

baby-boomer *n* a person born during a baby boom, esp (in Britain and the US) one born during the years 1945–55

Baby-bouncer *n trademark* a seat on springs suspended from a door frame, etc, in which a baby may be placed for exercise

baby broker *n* an adoption service, esp on the internet

Baby Buggy *n* **1** *trademark Brit* a kind of child's light pushchair **2** *US and Canadian informal* a small pram

baby carriage *n* Also: **baby buggy** *US and Canadian* a cot-like four-wheeled carriage for a baby. British term: **pram**

baby-face *n* **1** a smooth round face like a baby's **2** a person with such a face

baby grand *n* a small grand piano, approximately 5 feet long. Compare **boudoir grand, concert grand**

Babylon ('bæbɪlən) *n* **1** the chief city of ancient Mesopotamia: first settled around 3000 BC. See also **Hanging Gardens of Babylon 2** *derogatory* (in Protestant polemic) the Roman Catholic Church, regarded as the seat of luxury and corruption **3** *derogatory* any society or group in a society considered as corrupt or as a place of exile by another society or group, esp White Britain as

viewed by some West Indians [via Latin and Greek from Hebrew *Bābhel*; see BABEL]

Babylonia (,bæbɪ'ləʊnɪə) *n* the southern kingdom of ancient Mesopotamia: a great empire from about 2200–538 BC, when it was conquered by the Persians

Babylonian (,bæbɪ'ləʊnɪən) *n* **1** an inhabitant of ancient Babylon or Babylonia **2** the extinct language of Babylonia, belonging to the E Semitic subfamily of the Afro-Asiatic family: a dialect of Akkadian ▷ *adj* **3** of, relating to, or characteristic of ancient Babylon or Babylonia, its people, or their language **4** decadent or depraved

Babylonian captivity *n* **1** the exile of the Jews in Babylonia from about 586 to about 538 BC **2** the exile of the seven popes in Avignon (1309–77)

baby-minder *n* a person who is paid to look after other people's babies or very young children > 'baby-,minding *n*

baby-mother *n* a young mother who has been abandoned by the baby's father just before or after the birth

baby's-breath *or* **babies'-breath** *n* **1** a tall Eurasian caryophyllaceous plant, *Gypsophila paniculata*, bearing small white or pink fragrant flowers **2** any of several other plants, such as the grape hyacinth and certain bedstraws, that have small scented flowers

baby-sit *vb* -**sits, -sitting, -sat** (*intr*) to act or work as a baby-sitter > 'baby-,sitting *n, adj*

baby-sitter *n* a person who takes care of a child or children while the parents are out

baby snatcher *n informal* **1** a person who steals a baby from its pram **2** another name for **cradle snatcher**

baby talk *n* **1** the speech of very young children learning to talk **2** an adult's imitation of this

baby tooth *n* another term for **milk tooth**

baby-walker *n* a light frame on casters or wheels to help a baby learn to walk. US equivalent: **go-cart**

baby wipe *n* a disposable moistened medicated paper towel, usually supplied in a plastic drum or packet, used for cleaning babies

Bacău ('bækaʊ) *n* a city in E Romania on the River Bistrila: oil refining, textiles, paper. Pop: 128 000 (2005 est)

Baccalauréat (,bækə'lɔːrɪˌɑː) *n* (esp in France) a school-leaving examination that qualifies the successful candidates for entrance to university [C20 from French, from Medieval Latin *baccalaureus* bachelor]

baccalaureate (,bækə'lɔːrɪɪt) *n* **1** the university degree of Bachelor or Arts, Bachelor of Science, etc **2** an internationally recognized programme of study, comprising different subjects, offered as an alternative to a course of A levels in Britain **3** *US* a farewell sermon delivered at the commencement ceremonies in many colleges and universities [C17 from Medieval Latin *baccalaureātus*, from *baccalaureus* advanced student, alteration of *baccalārius* BACHELOR; influenced in folk etymology by Latin *bāca* berry + *laureus* laurel]

baccarat ('bækəˌrɑː, ,bækə'rɑː; *French* bakara) *n* a card game in which two or more punters gamble against the banker [C19 from French *baccara*, of unknown origin]

baccate ('bækeɪt) *adj botany* **1** like a berry in form, texture, etc **2** bearing berries [C19 from Latin *bāca* berry]

Bacchae ('bækiː) *pl n* the priestesses or female devotees of Bacchus [Latin, from Greek *Bakkhai*, plural of *Bakkhē* priestess of BACCHUS]

bacchanal ('bækən°l) *n* **1** a follower of Bacchus **2** a drunken and riotous celebration **3** a participant in such a celebration; reveller ▷ *adj* **4** of or relating to Bacchus [C16 from Latin *Bacchānālis*; see BACCHUS]

bacchanalia (,bækə'neɪlɪə) *pl n* **1** (*often capital*) orgiastic rites associated with Bacchus **2** any drunken revelry

bacchanalian (,bækə'neɪlɪən) *adj* **1** characterized

by or involving drunken revelry **2** (*often capital*) of or relating to the orgiastic rites associated with Bacchus

bacchant ('bækənt) *n, pl* **bacchants, bacchantes** (bə'kæntɪz) **1** a priest or votary of Bacchus **2** a drunken reveller [C17 from Latin *bacchāns*, from *bacchārī* to celebrate the BACCHANALIA]

bacchante (bə'kæntɪ) *n, pl* **bacchantes** (bə'kæntɪz) **1** a priestess or female votary of Bacchus **2** a drunken female reveller

Bacchic ('bækɪk) *adj* **1** of or relating to Bacchus **2** (*often not capital*) riotously drunk

bacchius (bæ'kaɪəs) *n, pl* -**chii** (-'kaɪaɪ) *prosody* a metrical foot of one short syllable followed by two long ones (˘--). Compare **dactyl** [C16 from Latin, from Greek *Bakkheios* (*pous*) a Bacchic (*foot*)]

Bacchus ('bækəs) *n* (in ancient Greece and Rome) a god of wine and giver of ecstasy, identified with Dionysus [C15 from Latin, from Greek *Bakkhos*; related to Latin *bāca* small round fruit, berry]

bacciferous (bæk'sɪfərəs) *adj* bearing berries [C17 from Latin *bācifer*, from *bāca* berry + *ferre* to bear]

bacciform ('bæksɪˌfɔːm) *adj botany* shaped like a berry

baccivorous (bæk'sɪvərəs) *adj* feeding on berries

baccy ('bækɪ) *n Brit* an informal name for **tobacco**

bach¹ (bax, baːk) *n Welsh* a term of friendly address: used esp after a person's name [Welsh, literally: little one]

bach² (bætʃ) *Austral and NZ* ▷ *vb* **1** a variant spelling of **batch²** ▷ *n* **2** a simple cottage, esp at the seaside

bacha ('bʌtʃə) *or* **bachcha** ('bʌtʃˌtʃə) *n Hinglish informal* a child or a young person [C21 from Hindi *baccā* a child]

bachelor ('bætʃələ, 'bætʃlə) *n* **1 a** an unmarried man **b** (*as modifier*): *a bachelor flat* **2 a** a person who holds the degree of Bachelor of Arts, Bachelor of Education, Bachelor of Science, etc **b** the degree itself **3** Also called: **bachelor-at-arms** (in the Middle Ages) a young knight serving a great noble **4 bachelor seal** a young male seal, esp a fur seal, that has not yet mated [C13 from Old French *bacheler* youth, squire, from Vulgar Latin *baccalāris* (unattested) farm worker, of Celtic origin; compare Irish Gaelic *bachlach* peasant] > 'bachelorhood *n*

bachelor apartment *n Canadian* a flat consisting of one room that is used as a sitting room and bedroom, as well as a kitchenette and a bathroom

bachelorette (,bætʃələ'rɛt) *n jocular* a young unmarried professional woman [C20 BACHELOR + -ETTE (sense 2)]

bachelor girl *n* a young unmarried woman, esp one who is self-supporting

Bachelor of Arts *n* **1** a degree conferred on a person who has successfully completed his or her undergraduate studies, usually in a branch of the liberal arts or humanities **2** a person who holds this degree

Bachelor of Science *n* **1** a degree conferred on a person who has successfully completed his or her undergraduate studies in a branch of the sciences **2** a person who holds this degree

bachelor's-buttons *n* (*functioning as singular or plural*) any of various plants of the daisy family with button-like flower heads

Bach flower remedy *n trademark* an alternative medicine consisting of a distillation from various flowers, designed to counteract negative states of mind and restore emotional balance [C20 after Dr E. *Bach* (1886–1936), homeopath who developed this system]

Bach trumpet (baːx) *n* a modern small three-valved trumpet for playing clarino passages in Bach's music

bacillaemia *or US* **bacillemia** (,bæsɪ'liːmɪə) *n pathol* the presence of bacilli in the blood

bacillary (bə'sɪlərɪ) *or* **bacillar** (bə'sɪlə) *adj* **1** of, relating to, or caused by bacilli **2** Also: **bacilliform** (bə'sɪlɪˌfɔːm) shaped like a short rod

bacilluria (ˌbæsɪˈljʊərɪə) *n pathol* the presence of bacilli in the urine

bacillus (bəˈsɪləs) *n, pl* -cilli (-ˈsɪlaɪ) **1** any rod-shaped bacterium, such as a clostridium bacterium. Compare **coccus** (sense 1), **spirillum** (sense 1) **2** any of various rodlike spore-producing bacteria constituting the family *Bacillaceae*, esp of the genus *Bacillus* [C19 from Latin: a small staff, from *baculum* walking stick]

bacitracin (ˌbæsɪˈtreɪsɪn) *n* an antibiotic used mainly in treating bacterial skin infections: obtained from the bacterium *Bacillus subtilis* [C20 BACI(LLUS) + *-trac-* from Margaret Tracy (born 1936), American girl in whose blood *Bacillus subtilis* was found; see -IN]

back¹ (bæk) *n* **1** the posterior part of the human body, extending from the neck to the pelvis. Related adjective: **dorsal 2** the corresponding or upper part of an animal **3** the spinal column **4** the part or side of an object opposite the front **5** the part or side of anything less often seen or used: *the back of a carpet; the back of a knife* **6** the part or side of anything that is furthest from the front or from a spectator: *the back of the stage* **7** the convex part of something: *the back of a hill; the back of a ship* **8** something that supports, covers, or strengthens the rear of an object **9** *ball games* **a** a mainly defensive player behind a forward **b** the position of such a player **10** the part of a book to which the pages are glued or that joins the covers **11** *mining* **a** the side of a passage or layer nearest the surface **b** the earth between that level and the next **12** the upper surface of a joist, rafter, slate, tile, etc, when in position. Compare **bed** (sense 13) **13 at one's back** behind, esp in support or pursuit **14 at the back of one's mind** not in one's conscious thoughts **15 behind one's back** without one's knowledge; secretly or deceitfully **16 break one's back** to overwork or work very hard **17 break the back of** to complete the greatest or hardest part of (a task) **18 (flat) on one's back** incapacitated, esp through illness **19 get off someone's back** *informal* to stop criticizing or pestering someone **20 have on one's back** to be burdened with **21 on someone's back** *informal* criticizing or pestering someone **22 put one's back into** to devote all one's strength to (a task) **23 put** (*or* **get**) **someone's back up** to annoy someone **24 see the back of** to be rid of **25 back of beyond a the.** a very remote place **b** *Austral* in such a place (esp in the phrase **out back of beyond**) **26 turn one's back on a** to turn away from in anger or contempt **b** to refuse to help; abandon **27 with one's back to the wall** in a difficult or desperate situation ▷ *vb* (*mainly tr*) **28** (*also intr*) to move or cause to move backwards **29** to provide support, money, or encouragement for (a person, enterprise, etc) **30** to bet on the success of: *to back a horse* **31** to provide with a back, backing, or lining **32** to provide with a music accompaniment: *a soloist backed by an orchestra* **33** to provide a background for; be at the back of: *mountains back the town* **34** to countersign or endorse **35** *archaic* to mount the back of **36** (*intr; foll by on or onto*) to have the back facing (towards): *the house backs onto a river* **37** (*intr*) (of the wind) to change direction in an anticlockwise direction. Compare **veer¹** (sense 3a) **38** *nautical* to position (a sail) so that the wind presses on its opposite side **39 back and fill a** *nautical* to manoeuvre the sails by alternately filling and emptying them of wind to navigate in a narrow place **b** to vacillate in one's opinion ▷ *adj* (*prenominal*) **40** situated behind: *a back lane* **41** of the past: *back issues of a magazine* **42** owing from an earlier date: *back rent* **43** *chiefly US, Austral, and NZ* remote: *back country* **44** (of a road) not direct **45** moving in a backward direction: *back current* **46** *phonetics* of, relating to, or denoting a vowel articulated with the tongue retracted towards the soft palate, as for the vowels in English *hard, fall, hot, full, fool* ▷ *adv* **47** at, to, or towards the rear;

away from something considered to be the front; backwards; behind **48** in, to, or towards the original starting point, place, or condition: *to go back home; put the book back; my headache has come back* **49** in or into the past: *to look back on one's childhood* **50** in reply, repayment, or retaliation: *to hit someone back; pay back a debt; to answer back* **51** in check: *the dam holds back the water* **52** in concealment; in reserve: *to keep something back; to hold back information* **53 back and forth** to and fro **54 back to front a** in reverse **b** in disorder ▷ See also **back down, back off, back out, back up** [Old English *bæc*; related to Old Norse *bak*, Old Frisian *bek*, Old High German *bah*]

back² *n* a large tub or vat, esp one used by brewers [C17 from Dutch *bak* tub, cistern, from Old French *bac*, from Vulgar Latin *bacca* (unattested) vessel for liquids]

backache (ˈbækˌeɪk) *n* an ache or pain in one's back

back bacon *n* lean bacon from the back of a pig's loin

backbeat (ˈbækˌbiːt) *n* the second and fourth beats in music written in even time or, in more complex time signatures, the last beat of the bar. Compare **downbeat** (sense 1)

backbencher (ˈbækˈbɛntʃə) *n Brit, Austral, and NZ* a Member of Parliament who does not hold office in the government or opposition

backbend (ˈbækˌbɛnd) *n* a gymnastic exercise in which the trunk is bent backwards until the hands touch the floor

backbite (ˈbækˌbaɪt) *vb* -**bites**, -**biting**, -**bit**; -**bitten** *or* -**bit** to talk spitefully about (an absent person) ▷ **ˈbackˌbiter** *n*

backblocks (ˈbækˌblɒks) *pl n Austral and NZ* bush or remote farming area far distant from city amenities ▷ **ˈbackˌblock** *adj* ▷ **ˈbackˌblocker** *n*

backboard (ˈbækˌbɔːd) *n* **1** a board that is placed behind something to form or support its back **2** a board worn to straighten or support the back, as after surgery **3** (in basketball) a flat upright surface supported on a high frame, under which the basket is attached

back boiler *n* a tank or series of pipes at the back of a fireplace for heating water. US name: **water back**

backbone (ˈbækˌbəʊn) *n* **1** a nontechnical name for **spinal column 2** something that resembles the spinal column in function, position, or appearance **3** strength of character; courage **4** the main or central mountain range of a country or region **5** *nautical* the main longitudinal members of a vessel, giving structural strength **6** *computing* (in computer networks) a large-capacity, high-speed central section by which other network segments are connected

backbreaker (ˈbækˌbreɪkə) *n* **1** a wrestling hold in which a wrestler uses his knee or shoulder as a fulcrum to bend his opponent's body backwards **2** *informal* an extremely arduous task

backbreaking (ˈbækˌbreɪkɪŋ) *adj* demanding great effort; exhausting

backburn (ˈbækˌbɜːn) *Austral and NZ* ▷ *vb* (*tr*) **1** to clear (an area of scrub, bush, etc) by creating a new fire that burns in the opposite direction to the line of advancing fire ▷ *n* **2** the act or result of backburning

back burner *n* **on the back burner** put aside for the time being, as a subject that is not of immediate concern but that may be activated later; postponed

backchat (ˈbækˌtʃæt) *n informal* the act of answering back, esp impudently

backcloth (ˈbækˌklɒθ) *n* a large painted curtain hanging at the back of a stage set. Also called: **backdrop**

backcomb (ˈbækˌkəʊm) *vb* to comb the under layers of (the hair) towards the roots to give more bulk to a hairstyle. Also: **tease**

back country *n Austral and NZ* land remote from a town or settled area

backcourt (ˈbækˌkɔːt) *n* **1** *tennis, chiefly US* the part of the court between the service line and the baseline **2** (in various court games) the area nearest the back boundary line

backcross (ˈbækˌkrɒs) *vb* **1** to mate (a hybrid of the first generation) with one of its parents ▷ *n* **2** the offspring so produced **3** the act or process of backcrossing

backdate (ˈbækˈdeɪt) *vb* (*tr*) to make effective from an earlier date: *the pay rise was backdated to August*

back door *n* **1** a door at the rear or side of a building **2 a** a means of entry to a job, position, etc, that is secret, underhand, or obtained through influence **b** (*as modifier*): *a backdoor way of making firms pay more*

back down *vb* **1** (*intr, adverb*) to withdraw an earlier claim **2** (*tr*) *rowing* to cause (a boat) to move backwards by pushing rather than pulling on the oars ▷ *n* **backdown 3** abandonment of an earlier claim

backdraught *or US and Canadian* **backdraft** (ˈbækˌdrɑːft) *n* **1** a reverse movement of air, gas, or liquid **2** an explosion that occurs when air reaches a fire that has used up all the available oxygen, often occurring when a door is opened to the room containing the fire

backdrop (ˈbækˌdrɒp) *n* **1** another name for **backcloth 2** the background to any scene or situation

backed (bækt) *adj* **a** having a back or backing **b** (*in combination*): *high-backed; black-backed*

back emf *n electrical engineering* an electromagnetic force appearing in an inductive circuit in such a direction as to oppose any change of current in the circuit

back emission *n electronics* the secondary emission of electrons from an anode

back end 1 *n Northern English dialect* autumn ▷ *adj* **back-end 2** (of money, costs, etc) required or incurred after a project has been completed [from the phrase *the back end of the year*]

back-end load *n* the final charges of commission and expenses made by an investment trust, insurance policy, etc, when the investor is paid out ▷ **back-end loading** *n*

backer (ˈbækə) *n* **1** a person who gives financial or other support **2** a person who bets on a competitor or contestant

backfield (ˈbækˌfiːld) *n American football* **1** (usually preceded by *the*) the quarterback and running backs in a team **2** the area behind the line of scrimmage from which the backfield begin each play

backfile (ˈbækˌfaɪl) *n* the archives of a newspaper or magazine

backfill (ˈbækˌfɪl) *vb* **1** (*tr*) to refill an excavated trench, esp (in archaeology) at the end of an investigation ▷ *n* **2** the soil used to do this

backfire (ˈbækˈfaɪə) *vb* (*intr*) **1** (of an internal-combustion engine) to emit a loud noise as a result of an explosion in the inlet manifold or exhaust system **2** to fail to have the desired or expected effect: *his plans backfired on him* **3** to start a controlled fire in order to halt an advancing forest or prairie fire by creating a barren area ▷ *n* **4** (in an internal-combustion engine) **a** an explosion of unburnt gases in the exhaust system **b** a premature explosion in a cylinder or inlet manifold **5** a controlled fire started to create a barren area that will halt an advancing forest or prairie fire

back foot *n* **on the back foot** at a disadvantage; outmanoeuvred or outclassed by an opponent

back formation *n* **1** the invention of a new word on the assumption that a familiar word is derived from it. The verbs *edit* and *burgle* in English were so created from *editor* and *burglar* **2** a word formed by this process

back four *n soccer* the defensive players in many modern team formations: usually two fullbacks and two centre backs

backgammon ('bæk,gæmən, bæk'gæmən) *n* **1** a game for two people played on a board with pieces moved according to throws of the dice **2** the most complete form of win in this game [C17 BACK[1] + *gammon*, variant of GAME[1]]

back green *n Central Scot urban dialect* grass or a garden at the back of a house, esp a tenement

background ('bæk,graʊnd) *n* **1** the part of a scene or view furthest from the viewer **2 a** an inconspicuous or unobtrusive position (esp in the phrase **in the background**) **b** (*as modifier*): *a background influence* **3** *art* **a** the plane or ground in a picture upon which all other planes or forms appear superimposed **b** the parts of a picture that appear most distant. Compare **foreground, middle-distance 4** a person's social class, education, training, or experience **5 a** the social, historical, or technical circumstances that lead up to or help to explain something: *the background to the French Revolution* **b** (*as modifier*): *background information* **6 a** a low level of sound, lighting, etc, whose purpose is to be an unobtrusive or appropriate accompaniment to something else, such as a social activity, conversation, or the action of a film **b** (*as modifier*): *background music* **7** Also called: **background radiation** *physics* low-intensity radiation as, for example, from small amounts of radioisotopes in soil, air, building materials, etc **8** *electronics* **a** unwanted effects, such as noise, occurring in a measuring instrument, electronic device, etc **b** (*as modifier*): *background interference*

background processing *n computing* the ability of a system to perform a low-priority task while, at the same time, dealing with a main application

backhand ('bæk,hænd) *n* **1** *sport* **a** a stroke made across the body with the back of the hand facing the direction of the stroke **b** (*as modifier*): *a backhand return* **2** the side on which backhand strokes are made **3** handwriting slanting to the left ▷ *adv* **4** with a backhand stroke ▷ *vb* (*tr*) **5** *sport* to play (a shot) backhand

backhanded (,bæk'hændɪd) *adj* **1** (of a blow, shot, stroke, etc) performed with the arm moving across the body **2** double-edged; equivocal: *a backhanded compliment* **3** (of handwriting) slanting to the left **4** (of a rope) twisted in the opposite way from the normal right-handed direction ▷ *adv* **5** in a backhanded manner > ,**back'handedly** *adv* > ,**back'handedness** *n*

backhander ('bæk,hændə) *n* **1** a backhanded stroke or blow **2** *informal* an indirect attack **3** *slang* a bribe

backie ('bækɪ) *n Brit informal* a ride on the back of someone's bicycle

backing ('bækɪŋ) *n* **1** support given to a person, cause, or enterprise **2** a body of supporters **3** something that forms, protects, supports, or strengthens the back of something **4** *theatre* a scenic cloth or flat placed behind a window, door, etc, in a set to mask the offstage space **5** *musical* accompaniment, esp for a pop singer **6** the support in gold or precious metals for a country's issue of money in notes **7** *meteorol* an anticlockwise change in wind direction **8** *Northern English* a passageway running behind a row of terraced houses

backing dog *n NZ and Austral* a dog that moves a flock of sheep by jumping on their backs

backing store *n* a computer storage device, usually a disk, that provides additional storage space for information so that it can be accessed and referred to when required and may be copied into the processor if needed

backlash ('bæk,læʃ) *n* **1** a reaction or recoil between interacting worn or badly fitting parts in a mechanism **2** the play between parts **3** a sudden and adverse reaction, esp to a political or social development: *a public backlash against the government is inevitable*

backless ('bæklɪs) *adj* (of a dress) low-cut at the back

back light *n* light falling on a photographic or television subject from the rear

backlist ('bæk,lɪst) *n* a publisher's previously published books that are still available. See also **front list, mid-list**

backlit (bæk'lɪt) *adj* illuminated from behind: *a backlit screen*

backlog ('bæk,lɒg) *n* **1** an accumulation of uncompleted work, unsold stock, etc, to be dealt with **2** *chiefly US and Canadian* a large log at the back of a fireplace

backlot ('bæk,lɒt) *n* an area outside a film or television studio used for outdoor filming

back marker *n* a competitor who is at the back of a field in a race

back matter *n* the parts of a book, such as the index and appendices, that follow the main text. Also called: **end matter**

backmost ('bæk,məʊst) *adj* furthest back

back mutation *n genetics* the reversion of a mutant to the original phenotype

back number *n* **1** an issue of a newspaper, magazine, etc, that appeared on a previous date **2** *informal* a person or thing considered to be old-fashioned

back o' Bourke (bɜːk) *adv Austral* in a remote or backward place [from *Bourke*, a town in New South Wales]

back off *vb* (*adverb*) *informal* **1** (*intr*) to retreat **2** (*tr*) to abandon (an intention, objective, etc)

back office *n* **a** the administrative and support staff of a financial institution or other business **b** (*as modifier*): *back-office operations*

back out *vb* (*intr, adverb; often foll by of*) to withdraw (from an agreement, etc)

backpack ('bæk,pæk) *n* **1** a rucksack or knapsack **2** a pack carried on the back of an astronaut, containing oxygen cylinders, essential supplies, etc ▷ *vb* **3** (*intr*) to travel about or go hiking with a backpack **4** (*tr*) to transport (food or equipment) by backpack > '**back,packer** *n* > '**back,packing** *n*

back passage *n* **1** the rectum **2** an interior passageway towards the back of a building

back pay *n* pay received by an employee from an increase awarded retrospectively

back-pedal *vb* -pedals, -pedalling, -pedalled *or US* -pedals, -pedaling, -pedaled (*intr*) **1** to turn the pedals of a bicycle backwards **2** to retract or modify a previous opinion, principle, etc **3** *boxing* to take backward steps

back pressure *n* **1** *engineering* **a** the pressure that opposes the motion of a piston on its exhaust stroke in an internal-combustion engine **b** the exhaust pressure in external combustion engines **2** *med* the local pressure that builds up when fluid flow is obstructed in the cardiovascular or urinary systems

back projection *n* a method of projecting pictures onto a translucent screen so that they are viewed from the opposite side, used esp in films to create the illusion that the actors in the foreground are moving. Also called: **background projection**

back rest *n* a support for the back of something

Back River *n* a river in N Canada, flowing northeast through Nunavut to the Arctic Ocean. Length: about 966 km (600 miles)

back room *n* **a** a place where research or planning is done, esp secret research in wartime **b** (*as modifier*): *back-room boys*

back row *n* (*functioning as singular or plural*) *rugby Union* **a** the forwards at the rear of a scrum **b** (*as modifier*): *an Australian back-row forward*

Backs (bæks) *pl n* **the**, the grounds between the River Cam and certain Cambridge colleges

back, sack, and crack *n informal* (cosmetic depilation of) the back, scrotum, and the area between the buttocks

back saw *n* a small handsaw stiffened along its upper edge by a metal section

back scatter *n physics* **1** the scattering of particles or radiation, such as sound waves, X-rays, or

alpha-particles, by the atoms of the medium through which they pass, in the backward direction **2** the radiation or particles so scattered **3** a technique whereby very long-range radars locate targets hidden by the curvature of the earth. Radar beams are reflected off the underside of the troposphere onto the target and the return beams, similarly reflected, are measured

backscratcher ('bæk,skrætʃə) *n* **1** an implement with a long handle, used for scratching one's own back **2** *informal* a person who provides a service, corporate or public money etc, for another, in order to receive a similar service or reward in return > '**back,scratching** *n*

back seat *n* **1** a seat at the back, esp of a vehicle **2** *informal* a subordinate or inconspicuous position (esp in the phrase **take a back seat**)

back-seat driver *n informal* **1** a passenger in a car who offers unwanted advice to the driver **2** a person who offers advice on or tries to direct matters that are not his or her concern

backsheesh ('bækʃiːʃ) *n* a variant spelling of **baksheesh**

back shift *n Brit* **1** a group of workers who work a shift from late afternoon to midnight in an industry or occupation where a day shift or a night shift is also worked **2** the period worked ▷ *US and Canadian name:* **swing shift**

backside (,bæk'saɪd) *n* **1** the back of something **2** ('bæk,saɪd) *informal* the buttocks

backsight ('bæk,saɪt) *n* **1** the sight of a rifle nearer the stock **2** *surveying* a reading taken looking backwards to a previously occupied station. Compare **foresight** (sense 4)

back slang *n* a type of slang in which words are spelled and, as far as possible, pronounced backwards

back-slapping *adj* energetically jovial; hearty

backslash *n* a slash which slopes to the left \

backslide ('bæk,slaɪd) *vb* -slides, -sliding, -slid; -slid *or* -slidden (*intr*) to lapse into bad habits or vices from a state of virtue, religious faith, etc > '**back,slider** *n*

backspace ('bæk,speɪs) *vb* **1** to move a (typewriter carriage) backwards ▷ *n* **2** a typewriter key that effects such a movement

backspin ('bæk,spɪn) *n sport* a backward spinning motion imparted to a ball to reduce its speed at impact. Compare **topspin**

back-stabbing *n* actions or remarks that are treacherous and likely to cause harm to a person, esp a friend or colleague

backstage (,bæk'steɪdʒ) *adv* **1** behind the part of the theatre in view of the audience; in the dressing rooms, wings, etc **2** towards the rear of the stage ▷ *adj* **3** situated backstage **4** *informal* away from public view

backstairs ('bæk,steəz) *pl n* **1** a secondary staircase in a house, esp one originally for the use of servants ▷ *adj* Also: **backstair 2** underhand: *backstairs gossip*

backstay ('bæk,steɪ) *n* **1** *nautical* a stay leading aft from the upper part of a mast to the deck or stern **2** *machinery* a supporting piece or arresting part **3** anything that supports or strengthens the back of something, such as leather covering the back seam of a shoe

backstitch ('bæk,stɪtʃ) *n* **1** a strong sewing stitch made by starting the next stitch at the middle or beginning of the preceding one ▷ *vb* **2** to sew using this stitch

backstop ('bæk,stɒp) *n* **1** *sport* a screen or fence to prevent balls leaving the playing area **2** a block or catch to prevent excessive backward movement, such as one on the sliding seat of a rowing boat ▷ *vb* -stops, -stopping, -stopped (*tr*) **3** *US* to provide with backing or support

back story *n* the events which take place before, and which help to bring about, the events portrayed in a film

back straight *n* a straight part of a circuit, esp of an athletics track or a racecourse, furthest from the finishing point

backstreet (ˈbækˌstriːt) *n* **1** a street in a town remote from the main roads **2** (*modifier*) denoting illicit activities regarded as likely to take place in such a street: *a backstreet abortion*

back stretch *n* a horse-racing term for **back straight**

backstroke (ˈbækˌstrəʊk) *n* **1** Also called: **back crawl** *swimming* **a** a stroke performed on the back, using backward circular strokes of each arm and flipper movements of the feet **b** (*as modifier*): *the backstroke champion* **2** a return stroke or blow **3** *chiefly US* a backhanded stroke **4** *bell-ringing* the upward movement of the bell rope as the bell swings back and forth. Compare **handstroke** ▷ *vb* **5** (*intr*) to swim the backstroke

backswept (ˈbækˌswɛpt) *adj* **1** slanting backwards **2** another word for **sweptback**

backsword (ˈbækˌsɔːd) *n* **1** another name for **broadsword 2** Also called: **backswordsman** a person who uses the backsword **3** a fencing stick with a basket-like protective hilt

back-to-back *adj* (*usually postpositive*) **1** facing in opposite directions, often with the backs touching **2** *chiefly Brit* (of urban houses) built so that their backs are joined or separated only by a narrow alley **3** *informal* consecutive **4** *commerce* **a** denoting a credit arrangement in which a finance house acts as an intermediary to conceal the identity of the seller from the buyer **b** denoting a loan from one company to another in a different country using a finance house to provide the loan but not the funding ▷ *n* **5** a house or terrace built in back-to-back style

backtrack (ˈbækˌtræk) *vb* (*intr*) **1** to return by the same route by which one has come **2** to retract or reverse one's opinion, action, policy, etc > ˈbackˌtracking *n*

back up *vb* (*adverb*) **1** (*tr*) to support or assist **2** (*intr*) *cricket* (of a nonstriking batsman) to move down the wicket in readiness for a run as a ball is bowled **3** (of water) to accumulate **4** (of traffic) to become jammed behind an accident or other obstruction **5** *computing* to make a copy of (a data file), esp for storage in another place as a security copy **6** *printing* to print the second side of (a sheet) **7** (*intr*, usually foll by *on*) *Austral* to repeat an action immediately ▷ *n* **backup 8** a support or reinforcement **9 a** a reserve or substitute **b** (*as modifier*): *backup troops* **10** the overflow from a blocked drain or pipe **11** *computing* a file or set of files copied for security purposes

back-up light *n* *US and Canadian* a light on the rear of a motor vehicle to warn others that the vehicle is being reversed. Also called: **reversing light**

backward (ˈbækwəd) *adj* **1** (*usually prenominal*) directed towards the rear: *a backward glance* **2** retarded in physical, material, or intellectual development: *backward countries; a backward child* **3 a** of or relating to the past; conservative or reactionary **b** (*in combination*): *backward-looking* **4** reluctant or bashful: *a backward lover* **5** *chess* (of a pawn) behind neighbouring pawns and unable to be supported by them ▷ *adv* **6** a variant of **backwards.** > ˈbackwardly *adv* > ˈbackwardness *n*

backwardation (ˌbækwəˈdeɪʃən) *n* *commerce* **1** the difference between the spot price for a commodity, including rent and interest, and the forward price **2** (formerly, on the Stock Exchange) postponement of delivery by a seller of securities until the next settlement period

backwards (ˈbækwədz) *or* **backward** *adv* **1** towards the rear **2** with the back foremost **3** in the reverse of usual order or direction **4** to or towards the past **5** into a worse state: *the patient was slipping backwards* **6** towards the point of origin **7** bend, lean, *or* fall over backwards *informal* to make a special effort, esp in order to please **8** know backwards *informal* to understand completely

backwash (ˈbækˌwɒʃ) *n* **1** a sucking movement of

water, such as that of retreating waves. Compare **swash 2** water washed backwards by the motion of oars or other propelling devices **3** the backward flow of air set up by an aircraft's engines **4** a condition resulting from a previous event; repercussion ▷ *vb* **5** (*tr*) to remove oil from (combed wool)

backwater (ˈbækˌwɔːtə) *n* **1** a body of stagnant water connected to a river **2** water held or driven back, as by a dam, flood, or tide **3** an isolated, backward, or intellectually stagnant place or condition ▷ *vb* **back water 4** (*intr*) to reverse the direction of a boat, esp to push the oars of a rowing boat

backwoods (ˈbækˌwʊdz) *pl n* **1** *chiefly US and Canadian* partially cleared, sparsely populated forests **2** any remote sparsely populated place **3** (*modifier*) of, from, or like the backwoods **4** (*modifier*) uncouth; rustic

backwoodsman (ˈbækˌwʊdzmən) *n, pl* **-men 1** a person from the backwoods **2** *US informal* an uncouth or rustic person **3** *Brit informal* a peer who rarely attends the House of Lords

backword (ˈbækˌwɜːd) *n Brit dialect* the act or an instance of failing to keep a promise or commitment (esp in the phrase **give** (**someone**) **backword**)

back yard *n* **1** a yard at the back of a house, etc **2** in one's own back yard **a** close at hand **b** involving or implicating one

baclava (ˈbɑːkləˌvɑː) *n* a variant spelling of **baklava**

Bacolod (bəˈkɒləd) *n* a town in the Philippines, on the NW coast of Negros Island. Pop: 468 000 (2005 est)

bacon (ˈbeɪkən) *n* **1** meat from the back and sides of a pig, dried, salted, and usually smoked **2** bring home the bacon *informal* **a** to achieve success **b** to provide material support **3** save (**someone's**) bacon *Brit informal* to help (someone) to escape from danger [C12 from Old French *bacon*, from Old High German *bahho*; related to Old Saxon *baco*; see BACK¹]

bacon-and-eggs *n* another name for **bird's-foot trefoil**

bacon beetle *n* See **dermestid**

baconer (ˈbeɪkənə) *n* a pig that weighs between 83 and 101 kg, from which bacon is cut

Baconian (beɪˈkəʊnɪən) *adj* **1** of or relating to Francis Bacon, Baron Verulam, Viscount St Albans (1561–1626), the English philosopher, statesman, and essayist, or to his inductive method of reasoning ▷ *n* **2** a follower of Bacon's philosophy **3** one who believes that plays attributed to Shakespeare were written by Bacon

BACS (bæks) *n acronym for* Bankers' Automated Clearing System; a method of making payments direct to a creditor's bank without using a cheque

bacteraemia *or US* **bacteremia** (ˌbæktəˈriːmɪə) *n pathol* the presence of bacteria in the blood

bacteria (bækˈtɪərɪə) *pl n, sing* **-rium** (-rɪəm) a very large group of microorganisms comprising one of the three domains of living organisms. They are prokaryotic, unicellular, and either free-living in soil or water or parasites of plants or animals. See also **prokaryote** [C19 plural of New Latin *bacterium*, from Greek *baktērion*, literally: a little stick, from *baktron* rod, staff] > bacˈterial *adj* > bacˈterially *adv*

bacteria bed *n* a layer of sand or gravel used to expose sewage effluent, in its final stages, to air and the action of microorganisms. Compare **filter bed** (sense 1)

bacterial plaque *n* another term for **dental plaque**

bactericide (bækˈtɪərɪˌsaɪd) *n* a substance able to destroy bacteria > bacˈteriˈcidal *adj*

bacterin (ˈbæktərɪn) *n obsolete* a vaccine prepared from bacteria

bacterio-, bacteri- *or sometimes before a vowel* **bacter-** *combining form* indicating bacteria or an action or condition relating to or characteristic of bacteria: *bacteriology; bactericide; bacteroid* [New Latin,

from BACTERIA]

bacteriol. *abbreviation for* **1** bacteriological **2** bacteriology

bacteriological warfare *n* another term for **germ warfare**

bacteriology (bækˌtɪərɪˈɒlədʒɪ) *n* the branch of science concerned with the study of bacteria > bacteriological (bækˌtɪərɪəˈlɒdʒɪkəl) *adj* > bacˌterioˈlogically *adv* > bacˌteriˈologist *n*

bacteriolysis (bækˌtɪərɪˈɒlɪsɪs) *n* the destruction or disintegration of bacteria > bacteriolytic (bækˌtɪərɪəˈlɪtɪk) *adj*

bacteriophage (bækˈtɪərɪəˌfeɪdʒ) *n* a virus that is parasitic in a bacterium and multiplies within its host, which is destroyed when the new viruses are released. Often shortened to: **phage** > bacteriophagic (bækˌtɪərɪəˈfædʒɪk) *adj* > bacteriophagous (bækˌtɪərɪˈɒfəgəs) *adj*

bacteriostasis (bækˌtɪərɪəʊˈsteɪsɪs, -ˈstæsɪs) *n, pl* **-stases** (-ˈsteɪsiːz, -ˈstæsiːz) inhibition of the growth and reproduction of bacteria, esp by the action of a chemical agent > **bacteriostatic** (bækˌtɪərɪəʊˈstætɪk) *adj* > bacˌterioˈstatically *adv*

bacteriostat (bækˈtɪərɪəʊˌstæt) *n* any substance that arrests the growth or reproduction of bacteria but does not kill them

bacteriotoxin (bækˌtɪərɪəʊˈtɒksɪn) *n* **1** any toxin that kills bacteria **2** a toxin produced by bacteria

bacterium (bækˈtɪərɪəm) *n* the singular of **bacteria**

bacteriuria (bækˌtɪərɪˈjʊərɪə) *or* **bacteruria** (ˌbæktəˈrjʊərɪə) *n* the presence of bacteria in the urine

bacteroid (ˈbæktəˌrɔɪd) *adj* **1** resembling a bacterium ▷ *n* **2** any rodlike bacterium of the genus *Bacteroides*, occurring in the gut of humans and animals

Bactria (ˈbæktrɪə) *n* an ancient country of SW Asia, between the Hindu Kush mountains and the Oxus River: forms the present Balkh region in N Afghanistan

Bactrian (ˈbæktrɪən) *adj* **1** of or relating to Bactria, ▷ *n* **2** a native or inhabitant of Bactria

Bactrian camel *n* a two-humped camel, *Camelus bactrianus*, used as a beast of burden in the cold deserts of central Asia. Compare **Arabian camel**

baculiform (bəˈkjuːlɪˌfɔːm, ˈbækjuː-) *adj biology* shaped like a rod: *baculiform fungal spores* [C19 from *baculi-*, from Latin *baculum* walking stick + -FORM]

baculum (ˈbækjʊləm) *n, pl* **-la** (-lə) *or* **-lums** a bony support in the penis of certain mammals, esp the carnivores [C20 New Latin, from Latin: stick, staff]

bad¹ (bæd) *adj* **worse**, **worst 1** not good; of poor quality; inadequate; inferior: *bad workmanship; bad soil; bad light for reading* **2** (often foll by *at*) lacking skill or talent; incompetent: *a bad painter; bad at sports* **3** (often foll by *for*) harmful: *bad air; smoking is bad for you* **4** immoral; evil: *a bad life* **5** naughty; mischievous; disobedient: *a bad child* **6** rotten; decayed; spoiled: *a bad egg* **7** severe; intense: *a bad headache* **8** incorrect; wrong; faulty: *bad pronunciation* **9** ill or in pain (esp in the phrase **feel bad**) **10** regretful, sorry, or upset (esp in the phrase **feel bad about**) **11** unfavourable; distressing: *bad news; a bad business* **12** offensive; unpleasant; disagreeable: *bad language; bad temper* **13** not valid or sound; void: *a bad cheque* **14** not recoverable: *a bad debt* **15** badder, baddest *slang* good; excellent **16** go from bad to worse to deteriorate even more **17** go bad to putrefy; spoil **18** in a bad way *informal* **a** seriously ill, through sickness or injury **b** in trouble of any kind **19** in someone's bad books See **book** (sense 21) **20** make the best of a bad job to manage as well as possible in unfavourable circumstances **21** not bad *or* not so bad *informal* passable; fair; fairly good **22** not half bad *informal* very good **23** too bad *informal* (often used dismissively) regrettable ▷ *n* **24** unfortunate or unpleasant events collectively (often in the phrase **take the bad with the good**) **25** an immoral or degenerate state (often in the phrase **go to the bad**) **26** the debit

b

side of an account: *£200 to the bad* ▷ *adv* **27** *not standard* badly: *to want something bad* [c13 probably from *bæd-*, as the first element of Old English *bǣddel* hermaphrodite, *bǣdling* sodomite] > '**baddish** *adj* > '**badness** *n*

bad² (bæd) *vb* a variant of **bade**

bada-bing (ˌbædəˈbɪŋ) *or* **bada-bing bada-boom** (ˌbædəˈbuːm) *sentence substitute US slang* an expression used to suggest that something can be done with no difficulty or delay [c20 perhaps imitative of the sound of something clicking into place]

Badajoz (ˈbædəˌhɒz; *Spanish* baˈðaxoθ) *n* a city in SW Spain: strategically positioned near the frontier with Portugal. Pop: 138 415 (2003 est)

Badalona (*Spanish* baðaˈlona) *n* a port in NE Spain: an industrial suburb of Barcelona. Pop: 214 440 (2003 est)

badass ('bædˌæs) *slang, chiefly US* ▷ *n* **1** a tough or aggressive person: *the meanest badass in town* ▷ *adj* **2** tough or aggressive: *a badass rock band* **3** excellent: *a real badass watch*

bad blood *n* a feeling of intense hatred or hostility; enmity

bad cholesterol *n* a nontechnical name for **low-density lipoprotein**

baddeleyite ('bædlɪˌaɪt) *n* a mineral consisting largely of zirconium dioxide: a source of zirconium. Formula: ZrO₂ [c19 named after J. *Baddeley*, British geologist]

badderlocks ('bædəˌlɒks) *n* a seaweed, *Alaria esculenta*, that has long brownish-green fronds and is eaten in parts of N Europe [c18 of unknown origin]

baddie *or* **baddy** ('bædɪ) *n, pl* **-dies** a bad character in a story, film, etc, esp an opponent of the hero

bade (bæd, beɪd) *or* **bad** *vb* past tense of **bid**

Baden ('baːdən) *n* a former state of West Germany, now part of Baden-Württemberg

Baden-Baden *n* a spa in SW Germany, in Baden-Württemberg. Pop: 53 938 (2003 est)

Baden-Württemberg (*German* 'baːdən'vyrtəmbɛrk) *n* a state of SW Germany; formerly in West Germany. Capital: Stuttgart. Pop: 53 938 (2003 est). Area: 35 742 sq km (13 800 sq miles)

bad faith *n* **1** intention to deceive; treachery or dishonesty (esp in the phrase **in bad faith**) **2** Also called: **mauvaise foi** (in the philosophy of the 20th-century French philosopher Jean-Paul Sartre) self-deception, as when an agent regards his actions as conditioned by circumstances or conventions in order to evade his own responsibility for choosing them freely

badge (bædʒ) *n* **1** a distinguishing emblem or mark worn to signify membership, employment, achievement, etc **2** any revealing feature or mark [c14 from Norman French *bage*; related to Anglo-Latin *bagia*]

badger ('bædʒə) *n* **1** any of various stocky omnivorous musteline mammals of the subfamily *Melinae*, such as *Meles meles* (**Eurasian badger**), occurring in Europe, Asia, and North America: order *Carnivora* (carnivores). They are typically large burrowing animals, with strong claws and a thick coat striped black and white on the head. Compare **ferret badger, hog badger 2** honey badger another name for **ratel** ▷ *vb* **3** (*tr*) to pester or harass [c16 variant of *badgeard*, probably from BADGE (from the white mark on its forehead) + -ARD]

Bad Godesberg (*German* baːt 'goːdəsbɛrk) *n* the official name for **Godesberg**

bad hair day *n informal* **1** a day on which one's hair is untidy and unmanageable **2** a day of mishaps and general irritation

badinage ('bædɪˌnɑːʒ) *n* playful or frivolous repartee or banter [c17 from French, from *badiner* to jest, banter, from Old Provençal *badar* to gape]

badinerie (bəˌdɪnəˈriː) *n music* a name given in the 18th century to a type of quick, light movement in a suite [French: a pleasantry]

badlands ('bædˌlændz) *pl n* any deeply eroded barren area

Bad Lands *pl n* a deeply eroded barren region of SW South Dakota and NW Nebraska

badly ('bædlɪ) *adv* worse, worst **1** poorly; defectively; inadequately: *the chair is badly made* **2** unfavourably; unsuccessfully; unfortunately: *our scheme worked out badly* **3** severely; gravely: *he was badly hurt* **4** incorrectly or inaccurately: *to speak German badly* **5** improperly; naughtily; wickedly: *to behave badly* **6** without humanity; cruelly: *to treat someone badly* **7** very much (esp in the phrases **need badly, badly in need of, want badly**) **8** regretfully: *he felt badly about it* **9 badly off** poor; impoverished ▷ *adj* **10** (*postpositive*) *Northern English dialect* ill; poorly

badman ('bædˌmæn) *n, pl* **-men** *chiefly US* a hired gunman, outlaw, or criminal

badmash (bʌˈmaːʃ) *Hinglish* ▷ *adj* **1** naughty or bad ▷ *n* **2** a hooligan [c21 from Urdu, from Persian *bad* evil + Arabic *ma'āš* livelihood]

badminton ('bædmɪntən) *n* **1** a game played with rackets and a shuttlecock, which is hit back and forth across a high net **2** Also called: **badminton cup** a long refreshing drink of claret with soda water and sugar [c19 named after BADMINTON House, where the game was first played]

Badminton ('bædmɪntən) *n* a village in SW England, in South Gloucestershire unitary authority, Gloucestershire: site of Badminton House, seat of the Duke of Beaufort; annual horse trials

bad-mouth *vb* (*tr*) *slang* to speak unfavourably about

bad news *n slang* someone or something regarded as undesirable: *he's bad news around here*

bad seed *n US, Canadian and Austral informal* a person who is seen as being congenitally disposed to wrongdoing and likely to be a bad influence on others

bad-tempered *adj* angry, irritable, or ungracious

bad trot *n Austral slang* a period of ill fortune

Baedeker ('beɪdɪkə) *n* **1** any of a series of travel guidebooks issued by the German publisher Karl Baedeker (1801–59) or his firm **2** any guidebook

Baedeker raid *n informal* one of the German air raids in 1942 on places of cultural and historical importance in England

bael ('beɪəl) *n* **1** a spiny Indian rutaceous tree, *Aegle marmelos* **2** the edible thick-shelled fruit of this tree [c17 from Hindi *bel*]

BAF *abbreviation for* British Athletic Federation

Bafana bafana (baˈfaːna) *pl n South African* the official name for the South African national soccer team [c20 from Nguni *bafana* the boys]

baffies ('bæfɪz) *pl n Scot dialect* slippers

Baffin Bay ('bæfɪn) *n* part of the Northwest Passage, situated between Baffin Island and Greenland [named after William *Baffin*, 17th-century English navigator]

Baffin Island *n* the largest island of the Canadian Arctic, between Baffin Island and Hudson Bay. Area: 476 560 sq km (184 000 sq miles)

baffle ('bæfᵊl) *vb* (*tr*) **1** to perplex; bewilder; puzzle **2** to frustrate (plans, efforts, etc) **3** to check, restrain, or regulate (the flow of a fluid or the emission of sound or light) **4** to provide with a baffle **5** *obsolete* to cheat or trick ▷ *n* Also called: **baffle board, baffle plate** a plate or mechanical device designed to restrain or regulate the flow of a fluid, the emission of light or sound, or the distribution of sound, esp in a loudspeaker or microphone [c16 perhaps from Scottish dialect *bachlen* to condemn publicly; perhaps related to French *bafouer* to disgrace] > '**bafflement** *n* > '**baffler** *n*

baffling ('bæflɪŋ) *adj* impossible to understand; perplexing; bewildering; puzzling > '**bafflingly** *adv*

BAFTA ('bæftə) *n acronym for* British Academy of Film and Television Arts

bag (bæg) *n* **1** a flexible container with an opening at one end **2** Also called: **bagful** the contents of or amount contained in such a container **3** any of various measures of quantity, such as a bag containing 1 hundredweight of coal **4** a piece of portable luggage **5** short for **handbag 6** anything that hangs loosely, sags, or is shaped like a bag, such as a loose fold of skin under the eyes or the bulging part of a sail **7** any pouch or sac forming part of the body of an animal, esp the udder of a cow **8** *hunting* the quantity of quarry taken in a single hunting trip or by a single hunter **9** *derogatory slang* an ugly or bad-tempered woman or girl (often in the phrase **old bag**) **10** *slang* a measure of marijuana, heroin, etc, in folded paper **11** *slang* a person's particular taste, field of skill, interest, activity, etc: *blues is his bag* **12 bag and baggage** *informal* **a** with all one's belongings **b** entirely **13 a bag of bones** a lean creature **14 in the bag** *slang* almost assured of succeeding or being obtained **15 the (whole) bag of tricks** *informal* every device; everything ▷ *vb* **bags, bagging, bagged 16** (*tr*) to put into a bag **17** to bulge or cause to bulge; swell **18** (*tr*) to capture or kill, as in hunting **19** (*tr*) to catch, seize, or steal **20** (*intr*) to hang loosely; sag **21** (*tr*) to achieve or accomplish: *she bagged seven birdies* **22** (*tr*) *Brit informal* to reserve or secure the right to do or to have something: *he bagged the best chair* **23** (*tr*) *Austral slang* to criticize; disparage. See also **bags** [c13 probably from Old Norse *baggi*; related to Old French *bague* bundle, pack, Medieval Latin *baga* chest, sack, Flemish *bagge*]

Baganda (bəˈgændə, -ˈgɑːn-) *n* (*functioning as plural*) a Negroid people of E Africa living chiefly in Uganda. See also **Ganda, Luganda**

bagasse (bəˈgæs) *n* **1** the pulp remaining after the extraction of juice from sugar cane or similar plants: used as fuel and for making paper, etc **2** Also called: **megass, megasse** a type of paper made from bagasse fibres [c19 from French, from Spanish *bagazo* dregs, refuse, from *baga* husk, from Latin *bāca* berry]

bagassosis (ˌbægəˈsəʊsɪs) *n* an allergic response to the dust of bagasse, causing breathlessness and fever

bagatelle (ˌbægəˈtɛl) *n* **1** something of little value or significance; trifle **2** a board game in which balls are struck into holes, with pins as obstacles; pinball **3** another name for **bar billiards 4** a short light piece of music, esp for piano [c17 from French, from Italian *bagattella*, from (dialect) *bagatta* a little possession, from *baga* a possession, probably from Latin *bāca* berry]

Bagdad (bæg'dæd) *n* a variant spelling of **Baghdad**

bagel *or* **beigel** ('beɪgᵊl) *n* a hard ring-shaped bread roll, characteristic of Jewish baking [c20 from Yiddish *beygel*, ultimately from Old High German *boug* ring]

baggage ('bægɪdʒ) *n* **1 a** suitcases, bags, etc, packed for a journey; luggage **b** *chiefly US and Canadian* (*as modifier*): *baggage car* **2** an army's portable equipment **3** *informal, old-fashioned* **a** a pert young woman **b** an immoral woman or prostitute **4** *Irish informal* a cantankerous old woman **5** *informal* previous knowledge and experience that a person may use or be influenced by in new circumstances: *cultural baggage* [c15 from Old French *bagage*, from *bague* a bundle, perhaps of Scandinavian origin; compare Old Norse *baggi* BAG]

bagging ('bægɪŋ) *n* coarse woven cloth; sacking

baggy¹ ('bægɪ) *adj* **-gier, -giest** (of clothes) hanging loosely; puffed out > '**baggily** *adv* > '**bagginess** *n*

baggy² ('bægɪ) *n, pl* **-gies** a variant spelling of **bagie**

baggy green *n Austral informal* **1** the Australian Test cricket cap **2 don** *or* **wear the baggy green** to represent Australia at Test cricket

bagh (baːg) *n* (in India and Pakistan) a garden [Urdu]

Baghdad *or* **Bagdad** (bæg'dæd) *n* the capital of

Iraq, on the River Tigris: capital of the Abbasid Caliphate (762–1258). Pop: 5 910 000 (2005 est)

bagie ('beɪgɪ) or **baggy** n, pl -gies Northumbrian dialect a turnip [perhaps from RUTABAGA]

bag lady n a woman who is homeless and wanders city streets with all her possessions in shopping bags. Also called (in full): **shopping bag lady**

bagless ('bæglɪs) adj (esp of a vacuum cleaner) not containing a bag

bagman ('bægmən) n, pl -men 1 Brit informal a travelling salesman 2 slang, chiefly US a person who collects or distributes money for racketeers 3 informal, chiefly Canadian a person who solicits money or subscriptions for a political party 4 Austral history a tramp or swagman, esp one on horseback 5 Also called: bagswinger Austral slang someone who takes money for a bookmaker

bag moth n NZ a moth, the larvae of which develop in bags or cases

bagna cauda (ˌbɑːnjə ˈkaʊdə) n a dip made from garlic, anchovies, butter, and olive oil, usually served hot over a spirit burner, with raw vegetables [from Italian bagno caldo, literally: hot bath]

bagnette ('bægnɛt) n a variant of **baguette** (sense 3)

bagnio ('bɑːnjəʊ) n, pl -ios 1 a brothel 2 obsolete an oriental prison for slaves 3 obsolete an Italian or Turkish bathhouse [c16 from Italian bagno, from Latin balneum bath, from Greek balaneion]

bagpipe ('bæg,paɪp) n (modifier) of or relating to the bagpipes: a bagpipe maker

bagpipes ('bæg,paɪps) pl n any of a family of musical wind instruments in which sounds are produced in reed pipes supplied with air from a bag inflated either by the player's mouth, as in the **Irish bagpipes** or **Highland bagpipes** of Scotland, or by arm-operated bellows, as in the **Northumbrian bagpipes**

Bagram ('bægrəm) n an air base in NE Afghanistan, near Kabul; now under the control of US forces

bags (bægz) pl n 1 informal a lot; a great deal 2 short for **Oxford bags** 3 Brit informal any pair of trousers ▷ interj 4 Also: bags I children's slang, Brit and Austral an indication of the desire to do, be, or have something 5 **rough as bags** or **sacks** Austral and NZ uncouth

bagswinger ('bæg,swɪŋə) n Austral slang another term for **bagman**

baguette or **baguet** (bæ'gɛt) n 1 a narrow French stick loaf 2 a small gem cut as a long rectangle 3 the shape of such a gem 4 architect a small moulding having a semicircular cross section [c18 from French, from Italian bacchetta a little stick, from bacchio rod, from Latin baculum walking stick]

Baguio ('bægɪˌəʊ) n a city in the N Philippines, on N Luzon: summer capital of the Republic. Pop: 287 000 (2005 est)

bagwash ('bæg,wɒʃ) n old-fashioned 1 a laundry that washes clothes without drying or pressing them 2 the clothes so washed

bagwig ('bæg,wɪg) n an 18th-century wig with hair pushed back into a bag

bagworm ('bæg,wɜːm) n 1 the larva of moths of the family Psychidae, which forms a protective case of silk covered with grass, leaves, etc 2 bagworm moth any moth of the family Psychidae

bah (bɑː, bæ) interj an expression of contempt or disgust

bahadur (bə'hɑːdə) n (often in combination) a title formerly conferred on the British on distinguished Indians [c18 from Hindi bahādur hero, from Persian: valiant]

Baha'í (bə'hɑːɪ) n 1 an adherent of the Baha'í Faith ▷ adj 2 of or relating to the Baha'í Faith [from Persian bahā'ī, literally: of glory, from bahā' u'llāh glory of God, from Arabic]

Baha'í Faith or **Baha'í** n a religious system founded in 1863 by Baha'ullah, based on Babism

and emphasizing the value of all religions and the spiritual unity of all mankind. Compare **Babism**. ▷ Ba'ha'ist or Ba'ha'ite adj, n

Baha'ísm (ba'hɑːˌɪzəm) n another name, not in Baha'í use, for the **Baha'í Faith**

Bahamas (bə'hɑːməz) or **Bahama Islands** pl n the a group of over 700 coral islands (about 20 of which are inhabited) in the Caribbean: a British colony from 1783 until 1964; an independent nation within the Commonwealth from 1973. Language: English. Currency: Bahamian dollar. Capital: Nassau. Pop: 317 000 (2004 est). Area: 13 939 sq km (5381 sq miles)

Bahamian (bə'heɪmɪən, -'hɑː-) adj 1 of or relating to the Bahamas ▷ n 2 a native or inhabitant of the Bahamas

Bahasa Indonesia (bɑː'hɑːsə) n the official language of Indonesia: developed from the form of Malay formerly widely used as a trade language in SE Asia

Bahawalpur (ˌbæhə'wɒlpə) n an industrial city in Pakistan: cotton, soap. Pop: 563 000 (2005 est)

Bahia (bə'hiːə; Portuguese bəˈiə) n 1 a state of E Brazil, on the Atlantic coast. Capital: Salvador. Pop: 13 323 212 (2002). Area: about 562 000 sq km (217 000 sq miles) 2 the former name of **San Salvador**

Bahía Blanca (Spanish ba'ia 'blanka) n a port in E Argentina. Pop: 276 000 (2005 est)

Bahia de los Cochinos (ba'ia de los ko'tʃinos) n the Spanish name for the **Bay of Pigs**

Bahrain or **Bahrein** (bɑː'reɪn) n an independent sheikhdom on the Persian Gulf, consisting of several islands: under British protection until the declaration of independence in 1971. It has large oil reserves. Language: Arabic. Religion: Muslim. Currency: dinar. Capital: Manama. Pop: 739 000 (2004 est). Area: 678 sq km (262 sq miles)

Bahraini or **Bahreini** (bɑː'reɪnɪ) adj 1 of or relating to Bahrain ▷ n 2 a native or inhabitant of Bahrain

baht (bɑːt) n, pl bahts or baht the standard monetary unit of Thailand, divided into 100 satang [from Thai bāt]

bahuvrihi (ˌbɑːhuː'vriːhiː) n linguistics 1 a class of compound words consisting of two elements the first of which is a specific feature of the second 2 a compound word of this type, such as hunchback, bluebell, highbrow [c19 from Sanskrit bahuvrīhi, itself this type of compound, from bahu much + vrīh rice]

Baikal (baɪ'kɑːl, -'kæl) n **Lake** a lake in Russia, in SE Siberia: the largest freshwater lake in Eurasia and the deepest in the world. Greatest depth: over 1500 m (5000 ft). Area: about 33 670 sq km (13 000 sq miles)

Baikonur (baɪ'kəʊnə) n a launching site for spacecraft in central Kazakhstan; formerly the centre for the Soviet space programme, now leased from Kazakhstan by Russia

bail¹ (beɪl) law ▷ n 1 a sum of money by which a person is bound to take responsibility for the appearance in court of another person or himself or herself, forfeited if the person fails to appear 2 the person or persons so binding themselves; surety 3 the system permitting release of a person from custody where such security has been taken: he was released on bail 4 **jump bail** or (formal) **forfeit bail** to fail to appear in court to answer to a charge 5 **stand** or **go bail** to act as surety (for someone) ▷ vb (tr) 6 (often foll by out) to release or obtain the release of (a person) from custody, security having been made ▷ See also **bail out** [c14 from Old French: custody, from baillier to hand over, from Latin bāiulāre to carry burdens, from bāiulus carrier, of obscure origin]

bail² or **bale** (beɪl) vb (often foll by out) to remove (water) from (a boat) [c13 from Old French baille bucket, from Latin bāiulus carrier] > 'bailer or 'baler n

bail³ (beɪl) n 1 cricket either of two small wooden bars placed across the tops of the stumps to form the wicket 2 agriculture a a partition between

stalls in a stable or barn, for horses b a portable dairy house built on wheels or skids 3 Austral and NZ a framework in a cowshed used to secure the head of a cow during milking ▷ vb 4 See **bail up** [c18 from Old French baile stake, fortification, probably from Latin baculum stick]

bail⁴ or **bale** (beɪl) n 1 the semicircular handle of a kettle, bucket, etc 2 a semicircular support for a canopy 3 a movable bar on a typewriter that holds the paper against the platen [c15 probably of Scandinavian origin; compare Old Norse beygja to bend]

bailable ('beɪləbəl) adj law 1 eligible for release on bail 2 admitting of bail: a bailable offence

bail bond n a document in which a prisoner and one or more sureties guarantee that the prisoner will attend the court hearing of the charges against him if he is released on bail

bail bondsman ('bɒndzmən) n law an individual or firm that lends bail money to defendants awaiting trial

Baile Átha Cliath (blɑː'klɪə) n the Irish Gaelic name for **Dublin**

bailee (beɪ'liː) n contract law a person to whom the possession of goods is transferred under a bailment

bailey ('beɪlɪ) n the outermost wall or court of a castle [c13 from Old French baille enclosed court, from bailler to enclose; see BAIL³]

Bailey bridge n a temporary bridge made of prefabricated steel panels that can be rapidly assembled [c20 named after Sir Donald Coleman Bailey (1901–85), its English designer]

bailie ('beɪlɪ) n 1 (in Scotland) a municipal magistrate 2 an obsolete or dialect spelling of **bailiff** [c13 from Old French bailli, from earlier baillif BAILIFF]

bailiff ('beɪlɪf) n 1 Brit the agent or steward of a landlord or landowner 2 a sheriff's officer who serves writs and summonses, makes arrests, and ensures that the sentences of the court are carried out 3 chiefly Brit (formerly) a high official having judicial powers 4 chiefly US an official having custody of prisoners appearing in court [c13 from Old French baillif, from bail custody; see BAIL¹]

bailiwick ('beɪlɪwɪk) n 1 law the area over which a bailiff has jurisdiction 2 a person's special field of interest, authority, or skill [c15 from BAILIE + WICK²]

bailment ('beɪlmənt) n 1 contract law a contractual delivery of goods in trust to a person for a specific purpose 2 criminal law the act of granting bail

bailor ('beɪlə, beɪ'lɔː) n contract law a person who retains ownership of goods but entrusts possession of them to another under a bailment

bail out or **bale out** vb (adverb) 1 (intr) to make an emergency parachute jump from an aircraft 2 (tr) informal to help (a person, organization, etc) out of a predicament: the government bailed the company out 3 (intr) informal to escape from a predicament

bail up vb (adverb) 1 Austral and NZ informal to confine (a cow) or (of a cow) to be confined by the head in a bail. See **bail³** 2 (tr) Austral history (of a bushranger) to hold under guard in order to rob 3 (intr) Austral to submit to robbery without offering resistance 4 (tr) Austral informal to accost or detain, esp in conversation; buttonhole

Baily ('beɪlɪ) n one of the largest craters on the moon, about 293 kilometres in diameter, lying in the SE quadrant

Baily's beads ('beɪlɪz) pl n the brilliant points of sunlight that appear briefly around the moon, just before and after a total eclipse [c19 named after Francis Baily (died 1844), English astronomer who described them]

báinín or **bawneen** ('bɑːniːn) n Irish 1 a collarless revers-less unlined man's jacket made of white close-woven wool 2 the material for such a jacket 3 báinín skirt a skirt made of this material 4 báinín wool white woollen thread [c20 from Irish Gaelic báinín, diminutive of bán white]

b

bainite ('beɪnaɪt) *n* a mixture of iron and iron carbide found in incompletely hardened steels, produced when austenite is transformed at temperatures between the pearlite and martensite ranges [c20 named after Edgar C. *Bain* (1891–1971), American physicist; see -ITE[1]]

bain-marie (*French* bɛ̃mari) *n, pl* ***bains-marie*** (bɛ̃mari) a vessel for holding hot water, in which sauces and other dishes are gently cooked or kept warm [c19 from French, from Medieval Latin *balneum Mariae*, literally: bath of Mary, inaccurate translation of Medieval Greek *kaminos Marios*, literally: furnace of *Miriam*, alleged author of a treatise on alchemy]

Bairam (baɪ'ræm, 'baɪræm) *n* either of two Muslim festivals, one (**Lesser Bairam**) falling at the end of Ramadan, the other (**Greater Bairam**) 70 days later at the end of the Islamic year [from Turkish *bayrām*]

bairn (bɛən; *Scot* bern) *n Scot and Northern English* a child [Old English *bearn*; related to *bearm* lap, Old Norse, Old High German *barn* child]

Baisakhi (baɪ'sæki:) *n* an annual Sikh festival commemorating the founding (1699) of the Order of the Khalsa by Gobind Singh [from Sanskrit, *Baisakh* (month of the year)]

bait[1] (beɪt) *n* **1** something edible, such as soft bread paste, worms, pieces of meat, etc, fixed to a hook or in a trap to attract fish or animals **2** an enticement; temptation **3** a variant spelling of **bate**[4] **4** *Northern English dialect* food, esp a packed lunch **5** *archaic* a short stop for refreshment during a journey ▷ *vb* **6** (*tr*) to put a piece of food on or in (a hook or trap) **7** (*tr*) to persecute or tease **8** (*tr*) to entice; tempt **9** (*tr*) to set dogs upon (a bear, etc) **10** (*tr*) *archaic* to feed (a horse), esp during a break in a journey **11** (*intr*) *archaic* to stop for rest and refreshment during a journey [c13 from Old Norse *beita* to hunt, persecute; related to Old English *bǣtan* to restrain, hunt, Old High German *beizen*]

> USAGE The phrase *with bated breath* is sometimes wrongly spelled *with baited breath*

bait[2] (beɪt) *vb* a variant spelling of **bate**[2]

baize (beɪz) *n* **1** a woollen fabric resembling felt, usually green, used mainly for the tops of billiard tables ▷ *vb* **2** (*tr*) to line or cover with such fabric [c16 from Old French *baies*, plural of *baie* baize, from *bai* reddish brown, BAY[5], perhaps the original colour of the fabric]

Baja California ('baehɑa) *n* **1** the Spanish name for **Lower California** **2** **Baja California Norte** ('nɔ:teɪ) ▷ *n* a state of NW Mexico, in the N part of the Lower California peninsula. Capital: Mexicali. Pop: 2 487 700 (2000). Area: about 71 500 sq km (27 600 sq miles)

Baja California Norte ('nɔ:teɪ) *n* a state of NW Mexico, in the N part of the Lower California peninsula. Capital: Mexicali. Pop: 2 487 700 (2000). Area: about 71 500 sq km (27 600 sq miles)

Baja California Sur *n* a state of NW Mexico, in the S part of the Lower California peninsula. Capital: La Paz. Pop: 423 516 (2000). Area: 73 475 sq km (28 363 sq miles)

bajada *Spanish* (ba'xada) *n rugby Union* a scrummaging technique, developed in Argentina, in which all eight forwards in a pack drive forward low and hard [c20 from Spanish *bajar* to go down]

Bajan ('beɪdʒən) *Caribbean informal* ▷ *n* **1** a native of Barbados ▷ *adj* **2** of or relating to Barbados or its inhabitants [c20 variant of *Badian*, a shortened form of *Barbadian*]

BAK *text messaging abbreviation for* back at keyboard

bake (beɪk) *vb* **1** (*tr*) to cook by dry heat in or as if in an oven **2** (*intr*) to cook bread, pastry, etc, in an oven **3** to make or become hardened by heat **4** (*intr*) *informal* to be extremely hot, as in the heat of the sun ▷ *n* **5** *US* a party at which the main dish is baked **6** a batch of things baked at one time **7** *Scot* a kind of biscuit **8** *Caribbean* a small flat fried cake [Old English *bacan*; related to Old Norse *baka*, Old High German *bahhan* to bake, Greek *phōgein* to parch, roast]

bakeapple ('beɪk,æpəl) *n Canadian* the fruit of the cloudberry

baked Alaska *n* a dessert consisting of cake and ice cream covered with meringue and cooked very quickly in a hot oven

baked beans *pl n* haricot beans, baked and tinned in tomato sauce

bakehouse ('beɪk,haʊs) *n* another word for **bakery**

Bakelite ('beɪkə,laɪt) *n trademark* any one of a class of thermosetting resins used as electric insulators and for making plastic ware, telephone receivers, etc [c20 named after L. H. *Baekeland* (1863–1944), Belgian-born US inventor; see -ITE[1]]

baker ('beɪkə) *n* **1** a person whose business or employment is to make or sell bread, cakes, etc **2** a portable oven **3** **on the baker's list** *Irish informal* in good health

baker's dozen *n* thirteen [c16 from the bakers' former practice of giving thirteen rolls where twelve were requested, to protect themselves against accusations of giving light weight]

bakery ('beɪkərɪ) *n, pl* **-eries** **1** Also called: **bakehouse** a room or building equipped for baking **2** a shop in which bread, cakes, etc, are sold

Bakewell tart ('beɪkwɛl) *n Brit* an open tart having a pastry base and a layer of jam and filled with almond-flavoured sponge cake [c19 named after *Bakewell*, Derbyshire]

Bakhtaran (,bæktə'rɑ:n, -'ræn) *n* a city in W Iran, in the valley of the Qareh Su: oil refinery. Pop: 832 000 (2005 est). Former name (until 1987): **Kermanshah**

baking ('beɪkɪŋ) *n* **1** **a** the process of cooking bread, cakes, etc **b** (*as modifier*): *a baking dish* **2** the bread, cakes, etc, cooked at one time ▷ *adj* **3** (esp of weather) very hot and dry

baking powder *n* any of various powdered mixtures that contain sodium bicarbonate, starch (usually flour), and one or more slightly acidic compounds, such as cream of tartar: used in baking as a substitute for yeast

bakkie ('bʌki:) *n South African* a small truck with an open body and low sides [c20 from Afrikaans *bak* container]

baklava *or* **baclava** ('bɑ:klə,vɑ:) *n* a rich cake of Middle Eastern origin consisting of thin layers of pastry filled with nuts and honey [from Turkish]

bakra ('bækrə) *Caribbean* ▷ *n, pl* **-ra** *or* **-ras** **1** a White person, esp one from Britain ▷ *adj* **2** (of people) White, esp British [of African origin]

baksheesh *or* **backsheesh** ('bækʃi:ʃ) (in some Eastern countries, esp formerly) *n* **1** money given as a tip, a present, or alms ▷ *vb* **2** to give such money to (a person) [c17 from Persian *bakhshīsh*, from *bakhshīdan* to give; related to Sanskrit *bhaksati* he enjoys]

Baku (*Russian* ba'ku) *or* **Baki** *n* the capital of Azerbaijan, a port on the Caspian Sea: important for its extensive oilfields. Pop: 1 830 000 (2005 est)

BAL *abbreviation for* British anti-lewisite. See **dimercaprol**

Bala ('bælə) *n* **Lake.** a narrow lake in Gwynedd: the largest natural lake in Wales. Length: 6 km (4 miles)

Balaam ('beɪlæm) *n Old Testament* a Mesopotamian diviner who, when summoned to curse the Israelites, prophesied future glories for them instead, after being reproached by his ass (Numbers 22–23)

Balaclava *or* **Balaclava helmet** (,bælə'klɑ:və) *n* (*often not capitals*) a close-fitting woollen hood that covers the ears and neck, as originally worn by soldiers in the Crimean War [c19 named after BALAKLAVA]

Balaklava *or* **Balaclava** (,bælə'klɑ:və; *Russian* bəla'klavə) *n* a small port in Ukraine, in S Crimea: scene of an inconclusive battle (1854), which included the charge of the Light Brigade, during the Crimean War

balalaika (,bælə'laɪkə) *n* a plucked musical instrument, usually having a triangular body and three strings: used chiefly for Russian folk music [c18 from Russian]

balance ('bæləns) *n* **1** a weighing device, generally consisting of a horizontal beam pivoted at its centre, from the ends of which two pans are suspended. The substance to be weighed is placed in one pan and known weights are placed in the other until the beam returns to the horizontal. See also **microbalance** **2** an imagined device for events, actions, motives, etc, in relation to each other (esp in the phrases **weigh in the balance, hang in the balance**) **3** a state of equilibrium **4** something that brings about such a state **5** equilibrium of the body; steadiness: *to lose one's balance* **6** emotional stability; calmness of mind **7** harmony in the parts of a whole: *balance in an artistic composition* **8** the act of weighing factors, quantities, etc, against each other **9** the power to influence or control: *he held the balance of power* **10** something that remains or is left: *let me have the balance of what you owe me* **11** *accounting* **a** equality of debit and credit totals in an account **b** a difference between such totals **12** *chem* the state of a chemical equation in which the number, kind, electrical charges, etc, of the atoms on opposite sides are equal **13** a balancing movement **14** short for **spring balance** **15** **in the balance** in an uncertain or undecided condition **16** **on balance** after weighing up all the factors **17** **strike a balance** to make a compromise ▷ *vb* **18** (*tr*) to weigh in or as if in a balance **19** (*intr*) to be or come into equilibrium **20** (*tr*) to bring into or hold in equilibrium **21** (*tr*) to assess or compare the relative weight, importance, etc, of **22** (*tr*) to act so as to equalize; be equal to **23** (*tr*) to compose or arrange so as to create a state of harmony **24** (*tr*) to bring (a chemical or mathematical equation) into balance **25** (*tr*) *accounting* **a** to compute the credit and debit totals of (an account) in order to determine the difference **b** to equalize the credit and debit totals of (an account) by making certain entries **c** to settle or adjust (an account) by paying any money due **26** (*intr*) (of a business account, balance sheet, etc) to have the debit and credit totals equal **27** to match or counter (one's dancing partner or his or her steps) by moving towards and away from him or her [c13 from Old French, from Vulgar Latin *bilancia* (unattested), from Late Latin *bilanx* having two scalepans, from BI-[1] + *lanx* scale]
> 'balanceable *adj*

Balance ('bæləns) *n* **the** the constellation Libra, the seventh sign of the zodiac

balance bridge *n* another name for **bascule bridge** (see **bascule** (sense1))

balanced ('bælənst) *adj* **1** having weight equally distributed **2** (of a person) mentally and emotionally stable **3** (of a discussion, programme, etc) presenting opposing points of view fairly and without bias **4** (of a diet) consisting of all essential nutrients in suitable form and amounts to maintain health **5** (of a budget) having expenditure no greater than income **6** *electronics* (of signals or circuitry) symmetrically disposed about earth or other reference potential **7** (of a chemical equation) having the correct relative number of moles of reactants and products

balance of nature *n* the stable state in which natural communities of animals and plants exist, maintained by adaptation, competition, and other interactions between members of the community and their nonliving environment

balance of payments *n* the difference over a given time between total payments to foreign nations, arising from imports of goods and services and transfers abroad of capital, interest, grants, etc, and total receipts from foreign nations, arising from exports of goods and services and transfers from abroad of capital, interest, grants, etc

balance of power *n* **1** the distribution of power among countries so that no one nation can seriously threaten the fundamental interests of another **2** any similar distribution of power or influence

balance of trade *n* the difference in value between total exports and total imports of goods. Also called: visible balance Compare **invisible balance**

balance pipe *n* *engineering* a pipe between two points used to equalize pressure

balancer ('bælənsə) *n* **1** a person or thing that balances **2** *entomol* another name for **haltere**

balance sheet *n* a statement that shows the financial position of a business enterprise at a specified date by listing the asset balances and the claims on such assets

balance weight *n* *engineering* a weight used in machines to counterbalance a part, as of a crankshaft. Also called: bobweight

balance wheel *n* a wheel oscillating against the hairspring of a timepiece, thereby regulating its beat

balancing act ('bælənsɪŋ) *n* **1** a circus act in which a performer displays his or her balancing ability **2** a situation requiring careful balancing of opposing groups, views, or activities: *a delicate balancing act between Greek and Turkish interests*

balanitis (,bælə'naɪtɪs) *n* *med* inflammation of the glans penis, usually due to infection [from New Latin *balanus*, from Greek *balanos* acorn + -ITIS]

balas ('bæləs, 'beɪ-) *n* a red variety of spinel, used as a gemstone. Also called: balas ruby [c15 from Old French *balais*, from Arabic *bālakhsh*, from *Badhakhshān*, region in Afghanistan where the gem is found]

balata ('bælətə) *n* **1** a tropical American sapotaceous tree, *Manilkara bidentata*, yielding a latex-like sap **2** a rubber-like gum obtained from this sap: used as a substitute for gutta-percha [from American Spanish, of Carib origin]

Balaton (*Hungarian* 'bɔlɔtɔn) *n* **Lake** a large shallow lake in W Hungary. Area: 689 sq km (266 sq miles)

balboa (bæl'bəʊə) *n* the standard currency unit of Panama, divided into 100 centesimos [named after Vasco Núñez de *Balboa* (?1475–1519), Spanish explorer]

Balboa (bæl'bəʊə; *Spanish* bal'βoa) *n* a port in Panama at the Pacific end of the Panama Canal: the administrative centre of the former Canal Zone. Pop: 2750 (1990)

balbriggan (bæl'brɪgən) *n* **1** a knitted unbleached cotton fabric **2** (*often plural*) underwear made of this [c19 from *Balbriggan*, Ireland, where it was originally made]

balconette (,bælkə'nɛt) *n* a lightly padded bra that is designed to lift and enhance the appearance of a woman's bust

balcony ('bælkənɪ) *n, pl* -nies **1** a platform projecting from the wall of a building with a balustrade or railing along its outer edge, often with access from a door or window **2** a gallery in a theatre or auditorium, above the dress circle **3** *US and Canadian* any circle or gallery in a theatre or auditorium including the dress circle [c17 from Italian *balcone*, probably from Old High German *balko* beam; see BALK] > **balconied** *adj*

bald (bɔːld) *adj* **1** having no hair or fur, esp (of a man) having no hair on all or most of the scalp **2** lacking natural growth **3** plain or blunt: *a bald statement* **4** bare or simple; unadorned **5** Also: baldfaced (of certain birds and other animals) having white markings on the head and face **6** (of a tyre) having a worn tread [c14 *ballede* (literally: having a white spot); related to Danish *bældet*, Greek *phalaros* having a white spot] > **baldish** *adj* > **baldly** *adv* > **baldness** *n*

baldachin, baldaquin ('bɔːldəkɪn) *or*

baldachino (,bɔːldə'kiːnəʊ) *n* **1** a richly ornamented silk and gold brocade **2** a canopy of fabric or stone over an altar, shrine, or throne in a Christian church or carried in Christian religious processions over an object of veneration [Old English *baldekin*, from Italian *baldacchino*, literally: stuff from Baghdad, from *Baldacco* Baghdad, noted for its brocades]

bald cypress *n* another name for **swamp cypress**

bald eagle *n* a large eagle, *Haliaeetus leucocephalus*, of North America, having a white head and tail, a yellow bill, and dark wings and body. It is the US national bird (see also **American eagle**)

Balder ('bɔːldə) *n* *Norse myth* a god, son of Odin and Frigg, noted for his beauty and sweet nature. He was killed by a bough of mistletoe thrown by the blind god Höd, misled by the malicious Loki

balderdash ('bɔːldə,dæʃ) *n* stupid or illogical talk; senseless rubbish [c16 of unknown origin]

baldhead ('bɔːld,hɛd) *n* a person with a bald head

baldheaded (,bɔːld'hɛdɪd) *adj* having a bald head

balding ('bɔːldɪŋ) *adj* somewhat bald or becoming bald

baldmoney ('bɔːld,mʌnɪ) *n* another name for **spignel**

baldpate ('bɔːld,peɪt) *n* **1** a person with a bald head **2** another name for the **American wigeon** (see **wigeon** (sense 2))

baldric ('bɔːldrɪk) *n* a wide silk sash or leather belt worn over the right shoulder to the left hip for carrying a sword, etc [c13 from Old French *baudrei*, of Frankish origin]

baldy ('bɔːldɪ) *informal* ▷ *adj* **1** bald ▷ *n, pl* baldies **2** a bald person

bale[1] (beɪl) *n* **1** a large bundle, esp of a raw or partially processed material, bound by ropes, wires, etc, for storage or transportation: *bale of hay* **2** a large package or carton of goods **3** *US* 500 pounds of cotton **4** a group of turtles **5** *Austral and NZ* See **wool bale** ▷ *vb* **6** to make (hay, etc) into a bale or bales **7** to put (goods) into packages or cartons **8** *Austral and NZ* to pack and compress (wool) into wool bales ▷ See also **bail out** [c14 probably from Old French *bale*, from Old High German *balla* BALL[1]]

bale[2] (beɪl) *n* **1** *archaic* evil; injury **2** woe; suffering; pain [Old English *bealu*; related to Old Norse *böl* evil, Gothic *balwa*, Old High German *balo*]

bale[3] (beɪl) *vb* a variant spelling of **bail**[2]

bale[4] (beɪl) *n* a variant spelling of **bail**[4]

Bâle (bal) *n* the French name for **Basle**

Balearic Islands (,bælɪ'ærɪk) *pl n* a group of islands in the W Mediterranean, consisting of Majorca, Minorca, Ibiza, Formentera, Cabrera, and 11 islets: a province of Spain. Capital: Palma, on Majorca. Pop: 1 071 500 (2003 est). Area: 5012 sq km (1935 sq miles). Spanish name: Baleares (bale'ares)

baleen (bə'liːn) *n* whalebone [c14 from Latin *bālaena* whale; related to Greek *phalaina* whale]

baleen whale *n* another name for **whalebone whale**

balefire ('beɪl,faɪə) *n* *archaic* **1** a bonfire **2** a beacon fire **3** a funeral pyre [c14 *bale*, from Old English *bǣl* pyre; related to Old Norse *bāl* flame, pyre, Sanskrit *bhāla* brightness]

baleful ('beɪlfʊl) *adj* **1** harmful, menacing, or vindictive **2** *archaic* dejected > **'balefully** *adv* > **'balefulness** *n*

baler ('beɪlə) *n* an agricultural machine for making bales of hay, etc. Also called: baling machine

Balfour Declaration ('bælfə) *n* the statement made by British foreign secretary Arthur Balfour (1848–1930) in 1917 of British support for the setting up of a national home for the Jews in Palestine, provided that the rights of "existing non-Jewish communities" in Palestine could be safeguarded

Bali ('bɑːlɪ) *n* an island in Indonesia, east of Java: mountainous, rising over 3000 m (10 000 ft). Capital: Denpasar. Pop: 2 902 200 (1995 est). Area:

5558 sq km (2146 sq miles)

balibuntal (,bælɪ'bʌntəl) *n* **1** closely woven fine straw, used for making hats in the Philippines **2** a hat of this straw [c20 changed from *Baliuag buntal*, from *Baliuag* in the Philippines, where such hats were made]

Balikpapan (,bɑːlɪk'pɑːpɑːn) *n* a city in Indonesia, on the SE coast of Borneo. Pop: 409 023 (2000)

Balinese (,bɑːlɪ'niːz) *adj* **1** of or relating to Bali, its people, or their language ▷ *n* **2** *pl* -nese a native or inhabitant of Bali **3** the language of the people of Bali, belonging to the Malayo-Polynesian family **4** See **Balinese cat**

Balinese cat *n* a breed of cat with medium-length silky hair, a plumed tail, blue eyes, large ears, and a dark mask, tail, and paws

balk *or* **baulk** (bɔːk, bɔːlk) *vb* **1** (*intr*; usually foll by *at*) to stop short, esp suddenly or unexpectedly; jib: *the horse balked at the jump* **2** (*intr*; foll by *at*) to turn away abruptly; recoil: *he balked at the idea of murder* **3** (*tr*) to thwart, check, disappoint, or foil: *he was balked in his plans* **4** (*tr*) to avoid deliberately: *he balked the question* **5** (*tr*) to miss unintentionally ▷ *n* **6** a roughly squared heavy timber beam **7** a timber tie beam of a roof **8** an unploughed ridge to prevent soil erosion or mark a division on common land **9** an obstacle; hindrance; disappointment **10** *baseball* an illegal motion by a pitcher towards the plate or towards the base when there are runners on base, esp without delivering the ball ▷ See also **baulk** [Old English *balca*; related to Old Norse *bálkr* partition, Old High German *balco* beam] > **'balker** *or* **'baulker** *n*

Balkan ('bɔːlkən) *adj* of, denoting, or relating to the Balkan States or their inhabitants, the Balkan Peninsula, or the Balkan Mountains

Balkanize *or* **Balkanise** ('bɔːlkə,naɪz) *vb* **1** (*tr*) to divide (a territory) into small warring states **2** to divide (a group or organization) into small factions > ,Balkani'zation *or* ,Balkani'sation *n* > 'Balka,nized *or* 'Balka,nised *adj*

Balkan Mountains *pl n* a mountain range extending across Bulgaria from the Black Sea to the eastern border. Highest peak: Mount Botev, 2376 m (7793 ft)

Balkan Peninsula *n* a large peninsula in SE Europe, between the Adriatic and Aegean Seas

Balkan States *pl n* the countries of the Balkan Peninsula: the former Yugoslavian Republics, Romania, Bulgaria, Albania, Greece, and the European part of Turkey. Also called: the Balkans

Balkh (bɑːlk) *n* a region of N Afghanistan, corresponding to ancient Bactria. Chief town: Mazar-i-Sharif

Balkhash (*Russian* bal'xaʃ) *n* **Lake** a salt lake in SE Kazakhstan: fed by the Ili River. Area: about 18 000 sq km (7000 sq miles)

balky *or* **baulky** ('bɔːkɪ, 'bɔːlkɪ) *adj* balkier, balkiest *or* baulkier, baulkiest inclined to stop abruptly and unexpectedly: *a balky horse* > 'balkily *or* 'baulkily *adv* > 'balkiness *or* 'baulkiness *n*

ball[1] (bɔːl) *n* **1** a spherical or nearly spherical body or mass: *a ball of wool* **2** a round or roundish body, either solid or hollow, of a size and composition suitable for any of various games, such as football, golf, billiards, etc **3** a ball propelled in a particular way in a sport: *a high ball* **4** any of various rudimentary games with a ball: *to play ball* **5** *cricket* a single delivery of the ball by the bowler to the batsman **6** *baseball* a single delivery of the ball by a pitcher outside certain limits and not swung at by the batter **7 a** a solid nonexplosive projectile for a firearm. Compare **shell** (sense 6) **b** such projectiles collectively **8** any more or less rounded part or protuberance: *the ball of the foot* **9** *slang* a testicle. See **balls 10** *vet science* another word for **bolus 11** *horticulture* the hard mass of roots and earth removed with the rest of the plant during transplanting **12 ball of muscle** *Austral* a very strong, fit, or forceful person **13 have the ball at one's feet** to have the chance of doing something **14 keep the ball rolling** to maintain

b

the progress of a project, plan, etc **15 on the ball** *informal* alert; informed **16 play ball** *informal* to cooperate **17 set** *or* **start the ball rolling** to open or initiate (an action, discussion, movement, etc) **18 the ball is in your court** you are obliged to make the next move ▷ *vb* **19** (*tr*) to make, form, wind, etc, into a ball or balls: *to ball wool* **20** (*intr*) to gather into a ball or balls **21** *taboo slang, chiefly US* to copulate (with) [c13 from Old Norse *böllr*; related to Old High German *balla*, Italian *palla* French *balle*]

USAGE Sense 9 of this word was formerly considered to be taboo, and it was labelled as such in previous editions of *Collins English Dictionary*. However, it has now become acceptable in speech, although some older or more conservative people may object to its use

ball² (bɔːl) *n* **1** a social function for dancing, esp one that is lavish or formal **2** *informal* a very enjoyable time (esp in the phrase **have a ball**) [c17 from French *bal* (n), from Old French *baller* (vb), from Late Latin *ballāre* to dance, from Greek *ballizein*]

ballad ('bæləd) *n* **1** a narrative song with a recurrent refrain **2** a narrative poem in short stanzas of popular origin, originally sung to a repeated tune **3** a slow sentimental song, esp a pop song [c15 from Old French *balade*, from Old Provençal *balada* song accompanying a dance, from *balar* to dance, from Late Latin *ballāre*; see BALL²]

ballade (bæ'lɑːd; *French* balad) *n* **1** *prosody* a verse form consisting of three stanzas and an envoy, all ending with the same line. The first three stanzas commonly have eight or ten lines each and the same rhyme scheme **2** *music* an instrumental composition, esp for piano, based on or intended to evoke a narrative

balladeer (,bælə'dɪə) *n* a singer of ballads
ballad metre *n* the metre of a ballad stanza
balladmonger ('bæləd,mʌŋgə) *n* **1** (formerly) a seller of ballads, esp on broadsheets **2** *derogatory* a writer of mediocre poetry

ballad opera *n* an opera consisting of popular tunes to which appropriate words have been set, interspersed with spoken dialogue

balladry ('bælədrɪ) *n* **1** ballad poetry or songs **2** the art of writing, composing, or performing ballads

ballad stanza *n* a four-line stanza, often used in ballads, in which the second and fourth lines rhyme and have three stresses each and the first and third lines are unrhymed and have four stresses each

ball ammunition *n* live small-arms ammunition
ball and chain *n* **1** (formerly) a heavy iron ball attached to a chain and fastened to a prisoner **2** a heavy restraint **3** *slang* one's wife

ball-and-socket joint *or* **ball joint** *n* **1** a coupling between two rods, tubes, etc, that consists of a spherical part fitting into a spherical socket, allowing free movement within a specific conical volume **2** Also called: **multiaxial joint** *anatomy* a bony joint, such as the hip joint, in which a rounded head fits into a rounded cavity, allowing a wide range of movement

Ballarat ('bælə,ræt, ,bælə'ræt) *n* a town in SE Australia, in S central Victoria: originally the centre of a gold-mining region. Pop: 72 999 (2001). See also **Eureka Stockade**

Ballardian (,bæl'ɑːdɪən) *adj* **1** of James Graham Ballard (born 1930), the British novelist, or his works **2** resembling or suggestive of the conditions described in Ballard's novels and stories, esp dystopian modernity, bleak man-made landscapes, and the psychological effects of technological, social or environmental developments

ballast ('bæləst) *n* **1** any dense heavy material, such as lead or iron pigs, used to stabilize a vessel,

esp one that is not carrying cargo **2** crushed rock, broken stone, etc, used for the foundation of a road or railway track **3** coarse aggregate of sandy gravel, used in making concrete **4** anything that provides stability or weight **5** *electronics* a device for maintaining the current in a circuit ▷ *vb* (*tr*) **6** to give stability or weight to [c16 probably from Low German; related to Old Danish, Old Swedish *barlast*, literally: bare load (without commercial value), from *bar* bare, mere + *last* load, burden]

ball bearing *n* **1** a bearing consisting of a number of hard steel balls rolling between a metal sleeve fitted over the rotating shaft and an outer sleeve held in the bearing housing, so reducing friction between moving parts while providing support for the shaft **2** a metal ball, esp one used in such a bearing

ball boy *or* **ball girl** *n* (esp in tennis) a person who retrieves balls that go out of play

ballbreaker ('bɔːl,breɪkə) *n* *slang* a person, esp a woman, whose character and behaviour may be regarded as threatening a man's sense of power [c20 from BALL¹ (in the sense: testicle) + BREAKER¹]

ball cock *n* a device for regulating the flow of a liquid into a tank, cistern, etc, consisting of a floating ball mounted at one end of an arm and a valve on the other end that opens and closes as the ball falls and rises

ballerina (,bælə'riːnə) *n* **1** a female ballet dancer **2** *US* the principal female dancer of a ballet company [c18 from Italian, feminine of *ballerino* dancing master, from *ballare* to dance, from Late Latin *ballāre*: see BALL²]

ballet ('bæleɪ, bæ'leɪ) *n* **1 a** a classical style of expressive dancing based on precise conventional steps with gestures and movements of grace and fluidity **b** (*as modifier*): *ballet dancer* **2** a theatrical representation of a story or theme performed to music by ballet dancers **3** a troupe of ballet dancers **4** a piece of music written for a ballet [c17 from French, from Italian *balletto* literally: a little dance, from *ballare* to dance; see BALL²] > **balletic** (bæ'lɛtɪk) *adj*

balletomania (,bælɪtəʊ'meɪnɪə) *n* passionate enthusiasm for ballet [c20 from BALLET + -O- + -MANIA] > **balletomane** ('bælɪtəʊ,meɪn) *n*

ballet-wrap cardigan *n* a cardigan with wrapover fronts which are fastened with wraparound ties

ballflower ('bɔːl,flaʊə) *n* *architect* a carved ornament in the form of a ball enclosed by the three petals of a circular flower

ball game *n* **1** any game played with a ball **2** *US and Canadian* a game of baseball **3** *informal* a situation; state of affairs (esp in the phrase **a whole new ball game**)

ball hockey *n* *Canadian* a game similar to ice hockey, but played on foot on a hard surface without ice, using a hard plastic ball instead of a puck

ballicatter (,bælɪ'kætə) *n* (in Newfoundland) ice that forms along a shore from waves and spray

ballista (bə'lɪstə) *n*, *pl* -**tae** (-tiː) **1** an ancient catapult for hurling stones, etc **2** an ancient form of large crossbow used to propel a spear [c16 from Latin, ultimately from Greek *ballein* to throw]

ballistic (bə'lɪstɪk) *adj* **1** of or relating to ballistics **2** denoting or relating to the flight of projectiles after power has been cut off, moving under their own momentum and the external forces of gravity and air resistance **3** (of a measurement or measuring instrument) depending on a brief impulse or current that causes a movement related to the quantity to be measured: *a ballistic pendulum* **4** **go ballistic** *informal* to become enraged or frenziedly violent **5** (of materials) strong enough to resist damage by projectile weapons: *ballistic nylon* > **bal'listically** *adv*

ballistic galvanometer *n* *physics* a type of galvanometer for measuring surges of current. After deflection the instrument returns slowly to its original reading

ballistic missile *n* a missile that has no wings or fins and that follows a ballistic trajectory when its propulsive power is discontinued

ballistics (bə'lɪstɪks) *n* (*functioning as singular*) the study of the flight dynamics of projectiles, either through the interaction of the forces of propulsion, the aerodynamics of the projectile, atmospheric resistance, and gravity (**exterior ballistics**), or through these forces along with the means of propulsion, and the design of the propelling weapon and projectile (**interior ballistics**)

ballistospore (bə'lɪstə,spɔː) *n* *botany* a spore, esp a fungal spore, that is forcefully ejected from its source

ball joint *n* another name for **ball-and-socket joint**

ball lightning *n* *meteorol* a luminous electrically charged ball occasionally seen during electrical storms

ball mill *n* *engineering* a horizontal cylinder or cone in which a substance, such as a mineral, is ground by rotation with steel or ceramic balls

ballocks ('bɒləks, 'bæl-) *pl n*, *interj*, *vb* a variant spelling of **bollocks**

ball of fire *n* *informal* a very lively person

ballon d'essai (bæ'lɔ̃ dɛ'seɪ) *n*, *pl* **ballons d'essai** (bæ'lɔ̃ dɛ'seɪ) a project or policy put forward experimentally to gauge reactions to it. Compare **trial balloon** [c19 from French, literally: trial balloon]

ballonet (,bælə'nɛt) *n* an air or gas compartment in a balloon or nonrigid airship, used to control buoyancy and shape [c20 from French *ballonnet* a little BALLOON]

balloon (bə'luːn) *n* **1** an inflatable rubber bag of various sizes, shapes, and colours: usually used as a plaything or party decoration **2** a large impermeable bag inflated with a lighter-than-air gas, designed to rise and float in the atmosphere. It may have a basket or gondola for carrying passengers, etc. See also **barrage balloon, hot-air balloon 3** a circular or elliptical figure containing the words or thoughts of a character in a cartoon **4** *Brit* **a** a kick or stroke that propels a ball high into the air **b** (*as modifier*): *a balloon shot* **5** *chem* a round-bottomed flask **6** a large rounded brandy glass **7** *commerce* **a** a large sum paid as an irregular instalment of a loan repayment **b** (*as modifier*): *a balloon loan* **8** *surgery* **a** an inflatable plastic tube used for dilating obstructed blood vessels or parts of the alimentary canal **b** (*as modifier*): *balloon angioplasty* **9 go down like a lead balloon** *informal* to be completely unsuccessful or unpopular **10 when the balloon goes up** *informal* when the trouble or action begins ▷ *vb* **11** (*intr*) to go up or fly in a balloon **12** (*intr*) to increase or expand significantly and rapidly: *losses ballooned to £278 million* **13** to inflate or be inflated; distend; swell: *the wind ballooned the sails* **14** (*tr*) *Brit* to propel (a ball) high into the air [c16 (in the sense: ball, ball game): from Italian dialect *ballone*, from *balla*, of Germanic origin; compare Old High German *balla* BALL¹] > **bal'looning** *n* > **bal'loonist** *n* > **bal'loon-,like** *adj*

balloon loan *n* a loan in respect of which interest and capital are paid off in instalments at irregular intervals

balloon payment *n* a large payment that concludes a series of smaller payments, for example in order to repay a loan

balloon sail *n* *nautical* a large light bellying sail used in light winds. Compare **spinnaker**

balloon sleeve *n* a sleeve fitting tightly from wrist to elbow and becoming fully rounded from elbow to shoulder

balloon tyre *n* a pneumatic tyre containing air at a relatively low pressure and having a wide tread

balloon vine *n* a tropical tendril-climbing sapindaceous plant, *Cardiospermum halicacabum*, cultivated for its ornamental balloon-like seed capsules

ballot ('bælət) *n* **1** the democratic practice of selecting a representative, a course of action, or deciding some other choice by submitting the options to a vote of all qualified persons **2** an instance of voting, usually in secret using ballot papers or a voting machine **3** the paper on which a vote is recorded **4** a list of candidates standing for office **5** the number of votes cast in an election **6** a random selection of successful applicants for something in which the demand exceeds the supply, esp for shares in an oversubscribed new issue **7** *NZ* the allocation by ballot of farming land among eligible candidates, such as ex-servicemen **8** *NZ* a low-interest housing loan allocated by building societies by drawing lots among its eligible members ▷ *vb* -lots, -loting, -loted **9** to vote or elicit a vote from: *we balloted the members on this issue* **10** (*tr*; usually foll by *for*) to select (officials, etc) by lot or ballot or to select (successful applicants) at random **11** (*tr*; often foll by *for*) to vote or decide (on an issue, etc) [c16 from Italian *ballotta*, literally: a little ball, from *balla* BALL¹]

ballot box *n* a box into which ballot papers are dropped after voting

ballotini (ˌbælə'ti:nɪ) *pl n* small glass beads used in reflective paints [c20 from Italian *ballottini* small balls]

ballot paper *n* a paper used for voting in a ballot, esp (in a parliamentary or local government election) one having the names of the candidates printed on it

ballottement (bə'lɒtmənt) *n med* a technique of feeling for a movable object in the body, esp confirmation of pregnancy by feeling the rebound of the fetus following a quick digital tap on the wall of the uterus [c19 from French, literally: a tossing, shaking, from *ballotter* to toss, from *ballotte* a little ball, from Italian *ballotta*; see BALLOT]

ballpark ('bɔ:lˌpɑ:k) *n* **1** *US and Canadian* a stadium used for baseball games **2** *informal* **a** approximate range: *in the right ballpark* **b** (*as modifier*): *a ballpark figure* **3** *informal* a situation; state of affairs: *it's a whole new ballpark for him*

ball-peen hammer *n* a hammer that has one end of its head shaped in a hemisphere for beating metal, etc

ballplayer ('bɔ:lˌpleɪə) *n* **1** a player, esp in soccer, with outstanding ability to control the ball **2** *US and Canadian* a baseball player, esp a professional

ballpoint, ballpoint pen ('bɔ:lˌpɔɪnt) *or* **ball pen** *n* a pen having a small ball bearing as a writing point. Also called (Brit): Biro

ball race *n engineering* **1** a ball bearing **2** one of the metal rings having a circular track within which the balls of the bearing roll

ballroom ('bɔ:lˌru:m, -ˌrʊm) *n* a large hall for dancing

ballroom dancing *n* social dancing, popular since the beginning of the 20th century, to dances in conventional rhythms (**ballroom dances**) such as the foxtrot and the quickstep

balls (bɔ:lz) *slang* ▷ *pl n* **1** the testicles **2** by the balls so as to be rendered powerless **3** nonsense; rubbish **4** courage; forcefulness ▷ *interj* **5** an exclamation of strong disagreement, contempt, annoyance, etc

USAGE Both its anatomical senses and its various extended senses nowadays have far less impact than they used to, and seen unlikely to cause offence, though some older or more conservative people may object. Interestingly, its use in the sense of courage is exactly paralleled in the Spanish term «cojones»

balls-up *or US* **ballup** ('bɔ:lʌp) *slang* ▷ *n* **1** something botched or muddled ▷ *vb* **balls up** *or US* **ball up 2** (*tr, adverb*) to muddle or botch

ballsy ('bɔ:lzɪ) *adj slang* courageous and spirited [c20 from BALLS meaning courage, forcefulness]

ball tearer *n Austral slang* something exceptional in its class, for good or bad qualities

ball valve *n* a one-way valve consisting of a metal ball with a cylindrical hole fitting into a concave seat over an opening

bally¹ ('bælɪ) *adj, adv* (intensifier) *Brit slang* a euphemistic word for **bloody** (sense 6)

bally² ('bælɪ) *n Northern English dialect* a thumb

ballyhoo (ˌbælɪ'hu:) *n informal* **1** a noisy, confused, or nonsensical situation or uproar **2** sensational or blatant advertising or publicity ▷ *vb* -hoos, -hooing, -hooed **3** (*tr*) *chiefly US* to advertise or publicize by sensational or blatant methods [c19 of uncertain origin]

Ballymena (ˌbælɪ'mi:nə) *n* a district in central Northern Ireland, in Co Antrim. Pop: 59 516 (2003 est). Area: 634 sq km (247 sq miles)

Ballymoney (ˌbælɪ'mʌnɪ) *n* a district in N Northern Ireland, in Co Antrim. Pop: 27 809 (2003 est). Area: 417 sq km (161 sq miles)

ballyrag ('bælɪˌræg) *vb* -rags, -ragging, -ragged a variant of **bullyrag**

balm (bɑ:m) *n* **1** any of various oily aromatic resinous substances obtained from certain tropical trees and used for healing and soothing. See also **balsam** (sense 1) **2** any plant yielding such a substance, esp the balm of Gilead **3** something comforting or soothing: *soft music is a balm* **4** any aromatic or oily substance used for healing or soothing **5** Also called: **lemon balm** an aromatic Eurasian herbaceous plant, *Melissa officinalis*, having clusters of small fragrant white two-lipped flowers: family *Lamiaceae* (labiates) **6** a pleasant odour [c13 from Old French *basme*, from Latin *balsamum* BALSAM] ▷ **'balm,like** *adj*

balmacaan (ˌbælmə'kɑ:n) *n* a man's knee-length loose flaring overcoat with raglan sleeves [c19 after *Balmacaan*, near Inverness, Scotland]

Balmain bug ('bælmeɪn) *n* a flattish edible Australian shellfish, *Ibacus peronii*, similar to the Moreton Bay bug [named after *Balmain*, a suburb of Sydney, Australia]

Balmer series (German 'balmər) *n* a series of lines in the hydrogen spectrum, discovered by Johann Jakob Balmer (1825–98) in 1885

balm of Gilead *n* **1** any of several trees of the burseraceous genus *Commiphora*, esp *C. opobalsamum* of Africa and W Asia, that yield a fragrant oily resin (see **balm** (sense 1)). Compare **myrrh** (sense 1) **2** the resin exuded by these trees **3** a North American hybrid female poplar tree, *Populus gileadensis* (or *P. candicans*), with broad heart-shaped leaves **4** a fragrant resin obtained from the balsam fir. See also **Canada balsam**

Balmoral¹ (bæl'mɒrəl) *n* (*sometimes not capital*) **1** a laced walking shoe **2** a 19th-century woollen petticoat, worn showing below the skirt **3** Also called: **bluebonnet** a Scottish brimless hat traditionally of dark blue wool with a cockade and plume on one side [c19 named after BALMORAL Castle]

Balmoral² (bæl'mɒrəl) *n* a castle in NE Scotland, in SW Aberdeenshire: a private residence of the British sovereign

Balmung ('bælmʊŋ) *or* **Balmunc** ('bælmʊŋk) *n* (in the *Nibelungenlied*) Siegfried's sword

balmy ('bɑ:mɪ) *adj* balmier, balmiest **1** (of weather) mild and pleasant **2** having the qualities of balm; fragrant or soothing **3** a variant spelling of **barmy** ▷ **'balmily** *adv* ▷ **'balminess** *n*

balneal ('bælnɪəl) *or* **balneary** ('bælnɪərɪ) *adj rare* of or relating to baths or bathing [c17 from Latin *balneum* bath, from Greek *balaneion*]

balneology (ˌbælnɪ'ɒlədʒɪ) *n* the branch of medical science concerned with the therapeutic value of baths, esp those taken with natural mineral waters [c19 from Latin *balneum* bath] ▷ **balneological** (ˌbælnɪə'lɒdʒɪkᵊl) *adj* ▷ **ˌbalne'ologist** *n*

balneotherapy (ˌbælnɪə'θɛrəpɪ) *n* the treatment of disease by bathing, esp to improve limb mobility in arthritic and neuromuscular disorders

baloney *or* **boloney** (bə'ləʊnɪ) *n* **1** *informal* foolish talk; nonsense **2** *chiefly US* another name for **bologna sausage** [c20 changed from *Bologna* (sausage)]

BALPA ('bælpə) *n acronym for* British Airline Pilots' Association

balsa ('bɔ:lsə) *n* **1** a bombacaceous tree, *Ochroma lagopus*, of tropical America **2** Also called: **balsawood** the very light wood of this tree, used for making rafts, etc **3** a light raft [c18 from Spanish: raft]

balsam ('bɔ:lsəm) *n* **1** any of various fragrant oleoresins, such as balm or tolu, obtained from any of several trees and shrubs and used as a base for medicines and perfumes **2** any of various similar substances used as medicinal or ceremonial ointments **3** any of certain aromatic resinous turpentines. See also **Canada balsam 4** any plant yielding balsam **5** Also called: **busy Lizzie** any of several balsaminaceous plants of the genus *Impatiens*, esp *I. balsamina*, cultivated for its brightly coloured flowers **6** anything healing or soothing [c15 from Latin *balsamum*, from Greek *balsamon*, from Hebrew *bāśām* spice] ▷ **balsamic** (bɔ:l'sæmɪk) *adj* ▷ **'balsamy** *adj*

balsam apple *n* an ornamental cucurbitaceous vine, *Momordica balsamina*, of the Old World tropics, with yellow flowers and orange egg-shaped fruits

balsam fir *n* a fir tree, *Abies balsamea*, of NE North America, that yields Canada balsam. Also called: **balsam, Canada balsam**. See also **balm of Gilead**

balsamic vinegar *n* a type of dark-coloured sweet Italian vinegar made from white grapes and aged in wooden barrels over a number of years

balsamiferous (ˌbɔ:lsə'mɪfərəs) *adj* yielding or producing balsam

balsaminaceous (ˌbɔ:lsəmɪ'neɪʃəs) *adj* of, relating to, or belonging to the *Balsaminaceae*, a family of flowering plants, including balsam and touch-me-not, that have irregular flowers and explosive capsules

balsam of Peru *n* an aromatic balsam that is obtained from the tropical South American leguminous tree *Myroxylon pereirae* and is similar to balsam of Tolu. Also called: **Peru balsam**

balsam of Tolu *n* the full name of **tolu**

balsam poplar *n* a poplar tree, *Populus balsamifera*, of NE North America, having resinous buds and broad heart-shaped leaves. See also **tacamahac**

balsam spruce *n* either of two North American coniferous trees of the genus *Picea*, *P. pungens* (the blue spruce) or *P. engelmanni*

Balt (bɔ:lt) *n* a member of any of the Baltic-speaking peoples of the Baltic States

Balthazar¹ ('bælθəˌzɑː, bæl'θæzə) *n* a wine bottle holding the equivalent of sixteen normal bottles (approximately 12 litres) [c20 named after Balthazar (BELSHAZZAR) from his drinking wine at a great feast (Daniel 5:1)]

Balthazar² ('bælθəˌzɑː, bæl'θæzə) *n* one of the Magi, the others being Caspar and Melchior

balti ('bɔ:ltɪ, 'bæltɪ) *n* **a** a spicy Indian dish, stewed until most of the liquid has evaporated, and served in a woklike pot **b** (*as modifier*): *a balti house* [from Urdu *bāltī* pail]

Baltic ('bɔ:ltɪk) *adj* **1** denoting or relating to the Baltic Sea or the Baltic States **2** of, denoting, or characteristic of Baltic as a group of languages **3** *Brit informal* extremely cold ▷ *n* **4** a branch of the Indo-European family of languages consisting of Lithuanian, Latvian, and Old Prussian **5** short for **Baltic Sea** Also called: Baltic Exchange a freight-chartering market in the City of London, which formerly also dealt in some commodities

Baltic Centre for Contemporary Art *n* an arts centre in Gateshead, NE England: formerly a 1950s grain warehouse: used for its present purpose since 2002. It has no permanent collection, but rather hosts a programme of temporary exhibitions and events

b

Baltics ('bɔːltɪks) *pl n* the another name for the **Baltic States**

Baltic Sea *n* a sea in N Europe, connected with the North Sea by the Skagerrak, Kattegat, and Öresund; shallow, with low salinity and small tides

Baltic Shield *n* the wide area of ancient rock in Scandinavia. Also called: **Scandinavian Shield**. See **shield** (sense 7)

Baltic States *pl n* the republics of Estonia, Latvia, and Lithuania, which became constituent republics of the former Soviet Union in 1940, regaining their independence in 1991. Sometimes shortened to: **the Baltics**

Baltimore ('bɔːltɪˌmɔː) *n* a port in N Maryland, on Chesapeake Bay. Pop: Pop: 628 670 (2003 est)

Baltimore oriole *n* a North American oriole, *Icterus galbula*, the male of which has orange and black plumage

Balto-Slavonic or **Balto-Slavic** *n* a hypothetical subfamily of Indo-European languages consisting of Baltic and Slavonic. It is now generally believed that similarities between them result from geographical proximity rather than any special relationship

Baluchi (bəˈluːtʃɪ) or **Balochi** (bəˈləʊtʃɪ) *n* **1** (*pl* -chis *or* -chi) a member of a Muslim people living chiefly in coastal Pakistan and Iran **2** the language of this people, belonging to the West Iranian branch of the Indo-European family ▷ *adj* **3** of or relating to Baluchistan, its inhabitants, or their language

Baluchistan (bəˈluːtʃɪˌstɑːn, -ˌstæn) or **Balochistan** (bəˈlɒtʃɪˌstɑːn, -ˌstæn) *n* **1** a mountainous region of SW Asia, in SW Pakistan and SE Iran **2** a province of SW Pakistan: a former territory of British India (until 1947). Capital: Quetta. Pop: Pop: 7 450 000 (2003 est)

balun ('bælən) *n electronics* a device for coupling two electrical circuit elements, such as an aerial and its feeder cable, where one is balanced and the other is unbalanced [c20 shortened from *bal(ance to) un(balance transformer)*]

baluster ('bæləstə) *n* **1** any of a set of posts supporting a rail or coping ▷ *adj* **2** (of a shape) swelling at the base and rising in a concave curve to a narrow stem or neck: *a baluster goblet stem* [c17 from French *balustre*, from Italian *balaustro* pillar resembling a pomegranate flower, ultimately from Greek *balaustion*]

balustrade ('bæləˌstreɪd) *n* an ornamental rail or coping with its supporting set of balusters [c17 from French, from *balustre* BALUSTER]

Bamako (ˌbæməˈkəʊ) *n* the capital of Mali, in the south, on the River Niger. Pop: 1 379 000 (2005 est)

Bambara (bɑːmˈbɑːrə) *n* **1** a member of a Negroid people of W Africa living chiefly in Mali and by the headwaters of the River Niger in Guinea **2** the language of this people, belonging to the Mande branch of the Niger-Congo family

Bamberg ('bæmbɜːɡ; *German* 'bambɛrk) *n* a town in S Germany, in N Bavaria: seat of independent prince-bishops of the Holy Roman Empire (1007–1802). Pop: 69 899 (2003 est)

bambi ('bæmbɪ) *n acronym for* born-again middle-aged biker: an affluent middle-aged man who rides a powerful motorbike

bambino (bæmˈbiːnəʊ) *n, pl* -nos *or* -ni (-niː) **1** *informal* a young child, esp an Italian one **2** a representation of the infant Jesus [c18 from Italian]

bamboo (bæmˈbuː) *n* **1** any tall treelike tropical or semitropical fast-growing grass of the genus *Bambusa*, having hollow woody-walled stems with ringed joints and edible young shoots (**bamboo shoots**) **2** the stem of any of these plants, used for building, poles, and furniture **3** any of various bamboo-like grasses of the genera *Arundinaria*, *Phyllostachys* or *Dendrocalamus* **4** (*modifier*) made of bamboo: *a bamboo fence* [c16 probably from Malay *bambu*]

bamboo curtain *n* (esp in the 1950s and 1960s) the political and military barrier to communications around the People's Republic of China

bamboo network *n* a network of close-knit Chinese entrepreneurs with large corporate empires in southeast Asia

bamboozle (bæmˈbuːzəl) *vb* (tr) *informal* **1** to cheat; mislead **2** to confuse [c18 of unknown origin] > **bam'boozler** *n* > **bam'boozlement** *n*

ban[1] (bæn) *vb* **bans**, **banning**, **banned** **1** (tr) to prohibit, esp officially, from action, display, entrance, sale, etc; forbid: *to ban a book; to ban smoking* **2** (tr) (formerly in South Africa) to place (a person suspected of illegal political activity) under a government order restricting his movement and his contact with other people **3** *archaic* to curse ▷ *n* **4** an official prohibition or interdiction **5** *law* an official proclamation or public notice, esp of prohibition **6** a public proclamation or edict, esp of outlawry **7** *archaic* public censure or condemnation **8** *archaic* a curse; imprecation [Old English *bannan* to proclaim; compare Old Norse *banna* to forbid, Old High German *bannan* to command]

ban[2] (bæn) *n* (in feudal England) the summoning of vassals to perform their military obligations [c13 from Old French *ban*, of Germanic origin; related to Old High German *ban* command, Old Norse *bann* BAN[1]]

ban[3] (bæn) *n, pl* **bani** ('bɑːnɪ) a monetary unit of Romania and Moldova worth one hundredth of a leu [from Romanian, from Serbo-Croat *bān* lord]

Banaba (bəˈnɑːbə) *n* an island in the SW Pacific, in the Republic of Kiribati. Phosphates were mined by Britain (1900–79). Area: about 5 sq km (2 sq miles). Pop: 284 (1990). Also called: **Ocean Island**

Banaban (bəˈnɑːbən) *adj* **1** of or relating to the SW Pacific island of Banaba ▷ *n* **2** a native or inhabitant of Banaba

banak ('bænæk) *n* **1** a tree of the genus *Virola*, of Central America: family *Myristicaceae* **2** the timber of this tree, used esp in Honduras for turning and construction [c20 Honduran name]

banal (bəˈnɑːl) *adj* lacking force or originality; trite; commonplace [c18 from Old French: relating to compulsory feudal service, hence common to all, commonplace, from *ban* BAN[2]] > **banality** (bəˈnælɪtɪ) *n* > **ba'nally** *adv*

banana (bəˈnɑːnə) *n* **1** any of several tropical and subtropical herbaceous treelike plants of the musaceous genus *Musa*, esp *M. sapientum*, a widely cultivated species propagated from suckers and having hanging clusters of edible fruit **2** the crescent-shaped fruit of any of these plants Compare **plantain**[2] [c16 from Spanish or Portuguese, of African origin]

banana belt *n Canadian informal* a region with a warm climate, esp one in Canada

Banana bender *n Austral slang, offensive* a native or inhabitant of Queensland. Also called: **Bananalander** (bəˈnɑːnəˌlændə)

banana oil *n* **1** a solution of cellulose nitrate in pentyl acetate or a similar solvent, which has a banana-like smell **2** a nontechnical name for **pentyl acetate**

banana plug *n electrical engineering* a small single-conductor electrical plug having a curved metal spring along its shank forming a clip to hold it in its socket

banana prawn *n Austral* a prawn of the genus *Penaeus*, fished commercially in tropical waters of N Australia

banana republic *n informal and derogatory* a small country, esp in Central America, that is politically unstable and has an economy dominated by foreign interest, usually dependent on one export, such as bananas

bananas (bəˈnɑːnəz) *adj slang* crazy (esp in the phrase **go bananas**)

banana skin *n* **1** the soft outer covering of a

banana **2** *informal* something unforeseen that causes an obvious and embarrassing mistake [sense 2 from the common slapstick joke of a person slipping after treading on a banana skin]

banana split *n* a dish of ice cream and banana cut in half lengthwise, usually topped with syrup, nuts, whipped cream, etc

Banaras (bəˈnɑːrəz) *n* a variant spelling of **Benares**

Banat ('bænɪt, 'bɑːnɪt) *n* a fertile plain extending through Hungary, Romania, and Serbia

banausic (bəˈnɔːsɪk) *adj* merely mechanical; materialistic; utilitarian [c19 from Greek *banausikos* for mechanics, from *baunos* forge]

Banbridge ('bænbrɪdʒ) *n* a district in S Northern Ireland, in Co Down. Pop: 43 083 (2003 est). Area: 442 sq km (170 sq miles)

Banbury ('bænbərɪ) *n* a town in central England, in N Oxfordshire: telecommunications, financial services. Pop: 43 867 (2001)

Banbury cake *n Brit* a cake consisting of a pastry base filled with currants, raisins, candied peel, and sugar, with a criss-cross pattern on the top

banc (bæŋk) *n* in banc *law* sitting as a full court [c18 from Anglo-French: bench]

bancassurance ('bæŋkəˌʃʊərəns) *n* the selling of insurance products by a bank to its customers [from French *banc* bank + *assurance* assurance]

bancassurer ('bæŋkəˌʃʊərə) *n* a bank that sells insurance products

banco ('bæŋkəʊ) *interj* a call in gambling games such as chemin de fer and baccarat by a player or bystander who wishes to bet against the entire bank [c18 from French from Italian: bank]

band[1] (bænd) *n* **1** a company of people having a common purpose; group: *a band of outlaws* **2** a group of musicians playing either brass and percussion instruments only (**brass band**) or brass, woodwind, and percussion instruments (**concert band** or **military band**) **3** a group of musicians who play popular music, jazz, etc, often for dancing **4** a group of instrumentalists generally; orchestra **5** *Canadian* a formally recognized group of Canadian Indians on a reserve **6** *anthropol* a division of a tribe; a family group or camp group **7** *US and Canadian* a flock or herd ▷ *vb* **8** (usually foll by *together*) to unite; assemble [c15 from French *bande* probably from Old Provençal *banda* of Germanic origin; compare Gothic *bandwa* sign, BANNER]

band[2] (bænd) *n* **1** a thin flat strip of some material, used esp to encircle objects and hold them together: *a rubber band* **2 a** a strip of fabric or other material used as an ornament, distinguishing mark, or to reinforce clothing **b** (in combination): *waistband; hairband; hatband* **3** a stripe of contrasting colour or texture. See also **chromosome band** **4** a driving belt in machinery **5** a range of values that are close or related in number, degree, or quality **6 a** *physics* a range of frequencies or wavelengths between two limits **b** *radio* such a range allocated to a particular broadcasting station or service **7** short for **energy band** **8** *computing* one or more tracks on a magnetic disk or drum **9** *anatomy* any structure resembling a ribbon or cord that connects, encircles, or binds different parts **10** the cords to which the folded sheets of a book are sewn **11** a thin layer or seam of ore **12** *architect* a strip of flat panelling, such as a fascia or plinth, usually attached to a wall **13** a large white collar, sometimes edged with lace, worn in the 17th century **14** either of a pair of hanging extensions of the collar, forming part of academic, legal, or (formerly) clerical dress **15** a ring for the finger (esp in phrases such as **wedding band**, **band of gold**, etc) ▷ *vb* (tr) **16** to fasten or mark with a band **17** *US and Canadian* to ring (birds). See **ring**[1] (sense 22) [c15 from Old French *bende*, of Germanic origin; compare Old High German *binda* fillet; see BAND[3]]

band[3] (bænd) *n* an archaic word for **bond** (senses

1, 3, 4) [c13 from Old Norse *band*; related to Old High German *bant* fetter; see BEND¹, BOND]

Banda Aceh ('bændə 'aːtʃeɪ) *n* a city in N Indonesia, in N Sumatra; the capital of Aceh region; suffered badly in the Indian Ocean tsunami of December 2004. Pop: 154 767 (2000)

bandage ('bændɪdʒ) *n* **1** a piece of material used to dress a wound, bind a broken limb, etc **2** a strip of any soft material used for binding, etc ▷ *vb* **3** to cover or bind with a bandage [c16 from French, from *band* strip, BAND²]

bandanna or **bandana** (bæn'dænə) *n* a large silk or cotton handkerchief or neckerchief [c18 from Hindi *bāndhnū* tie-dyeing, from *bāndhnā* to tie, from Sanskrit *bandhnāti* he ties]

bandar ('bændaːr) *n Hinglish* **1** a male monkey **2** *informal* an impudent or mischievous man or boy [c21 Hindi]

bandari ('bændaːˌriː) *n Hinglish* **1** a female monkey **2** *informal* an impudent or mischievous girl or woman [c21 Hindi]

Bandar Seri Begawan ('baːndaː 'sɛrɪ bə'gaːwən) *n* the capital of Brunei. Pop: 64 000 (2005 est). Former name: Brunei

Banda Sea *n* a part of the Pacific in Indonesia, between Sulawesi and New Guinea

B & B *abbreviation for* bed and breakfast

bandbox ('bænd,bɒks) *n* a lightweight usually cylindrical box used for holding small articles, esp hats

bandeau ('bændəʊ) *n, pl* -deaux (-dəʊz) a narrow band of ribbon, velvet, etc, worn round the head [c18 from French, from Old French *bandel* a little BAND²]

banderilla (ˌbændə'riːə, -'riːljə) *n bullfighting* a decorated barbed dart, thrust into the bull's neck or shoulder [Spanish, literally: a little banner, from *bandera* banner]

banderillero (ˌbændəri:'ɛərəʊ, -ri:'ljɛərəʊ) *n, pl* -ros a bullfighter's assistant who sticks banderillas into the bull

banderole, banderol ('bændə,rəʊl) or **bannerol** *n* **1** a long narrow flag, usually with forked ends, esp one attached to the masthead of a ship; pennant **2** a square flag draped over a tomb or carried at a funeral **3** a ribbon-like scroll or sculptured band bearing an inscription, found esp in Renaissance architecture **4** a streamer on a knight's lance [c16 from Old French, from Italian *banderuola*, literally: a little banner, from *bandiera* BANNER]

band-gala ('bʌndgələ:) *adj* (in India) (of a coat) closed at the neck [from Hindi]

bandh or **bundh** (bʌnd) *n* (in India) a general strike [Hindi, literally: a tying up]

bandicoot ('bændɪˌkuːt) *n* **1** any agile terrestrial marsupial of the family Peramelidae of Australia and New Guinea. They have a long pointed muzzle and a long tail and feed mainly on small invertebrates **2** bandicoot rat Also called: mole rat any of three burrowing rats of the genera *Bandicota* and *Nesokia*, of S and SE Asia: family Muridae [c18 from Telugu *pandikokku*, from *pandi* pig + *kokku* bandicoot]

banding ('bændɪŋ) *n Brit* the practice of grouping schoolchildren according to ability to ensure a balanced intake at different levels of ability to secondary school

bandit ('bændɪt) *n, pl* -dits or -ditti (-'dɪtɪ) a robber, esp a member of an armed gang; brigand [c16 from Italian *bandito*, literally: banished man, from *bandire* to proscribe, from *bando* edict, BAN¹]
▷ 'banditry *n*

Bandjarmasin or **Bandjermasin** (ˌbændʒə'maːsɪn) *n* variant spellings of **Banjarmasin**

bandmaster ('bænd,maːstə) *n* the conductor of a band

bandobust or **bundobust** ('bʌndəʊbəst) *n* (in India and Pakistan) an arrangement [Hindi *band-o-bast* tying and binding, from Persian]

Band of Hope *n* a society promoting lifelong abstention from alcohol among young people: founded in Britain in 1847

bandolier or **bandoleer** (ˌbændə'lɪə) *n* a soldier's broad shoulder belt having small pockets or loops for cartridges [c16 from Old French *bandouliere*, from Old Spanish *bandolera*, *bandolero* guerrilla, from Catalan *bandoler*, from *bandol* band, from Spanish *bando*; see BAND¹]

bandoline ('bændə,liːn) *n* a glutinous hair dressing, used (esp formerly) to keep the hair in place [c19 *bando-*, from French BANDEAU + -*line*, from Latin *linere* to smear]

bandoneon (bæn'dəʊnɪən) *n* a type of square concertina, esp used in Argentina [c20 from Spanish, from German *Bandonion*, from Heinrich *Band*, its inventor]

bandore (bæn'dɔː, 'bændɔː) *n* a 16th-century plucked musical instrument resembling a lute but larger and fitted with seven pairs of metal strings. Also called: pandore, pandora [c16 from Spanish *bandurria*, from Late Latin *pandūra* three-stringed instrument, from Greek *pandoura*]

band-pass filter *n* **1** *electronics* a filter that transmits only those currents having a frequency lying within specified limits. Compare **high-pass filter, low-pass filter 2** an optical device, consisting of absorbing filters, for transmitting electromagnetic waves of predetermined wavelengths

B and S *n Austral informal* a dance held for young people in country areas, usually in a field or barn [abbreviation for BACHELOR AND SPINSTER]

band saw *n* a power-operated saw consisting of an endless toothed metal band running over and driven by two wheels

bandsman ('bændzmən) *n, pl* -men a player in a musical band, esp a brass or military band

band spectrum *n* a spectrum consisting of a number of bands of closely spaced lines that are associated with emission or absorption of radiation by molecules

bandspreading ('bænd,sprɛdɪŋ) *n* an additional tuning control in some radio receivers whereby a selected narrow band of frequencies can be spread over a wider frequency band, in order to give finer control of tuning

bandstand ('bænd,stænd) *n* a platform for a band, usually out of doors and roofed

band theory *n physics* a theory of the electrical properties of metals, semiconductors, and insulators based on energy bands

Bandung ('bændʊŋ) *n* a city in Indonesia, in SW Java. Pop: 2 136 260 (2000)

B & W *abbreviation for* black and white

bandwagon ('bænd,wægən) *n* **1** US a wagon, usually high and brightly coloured, for carrying the band in a parade **2** jump, climb, or get on the bandwagon to join or give support to a party or movement that seems to be assured of success

bandwidth ('bænd,wɪdθ) *n* **1** the range of frequencies within a given waveband used for a particular transmission **2** the range of frequencies over which a receiver or amplifier should not differ by more than a specified amount **3** the range of frequencies used in a specific telecommunications signal

bandy ('bændɪ) *adj* -dier, -diest **1** Also: bandy-legged having legs curved outwards at the knees **2** (of legs) curved outwards at the knees **3** knock (someone) bandy *Austral informal* to amaze or astound ▷ *vb* -dies, -dying, -died (*tr*) **4** to exchange (words) in a heated or hostile manner **5** to give and receive (blows) **6** (often foll by *about*) to circulate (a name, rumour, etc) **7** to throw or strike to and fro; toss about ▷ *n, pl* -dies **8** an early form of hockey, often played on ice **9** a stick, curved at one end, used in the game of bandy **10** an old form of tennis [c16 probably from Old French *bander* to hit the ball back and forth at tennis]

bandy-bandy ('bændɪ'bændɪ) *n, pl* -bandies a small Australian elapid snake, *Vermicella annulata*, ringed with black and yellow

bandy legs *pl n* another term for **bow legs**

Bandywallop ('bændɪ,wɒləp) *n Austral informal* an imaginary town, far from civilization

bane¹ (beɪn) *n* **1** a person or thing that causes misery or distress (esp in the phrase **bane of one's life**) **2** something that causes death or destruction **3 a** a fatal poison **b** (in combination): *ratsbane* **4** *archaic* ruin or distress [Old English *bana*; related to Old Norse *bani* death, Old High German *bano* destruction, death]

bane² (ben, beɪn) *n* a Scot word for **bone**

baneberry ('beɪnbərɪ) *n, pl* -ries **1** Also called (Brit): herb Christopher, (US) cohosh any ranunculaceous plant of the genus *Actaea*, esp *A. spicata*, which has small white flowers and red or white poisonous berries **2** a berry of any of these plants

baneful ('beɪnfʊl) *adj archaic* destructive, poisonous, or fatal ▷ 'banefully *adv* ▷ 'banefulness *n*

Banff (bæmf) *n* **1** a town in NE Scotland, in Aberdeenshire. Pop: 3991 (2001) **2** a town in Canada, in SW Alberta, in the Rocky Mountains: surrounded by **Banff National Park**. Pop: 7135 (2001)

Banffshire ('bæmfʃɪə, -ʃə) *n* (until 1975) a county of NE Scotland: formerly (1975–96) part of Grampian region, now part of Aberdeenshire

bang¹ (bæŋ) *n* **1** a short loud explosive noise, as of the bursting of a balloon or the report of a gun **2** a hard blow or knock, esp a noisy one; thump: *he gave the ball a bang* **3** *informal* a startling or sudden effect: *he realized with a bang that he was late* **4** *slang* an injection of heroin or other narcotic **5** *taboo slang* an act of sexual intercourse **6** get a bang out of *US and Canadian slang* to experience a thrill or excitement from **7** with a bang successfully: *the party went with a bang* ▷ *vb* **8** to hit or knock, esp with a loud noise; bump: *to bang one's head* **9** to move noisily or clumsily: *to bang about the house* **10** to close (a door, window, etc) or (of a door, etc) be closed noisily; slam **11** (*tr*) to cause to move by hitting vigorously: *he banged the ball over the fence* **12** to make or cause to make a loud noise, as of an explosion **13** (*tr*) *Brit* **a** to cause (stock prices) to fall by rapid selling **b** to sell rapidly in (a stock market), thus causing prices to fall **14** *taboo slang* to have sexual intercourse with **15** (*intr*) *slang* to inject heroin, etc **16** bang for one's buck *informal* value for money: *this option offers more bang for your buck* **17** bang goes *informal* that is the end of: *bang goes my job in Wapping* **18** bang one's head against a brick wall to try to achieve something impossible ▷ *adv* **19** with a sudden impact or effect: *bang went his hopes of winning; the car drove bang into a lamp-post* **20** precisely: *bang in the middle of the road* **21** bang to rights *slang* caught red-handed **22** go bang to burst, shut, etc, with a loud noise. See also **bang up** [c16 from Old Norse *bang*, *banga* hammer; related to Low German *bangen* to beat; all of imitative origin]

bang² (bæŋ) *n* **1** a fringe or section of hair cut straight across the forehead ▷ *vb* (*tr*) **2** to cut (the hair) in such a style **3** to dock (the tail of a horse, etc) [c19 probably short for *bangtail* short tail]

bang³ (bæŋ) *n* a variant spelling of **bhang**

bangalay ('bæŋgələɪ, bæŋ'gælɪ) *n* a myrtaceous Australian tree, *Eucalyptus botryoides*, valued for its hard red wood [from a native Australian language]

Bangalore (ˌbæŋgə'lɔː) *n* a city in S India, capital of Karnataka state: printing, textiles, pharmaceuticals. Pop: 4 292 223 (2001)

bangalore torpedo *n* an explosive device in a long metal tube, used to blow gaps in barbed-wire barriers [c20 named after BANGALORE, where it was developed]

bangalow ('bæŋgələʊ) *n* an Australian palm, *Archontophoenix cunninghamiana*, native to New South Wales and Queensland. Also called: bangalow palm [from a native Australian language]

b

bang-bang *n informal* war and fighting, esp involving ammunition

banger ('bæŋə) *n Brit* **1** *slang* a sausage **2** *informal* **a** an old decrepit car **b** (*as modifier*): *banger racing* **3** a type of firework that explodes loudly

bangin' ('bæŋɪn) *or* **banging** ('bæŋɪn) *adj slang* excellent: *the island boasts a bangin' selection of clubs*

Bangka *or* **Banka** ('bæŋkə) *n* an island in Indonesia, separated from Sumatra by the **Bangka Strait**. Chief town: Pangkalpinang. Area: about 11 914 sq km (4600 sq miles)

Bangkok ('bæŋkɒk, bæŋ'kɒk) *n* the capital and chief port of Thailand, on the Chao Phraya River: became a royal city and the capital in 1782. Pop: 6 604 000 (2005 est). Thai name: **Krung Thep** ('krʊŋ 'teɪp)

Bangla ('bæŋlə) *n* another name for **Bengali** (sense 2)

Bangladesh (,bɑːŋglə'dɛʃ, ,bæŋ-) *n* a republic in S Asia: formerly the Eastern Province of Pakistan; became independent in 1971 after civil war and the defeat of Pakistan by India; consists of the plains and vast deltas of the Ganges and Brahmaputra Rivers; prone to flooding: economy based on jute and jute products (over 70 per cent of world production); a member of the Commonwealth. Language: Bengali. Religion: Muslim. Currency: taka. Capital: Dhaka. Pop: 149 665 000 (2004 est). Area: 142 797 sq km (55 126 sq miles)

Bangladeshi (,bɑːŋglə'dɛʃɪ, ,bæŋ-) *adj* **1** of or relating to Bangladesh ▷ *n* **2** a native or inhabitant of Bangladesh

bangle ('bæŋgəl) *n* **1** a bracelet, usually without a clasp, often worn high up round the arm or sometimes round the ankle **2** a disc or charm hanging from a bracelet, necklace, etc [c19 from Hindi *bangrī*]

bang on *adj, adv Brit informal* **1** with absolute accuracy **2** excellent or excellently ▷ Also (US): **bang up**

Bangor ('bæŋgɔː, -gə) *n* **1** a university town in NW Wales, in Gwynedd, on the Menai Strait. Pop: 15 280 (2001) **2** a town in SE Northern Ireland, in North Down district, Co Down, on Belfast Lough. Pop: 58 388 (2001)

bangtail ('bæŋ,teɪl) *n* **1** a horse's tail cut straight across but not through the bone **2** a horse with a tail cut in this way **3** *marketing* a type of envelope used in direct marketing in which a perforated tail can be used as an order form or response note [c19 from *bangtail* short tail]

bangtail muster *n Austral history* a roundup of cattle to be counted, each one having the hairs on its tail docked as it is counted

Bangui (*French* bāgi) *n* the capital of the Central African Republic, in the south part, on the Ubangi River. Pop: 732 000 (2005 est)

bang up *vb* (*tr, adverb*) *prison slang* to lock up (a prisoner) in his or her cell, esp for the night

Bangweulu (,bæŋwɪ'uːlʊ) *Lake* a shallow lake in NE Zambia, discovered by David Livingstone, who died there in 1873. Area: about 9850 sq km (3800 sq miles), including swamps

bani ('bɑːnɪ) *n* the plural of **ban³**

banian ('bænjən) *n* a variant spelling of **banyan**

banish ('bænɪʃ) *vb* (*tr*) **1** to expel from a place, esp by an official decree as a punishment **2** to drive away: *to banish gloom* [c14 from Old French *banir*, of Germanic origin; compare Old High German *ban* BAN²] > **banishment** *n*

banisters *or* **bannisters** ('bænɪstəz) *pl n* the railing and supporting balusters on a staircase; balustrade [c17 altered from BALUSTER]

Banja Luka (*Serbo-Croat* 'baːnja: ,luːka) *n* a city in NW Bosnia-Herzegovina, on the Vrbas River: scene of battles between the Austrians and Turks in 1527, 1688, and 1737; besieged by Serb forces (1992–95). Pop: 182 000 (2004)

Banjarmasin, Banjermasin, Bandjarmasin *or* **Bandjermasin** (,bændʒə'mɑːsɪn) *n* a port in Indonesia, in SW Borneo. Pop: 527 415 (2000)

banjo ('bændʒəʊ) *n, pl* **-jos** *or* **-joes** **1** a stringed musical instrument with a long neck (usually fretted) and a circular drumlike body overlaid with parchment, plucked with the fingers or a plectrum **2** *slang* any banjo-shaped object, esp a frying pan **3** *Austral and NZ slang* a long-handled shovel with a wide blade **4** (*modifier*) banjo-shaped: *a banjo clock* [c18 variant (US Southern pronunciation) of BANDORE] > **banjoist** *n*

Banjul (bæn'dʒuːl) *n* the capital of The Gambia, a port at the mouth of the Gambia River. Pop: 392 000 (2005 est). Former name (until 1973): Bathurst

bank¹ (bæŋk) *n* **1** an institution offering certain financial services, such as the safekeeping of money, conversion of domestic into and from foreign currencies, lending of money at interest, and acceptance of bills of exchange **2** the building used by such an institution **3** a small container used at home for keeping money **4** the funds held by a gaming house or a banker or dealer in some gambling games **5** (in various games) **a** the stock, as of money, pieces, tokens, etc, on which players may draw **b** the player holding this stock **6** any supply, store, or reserve, for future use: *a data bank; a blood bank* ▷ *vb* **7** (*tr*) to deposit (cash, cheques, etc) in a bank **8** (*intr*) to transact business with a bank **9** (*intr*) to engage in the business of banking **10** (*intr*) to hold the bank in some gambling games ▷ See also **bank on** [c15 probably from Italian *banca* bench, moneychanger's table, of Germanic origin; compare Old High German *banc* BENCH]

bank² (bæŋk) *n* **1** a long raised mass, esp of earth; mound; ridge **2** a slope, as of a hill **3** the sloping side of any hollow in the ground, esp when bordering a river: *the left bank of a river is on a spectator's left looking downstream* **4** **a** an elevated section, rising to near the surface, of the bed of a sea, lake, or river **b** (*in combination*): *sandbank; mudbank* **5** **a** the area around the mouth of the shaft of a mine **b** the face of a body of ore **6** the lateral inclination of an aircraft about its longitudinal axis during a turn **7** Also called: **banking, camber, cant, superelevation** a bend on a road or on a railway, athletics, cycling, or other track having the outside built higher than the inside in order to reduce the effects of centrifugal force on vehicles, runners, etc, rounding it at speed and in some cases to facilitate drainage **8** the cushion of a billiard table ▷ *vb* **9** (when *tr*, often foll by *up*) to form into a bank or mound **10** (*tr*) to border or enclose (a road, etc) with a bank **11** (*tr*, sometimes foll by *up*) to cover (a fire) with ashes, fresh fuel, etc, so that it will burn slowly **12** to cause (an aircraft) to tip laterally about its longitudinal axis or (of an aircraft) to tip in this way, esp while turning **13** to travel round a bank, esp at high speed **14** (*tr*) *billiards* to drive (a ball) into the cushion [c12 of Scandinavian origin; compare Old Icelandic *bakki* hill, Old Danish *banke*, Swedish *backe*]

bank³ (bæŋk) *n* **1** an arrangement of objects, esp similar objects, in a row or in tiers: *a bank of dials* **2** **a** a tier of oars in a galley **b** a bench for the rowers in a galley **3** a grade of lightweight writing and printing paper used for airmail letters, etc **4** *telephony* (in automatic switching) an assembly of fixed electrical contacts forming a rigid unit in a selector or similar device ▷ *vb* **5** (*tr*) to arrange in a bank [c17 from Old French *banc* bench, of Germanic origin; see BANK¹]

Banka ('bæŋkə) *n* a variant spelling of **Bangka**

bankable ('bæŋkəbəl) *adj* **1** appropriate for receipt by a bank **2** dependable or reliable: *a bankable promise* **3** (esp of a star) likely to ensure the financial success of a film > **,banka'bility** *n*

bank acceptance *n* a bill of exchange or draft drawn on and endorsed by a bank. Also called: **banker's acceptance**

bank account *n* **1** an account created by the deposit of money at a bank by a customer **2** the amount of money credited to a depositor at a bank

bank annuities *pl n* another term for **consols**

bank bill *n* **1** Also called: **bank draft** a bill of exchange drawn by one bank on another **2** Also called: **banker's bill** *US* a banknote

bankbook ('bæŋk,bʊk) *n* a book held by depositors at certain banks, in which the bank enters a record of deposits, withdrawals, and earned interest. Also called: **passbook**

bank clerk *n Brit* an employee of a bank

bank discount *n* interest on a loan deducted from the principal amount when the loan is made and based on the loan's face value

bank draft *n* a cheque drawn by a bank on itself, which is bought by a person to pay a supplier unwilling to accept a normal cheque. Also called: **banker's cheque**

banker¹ ('bæŋkə) *n* **1** a person who owns or is an executive in a bank **2** an official or player in charge of the bank in any of various games, esp gambling games **3** a result that has been forecast identically in a series of entries on a football pool coupon **4** a person or thing that appears certain to win or be successful

banker² ('bæŋkə) *n* **1** a fishing vessel of Newfoundland **2** a fisherman in such a vessel **3** *Austral and NZ informal* a stream almost overflowing its banks (esp in the phrase **run a banker**) **4** Also called: **bank engine** *Brit* a locomotive that is used to help a heavy train up a steep gradient

banker³ ('bæŋkə) *n* **1** a craftsman's workbench **2** a timber board used as a base for mixing building materials

banker's order *n* another name for **standing order** (sense 1)

banket ('bæŋkɪt) *n* a gold-bearing conglomerate found in South Africa [c19 from Dutch: a kind of almond hardbake, alluding to its appearance]

Bank Giro *n* a British giro system operated by clearing banks to enable customers to pay sums of money to others by credit transfer

bank holiday *n* (in Britain) any of several weekdays on which banks are closed by law and which are observed as national holidays

banking¹ ('bæŋkɪŋ) *n* the business engaged in by a bank

banking² ('bæŋkɪŋ) *n* **1** an embankment of a river **2** another word for **bank¹** (sense 7) **3** fishing on a sea bank, esp off the coast of Newfoundland **4** the manoeuvre causing an aircraft to bank

bank manager *n* a person who directs the business of a local branch of a bank

banknote ('bæŋk,nəʊt) *n* a promissory note issued by a central bank, serving as money

Bank of England *n* the central bank of the United Kingdom, which acts as banker to the government and the commercial banks. It is responsible for managing the government's debt and implementing its policy on other monetary matters: established in 1694, nationalized in 1946; in 1997 the government restored the authority to set interest rates to the Bank

bank on *vb* (*intr, preposition*) to expect or rely with confidence on: *you can bank on him always arriving on time*

bank rate *n* another name for **base rate** (sense 2)

bankroll ('bæŋk,rəʊl) *chiefly US and Canadian* ▷ *n* **1** a roll of currency notes **2** the financial resources of a person, organization, etc ▷ *vb* **5** (*tr*) *slang* to provide the capital for; finance

bankroller ('bæŋk,rəʊlə) *n* the person or organization that provides the finance for a project, business, etc

bankrupt ('bæŋkrʌpt, -rəpt) *n* **1** a person adjudged insolvent by a court, his or her property being transferred to a trustee and administered for the benefit of his creditors **2** any person unable to discharge all his or her debts **3** a person whose resources in a certain field are exhausted or nonexistent: *a spiritual bankrupt* ▷ *adj* **4** adjudged insolvent **5** financially ruined **6**

depleted in resources or having completely failed: *spiritually bankrupt* **7** (foll by *of*) *Brit* lacking: *bankrupt of intelligence* ▷ *vb* **8** (*tr*) to make bankrupt [C16 from Old French *banqueroute*, from Old Italian *bancarotta*, from *banca* BANK¹ + *rotta* broken, from Latin *ruptus*, from *rumpere* to break]

bankruptcy (ˈbæŋkrʌptsɪ, -rəptsɪ) *n, pl* **-cies** the state, condition, or quality of being or becoming bankrupt

bankruptcy order *n law* a court order appointing a receiver to manage the property of a debtor or bankrupt. Former name: **receiving order**

banksia (ˈbæŋksɪə) *n* any shrub or tree of the Australian genus *Banksia*, having long leathery evergreen leaves and dense cylindrical heads of flowers that are often red or yellowish: family *Proteaceae*. See also **honeysuckle** (sense 3) [C19 New Latin, named after Sir Joseph Banks (1743–1820), British botanist and explorer]

Banks Island *n* **1** an island of N Canada, in the Northwest Territories: the westernmost island of the Arctic Archipelago. Area: about 67 340 sq km (26 000 sq miles) **2** an island of W Canada, off British Columbia. Length: about 72 km (45 miles)

banksman (ˈbæŋksmən) *n* a crane driver's helper, who signals instructions to the driver for the movement of the crane and its jib

bank statement *n* a statement of transactions in a bank account, esp one of a series sent at regular intervals to the depositor

banlieue (*French* bɑ̃ljø) *n* a suburb of a city

banner (ˈbænə) *n* **1** a long strip of flexible material displaying a slogan, advertisement, etc, esp one suspended between two points **2** a placard or sign carried in a procession or demonstration **3** something that represents a belief or principle: *a commitment to nationalization was the banner of British socialism* **4** the flag of a nation, army, etc, used as a standard or ensign **5** (formerly) the standard of an emperor, knight, etc **6** Also called: **banner headline** a large headline in a newspaper, etc, extending across the page, esp the front page **7** an advertisement, often animated, that extends across the width of a web page **8** a square flag, often charged with the arms of its bearer ▷ *vb* **9** (*tr*) (of a newspaper headline) to display (a story) prominently ▷ *adj* **10** *US* outstandingly successful: *a banner year for orders* [C13 from Old French *baniere*, of Germanic origin; compare Gothic *bandwa* sign; influenced by Medieval Latin *bannum* BAN¹, *bannīre* to BANISH] > ˈ**bannered** *adj*

banner ad *n* **1** a banner advertising a product **2** an advert along the top of a page of a website

banneret (ˈbænərɪt, -əˌrɛt) *n* (in the Middle Ages) **1** Also called: **knight banneret** a knight who was entitled to command other knights and men-at-arms under his own banner **2** a title of knighthood conferred by the king for valour on the battlefield [C14 from Old French *banerete* a small BANNER]

bannerette *or* **banneret** (ˌbænəˈrɛt) *n* a small banner [C13 from Old French *baneret*, from *banere* BANNER]

bannerol (ˈbænəˌrəʊl) *n* a variant of **banderole**

bannisters (ˈbænɪstəz) *pl n* a variant spelling of **banisters**

bannock (ˈbænək) *n* a round flat unsweetened cake originating in Scotland, made from oatmeal or barley and baked on a griddle [Old English *bannuc*; of Celtic origin; compare Gaelic *bannach*, Cornish *banna* a drop, bit; perhaps related to Latin *pānicium*, from *pānis* bread]

Bannockburn (ˈbænəkˌbɜːn) *n* a village in central Scotland, south of Stirling: nearby is the site of a victory (1314) of the Scots, led by Robert the Bruce, over the English. Pop: 7396 (2001)

banns *or* **bans** (bænz) *pl n* **1** the public declaration of an intended marriage, usually formally announced on three successive Sundays in the parish churches of both the betrothed **2** **forbid the banns** to raise an objection to a marriage announced in this way [C14 plural of *bann* proclamation; see BAN¹]

banoffee *or* **banoffi** (bəˈnɒfɪ) *n* a filling for a pie, consisting of toffee and banana [C20 from BAN(ANA) + (T)OFFEE]

banquet (ˈbæŋkwɪt) *n* **1** a lavish and sumptuous meal; feast **2** a ceremonial meal for many people, often followed by speeches ▷ *vb* **-quets, -queting, -queted** **3** (*intr*) to hold or take part in a banquet **4** (*tr*) to entertain or honour (a person) with a banquet [C15 from Old French, from Italian *banchetto*, from *banco* a table, of Germanic origin; see BANK¹] > ˈ**banqueter** *n*

banquette (bæŋˈkɛt) *n* **1** an upholstered bench **2** (formerly) a raised part behind a parapet **3** a footbridge [C17 from French, from Provençal *banqueta*, literally: a little bench, from *banc* bench; see BANK³]

bans (bænz) *pl n* a variant spelling of **banns**

bansela (banˈsɛlə) *n* a variant of **bonsela**

banshee (ˈbænʃiː, bænˈʃiː) *n* (in Irish folklore) a female spirit whose wailing warns of impending death [C18 from Irish Gaelic *bean sídhe*, literally: woman of the fairy mound]

Banstead (ˈbænˌstɛd) *n* a town in S England, in NE Surrey. Pop: 19 332 (2001)

bant (bænt) *n Lancashire dialect* **1** string **2** strength or springiness of material [probably a dialect pronunciation of BAND²]

bantam (ˈbæntəm) *n* **1** any of various very small breeds of domestic fowl **2** a small but aggressive person **3** *boxing* short for **bantamweight** **4** *Canadian* **a** an age level of between 13 and 15 in amateur sport, esp ice hockey **b** (*as modifier*): *bantam hockey* [C18 after *Bantam* village in Java, said to be the original home of this fowl]

bantamweight (ˈbæntəmˌweɪt) *n* **1** **a** a professional boxer weighing 112–118 pounds (51–53.5 kg) **b** an amateur boxer weighing 51–54 kg (112–119 pounds) **c** (*as modifier*): *the bantamweight champion* **2** a wrestler in a similar weight category (usually 115–126 pounds (52–57 kg))

banter (ˈbæntə) *vb* **1** to speak to or tease lightly or jokingly ▷ *n* **2** light, teasing, or joking language or repartee [C17 of unknown origin] > ˈ**banterer** *n*

banting (ˈbæntɪŋ) *n obsolete* slimming by avoiding eating sugar, starch, and fat [C19 named after William *Banting* (1797–1878), London undertaker who popularized this diet]

bantling (ˈbæntlɪŋ) *n archaic, disparaging* a young child; brat [C16 perhaps from German *Bänkling* illegitimate child, from *Bank* bench + -LING¹]

Bantoid (ˈbɑːntɔɪd, ˈbæn-) *adj* denoting or relating to languages, esp in Cameroon and Nigeria, that possess certain Bantu characteristics. See also **Semi-Bantu**

Bantu (ˈbɑːntʊ, ˈbæntuː, bænˈtuː) *n* **1** a group of languages of Africa, including most of the principal languages spoken from the equator to the Cape of Good Hope, but excluding the Khoisan family: now generally regarded as part of the Benue-Congo branch of the Niger-Congo family **2** *pl* **-tu** *or* **-tus** *South African derogatory* a Black speaker of a Bantu language ▷ *adj* **3** denoting, relating to, or belonging to this group of peoples or to any of their languages [C19 from Bantu *Ba-ntu* people]

Bantu beer *n South African* a malted drink made from partly fermented and germinated millet

Bantustan (ˈbɑːntʊˌstɑːn, ˌbæntʊˈstɑːn) *n* (formerly, in South Africa) an area reserved for occupation by a Black African people, with limited self-government; abolished in 1993. Official name: **homeland**

banyan *or* **banian** (ˈbænjən) *n* **1** a moraceous tree, *Ficus benghalensis*, of tropical India and the East Indies, having aerial roots that grow down into the soil forming additional trunks **2** a member of the Hindu merchant caste of N and W India **3** a loose-fitting shirt, jacket, or robe, worn originally in India [C16 from Hindi *baniyā*, from Sanskrit *vānija* merchant]

Banyana banyana (bəˈnjɑːnə bəˈnjɑːnə) *pl n* the South Africa women's national soccer team [C20 from Nguni *banyana* the girls]

banzai (ˈbɑːnzaɪ, bɑːˈnzaɪ) *interj* a patriotic cheer, battle cry, or salutation [Japanese: literally, (may you live for) ten thousand years]

banzai attack *n* a mass attack of troops, without concern for casualties, as practised by the Japanese in World War II

baobab (ˈbeɪəʊˌbæb) *n* a bombacaceous tree, *Adansonia digitata*, native to Africa, that has a very thick trunk, large white flowers, and a gourdlike fruit with an edible pulp called monkey bread. Also called: **bottle tree, monkey bread tree** [C17 probably from a native African word]

Baoding (ˈbaʊˈdɪŋ), **Paoting** *or* **Pao-ting** *n* a city in NE China, in N Hebei province. Pop: 810 000 (2005 est). Former name: **Ch'ing-yüan** *or* **Tsingyuan**

BAOR *abbreviation for* British Army of the Rhine

Baotou (ˈbaʊˈtuː) *or* **Paotow** *n* an industrial city in N China, in the central Inner Mongolia AR on the Yellow River. Pop: 1 367 000 (2005 est)

bap (bæp) *n Brit* a large soft bread roll [C16 of unknown origin]

bapt. *abbreviation for* **1** baptism **2** baptized

baptism (ˈbæpˌtɪzəm) *n* **1** a Christian religious rite consisting of immersion in or sprinkling with water as a sign that the subject is cleansed from sin and constituted as a member of the Church **2** the act of baptizing or of undergoing baptism **3** any similar experience of initiation, regeneration, or dedication > bapˈ**tismal** *adj* > bapˈ**tismally** *adv*

baptism of fire *n* **1** a soldier's first experience of battle **2** any initiating ordeal or experience **3** *Christianity* the penetration of the Holy Ghost into the human spirit to purify, consecrate, and strengthen it, as was believed to have occurred initially at Pentecost

Baptist (ˈbæptɪst) *n* **1** a member of any of various Christian sects that affirm the necessity of baptism (usually of adults and by immersion) following a personal profession of the Christian faith **2** **the Baptist** See **John the Baptist** ▷ *adj* **3** denoting, relating to, or characteristic of any Christian sect that affirms the necessity of baptism following a personal profession of the Christian faith

baptistry *or* **baptistery** (ˈbæptɪstrɪ) *n, pl* **-ries** *or* **-eries** **1** a part of a Christian church in which baptisms are carried out **2** a tank in a Baptist church in which baptisms are carried out

baptize *or* **baptise** (bæpˈtaɪz) *vb* **1** *Christianity* to immerse (a person) in water or sprinkle water on (a person) as part of the rite of baptism **2** (*tr*) to give a name to; christen **3** (*tr*) to cleanse; purify [C13 from Late Latin *baptīzāre*, from Greek *baptizein*, from *baptein* to bathe, dip]

bar¹ (bɑː) *n* **1** a rigid usually straight length of metal, wood, etc, that is longer than it is wide or thick, used esp as a barrier or as a structural or mechanical part: *a bar of a gate* **2** a solid usually rectangular block of any material: *a bar of soap* **3** anything that obstructs or prevents **4** **a** an offshore ridge of sand, mud, or shingle lying near the shore and parallel to it, across the mouth of a river, bay, or harbour, or linking an island to the mainland **b** *US and Canadian* an alluvial deposit in a stream, river, or lake **5** a counter or room where alcoholic drinks are served **6** a counter, room, or establishment where a particular range of goods, food, services, etc, are sold: *a coffee bar; a heel bar* **7** a narrow band or stripe, as of colour or light **8** a heating element in an electric fire **9** (in England) the area in a court of law separating the part reserved for the bench and Queen's Counsel from the area occupied by junior barristers, solicitors, and the general public. See also **Bar** **10** the place in a court of law where the accused stands during his trial: *the prisoner at the bar* **11** a particular court of law **12** *Brit* (in the House of Lords and House of Commons) the boundary where nonmembers wishing to address either House appear and

b

where persons are arraigned **13** a plea showing that a plaintiff has no cause of action, as when the case has already been adjudicated upon or the time allowed for bringing the action has passed **14** anything referred to as an authority or tribunal: *the bar of decency* **15** Also called: **measure music a** a group of beats that is repeated with a consistent rhythm throughout a piece or passage of music. The number of beats in the bar is indicated by the time signature **b** another word for **bar line 16 a** *Brit* insignia added to a decoration indicating a second award **b** *US* a strip of metal worn with uniform, esp to signify rank or as an award for service **17** a variant spelling of **barre 18** *sport* See **crossbar 19** *gymnastics* See **horizontal bar 20 a** part of the metal mouthpiece of a horse's bridle **b** the space between the horse's teeth in which such a part fits **21** either of two horny extensions that project forwards and inwards from the rear of the outer layer of a horse's hoof **22** See **crowbar** and **glazing-bar 23** *lacemaking, needlework* another name for **bride² 24** *heraldry* an ordinary consisting of a horizontal line across a shield, typically narrower than a fesse, and usually appearing in twos or threes **25** *maths* a superscript line ‾ placed over a letter symbol to indicate, for example, a mean value or the complex conjugate of a complex number **26 behind bars** in prison **27 won't** (*or* **wouldn't**) **have a bar of** *Austral and NZ informal* cannot tolerate; dislike ▷ *vb* **bars, barring, barred** (*tr*) **28** to fasten or secure with a bar: *to bar the door* **29** to shut in or out with or as if with barriers: *to bar the entrances* **30** to obstruct; hinder: *the fallen tree barred the road* **31** (usually foll by *from*) to prohibit; forbid: *to bar a couple from meeting* **32** (usually foll by *from*) to keep out; exclude: *to bar a person from membership* **33** to mark with a bar or bars **34** *law* to prevent or halt (an action) by showing that the claimant has no cause **35** to mark off (music) into bars with bar lines ▷ *prep* **36** except for: *the best recital bar last night's* **37 bar none** without exception [c12 from Old French *barre*, from Vulgar Latin *barra* (unattested) bar, rod, of unknown origin]

bar² (bɑː) *n* a cgs unit of pressure equal to 10⁶ dynes per square centimetre. 1 bar is equivalent to 10⁵ newtons per square metre [c20 from Greek *baros* weight]

bar³ (bɑː) *Southwest English dialect* ▷ *n* **1** immunity from being caught or otherwise penalized in a game ▷ *interj* **2** a cry for such immunity [variant of BARLEY²]

Bar (bɑː) *n* **the 1** (in England and elsewhere) barristers collectively **2** *US* the legal profession collectively **3 be called to** *or* **go to the Bar** *Brit* to become a barrister **4 be called within the Bar** *Brit* to be appointed as a Queen's Counsel

BAR *abbreviation for* Browning Automatic Rifle

bar. *abbreviation for* **1** barometer **2** barometric **3** barrel (container or unit of measure) **4** barrister

Bar- (bar, bɑː) *prefix* (before Jewish patronymic names) son of: *Bar-Kochba*

Barabbas (bəˈræbəs) *n New Testament* a condemned robber who was released at the Passover instead of Jesus (Matthew 27:16)

barachois (ˌbærəˈʃwɑː) *n* (in the Atlantic Provinces of Canada) a shallow lagoon formed by a sand bar [French]

baraesthesia *or US* **baresthesia** (ˌbærɪsˈθiːzɪə) *n physiol* the ability to sense pressure [c20 from Greek *baros* weight + AESTHESIA]

Baranof Island (ˈbærənəf) *n* an island off SE Alaska, in the western part of the Alexander Archipelago. Area: 4162 sq km (1607 sq miles)

Bárány test (*German* ˈbɑːranɪ) *n* a test which detects diseases of the semicircular canals of the inner ear, devised by Robert Bárány (1876–1936)

barathea (ˌbærəˈθɪə) *n* a fabric made of silk and wool or cotton and rayon, used esp for coats [c19 of unknown origin]

baraza (baˈraza) *n E African* **1** a place where public

meetings are held **2** a palaver or meeting [c19 from Swahili]

barb¹ (bɑːb) *n* **1** a subsidiary point facing in the opposite direction to the main point of a fish-hook, harpoon, arrow, etc, intended to make extraction difficult **2** any of various pointed parts, as on barbed wire **3** a cutting remark; gibe **4** any of the numerous hairlike filaments that form the vane of a feather **5** a beardlike growth in certain animals **6** a hooked hair or projection on certain fruits **7** any small cyprinid fish of the genus *Barbus* (or *Puntius*) and related genera, such as *B. conchonius* (**rosy barb**) **8** (*usually plural*) any of the small fleshy protuberances beneath the tongue in horses and cattle **9** a white linen cloth forming part of a headdress extending from the chin to the upper chest, originally worn by women in the Middle Ages, now worn by nuns of some orders **10** *obsolete* a beard ▷ *vb* **11** (*tr*) to provide with a barb or barbs [c14 from Old French *barbe* beard, point, from Latin *barba* beard] ▷ **barbed** *adj*

barb² (bɑːb) *n* a breed of horse of North African origin, similar to the Arab but less spirited [c17 from French *barbe*, from Italian *barbero* a Barbary (horse)]

barb³ (bɑːb) *n Austral* a black kelpie (see **kelpie¹**) [c19 named after one that was named *Barb* after a winning racehorse]

BARB (bɑːb) *n* (in Britain) ▷ *acronym for* Broadcasters' Audience Research Board

Barbadian (bɑːˈbeɪdɪən) *adj* **1** of or relating to Barbados or its inhabitants ▷ *n* **2** a native or inhabitant of Barbados

Barbados (bɑːˈbeɪdɒs, -dəʊz, -dɒs) *n* an island in the Caribbean, in the E Lesser Antilles: a British colony from 1628 to 1966, now an independent state within the Commonwealth. Language: English. Currency: Barbados dollar. Capital: Bridgetown. Pop: 271 000 (2004 est.). Area: 430 sq km (166 sq miles)

Barbados earth *n* a diatomaceous marl found in Barbados

barbarian (bɑːˈbɛərɪən) *n* **1** a member of a primitive or uncivilized people **2** a coarse, insensitive, or uncultured person **3** a vicious person ▷ *adj* **4** of an uncivilized culture **5** insensitive, uncultured, or brutal [c16 see BARBAROUS] ▷ **barˈbarianism** *n*

barbaric (bɑːˈbærɪk) *adj* **1** of or characteristic of barbarians **2** primitive or unsophisticated; unrestrained **3** brutal [c15 from Latin *barbaricus* foreign, outlandish; see BARBAROUS] ▷ **barˈbarically** *adv*

barbarism (ˈbɑːbəˌrɪzəm) *n* **1** a brutal, coarse, or ignorant act **2** the condition of being backward, coarse, or ignorant **3** a substandard or erroneously constructed or derived word or expression; solecism **4** any act or object that offends against accepted taste [c16 from Latin *barbarismus* error of speech, from Greek *barbarismos*, from *barbaros* BARBAROUS]

barbarity (bɑːˈbærɪtɪ) *n, pl* **-ties 1** the state or condition of being barbaric or barbarous **2** a brutal or vicious act **3** a crude or unsophisticated quality, style, expression, etc

barbarize *or* **barbarise** (ˈbɑːbəˌraɪz) *vb* **1** to make or become barbarous **2** to use barbarisms in (language) ▷ ˌbarbariˈzation *or* ˌbarbariˈsation *n*

barbarous (ˈbɑːbərəs) *adj* **1** uncivilized; primitive **2** brutal or cruel **3** lacking refinement [c15 via Latin from Greek *barbaros* barbarian, non-Greek, in origin imitative of incomprehensible speech; compare Sanskrit *barbara* stammering, non-Aryan] ▷ ˈbarbarously *adv* ▷ **barbarousness** *n*

Barbary (ˈbɑːbərɪ) *n* a historic name for a region of N Africa extending from W Egypt to the Atlantic and including the **Barbary States** of Tripolitania, Tunisia, Algeria, and Morocco

Barbary ape *n* a tailless macaque, *Macaca sylvana*, that inhabits rocky cliffs and forests in NW Africa and Gibraltar: family *Cercopithecidae*, order *Primates*

Barbary Coast *n* **the** the Mediterranean coast of North Africa: a centre of piracy against European shipping from the 16th to the 19th centuries

barbastelle (ˌbɑːbəˈstɛl) *n* an insectivorous forest bat, *Barbastella barbastellus*, widely distributed across Eurasia, having a wrinkled face and prominent ears: roosts in trees or caves [French: from Italian *barbastello*, from Latin *vespertilio* bat; see PIPISTRELLE]

barbate (ˈbɑːbeɪt) *adj chiefly biology* having tufts of long hairs; bearded [c19 from Latin *barba* a beard]

barbecue (ˈbɑːbɪˌkjuː) *n* **1** a meal cooked out of doors over an open fire **2** an outdoor party or picnic at which barbecued food is served **3** a grill or fireplace used in barbecuing **4** the food so cooked ▷ *vb* **-cues, -cuing, -cued** (*tr*) **5** to cook (meat, fish, etc) on a grill, usually over charcoal and often with a highly seasoned sauce **6** to cook (meat, fish, etc) in a highly seasoned sauce [c17 from American Spanish *barbacoa*, probably from Taino: frame made of sticks]

barbed wire *n* strong wire with sharply pointed barbs at close intervals. Also called (US): **barbwire**

barbed-wire grass *n Austral* an aromatic grass, *Cymbopogon refractus*, with groups of seed heads resembling barbed wire

barbel (ˈbɑːbəl) *n* **1** any of several slender tactile spines or bristles that hang from the jaws of certain fishes, such as the catfish and carp **2** any of several European cyprinid fishes of the genus *Barbus*, esp *B. barbus*, that resemble the carp but have a longer body and pointed snout [c14 from Old French, from Latin *barbus*, from *barba* beard]

barbell (ˈbɑːˌbɛl) *n* a metal rod to which heavy discs are attached at each end for weightlifting exercises

barbellate (ˈbɑːbɪˌleɪt, bɑːˈbɛlɪt, -eɪt) *adj* **1** (of plants or plant organs) covered with barbs, hooks, or bristles **2** (of animals) possessing bristles or barbels [c19 from New Latin *barbellātus*, from *barbella* short stiff hair, from Latin *barbula* a little beard, from *barba* beard]

barber (ˈbɑːbə) *n* **1** a person whose business is cutting men's hair and shaving or trimming beards ▷ *vb* (*tr*) **2** to cut the hair of **3** to shave or trim the beard of [c13 from Old French *barbeor*, from *barbe* beard, from Latin *barba*]

barberry (ˈbɑːbərɪ) *n, pl* **-ries 1** any spiny berberidaceous shrub of the widely distributed genus *Berberis*, esp *B. vulgaris*, having clusters of yellow flowers and orange or red berries: widely cultivated as hedge plants **2** the fruit of any of these plants [c15 from Old French *berberis*, from Arabic *barbāris*]

barbershop (ˈbɑːbəˌʃɒp) *n* **1** now chiefly US the premises of a barber **2** (*modifier*) denoting or characterized by a type of close four-part harmony for male voices, popular in romantic and sentimental songs of the 1920s and 1930s: *a barbershop quartet*

barber's itch *or* **rash** *n* any of various fungal infections of the bearded portion of the neck and face. Technical name: **tinea barbae**

barber's pole *n* a sign outside a barber's shop consisting of a pole painted with red and white spiral stripes

Barberton daisy (ˈbɑːbətən) *n* See **gerbera** [from *Barberton*, a town in Mpumulanga Province, South Africa]

barbet (ˈbɑːbɪt) *n* any small tropical brightly coloured bird of the family *Capitonidae*, having short weak wings and a sharp stout bill with tuftlike feathers at its base: order *Piciformes* (woodpeckers, etc) [c18 from French, ultimately from Latin *barbātus* bearded, BARBATE]

barbette (bɑːˈbɛt) *n* **1** (formerly) an earthen platform inside a parapet, from which heavy guns could fire over the top **2** an armoured cylinder below a turret on a warship that protects the revolving structure and foundation of the turret [c18 from French, diminutive of *barbe* a nun's BARB¹, from a fancied similarity between the earthwork around a cannon and this part of a nun's habit]

barbican (ˈbɑːbɪkən) *n* **1** a walled outwork or tower to protect a gate or drawbridge of a fortification **2** a watchtower projecting from a fortification [c13 from Old French *barbacane*, from Medieval Latin *barbacana*, of unknown origin]

Barbican (ˈbɑːbɪkən) *n* **the.** a building complex in the City of London: includes residential developments and the Barbican Arts Centre (completed 1982) housing concert and exhibition halls, theatres, cinemas, etc

barbicel (ˈbɑːbɪˌsɛl) *n ornithol* any of the minute hooks on the barbules of feathers that interlock with those of adjacent barbules [c19 from New Latin *barbicella*, literally: a small beard, from Latin *barba* beard]

barbie *or* **barby** (ˈbɑːbɪ) *n informal, chiefly Austral* short for **barbecue**

Barbie doll *or* **Barbie** (ˈbɑːbɪ) *n* **1** *trademark* a teenage doll with numerous sets of clothes and accessories **2** *slang, usually derogatory* a superficially attractive but insipid young woman

bar billiards *n* (*functioning as singular*) *Brit* a table game in pubs, etc, in which short cues are used to pocket balls into holes scoring various points and guarded by wooden pegs that incur penalties if they are knocked over

barbitone (ˈbɑːbɪˌtəʊn) *or US* **barbital** (ˈbɑːbɪˌtæl) *n* a long-acting barbiturate used medicinally, usually in the form of the sodium salt, as a sedative or hypnotic [c20 from BARBIT(URIC ACID) + -ONE]

barbiturate (bɑːˈbɪtjʊrɪt, -ˌreɪt) *n* a derivative of barbituric acid, such as phenobarbital, used in medicine as a sedative, hypnotic, or anticonvulsant

barbituric acid (ˌbɑːbɪˈtjʊərɪk) *n* a white crystalline solid used in the preparation of barbiturate drugs. Formula: $C_4H_4N_2O_3$. Systematic name: 2,4,6-trioxypyrimidine Also called: malonylurea [c19 partial translation of German *Barbitursäure*, perhaps from the name *Barbara* + URIC + *Säure* acid]

Barbizon School (ˈbɑːbɪˌzɒn) *n* a group of French painters of landscapes of the 1840s, including Théodore Rousseau, Daubigny, Diaz, Corot, and Millet [c19 from *Barbizon* a village near Paris and a favourite haunt of the painters]

Barbour jacket *or* **Barbour** (ˈbɑːbə) *n trademark* a hard-wearing waterproof waxed jacket

Barbuda (bɑːˈbuːdə) *n* a coral island in the E Caribbean, in the Leeward Islands: part of the independent state of Antigua and Barbuda. Area: 160 sq km (62 sq miles)

barbule (ˈbɑːbjuːl) *n* **1** a very small barb **2** *ornithol* any of the minute hairs that project from a barb and in some feathers interlock by hooks and grooves, forming a flat vane [c19 from Latin *barbula* a little beard, from *barba* beard]

Barca (ˈbɑːkə) *n* the surname of several noted Carthaginian generals, including Hamilcar, Hasdrubal, and Hannibal > ˈBarcan *adj*

barcarole *or* **barcarolle** (ˈbɑːkəˌrəʊl, -ˌrɒl, ˌbɑːkəˈrəʊl) *n* **1** a Venetian boat song in a time of six or twelve quaver beats to the bar **2** an instrumental composition resembling this [c18 from French, from Italian *barcarola*, from *barcaruolo* boatman, from *barca* boat; see BARQUE]

Barce (ˈbɑːtʃe) *or* **Barca** (ˈbarka) *n* the Italian name for **Al Marj**

Barcelona (ˌbɑːsɪˈləʊnə) *n* the chief port of Spain, on the NE Mediterranean coast: seat of the Republican government during the Civil War (1936–39); the commercial capital of Spain. Pop: 1 582 738 (2003 est). Ancient name: Barcino (bɑːˈsiːnəʊ)

BArch *abbreviation for* Bachelor of Architecture

barchan, barkhan, barchane *or* **barkan** (bɑːˈkɑːn) *n* a crescent-shaped shifting sand dune, convex on the windward side and steeper and concave on the leeward

bar chart *n* another name for **bar graph**

bar code *n commerce* a machine-readable arrangement of numbers and parallel lines of different widths printed on a package, which can be electronically scanned at a checkout to register the price of the goods and to activate computer stock-checking and reordering. Also called: Universal Product Code, UPC

Barcoo River (bɑːˈkuː) *n* a river in E central Australia, in SW Queensland: joins with the Thomson River to form Cooper Creek

Barcoo salute *n Austral informal* a movement of the hand to brush flies away from the face

bard¹ (bɑːd) *n* **1 a** (formerly) one of an ancient Celtic order of poets who recited verses about the exploits, often legendary, of their tribes **b** (in modern times) a poet who wins a verse competition at a Welsh eisteddfod **2** *archaic or literary* any poet, esp one who writes lyric or heroic verse or is of national importance [c14 from Scottish Gaelic; related to Welsh *bardd*] > ˈbardic *adj* > ˈbardism *n*

bard² *or* **barde** (bɑːd) *n* **1** a piece of larding bacon or pork fat placed on game or lean meat during roasting to prevent drying out **2** an ornamental caparison for a horse ▷ *vb* (*tr*) **3** to place a bard on [c15 from Old French *barde*, from Old Italian *barda*, from Arabic *barda'ah* packsaddle]

Bard (bɑːd) *n* **the.** an epithet of William Shakespeare (1564–1616), the English dramatist and poet

bar diagram *n* another name for **bar graph**

bardie (ˈbɑːdiː) *n* **1** an edible white wood-boring grub of Australia **2** starve the bardies! *Austral slang* an exclamation of surprise or protest [from a native Australian language]

bardo (ˈbɑːdəʊ) *n* (*often capital*) (in Tibetan Buddhism) the state of the soul between its death and its rebirth [Tibetan *bardo* between two]

bardolatry (bɑːˈdɒlətrɪ) *n facetious* idolatry or excessive admiration of William Shakespeare (1564–1616), the English dramatist and poet

Bardolino (ˌbɑːdəˈliːnəʊ) *n, pl* -nos a light dry red wine produced around Verona in NE Italy

bare¹ (bɛə) *adj* **1** unclothed; exposed: used esp of a part of the body **2** without the natural, conventional, or usual covering or clothing: *a bare tree* **3** lacking appropriate furnishings, etc: *a bare room* **4** unembellished; simple: *the bare facts* **5** (*prenominal*) just sufficient; mere: *he earned the bare minimum* **6** with one's bare hands without a weapon or tool ▷ *vb* **7** (*tr*) to make bare; uncover; reveal [Old English *bær*; compare Old Norse *berr*, Old High German *bar* naked, Old Slavonic *bosŭ* barefoot] > ˈbareness *n*

bare² (bɛə) *vb archaic* a past tense of **bear¹**

bareback (ˈbɛəˌbæk) *or* **barebacked** *adj* ▷ *adv* **1** (of horse-riding) without a saddle **2** *slang* (of sex) without a condom ▷ *vb slang* **3** (*intr*) to practise unprotected sex

barefaced (ˈbɛəˌfeɪst) *adj* **1** unconcealed or shameless: *a barefaced lie* **2** with the face uncovered or shaven > barefacedly (ˈbɛəˌfeɪsɪdlɪ) *adv* > bare facedness *n*

barefoot (ˈbɛəˌfʊt) *or* **barefooted** *adj* ▷ *adv* with the feet uncovered

barefoot doctor *n* (esp in developing countries) a worker trained as a medical auxiliary in a rural area who dispenses medicine, gives first aid, assists at childbirth, etc [c20 translation of Chinese *chijiao yisheng*, officially translated as primary health worker]

barège (French barɛʒ) *n* **1** a light silky gauze fabric made of wool **2** made of such a fabric [c19 named after *Barèges*, France, where it was originally made]

barehanded (ˌbɛəˈhændɪd) *adv, adj* **1** without weapons, tools, etc **2** with hands uncovered

bareheaded (ˌbɛəˈhɛdɪd) *adj, adv* with head uncovered

Bareilly (bəˈreɪlɪ) *n* a city in N India, in N central Uttar Pradesh. Pop: 699 839 (2001)

bare-knuckle *adj* **1** without boxing gloves: *a bare-knuckle fight* **2** aggressive and without reservations: *a bare-knuckle confrontation*

barely (ˈbɛəlɪ) *adv* **1** only just; scarcely: *barely enough for their needs* **2** *informal* nearly: *barely old enough* **3** scantily; poorly: *barely furnished* **4** *archaic* openly

◼ USAGE See at **hardly**

Barents Sea (ˈbærənts) *n* a part of the Arctic Ocean, bounded by Norway, Russia, and the islands of Novaya Zemlya, Spitsbergen, and Franz Josef Land [named after Willem *Barents* (1550–97) Dutch navigator and explorer]

baresark (ˈbɛəˌsɑːk) *n* another word for **berserk** (sense 2) [c19 literally: bare shirt]

barf (bɑːf) *slang* ▷ *vb* (*tr*) **1** to vomit ▷ *n* **2** the act of vomiting **3** the matter ejected in vomiting [c20 probably of imitative origin]

barfly (ˈbɑːˌflaɪ) *n, pl* -flies *informal* a person who frequents bars

bargain (ˈbɑːgɪn) *n* **1** an agreement or contract establishing what each party will give, receive, or perform in a transaction between them **2** something acquired or received in such an agreement **3 a** something bought or offered at a low price: *a bargain at an auction* **b** (*as modifier*): *a bargain price* **4** into *or* (*US*) in the bargain in excess of what has been stipulated; besides **5** make *or* strike a bargain to agree on terms ▷ *vb* **6** (*intr*) to negotiate the terms of an agreement, transaction, etc **7** (*tr*) to exchange, as in a bargain **8** to arrive at (an agreement or settlement) [c14 from Old French *bargaigne*, from *bargaignier* to trade, of Germanic origin; compare Medieval Latin *barcāniāre* to trade, Old English *borgian* to borrow] > ˈbargainer *n* > ˈbargaining *n, adj*

bargain away *vb* (*tr, adverb*) to lose or renounce (freedom, rights, etc) in return for something valueless or of little value

bargain basement *n* part of a shop where goods are sold at reduced prices

bargain bin *n* a container in a shop from which customers can buy goods that may be old or imperfect at greatly reduced prices

bargain for *vb* (*intr, preposition*) to expect; anticipate (a style of behaviour, change in fortune, etc): *he got more than he bargained for*

bargaining agent *n* an organization, usually a trade union, that acts or bargains on behalf of a group of employees in collective bargaining

bargaining level *n* the level within an organizational hierarchy, such as company level, national level, etc, at which collective bargaining takes place

bargaining scope *n* the range of topics within the scope of a particular set of negotiations leading to a collective agreement

bargaining unit *n* a specific group of employees who are covered by the same collective agreement or set of agreements and represented by the same bargaining agent or agents

bargain on *vb* (*intr, preposition*) to rely or depend on (something): *he bargained on her support*

barge (bɑːdʒ) *n* **1** a vessel, usually flat-bottomed and with or without its own power, used for transporting freight, esp on canals **2** a vessel, often decorated, used in pageants, for state occasions, etc **3** *navy* a boat allocated to a flag officer, used esp for ceremonial occasions and often carried on board his flagship **4** *informal and derogatory* any vessel, esp an old or clumsy one **5** *Austral informal* a heavy or cumbersome surfboard ▷ *vb* **6** (*intr; foll by into*) *informal* to bump (into) **7** (*tr*) *informal* to push (someone or one's way) violently **8** (*intr; foll by into or in*) *informal* to interrupt rudely or clumsily: *to barge into a conversation* **9** (*tr*) *sailing* to bear down on (another boat or boats) at the start of a race **10** (*tr*) to transport by barge **11** (*intr*) *informal* to move slowly or clumsily [c13 from Old French, from Medieval Latin *barga*, probably from Late Latin *barca* a small boat; see BARQUE]

b

bargeboard ('bɑːdʒ,bɔːd) *n* a board, often decorated with carved ornaments, placed along the gable end of a roof. Also called: vergeboard

barge couple *n* either of a pair of outside rafters along the gable end of a roof

barge course *n* **1** the overhang of the gable end of a roof **2** a course of bricks laid on edge to form the coping of a wall

bargee (bɑːˈdʒiː) *or US and Canadian* **bargeman** ('bɑːdʒmən) *n*, *pl* bargees *or* bargemen a person employed on or in charge of a barge

bargepole ('bɑːdʒ,pəʊl) *n* **1** a long pole used to propel a barge **2** not touch with a bargepole *informal* to refuse to have anything to do with

bar girl *n* *chiefly US* an attractive girl employed by the management of a bar to befriend male customers and encourage them to buy drinks

bargoon (,bɑːˈguːn) *n* *Canadian slang* a bargain [c20 humorous alteration of BARGAIN]

bar graph *n* a graph consisting of vertical or horizontal bars whose lengths are proportional to amounts or quantities. Also called: bar chart, bar diagram

Bari ('bɑːrɪ) *n* a port in SE Italy, capital of Apulia, on the Adriatic coast. Pop: 316 532 (2001)

bariatric (,bærɪˈætrɪk) *adj* of or relating to the treatment of obesity: *bariatric surgery* [c20 from BARO + IATRIC]

baric[1] ('bεərɪk, 'bærɪk) *adj* of or containing barium

baric[2] ('bærɪk) *adj* of or concerned with weight, esp that of the atmosphere as indicated by barometric pressure

barilla (bəˈrɪlə) *n* **1** an impure mixture of sodium carbonate and sodium sulphate obtained from the ashes of certain plants, such as the saltworts **2** either of two chenopodiaceous plants, *Salsola kali* (or *soda*) or *Halogeton soda*, formerly burned to obtain a form of sodium carbonate. See also **saltwort** [c17 from Spanish *barrilla*, literally: a little bar, from *barra* BAR[1]]

barista (bəˈrɪstə) *n* a person who makes and serves coffee in a coffee bar [c20 Italian: literally, bartender]

barit. *abbreviation for* baritone

barite ('bεəraɪt) *n* *US and Canadian* a colourless or white mineral consisting of barium sulphate in orthorhombic crystalline form, occurring in sedimentary rocks and with sulphide ores: a source of barium. Formula: $BaSO_4$. Also called: barytes, heavy spar [c18 from BAR(IUM) + -ITE[1]]

baritone ('bærɪ,təʊn) *n* **1** the second lowest adult male voice, having a range approximately from G an eleventh below middle C to F a fourth above it **2** a singer with such a voice **3** the second lowest instrument in the families of the saxophone, horn, oboe, etc ▷ *adj* **4** relating to or denoting a baritone: *a baritone part* **5** denoting the second lowest instrument in a family: *the baritone horn* [c17 from Italian *baritono* a deep voice, from Greek *barutonos* deep-sounding, from *barus* heavy, low + *tonos* TONE]

barium ('bεərɪəm) *n* a soft silvery-white metallic element of the alkaline earth group. It is used in bearing alloys and compounds used as pigments. Symbol: Ba; atomic no.: 56; atomic wt.: 137.327; valency: 2; relative density: 3.5; melting pt.: 729°C; boiling pt.: 1805°C [c19 from BAR(YTA) + -IUM]

barium enema *n* an injection into the rectum of a preparation of barium sulphate, which is opaque to X-rays, before X-raying the lower alimentary canal

barium hydroxide *n* a white poisonous crystalline solid, used in the manufacture of organic compounds and in the preparation of beet sugar. Formula: $Ba(OH)_2$. Also called: baryta

barium meal *n* a preparation of barium sulphate, which is opaque to X-rays, swallowed by a patient before X-ray examination of the upper part of the alimentary canal

barium oxide *n* a white or yellowish-white poisonous heavy powder used esp as a dehydrating agent. Formula: BaO. Also called: baryta

barium sulphate *n* a white insoluble fine dense powder, used as a pigment, as a filler for paper, rubber, etc, and in barium meals. Formula: $BaSO_4$. Also called: blanc fixe

barium titanate *n* a crystalline ceramic used in capacitors and piezoelectric devices. Formula: $BaTiO_3$

bark[1] (bɑːk) *n* **1** the loud abrupt usually harsh or gruff cry of a dog or any of certain other animals **2** a similar sound, such as one made by a person, gun, etc **3** his bark is worse than his bite he is bad-tempered but harmless ▷ *vb* **4** (*intr*) (of a dog or any of certain other animals) to make its typical loud abrupt cry **5** (*intr*) (of a person, gun, etc) to make a similar loud harsh sound **6** to say or shout in a brusque, peremptory, or angry tone: *he barked an order* **7** *US informal* to advertise (a show, merchandise, etc) by loudly addressing passers-by **8** bark up the wrong tree *informal* to misdirect one's attention, efforts, etc; be mistaken [Old English *beorcan*; related to Lithuanian *burgěti* to quarrel, growl]

bark[2] (bɑːk) *n* **1** a protective layer of dead corky cells on the outside of the stems of woody plants **2** any of several varieties of this substance that can be used in tanning, dyeing, or in medicine **3** an informal name for **cinchona** ▷ *vb* (*tr*) **4** to scrape or rub off skin, as in an injury **5** to remove the bark or a circle of bark from (a tree or log) **6** to cover or enclose with bark **7** to tan (leather), principally by the tannins in barks [c13 from Old Norse *börkr*; related to Swedish, Danish *bark*, German *Borke*; compare Old Norse *bjòrkr* BIRCH]

bark[3] (bɑːk) *n* a variant spelling (esp US) of **barque**

bark beetle *n* any small beetle of the family *Scolytidae*, which bore tunnels in the bark and wood of trees, causing great damage. They are closely related to the weevils

bark cloth *n* a papery fabric made from the fibrous inner bark of various trees, esp of the moraceous genus *Ficus* and the leguminous genus *Brachystegia*

barkeeper ('bɑː,kiːpə) *n* another name (esp US) for **barman**

barkentine *or* **barkantine** ('bɑːkən,tiːn) *n* *US and Canadian* a sailing ship of three or more masts rigged square on the foremast and fore-and-aft on the others. British spellings: barquentine, barquantine [c17 from BARQUE + (BRIG)ANTINE]

barker[1] ('bɑːkə) *n* **1** an animal or person that barks **2** a person who stands at a show, fair booth, etc, and loudly addresses passers-by to attract customers

barker[2] ('bɑːkə) *n* a person or machine that removes bark from trees or logs or prepares it for tanning

barkhan *or* **barkan** (bɑːˈkɑːn) *n* variant spellings of **barchan**

Barkhausen effect (*German* 'bɑːrkhaʊzᵊn) *n* the phenomenon that ferromagnetic material in an increasing magnetic field becomes magnetized in discrete jumps, discovered by Heinrich Georg Barkhausen (1881–1956)

barking ('bɑːkɪŋ) *slang* ▷ *adj* **1** mad; crazy ▷ *adv* **2** (*intensifier*): *barking mad*

Barking and Dagenham ('bɑːkɪŋ) *n* a borough of E Greater London. Pop: 165 900 (2003 est). Area: 34 sq km (13 sq miles)

barking deer *n* another name for **muntjac**

Barletta (*Italian* barˈletta) *n* a port in SE Italy, in Apulia. Pop: 92 094 (2001)

barley[1] ('bɑːlɪ) *n* **1** any of various erect annual temperate grasses of the genus *Hordeum*, esp *H. vulgare*, that have short leaves and dense bristly flower spikes and are widely cultivated for grain and forage **2** the grain of any of these grasses, used in making beer and whisky and for soups, puddings, etc. See also **pearl barley** [Old English *bærlic* (adj); related to *bere* barley, Old Norse *barr* barley, Gothic *barizeins* of barley, Latin *farīna* flour]

barley[2] ('bɑːlɪ) *sentence substitute dialect* a cry for truce or respite from the rules of a game [c18 probably changed from PARLEY]

barleycorn ('bɑːlɪ,kɔːn) *n* **1** a grain of barley, or barley itself **2** an obsolete unit of length equal to one third of an inch

barley sandwich *n* *US and Canadian informal* a drink of beer, esp at lunch time

barley sugar *n* a brittle clear amber-coloured sweet made by boiling sugar, originally with a barley extract

barley water *n* a drink made from an infusion of barley, usually flavoured with lemon or orange

barley wine *n* *Brit* an exceptionally strong beer

bar line *or* **bar** *n* *music* the vertical line marking the boundary between one bar and the next

barm (bɑːm) *n* **1** the yeasty froth on fermenting malt liquors **2** an archaic or dialect word for **yeast** [Old English *beorm*; related to *beran* to BEAR, Old Norse *barmr* barm, Gothic *barms*, Old High German *barm* see FERMENT]

barmaid ('bɑː,meɪd) *n* a woman who serves in a pub

barman ('bɑːmən) *n*, *pl* -men a man who serves in a pub

barmbrack ('bɑːm,bræk) *n* *Irish* a loaf of bread with currants in it. Also: barnbrack Often shortened to: brack [from Irish Gaelic *bairín breac* speckled loaf]

barm cake *n* *Lancashire dialect* a round flat soft bread roll

Barmecide ('bɑːmɪ,saɪd) *or* **Barmecidal** *adj* lavish or plentiful in imagination only; illusory; sham: *a Barmecide feast* [c18 from the name of a prince in *The Arabian Nights* who served empty plates to beggars, alleging that they held sumptuous food]

Bar Mitzvah (bɑː ˈmɪtsvə) (*sometimes not capitals*) *Judaism* ▷ *adj* **1** (of a Jewish boy) having assumed full religious obligations, being at least thirteen years of age ▷ *n* **2** the occasion, ceremony, or celebration of that event **3** the boy himself on that day [Hebrew: son of the law]

barmy ('bɑːmɪ) *adj* -mier, -miest *slang* insane. Also: balmy [c16 originally, full of BARM, hence frothing, excited, flighty, etc]

barn[1] (bɑːn) *n* **1** a large farm outbuilding, used chiefly for storing hay, grain, etc, but also for housing livestock **2** *US and Canadian* a large shed for sheltering railroad cars, trucks, etc **3** any large building, esp an unattractive one **4** (*modifier*) relating to a system of poultry farming in which birds are allowed to move freely within a barn: *barn eggs* [Old English *beren*, from *bere* barley + *ærn* room; see BARLEY[1]]

barn[2] (bɑːn) *n* a unit of nuclear cross section equal to 10^{-28} square metre. Symbol: b [c20 from BARN[1]; so called because of the relatively large cross section]

Barnabas ('bɑːnəbəs) *n* Saint *New Testament* original name *Joseph*. a Cypriot Levite who supported Saint Paul in his apostolic work (Acts 4:36, 37). Feast day: June 11

barnacle ('bɑːnəkᵊl) *n* **1** any of various marine crustaceans of the subclass *Cirripedia* that, as adults, live attached to rocks, ship bottoms, etc They have feathery food-catching cirri protruding from a hard shell. See **acorn barnacle**, **goose barnacle 2** a person or thing that is difficult to get rid of [c16 related to Late Latin *bernicla*, of obscure origin] ▷ 'barnacled *adj*

barnacle goose *n* **1** a N European goose, *Branta leucopsis*, that has a black-and-white head and body and grey wings **2** a former name for **brent goose** [c13 *bernekke*, related to Late Latin *bernaca*, from the belief that the goose developed from a shellfish; ultimate origin obscure]

Barnard's star *n* a red dwarf star in the constellation Ophiuchus having the largest proper motion known [c20 named after Edward Emerson Barnard (1857–1923), US astronomer]

Barnaul (*Russian* bərnaˈul) *n* a city in S Russia, on

the River Ob. Pop: 605 000 (2005 est)

barn dance *n* **1** *Brit* a progressive round country dance **2** *US and Canadian* a party with hoedown music and square-dancing **3** a party featuring country dancing **4** a disco or party held in a barn

barn door *n* **1** the door of a barn **2** *informal* a target so large that it cannot be missed **3** *photog, television, theatre* an adjustable flap over the front of a studio or theatre lamp

barnet or **barnet fair** ('ba:nɪt) *n Brit slang* hair [C19 from rhyming slang *Barnet Fair* hair]

Barnet ('ba:nɪt) *n* a borough of N Greater London: scene of a Yorkist victory (1471) in the Wars of the Roses. Pop: 324 400 (2003 est). Area: 89 sq km (34 sq miles)

barney ('ba:nɪ) *informal* ▷ *n* **1** a noisy argument ▷ *vb* (*intr*) **2** *chiefly Austral and NZ* to argue or quarrel [C19 of unknown origin]

barn owl *n* any owl of the genus *Tyto*, esp *T. alba*, having a pale brown and white plumage, long slender legs, and a heart-shaped face: family *Tytonidae*

Barnsley ('ba:nzlɪ) *n* **1** an industrial town in N England, in Barnsley unitary authority, South Yorkshire. Pop: 71 599 (2001) **2** a unitary authority in N England, in South Yorkshire. Pop: 220 200 (2003 est). Area: 329 sq km (127 sq miles)

Barnstaple ('ba:nstəpᵊl) *n* a town in SW England, in Devon, on the estuary of the River Taw: tourism, agriculture. Pop: 30 765 (2001)

barnstorm ('ba:n,stɔ:m) *vb* (*intr*) **1** to tour rural districts putting on shows, esp theatrical, athletic, or acrobatic shows **2** *chiefly US and Canadian* to tour rural districts making speeches in a political campaign [C19 from BARN¹ + STORM (*vb*); from the performances often being in barns] > **barn,stormer** *n* > **barn,storming** *n, adj*

barn swallow *n* the US and Canadian name for the common swallow, *Hirundo rustica*. See **swallow²**

barnyard ('ba:n,ja:d) *n* **1** a yard adjoining a barn, in which farm animals are kept **2** (*modifier*) belonging to or characteristic of a barnyard **3** (*modifier*) crude or earthy: *barnyard humour*

baro *combining form* indicating weight or pressure: *barometer* [from Greek *baros* weight; related to Latin *gravis* heavy]

Baroda (bə'rəʊdə) *n* **1** a former state of W India, part of Gujarat since 1960 **2** the former name (until 1976) of **Vadodara**

barognosis (,bærəg'nəʊsɪs) *n physiol* the ability to judge weight [C20 from Greek *baros* weight + *gnosis* knowledge]

barogram ('bærə,græm) *n meteorol* the record of atmospheric pressure traced by a barograph or similar instrument

barograph ('bærə,gra:f, -,græf) *n meteorol* a self-recording aneroid barometer > **barographic** (,bærə'græfɪk) *adj*

Barolo (bə'rəʊləʊ) *n* (*sometimes not capital*) a dry red wine produced in the Piedmont region of Italy

barometer (bə'rɒmɪtə) *n* **1** an instrument for measuring atmospheric pressure, usually to determine altitude or weather changes **2** anything that shows change or impending change: *the barometer of social change* > **barometric** (,bærə'mɛtrɪk) or **,baro'metrical** *adj* > **,baro'metrically** *adv* > **ba'rometry** *n*

barometric pressure *n* atmospheric pressure as indicated by a barometer

baron ('bærən) *n* **1** a member of a specific rank of nobility, esp the lowest rank in the British Isles **2** (in Europe from the Middle Ages) originally any tenant-in-chief of a king or other overlord, who held land from his superior by honourable service; a land-holding nobleman **3** a powerful businessman or financier: *a press baron* **4** *English law* (formerly) the title held by judges of the Court of Exchequer **5** short for **baron of beef** [C12 from Old French, of Germanic origin; compare Old High German *baro* freeman, Old Norse *berjask* to fight]

baronage ('bærənɪdʒ) *n* **1** barons collectively **2**

the rank or dignity of a baron

baroness ('bærənɪs) *n* **1** the wife or widow of a baron **2** a woman holding the rank of baron in her own right

baronet ('bærənɪt, -,nɛt) *n* (in Britain) a commoner who holds the lowest hereditary title of honour, ranking below a baron. Abbreviations: Bart. or Bt [C15 order instituted 1611, from BARON + -ET]

baronetage ('bærənɪtɪdʒ) *n* **1** the order of baronets; baronets collectively **2** the rank of a baronet; baronetcy

baronetcy ('bærənɪtsɪ, -,nɛt-) *n, pl* **-cies** the rank, position, or patent of a baronet

barong (bæ'rɒŋ) *n* a broad-bladed cleaver-like knife used in the Philippines [from Moro; see PARANG]

baronial (bə'rəʊnɪəl) *adj* of, relating to, or befitting a baron or barons

baron of beef *n* a cut of beef consisting of a double sirloin joined at the backbone

Barons' War *n* either of two civil wars in 13th-century England. The **First Barons' War** (1215–17) was precipitated by King John's failure to observe the terms of Magna Carta: many of the Barons' grievances were removed by his death (1216) and peace was concluded in 1217. The **Second Barons' War** (1264–67) was caused by Henry III's refusal to accept limitations on his authority: the rebel Barons (led (1264–65) by Simon de Montfort), initially successful, were defeated at the battle of Evesham (1265); sporadic resistance continued until 1267

barony ('bærənɪ) *n, pl* **-nies 1 a** the domain of a baron **b** (in Ireland) a division of a county **c** (in Scotland) a large estate or manor **2** the rank or dignity of a baron **3** a sphere of influence dominated by an industrial magnate or other powerful individual

barophilic (,bærə'fɪlɪk) *adj* (of living organisms) growing best in conditions of high atmospheric pressure > **barophile** ('bærə,faɪl) *n*

barophoresis (,bærəfə'ri:sɪs) *n chem* the diffusion of suspended particles at a rate dependent on external forces

baroque (bə'rɒk, bə'rəʊk) *n* (*often capital*) **1** a style of architecture and decorative art that flourished throughout Europe from the late 16th to the early 18th century, characterized by extensive ornamentation **2** a 17th-century style of music characterized by extensive use of the thorough bass and of ornamentation **3** any ornate or heavily ornamented style ▷ *adj* **4** denoting, being in, or relating to the baroque **5** (of pearls) irregularly shaped [C18 from French, from Portuguese *barroco* a rough or imperfectly shaped pearl]

baroreceptor ('bærəʊrɪ,sɛptə) or **baroceptor** *n* a collection of sensory nerve endings, principally in the carotid sinuses and the aortic arch, that monitor blood pressure changes in the body

baroscope ('bærə,skəʊp) *n* any instrument for measuring atmospheric pressure, esp a manometer with one side open to the atmosphere > **baroscopic** (,bærə'skɒpɪk) *adj*

barostat ('bærəʊ,stæt) *n* a device for maintaining constant pressure, such as one used in an aircraft cabin

barotrauma ('bærəʊ,trɔ:mə) *n* an injury caused by changes in atmospheric pressure, esp to the eardrums or lungs

Barotse (bæ'rɒtsɪ) *n* **1** (*pl* **-se** or **-ses**) a member of a Negroid people of central Africa living chiefly in SW Zambia **2** the language spoken by this people; Lozi

barouche (bə'ru:ʃ) *n* a four-wheeled horse-drawn carriage, popular in the 19th century, having a retractable hood over the rear half, seats inside for two couples facing each other, and a driver's seat outside at the front [C19 from German (dialect) *Barutsche*, from Italian *baroccio*, from Vulgar Latin *birotium* (unattested) vehicle with two wheels,

from Late Latin *birotus* two-wheeled, from BI-¹ + *rota* wheel]

barperson ('ba:,pɜ:sᵊn) *n, pl* **-persons** a person who serves in a pub: used esp in advertisements

barque or esp US **bark** (ba:k) *n* **1** a sailing ship of three or more masts having the foremasts rigged square and the aftermast rigged fore-and-aft **2** *poetic* any boat, esp a small sailing vessel [C15 from Old French, from Old Provençal *barca*, from Latin, of unknown origin]

barquentine or **barquantine** ('ba:kən,ti:n) *n* a sailing ship of three or more masts rigged square on the foremast and fore-and-aft on the others. Usual Australian and Canadian spelling: barkentine [C17 from BARQUE + (BRIG)ANTINE]

Barquisimeto (*Spanish* barkisi'meto) *n* a city in NW Venezuela. Pop: 1 009 000 (2005 est)

barra ('bærə) *n Austral informal* a barramundi

Barra ('bærə) *n* an island in NW Scotland, in the Outer Hebrides: fishing, crofting, tourism. Pop: 1078 (2001)

barrack¹ ('bærək) *vb* to house (people, esp soldiers) in barracks

barrack² ('bærək) *vb Brit, Austral, and NZ informal* **1** to criticize loudly or shout against (a player, team, speaker, etc); jeer **2** (*intr*; foll by *for*) to shout support (for) [C19 from northern Irish: to boast] > **barracker** *n* > **barracking** *n, adj*

barrack-room lawyer *n* a person who freely offers opinions, esp in legal matters, that he or she is unqualified to give

barracks ('bærəks) *pl n* (*sometimes singular; when plural, sometimes functions as singular*) **1** a building or group of buildings used to accommodate military personnel **2** any large building used for housing people, esp temporarily **3** a large and bleak building [C17 from French *baraque*, from Old Catalan *barraca* hut, of uncertain origin]

barracoon (,bærə'ku:n) *n* (formerly) a temporary place of confinement for slaves or convicts, esp those awaiting transportation [C19 from Spanish *barracón*, from *barraca* hut, from Catalan]

barracouta (,bærə'ku:tə) *n* a large predatory Pacific fish, *Thyrsites atun*, with a protruding lower jaw and strong teeth: family *Gempylidae* [C17 variant of BARRACUDA]

barracuda (,bærə'kju:də) *n, pl* **-da** or **-das** any predatory marine teleost fish of the mostly tropical family *Sphyraenidae*, esp *Sphyraena barracuda*. They have an elongated body, strong teeth, and a protruding lower jaw [C17 from American Spanish, of unknown origin]

barrage ('bæra:ʒ) *n* **1** *military* the firing of artillery to saturate an area, either to protect against an attack or to support an advance **2** an overwhelming and continuous delivery of something, as words, questions, or punches **3** a usually gated construction, similar to a low dam, across a watercourse, esp one to increase the depth of water to assist navigation or irrigation **4** *fencing* a heat or series of bouts in a competition ▷ *vb* **5** (*tr*) to attack or confront with a barrage: *the speaker was barraged with abuse* [C19 from French, from *barrer* to obstruct; see BAR¹]

barrage balloon *n* one of a number of tethered balloons with cables or net suspended from them, used to deter low-flying air attack

barramunda (,bærə'mʌndə) *n, pl* **-das** or **-da** the edible Australian lungfish, *Neoceratodus forsteri*, having paddle-like fins and a long body covered with large scales [from a native Australian language]

barramundi (,bærə'mʌndɪ) *n, pl* **-dis, -dies** or **-di** any of several large edible Australian fishes esp the percoid species *Lates calcarifer* (family Centropomidae) of NE coastal waters or the freshwater species *Scleropages leichardti* (family Osteoglossidae) of Queensland

barranca (bə'ræŋkə) or **barranco** (bə'ræŋkəʊ) *n, pl* **-cas** or **-cos** *Southwestern US* a ravine or precipice [C19 from Spanish, of uncertain origin]

Barranquilla (*Spanish* barran'kiʎa) *n* a port in N

b

Colombia, on the Magdalena River. Pop: 1 918 000 (2005 est)

barrator ('bærətə) *n* a person guilty of barratry [c14 from Old French *barateor*, from *barater* to BARTER]

barratry *or* **barretry** ('bærətrɪ) *n* **1** *criminal law* (formerly) the vexatious stirring up of quarrels or bringing of lawsuits **2** *maritime law* a fraudulent practice committed by the master or crew of a ship to the prejudice of the owner or charterer **3** *Scots law* the crime committed by a judge in accepting a bribe **4** the purchase or sale of public or Church offices [c15 from Old French *baraterie* deception, from *barater* to BARTER] ▷ 'barratrous *or* 'barretrous *adj* ▷ 'barratrously *or* 'barretrously *adv*

barre (French *bar*) *n* a rail at hip height used for ballet practice and leg exercises [literally: bar]

barré ('bæreɪ) *n* **1** the act of laying the index finger over some or all of the strings of a guitar, lute, or similar instrument, so that the pitch of each stopped string is simultaneously raised. Compare **capo¹ 2** the playing of chords in this manner ▷ *vb* **3** to execute (chords) in this manner ▷ *adv* **4** by using the barré [c19 from French, from *barrer* BAR¹]

barrel ('bærəl) *n* **1** a cylindrical container usually bulging outwards in the middle and held together by metal hoops; cask **2** Also called: **barrelful** the amount that a barrel can hold **3** a unit of capacity used in brewing, equal to 36 Imperial gallons **4** a unit of capacity used in the oil and other industries, normally equal to 42 US gallons or 35 Imperial gallons **5** a thing or part shaped like a barrel, esp a tubular part of a machine **6** the tube through which the projectile of a firearm is discharged **7** *horology* the cylindrical drum in a watch or clock that is rotated by the mainspring **8** the trunk of a four-legged animal: *the barrel of a horse* **9** the quill of a feather **10** *informal* a large measure; a great deal (esp in the phrases **barrel of fun, barrel of laughs**) **11** *Austral informal* the hollow inner side of a wave **12** **over a barrel** *informal* powerless **13** **scrape the barrel** *informal* to be forced to use one's last and weakest resource ▷ *vb* **-rels, -relling, -relled** *or US* **-rels, -reling, -reled 14** (*tr*) to put into a barrel or barrels **15** (*intr*; foll by *along, in, etc*) *informal* to travel or move very fast (*intr*) **16** *Austral informal* to ride on the inside of a wave [c14 from Old French *baril* perhaps from *barre* BAR¹]

barrel-chested *adj* having a large rounded chest

barrel distortion *n* *photog* distortion of an image produced by an optical system that causes straight lines at image margins to bulge outwards

barrelhouse ('bærəl,haʊs) *n* **1** *US* a cheap and disreputable drinking establishment **2 a** a vigorous and unpolished style of jazz for piano, originating in the barrelhouses of New Orleans **b** (*as modifier*): *barrelhouse blues*

barrel organ *n* **1** an instrument consisting of a cylinder turned by a handle and having pins on it that interrupt the air flow to certain pipes, thereby playing any of a number of tunes. See also **hurdy-gurdy 2** a similar instrument in which the projections on a rotating barrel pluck a set of strings

barrel roll *n* **1** a flight manoeuvre in which an aircraft rolls about its longitudinal axis while following a spiral course in line with the direction of flight ▷ *vb* **barrel-roll 2** (*intr*) (of an aircraft) to perform a barrel roll

barrel vault *n* *architect* a vault in the form of a half cylinder. Also called: **wagon vault, tunnel vault**

barren ('bærən) *adj* **1** incapable of producing offspring, seed, or fruit; sterile: *a barren tree* **2** unable to support the growth of crops, etc; unproductive; bare: *barren land* **3** lacking in stimulation or ideas; dull: *a rather barren play* **4** not producing worthwhile results; unprofitable: *a barren period in a writer's life* **5** (foll by *of*) totally lacking (in); devoid (of): *his speech was barren of wit* **6**

(of rock strata) having no fossils [c13 from Old French *brahain*, of uncertain origin] ▷ 'barrenly *adv* ▷ 'barrenness *n*

Barren Lands *pl n* **the.** a region of tundra in N Canada, extending westwards from Hudson Bay: sparsely inhabited, chiefly by Inuit. Also called: **Barren Grounds**

barrens ('bærənz) *pl n* (*sometimes singular*) (in North America) a stretch of usually level land that is sparsely vegetated or barren

barrenwort ('bærən,wɜːt) *n* a herbaceous European berberidaceous plant, *Epimedium alpinum*, having red-and-yellow star-shaped flowers

barret ('bærɪt) *n* a small flat cap resembling a biretta [c19 from French *barrette*, from Italian *berretta* BIRETTA; compare BERET]

barrette (bə'rɛt) *n* a clasp or pin for holding women's hair in place [c20 from French: a little bar, from *barre* BAR¹]

barricade (,bærɪ'keɪd, 'bærɪ,keɪd) *n* **1** a barrier for defence, esp one erected hastily, as during street fighting ▷ *vb* (*tr*) **2** to erect a barricade across (an entrance, passageway, etc) or at points of access to (a room, district of a town, etc): *they barricaded the door* **3** (*usually passive*) to obstruct; block: *his mind was barricaded against new ideas* [c17 from Old French, from *barriquer* to barricade, from *barrique* a barrel, from Spanish *barrica*, from *barril* BARREL] ▷ 'barri,cader *n*

barrie ('bærɪ) *adj Scot dialect* very good; attractive [from Romany]

barrier ('bærɪə) *n* **1** anything serving to obstruct passage or to maintain separation, such as a fence or gate **2** anything that prevents or obstructs passage, access, or progress: *a barrier of distrust* **3** anything that separates or hinders union: *a language barrier* **4** an exposed offshore sand bar separated from the shore by a lagoon **b** (*as modifier*): *a barrier beach* **5** (*sometimes capital*) that part of the Antarctic icecap extending over the sea [c14 from Old French *barriere*, from *barre* BAR¹]

barrier cream *n* a cream used to protect the skin, esp the hands, from dirt and from the action of oils or solvents

barrier-nurse *vb* (*tr*) to tend (infectious patients) in isolation, to prevent the spread of infection ▷ barrier nursing *n*

barrier of ideas *n philosophy* the representations of objects which certain accounts of perception interpose between the objects themselves and our awareness of them, so that, as critics argue, we can never know whether there is in reality anything which resembles our perceptions. See **representationalism** (sense 1)

barrier reef *n* a long narrow coral reef near and lying parallel to the shore, separated from it by deep water. See **Great Barrier Reef**

barring ('bɑːrɪŋ) *prep* unless (something) occurs; except for: *barring rain, the match will be held tomorrow*

barrio ('bærɪəʊ; *Spanish* 'barrjo) *n, pl* **-rios 1** a Spanish-speaking quarter in a town or city, esp in the US **2** a Spanish-speaking community [from Spanish, from Arabic *barrī* of open country, from *barr* open country]

barrister ('bærɪstə) *n* **1** Also called: **barrister-at-law** (in England) a lawyer who has been called to the bar and is qualified to plead in the higher courts. Compare **solicitor** See also **advocate, counsel 2** (in Canada) a lawyer who pleads in court **3** *US* a less common word for **lawyer** [c16 from BAR¹]

barro ('bærəʊ) *adj Austral slang* embarrassing

barroom ('bɑː,ruːm, -,rʊm) *n US* a room or building where alcoholic drinks are served over a counter

barrow¹ ('bærəʊ) *n* **1** See **wheelbarrow, handbarrow 2** Also called: **barrowful** the amount contained in or on a barrow **3** *chiefly Brit* a handcart, typically having two wheels and a canvas roof, used esp by street vendors **4** *Northern English dialect* concern or business (esp in the phrases **that's not my barrow, that's just my**

barrow) 5 **into one's barrow** *Irish and Scot dialect* suited to one's interests or desires [Old English *bearwe*; related to Old Norse *barar* BIER, Old High German *bāra*]

barrow² ('bærəʊ) *n* a heap of earth placed over one or more prehistoric tombs, often surrounded by ditches. **Long barrows** are elongated Neolithic mounds usually covering stone burial chambers; **round barrows** are Bronze Age, covering burials or cremations [Old English *beorg*; related to Old Norse *bjarg*, Gothic *bairgahei* hill, Old High German *berg* mountain]

barrow³ ('bærəʊ) *n* a castrated pig [Old English *bearg*; related to Old Norse *börgr*, Old High German *barug*]

Barrow ('bærəʊ) *n* **1** a river in SE Ireland, rising in the Slieve Bloom Mountains and flowing south to Waterford Harbour. Length: about 193 km (120 miles) **2** See **Barrow-in-Furness** and **Barrow Point**

barrow boy *n Brit* a man who sells his wares from a barrow; street vendor

Barrow-in-Furness *n* an industrial town in NW England, in S Cumbria. Pop: 47 194 (2001)

Barrow Point *n* the northernmost tip of Alaska, on the Arctic Ocean

barry *or* **Barry Crocker** ('bærɪ) *n Austral slang* a mistake or blunder; a disappointing performance [rhyming slang for SHOCKER]

Barry ('bærɪ) *n* a port in SE Wales, in Vale of Glamorgan county borough on the Bristol Channel. Pop: 50 661 (2001)

Barsac ('bɑːsæk; *French* barsak) *n* a sweet French white wine produced around the town of Barsac in the Gironde

bar sinister *n* **1** (not in heraldic usage) another name for **bend sinister 2** the condition, implication, or stigma of being of illegitimate birth

Bart. *abbreviation for* Baronet

bartender ('bɑː,tɛndə) *n chiefly US and Canadian* a man who serves in a bar. Also called: **barman**

barter ('bɑːtə) *vb* **1** to trade (goods, services, etc) in exchange for other goods, services, etc, rather than for money: *the refugees bartered for food* **2** (*intr*) to haggle over the terms of such an exchange; bargain ▷ *n* **3** trade by the exchange of goods [c15 from Old French *barater* to cheat; perhaps related to Greek *prattein* to do] ▷ 'barterer *n*

Barthian ('bɑːtɪən, -θɪən) *adj* **1** of or relating to Karl Barth (1886–1968), the Swiss Protestant theologian, or his ideas ▷ *n* **2** a person who supports or believes in the ideas of Karl Barth

Bartholin's glands ('bɑːθəlɪnz) *pl n anatomy* two small reddish-yellow glands, one on each side of the vaginal orifice, that secrete a mucous lubricating substance during sexual stimulation in females. Compare **Cowper's glands** [named by Caspar *Bartholin* (1655–1738), Danish anatomist, in honour of his father, Thomas]

Bartholomew (bɑː'θɒlə,mjuː) *n* Saint *New Testament* one of the twelve apostles (Matthew 10:3). Feast day: Aug 24 or June 11

bartizan ('bɑːtɪzən, ,bɑːtɪ'zæn) *n* a small turret projecting from a wall, parapet, or tower [c19 variant of *bertisene*, erroneously for *bretising*, from *bretasce* parapet; see BRATTICE] ▷ bartizaned ('bɑːtɪzənd, ,bɑːtɪ'zænd) *adj*

Bartlett *or* **Bartlett pear** ('bɑːtlɪt) *n* another name for **Williams pear**: used esp in the US and generally of tinned pears [named after Enoch *Bartlett* (1779–1860), of Dorchester, Mass., who marketed it in the US]

barton ('bɑːtᵊn) *n archaic* a farmyard [Old English *beretūn*, from *bere* barley + *tūn* stockade; see TOWN]

bartsia ('bɑːtsɪə) *n* any of several species of semiparasitic scrophulariaceous plants, including **red bartsia** (*Odontites verna*), a pink-flowered weed of cornfields [c18 New Latin, named after Johann *Bartsch* (died 1738), German botanist]

Baruch ('bɛərʊk, 'bɑː-) *n Bible* **a** a disciple of Jeremiah (Jeremiah 32–36) **b** the book of the Apocrypha said to have been written by him

barycentre (ˈbærɪˌsɛntə) *n* a centre of mass, esp of the earth-moon system or the solar system [c20 from Greek *barus* heavy + CENTRE] ▷ ˌbaryˈcentric *adj*

barye (ˈbærɪ) *n* a unit of pressure in the cgs system equal to one dyne per square centimetre. 1 barye is equivalent to 1 microbar [c19 from French, from Greek *barus* heavy]

baryon (ˈbærɪˌɒn) *n* any of a class of elementary particles that have a mass greater than or equal to that of the proton, participate in strong interactions, and have a spin of ½. Baryons are either nucleons or hyperons. The **baryon number** is the number of baryons in a system minus the number of antibaryons [c20 *bary-*, from Greek *barus* heavy + -ON]

baryonic (ˌbærɪˈɒnɪk) *adj* of or relating to a baryon

barysphere (ˈbærɪˌsfɪə) *n* a former name for **core** (sense 4) [c20 from Greek *barus* heavy + SPHERE]

baryta (bəˈraɪtə) *n* another name for **barium oxide** *or* **barium hydroxide** [c19 New Latin, from Greek *barutēs* weight, from *barus* heavy] ▷ **barytic** (bəˈrɪtɪk) *adj*

barytes (bəˈraɪtiːz) *n* a colourless or white mineral consisting of barium sulphate in orthorhombic crystalline form, occurring in sedimentary rocks and with sulphide ores: a source of barium. Formula: BaSO₄ Also called (esp US and Canadian): **barite, heavy spar** [c18 from Greek *barus* heavy + -itēs -ITE¹]

baryton (ˈbærɪˌtəʊn) *n* a bass viol with sympathetic strings as well as its six main strings [c18 from French: BARITONE]

barytone¹ (ˈbærɪˌtəʊn) *n* a less common spelling of **baritone**

barytone² (ˈbærɪˌtəʊn) (in ancient Greek) *adj* **1** having the last syllable unaccented ▷ *n* **2** a word in which the last syllable is unaccented. Compare **oxytone** [c19 from Greek *barutonos* heavy-sounding, from *barus* heavy + *tonos* TONE]

basal (ˈbeɪsᵊl) *adj* **1** at, of, or constituting a base **2** of or constituting a foundation or basis; fundamental; essential ▷ ˈbasally *adv*

basal anaesthesia *n* preliminary and incomplete anaesthesia induced to prepare a surgical patient for total anaesthesia with another agent

basal ganglia *pl n* the thalamus together with other closely related masses of grey matter, situated near the base of the brain

basal metabolic rate *n* the rate at which heat is produced by the body at rest, 12 to 14 hours after eating, measured in kilocalories per square metre of body surface per hour. Abbreviation: BMR

basal metabolism *n* the amount of energy required by an individual in the resting state, for such functions as breathing and circulation of the blood. See **basal metabolic rate**

basalt (ˈbæsɔːlt) *n* **1** a fine-grained dark basic igneous rock consisting of plagioclase feldspar, a pyroxene, and olivine: the most common volcanic rock and usually extrusive. See **flood basalt** **2** a form of black unglazed pottery resembling basalt [c18 from Late Latin *basaltēs*, variant of *basanītēs*, from Greek *basanītēs* touchstone, from *basanos*, of Egyptian origin] ▷ baˈsaltic *adj*

basaltware (ˈbæsɔːltˌwɛə, ˈbeɪsɔːlt-) *n* hard fine-grained black stoneware, made in Europe, esp in England, in the late 18th century

basanite (ˈbæsəˌnaɪt) *n* a black basaltic rock containing plagioclase, augite, olivine, and nepheline, leucite, or analcite, formerly used as a touchstone [c18 see BASALT]

bas bleu (French ba blø) *n, pl bas bleus* (ba blø) a bluestocking; intellectual woman [c10 from French translation of English BLUESTOCKING]

bascinet (ˌbæsɪˈnɛt, ˈbæsɪˌnɛt) *n* armour a variant spelling of **basinet**

bascule (ˈbæskjuːl) *n* **1** Also called: **balance bridge, counterpoise bridge** a bridge with a movable section hinged about a horizontal axis

and counterbalanced by a weight. Compare **drawbridge** **2** a movable roadway forming part of such a bridge: *Tower Bridge has two bascules* [c17 from French: seesaw, from *bas* low + *cul* rump; see BASE², CULET]

base¹ (beɪs) *n* **1** the bottom or supporting part of anything **2** the fundamental or underlying principle or part, as of an idea, system, or organization; basis **3 a** a centre of operations, organization, or supply: *the climbers made a base at 8000 feet* **b** (*as modifier*): *base camp* **4** a centre from which military activities are coordinated **5** anything from which a process, as of measurement, action, or thought, is or may be begun; starting point: *the new discovery became the base for further research* **6** the main ingredient of a mixture: *to use rice as a base in cookery* **7** a chemical compound that combines with an acid to form a salt and water. A solution of a base in water turns litmus paper blue, produces hydroxyl ions, and has a pH greater than 7. Bases are metal oxides or hydroxides or amines. See also **Lewis base** **8** *biochem.* any of the nitrogen-containing constituents of nucleic acids: adenine, thymine (in DNA), uracil (in RNA), guanine, or cytosine **9** a medium such as oil or water in which the pigment is dispersed in paints, inks, etc; vehicle **10** the inorganic material on which the dye is absorbed in lake pigments; carrier **11** *biology* **a** the part of an organ nearest to its point of attachment **b** the point of attachment of an organ or part **12** the bottommost layer or part of anything **13** *architect* **a** the lowest division of a building or structure **b** the lower part of a column or pier **14** another word for **baseline** (sense 2) **15** the lower side or face of a geometric construction **16** *maths* **a** the number of distinct single-digit numbers in a counting system, and so the number represented as 10 in a place-value system: *the binary system has two digits, 0 and 1, and 10 to base two represents 2.* See **place-value** **b** (of a logarithm or exponential) the number whose powers are expressed: *since 1000 = 10³, the logarithm of 1000 to base 10 is 3* **c** (of a mathematical structure) a substructure from which the given system can be generated **d** the initial instance from which a generalization is proven by mathematical induction **17** *logic, maths* Also called: **base clause** the initial element of a recursive definition, that defines the first element of the infinite sequence generated thereby **18** *linguistics* **a** a root or stem **b** See **base component** **19** *electronics* the region in a transistor between the emitter and collector **20** *photog* the glass, paper, or cellulose-ester film that supports the sensitized emulsion with which it is coated **21** *heraldry* the lower part of the shield **22** *jewellery* the quality factor used in pricing natural pearls **23** a starting or finishing point in any of various games **24** *baseball* any of the four corners of the diamond, which runners have to reach in order to score **25** the main source of a certain commodity or element: *a customer base; their fan base* **26** **get to first base** *US and Canadian informal* to accomplish the first stage in a project or a series of objectives **27** **off base** *US and Canadian informal* wrong or badly mistaken **28** **touch base** to make contact ▷ *vb* **29** (*tr; foll by on or upon*) to use as a basis (for); found (on): *your criticisms are based on ignorance* **30** (often foll by *at* or *in*) to station, post, or place (a person or oneself) [c14 from Old French, from Latin *basis* pedestal; see BASIS]

base² (beɪs) *adj* **1** devoid of honour or morality; ignoble; contemptible **2** of inferior quality or value **3** debased; alloyed; counterfeit: *base currency* **4** *English history* **a** (of land tenure) held by villein or other ignoble service **b** holding land by villein or other ignoble service **5** *archaic* born of humble parents; plebeian **6** *archaic* illegitimate ▷ *adj* ▷ **7** *music* an obsolete spelling of **bass** [c14 from Old French *bas*, from Late Latin *bassus* of low height, perhaps from Greek *bassōn* deeper] ▷ ˈbasely *adv* ▷ ˈbaseness *n*

baseball (ˈbeɪsˌbɔːl) *n* **1** a team game with nine players on each side, played on a field with four bases connected to form a diamond. The object is to score runs by batting the ball and running round the bases **2** the hard rawhide-covered ball used in this game

baseball cap *n* a close-fitting thin cap with a deep peak

baseband (ˈbeɪsˌbænd) *n* a transmission technique using a narrow range of frequencies that allows only one message to be telecommunicated at a time. See also **broadband**

baseboard (ˈbeɪsˌbɔːd) *n* **1** a board functioning as the base of anything **2** US and Canadian a skirting made of wood. Also called: **skirting board**

baseborn (ˈbeɪsˌbɔːn) *adj archaic* **1** born of humble parents **2** illegitimate **3** mean; contemptible

baseburner (ˈbeɪsˌbɜːnə) *n* US a stove into which coal is automatically fed from a hopper above the fire chamber

base component *n* the system of rules in a transformational grammar that specify the deep structure of the language

base head *n slang* a person who is addicted to cocaine

base hospital *n Austral* a hospital serving a large rural area

base jumping *n* a sport in which a participant parachutes from any of a variety of fixed objects such as high buildings, cliffs, etc [c20 *b(uilding)*, *a(ntennae)*, *s(pan, and)* *e(arthbound object)*]

Basel (ˈbɑːzᵊl) *n* a variant spelling of **Basle**

baseless (ˈbeɪslɪs) *adj* not based on fact; unfounded: *a baseless supposition* ▷ ˈbaselessly *adv* ▷ ˈbaselessness *n*

base level *n* the lowest level to which a land surface can be eroded by streams, which is, ultimately, sea level

baseline (ˈbeɪsˌlaɪn) *n* **1** *surveying* a measured line through a survey area from which triangulations are made **2** an imaginary line, standard of value, etc, by which things are measured or compared **3** a line at each end of a tennis court that marks the limit of play

baseliner (ˈbeɪsˌlaɪnə) *n tennis* a player who plays most of his or her shots from the back of court

base load *n* the more or less constant part of the total load on an electrical power-supply system. Compare **peak load**

baseman (ˈbeɪsmən) *n, pl* -men *baseball* a fielder positioned near a base

basement (ˈbeɪsmənt) *n* **1 a** a partly or wholly underground storey of a building, esp the one immediately below the main floor. Compare **cellar** **b** (*as modifier*): *a basement flat* **2** the foundation or substructure of a wall or building **3** *geology* a part of the earth's crust formed of hard igneous or metamorphic rock that lies beneath the cover of soft sedimentary rock, sediment, and soil

base metal *n* any of certain common metals such as copper, lead, zinc, and tin, as distinct from the precious metals, gold, silver, and platinum

basenji (bəˈsɛndʒɪ) *n* a small smooth-haired breed of dog of African origin having a tightly curled tail and an inability to bark [c20 from a Bantu language]

base pairing *n biochem* the hydrogen bonding that occurs between complementary nitrogenous bases in the two polynucleotide chains of a DNA molecule

base period *n statistics* a neutral period used as a standard for comparison in constructing an index to express a variable factor: 100 is usually taken as the index number for the variable in the base period

base rate *n* **1** *Brit* the rate of interest used by individual commercial banks as a basis for their lending rates **2** *Brit informal* the rate at which the Bank of England lends to the discount houses, which effectively controls the interest rates charged throughout the banking system **3** *statistics* the average number of times an event

b

occurs divided by the average number of times on which it might occur

base rate fallacy *n statistics* the tendency, when making judgments of the probability with which an event will occur, to ignore the base rate and to concentrate on other information

bases[1] ('beɪsɪːz) *n* the plural of **basis**

bases[2] ('beɪsɪz) *n* the plural of **base**[1]

base speed *n slang* a pure pinkish-grey form of the drug amphetamine with a putty-like consistency

base station *n* a fixed transmitter that forms part of an otherwise mobile radio network

base unit *n physics* any of the fundamental units in a system of measurement. The base SI units are the metre, kilogram, second, ampere, kelvin, candela, and mole

bash (bæʃ) *informal* ▷ *vb* **1** (*tr*) to strike violently or crushingly **2** (*tr; often foll by in, down, etc*) to smash, break, etc, with a crashing blow: *to bash a door down* **3** (*intr; foll by into*) to crash (into); collide (with): *to bash into a lamppost* **4** to dent or be dented: *this tin is bashed; this cover won't bash easily* ▷ *n* **5** a heavy blow, as from a fist **6** a dent; indentation **7** a party **8** **have a bash** *informal* to make an attempt ▷ See also **bash up** [C17 of uncertain origin]

Bashan ('beɪʃæn) *n Old Testament* a region to the east of the Jordan, renowned for its rich pasture (Deuteronomy 32:14)

bashaw (bə'ʃɔ:) *n* **1** a rare spelling of **pasha** **2** an important or pompous person [C16 from Turkish *başa*, from *bas* head, chief]

bashful ('bæʃfʊl) *adj* **1** disposed to attempt to avoid notice through shyness or modesty; diffident; timid **2** indicating or characterized by shyness or modesty [C16 from *bash*, short for ABASH + -FUL] > **'bashfully** *adv* > **'bashfulness** *n*

bashibazouk (ˌbæʃɪbə'zu:k) *n* (in the 19th century) one of a group of irregular Turkish soldiers notorious for their brutality [C19 from Turkish *başibozuk* irregular soldier, from *bas* head + *bozuk* corrupt]

-bashing *n and adj combining form informal or slang* **a** indicating a malicious attack on members of a particular group: *queer-bashing; union-bashing* **b** indicating any of various other activities: *Bible-bashing; spud-bashing; square-bashing* > **-basher** *n combining form*

Bashkir (bæʃ'kɪə) *n* **1** (*pl* -**kir** *or* -**kirs**) a member of a Mongoloid people of E central Russia, living chiefly in the Bashkir Republic **2** the language of this people, belonging to the Turkic branch of the Altaic family

Bashkir Republic *n* a constituent republic of E central Russia, in the S Urals: established as the first Soviet autonomous republic in 1919; rich mineral resources. Capital: Ufa. Pop: 4 012 900 (2002). Area: 143 600 sq km (55 430 sq miles). Also called: **Bashkiria** (bæʃ'kɪərɪə), **Bashkortostan** (bæʃˈkɔːtəˌstaːn; *Russian* baʃkortoˈstaːn)

basho ('bæʃəʊ) *n, pl* **basho** a grand tournament in sumo wrestling [C20 from Japanese]

bash up *vb* (*tr, adverb*) *Brit slang* to thrash; beat violently

basic ('beɪsɪk) *adj* **1** of, relating to, or forming a base or basis; fundamental; underlying **2** elementary or simple: *a few basic facts* **3** excluding additions or extras: *basic pay* **4** *chem* **a** of, denoting, or containing a base; alkaline **b** (of a salt) containing hydroxyl or oxide groups not all of which have been replaced by an acid radical: *basic lead carbonate, 2PbCO₃.Pb(OH)₂* **5** *metallurgy* of, concerned with, or made by a process in which the furnace or converter is made of a basic material, such as magnesium oxide **6** (of such igneous rocks as basalt) containing between 52 and 45 per cent silica **7** *military* primary or initial: *basic training* ▷ *adj* **8** (*usually plural*) a fundamental principle, fact, etc

BASIC *or* **Basic** ('beɪsɪk) *n* a computer programming language that uses common

English terms [C20 acronym of *b(eginner's)* *a(ll-purpose)* *s(ymbolic)* *i(nstruction)* *c(ode)*]

basically ('beɪsɪklɪ) *adv* **1** in a fundamental or elementary manner; essentially: *strident and basically unpleasant* **2** (*sentence modifier*) in essence; in summary; put simply: *basically we had underestimated mother nature*

Basic Curriculum *n Brit education* in England and Wales, the National Curriculum plus religious education

basic education *n* (in India) education in which all teaching is correlated with the learning of a craft

basic English *n* a simplified form of English, proposed by C. K. Ogden and I. A. Richards, containing a vocabulary of approximately 850 of the commonest English words, intended as an international language

basic industry *n* an industry which is highly important in a nation's economy

basicity (beɪ'sɪsɪtɪ) *n chem* **a** the state of being a base **b** the extent to which a substance is basic

basicranial (ˌbeɪsɪ'kreɪnɪəl) *adj anatomy* of or relating to the base of the skull

basic rate *n* the standard or lowest level on a scale of money payable, esp in taxation

basic slag *n* a furnace slag produced in steel-making, containing large amounts of calcium phosphate: used as a fertilizer

basidiocarp (bæ'sɪdɪəʊˌkɑːp) *n* the fruiting body of basidiomycetous fungi; the mushroom of agarics

basidiomycete (bæˌsɪdɪəʊmaɪ'siːt) *n* any fungus of the phylum Basidiomycota (formerly class *Basidiomycetes*), in which the spores are produced in basidia. The group includes boletes, puffballs, smuts, and rusts [C19 from BASIDI(UM) + -MYCETE] > **baˌsidiomy'cetous** *adj*

basidiospore (bæ'sɪdɪəʊˌspɔː) *n* one of the spores, usually four in number, produced in a basidium > **baˌsidio'sporous** *adj*

basidium (bæ'sɪdɪəm) *n, pl* **-ia** (-ɪə) the structure, produced by basidiomycetous fungi after sexual reproduction, in which spores are formed at the tips of projecting slender stalks [C19 from New Latin, from Greek *basidion*; see BASIS, -IUM] > **ba'sidial** *adj*

basifixed ('beɪsɪˌfɪkst) *adj botany* (of an anther) attached to the filament by its base

basifugal (beɪ'sɪfjʊɡᵊl) *adj botany* a less common word for **acropetal**

basify ('beɪsɪˌfaɪ) *vb* **-fies, -fying, -fied** (*tr*) to make basic

basil ('bæzᵊl) *n* **1** Also called: **sweet basil** a Eurasian plant, *Ocimum basilicum*, having spikes of small white flowers and aromatic leaves used as herbs for seasoning: family *Lamiaceae* (labiates) **2** Also called: **wild basil** a European plant, *Satureja vulgaris* (or *Clinopodium vulgare*), with dense clusters of small pink or whitish flowers: family *Lamiaceae* **3** **basil-thyme** a European plant, *Acinos arvensis*, having clusters of small violet-and-white flowers: family *Lamiaceae* [C15 from Old French *basile*, from Late Latin *basilicum*, from Greek *basilikon*, from *basilikos* royal, from *basileus* king]

Basilan (bə'siːlɑːn, bæ'siːlæn) *n* **1** a group of islands in the Philippines, SW of Mindanao **2** the main island of this group, separated from Mindanao by the **Basilan Strait**. Area: 1282 sq km (495 sq miles) **3** a city on Basilan Island. Pop: 381 000 (2005 est)

basilar ('bæsɪlə) *adj chiefly anatomy* of or situated at a base: *basilar artery* (at the base of the skull) Also: **basilary** ('bæsɪlərɪ, -sɪlrɪ) [C16 from New Latin *basilaris*, from Latin *basis* BASE[1]; compare Medieval Latin *basile* pelvis]

Basildon ('bæzɪldən) *n* a town in SE England, in S Essex: designated a new town in 1955. Pop: 99 876 (2001)

Basilian (bə'zɪlɪən) *n* a monk of the Eastern Christian order of St Basil, founded in Cappadocia in the 4th century AD

basilica (bə'zɪlɪkə) *n* **1** a Roman building, used for public administration, having a large rectangular central nave with an aisle on each side and an apse at the end **2** a rectangular early Christian or medieval church, usually having a nave with clerestories, two or four aisles, one or more vaulted apses, and a timber roof **3** a Roman Catholic church having special ceremonial rights [C16 from Latin, from Greek *basilikē* hall, from *basilikē oikia* the king's house, from *basileus* king; see BASIL] > **ba'silican** *or* **ba'silic** *adj*

Basilicata (*Italian* bazili'kata) *n* a region of S Italy, between the Tyrrhenian Sea and the Gulf of Taranto. Capital: Potenza. Pop: 596 821 (2003 est). Area: 9985 sq km (3855 sq miles)

basilic vein (bə'zɪlɪk) *n* a large vein situated on the inner side of the arm [C18 from Latin *basilicus* kingly; see BASIL]

basilisk ('bæzɪˌlɪsk) *n* **1** (in classical legend) a serpent that could kill by its breath or glance **2** any small arboreal semiaquatic lizard of the genus *Basiliscus* of tropical America: family *Iguanidae* (iguanas). The males have an inflatable head crest, used in display **3** a 16th-century medium cannon, usually made of brass [C14 from Latin *basiliscus*, from Greek *basiliskos* royal child, from *basileus* king]

basin ('beɪsᵊn) *n* **1** a round container open and wide at the top with sides sloping inwards towards the bottom or base, esp one in which liquids are mixed or stored **2** Also called: **basinful** the amount a basin will hold **3** a washbasin or sink **4** any partially enclosed or sheltered area where vessels may be moored or docked **5** the catchment area of a particular river and its tributaries or of a lake or sea **6** a depression in the earth's surface **7** *geology* a part of the earth's surface consisting of rock strata that slope down to a common centre [C13 from Old French *bacin*, from Late Latin *bacchīnon*, from Vulgar Latin *bacca* (unattested) container for water; related to Latin *bāca* berry]

basinet *or* **bascinet** ('bæsɪnɪt, -ˌnɛt) *n* a close-fitting medieval helmet of light steel usually with a visor [C14 from Old French *bacinet*, a little basin, from *bacin* BASIN]

Basingstoke ('beɪzɪŋˌstəʊk) *n* a town in S England, in N Hampshire. Pop: 90 171 (2001)

basion ('beɪsɪən) *n anatomy* the midpoint on the forward border of the foramen magnum [C19 from New Latin, from Latin *basis* BASE[1]]

basipetal (beɪ'sɪpɪtᵊl) *adj* (of leaves and flowers) produced in order from the apex downwards so that the youngest are at the base. Compare **acropetal**

basis ('beɪsɪs) *n, pl* **-ses** (-siːz) **1** something that underlies, supports, or is essential to something else, esp an abstract idea **2** a principle on which something depends or from which something has issued **3** *maths* (of a vector space) a maximal set of linearly independent vectors, in terms of which all the elements of the space are uniquely expressible, and the number of which is the dimension of the space: *the vectors* **x**, **y** *and* **z** *form a basis of the 3-dimensional space all members of which can be written as* a**x** + b**y** + c**z** [C14 via Latin from Greek: step, from *bainein* to step, go]

basis point *n* a measure used for describing interest rates, equal to one hundredth of a percentage point (0.01%)

bask (bɑːsk) *vb* (*intr; usually foll by in*) **1** to lie in or be exposed to pleasant warmth, esp that of the sun **2** to flourish or feel secure under some benevolent influence or favourable condition [C14 from Old Norse *bathask* to BATHE]

Baskerville ('bæskəˌvɪl) *n* a style of type [C18 named after John *Baskerville* (1706–1775), English printer]

basket ('bɑːskɪt) *n* **1** a container made of interwoven strips of pliable materials, such as cane, straw, thin wood, or plastic, and often carried by means of a handle or handles **2** Also called: **basketful** the amount a basket will hold **3** something resembling such a container in appearance or function, such as the structure suspended from a balloon **4** *basketball* **a** an open horizontal metal hoop fixed to the backboard, through which a player must throw the ball to score points **b** a point or points scored in this way **5** a group or collection of similar of related things: *a basket of currencies* **6** *informal* a euphemism for **bastard** (senses 1, 2) **7** the list of items an internet shopper chooses to buy at one time from a website: *add these items to your basket* [C13 probably from Old Northern French *baskot* (unattested), from Latin *bascauda* basketwork holder, of Celtic origin]

basketball ('bɑːskɪt,bɔːl) *n* **1** a game played by two opposing teams of five men (or six women) each, usually on an indoor court. Points are scored by throwing the ball through an elevated horizontal metal hoop **2** the inflated ball used in this game

basket case *n slang* **1** *offensive, chiefly US and Canadian* a person who has had both arms and both legs amputated **2** a person who is suffering from extreme nervous strain; nervous wreck **3 a** someone or something that is incapable of functioning normally **b** (*as modifier*): *a basket-case economy*

basket chair *n* a chair made of wickerwork; a wicker chair

basket clause *n* an all-inclusive or comprehensive clause in a contract

basket hilt *n* a hilt fitted to a broadsword, with a generally padded basket-shaped guard to protect the hand > '**basket-,hilted** *adj*

Basket Maker *n* a member of an early Native American people of the southwestern US, preceding the Pueblo people, known for skill in basket-making

basketry ('bɑːskɪtrɪ) *n* **1** the art or practice of making baskets **2** baskets collectively

basket-star *n* any of several echinoderms of the genus *Gorgonocephalus*, in which long slender arms radiate from a central disc: order *Ophiuroidea* (brittle-stars)

basket weave *n* a weave of two or more yarns together, resembling that of a basket, esp in wool or linen fabric

basketweaver ('bɑːskɪt,wiːvə) *n Austral derogatory slang* a person who advocates simple, natural, and unsophisticated living

basketwork ('bɑːskɪt,wɜːk) *n* another word for **wickerwork**

basking shark *n* a very large plankton-eating shark, *Cetorhinus maximus*, often floating at the sea surface: family *Cetorhinidae*. Also called: sailfish

Basle (bɑːl) or **Basel** ('bɑːzəl) *n* **1** a canton of NW Switzerland, divided into the demicantons of **Basle-Landschaft** and **Basle-Stadt**. Pops.: 263 200 and 186 900 (2002 est). Areas: 427 sq km (165 sq miles) and 36 sq km (14 sq miles) respectively **2** a city in NW Switzerland, capital of Basle canton, on the Rhine: oldest university in Switzerland. Pop: 165 000 (2002 est). French name: Bâle

basmati rice (bəz'mætɪ) *n* a variety of long-grain rice with slender aromatic grains, used for savoury dishes [from Hindi, literally: aromatic]

Bas Mitzvah (bɑːs 'mɪtsvə) *n* (*sometimes not capitals*) a variant of **Bat Mitzvah**

basophil ('beɪsəfɪl) or **basophile** *adj also* **basophilic** (,beɪsə'fɪlɪk) **1** (of cells or cell contents) easily stained by basic dyes ▷ *n* **2** a basophil cell, esp a leucocyte [C19 from Greek; see BASE[1] + -PHILE]

basophilia (,beɪsə'fɪlɪə) *n* **1** an abnormal increase of basophil leucocytes in the blood **2** the affinity of a biological specimen for basic dyes

Basotho (bə'suːtuː, -'səʊtəʊ) *n, pl* -tho or -thos a member of the subgroup of the Sotho people who chiefly inhabit Lesotho. Former name: Basuto

Basotho-Qwaqwa (bə'suːtuː'kwɑːkwə, -'səʊtəʊ-) *n* (formerly) a Bantustan in South Africa, in the Orange Free State; the only Bantustan without

exclaves: abolished in 1993. Also called: Qwaqwa Former name (until 1972): Basotho-Ba-Borwa

basque (bæsk, bɑːsk) *n* **1** a short extension below the waist to the bodice of a woman's jacket, etc **2** a tight-fitting bodice for women [C19 perhaps from Basque]

Basque (bæsk, bɑːsk) *n* **1** a member of a people of unknown origin living around the W Pyrenees in France and Spain **2** the language of this people, of no known relationship with any other language ▷ *adj* **3** relating to, denoting, or characteristic of this people or their language [C19 from French, from Latin *Vascō* a Basque]

Basque Provinces *n* an autonomous region of N Spain, comprising the provinces of Álava, Guipúzcoa, and Vizcaya: inhabited mainly by Basques, who retained virtual autonomy from the 9th to the 19th century. Pop: 1 840 700 (2003 est). Area: about 7250 sq km (2800 sq miles)

Basra, Basrah ('bæzrə) or **Busra, Busrah** ('bʌsrə) *n* a port in SE Iraq, on the Shatt-al-Arab. Pop: 1 187 000 (2005 est)

bas-relief (,bɑːrɪ'liːf, ,bæs-, 'bɑːrɪ,liːf, 'bæs-) *n* sculpture in low relief, in which the forms project slightly from the background but no part is completely detached from it. Also called (Italian): basso rilievo [C17 from French, from Italian *basso rilievo* low relief; see BASE[2], RELIEF]

Bas-Rhin (*French* barɛ̃) *n* a department of NE France in Alsace region. Capital: Strasbourg. Pop: 1 052 698 (2003 est). Area: 4793 sq km (1869 sq miles)

bass[1] (beɪs) *n* **1** the lowest adult male voice usually having a range from E a 13th below middle C to D a tone above it **2** a singer with such a voice **3** the bass the lowest part in a piece of harmony. See also **thorough bass 4** *informal* short for **bass guitar, double bass 5 a** the low-frequency component of an electrical audio signal, esp in a record player or tape recorder **b** the knob controlling this on such an instrument ▷ *adj* **6** relating to or denoting the bass: *bass pitch; the bass part* **7** denoting the lowest and largest instrument in a family: *a bass trombone* [C15 *bas* BASE[1]; modern spelling influenced by BASSO]

bass[2] (bæs) *n* **1** any of various sea perches, esp *Morone labrax*, a popular game fish with one large spiny dorsal fin separate from a second smaller one. See also **sea bass, stone bass 2** another name for the **European perch** (see **perch[2]** (sense 1)) **3** any of various predatory North American freshwater percoid fishes, such as *Micropterus salmoides*, (**largemouth bass**): family *Centrarchidae* (sunfishes, etc). ▷ See also **black bass, rock bass** [C15 changed from BASE[2], influenced by Italian *basso* low]

bass[3] (bæs) *n* **1** another name for **bast** (sense 1) **2** short for **basswood 3** Also called: **fish bass** a bast fibre bag for holding an angler's catch [C17 changed from BAST]

bass clef (beɪs) *n* the clef that establishes F a fifth below middle C on the fourth line of the staff. Symbol: 𝄢. Also called: F clef

bass drum (beɪs) *n* a large shallow drum of low and indefinite pitch. Also called: gran cassa

Bassein (bɑː'seɪn) *n* a city in Myanmar, on the Irrawaddy delta: a port on the **Bassein River** (the westernmost distributary of the Irrawaddy). Pop: 231 000 (2005 est)

Basse-Normandie (*French* basnɔrmɑ̃di) *n* a region of NW France, on the English Channel: consists of the Cherbourg peninsula in the west rising to the Normandy hills in the east; mainly agricultural

Bassenthwaite ('bæsⁿn,θweɪt) *n* a lake in NW England, in Cumbria near Keswick. Length: 6 km (4 miles)

Basses-Alpes (*French* basalp) *n* the former name for **Alpes-de-Haute-Provence**

Basses-Pyrénées (*French* baspirene) *pl n* the former name for **Pyrénées-Atlantiques**

basset[1] ('bæsɪt) *n* a long low smooth-haired breed

of hound with short strong legs and long ears. Also called: basset hound [C17 from French, from *basset* short, from *bas* low; see BASE[2]]

basset[2] ('bæsɪt) *vb* -sets, -seting, -seted, *n* a rare word for **outcrop** [C17 perhaps from French: low stool, see BASSET[1]]

Basseterre (bæs'tɛə; *French* bastɛr) *n* a port in the Caribbean, on St Kitts: the capital of St Kitts-Nevis. Pop: 13 220 (2001)

Basse-Terre ('bæs'tɛə; *French* bastɛr) *n* **1** a mountainous island in the Caribbean, in the Leeward Islands, comprising part of Guadeloupe. Area: 848 sq km (327 sq miles) **2** a port in W Guadeloupe, on Basse-Terre Island: the capital of the French Overseas Department of Guadeloupe. Pop: 12 410 (1999)

basset horn *n* an obsolete woodwind instrument of the clarinet family [C19 probably from German *Bassetthorn*, from Italian *bassetto*, diminutive of BASSO + HORN]

bass guitar (beɪs) *n* a guitar that has the same pitch and tuning as a double bass, usually electrically amplified

bassinet (,bæsɪ'nɛt) *n* a wickerwork or wooden cradle or pram, usually hooded [C19 from French: little basin, from *bassin* BASIN; associated in folk etymology with French *barcelonnette* a little cradle, from *berceau* cradle]

bassist ('beɪsɪst) *n* a player of a double bass, esp in a jazz band

basso ('bæsəʊ) *n, pl* -sos or -si (-sɪ) (esp in operatic or solo singing) a singer with a bass voice [C19 from Italian, from Late Latin *bassus* low; see BASE[2]]

basso continuo *n* another term for **thorough bass**. Often shortened to: continuo [Italian, literally: continuous bass]

bassoon (bə'suːn) *n* **1** a woodwind instrument, the tenor of the oboe family. Range: about three and a half octaves upwards from the B flat below the bass staff **2** an orchestral musician who plays the bassoon [C18 from French *basson*, from Italian *bassone*, from *basso* deep; see BASE[2]] > bas'soonist *n*

basso profundo (prəʊ'fʌndəʊ; *Italian* pro'fundo) *n, pl* -dos (esp in operatic solo singing) a singer with a very deep bass voice [Italian, literally: deep bass]

basso rilievo (*Italian* 'basso ri'ljevo) *n, pl* -vos Italian name for **bas-relief**

bass response (beɪs) *n* the response of an audio reproduction system or component to low frequencies

Bass Strait (bæs) *n* a channel between mainland Australia and Tasmania, linking the Indian Ocean and the Tasman Sea

bass viol (beɪs) *n* **1** another name for **viola da gamba 2** *US* a less common name for **double bass** (sense 1)

basswood ('bæs,wʊd) *n* **1** any of several North American linden trees, esp *Tilia americana*. Sometimes shortened to: bass **2** the soft light-coloured wood of any of these trees, used for furniture [C19 from BASS[3]; see BAST]

bast (bæst) *n* **1** Also called: bass fibrous material obtained from the phloem of jute, hemp, flax, lime, etc, used for making rope, matting, etc **2** *botany* another name for **phloem** [Old English *bæst*; related to Old Norse, Middle High German *bast*]

bastard ('bɑːstəd, 'bæs-) *n* **1** *informal, offensive* an obnoxious or despicable person **2** *informal, often humorous or affectionate* a person, esp a man: *lucky bastard* **3** *informal* something extremely difficult or unpleasant: *that job is a real bastard* **4** *old-fashioned or offensive* a person born of unmarried parents; an illegitimate baby, child, or adult **5** something irregular, abnormal, or inferior **6** a hybrid, esp an accidental or inferior one ▷ *adj* (*prenominal*) **7** *old-fashioned or offensive* illegitimate by birth **8** irregular, abnormal, or inferior in shape, size, or appearance **9** resembling a specified thing, but not actually being such: *a bastard cedar* **10** counterfeit; spurious [C13 from Old French *bastart*, perhaps from *bast* in the phrase *fils de bast* son of

b

the packsaddle (that is, of an unlawful and not the marriage bed), from Medieval Latin *bastum* packsaddle, of uncertain origin) ▷ 'bastardly *adj*

bastard cut *adj mechanical engineering* (of a file) having medium teeth; intermediate between a coarse cut and a fine cut

bastardization or **bastardisation** (ˌbɑːstədaɪˈzeɪʃən, ˌbæs-) *n* 1 the act of bastardizing 2 *Austral* an initiation ceremony in a school or military unit, esp one involving brutality b brutality or bullying

bastardize or **bastardise** ('bɑːstəˌdaɪz, 'bæs-) *vb* (tr) 1 to debase; corrupt 2 *archaic* to declare illegitimate

bastard measles *n pathol* an informal name for **rubella**

bastardry ('bɑːstədrɪ, 'bæs-) *n slang, chiefly Austral* malicious or cruel behaviour

bastard title *n* another name for **half-title** (of a book)

bastard wing *n* a tuft of feathers attached to the first digit of a bird, distinct from the wing feathers attached to the other digits and the ulna. Also called: **alula**

bastardy ('bɑːstədɪ, 'bæs-) *n archaic* the condition of being a bastard; illegitimacy

baste[1] ('beɪst) *vb* (tr) to sew with loose temporary stitches [c14 from Old French *bastir* to build, of Germanic origin; compare Old High German *besten* to sew with BAST]

baste[2] ('beɪst) *vb* to moisten (meat) during cooking with hot fat and the juices produced [c15 of uncertain origin]

baste[3] ('beɪst) *vb* (tr) to beat thoroughly; thrash [c16 probably from Old Norse *beysta*]

basti, bustee or **busti** ('bɑːstɪ) *n* (in India) a slum inhabited by poor people [Urdu: settlement]

Bastia ('bɑːstjə) *n* a port in NE Corsica: the main commercial and industrial town of the island: capital of Haute-Corse department. Pop: 37 884 (1999)

Bastille (bæˈstiːl; *French* bastij) *n* a fortress in Paris, built in the 14th century: a prison until its destruction in 1789, at the beginning of the French Revolution [c14 from Old French *bastile* fortress, from Old Provençal *bastida*, from *bastir* to build, of Germanic origin; see BASTE[1]]

Bastille Day *n* (in France) an annual holiday on July 14, commemorating the fall of the Bastille

bastinado (ˌbæstɪˈneɪdəʊ) *n, pl* -does 1 punishment or torture in which the soles of the feet are beaten with a stick 2 a blow or beating with a stick 3 a stick; cudgel ▷ *vb* -does, -doing, -doed (tr) 4 to beat (a person) on the soles of the feet [c16 from Spanish *bastonada*, from *baston* stick, from Late Latin *bastum* see BATON]

basting ('beɪstɪŋ) *n* 1 loose temporary stitches; tacking 2 sewing with such stitches

bastion ('bæstɪən) *n* 1 a projecting work in a fortification designed to permit fire to the flanks along the face of the wall 2 any fortified place 3 a thing or person regarded as upholding or defending an attitude, principle, etc: *the last bastion of opposition* [c16 from French, from earlier *bastillon* bastion, from *bastille* BASTILLE]

bastnaesite or **bastnasite** ('bæstnəˌsaɪt) *n* a rare yellow to reddish-brown mineral consisting of a carbonate of fluorine and several lanthanide metals. It occurs in association with zinc and is a source of the lanthanides. Formula: LaFCO₃ [c19 from Swedish *bastnäsit*, after *Bastnäs*, Sweden, where it was found]

Bastogne (bæˈstəʊn; *French* bastɔɲ) *n* a town in SE Belgium: of strategic importance to Allied defences during the Battle of the Bulge; besieged by the Germans during the winter of 1944–45. Pop: 14 070 (2004 est)

Basuto (bəˈsuːtəʊ) *n, pl* -tos or -to a former name for **Sotho** (senses 3, 4)

Basutoland (bəˈsuːtəʊˌlænd) *n* the former name (until 1966) of **Lesotho**

BASW ('bæzwə) *n* (in Britain) ▷ *acronym for* British

Association of Social Workers

bat[1] (bæt) *n* 1 any of various types of club with a handle, used to hit the ball in certain sports, such as cricket, baseball, or table tennis 2 a flat round club with a short handle, resembling a table-tennis bat, used by a man on the ground to guide the pilot of an aircraft when taxiing 3 *cricket* short for **batsman** 4 any stout stick, esp a wooden one 5 *informal* a blow from such a stick 6 *Austral* a small board used for tossing the coins in the game of two-up 7 *US and Canadian slang* a drinking spree; binge 8 *slang* speed; rate; pace: *they went at a fair bat* 9 another word for **batting** (sense 1) 10 carry one's bat *cricket* (of an opening batsman) to reach the end of an innings without being dismissed 11 off one's own bat a of one's own accord; without being prompted by someone else b by one's own unaided efforts 12 (right) off the bat *US and Canadian informal* immediately; without hesitation ▷ *vb* bats, batting, batted 13 (tr) to strike with or as if with a bat 14 (intr) *sport* (of a player or a team) to take a turn at batting ▷ See also **bat around** [Old English *batt* club, probably of Celtic origin; compare Gaelic *bat*, Russian *bat*]

bat[2] (bæt) *n* 1 any placental mammal of the order Chiroptera, being a nocturnal mouselike animal flying with a pair of membranous wings (patagia). The group is divided into the *Megachiroptera* (**fruit bats**) and *Microchiroptera* (**insectivorous bats**). Related adjective: **chiropteran** 2 *slang* an irritating or eccentric woman (esp in the phrase **old bat**) 3 blind as a bat having extremely poor eyesight 4 have bats in the (or one's) belfry *informal* to be mad or eccentric; have strange ideas 5 like a bat out of hell *slang* very quickly [c14 *bakke*, probably of Scandinavian origin; compare Old Norse *ledhrblaka* leather-flapper, Swedish dialect *natt-batta* night bat] ▷ 'batlike *adj*

bat[3] (bæt) *vb* bats, batting, batted (tr) 1 to wink or flutter (one's eyelids) 2 not bat an eye or eyelid *informal* to show no surprise or concern [c17 probably a variant of BATE[2]]

Bataan (bɑːˈtæn, -ˈtɑːn) *n* a peninsula in the Philippines, in W Luzon: scene of the surrender of US and Philippine forces to the Japanese during World War II, later retaken by American forces

Batangas (bəˈtæŋɡæs) *n* a port in the Philippines, in SW Luzon. Pop: 293 000 (2005 est)

Batan Islands (bəˈtɑːn) *pl n* a group of islands in the Philippines, north of Luzon. Capital: Basco. Pop: 12 091 (latest est). Area: 197 sq km (76 sq miles)

bat around *vb* 1 (tr, adverb) *US and Canadian slang* to discuss (an idea, proposition, etc) informally 2 (intr) Also: bat along *dialect*, *US and Canadian slang* to wander or move about

batata (bəˈtɑːtə) *n* another name for **sweet potato** [c16 from Spanish, from Taino]

batavia (bəˈteɪvɪə) *n* a variety of lettuce with smooth pale green leaves. Also called: Batavian endive, Batavian lettuce

Batavia (bəˈteɪvɪə) *n* 1 an ancient district of the Netherlands, on an island at the mouth of the Rhine 2 an archaic or literary name for **Holland**[1] 3 a former name for **Jakarta**

Batavian (bəˈteɪvɪən) *adj* 1 of or relating to Batavia (a former name for Holland or Jakarta) or its inhabitants ▷ *n* 2 a native or inhabitant of Batavia

batch[1] (bætʃ) *n* 1 a group or set of usually similar objects or people, esp if sent off, handled, or arriving at the same time 2 the bread, cakes, etc, produced at one baking 3 the amount of a material needed for an operation 4 Also called: batch loaf a tall loaf having a close texture and a thick crust on the top and bottom, baked as part of a batch: the sides of each loaf are greased so that they will pull apart after baking to have pale crumby sides; made esp in Scotland and Ireland. Compare **pan loaf** ▷ *vb* (tr) 5 to group (items) for efficient processing 6 to handle by batch

processing [c15 *bache*; related to Old English *bacan* to BAKE; compare Old English *gebæc* batch, German *Gebäck*]

batch[2] or **bach** (bætʃ) *vb* *Austral and NZ informal* 1 (intr) (of a man) to do his own cooking and housekeeping 2 to live alone

Bat Chayil (bɑːt ˈxajil) *n* (sometimes not capitals) *Judaism* 1 (in some congregations) a ceremony of confirmation for a girl of at least Bat Mitzvah age 2 the girl herself ▷ Also: Bat Hayil [from Hebrew, literally: daughter of valour]

batch processing *n* 1 manufacturing products or treating materials in batches, by passing the output of one process to subsequent processes. Compare **continuous processing** 2 a system by which the computer programs of a number of individual users are submitted to the computer as a single batch. Compare **time sharing** (sense 2)

bate[1] (beɪt) *vb* 1 another word for **abate** 2 with bated breath holding one's breath in suspense or fear

bate[2] (beɪt) *vb* (intr) (of hawks) to jump violently from a perch or the falconer's fist, often hanging from the leash while struggling to escape [c13 from Old French *batre* to beat, from Latin *battuere*; related to BAT[1]]

bate[3] (beɪt) *vb* (tr) 1 to soak (skin or hides) in a special solution to soften them and remove chemicals used in previous treatments ▷ *n* 2 the solution used [Old English *bætan* to BAIT[1]]

bate[4] (beɪt) *n Brit slang* a bad temper or rage [c19 from BAIT[1], alluding to the mood of a person who is being baited]

bateau (bæˈtəʊ; *French* bato) *n, pl* -teaux (-təʊz; *French* -to) a light flat-bottomed boat used on rivers in Canada and the northern US [c18 from French: boat, from Old French *batel*, from Old English *bāt*; see BOAT]

bateleur eagle ('bætəlɜː) *n* an African crested bird of prey, *Terathopius ecaudatus*, with a short tail and long wings: subfamily *Circaetinae*, family *Accipitridae* (hawks, etc) [c19 from French *bateleur* juggler]

Batesian mimicry ('beɪtsɪən) *n zoology* mimicry in which a harmless species is protected from predators by means of its resemblance to a harmful or inedible species [c19 named after H. W. *Bates* (1825–92), British naturalist and explorer]

batfish ('bætˌfɪʃ) *n, pl* -fish or -fishes any angler of the family *Ogcocephalidae*, having a flattened scaleless body and moving on the sea floor by means of fleshy pectoral and pelvic fins

batfowl ('bætˌfaʊl) *vb* (intr) to catch birds by temporarily blinding them with light ▷ 'bat,fowler *n*

bath[1] (bɑːθ) *n, pl* baths (bɑːðz) 1 a large container, esp one made of enamelled iron or plastic, used for washing or medically treating the body. Related adjective: **balneal** 2 the act or an instance of washing in such a container 3 the amount of liquid contained in a bath 4 run a bath to turn on the taps to fill a bath with water for bathing oneself 5 (usually plural) a place that provides baths or a swimming pool for public use 6 a a vessel in which something is immersed to maintain it at a constant temperature, to process it photographically, electrolytically, etc, or to lubricate it b the liquid used in such a vessel ▷ *vb* 7 *Brit* to wash in a bath [Old English *bæth*; compare Old High German *bad*, Old Norse *bath*; related to Swedish *basa* to clean with warm water, Old High German *bāen* to warm]

bath[2] (bæθ) *n* an ancient Hebrew unit of liquid measure equal to about 8.3 Imperial gallons or 10 US gallons [Hebrew]

Bath (bɑːθ) *n* a city in SW England, in Bath and North East Somerset unitary authority, Somerset, on the River Avon: famous for its hot springs; a fashionable spa in the 18th century; Roman remains, notably the baths; university (1966). Pop: 90 144 (2001). Latin name: Aquae Sulis ('ækwiˈsuːlɪs)

Ba'th (bɑːθ) or **Ba'ath** n an Arab Socialist party, esp in Iraq and Syria, founded by Michel Aflaq in 1941. It attempts to combine Marxism with pan-Islamic nationalism [c20 from Arabic: resurgence] > **'Ba'thi** adj > **'Ba'thism** n > **'Ba'thist** n

Bath and North East Somerset (ˈsʌməsɛt) n a unitary authority in SW England, in Somerset; formerly (1974–96) part of the county of Avon. Pop: 170 900 (2003 est). Area: 351 sq km (136 sq miles)

Bat Hayil (bɑːt ˈxajil) n a variant spelling of **Bat Chayil**

bath bun n Brit a sweet bun containing spices and dried fruit [c19 from BATH, where it was originally made]

Bath chair n a wheelchair for invalids, often with a hood

Bath chap n the lower part of the cheek of a pig, cooked and eaten, usually cold

bath cube n a cube of soluble scented material for use in a bath

bathe (beɪð) vb 1 (intr) to swim or paddle in a body of open water or a river, esp for pleasure 2 (tr) to apply liquid to (skin, a wound, etc) in order to cleanse or soothe 3 to immerse or be immersed in a liquid: to bathe machine parts in oil 4 chiefly US and Canadian to wash in a bath 5 (tr; often passive) to suffuse: her face was bathed with radiance 6 (tr) (of water, the sea, etc) to lap; wash: waves bathed the shore ▷ n 7 Brit a swim or paddle in a body of open water or a river [Old English bathian; related to Old Norse batha, Old High German badōn] > **'bather** n

bathers (ˈbeɪðəz) pl n Austral a swimming costume

bathetic (bəˈθɛtɪk) adj containing or displaying bathos

bathhouse (ˈbɑːθˌhaʊs) n a building containing baths, esp for public use

bathing beauty (ˈbeɪðɪŋ) n an attractive girl in a swimming costume. Also called (old-fashioned): **bathing belle**

bathing cap (ˈbeɪðɪŋ) n a tight rubber cap worn by a swimmer to keep the hair dry

bathing costume (ˈbeɪðɪŋ) n another name for **swimming costume**

bathing machine (ˈbeɪðɪŋ) n a small hut, on wheels so that it could be pulled to the sea, used in the 18th and 19th centuries for bathers to change their clothes

bathing suit (ˈbeɪðɪŋ) n 1 a garment worn for bathing, esp an old-fashioned one that covers much of the body 2 another name for **swimming costume**

batho- combining form a variant of **bathy-**

bathochromic (ˌbæθəˈkrəʊmɪk) adj chem denoting or relating to a shift to a longer wavelength in the absorption spectrum of a compound > **'batho,chrome** n

batholith (ˈbæθəlɪθ) or **batholite** (ˈbæθəˌlaɪt) n a very large irregular-shaped mass of igneous rock, esp granite, formed from an intrusion of magma at great depth, esp one exposed after erosion of less resistant overlying rocks > ˌbatho'lithic or ˌbatho'litic adj

Bath Oliver n Brit a kind of unsweetened biscuit [c19 named after William Oliver (1695–1764), a physician at Bath]

bathometer (bəˈθɒmɪtə) n an instrument for measuring the depth of water > **bathometric** (ˌbæθəˈmɛtrɪk) adj > ˌbatho'metrically adv > **bathometry** (bəˈθɒmɪtrɪ) n

Bathonian (bəˈθəʊnɪən) adj 1 of or relating to Bath 2 geology of or denoting a stage of the Jurassic system in NW Europe ▷ n 3 a native or resident of Bath 4 the Bathonian period or rock system

bathophilous (bæˈθɒfɪləs) adj (of an organism) living in very deep water

bathos (ˈbeɪθɒs) n 1 a sudden ludicrous descent from exalted to ordinary matters or style in speech or writing 2 insincere or excessive pathos 3 triteness; flatness 4 the lowest point; nadir [c18 from Greek: depth, from bathus deep]

bathrobe (ˈbɑːθˌrəʊb) n 1 a loose-fitting garment of towelling, for wear before or after a bath or swimming 2 US and Canadian a dressing gown

bathroom (ˈbɑːθˌruːm, -ˌrʊm) n 1 a room containing a bath or shower and usually a washbasin and lavatory 2 US and Canadian another name for **lavatory**

bath salts pl n soluble scented salts for use in a bath

Bathsheba (bæθˈʃiːbə, ˈbæθʃɪbə) n Old Testament the wife of Uriah, who committed adultery with David and later married him and became the mother of his son Solomon (II Samuel 11–12)

Bath stone n Brit a kind of limestone used as a building material, esp at Bath in England

bathtub (ˈbɑːθˌtʌb) n a bath, esp one not permanently fixed

bathtub race n Canadian a sailing race between bathtubs fitted with outboard motors

Bathurst (ˈbæθəst) n 1 a city in SE Australia, in E New South Wales: scene of a gold rush in 1851. Pop: 27 036 (2001) 2 a port in E Canada, in NE New Brunswick: rich mineral resources discovered in 1953. Pop: 16 427 (2001) 3 the former name (until 1973) of **Banjul**

Bathurst burr n an Australian plant, Xanthium spinosum, having numerous hooked burrs that became entangled in sheep's wool [c19 from Bathurst region of New South Wales]

bathy- or **batho-** combining form indicating depth: bathysphere; bathometer [from Greek bathus deep]

bathyal (ˈbæθɪəl) adj denoting or relating to an ocean depth of between 200 and 2000 metres (about 100 and 1000 fathoms), corresponding to the continental slope

bathylimnetic (ˌbæθɪlɪmˈnɛtɪk) adj (of an organism) living in the depths of lakes and marshes

bathymetry (bəˈθɪmɪtrɪ) n measurement of the depth of an ocean or other large body of water > bathymetric (ˌbæθɪˈmɛtrɪk) adj > ˌbathy'metrically adv

bathypelagic (ˌbæθɪpəˈlædʒɪk) adj of, relating to, or inhabiting the lower depths of the ocean between approximately 1000 and 4000 metres

bathyscaph (ˈbæθɪˌskæf) or **bathyscaphe** (ˈbæθɪˌskeɪf, -ˌskæf) or **bathyscape** (ˈbæθɪˌskæp) n a submersible vessel having a flotation compartment with an observation capsule underneath, capable of reaching ocean depths of over 10 000 metres (about 5000 fathoms) [c20 from BATHY- + -scaph, from Greek skaphē light boat]

bathysphere (ˈbæθɪˌsfɪə) n a strong steel deep-sea diving sphere, lowered by cable

batik or **battik** (ˈbætɪk) n a a process of printing fabric in which parts not to be dyed are covered by wax b fabric printed in this way c (as modifier): a batik shirt [c19 via Malay from Javanese: painted]

batiste (bæˈtiːst) n a fine plain-weave cotton fabric: used esp for shirts and dresses [c17 from French, from Old French toile de baptiste, probably after Baptiste of Cambrai, 13th-century French weaver, its reputed inventor]

Batley (ˈbætlɪ) n a town in N England, in Kirklees unitary authority, West Yorkshire. Pop: 49 448 (2001)

batman (ˈbætmən) n, pl -men an officer's personal servant in any of the armed forces [c18 from Old French bat, bast, from Medieval Latin bastum packsaddle]

Batman (ˈbætˌmæn) n a character in an American comic strip and several films who secretly assumes a batlike costume in order to fight crime

Bat Mitzvah (bɑːt ˈmɪtsvə) (sometimes not capitals) Judaism ▷ adj 1 (of a Jewish girl) having attained religious majority at the age of twelve ▷ n 2 the date of, or, in some congregations, a ceremony marking, this event 3 the girl herself on that day ▷ Also called: **Bas Mitzvah** [from Hebrew, literally: daughter of the commandment]

baton (ˈbætən, -tɒn) n 1 a thin stick used by the conductor of an orchestra, choir, etc, to indicate rhythm or expression 2 a a short stick carried for use as a weapon, as by a policeman; truncheon b (as modifier): a baton charge 3 athletics a short bar carried by a competitor in a relay race and transferred to the next runner at the end of each stage 4 a long stick with a knob on one end, carried, twirled, and thrown up and down by a drum major or drum majorette, esp at the head of a parade 5 a staff or club carried by an official as a symbol of authority 6 heraldry a single narrow diagonal line superimposed on all other charges, esp one curtailed at each end, signifying a bastard line [c16 from French bâton, from Late Latin bastum rod, probably ultimately from Greek bastazein to lift up, carry]

bâton de commandement (French batɔ̃ də kɔmɑ̃dmɑ̃) n an antler object found in Upper Palaeolithic sites from the Aurignacian period onwards, consisting of a rod, often ornately decorated, with a hole through the thicker end [literally: baton of command, although the object was probably actually used in making shafts for arrows and spears]

Baton Rouge (ˈbætⁿn ˈruːʒ) n the capital of Louisiana, in the SE part on the Mississippi River. Pop: 225 090 (2003 est)

baton round n the official name for **plastic bullet**

batrachian (bəˈtreɪkɪən) n 1 any amphibian, esp a frog or toad ▷ adj 2 of or relating to the frogs and toads [c19 from New Latin Batrachia, from Greek batrakhos frog]

bats (bæts) adj informal crazy; very eccentric [from BATS-IN-THE-BELFRY (sense 2)]

bats-in-the-belfry n (functioning as singular) 1 a hairy Eurasian campanulaceous plant, Campanula trachelium, with bell-shaped blue-purple flowers ▷ adj 2 slang mad; demented

batsman (ˈbætsmən) n, pl -men 1 cricket a a person who bats or whose turn it is to bat b a player who specializes in batting 2 a person on the ground who uses bats to guide the pilot of an aircraft when taxiing > **'batsman,ship** n

bats-wing coral-tree n a small tree, Erythrina verspertilio, of tropical and subtropical Australia with red flowers and leaves shaped like the wings of a bat

batt (bæt) n 1 textiles another word for **batting** (sense 1) 2 Austral and NZ a slab-shaped piece of insulating material used in building houses

battalion (bəˈtæljən) n 1 a military unit comprised of three or more companies or formations of similar size 2 (usually plural) any large array [c16 from French bataillon, from Old Italian battaglione, from battaglia company of soldiers, BATTLE]

battels (ˈbætⁿlz) pl n (at some universities) the account of a member of a college for board, provisions, and other college expenses [c16 perhaps from obsolete battle to feed, fatten, of uncertain origin]

battement (French batmɑ̃) n ballet extension of one leg forwards, sideways, or backwards, either once or repeatedly [c19 French, literally: beating]

batten¹ (ˈbætⁿn) n 1 a sawn strip of wood used in building to cover joints, provide a fixing for tiles or slates, support lathing, etc 2 a long narrow board used for flooring 3 a narrow flat length of wood or plastic inserted in pockets of a sail to give it proper shape 4 a lath used for holding a tarpaulin along the side of a raised hatch on a ship 5 theatre a a row of lights b the strip or bar supporting them 6 Also called: **dropper** NZ an upright part of a fence made of wood or other material, designed to keep wires at equal distances apart ▷ vb 7 (tr) to furnish or strengthen with battens 8 **batten down the hatches a** to use battens in nailing a tarpaulin over a hatch on a ship to make it secure **b** to prepare for action, a crisis, etc [c15 from French bâton stick; see BATON] > **'battening** n

batten² (ˈbætⁿn) vb (intr; usually foll by on) to thrive, esp at the expense of someone else: to *batten on the needy* [C16 probably from Old Norse *batna* to improve; related to Old Norse *betr* BETTER[1], Old High German *bazzen* to get better]

Battenburg ('bætᵊn,bɜːɡ) *n* an oblong sponge cake divided longitudinally into four square sections, two coloured pink and two yellow, with an outer coating of marzipan [perhaps named after *Battenberg*, a village in Prussia]

batten plate *n* (in structural design) a horizontal rectangular plate that is used to connect pairs of steel sections by being riveted or welded across them to form a composite section

Batten's disease ('bætᵊnz) *n* a rare hereditary disease in which lipids accumulate in the nervous system, leading to mental deterioration, spasticity, and blindness that start in early childhood [C20 named after F. E. Batten (1865–1918), British neurologist]

batter[1] ('bætə) *vb* **1** to hit (someone or something) repeatedly using heavy blows, as with a club or other heavy instrument; beat heavily **2** (*tr; often passive*) to damage or injure, as by blows, heavy wear, etc **3** (*tr*) *social welfare* to subject (a person, esp a close relative living in the same house) to repeated physical violence **4** (*tr*) to subject (a person, opinion, or theory) to harsh criticism; attack [C14 *bateren*, probably from *batten* to BAT[1]]

batter[2] ('bætə) *n* a mixture of flour, eggs, and milk, used to make cakes, pancakes, etc, and to coat certain foods before frying [C15 *bater*, probably from *bateren* to BATTER[1]]

batter[3] ('bætə) *n sport* a player who bats

batter[4] ('bætə) *n* **1** the slope of the face of a wall that recedes gradually backwards and upwards ▷ *vb* **2** (*intr*) to have such a slope [C16 (*vb:* to incline): of uncertain origin]

batter[5] ('bætə) *n* a spree or debauch [C19 of unknown origin]

battered ('bætəd) *adj* subjected to persistent physical violence, esp by a close relative living in the same house: *a battered baby*

batterer ('bætərə) *n* **a** a person who batters someone **b** (*in combination*): *baby-batterer; wife-batterer*

batterie de cuisine (*French* batri də kɥizin) *n* cooking utensils collectively; pots and pans, etc [C18 literally: battery of kitchen]

battering ('bætərɪŋ) *n* **a** the act or practice of battering someone **b** (*in combination*): *baby-battering; granny-battering*

battering ram *n* (esp formerly) a large beam used to break down the walls or doors of fortifications

Battersea ('bætəsɪ) *n* a district in London, in Wandsworth: noted for its dogs' home, power station (now a leisure centre), and park

battery ('bætərɪ) *n, pl* -teries **1 a** two or more primary cells connected together, usually in series, to provide a source of electric current **b** short for **dry battery 2** another name for **accumulator** (sense 1) **3** a number of similar things occurring together: *a battery of questions* **4** *criminal law* unlawful beating or wounding of a person or mere touching in a hostile or offensive manner. See also **assault and battery 5** a fortified structure on which artillery is mounted **6** a group of guns, missile launchers, searchlights, or torpedo tubes of similar type or size operated as a single entity **7** a small tactical unit of artillery usually consisting of two or more troops, each of two, three or four guns **8** *chiefly Brit* **a** a large group of cages for intensive rearing of poultry **b** (*as modifier*): *battery hens* **9** *psychol* a series of tests **10** *chess* two pieces of the same colour placed so that one can unmask an attack by the other by moving **11** the percussion section in an orchestra **12** *baseball* the pitcher and the catcher considered together [C16 from Old French *batterie* beating, from *battre* to beat, from Latin *battuere*]

battik ('bætɪk) *n* a variant spelling of **batik**

batting ('bætɪŋ) *n* **1** Also called: **batt** cotton or woollen wadding used in quilts, mattresses, etc **2** the action of a person or team that hits with a

bat, esp in cricket or baseball

battle ('bætᵊl) *n* **1** a fight between large armed forces; military or naval engagement; combat **2** conflict; contention; struggle: *his battle for recognition* **3** do, give, *or* join battle to start fighting ▷ *vb* **4** (when *intr*, often foll by *against, for,* or *with*) to fight in or as if in military combat; contend (with): *she battled against cancer* **5** to struggle in order to achieve something or arrive somewhere: *he battled through the crowd* **6** (*intr*) *Austral* to scrape a living, esp by doing odd jobs [C13 from Old French *bataile*, from Late Latin *battālia* exercises performed by soldiers, from *battuere* to beat] > 'battler *n*

Battle ('bætᵊl) *n* a town in SE England, in East Sussex: site of the Battle of Hastings (1066); medieval abbey. Pop: 5190 (2001)

battle-axe *n* **1** (formerly) a large broad-headed axe **2** *informal* an argumentative domineering woman

battle-axe block *n Austral* a block of land behind another, with access from the street through a narrow drive

battlebus ('bætᵊl,bʌs) *n* the coach that transports politicians and their advisers round the country during an election campaign

battle cruiser *n* a warship of battleship size but with lighter armour and fewer guns and capable of high speed

battle cry *n* **1** a shout uttered by soldiers going into battle **2** a slogan used to rally the supporters of a campaign, movement, etc

battledore ('bætᵊl,dɔː) *n* **1** Also called: **battledore and shuttlecock** an ancient racket game **2** a light racket, smaller than a tennis racket, used for striking the shuttlecock in this game **3** (formerly) a wooden utensil used for beating clothes, in baking, etc [C15 *batyldoure*, perhaps from Old Provençal *batedor* a beater, from Old French *battre* to beat, BATTER[1]]

battledress ('bætᵊl,drɛs) *n* the ordinary uniform of a soldier, consisting of tunic and trousers

battle fatigue *n psychol* a type of mental disorder, characterized by anxiety, depression, and loss of motivation, caused by the stress of active warfare. Also called: **combat fatigue**. See also **shell shock**

battlefield ('bætᵊl,fiːld) *or* **battleground** ('bætᵊl,graʊnd) *n* the place where a battle is fought; an area of conflict

battle group *n* a group of warships usu. consisting of at least one aircraft carrier, other surface ships, submarines, landing craft, etc

battle line *n* **1** the line along which troops are positioned for battle **2** the battle lines are drawn conflict or argument is about to occur between opposing people or groups

battlement ('bætᵊlmənt) *n* a parapet or wall with indentations or embrasures, originally for shooting through [C14 from Old French *batailles*, plural of *bataille* BATTLE] > 'battlemented *adj*

Battle of Britain *n* the. from August to October 1940, the prolonged bombing of S England by the German Luftwaffe and the successful resistance by the RAF Fighter Command, which put an end to the German plan of invading Britain

Battle of the Atlantic *n* the struggle for control of the sea routes around the United Kingdom during World War II, esp 1940–43

battlepiece ('bætᵊl,piːs) *n* a painting, relief, mosaic, etc, depicting a battle, usually commemorating an actual event

battle royal *n* **1** a fight, esp with fists or cudgels, involving more than two combatants; melee **2** a long violent argument

battleship ('bætᵊl,ʃɪp) *n* **1** a heavily armoured warship of the largest type having many large-calibre guns **2** (formerly) a warship of sufficient size and armament to take her place in the line of battle; ship of the line

battue (bæ'tuː, -'tjuː; *French* baty) *n* **1** the beating of woodland or cover to force game to flee in the direction of hunters **2 a** an organized shooting

party using this method **b** the game disturbed or shot by this method **3** indiscriminate slaughter, as of a defenceless crowd [C19 from French, feminine of *battu* beaten, from *battre* to beat, from Latin *battuere*]

batty ('bætɪ) *adj* -tier, -tiest *slang* **1** insane; crazy **2** odd; eccentric [C20 from BAT[2]; compare the phrase *have bats in the belfry*]

batty boy *or* **man** *n chiefly Brit derogatory slang* a male homosexual [C20 from Caribbean slang *batty* bottom, buttocks]

Batum (baː'tuːm) *or* **Batumi** (baː'tuːmɪ) *n* a city in Georgia: capital of the Adzhar Autonomous Republic; a major Black Sea port. Pop: 118 000 (2005 est)

batwing ('bæt,wɪŋ) *adj* shaped like the wings of a bat, as a black tie, collar, etc

batwing sleeve *n* a sleeve of a garment with a deep armhole and a tight wrist

batwoman ('bæt,wʊmən) *n, pl* -women a female servant in any of the armed forces

bauble ('bɔːbᵊl) *n* **1** a showy toy or trinket of little value; trifle **2** (formerly) a mock staff of office carried by a court jester [C14 from Old French *baubel* plaything, of obscure origin]

Bauchi ('baʊtʃɪ) *n* **1** a state of N Nigeria: formed in 1976 from part of North-Eastern State; tin mining. Capital: Bauchi. Pop: 446 000 (2005 est). Area: 64 605 sq km (24 944 sq miles) **2** a town in N central Nigeria, capital of Bauchi state. Pop: 76 070 (1991 est)

bauchle ('bɒxᵊl) *n Scot* **1** an old worn shoe **2** a worthless or clumsy person **3** a useless object **4** a trout-fisher's term for a **perch[2]** [C18 of unknown origin]

Baucis ('bɔːsɪs) *n Greek myth* a poor peasant woman who, with her husband Philemon, was rewarded for hospitality to the disguised gods Zeus and Hermes

baud (bɔːd) *n* a unit used to measure the speed of electronic code transmissions, equal to one unit interval per second [C20 named after J. M. E. Baudot (1845–1903), French inventor]

bauera ('baʊərə) *n* any small evergreen Australian shrub of the genus *Bauera*, having pink or purple flowers [C19 named after Franz (1758–1840) and Ferdinand (1760–1826) *Bauer*, Australian botanical artists]

Bauhaus ('baʊ,haʊs) *n* **a** a German school of architecture and applied arts founded in 1919 by Walter Gropius on experimental principles of functionalism and truth to materials. After being closed by the Nazis in 1933, its ideas were widely disseminated by its students and staff, including Kandinsky, Klee, Feininger, Moholy-Nagy, and Mies van der Rohe **b** (*as modifier*): *Bauhaus wallpaper* [C20 German, literally: building house]

bauhinia (bɔː'hɪnɪə, bəʊ-) *n* any climbing or shrubby leguminous plant of the genus *Bauhinia*, of tropical and warm regions, widely cultivated for ornament [C18 New Latin, named after Jean and Gaspard *Bauhin*, 16th-century French herbalists]

baulk (bɔːk; *usually for sense* 1 bɔːlk) *n* **1** Also (US): balk *billiards* **a** (in billiards) the space, usually 29 inches deep, between the baulk line and the bottom cushion **b** (in baulk-line games) one of the spaces between the cushions and the baulk lines **c** in baulk inside one of these spaces **2** *archaeol* a strip of earth left between excavation trenches for the study of the complete stratigraphy of a site **3** *croquet* either of two lines (A baulk and B baulk) at diagonally opposite ends of the court, from which the ball is struck into play ▷ *vb,* **n 4** a variant spelling of **balk**

baulk line *or US* **balk line** *n billiards* **1** Also called: **string line** a straight line across a billiard table behind which the cue balls are placed at the start of a game **2 a** one of four lines parallel to the cushions dividing the table into a central panel and eight smaller ones (the baulks) **b** a type of game using these lines as restrictions

Baumé scale (bəʊˈmeɪ, ˈbəʊmeɪ) *n* a scale for calibrating hydrometers used for measuring the specific gravity of liquids. 1 degree Baumé is equal to 144.3$(s-1)/s$), where *s* is specific gravity [c19 named after Antoine *Baumé* (1728–1804), French chemist]

Bautzen (ˈbaʊtsən) *n* a city in E Germany, in Saxony: site of an indecisive battle in 1813 between Napoleon's army and an allied army of Russians and Prussians. Pop: 42 160 (2003 est)

bauxite (ˈbɔːksaɪt) *n* a white, red, yellow, or brown amorphous claylike substance comprising aluminium oxides and hydroxides, often with such impurities as iron oxides. It is the chief ore of aluminium. General formula: $Al_2O_3.nH_2O$ [c19 from French, from (*Les*) *Baux* in southern France, where it was originally found]

Bavaria (bəˈvɛərɪə) *n* a state of S Germany: a former duchy and kingdom; mainly wooded highland, with the Alps in the south. Capital: Munich. Pop: 12 155 000 (2000 est). Area: 70 531 sq km (27 232 sq miles). German name: **Bayern**

Bavarian (bəˈvɛərɪən) *adj* 1 of or relating to Bavaria or its inhabitants ▷ *n* 2 a native or inhabitant of Bavaria

Bavarian cream *n* a cold dessert consisting of a rich custard set with gelatine and flavoured in various ways. Also called: bavarois (*French* bavarwa)

bawbee (bɔːˈbiː) *n* 1 a former Scottish silver coin 2 *Scot* an informal word for **halfpenny** (sense 2) [c16 named after Alexander Orok of *Sillebawby*, master of the mint]

bawcock (ˈbɔːˌkɒk) *n archaic* a fine fellow [c16 from French *beau coq*, from *beau* handsome + *coq* COCK[1]]

bawd (bɔːd) *n archaic* 1 a person who runs a brothel, esp a woman 2 a prostitute [c14 from Old French *baude*, feminine of *baud* merry, of Germanic origin; compare Old High German *bald* BOLD]

bawdry (ˈbɔːdrɪ) *n archaic* obscene talk or language

bawdy (ˈbɔːdɪ) *adj* bawdier, bawdiest 1 (of language, plays, etc) containing references to sex, esp to be humorous ▷ *n* 2 obscenity or eroticism, esp in writing or drama > **ˈbawdily** *adv* > **ˈbawdiness** *n*

bawdyhouse (ˈbɔːdɪˌhaʊs) *n* an archaic word for **brothel**

bawl (bɔːl) *vb* 1 (*intr*) to utter long loud cries, as from pain or frustration; wail 2 to shout loudly, as in anger ▷ *n* 3 a loud shout or cry [c15 probably from Icelandic *baula* to low; related to Medieval Latin *baulāre* to bark, Swedish *böla* to low; all of imitative origin] > **ˈbawler** *n* > **ˈbawling** *n*

bawl out *vb* (*tr, adverb*) *informal* to scold loudly

bawneen (ˈbɑːniːn) *n Irish* a variant spelling of **báinín**

bay[1] (beɪ) *n* 1 a wide semicircular indentation of a shoreline, esp between two headlands or peninsulas 2 an extension of lowland into hills that partly surround it 3 *US* an extension of prairie into woodland [c14 from Old French *baie*, perhaps from Old French *baer* to gape, from Medieval Latin *batāre* to yawn]

bay[2] (beɪ) *n* 1 an alcove or recess in a wall 2 any partly enclosed compartment, as one in which hay is stored in a barn 3 See **bay window** 4 an area off a road in which vehicles may park or unload, esp one adjacent to a shop, factory, etc 5 a compartment in an aircraft, esp one used for a specified purpose: *the bomb bay* 6 *nautical* a compartment in the forward part of a ship between decks, often used as the ship's hospital 7 *Brit* a tracked recess in the platform of a railway station, esp one forming the terminus of a branch line [c14 from Old French *baee* gap or recess in a wall, from *baer* to gape; see BAY[1]]

bay[3] (beɪ) *n* 1 a deep howl or growl, esp of a hound on the scent 2 at bay a (of a person or animal) forced to turn and face attackers: *the dogs held the deer at bay* b at a distance: *to keep a disease at* bay 3 bring to bay to force into a position from which retreat is impossible ▷ *vb* 4 (*intr*) to howl (at) in deep prolonged tones 5 (*tr*) to utter in a loud prolonged tone 6 (*tr*) to drive to or hold at bay [c13 from Old French *abaiier* to bark, of imitative origin]

bay[4] (beɪ) *n* 1 Also called: bay laurel, sweet bay a small evergreen Mediterranean laurel, *Laurus nobilis*, with glossy aromatic leaves, used for flavouring in cooking, and small blackish berries. See **laurel** (sense 1) 2 any of various other trees with strongly aromatic leaves used in cooking, esp a member of the genera *Myrica* or *Pimenta* 3 any of several magnolias. See **sweet bay** 4 any of certain other trees or shrubs, esp bayberry 5 (*plural*) a wreath of bay leaves. See **laurel** (sense 6) [c14 from Old French *baie* laurel berry, from Latin *bāca* berry]

bay[5] (beɪ) *n* 1 a a moderate reddish-brown colour b (*as adjective*): *a bay horse* 2 an animal of this colour, esp a horse [c14 from Old French *bai*, from Latin *badius*]

bayadere (ˌbaɪəˈdɪə, -ˈdɛə) *n* 1 a dancing girl, esp one serving in a Hindu temple 2 a fabric or design with horizontal stripes, esp of a bright colour ▷ *adj* 3 (of fabric, etc) having horizontal stripes [c18 via French from Portuguese *bailadeira* dancing girl, from *bailar* to dance, from Latin *ballāre*; see BALL[2]]

Bayamón (*Spanish* baja'mon) *n* a city in NE central Puerto Rico, south of San Juan. Pop: 224 915 (2003 est)

Bayard (ˈbeɪəd) *n* a legendary horse that figures prominently in medieval romance

bayberry (ˈbeɪbərɪ) *or* **bay** *n, pl* -ries 1 any of several North American aromatic shrubs or small trees of the genus *Myrica*, that bear grey waxy berries: family *Myricaceae*. See also **wax myrtle** 2 Also called: bay rum tree a tropical American myrtaceous tree, *Pimenta racemosa*, that yields an oil used in making bay rum 3 the fruit of any of these plants

Bayern (ˈbaɪərn) *n* the German name for **Bavaria**

Bayesian (ˈbeɪzɪən) *adj* (of a theory) presupposing known a priori probabilities which may be subjectively assessed and which can be revised in the light of experience in accordance with Bayes' theorem. A hypothesis is thus confirmed by an experimental observation which is likely given the hypothesis and unlikely without it. Compare **maximum likelihood**

Bayes' theorem (beɪz) *n statistics* the fundamental result which expresses the conditional probability $P(E/A)$ of an event *E* given an event *A* as $P(A/E).P(E)/P(A)$; more generally, where E_n is one of a set of values E_i which partition the sample space, $P(E_n/A) = P(A/E_n)P(E_n)/\Sigma P(A/E_i)P(E_i)$. This enables prior estimates of probability to be continually revised in the light of observations [c20 named after Thomas *Bayes* (1702–61), English mathematician and Presbyterian minister]

Bayeux (*French* bajø) *n* a town in NW France, on the River Aure: its museum houses the Bayeux tapestry and there is a 13th-century cathedral: dairy foods, plastic. Pop: 14 961 (1999)

Bayeux tapestry *n* an 11th- or 12th-century embroidery in Bayeux, nearly 70.5 m (231 ft) long by 50 cm (20 inches) high, depicting the Norman conquest of England

bay leaf *n* a leaf, usually dried, of the Mediterranean laurel, *Laurus nobilis*, used in cooking to flavour soups and stews

bay lynx *n* another name for **bobcat**

Bay of Pigs *n* a bay on the SW coast of Cuba: scene of an unsuccessful invasion of Cuba by US-backed troops (April 17, 1961). Spanish name: Bahia de los Cochinos

bayonet (ˈbeɪənɪt) *n* 1 a blade that can be attached to the muzzle of a rifle for stabbing in close combat 2 a type of fastening in which a cylindrical member is inserted into a socket against spring pressure and turned so that pins on its side engage in slots in the socket ▷ *vb* -nets, -neting, -neted *or* -nets, -netting, -netted 3 (*tr*) to stab or kill with a bayonet [c17 from French *baïonnette*, from BAYONNE where it originated]

Bayonne (*French* bajɔn) *n* a port in SW France: a commercial centre for the Basque region. Pop: 40 078 (1999)

bayou (ˈbaɪjuː) *n* (in the southern US) a sluggish marshy tributary of a lake or river [c18 from Louisiana French, from Choctaw *bayuk*]

Bayreuth (*German* baiˈrɔyt) *n* a city in E Germany, in NE Bavaria: home and burial place of Richard Wagner; annual festivals of his music. Pop: 74 818 (2003 est)

bay rum *n* 1 an aromatic liquid, used in medicines and cosmetics, originally obtained by distilling the leaves of the bayberry tree (*Pimenta racemosa*) with rum: now also synthesized from alcohol, water, and various oils 2 bay rum tree another name for **bayberry** (sense 2)

Bay Street *n* (in Canada) 1 the financial centre of Toronto, in which Canada's largest stock exchange is situated 2 the financial interests and powers of Toronto

bay tree *n* another name for **bay**[4] (sense 1)

bay window *n* a window projecting from the wall of a building and forming an alcove of a room. Sometimes shortened to: bay See also **bow window, oriel window**

baywood (ˈbeɪˌwʊd) *n* the light soft wood of a tropical American mahogany tree, *Swietenia macrophylla*, of the bay region of SE Mexico

bayyan (baɪˈjaːn) *n Islam* an official declaration [c21 from Arabic]

bazaar *or* **bazar** (bəˈzɑː) *n* 1 (esp in the Orient) a market area, esp a street of small stalls 2 a sale in aid of charity, esp of miscellaneous secondhand or handmade articles 3 a shop where a large variety of goods is sold [c16 from Persian *bāzār*, from Old Persian *abēcharish*]

bazoo (bəˈzuː) *n* a US slang word for **mouth** [c19 of unknown origin]

bazooka (bəˈzuːkə) *n* a portable tubular rocket-launcher that fires a projectile capable of piercing armour: used by infantrymen as a short-range antitank weapon [c20 named after a pipe instrument invented by Bob Burns (1896–1956), American comedian]

bb *the internet domain name for* Barbados

BB 1 *abbreviation for* Boys' Brigade 2 (on Brit pencils) *symbol for* double black: denoting a very soft lead

B2B *abbreviation for* business-to-business; denoting trade between commercial organizations rather than between businesses and private customers. Compare **B2C, B2E**

BBBC *abbreviation for* British Boxing Board of Control

BBC *abbreviation for* British Broadcasting Corporation

BBFC *abbreviation for* British Board of Film Classification

BBL *text messaging abbreviation for* be back later

B-boy (ˈbiːˌbɔɪ) *n* a male rap-music fan, who typically can be identified by his casual style of dress [c20 from *Bronx boy*]

BBQ *abbreviation for* barbecue

BBS *text messaging abbreviation for* be back soon

BBSRC (in Britain) *abbreviation for* Biotechnology and Biological Sciences Research Council

B bursary *n NZ* the lower of two bursaries available for students entering university, polytechnic, etc. Compare **A bursary**

BC *abbreviation for* 1 Also: B.C. (indicating years numbered back from the supposed year of the birth of Christ) before Christ: *in 54 BC Caesar came.* Compare **AD**

▪ USAGE See at **AD**

2 British Columbia

B2C *abbreviation for* business to consumer: denoting

an internet communication channel between a business and consumers. Compare **B2B, B2E**

BCA (in New Zealand) *abbreviation for* Bachelor of Commerce and Administration

BCAR *abbreviation for* **British Civil Airworthiness Requirements**

BCC *abbreviation for* British Coal Corporation (formerly the National Coal Board)

BCD *abbreviation for* **binary-coded decimal**

BCE *abbreviation for* Before Common Era (used, esp by non-Christians, in numbering years BC)

B-cell *n* another name for **B-lymphocyte**

BCF *abbreviation for* 1 British Chess Federation 2 British Cycling Federation

BCG *abbreviation for* bacille Calmette-Guérin (antituberculosis vaccine)

BCh *abbreviation for* Bachelor of Surgery [from Latin *Baccalaureus Chirurgiae*]

BCL *abbreviation for* Bachelor of Civil Law

BCNU *text messaging abbreviation for* be seeing you

BCNZ *abbreviation for* (the former) Broadcasting Corporation of New Zealand

BCom *abbreviation for* Bachelor of Commerce

B complex *n* short for **vitamin B complex**

B.C.S. (in the US and Canada) *abbreviation for* Bachelor of Computer Science

bd¹ *abbreviation for* 1 board 2 *insurance, finance* bond

bd² *the internet domain name for* Bangladesh

BD *abbreviation for* 1 Bachelor of Divinity 2 *commerce* bills discounted 3 ▷ *international car registration for* Bangladesh

B/D *abbreviation for* 1 bank draft 2 *commerce* bills discounted 3 Also: b/d *book-keeping* brought down

BDA *abbreviation for* British Dental Association

Bde *or* **bde** *abbreviation for* brigade

bdellium ('dɛlɪəm) *n* 1 any of several African or W Asian trees of the burseraceous genus *Commiphora* that yield a gum resin 2 the aromatic gum resin, similar to myrrh, produced by any of these trees [C16 from Latin, from Greek *bdellion*, perhaps from Hebrew *bĕdhōlah*]

bdl *abbreviation for* bundle

bds *abbreviation for* bundles

BDS 1 *abbreviation for* Bachelor of Dental Surgery 2 *international car registration for* Barbados

be¹ (biː; *unstressed* bɪ) *vb, pres sing 1st pers* am; *2nd pers* are; *3rd pers is pres pl* are *past sing 1st pers* was; *2nd pers* were; *3rd pers* was *past pl* were *pres part* being *past part* been (*intr*) 1 to have presence in the realm of perceived reality; exist; live: *I think, therefore I am; not all that is can be understood* 2 (*used in the perfect or past perfect tenses only*) to pay a visit; go: *have you been to Spain?* 3 to take place; occur: *my birthday was last Thursday* 4 (*copula*) used as a linking verb between the subject of a sentence and its noun or adjective complement or complementing phrase. In this case *be* expresses the relationship of either essential or incidental equivalence or identity (*John is a man; John is a musician*) or specifies an essential or incidental attribute (*honey is sweet; Susan is angry*). It is also used with an adverbial complement to indicate a relationship of location in space or time (*Bill is at the office; the dance is on Saturday*) 5 (*takes a present participle*) forms the progressive present tense: *the man is running* 6 (*takes a past participle*) forms the passive voice of all transitive verbs and (archaically) certain intransitive ones: *a good film is being shown on television tonight; I am done* 7 (*takes an infinitive*) expresses intention, expectation, supposition, or obligation: *the president is to arrive at 9.30; you are not to leave before I say so* 8 (*takes a past participle*) forms the perfect or past perfect tense of certain intransitive verbs of motion, such as **go** or **come**: *the last train is gone* 9 be that as it may the facts concerning (something) are of no importance [Old English *bēon*; related to Old High German *bim* am, Latin *fui* I have been, Greek *phuein* to bring forth, Sanskrit *bhavati* he is]

be² *the internet domain name for* Belgium

Be *the chemical symbol for* beryllium

Bé *abbreviation for* Baumé

BE *abbreviation for* 1 bill of exchange 2 (in the US) Board of Education 3 Bachelor of Education 4 Bachelor of Engineering

B2E *abbreviation for* business to employee: denoting an internet communication channel between a company and its employers. Compare **B2B, B2C**

be- *prefix forming transitive verbs* 1 (*from nouns*) to surround completely; cover on all sides: *befog* 2 (*from nouns*) to affect completely or excessively: *bedazzle* 3 (*from nouns*) to consider as or cause to be: *befool; befriend* 4 (*from nouns*) to provide or cover with: *bejewel* 5 (*from verbs*) at, for, against, on, or over: *bewail; berate* [Old English *be-, bi-*, unstressed variant of *bī* BY]

B/E, BE *or* **b.e.** *abbreviation for* bill of exchange

BEA (formerly) *abbreviation for* British European Airways

beach (biːtʃ) *n* 1 an extensive area of sand or shingle sloping down to a sea or lake, esp the area between the high- and low-water marks on a seacoast. Related adjective: **littoral** ▷ *vb* 2 to run or haul (a boat) onto a beach [C16 perhaps related to Old English *bæce* river, BECK²]

beach ball *n* a large light brightly coloured ball for playing with on a beach

beach buggy *n* a low car, often open and with balloon tyres, for driving on sand. Also called: dune buggy

beachcomber ('biːtʃˌkəʊmə) *n* 1 a person who searches shore debris for anything of worth, esp a vagrant living on a beach 2 *Canadian* (in British Columbia) a person who is paid for salvaging loose logs and returning them to logging companies 3 a long high wave rolling onto a beach > 'beach,combing *n*

beach flea *n* another name for the **sand hopper**

beachhead ('biːtʃˌhɛd) *n military* 1 an area on a beach that has been captured from the enemy and on which troops and equipment are landed 2 the object of an amphibious operation [C20 modelled on BRIDGEHEAD]

Beach-la-Mar (ˌbiːtʃləˈmɑː) *n* an English-based creole language spoken in Vanuatu and Fiji, and formerly much more widespread. Also called: Biche-la-mar [C19 quasi-French, from BÊCHE-DE-MER (trepang, this being a major trading commodity in the SW Pacific; hence the name was applied to the trading language)]

beach plum *n* 1 a rosaceous shrub, *Prunus maritima*, of coastal regions of E North America 2 its edible plumlike fruit

Beachy Head ('biːtʃɪ) *n* a headland in East Sussex, on the English Channel, consisting of chalk cliffs 171 m (570 ft) high

beacon ('biːkən) *n* 1 a signal fire or light on a hill, tower, etc, esp one used formerly as a warning of invasion 2 a hill on which such fires were lit 3 a lighthouse, signalling buoy, etc, used to warn or guide ships in dangerous waters 4 short for **radio beacon** 5 a radio or other signal marking a flight course in air navigation 6 short for **Belisha beacon** 7 a person or thing that serves as a guide, inspiration, or warning 8 a stone set by a surveyor to mark a corner or line of a site boundary, etc ▷ *vb* 9 to guide or warn 10 (*intr*) to shine [Old English *beacen* sign; related to Old Frisian *bāken*, Old Saxon *bōcan*, Old High German *bouhhan*]

beacon school *n Brit* a notably successful school whose methods and practices are brought to the attention of the education service as a whole in order that they may be adopted by other schools

Beaconsfield ('bɛkənzˌfiːld, 'biːk-) *n* a town in SE England, in Buckinghamshire. Pop: 12 292 (2001)

beacon status *n Brit* a ranking awarded by the government to an organization, rendering it eligible for extra funding, and aimed at encouraging organizations to share good practice with each other

bead (biːd) *n* 1 a small usually spherical piece of glass, wood, plastic, etc, with a hole through it by means of which it may be strung with others to

form a necklace, etc 2 a small drop of moisture: *a bead of sweat* 3 a small bubble in or on a liquid 4 a small metallic knob acting as the sight of a firearm 5 draw a bead on to aim a rifle or pistol at 6 Also called: astragal *architect, furniture* a small convex moulding having a semicircular cross section 7 *chem* a small solid globule made by fusing a powdered sample with borax or a similar flux on a platinum wire. The colour of the globule serves as a test for the presence of certain metals (**bead test**) 8 *metallurgy* a deposit of welding metal on the surface of a metal workpiece, often used to examine the structure of the weld zone 9 *RC Church* one of the beads of a rosary 10 count, say, *or* tell one's beads to pray with a rosary ▷ *vb* 11 (*tr*) to decorate with beads 12 to form into beads or drops [Old English *bed* prayer; related to Old High German *gibet* prayer] > 'beaded *adj*

beadblast ('biːdˌblɑːst) *n* 1 a jet of small glass beads blown from a nozzle under air or steam pressure ▷ *vb* 2 (*tr*) to clean or treat (a surface) with a beadblast > 'bead,blaster *n*

beading ('biːdɪŋ) *n* 1 another name for **bead** (sense 6) 2 Also called: beadwork ('biːdˌwɜːk) a narrow strip of some material used for edging or ornamentation

beadle ('biːdᵊl) *n* 1 (formerly, in the Church of England) a minor parish official who acted as an usher and kept order 2 (in Scotland) a church official attending on the minister 3 *Judaism* a synagogue attendant. See also **shammes** 4 an official in certain British universities and other institutions [Old English *bydel*; related to Old High German *butil* bailiff] > 'beadleship *n*

beadledom ('biːdᵊldəm) *n* petty officialdom

beadroll ('biːdˌrəʊl) *n archaic* a list of persons for whom prayers are to be offered

bead-ruby *n, pl* -bies a N temperate liliaceous plant with small white bell-shaped flowers and small red berries

beadsman *or* **bedesman** ('biːdzmən) *n, pl* -men 1 a person who prays for another's soul, esp one paid or fed for doing so 2 a person kept in an almshouse

beady ('biːdɪ) *adj* beadier, beadiest 1 small, round, and glittering: used esp of eyes 2 resembling or covered with beads > 'beadily *adv* > 'beadiness *n*

beady eye *n informal* keen watchfulness that may be somewhat hostile: *he's got his beady eye on you* > ,beady-'eyed *adj*

beagle ('biːgᵊl) *n* 1 a small sturdy breed of hound, having a smooth dense coat usually of white, tan, and black; often used (esp formerly) for hunting hares 2 *archaic* a person who spies on others ▷ *vb* 3 (*intr*) to hunt with beagles, normally on foot [C15 of uncertain origin]

beak¹ (biːk) *n* 1 the projecting jaws of a bird, covered with a horny sheath; bill 2 any beaklike mouthpart in other animals, such as turtles 3 *slang* a person's nose, esp one that is large, pointed, or hooked 4 any projecting part, such as the pouring lip of a bucket 5 *architect* the upper surface of a cornice, which slopes out to throw off water 6 *chem* the part of a still or retort through which vapour passes to the condenser 7 *nautical* another word for **ram** (sense 5) [C13 from Old French *bec*, from Latin *beccus*, of Gaulish origin] > beaked (biːkt) *adj* > 'beakless *adj* > 'beak,like *adj* > 'beaky *adj*

beak² (biːk) *n* a Brit slang word for **judge, magistrate, headmaster** *or* **schoolmaster** [C19 originally thieves' jargon]

beaker ('biːkə) *n* 1 a cup usually having a wide mouth: *a plastic beaker* 2 a cylindrical flat-bottomed container used in laboratories, usually made of glass and having a pouring lip 3 the amount a beaker holds [C14 from Old Norse *bikarr*; related to Old High German *behhāri*, Middle Dutch *bēker* beaker, Greek *bikos* earthenware jug]

Beaker folk *n* a prehistoric people thought to

have originated in the Iberian peninsula and spread to central Europe and Britain during the second millennium BC [C20 named after the beakers found among their remains]

beaky-nosed *adj* having a nose that is large, pointed, or hooked

be-all and end-all *n informal* 1 the ultimate aim or justification: *to provide help for others is the be-all and end-all of this group* 2 *often humorous* a person or thing considered to be beyond improvement

beam (biːm) *n* 1 a long thick straight-sided piece of wood, metal, concrete, etc, esp one used as a horizontal structural member 2 any rigid member or structure that is loaded transversely 3 the breadth of a ship or boat taken at its widest part, usually amidships 4 a ray or column of light, as from a beacon 5 a broad smile 6 one of the two cylindrical rollers on a loom, one of which holds the warp threads before weaving, the other the finished work 7 the main stem of a deer's antler from which the smaller branches grow 8 the central shaft of a plough to which all the main parts are attached 9 a narrow unidirectional flow of electromagnetic radiation or particles: *a beam of light; an electron beam* 10 the horizontal centrally pivoted bar in a balance 11 *informal* the width of the hips (esp in the phrase **broad in the beam**) 12 **a beam in one's eye** a fault or grave error greater in oneself than in another person 13 **off (the) beam a** not following a radio beam to maintain a course **b** *informal* wrong, mistaken, or irrelevant 14 **on the beam a** following a radio beam to maintain a course **b** *nautical* opposite the beam of a vessel; abeam **c** *informal* correct, relevant, or appropriate ▷ *vb* 15 to send out or radiate (rays of light) 16 (*tr*) to divert or aim (a radio signal or broadcast, light, etc) in a certain direction: *to beam a programme to Tokyo* (*tr*) 17 to pass (data, esp business card details, etc) from one hand-held computer to another by means of infrared beams 18 (*intr*) to smile broadly with pleasure or satisfaction [Old English *beam*; related to Gothic *bagms* tree, Old High German *boum* tree] > **beamed** *adj* > **'beaming** *adj, n* > **'beamless** *adj* > **'beam,like** *adj* > **'beamy** *adj*

beam aerial *n* an aerial system, such as a Yagi aerial, having directional properties. Also called (esp US): **beam antenna**

beam compass *n* an instrument for drawing large circles or arcs, consisting of a horizontal beam along which two vertical legs slide. Also called: **trammel**

beam-ends *pl n* 1 the ends of a vessel's beams 2 **on her beam-ends** (of a vessel) heeled over through an angle of 90° 3 **on one's beam-ends a** out of resources; destitute **b** desperate

beam engine *n* an early type of steam engine, in which a pivoted beam is vibrated by a vertical steam cylinder at one end, so that it transmits motion to the workload, such as a pump, at the other end

beamer ('biːmə) *n cricket* a full-pitched ball bowled at the batsman's head

beam hole *n* a hole in the shield of a nuclear reactor through which a beam of radiation, esp of neutrons, is allowed to escape for experimental purposes

beam riding *n* a method of missile guidance in which the missile steers itself along the axis of a conically scanned microwave beam > **beam rider** *n*

beam splitter *n* a system that divides a beam of light, electrons, etc, into two or more paths

bean (biːn) *n* 1 any of various leguminous plants of the widely cultivated genus *Phaseolus* producing edible seeds in pods. See **French bean, lima bean, scarlet runner, string bean** 2 any of several other leguminous plants that bear edible pods or seeds, such as the broad bean and soya bean 3 any of various other plants whose seeds are produced in pods or podlike fruits 4 the seed or pod of any of these plants 5 any of various beanlike seeds, such as coffee 6 *US and Canadian slang* another word for head 7 **not have a bean** *slang* to be without money: *I haven't got a bean* 8 **full of beans** *informal* **a** full of energy and vitality **b** *US* mistaken; erroneous 9 **spill the beans** *informal* to disclose something confidential ▷ *vb* 10 *chiefly US and Canadian slang* (*tr*) to hit (a person) on the head [Old English *bēan*; related to Old Norse *baun*, Old Frisian *bāne*, Old High German *bōna* bean]

beanbag ('biːn,bæg) *n* 1 a small cloth bag filled with dried beans and thrown in games 2 Also called: **sag bag** a very large cushion loosely filled with foam rubber or polystyrene granules so that it moulds into a comfortable shape: used as an informal low seat

beanbag gun *n* a gun that fires a fabric bag containing lead shot, designed to stun or knock the target to the ground

bean caper *n* a shrub, *Zygophyllum fabago*, of E Mediterranean regions, whose flower buds are eaten as a substitute for capers: family *Zygophyllaceae*

bean-counter *n informal* an accountant

bean curd *n* another name for **tofu**

beanery ('biːnərɪ) *n, pl* **-eries** *US informal* a cheap restaurant

beanfeast ('biːn,fiːst) *n Brit informal* 1 an annual dinner given by employers to employees 2 any festive or merry occasion

beanie *or* **beany** ('biːnɪ) *n, pl* **beanies** a round close-fitting hat resembling a skullcap

beano ('biːnəʊ) *n, pl* **beanos** *Brit slang* a celebration, party, or other enjoyable time

beanpole ('biːn,pəʊl) *n* 1 a tall stick or pole used to support bean plants 2 *slang* a tall thin person

bean sprout *n* the sprout of a newly germinated mung bean, eaten as a vegetable, esp in Chinese dishes

beanstalk ('biːn,stɔːk) *n* the stem of a bean plant

bean tree *n* any of various trees having beanlike pods, such as the catalpa and carob

bear[1] (bɛə) *vb* **bears, bearing, bore, borne** (*mainly tr*) 1 to support or hold up; sustain 2 to bring or convey: *to bear gifts* 3 to take, accept, or assume the responsibility of: *to bear an expense* 4 (*past participle* **born** in passive use except when foll by *by*) to give birth to: *to bear children* 5 (*also intr*) to produce by or as if by natural growth: *to bear fruit* 6 to tolerate or endure: *she couldn't bear him* 7 to admit of; sustain: *his story does not bear scrutiny* 8 to hold in the conscious mind or in one's feelings: *to bear a grudge; I'll bear that idea in mind* 9 to show or be marked with: *he still bears the scars* 10 to transmit or spread: *to bear gossip* 11 to render or supply (esp in the phrase **bear witness**) 12 to conduct or manage (oneself, the body, etc): *she bore her head high* 13 to have, be, or stand in (relation or comparison): *his account bears no relation to the facts* 14 (*intr*) to move, be located, or lie in a specified direction: *the way bears east* 15 to have by right; be entitled to (esp in the phrase **bear title**) 16 **bear a hand** to give assistance 17 **bring to bear** to bring into operation or effect: *he brought his knowledge to bear on the situation* ▷ See also **bear down, bear off, bear on, bear out, bear up, bear with, born** [Old English *beran*; related to Old Norse *bera*, Old High German *beran* to carry, Latin *ferre*, Greek *pherein* to bear, Sanskrit *bharati* he carries]

bear[2] (bɛə) *n, pl* **bears** *or* **bear** 1 any plantigrade mammal of the family *Ursidae*: order *Carnivora* (carnivores). Bears are typically massive omnivorous animals with a large head, a long shaggy coat, and strong claws. See also **black bear, brown bear, polar bear** Related adjective: **ursine** 2 any of various bearlike animals, such as the koala and the ant bear 3 a clumsy, churlish, or ill-mannered person 4 a teddy bear 5 *stock exchange* **a** a speculator who sells in anticipation of falling prices to make a profit on repurchase **b** (*as modifier*): *a bear market*. Compare **bull[1]** (sense 5) ▷ *vb* **bears, bearing, beared** 6 (*tr*) to lower or attempt to lower the price or prices of (a stock market or a security) by speculative selling [Old English *bera*; related to Old Norse *bjorn*, Old High German *bero*]

Bear (bɛə) *n* **the** 1 the English name for either **Ursa Major** (**Great Bear**) or **Ursa Minor** (**Little Bear**) 2 an informal name for **Russia**

bearable ('bɛərəbᵊl) *adj* endurable; tolerable > **'bearably** *adv*

bear-baiting *n* (formerly) an entertainment in which dogs attacked and enraged a chained bear

bearberry ('bɛəbərɪ) *n, pl* **-ries** 1 a trailing evergreen ericaceous shrub, *Arctostaphylos uva-ursi*, with small pinkish-white flowers, red berries, and astringent leaves 2 **alpine** *or* **black bearberry** a related species, *A. alpina* of European mountains, having black berries

bearcat ('bɛə,kæt) *n* another name for **lesser panda**. See **panda** (sense 2)

beard (bɪəd) *n* 1 the hair growing on the lower parts of a man's face 2 any similar growth in animals 3 a tuft of long hairs in plants such as barley and wheat; awn 4 the gills of an oyster 5 a barb, as on an arrow or fish-hook 6 *slang* a woman who accompanies a homosexual man to give the impression that he is heterosexual 7 *printing* the part of a piece of type that connects the face with the shoulder ▷ *vb* (*tr*) 8 to oppose boldly or impertinently 9 to pull or grasp the beard of [Old English *beard*; related to Old Norse *barth*, Old High German *bart*, Latin *barba*] > **'bearded** *adj*

bearded collie *n* a medium-sized breed of dog having a profuse long straight coat, usually grey or fawn and often with white on the head, legs, and chest, a long tail, and a distinctive beard

bearded dragon *n* 1 a large Australian lizard, *Amphibolurus barbatus*, with an erectile frill around the neck. Also called: **bearded lizard, jew lizard** 2 another name for **frill-necked lizard**

bearded tit *n* another name for **reedling**

bearded vulture *n* another name for **lammergeier**

beardless ('bɪədlɪs) *adj* 1 without a beard 2 too young to grow a beard; immature > **'beardlessness** *n*

bear down *vb* (*intr, adverb; often foll by* on *or* upon) 1 to press or weigh down 2 to approach in a determined or threatening manner 3 (of a vessel) to make an approach (to another vessel, obstacle, etc) from windward 4 (of a woman during childbirth) to exert a voluntary muscular pressure to assist delivery

beard-stroking *n* 1 deep thought: *the response involved much beard-stroking* ▷ *adj* 2 boringly intellectual: *a beard-stroking bore*

beardy ('bɪədɪ) *adj* **-dier, -diest** 1 wearing a beard ▷ *n, pl* **-dies** 2 a person who has a beard

bearer ('bɛərə) *n* 1 a person or thing that bears, presents, or upholds 2 a person who presents a note or bill for payment 3 (formerly, in Africa, India, etc) **a** a native carrier, esp on an expedition **b** a native servant 4 See **pallbearer** 5 the holder of a rank, position, office, etc 6 (*modifier*) *finance* payable to the person in possession: *bearer bonds*

bear garden *n* 1 (formerly) a place where bears were exhibited and where bear-baiting took place 2 a place or scene of tumult and disorder

bear hug *n* 1 a wrestling hold in which the arms are locked tightly round an opponent's chest and arms 2 any similar tight embrace 3 *commerce* an approach to the board of one company by another to indicate that an offer is to be made for their shares

bearing ('bɛərɪŋ) *n* 1 a support, guide, or locating piece for a rotating or reciprocating mechanical part 2 (foll by *on* or *upon*) relevance (to): *it has no bearing on this problem* 3 a person's general social conduct, esp in manners, dress, and behaviour 4 **a** the act, period, or capability of producing fruit or young **b** an amount produced; yield 5 the part of a beam or lintel that rests on a support 6 anything that carries weight or acts as a support 7 the angular direction of a line, point, or course measured from true north or south (**true bearing**),

b

magnetic north or south (**magnetic bearing**), or one's own position **8** (*usually plural*) the position or direction, as of a ship, fixed with reference to two or more known points **9** (*usually plural*) a sense of one's relative position or situation; orientation (esp in the phrases **lose, get,** *or* **take one's bearings**) **10** *heraldry* **a** a device or emblem on a heraldic shield; charge **b** another name for **coat of arms**

bearing pedestal *n* an independent support for a bearing, usually incorporating a bearing housing

bearing pile *n* a foundation pile that supports weight vertically. Compare **sheet pile**

bearing rein *n chiefly Brit* a rein from the bit to the saddle, designed to keep the horse's head in the desired position. Usual US word: **checkrein**

bearish ('bɛərɪʃ) *adj* **1** like a bear; rough; clumsy; churlish **2** *stock exchange* causing, expecting, or characterized by a fall in prices: *a bearish market* > **'bearishly** *adv* > **'bearishness** *n*

Béarnaise (ˌbeɪə'neɪz) *n* a rich sauce made from egg yolks, lemon juice or wine vinegar, butter, shallots, herbs, and seasoning [c19 French, from *Béarn* in SW France]

bear off *vb* (*adverb*) *nautical* (of a vessel) to avoid hitting an obstacle, another vessel, etc, by swerving onto a different course

bear on *vb* (*intr, preposition*) **1** to be relevant to; relate to **2** to be burdensome to or afflict: *his misdeeds bore heavily on his conscience*

bear out *vb* (*tr, adverb*) to show to be true or truthful; confirm: *the witness will bear me out*

bear paw *n Canadian* a type of small round snowshoe

bear raid *n* an attempt to force down the price of a security or commodity by sustained selling

bear's-breech *or* **bear's-breeches** *n* a widely cultivated S European acanthus plant, *Acanthus mollis*, having whitish purple-veined flowers

bear's-ear *n* another name for **auricula** (sense 1)

bear's-foot *n* either of two Eurasian hellebore plants, *Helleborus foetidus* or *H. viridis*, having leaves shaped like the foot and claws of a bear

bearskin ('bɛəˌskɪn) *n* **1** the pelt of a bear, esp when used as a rug **2** a tall helmet of black fur worn by certain regiments in the British Army **3** a rough shaggy woollen cloth, used for overcoats

bear up *vb* (*intr, adverb*) to endure cheerfully

bear with *vb* (*intr, preposition*) to be patient with: *bear with me while I tell you my story*

bearwood ('bɛəˌwʊd) *n* another name for **cascara** (sense 2)

beast (bi:st) *n* **1** any animal other than man, esp a large wild quadruped **2** savage nature or characteristics: *the beast in man* **3** a brutal, uncivilized, or filthy person [c13 from Old French *beste*, from Latin *bestia*, of obscure origin]

beastie ('bi:stɪ) *n* **1** *Scot* a small animal **2** *informal* an insect

beastings ('bi:stɪŋz) *n* a US spelling of **beestings**

beastly ('bi:stlɪ) *adj* **-lier, -liest 1** *informal* unpleasant; disagreeable; nasty: *beastly weather* **2** *obsolete* of or like a beast; bestial ▷ *adv* **3** *informal* (intensifier): *the weather is so beastly hot* > **'beastliness** *n*

beast of burden *n* an animal, such as a donkey or ox, used for carrying loads

beast of prey *n* any animal that hunts other animals for food

beat (bi:t) *vb* **beats, beating, beat; beaten** *or* **beat 1** (when *intr*, often foll by *against, on*, etc) to strike with or as if with a series of violent blows; dash or pound repeatedly (against) **2** (*tr*) to punish by striking; flog **3** to move or cause to move up and down; flap: *the bird beat its wings heavily* **4** (*intr*) to throb rhythmically; pulsate: *her heart beat fast* **5** (*tr*) to make (one's way) by or as if by blows: *she beat her way out of the crowd* **6** (*tr*; sometimes foll by *up*) *cookery* to stir or whisk (an ingredient or mixture) vigorously **7** (*tr*; sometimes foll by *out*) to shape, make thin, or flatten (a piece of metal) by repeated blows **8** (*tr*) *music* to indicate (time) by the motion of one's hand, baton, etc, or by the action of a metronome **9** (when *tr*, sometimes foll by *out*) to produce (a sound or signal) by or as if by striking a drum **10** to sound or cause to sound, by or as if by beating: *beat the drums!* **11** to overcome (an opponent) in a contest, battle, etc **12** (*tr*; often foll by *back, down, off* etc) to drive, push, or thrust **13** (*tr*) to arrive or finish before (someone or something);anticipate or forestall: *they set off early to beat the rush hour* **14** (*tr*) to form (a path or track) by repeatedly walking or riding over it **15** to scour (woodlands, coverts, or undergrowth) so as to rouse game for shooting **16** (*tr*) *slang* to puzzle or baffle: *it beats me how he can do that* **17** (*intr*) *physics* (of sounds or electrical signals) to combine and produce a pulsating sound or signal **18** (*intr*) *nautical* to steer a sailing vessel as close as possible to the direction from which the wind is blowing **19** (*tr*) *slang, chiefly US* to cheat or defraud: *he beat his brother out of the inheritance* **20 beat about the bush** to avoid the point at issue; prevaricate **21 beat a retreat** to withdraw or depart in haste **22 beat it** *slang* (*often imperative*) to go away **23 beat one's breast** See **breast** (sense 10) **24 beat someone's brains out** *slang* to kill by knocking severely about the head **25 beat someone to it** *informal* to reach a place or achieve an objective before someone else **26 beat the bounds** *Brit* (formerly) to define the boundaries of a parish by making a procession around them and hitting the ground with rods **27 can you beat it** *or* **that?** *slang* an expression of utter amazement or surprise ▷ *n* **28** a stroke or blow **29** the sound made by a stroke or blow **30** a regular sound or stroke; throb **31 a** an assigned or habitual round or route, as of a policeman or sentry **b** (*as modifier*): *beat police officers* **32** the basic rhythmic unit in a piece of music, usually grouped in twos, threes, or fours **33 a** pop or rock music characterized by a heavy rhythmic beat **b** (*as modifier*): *a beat group* **34** *physics* the low regular frequency produced by combining two sounds or electrical signals that have similar frequencies **35** *horology* the impulse given to the balance wheel by the action of the escapement **36** *prosody* the accent, stress, or ictus in a metrical foot **37** *nautical* a course that steers a sailing vessel as close as possible to the direction from which the wind is blowing **38 a** the act of scouring for game by beating **b** the organized scouring of a particular woodland so as to rouse the game in it **c** the woodland where game is so roused **39** short for **beatnik 40** *fencing* a sharp tap with one's blade on an opponent's blade to deflect it **41** (*modifier, often capital*) of, characterized by, or relating to the Beat Generation: *a beat poet; beat philosophy* ▷ *adj* **42** (*postpositive*) *slang* totally exhausted. ▷ See also **beat down, beat up** [Old English *bēatan*; related to Old Norse *bauta*, Old High German *bōzan*] > **'beatable** *adj*

beatbox ('bi:tˌbɒks) *n informal* a drum machine

beat down *vb* (*adverb*) **1** (*tr*) *informal* to force or persuade (a seller) to accept a lower price: *I beat him down three pounds* **2** (*intr*) (of the sun) to shine intensely; be very hot

beaten ('bi:tᵊn) *adj* **1** defeated or baffled **2** shaped or made thin by hammering: *a bowl of beaten gold* **3** much travelled; well trodden (esp in the phrase **the beaten track**) **4 off the beaten track a** in or into unfamiliar territory **b** out of the ordinary; unusual **5** (of food) mixed by beating; whipped **6** tired out; exhausted **7** *hunting* (of woods, undergrowth, etc) scoured so as to rouse game

beater ('bi:tə) *n* **1** a person who beats or hammers: *a panel beater* **2** an instrument or device used for beating: *a carpet beater* **3** a person who rouses wild game from woodland, undergrowth, etc

Beat Generation *n* (*functioning as singular or plural*) **1** members of the generation that came to maturity in the 1950s, whose rejection of the social and political systems of the West was expressed through contempt for regular work, possessions, traditional dress, etc, and espousal of anarchism, communal living, drugs, etc **2** a group of US writers, notably Jack Kerouac, Allen Ginsberg, and William Burroughs, who emerged in the 1950s

beatific (ˌbi:ə'tɪfɪk) *adj* **1** displaying great happiness, calmness, etc: *a beatific smile* **2** of, conferring, or relating to a state of celestial happiness [c17 from Late Latin *beātificus*, from Latin *beātus*, from *beāre* to bless + *facere* to make] > ˌ**bea'tifically** *adv*

beatify (bɪ'ætɪˌfaɪ) *vb* **-fies, -fying, -fied 1** (*tr*) *RC Church* (of the pope) to declare formally that (a deceased person) showed a heroic degree of holiness in his or her life and therefore is worthy of public veneration: the first step towards canonization **2** (*tr*) to make extremely happy [c16 from Old French *beatifier*, from Late Latin *beātificāre* to make blessed; see BEATIFIC] > **beatification** (bɪˌætɪfɪ'keɪʃən) *n*

beating ('bi:tɪŋ) *n* **1** a whipping or thrashing, as in punishment **2** a defeat or setback **3 take some** *or* **a lot of beating** to be difficult to improve upon

beatitude (bɪ'ætɪˌtju:d) *n* **1** supreme blessedness or happiness **2** an honorific title of the Eastern Christian Church, applied to those of patriarchal rank [c15 from Latin *beātitūdō*, from *beātus* blessed; see BEATIFIC]

Beatitude (bɪ'ætɪˌtju:d) *n New Testament* any of eight distinctive sayings of Jesus in the Sermon on the Mount (Matthew 5:3–11) in which he declares that the poor, the meek, those that mourn, the merciful, the peacemakers, the pure of heart, those that thirst for justice, and those that are persecuted will, in various ways, receive the blessings of heaven

beatnik ('bi:tnɪk) *n* **1** a member of the Beat Generation (sense 1) **2** *informal* any person with long hair and shabby clothes [c20 from BEAT (n) + -NIK, by analogy with SPUTNIK]

beat up *informal* ▷ *vb* **1** (*tr, adverb*) to strike or kick (a person), usually repeatedly, so as to inflict severe physical damage **2 beat oneself up** *informal* to reproach oneself ▷ *adj* **beat-up 3** worn-out; dilapidated

beaty ('bi:tɪ) *adj informal* (of music) having a strong rhythm: *funky, beaty rock tracks*

beau (bəʊ) *n, pl* **beaux** (bəʊ, bəʊz) *or* **beaus** (bəʊz) **1** a lover, sweetheart, or escort of a girl or woman **2** a man who is greatly concerned with his clothes and appearance; dandy [c17 from French, from Old French *biau*, from Latin *bellus* handsome, charming]

Beaufort scale *n meteorol* an international scale of wind velocities ranging for practical purposes from 0 (calm) to 12 (hurricane force). In the US an extension of the scale, from 13 to 17 for winds over 64 knots, is used [c19 after Sir Francis *Beaufort* (1774–1857), British admiral and hydrographer who devised it]

Beaufort Sea *n* part of the Arctic Ocean off the N coast of North America

beau geste (*French* bo ʒɛst) *n, pl* ***beaux gestes*** (bo ʒɛst) a noble or gracious gesture or act, esp one that is meaningless [literally: beautiful gesture]

beau idéal (*French* bo ideal) *n, pl* ***beaux idéals*** (boz ideal) perfect beauty or excellence [literally: ideal beauty]

beaujolais ('bəʊʒəˌleɪ) *n* (*sometimes capital*) a popular fresh-tasting red or white wine from southern Burgundy in France

Beaulieu ('bju:lɪ) *n* a village in S England, in Hampshire: site of Palace House, seat of Lord Montagu and once the gatehouse of the ruined 13th-century abbey; the National Motor Museum is in its grounds. Pop: 1200 (latest est)

Beaumaris (bəʊ'mærɪs) *n* a resort in N Wales, on the island of Anglesey: 13th-century castle. Pop: 1513 (2001)

beau monde ('bəʊ 'mɒnd; *French* bo mɔ̃d) *n* the world of fashion and society [c18 French, literally: fine world]

Beaumont (ˈbəʊmɒnt) *n* a city in SE Texas. Pop: 112 434 (2003 est)
Beaune (bəʊn) *n* **1** a city in E France, near Dijon: an important trading centre for Burgundy wines. Pop: 21 923 (1999) **2** a wine produced in this district
beaut (bjuːt) *slang, chiefly Austral and NZ* ▷ *n* **1** a person or thing that is outstanding or distinctive **2** a kind, friendly, or trustworthy person ▷ *adj* **3** good or excellent ▷ *interj* **4** Also: **you beaut!** an exclamation of joy or pleasure
beauteous (ˈbjuːtɪəs) *adj* a poetic word for **beautiful**. > ˈ**beauteously** *adv* > ˈ**beauteousness** *n*
beautician (bjuːˈtɪʃən) *n* a person who works in or manages a beauty salon
beautiful (ˈbjuːtɪfʊl) *adj* **1** possessing beauty; aesthetically pleasing **2** highly enjoyable; very pleasant: *the party was beautiful* > ˈ**beautifulness** *n*
beautifully (ˈbjuːtɪflɪ) *adv* **1** in a beautiful manner **2** *informal* (intensifier): *you did beautifully well in the race*
beautiful people *pl n* (*sometimes capitals*; preceded by *the*) rich, fashionable people in international high society
beautify (ˈbjuːtɪˌfaɪ) *vb* **-fies, -fying, -fied** to make or become beautiful > **beautification** (ˌbjuːtɪfɪˈkeɪʃən) *n* > ˈ**beautiˌfier** *n*
beauty (ˈbjuːtɪ) *n, pl* **-ties 1** the combination of all the qualities of a person or thing that delight the senses and please the mind **2** a very attractive and well-formed girl or woman **3** *informal* an outstanding example of its kind: *the horse is a beauty* **4** *informal* an advantageous feature: *one beauty of the job is the short hours* **5** *informal, old-fashioned* a light-hearted and affectionate term of address: *hello, my old beauty!* ▷ *interj* **6** (NZ ˈbjuːdɪ) an expression of approval or agreement. Also (Scot, Austral, and NZ): **you beauty** [C13 from Old French *biauté*, from *biau* beautiful; see BEAU]
beauty contest *n* **1** a competition in which the participants, usually women, are judged on their attractiveness, with a prize, and often a title, awarded to the winner **2** *informal* any contest decided on the basis of superficial attractiveness, popularity, etc: *the referendum might turn into a party political beauty contest*
beauty queen *n* an attractive young woman, esp one who has won a beauty contest
beauty salon *or* **parlour** *n* an establishment providing women with services to improve their beauty, such as hairdressing, manicuring, facial treatment, and massage
beauty sleep *n informal* sleep, esp sleep before midnight
beauty spot *n* **1** a place of outstanding beauty **2** a small dark-coloured patch or spot worn on a lady's face as an adornment or as a foil to her complexion **3** a mole or other similar natural mark on the skin
beauty therapist *n* a person whose job is to carry out treatments to improve a person's appearance, such as facials, manicures, removal of unwanted hair, etc
Beauvais (*French* bovɛ) *n* a market town in N France, 64 km (40 miles) northwest of Paris. Pop: 55 392 (1999)
beaux (bəʊ, bəʊz) *n* a plural of **beau**
beaux-arts (bəʊˈzɑː) *pl n* **1** another word for **fine art 2** (*modifier*) relating to the classical decorative style, esp that of the École des Beaux-Arts in Paris: *beaux-arts influences* [C19 French, literally: fine arts]
beaver[1] (ˈbiːvə) *n* **1** a large amphibious rodent, *Castor fiber*, of Europe, Asia, and North America: family *Castoridae*. It has soft brown fur, a broad flat hairless tail, and webbed hind feet, and constructs complex dams and houses (lodges) in rivers **2** the fur of this animal **3** **mountain beaver** a burrowing rodent, *Aplodontia rufa*, of W North America: family *Aplodontidae* **4** a tall hat of beaver fur or a fabric resembling it, worn, esp by men, during the 19th century **5** a woollen napped cloth resembling beaver fur, formerly much used for overcoats, etc **6** a greyish- or yellowish-brown **7** *obsolete* a full beard **8** a bearded man **9** (*modifier*) having the colour of beaver or made of beaver fur or some similar material: *a beaver lamb coat; a beaver stole* ▷ *vb* **10** (*intr*; usually foll by *away*) to work industriously or steadily [Old English *beofor*; compare Old Norse *biōrr*, Old High German *bibar*, Latin *fiber*, Sanskrit *babhrú* red-brown]
beaver[2] (ˈbiːvə) *n* a movable piece on a medieval helmet used to protect the lower part of the face [C15 from Old French *baviere*, from *baver* to dribble]
Beaver (ˈbiːvə) *n* a member of a **Beaver Colony**, the youngest group of boys (aged 6–8 years) in the Scout Association
beaverboard (ˈbiːvəˌbɔːd) *n* a stiff light board of compressed wood fibre, used esp to surface partitions
beaver fever *n Canadian* an infectious disease caused by drinking water that has been contaminated by wildlife
Beaver Tail *n trademark* a flat oval doughnut served fried and sugared
bebeerine (bəˈbɪəriːn, -rɪn) *n* an alkaloid, resembling quinine, obtained from the bark of the greenheart and other plants [C19 from German *Bebeerin*; see BEBEERU, -INE[2]]
bebeeru (bəˈbɪəruː) *n* another name for **greenheart** (sense 1) [C19 from Spanish *bibirú*, of Carib origin]
Bebington (ˈbɛbɪŋtən) *n* a town in NW England, in Wirral unitary authority, Merseyside: docks and chemical works. Pop: 57 066 (2001)
bebop (ˈbiːbɒp) *n* the full name for **bop**[1] (sense 1) [C20 imitative of the rhythm of the music] > ˈ**bebopper** *n*
becalmed (bɪˈkɑːmd) *adj* (of a sailing boat or ship) motionless through lack of wind
became (bɪˈkeɪm) *vb* the past tense of **become**
because (bɪˈkɒz, -ˈkəz) *conj* **1** (*subordinating*) on account of the fact that; on account of being; since: *because it's so cold we'll go home* **2** **because of** (*preposition*) on account of: *I lost my job because of her* [C14 *bi cause*, from *bi* BY + CAUSE]
USAGE See at **reason**
beccafico (ˌbɛkəˈfiːkəʊ) *n, pl* **-cos** any of various European songbirds, esp warblers of the genus *Sylvia*, eaten as a delicacy in Italy and other countries [C17 from Italian, from *beccare* to peck + *fico* fig, from Latin *ficus*]
béchamel sauce (ˌbeɪʃəˈmɛl) *n* a thick white sauce flavoured with onion and seasonings [C18 named after the Marquis of *Béchamel*, steward of Louis XIV of France and its creator]
bechance (bɪˈtʃɑːns) *vb* (*intr*) *archaic* to happen (to)
Béchar (*French* beʃar) *n* a city in NW Algeria: an oasis. Pop: 149 000 (2005 est). Former name: **Colomb-Béchar**
bêche-de-mer (ˌbɛʃdəˈmɛə) *n, pl* **bêches-de-mer** (ˌbɛʃdəˈmɛə) *or* **bêche-de-mer 1** another name for **trepang 2** See **Beach-la-Mar** [C19 quasi-French, from earlier English *biche de mer*, from Portuguese *bicho do mar* worm of the sea]
Bechuana (bɛˈtʃwɑːnə, ˌbɛtʃʊˈɑːnə, ˌbɛkjʊ-) *n, pl* **-na** *or* **-nas 1** a former name for **Tswana 2** a former name for a member of the Bantu people of Botswana
Bechuanaland (bɛˈtʃwɑːnəˌlænd, ˌbɛtʃʊˈɑːnəˌlænd, ˌbɛkjʊ-) *n* the former name (until 1966) of **Botswana**
beck[1] (bɛk) *n* **1** a nod, wave, or other gesture or signal **2** **at (someone's) beck and call** ready to obey (someone's) orders instantly; subject to (someone's) slightest whim [C14 short for *becnen* to BECKON]
beck[2] (bɛk) *n* (in N England) a stream, esp a swiftly flowing one [Old English *becc*, from Old Norse *bekkr*; related to Old English *bece*, Old Saxon *beki*, Old High German *bah* brook, Sanskrit *bhanga* wave]
becket (ˈbɛkɪt) *n nautical* **1** a clevis forming part of one end of a sheave, used for securing standing lines by means of a thimble **2** a short line with a grommet or eye at one end and a knot at the other, used for securing spars or other gear in place [C18 of unknown origin]
becket bend *n* another name for **sheet bend**
beckon (ˈbɛkən) *vb* **1** to summon with a gesture of the hand or head **2** to entice or lure ▷ *n* **3** a summoning gesture [Old English *bīecnan*, from *bēacen* sign; related to Old Saxon *bōknian*; see BEACON] > ˈ**beckoner** *n* > ˈ**beckoning** *adj, n*
becloud (bɪˈklaʊd) *vb* (*tr*) **1** to cover or obscure with a cloud **2** to confuse or muddle: *to becloud the issues*
become (bɪˈkʌm) *vb* **-comes, -coming, -came, -come** (*mainly intr*) **1** (*copula*) to come to be; develop or grow into: *he became a monster* **2** (foll by *of; usually used in a question*) to fall to or be the lot (of); happen (to): *what became of him?* **3** (*tr*) (of clothes, etc) to enhance the appearance of (someone); suit: *that dress becomes you* **4** (*tr*) to be appropriate; befit: *it ill becomes you to complain* [Old English *becuman* to happen; related to Old High German *biqueman* to come to, Gothic *biquiman* to appear suddenly]
becoming (bɪˈkʌmɪŋ) *adj* **1** suitable; appropriate ▷ *n* **2** any process of change **3** (in the philosophy of Aristotle) any change from the lower level of potentiality to the higher level of actuality > **beˈcomingly** *adv* > **beˈcomingness** *n*
becquerel (ˌbɛkəˈrɛl) *n* the derived SI unit of radioactivity equal to one disintegration per second. Symbol: Bq [C20 named after Antoine Henri Becquerel (1852–1908), French physicist]
BECTU (ˈbɜktuː) (in Britain) *n abbreviation or acronym for* Broadcasting, Entertainment, Cinematograph and Theatre Union
bed (bɛd) *n* **1** a piece of furniture on which to sleep **2** the mattress and bedclothes on such a piece of furniture: *an unmade bed* **3** sleep or rest: *time for bed* **4** any place in which a person or animal sleeps or rests **5** *med* a unit of potential occupancy in a hospital or residential institution **6** *informal* a place for sexual intercourse **7** *informal* sexual intercourse **8** a plot of ground in which plants are grown, esp when considered together with the plants in it: *a flower bed* **9** the bottom of a river, lake, or sea **10** a part of this used for cultivation of a plant or animal: *oyster beds* **11** a layer of crushed rock, gravel, etc, used as a foundation for a road, railway, etc **12** a layer of mortar in a masonry wall **13** the underside of a brick, tile, slate, etc, when in position. Compare **back**[1] (sense 12) **14** any underlying structure or part **15** a layer of rock, esp sedimentary rock **16** the flat part of a letterpress printing press onto or against which the type forme is placed **17** a layer of solid particles of an absorbent, catalyst, or reagent through which a fluid is passed during the course of a chemical reaction or other process **18** a machine base on which a moving part carrying a tool or workpiece slides: *lathe bed* **19** **a bed of roses** a situation of comfort or ease **20** **to be brought to bed (of)** *archaic* to give birth (to) **21** **bed of nails a** a situation or position of extreme difficulty **b** a bed studded with nails on which a fakir lies **22** **get out of bed on the wrong side** *informal* to be ill-tempered from the start of the day **23** **go to bed a** (often foll by *with*) to have sexual intercourse (with) **b** *journalism, printing* (of a newspaper, magazine, etc) to go to press; start printing **24** **put to bed a** *journalism* to finalize work on (a newspaper, magazine, etc) so that it is ready to go to press **b** *printing* to lock up the type forme of (a publication) in the press before printing **25** **take to one's bed** to remain in bed, esp because of illness ▷ *vb* **beds, bedding, bedded 26** (usually foll by *down*) to go to or put into a place to sleep or rest **27** (*tr*) to have sexual intercourse with **28** (*tr*) to place, fix, or sink firmly into position; embed **29** *geology* to form or be arranged in a distinct layer; stratify **30** (*tr*; often foll by *out*) to plant in a bed of soil. ▷ See also **bed in** [Old English *bedd*; related to Old Norse *bethr*, Old High German *betti*, Gothic *badi*]

BEd *abbreviation for* Bachelor of Education

bed and board *n* **1** sleeping accommodation and meals **2** divorce from bed and board *US law* a form of divorce whereby the parties are prohibited from living together but the marriage is not dissolved

bed and breakfast *chiefly Brit* ▷ *n* **1** (in a hotel, boarding house, etc) overnight accommodation and breakfast ▷ *adj* **2** (of a stock-exchange transaction) establishing a loss for tax purposes, shares being sold after hours one evening and bought back the next morning when the market opens

bed and PEP *adj Brit* (of a stock-exchange transaction) complying with regulations for self-select PEPs, a shareholding being sold in the evening and bought back the next morning for the shareholder's own PEP

bedaub (bɪˈdɔːb) *vb* (*tr*) **1** to smear all over with something thick, sticky, or dirty **2** to ornament in a gaudy or vulgar fashion

bedazzle (bɪˈdæzʲl) *vb* (*tr*) to dazzle or confuse, as with brilliance ▷ **beˈdazzlement** *n*

bed bath *n* another name for **blanket bath**

bed-blocking *n Brit* the use of hospital beds by elderly patients who cannot leave hospital because they have no place in a residential care home ▷ **ˈbed-ˌblocker** *n*

bedbug (ˈbɛdˌbʌg) *n* any of several bloodsucking insects of the heteropterous genus *Cimex*, esp *C. lectularius* of temperate regions, having an oval flattened wingless body and infesting dirty houses: family *Cimicidae*

bedchamber (ˈbɛdˌtʃeɪmbə) *n* an archaic word for **bedroom**

bedclothes (ˈbɛdˌkləʊðz) *pl n* sheets, blankets, and other coverings of a bed

beddable (ˈbɛdəbʲl) *adj* sexually attractive

bedder (ˈbɛdə) *n* **1** *Brit* (at some universities) a college servant employed to keep students' rooms in order **2** a plant that may be grown in a garden bed

bedding (ˈbɛdɪŋ) *n* **1** bedclothes, sometimes considered together with a mattress **2** litter, such as straw, for animals **3** something acting as a foundation, such as mortar under a brick **4** the arrangement of a mass of rocks into distinct layers; stratification

bedding plant *n* a plant that may be grown in a garden bed

bedeck (bɪˈdɛk) *vb* (*tr*) to cover with decorations; adorn

bedel *or* **bedell** (ˈbiːdʲl) *n* archaic spellings of **beadle** (sense 4)

bedesman (ˈbiːdzmən) *n, pl* -men a variant spelling of **beadsman**

bedevil (bɪˈdɛvʲl) *vb* -ils, -illing, -illed *or US* -ils, -iling, -iled (*tr*) **1** to harass or torment **2** to throw into confusion **3** to possess, as with a devil ▷ **beˈdevilment** *n*

bedew (bɪˈdjuː) *vb* (*tr*) to wet or cover with or as if with drops of dew

bedfast (ˈbɛdˌfɑːst) *adj* an archaic word for **bedridden**

bedfellow (ˈbɛdˌfɛləʊ) *n* **1** a person with whom one shares a bed **2** a temporary ally or associate

Bedford (ˈbɛdfəd) *n* **1** a town in SE central England, administrative centre of Bedfordshire, on the River Ouse. Pop: 82 488 (2001) **2** short for **Bedfordshire**

Bedford cord *n* a heavy corded cloth, similar to corduroy [c19 named after Bedford]

Bedfordshire (ˈbɛdfədˌʃɪə, -ʃə) *n* a county of S central England: mainly low-lying, with the Chiltern Hills in the south: the geographical county includes Luton, which became a separate unitary authority in 1997. Administrative centre: Bedford. Pop (excluding Luton): 388 600 (2003 est). Area (excluding Luton): 1192 sq km (460 sq miles). Abbreviation: **Beds**

bedight (bɪˈdaɪt) *archaic* ▷ *vb* -dights, -dighting, -dight *or* -dighted **1** (*tr*) to array or adorn ▷ *adj* **2**

(*past participle of the verb*) adorned or bedecked [c14 from DIGHT]

bedim (bɪˈdɪm) *vb* -dims, -dimming, -dimmed (*tr*) to make dim or obscure

bed in *vb* **1** (*preposition*) *engineering* to fit (parts) together accurately or (of parts) to be fitted together, either through machining or use, as in fitting a bearing to its shaft **2** (*preposition*) to make or become settled and able to work efficiently in harmony

Bedivere (ˈbɛdɪˌvɪə) *n* **Sir**. (in Arthurian legend) a knight who took the dying King Arthur to the barge in which he was carried to Avalon

bedizen (bɪˈdaɪzʲn, -ˈdɪzʲn) *vb* (*tr*) *archaic* to dress or decorate gaudily or tastelessly [c17 from BE- + obsolete *dizen* to dress up, of uncertain origin] ▷ **beˈdizenment** *n*

bed jacket *n* a woman's short upper garment worn over a nightgown when sitting up in bed

bedlam (ˈbɛdləm) *n* **1** a noisy confused place or situation; state of uproar: *his speech caused bedlam* **2** *archaic* a lunatic asylum; madhouse [c13 *bedlem*, *bethlem*, after the Hospital of St Mary of *Bethlehem* in London]

bedlamite (ˈbɛdləˌmaɪt) *n archaic* a lunatic; insane person

bed linen *n* sheets and pillowcases for a bed

Bedlington terrier (ˈbɛdlɪŋtən) *n* a lithe, graceful breed of terrier having a long tapering head with no stop and a thick fleecy coat. Often shortened to: **Bedlington** [c19 named after the town *Bedlington* in Northumberland, where they were first bred]

Bedloe's Island (ˈbɛdləʊz) *or* **Bedloe Island** *n* the former name (until 1956) of **Liberty Island**

bed moulding *n architect* **1** a moulding in an entablature between the corona and the frieze **2** any moulding below a projection

Bedouin *or* **Beduin** (ˈbɛdʊɪn) *n* **1** (*pl* -ins *or* -in) a member of any of the nomadic tribes of Arabs inhabiting the deserts of Arabia, Jordan, and Syria, as well as parts of the Sahara **2** a wanderer or rover ▷ *adj* **3** of or relating to the Bedouins **4** wandering or roving [c14 from Old French *beduin*, from Arabic *badāwi*, plural of *badwi*, from *badw* desert]

bedpan (ˈbɛdˌpæn) *n* **1** a shallow vessel placed under a bedridden patient to collect faeces and urine **2** another name for **warming pan**

bedplate (ˈbɛdˌpleɪt) *n* a heavy metal platform or frame to which an engine or machine is attached

bedpost (ˈbɛdˌpəʊst) *n* **1** any of the four vertical supports at the corners of a bedstead **2** between you and me and the bedpost *informal* confidentially; in secret

bedraggle (bɪˈdrægʲl) *vb* (*tr*) to make (hair, clothing, etc) limp, untidy, or dirty, as with rain or mud

bedraggled (bɪˈdrægʲld) *adj* (of hair, clothing, etc) limp, untidy, or dirty, as with rain or mud

bedrail (ˈbɛdˌreɪl) *n* a rail or board along the side of a bed that connects the headboard with the footboard

bedridden (ˈbɛdˌrɪdʲn) *adj* confined to bed because of illness, esp for a long or indefinite period [Old English *bedreda*, from *bedd* BED + *-rida* rider, from *rīdan* to RIDE]

bedrock (ˈbɛdˌrɒk) *n* **1** the solid unweathered rock that lies beneath the loose surface deposits of soil, alluvium, etc **2** basic principles or facts (esp in the phrase **get down to bedrock**) **3** the lowest point, level, or layer

bedroll (ˈbɛdˌrəʊl) *n* a portable roll of bedding, such as a sleeping bag, used esp for sleeping in the open

bedroom (ˈbɛdˌruːm, -ˌrʊm) *n* **1** a room furnished with beds and used for sleeping **2** (*modifier*) containing references to sex: *a bedroom comedy*

Beds *abbreviation for* Bedfordshire

bedside (ˈbɛdˌsaɪd) *n* **a** the space by the side of a bed, esp of a sick person **b** (*as modifier*): *a bedside lamp; a doctor's bedside manner*

bedsit (ˈbɛdˌsɪt) *n* a furnished sitting room containing sleeping accommodation and sometimes cooking and washing facilities. Also called: **bedsitter**, **bedsitting room**

bedsore (ˈbɛdˌsɔː) *n* the nontechnical name for **decubitus ulcer**

bedspread (ˈbɛdˌsprɛd) *n* a top cover on a bed over other bedclothes

bedstead (ˈbɛdˌstɛd) *n* the framework of a bed, usually including a headboard and springs but excluding the mattress and other coverings

bedstraw (ˈbɛdˌstrɔː) *n* any of numerous rubiaceous plants of the genus *Galium*, which have small white or yellow flowers and prickly or hairy fruits: some species formerly used as straw for beds as they are aromatic when dry. See also **lady's bedstraw**

bed tea *n* (in some Asian countries) tea served to a guest in bed in the morning

bedtime (ˈbɛdˌtaɪm) *n* **a** the time when one usually goes to bed **b** (*as modifier*): *a bedtime story*

bedwarmer (ˈbɛdˌwɔːmə) *n* a metal pan containing hot coals, formerly used to warm a bed

bed-wetting *n* the act or habit of involuntarily urinating in bed. Technical term: enuresis ▷ **ˈbed-ˌwetter** *n*

Bedworth (ˈbɛdwəθ) *n* a town in central England, in N Warwickshire. Pop: 30 001 (2001)

bee¹ (biː) *n* **1** any hymenopterous insect of the superfamily *Apoidea*, which includes social forms such as the honeybee and solitary forms such as the carpenter bee. See also **bumblebee**, **mason bee** Related adjective: **apian** **2** busy bee a person who is industrious or has many things to do **3** have a bee in one's bonnet to be preoccupied or obsessed with an idea [Old English *bīo*; related to Old Norse *bȳ*, Old High German *bīa*, Dutch *bij*, Swedish *bi*]

bee² (biː) *n* **1** a social gathering for a specific purpose, as to carry out a communal task or hold competitions: *quilting bee* **2** See **spelling bee** [c18 perhaps from dialect *bean* neighbourly help, from Old English *bēn* boon]

bee³ (biː) *n nautical* a small sheave with one cheek removed and the pulley and other cheek fastened flat to a boom or another spar, used for reeving outhauls or stays [Old English *bēag*; related to Old High German *boug* ring, Old Norse *bogi* a bow]

BEE (in South Africa) *abbreviation for* Black Economic Empowerment: a government policy aimed at encouraging and supporting shareholding by black people

Beeb (biːb) *n* **the**. an informal name for the **BBC**

bee beetle *n* a European beetle, *Trichodes apiarius*, that is often parasitic in beehives: family *Cleridae*

beebread (ˈbiːˌbrɛd) *n* a mixture of pollen and nectar prepared by worker bees and fed to the larvae. Also called: ambrosia

beech (biːtʃ) *n* **1** any N temperate tree of the genus *Fagus*, esp *F. sylvatica* of Europe, having smooth greyish bark: family *Fagaceae* **2** any tree of the related genus *Nothofagus*, of temperate Australasia and South America **3** the hard wood of any of these trees, used in making furniture, etc **4** See **copper beech** [Old English *bēce*; related to Old Norse *bók*, Old High German *buohha*, Middle Dutch *boeke*, Latin *fāgus* beech, Greek *phēgos* edible oak] ▷ **ˈbeechen** *or* **ˈbeechy** *adj*

beech fern *n* a fern, *Thelypteris phegopteris*, that grows in damp N temperate woods and hills: family *Polypodiaceae*

beech marten *n* another name for **stone marten**

beechnut (ˈbiːtʃˌnʌt) *n* the small brown triangular edible nut of the beech tree. Collectively, the nuts are often termed **beech mast**, esp when lying on the ground

bee-eater *n* any insectivorous bird of the family *Meropidae* of tropical and subtropical regions of the Old World, having a long downward-curving bill and long pointed wings and tail: order *Coraciiformes* (kingfishers, etc)

beef (biːf) *n* **1** the flesh of various bovine animals, esp the cow, when killed for eating **2** (*pl* beeves (bi:vz) an adult ox, bull, cow, etc, reared for its meat **3** *informal* human flesh, esp when muscular **4** (*pl* beefs) a complaint ▷ *vb* **5** (*intr*) *slang* to complain, esp repeatedly: *he was beefing about his tax* **6** (*tr*; often foll by *up*) *informal* to strengthen; reinforce [c13 from Old French *boef*, from Latin *bōs* ox; see COW¹]

beefburger ('bi:f,bɜːɡə) *n* a flat fried cake of minced beef; hamburger

beefcake ('bi:f,keɪk) *n slang* men displayed for their muscular bodies, esp in photographs. Compare **cheesecake** (sense 2)

beefeater ('bi:f,i:tə) *n* a nickname often applied to the Yeomen of the Guard and the Yeomen Warders at the Tower of London

Beefheartian (,bi:f'hɑːtɪən) *adj* of or recalling the music of Captain Beefheart and his Magic Band, an avant-garde rock/blues band (1966–1982); incorporating strange rhythms, free jazz elements, bizarre lyrics, and growling vocals [c20 from Captain *Beefheart*, stage/recording name of Don *Van Vliet* (born 1941), US musician]

bee fly *n* any hairy beelike nectar-eating dipterous fly of the family *Bombyliidae*, whose larvae are parasitic on those of bees and related insects

beef road *n Austral* a road used for transporting cattle

beefsteak ('bi:f,steɪk) *n* a piece of beef that can be grilled, fried, etc, cut from any lean part of the animal

beefsteak fungus *n* an edible reddish bracket fungus, *Fistulina hepatica*, that grows esp on oak trees and oozes a bloodlike juice

beefsteak plant *n* an Asian plant, *Perilla frutescens crispa*, with aromatic red or green leaves which are used in cooking: family *Lamiaceae*. Also called: shiso, Japanese basil

beef stroganoff *n* a dish of thin strips of beef cooked with onions, mushrooms, and seasonings, served in a sour-cream sauce [c19 named after Count Paul *Stroganoff*, 19th-century Russian diplomat]

beef tea *n* a drink made by boiling pieces of lean beef: often given to invalids to stimulate the appetite

beef tomato *n* a very large fleshy variety of tomato. Also called: beefsteak tomato

beefwood ('bi:f,wʊd) *n* **1** any of various trees that produce very hard wood, esp the Australian tree *Casuarina equisetifolia* (see **casuarina**), widely planted in warm regions **2** the wood of any of these trees [from the red colour and grain]

beefy ('bi:fɪ) *adj* beefier, beefiest **1** like beef **2** *informal* muscular; brawny **3** *informal* fleshy; obese > 'beefily *adv* > 'beefiness *n*

bee glue *n* another name for **propolis**

beehive ('bi:,haɪv) *n* **1** a man-made receptacle used to house a swarm of bees **2** a dome-shaped hair style in which the hair is piled high on the head **3** a place where busy people are assembled

Beehive ('bi:,haɪv) *n* the *informal* **1** the dome-shaped building that houses sections of Parliament in Wellington, New Zealand **2** the New Zealand government

beehive house *n* a prehistoric circular building found in various parts of Europe, usually of stone and having a dome-shaped roof

beekeeper ('bi:,ki:pə) *n* a person who keeps bees for their honey; apiarist > 'bee,keeping *n*

bee killer *n* another name for **robber fly**

beeline ('bi:,laɪn) *n* the most direct route between two places *esp* in the phrase **make a beeline for**)

Beelzebub (bɪˈɛlzɪ,bʌb) *n* **1** *Old Testament* a god of the Philistines (2 Kings 1:2) **2** Satan or any devil or demon [Old English *Belzebub*, ultimately from Hebrew *bá'al zebūb*, literally: lord of flies]

bee moth *n* any of various pyralid moths, such as the wax moth, whose larvae live in the nests of bees or wasps, feeding on nest materials and host larvae

been (bi:n, bɪn) *vb* the past participle of **be**

been-there done-that *interj* an exclamation expressing familiarity and boredom with a situation, experience, etc

beento ('bi:ntu:, 'bɪntʊ) *W African informal* ▷ *n, pl* -tos **1** a person who has resided in Britain, esp during part of his or her education ▷ *adj* **2** of, relating to, or characteristic of such a person [c20 from BEEN + TO]

bee orchid *n* **1** a European orchid, *Ophrys apifera*, whose flower resembles a bumble bee in shape and colour **2** any of several other orchids with beelike flowers

beep (bi:p) *n* **1** a short high-pitched sound, esp one made by the horn of a car, bicycle, etc, or by electronic apparatus ▷ *vb* **2** to make or cause to make such a noise [c20 of imitative origin] > 'beeper *n*

bee plant *n* any of various plants much visited by bees for nectar and pollen

beer (bɪə) *n* **1** an alcoholic drink brewed from malt, sugar, hops, and water and fermented with yeast. Compare **ale 2** a slightly fermented drink made from the roots or leaves of certain plants: *ginger beer; nettle beer* **3** (*modifier*) relating to or used in the drinking of beer: *beer glass; beer mat* **4** (*modifier*) in which beer is drunk, esp (of licensed premises) having a licence to sell beer: *beer house; beer cellar; beer garden* [Old English *beor*; related to Old Norse *bjórr*, Old Frisian *biār*, Old High German *bior*]

beer and skittles *n* (*functioning as singular*) *informal* enjoyment or pleasure

beer belly *n informal* a protruding belly caused by excessive beer drinking. Also called: beer gut

beer goggles *pl n* with one's beer goggles on *informal* seeing people and things as becoming increasingly attractive as one's alcohol intake rises

beer parlour *or* **parlor** *n Canadian* a room in a tavern, hotel, etc in which beer is served

Beersheba (bɪə'ʃiːbə) *n* a town in S Israel: commercial centre of the Negev. In biblical times it marked the southern limit of Palestine. Pop: 183 000 (2003 est)

beer-up *n Austral dated slang* a drinking bout

beery ('bɪərɪ) *adj* beerier, beeriest **1** smelling or tasting of beer **2** given to drinking beer > 'beerily *adv* > 'beeriness *n*

bee's knees *n* the (*functioning as singular*) *informal* an excellent or ideally suitable person or thing

beestings, biestings *or US* **beastings** ('bi:stɪŋz) *n* (*functioning as singular*) the first milk secreted by the mammary glands of a cow or similar animal immediately after giving birth; colostrum [Old English *bȳsting*, from *bēost* beestings; related to Middle Dutch *biest*]

bee-stung *adj* (of the lips) pouting and sensuous

beeswax ('bi:z,wæks) *n* **1 a** a yellowish or dark brown wax secreted by honeybees for constructing honeycombs **b** this wax after refining, purifying, etc, used in polishes, ointments, and for modelling ▷ *vb* **2** (*tr*) to polish with such wax

beeswing ('bi:z,wɪŋ) *n* **1** a light filmy crust of tartar that forms in port and some other wines after long keeping in the bottle **2** a port or other wine containing beeswing

beet (bi:t) *n* **1** any chenopodiaceous plant of the genus *Beta*, esp the Eurasian species *B. vulgaris*, widely cultivated in such varieties as the sugar beet, mangelwurzel, beetroot, and spinach beet. See also **chard 2** the leaves of any of several varieties of this plant, which are cooked and eaten as a vegetable **3** red beet the US name for beetroot [Old English *bēte*, from Latin *bēta*]

beetfly ('bi:t,flaɪ) *n, pl* -flies a muscid fly, *Pegomyia hyoscyami*: a common pest of beets and mangel-wurzels. Also called: mangold fly

beetle¹ ('bi:t²l) *n* **1** any insect of the order *Coleoptera*, having biting mouthparts and forewings modified to form shell-like protective elytra. Related adjective: **coleopteran 2** a game

played with dice in which the players draw or assemble a beetle-shaped form ▷ *vb* (*intr*; foll by *along, off*, etc) **3** *informal* to scuttle or scurry; hurry [Old English *bitela*; related to *bitol* teeth, BIT, *bītan* to BITE]

beetle² ('bi:t²l) *n* **1** a heavy hand tool, usually made of wood, used for ramming, pounding, or beating **2** a machine used to finish cloth by stamping it with wooden hammers ▷ *vb* (*tr*) **3** to beat or pound with a beetle **4** to finish (cloth) by means of a beetle [Old English *bietel*, from *bēatan* to BEAT; related to Middle Low German *bētel* chisel, Old Norse *beytill* penis]

beetle³ ('bi:t²l) *vb* **1** (*intr*) to overhang; jut ▷ *adj* **2** overhanging; prominent [c14 perhaps related to BEETLE¹] > 'beetling *adj*

beetle-browed *adj* **1** having bushy or overhanging eyebrows **2** sullen in appearance; scowling

beetle drive *n* a social occasion at which a progressive series of games of beetle is played. See **beetle¹** (sense 2)

beetroot ('bi:t,ru:t) *n* **1** a variety of the beet plant, *Beta vulgaris*, that has a bulbous dark red root that may be eaten as a vegetable, in salads, or pickled **2** the root of this plant ▷ US name: red beet

beet sugar *n* the sucrose obtained from sugar beet, identical in composition to cane sugar

beeves (bi:vz) *n archaic* the plural of **beef** (sense 2)

beezer ('bi:zə) *slang* ▷ *n* **1** *Brit old-fashioned* a person or chap **2** *Brit old-fashioned* the nose **3** *Scot* an extreme example of its kind ▷ *adj* **4** *Brit old-fashioned* excellent; most attractive [c20 of uncertain origin]

BEF *abbreviation for* British Expeditionary Force, the British armies that served in France and Belgium 1914–18 and in France 1939–40

befall (bɪˈfɔːl) *vb* -falls, -falling, -fell, -fallen *archaic or literary* **1** (*intr*) to take place; come to pass **2** (*tr*) to happen to **3** (*intr*; usually foll by *to*) to be due, as by right [Old English *befeallan*; related to Old High German *bifallan*, Dutch *bevallen*; see BE-, FALL]

befit (bɪˈfɪt) *vb* -fits, -fitting, -fitted (*tr*) to be appropriate to or suitable for [c15 from BE- + FIT¹] > be'fitting *adj* > be'fittingly *adv*

befog (bɪˈfɒɡ) *vb* -fogs, -fogging, -fogged (*tr*) **1** to surround with fog **2** to make confused, vague, or less clear

befool (bɪˈfuːl) *vb* (*tr*) to make a fool of

before (bɪˈfɔː) *conj* (*subordinating*) **1** earlier than the time when **2** rather than: *he'll resign before he agrees to it* ▷ *prep* **3** preceding in space or time; in front of; ahead of: *standing before the altar* **4** when confronted by: *to withdraw before one's enemies* **5** in the presence of: *to be brought before a judge* **6** in preference to: *to put friendship before money* ▷ *adv* **7** at an earlier time; previously; beforehand; in front [Old English *beforan*; related to Old Frisian *befara*, Old High German *bifora*]

beforehand (bɪˈfɔː,hænd) *adj* (*postpositive*), *adv* early; in advance; in anticipation: *she came an hour beforehand*

beforetime (bɪˈfɔː,taɪm) *adv archaic* formerly

befoul (bɪˈfaʊl) *vb* (*tr*) to make dirty or foul; soil; defile > be'fouler *n* > be'foulment *n*

befriend (bɪˈfrɛnd) *vb* (*tr*) to be a friend to; assist; favour

befuddle (bɪˈfʌd²l) *vb* (*tr*) **1** to confuse, muddle, or perplex **2** to make stupid with drink > be'fuddlement *n*

beg¹ (bɛɡ) *vb* begs, begging, begged **1** (when *intr*, often foll by *for*) to solicit (for money, food, etc), esp in the street **2** to ask (someone) for (something or leave to do something) formally, humbly, or earnestly: *I beg forgiveness; I beg to differ* **3** (*intr*) (of a dog) to sit up with forepaws raised expectantly **4** to leave unanswered or unresolved: *to beg a question* **5** beg the question **a** to evade the issue **b** to assume the thing under examination as proved **c** to suggest that a question needs to be asked: *the firm's success begs the question: why aren't more companies doing the same?* **6** go (a-)begging to

b

be unwanted or unused. ▷ See also **beg off** [C13 probably from Old English *bedecian*; related to Gothic *bidagwa* BEGGAR]

> **USAGE** The use of *beg the question* to mean that a question needs to be asked is considered by some people to be incorrect

beg² (bɛg) *n* a variant of **bey**

begad (bɪˈgæd) *interj archaic slang* an emphatic exclamation [C18 euphemistic alteration of *by God!*]

began (bɪˈgæn) *vb* the past tense of **begin**

begat (bɪˈgæt) *archaic* a past tense of **beget**

beget (bɪˈgɛt) *vb* -gets, -getting, -got *or* -gat; -gotten *or* -got (*tr*) **1** to father **2** to cause or create [Old English *begietan*; related to Old Saxon *bigetan*, Old High German *pigezzan*, Gothic *bigitan* to find; see BE-, GET] > be'getter *n*

beggar ('bɛgə) *n* **1** a person who begs, esp one who lives by begging **2** a person who has no money or resources; pauper **3** *ironic or jocular, chiefly Brit* fellow: *lucky beggar!* ▷ *vb* (*tr*) **4** to be beyond the resources of (esp in the phrase **to beggar description**) **5** to impoverish; reduce to begging > 'beggar,hood *or* 'beggardom *n*

beggarly ('bɛgəlɪ) *adj* meanly inadequate; very poor: *beggarly living conditions* > 'beggarliness *n*

beggar-my-neighbour *n* **1** a card game in which one player tries to win all the cards of the other player **2** (*modifier*) relating to or denoting an advantage gained by one side at the expense of the other: *beggar-my-neighbour policies*

beggar's-lice *n* (*functioning as singular*) **1** any of several plants, esp the stickseed, having small prickly fruits that adhere to clothing, fur, etc **2** the seed or fruit of any of these plants

beggar-ticks *or* **beggar's-ticks** *n* (*functioning as singular*) **1** any of various plants, such as the bur marigold and tick trefoil, having fruits or seeds that cling to clothing, fur, etc **2** the seed or fruit of any of these plants

beggarweed ('bɛgəˌwiːd) *n* any of various leguminous plants of the genus *Desmodium*, esp *D. purpureum* of the Caribbean, grown in the southern US as forage plants and to improve the soil. See also **tick trefoil**

beggary ('bɛgərɪ) *n* **1** extreme poverty or need **2** the condition of being a beggar

begging bowl *n* a bowl carried by a beggar, esp a Franciscan or other friar or a Buddhist monk, to receive food or alms

begging letter *n* a letter asking for money sent esp by a stranger to someone known to be rich

Beghard ('bɛgəd, bɪˈgɑːd) *n* a member of a Christian brotherhood that was founded in Flanders in the 13th century and followed a life based on that of the Beguines. Also called: Beguin [C17 from Medieval Latin *beghardus*, from BEG(UINE) + -ARD; compare Old French *bégard*, Middle Dutch *beggaert*, Middle High German *beghart*]

begin (bɪˈgɪn) *vb* -gins, -ginning, -gan, -gun **1** to start or cause to start (something or to do something) **2** to bring or come into being for the first time; arise or originate **3** to start to say or speak **4** (*used with a negative*) to have the least capacity (to do something): *he couldn't begin to compete with her* **5** to begin with in the first place [Old English *beginnan*; related to Old High German *biginnan*, Gothic *duginnan*]

beginner (bɪˈgɪnə) *n* a person who has just started to do or learn something; novice

beginning (bɪˈgɪnɪŋ) *n* **1** a start; commencement **2** (*often plural*) a first or early part or stage **3** the place where or time when something starts **4** an origin; source

begird (bɪˈgɜːd) *vb* -girds, -girding, -girt *or* -girded (*tr*) *poetic* **1** to surround; gird around **2** to bind [Old English *begierdan*; see BE-, GIRD¹]

beg off *vb* (*intr, adverb*) to ask to be released from an engagement, obligation, etc

begone (bɪˈgɒn) *sentence substitute* go away! [C14 from BE (imperative) + GONE]

begonia (bɪˈgəʊnjə) *n* any plant of the genus *Begonia*, of warm and tropical regions, widely grown for their ornamental leaves and waxy flowers: family *Begoniaceae* [C18 New Latin, named after Michel Bégon (1638–1710), French patron of science]

begorra (bɪˈgɒrə) *interj* an emphatic exclamation, regarded as a characteristic utterance of Irish people [C19 euphemistic alteration of *by God!*]

begot (bɪˈgɒt) *vb* a past tense and past participle of **beget**

begotten (bɪˈgɒtᵊn) *vb* a past participle of **beget**

begrime (bɪˈgraɪm) *vb* (*tr*) to make dirty; soil

begrudge (bɪˈgrʌdʒ) *vb* (*tr*) **1** to give, admit, or allow unwillingly or with a bad grace **2** to envy (someone) the possession of (something) > be'grudgingly *adv*

begrudgery (bɪˈgrʌdʒərɪ) *n Irish informal* resentment of any person who has achieved success or wealth

beguile (bɪˈgaɪl) *vb* -guiles, -guiling, -guiled (*tr*) **1** to charm; fascinate **2** to delude; influence by slyness **3** (*often foll by of or out of*) to deprive (someone) of something by trickery; cheat (someone) of **4** to pass pleasantly; while away > be'guilement *n* > be'guiler *n*

beguiling (bɪˈgaɪlɪŋ) *adj* **1** charming or fascinating **2** using slyness to delude someone > be'guilingly *adv*

Beguin ('bɛgɪn; *French* begɛ̃) *n* another word for **Beghard**

beguine (bɪˈgiːn) *n* **1** a dance of South American origin in bolero rhythm **2** a piece of music in the rhythm of this dance **3** a variant of **biggin¹** [C20 from Louisiana French, from French *béguin* flirtation]

Beguine ('bɛgiːn) *n* a member of a Christian sisterhood that was founded in Liège in the 12th century, and, though not taking religious vows, followed an austere life [C15 from Old French, perhaps after *Lambert le Bègue* (the Stammerer), 12th-century priest of Liège, who founded the sisterhood]

begum ('beɪgəm) *n* (in Pakistan and certain other Muslim countries) a woman of high rank, esp the widow of a prince [C18 from Urdu *begam*, from Turkish *begim*; see BEY]

begun (bɪˈgʌn) *vb* the past participle of **begin**

behalf (bɪˈhɑːf) *n* interest, part, benefit, or respect (only in the phrases **on** (someone's) **behalf**, *or US and Canadian* **in behalf of**, **in this** (*or that*) **behalf**) [Old English *be halfe* from *by* + *halfe* side; compare Old Norse *af halfu*]

> **USAGE** *On behalf of* is sometimes wrongly used where *on the part of* is intended. The distinction is that *on behalf of someone* means 'for someone's benefit' or 'representing someone', while *on the part of someone* can be roughly paraphrased as 'by someone'. So, the following example is incorrect: *another act of apparent negligence, this time not on behalf of the company itself, but on behalf of its banker, when what was meant was there was negligence by the company and its banker*

behave (bɪˈheɪv) *vb* **1** (*intr*) to act or function in a specified or usual way **2** to conduct (oneself) in a specified way: *he behaved badly towards her* **3** to conduct (oneself) properly or as desired: *the child behaved himself all day* [C15 see BE-, HAVE]

behaviour *or US* **behavior** (bɪˈheɪvjə) *n* **1** manner of behaving or conducting oneself **2** on one's best behaviour behaving with careful good manners **3** *psychol* **a** the aggregate of all the responses made by an organism in any situation **b** a specific response of a certain organism to a specific stimulus or group of stimuli **4** the action, reaction, or functioning of a system, under normal or specified circumstances [C15 from BEHAVE; influenced in form by Middle

English *havior*, from Old French *havoir*, from Latin *habēre* to have] > be'havioural *or US* be'havioral *adj*

behavioural contagion *n* the spread of a particular type of behaviour, such as crying, through a crowd or group of people

behavioural science *n* the application of scientific methods to the study of the behaviour of organisms

behavioural sink *n psychol* a small area in which people or animals live in overcrowded conditions

behaviourism *or US* **behaviorism** (bɪˈheɪvjəˌrɪzəm) *n* **1** a school of psychology that regards the objective observation of the behaviour of organisms (usually by means of automatic recording devices) as the only proper subject for study and that often refuses to postulate any intervening mechanisms between the stimulus and the response **2** the doctrine that the mind has no separate existence but that statements about the mind and mental states can be analysed into statements about actual and potential behaviour. Compare **materialism** (sense 2) See also **mind-body problem**. > be'haviourist *or US* be'haviorist *adj, n* > be,haviour'istic *or US* be,havior'istic *adj*

behaviour therapy *n* any of various means of treating psychological disorders, such as desensitization, aversion therapy, and instrumental conditioning, that depend on the patient systematically learning new modes of behaviour

behead (bɪˈhɛd) *vb* (*tr*) to remove the head from; decapitate [Old English *behēafdian*, from BE- + *heafod* HEAD; related to Middle High German *behoubeten*]

beheld (bɪˈhɛld) *vb* the past tense and past participle of **behold**

behemoth (bɪˈhiːmɒθ) *n* **1** *Old Testament* a gigantic beast, probably a hippopotamus, described in Job 40:15 **2** a huge or monstrous person or thing [C14 from Hebrew *běhēmōth*, plural of *běhēmāh* beast]

behest (bɪˈhɛst) *n* an authoritative order or earnest request [Old English *behǣs*, from *behātan*; see BE-, HEST]

behind (bɪˈhaɪnd) *prep* **1** in or to a position further back than; at the rear of; at the back of **2** in the past in relation to: *I've got the exams behind me now* **3** late according to; not keeping up with: *running behind schedule* **4** concerning the circumstances surrounding: *the reasons behind his departure* **5** backing or supporting: *I'm right behind you in your application* ▷ *adv* **6** in or to a position further back; following **7** remaining after someone's departure: *he left it behind* **8** in debt; in arrears: *to fall behind with payments* ▷ *adj* **9** (*postpositive*) in a position further back; retarded: *the man behind prodded me* ▷ *n* **10** *informal* the buttocks **11** *Australian rules football* a score of one point made by kicking the ball over the **behind line** between a goalpost and one of the smaller outer posts (**behind posts**) [Old English *behindan*]

behindhand (bɪˈhaɪndˌhænd) *adj* (*postpositive*), *adv* **1** remiss in fulfilling an obligation **2** in debt; in arrears **3** delayed in development; backward **4** late; behind time

Behistun (ˌbeɪhɪˈstuːn), **Bisitun** *or* **Bisutun** *n* a village in W Iran on the ancient road from Ecbatana to Babylon. On a nearby cliff is an inscription by Darius in Old Persian, Elamite, and Babylonian describing his enthronement

behold (bɪˈhəʊld) *vb* -holds, -holding, -held (often used in the imperative to draw attention to something) *archaic or literary* to look (at); observe [Old English *bihealdan*; related to Old High German *bihaltan*, Dutch *behouden*; see BE-, HOLD] > be'holder *n*

beholden (bɪˈhəʊldᵊn) *adj* indebted; obliged; under a moral obligation [Old English *behealden*, past participle of *behealdan* to BEHOLD]

behoof (bɪˈhuːf) *n, pl* -hooves *rare* advantage or profit [Old English *behōf*; related to Middle High

German *behuof* something useful; see BEHOVE]

behove (bɪ'həʊv) *or US* **behoove** (bɪ'hu:v) *vb* (*tr; impersonal*) *archaic* to be necessary or fitting for: *it behoves me to arrest you* [Old English *behōfian*; related to Middle Low German *behōven*]

beige (beɪʒ) *n* **1 a** a very light brown, sometimes with a yellowish tinge, similar to the colour of undyed wool **b** (*as adjective*): *beige gloves* **2** a fabric made of undyed or unbleached wool [c19 from Old French, of obscure origin]

beigel ('beɪɡ³l) *n* a variant spelling of **bagel**

beignet ('bɛnjeɪ) *n chiefly US and Canadian* a square deep-fried pastry served hot and sprinkled with icing sugar [c19 French *bignet* filled pastry, from *buyne*, literally: bump or lump]

Beijing ('beɪ'dʒɪŋ) *n* the capital of the People's Republic of China, in the northeast in central Hebei province: dates back to the 12th century BC; consists of two central walled cities, the Outer City (containing the commercial quarter) and the Inner City, which contains the Imperial City, within which is the Purple or Forbidden City; three universities. Pop: 10 849 000 (2005 est). Former English name: Peking

being ('bi:ɪŋ) *n* **1** the state or fact of existing; existence **2** essential nature; self: *she put her whole being into the part* **3** something that exists or is thought to exist, esp something that cannot be assigned to any category: *a being from outer space* **4** a person; human being **5** (in the philosophy of Aristotle) actuality. Compare **becoming** (sense 3)

Beira ('baɪərə) *n* a port in E Mozambique: terminus of a transcontinental railway from Lobito, Angola, through the Democratic Republic of Congo (formerly Zaïre), Zambia, and Zimbabwe. Pop: 566 000 (2005 est).

Beirut *or* **Beyrouth** (,beɪ'ru:t) *n* the capital of Lebanon, a port on the Mediterranean: part of the Ottoman Empire from the 16th century until 1918; four universities (Lebanese, American, French, and Arab). Pop: 1 875 000 (2005 est).

Beit Knesset *or* **Beth Knesseth** (bɛt 'knɛsɛt) *n* a synagogue: often used in the names of congregations [from Hebrew, literally: house of assembly]

bejesus (bɪ'dʒeɪzəz) *informal* ▷ *interj* **1** an exclamation of surprise, emphasis, etc, regarded as a characteristic utterance of Irish people ▷ *n* **2** the bejesus (intensifier) used in such phrases as **beat the bejesus out of, scare the bejesus out of,** etc [c20 alteration of *by Jesus*]

bejewel (bɪ'dʒu:əl) *vb* **-els, -elling, -elled** *or US* **-els, -eling, -eled** (*tr*) to decorate with or as if with jewels

bejewelled *or US* **bejeweled** (bɪ'dʒu:əld) *adj* decorated with or as if with jewels

Bekaa *or* **Beqaa** (bɪ'kɑ:) *n* a broad valley in central Lebanon, between the Lebanon and Anti-Lebanon Mountains. Ancient name: **Coelesyria** (,si:li:'sɪrɪə)

bel (bɛl) *n* a unit for comparing two power levels, equal to the logarithm to the base ten of the ratio of the two powers. Symbols: B, b See also **decibel** [c20 named after Alexander Graham Bell (1847–1922), Scots-born US scientist]

Bel (beɪl) *n* (in Babylonian and Assyrian mythology) the god of the earth

belabour *or US* **belabor** (bɪ'leɪbə) *vb* (*tr*) **1** to beat severely; thrash **2** to attack verbally; criticize harshly **3** an obsolete word for **labour**

belah *or* **belar** ('bi:lɑ:) *n* an Australian casuarina tree, *Casuarina glauca*, yielding a useful timber

Belarus ('bɛlə,rʌs, -,rʊs) *or* **Byelorussia, Belorussia** (,bjɛləʊ'rʌʃə, ,bɛl-) *n* a republic in E Europe; part of the medieval Lithuanian and Polish empires before occupied by Russia; a Soviet republic (1919–91); in 1997 formed a close political and economic union with Russia: mainly low-lying and forested. Languages: Belarussian; Russian. Religion: believers are mostly Christian. Currency: rouble. Capital: Minsk. Pop: 9 851 000 (2004 est). Area: 207 600 sq km (80 134 sq miles).

Also called: Byelorussian Republic, Bielorussia, White Russia

Belarussian, Belarusian, Byelorussian *or* **Belorussian** (,bɛləʊ'rʌʃən, ,bjɛl-) *adj* **1** of, relating to, or characteristic of Belarus, its people, or their language ▷ *n* **2** the official language of Belarus: an East Slavonic language closely related to Russian **3** a native or inhabitant of Belarus. Also called: **White Russian**

belated (bɪ'leɪtɪd) *adj* late or too late: *belated greetings* > be'latedly *adv* > be'latedness *n*

Belau (bə'laʊ) *n* an alternative name for the (Republic of) **Palau**

belay (bɪ'leɪ) *vb* **-lays, -laying, -layed 1** *nautical* to make fast (a line) by securing to a pin, cleat, or bitt **2** (*usually imperative*) *nautical* to stop; cease **3** ('bi:,leɪ) *mountaineering* to secure (a climber) to a mountain by tying the rope off round a rock spike, piton, nut, etc ▷ *n* **4** ('bi:,leɪ) *mountaineering* the attachment (of a climber) to a mountain by tying the rope off round a rock spike, piton, nut, etc, to safeguard the party in the event of a fall. See also **running belay** [Old English *belecgan*; related to Old High German *bileggan*, Dutch *beleggen*]

belaying pin *n nautical* a cylindrical, sometimes tapered pin, usually of metal or wood, that fits into a hole in a pin or fife rail: used for belaying

bel canto ('bɛl 'kæntəʊ) *n music* **a** a style of singing characterized by beauty of tone rather than dramatic power **b** (*as modifier*): *a bel canto aria* [c19 Italian, literally: beautiful singing]

belch (bɛltʃ) *vb* **1** (*usually intr*) to expel wind from the stomach noisily through the mouth; eructate **2** to expel or be expelled forcefully from inside: *smoke belching from factory chimneys* **3** to say (curses, insults, etc) violently or bitterly ▷ *n* **4** an act of belching; eructation [Old English *bialcan*; related to Middle Low German *belken* to shout, Dutch *balken* to bray]

beldam *or* **beldame** ('bɛldəm) *n* **1** *archaic* an old woman, esp an ugly or malicious one; hag **2** an obsolete word for **grandmother** [c15 from *belgrand* (as in *grandmother*), from Old French *bel* beautiful, from Latin *bellus* + *dam* mother, variant of DAME]

beleaguer (bɪ'li:ɡə) *vb* (*tr*) **1** to trouble persistently; harass **2** to lay siege to [c16 from BE- + LEAGUER[1]]

Belém (*Portuguese* bə'lẽĩ) *n* a port in N Brazil, the capital of Pará state, on the Pará River: major trading centre for the Amazon basin. Pop: 2 097 000 (2005 est)

belemnite ('bɛləm,naɪt) *n* **1** any extinct marine cephalopod mollusc of the order *Belemnoidea*, related to the cuttlefish **2** the long pointed conical internal shell of any of these animals: a common Mesozoic fossil [c17 from Greek *belemnon* dart]

belemnoid ('bɛləm,nɔɪd) *adj anatomy, zoology* shaped like a dart

bel esprit *French* (bɛl ɛspri) *n, pl beaux esprits* (boz ɛspri) a witty or clever person [literally: fine wit]

Belfast ('bɛlfɑ:st, bɛl'fɑ:st) *n* **1** the capital of Northern Ireland, a port on Belfast Lough in Belfast district, Co Antrim and Co Down: became the centre of Irish Protestantism and of the linen industry in the 17th century; seat of the Northern Ireland assembly and executive. Pop: 276 459 (2001) **2** a district of W Northern Ireland, in Co Antrim and Co Down. Pop: 271 596 (2003 est). Area: 115 sq km (44 sq miles)

Belfort (*French* bɛlfɔr) *n* **1 Territoire de** (tɛritwar də) a department of E France, now in Franche-Comté region: the only part of Alsace remaining to France after 1871. Capital: Belfort. Pop: Pop: 139 383 (2003 est). Area: 608 sq km (237 sq miles) **2** a fortress town in E France: strategically situated in the **Belfort Gap** between the Vosges and the Jura mountains. Pop: 50 417 (1999)

belfry ('bɛlfrɪ) *n, pl* **-fries 1** the part of a tower or steeple in which bells are hung **2** a tower or

steeple. Compare **campanile 3** the timber framework inside a tower or steeple on which bells are hung **4** (formerly) a movable tower for attacking fortifications [c13 from Old French *berfrei*, of Germanic origin; compare Middle High German *bercfrit* fortified tower, Medieval Latin *berfredus* tower]

Belg. *or* **Bel.** *abbreviation for* **1** Belgian **2** Belgium

belga ('bɛlɡə) *n* a former Belgian monetary unit worth five francs

Belgae ('bɛldʒi:, 'bɛlɡaɪ) *n* an ancient Celtic people who in Roman times inhabited present-day Belgium and N France > 'Belgic *adj*

Belgaum (bɛl'ɡaʊm) *n* a city in India, in Karnataka: cotton, furniture, leather. Pop: 399 600 (2001)

Belgian ('bɛldʒən) *n* **1** a native, citizen, or inhabitant of Belgium. See also **Fleming[1]**, **Walloon** ▷ *adj* **2** of, relating to, or characteristic of Belgium or the Belgians **3** of or relating to the Walloon French or the Flemish languages

Belgian Congo *n* a former name (1908–60) of (Democratic Republic of) **Congo** (sense 1)

Belgian hare *n* a large red breed of domestic rabbit

Belgian shepherd dog *n* a medium-sized well-proportioned dog of a breed that resembles an Alsatian in appearance and is often used as a sheepdog or a guard dog

Belgium ('bɛldʒəm) *n* a federal kingdom in NW Europe: at various times under the rulers of Burgundy, Spain, Austria, France, and the Netherlands before becoming an independent kingdom in 1830. It formed the Benelux customs union with the Netherlands and Luxembourg in 1948 and was a founder member of the Common Market, now the European Union. It consists chiefly of a low-lying region of sand, woods, and heath (the Campine) in the north and west, and a fertile undulating central plain rising to the Ardennes Mountains in the southeast. Languages: French, Flemish (Dutch), German. Religion: Roman Catholic majority. Currency: euro. Capital: Brussels. Pop: 10 339 000 (2004 est). Area: 30 513 sq km (11 778 sq miles)

Belgorod-Dnestrovski *or* **Byelgorod-Dnestrovski** (*Russian* 'bjɛlɡərət-dnjɪ'strɔfskɪj) *n* a port in SW Ukraine, on the Dniester estuary: belonged to Romania from 1918 until 1940; under Soviet rule (1944–91). Pop: 56 800 (1991 est). Romanian name: **Cetatea Albă** Former name (until 1946): **Akkerman**

Belgrade (bɛl'ɡreɪd, 'bɛlɡreɪd) *n* the capital of the Union of Serbia and Montenegro and of Serbia, in the E part at the confluence of the Danube and Sava Rivers: became the capital of Serbia in 1878 and of Yugoslavia in 1929. Pop: 1 280 639 (2002). Serbo-Croat name: **Beograd**

Belgravia (bɛl'ɡreɪvɪə) *n* a fashionable residential district of W central London, around Belgrave Square

Belial ('bi:lɪəl) *n* **1** a demon mentioned frequently in apocalyptic literature: identified in the Christian tradition with the devil or Satan **2** (in the Old Testament and rabbinical literature) worthlessness or wickedness [c13 from Hebrew *belīyya'al*, from *belīy* without + *ya'al* worth]

belie (bɪ'laɪ) *vb* **-lies, -lying, -lied** (*tr*) **1** to show to be untrue; contradict **2** to misrepresent; disguise the nature of: *the report belied the real extent of the damage* **3** to fail to justify; disappoint [Old English *belēogan*; related to Old Frisian *biliuga*, Old High German *biliugan*; see BE-, LIE[1]] > be'lier *n*

belief (bɪ'li:f) *n* **1** a principle, proposition, idea, etc, accepted as true **2** opinion; conviction **3** religious faith **4** trust or confidence, as in a person or a person's abilities, probity, etc

believe (bɪ'li:v) *vb* **1** (*tr; may take a clause as object*) to accept (a statement, supposition, or opinion) as true: *I believe God exists* **2** (*tr*) to accept the statement or opinion of (a person) as true **3** (*intr; foll by in*) to be convinced of the truth or existence

b

(of): to believe in fairies **4** (*intr*) to have religious faith **5** (*when tr, takes a clause as object*) to think, assume, or suppose: *I believe that he has left already* **6** (*tr; foll by* of; *used with* can, could, would, *etc*) to think that someone is able to do (a particular action): *I wouldn't have believed it of him* [Old English *beliefan*] > be'lieva,bility *n* > be'lievable *adj* > be'lievably *adv* > be'liever *n* > be'lieving *n, adj*

belike (bɪˈlaɪk) *adv archaic or dialect* perhaps; maybe

Belisha beacon (bəˈliːʃə) *n* a flashing light in an orange globe mounted on a post, indicating a pedestrian crossing on a road [c20 named after Leslie Hore-*Belisha* (1893–1957), British politician]

belittle (bɪˈlɪtˀl) *vb* (*tr*) **1** to consider or speak of (something) as less valuable or important than it really is; disparage **2** to cause to make small; dwarf > be'littlement *n* > be'littler *n* > be'littlingly *adv*

Belitung (bɪˈliːtʊŋ) *n* another name for **Billiton**

Belize (bəˈliːz) *n* a state in Central America, on the Caribbean Sea: site of a Mayan civilization until the 9th century AD; colonized by the British from 1638; granted internal self-government in 1964; became an independent state within the Commonwealth in 1981. Official language: English; Carib and Spanish are also spoken. Currency: Belize dollar. Capital: Belmopan. Pop: 261 000 (2004 est). Area: 22 965 sq km (8867 sq miles). Former name (until 1973): British Honduras

Belizean (bəˈliːzən) *adj* **1** of or relating to Belize or its inhabitants ▷ *n* **2** a native or inhabitant of Belize

Belize City *n* a port and the largest city in Belize, on the Caribbean coast: capital until 1973, when that function was transferred inland to Belmopan owing to hurricane risk. Pop: 53 000 (2005 est)

bell¹ (bɛl) *n* **1** a hollow, usually metal, cup-shaped instrument that emits a musical ringing sound when struck, often by a clapper hanging inside it **2** the sound made by such an instrument or device, as for showing the hours or marking the beginning or end of a period of time **3** an electrical device that rings or buzzes as a signal **4** the bowl-shaped termination of the tube of certain musical wind instruments, such as the trumpet or oboe **5** any musical percussion instrument emitting a ringing tone, such as a glockenspiel, one of a set of hand bells, etc. Compare **chime¹** (sense 3) **6** *nautical* a signal rung on a ship's bell to count the number of half-hour intervals during each of six four-hour watches reckoned from midnight. Thus, one bell may signify 12.30, 4.30, or 8.30 a.m or p.m **7** See **diving bell 8** *biology* a structure resembling a bell in shape, such as the corolla of certain flowers or the body of a jellyfish **9** *Brit slang* a telephone call (esp in the phrase **give someone a bell**) **10** *beat or knock seven bells out of Brit informal* to give a severe beating to **11** **bell, book, and candle a** instruments used formerly in excommunications and other ecclesiastical acts **b** *informal* the solemn ritual ratification of such acts **12** **ring a bell** to sound familiar; recall to the mind something previously experienced, esp indistinctly **13** **sound as a bell** in perfect condition **14** **the bells** the ringing of bells, in a church or other public building, at midnight on December 31st, symbolizing the beginning of a new year ▷ *vb* **15** to be or cause to be shaped like a bell **16** (*tr*) to attach a bell or bells to **17** **bell the cat** to undertake a dangerous mission [Old English *belle*; related to Old Norse *bjalla*, Middle Low German *bell*; see BELL²]

bell⁴ (bɛl) *n* **1** a bellowing or baying cry, esp that of a hound or a male deer in rut ▷ *vb* **2** to utter (such a cry) [Old English *bellan*; related to Old Norse *belja* to bellow, Old High German *bellan* to roar, Sanskrit *bhāsate* he talks; see BELLOW]

belladonna (ˌbɛləˈdɒnə) *n* **1** either of two alkaloid drugs, atropine or hyoscyamine, obtained from the leaves and roots of the deadly nightshade **2**

another name for **deadly nightshade** [c16 from Italian, literally: beautiful lady; supposed to refer to its use by women as a cosmetic]

belladonna lily *n* another name for **amaryllis**

bellarmine (ˈbɛləˌmiːn) *n* a large stoneware or earthenware jug for ale or spirits, bearing a bearded mask [c18 named after Saint Robert Bellarmine (1542–1621), Italian Jesuit theologian and cardinal, whom these jugs were intended to caricature]

Bellatrix (ˈbɛlətrɪks) *n* the third brightest star in the constellation Orion

bellbird (ˈbɛlˌbɜː) *n* **1** any of several tropical American passerine birds of the genus *Procnias* having a bell-like call: family *Cotingidae* (cotingas) **2** either of two other birds with a bell-like call: an Australian flycatcher, *Oreoica gutturalis* (**crested bellbird**), or a New Zealand honeyeater, *Anthornis melanura*

bell-bottoms *pl n* trousers that flare from the knee and have wide bottoms > 'bell-,bottomed *adj*

bellboy (ˈbɛlˌbɔɪ) *n* a man or boy employed in a hotel, club, etc, to carry luggage and answer calls for service; page; porter. Also called (US and Canadian): **bellhop**

bell bronze *n* an alloy of copper and tin that contains a high proportion (at least 20 per cent) of tin: used for bell founding

bell buoy *n* a navigational buoy fitted with a bell, the clapper of which strikes when the waves move the buoy

bell captain *n US and Canadian* another name for **captain** (sense 9)

bell crank *n engineering* a lever with two arms having a common fulcrum at their junction

belle (bɛl) *n* **1** a beautiful girl or woman **2** the most attractive or admired girl or woman at a place, function, etc (esp in the phrase **the belle of the ball**) [c17 from French, feminine of BEAU]

Belleau Wood (ˈbɛləʊ; *French* bɛlo) *n* a forest in N France: site of a battle (1918) in which the US Marines halted a German advance on Paris

Belleek (bəˈliːk) *n trademark* **a** a kind of thin fragile porcelain with a lustrous glaze **b** (*as modifier*): *a Belleek vase* [named after *Belleek*, a town in Northern Ireland where such porcelain is made]

belle époque (*French* bɛl epɔk) *n* the period of comfortable well-established life in Europe before World War I [literally: fine period]

Belle Isle *n* an island in the Atlantic, at the N entrance to the **Strait of Belle Isle**, between Labrador and Newfoundland. Area: about 39 sq km (15 sq miles)

Bellerophon (bəˈlɛrəˌfɒn) *n Greek myth* a hero of Corinth who performed many deeds with the help of the winged horse Pegasus, notably the killing of the monster Chimera

belles-lettres (*French* bɛlˈlɛtrə) *n* (*functioning as singular*) literary works, esp essays and poetry, valued for their aesthetic rather than their informative or moral content [c17 from French: fine letters]

belletrist (bɛlˈlɛtrɪst) *n* a writer of belles-lettres > bel'letrism *n* > belletristic (ˌbɛlɪˈtrɪstɪk) *adj*

bellflower (ˈbɛlˌflaʊə) *n* another name for **campanula**

bellfounder (ˈbɛlˌfaʊndə) *n* a foundry worker who casts bells > 'bell,foundry *n*

bell glass *n* another name for **bell jar**

bell heather *n* an ericaceous shrub, *Erica cinerea*. See **heath** (sense 2)

bellhop (ˈbɛlˌhɒp) *n US and Canadian* another name for **bellboy**

bellicose (ˈbɛlɪˌkəʊs, -ˌkəʊz) *adj* warlike; aggressive; ready to fight [c15 from Latin *bellicōsus*, from *bellum* war] > 'belli,cosely *adv* > bellicosity (ˌbɛlɪˈkɒsɪtɪ) *n*

belligerati (bɪˌlɪdʒəˈrɑːtɪ) *pl n* intellectuals, such as writers, who advocate war or imperialism [c20 from bellig(erent) + -*ati* as in LITERATI]

belligerence (bɪˈlɪdʒərəns) *n* the act or quality of

being belligerent or warlike; aggressiveness

belligerency (bɪˈlɪdʒərənsɪ) *n* the state of being at war

belligerent (bɪˈlɪdʒərənt) *adj* **1** marked by readiness to fight or argue; aggressive: *a belligerent tone* **2** relating to or engaged in a legally recognized war or warfare ▷ *n* **3** a person or country engaged in fighting or war [c16 from Latin *belliger*, from *bellum* war + *gerere* to wage]

Bellingshausen Sea (ˈbɛlɪŋzˌhaʊzˀn) *n* an area of the S Pacific Ocean off the coast of Antarctica [named after Fabian Gottlieb *Bellingshausen* (1778–1852), Russian explorer]

Bellinzona (*Italian* bellinˈtsona) *n* a town in SE central Switzerland, capital of Ticino canton. Pop: 16 463 (2000)

bell jar *n* a bell-shaped glass cover used to protect flower arrangements or fragile ornaments or to cover apparatus in experiments, esp to prevent gases escaping

bell magpie *n* another name for **currawong**

bellman (ˈbɛlmən) *n, pl* -men a man who rings a bell, esp (formerly) a town crier

bell metal *n* an alloy of copper and tin, with some zinc and lead, used in casting bells

bell moth *n* any moth of the family *Tortricidae*, which when at rest resemble the shape of a bell

bellock (ˈbɛlək) *vb Midland English dialect* to shout

Bellona (bəˈləʊnə) *n* the Roman goddess of war

bellow (ˈbɛləʊ) *vb* **1** (*intr*) to make a loud deep raucous cry like that of a bull; roar **2** to shout (something) unrestrainedly, as in anger or pain; bawl ▷ *n* **3** the characteristic noise of a bull **4** a loud deep sound, as of pain or anger [c14 probably from Old English *bylgan*; related to *bellan* to BELL²] > 'bellower *n*

bellows (ˈbɛləʊz) *n* (*functioning as singular or plural*) **1** Also called: **pair of bellows** an instrument consisting of an air chamber with flexible sides or end, a means of compressing it, an inlet valve, and a constricted outlet that is used to create a stream of air, as for producing a draught for a fire or for sounding organ pipes **2** *photog* a telescopic light-tight sleeve, connecting the lens system of some cameras to the body of the instrument **3** a flexible corrugated element used as an expansion joint, pump, or means of transmitting axial motion [c16 from plural of Old English *belig* BELLY]

bellows fish *n* another name for **snipefish**

bell pull *n* a handle, rope, or cord pulled to operate a doorbell or servant's bell

bell punch *n* a machine that issues or stamps a ticket, etc, ringing a bell as it does so

bell push *n* a button pressed to operate an electric bell

bell-ringer *n* **1** a person who rings church bells **2** a person who plays musical handbells > 'bell-,ringing *n*

bells and whistles *pl n* **1** additional features or accessories which are nonessential but very attractive: *my car has all the latest bells and whistles* **2** additions, such as options or warranties, made to a financial product to increase its market appeal [c20 from the bells and whistles which used to decorate fairground organs]

bell sheep *n Austral* a sheep that a shearer is just starting to shear (and which he is allowed to finish) as the bell rings for the end of a work period

bells of Ireland *n* (*functioning as singular*) an annual garden plant, *Moluccella laevis*, whose flowers have a green cup-shaped calyx: family *Lamiaceae* (labiates)

Bell's palsy *n* a usually temporary paralysis of the muscles of the face, normally on one side [c19 named after Sir Charles *Bell* (1774–1842), British anatomist]

bell tent *n* a cone-shaped tent having a single central supporting pole

bell-topper *n NZ obsolete, informal* a tall silk hat

bellwether (ˈbɛlˌwɛðə) *n* **1** a sheep that leads the herd, often bearing a bell **2** a leader, esp one followed unquestioningly

bellwort (ˈbɛlˌwɜːt) *n US* **1** any plant of the North American liliaceous genus *Uvularia*, having slender bell-shaped yellow flowers **2** another name for **campanula**

belly (ˈbɛlɪ) *n*, *pl* **-lies 1** the lower or front part of the body of a vertebrate, containing the intestines and other abdominal organs; abdomen. Related adjective: **ventral 2** the stomach, esp when regarded as the seat of gluttony **3** a part, line, or structure that bulges deeply: *the belly of a sail* **4** the inside or interior cavity of something: *the belly of a ship* **5** the front or inner part or underside of something **6** the surface of a stringed musical instrument over which the strings are stretched **7** the thick central part of certain muscles **8** *Austral and NZ* the wool from a sheep's belly **9** *tanning* the portion of a hide or skin on the underpart of an animal **10** *archery* the surface of the bow next to the bowstring **11** *archaic* the womb **12 go belly up** *informal* to die, fail, or come to an end ⊳ *vb* **-lies, -lying, -lied 13** to swell out or cause to swell out; bulge [Old English *belig*; related to Old High German *balg*, Old Irish *bolg* sack, Sanskrit *barhi* chaff]

bellyache (ˈbɛlɪˌeɪk) *n* **1** an informal term for **stomachache** ⊳ *vb* **2** (*intr*) *slang* to complain repeatedly > ˈbellyˌacher *n*

bellyband (ˈbɛlɪˌbænd) *n* a strap around the belly of a draught animal, holding the shafts of a vehicle

bellybutton (ˈbɛlɪˌbʌtᵊn) *n* an informal name for the **navel**

belly dance *n* a sensuous and provocative dance of Middle Eastern origin, performed by women, with undulating movements of the hips and abdomen ⊳ *vb* **belly-dance 2** (*intr*) to perform such a dance > **belly dancer** *n*

belly flop *n* **1** a dive into water in which the body lands horizontally **2** another name for **belly landing** ⊳ *vb* **belly-flop -flops, -flopping, -flopped 3** (*intr*) to perform a belly flop

bellyful (ˈbɛlɪˌfʊl) *n* **1** as much as one wants or can eat **2** *slang* more than one can tolerate

belly landing *n* the landing of an aircraft on its fuselage without use of its landing gear

belly laugh *n* a loud deep hearty laugh

Belmopan (ˌbɛlməˈpæn) *n* (since 1973) the capital of Belize, about 50 miles inland: founded in 1970. Pop: 10 000 (2005 est)

Belo Horizonte (Portuguese ˈbɛːloriˈzõːntə) *n* a city in SE Brazil, the capital of Minas Gerais state. Pop: 5 304 000 (2005 est)

belong (bɪˈlɒŋ) *vb* (*intr*) **1** (foll by *to*) to be the property or possession (of) **2** (foll by *to*) to be bound to (a person, place, or club) by ties of affection, dependence, allegiance, or membership **3** (foll by *to, under, with*, etc) to be classified (with): *this plant belongs to the daisy family* **4** (foll by *to*) to be a part or adjunct (of): *this top belongs to the smaller box* **5** to have a proper or usual place: *that plate belongs in the cupboard* **6** *informal* to be suitable or acceptable, esp socially: *although they were rich, they just didn't belong* [C14 *belongen*, from BE- (intensive) + *longen*; related to Old High German *bilangēn* to reach; see LONG³]

belonging (bɪˈlɒŋɪŋ) *n* secure relationship; affinity (esp in the phrase **a sense of belonging**)

belongings (bɪˈlɒŋɪŋz) *pl n* (*sometimes singular*) the things that a person owns or has with him; possessions; effects

Belorussia (ˌbjɛləʊˈrʌʃə, ˌbɛl-) *n* a variant spelling of **Belarus**

Belorussian *n, adj* a variant spelling of **Belarussian**

Belostok (bjɪlaˈstɔk) *n* transliteration of the Russian name for **Białystok**

beloved (bɪˈlʌvɪd, -ˈlʌvd) *adj* **1** dearly loved ⊳ *n* **2** a person who is dearly loved, such as a wife or husband

Belovo (*Russian* ˈbjɛləvə) *n* a variant spelling of **Byelovo**

below (bɪˈləʊ) *prep* **1** at or to a position lower than; under **2** less than in quantity or degree **3** south of **4** downstream of **5** unworthy of; beneath ⊳ *adv* **6** at or to a lower position or place **7** at a later place (in something written): *see below* **8** *archaic* beneath heaven; on earth or in hell [C14 *bilooghe*, from *bi* BY + *looghe* LOW¹]

below stairs *adv* (formerly) at or in the basement of a large house, considered as the place where the servants live and work

below-the-line *adj* **1** denoting the entries printed below the horizontal line on a company's profit-and-loss account that show how any profit is to be distributed **2** (of an advertising campaign) employing sales promotions, direct marketing, in-store exhibitions and displays, trade shows, sponsorship, and merchandising that do not involve an advertising agency **3** (in national accounts) below the horizontal line separating revenue from capital transactions. Compare **above-the-line**

Bel Paese (ˈbɛl pɑːˈeɪzɪ) *n* a mild creamy Italian cheese [C20 from Italian, literally: beautiful country]

Belsen (ˈbɛlsᵊn; *German* ˈbɛlzən) *n* a village in NE Germany: with Bergen, the site of a Nazi concentration camp (1943–45)

Belshazzar (bɛlˈʃæzə) *n* 6th century BC, the son of Nabonidus, coregent of Babylon with his father for eight years: referred to as king and son of Nebuchadnezzar in the Old Testament (Daniel 5:1, 17; 8:1); described as having received a divine message of doom written on a wall at a banquet (**Belshazzar's Feast**)

belt (bɛlt) *n* **1** a band of cloth, leather, etc, worn, usually around the waist, to support clothing, carry tools, weapons, or ammunition, or as decoration **2** a narrow band, circle, or stripe, as of colour **3** an area, esp an elongated one, where a specific thing or specific conditions are found; zone: *the town belt; a belt of high pressure* **4** a belt worn as a symbol of rank (as by a knight or an earl), or awarded as a prize (as in boxing or wrestling), or to mark particular expertise (as in judo or karate) **5** See **seat belt 6** a band of flexible material between rotating shafts or pulleys to transfer motion or transmit goods: *a fan belt; a conveyer belt* **7** short for **beltcourse** (see **cordon** (sense 4)) **8** *informal* a sharp blow, as with a bat or the fist **9 below the belt a** *boxing* below the waist, esp in the groin **b** *informal* in an unscrupulous or cowardly way **10 tighten one's belt** to take measures to reduce expenditure **11 under one's belt a** (of food or drink) in one's stomach **b** in one's possession **c** as part of one's experience: *he had a linguistics degree under his belt* ⊳ *vb* **12** (*tr*) to fasten or attach with or as if with a belt **13** (*tr*) to hit with a belt **14** (*tr*) *slang* to give a sharp blow; punch **15** (*intr*; foll by *along*) *slang* to move very fast, esp in a car: *belting down the motorway* **16** (*tr*) *rare* to mark with belts, as of colour **17** (*tr*) *rare* to encircle; surround ⊳ See also **belt out, belt up** [Old English, from Latin *balteus*]

belt-and-braces *adj* providing double security, in case one security measure should fail: *a belt-and-braces policy*

Beltane (ˈbɛlteɪn, -tən) *n* an ancient Celtic festival with a sacrificial bonfire on May Day. It is also celebrated by modern pagans [C15 from Scottish Gaelic *bealltainn*]

beltcourse (ˈbɛltˌkɔːs) *n* another name for **cordon** (sense 4)

belt drive *n engineering* a transmission system using a flexible belt to transfer power

belter (ˈbɛltə) *n informal* **1** an event, person, quality, etc, that is admirable, outstanding, or thrilling: *a real belter of a match* **2 a** a rousing or spirited popular song that is sung loudly and enthusiastically **b** a person who sings popular songs in a loud and spirited manner

belting (ˈbɛltɪŋ) *n* **1** the material used to make a belt or belts **2** belts collectively **3** *informal* a

beating ⊳ *adj* **4** *Brit informal* excellent; first-class

belt man *n Austral and NZ* (formerly) the member of a beach life-saving team who swam out with a line attached to his belt

belt out *vb* (*tr, adverb*) *informal* to sing loudly or emit (sound, esp pop music) loudly: *a jukebox belting out the latest hits*

belt up *vb* (*adverb*) **1** *slang* to become silent or cause to become silent; stop talking: often used in the imperative **2** to fasten with or by a belt, esp a seat belt

beltway (ˈbɛltˌweɪ) *n* **1** the usual US name for a **ring road 2** (*usually with capital*) **a** the people and institutions located in the area bounded by the Washington Beltway, taken to be politically and socially out of touch with the rest of America and much given to political intrigue **b** (*as modifier*): *Beltway Cassandras*

beluga (bɪˈluːgə) *n* **1** a large white sturgeon, *Acipenser* (or *Huso*) *huso*, of the Black and Caspian Seas: a source of caviar and isinglass **2** another name for **white whale** [C18 from Russian *byeluga*, from *byely* white]

belvedere (ˈbɛlvɪˌdɪə, ˌbɛlvɪˈdɪə) *n* a building, such as a summerhouse or roofed gallery, sited to command a fine view. See also **gazebo** [C16 from Italian: beautiful sight]

Belvoir Castle (ˈbiːvə) *n* a castle in Leicestershire, near Grantham (in Lincolnshire): seat of the Dukes of Rutland; rebuilt by James Wyatt in 1816

BEM *abbreviation for* British Empire Medal

bema, bimah or **bima** (ˈbiːmə) *n* **1** the speaker's platform in the assembly in ancient Athens **2** *christian Orthodox Church* a raised area surrounding the altar in a church; the sanctuary **3** *Judaism* another word for **almemar** [C17 via Late Latin, from Greek *bēma*, from *bainein* to go]

Bemba (ˈbɛmbə) *n* (*pl* **-ba** or **-bas**) a member of a Negroid people of Africa, living chiefly in Zambia on a high infertile plateau **2** the language of this people, belonging to the Bantu group of the Niger-Congo family

Bembo (ˈbɛmbəʊ) *n* a style of type [C20 named after Pietro *Bembo* (1470–1547), Italian scholar, poet, and cardinal, because the design of the typeface was based on one used for an edition of his tract *De ætna* by the printer Aldus Manutius]

bemean (bɪˈmiːn) *vb* a less common word for **demean**

bemire (bɪˈmaɪə) *vb* (*tr*) **1** to soil with or as if with mire **2** (*usually passive*) to stick fast in mud or mire

bemoan (bɪˈməʊn) *vb* to grieve over (a loss, etc); mourn; lament (esp in the phrase **bemoan one's fate**) [Old English *bemǣnan*; see BE-, MOAN]

bemuse (bɪˈmjuːz) *vb* (*tr*) to confuse; bewilder > be'musement *n* > be'musing *adj*

bemused (bɪˈmjuːzd) *adj* preoccupied; lost in thought > bemusedly (bɪˈmjuːzɪdlɪ) *adv*

ben¹ (bɛn) *Scot* ⊳ *n* **1** an inner room in a house or cottage ⊳ *prep* ⊳ *adv* **2** in; within; inside; into the inner part (of a house) ⊳ *adj* **3** inner. Compare **but²** [Old English *binnan*, from BE- + *innan* inside]

ben² (bɛn) *n* **1** any of several Asiatic trees of the genus *Moringa*, esp *M. oleifera* of Arabia and India, whose seeds yield **oil of ben**, used in manufacturing perfumes and cosmetics, lubricating delicate machinery, etc: family *Moringaceae* **2** the seed of such a tree [C15 from Arabic *bān*]

ben³ (bɛn) *n Scot, Irish* a mountain peak (esp in place names): *Ben Lomond* [C18 from Gaelic *beinn*, from *beann*]

Benadryl (ˈbɛnədrɪl) *n trademark* an antihistamine drug used in sleeping tablets; diphenhydramine. Formula: $C_{17}H_{21}NO$

bename (bɪˈneɪm) *vb* **-names, -naming, -named; -named** or **-nempt** an archaic word for **name** (sense 12) [Old English *benemnan*; see BE-, NAME]

Benares (bɪˈnɑːrɪz) or **Banaras** *n* the former name of **Varanasi**

bench (bɛntʃ) *n* **1** a long seat for more than one person, usually lacking a back or arms **2** a plain

b

stout worktable **3 the bench** (*sometimes capital*) **a** a judge or magistrate sitting in court in a judicial capacity **b** judges or magistrates collectively **4** *sport* the seat on which reserve players and officials sit during a game **5** *geology* a flat narrow platform of land, esp one marking a former shoreline **6** a ledge in a mine or quarry from which work is carried out **7** a platform on which dogs or other domestic animals are exhibited at shows **8** *NZ* a hollow on a hillside formed by sheep ▷ *vb* (*tr*) **9** to provide with benches **10** to exhibit (a dog, etc) at a show **11** *NZ* to form (a track) up a hill by excavating a flattened area **12** *US and Canadian sport* to take or keep (a player) out of a game, often for disciplinary reasons [Old English *benc*; related to Old Norse *bekkr*, Old High German *bank*, Danish, Swedish *bänk*; see BANK³]

bencher (ˈbɛntʃə) *n* (*often plural*) *Brit* **1** a member of the governing body of one of the Inns of Court, usually a judge or a Queen's Counsel **2** See **backbencher**

benchmark (ˈbɛntʃˌmɑːk) *n* **1** a mark on a stone post or other permanent feature, at a point whose exact elevation and position is known: used as a reference point in surveying. Abbreviation: **BM 2 a** a criterion by which to measure something; standard; reference point **b** (*as modifier*): *a benchmark test* ▷ *vb* **3** to measure or test against a benchmark: *the firm benchmarked its pay against that in industry*

benchmark position *n NZ* a public service job used for comparison with a similar position, such as a position in commerce, for wage settlements

bench press *n* **1** a weight-training exercise in which a person lies on a bench and pushes a barbell upwards with both hands from chest level until the arms are straight, then lowers it again ▷ *vb* **bench-press 2** (*intr*) to carry out one or more bench presses

bench test *n* the critical evaluation of a new or repaired component, device, apparatus, etc, prior to installation to ensure that it is in perfect condition

bench warrant *n* a warrant issued by a judge or court directing that an offender be apprehended

benchy (ˈbɛntʃɪ) *adj NZ* (of a hillside) hollowed out in benches

bend¹ (bɛnd) *vb* **bends, bending, bent 1** to form or cause to form a curve, as by pushing or pulling **2** to turn or cause to turn from a particular direction: *the road bends left past the church* **3** (*intr*; often foll by *down*, etc) to incline the body; stoop; bow **4** to submit or cause to submit: *to bend before superior force* **5** (*tr*) to turn or direct (one's eyes, steps, attention, etc) **6** (*tr*) to concentrate (the mind); apply oneself closely **7** (*tr*) *nautical* to attach or fasten, as a sail to a boom or a line to a cleat **8 bend over backwards** *informal* to make a special effort, esp in order to please: *he bends over backwards to accommodate his customers* **9 bend (someone's) ear** *informal* to speak at length to an unwilling listener, esp to voice one's troubles **10 bend the rules** *informal* to ignore rules or change them to suit one's own convenience ▷ *n* **11** a curved part, as in a road or river **12** *nautical* a knot or eye in a line for joining it to another or to an object **13** the act or state of bending **14** *Brit slang* **round the bend** mad; crazy; eccentric ▷ See also **bends** [Old English *bendan*; related to Old Norse *benda*, Middle High German *benden*; see BIND, BAND³]

bend² (bɛnd) *n heraldry* an ordinary consisting of a diagonal line traversing a shield [Old English *bend* BAND²; see BEND¹]

Ben Day process *n printing* a method of adding texture, shading, or detail to line drawings by overlaying a transparent sheet of dots or any other pattern during platemaking [c20 named after *Benjamin Day* (1838–1916), American printer]

bender (ˈbɛndə) *n* **1** *informal* a drinking bout **2** *Brit derogatory slang* a male homosexual **3** *informal* a makeshift shelter constructed by placing tarpaulin or plastic sheeting over bent saplings or woven branches

Bendigo (ˈbɛndɪˌɡəʊ) *n* a city in SE Australia, in central Victoria: founded in 1851 after the discovery of gold. Pop: 68 715 (2001)

bending moment *n* the algebraic sum of all the moments to one side of a cross-section of a beam or other structural support

bends (bɛndz) *pl n* **the** (*functioning as singular or plural*) a nontechnical name for **decompression sickness**

bend sinister *n heraldry* a diagonal line bisecting a shield from the top right to the bottom left, typically indicating a bastard line

bendy¹ (ˈbɛndɪ) *adj* **bendier, bendiest 1** flexible or pliable **2** having many bends: *a bendy road*

bendy² *or* **bendee** (ˈbɛndɪ) *adj* (*usually postpositive*) *heraldry* striped diagonally

beneath (bɪˈniːθ) *prep* **1** below, esp if covered, protected, or obscured by **2** not as great or good as would be demanded by: *beneath his dignity* ▷ *adv* **3** below; underneath [Old English *beneothan*, from BE- + *neothan* low; see NETHER]

benedicite (ˌbɛnɪˈdaɪsɪtɪ) *n* **1** (esp in Christian religious orders) a blessing or grace ▷ *interj* **2** *obsolete* an expression of surprise [c13 from Latin, from *benedīcere*, from *bene* well + *dīcere* to speak]

Benedicite (ˌbɛnɪˈdaɪsɪtɪ) *n Christianity* a canticle that originated as part of the *Song of the Three Holy Children* in the secondary addition to the Book of Daniel, beginning *Benedicite omnia opera Domini Domino* in Latin, and *O all ye Works of the Lord* in English

Benedictine *n* **1** (ˌbɛnɪˈdɪktɪn, -taɪn) a monk or nun who is a member of a Christian religious community founded by or following the rule of Saint Benedict (?480–?547 AD), the Italian monk **2** (ˌbɛnɪˈdɪktiːn) a greenish-yellow liqueur made from a secret formula developed at the Benedictine monastery at Fécamp in France in about 1510 ▷ *adj* **3** (ˌbɛnɪˈdɪktɪn, -taɪn) of or relating to Saint Benedict, his order, or his rule

benediction (ˌbɛnɪˈdɪkʃən) *n* **1** an invocation of divine blessing, esp at the end of a Christian religious ceremony **2** a Roman Catholic service in which the congregation is blessed with the sacrament **3** the state of being blessed [c15 from Latin *benedictio*, from *benedīcere* to bless; see BENEDICITE] > ˌ**beneˈdictory** *adj*

Benedict's solution *or* **reagent** *n* a chemical solution used to detect the presence of glucose and other reducing sugars. Medically, it is used to test the urine of diabetics [named after S. R. *Benedict* (1884–1936), US chemist]

Benedictus (ˌbɛnɪˈdɪktəs) *n* (*sometimes not capital*) *Christianity* **1** a short canticle beginning *Benedictus qui venit in nomine Domini* in Latin and *Blessed is he that cometh in the name of the Lord* in English **2** a canticle beginning *Benedictus Dominus Deus Israel* in Latin and *Blessed be the Lord God of Israel* in English

benefaction (ˌbɛnɪˈfækʃən) *n* **1** the act of doing good, esp by giving a donation to charity **2** the donation or help given [c17 from Late Latin *benefactiō*, from Latin *bene* well + *facere* to do]

benefactor (ˈbɛnɪˌfæktə, ˌbɛnɪˈfæk-) *n* a person who supports or helps a person, institution, etc, esp by giving money; patron > ˈ**beneˌfactress** *fem n*

benefic (bɪˈnɛfɪk) *adj* a rare word for **beneficent**

benefice (ˈbɛnɪfɪs) *n* **1** *Christianity* an endowed Church office yielding an income to its holder; a Church living **2** the property or revenue attached to such an office **3** (in feudal society) a tenement (piece of land) held by a vassal from a landowner on easy terms or free, esp in return for military support. See also **vassalage** ▷ *vb* **4** (*tr*) to provide with a benefice [c14 from Old French, from Latin *beneficium* benefit, from *beneficus*, from *bene* well + *facere* to do]

beneficence (bɪˈnɛfɪsəns) *n* **1** the act of doing good; kindness **2** a charitable act or gift

beneficent (bɪˈnɛfɪsᵊnt) *adj* charitable; generous [c17 from Latin *beneficent-*, from *beneficus*; see BENEFICE] > beˈ**neficently** *adv*

beneficial (ˌbɛnɪˈfɪʃəl) *adj* **1** (sometimes foll by *to*) causing a good result; advantageous **2** *law* entitling a person to receive the profits or proceeds of property: *a beneficial interest in land* [c15 from Late Latin *beneficiālis*, from Latin *beneficium* kindness] > ˌ**beneˈficially** *adv*

beneficiary (ˌbɛnɪˈfɪʃərɪ) *n, pl* **-ciaries 1** a person who gains or benefits in some way from something **2** *law* a person entitled to receive funds or other property under a trust, will, or insurance policy **3** the holder of an ecclesiastical or other benefice **4** *NZ* a person who receives government assistance: *social security beneficiary* ▷ *adj* **5** of or relating to a benefice or the holder of a benefice

benefit (ˈbɛnɪfɪt) *n* **1** something that improves or promotes **2** advantage or sake: *this is for your benefit* **3** *Brit* **a** an allowance paid by the government as for sickness, unemployment, etc, to which a person is entitled under social security or the national insurance scheme **b** any similar allowance in various other countries **4** (*sometimes plural*) a payment or series of payments made by an institution, such as an insurance company or trade union, to a person who is ill, unemployed, etc **5** a theatrical performance, sports event, etc, to raise money for a charity ▷ *vb* **-fits, -fiting, -fited** *or esp US* **-fits, -fitting, -fitted 6** to do or receive good; profit [c14 from Anglo-French *benfet*, from Latin *benefactum*, from *bene facere* to do well]

benefit in kind *n* a nonpecuniary benefit, such as a company car or medical insurance, given to an employee

benefit of clergy *n Christianity* **1** sanction by the church: *marriage without benefit of clergy* **2** (in the Middle Ages) a privilege that placed the clergy outside the jurisdiction of secular courts and entitled them to trial in ecclesiastical courts

benefit society *n* a US term for **friendly society**

Benelux (ˈbɛnɪˌlʌks) *n* **1** the customs union formed by Belgium, the Netherlands, and Luxembourg in 1948; became an economic union in 1960 **2** these countries collectively

benempt (bɪˈnɛmpt) *vb archaic* a past participle of **bename**

Benevento (ˌbɛnəˈvɛntəʊ) *n* a city in S Italy, in N Campania: at various times under Samnite, Roman, Lombard, Saracen, Norman, and papal rule. Pop: 61 791 (2001). Ancient name: **Beneventum** (ˌbɛnəˈvɛntʊm)

benevolence (bɪˈnɛvələns) *n* **1** inclination or tendency to help or do good to others; charity **2** an act of kindness **3** (in the Middle Ages) a forced loan or contribution exacted by English kings from their nobility and subjects

benevolent (bɪˈnɛvələnt) *adj* **1** intending or showing goodwill; kindly; friendly: *a benevolent smile; a benevolent old man* **2** doing good or giving aid to others, rather than making profit; charitable: *a benevolent organization* [c15 from Latin *benevolēns*, from *bene* well + *velle* to wish] > beˈ**nevolently** *adv*

Benfleet (ˈbɛnˌfliːt) *n* a town in SE England, in S Essex on an inlet of the Thames estuary. Pop: 48 539 (2001)

BEng *abbreviation for* Bachelor of Engineering

Bengal (bɛnˈɡɔːl, bɛŋ-) *n* **1** a former province of NE India, in the great deltas of the Ganges and Brahmaputra Rivers: in 1947 divided into West Bengal (belonging to India) and East Bengal (Bangladesh) **2 Bay of.** a wide arm of the Indian Ocean, between India and Myanmar **3** a breed of medium-large cat with a spotted or marbled coat

Bengali (bɛnˈɡɔːlɪ, bɛŋ-) *n* **1** a member of a people living chiefly in Bangladesh and in West Bengal. The West Bengalis are mainly Hindus; the East Bengalis of Bangladesh are mainly Muslims **2** the language of this people: the official language of Bangladesh and the chief language of West Bengal; it belongs to the Indic branch of the Indo-European family. Also called: **Bangla** ▷ *adj* **3** of or relating to Bengal, the Bengalis, or their language

bengaline ('bɛŋgə,liːn, ,bɛŋgə'liːn) *n* a heavy corded fabric, esp silk with woollen or cotton cord [c19 from French; see BENGAL, -INE¹; first produced in Bengal]

Bengal light *n* a firework or flare that burns with a steady bright blue light, formerly used as a signal

Bengbu ('bɛŋ'buː), **Pengpu** or **Pang-fou** *n* a city in E China, in Anhui province. Pop: 779 000 (2005 est)

Benghazi or **Bengasi** (bɛn'gɑːzɪ) *n* a port in N Libya, on the Gulf of Sidra: centre of Italian colonization (1911–42); scene of much fighting in World War II. Pop: 1 080 500 (2002 est). Ancient names: Hesperides, Berenice (bɛrə'naɪsɪ)

Benguela (bɛŋ'gwɛlə) *n* a port in W Angola: founded in 1617; a terminus (with Lobito) of the railway that runs from Beira in Mozambique through the Copper Belt of Zambia and Zimbabwe. Pop: 41 000 (latest est)

Beni (*Spanish* 'beni) *n* a river in N Bolivia, rising in the E Cordillera of the Andes and flowing north to the Marmoré River. Length: over 1600 km (1000 miles)

Benidorm ('bɛnɪdɔːm) *n* a a coastal resort town in W Spain, on the Costa Blanca

benighted (bɪ'naɪtɪd) *adj* **1** lacking cultural, moral, or intellectual enlightenment; ignorant **2** *archaic* overtaken by night > **be'nightedly** *adv* > **be'nightedness** *n*

benign (bɪ'naɪn) *adj* **1** showing kindliness; genial **2** (of soil, climate, etc) mild; gentle **3** favourable; propitious **4** *pathol* (of a tumour, etc) not threatening to life or health; not malignant [c14 from Old French *benigne*, from Latin *benignus*, from *bene* well + *gignere* to produce] > **be'nignly** *adv*

benignant (bɪ'nɪgnənt) *adj* **1** kind; gracious, as a king to his subjects **2** a less common word for **benign** (senses 3, 4) > **be'nignancy** *n* > **be'nignantly** *adv*

benignity (bɪ'nɪgnɪtɪ) *n*, *pl* **-ties 1** the quality of being benign; favourable attitude **2** a kind or gracious act

Beni Hasan ('bɛnɪ hæ'sɑːn) *n* a village in central Egypt, on the Nile, with cliff-cut tombs dating from 2000 BC

Benin (bɛ'niːn) *n* **1** a republic in W Africa, on the **Bight of Benin**, a section of the Gulf of Guinea: in the early 19th century a powerful kingdom, famed for its women warriors; became a French colony in 1893, gaining independence in 1960. It consists chiefly of coastal lagoons and swamps in the south, a fertile plain and marshes in the centre, and the Atakora Mountains in the northwest. Official language: French. Religion: animist majority. Currency: franc. Capital: Porto Novo (the government is based in Cotonou). Pop: 6 918 000 (2004 est). Area: 112 622 sq km (43 474 sq miles). Former name (until 1975): Dahomey **2** a former kingdom of W Africa, powerful from the 14th to the 17th centuries: now a province of S Nigeria: noted for its bronzes

Benin City *n* a city in S Nigeria, capital of Edo state: former capital of the kingdom of Benin. Pop: 1 022 000 (2005 est)

Beninese (,bɛni'niːz) *adj* **1** of or relating to Benin or its people ▷ *n* **2** a native or inhabitant of Benin. Also: Beninois (,bɛni'nwɑː)

Benioff zone ('bɛnɪɒf) *n* a long narrow region, usually adjacent to a continent, along which earthquake foci lie on a plane which dips downwards at about 45° and along which the oceanic lithosphere is thought to be descending into the earth's interior. Compare **subduction zone** [c20 named after Hugo *Benioff* (1899–1968), American seismologist, who first discovered the phenomenon]

benison ('bɛnɪzªn, -sªn) *n archaic* a blessing, esp a spoken one [c13 from Old French *beneison*, from Latin *benedictiō* BENEDICTION]

benjamin ('bɛndʒəmɪn) *n* **1** another name for

benzoin (sense 1) **2** **benjamin bush** another name for **spicebush** [c16 variant of *benzoin*; influenced in form by the name *Benjamin*]

Benjamin ('bɛndʒəmɪn) *n* **1** *Old Testament* **a** the youngest and best-loved son of Jacob and Rachel (Genesis 35:16–18; 42:4) **b** the tribe descended from this patriarch **c** the territory of this tribe, northwest of the Dead Sea **2** *archaic* a youngest and favourite son

Ben Lomond (bɛn 'ləʊmənd) *n* **1** a mountain in W central Scotland, on the E side of Loch Lomond. Height: 973 m (3192 ft) **2** a mountain in NE Tasmania. Height: 1527 m (5010 ft) **3** a mountain in SE Australia, in NE New South Wales. Height: 1520 m (4986 ft)

benne ('bɛnɪ) *n* **1** another name for **sesame 2** **benne oil** the edible oil obtained from sesame seeds [c18 from Malay *bene*; compare Bambara *bene*]

bennet ('bɛnɪt) *n* short for **herb bennet**

Ben Nevis (bɛn 'nɛvɪs) *n* a mountain in W Scotland, in the Grampian mountains: highest peak in Great Britain. Height: 1344 m (4408 ft)

Bennington ('bɛnɪŋtən) *n* a town in SW Vermont: the site of a British defeat (1777) in the War of American Independence. Pop: 15 637 (2003 est)

benny¹ ('bɛnɪ) *n*, *pl* **-nies** *dated slang* an amphetamine tablet, esp benzedrine: a stimulant [c20 shortened from BENZEDRINE]

benny² ('bɛnɪ) *n*, *pl* **-nies** US *slang* a man's overcoat [c19 from *Benjamin*, perhaps from a tailor's name]

benomyl ('bɛnəmɪl) *n* a fungicide, derived from imidazole, used on cereal and fruit crops: suspected of being carcinogenic

Benoni (bɪ'nəʊnɪ) *n* a city in NE South Africa: gold mines. Pop: 94 341 (2001)

bent¹ (bɛnt) *adj* **1** not straight; curved **2** (foll by *on*) fixed (on a course of action); resolved (to); determined (to) **3** *slang* **a** dishonest; corrupt **b** (of goods) stolen **c** crazy; mad **d** sexually deviant, esp homosexual ▷ *n* **4** personal inclination, propensity, or aptitude **5** capacity of endurance (esp in the phrase **to the top of one's bent**) **6** *civil engineering* a framework placed across a structure to stiffen it

bent² (bɛnt) *n* **1** short for **bent grass 2** a stalk of bent grass **3** *archaic* any stiff grass or sedge **4** *Scot and Northern English dialect* heath or moorland [Old English *bionot*; related to Old Saxon *binet*, Old High German *binuz* rush]

bent grass *n* any perennial grass of the genus *Agrostis*, esp *A. tenuis*, which has a spreading panicle of tiny flowers. Some species are planted for hay or in lawns. Sometimes shortened to: bent

Benthamism ('bɛnθə,mɪzəm) *n* the philosophy of utilitarianism as first expounded by the British philosopher and jurist Jeremy Bentham (1748–1832) in terms of an action being good that has a greater tendency to augment the happiness of the community than to diminish it > **Bentha,mite** *n*, *adj*

benthos ('bɛnθɒs) or **benthon** *n* **1** the animals and plants living at the bottom of a sea or lake **2** the bottom of a sea or lake [c19 from Greek: depth; related to *bathus* deep] > **'benthic**, **'benthal** or **ben'thonic** *adj*

bento or **bento box** ('bɛntəʊ) *n*, *pl* **-tos** a thin box, made of plastic or lacquered wood, divided into compartments which contain small separate dishes comprising a Japanese meal, esp lunch [Japanese *bentō* box lunch]

bentonite ('bɛntə,naɪt) *n* a valuable clay, formed by the decomposition of volcanic ash, that swells as it absorbs water: used as a filler in the building, paper, and pharmaceutical industries [c19 from Fort *Benton*, Montana, USA, where found, + -ITE¹]

bentwood ('bɛnt,wʊd) *n* **a** wood bent in moulds after being heated by steaming, used mainly for furniture **b** (*as modifier*): *a bentwood chair*

Benue ('bɛnʊ,eɪ) *n* **1** a state of SE Nigeria, formed in 1976 from part of Benue-Plateau state. Capital: Makurdi. Pop: 3 108 754 (1995 est). Area: 34 059 sq km (13 150 sq miles) **2** a river in W Africa, rising in N Cameroon and flowing west across Nigeria: chief tributary of the River Niger. Length: 1400 km (870 miles)

Benue-Congo *n* **1** a branch of the Niger-Congo family of African languages, consisting of the Bantu languages together with certain other languages of W Africa ▷ *adj* **2** relating or belonging to this group of languages

benumb (bɪ'nʌm) *vb* (*tr*) **1** to make numb or powerless; deaden physical feeling in, as by cold **2** (*usually passive*) to make inactive; stupefy (the mind, senses, will, etc) > **be'numbingly** *adv*

Benxi ('bɛn'ʃiː), **Penchi** or **Penki** *n* an industrial city in NE China, in S Liaoning province. Pop: 967 000 (2005 est)

benzaldehyde (bɛn'zældɪ,haɪd) *n* a yellowish fragrant volatile oil occurring in almond kernels and used in the manufacture of dyes, perfumes, and flavourings and as a solvent for oils and resins. Formula: C_6H_5CHO. Systematic name: benzenecarbaldehyde

Benzedrine ('bɛnzɪ,driːn, -drɪn) *n* a trademark for amphetamine

benzene ('bɛnziːn, bɛn'ziːn) *n* a colourless flammable toxic aromatic liquid used in the manufacture of styrene, phenol, etc, as a solvent for fats, resins, etc, and as an insecticide. Formula: C_6H_6. See also **benzene ring**

benzenecarbaldehyde (,bɛnziː,nkɑː'bældɪ,haɪd) *n* the systematic name for **benzaldehyde**

benzenecarbonyl (,bɛnziː'nkɑː,bɒnaɪl) *n* (*modifier*) the systematic name for **benzoyl**

benzenecarboxylate (,bɛnziː,nkɑː'bɒksɪ,leɪt) *n* the systematic name for **benzoate**

benzenecarboxylic acid (,bɛnziː,nkɑː,bɒk'sɪlɪk) *n* the systematic name for **benzoic acid**

benzene hexachloride *n* another name for hexachlorocyclohexane

benzene ring *n* the hexagonal ring of bonded carbon atoms in the benzene molecule or its derivatives. Also called: benzene nucleus See also **Kekulé formula**

benzidine ('bɛnzɪ,diːn, -dɪn) *n* a grey or reddish poisonous crystalline powder that is used mainly in the manufacture of dyes, esp Congo red. Formula: $NH_2(C_6H_4)_2NH_2$

benzine ('bɛnziːn, bɛn'ziːn) or **benzin** ('bɛnzɪn) *n* a volatile mixture of the lighter aliphatic hydrocarbon constituents of petroleum. See **ligroin, petroleum ether**

benzo- or *sometimes before a vowel* **benz-** *combining form* **1** indicating a benzene ring fused to another ring in a polycyclic compound: *benzofuran* **2** indicating derivation from benzene or benzoic acid or the presence of phenyl groups: *benzophenone* [from BENZOIN]

benzoate ('bɛnzəʊ,eɪt, -ɪt) *n* any salt or ester of benzoic acid, containing the group C_6H_5COO- or the ion $C_6H_5COO^-$. Systematic name: benzenecarboxylate

benzoate of soda *n* another name for **sodium benzoate**

benzocaine ('bɛnzəʊ,keɪn) *n* a white crystalline ester used as a local anaesthetic; ethyl *para*-aminobenzoate. Formula: $C_9H_{11}NO_2$

benzodiazepine (,bɛnzəʊdaɪ'eɪzə,piːn) *n* any of a group of chemical compounds that are used as minor tranquillizers, such as diazepam (Valium) and chlordiazepoxide (Librium) [c20 from BENZO- + DI-¹ + AZA- + EP- + -INE²]

benzofuran (,bɛnzəʊ'fjʊəræn) *n* a colourless insoluble aromatic liquid obtained from coal tar and used in the manufacture of synthetic resins. Formula: C_8H_6O. Also called: coumarone, cumarone

benzoic (bɛn'zəʊɪk) *adj* of, containing, or derived from benzoic acid or benzoin

benzoic acid *n* a white crystalline solid occurring

b

in many natural resins, used in the manufacture of benzoates, plasticizers, and dyes and as a food preservative (E210). Formula: C_6H_5COOH. Systematic name: benzenecarboxylic acid

benzoin ('benzɔɪn, -zəʊɪn, bɛn'zəʊɪn) n **1** Also called: benjamin a gum resin containing benzoic acid, obtained from various trees of the genus *Styrax*, esp *S. benzoin* of Java and Sumatra, and used in ointments, perfume, etc **2** a white or yellowish crystalline compound with a camphor-like odour used as an antiseptic and flavouring; 2-hydroxy-2-phenylacetophenone. Formula: $C_6H_5CHOHCOC_6H_5$ **3** any lauraceous aromatic shrub or tree of the genus *Lindera*, esp *L. benzoin* (spicebush) [c16 from French *benjoin*, from Old Catalan *benjui*, from Arabic *lubān jāwī*, literally: frankincense of Java]

benzol *or* **benzole** ('benzɒl) n **1** a crude form of benzene, containing toluene, xylene, and other hydrocarbons, obtained from coal tar or coal gas and used as a fuel **2** an obsolete name for **benzene**

benzophenone (,benzəʊfɪ'nəʊn) n a white sweet-smelling crystalline solid used mainly in the manufacture of organic compounds and in perfume. Formula: $C_6H_5COC_6H_5$. Also called: diphenylketone

benzoquinone (,benzəʊkwɪ'nəʊn, -'kwɪnəʊn) n a yellow crystalline water-soluble unsaturated ketone manufactured from aniline and used in the production of dyestuffs. Formula: $C_6H_4O_2$. Also called: quinone Systematic name: cyclohexadiene-1,4-quinone

benzoyl ('benzəʊɪl) n (*modifier*) of, consisting of, or containing the monovalent group C_6H_5CO-: *benzoyl group or radical*. Systematic name: benzenecarbonyl

benzyl ('benzaɪl) n (*modifier*) of, consisting of, or containing the monovalent group $C_6H_5CH_2$-: *benzyl alcohol*. Systematic name: phenylmethyl

Beograd (bɛ'ɔgrad) n the Serbo-Croat name for **Belgrade**

Beothuk (bɪ'ɒθʊk) n a member of an extinct Native Canadian people formerly living in Newfoundland

Beowulf ('beɪə,wʊlf) n an anonymous Old English epic poem in alliterative verse, believed to have been composed in the 8th century AD

bequeath (bɪ'kwi:ð, -'kwi:θ) vb (*tr*) **1** *law* to dispose of (property, esp personal property) by will. Compare **devise** (sense 2) **2** to hand down; pass on, as to following generations [Old English *becwethan*; related to Old Norse *kvetha* to speak, Gothic *qithan*, Old High German *quethan*] ▷ be'queather n

bequest (bɪ'kwɛst) n **1 a** the act of bequeathing **b** something that is bequeathed **2** *law* a gift of property by will, esp personal property. Compare **devise** (senses 4, 5) [c14 BE- + Old English *-cwiss* degree; see BEQUEATH]

Berar (bɛ'rɑ:) n a region of W central India: part of Maharashtra state since 1956; important for cotton growing

berate (bɪ'reɪt) vb (*tr*) to scold harshly

Berber ('bɜ:bə) n **1** a member of a Caucasoid Muslim people of N Africa **2** the language of this people, forming a subfamily of the Afro-Asiatic family of languages. There are extensive differences between dialects ▷ adj **3** of or relating to this people or their language

Berbera ('bɜ:bərə) n a port in N Somalia, on the Gulf of Aden. Pop: 70 000 (1990 est)

berbere (beə'beə) n a hot-tasting Ethiopian paste made from garlic, cayenne pepper, coriander, and other spices, often used in stews [French]

berberidaceous (,bɜ:bərɪ'deɪʃəs) adj of, relating to, or belonging to the *Berberidaceae*, a mainly N temperate family of flowering plants (mostly shrubs), including barberry and barrenwort [c19 from Medieval Latin *berberis*, from Arabic *barbārīs* BARBERRY]

berberine ('bɜ:bə,ri:n) n a yellow bitter-tasting alkaloid obtained from barberry and other plants

and used medicinally, esp in tonics. Formula: $C_{20}H_{19}NO_5$ [c19 from German *Berberin*, from New Latin *berberis* BARBERRY]

berberis ('bɜ:bərɪs) n any shrub of the berberidaceous genus *Berberis* See **barberry** [c19 from Medieval Latin, of unknown origin]

berbice chair ('bɜ:bi:s) n a large armchair with long arms that can be folded inwards to act as leg rests [c20 named after *Berbice*, a river and former county in Guyana]

berceuse (*French* bɛrsøz) n **1** a cradlesong or lullaby **2** an instrumental piece suggestive of this, in six-eight time [c19 from French: lullaby, from *bercer* to rock]

Berchtesgaden (*German* 'bɛrçtəsga:dən) n a town in Germany, in SE Bavaria: site of the fortified mountain retreat of Adolf Hitler. Pop: 7667 (2003 est)

bereave (bɪ'ri:v) vb (*tr*) **1** (usually foll by *of*) to deprive (of) something or someone valued, esp through death **2** *obsolete* to remove by force ▷ See also **bereft** [Old English *bereafian*; see REAVE[1]]

bereaved (bɪ'ri:vd) adj having been deprived of something or someone valued, esp through death

bereavement (bɪ'ri:vmənt) n **1** the condition having been deprived of something or someone valued, esp through death **2** a death

bereft (bɪ'rɛft) adj (usually foll by *of*) deprived; parted (from): *bereft of hope*

beret ('bɛreɪ) n a round close-fitting brimless cap of soft wool material or felt [c19 from French *béret*, from Old Provençal *berret*, from Medieval Latin *birrettum* cap; see BIRETTA]

Berezina (*Russian* bɪrɪzi'na) n a river in Belarus, rising in the north and flowing south to the River Dnieper: linked with the River Dvina and the Baltic Sea by the **Berezina Canal**. Length: 563 km (350 miles)

Berezniki (*Russian* bɪrɪzni'ki) n a city in E Russia: chemical industries. Pop: 169 000 (2005 est)

berg[1] (bɜ:g) n short for **iceberg**

berg[2] (bɜ:g) n a South African word for **mountain**

Bergamo (*Italian* 'bɛrgamo) n a walled city in N Italy, in Lombardy. Pop: 113 143 (2001)

bergamot ('bɜ:gə,mɒt) n **1** Also called: bergamot orange a small Asian spiny rutaceous tree, *Citrus bergamia*, having sour pear-shaped fruit **2** essence of bergamot a fragrant essential oil from the fruit rind of this plant, used in perfumery and some teas (including Earl Grey) **3** a Mediterranean mint, *Mentha citrata*, that yields an oil similar to essence of bergamot **4 a** wild bergamot a North American plant, *Monarda fistulosa*, with clusters of purple flowers: family Lamiaceae (labiates) **b** a garden plant of the same genus, usually *M. didyma* (bee balm), grown for its scarlet or pink flowers **5** a variety of pear [c17 from French *bergamote*, from Italian *bergamotta*, of Turkic origin; related to Turkish *bey-armudu* prince's pear; see BEY]

Bergdama (,bɜ:g'dɑ:mə) n another name for a **Damara**

bergen ('bɜ:gən) n a large rucksack with a capacity of over 50 litres

Bergen n **1** (*Norwegian* 'bærgən) a port in SW Norway: chief city in medieval times. Pop: 237 430 (2004 est) **2** ('bɛrxən) the Flemish name for **Mons**

bergère (bɜ:'ʒɛə) n **1** a type of French armchair made from about 1725 having a wide deep seat and upholstered sides and back. In later examples, woven cane is often used instead of upholstery **2** a sofa of a similar design [French, literally: shepherdess]

Bergie ('bɜ:gɪ) n *South African informal* a vagabond, esp one living on the slopes of Table Mountain in the Western Cape province of South Africa [from Afrikaans *berg* mountain]

bergschrund ('bɛrkʃrʊnt, 'bɜ:gʃru:nd) n a crevasse at the head of a glacier. Also called: rimaye [c19 German: mountain crack]

Bergsonian (bɜ:g'səʊnɪən) adj **1** of or relating to Henri Bergson, the French philosopher (1859–1941)

▷ n **2** a follower or admirer of Bergson

Bergsonism ('bɜ:gsə,nɪzəm) n the philosophy of Henri Bergson, the French philosopher (1859–1941), which emphasizes duration as the basic element of experience and asserts the existence of a life-giving force that permeates the entire natural order. Compare **élan vital**

berg wind n a hot dry wind in South Africa blowing from the plateau down to the coast

beriberi (,bɛrɪ'bɛrɪ) n a disease, endemic in E and S Asia, caused by dietary deficiency of thiamine (vitamin B_1). It affects the nerves to the limbs, producing pain, paralysis, and swelling [c19 from Sinhalese, by reduplication from *beri* weakness]

berimbau (berɪ'bʊw) n a Brazilian single-stringed bowed instrument, used to accompany capoeira [from the quimbundo (an Angolan language) word *mbirimbau*]

Bering Sea n a part of the N Pacific Ocean, between NE Siberia and Alaska. Area: about 2 275 000 sq km (878 000 sq miles)

Bering Strait n a strait between Alaska and Russia, connecting the Bering Sea and the Arctic Ocean

berk *or* **burk** (bɜ:k) n *Brit slang* a stupid person; fool [c20 shortened from *Berkeley* or *Berkshire Hunt* rhyming slang for *cunt*]

Berkeleian (bɑː'kliːən) adj **1** denoting or relating to the philosophy of George Berkeley, the Irish philosopher and Anglican bishop (1685–1753) ▷ n **2** a follower of his teachings

Berkeleianism (bɑː'kliːə,nɪzəm) n the philosophical system of George Berkeley, the Irish philosopher and Anglican bishop (1685–1753), holding that objects exist only when perceived, that God's perception sustains the universe, and that there is no independent substratum or substance in which these perceptions inhere

Berkeley ('bɜ:klɪ) n a city in W California, on San Francisco Bay: seat of the University of California. Pop: 102 049 (2003 est)

Berkeley Castle ('bɑːklɪ) n a castle in Gloucestershire: scene of the murder of Edward II in 1327

berkelium (bɜ:'ki:lɪəm, 'bɜ:klɪəm) n a metallic transuranic element produced by bombardment of americium. Symbol: Bk; atomic no.: 97; half-life of most stable isotope, [247]Bk: 1400 years; valency: 3 or 4; relative density: 14 (est) [c20 named after BERKELEY, where it was discovered]

berko ('bɜ:kəʊ) adj *Austral slang* berserk

Berks (bɑːks) abbreviation for **Berkshire**

Berkshire ('bɑːkʃɪə, -ʃə) n **1** a historic county of S England: since reorganization in 1974 the River Thames has marked the N boundary while the **Berkshire Downs** occupy central parts; the county council was replaced by six unitary authorities in 1998. Area: 1259 sq km (486 sq miles). Abbreviation: Berks **2** a rare breed of pork and bacon pig having a black body and white points

berley *or* **burley** ('bɜːlɪ) *Austral* ▷ n **1** bait scattered on water to attract fish **2** *slang* rubbish; nonsense ▷ vb (*tr*) **3** to scatter (bait) on water **4** to hurry (someone); urge on [origin unknown]

berlin (bə'lɪn, 'bɜːlɪn) n **1** (*sometimes capital*) Also called: berlin wool a fine wool yarn used for tapestry work, etc **2** a four-wheeled two-seated covered carriage, popular in the 18th century **3** a limousine with a glass partition between the front and rear seats ▷ Also called (for senses 2, 3): berline (bə'li:n, 'bɜ:li:n) [c18 named after BERLIN]

Berlin (bɜ:'lɪn; *German* bɛr'li:n) n the capital of Germany (1871–1945 and from 1990), formerly divided (1945–90) into the eastern sector, capital of East Germany, and the western sectors, which formed an exclave in East German territory closely affiliated with West Germany: a wall dividing the sectors was built in 1961 by the East German authorities to stop the flow of refugees from east to west; demolition of the wall began in 1989 and the city was formally reunited in 1990: formerly (1618–1871) the capital of Brandenburg and Prussia. Pop: 3 388 477 (2003 est)

Berliner (bɜːˈliːnə) *n* a native or inhabitant of Berlin

berm *or* **berme** (bɜːm) *n* **1** a narrow path or ledge at the edge of a slope, road, or canal **2** NZ the grass verge of a suburban street, usually kept mown **3** *fortifications* a narrow path or ledge between a moat and a rampart **4** *military* a man-made ridge of sand, designed as an obstacle to tanks, which, in crossing it, have to expose their vulnerable underparts [c18 from French *berme*, from Dutch *berm*, probably from Old Norse *barmr* BRIM]

Bermejo (Spanish berˈmexo) *n* a river in Argentina, rising in the northwest and flowing southeast to the Paraguay River. Length: about 1600 km (1000 miles)

Bermuda (bəˈmjuːdə) *n* a UK Overseas Territory consisting of a group of over 150 coral islands (**the Bermudas**) in the NW Atlantic: discovered in about 1503, colonized by the British by 1612, although not acquired by the British crown until 1684. Capital: Hamilton. Pop: 82 000 (2003 est). Area: 53 sq km (20 sq miles)

Bermuda grass *n* a widely distributed grass, *Cynodon dactylon*, with wiry creeping rootstocks and several purplish spikes of flowers arising from a single point: used for lawns, pasturage, binding sand dunes, etc. Also called: **scutch grass, wire grass**

Bermuda rig *n* a fore-and-aft sailing boat rig characterized by a tall mainsail (**Bermudian mainsail**) that tapers to a point > **Berˈmuda-ˈrigged** *adj*

Bermuda shorts *pl n* close-fitting shorts that come down to the knees. Also called: **Bermudas**

Bermuda Triangle *n* an area in the Atlantic Ocean bounded by Bermuda, Puerto Rico, and Florida where ships and aeroplanes are alleged to have disappeared mysteriously

Bermudian (bəˈmjuːdɪən) *n* **1** a native or inhabitant of Bermuda ▷ *adj* **2** of or relating to Bermuda or its inhabitants

Bern (bɜːn; German bɛrn) *n* **1** the capital of Switzerland, in the W part, on the Aar River: entered the Swiss confederation in 1353 and became the capital in 1848. Pop: 122 700 (2002 est) **2** a canton of Switzerland, between the French frontier and the Bernese Alps. Capital: Bern. Pop: 950 200 (2002 est). Area: 6884 sq km (2658 sq miles). French name: **Berne** (bɛrn)

Bernardine (ˈbɜːnədɪn, -diːn) *n* **1** a monk of one of the reformed and stricter branches of the Cistercian order ▷ *adj* **2 a** of or relating to this branch of the Cistercians **b** of or relating to Saint Bernard of Clairvaux (?1090–1153), French abbot and theologian

Bernese Alps *or* **Oberland** (ˈbɜːniːz) *n* a mountain range in SW Switzerland, the N central part of the Alps. Highest peak: Finsteraarhorn, 4274 m (14 022 ft)

Bernese mountain dog *n* a strong sturdy dog of a breed with a bushy tail and a long silky black coat with reddish-brown and white markings, often used as a working farm dog

bernicle goose (ˈbɜːnɪkᵊl) *n* a former name for the **brent goose** *or* **barnacle goose**

Bernina (bəˈniːnə; Italian berˈnina) *n* **Piz a** mountain in SE Switzerland, the highest peak of the **Bernina Alps** in the S Rhaetian Alps. Height: 4049 m (13 284 ft)

Bernina Pass *n* a pass in the Alps between SE Switzerland and N Italy, east of Piz Bernina. Height: 2323 m (7622 ft)

Bernoulli's principle *or* **law** *n physics* the principle that in a liquid flowing through a pipe the pressure difference that accelerates the flow when the bore changes is equal to the product of half the density times the change of the square of the speed, provided friction is negligible [c19 named after Daniel Bernoulli (1700–82), Swiss mathematician and physicist]

Bernoulli trial *n statistics* one of a sequence of independent experiments each of which has the same probability of success, such as successive throws of a die, the outcome of which is described by a binomial distribution. See also **binomial experiment, geometric distribution** [named after Jacques Bernoulli (1654–1705), Swiss mathematician]

berretta (bɪˈrɛtə) *n* a variant spelling of **biretta**

berrigan (ˈbɛrɪgən) *n* an Australian tree, *Pittosporum phylliraeoides*, with hanging branches

berry (ˈbɛrɪ) *n, pl* -ries **1** any of various small edible fruits such as the blackberry and strawberry **2** *botany* an indehiscent fruit with two or more seeds and a fleshy pericarp, such as the grape or gooseberry **3** any of various seeds or dried kernels, such as a coffee bean **4** the egg of a lobster, crayfish, or similar animal ▷ *vb* -ries, -rying, -ried (intr) **5** to bear or produce berries **6** to gather or look for berries [Old English *berie*; related to Old High German *beri*, Dutch *bezie*] > ˈberried *adj*

berryfruit (ˈbɛrɪˌfruːt) *n Austral and NZ* any edible berry such as a raspberry, boysenberry, blackcurrant, or strawberry

bersagliere (ˌbɛəsɑːˈljɛərɪ) *n, pl* -ri (-riː) a member of a rifle regiment in the Italian Army [c19 from Italian, from *bersaglio* target, from Old French *bersail*, from *berser* to fire at]

berseem (bɜːˈsiːm) *n* a Mediterranean clover, *Trifolium alexandrinum*, grown as a forage crop and to improve the soil in the southwestern US and the Nile valley. Also called: Egyptian clover [c20 from Arabic *barsīm*, from Coptic *bersīm*]

berserk (bəˈzɜːk, -ˈsɜːk) *adj* **1** frenziedly violent or destructive (esp in the phrase **go berserk**) ▷ *n* **2** Also called: **berserker** a member of a class of ancient Norse warriors who worked themselves into a frenzy before battle and fought with insane fury and courage [c19 Icelandic *berserkr*, from *björn* bear + *serkr* shirt]

berth (bɜːθ) *n* **1** a bed or bunk in a vessel or train, usually narrow and fixed to a wall **2** *nautical* a place assigned to a ship at a mooring **3** *nautical* sufficient distance from the shore or from other ships or objects for a ship to manoeuvre **4** give a wide berth to to keep clear of; avoid **5** *nautical* accommodation on a ship **6** *informal* a job, esp as a member of a ship's crew ▷ *vb* **7** (tr) *nautical* to assign a berth to (a vessel) **8** *nautical* to dock (a vessel) **9** (tr) to provide with a sleeping place, as on a vessel or train **10** (intr) *nautical* to pick up a mooring in an anchorage [c17 probably from BEAR¹ + -TH¹]

bertha (ˈbɜːθə) *n* a wide deep capelike collar, often of lace, usually to cover up a low neckline [c19 from French *berthe*, from *Berthe*, 8th-century Frankish queen, mother of Charlemagne]

Bertillon system (ˈbɜːtɪˌlɒn; French bɛrtijɔ̃) *n* a system formerly in use for identifying persons, esp criminals, by means of a detailed record of physical characteristics [c19 named after Alphonse *Bertillon* (1853–1914), French criminal investigator]

Berwickshire (ˈbɛrɪkʃɪə, -ʃə) *n* (until 1975) a county of SE Scotland: part of the Borders region from 1975 to 1996, now part of Scottish Borders council area

Berwick-upon-Tweed (twiːd) *n* a town in N England, in N Northumberland at the mouth of the Tweed: much involved in border disputes between England and Scotland between the 12th and 16th centuries; neutral territory 1551–1885. Pop: 12 870 (2001). Also called: **Berwick**

beryl (ˈbɛrɪl) *n* a white, blue, yellow, green, or pink mineral, found in coarse granites and igneous rocks. It is a source of beryllium and is sometimes used as a gemstone: the green variety is emerald, the blue is aquamarine. Composition: beryllium aluminium silicate. Formula: $Be_3Al_2Si_6O_{18}$. Crystal structure: hexagonal [c13 from Old French, from Latin *bēryllus*, from Greek *bērullos*, of Indic origin] > ˈberyline *adj*

beryllium (bɛˈrɪlɪəm) *n* a corrosion-resistant toxic silvery-white metallic element that occurs chiefly in beryl and is used mainly in X-ray windows and in the manufacture of alloys. Symbol: Be; atomic no.: 4; atomic wt.: 9.012; valency: 2; relative density: 1.848; melting pt.: 1289°C; boiling pt.: 2472°C. Former names: glucinum, glucinium [c19 from Latin *bēryllus*, from Greek *bērullos*]

Bes (bɛs) *n* an ancient Egyptian god represented as a grotesque hairy dwarf: the patron of music and pleasure

Besançon (French bəzɑ̃sɔ̃) *n* a city in E France, on the Doubs River: university (1422). Pop: 117 733 (1999)

beseech (bɪˈsiːtʃ) *vb* -seeches, -seeching, -sought *or* -seeched (tr) to ask (someone) earnestly (to do something or for something); beg [c12 see BE-, SEEK; related to Old Frisian *besēka*] > beˈseecher *n* > beˈseeching *adj* > beˈseechingly *adv*

beseem (bɪˈsiːm) *vb archaic* to be suitable for; befit

beset (bɪˈsɛt) *vb* -sets, -setting, -set (tr) **1** (esp of dangers, temptations, or difficulties) to trouble or harass constantly **2** to surround or attack from all sides **3** *archaic* to cover with, esp with jewels > beˈsetter *n*

besetting (bɪˈsɛtɪŋ) *adj* tempting, harassing, or assailing (esp in the phrase **besetting sin**)

beshrew (bɪˈʃruː) *vb* (tr) *archaic* to wish evil on; curse (used in mild oaths such as **beshrew me**) [c14 see BE-, SHREW]

beside (bɪˈsaɪd) *prep* **1** next to; at, by, or to the side of **2** as compared with **3** away from; wide of: *beside the point* **4** *archaic* besides **5** beside oneself (postpositive; often foll by with) overwhelmed; overwrought: *beside oneself with grief* ▷ *adv* **6** at, by, to, or along the side of something or someone [Old English *be sīdan*; see BY, SIDE]

besides (bɪˈsaɪdz) *prep* **1** apart from; even considering: *besides costing too much, the scheme is impractical* ▷ *sentence connector* **2** anyway; moreover ▷ *adv* **3** as well

besiege (bɪˈsiːdʒ) *vb* (tr) **1** to surround (a fortified area, esp a city) with military forces to bring about its surrender **2** to crowd round; hem in **3** to overwhelm, as with requests or queries > beˈsieger *n*

besmear (bɪˈsmɪə) *vb* (tr) **1** to smear over; daub **2** to sully; defile (often in the phrase **besmear (a person's) reputation**)

besmirch (bɪˈsmɜːtʃ) *vb* (tr) **1** to make dirty; soil **2** to reduce the brightness or lustre of **3** to sully (often in the phrase **besmirch (a person's) name**)

besom¹ (ˈbiːzəm) *n* **1** a broom, esp one made of a bundle of twigs tied to a handle **2** *curling* a broom or brush used to sweep the ice in front of the stone to make it slide farther ▷ *vb* (tr) **3** to sweep with a besom [Old English *besma*; related to Old High German *besmo* broom]

besom² (ˈbɪzəm, ˈbizəm) *n Scot and Northern English dialect* a derogatory term for a **woman** [perhaps from Old English *bysen* example; related to Old Norse *bysn* wonder]

besotted (bɪˈsɒtɪd) *adj* **1** stupefied with drink; intoxicated **2** infatuated; doting **3** foolish; muddled

besought (bɪˈsɔːt) *vb* the past tense and past participle of **beseech**

bespangle (bɪˈspæŋɡᵊl) *vb* (tr) to cover or adorn with or as if with spangles

bespatter (bɪˈspætə) *vb* (tr) **1** to splash all over, as with dirty water **2** to defile; slander; besmirch

bespeak (bɪˈspiːk) *vb* -speaks, -speaking, -spoke, -spoken *or* -spoke (tr) **1** to engage, request, or ask for in advance **2** to indicate or suggest: *this act bespeaks kindness* **3** *poetic* to speak to; address **4** *archaic* to foretell

bespectacled (bɪˈspɛktəkᵊld) *adj* wearing spectacles

bespoke (bɪˈspəʊk) *adj chiefly Brit* **1** (esp of clothing or a website, computer program, etc) made to the customer's specifications **2** making or selling such suits, jackets, etc: *a bespoke tailor*

bespread (bɪˈsprɛd) *vb* **-spreads, -spreading, -spread** (*tr*) to cover (a surface) with something

besprent (bɪˈsprɛnt) *adj poetic* sprinkled over [C14 past participle of Old English *besprengan* to BESPRINKLE]

besprinkle (bɪˈsprɪŋkˀl) *vb* (*tr*) to sprinkle all over with liquid, powder, etc

Bessarabia (ˌbɛsəˈreɪbɪə) *n* a region in E Europe, mostly in Moldova and Ukraine: long disputed by the Turks and Russians; a province of Romania from 1918 until 1940. Area: about 44 300 sq km (17 100 sq miles)

Bessemer converter (ˈbɛsɪmə) *n* a refractory-lined furnace used to convert pig iron into steel by the Bessemer process

Bessemer process *n* **1** (formerly) a process for producing steel by blowing air through molten pig iron at about 1250°C in a Bessemer converter: silicon, manganese, and phosphorus impurities are removed and the carbon content is controlled **2** a similar process for removing sulphur and iron from copper matte [C19 named after Sir Henry *Bessemer* (1813–98), English engineer]

best (bɛst) *adj* **1** the superlative of **good 2** most excellent of a particular group, category, etc **3** most suitable, advantageous, desirable, attractive, etc **4** the best part of most of: *the best part of an hour* **5** put one's best foot forward **a** to do one's utmost to make progress **b** to hurry ▷ *adv* **6** the superlative of **well 7** in a manner surpassing all others; most excellently, advantageously, attractively, etc **8** (*in combination*) in or to the greatest degree or extent; most: *the best-loved hero* **9** as best one can *or* may as effectively as possible within one's limitations **10** had best would be wise, sensible, etc, to: *you had best go now* ▷ *n* **11** the best the most outstanding or excellent person, thing, or group in a category **12** (often preceded by *at*) the most excellent, pleasing, or skilled quality or condition: *journalism at its best* **13** the most effective effort of which a person or group is capable: *even their best was inadequate* **14** a winning majority: *the best of three games* **15** Also: all the best best wishes: *she sent him her best* **16** a person's smartest outfit of clothing **17** at best **a** in the most favourable interpretation **b** under the most favourable conditions **18** for the best **a** for an ultimately good outcome **b** with good intentions: *he meant it for the best* **19** get *or* have the best of to surpass, defeat, or outwit; better **20** give (someone) the best to concede (someone's) superiority **21** make the best of to cope as well as possible in the unfavourable circumstances (often in the phrases **make the best of a bad job, make the best of it**) **22** six of the best *informal* six strokes with a cane on the buttocks or hand ▷ *vb* **23** (*tr*) to gain the advantage over or defeat [Old English *betst*; related to Gothic *batista*, Old High German *bezzist*]

best-ball *adj golf* of, relating to, or denoting a match in which one player competes against the best individual totals of two or more other players at each hole

best boy *n chiefly US* the assistant to the senior electrician or to the key grip in a film crew

best end *n* the end of the neck of lamb, pork, etc, nearest to the ribs

best girl *n archaic* one's sweetheart

besti (ˈbeɪstiː) *n Hinglish* shame; embarrassment [C21 Hindi *be-izzat* dishonour]

bestial (ˈbɛstɪəl) *adj* **1** brutal or savage **2** sexually depraved; carnal **3** lacking in refinement; brutish **4** of or relating to a beast [C14 from Late Latin *bestiālis*, from Latin *bestia* BEAST] > **ˈbestially** *adv*

bestiality (ˌbɛstɪˈælɪtɪ) *n, pl* **-ties 1** bestial behaviour, character, or action **2** sexual activity between a person and an animal

bestialize *or* **bestialise** (ˈbɛstɪəˌlaɪz) *vb* (*tr*) to make bestial or brutal

bestiary (ˈbɛstɪərɪ) *n, pl* **-aries** a moralizing medieval collection of descriptions (and often illustrations) of real and mythical animals

bestir (bɪˈstɜː) *vb* **-stirs, -stirring, -stirred** (*tr*) to cause (oneself, or, rarely, another person) to become active; rouse

best man *n* the (male) attendant of the bridegroom at a wedding

bestow (bɪˈstəʊ) *vb* (*tr*) **1** to present (a gift) or confer (an award or honour) **2** *archaic* to apply (energy, resources, etc) **3** *archaic* to house (a person) or store (goods) > **beˈstowal** *or* **beˈstowment** *n* > **beˈstower** *n*

best practice *n* the recognized methods of correctly running businesses or providing services

bestrew (bɪˈstruː) *vb* **-strews, -strewing, -strewed; -strewn** *or* **-strewed** (*tr*) to scatter or lie scattered over (a surface)

bestride (bɪˈstraɪd) *vb* **-strides, -striding, -strode** *or archaic* **-strid, -stridden** *or archaic* **-strid** (*tr*) **1** to have or put a leg on either side of **2** to extend across; span **3** to stride over or across

bestseller (ˌbɛstˈsɛlə) *n* **1** a book, record, CD, or other product that has sold in great numbers, esp over a short period **2** the author of one or more such books, etc > **ˌbestˈselling** *adj*

bet (bɛt) *n* **1** an agreement between two parties that a sum of money or other stake will be paid by the loser to the party who correctly predicts the outcome of an event **2** the money or stake risked **3** the predicted result in such an agreement: *his bet was that the horse would win* **4** a person, event, etc, considered as likely to succeed or occur: *it's a good bet that they will succeed* **5** a course of action (esp in the phrase **one's best bet**) **6** *informal* an opinion; view: *my bet is that you've been up to no good* ▷ *vb* **bets, betting, bet** *or* **betted 7** (when *intr* foll by *on or against*) to make or place a bet with (a person or persons) **8** (*tr*) to stake (money, etc) in a bet **9** (*tr; may take a clause as object*) *informal* to predict (a certain outcome): *I bet she fails* **10** you bet *informal* of course; naturally [C16 probably short for ABET]

beta (ˈbiːtə) *n* **1** the second letter in the Greek alphabet (Β or β), a consonant, transliterated as *b* **2** the second highest grade or mark, as in an examination **3** (*modifier*) **a** involving or relating to electrons: *beta emitter* **b** relating to one of two or more allotropes or crystal structures of a solid: *beta iron* **c** relating to one of two or more isomeric forms of a chemical compound [from Greek *bēta*, from Hebrew; see BETH]

Beta (ˈbiːtə) *n* (*foll by the genitive case of a specified constellation*) a star in a constellation, usually the second brightest: *Beta Persei*

beta-blocker *n* any of a class of drugs, such as propranolol, that inhibit the activity of the nerves that are stimulated by adrenaline; they therefore decrease the contraction and speed of the heart: used in the treatment of high blood pressure and angina pectoris

Betacam (ˈbiːtəˌkæm) *n trademark* a high-quality professional video system

betacarotene (ˌbiːtəˈkærəˌtiːn) *n* the most important form of the plant pigment carotene, which occurs in milk, vegetables, and other foods and, when eaten by man and animals, is converted in the body to vitamin A

beta coefficient *n stock exchange* a measure of the extent to which a particular security rises or falls in value in response to market movements

betacyanin (ˌbiːtəˈsaɪənɪn) *n* any one of a group of red nitrogenous pigments found in certain plants, such as beetroot

beta decay *n* the radioactive transformation of an atomic nucleus accompanying the emission of an electron. It involves unit change of atomic number but none in mass number. Also called: beta transformation *or* process

beta globulin *n* another name for **transferrin**

betaine (ˈbiːtəˌiːn, -ɪn, bɪˈteiiːn, -ɪn) *n* **1** a sweet-tasting alkaloid that occurs in the sugar beet and other plants and in animals. Formula: $C_5H_{11}NO_2$ **2** (*plural*) a group of chemical compounds that resemble betaine and are slightly basic zwitterions [C19 from New Latin *Bēta* beet + -INE²]

beta iron *n* a nonmagnetic allotrope of pure iron stable between 770°C and 910°C

betake (bɪˈteɪk) *vb* **-takes, -taking, -took, -taken** (*tr*) **1** betake oneself to go; move **2** *archaic* to apply (oneself) to

beta particle *n* a high-speed electron or positron emitted by a nucleus during radioactive decay or nuclear fission

beta ray *n* a stream of beta particles

beta rhythm *or* **wave** *n physiol* the normal electrical activity of the cerebral cortex, occurring at a frequency of 13 to 30 hertz and detectable with an electroencephalograph. See also **brain wave**

beta stock *n* any of the second rank of active securities on the Stock Exchange, of which there are about 500. Continuous display of prices by market makers is required but not immediate publication of transactions

beta-test *n* **1** a test of a new or modified piece of computer software by customers who volunteer to do so ▷ *vb* (*tr*) **2** to test (software) in this way. Compare **alpha-test**

betatopic (ˌbiːtəˈtɒpɪk) *adj* (of atoms) differing in proton number by one, theoretically as a result of emission of a beta particle

betatron (ˈbiːtəˌtrɒn) *n* a type of particle accelerator for producing high-energy beams of electrons, having an alternating magnetic field to keep the electrons in a circular orbit of fixed radius and accelerate them by magnetic induction. It produces energies of up to about 300 MeV

betel (ˈbiːtˀl) *n* an Asian piperaceous climbing plant, *Piper betle*, the leaves of which are chewed, with the betel nut, by the peoples of SE Asia [C16 from Portuguese, from Malayalam *vettila*]

Betelgeuse *or* **Betelgeux** (ˌbiːtˀlˈdʒɜːz, ˈbiːtˀlˌdʒɜːz) *n* a very remote luminous red supergiant, Alpha Orionis: the second brightest star in the constellation Orion. It is a variable star [C18 from French, from Arabic *bīt al-jauzā'* literally: shoulder of the giant, that is, of Orion]

betel nut *n* the seed of the betel palm, chewed with betel leaves and lime by people in S and SE Asia as a digestive stimulant and narcotic

betel palm *n* a tropical Asian feather palm, *Areca catechu*, with scarlet or orange fruits. See **betel nut**

bête noire (*French* bɛt nwaʀ) *n, pl* **bêtes noires** (bɛt nwaʀ) a person or thing that one particularly dislikes or dreads [literally: black beast]

beth (bɛt) *n* the second letter of the Hebrew alphabet (ב) transliterated as *b* [from Hebrew *bēth-, bayith* house]

Bethany (ˈbɛθənɪ) *n* a village in the West Bank, near Jerusalem at the foot of the Mount of Olives: in the New Testament, the home of Lazarus and the lodging place of Jesus during Holy Week

Beth Din *or* **Bet Din** (bɛθ dɪn; *Hebrew* bet dɪn) *n Judaism* a rabbinical court, consisting of at least three dayanim, and having authority over such matters as divorce and conversion and other communal ecclesiastical matters such as Kashruth. It may also try civil disputes with the consent of both parties [from Hebrew, literally: house of judgment]

Bethel (ˈbɛθəl) *n* **1** an ancient town in the West Bank, near Jerusalem: in the Old Testament, the place where the dream of Jacob occurred (Genesis 28:19) **2** a chapel of any of certain Nonconformist Christian sects **3** a seamen's chapel [C17 from Hebrew *bēth 'ēl* house of God]

Bethesda (bəˈθɛzdə) *n* **1** *New Testament* a pool in Jerusalem reputed to have healing powers, where a paralytic was healed by Jesus (John 5:2) **2** a chapel of any of certain Nonconformist Christian sects

bethink (bɪˈθɪŋk) *vb* **-thinks, -thinking, -thought** *archaic or dialect* **1** to cause (oneself) to consider or meditate **2** (*tr; often foll by of*) to remind (oneself)

Bethlehem ('bɛθlɪˌhɛm, -lɪəm) *n* a town in the West Bank, near Jerusalem: birthplace of Jesus and early home of King David

bethought (bɪ'θɔːt) *vb* the past tense and past participle of **bethink**

Bethsaida (bɛθ'seɪdə) *n* a ruined town in N Israel, near the N shore of the Sea of Galilee

betide (bɪ'taɪd) *vb* to happen or happen to; befall (often in the phrase **woe betide (someone)**) [c13 see BE-, TIDE²]

betimes (bɪ'taɪmz) *adv archaic* **1** in good time; early **2** in a short time; soon [c14 *bitimes*; see BY, TIME]

bêtise (be'tiːz) *n rare* folly or lack of perception [French, from *bête* foolish, from *bête* (n) stupid person, BEAST]

betoken (bɪ'təʊkən) *vb* (*tr*) **1** to indicate; signify: *black clothes betoken mourning* **2** to portend; augur

betony ('bɛtənɪ) *n, pl* **-nies 1** a Eurasian plant, *Stachys* (or *Betonica*) *officinalis*, with a spike of reddish-purple flowers, formerly used in medicine and dyeing: family *Lamiaceae* (labiates) **2** any of several related plants of the genus *Stachys* **3** wood betony a North American scrophulariaceous plant, *Pedicularis canadensis*. See also **lousewort** [c14 from Old French *betoine*, from Latin *betonica*, variant of *vettonica*, probably named after the *Vettones*, an ancient Iberian tribe]

betook (bɪ'tʊk) *vb* the past tense of **betake**

betray (bɪ'treɪ) *vb* (*tr*) **1** to aid an enemy of (one's nation, friend, etc); be a traitor to: *to betray one's country* **2** to hand over or expose (one's nation, friend, etc) treacherously to an enemy **3** to disclose (a secret, confidence, etc) treacherously **4** to break (a promise) or be disloyal to (a person's trust) **5** to disappoint the expectations of; fail: *his tired legs betrayed him* **6** to show signs of; indicate: *if one taps china, the sound betrays any faults* **7** to reveal unintentionally: *his grin betrayed his satisfaction* **8** betray oneself to reveal one's true character, intentions, etc **9** to lead astray; deceive **10** *euphemistic* to seduce and then forsake (a woman) [c13 from BE- + *trayen* from Old French *trair*, from Latin *trādere*] > be'trayal *n* > be'trayer *n*

betroth (bɪ'trəʊð) *vb* (*tr*) *archaic* to promise to marry or to give in marriage [c14 *betreuthen*, from BE- + *treuthe* TROTH, TRUTH]

betrothal (bɪ'trəʊðəl) *n* **1** engagement to be married **2** a mutual promise to marry

betrothed (bɪ'trəʊðd) *adj* **1** engaged to be married: *he was betrothed to her* ▷ *n* **2** the person to whom one is engaged; fiancé or fiancée

betta ('bɛtə) *n* another name for **fighting fish** [c19 from New Latin, of unknown origin]

better¹ ('bɛtə) *adj* **1** the comparative of **good 2** more excellent than other members of a particular group, category, etc **3** more suitable, advantageous, attractive, etc **4** improved in health **5** fully recovered in health **6** in more favourable circumstances, esp financially **7** the better part of a large part of: *the better part of a day* ▷ *adv* **8** the comparative of **well 9** in a more excellent manner; more advantageously, attractively, etc **10** in or to a greater degree or extent; more: *she is better loved than her sister* **11** go one better (*Brit intr; US tr*) to outdo (a person) or improve upon (someone else's effort) **12** had better would be wise, sensible, etc to: *I had better be off* **13** know better than to not to be so stupid as to **14** think better of **a** to change one's course of action after reconsideration **b** to rate (a person) more highly ▷ *n* **15** the better something that is the more excellent, useful, etc, of two such things **16** (*usually plural*) a person who is superior, esp in social standing or ability **17** all the better for improved as a result of **18** all the better to more suitable to **19** for better for worse whatever the subsequent events or changes may be **20** for the better by way of improvement: *a change for the better* **21** get the better of to defeat, outwit, or surpass **22** the better of *Irish* having recovered from: *I'm not the better of it yet* ▷ *vb* **23** to make or

become better **24** (*tr*) to improve upon; surpass [Old English *betera*; related to Old Norse *betri*, Gothic *batiza*, Old High German *beziro*]

better² *or esp US* **bettor** ('bɛtə) *n* a person who bets

better half *n humorous* one's spouse

betterment ('bɛtəmənt) *n* **1** a change for the better; improvement **2** *property law* an improvement effected on real property that enhances the value of the property

betting shop *n* (in Britain) a licensed bookmaker's premises not on a racecourse

bettong (be'tɒŋ) *n* a species of rat kangaroo of Australia having a short nose [c19 from a native Australian language]

betulaceous (ˌbɛtjʊ'leɪʃəs) *adj* of, relating to, or belonging to the *Betulaceae*, a family of mostly N temperate catkin-bearing trees and shrubs such as birch and alder, some species of which reach the northern limits of tree growth [c19 from Latin *betula* birch]

between (bɪ'twiːn) *prep* **1** at a point or in a region intermediate to two other points in space, times, degrees, etc **2** in combination; together: *between them, they saved enough money to buy a car* **3** confined or restricted to: *between you and me* **4** indicating a reciprocal relation or comparison: *an argument between a man and his wife* **5** indicating two or more alternatives: *a choice between going now and staying all night* ▷ *adv* Also: **in between 6** between one specified thing and another: *two houses with a garage between* [Old English *betwēonum*; related to Gothic *tweihnai* two together; see TWO, TWAIN]

> USAGE After *distribute* and words with a similar meaning, *among* should be used rather than *between*: *this enterprise issued shares which were distributed among its workers*

between-subjects design *n* (*modifier*) *statistics* (of an experiment) concerned with measuring the value of the dependent variable for distinct and unrelated groups subjected to each of the experimental conditions. Compare **within-subjects design, matched-pairs design**

betweentimes (bɪ'twiːnˌtaɪmz) *or* **betweenwhiles** (bɪ'twiːnˌwaɪlz) *adv* between other activities; during intervals

betwixt (bɪ'twɪkst) *prep, adv* **1** *archaic* another word for **between 2 betwixt and between** in an intermediate, indecisive, or middle position [Old English *betwix*; related to Old High German *zwiski* two each]

Betws-y-Coed (ˌbɛtsɪ'kɔɪd) *n* a village in N Wales, in Conwy county borough, on the River Conwy: noted for its scenery. Pop: 2860 (1991)

Beulah ('bjuːlə) *n Old Testament* the land of Israel (Isaiah 62:4) [Hebrew, literally: married woman]

Beuthen ('bɔytən) *n* the German name for **Bytom**

BeV (in the US) *abbreviation for* gigaelectronvolts (GeV) [c20 from *b(illion) e(lectron) v(olts)*]

Bevan ('bɛvən) *or* **Bev** (bɛv) *n Austral slang, derogatory* **1** a stupid or unfashionable male **2** an aggressive and surly youth [from the boy's name *Bevan*]

bevatron ('bɛvəˌtrɒn) *n* a proton synchrotron at the University of California [c20 from BeV + -TRON]

Bev curls (bɛv) *pl n Austral slang* long locks of hair, considered to be typical of a certain kind of unfashionable male [c20 see BEVAN]

bevel ('bɛvᵊl) *n* **1 a** Also called: **cant** a surface that meets another at an angle other than a right angle. Compare **chamfer** (sense 1) **b** (*as modifier*): *a bevel edge; bevel square* ▷ *vb* **-els, -elling, -elled** *or US* **-els, -eling, -eled 2** (*intr*) to be inclined; slope **3** (*tr*) to cut a bevel on (a piece of timber, etc) [c16 from Old French *bevel* (unattested), from *baïf*, from *baer* to gape; see BAY¹] > 'bevelled *or US* 'beveled *adj* > 'beveller *n or US* 'beveler *n*

bevel gear *n* a gear having teeth cut into a conical surface known as the pitch zone. Two such gears mesh together to transmit power

between two shafts at an angle to each other

bevel square *n* a woodworker's square with an adjustable arm that can be set to mark out an angle or to check the slope of a surface

beverage ('bɛvərɪdʒ, 'bɛvrɪdʒ) *n* any drink, usually other than water [c13 from Old French *bevrage*, from *beivre* to drink, from Latin *bibere*]

beverage room *n Canadian* a room in a tavern, hotel, etc, in which alcoholic drinks are served

Beverley ('bɛvəlɪ) *n* a market town in NE England, the administrative centre of the East Riding of Yorkshire. Pop: 29 110 (2001)

Beverly Hills ('bɛvəlɪ) *n* a city in SW California, near Los Angeles: famous as the home of film stars. Pop: 34 941 (2003 est)

Bevin boy *n* (in Britain during World War II) a young man selected by ballot to work in a coal mine instead of doing conventional military service [c20 named after Ernest Bevin (1881–1951), British Labour statesman and trade unionist, who originated the scheme]

bevvy ('bɛvɪ) *informal* ▷ *n, pl* **-vies 1** a drink, esp an alcoholic one: *we had a few bevvies last night* **2** a session of drinking ▷ *vb* **-vies, -vying, -vied** (*intr*) **3** to drink alcohol [probably from Old French *bevee, buvee* drinking] > 'bevvied *adj*

bevy ('bɛvɪ) *n, pl* **bevies 1** a flock of quails **2** a group, esp of girls **3** a group of roedeer [c15 of uncertain origin]

bewail (bɪ'weɪl) *vb* to express great sorrow over (a person or thing); lament > be'wailed *adj* > be'wailer *n* > be'wailing *n, adj*

beware (bɪ'wɛə) *vb* (*usually used in the imperative or infinitive, often foll by of*) to be cautious or wary (of); be on one's guard (against) [c13 *be war*, from BE (imperative) + *war* WARY]

bewhiskered (bɪ'wɪskəd) *adj* having whiskers on the cheeks

Bewick's swan *n* a white Old World swan, *Cygnus bewickii*, having a black bill with a small yellow base [named after Thomas *Bewick* (1753–1828), English engraver noted esp for his woodcuts of birds]

bewilder (bɪ'wɪldə) *vb* (*tr*) **1** to confuse utterly; puzzle **2** *archaic* to cause to become lost [c17 see BE-, WILDER]

bewildering (bɪ'wɪldərɪŋ) *adj* causing utter confusion; puzzling > be'wilderingly *adv*

bewitch (bɪ'wɪtʃ) *vb* (*tr*) **1** to attract and fascinate; enchant **2** to cast a spell over [c13 *bewicchen*; see BE-, WITCH] > be'witching *adj* > be'witching *adv*

bewray (bɪ'reɪ) *vb* (*tr*) an obsolete word for **betray** [c13 from BE- + Old English *wrēgan* to accuse; related to Gothic *wrōhjan*] > be'wrayer *n*

Bexhill(-on-Sea) (ˌbɛks'hɪl) *n* a resort in S England, in East Sussex on the English Channel. Pop: 39 451 (2001)

Bexley ('bɛkslɪ) *n* a borough of SE Greater London. Pop: 219 100 (2003 est). Area: 61 sq km (23 sq miles)

bey (beɪ) *n* **1** (in the Ottoman Empire) a title given to senior officers, provincial governors, certain other officials or nobles, and (sometimes) Europeans **2** (in modern Turkey) a title of address, corresponding to *Mr.* Also called: **beg** [c16 Turkish: lord]

Beyoğlu ('beɪɔːluː) *n* a district of Istanbul, north of the Golden Horn: the European quarter. Former name: Pera

beyond (bɪ'jɒnd) *prep* **1** at or to a point on the other side of; at or to the further side of: *beyond those hills there is a river* **2** outside the limits or scope of: *beyond this country's jurisdiction* ▷ *adv* **3** at or to the other or far side of something **4** outside the limits of something ▷ *n* **5** the beyond the unknown; the world outside the range of human perception, esp life after death in certain religious beliefs [Old English *begeondan*; see BY, YONDER]

Beyrouth (beɪ'ruːt, 'beɪruːt) *n* a variant spelling of **Beirut**

bezant, bezzant ('bɛzᵊnt, bɪ'zænt) *or* **byzant** *n* **1** a medieval Byzantine gold coin **2** *architect* an ornament in the form of a flat disc **3** *heraldry* a

b

small gold circle [C13 from Old French *besant*, from Medieval Latin *Byzantius* Byzantine (coin)]

bezel ('bɛzªl) *n* **1** the sloping face adjacent to the working edge of a cutting tool **2** the upper oblique faces of a cut gem **3** a grooved ring or part holding a gem, watch crystal, etc **4** a retaining outer rim used in vehicle instruments, eg in tachometers and speedometers **5** a small indicator light used in vehicle instrument panels [C17 probably from French *biseau*, perhaps from Latin *bis* twice]

Béziers (*French* bezje) *n* a city in S France: scene of a massacre (1209) during the Albigensian Crusade. It is a centre of the wine trade. Pop: 69153 (1999)

bezique (bɪ'ziːk) *n* **1** a card game for two or more players with tricks similar to whist but with additional points scored for honours and sequences: played with two packs with nothing below a seven **2** (in this game) the queen of spades and jack of diamonds declared together [C19 from French *bésigue*, of unknown origin]

bezoar ('biːzɔː) *n* a hard mass, such as a stone or hairball, in the stomach and intestines of animals, esp ruminants, and man: formerly thought to be an antidote to poisons [C15 from Old French *bézoard*, from Arabic *bāzahr*, from Persian *bādzahr*, from *bād* against + *zahr* poison]

bezonian (bɪ'zəʊnɪən) *n archaic* a knave or rascal [C16 from Italian *bisogno* ill-equipped raw recruit; literally, need]

Bezwada ('beɪzˌwɑːdə) *n* the former name of **Vijayawada**

bf *the internet domain name for* Burkina Faso

B/F *or* **b/f** *book-keeping abbreviation for* brought forward

B.F.A. (in the US and Canada) *abbreviation for* Bachelor of Fine Arts

BFI *abbreviation for* British Film Institute

BFN *text messaging abbreviation for* bye for now

BFPO *abbreviation for* British Forces Post Office

bg *the internet domain name for* Bulgaria

BG *international car registration for* Bulgaria

B2G *abbreviation for* business to government: referring to a business dealing with government rather than individuals or companies

bh *the internet domain name for* Bahrain

BH *international car registration for* Belize [from *British Honduras*]

Bhagalpur ('bɑːgəlˌpʊə) *n* a city in India, in Bihar: agriculture, textiles, university (1960). Pop: 340349 (2001)

Bhagavad-Gita ('bʌgəvədˈgiːtə) *n* a sacred Hindu text composed about 200 BC and incorporated into the *Mahabharata*, a Sanskrit epic [from Sanskrit: song of the Blessed One, from *bhaga* blessing + *gītā* a song]

Bhai (baɪ) *n* a title or form of address prefixed to the names of distinguished Sikhs [from Hindi *bhāi*, from Sanskrit *bhrātr* BROTHER]

bhajan ('bʌdʒən) *n Hinduism, Sikhism* the singing of devotional songs and hymns [from Sanskrit, literally: adoration, worship]

bhaji ('bɑːdʒɪ) *n* an Indian savoury made of chopped vegetables mixed in a spiced batter and deep-fried [C19 from Hindi *bhājī* fried vegetables]

bhakti ('bʌktɪ) *n Hinduism* loving devotion to God leading to nirvana [from Sanskrit: portion, from *bhajati* he allocates]

bhang *or* **bang** (bæŋ) *n* a preparation of the leaves and flower tops of Indian hemp, which has psychoactive properties: much used in India. See also **cannabis** [C16 from Hindi *bhāng*]

bhangra ('bæŋgrə) *n* a type of Asian pop music that combines elements of traditional Punjabi music with Western pop [C20 from Hindi]

bharal *or* **burhel** ('bʌrəl) *n* a wild Himalayan sheep, *Pseudois nayaur*, with a bluish-grey coat and round backward-curving horns [Hindi]

Bharat ('bʌrʌt) *n* transliteration of the Hindi name for India

Bharatiya ('bɑːrəˌtiːjə) *adj* of or relating to India

Bharat Natyam ('bʌrət 'nɑːtjəm) *n* a form of

Indian classical ballet [from Sanskrit *bharatanātya* Bharata's dancing, from *Bharata* the sage supposed to have written of dramatic art and dancing + *nātya* dancing]

bhat (bɑːt) *n, pl* bhat the standard monetary unit of Thailand

Bhatpara (bɑːt'pɑːrə) *n* a city in NE India, in West Bengal on the Hooghly River: jute and cotton mills. Pop: 441956 (2001)

bhavan ('bʌvən) *or* **bhawan** *n* (in India) a large house or building

Bhavnagar ('bɑːvnəgə) *n* a port in W India, in S Gujarat. Pop: 510958 (2001)

bhikhu ('biːˌku) *n* a fully ordained Buddhist monk [Pali, literally: beggar]

bhikkhuni ('biːkuˌni) *n* a fully ordained Buddhist nun [Pali, literally: beggar]

bhindi ('bɪndɪ) *n* the okra as used in Indian cooking: its green pods are eaten as vegetables. Also called: **lady's finger** [Hindi]

bhishti *or* **bheesty** ('biːstɪ) *n, pl* -ties (formerly in India) a water-carrier [C18 from Hindi *bhīstī*, from Persian *bihishtī* heavenly one, from *bihisht* paradise]

Bhopal (bəʊ'pɑːl) *n* a city in central India, the capital of Madhya Pradesh state and of the former state of Bhopal: site of a poisonous gas leak from a US-owned factory, which killed over 7000 people in 1984 and was implicated in a further 15000 deaths afterwards. Pop: 1433875 (2001)

B horizon *n* the layer of a soil profile immediately below the A horizon, containing deposits of leached material

bhp *abbreviation for* brake horsepower

BHP (in Australia) *abbreviation for* Broken Hill Proprietary

BHS *abbreviation for* (in Britain) British Horse Society

Bhubaneswar (ˌbʊbə'neɪʃwə) *n* an ancient city in E India, the capital of Orissa state: many temples built between the 7th and 16th centuries. Pop: 647302 (2001)

bhuna ('buːnə) *n* an Indian dish or sauce in which spices are dry-roasted in a pan and then combined with a moistening agent such as yogurt or water [from Urdu]

Bhutan (buː'tɑːn) *n* a kingdom in central Asia: disputed by Tibet, China, India, and Britain since the 18th century, the conflict now being chiefly between China and India (which is responsible for Bhutan's external affairs); contains inaccessible stretches of the E Himalayas in the north. Official language: Dzongka; Nepali is also spoken. Official religion: Mahayana Buddhist. Currencies: ngultrum and Indian rupee. Capital: Thimbu. Pop: 2325000 (2005 est). Area: about 46600 sq km (18000 sq miles)

Bhutanese (ˌbuːtɑːn'iːz) *n* **1** a native or inhabitant of Bhutan ▷ *adj* **2** of or relating to Bhutan or its inhabitants

bi¹ (baɪ) *adj, n slang* short for **bisexual** (senses 1, 6)

bi² *the internet domain name for* Burundi

Bi *the chemical symbol for* bismuth

bi-¹ *or sometimes before a vowel* **bin-** *combining form* **1** two; having two: *bifocal* **2** occurring every two; lasting for two: *biennial* **3** on both sides, surfaces, directions, etc: *bilateral* **4** occurring twice during: *biweekly* **5 a** denoting an organic compound containing two identical cyclic hydrocarbon systems: *biphenyl* **b** (rare in technical usage) indicating an acid salt of a dibasic acid: *sodium bicarbonate* **c** (not in technical usage) equivalent of **di-¹** (sense 2a) [from Latin, from *bis* TWICE]

bi-² *combining form* a variant of bio-

Biafra (bɪ'æfrə) *n* **1** a region of E Nigeria, formerly a local government region: seceded as an independent republic (1967–70) during the Civil War, but defeated by Nigerian government forces **2 Bight of** former name (until 1975) of (the Bight of) **Bonny**

Biafran (bɪ'æfrən) *adj* **1** of or relating to Biafra or its inhabitants ▷ *n* **2** a native or inhabitant of Biafra

Biak (bi'jɑːk) *n* an island in Indonesia, north of West Irian: the largest of the Schouten Islands. Area: 2455 sq km (948 sq miles)

Białystok (*Polish* bja'wɪstɔk) *n* a city in E Poland: belonged to Prussia (1795–1807) and to Russia (1807–1919). Pop: 315000 (2005 est). Russian name: Belostok

biannual (baɪ'ænjʊəl) *adj* occurring twice a year. Compare **biennial**. > bi'annually *adv*

biannulate (baɪ'ænjʊlɪt, -ˌleɪt) *adj zoology* having two bands, esp of colour

Biarritz ('bɪərɪts, bɪə'rɪts; *French* bjarits) *n* a town in SW France, on the Bay of Biscay: famous resort, patronized by Napoleon III and by Queen Victoria and Edward VII of Great Britain and Ireland. Pop: 30055 (1999)

bias ('baɪəs) *n* **1** mental tendency or inclination, esp an irrational preference or prejudice **2** a diagonal line or cut across the weave of a fabric **3** *electronics* the voltage applied to an electronic device or system to establish suitable working conditions **4** *bowls* **a** a bulge or weight inside one side of a bowl **b** the curved course of such a bowl on the green **5** *statistics* **a** an extraneous latent influence on, unrecognized conflated variable in, or selectivity in a sample which influences its distribution and so renders it unable to reflect the desired population parameters **b** if T is an estimator of the parameter θ, the expected value of (T–θ) **6** an inaudible high-frequency signal used to improve the quality of a tape recording ▷ *adj* **7** slanting obliquely; diagonal: *a bias fold* ▷ *adv* **8** obliquely; diagonally ▷ *vb* -ases, -asing, -ased *or* -asses, -assing, -assed (tr) **9** (*usually passive*) to cause to have a bias; prejudice; influence: *his writing was biased against the left* [C16 from Old French *biais*, from Old Provençal, perhaps ultimately from Greek *epikarsios* oblique] > 'biased *or* 'biassed *adj*

bias binding *n* a strip of material cut on the bias for extra stretch and often doubled, used for binding hems, interfacings, etc, or for decoration

biathlon (baɪ'æθlən, -lɒn) *n sport* a contest in which skiers with rifles shoot at four targets along a 20-kilometre (12.5-mile) cross-country course

biauriculate (ˌbaɪɔː'rɪkjʊlɪt, -ˌleɪt) *or* **biauricular** *adj* having two auricles or earlike parts

biaxial (baɪ'æksɪəl) *adj* (esp of a crystal) having two axes

bib (bɪb) *n* **1** a piece of cloth or plastic worn, esp by babies, to protect their clothes while eating **2** the upper part of some aprons, dungarees, etc, that covers the upper front part of the body **3** Also called: **pout, whiting pout** a light-brown European marine gadoid food fish, *Gadus* (or *Trisopterus*) *luscus*, with a barbel on its lower jaw **4** short for **bibcock 5** stick one's bib in *Austral informal* to interfere ▷ *vb* **bibs, bibbing, bibbed 6** *archaic* to drink (something); tipple [C14 *bibben* to drink, probably from Latin *bibere*]

bib and brace *n* a work garment consisting of trousers and an upper front part supported by straps over the shoulders

bib and tucker *n informal* an outfit of clothes (esp in the phrase **best bib and tucker**)

bibb (bɪb) *n nautical* a wooden support on a mast for the trestletrees [C18 variant of BIB]

bibber ('bɪbə) *n* a drinker; tippler (esp in the expression **wine-bibber**)

bibble ('bɪbªl) *n Midland English dialect* a pebble

bibcock ('bɪbˌkɒk) *or* **bib** *n* a tap having a nozzle bent downwards and supplied from a horizontal pipe

bibelot ('bɪbləʊ; *French* biblo) *n* **1** an attractive or curious trinket **2** a miniature book [C19 from French, from Old French *beubelet*, perhaps from a reduplication of *bel* beautiful]

Bible ('baɪbªl) *n* **1 a the**. the sacred writings of the Christian religion, comprising the Old and New Testaments and, in the Roman Catholic Church, the Apocrypha **b** (*as modifier*): *a Bible reading* **2** (*often* *not capital*) any book containing the sacred writings of a religion **3** (*usually not capital*) a book regarded as authoritative: *the angler's bible* [c13 from Old French, from Medieval Latin *biblia* books, from Greek, plural of *biblion* book, diminutive of *biblos* papyrus, from *Bublos* Phoenician port from which Greece obtained Egyptian papyrus]

Bible Belt *n* **the.** those states of the S US where Protestant fundamentalism is dominant

Bible paper *n* **1** a thin tough opaque paper used for Bibles, prayer books, and reference books **2** (not in technical usage) another name for **India paper**

Bible-thumper *n slang* an enthusiastic or aggressive exponent of the Bible. Also called: Bible-basher, Bible-pounder, Bible-puncher > 'Bible-,thumping *n, adj*

biblical ('bıblık³l) *adj* **1** of, occurring in, or referring to the Bible **2** resembling the Bible in written style > 'biblically *adv*

Biblical Aramaic *n* the form of Aramaic that was the common language of Palestine in New Testament times. It was widespread throughout the Persian Empire from the 5th century and is found in the later books of the Old Testament (esp Daniel 2:4–7:28)

Biblical Latin *n* the form of Latin used in versions of the Bible, esp the form used in the Vulgate. See also **Late Latin**

Biblicist ('bıblısıst) *or* **Biblist** *n* **1** a biblical scholar **2** a person who takes the Bible literally

biblio- *combining form* indicating book or books: *bibliography; bibliomania* [from Greek *biblion* book]

bibliog. *abbreviation for* **1** bibliographer **2** bibliography

bibliography (,bıblı'ɒgrəfı) *n, pl* -phies **1** a list of books or other material on a subject **2** a list of sources used in the preparation of a book, thesis, etc **3** a list of the works of a particular author or publisher **4 a** the study of the history, classification, etc, of literary material **b** a work on this subject > ,bibli'ographer *n* > bibliographic (,bıblıəʊ'græfık) *or* ,biblio'graphical *adj* > ,biblio'graphically *adv*

bibliolatry (,bıblı'ɒlətrı) *n* **1** excessive devotion to or reliance on the Bible **2** extreme fondness for books

bibliomancy ('bıblıəʊ,mænsı) *n* prediction of the future by interpreting a passage chosen at random from a book, esp the Bible

bibliomania (,bıblıəʊ'meınıə) *n* extreme fondness for books > ,biblio'mani,ac *n, adj*

bibliophile ('bıblıə,faıl) *or* **bibliophil** ('bıblıəfıl) *n* a person who collects or is fond of books > bibliophilism (,bıblı'ɒfə,lızəm) *n* > ,bibli'ophi'listic *adj*

bibliopole ('bıblıəʊ,pəʊl) *or* **bibliopolist** (,bıblı'ɒpəlıst) *n* a dealer in books, esp rare or decorative ones [c18 from Latin *bibliopōla*, from Greek *bibliopōlēs* bookseller, from BIBLIO- + *pōlein* to sell] > ,bibli'opoly *n*

bibliotheca (,bıblıəʊ'θiːkə) *n, pl* -cas *or* -cae (-kiː) **1** a library or collection of books **2** a printed catalogue compiled by a bibliographer [Latin: library, from Greek *bibliothēkē*, from BIBLIO- + *thēkē* receptacle]

bibulous ('bıbjʊləs) *adj* addicted to alcohol [c17 from Latin *bibulus*, from *bibere* to drink] > 'bibulously *adv* > 'bibulousness *n*

bicameral (baı'kæmərəl) *adj* (of a legislature) consisting of two chambers [c19 from BI-¹ + Latin *camera* CHAMBER] > bi'cameral,ism *n* > bi'cameralist *n*

bicapsular (baı'kæpsjʊlə) *adj* (of plants) having two capsules or one capsule with two chambers

bicarb ('baıka:b) *n* short for **bicarbonate of soda**. See **sodium bicarbonate**

bicarbonate (baı'ka:bənıt, -,neıt) *n* **1** a salt of carbonic acid containing the ion HCO₃⁻; an acid carbonate **2** (*modifier*) consisting of, containing, or concerned with the ion HCO₃⁻: *a bicarbonate compound*. Systematic name: hydrogen carbonate **3**

short for **bicarbonate of soda**

bicarbonate of soda *n* sodium bicarbonate, esp when used as a medicine or as a raising agent in baking

bicarpellary (,baıka:'pelərı) *adj botany* (of an ovary) having two carpels

bice (baıs) *n* **1** Also called: **bice blue** a medium blue colour; azurite **2** Also called: **bice green** a yellowish-green colour; malachite [c14 from Old French *bis* dark grey, of uncertain origin]

bicentenary (,baısen'tiːnərı) *or US* **bicentennial** (,baısen'tenıəl) *adj* **1** marking a 200th anniversary **2** occurring every 200 years **3** lasting 200 years ▷ *n, pl* -naries **4** a 200th anniversary

bicephalous (baı'sefələs) *adj* **1** *biology* having two heads **2** crescent-shaped

biceps ('baıseps) *n, pl* -ceps *anatomy* any muscle having two heads or origins, esp the muscle that flexes the forearm. Related adjective: **bicipital** [c17 from Latin: having two heads, from BI-¹ *caput* head]

Biche-la-mar (,biːtʃlə'ma:) *n* another name for **Beach-la-Mar**

bichloride (baı'klɔːraıd) *n* another name for **dichloride**

bichloride of mercury *n* another name for **mercuric chloride**

bichon frise ('biːʃɒn 'friːzeı) *n, pl* bichon frises a small white poodle-like dog of European origin, with a silky, loosely curling coat [c20 French, literally: curly toy dog]

bichromate (baı'krəʊ,meıt, -mıt) *n* another name for **dichromate**

bicipital (baı'sıpıt³l) *adj* **1** having two heads **2** of or relating to a biceps muscle [c17 see BICEPS, -AL¹]

bicker ('bıkə) *vb* (*intr*) **1** to argue over petty matters; squabble **2** *poetic* **a** (esp of a stream) to run quickly **b** to flicker; glitter ▷ *n* **3** a petty squabble [c13 of unknown origin] > 'bickerer *n* > 'bickering *n, adj*

bickie *or* **bikkie** ('bıkı) *n informal* **1** short for **biscuit** (sense 1) **2** big bickies *Austral slang* a large sum of money

bicoastal (baı'kəʊst³l) *adj* relating to both the east and west coasts of the US: *she had a bicoastal upbringing*

bicollateral (,baıkɒ'lætərəl) *adj botany* (of a vascular bundle) having two phloem groups to the inside and outside, respectively, of the xylem

bicolour ('baı,kʌlə), **bicoloured**, *US* **bicolor**, **bicolored** *adj* two-coloured

biconcave (baı'kɒnkeıv, ,baıkɒn'keıv) *adj* (of a lens) having concave faces on both sides; concavo-concave > biconcavity (,baıkɒn'kævıtı) *n*

biconditional (,baıkən'dıʃən³l) *n* another name for **equivalence** (sense 2)

biconvex (baı'kɒnveks, ,baıkɒn'veks) *adj* (of a lens) having convex faces on both sides; convexo-convex

bicorn ('baıkɔːn), **bicornate** (baı'kɔːnıt, -,neıt) *or* **bicornuate** (baı'kɔːnjʊıt, -,eıt) *adj* having two horns or hornlike parts [c19 from Latin *bicornis*, from BI-¹ + *cornu* horn]

bi-curious *adj* considering experimenting with bisexuality

bicuspid (baı'kʌspıd) *or* **bicuspidate** (baı'kʌspı,deıt) *adj* **1** having or terminating in two cusps or points ▷ *n* **2** a bicuspid tooth; premolar

bicuspid valve *n* another name for **mitral valve**

bicycle ('baısık³l) *n* **1** a vehicle with a tubular metal frame mounted on two spoked wheels, one behind the other. The rider sits on a saddle, propels the vehicle by means of pedals that drive the rear wheel through a chain, and steers with handlebars on the front wheel. Often shortened to: cycle, (*informal*) bike ▷ *vb* **2** (*intr*) to ride a bicycle; cycle [c19 from BI-¹ + Late Latin *cyclus*, from Greek *kuklos* wheel] > 'bicyclist *or* 'bicycler *n*

bicycle chain *n* a chain that transmits power from the pedals to the driving wheel of a bicycle

bicycle clip *n* one of a pair of clips worn around the ankles by cyclists to keep the trousers tight

and out of the chain

bicycle pump *n* a hand pump for pumping air into the tyres of a bicycle

bicyclic (baı'saıklık, -'sıklık) *or* **bicyclical** *adj* **1** of, forming, or formed by two circles, cycles, etc **2** (of stamens, petals, etc) arranged in two whorls **3** (of a chemical compound) having atoms arranged in two rings fused together with at least two atoms common to each ring: *naphthalene is bicyclic*

bid (bıd) *vb* bids; bidding; bad, bade *or esp for senses* 1, 2, 5, 7 bid; bidden *or esp for senses* 1, 2, 5, 7 bid **1** (often foll by *for* or *against*) to offer (an amount) in attempting to buy something, esp in competition with others as at an auction **2** *commerce* to respond to an offer by a seller by stating (the more favourable terms) on which one is willing to make a purchase **3** (*tr*) to say (a greeting, blessing, etc): *to bid farewell* **4** to order; command: *do as you are bid!* **5** (*intr*; usually foll by *for*) to attempt to attain power, etc **6** (*tr*) to invite; ask kindly: *she bade him sit down* **7** *bridge* to declare in the auction before play how many tricks one expects to make **8** bid defiance to resist boldly **9** bid fair to seem probable ▷ *n* **10** an offer of a specified amount, as at an auction **b** the price offered **11** *commerce* **a** a statement by a buyer, in response to an offer by a seller, of the more favourable terms that would be acceptable **b** the price or other terms so stated **12** an attempt, esp an attempt to attain power **13** *bridge* **a** the number of tricks a player undertakes to make **b** a player's turn to make a bid **14** short for **bid price** ▷ See also **bid in**, **bid up** [Old English *biddan*; related to German *bitten*] > 'bidder *n*

b.i.d. (in prescriptions) *abbreviation for* bis in die [Latin: twice a day]

Bida ('baıda:) *or* **El Beda** (el 'beıda:) *n* the former name of **Doha**

bidarka (baı'da:kə) *or* **bidarkee** (baı'da:kiː) *n* a canoe covered in animal skins, esp sealskin, used by the Inuit of Alaska [c19 from Russian *baidarka*, diminutive of *baidara* umiak]

biddable ('bıdəb³l) *adj* **1** having sufficient value to be bid on, as a hand or suit at bridge **2** docile; obedient > 'biddableness *n* > 'biddably *adv*

bidden ('bıd³n) *vb* a past participle of **bid**

bidding ('bıdıŋ) *n* **1** an order; command (often in the phrases do or follow the bidding of, at someone's bidding) **2** an invitation; summons **3** the act of making bids, as at an auction or in bridge **4** *bridge* a group of bids considered collectively, esp those made on a particular deal

biddy¹ ('bıdı) *n, pl* -dies a dialect word for **chicken** *or* **hen** [c17 perhaps imitative of calling chickens]

biddy² ('bıdı) *n, pl* -dies *informal* a woman, esp an old gossip or interfering one [c18 from pet form of *Bridget*]

biddy-biddy *or* **biddi-biddi** ('bıdı,bıdı) *n, pl* -biddies **1** a low-growing rosaceous plant, *Acaena viridior* of New Zealand, having prickly burs **2** the burs of this plant ▷ Also (NZ) biddy-bid, (Austral) bidgee-widgee ('bıdʒı,wıdʒı) [from Māori *piri piri*]

bide (baıd) *vb* bides, biding, bided *or* bode, bided **1** (*intr*) *archaic or dialect* to continue in a certain place or state; stay **2** (*intr*) *archaic or dialect* to live; dwell **3** (*tr*) *archaic or dialect* to tolerate; endure **4** bide a wee *Scot* to stay a little **5** bide by *Scot* to abide by **6** bide one's time to wait patiently for an opportunity ▷ Also (Scot) byde [Old English *bīdan*; related to Old Norse *bītha* to wait, Gothic *beidan*, Old High German *bītan*]

bidentate (baı'den,teıt) *adj* **1** having two teeth or toothlike parts or processes **2** *chem* (of a ligand) having two atoms from which electrons can be donated to the central coordinated atom

bidet ('biːdeı) *n* a small low basin for washing the genitals and anal area [c17 from French: small horse, probably from Old French *bider* to trot]

bidie-in (,baıdı'ın) *n Scot* a live-in sexual partner

bid in *vb* (*adverb*) (in an auction) to outbid all previous offers for (one's own property) to retain ownership or increase the final selling price

b

bidirectional (ˌbaɪdɪˈrɛkʃənʰl) *adj computing* (of a printhead) capable of printing from left to right and from right to left

bid price *n stock exchange* the price at which a stockjobber is prepared to purchase a specific security. Compare **offer price**

bid up *vb* (*adverb*) to increase the market price of (a commodity) by making artificial bids

Biedermeier (ˈbiːdəˌmaɪə) *adj* **1** of or relating to a decorative and furnishing style in mid-19th-century Germany, characterized by solidity and conventionality **2** boringly conventional in outlook; bourgeois [C19 after Gottlieb *Biedermeier*, a fictitious character portrayed as a conventional unimaginative bourgeois and the author of poems actually written by several satirical poets]

Biel (biːl) *n* **1** a town in NW Switzerland, on Lake Biel. Pop: 48 655 (2000). French name: **Bienne 2 Lake** a lake in NW Switzerland: remains of lake dwellings were discovered here in the 19th century. Area: 39 sq km (15 sq miles). German name: **Bielersee**

bield (biːld) *Scot and Northern English dialect* ▷ *n* **1** a shelter; house ▷ *vb* **2** to shelter or take shelter [Old English *bieldo, byldo* boldness (hence: refuge); related to Gothic *balthei*, Old English *beald* BOLD]

Bielefeld (*German* ˈbiːləfɛlt) *n* a city in Germany, in NE North Rhine-Westphalia: food, textiles. Pop: 328 452 (2003 est)

Bielsko-Biała (*Polish* ˈbjɛlskɔˈbjawa) *n* a town in S Poland: created in 1951 by the union of Bielsko and Biala Krakowska; a leading textile centre since the 16th century. Pop: 356 000 (2005 est)

Bien Hoa (ˈbjɛn ˈhəʊə) *n* a town in S Vietnam: a former capital of Cambodia. Pop: 520 000 (2005 est)

Bienne (bjɛn) *n* the French name for **Biel**

biennial (baɪˈɛnɪəl) *adj* **1** occurring every two years **2** lasting two years. Compare **biannual** ▷ *n* **3** a plant, such as the carrot, that completes its life cycle within two years, developing vegetative storage parts during the first year and flowering and fruiting in its second year. Compare **annual** (sense 3), **perennial** (sense 3) **4** an event that takes place every two years ▷ **bi'ennially** *adv*

bien-pensant (*French* bjɛ̃pɑ̃sɑ̃) *adj* **1** right-thinking; orthodox ▷ *n* **bien pensant, pl bien pensants** (bjɛ̃pɑ̃sɑ̃) **2** a right-thinking person [literally: well-thinking]

bier (bɪə) *n* a platform or stand on which a corpse or a coffin containing a corpse rests before burial [Old English *bēr*; related to *beran* to BEAR[1], Old High German *bāra* bier, Sanskrit *bhārā* a burden]

bierkeller (ˈbɪəˌkɛlə) *n Brit* a public house decorated in German style, selling German beers [C20 German, literally: beer cellar]

biestings (ˈbiːstɪŋz) *n* a variant spelling of **beestings**

bifacial (baɪˈfeɪʃəl) *adj* **1** having two faces or surfaces **2** *botany* (of leaves, etc) having upper and lower surfaces differing from each other **3** *archaeol* (of flints) flaked by percussion from two sides along the chopping edge

bifarious (baɪˈfɛərɪəs) *adj botany* having parts arranged in two rows on either side of a central axis [C17 from Latin *bifārius* double] ▷ **bi'fariously** *adv*

biff (bɪf) *slang* ▷ *n* **1** a blow with the fist **2** *Irish school slang* a blow to the palm of the hand with a strap or cane as a punishment ▷ *vb* **3** (*tr*) to give (someone) such a blow [C20 probably of imitative origin]

biffer (ˈbɪfə) *n informal* **1** someone, such as a sportsperson, who has a reputation for hitting hard **2** an implement used to serve blows

BIFFEX (ˈbɪfɛks) *acronym* Baltic International Freight Futures Exchange, inaugurated in London in 1985

biffin (ˈbɪfɪn) *n Brit* a variety of red cooking apple [C18 from *beefin* ox for slaughter, from BEEF; referring to the apple's colour]

biffo (ˈbɪfəʊ) *Austral slang* ▷ *n* **1** fighting or aggressive behaviour: *he enjoys a bit of biffo now and then* ▷ *adj* **2** aggressive; pugnacious

bifid (ˈbaɪfɪd) *adj* divided into two lobes by a median cleft: *bifid leaves* [C17 from Latin *bifidus* from BI-[1] + *-fidus*, from *findere* to split] ▷ **bi'fidity** *n* ▷ **'bifidly** *adv*

bifilar (baɪˈfaɪlə) *adj* **1** having two parallel threads, as in the suspension of certain measuring instruments **2** of or relating to a resistor in which the wire is wound in a loop around a coil, the two leads being parallel, to reduce the inductance ▷ **bi'filarly** *adv*

biflagellate (baɪˈflædʒɪˌleɪt, -lɪt) *adj biology* having two flagella: *biflagellate protozoans*

bifocal (baɪˈfəʊkʰl) *adj* **1** *optics* having two different focuses **2** relating to a compound lens permitting near and distant vision

bifocals (baɪˈfəʊkʰlz) *pl n* a pair of spectacles with bifocal lenses

bifoliate (baɪˈfəʊlɪˌeɪt, -ɪt) *adj* having only two leaves

bifoliolate (baɪˈfəʊlɪəˌleɪt, -lɪt) *adj* (of compound leaves) consisting of two leaflets

biforate (ˈbaɪfəˌreɪt) *adj biology* having two openings, pores, or perforations [C19 from New Latin *biforātus*, from BI-[1] + *forāre* to pierce]

biform (ˈbaɪˌfɔːm) *or* **biformed** *adj* having or combining the characteristics of two forms, as a centaur

Bifrost (ˈbɪvrɒst, ˈbiːfrɒst) *n Norse myth* the rainbow bridge of the gods from their realm Asgard to earth [from Icelandic, from *bifa* to shake + *rost* path]

bifter (ˈbɪftə) *n slang* a cannabis cigarette

bifurcate *vb* (ˈbaɪfəˌkeɪt) **1** to fork or divide into two parts or branches ▷ *adj* (ˈbaɪfəˌkeɪt, -kɪt) **2** forked or divided into two sections or branches [C17 from Medieval Latin *bifurcātus*, from Latin *bifurcus*, from BI-[1] + *furca* fork] ▷ **ˌbifur'cation** *n*

big[1] (bɪg) *adj* **bigger, biggest 1** of great or considerable size, height, weight, number, power, or capacity **2** having great significance; important: *a big decision* **3** important through having power, influence, wealth, authority, etc: *the big four banks* **4** (intensifier usually qualifying something undesirable): *a big dope* **5** *informal* considerable in extent or intensity (esp in the phrase **in a big way**) **6 a** elder: *my big brother* **b** grown-up: *when you're big, you can stay up later* **7 a** generous; magnanimous: *that's very big of you* **b** (*in combination*): *big-hearted* **8** (often foll by *with*) brimming; full: *my heart is big with sadness* **9** extravagant; boastful: *he's full of big talk* **10** (of wine) full-bodied, with a strong aroma and flavour **11 too big for one's boots** *or* **breeches** conceited; unduly self-confident **12** in an advanced stage of pregnancy (esp in the phrase **big with child**) **13 big on** *informal* enthusiastic about: *that company is big on* ▷ *adv informal* **14** boastfully; pretentiously (esp in the phrase **talk big**) **15** in an exceptional way; well: *his talk went over big with the audience* **16** on a grand scale (esp in the phrase **think big**). ▷ See also **big up** [C13 perhaps of Scandinavian origin; compare Norwegian dialect *bugge* big man] ▷ **'biggish** *adj* ▷ **'bigness** *n*

big[2] (bɪg) *vb* **bigs, bigging, bigged** *or* **bug** (bʌg) *Scot* **1** to build **2** to excavate (earth) into a pile [from Old Norse *byggja*; related to Old English *būian* to inhabit]

bigamy (ˈbɪgəmɪ) *n, pl* **-mies** the crime of marrying a person while one is still legally married to someone else [C13 via French from Medieval Latin *bigamus*; see BI-[1], -GAMY] ▷ **'bigamist** *n* ▷ **'bigamous** *adj* ▷ **'bigamously** *adv*

Big Apple *n* **the** *informal* New York City [C20 probably from US jazzmen's earlier use to mean any big, esp northern, city; of obscure origin]

bigarreau (ˈbɪgəˌrəʊ, ˌbɪgəˈrəʊ) *n* any of several heart-shaped varieties of sweet cherry that have firm flesh [C17 from French, from *bigarré* mottled]

big band *n* a large jazz or dance band, popular esp in the 1930s to the 1950s

big bang *n* **1** any sudden forceful beginning or radical change **2** (*modifier*) of or relating to the big-bang theory **3** (*sometimes capitals*) the major modernization that took place on the London Stock Exchange on Oct 27 1986, after which the distinction between jobbers and brokers was abolished and operations became fully computerized

big-bang theory *n* a cosmological theory postulating that approximately 12 billion years ago all the matter of the universe, packed into a small superdense mass, was hurled in all directions by a cataclysmic explosion. As the fragments slowed down, the galaxies and stars evolved but the universe is still expanding. Compare **steady-state theory**

big beast *n informal* an important or powerful person

big beat *n* **a** an eclectic type of dance music in which heavy beats and samples are layered over the songs or instrumental tracks of other performers or bands **b** (*as modifier*): *a big-beat compilation*

Big Ben *n* **1** the bell in the clock tower of the Houses of Parliament, London **2** the clock in this tower **3** the tower [C19 named after Sir *Benjamin Hall*, Chief Commissioner of Works in 1856 when it was cast]

Big Bertha *n* any of three large German guns of World War I used to bombard Paris [C20 approximate translation of German *dicke Bertha*: fat Bertha; named after *Bertha* Krupp, at whose works in Essen a very effective 42 cm mortar was made]

Big Board *n US informal* **1** the quotation board in the New York Stock Exchange **2** the New York Stock Exchange

Big Brother *n* **1** a person, organization, etc, that exercises total dictatorial control **2** a television gameshow format in which a small number of people living in accommodation sealed off from the outside world are constantly monitored by TV cameras. Viewers vote each week to expel a person from the group until there is only one person left, who wins a cash prize [C20 after a character in the novel *1984* (1949) by English writer George Orwell (1903–1950)]

big bucks *pl n informal, chiefly US* **1** large quantities of money **2** the power and influence of people or organizations that control large quantities of money

big bud *n* a serious disease of plants, esp of blackcurrants, in which the buds swell up as a result of attack by the gall mite *Cecidophyopsis ribis*

big business *n* large commercial organizations collectively, esp when considered as exploitative or socially harmful

big cheese *n slang* an important person

big Chief *or* **big Daddy** *n informal* other terms for **big White Chief**

big deal *interj slang* an exclamation of scorn, derision, etc, used esp to belittle a claim or offer

big dipper *n* **1** (in amusement parks) a narrow railway with open carriages that run swiftly over a route of sharp curves and steep inclines. Also called: roller coaster

Big Dipper *n* the US and Canadian name for the **Plough** (constellation)

big end *n Brit* **1** Also called (in vertical engines): **bottom end** the larger end of a connecting rod in an internal-combustion engine. Compare **little end 2** the bearing surface between the larger end of a connecting rod and the crankpin of the crankshaft

bigener (ˈbaɪdʒɪnə) *n biology* a hybrid between individuals of different genera [C20 back formation from *bigeneric*; see BI-[1], GENUS]

bigeneric (ˌbaɪdʒəˈnɛrɪk) *adj* (of a hybrid plant) derived from parents of two different genera

bigeye (ˈbɪgˌaɪ) *n, pl* **-eye** *or* **-eyes** any tropical or subtropical red marine percoid fish of the family

Priacanthidae, having very large eyes and rough scales

big fish *n informal* **1** an important or powerful person **2** a big fish in a small pond the most important or powerful person in a small group

Big Five *n the* **1** the five countries considered to be the major world powers. In the period immediately following World War II, the US, Britain, the Soviet Union, China, and France were regarded as the Big Five **2** the lion, the elephant, the rhinoceros, the buffalo, and the leopard: considered to be the five principal African wild animals, esp as sought by those on safari **3** a small powerful group, as of banks, companies, etc. Also: Big Four, Big Three

big game *n* **1** large animals that are hunted or fished for sport **2** *informal* the objective of an important or dangerous undertaking

biggin[1] *or* **biggon** (ˈbɪgɪn) *n* a plain close-fitting cap, often tying under the chin, worn in the Middle Ages and by children in the 17th century [c16 from French *béguin*; see BEGUINE]

biggin[2] (ˈbɪgən) *n Scot* a construction, esp a house or cottage [see BIG[2]]

big gun *n informal* an important or influential person

big hair *n* a hairstyle with volume created by hair products or styling techniques such as backcombing, etc

bighead (ˈbɪɡˌhɛd) *n* **1** *informal* a conceited person **2** *US and Canadian informal* conceit; egotism **3** *vet science* **a** an abnormal bulging or increase in the size of an animal's skull, as from osteomalacia **b** any of various diseases of sheep characterized by swelling of the head, esp any caused by infection with *Clostridium* bacteria > ˌbigˈheaded *adj* > ˌbigˈheadedly *adv* > ˌbigˈheadedness *n*

big-hearted *adj* warmly generous > ˌbig-ˈheartedness *n*

big hitter *n* **1** a sportsperson who is capable of hitting the ball long or hard **2** *informal* an influential and important person: *one of the government's big hitters*

bighorn (ˈbɪɡˌhɔːn) *n, pl* -horns *or* -horn a large wild sheep, *Ovis canadensis*, inhabiting mountainous regions in North America and NE Asia: family *Bovidae*, order *Artiodactyla*. The male has massive curved horns, and the species is well adapted for climbing and leaping

bight (baɪt) *n* **1** a wide indentation of a shoreline, or the body of water bounded by such a curve **2** the slack middle part of an extended rope **3** a curve or loop in a rope ▷ *vb* **4** (*tr*) to fasten or bind with a bight [Old English *byht*; see BOW[2]]

Bight *n the Austral informal* the major indentation of the S coast of Australia, from Cape Pasley in W Australia to the Eyre Peninsula in S Australia. In full: the Great Australian Bight

big money *n* large sums of money: *there's big money in professional golf*

bigmouth (ˈbɪɡˌmaʊθ) *n slang* a noisy, indiscreet, or boastful person > ˈbig-ˌmouthed *adj*

big name *n informal* **a** a famous person **b** (*as modifier*): *a big-name performer*

big noise *n informal* an important person

bignonia (bɪɡˈnəʊnɪə) *n* any tropical American bignoniaceous climbing shrub of the genus *Bignonia* (or *Doxantha*), cultivated for their trumpet-shaped yellow or reddish flowers. See also **cross vine** [c19 from New Latin, named after the Abbé Jean-Paul *Bignon* (1662–1743)]

bignoniaceous (bɪɡˌnəʊnɪˈeɪʃəs) *adj* of, relating to, or belonging to the *Bignoniaceae*, a chiefly tropical family of trees, shrubs, and lianas, including jacaranda, bignonia, and catalpa

big-note *vb Austral informal* to boast about (oneself)

bigot (ˈbɪɡət) *n* a person who is intolerant of any ideas other than his or her own, esp on religion, politics, or race [c16 from Old French: name applied contemptuously to the Normans by the French, of obscure origin] > ˈbigoted *adj*

bigotry (ˈbɪɡətrɪ) *n, pl* -ries the attitudes, behaviour, or way of thinking of a bigot; prejudice; intolerance

big science *n* scientific research that requires a large investment of capital

big screen *n* an informal name for the **cinema**

big shot *n informal* an important or influential person

Big Smoke *n the informal* a large city, esp London

big stick *n informal* force or the threat of using force

big tent *n* **a** a political approach in which a party claims to be open to a wide spectrum of constituents and groups **b** (*as modifier*): big-tent politics

big time *n informal* **a** the the highest or most profitable level of an occupation or profession, esp the entertainment business **b** (*as modifier*): *a big-time comedian* > ˈbig-ˌtimer *n*

big top *n informal* **1** the main tent of a circus **2** the circus itself

big tree *n* a giant Californian coniferous tree, *Sequoiadendron giganteum*, with a wide tapering trunk and thick spongy bark: family *Taxodiaceae*. It often reaches a height of 90 metres. Also called: giant sequoia, wellingtonia. See also **sequoia**

biguanide (baɪˈɡwɑːnaɪd) *n* any of a class of compounds some of which are used in the treatment of certain forms of diabetes. See also **phenformin** [c19 from BI-[1] + GUANIDINE + -IDE]

big up *vb* bigs, bigging, bigged (*tr, adverb*) *slang* to make important, prominent, or famous: *we'll do our best to big you up*

big wheel *n* **1** another name for a **Ferris wheel 2** *informal* an important person

big White Chief *n informal* an important person, boss, or leader. Also called: big Chief, big Daddy

bigwig (ˈbɪɡˌwɪɡ) *n informal* an important person

Bihar (bɪˈhɑː) *n* a state of NE India: consists of part of the Ganges plain; important for rice: lost the S to the new state of Jharkhand in 2000. Capital: Patna. Pop: 82 878 796 (2001). Area: 99 225 sq km (38 301 sq miles)

Bihari (bɪˈhɑːrɪ) *n* **1** (*pl* Bihari *or* Biharis) a member of an Indian people living chiefly in Bihar but also in other parts of NW India and Bangladesh **2** the language of this people, comprising a number of highly differentiated dialects, belonging to the Indic branch of the Indo-European family ▷ *adj* **3** of or relating to this people, their language, or Bihar

Biisk (*Russian* bijsk) *n* a variant spelling of **Biysk**

Bijapur (bɪˈdʒɑːpʊə) *n* an ancient city in W India, in N Mysore: capital of a former kingdom, which fell at the end of the 17th century: cotton. Pop: 245 946 (2001)

bijection (baɪˈdʒɛkʃən) *n* a mathematical function or mapping that is both an injection and a surjection and therefore has an inverse. See also **injection** (sense 5), **surjection**

bijective (baɪˈdʒɛktɪv) *adj maths* (of a function, relation, etc) associating two sets in such a way that every member of each set is uniquely paired with a member of the other: *the mapping from the set of married men to the set of married women is bijective in a monogamous society*

bijou (ˈbiːʒuː) *n, pl* -joux (-ʒuːz) **1** something small and delicately worked, such as a trinket **2** (*modifier*) *often ironic* small but elegant and tasteful: *a bijou residence* [c19 from French, from Breton *bizou* finger ring, from *biz* finger; compare Welsh *bys* finger, Cornish *bis*]

bijouterie (biːˈʒuːtərɪ) *n* **1** jewellery esteemed for the delicacy of the work rather than the value of the materials **2** a collection of such jewellery

bijugate (ˈbaɪdʒʊˌɡeɪt, baɪˈdʒuːɡeɪt) *or* **bijugous** *adj* (of compound leaves) having two pairs of leaflets

Bikaner (ˈbiːkəˌnɪə) *n* a walled city in NW India, in Rajasthan: capital of the former state of Bikaner, on the edge of the Thar Desert. Pop: 529 007 (2001)

bike[1] (baɪk) *n, vb* **1** *informal* short for **bicycle** *or* **motorcycle 2** on your bike *Brit slang* away you go **3** get off one's bike *Austral and NZ slang* to lose one's self-control ▷ *n* **4** *slang* a promiscuous woman: *the town bike*

bike[2] *or* **byke** (bəɪk, baɪk) *Scot* ▷ *n* **1** a wasps' or bees' nest ▷ *vb* (*intr*) **2** to swarm [c14 of uncertain origin]

biker (ˈbaɪkə) *n informal* a member of a motorcycle gang

biker jacket *n* a short, close-fitting leather jacket with zips and studs, often worn by motorcyclists

bikie (ˈbaɪkɪ) *n Austral and NZ slang* a member of a motorcycle gang

bikini (bɪˈkiːnɪ) *n, pl* -nis a woman's very brief two-piece swimming costume [c20 after Bikini atoll, from a comparison between the devastating effect of the atomic-bomb test and the effect caused by women wearing bikinis]

Bikini (bɪˈkiːnɪ) *n* an atoll in the N Pacific; one of the Marshall Islands: site of a US atomic-bomb test in 1946

bikkie (ˈbɪkɪ) *n* a variant spelling of **bickie**

bilabial (baɪˈleɪbɪəl) *adj* **1** of, relating to, or denoting a speech sound articulated using both lips: (*p*) is a bilabial stop, (*w*) a bilabial semivowel ▷ *n* **2** a bilabial speech sound

bilabiate (baɪˈleɪbɪˌeɪt, -ɪt) *adj botany* divided into two lips: *the snapdragon has a bilabiate corolla*

bilander (ˈbɪləndə) *n* a small two-masted cargo ship [c17 from Dutch, literally: by-lander, because used on canals]

bilateral (baɪˈlætərəl) *adj* **1** having or involving two sides **2** affecting or undertaken by two parties; mutual: *a bilateral treaty* **3** denoting or relating to bilateral symmetry **4** having identical sides or parts on each side of an axis; symmetrical **5** *sociol* relating to descent through both maternal and paternal lineage. Compare **unilateral** (sense 5) **6** *Brit* relating to an education that combines academic and technical courses **7** a bilateral meeting > biˈlaterally *adv*

bilateral symmetry *n* the property of an organism or part of an organism such that, if cut in only one plane, the two cut halves are mirror images of each other. See also **radial symmetry**

bilateral trade *n* a system of trading between two countries in which each country attempts to balance its trade with that of the other

Bilbao (bɪlˈbɑːəʊ; *Spanish* bilˈβau) *n* a port in N Spain, on the Bay of Biscay: the largest city in the Basque Provinces: famous since medieval times for the production of iron and steel goods: modern buildings include the Guggenheim Art Museum (1997). Pop: 353 567 (2003 est). Basque name: Bilbo

bilberry (ˈbɪlbərɪ) *n, pl* -ries **1** any of several ericaceous shrubs of the genus *Vaccinium*, having edible blue or blackish berries. See also **blueberry 2 a** the fruit of any of these plants **b** (*as modifier*): *bilberry pie* [c16 probably of Scandinavian origin; compare Danish *bøllebær*, from *bølle* bilberry + *bær* BERRY]

bilbo (ˈbɪlbəʊ) *n, pl* -bos *or* -boes (formerly) a sword with a marked temper and elasticity [c16 from *Bilboa*, variant (in English) of *Bilbao*, Spain, noted for its blades]

bilboes (ˈbɪlbəʊz) *pl n* a long iron bar with two sliding shackles, formerly used to confine the ankles of a prisoner [c16 perhaps changed from BILBAO]

bilby (ˈbɪlbɪ) *n, pl* -bies a burrowing marsupial of the genus *Macrotis* of Australia having long pointed ears and grey fur. Also called: rabbit bandicoot, dalgyte

Bildungsroman (*German* ˈbɪldʊŋsroˌmaːn) *n* a novel concerned with a person's formative years and development [literally: education novel]

bile[1] (baɪl) *n* **1** a bitter greenish to golden brown alkaline fluid secreted by the liver and stored in the gall bladder. It is discharged during digestion into the duodenum, where it aids the emulsification and absorption of fats **2**

irritability or peevishness **3** *archaic* either of two bodily humours, one of which (**black bile**) was thought to cause melancholy and the other (**yellow bile**) anger [C17 from French, from Latin *bīlis*, probably of Celtic origin; compare Welsh *bustl* bile]

bile² ('baɪl) *vb* a Scot word for **boil**

bilection (baɪ'lɛkʃən) *n* another word for **bolection**

bilestone ('baɪlˌstəʊn) *n* another name for **gallstone**

bilge (bɪldʒ) *n* **1** *nautical* the parts of a vessel's hull where the vertical sides curve inwards to form the bottom **2** (*often plural*) the parts of a vessel between the lowermost floorboards and the bottom **3** Also called: **bilge water** the dirty water that collects in a vessel's bilge **4** *informal* silly rubbish; nonsense **5** the widest part of the belly of a barrel or cask ▷ *vb* **6** (*intr*) *nautical* (of a vessel) to take in water at the bilge **7** (*tr*) *nautical* to damage (a vessel) in the bilge, causing it to leak [C16 probably a variant of BULGE] > **'bilgy** *adj*

bilge keel *n* one of two keel-like projections along the bilges of some vessels to improve sideways stability

bilharzia (bɪl'hɑːtsɪə) *n* **1** another name for a **schistosome 2** another name for **schistosomiasis** [C19 New Latin, named after Theodor *Bilharz* (1825–62), German parasitologist who discovered schistosomes]

bilharziasis (ˌbɪlhɑːˈtsaɪəsɪs) *or* **bilharziosis** (bɪlˌhɑːtsɪˈəʊsɪs) *n* another name for **schistosomiasis**

biliary ('bɪlɪərɪ) *adj* of or relating to bile, to the ducts that convey bile, or to the gall bladder

bilinear (baɪ'lɪnɪə) *adj* **1** of or referring to two lines **2** of or relating to a function of two variables that is linear in each independently, as $f(x, y) = xy$

bilingual (baɪ'lɪŋgwəl) *adj* **1** able to speak two languages, esp with fluency **2** written or expressed in two languages ▷ *n* **3** a bilingual person > **bi'lingualˌism** *n* > **bi'lingually** *adv*

bilious ('bɪlɪəs) *adj* **1** of or relating to bile **2** affected with or denoting any disorder related to excess secretion of bile **3** *informal* (esp of colours) extremely distasteful; nauseating: *a bilious green* **4** *informal* bad-tempered; irritable [C16 from Latin *bīliōsus* full of BILE¹] > **'biliousness** *n*

bilirubin (ˌbɪlɪ'ruːbɪn, ˌbaɪ-) *n* an orange-yellow pigment in the bile formed as a breakdown product of haemoglobin. Excess amounts in the blood produce the yellow appearance associated with jaundice. Formula: $C_{32}H_{36}O_6N_4$ [C19 from BILE¹ + Latin *ruber* red + -IN]

biliverdin (ˌbɪlɪ'vɜːdɪn) *n* a dark green pigment in the bile formed by the oxidation of bilirubin. Formula: $C_{33}H_{34}O_6N_4$ [C19 coined in Swedish, from Latin *bīlis* bile + Old French *verd* green + -IN]

bilk (bɪlk) *vb* (*tr*) **1** to balk; thwart **2** (often foll by *of*) to cheat or deceive, esp to avoid making payment to **3** to escape from; elude **4** *cribbage* to play a card that hinders (one's opponent) from scoring in his or her crib ▷ *n* **5** a swindle or cheat **6** a person who swindles or cheats [C17 perhaps variant of BALK] > **'bilker** *n*

bill¹ (bɪl) *n* **1** money owed for goods or services supplied: *an electricity bill* **2** a written or printed account or statement of money owed **3** *chiefly Brit* such an account for food and drink in a restaurant, hotel, etc. Usual US and Canadian word: **check 4** any printed or written list of items, events, etc, such as a theatre programme: *who's on the bill tonight?* **5** *fit* or *fill the bill informal* to serve or perform adequately **6** a statute in draft, before it becomes law **7** a printed notice or advertisement; poster **8** *US and Canadian* a piece of paper money; note **9** an obsolete name for **promissory note 10** *law* See **bill of indictment 11** See **bill of exchange 12** See **bill of fare 13** *archaic* any document ▷ *vb* (*tr*) **14** to send or present an account for payment to (a person) **15** to enter

(items, goods, etc) on an account or statement **16** to advertise by posters **17** to schedule as a future programme: *the play is billed for next week* [C14 from Anglo-Latin *billa*, alteration of Late Latin *bulla* document, BULL³]

bill² (bɪl) *n* **1** the mouthpart of a bird, consisting of projecting jaws covered with a horny sheath; beak. It varies in shape and size according to the type of food eaten and may also be used as a weapon **2** any beaklike mouthpart in other animals **3** a narrow promontory: *Portland Bill* **4** *nautical* the pointed tip of the fluke of an anchor ▷ *vb* (*intr*) (esp in the phrase **bill and coo**) **5** (of birds, esp doves) to touch bills together **6** (of lovers) to kiss and whisper amorously [Old English *bile*; related to *bill* BILL³]

bill³ (bɪl) *n* **1** a pike or halberd with a narrow hooked blade **2** short for **billhook** [Old English *bill* sword, related to Old Norse *bīldr* instrument used in blood-letting, Old High German *bil* pickaxe]

bill⁴ (bɪl) *n* *ornithol* another word for **boom¹** (sense 4) [C18 from dialect *beel* BELL² (vb)]

billable ('bɪləb°l) *adj* referring to time worked, esp by a lawyer, on behalf of a particular client and for which that client will be expected to pay: *a timesheet of my billable hours*

billabong ('bɪləˌbɒŋ) *n* *Austral* **1** a backwater channel that forms a lagoon or pool **2** a branch of a river running to a dead end [C19 from a native Australian language, from *billa* river + *bong* dead]

billboard¹ ('bɪlˌbɔːd) *n* another name for **hoarding** [C19 from BILL¹ + BOARD]

billboard² ('bɪlˌbɔːd) *n* a fitting at the bow of a vessel for securing an anchor [C19 from BILL² + BOARD]

bill broker *n* a person whose business is the purchase and sale of bills of exchange

biller ('bɪlə) *n* *Southwest English dialect* the stem of a plant

billet¹ ('bɪlɪt) *n* **1** accommodation, esp for a soldier, in civilian lodgings **2** the official requisition for such lodgings **3** a space or berth allocated, esp for slinging a hammock, in a ship **4** *informal* a job **5** *archaic* a brief letter or document ▷ *vb* **-lets, -leting, -leted 6** (*tr*) to assign a lodging to (a soldier) **7** (*tr*) *informal* to assign to a post or job **8** to lodge or be lodged [C15 from Old French *billette*, from *bulle* a document; see BULL³] > **ˌbillet'ee** *n* > **'billeter** *n*

billet² ('bɪlɪt) *n* **1** a chunk of wood, esp for fuel **2** *metallurgy* **a** a metal bar of square or circular cross section **b** an ingot cast into the shape of a prism **3** *architect* a carved ornament in a moulding, with short cylinders or blocks evenly spaced [C15 from Old French *billette* a little log, from *bille* log, probably of Celtic origin]

billet-doux (ˌbɪlɪ'duː; French bijɛdu) *n, pl* **billets-doux** (ˌbɪlɪ'duːz; French bijɛdu) *old-fashioned or jocular* a love letter [C17 from French, literally: a sweet letter, from *billet* (see BILLET¹) + *doux* sweet, from Latin *dulcis*]

billfish ('bɪlˌfɪʃ) *n, pl* **-fish, -fishes** *US* any of various fishes having elongated jaws, esp any fish of the family *Istiophoridae*, such as the spearfish and marlin

billfold ('bɪlˌfəʊld) *n* *US and Canadian* a small folding case, usually of leather, for holding paper money, documents, etc. Also called (in Britain and other countries): **wallet**

billhook ('bɪlˌhʊk) *n* a cutting tool with a wooden handle and a curved blade terminating in a hook at its tip, used for pruning, chopping, etc. Also called: **bill**

billiard ('bɪljəd) *n* (*modifier*) of or relating to billiards: *a billiard table; a billiard cue; a billiard ball*

billiards ('bɪljədz) *n* (*functioning as singular*) **1** any of various games in which long cues are used to drive balls now made of composition or plastic. It is played on a rectangular table covered with a smooth tight-fitting cloth and having raised cushioned edges **2** a version of this, played on a rectangular table having six pockets let into the

corners and the two longer sides. Points are scored by striking one of three balls with the cue to contact the other two or one of the two. Compare **pool²** (sense 5), **snooker** [C16 from Old French *billard* curved stick, from Old French *bille* log; see BILLET²]

billing ('bɪlɪŋ) *n* **1** *theatre* the relative importance of a performer or act as reflected in the prominence given in programmes, advertisements, etc **2** *chiefly US and Canadian* public notice or advertising (esp in the phrase **advance billing**)

billingsgate ('bɪlɪŋzˌgeɪt) *n* obscene or abusive language [C17 after BILLINGSGATE, which was notorious for such language]

Billingsgate ('bɪlɪŋzˌgeɪt) *n* the largest fish market in London, on the N bank of the River Thames; moved to new site on the Isle of Dogs in 1982

Billings method *n* a natural method of birth control that involves examining the colour and viscosity of the cervical mucus to discover when ovulation is occurring. Also called: **ovulation method, mucus method** [C20 devised by Drs John and Evelyn *Billings* in the 1960s]

billion ('bɪljən) *n, pl* **-lions** *or* **-lion 1** one thousand million: it is written as 1 000 000 000 or 10⁹ **2** (formerly, in Britain) one million million: it is written as 1 000 000 000 000 or 10¹² **3** (*often plural*) any exceptionally large number ▷ *determiner* **4** (preceded by *a* or a cardinal number) **a** amounting to a billion: *it seems like a billion years ago* **b** (*as pronoun*): *we have a billion here* [C17 from French, from BI-¹ + -*llion* as in *million*] > **'billionth** *adj, n*

billionaire (ˌbɪljə'nɛə) *n* a person whose assets are worth over a billion of the monetary units of his country

Billiton ('bɪlɪtɒn, bɪ'liːtɒn) *n* an island of Indonesia, in the Java Sea between Borneo and Sumatra. Chief town: Tanjungpandan. Area: 4833 sq km (1866 sq miles). Also called: **Belitung**

bill of adventure *n* a certificate made out by a merchant to show that goods handled by him and his agents are the property of another party at whose risk the dealing is done

bill of attainder *n* (formerly) a legislative act finding a person guilty without trial of treason or felony and declaring him attainted. See also **attainder** (sense 1)

bill of exchange *n* (now chiefly in foreign transactions) a document, usually negotiable, containing an instruction to a third party to pay a stated sum of money at a designated future date or on demand

bill of fare *n* another name for **menu**

bill of health *n* **1** a certificate, issued by a port officer, that attests to the health of a ship's company **2 clean bill of health** *informal* **a** a good report of one's physical condition **b** a favourable account of a person's or a company's financial position

bill of indictment *n* *criminal law* a formal document accusing a person or persons of crime, formerly presented to a grand jury for certification as a true bill but now signed by a court official

bill of lading *n* (in foreign trade) a document containing full particulars of goods shipped or for shipment. Usual US and Canadian name: **waybill**

bill of quantities *n* a document drawn up by a quantity surveyor providing details of the prices, dimensions, etc, of the materials required to build a large structure, such as a factory

Bill of Rights *n* **1** an English statute of 1689 guaranteeing the rights and liberty of the individual subject **2** the first ten amendments to the US Constitution, added in 1791, which guarantee the liberty of the individual **3** (in Canada) a statement of basic human rights and freedoms enacted by Parliament in 1960 **4** (*usually not capitals*) any charter or summary of basic human rights

bill of sale *n law* a deed transferring personal property, either outright or as security for a loan or debt

billon ('bɪlən) *n* **1** an alloy consisting of gold or silver and a base metal, usually copper, used esp for coinage **2** any coin made of such an alloy [C18 from Old French: ingot, from *bille* log; see BILLET²]

billow ('bɪləʊ) *n* **1** a large sea wave **2** a swelling or surging mass, as of smoke or sound **3** a large atmospheric wave, usually in the lee of a hill **4** (*plural*) *poetic* the sea itself ▷ *vb* **5** to rise up, swell out, or cause to rise up or swell out [C16 from Old Norse *bylgja*; related to Swedish *bölja*, Danish *bölg*, Middle High German *bulge*; see BELLOW, BELLY] > 'billowing *adj, n*

billowy ('bɪləʊɪ) *adj* full of or forming billows: *a billowy sea* > 'billowiness *n*

billposter ('bɪl,pəʊstə) *or* **billsticker** *n* a person who is employed to stick advertising posters to walls, fences, etc > 'bill,posting *or* 'bill,sticking *n*

billy¹ ('bɪlɪ) *n, pl* -lies *US and Canadian* a wooden club esp a police officer's truncheon [C19 special use of the name *Billy*, pet form of *William*]

billy² ('bɪlɪ), **billycan** ('bɪlɪ,kæn) *n, pl* -lies *or* -lycans **1** a metal can or pot for boiling water, etc, over a campfire **2** *Austral and NZ* (*as modifier*): *billy-tea* **3** *Austral and NZ informal* to make tea [C19 from Scot *billypot* cooking vessel]

billy-bread *n NZ* bread baked in a billy over a camp fire

billycock ('bɪlɪkɒk) *n rare, chiefly Brit* any of several round-crowned brimmed hats of felt, such as the bowler [C19 named after *William Coke*, Englishman for whom it was first made]

billy goat *n* a male goat. Compare **nanny goat**

Billy No-Mates *n slang* a person with no friends

billyo *or* **billyoh** ('bɪlɪ,əʊ) *n* like billyo *informal* (intensifier): *snowing like billyo* [C19 of unknown origin]

bilobate (baɪ'ləʊ,beɪt) *or* **bilobed** ('baɪ,ləʊbd) *adj* divided into or having two lobes: *a bilobate leaf*

bilocular (baɪ'lɒkjʊlə) *or* **biloculate** *adj biology* divided into two chambers or cavities: *some flowering plants have bilocular ovaries*

biltong ('bɪl,tɒŋ) *n South African* strips of meat dried and cured in the sun [C19 Afrikaans, from Dutch *bil* buttock + *tong* TONGUE]

Bim (bɪm) *n informal* a native or inhabitant of Barbados [C19 of unknown origin]

BIM *abbreviation for* British Institute of Management

bimah *or* **bima** ('biːmə) *n* variant spellings of **bema**

bimanous ('bɪmənəs, baɪ'meɪ-) *adj* (of man and the higher primates) having two hands distinct in form and function from the feet [C19 from New Latin *bimana* two handed, from BI-¹ + Latin *manus* hand]

bimanual (baɪ'mænjʊəl) *adj* using or requiring both hands > bi'manually *adv*

bimble box ('bɪmb⁰l) *n* a dense Australian tree, *Eucalyptus populnea*, with shiny green leaves, valued for its hard wood [*bimble* from a native Australian language + BOX³]

bimbo ('bɪmbəʊ) *n, pl* -bos *or* -boes **1** an attractive but empty-headed young woman **2** a fellow; person esp a foolish one [C20 from Italian: little child, perhaps via Polari]

bimestrial (baɪ'mɛstrɪəl) *adj* **1** lasting for two months **2** a less common word for **bimonthly** (sense 1) [C19 from Latin *bimēstris*, from BI-¹ + *mēnsis* month] > bi'mestrially *adv*

bimetallic (,baɪmɪ'tælɪk) *adj* **1** consisting of two metals **2** of, relating to, or based on bimetallism

bimetallic strip *n* a strip consisting of two metals of different coefficients of expansion welded together so that it buckles on heating: used in thermostats, etc

bimetallism (baɪ'mɛtə,lɪzəm) *n* **1** the use of two metals, esp gold and silver, in fixed relative values as the standard of value and currency **2** the economic policies or doctrine supporting a

bimetallic standard > bi'metallist *n*

bimillenary (,baɪmɪ'liːnərɪ, baɪ'mɪlɪnərɪ) *adj* **1** marking a two-thousandth anniversary ▷ *n, pl* -naries **2** a two-thousandth anniversary

bimodal distribution (baɪ'məʊd⁰l) *n statistics* a frequency distribution with two modes

bimolecular (,baɪmə'lɛkjʊlə) *adj* (of a chemical complex, collision, etc) having or involving two molecules

bimonthly (baɪ'mʌnθlɪ) *adj, adv* **1** every two months **2** (often avoided because of confusion with sense 1) twice a month; semimonthly. See **bi-¹** ▷ *n, pl* -lies **3** a periodical published every two months

bimorph ('baɪmɔːf) *or* **bimorph cell** *n electronics* an assembly of two piezoelectric crystals cemented together so that an applied voltage causes one to expand and the other to contract, converting electrical signals into mechanical energy. Conversely, bending can generate a voltage: used in loudspeakers, gramophone pick-ups, etc

bin (bɪn) *n* **1** a large container or enclosed space for storing something in bulk, such as coal, grain, or wool **2** Also called: **bread bin** a small container for bread **3** Also called: **dustbin, rubbish bin** a container for litter, rubbish, etc **4** *Brit* **a** a storage place for bottled wine **b** one particular bottling of wine ▷ *vb* **bins, binning, binned** **5** (*tr*) to store in a bin **6** (*tr*) to put in a wastepaper bin [Old English *binne* basket, probably of Celtic origin; related to *bindan* to BIND]

bin- *prefix* a variant, esp before a vowel, of **bi-¹**: *binocular*

binal ('baɪn⁰l) *adj* twofold; double [C17 from New Latin *bīnālis*; see BIN-]

binary ('baɪnərɪ) *adj* **1** composed of, relating to, or involving two; dual **2** *maths, computing* of, relating to, or expressed in binary notation or binary code **3** (of a compound or molecule) containing atoms of two different elements **4** *metallurgy* (of an alloy) consisting of two components or phases **5** (of an educational system) consisting of two parallel forms of education such as the grammar school and the secondary modern in Britain **6** *maths, logic* (of a relation, expression, or operation) applying to two elements of its domain; having two argument places; dyadic ▷ *n, pl* -ries **7** something composed of two parts or things **8** *astronomy* See **binary star** **9** short for **binary weapon** [C16 from Late Latin *bīnārius*; see BIN-]

binary code *n computing* the representation of each one of a set of numbers, letters, etc, as a unique sequence of bits, as in ASCII

binary-coded decimal *n* a number in binary code written in groups of four bits, each group representing one digit of the corresponding decimal number. Abbreviation: BCD

binary digit *n* either of the two digits 0 or 1, used in binary notation. See also **bit⁴**

binary fission *n* asexual reproduction in unicellular organisms by division into two daughter cells

binary form *n music* a structure consisting of two sections, each being played twice

binary notation *or* **system** *n* a number system having a base of two, numbers being expressed by sequences of the digits 0 and 1: used in computing, as 0 and 1 can be represented electrically as *off* and *on*

binary number *n* a number expressed in binary notation, as 1101.101 = $1 \times 2^3 + 1 \times 2^2 + 0 \times 2^1 + 1 \times 2^0 + 1 \times 2^{-1} + 0 \times 2^{-2} + 1 \times 2^{-3} = 13\frac{5}{8}$

binary star *n* a double star system comprising two stars orbiting around their common centre of mass. A **visual binary** can be seen through a telescope. A **spectroscopic binary** can only be observed by the spectroscopic Doppler shift as each star moves towards or away from the earth. Sometimes shortened to: **binary**. See also **optical double star, eclipsing binary**

binary weapon *n* a chemical weapon consisting of a projectile containing two substances separately that mix to produce a lethal agent when the projectile is fired

binate ('baɪneɪt) *adj botany* occurring in two parts or in pairs: *binate leaves* [C19 from New Latin *bīnātus*, probably from Latin *combīnātus* united] > 'bi,nately *adv*

binaural (baɪ'nɔːrəl, bɪn-) *adj* **1** relating to, having, or hearing with both ears **2** employing two separate channels for recording or transmitting sound; so creating an impression of depth: *a binaural recording* > bin'aurally *adv*

bind (baɪnd) *vb* **binds, binding, bound** **1** to make or become fast or secure with or as if with a tie or band **2** (*tr; often foll by up*) to encircle or enclose with a band: *to bind the hair* **3** (*tr*) to place (someone) under obligation; oblige **4** (*tr*) to impose legal obligations or duties upon (a person or party to an agreement) **5** (*tr*) to make (a bargain, agreement, etc) irrevocable; seal **6** (*tr*) to restrain or confine with or as if with ties, as of responsibility or loyalty **7** (*tr*) to place under certain constraints; govern **8** (*tr; often foll by up*) to bandage or swathe: *to bind a wound* **9** to cohere or stick or cause to cohere or stick: *egg binds fat and flour* **10** to make or become compact, stiff, or hard: *frost binds the earth* **11 a** (*tr*) to enclose and fasten (the pages of a book) between covers **b** (*intr*) (of a book) to undergo this process **12** (*tr*) to provide (a garment, hem, etc) with a border or edging, as for decoration or to prevent fraying **13** (*tr; sometimes foll by out or over*) to employ as an apprentice; indenture **14** (*intr*) *slang* to complain **15** (*tr*) *logic* to bring (a variable) into the scope of an appropriate quantifier. See also **bound¹** (sense 9) ▷ *n* **16** something that binds **17** the act of binding or state of being bound **18** *informal* a difficult or annoying situation **19** another word for **bine** **20** *music* another word for **tie** (sense 17) **21** *mining* clay between layers of coal **22** *fencing* a pushing movement with the blade made to force one's opponent's sword from one line into another **23** *chess* a position in which one player's pawns have a hold on the centre that makes it difficult for the opponent to advance there ▷ See also **bind over** [Old English *bindan*; related to Old Norse *binda*, Old High German *bintan*, Latin *offendix* BAND², Sanskrit *badhnāti* he binds]

binder ('baɪndə) *n* **1** a firm cover or folder with rings or clasps for holding loose sheets of paper together **2** a material used to bind separate particles together, give an appropriate consistency, or facilitate adhesion to a surface **3 a** a person who binds books; bookbinder **b** a machine that is used to bind books **4** something used to fasten or tie, such as rope or twine **5** *NZ informal* a square meal **6** Also called: **reaper binder** *obsolete* a machine for cutting grain and binding it into bundles or sheaves. Compare **combine harvester** **7** an informal agreement giving insurance coverage pending formal issue of a policy **8** a tie, beam, or girder, used to support floor joists **9** a stone for binding masonry; bondstone **10** the nonvolatile component of the organic media in which pigments are dispersed in paint **11** (in systemic grammar) a word that introduces a bound clause; a subordinating conjunction or a relative pronoun. Compare **linker** (sense 2)

bindery ('baɪndərɪ) *n, pl* -eries a place in which books are bound

bindi *or* **bindhi** ('bɪndɪ) *n* a decorative dot worn in the middle of the forehead, esp by Hindu women [Hindi]

bindi-eye ('bɪndɪ,aɪ) *n Austral* **1** any of various small weedy Australian herbaceous plants of the genus *Calotis*, with burlike fruits: family *Asteraceae* (composites) **2** any bur or prickle [C20 perhaps from a native Australian language]

binding ('baɪndɪŋ) *n* **1** anything that binds or fastens **2** the covering within which the pages of

b

a book are bound **3** the material or tape used for binding hems, etc ▷ *adj* **4** imposing an obligation or duty: *a binding promise* **5** causing hindrance; restrictive

binding energy *n physics* **1** the energy that must be supplied to a stable nucleus before it can undergo fission. It is equal to the mass defect **2** the energy required to remove a particle from a system, esp an electron from an atom

bind over *vb* (*tr, adverb*) to place (a person) under a legal obligation, such as one to keep the peace

bindweed ('baɪnd,wiːd) *n* **1** any convolvulaceous plant of the genera *Convolvulus* and *Calystegia* that twines around a support. See also **convolvulus 2** any of various other trailing or twining plants, such as black bindweed

bine (baɪn) *n* **1** the climbing or twining stem of any of various plants, such as the woodbine or bindweed **2** any plant with such a stem [c19 variant of BIND]

Binet-Simon scale ('biːneɪ'saɪmən) *n psychol* a test comprising questions and tasks, used to determine the mental age of subjects, usually children. Also called: **Binet scale** *or* **test**. See also **Stanford-Binet test** [c20 named after Alfred *Binet* (1857–1911) + Théodore *Simon* (1873–1961), French psychologists]

bing (bɪŋ) *n dialect* a heap or pile, esp of spoil from a mine [c16 from Old Norse *bingr* heap]

binge (bɪndʒ) *n informal* **1** a bout of excessive eating or drinking **2** excessive indulgence in anything: *a shopping binge* ▷ *vb* **binges, bingeing** *or* **binging, binged** (*intr*) **3** to indulge in a binge (esp of eating or drinking) [c19 probably Lincolnshire dialect *binge* to soak]

binge drinking *n* the practice of drinking excessive amounts of alcohol regularly ▷ **binge drinker** *n*

Bingen ('bɪŋən) *n* a town in W Germany on the Rhine: wine trade and tourist centre. Pop: 24 716 (2003 est)

bingle ('bɪŋgəl) *n Austral old-fashioned informal* a minor crash or upset, as in a car or on a surfboard [c20 of uncertain origin]

bingo ('bɪŋgəʊ) *n, pl* **-gos 1** a gambling game, usually played with several people, in which numbers selected at random are called out and the players cover the numbers on their individual cards. The first to cover a given arrangement of numbers is the winner. Compare **lotto** ▷ *sentence substitute* **2** a cry by the winner of a game of bingo **3** an expression of surprise at a sudden occurrence or the successful completion of something: *and bingo! the lights went out* [c19 perhaps from *bing*, imitative of a bell ringing to mark the win]

Bini *or* **Beni** (bə'niː) *n, pl* **-ni** *or* **-nis** other names for **Edo**

biniou (binju) *n* a small high-pitched Breton bagpipe [from Breton *beniou*]

bin liner *n* a plastic bag used to line the inside of a rubbish bin

binman ('bɪn,mæn, 'bɪnmən) *n, pl* **-men** another name for **dustman**

binnacle ('bɪnəkəl) *n* a housing for a ship's compass [c17 changed from c15 *bitakle*, from Portuguese *bitácula*, from Late Latin *habitáculum* dwelling-place, from Latin *habitāre* to inhabit; spelling influenced by BIN]

binocular (bɪ'nɒkjʊlə, baɪ-) *adj* involving, relating to, seeing with or intended for both eyes: *binocular vision* [c18 from BI-¹ + Latin *oculus* eye]

binocular disparity *n physiol* the small differences in the positions of the parts of the images falling on each eye that results when each eye views the scene from a slightly different position; these differences make stereoscopic vision possible

binocular rivalry *n psychol* the phenomenon whereby one is unable to see simultaneously different images presented one to each eye; usually in some areas of the eye the image presented to the left eye is seen, in others that

presented to the right eye. Also called: **retinal rivalry**

binoculars (bɪ'nɒkjʊləz, baɪ-) *pl n* an optical instrument for use with both eyes, consisting of two small telescopes joined together. Also called: **field glasses**

binomial (baɪ'nəʊmɪəl) *n* **1** a mathematical expression consisting of two terms, such as *3x + 2y* **2** a two-part taxonomic name for an animal or plant. See **binomial nomenclature** ▷ *adj* **3** referring to two names or terms [c16 from Medieval Latin *binōmius* from BI-¹ + Latin *nōmen* NAME] ▷ **bi'nomially** *adv*

binomial coefficient *n maths* any of the numerical factors which multiply the successive terms in a binomial expansion; any term of the form *n!/(n–k)!k!*: written (ⁿₖ), ⁿCₖ, or Cⁿₖ. See also **combination** (sense 6)

binomial distribution *n* a statistical distribution giving the probability of obtaining a specified number of successes in a specified number of independent trials of an experiment with a constant probability of success in each. Symbol: *Bi (n, p)*, where *n* is the number of trials and *p* the probability of success in each

binomial experiment *n statistics* an experiment consisting of a fixed number of independent trials each with two possible outcomes, success and failure, and the same probability of success. The probability of a given number of successes is described by a binominal distribution. See also **Bernoulli trial**

binomial nomenclature *or* **binominal nomenclature** *n* a system for naming plants and animals by means of two Latin names: the first indicating the genus and the second the species to which the organism belongs, as in *Panthera leo* (the lion)

binomial theorem *n* a mathematical theorem that gives the expansion of any binomial raised to a positive integral power, *n*. It contains *n + 1* terms: $(x + a)^n = x^n + nx^{n-1}a + [n(n-1)/2]x^{n-2}a^2 + ... + (^n_k)x^{n-k}a^k + ... + a^n$, where $(^n_k) = n!/(n-k)!k!$, the number of combinations of *k* items selected from *n*

binominal (baɪ'nɒmɪnəl) *biology* ▷ *adj* **1** of or denoting the binomial nomenclature ▷ *n* **2** a two-part taxonomic name; binomial

binovular (bɪ'nɒvjʊlə) *adj* relating to or derived from two different ova: *binovular fertilization*

bins (bɪnz) *pl n Northern English dialect* a pair of glasses

bint (bɪnt) *n slang* a derogatory term for **girl** *or* **woman** [c19 from Arabic, literally: daughter]

binturong ('bɪntjʊ,rɒŋ, bɪn'tjʊərɒn) *n* an arboreal SE Asian viverrine mammal, *Arctictis binturong*, closely related to the palm civets but larger and having long shaggy black hair [from Malay]

binucleate (baɪ'njuːklɪ,eɪt, -ɪt) *adj biology* having two nuclei: *a binucleate cell*. Also: **binuclear, binucleated**

bio ('baɪəʊ) *n, pl* **bios** short for **biography**

bio- *or before a vowel* **bi-** *combining form* **1** indicating or involving life or living organisms: *biogenesis; biolysis* **2** indicating a human life or career: *biography; biopic* [from Greek *bios* life]

bioaccumulate (,baɪəˈkjuːmjʊ,leɪt) *vb* (*intr*) (of substances, esp toxins) to build up within the tissues of organisms > ,bioac,cumu'lation *n*

bioactive (,baɪəʊˈæktɪv) *adj* (of a substance) having or producing an effect on living tissue > ,bioac'tivity *n*

bioaeration (,baɪəʊɛəˈreɪʃən) *n* the oxidative treatment of raw sewage by aeration

bioaeronautics (,baɪəʊˌɛərəˈnɔːtɪks) *n* (*functioning as singular*) the use of aircraft in the discovery, development, and protection of natural and biological resources

bioassay *n* (,baɪəʊəˈseɪ, -ˈæseɪ) **1** a method of determining the concentration, activity, or effect of a change to substance by testing its effect on a living organism and comparing this with the

activity of an agreed standard ▷ *vb* (,baɪəʊəˈseɪ) **2** (*tr*) to subject to a bioassay

bioastronautics (,baɪəʊ,æstrəˈnɔːtɪks) *n* (*functioning as singular*) the study of the effects of space flight on living organisms. See **space medicine**

bioavailability (,baɪəʊə,veɪləˈbɪlɪtɪ) *n* the extent to which a drug or other substance is taken up by a specific tissue or organ after administration; the proportion of the dose of a drug that reaches the systemic circulation intact after administration by a route other than intravenous. Also called: **systemic availability** > ,bioa'vailable *adj*

Bío-Bío (Spanish 'biːoˈbiːo) *n* a river in central Chile, rising in the Andes and flowing northwest to the Pacific. Length: about 390 km (240 miles)

biocatalyst (,baɪəʊˈkætəlɪst) *n* a chemical, esp an enzyme, that initiates or increases the rate of a biochemical reaction > **biocatalytic** (,baɪəʊ,kætəˈlɪtɪk) *adj*

biocellate (baɪˈɒsɪ,leɪt, ,baɪəʊˈsɛlɪt) *adj* (of animals and plants) marked with two eyelike spots or ocelli [c19 from BI-¹ + *ocellate*, from Latin *ocellus*, diminutive of *oculus* eye]

biochemical oxygen demand *n* a measure of the organic pollution of water: the amount of oxygen, in mg per litre of water, absorbed by a sample kept at 20°C for five days. Abbreviation: **BOD**

biochemistry (,baɪəʊˈkɛmɪstrɪ) *n* the study of the chemical compounds, reactions, etc, occurring in living organisms > **biochemical** (,baɪəʊˈkɛmɪkəl) *adj* > ,bio'chemically *adv* > ,bio'chemist *n*

biochip ('baɪə,tʃɪp) *n* a small glass or silicon plate containing an array of biochemical molecules or structures, used as a biosensor or in gene sequencing. Also called: **microarray**

biocide ('baɪə,saɪd) *n* a chemical, such as a pesticide, capable of killing living organisms > ,bio'cidal *adj*

bioclastic (,baɪəʊˈklæstɪk) *adj* (of deposits, esp limestones) derived from shell fragments or similar organic remains

bioclimatology (,baɪəʊ,klaɪməˈtɒlədʒɪ) *n* the study of the effects of climatic conditions on living organisms > ,bio,clima'tologist *n*

biocoenology *or* **biocenology** (,baɪəʊsɪˈnɒlədʒɪ) *n* the branch of ecology concerned with the relationships and interactions between the members of a natural community [c20 from BIO- + ceno-, from Greek *koinos* common + -LOGY]

biocoenosis *or* **biocenosis** (,baɪəʊsɪˈnəʊsɪs) *n* a diverse community inhabiting a single biotope > ,biocoe'notic *or* ,bioce'notic *adj*

biocomputing (,baɪəʊkəmˈpjuːtɪŋ) *n* the application of computing to problems in biology, biochemistry, and genetics

bioconversion (,baɪəʊkənˈvɜːʃən) *n* the use of biological processes or materials to change organic substances into a new form, such as the conversion of waste into methane by fermentation

biocycle (,baɪəʊˈsaɪkəl) *n ecology* the cycling of chemicals through the biosphere

biodata ('baɪəʊ,deɪtə, -,dɑːtə) *n* information regarding an individual's education and work history, esp in the context of a selection process [c20 from BIO(GRAPHICAL) + DATA]

biodegradable (,baɪəʊdɪˈgreɪdəbəl) *adj* (of sewage constituents, packaging material, etc) capable of being decomposed by bacteria or other biological means > **biodegradation** (,baɪəʊ,dɛgrəˈdeɪʃən) *n* > **biodegradability** (,baɪəʊ,dɛgrɛdɪˈbɪlɪtɪ) *n*

biodiesel ('baɪəʊ,diːzəl) *n* a biofuel intended for use in diesel engines

biodiversity (,baɪəʊdaɪˈvɜːsɪtɪ) *n* the existence of a wide variety of plant and animal species in their natural environments, which is the aim of conservationists concerned about the indiscriminate destruction of rainforests and other habitats

biodot ('baɪə,dɒt) *n* a temperature-sensitive

device stuck to the skin in order to monitor stress

biodynamics (ˌbaɪəʊdaɪˈnæmɪks, -dɪ-) *n* (*functioning as singular*) the branch of biology that deals with the energy production and activities of organisms > ˌbiodyˈnamic *or* ˌbiodyˈnamical *adj*

bioecology (ˌbaɪəʊɪˈkɒlədʒɪ) *n* another word for **ecology** (sense 1) > bioecological (ˌbaɪəʊˌiːkəˈlɒdʒɪkᵊl) *adj* > ˌbioˌecoˈlogically *adv* > ˌbioˈecologist *n*

bioelectricity (ˌbaɪəʊˌɪlɛkˈtrɪsɪtɪ) *n* electricity generated by a living organism > ˌbioeˈlectric *adj*

bioenergetics (ˌbaɪəʊˌenəˈdʒetɪks) *n* (*functioning as singular*) the study of energy transformations in living organisms and systems > ˌbioˌenerˈgetic *adj*

bioengineering (ˌbaɪəʊˌendʒɪˈnɪərɪŋ) *n* **1** the design and manufacture of aids, such as artificial limbs, to rectify defective body functions **2** the design, manufacture, and maintenance of engineering equipment used in biosynthetic processes, such as fermentation > ˌbioˌengiˈneer *n*

bioethics (ˌbaɪəʊˈɛθɪks) *n* (*functioning as singular*) the study of ethical problems arising from biological research and its applications in such fields as organ transplantation, genetic engineering, or artificial insemination > ˌbioˈethical *adj* > bioethicist (ˌbaɪəʊˈɛθɪsɪst) *n*

biofact (ˈbaɪəʊfækt) *n* **1** an item of biological information **2** an item of biographical information

biofeedback (ˌbaɪəʊˈfiːdbæk) *n physiol, psychol* a technique for teaching the control of autonomic functions, such as the rate of heartbeat or breathing, by recording the activity and presenting it (usually visually) so that the person can know the state of the autonomic function he or she is learning to control. Compare **neurofeedback**

bioflavonoid (ˌbaɪəʊˈfleɪvəˌnɔɪd) *n* another name for **vitamin P**

biofuel (ˈbaɪəʊˌfjʊəl) *n* a gaseous, liquid, or solid substance of biological origin that is used as a fuel

biog. abbreviation for **1** biographical **2** biography

biogas (ˈbaɪəʊˌgæs) *n* a gas that is produced by the action of bacteria on organic waste matter: used as a fuel

biogen (ˈbaɪədʒən) *n* a hypothetical protein assumed to be the basis of the formation and functioning of body cells and tissues

biogenesis (ˌbaɪəʊˈdʒɛnɪsɪs) *n* the principle that a living organism must originate from a parent organism similar to itself. Compare **abiogenesis** > ˌbiogeˈnetic, ˌbiogeˈnetical *or* biogenous (baɪˈɒdʒənəs) *adj* > ˌbiogeˈnetically *adv*

biogenetics (ˌbaɪəʊdʒɪˈnetɪks) *n* (*functioning as singular*) the branch of biology concerned with altering the genomes of living organisms

biogenic (ˌbaɪəʊˈdʒɛnɪk) *adj* produced or originating from a living organism

biogeography (ˌbaɪəʊdʒɪˈɒɡrəfɪ) *n* the branch of biology concerned with the geographical distribution of plants and animals > biogeographical (ˌbaɪəʊˌdʒɪəˈɡræfɪkᵊl) *adj* > ˌbioˌgeoˈgraphically *adv*

biographee (ˌbaɪɒɡræˈfiː) *n* a person whose biography has been written

biographize *or* **biographise** (baɪˈɒɡrəˌfaɪz) *vb* (*tr*) to write a biography of: *the maverick duo were not easy to biographize*

biography (baɪˈɒɡrəfɪ) *n, pl* -phies **1** an account of a person's life by another **2** such accounts collectively > biˈographer *n* > biographical (ˌbaɪəˈɡræfɪkᵊl) *or archaic* ˌbioˈgraphic *adj* > ˌbioˈgraphically *adv*

biohazard (ˌbaɪəʊˈhæzəd) *n* material of biological origin that is hazardous to humans > ˌbioˈhazardous *adj*

bioherm (ˈbaɪəʊˌhɜːm) *n* **1** a mound of material laid down by sedentary marine organisms, esp a coral reef **2** the fossilized remains of such a mound [c20 from BIO- + Greek *herma* submerged rock]

bioindustry (ˈbaɪəʊˌɪndəstrɪ) *n, pl* -tries an

industry that makes use of biotechnology and other advanced life science methodologies in the creation or alteration of life forms or processes

bioinformatics (ˌbaɪəʊˌɪnfəˈmætɪks) *n* (*functioning as singular*) the branch of information science concerned with large databases of biochemical or pharmaceutical information

Bioko (baɪˈəʊkəʊ) *n* an island in the Gulf of Guinea, off the coast of Cameroon: part of Equatorial Guinea. Capital: Malabo. Area: 2017 sq km (786 sq miles). Former names: Fernando Po (until 1973), Macías Nguema (1973–79)

biol. abbreviation for **1** biological **2** biology

biological (ˌbaɪəˈlɒdʒɪkᵊl) *or archaic* **biologic** *adj* **1** of or relating to biology **2** (of a detergent) containing enzymes said to be capable of removing stains of organic origin from items to be washed ⊳ *n* **3** (*usually plural*) a drug, such as a vaccine, that is derived from a living organism > ˌbioˈlogically *adv*

biological clock *n* **1** an inherent periodicity in the physiological processes of living organisms that is not dependent on the periodicity of external factors **2** the hypothetical mechanism responsible for this periodicity ⊳ See also **circadian**

biological control *n* the control of destructive organisms by the use of other organisms, such as the natural predators of the pests

biological marker *n* a substance, physiological characteristic, gene, etc that indicates, or may indicate, the presence of disease, a physiological abnormality or a psychological condition. Also called: **biomarker**

biological shield *n* a protective shield impervious to radiation, esp the thick concrete wall surrounding the core of a nuclear reactor

biological warfare *n* the use of living organisms or their toxic products to induce death or incapacity in humans and animals and damage to plant crops, etc. Abbreviation: **BW**

biology (baɪˈɒlədʒɪ) *n* **1** the study of living organisms, including their structure, functioning, evolution, distribution, and interrelationships **2** the structure, functioning, etc, of a particular organism or group of organisms **3** the animal and plant life of a particular region > biˈologist *n*

bioluminescence (ˌbaɪəʊˌluːmɪˈnɛsəns) *n* the production of light by living organisms as a result of the oxidation of a light-producing substance (luciferin) by the enzyme luciferase: occurs in many marine organisms, insects such as the firefly, etc > ˌbioˌlumiˈnescent *adj*

biolysis (baɪˈɒlɪsɪs) *n* **1** the death and dissolution of a living organism **2** the disintegration of organic matter by the action of bacteria etc > biolytic (ˌbaɪəˈlɪtɪk) *adj*

biomarker (ˈbaɪəʊˌmɑːkə) *n* another name for **biological marker**

biomass (ˈbaɪəʊˌmæs) *n* **1** the total number of living organisms in a given area, expressed in terms of living or dry weight per unit area **2** vegetable matter used as a source of energy

biomathematics (ˌbaɪəʊˌmæθəˈmætɪks, -ˌmæθˈmæt-) *n* (*functioning as singular*) the study of the application of mathematics to biology

biome (ˈbaɪˌəʊm) *n* a major ecological community, extending over a large area and usually characterized by a dominant vegetation. See **formation** (sense 6) [c20 from BIO- + -OME]

biomechanics (ˌbaɪəʊmɪˈkænɪks) *n* (*functioning as singular*) the study of the mechanics of the movement of living organisms

biomedical (ˌbaɪəʊˈmɛdɪkᵊl) *adj* of or relating to biology and medicine or biomedicine

biomedicine (ˌbaɪəʊˈmɛdɪsɪn, -ˈmɛdsɪn) *n* **1** the medical study of the effects of unusual environmental stress on human beings, esp in connection with space travel **2** the study of herbal remedies

biometeorology (ˌbaɪəʊˌmiːtɪəˈrɒlədʒɪ) *n* the

study of the effect of weather conditions on living organisms

biometric (ˌbaɪəʊˈmɛtrɪk) *adj* **1 a** relating to the analysis of biological data using mathematical and statistical methods **b** relating to digital scanning of the physiological or behavioural characteristics of individuals as a means of identification: *biometric fingerprinting* **2** relating to the statistical calculation of the probable duration of human life

biometry (baɪˈɒmɪtrɪ) *or* **biometrics** (ˌbaɪəˈmɛtrɪks) *n* (*functioning as singular*) **1 a** the analysis of biological data using mathematical and statistical methods **b** the practice of digitally scanning the physiological or behavioural characteristics of individuals as a means of identification **2** the statistical calculation of the probable duration of human life > ˌbioˈmetrically *adv*

biomimetic (ˌbaɪəʊmɪˈmɛtɪk) *adj* (of a human-made product) imitating nature or a natural process

biomimicry (ˌbaɪəʊˈmɪmɪkrɪ) *n* the mimicking of life using imitation biological systems

biomorph (ˈbaɪəʊˌmɔːf) *n* a set of two-dimensional branching biomorphic images that can be used to illustrate evolutionary concepts

biomorphic (ˌbaɪəʊˈmɔːfɪk) *adj* having the form of a living organism

bionic (baɪˈɒnɪk) *adj* **1** of or relating to bionics **2** (in science fiction) having certain physiological functions augmented or replaced by electronic equipment: *the bionic man*

bionics (baɪˈɒnɪks) *n* (*functioning as singular*) **1** the study of certain biological functions, esp those relating to the brain, that are applicable to the development of electronic equipment, such as computer hardware, designed to operate in a similar manner **2** the technique of replacing a limb or body part by an artificial limb or part that is electronically or mechanically powered [c20 from BIO- + (ELECTR)ONICS]

bionomics (ˌbaɪəˈnɒmɪks) *n* (*functioning as singular*) a less common name for **ecology** (senses 1, 2) [c19 from BIO- + *nomics* on pattern of ECONOMICS] > ˌbioˈnomic *adj* > ˌbioˈnomically *adv* > bionomist (baɪˈɒnəmɪst) *n*

bio-organism *n* a dangerous fast-proliferating organism that could be used as the basis of a biological weapon

biopesticide (ˌbaɪəʊˈpɛstɪˌsaɪd) *n* a naturally occurring or derived substance or an organism that controls pests by nontoxic means > ˌbioˌpestiˈcidal *adj*

biopharmaceutical (ˌbaɪəʊˌfɑːməˈsjuːtɪkᵊl) *adj* of or relating to drugs produced using biotechnology

biophilia (ˌbaɪəʊˈfɪlɪə) *n* an innate love for the natural world, supposed to be felt universally by humankind [c20 BIO + -PHILIA]

biophysics (ˌbaɪəʊˈfɪzɪks) *n* (*functioning as singular*) the physics of biological processes and the application of methods used in physics to biology > ˌbioˈphysical *adj* > ˌbioˈphysically *adv* > biophysicist (ˌbaɪəʊˈfɪzɪsɪst) *n*

biopic (ˈbaɪəʊˌpɪk) *n informal* a film based on the life of a famous person, esp one giving a popular treatment [c20 from *bio(graphical)* + *pic(ture)*]

biopiracy (ˈbaɪəʊˌpaɪrəsɪ) *n* the use of wild plants by international companies to develop medicines, without recompensing the countries from which they are taken

bioplasm (ˈbaɪəʊˌplæzəm) *n now rare* living matter; protoplasm > ˌbioˈplasmic *adj*

biopoiesis (ˌbaɪəʊpɔɪˈiːsɪs) *n* the development of living matter from nonliving matter, esp considered as an evolutionary process

bioprospecting (ˌbaɪəʊˈprɒspɛktɪŋ) *n* searching for plant or animal species for use as a source of commercially exploitable products, such as medicinal drugs

biopsy (ˈbaɪɒpsɪ) *n, pl* -sies **1** examination, esp under a microscope, of tissue from a living body

b

to determine the cause or extent of a disease **2** the sample taken for such an examination [c20 from BIO- + Greek *opsis* sight] ▷ **bioptic** (baɪˈɒptɪk) *adj*

bioreagent (ˌbaɪəʊriːˈeɪdʒənt) *n* a reagent of biological origin, such as an enzyme

bioremediation (ˌbaɪəʊrɪˌmiːdɪˈeɪʃən) *n* the use of plants to extract heavy metals from contaminated soils and water. Also called: **phytoremediation**

biorhythm (ˈbaɪəʊˌrɪðəm) *n* a cyclically recurring pattern of physiological states in an organism or organ, such as alpha rhythm or circadian rhythm; believed by some to affect physical and mental states and behaviour ▷ ˌbioˈrhythmic *adj* ▷ ˌbioˈrhythmically *adv*

biorhythmics (ˌbaɪəʊˈrɪðmɪks) *n* (*functioning as singular*) the study of biorhythms

biosafety (ˌbaɪəʊˈseɪftɪ) *n* the precautions taken to control the cultivation and distribution of genetically modified crops and products

bioscience (ˈbaɪəʊˌsaɪəns) *n* **1** another name for a **life science 2** the life sciences collectively ▷ ˌbioˈscientific *adj* ▷ ˌbioˈscientist *n*

bioscope (ˈbaɪəˌskəʊp) *n* **1** a kind of early film projector **2** a South African word for **cinema**

bioscopy (baɪˈɒskəpɪ) *n*, *pl* **-pies** examination of a body to determine whether it is alive

bio-security *n* the precautions taken to protect against the spread of lethal or harmful organisms and diseases ▷ ˌbio-seˈcure *adj*

-biosis *n combining form* indicating a specified mode of life: *symbiosis* [New Latin, from Greek *biōsis*; see BIO-, -OSIS] ▷ **-biotic** *adj combining form*

biosolids (ˈbaɪəʊˌsɒlɪdz) *pl n* semisolid or solid organic material obtained from the recycling of sewage, used esp as a fertilizer

biosphere (ˈbaɪəˌsfɪə) *n* the part of the earth's surface and atmosphere inhabited by living things

biostatics (ˌbaɪəʊˈstætɪks) *n* (*functioning as singular*) the branch of biology that deals with the structure of organisms in relation to their function ▷ ˌbioˈstatic *adj* ▷ ˌbioˈstatically *adv*

biostrome (ˈbaɪəˌstrəʊm) *n* a rock layer consisting of a deposit of organic material, such as fossils [c20 from BIO- + Greek *strōma* covering]

biosurgery (ˈbaɪəʊˌsɜːdʒərɪ) *n* the use of live sterile maggots to treat patients with infected wounds

biosynthesis (ˌbaɪəʊˈsɪnθɪsɪs) *n* the formation of complex compounds from simple substances by living organisms ▷ **biosynthetic** (ˌbaɪəʊsɪnˈθɛtɪk) *adj* ▷ ˌbiosynˈthetically *adv*

biosystematics (ˌbaɪəʊˌsɪstɪˈmætɪks) *n* (*functioning as singular*) the study of the variation and evolution of a population of organisms in relation to their taxonomic classification

biota (baɪˈəʊtə) *n* the plant and animal life of a particular region or period [c20 from New Latin, from Greek *biotē* way of life, from *bios* life]

biotech (ˈbaɪəʊˌtɛk) *n* **a** short for **biotechnology b** (*as modifier*): *a biotech company*

biotechnology (ˌbaɪəʊtɛkˈnɒlədʒɪ) *n* **1** (in industry) the technique of using microorganisms, such as bacteria, to perform chemical processing, such as waste recycling, or to produce other materials, such as beer and wine, cheese, antibiotics, and (using genetic engineering) hormones, vaccines, etc **2** another name for **ergonomics**. ▷ **biotechnological** (ˌbaɪəʊˌtɛknəˈlɒdʒɪkˀl) *adj* ▷ ˌbioˌtechnoˈlogically *adv* ▷ ˌbiotechˈnologist *n*

biotelemetry (ˌbaɪəʊtɪˈlɛmɪtrɪ) *n* the monitoring of biological functions in humans or animals by means of a miniature transmitter that sends data to a distant point to be read by electronic instruments ▷ **biotelemetric** (ˌbaɪəʊtɛlɪˈmɛtrɪk) *adj*

bio-terrorism or **bio-terror** *n* the use of living organisms and their toxic products to kill or incapacitate, esp as a political weapon ▷ ˈbio-ˌterrorist *adj*, *n*

biotic (baɪˈɒtɪk) *adj* **1** of or relating to living

organisms **2** (of a factor in an ecosystem) produced by the action of living organisms. Compare **edaphic** [c17 from Greek *biotikos*, from *bios* life]

biotin (ˈbaɪətɪn) *n* a vitamin of the B complex, abundant in egg yolk and liver, deficiency of which causes dermatitis and loss of hair. Formula: $C_{10}H_{16}N_2O_3S$. See also **avidin** [c20 *biot-* from Greek *biotē* life, way of life + -IN]

biotite (ˈbaɪəˌtaɪt) *n* a black or dark green mineral of the mica group, found in igneous and metamorphic rocks. Composition: hydrous magnesium iron potassium aluminium silicate. Formula: $K(Mg,Fe)_3(Al,Fe)Si_3O_{10}(OH)_2$. Crystal structure: monoclinic ▷ **biotitic** (ˌbaɪəˈtɪtɪk) *adj*

biotope (ˈbaɪəˌtəʊp) *n* *ecology* a small area, such as the bark of a tree, that supports its own distinctive community [c20 from BIO- + Greek *topos* place]

biotroph (ˈbaɪəʊˌtrəʊf) *n* a parasitic organism, esp a fungus

biotype (ˈbaɪəˌtaɪp) *n* a group of genetically identical plants within a species, produced by apomixis. Also called: **microspecies** ▷ **biotypic** (ˌbaɪəˈtɪpɪk) *adj*

bio-warfare *n* another name for **biological warfare**

bioweapon (ˈbaɪəʊˌwɛpən) *n* a living organism or a toxic product manufactured from it, used to kill or incapacitate

biparietal (ˌbaɪpəˈraɪɪtˀl) *adj* *anatomy* relating to or connected to both parietal bones

biparous (ˈbɪpərəs) *adj* **1** *zoology* producing offspring in pairs **2** *botany* (esp of an inflorescence) producing two branches from one stem

bipartisan (ˌbaɪpɑːtɪˈzæn, baɪˈpɑːtɪˌzæn) *adj* consisting of or supported by two political parties ▷ ˌbipartiˈsanship *n*

bipartite (baɪˈpɑːtaɪt) *adj* **1** consisting of or having two parts **2** affecting or made by two parties; bilateral: *a bipartite agreement* **3** *botany* (esp of some leaves) divided into two parts almost to the base ▷ biˈpartitely *adv* ▷ **bipartition** (ˌbaɪpɑːˈtɪʃən) *n*

biped (ˈbaɪpɛd) *n* **1** any animal with two feet ▷ *adj* also **bipedal** (baɪˈpiːdˀl, -ˈpɛdˀl) **2** having two feet

bipetalous (baɪˈpɛtələs) *adj* having two petals

biphasic (baɪˈfeɪzɪk) *adj* **1** having two phases **2** See **two-phase**

biphenyl (baɪˈfɛnˀl, -ˈfiː-) *n* **1** a white or colourless crystalline solid used as a heat-transfer agent, as a fungicide, as an antifungal food preservative (**E230**) on the skins of citrus fruit, and in the manufacture of dyes, etc. Formula: $C_6H_5C_6H_5$ **2** any substituted derivative of biphenyl. Also called: **diphenyl**

bipinnate (baɪˈpɪnˌeɪt) *adj* (of pinnate leaves) having the leaflets themselves divided into smaller leaflets ▷ biˈpinˌnately *adv*

biplane (ˈbaɪˌpleɪn) *n* a type of aeroplane having two sets of wings, one above the other. Compare **monoplane**

bipod (ˈbaɪpɒd) *n* a two-legged support or stand

bipolar (baɪˈpəʊlə) *adj* **1** having two poles: *a bipolar dynamo; a bipolar neuron* **2** relating to or found at the North and South Poles **3** having or characterized by two opposed opinions, natures, etc **4** (of a transistor) utilizing both majority and minority charge carriers **5** suffering from bipolar manic-depressive disorder ▷ bipoˈlarity *n*

bipolar manic-depressive disorder or **bipolar syndrome** *n* See **manic-depressive**

biprism (ˈbaɪˌprɪzəm) *n* a prism having a highly obtuse angle to facilitate beam splitting

bipropellant (ˌbaɪprəˈpɛlənt) *n* a rocket propellant consisting of two substances, usually a fuel and an oxidizer. Also called: **dipropellant**. Compare **monopropellant**

bipyramid (ˌbaɪˈpɪrəmɪd) *n* a geometrical form consisting of two pyramids with a common polygonal base

biquadrate (baɪˈkwɒdreɪt, -rɪt) *n* *maths* the fourth power

biquadratic (ˌbaɪkwɒˈdrætɪk) *maths* ▷ *adj* Also **quartic 1** of or relating to the fourth power ▷ *n* **2** a biquadratic equation, such as $x^4 + x + 6 = 0$

biquarterly (baɪˈkwɔːtəlɪ) *adj* occurring twice every three months

biracial (baɪˈreɪʃəl) *adj* for, representing, or including members of two races, esp White and Black ▷ biˈracialism *n* ▷ biˈracially *adv*

biradial (baɪˈreɪdɪəl) *adj* showing both bilateral and radial symmetry, as certain sea anemones

biramous (ˈbaɪrəməs) *adj* divided into two parts, as the appendages of crustaceans

birch (bɜːtʃ) *n* **1** any betulaceous tree or shrub of the genus *Betula*, having thin peeling bark. See also **silver birch 2** the hard close-grained wood of any of these trees **3 the birch** a bundle of birch twigs or a birch rod used, esp formerly, for flogging offenders ▷ *adj* **4** of, relating to, or belonging to the birch **5** consisting or made of birch ▷ *vb* **6** (*tr*) to flog with a birch [Old English *bierce*; related to Old High German *birihha*, Sanskrit *bhūrja*] ▷ ˈbirchen *adj*

birchbark biting (ˈbɜːtʃˌbɑːk) *n* a Native Canadian craft in which designs are bitten onto bark from birch trees

Bircher (ˈbɜːtʃə), **Birchist** or **Birchite** *n* a member or supporter of the John Birch Society ▷ ˈBirchˌism *n*

bird (bɜːd) *n* **1** any warm-blooded egg-laying vertebrate of the class *Aves*, characterized by a body covering of feathers and forelimbs modified as wings. Birds vary in size between the ostrich and the humming bird. Related adjectives: **avian, ornithic 2** *informal* a person (usually preceded by a qualifying adjective, as in the phrases **rare bird, odd bird, clever bird**) **3** *slang, chiefly Brit* a girl or young woman, esp one's girlfriend **4** *slang* prison or a term in prison (esp in the phrase **do bird**; shortened from *birdlime*, rhyming slang for *time*) **5 a bird in the hand** something definite or certain **6 the bird has flown** *informal* the person in question has fled or escaped **7 the birds and the bees** *euphemistic* or *jocular* sex and sexual reproduction **8 birds of a feather** people with the same characteristics, ideas, interests, etc **9 get the bird** *informal* **a** to be fired or dismissed **b** (esp of a public performer) to be hissed at, booed, or derided **10 give (someone) the bird** *informal* to tell (someone) rudely to depart; scoff at; hiss **11 kill two birds with one stone** to accomplish two things with one action **12 like a bird** without resistance or difficulty **13 a little bird** a (supposedly) unknown informant: *a little bird told me it was your birthday* **14** (**strictly**) **for the birds** *informal* deserving of disdain or contempt; not important [Old English *bridd*, of unknown origin] ▷ ˈbirdlike *adj*

birdbath (ˈbɜːdˌbɑːθ) *n* a small basin or trough for birds to bathe in, usually in a garden

bird-brained *adj informal* silly; stupid

birdcage (ˈbɜːdˌkeɪdʒ) *n* **1** a wire or wicker cage in which captive birds are kept **2** any object of a similar shape, construction, or purpose **3** *Austral and NZ* an area on a racecourse where horses parade before a race

bird call *n* **1** the characteristic call or song of a bird **2** an imitation of this **3** an instrument imitating the call of a bird, used esp by hunters or bird-catchers

bird-catcher tree *n* another name for **parapara**

bird cherry *n* a small Eurasian rosaceous tree, *Prunus padus*, with clusters of white flowers and small black fruits. See also **cherry** (sense 1)

bird colonel *n* *US military slang* a full colonel in the US Army [from the eagle insignia of rank]

bird dog *US and Canadian* ▷ *n* **1** *hunting* a dog used or trained to retrieve game birds after they are shot ▷ *vb* **bird-dog -dogs, -dogging, -dogged 2** *informal* to control closely with unceasing vigilance

bird flu *n* a form of influenza occurring in poultry mainly in Japan, China and Southeast Asia, caused by a virus capable of spreading to humans. Also called: avian flu

birdhouse ('bɜːd,haʊs) *n US* **1** a small shelter or box for birds to nest in **2** an enclosure or large cage for captive birds; aviary

birdie ('bɜːdɪ) *n* **1** *golf* a score of one stroke under par for a hole **2** *informal* a bird, esp a small bird ▷ *vb* **3** (*tr*) *golf* to play (a hole) in one stroke under par

birding ('bɜːdɪŋ) *n* another name for **bird-watching**. > 'birder *n*

birdlime ('bɜːd,laɪm) *n* **1** a sticky substance, prepared from holly, mistletoe, or other plants, smeared on twigs to catch small birds ▷ *vb* **2** (*tr*) to smear (twigs) with birdlime to catch (small birds)

birdman ('bɜːd,mæn, -mən) *n, pl* **-men 1** a man concerned with birds, such as a fowler or ornithologist **2** a man who attempts to fly using his own muscle power **3** an obsolete informal name for **airman**

bird-nesting *or* **birds'-nesting** *n* searching for birds' nests as a hobby, often to steal the eggs

bird of paradise *n* **1** any songbird of the family *Paradisaeidae* of New Guinea and neighbouring regions, the males of which have brilliantly coloured ornate plumage **2** **bird-of-paradise flower** any of various banana-like plants of the genus *Strelitzia*, esp *S. reginae*, that are native to tropical southern Africa and South America and have purple bracts and large orange or yellow flowers resembling birds' heads: family *Strelitziaceae*

bird of passage *n* **1** a bird that migrates seasonally **2** a transient person or one who roams about

bird of peace *n* a figurative name for **dove¹** (sense 1)

bird of prey *n* a bird, such as a hawk, eagle, or owl, that hunts and kills other animals, esp vertebrates, for food. It has strong talons and a sharp hooked bill. Related adjective: **raptorial**

bird pepper *n* **1** a tropical solanaceous plant, *Capsicum frutescens*, thought to be the ancestor of the sweet pepper and many hot peppers **2** the narrow podlike hot-tasting fruit of this plant

birdseed ('bɜːd,siːd) *n* a mixture of various kinds of seeds for feeding cagebirds. Also called: canary seed

bird's-eye *adj* **1 a** seen or photographed from high above **b** summarizing the main points of a topic; summary (esp in the phrase **bird's-eye view**) **2** having markings resembling birds' eyes ▷ *n* **3** **bird's-eye primrose** a Eurasian primrose, *Primula farinosa*, having clusters of purplish flowers with yellow centres **4** **bird's-eye speedwell** the usual US name for **germander speedwell 5** any of several other plants having flowers of two contrasting colours **6** a pattern in linen and cotton fabrics, made up of small diamond shapes with a dot in the centre of each **7** a linen or cotton fabric with such a pattern

bird's-eye chilli *n* a small red hot-tasting chilli

bird's-foot *or* **bird-foot** *n, pl* **-foots 1** a European leguminous plant, *Ornithopus perpusillus*, with small red-veined white flowers and curved pods resembling a bird's claws **2** any of various other plants whose flowers, leaves, or pods resemble a bird's foot or claw

bird's-foot trefoil *n* any of various creeping leguminous Eurasian plants of the genus *Lotus*, esp *L. corniculatus*, with red-tipped yellow flowers and seed pods resembling the claws of a bird. Also called: bacon-and-eggs

birdshot ('bɜːd,ʃɒt) *n* small pellets designed for shooting birds

bird's-nest *vb* (*intr*) to search for the nests of birds in order to collect the eggs

bird's-nest fungus *n* any fungus of the family *Nidulariaceae*, having a nestlike spore-producing

body containing egglike spore-filled structures

bird's-nest orchid *n* **1** a brown parasitic Eurasian orchid, *Neottia nidus-avis*, whose thick fleshy roots resemble a bird's nest and contain a fungus on which the orchid feeds **2** a parasitic Eurasian plant, *Monotropa hypopitys*, whose thick fleshy roots resemble a bird's nest and contain a fungus on which the plant feeds: family *Monotropaceae*

bird's-nest soup *n* a rich spicy Chinese soup made from the outer part of the nests of SE Asian swifts of the genus *Collocalia*

birdsong ('bɜːd,sɒŋ) *n* the musical call of a bird or birds

bird spider *n* any large hairy predatory bird-eating spider of the family *Aviculariidae*, of tropical America

bird strike *n* a collision of an aircraft with a bird

bird table *n* a table or platform in the open on which food for birds may be placed

bird-watcher *n* a person who studies wild birds in their natural surroundings > 'bird-,watching *n*

birefringence (,baɪrɪ'frɪndʒəns) *n* another name for **double refraction**. > ,bire'fringent *adj*

bireme ('baɪriːm) *n* an ancient galley having two banks of oars [c17 from Latin *birēmus*, from BI-¹ + -*rēmus* oar]

biretta *or* **berretta** (bɪ'rɛtə) *n RC Church* a stiff clerical cap having either three or four upright pieces projecting outwards from the centre to the edge: coloured black for priests, purple for bishops, red for cardinals, and white for certain members of religious orders [c16 from Italian *berretta*, from Old Provençal *berret*, from Late Latin *birrus* hooded cape]

biriani (,bɪrɪ'ɑːnɪ) *n* a variant spelling of **biryani**

birk (bɪrk, bɜːk) *chiefly Scot* ▷ *n* **1** a birch tree **2** (*plural*) a birch wood ▷ *adj* **3** consisting of or made of birch [c14 from Old Norse; compare BIRCH]

Birkenhead (,bɜːkən'hɛd) *n* a port in NW England, in Wirral unitary authority, Merseyside: former shipbuilding centre. Pop: 83 729 (2001)

birkie ('bɪrkɪ) *n Scot* **1** a spirited or lively person **2** a foolish posturer [c18 perhaps related to Old English *beorcan* to bark; compare Old Norse *berkia*]

birl¹ (bɜːl; *Scot* bɪrl) *vb* **1** *Scot* to spin; twirl **2** *US and Canadian* to cause (a floating log) to spin using the feet while standing on it, esp as a sport among lumberjacks ▷ *n* **3** a variant spelling of **burl²** [c18 probably imitative and influenced by WHIRL and HURL] > 'birling *n*

birl² (bɜːl; *Scot* bɪrl) *vb archaic, Scot* to ply (one's guests, etc) with drink [Old English *byrelian*; related to *byrele* cup-bearer]

Birman ('bɜːmən) *n* a breed of large long-haired cat having a light-coloured coat with dark face, tail, and legs, and white feet [variant of *Burman*, a Burmese cat]

Birmingham ('bɜːmɪŋəm) *n* **1** an industrial city in central England, in Birmingham unitary authority, in the West Midlands: the second largest city in Great Britain; two cathedrals; three universities (1900, 1966, 1992). Pop: 970 892 (2001). Related adjective: (*informal*) **Brummie 2** a unitary authority in central England, in the West Midlands. Pop: 992 100 (2003 est). Area: 283 sq km (109 sq miles) **3** ('bɜːmɪŋ,hæm) an industrial city in N central Alabama: rich local deposits of coal, iron ore, and other minerals. Pop: 236 620 (2003 est)

Biro ('baɪrəʊ) *n, pl* **-ros** *trademark Brit* a kind of ballpoint [c20 named after Laszlo *Bíró* (1900–85), Hungarian inventor]

Birobidzhan *or* **Birobijan** (*Russian* birəbid'ʒan) *n* **1** a city in SE Russia: capital of the Jewish Autonomous Region. Pop: 82 000 (1994) **2** another name for the **Jewish Autonomous Region**

birr¹ (bɜː) *chiefly US and Scot* ▷ *vb* **1** to make or cause to make a whirring sound ▷ *n* **2** a whirring sound **3** force, as of wind **4** vigour; energy [Old English *byre* storm, related to Old Norse *byrr* favourable wind]

birr² (bɜː) *n* the standard monetary unit of

Ethiopia, divided into 100 cents [c20 from Amharic]

birth (bɜːθ) *n* **1** the process of bearing young; parturition; childbirth. Related adjective: **natal 2** the act or fact of being born; nativity **3** the coming into existence of something; origin **4** ancestry; lineage: *of high birth* **5** noble ancestry: *a man of birth* **6** natural or inherited talent: *an artist by birth* **7** *archaic* the offspring or young born at a particular time or of a particular mother **8** **give birth (to) a** to bear (offspring) **b** to produce, originate, or create (an idea, plan, etc) ▷ *vb* (*tr*) *rare* **9** to bear or bring forth (a child) [c12 from Old Norse *byrth*; related to Gothic *gabaurths*, Old Swedish *byrdh*, Old High German *berd* child; see BEAR¹, BAIRN]

birth certificate *n* an official form giving details of the time and place of a person's birth, and his or her name, sex, mother's name and (usually) father's name

birth control *n* limitation of child-bearing by means of contraception. See also **family planning**

birthday ('bɜːθ,deɪ) *n* **1 a** an anniversary of the day of one's birth **b** (*as modifier*): *birthday present* **2** the day on which a person was born **3** any anniversary

Birthday honours *pl n* (in Britain) honorary titles conferred on the official birthday of the sovereign

birthday suit *n informal, humorous* a state of total nakedness, as at birth

birthing ball *n* a large soft rubber ball used by women during childbirth to give support and to aid pain relief

birthing centre ('bɜːθɪŋ) *n NZ* a private maternity hospital

birthing chair *n* a chair constructed to allow a woman in labour to give birth in a sitting position

birthing pool *n* a large bath in which a woman can give birth

birthmark ('bɜːθ,mɑːk) *n* a blemish or new growth on skin formed before birth, usually brown or dark red; naevus

birth mother *n* the woman who gives birth to a child, regardless of whether she is the genetic mother or subsequently brings up the child

birthplace ('bɜːθ,pleɪs) *n* the place where someone was born or where something originated

birth rate *n* the ratio of live births in a specified area, group, etc, to the population of that area, etc, usually expressed per 1000 population per year

birthright ('bɜːθ,raɪt) *n* **1** privileges or possessions that a person has or is believed to be entitled to as soon as he is born **2** the privileges or possessions of a first-born son **3** inheritance; patrimony

birthroot ('bɜːθ,ruːt) *n* any of several North American plants of the genus *Trillium*, esp *T. erectum*, whose tuber-like roots were formerly used by the Native Americans as an aid in childbirth: family *Trilliaceae*

birthstone ('bɜːθ,stəʊn) *n* a precious or semiprecious stone associated with a month or sign of the zodiac and thought to bring luck if worn by a person born in that month or under that sign

birthwort ('bɜːθ,wɜːt) *n* any of several climbing plants of the genus *Aristolochia*, esp *A. clematitis* of Europe, once believed to ease childbirth: family *Aristolochiaceae*

biryani *or* **biriani** (,bɪrɪ'ɑːnɪ) *n* any of a variety of Indian dishes made with rice, highly flavoured and coloured with saffron or turmeric, mixed with meat or fish [from Urdu]

bis (bɪs) *adv* **1** twice; for a second time (used in musical scores to indicate a part to be repeated) ▷ *sentence substitute* **2** encore! again! [c19 via Italian from Latin, from Old Latin *duis*]

BIS 1 *abbreviation for* Bank for International Settlements: an institution, based in Basel, Switzerland, that accepts deposits, makes loans

b

for national central banks, and assists in offsetting speculative movements of funds between the major currencies; set up in 1930 **2** *International car registration for* Bosnia-Herzegovina

Bisayan (bɪˈsɑːjən) *n* a variant of **Visayan**

Bisayas (biˈsajas) *pl n* the Spanish name for the **Visayan Islands**

Biscay (ˈbɪskeɪ, -kɪ) *n* **Bay of**. a large bay of the Atlantic Ocean between W France and N Spain: notorious for storms

biscuit (ˈbɪskɪt) *n* **1** *Brit* a small flat dry sweet or plain cake of many varieties, baked from a dough. US and Canadian word: **cookie 2** *US and Canadian* a kind of small roll similar to a muffin **3 a** a pale brown or yellowish-grey colour **b** (*as adjective*): *biscuit gloves* **4** Also called: **bisque** earthenware or porcelain that has been fired but not glazed **5** **take the biscuit** *slang* to be regarded (by the speaker) as the most surprising thing that could have occurred [C14 from Old French, from (*pain*) *bescuit* twice-cooked (bread), from *bes* BIS + *cuire* to cook, from Latin *coquere*]

bise (biːz) *n* a cold dry northerly wind in Switzerland and the neighbouring parts of France and Italy, usually in the spring [C14 from Old French, of Germanic origin; compare Old Swedish *bisa* whirlwind]

bisect (baɪˈsɛkt) *vb* **1** (*tr*) *maths* to divide into two equal parts **2** to cut or split into two [C17 BI-¹ + *-sect* from Latin *secāre* to cut] > **bisection** (baɪˈsɛkʃən) *n*

bisector (baɪˈsɛktə) *n maths* **1** a straight line or plane that bisects an angle **2** a line or plane that bisects another line

bisectrix (baɪˈsɛktrɪks) *n, pl* **bisectrices** (baɪˈsɛktrɪˌsiːz) **1** another name for **bisector 2** the bisector of the angle between the optic axes of a crystal

biseriate (ˌbaɪˈsɪərɪɪt) *adj* (of plant parts, such as petals) arranged in two whorls, cycles, rows, or series

biserrate (baɪˈsɛreɪt, -ɪt) *adj* **1** *botany* (of leaf margins, etc) having serrations that are themselves serrate **2** *zoology* serrated on both sides, as the antennae of some insects

bi sex *n* sex with both male and female partners

bisexual (baɪˈsɛksjʊəl) *adj* **1** sexually attracted by both men and women **2** showing characteristics of both sexes: *a bisexual personality* **3** (of some plants and animals) having both male and female reproductive organs **4** of or relating to both sexes ▷ *n* **5** a bisexual organism; a hermaphrodite **6** a bisexual person > **bisexuality** (baɪˌsɛksjʊˈælɪtɪ) *or esp US* bi**'sexualism** *n* > bi**'sexually** *adv*

bish (bɪʃ) *n Brit slang* a mistake [C20 of unknown origin]

Bishkek (bɪʃˈkɛk) *n* the capital of Kyrgyzstan. Pop: 828 000 (2005 est). Also called: **Pishpek**. Former name (1926–91): **Frunze**

Bisho (ˈbɪʃəʊ) *n* a new town in S S Africa, on the Buffalo River adjacent to King Williams Town; the capital of Eastern Cape, it was formerly the capital of the Ciskei Bantustan: it is the centre of a sheep and cattle ranching area with various industries

bishop (ˈbɪʃəp) *n* **1** (in the Roman Catholic, Anglican, and Greek Orthodox Churches) a clergyman having spiritual and administrative powers over a diocese or province of the Church. See also **suffragan**. Related adjective: **episcopal 2** (in some Protestant Churches) a spiritual overseer of a local church or a number of churches **3** a chesspiece, capable of moving diagonally over any number of unoccupied squares of the same colour **4** mulled wine, usually port, spiced with oranges, cloves, etc [Old English *biscop*, from Late Latin *epīscopus*, from Greek *episkopos*, from EPI- + *skopos* watcher]

Bishop Auckland *n* a town in N England, in central Durham: seat of the bishops of Durham since the 12th century: light industries. Pop: 24 764 (2001)

bishopbird (ˈbɪʃəpˌbɜːd) *n* any African weaverbird of the genus *Euplectes* (or *Pyromelana*), the males of which have black plumage marked with red or yellow

bishopric (ˈbɪʃəprɪk) *n* the see, diocese, or office of a bishop

bishop's-cap *n* another name for **mitrewort**

bishop sleeve *n* a full sleeve gathered at the wrist

bishop's mitre *n* a European heteropterous bug, *Aelia acuminata*, whose larvae are a pest of cereal grasses: family *Pentatomidae*

bishop's weed *n* another name for **goutweed**

Bisitun (ˌbiːsɪˈtuːn) *n* another name for **Behistun**

bisk (bɪsk) *n* a less common spelling of **bisque**¹

Bisk (*Russian* bijsk) *n* a variant spelling of **Biysk**

Biskra (ˈbɪskrɑː) *n* a town and oasis in NE Algeria, in the Sahara. Pop: 204 000 (2005 est)

Bisley (ˈbɪzlɪ) *n* a village in SE England, in Surrey: annual meetings of the National Rifle Association

Bismarck (ˈbɪzmɑːk) *n* a city in North Dakota, on the Missouri River: the state capital. Pop: 56 344 (2003 est)

Bismarck Archipelago *n* a group of over 200 islands in the SW Pacific, northeast of New Guinea: part of Papua New Guinea. Main islands: New Britain, New Ireland, Lavongai, and the Admiralty Islands. Chief town: Rabaul, on New Britain. Pop: 424 000 (1995 est). Area: 49 658 sq km (19 173 sq miles)

Bismarck herring *n* marinaded herring, served cold

Bismillah (ˌbɪsmɪˈlɑː) *interj* the words which preface all except one of the surahs of the Koran, used by Muslims as a blessing before eating or some other action [shortened from *Bismillah-ir-Rahman-ir-Rahim*, from Arabic, literally: in the name of God, the merciful and compassionate]

bismuth (ˈbɪzməθ) *n* a brittle pinkish-white crystalline metallic element having low thermal and electrical conductivity, which expands on cooling. It is widely used in alloys, esp low-melting alloys in fire safety devices; its compounds are used in medicines. Symbol: Bi; atomic no.: 83; atomic wt.: 208.98037; valency: 3 or 5; relative density: 9.747; melting pt.: 271.4°C; boiling pt.: 1564±5°C [C17 from New Latin *bisemūtum*, from German *Wismut*, of unknown origin] > **bismuthal** (ˈbɪzməθəl) *adj*

bismuthic (bɪzˈmjuːθɪk, -ˈmʌθɪk) *adj* of or containing bismuth in the pentavalent state

bismuthinite (bɪzˈmʌθɪˌnaɪt) *or* **bismuth glance** *n* a grey mineral consisting of bismuth sulphide in orthorhombic crystalline form. It occurs in veins associated with tin, copper, silver, lead, etc, and is a source of bismuth. Formula: Bi_2S_3

bismuthous (ˈbɪzməθəs) *adj* of or containing bismuth in the trivalent state

bison (ˈbaɪsən) *n, pl* **-son 1** Also called: **American bison, buffalo** a member of the cattle tribe, *Bison bison*, formerly widely distributed over the prairies of W North America but now confined to reserves and parks, with a massive head, shaggy forequarters, and a humped back **2** Also called: **wisent, European bison** a closely related and similar animal, *Bison bonasus*, formerly widespread in Europe [C14 from Latin *bisōn*, of Germanic origin; related to Old English *wesand*, Old Norse *vīsundr*]

bisphosphonate (ˌbɪsˈfɒsfəneɪt) *n* any drug of a class that inhibits the resorption of bone; used in treating certain bone disorders, esp osteoporosis

bisque¹ (bɪsk) *n* a thick rich soup made from shellfish [C17 from French]

bisque² (bɪsk) *n* **1 a** a pink to yellowish tan colour **b** (*as modifier*): *a bisque tablecloth* **2** *ceramics* another name for **biscuit** (sense 4) [C20 shortened from BISCUIT]

bisque³ (bɪsk) *n tennis, golf, croquet* an extra point, stroke, or turn allowed to an inferior player, usually taken when desired [C17 from French, of obscure origin]

Bissau (bɪˈsaʊ) *or* **Bissão** (*Portuguese* biˈs[˜ə]ʊ) *n* a port on the Atlantic, the capital of Guinea-Bissau (until 1974 Portuguese Guinea). Pop: 369 000 (2005 est)

bissextile (bɪˈsɛkstaɪl) *adj* **1** (of a month or year) containing the extra day of a leap year ▷ *n* **2** a rare name for **leap year** [C16 from Late Latin *bissextilis annus* leap year, from Latin *bissextus*, from BI-¹ + *sextus* sixth; referring to February 24, the 6th day before the Calends of March]

bist (bɪst) *vb archaic or dialect* a form of the second person singular of **be**

bistable (baɪˈsteɪbᵊl) *adj* **1** having two stable states: *bistable circuit* ▷ *n* **2** *computing* another name for **flip-flop** (sense 2)

Bisto (ˈbɪstəʊ) *n trademark* a preparation for thickening, flavouring, and browning gravy

bistort (ˈbɪstɔːt) *n* **1** Also called: **snakeroot, snakeweed, Easter-ledges** a Eurasian polygonaceous plant, *Polygonum bistorta*, having leaf stipules fused to form a tube around the stem and a spike of small pink flowers **2** Also called: **snakeroot** a related plant, *Polygonum bistortoides*, of W North America, with oval clusters of pink or white flowers **3** any of several other plants of the genus *Polygonum* [C16 from French *bistorte*, from Latin *bis* twice + *tortus* from *torquēre* to twist]

bistoury (ˈbɪstərɪ) *n, pl* **-ries** a long surgical knife with a narrow blade [C15 from Old French *bistorie* dagger, of unknown origin]

bistre *or US* **bister** (ˈbɪstə) *n* **1** a transparent water-soluble brownish-yellow pigment made by boiling the soot of wood, used for pen and wash drawings **2 a** a yellowish-brown to dark brown colour **b** (*as modifier*): *bistre paint* [C18 from French, of unknown origin]

bistro (ˈbiːstrəʊ) *n, pl* **-tros** a small restaurant [French: of obscure origin; perhaps from Russian *bistro* fast]

bisulcate (baɪˈsʌlˌkeɪt) *adj* **1** marked by two grooves **2** *zoology* **a** cleft or cloven, as a hoof **b** having cloven hoofs

bisulphate (baɪˈsʌlˌfeɪt) *n* **1** a salt or ester of sulphuric acid containing the monovalent group $-HSO_4$ or the ion HSO_4^- **2** (*modifier*) consisting of, containing, or concerned with the group $-HSO_4$ or the ion HSO_4^-: *bisulphate ion* ▷ Systematic name: **hydrogen sulphate**

bisulphide (baɪˈsʌlfaɪd) *n* another name for **disulphide**

bisulphite (baɪˈsʌlfaɪt) *n* **1** a salt or ester of sulphurous acid containing the monovalent group $-HSO_3$ or the ion HSO_3^- **2** (*modifier*) consisting of or containing the group $-HSO_3$ or the ion HSO_3^-: *bisulphite ion* ▷ Systematic name: **hydrogen sulphite**

Bisutun (ˌbiːsʊˈtuːn) *n* another name for **Behistun**

bisymmetric (ˌbaɪsɪˈmɛtrɪk) *or* **bisymmetrical** *adj* **1** *botany* showing symmetry in two planes at right angles to each other **2** (of plants and animals) showing bilateral symmetry > ˌbisym'metrically *adv* > **bisymmetry** (baɪˈsɪmɪtrɪ) *n*

bit¹ (bɪt) *n* **1** a small piece, portion, or quantity **2** a short time or distance **3** *US and Canadian informal* the value of an eighth of a dollar: spoken of only in units of two: *two bits* **4** any small coin **5** short for **bit part 6** *informal* way of behaving, esp one intended to create a particular impression: *she's doing the prima donna bit* **7** **a bit** rather; somewhat: *a bit dreary* **8 a bit of a** rather: *a bit of a dope* **b** a considerable amount: *that must take quite a bit of courage* **9 a bit of all right, bit of crumpet, bit of stuff,** *or* **bit of tail** *Brit slang* a sexually attractive woman **10 bit by bit** gradually **11 bit on the side** *informal* an extramarital affair **12 do one's bit** to make one's expected contribution **13 every bit** (foll by *as*) to the same degree: *she was every bit as clever as her brother* **14 not a bit (of it)** not in the slightest; not at all **15 to bits** completely apart: *to fall to bits* [Old English *bite* action of biting; see BITE]

bit² (bɪt) *n* **1** a metal mouthpiece, for controlling a horse on a bridle **2** anything that restrains or curbs **3** take *or* have the bit in *or* between one's teeth **a** to undertake a task with determination **b** to rebel against control **4** a cutting or drilling tool, part, or head in a brace, drill, etc **5** the blade of a woodworking plane **6** the part of a pair of pincers designed to grasp an object **7** the copper end of a soldering iron **8** the part of a key that engages the levers of a lock ▷ *vb* bits, bitting, bitted (*tr*) **9** to put a bit in the mouth of (a horse) **10** to restrain; curb [Old English *bita*; related to Old English *bītan* to BITE]

bit³ (bɪt) *vb* the past tense and (archaic) past participle of **bite**

bit⁴ (bɪt) *n* *maths, computing* **1** a single digit of binary notation, represented either by 0 or by 1 **2** the smallest unit of information, indicating the presence or absence of a single feature **3** a unit of capacity of a computer, consisting of an element of its physical structure capable of being in either of two states, such as a switch with *on* and *off* positions, or a microscopic magnet capable of alignment in two directions [C20 from abbreviation of BINARY DIGIT]

bitartrate (baɪ'tɑːˌtreɪt) *n* (not in technical usage) a salt or ester of tartaric acid containing the monovalent group $-HC_4H_4O_6$ or the ion $HC_4H_4O_6^-$. Also called: hydrogen tartrate

bitch (bɪtʃ) *n* **1** a female dog or other female canine animal, such as a wolf **2** *slang, derogatory* a malicious, spiteful, or coarse woman **3** *informal* a complaint **4** *informal* a difficult situation or problem ▷ *vb informal* **5** (*intr*) to complain; grumble **6** to behave (towards) in a spiteful or malicious manner **7** (*tr*, often foll by *up*) to botch; bungle [Old English *bicce*]

bitchfest ('bɪtʃˌfɛst) *n* *slang* a malicious and spiteful discussion of people, events, etc

bitchin' ('bɪtʃɪn) *or* **bitching** ('bɪtʃɪŋ) *US slang* ▷ *adj* **1** wonderful or excellent ▷ *adv* **2** extremely: *bitchin' good*

bitch-slap *vb* -slaps, -slapped, -slapping (*tr*) *slang* to strike (someone) with one's open hand

bitchy ('bɪtʃɪ) *adj* bitchier, bitchiest *informal* characteristic of or behaving like a bitch; malicious; snide: *a bitchy put-down* > 'bitchily *adv* > 'bitchiness *n*

bite (baɪt) *vb* bites, biting, bit, bitten **1** to grip, cut off, or tear with or as if with the teeth or jaws **2** (of animals, insects, etc) to injure by puncturing or tearing (the skin or flesh) with the teeth, fangs, etc, esp as a natural characteristic **3** (*tr*) to cut or penetrate, as with a knife **4** (of corrosive material such as acid) to eat away or into **5** to smart or cause to smart; sting: *mustard bites the tongue* **6** (*intr*) *angling* (of a fish) to take or attempt to take the bait or lure **7** to take firm hold of or act effectively upon **8** to grip or hold (a workpiece) with a tool or chuck **9** (of a screw, thread, etc) to cut into or grip (an object, material, etc) **10** (*tr*) *informal* to annoy or worry: *what's biting her?* **11** (*often passive*) *slang* to cheat **12** (*tr*; often foll by *for*) *Austral and NZ slang* to ask (for); scrounge from **13** bite off more than one can chew *informal* to attempt a task beyond one's capability **14** bite the bullet to face up to (pain, trouble, etc) with fortitude; be stoical **15** bite someone's head off to respond harshly and rudely (to) **16** bite the dust See **dust** (sense 11) **17** bite the hand that feeds one to repay kindness with injury or ingratitude **18** once bitten, twice shy after an unpleasant experience one is cautious in similar situations **19** put the bite on (someone) *Austral slang* to ask (someone) for money ▷ *n* **20** the act of biting **21** a thing or amount bitten off **22** a wound, bruise, or sting inflicted by biting **23** *angling* an attempt by a fish to take the bait or lure **24** *informal* an incisive or penetrating effect or quality: *tthat's a question with a bite* **25** a light meal; snack **26** a cutting, stinging, or smarting sensation **27** the depth of cut of a machine tool **28** the grip or hold applied by a tool or chuck to a workpiece **29** *dentistry* the angle or manner of contact between the upper and lower teeth when the mouth is closed naturally **30** the surface of a file or rasp with cutting teeth **31** the corrosive action of acid, as on a metal etching plate [Old English *bītan*; related to Latin *findere* to split, Sanskrit *bhedati* he splits] > 'biter *n*

bite back *vb* (*tr, adverb*) to restrain (a hurtful, embarrassing, or indiscreet remark); avoid saying

Bithynia (bɪ'θɪnɪə) *n* an ancient country on the Black Sea in NW Asia Minor

biting ('baɪtɪŋ) *adj* **1** piercing; keen: *a biting wind* **2** sarcastic; incisive: *a biting comment* > 'bitingly *adv*

biting *or* **bird louse** *n* See **louse** (sense 2)

biting midge *n* any small fragile dipterous fly of the family *Ceratopogonidae*, most of which suck the blood of mammals, birds, or other insects

biting point *n* **1** (in driving) the point at which the plates of the clutch connect as the clutch pedal is released **2** a point at which success is achieved

bitmap ('bɪtˌmæp) *n* *computing* **1** a picture created on a visual display unit where each pixel corresponds to one or more bits in memory, the number of bits per pixel determining the number of available colours ▷ *vb* -maps, -mapping, -mapped **2** (*tr*) to create a bitmap of

bitmap font *n* *computing* a font format in which letters and symbols are stored as a pattern of dots. Compare **outline font**

Bitolj (*Serbo-Croat* 'bitolj) *or* **Bitola** ('biːtəʊlə) *n* a city in SW Macedonia: under Turkish rule from 1382 until 1913 when it was taken by the Serbs. Pop: 77 000 (2005 est)

bitou bush ('biːtəʊ) *n* a sprawling woody shrub, *Chrysanthemoides monilifera rotundata*, with oval green leaves and yellow daisy-like flowers. It is native to South Africa and considered an invasive species in Australia [from the *Bitou* river in South Africa]

bit part *n* a very small acting role with few lines to speak

bit rate *n* *computing* the rate of flow of binary digits in a digital data-processing system, usually expressed as the number of bits per second

bitser ('bɪtsə) *n* *Austral informal* a mongrel dog [C20 from *bits o'* bits of, as in *his dog is bits o' this and bits o' that*]

bit slice *adj* *computing* (of central processing units) able to be built up in sections to form complete central processing units with various word lengths

bitstock ('bɪtˌstɒk) *n* the handle or stock of a tool into which a drilling bit is fixed

bitstream ('bɪtˌstriːm) *n* *computing* a sequence of digital data transmitted electronically

bitt (bɪt) *nautical* ▷ *n* **1** one of a pair of strong posts on the deck of a ship for securing mooring and other lines **2** another word for **bollard** (sense 1) ▷ *vb* **3** (*tr*) to secure (a line) by means of a bitt [C14 probably of Scandinavian origin; compare Old Norse *biti* cross beam, Middle High German *bizze* wooden peg]

bitten ('bɪtᵊn) *vb* the past participle of **bite**

bitter ('bɪtə) *adj* **1** having or denoting an unpalatable harsh taste, as the peel of an orange or coffee dregs. Compare **sour** (sense 1) **2** showing or caused by strong unrelenting hostility or resentment: *he was still bitter about the divorce* **3** difficult or unpleasant to accept or admit: *a bitter blow* **4** cutting; sarcastic: *bitter words* **5** bitingly cold: *a bitter night* ▷ *adv* **6** very; extremely (esp in the phrase **bitter cold**) ▷ *n* **7** a thing that is bitter **8** *Brit* beer with a high hop content, with a slightly bitter taste ▷ *vb* **9** to make or become bitter ▷ See also **bitters** [Old English *biter*; related to *bītan* to BITE] > 'bitterly *adv* > 'bitterness *n*

bitter apple *n* another name for **colocynth**

bitterbark ('bɪtəˌbɑːk) *n* an Australian tree, *Alstonia constricta*, with bitter-tasting bark that is used in preparing tonic medicines

bittercress ('bɪtəˌkrɛs) *n* one of several perennial or annual plants of the genus *Cardamine*, that are related to lady's-smock, including **hairy bittercress** (*C. hirsuta*), a common weed resembling shepherd's purse, with which it is often confused: family: *Brassicaceae* (crucifers)

bitter end *n* **1** *nautical* the end of a line, chain, or cable, esp the end secured in the chain locker of a vessel **2** **a** to the bitter end until the finish of a task, job, or undertaking, however unpleasant or difficult **b** until final defeat or death [C19 in both senses perhaps from BITT]

Bitter Lakes *pl n* two lakes, the **Great Bitter Lake** and **Little Bitter Lake** in NE Egypt: part of the Suez Canal

bitterling ('bɪtəlɪŋ) *n* a small brightly coloured European freshwater cyprinid fish, *Rhodeus sericeus*: a popular aquarium fish [C19 from German; see BITTER + -LING¹]

bittern¹ ('bɪtən) *n* any wading bird of the genera *Ixobrychus* and *Botaurus*, related and similar to the herons but with shorter legs and neck, a stouter body, and a booming call: family *Ardeidae*, order *Ciconiiformes* [C14 from Old French *butor*, perhaps from Latin *būtiō* bittern + *taurus* bull; referring to its cry]

bittern² ('bɪtən) *n* the bitter liquid remaining after common salt has been crystallized out of sea water: a source of magnesium, bromine, and iodine compounds [C17 variant of *bittering*; see BITTER]

bitternut ('bɪtəˌnʌt) *n* **1** an E North American hickory tree, *Carya cordiformis*, with thin-shelled nuts and bitter kernels **2** the nut of this plant

bitter orange *n* another name for **Seville orange**

bitter principle *n* any of various bitter-tasting substances, such as aloin, usually extracted from plants

bitters ('bɪtəz) *pl n* **1** bitter-tasting spirits of varying alcoholic content flavoured with plant extracts **2** a similar liquid containing a bitter-tasting substance, used as a tonic to stimulate the appetite or improve digestion

bittersweet ('bɪtəˌswiːt) *n* **1** any of several North American woody climbing plants of the genus *Celastrus*, esp *C. scandens*, having orange capsules that open to expose scarlet-coated seeds: family *Celastraceae* **2** another name for **woody nightshade** ▷ *adj* **3** tasting of or being a mixture of bitterness and sweetness **4** pleasant but tinged with sadness

bitterweed ('bɪtəˌwiːd) *n* any of various plants that contain a bitter-tasting substance

bitterwood ('bɪtəˌwʊd) *n* any of several simaroubaceous trees of the genus *Picrasma* of S and SE Asia and the Caribbean, whose bitter bark and wood are used in medicine as a substitute for quassia

bitty ('bɪtɪ) *adj* -tier, -tiest **1** lacking unity; disjointed **2** containing bits, sediment, etc > 'bittiness *n*

bitumen ('bɪtjʊmɪn) *n* **1** any of various viscous or solid impure mixtures of hydrocarbons that occur naturally in asphalt, tar, mineral waxes, etc: used as a road surfacing and roofing material **2** the constituents of coal that can be extracted by an organic solvent **3** any liquid suitable for coating aggregates **4** the bitumen **a** *Austral and NZ informal* any road with a bitumen surface **b** (*capital*) *Austral informal* the road in the Northern Territory between Darwin and Alice Springs **5** a transparent brown pigment or glaze made from asphalt [C15 from Latin *bitūmen*, perhaps of Celtic origin] > bituminous (bɪ'tjuːmɪnəs) *adj*

bituminize *or* **bituminise** (bɪ'tjuːmɪˌnaɪz) *vb* (*tr*) to treat with or convert into bitumen > biˌtumini'zation *or* biˌtumini'sation *n*

bituminous coal *n* a soft black coal, rich in volatile hydrocarbons, that burns with a smoky yellow flame. Fixed carbon content: 46–86 per cent; calorific value: $1.93 \times 10^7 - 3.63 \times 10^7$ J/kg. Also called: soft coal

bivalence (baɪ'veɪləns, 'bɪvə-) *n* *logic, philosophy*

b

the semantic principle that there are exactly two truth values, so that every meaningful statement is either true or false. Compare **many-valued logic**

bivalent (baɪˈveɪlənt, ˈbɪvə-) *adj* **1** *chem* another word for **divalent 2** (of homologous chromosomes) associated together in pairs ▷ *n* **3** a structure formed during meiosis consisting of two homologous chromosomes associated together ▷ biˈvalency *n*

bivalve (ˈbaɪˌvælv) *n* **1** Also called: **pelecypod, amellibranch** any marine or freshwater mollusc of the class *Pelecypoda* (formerly *Bivalvia* or *Lamellibranchia*), having a laterally compressed body, a shell consisting of two hinged valves, and gills for respiration. The group includes clams, cockles, oysters, and mussels ▷ *adj* **2** Also: **pelecypod, lamellibranch** of, relating to, or belonging to the *Pelecypoda* **3** Also: **bivalvate** (baɪˈvælveɪt) *biology* having or consisting of two valves or similar parts: *a bivalve seed capsule* ▷ biˈvalvular *adj*

bivariate (baɪˈvɛərɪɪt) *adj statistics* (of a distribution) involving two random variables, not necessarily independent of one another

bivouac (ˈbɪvʊˌæk, ˈbɪvwæk) *n* **1** a temporary encampment with few facilities, as used by soldiers, mountaineers, etc ▷ *vb* **-acs, -acking, -acked 2** (*intr*) to make such an encampment [c18 from French *bivuac*, probably from Swiss German *Beiwacht*, literally: BY + WATCH]

bivvy (ˈbɪvɪ) *n, pl* **-vies** *slang* a small tent or shelter [c20 shortened from BIVOUAC]

biweekly (baɪˈwiːklɪ) *adj, adv* **1** every two weeks **2** (often avoided because of confusion with sense 1) twice a week; semiweekly. See **bi-¹** ▷ *n, pl* **-lies 3** a periodical published every two weeks

biyearly (baɪˈjɪəlɪ) *adj, adv* **1** every two years; biennial or biennially **2** (often avoided because of confusion with sense 1) twice a year; biannual or biannually. See **bi-¹**

Biysk, Biisk *or* **Bisk** (*Russian* bijsk) *n* a city in SW Russia, at the foot of the Altai Mountains. Pop: 216 000 (2005 est)

biz¹ (bɪz) *n informal* short for **business**

biz² *an internet domain name for* a business

bizarre (bɪˈzɑː) *adj* odd or unusual, esp in an interesting or amusing way [c17 from French: from Italian *bizzarro* capricious, of uncertain origin] ▷ biˈzarrely *adv* ▷ biˈzarreness *n*

bizarrerie (bɪˈzɑːrərɪ) *n* **1** the quality of being bizarre **2** a bizarre act

Bizerte (bɪˈzɜːtə; *French* bizɛrt) *or* **Bizerta** *n* a port in N Tunisia, on the Mediterranean at the canalized outlet of **Lake Bizerte**. Pop: 118 000 (2005 est)

bizzo (ˈbɪzəʊ) *n Austral informal* **1** empty and irrelevant talk or ideas; nonsense: *all that bizzo* **2** a businessman's club

bizzy (ˈbɪzɪ) *n, pl* **-zies** *Brit slang, chiefly Liverpudlian* a policeman [c20 from BUSY]

bj *the internet domain name for* Benin

B.J. (in the US and Canada) *abbreviation for* Bachelor of Journalism

Björneborg (bjœrnəˈbɔrj) *n* the Swedish name for **Pori**

bk *abbreviation for* **1** bank **2** book

Bk *the chemical symbol for* berkelium

bkcy *abbreviation for* bankruptcy

bkg *abbreviation for* banking

bkpt *abbreviation for* bankrupt

bks *abbreviation for* **1** barracks **2** books

bl *abbreviation for* barrel

BL *abbreviation for* **1** Bachelor of Law **2** Bachelor of Letters **3** Barrister-at-Law **4** British Library

B/L, b/l *or* **b.l.** *pl* Bs/L, bs/l *or* bs.l *abbreviation for* bill of lading

blab (blæb) *vb* blabs, blabbing, blabbed **1** to divulge (secrets) indiscreetly **2** (*intr*) to chatter thoughtlessly; prattle ▷ *n* **3** a less common word for **blabber** (senses 1, 2) [c14 of Germanic origin; compare Old High German *blabbizōn*, Icelandic *blabbra*] ▷ ˈblabbing *n, adj*

blabber (ˈblæbə) *n* **1** a person who blabs **2** idle chatter ▷ *vb* **3** (*intr*) to talk without thinking; chatter [c15 *blabberen*, probably of imitative origin]

blabbermouth (ˈblæbəˌmaʊθ) *n informal* a person who talks too much or indiscreetly

black (blæk) *adj* **1** of the colour of jet or carbon black, having no hue due to the absorption of all or nearly all incident light. Compare **white** (sense 1) **2** without light; completely dark **3** without hope or alleviation; gloomy: *the future looked black* **4** very dirty or soiled: *black factory chimneys* **5** angry or resentful: *she gave him black looks* **6** (of a play or other work) dealing with the unpleasant realities of life, esp in a pessimistic or macabre manner: *black comedy* **7** (of coffee or tea) without milk or cream **8** causing, resulting from, or showing great misfortune: *black areas of unemployment* **9 a** wicked or harmful: *a black lie* **b** (*in combination*): *black-hearted* **10** causing or deserving dishonour or censure: *a black crime* **11** (of the face) purple, as from suffocation **12** *Brit* (of goods, jobs, works, etc) being subject to boycott by trade unionists, esp in support of industrial action elsewhere ▷ *n* **13** a black colour **14** a dye or pigment of or producing this colour **15** black clothing, worn esp as a sign of mourning **16** *chess, draughts* **a** a black or dark-coloured piece or square **b** (*usually capital*) the player playing with such pieces **17** complete darkness: *the black of the night* **18** a black ball in snooker, etc **19** (in roulette and other gambling games) one of two colours on which players may place even bets, the other being red **20** **in the black** in credit or without debt **21** *archery* a black ring on a target, between the outer and the blue, scoring three points ▷ *vb* **22** another word for **blacken 23** (*tr*) to polish (shoes, etc) with blacking **24** (*tr*) to bruise so as to make black: *he blacked her eye* **25** (*tr*) *Brit, Austral, and NZ* (of trade unionists) to organize a boycott of (specified goods, jobs, work, etc), esp in support of industrial action elsewhere. ▷ See also **blackout** [Old English *blæc*; related to Old Saxon *blak* ink, Old High German *blakra* to blink] ▷ ˈblackish *adj* ▷ ˈblackishly *adv* ▷ ˈblackly *adv* ▷ ˈblackness *n*

Black (blæk) *n* **1** sometimes derogatory a member of a dark-skinned race, esp someone of Negroid or Australoid origin ▷ *adj* **2** of or relating to a Black or Blacks: *a Black neighbourhood*

blackamoor (ˈblækəˌmʊə, -ˌmɔː) *n archaic* a Black or other person with dark skin [c16 see BLACK, MOOR]

black-and-blue *adj* **1** (of the skin) discoloured, as from a bruise **2** feeling pain or soreness, as from a beating

black and tan *n* a mixture of stout or porter and ale

Black and Tans *pl n* **the.** a specially recruited armed auxiliary police force sent to Ireland in 1921 by the British Government to combat Sinn Féin [name suggested by the colour of their uniforms and the *Black and Tans* hunt in Munster]

black-and-tan terrier *n* a less common name for **Manchester terrier**

black-and-white *adj* **1 a** a photograph, picture, sketch, etc, in black, white, and shades of grey rather than in colour **b** (*as modifier*): *black-and-white film* **2** the neutral tones of black, white, and intermediate shades of grey. Compare **colour** (sense 2) **3 in black and white a** in print or writing **b** in extremes: *he always saw things in black and white*

black art *n* **the** another name for **black magic**

black-backed gull *n* either of two common black and-white European coastal gulls, *Larus fuscus* (**lesser black-backed gull**) and *L. marinus* (**great black-backed gull**) **2** Also called: **karoro** a southern gull, *larus dominicanus*, with black feathers on its back

blackball (ˈblækˌbɔːl) *n* **1** a negative vote or veto **2** a black wooden ball used to indicate disapproval or to veto in a vote **3** *NZ* a hard boiled sweet with black-and-white stripes ▷ *vb* (*tr*) **4** to vote against

in a ballot **5** to exclude (someone) from a group, profession, etc; ostracize [c18 see sense 2]

black bass (bæs) *n* any of several predatory North American percoid freshwater game fishes of the genus *Micropterus*: family *Centrarchidae* (sunfishes, etc)

black bean *n* an Australian leguminous tree, *Castanospermum australe*, having thin smooth bark and yellow or reddish flowers: used in furniture manufacture. Also called: **Moreton Bay chestnut**

black bear *n* **1 American black bear** a bear, *Euarctos* (or *Ursus*) *americanus*, inhabiting forests of North America. It is smaller and less ferocious than the brown bear **2 Asiatic black bear** a bear, *Selenarctos thibetanus*, of central and E Asia, whose coat is black with a pale V-shaped mark on the chest

black beetle *n* **1** another name for the **oriental cockroach** (see **cockroach**) **2** *NZ* another name for **Māori bug**

black belt *n* **1** *martial Arts* **a** a black belt worn by an instructor or expert competitor in the dan grades, usually from first to fifth dan **b** a person entitled to wear this **2 the** a region of the southern US extending from Georgia across central Alabama and Mississippi, in which the population contains a large number of Blacks: also noted for its fertile black soil

blackberry (ˈblækbərɪ) *n, pl* **-ries 1** Also called: **bramble** any of several woody plants of the rosaceous genus *Rubus*, esp *R. fruticosus*, that have thorny stems and black or purple glossy edible berry-like fruits (drupelets) **2 a** the fruit of any of these plants **b** (*as modifier*): *blackberry jam* **3 blackberry lily** an ornamental Chinese iridaceous plant, *Belamcanda chinensis*, that has red-spotted orange flowers and clusters of black seeds that resemble blackberries ▷ *vb* **-ries, -rying, -ried 4** (*intr*) to gather blackberries

BlackBerry *or* **Blackberry** *n trademark* a handheld device for sending and receiving e-mail

black bile *n archaic* one of the four bodily humours; melancholy. See **humour** (sense 8)

black bindweed *n* a twining polygonaceous European plant, *Polygonum convolvulus*, with heart-shaped leaves and triangular black seed pods

blackbird (ˈblækˌbɜːd) *n* **1** a common European thrush, *Turdus merula*, in which the male has a black plumage and yellow bill and the female is brown **2** any of various American orioles having a dark plumage, esp any of the genus *Agelaius* **3** *history* a person, esp a South Sea Islander, who was kidnapped and sold as a slave, esp in Australia ▷ *vb* **4** (*tr*) (formerly) to kidnap and sell into slavery

Black Bloc *or* **Black Block** *n* an informal grouping of militant, mainly anarchist, protesters who act together during anti-capitalism, anti-war, etc, protests, often wearing black hoods and black clothing

blackboard (ˈblækˌbɔːd) *n* a hard or rigid surface made of a smooth usually dark substance, used for writing or drawing on with chalk, esp in teaching

black body *n physics* a hypothetical body that would be capable of absorbing all the electromagnetic radiation falling on it. Also called: **full radiator**

black book *n* **1** a book containing the names of people to be punished, blacklisted, etc **2 in someone's black books** *informal* out of favour with someone

black bottom *n* a dance of the late 1920s that originated in America, involving a sinuous rotation of the hips

black box *n* **1** a self-contained unit in an electronic or computer system whose circuitry need not be known to understand its function **2** an informal name for **flight recorder**

black boy *or* **blackboy** (ˈblækˌbɔɪ) *n* another name for **grass tree** (sense 1)

black bread *n* a kind of very dark coarse rye bread

black bream *n* **1** another name for **luderick** **2** a dark-coloured food and game fish, *Acanthopagrus australis*, of E Australian seas

black bryony *n* a climbing herbaceous Eurasian plant, *Tamus communis*, having small greenish flowers and poisonous red berries: family *Dioscoreaceae*

blackbuck ('blæk,bʌk) *n* an Indian antelope, *Antilope cervicapra*, the male of which has spiral horns, a dark back, and a white belly

black bun *n Scot* a very rich dark fruitcake, usually in a pastry case. Also called: **currant bun**

Blackburn ('blækbɜːn) *n* **1** a city in NW England, in Blackburn with Darwen unitary authority, Lancashire: formerly important for textiles, now has mixed industries. Pop: 105 085 (2001) **2** **Mount.** a mountain in SE Alaska, the highest peak in the Wrangell Mountains. Height: 5037 m (16 523 ft)

Blackburn with Darwen ('dɑːwɛn) *n* a unitary authority in NW England, in Lancashire. Pop: 139 800 (2003 est). Area: 137 sq km (53 sq miles)

blackbutt ('blæk,bʌt) *n* any of various Australian eucalyptus trees having rough fibrous bark and hard wood used as timber

blackcap ('blæk,kæp) *n* **1** a brownish-grey Old World warbler, *Sylvia atricapilla*, the male of which has a black crown **2** any of various similar birds, such as the black-capped chickadee (*Parus atricapillus*) **3** *US* a popular name for **raspberry** (sense 3) **4** *Brit* (formerly) the cap worn by a judge when passing a death sentence

black cap *n* another name for **white-fronted tern**

Black Caps *pl n* **the.** the international cricket team of New Zealand [c20 so named because of the players' black caps]

black-coated *adj Brit* (esp formerly) (of a worker) clerical or professional, as distinguished from commercial or industrial

blackcock ('blæk,kɒk) *n* the male of the black grouse. Also called: **heath cock** Compare **greyhen**

Black Country *n* **the.** the formerly heavily industrialized region of central England, northwest of Birmingham

black cuckoo *n Austral* another name for **koel**

blackcurrant (,blæk'kʌrənt) *n* **1** a N temperate shrub, *Ribes nigrum*, having red or white flowers and small edible black berries: family *Grossulariaceae* **2 a** the fruit of this shrub **b** (*as modifier*): *blackcurrant jelly*

blackdamp ('blæk,dæmp) *n* air that is low in oxygen content and high in carbon dioxide as a result of an explosion in a mine. Also called: **chokedamp**

Black Death *n* **the.** a form of bubonic plague pandemic in Europe and Asia during the 14th century, when it killed over 50 million people. See **bubonic plague**

black diamond *n* **1** another name for **carbonado²** **2** (*usually plural*) a figurative expression for **coal**

black disc *n* a conventional black vinyl gramophone record as opposed to a compact disc

black disease *n vet science* an infectious necrotic hepatitis in sheep and occasionally cattle caused by to toxins produced by infection with species of *Clostridial*. Secondary to liver fluke infestation, the disease is characterized by sudden death. So-called because of the black discolouration of subcutaneous tissues due to congestion and haemorrhage seen at post-mortem

black dog *n informal* depression or melancholy

black earth *n* another name for **chernozem**

black economy *n* that portion of the income of a nation that remains illegally undeclared either as a result of payment in kind or as a means of tax avoidance

blacken ('blækən) *vb* **1** to make or become black or dirty **2** (*tr*) to defame; slander (esp in the phrase **blacken someone's name**)

black eye *n* bruising round the eye

black-eyed pea *n* another name for **cowpea** (sense 2)

black-eyed Susan *n* **1** any of several North American plants of the genus *Rudbeckia*, esp *R. hirta*, having flower heads of orange-yellow rays and brown-black centres: family *Asteraceae* (composites) **2** a climbing plant, *Thunbergia alata*, native to tropical Africa but widely naturalized elsewhere, having yellow flowers with purple centres, grown as a greenhouse annual

blackface ('blæk,feɪs) *n* **1 a** a performer made up to imitate a Black person **b** the make-up used by such a performer, usually consisting of burnt cork **2** a breed of sheep having a dark face

Black Ferns *pl n* **the** the women's international Rugby Union football team of New Zealand

blackfish ('blæk,fɪʃ) *n, pl* -fish, -fishes **1** a minnow-like Alaskan freshwater fish, *Dallia pectoralis*, related to the pikes and thought to be able to survive prolonged freezing **2** a female salmon that has recently spawned. Compare **redfish** (sense 1) **3** any of various other dark fishes, esp the luderick, a common edible Australian estuary fish **4** another name for **pilot whale**

black flag *n* another name for the **Jolly Roger**

blackfly ('blæk,flaɪ) *n, pl* -flies a black aphid, *Aphis fabae*, that infests beans, sugar beet, and other plants. Also called: **bean aphid**

black fly *n* any small blackish stout-bodied dipterous fly of the family *Simuliidae*, which sucks the blood of man, mammals, and birds. See also **buffalo gnat**

Blackfoot ('blæk,fʊt) *n* **1** (*pl* -feet or -foot) a member of a group of Native American peoples formerly living in the northwestern Plains **2** any of the languages of these peoples, belonging to the Algonquian family [c19 translation of Blackfoot *Siksika*]

Black Forest *n* **the.** a hilly wooded region of SW Germany, in Baden-Württemberg: a popular resort area. German name: **Schwarzwald**

Black Friar *n* a Dominican friar

black frost *n* a frost without snow or rime that is severe enough to blacken vegetation

black game *n* another name for **black grouse** (sense 1)

black grouse *n* **1** Also called: **black game** a large N European grouse, *Lyrurus tetrix*, the male of which has a bluish-black plumage and lyre-shaped tail **2** a related and similar species, *Lyrurus mlokosiewiczi*, of W Asia

blackguard ('blægɑːd, -gəd) *n* **1 a** an unprincipled contemptible person; scoundrel **b** (*as modifier*): *blackguard language* ▷ *vb* **2** (*tr*) to ridicule or denounce with abusive language **3** (*intr*) to behave like a blackguard [c16 originally a collective noun referring to the lowest menials in court, camp followers, vagabonds; see BLACK, GUARD] ▷ **'blackguardism** *n* ▷ **'blackguardly** *adj*

black guillemot *n* a common guillemot, *Cepphus grylle*: its summer plumage is black with white wing patches and its winter plumage white with greyish wings

Black Hand *n* **1** a group of Sicilian blackmailers and terrorists formed in the 1870s and operating in the US in the early 20th century **2** (in 19th-century Spain) an organization of anarchists

black hat *n informal* **a** a computer hacker who carries out illegal malicious hacking work **b** (*as modifier*): *black-hat hackers*. Compare **white hat**

blackhead ('blæk,hɛd) *n* **1** a black-tipped plug of fatty matter clogging a pore of the skin, esp the duct of a sebaceous gland. Technical name: **comedo** **2** an infectious and often fatal disease of turkeys and some other fowl caused by the parasitic protozoa *Histomonas meleagridis*. Technical name: **infectious enterohepatitis** **3** any of various birds, esp gulls or ducks, with black plumage on the head

blackheart ('blæk,hɑːt) *n* **1** an abnormal darkening of the woody stems of some plants, thought to be caused by extreme cold **2** any of various diseases of plants, such as the potato, in which the central tissues are blackened **3** a variety of cherry that has large sweet fruit with purplish flesh and an almost black skin

black heat *n* heat emitted by an electric element made from low-resistance thick wire that does not glow red

Blackheath ('blækhiːθ) *n* a residential district in SE London, mainly in the boroughs of Lewisham and Greenwich: a large heath formerly notorious for highwaymen

Black Hills *pl n* a group of mountains in W South Dakota and NE Wyoming: famous for the gigantic sculptures of US presidents on the side of Mount Rushmore Highest peak: Harney Peak, 2207 m (7242 ft)

black hole *astronomy n* **1** an object in space so dense that its escape velocity exceeds the speed of light **2** any place regarded as resembling a black hole in that items or information entering it cannot be retrieved

Black Hole of Calcutta *n* **1** a small dungeon in which in 1756 the Nawab of Bengal reputedly confined 146 English prisoners, of whom only 23 survived **2** *informal, chiefly Brit* any uncomfortable or overcrowded place

black horehound *n* a hairy unpleasant-smelling chiefly Mediterranean plant, *Ballota nigra*, having clusters of purple flowers: family *Lamiaceae* (labiates)

black house *n* a type of thatched house, usually made of turf, formerly found in the highlands and islands of Scotland

black ice *n* a thin transparent layer of new ice on a road or similar surface

blacking ('blækɪŋ) *n* any preparation, esp one containing lampblack, for giving a black finish to shoes, metals, etc

Black Isle *n* **the** a peninsula in NE Scotland, in Highland council area, between the Cromarty and Moray Firths [so called because until the late 18th century much of it was uncultivated black moor]

blackjack¹ ('blæk,dʒæk) *chiefly US and Canadian* ▷ *n* **1** a truncheon of leather-covered lead with a flexible shaft ▷ *vb* **2** (*tr*) to hit with or as if with a blackjack **3** (*tr*) to compel (a person) by threats [c19 from BLACK + JACK¹ (implement)]

blackjack² ('blæk,dʒæk) *n cards* **1** pontoon or any of various similar card games **2** the ace of spades [c20 from BLACK + JACK¹ (the knave)]

blackjack³ ('blæk,dʒæk) *n* a dark iron-rich variety of the mineral sphalerite [c18 from BLACK + JACK¹ (originally a miner's name for this useless ore)]

blackjack⁴ ('blæk,dʒæk) *n* a small oak tree, *Quercus marilandica*, of the southeastern US, with blackish bark and fan-shaped leaves. Also called: **blackjack oak** [c19 from BLACK + JACK¹ (from the proper name, popularly used in many plant names)]

blackjack⁵ ('blæk,dʒæk) *n* a tarred leather tankard or jug [c16 from BLACK + JACK³]

black japan *n* a black bituminous varnish

black knight *n commerce* a person or firm that makes an unwelcome takeover bid for a company. Compare **grey knight, white knight**

black knot *n* a fungal disease of plums and cherries caused by *Dibotryon morbosum*, characterized by rough black knotlike swellings on the twigs and branches

black lead (lɛd) *n* another name for **graphite**

blackleg ('blæk,lɛg) *n* **1** Also called: **scab** **a** a person who acts against the interests of a trade union, as by continuing to work during a strike or taking over a striker's job **b** (*as modifier*): *blackleg labour* **2** Also called: **black quarter** an acute infectious disease of cattle, sheep, and pigs, characterized by gas-filled swellings, esp on the legs, caused by *Clostridium* bacteria **3** *plant pathol* **a** a fungal disease of cabbages and related plants caused by *Phoma lingam*, characterized by blackening and decay of the lower stems **b** a similar disease of potatoes, caused by bacteria **4** a person who cheats in gambling, esp at cards or in racing ▷ *vb* -legs, -legging, -legged **5** *Brit* to act

b

against the interests of a trade union, esp by refusing to join a strike

black letter *n printing* another name for **Gothic** (sense 10)

black light *n* the invisible electromagnetic radiation in the ultraviolet and infrared regions of the spectrum

blacklist ('blæk,lɪst) *n* **1** a list of persons or organizations under suspicion, or considered untrustworthy, disloyal, etc, esp one compiled by a government or an organization ▷ *vb* **2** (*tr*) to put on a blacklist > 'black,listing *n*

black lung *n* another name for **pneumoconiosis**

black magic *n* magic used for evil purposes by invoking the power of the devil

blackmail ('blæk,meɪl) *n* **1** the act of attempting to obtain money by intimidation, as by threats to disclose discreditable information **2** the exertion of pressure or threats, esp unfairly, in an attempt to influence someone's actions ▷ *vb* (*tr*) **3** to exact or attempt to exact (money or anything of value) from (a person) by threats or intimidation; extort **4** to attempt to influence the actions of (a person), esp by unfair pressure or threats [C16 see BLACK, MAIL³] > 'blackmailer *n*

black maire *n* another name for **maire**

Black Maria (mə'raɪə) *n* a police van for transporting prisoners

black mark *n* an indication of disapproval, failure, etc

black market *n* **1 a** any system in which goods or currencies are sold and bought illegally, esp in violation of controls or rationing **b** (*as modifier*): *black market lamb* **2** the place where such a system operates ▷ *vb* black-market **3** to sell (goods) on the black market > black marketeer *n*

black mass *n* (*sometimes capitals*) a blasphemous travesty of the Christian Mass, performed by practitioners of black magic

black matipo (mɑː'tiːpɒ) *n* another name for **tawhiri** [Māori]

black measles *pl n* (*often functioning as singular*) a severe form of measles characterized by dark eruptions caused by bleeding under the skin

black medick *n* a small European leguminous plant, *Medicago lupulina*, with trifoliate leaves, small yellow flowers, and black pods. Also called: nonesuch

black money *n* **1** that part of a nation's income that relates to its black economy **2** any money that a person or organization acquires illegally, as by a means that involves tax evasion **3** *US* money to fund a government project that is concealed in the cost of some other project

Black Monk *n* a Benedictine monk

black mould *n* another name for **bread mould**

Black Mountain *n* **the**. a mountain range in S Wales, in E Carmarthenshire and W Powys. Highest peak: Carmarthen Van, 802 m (2632 ft)

Black Mountains *pl n* a mountain range running from N Monmouthshire and SE Powys (Wales) to SW Herefordshire (England). Highest peak: Waun Fach, 811 m (2660 ft)

Black Muslims *n* (esp in the US) a political and religious movement of Black people who adopt the religious practices of Islam and seek to establish a new Black nation. Official name: Nation of Islam

black mustard *n* a Eurasian plant, *Brassica* (or *Sinapis*) *nigra*, with clusters of yellow flowers and pungent seeds from which the condiment mustard is made: family *Brassicaceae* (crucifers)

black nightshade *n* a poisonous solanaceous plant, *Solanum nigrum*, a common weed in cultivated land, having small white flowers with backward-curved petals and black berry-like fruits

black-on-black *adj* concerning black people exclusively: *black-on-black violence*

black opal *n* any opal of a dark coloration, not necessarily black

blackout ('blæk,aʊt) *n* **1** the extinguishing or hiding of all artificial light, esp in a city visible to an enemy attack from the air **2** a momentary loss of consciousness, vision, or memory **3** a temporary electrical power failure or cut **4** *electronics* a temporary loss of sensitivity in a valve following a short strong pulse **5** a temporary loss of radio communications between a spacecraft and earth, esp on re-entry into the earth's atmosphere **6** the suspension of radio or television broadcasting, as by a strike or for political reasons ▷ *vb* black out (*adverb*) **7** (*tr*) to obliterate or extinguish (lights) **8** (*tr*) to create a blackout in (a city etc) **9** (*intr*) to lose vision, consciousness, or memory temporarily **10** (*tr, adverb*) to stop (news, a television programme) from being released or broadcast

black pad *n Midland English dialect* a rough road or track

Black Panther *n* (in the US) a member of a militant Black political party founded in 1965 to end the political dominance of Whites

black pepper *n* a pungent condiment made by grinding the dried unripe berries, together with their black husks, of the pepper plant *Piper nigrum*

black pine *n* See **matai**

blackpoll ('blæk,pəʊl) *n* a North American warbler, *Dendroica striata*, the male of which has a black-and-white head

Blackpool ('blæk,puːl) *n* **1** a town and resort in NW England, in Blackpool unitary authority, Lancashire on the Irish Sea: famous for its tower, 158 m (518 ft) high, and its illuminations. Pop: 142 283 (2001) **2** a unitary authority in NW England, in Lancashire. Pop: 142 400 (2003 est). Area: 35 sq km (13 sq miles)

black powder *n* another name for **gunpowder**

Black Power *n* a social, economic, and political movement of Black people, esp in the US, to obtain equality with Whites

black propaganda *n* propaganda that does not come from the source it claims to come from. Compare **grey propaganda, white propaganda**

black pudding *n* a kind of black sausage made from minced pork fat, pig's blood, and other ingredients. Also called: blood pudding. Usual US and Canadian name: blood sausage

black quarter *n* another name for **blackleg** (sense 2)

black rat *n* a common rat, *Rattus rattus*: a household pest that has spread from its native Asia to all countries

Black Rod *n* **1** (in Britain) an officer of the House of Lords and of the Order of the Garter, whose main duty is summoning the Commons at the opening and proroguing of Parliament **2** a similar officer in any of certain other legislatures

black rot *n* any of various plant diseases of fruits and vegetables, producing blackening, rotting, and shrivelling and caused by bacteria (including *Xanthomonas campestris*) and fungi (such as *Physalospora malorum*)

black run *n skiing* an extremely difficult run, suitable for expert skiers

black rust *n* a stage in any of several diseases of cereals and grasses caused by rust fungi in which black masses of spores appear on the stems or leaves

Black Sash *n* (formerly, in South Africa) an organization of women opposed to apartheid

Black Sea *n* an inland sea between SE Europe and Asia: connected to the Aegean Sea by the Bosporus, the Sea of Marmara, and the Dardanelles, and to the Sea of Azov by the Kerch Strait. Area: about 415 000 sq km (160 000 sq miles). Ancient names: Pontus Euxinus, Euxine Sea

black section *n* (in Britain) an unofficial group within the Labour Party in any constituency that represents the interests of local Black people

black shag *n* a large dark-coloured shag, *Phalacrocorax carbo novaehollandis*, of Australasian waters. Also called (NZ): kawau

black sheep *n* a person who is regarded as a disgrace or failure by his family or peer group

Blackshirt ('blæk,ʃɜːt) *n* (in Europe) a member of a fascist organization, esp a member of the Italian Fascist party before and during World War II

blacksmith ('blæk,smɪθ) *n* an artisan who works iron with a furnace, anvil, hammer, etc [C14 see BLACK, SMITH]

blacksnake ('blæk,sneɪk) *n* **1** any of several Old World black venomous elapid snakes, esp *Pseudechis porphyriacus* (**Australian blacksnake**) **2** any of various dark nonvenomous snakes, such as *Coluber constrictor* (black racer) **3** *US and Canadian* a long heavy pliant whip of braided leather or rawhide

black spot *n* **1** a place on a road where accidents frequently occur **2** any dangerous or difficult place **3** a disease of roses, *Diplocarpon rosae*, that causes circular black blotches on the leaves

black spruce *n* a coniferous tree, *Picea mariana*, of the northern regions of North America, growing mostly in cold bogs and having dark green needles. Also called: spruce pine

blackstrap molasses ('blæk,stræp) *pl n* (*functioning as singular*) the molasses remaining after the maximum quantity of sugar has been extracted from the raw material

black stump *n* **1** the *Austral* an imaginary marker of the extent of civilization (esp in the phrase **beyond the black stump**) **2** *NZ* a long way off

black swan *n* a large Australian swan, *Cygnus atratus*, that has a black plumage and red bill

blacktail ('blæk,teɪl) *n* a variety of mule deer having a black tail

blackthorn ('blæk,θɔːn) *n* **1** Also called: sloe a thorny Eurasian rosaceous shrub, *Prunus spinosa*, with black twigs, white flowers, and small sour plumlike fruits **2** a walking stick made from its wood

black tie *n* **1** a black bow tie worn with a dinner jacket **2** (*modifier*) denoting an occasion when a dinner jacket should be worn ▷ Compare **white tie**

blacktop ('blæk,tɒp) *n chiefly US and Canadian* **1** a bituminous mixture used for paving **2** a road paved with this mixture

black tracker *n Austral* an Aboriginal tracker working for the police

black treacle *n Brit* another term for **treacle** (sense 1)

black tree fern *n* another name for **mamaku**

black velvet *n* **1** a mixture of stout and champagne in equal proportions **2** *Austral slang* Aboriginal women as sexual partners

Black Volta *n* a river in W Africa, rising in SW Burkina-Faso and flowing northeast, then south into Lake Volta: forms part of the border of Ghana with Burkina-Faso and with the Ivory Coast. Length: about 800 km (500 miles)

black vomit *n* **1** vomit containing blood, often a manifestation of disease, such as yellow fever **2** *informal* yellow fever

Blackwall hitch ('blæk,wɔːl) *n* a knot for hooking tackle to the end of a rope, holding fast when pulled but otherwise loose [C19 named after *Blackwall*, former docks in London]

black walnut *n* **1** a North American walnut tree, *Juglans nigra*, with hard dark wood and edible oily nuts **2** the valuable wood of this tree, used for cabinet work **3** the nut of this tree ▷ Compare **butternut** (senses 1–4)

blackwash ('blæk,wɒʃ) *vb* (*tr*) *informal* to present (someone or something) in the worst possible light [C21 coined as an opposite to WHITEWASH]

Black Watch *n* **the**. the Royal Highland Regiment in the British army [so called for their dark tartan]

black-water fever *n vet science* a form of babesiosis seen in cattle, deer, bison, water buffalo, African buffalo, and reindeer; characterized by fever, depression, jaundice, dark red-black discolouration of the urine, anaemia, and death. Also called: Texas fever

blackwater rafting *n NZ* the sport of riding through underground caves on a large rubber tube. Also called: **cave tubing**

black wattle *n* **1** a small Australian acacia tree, *A. mearnsii*, with yellow flowers **2** a tall Australian shrub, *Callicoma serratifolia*

black whale *n* another name for **pilot whale**

black widow *n* an American spider, *Latrodectus mactans*, the female of which is black with red markings, highly venomous, and commonly eats its mate

blackwood (ˈblækˌwʊd) *n* **1** Also called: **Sally Wattle** a tall Australian acacia tree, *A. melanoxylon*, having small clusters of flowers and curved pods and yielding highly valued black timber **2** any of various trees or shrubs of the leguminous genus *Dalbergia*, esp *D. melanoxylon* (of Africa) or *D. latifolia* (of India), yielding black wood used for carving and musical instruments **3** the wood of any of these trees

Blackwood (ˈblækˌwʊd) *n bridge* a conventional bidding sequence of four and five no-trumps, which are requests to the partner to show aces and kings respectively [C20 named after Easeley F. *Blackwood*, its American inventor]

bladder (ˈblædə) *n* **1** *anatomy* a distensible membranous sac, usually containing liquid or gas, esp the urinary bladder. Related adjective: **vesical** **2** an inflatable part of something **3** a blister, cyst, vesicle, etc, usually filled with fluid **4** a hollow vesicular or saclike part or organ in certain plants, such as the bladderwort or bladderwrack [Old English *blǣdre*] > ˈ**bladdery** *adj*

bladder campion *n* a European caryophyllaceous plant, *Silene vulgaris*, having white flowers with an inflated calyx

bladdered (ˈbladəd) *adj slang* intoxicated; drunk

bladder fern *n* a small fern, *Cystoperis fragilis*, with graceful lanceolate leaves, typically growing on limestone rocks and walls [C19 named from the bladder-shaped indusium]

bladder ketmia (ˈkɛtmɪə) *n* another name for **flower-of-an-hour**

bladdernose (ˈblædəˌnəʊz) *n* another name for **hooded seal**

bladdernut (ˈblædəˌnʌt) *n* **1** any temperate shrub or small tree of the genus *Staphylea*, esp *S. pinnata* of S Europe, that has bladder-like seed pods: family *Staphyleaceae* **2** the pod of any such tree

bladder senna *n* a Eurasian leguminous plant, *Colutea arborescens*, with yellow and red flowers and membranous inflated pods

bladder worm *n* an encysted saclike larva of the tapeworm. The main types are cysticercus, hydatid and coenurus

bladderwort (ˈblædəˌwɜːt) *n* any aquatic plant of the genus *Utricularia*, some of whose leaves are modified as small bladders to trap minute aquatic animals: family *Lentibulariaceae*

bladderwrack (ˈblædəˌræk) *n* any of several seaweeds of the genera *Fucus* and *Ascophyllum*, esp *F. vesiculosus*, that grow in the intertidal regions of rocky shores and have branched brown fronds with air bladders

blade (bleɪd) *n* **1** the part of a sharp weapon, tool, etc, that forms the cutting edge **2** (*plural*) *Austral and NZ* hand shears used for shearing sheep **3** the thin flattish part of various tools, implements, etc, as of a propeller, turbine, etc **4** the flattened expanded part of a leaf, sepal, or petal **5** the long narrow leaf of a grass or related plant **6** the striking surface of a bat, club, stick, or oar **7** the metal runner on an ice skate **8** *archaeol* a long thin flake of flint, possibly used as a tool **9** the upper part of the tongue lying directly behind the tip **10** *archaic* a dashing or swaggering young man **11** short for **shoulder blade** **12** a poetic word for a **sword** *or* **swordsman** [Old English *blæd*; related to Old Norse *blath* leaf, Old High German *blat*, Latin *folium* leaf] > ˈ**bladed** *adj*

blade grader *n* another name for **grader** (sense 2)

blade-shearing *n NZ* the shearing of sheep using hand shears > ˈ**blade-ˌshearer** *n*

blade slap *n* the regular noise beat generated by the rotor blades of a helicopter

blading *n* the act or an instance of skating with in-line skates

blady grass (ˈbleɪdɪ) *n* a coarse leafy Australasian grass, *Imperata cylindrica*

blae (ble, bleɪ) *adj Scot* bluish-grey; slate-coloured [from Old Norse *blár*]

blaeberry (ˈbleɪbərɪ) *n, pl* **-ries** *Brit* another name for **bilberry** (senses 1, 2) [C15 from BLAE + BERRY]

Blaenau Gwent (ˈblaɪnaʊ ˈgwɛnt) *n* a county borough of SE Wales, created in 1996 from NW Gwent. Administrative centre: Ebbw Vale. Pop: 68 900 (2003 est). Area: 109 sq km (42 sq miles)

blaes (blez, bleɪz) *n Scot* **a** hardened clay or shale, esp when crushed and used to form the top layer of a sports pitch: bluish-grey or reddish in colour **b** (*as modifier*): *a blaes pitch* [C18 from BLAE]

blag (blæg) *slang* ▷ *n* **1** a robbery, esp with violence ▷ *vb* **blags, blagging, blagged** (*tr*) **2** to obtain by wheedling or cadging: *she blagged free tickets from her mate* **3** to snatch (wages, someone's handbag, etc); steal **4** to rob (esp a bank or post office) [C19 of unknown origin] > ˈ**blagger** *n*

Blagoveshchensk (*Russian* bləgaˈvjeʃtʃɪnsk) *n* a city and port in E Russia, in Siberia on the Amur River. Pop: 222 000 (2005 est)

blague (blɑːg) *n* pretentious but empty talk; nonsense [C19 from French] > ˈ**blaguer** *n*

blah *or* **blah blah** (blɑː) *slang* ▷ *n* **1** worthless or silly talk; claptrap ▷ *adj* **2** uninteresting; insipid ▷ *vb* **3** (*intr*) to talk nonsense or boringly

blain (bleɪn) *n* a blister, blotch, or sore on the skin [Old English *blegen*; related to Middle Low German *bleine*]

Blairite (ˈblɛəraɪt) *adj* **1** of or relating to the modernizing policies of Tony Blair (full name *Anthony Charles Lynton Blair*; born 1953), British Labour politician and prime minister from 1997 ▷ *n* **2** a supporter of the modernizing policies of Tony Blair

Blair's babes *pl n informal* (in Britain) the female Members of Parliament elected as part of Prime Minister Tony Blair's Labour government in 1997

blame (bleɪm) *n* **1** responsibility for something that is wrong or deserving censure; culpability **2** an expression of condemnation; reproof **3** **be to blame** to be at fault or culpable ▷ *vb* (*tr*) **4** (usually foll by *for*) to attribute responsibility to; accuse: *I blame him for the failure* **5** (usually foll by *on*) to ascribe responsibility for (something) to: *I blame the failure on him* **6** to find fault with [C12 from Old French *blasmer*, ultimately from Late Latin *blasphēmāre* to BLASPHEME] > ˈ**blamable** *or* ˈ**blameable** *adj* > ˈ**blamably** *or* ˈ**blameably** *adv*

blame culture *n* the tendency to look for one person or organization that can be held responsible for a bad state of affairs, an accident, etc

blamed (bleɪmd) *adj, adv chiefly US* a euphemistic word for **damned** (senses 2, 3)

blameful (ˈbleɪmfʊl) *adj* deserving blame; guilty > ˈ**blamefully** *adv* > ˈ**blamefulness** *n*

blameless (ˈbleɪmlɪs) *adj* free from blame; innocent > ˈ**blamelessly** *adv* > ˈ**blamelessness** *n*

blameworthy (ˈbleɪmˌwɜːðɪ) *adj* deserving disapproval or censure > ˈ**blameˌworthiness** *n*

Blanc (*French* blɑ̃) *n* **1** **Mont**. See **Mont Blanc** **2** **Cape**. a headland in N Tunisia: the northernmost point of Africa **3** **Cape** Also called: **Cape Blanco** (ˈblæŋkəʊ) a peninsula in Mauritania, on the Atlantic coast

blanc fixe (*French* blɑ̃ fiks) *n* another name for **barium sulphate** [literally: fixed white]

blanch (blɑːntʃ) *vb* (*mainly tr*) **1** (*also intr*) to remove colour from, or (of colour) to be removed; whiten; fade: *the sun blanched the carpet; over the years the painting blanched* **2** (*usually intr*) to become or cause to become pale, as with sickness or fear **3** to plunge tomatoes, nuts, etc, into boiling water to loosen the skin **4** to plunge (meat, green vegetables, etc) in boiling water or bring to the boil in water in order to whiten, preserve the natural colour, or reduce or remove a bitter or salty taste **5** to cause (celery, chicory, etc) to grow free of chlorophyll by the exclusion of sunlight **6** *metallurgy* to whiten (a metal), usually by treating it with an acid or by coating it with tin **7** (*tr*, usually foll by *over*) to attempt to conceal something [C14 from Old French *blanchir* from *blanc* white; see BLANK]

blancmange (bləˈmɒnʒ) *n* a jelly-like dessert, stiffened usually with cornflour and set in a mould [C14 from Old French *blanc manger*, literally: white food]

bland (blænd) *adj* **1** devoid of any distinctive or stimulating characteristics; uninteresting; dull: *bland food* **2** gentle and agreeable; suave **3** (of the weather) mild and soothing **4** unemotional or unmoved: *a bland account of atrocities* ▷ See also **bland out** [C15 from Latin *blandus* flattering] > ˈ**blandly** *adv* > ˈ**blandness** *n*

blandish (ˈblændɪʃ) *vb* (*tr*) to seek to persuade or influence by mild flattery; coax [C14 from Old French *blandir* from Latin *blandīrī*]

blandishments (ˈblændɪʃmənts) *pl n* (*rarely singular*) flattery intended to coax or cajole

bland out *vb* (*intr, adverb*) *informal* to become bland

blank (blæŋk) *adj* **1** (of a writing surface) bearing no marks; not written on **2** (of a form, etc) with spaces left for details to be filled in **3** without ornament or break; unrelieved: *a blank wall* **4** not filled in; empty; void: *a blank space* **5** exhibiting no interest or expression: *a blank look* **6** lacking understanding; confused: *he looked blank even after the explanations* **7** absolute; complete: *blank rejection* **8** devoid of ideas or inspiration: *his mind went blank in the exam* **9** unproductive; barren ▷ *n* **10** an emptiness; void; blank space **11** an empty space for writing in, as on a printed form **12** a printed form containing such empty spaces **13** something characterized by incomprehension or mental confusion: *my mind went a complete blank* **14** a mark, often a dash, in place of a word, esp a taboo word **15** short for **blank cartridge** **16** a plate or plug used to seal an aperture **17** a piece of material prepared for stamping, punching, forging, etc **18** *archery* the white spot in the centre of a target **19** **draw a blank** **a** to choose a lottery ticket that fails to win **b** to get no results from something ▷ *vb* (*tr*) **20** (usually foll by *out*) to cross out, blot, or obscure **21** *slang* to ignore or be unresponsive towards (someone): *the crowd blanked her for the first four numbers* **22** to forge, stamp, punch, or cut (a piece of material) in preparation for forging, die-stamping, or drawing operations **23** (often foll by *off*) to seal (an aperture) with a plate or plug **24** *US and Canadian informal* to prevent (an opponent) from scoring in a game [C15 from Old French *blanc* white, of Germanic origin; related to Old English *blanca* a white horse] > ˈ**blankly** *adv* > ˈ**blankness** *n*

b

blank cartridge *n* a cartridge containing powder but no bullet: used in battle practice or as a signal

blank cheque *n* **1** a signed cheque on which the amount payable has not been specified **2** complete freedom of action

blank endorsement *n* an endorsement on a bill of exchange, cheque, etc, naming no payee and thus making the endorsed sum payable to the bearer. Also called: **endorsement in blank**

blanket (ˈblæŋkɪt) *n* **1** a large piece of thick cloth for use as a bed covering, animal covering, etc, enabling a person or animal to retain natural body heat **2** a concealing cover or layer, as of smoke, leaves, or snow **3** a rubber or plastic sheet wrapped round a cylinder, used in offset printing to transfer the image from the plate, stone, or forme to the paper **4** *physics* a layer of a fertile substance placed round the core of a nuclear reactor as a reflector or absorber and often to breed new fissionable fuel **5** (*modifier*) applying to or covering a wide group or variety of people, conditions, situations, etc: *blanket insurance against loss, injury, and theft* **6** (**born**) **on the wrong side of the blanket** *informal* illegitimate ▷ *vb* (*tr*) **7** to cover with or as if with a blanket; overlie **8** to cover a very wide area, as in a publicity campaign; give blanket coverage **9** (usually foll by *out*) to obscure or suppress: *the storm blanketed out the TV picture* **10** *nautical* to prevent wind from reaching the sails of (another sailing vessel) by passing to windward of it [c13 from Old French *blancquete*, from *blanc*; see BLANK]

blanket bath *n* an all-over wash given to a person confined to bed

blanket bog *n* a very acid peat bog, low in nutrients, extending widely over a flat terrain, found in cold wet climates

blanket finish *n athletics, horse racing* a finish so close that a blanket would cover all the contestants involved

blanket stitch *n* a strong reinforcing stitch for the edges of blankets and other thick material

blankety ('blæŋkɪtɪ) *adj, adv* a euphemism for any taboo word [c20 from BLANK]

blank verse *n prosody* unrhymed verse, esp in iambic pentameters

blanquette de veau (blæŋ'kɛt də 'vəʊ) *n* a ragout or stew of veal in a white sauce [French]

Blantyre-Limbe (blæn'taɪə'lɪmbeɪ) *n* a city in S Malawi: largest city in the country; formed in 1956 from the adjoining towns of Blantyre and Limbe. Pop: 647 000 (2005 est)

blare (blɛə) *vb* **1** to sound loudly and harshly **2** to proclaim loudly and sensationally ▷ *n* **3** a loud and usually harsh or grating noise [c14 from Middle Dutch *bleren*; of imitative origin]

blarney ('blɑːnɪ) *n* **1** flattering talk ▷ *vb* **2** to cajole with flattery; wheedle [c19 after the BLARNEY STONE]

Blarney Stone *n* a stone in **Blarney Castle**, in the SW Republic of Ireland, said to endow whoever kisses it with skill in flattery

blart (blɑːt) *vb* (*intr*) *English dialect* to sound loudly and harshly

blasé ('blɑːzeɪ) *adj* **1** indifferent to something because of familiarity or surfeit **2** lacking enthusiasm; bored [c19 from French, past participle of *blaser* to cloy]

blaspheme (blæs'fiːm) *vb* **1** (*tr*) to show contempt or disrespect for (God, a divine being, or sacred things), esp in speech **2** (*intr*) to utter profanities, curses, or impious expressions [c14 from Late Latin *blasphēmāre*, from Greek *blasphēmein* from *blasphēmos* BLASPHEMOUS] > blas'phemer *n*

blasphemous ('blæsfɪməs) *adj* expressing or involving impiousness or gross irreverence towards God, a divine being, or something sacred [c15 via Late Latin, from Greek *blasphēmos* evil-speaking, from *blapsis* evil + *phēmē* speech] > 'blasphemously *adv*

blasphemy ('blæsfɪmɪ) *n, pl* -mies **1** blasphemous behaviour or language **2** Also called: **blasphemous libel** *law* the crime committed if a person insults, offends, or vilifies the deity, Christ, or the Christian religion

blast (blɑːst) *n* **1** an explosion, as of dynamite **2 a** the rapid movement of air away from the centre of an explosion, combustion of rocket fuel, etc **b** a wave of overpressure caused by an explosion; shock wave **3** the charge of explosive used in a single explosion **4** a sudden strong gust of wind or air **5** a sudden loud sound, as of a trumpet **6** a violent verbal outburst, as of criticism **7** a forcible jet or stream of air, esp one used to intensify the heating effect of a furnace, increase the draught in a steam engine, or break up coal at a coalface **8** any of several diseases of plants and animals, esp one producing withering in plants **9** *US slang* a very enjoyable or thrilling experience: *the party was a blast* **10** (**at**) **full blast** at maximum speed, volume etc ▷ *interj* **11** *slang* an exclamation of annoyance (esp in phrases such as **blast it! blast**

him!) ▷ *vb* **12** to destroy or blow up with explosives, shells, etc **13** to make or cause to make a loud harsh noise **14** (*tr*) to remove, open, etc, by an explosion: *to blast a hole in a wall* **15** (*tr*) to ruin; shatter: *the rain blasted our plans for a picnic* **16** to wither or cause to wither; blight or be blighted **17** to criticize severely **18** to shoot or shoot at: *he blasted the hat off her head; he blasted away at the trees* ▷ See also **blastoff** [Old English *blǣst*, related to Old Norse *blāstr*] > 'blaster *n*

-blast *n combining form* (in biology) indicating an embryonic cell or formative layer: *mesoblast* [from Greek *blastos* bud]

blasted ('blɑːstɪd) *adj* **1** blighted or withered ▷ *adj* (*prenominal*) ▷ *adv* **2** *slang* (intensifier): *a blasted idiot*

blastema (blæ'stiːmə) *n, pl* -mas or -mata (-mətə) a mass of undifferentiated animal cells that will develop into an organ or tissue: present at the site of regeneration of a lost part [c19 from New Latin, from Greek: offspring, from *blastos* bud] > blastemic (blæ'stiːmɪk, -'stɛm-) *adj*

blast furnace *n* a vertical cylindrical furnace for smelting iron, copper, lead, and tin ores. The ore, scrap, solid fuel, and slag-forming materials are fed through the top and a blast of preheated air is forced through the charge from the bottom. Metal and slag are run off from the base

blast-furnace cement *n* a type of cement made from a blend of ordinary Portland cement and crushed slag from a blast furnace. It has lower setting properties than ordinary Portland cement

blasting ('blɑːstɪŋ) *n* a distortion of sound caused by overloading certain components of a radio system

blast injection *n* the injection of liquid fuel directly into the cylinder of an internal-combustion engine using a blast of high-pressure air to atomize the spray of fuel. Compare **solid injection**

blasto- *combining form* (in biology) indicating an embryo or bud or the process of budding: *blastoderm* [from Greek *blastos*. See -BLAST]

blastochyle ('blæstəʊ,kaɪl) *n embryol* the fluid in a blastocoel

blastocoel or **blastocoele** ('blæstəʊ,siːl) *n embryol* the cavity within a blastula. Also called: **segmentation cavity**

blastocyst ('blæstəʊ,sɪst) *n embryol* **1** Also called: **blastosphere** the blastula of mammals: a sphere of cells (**trophoblast**) enclosing an inner mass of cells and a fluid-filled cavity (**blastocoel**) **2** another name for **germinal vesicle**

blastoderm ('blæstəʊ,dɜːm) *n embryol* **1** the layer of cells that surrounds the blastocoel of a blastula **2** a flat disc of cells formed after cleavage in a heavily yolked egg, such as a bird's egg. Also called: blastodisc > ,blasto'dermic *adj*

blastodisc ('blæstəʊ,dɪsk) *n* another name for **blastoderm**

blastoff ('blɑːst,ɒf) *n* **1** the launching of a rocket under its own power **2** the time at which this occurs ▷ *vb* **blast off 3** (*adverb; when tr, usually passive*) (of a rocket, spacemen, etc) to be launched

blastogenesis (,blæstəʊ'dʒɛnɪsɪs) *n* **1** the theory that inherited characteristics are transmitted only by germ plasm. See also **pangenesis 2** asexual reproduction, esp budding > ,blasto'genic or ,blasto'genetic *adj*

blastoma (blæ'stəʊmə) *n, pl* -mata or -mas *pathol* **a** a tumour composed of embryonic tissue that has not yet developed a specialized function **b** (in combination): *neuroblastoma* [c20 New Latin, from BLASTO- + -OMA]

blastomere ('blæstəʊ,mɪə) *n embryol* any of the cells formed by cleavage of a fertilized egg > blastomeric (,blæstəʊ'mɛrɪk) *adj*

blastopor ('blæstəʊ,pɔː) *n embryol* the opening of the archenteron in the gastrula that develops into the anus of some animals > ,blasto'poric or ,blasto'poral *adj*

blastosphere ('blæstəʊ,sfɪə) *n* **1** another name

for **blastula 2** another name for **blastocyst** (sense 1)

blastospore ('blæstəʊ,spɔː) *n botany* a spore formed by budding, as in certain fungi

blastula ('blæstjʊlə) *n, pl* -las or -lae (-liː) an early form of an animal embryo that develops from a morula, consisting of a sphere of cells with a central cavity. Also called: blastosphere [c19 New Latin; see BLASTO-] > 'blastular *adj*

blastulation (,blæstjʊ'leɪʃən) *n embryol* the process of blastula formation

blat (blæt) *vb* blats, blatting, blatted *US and Canadian* **1** (*intr*) to cry out or bleat like a sheep **2** (*tr*) to utter indiscreetly in a loud voice [c19 of imitative origin]

blatant ('bleɪtᵊnt) *adj* **1** glaringly conspicuous or obvious: *a blatant lie* **2** offensively noticeable: *blatant disregard for a person's feelings* **3** offensively noisy [c16 coined by Edmund Spenser; probably influenced by Latin *blatīre* to babble; compare Middle Low German *pladderen*] > 'blatancy *n* > 'blatantly *adv*

blather ('blæðə) or *Scot* **blether** *vb* **1** (*intr*) to speak foolishly ▷ *n* **2** foolish talk; nonsense **3** a person who blathers [c15 from Old Norse *blathra*, from *blathr* nonsense]

blatherskite ('blæðə,skaɪt) *n* **1** a talkative silly person **2** foolish talk; nonsense [c17 see BLATHER, SKATE³]

blatted ('blætɪd) *adj slang* drunk [c20 of uncertain origin]

Blaue Reiter (*German* 'blauə 'raɪtər) *n der* a group of German expressionist painters formed in Munich in 1911, including Kandinsky and Klee, who sought to express the spiritual side of man and nature, which they felt had been neglected by impressionism [c20 literally: blue rider, name adopted by Kandinsky and Marc because they liked the colour blue, horses, and riders]

blaxploitation (,blæksplɔɪ'teɪʃən) *n* a genre of films featuring Black stereotypes [c20 from BLA(CK) + (E)XPLOITATION]

Blaydon ('bleɪdᵊn) *n* an industrial town in NE England, in Gateshead unitary authority, Tyne and Wear. Pop: 14 648 (2001)

blaze¹ (bleɪz) *n* **1** a strong fire or flame **2** a very bright light or glare **3** an outburst (of passion, acclaim, patriotism, etc) **4** brilliance; brightness ▷ *vb* (*intr*) **5** to burn fiercely **6** to shine brightly **7** (often foll by *up*) to become stirred, as with anger or excitement **8** (usually foll by *away*) to shoot continuously ▷ See also **blazes** [Old English *blæse*]

blaze² (bleɪz) *n* **1** a mark, usually indicating a path, made on a tree, esp by chipping off the bark **2** a light-coloured marking on the face of a domestic animal, esp a horse ▷ *vb* (*tr*) **3** to indicate or mark (a tree, path, etc) with a blaze **4** blaze a trail to explore new territories, areas of knowledge, etc, in such a way that others can follow [c17 probably from Middle Low German *bles* white marking; compare BLEMISH]

blaze³ (bleɪz) *vb* (*tr*; often foll by *abroad*) to make widely known; proclaim [c14 from Middle Dutch *blāsen*, from Old High German *blāsan*; related to Old Norse *blāsa*]

blazer ('bleɪzə) *n* a fairly lightweight jacket, often striped or in the colours of a sports club, school, etc

blazes ('bleɪzɪz) *pl n* **1** *slang* a euphemistic word for **hell** (esp in the phrase **go to blazes**) **2** *informal* (intensifier): *to run like blazes; what the blazes are you doing?*

blazing star *n US* **1** a North American liliaceous plant, *Chamaelirium luteum*, with a long spike of small white flowers **2** any plant of the North American genus *Liatris*, having clusters of small red or purple flowers: family *Asteraceae* (composites)

blazon ('bleɪzᵊn) *vb* (*tr*) **1** (often foll by *abroad*) to proclaim loudly and publicly **2** *heraldry* to describe (heraldic arms) in proper terms **3** to draw and colour (heraldic arms) conventionally

▷ *n* **4** *heraldry* a conventional description or depiction of heraldic arms **5** any description or recording, esp of good qualities [c13 from Old French *blason* coat of arms] > ˈblazoner *n*

blazonry (ˈbleɪzənrɪ) *n, pl* -ries **1** the art or process of describing heraldic arms in proper form **2** heraldic arms collectively **3** colourful or ostentatious display

bldg *abbreviation for* building

bleach (bliːtʃ) *vb* **1** to make or become white or colourless, as by exposure to sunlight, by the action of chemical agents, etc ▷ *n* **2** a bleaching agent **3** the degree of whiteness resulting from bleaching **4** the act of bleaching [Old English *blǣcan*; related to Old Norse *bleikja*, Old High German *bleih* pale] > ˈbleachable *adj* > ˈbleacher *n*

bleachers (ˈbliːtʃəz) *pl n* **1** (*sometimes singular*) a tier of seats in a sports stadium, etc, that are unroofed and inexpensive **2** the people occupying such seats

bleaching powder *n* a white powder with the odour of chlorine, consisting of chlorinated calcium hydroxide with an approximate formula CaCl(OCl).4H₂O. It is used in solution as a bleaching agent and disinfectant. Also called: chloride of lime, chlorinated lime

bleak¹ (bliːk) *adj* **1** exposed and barren; desolate **2** cold and raw **3** offering little hope or excitement; dismal: *a bleak future* [Old English *blāc* bright, pale; related to Old Norse *bleikr* white, Old High German *bleih* pale] > ˈbleakly *adv* > ˈbleakness *n*

bleak² (bliːk) *n* any slender silvery European cyprinid fish of the genus *Alburnus*, esp *A. lucidus*, occurring in slow-flowing rivers [c15 probably from Old Norse *bleikja* white colour; related to Old High German *bleiche* BLEACH]

blear (blɪə) *archaic* ▷ *vb* **1** (*tr*) to make (eyes or sight) dim with or as if with tears; blur ▷ *adj* **2** a less common word for **bleary** [c13 *blere* to make dim; related to Middle High German *blerre* blurred vision]

bleary (ˈblɪərɪ) *adj* blearier, bleariest **1** (of eyes or vision) dimmed or blurred, as by tears or tiredness **2** indistinct or unclear **3** exhausted; tired > ˈblearily *adv* > ˈbleariness *n*

bleary-eyed *or* **blear-eyed** *adj* **1** with eyes blurred, as with old age or after waking **2** physically or mentally unperceptive

bleat (bliːt) *vb* **1** (*intr*) (of a sheep, goat, or calf) to utter its characteristic plaintive cry **2** (*intr*) to speak with any similar sound **3** to whine; whimper ▷ *n* **4** the characteristic cry of sheep, goats, and young calves **5** any sound similar to this **6** a weak complaint or whine [Old English *blǣtan*; related to Old High German *blāzen*, Dutch *blaten*, Latin *flēre* to weep; see BLARE] > ˈbleater *n* > ˈbleating *n, adj*

bleb (blɛb) *n* **1** a fluid-filled blister on the skin **2** a small air bubble [c17 variant of BLOB] > ˈblebby *adj*

Bledisloe Cup (ˈblɛdɪsləʊ) *n rugby Union* a trophy competed for, usually annually, by New Zealand and Australia since 1932 [c20 after Charles Bathurst, 1st Viscount *Bledisloe* (1867–1958), Governor General of New Zealand who donated the trophy]

bleed (bliːd) *vb* bleeds, bleeding, bled **1** (*intr*) to lose or emit blood **2** (*tr*) to remove or draw blood from (a person or animal) **3** (*intr*) to be injured or die, as for a cause or one's country **4** (of plants) to exude (sap or resin), esp from a cut **5** (*tr*) *informal* to obtain relatively large amounts of money, goods, etc, esp by extortion **6** (*tr*) to draw liquid or gas from (a container or enclosed system): *to bleed the hydraulic brakes* **7** (*intr*) (of dye or paint) to run or become mixed, as when wet **8** to print or be printed so that text, illustrations, etc, run off the trimmed page **9** (*tr*) to trim (the edges of a printed sheet) so closely as to cut off some of the printed matter **10** (*intr*) *civil engineering, building trades* (of a mixture) to exude (a liquid) during compaction, such as water from cement **11** bleed

(someone or something) dry to extort gradually all the resources of (a person or thing) **12** one's heart bleeds used to express sympathetic grief, but often used ironically ▷ *n* **13** *printing* **a** an illustration or sheet trimmed so that some matter is bled **b** (*as modifier*): *a bleed page* **14** *printing* the trimmings of a sheet that has been bled [Old English *blēdan*; see BLOOD]

bleeder (ˈbliːdə) *n* **1** *slang* **a** *derogatory* a despicable person: *a rotten bleeder* **b** any person; fellow: *where's the bleeder gone?* **2** *pathol* a nontechnical name for a **haemophiliac**

bleeder resistor *n* a resistor connected across the output terminals of a power supply in order to improve voltage regulation and to discharge filter capacitors

bleeder's disease *n* a nontechnical name for **haemophilia**

bleeding (ˈbliːdɪŋ) *adj, adv Brit slang* (intensifier): *a bleeding fool; it's bleeding beautiful*

bleeding edge *n* the very forefront of technological development

bleeding heart *n* **1** any of several plants of the genus *Dicentra*, esp the widely cultivated Japanese species *D. spectabilis*, which has finely divided leaves and heart-shaped nodding pink flowers: family *Fumariaceae* **2** *informal* **a** a person who is excessively softhearted **b** (*as modifier*): *a bleeding-heart liberal*

bleed valve *n* a valve for running off a liquid from a tank, tube, etc, or for allowing accumulations of gas in a liquid to blow off. Also called: bleed nipple

bleep (bliːp) *n* **1** a short high-pitched signal made by an electronic apparatus; beep **2** another word for **bleeper** ▷ *vb* **3** (*intr*) to make such a noise **4** (*tr*) to call (someone) by triggering the bleeper he or she is wearing [c20 of imitative origin]

bleeper (ˈbliːpə) *n* a small portable radio receiver, carried esp by doctors, that sounds a coded bleeping signal to call the carrier. Also called: bleep

blemish (ˈblɛmɪʃ) *n* **1** a defect; flaw; stain ▷ *vb* **2** (*tr*) to flaw the perfection of; spoil; tarnish [c14 from Old French *blemir* to make pale, probably of Germanic origin]

blench¹ (blɛntʃ) *vb* (*intr*) to shy away, as in fear; quail [Old English *blencan* to deceive]

blench² (blɛntʃ) *vb* to make or become pale or white [c19 variant of BLANCH]

blend (blɛnd) *vb* **1** to mix or mingle (components) together thoroughly **2** (*tr*) to mix (different grades or varieties of tea, whisky, tobacco, etc) to produce a particular flavour, consistency, etc **3** (*intr*) to look good together; harmonize **4** (*intr*) (esp of colours) to shade imperceptibly into each other ▷ *n* **5** a mixture or type produced by blending **6** the act of blending **7** Also called: portmanteau word a word formed by joining together the beginning and the end of two other words: *"brunch" is a blend of "breakfast" and "lunch"* [Old English *blandan*; related to *blendan* to deceive, Old Norse *blanda*, Old High German *blantan*]

blende (blɛnd) *n* **1** another name for **sphalerite 2** any of several sulphide ores, such as antimony sulphide [c17 German *Blende*, from *blenden* to deceive, BLIND; so called because it is easily mistaken for galena]

blended learning *n education* the use of both classroom teaching and on-line learning in education

blender (ˈblɛndə) *n* **1** a person or thing that blends **2** Also called: liquidizer a kitchen appliance with blades used for puréeing vegetables, blending liquids, etc

Blenheim¹ (ˈblɛnɪm) *n* a village in SW Germany, site of a victory of Anglo-Austrian forces under the Duke of Marlborough and Prince Eugène of Savoy that saved Vienna from the French and Bavarians (1704) during the War of the Spanish Succession. Modern name: Blindheim

Blenheim² (ˈblɛnɪm) *n* **1** a type of King Charles

spaniel having red-and-white markings **2** Also called: Blenheim orange **a** a type of apple tree bearing gold-coloured apples **b** the fruit of this tree [c19 named after BLENHEIM PALACE]

Blenheim Palace *n* a palace in Woodstock in Oxfordshire: built (1705–22) by Sir John Vanbrugh for the 1st Duke of Marlborough as a reward from the nation for his victory at Blenheim; gardens laid out by Henry Wise and Capability Brown; birthplace of Sir Winston Churchill (1874)

blennioid (ˈblɛnɪˌɔɪd) *adj* **1** of, relating to, or belonging to the *Blennioidea*, a large suborder of small mainly marine spiny-finned fishes having an elongated body with reduced pelvic fins. The group includes the blennies, butterfish, and gunnel ▷ *n* **2** any fish belonging to the *Blennioidea*

blennorrhoea *or US* **blennorrhea** (ˌblɛnəˈrɪə) *n pathol* an excessive discharge of watery mucus, esp from the urethra or the vagina

blenny (ˈblɛnɪ) *n, pl* -nies **1** any blennioid fish of the family *Blenniidae* of coastal waters, esp the genus *Blennius*, having a tapering scaleless body, a long dorsal fin, and long raylike pelvic fins **2** any of various related fishes [c18 from Latin *blennius*, from Greek *blennos* slime; from the mucus that coats its body]

blent (blɛnt) *vb archaic or literary* a past participle of **blend**

blepharism (ˈblɛfərɪzəm) *n* spasm of the eyelids, causing rapid involuntary blinking

blepharitis (ˌblɛfəˈraɪtɪs) *n* inflammation of the eyelids [c19 from Greek *blephar(on)* eyelid + -ITIS] > blepharitic (ˌblɛfəˈrɪtɪk) *adj*

blepharoplasty (ˈblɛfərəʊˌplæstɪ) *n* cosmetic surgery performed on the eyelid [c20 from Greek *blepharo(n)* eyelid + -PLASTY]

blepharospasm (ˈblɛfərəʊˌspæzəm) *n* spasm of the muscle of the eyelids, causing the eyes to shut tightly, either as a response to painful stimuli or occurring as a form of dystonia [c19 from Greek *blepharo(n)* eyelid + SPASM]

blert (blɜːt) *n Northern English dialect* a fool

blesbok *or* **blesbuck** (ˈblɛsˌbʌk) *n, pl* -boks, -bok *or* -bucks, -buck an antelope, *Damaliscus dorcas* (or *albifrons*), of southern Africa. The coat is a deep reddish-brown with a white blaze between the eyes; the horns are lyre-shaped [c19 Afrikaans, from Dutch *bles* BLAZE² + *bok* goat, BUCK¹]

bless (blɛs) *vb* blesses, blessing, blessed *or* blest (*tr*) **1** to consecrate or render holy, beneficial, or prosperous by means of a religious rite **2** to give honour or glory to (a person or thing) as divine or holy **3** to call upon God to protect; give a benediction to **4** to worship or adore (God); call or hold holy **5** (*often passive*) to grant happiness, health, or prosperity to: *they were blessed with perfect peace* **6** (*usually passive*) to endow with a talent, beauty, etc: *she was blessed with an even temper* **7** *rare* to protect against evil or harm **8** bless! (*interjection*) an exclamation of well-wishing **9** bless you! (*interjection*) **a** a traditional phrase said to a person who has just sneezed **b** an exclamation of well-wishing or surprise **10** bless me! *or* (God) bless my soul! (*interjection*) an exclamation of surprise **11** not have a penny to bless oneself with to be desperately poor [Old English *blētsian* to sprinkle with sacrificial blood; related to *blōd* BLOOD]

blessed (ˈblɛsɪd, blɛst) *adj* **1** made holy by religious ceremony; consecrated **2** worthy of deep reverence or respect **3** *RC Church* (of a person) beatified by the pope **4** characterized by happiness or good fortune: *a blessed time* **5** bringing great happiness or good fortune **6** a euphemistic word for **damned**, used in mild oaths: *I'm blessed if I know* ▷ *n* **7** the blessed *Christianity* the dead who are already enjoying heavenly bliss > ˈblessedly *adv* > ˈblessedness *n*

Blessed Sacrament *n chiefly RC Church* the consecrated elements of the Eucharist

Blessed Virgin *n chiefly RC Church* another name for **Mary** (sense 1a)

b

blessing ('blɛsɪŋ) n 1 the act of invoking divine protection or aid 2 the words or ceremony used for this 3 a short prayer of thanksgiving before or after a meal; grace 4 *Judaism* Also called: **brachah, brocho a** a short prayer prescribed for a specific occasion and beginning "Blessed art thou, O Lord..." **b** a section of the liturgy including a similar formula 5 approval; good wishes: *her father gave his blessing to the marriage* 6 the bestowal of a divine gift or favour 7 a happy event or state of affairs: *a blessing in disguise*

blest (blɛst) vb a past tense and past participle of **bless**

blet (blɛt) n a state of softness or decay in certain fruits, such as the medlar, brought about by overripening [c19 from French *blettir* to become overripe]

Bletchley Park ('blɛtʃlɪ) n the Buckinghamshire estate which was the centre of British code-breaking operations during World War II

blether ('blɛðə) vb, n *Scot* a variant spelling of **blather** [c16 from Old Norse *blathra*, from *blathr* nonsense]

blethered ('blɛðəd) adj *Northern English dialect* weary

blew (blu:) vb the past tense of **blow¹**

blewits ('blu:ɪts) n (*functioning as singular*) an edible saprotroph agaricaceous fungus, *Tricholoma saevum*, having a pale brown cap and bluish stalk [c19 probably based on BLUE]

Blida ('bli:də) n a city in N Algeria, on the edge of the Mitidja Plain. Pop: 269 000 (2005 est)

blight (blaɪt) n 1 any plant disease characterized by withering and shrivelling without rotting. See also **potato blight** 2 any factor, such as bacterial attack or air pollution, that causes the symptoms of blight in plants 3 a person or thing that mars or prevents growth, improvement, or prosperity 4 an ugly urban district 5 the state or condition of being blighted or spoilt ▷ vb 6 to cause or suffer a blight 7 (tr) to frustrate or disappoint 8 (tr) to spoil; destroy [c17 perhaps related to Old English *blæce* rash; compare BLEACH]

blighter ('blaɪtə) n *Brit informal* 1 a fellow: *where's the blighter gone?* 2 a despicable or irritating person or thing

blighty *or* **blighty bird** ('blaɪtɪ) n *NZ* another name for **white-eye**

Blighty ('blaɪtɪ) n (*sometimes not capital*) *Brit slang* (used esp by troops serving abroad) 1 England; home 2 (esp in World War I) **a** Also called: **a blighty one** a slight wound that causes the recipient to be sent home to England **b** leave in England [c20 from Hindi *bilāyatī* foreign land, England, from Arabic *wilāyat* country, from *waliya* he rules]

bliksem ('blɪksəm) interj *South African* an exclamation expressive of surprise, shock, displeasure, etc [from Afrikaans: lightning]

blimey ('blaɪmɪ) interj *Brit slang* an exclamation of surprise or annoyance [c19 short for *gorblimey* God blind me]

blimp¹ (blɪmp) n 1 a small nonrigid airship, esp one used for observation or as a barrage balloon 2 *films* a soundproof cover fixed over a camera during shooting ▷ See also **blimp out** [c20 probably from (type) B-limp]

blimp² (blɪmp) n (*often capital*) *chiefly Brit* a person, esp a military officer, who is stupidly complacent and reactionary. Also called: **Colonel Blimp** [c20 after a character created by Sir David Low (1891–1963), New Zealand-born British political cartoonist]

blimp out vb (*intr, adverb*) *slang* to become greatly overweight

blin (blɪn) adj a Scot word for **blind**

blind (blaɪnd) adj 1 **a** unable to see; sightless **b** (*as collective noun; preceded by the*): *the blind* 2 (usually foll by *to*) unable or unwilling to understand or discern 3 not based on evidence or determined by reason: *blind hatred* 4 acting or performed without control or preparation 5 done

without being able to see, relying on instruments for information 6 hidden from sight: *a blind corner; a blind stitch* 7 closed at one end: *a blind alley* 8 completely lacking awareness or consciousness: *a blind stupor* 9 *informal* very drunk 10 having no openings or outlets: *a blind wall* 11 without having been seen beforehand: *a blind purchase* 12 (of cultivated plants) having failed to produce flowers or fruits 13 (intensifier): *not a blind bit of notice* 14 **turn a blind eye (to)** to disregard deliberately or pretend not to notice (something, esp an action of which one disapproves) ▷ adv 15 without being able to see ahead or using only instruments: *to drive blind; flying blind* 16 without adequate knowledge or information; carelessly: *to buy a house blind* 17 (intensifier) (in the phrase **blind drunk**) 18 **bake blind** to bake (the empty crust of a pie, pastry, etc) by half filling with dried peas, crusts of bread, etc, to keep it in shape ▷ vb (*mainly tr*) 19 to deprive of sight permanently or temporarily 20 to deprive of good sense, reason, or judgment 21 to darken; conceal 22 (foll by *with*) to overwhelm by showing detailed knowledge: *to blind somebody with science* 23 (intr) *Brit slang* to drive very fast 24 (intr) *Brit slang* to curse (esp in the phrase **effing and blinding**) ▷ n 25 (*modifier*) for or intended to help the blind: *a blind school* 26 a shade for a window, usually on a roller 27 any obstruction or hindrance to sight, light, or air 28 a person, action, or thing that serves to deceive or conceal the truth 29 a person who acts on behalf of someone whose identity or actions to be known 30 *Brit slang* Also called: **blinder** a drunken orgy; binge 31 *poker* a stake put up by a player before he examines his cards 32 *hunting, chiefly US and Canadian* a screen of brush or undergrowth, in which hunters hide to shoot their quarry. Brit name: **hide** 33 *military* a round or demolition charge that fails to explode [Old English *blind*; related to Old Norse *blindr*, Old High German *blint*; Lettish *blendu* to see dimly; see BLUNDER] ▷ **'blindly** adv ▷ **'blindness** n

🔲 USAGE See at **disabled**

blindage ('blaɪndɪdʒ) n *military* (esp formerly) a protective screen or structure, as over a trench

blind alley n 1 an alley open at one end only; cul-de-sac 2 *informal* a situation in which no further progress can be made

blind blocking n *bookbinding* another name for **blind stamping**

blind date n *informal* 1 a social meeting between two people who have not met before 2 either of the persons involved

blinder ('blaɪndə) n 1 an outstanding performance in sport 2 *Brit slang* another name for **blind** (sense 30)

blinders ('blaɪndəz) pl n *US and Canadian* leather sidepieces attached to a horse's bridle to prevent sideways vision. Also called (in Britain and other countries): **blinkers**

blindfish ('blaɪnd,fɪʃ) n, pl **-fish** *or* **-fishes** any of various small fishes, esp the cavefish, that have rudimentary or functionless eyes and occur in subterranean streams

blindfold ('blaɪnd,fəʊld) vb (tr) 1 to prevent (a person or animal) from seeing by covering (the eyes) 2 to prevent from perceiving or understanding ▷ n 3 a piece of cloth, bandage, etc, used to cover the eyes 4 any interference to sight ▷ adj, adv 5 having the eyes covered with a cloth or bandage 6 *chess* not seeing the board and pieces 7 rash; inconsiderate [changed (c16) through association with FOLD¹ from Old English *blindfellian* to strike blind; see BLIND, FELL²]

Blind Freddie n *Austral informal* an imaginary person representing the highest degree of incompetence (esp in the phrase **Blind Freddie could see that!**)

blind gut n *informal* another name for the **caecum**

Blindheim ('blɪnt,haɪm) n the German name for **Blenheim¹**

blinding ('blaɪndɪŋ) n 1 sand or grit spread over a

road surface to fill up cracks 2 the process of laying blinding 3 Also called: **mattress** a layer of concrete made with little cement spread over soft ground to seal it so that reinforcement can be laid on it ▷ adj 4 making one blind or as if blind: *blinding snow* 5 most noticeable; brilliant or dazzling: *a blinding display of skill* ▷ **'blindingly** adv

blind man's buff n a game in which a blindfolded person tries to catch and identify the other players [c16 buff, perhaps from Old French *buffe* a blow; see BUFFET²]

blind register n (in the United Kingdom) a list of those who are blind and are therefore entitled to financial and other benefits

blind side n 1 *rugby* the side of the field between the scrum and the nearer touchline 2 the side on which a person's vision is obscured ▷ vb **blind-side** 3 (tr) *US* to take (someone) by surprise

blindsight ('blaɪnd,saɪt) n the ability to respond to visual stimuli without having any conscious visual experience; it can occur after some forms of brain damage

blind snake n any burrowing snake of the family *Typhlopidae* and related families of warm and tropical regions, having very small or vestigial eyes

blind spot n 1 a small oval-shaped area of the retina in which vision is not experienced. It marks the nonphotosensitive site of entrance into the eyeball of the optic nerve. See **optic disc** 2 a place or area, as in an auditorium or part of a road, where vision is completely or partially obscured or hearing is difficult or impossible 3 a subject about which a person is ignorant or prejudiced, or an occupation in which he is inefficient 4 a location within the normal range of a radio transmitter with weak reception

blind staggers n (*functioning as singular*) *vet science* another name for **staggers**

blind stamping n *bookbinding* an impression on a book cover without using colour or gold leaf. Also called: **blind blocking**

blindstorey *or* **blindstory** ('blaɪnd,stɔːrɪ) n, pl **-reys** *or* **-ries** a storey without windows, such as a gallery in a Gothic church. Compare **clerestory**

blind trust n a trust fund that manages the financial affairs of a person without informing him or her of any investments made, usually so that the beneficiary cannot be accused of using public office for private gain

blindworm ('blaɪnd,wɜːm) n another name for **slowworm**

bling-bling ('blɪŋ,blɪŋ) *or* **bling** adj 1 *slang* flashy; ostentatious; glitzy ▷ n 2 ostentatious jewellery [c20 imitative of jewellery clashing together or of light reflecting off jewellery]

blinging ('blɪŋɪŋ) adj *slang* 1 flashy and expensive 2 very good [c20 from BLING-BLING]

blinglish ('blɪŋlɪʃ) n *informal* a form of spoken English that blends British English with Black youth slang [c21 from BLING(-BLING) + (ENG)LISH, a reference to the jewellery favoured by some Black rappers and singers]

blini ('blɪnɪ) *or* **bliny, blinis** ('blɪnɪz) pl n Russian pancakes made of buckwheat flour and yeast [c19 from Russian: plural of *blin*, from Old Russian *mlinŭ*, related to Russian *molot'* to grind]

blink (blɪŋk) vb 1 to close and immediately reopen (the eyes or an eye), usually involuntarily 2 (intr) to look with the eyes partially closed, as in strong sunlight 3 to shine intermittently, as in signalling, or unsteadily 4 (tr; foll by *away, from, etc*) to clear the eyes of (dust, tears, etc) 5 (when tr, usually foll by *at*) to be surprised or amazed: *he blinked at the splendour of the ceremony* 6 (when intr, foll by *at*) to pretend not to know or see (a fault, injustice, etc) ▷ n 7 the act or an instance of blinking 8 a glance; glimpse 9 short for **iceblink** (sense 1) 10 **on the blink** *slang* not working properly [c14 variant of BLENCH¹; related to Middle Dutch *blinken* to glitter, Danish *blinke* to wink, Swedish *blinka*]

blinker ('blɪŋkə) n 1 a flashing light for sending messages, as a warning device, etc, such as a direction indicator on a road vehicle 2 (often plural) a slang word for **eye¹** ▷ vb (tr) 3 to provide (a horse) with blinkers 4 to obscure with or as if with blinkers

blinkered ('blɪŋkəd) adj 1 considering only a narrow point of view 2 (of a horse) wearing blinkers

blinkers ('blɪŋkəz) pl n 1 (sometimes singular) chiefly Brit leather sidepieces attached to a horse's bridle to prevent sideways vision. Usual US and Canadian word: blinders 2 a slang word for **goggle** (sense 4)

blinking ('blɪŋkɪŋ) adj, adv informal (intensifier): a blinking fool; a blinking good film

blinks (blɪŋks) n (functioning as singular) a small temperate portulacaceous plant, Montia fontana with small white flowers [C19 from BLINK, because the flowers do not fully open and thus seem to blink at the light]

blintz or **blintze** (blɪnts) n a thin pancake folded over a filling usually of apple, cream cheese, or meat [C20 from Yiddish blintse, from Russian blinyets little pancakes; see BLINI]

blip (blɪp) n 1 a repetitive sound, such as that produced by an electronic device, by dripping water, etc 2 Also called: pip the spot of light or a sharply peaked pulse on a radar screen indicating the position of an object 3 a temporary irregularity recorded in performance of something ▷ vb blips, blipping, blipped 4 (intr) to produce such a noise [C20 of imitative origin]

blipvert ('blɪp,vɜːt) n a very short television advertisement [(C20 from BLIP + (AD)VERT]

bliss (blɪs) n 1 perfect happiness; serene joy 2 the ecstatic joy of heaven [Old English bliss; related to blīthe BLITHE, Old Saxon blīdsea bliss] > 'blissless adj

blissful ('blɪsfʊl) adj 1 serenely joyful or glad 2 blissful ignorance unawareness or inexperience of something unpleasant > 'blissfully adv > 'blissfulness n

B list n a a category considered to be slightly below the most socially desirable b (as modifier): B-list celebrities ▷ Compare **A list**

blister ('blɪstə) n 1 a small bubble-like elevation of the skin filled with serum, produced as a reaction to a burn, mechanical irritation, etc 2 a swelling containing air or liquid, as on a painted surface 3 a transparent dome or any bulge on the fuselage of an aircraft, such as one used for observation 4 slang an irritating person 5 NZ slang a rebuke ▷ vb 6 to have or cause to have blisters 7 (tr) to attack verbally with great scorn or sarcasm [C13 from Old French blestre, probably from Middle Dutch bluyster blister; see BLAST] > 'blistered adj > 'blistery adj

blister beetle n any beetle of the family Meloidae, many of which produce a secretion that blisters the skin. See also **Spanish fly**

blister copper n an impure form of copper having a blister-like surface due to the release of gas during cooling

blistering ('blɪstərɪŋ, -trɪŋ) adj 1 (of weather) extremely hot 2 (of criticism) extremely harsh > 'blisteringly adv

blister pack n a type of packet in which small items are displayed and sold, consisting of a transparent dome or plastic or similar material mounted on a firm backing such as cardboard. Also called: bubble pack

blister rust n a disease of certain pines caused by rust fungi of the genus Cronartium, causing swellings on the bark from which orange masses of spores are released

BLit abbreviation for Bachelor of Literature

blithe (blaɪð) adj 1 very happy or cheerful 2 heedless; casual and indifferent [Old English blīthe] > 'blithely adv > 'blitheness n

blithering ('blɪðərɪŋ) adj 1 talking foolishly; jabbering 2 informal stupid; foolish: you blithering idiot [C19 variant of BLATHER + -ING²]

blithesome ('blaɪðsəm) adj literary cheery; merry > 'blithesomely adv > 'blithesomeness n

BLitt abbreviation for Bachelor of Letters [Latin Baccalaureus Litterarum]

blitz (blɪts) n 1 a violent and sustained attack, esp with intensive aerial bombardment 2 any sudden intensive attack or concerted effort 3 American football a defensive charge on the quarterback ▷ vb 4 (tr) to attack suddenly and intensively [C20 shortened from German Blitzkrieg lightning war]

Blitz (blɪts) n the. the systematic night-time bombing of Britain in 1940–41 by the German Luftwaffe

blitzkrieg ('blɪts,kriːg) n a swift intensive military attack, esp using tanks supported by aircraft, designed to defeat the opposition quickly [C20 from German: lightning war]

blizzard ('blɪzəd) n a strong bitterly cold wind accompanied by a widespread heavy snowfall [C19 of uncertain origin]

BLL abbreviation for Bachelor of Laws

BL Lac object n an extremely compact violently variable form of active galaxy [C20 named after BL Lacertae, first identified example found in the constellation Lacerta and originally thought to be a variable star]

bloat (bləʊt) vb 1 to swell or cause to swell, as with a liquid, air, or wind 2 to become or cause to be puffed up, as with conceit 3 (tr) to cure (fish, esp herring) by half-drying in smoke ▷ n 4 vet science an abnormal distention of the abdomen in cattle, sheep, etc, caused by accumulation of gas in the stomach [C17 probably related to Old Norse blautr soaked, Old English blāt pale]

bloated ('bləʊtɪd) adj 1 swollen, as with a liquid, air, or wind 2 puffed up, as with conceit

bloater ('bləʊtə) n 1 a herring, or sometimes a mackerel, that has been salted in brine, smoked, and cured 2 Brit slang a fat or greedy person

blob (blɒb) n 1 a soft mass or drop, as of some viscous liquid 2 a spot, dab, or blotch of colour, ink, etc 3 a indistinct or shapeless form or object 4 a slang word for **condom** ▷ vb blobs, blobbing, blobbed 5 (tr) to put blobs, as of ink or paint, on [C15 perhaps of imitative origin; compare BUBBLE] > 'blobby adj

bloc (blɒk) n a group of people or countries combined by a common interest or aim: the Soviet bloc [C20 from French: BLOCK]

block (blɒk) n 1 a large solid piece of wood, stone, or other material with flat rectangular sides, as for use in building 2 any large solid piece of wood, stone, etc, usually having at least one face fairly flat 3 such a piece on which particular tasks may be done, as chopping, cutting, or beheading 4 Also called: building block one of a set of wooden or plastic cubes as a child's toy 5 a form on which things are shaped or displayed: a wig block 6 slang a person's head (esp in the phrase knock someone's block off) 7 do one's block Austral and NZ slang to become angry 8 a dull, unemotional, or hardhearted person 9 a large building of offices, flats, etc 10 a group of buildings in a city bounded by intersecting streets on each side b the area or distance between such intersecting streets 11 Austral and NZ an area of land for a house, farm, etc 12 Austral and NZ a log, usually a willow, fastened to a timber base and used in a wood-chopping competition 13 an area of land, esp one to be divided for building or settling 14 See cylinder block 15 a a piece of wood, metal, or other material having an engraved, cast, or carved design in relief, used either for printing or for stamping book covers, etc b Brit a letterpress printing plate, esp one mounted type-high on wood or metal 16 a casing housing one or more freely rotating pulleys. See also block and tackle 17 on the block chiefly US and Canadian up for auction 18 the act of obstructing or condition of being obstructed, as in sports 19 an obstruction or hindrance 20 pathol a

interference in the normal physiological functioning of an organ or part b See heart block c See nerve block 21 psychol a short interruption of perceptual or thought processes 22 obstruction of an opponent in a sport 23 a a section or quantity, as of tickets or shares, handled or considered as a single unit b (as modifier): a block booking; block voting 24 a a stretch of railway in which only one train may travel at a time b (as modifier): a block signal 25 an unseparated group of four or more postage stamps. Compare strip¹ (sense 3) 26 a pad of paper 27 computing a group of words treated as a unit of data on a tape, disk, etc 28 athletics short for starting block 29 cricket a mark made near the popping crease by a batsman to indicate his position in relation to the wicket 30 a chip off the old block informal a person who resembles one of his or her parents in behaviour ▷ vb (mainly tr) 31 to shape or form (something) into a block 32 to fit with or mount on a block 33 to shape by use of a block: to block a hat 34 (often foll by up) to obstruct (a passage, channel, etc) or prevent or impede the motion or flow of (something or someone) by introducing an obstacle: to block the traffic; to block up a pipe 35 to impede, retard, or prevent (an action, procedure, etc) 36 to stamp (a title, design, etc) on (a book cover, etc) by means of a block (see sense 15a), esp using gold leaf or other foil 37 (esp of a government or central bank) to limit the use or conversion of assets or currency 38 (also intr) sport to obstruct or impede movement by (an opponent) 39 (intr) to suffer a psychological block 40 to interrupt a physiological function, as by use of an anaesthetic 41 (also intr) cricket to play (a ball) defensively. ▷ See also block in, block out [C14 from Old French bloc, from Dutch blok; related to Old High German bloh] > 'blocker n

blockade (blɒ'keɪd) n 1 military the interdiction of a nation's sea lines of communications, esp of an individual port by the use of sea power 2 something that prevents access or progress 3 med the inhibition of the effect of a hormone or a drug, a transport system, or the action of a nerve by a drug ▷ vb (tr) 4 to impose a blockade on 5 to obstruct the way to [C17 from BLOCK + -ade, as in AMBUSCADE] > block'ader n

blockage ('blɒkɪdʒ) n 1 the act of blocking or state of being blocked 2 an object causing an obstruction

block and tackle n a hoisting device in which a rope or chain is passed around a pair of blocks containing one or more pulleys. The upper block is secured overhead and the lower block supports the load, the effort being applied to the free end of the rope or chain

blockboard ('blɒk,bɔːd) n a type of plywood in which soft wood strips are bonded together and sandwiched between two layers of veneer

blockbuster ('blɒk,bʌstə) n informal 1 a large bomb used to demolish extensive areas or strengthened targets 2 a very successful, effective, or forceful person, thing, etc

blockbusting ('blɒk,bʌstɪŋ) n US informal the act or practice of inducing the sale of property cheaply by exploiting the owners' fears of lower prices if racial minorities live in the area

block capital n another term for block letter

block diagram n 1 a diagram showing the interconnections between the parts of an industrial process 2 a three-dimensional drawing representing a block of the earth's crust, showing geological structure 3 computing a diagram showing the interconnections between electronic components or parts of a program

blocked (blɒkt) adj slang functionally impeded by amphetamine

blocked shoe n a dancing shoe with a stiffened toe that enables a ballet dancer to dance on the tips of the toes

blocker n 1 a person or thing that acts as a block 2 physiol an agent that blocks a physiological

b

function, such as the transport of an ion across an ion channel

block grant *n* (in Britain) an annual grant made by the government to a local authority to help to pay for the public services it provides, such as health, education, and housing

blockhead ('blɒk,hɛd) *n derogatory* a stupid person > ,block'headed *adj* > ,block'headedly *adv* > ,block'headedness *n*

blockhouse ('blɒk,haʊs) *n* **1** (formerly) a wooden fortification with ports or loopholes for defensive fire, observation, etc **2** a concrete structure strengthened to give protection against enemy fire, with apertures to allow defensive gunfire **3** a building constructed of logs or squared timber **4** a reinforced concrete building close to a rocket-launching site for protecting personnel and equipment during launching

blockie ('blɒkɪ) *n Austral informal* an owner of a small property, esp a farm

block in *vb* (*tr, adverb*) to sketch in outline, with little detail

blocking ('blɒkɪŋ) *n* **1** *electronics* the interruption of anode current in a valve because of the application of a high negative voltage to the grid **2** internal congestion in a communication system that prevents the transmission of information

blockish ('blɒkɪʃ) *adj* lacking vivacity or imagination; stupid > 'blockishly *adv* > 'blockishness *n*

block lava *n* volcanic lava occurring as rough-surfaced jagged blocks

block letter *n* Also called: **block capital** a plain capital letter

block out *vb* (*tr, adverb*) **1** to plan or describe (something) in a general fashion **2** to prevent the entry or consideration of (something) **3** *photog, printing* to mask part of (a negative), in order that light may not pass through it

Block Parent Program of Canada *n* the (in Canada) a registered charity and child-safety organization

block plane *n* a carpenter's small plane used to cut across the end grain of wood

block printing *n* printing from hand engraved or carved blocks of wood or linoleum

block release *n Brit* the release of industrial trainees from work for study at a college for several weeks

block sampling *n* the selection of a corpus for statistical literary analysis by random selection of a starting point and consideration of the continuous passage following it. Compare **spread sampling**

block tin *n* pure tin, esp when cast into ingots

block vote *n Brit* (at a conference, esp of trade unionists) the system whereby each delegate's vote has a value in proportion to the number of people he or she represents. Compare **OMOV**

blocky *adj* like a block, esp in shape and solidity > 'blockiness *n*

Bloc Québécois (blɒk keɪbeˈkwɑ:) *n* (in Canada) a political party that advocates autonomy for Quebec

Bloemfontein ('blu:mfɒn,teɪn) *n* a city in central South Africa: capital of Free State province and judicial capital of the country. Pop: 111 698 (2001)

blog (blɒg) *n informal* a journal written on-line and accessible to users of the internet. Full name: weblog > 'blogger *n* > 'blogging *n*

Blois (*French* blwa) *n* a city in N central France, on the Loire: 13th-century castle. Pop: 49 171 (1999)

bloke (bləʊk) *n Brit and Austral* an informal word for **man** [c19 from Shelta]

blowkart ('bləʊ,kɑ:t) *n* a single-seat three-wheeled vehicle with a sail, built to be propelled over land by the wind [c20 from BLO(W) + (GO-)KART] > 'blow,karting *n*

blokeish or **blokish** ('bləʊkɪʃ) *adj informal, sometimes derogatory* denoting or exhibiting the characteristics believed typical of an ordinary man: *blokeish nudges and winks*. Also: **blokey** ('bləʊkɪ)

> 'blokeishness or 'blokishness *n*

blond (blɒnd) *adj* **1** (of men's hair) of a light colour; fair **2** (of a person, people or a race) having fair hair, a light complexion, and, typically, blue or grey eyes **3** (of soft furnishings, wood, etc) light in colour ▷ *n* **4** a person, esp a man, having light-coloured hair and skin [c15 from Old French *blond*, probably of Germanic origin; related to Late Latin *blundus* yellow, Italian *biondo*, Spanish *blondo*] > 'blondness *n*

USAGE Although *blond* and *blonde* correspond to masculine and feminine forms in French, this distinction is not consistently made in English. *Blonde* is the commoner form both as a noun and an adjective, and is more frequently used to refer to women than men. The less common variant *blond* occurs usually as an adjective, occasionally as a noun, and is the preferred form when referring to men with fair hair

blonde (blɒnd) *adj* **1** (of women's hair) of a light colour; fair **2** (of a person, people or a race) having fair hair, a light complexion, and, typically, blue or grey eyes **3** (of soft furnishings, wood, etc) light in colour ▷ *n* **4** a person, esp a woman, having light-coloured hair and skin **5** Also called: **blonde lace** a French pillow lace, originally of unbleached cream-coloured Chinese silk, later of bleached or black-dyed silk [c15 from Old French *blond* (fem *blonde*), probably of Germanic origin; related to Late Latin *blundus* yellow, Italian *biondo*, Spanish *blondo*] > 'blondeness *n*

blonding ('blɒndɪŋ) *n* **a** the act or an instance of dyeing hair blonde **b** (*as modifier*): *blonding sprays*

blood (blʌd) *n* **1** a reddish fluid in vertebrates that is pumped by the heart through the arteries and veins, supplies tissues with nutrients, oxygen, etc, and removes waste products. It consists of a fluid (see **blood plasma**) containing cells (erythrocytes, leucocytes, and platelets). Related adjectives: **haemal, haematic, sanguineous 2** a similar fluid in such invertebrates as annelids and arthropods **3** bloodshed, esp when resulting in murder **4** the guilt or responsibility for killing or injuring (esp in the phrase **to have blood on one's hands** or **head**) **5** life itself; lifeblood **6** relationship through being of the same family, race, or kind; kinship **7** blood, sweat and tears *informal* hard work and concentrated effort **8** **flesh and blood a** near kindred or kinship, esp that between a parent and child **b** human nature (esp in the phrase **it's more than flesh and blood can stand**) **9** ethnic or national descent: *of Spanish blood* **10** **in one's blood** as a natural or inherited characteristic or talent **11** **the blood** royal or noble descent: *a prince of the blood* **12** temperament; disposition; temper **13** a of pure or pure breeding; pedigree **b** (*as modifier*): *blood horses* **14** people viewed as members of a group, esp as an invigorating force (in the phrases **new blood, young blood**) **15** *chiefly Brit rare* a dashing young man; dandy; rake **16** the sensual or carnal nature of man **17** *obsolete* one of the four bodily humours. See **humour** (sense 8) **18** **bad blood** hatred; ill feeling **19** **blood is thicker than water** family duties and loyalty outweigh other ties **20** **have** or **get one's blood up** to be or cause to be angry or inflamed **21** **in cold blood** showing no passion; deliberately; ruthlessly **22** **make one's blood boil** to cause to be angry or indignant **23** **make one's blood run cold** to fill with horror ▷ *vb* **24** *hunting* to cause (young hounds) to taste the blood of a freshly killed quarry and so become keen to hunt **25** *hunting* to smear the cheeks or forehead of (a person) with the blood of the kill as an initiation in hunting **26** to initiate (a person) to war [Old English *blōd*; related to Old Norse *blōth*, Old High German *bluot*]

blood-and-thunder *adj* denoting or relating to a melodramatic adventure story

blood bank *n* a place where whole blood, blood plasma, or other blood products are stored until required in transfusion

blood bath *n* indiscriminate slaughter; a massacre

blood brother *n* **1** a brother by birth **2** a man or boy who has sworn to treat another as his brother, often in a ceremony in which their blood is mingled

blood cell *n* any of the cells that circulate in the blood. See **erythrocyte, leucocyte**

blood count *n* the number of red and white blood corpuscles and platelets in a specific sample of blood. See **haemocytometer**

bloodcurdling ('blʌd,kɜ:dlɪŋ) *adj* terrifying; horrifying > 'blood,curdlingly *adv*

blood donor *n* a person who gives his or her blood to be used for transfusion

blood doping *n* the illegal practice of removing a quantity of blood from an athlete long before a race and reinjecting it shortly before a race, so boosting oxygenation of the blood

blood-drop emlets ('ɛmlɪts) *n* (*functioning as singular*) a Chilean scrophulariaceous plant, *Mimulus luteus*, naturalized in Europe, having red-spotted yellow flowers. See also **monkey flower, musk** (sense 3)

blooded ('blʌdɪd) *adj* **1** (of horses, cattle, etc) of good breeding **2** (*in combination*) having blood or temperament as specified: *hot-blooded, cold-blooded, warm-blooded, red-blooded, blue-blooded*

blood feud *n* a feud in which the members of hostile families or clans murder each other

bloodfin ('blʌd,fɪn) *n* a silvery red-finned South American freshwater fish, *Aphyocharax rubripinnis*: a popular aquarium fish: family *Characidae* (characins)

blood fluke *n* any parasitic flatworm, such as a schistosome, that lives in the blood vessels of man and other vertebrates: class *Digenea*. See also **trematode**

blood group *n* any one of the various groups into which human blood is classified on the basis of its agglutinogens. Also called: **blood type**

blood guilt *n* guilt of murder or shedding blood > 'blood-,guilty *adj* > 'blood-,guiltiness *n*

blood heat *n* the normal temperature of the human body, 98.4°F or 37°C

bloodhound ('blʌd,haʊnd) *n* **1** a large breed of hound having a smooth glossy coat of red, tan, or black and loose wrinkled skin on its head: formerly much used in tracking and police work **2** *informal* a detective

bloodless ('blʌdlɪs) *adj* **1** without blood **2** conducted without violence (esp in the phrase **bloodless revolution**) **3** anaemic-looking; pale **4** lacking vitality; lifeless **5** lacking in emotion; cold; unfeeling > 'bloodlessly *adv* > 'bloodlessness *n*

Bloodless Revolution *n* the. another name for the **Glorious Revolution**

blood-letting ('blʌd,lɛtɪŋ) *n* **1** the therapeutic removal of blood, as in relieving congestive heart failure. See also **phlebotomy 2** bloodshed, esp in a blood feud

bloodline ('blʌd,laɪn) *n* all the members of a family group over generations, esp regarding characteristics common to that group; pedigree

bloodmobile ('blʌdmə,bi:l) *n US* a motor vehicle equipped for collecting blood from donors

blood money *n* **1** compensation paid to the relatives of a murdered person **2** money paid to a hired murderer **3** a reward for information about a criminal, esp a murderer

blood orange *n* a variety of orange all or part of the pulp of which is dark red when ripe

blood plasma *n* **1** the pale yellow fluid portion of the blood; blood from which red and white blood cells and platelets have been removed **2** a sterilized preparation of this fluid for use in transfusions

blood poisoning *n* a nontechnical term for **septicaemia**

blood pressure *n* the pressure exerted by the blood on the inner walls of the arteries, being relative to the elasticity and diameter of the vessels and the force of the heartbeat

blood pudding *n* another name for **black pudding**

blood red *n* **a** a deep red colour **b** (*as adjective*): *blood-red roses*

blood relation or **relative** *n* a person related to another by birth, as distinct from one related by marriage

bloodroot (ˈblʌdˌruːt) *n* **1** Also called: **red puccoon** a North American papaveraceous plant, *Sanguinaria canadensis*, having a single whitish flower and a fleshy red root that yields a red dye **2** another name for **tormentil**

blood sausage *n* *US and Canadian* a kind of black sausage made from minced pork fat, pig's blood, and other ingredients. Also called (in Britain and certain other countries): **black pudding**

blood serum *n* blood plasma from which the clotting factors have been removed

bloodshed (ˈblʌdˌʃɛd) *n* slaughter; killing

bloodshot (ˈblʌdˌʃɒt) *adj* (of an eye) inflamed

blood sport *n* any sport involving the killing of an animal, esp hunting

bloodstain (ˈblʌdˌsteɪn) *n* a dark discoloration caused by blood, esp dried blood

bloodstained (ˈblʌdˌsteɪnd) *adj* stained by or covered with blood

bloodstock (ˈblʌdˌstɒk) *n* thoroughbred horses, esp those bred for racing

bloodstock industry *n* the breeding and training of racehorses

bloodstone (ˈblʌdˌstəʊn) *n* a dark-green variety of chalcedony with red spots: used as a gemstone. Also called: **heliotrope**

bloodstream (ˈblʌdˌstriːm) *n* the flow of blood through the vessels of a living body

blood substitute *n* a substance such as plasma, albumin, or dextran, used to replace lost blood or increase the blood volume

bloodsucker (ˈblʌdˌsʌkə) *n* **1** an animal that sucks blood, esp a leech or mosquito **2** a person or thing that preys upon another person, esp by extorting money

blood sugar *n* *med* the glucose concentration in the blood: the normal fasting value is between 3.9 and 5.6 mmol/l

blood test *n* analysis of a blood sample to determine blood group, alcohol concentration, etc

bloodthirsty (ˈblʌdˌθɜːstɪ) *adj* **-thirstier, -thirstiest** **1** murderous; cruel **2** taking pleasure in bloodshed or violence **3** describing or depicting killing and violence; gruesome: *a bloodthirsty film* > ˈblood.thirstily *adv* > ˈblood.thirstiness *n*

blood type *n* another name for **blood group**

blood vessel *n* an artery, capillary, or vein

blood volume *n* *med* the total quantity of blood in the body

bloodwood (ˈblʌdˌwʊd) *n* any of several species of Australian eucalyptus that exude a red sap

bloodworm (ˈblʌdˌwɜːm) *n* **1** the red wormlike aquatic larva of the midge, *Chironomus plumosus*, which lives at the bottom of stagnant pools and ditches **2** a freshwater oligochaete tubifex worm **3** any of several small reddish worms used as angling bait

bloody (ˈblʌdɪ) *adj* **bloodier, bloodiest 1** covered or stained with blood **2** resembling or composed of blood **3** marked by much killing and bloodshed: *a bloody war* **4** cruel or murderous: *a bloody tyrant* **5** of a deep red colour; blood-red ▷ *adv* ▷ *adj* **6** *slang, chiefly Brit (intensifier)*: *a bloody fool; bloody fine food* ▷ *vb* **bloodies, bloodying, bloodied 7** (*tr*) to stain with blood > ˈbloodily *adv* > ˈbloodiness *n*

Bloody Caesar *n* a drink consisting of vodka, juice made from clams and tomatoes, Worcester sauce, and Tabasco

Bloody Mary *n* a drink consisting of tomato juice and vodka

bloody-minded *adj Brit informal* deliberately obstructive and unhelpful > ˌbloody-ˈmindedness *n* > ˌbloody-ˈmindedly *adv*

bloody-nosed beetle *n* a beetle, *Timarcha tenebricosa*, that exudes bright red blood when alarmed: family *Chrysomelidae*

bloom¹ (bluːm) *n* **1** a blossom on a flowering plant; a flower **2** the state, time, or period when flowers open (esp in the phrases **in bloom, in full bloom**) **3** open flowers collectively: *a tree covered with bloom* **4** a healthy, vigorous, or flourishing condition; prime (esp in the phrase **the bloom of youth**) **5** youthful or healthy rosiness in the cheeks or face; glow **6** a fine whitish coating on the surface of fruits, leaves, etc, consisting of minute grains of a waxy substance **7** any coating similar in appearance, such as that on new coins **8** *ecology* a visible increase in the algal constituent of plankton, which may be seasonal or due to excessive organic pollution **9** Also called: **chill** a dull area formed on the surface of gloss paint, lacquer, or varnish ▷ *vb (mainly intr)* **10** (of flowers) to open; come into flower **11** to bear flowers; blossom **12** to flourish or grow **13** to be in a healthy, glowing, or flourishing condition **14** (*tr*) *physics* to coat (a lens) with a thin layer of a substance, often magnesium fluoride, to eliminate surface reflection [C13 of Germanic origin; compare Old Norse *blōm* flower, Old High German *bluomo*, Middle Dutch *bloeme*; see BLOW³]

bloom² (bluːm) *n* **1** a rectangular mass of metal obtained by rolling or forging a cast ingot. See also **billet¹** (sense 2) ▷ *vb* **2** (*tr*) to convert (an ingot) into a bloom by rolling or forging [Old English *blōma* lump of metal]

bloomed (bluːmd) *adj photog, optics* (of a lens) coated with a thin film of magnesium fluoride or some other substance to reduce the amount of light lost by reflection. Also called: **coated**

bloomer¹ (ˈbluːmə) *n* a plant that flowers, esp in a specified way: *a night bloomer*

bloomer² (ˈbluːmə) *n Brit informal* a stupid mistake; blunder [C20 from BLOOMING]

bloomer³ (ˈbluːmə) *n Brit* a medium-sized loaf, baked on the sole of the oven, glazed and notched on top [C20 of uncertain origin]

bloomers (ˈbluːməz) *pl n* **1** *informal* women's or girls' baggy knickers **2** (formerly) loose trousers gathered at the knee worn by women for cycling and athletics **3** *history* Also called: **rational dress** long loose trousers gathered at the ankle and worn under a shorter skirt [from *bloomer*, a garment introduced in about 1850 and publicized by Mrs A. Bloomer (1818–94), US social reformer]

bloomery (ˈbluːmərɪ) *n, pl* **-eries** a place in which malleable iron is produced directly from iron ore

blooming (ˈbluːmɪŋ) *adv, adj Brit informal* (intensifier): *a blooming genius; blooming painful* [C19 euphemistic for BLOODY]

Bloomington (ˈbluːmɪŋtən) *n* a city in central Indiana: seat of the University of Indiana (1820). Pop: 70 642 (2003 est)

Bloomsbury (ˈbluːmzbərɪ, -brɪ) *n* **1** a district of central London in the borough of Camden: contains the British Museum, part of the University of London, and many publishers' offices ▷ *adj* **2** relating to or characteristic of the Bloomsbury Group

Bloomsbury Group *n* a group of writers, artists, and intellectuals living and working in and around Bloomsbury in London from about 1907 to 1930. Influenced by the philosophy of G. E. Moore, they included Leonard and Virginia Woolf, Clive and Vanessa Bell, Roger Fry, E. M. Forster, Lytton Strachey, Duncan Grant, and John Maynard Keynes

Bloomsday (ˈbluːmzdeɪ) *n* an annual celebration in Dublin on June 16th of the life of the Irish author James Joyce (1882–1941) and in particular, his novel *Ulysses*, which is entirely set in Dublin on June 16th, 1904 [C20 Leopold Bloom, the central character in *Ulysses*]

bloomy (ˈbluːmɪ) *adj* **bloomier, bloomiest** having a fine whitish coating on the surface, such as on the rind of a cheese

blooper (ˈbluːpə) *n informal, chiefly US and Canadian* a blunder; bloomer; stupid mistake [C20 from *bloop* (imitative of an embarrassing sound) + -ER¹]

bloquiste (blɒkˈiːst) *n* (in Canada) a member or supporter of the Bloc Québécois

blossom (ˈblɒsəm) *n* **1** the flower or flowers of a plant, esp conspicuous flowers producing edible fruit **2** the time or period of flowering (esp in the phrases **in blossom, in full blossom**) ▷ *vb* **3** (of plants) to come into flower **4** to develop or come to a promising stage: *youth had blossomed into maturity* [Old English *blōstm*; related to Middle Low German *blōsem*, Latin *flōs* flower] > ˈblossoming *n, adj* > ˈblossomless *adj* > ˈblossomy *adj*

blot¹ (blɒt) *n* **1** a stain or spot of ink, paint, dirt, etc **2** something that spoils or detracts from the beauty or worth of something **3** a blemish or stain on one's character or reputation ▷ *vb* **blots, blotting, blotted 4** (of ink, dye, etc) to form spots or blobs on (a material) or (of a person) to cause such spots or blobs to form on (a material) **5** **blot one's copybook** *informal* to spoil one's reputation by making a mistake, offending against social customs, etc **6** (*intr*) to stain or become stained or spotted **7** (*tr*) to cause a blemish or in on; disgrace **8** to soak up (excess ink, etc) by using blotting paper or some other absorbent material **9** (of blotting paper or some other absorbent material) to absorb (excess ink, etc) **10** (*tr; often foll by out*) **a** to darken or hide completely; obscure; obliterate **b** to destroy; annihilate [C14 probably of Germanic origin; compare Middle Dutch *bluyster* BLISTER]

blot² (blɒt) *n* **1** *backgammon* a man exposed by being placed alone on a point and therefore able to be taken by the other player **2** *archaic* a weak spot [C16 perhaps from Middle Dutch *bloot* poor]

blot analysis *n biochem* a technique for analysing biological molecules, such as proteins (**Western blot analysis**), DNA (**Southern blot analysis**), and RNA (**Northern blot analysis**), involving their separation by gel electrophoresis, transfer to a nitrocellulose sheet, and subsequent analysis by autoradiography. Also called: **blotting**

blotch (blɒtʃ) *n* **1** an irregular spot or discoloration, esp a dark and relatively large one such as an ink stain ▷ *vb* **2** to become or cause to become marked by such discoloration **3** (*intr*) (of a pen or ink) to write or flow unevenly in blotches [C17 probably from BOTCH, influenced by BLOT¹]

blotchy (ˈblɒtʃɪ) *adj* covered in or marked by blotches > ˈblotchily *adv* > ˈblotchiness *n*

blotter (ˈblɒtə) *n* **1** something used to absorb excess ink or other liquid, esp a sheet of blotting paper with a firm backing **2** *US* a daily record of events, such as arrests, in a police station (esp in the phrase **police blotter**)

blotting paper *n* a soft absorbent unsized paper, used esp for soaking up surplus ink

blotto (ˈblɒtəʊ) *adj slang* unconscious, esp through drunkenness [C20 from BLOT¹ (vb); compare *blot out*]

blouse (blaʊz) *n* **1** a woman's shirtlike garment made of cotton, nylon, etc **2** a loose-fitting smocklike garment, often knee length and belted, worn esp by E European peasants **3** a loose-fitting waist-length belted jacket worn by soldiers ▷ *vb* **4** to hang or make so as to hang in full loose folds [C19 from French, of unknown origin]

blouson (ˈbluːzɒn) *n* a short jacket or top having the shape of a blouse [C20 French]

blow¹ (bləʊ) *archaic* ▷ *vb* **blows, blowing, blew, blown 1** (of a current of air, the wind, etc) to be or cause to be in motion **2** (*intr*) to move or be carried by or as if by wind or air: *a feather blew in through the window* **3** to expel (air, cigarette smoke, etc) through the mouth or nose **4** to force or cause

b

(air, dust, etc) to move (into, in, over, etc) by using an instrument or by expelling breath **5** (*intr*) to breathe hard; pant **6** (sometimes foll by *up*) to inflate with air or the breath **7** (*intr*) (of wind, a storm, etc) to make a roaring or whistling sound **8** to cause (a whistle, siren, etc) to sound by forcing air into it, as a signal, or (of a whistle, etc) to sound thus **9** (*tr*) to force air from the lungs through (the nose) to clear out mucus or obstructing matter **10** (often foll by *up, down, in,* etc) to explode, break, or disintegrate completely: *the bridge blew down in the gale* **11** *electronics* to burn out (a fuse, valve, etc) because of excessive current or (of a fuse, valve, etc) to burn out **12** **blow a fuse** *slang* to lose one's temper **13** (*intr*) (of a whale) to spout water or air from the lungs **14** (*tr*) to wind (a horse) by making it run excessively **15** to cause (a wind instrument) to sound by forcing one's breath into the mouthpiece, or (of such an instrument) to sound in this way **16** (*intr*) *jazz slang* to play in a jam session **17** (*intr*) (of flies) to lay eggs (in) **18** to shape (glass, ornaments, etc) by forcing air or gas through the material when molten **19** (*intr*) *chiefly Scot, Austral, and NZ* to boast or brag **20** (*tr*) *slang* **a** to spend (money) freely **b** *US* to treat or entertain **21** (*tr*) *slang* to use (an opportunity) ineffectively **22** *slang* to go suddenly away (from) **23** (*tr*) *slang* to expose or betray (a person or thing meant to be kept secret) **24** (*tr*) *US slang* to inhale (a drug) **25** (*intr*) *slang* to masturbate **26** *past participle* **blowed** *informal* another word for **damn** (esp in the phrases **I'll be blowed, blow it!, blow me down!**) **27** *draughts* another word for **huff** (sense 4) **28** **blow hot and cold** to vacillate **29** **blow a kiss** *or* **kisses** to kiss one's hand, then blow across it as if to carry the kiss through the air to another person **30** **blow one's own trumpet** to boast of one's own skills or good qualities **31** **blow someone's mind** *slang* **a** (of a drug, esp LSD) to alter someone's mental state **b** to astound or surprise someone **32** **blow one's top** *or* (*esp US and Canadian*) **lid** *or* **stack** *informal* to lose one's temper ▷ *n* **33** the act or an instance of blowing **34** the sound produced by blowing **35** a blast of air or wind **36** *metallurgy* **a** a stage in the Bessemer process in which air is blasted upwards through molten pig iron **b** the quantity of metal treated in a Bessemer converter **37** *mining* **a** a rush of air into a mine **b** the collapse of a mine roof **38** *jazz slang* a jam session **39** **a** *Brit* a slang name for **cannabis** (sense 2) **b** *US* a slang name for **cocaine** ▷ See also **blow away, blow in, blow into, blow off, blow on, blow out, blow over, blow through, blow up** [Old English *blāwan*, related to Old Norse *blǣr* gust of wind, Old High German *blāen*, Latin *flāre*]

blow[2] (bləʊ) *n* **1** a powerful or heavy stroke with the fist, a weapon, etc **2** **at one** *or* **a blow** by or with only one action; all at one time **3** a sudden setback; unfortunate event: *to come as a blow* **4** **come to blows** **a** to fight **b** to result in a fight **5** an attacking action: *a blow for freedom* **6** *Austral and NZ* a stroke of the shears in sheep-shearing [c15 probably of Germanic origin; compare Old High German *bliuwan* to beat]

blow[3] (bləʊ) *vb* **blows, blowing, blew, blown** **1** (*intr*) (of a plant or flower) to blossom or open out **2** (*tr*) to produce (flowers) ▷ *n* **3** a mass of blossoms **4** the state or period of blossoming (esp in the phrase **in full blow**) [Old English *blōwan*; related to Old Frisian *blōia* to bloom, Old High German *bluoen*, Latin *flōs* flower; see BLOOM[1]]

blow away *vb* (*tr, adverb*) *slang, chiefly US* **1** to kill (someone) by shooting **2** to defeat decisively

blowback (ˈbləʊˌbæk) *n* **1** the escape to the rear of gases formed during the firing of a weapon or in a boiler, internal-combustion engine, etc **2** the action of a light automatic weapon in which the expanding gases of the propellant force back the bolt, thus reloading the weapon

blow-by *n* the leakage of gas past the piston of an engine at maximum pressure

blow-by-blow *adj* (*prenominal*) explained in great detail: *a blow-by-blow account of the argument*

blowdown (ˈbləʊˌdaʊn) *n* **1** an accident in a nuclear reactor in which a cooling pipe bursts causing the loss of essential coolant ▷ *vb* **2** to open a valve in a steam boiler to eject any sediment that has collected

blow-dry *vb* **-dries, -drying, -dried** (*tr*) **1** to style (hair) while drying it with a hand-held hairdryer ▷ *n* **2** this method of styling the hair

blower (ˈbləʊə) *n* **1** a mechanical device, such as a fan, that blows **2** a low-pressure rotary compressor, esp in a furnace or internal-combustion engine. See also **supercharger** **3** an informal name for **telephone** **4** an informal name for **speaking tube** **5** an informal name for a **whale** **6** *mining* a discharge of firedamp from a crevice

blowfish (ˈbləʊˌfɪʃ) *n, pl* **-fish** *or* **-fishes** a popular name for **puffer** (sense 2)

blowfly (ˈbləʊˌflaɪ) *n, pl* **-flies** any of various dipterous flies of the genus *Calliphora* and related genera that lay their eggs in rotting meat, dung, carrion, and open wounds: family *Calliphoridae*. Also called: **bluebottle**

blowgun (ˈbləʊˌɡʌn) *n* the US word for **blowpipe** (sense 1)

blowhard (ˈbləʊˌhɑːd) *informal* ▷ *n* **1** a boastful person ▷ *adj* **2** blustering or boastful

blowhole (ˈbləʊˌhəʊl) *n* **1** the nostril, paired or single, of whales, situated far back on the skull **2** a hole in ice through which whales, seals, etc, breathe **3** **a** a vent for air or gas, esp to release fumes from a tunnel, passage, etc **b** *NZ* a hole emitting gas or steam in a volcanic region **4** a bubble-like defect in an ingot resulting from gas being trapped during solidification **5** *geology* a hole in a cliff top leading to a sea cave through which air is forced by the action of the sea

blowie (ˈbləʊɪ) *n* *Austral informal* a blowfly

blow in *vb* (*intr, adverb*) *informal* to arrive or enter suddenly

blow-in *n* *Austral informal* an unwelcome newcomer or stranger

blow into *vb* (*intr, preposition*) *informal* to arrive in or enter (a room, etc) suddenly

blow job *n* a slang term for **fellatio**

> USAGE This word was formerly considered to be taboo, and it was labelled as such in previous editions of *Collins English Dictionary*. However, it has now become acceptable in speech, although some older or more conservative people may object to its use

blowlamp (ˈbləʊˌlæmp) *n* another name for **blowtorch**

blow moulding *n* a process for moulding single-piece plastic objects in which a thermoplastic is extruded into a split mould and blown against its sides

blown (bləʊn) *vb* the past participle of **blow[1]** and **blow[3]**

blow off *vb* (*adverb*) **1** to permit (a gas under pressure, esp steam) to be released **2** (*intr*) *Brit slang* to emit wind noisily from the anus **3** (*tr*) *informal* to reject or jilt (someone) **4** **blow off steam** See **steam** (sense 6) ▷ *n* **blow-off** **5** a discharge of a surplus fluid, such as steam, under pressure **6** a device through which such a discharge is made

blow on *vb* (*intr, preposition*) to defame or discredit (a person)

blow out *vb* (*adverb*) **1** to extinguish (a flame, candle, etc) or (of a flame, candle, etc) to become extinguished **2** (*intr*) (of a tyre) to puncture suddenly, esp at high speed **3** (*intr*) (of a fuse) to melt suddenly **4** (*tr; often reflexive*) to diminish or use up the energy of: *the storm blew itself out* **5** (*intr*) (of an oil or gas well) to lose oil or gas in an uncontrolled manner **6** (*tr*) *slang* to cancel: *the band had to blow out the gig* **7** **blow one's brains out** to kill oneself by shooting oneself in the head ▷ *n* **blowout** **8** the sudden melting of an electrical fuse **9** a sudden burst in a tyre **10** the uncontrolled escape of oil or gas from an oil or gas well **11** the failure of a jet engine, esp when in flight **12** *slang* a large filling meal or lavish entertainment

blow over *vb* (*intr, adverb*) **1** to cease or be finished: *the storm blew over* **2** to be forgotten: *the scandal will blow over*

blowpipe (ˈbləʊˌpaɪp) *n* **1** a long tube from which pellets, poisoned darts, etc, are shot by blowing. US word: **blowgun** **2** Also called: **blow tube** a tube for blowing air or oxygen into a flame to intensify its heat and direct it onto a small area **3** a long narrow iron pipe used to gather molten glass and blow it into shape

blowsy *or* **blowzy** (ˈblaʊzɪ) *adj* **blowsier, blowsiest** *or* **blowzier, blowziest** **1** (esp of a woman) untidy in appearance; slovenly or sluttish **2** (of a woman) ruddy in complexion; red-faced [c18 from dialect *blowze* beggar girl, of unknown origin] > ˈ**blowsily** *or* ˈ**blowzily** *adv* > ˈ**blowsiness** *or* ˈ**blowziness** *n*

blow through *vb* (*intr, adverb*) *Austral informal* to leave; make off

blowtorch (ˈbləʊˌtɔːtʃ) *n* a small burner that produces a very hot flame, used to remove old paint, melt soft metal, etc

blow up *vb* (*adverb*) **1** to explode or cause to explode **2** (*tr*) to increase the importance of (something): *they blew the whole affair up* **3** (*intr*) to come into consideration: *we lived well enough before this thing blew up* **4** (*intr*) to come into existence with sudden force: *a storm had blown up* **5** *informal* to lose one's temper (with a person) **6** (*tr*) *informal* to reprimand (someone) **7** (*tr*) *informal* to enlarge the size or detail of (a photograph) ▷ *n* **blow-up** **8** an explosion **9** *informal* an enlarged photograph or part of a photograph **10** *informal* a fit of temper or argument **11** Also called: **blowing up** *informal* a reprimand

blowy (ˈbləʊɪ) *adj* **blowier, blowiest** another word for **windy** (sense 1)

blub (blʌb) *vb* **blubs, blubbing, blubbed** *Brit* a slang word for **blubber** (senses 1–3)

blubber (ˈblʌbə) *vb* **1** to sob without restraint **2** to utter while sobbing **3** (*tr*) to make (the face) wet and swollen or disfigured by crying ▷ *n* **4** a thick insulating layer of fatty tissue below the skin of aquatic mammals such as the whale: used by man as a source of oil **5** *informal* excessive and flabby body fat **6** the act or an instance of weeping without restraint **7** *Austral* an informal name for **jellyfish** ▷ *adj* **8** (*often in combination*) swollen or fleshy: *blubber-faced; blubber-lips* [c12 perhaps from Low German *blubbern* to BUBBLE, of imitative origin] > ˈ**blubberer** *n*

blubbery (ˈblʌbərɪ) *adj* **-ier, -iest** **1** of, containing, or like blubber; fat **2** weeping or with the face disfigured by weeping

blucher (ˈbluːkə, -tʃə) *n* *obsolete* a high shoe with laces over the tongue [c19 named after Gebhard Leberecht von Blücher (1742–1819), Prussian field marshal, who commanded the Prussian army against Napoleon at Waterloo (1815)]

bludge (blʌdʒ) *Austral and NZ informal* ▷ *vb* **1** (when *intr*, often foll by *on*) to scrounge from (someone) **2** (*intr*) to evade work **3** (*intr*) *archaic* to act as a pimp ▷ *n* **4** a very easy task; undemanding employment [c19 back formation from slang *bludger* pimp, from BLUDGEON]

bludgeon (ˈblʌdʒən) *n* **1** a stout heavy club, typically thicker at one end **2** a person, line of argument, etc, that is effective but unsubtle ▷ *vb* (*tr*) **3** to hit or knock down with or as with a bludgeon **4** (often foll by *into*) to force; bully; coerce: *they bludgeoned him into accepting the job* [c18 of uncertain origin] > ˈ**bludgeoner** *n*

bludger (ˈblʌdʒə) *n* *Austral and NZ informal* **1** a person who scrounges **2** a person who avoids work **3** a person in authority regarded as ineffectual by those working under him

blue (bluː) n **1** any of a group of colours, such as that of a clear unclouded sky, that have wavelengths in the range 490–445 nanometres. Blue is the complementary colour of yellow and with red and green forms a set of primary colours. Related adjective: **cyanic 2** a dye or pigment of any of these colours **3** blue cloth or clothing: *dressed in blue* **4 a** a sportsperson who represents or has represented Oxford or Cambridge University and has the right to wear the university colour (dark blue for Oxford, light blue for Cambridge): *an Oxford blue* **b** the honour of so representing one's university **5** *Brit* an informal name for **Tory 6** any of numerous small blue-winged butterflies of the genera *Lampides, Polyommatus*, etc: family *Lycaenidae* **7** *archaic* short for **bluestocking 8** *slang* a policeman **9** *archery* a blue ring on a target, between the red and the black, scoring five points **10** a blue ball in snooker, etc **11** another name for **blueing 12** *Austral and NZ slang* an argument or fight: *he had a blue with a taxi driver* **13** Also: **bluey** *Austral and NZ slang* a court summons, esp for a traffic offence **14** *Austral and NZ informal* a mistake; error **15 out of the blue** apparently from nowhere; unexpectedly: *the opportunity came out of the blue* **16 into the blue** into the unknown or the far distance ▷ *adj* **bluer, bluest 17** of the colour blue **18** (of the flesh) having a purple tinge, as from cold or contusion **19** depressed, moody, or unhappy **20** dismal or depressing: *a blue day* **21** indecent, titillating, or pornographic: *blue films* **22** bluish in colour or having parts or marks that are bluish: *a blue fox; a blue whale* **23** *rare* aristocratic; noble; patrician: *a blue family.* See **blue blood** ▷ *vb* **blues, blueing** or **bluing, blued 24** to make, dye, or become blue **25** (tr) to treat (laundry) with blueing **26** (tr) *slang* to spend extravagantly or wastefully; squander ▷ See also **blues** [c13 from Old French *bleu*, of Germanic origin; compare Old Norse *blār*, Old High German *blāo*, Middle Dutch *blā*; related to Latin *flāvus* yellow] > **'bluely** *adv* > **'blueness** *n*

Blue (bluː) or **Bluey** *n Austral informal* a person with red hair

blue-arsed fly n **1** *informal* a blowfly; bluebottle **2 like a blue-arsed fly** *informal* in a state of frenzied activity

blue baby n a baby born with a bluish tinge to the skin because of lack of oxygen in the blood, esp caused by a congenital defect of the heart

blue bag n (in Britain) **1** a fabric bag for a barrister's robes **2** a small bag containing blueing for laundering

Bluebeard ('bluːˌbɪəd) n **1** a villain in European folk tales who marries several wives and murders them in turn. In many versions the seventh and last wife escapes the fate of the others **2** a man who has had several wives

bluebeat ('bluːˌbiːt) n a type of West Indian pop music of the 1960s; a precursor of reggae

bluebell ('bluːˌbɛl) n **1** Also called: **wild** or **wood hyacinth** a European liliaceous woodland plant, *Hyacinthoides* (or *Endymion*) *non-scripta*, having a one-sided cluster of blue bell-shaped flowers **2** Also called: **Spanish bluebell** a similar and related plant, *hispanica*, widely grown in gardens and becoming naturalized **3** a Scot name for **harebell 4** any of various other plants with blue bell-shaped flowers

blue beret n an informal name for a soldier of a United Nations peacekeeping force

blueberry ('bluːbərɪ, -brɪ) n, pl **-ries 1** Also called: **huckleberry** any of several North American ericaceous shrubs of the genus *Vaccinium*, such as *V. pennsylvanicum*, that have blue-black edible berries with tiny seeds. See also **bilberry 2 a** the fruit of any of these plants **b** (*as modifier*): *blueberry pie*

bluebill ('bluːˌbɪl) n *US* another name for **scaup**

blue billy n *NZ* an informal name for **dove prion** [probably from the name *Billy*]

bluebird ('bluːˌbɜːd) n **1** any North American songbird of the genus *Sialia*, having a blue or partly blue plumage: subfamily *Turdinae* (thrushes) **2 fairy bluebird** any songbird of the genus *Irena*, of S and SE Asia, having a blue-and-black plumage: family *Irenidae* **3** any of various other birds having a blue plumage

blue blood n royal or aristocratic descent [c19 translation of Spanish *sangre azul*] > **'blue-'blooded** *adj*

bluebonnet ('bluːˌbɒnɪt) or **bluecap** ('bluːˌkæp) n other names for **Balmoral¹** (sense 3)

bluebook n **1** (in Britain) a government publication bound in a stiff blue paper cover: usually the report of a royal commission or a committee **2** *informal, chiefly US* a register of well-known people **3** (in Canada) an annual statement of government accounts

bluebottle ('bluːˌbɒtᵊl) n **1** another name for the **blowfly 2** any of various blue-flowered plants, esp the cornflower **3** *Brit* an informal word for a **policeman 4** *Austral and NZ* an informal name for **Portuguese man-of-war**

blue box n *Canadian* a blue plastic container for domestic refuse that is to be collected and recycled

blue buck n another name for the **blaubok**

bluebush ('bluːˌbʊʃ) n any of various blue-grey herbaceous Australian shrubs of the genus *Maireana*

blue cattle dog n an Australian breed of dog with a bluish coat, developed for herding cattle. Also called: **Australian cattle dog, blue heeler**

blue cheese n cheese containing a blue mould, esp Stilton, Roquefort, or Danish blue. Also called (Austral and NZ): **blue vein**

blue chip n **1** a gambling chip with the highest value **2** *finance* **a** a stock considered reliable with respect to both dividend income and capital value **b** (*as modifier*): *a blue-chip company* **3** (*modifier*) denoting something considered to be a valuable asset

blue cod n a common marine spiny-finned food fish, *Parapercis colias*, of the sub-Antarctic waters of New Zealand, esp at the Chatham Islands, which is greenish blue with brown marbling and inhabits rocky bottoms. Its smoked flesh is considered a delicacy. Also called: **rock cod, pakirikiri, patutuki, rawaru**

blue-collar *adj* of, relating to, or designating manual industrial workers: *a blue-collar union.* Compare **white-collar, pink-collar**

blue devils pl n **1** a fit of depression or melancholy **2** an attack of delirium tremens

blue duck n a mountain duck, *Hymenolaimus malacorhynchos*, of New Zealand having a mostly lead-blue plumage. Also called (NZ): **whio**

Blue Ensign n an ensign having the Union Jack on a blue background at the upper corner of the vertical edge alongside the hoist: flown by Royal Navy auxiliary vessels, and, with some extra distinguishing mark or insignia, by certain yacht clubs. Compare **Red Ensign, White Ensign**

blue-eyed boy n *informal, chiefly Brit* the favourite or darling of a person or group. Usual US equivalent: **fair-haired boy**

blue-eyed grass n any of various mainly North American iridaceous marsh plants of the genus *Sisyrinchium* that have grasslike leaves and small flat starlike blue flowers

blue-eyed Mary n a blue-flowered boraginaceous plant, *Omphalodes verna*, native to S Europe and cultivated in Britain

blue-eyed soul n *informal* soul music written and performed by White singers in a style derived from the blues

bluefin ('bluːˌfɪn) or **bluefin tuna** n another name for **tunny**

bluefish ('bluːˌfɪʃ) n, pl **-fish** or **-fishes 1** Also called: **snapper** a predatory bluish marine percoid food and game fish, *Pomatomus saltatrix*, related to the horse mackerel: family *Pomatomidae* **2** any of

various other bluish fishes

Blue Flag n an award given to a seaside resort that meets EU standards of cleanliness of beaches and purity of water in bathing areas

blue fox n **1** a variety of the arctic fox that has a pale grey winter coat and is bred for its fur **2** the fur of this animal

blue funk n *slang* a state of great terror or loss of nerve

bluegill ('bluːˌgɪl) n a common North American freshwater sunfish, *Lepomis macrochirus*: an important food and game fish

blue goose n a variety of the snow goose that has a bluish-grey body and white head and neck

bluegrass ('bluːˌgrɑːs) n **1** any of several North American bluish-green grasses of the genus *Poa*, esp *P. pratensis* (**Kentucky bluegrass**), grown for forage **2** a type of folk music originating in Kentucky, characterized by a simple harmonized accompaniment

blue-green algae pl n the former name for **cyanobacteria**

blue ground n *mineralogy* another name for **kimberlite**

blue grouse n a grouse, *Dendragapus obscurus*, of W North America, having a bluish-grey plumage with a black tail

blue gum n **1** a tall fast-growing widely cultivated Australian myrtaceous tree, *Eucalyptus globulus*, having aromatic leaves containing a medicinal oil, bark that peels off in shreds, and hard timber. The juvenile leaves are bluish in colour **2** any of several other eucalyptus trees ▷ See also **red gum** (sense 1)

blue heeler n *Austral and NZ* a cattle dog that controls cattle by biting their heels. Also called: **heeler**

blueing or **bluing** ('bluːɪŋ) n **1** a blue material, such as indigo, used in laundering to counteract yellowing **2** the formation of a film of blue oxide on a steel surface

bluejacket ('bluːˌdʒækɪt) n a sailor in the Navy

bluejacking ('bluːˌdʒækɪŋ) n the practice of using one Bluetooth-enabled mobile phone to gain access to another, esp in order to send anonymous text messages [c21 from BLUE(TOOTH) + (HIGH)JACKING]

blue jay n a common North American jay, *Cyanocitta cristata*, having bright blue plumage with greyish-white underparts

blue john n a blue or purple fibrous variety of fluorspar occurring only in Derbyshire: used for vases, etc

blue laws pl n *US history* a number of repressive puritanical laws of the colonial period, forbidding any secular activity on Sundays

blue lias n a type of rock composed of alternating layers of bluish shale or clay and grey argillaceous limestone. See also **Lias**

Blue Mantle n one of the four pursuivants of the British College of Arms

blue merle n See **merle²**

blue moon n **1** the second full moon occurring within a calendar month **2 once in a blue moon** *informal* very rarely; almost never

blue mould n **1** Also called: **green mould** any fungus of the genus *Penicillium* that forms a bluish mass on decaying food, leather, etc **2** any fungal disease of fruit trees characterized by necrosis and a bluish growth on the affected tissue: mostly caused by *Penicillium* species

Blue Mountains pl n **1** a mountain range in the US, in NE Oregon and SE Washington. Highest peak: Rock Creek Butte, 2773 m (9097 ft) **2** a mountain range in the Caribbean, in E Jamaica: Blue Mountain coffee is grown on its slopes. Highest peak: Blue Mountain Peak, 2256 m (7402 ft) **3** a plateau in SE Australia, in E New South Wales: part of the Great Dividing Range. Highest part: about 1134 m (3871 ft)

blue murder n *informal* a great outcry, noise; horrible din (esp in such phrases as **cry, howl,**

b

scream, etc, **blue murder**)

Blue Nile *n* a river in E Africa, rising in central Ethiopia as the Abbai and flowing southeast, then northwest to join the White Nile. Length: about 1530 km (950 miles)

bluenose ('bluː,nəʊz) *n* **1** *US slang* a puritanical or prudish person **2** (*often capital*) *informal* a native or inhabitant of Nova Scotia

blue note *n jazz* a flattened third or seventh, used frequently in the blues

blue-on-blue *adj military* of or relating to friendly fire: *blue-on-blue contacts* [c20 from the colour used to mark a country's own troops and allies on a military map]

blue pencil *n* **1** deletion, alteration, or censorship of the contents of a book or other work ▷ *vb* **blue-pencil -cils, -cilling, -cilled** or *US* **-cils, -ciling, -ciled 2** (*tr*) to alter or delete parts of (a book, film, etc), esp to censor

blue peter *n* a signal flag of blue with a white square at the centre, displayed by a vessel about to leave port [c19 from the name *Peter*]

blue pointer *n* a large shark, *Isuropsis mako*, of Australian coastal waters, having a blue back and pointed snout

blueprint ('bluː,prɪnt) *n* **1** Also called: **cyanotype** a photographic print of plans, technical drawings, etc, consisting of white lines on a blue background **2** an original plan or prototype that influences subsequent design or practice: *the Montessori method was the blueprint for education in the 1940s* ▷ *vb* **3** (*tr*) to make a blueprint of (a plan)

blue racer *n* a long slender blackish-blue fast-moving colubrid snake, *Coluber constrictor flaviventris*, of the US

blue riband or **ribband** *n* **1** (*sometimes capitals*) Also called (esp US): **blue ribbon** the record for the fastest sea journey between two places, esp (in the 1920s and 30s) for a passenger liner between New York and Southampton **2 a** the most distinguished achievement in any field **b** (*as modifier*): *the blue-riband event of the meeting*

blue ribbon *n* **1** (in Britain) a badge of blue silk worn by members of the Order of the Garter **2** a badge awarded as the first prize in a competition **3** *US* a badge worn by a member of a temperance society

blue-ribbon jury *n* a US name for a **special jury**

Blue Ridge Mountains *pl n* a mountain range in the eastern US, extending from West Virginia into Georgia: part of the Appalachian mountains. Highest peak: Mount Mitchell, 2038 m (6684 ft)

blue-ringed octopus *n* a highly venomous octopus, *Octopus maculosus*, of E Australia which exhibits blue bands on its tentacles when disturbed

blue rinse *n* **1** a rinse for tinting grey hair a silvery-blue colour ▷ *adj* **blue-rinse 2** denoting or typifying an elderly, well-groomed, socially active, and comparatively wealthy woman

Blue Rod *n Brit* officer of the Order of St Michael and St George. Full title: **Gentleman Usher of the Blue Rod**

blue run *n skiing* an easy run, suitable for beginners

blues (bluːz) *pl n* (*sometimes functioning as singular*) **the 1** a feeling of depression or deep unhappiness **2** a type of folk song devised by Black Americans at the beginning of the 20th century, usually employing a basic 12-bar chorus, the tonic, subdominant, and dominant chords, frequent minor intervals, and blue notes > **'bluesy** *adj*

Blues (bluːz) *pl n* **the** *Brit* the Royal Horse Guards

blue schist *n* a metamorphic rock formed under conditions of high pressure and relatively low temperature

blue screen *n* a special effects film technique involving filming actors against a blue screen on which effects such as computerized graphics can be added later and integrated into a single sequence

blueshift ('bluː,ʃɪft) *n* a shift in the spectral lines of a stellar spectrum towards the blue end of the visible region relative to the wavelengths of these lines in the terrestrial spectrum: a result of the **Doppler effect** caused by stars approaching the solar system. Compare **redshift**

blue-singlet *adj Austral* working-class

blue-sky or **blue-skies** *n* (*modifier*) of or denoting theoretical research without regard to any future application of its result: *a blue-sky project*

blue-sky law *n US* a state law regulating the trading of securities: intended to protect investors from fraud

blue-sky thinking *n* creative ideas that are not limited by current thinking or beliefs

bluesnarfing ('bluː,snɑːfɪŋ) *n* the practice of using one Bluetooth-enabled mobile phone to steal contact details, ring tones, images, etc from another [c21 from BLUE(TOOTH) + SNARF]

blue spruce *n* a spruce tree, *Picea pungens glauca*, native to the Rocky Mountains of North America, having blue-green needle-like leaves. Also called: **balsam spruce**

blue stain *n forestry* a bluish discoloration of sapwood caused by growth of fungi

bluestocking ('bluː,stɒkɪŋ) *n usually disparaging* a scholarly or intellectual woman [from the blue worsted stockings worn by members of a C18 literary society]

bluestone ('bluː,stəʊn) *n* **1** a blue-grey sandstone containing much clay, used for building and paving **2** the blue crystalline form of copper sulphate **3** a blue variety of basalt found in Australia and used as a building stone

blue swimmer *n* **1** an edible bluish Australian swimming crab, *Portunus pelagicus* **2** *Austral informal* an Australian ten-dollar note

bluet ('bluːɪt) *n* a North American rubiaceous plant, *Houstonia caerulea*, with small four-petalled blue flowers

bluethroat ('bluː,θrəʊt) *n* a small brownish European songbird, *Cyanosylvia svecica*, related to the thrushes, the male of which has a blue throat: family *Muscicapidae*

bluetit ('bluː,tɪt) *n* a common European tit, *Parus caeruleus*, having a blue crown, wings, and tail, yellow underparts, and a black and grey head

bluetongue[1] (,bluː'tʌŋ) *n* an Australian lizard, *Tiliqua scincoides*, having a cobalt-blue tongue

bluetongue[2] (,bluː'tʌŋ) *n vet science* a viral disease of domestic and wild ruminants transmitted by arthropods and characterized by reproductive problems or vasculitis. Sheep, which are most frequently affected, develop swelling of the face and a cyanotic tongue

Bluetooth ('bluː,tuːθ) *n* a short-range radio technology that allows wireless communication between a computer and a keyboard, between mobile phones, etc [c20: after the 10th-century Danish King Harald Blatand (Harold Bluetooth), instrumental in uniting warring factions in Scandinavia]

blue vein *n Austral and NZ* another name for **blue cheese**

blue vitriol *n* the fully hydrated blue crystalline form of copper sulphate

blueweed ('bluː,wiːd) *n US* another name for **viper's bugloss**

blue whale *n* the largest mammal: a widely distributed bluish-grey whalebone whale, *Sibbaldus* (or *Balaenoptera*) *musculus*, closely related and similar to the rorquals: family *Balaenopteridae*. Also called: **sulphur-bottom**

bluey ('bluːɪ) *n Austral informal* **1** a blanket **2** a swagman's bundle **3 hump (one's) bluey** to carry one's bundle; tramp **4** *slang* a variant of **blue** (sense 13) **5** a cattle dog **6** a red-headed person [(for senses 1, 2, 5) c19 from BLUE (on account of their colour) + -Y[2]]

Bluey ('bluːɪ) *n* a variant of **Blue**

bluff[1] (blʌf) *vb* **1** to pretend to be confident about an uncertain issue or to have undisclosed resources, in order to influence or deter (someone) ▷ *n* **2** deliberate deception intended to create the impression of a stronger position or greater resources than one actually has **3 call someone's bluff** to challenge someone to give proof of his claims [c19 originally US poker-playing term, from Dutch *bluffen* to boast] > **bluffer** *n*

bluff[2] (blʌf) *n* **1** a steep promontory, bank, or cliff, esp one formed by river erosion on the outside bend of a meander **2** *Canadian* a clump of trees on the prairie; copse ▷ *adj* **3** good-naturedly frank and hearty **4** (of a bank, cliff, etc) presenting a steep broad face [c17 (in the sense: nearly perpendicular): perhaps from Middle Dutch *blaf* broad] > **bluffly** *adv* > **bluffness** *n*

bluish or **blueish** ('bluːɪʃ) *adj* somewhat blue > **'bluishness** or **'blueishness** *n*

blunder ('blʌndə) *n* **1** a stupid or clumsy mistake **2** a foolish tactless remark ▷ *vb* (*mainly intr*) **3** to make stupid or clumsy mistakes **4** to make foolish tactless remarks **5** (*often foll by about, into*, etc) to act clumsily; stumble: *he blundered into a situation he knew nothing about* **6** (*tr*) to mismanage; botch [c14 of Scandinavian origin; compare Old Norse *blunda* to close one's eyes, Norwegian dialect *blundra*; see BLIND] > **blunderer** *n* > **blundering** *n, adj* > **blunderingly** *adv*

blunderbuss ('blʌndə,bʌs) *n* **1** an obsolete short musket with large bore and flared muzzle, used to scatter shot at short range **2** *informal* a clumsy unsubtle person [c17 changed (through the influence of BLUNDER) from Dutch *donderbus*; from *donder* THUNDER + obsolete *bus* gun]

blunge (blʌndʒ) *vb* (*tr*) to mix (clay or a similar substance) with water in order to form a suspension for use in ceramics [c19 probably from BLEND + PLUNGE]

blunger ('blʌndʒə) *n* a large vat in which the contents, esp clay and water, are mixed by rotating arms

blunt (blʌnt) *adj* **1** (esp of a knife or blade) lacking sharpness or keenness; dull **2** not having a sharp edge or point: *a blunt instrument* **3** (of people, manner of speaking, etc) lacking refinement or subtlety; straightforward and uncomplicated **4** outspoken; direct and to the point: *a blunt Yorkshireman* ▷ *vb* (*tr*) **5** to make less sharp **6** to diminish the sensitivity or perception of; make dull ▷ *n* **7** *slang* a cannabis cigarette [c12 probably of Scandinavian origin; compare Old Norse *blundr* dozing, *blunda* to close one's eyes; see BLUNDER, BLIND] > **bluntly** *adv* > **bluntness** *n*

blunthead ('blʌnt,hed) *n slang* a frequent recreational user of marijuana [c20 from BLUNT (sense 7) + -HEAD]

blur (blɜː) *vb* **blurs, blurring, blurred 1** to make or become vague or less distinct: *heat haze blurs the hills; education blurs class distinctions* **2** to smear or smudge **3** (*tr*) to make (the judgment, memory, or perception) less clear; dim ▷ *n* **4** something vague, hazy, or indistinct **5** a smear or smudge [c16 perhaps variant of BLEAR] > **blurred** (blɜːd) *adj* > **blurredly** ('blɜːrɪdlɪ, 'blɜːd-) *adv* > **blurredness** *n* > **blurriness** *n* > **blurry** *adj*

blurb (blɜːb) *n* a promotional description, as found on the jackets of books [c20 coined by Gelett Burgess (1866–1951), US humorist and illustrator]

blurt (blɜːt) *vb* (*tr; often foll by out*) to utter suddenly and involuntarily [c16 probably of imitative origin]

blush (blʌʃ) *vb* **1** (*intr*) to become suddenly red in the face from embarrassment, shame, modesty, or guilt; redden **2** to make or become reddish or rosy ▷ *n* **3** a sudden reddening of the face from embarrassment, shame, modesty, or guilt **4** a rosy glow: *the blush of a peach* **5** a reddish or pinkish tinge **6** a cloudy area on the surface of freshly applied gloss paint **7 at first blush** when first seen; as a first impression [Old English *blȳscan*; related to *blȳsian* to burn, Middle Low German *blüsen* to light a fire] > **'blushful** *adj* > **'blushing** *n, adj* > **'blushingly** *adv*

blusher ('blʌʃə) *n* a cosmetic applied to the face to

imbue it with a rosy colour

bluster ('blʌstə) *vb* **1** to speak or say loudly or boastfully **2** to act in a bullying way **3** (*tr*, foll by *into*) to force or attempt to force (a person) into doing something by behaving thus **4** (*intr*) (of the wind) to be noisy or gusty ▷ *n* **5** boisterous talk or action; swagger **6** empty threats or protests **7** a strong wind; gale [c15 probably from Middle Low German *blüsteren* to storm, blow violently] > 'blusterer *n* > 'blustering *n*, *adj* > 'blusteringly or 'blusterously *adv* > 'blustery or 'blusterous *adj*

Blu-tack ('bluːtæk) *n* **1** *trademark* a type of blue, malleable, sticky material used to attach paper, card, etc to walls and other surfaces ▷ *vb* **2** (*tr*) to attach (paper, card, etc) to a wall or other surface by means of this material

Blvd *abbreviation for* Boulevard

B-lymphocyte *n* a type of lymphocyte, originating in bone marrow, that produces antibodies. Also called: **B-cell**. See also **T-lymphocyte**

Blyth (blaɪð) *n* a port in N England, in SE Northumberland, on the North Sea. Pop: 35 691 (2001)

bm¹ *abbreviation for* **1** board measure **2** bowel movement

bm² *the internet domain name for* Bermuda

BM *abbreviation for* **1** Bachelor of Medicine **2** *surveying* benchmark **3** British Museum

BMA *abbreviation for* British Medical Association

BMI *abbreviation for* **1** body mass index **2** Broadcast Music Incorporated

BMJ *abbreviation for* British Medical Journal

B-movie *n* a film originally made (esp in Hollywood in the 1940s and 50s) as a supporting film, now often considered as a genre in its own right

BMR *abbreviation for* basal metabolic rate

BMus *abbreviation for* Bachelor of Music

BMX *abbreviation for* **1** bicycle motocross; stunt riding on rough ground or over an obstacle course on a bicycle **2** a bicycle designed for bicycle motocross

bn¹ *abbreviation for* billion

bn² *the internet domain name for* Brunei Darussalam

Bn *abbreviation for* **1** Baron **2** Also: **bn** Battalion

B4N *text messaging abbreviation for* bye for now

BNA (in Canada) *abbreviation for* British North America

B'nai B'rith (bə'neɪ bə'riːθ, briθ) *n* a Jewish fraternal organization founded in New York in 1843, having moral, philanthropic, social, educational, and political aims [from Hebrew *benē brīth* sons of the covenant]

BNFL *abbreviation for* British Nuclear Fuels Limited

BNP *abbreviation for* British National Party

bo or **boh** (bəʊ) *interj* **1** Also: **boh** an exclamation uttered to startle or surprise someone, esp a child in a game **2** *slang* an exclamation of encouragement or an expression of enthusiasm

bo *the internet domain name for* Bolivia

BO *abbreviation for* **1** *informal* body odour **2** box office

b.o. *abbreviation for* **1** back order **2** branch office **3** broker's order **4** buyer's option

B/O *abbreviation for* **1** book-keeping brought over **2** buyer's option

boa ('bəʊə) *n* **1** any large nonvenomous snake of the family *Boidae*, most of which occur in Central and South America and the Caribbean. They have vestigial hind limbs and kill their prey by constriction **2** a woman's long thin scarf, usually of feathers or fur [c19 from New Latin, from Latin: a large Italian snake, water snake]

boab ('bəʊæb) *n Austral* short for **baobab**

BOAC (formerly) *abbreviation for* British Overseas Airways Corporation

boa constrictor *n* a very large snake, *Constrictor constrictor*, of tropical America and the Caribbean, that kills its prey by constriction: family *Boidae* (boas)

boak (bok, bəʊk) *vb, n* a variant spelling of **boke**

Boanerges (ˌbəʊə'nɜːdʒiːz) *n* **1** *New Testament* a nickname applied by Jesus to James and John in Mark 3:17 **2** a fiery preacher, esp one with a powerful voice [c17 from Hebrew *benē reghesh* sons of thunder]

boar (bɔː) *n* **1** an uncastrated male pig **2** See **wild boar** [Old English *bār*; related to Old High German *bēr*]

board (bɔːd) *n* **1** a long wide flat relatively thin piece of sawn timber **2 a** a smaller flat piece of rigid material for a specific purpose: *ironing board* **b** (*in combination*): *breadboard; cheeseboard* **3** a person's food or meals, provided regularly for money or sometimes as payment for work done (esp in the phrases **full board, board and lodging**) **4** *archaic* a table, esp one used for eating at, and esp when laden with food **5 a** (*sometimes functioning as plural*) a group of people who officially administer a company, trust, etc: *a board of directors* **b** (*as modifier*): *a board meeting* **6** any other committee or council: *a board of interviewers* **7** the boards (*plural*) the acting profession; the stage **8** short for **blackboard, chessboard, notice board, printed circuit board** (see **printed circuit**), **springboard, surfboard 9** stiff cardboard or similar material covered with paper, cloth, etc, used for the outside covers of a book **10** a flat thin rectangular sheet of composite material, such as plasterboard or chipboard **11** *chiefly US* **a** a list on which stock-exchange securities and their prices are posted **b** *informal* the stock exchange itself **12** *nautical* **a** the side of a ship **b** the leg that a sailing vessel makes on a beat to windward **13** *Austral and NZ* the part of the floor of a sheep-shearing shed, esp a raised part, where the shearers work **14** *NZ* the killing floor of an abattoir or freezing works **15 a** any of various portable surfaces specially designed for indoor games such as chess, backgammon, etc **b** (*as modifier*): *board games* **16 a** a set of hands in duplicate bridge **b** a wooden or metal board containing four slots, or often nowadays, a plastic wallet, in which the four hands are placed so that the deal may be replayed with identical hands **17** the hull of a sailboard, usually made of plastic, to which the mast is jointed and on which a windsurfer stands **18** See **above board 19** go by the board to fall into disuse, neglected, or lost: *in these days courtesy goes by the board* **20** on board on or in a ship, boat, aeroplane, or other vehicle **21** sweep the board **a** (in gambling) to win all the cards or money **b** to win every event or prize in a contest **22** take on board to accept (new ideas, situations, theories, etc) ▷ *vb* **23** to go aboard (a vessel, train, aircraft, or other vehicle) **24** *nautical* to come alongside (a vessel) before attacking or going aboard **25** to attack (a ship) by forcing one's way aboard **26** (*tr*; often foll by *up, in*, etc) to cover or shut with boards **27** (*intr*) to give or receive meals or meals and lodging in return for money or work **28** (sometimes foll by *out*) to receive or arrange for (someone, esp a child) to receive food and lodging away from home, usually in return for payment [Old English *bord*; related to Old Norse *borth* ship's side, table, Old High German *bort* ship's side, Sanskrit *bardhaka* a cutting off] > 'boardable *adj*

board-and-shingle *n Caribbean* a small dwelling with wooden walls and a shingle roof

board bridge *n* another name for **duplicate bridge**

boarder ('bɔːdə) *n* **1** *Brit* a pupil who lives at school during term time **2** *US* a child who lives away from its parents and is cared for by a person or organization receiving payment **3** another word for **lodger 4** a person who boards a ship, esp one who forces his way aboard in an attack: *stand by to repel boarders* **5** *informal* a person who takes part in sailboarding or snowboarding

board foot *n* a unit of board measure: the cubic content of a piece of wood one foot square and one inch thick

boarding ('bɔːdɪŋ) *n* **1** a structure of boards, such

as a floor or fence **2** timber boards collectively **3 a** the act of embarking on an aircraft, train, ship, etc **b** (*as modifier*): *a boarding pass* **4** a process used in tanning to accentuate the natural grain of hides, in which the surface of a softened leather is lightly creased by folding grain to grain and the fold is worked to and fro across the leather

boarding house *n* a private house in which accommodation and meals are provided for paying guests **2** *Austral* a house for boarders at a school. See also **house** (sense 10)

boarding out *n social welfare, Brit* **a** the local-authority practice of placing a client in a foster family or voluntary establishment and paying for it **b** (*as modifier*): *boarding-out allowances*

boarding school *n* a school providing living accommodation for some or all of its pupils

board measure *n* a system of units for measuring wood based on the board foot. 1980 board feet equal one standard

board of trade *n US and Canadian* another name for a **chamber of commerce**

Board of Trade *n* (in the United Kingdom) a ministry within the Department of Trade: responsible for the supervision of commerce and the promotion of export trade

Board of Trade Unit *n* a unit of electrical energy equal to 1 kilowatt-hour. Abbreviation: BTU

boardroom ('bɔːdˌruːm, -ˌrʊm) *n* **a** a room where the board of directors of a company meets **b** (*as modifier*): *a boardroom power struggle*

board rule *n* a measuring device for estimating the number of board feet in a quantity of wood

boardsailing ('bɔːdˌseɪlɪŋ) *n* another name for **windsurfing**. > 'board,sailor *n*

board school *n Brit* (formerly) a school managed by a board elected by local ratepayers

board shorts *pl n* shorts with longer legs, originally meant to protect a surfer's legs against the surfboard

boardwalk ('bɔːdˌwɔːk) *n US and Canadian* a promenade, esp along a beach, usually made of planks

boarfish ('bɔːˌfɪʃ) *n, pl* **-fish** or **-fishes** any of various spiny-finned marine teleost fishes of the genera *Capros, Antigonia*, etc, related to the dories, having a deep compressed body, a long snout, and large eyes

boarish ('bɔːrɪʃ) *adj* coarse, cruel, or sensual > 'boarishly *adv* > 'boarishness *n*

boart (bɔːt) *n* a variant spelling of **bort**

boast¹ (bəʊst) *vb* **1** (*intr*; sometimes foll by *of* or *about*) to speak in exaggerated or excessively proud terms of one's possessions, skills, or superior qualities; brag **2** (*tr*) to possess (something to be proud of): *the city boasts a fine cathedral* ▷ *n* **3** a bragging statement **4** a possession, attribute, attainment, etc, that is or may be bragged about [c13 of uncertain origin] > 'boaster *n* > 'boasting *n, adj* > 'boastingly *adv*

boast² (bəʊst) *vb* (*tr*) to shape or dress (stone) roughly with a broad chisel [c19 of unknown origin]

boast³ (bəʊst) *squash* ▷ *n* **1** a stroke in which the ball is hit on to one of the side walls before hitting the front wall ▷ *vb* **2** to hit (the ball) in this way or make such a stroke [c19 perhaps from French *bosse* the place where the ball hits the wall] > 'boasted *adj*

boastful ('bəʊstfʊl) *adj* tending to boast; characterized by boasting > 'boastfully *adv* > 'boastfulness *n*

boat (bəʊt) *n* **1** a small vessel propelled by oars, paddle, sails, or motor for travelling, transporting goods, etc, esp one that can be carried aboard a larger vessel **2** (not in technical use) another word for **ship 3** *navy* a submarine **4** a container for gravy, sauce, etc **5** a small boat-shaped container for incense, used in some Christian churches **6** in the same boat sharing the same problems **7** burn one's boats See **burn¹** (sense 19) **8** miss the boat to lose an opportunity **9** push

b

the **boat out** *Brit informal* to celebrate, esp lavishly and expensively **10 rock the boat** *informal* to cause a disturbance in the existing situation ▷ *vb* **11** (*intr*) to travel or go in a boat, esp as a form of recreation **12** (*tr*) to transport or carry in a boat [Old English *bāt*; related to Old Norse *beit* boat]

boatbill ('bəʊt,bɪl) *or* **boat-billed heron** *n* a nocturnal tropical American wading bird, *Cochlearius cochlearius*, similar to the night herons but with a broad flattened bill: family *Ardeidae*, order *Ciconiiformes*

boat deck *n* the deck of a ship on which the lifeboats are kept

boat drill *n* practice in launching the lifeboats and taking off the passengers and crew of a ship

boatel *or* **botel** (bəʊ'tɛl) *n* **1** a waterside hotel catering for boating people **2** a ship that functions as a hotel [C20 from BOAT + (HOT)EL]

boater ('bəʊtə) *n* a stiff straw hat with a straight brim and flat crown

boathook ('bəʊt,hʊk) *n* a pole with a hook at one end, used aboard a vessel for fending off other vessels or obstacles or for catching a line or mooring buoy

boathouse ('bəʊt,haʊs) *n* a shelter by the edge of a river, lake, etc, for housing boats

boatie ('bəʊtɪ) *n Austral and NZ informal* a boating enthusiast

boating ('bəʊtɪŋ) *n* the practice of rowing, sailing, or cruising in boats as a form of recreation

boatload ('bəʊt,ləʊd) *n* the amount of cargo or number of people held by a boat or ship

boatman ('bəʊtmən) *n, pl* **-men 1** a man who works on, hires out, repairs, or operates a boat or boats **2** short for **water boatman**

boat neck *n* a high slitlike neckline of a garment that extends onto the shoulders. Also called: **bateau neckline**

boat people *pl n* refugees, esp from Vietnam in the late 1970s, who leave by boat hoping to be picked up by ships of another country

boat race *n* the *Brit* a rowing event held annually in the spring, in which an eight representing Oxford University rows against one representing Cambridge University on the Thames between Putney and Mortlake

boatswain, bosun *or* **bo's'n** ('bəʊs°n) *n* a petty officer on a merchant ship or a warrant officer on a warship who is responsible for the maintenance of the ship and its equipment [Old English *bātswegen*; see BOAT, SWAIN]

boatswain's chair *n nautical* a seat consisting of a short flat board slung from ropes, used to support a person working on the side of a vessel or in its rigging

boat train *n* a train scheduled to take passengers to or from a particular ship

Boa Vista (*Portuguese* 'bo:ə 'viʃtə) *n* a town in N Brazil, capital of the state of Roraima, on the Rio Branco. Pop: 275 000 (2005 est)

Boaz ('bəʊæz) *n Old Testament* a kinsman of Naomi, who married her daughter-in-law Ruth (Ruth 2–4); one of David's ancestors

bob¹ (bɒb) *vb* **bobs, bobbing, bobbed 1** to move or cause to move up and down repeatedly, as while floating in water **2** to move or cause to move with a short abrupt movement, as of the head **3** to make (a bow or curtsy): *the little girl bobbed before the visitor* **4** (*intr*; usually foll by *up*) to appear or emerge suddenly **5** (*intr*; foll by *under, below,* etc) to disappear suddenly, as beneath a surface **6** (*intr*; usually foll by *for*) to attempt to get hold (of a floating or hanging object, esp an apple) in the teeth as a game ▷ *n* **7** a short abrupt movement, as of the head **8** a quick curtsy or bow **9** *bell-ringing* a particular set of changes **10** *angling* **a** short for **bobfloat b** the topmost fly on a cast of three, often fished bobbing at the surface **c** this position on a wet-fly cast [C14 of uncertain origin]

bob² (bɒb) *n* **1** a hairstyle for women and children in which the hair is cut short evenly all round the head **2** a dangling or hanging object, such as the

weight on a pendulum or on a plumb line **3** a polishing disc on a rotating spindle. It is usually made of felt, leather, etc, impregnated with an abrasive material **4** short for **bob skate** *or* **bobsleigh 5** a runner or pair of runners on a bobsled **6** *angling* a small knot of worms, maggots, etc, used as bait **7** a very short line of verse at the end of a stanza or preceding a rhyming quatrain (the wheel) at the end of a stanza **8** a refrain or burden with such a short line or lines **9** a docked tail, esp of a horse **10** *Brit dialect* a hanging cluster, as of flowers or ribbons ▷ *vb* **bobs, bobbing, bobbed 11** (*tr*) to cut (the hair) in a bob **12** (*tr*) to cut short, sometimes, esp the tail of an animal); dock or crop **13** (*intr*) to ride on a bobsled [C14 *bobbe* bunch of flowers, perhaps of Celtic origin]

bob³ (bɒb) *vb* **bobs, bobbing, bobbed 1** to tap or cause to tap or knock lightly (against) ▷ *n* **2** a light knock; tap [C13 *bobben* to rap, beat; see BOP²]

bob⁴ (bɒb) *n, pl* **bob** *Brit* (formerly) an informal word for a **shilling** [C19 of unknown origin]

Bob (bɒb) *n* **Bob's your uncle** *slang* everything is or will turn out all right [C19 perhaps from pet form of *Robert*]

bobbejaan ('bɒbə,jɑːn) *n South African* **1** a baboon **2** a large black spider **3** a monkey wrench [Afrikaans]

bobbery ('bɒbərɪ) *n, pl* **-beries 1** Also called: **bobbery pack** a mixed pack of hunting dogs, often not belonging to any of the hound breeds **2** *informal* a noisy commotion ▷ *adj* **3** *informal* noisy or excitable [C19 from Hindi *bāp re*, literally: oh father!]

bobbin ('bɒbɪn) *n* **1** a spool or reel on which thread or yarn is wound, being unwound as required; spool; reel **2** narrow braid or cord used as binding or for trimming **3** a device consisting of a short bar and a length of string, used to control a wooden door latch **4 a** a spool on which insulated wire is wound to form the coil of a small electromagnetic device, such as a bell or buzzer **b** the coil of such a spool **5** (*plural*) *Brit slang* matter that is worthless or of inferior quality; rubbish [C16 from Old French *bobine*, of unknown origin]

bobbinet (,bɒbɪ'nɛt) *n* a netted fabric of hexagonal mesh, made on a lace machine [C19 see BOBBIN, NET¹]

bobbin lace *n* lace made with bobbins rather than with needle and thread (needlepoint lace); pillow lace

bobble ('bɒb°l) *n* **1** a short jerky motion, as of a cork floating on disturbed water; bobbing movement **2** a tufted ball, usually for ornament, as on a knitted hat **3** any small dangling ball or bundle ▷ *vb* **4** (*intr*) *sport* (of a ball) to bounce with a rapid erratic motion due to an uneven playing surface **5** *US informal* to handle (something) ineptly; muff; bungle: *he bobbled the ball and lost the game* [C19 from BOB¹ (vb)]

bobble hat *n* a knitted hat with a tufted woollen ball on top

bobby ('bɒbɪ) *n, pl* **-bies** *informal* a British policeman [C19 from *Bobby* after Sir *Robert* Peel (1788–1850), British Conservative statesman, who, as Home Secretary, set up the Metropolitan Police Force in 1828]

bobby calf *n* an unweaned calf culled for slaughter

bobby-dazzler *n dialect* anything outstanding, striking, or showy, esp an attractive girl [C19 expanded form of *dazzler* something striking or attractive]

bobby pin *n US, Canadian, Austral and NZ* a metal hairpin bent in order to hold the hair in place. Brit terms: **hairgrip, kirby grip**

bobby socks *pl n* ankle-length socks worn by teenage girls, esp in the US in the 1940s

bobbysoxer ('bɒbɪ,sɒksə) *n informal, chiefly US* an adolescent girl wearing bobby socks, esp in the 1940s

bobcat ('bɒb,kæt) *n* a North American feline

mammal, *Lynx rufus*, closely related to but smaller than the lynx, having reddish-brown fur with dark spots or stripes, tufted ears, and a short tail. Also called: **bay lynx** [C19 from BOB² (referring to its short tail) + CAT¹]

bobfloat ('bɒb,fləʊt) *n angling* a small buoyant float, usually consisting of a quill stuck through a piece of cork

boblet ('bɒblɪt) *n* a two-man bobsleigh [C20 from BOB² + -LET]

Bobo-Dioulasso ('bəʊbədju:'læsəʊ) *n* a city in W Burkina-Faso. Pop: 396 000 (2005 est)

bobol ('bʌbɔ:l) *E Caribbean* ▷ *n* **1** a fraud carried out by one or more persons with access to public funds in collusion with someone in a position of authority ▷ *vb* **2** (*intr*) to commit a bobol [C20 of uncertain origin]

bobolink ('bɒbə,lɪŋk) *n* an American songbird, *Dolichonyx oryzivorus*, the male of which has a white back and black underparts in the breeding season: family *Icteridae* (American orioles). Also called (US): **reedbird, ricebird** [C18 of imitative origin]

bobotie (bʊ'bʊtɪ) *n* a South African dish consisting of curried mincemeat with a topping of beaten egg baked to a crust [C19 from Afrikaans, probably from Malay]

bobowler ('bɒb,aʊlə) *n Midland English dialect* a large moth [of uncertain origin]

Bobruisk *or* **Bobruysk** (bə'bru:ɪsk) *n* a port in Belarus, on the River Berezina: engineering, timber, tyre manufacturing. Pop: 219 000 (2005 est)

bob skate *n chiefly US and Canadian* an ice skate with two parallel blades [C20 from *bob*(sled) + SKATE¹]

bobsleigh ('bɒb,sleɪ) *n* **1** a racing sledge for two or more people, with a steering mechanism enabling the driver to direct it down a steeply banked ice-covered run **2** (esp formerly) **a** a sleigh made of two short sledges joined one behind the other **b** one of these two short sledges ▷ *vb* **3** (*intr*) to ride on a bobsleigh. Also called (esp US and Canadian): **bobsled** ('bɒb,slɛd) [C19 BOB² + SLEIGH]

bobstay ('bɒb,steɪ) *n* a strong stay between a bowsprit and the stem of a vessel for holding down the bowsprit [C18 perhaps from BOB¹ + STAY³]

bobsy-die ('bɒbzɪ,daɪ) *n NZ informal* fuss; confusion; pandemonium (esp in the phrases **kick up bobsy-die, play bobsy-die**) [from C19 *bob's a-dying*]

bobtail ('bɒb,teɪl) *n* **1** a docked or diminutive tail **2** an animal with such a tail ▷ *adj also* **bobtailed 3** having the tail cut short ▷ *vb* (*tr*) **4** to dock the tail of **5** to cut short; curtail [C16 from BOB² + TAIL¹]

bobweight ('bɒb,weɪt) *n* another name for **balance weight**

bobwhite ('bɒb,waɪt) *n* a brown North American quail, *Colinus virginianus*, the male of which has white markings on the head: a popular game bird [C19 of imitative origin]

bocage (bɒ'kɑːʒ) *n* **1** the wooded countryside characteristic of northern France, with small irregular-shaped fields and many hedges and copses **2** woodland scenery represented in ceramics [C17 from French, from Old French *bosc*; see BOSCAGE]

boccie, bocci, bocce ('bɒtʃi:) *or* **boccia** ('bɒtʃə) *n* an Italian version of bowls played on a lawn smaller than a bowling green [from Italian *bocce* bowls, plural of *boccia* ball; see BOSS²]

bocconcini *or* **boconcini** (*Italian* bokontʃini) *pl n* small bite-sized pieces of mozzarella cheese [C21 Italian: mouthful]

Boche (bɒʃ) *n derogatory slang* (esp in World Wars I and II) **1** a German, esp a German soldier **2** the (usually functioning as plural) Germans collectively, esp German soldiers regarded as the enemy [C20 from French, probably shortened from *alboche* German, from *allemand* German + *caboche* pate]

Bochum (*German* 'bo:xum) *n* an industrial city in

NW Germany, in W North Rhine-Westphalia: university (1965). Pop: 387 283 (2003 est)

bock (bok, bəʊk) *vb, n* a variant spelling of **boke**

bock beer *or* **bock** (bɒk) *n* **1** *US and Canadian* heavy dark strong beer **2** (in France) a light beer [c19 from German *Bock bier*, literally: buck beer, name given through folk etymology to beer brewed in *Einbeck*, near Hanover]

bockedy ('bɒkədı) *adj Irish* (of a structure, piece of furniture, etc) unsteady [from Irish Gaelic *bacaideach* limping]

bod (bɒd) *n informal* **1** a fellow; chap: *he's a queer bod* **2** another word for **body** (sense 1) [c18 short for **body**]

BOD *abbreviation for* biochemical oxygen demand

bodacious (bəʊ'deɪʃəs) *adj slang, chiefly US* impressive or remarkable; excellent [c19 from English dialect; blend of BOLD + AUDACIOUS]

bode[1] (bəʊd) *vb* **1** to be an omen of (good or ill, esp of ill); portend; presage **2** (*tr*) *archaic* to predict; foretell [Old English *bodian*; related to Old Norse *botha* to proclaim, Old Frisian *bodia* to invite] > **boding** *n, adj* > **bodement** *n*

bode[2] (bəʊd) *vb* the past tense of **bide**

bodega (bəʊ'di:gə; *Spanish* bo'ðeɣa) *n* a shop selling wine and sometimes groceries, esp in a Spanish-speaking country [c19 from Spanish, ultimately from Greek *apothēkē* storehouse, from *apothenai* to store, put away]

Bodensee ('bo:dənze:) *n* the German name for (Lake) **Constance**

Bode's law (bəʊdz) *n astronomy* an empirical rule relating the distances of the planets from the sun, based on the numerical sequence 0, 3, 6, 12, 24,.... Adding 4 to each number and dividing by 10 gives the sequence 0.4, 0.7, 1, 1.6, 2.8,..., which is a reasonable representation of distances in astronomical units for most planets if the minor planets are counted as a single entity at 2.8 [named after Johann Elert *Bode* (1747–1826), who in 1772 published the law, formulated by Johann Titius in 1766]

bodge (bɒdʒ) *vb* **1** *informal* to make a mess of; botch **2** *Austral informal* to make or adjust in a false or clumsy way: *I bodged the figures* [c16 changed from BOTCH]

bodger ('bɒdʒə) *adj* **1** *Austral informal* worthless or second-rate **2** a labourer who traditionally lived and worked in the forest, making chairs from felling trees [c20 from BODGE]

bodgie ('bɒdʒı) *Austral and NZ* ▷ *n* **1** an unruly or uncouth young man, esp in the 1950s; teddy boy ▷ *adj* **2** inferior; worthless [c20 from BODGE]

Bodh Gaya ('bɒd gə'jɑ:) *n* a variant spelling of **Buddh Gaya**

Bodhisattva (ˌbəʊdɪ'sætvə, -wə, ˌbɒd-, ˌbəʊdi:'sʌtvə) *n* (in Mahayana Buddhism) a divine being worthy of nirvana who remains on the human plane to help men to salvation. Compare **arhat** [Sanskrit, literally: one whose essence is enlightenment, from *bodhi* enlightenment + *sattva* essence]

Bodhi Tree (ˌbəʊdı) *n* the sacred peepul at Buddh Gaya under which Gautama Siddhartha attained enlightenment and became the Buddha [Sanskrit *bodhi* enlightenment]

bodhrán (bəʊ'rɑ:n, 'bɒ:rɑ:n) *n* a shallow one-sided drum popular in Irish and Scottish folk music [Irish Gaelic]

bodice ('bɒdɪs) *n* **1** the upper part of a woman's dress, from the shoulder to the waist **2** a tight-fitting corset worn laced over a blouse, as in certain national costumes, or (formerly) as a woman's undergarment [c16 originally Scottish *bodies*, plural of BODY]

bodice ripper *n informal* a romantic novel, usually on a historical theme, that involves some sex and violence

Bo Diddley beat (ˌbəʊ 'dɪdlı 'bi:t) *n* a type of syncopated Black rhythm, frequently used in rock music [c20 named after *Bo Diddley* (born 1929), US rhythm-and-blues performer and songwriter]

-bodied *adj* (*in combination*) having a body or bodies as specified: *able-bodied; long-bodied; many-bodied*

bodiless ('bɒdɪlɪs) *adj* having no body or substance; incorporeal or insubstantial

bodily ('bɒdɪlı) *adj* **1** relating to or being a part of the human body ▷ *adv* **2** by taking hold of the body: *he threw him bodily from the platform* **3** in person; in the flesh

bodkin ('bɒdkın) *n* **1** a blunt large-eyed needle used esp for drawing tape through openwork **2** *archaic* a dagger **3** *printing* a pointed steel tool used for extracting characters when correcting metal type **4** *archaic* a long ornamental hairpin [c14 probably of Celtic origin; compare Gaelic *biodag* dagger]

Bodleian (bɒd'li:ən, 'bɒdlı-) *n* the principal library of Oxford University: a copyright deposit library [c17 named after Sir Thomas *Bodley* (1545–1613), English scholar who founded it in 1602]

Bodmin ('bɒdmın) *n* a market town in SW England, in Cornwall, near **Bodmin Moor**, a granite upland rising to 420 m (1375 ft). Pop: 12 778 (2001)

Bodoni (bə'dəʊnı) *n* a style of type designed by the Italian printer Giambattista *Bodoni* (1740–1813)

body ('bɒdı) *n, pl* **bodies 1 a** the entire physical structure of an animal or human being. Related adjectives: **corporeal, physical b** (*as modifier*): *body odour* **2** the flesh, as opposed to the spirit: *while we are still in the body* **3** the trunk or torso, not including the limbs, head, or tail **4** a dead human or animal; corpse **5** the largest or main part of anything: *the body of a vehicle; the body of a plant* **6** a separate or distinct mass of water or land **7** the main part; majority: *the body of public opinion* **8** the central part of a written work: *the body of a thesis as opposed to the footnotes* **9** a number of individuals regarded as a single entity; group: *the student body; they marched in a body* **10** *maths* a three-dimensional region with an interior **11** *physics* an object or substance that has three dimensions, a mass, and is distinguishable from surrounding objects **12** fullness in the appearance of the hair **13** the characteristic full quality of certain wines, depending on the density and the content of alcohol or tannin: *a Burgundy has a heavy body* **14** substance or firmness, esp of cloth **15** the sound box of a guitar, violin, or similar stringed instrument **16** a woman's close-fitting one-piece garment for the torso **17** the part of a dress covering the body from the shoulders to the waist **18** another name for **shank** (sense 11) **19 a** the pigment contained in or added to paint, dye, etc **b** the opacity of a paint in covering a surface **c** the apparent viscosity of a paint **20** (in watercolour painting) **a** a white filler mixed with pigments to make them opaque **b** (*as modifier*): *body colour*. See also **gouache 21** *printing* the measurement from top to bottom of a piece of type, usually ascender to descender **22** an informal or dialect word for a **person 23 keep body and soul together** to manage to keep alive; survive **24** (*modifier*) of or relating to the main reading matter of a book as distinct from headings, illustrations, appendices, etc: *the body text* ▷ *vb* **bodies, bodying, bodied** (*tr*) **25** (usually foll by *forth*) to give a body or shape to [Old English *bodig*; related to Old Norse *buthkr* box, Old High German *botah* body]

body bag *n military* a large heavy-duty plastic bag used to contain and transport human remains, esp those of battle casualties

body beautiful *n* (usually with *the*) **a** a beautiful body **b** idealized physical beauty

body blow *n* **1** *boxing* Also called: **body punch** a blow to the body of an opponent **2** a severe disappointment or setback: *unavailability of funds was a body blow to the project*

bodyboard ('bɒdı,bɔ:d) *n* a surfboard that is shorter and blunter than the standard board and on which the surfer lies rather than stands. Also

called: boogie board

bodyboarding ('bɒdı,bɔ:dın) *n* the sport of surfing using a bodyboard

body building *n* the practice of performing regular exercises designed to make the muscles of the body conspicuous

body cavity *n* the internal cavity of any multicellular animal that contains the digestive tract, heart, kidneys, etc. In vertebrates it develops from the coelom

body-centred *adj* (of a crystal) having a lattice point at the centre of each unit cell as well as at the corners. Compare **face-centred**

bodycheck ('bɒdı,tʃɛk) *n* **1** *sport* obstruction of another player **2** *wrestling* the act of blocking a charging opponent with the body ▷ *vb* **3** (*tr*) to deliver a bodycheck to (an opponent)

body combat *n* a type of fitness programme in which individuals perform non-contact martial arts moves to music

body corporate *n law* a group of persons incorporated to carry out a specific enterprise. See **corporation** (sense 1)

body double *n films* a person who substitutes for a star for the filming of a scene that involves shots of the body rather than the face

body dysmorphic disorder *n* a psychological disorder characterized by a strong feeling that one's appearance or health would be improved by the removal of a healthy body part

bodyguard ('bɒdı,gɑ:d) *n* a person or group of people who escort and protect someone, esp a political figure

body horror *n* a horror film genre in which the main feature is the graphically depicted destruction or degeneration of a human body or bodies

body image *n psychol* an individual's concept of his or her own body

body language *n* the nonverbal imparting of information by means of conscious or subconscious bodily gestures, posture, etc

body-line *adj cricket* denoting or relating to fast bowling aimed at the batsman's body

body mass index *n* an index used to indicate whether a person is over- or underweight. It is obtained by dividing a person's weight in kilograms by the square of their height in metres. An index of 20–25 is normal. Abbreviation: BMI

body modification *n* any method of permanently adorning the body, including tattooing and piercing

Body of Christ *n* the Christian Church

body-packer *n* a person who smuggles illicit drugs in balloons, condoms, or similar plastic bags which have either been swallowed or inserted in the rectum or vagina

body politic *n* the. the people of a nation or the nation itself considered as a political entity; the state

body search *n* **1** a form of search by police, customs officials, etc, that involves examination of a prisoner's or suspect's bodily orifices ▷ *vb* **body-search 2** (*tr*) to search (a prisoner or suspect) in this manner

bodyshell ('bɒdı,ʃɛl) *n* the external shell of a motor vehicle

body shop *n* a place where the bodywork of motor vehicles is built or repaired

body snatcher *n* (formerly) a person who robbed graves and sold the corpses for dissection > **body snatching** *n*

body stocking *n* a one-piece undergarment for women, usually of nylon, covering the torso

bodysuit ('bɒdı,su:t, -,sju:t) *n* **1** another name for **body** (sense 16) **2** a one-piece undergarment for a baby

body-surf *vb* (*intr*) **1** to ride a wave by lying on it without a surfboard **2** (*intr*) *informal* to fling oneself prone onto a crowd of people, for example on a dance floor or at a rock concert, and move or be carried over their heads

b

> 'body,surfer n > 'body,surfing n

body swerve n **1** sport (esp in football games) the act or an instance of swerving past an opponent **2** Scot the act or an instance of avoiding (a situation considered unpleasant): I think I'll give the meeting a body swerve ▷ vb **body-swerve 3** sport (esp in football games) to pass (an opponent) using a body swerve **4** Scot to avoid (a situation or person considered unpleasant)

body warmer n a sleeveless type of jerkin, usually quilted, worn as an outer garment for extra warmth

bodywork ('bɒdɪ,wɜːk) n **1** the external shell of a motor vehicle **2** any form of therapy in which parts of the body are manipulated, such as massage

body wrap n a beauty treatment in which the body is covered in lotion and wrapped tightly in strips of cloth in order to promote weight loss or improve skin tone

Boehmite ('bɜːmaɪt) n a grey, red, or brown mineral that consists of alumina in rhombic crystalline form and occurs in bauxite. Formula: AlO(OH) [c20 from German Böhmit, after J. Böhm, 20th-century German scientist]

Boeotia (bɪ'əʊʃɪə) n a region of ancient Greece, northwest of Athens. It consisted of ten city-states, which formed the Boeotian League, led by Thebes: at its height in the 4th century BC. Modern Greek name: Voiotia

Boeotian (bɪ'əʊʃɪən) n **1** a native or inhabitant of Boeotia, a region of ancient Greece ▷ adj **2** of or relating to Boeotia or its inhabitants

boep (bup) n South African a protruding or distended belly: beer boep [Afrikaans]

Boer (bʊə, 'bəʊə, bɔː) n, adj **a** a descendant of any of the Dutch or Huguenot colonists who settled in South Africa, mainly in Cape Colony, the Orange Free State, and the Transvaal **b** (as modifier): a Boer farm [c19 from Dutch Boer; see BOOR]

boerbul ('bʊə,bʌl) n South African a crossbred mastiff used esp as a watchdog [from Afrikaans boerboel a breed of mastiff]

boere- (bʊə, 'bəʊə, bɔː) combining form South African rustic or country-style: boeremusiek [Afrikaans]

boeremusiek ('bʊərə,mjuːzɪk) n South African a special variety of light music associated with the culture of the Afrikaners [Afrikaans]

boerewors ('bʊərə,vɒs) n South African a highly seasoned traditional sausage made from minced or pounded meat [Afrikaans]

boertjie ('bʊətʃɪ) n South African a person, esp a friend, often used as a term of address [Afrikaans: little farmer]

Boer War n either of two conflicts between Britain and the South African Boers, the first (1880–1881) when the Boers sought to regain the independence given up for British aid against the Zulus, the second (1899–1902) when the Orange Free State and Transvaal declared war on Britain. Also called: Anglo-Boer War, South African War

boet (but) n South African brother; mate, chum [Afrikaans]

boeuf bourguignon (French bœf burgiɲɔ̃) n a casserole of beef, vegetables, herbs, etc, cooked in red wine. Also called: boeuf à la bourguignonne [French: Burgundy beef]

boff (bɒf) n informal short for **boffin**

boffin ('bɒfɪn) n **1** Brit informal a scientist, esp one carrying out military research **2** a person who has extensive skill or knowledge in a particular field: a Treasury boffin **3** informal someone who is considered to be very clever, often to the exclusion of all non-academic interests [c20 of uncertain origin]

boffo ('bɒfəʊ) adj **1** slang very good; highly successful **2** a person who has extensive skill or knowledge in a particular field [c20 of uncertain origin]

Bofors gun ('bəʊfəz) n an automatic single- or double-barrelled anti-aircraft gun with 40 millimetre bore [c20 named after Bofors, Sweden,

where it was first made]

bog (bɒg) n **1** wet spongy ground consisting of decomposing vegetation, which ultimately forms peat **2** an area of such ground **3** a place or thing that prevents or slows progress or improvement **4** a slang word for **lavatory** (sense 1) **5** Austral slang the act or an instance of defecating. ▷ See also **bog down, bog in, bog off** [c13 from Gaelic bogach swamp, from bog soft] > 'boggy adj > 'bogginess n

bogan[1] ('bəʊgən) n Canadian (esp in the Maritime Provinces) a sluggish side stream. Also called: logan, pokelogan [of Algonquian origin]

bogan[2] ('bəʊgən) n Austral informal **1** a fool **2** a hooligan [c20 of unknown origin]

bogart ('bəʊgɑːt) vb (tr) slang to monopolize or keep (something, esp a marijuana cigarette) to oneself selfishly [c20 after the US film actor Humphrey Bogart (1899–1957), on account of his alleged greed for marijuana]

bog asphodel n either of two liliaceous plants, Narthecium ossifragum of Europe or N. americanum of North America, that grow in boggy places and have small yellow flowers and grasslike leaves

Boğazköy (Turkish bɔ:'ɑzkœi) n a village in central Asia Minor: site of the ancient Hittite capital

bogbean ('bɒg,biːn) n another name for **buckbean**

bog cotton n another name for **cotton grass**

bog deal n pine wood found preserved in peat bogs

bog down vb bogs, bogging, bogged (adverb; when tr, often passive) to impede or be impeded physically or mentally

bogey[1] or **bogy** ('bəʊgɪ) n **1** an evil or mischievous spirit **2** something that worries or annoys **3** golf **a** a score of one stroke over par on a hole. Compare **par** (sense 5) **b** obsolete a standard score for a hole or course, regarded as one that a good player should make **4** slang a piece of dried mucus discharged from the nose **5** air force slang an unidentified or hostile aircraft **6** slang a detective; policeman ▷ vb **7** (tr) golf to play (a hole) in one stroke over par [c20 probably related to BUG[2] and BOGLE[1]; compare BUGABOO]

bogey[2] or **bogie** ('bəʊgɪ) Austral ▷ vb **1** to bathe or swim ▷ n **2** a bathe or swim [c19 from a native Australian language]

bogey hole n Austral a natural pool used for swimming

bogeyman ('bəʊgɪ,mæn) n, pl -men a person, real or imaginary, used as a threat, esp to children

boggart ('bɒgət) n Northern English dialect a ghost or poltergeist [perhaps from bog, variant of BUG[2] + -ARD]

bogger (bɒgə) n Austral slang a lavatory

bogging ('bɒgɪn) adj Scot informal filthy; covered in dirt and grime

boggle ('bɒgᵊl) vb (intr; often foll by at) **1** to be surprised, confused, or alarmed (esp in the phrase **the mind boggles**) **2** to hesitate or be evasive when confronted with a problem **3** (tr) to baffle; bewilder; puzzle [c16 probably variant of BOGLE[1]]

bogie[1] or **bogy** ('bəʊgɪ) n **1** an assembly of four or six wheels forming a pivoted support at either end of a railway coach. It provides flexibility on curves **2** chiefly Brit a small railway truck of short wheelbase, used for conveying coal, ores, etc **3** a Scot word for **soapbox** (sense 3) [c19 of unknown origin]

bogie[2] ('bəʊgɪ) n a variant spelling of **bogey**[2]

bog in vb bogs, bogging, bogged (intr, adverb) Austral and NZ informal **1** to start energetically on a task **2** to start eating; tuck in ▷ Also (preposition): **bog into**

bogle[1] ('bəʊgᵊl, 'bɒg-) n **1** a dialect or archaic word for **bogey**[1] (sense 1) **2** Scot a scarecrow [c16 from Scottish bogill, perhaps from Gaelic; compare Welsh bygel; see BUG[2]]

bogle[2] ('bəʊgᵊl) n a rhythmic dance, originating in the early 1990s, performed to ragga music ▷ vb **2** (intr) to perform such a dance

bogman ('bɒg,mæn) n, pl -men archaeol the body of a person found preserved in a peat bog

bog moss n another name for **peat moss**

bog myrtle n another name for **sweet gale**

Bognor Regis ('bɒgnə 'riːdʒɪs) n a resort in S England, in West Sussex on the English Channel: electronics industries. Regis was added to the name after King George V's convalescence there in 1929. Pop: 62 141 (2001)

bog oak n oak or other wood found preserved in peat bogs; bogwood

BOGOF ('bɒgɒf) acronym for buy one, get one free

bog off Brit slang ▷ interj **1** go away! ▷ vb bogs, bogging, bogged **2** (intr, adverb) to go away

bogong ('bəʊ,gɒŋ) or **bugong** ('buː,gɒŋ) n an edible dark-coloured Australian noctuid moth, Agrotis infusa

Bogor ('bəʊgɔː) n a city in Indonesia, in W Java: botanical gardens and research institutions. Pop: 750 819 (2000). Former name: Buitenzorg

bog orchid n an orchid, Hammarbya (or Malaxis) paludosa, growing in sphagnum bogs in the N hemisphere. It has greenish-yellow flowers and its leaves bear a fringe of tiny bulbils

Bogotá (,bəʊgə'tɑː; Spanish boɣo'ta) n the capital of Colombia, on a central plateau of the E Andes: originally the centre of Chibcha civilization; founded as a city in 1538 by the Spaniards. Pop: 7 594 000 (2005 est)

bog rosemary n another name for **marsh andromeda**

bog rush n a blackish tufted cyperaceous plant, Schoenus nigricans, growing on boggy ground

bog-standard n informal completely ordinary; run-of-the-mill

bogtrotter ('bɒg,trɒtə) n a derogatory term for an Irish person, esp an Irish peasant

bogus ('bəʊgəs) adj spurious or counterfeit; not genuine: a bogus note [c19 from bogus apparatus for making counterfeit money; perhaps related to BOGEY[1]] > 'bogusly adv > 'bogusness n

bogwood ('bɒg,wʊd) n another name for **bog oak**

bogy ('bəʊgɪ) n, pl -gies a variant spelling of **bogey**[1] or **bogie**[1]

boh (bəʊ) interj a variant spelling of **bo**

Bohai ('bɔː'haɪ) or **Pohai** n a large inlet of the Yellow Sea on the coast of NE China. Also called: (Gulf of) Chihli

bohea (bəʊ'hiː) n a black Chinese tea, once regarded as the choicest, but now as an inferior grade [c18 from Chinese (Fukien dialect) bu-i, from Mandarin Chinese Wu-i Shan range of hills on which this tea was grown]

Bohemia (bəʊ'hiːmɪə) n **1** a former kingdom of central Europe, surrounded by mountains: independent from the 9th to the 13th century; belonged to the Hapsburgs from 1526 until 1918 **2** an area of the W Czech Republic, formerly a province of Czechoslovakia (1918–1949). From 1939 until 1945 it formed part of the German protectorate of Bohemia-Moravia. Czech name: Čechy. German name: Böhmen ('bøːmən) **3** a district frequented by unconventional people, esp artists or writers

Bohemian (bəʊ'hiːmɪən) n **1** a native or inhabitant of Bohemia, esp of the old kingdom of Bohemia; a Czech **2** (often not capital) a person, esp an artist or writer, who lives an unconventional life **3** the Czech language ▷ adj **4** of, relating to, or characteristic of Bohemia, its people, or their language **5** unconventional in appearance, behaviour, etc

Bohemian Brethren pl n a Protestant Christian sect formed in the 15th century from various Hussite groups, which rejected oaths and military service and advocated a pure and disciplined spiritual life. It was reorganized in 1722 as the Moravian Church. Also called: Unitas Fratrem ('juːnɪtæs 'frætrɛm)

Bohemian Forest n a mountain range between the SW Czech Republic and SE Germany. Highest peak: Arber, 1457 m (4780 ft). Czech name: Český Les ('tʃɛski 'lɛs). German name: Böhmerwald ('bøːmər,valt)

Bohemianism (bəʊˈhiːmɪəˌnɪzəm) *n* unconventional behaviour or appearance, esp of an artist

Böhm flute *n* a type of flute in which the holes are covered with keys; the standard type of modern flute [c19 named after Theobald *Böhm* (1793–1881), German flautist who invented it]

boho (ˈbəʊhəʊ) *n, pl* **-hos**, *adj informal* short for **Bohemian** (senses 2, 5)

Bohol (bəʊˈhɔːl) *n* an island of the central Philippines. Chief town: Tagbilaran. Pop: 1 139 130 (2000). Area: about 3900 sq km (1500 sq miles)

bohrium (ˈbɔːrɪəm) *n* a transuranic element artificially produced in minute quantities by bombarding ²⁰⁴Bi atoms with ⁵⁴Cr nuclei. Symbol: Bh; atomic no.: 107. Former names: **element 107**, **unnilheptium** [c20 after Neils *Bohr* (1885–1962), Danish physicist]

Bohr theory *n* a theory of atomic structure that explains the spectrum of hydrogen atoms. It assumes that the electron orbiting around the nucleus can exist only in certain energy states, a jump from one state to another being accompanied by the emission or absorption of a quantum of radiation [c20 after Niels *Bohr* (1885–1962), Danish physicist]

bohunk (ˈbəʊˌhʌŋk) *n US and Canadian derogatory slang* a labourer from east or central Europe [c20 blend of *Bo(hemian)* + *Hung(arian)*, with alteration of *g* to *k*]

boi (bɔɪ) *n informal* a lesbian who adopts a boyish appearance or manner [c20 modified spelling of BOY]

boil¹ (bɔɪl) *vb* **1** to change or cause to change from a liquid to a vapour so rapidly that bubbles of vapour are formed copiously in the liquid. Compare **evaporate 2** to reach or cause to reach boiling point **3** to cook or be cooked by the process of boiling **4** (*intr*) to bubble and be agitated like something boiling; seethe: *the ocean was boiling* **5** (*intr*) to be extremely angry or indignant (esp in the phrase **make one's blood boil**): *she was boiling at his dishonesty* **6** (*intr*) to contain a boiling liquid: *the pot is boiling* ▷ *n* **7** the state or action of boiling (esp in the phrases **on the boil, off the boil**) ▷ See also **boil away, boil down, boil off, boil over, boil up** [c13 from Old French *boillir*, from Latin *bullīre* to bubble, from *bulla* a bubble] > ¹**boilable** *adj*

boil² (bɔɪl) *n* a red painful swelling with a hard pus-filled core caused by bacterial infection of the skin and subcutaneous tissues, esp at a hair follicle. Technical name: **furuncle** [Old English *bȳle*; related to Old Norse *beyla* swelling, Old High German *būlla* bladder, Gothic *ufbauljan* to inflate]

boil away *vb* (*adverb*) to cause (liquid) to evaporate completely by boiling or (of liquid) to evaporate completely

boil down *vb* (*adverb*) **1** to reduce or be reduced in quantity and usually altered in consistency by boiling: *to boil a liquid down to a thick glue* **2 boil down to a** (*intr*) to be the essential element in something **b** (*tr*) to summarize; reduce to essentials

boiled shirt *n informal* a dress shirt with a stiff front

boiled sweet *n Brit* a hard sticky sweet of boiled sugar with any of various flavourings

boiler (ˈbɔɪlə) *n* **1** a closed vessel or arrangement of enclosed tubes in which water is heated to supply steam to drive an engine or turbine or provide heat **2** a domestic device burning solid fuel, gas, or oil, to provide hot water, esp for central heating **3** a large tub for boiling laundry **4** a tough old chicken for cooking by boiling

boilermaker (ˈbɔɪləˌmeɪkə) *n* **1** a person who works with metal in heavy industry; plater or welder **2** *Brit slang* a beer drink consisting of half of draught mild and half of bottled brown ale **3** *US slang* a drink of whisky followed by a beer chaser

boilerplate (ˈbɔɪləˌpleɪt) *n* **1** a form of mild-steel plate used in the production of boiler shells **2** a copy made with the intention of making other copies from it **3** a set of instructions incorporated in several places in a computer program or a standard form of words used repeatedly in drafting contracts, guarantees, etc **4** a draft contract that can easily be modified to cover various types of transaction ▷ *vb* **5** to incorporate standard material automatically in a text

boiler room *n* **1** any room in a building (often in the basement) that contains a boiler for central heating, etc **2** the part of a steam ship that houses the boilers and furnaces **3** the room or department in which the real work of an organization goes on unseen **4** (*chiefly US*) an office used by a team of telephone salespeople, esp of stocks and shares, operating under high pressure **5 a** a fraudulent scheme in which investors are encouraged to buy non-existent, worthless, or over-priced shares **b** (*as modifier*): *a boiler-room scam*

boiler suit *n Brit* a one-piece work garment consisting of overalls and a shirt top usually worn over ordinary clothes to protect them

boiling (ˈbɔɪlɪŋ) *adj, adv* **1** very warm: *a boiling hot day* ▷ *n* **2 the whole boiling** *slang* the whole lot

boiling point *n* **1** the temperature at which a liquid boils at a given pressure, usually atmospheric pressure at sea level; the temperature at which the vapour pressure of a liquid equals the external pressure **2** *informal* the condition of being angered or highly excited

boiling-water reactor *n* a nuclear reactor using water as coolant and moderator, steam being produced in the reactor itself: enriched uranium oxide cased in zirconium is the fuel. Abbreviation: **BWR**

boil off *vb* to remove or be removed (from) by boiling: *to boil off impurities*

boilover (ˈbɔɪlˌəʊvə) *n Austral* **1** a surprising result in a sporting event, esp in a horse race **2** a sudden conflict

boil over *vb* (*adverb*) **1** to overflow or cause to overflow while boiling **2** (*intr*) to burst out in anger or excitement: *she boiled over at the mention of his name*

boil up *vb* (*intr, adverb*) *Austral and NZ* to make tea

bois-brûlé (ˌbwɑːbruːˈleɪ) *n* (*sometimes capital*) *Canadian archaic* a mixed-race person of Canadian Indian and White (usually French Canadian) ancestry; Métis. Also called: **Brule** [French, literally: burnt wood]

Bois de Boulogne (*French* bwa də bulɔɲ) *n* a large park in W Paris, formerly a forest: includes the racecourses of Auteuil and Longchamp

Boise or **Boise City** (ˈbɔɪzɪ, -sɪ) *n* a city in SW Idaho: the state capital. Pop: 190 117 (2003 est)

Bois-le-Duc (bwa lə dyk) *n* the French name for **'s Hertogenbosch**

boisterous (ˈbɔɪstərəs, -strəs) *adj* **1** noisy and lively; unrestrained or unruly **2** (of the wind, sea, etc) turbulent or stormy [c13 *boistuous*, of unknown origin] > ˈ**boisterously** *adv* > ˈ**boisterousness** *n*

Bok (bɒk) *n mainly S. African* short for **Springbok**

bok choy (ˈbɒk ˈtʃɔɪ) *n* a Chinese plant, *Brassica chinensis*, that is related to the cabbage and has edible stalks and leaves. Also called: **Chinese cabbage, Chinese leaf, pak-choi cabbage** [from Chinese dialect, literally: white vegetable]

boke, boak or **bock** (bɒk, bəʊk) *Scot* ▷ *vb* **1** to retch or vomit ▷ *n* **2** a retch; vomiting fit [Middle English *bolken*; related to BELCH, German *bölken* to roar]

Bokhara (bʊˈxɑːrə) *n* a variant spelling of **Bukhara**

bokmakierie (ˌbɒkməˈkɪərɪ) *n South African* a large yellow shrike, *Telophorus zeylonus*, of southern Africa, known for its melodious song [c19 from Afrikaans, imitative of its call]

Bokmål (*Norwegian* ˈbuːkmɔːl) *n* one of the two official forms of written Norwegian, closely related to Danish. Also called: **Dano-Norwegian**. Formerly called: **Riksmål**. Compare **Nynorsk** [Norwegian, literally: book language]

BOL *international car registration for* Bolivia

Bol. *abbreviation for* Bolivia(n)

bola (ˈbəʊlə) or **bolas** (ˈbəʊləs) *n, pl* **-las** or **-lases** a missile used by gauchos and Indians of South America, consisting of two or more heavy balls on a cord. It is hurled at a running quarry, such as an ox or rhea, so as to entangle its legs [Spanish: ball, from Latin *bulla* knob]

Boland (ˈbʊəlant) *n* an area of high altitude in S South Africa

Bolan Pass (bəʊˈlɑːn) *n* a mountain pass in W central Pakistan through the Brahui Range, between Sibi and Quetta, rising to 1800 m (5900 ft)

bold (bəʊld) *adj* **1** courageous, confident, and fearless; ready to take risks **2** showing or requiring courage: *a bold plan* **3** immodest or impudent: *she gave him a bold look* **4** standing out distinctly; conspicuous: *a figure carved in bold relief* **5** very steep: *the bold face of the cliff* **6** imaginative in thought or expression: *the novel's bold plot* **7** printing set in bold face ▷ *n* **8** printing short for **bold face** [Old English *beald*; related to Old Norse *ballr* dangerous, terrible, *baldinn* defiant, Old High German *bald* bold] > ˈ**boldly** *adv* > ˈ**boldness** *n*

bold face *n* **1** printing a weight of type characterized by thick heavy lines, as the entry words in this dictionary. Compare **light face** ▷ *adj* **boldface 2** (of type) having this weight

bole¹ (bəʊl) *n* the trunk of a tree [c14 from Old Norse *bolr*; related to Middle High German *bole* plank]

bole² (bəʊl) or **bolus** *n* **1** a reddish soft variety of clay used as a pigment **2** a moderate reddish-brown colour [c13 from Late Latin *bōlus* lump, from Greek *bōlos*]

bolection (bəʊˈlɛkʃən) *n architect* a stepped moulding covering and projecting beyond the joint between two members having surfaces at different levels. Also called: **bilection** [c18 of unknown origin]

bolero (bəˈlɛərəʊ) *n, pl* **-ros 1** a Spanish dance, often accompanied by the guitar and castanets, usually in triple time **2** a piece of music composed for or in the rhythm of this dance **3** (*also* ˈbɒlərəʊ) a kind of short jacket not reaching the waist, with or without sleeves and open at the front: worn by men in Spain and by women elsewhere [c18 from Spanish; perhaps related to *bola* ball]

boletus (bəʊˈliːtəs) *n, pl* **-tuses** or **-ti** (-ˌtaɪ) any saprotroph basidiomycetous fungus of the genus *Boletus*, having a brownish umbrella-shaped cap with spore-bearing tubes in the underside: family *Boletaceae*. Many species are edible [c17 from Latin: variety of mushroom, from Greek *bōlitēs*; perhaps related to Greek *bōlos* lump]

bolide (ˈbəʊlaɪd, -lɪd) *n* a large exceptionally bright meteor that often explodes. Also called: **fireball** [c19 from French, from *bolis* missile; see BALLISTA]

boline (ˈbəʊliːn) *n* (in Wicca) a knife, usually sickle-shaped and with a white handle, used for gathering herbs and carving symbols

bolívar (ˈbɒlɪˌvɑː; *Spanish* boˈliβar) *n, pl* **-vars** or **-vares** (-βares) the standard monetary unit of Venezuela, equal to 100 céntimos [named after Simon Bolivar (1783–1830), South American soldier and liberator]

Bolivia (bəˈlɪvɪə) *n* an inland republic in central S America: original Aymará Indian population conquered by the Incas in the 13th century; colonized by Spain from 1538; became a republic in 1825; consists of low plains in the east, with ranges of the Andes rising to over 6400 m (21 000 ft) and the Altiplano, a plateau averaging 3900 m (13 000 ft) in the west; contains some of the world's highest inhabited regions; important producer of tin and other minerals. Official languages: Spanish, Quechua, and Aymara.

b

Religion: Roman Catholic. Currency: boliviano. Capital: La Paz (administrative); Sucre (judicial). Pop: 8 973 000 (2004 est). Area: 1 098 580 sq km (424 260 sq miles)

Bolivian (bəˈlɪvɪən) *adj* **1** of or relating to Bolivia or its inhabitants ▷ *n* **2** a native or inhabitant of Bolivia

boliviano (bəˌlɪvɪˈɑːnəʊ; *Spanish* boliˈvjano) *n, pl* **-nos** (-nəʊz; *Spanish* -nos) (until 1963 and from 1987) the standard monetary unit of Bolivia, equal to 100 centavos

boll (bəʊl) *n* the fruit of such plants as flax and cotton, consisting of a rounded capsule containing the seeds [c13 from Dutch *bolle*; related to Old English *bolla* BOWL[1]]

bollard (ˈbɒlɑːd, ˈbɒləd) *n* **1** a strong wooden or metal post mounted on a wharf, quay, etc, used for securing mooring lines **2** *Brit* a small post or marker placed on a kerb or traffic island to make it conspicuous to motorists **3** *mountaineering* an outcrop of rock or pillar of ice that may be used to belay a rope [c14 perhaps from BOLE[1] + -ARD]

bollocking (ˈbɒləkɪŋ) *n slang* a severe telling-off; dressing-down [from *bollock* (vb) (in the sense: to reprimand)]

bollocks (ˈbɒləks), **ballocks** *or US* **bollix** (ˈbɒlɪks) *slang* ▷ *pl n* **1** another word for **testicles** **2** nonsense; rubbish ▷ *interj* **3** an exclamation of annoyance, disbelief, etc **4** **the (dog's) bollocks** something excellent ▷ *vb* (usually foll by *up*) **5** to muddle or botch [Old English *beallucas*, diminutive (pl) of *beallu* (unattested); see BALL[1]]

> USAGE Both its anatomical senses and its various extended senses nowadays have far less impact than they used to, and seem unlikely to cause offence, though some older or more conservative people may object. The fact that shops displaying the Sex Pistols' album containing this word were charged with offences defined in 19th-century Indecent Advertisement and Vagrancy Acts now seems hard to credit

boll weevil *n* a greyish weevil, *Anthonomus grandis*, of the southern US and Mexico, whose larvae live in and destroy cotton bolls. See also **weevil** (sense 1)

bollworm (ˈbəʊlˌwɜːm) *n* any of various moth caterpillars, such as *Pectinophora* (or *Platyedra*) *gossypiella* (**pink bollworm**), that feed on and destroy cotton bolls

Bollywood (ˈbɒlɪˌwʊd) *n informal* **a** the Indian film industry **b** (*as modifier*): *a Bollywood star* [c20 from BO(MBAY) + (HO)LLYWOOD]

bolo (ˈbəʊləʊ) *n, pl* **-los** a large single-edged knife, originating in the Philippines [Philippine Spanish, probably from a native word]

Bologna (bəˈləʊnjə; *Italian* boˈloɲɲa) *n* a city in N Italy, at the foot of the Apennines: became a free city in the Middle Ages; university (1088). Pop: 371 217 (2001). Ancient name: **Bononia** (bəˈnəʊnɪə)

bologna sausage *n chiefly US and Canadian* a large smoked sausage made of seasoned mixed meats. Also called: **baloney, boloney,** (esp Brit) **polony**

Bolognese (ˌbɒləˈniːz, -ˈneɪz) *adj* **1** of or relating to Bologna or its inhabitants ▷ *n* **2** a native or inhabitant of Bologna

bolometer (bəʊˈlɒmɪtə) *n* a sensitive instrument for measuring radiant energy by the increase in the resistance of an electrical conductor [c19 from *bol-*, from Greek *bolē* ray of light, stroke, from *ballein* to throw + -METER] > **bolometric** (ˌbəʊləˈmɛtrɪk) *adj* > ˌ**boloˈmetrically** *adv* > **boˈlometry** *n*

boloney (bəˈləʊnɪ) *n* **1** a variant spelling of **baloney** **2** *chiefly US* another name for **bologna sausage**

Bolshevik (ˈbɒlʃɪvɪk) *n, pl* **-viks** *or* **-viki** (-ˈviːkɪ) **1** (formerly) a Russian Communist. Compare **Menshevik** **2** any Communist **3** (*often not capital*) *informal and derogatory* any political radical, esp a revolutionary [c20 from Russian *Bol'shevik* majority, from *bol'shoi* great; from the fact that this group formed a majority of the Russian Social Democratic Party in 1903] > ˈ**Bolsheˌvism** *n* > ˈ**Bolshevist** *adj, n* > ˌ**Bolsheˈvistic** *adj*

bolshie *or* **bolshy** (ˈbɒlʃɪ) (*sometimes capital*) *Brit informal* ▷ *adj* **1** difficult to manage; rebellious **2** politically radical or left-wing ▷ *n, pl* **-shies** **3** *derogatory* any political radical [c20 shortened from BOLSHEVIK]

bolson (bəʊlˈsəʊn) *n Southwestern US* a desert valley surrounded by mountains, with a shallow lake at the centre [c19 from American Spanish *bolsón*, from Spanish *bolsa* purse, from Late Latin *bursa* bag; see PURSE]

bolster (ˈbəʊlstə) *vb* (*tr*) **1** (often foll by *up*) to support or reinforce; strengthen: *to bolster morale* **2** to prop up with a pillow or cushion **3** to add padding to: *to bolster a dress* ▷ *n* **4** a long narrow pillow or cushion **5** any pad or padded support **6** *architect* a short horizontal length of timber fixed to the top of a post to increase the bearing area and reduce the span of the supported beam **7** a cold chisel having a broad blade splayed towards the cutting edge, used for cutting stone slabs, etc [Old English *bolster*; related to Old Norse *bolstr*, Old High German *bolstar*, Dutch *bulster*] > ˈ**bolsterer** *n* > ˈ**bolstering** *n, adj*

bolt[1] (bəʊlt) *n* **1** a bar that can be slid into a socket to lock a door, gate, etc **2** a bar or rod that forms part of a locking mechanism and is moved by a key or a knob **3** a metal rod or pin that has a head at one end and a screw thread at the other to take a nut **4** a sliding bar in a breech-loading firearm that ejects the empty cartridge, replaces it with a new one, and closes the breech **5** a flash of lightning **6** a sudden start or movement, esp in order to escape: *they made a bolt for the door* **7** *US* a sudden desertion, esp from a political party **8** a roll of something, such as cloth, wallpaper, etc **9** an arrow, esp for a crossbow **10** *printing* a folded edge on a sheet of paper that is removed when cutting to size **11** *mechanical engineering* short for **expansion bolt** **12** **a bolt from the blue** a sudden, unexpected, and usually unwelcome event **13** **shoot one's bolt** to exhaust one's effort: *the runner had shot his bolt* ▷ *vb* **14** (*tr*) to secure or lock with or as with a bolt or bolts: *bolt your doors* **15** (*tr*) to eat hurriedly: *don't bolt your food* **16** (*intr;* usually foll by *from* or *out*) to move or jump suddenly: *he bolted from the chair* **17** (*intr*) (esp of a horse) to start hurriedly and run away without warning **18** (*tr*) to roll or make (cloth, wallpaper, etc) into bolts **19** *US* to desert (a political party, etc) **20** (*intr*) (of cultivated plants) to produce flowers and seeds prematurely **21** (*tr*) to cause (a wild animal) to leave its lair; start: *terriers were used for bolting rats* ▷ *adv* **22** stiffly, firmly, or rigidly (archaic except in the phrase **bolt upright**) [Old English *bolt* arrow; related to Old High German *bolz* bolt for a crossbow]

bolt[2] *or* **boult** (bəʊlt) *vb* (*tr*) **1** to pass (flour, a powder, etc) through a sieve **2** to examine and separate [c13 from Old French *bulter*, probably of Germanic origin; compare Old High German *būtil* bag] > ˈ**bolter** *or* ˈ**boulter** *n*

bolter (ˈbəʊltə) *n Austral informal* **1** an outsider in a contest or race **2** *history* an escaped convict; bushranger

bolt hole *n* a place of escape from danger

Bolton (ˈbəʊltən) *n* **1** a town in NW England, in Bolton unitary authority, Greater Manchester: centre of the woollen trade since the 14th century; later important for cotton. Pop: 139 403 (2001) **2** a unitary authority in NW England, in Greater Manchester. Pop: 263 800 (2003 est). Area: 140 sq km (54 sq miles)

bolt-on *adj* supplementary or additional: *a bolt-on prologue*

boltonia (bəʊlˈtəʊnɪə) *n* any North American plant of the genus *Boltonia*, having daisy-like flowers with white, violet, or pinkish rays: family *Compositae* (composites) [c18 New Latin, named after James *Bolton*, C18 English botanist]

boltrope (ˈbəʊltˌrəʊp) *n nautical* a rope sewn to the foot or luff of a sail to strengthen it [c17 from BOLT[1] + ROPE]

Boltzmann constant *n physics* the ratio of the gas constant to the Avogadro constant, equal to $1.380\,650 \times 10^{-23}$ joule per kelvin. Symbol: *k*

bolus (ˈbəʊləs) *n, pl* **-luses** **1** a small round soft mass, esp of chewed food **2** an intravenous injection of a single dose of a drug over a short period **3** *obsolete* a large pill or tablet used in veterinary and clinical medicine **4** another word for **bole**[2] [c17 from New Latin, from Greek *bōlos* clod, lump]

Bolzano (*Italian* bolˈtsano) *n* a city in NE Italy, in Trentino-Alto Adige: belonged to Austria until 1919. Pop: 94 989 (2001). German name: **Bozen**

boma (ˈboːma) *n* (in central and E Africa) **1** an enclosure, esp a palisade or fence of thorn bush, set up to protect a camp, herd of animals, etc **2** **a** a police post **b** a magistrate's office [c19 from Swahili]

Boma (ˈbəʊmə) *n* a port in the Democratic Republic of Congo (formerly Zaïre), on the Congo River, capital of the Belgian Congo until 1926: forest products. Pop: 607 000 (2005 est)

bomb (bɒm) *n* **1** **a** a hollow projectile containing explosive, incendiary, or other destructive substance, esp one carried by aircraft **b** (*as modifier*): *bomb disposal; a bomb bay* **c** (*in combination*): *a bombload; bombproof* **2** any container filled with explosive: *a car bomb; a letter bomb* **3** **the bomb** **a** a hydrogen or atomic bomb considered as the ultimate destructive weapon **b** *slang* something excellent: *it's the bomb* **4** a round or pear-shaped mass of volcanic rock, solidified from molten lava that has been thrown into the air **5** *med* a container for radioactive material, applied therapeutically to any part of the body: *a cobalt bomb* **6** *Brit slang* a large sum of money (esp in the phrase **make a bomb**) **7** *US and Canadian slang* a disastrous failure: *the new play was a total bomb* **8** *Austral and NZ slang* an old or dilapidated motorcar **9** *American football* a very long high pass **10** (in rugby union) another term for **up-and-under** **11** **like a bomb** *Brit and NZ informal* with great speed or success; very well (esp in the phrase **go like a bomb**) ▷ *vb* **12** to attack with or as if with a bomb or bombs; drop bombs (on) **13** (*intr;* often foll by *off, along,* etc) *informal* to move or drive very quickly **14** (*intr*) *slang* to fail disastrously; be a flop: *the new play bombed.* See also **bomb out** [c17 from French *bombe*, from Italian *bomba*, probably from Latin *bombus* a booming sound, from Greek *bombos*, of imitative origin; compare Old Norse *bumba* drum]

bombacaceous (ˌbɒmbəˈkeɪʃəs) *adj* of, relating to, or belonging to the *Bombacaceae*, a family of tropical trees, including the kapok tree and baobab, that have very thick stems, often with water-storing tissue [c19 from New Latin *Bombācāceae*, from Medieval Latin *bombāx* cotton, from Latin *bombyx* silkworm, silk, from Greek *bombux*]

bombard *vb* (bɒmˈbɑːd) (*tr*) **1** to attack with concentrated artillery fire or bombs **2** to attack with vigour and persistence: *the boxer bombarded his opponent with blows to the body* **3** to attack verbally, esp with questions: *the journalists bombarded her with questions* **4** *physics* to direct high-energy particles or photons against (atoms, nuclei, etc) esp to produce ions or nclear transformations ▷ *n* (ˈbɒmbɑːd) **5** an ancient type of cannon that threw stone balls [c15 from Old French *bombarder* to pelt, from *bombarde* stone-throwing cannon, probably from Latin *bombus* booming sound; see BOMB] > **bomˈbardment** *n*

bombarde (ˈbɒmˌbɑːd) *n* an alto wind instrument similar to the oboe or medieval shawm, used mainly in Breton traditional music [French, from BOMBARD, in the sense of booming sound]

bombardier (ˌbɒmbəˈdɪə) *n* **1** the member of a bomber aircrew responsible for aiming and releasing the bombs **2** *Brit* a noncommissioned rank below the rank of sergeant in the Royal Artillery **3** Also called: **bombardier beetle** any of various small carabid beetles of the genus *Brachinus*, esp *B. crepitans* of Europe, which defend themselves by ejecting a jet of volatile fluid [c16 from Old French: one directing a bombard; see BOMBARD]

Bombardier (ˌbɒmbəˈdɪə) *n trademark Canadian* a snow tractor, typically having caterpillar tracks at the rear and skis at the front [c20 named after J. A. *Bombardier*, Canadian inventor and manufacturer]

bombardon (ˈbɒmbədən, bɒmˈbɑːdən) *n* **1** a brass instrument of the tuba type, similar to a sousaphone **2** a 16-foot bass reed stop on an organ [c19 from Italian *bombardone*; see BOMBARD]

bombast (ˈbɒmbæst) *n* **1** pompous and grandiloquent language **2** *obsolete* material used for padding [c16 from Old French *bombace*, from Medieval Latin *bombāx* cotton; see BOMBACACEOUS] > bomˈbastic *adj* > bomˈbastically *adv*

Bombay (bɒmˈbeɪ) *n* **1** a port in W India, capital of Maharashtra state, on the Arabian Sea: ceded by Portugal to England in 1661 and of major importance in British India; commercial and industrial centre, esp for cotton. Pop: 11 914 398 (2001). Official and Hindi name: Mumbai **2** a breed of black short-haired medium-sized cat

Bombay duck *n* a teleost fish, *Harpodon nehereus*, that resembles and is related to the lizard fishes: family *Harpodontidae*. It is eaten dried with curry dishes as a savoury. Also called: bummalo [c19 changed from *bombil* (see BUMMALO) through association with Bombay, from which it was exported]

Bombay Hills *pl n* a row of hills marking the southern boundary of greater Auckland on the North Island, New Zealand

bombazine or **bombasine** (ˌbɒmbəˈziːn, ˈbɒmbəˌziːn) *n* a twilled fabric, esp one with a silk warp and worsted weft, formerly worn dyed black for mourning [c16 from Old French *bombasin*, from Latin *bombȳcinus* silken, from *bombyx* silkworm, silk; see BOMBACACEOUS]

bomb calorimeter *n chem* a device for determining heats of combustion by igniting a sample in a high pressure of oxygen in a sealed vessel and measuring the resulting rise in temperature: used for measuring the calorific value of foods

bombe (bɒmb) *n* **1** Also called: bombe glacée a dessert of ice cream lined or filled with custard, cake crumbs, etc **2** a mould shaped like a bomb in which this dessert is made [c19 from French, literally: BOMB; from its rounded shape]

bombé (bɒmˈbeɪ; *French* bɔ̃be) *adj* (of furniture) having a projecting swollen shape [French, literally: bomb-shaped, from *bombe* BOMB]

bombed (bɒmd) *adj slang* under the influence of alcohol or drugs (esp in the phrase **bombed out of one's mind** or **skull**)

bomber (ˈbɒmə) *n* **1** a military aircraft designed to carry out bombing missions **2** a person who plants bombs **3** *navy slang* a Polaris submarine

bomber jacket *n* a short jacket finishing at the waist with an elasticated band, usually having a zip front and cuffed sleeves

bombinate (ˈbɒmbɪˌneɪt) *vb* (*intr*) *literary* to make a buzzing noise. Also (*rare*): bombilate [c19 from Latin *bombināre*, variant of *bombilāre* to buzz] > ˌbombiˈnation *n*

bombing run *n* the part of a flight of a bomber aircraft that brings it to the point over a target at which its bombs are released

bomblet (ˈbɒmlɪt) *n* one of a number of small bombs contained in a larger bomb

bombora (bɒmˈbɔːrə) *n Austral* **1** a submerged reef **2** a turbulent area of sea over such a reef [from a native Australian language]

bomb out *vb* (*adverb; tr, usually passive*) to make homeless by bombing: *24 families in this street have been bombed out*

bombshell (ˈbɒmˌʃɛl) *n* **1** (esp formerly) a bomb or artillery shell **2** a shocking or unwelcome surprise: *the news of his death was a bombshell* **3** *informal* an attractive girl or woman (esp in the phrase **blonde bombshell**)

bombsight (ˈbɒmˌsaɪt) *n* a mechanical or electronic device in an aircraft for aiming bombs

bomb site *n* an area where the buildings have been destroyed by bombs

bombycid (ˈbɒmbɪsɪd) *n* **1** any moth, including the silkworm moth, of the family *Bombycidae*, most of which occur in Africa and SE Asia ▷ *adj* **2** of, relating to, or belonging to the *Bombycidae* [c19 from Latin *bombyx* silkworm]

bommie (ˈbɒmɪ) *n Austral* an outcrop of coral reef, often resembling a column, that is higher than the surrounding platform of reef and which may be partially exposed at low tide [from *bombora*, from a native Australian language]

Bomu (ˈbəʊmuː) or **Mbomu** (əmˈbəʊmuː) *n* a river in central Africa, rising in the SE Central African Republic and flowing west into the Uele River, forming the Ubangi River. Length: about 800 km (500 miles)

Bon[1] (bɔːn) *n* **1** Also called: Feast (*or* Festival) of Lanterns an annual festival celebrated by Japanese Buddhists **2 a** the pre-Buddhist priests of Tibet or one such priest **b** their religion [from Japanese *bon*, originally *Urabon*, from Sanskrit *ullambana* hanging upside down]

Bon[2] (bɒn) *n* **Cape** a peninsula of NE Tunisia

Bona (ˈbəʊnə) *n* **Mount** a mountain in S Alaska, in the Wrangell Mountains. Height: 5005 m (16 420 ft)

bona fide *adj* (ˈbəʊnə ˈfaɪdɪ) **1** real or genuine: *a bona fide manuscript* **2** undertaken in good faith: *a bona fide agreement* ▷ *n* (ˈbɔːnə faɪd) **3** *Irish informal* a public house licensed to remain open after normal hours to serve bona fide travellers [c16 from Latin]

bona fides (ˈbəʊnə ˈfaɪdiːz) *n law* good faith; honest intention [Latin]

Bonaire (bɒnˈɛə) *n* an island in the S Caribbean, in the E Netherlands Antilles: one of the Leeward Islands. Chief town: Kralendijk. Pop: 10 185 (2004 est). Area: about 288 sq km (111 sq miles)

bonanza (bəˈnænzə) *n* **1** a source, usually sudden and unexpected, of luck or wealth **2** *US and Canadian* a mine or vein rich in ore [c19 from Spanish, literally: calm sea, hence, good luck, from Medieval Latin *bonacia*, from Latin *bonus* good + *malacia* dead calm, from Greek *malakia* softness]

Bonapartism (ˈbəʊnəpɑːˌtɪzəm) *n* **1** a political system resembling the rules of the Bonapartes, esp Napoleon I (1769–1821; Emperor of the French 1804–15) and Napoleon III (1808–73; Emperor of the French 1852–70): centralized government by a military dictator, who enjoys popular support given expression in plebiscites **2** (esp in France) support for the government or dynasty of Napoleon Bonaparte > ˈBonaˌpartist *n*

bona vacantia (ˈbəʊnə vəˈkæntɪə) *pl n law* unclaimed goods

bonbon (ˈbɒnbɒn) *n* a sweet [c19 from French, originally a children's word from *bon* good]

bonce (bɒns) *n Brit slang* the head [c19 (originally: a type of large playing marble): of unknown origin]

bond (bɒnd) *n* **1** something that binds, fastens, or holds together, such as a chain or rope **2** (*often plural*) something that brings or holds people together; tie: *a bond of friendship* **3** (*plural*) something that restrains or imprisons; captivity or imprisonment **4** something that governs behaviour; obligation; duty **5** a written or spoken agreement, esp a promise. *marriage bond* **6** adhesive quality or strength **7** *finance* a certificate of debt issued in order to raise funds. It carries a fixed rate of interest and is repayable with or without security at a specified future date **8** *law* a written acknowledgment of an obligation to pay a sum or to perform a contract **9** *insurance, US and*

Canadian a policy guaranteeing payment of a stated sum to an employer in compensation for financial losses incurred through illegal or unauthorized acts of an employee **10** any of various arrangements of bricks or stones in a wall in which they overlap so as to provide strength **11** See **chemical bond 12** See **bond paper 13** in bond *commerce* deposited in a bonded warehouse ▷ *vb* (*mainly tr*) **14** (*also intr*) to hold or be held together, as by a rope or an adhesive; bind; connect **15** *aeronautics* to join (metallic parts of an aircraft) together such that they are electrically interconnected **16** to put or hold (goods) in bond **17** *law* to place under bond **18** *finance* to issue bonds on; mortgage **19** to arrange (bricks, etc) in a bond [c13 from Old Norse *band*; see BAND[2]]

bondage (ˈbɒndɪdʒ) *n* **1** slavery or serfdom; servitude **2** Also called: villeinage (in medieval Europe) the condition and status of unfree peasants who provided labour and other services for their lord in return for holdings of land **3** a sexual practice in which one partner is physically bound

bonded (ˈbɒndɪd) *adj* **1** *finance* consisting of, secured by, or operating under a bond or bonds **2** *commerce* deposited in a bonded warehouse; placed or stored in bond

bonded warehouse *n* a warehouse in which dutiable goods are deposited until duty is paid or the goods are cleared for export

bondholder (ˈbɒndˌhəʊldə) *n* an owner of one or more bonds issued by a company or other institution

Bondi Beach (ˈbɒndaɪ) *n* a beach in Sydney, Australia, popular with surfers

bonding (ˈbɒndɪŋ) *n* the process by which individuals become emotionally attached to one another. See also **pair bond**

bondmaid (ˈbɒndˌmeɪd) *n* an unmarried female serf or slave

bond paper *n* a superior quality of strong white paper, used esp for writing and typing

bondservant (ˈbɒndˌsɜːvənt) *n* a serf or slave

bondsman (ˈbɒndzmən) *n, pl* -men **1** *law* a person bound by bond to act as surety for another **2** another word for **bondservant**

bondstone (ˈbɒndˌstəʊn) *n* a long stone or brick laid in a wall as a header. Also called: bonder

bond washing *n* a series of deals in bonds made with the intention of avoiding taxation

bone (bəʊn) *n* **1** any of the various structures that make up the skeleton in most vertebrates **2** the porous rigid tissue of which these parts are made, consisting of a matrix of collagen and inorganic salts, esp calcium phosphate, interspersed with canals and small holes. Related adjectives: **osseous, osteal 3** something consisting of bone or a bonelike substance **4** (*plural*) the human skeleton or body: *they laid his bones to rest; come and rest your bones* **5** a thin strip of whalebone, light metal, plastic, etc, used to stiffen corsets and brassieres **6** (*plural*) the essentials (esp in the phrase **the bare bones**): *to explain the bones of a situation* **7** (*plural*) dice **8** (*plural*) an informal nickname for a **doctor 9** close to *or* near the bone **a** risqué or indecent: *his jokes are rather close to the bone* **b** in poverty; destitute **10** feel in one's bones to have an intuition of **11** have a bone to pick to have grounds for a quarrel **12** make no bones about **a** to be direct and candid about **b** to have no scruples about **13** point the bone (often foll by at) *Austral* **a** to wish bad luck (on) **b** to threaten to bring about the downfall (of) ▷ *vb* (*mainly tr*) **14** to remove the bones from (meat for cooking, etc) **15** to stiffen (a corset, etc) by inserting bones **16** to fertilize with bone meal **17** *taboo slang* to have sexual intercourse with **18** *Brit* a slang word for **steal** ▷ See also **bone up** [Old English *bān*; related to Old Norse *béin*, Old Frisian *bēn*, Old High German *bein*] > ˈboneless *adj*

Bône (*French* bon) *n* a former name of **Annaba**

bone ash *n* the residue obtained when bones are

burned in air, consisting mainly of calcium phosphate. It is used as a fertilizer and in the manufacture of bone china

bone bed *n geology* a sediment containing large quantities of fossilized animal remains, such as bones, teeth, scales, etc

boneblack ('bəʊn,blæk) *n* a black residue from the destructive distillation of bones, containing about 10 per cent carbon and 80 per cent calcium phosphate, used as a decolorizing agent and pigment

bone china *n* porcelain containing bone ash

bone-dry *adj informal* **a** completely dry: *a bone-dry well* **b** (*postpositive*): *the well was bone dry*

bonefish ('bəʊn,fɪʃ) *n, pl* **-fish** *or* **-fishes 1** a silvery marine clupeoid game fish, *Albula vulpes*, occurring in warm shallow waters: family *Albulidae* **2** a similar related fish, *Dixonina nemoptera*, of the Pacific Ocean

bonehead ('bəʊn,hɛd) *n slang* a stupid or obstinate person > ,bone'headed *adj*

bone idle *adj* very idle; extremely lazy

bone marrow *n* See **marrow¹** (sense 1)

bone meal *n* the product of dried and ground animal bones, used as a fertilizer or in stock feeds

bone of contention *n* the grounds or subject of a dispute

bone oil *n* a dark brown pungent oil, containing pyridine and hydrocarbons, obtained by the destructive distillation of bones

boner ('bəʊnə) *n* **1** *slang* a blunder **2** *slang* an erection of the penis **3** *NZ* a low-grade slaughtered animal suitable for use in pies, sausages, etc

boneset ('bəʊn,sɛt) *n* any of various North American plants of the genus *Eupatorium*, esp *E. perfoliatum*, which has flat clusters of small white flowers: family *Asteraceae* (composites). Also called: **agueweed, feverwort, thoroughwort**

bonesetter ('bəʊn,sɛtə) *n* a person who sets broken or dislocated bones, esp one who has no formal medical qualifications

boneshaker ('bəʊn,ʃeɪkə) *n* **1** an early type of bicycle having solid tyres and no springs **2** *slang* any decrepit or rickety vehicle

bone turquoise *n* fossilized bone or tooth stained blue with iron phosphate and used as a gemstone. Also called: **odontolite**

bone up *vb* (*adverb; when intr, usually foll by on*) *informal* to study intensively

boneyard ('bəʊn,jɑːd) *n* an informal name for a cemetery

bonfire ('bɒn,faɪə) *n* a large outdoor fire [c15 alteration (through influence of French *bon* good) of *bone-fire*; from the use of bones as fuel]

bong¹ (bɒŋ) *n* **1** a deep reverberating sound, as of a large bell ▷ *vb* (*intr*) **2** to make a deep reverberating sound [c20 of imitative origin]

bong² (bɒŋ) *n* a type of water pipe for smoking marijuana, crack, etc [c20 of unknown origin]

bongo¹ ('bɒŋɡəʊ) *n, pl* **-go** *or* **-gos** a rare spiral-horned antelope, *Boocercus* (or *Taurotragus*) *eurycerus*, inhabiting forests of central Africa. The coat is bright red-brown with narrow cream stripes [of African origin]

bongo² ('bɒŋɡəʊ) *n, pl* **-gos** *or* **-goes** a small bucket-shaped drum, usually one of a pair, played by beating with the fingers [American Spanish, probably of imitative origin]

bonham ('bɒnəv) *n* Irish a piglet [c19 from Irish Gaelic *banbh*]

bonhomie ('bɒnəmɪ; *French* bɔnɔmi) *n* exuberant friendliness [c18 from French, from *bonhomme* good-humoured fellow, from *bon* good + *homme* man]

bonhomous ('bɒnəməs) *adj* exhibiting bonhomie

Bonin Islands ('bəʊnɪn) *pl n* a group of 27 volcanic islands in the W Pacific: occupied by the US after World War II; returned to Japan in 1968. Largest island: Chichijima. Area: 103 sq km (40 sq miles). Japanese name: Ogasawara Gunto

bonism ('bəʊ,nɪzəm) *n* the doctrine that the

world is good, although not the best of all possible worlds [c19 from Latin *bonus* good + -ISM] > 'bonist *n, adj*

bonito (bə'niːtəʊ) *n, pl* **-tos 1** any of various small tunny-like marine food fishes of the genus *Sarda*, of warm Atlantic and Pacific waters: family *Scombridae* (tunnies and mackerels) **2** any of various similar or related fishes, such as *Katsuwonus pelamis* (**oceanic bonito**), the flesh of which is dried and flaked and used in Japanese cookery [c16 from Spanish *bonito*, from Latin *bonus* good]

bonk (bɒŋk) *vb informal* **1** (*tr*) to hit **2** to have sexual intercourse (with) [c20 probably of imitative origin] > **'bonking** *n*

bonkbuster *n* ('bɒŋk,bʌstə) *informal* a novel characterized by graphic descriptions of the heroine's frequent sexual encounters [c20 from BONK (sense 2) + (BLOCK)BUSTER]

bonkers ('bɒŋkəz) *adj slang, chiefly Brit* mad; crazy [c20 (originally in the sense: slightly drunk, tipsy): of unknown origin]

bon mot (*French* bɔ̃ mo) *n, pl* **bons mots** (bɔ̃ mo) a clever and fitting remark [French, literally: good word]

Bonn (bɒn; *German* bɔn) *n* a city in W Germany, in North Rhine-Westphalia on the Rhine: the former capital (1949–90) of West Germany; university (1786). Pop: 311 052 (2003 est)

bonne (*French* bɔn) *n* a housemaid or female servant [c18 from feminine of *bon* good]

bonne bouche (*French* bɔn buʃ) *n, pl* **bonnes bouches** (bɔn buʃ) a tasty titbit or morsel [literally: good mouth(ful)]

bonnet ('bɒnɪt) *n* **1** any of various hats worn, esp formerly, by women and girls, usually framing the face and tied with ribbons under the chin **2** (in Scotland) Also called: **bunnet** ('bʌnɪt) **a** a soft cloth cap **b** formerly, a flat brimless cap worn by men **3** the hinged metal part of a motor vehicle body that provides access to the engine, or to the luggage space in a rear-engined vehicle **4** a cowl on a chimney **5** *nautical* a piece of sail laced to the foot of a foresail to give it greater area in light winds **6** (in the US and Canada) a headdress of feathers worn by some tribes of American Indians, esp formerly as a sign of war [c14 from Old French *bonet*, from Medieval Latin *abonnis*, of unknown origin]

bonnet monkey *n* an Indian macaque, *Macaca radiata*, with a bonnet-like tuft of hair

bonnet rouge (*French* bɔnɛ ruʒ) *n* **1** a red cap worn by ardent supporters of the French Revolution **2** an extremist or revolutionary [literally: red cap]

bonny ('bɒnɪ) *adj* **-nier, -niest 1** *Scot and Northern English dialect* beautiful or handsome: *a bonny lass* **2** merry or lively: *a bonny family* **3** good or fine: *a bonny house* **4** (esp of babies) plump **5** *Scot and Northern English dialect* considerable; to be reckoned with: *cost a bonny penny* > *adv* **6** *informal* agreeably or well: *to speak bonny* [c15 of uncertain origin; perhaps from Old French *bon* good, from Latin *bonus*] > **'bonnily** *adv*

Bonny ('bɒnɪ) *n* **Bight of** a wide bay at the E end of the Gulf of Guinea off the coasts of Nigeria and Cameroon. Former name (until 1975): **Bight of Biafra**

bonobo ('bɒnəbəʊ) *n* an anthropoid ape, *Pan paniscus*, of central W Africa: similar to the chimpanzee but much smaller and having a black face. Also called: **pygmy chimpanzee** [c20 from W African language]

bonsai ('bɒnsaɪ) *n, pl* **-sai 1** the art of growing dwarfed ornamental varieties of trees or shrubs in small shallow pots or trays by selective pruning, etc **2** a tree or shrub grown by this method [c20 Japanese: plant grown in a pot, from *bon* basin, bowl + *sai* to plant]

bonsela (bɒn'sɛlə) *n South African informal* a present or gratuity. Also called: **bansela, pasela** (pə'sɛlə) [from Zulu *ibanselo* a gift]

bonspiel ('bɒn,spiːl, -spəl) *n* a curling match [c16

probably from Low German; compare Flemish *bonespel* children's game; see SPIEL]

bontebok ('bɒntɪ,bʌk) *n, pl* **-boks** *or* **-bok** an antelope, *Damaliscus pygargus* (or *dorcas*), of southern Africa, having a deep reddish-brown coat with a white blaze, tail, and rump patch [c18 Afrikaans, from *bont* pied + *bok* BUCK¹]

bon ton (*French* bɔ̃ tɔ̃) *n literary* **1** sophisticated manners or breeding **2** fashionable society [literally: good tone]

bonus ('bəʊnəs) *n* **1** something given, paid, or received above what is due or expected: *a Christmas bonus for all employees* **2** *chiefly Brit* an extra dividend allotted to shareholders out of profits **3** *insurance, Brit* a dividend, esp a percentage of net profits, distributed to policyholders either annually or when the policy matures **4** *Brit* a slang word for a **bribe** [c18 from Latin *bonus* (adj) good]

bonus issue *n Brit* an issue of shares made by a company without charge and distributed pro rata among existing shareholders. Also called: **scrip issue**

bon vivant (*French* bɔ̃ vivɑ̃) *n, pl* **bons vivants** (bɔ̃ vivɑ̃) a person who enjoys luxuries, esp good food and drink. Also called (but not in French): **bon viveur** (,bɒn viːˈvɜː) [literally: good living (man)]

bon voyage (*French* bɔ̃ vwajaʒ) *sentence substitute* a phrase used to wish a traveller a pleasant journey [French, literally: good journey]

bonxie ('bɒŋksɪ) *n* a name, originally Shetland, for the **great skua** (see **skua**) [c19 probably of Scandinavian origin: compare Norwegian *bunke* heap, something dumpy]

bony ('bəʊnɪ) *adj* **bonier, boniest 1** resembling or consisting of bone or bones **2** having many bones **3** having prominent bones: *bony cheeks* **4** thin or emaciated: *a bony old woman* > **'boniness** *n*

bony bream *n* an Australian freshwater clupeid fish, *Fluvialosa richardsonii*

bony fish *n, n* any fish of the class *Osteichthyes*, including most of the extant species, having a skeleton of bone rather than cartilage

bonze (bɒnz) *n* a Chinese or Japanese Buddhist priest or monk [c16 from French, from Portuguese *bonzo*, from Japanese *bonsō*, from Sanskrit *bon* + *sō* priest or monk]

bonzer ('bɒnzə) *adj Austral and NZ slang, archaic* excellent; very good [c20 of uncertain origin; perhaps from BONANZA]

boo (buː) *interj* **1** an exclamation uttered to startle or surprise someone, esp a child **2** a shout uttered to express disgust, dissatisfaction, or contempt, esp at a theatrical production, political meeting, etc **3 would not say boo to a goose** is extremely timid or diffident ▷ *vb* **boos, booing, booed 4** to shout "boo" at (someone or something), esp as an expression of disgust, dissatisfaction, or disapproval: *to boo the actors*

boob¹ (buːb) *slang* ▷ *n* **1** an ignorant or foolish person; booby **2** *Brit* an embarrassing mistake; blunder **3** a female breast ▷ *vb* **4** (*intr*) *Brit* to make a blunder [c20 back formation from BOOBY]

boob² (buːb) *n Austral slang* **1** a prison ▷ *adj* **2** of poor quality, similar to that provided in prison: *boob coffee* [from the US colloquial sense of *booby hatch* meaning jail]

boob happy *adj Austral slang* suffering from the mental strain caused by the difficulties of prison life

boobhead ('buːb,hɛd) *n Austral slang* a repeat offender in a prison

boobialla (,buːbɪˈælə) *n Austral* **1** another name for **golden wattle** (sense 2) **2** any of various trees or shrubs of the genus *Myoporum*, esp *M. insulare* [from a native Australian language]

boo-boo *n, pl* **-boos** *informal* an embarrassing mistake; blunder [c20 perhaps from nursery talk; compare BOOHOO]

boobook ('buːbʊk) *n* a small spotted brown Australian owl, *Ninox boobook*

boob tube *n slang* **1** a close-fitting strapless top, worn by women **2** *Austral* a strapless, boneless, shapeless brassiere made of a stretch fabric **3** *chiefly US and Canadian* a television receiver

booby (ˈbuːbɪ) *n, pl* -bies **1** an ignorant or foolish person **2** *Brit* the losing player in a game **3** any of several tropical marine birds of the genus *Sula*: family *Sulidae*, order *Pelecaniformes* (pelicans, cormorants, etc). They have a straight stout bill and the plumage is white with darker markings. Compare **gannet** [c17 from Spanish *bobo*, from Latin *balbus* stammering]

booby hatch *n* **1** a hoodlike covering for a hatchway on a ship **2** *US slang* a mental hospital

booby prize *n* a mock prize given to the person having the lowest score or giving the worst performance in a competition

booby trap *n* **1** a hidden explosive device primed in such a way as to be set off by an unsuspecting victim **2** a trap for an unsuspecting person, esp one intended as a practical joke, such as an object balanced above a door to fall on the person who opens it ▷ *vb* booby-trap, traps, -trapping, -trapped **3** (*tr*) to set a booby trap in or on (a building or object) or for (a person)

boodie (ˈbuːdɪ) *n* a burrowing rat kangaroo, *Bettongia lesueur*, found on islands off Western Australia [from Nyungar (an extinct native language of SW Australia) *burdi*]

boodle (ˈbuːd³l) *slang* ▷ *n* **1** money or valuables, esp when stolen, counterfeit, or used as a bribe **2** *chiefly US* another word for **caboodle** ▷ *vb* **3** to give or receive money corruptly or illegally [c19 from Dutch *boedel* all one's possessions, from Old Frisian *bōdel* movable goods, inheritance; see CABOODLE]

boofhead (ˈbuːfhɛd) *n slang, chiefly Austral* **1** a stupid person **2** a person or animal with a large head

boofy (ˈbuːfɪ) *adj Austral informal* **1** muscular and strong but stupid **2** (of the hair) voluminous **3** puffed out: *boofy sleeves*

boogie (ˈbuːgɪ) *slang* ▷ *vb* -gies, -gieing, -gied (*intr*) **1** to dance to pop music **2** to make love ▷ *n* **3** a session of dancing to pop music [c20 originally African-American slang, perhaps from Kongo *mbugi* devilishly good]

boogie board *n* another name for **bodyboard**

boogie-woogie (ˈbuːgɪˈwuːgɪ, ˈbuːgɪˈwuːgɪ) *n* a style of piano jazz using a dotted bass pattern, usually with eight notes in a bar and the harmonies of the 12-bar blues

boohai (buːˈhaɪ) *n* up the boohai NZ *informal* thoroughly lost [from the remote township of *Puhoi*]

boohoo (ˌbuːˈhuː) *vb* -hoos, -hooing, -hooed **1** to sob or pretend to sob noisily ▷ *n, pl* -hoos **2** (*sometimes plural*) distressed or pretended sobbing [c20 nursery talk]

boo-hurrah theory *n philosophy* an informal term for **emotivism**

book (bʊk) *n* **1** a number of printed or written pages bound together along one edge and usually protected by thick paper or stiff pasteboard covers. See also **hardback, paperback 2 a** a written work or composition, such as a novel, technical manual, or dictionary **b** (*as modifier*): *the book trade; book reviews* **c** (*in combination*): *bookseller; bookshop; bookshelf; bookrack* **3** a number of blank or ruled sheets of paper bound together, used to record lessons, keep accounts, etc **4** (*plural*) a record of the transactions of a business or society **5** the script of a play or the libretto of an opera, musical, etc **6** a major division of a written composition, as of a long novel or of the Bible **7** a number of tickets, sheets, stamps, etc, fastened together along one edge **8** *bookmaking* a record of the bets made on a horse race or other event **9** (*in card games*) the number of tricks that must be taken by a side or player before any trick has a scoring value: *in bridge, six of the 13 tricks form the book* **10** strict or rigid regulations, rules, or standards (esp in the phrases **according to the book, by the book**) **11** a source of knowledge or authority: *the*

book of life 12 a telephone directory (in the phrase **in the book**) **13** the book (*sometimes capital*) the Bible **14** an open book a person or subject that is thoroughly understood **15** a closed book a person or subject that is unknown or beyond comprehension: *chemistry is a closed book to him* **16** bring to book to reprimand or require (someone) to give an explanation of his conduct **17** close the book on to bring to a definite end: *we have closed the book on apartheid* **18** close the books *book-keeping* to balance accounts in order to prepare a statement or report **19** cook the books *informal* to make fraudulent alterations to business or other accounts **20** in my book according to my view of things **21** in someone's good *or* bad books regarded by someone with favour (or disfavour) **22** keep the books to keep written records of the finances of a business or other enterprise **23** on the books **a** enrolled as a member **b** registered or recorded **24** read (someone) like a book to understand (a person, his motives, character, etc) thoroughly and clearly **25** throw the book at **a** to charge with every relevant offence **b** to inflict the most severe punishment on ▷ *vb* **26** to reserve (a place, passage, etc) or engage the services of (a performer, driver, etc) in advance: *to book a flight; to book a band* **27** (*tr*) to take the name and address of (a person guilty of a minor offence) with a view to bringing a prosecution: *he was booked for ignoring a traffic signal* **28** (*tr*) (of a football referee) to take the name of (a player) who grossly infringes the rules while playing, two such acts resulting in the player's dismissal from the field **29** (*tr*) *archaic* to record in a book ▷ See also **book in, book into, book out, book up** [Old English *bōc*; related to Old Norse *bōk*, Old High German *buoh* book, Gothic *bōka* letter; see BEECH (the bark of which was used as a writing surface)]

bookbinder (ˈbʊkˌbaɪndə) *n* a person whose business or craft is binding books ▷ ˈbookˌbinding *n*

bookbindery (ˈbʊkˌbaɪndərɪ) *n, pl* -eries a place in which books are bound. Often shortened to: bindery

bookcase (ˈbʊkˌkeɪs) *n* a piece of furniture containing shelves for books, often fitted with glass doors

book club *n* a club that sells books at low prices to members, usually by mail order, esp on condition that they buy a minimum number

bookcrossing (ˈbʊkˌkrɒsɪŋ) *n* the practice of deliberately leaving books in places where they will be found and read by other people

booked up *adj* unable to offer any appointments or accept any reservations, etc; fully booked; full up

book end *n* one of a pair of usually ornamental supports for holding a row of books upright

Booker Prize (ˈbʊkə) *n* the former name for **Man Booker Prize**

book group *n* another name for **reading group**

bookie (ˈbʊkɪ) *n informal* short for **bookmaker**

book in *vb* (*adverb*) **1** to reserve a room for (oneself or someone else) at a hotel **2** *chiefly Brit* to record something in a book or register, esp one's arrival at a hotel

booking (ˈbʊkɪŋ) *n* **1** *chiefly Brit* **a** a reservation, as of a table or room in a hotel, seat in a theatre, or seat on a train, aircraft, etc **b** (*as modifier*): *the booking office at a railway station* **2** *theatre* an engagement for the services of an actor or acting company

book into *vb* (*preposition*) to reserve a room for (oneself or someone else) at (a hotel)

bookish (ˈbʊkɪʃ) *adj* **1** fond of reading; studious **2** consisting of or forming opinions or attitudes through reading rather than direct personal experience; academic: *a bookish view of life* **3** of or relating to books: *a bookish career in publishing* ▷ ˈbookishly *adv* ▷ ˈbookishness *n*

book-keeping *n* the skill or occupation of maintaining accurate records of business

transactions ▷ ˈbook-ˌkeeper *n*

book-learning *n* **1** knowledge gained from books rather than from direct personal experience **2** formal education

booklet (ˈbʊklɪt) *n* a thin book, esp one having paper covers; pamphlet

booklight (ˈbʊkˌlaɪt) *n* a small light that can be clipped onto a book for reading by

booklouse (ˈbʊkˌlaʊs) *n, pl* -lice any small insect of the order *Psocoptera*, esp *Trogium pulsatorium* (**common booklouse**), a wingless species that feeds on bookbinding paste, etc

bookmaker (ˈbʊkˌmeɪkə) *n* a person who as an occupation accepts bets, esp on horseraces, and pays out to winning betters ▷ ˈbookˌmaking *n*

bookmark (ˈbʊkˌmɑːk) *n* **1** Also called: bookmarker a strip or band of some material, such as leather or ribbon, put between the pages of a book to mark a place **2** *computing* **a** an address for a website stored on a computer so that the user can easily return to the site **b** an identifier placed in a document so that part of the document can be accessed easily ▷ *vb* **3** (*tr*) *computing* **a** to identify and store (a website) so that one can return to it easily **b** to place a bookmark in (a document)

bookmobile (ˈbʊkməˌbiːl) *n US and Canadian* a vehicle providing lending library facilities. Also called (in Britain and certain other countries): mobile library

book of account *n* another name for **journal** (sense 4a)

Book of Changes *n* another name for the **I Ching**

Book of Common Prayer *n* the official book of church services of the Church of England, until 1980, when the Alternative Service Book was sanctioned

book of hours *n* (*often capitals*) a book used esp in monasteries during the Middle Ages that contained the prayers and offices of the canonical hours

Book of Kells *n* See **Kells**

Book of Mormon *n* a sacred book of the Mormon Church, believed by Mormons to be a history of certain ancient peoples in America, written on golden tablets (now lost) and revealed by the prophet Mormon to Joseph Smith

book of original entry *n* another name for **journal** (sense 4a)

book out *vb* (*usually intr, adverb*) to leave or cause to leave a hotel

bookplate (ˈbʊkˌpleɪt) *n* a label bearing the owner's name and an individual design or coat of arms, pasted into a book

book rest *n* a cradle for holding an open book so that it may be read comfortably

book scorpion *n* any of various small arachnids of the order *Pseudoscorpionida* (false scorpions), esp *Chelifer cancroides*, which are sometimes found in old books, etc

bookstall (ˈbʊkˌstɔːl) *n* a stall or stand where periodicals, newspapers, or books are sold. US word: newsstand

booksy (ˈbʊksɪ) *adj* inclined to be bookish or literary

book token *n Brit* a gift token to be exchanged for books

book up *vb* (*adverb*) **1** to make a reservation (for); book **2** See **booked up**

book value *n* **1** the value of an asset of a business according to its books **2 a** the net capital value of an enterprise as shown by the excess of book assets over book liabilities **b** the value of a share computed by dividing the net capital value of an enterprise by its issued shares. Compare **par value, market value**

bookwork (ˈbʊkˌwɜːk) **1** the keeping of accounts **2** learning through the study of books rather than from practical experience

bookworm (ˈbʊkˌwɜːm) *n* **1** a person excessively devoted to studying or reading **2** any of various small insects that feed on the binding paste of

b

books, esp the book louse

bool (buːl) *Scot* ▷ *n* **1** a bowling bowl **2** a playing marble **3** (*plural*) the game of bowls or marbles ▷ *vb* (*intr*) **4** to play bowls [Scot variant of BOWL²]

Boolean algebra (ˈbuːlɪən) *n* a system of symbolic logic devised by George Boole to codify logical operations. It is used in computers

boom¹ (buːm) *vb* **1** to make a deep prolonged resonant sound, as of thunder or artillery fire **2** to prosper or cause to prosper vigorously and rapidly: *business boomed* ▷ *n* **3** a deep prolonged resonant sound: *the boom of the sea* **4** the cry of certain animals, esp the bittern **5** a period of high economic growth characterized by rising wages, profits, and prices, full employment, and high levels of investment, trade, and other economic activity. Compare **depression** (sense 5) [c15 perhaps from Dutch *bommen*, of imitative origin]

boom² (buːm) *n* **1** *nautical* a spar to which a sail is fastened to control its position relative to the wind **2** a beam or spar pivoting at the foot of the mast of a derrick, controlling the distance from the mast at which a load is lifted or lowered **3** a pole, usually extensible, carrying an overhead microphone and projected over a film or television set **4 a** a barrier across a waterway, usually consisting of a chain of connected floating logs, to confine free-floating logs, protect a harbour from attack, etc **b** the area so barred off [c16 from Dutch *boom* tree, BEAM]

boomer (ˈbuːmə) *n* **1** *Austral* a large male kangaroo **2** *Austral and NZ informal* anything exceptionally large [from English dialect]

boomerang (ˈbuːməˌræŋ) *n* **1** a curved flat wooden missile of native Australians, which can be made to return to the thrower **2** an action or statement that recoils on its originator ▷ *vb* **3** (*intr*) to recoil or return unexpectedly, causing harm to its originator; backfire [c19 from a native Australian language]

boomerang kid *n* a young adult who, after having lived on his or her own for a time, returns to live in the parental home, usually due to financial problems caused by unemployment or the high cost of living independently

boomkin (ˈbuːmkɪn) *n nautical* a short boom projecting from the deck of a ship, used to secure the main-brace blocks or to extend the lower edge of the foresail [c17 from Dutch *boomken*, from *boom* tree; see BEAM, -KIN]

boomslang (ˈbuːmˌslæŋ) *n* a large greenish venomous arboreal colubrid snake, *Dispholidus typus*, of southern Africa [c18 from Afrikaans, from *boom* tree + *slang* snake]

boom town *n* a town that is enjoying sudden prosperity or has grown rapidly

boon¹ (buːn) *n* **1** something extremely useful, helpful, or beneficial; a blessing or benefit: *the car was a boon to him* **2** *archaic* a favour; request: *he asked a boon of the king* [c12 from Old Norse *bōn* request; related to Old English *bēn* prayer]

boon² (buːn) *adj* **1** close, special, or intimate (in the phrase **boon companion**) **2** *archaic* jolly or convivial [c14 from Old French *bon* from Latin *bonus* good]

boondocks (ˈbuːnˌdɒks) *pl n* the *US and Canadian slang* **1** wild, desolate, or uninhabitable country **2** a remote rural or provincial area. Sometimes shortened to: **the Boonies** [c20 from Tagalog *bundok* mountain]

boondoggle (ˈbuːnˌdɒgəl) *informal, chiefly US and Canadian* ▷ *vb* **1** (*intr*) to do futile and unnecessary work ▷ *n* **2** a futile and unnecessary project or work [c20 said to have been coined by R. H. Link, American scoutmaster] > **ˈboonˌdoggler** *n*

booner (ˈbuːnə) *or* **boon** *n Austral informal* a young working-class person from Canberra [c20 of unknown origin]

boong (buːŋ) *n Austral offensive* a Black person [c20 perhaps of native Australian origin]

boonga (ˈbuːŋə) *n NZ offensive* a Pacific Islander

[perhaps of native Australian origin, from BOONG]

boongary (ˈbuːŋgærɪ) *n* a tree kangaroo, *Dendrolagus lumholtzi*, of northeastern Queensland [from a native Australian language]

boor (bʊə) *n* an ill-mannered, clumsy, or insensitive person [Old English *gebūr*; related to Old High German *gibūr* farmer, dweller, Albanian *būr* man; see NEIGHBOUR]

boorish (ˈbʊərɪʃ) *adj* ill-mannered, clumsy, or insensitive; rude > **ˈboorishly** *adv* > **ˈboorishness** *n*

booshit (ˈbuːʃɪt) *adj Austral slang* very good; excellent

boost (buːst) *n* **1** encouragement, improvement, or help: *a boost to morale* **2** an upward thrust or push: *he gave him a boost over the wall* **3** an increase or rise: *a boost in salary* **4** a publicity campaign; promotion **5** the amount by which the induction pressure of a supercharged internal-combustion engine exceeds that of the ambient pressure ▷ *vb* (*tr*) **6** to encourage, assist, or improve: *to boost morale* **7** to lift by giving a push from below or behind **8** to increase or raise: *to boost the voltage in an electrical circuit* **9** to cause to rise; increase: *to boost sales* **10** to advertise on a big scale **11** to increase the induction pressure of (an internal-combustion engine) above that of the ambient pressure; supercharge [c19 of unknown origin]

booster (ˈbuːstə) *n* **1** a person or thing that supports, assists, or increases power or effectiveness **2** *Also called:* **launch vehicle** the first stage of a multistage rocket **3** *radio, television* **a** a radio-frequency amplifier connected between an aerial and a receiver to amplify weak incoming signals **b** a radio-frequency amplifier that amplifies incoming signals, retransmitting them at higher power **4** another name for **supercharger 5** short for **booster dose 6** *slang, chiefly US* a shoplifter

booster dose *n* a supplementary injection of a vaccine given to maintain the immunization provided by an earlier dose

boosterish (ˈbuːstərɪʃ) *adj* designed to boost business; optimistic

boosterism (ˈbuːstəˌrɪzəm) *n* the practice of actively promoting a city, region, etc, and its local businesses

boot¹ (buːt) *n* **1** a strong outer covering for the foot; shoe that extends above the ankle, often to the knee. See also **chukka boot, top boot, Wellington boot, surgical boot 2** an enclosed compartment of a car for holding luggage, etc, usually at the rear. US and Canadian name: **trunk 3** a protective covering over a mechanical device, such as a rubber sheath protecting a coupling joining two shafts **4** *US and Canadian* a rubber patch used to repair a puncture in a tyre **5** an instrument of torture used to crush the foot and lower leg **6** a protective covering for the lower leg of a horse **7** a kick: *he gave the door a boot* **8** *Brit slang* an ugly person (esp in the phrase **old boot**) **9** *US slang* a navy or marine recruit, esp one in training **10** *computing* short for **bootstrap** (sense 4a) **11 bet one's boots** to be certain: *you can bet your boots he'll come* **12** See **boots and all 13 die with one's boots on** to die while still active **b** to die in battle **14 lick the boots of** to be servile, obsequious, or flattering towards **15 put the boot in** *slang* **a** to kick a person, esp when he or she is already down **b** to harass someone or aggravate a problem **c** to finish off (something) with unnecessary brutality **16 the boot** *slang* dismissal from employment; the sack **17 the boot is on the other foot** *or* **leg** the situation is or has now reversed **18 too big for one's boots** self-important or conceited ▷ *vb* **19** (*tr*) (esp in football) to kick **20** (*tr*) to equip with boots **21** (*tr*) *informal* **a** (often foll by *out*) to eject forcibly **b** to dismiss from employment **22** *Also* **boot up**. to start up the operating system of (a computer) or (of a computer) to begin operating ▷ *See also* **boots** [c14 *bote*, from Old French, of uncertain origin]

boot² (buːt) *vb* (*usually impersonal*) **1** *archaic* to be of advantage or use to (a person): *what boots it to complain?* ▷ *n* **2** *obsolete* an advantage **3** *dialect* something given in addition, esp to equalize an exchange: *a ten pound boot to settle the bargain* **4 to boot** as well; in addition: *it's cold and musty, and damp to boot* [Old English *bōt* compensation; related to Old Norse *bōt* remedy, Gothic *bōta*, Old High German *buoza* improvement]

bootblack (ˈbuːtˌblæk) *n chiefly US* another word for **shoeblack**

boot boy *n* a member of a gang of hooligans who usually wear heavy boots

boot camp *n* **1** *US slang* a basic training camp for new recruits to the US Navy or Marine Corps **2** a centre for juvenile offenders, with a strict disciplinary regime, hard physical exercise, and community labour programmes

boot-cut *adj* (of trousers) slightly flared at the bottom of the legs

booted (ˈbuːtɪd) *adj* **1** wearing boots **2** *ornithol* **a** (of birds) having an undivided tarsus covered with a horny sheath **b** (of poultry) having a feathered tarsus

bootee (ˈbuːtiː, buːˈtiː) *n* **1** a soft shoe for a baby, esp a knitted one **2** a boot for women and children, esp an ankle-length one

Boötes (bəʊˈəʊtiːz) *n, Latin genitive* **Boötis** (bəʊˈəʊtɪs) a constellation in the N hemisphere lying near Ursa Major and containing the first magnitude star Arcturus [c17 via Latin from Greek: ploughman, from *boōtein* to plough, from *bous* ox]

booth (buːð, buːθ) *n, pl* **booths** (buːðz) **1** a stall for the display or sale of goods, esp a temporary one at a fair or market **2** a small enclosed or partially enclosed room or cubicle, such as one containing a telephone (**telephone booth**) or one in which a person casts his or her vote at an election (**polling booth**) **3** two long high-backed benches with a long table between, used esp in bars and inexpensive restaurants **4** (*formerly*) a temporary structure for shelter, dwelling, storage, etc [c12 of Scandinavian origin; compare Old Norse *buth*, Swedish, Danish *bod* shop, stall; see BOWER¹]

Boothia Peninsula (ˈbuːθɪə) *n* a peninsula of N Canada: the northernmost part of the mainland of North America, lying west of the **Gulf of Boothia**, an arm of the Arctic Ocean

bootie (ˈbuːtɪ) *n Brit slang* a Royal Marine [c20 from *bootneck*, so called from the leather tab used to close their tunic collars]

bootjack (ˈbuːtˌdʒæk) *n* a device that grips the heel of a boot to enable the foot to be withdrawn easily

bootlace (ˈbuːtˌleɪs) *n* a strong lace for fastening a boot

bootlace fungus *n* another name for **honey fungus**

bootlace worm *n* a nemertean worm, *Linens longissimus*, that inhabits shingly shores and attains lengths of over 6 m (20 ft)

Bootle (ˈbuːtəl) *n* a port in NW England, in Sefton unitary authority, Merseyside; on the River Mersey adjoining Liverpool. Pop: 59 123 (2001)

bootleg (ˈbuːtˌleg) *vb* **-legs, -legging, -legged 1** to make, carry, or sell (illicit goods, esp alcohol) ▷ *n* **2** something made or sold illicitly, such as alcohol during Prohibition in the US **3** an illegally made copy of a CD, tape, etc ▷ *adj* **4** produced, distributed, or sold illicitly: *bootleg whisky; bootleg tapes* [c17 see BOOT¹, LEG; from the practice of smugglers of carrying bottles of liquor concealed in their boots] > **ˈbootˌlegger** *n*

bootless (ˈbuːtlɪs) *adj* of little or no use; vain; fruitless: *a bootless search* [Old English *bōtlēas*, from *bōt* compensation; Old Norse *bótalauss*] > **ˈbootlessly** *adv*

bootlick (ˈbuːtˌlɪk) *vb informal* to seek favour by servile or ingratiating behaviour towards (someone, esp someone in authority); toady > **ˈbootˌlicker** *n*

bootloader ('buːtˌləʊdə) *n computing* short for **bootstrap loader**. See **bootstrap** (sense 4)

boot money *n informal* unofficial bonuses in the form of illegal cash payments made by a professional sports club to its players

boots (buːts) *n, pl* **boots** *Brit* (formerly) a shoeblack who cleans the guests' shoes in a hotel

boots and all *Austral and NZ informal* ▷ *adv* **1** making every effort; with no holds barred ▷ *adj* (**boots-and-all** *when prenominal*) **2** behaving or conducted in such a manner

boots and saddles *n* a bugle call formerly used in the US Cavalry to summon soldiers to mount

bootstrap ('buːtˌstræp) *n* **1** a leather or fabric loop on the back or side of a boot for pulling it on **2** by one's (own) bootstraps by one's own efforts; unaided **3** (*modifier*) self-acting or self-sufficient, as an electronic amplifier that uses its output voltage to bias its input **4** a *Also called* **boot** a technique for loading the first few program instructions into a computer main store to enable the rest of the program to be introduced from an input device **b** (*as modifier*): *a bootstrap loader* **5** *commerce* an offer to purchase a controlling interest in a company, esp with the intention of purchasing the remainder of the equity at a lower price

boot topping *n nautical* **1** the part of a ship's hull that is between the load line and the water line when the ship is not loaded **2** a coating applied to this part of a ship to remove marine growth

boot tree *n* **1** a shoetree for a boot, often having supports to stretch the leg of the boot **2** a last for making boots

booty[1] ('buːtɪ) *n, pl* -ties any valuable article or articles, esp when obtained as plunder [c15 from Old French *butin*, from Middle Low German *buite* exchange; related to Old Norse *býta* to exchange, *býti* barter]

booty[2] ('buːtɪ) *n slang* the buttocks [c20 from BUTT[1] buttocks]

booty call *n slang* a meeting arranged for the purpose of having sex

bootylicious (ˌbuːtɪ'lɪʃəs) *adj slang* sexually attractive, esp with curvaceous buttocks [c20 from BOOTY[2] + (DE)LICIOUS]

boo-word ('buːˌwɜːd) *n* any word that seems to cause irrational fear: *"communism" became a boo-word in the McCarthy era*

booze (buːz) *informal* ▷ *n* **1** alcoholic drink **2** a drinking bout or party ▷ *vb* **3** (*usually intr*) to drink (alcohol), esp in excess [c13 from Middle Dutch *būsen*] > **boozed** *adj* > **'boozing** *n*

booze cruise *n Brit informal* a day trip to a foreign country, esp from England across the English Channel to France, for the purposes of buying cheap alcohol, cigarettes, etc

boozed-up *adj slang* intoxicated; drunk

booze hag *n NZ slang* a girl or woman who drinks to excess

boozer ('buːzə) *n informal* **1** a person who is fond of drinking **2** *Brit, Austral, and NZ* a bar or pub

booze-up *n Brit, Austral, and NZ slang* a drinking spree

boozy ('buːzɪ) *adj* **boozier, booziest** *informal* inclined to or involving excessive drinking of alcohol; drunken: *a boozy lecturer; a boozy party* > **'booziness** *n*

bop[1] (bɒp) *n* **1** a form of jazz originating in the 1940s, characterized by rhythmic and harmonic complexity and instrumental virtuosity. Originally called: **bebop 2** *informal* a session of dancing to pop music ▷ *vb* **bops, bopping, bopped 3** (*intr*) *informal* to dance to pop music [c20 shortened from BEBOP] > **'bopper** *n*

bop[2] (bɒp) *informal* ▷ *vb* **bops, bopping, bopped 1** (*tr*) to strike; hit ▷ *n* **2** a blow [c19 of imitative origin]

bo-peep (ˌbəʊ'piːp) *n* **1** a game for very young children, in which one hides (esp hiding one's face in one's hands) and reappears suddenly **2** *Austral and NZ informal* a quick look (esp in the phrase **have a bo-peep**)

Bophuthatswana (ˌbəʊpuːtɑːt'swɑːnə) *n* (formerly) a Bantu homeland in N South Africa: consisted of six separate areas; granted independence by South Africa in 1977 although this was not internationally recognized; abolished in 1993. Capital: Mmabatho

bora[1] ('bɔːrə) *n* (*sometimes capital*) a violent cold north wind blowing from the mountains to the E coast of the Adriatic, usually in winter [c19 from Italian (Venetian dialect), from Latin *boreas* the north wind]

bora[2] ('bɔːrə) *n* an initiation ceremony of native Australians, introducing youths to manhood [from a native Australian language]

Bora Bora ('bɔːrə 'bɔːrə) *n* an island in the S Pacific, in French Polynesia, in the Society Islands: one of the Leeward Islands. Area: 39 sq km (15 sq miles)

boracic (bə'ræsɪk) *adj* another word for **boric**

boracite ('bɔːrəˌsaɪt) *n* a white mineral that forms salt deposits of magnesium borate and chloride in orthorhombic crystalline form. Formula: $Mg_3ClB_7O_{13}$

borage ('bɒrɪdʒ, 'bʌrɪdʒ) *n* **1** a European boraginaceous plant, *Borago officinalis*, with star-shaped blue flowers. The young leaves have a cucumber-like flavour and are sometimes used in salads or as seasoning **2** any of several related plants [c13 from Old French *bourage*, perhaps from Arabic *abū 'āraq* literally: father of sweat, from its use as a diaphoretic]

boraginaceous (bəˌrædʒɪ'neɪʃəs) *adj* of, relating to, or belonging to the *Boraginaceae*, a family of temperate and tropical typically hairy-leaved flowering plants that includes forget-me-not, lungwort, borage, comfrey, and heliotrope [c19 from New Latin *Borāgināceae*, from *Borāgō* genus name; see BORAGE]

borak ('bɒrək) or **borax** ('bɔːræks) *n Austral and NZ slang, archaic* **1** rubbish; nonsense **2** poke borak at (someone) to jeer at (someone) [from a native Australian language]

borane ('bɔːreɪn) *n* any compound of boron and hydrogen, used in the synthesis of other boron compounds and as high-energy fuels [c20 from BOR(ON) + -ANE]

Borås (*Swedish* bu'roːs) *n* a city in SW Sweden, chiefly producing textiles. Pop: 98 831 (2004 est)

borate *n* ('bɔːreɪt, -ɪt) **1** a salt or ester of boric acid. Salts of boric acid consist of BO_3 and BO_4 units linked together ▷ *vb* ('bɔːreɪt) **2** (*tr*) to treat with borax, boric acid, or borate

borax ('bɔːræks) *n, pl* -raxes, -races (-rəˌsiːz) **1** *Also called:* tincal a soluble readily fusible white mineral consisting of impure hydrated disodium tetraborate in monoclinic crystalline form, occurring in alkaline soils and salt deposits. Formula: $Na_2B_4O_7.10H_2O$ **2** pure disodium tetraborate [c14 from Old French *boras*, from Medieval Latin *borax*, from Arabic *būraq*, from Persian *būrah*]

borazon ('bɔːrəˌzɒn, -zᵊn) *n* an extremely hard form of boron nitride [c20 from BOR(ON) + AZO- + -ON]

borborygmus (ˌbɔːbə'rɪgməs) *n, pl* -mi (-maɪ) rumbling of the stomach [c18 from Greek] > ˌborbo'rygmal or ˌborbo'rygmic *adj*

Bordeaux (bɔː'dəʊ; *French* bɔrdo) *n* **1** a port in SW France, on the River Garonne: a major centre of the wine trade. Pop: 215 363 (1999) **2** any of several red, white, or rosé wines produced around Bordeaux. Related adjective: **Bordelais**

Bordeaux mixture *n horticulture* a fungicide consisting of a solution of equal quantities of copper sulphate and quicklime [c19 loose translation of French *bouillie bordelaise*, from *bouillir* to boil + *bordelais* of BORDEAUX]

Bordelaise (ˌbɔːdə'leɪz; *French* bɔrdəlɛz) *adj cookery* denoting a brown sauce flavoured with red wine and sometimes mushrooms [French: of BORDEAUX]

bordello (bɔː'dɛləʊ) *n, pl* -los a brothel. Also called (archaic): **bordel** ('bɔːdᵊl) [c16 from Italian, from Old French *borde* hut, cabin]

border ('bɔːdə) *n* **1** a band or margin around or along the edge of something **2** the dividing line or frontier between political or geographic regions **3** a a region straddling such a boundary **b** (*as modifier*): *border country* **4** a a design or ornamental strip around the edge or rim of something, such as a printed page or dinner plate **b** (*as modifier*): *a border illustration* **5** a long narrow strip of ground planted with flowers, shrubs, trees, etc, that skirts a path or wall or surrounds a lawn or other area: *a herbaceous border* ▷ *vb* **6** (*tr*) to decorate or provide with a border **7** (when *intr*, foll by *on* or *upon*) **a** to be adjacent (to); lie along the boundary (of): *his land borders on mine* **b** to be nearly the same (as); verge (on): *his stupidity borders on madness* [c14 from Old French *bordure*, from *border* to border, from *bort* side of a ship, of Germanic origin; see BOARD]

Border ('bɔːdə) *n* the **1** (*often plural*) the area straddling the border between England and Scotland **2** the area straddling the border between Northern Ireland and the Republic of Ireland **3** the region in S South Africa around East London

Border collie *n* a medium-sized breed of collie with a silky usually black-and-white coat: used mainly as sheepdogs

border disease *n vet science* a congenital infectious disease of sheep and goats caused by a *Togavirus* and characterized by abortion, infertility, and deformity of lambs

bordereau (ˌbɔːdə'rəʊ; *French* bɔrdəro) *n, pl* -reaux (-'rəʊ, -'rəʊz; *French* -ro) a memorandum or invoice prepared for a company by an underwriter, containing a list of reinsured risks [c20 from French]

borderer ('bɔːdərə) *n* a person who lives in a border area, esp the border between England and Scotland

borderland ('bɔːdəˌlænd) *n* **1** land located on or near a frontier or boundary **2** an indeterminate region: *the borderland between intellect and intelligence*

Border Leicester *n* a breed of sheep originally developed in the border country between Scotland and England by crossing English Leicesters with Cheviots: large numbers in Scotland, Australia, and New Zealand. It has a long white fleece with no wool on the head

borderless ('bɔːdəˌlɪs) *adj* **1** without a band or margin around or along the edge: *borderless prints* **2** (of an island) not divided by a national border **3** without limits: *an intellectual curiosity that seems borderless* **4** (of trade, travel, etc) not constrained by the presence of international borders: *a borderless business world*

borderline ('bɔːdəˌlaɪn) *n* **1** a border; dividing line; line of demarcation **2** an indeterminate position between two conditions or qualities: *the borderline between friendship and love* ▷ *adj* **3** on the edge of one category and verging on another: *a borderline failure in the exam*

borderline personality disorder *n psychiatry* a mental condition on the dividing line between a psychiatric disorder and normality characterized by impulsiveness, extreme mood swings, and often aggressiveness

Borders Region *n* a former local government region in S Scotland, formed in 1975 from Berwick, Peebles, Roxburgh, Selkirk, and part of Midlothian; replaced in 1996 by Scottish Borders council area

border terrier *n* a small rough-coated breed of terrier that originated in Britain

bordure ('bɔːdjʊə) *n heraldry* the outer edge of a shield, esp when decorated distinctively [c15 from Old French; see BORDER]

bore[1] (bɔː) *vb* **1** to produce (a hole) in (a material) by use of a drill, auger, or other cutting tool **2** to increase the diameter of (a hole), as by an internal

b

turning operation on a lathe or similar machine **3** (*tr*) to produce (a hole in the ground, tunnel, mine shaft, etc) by digging, drilling, cutting, etc **4** (*intr*) *informal* (of a horse or athlete in a race) to push other competitors, esp in order to try to get them out of the way ▷ *n* **5** a hole or tunnel in the ground, esp one drilled in search of minerals, oil, etc **6 a** a circular hole in a material produced by drilling, turning, or drawing **b** the diameter of such a hole **7 a** the hollow part of a tube or cylinder, esp of a gun barrel **b** the diameter of such a hollow part; calibre **8** *Austral* an artesian well [Old English *borian*; related to Old Norse *bora*, Old High German *borōn* to bore, Latin *forāre* to pierce, Greek *pharos* ploughing, *phárunx* PHARYNX]

bore² (bɔː) *vb* **1** (*tr*) to tire or make weary by being dull, repetitious, or uninteresting ▷ *n* **2** a dull, repetitious, or uninteresting person, activity, or state [c18 of unknown origin] > **bored** *adj*

bore³ (bɔː) *n* a high steep-fronted wave moving up a narrow estuary, caused by the tide [c17 from Old Norse *bāra* wave, billow]

bore⁴ (bɔː) *vb* the past tense of **bear¹**

boreal ('bɔːrɪəl) *adj* of or relating to the north or the north wind [c15 from Latin *boreās* the north wind]

Boreal ('bɔːrɪəl) *adj* **1** of or denoting the coniferous forests in the north of the N hemisphere **2** designating a climatic zone having snowy winters and short summers **3** designating a dry climatic period from about 7500 to 5500 BC, characterized by cold winters, warm summers, and a flora dominated by pines and hazels

Boreas ('bɔːrɪəs) *n Greek myth* the god personifying the north wind [c14 via Latin from Greek]

borecole ('bɔːkəʊl) *n* another name for **kale**

boredom ('bɔːdəm) *n* the state of being bored; tedium

boree ('bɔːriː) *n Austral* another name for **myall** [from a native Australian language]

boreen ('bɔːriːn) *n Irish* a country lane or narrow road [c19 from Irish Gaelic *bóithrín*, diminutive of *bóthar* road]

borehole ('bɔːˌhəʊl) *n* a hole driven into the ground to obtain geological information, release water, etc

borer ('bɔːrə) *n* **1** a machine or hand tool for boring holes **2** any of various insects, insect larvae, molluscs, or crustaceans that bore into rock or plant material, esp wood. See also **woodborer, corn borer, marine borer, rock borer**

borer bomb *n NZ* a device that emits pesticide fumes

Borgerhout (*Flemish* bɔrxər'hɑut) *n* a city in N Belgium, near Antwerp. Pop: 40 142 (2002 est)

Borgesian (ˌbɔːˈhesɪən) *adj* **1** of the Argentinian writer and poet Jorge Luis Borges (1899–1986) or his works **2** reminiscent of elements of Borges' stories and essays, esp labyrinths, mirrors, reality, identity, the nature of time, and infinity

boric ('bɔːrɪk) *adj* of or containing boron. Also: **boracic**

boric acid *n* **1** Also called: **orthoboric acid** Systematic name: **trioxoboric(III) acid** a white soluble weakly acid crystalline solid used in the manufacture of heat-resistant glass and porcelain enamels, as a fireproofing material, and as a mild antiseptic. Formula: H_3BO_3 **2** any other acid containing boron

boride ('bɔːraɪd) *n* a compound in which boron is the most electronegative element, esp a compound of boron and a metal [c19 from BOR(ON) + -IDE]

boring¹ ('bɔːrɪŋ) *n* **1 a** the act or process of making or enlarging a hole **b** the hole made in this way **2** (*often plural*) a fragment, particle, chip, etc, produced during boring

boring² ('bɔːrɪŋ) *adj* dull; repetitious; uninteresting > '**boringly** *adv*

boring mill *n engineering* a large vertical lathe having a rotating table on which work is secured.

Tools are held on a fixed post and the work is rotated around it. Also called (*informal*): **roundabout**

borlotti bean (bɔːˈlɒtɪ) *n* a variety of kidney bean with a pinkish-brown speckled skin that turns brown when cooked: grown in southern Europe, East Africa, and Taiwan [from Italian, plural of *borlotto* kidney bean]

borm (bɔːm) *vb* (*tr*) *Midland English dialect* to smear with paint, oil, etc

born (bɔːn) *vb* **1** the past participle (in most passive uses) of **bear¹** (sense 4) **2 was not born yesterday** is not gullible or foolish ▷ *adj* **3** possessing or appearing to have possessed certain qualities from birth: *a born musician* **4 a** being at birth in a particular social status or other condition as specified: *ignobly born* **b** (*in combination*): *lowborn* **5** in **all one's born days** *informal* so far in one's life

> ▌ **USAGE** Care should be taken not to use *born* where *borne* is intended: *he had borne* (not *born*) *his ordeal with great courage; the following points should be borne in mind*

borna disease ('bɔːnə) *n vet science* a viral disease of mammals, especially horses, caused by a member of the *Flaviviridae* and characterized by the development of encephalitis

born-again ('bɔːnəˌɡɛn) *adj* **1** having experienced conversion, esp evangelical Christianity **2** showing the enthusiasm of one newly converted to any cause: *a born-again monetarist* ▷ *n* **3** a person who shows fervent enthusiasm for a new-found cause, belief, etc

borne (bɔːn) *vb* **1** the past participle of **bear¹** (for all active uses of the verb; also for all passive uses except sense 4 unless followed by *by*) **2** be **borne in on** or **upon** (of a fact) to be realized by (someone): *it was borne in on us how close we had been to disaster*

Bornean ('bɔːnɪən) *adj* **1** of or relating to Borneo or its inhabitants ▷ *n* **2** a native or inhabitant of Borneo

Borneo ('bɔːnɪˌəʊ) *n* an island in the W Pacific, between the Sulu and Java Seas, part of the Malay Archipelago: divided into Kalimantan (**Indonesian Borneo**), the Malaysian states of Sarawak and Sabah, and the sultanate of Brunei; mountainous and densely forested. Area: about 750 000 sq km (290 000 sq miles)

borneol ('bɔːnɪˌɒl) *n* a white solid terpene alcohol extracted from the Malaysian tree *Dryobalanops aromatica*, used in perfume and in the manufacture of organic esters. Formula: $C_{10}H_{17}OH$. Also called: **bornyl alcohol** [c19 from BORNE(O) + -OL¹]

born-free *n* **1** (in South Africa) a person who was born or grew up after the end of the Apartheid era **2** (in Zimbabwe) a person who was born or grew up after the end of White minority rule

Bornholm (*Danish* bɔːnˈhɔlm) *n* an island in the Baltic Sea, south of Sweden: administratively part of Denmark. Chief town: Rønne. Pop: 43 956 (2003 est). Area: 588 sq km (227 sq miles)

Bornholm disease ('bɔːnˌhɒlm) *n* an epidemic virus infection characterized by pain round the base of the chest [c20 named after BORNHOLM, where it was first described]

bornite ('bɔːnaɪt) *n* a mineral consisting of a sulphide of copper and iron that tarnishes to purple or dark red. It occurs in copper deposits. Formula: Cu_5FeS_4 Also called: **peacock ore** [c19 named after I. von Born (1742–91), Austrian mineralogist; see -ITE¹]

Borno ('bɔːnəʊ) *n* a state of NE Nigeria, on Lake Chad: the second largest state, formed in 1976 from part of North-Eastern State. Capital: Maiduguri. Pop: 2 903 238 (1995 est). Area: 70 898 sq km (27 374 sq miles)

Borodino (ˌbɒrəˈdiːnəʊ; *Russian* bərədɪˈnɔ) *n* a village in E central Russia, about 110 km (70 miles) west of Moscow: scene of a battle (1812) in

which Napoleon defeated the Russians but irreparably weakened his army

boron ('bɔːrɒn) *n* a very hard almost colourless crystalline metalloid element that in impure form exists as a brown amorphous powder. It occurs principally in borax and is used in hardening steel. The naturally occurring isotope **boron-10** is used in nuclear control rods and neutron detection instruments. Symbol: B; atomic no.: 5; atomic wt.: 10.81; valency: 3; relative density: 2.34 (crystalline), 2.37 (amorphous); melting pt.: 2092°C; boiling pt.: 4002°C [c19 from BOR(AX) + (CARB)ON]

boron carbide *n* a black extremely hard inert substance having a high capture cross section for thermal neutrons. It is used as an abrasive and refractory and in control rods in nuclear reactors. Formula: B_4C

boronia (bəˈrəʊnɪə) *n* any aromatic rutaceous shrub of the Australian genus *Boronia*

boron nitride *n* a white inert crystalline solid existing both in a graphite-like form and in an extremely hard diamond-like form (borazon). It is used as a refractory, high temperature lubricant and insulator, and heat shield. Formula: BN

borosilicate (ˌbɔːrəʊˈsɪlɪkɪt, -ˌkeɪt) *n* a salt of boric and silicic acids

borosilicate glass *n* any of a range of heat- and chemical-resistant glasses, such as Pyrex, prepared by fusing together boron(III) oxide, silicon dioxide, and, usually, a metal oxide

borough ('bʌrə) *n* **1** a town, esp (in Britain) one that forms the constituency of an MP or that was originally incorporated by royal charter. See also **burgh 2** any of the 32 constituent divisions that together with the City of London make up Greater London **3** any of the five constituent divisions of New York City **4** (in the US) a self-governing incorporated municipality **5** (in medieval England) a fortified town or village or a fort **6** (in New Zealand) a small municipality with a governing body [Old English *burg*; related to *beorgan* to shelter, Old Norse *borg* wall, Gothic *baurgs* city, Old High German *burg* fortified castle]

borough-English *n English law* (until 1925) a custom in certain English boroughs whereby the youngest son inherited land to the exclusion of his older brothers. Compare **primogeniture, gavelkind** [c14 from Anglo-French *tenure en burgh Engloys* tenure in an English borough; so called because the custom was unknown in France]

borrow ('bɒrəʊ) *vb* **1** to obtain or receive (something, such as money) on loan for temporary use, intending to give it, or something equivalent or identical, back to the lender **2** to adopt (ideas, words, etc) from another source; appropriate **3** *not standard* to lend **4** *golf* to putt the ball uphill of the direct path to the hole **5** (*intr*) *golf* (of a ball) to deviate from a straight path because of the slope of the ground ▷ *n* **6** *golf* a deviation of a ball from a straight path because of the slope of the ground: *a left borrow* **7** material dug from a borrow pit to provide fill at another **8** living on **borrowed time a** living an unexpected extension of life **b** close to death [Old English *borgian*; related to Old High German *borgēn* to take heed, give security] > '**borrower** *n*

> ▌ **USAGE** The use of *off* after *borrow* was formerly considered incorrect, but is now acceptable in informal contexts

borrow pit *n civil engineering* an excavation dug to provide fill to make up ground elsewhere

Bors (bɔːs) *n* Sir (in Arthurian legend) **1** one the knights of the Round Table, nephew of Lancelot **2** an illegitimate son of King Arthur

borscht (bɔːʃt), **borsch** (bɔːʃ) or **borshch** (bɔːʃtʃ) *n* a Russian and Polish soup based on beetroot [c19 from Russian *borshch*]

borsic ('bɔːsɪk) *n aeronautics* a strong light composite material of boron fibre and silicon carbide used in aviation

borstal ('bɔːstəl) *n* **1** (formerly in Britain) an

informal name for an establishment in which offenders aged 15 to 21 could be detained for corrective training. Since the Criminal Justice Act 1982, they have been replaced by **youth custody centres** (now known as **young offender institutions**) **2** (formerly) a similar establishment in Australia and New Zealand [c20 named after *Borstal*, village in Kent where the first institution was founded]

bort, boart ('bɔːt) *or* **bortz** (bɔːts) *n* an inferior grade of diamond used for cutting and drilling or, in powdered form, as an industrial abrasive [Old English *gebrot* fragment; related to Old Norse *brot* piece, Old High German *broz* bud] > '**borty** *adj*

borzoi ('bɔːzɔɪ) *n, pl* -**zois** a tall graceful fast-moving breed of dog with a long silky coat, originally used in Russia for hunting wolves. Also called: **Russian wolfhound** [c19 from Russian *borzoi*, literally: swift; related to Old Slavonic *brŭzŭ* swift]

bosberaad ('bɒsbə,rɑːd) *n South African* a meeting in an isolated venue to break a political deadlock [c20 Afrikaans, from *bos* bush + *beraad* council]

boscage *or* **boskage** ('bɒskɪdʒ) *n literary* a mass of trees and shrubs; thicket [c14 from Old French *bosc*, probably of Germanic origin; see BUSH¹, -AGE]

Bosch process *n obsolete* an industrial process for manufacturing hydrogen by the catalytic reduction of steam with carbon monoxide [c20 named after Carl *Bosch* (1874–1940), German chemist]

boschvark ('bɒʃ,vɑːk) *n South African* another name for **bushpig** [Afrikaans]

Bose-Einstein statistics *pl n* (*functioning as singular*) *physics* the branch of quantum statistics applied to systems of particles of zero or integral spin that do not obey the exclusion principle. Compare **Fermi-Dirac statistics**

bosh¹ (bɒʃ) *n informal* empty or meaningless talk or opinions; nonsense [c19 from Turkish *boş* empty]

bosh² (bɒʃ) *n* **1** the lower tapering portion of a blast furnace, situated immediately above the air-inlet tuyères **2** the deposit of siliceous material that occurs on the surfaces of vessels in which copper is refined **3** a water tank for cooling glass-making tools, etc **4** *South Wales dialect* a kitchen sink or wash basin [c17 probably from German; compare *böschen* to slope, *Böschung* slope]

bosk (bɒsk) *n literary* a small wood of bushes and small trees [c13 variant of *busk* BUSH¹]

bosket *or* **bosquet** ('bɒskɪt) *n* a clump of small trees or bushes; thicket [c18 from French *bosquet*, from Italian *boschetto*, from *bosco* wood, forest; see BUSH¹]

Boskop ('bɒskɒp) *n* **a** a prehistoric race of the late Pleistocene period in sub-Saharan Africa **b** (*as modifier*): *Boskop man* [c20 named after *Boskop*, in the Transvaal, where remains of this race were first discovered]

bosky ('bɒskɪ) *adj* **boskier, boskiest** *literary* containing or consisting of bushes or thickets: *a bosky wood*

Bosman ruling ('bɒzmən) *n soccer* an EU ruling that allows out-of-contract footballers to leave their clubs without the clubs receiving a transfer fee [c20 named after Jean-Marc *Bosman* (born 1964), Belgian footballer whose court case brought about the ruling]

bo's'n ('bəʊsᵊn) *n nautical* a variant spelling of **boatswain**

Bosnia ('bɒznɪə) *n* a region of central Bosnia-Herzegovina: belonged to Turkey (1463–1878), to Austria-Hungary (1879–1918), then to Yugoslavia (1918–91)

Bosnia Herzegovina *or esp US* **Bosnia and Herzegovina** *n* a country in SW Europe; a constituent republic of Yugoslavia until 1991; in a state of civil war (1992–95); Serbian and Croatian forces were also involved: mostly barren and mountainous, with forests in the east. Language: Serbo-Croatian (sometimes now divided into

Serbian, Croatian and Bosnian). Religion: Muslim, Serbian Orthodox, and Roman Catholic. Currency: marka (pegged to the euro). Capital: Sarajevo. Pop: 4 186 000 (2004 est). Area: 51 129 sq km (19 737 sq miles)

Bosnian ('bɒznɪən) *adj* **1** of or relating to Bosnia or its inhabitants ▷ *n* **2** a native or inhabitant of Bosnia

bosom ('bʊzəm) *n* **1** the chest or breast of a person, esp the female breasts **2** the part of a woman's dress, coat, etc, that covers the chest **3** a protective centre or part: *the bosom of the family* **4** the breast considered as the seat of emotions **5** (*modifier*) very dear; intimate: *a bosom friend* ▷ *vb* (*tr*) **6** to embrace **7** to conceal or carry in the bosom [Old English *bōsm*; related to Old High German *buosam*]

bosomy ('bʊzəmɪ) *adj* (of a woman) having large breasts

boson ('bəʊzɒn) *n* any of a group of elementary particles, such as a photon or pion, that has zero or integral spin and obeys the rules of Bose-Einstein statistics. Compare **fermion** [c20 named after Satyendra Nath *Bose* (1894–1974), Indian physicist; see -ON]

Bosporus ('bɒspərəs) *or* **Bosphorus** ('bɒsfərəs) *n* **the** a strait between European and Asian Turkey, linking the Black Sea and the Sea of Marmara

bosquet ('bɒskɪt) *n* a variant spelling of **bosket**

boss¹ (bɒs) *informal* ▷ *n* **1** a person in charge of or employing others **2** *chiefly US* a professional politician who controls a party machine or political organization, often using devious or illegal methods ▷ *vb* **3** to employ, supervise, or be in charge of **4** (usually foll by *around* or *about*) to be domineering or overbearing towards (others) ▷ *adj* **5** *slang* excellent; fine: *a boss hand at carpentry; that's boss!* [c19 from Dutch *baas* master; probably related to Old High German *basa* aunt, Frisian *baes* master]

boss² (bɒs) *n* **1** a knob, stud, or other circular rounded protuberance, esp an ornamental one on a vault, a ceiling, or a shield **2** *biology* any of various protuberances or swellings in plants and animals **3 a** an area of increased thickness, usually cylindrical, that strengthens or provides room for a locating device on a shaft, hub of a wheel, etc **b** a similar projection around a hole in a casting or fabricated component **4** an exposed rounded mass of igneous or metamorphic rock, esp the uppermost part of an underlying batholith ▷ *vb* (*tr*) **5** to ornament with bosses; emboss [c13 from Old French *boce*, from Vulgar Latin *bottia* (unattested); related to Italian *bozza* metal knob, swelling]

boss³ (bɒs) *or* **bossy** *n, pl* **bosses** *or* **bossies** a calf or cow [c19 from dialect *buss* calf, perhaps ultimately from Latin *bōs* cow, ox]

BOSS (bɒs) *n* (formerly) ▷ *acronym for* Bureau of State Security; a branch of the South African security police

bossa nova ('bɒsə 'nəʊvə) *n* **1** a dance similar to the samba, originating in Brazil **2** a piece of music composed for or in the rhythm of this dance [c20 Portuguese, literally: new voice]

bossboy ('bɒs,bɔɪ) *n South African* a Black African foreman of a gang of workers

boss cocky *n Austral informal* a boss or person in power

bosset ('bɒsɪt) *n* either of the rudimentary antlers found in young deer [c19 from French *bossette* a small protuberance, from *bosse* BOSS²]

boss-eyed *adj informal* having a squint [c19 from *boss* to miss or bungle a shot at a target (dialect)]

bossing ('bɒsɪŋ) *n civil engineering* the act of shaping malleable metal, such as lead cladding, with mallets to fit a surface

bossism ('bɒs,ɪzəm) *n US* the domination or the system of domination of political organizations by bosses

boss screen *n* a screen image within a computer game that can be activated instantly, designed to

hide the evidence of game-playing, especially at work

bossy¹ ('bɒsɪ) *adj* **bossier, bossiest** *informal* domineering, overbearing, or authoritarian > '**bossily** *adv* > '**bossiness** *n*

bossy² ('bɒsɪ) *adj* (of furniture) ornamented with bosses

bosthoon ('bɒsduːn) *n Irish* a boor [c19 from Irish Gaelic *bastún*, from Old French *baston* penis]

boston ('bɒstən) *n* **1** a card game for four, played with two packs **2** *chiefly US* a slow gliding dance, a variation of the waltz

Boston ('bɒstən) *n* **1** a port in E Massachusetts, the state capital. Pop: 581 616 (2003 est) **2** a port in E England, in SE Lincolnshire. Pop: 35 124 (2001)

Boston bluefish *n Canadian* another name for **pollack**

Boston crab *n* a wrestling hold in which a wrestler seizes both or one of his opponent's legs, turns him face downwards, and exerts pressure over his back

Boston ivy *n* the US name for **Virginia creeper** (sense 2)

Boston matrix *n* a two-dimensional matrix, used in planning the business strategy of a large organization, that identifies those business units in the organization that generate cash and those that use it [c20 from the Boston Consultancy Group, a leading firm of strategic consultants, who developed it]

Boston Tea Party *n US history* a raid in 1773 made by citizens of Boston (disguised as Indians) on three British ships in the harbour as a protest against taxes on tea and the monopoly given to the East India Company. The contents of several hundred chests of tea were dumped into the harbour

Boston terrier *or* **Boston bull terrier** *n* a short stocky smooth-haired breed of terrier with a short nose, originally developed by crossing the French and English bulldogs with the English bull terrier

bosun ('bəʊsᵊn) *n nautical* a variant spelling of **boatswain**

Boswellian (bɒz'wɛlɪən) *adj* of or relating to James Boswell, the Scottish author and lawyer (1740–97)

Bosworth Field ('bɒzwɜːθ, -wəθ) *n English history* the site, two miles south of Market Bosworth in Leicestershire, of the battle that ended the Wars of the Roses (August 1485). Richard III was killed and Henry Tudor was crowned king as Henry VII

bot¹ *or* **bott** (bɒt) *n* **1** the larva of a botfly, which typically develops inside the body of a horse, sheep, or man **2** any similar larva **3** *NZ informal* a mild illness in humans ▷ See also **bots** [c15 probably from Low German; related to Dutch *bot*, of obscure origin]

bot² (bɒt) *Austral informal* ▷ *vb* **1** to scrounge or borrow **2** (*intr*; often foll by *on*) to scrounge (from); impose (on) ▷ *n* **3** a scrounger **4** **on the bot** (for) wanting to scrounge: *he's on the bot for a cigarette* [c20 perhaps from BOTFLY, alluding to the creature's bite; see BITE (sense 12)]

bot³ (bɒt) *n computing* an autonomous computer program that performs time-consuming tasks, esp on the internet [c20 from (RO)BOT]

BOT *abbreviation for* Board of Trade

bot. *abbreviation for* **1** botanical **2** botany

botanical (bə_tænɪkᵊl) *or* **botanic** *adj* **1** of or relating to botany or plants ▷ *n* **2** any drug or pesticide that is made from parts of a plant [c17 from Medieval Latin *botanicus*, from Greek *botanikos* relating to plants, from *botanē* plant, pasture, from *boskein* to feed; perhaps related to Latin *bōs* ox, cow] > bo'**tanically** *adv*

botanic garden *n* a place in which plants are grown, studied, and exhibited

botanize *or* **botanise** ('bɒtə,naɪz) *vb* **1** (*intr*) to collect or study plants **2** (*tr*) to explore and study the plants in (an area or region)

botany ('bɒtənɪ) *n, pl* -**nies** **1** the study of plants, including their classification, structure,

b

physiology, ecology, and economic importance **2** the plant life of a particular region or time **3** the biological characteristics of a particular group of plants [c17 from BOTANICAL; compare ASTRONOMY, ASTRONOMICAL] > 'botanist *n*

Botany Bay *n* **1** an inlet of the Tasman Sea, on the SE coast of Australia: surrounded by the suburbs of Sydney **2** (in the 19th century) a British penal settlement that was in fact at Port Jackson, New South Wales

Botany wool *n* a fine wool from the merino sheep [c19 from BOTANY BAY, where the wool came from originally]

botargo (bə'tɑ:gəʊ) *n, pl* -gos *or* -goes a relish consisting of the roe of mullet or tunny, salted and pressed into rolls [c15 from obsolete Italian, from Arabic *butarkhah*]

botch (bɒtʃ) *vb* (*tr*; often foll by *up*) **1** to spoil through clumsiness or ineptitude **2** to repair badly or clumsily ▷ *n* **3** Also called: **botch-up** a badly done piece of work or repair (esp in the phrase **make a botch of** (**something**)) [c14 of unknown origin] > 'botcher *n*

botchy ('bɒtʃɪ) *adj* botchier, botchiest clumsily done or made > 'botchily *adv* > 'botchiness *n*

botel (bəʊ'tɛl) *n* a variant spelling of **boatel**

botfly ('bɒt,flaɪ) *n, pl* -flies any of various stout-bodied hairy dipterous flies of the families *Oestridae* and *Gasterophilidae*, the larvae of which are parasites of man, sheep, and horses

both (bəʊθ) *determiner* **1 a** the two; two considered together: *both dogs were dirty* **b** (*as pronoun*): *both are to blame* ▷ *conj* **2** (*coordinating*) used preceding words, phrases, or clauses joined by *and*, used to emphasize that not just one, but also the other of the joined elements is included: *both Ellen and Keith enjoyed the play; both new and exciting* [c12 from Old Norse *bāthir*; related to Old High German *bēde*, Latin *ambō*, Greek *amphō*]

bother ('bɒðə) *vb* **1** (*tr*) to give annoyance, pain, or trouble to; irritate: *his bad leg is bothering him again* **2** (*tr*) to trouble (a person) by repeatedly disturbing; pester: *stop bothering your father!* **3** (*intr*) to take the time or trouble; concern oneself: *don't bother to come with me* **4** (*tr*) to make (a person) alarmed or confused: *the thought of her husband's return clearly bothered her* ▷ *n* **5** a state of worry, trouble, or confusion **6** a person or thing that causes fuss, trouble, or annoyance **7** *informal* a disturbance or fight; trouble (esp in the phrase **a spot of bother**) ▷ *interj* **8** *chiefly Brit* an exclamation of slight annoyance [c18 perhaps from Irish Gaelic *bodhar* deaf, vexed; compare Irish Gaelic *buairim* I vex]

botheration (,bɒðə'reɪʃən) *n, interj informal* another word for **bother** (senses 5, 8)

bothersome ('bɒðəsəm) *adj* causing bother; troublesome

Bothnia ('bɒθnɪə) *n* Gulf of. an arm of the Baltic Sea, extending north between Sweden and Finland

both ways *adj, adv* **1** another term for **each way 2 have it both ways** (*usually with a negative*) to try to get the best of a situation, argument, etc, by chopping and changing between alternatives or opposites

bothy ('bɒθɪ) *n, pl* bothies *chiefly Scot* **1** a cottage or hut **2** (esp in NE Scotland) a farmworker's summer quarters **3** a mountain shelter [c18 perhaps related to BOOTH]

bothy ballad *n Scot* a folk song, esp one from the farming community of NE Scotland

botnet ('bɒt,nɛt) *n* (sometimes with a capital) a network of computers infected by a program that communicates with its creator in order to send unsolicited emails, attack websites, etc [c20 from (RO)BOT + NET(WORK)]

Botox ('bəʊtɒks) *n trademark* a preparation of botulinum toxin used to treat muscle spasm and to remove wrinkles [c20 from BOT(ULINUM) (T)OX(IN)]

bo tree (bəʊ) *n* another name for the **peepul** [c19 from Sinhalese, from Pali *bodhitaru* tree of wisdom,

from Sanskrit *bodhi* wisdom, awakening; see BODHISATTVA]

botryoidal (,bɒtrɪ'ɔɪd²l) *or* **botryose** ('bɒtrɪ,əʊs, -,əʊz) *adj* (of minerals, parts of plants, etc) shaped like a bunch of grapes [c18 from Greek *botruoeidēs*, from *botrus* cluster of grapes; see -OID]

botrytis (bɒt'raɪtɪs) *n* **1** any of a group of fungi of the genus *Botrytis*, several of which cause plant diseases **2** *winemaking* a fungus of this genus, *Botrytis cinerea*, which causes noble rot

bots (bɒts) *n* (*functioning as singular*) a digestive disease of horses and some other animals caused by the presence of botfly larvae in the stomach

Botswana (bʊ'tʃwɑ:nə, bʊt'swɑ:nə, bɒt-) *n* a republic in southern Africa: established as the British protectorate of Bechuanaland in 1885 as a defence against the Boers; became an independent state within the Commonwealth in 1966; consists mostly of a plateau averaging 1000 m (3300 ft), with the extensive Okavango swamps in the northwest and the Kalahari Desert in the southwest. Languages: English and Tswana. Religion: animist majority. Currency: pula. Capital: Gaborone. Pop: 1 795 000 (2004 est). Area: about 570 000 sq km (220 000 sq miles)

bott (bɒt) *n* a variant spelling of **bot**[1]

botte (French *bot*) *n fencing* a thrust or hit

bottine (bɒ'ti:n) *n* a light boot for women or children; half-boot [c19 from French: little boot, from *botte* boot]

bottle[1] ('bɒt²l) *n* **1 a** a vessel, often of glass and typically cylindrical with a narrow neck that can be closed with a cap or cork, for containing liquids **b** (*as modifier*): *a bottle rack* **2** Also called: **bottleful** the amount such a vessel will hold **3 a** a container equipped with a teat that holds a baby's milk or other liquid; nursing bottle **b** the contents of such a container: *the baby drank his bottle* **4** short for **magnetic bottle 5** *Brit slang* nerve; courage (esp in the phrase **lose one's bottle**) **6** *Brit slang* money collected by street entertainers or buskers **7 full bottle** *Austral slang* well-informed and enthusiastic about something **8 the bottle** *informal* drinking of alcohol, esp to excess ▷ *vb* (*tr*) **9** to put or place (wine, beer, jam, etc) in a bottle or bottles **10** to store (gas) in a portable container under pressure **11** *slang* to injure by thrusting a broken bottle into (a person) **12** *Brit slang* (of a busker) to collect money from the bystanders. ▷ See also **bottle out, bottle up** [c14 from Old French *botaille*, from Medieval Latin *butticula* literally: a little cask, from Late Latin *buttis* cask, BUTT[4]]

bottle[2] ('bɒt²l) *n dialect* a bundle, esp of hay [c14 from Old French *botel*, from *botte* bundle, of Germanic origin]

bottle bank *n* a large container into which the public may throw glass bottles for recycling

bottlebrush ('bɒt²l,brʌʃ) *n* **1** a cylindrical brush on a thin shaft, used for cleaning bottles **2** Also called: **callistemon** any of various Australian myrtaceous shrubs or trees of the genera *Callistemon* and *Melaleuca*, having dense spikes of large red flowers with protruding brushlike stamens **3** any of various similar trees or shrubs

bottled *or* **bottle gas** *n* butane or propane gas liquefied under pressure in portable containers and used in camping stoves, blowtorches, etc

bottle-feed *vb* -feeds, -feeding, -fed to feed (a baby) with milk from a bottle instead of breastfeeding

bottle glass *n* glass used for making bottles, consisting of a silicate of sodium, calcium, and aluminium

bottle gourd *n* **1** an Old World cucurbitaceous climbing plant, *Lagenaria siceraria*, having large hard-shelled gourds as fruits **2** the fruit of this plant ▷ Also called: **calabash**

bottle green *n, adj* **a** a dark green colour **b** (*as adjective*): *a bottle-green car*

bottle-jack *n NZ* a large jack used for heavy lifts

bottleneck ('bɒt²l,nɛk) *n* **1 a** a narrow stretch of

road or a junction at which traffic is or may be held up **b** the hold up **2** something that holds up progress, esp of a manufacturing process **3** *music* **a** the broken-off neck of a bottle placed over a finger and used to produce a buzzing effect in a style of guitar-playing originally part of the American blues tradition **b** the style of guitar playing using a bottleneck ▷ *vb* **4** (*tr*) US to be or cause an obstruction in

bottlenose dolphin ('bɒt²l,nəʊz) *n* any dolphin of the genus *Tursiops*, esp *T. truncatus*, some of which have been kept in captivity and trained to perform tricks

bottle-o *or* **bottle-oh** *n Austral and NZ history informal* a dealer in empty bottles

bottle out *vb* (*intr, adverb*) *Brit slang* to lose one's nerve

bottle party *n* a party to which guests bring drink

bottler ('bɒt²lə) *n Austral and NZ informal* an excellent or outstanding person or thing

bottle shop *n Austral and NZ* a shop or part of a hotel where alcohol is sold in unopened containers for consumption elsewhere. Also called: **bottle store**

bottle tree *n* **1** any of several Australian sterculiaceous trees of the genus *Sterculia* (or *Brachychiton*) that have a bottle-shaped swollen trunk **2** another name for **baobab**

bottle up *vb* (*tr, adverb*) **1** to restrain (powerful emotion) **2** to keep (an army or other force) contained or trapped: *the French fleet was bottled up in Le Havre*

bottle-washer *n informal* a menial or factotum

bottom ('bɒtəm) *n* **1** the lowest, deepest, or farthest removed part of a thing: *the bottom of a hill* **2** the least important or successful position: *the bottom of a class* **3** the ground underneath a sea, lake, or river **4 touch bottom** to run aground **5** the inner depths of a person's true feelings (esp in the phrase **from the bottom of one's heart**) **6** the underneath part of a thing **7** *nautical* the parts of a vessel's hull that are under water **8** (in literary or commercial contexts) a boat or ship **9** *billiards, snooker* a strike in the centre of the cue ball **10** a dry valley or hollow **11** (*often plural*) US and Canadian the low land bordering a river **12** the lowest level worked in a mine **13** (esp of horses) staying power; stamina **14** importance, seriousness, or influence: *his views all have weight and bottom* **15** *informal* the buttocks **16** at bottom in reality; basically or despite appearances to the contrary: *he's a kind man at bottom* **17 be at the bottom of** to be the ultimate cause of **18 get to the bottom of** to discover the real truth about **19 knock the bottom out of** to destroy or eliminate ▷ *adj* (*prenominal*) **20** lowest or last: *the bottom price* **21 bet** (*or* **put**) **one's bottom dollar on** to be absolutely sure of (one's opinion, a person, project, etc) **22** of, relating to, or situated at the bottom or a bottom: *the bottom shelf* **23** fundamental; basic ▷ *vb* **24** (*tr*) to provide (a chair, etc) with a bottom or seat **25** (*tr*) to discover the full facts or truth of; fathom **26** (*usually foll by* *on or upon*) to base or be founded (on an idea, etc) **27** (*intr*) *nautical* to strike the ground beneath the water with a vessel's bottom **28** *Austral mining* **a** to mine (a hole, claim, etc) deep enough to reach any gold there is **b** (*intr; foll by on*) to reach (gold, mud, etc) on bottoming **29** *electronics* to saturate a transistor so that further increase of input produces no change in output ▷ See also **bottom out** [Old English *botm*; related to Old Norse *botn*, Old High German *bodam*, Latin *fundus*, Greek *puthmēn*]

bottom dead centre *n engineering* the position of the crank of a reciprocating engine when the piston is at its nearest point to the crankshaft. Also called: **outer dead centre**

bottom drawer *n Brit* a young woman's collection of clothes, linen, cutlery, etc, in anticipation of marriage. US & Canadian equivalent: hope chest

bottom end *n* (in vertical engines) another name for **big end** (sense 1)

bottom feeder *n* **1** a fish that feeds on material at the bottom of a river, lake, sea, etc **2** an objectionable and unimpressive person or thing **3** Also called: **bottom fisher** a speculator who buys shares in companies that are performing poorly in anticipation of improved performance

bottom fishing *n* investing in low-priced shares that show prospects of recovery or in shares that are low-priced because of a general market decline in the hope of making a profit ▷ **bottom fisher** *n*

bottom house *n* Caribbean **1** the open space beneath a house built upon high pillars **2** such a space partially enclosed and floored for use as servants' quarters

bottoming ('bɒtəmɪŋ) *n* the lowest level of foundation material for a road or other structure

bottomless ('bɒtəmlɪs) *adj* **1** having no bottom **2** unlimited; inexhaustible **3** very deep

bottom line *n* **1** the last line of a financial statement that shows the net profit or loss of a company or organization **2** the final outcome of a process, discussion, etc **3** the most important or fundamental aspect of a situation

bottommost ('bɒtəm,məʊst) *adj* lowest or most fundamental

bottom out *vb* (intr, adverb) to reach the lowest point and level out: *the recession shows no sign of bottoming out*

bottomry ('bɒtəmrɪ) *n, pl* -ries maritime law a contract whereby the owner of a ship borrows money to enable the vessel to complete the voyage and pledges the ship as security for the loan [c16 from Dutch *bodemerij*, from *bodem* BOTTOM (hull of a ship) + -*erij* -RY]

bottomset bed ('bɒtəm,sɛt) *n* the fine sediment deposited at the front of a growing delta

bottoms up *interj* an informal drinking toast

bottom-up *adj* from the lowest level of a hierarchy or process to the top: *a bottom-up approach to corporate decision-making*

bottom-up processing *n* a processing technique, either in the brain or in a computer, in which incoming information is analysed in successive steps and later-stage processing does not affect processing in earlier stages

Bottrop (German 'bɔtrɔp) *n* an industrial city in W Germany, in North Rhine-Westphalia in the Ruhr. Pop: 120 324 (2003 est)

botulin ('bɒtjʊlɪn) *n* a potent toxin produced by the bacterium *Clostridium botulinum* in imperfectly preserved food, etc, causing botulism [c19 from BOTULINUS]

botulinum toxin (,bɒtjʊ'laɪnəm) *n* a pharmaceutical formulation of botulin used in minute doses to treat various forms of muscle spasm and for the cosmetic removal of wrinkles. See **Botox**

botulinus (,bɒtjʊ'laɪnəs) *n, pl* -nuses an anaerobic bacterium, *Clostridium botulinum*, whose toxins (botulins) cause botulism: family *Bacillaceae* [c19 from New Latin, from Latin *botulus* sausage]

botulism ('bɒtjʊ,lɪzəm) *n* severe poisoning from ingestion of botulin, which affects the central nervous system producing difficulty in swallowing, visual disturbances, and respiratory paralysis: often fatal [c19 first formed as German *Botulismus* literally: sausage poisoning, from Latin *botulus* sausage]

Bouaké (French bwake) *n* a market town in S central Côte d'Ivoire. Pop: 521 000 (2005 est)

boubou *or* **bubu** ('bu:bu:) *n* a long flowing garment worn by men and women in Mali, Nigeria, Senegal, and some other parts of Africa [a native name in Mali]

bouchée (bu:'ʃeɪ) *n* a small pastry case filled with a savoury mixture, served hot with cocktails or as an hors d'oeuvre [c19 from French: mouthful]

Bouches-du-Rhône (French buʃdyrɔn) *n* a

department of S central France, in Provence-Alpes-Côte d'Azur region. Capital: Marseille. Pop: 1 883 645 (2003 est). Area: 5284 sq km (2047 sq miles)

bouclé ('bu:kleɪ) *n* **1** a curled or looped yarn or fabric giving a thick knobbly effect ▷ *adj* **2** of or designating such a yarn or fabric: *a bouclé wool coat* [c19 from French *bouclé* curly, from *boucle* a curl, BUCKLE]

bouclée ('bu:kleɪ) *n* a support for a cue in billiards formed by doubling the first finger so that its tip is aligned with the thumb at its second joint, to form a loop through which the cue may slide [from French, literally: curled]

boudin (French budɛ̃) *n* a French version of a black pudding [c20 French]

boudoir ('bu:dwa:, -dwɔ:) *n* a woman's bedroom or private sitting room [c18 from French, literally: room for sulking in, from *bouder* to sulk]

boudoir grand *n* a domestic grand piano between 5 and 6 feet in length. Compare **baby grand, concert grand**

bouffant ('bu:fɒŋ) *adj* **1** (of a hair style) having extra height and width through back-combing; puffed out **2** (of sleeves, skirts, etc) puffed out ▷ *n* **3** a bouffant hair style [c20 from French, from *bouffer* to puff up]

bouffe (bu:f) *n* See **opéra bouffe**

Bougainville ('bu:gən,vɪl) *n* an island in the W Pacific, in Papua New Guinea: the largest of the Solomon Islands: unilaterally declared independence in 1990; occupied by government troops in 1992, and granted autonomy in 2001. Chief town: Kieta. Area: 10 049 sq km (3880 sq miles)

bougainvillea *or* **bougainvillaea** (,bu:gən'vɪlɪə) *n* any tropical woody nyctaginaceous widely cultivated climbing plant of the genus *Bougainvillea*, having inconspicuous flowers surrounded by showy red or purple bracts [c19 New Latin, named after Louis Antoine de *Bougainville* (1729–1811), French navigator]

bough (baʊ) *n* any of the main branches of a tree [Old English *bōg* arm, twig; related to Old Norse *bōgr* shoulder, ship's bow, Old High German *buog* shoulder, Greek *pēkhus* forearm, Sanskrit *bāhu*; see BOW³, ELBOW]

bought (bɔ:t) *vb* **1** the past tense and past participle of **buy** ▷ *adj* **2** purchased from a shop; not homemade

boughten ('bɔ:t³n) *adj* a dialect word for **bought** (sense 2)

bougie ('bu:ʒi:, bu:'ʒi:) *n* med a long slender semiflexible cylindrical instrument for inserting into body passages, such as the rectum or urethra, to dilate structures, introduce medication, etc [c18 from French, originally a wax candle from *Bougie* (Bujiya), Algeria]

bouillabaisse (,bu:jə'bɛs) *n* a rich stew or soup of fish and vegetables flavoured with spices, esp saffron [c19 from French, from Provençal *bouiabaisso*, literally: boil down]

bouillon ('bu:jɒn) *n* a plain unclarified broth or stock [c18 from French, from *bouillir* to BOIL¹]

boulder ('bəʊldə) *n* **1** a smooth rounded mass of rock that has a diameter greater than 25cm and that has been shaped by erosion and transported by ice or water from its original position **2** geology a rock fragment with a diameter greater than 256 mm and thus bigger than a cobble [c13 probably of Scandinavian origin; compare Swedish dialect *bullersten*, from Old Swedish *bulder* rumbling + *sten* STONE] ▷ 'bouldery *adj*

boulder clay *n* an unstratified glacial deposit consisting of fine clay, boulders, and pebbles. See also **till⁴**

Boulder Dam *n* the former name (1933–47) of Hoover Dam

bouldering ('bəʊldərɪŋ) *n* rock climbing on large boulders or small outcrops either as practice or as a sport in its own right

boule¹ ('bu:li:) *n* **1** the parliament in modern

Greece **2** the senate of an ancient Greek city-state [c19 from Greek *boulē* senate]

boule² (bu:l) *n* a pear-shaped imitation ruby, sapphire, etc, made from synthetic corundum [c19 from French: ball]

boule³ (bu:l) *n* a round loaf of white bread [c20 from French: a ball]

boules (French bul) *pl n* (functioning as singular) a game, popular in France, in which metal bowls are thrown to land as near as possible to a target ball. It is played on rough surfaces [plural of *boule* BALL¹; see BOWL²]

boulevard ('bu:lva:, -va:d) *n* **1 a** a wide usually tree-lined road in a city, often used as a promenade **b** (capital as part of a street name): *Sunset Boulevard* **2** chiefly Canadian **a** a grass strip between the pavement and road **b** the strip of ground between the edge of a private property and the road **c** the centre strip of a road dividing traffic travelling in different directions [c18 from French, from Middle Dutch *bolwerc* BULWARK; so called because originally often built on the ruins of an old rampart]

boulevardier (bu:l'va:dɪ,eɪ) *n* (originally in Paris) a fashionable man, esp one who frequents public places

boulle, boule *or* **buhl** (bu:l) *adj* **1** denoting or relating to a type of marquetry of patterned inlays of brass and tortoiseshell, occasionally with other metals such as pewter, much used on French furniture from the 17th century ▷ *n* **2** Also called: **boullework** something ornamented with such marquetry [c18 named after André Charles *Boulle* (1642–1732), French cabinet-maker]

Boulogne (bu'lɔɪn; French bulɔɲ) *n* a port in N France, on the English Channel. Pop: 44 859 (1999). Official name: **Boulogne-sur-Mer** (French bulɔɲsyrmɛr)

Boulogne-Billancourt (French bulɔɲbijɑ̃kur) *n* an industrial suburb of SW Paris. Pop: 106 367 (1999). Also called: **Boulogne-sur-Seine** (French bulɔɲsyrsɛn)

boult (bəʊlt) *vb* a variant spelling of **bolt²**

bounce (baʊns) *vb* **1** (intr) (of an elastic object, such as a ball) to rebound from an impact **2** (tr) to cause (such an object) to hit a solid surface and spring back **3** to rebound or cause to rebound repeatedly **4** to move or cause to move suddenly, excitedly, or violently; spring: *she bounced up from her chair* **5** slang (of a bank) to send (a cheque) back or (of a cheque) to be sent back unredeemed because of lack of funds in the drawer's account **6** (of an internet service provider) to send (an email message) back or (of an email message) to be sent back to the sender, for example because the recipient's email account is full **7** (tr) slang to force (a person) to leave (a place or job); throw out; eject **8** (tr) Brit to hustle (a person) into believing or doing something ▷ *n* **9** the action of rebounding from an impact **10** a leap; jump; bound **11** the quality of being able to rebound; springiness **12** informal vitality; vigour; resilience **13** Brit swagger or impudence **14** the bounce Australian rules football the start of play at the beginning of each quarter or after a goal **15** get or give the bounce US informal to dismiss or be dismissed from a job **16** on the bounce informal in succession; one after the other: *they have lost nine games on the bounce* [c13 probably of imitative origin; compare Low German *bunsen* to beat, Dutch *bonken* to thump]

bounce back *vb* **1** (intr, adverb) to recover one's health, good spirits, confidence, etc, easily after a setback ▷ *n* **bounce-back 2** a recovery following a setback

bouncebackability (,baʊns,bækə'bɪlɪtɪ) *n* informal the ability to recover after a setback, esp in sport

bounce game *n* (esp in soccer) a non-competitive game played as part of training

bouncer ('baʊnsə) *n* **1** slang a man employed at a club, pub, disco, etc, to throw out drunks or troublemakers and stop those considered

b

undesirable from entering **2** *slang* a dishonoured cheque **3** *cricket* another word for **bumper¹ 4** a person or thing that bounces

bouncing ('baʊnsɪŋ) *adj* (when *postpositive*, foll by *with*) vigorous and robust (esp in the phrase **a bouncing baby**)

bouncing Bet (bɛt) *n* another name for **soapwort**

bouncy ('baʊnsɪ) *adj* **bouncier, bounciest 1** lively, exuberant, or self-confident **2** having the capability or quality of bouncing: *a bouncy ball* **3** responsive to bouncing; springy: *a bouncy bed* > **'bouncily** *adv* > **'bounciness** *n*

bouncy castle *n* a very large inflatable model, usually of a castle, on which children may bounce at fairs, etc

bound¹ (baʊnd) *vb* **1** the past tense and past participle of **bind** ▷ *adj* **2** in bonds or chains; tied with or as if with a rope: *a bound prisoner* **3** (*in combination*) restricted; confined: *housebound; fogbound* **4** (*postpositive*, foll by an infinitive) destined; sure; certain: *it's bound to happen* **5** (*postpositive*, often foll by *by*) compelled or obliged to act, behave, or think in a particular way, as by duty, circumstance, or convention **6** (of a book) secured within a cover or binding: *to deliver bound books.* See also **half-bound 7** (*postpositive*, foll by *on*) *US* resolved; determined: *bound on winning* **8** *linguistics* **a** denoting a morpheme, such as the prefix *non-*, that occurs only as part of another word and not as a separate word in itself. Compare **free** (sense 21) **b** (in systemic grammar) denoting a clause that has a nonfinite predicator or that is introduced by a binder, and that occurs only together with a freestanding clause. Compare **freestanding 9** *logic* (of a variable) occurring within the scope of a quantifier that indicates the degree of generality of the open sentence in which the variable occurs: in (*x*) (*Fx* → *bxy*), *x* is bound and *y* is free. Compare **free** (sense 22) **10 bound up with** closely or inextricably linked with: *his irritability is bound up with his work* **11 I'll be bound** I am sure (something) is true

bound² (baʊnd) *vb* **1** to move forwards or make (one's way) by leaps or jumps **2** to bounce; spring away from an impact ▷ *n* **3** a jump upwards or forwards **4 by leaps and bounds** with unexpectedly rapid progess: *her condition improved by leaps and bounds* **5** a sudden pronounced sense of excitement: *his heart gave a sudden bound when he saw her* **6** a bounce, as of a ball [C16 from Old French *bond* a leap, from *bondir* to jump, resound, from Vulgar Latin *bombitīre* (unattested) to buzz, hum, from Latin *bombus* booming sound]

bound³ (baʊnd) *vb* **1** (*tr*) to place restrictions on; limit **2** (when *intr*, foll by *on*) to form a boundary of (an area of land or sea, political or administrative region, etc) ▷ *n* **3** *maths* **a** a number which is greater than all the members of a set of numbers (an **upper bound**), or less than all its members (a **lower bound**). See also **bounded** (sense 1) **b** more generally, an element of an ordered set that has the same ordering relation to all the members of a given subset **c** whence, an estimate of the extent of some set **4** See **bounds** [C13 from Old French *bonde*, from Medieval Latin *bodina*, of Gaulish origin]

bound⁴ (baʊnd) *adj* **a** (*postpositive*, often foll by *for*) going or intending to go towards; on the way to: *a ship bound for Jamaica; homeward bound* **b** (*in combination*): *northbound traffic* [C13 from Old Norse *buinn*, past participle of *būa* to prepare]

boundary ('baʊndərɪ, -drɪ) *n, pl* **-ries 1** something that indicates the farthest limit, as of an area; border **2** *cricket* **a** the marked limit of the playing area **b** a stroke that hits the ball beyond this limit **c** the four runs scored with such a stroke, or the six runs if the ball crosses the boundary without touching the ground

Boundary Commission *n* (in Britain) a body established by statute to undertake periodic reviews of the boundaries of parliamentary constituencies and to recommend changes to take account of population shifts

boundary layer *n* the layer of fluid closest to the surface of a solid past which the fluid flows: it has a lower rate of flow than the bulk of the fluid because of its adhesion to the solid

boundary rider *n* *Austral* an employee on a sheep or cattle station whose job is to maintain fences in good repair and to prevent stock from straying

bounded ('baʊndɪd) *adj maths* **1** (of a set) having a bound, esp where a measure is defined in terms of which all the elements of the set, or the differences between all pairs of members, are less than some value, or else all its members lie within some other well-defined set **2** (of an operator, function, etc) having a bounded set of values

bounden ('baʊndən) *adj* morally obligatory (archaic except in the phrase **bounden duty**)

bounder ('baʊndə) *n* **1** *old-fashioned, Brit slang* a morally reprehensible person; cad **2** a person or animal that bounds

boundless ('baʊndlɪs) *adj* unlimited; vast: *boundless energy* > **'boundlessly** *adv* > **'boundlessness** *n*

bounds (baʊndz) *pl n* **1** (*sometimes singular*) a limit; boundary (esp in the phrase **know no bounds**) **2** something that restrains or confines, esp the standards of a society: *within the bounds of modesty* **3 beat the bounds** See **beat** (sense 26) ▷ See also **out of bounds**

bounteous ('baʊntɪəs) *adj literary* **1** giving freely; generous: *the bounteous goodness of God* **2** plentiful; abundant > **'bounteously** *adv* > **'bounteousness** *n*

bountiful ('baʊntɪfʊl) *adj* **1** plentiful; ample (esp in the phrase **a bountiful supply**) **2** giving freely; generous > **'bountifully** *adv* > **'bountifulness** *n*

bounty ('baʊntɪ) *n, pl* **-ties 1** generosity in giving to others; liberality **2** a generous gift; something freely provided **3** a payment made by a government, as, formerly, to a sailor on enlisting or to a soldier after a campaign **4** any reward or premium: *a bounty of 20p for every rat killed* [C13 (in the sense: goodness): from Old French *bontet*, from Latin *bonitās* goodness, from *bonus* good]

Bounty ('baʊntɪ) *n* a British naval ship commanded by Captain William Bligh, which was on a scientific voyage in 1789 between Tahiti and the West Indies when her crew mutinied

bounty bag *n* a set of free samples, such as nappies and creams, given to mothers leaving hospital with a new baby

bouquet *n* **1** (bəʊˈkeɪ, buː-) a bunch of flowers, esp a large carefully arranged one **2** (buːˈkeɪ) Also called: **nose** the characteristic aroma or fragrance of a wine or liqueur **3** a compliment or expression of praise [C18 from French: thicket, from Old French *bosc* forest, wood, probably of Germanic origin; see BUSH¹]

bouquet garni ('buːkeɪ gɑːˈniː) *n, pl* bouquets garnis ('buːkeɪz gɑːˈniː) a bunch of herbs tied together and used for flavouring soups, stews, etc [C19 from French, literally: garnished bouquet]

Bourbaki ('bɔːbəkɪ) *n* **Nicholas** the pseudonym of a group of mainly French mathematicians that, since 1939, has been producing a monumental work on advanced mathematics, *Eléments de Mathématique*

bourbon ('bɜːbən) *n* a whiskey distilled, chiefly in the US, from maize, esp one containing at least 51 per cent maize (the rest being malt and rye) and aged in charred white-oak barrels [C19 named after *Bourbon* county, Kentucky, where it was first made]

Bourbon biscuit *n* a rich chocolate-flavoured biscuit with a chocolate-cream filling

Bourbonism ('bʊəbəˌnɪzəm) *n* **1** support for the rule of the Bourbons, the European royal line that ruled in France from 1589 to 1793 and 1815–48, and in Spain (1700–1808; 1813–1931) and Naples and Sicily (1734–1806; 1815–1860) **2** *US* extreme political and social conservatism

bourdon ('bʊədⁿn, 'bɔːdⁿn) *n* **1** a 16-foot organ stop of the stopped diapason type **2** the drone of a bagpipe **3** a drone or pedal point in the bass of a harmonized melody [C14 from Old French: drone (of a musical instrument), of imitative origin]

Bourdon gauge *n* a type of aneroid pressure gauge consisting of a flattened curved tube attached to a pointer that moves around a dial. As the pressure in the tube increases the tube tends to straighten and the pointer indicates the applied pressure [C19 named after Eugène *Bourdon* (1808–84), French hydraulic engineer, who invented it]

bourg (bʊəg; *French* bur) *n* a French market town, esp one beside a castle [C15 French, from Old French *borc*, from Late Latin *burgus* castle, of Germanic origin; see BOROUGH]

bourgeois¹ ('bʊəʒwɑː, bʊəˈʒwɑː) *often disparaging* ▷ *n, pl* **-geois 1** a member of the middle class, esp one regarded as being conservative and materialistic or (in Marxist thought) a capitalist exploiting the working class **2** a mediocre, unimaginative, or materialistic person ▷ *adj* **3** characteristic of, relating to, or comprising the middle class **4** conservative or materialistic in outlook: *a bourgeois mentality* **5** (in Marxist thought) dominated by capitalists or capitalist interests [C16 from Old French *borjois, burgeis* burgher, citizen, from *bourg* town; see BURGESS] > **bourgeoise** ('bʊəʒwɑːz, bʊəˈʒwɑːz) *fem n*

bourgeois² (bəˈdʒɔɪs) *n* (formerly) a size of printer's type approximately equal to 9 point [C19 perhaps from its size, midway between long primer and brevier]

bourgeoisie (ˌbʊəʒwɑːˈziː) *n* **the 1** the middle classes **2** (in Marxist thought) the ruling class of the two basic classes of capitalist society, consisting of capitalists, manufacturers, bankers, and other employers. The bourgeoisie owns the most important of the means of production, through which it exploits the working class

bourgeon ('bɜːdʒən) *n, vb* a variant spelling of **burgeon**

Bourges (*French* burʒ) *n* a city in central France. Pop: 72 480 (1999)

Bourgogne (burɡɔɲ) *n* the French name for **Burgundy**

bourn¹ *or* **bourne** (bɔːn) *n archaic* **1** a destination; goal **2** a boundary [C16 from Old French *borne*; see BOUND³]

bourn² (bɔːn) *n chiefly Southern Brit* a stream, esp an intermittent one in chalk areas. Compare **burn²** [C16 from Old French *bodne* limit; see BOUND³]

Bournemouth ('bɔːnməθ) *n* **1** a resort in S England, in Bournemouth unitary authority, Dorset, on the English Channel. Pop: 167 527 (2001) **2** a unitary authority in SE Dorset. Pop: 163 700 (2003 est). Area: 46 sq km (17 sq miles)

bourrée ('bʊəreɪ) *n* **1** a traditional French dance in fast duple time, resembling a gavotte **2** a piece of music composed in the rhythm of this dance [C18 from French *bourrée* a bundle of faggots (it was originally danced round a fire of faggots)]

Bourse (bʊəs) *n* a stock exchange of continental Europe, esp Paris [C19 from French, literally: purse, from Medieval Latin *bursa*, ultimately from Greek: leather]

bouse *or* **bowse** (baʊz) *vb* (*tr*) *nautical* to raise or haul with a tackle [C16 of unknown origin]

boustrophedon (ˌbuːstrəˈfiːdⁿn, ˌbaʊ-) *adj* having alternate lines written from right to left and from left to right [C17 from Greek, literally: turning as in ploughing with oxen, from *bous* ox + *-strophēdon* from *strephein* to turn; see STROPHE]

bout (baʊt) *n* **1 a** a period of time spent doing something, such as drinking **b** a period of illness **2** a contest or fight, esp a boxing or wrestling match [C16 variant of obsolete *bought* turn; related to German *Bucht* BIGHT; see ABOUT]

boutade (buːˈtɑːd) *n* an outburst; sally [C17 from French, from *bouter* to thrust]

boutique (buːˈtiːk) *n* **1** a shop, esp a small one

selling fashionable clothes and other items **2 a** of or denoting a small specialized producer or business **b** (*as modifier*): *a boutique winery* **3** a small specialized stall or shopping area within a supermarket, esp selling fresh meat, seafood, etc [C18 from French, probably from Old Provençal *botica*, ultimately from Greek *apothēkē* storehouse; see APOTHECARY]

boutonniere (ˌbuːtɒnɪˈɛə) *n* another name for **buttonhole** (sense 2) [C19 from French: buttonhole, from *bouton* BUTTON]

bouvier (ˈbuːvɪeɪ) *n* a large powerful dog of a Belgian breed, having a rough shaggy coat: used esp for cattle herding and guarding [C20 from French, literally: cowherd]

bouzouki (buːˈzuːkɪ) *n* a Greek long-necked stringed musical instrument related to the mandolin [C20 from Modern Greek *mpouzouki*, perhaps from Turkish *büjük* large]

bovid (ˈbəʊvɪd) *adj* **1** of, relating to, or belonging to the *Bovidae*, a family of ruminant artiodactyl hollow-horned mammals including sheep, goats, cattle, antelopes, and buffalo ▷ *n* **2** any bovid animal [C19 from New Latin *Bovidae*, from Latin *bōs* ox]

bovine (ˈbəʊvaɪn) *adj* **1** of, relating to, or belonging to the *Bovini* (cattle), a bovid tribe including domestic cattle **2** (of people) dull; sluggish; stolid ▷ *n* **3** any animal belonging to the *Bovini* [C19 from Late Latin *bovīnus* concerning oxen or cows, from Latin *bōs* ox, cow]
> **bovinely** *adv*

bovine somatotrophin *n* the full name for **BST** (sense 1)

bovine spongiform encephalopathy *n* the full name for **BSE**

Bovril (ˈbɒvrɪl) *n trademark* a concentrated beef extract, used for flavouring, as a stock, etc

bovver (ˈbɒvə) *n Brit slang* **a** rowdiness, esp caused by gangs of teenage youths **b** (*as modifier*): *a bovver boy* [C20 slang pronunciation of BOTHER]

bovver boots *pl n Brit slang* heavy boots worn by some teenage youths in Britain, used in gang fights

bow¹ (baʊ) *vb* **1** to lower (one's head) or bend (one's knee or body) as a sign of respect, greeting, assent, or shame **2** to bend or cause to bend; incline downwards **3** (*intr*; usually foll by *to* or *before*) to comply or accept: *bow to the inevitable* **4** (*tr*; foll by *in*, *out*, *to* etc) to usher (someone) into or out of a place with bows and deference: *the manager bowed us to our car* **5** (*tr*; usually foll by *down*) to bring (a person, nation, etc) to a state of submission **6 bow and scrape** to behave in an excessively deferential or obsequious way ▷ *n* **7** a lowering or inclination of the head or body as a mark of respect, greeting, or assent **8 take a bow** to acknowledge or receive applause or praise ▷ See also **bow out** [Old English *būgan*, related to Old Norse *bjūgr* bent, Old High German *biogan* to bend, Dutch *buigen*]

bow² (bəʊ) *n* **1** a weapon for shooting arrows, consisting of an arch of flexible wood, plastic, metal, etc bent by a string (**bowstring**) fastened at each end. See also **crossbow 2** (*of a violin*) a long slightly curved stick across which are stretched strands of horsehair, used for playing the strings of a violin, viola, cello, or related instrument **b** a stroke with such a stick **3 a** a decorative interlacing of ribbon or other fabrics, usually having two loops and two loose ends **b** the knot forming such an interlacing; bowknot **4 a** something that is curved, bent, or arched **b** (*in combination*): *rainbow*; *oxbow*; *saddlebow* **5** a person who uses a bow and arrow; archer **6** *US* **a** a frame of a pair of spectacles **b** a sidepiece of the frame of a pair of spectacles that curls round behind the ear **7** a metal ring forming the handle of a pair of scissors or of a large old-fashioned key **8** *architect* part of a building curved in the form of a bow. See also **bow window** ▷ *vb* **9** to form or cause to form a curve or curves **10** to make strokes of a bow across (violin

strings) [Old English *boga* arch, bow; related to Old Norse *bogi* a bow, Old High German *bogo*, Old Irish *bocc*, and BOW¹]

bow³ (baʊ) *n* **1** *chiefly nautical* **a** (*often plural*) the forward end or part of a vessel **b** (*as modifier*): *the bow mooring line* **2** *rowing* short for **bowman² 3** *on* the port (*or starboard*) bow *nautical* within 45 degrees to the port (or starboard) of straight ahead **4** a shot across someone's bows *informal* a warning [C15 probably from Low German *boog*; related to Dutch *boeg*, Danish *bov* ship's bow, shoulder; see BOUGH]

bow collector (bəʊ) *n* a sliding current collector, consisting of a bow-shaped spring mounted on a hinged framework, used on trains, etc, to collect current from an overhead-wire. Compare **skate¹** (sense 4)

bow compass (bəʊ) *n* a compass for drawing, in which the legs are joined by a flexible metal bow-shaped spring rather than a hinge, the angle being adjusted by a screw. Also called: **bow-spring compass**

bowdlerize or **bowdlerise** (ˈbaʊdləˌraɪz) *vb* (*tr*) to remove passages or words regarded as indecent from (a play, novel, etc); expurgate [C19 after Thomas *Bowdler* (1754–1825), English editor who published an expurgated edition of Shakespeare]
> ˌbowdleriˈzation or ˌbowdleriˈsation *n*
> ˈbowdlerˌizer or ˈbowdlerˌiser *n* > ˈbowdlerism *n*

bowed (baʊd) *adj* **1** lowered; bent forward; curved: *bowed head*; *bowed back* **2 bowed down** (foll by *by* or *with*) weighed down; troubled: *bowed down by grief*

bowel (ˈbaʊəl) *n* **1** an intestine, esp the large intestine in man **2** (*plural*) innards; entrails **3** (*plural*) the deep or innermost part (esp in the phrase **the bowels of the earth**) **4** (*plural*) *archaic* the emotions, esp of pity or sympathy [C13 from Old French *bouel*, from Latin *botellus* a little sausage, from *botulus* sausage]

bowel movement *n* **1** the discharge of faeces; defecation **2** the waste matter discharged; faeces

bower¹ (ˈbaʊə) *n* **1** a shady leafy shelter or recess, as in a wood or garden; arbour **2** *literary* a lady's bedroom or apartments, esp in a medieval castle; boudoir **3** *literary* a country cottage, esp one regarded as charming or picturesque [Old English *būr* dwelling; related to Old Norse *būr* pantry, Old High German *būr* dwelling] > ˈbowery *adj*

bower² (ˈbaʊə) *n nautical* a vessel's bow anchor [C18 from BOW³ + -ER¹]

bower³ (ˈbaʊə) *n* a jack in euchre and similar card games [C19 from German *Bauer* peasant, jack (in cards)]

bowerbird (ˈbaʊəˌbɜːd) *n* **1** any of various songbirds of the family *Ptilonorhynchidae*, of Australia and New Guinea. The males build bower-like display grounds in the breeding season to attract the females **2** *informal, chiefly Austral* a person who collects miscellaneous objects

Bowery (ˈbaʊərɪ) *n* **the**. a street in New York City noted for its cheap hotels and bars, frequented by vagrants and drunks [C17 from Dutch *bouwerij*, from *bouwen* to farm + *erij* -ERY; see BOOR, BOER]

bowfin (ˈbəʊˌfɪn) *n* a primitive North American freshwater bony fish, *Amia calva*, with an elongated body and a very long dorsal fin: family *Amiidae*

bowhead (ˈbəʊˌhɛd) *n* a large-mouthed arctic whale, *Balaena mysticetus*, that has become rare through overfishing but is now a protected species

bowie knife (ˈbəʊɪ) *n* a stout hunting knife with a short hilt and a guard for the hand [C19 named after Jim *Bowie* (1796–1836), US frontiersman, who popularized it]

bowing (ˈbəʊɪŋ) *n* the technique of using the bow in playing a violin, viola, cello, or related instrument

bowknot (ˈbəʊˌnɒt) *n* a decorative knot usually having two loops and two loose ends; bow

bowl¹ (bəʊl) *n* **1** a round container open at the

top, used for holding liquid, keeping fruit, serving food, etc **2** Also: **bowlful** the amount a bowl will hold **3** the rounded or hollow part of an object, esp of a spoon or tobacco pipe **4** any container shaped like a bowl, such as a sink or lavatory **5** *chiefly US* a bowl-shaped building or other structure, such as a football stadium or amphitheatre **6** a bowl-shaped depression of the land surface. See also **dust bowl 7** *literary* **a** a drinking cup **b** intoxicating drink [Old English *bolla*; related to Old Norse *bolli*, Old Saxon *bollo*]

bowl² (bəʊl) *n* **1** a wooden ball used in the game of bowls, having flattened sides, one side usually being flatter than the other in order to make it run on a curved course **2** a large heavy ball with holes for gripping with the fingers and thumb, used in tenpin bowling ▷ *vb* **3** to roll smoothly or cause to roll smoothly, esp by throwing underarm along the ground **4** (*intr*; usually foll by *along*) to move easily and rapidly, as in a car **5** *cricket* **a** to send (a ball) down the pitch from one's hand towards the batsman, keeping the arm straight while doing so **b** Also: **bowl out** to dismiss (a batsman) by delivering a ball that breaks his wicket **6** (*intr*) to play bowls or tenpin bowling **7** (*tr*) (in tenpin bowling) to score (a specified amount): *he bowled 120* ▷ See also **bowl over**, **bowls** [C15 from French *boule*, ultimately from Latin *bulla* bubble]

bow legs (bəʊ) *pl n* a condition in which the legs curve outwards like a bow between the ankle and the thigh. Also called: **bandy legs** > **bow-legged** (ˈbəʊˈlɛgɪd, ˈbəʊˈlɛgd) *adj*

bowler¹ (ˈbəʊlə) *n* **1** one who bowls in cricket **2** a player at the game of bowls

bowler² (ˈbəʊlə) *n* a stiff felt hat with a rounded crown and narrow curved brim. US and Canadian name: **derby** [C19 named after John *Bowler*, 19th-century London hatter]

bowler³ (ˈbəʊlə) *n Dublin dialect* a dog [perhaps from B(OW-WOW) + (H)OWLER]

bowline (ˈbəʊlɪn) *n nautical* **1** a line for controlling the weather leech of a square sail when a vessel is close-hauled **2 on a bowline** beating close to the wind **3** a knot used for securing a loop that will not slip at the end of a piece of rope [C14 probably from Middle Low German *bōline*, equivalent to BOW³ + LINE¹]

bowling (ˈbəʊlɪŋ) *n* **1** any of various games in which a heavy ball is rolled down a special alley, usually made of wood, at a group of wooden pins, esp the games of tenpin bowling (tenpins) and skittles (ninepins) **2** the game of bowls **3** *cricket* the act of delivering the ball to the batsman **4** (*modifier*) of or relating to bowls or bowling: *a bowling team*

bowling alley *n* **1 a** a long narrow wooden lane down which the ball is rolled in tenpin bowling **b** a similar lane or alley, usually with raised sides, for playing skittles (ninepins) **2** a building having several lanes for tenpin bowling

bowling crease *n cricket* a line marked at the wicket, over which a bowler must not advance fully before delivering the ball

bowling green *n* an area of closely mown turf on which the game of bowls is played

bowl over *vb* (*tr, adverb*) **1** *informal* to surprise (a person) greatly, esp in a pleasant way; astound; amaze: *he was bowled over by our gift* **2** to knock (a person or thing) down; cause to fall over

bowls (bəʊlz) *n* (*functioning as singular*) **1 a** a game played on a bowling green in which a small bowl (the jack) is pitched from a mark and two opponents or opposing teams take turns to roll biased wooden bowls towards it, the object being to finish as near the jack as possible **b** (*as modifier*): *a bowls tournament* **2** skittles or tenpin bowling

bowman¹ (ˈbəʊmən) *n*, *pl* -men an archer
bowman² (ˈbaʊmən) *n*, *pl* -men *nautical* an oarsman at the bow of a boat. Also called: **bow oar**
bow out (baʊ) *vb* (*adverb; usually tr; often foll by of*)

b

to retire or withdraw gracefully

bowsaw ('bəʊˌsɔ:) *n* a saw with a thin blade in a bow-shaped frame

bowse (baʊz) *vb* a variant spelling of **bouse**

bowser ('baʊzə) *n* **1** a tanker containing fuel for aircraft, military vehicles, etc **2** *Austral and NZ obsolete* a petrol pump [originally a US proprietary name, from S. F. *Bowser*, US inventor, who made the first one in 1885]

bowshot ('bəʊˌʃɒt) *n* the distance an arrow travels from the bow

bowsie ('baʊzi:) *or* **bowsey** *n Irish informal* **1** a low-class mean or obstreperous person **2** a drunkard [of unknown origin]

bowsprit ('bəʊsprɪt) *n nautical* a spar projecting from the bow of a vessel, esp a sailing vessel, used to carry the headstay as far forward as possible [c13 from Middle Low German *bōchsprēt*, from *bōch* BOW³ + *sprēt* pole]

Bow Street runner (bəʊ) *n* (in Britain from 1749 to 1829) an officer at Bow Street magistrates' court, London, whose duty was to pursue and arrest criminals

bowstring ('bəʊˌstrɪŋ) *n* the string of an archer's bow, usually consisting of three strands of hemp

bowstring hemp *n* a hemplike fibre obtained from the sansevieria

bow tie (bəʊ) *n* a man's tie tied in a bow, now chiefly in plain black for formal evening wear

bow weight (bəʊ) *n archery* the poundage required to draw a bow to the full length of the arrow

bow window (bəʊ) *n* a bay window in the shape of a curve

bow-wow ('baʊˌwaʊ, -'waʊ) *n* **1** a child's word for **dog 2** an imitation of the bark of a dog ▷ *vb* **3** (*intr*) to bark or imitate a dog's bark

bowyangs ('bəʊjæŋz) *pl n Austral and NZ history* a pair of strings or straps secured round each trouser leg below the knee, worn esp by sheep-shearers and other labourers [c19 from English dialect *bowy-yanks* leggings]

bowyer ('bəʊjə) *n* a person who makes or sells archery bows

box¹ (bɒks) *n* **1** a receptacle or container made of wood, cardboard, etc, usually rectangular and having a removable or hinged lid **2** Also called: **boxful** the contents of such a receptacle or the amount it can contain: *he ate a whole box of chocolates* **3** any of various containers for a specific purpose: *a money box; letter box* **4** (*often in combination*) any of various small cubicles, kiosks, or shelters: *a telephone box or callbox; a sentry box; a signal box on a railway* **5** a separate compartment in a public place for a small group of people, as in a theatre or certain restaurants **6** an enclosure within a courtroom. See **jury box, witness box 7** a compartment for a horse in a stable or a vehicle. See **loosebox, horsebox 8** *Brit* a small country house occupied by sportsmen when following a field sport, esp shooting **9 a** a protective housing for machinery or mechanical parts **b** the contents of such a box **c** (*in combination*): *a gearbox* **10** a shaped device of light tough material worn by sportsmen to protect the genitals, esp in cricket **11** a section of printed matter on a page, enclosed by lines, a border, or white space **12** a central agency to which mail is addressed and from which it is collected or redistributed: *a post-office box; to reply to a box number in a newspaper advertisement* **13** the central part of a computer or the casing enclosing it **14** short for **penalty box 15** *baseball* either of the designated areas for the batter or the pitcher **16** the raised seat on which the driver sits in a horse-drawn coach **17** *NZ* a wheeled container for transporting coal in a mine **18** *Austral and NZ* an accidental mixing of herds or flocks **19** a hole cut into the base of a tree to collect the sap **20** short for **Christmas box 21** a device for dividing water into two or more ditches in an irrigation system **22** an informal name for a **coffin 23** *taboo slang* the female genitals **24** be

a box of birds *NZ* to be very well indeed **25** the box *Brit informal* television **26** think out of the box to think in a different, innovative, or original manner, esp with regard to business practices, products, systems, etc **27** out of the box *Austral informal* outstanding or excellent: *a day out of the box* ▷ *vb* **28** (*tr*) to put into a box **29** (*tr*; usually foll by *in* or *up*) to prevent from moving freely; confine **30** (*tr*; foll by *in*) *printing* to enclose (text) within a ruled frame **31** (*tr*) to make a cut in the base of (a tree) in order to collect the sap **32** (*tr*) *Austral and NZ* to mix (flocks or herds) accidentally **33** (*tr*; sometimes foll by *up*) *NZ* to confuse: *I am all boxed up* **34** *nautical* short for **boxhaul 35** box the compass *nautical* to name the compass points in order [Old English *box*, from Latin *buxus* from Greek *puxos* BOX³] > 'box,like *adj*

box² (bɒks) *vb* **1** (*tr*) to fight (an opponent) in a boxing match **2** (*intr*) to engage in boxing **3** (*tr*) to hit (a person) with the fist; punch or cuff **4** box clever to behave in a careful and cunning way ▷ *n* **5** a punch with the fist, esp on the ear [c14 of uncertain origin; perhaps related to Dutch *boken* to shunt, push into position]

box³ (bɒks) *n* **1** a dense slow-growing evergreen tree or shrub of the genus *Buxus*, esp *B. sempervirens*, which has small shiny leaves and is used for hedges, borders, and garden mazes: family *Buxaceae* **2** the wood of this tree. See **boxwood** (sense 1) **3** any of several trees the timber or foliage of which resembles this tree, esp various species of *Eucalyptus* with rough bark [Old English, from Latin *buxus*]

box beam *n* another name for **box girder**

boxberry ('bɒksbəri) *n, pl* -**ries 1** the fruit of the partridgeberry or wintergreen **2** another name for **partridgeberry** and **wintergreen** (sense 1)

boxboard ('bɒksˌbɔ:d) *n* a tough paperboard made from wood and wastepaper pulp: used for making boxes, etc

box calf *n* black calfskin leather, tanned with chromium salts, having a pattern of fine creases formed by boarding [c20 named after Joseph *Box*, London shoemaker]

box camera *n* a simple box-shaped camera having an elementary lens, shutter, and viewfinder

box canyon *n Western US* a canyon with vertical or almost vertical walls

boxcar ('bɒksˌkɑ:) *n US and Canadian* a closed railway freight van

box chronometer *n nautical* a ship's chronometer, supported on gimbals in a wooden box

box coat *n* **1** a plain short coat that hangs loosely from the shoulders **2** a heavy overcoat, worn formerly by coachmen

box cutter *n* a knife-like tool with a short retractable blade

box elder *n* a medium-sized fast-growing widely cultivated North American maple, *Acer negundo*, which has compound leaves with lobed leaflets. Also called: **ash-leaved maple**

boxer ('bɒksə) *n* **1** a person who boxes, either professionally or as a hobby; pugilist **2** a medium-sized smooth-haired breed of dog with a short nose and a docked tail

Boxer ('bɒksə) *n* **a** a member of a nationalistic Chinese secret society that led an unsuccessful rebellion in 1900 against foreign interests in China **b** (*as modifier*): *the Boxer Rebellion* [c18 rough translation of Chinese *I Ho Ch'üan*, literally: virtuous harmonious fist, altered from *I Ho T'uan* virtuous harmonious society]

boxercise ('bɒksəˌsaɪz) *n* a system of sustained exercises combining boxing movements with aerobic activities

boxer shorts *pl n* men's underpants shaped like shorts but having a front opening. Also called: **boxers**

boxfish ('bɒksˌfɪʃ) *n, pl* -**fish** *or* -**fishes** another name for **trunkfish**

box-fresh *adj* unused or unspoiled; straight from the packaging

box girder *n* **a** a girder that is hollow and square or rectangular in shape **b** (*as modifier*): *a box-girder bridge*. Also called: **box beam**

Boxgrove man ('bɒksgrəʊv) *n* a type of primitive man, probably *Homo heidelbergensis* (see **Heidelberg man**) and probably dating from the Middle Palaeolithic period some 500 000 years ago; remains were found at Boxgrove in West Sussex in 1993 and 1995

boxhaul ('bɒksˌhɔ:l) *vb nautical* to bring (a square-rigger) onto a new tack by backwinding the foresails and steering hard round

boxing ('bɒksɪŋ) *n* **a** the act, art, or profession of fighting with the fists, esp the modern sport practised under Queensberry rules **b** (*as modifier*): *a boxing enthusiast*

Boxing Day *n Brit* the first day (traditionally and strictly, the first weekday) after Christmas, observed as a holiday [c19 from the custom of giving Christmas boxes to tradesmen and staff on this day]

boxing glove *n* one of a pair of thickly padded mittens worn for boxing

box jellyfish *n* any of various highly venomous jellyfishes of the order *Cubomedusae*, esp *Chironex fleckeri*, of Australian tropical waters, having a cuboidal body with tentacles hanging from each of the lower corners. Also called (Austral): **sea wasp**

box junction *n* (in Britain) a road junction having yellow cross-hatching painted on the road surface. Vehicles may only enter the hatched area when their exit is clear

box kite *n* a kite with a boxlike frame open at both ends

box number *n* **1** the number of an individual pigeonhole at a newspaper to which replies to an advertisement may be addressed **2** the number of an individual pigeonhole at a post office from which mail may be collected

box office *n* **1** an office at a theatre, cinema, etc, where tickets are sold **2** the receipts from a play, film, etc **3 a** the public appeal of an actor or production: *the musical was bad box office* **b** (*as modifier*): *a box-office success*

box pleat *n* a flat double pleat made by folding under the fabric on either side of it

boxroom ('bɒksˌru:m, -ˌrʊm) *n* a small room or large cupboard in which boxes, cases, etc, may be stored

box seat *n* **1** a seat in a theatre box **2** in the box seat *Brit, Austral, and NZ* in the best position

box spanner *n* a spanner consisting of a steel cylinder with a hexagonal end that fits over a nut: used esp to turn nuts in positions that are recessed or difficult of access

box spring *n* a coiled spring contained in a boxlike frame, used as base for mattresses, chairs, etc

boxthorn ('bɒksˌθɔ:n) *n* another name for **matrimony vine**

boxwood ('bɒksˌwʊd) *n* **1** the hard close-grained yellow wood of the box tree, used to make tool handles, small turned or carved articles, etc **2** the box tree

boxy ('bɒksɪ) *adj* squarish or chunky in style or appearance: *a boxy square-cut jacket*

boy (bɔɪ) *n* **1** a male child; lad; youth **2** a man regarded as immature or inexperienced: *he's just a boy when it comes to dealing with women* **3** See **old boy 4** *informal* a group of men, esp a group of friends **5** *usually derogatory* (esp in former colonial territories) a Black or native male servant of any age **6** *Austral* a jockey or apprentice **7** short for **boyfriend 8** boys will be boys youthful indiscretion or exuberance must be expected and tolerated **9** jobs for the boys *informal* appointment of one's supporters to posts, without reference to their qualifications or ability **10** the boy *Irish informal* the right tool for a particular task: *that's the boy to cut it* ▷ *interj* **11** an exclamation of surprise, pleasure, contempt, etc: *boy, is he going to be sorry!* [c13 (in the sense: male servant; c14 young male): of uncertain origin; perhaps from Anglo-French *abuié* fettered (unattested), from Latin *boia* fetter]

boyar ('bəʊjɑː, 'bɔɪə) *n* a member of an old order of Russian nobility, ranking immediately below the princes: abolished by Peter the Great [c16 from Old Russian *boyarin*, from Old Slavonic *boljarinŭ*, probably from Old Turkic *boila* a title]

boy band *n* an all-male vocal pop group created to appeal to a young audience

boycott ('bɔɪkɒt) *vb* **1** (*tr*) to refuse to have dealings with (a person, organization, etc) or refuse to buy (a product) as a protest or means of coercion: *to boycott foreign produce* ▷ *n* **2** an instance or the use of boycotting [c19 after Captain C. C. *Boycott* (1832–97), Irish land agent for the Earl of Erne, County Mayo, Ireland, who was a victim of such practices for refusing to reduce rents]

boyf (bɔɪf) *n* slang a boyfriend

boyfriend ('bɔɪˌfrɛnd) *n* a male friend with whom a person is romantically or sexually involved; sweetheart or lover

boyhood ('bɔɪhʊd) *n* the state or time of being a boy: *his boyhood was happy*

boyish ('bɔɪɪʃ) *adj* of or like a boy in looks, behaviour, or character, esp when regarded as attractive or endearing: *a boyish smile* > 'boyishly *adv* > 'boyishness *n*

Boyle's law *n* the principle that the pressure of a gas varies inversely with its volume at constant temperature [c18 named after Robert *Boyle* (1627–91), Irish scientist]

boy-meets-girl *adj* conventionally or trivially romantic: *a boy-meets-girl story*

Boyne (bɔɪn) *n* a river in the E Republic of Ireland, rising in the Bog of Allen and flowing northeast to the Irish Sea: William III of England defeated the deposed James II in a battle (**Battle of the Boyne**) on its banks in 1690, completing the overthrow of the Stuart cause in Ireland. Length: about 112 km (70 miles)

boyo ('bɔɪəʊ) *n* Brit informal a boy or young man: often used in direct address [from Irish and Welsh]

Boyoma Falls (bɔɪ'əʊmə) *pl n* a series of seven cataracts in the NE Democratic Republic of Congo (formerly Zaïre), on the upper River Congo: forms an unnavigable stretch of 90 km (56 miles), which falls 60 m (200 ft). Former name: **Stanley Falls**

boy racer *n* informal **a** a young man who drives his car aggressively and at inappropriately high speeds ▷ *b* (*as modifier*): *the boy-racer market*

Boys' Brigade *n* (in Britain) an organization for boys, founded in 1883, with the aim of promoting discipline and self-respect

boy scout *n* See **Scout**

boysenberry ('bɔɪzˀnbəri) *n, pl* -ries **1** a type of bramble: a hybrid of the loganberry and various blackberries and raspberries **2** the large red edible fruit of this plant [c20 named after Rudolph *Boysen*, American botanist who developed it]

boysy ('bɔɪzɪ) *adj* informal suited to or typical of boys or young men: *done in a matey, boysy way*

Bozcaada (ˌbɒzdʒaːˈda) *n* the Turkish name for **Tenedos**

Bozen ('boːtsən) *n* the German name for **Bolzano**

bozo ('bəʊzəʊ) *n, pl* -zos US slang a man, esp a stupid one [c20 of uncertain origin; perhaps based on BEAU]

bp abbreviation for **1** (of alcoholic density) below proof **2** boiling point **3** bishop

BP abbreviation for **1** blood pressure **2** British Pharmacopoeia

BPC abbreviation for British Pharmaceutical Codex

B.P.E. (in the US and Canada) abbreviation for Bachelor of Physical Education

BPharm abbreviation for Bachelor of Pharmacy

BPhil abbreviation for Bachelor of Philosophy

bpi abbreviation for bits per inch (used of a computer tape or disk surface)

BPR abbreviation for **business process re-engineering**

bps computing abbreviation for bits per second (of transmitted information)

b.pt. abbreviation for boiling point

Bq symbol for becquerel(s)

br abbreviation for **1** brother **2** Also: B/R bills receivable **3** the internet domain name for Brazil

Br 1 abbreviation for (in a religious order) Brother **2** ▷ the chemical symbol for bromine

BR 1 (formerly) abbreviation for British Rail **2** international car registration for Brazil

Br. abbreviation for **1** Britain **2** British

B/R or **br** abbreviation for bills receivable

bra¹ (brɑː) *n* short for **brassiere**

bra² (brɑː) South African informal another word for **bro²**

braai (braɪ) South African ▷ *vb* **1** to grill or roast (meat) over open coals ▷ *n* **2** short for **braaivleis** [Afrikaans]

braaivleis ('braɪˌfleɪs) *n* South African **1** a picnic at which meat is cooked over an open fire; a barbecue **2** the meat cooked at such a barbecue [from Afrikaans *braai* roast + *vleis* meat]

braata ('brɑːtə) or **braatas** ('brɑːtəs) *n* Caribbean a small portion added to a purchase of food by a market vendor, to encourage the customer to return. Also called: **broughta, broughtas** [perhaps from Spanish *barata* a bargain]

Brabant (brə'bænt) *n* **1** a former duchy of W Europe: divided when Belgium became independent (1830), the south forming the Belgian provinces of Antwerp and Brabant and the north forming the province of North Brabant in the Netherlands **2** a former province of central Belgium; replaced in 1995 by the provinces **Flemish Brabant** and **Walloon Brabant**

brabble ('bræbˀl) *vb, n* a rare word for **squabble** [c16 from Middle Dutch *brabbelen* to jabber] > 'brabbler *n*

braccate ('brækeɪt) *adj* (of birds) having feathered legs [from Latin *braccātus*, from *brāccae* breeches + -ATE¹]

brace (breɪs) *n* **1** In full: **hand brace** a hand tool for drilling holes, with a socket to hold the drill at one end and a cranked handle by which the tool can be turned. See also **brace and bit 2** something that steadies, binds, or holds up another thing **3** a structural member, such as a beam or prop, used to stiffen a framework **4** a sliding loop, usually of leather, attached to the cords of a drum: used to change its tension **5** a pair; two, esp of game birds: *a brace of partridges* **6** either of a pair of characters, { }, used for connecting lines of printing or writing or as a third sign of aggregation in complex mathematical or logical expressions that already contain parentheses and square brackets **7** Also called: **accolade** a line or bracket connecting two or more staves of music **8** (*often plural*) an appliance of metal bands and wires that can be tightened to maintain steady pressure on the teeth for correcting uneven alignment **9** *med* any of various appliances for supporting the trunk, a limb, or teeth **10** another word for **bracer² 11** (in square-rigged sailing ships) a rope that controls the movement of a yard and thus the position of a sail **12** See **braces** ▷ *vb* (*mainly tr*) **13** to provide, strengthen, or fit with a brace **14** to steady or prepare (oneself or something) as before an impact **15** (*also intr*) to stimulate; freshen; invigorate: *sea air is bracing* **16** to control the horizontal movement of (the yards of a square-rigged sailing ship) [c14 from Old French: the two arms, from Latin *bracchia* arms]

brace and bit *n* a hand tool for boring holes, consisting of a cranked handle into which a drilling bit is inserted

bracelet ('breɪslɪt) *n* **1** an ornamental chain worn around the arm or wrist **2** an expanding metal band for a wristwatch. Related adjective:

armillary [c15 from Old French, from *bracel*, literally: a little arm, from Latin *bracchium* arm; see BRACE]

bracelets ('breɪslɪts) *pl n* a slang name for **handcuffs**

bracer¹ ('breɪsə) *n* **1** a person or thing that braces **2** informal a tonic, esp an alcoholic drink taken as a tonic

bracer² ('breɪsə) *n* archery, fencing a leather guard worn to protect the arm [c14 from Old French *braciere*, from *braz* arm, from Latin *bracchium* arm]

braces ('breɪsɪz) *pl n* Brit a pair of straps worn over the shoulders by men for holding up the trousers. US and Canadian word: **suspenders**

brach (brætʃ) or **brachet** ('brætʃɪt) *n* archaic a bitch hound [c14 back formation from *brachez* hunting dogs, from Old French, plural of *brachet*, of Germanic origin; compare Old High German *braccho* hound]

brachah (bra'xa) or **brocho** *n* Judaism Hebrew terms usually translated as "blessing". See **blessing** (sense 4)

brachial ('breɪkɪəl, 'bræk-) *adj* of or relating to the arm or to an armlike part or structure

brachiate *adj* ('breɪkɪɪt, -ˌeɪt, 'bræk-) **1** botany having widely divergent paired branches ▷ *vb* ('breɪkɪˌeɪt, 'bræk-) **2** (*intr*) (of some arboreal apes and monkeys) to swing by the arms from one hold to the next [c19 from Latin *bracchiātus* with armlike branches] > ˌbrachi'ation *n*

brachio- or before a vowel **brachi-** combining form indicating a brachium: *brachiopod*

brachiocephalic (ˌbreɪkɪəʊsɪ'fælɪk) *adj* of, relating to, or supplying the arm and head: *brachiocephalic artery*

brachiopod ('breɪkɪəˌpɒd, 'bræk-) *n* any marine invertebrate animal of the phylum *Brachiopoda*, having a ciliated feeding organ (lophophore) and a shell consisting of dorsal and ventral valves. Also called: **lamp shell**. See also **bryozoan** [c19 from New Latin *Brachiopoda*; see BRACHIUM, -POD]

brachiosaurus (ˌbreɪkɪə'sɔːrəs) *n* a dinosaur of the genus *Brachiosaurus*, up to 30 metres long: the largest land animal ever known. See also **sauropod**

brachistochrone (brə'kɪstəˌkrəʊn) *n* maths the curve between two points through which a body moves under the force of gravity in a shorter time than for any other curve; the path of quickest descent [c18 from Greek *brakhistos*, superlative of *brakhus* short + *chronos* time]

brachium ('breɪkɪəm, 'bræk-) *n, pl* -chia (-kɪə) **1** anatomy the arm, esp the upper part **2** a corresponding part, such as a wing, in an animal **3** biology a branching or armlike part [c18 New Latin, from Latin *bracchium* arm, from Greek *brakhīōn*]

brachy- combining form indicating something short: *brachycephalic* [from Greek *brakhus* short]

brachycephalic (ˌbrækɪsɪ'fælɪk) *adj* also **brachycephalous** (ˌbrækɪ'sɛfələs) **1** having a head nearly as broad from side to side as from front to back, esp one with a cephalic index over 80 ▷ *n* **2** an individual with such a head ▷ Compare **dolichocephalic, mesocephalic**. > ˌbrachy'cephaly or ˌbrachy'cephalism *n*

brachycerous (bræ'kɪsərəs) *adj* (of insects) having short antennae

brachydactylic (ˌbrækɪdæk'tɪlɪk) or **brachydactylous** (ˌbrækɪ'dæktɪləs) *adj* having abnormally short fingers or toes > ˌbrachy'dactyly or ˌbrachy'dactyl,ism *n*

brachylogy (bræ'kɪlədʒɪ) *n, pl* -gies **1** a concise style in speech or writing **2** a colloquial shortened form of expression that is not the result of a regular grammatical process. *the omission of "good" in the expression "Afternoon" is a brachylogy* > bra'chylogous *adj*

brachyodont ('brækɪəˌdɒnt) *adj* (of mammals, such as humans) having teeth with short crowns

brachypterous (bræ'kɪptərəs) *adj* having very short or incompletely developed wings:

b

brachypterous insects > bra'chypterism *n*

brachytherapy (ˌbrækɪ'θɛrəpɪ) *n* a form of radiotherapy in which sealed sources of radioactive material are inserted temporarily into body cavities or directly into tumours

brachyuran (ˌbrækɪ'jʊərən) *n* **1** any decapod crustacean of the group (formerly suborder) *Brachyura*, which includes the crabs ▷ *adj* **2** of, relating to, or belonging to the *Brachyura* [C19 from New Latin *Brachyura* (literally: short-tailed creatures), from BRACHY- + Greek *oura* tail]

bracing ('breɪsɪŋ) *adj* **1** refreshing; stimulating; invigorating: *the air here is bracing* ▷ *n* **2** a system of braces used to strengthen or support: *the bracing supporting the building is perfectly adequate* > 'bracingly *adv*

bracken ('brækən) *n* **1** Also called: **brake** any of various large coarse ferns, esp *Pteridium aquilinum*, having large fronds with spore cases along the undersides and extensive underground stems **2** a clump of any of these ferns [C14 of Scandinavian origin; compare Swedish *bräken*, Danish *bregne*]

bracket ('brækɪt) *n* **1** an L-shaped or other support fixed to a wall to hold a shelf, etc **2** one or more wall shelves carried on brackets **3** *architect* a support projecting from the side of a wall or other structure. See also **corbel, ancon, console² 4** Also called: **square bracket** either of a pair of characters, [ ], used to enclose a section of writing or printing to separate it from the main text **5** a general name for **parenthesis, square bracket** and **brace** (sense 6) **6** a group or category falling within or between certain defined limits: *the lower income bracket* **7** the distance between two preliminary shots of artillery fire in range-finding **8** a skating figure consisting of two arcs meeting at a point, tracing the shape ⅄ ▷ *vb* (*tr*) **-kets, -keting, -keted 9** to fix or support by means of a bracket or brackets **10** to put (written or printed matter) in brackets, esp as being irrelevant, spurious, or bearing a separate relationship of some kind to the rest of the text **11** to couple or join (two lines of text, etc) with a brace **12** (often foll by *with*) to group or class together: *to bracket Marx with the philosophers* **13** to adjust (artillery fire) until the target is hit [C16 from Old French *braguette* codpiece, diminutive of *bragues* breeches, from Old Provençal *braga*, from Latin *brāca* breeches]

bracket fungus *n* any saprotroph or parasitic fungus of the basidiomycetous family *Polyporaceae*, growing as a shelflike mass (bracket) from tree trunks and producing spores in vertical tubes in the bracket

bracketing ('brækɪtɪŋ) *n* **1** a set of brackets **2** *photog* a technique in which a series of test pictures are taken at different exposure levels in order to obtain the optimum exposure

brackish ('brækɪʃ) *adj* (of water) slightly briny or salty [C16 from Middle Dutch *brac* salty; see -ISH] > 'brackishness *n*

Bracknell ('bræknəl) *n* a town in SE England, in Bracknell Forest unitary authority, Berkshire, designated a new town in 1949. Pop: 70 795 (2001)

Bracknell Forest *n* a unitary authority in SE England, in E Berkshire. Pop: 110 100 (2003 est). Area: 109 sq km (42 sq miles)

bract (brækt) *n* a specialized leaf, usually smaller than the foliage leaves, with a single flower or inflorescence growing in its axil [C18 from New Latin *bractea*, Latin: thin metal plate, gold leaf, variant of *brattea*, of obscure origin] > 'bracteal *adj* > 'bractless *adj*

bracteate ('bræktɪɪt, -ˌeɪt) *adj* **1** (of a plant) having bracts ▷ *n* **2** *archaeol* a fine decorated dish or plate of precious metal [C19 from Latin *bracteātus* gold-plated; see BRACT]

bracteole ('bræktɪˌəʊl) *n* a secondary bract subtending a flower within an inflorescence. Also called: 'bractlet [C19 from New Latin *bracteola*, from *bractea* thin metal plate; see BRACT] > 'bracteolate *adj*

brad (bræd) *n* a small tapered nail having a small head that is either symmetrical or formed on one side only [Old English *brord* point, prick; related to Old Norse *broddr* spike, sting, Old High German *brort* edge]

bradawl ('bræd,ɔːl) *n* an awl used to pierce wood, leather, or other materials for the insertion of brads, screws, etc

Bradford ('brædfəd) *n* **1** an industrial city in N England, in Bradford unitary authority, West Yorkshire: a centre of the woollen industry from the 14th century and of the worsted trade from the 18th century; university (1966). Pop: 293 717 (2001) **2** a unitary authority in West Yorkshire. Pop: 477 800 (2003 est). Area: 370 sq km (143 sq miles)

Bradford score *n* a measure of the amount of time during which an employee is absent from work, based on assigning a number of points according to the frequency and length of absences

Bradshaw ('brædˌʃɔː) *n* a British railway timetable, published annually from 1839 to 1961 [C19 named after its original publisher, George Bradshaw (1801–53)]

brady- *combining form* indicating slowness: *bradycardia* [from Greek *bradus* slow]

bradycardia (ˌbrædɪ'kɑːdɪə) *n pathol* an abnormally low rate of heartbeat. Compare **tachycardia**. > **bradycardiac** (ˌbrædɪ'kɑːdɪˌæk) *adj*

bradykinesia (ˌbrædɪkɪ'niːzɪə) *n physiol* abnormal slowness of physical movement, esp as an effect of Parkinson's disease [C20 from BRADY- + Greek *kinēsis* motion]

bradykinin (ˌbrædɪ'kaɪnɪn, ˌbreɪdɪ-) *n* a peptide in blood plasma that dilates blood vessels and causes contraction of smooth muscles. Formula: $C_{50}H_{73}N_{15}O_{11}$ [C20 from BRADY- + Greek *kin(ēsis)* motion + -IN]

brae (breɪ; *Scot* bre) *n Scot* **1** a hill or hillside; slope **2** (*plural*) an upland area: *the Gleniffer Braes* [C14 *bra*; related to Old Norse *brā* eyelash, Old High German *brāwa* eyelid, eyebrow; compare BROW]

Braeburn ('breɪˌbɜːn) *n* a variety of eating apple from New Zealand having sweet flesh and green and red skin

braeheid (bre'hiːd) *n Scot* the summit of a hill

Braemar (ˌbreɪ'mɑː) *n* a village in NE Scotland, in Aberdeenshire; Balmoral Castle is nearby: site of the Royal Braemar Gathering, an annual Highland Games meeting

brag (bræg) *vb* **brags, bragging, bragged 1** to speak of (one's own achievements, possessions, etc) arrogantly and boastfully ▷ *n* **2** boastful talk or behaviour, or an instance of this **3** something boasted of: *his brag was his new car* **4** a braggart; boaster **5** a card game: an old form of poker [C13 of unknown origin] > 'bragger *n* > 'bragging *n, adj* > 'braggingly *adv*

Braga (*Portuguese* 'bra:gə) *n* a city in N Portugal: capital of the Roman province of Lusitania; 12th-century cathedral, seat of the Primate of Portugal. Pop: 164 193 (2001). Ancient name: Bracara Augusta

braggadocio (ˌbrægə'dəʊtʃɪˌəʊ) *n, pl* **-os 1** vain empty boasting **2** a person who boasts; braggart [C16 from *Braggadocchio*, name of a boastful character in Spenser's *Faerie Queene*; probably from BRAGGART + Italian *-occhio* (augmentative suffix)]

braggadocious (ˌbrægə'dəʊʃəs) *adj US informal* boastful [C20 from BRAGGADOCIO]

braggart ('brægət) *n* **1** a person who boasts loudly or exaggeratedly; bragger ▷ *adj* **2** boastful [C16 see BRAG]

Bragg's law *n* the principle that when a beam of X-rays of wavelength λ enters a crystal, the maximum intensity of the reflected ray occurs when sin θ = *n*λ/2*d*, where θ is the complement of the angle of incidence, *n* is a whole number, and *d* is the distance between layers of atoms [C20 named after Sir William Henry Bragg (1862–1942), and his son, Sir Lawrence Bragg (1890–1971), British physicists]

Bragi ('brɑːgɪ) or **Brage** ('brɑːgə) *n Norse myth* the god of poetry and music, son of Odin

Brahma¹ ('brɑːmə) *n* **1** a Hindu god: in later Hindu tradition, the Creator who, with Vishnu, the Preserver, and Shiva, the Destroyer, constitutes the triad known as the Trimurti **2** another name for **Brahman** (sense 2) [from Sanskrit, from *brahman* praise]

Brahma² ('brɑːmə, 'breɪ-) *n* a heavy breed of domestic fowl with profusely feathered legs and feet [C19 shortened from *Brahmaputra* (river); from its having been imported originally from Lakhimpur, a town on the Brahmaputra]

Brahman ('brɑːmən) *n, pl* **-mans 1** (*sometimes not capital*) Also called (esp formerly): **Brahmin** a member of the highest or priestly caste in the Hindu caste system **2** *Hinduism* the ultimate and impersonal divine reality of the universe, from which all being originates and to which it returns **3** another name for **Brahma¹** [C14 from Sanskrit *brāhmana*, from *brahman* prayer] > Brahmanic (brɑː'mænɪk) or Brah'manical *adj*

Brahmana ('brɑːmənə) *n Hinduism* any of a number of sacred treatises added to each of the Vedas

Brahmani ('brɑːmənɪ) *n, pl* **-nis** (*sometimes not capital*) a woman of the Brahman caste

Brahmanism ('brɑːməˌnɪzəm) or **Brahminism** *n* (*sometimes not capital*) **1** the religious and social system of orthodox Hinduism, characterized by diversified pantheism, the caste system, and the sacrifices and family ceremonies of Hindu tradition **2** the form of Hinduism prescribed in the Vedas, Brahmanas, and Upanishads > 'Brahmanist or 'Brahminist *n*

Brahmaputra (ˌbrɑːmə'puːtrə) *n* a river in S Asia, rising in SW Tibet as the Tsangpo and flowing through the Himalayas and NE India to join the Ganges at its delta in Bangladesh. Length: about 2900 km (1800 miles)

Brahmin ('brɑːmɪn) *n, pl* **-min** or **-mins 1** the older spelling of **Brahman** (a Hindu priest) **2** (in the US) a highly intelligent or socially exclusive person, esp a member of one of the older New England families **3** an intellectual or social snob > Brah'minic or Brah'minical *adj*

Brahui (brɑː'huːɪ) *n* **1** a language spoken in Pakistan, forming an isolated branch of the Dravidian family **2** (*pl* **-hui** or **-huis**) a member of the people that speaks this language

braid¹ (breɪd) *vb* (*tr*) **1** to interweave several strands of (hair, thread, etc); plait **2** to make by such weaving: *to braid a rope* **3** to dress or bind (the hair) with a ribbon, etc **4** to decorate with an ornamental trim or border: *to braid a skirt* ▷ *n* **5** a length of hair, fabric, etc, that has been braided; plait **6** narrow ornamental tape of woven silk, wool, etc [Old English *bregdan* to move suddenly, weave together; compare Old Norse *bregtha*, Old High German *brettan* to draw a sword] > 'braider *n*

braid² (bred, breɪd) *Scot* ▷ *adj* **1** broad ▷ *adv* **2** broadly; frankly [Scot variant of BROAD]

braided ('breɪdɪd) *adj* (of a river or stream) flowing in several shallow interconnected channels separated by banks of deposited material

braiding ('breɪdɪŋ) *n* **1** braids collectively **2** work done in braid **3** a piece of braid

brail (breɪl) *nautical* ▷ *n* **1** one of several lines fastened to the leech of a fore-and-aft sail to aid in furling it ▷ *vb* **2** (*tr*; sometimes foll by *up*) to furl (a fore-and-aft sail) using brails [C15 from Old French *braiel*, from Medieval Latin *brācāle* belt for breeches, from Latin *brāca* breeches]

Brăila (*Romanian* brə'ila) *n* a port in E Romania: belonged to Turkey (1544–1828). Pop: 192 000 (2005 est)

Braille (breɪl) *n* **1** a system of writing for the blind consisting of raised dots that can be interpreted by touch, each dot or group of dots representing a letter, numeral, or punctuation mark **2** any writing produced by this method. Compare **Moon¹**

▷ *vb* **3** (*tr*) to print or write using this method
brain (breɪn) *n* **1** the soft convoluted mass of nervous tissue within the skull of vertebrates that is the controlling and coordinating centre of the nervous system and the seat of thought, memory, and emotion. It includes the cerebrum, brainstem, and cerebellum. Technical name: **encephalon**. Related adjectives: **cerebral, encephalic 2** the main neural bundle or ganglion of certain invertebrates **3** (*often plural*) *informal* intellectual ability: *he's got brains* **4** *informal* shrewdness or cunning **5** *informal* an intellectual or intelligent person **6** (*usually plural; functioning as singular*) *informal* a person who plans and organizes an undertaking or is in overall control of an organization, etc **7** an electronic device, such as a computer, that performs apparently similar functions to the human brain **8** **on the brain** constantly in mind: *I had that song on the brain* **9** **pick someone's brain** to obtain information or ideas from someone ▷ *vb* (*tr*) **10** to smash the skull of **11** *slang* to hit hard on the head [Old English *brægen*; related to Old Frisian *brein*, Middle Low German *bregen*, Greek *brekhmos* forehead]
brainbox ('breɪn,bɒks) *n slang* **1** the skull **2** a clever person
brain candy *n informal* something that is entertaining or enjoyable but lacks depth or significance
brainchild ('breɪn,tʃaɪld) *n, pl* **-children** *informal* an idea or plan produced by creative thought; invention
brain coral *n* a stony coral of the genus *Meandrina*, in which the polyps lie in troughlike thecae resembling the convoluted surface of a human brain
braindead ('breɪn,dɛd) *adj* **1** having suffered brain death **2** *informal* not using or showing intelligence; stupid
brain death *n* irreversible cessation of respiration due to irreparable brain damage, even though the heart may continue beating with the aid of a mechanical ventilator: widely considered as the criterion of death
brain drain *n informal* the emigration of scientists, technologists, academics, etc, for better pay, equipment, or conditions
brainfart ('breɪn,fɑːt) *n informal* an idea that a person voices without much consideration, such as during a brainstorming session
brain fever *n* inflammation of the brain or its covering membranes
brain-fever bird *n* an Indian cuckoo, *Cuculus varius*, that utters a repetitive call
brain fingerprinting *n* a technique in which sensors worn on the head are used to measure the involuntary brain activity of someone in response to certain images or pieces of evidence pertaining to a crime
brain gain *n informal* the immigration into a country of scientists, technologists, academics, etc, attracted by better pay, equipment, or conditions
brainiac ('breɪnɪ,æk) *n informal* a highly intelligent person [c20 from a super-intelligent character in an American comic strip]
brainless ('breɪnlɪs) *adj* stupid or foolish ▷ 'brainlessly *adv* ▷ 'brainlessness *n*
brainpan ('breɪn,pæn) *n informal* the skull
brainpower ('breɪn,paʊə) *n* intelligence; mental ability
brainsick ('breɪn,sɪk) *adj* relating to or caused by insanity; crazy; mad ▷ 'brain,sickly *adv* ▷ 'brain,sickness *n*
brainstem ('breɪn,stɛm) *n* the stalklike part of the brain consisting of the medulla oblongata, the midbrain, and the pons Varolii
brainstorm ('breɪn,stɔːm) *n* **1** a severe outburst of excitement, often as the result of a transitory disturbance of cerebral activity **2** *Brit informal* a sudden mental aberration **3** *informal* another word for **brainwave**

brainstorming ('breɪn,stɔːmɪŋ) *n* intensive discussion to solve problems or generate ideas
brains trust *n* **1** a group of knowledgeable people who discuss topics in public or on radio or television **2** Also called: **brain trust** *US* a group of experts who advise the government
brain-teaser or **brain-twister** *n informal* a difficult problem
brain up *vb* (*tr*) to make more intellectually demanding or sophisticated: *we need to brain up the curriculum*
brainwash ('breɪn,wɒʃ) *vb* (*tr*) to effect a radical change in the ideas and beliefs of (a person), esp by methods based on isolation, sleeplessness, hunger, extreme discomfort, pain, and the alternation of kindness and cruelty ▷ 'brain,washer *n* ▷ 'brain,washing *n*
brainwave ('breɪn,weɪv) *n informal* a sudden inspiration or idea. Also called: **brainstorm**
brain wave *n* any of the fluctuations of electrical potential in the brain as represented on an electroencephalogram. They vary in frequency from 1 to 30 hertz. See also **alpha rhythm, beta rhythm, delta rhythm**
brainy ('breɪnɪ) *adj* **brainier, brainiest** *informal* clever; intelligent ▷ 'brainily *adv* ▷ 'braininess *n*
braise (breɪz) *vb* to cook (meat, vegetables, etc) by lightly browning in fat and then cooking slowly in a closed pan with a small amount of liquid [c18 from French *braiser*, from Old French *brese* live coals, probably of Germanic origin; compare Old English *brædan*, Old High German *brātan* to roast]
brak[1] (brak) *adj South African* (of water) brackish or salty [c19 Afrikaans]
brak[2] (brak) *n South African* a mongrel dog [c20 from Afrikaans, literally: setter]
brake[1] (breɪk) *n* **1** a (*often plural*) a device for slowing or stopping a vehicle, wheel, shaft, etc, or for keeping it stationary, esp by means of friction. See also **drum brake, disc brake, hydraulic brake, air brake, handbrake** b (*as modifier*): *the brake pedal* **2** a machine or tool for crushing or breaking flax or hemp to separate the fibres **3** Also called: **brake harrow** a heavy harrow for breaking up clods **4** short for **brake van 5** short for **shooting brake 6** Also spelt: **break** an open four-wheeled horse-drawn carriage **7** an obsolete word for the **rack** (an instrument of torture) ▷ *vb* **8** to slow down or cause to slow down, by or as if by using a brake **9** (*tr*) to crush or break up using a brake [c18 from Middle Dutch *braeke*; related to *breken* to BREAK] ▷ 'brakeless *adj*
brake[2] (breɪk) *n* an area of dense undergrowth, shrubs, brushwood, etc; thicket [Old English *bracu*; related to Middle Low German *brake*, Old French *bracon* branch]
brake[3] (breɪk) *n* another name for **bracken** (sense 1). See also **rock brake**
brake[4] (breɪk) *vb archaic, chiefly biblical* a past tense of **break**
brake band *n* a strip of fabric, leather, or metal tightened around a pulley or shaft to act as a brake
brake drum *n* the cast-iron drum attached to the hub of a wheel of a motor vehicle fitted with drum brakes. See also **brake shoe**
brake-fade *n* the decrease in efficiency of braking of a motor vehicle due to overheating of the brakes
brake fluid *n* an oily liquid used to transmit pressure in a hydraulic brake or clutch system
brake horsepower *n* the rate at which an engine does work, expressed in horsepower. It is measured by the resistance of an applied brake. Abbreviation: **bhp**
brake light *n* a red light attached to the rear of a motor vehicle that lights up when the brakes are applied, serving as a warning to following drivers. Also called: **stoplight**
brake lining *n* a curved thin strip of an asbestos composition riveted to a brake shoe to provide it with a renewable surface

brakeman ('breɪkmən) *n, pl* **-men 1** *US and Canadian* a crew member of a goods or passenger train. His duties include controlling auxiliary braking power and inspecting the train **2** the person at the back of a two- or four-man bobsleigh, who operates the brake
brake pad *n* the flat metal casting, together with the bound friction material, in a disc brake
brake parachute *n* a parachute attached to the rear of a vehicle and opened to assist braking. Also called: **brake chute, parachute brake, parabrake**
brake shoe *n* **1** the curved metal casting to which the brake lining is riveted in a drum brake **2** the curved metal casting together with the attached brake lining. Sometimes (for both senses) shortened to: **shoe**
brakesman ('breɪksmən) *n, pl* **-men** a pithead winch operator
brake van *n railways, Brit* the coach or vehicle from which the guard applies the brakes; guard's van
Brakpan ('bræk,pæn) *n* a city in E South Africa: gold-mining centre. Pop: 62 116 (2001)
bramble ('bræmbəl) *n* **1** any of various prickly herbaceous plants or shrubs of the rosaceous genus *Rubus*, esp the blackberry. See also **stone bramble 2** *Scot* a blackberry b (*as modifier*): *bramble jelly* **3** any of several similar and related shrubs ▷ *vb* (*intr*) **4** to gather blackberries [Old English *brǣmbel*; related to Old Saxon *brāmal*, Old High German *brāmo*] ▷ 'brambly *adj*
brambling ('bræmblɪŋ) *n* a Eurasian finch, *Fringilla montifringilla*, with a speckled head and back and, in the male, a reddish brown breast and darker wings and tail
Bramley ('bræmlɪ) or **Bramley's seedling** *n* a variety of cooking apple having juicy firm flesh [c19 named after Matthew Bramley, 19th-century English butcher, said to have first grown it]
bran (bræn) *n* **1** husks of cereal grain separated from the flour by sifting **2** food prepared from these husks. Related adjective: **furfuraceous** [c13 from Old French, probably of Gaulish origin]
branch (brɑːntʃ) *n* **1** a secondary woody stem arising from the trunk or bough of a tree or the main stem of a shrub **2** a subdivision of the stem or root of any other plant **3** an offshoot or secondary part: *a branch of a deer's antlers* **4** a a subdivision or subsidiary section of something larger or more complex: *branches of learning; branch of the family* b (*as modifier*): *a branch office* **5** *US* any small stream **6** *maths* a section of a curve separated from the rest of the curve by discontinuities or special points **7** Also called: **jump** *computing* a departure from the normal sequence of programmed instructions into a separate program area **8** an alternative route in an atomic or nuclear decay series ▷ *vb* **9** (*intr*) (of a tree or other plant) to produce or possess branches **10** (*intr*; usually foll by *from*) (of stems, roots, etc) to grow and diverge (from another part) **11** to divide or be divided into subsidiaries or offshoots **12** (*intr*; often foll by *off*) to diverge from the main way, road, topic, etc ▷ See also **branch out** [c13 from Old French *branche*, from Late Latin *branca* paw, foot] ▷ 'branchless *adj* ▷ 'branch,like *adj* ▷ 'branchy *adj*
branch- *adj and n combining form* (in zoology) indicating gills: *lamellibranch* [from Latin: BRANCHIA]
branched chain *n chem* an open chain of atoms with one or more side chains attached to it. Compare **straight chain**
branchia ('bræŋkɪə) *n, pl* **-chiae** (-kɪ,iː) a gill in aquatic animals ▷ 'branchi,ate *adj*
branchial ('bræŋkɪəl) *adj* **1** of or relating to the gills of an aquatic animal, esp a fish **2** of or relating to homologous structures in higher vertebrates: *branchial cyst*
branching ('brɑːntʃɪŋ) *n physics* the occurrence of several decay paths (**branches**) in the disintegration of a particular nuclide or the

b

de-excitation of an excited atom. The **branching fraction** (nuclear) or **branching ratio** (atomic) is the proportion of the disintegrating nuclei that follow a particular branch to the total number of disintegrating nuclides

branch instruction *n computing* a machine-language or assembly-language instruction that causes the computer to branch to another instruction

branchiopod ('bræŋkɪəˌpɒd) *n* any crustacean of the mainly freshwater subclass *Branchiopoda*, having flattened limblike appendages for swimming, feeding, and respiration. The group includes the water fleas

branchiostegal (ˌbræŋkɪə'stiːgəl) *adj zoology* of or relating to the operculum covering the gill slits of fish: *branchiostegal membrane; branchiostegal rays* [from BRANCHIA + Greek *stegos* roof]

branch line *n railways* a secondary route to a place or places not served by a main line

branch officer *n* (in the British navy since 1949) any officer who holds warrant

branch out *vb* (*intr, adverb*; often foll by *into*) to expand or extend one's interests: *our business has branched out into computers now*

branch plant *or* **factory** *n Canadian* a plant or factory in Canada belonging to a company whose headquarters are in another country

brand (brænd) *n* **1** a particular product or a characteristic that serves to identify a particular product **2** a trade name or trademark **3** a particular kind or variety: *he had his own brand of humour* **4** an identifying mark made, usually by burning, on the skin of animals or (formerly) slaves or criminals, esp as a proof of ownership **5** an iron heated and used for branding animals, etc **6** a mark of disgrace or infamy; stigma: *he bore the brand of a coward* **7** a burning or burnt piece of wood, as in a fire **8** *archaic or poetic* **a** a flaming torch **b** a sword **9** a fungal disease of garden plants characterized by brown spots on the leaves, caused by the rust fungus *Puccinia arenariae* ▷ *vb* (*tr*) **10** to label, burn, or mark with or as with a brand **11** to place indelibly in the memory: *the scene of slaughter was branded in their minds* **12** to denounce; stigmatize: *they branded him a traitor* **13** to give a product a distinctive identity by means of characteristic design, packaging, etc [Old English *brand-*, related to Old Norse *brandr*, Old High German *brant*; see BURN¹] > 'brander *n*

brandade (*French* brɑ̃ˈdad) *n* a Provençal dish of salt cod puréed with olive oil and milk [French, from Modern Provençal *brandado*, literally, something that has been shaken]

brand awareness *n marketing* the extent to which consumers are aware of a particular product or service

brand contamination *n* the process by which the reputation of a particular brand or product becomes tarnished by adverse publicity

branded ('brændɪd) *adj* identifiable as being the product of a particular manufacturer or marketing company

Brandenburg ('brændənˌbɜːɡ; *German* 'brandənburk) *n* **1** a state in NE Germany, part of East Germany until 1990. A former electorate, it expanded under the Hohenzollerns to become the kingdom of Prussia (1701). The district east of the Oder River became Polish in 1945. Capital: Potsdam. Pop: 2 575 000 (2003 est). Area: 29 481 sq km (11 219 sq miles) **2** a city in NE Germany: former capital of the Prussian province of Brandenburg. Pop: 75 485 (2003 est)

brand extension *n marketing* the practice of using a well-known brand name to promote new products or services in unrelated fields. Also called: **brand stretching**

brand image *n* the attributes of a brand as perceived by potential and actual customers

brandish ('brændɪʃ) *vb* (*tr*) **1** to wave or flourish (a weapon) in a triumphant, threatening, or ostentatious way ▷ *n* **2** a threatening or defiant

flourish [c14 from Old French *brandir*, from *brand* sword, of Germanic origin; compare Old High German *brant* weapon] > 'brandisher *n*

brand leader *n marketing* a product with the highest number of total sales within its category

brandling ('brændlɪŋ) *n* a small red earthworm, *Eisenia foetida* (or *Helodrilus foetidus*), found in manure and used as bait by anglers [c17 from BRAND + -LING¹]

brand name *n* another name for **brand** (sense 2)

brand Nazi *n informal* a person who insists on buying one particular brand of clothing or other commodity

brand-new *adj* absolutely new [c16 from BRAND (n) + -NEW, likened to newly forged iron]

brand stretching *n marketing* another name for **brand extension**

brandy ('brændɪ) *n, pl* -dies **1** an alcoholic drink consisting of spirit distilled from grape wine **2** a distillation of wines made from other fruits: *plum brandy* [c17 from earlier *brandewine*, from Dutch *brandewijn* burnt wine, from *bernen* to burn or distil + *wijn* WINE; compare German *Branntwein*]

brandy bottle *n* another name for a **yellow water lily**

brandy butter *n* butter and sugar creamed together with brandy and served with Christmas pudding, etc

brandy snap *n* a crisp sweet biscuit, rolled into a cylinder after baking and often filled with whipped cream

branks (bræŋks) *pl n* (formerly) an iron bridle used to restrain scolding women [c16 of unknown origin]

branle ('bræn°l) *n* an old French country dance performed in a linked circle [c17 from Old French *branler* to shake, variant of *brandir* to BRANDISH]

brant (brænt) *n, pl* **brants** *or* **brant** *US and Canadian* a small goose, *Branta bernicla*, that has a dark grey plumage and short neck and occurs in most northern coastal regions. Also called (in Britain and certain other countries): **brent goose**

Brantford ('bræntfəd) *n* a city in central Canada, in SW Ontario. Pop: 86 417 (2001)

bran tub *n* (in Britain) a tub containing bran in which small wrapped gifts are hidden, used at parties, fairs, etc

brasco ('bræskəʊ) *n Austral slang* a lavatory [from a toilet manufacturer named *Brass Co*]

brash¹ (bræʃ) *adj* **1** tastelessly or offensively loud, showy, or bold **2** hasty; rash **3** impudent [c19 perhaps influenced by RASH¹] > 'brashly *adv* > 'brashness *n*

brash² (bræʃ) *n* loose rubbish, such as broken rock, hedge clippings, etc; debris [c18 of unknown origin]

brash³ (bræʃ) *n pathol* another name for **heartburn** [c16 perhaps of imitative origin]

brashy ('bræʃɪ) *adj* brashier, brashiest **1** loosely fragmented; rubbishy **2** (of timber) brittle > 'brashness *n*

brasier ('breɪzɪə) *n* a less common spelling of **brazier**

brasil (brə'zɪl) *n* a variant spelling of **brazil**

Brasil (brə'ziːl) *n* the Portuguese spelling of **Brazil**

brasilein (brə'zɪlɪɪn) *n* a variant spelling of **brazilein**

Brasília (brə'zɪljə; *Portuguese* brəzi'liːa) *n* the capital of Brazil (since 1960), on the central plateau: the former capital was Rio de Janeiro. Pop: 3 341 000 (2005 est)

brasilin ('bræzɪlɪn) *n* a variant spelling of **brazilin**

Braşov (*Romanian* bra'ʃov) *n* an industrial city in central Romania: formerly a centre for expatriate Germans, ceded by Hungary to Romania in 1920. Pop: 249 000 (2005 est). Former name (1950–61): Stalin. German name: Kronstadt. Hungarian name: Brassó

brass (brɑːs) *n* **1** an alloy of copper and zinc containing more than 50 per cent of copper. **Alpha brass** (containing less than 35 per cent of zinc) is used for most engineering materials requiring

forging, pressing, etc **Alpha-beta brass** (35–45 per cent zinc) is used for hot working and extrusion. **Beta brass** (45–50 per cent zinc) is used for castings. Small amounts of other metals, such as lead or tin, may be added. Compare **bronze** (sense 1) **2** an object, ornament, or utensil made of brass **3 a** the large family of wind instruments including the trumpet, trombone, French horn, etc, each consisting of a brass tube blown directly by means of a cup- or funnel-shaped mouthpiece **b** (*sometimes functioning as plural*) instruments of this family forming a section in an orchestra **c** (*as modifier*): *a brass ensemble* **4** a renewable sleeve or bored semicylindrical shell made of brass or bronze, used as a liner for a bearing **5** (*functioning as plural*) *informal* important or high-ranking officials, esp military officers: *the top brass*. See also **brass hat 6** *Northern English dialect* money: *where there's muck, there's brass!* **7** *Brit* an engraved brass memorial tablet or plaque, set in the wall or floor of a church **8** *informal* bold self-confidence; cheek; nerve: *he had the brass to ask for more time* **9** *slang* a prostitute **10** (*modifier*) of, consisting of, or relating to brass or brass instruments: *a brass ornament; a brass band*. Related adjective: **brazen** [Old English *bræs*; related to Old Frisian *bres* copper, Middle Low German *bras* metal]

brassard ('bræsɑːd) *or* **brassart** ('bræsət) *n* **1** an identifying armband or badge **2** a piece of armour for the upper arm [c19 from French, from *bras* arm, from Latin BRACHIUM]

brass band *n* See **band¹** (sense 2)

brassbound ('brɑːsˌbaʊnd) *adj* inflexibly entrenched: *brassbound traditions*

brassed off *adj Brit slang* fed up; disgruntled

brasserie ('bræsərɪ) *n* **1** a bar in which drinks and often food are served **2** a small and usually cheap restaurant [c19 from French, from *brasser* to stir, brew]

brass farthing *n Brit informal* something of little or no value: *his opinion isn't worth a brass farthing* [c18 probably coined when farthings were first minted in bronze rather than silver]

brass hat *n Brit informal* a top-ranking official, esp a military officer [c20 from the gold leaf decoration on the peaks of caps worn by officers of high rank]

brassica ('bræsɪkə) *n* any plant of the genus *Brassica*, such as cabbage, rape, turnip, and mustard: family *Brassicaceae* (crucifers) [c19 from Latin: cabbage] > **brassicaceous** (ˌbræsɪ'keɪʃəs) *adj*

brassie *or* **brassy** ('bræsɪ, 'brɑː-) *n, pl* **brassies** *golf* a former name for a club, a No. 2 wood, originally having a brass-plated sole and with a shallower face than a driver to give more loft

brassiere ('bræsɪə, 'bræz-) *n* a woman's undergarment for covering and supporting the breasts. Often shortened to: **bra** [c20 from C17 French: bodice, from Old French *braciere* a protector for the arm, from *braz* arm]

brass neck *n Brit informal* effrontery; nerve

Brassó ('brɒʃoː) *n* the Hungarian name for **Braşov**

brass rubbing *n* **1** the taking of an impression of an engraved brass tablet or plaque by placing a piece of paper over it and rubbing the paper with graphite, heelball, or chalk **2** an impression made in this way

brass tacks *pl n informal* basic realities; hard facts (esp in the phrase **get down to brass tacks**)

brassy ('brɑːsɪ) *adj* brassier, brassiest **1** insolent; brazen **2** flashy; showy **3** (of sound) harsh, strident, or resembling the sound of a brass instrument **4** like brass, esp in colour **5** decorated with or made of brass **6** a variant spelling of **brassie**. > 'brassily *adv* > 'brassiness *n*

brat¹ (bræt) *n* a child, esp one who is ill-mannered or unruly: used contemptuously or playfully [c16 perhaps special use of earlier *brat* rag, from Old English *bratt* cloak, of Celtic origin; related to Old Irish *bratt* cloth, BRAT²]

brat² (bræt) *n Northern English dialect* an apron or overall [from Old English *brat* cloak; related to Old

Irish *bratt* cloth used to cover the body]

Bratislava (ˌbrætɪˈslɑːvə) *n* the capital of Slovakia since 1918, a port on the River Danube; capital of Hungary (1541–1784) and seat of the Hungarian parliament until 1848. Pop: 428 672 (2001). German name: Pressburg. Hungarian name: Pozsony

bratpack (ˈbrætˌpæk) *n* **1** a group of precocious and successful young actors, writers, etc **2** a group of ill-mannered young people > ˈbratˌpacker *n*

brattice (ˈbrætɪs) *n* **1** a partition of wood or treated cloth used to control ventilation in a mine **2** *medieval fortifications* a fixed wooden tower or parapet ▷ *vb* **3** (*tr*) *mining* to fit with a brattice [c13 from Old French *bretesche* wooden tower, from Medieval Latin *breteschia*, probably from Latin *Britō* a Briton]

brattishing (ˈbrætɪʃɪŋ) *n architect* decorative work along the coping or on the cornice of a building [c16 variant of *bratticing*; see BRATTICE]

bratwurst (ˈbrɑːtˌwɜːst; *German* ˈbrɑːtvʊrst) *n* a type of small pork sausage [c20 German, from Old High German, from *brāto* meat + *wurst* sausage; related to Old Saxon *brādo* ham]

braunite (ˈbraʊnaɪt) *n* a brown or black mineral that consists of manganese oxide and silicate and is a source of manganese. Formula: $3Mn_2O_3.MnSiO_3$ [c19 named after A. E. *Braun* (1809–56), German official in the treasury at Gotha]

Braunschweig (ˈbraʊnʃvaik) *n* the German name for **Brunswick**

bravado (brəˈvɑːdəʊ) *n, pl* -**does** *or* -**dos** vaunted display of courage or self-confidence; swagger [c16 from Spanish *bravada* (modern *bravata*), from Old Italian *bravare* to challenge, provoke, from *bravo* wild, BRAVE]

Bravais lattice (ˈbræveɪ, brəˈveɪ) *n crystallog* any of 14 possible space lattices found in crystals [named after Auguste *Bravais*, 19th-century French physicist]

brave (breɪv) *adj* **1 a** having or displaying courage, resolution, or daring; not cowardly or timid **b** (*as collective noun* preceded by the): the brave **2** fine; splendid: *a brave sight; a brave attempt* **3** *archaic* excellent or admirable ▷ *n* **4** a warrior of a Native American tribe **5** an obsolete word for **bully** ▷ *vb* (*tr*) **6** to dare or defy: *to brave the odds* **7** to confront with resolution or courage: *to brave the storm* **8** *obsolete* to make splendid, esp in dress [c15 from French, from Italian *bravo* courageous, wild, perhaps ultimately from Latin *barbarus* BARBAROUS] > ˈbravely *adv* > ˈbraveness *n* > ˈbravery *n*

bravissimo (brɑːˈvɪsɪˌməʊ) *interj* very well done! excellent! [c18 from Italian, superlative of BRAVO]

bravo *interj* **1** (brɑːˈvəʊ) well done! ▷ *n* **2** (brɑːˈvəʊ) *pl* -**vos** a cry of "bravo" **3** (ˈbrɑːvəʊ) *pl* -**voes** *or* -**vos** a hired killer or assassin [c18 from Italian: splendid!; see BRAVE]

Bravo (ˈbrɑːvəʊ) *n communications* a code word for the letter b

bravura (brəˈvjʊərə, -ˈvʊərə) *n* **1** a display of boldness or daring **2** *music* **a** brilliance of execution **b** (*as modifier*): *a bravura passage* [c18 from Italian: spirit, courage, from *bravare* to show off, see BRAVADO]

braw (brɔː, brɑː) *chiefly Scot* ▷ *adj* **1** fine or excellent, esp in appearance or dress ▷ *pl n* **2** best clothes [c16 Scottish variant of BRAVE] > ˈbrawly *adv*

brawl[1] (brɔːl) *n* **1** a loud disagreement or fight **2** *US slang* an uproarious party ▷ *vb* (*intr*) **3** to quarrel or fight noisily; squabble **4** (esp of water) to flow noisily [c14 probably related to Dutch *brallen* to boast, behave aggressively] > ˈbrawler *n* > ˈbrawling *n, adj*

brawl[2] (brɔːl) *n* a dance: the English version of the branle

brawn (brɔːn) *n* **1** strong well-developed muscles **2** physical strength, esp as opposed to intelligence **3** *Brit* a seasoned jellied loaf made

from the head and sometimes the feet of a pig or calf [c14 from Old French *braon* slice of meat, of Germanic origin; compare Old High German *brāto*, Old English *bræd* flesh]

brawny (ˈbrɔːnɪ) *adj* brawnier, brawniest muscular and strong > ˈbrawnily *adv* > ˈbrawniness *n*

Braxton Hicks contractions (ˈbrækstən ˈhɪks) *pl n* painless intermittent contractions of the womb that occur in pregnancy, becoming stronger towards full term [c19 named after J. *Braxton Hicks* (1823–97), British obstetrician]

braxy (ˈbræksɪ) *n* an acute and usually fatal bacterial disease of sheep characterized by high fever, coma, and inflammation of the fourth stomach, caused by infection with *Clostridium septicum* [c18 of unknown origin]

bray[1] (breɪ) *vb* **1** (*intr*) (of a donkey) to utter its characteristic loud harsh sound; heehaw **2** (*intr*) to make a similar sound, as in laughing: *he brayed at the joke* **3** (*tr*) to utter with a loud harsh sound ▷ *n* **4** the loud harsh sound uttered by a donkey **5** a similar loud cry or uproar: *a bray of protest* [c13 from Old French *braire*, probably of Celtic origin] > ˈbrayer *n*

bray[2] (breɪ) *vb* **1** (*tr*) to distribute (ink) over printing type or plates **2** (*tr*) to pound into a powder, as in a mortar **3** *Northern English dialect* to hit or beat (someone or something) hard; bang [c14 from Old French *breier* of Germanic origin; see BREAK] > ˈbrayer *n*

Braz. *abbreviation for* Brazil(ian)

braze[1] (breɪz) *vb* **1** to decorate with, make like, or make of brass **2** to make like brass, as in hardness [Old English *bræsen*, from *bræs* BRASS]

braze[2] (breɪz) *vb* **1** (*tr*) to make a joint between (two metal surfaces) by fusing a layer of brass or high-melting solder between them **2** ▷ *n* the high-melting solder or alloy used in brazing [c16 from Old French: to burn, of Germanic origin; see BRAISE] > ˈbrazer *n*

brazen (ˈbreɪz[ə]n) *adj* **1** shameless and bold **2** made of or resembling brass **3** having a ringing metallic sound like that of a brass trumpet ▷ *vb* (*tr*) **4** (usually foll by *out* or *through*) to face and overcome boldly or shamelessly: *the witness brazened out the prosecutor's questions* **5** to make (oneself, etc) bold or brash [Old English *bræsen*, from *bræs* BRASS] > ˈbrazenly *adv* > ˈbrazenness *n*

brazen-faced *adj* shameless or impudent

brazier[1] *or* **brasier** (ˈbreɪzɪə) *n* a person engaged in brass-working or brass-founding [c14 from Old English *bræsian* to work in brass + -ER[1]] > ˈbraziery *n*

brazier[2] *or* **brasier** (ˈbreɪzɪə) *n* a portable metal receptacle for burning charcoal or coal, used for cooking, heating, etc [c17 from French *brasier*, from *braise* live coals; see BRAISE]

brazil *or* **brasil** (brəˈzɪl) *n* **1** Also called: brazil wood the red wood obtained from various tropical leguminous trees of the genus *Caesalpinia*, such as C. *echinata* of America: used for cabinetwork **2** the red or purple dye extracted from any of these woods. See also **brazilin 3** short for **brazil nut** [c14 from Old Spanish *brasil*, from *brasa* glowing coals, of Germanic origin; referring to the redness of the wood; see BRAISE]

Brazil (brəˈzɪl) *n* a republic in South America, comprising about half the area and half the population of South America: colonized by the Portuguese from 1500 onwards; became independent in 1822 and a republic in 1889; consists chiefly of the tropical Amazon basin in the north, semiarid scrub in the northeast, and a vast central tableland; an important producer of coffee and minerals, esp iron ore. Official language: Portuguese. Religion: Roman Catholic majority. Currency: real. Capital: Brasília. Pop: 180 655 000 (2004 est). Area: 8 511 957 sq km (3 286 470 sq miles)

brazilein *or* **brasilein** (brəˈzɪlɪɪn) *n* a red crystalline solid obtained by the oxidation of brazilin and used as a dye. Formula: $C_{16}H_{12}O_5$ [c19

from German *Brasilein*, from BRAZILIN]

Brazilian (brəˈzɪljən) *adj* **1** of or relating to Brazil or its inhabitants ▷ *n* **2** a native or inhabitant of Brazil

Brazilian bikini wax (brəˈzɪlɪən) *n* the act or instance of removing all or almost all of a woman's pubic hair for cosmetic reasons [c20 reference to the popularity of this treatment in Brazil]

brazilin *or* **brasilin** (ˈbræzɪlɪn) *n* a pale yellow soluble crystalline solid, turning red in alkaline solution, extracted from brazil wood and sappanwood and used in dyeing and as an indicator. Formula: $C_{16}H_{14}O_5$ [c19 from French *brésiline*, from *brésil* brazil wood]

brazil nut *n* **1** a tropical South American tree, *Bertholletia excelsa*, producing large globular capsules, each containing several closely packed triangular nuts: family *Lecythidaceae* **2** the nut of this tree, having an edible oily kernel and a woody shell ▷ Often shortened to: **brazil**

Brazzaville (*French* brazavil) *n* the capital of Congo-Brazzaville, in the south on the River Congo. Pop: 1 153 000 (2005 est) [c19 named after Pierre de *Brazza* (1852–1905), French explorer]

BRB *text messaging abbreviation for* be right back

BRCS *abbreviation for* British Red Cross Society

BRE (in Britain) *abbreviation for* Building Research Establishment

breach (briːtʃ) *n* **1** a crack, break, or rupture **2** a breaking, infringement, or violation of a promise, obligation, etc **3** any severance or separation: *there was a breach between the two factions of the party* **4** a gap in an enemy's fortifications or line of defence created by bombardment or attack **5** the act of a whale in breaking clear of the water **6** the breaking of sea waves on a shore or rock **7** an obsolete word for **wound**[1] ▷ *vb* **8** (*tr*) to break through or make an opening, hole, or incursion in **9** (*tr*) to break a promise, law, etc **10** (*intr*) (of a whale) to break clear of the water [Old English *bræc*; influenced by Old French *brèche*, from Old High German *brecha*, from *brechan* to BREAK]

breach of promise *n law* (formerly) failure to carry out one's promise to marry

breach of the peace *n law* an offence against public order causing an unnecessary disturbance of the peace

breach of trust *n law* a violation of duty by a trustee or any other person in a fiduciary position

bread (brɛd) *n* **1** a food made from a dough of flour or meal mixed with water or milk, usually raised with yeast or baking powder and then baked **2** necessary food; nourishment: *give us our daily bread* **3** a slang word for **money 4** *Christianity* a small loaf, piece of bread, or wafer of unleavened bread used in the Eucharist **5** bread and circuses something offered as a means of distracting attention from a problem or grievance **6** break bread See **break** (sense 46) **7** cast one's bread upon the waters to do good without expectation of advantage or return **8** to know which side one's bread is buttered to know what to do in order to keep one's advantages **9** take the bread out of (someone's) mouth to deprive (someone) of a livelihood ▷ *vb* **10** (*tr*) to cover with breadcrumbs before cooking: *breaded veal* [Old English *brēad*; related to Old Norse *braud*, Old Frisian *brād*, Old High German *brōt*]

bread and butter *informal* ▷ *n* **1** a means of support or subsistence; livelihood: *the inheritance was their bread and butter* (*modifier*) **2** bread-and-butter **a** providing a basic means of subsistence: *a bread-and-butter job* **b** solid, reliable, or practical: *a bread-and-butter player* **c** expressing gratitude, as for hospitality (esp in the phrase **bread-and-butter letter**)

bread and honey *n Brit slang* money [c20 rhyming slang]

breadbasket (ˈbrɛdˌbɑːskɪt) *n* **1** a basket for carrying bread or rolls **2** a slang word for **stomach**

b

breadboard ('brɛd,bɔ:d) *n* **1** a wooden board on which dough is kneaded or bread is sliced **2** an experimental arrangement of electronic circuits giving access to components so that modifications can be carried out easily
breadcrumb ('brɛd,krʌm) *n* **1** the soft inner part of bread **2** (*plural*) bread crumbled into small fragments, as for use in cooking ▷ *vb* (*tr*) **3** to coat (food) with breadcrumbs: *egg and breadcrumb the escalopes*
breadfruit ('brɛd,fru:t) *n, pl* **-fruits** *or* **-fruit** **1** a moraceous tree, *Artocarpus communis* (or *A. altilis*), of the Pacific Islands, having large round edible starchy usually seedless, fruit **2** the fruit of this tree, which is eaten baked or roasted and has a texture like bread
breadline ('brɛd,laɪn) *n* **1** a queue of people waiting for free food given out by a government agency or a charity organization **2** **on the breadline** impoverished; living at subsistence level
bread mould *or* **black mould** *n* a black saprotrophic zygomycete fungus, *Rhizopus nigricans*, occurring on decaying bread and vegetable matter
breadnut ('brɛd,nʌt) *n* **1** a moraceous tree, *Brosimum alicastrum*, of Central America and the Caribbean **2** the nutlike fruit of this tree, ground to produce a substitute for wheat flour, esp in the West Indies
breadroot ('brɛd,ru:t) *n* a leguminous plant, *Psoralea esculenta*, of central North America, having an edible starchy root. Also called: **prairie turnip**
bread sauce *n* a milk sauce thickened with breadcrumbs and served with roast poultry, esp chicken
breadsticks ('brɛd,stɪks) *pl n* bread baked in long thin crisp sticks
breadth (brɛdθ, brɛtθ) *n* **1** the linear extent or measurement of something from side to side; width **2** a piece of fabric having a standard or definite width **3** distance, extent, size, or dimension **4** openness and lack of restriction, esp of viewpoint or interest; liberality [C16 from obsolete *brēde* (from Old English *brǣdu*, from *brād* BROAD) + -TH[1]; related to Gothic *braidei*, Old High German *breitī*]
breadthways ('brɛdθ,weɪz, 'brɛtθ-) *or esp US* **breadthwise** ('brɛdθ,waɪz, 'brɛtθ-) *adv* from side to side
breadwinner ('brɛd,wɪnə) *n* a person supporting a family with his or her earnings > **'bread,winning** *n, adj*
break (breɪk) *vb* **breaks, breaking, broke, broken** **1** to separate or become separated into two or more pieces: *this cup is broken* **2** to damage or become damaged so as to be inoperative: *my radio is broken* **3** to crack or become cracked without separating **4** to burst or cut the surface of (skin, etc) **5** to discontinue or become discontinued: *they broke for lunch; to break a journey* **6** to disperse or become dispersed: *the clouds broke* **7** (*tr*) to fail to observe (an agreement, promise, law, etc): *to break one's word* **8** (foll by *with*) to discontinue an association (with) **9** to disclose or be disclosed: *he broke the news gently* **10** (*tr*) to fracture (a bone) in (a limb, etc) **11** (*tr*) to divide (something complete or perfect): *to break a set of books* **12** to bring or come to an end: *the summer weather broke at last* **13** (*tr*) to bring to an end by or as if by force: *to break a strike* **14** (when *intr*, often foll by *out*) to escape (from): *he broke jail; he broke out of jail* **15** to weaken or overwhelm or be weakened or overwhelmed, as in spirit **16** (*tr*) to cut through or penetrate: *a cry broke the silence* **17** (*tr*) to improve on or surpass: *to break a record* **18** (*tr*; often foll by *in*) to accustom (a horse) to the bridle and saddle, to being ridden, etc **19** (*tr*; often foll by *of*) to cause (a person) to give up (a habit): *this cure will break you of smoking* **20** (*tr*) to weaken the impact or force of: *this net will break his fall* **21** (*tr*) to decipher: *to break a code* **22** (*tr*) to lose the order of: *to break ranks* **23** (*tr*) to reduce to poverty or the state of bankruptcy **24** (when *intr*, foll by *into*) to obtain, give, or receive smaller units in exchange for; change: *to break a pound note* **25** (*tr*) *chiefly military* to demote to a lower rank **26** (*intr*; often foll by *from* or *out of*) to proceed suddenly **27** (*intr*) to come into being: *light broke over the mountains* **28** (*intr*; foll by *into* or *out into*) to burst into song, laughter, etc **29** (*tr*) to open with explosives: *to break a safe* **30** (*intr*) (of waves) **a** (often foll by *against*) to strike violently **b** to collapse into foam or surf **31** (*intr*) (esp of fish) to appear above the surface of the water **32** (*intr*) (of the amniotic fluid surrounding an unborn baby) to be released when the amniotic sac ruptures in the first stage of labour: *her waters have broken* **33** (*intr*) *informal, chiefly US* to turn out in a specified manner: *things are breaking well* **34** (*intr*) (of prices, esp stock exchange quotations) to fall sharply **35** (*intr*) to make a sudden effort, as in running, horse racing, etc **36** (*intr*) *cricket* (of a ball) to change direction on bouncing **37** (*tr*) *cricket* (of a player) to knock down at least one bail from (a wicket) **38** (*intr*) *billiards, snooker* to scatter the balls at the start of a game **39** (*intr*) *horse racing* to commence running in a race: *they broke even* **40** (*intr*) *boxing, wrestling* (of two fighters) to separate from a clinch **41** (*intr*) *music* **a** (of the male voice) to undergo a change in register, quality, and range at puberty **b** (of the voice or some instruments) to undergo a change in tone, quality, etc, when changing registers **42** (*intr*) *phonetics* (of a vowel) to turn into a diphthong, esp as a development in the language **43** (*tr*) to open the breech of (certain firearms) by snapping the barrel away from the butt on its hinge **44** (*tr*) to interrupt the flow of current in (an electrical circuit). Compare **make**[1] (sense 27) **45** (*intr*) *informal, chiefly US* to become successful; make a breakthrough **46** **break bread** **a** to eat a meal, esp with others **b** *Christianity* to administer or participate in Holy Communion **47** **break camp** to pack up equipment and leave a camp **48** **break (new) ground** to do something that has not been done before **49**. **break one's back** *or* (*slang*) **balls** to overwork or work very hard **50** **break the back of** to complete the greatest or hardest part of (a task) **51** **break the bank** to ruin financially or deplete the resources of a bank (as in gambling) **52** **break the ice** **a** to relieve shyness or reserve, esp between strangers **b** to be the first of a group to do something **53** **break the mould** to make a change that breaks an established habit, pattern, etc **54** **break service** *tennis* to win a game in which an opponent is serving **55** **break wind** to emit wind from the anus ▷ *n* **56** the act or result of breaking; fracture **57** a crack formed as the result of breaking **58** a brief respite or interval between two actions: *a break from one's toil* **59** a sudden rush, esp to escape: *to make a break for freedom* **60** a breach in a relationship: *she has made a break from her family* **61** any sudden interruption in a continuous action **62** *Brit* a short period between classes at school. US and Canadian equivalent: **recess** **63** *informal* a fortunate opportunity, esp to prove oneself **64** *informal* a piece of (good or bad) luck **65** (esp in a stock exchange) a sudden and substantial decline in prices **66** *prosody* a pause in a line of verse; caesura **67** *billiards, snooker* **a** a series of successful shots during one turn **b** the points scored in such a series **68** *billiards, snooker* **a** the opening shot with the cue ball that scatters the placed balls **b** the right to take this first shot **69** Also called: **service break, break of serve** *tennis* the act or instance of breaking an opponent's service **70** one of the intervals in a sporting contest **71** *horse racing* the start of a race: *an even break* **72** (in tenpin bowling) failure to knock down all the pins after the second attempt **73** **a** *jazz* a short usually improvised solo passage **b** an instrumental passage in a pop song **74** a discontinuity in an electrical circuit **75** access to a radio channel by a citizens' band operator **76** a variant spelling of **brake**[1] (sense 6) ▷ *interj* **77** *boxing, wrestling* a command by a referee for two opponents to separate ▷ See also **breakaway, break down, break even, break in, break into, break off, break out, break through, break up, break with** [Old English *brecan*; related to Old Frisian *breka*, Gothic *brikan*, Old High German *brehhan*, Latin *frangere* Sanskrit *bhráj* bursting forth]
breakable ('breɪkəbᵊl) *adj* **1** capable of being broken ▷ *n* **2** (*usually plural*) a fragile easily broken article
breakage ('breɪkɪdʒ) *n* **1** the act or result of breaking **2** the quantity or amount broken: *the total breakage was enormous* **3** compensation or allowance for goods damaged while in use, transit, etc
breakaway ('breɪkə,weɪ) *n* **1** **a** loss or withdrawal of a group of members from an association, club, etc **b** (*as modifier*): *a breakaway faction* **2** *sport* **a** a sudden attack, esp from a defensive position, in football, hockey, etc **b** an attempt to get away from the rest of the field in a race **3** *Austral* a stampede of cattle, esp at the smell of water ▷ *vb* **break away** (*intr, adverb*) **4** (often foll by *from*) to leave hastily or escape **5** to withdraw or secede **6** *sport* to make a breakaway **7** *horse racing* to start prematurely
breakbeat ('breɪk,bi:t) *n* a type of electronic dance music
breakbone fever ('breɪk,bəʊn) *n* another name for **dengue**
break dance *n* **1** an acrobatic dance style originating in the 1980s ▷ *vb* **break-dance** **2** (*intr*) to perform a break dance > **break dancer** *n* > **break dancing** *n*
break down *vb* (*adverb*) **1** (*intr*) to cease to function; become ineffective: *communications had broken down* **2** to yield or cause to yield, esp to strong emotion or tears: *she broke down in anguish* **3** (*tr*) to crush or destroy **4** (*intr*) to have a nervous breakdown **5** to analyse or be subjected to analysis **6** to separate or cause to separate into simpler chemical elements; decompose **7** (*tr*) *NZ* to saw (a large log) into planks **8** **break it down** *Austral and NZ informal* **a** stop it **b** don't expect me to believe that; come off it ▷ *n* **breakdown** **9** an act or instance of breaking down; collapse **10** short for **nervous breakdown** **11** an analysis or classification of something into its component parts: *he prepared a breakdown of the report* **12** the sudden electrical discharge through an insulator or between two electrodes in a vacuum or gas discharge tube **13** *electrical engineering* the sudden transition, dependent on the bias magnitude, from a high to a low dynamic resistance in a semiconductor device **14** a lively American country dance
breakdown van *or* **truck** *n* *chiefly Brit* another name for a **tow truck**
breaker[1] ('breɪkə) *n* **1** a person or thing that breaks something, such as a person or firm that breaks up old cars, etc **2** a large wave with a white crest on the open sea or one that breaks into foam on the shore **3** *electronics* short for **circuit breaker** **4** a machine or plant for crushing rocks or coal **5** Also called: **breaking plough** a plough with a long shallow mouldboard for turning virgin land or sod land **6** *textiles* a machine for extracting fibre preparatory to carding **7** an operator on citizens' band radio
breaker[2] ('breɪkə) *n* a small water cask for use in a boat [C19 anglicized variant of Spanish *barrica*, from French (Gascon dialect) *barrique*]
break even *vb* **1** (*intr, adverb*) to attain a level of activity, as in commerce, or a point of operation, as in gambling, at which there is neither profit nor loss ▷ *n* **breakeven** **2** *accounting* **a** the level of commercial activity at which the total cost and total revenue of a business enterprise are equal **b** (*as modifier*): *breakeven prices*
breakeven chart ('breɪk,i:vᵊn) *n* *accounting* a graph measuring the value of an enterprise's revenue and costs against some index of its

activity, such as percentage capacity. The intersection of the total revenue and total cost curves gives the breakeven point

breakfast ('brɛkfəst) n 1 a the first meal of the day b (as modifier): breakfast cereal; a breakfast room 2 the food at this meal 3 (in the Caribbean) a midday meal ▷ vb 4 to eat or supply with breakfast [C15 from BREAK + FAST²] > 'breakfaster n

breakfast club n a service that provides a breakfast for children who arrive early at school

break feeding n NZ the feeding of animals on paddocks where feeding space is controlled by the frequent movement of an electric fence

breakfront ('breɪkˌfrʌnt) adj (prenominal) (of a bookcase, bureau, etc) having a slightly projecting central section

break in vb (adverb) 1 (sometimes foll by on) to interrupt 2 (intr) to enter a house, etc, illegally, esp by force 3 (tr) to accustom (a person or animal) to normal duties or practice 4 (tr) to use or wear (shoes, new equipment, etc) until comfortable or running smoothly 5 (tr) Austral and NZ to bring (new land) under cultivation ▷ n break-in 6 a the illegal entering of a building, esp by thieves b (as modifier): the break-in plans

breaking ('breɪkɪŋ) n linguistics (in Old English, Old Norse, etc) the change of a vowel into a diphthong [C19 translation of German Brechung]

breaking and entering n (formerly) the gaining of unauthorized access to a building with intent to commit a crime or, having committed the crime, the breaking out of the building

breaking point n 1 the point at which something or someone gives way under strain 2 the moment of crisis in a situation

break into vb (intr, preposition) 1 to enter (a house, etc) illegally, esp by force 2 to change abruptly from a slower to a faster speed: the horse broke into a gallop 3 to consume (supplies held in reserve): at the end of the exercise the soldiers had to break into their iron rations

breakneck ('breɪkˌnɛk) adj (prenominal) (of speed, pace, etc) excessive and dangerous

break of day n another term for dawn (sense 1)

break off vb 1 to sever or detach or be severed or detached: it broke off in my hands; he broke a piece off the bar of chocolate 2 (adverb) to end (a relationship, association, etc) or (of a relationship, etc) to be ended 3 (intr, adverb) to stop abruptly; halt: he broke off in the middle of his speech ▷ n breakoff 4 the act or an instance of breaking off or stopping

break out vb 1 (intr, adverb) to begin or arise suddenly: panic broke out 2 (intr, adverb) to make an escape, esp from prison or confinement 3 (intr, adverb, foll by in) (of the skin) to erupt (in a rash, pimples, etc) 4 (tr, adverb) to launch or introduce (a new product) 5 (tr, adverb) to open and start using: break out the champagne ▷ n break-out 6 an escape, esp from prison or confinement 7 a a great success, esp following relatively disappointing performance b (as modifier): a breakout year

break-out group n a group of people who detach themselves from a larger group or meeting in order to hold separate discussions

breakpoint ('breɪkˌpɔɪnt) n computing a an instruction inserted by a debug program causing a return to the debug program b the point in a program at which such an instruction operates

break point n tennis a point which allows the receiving player to break the service of the server

break through vb 1 (intr) to penetrate 2 (intr, adverb) to achieve success, make a discovery, etc, esp after lengthy efforts ▷ n breakthrough 3 a significant development or discovery, esp in science 4 the penetration of an enemy's defensive position or line in depth and strength

break up vb (adverb) 1 to separate or cause to separate 2 to put an end to (a relationship) or (of a relationship) to come to an end 3 to dissolve or cause to dissolve; disrupt or be disrupted: the meeting broke up at noon 4 (intr) Brit (of a school) to

close for the holidays 5 (intr) (of a person making a telephone call) to be inaudible at times, owing to variations in the signal: you're breaking up 6 informal to lose or cause to lose control of the emotions: the news of his death broke her up 7 slang to be or cause to be overcome with laughter ▷ n break-up 8 a separation or disintegration

break-up value n commerce 1 the value of an organization assuming that it will not continue to trade 2 the value of a share in a company based only on the value of its assets

breakwater ('breɪkˌwɔːtə) n 1 Also called: mole a massive wall built out into the sea to protect a shore or harbour from the force of waves 2 another name for groyne

break with vb (intr, preposition) to end a relationship or association with (someone or an organization or social group)

bream¹ (briːm; Austral brɪm) or Austral **brim** (brɪm) n, pl bream or brim 1 any of several Eurasian freshwater cyprinid fishes of the genus Abramis, esp A. brama, having a deep compressed body covered with silvery scales 2 white or silver bream a similar cyprinid, Blicca bjoerkna 3 short for sea bream [C14 from Old French bresme, of Germanic origin; compare Old High German brahsema; perhaps related to brehan to glitter]

bream² (briːm) vb nautical (formerly) to clean debris from (the bottom of a vessel) by heating to soften the pitch [C15 probably from Middle Dutch bremme broom; from using burning broom as a source of heat]

breast (brɛst) n 1 the front part of the body from the neck to the abdomen; chest 2 either of the two soft fleshy milk-secreting glands on the chest in sexually mature human females. adjective mammary 3 a similar organ in certain other mammals 4 anything that resembles a breast in shape or position: the breast of the hill 5 a source of nourishment: the city took the victims to its breast 6 the source of human emotions 7 the part of a garment that covers the breast 8 a projection from the side of a wall, esp that formed by a chimney 9 mining the face being worked at the end of a tunnel 10 beat one's breast to display guilt and remorse publicly or ostentatiously 11 make a clean breast of to make a confession of ▷ vb (tr) 12 to confront boldly; face: breast the storm 13 to oppose with the breast or meet at breast level: breasting the waves 14 to come alongside of: breast the ship 15 to reach the summit of: breasting the mountain top [Old English brēost; related to Old Norse brjōst, Old High German brust, Dutch borst, Swedish bräss, Old Irish brū belly, body]

breastbone ('brɛstˌbəʊn) n the nontechnical name for sternum

breast-feed vb -feeds, -feeding, -fed to feed (a baby) with milk from the breast; suckle > 'breast-ˌfed adj > 'breast-ˌfeeding n

breastpin ('brɛstˌpɪn) n a brooch worn on the breast, esp to close a garment

breastplate ('brɛstˌpleɪt) n 1 a piece of armour covering the chest 2 the strap of a harness covering a horse's breast 3 Judaism an ornamental silver plate hung on the scrolls of the Torah 4 Old Testament a square vestment ornamented with 12 precious stones, representing the 12 tribes of Israel, worn by the high priest when praying before the holy of holies 5 zoology a nontechnical name for plastron

breast pump n a device for extracting and collecting milk from the breast during lactation

breaststroke ('brɛstˌstrəʊk) n a swimming stroke in which the arms are extended in front of the head and swept back on either side while the legs are drawn up beneath the body and thrust back together

breastwork ('brɛstˌwɜːk) n fortifications a temporary defensive work, usually breast-high. Also called: parapet

breath (brɛθ) n 1 the intake and expulsion of air during respiration 2 the air inhaled or exhaled

during respiration 3 a single respiration or inhalation of air, etc 4 the vapour, heat, or odour of exhaled air: his breath on the window melted the frost 5 a slight gust of air 6 a short pause or rest: take a breath for five minutes 7 a brief time: it was done in a breath 8 a suggestion or slight evidence; suspicion: a breath of scandal 9 a whisper or soft sound 10 life, energy, or vitality: the breath of new industry 11 phonetics the passage of air through the completely open glottis without vibration of the vocal cords, as in exhaling or pronouncing fricatives such as (f) or (h) or stops such as (p) or (k). Compare voice (sense 11) 12 a breath of fresh air a refreshing change from what one is used to 13 catch one's breath to rest until breathing is normal, esp after exertion 14 hold one's breath to wait expectantly or anxiously 15 in the same breath done or said at the same time 16 out of breath gasping for air after exertion 17 save one's breath to refrain from useless talk 18 take one's breath away to overwhelm with surprise, etc 19 under or below one's breath in a quiet voice or whisper [Old English brǣth; related to brǣdan to burn, Old High German brādam heat, breath]

breathable ('briːðəb°l) adj 1 (of air) fit to be breathed 2 (of a material) allowing air to pass through so that perspiration can evaporate

breathalyse or US **breathalyze** ('brɛθəˌlaɪz) vb (tr) to apply a Breathalyser test to (someone)

Breathalyser or **Breathalyzer** ('brɛθəˌlaɪzə) n trademark a device for estimating the amount of alcohol in the breath: used in testing people suspected of driving under the influence of alcohol [C20 BREATH + (AN)ALYSER]

breatharian (ˌbrɛθ'ɛərɪən) n 1 a person who believes that it is possible to subsist healthily on air alone ▷ adj 2 of or relating to a breatharian: a breatharian purification programme > breath'arianˌism n

breathe (briːð) vb 1 to take in oxygen from (the surrounding medium, esp air) and give out carbon dioxide; respire 2 (intr) to exist; be alive: every animal that breathes on earth 3 (intr) to rest to regain breath, composure, etc: stop your questions, and give me a chance to breathe 4 (intr) (esp of air) to blow lightly: the wind breathed through the trees 5 (intr) machinery a to take in air, esp for combustion: the engine breathes through this air filter b to equalize the pressure within a container, chamber, etc, with atmospheric pressure: the crankcase breathes through this duct 6 (tr) phonetics to articulate (a speech sound) without vibration of the vocal cords. Compare voice (sense 19) 7 to exhale or emit: the dragon breathed fire 8 (tr) to impart; instil: to breathe confidence into the actors 9 (tr) to speak softly; whisper: to breathe words of love 10 (tr) to permit to rest: to breathe a horse 11 (intr) (of a material) to allow air to pass through so that perspiration can evaporate 12 breathe again, freely or easily to feel relief: I could breathe again after passing the exam 13 breathe down (someone's) neck to stay close to (someone), esp to oversee what they are doing: the cops are breathing down my neck 14 breathe one's last to die or be finished or defeated [C13 from BREATH]

breathed (brɛθt, briːðd) adj phonetics relating to or denoting a speech sound for whose articulation the vocal cords are not made to vibrate. Compare voiced

breather ('briːðə) n 1 informal a short pause for rest 2 a person who breathes in a specified way: a deep breather 3 a vent in a container to equalize internal and external pressure, such as the pipe in the crankcase of an internal-combustion engine 4 a small opening in a room, container, cover, etc, supplying air for ventilation

breathing ('briːðɪŋ) n 1 the passage of air into and out of the lungs to supply the body with oxygen 2 a single breath: a breathing between words 3 an utterance: a breathing of hate 4 a soft movement, esp of air 5 a rest or pause 6 phonetics a expulsion of breath (rough breathing) or

b

absence of such expulsion (**smooth breathing**) preceding the pronunciation of an initial vowel or rho in ancient Greek **b** either of two symbols indicating this

breathing space *n* **1** enough area to permit freedom of movement: *the country gives us some breathing space* **2** a pause for rest, etc: *a coffee break was their only breathing space*

breathless ('brɛθlɪs) *adj* **1** out of breath; gasping, etc **2** holding one's breath or having it taken away by excitement, etc: *a breathless confrontation* **3** (esp of the atmosphere) motionless and stifling **4** *rare* lifeless; dead > '**breathlessly** *adv* > '**breathlessness** *n*

breathtaking ('brɛθ,teɪkɪŋ) *adj* causing awe or excitement: *a breathtaking view* > '**breath,takingly** *adv*

breath test *n Brit* a chemical test of a driver's breath to determine the amount of alcohol he has consumed

breathy ('brɛθɪ) *adj* **breathier, breathiest** **1** (of the speaking voice) accompanied by an audible emission of breath **2** (of the singing voice) lacking resonance > '**breathily** *adv* > '**breathiness** *n*

breccia ('brɛtʃɪə) *n* a rock consisting of angular fragments embedded in a finer matrix, formed by erosion, impact, volcanic activity, etc [c18 from Italian, from Old High German *brecha* a fragment; see BREACH] > '**brecci,ated** *adj*

Brechtian ('brɛxtɪən) *adj* **1** of or relating to Bertolt Brecht, the German dramatist, theatrical producer, and poet (1898–1956) ▷ *n* **2** a follower or admirer of Brecht

Brecon ('brɛkən) *or* **Brecknock** ('brɛknɒk) *n* **1** a town in SE Wales, in Powys: textile and leather industries. Pop: 7901 (2001) **2** short for **Breconshire**

Breconshire ('brɛkən,ʃɪə, -ʃə) *or* **Brecknockshire** ('brɛknɒk,ʃɪə, -ʃə) *n* (until 1974) a county of SE Wales, now mainly in Powys: over half its area forms the **Brecon Beacons National Park**

bred (brɛd) *vb* **1** the past tense and past participle of **breed** ▷ *n* **2** *Austral slang* a person who lives in a small remote place [sense 2: diminutive form of *inbred*]

Breda ('breɪdə; *Dutch* bre'da:) *n* a city in the S Netherlands, in North Brabant province: residence of Charles II of England during his exile. Pop: 164 000 (2003 est)

brede (bri:d) *n, vb* an archaic spelling of **braid**[1]

bredie ('bri:dɪ) *n South African* a meat and vegetable stew [c19 from Portuguese *bredo* ragout]

bree[1] *or* **brie** (bri:) *n Scot* broth, stock, or juice [Old English *brīg*, variant of *brīw* pottage; related to Old High German *brīo* soup, Old English *brīwan* to cook, Middle Irish *brēo* flame]

bree[2] (bri:) *n* a Scot word for **brunt** [c19 perhaps from earlier *bree* brow]

breech *n* (bri:tʃ) **1** the lower dorsal part of the human trunk; buttocks **2** the lower part or bottom of something: *the breech of the bridge* **3** the lower portion of a pulley block, esp the part to which the rope or chain is secured **4** the part of a firearm behind the barrel or bore **5** *obstetrics* short for **breech delivery** ▷ *vb* (bri:tʃ, brɪtʃ) (*tr*) **6** to fit (a gun) with a breech **7** *archaic* to clothe in breeches or any other clothing ▷ See also **breeches** [Old English *brēc*, plural of *brōc* leg covering; related to Old Norse *brōk*, Old High German *bruoh*]

USAGE *Breech* is sometimes wrongly used as a verb where *breach* is meant: *the barrier/agreement was breached* (not *breeched*)

breechblock ('bri:tʃ,blɒk) *n* a metal block in breech-loading firearms that is withdrawn to insert the cartridge and replaced to close the breech before firing

breechcloth ('bri:tʃ,klɒθ) *or* **breechclout** ('bri:tʃ,klaʊt) *n* other names for **loincloth**

breech delivery *n* birth of a baby with the feet or buttocks appearing first

breeches ('brɪtʃɪz, 'bri:-) *pl n* **1** trousers extending

to the knee or just below, worn for riding, mountaineering, etc **2** *informal or dialect* any trousers **3** too big for one's breeches conceited; unduly self-confident

breeches buoy *n* a ring-shaped life buoy with a support in the form of a pair of short breeches, in which a person is suspended for safe transfer from a ship

breeching ('brɪtʃɪŋ, 'bri:-) *n* **1** the strap of a harness that passes behind a horse's haunches **2** *naval* (formerly) the rope used to check the recoil run of a ship's guns or to secure them against rough weather **3** the parts comprising the breech of a gun

breech-loader ('bri:tʃ,ləʊdə) *n* a firearm that is loaded at the breech

breech-loading ('bri:tʃ,ləʊdɪŋ) *adj* (of a firearm) loaded at the breech

breed (bri:d) *vb* **breeds, breeding, bred** **1** to bear (offspring) **2** (*tr*) to bring up; raise **3** to produce or cause to produce by mating; propagate **4** to produce and maintain new or improved strains of (domestic animals and plants) **5** to produce or be produced; generate: *to breed trouble; violence breeds in densely populated areas* ▷ *n* **6** a group of organisms within a species, esp a group of domestic animals, originated and maintained by man and having a clearly defined set of characteristics **7** a lineage or race: *a breed of Europeans* **8** a kind, sort, or group: *a special breed of hatred* [Old English *brēdan*, of Germanic origin; related to BROOD]

breeder ('bri:də) *n* **1** a person who breeds plants or animals **2** something that reproduces, esp to excess: *rabbits are persistent breeders* **3** an animal kept for breeding purposes **4** a source or cause: *a breeder of discontent* **5** short for **breeder reactor**

breeder reactor *n* a type of nuclear reactor that produces more fissionable material than it consumes. Compare **converter reactor**. See also **fast-breeder reactor**

breeding ('bri:dɪŋ) *n* **1** the process of bearing offspring; reproduction **2** the process of producing plants or animals by sexual reproduction **3** the result of good training, esp the knowledge of correct social behaviour; refinement: *a man of breeding* **4** a person's line of descent: *his breeding was suspect* **5** *physics* a process occurring in a nuclear reactor as a result of which more fissionable material is produced than is used up

Breed's Hill (bri:dz) *n* a hill in E Massachusetts, adjoining Bunker Hill: the true site of the Battle of Bunker Hill (1775)

breeks (bri:ks) *pl n Scot* trousers [Scot variant of BREECHES]

breenge *or* **breinge** (bri:ndʒ) *Scot* ▷ *vb* (*intr*) **1** to lunge forward; move violently or dash ▷ *n* **2** a violent movement [of unknown origin]

breeze[1] (bri:z) *n* **1** a gentle or light wind **2** *meteorol* a wind of force two to six inclusive on the Beaufort scale **3** *informal* an easy task or state of ease: *being happy here is a breeze* **4** *informal, chiefly Brit* a disturbance, esp a lively quarrel **5** shoot the breeze *informal* to chat ▷ *vb* (*intr*) **6** to move quickly or casually: *he breezed into the room* **7** (of wind) to blow: *the south wind breezed over the fields* [c16 probably from Old Spanish *briza* northeast wind]

breeze[2] (bri:z) *n* an archaic or dialect name for the **gadfly** [Old English *briosa*, of unknown origin]

breeze[3] (bri:z) *n* ashes of coal, coke, or charcoal used to make breeze blocks [c18 from French *braise* live coals; see BRAISE]

breeze block *n* a light building brick made from the ashes of coal, coke, etc, bonded together by cement and used esp for walls that bear relatively small loads. Usual US names: **cinder block, clinker block**

breezeway ('bri:z,weɪ) *n* a roofed passageway connecting two buildings, sometimes with the sides enclosed

breezy ('bri:zɪ) *adj* **breezier, breeziest** **1** fresh;

windy: *a breezy afternoon* **2** casual or carefree; lively; light-hearted: *her breezy nature* **3** lacking substance; light: *a breezy conversation* > '**breezily** *adv* > '**breeziness** *n*

Bregenz (*German* bre'gɛnts) *n* a resort in W Austria, the capital of Vorarlberg province. Pop: 26 752 (2001)

bregma ('brɛgmə) *n, pl* -**mata** (-mətə) the point on the top of the skull where the coronal and sagittal sutures meet: in infants this corresponds to the anterior fontanelle [c16 New Latin from Greek: front part of the head]

brei (breɪ) *vb* **breis, breiing, breid** (*intr*) *South African informal* to speak with a uvular *r*, esp in Afrikaans. Also: **brey**. Compare **burr**[2] [c20 from Afrikaans; compare BRAY[1]]

breid (bri:d) *n* a Scot word for **bread**

breist *or* **breest** (bri:st) *n* a Scot word for **breast**

brekky ('brɛkɪ) *n* a slang word for **breakfast**

Bremen ('breɪmən) *n* **1** a state of NW Germany, centred on the city of Bremen and its outport Bremerhaven; formerly in West Germany. Pop: 663 000 (2003 est). Area: 404 sq km (156 sq miles) **2** an industrial city and port in NW Germany, on the Weser estuary. Pop: 544 853 (2003 est)

Bremerhaven (*German* bre:mər'ha:fən) *n* a port in NW Germany: an outport for Bremen. Pop: 118 276 (2003 est). Former name (until 1947): **Wesermünde**

bremsstrahlung ('brɛmz,ʃtra:lən) *n* the radiation produced when an electrically charged particle, especially an electron, is slowed down by the electric field of an atomic nucleus or an atomic ion [c20 German: braking radiation]

Bren gun (brɛn) *n* an air-cooled gas-operated light machine gun taking .303 calibre ammunition: used by British and Commonwealth forces in World War II [c20 after Br(no), now in the Czech Republic, where it was first made and En(field), England, where manufacture was continued]

Brenner Pass ('brɛnə) *n* a pass over the E Alps, between Austria and Italy. Highest point: 1372 m (4501 ft)

Brent (brɛnt) *n* a borough of NW Greater London. Pop: 267 800 (2003 est). Area: 44 sq km (17 sq miles)

brent goose (brɛnt) *n* a small goose, *Branta bernicla*, that has a dark grey plumage and short neck and occurs in most northern coastal regions. Also called: **brent**, (esp US and Canadian) **brant** [c16 perhaps of Scandinavian origin; compare Old Norse *brandgās* sheldrake]

Brentwood ('brɛnt,wʊd) *n* a residential town in SE England, in SW Essex near London. Pop: 47 593 (2001)

br'er (brɜ:, brɛə) *n Southern African-American dialect* brother: usually prefixed to a name: *Br'er Jones*

Brescia (*Italian* 'brɛʃʃa) *n* a city in N Italy, in Lombardy: at its height in the 16th century. Pop: 187 567 (2001). Ancient name: **Brixia** ('brɪksɪə)

Breslau ('brɛzlau) *n* the German name for **Wrocław**

Brest (brɛst) *n* **1** a port in NW France, in Brittany: chief naval station of the country, planned by Richelieu in 1631 and fortified by Vauban. Pop: 149 634 (1999) **2** a city in SW Belarus: Polish until 1795 and from 1921 to 1945. Pop: 299 000 (2005 est). Former name (until 1921): **Brest Litovsk** (brɛst li'tɒfsk). Polish name: **Brześć nad Bugiem**

Bretagne (brətaɲ) *n* the French name for **Brittany**

brethren ('brɛðrɪn) *pl n archaic except when referring to fellow members of a religion, sect, society, etc* a plural of **brother**

Breton ('brɛt⁰n; *French* brətɔ̃) *adj* **1** of, relating to, or characteristic of Brittany, its people, or their language ▷ *n* **2** a native or inhabitant of Brittany, esp one who speaks the Breton language **3** the indigenous language of Brittany, belonging to the Brythonic subgroup of the Celtic family of languages

Bretton Woods Conference ('brɛt⁰n) *n* an international monetary conference held in 1944 at

Bretton Woods in New Hampshire, which resulted in the establishment of the World Bank and the International Monetary Fund

breunnerite ('brɔɪnəˌraɪt) *n* an iron-containing type of magnesite used in the manufacture of refractory bricks [c19 named after Count *Breunner*, Austrian nobleman, + -ITE[1]]

breve (briːv) *n* 1 an accent, (˘), placed over a vowel to indicate that it is of short duration or is pronounced in a specified way 2 *music* a note, now rarely used, equivalent in time value to two semibreves 3 *RC Church* a less common word for **brief** (papal letter) [c13 from Medieval Latin *breve*, from Latin *brevis* short; see BRIEF]

brevet ('brɛvɪt) *n* 1 a document entitling a commissioned officer to hold temporarily a higher military rank without the appropriate pay and allowances ▷ *vb* -vets, -vetting, -vetted *or* -vets, -veting, -veted 2 (*tr*) to promote by brevet [c14 from Old French *brievet* a little letter, from *brief* letter; see BRIEF] ▷ 'brevetcy *n*

breviary ('briːvjərɪ) *n*, *pl* -ries 1 *RC Church* a book of psalms, hymns, prayers, etc, to be recited daily by clerics in major orders and certain members of religious orders as part of the divine office 2 a similar book in the Orthodox Church [c16 from Latin *breviārium* an abridged version, from *breviāre* to shorten, from *brevis* short]

brevier (brə'vɪə) *n* (formerly) a size of printer's type approximately equal to 8 point [c16 probably from Dutch, literally: BREVIARY; so called because this type size was used for breviaries]

brevity ('brɛvɪtɪ) *n*, *pl* -ties 1 conciseness of expression; lack of verbosity 2 a short duration; brief time [c16 from Latin *brevitās* shortness, from *brevis* BRIEF]

brew[1] (bruː) *vb* 1 to make (beer, ale, etc) from malt and other ingredients by steeping, boiling, and fermentation 2 to prepare (a drink, such as tea) by boiling or infusing 3 (*tr*) to devise or plan: *to brew a plot* 4 (*intr*) to be in the process of being brewed: *the tea was brewing in the pot* 5 (*intr*) to be impending or forming: *there's a storm brewing* ▷ *n* 6 a beverage produced by brewing, esp tea or beer: *a strong brew* 7 an instance or time of brewing: *last year's brew* 8 a mixture: *an eclectic brew of mysticism and political discontent*. ▷ See also **brew up** [Old English *brēowan*; related to Old Norse *brugga*, Old Saxon *breuwan*, Old High German *briuwan*] ▷ 'brewer *n*

brew[2] (bruː) *n Northern English dialect* a hill

brewage ('bruːɪdʒ) *n* 1 a product of brewing; brew 2 the process of brewing

brewer's grain *n* an exhausted malt occurring as a by-product of brewing and used as a feedstuff for cattle, pigs, and sheep

brewer's yeast *n* 1 a yeast, *Saccharomyces cerevisiae*, used in brewing. See **yeast** (sense 3) 2 yeast obtained as a by-product of brewing

brewery ('bruərɪ) *n*, *pl* -eries a place where beer, ale, etc, is brewed

brewing ('bruːɪŋ) *n* a quantity of a beverage brewed at one time

brewis ('bruːɪs) *or* **brevis** ('brɛvɪs) *n dialect, chiefly Northern English, Canadian, and US* 1 bread soaked in broth, gravy, etc 2 thickened broth 3 (bruːz) *Canadian* a Newfoundland stew of cod or pork, hardtack, and potatoes [c16 from Old French *broez*, from *broet*, diminutive of *breu* BROTH]

brewpub ('bruːˌpʌb) *n* a pub that incorporates a brewery on its premises

brew up *Brit and NZ informal* ▷ *vb* (*intr, adverb*) 1 to make tea, esp out of doors or in informal circumstances ▷ *n* **brew-up** 2 a making of tea

brey (breɪ) *vb* (*intr*) *South African informal* a variant spelling of **brei**

briar[1] *or* **brier** ('braɪə) *n* 1 Also called: **tree heath** an ericaceous shrub, *Erica arborea*, of S Europe, having a hard woody root (briarroot) 2 a tobacco pipe made from the root of this plant [c19 from French *bruyère* heath, from Late Latin *brūcus*, of Gaulish origin] ▷ 'briary *or* 'briery *adj*

briar[2] ('braɪə) *n* a variant spelling of **brier**[1]

briard (briː'ɑːd, briː'ɑː) *n* a medium-sized dog of an ancient French sheep-herding breed having a long rough coat of a single colour [French, literally: of Brie (region in N France)]

Briareus (braɪˈɛərɪəs) *n Greek myth* a giant with a hundred arms and fifty heads who aided Zeus and the Olympians against the Titans ▷ Bri'arean *adj*

briarroot *or* **brierroot** ('braɪəˌruːt) *n* 1 the hard woody root of the briar, used for making tobacco pipes 2 any of several other woods used to make tobacco pipes Also called: **briarwood, brierwood**

bribe (braɪb) *vb* 1 to promise, offer, or give something, usually money, to (a person) to procure services or gain influence, esp illegally ▷ *n* 2 a reward, such as money or favour, given or offered for this purpose 3 any persuasion or lure 4 a length of flawed or damaged cloth removed from the main piece [c14 from Old French *briber* to beg, of obscure origin] ▷ 'bribable *or* 'bribeable *adj* ▷ 'briber *n*

bribery ('braɪbərɪ) *n*, *pl* -eries the process of giving or taking bribes

bric-a-brac ('brɪkəˌbræk) *n* miscellaneous small objects, esp furniture and curios, kept because they are ornamental or rare [c19 from French; phrase based on *bric* piece]

bricht (brɪxt) *adj* a Scot word for **bright**

brick (brɪk) *n* 1 a a rectangular block of clay mixed with sand and fired in a kiln or baked by the sun, used in building construction b (*as modifier*): *a brick house* 2 the material used to make such blocks 3 any rectangular block: *a brick of ice* 4 bricks collectively 5 *informal* a reliable, trustworthy, or helpful person 6 *Brit* a child's building block 7 short for **brick red** 8 **drop a brick** *Brit* to make a tactless or indiscreet remark 9 **like a ton of bricks** *informal* (used esp of the manner of punishing or reprimanding someone) with great force; severely: *when he spotted my mistake he came down on me like a ton of bricks* ▷ *vb* (*tr*) 10 (usually foll by *in, up* or *over*) to construct, line, pave, fill, or wall up with bricks: *to brick up a window; brick over a patio* 11 *slang* to attack (a person) with a brick or bricks [c15 from Old French *brique*, from Middle Dutch *bricke*; related to Middle Low German *brike*, Old English *brecan* to BREAK]

brickbat ('brɪkˌbæt) *n* 1 a piece of brick or similar material, esp one used as a weapon 2 blunt criticism: *the critic threw several brickbats at the singer*

brickearth ('brɪkˌɜːθ) *n* a clayey alluvium suitable for the making of bricks: specifically, such a deposit in southern England, yielding a fertile soil

brickie *or* **bricky** ('brɪkɪ) *n Brit informal* a bricklayer

bricking ('brɪkɪŋ) *n Austral slang* the falsification of evidence in order to bring a criminal charge

bricklayer ('brɪkˌleɪə) *n* a person trained or skilled in laying bricks

bricklaying ('brɪkˌleɪɪŋ) *n* the technique or practice of laying bricks

brick red *n, adj* a a reddish-brown colour b (*as adjective*): *a brick-red carpet*

bricks and clicks *n* 1 a combination of traditional business carried out on physical premises and internet trading ▷ *modifier* bricks-and-clicks 2 combining traditional business carried out on physical premises and internet trading: *bricks-and-clicks companies* [c20 from BRICKS AND MORTAR and *click*, meaning an act of pressing and releasing a computer mouse button]

bricks and mortar *n* 1 a a building or buildings: *he invested in bricks and mortar rather than stocks and shares* b (*modifier*) bricks-and-mortar 2 a physical business premises rather than an internet presence: *bricks-and-mortar firms*

brick veneer *n* (in Australia) a timber-framed house with a brick exterior

brickwork ('brɪkˌwɜːk) *n* 1 a structure, such as a wall, built of bricks 2 construction using bricks

bricky ('brɪkɪ) *adj* 1 made of bricks, or like a brick ▷ *n* 2 a variant spelling of **brickie**

brickyard ('brɪkˌjɑːd) *n* a place in which bricks are made, stored, or sold

bricolage ('brɪkəˌlɑːʒ; *French* brɪkɔlaʒ) *n architect* 1 the jumbled effect produced by the close proximity of buildings from different periods and in different architectural styles 2 the deliberate creation of such an effect in certain modern developments: *the post-modernist bricolage of the new shopping centre*

bricole (brɪ'kəʊl, 'brɪk°l) *n* 1 *billiards* a shot in which the cue ball touches a cushion after striking the object ball and before touching another ball 2 (in ancient and medieval times) a military catapult for throwing stones, etc 3 (esp formerly) a harness worn by soldiers for dragging guns or carrying stretchers 4 an indirect or unexpected action [c16 from Old French: catapult, from Medieval Latin *bricola*, of uncertain origin]

BRICs (brɪks) *n acronym for* Brazil, Russia, India, and China: seen collectively as the most important emerging economies with large potential markets

bridal ('braɪd°l) *adj* 1 of or relating to a bride or a wedding; nuptial ▷ *n* 2 *obsolete* a wedding or wedding feast [Old English *brýdealu*, literally: "bride ale", that is, wedding feast]

bridal wreath *n* any of several N temperate rosaceous shrubs of the genus *Spiraea*, esp *S. prunifolia*, cultivated for their sprays of small white flowers

bride[1] (braɪd) *n* a woman who has just been or is about to be married [Old English *brýd*; related to Old Norse *brúthr*, Gothic *brúths* daughter-in-law, Old High German *brūt*]

bride[2] (braɪd) *n lacemaking, needlework* a thread or loop that joins parts of a pattern. Also called: **bar** [c19 from French, literally: BRIDLE, probably of Germanic origin]

bridegroom ('braɪdˌgruːm, -ˌgrʊm) *n* a man who has just been or is about to be married [c14 changed (through influence of GROOM) from Old English *brýdguma*, from *brýd* BRIDE[1] + *guma* man; related to Old Norse *brúthgumi*, Old High German *brūtigomo*]

bride price *or* **wealth** *n* (in some societies) money, property, or services given by a bridegroom to the kinsmen of his bride in order to establish his rights over the woman

bridesmaid ('braɪdzˌmeɪd) *n* a girl or young unmarried woman who attends a bride at her wedding. Compare **matron of honour, maid of honour**

bridewell ('braɪdˌwɛl, -wəl) *n* a house of correction; jail, esp for minor offences [c16 after *Bridewell* (originally, St Bride's Well), a house of correction in London]

bridge[1] (brɪdʒ) *n* 1 a structure that spans and provides a passage over a road, railway, river, or some other obstacle 2 something that resembles this in shape or function: *his letters provided a bridge across the centuries* 3 a the hard ridge at the upper part of the nose, formed by the underlying nasal bones b an anatomical ridge or connecting structure. Compare **pons** 4 the part of a pair of glasses that rests on the nose 5 Also called: **bridgework** a dental plate containing one or more artificial teeth that is secured to the surrounding natural teeth 6 a platform athwartships and above the rail, from which a ship is piloted and navigated 7 a piece of wood, usually fixed, supporting the strings of a violin, guitar, etc, and transmitting their vibrations to the sounding board 8 Also called: **bridge passage** a passage in a musical, literary, or dramatic work linking two or more important sections 9 Also called: **bridge circuit** *electronics* any of several networks, such as a Wheatstone bridge, consisting of two branches across which a measuring device is connected. The resistance, capacitance, etc, of one component can be determined from the known values of the others when the voltage in each

b

branch is balanced **10** *computing* a device that connects networks and sends packets between them **11** *billiards, snooker* **a** a support for a cue made by placing the fingers on the table and raising the thumb **b** a cue rest with a notched end for shots beyond normal reach **12** *theatre* **a** a platform of adjustable height above or beside the stage for the use of stagehands, light operators, etc **b** *chiefly Brit* a part of the stage floor that can be raised or lowered **13** a partition in a furnace or boiler to keep the fuel in place **14** **build bridges** to promote reconciliation or cooperation between hostile groups or people **15** **burn one's bridges** See **burn¹** (sense 19) **16** **cross a bridge when (one) comes to it** to deal with a problem only when it arises; not to anticipate difficulties ▷ *vb* (*tr*) **17** to build or provide a bridge over something; span: *to bridge a river* **18** to connect or reduce the distance between: *let us bridge our differences* [Old English *brycg*; related to Old Norse *bryggja* gangway, Old Frisian *bregge*, Old High German *brucka*, Danish, Swedish *bro*] > **ˈbridgeable** *adj* > **ˈbridgeless** *adj*

bridge² (brɪdʒ) *n* a card game for four players, based on whist, in which one hand (the dummy) is exposed and the trump suit decided by bidding between the players. See also **contract bridge, duplicate bridge, rubber bridge, auction bridge** [c19 of uncertain origin, but compare Turkish *bir-üç* (unattested phrase) one-three (said perhaps to refer to the one exposed hand and the three players' hands)]

bridgeboard (ˈbrɪdʒˌbɔːd) *n* a board on both sides of a staircase that is cut to support the treads and risers. Also called: **cut string**

bridgehead (ˈbrɪdʒˌhɛd) *n military* **1** an area of ground secured or to be taken on the enemy's side of an obstacle, esp a defended river **2** a fortified or defensive position at the end of a bridge nearest to the enemy **3** an advantageous position gained for future expansion

Bridgend (ˌbrɪdʒˈɛnd) *n* a county borough in S Wales, created in 1996 from S Mid Glamorgan. Administrative centre: Bridgend. Pop: 129 900 (2003 est). Area: 264 sq km (102 sq miles)

Bridge of Sighs *n* a covered 16th-century bridge in Venice, between the Doges' Palace and the prisons, through which prisoners were formerly led to trial or execution

bridge passage *n* See **bridge¹** (sense 8)

Bridgeport (ˈbrɪdʒˌpɔːt) *n* a port in SW Connecticut, on Long Island Sound. Pop: 139 664 (2003 est)

bridge rectifier *n electrical engineering* a full-wave rectifier consisting of a bridge with a similar rectifier in each of the four arms

bridge roll *n Brit* a soft bread roll in a long thin shape [c20 from BRIDGE² or perhaps BRIDGE¹]

Bridgetown (ˈbrɪdʒˌtaʊn) *n* the capital of Barbados, a port on the SW coast. Pop: 144 000 (2005 est)

bridgework (ˈbrɪdʒˌwɜːk) *n* **1 a** a partial denture attached to the surrounding teeth. See **bridge¹** (sense 5) **b** the technique of making such appliances **2** the process or occupation of constructing bridges

bridging (ˈbrɪdʒɪŋ) *n* **1** one or more timber struts fixed between floor or roof joists to stiffen the construction and distribute the loads **2** *mountaineering* a technique for climbing a wide chimney by pressing left hand and foot against one side of it and right hand and foot against the other side **3** *rugby Union* an illegal move in which a player leans down and forward onto the body of a prone player in a ruck, thereby preventing opposing players from winning the ball by fair rucking

bridging loan *n* a loan made to cover the period between two transactions, such as the buying of another house before the sale of the first is completed

Bridgwater (ˈbrɪdʒˌwɔːtə) *n* a town in SW England, in central Somerset. Pop: 36 563 (2001)

bridie (ˈbraɪdɪ; *Scot* ˈbrɪdɪ) *n Scot* a semicircular pie containing meat and onions [of unknown origin]

bridle (ˈbraɪdəl) *n* **1** a headgear for a horse, etc, consisting of a series of buckled straps and a metal mouthpiece (bit) by which the animal is controlled through the reins **2** something that curbs or restrains; check **3** a Y-shaped cable, rope, or chain, used for holding, towing, etc **4** *machinery* a device by which the motion of a component is limited, often in the form of a linkage or flange ▷ *vb* **5** (*tr*) to put a bridle on (a horse, mule, etc) **6** (*intr*) (of a horse) to respond correctly to the pull of the reins **7** (*tr*) to restrain; curb: *he bridled his rage* **8** (*intr*; often foll by *at*) to show anger, scorn, or indignation [Old English *brigdels*; related to *bregdan* to BRAID¹, Old High German *brittil*, Middle Low German *breidel*] > **ˈbridler** *n*

bridle path *or* **bridleway** (ˈbraɪdəlˌweɪ) *n* a path suitable for riding or leading horses. Also called (NZ): **bridle track**

bridlewise (ˈbraɪdəlˌwaɪz) *adj US* (of a horse) obedient to the pressure of the reins on the neck rather than to the bit

bridoon (brɪˈduːn) *n* a horse's bit: a small snaffle used in double bridles [c18 from French *bridon*, from *bride* bridle; compare Middle English *bride*]

brie (briː) *n* a variant spelling of **bree¹**

Brie (briː) *n* **1** a soft creamy white cheese, similar to Camembert but milder **2** a mainly agricultural area in N France, between the Rivers Marne and Seine: noted esp for its cheese

brief (briːf) *adj* **1** short in duration: *a brief holiday* **2** short in length or extent; scanty: *a brief bikini* **3** abrupt in manner; brusque: *the professor was brief with me this morning* **4** terse or concise; containing few words: *he made a brief statement* ▷ *n* **5** a condensed or short statement or written synopsis; abstract **6** *law* a document containing all the facts and points of law of a case by which a solicitor instructs a barrister to represent a client **7** *RC Church* a letter issuing from the Roman court written in modern characters, as contrasted with a papal bull; papal brief **8** short for **briefing 9** a paper outlining the arguments and information on one side of a debate **10** *Brit slang* a lawyer, esp a barrister **11** **hold a brief for** to argue for; champion **12** **in brief** in short; to sum up ▷ *vb* (*tr*) **13** to prepare or instruct by giving a summary of relevant facts **14** to make a summary or synopsis of **15** *English law* **a** to instruct (a barrister) by brief **b** to retain (a barrister) as counsel **16** (*intr*; foll by *against*) to supply potentially damaging or negative information regarding somone, as to the media, a politician, etc. See also **briefs** [c14 from Old French *bref*, from Latin *brevis*; related to Greek *brakhus*] > **ˈbriefly** *adv* > **ˈbriefness** *n*

briefcase (ˈbriːfˌkeɪs) *n* a flat portable case, often of leather, for carrying papers, books, etc

briefing (ˈbriːfɪŋ) *n* **1** a meeting at which detailed information or instructions are given, as for military operations, etc **2** the facts presented during such a meeting

briefless (ˈbriːflɪs) *adj* (said of a barrister) without clients

briefs (briːfs) *pl n* men's underpants or women's pants without legs

brier¹ *or* **briar** (ˈbraɪə) *n* any of various thorny shrubs or other plants, such as the sweetbrier and greenbrier [Old English *brēr*, *brǣr*, of obscure origin] > **ˈbriery** *or* **ˈbriary** *adj*

brier² (ˈbraɪə) *n* a variant spelling of **briar¹**

brierroot (ˈbraɪəˌruːt) *n* a variant spelling of **briarroot** Also called: **brier"wood**

brig¹ (brɪg) *n* **1** *nautical* a two masted square rigger **2** *chiefly US* a prison, esp in a navy ship [c18 shortened from BRIGANTINE]

brig² (brɪg) *n* a Scot and northern English word for a **bridge¹**

Brig. *abbreviation for* Brigadier

brigade (brɪˈɡeɪd) *n* **1** a formation of fighting units, together with support arms and services,

smaller than a division and usually commanded by a brigadier **2** a group of people organized for a certain task: *a rescue brigade* ▷ *vb* (*tr*) **3** to organize into a brigade **4** to put or group together [c17 from Old French, from Old Italian, from *brigare* to fight, perhaps of Celtic origin; see BRIGAND]

brigadier (ˌbrɪɡəˈdɪə) *n* **1** an officer of the British Army or Royal Marines who holds a rank junior to a major general but senior to a colonel, usually commanding a brigade **2** an equivalent rank in other armed forces **3** *US army* short for **brigadier general 4** *history* a noncommissioned rank in the armies of Napoleon I [c17 from French, from BRIGADE]

brigadier general *n, pl* brigadier generals **1** an officer of the US Army, Air Force, or Marine Corps who holds a rank junior to a major general but senior to a colonel, usually commanding a brigade **2** the former name for a **brigadier** (sense 1)

brigalow (ˈbrɪɡələʊ) *n Austral* **a** any of various acacia trees **b** (*as modifier*): *brigalow country* [c19 from a native Australian language]

brigand (ˈbrɪɡənd) *n* a bandit or plunderer, esp a member of a gang operating in mountainous areas [c14 from Old French, from Old Italian *brigante* fighter, from *brigare* to fight, from *briga* strife, of Celtic origin] > **ˈbrigandage** *or* **ˈbrigandry** *n*

brigandine (ˈbrɪɡənˌdiːn, -ˌdaɪn) *n* a coat of mail, invented in the Middle Ages to increase mobility, consisting of metal rings or sheets sewn on to cloth or leather [c15 from Old French, from BRIGAND + -INE¹]

brigantine (ˈbrɪɡənˌtiːn, -ˌtaɪn) *n* a two-masted sailing ship, rigged square on the foremast and fore-and-aft with square topsails on the mainmast [c16 from Old Italian *brigantino* pirate ship, from *brigante* BRIGAND]

Brig. Gen. *abbreviation for* brigadier general

Brighouse (ˈbrɪɡˌhaʊs) *n* a town in N England, in Calderdale unitary authority, West Yorkshire: machine tools, textiles, engineering. Pop: 32 360 (2001)

bright (braɪt) *adj* **1** emitting or reflecting much light; shining **2** (of colours) intense or vivid **3** full of promise: *a bright future* **4** full of animation; cheerful: *a bright face* **5** *informal* quick witted or clever: *a bright child* **6** magnificent; glorious: *a bright victory* **7** polished; glistening: *a bright finish* **8** (of the voice) distinct and clear **9** (of a liquid) translucent and clear: *a circle of bright water* **10** **bright and early** very early in the morning ▷ *n* **11** a thin flat paintbrush with a straight sharp edge used for highlighting in oil painting **12** *poetic* brightness or splendour: *the bright of his armour* ▷ *adv* **13** brightly: *the fire was burning bright* ▷ See also **brights** [Old English *beorht*; related to Old Norse *bjartr*, Gothic *bairhts* clear, Old High German *beraht*, Norwegian *bjerk*, Swedish *brokig* pied] > **ˈbrightly** *adv*

bright-blindness *n vet science* blindness occurring in sheep grazing pastures heavily infested with bracken

brighten (ˈbraɪtən) *vb* **1** to make or become bright or brighter **2** to make or become cheerful > **ˈbrightener** *n*

brightening agent *n* a compound applied to a textile to increase its brightness by the conversion of ultraviolet radiation to visible (blue) light, used in detergents

bright-eyed *adj* **1** eager; fresh and enthusiastic **2** **bright-eyed and bushy-tailed** *informal* keen, confident, and alert

bright lights *pl n* **the.** places of entertainment in a city

brightness (ˈbraɪtnɪs) *n* **1** the condition of being bright **2** *physics* a former name for **luminosity** (sense 4) **3** *psychol* the experienced intensity of light

Brighton (ˈbraɪtən) *n* a coastal resort in S England, in Brighton and Hove unitary authority, East Sussex: patronized by the Prince Regent, who had the Royal Pavilion built (1782); seat of the University of Sussex (1966) and the University of Brighton (1992). Pop: 134 293 (2001)

Brighton and Hove (ˈhəʊv) *n* a city and unitary authority in S England, in East Sussex. Pop: 251 500 (2003 est.). Area: 72 sq km (28 sq miles)

brights (braɪts) *pl n US* the high beam of the headlights of a motor vehicle

Bright's disease (braɪts) *n* chronic inflammation of the kidneys; chronic nephritis [c19 named after Richard *Bright* (1789–1858), British physician]

brightwork (ˈbraɪtˌwɜːk) *n* **1** shiny metal trimmings or fittings on ships, cars, etc **2** varnished or plain woodwork on a vessel

brik (brɪk) *n* a Tunisian deep-fried spicy pastry filled with fish or meat and sometimes an egg [Arabic]

brill (brɪl) *n, pl* **brill** or **brills** a European food fish, *Scophthalmus rhombus*, a flatfish similar to the turbot but lacking tubercles on the body: family *Bothidae* [c15 probably from Cornish *brỹthel* mackerel, from Old Cornish *brỹth* speckled; related to Welsh *brith* spotted]

brilliance (ˈbrɪljəns) or **brilliancy** *n* **1** great brightness; radiance **2** excellence or distinction in physical or mental ability; exceptional talent **3** splendour; magnificence: *the brilliance of the royal court* **4** *physics* a former term for **luminance**

brilliant (ˈbrɪljənt) *adj* **1** shining with light; sparkling **2** (of a colour) having a high saturation and reflecting a considerable amount of light; vivid **3** outstanding; exceptional: *a brilliant success* **4** splendid; magnificent: *a brilliant show* **5** of outstanding intelligence or intellect: *a brilliant mind; a brilliant idea* **6** *music* **a** (of the tone of an instrument) having a large proportion of high harmonics above the fundamental **b** Also: brilliant (*French* brijɑ̃) brillante (*French* brijɑ̃t) with spirit; lively ▷ *n* **7** Also called: brilliant cut **a** a popular circular cut for diamonds and other gemstones in the form of two many-faceted pyramids (the top one truncated) joined at their bases **b** a diamond of this cut **8** (formerly) a size of a printer's type approximately equal to 4 point [c17 from French *brillant* shining, from *briller* to shine, from Italian *brillare*, from *brillo* BERYL] ▷ ˈbrilliantly *adv*

brilliantine (ˈbrɪljənˌtiːn) *n* **1** a perfumed oil used to make the hair smooth and shiny **2** *chiefly US* a glossy fabric made of mohair and cotton [c19 from French, from *brillant* shining]

brim (brɪm) *n* **1** the upper rim of a vessel: *the brim of a cup* **2** a projecting rim or edge: *the brim of a hat* **3** the brink or edge of something ▷ *vb* **brims, brimming, brimmed 4** to fill or be full to the brim: *eyes brimming with tears* [c13 from Middle High German *brem*, probably from Old Norse *barmr*; see BERM] ▷ ˈbrimless *adj*

brimful or **brimfull** (ˌbrɪmˈfʊl) *adj* (*postpositive*, foll by *of*) filled up to the brim (with)

brimmer (ˈbrɪmə) *n* a vessel, such as a glass or bowl, filled to the brim

brimstone (ˈbrɪmˌstəʊn) *n* **1** an obsolete name for **sulphur 2** a common yellow butterfly, *Gonepteryx rhamni*, of N temperate regions of the Old World: family *Pieridae* **3** *archaic* a scolding nagging woman; virago [Old English *brynstān*; related to Old Norse *brennistein*; see BURN[1], STONE]

Brindisi (*Italian* ˈbrindizi) *n* a port in SE Italy, in SE Apulia: important naval base in Roman times and a centre of the Crusades in the Middle Ages. Pop: 89 081 (2001). Ancient name: **Brundisium**

brindle (ˈbrɪndᵊl) *n* **1** a brindled animal **2** a brindled colouring [c17 back formation from BRINDLED]

brindled (ˈbrɪndᵊld) *adj* brown or grey streaked or patched with a darker colour: *a brindled dog* [c17 changed from c15 *brended*, literally: branded, probably of Scandinavian origin; compare Old Norse *bröndóttr*; see BRAND]

brine (braɪn) *n* **1** a strong solution of salt and

water, used for salting and pickling meats, etc **2** the sea or its water **3** *chem* **a** a concentrated solution of sodium chloride in water **b** any solution of a salt in water: *a potassium chloride brine* ▷ *vb* **4** (*tr*) to soak in or treat with brine [Old English *brīne*; related to Middle Dutch *brīne*, Old Slavonic *bridŭ* bitter, Sanskrit *bibhrāya* burnt] ▷ ˈbrinish *adj*

Brinell hardness number or **Brindell (hardness) number** (brɪˈnɛl) *n* a measure of the hardness of a material obtained by pressing a hard steel ball into its surface; it is expressed as the ratio of the load on the ball in kilograms to the area of the depression made by the ball in square millimetres [c19 named after Johann A. *Brinell* (1849–1925), Swedish engineer]

brinelling (ˈbrɪnɛlɪŋ) *n* a localized surface corrosion; a cause of damage to bearings

bring (brɪŋ) *vb* **brings, bringing, brought** (*tr*) **1** to carry, convey, or take (something or someone) to a designated place or person: *bring that book to me; will you bring Jessica to Tom's party?* **2** to cause to happen or occur to (oneself or another): *to bring disrespect on oneself* **3** to cause to happen as a consequence: *responsibility brings maturity* **4** to cause to come to mind: *it brought back memories* **5** to cause to be in a certain state, position, etc: *the punch brought him to his knees* **6** to force, persuade, or make (oneself): *I couldn't bring myself to do it* **7** to sell for; fetch: *the painting brought 20 pounds* **8** *law* **a** to institute (proceedings, charges, etc) **b** to put (evidence, etc) before a tribunal **9 bring forth** to give birth to **10 bring home to a** to convince of: *his account brought home to us the gravity of the situation* **b** to place the blame on **11 bring to bear** See **bear**[1] (sense 17) ▷ See also **bring about, bring down, bring forward, bring in, bring off, bring on, bring out, bring over, bring round, bring to, bring up** [Old English *bringan*; related to Gothic *briggan*, Old High German *bringan*] ▷ ˈbringer *n*

bring about *vb* (*tr, adverb*) **1** to cause to happen: *to bring about a change in the law* **2** to turn (a ship) around

bring-and-buy sale *n Brit and NZ* an informal sale, often conducted for charity, to which people bring items for sale and buy those that others have brought

bring down *vb* (*tr, adverb*) **1** to cause to fall: *the fighter aircraft brought the enemy down; the ministers agreed to bring down the price of oil* **2** (*usually passive*) *slang* to cause to be elated and then suddenly depressed, as from using drugs

bring forward *vb* (*tr, adverb*) **1** to present or introduce (a subject) for discussion **2** *book-keeping* to transfer (a figure representing the sum of the figures on a page or in a column) to the top of the next page or column **3** to move to an earlier time or date: *the kickoff has been brought forward to 2 p.m.*

bring in *vb* (*tr, adverb*) **1** to yield (income, profit, or cash): *his investments brought him in £100* **2** to produce or return (a verdict) **3** to put forward or introduce (a legislative bill, etc)

bringing-up *n* another term for **upbringing**

bring off *vb* (*tr, adverb*) **1** to succeed in achieving (something), esp with difficulty or contrary to expectations: *he managed to bring off the deal* **2** *slang* to cause to have an orgasm

| USAGE The second sense of this word was formerly considered to be taboo, and it was labelled as such in previous editions of *Collins English Dictionary*. However, it has now become acceptable in speech, although some older or more conservative people may object to its use

bring on *vb* (*tr, adverb*) **1** to induce or cause: *these pills will bring on labour* **2** *slang* to cause sexual excitement in; stimulate

| USAGE The second sense of this word was formerly considered to be taboo, and it was labelled as such in

previous editions of *Collins English Dictionary*. However, it has now become acceptable in speech, although some older or more conservative people may object to its use

bring out *vb* (*tr, adverb*) **1** to produce or publish or have published: *when are you bringing out a new dictionary?* **2** to expose, reveal, or cause to be seen: *she brought out the best in me* **3** to encourage (a shy person) to be less reserved (often in the phrase **bring (someone) out of himself** or **herself**) **4** *Brit* (of a trade union, provocative action by management, misunderstanding, etc) to cause (workers) to strike **5** (foll by *in*) to cause (a person) to become covered (with spots, a rash, etc) **6** *Brit* to introduce (a girl) formally into society as a debutante

bring over *vb* (*tr, adverb*) to cause (a person) to change allegiances

bring round or **around** *vb* (*tr, adverb*) **1** to restore (a person) to consciousness, esp after a faint **2** to convince (another person, usually an opponent) of an opinion or point of view

bring to *vb* (*tr*) **1** (*adverb*) to restore (a person) to consciousness **2** (*adverb*) to cause (a ship) to turn into the wind and reduce her headway **3** (*preposition*) to make (something) equal to (an amount of money): *that brings your bill to £17*

bring up *vb* (*tr, adverb*) **1** to care for and train (a child); rear: *we had been brought up to go to church* **2** to raise (a subject) for discussion; mention **3** to vomit (food) **4** (foll by *against*) to cause (a person) to face or confront **5** (foll by *to*) to cause (something) to be of a required standard

brinjal (ˈbrɪndʒəl) *n* (in India and Africa) another name for the **aubergine** [c17 from Portuguese *berinjela*, from Arabic; see AUBERGINE]

brink (brɪŋk) *n* **1** the edge, border, or verge of a steep place: *the brink of the precipice* **2** the highest point; top: *the sun fell below the brink of the hill* **3** the land at the edge of a body of water **4** the verge of an event or state: *the brink of disaster* [c13 from Middle Dutch *brinc*, of Germanic origin; compare Old Norse *brekka* slope, Middle Low German *brink* edge of a field]

brinkmanship (ˈbrɪŋkmənˌʃɪp) *n* the art or practice of pressing a dangerous situation, esp in international affairs, to the limit of safety and peace in order to win an advantage from a threatening or tenacious foe

brinny (ˈbrɪnɪ) *n, pl* -**nies** *Austral children's slang, old-fashioned* a stone, esp when thrown

briny (ˈbraɪnɪ) *adj* **brinier, briniest 1** of or resembling brine; salty ▷ *n* **2** (preceded by *the*) an informal name for the **sea**. ▷ ˈbrininess *n*

brio (ˈbriːəʊ) *n* liveliness or vigour; spirit. See also **con brio** [c19 from Italian, of Celtic origin]

brioche (ˈbriːəʊʃ, -ɒʃ; *French* briɔʃ) *n* a soft roll or loaf made from a very light yeast dough, sometimes mixed with currants [c19 from Norman dialect, from *brier* to knead, of Germanic origin; compare French *broyer* to pound, BREAK]

briolette (ˌbriːəʊˈlɛt) *n* a pear-shaped gem cut with long triangular facets [c19 from French, alteration of *brillolette*, from *brignolette* little dried plum, after *Brignoles*, France, where these plums are produced]

briony (ˈbraɪənɪ) *n, pl* -**nies** a variant spelling of **bryony**

briquette or **briquet** (brɪˈkɛt) *n* **1** a small brick made of compressed coal dust, sawdust, charcoal, etc, used for fuel **2** a small brick of any substance: *an ice-cream briquette* ▷ *vb* **3** (*tr*) to make into the form of a brick or bricks: *to briquette clay* [c19 from French: a little brick, from *bique* BRICK]

bris (ˈbrɪs) or **brith** (ˈbrɪt) *n Judaism* ritual circumcision of male babies, usually at eight days old, regarded as the formal entry of the child to the Jewish community [from Hebrew, literally: covenant]

brisance (ˈbriːzəns; *French* brizɑ̃s) *n* the shattering

b

effect or power of an explosion or explosive [c20 from French, from *briser* to break, ultimately of Celtic origin; compare Old Irish *brissim* I break] > ˈ**brisant** *adj*

Brisbane (ˈbrɪzbən) *n* a port in E Australia, the capital of Queensland: founded in 1824 as a penal settlement; vast agricultural hinterland. Pop: 1 508 161 (2001)

brise-soleil (ˌbriːzsəʊˈleɪ) *n* a structure used in hot climates to protect a window from the sun, usually consisting of horizontal or vertical strips of wood, concrete, etc [c20 French: break-sun, from *briser* to break + *soleil* sun]

brisk (brɪsk) *adj* 1 lively and quick; vigorous: *a brisk walk; trade was brisk* 2 invigorating or sharp: *brisk weather* ▷ *vb* 3 (often foll by *up*) to enliven; make or become brisk [c16 probably variant of BRUSQUE] > ˈ**briskly** *adv* > ˈ**briskness** *n*

brisken (ˈbrɪskən) *vb* to make or become more lively or brisk

brisket (ˈbrɪskɪt) *n* 1 the breast of a four-legged animal 2 the meat from this part, esp of beef [c14 probably of Scandinavian origin; related to Old Norse *brjōsk* gristle, Norwegian and Danish *brusk*]

brisling (ˈbrɪslɪŋ) *n* another name for a **sprat**, esp a Norwegian sprat seasoned, smoked, and canned in oil [c20 from Norwegian; related to obsolete Danish *bretling*, German *Breitling*]

Brisso (ˈbrɪzəʊ) *n Austral informal* a person who lives in Brisbane

bristle (ˈbrɪsəl) *n* 1 any short stiff hair of an animal or plant 2 something resembling these hair: *toothbrush bristle* ▷ *vb* 3 (when *intr*, often foll by *up*) to stand up or cause to stand up like bristles: *the angry cat's fur bristled* 4 (*intr*; sometimes foll by *up*) to show anger, indignation, etc: *she bristled at the suggestion* 5 (*intr*) to be thickly covered or set: *the target bristled with arrows* 6 (*intr*) to be in a state of agitation or movement: *the office was bristling with activity* 7 (*tr*) to provide with a bristle or bristles [c13 *bristil, brustel* from earlier *brust*, from Old English *byrst*; related to Old Norse *burst*, Old High German *borst*] > ˈ**bristly** *adj*

bristlecone pine (ˈbrɪsəlˌkəʊn) *n* a coniferous tree, *Pinus aristata*, of the western US, bearing cones with bristle-like prickles: one of the longest-lived trees, useful in radiocarbon dating

bristle-grass *n* any of various grasses of the genus *Setaria*, such as *S. viridis*, having a bristly inflorescence

bristletail (ˈbrɪsəlˌteɪl) *n* any primitive wingless insect of the orders *Thysanura* and *Diplura*, such as the silverfish and firebrat, having a flattened body and long tail appendages

bristle worm *n* a popular name for a **polychaete**

Bristol (ˈbrɪstəl) *n* 1 **City of** a port and industrial city in SW England, mainly in Bristol unitary authority, on the River Avon seven miles from its mouth on the Bristol Channel: a major port, trading with America, in the 17th and 18th centuries; the modern port consists chiefly of docks at Avonmouth and Portishead; noted for the **Clifton Suspension Bridge** (designed by I. K. Brunel, 1834) over the Avon gorge; Bristol university (1909) and University of the West of England (1992). Pop: 420 556 (2001) 2 **City of** a unitary authority in SW England, created in 1996 from part of Avon county. Pop: 391 500 (2003 est). Area: 110 sq km (42 sq miles)

Bristol board *n* a heavy smooth cardboard of fine quality, used for printing and drawing

Bristol Channel *n* an inlet of the Atlantic, between S Wales and SW England, merging into the Severn estuary. Length: about 137 km (85 miles)

Bristol fashion *adv, adj* (*postpositive*) 1 *nautical* clean and neat, with newly painted and scrubbed surfaces, brass polished, etc 2 shipshape and Bristol fashion in good order; efficiently arranged

bristols (ˈbrɪstəlz) *pl n Brit slang* a woman's breasts [c20 short for *Bristol Cities*, rhyming slang for *titties*]

brit (brɪt) *n* (*functioning as singular or plural*) 1 the young of a herring, sprat, or similar fish 2 minute marine crustaceans, esp copepods, forming food for many fishes and whales [c17 perhaps from Cornish *brȳthel* mackerel; see BRILL]

Brit (brɪt) *n informal* a British person

Brit *abbreviation for* 1 Britain 2 British

Britain (ˈbrɪtən) *n* another name for **Great Britain** or the **United Kingdom**

Britannia (brɪˈtænɪə) *n* 1 a female warrior carrying a trident and wearing a helmet, personifying Great Britain or the British Empire 2 (in the ancient Roman Empire) the S part of Great Britain 3 short for **Britannia coin**

Britannia coin *n* any of four British gold coins introduced in 1987 for investment purposes; their denominations are £100, £50, £25, and £10

Britannia metal *n* an alloy of low melting point consisting of tin with 5–10 per cent antimony, 1–3 per cent copper, and sometimes small quantities of zinc, lead, or bismuth: used for decorative purposes and for bearings

Britannic (brɪˈtænɪk) *adj* of Britain; British (esp in the phrases **His** or **Her Britannic Majesty**)

Britart (ˈbrɪtˌɑːt) *n* a movement in modern British art beginning in the late 1980s, often conceptual or using controversial materials, including such artists as Damien Hirst and Rachel Whiteread [c20 *Brit* short for *British*]

britches (ˈbrɪtʃɪz) *pl n* a variant spelling of **breeches**

brith (brɪt) *n* a variant of **bris**

Briticism (ˈbrɪtɪˌsɪzəm) *n* a custom, linguistic usage, or other feature peculiar to Britain or its people

British (ˈbrɪtɪʃ) *adj* 1 relating to, denoting, or characteristic of Britain or any of the natives, citizens, or inhabitants of the United Kingdom 2 relating to or denoting the English language as spoken and written in Britain, esp the S dialect generally regarded as standard. See also **Southern British English, Received Pronunciation** 3 relating to or denoting the ancient Britons ▷ *n* 4 (*functioning as plural*) the natives or inhabitants of Britain 5 the extinct Celtic language of the ancient Britons. See also **Brythonic.** > ˈ**Britishness** *n*

British Antarctic Territory *n* a UK Overseas Territory in the S Atlantic (claims are suspended under the Antarctic Treaty): created in 1962 and consisting of the South Shetland Islands, the South Orkney Islands, and Graham Land; formerly part of the Falkland Islands Dependencies

British Association screw thread *n engineering* a system of screw sizes designated from 0 to 25. Now superseded by standard metric sizes. Abbreviation: BA

British Cameroons *pl n* a former British trust territory of West Africa. See **Cameroon**

British Civil Airworthiness Requirements *pl n* (in Britain) documents specifying aerodynamic, engineering design, construction, and performance requirements, which must be met before an aircraft is given permission to fly

British Columbia *n* a province of W Canada, on the Pacific coast: largely mountainous with extensive forests, rich mineral resources, and important fisheries. Capital: Victoria. Pop: 4 196 383 (2004 est). Area: 930 532 sq km (359 279 sq miles). Abbreviation: BC

British Columbian *adj* 1 of or relating to British Columbia or its inhabitants ▷ *n* 2 a native or inhabitant of British Columbia

British Commonwealth of Nations *n* the former name of the Commonwealth

British Council *n* an organization founded (1934) to extend the influence of British culture and education throughout the world

British disease *n* (usually preceded by *the*) the pattern of strikes and industrial unrest in the 1970s and early 1980s supposed by many during this time to be endemic in Britain and to weaken the British economy

British East Africa *n* the former British possessions of Uganda, Kenya, Tanganyika, and Zanzibar, before their independence in the 1960s

British Empire *n* (formerly) the United Kingdom and the territories under its control, which reached its greatest extent at the end of World War I when it embraced over a quarter of the world's population and more than a quarter of the world's land surface

Britisher (ˈbrɪtɪʃə) *n* (not used by the British) 1 a native or inhabitant of Great Britain 2 any British subject

British Guiana *n* the former name (until 1966) of **Guyana**

British Honduras *n* the former name of **Belize**

British India *n* the 17 provinces of India formerly governed by the British under the British sovereign: ceased to exist in 1947 when the independent states of India and Pakistan were created

British Indian Ocean Territory *n* a UK Overseas Territory in the Indian Ocean: consists of the Chagos Archipelago (formerly a dependency of Mauritius) and formerly included (until 1976) Aldabra, Farquhar, and Des Roches, now administratively part of the Seychelles. Diego Garcia is an important US naval base

British Isles *pl n* a group of islands in W Europe, consisting of Great Britain, Ireland, the Isle of Man, Orkney, Shetland, the Channel Islands belonging to Great Britain, and the islands adjacent to these

Britishism (ˈbrɪtɪˌʃɪzəm) *n* a variant of **Briticism**

British Israelite *n* a member of a religious movement claiming that the British people are descended from the lost tribes of Israel

British Legion *n Brit* a shortened form of **Royal British Legion**

British Library *n* the British national library, formed in 1973 from the British Museum library and other national collections: housed mainly in the British Museum until 1997 when a purpose-built library in St Pancras, London, was completed

British List *n* a list, maintained by the British Ornithologists' Union, of birds accepted as occurring at least once in the British Isles

British longhair (ˈlɒŋˌheə) *n* a breed of large cat with a semi-long thick soft coat

British lop *n* a breed of large white pig with large drooping ears, originating from Wales, Cumberland, and Ulster. Former name: **long white lop-eared**

British Museum *n* a museum in London, founded in 1753: contains one of the world's richest collections of antiquities and (until 1997) most of the British Library

British National Party *n* (in Britain) a neo-Nazi political party. Abbreviation: BNP

British North America *n* (formerly) Canada or its constituent regions or provinces that formed part of the British Empire

British shorthair (ˈʃɔːtˌheə) *n* a breed of large cat with a short dense coat

British Somaliland *n* a former British protectorate (1884–1960) in E Africa, on the Gulf of Aden: united with Italian Somaliland in 1960 to form the Somali Republic

British Standard brass thread *n engineering* a Whitworth screw thread having 26 threads per inch, used for thin-walled tubing and designated by the diameter of the tubing. Abbreviation: BSB

British Standard fine thread *n engineering* a screw thread having a Whitworth profile but a finer pitch for a given diameter. Abbreviation: BSF

British Standard pipe thread *n engineering* a screw thread of Whitworth profile used for piping and designated by the bore of the pipe. Abbreviation: BSP

British Standards Institution *n* an association, founded in London in 1901, that establishes and maintains standards for units of measurements, clothes sizes, technical terminology, etc, as used in Britain. Abbreviation: BSI. Compare **National Bureau of Standards, International Standards Organization**

British Standard Time *n* the standard time used in Britain all the year round from 1968 to 1971, set one hour ahead of Greenwich Mean Time and equalling Central European Time

British Standard Whitworth thread *n* See **Whitworth screw thread**. Abbreviation: BSW

British Summer Time *n* time set one hour ahead of Greenwich Mean Time: used in Britain from the end of March to the end of October, providing an extra hour of daylight in the evening. Abbreviation: BST. Compare **daylight-saving time**

British Technology Group *n* an organization formed in 1981 by the merger of the National Enterprise Board and the National Research and Development Corporation to encourage and finance technological innovation: privatized in 2000. Abbreviation: BTG

British thermal unit *n* a unit of heat in the fps system equal to the quantity of heat required to raise the temperature of 1 pound of water by 1°F. 1 British thermal unit is equivalent to 1055.06 joules or 251.997 calories. Abbrevs: btu, BThU

British Union of Fascists *n* the British fascist party founded by Sir Oswald Mosley (1932), which advocated a strong corporate state and promoted anti-Semitism

British Virgin Islands *pl n* a UK Overseas Territory in the Caribbean, consisting of 36 islands in the E Virgin Islands: formerly part of the Federation of the Leeward Islands (1871–1956). Capital: Road Town, on Tortola. Pop: 21 000 (2003 est). Area: 153 sq km (59 sq miles)

British warm *n* an army officer's short thick overcoat

British West Africa *n* the former British possessions of Nigeria, The Gambia, Sierra Leone, and the Gold Coast, and the former trust territories of Togoland and Cameroons

British West Indies *pl n* a former name for the states in the Caribbean that are members of the Commonwealth: the Bahamas, Barbados, Jamaica, Trinidad and Tobago, Antigua and Barbuda, Saint Kitts-Nevis, Dominica, Grenada, Saint Lucia, and Saint Vincent and the Grenadines; along with the islands which remain as United Kingdom dependencies: Anguilla, the Cayman Islands, Montserrat, the Turks and Caicos Islands and the British Virgin Islands

British White *n* a British breed of medium-sized white cattle with black points, bred mainly for meat

Brit Lit *or* **Britlit** ('brɪt,lɪt) *n* British literature, esp current fashionable writing

brit milah ('brit mi'laː, 'milə) *n Judaism* a Hebrew term usually translated as **circumcision**

Britneyfication (,brɪtnɪfɪ'keɪʃən) *n* the effect on clothes and fashions of following the revealing styles favoured by the US pop singer Britney Spears (born 1981)

Briton ('brɪtªn) *n* 1 a native or inhabitant of Britain 2 a citizen of the United Kingdom 3 *history* any of the early Celtic inhabitants of S Britain who were largely dispossessed by the Anglo-Saxon invaders after the 5th century AD [c13 from Old French *Breton*, from Latin *Britto*, of Celtic origin]

Britpack ('brɪt,pæk) *n* **a** a group of young and successful British actors, directors, artists, etc **b** (*as modifier*): *Britpack talent* [c20 a play on BRATPACK]

Britpop ('brɪt,pɒp) *n* the characteristic pop music performed by some British bands of the mid 1990s

Brittany¹ ('brɪtənɪ) *n* a region of NW France, the peninsula between the English Channel and the Bay of Biscay: settled by Celtic refugees from Wales and Cornwall during the Anglo-Saxon invasions; disputed between England and France until 1364. Breton name: **Breiz** (braɪz) French

name: Bretagne. Related adjective: **Breton**

Brittany² *n, pl* **-nies** a medium-sized strongly-built variety of retriever with a slightly wavy coat usu. in tan and white, liver and white, or black and white

brittle ('brɪtªl) *adj* 1 easily cracked, snapped, or broken; fragile 2 curt or irritable: *a brittle reply* 3 hard or sharp in quality ▷ *n* 4 a crunchy sweet made with treacle and nuts: *peanut brittle* [c14 from Old English *brytel* (unattested); related to *brytsen* fragment, *brēotan* to break] > 'brittely *or* 'brittly *adv*

brittle bone disease *n* the nontechnical name for **osteogenesis imperfecta**

brittleness ('brɪtªlnɪs) *n* 1 the quality of being brittle 2 *metallurgy* the tendency of a metal to break without being significantly distorted or exposed to a high level of stress. Compare **toughness** (sense 2), **softness** (sense 2)

brittle-star *n* any echinoderm of the class *Ophiuroidea*, occurring on the sea bottom and having five long slender arms radiating from a small central disc. See also **basket-star**

Brittonic (brɪ'tɒnɪk) *n, adj* another word for **Brythonic**

britzka *or* **britska** ('brɪtskə) *n* a long horse-drawn carriage with a folding top over the rear seat and a rear-facing front seat [c19 from German, variant of *Britschka*, from Polish *bryczka* a little cart, from *bryka* cart]

Brix scale (brɪks) *n* a scale for calibrating hydrometers used for measuring the concentration and density of sugar solutions at a given temperature [c19 named after A. F. W. Brix, 19th-century German inventor]

BRN *international car registration for* Bahrain

Brno ('bɜːnəʊ; *Czech* 'brnɔ) *n* a city in the Czech Republic; formerly the capital of Moravia: the country's second largest city. Pop: 375 000 (2005 est). German name: **Brünn**

bro¹ (brəʊ) *n* 1 NZ a family member 2 a close associate

bro² (bruː), **bra** *or* **bru** *n South African informal* a friend, often used in direct address [c20 from Afrikaans *broer* brother]

bro. (brəʊ) *abbreviation for* brother

broach¹ (brəʊtʃ) *vb* 1 (*tr*) to initiate (a topic) for discussion: *to broach a dangerous subject* 2 (*tr*) to tap or pierce (a container) to draw off (a liquid): *to broach a cask; to broach wine* 3 (*tr*) to open in order to begin to use: *to broach a shipment* 4 (*intr*) to break the surface of the water: *the trout broached after being hooked* 5 (*tr*) *machinery* to enlarge and finish (a hole) by reaming ▷ *n* 6 a long tapered toothed cutting tool for enlarging holes 7 a spit for roasting meat, etc 8 a roof covering the corner triangle on the top of a square tower having an octagonal spire 9 a pin, forming part of some types of lock, that registers in the hollow bore of a key 10 a tool used for tapping casks 11 a less common spelling of **brooch** [c14 from Old French *broche*, from Vulgar Latin *brocca* (unattested), from Latin *brochus* projecting] > 'broacher *n*

broach² (brəʊtʃ) *vb nautical* (usually foll by *to*) to cause (a sailing vessel) to swerve sharply and dangerously or (of a sailing vessel) to swerve sharply and dangerously in a following sea, so as to be broadside to the waves [c18 perhaps from BROACH¹ in obsolete sense of turn on a spit]

broad (brɔːd) *adj* 1 having relatively great breadth or width 2 of vast extent; spacious: *a broad plain* 3 (*postpositive*) from one side to the other: *four miles broad* 4 of great scope or potential: *that invention had broad applications* 5 not detailed; general: *broad plans* 6 clear and open; full (esp in the phrase **broad daylight**) 7 obvious or plain: *broad hints* 8 liberal; tolerant: *a broad political stance* 9 widely spread; extensive: *broad support* 10 outspoken or bold: *a broad manner* 11 vulgar; coarse; indecent: *a broad joke* 12 unrestrained; free: *broad laughter* 13 (of a dialect or pronunciation) consisting of a large number of speech sounds characteristic of a particular geographical area: *a broad Yorkshire accent*

14 *finance* denoting an assessment of liquidity as including notes and coin in circulation with the public, banks' till money and balances, most private-sector bank deposits, and sterling bank-deposit certificates: *broad money*. Compare **narrow** (sense 7) 15 *phonetics* **a** of or relating to a type of pronunciation transcription in which symbols correspond approximately to phonemes without taking account of allophonic variations **b** broad a the long vowel in English words such as *father*, *half*, as represented in the received pronunciation of Southern British English 16 **as broad as it is long** amounting to the same thing; without advantage either way ▷ *n* 17 the broad part of something 18 *slang, chiefly US and Canadian* **a** a girl or woman **b** a prostitute 19 *Brit dialect* a river spreading over a lowland. See also **Broads** 20 *East Anglian dialect* a shallow lake 21 a wood-turning tool used for shaping the insides and bottoms of cylinders ▷ *adv* 22 widely or fully: *broad awake* [Old English *brād*; related to Old Norse *breithr*, Old Frisian *brēd*, Old High German *breit*, Gothic *braiths*] > 'broadly *adv* > 'broadness *n*

B-road *n* (in Britain) a secondary road

broad arrow *n* 1 a mark shaped like a broad arrowhead designating British government property and formerly used on prison clothing 2 an arrow with a broad head

broadband ('brɔːd,bænd) *n* a transmission technique using a wide range of frequencies that enables messages to be sent simultaneously, used in fast internet connections. See also **baseband**

broad bean *n* 1 an erect annual Eurasian bean plant, *Vicia faba*, cultivated for its large edible flattened seeds, used as a vegetable 2 the seed of this plant Also called: **horse bean**

broadbill ('brɔːd,bɪl) *n* 1 any passerine bird of the family *Eurylaimidae*, of tropical Africa and Asia, having bright plumage and a short wide bill 2 *US* any of various wide-billed birds, such as the scaup and shoveler 3 *US* another name for **swordfish**

broadbrim ('brɔːd,brɪm) *n* a broad-brimmed hat, esp one worn by the Quakers in the 17th century

broadbrush ('brɔːd,brʌʃ) *adj* lacking full detail or information; incomplete or rough: *anything other than a broadbrush strategy for the industry will be overloaded with detail*

broadcast ('brɔːd,kɑːst) *vb* **-casts**, **-casting**, **-cast** *or* **-casted** 1 to transmit (announcements or programmes) on radio or television 2 (*intr*) to take part in a radio or television programme 3 (*tr*) to make widely known throughout an area: *to broadcast news* 4 (*tr*) to scatter (seed, etc) over an area, esp by hand ▷ *n* 5 **a** a transmission or programme on radio or television **b** (*as modifier*): *a broadcast signal* 6 **a** the act of scattering seeds **b** (*as modifier*): *the broadcast method of sowing* ▷ *adj* 7 dispersed over a wide area: *broadcast seeds* ▷ *adv* 8 far and wide: *seeds to be sown broadcast* > 'broad,caster *n* > 'broad,casting *n*

Broad Church *n* 1 a party within the Church of England which favours a broad and liberal interpretation of Anglican formularies and rubrics and objects to positive definition in theology. Compare **High Church, Low Church** 2 (*usually not capitals*) a group or movement which embraces a wide and varied number of views, approaches, and opinions ▷ *adj* Broad-Church 3 of or relating to this party in the Church of England

broadcloth ('brɔːd,klɒθ) *n* 1 fabric woven on a wide loom 2 a closely woven fabric of wool, worsted, cotton, or rayon with lustrous finish, used for clothing

broaden ('brɔːdªn) *vb* to make or become broad or broader; widen

broad gauge *n* 1 a railway track with a greater distance between the lines than the standard gauge of 56½ inches (about 1.44 metres) used now by most mainline railway systems ▷ *adj* broad-gauge 2 of, relating to, or denoting a railway having this track

b

broad jump *n US and Canadian* an athletic contest in which competitors try to cover the farthest distance possible with a running jump from a fixed board or mark. Also called (in Britain and certain other countries): **long jump**

Broadlands ('brɔːdlənds) *n* a Palladian mansion near Romsey in Hampshire: formerly the home of Lord Palmerston and Lord Mountbatten

broadleaf ('brɔːdˌliːf) *n, pl* -**leaves 1** any tobacco plant having broad leaves, used esp in making cigars **2** Also called: **kapuka, papauma, puka** NZ an evergreen tree with large glossy leaves

broad-leaved *adj* denoting trees other than conifers, most of which have broad rather than needle-shaped leaves

broadline ('brɔːdˌlaɪn) *n chiefly US* **a** a company that deals in high volume at the cheaper end of a product line **b** (*as modifier*): *broadline distributors*

broadloom ('brɔːdˌluːm) *n* (*modifier*) of or designating carpets or carpeting woven on a wide loom to obviate the need for seams

broad-minded *adj* **1** tolerant of opposing viewpoints; not prejudiced; liberal **2** not easily shocked by permissive sexual habits, pornography, etc > **broad-'mindedly** *adv* > ,**broad-'mindedness** *n*

Broadmoor ('brɔːdˌmɔː) *n* an institution in Berkshire, England, for housing and treating mentally ill criminals

Broads (brɔːdz) *pl n* **the 1** a group of shallow navigable lakes, connected by a network of rivers, in E England, in Norfolk and Suffolk **2** the region around these lakes: a tourist centre; several bird sanctuaries

broad seal *n* the official seal of a nation and its government

broadsheet ('brɔːdˌʃiːt) *n* **1** a newspaper having a large format, approximately 15 by 24 inches (38 by 61 centimetres). Compare **tabloid 2** another word for **broadside** (sense 4)

broadside ('brɔːdˌsaɪd) *n* **1** *nautical* the entire side of a vessel, from stem to stern and from waterline to rail **2** *naval* **a** all the armament fired from one side of a warship **b** the simultaneous discharge of such armament **3** a strong or abusive verbal or written attack **4** Also called: **broadside ballad** a ballad or popular song printed on one side of a sheet of paper and sold by hawkers, esp in 16th-century England **5** any standard size of paper before cutting or folding: *demy broadside* **6** another name for **broadsheet** (sense 1) **7** a large flat surface: *the broadside of the barn* ▷ *adv* **8** with a broader side facing an object; sideways: *the train hit the lorry broadside*

broad-spectrum *n* (*modifier*) effective against a wide variety of diseases or microorganisms: *a broad-spectrum antibiotic*

broadsword ('brɔːdˌsɔːd) *n* a broad-bladed sword used for cutting rather than stabbing. Also called: **backsword**

broadtail ('brɔːdˌteɪl) *n* **1** the highly valued black wavy fur obtained from the skins of newly born karakul lambs; caracul **2** another name for **karakul**

Broadway ('brɔːdˌweɪ) *n* **1** a thoroughfare in New York City, famous for its theatres: the centre of the commercial theatre in the US ▷ *adj* **2** of or relating to or suitable for the commercial theatre, esp on Broadway

Brobdingnagian (,brɒbdɪŋˈnægɪən) *adj* gigantic; huge; immense [C18 from *Brobdingnag*, an imaginary country of giants in Swift's *Gulliver's Travels* (1726)]

brocade (brəʊˈkeɪd) *n* **1 a** a rich fabric woven with a raised design, often using gold or silver threads **b** (*as modifier*): *brocade curtains* ▷ *vb* **2** (*tr*) to weave with such a design [C17 from Spanish *brocado*, from Italian *broccato* embossed fabric, from *brocco* spike, from Latin *brochus* projecting; see BROACH[1]]

Broca's area *or* **centre** ('brɒkəz) *n* the region of the cerebral cortex of the brain concerned with

speech; the speech centre [C19 named after Paul *Broca* (1824–80), French surgeon and anthropologist]

brocatelle *or US* **brocatel** (,brɒkəˈtɛl) *n* **1** a heavy brocade with the design in deep relief, used chiefly in upholstery **2** a type of variegated marble from France and Italy [C17 from French, from Italian *broccatello*, diminutive of *broccato* BROCADE]

broccoli ('brɒkəlɪ) *n* **1** a cultivated variety of cabbage, *Brassica oleracea italica*, having branched greenish flower heads **2** the flower head of this plant, eaten as a vegetable before the buds have opened **3** a variety of this plant that does not form a head, whose stalks are eaten as a vegetable [C17 from Italian, plural of *broccolo* a little sprout, from *brocco* sprout, spike; see BROCADE]

broch (brɒk, brɒx) *n* (in Scotland) a circular dry-stone tower large enough to serve as a fortified home; they date from the Iron Age and are found esp in the north and the islands [C17 from Old Norse *borg*; related to Old English *burh* settlement, *burgh*]

broché (brəʊˈʃeɪ; *French* brɔʃe) *adj* woven with a raised design, as brocade [C19 from French *brocher* to brocade, stitch; see BROACH[1]]

brochette (brɒˈʃɛt; *French* brɔʃɛt) *n* a skewer or small spit, used for holding pieces of meat, etc, while roasting or grilling [C19 from Old French *brochete* small pointed tool; see BROACH[1]]

brocho ('brɒxɔ) *n* a variant of **brachah**

brochure ('brəʊʃjʊə, -fə) *n* a pamphlet or booklet, esp one containing summarized or introductory information or advertising [C18 from French, from *brocher* to stitch (a book)]

brock (brɒk) *n* a Brit name for **badger** (sense 1): used esp as a form of address in stories, etc [Old English *broc*, of Celtic origin; compare Welsh *broch*]

Brocken (*German* 'brɔkən) *n* a mountain in central Germany, formerly in East Germany: the highest peak of the Harz Mountains; important in German folklore. Height: 1142 m (3747 ft). The **Brocken Bow** or **Brocken Spectre** is an atmospheric phenomenon in which an observer, when the sun is low, may see his enlarged shadow against the clouds, often surrounded by coloured lights

brocket ('brɒkɪt) *n* any small deer of the genus *Mazama*, of tropical America, having small unbranched antlers [C15 from Anglo-French *broquet*, from *broque* horn, from Vulgar Latin *brocca* (unattested); see BROACH[1]]

broddle ('brɒdəl) *vb* (*tr*) Yorkshire *dialect* to poke or pierce (something) [perhaps from BRADAWL]

broderie anglaise (,brəʊdərɪ aːnˈglɛz) *n* open embroidery on white cotton, fine linen, etc [C19 French: English embroidery]

Broederbond ('bruːdəˌbɔːnt, 'bruːdəˌbɒnt) *n* (in South Africa) a secret society of Afrikaner Nationalists committed to securing and maintaining Afrikaner control over important areas of government [Afrikaans: band of brothers]

broekies ('bruːkiːz) *pl n* South African *informal* underpants [C19 Afrikaans]

brog (brɒg, brɔːg, brɒg) *n* Scot a bradawl [C19 of uncertain origin]

brogan ('brəʊgən) *n* a heavy laced usually ankle-high work boot [C19 from Gaelic *brōgan* a little shoe, from *brōg* shoe; see BROGUE[2]]

brogue[1] (brəʊg) *n* a broad gentle-sounding dialectal accent, esp that used by the Irish in speaking English [C18 probably from BROGUE[2], alluding to the footwear of the peasantry]

brogue[2] (brəʊg) *n* **1** a sturdy walking shoe, often with ornamental perforations **2** an untanned shoe worn formerly in Ireland and Scotland [C16 from Irish Gaelic *bróg* boot, shoe, probably from Old Norse *brōk* leg covering]

broider ('brɔɪdə) *vb* (*tr*) an archaic word for **embroider** [C15 from Old French *brosder*, of Germanic origin; see EMBROIDER]

broil[1] (brɔɪl) *vb* **1** *chiefly US and Canadian* to cook (meat, fish, etc) by direct heat, as under a grill or over a hot fire, or (of meat, fish, etc) to be cooked in this way. Usual equivalent (in Britain and other countries): **grill 2** to become or cause to become extremely hot **3** (*intr*) to be furious ▷ *n* **4** the process of broiling **5** something broiled [C14 from Old French *bruillir* to burn, of uncertain origin]

broil[2] (brɔɪl) *archaic* ▷ *n* **1** a loud quarrel or disturbance; brawl ▷ *vb* **2** (*intr*) to brawl; quarrel [C16 from Old French *brouiller* to mix, from *breu* broth; see BREWIS, BROSE]

broiler ('brɔɪlə) *n* **1** a young tender chicken suitable for roasting **2** *chiefly US* a pan, grate, etc for broiling food **3** a very hot day

broiler house *n* a building in which broiler chickens are reared in confined conditions

broke (brəʊk) *vb* **1** the past tense of **break** ▷ *adj* **2** *informal* having no money; bankrupt **3** **go for broke** *slang* to risk everything in a gambling or other venture

broken ('brəʊkən) *vb* **1** the past participle of **break** ▷ *adj* **2** fractured, smashed, or splintered: *a broken vase* **3** imperfect or incomplete; fragmentary: *a broken set of books* **4** interrupted; disturbed; disconnected: *broken sleep* **5** intermittent or discontinuous: *broken sunshine* **6** varying in direction or intensity, as of pitch: *a broken note; a broken run* **7** not functioning: *a broken radio* **8** spoilt or ruined by divorce (esp in the phrases **broken home, broken marriage**) **9** (of a trust, promise, contract, etc) violated; infringed **10** overcome with grief or disappointment: *a broken heart* **11** (of the speech of a foreigner) imperfect in grammar, vocabulary, and pronunciation: *broken English* **12** *Also* **broken-in** made tame or disciplined by training: *a broken horse; a broken recruit* **13** exhausted or weakened as through ill-health or misfortune **14** confused or disorganized: *broken ranks of soldiers* **15** breached or opened: *broken defensive lines* **16** irregular or rough; uneven: *broken ground* **17** bankrupt or out of money: *a broken industry* **18** (of colour) having a multicoloured decorative effect, as by stippling paint onto a surface **19** *South African informal* drunk > '**brokenly** *adv*

broken chord *n music* a chord played as an arpeggio

broken consort *n* See **consort** (sense 4)

broken-down *adj* **1** worn out, as by age or long use; dilapidated: *a broken-down fence* **2** not in working order: *a broken-down tractor* **3** physically or mentally ill

brokenhearted (,brəʊkənˈhɑːtɪd) *adj* overwhelmed by grief or disappointment > ,**broken'heartedly** *adv* > ,**broken'heartedness** *n*

Broken Hill *n* a city in SE Australia, in W New South Wales: mining centre for lead, silver, and zinc. Pop: 19 834 (2001)

broken wind (wɪnd) *n vet science* another name for **heaves** (sense 1)

broker ('brəʊkə) *n* **1** an agent who, acting on behalf of a principal, buys or sells goods, securities, etc, in return for a commission: *insurance broker* **2** (formerly) short for **stockbroker 3** a dealer in second-hand goods ▷ *vb* **4** to act as a broker (in) [C14 from Anglo-French *brocour* broacher (of casks, hence, one who sells, agent), from Old Northern French *broquier* to tap a cask, from *broque* tap of a cask; see BROACH[1]]

brokerage ('brəʊkərɪdʒ) *n* **1** commission charged by a broker to his principals **2** a broker's business or office

broker-dealer *n* another name for **stockbroker**

broking ('brəʊkɪŋ) *adj* **1** acting as a broker ▷ *n* **2** the business of a broker [C16 from obsolete verb *broke*; see BROKER]

brolga ('brɒlgə) *n* a large grey Australian crane, *Grus rubicunda*, having a red-and-green head and a trumpeting call. Also called: **Australian crane, native companion** [C19 from a native Australian language]

brolly ('brɒlɪ) *n, pl* -**lies** an informal Brit name for **umbrella** (sense 1)

bromal ('brəʊməl) *n* a yellowish oily synthetic liquid formerly used medicinally as a sedative and hypnotic; tribromoacetaldehyde. Formula: Br₃CCHO [C19 from BROM(INE) + AL(COHOL)]

bromate ('brəʊmeɪt) *n* **1** any salt or ester of bromic acid, containing the monovalent group -BrO₂ or ion BrO₃⁻ ▷ *vb* **2** to add bromate to (a product), as in the treatment of flour [C19 probably from German *Bromat*; see BROMO-, -ATE¹]

Bromberg ('brɒmbɛrk) *n* the German name for **Bydgoszcz**

brome grass *or* **brome** (brəʊm) *n* any of various grasses of the genus *Bromus*, having small flower spikes in loose drooping clusters. Some species are used for hay [C18 via Latin from Greek *bromos* oats, of obscure origin]

bromeliad (brəʊ'miːlɪˌæd) *n* any plant of the tropical American family *Bromeliaceae*, typically epiphytes with a rosette of fleshy leaves. The family includes the pineapple and Spanish moss [C19 from New Latin *Bromelia* type genus, after Olaf *Bromelius* (1639–1705), Swedish botanist] ▷ bro,meli'aceous *adj*

bromelin ('brəʊməlɪn) *n* a protein-digesting enzyme (see **endopeptidase**) found in pineapple and extracted for use in treating joint pain and inflammation, hay fever, and various other conditions [C19 from *Bromelia* type genus of pineapple family (see BROMELIAD) + -IN]

bromeosin (brəʊ'miːəsɪn) *n chem* another name for **eosin** [C20 from BROMO- + EOSIN]

bromic ('brəʊmɪk) *adj* of or containing bromine in the trivalent or pentavalent state

bromic acid *n* a colourless unstable water-soluble liquid used as an oxidizing agent in the manufacture of dyes and pharmaceuticals. Formula: HBrO₃

bromide ('brəʊmaɪd) *n* **1** any salt of hydrobromic acid, containing the monovalent ion Br⁻ (**bromide ion**) **2** any compound containing a bromine atom, such as methyl bromide **3** a dose of sodium or potassium bromide given as a sedative **4 a** a trite saying; platitude **b** a dull or boring person [C19, C20 (cliché): from BROM(INE) + -IDE]

bromide paper *n* a type of photographic paper coated with an emulsion of silver bromide usually containing a small quantity of silver iodide

bromidic (brəʊ'mɪdɪk) *adj* ordinary; dull

brominate ('brəʊmɪˌneɪt) *vb* to treat or react with bromine. Also: **bromate** ▷ ,bromin'ation *n*

bromine ('brəʊmiːn, -mɪn) *n* a pungent dark red volatile liquid element of the halogen series that occurs in natural brine and is used in the production of chemicals, esp ethylene dibromide. Symbol: Br; atomic no.: 35; atomic wt.: 79.904; valency: 1, 3, 5, or 7; relative density 3.12; density (gas): 7.59 kg/m³; melting pt.: –7.2°C; boiling pt.: 58.78°C [C19 from French *brome* bromine, from Greek *brōmos* bad smell + -INE², of uncertain origin]

bromism ('brəʊˌmɪzəm) *or US* **brominism** *n* poisoning caused by the excessive intake of bromine or compounds containing bromine

Bromley ('brɒmlɪ) *n* a borough of SE Greater London. Pop: 298 300 (2003 est). Area: 153 sq km (59 sq miles)

bromo- *or before a vowel* **brom-** *combining form* indicating the presence of bromine: *bromoform*

bromoform ('brəʊməˌfɔːm) *n* a heavy colourless liquid substance with a sweetish taste and an odour resembling that of chloroform. Formula: CHBr₃. Systematic name: **tribromomethane**

Bromsgrove ('brɒmzˌgrəʊv) *n* a town in W central England, in N Worcestershire. Pop: 29 237 (2001)

bronchi ('brɒŋkaɪ) *n* the plural of **bronchus**

bronchia ('brɒŋkɪə) *pl n* another name for **bronchial tubes** [C17 from Late Latin, from Greek *bronkhia*, plural of *bronkhion*, diminutive of *bronkhus* windpipe, throat]

bronchial ('brɒŋkɪəl) *adj* of or relating to the bronchi or the bronchial tubes ▷ 'bronchially *adv*

bronchial tubes *pl n* the bronchi or their smaller divisions

bronchiectasis (ˌbrɒŋkɪ'ɛktəsɪs) *n* chronic dilation of the bronchi or bronchial tubes, which often become infected [C19 from BRONCHO- + Greek *ektasis* a stretching]

bronchiole ('brɒŋkɪˌəʊl) *n* any of the smallest bronchial tubes, usually ending in alveoli [C19 from New Latin *bronchiolum*, diminutive of Late Latin *bronchium*, singular of BRONCHIA] ▷ bronchiolar (ˌbrɒŋkɪ'əʊlə) *adj*

bronchiolitis (ˌbrɒŋkɪəʊ'laɪtɪs) *n* a condition in which the small airways in the lungs become inflamed by a virus. It is most common in infants, who become breathless in severe cases. Recurrent attacks may lead to asthma

bronchitis (brɒŋ'kaɪtɪs) *n* inflammation of the bronchial tubes, characterized by coughing, difficulty in breathing, etc, caused by infection or irritation of the respiratory tract ▷ bronchitic (brɒŋ'kɪtɪk) *adj, n*

broncho- *or before a vowel* **bronch-** *combining form* indicating or relating to the bronchi: *bronchitis* [from Greek: BRONCHUS]

bronchodilator ('brɒŋkəʊdaɪˌleɪtə) *n* any drug or other agent that causes dilation of the bronchial tubes by relaxing bronchial muscle: used, esp in the form of aerosol sprays, for the relief of asthma

bronchography (brɒŋ'kɒgrəfɪ) *n* radiography of the bronchial tubes after the introduction of a radiopaque medium into the bronchi

bronchopneumonia (ˌbrɒŋkəʊnjuː'məʊnɪə) *n* inflammation of the lungs, originating in the bronchioles

bronchoscope ('brɒŋkəˌskəʊp) *n* an instrument for examining and providing access to the interior of the bronchial tubes ▷ bronchoscopic (ˌbrɒŋkə'skɒpɪk) *adj* ▷ bronchoscopist (brɒŋ'kɒskəpɪst) *n* ▷ bron'choscopy *n*

bronchus ('brɒŋkəs) *n, pl* **-chi** (-kaɪ) either of the two main branches of the trachea, which contain cartilage within their walls [C18 from New Latin, from Greek *bronkhos* windpipe]

bronco *or* **broncho** ('brɒŋkəʊ) *n, pl* **-cos** *or* **-chos** (in the US and Canada) a wild or partially tamed pony or mustang of the western plains [C19 from Mexican Spanish, short for Spanish *potro bronco* unbroken colt, probably from Latin *broccus* projecting (as knots on wood), hence, rough, wild]

broncobuster ('brɒŋkəʊˌbʌstə) *n* (in the western US and Canada) a cowboy who breaks in broncos or wild horses

brontobyte ('brɒntəʊˌbaɪt) *n computing not standard* 10²⁷ or 2⁹⁰ bytes [C21 probably from BRONTOSAURUS]

brontosaurus (ˌbrɒntə'sɔːrəs) *or* **brontosaur** ('brɒntəˌsɔː) *n* any very large herbivorous quadrupedal dinosaur of the genus *Apatosaurus*, common in North America during Jurassic times, having a long neck and long tail: suborder *Sauropoda* (sauropods) [C19 from New Latin, from Greek *brontē* thunder + *sauros* lizard]

Bronx (brɒŋks) *n* **the** a borough of New York City, on the mainland, separated from Manhattan by the Harlem River. Pop: 1 363 198 (2003 est)

Bronx cheer *n chiefly US* a loud noise, imitating a fart, made with the lips and tongue and expressing derision or contempt; raspberry

bronze (brɒnz) *n* **1 a** any hard water-resistant alloy consisting of copper and smaller proportions of tin and sometimes zinc and lead **b** any similar copper alloy containing other elements in place of tin, such as aluminium bronze, beryllium bronze, etc. See also **phosphor bronze, gunmetal** Compare **brass** (sense 1) **2** a yellowish-brown colour or pigment **3** a statue, medal, or other object made of bronze **4** short for **bronze medal** ▷ *adj* **5** made of or resembling bronze **6** of a yellowish-brown colour: *a bronze skin* ▷ *vb* **7** (esp of the skin) to make or become brown; tan **8** (*tr*) to give the appearance of bronze to [C18 from French, from Italian *bronzo*, perhaps ultimately from Latin

Brundisium Brindisi, famed for its bronze] ▷ 'bronzy *adj*

bronze age *n classical myth* a period of human existence marked by war and violence, following the golden and silver ages and preceding the iron age

Bronze Age *n archaeol* **a** a technological stage between the Stone and Iron Ages, beginning in the Middle East about 4500 BC and lasting in Britain from about 2000 to 500 BC, during which weapons and tools were made of bronze and there was intensive trading **b** (*as modifier*): *a Bronze-Age tool*

bronze medal *n* a medal of bronze, awarded to a competitor who comes third in a contest or race. Compare **gold medal, silver medal**

bronzer ('brɒnzə) *n* a cosmetic applied to the skin to simulate a sun tan

bronze whaler *n* a shark, *Carcharhinus brachyurus*, of southern Australian waters, having a bronze-coloured back

bronzing ('brɒnzɪŋ) *n building trades* **1** blue pigment producing a metallic lustre when ground into paint media at fairly high concentrations **2** the application of a mixture of powdered metal or pigments of a metallic lustre, and a binding medium, such as gold size, to a surface

bronzite ('brɒnzaɪt) *n* a type of orthopyroxene often having a metallic or pearly appearance

brooch (brəʊtʃ) *n* an ornament with a hinged pin and catch, worn fastened to clothing [C13 from Old French *broche*; see BROACH¹]

brood (bruːd) *n* **1** a number of young animals, esp birds, produced at one hatching **2** all the offspring in one family: often used jokingly or contemptuously **3** a group of a particular kind; breed **4** (*as modifier*) kept for breeding: *a brood mare* ▷ *vb* **5** (of a bird) **a** to sit on or hatch (eggs) **b** (*tr*) to cover (young birds) protectively with the wings **6** (when *intr*, often foll by *on, over* or *upon*) to ponder morbidly or persistently [Old English *brōd*; related to Middle High German *bruot*, Dutch *broed*; see BREED] ▷ 'brooding *n, adj* ▷ 'broodingly *adv*

brooder ('bruːdə) *n* **1** an enclosure or other structure, usually heated, used for rearing young chickens or other fowl **2** a person or thing that broods

brood pouch *n* **1** a pouch or cavity in certain animals, such as frogs and fishes, in which their eggs develop and hatch **2** another name for **marsupium**

broody ('bruːdɪ) *adj* **broodier, broodiest 1** moody; meditative; introspective **2** (of poultry) wishing to sit on or hatch eggs **3** *informal* (of a woman) wishing to have a baby of her own ▷ 'broodiness *n*

brook¹ (brʊk) *n* a natural freshwater stream smaller than a river [Old English *brōc*; related to Old High German *bruoh* swamp, Dutch *broek*]

brook² (brʊk) *vb* (*tr; usually used with a negative*) to bear; tolerate [Old English *brūcan*; related to Gothic *brūkjan* to use, Old High German *brūhhan*, Latin *fruī* to enjoy] ▷ 'brookable *adj*

Brook Farm *n* an experimental communist community established by writers and scholars in West Roxbury, Massachusetts, from 1841 to 1847

brookite ('brʊkaɪt) *n* a reddish-brown to black mineral consisting of titanium oxide in orthorhombic crystalline form: occurs in silica veins. Formula: TiO₂ [C19 named after Henry J. *Brooke* (died 1857), English mineralogist]

brooklet ('brʊklɪt) *n* a small brook

brooklime ('brʊkˌlaɪm) *n* either of two blue-flowered scrophulariaceous trailing plants, *Veronica americana* of North America or *V. beccabunga* of Europe and Asia, growing in moist places. See also **speedwell** [C16 variant of C15 *brokelemk* speedwell, from BROOK¹ + -*lemk*, from Old English *hleomoce*; influenced by *lime*]

Brooklyn ('brʊklɪn) *n* a borough of New York City, on the SW end of Long Island. Pop: 2 465 326 (2000)

Brooks Range (brʊks) *n* a mountain range in N Alaska. Highest peak: Mount Isto, 2761 m (9058 ft)

b

brook trout *n* a North American freshwater trout, *Salvelinus fontinalis*, introduced in Europe and valued as a food and game fish. Also called: **speckled trout**

brookweed ('brʊkˌwiːd) *n* either of two white-flowered primulaceous plants, *Samolus valerandi* of Europe or *S. floribundus* of North America, growing in moist places. Also called: **water pimpernel**. See also **pimpernel**

broom (bruːm, brʊm) *n* **1** an implement for sweeping consisting of a long handle to which is attached either a brush of straw, bristles, or twigs, bound together, or a solid head into which are set tufts of bristles or fibres **2** any of various yellow-flowered Eurasian leguminous shrubs of the genera *Cytisus*, *Genista*, and *Spartium*, esp *C. scoparius* **3** any of various similar Eurasian plants of the related genera *Genista* and *Spartium* **4** **new broom** a newly appointed official, etc, eager to make changes ▷ *vb* **5** (*tr*) to sweep with a broom [Old English *brōm*; related to Old High German *brāmo*, Middle Dutch *bremme*]

broomcorn ('bruːmˌkɔːn, 'brʊm-) *n* a variety of sorghum, *Sorghum vulgare technicum*, the long stiff flower stalks of which have been used for making brooms

broomrape ('bruːmˌreɪp, 'brʊm-) *n* any orobanchaceous plant of the genus *Orobanche*: brownish small-flowered leafless parasites on the roots of other plants, esp on legumes [c16 adaptation and partial translation of Medieval Latin *rāpum genistae* tuber (hence: root nodule) of Genista (a type of broom plant)]

broomstick ('bruːmˌstɪk, 'brʊm-) *n* the long handle of a broom

bros. *or* **Bros.** *abbreviation for* brothers

brose (brəʊz) *n* *Scot* oatmeal or pease porridge, sometimes with butter or fat added. See also **Atholl brose** [c13 *broys*, from Old French *broez*, from *breu* broth, of Germanic origin]

bro talk *n* **1** NZ Māori English **2** NZ English spoken with a Māori accent [c20 BRO[1] (sense 1) + TALK]

broth (brɒθ) *n* **1** a soup made by boiling meat, fish, vegetables, etc, in water **2** another name for **stock** (sense 19) [Old English *broth*; related to Old Norse *broth*, Old High German *brod*, German *brodeln* to boil; see BREW]

brothel ('brɒθəl) *n* **1** a house or other place where men pay to have sexual intercourse with prostitutes **2** *Austral informal* any untidy or messy place [c16 short for *brothel-house*, from c14 *brothel* useless person, from Old English *brēothan* to deteriorate; related to *briethel* worthless]

brother ('brʌðə) *n*, *pl* **brothers** *or* (*archaic except when referring to fellow members of a religion, sect, society, etc*) **brethren** **1** a male person having the same parents as another person **2** short for **half-brother** *or* **stepbrother** **3 a** a male person belonging to the same group, profession, nationality, trade union, etc, as another or others; fellow member **b** (*as modifier*): **brother workers 4** comrade; friend: used as a form of address **5** *Christianity* **a** a member of a male religious order who undertakes work for the order without actually being in holy orders **b** a lay member of a male religious order Related adjective: **fraternal** ▷ *interj* **6** *slang* an exclamation of amazement, disgust, surprise, disappointment, etc [Old English *brōthor*; related to Old Norse *brōthir*, Old High German *bruoder*, Latin *frāter*, Greek *phratēr*, Sanskrit *bhrātar*]

brotherhood ('brʌðəˌhʊd) *n* **1** the state of being related as a brother or brothers **2** an association or fellowship, such as a trade union **3** all persons engaged in a particular profession, trade, etc **4** the belief, feeling, or hope that all men should regard and treat one another as brothers: *the brotherhood of man is a myth*

brother-in-law *n*, *pl* **brothers-in-law 1** the brother of one's wife or husband **2** the husband of one's sister

brotherly ('brʌðəlɪ) *adj* **1** of, resembling, or suitable to a brother, esp in showing loyalty and affection; fraternal ▷ *adv* **2** in a brotherly way; fraternally > **'brotherliness** *n*

brougham ('bruːəm, bruːm) *n* **1** a four-wheeled horse-drawn closed carriage having a raised open driver's seat in front **2** *obsolete* a large car with an open compartment at the front for the driver **3** *obsolete* an early electric car [c19 named after Henry Peter, Lord Brougham (1778–1868)]

brought (brɔːt) *vb* the past tense and past participle of **bring**

broughta ('brɔːtə) *or* **broughtas** ('brɔːtəs) *n* variants of **braata**

brouhaha ('bruːhɑːˌhɑː) *n* a loud confused noise; commotion; uproar [French, of imitative origin]

brow (braʊ) *n* **1** the part of the face from the eyes to the hairline; forehead **2** short for **eyebrow 3** the expression of the face; countenance: *a troubled brow* **4** the top of a mine shaft; pithead **5** the jutting top of a hill, etc **6** *Northern English dialect* a steep slope on a road [Old English *brū*; related to Old Norse *brūn* eyebrow, Lithuanian *bruvis*, Greek *ophrus*, Sanskrit *bhrūs*]

browband ('braʊˌbænd) *n* the strap of a horse's bridle that goes across the forehead

browbeat ('braʊˌbiːt) *vb* **-beats, -beating, -beat, -beaten** (*tr*) to discourage or frighten with threats or a domineering manner; intimidate > **'brow,beater** *n*

-browed *adj* (*in combination*) having a brow or brows as specified: *dark-browed*

brown (braʊn) *n* **1** any of various colours, such as those of wood or earth, produced by low intensity light in the wavelength range 620–585 nanometres **2** a dye or pigment producing these colours **3** brown cloth or clothing: *dressed in brown* **4** any of numerous mostly reddish-brown butterflies of the genera *Maniola*, *Lasiommata*, etc, such as *M. jurtina* (**meadow brown**): family *Satyridae* ▷ *adj* **5** of the colour brown **6** (of bread) made from a flour that has not been bleached or bolted, such as wheatmeal or wholemeal flour **7** deeply tanned or sunburnt ▷ *vb* **8** to make (esp food as a result of cooking) brown or (esp of food) to become brown [Old English *brūn*; related to Old Norse *brūnn*, Old High German *brūn*, Greek *phrunos* toad, Sanskrit *babhru* reddish-brown] > **'brownish** *or* **'browny** *adj* > **'brownness** *n*

brown algae *pl n* any algae of the phylum *Phaeophyta*, such as the wracks and kelps, which contain a brown pigment in addition to chlorophyll

brown bag *US* ▷ *n* **1** a bag made of brown paper, often used for carrying a packed lunch or alcohol ▷ *vb* **brown-bag -bags, -bagging, -bagged** (*intr*) **2** to take a packed lunch in a brown bag **3** to carry alcohol in a brown bag

brown bagging *n* the practice of eating one's lunch or drinking a bottle of alcohol from a brown bag

brown bear *n* a large ferocious brownish bear, *Ursus arctos*, inhabiting temperate forests of North America, Europe, and Asia. See also **grizzly bear, Kodiak bear**

brown coal *n* a low-quality coal intermediate in grade between peat and lignite

brown cow *n* *South African* a drink made by mixing cola and milk

brown creeper *n* a small bush bird, *Finschia novaeseelandiae*, of South Island, New Zealand. Also called: **bush canary**

brown dwarf *n* a type of celestial body midway in mass between a large planet and a small star

brown earth *n* an intrazonal soil of temperate humid regions typically developed under deciduous forest into a dark rich layer (mull): characteristic of much of southern and central England

browned-off *adj informal* thoroughly discouraged or disheartened; fed up

brown fat *n* tissue composed of a type of fat cell

that dissipates as heat most of the energy released when food is oxidized; brown adipose tissue. It is present in hibernating animals and human babies and is thought to be important in adult weight control

brownfield ('braʊnˌfiːld) *n* (*modifier*) denoting or located in an urban area that has previously been built on: *Hampshire has many brownfield developments*

brown goods *pl n* *marketing* consumer goods such as televisions, radios, or videos. Compare **white goods** (sense 1)

Brownian movement ('braʊnɪən) *n* random movement of microscopic particles suspended in a fluid, caused by bombardment of the particles by molecules of the fluid. First observed in 1827, it provided strong evidence in support of the kinetic theory of molecules [c19 named after Robert *Brown* (1773–1858), Scottish botanist]

brownie ('braʊnɪ) *n* **1** (in folklore) an elf said to do helpful work at night, esp household chores **2** a small square nutty chocolate cake **3** *Austral history* a bread made with currants [c16 diminutive of BROWN (that is, a small brown man)]

Brownie ('braʊnɪ) *n* **1** another name for **Brownie Guide 2** *trademark* (formerly) a popular make of simple box camera

Brownie Guide *or* **Brownie** ('braʊnɪ) *n* a member of the Brownie Guides, one of the junior branches (aged 7–10 years) in The Guide Association

Brownie Guider *n* the adult leader of a pack of Brownie Guides. Former name: **Brown Owl**

Brownie point *n* a notional mark to one's credit earned for being seen to do the right thing [c20 from the mistaken notion that Brownie Guides earn points for good deeds]

browning ('braʊnɪŋ) *n* *Brit* a substance used to darken soups, gravies, etc

Browning ('braʊnɪŋ) *n* **1** Also called: Browning automatic rifle a portable gas-operated air-cooled automatic rifle using .30 calibre ammunition and capable of firing between 200 and 350 rounds per minute. Abbreviation: BAR **2** Also called: Browning machine gun a water-cooled automatic machine gun using .30 or .50 calibre ammunition and capable of firing over 500 rounds per minute [c20 named after John M. *Browning* (1855–1926), American designer of firearms]

Brownist ('braʊnɪst) *n* a person who supported the principles of church government advocated by Robert Browne and adopted in modified form by the Independents or Congregationalists [c16 named after Robert *Browne* (?1550–1633), English Puritan] > **'Brownism** *n*

brown lung disease *n* another name for **byssinosis**

brown nose *n* *vet science* a form of light sensitization in cattle

brown-nose *slang* ▷ *vb* **1** to be abjectly subservient (to); curry favour (with) ▷ *n* **2** an abjectly subservient person; sycophant [c20 from the notion that a subservient person kisses the backside of the person with whom he or she is currying favour]

brownout ('braʊnˌaʊt) *n* *chiefly US* **1** a dimming or reduction in the use of electric lights in a city, esp to conserve electric power or as a defensive precaution in wartime **2** a temporary reduction in electrical power. Compare **blackout** (sense 3) **3** a temporary slowing down of the workings of the internet caused when too many users attempt to access it at the same time

brown owl *n* another name for **tawny owl**

Brown Owl *n* a name (no longer in official use) for **Brownie Guider**

brown paper *n* a coarse unbleached paper used for wrapping

brown rat *n* a common brownish rat, *Rattus norvegicus*: a serious pest in all parts of the world. Also called: Norway rat

brown rice *n* unpolished rice, in which the

grains retain the outer yellowish-brown layer (bran)

brown rot *n* **1** a disease of apples, peaches, etc, caused by fungi of the genus *Sclerotinia* and characterized by yellowish-brown masses of spores on the plant surface **2** decay of timber caused by the action of fungi on the cellulose

brown seaweed *n* another term for **brown algae**

Brown Shirt *n* **1** (in Nazi Germany) a storm trooper **2** a member of any fascist party or group

brown snake *n Austral* any of various common venomous snakes of the genus *Pseudonaja*

brown-state *adj* (of linen and lace fabrics) undyed

brownstone ('braʊn,stəʊn) *n US* **1** a reddish-brown iron-rich sandstone used for building **2** a house built of or faced with this stone

brown study *n* a mood of deep absorption or thoughtfulness; reverie

brown sugar *n* sugar that is unrefined or only partially refined

brown-tail moth *n* a small brown-and-white European moth, *Euproctis phaeorrhoea*, naturalized in the eastern US where it causes damage to shade trees: family *Lymantriidae* (or *Liparidae*). See also **tussock moth**

brown toast *n Canadian* toasted wholemeal bread

brown trout *n* a common brownish variety of the trout *Salmo trutta* that occurs in the rivers of N Europe and has been successfully introduced in North America. Compare **sea trout** (sense 1)

browse (braʊz) *vb* **1** to look through (a book, articles for sale in a shop, etc) in a casual leisurely manner **2** *computing* to search for and read hypertext, esp on the World Wide Web **3** (of deer, goats, etc) to feed upon (vegetation) by continual nibbling ▷ *n* **4** the act or an instance of browsing **5** the young twigs, shoots, leaves, etc, on which certain animals feed [c15 from French *broust, brost* (modern French *brout*) bud, of Germanic origin; compare Old Saxon *brustian* to bud]

browser ('braʊzə) *n* **1** a person or animal that browses **2** *computing* a software package that enables a user to find and read hypertext files, esp on the World Wide Web

browser skin *n computing* a changeable decorative background for a browser

BRT *text messaging abbreviation for* be right there

bru (bru:) *n South African informal* another word for **bro²**

BRU *international car registration for* Brunei

Bruce (bru:s) *n Brit* a jocular name for an Australian man

brucellosis (,bru:sɪ'ləʊsɪs) *n* an infectious disease of cattle, goats, dogs, and pigs, caused by bacteria of the genus *Brucella* and transmittable to man (eg by drinking contaminated milk): symptoms include fever, chills, and severe headache. Also called: undulant fever [c20 from New Latin *Brucella*, named after Sir David *Bruce* (1855–1931), Australian bacteriologist and physician]

brucine ('bru:si:n, -sɪn) *n* bitter poisonous alkaloid resembling strychnine and obtained from the tree *Strychnos nuxvomica*: used mainly in the denaturation of alcohol. Formula: $C_{23}H_{26}N_2O_4$ [c19 named after James *Bruce* (1730–94), Scottish explorer of Africa]

Brücke (*German* 'brykə) *n* **die** (di:) a group of German Expressionist painters (1905–13), including Karl Schmidt-Rottluff, Fritz Bleyl, Erich Heckel, and Ernst Ludwig Kirchner. In 1912 they exhibited with *der Blaue Reiter* [German: literally, the bridge]

Bruges (bru:ʒ; *French* bryʒ) *n* a city in NW Belgium, capital of West Flanders province: centre of the medieval European wool and cloth trade. Pop: 117 025 (2004 est). Flemish name: Brugge ('bryxə)

brugmansia (brʊg'mænsɪə) *n* any of various solanaceous plants of the genus *Brugmansia*, native to tropical American regions and closely related to daturas, having sweetly scented flowers

bruin ('bru:ɪn) *n* a name for a bear, used in children's tales, fables, etc [c17 from Dutch *bruin* brown, the name of the bear in the epic *Reynard the Fox*]

bruise (bru:z) *vb* (*mainly tr*) **1** (*also intr*) to injure (tissues) without breaking the skin, usually with discoloration, or (of tissues) to be injured in this way **2** to offend or injure (someone's feelings) by an insult, unkindness, etc **3** to damage the surface of (something), as by a blow **4** to crush (food, etc) by pounding or pressing ▷ *n* **5** a bodily injury without a break in the skin, usually with discoloration; contusion [Old English *brȳsan*, of Celtic origin; compare Irish *brúigim* I bruise]

bruiser ('bru:zə) *n* a strong tough person, esp a boxer or a bully

bruising ('bru:zɪŋ) *adj* **1** causing bruises, as by a blow **2** aggressively antagonistic; hurtful: *four months of bruising negotiation* ▷ *n* **3** a bruise or bruises

bruit (bru:t) *vb* **1** (*tr; often passive*; usually foll by *about*) to report; rumour: *it was bruited about that the king was dead* ▷ *n* **2** *med* an abnormal sound heard within the body during auscultation, esp a heart murmur **3** *archaic* **a** a rumour **b** a loud outcry; clamour [c15 via French from Medieval Latin *brūgitus*, probably from Vulgar Latin *bragere* (unattested) to yell + Latin *rugīre* to roar]

Brule or **Brûlé** (bru:'leɪ) *n* (*sometimes not capital*) short for **bois-brûlé**

Brumaire (*French* brymɛr) *n* the month of mist: the second month of the French revolutionary calendar, extending from Oct 23 to Nov 21 [c19 from *brume* mist, from Latin *brūma* winter; see BRUME]

brumal ('bru:məl) *adj* of, characteristic of, or relating to winter; wintry

brumby ('brʌmbɪ) *n, pl* -bies *Austral* **1** a wild horse, esp one descended from runaway stock **2** *informal* a wild or unruly person [c19 of unknown origin]

brume (bru:m) *n poetic* heavy mist or fog [c19 from French: mist, winter, from Latin *brūma*, contracted from *brevissima diēs* the shortest day] ▷ 'brumous *adj*

Brummagem ('brʌmədʒəm) *n* **1** an informal name for **Birmingham**. Often shortened to: Brum **2** (*sometimes not capital*) something that is cheap and flashy, esp imitation jewellery ▷ *adj* **3** (*sometimes not capital*) cheap and gaudy; tawdry [c17 from earlier *Bromecham*, local variant of BIRMINGHAM]

Brummie ('brʌmɪ) *n* **1** *informal* a native or inhabitant of Birmingham ▷ *adj* **2** of or relating to Birmingham [c20 from BRUMMAGEM]

brunch (brʌntʃ) *n* a meal eaten late in the morning, combining breakfast with lunch [c20 from BR(EAKFAST) + (L)UNCH]

Brundisium (brʌn'dɪzɪəm) *n* the ancient name for **Brindisi**

Brunei (bru:'naɪ, 'bru:naɪ) *n* **1** a sultanate in NW Borneo, consisting of two separate areas on the South China Sea, otherwise bounded by Sarawak: controlled all of Borneo and parts of the Philippines and the Sulu Islands in the 16th century; under British protection since 1888; internally self-governing since 1971; became fully independent in 1984 as a member of the Commonwealth. The economy depends chiefly on oil and natural gas. Official language: Malay; English is also widely spoken. Religion: Muslim. Currency: Brunei dollar. Capital: Bandar Seri Begawan. Pop: 366 000 (2004 est). Area: 5765 sq km (2226 sq miles) **2** the former name of **Bandar Seri Begawan**

brunette (bru:'nɛt) *n* **1** a girl or woman with dark brown hair ▷ *adj also* **brunet 2** dark brown: *brunette hair* [c17 from French, feminine of *brunet* dark, brownish, from *brun* brown, of Germanic origin; see BROWN]

Brunhild ('brʊnhɪld, -hɪlt) or **Brünnhilde** (*German* bryn'hɪldə) *n* (in the *Nibelungenlied*) a legendary

queen won for King Gunther by the magic of Siegfried: corresponds to Brynhild in Norse mythology

Brünn (bryn) *n* the German name for **Brno**

Brunswick ('brʌnzwɪk) *n* **1** a former duchy (1635–1918) and state (1918–46) of central Germany, now part of the state of Lower Saxony; formerly (1949–90) part of West Germany **2** a city in central Germany: formerly capital of the duchy and state of Brunswick. Pop: 245 076 (2003 est). German name: Braunschweig

brunt (brʌnt) *n* the main force or shock of a blow, attack, etc (esp in the phrase **bear the brunt of**) [c14 of unknown origin]

Brusa (*Turkish* 'bru:sɑ:) *n* the former name of **Bursa**

bruschetta (bru'ʃɛtə) *n* an Italian open sandwich of toasted bread topped with olive oil and tomatoes, olives, etc [c20 from Italian *bruscare*, from *abbrustolire* to toast]

brush¹ (brʌʃ) *n* **1** a device made of bristles, hairs, wires, etc, set into a firm back or handle: used to apply paint, clean or polish surfaces, groom the hair, etc **2** the act or an instance of brushing **3** a light stroke made in passing; graze **4** a brief encounter or contact, esp an unfriendly one; skirmish **5** the bushy tail of a fox, often kept as a trophy after a hunt, or of certain breeds of dog **6** an electric conductor, esp one made of carbon, that conveys current between stationary and rotating parts of a generator, motor, etc **7** a dark brush-shaped region observed when a biaxial crystal is viewed through a microscope, caused by interference between beams of polarized light ▷ *vb* **8** (*tr*) to clean, polish, scrub, paint, etc, with a brush **9** (*tr*) to apply or remove with a brush or brushing movement: *brush the crumbs off the table* **10** (*tr*) to touch lightly and briefly **11** (*intr*) to move so as to graze or touch something lightly ▷ See also **brush aside, brush off, brush up** [c14 from Old French *broisse*, perhaps from *broce* BRUSH²] ▷ 'brusher *n* ▷ 'brush,like *adj*

brush² (brʌʃ) *n* **1** a thick growth of shrubs and small trees; scrub **2** land covered with scrub **3** broken or cut branches or twigs; brushwood **4** wooded sparsely populated country; backwoods [c16 (dense undergrowth), c14 (cuttings of trees): from Old French *broce*, from Vulgar Latin *bruscia* (unattested) brushwood]

brush aside or **away** *vb* (*tr, adverb*) to dismiss without consideration; disregard

brush border *n physiol* a layer of tightly packed minute finger-like protuberances on cells that line absorptive surfaces, such as those of the intestine and kidney. See also **microvillus**

brush discharge *n* a slightly luminous electrical discharge between points of high charge density when the charge density is insufficient to cause a spark or around sharp points on a highly charged conductor because of ionization of air molecules in their vicinity

brushed (brʌʃt) *adj textiles* treated with a brushing process to raise the nap and give a softer, warmer finish: *brushed nylon*

brush fire *n* **1** a fire in bushes and scrub **2** a minor local war

brush flower *n* a flower or inflorescence with numerous long stamens, usually pollinated by birds or bats

brushmark ('brʌʃ,mɑ:k) *n* the indented lines sometimes left by the bristles of a brush on a painted surface

brush off *slang* ▷ *vb* (*tr, adverb*) **1** to dismiss and ignore (a person), esp curtly ▷ *n* **brushoff 2** an abrupt dismissal or rejection

brush-tailed phalanger *n Austral* another name for **tuan²**

brush-tailed possum or **brush-tail possum** *n* any of several widely-distributed Australian possums of the genus *Trichosurus*

brush turkey *n* any of several gallinaceous birds, esp *Alectura lathami*, of New Guinea and Australia,

b

having a black plumage: family *Megapodidae* (megapodes)

brush up *vb* (*adverb*) **1** (*tr*; often foll by *on*) to refresh one's knowledge, skill, or memory of (a subject) **2** to make (a person or oneself) tidy, clean, or neat as after a journey ▷ *n* **brush-up 3** *Brit* the act or an instance of tidying one's appearance (esp in the phrase **wash and brush-up**)

brushwood ('brʌʃ,wʊd) *n* **1** cut or broken-off tree branches, twigs, etc **2** another word for **brush²** (sense 1)

brushwork ('brʌʃ,wɜːk) *n* **1** a characteristic manner of applying paint with a brush: *that is not Rembrandt's brushwork* **2** work done with a brush

brushy¹ ('brʌʃɪ) *adj* **brushier, brushiest** like a brush; thick and furry

brushy² ('brʌʃɪ) *adj* **brushier, brushiest** covered or overgrown with brush

brusque (bruːsk, brʊsk) *adj* blunt or curt in manner or speech [c17 from French, from Italian *brusco* sour, rough, from Medieval Latin *bruscus* butcher's broom] > **brusquely** *adv* > **brusqueness** *or less commonly* **brusquerie** ('bruːskərɪ) *n*

Brussels ('brʌsəlz) *n* the capital of Belgium, in the central part: became capital of Belgium in 1830; seat of the European Commission. Pop: 999 899 (2004 est). Flemish name: **Brussel** ('brysəl). French name: **Bruxelles**

Brussels carpet *n* a worsted carpet with a heavy pile formed by uncut loops of wool on a linen warp

Brussels lace *n* a fine lace with a raised or appliqué design

Brussels sprout *n* **1** a variety of cabbage, *Brassica oleracea gemmifera*, having a stout stem studded with budlike heads of tightly folded leaves, resembling tiny cabbages **2** the head of this plant, eaten as a vegetable

brussen ('brʌsən) *adj Northern English dialect* bold

brut (bruːt; *French* bryt) *adj* (of champagne) not sweet; dry [c19 from French raw, rough, from Latin *brūtus* heavy; see BRUTE]

brutal ('bruːtəl) *adj* **1** cruel; vicious; savage **2** extremely honest or coarse in speech or manner **3** harsh; severe; extreme: *brutal cold* > **bru'tality** *n* > **'brutally** *adv*

brutalism ('bruːtə,lɪzəm) *n* an austere style of architecture characterized by emphasis on such structural materials as undressed concrete and unconcealed service pipes. Also called: **new brutalism** > **'brutalist** *n, adj*

brutalize *or* **brutalise** ('bruːtə,laɪz) *vb* **1** to make or become brutal **2** (*tr*) to treat brutally > ,**brutali'zation** *or* ,**brutali'sation** *n*

brute (bruːt) *n* **1 a** any animal except man; beast; lower animal **b** (*as modifier*): *brute nature* **2** a brutal person ▷ *adj* (*prenominal*) **3** wholly instinctive or physical (esp in the phrases **brute strength, brute force**) **4** without reason or intelligence **5** coarse and grossly sensual [c15 from Latin *brūtus* heavy, irrational; related to *gravis* heavy]

brutify ('bruːtɪ,faɪ) *vb* **-fies, -fying, -fied** a less common word for **brutalize** (sense 1)

brutish ('bruːtɪʃ) *adj* **1** of, relating to, or resembling a brute or brutes; animal **2** coarse; cruel; stupid > **'brutishly** *adv* > **'brutishness** *n*

Bruxelles (brysɛl) *n* the French name for **Brussels**

bruxism ('brʌksɪzəm) *n* the habit of grinding the teeth, esp unconsciously [irregularly formed from Greek *brykein* to gnash the teeth + -ISM]

Bryansk (brɪ'ænsk; *Russian* brjansk) *n* a city in W Russia. Pop: 428 000 (2005 est)

Brynhild ('brɪnhɪld) *n Norse myth* a Valkyrie won as the wife of Gunnar by Sigurd who wakes her from an enchanted sleep: corresponds to Brunhild in the *Nibelungenlied*

bryology (braɪ'ɒlədʒɪ) *n* the branch of botany concerned with the study of bryophytes > **bryological** (,braɪə'lɒdʒɪk²l) *adj* > **bry'ologist** *n*

bryony *or* **briony** ('braɪənɪ) *n, pl* **-nies** any of several herbaceous climbing plants of the cucurbitaceous genus *Bryonia*, of Europe and N

Africa. See also **black bryony, white bryony** [Old English *bryōnia*, from Latin, from Greek *bruōnia*]

bryophyte ('braɪə,faɪt) *n* any plant of the phyla *Bryophyta* (mosses), *Hepatophyta* (liverworts), or *Anthocerophyta* (hornworts), having stems and leaves but lacking true vascular tissue and roots and reproducing by spores [c19 New Latin, from Greek *bruon* moss + -PHYTE] > **bryophytic** (,braɪə'fɪtɪk) *adj*

bryozoan (,braɪə'zəʊən) *n* **1** any aquatic invertebrate animal of the phylum *Bryozoa*, forming colonies of polyps each having a ciliated feeding organ (lophophore). Popular name: **sea mat** ▷ *adj* **2** of, relating to, or belonging to the *Bryozoa* ▷ Also called: **polyzoan, ectoproct** [c19 from Greek *bruon* moss + *zōion* animal]

Brython ('brɪθən) *n* a Celt who speaks a Brythonic language. Compare **Goidel** [c19 from Welsh; see BRITON]

Brythonic (brɪ'θɒnɪk) *n* **1** the S group of Celtic languages, consisting of Welsh, Cornish, and Breton ▷ *adj* **2** of, relating to, or characteristic of this group of languages ▷ Also called: **Brittonic**

Brześć nad Bugiem (bʒɛʃtʃ nad 'bugjɛm) *n* the Polish name for **Brest** (sense 2)

bs the internet domain name for Bahamas

BS *abbreviation for* **1** Bachelor of Surgery **2** British Standard(s) (indicating the catalogue or publication number of the British Standards Institution) **3** *international car registration for* Bahamas

B.S. (in the US and Canada) *abbreviation for* Bachelor of Science

B/S *or* **b/s** *abbreviation for* **1** bags **2** bales **3** bill of sale

BSB *abbreviation for* **1** British Sky Broadcasting (formerly for British Satellite Broadcasting) **2** British Standard brass thread

BSc *abbreviation for* Bachelor of Science

BSC *abbreviation for* **1** (the former) British Steel Corporation **2** (in Britain) Broadcasting Standards Commission

BSE *abbreviation for* bovine spongiform encephalopathy: a fatal slow-developing disease of cattle, affecting the nervous system. It is caused by a prion protein and is thought to be transmissable to humans, causing a variant form of Creutzfeldt-Jakob disease. Informal name: **mad cow disease**

B-setting *n photog* a shutter setting in which the shutter remains open until the shutter control is released

BSF *abbreviation for* British Standard fine thread

BSI *abbreviation for* British Standards Institution

B-side *n* the less important side of a gramophone record. Also called: **flip side**

BSJA *abbreviation for* (in Britain) British Show Jumping Association

bsl *abbreviation for* below sea level

BSL *abbreviation for* British Sign Language

Bs/L *abbreviation for* bills of lading

BSP *abbreviation for* British Standard pipe thread

B Special *n* a member of a part-time largely Protestant police force formerly functioning in Northern Ireland

BSS *abbreviation for* British Standards Specification

BSSc *or* **BSocSc** *abbreviation for* Bachelor of Social Science

BST *abbreviation for* **1** bovine somatotrophin: a growth hormone that can be used to increase milk production in dairy cattle **2** British Summer Time

BSW *abbreviation for* British Standard Whitworth thread

bt the internet domain name for Bhutan

Bt *abbreviation for* Baronet

BT *abbreviation for* British Telecom [c20 shortened from TELECOMMUNICATIONS]

BTEC ('bɪ,tɛk) (in Britain) *n acronym for* **1** Business and Technology Council **2** a certificate or diploma in a vocational subject awarded by this body

BTG *abbreviation for* British Technology Group

B.Th. (in the US and Canada) *abbreviation for* Bachelor of Theology

btl. *abbreviation for* bottle

btu *or* **BThU** *abbreviation for* British thermal unit. US abbreviation: BTU

BTU *abbreviation for* **Board of Trade Unit**

BTW *abbreviation for* by the way: used esp in emails, text messages, etc

bty *or* **btry.** *military abbreviation for* battery

bub (bʌb) *n* **1** *US informal* fellow; youngster: used as a form of address **2** *Austral and NZ slang* **a** a baby **b** **bubs grade** the first grade of schooling; nursery school [c20 perhaps from German *Bube* boy]

bubal ('bjuːb²l) *or* **bubalis** ('bjuːbəlɪs) *n* any of various antelopes, esp an extinct N African variety of hartebeest [c15 from Latin *būbalus* African gazelle, from Greek *boubalos*, from Greek *bous* ox]

bubaline ('bjuːbə,laɪn, -lɪn) *adj* **1** (of antelopes) related to or resembling the bubal **2** resembling or relating to the buffalo [c19 from New Latin, from Latin *būbalus*; see BUBAL]

bubble ('bʌb²l) *n* **1** a thin film of liquid forming a hollow globule around air or a gas: *a soap bubble* **2** a small globule of air or a gas in a liquid or a solid, as in carbonated drinks, glass, etc **3** the sound made by a bubbling liquid **4** something lacking substance, stability, or seriousness **5** an unreliable scheme or enterprise **6** a dome, esp a transparent glass or plastic one ▷ *vb* **7** to form or cause to form bubbles **8** (*intr*) to move or flow with a gurgling sound **9** (*intr*; often foll by *over*) to overflow (with excitement, anger, etc) **10** (*intr*) *Scot* to snivel; blubber ▷ See also **bubble under** [c14 probably of Scandinavian origin; compare Swedish *bubbla*, Danish *boble*, Dutch *bobbel*, all of imitative origin]

bubble and squeak *n* (in Britain and Australia) a dish of leftover boiled cabbage, potatoes, and sometimes cooked meat fried together [c18 so called from the sounds of this dish cooking]

bubble bath *n* **1** a powder, liquid, or crystals used to scent, soften, and foam in bath water **2** a bath to which such a substance has been added

bubble car *n* (in Britain, formerly) a small car, often having three wheels, with a transparent bubble-shaped top

bubble chamber *n* a device that enables the tracks of ionizing particles to be photographed as a row of bubbles in a superheated liquid. Immediately before the particles enter the chamber the pressure is reduced so that the ionized particles act as centres for small vapour bubbles

bubble float *n angling* a hollow spherical float that can be weighted with water to aid casting

bubble gum *n* **1** a type of chewing gum that can be blown into large bubbles **2** *slang* **a** crassly commercial pop music aimed at the very young **b** (*as modifier*): *a bubble-gum hit*

bubble-jet printer *n computing* an ink-jet printer that heats the ink before printing

bubble memory *n computing* a method of storing high volumes of data by the use of minute pockets of magnetism (bubbles) in a semiconducting material: the bubbles may be caused to migrate past a read head or to a buffer area for storage

bubble pack *n* another term for **blister pack**

bubble point *n chem* the temperature at which bubbles just start to appear in a heated liquid mixture

bubbler ('bʌblə) *n* **1** a drinking fountain in which the water is forced in a stream from a small vertical nozzle **2** *chem* any device for bubbling gas through a liquid

bubble tea *n* a cold drink, originally from Taiwan, of tea infused with fruit flavouring, shaken to produce bubbles, and served over tapioca pearls in a clear cup. It is usually drunk through a very wide straw

bubble under *vb* (*intr, adverb*) **1** to remain just

beneath a particular level **2** to continue in the background or under the surface

bubble wrap *n* a type of polythene wrapping containing many small air pockets, used as a protective covering when transporting breakable goods

bubbly ('bʌblɪ) *adj* -blier, -bliest **1** full of or resembling bubbles **2** lively; animated; excited: *a bubbly personality* ▷ *n* **3** an informal name for champagne

bubo ('bju:bəʊ) *n, pl* -boes *pathol* inflammation and swelling of a lymph node, often with the formation of pus, esp in the region of the armpit or groin [c14 from Medieval Latin *bubō* swelling, from Greek *boubōn* groin, glandular swelling] > **bubonic** (bju:'bɒnɪk) *adj*

bubonic plague *n* an acute infectious febrile disease characterized by chills, prostration, delirium, and formation of buboes: caused by the bite of a rat flea infected with the bacterium *Yersinia pestis*. See also **plague**

bubonocele (bju:'bɒnə,si:l) *n* an incomplete hernia in the groin; partial inguinal hernia [c17 from Greek *boubōn* groin + *kēlē* tumour]

bubu ('bu:bu:) *n* a variant spelling of **boubou**

Bucaramanga (*Spanish* bukara'maŋga) *n* a city in N central Colombia, in the Cordillera Oriental: centre of a district growing coffee, tobacco, and cotton. Pop: 1 069 000 (2005 est)

buccal ('bʌkəl) *adj* **1** of or relating to the cheek **2** of or relating to the mouth; oral: *buccal lesion* [c19 from Latin *bucca* cheek]

buccaneer (,bʌkə'nɪə) *n* **1** a pirate, esp one who preyed on the Spanish colonies and shipping in America and the Caribbean in the 17th and 18th centuries ▷ *vb* (*intr*) **2** to be or act like a buccaneer [c17 from French *boucanier*, from *boucaner* to smoke meat, from Old French *boucan* frame for smoking meat, of Tupian origin; originally applied to French and English hunters of wild oxen in the Caribbean]

buccinator ('bʌksɪ,neɪtə) *n* a thin muscle that compresses the cheeks and holds them against the teeth during chewing, etc [c17 from Latin, from *buccināre* to sound the trumpet, from *buccina* trumpet]

bucentaur (bju:'sɛntɔ:) *n* the state barge of Venice from which the doge and other officials dropped a ring into the sea on Ascension Day to symbolize the ceremonial marriage of the state with the Adriatic [c17 from Italian *bucentoro*, of uncertain origin]

Bucephalus (bju:'sɛfələs) *n* the favourite horse of Alexander the Great [c17 from Latin, from Greek *Boukephalos*, from *bous* ox + *kephalē* head]

Bucharest (,bu:kə'rɛst, ,bju:-) *n* the capital of Romania, in the southeast. Pop: 1 764 000 (2005 est). Romanian name: Bucureşti

Buchenwald (*German* 'bu:xənvalt) *n* a village in E central Germany, near Weimar; site of a Nazi concentration camp (1937–45)

Buchmanism ('bʊkmə,nɪzəm) *n* another name for **Moral Rearmament** [c20 named after Frank *Buchman* (1878–1961), US evangelist who founded it] > 'Buchman,ite *n, adj*

Buchner funnel ('bʌknə) *n* a laboratory filter funnel used under reduced pressure. It consists of a shallow porcelain cylinder with a flat perforated base [named after its inventor, Eduard *Buchner* (1860–1917), German chemist]

buchu ('bu:ku:) *n* any of several S. African rutaceous shrubs of the genus *Barosma*, esp *B. betulina*, whose leaves are used as an antiseptic and diuretic [c18 from a South African Bantu name]

buck[1] (bʌk) *n* **1 a** the male of various animals including the goat, hare, kangaroo, rabbit, and reindeer **b** (*as modifier*): *a buck antelope* **2** *South African* an antelope or deer of either sex **3** *US informal* a young man **4** *archaic* a robust spirited young man **5** *archaic* a dandy; fop **6** the act of bucking ▷ *vb* **7** (*intr*) (of a horse or other animal)

to jump vertically, with legs stiff and back arched **8** (*tr*) (of a horse, etc) to throw (its rider) by bucking **9** (when *intr*, often foll by *against*) *informal, chiefly US and Canadian* to resist or oppose obstinately: *to buck against change; to buck change* **10** (*tr; usually passive*) *informal* to cheer or encourage: *I was very bucked at passing the exam* **11** *US and Canadian Informal* (esp of a car) to move forward jerkily; jolt **12** *US and Canadian* to charge against (something) with the head down; butt ▷ See also **buck up** [Old English *bucca* he-goat; related to Old Norse *bukkr*, Old High German *bock*, Old Irish *bocc*] > 'bucker *n*

buck[2] (bʌk) *n* **1** *US, Canadian and Austral informal* a dollar **2** *South African informal* a rand **3** a fast buck easily gained money **4** bang for one's buck See **bang**[1] (sense 15) [c19 of obscure origin]

buck[3] (bʌk) *n* **1** *gymnastics* a type of vaulting horse **2** *US and Canadian* a stand for timber during sawing. Also called (in Britain and certain other countries): **sawhorse** ▷ *vb* **3** (*tr*) *US and Canadian* to cut (a felled or fallen tree) into lengths [c19 short for SAWBUCK]

buck[4] (bʌk) *n* **1** *poker* a marker in the jackpot to remind the winner of some obligation when his turn comes to deal **2** pass the buck *informal* to shift blame or responsibility onto another **3** the buck stops here *informal* the ultimate responsibility lies here [c19 probably from *buckhorn knife*, placed before a player in poker to indicate that he was the next dealer]

buck and wing *n* *US* a boisterous tap dance, derived from Black and Irish clog dances

buckaroo (,bʌkə'ru:, ,bʌkə'ru:) *n, pl* -roos *Southwestern US* a cowboy [c19 variant of Spanish *vaquero*, from *vaca* cow, from Latin *vacca*]

buckbean ('bʌk,bi:n) *n* a marsh plant, *Menyanthes trifoliata*, with white or pink flowers: family *Menyanthaceae*. Also called: **bogbean**

buckboard ('bʌk,bɔ:d) *n* *US and Canadian* an open four-wheeled horse-drawn carriage with the seat attached to a flexible board between the front and rear axles

buckeen (bʌ'ki:n) *n* (in Ireland) a poor young man who aspires to the habits and dress of the wealthy [c18 from Irish Gaelic *boicín*, diminutive of *boc* an important person]

bucket ('bʌkɪt) *n* **1** an open-topped roughly cylindrical container; pail **2** Also called: **bucketful** the amount a bucket will hold **3** any of various bucket-like parts of a machine, such as the scoop on a mechanical shovel **4** a cupped blade or bucket-like compartment on the outer circumference of a water wheel, paddle wheel, etc **5** *computing* a unit of storage on a direct-access device from which data can be retrieved **6** *chiefly US* a turbine rotor blade **7** *Austral and NZ* an ice cream container **8** kick the bucket *slang* to die ▷ *vb* -kets, -keting, -keted **9** (*tr*) to carry in or put into a bucket **10** (*intr; often foll by down*) (of rain) to fall very heavily: *it bucketed all day* **11** (*intr; often foll by along*) *chiefly Brit* to travel or drive fast **12** (*tr*) *chiefly Brit* to ride (a horse) hard without consideration **13** (*tr*) *Austral slang* to criticize severely [c13 from Anglo-French *buket*, from Old English *būc*; compare Old High German *būh* belly, German *Bauch* belly]

bucket about *vb* (*intr*) *Brit* (esp of a boat in a storm) to toss or shake violently

bucket ladder *n* **a** a series of buckets that move in a continuous chain, used to dredge riverbeds, etc, or to excavate land **b** (*as modifier*): *a bucket-ladder dredger*

bucket out *vb* (*tr*) to empty out with or as if with a bucket

bucket seat *n* a seat in a car, aircraft, etc, having curved sides that partially enclose and support the body

bucket shop *n* **1** an unregistered firm of stockbrokers that engages in speculation with clients' funds **2** *chiefly Brit* any small business that cannot be relied upon, esp one selling cheap airline tickets

buckeye ('bʌk,aɪ) *n* any of several North American trees of the genus *Aesculus*, esp *A. glabra* (Ohio buckeye), having erect clusters of white or red flowers and prickly fruits: family *Hippocastanaceae*. See also **horse chestnut**

Buckfast ('bʌk,fɑ:st) *n* *trademark* a fortified tonic wine. Informal name: **Buckie** [from *Buckfast* Abbey, Devon, England where it is produced]

buck fever *n* nervous excitement felt by inexperienced hunters at the approach of game

buckhorn ('bʌk,hɔ:n) *n* **1 a** a horn from a buck, used for knife handles, etc **b** (*as modifier*): *a buckhorn knife* **2** Also called: **buck's horn plantain** a Eurasian plant, *Plantago coronopus*, having leaves resembling a buck's horn: family *Plantaginaceae*

buckhound ('bʌk,haʊnd) *n* a hound, smaller than a staghound, used for hunting the smaller breeds of deer, esp fallow deer

buckie ('bʌkɪ) *n* *Scot* **1** a whelk or its shell **2** a lively or boisterous person, esp a youngster [related to Latin *buc(c)inum* whelk, from *buc(c)ina* trumpet, horn]

Buckie ('bʌkɪ) *n* *informal* short for **Buckfast**

Buckingham ('bʌkɪŋəm) *n* a town in S central England, in Buckinghamshire; university (1975). Pop: 12 512 (2001)

Buckingham Palace *n* the London residence of the British sovereign: built in 1703, rebuilt by John Nash in 1821–36 and partially redesigned in the early 20th century

Buckinghamshire ('bʌkɪŋəm,ʃɪə, -ʃə) *n* a county in SE central England, containing the Vale of Aylesbury and parts of the Chiltern Hills: the geographic and ceremonial county includes Milton Keynes, which became an independent unitary authority in 1997. Administrative centre: Aylesbury. Pop (excluding Milton Keynes): 478 000 (2003 est). Area (excluding Milton Keynes): 1568 sq km (605 sq miles). Abbreviation: **Bucks**

buckjumper ('bʌk,dʒʌmpə) *n* *Austral* an untamed horse

buckjumping ('bʌk,dʒʌmpɪŋ) *n* *Austral* a competitive event for buckjumpers in a rodeo

buckle ('bʌkəl) *n* **1** a clasp for fastening together two loose ends, esp of a belt or strap, usually consisting of a frame with an attached movable prong **2** an ornamental representation of a buckle, as on a shoe **3** a kink, bulge, or other distortion: *a buckle in a railway track* ▷ *vb* **4** to fasten or be fastened with a buckle **5** to bend or cause to bend out of shape, esp as a result of pressure or heat [c14 from Old French *bocle*, from Latin *buccula* a little cheek, hence, cheek strap of a helmet, from *bucca* cheek]

buckle down *vb* (*intr, adverb*) *informal* to apply oneself with determination: *to buckle down to a job*

buckler ('bʌklə) *n* **1** a small round shield worn on the forearm or held by a short handle **2** a means of protection; defence ▷ *vb* **3** (*tr*) *archaic* to defend [c13 from Old French *bocler*, from *bocle* shield boss; see BUCKLE, BOSS[2]]

buckler fern *n* any of various ferns of the genus *Dryopteris*, such as *D. dilatata* (broad buckler fern): family *Polypodiaceae*

Buckley's chance ('bʌklɪz) *n* *Austral and NZ slang* no chance at all. Often shortened to: **Buckley's** [c19 of obscure origin]

buckling ('bʌklɪŋ) *n* another name for a **bloater** [c20 from German *Bückling*]

buckminsterfullerene (,bʌkmɪnstə'fʊlə,ri:n) *n* a form of carbon that contains molecules having 60 carbon atoms arranged at the vertices of a polyhedron with hexagonal and pentagonal faces. It is produced in carbon arcs and occurs naturally in small amounts in certain minerals. Also called: **fullerene** [c20 named after (Richard) *Buckminster Fuller* (1895–1983), US architect and engineer]

bucko ('bʌkəʊ) *n, pl* -oes *Irish* a lively young fellow: often a term of address

buckra ('bʌkrə) *n* (used contemptuously by Black people, esp in the US) a White man [c18 probably from Efik *mba-ka-ra* master]

b

buck rabbit *or* **rarebit** *n Brit* Welsh rabbit with either an egg or a piece of toast on top

buckram ('bʌkrəm) *n* **1 a** cotton or linen cloth stiffened with size, etc, used in lining or stiffening clothes, bookbinding, etc **b** (*as modifier*): *a buckram cover* **2** *archaic* stiffness of manner ▷ *vb* **-rams, -raming, -ramed 3** (*tr*) to stiffen with buckram [c14 from Old French *boquerant*, from Old Provençal *bocaran*, ultimately from BUKHARA, once an important source of textiles]

Bucks (bʌks) *abbreviation for* Buckinghamshire

bucksaw ('bʌkˌsɔː) *n* a woodcutting saw having its blade set in a frame and tensioned by a turnbuckle across the back of the frame

buck's fizz *n* a cocktail made of champagne and orange juice

buckshee (ˌbʌkˈʃiː) *adj Brit slang* without charge; free [c20 from BAKSHEESH]

buckshot ('bʌkˌʃɒt) *n* lead shot of large size used in shotgun shells, esp for hunting game [c15 (original sense: the distance at which a buck can be shot)]

buckskin ('bʌkˌskɪn) *n* **1** the skin of a male deer **2 a** a strong greyish-yellow suede leather, originally made from deerskin but now usually made from sheepskin **b** (*as modifier*): *buckskin boots* **3** *US* (*sometimes capital*) a person wearing buckskin clothes, esp an American soldier of the Civil War **4** a stiffly starched cotton cloth **5** a strong satin-woven woollen fabric ▷ *adj* **6** greyish-yellow

buckskins ('bʌkˌskɪnz) *pl n* (in the US and Canada) breeches, shoes, or a suit of buckskin

buck's party *or* **night** *n Austral* a party for men only, esp one held for a man before he is married. Also called (in Britain and certain other countries): **stag night, stag party**

buckthorn ('bʌkˌθɔːn) *n* any of several thorny small-flowered shrubs of the genus *Rhamnus*, esp the Eurasian species *R. cathartica*, whose berries were formerly used as a purgative: family *Rhamnaceae*. See also **sea buckthorn** [c16 from BUCK¹ (from the spiny branches, imagined as resembling antlers) + THORN]

bucktooth ('bʌkˌtuːθ) *n, pl* **-teeth** *derogatory* a projecting upper front tooth [c18 from BUCK¹ (deer) + TOOTH] > **'buck-toothed** *adj*

buck up *vb* (*adverb*) *informal* **1** to make or cause to make haste **2** to make or become more cheerful, confident, etc

buckwheat ('bʌkˌwiːt) *n* **1** any of several polygonaceous plants of the genus *Fagopyrum*, esp *F. esculentum*, which has fragrant white flowers and is cultivated, esp in the US, for its seeds **2** the edible seeds of this plant, ground into flour or used as animal fodder **3** the flour obtained from these seeds [c16 from Middle Dutch *boecweite*, from *boeke* BEECH + *weite* WHEAT, from the resemblance of their seeds to beechnuts]

buckyball ('bʌkɪˌbɔːl) *n informal* a ball-like polyhedral carbon molecule of the type found in buckminsterfullerene and other fullerenes [c20 from BUCK(MINSTERFULLERENE) + Y² + BALL¹]

buckytube ('bʌkɪˌtjuːb) *n informal* a tube of carbon atoms structurally similar to buckminsterfullerene

bucolic (bjuːˈkɒlɪk) *adj also* **bucolical 1** of or characteristic of the countryside or country life; rustic **2** of or relating to shepherds; pastoral ▷ *n* **3** (*sometimes plural*) a pastoral poem, often in the form of a dialogue **4** a rustic; farmer or shepherd [c16 from Latin *būcolicus*, from Greek *boukolikos*, from *boukolos* cowherd, from *bous* ox] > **buˈcolically** *adv*

Bucovina (ˌbuːkəˈviːnə) *n* a variant spelling of **Bukovina**

Bucureşti (bukuˈreʃtj) *n* the Romanian name for **Bucharest**

bud¹ (bʌd) *n* **1** a swelling on a plant stem consisting of overlapping immature leaves or petals **2 a** a partially opened flower **b** (*in combination*): *rosebud* **3** any small budlike outgrowth: *taste buds* **4** something small or

immature **5** an asexually produced outgrowth in simple organisms, such as yeasts, and the hydra that develops into a new individual **6** a slang word for **marijuana 7 in bud** at the stage of producing buds **8 nip in the bud** to put an end to (an idea, movement, etc) in its initial stages ▷ *vb* **buds, budding, budded 9** (*intr*) (of plants and some animals) to produce buds **10** (*intr*) to begin to develop or grow **11** (*tr*) *horticulture* to graft (a bud) from one plant onto another, usually by insertion under the bark [c14 *budde*, of Germanic origin; compare Icelandic *budda* purse, Dutch *buidel*]

bud² (bʌd) *n informal, chiefly US* short for **buddy**: used as a term of address

buda ('budə) *n Hinglish derogatory* an old man [c21 Hindi]

Budapest (ˌbjuːdəˈpɛst; *Hungarian* 'budɒpeʃt) *n* the capital of Hungary, on the River Danube: formed in 1873 from the towns of Buda and Pest. Traditionally Buda, the old Magyar capital, was the administrative and Pest the trade centre: suffered severely in the Russian siege of 1945 and in the unsuccessful revolt against the Communist regime (1956). Pop: 1 719 342 (2003 est)

buddha ('budə) *n* **1** *Buddhism* (*often capital*) a person who has achieved a state of perfect enlightenment **2** an image or picture of the Buddha [c17 from Sanskrit: awakened, enlightened, from *budh* to awake, know]

Buddha ('budə) *n* **the** ?563–483 BC, a title applied to Gautama Siddhartha, a nobleman and religious teacher of N India, regarded by his followers as the most recent rediscoverer of the path to enlightenment: the founder of Buddhism

Buddh Gaya ('bud gə'jɑː), **Buddha Gaya** *or* **Bodh Gaya** *n* a town in NE India, in Bihar: site of the sacred bo tree under which Gautama Siddhartha attained enlightenment and became the Buddha; pilgrimage centre. Pop: 30 883 (2001)

Buddhism ('budɪzəm) *n* a religious teaching propagated by the Buddha and his followers, which declares that by destroying greed, hatred, and delusion, which are the causes of all suffering, man can attain perfect enlightenment. See nirvana. > **'Buddhist** *n, adj*

budding ('bʌdɪŋ) *adj* at an early stage of development but showing promise or potential: *a budding genius*

buddle ('bʌdᵊl) *n* **1** a sloping trough in which ore is washed ▷ *vb* **2** (*tr*) to wash (ore) in a buddle [c16 of unknown origin]

buddleia ('bʌdlɪə) *n* any ornamental shrub of the genus *Buddleia*, esp *B. davidii*, which has long spikes of mauve flowers and is frequently visited by butterflies: family *Buddleiaceae*. Also called: **butterfly bush** [c19 named after A. *Buddle* (died 1715), British botanist]

buddy ('bʌdɪ) *n, pl* **-dies 1** *chiefly US and Canadian* an informal word for **friend** Also called (as a term of address): **bud 2** a volunteer who visits and gives help and support to a person suffering from AIDS **3** a volunteer who gives help and support to a person who has become disabled but is returning to work ▷ *vb* **-dying, -died 4** (*intr*) to act as a buddy to a person suffering from AIDS [c19 probably a baby-talk variant (US) of BROTHER]

buddy-buddy *adj informal, chiefly US* on friendly or intimate terms

buddy movie *or* **film** *n* a genre of film dealing with the relationship and adventures of two friends

budge¹ (bʌdʒ) *vb* (*usually used with a negative*) **1** to move, however slightly: *the car won't budge* **2** to change or cause to change opinions, etc [c16 from Old French *bouger*, from Vulgar Latin *bullicāre* (unattested) to bubble, from Latin *bullīre* to boil, from *bulla* bubble]

budge² (bʌdʒ) *n* a lambskin dressed for the fur to be worn on the outer side [c14 from Anglo-French *bogee*, of obscure origin]

budgerigar ('bʌdʒərɪˌgɑː) *n* a small green

Australian parrot, *Melopsittacus undulatus*: a popular cagebird that is bred in many different coloured varieties. Often (informal) shortened to: **budgie** [c19 from a native Australian language]

budget ('bʌdʒɪt) *n* **1** an itemized summary of expected income and expenditure of a country, company, etc, over a specified period, usually a financial year **2** an estimate of income and a plan for domestic expenditure of an individual or a family, often over a short period, such as a month or a week **3** a restriction on expenditure (esp in the phrase **on a budget**) **4** (*modifier*) economical; inexpensive: *budget meals for a family* **5** the total amount of money allocated for a specific purpose during a specified period **6** *archaic* a stock, quantity, or supply ▷ *vb* **-gets, -geting, -geted 7** (*tr*) to enter or provide for in a budget **8** to plan the expenditure of (money, time, etc) **9** (*intr*) to make a budget [c15 (meaning: leather pouch, wallet): from Old French *bougette*, diminutive of *bouge*, from Latin *bulga*, of Gaulish origin; compare Old English *bælg* bag] > **'budgetary** *adj*

Budget ('bʌdʒɪt) *n* **the.** an estimate of British government expenditures and revenues and the financial plans for the ensuing fiscal year presented annually to the House of Commons by the Chancellor of the Exchequer

budget account *n* **1** an account with a department store, etc, enabling a customer to make monthly payments to cover his past and future purchases **2** a bank account for paying household bills, being credited with regular or equal monthly payments from the customer's current account

budgetary control *n* a system of managing a business by applying a financial value to each forecast activity. Actual performance is subsequently compared with the estimates

budget deficit *n* the amount by which government expenditure exceeds income from taxation, customs duties, etc, in any one fiscal year

budget for *vb* (*tr, preposition*) to allocate, save, or set aside money for (a particular purpose, period, etc): *we need to budget for a fuel increase this winter*

budgie ('bʌdʒɪ) *n informal* short for **budgerigar**

budi ('budiː) *n Hinglish derogatory* an old woman [c21 Hindi]

bud scale *n* one of the hard protective sometimes hairy or resinous specialized leaves surrounding the buds of certain plants, such as the rhododendron

bud sport *n horticulture* a shoot, inflorescence, etc, that differs from another such structure on a plant and is caused by a somatic mutation; the differences can be retained by vegetative propagation

Budweis ('butvais) *n* the German name for **České Budějovice**

Buenaventura (*Spanish* bwenaβenˈtura) *n* a major port in W Colombia, on the Pacific coast. Pop: 250 000 (2005 est)

Buena Vista (*Spanish* 'bwena 'vista) *n* a village in NE Mexico, near Saltillo: site of the defeat of the Mexicans by US forces (1847)

Buenos Aires ('bweɪnɒs 'aɪrɪz; *Spanish* 'bwenos 'aires) *n* the capital of Argentina, a major port and industrial city on the Río de la Plata estuary: became capital in 1880; university (1821). Pop: 13 349 000 (2005 est)

BUF *abbreviation for* (formerly) **British Union of Fascists**

buff¹ (bʌf) *n* **1 a** a soft thick flexible undyed leather made chiefly from the skins of buffalo, oxen, and elk **b** (*as modifier*): *a buff coat* **2 a** a dull yellow or yellowish-brown colour **b** (*as adjective*): *buff paint* **3** Also called: **buffer a** a cloth or pad of material used for polishing an object **b** a flexible disc or wheel impregnated with a fine abrasive for polishing metals, etc, with a power tool **4** *informal* one's bare skin (esp in the phrase **in the buff**) ▷ *vb* **5** to clean or polish (a metal, floor, shoes, etc) with a buff **6** to remove the grain surface of (a leather) ▷ *adj* **7** *US informal* in a condition of high physical fitness and body tone, maintained by regular exercise [C16 from Old French *buffle*, from Old Italian *bufalo*, from Late Latin *būfalus* BUFFALO]

buff[2] (bʌf) *vb* **1** (*tr*) to deaden the force of ▷ *n* **2** *archaic* a blow or buffet (now only in the phrase **blind man's buff**) [C15 back formation from BUFFET[2]]

buff[3] (bʌf) *n informal* an expert on or devotee of a given subject: *a cheese buff* [C20 originally US: an enthusiastic fire watcher, from the buff-coloured uniforms worn by volunteer firemen in New York City]

buffalo (ˈbʌfəˌləʊ) *n, pl* **-loes** *or* **-lo 1** Also called: **Cape buffalo** a member of the cattle tribe, *Syncerus caffer*, mostly found in game reserves in southern and eastern Africa and having upward-curving horns **2** short for **water buffalo 3** *US and Canadian* a member of the cattle tribe, *Bison bison*, formerly widely distributed over the prairies of W North America but now confined to reserves and parks, with a massive head, shaggy forequarters, and a humped back. Also called: **bison** (sense 1) Related adjective: **bubaline** ▷ *vb* (*tr*) *US and Canadian informal* **4** (*often passive*) to confuse **5** to intimidate [C16 from Italian *bufalo*, from Late Latin *būfalus*, alteration of Latin *būbalus*; see BUBAL]

Buffalo (ˈbʌfəˌləʊ) *n* a port in W New York State, at the E end of Lake Erie. Pop: 285 018 (2003 est)

buffalo fish *n* any of several freshwater North American hump-backed cyprinoid fishes of the genus *Ictiobus*: family *Catostomidae* (suckers)

buffalo gnat *n* any of various small North American blood-sucking dipterous insects of the genus *Simulium* and related genera: family *Simuliidae*. Also called: **black fly**

buffalo grass *n* **1** a short grass, *Buchloë dactyloides*, growing on the dry plains of the central US **2** *Austral* a grass, *Stenotaphrum americanum*, introduced from North America

buffel grass (ˈbʌfəl) *n Austral* a pasture grass, *Cenchrus ciliaris*, native to Africa and India, introduced in N Australia

buffer[1] (ˈbʌfə) *n* **1** one of a pair of spring-loaded steel pads attached at both ends of railway vehicles and at the end of a railway track to reduce shock due to contact **2** a person or thing that lessens shock or protects from damaging impact, circumstances, etc **3** *chem* **a** an ionic compound, usually a salt of a weak acid or base, added to a solution to resist changes in its acidity or alkalinity and thus stabilize its pH **b** Also called: **buffer solution** a solution containing such a compound **4** *computing* a memory device for temporarily storing data **5** *electronics* an isolating circuit used to minimize the reaction between a driving and a driven circuit **6** short for **buffer state 7 hit the buffers** *informal* to finish or be stopped, esp unexpectedly ▷ *vb* (*tr*) **8** to insulate against or protect from shock; cushion **9** *chem* to add a buffer to (a solution) [C19 from BUFF[2]]

buffer[2] (ˈbʌfə) *n* **1** any device used to shine, polish, etc; buff **2** a person who uses such a device

buffer[3] (ˈbʌfə) *n Brit informal* a stupid or bumbling man (esp in the phrase **old buffer**) [C18 perhaps from Middle English *buffer* stammerer]

buffer state *n* a small neutral state between two rival powers

buffer stock *n commerce* a stock of a commodity built up by a government or trade organization with the object of using it to stabilize prices

buffet[1] *n* **1** (ˈbʊfeɪ) a counter where light refreshments are served **2** (ˈbʊfeɪ) **a** a meal at which guests help themselves from a number of dishes and often eat standing up **b** (*as modifier*): *a buffet lunch* **3** (ˈbʌfɪt, ˈbʊfeɪ) a piece of furniture used from medieval times to the 18th century for displaying plates, etc and typically comprising one or more cupboards and some open shelves **4** (ˈbʌfɪ) *Scot and Northern English dialect* a kind of low stool, pouffe, or hassock [C18 from French, of unknown origin]

buffet[2] (ˈbʌfɪt) *vb* **-fets, -feting, -feted 1** (*tr*) to knock against or about; batter: *the wind buffeted the boat* **2** (*tr*) to hit, esp with the fist; cuff **3** to force (one's way), as through a crowd **4** (*intr*) to struggle; battle ▷ *n* **5** a blow, esp with a fist or hand **6** aerodynamic excitation of an aircraft structure by separated flows [C13 from Old French *buffeter*, from *buffet* a light blow, from *buffe*, of imitative origin] > ˈ**buffeter** *n*

buffet car (ˈbʊfeɪ) *n Brit* a railway coach where light refreshments are served

buffeting (ˈbʌfɪtɪŋ) *n* response of an aircraft structure to buffet, esp an irregular oscillation of the tail

buffing wheel *n* a wheel covered with a soft material, such as lamb's wool or leather, used for shining and polishing. Also called: **buff wheel**

bufflehead (ˈbʌfəlˌhɛd) *n* a small North American diving duck, *Bucephala* (or *Glaucionetta*) *albeola*: the male has black-and-white plumage and a fluffy head. Also called: **butterball** [C17 *buffle* from obsolete *buffle* wild ox (see BUFF[1]), referring to the duck's head]

buffo (ˈbʊfəʊ; *Italian* ˈbuffo) *n, pl* **-fi** (-fɪ) *or* **-fos 1** (in Italian opera of the 18th century) a comic part, esp one for a bass **2** Also called: **buffo bass, basso buffo** (*Italian* ˈbasso ˈbuffo) a bass singer who performs such a part [C18 from Italian (adj): comic, from *buffo* (n) BUFFOON]

buffoon (bəˈfuːn) *n* **1** a person who amuses others by ridiculous or odd behaviour, jokes, etc **2** a foolish person [C16 from French *bouffon*, from Italian *buffone*, from Medieval Latin *būfō*, from Latin: toad] > **bufˈfoonery** *n*

Buffs (bʌfs) *pl n* **the** the Third Regiment of Foot, esp the Royal East Kent Regiment [C19 from their buff-coloured facings]

buff-tip moth *n* a large European moth, *Phalera bucephala*, having violet-brown buff-tipped forewings held at rest around the body so that it resembles a snapped-off twig

bufotalin (ˌbuːfəʊˈtælɪn) *n* the principal poisonous substance in the skin and saliva of the common European toad

bug[1] (bʌɡ) *n* **1** any insect of the order *Hemiptera*, esp any of the suborder *Heteroptera*, having piercing and sucking mouthparts specialized as a beak (rostrum). See also **assassin bug, bedbug, chinch bug 2** *chiefly US and Canadian* any insect, such as the June bug or the Croton bug **3** *informal* **a** a microorganism, esp a bacterium, that produces disease **b** a disease, esp a stomach infection, caused by a microorganism **4** *informal* an obsessive idea, hobby, etc; craze (esp in the phrases **get the bug, be bitten by the bug, the bug bites,** etc) **5** *informal* a person having such a craze; enthusiast **6** (*often plural*) *informal* an error or fault, as in a machine or system, esp in a computer or computer program **7** *informal* a concealed microphone used for recording conversations, as in spying **8** *US* (in poker) a joker used as an ace or wild card to complete a straight or flush ▷ *vb* **bugs, bugging, bugged** *informal* **9** (*tr*) to irritate; bother **10** (*tr*) to conceal a microphone in (a room, etc) **11** (*intr*) *US* (of eyes) to protrude. ▷ See also **bug out** [C16 of uncertain origin; perhaps related to Old English *budda* beetle]

bug[2] (bʌɡ) *n obsolete* an evil spirit or spectre; hobgoblin [C14 *bugge*, perhaps from Middle Welsh *bwg* ghost. See also BUGBEAR, BUGABOO]

bug[3] (bʌɡ) *vb* a past tense and past participle of **big**[2]

Bug (*Russian* buk) *n* **1** Also called: **Southern Bug** a river in E Europe, rising in W Ukraine and flowing southeast to the Dnieper estuary and the Black Sea. Length: 853 km (530 miles) **2** Also called: **Western Bug** a river in E Europe, rising in SW Ukraine and flowing northwest to the River Vistula in Poland, forming part of the border between Poland and Ukraine. Length: 724 km (450 miles)

bugaboo (ˈbʌɡəˌbuː) *n, pl* **-boos** an imaginary source of fear; bugbear; bogey [C18 probably of Celtic origin; compare Cornish *buccaboo* the devil]

Buganda (bʊˈɡændə) *n* a region of Uganda: a powerful Bantu kingdom from the 17th century

bugbane (ˈbʌɡˌbeɪn) *n* any of several ranunculaceous plants of the genus *Cimicifuga*, esp *C. foetida* of Europe, whose flowers are reputed to repel insects

bugbear (ˈbʌɡˌbɛə) *n* **1** a thing that causes obsessive fear or anxiety **2** (in English folklore) a goblin said to eat naughty children and thought to be in the form of a bear [C16 from BUG[2] + BEAR[2]; compare BUGABOO]

bugger (ˈbʌɡə) *n* **1** a person who practises buggery **2** *slang* a person or thing considered to be contemptible, unpleasant, or difficult **3** *slang* a humorous or affectionate term for a man or child: *a silly old bugger; a friendly little bugger* **4 bugger all** *slang* nothing **5 play silly buggers** *slang* to fool around and waste time ▷ *vb* **6** to practise buggery (with) **7** (*tr*) *slang, chiefly Brit* to ruin, complicate, or frustrate **8** *slang* to tire; weary: *he was absolutely buggered* ▷ *interj* **9** *slang* an exclamation of annoyance or disappointment [C16 from Old French *bougre*, from Medieval Latin *Bulgarus* Bulgarian; from the condemnation of the dualist heresy rife in Bulgaria from the tenth century to the fifteenth]

bugger about *or* **around** *vb* (*adverb*) *Brit slang* **1** (*intr*) to fool about and waste time **2** (*tr*) to create difficulties or complications for (a person)

bugger off *vb* (*intr, adverb*) *Brit slang* to go away; depart

buggery (ˈbʌɡərɪ) *n* anal intercourse between a man and another man, a woman, or an animal. Compare **sodomy**

Buggins' turn (ˈbʌɡɪnz) *or* **Buggins's turn** *n Brit slang* the principle of awarding an appointment to members of a group in turn, rather than according to merit [C20 origin unknown]

buggy[1] (ˈbʌɡɪ) *n, pl* **-gies 1** a light horse-drawn carriage having either four wheels (esp in the US and Canada) or two wheels (esp in Britain and India) **2** short for **beach buggy 3** short for **baby buggy 4** a small motorized vehicle designed for a particular purpose: *golf buggy; moon buggy* [C18 of unknown origin]

buggy[2] (ˈbʌɡɪ) *adj* **-gier, -giest 1** infested with bugs **2** *US slang* insane > ˈ**bugginess** *n*

bughouse (ˈbʌɡˌhaʊs) *offensive slang, chiefly US* ▷ *n* **1** a mental hospital or asylum ▷ *adj* **2** insane; crazy [C20 from BUG[1] + (MAD)HOUSE]

bugle[1] (ˈbjuːɡəl) *n* **1** *music* a brass instrument similar to the cornet but usually without valves: used for military fanfares, signal calls, etc ▷ *vb* **2** (*intr*) to play or sound (on) a bugle [C14 short for *bugle horn* ox horn (musical instrument), from Old French *bugle*, from Latin *būculus* young bullock, from *bōs* ox] > ˈ**bugler** *n*

bugle[2] (ˈbjuːɡəl) *n* any of several Eurasian plants of the genus *Ajuga*, esp *A. reptans*, having small blue or white flowers: family *Lamiaceae* (labiates). Also called: **bugleweed** See also **ground pine** [C13 from Late Latin *bugula*, of uncertain origin]

bugle[3] (ˈbjuːɡəl) *n* a tubular glass or plastic bead sewn onto clothes for decoration [C16 of unknown origin]

bugleweed (ˈbjuːɡəlˌwiːd) *n* **1** Also called: **water horehound** *US* any aromatic plant of the genus *Lycopus*, having small whitish or pale blue flowers: family *Lamiaceae* (labiates). See also **gipsywort 2** another name for **bugle**[2]

bugloss (ˈbjuːɡlɒs) *n* any of various hairy Eurasian boraginaceous plants of the genera *Anchusa, Lycopsis*, and *Echium*, esp *L. arvensis*, having clusters of blue flowers. See also **viper's bugloss** [C15 from Latin *būglōssa*, from Greek *bouglōssos* ox-tongued, from *bōs* ox + *glōssa* tongue]

bugong (ˈbuːɡɒŋ) *n* another name for **bogong**

bug out *vb* (*intr, adverb*) *slang, chiefly US* to depart hurriedly; run away; retreat

buhl (buːl) *adj, n* the usual US spelling of **boulle**

buhrstone, burstone *or* **burrstone** ('bɜːˌstəʊn) *n* **1** a hard tough rock containing silica, fossils, and cavities, formerly used as a grindstone **2** a grindstone or millstone made of this rock [c18 *burr*, perhaps identical to BURR[1] (alluding to roughness)]

BUI *International car registration for* (British) Virgin Islands

buibui ('bʊɪ'bʊɪ) *n* a piece of black cloth worn as a shawl by Muslim women, esp on the E African coast [from Swahili]

build (bɪld) *vb* **builds, building, built 1** to make, construct, or form by joining parts or materials: *to build a house* **2** (*intr*) to be a builder by profession **3** (*tr*) to order the building of: *the government builds most of our hospitals* **4** (foll by *on* or *upon*) to base; found: *his theory was not built on facts* **5** (*tr*) to establish and develop: *it took ten years to build a business* **6** (*tr*) to make in a particular way or for a particular purpose: *the car was not built for speed* **7** (*intr*; often foll by *up*) to increase in intensity: *the wind was building* **8** *cards* **a** to add cards to each other to form (a sequence or set) **b** (*intr*) to add to the layout of cards on the table from one's hand ▷ *n* **9** physical form, figure, or proportions: *a man with an athletic build.* ▷ See also **build in, build into, build up** [Old English *byldan*; related to *bylda* farmer, *bold* building, Old Norse *bōl* farm, dwelling; see BOWER[1]]

buildable ('bɪldəbəl) *adj* suitable for building on

builder ('bɪldə) *n* **1** a person who builds, esp one who contracts for and supervises the construction or repair of buildings **2** a substance added to a soap or detergent as a filler or abrasive

build in *vb* (*tr, adverb*) to incorporate or construct as an integral part: *to build in safety features*

building ('bɪldɪŋ) *n* **1** something built with a roof and walls, such as a house or factory **2** the act, business, occupation, or art of building houses, boats, etc

building and loan association *n* a US name for **building society**

building block *n* **1** a block of stone or other material, larger than a brick, used in building **2** a component that fits with others to form a whole: *standardized software building blocks* **3** another name for (the child's toy) **block**

building line *n* the boundary line along a street beyond which buildings must not project

building paper *n* any of various types of heavy-duty paper that usually consist of bitumen reinforced with fibre sandwiched between two sheets of kraft paper: used in damp-proofing or as insulation between the soil and a road surface

building society *n* a cooperative organization that accepts deposits of money from savers and uses them to make loans, secured by mortgages, to house buyers. Since 1986 they have been empowered to offer banking services

build into *vb* (*tr, preposition*) to make (something) a definite part of (a contract, agreement, etc)

build up *vb* (*adverb*) **1** (*tr*) to construct gradually, systematically, and in stages **2** to increase, accumulate, or strengthen, esp by degrees: *the murmur built up to a roar* **3** (*intr*) to prepare for or gradually approach a climax **4** (*tr*) to improve the health or physique of (a person) **5** (*tr, usually passive*) to cover (an area) with buildings **6** (*tr*) to cause (a person, enterprise, etc) to become better known; publicize: *they built several actresses up into stars* ▷ *n* **7** progressive increase in number, size, etc: *the build-up of industry* **8** a gradual approach to a climax or critical point **9** the training and practice that constitutes the preparation for a particular event or competition: *the team's Olympic build-up* **10** extravagant publicity or praise, esp in the form of a campaign **11** *military* the process of attaining the required strength of forces and equipment, esp prior to an operation

built (bɪlt) *vb* the past tense and past participle of **build**

built cane *n* *angling* another name for **split cane**

built-in *adj* **1** made or incorporated as an integral part: *a built-in cupboard; a built-in escape clause* **2** essential; inherent ▷ *n* **3** *Austral* a built-in cupboard or wardrobe

built-in obsolescence *n* See **planned obsolescence**

built-up *adj* **1** having many buildings (esp in the phrase **built-up area**) **2** denoting a beam, girder, or stanchion constructed of sections welded, riveted, or bolted together, etc **3** increased by the addition of parts: *built-up heels*

Buitenzorg (*Dutch* 'bœitənzɔrx) *n* the former name of **Bogor**

Bujumbura (ˌbuːdʒəm'bʊərə) *n* the capital of Burundi, a port at the NE end of Lake Tanganyika. Pop: 419 000 (2005 est). Former name: **Usumbura**

Bukavu (buː'kɑːvuː) *n* a port in E Democratic Republic of Congo (formerly Zaïre), on Lake Kivu: commercial and industrial centre. Pop: 294 000 (2005 est). Former name (until 1966): Costermansville

Bukhara *or* **Bokhara** (bʊ'xɑːrə) *n* **1** a city in S Uzbekistan. Pop: 299 000 (2005 est) **2** a former emirate of central Asia: a powerful kingdom and centre of Islam; became a territory of the Soviet Union (1920) and was divided between the former Uzbek, Tajik, and Turkmen Soviet Socialist Republics

Bukhara rug *or* **Bokhara rug** *n* a kind of rug, typically having a black-and-white geometrical pattern on a reddish ground

bukkake (ˌbuː'kækɪ) *n* a sexual practice in which several men ejaculate on the face of an individual woman [c21 Japanese *bukkakeru* to dash (water)]

Bukovina *or* **Bucovina** (ˌbuːkə'viːnə) *n* a region of E central Europe, part of the NE Carpathians: the north was seized by the Soviet Union (1940) and later became part of Ukraine; the south remained Romanian

Bul (buːl) *n* the eighth month of the Old Hebrew calendar, corresponding to Heshvan of the Babylonian or post-exilic Jewish calendar: a period from mid-October to mid-November [from Hebrew *būl*, of Canaanite origin]

bul. *abbreviation for* bulletin

Bulawayo (ˌbʊlə'weɪəʊ) *n* a city in SW Zimbabwe founded (1893) on the site of the kraal of Lobengula, the last Matabele king; the country's main industrial centre. Pop: 693 000 (2005 est)

bulb (bʌlb) *n* **1** a rounded organ of vegetative reproduction in plants such as the tulip and onion: a flattened stem bearing a central shoot surrounded by fleshy nutritive inner leaves and thin brown outer leaves. Compare **corm 2** a plant, such as a hyacinth or daffodil, that grows from a bulb **3** See **light bulb 4** a rounded part of an instrument such as a syringe or thermometer **5** *anatomy* a rounded expansion of a cylindrical organ or part, such as the medulla oblongata **6** Also called: **bulbous bow** a bulbous protuberance at the forefoot of a ship to reduce turbulence [c16 from Latin *bulbus*, from Greek *bolbos* onion]

bulbar ('bʌlbə) *adj chiefly anatomy* of or relating to a bulb, esp the medulla oblongata

bulb fly *n* a hoverfly the larvae of which live in bulbs and are pests, esp the yellow and black **narcissus bulb fly** (*Meridon equestris*)

bulbiferous (bʌl'bɪfərəs) *adj* (of plants) producing bulbs

bulbil ('bʌlbɪl) *or* **bulbel** ('bʌlbəl) *n* **1** a small bulblike organ of vegetative reproduction growing in leaf axils or on flower stalks of plants such as the onion and tiger lily **2** any small bulb of a plant **3** any small bulblike structure in an animal [c19 from New Latin *bulbillus*, from Latin *bulbus* BULB]

bulb mite *n* a widespread mite, *Rhizaglophus eclinops*, that tunnels in the bulbs of lilies and other plants

bulbous ('bʌlbəs) *adj* **1** shaped like a bulb; swollen; bulging **2** growing from or bearing bulbs > 'bulbously *adv*

bulbul ('bʊlbʊl) *n* **1** any songbird of the family Pycnonotidae of tropical Africa and Asia, having brown plumage and, in many species, a distinct crest **2** a songbird, taken to be the nightingale, often mentioned in Persian poetry [c18 via Persian from Arabic]

Bulg. *abbreviation for* Bulgaria(n)

Bulgar ('bʌlgɑː, 'bʊl-) *n* **1** a member of a group of non-Indo-European peoples that settled in SE Europe in the late 7th century AD and adopted the language and culture of their Slavonic subjects **2** a rare name for a **Bulgarian**

Bulgaria (bʌl'gɛərɪə, bʊl-) *n* a republic in SE Europe, on the Balkan Peninsula on the Black Sea: under Turkish rule from 1395 until 1878; became an independent kingdom in 1908 and a republic in 1946; consists chiefly of the Danube valley in the north and the Balkan Mountains in the central part, separated from the Rhodope Mountains of the south by the valley of the Maritsa River. Language: Bulgarian. Religion: Christian (Bulgarian Orthodox) majority. Currency: lev. Capital: Sofia. Pop: 7 829 000 (2004 est). Area: 110 911 sq km (42 823 sq miles)

Bulgarian (bʌl'gɛərɪən, bʊl-) *adj* **1** of, relating to, or characteristic of Bulgaria, its people, or their language ▷ *n* **2** the official language of Bulgaria, belonging to the S Slavonic branch of the Indo-European family **3** a native, inhabitant, or citizen of Bulgaria

bulge (bʌldʒ) *n* **1** a swelling or an outward curve **2** a sudden increase in number or volume, esp of population **3** *Brit* another name for **baby boom 4** *Brit* the projecting part of an army's front line; salient ▷ *vb* **5** to swell outwards [c13 from Old French *bouge*, from Latin *bulga* bag, probably of Gaulish origin] > 'bulging *adj* > 'bulgingly *adv* > 'bulgy *adj* > 'bulginess *n*

Bulge (bʌldʒ) *n* **Battle of the** (in World War II) the final major German counteroffensive in 1944 when the Allied forces were pushed back into NE Belgium; the Germans were repulsed by Jan 1945

bulgur ('bʌlgə) *n* Also called: **burghul** a kind of dried cracked wheat [c20 from Turkish, from Arabic *burghul*, from Persian]

bulimia (bjuː'lɪmɪə) *n* **1** pathologically insatiable hunger, esp when caused by a brain lesion **2** Also called: **bulimia nervosa** a disorder characterized by compulsive overeating followed by vomiting: sometimes associated with anxiety about gaining weight [c17 from New Latin, from Greek *boulimia*, from *bous* ox + *limos* hunger] > bu'limic *n, adj*

bulk (bʌlk) *n* **1** volume, size, or magnitude, esp when great **2** the main part: *the bulk of the work is repetitive* **3** a large body, esp of a person: *he eased his bulk out of the chair* **4** unpackaged cargo or goods **5** a ship's cargo or hold **6** printing **a** the thickness of a number of sheets of paper or cardboard **b** the thickness of a book excluding its covers **7** (*plural*) copies of newspapers sold in bulk at a discounted price to hotels, airlines, etc which issue them free to their customers **8** in bulk **a** in large quantities **b** (of a cargo, etc) unpackaged ▷ *vb* **9** to cohere or cause to cohere in a mass **10** to place, hold, or transport (several cargoes of goods) in bulk **11** **bulk large** to be or seem important or prominent: *the problem bulked large in his mind* [c15 from Old Norse *bulki* cargo]

▌ **USAGE** The use of a plural noun after *bulk* was formerly considered incorrect, but is now acceptable

bulk buying *n* **1** the purchase at one time, and often at a reduced price, of a large quantity of a particular commodity **2** the purchase of the whole or greater part of the output of a commodity of a country or state by a single buyer, usually another country or state; state trading

bulk carrier *n* a ship that carries unpackaged cargo, usually consisting of a single dry commodity, such as coal or grain. Also called: **bulker**

bulkhead ('bʌlk,hɛd) *n* **1** any upright wall-like partition in a ship, aircraft, vehicle, etc **2** a wall or partition built to hold back earth, fire, water, etc [c15 probably from *bulk* projecting framework, from Old Norse *bálkr* partition + HEAD]

bulking ('bʌlkɪŋ) *n* **1** the expansion of excavated material to a volume greater than that of the excavation from which it came **2** an increase in the volume of dry sand when its moisture content is increased

bulk modulus *n* a coefficient of elasticity of a substance equal to minus the ratio of the applied stress (*p*) to the resulting fractional change in volume (d*V/V*) in a specified reference state (d*V/V* is the **bulk strain**). Symbol: *K*

bulk up (*adverb*) to increase or cause to increase in size or importance

bulky ('bʌlkɪ) *adj* **bulkier, bulkiest** very large and massive, esp so as to be unwieldy > '**bulkily** *adv* > '**bulkiness** *n*

bull¹ (bʊl) *n* **1** any male bovine animal, esp one that is sexually mature. Related adjective: **taurine 2** the uncastrated adult male of any breed of domestic cattle **3** the male of various other animals including the elephant and whale **4** a very large, strong, or aggressive person **5** *stock exchange* **a** a speculator who buys in anticipation of rising prices in order to make a profit on resale **b** (*as modifier*): *a bull market*. Compare **bear¹** (sense 5) **6** *chiefly Brit* short for **bull's-eye** (senses 1, 2) **7** *slang* short for **bullshit 8** short for **bulldog, bull terrier 9 a bull in a china shop** a clumsy person **10 shoot the bull** *US and Canadian slang* **a** to pass time talking lightly **b** to boast or exaggerate **11 take the bull by the horns** to face and tackle a difficulty without shirking ▷ *adj* **12** male; masculine: *a bull elephant* **13** large; strong ▷ *vb* **14** (*tr*) to raise or attempt to raise the price or prices of (a stock market or a security) by speculative buying **15** (*intr*) (of a cow) to be on heat **16** (*intr*) *US slang* to talk lightly or foolishly [Old English *bula*, from Old Norse *boli*; related to Middle Low German *bulle*, Middle Dutch *bolle*]

bull² (bʊl) *n* a ludicrously self-contradictory or inconsistent statement. Also called: **Irish bull** [c17 of uncertain origin]

bull³ (bʊl) *n* a formal document issued by the pope, written in antiquated characters and often sealed with a leaden bulla [c13 from Medieval Latin *bulla* seal attached to a bull, from Latin: round object]

Bull¹ (bʊl) *n* **the.** the constellation Taurus, the second sign of the zodiac

Bull² (bʊl) *n* See **John Bull**

bulla ('bʊlə, 'bʌlə) *n*, *pl* -**lae** (-liː) **1** a leaden seal affixed to a papal bull, having a representation of Saints Peter and Paul on one side and the name of the reigning pope on the other **2** an ancient Roman rounded metal or leather box containing an amulet, worn around the neck **3** *pathol* another word for **blister** (sense 1) **4** *anatomy* a rounded bony projection [c19 from Latin: round object, bubble]

bullace ('bʊlɪs) *n* a small Eurasian rosaceous tree, *Prunus domestica insititia* (or *P. insititia*), of which the damson is the cultivated form. See also **plum¹** (sense 1) [from Old French *beloce*, from Medieval Latin *bolluca*, perhaps of Gaulish origin]

Bullamakanka (,buːləmə'kæŋkə) *n Austral slang* an imaginary very remote and backward place

bull ant *n* any large Australian ant of the genus *Myrmecia*, having a powerful stinging bite: subfamily *Ponerinae*. Also called: **bulldog ant**

bullate ('bʌleɪt, -ɪt, 'bʊl-) *adj botany, anatomy* puckered or blistered in appearance: *the bullate leaves of the primrose* [c19 from Medieval Latin *bullātus* inflated, from Latin *bulla* bubble]

bull bars *pl n* a large protective metal grille on the front of some vehicles, esp four-wheel-drive vehicles

bullbat ('bʊl,bæt) *n* another name for **nighthawk** (sense 1)

bulldog ('bʊl,dɒg) *n* **1** a sturdy thickset breed of dog with an undershot jaw, short nose, broad head, and a muscular body **2** (at Oxford University) an official who accompanies the proctors on ceremonial occasions **3** *commerce* a fixed-interest bond issued in Britain by a foreign borrower

bulldog ant *n* another name for **bull ant**

bulldog clip *n trademark* a clip for holding papers together, consisting of two T-shaped metal clamps held in place by a cylindrical spring

bulldoze ('bʊl,dəʊz) *vb* (*tr*) **1** to move, demolish, flatten, etc, with a bulldozer **2** *informal* to force; push: *he bulldozed his way through the crowd* **3** *informal* to intimidate or coerce [c19 probably from BULL¹ + DOSE]

bulldozer ('bʊl,dəʊzə) *n* **1** a powerful tractor fitted with caterpillar tracks and a blade at the front, used for moving earth, rocks, etc **2** *informal* a person who bulldozes

bull dust *n* **1** *Austral* fine dust **2** *slang* nonsense

bull dyke *n slang* a lesbian who is markedly masculine

bullet ('bʊlɪt) *n* **1 a** a small metallic missile enclosed in a cartridge, used as the projectile of a gun, rifle, etc **b** the entire cartridge **2** something resembling a bullet, esp in shape or effect **3** *stock exchange* a fixed interest security with a single maturity date **4** *commerce* a security that offers a fixed interest and matures on a fixed date **5** *commerce* **a** the final repayment of a loan that repays the whole of the sum borrowed, as interim payments have been for interest only **b** (*as modifier*): *a bullet loan* **6** *Brit slang* dismissal, sometimes without notice (esp in the phrases **get** or **give the bullet**) **7** *printing* See **centred dot 8 bite the bullet** See **bite** (sense 14) [c16 from French *boulette*, diminutive of *boule* ball; see BOWL²] > '**bullet-like** *adj*

bulletin ('bʊlɪtɪn) *n* **1** an official statement on a matter of public interest, such as the illness of a public figure **2** a broadcast summary of the news **3** a periodical publication of an association, etc ▷ *vb* **4** (*tr*) to make known by bulletin [c17 from French, from Italian *bullettino*, from *bulletta*, diminutive of *bulla* papal edict, BULL³]

bulletin board *n* **1** *US and Canadian* a board on which notices, advertisements, bulletins, etc, are displayed. Also called (in Britain and certain other countries): **notice board 2** *computing* a facility on a computer network allowing any user to leave messages that can be read by any other user, and to download software and information to the user's own computer

bullet point *n* any of a number of items printed in a list, each after a centred dot, usually the most important points in a longer piece of text

bulletproof ('bʊlɪt,pruːf) *adj* **1** not penetrable by bullets: *bulletproof glass* ▷ *vb* **2** (*tr*) to make bulletproof

bulletwood ('bʊlɪt,wʊd) *n* the wood of a tropical American sapotaceous tree, *Manilkara bidentata*, widely used for construction due to its durability and toughness

bullfight ('bʊl,faɪt) *n* a traditional Spanish, Portuguese, and Latin American spectacle in which a matador, assisted by banderilleros and mounted picadors, baits and usually kills a bull in an arena > '**bull,fighter** *n* > '**bull,fighting** *n*

bullfinch¹ ('bʊl,fɪntʃ) *n* **1** a common European finch, *Pyrrhula pyrrhula*: the male has a bright red throat and breast, black crown, wings, and tail, and a grey and white back **2** any of various similar finches [c14 see BULL¹, FINCH; probably so called from its stocky shape and thick neck]

bullfinch² ('bʊl,fɪntʃ) *n Brit* a high thick hedge too difficult for a horse and rider to jump [c19 perhaps changed from the phrase *bull fence*]

bullfrog ('bʊl,frɒg) *n* any of various large frogs, such as *Rana catesbeiana* (**American bullfrog**),

having a loud deep croak

bullhead ('bʊl,hɛd) *n* **1** any of various small northern mainly marine scorpaenoid fishes of the family *Cottidae* that have a large head covered with bony plates and spines **2** any freshwater North American catfish of the genus *Ameiurus* (or *Ictalurus*), having a large head bearing several long barbels **3** a scorpion fish, *Scorpaena guttata*, of North American Pacific coastal waters **4** *informal* a stupidly stubborn or unintelligent person

bull-headed *adj* blindly obstinate; stubborn, headstrong, or stupid > ,bull-'headedly *adv* > ,bull-'headedness *n*

bullhead rail *n railways* a rail having a cross section with a bulbous top and bottom, the top being larger. Now largely superseded by **flat-bottomed rail**

bullhorn ('bʊl,hɔːn) *n US and Canadian* a portable loudspeaker having a built-in amplifier and microphone. Also called (in Britain and certain other countries): **loud-hailer**

bullion ('bʊljən) *n* **1** gold or silver in mass **2** gold or silver in the form of bars and ingots, suitable for further processing **3** Also called: **bullion fringe** a thick gold or silver wire or fringed cord used as a trimming, as on military uniforms [c14 (in the sense: melted gold or silver): from Anglo-French: mint, probably from Old French *bouillir* to boil, from Latin *bullīre*]

bullish ('bʊlɪʃ) *adj* **1** like a bull **2** *stock exchange* causing, expecting, or characterized by a rise in prices: *a bullish market* **3** *informal* cheerful and optimistic: *the prime minister was in a bullish mood* > '**bullishness** *n*

bull kelp *n* any of various large brown seaweeds of Pacific and Antarctic waters

bull mastiff *n* a large powerful breed of dog with a short usually fawn or brindle coat, developed by crossing the bulldog with the mastiff

bull-necked *adj* having a short thick neck

bull nose *n* **1** Also called: **atrophic rhinitis** a disease of pigs resulting in deformity of the nose, caused by infection with the bacterium *Bordatella bronchiseptica* **2** a rounded edge of a brick, step, etc **3** a rounded exterior angle, as where two walls meet

bull-nosed *adj* having a rounded end

bullock ('bʊlək) *n* **1** a gelded bull; steer **2** *archaic* a bull calf ▷ *vb* **3** (*intr*) *Austral and NZ informal* to work hard and long [Old English *bulluc*; see BULL¹, -OCK]

bullock's heart *n* another name for **custard apple** (senses 1, 2)

bullocky ('bʊləkɪ) *n*, *pl* -ockies *Austral and NZ informal* the driver of a team of bullocks

bullpen ('bʊl,pɛn) *n* **1** *US informal* a large cell where prisoners are confined together temporarily **2** *baseball* a part of a baseball field where relief pitchers warm up

bullring ('bʊl,rɪŋ) *n* an arena for bullfighting

bullroarer ('bʊl,rɔːrə) *n* a wooden slat attached to a thong that makes a roaring sound when the thong is whirled: used esp by native Australians in religious rites

Bull Run *n* **Battles of** two battles fought at Manassas Junction near a stream named Bull Run, during the American Civil War (July, 1861 and August, 1862), in both of which the Federal army was routed by the Confederates. Also called: **First and Second Manassas**. See also **Manassas**

bull session *n informal, chiefly US and Canadian* an informal discussion, often among men [c20 from BULL²]

bull's-eye *n* **1** the small central disc of a target, usually the highest valued area **2** a shot hitting this **3** *informal* something that exactly achieves its aim **4** a small circular or oval window or opening **5** a thick disc of glass set into a ship's deck, etc, to admit light **6** the glass boss at the centre of a sheet of blown glass **7 a** a small thick plano-convex lens used as a condenser **b** a lamp or lantern containing such a lens **8** a

b

peppermint-flavoured, usually striped, boiled sweet **9** *nautical* a circular or oval wooden block with a groove around it for the strop of a shroud and a hole at its centre for a line. Compare **deadeye 10** *meteorol* the eye or centre of a cyclone

bullshit ('bʊlʃɪt) *slang* ▷ *n* **1** exaggerated or foolish talk; nonsense **2** (in the British Army) exaggerated zeal, esp for ceremonial drill, cleaning, polishing, etc. Usually shortened to: **bull** ▷ *vb* **-shits**, **-shitting**, **-shitted 3** (*intr*) to talk in an exaggerated or foolish manner > **'bullshitter** *n*

> **USAGE** This word was formerly considered to be taboo, and it was labelled as such in previous editions of Collins English Dictionary. However, it has now become acceptable in speech, although some older or more conservative people may object to its use

bull snake *n* any burrowing North American nonvenomous colubrid snake of the genus *Pituophis*, typically having yellow and brown markings. Also called: **gopher snake**

bull's wool *n* *Austral and NZ informal* nonsense

bull terrier *n* a breed of terrier having a muscular body and thick neck, with a short smooth often white coat: developed by crossing the bulldog with various terriers. See also **pit bull terrier, Staffordshire bull terrier**

bull tongue *n* *chiefly US* **1** a heavy plough used in growing cotton, having an almost vertical mouldboard **2** a plough or cultivator with a single shovel

bull trout *n* any large trout, esp the salmon trout

bullwaddy, bullwaddy, bullwaddie, bulwaddee *or* **bullwaddy** (bʊl'wɒdɪ) *n* a N Australian tree, *Macropteranthes kekwickii*, growing in dense thickets [of uncertain origin]

bullwhip ('bʊl,wɪp) *n* **1** a long tapering heavy whip, esp one of plaited rawhide ▷ *vb* **-whips**, **-whipping**, **-whipped 2** (*tr*) to whip with a bullwhip

bully¹ ('bʊlɪ) *n, pl* **-lies 1** a person who hurts, persecutes, or intimidates weaker people **2** *archaic* a hired ruffian **3** *obsolete* a procurer; pimp **4** *obsolete* a fine fellow or friend **5** *obsolete* a sweetheart; darling ▷ *vb* **-lies**, **-lying**, **-lied 6** (when *tr*, often foll by *into*) to hurt, intimidate, or persecute (a weaker or smaller person), esp to make him do something ▷ *adj* **7** dashing; jolly: *my bully boy* **8** *informal* very good; fine ▷ *interj* **9** Also: **bully for you**, **him**, etc *informal* well done! bravo! [c16 (in the sense: sweetheart, hence fine fellow, hence swaggering coward): probably from Middle Dutch *boele* lover, from Middle High German *buole*, perhaps childish variant of *bruoder* BROTHER]

bully² ('bʊlɪ) *n* any of various small freshwater fishes of the genera *Gobiomorphus* and *Philynodon* of New Zealand. Also called (NZ): **pakoko, titarakura, toitoi** [c20 short for COCKABULLY]

bully beef *n* tinned corned beef. Often shortened to: **bully** [c19 *bully*, anglicized version of French *bouilli*, from *boeuf bouilli* boiled beef]

bullyboy ('bʊlɪ,bɔɪ) *n* **a** a ruffian or tough, esp a hired one **b** (*as modifier*): *bullyboy tactics*

bully-off *hockey* ▷ *n* **1** a method by which a game is restarted after a stoppage. Two opposing players stand with the ball between them and alternately strike their sticks together and against the ground three times before trying to hit the ball ▷ *vb* **bully off 2** (*intr, adverb*) to restart play after a stoppage with a bully-off ▷ Often shortened to: **bully**. Compare **face-off** [c19 perhaps from *bully scrum* in Eton football; of unknown origin]

bullyrag ('bʊlɪ,ræg) *vb* **-rags**, **-ragging**, **-ragged** (*tr*) to bully, esp by means of cruel practical jokes. Also: **ballyrag** [c18 of unknown origin]

bulnbuln ('bʊln,bʊln) *n* *Austral* another name for **lyrebird** [c19 from a native Australian language]

bulrush ('bʊl,rʌʃ) *n* **1** a grasslike cyperaceous marsh plant, *Scirpus lacustris*, used for making

mats, chair seats, etc **2** a popular name for **reed mace** (sense 1): the name derived from Alma-Tadema's painting of the finding of the infant Moses in the "bulrushes" — actually reed mace **3** a biblical word for **papyrus** (the plant) [c15 *bulrish*, *bul-* perhaps from BULL¹ + *rish* RUSH², referring to the largeness of the plant]

bulwark ('bʊlwək) *n* **1** a wall or similar structure used as a fortification; rampart **2** a person or thing acting as a defence against injury, annoyance, etc **3** (*often plural*) *nautical* a solid vertical fencelike structure along the outward sides of a deck **4** a breakwater or mole ▷ *vb* **5** (*tr*) to defend or fortify with or as if with a bulwark [c15 via Dutch from Middle High German *bolwerk*, from *bol* plank, BOLE¹ + *werk* WORK]

bum¹ (bʌm) *n* *Brit slang* the buttocks or anus [c14 of uncertain origin]

bum² (bʌm) *informal* ▷ *n* **1** a disreputable loafer or idler **2** a tramp; hobo **3** an irresponsible, unpleasant, or mean person **4** a person who spends a great deal of time on a specified sport: *baseball bum* **5** on the bum **a** living as a loafer or vagrant **b** out of repair; broken ▷ *vb* **bums**, **bumming**, **bummed 6** (*tr*) to get by begging; cadge: *to bum a lift* **7** (*intr; often foll by around*) to live by begging or as a vagrant or loafer **8** (*intr*; usually foll by *around*) to spend time to no good purpose; loaf; idle **9** bum (someone) off *US and Canadian slang* to disappoint, annoy, or upset (someone) ▷ *adj* **10** (*prenominal*) of poor quality; useless **11** wrong or inappropriate: *a bum note* [c19 probably shortened from earlier *bummer* a loafer, probably from German *bummeln* to loaf]

bum bag *n* a small bag worn on a belt, round the waist

bumbailiff (,bʌm'beɪlɪf) *n* *Brit derogatory* (formerly) an officer employed to collect debts and arrest debtors for nonpayment [c17 from BUM¹ + *bailiff*, so called because he follows hard behind debtors]

bumble¹ ('bʌmb³l) *vb* **1** to speak or do in a clumsy, muddled, or inefficient way: *he bumbled his way through his speech* **2** (*intr*) to proceed unsteadily; stumble ▷ *n* **3** a blunder or botch [c16 perhaps a blend of BUNGLE + STUMBLE] > **'bumbler** *n* > **'bumbling** *n, adj*

bumble² ('bʌmb³l) *vb* (*intr*) to make a humming sound [c14 *bomblen* to buzz, boom, of imitative origin]

bumblebee ('bʌmb³l,biː) *or* **humblebee** *n* any large hairy social bee of the genus *Bombus* and related genera, of temperate regions: family *Apidae* [c16 from BUMBLE² + BEE¹]

bumbledom ('bʌmbəldəm) *n* self-importance in a minor office [c19 after *Bumble*, name of the beadle in Dickens' *Oliver Twist* (1837–38)]

bumble-foot *n* *vet science* an inflammatory condition of the feet of birds, usually caused by an infection

bumble-puppy *n* **1** a game in which a ball, attached by string to a post, is hit so that the string winds round the post **2** (*modifier*) (of whist or bridge) played unskilfully

bumboat ('bʌm,bəʊt) *n* any small boat used for ferrying supplies or goods for sale to a ship at anchor or at a mooring [c17 (in the sense: scavenger's boat) *bum*, from Dutch *boomschip* canoe (from *bom* tree) + BOAT]

bumf *or* **bumph** (bʌmf) *n* *Brit* **1** *informal, derogatory* superfluous documents, forms, publicity material, etc **2** *slang* toilet paper [c19 short for earlier *bumfodder*; see BUM¹]

bumfluff ('bʌm,flʌf) *n* *informal* the soft and fluffy growth of hair on the chin of an adolescent

bumfreezer ('bʌm,friːzə) *n* **1** a slang name for an **Eton jacket 2** *slang* any of various similar styles of short jacket worn by men

bumkin ('bʌmkɪn) *n* a variant spelling of **boomkin**

bummalo ('bʌmə,ləʊ) *n, pl* **-lo** another name for **Bombay duck** [c17 from Marathi *bombīla*]

bummaree (,bʌmə'riː) *n* *Brit* (formerly) **1** a dealer at Billingsgate fish market **2** a porter at Smithfield meat market [c18 of unknown origin]

bummer ('bʌmə) *n* *slang* **1** an unpleasant or disappointing experience **2** *chiefly US* a vagrant or idler **3** an adverse reaction to a drug, characterized by panic or fear

bump (bʌmp) *vb* **1** (when *intr*, usually foll by *against* or *into*) to knock or strike with a jolt **2** (*intr*; often foll by *along*) to travel or proceed in jerks and jolts **3** (*tr*) to hurt by knocking: *he bumped his head on the ceiling* **4** (*tr*) to knock out of place; dislodge: *the crash bumped him from his chair* **5** (*tr*) *Brit* to throw (a child) into the air, one other child holding each limb, and let him down again to touch the ground **6** (in rowing races, esp at Oxford and Cambridge) to catch up with and touch (another boat that started a fixed distance ahead) **7** *cricket* to bowl (a ball) so that it bounces high on pitching or (of a ball) to bounce high when bowled **8** (*intr*) *chiefly US and Canadian* to dance erotically by thrusting the pelvis forward (esp in the phrase **bump and grind**) **9** (*tr*) *poker* to raise (someone) **10** (*tr*) *informal* to exclude a ticket-holding passenger from a flight as a result of overbooking **11** (*tr*) *informal* to displace (someone or something) from a previously allocated position: *the story was bumped from the front page* **12** bump uglies *US slang* to have sexual intercourse ▷ *n* **13** an impact; knock; jolt; collision **14** a dull thud or other noise from an impact or collision **15** the shock of a blow or collision **16** a lump on the body caused by a blow **17** a protuberance, as on a road surface **18** any of the natural protuberances of the human skull, said by phrenologists to indicate underlying faculties and character **19** a rising current of air that gives an aircraft a severe upward jolt **20** (*plural*) the act of bumping a child. See sense 5 **21** *rowing* the act of bumping. See **bumping race 22** *cricket* bump ball a ball that bounces into the air after being hit directly into the ground by the batsman ▷ See also **bump into, bump off, bump up** [c16 probably of imitative origin]

bumper¹ ('bʌmpə) *n* **1** a horizontal metal bar attached to the front or rear end of a car, lorry, etc, to protect against damage from impact **2** a person or machine that bumps **3** *cricket* a ball bowled so that it bounces high on pitching; bouncer

bumper² ('bʌmpə) *n* **1** a glass, tankard, etc, filled to the brim, esp as a toast **2** an unusually large or fine example of something ▷ *adj* **3** unusually large, fine, or abundant: *a bumper crop* ▷ *vb* **4** (*tr*) to toast with a bumper **5** (*tr*) to fill to the brim **6** (*intr*) to drink bumpers [c17 (in the sense: a brimming glass): probably from *bump* (obsolete *vb*) to bulge; see BUMP]

bumper³ ('bʌmpə) *n* *Austral old-fashioned informal* a cigarette end [c19 perhaps from a blend of BUTT¹ and STUMP]

bumper car *n* a low-powered electrically propelled vehicle driven and bumped against similar cars in a special rink at a funfair. Also called: **Dodgem**

bumper sticker *n* a label affixed to the rear windscreen or bumper of a motor vehicle displaying an advertisement or slogan

bumph (bʌmf) *n* a variant spelling of **bumf**

bumping race *n* (esp at Oxford and Cambridge) a race in which rowing eights start an equal distance one behind the other and each tries to bump the boat in front

bump into *vb* (*intr, preposition*) *informal* to meet by chance; encounter unexpectedly

bumpkin¹ ('bʌmpkɪn) *n* an awkward simple rustic person (esp in the phrase **country bumpkin**) [c16 (perhaps originally applied to Dutchmen): perhaps from Dutch *boomken* small tree, or from Middle Dutch *boomekijn* small barrel, alluding to a short or squat person]

bumpkin² ('bʌmpkɪn) *or* **bumkin** *n* variant

spellings of **boomkin**

bump off *vb* (*tr, adverb*) *slang* to murder; kill

bump start *Brit* ▷ *n* **1** a method of starting a motor vehicle by engaging a low gear with the clutch depressed and pushing it or allowing it to run down a hill until sufficient momentum has been acquired to turn the engine by releasing the clutch ▷ *vb* **bump-start 2** (*tr*) to start (a motor vehicle) using this method

bumptious ('bʌmpʃəs) *adj* offensively self-assertive or conceited [c19 perhaps a blend of BUMP + FRACTIOUS] > **'bumptiously** *adv* > **'bumptiousness** *n*

bump up *vb* (*tr, adverb*) *informal* to raise or increase: *prices are being bumped up daily*

bumpy ('bʌmpɪ) *adj* **bumpier, bumpiest 1** having an uneven surface: *a bumpy road* **2** full of jolts; rough: *a bumpy flight* > **'bumpily** *adv* > **'bumpiness** *n*

bum rap *n US slang* **1** a trumped-up or false charge **2** an unjust punishment

bum's rush *n slang* **1** forcible ejection, as from a gathering **2** rapid dismissal, as of an idea

bum steer *n slang, chiefly US* false or misleading information or advice

bumsters ('bʌmstəz) *pl n Brit* trousers cut so that the top lies just above the cleft of the buttocks

bumsucking ('bʌm,sʌkɪŋ) *n Brit slang* obsequious behaviour; toadying > **'bum,sucker** *n*

bun (bʌn) *n* **1** a small roll, similar to bread but usually containing sweetening, currants, spices, etc **2** any of various types of small round sweet cakes **3** a hairstyle in which long hair is gathered into a bun shape at the back of the head **4 have a bun in the oven** *slang* to be pregnant [c14 of unknown origin]

Buna ('bu:nə, 'bju:-) *n trademark* a synthetic rubber formed by polymerizing butadiene or by copolymerizing it with such compounds as acrylonitrile or styrene

bunch (bʌntʃ) *n* **1** a number of things growing, fastened, or grouped together: *a bunch of grapes*; *a bunch of keys* **2** a collection; group: *a bunch of queries* **3** *informal* a group or company: *a bunch of boys* **4** *archaic* a protuberance ▷ *vb* **5** (sometimes foll by *up*) to group or be grouped into a bunch ▷ See also **bunches** [c14 of obscure origin]

bunchberry ('bʌntʃ,bɛrɪ) *n, pl* **-ries** a dwarf variety of dogwood native to North America, *Cornus canadensis*, having red berries

bunches ('bʌntʃɪz) *pl n Brit* a hairstyle in which hair is tied into two sections on either side of the head at the back

bunchy ('bʌntʃɪ) *adj* **bunchier, bunchiest 1** composed of or resembling bunches **2** bulging > **'bunchiness** *n*

bunco *or* **bunko** ('bʌŋkəʊ) *US informal* ▷ *n, pl* **-cos** *or* **-kos 1** a swindle, esp one by confidence tricksters ▷ *vb* **-cos, -coing, -coed** *or* **-kos, -koing, -koed 2** (*tr*) to swindle; cheat [c19 perhaps from Spanish *banca* bank (in gambling), from Italian *banca* BANK¹]

buncombe ('bʌŋkəm) *n* a variant spelling (esp US) of **bunkum**

bund (bʌnd) *n* (in India and the Far East) **1** an embankment; dyke **2** an embanked road or quay [c19 from Hindi *band*, from Persian; related to Sanskrit *bandha* BAND¹]

Bund (bʊnd; *German* bʊnt) *n, pl* **Bunds** *or* **Bünde** (*German* 'bʏndə) **1** (*sometimes not capital*) a federation or league **2** short for **German American Bund**, an organization of US Nazis and Nazi sympathizers in the 1930s and 1940s **3** an organization of socialist Jewish workers in Russia founded in 1897 **4** the confederation of N German states, which existed from 1867–71 [c19 German; related to BAND², BIND]

Bundaberg ('bʌndə,bɜːg) *n* a city in E Australia, near the E coast of Queensland: centre of a sugar-growing area, with a nearby deep-water port. Pop: 44 556 (2001)

Bundelkhand (,bʌnd²l'kʌnd, -'xʌnd) *n* a region of central India: formerly native states, now mainly part of Madhya Pradesh

Bundesrat ('bʊndəs,rɑːt) *n* **1** (in Germany and formerly in West Germany) the council of state ministers with certain legislative and administrative powers, representing the state governments at federal level **2** (in Austria) an assembly with some legislative power that represents state interests at the federal level **3** (in Switzerland) the executive council of the confederation **4** (in the German empire from 1871–1918) the council representing the governments of the constituent states, with administrative, judicial, and legislative powers [c19 German, from *Bund* federation + *Rat* council]

Bundestag ('bʊndəs,tɑːg) *n* (in Germany and formerly in West Germany) the legislative assembly, which is elected by universal adult suffrage and elects the federal chancellor [c19 German, from *Bund* federation + *-tag*, from *tagen* to meet]

bundh (bʌnd) *n* a variant spelling of **bandh**

bundle ('bʌnd²l) *n* **1** a number of things or a quantity of material gathered or loosely bound together: *a bundle of sticks*. Related adjective: **fascicular 2** something wrapped or tied for carrying; package **3** *slang* a large sum of money **4 go a bundle on** *slang* to be extremely fond of **5** *biology* a collection of strands of specialized tissue such as nerve fibres **6** *botany* short for **vascular bundle 7** *textiles* a measure of yarn or cloth; 60 000 yards of linen yarn; 5 or 10 pounds of cotton hanks **8 drop one's bundle** *Austral and NZ slang* to panic or give up hope ▷ *vb* **9** (*tr*; often foll by *up*) to make into a bundle **10** (foll by *out, off, into* etc) to go or cause to go, esp roughly or unceremoniously: *we bundled him out of the house* **11** (*tr*; usually foll by *into*) to push or throw, esp quickly and untidily: *to bundle shirts into a drawer* **12** (*tr*) to sell (computer hardware and software) as one indivisible package **13** (*tr*) to give away (a relatively cheap one) to attract business: *several free CDs are often bundled with music centres* **14** (*intr*) to sleep or lie in one's clothes on the same bed as one's betrothed: formerly a custom in New England, Wales, and elsewhere [c14 probably from Middle Dutch *bundel*; related to Old English *bindele* bandage; see BIND, BOND] > **'bundler** *n*

bundle up *vb* (*adverb*) **1** to dress (somebody) warmly and snugly **2** (*tr*) to make (something) into a bundle or bundles, esp by tying

bundobust ('bʌndəbʌst) *n* a variant spelling of **bandobust**

bundu ('bʊndu) *n South African and Zimbabwean slang* **a** a largely uninhabited wild region far from towns **b** (*as modifier*): *a bundu hat* [c20 from a Bantu language]

bundwall ('bʌnd,wɔːl) *n* a concrete or earth wall surrounding a storage tank containing crude oil or its refined product, designed to hold the contents of the tank in the event of a rupture or leak [c20 from BUND + WALL]

bundy ('bʌndɪ) *n, pl* **-dies** *Austral* **1** a time clock **2** *informal* **punch the bundy a** to start work **b** to be in regular employment ▷ *vb* **3** (*intr*; foll by *on* or *off*) to arrive or depart from work, esp when it involves registering the time of arrival or departure on a card [from a trademark]

bunfight ('bʌn,faɪt) *n Brit slang* **1** a tea party **2** *ironic* an official function **3** a petty squabble or argument

bung¹ (bʌŋ) *n* **1** a stopper, esp of cork or rubber, for a cask, piece of laboratory glassware, etc **2** short for **bunghole** ▷ *vb* (*tr*) **3** (often foll by *up*) to close or seal with or as with a bung: *the car's exhaust was bunged up with mud* **4** *Brit slang* to throw; sling [c15 from Middle Dutch *bonghe*, from Late Latin *puncta* PUNCTURE]

bung² (bʌŋ) *Brit slang* ▷ *n* **1** a gratuity; tip **2** a bribe ▷ *vb* **3** (*tr*) to give (someone) a tip or bribe [c16 (originally in the sense: a purse): perhaps from Old English *pung*, changed over time through the influence of BUNG¹]

bung³ (bʌŋ) *adj Austral and NZ informal* **1** useless **2 go bung** to fail or collapse [c19 from a native Australian language]

bungalow ('bʌŋgə,ləʊ) *n* **1** a one-storey house, sometimes with an attic **2** (in India) a one-storey house, usually surrounded by a veranda [c17 from Hindi *banglā* (house) of the Bengal type]

bungee jumping *or* **bungy jumping** ('bʌndʒɪ) *n* a sport in which a participant jumps from a high bridge, building, etc, secured only by a rubber cord attached to the ankles [c20 from *bungie*, slang for India rubber, of unknown origin]

bunger ('bʌŋə) *n Austral slang* a firework

bunghole ('bʌŋ,həʊl) *n* a hole in a cask, barrel, etc, through which liquid can be poured or drained

bungle ('bʌŋg²l) *vb* **1** (*tr*) to spoil (an operation) through clumsiness, incompetence, etc; botch ▷ *n* **2** a clumsy or unsuccessful performance or piece of work; mistake; botch [c16 perhaps of Scandinavian origin; compare dialect Swedish *bangla* to work without results] > **'bungler** *n* > **'bungling** *adj, n*

bungwall ('bʌŋwɔl) *n* an Australian fern, *Blechnum indicum*, having an edible rhizome [from a native Australian language]

bunion ('bʌnjən) *n* swelling of the first joint of the big toe, which is displaced to one side. An inflamed bursa forms over the joint [c18 perhaps from obsolete *bunny* a swelling, of uncertain origin]

bunk¹ (bʌŋk) *n* **1** a narrow shelflike bed fixed along a wall **2** short for **bunk bed 3** *informal* any place where one sleeps ▷ *vb* **4** (*intr*; often foll by *down*) to prepare to sleep: *he bunked down on the floor* **5** (*intr*) to occupy a bunk or bed **6** (*tr*) to provide with a bunk or bed [c19 probably short for BUNKER]

bunk² (bʌŋk) *n informal* short for **bunkum** (sense 1)

bunk³ (bʌŋk) *Brit slang* ▷ *n* **1** a hurried departure, usually under suspicious circumstances (esp in the phrase **do a bunk**) ▷ *vb* **2** (usually foll by *off*) to play truant from (school, work, etc) [c19 perhaps from BUNK¹ (in the sense: to occupy a bunk, hence a hurried departure, as on a ship)]

bunk bed *n* one of a pair of beds constructed one above the other

bunker ('bʌŋkə) *n* **1** a large storage container or tank, as for coal **2** Also called (esp US and Canadian): **sand trap** an obstacle on a golf course, usually a sand-filled hollow bordered by a ridge **3** an underground shelter, often of reinforced concrete and with a bank and embrasures for guns above ground ▷ *vb* **4** *golf* **a** to drive (the ball) into a bunker **b** (*passive*) to have one's ball trapped in a bunker **5** (*tr*) *nautical* **a** to fuel (a ship) **b** to transfer (cargo) from a ship to a storehouse [c16 (in the sense: chest, box): from Scottish *bonkar*, of unknown origin]

Bunker Hill *n* the first battle of the American Revolution, actually fought on Breed's Hill, next to Bunker Hill, near Boston, on June 17, 1775. Though defeated, the colonists proved that they could stand against British regular soldiers

bunkhouse ('bʌŋk,haʊs) *n* (in the US and Canada) a building containing the sleeping quarters of workers on a ranch

bunko ('bʌŋkəʊ) *n, vb* a variant spelling of **bunco**

bunkum *or* **buncombe** ('bʌŋkəm) *n* **1** empty talk; nonsense **2** *chiefly US* empty or insincere speechmaking by a politician to please voters or gain publicity [c19 after *Buncombe*, a county in North Carolina, alluded to in an inane speech by its Congressional representative Felix Walker (about 1820)]

bunny ('bʌnɪ) *n, pl* **-nies 1** Also called: **bunny rabbit** a child's word for **rabbit** (sense 1) **2** Also called: **bunny girl** a night-club hostess whose costume includes rabbit-like tail and ears **3** *Austral informal* a mug; dupe **4** *slang* a devotee of a specified pastime or activity: *gym bunny; disco bunny*

b

5 *Brit slang* talk, esp when inconsequential; chatter **6 not a happy bunny** *Brit slang* deeply dissatisfied or discontented [c17 from Scottish Gaelic *bun* scut of a rabbit; sense 5 from RABBIT (sense 4)]

bunny boiler *n slang* a woman who is considered to be emotionally unstable and likely to be dangerously vengeful [c20 from the 1987 film *Fatal Attraction*, in which a female character boils a pet rabbit to terrorize the family of the lover who spurns her]

bunny hop *n* **1** a jump executed with the feet held tightly together and the knees bent **2** a jump over an obstacle executed by a person riding a bicycle and standing up on the pedals **3** *US* a dance performed by a line of people holding onto each other from behind and moving around the room tapping and stepping with each foot separately and then jumping with both feet held together ▷ *vb* **bunny-hop** (*intr*) **4** to jump with the feet held tightly together and the knees bent **5** to jump a bicycle over an obstacle without dismounting

bunny hug *n* **1** a ballroom dance with syncopated rhythm, popular in America in the early 20th century **2** a piece of music in the rhythm of this dance

bunodont ('bjuːnəˌdɒnt) *adj* (of the teeth of certain mammals) having cusps that are separate and rounded [from Greek *bounos* hill + -ODONT]

bunraku (bʊnˈrɑːkuː) *n* a Japanese form of puppet theatre in which the puppets are usually about four feet high, with moving features as well as limbs and each puppet is manipulated by up to three puppeteers who remain onstage [c20 Japanese]

buns (bʌnz) *pl n informal, chiefly US* the buttocks

Bunsen burner ('bʌnsən) *n* a gas burner, widely used in scientific laboratories, consisting of a metal tube with an adjustable air valve at the base [c19 named after its inventor Robert Wilhelm *Bunsen* (1811–99), German chemist]

bunt¹ (bʌnt) *vb* **1** (of an animal) to butt (something) with the head or horns **2** to cause (an aircraft) to fly in part of an inverted loop or (of an aircraft) to fly in such a loop **3** *US and Canadian* (in baseball) to hit (a pitched ball) very gently ▷ *n* **4** the act or an instance of bunting [c19 perhaps nasalized variant of BUTT³]

bunt² (bʌnt) *n nautical* the baggy centre of a fishing net or other piece of fabric, such as a square sail [c16 perhaps from Middle Low German *bunt* BUNDLE]

bunt³ (bʌnt) *n* a disease of cereal plants caused by smut fungi (genus *Tilletia*) [c17 of unknown origin]

buntal ('bʌntˀl) *n* straw obtained from leaves of the talipot palm [c20 from Tagalog]

bunting¹ ('bʌntɪŋ) *n* **1** a coarse, loosely woven cotton fabric used for flags, etc **2** decorative flags, pennants, and streamers **3** flags collectively, esp those of a boat [c18 of unknown origin]

bunting² ('bʌntɪŋ) *n* any of numerous seed-eating songbirds of the families *Fringillidae* (finches, etc) or *Emberizidae*, esp those of the genera *Emberiza* of the Old World and *Passerina* of North America. They all have short stout bills [c13 of unknown origin]

buntline ('bʌntlɪn, -ˌlaɪn) *n nautical* one of several lines fastened to the foot of a square sail for hauling it up to the yard when furling [c17 from BUNT² + LINE¹]

bunya ('bʌnjə) *n* a tall dome-shaped Australian coniferous tree, *Araucaria bidwillii*, having edible cones (**bunya nuts**) and thickish flattened needles. Also called: **bunya-bunya, bunya-bunya pine** [c19 from a native Australian language]

bunyip ('bʌnjɪp) *n Austral* a legendary monster said to inhabit swamps and lagoons of the Australian interior [c19 from a native Australian language]

buoy (bɔɪ; *US* 'buːɪ) *n* **1** a distinctively shaped and coloured float, anchored to the bottom, for designating moorings, navigable channels, or obstructions in a body of water. See also **life buoy** ▷ *vb* **2** (*tr*; usually foll by *up*) to prevent from sinking: *the belt buoyed him up* **3** (*tr*; usually foll by *up*) to raise the spirits of; hearten **4** (*tr*) *nautical* to mark (a channel or obstruction) with a buoy or buoys **5** (*intr*) to rise to the surface [c13 probably of Germanic origin; compare Middle Dutch *boeie, boeye*; see BEACON]

buoyage ('bɔɪɪdʒ) *n* **1** a system of buoys **2** the buoys used in such a system **3** the providing of buoys

buoyancy ('bɔɪənsɪ) *n* **1** the ability to float in a liquid or to rise in a fluid **2** the property of a fluid to exert an upward force (upthrust) on a body that is wholly or partly submerged in it **3** the ability to recover quickly after setbacks; resilience **4** cheerfulness

buoyancy bags *pl n* another term for **flotation bags**

buoyant ('bɔɪənt) *adj* **1** able to float in or rise to the surface of a liquid **2** (of a liquid or gas) able to keep a body afloat or cause it to rise **3** cheerful or resilient [c16 probably from Spanish *boyante*, from *boyar* to float, from *boya* buoy, ultimately of Germanic origin]

BUPA ('buːpə) *n acronym for* The British United Provident Association Limited: a company which provides private medical insurance

bupivacaine (bjuːˈpɪvəkeɪn) *n* a local anaesthetic of long duration, used for nerve blocks [c20 perhaps from BU(TYL) + *pi*(*pecoloxylidide*), the drug's chemical components + -*vacaine*, from (NO)VOCAINE]

buppie ('bʌpɪ) *n informal* (*sometimes capital*) an affluent young Black person [c20 from B(LACK) + (Y)UPPIE]

buprenorphine (bjuːˈprɛnɔːfiːn) *n* an opiate used medicinally as a powerful analgesic

buprestid (bjuːˈprɛstɪd) *n* **1** any beetle of the mainly tropical family *Buprestidae*, the adults of which are brilliantly coloured and the larvae of which bore into and cause damage to trees, roots, etc ▷ *adj* **2** of, relating to, or belonging to the family *Buprestidae* [c19 from Latin *buprestis* poisonous beetle, causing the cattle who eat it to swell up, from Greek, from *bous* ox + *prēthein* to swell up]

bur (bɜː) *n* **1** a seed vessel or flower head, as of burdock, having hooks or prickles **2** any plant that produces burs **3** a person or thing that clings like a bur **4** a small surgical or dental drill **5** a variant spelling of **burr¹, burr³** ▷ *vb* **burs, burring, burred 6** (*tr*) to remove burs from ▷ Also (for senses 1–4, 6): **burr** [c14 probably of Scandinavian origin; compare Danish *burre* bur, Swedish *kardborre* burdock]

BUR *international car registration for* Myanmar (Burma)

Bur. *abbreviation for* Myanmar (Burma)

buran (buˈrɑːn) *or* **bura** (buˈrɑː) *n* (in central Asia) **1** a blizzard, with the wind blowing from the north and reaching gale force **2** a summer wind from the north, causing dust storms [c19 from Russian, of Turkic origin; related to Kazan Tatar *buran*]

Buraydah *or* **Buraida** (buˈraɪdə) *n* a town and oasis in central Saudi Arabia. Pop: 462 000 (2005 est)

Burberry ('bɜːbərɪ) *n, pl* **-ries** *trademark* a light good-quality raincoat, esp of gabardine

burble ('bɜːbˀl) *vb* **1** to make or utter with a bubbling sound; gurgle **2** (*intr*; often foll by *away* or *on*) to talk quickly and excitedly **3** (*intr*) (of the airflow around a body) to become turbulent ▷ *n* **4** a bubbling or gurgling sound **5** a flow of excited speech **6** turbulence in the airflow around a body [c14 probably of imitative origin; compare Spanish *borbollar* to bubble, gush, Italian *borbugliare*] > **'burbler** *n*

burbot ('bɜːbət) *n, pl* **-bots** *or* **-bot** a freshwater gadoid food fish, *Lota lota*, that has barbels around its mouth and occurs in Europe, Asia, and North America [c14 from Old French *bourbotte*, from *bourbeter* to wallow in mud, from *bourbe* mud, probably of Celtic origin]

'burb *or* **burb** (bɜːb) *n informal usually plural* short for **suburb**

burden¹ ('bɜːdˀn) *n* **1** something that is carried; load **2** something that is exacting, oppressive, or difficult to bear: *the burden of responsibility*. Related adjective: **onerous 3** *nautical* **a** the cargo capacity of a ship **b** the weight of a ship's cargo ▷ *vb* (*tr*) **4** (sometimes foll by *up*) to put or impose a burden on; load **5** to weigh down; oppress: *the old woman was burdened with cares* [Old English *byrthen*; related to *beran* to BEAR¹, Old Frisian *berthene* burden, Old High German *burdin*]

burden² ('bɜːdˀn) *n* **1** a line of words recurring at the end of each verse of a ballad or similar song; chorus or refrain **2** the principal or recurrent theme of a speech, book, etc **3** another word for **bourdon** [c16 from Old French *bourdon* bass horn, droning sound, of imitative origin]

burden of proof *n law* the obligation, in criminal cases resting initially on the prosecution, to provide evidence that will convince the court or jury of the truth of one's contention

burdensome ('bɜːdˀnsəm) *adj* hard to bear; onerous

burdizzo (bɜːˈdɪzəʊ) *n vet science* a surgical instrument used to castrate animals

burdock ('bɜːˌdɒk) *n* a coarse weedy Eurasian plant of the genus *Arctium*, having large heart-shaped leaves, tiny purple flowers surrounded by hooked bristles, and burlike fruits: family *Asteraceae* (composites) [c16 from BUR + DOCK⁴]

bureau ('bjʊərəʊ) *n, pl* **-reaus** *or* **-reaux** (-rəʊz) **1** *chiefly Brit* a writing desk with pigeonholes, drawers, etc, against which the writing surface can be closed when not in use **2** *US* a chest of drawers **3** an office or agency, esp one providing services for the public **4 a** a government department **b** a branch of a government department [c17 from French: desk, office, originally: type of cloth used for covering desks and tables, from Old French *burel*, from Late Latin *burra* shaggy cloth]

bureaucracy (bjʊəˈrɒkrəsɪ) *n, pl* **-cies 1** a system of administration based upon organization into bureaus, division of labour, a hierarchy of authority, etc: designed to dispose of a large body of work in a routine manner **2** government by such a system **3** government or other officials collectively **4** any administration in which action is impeded by unnecessary official procedures and red tape

bureaucrat ('bjʊərəˌkræt) *n* **1** an official in a bureaucracy **2** an official who adheres to bureaucracy, esp rigidly > **bureaucratism** (bjʊəˈrɒkrəˌtɪzəm) *n*

bureaucratic (ˌbjʊərəˈkrætɪk) *adj* of or relating to bureaucrats; characterized by bureaucracy > ˌbureau'cratically *adv*

bureaucratize *or* **bureaucratise** (bjʊəˈrɒkrəˌtaɪz) *vb* (*tr*) to administer by or transform into a bureaucracy > bu,reaucrati'zation *or* bu,reaucrati'sation *n*

burette *or US* **buret** (bjʊˈrɛt) *n* a graduated glass tube with a stopcock on one end for dispensing and transferring known volumes of fluids, esp liquids [c15 from French: cruet, oil can, from Old French *buire* ewer, of Germanic origin; compare Old English *būc* pitcher, belly]

burg (bɜːg) *n* **1** *history* a fortified town **2** *US informal* a town or city [c18 (in the sense: fortress); from Old High German *burg* fortified town; see BOROUGH]

burgage ('bɜːgɪdʒ) *n history* **1** (in England) tenure of land or tenement in a town or city, which originally involved a fixed money rent **2** (in Scotland) the tenure of land direct from the crown in Scottish royal burghs in return for watching and warding [c14 from Medieval Latin *burgāgium*, from *burgus*, from Old English *burg*; see BOROUGH]

Burgas (*Bulgarian* bur'gas) *n* a port in SE Bulgaria on an inlet of the Black Sea. Pop: 177 000 (2005 est)

burgee ('bɜːdʒiː) *n nautical* a triangular or swallow-tailed flag flown from the mast of a merchant ship for identification and from the mast of a yacht to indicate its owner's membership of a particular yacht club [c18 perhaps from French (Jersey dialect) *bourgeais* shipowner, from Old French *borgeis*; see BOURGEOIS¹, BURGESS]

Burgenland (*German* 'burgən,lant) *n* a state of E Austria. Capital: Eisenstadt. Pop: 276 419 (2003 est). Area: 3965 sq km (1531 sq miles)

burgeon or **bourgeon** ('bɜːdʒən) *vb* 1 (often foll by *forth* or *out*) (of a plant) to sprout (buds) 2 (*intr*; often foll by *forth* or *out*) to develop or grow rapidly; flourish ▷ *n* 3 a bud of a plant [c13 from Old French *burjon*, perhaps ultimately from Late Latin *burra* shaggy cloth; from the downiness of certain buds]

burger ('bɜːgə) *n informal* **a** short for **hamburger** **b** (*in combination*): *a cheeseburger*

burgess ('bɜːdʒɪs) *n* 1 (in England) **a** a citizen or freeman of a borough **b** any inhabitant of a borough 2 *English history* a Member of Parliament from a borough, corporate town, or university 3 a member of the colonial assembly of Maryland or Virginia [c13 from Old French *burgeis*, from *borc* town, from Late Latin *burgus*, of Germanic origin; see BOROUGH]

Burgess Shale *n* a bed of Cambrian sedimentary rock in the Rocky Mountains in British Columbia containing many unique invertebrate fossils [named after the *Burgess* Pass, where the bed is exposed]

burgh ('bʌrə) *n* 1 (in Scotland) a town, esp one incorporated by charter, that enjoyed a degree of self-government until the local-government reorganization of 1975 2 an archaic form of **borough** (sense 1) [c14 Scottish form of BOROUGH] ▷ **burghal** ('bɜːgəl) *adj*

burgher ('bɜːgə) *n* 1 a member of the trading or mercantile class of a medieval city 2 a respectable citizen; bourgeois 3 *archaic* a citizen or inhabitant of a corporate town, esp on the Continent 4 *South African history* **a** a citizen of the Cape Colony or of one of the Transvaal and Free State republics **b** (*as modifier*): *burgher troops* [c16 from German *Bürger*, or Dutch *burger* freeman of a BOROUGH]

Burghley House *n* an Elizabethan mansion near Stamford in Lincolnshire: seat of the Cecil family; site of the annual Burghley Horse Trials

burghul (bɜː'guːl) *n* another name for **bulgur**

burglar ('bɜːglə) *n* a person who commits burglary; housebreaker [c15 from Anglo-French *burgler*, from Medieval Latin *burglātor*, probably from *burgāre* to thieve, from Latin *burgus* castle, fortress, of Germanic origin]

burglarize or **burglarise** ('bɜːglə,raɪz) *vb* (*tr*) *US and Canadian* to break into (a place) and steal from (someone); burgle

burglary ('bɜːglərɪ) *n, pl* -ries *English criminal law* the crime of either entering a building as a trespasser with the intention of committing theft, rape, grievous bodily harm, or damage, or, having entered as a trespasser, of committing one or more of these offences ▷ **burglarious** (bɜːˈglɛərɪəs) *adj*

burgle ('bɜːgəl) *vb* to commit burglary upon (a house, etc)

burgomaster ('bɜːgə,mɑːstə) *n* 1 the chief magistrate of a town in Austria, Belgium, Germany, or the Netherlands; mayor 2 a popular name for the **glaucous gull** [c16 partial translation of Dutch *burgemeester*; see BOROUGH, MASTER]

burgonet ('bɜːgə,nɛt) *n* a light 16th-century helmet, usually made of steel, with hinged cheekpieces [c16 from French *bourguignotte*, from *bourguignot* of Burgundy, from *Bourgogne* Burgundy]

burgoo ('bɜːguː, bɜː'guː) *n, pl* -goos 1 *nautical slang* porridge 2 *Southern US* **a** a thick highly seasoned soup or stew of meat and vegetables **b** a picnic or gathering at which such soup is served [c18 perhaps from Arabic *burghul* crushed grain]

Burgos ('bɜːgɒs) *n* a city in N Spain, in Old Castile: cathedral. Pop: 169 317 (2003 est)

burgrave ('bɜːgreɪv) *n* 1 the military governor of a German town or castle, esp in the 12th and 13th centuries 2 a nobleman ruling a German town or castle by hereditary right [c16 from German *Burggraf*, from Old High German *burg* BOROUGH + *grāve* count]

Burgundian (bɜːˈgʌndɪən) *adj* 1 of or relating to Burgundy or its inhabitants ▷ *n* 2 a native or inhabitant of Burgundy

Burgundy ('bɜːgəndɪ) *n, pl* -dies 1 a region of E France famous for its wines, lying west of the Saône: formerly a semi-independent duchy; annexed to France in 1482. French name: Bourgogne 2 **Free County of**. another name for **Franche-Comté** 3 a monarchy (1384–1477) of medieval Europe, at its height including the Low Countries, the duchy of Burgundy, and Franche-Comté 4 **Kingdom of**. a kingdom in E France, established in the early 6th century AD, eventually including the later duchy of Burgundy, Franche-Comté, and the Kingdom of Provence: known as the Kingdom of Arles from the 13th century 5 **a** any red or white wine produced in the region of Burgundy, around Dijon **b** any heavy red table wine 6 (*often not capital*) a blackish-purple to purplish-red colour

burhel ('bʌrəl) *n* a variant spelling of **bharal**

burial ('bɛrɪəl) *n* the act of burying, esp the interment of a dead body [Old English *byrgels* burial place, tomb; see BURY, -AL²]

burial ground *n* a graveyard or cemetery

Buridan's ass ('bjʊərɪdænz) *n philosophy* an example intended to show the deficiency of reason. An ass standing equidistant from two identical heaps of oats starves to death because reason provides no grounds for choosing to eat one rather than the other [named after Jean *Buridan*, 14th-century French philosopher, to whom it was incorrectly attributed]

burier ('bɛrɪə) *n* a person or thing that buries

burin ('bjʊərɪn) *n* 1 a chisel of tempered steel with a sharp lozenge-shaped point, used for engraving furrows in metal, wood, or marble 2 an engraver's individual style 3 *archaeol* a prehistoric flint tool with a very small transverse edge [c17 from French, perhaps from Italian *burino*, of Germanic origin: compare Old High German *boro* auger; see BORE¹]

burk (bɜːk) *n Brit slang* a variant spelling of **berk**

burka ('bɜːkə) *n* a variant spelling of **burqa** [c19 from Arabic]

burke (bɜːk) *vb* (*tr*) 1 to murder in such a way as to leave no marks on the body, usually by suffocation 2 to get rid of, silence, or suppress [c19 named after William *Burke* (1792–1829), Irish murderer and body snatcher, associate of William Hare; executed in Edinburgh for a murder of this type]

Burkinabé (,bɜːkɪnə'beɪ) *adj* 1 of or relating to Burkina-Faso or its inhabitants ▷ *n* 2 a native or inhabitant of Burkina-Faso

Burkina-Faso (bɜː'kiːnə'fæsəʊ) *n* an inland republic in W Africa: dominated by Mossi kingdoms (10th–19th centuries); French protectorate established in 1896; became an independent republic in 1960; consists mainly of a flat savanna plateau. Official language: French; Mossi and other African languages also widely spoken. Religion: mostly animist, with a large Muslim minority. Currency: franc. Capital: Ouagadougou. Pop: 13 393 000 (2004 est). Area: 273 200 sq km (105 900 sq miles). Former name (until 1984): Upper Volta

Burkitt lymphoma ('bɜːkɪt) or **Burkitt's lymphoma** ('bɜːkɪts) *n* a rare type of tumour of the white blood cells, occurring mainly in Africa and associated with infection by Epstein-Barr virus [named after Dennis *Burkitt* (1911–93), British surgeon who first described the tumour]

burl¹ (bɜːl) *n* 1 a small knot or lump in wool 2 a roundish warty outgrowth from the trunk, roots, or branches of certain trees ▷ *vb* 3 (*tr*) to remove the burls from (cloth) [c15 from Old French *burle* tuft of wool, probably ultimately from Late Latin *burra* shaggy cloth] ▷ **'burler** *n*

burl² or **birl** (bɜːl) *n informal* 1 *Scot, Austral and NZ* an attempt; try (esp in the phrase **give it a burl**) 2 *Austral and NZ* a ride in a car [c20 perhaps from BIRL¹ in the Scot sense: a twist or turn]

burlap ('bɜːlæp) *n* a coarse fabric woven from jute, hemp, or the like [c17 from *borel* coarse cloth, from Old French *burel* (see BUREAU) + LAP¹]

burlesque (bɜː'lɛsk) *n* 1 an artistic work, esp literary or dramatic, satirizing a subject by caricaturing it 2 a ludicrous imitation or caricature 3 a play of the 17th–19th centuries that parodied some contemporary dramatic fashion or event 4 Also: burlesk *US and Canadian theatre* a bawdy comedy show of the late 19th and early 20th centuries: the striptease eventually became one of its chief elements. Slang name: burleycue ▷ *adj* 5 of, relating to, or characteristic of a burlesque ▷ *vb* -lesques, -lesquing, -lesqued 6 to represent or imitate (a person or thing) in a ludicrous way; caricature [c17 from French, from Italian *burlesco*, from *burla* a jest, piece of nonsense] ▷ **bur'lesquer** *n*

burley¹ ('bɜːlɪ) *n, vb* a variant spelling of **berley**

burley² ('bɜːlɪ) *n* a light thin-leaved tobacco, grown esp in Kentucky [c19 probably from the name *Burley*]

Burlington ('bɜːlɪŋtən) *n* 1 a city in S Canada on Lake Ontario, northeast of Hamilton. Pop: 150 836 (2001) 2 a city in NW Vermont on Lake Champlain: largest city in the state; University of Vermont (1791). Pop: 39 148 (2003 est)

burly ('bɜːlɪ) *adj* -lier, -liest large and thick of build; sturdy; stout [c13 of Germanic origin; compare Old High German *burlīh* lofty] ▷ **'burliness** *n*

Burma ('bɜːmə) *n* the former name (until 1989) of **Myanmar**

bur marigold *n* any plant of the genus *Bidens* that has yellow flowers and pointed fruits that cling to fur and clothing: family *Asteraceae* (composites). Also called: beggar-ticks, sticktight

Burma Road *n* the route extending from Lashio in Burma (now Myanmar) to Chongqing in China, which was used by the Allies during World War II to supply military equipment to Chiang Kai-shek's forces in China

Burmese (bɜːˈmiːz) *adj also* Burman 1 of, relating to, or characteristic of Burma (Myanmar), its people, or their language ▷ *n, pl* -mese 2 a native or inhabitant of Burma (Myanmar) 3 the official language of Burma (Myanmar), belonging to the Sino-Tibetan family

Burmese cat *n* a breed of cat similar in shape to the Siamese but typically having a dark brown or blue-grey coat

burn¹ (bɜːn) *vb* burns, burning, burnt *or* burned 1 to undergo or cause to undergo combustion 2 to destroy or be destroyed by fire 3 (*tr*) to damage, injure, or mark by heat: *he burnt his hand; she was burnt by the sun* 4 to die or put to death by fire: *to burn at the stake* 5 (*intr*) to be or feel hot: *my forehead burns* 6 to smart or cause to smart: *brandy burns one's throat* 7 (*intr*) to feel strong emotion, esp anger or passion 8 (*tr*) to use for the purposes of light, heat, or power: *to burn coal* 9 (*tr*) to form by or as if by fire: *to burn a hole* 10 to char or become charred: *the potatoes are burning in the saucepan* 11 (*tr*) to brand or cauterize 12 (*tr*) to cut (metal) with an oxygen-rich flame 13 to produce by or subject to heat as part of a process: *to burn charcoal* 14 (*tr*) to copy information onto (a CD-ROM) 15 *astronomy* to convert (a lighter element) to a heavier one by nuclear fusion in a star: *to burn hydrogen* 16 *cards,*

b

chiefly Brit to discard or exchange (one or more useless cards) **17** *(tr; usually passive) informal* to cheat, esp financially **18** *slang, chiefly US* to electrocute or be electrocuted **19** *(tr) Austral slang* to drive fast (esp in the phrase **go for a burn**) **20 burn one's bridges** *or* **boats** to commit oneself to a particular course of action with no possibility of turning back **21 burn the candle at both ends** See **candle** (sense 3) **22 burn one's fingers** to suffer from having meddled or been rash ▷ *n* **23** an injury caused by exposure to heat, electrical, chemical, or radioactive agents. Burns are classified according to the depth of tissue affected: **first-degree burn**: skin surface painful and red; **second-degree burn**: blisters appear on the skin; **third-degree burn**: destruction of both epidermis and dermis **24** a mark, eg on wood, caused by burning **25** a controlled use of rocket propellant, esp for a course correction **26** a hot painful sensation in a muscle, experienced during vigorous exercise: *go for the burn!* **27** *Austral and NZ* a controlled fire to clear an area of scrub **28** *slang* tobacco or a cigarette ▷ See also **burn in, burn off, burn out** [Old English *beornan* (intr), *bærnan* (tr); related to Old Norse *brenna* (tr or intr), Gothic *brinnan* (intr), Latin *fervēre* to boil, seethe]

burn² (bɜːn; *Scot* bʌrn) *n Scot and Northern English* a small stream; brook [Old English *burna*; related to Old Norse *brunnr* spring, Old High German *brunno*, Lithuanian *briáutis* to burst forth]

burned (bɜːnd) *adj slang* having been cheated in a sale of drugs

burner ('bɜːnə) *n* **1** the part of a stove, lamp, etc, that produces flame or heat **2** an apparatus for burning something, as fuel or refuse: *an oil burner*

burnet ('bɜːnɪt) *n* **1** a plant of the rosaceous genus *Sanguisorba* (or *Poterium*), such as *S. minor* (or *P. sanguisorba*), which has purple-tinged green flowers and leaves that are sometimes used for salads **2 burnet rose** Also called: **Scotch rose** a very prickly Eurasian rose, *Rosa pimpinellifolia*, with white flowers and purplish-black fruits **3 burnet saxifrage** a Eurasian umbelliferous plant of the genus *Pimpinella*, having umbrella-like clusters of white or pink flowers **4** a moth of the genus *Zygaena*, having red-spotted dark green wings and antennae with enlarged tips: family *Zygaenidae* [c14 from Old French *burnete*, variant of *brunete* dark brown (see BRUNETTE); so called from the colour of the flowers of some of the plants]

Burnham scale ('bɜːnəm) *n* the salary scale for teachers in English state schools, which is revised periodically [c20 named after Lord *Burnham* (1862–1933), chairman of the committee that originally set it up]

burn in *vb (tr, adverb)* to darken (areas on a photographic print) by exposing them to light while masking other regions

burning ('bɜːnɪŋ) *adj* **1** intense; passionate **2** urgent; crucial: *a burning problem* ▷ *n* **3** a form of heat treatment used to harden and finish ceramic materials or to prepare certain ores for further treatment by calcination **4** overheating of an alloy during heat treatment in which local fusion or excessive oxide formation and penetration occur, weakening the alloy **5** the heat treatment of particular kinds of gemstones to change their colour > 'burningly *adv*

burning bush *n* **1** a rutaceous shrub, *Dictamnus fraxinella*, of S Europe and Asia, whose glands release a volatile inflammable oil that can burn without harming the plant: identified as the bush from which God spoke to Moses (Exodus 3:2–4) **2** any of several shrubs or trees, esp the wahoo, that have bright red fruits or seeds **3** another name for **gas plant 4** any of several plants, esp kochia, with a bright red autumn foliage **5** *Old Testament* the bush that burned without being consumed, from which God spoke to Moses (Exodus 3:2–4)

burning glass *n* a convex lens for concentrating the sun's rays into a small area to produce heat or fire

burnish ('bɜːnɪʃ) *vb* **1** to make or become shiny or smooth by friction; polish ▷ *n* **2** a shiny finish; lustre [c14 *burnischen*, from Old French *brunir* to make brown, from *brun* BROWN] > 'burnishable *adj* > 'burnisher *n*

Burnley ('bɜːnlɪ) *n* an industrial town in NW England, in E Lancashire. Pop: 73 021 (2001)

burn off *vb (tr, adverb)* **1** to burn (land) of vegetation by burning **2** to get rid of (unwanted gas at an oil well, etc) by burning ▷ *n* **burn-off 3** an act or the process of burning off

burnous, burnouse *or US* **burnoose** (bɜːˈnuːs, -ˈnuːz) *n* a long circular cloak with a hood attached, worn esp by Arabs [c17 via French *burnous* from Arabic *burnus*, from Greek *birros* cloak] > bur'noused *or U.S* bur'noosed *adj*

burn out *vb (adverb)* **1** to become or cause to become worn out or inoperative as a result of heat or friction: *the clutch burnt out* **2** *(intr)* (of a rocket, jet engine, etc) to cease functioning as a result of exhaustion of the fuel supply **3** *(tr; usually passive)* to destroy by fire **4** to become or cause to become exhausted through overwork or dissipation ▷ *n* **burnout 5** the failure of a mechanical device from excessive heating **6** a total loss of energy and interest and an inability to function effectively, experienced as a result of excessive demands upon one's resources or chronic overwork

burnsides ('bɜːnˌsaɪdz) *pl n US* thick side whiskers worn with a moustache and clean-shaven chin [c19 named after General A. E. *Burnside* (1824–81), Union general in the US Civil War]

burnt (bɜːnt) *vb* **1** a past tense and past participle of **burn¹** ▷ *adj* **2** affected by or as if by burning; charred **3** (of various pigments, such as ochre and orange) calcined, with a resultant darkening of colour

burnt almond *n* a sweet consisting of an almond enclosed in burnt sugar

burnt offering *n* a sacrificial offering burnt, usually on an altar, to honour, propitiate, or supplicate a deity

burnt shale *n* carbonaceous shale formed by destructive distillation of oil shale or by spontaneous combustion of shale after it has been some years in a tip: sometimes used in road making

burnt sienna *n* **1** a reddish-brown dye or pigment obtained by roasting raw sienna in a furnace **2** a dark reddish-orange to reddish-brown colour

burnt-tip orchid *n* a small orchid, *Orchis ustulata*, resembling the lady orchid, having dark reddish-brown hoods that give a burnt look to the tip of the flower spike

burnt umber *n* **1** a brown pigment obtained by heating umber **2** a dark brown colour

burn-up *n slang* a period of fast driving

bur oak *n* an E North American oak, *Quercus macrocarpa*, having fringed acorn cups and durable timber

buroo (bəˈruː, bruː) *n, pl* **-roos** *Scot and Irish dialect* **1** the government office from which unemployment benefit is distributed **2** the unemployment benefit itself (esp in the phrase **on the buroo**) [c20 from BUREAU]

burp (bɜːp) *n* **1** *informal* a belch ▷ *vb* **2** *(intr) informal* to belch **3** *(tr)* to cause (a baby) to burp to relieve flatulence after feeding [c20 of imitative origin]

burpee ('bɜːpiː) *n* **1** a squat thrust that starts and ends in a standing position **2** *US* a piece of absorbent material placed on the shoulder while burping a baby [c20 sense 1 from *Burpee test*, a measure of endurance and coordination devised by R.H. *Burpee*, US psychologist]

burp gun *n US slang* an automatic pistol or submachine gun

burqa *or* **burka** ('bɜːkə) *n* a long enveloping garment worn by Muslim women in public [c19 from Arabic]

burr¹ (bɜː) *n* **1** a small power-driven hand-operated rotary file, esp for removing burrs or for machining recesses **2** a rough edge left on a workpiece after cutting, drilling, etc **3** a rough or irregular protuberance, such as a burl on a tree **4** *Brit* a burl on the trunk or root of a tree, sliced across for use as decorative veneer ▷ *n* ▷ *vb* **5** a variant spelling of **bur** ▷ *vb* (*tr*) **6** to form a rough edge on (a workpiece) **7** to remove burrs from (a workpiece) by grinding, filing, etc; deburr [c14 variant of BUR]

burr² (bɜː) *n* **1** *phonetics* an articulation of (r) characteristic of certain English dialects, esp the uvular fricative trill of Northumberland or the retroflex r of the West of England **2** a whirring sound ▷ *vb* **3** to pronounce (words) with a burr **4** to make a whirring sound [c18 either special use of BUR (in the sense: rough sound) or of imitative origin]

burr³ *or* **bur** (bɜː) *n* **1** a washer fitting around the end of a rivet **2** a blank punched out of sheet metal [c16 (in the sense: broad ring on a spear): variant of *burrow* (in obsolete sense: BOROUGH)]

burr⁴, buhr *or* **bur** (bɜː) *n* **1** short for **buhrstone 2** a mass of hard siliceous rock surrounded by softer rock [c18 probably from BUR, from its qualities of roughness]

burramys ('bʌrəmɪs) *n* the very rare mountain pigmy possum, *Burramys parvus*, of Australia. It is about the size of a rat and restricted in habitat to very high altitudes, mainly Mt Hotham, Victoria. Until 1966 it was known only as a fossil

burrawang ('bʌrəwæŋ) *n* any of several Australian cycads of the genus *Macrozamia*, having an edible nut [c19 from Mount *Budawang*, New South Wales]

bur reed *n* a marsh plant of the genus *Sparganium*, having narrow leaves, round clusters of small green flowers, and round prickly fruit: family *Sparganiaceae*

Burrell Collection ('bʌrəl) *n* a gallery in Glasgow, noted for its collection of paintings, textiles, furniture, ceramics, etc [c20 named after Sir William *Burrell* (1861–1958), Scottish shipping magnate, and his wife Constance, who founded the collection]

Burren ('bʌrən) *n* **the** a limestone area on the North Clare coast in the Irish Republic, famous for its wild flowers, caves, and dolmens

burrito (bəˈriːtəʊ) *n, pl* **-tos** *Mexican cookery* a tortilla folded over a filling of minced beef, chicken, cheese, or beans [c20 from Mexican Spanish, from Spanish: literally, a young donkey]

burro ('bʊrəʊ) *n, pl* **-ros** a donkey, esp one used as a pack animal [c19 Spanish, from Portuguese, from *burrico* donkey, ultimately from Latin *burrīcus* small horse]

burrow ('bʌrəʊ) *n* **1** a hole or tunnel dug in the ground by a rabbit, fox, or other small animal, for habitation or shelter **2** a small snug place affording shelter or retreat ▷ *vb* **3** to dig (a burrow) in, through, or under (ground) **4** *(intr; often foll by through)* to move through or by as by digging: *to burrow through the forest* **5** *(intr)* to hide or live in a burrow **6** *(intr)* to delve deeply: *he burrowed into his pockets* **7** to hide (oneself) [c13 probably a variant of BOROUGH] > 'burrower *n*

burrstone ('bɜːˌstəʊn) *n* a variant spelling of **buhrstone**

burry ('bɜːrɪ) *adj* **-rier, -riest 1** full of or covered in burs **2** resembling burs; prickly

bursa ('bɜːsə) *n, pl* **-sae** (-siː) *or* **-sas 1** a small fluid-filled sac that reduces friction between movable parts of the body, esp at joints **2** *zoology* any saclike cavity or structure [c19 from Medieval Latin: bag, pouch, from Greek: skin, hide; see PURSE] > 'bursal *adj*

Bursa ('bɜːsə) *n* a city in NW Turkey: founded in the 2nd century BC; seat of Bithynian kings. Pop: 1 413 000 (2005 est). Former name: Brusa

bursar ('bɜːsə) *n* **1** an official in charge of the financial management of a school, college, or university **2** *chiefly Scot and NZ* a student holding a bursary [c13 from Medieval Latin *bursārius* keeper of the purse, from *bursa* purse]

bursarial (bɜːˈsɛərɪəl) *adj* of, relating to, or paid by a bursar or bursary

bursary ('bɜːsərɪ) *n, pl* -ries **1** Also called: **bursarship** a scholarship or grant awarded esp in Scottish and New Zealand schools, universities etc **2** *Brit* **a** the treasury of a college, etc **b** the bursar's room in a college

Burschenschaft (*German* 'burʃənʃaft) *n* a students' fraternity, originally one concerned with Christian ideals, patriotism, etc [literally: youth association]

burse (bɜːs) *n* **1** *chiefly RC Church* a flat case used at Mass as a container for the corporal **2** *Scot* **a** a fund providing allowances for students **b** the allowance provided [c19 from Medieval Latin *bursa* purse]

burseraceous (ˌbɜːsəˈreɪʃəs) *adj* of, relating to, or belonging to the *Burseraceae*, a tropical family of trees and shrubs having compound leaves and resin or balsam in their stems. The family includes bdellium and some balsams [c19 from New Latin *Bursera* type genus, named after J. *Burser* (1593–1649), German botanist]

bursicon ('bɜːsɪkɒn) *n* a hormone, produced by the insect brain, that regulates processes associated with ecdysis, such as darkening of the cuticle

bursiform ('bɜːsɪˌfɔːm) *adj* shaped like a pouch or sac [c19 from Latin *bursa* bag + -FORM]

bursitis (bɜːˈsaɪtɪs) *n* inflammation of a bursa, esp one in the shoulder joint

burst (bɜːst) *vb* **bursts, bursting, burst 1** to break or cause to break open or apart suddenly and noisily, esp from internal pressure; explode **2** (*intr*) to come, go, etc, suddenly and forcibly: *he burst into the room* **3** (*intr*) to be full to the point of breaking open **4** (*intr*) to give vent (to) suddenly or loudly: *to burst into song* **5** to cause or suffer the rupture of: *to burst a blood vessel* ▷ *n* **6** a sudden breaking open or apart; explosion **7** a break; breach; rupture **8** a sudden display or increase of effort or action; spurt: *a burst of speed* **9** a sudden and violent emission, occurrence, or outbreak: *a burst of heavy rain; a burst of applause* **10** a volley of fire from a weapon or weapons ▷ *adj* **11** broken apart; ruptured: *a burst pipe* [Old English *berstan*; related to Old Norse *bresta*, Old Frisian *bersta*, Old High German *brestan*; compare BREAK] > 'burster *n*

burstone ('bɜːˌstəʊn) *n* a variant spelling of **buhrstone**

burthen ('bɜːðən) *n, vb* an archaic word for **burden**¹ > 'burthensome *adj*

burton ('bɜːtⁿn) *n* **1** *nautical* a kind of light hoisting tackle **2 go for a burton** *Brit slang* **a** to be broken, useless, or lost **b** to die [c15 of uncertain origin]

Burton-upon-Trent *n* a town in W central England, in E Staffordshire: famous for brewing. Pop: 43 784 (2001)

Burundi (bəˈrʊndɪ) *n* a republic in E central Africa: inhabited chiefly by the Hutu, Tutsi, and Twa (Pygmy); made part of German East Africa in 1899; part of the Belgian territory of Ruanda-Urundi from 1923 until it became independent in 1962; ethnic violence has erupted at times; consists mainly of high plateaus along the main Nile-Congo dividing range, dropping rapidly to the Great Rift Valley in the west. Official languages: Kirundi and French. Religion: Christian majority. Currency: Burundi franc. Capital: Bujumbura. Pop: 7 068 000 (2004 est). Area: 27 731 sq km (10 707 sq miles). Former name (until 1962): Urundi

Burundian (bəˈrʊndɪən) *adj* **1** of or relating to Burundi or its inhabitants ▷ *n* **2** a native or inhabitant of Burundi

burweed ('bɜːˌwiːd) *n* any of various plants that bear burs, such as the burdock

bury ('bɛrɪ) *vb* **buries, burying, buried** (*tr*) **1** to place (a corpse) in a grave, usually with funeral rites; inter **2** to place in the earth and cover with soil **3** to lose through death **4** to cover from sight; hide **5** to embed; sink: *to bury a nail in plaster* **6** to occupy (oneself) with deep concentration; engross: *to be buried in a book* **7** to dismiss from the mind; abandon: *to bury old hatreds* **8 bury the hatchet** to cease hostilities and become reconciled **9 bury one's head in the sand** to refuse to face a problem [Old English *byrgan* to bury, hide; related to Old Norse *bjarga* to save, preserve, Old English *beorgan* to defend]

Bury ('bɛrɪ) *n* **1** a town in NW England, in Bury unitary authority, Greater Manchester: an early textile centre. Pop: 60 178 (2001) **2** a unitary authority in NW England, in Greater Manchester. Pop: 181 900 (2003 est). Area: 99 sq km (38 sq miles)

Buryat or **Buriat** (buəˈjɑːt, buərɪˈɑːt) *n* **1** a member of a Mongoloid people living chiefly in the Buryat Republic **2** the language of this people, belonging to the Mongolic branch of the Altaic family

Buryat Republic or **Buryatia** (buəˈjɑːtɪə; *Russian* buˈrjatija) *n* a constituent republic of SE central Russia, on Lake Baikal: mountainous, with forests covering over half the total area. Capital: Ulan-Ude. Pop: 981 000 (2002). Area: 351 300 sq km (135 608 sq miles)

burying beetle *n* a beetle of the genus *Necrophorous*, which buries the dead bodies of small animals by excavating beneath them, using the corpses as food for themselves and their larvae: family *Silphidae*. Also called: **sexton**

Bury St Edmunds ('bɛrɪ sənt 'ɛdməndz) *n* a market town in E England, in Suffolk. Pop: 36 218 (2001)

bus (bʌs) *n, pl* **buses** or **busses 1** a large motor vehicle designed to carry passengers between stopping places along a regular route. More formal name: **omnibus**. Sometimes called: **motorbus 2** short for **trolleybus 3** (*modifier*) of or relating to a bus or buses: *a bus driver; a bus station* **4** *informal* a car or aircraft, esp one that is old and shaky **5** *electronics, computing* short for **busbar 6** the part of a MIRV missile payload containing the re-entry vehicles and guidance and thrust devices **7** *astronautics* a platform in a space vehicle used for various experiments and processes **8 miss the bus** to miss an opportunity; be too late ▷ *vb* **buses, busing, bused** or **busses, bussing, bussed 9** to travel or transport by bus **10** *chiefly US and Canadian* to transport (children) by bus from one area to a school in another in order to create racially integrated classes [c19 short for OMNIBUS]

bus boy *n US and Canadian* a waiter's assistant

busbar ('bʌzˌbɑː) *n* **1** an electrical conductor, maintained at a specific voltage and capable of carrying a high current, usually used to make a common connection between several circuits in a system **2** a group of such electrical conductors at a low voltage, used for carrying data in binary form between the various parts of a computer or its peripherals ▷ Sometimes shortened to: **bus**

busby ('bʌzbɪ) *n, pl* -bies **1** a tall fur helmet with a bag hanging from the top to the right side, worn by certain soldiers, usually hussars, as in the British Army **2** (not in official usage) another name for **bearskin** (the hat) [c18 (in the sense: large bushy wig): perhaps from a proper name]

busera (buˈsɛrə) *n* a Ugandan alcoholic drink made from millet: sometimes mixed with honey **2** a porridge made out of millet [from Rukiga, a language of SW Uganda]

bush¹ (buʃ) *n* **1** a dense woody plant, smaller than a tree, with many branches arising from the lower part of the stem; shrub **2** a dense cluster of such shrubs; thicket **3** something resembling a bush, esp in density: *a bush of hair* **4 a** (often preceded by *the*) an uncultivated or sparsely settled area, esp in Africa, Australia, New Zealand, or Canada: usually covered with trees or shrubs, varying from open shrubby country to dense rainforest **b** (*as modifier*): *bush flies* **5** *Canadian* an area of land on a farm on which timber is grown and cut. Also called: **bush lot, woodlot 6** a forested area; woodland **7** (often preceded by *the*) *informal* the countryside, as opposed to the city: *out in the bush* **8** a fox's tail; brush **9** *obsolete* **a** a bunch of ivy hung as a vintner's sign in front of a tavern **b** any tavern sign **10 beat about the bush** to avoid the point at issue; prevaricate ▷ *adj* **11** *West African informal* ignorant or stupid, esp as considered typical of unwesternized rustic life **12** *US and Canadian informal* unprofessional, unpolished, or second-rate **13 go bush** *informal, Austral and NZ* **a** to abandon city amenities and live rough **b** to run wild ▷ *vb* **14** (*intr*) to grow thick and bushy **15** (*tr*) to cover, decorate, support, etc, with bushes [c13 of Germanic origin; compare Old Norse *buski*, Old High German *busc*, Middle Dutch *bosch*; related to Old French *bosc* wood, Italian *bosco*]

bush² (buʃ) *n* **1** Also called (esp US and Canadian): **bushing** a thin metal sleeve or tubular lining serving as a bearing or guide ▷ *vb* **2** to fit a bush to (a casing, bearing, etc) [c15 from Middle Dutch *busse* box, bush; related to German *Büchse* tin, Swedish *hjulbössa* wheel-box, Late Latin *buxis* BOX¹]

bushbaby ('buʃˌbeɪbɪ) *n, pl* -babies any agile nocturnal arboreal prosimian primate of the genera *Galago* and *Euoticus*, occurring in Africa south of the Sahara: family *Lorisidae* (lorises). They have large eyes and ears and a long tail. Also called: **galago**

bush ballad *n* an old Australian bush poem in a ballad metre dealing with aspects of life and characters in the bush

bush-bash *vb Austral slang* (*intr*) **1** to clear scrubland **2** to drive through thick scrubland ▷ Also called: **scrub-bash**

bushbashing ('buʃˌbæʃɪŋ) *n Austral and NZ slang* the process of forcing a path through the bush

bushbuck ('buʃˌbʌk) or **boschbok** *n, pl* -bucks, -buck or -boks, -bok a small nocturnal spiral-horned antelope, *Tragelaphus scriptus*, of the bush and tropical forest of Africa. Its coat is reddish-brown with a few white markings

bush canary *n NZ* another name for **brown creeper**

bush carpenter *n Austral and NZ slang* a rough-and-ready unskilled workman

bushcraft ('buʃˌkrɑːft) *n Austral and NZ* ability and experience in matters concerned with living in the bush

bushed (buʃt) *adj informal* **1** (*postpositive*) extremely tired; exhausted **2** *Canadian* mentally disturbed from living in isolation, esp in the north **3** *Austral and NZ* lost or bewildered, as in the bush

bushel¹ ('buʃəl) *n* **1** a Brit unit of dry or liquid measure equal to 8 Imperial gallons. 1 Imperial bushel is equivalent to 0.036 37 cubic metres **2** a US unit of dry measure equal to 64 US pints. 1 US bushel is equivalent to 0.035 24 cubic metres **3** a container with a capacity equal to either of these quantities **4** *US informal* a large amount; great deal **5 hide one's light under a bushel** to conceal one's abilities or good qualities [c14 from Old French *boissel*, from *boisse* one sixth of a bushel, of Gaulish origin]

bushel² ('buʃəl) *vb* -els, -elling, -elled or -els, -eling, -eled (*tr*) *US* to alter or mend (a garment) [c19 probably from German *bosseln* to do inferior work, patch, from Middle High German *bōzeln* to beat, from Old High German *bōzan*] > 'busheller, 'busheler or 'bushelman *n*

bushfire ('buʃˌfaɪə) *n* an uncontrolled fire in the bush; a scrub or forest fire

bushfly ('buʃˌflaɪ) *n, pl* -flies any of various small black dipterous flies of Australia, esp *Musca vetustissima*, that breed in faeces and dung: family *Calliphoridae*

bush grass *n* a coarse reedlike grass, *Calamagrostis*

b

epigejos, 1–1½ metres (3–4½ ft) high that grows on damp clay soils in Europe and temperate parts of Asia

bushhammer ('bʊʃˌhæmə) *n* a hammer with small pyramids projecting from its working face, used for dressing stone [C19 from German *Bosshammer*, from *bossen* to beat + HAMMER]

bush-hawk *n* another name for **karearea**

bush house *n chiefly Austral* a shed or hut in the bush or a garden

Bushido (ˌbuːʃɪˈdəʊ) *n* (*sometimes not capital*) the feudal code of the Japanese samurai, stressing self-discipline, courage and loyalty [C19 from Japanese *bushi* warrior (from Chinese *wushih*) + *dō* way (from Chinese *tao*)]

bushie ('bʊʃɪ) *n* a variant spelling of **bushy²**

Bushie ('bʊʃɪ) *n* a supporter of US President George W. Bush or a member of his administration

bushing ('bʊʃɪŋ) *n* 1 another word for **bush²** (sense 1) 2 an adaptor having ends of unequal diameters, often with internal screw threads, used to connect pipes of different sizes 3 a layer of electrical insulation enabling a live conductor to pass through an earthed wall, etc

Bushire (bjuːˈʃaɪə) *n* a port in SW Iran, on the Persian Gulf. Pop: 166 000 (2005 est). Persian name: Bushehr (buˈʃehr)

Bushism ('bʊʃɪzəm) *n* an apparently fatuous statement attributed to George W. Bush (born 1946), 43rd Presidnt of the USA

bush jacket *or* **shirt** *n* a casual jacket or shirt having four patch pockets and a belt

bush knife *n Austral* a large heavy knife suitable for outdoor use

bushland ('bʊʃˌlænd) *n* uncultivated land (esp in Australia) that is covered with trees, shrubs, or other natural vegetation

bush lawyer *n Austral and NZ* 1 any of several prickly trailing plants of the genus *Rubus* 2 *informal* a person who gives opinions but is not qualified to do so

bush-line *n NZ* the contour at which the growth of the bush ceases

bush lot *n Canadian* another name for **bush¹** (sense 5)

bushman ('bʊʃmən) *n, pl* -men *Austral and NZ* a person who lives or travels in the bush, esp one versed in bush lore

Bushman ('bʊʃmən) *n, pl* -man *or* -men 1 a member of a hunting and gathering people of southern Africa, esp the Kalahari region, typically having leathery yellowish skin, short stature, and prominent buttocks 2 any language of this people, belonging to the Khoisan family [C18 from Afrikaans *boschjesman*]

bushman's singlet *n NZ* a sleeveless heavy black woollen singlet, used as working clothing by timber fellers

bushmaster ('bʊʃˌmɑːstə) *n* a large greyish-brown highly venomous snake, *Lachesis muta*, inhabiting wooded regions of tropical America: family *Crotalidae* (pit vipers)

bushmeat ('bʊʃˌmiːt) *n* meat taken from any animal native to African forests, including species that may be endangered or not usually eaten outside Africa

bush oyster *n Austral euphemistic* a bull's testicle when cooked and eaten

bushpig ('bʊʃˌpɪg) *n* a wild pig, *Potamochoerus porcus*, inhabiting forests in tropical Africa and Madagascar. It is brown or black, with pale markings on the face. Also called: **boschvark**

bushranger ('bʊʃˌreɪndʒə) *n* 1 *Austral history* an escaped convict or robber living in the bush 2 *US* a person who lives away from civilization; backwoodsman

bush shrike *n* 1 any shrike of the African subfamily *Malaconotinae*, such as *Chlorophoneus nigrifrons* (**black-fronted bush shrike**) 2 another name for **ant bird**

bush sickness *n NZ and Austral* an animal disease

caused by a cobalt deficiency in old bush country > 'bush-ˌsick *adj*

bush tea *n* 1 a leguminous shrub of the genus *Cyclopia*, of southern Africa 2 a beverage prepared from the dried leaves of any of these plants

bush telegraph *n* 1 a means of communication between primitive peoples over large areas, as by drum beats 2 a means of spreading rumour, gossip, etc

bushtit ('bʊʃˌtɪt) *n* any small grey active North American songbird of the genus *Psaltriparus*, such as *P. minimus* (**common bushtit**): family *Paridae* (titmice)

bush tram *n NZ* a railway line in the bush to facilitate the entry of workers and the removal of timber

bush tucker *n Austral* **a** any wild animal, insect, plant or plant extract, etc traditionally used as food by native Australians **b** cooking based around ingredients taken from the Australian wilderness

bushveld ('bʊʃˌfɛlt, -ˌvɛlt) *n* **the** an area of low altitude in N South Africa, having scrub vegetation. Also called: **lowveld**

bushwalking ('bʊʃˌwɔːkɪŋ) *n Austral* an expedition on foot in the bush

bushwhack ('bʊʃˌwæk) *vb* 1 (*tr*) *US, Canadian and Austral* to ambush 2 (*tr*) *US, Canadian and Austral* to cut or beat one's way through thick woods 3 (*intr*) *US, Canadian and Austral* to range or move around in woods or the bush 4 (*intr*) *US and Canadian* to fight as a guerrilla in wild or uncivilized regions 5 (*intr*) *NZ* to work in the bush, esp at timber felling

bushwhacker ('bʊʃˌwækə) *n* 1 *US, Canadian and Austral* a person who travels around or lives in thinly populated woodlands 2 *Austral informal* an unsophisticated person; boor 3 a Confederate guerrilla during the American Civil War 4 *US* any guerrilla 5 *NZ* a person who works in the bush, esp at timber felling

bush wren *n* a wren, *Xenicus longipes*, occurring in New Zealand: family *Xenicidae*. See also **rifleman** (sense 2)

bushy¹ ('bʊʃɪ) *adj* bushier, bushiest 1 covered or overgrown with bushes 2 thick and shaggy: *bushy eyebrows* > 'bushily *adv* > 'bushiness *n*

bushy² *or* **bushie** ('bʊʃɪ) *n, pl* bushies *Austral informal* 1 a person who lives in the bush 2 an unsophisticated uncouth person 3 a member of a bush fire brigade

busily ('bɪzɪlɪ) *adv* in a busy manner; industriously

business ('bɪznɪs) *n* 1 a trade or profession 2 an industrial, commercial, or professional operation; purchase and sale of goods and services: *the tailoring business* 3 a commercial or industrial establishment, such as a firm or factory 4 commercial activity; dealings (esp in the phrase **do business**) 5 volume or quantity of commercial activity: *business is poor today* 6 commercial policy or procedure: *overcharging is bad business* 7 proper or rightful concern or responsibility (often in the phrase **mind one's own business**) 8 a special task; assignment 9 a matter or matters to be attended to: *the business of the meeting* 10 an affair; matter: *a queer business; I'm tired of the whole business* 11 serious work or activity: *get down to business* 12 a complicated affair; rigmarole 13 *informal* a vaguely defined collection or area: *jets, fast cars, and all that business* 14 Also called: **stage business** *theatre* an incidental action, such as lighting a pipe, performed by an actor for dramatic effect 15 a group of ferrets 16 like nobody's business *informal* extremely well or fast 17 mean business to be in earnest 18 do the business *informal* to achieve what is required: *it tastes vile, but it does the business* 19 a euphemistic word for **defecation** (esp in the phrase **do one's business**) 20 a slang word for **prostitution** [Old English *bisignis* solicitude, attentiveness, from *bisig* BUSY + *-nis* -NESS]

business angel *n informal* an investor in a

business venture, esp one in its early stages. Also called: **angel investor**

business casual *n informal* a style of casual clothing worn by businesspeople at work instead of more formal attire

business class *n* 1 a class of air travel which is less luxurious than first class but superior to economy class, intended for business passengers ▷ *adj* **business-class** 2 of or relating to this class of travel

business college *n* a college providing courses in secretarial studies, business management, accounting, commerce, etc

business cycle *n chiefly US and Canadian* the recurrent fluctuation between boom and depression in the economic activity of a capitalist country. Also called: **trade cycle**

business end *n informal* the part of a tool or weapon that does the work, as contrasted with the handle

businesslike ('bɪznɪsˌlaɪk) *adj* 1 efficient and methodical 2 earnest or severe

businessman ('bɪznɪsˌmæn, -mən) *n, pl* -men a person, esp a man, engaged in commercial or industrial business, esp as an owner or executive

business park *n* an area specially designated and landscaped to accommodate business offices, warehouses, light industry, etc

businessperson ('bɪznɪsˌpɜːsən) *n, pl* -people *or* -persons a person engaged in commercial or industrial business, esp as an owner or executive

business plan *n* a detailed plan setting out the objectives of a business, the strategy and tactics planned to achieve them, and the expected profits, usually over a period of three to ten years

business process re-engineering *n* restructuring an organization by means of a radical reassessment of its core processes and predominant competencies. Abbreviation: BPR

businesswoman ('bɪznɪsˌwʊmən) *n, pl* -women a woman engaged in commercial or industrial business, esp as an owner or executive

businessy ('bɪznɪsɪ) *adj* of, relating to, typical of, or suitable for the world of commercial or industrial business: *well-heeled, businessy types*

busk¹ (bʌsk) *n* 1 a strip of whalebone, wood, steel, etc, inserted into the front of a corset to stiffen it 2 *archaic or dialect* the corset itself [C16 from Old French *busc*, probably from Old Italian *busco* splinter, stick, of Germanic origin]

busk² (bʌsk) *vb* (*intr*) *Brit* to make money by singing, dancing, acting, etc, in public places, as in front of theatre queues [C20 perhaps from Spanish *buscar* to look for] > 'busker *n* > 'busking *n*

busk³ (bʌsk) *vb* (*tr*) *Scot* 1 to make ready; prepare 2 to dress or adorn [C14 from Old Norse *būask*, from *būa* to make ready, dwell; see BOWER]

buskin ('bʌskɪn) *n* 1 (formerly) a sandal-like covering for the foot and leg, reaching the calf and usually laced 2 Also called: **cothurnus** a thick-soled laced half boot resembling this, worn esp by actors of ancient Greece 3 (usually preceded by *the*) *chiefly literary* tragic drama [C16 perhaps from Spanish *borzeguí*; related to Old French *bouzequin*, Italian *borzacchino*, of obscure origin]

bus lane *n* one track of a road marked for use by buses only

busman's holiday ('bʌsmənz) *n informal* a holiday spent doing the same sort of thing as one does at work [C20 alluding to a bus driver having a driving holiday]

Busra *or* **Busrah** ('bʌsrə) *n* variant spellings of **Basra**

buss (bʌs) *n, vb* an archaic or dialect word for **kiss** [C16 probably of imitative origin; compare French *baiser*, German dialect *Bussi* little kiss]

bus shelter *n* a covered structure at a bus stop providing protection against the weather for people waiting for a bus

bus stop *n* a place on a bus route, usually marked by a sign, at which buses regularly stop for passengers to alight and board

bust¹ (bʌst) n **1** the chest of a human being, esp a woman's bosom **2** a sculpture of the head, shoulders, and upper chest of a person [c17 from French *buste*, from Italian *busto* a sculpture, of unknown origin]

bust² (bʌst) *informal* ▷ vb busts, busting, busted *or* bust **1** to burst or break **2** to make or become bankrupt **3** (tr) (of the police) to raid, search, or arrest: *the girl was busted for drugs* **4** (tr) US and Canadian to demote, esp in military rank **5** (tr) US and Canadian to break or tame (a horse, etc) **6** (tr) chiefly US to punch; hit **7 bust a gut** See **gut** (sense 9) ▷ n **8** a raid, search, or arrest by the police **9** chiefly US a punch; hit **10** US and Canadian a failure, esp a financial one; bankruptcy **11** a drunken party ▷ adj **12** broken **13** bankrupt **14 go bust** to become bankrupt [c19 from a dialect pronunciation of BURST]

bustard (ˈbʌstəd) n any terrestrial bird of the family *Otididae*, inhabiting open regions of the Old World: order *Gruiformes* (cranes, rails, etc). They have long strong legs, a heavy body, a long neck, and speckled plumage [c15 from Old French *bistarde*, influenced by Old French *oustarde*, both from Latin *avis tarda* slow bird]

busted (ˈbʌstəd) adj informal caught out doing something wrong and therefore in trouble: *you are so busted*

bustee *or* **busti** (ˈbʌstiː) n variant spellings of **basti**

buster (ˈbʌstə) n slang **1** (in combination) a person or thing destroying something as specified: *dambuster* **2** US and Canadian a term of address for a boy or man **3** US and Canadian a person who breaks horses **4** chiefly US and Canadian a spree, esp a drinking bout

buster collar n a round collar, similar to a lampshade in shape, that is fitted round the neck of an animal or bird, for example to prevent it removing or interfering with a dressing or other treatment

bustier (ˈbuːstɪeɪ) n a type of close-fitting usually strapless top worn by women

bustle¹ (ˈbʌsəl) vb **1** (when intr, often foll by about) to hurry or cause to hurry with a great show of energy or activity ▷ n **2** energetic and noisy activity [c16 probably from obsolete *buskle* to make energetic preparation, from dialect *busk* from Old Norse *būask* to prepare] > ˈbustler n > ˈbustling adj

bustle² (ˈbʌsəl) n a cushion or a metal or whalebone framework worn by women in the late 19th century at the back below the waist in order to expand the skirt [c18 of unknown origin]

bust-up informal ▷ n **1** a quarrel, esp a serious one ending a friendship, etc **2** Brit a disturbance or brawl ▷ vb bust up (adverb) **3** (intr) to quarrel and part **4** (tr) to disrupt (a meeting), esp violently

busty (ˈbʌstɪ) adj bustier, bustiest (of a woman) having a prominent bust

busuuti (buːˈsuːtɪ) n a long garment with short sleeves and a square neckline, worn by Ugandan women, esp in S Uganda [c20 from Luganda]

busy (ˈbɪzɪ) adj busier, busiest **1** actively or fully engaged; occupied **2** crowded with or characterized by activity: *a busy day* **3** chiefly US and Canadian (of a room, telephone line, etc) in use; engaged **4** overcrowded with detail: *a busy painting* **5** meddlesome; inquisitive; prying ▷ vb busies, busying, busied **6** (tr) to make or keep (someone, esp oneself) busy; occupy [Old English *bisig*; related to Middle Dutch *besich*, perhaps to Latin *festīnāre* to hurry] > ˈbusyness n

busybody (ˈbɪzɪˌbɒdɪ) n, pl -bodies a meddlesome, prying, or officious person > ˈbusyˌbodying n

busy Lizzie (ˈlɪzɪ) n a balsaminaceous plant, *Impatiens balsamina*, that has pink, red, or white flowers and is often grown as a pot plant

busy signal n US and Canadian a repeated single note heard on a telephone when the number called is already in use. Also called (especially in Britain): **engaged tone**

but¹ (bʌt; unstressed bət) conj (coordinating) **1** contrary to expectation: *he cut his knee but didn't cry* **2** in contrast; on the contrary: *I like opera but my husband doesn't* **3** (usually used after a negative) other than: *we can't do anything but wait* ▷ conj (subordinating) **4** (usually used after a negative) without it happening or being the case that: *we never go out but it rains* **5** (foll by that) except that: *nothing is impossible but that we live forever* **6** archaic if not; unless ▷ sentence connector **7** informal used to introduce an exclamation: *my, but you're nice* ▷ prep **8** except; save: *they saved all but one of the pigs* **9** but for were it not for: *but for you, we couldn't have managed* ▷ adv **10** just; merely; only: *he was but a child; I can but try* **11** Scot, Austral and NZ informal though; however: *it's a rainy day: warm, but* **12** all but almost; practically: *he was all but dead when we found him* ▷ n **13** an objection (esp in the phrase **ifs and buts**) [Old English *būtan* without, outside, except, from *be* BY + *ūtan* OUT; related to Old Saxon *biūtan*, Old High German *biūzan*]

but² (bʌt) Scot ▷ n **1** the outer room of a two-roomed cottage: usually the kitchen ▷ prep, adv **2** in or into the outer part (of a house). Compare **ben¹** [c18 from *but* (adv) outside, hence, outer room; see BUT¹]

butadiene (ˌbjuːtəˈdaɪiːn) n a colourless easily liquefiable flammable gas that polymerizes readily and is used mainly in the manufacture of synthetic rubbers. Formula: $CH_2{:}CHCH{:}CH_2$. Systematic name: buta-1,3-diene [c20 from BUTA(NE) + DI-¹ + -ENE]

but and ben n Scot a two-roomed cottage consisting of an outer room or kitchen (**but**) and an inner room (**ben**)

butane (ˈbjuːteɪn, bjuːˈteɪn) n a colourless flammable gaseous alkane that exists in two isomeric forms, both of which occur in natural gas. The stable isomer, *n*-butane, is used mainly in the manufacture of rubber and fuels (such as Calor Gas). Formula: C_4H_{10} [c19 from BUT(YL) + -ANE]

butanol (ˈbjuːtəˌnɒl) n a colourless substance existing in four isomeric forms. The three liquid isomers are used as solvents for resins, lacquers, etc, and in the manufacture of organic compounds. Formula: C_4H_9OH. Also called: **butyl alcohol** [c19 from BUTAN(E) + -OL¹]

butanone (ˈbjuːtəˌnəʊn) n a colourless soluble flammable liquid used mainly as a solvent for resins, as a paint remover, and in lacquers, cements, and adhesives. Formula: $CH_3COC_2H_5$. Also called: **methyl ethyl ketone** [c20 from BUTAN(E) + -ONE]

butch (bʊtʃ) slang ▷ adj **1** (of a woman or man) markedly or aggressively masculine ▷ n **2** a lesbian who is noticeably masculine **3** a strong rugged man [c18 back formation from BUTCHER]

butcher (ˈbʊtʃə) n **1** a retailer of meat **2** a person who slaughters or dresses meat for market **3** an indiscriminate or brutal murderer **4** a person who destroys, ruins, or bungles something ▷ vb (tr) **5** to slaughter or dress (animals) for meat **6** to kill brutally or indiscriminately **7** to make a mess of; botch; ruin [c13 from Old French *bouchier*, from *bouc* he-goat, probably of Celtic origin; see BUCK¹; compare Welsh *bwch* he-goat]

butcherbird (ˈbʊtʃəˌbɜːd) n **1** a shrike, esp one of the genus *Lanius* **2** any of several Australian magpies of the genus *Cracticus* that impale their prey on thorns

butcher's (ˈbʊtʃəz) or **butcher's hook** n Brit slang a look [c19 rhyming slang]

butcher's-broom n a liliaceous evergreen shrub, *Ruscus aculeatus*, that has stiff prickle-tipped flattened green stems, which resemble and function as true leaves. The plant was formerly used for making brooms

butchery (ˈbʊtʃərɪ) n, pl -eries **1** the business or work of a butcher **2** wanton and indiscriminate slaughter; carnage **3** a less common word for **slaughterhouse**

Bute (bjuːt) n an island off the coast of SW Scotland, in Argyll and Bute council area: situated in the Firth of Clyde, separated from the Cowal peninsula by the **Kyles of Bute**. Chief town: Rothesay. Pop: 7228 (2001). Area: 121 sq km (47 sq miles)

butene (ˈbjuːtiːn) n a pungent colourless gas existing in four isomeric forms, all of which are used in the manufacture of organic compounds. Formula: C_4H_8. Also called: butylene [c20 from BUT(YL) + -ENE]

butenedioic acid (ˌbjuːtiːndaɪˈəʊɪk) n either of two geometrical isomers with the formula HOOCCH:CHCOOH. See **fumaric acid, maleic acid**

Buteshire (ˈbjuːtʃɪə, -ʃə) n (until 1975) a county of SW Scotland, consisting of islands in the Firth of Clyde and Kilbrannan Sound: formerly part of Strathclyde region (1975–96), now part of Argyll and Bute council area

Buteyko method (ˌbuːˈteɪkəʊ) n a breath control technique used to prevent hyperventilation and treat asthma without drugs [c20 named after Konstantin P. *Buteyko* (born 1923), Russian physician]

butler (ˈbʌtlə) n the male servant of a household in charge of the wines, table, etc: usually the head servant [c13 from Old French *bouteillier*, from *bouteille* BOTTLE¹]

butlery (ˈbʌtlərɪ) n, pl -leries **1** a butler's room **2** another name for **buttery²** (sense 1)

butsudan (ˈbʌtsəˌdæn) n, pl butsudan, -dans **1** (in Buddhism) a small household altar **2** (in Nichiren Buddhism) an ornate cabinet which holds the Gohonzon [from Japanese *butsu* Buddha (from Chinese *fu*) + *dan* shelf]

butt¹ (bʌt) n **1** the thicker or blunt end of something, such as the end of the stock of a rifle **2** the unused end of something, esp of a cigarette; stub **3** tanning the portion of a hide covering the lower backside of the animal **4** US and Canadian informal the buttocks **5** US a slang word for **cigarette 6** building trades short for **butt joint** or **butt hinge** [c15 (in the sense: thick end of something, buttock): related to Old English *buttuc* end, ridge, Middle Dutch *bot* stumpy]

butt² (bʌt) n **1** a person or thing that is the target of ridicule, wit, etc **2** shooting, archery **a** a mound of earth behind the target on a target range that stops bullets or wide shots **b** the target itself **c** (plural) the target range **3** a low barrier, usually of sods or peat, behind which sportsmen shoot game birds, esp grouse **4** archaic goal; aim ▷ vb **5** (usually foll by on or against) to lie or be placed end on to; abut: *to butt a beam against a wall* [c14 (in the sense: mark for archery practice): from Old French *but*; related to French *butte* knoll, target]

butt³ (bʌt) vb **1** to strike or push (something) with the head or horns **2** (intr) to project; jut **3** (intr; foll by in or into) to intrude, esp into a conversation; interfere; meddle **4 butt out** informal, chiefly US and Canadian to stop interfering or meddling ▷ n **5** a blow with the head or horns [c12 from Old French *boter*, of Germanic origin; compare Middle Dutch *botten* to strike; see BEAT, BUTTON] > ˈbutter n

butt⁴ (bʌt) n **1** a large cask, esp one with a capacity of two hogsheads, for storing wine or beer **2** a US unit of liquid measure equal to 126 US gallons [c14 from Old French *botte*, from Old Provençal *bota*, from Late Latin *buttis* cask, perhaps from Greek *butinē* chamber pot]

butt bra n chiefly US and Canadian an undergarment for supporting the buttocks

butte (bjuːt) n Western US and Canadian an isolated steep-sided flat-topped hill [c19 from French, from Old French *bute* mound behind a target, from *but* target; see BUTT²]

butter (ˈbʌtə) n **1 a** an edible fatty whitish-yellow solid made from cream by churning, for cooking and table use **b** (as modifier): *butter icing*. Related adjective: **butyraceous 2** any substance with a butter-like consistency, such as peanut

b

butter or vegetable butter **3 look as if butter wouldn't melt in one's mouth** to look innocent, although probably not so ▷ *vb* (*tr*) **4** to put butter on or in **5** to flatter ▷ See also **butter up** [Old English *butere*, from Latin *būtyrum*, from Greek *bouturon*, from *bous* cow + *turos* cheese]

butter-and-eggs *n* (*functioning as singular*) any of various plants, such as toadflax, the flowers of which are of two shades of yellow

butterball ('bʌtə,bɔːl) *n US* **1** another name for **bufflehead 2** *informal* a chubby or fat person

butter bean *n* a variety of lima bean that has large pale flat edible seeds and is grown in the southern US

butterbur ('bʌtə,bɜː) *n* a plant of the Eurasian genus *Petasites* with fragrant whitish or purple flowers, woolly stems, and leaves formerly used to wrap butter: family *Asteraceae* (composites)

buttercup ('bʌtə,kʌp) *n* any of various yellow-flowered ranunculaceous plants of the genus *Ranunculus*, such as *R. acris* (meadow buttercup), which is native to Europe but common throughout North America. See also **crowfoot, goldilocks** (sense 2), **spearwort, lesser celandine**

butterfat ('bʌtə,fæt) *n* the fatty substance of milk from which butter is made, consisting of a mixture of glycerides, mainly butyrin, olein, and palmitin

butterfat cheque *n* the *NZ* the total annual cash return for operations on a dairy farm

butterfingers ('bʌtə,fɪŋgəz) *n* (*functioning as singular*) *informal* a person who drops things inadvertently or fails to catch things > 'butter,fingered *adj*

butterfish ('bʌtə,fɪʃ) *n, pl* **-fish** or **-fishes 1** an eel-like blennioid food fish, *Pholis gunnellus*, occurring in North Atlantic coastal regions: family *Pholidae* (gunnels). It has a slippery scaleless golden brown skin with a row of black spots along the base of the long dorsal fin **2** Also called: **greenbone**, (Māori) **marari** an edible reef fish, *Coridodax pullus*, of esp S New Zealand. It has a slippery purplish-grey to olive-green skin and is often found browsing on kelp

butterflies ('bʌtə,flaɪz) *pl n informal* tremors in the stomach region due to nervousness

butterfly ('bʌtə,flaɪ) *n, pl* **-flies 1** any diurnal insect of the order *Lepidoptera* that has a slender body with clubbed antennae and typically rests with the wings (which are often brightly coloured) closed over the back. Compare **moth. 2** a person who never settles with one group, interest, or occupation for long **3** a swimming stroke in which the arms are plunged forward together in large circular movements **4** *commerce* the simultaneous purchase and sale of traded call options, at different exercise prices or with different expiry dates, on a stock exchange or commodity market [Old English *buttorflēoge*; the name perhaps is based on a belief that butterflies stole milk and butter]

butterfly ballot *n US* a ballot paper in the form of two leaves extending from a central spine [c20 from its resemblance to a butterfly's wings]

butterfly bush *n* another name for **buddleia**

butterfly collar *n* the Irish name for **wing collar**

butterfly diagram *n astronomy* a graphical butterfly-shaped representation of the sunspot density on the solar disc in the 11-year sunspot cycle

butterfly effect *n* the idea, used in chaos theory, that a very small difference in the initial state of a physical system can make a significant difference to the state at some later time [c20 from the theory that a butterfly flapping its wings in one part of the world might ultimately cause a hurricane in another part of the world]

butterfly fish *n* any small tropical marine percoid fish of the genera *Chaetodon, Chelmon*, etc, that has a deep flattened brightly coloured or strikingly marked body and brushlike teeth:

family *Chaetodontidae*. See also **angelfish** (sense 1)

butterfly nut *n* another name for **wing nut**

butterfly valve *n* **1** a disc that acts as a valve by turning about a diameter, esp one used as the throttle valve in a carburettor **2** a non-return valve consisting of two semicircular plates hinged about a common central spindle

butterfly weed *n* a North American asclepiadaceous plant, *Asclepias tuberosa* (or *A. decumbens*), having flat-topped clusters of bright orange flowers. Also called: **orange milkweed, pleurisy root**

butterine ('bʌtə,riːn, -rɪn) *n* an artificial butter made partly from milk

Buttermere ('bʌtə,mɪə) *n* a lake in NW England, in Cumbria, in the Lake District, southwest of Keswick. Length: 2 km (1.25 miles)

buttermilk ('bʌtə,mɪlk) *n* the sourish liquid remaining after the butter has been separated from milk, often used for making scones and soda bread

butter muslin *n* a fine loosely woven cotton material originally used for wrapping butter

butternut ('bʌtə,nʌt) *n* **1** a walnut tree, *Juglans cinerea* of E North America. Compare **black walnut 2** the oily edible egg-shaped nut of this tree **3** the hard brownish-grey wood of this tree **4** the bark of this tree or an extract from it, formerly used as a laxative **5** a brownish colour or dye **6** NZ short for **butternut pumpkin** ▷ Also called (for senses 1–4): **white walnut**

butternut pumpkin *n Austral* a variety of pumpkin, eaten as vegetable. Also called (NZ): **butternut**

butterscotch ('bʌtə,skɒtʃ) *n* **1** a kind of hard brittle toffee made with butter, brown sugar, etc **2 a** a flavouring made from these ingredients **b** (*as modifier*): *butterscotch icing* [c19 perhaps first made in Scotland]

butter tart *n Canadian* a kind of tart made with butter, brown sugar, and raisins

butter up *vb* (*tr, adverb*) to flatter

butterwort ('bʌtə,wɜːt) *n* a plant of the genus *Pinguicula*, esp *P. vulgaris*, that grows in wet places and has violet-blue spurred flowers and fleshy greasy glandular leaves on which insects are trapped and digested: family *Lentibulariaceae*

buttery[1] ('bʌtərɪ) *adj* **1** containing, like, or coated with butter **2** *informal* grossly or insincerely flattering; obsequious > 'butteriness *n*

buttery[2] ('bʌtərɪ) *n, pl* **-teries 1** a room for storing foods or wines **2** *Brit* (in some universities) a room in which food is supplied or sold to students [c14 from Anglo-French *boterie*, from Anglo-Latin *buteria*, probably from *butta* cask, BUTT[4]]

butt hinge *n* a hinge made of two matching leaves, one recessed into a door and the other into the jamb so that they are in contact when the door is shut. sometimes shortened to: **butt**

butt joint *n* a joint between two plates, planks, bars, sections, etc, when the components are butted together and do not overlap or interlock. The joint may be strapped with jointing plates laid across it or welded (**butt weld**). Sometimes shortened to: **butt**

buttock ('bʌtək) *n* **1** either of the two large fleshy masses of thick muscular tissue that form the human rump. See also **gluteus**. Related adjectives: **gluteal, natal 2** the analogous part in some mammals [c13 perhaps from Old English *buttuc* round slope, diminutive of *butt* (unattested) strip of land; see BUTT[1] -OCK]

buttock-clenching *adj informal* making one tighten the buttocks through extreme fear or embarrassment: *buttock-clenching embarrassment*

button ('bʌtən) *n* **1** a disc or knob of plastic, wood, etc, attached to a garment, etc, usually for fastening two surfaces together by passing it through a buttonhole or loop **2** a small round object, such as any of various sweets, decorations, or badges **3** a small disc that completes an electric circuit when pushed, as one that operates

a doorbell or machine **4** a symbolic representation of a button on the screen of a computer that is notionally depressed by manipulating the mouse to initiate an action **5** *biology* any rounded knoblike part or organ, such as an unripe mushroom **6** *fencing* the protective knob fixed to the point of a foil **7** a small amount of metal, usually lead, with which gold or silver is fused, thus concentrating it during assaying **8** the piece of a weld that pulls out during the destructive testing of spot welds **9** *rowing* a projection around the loom of an oar that prevents it slipping through the rowlock **10** *Brit* an object of no value (esp in the phrase **not worth a button**) **11** *slang* intellect; mental capacity (in such phrases as **a button short, to have all one's buttons**, etc) **12 on the button** *informal* exactly; precisely ▷ *vb* **13** to fasten with a button or buttons **14** (*tr*) to provide with buttons **15** (*tr*) *fencing* to hit (an opponent) with the button of one's foil **16 button (up) one's lip** *or* **mouth** to stop talking: often imperative ▷ See also **buttons, button up** [c14 from Old French *boton*, from *boter* to thrust, butt, of Germanic origin; see BUTT[3]] > 'buttoner *n* > 'buttonless *adj* > 'buttony *adj*

buttonball ('bʌtən,bɔːl) *n US and Canadian* a North American plane tree, *Platanus occidentalis*. See **plane tree**

button-down *adj* **1** (of a collar) having points that are fastened to the garment with buttons **2** (of a shirt) having a button-down collar **3** Also: **buttoned-down** conventional or conservative: *a button-down corporate culture*

buttonhole ('bʌtən,həʊl) *n* **1** a slit in a garment, etc, through which a button is passed to fasten two surfaces together **2** a flower or small bunch of flowers worn pinned to the lapel or in the buttonhole, esp at weddings, formal dances, etc. US name: **boutonniere** ▷ *vb* (*tr*) **3** to detain (a person) in conversation **4** to make buttonholes in **5** to sew with buttonhole stitch

buttonhole stitch *n* a reinforcing looped stitch for the edge of material, such as around a buttonhole

buttonhook ('bʌtən,hʊk) *n* a thin tapering hooked instrument formerly used for pulling buttons through the buttonholes of gloves, shoes, etc

buttonmould ('bʌtən,məʊld) *n* the small core of plastic, wood, or metal that is the base for buttons covered with fabric, leather, etc

button quail *n* any small quail-like terrestrial bird of the genus *Turnix*, such as *T. sylvatica* (striped button quail), occurring in tropical and subtropical regions of the Old World: family *Turnicidae*, order *Gruiformes* (cranes, rails, etc). Also called: **hemipode**

buttons ('bʌtənz) *n* (*functioning as singular*) *Brit informal* a page boy

button-through *adj* (of a dress or skirt) fastened with buttons from top to hem

button tow *n* a kind of ski lift for one person consisting of a pole that has a circular plate at the bottom and is attached to a moving cable. The person places the pole between his or her legs so that the plate takes his or her weight

button up *vb* (*tr, adverb*) **1** to fasten (a garment) with a button or buttons **2** *informal* to conclude (business) satisfactorily **3 buttoned up** *slang* taciturn; silent and somewhat tense

buttonwood ('bʌtən,wʊd) *or* **button tree** *n* **1** Also called: **buttonball** a North American plane tree, *Platanus occidentalis*. See **plane tree 2** a small West Indian tree, *Conocarpus erectus*, with button-like fruits and heavy hard compact wood: family *Combretaceae*

butt plate *n* a plate made usually of metal and attached to the butt end of a gunstock

buttress ('bʌtrɪs) *n* **1** Also called: **pier** a construction, usually of brick or stone, built to support a wall. See also **flying buttress 2** any support or prop **3** something shaped like a buttress, such as a projection from a mountainside **4** either of the two pointed rear parts of a horse's hoof ▷ *vb* (*tr*) **5** to support (a wall) with a buttress **6** to support or sustain [c13 from Old French *bouterez*, short for *ars bouterez* thrusting arch, from *bouter* to thrust, BUTT³]

buttress root *n* a tree root that extends above ground as a platelike outgrowth of the trunk supporting the tree. Buttress roots are mainly found in trees of tropical rain forests

buttress thread *n* a screw thread having one flank that is vertical while the other is inclined, and a flat top and bottom: used in machine tools and designed to withstand heavy thrust in one direction

butt shaft *n* a blunt-headed unbarbed arrow

butt weld *n* See **butt joint**

butty¹ ('bʌtɪ) *n, pl* **-ties** *chiefly Northern English dialect* a sandwich: *a jam butty* [c19 from *buttered* (bread)]

butty² ('bʌtɪ) *n, pl* **-ties** *English dialect* (esp in mining parlance) a friend or workmate [c19 perhaps from obsolete *booty* sharing, from BOOT², later applied to a middleman in a mine]

Butung ('buːtʊŋ) *n* an island of Indonesia, southeast of Sulawesi: hilly and forested. Chief town: Baubau. Pop: 317 124 (latest est). Area: 4555 sq km (1759 sq miles)

butut (buˈtʊt) *n* a Gambian monetary unit worth one hundredth of a dalasi

butyl ('bjuːˌtaɪl, -tɪl) *n* (*modifier*) of, consisting of, or containing any of four isomeric forms of the group C_4H_9-: *butyl rubber* [c19 from BUT(YRIC ACID) + -YL]

butyl acetate *n* a colourless liquid with a fruity odour, existing in four isomeric forms. Three of the isomers are important solvents for cellulose lacquers. Formula: $CH_3COOC_4H_9$

butyl alcohol *n* another name for **butanol**

butylene ('bjuːtɪˌliːn) *n* another name for **butene**

butyl rubber *n* a copolymer of isobutene and isoprene, used in tyres and as a waterproofing material

butyraceous (ˌbjuːtɪˈreɪʃəs) *adj* of, containing, or resembling butter [c17 *butyr-*, from Latin *būtyrum* BUTTER + -ACEOUS]

butyraldehyde (ˌbjuːtɪˈrældɪˌhaɪd) *n* a colourless flammable pungent liquid used in the manufacture of resins. Formula: $CH_3(CH_2)_2CHO$ [c20 from BUTYR(IC ACID) + ALDEHYDE]

butyrate ('bjuːtɪˌreɪt) *n* any salt or ester of butyric acid, containing the monovalent group C_3H_7COO- or ion $C_3H_7COO^-$

butyric acid (bjuːˈtɪrɪk) *n* a carboxylic acid existing in two isomeric forms, one of which produces the smell in rancid butter. Its esters are used in flavouring. Formula: $C_3(CH_2)_2COOH$ [c19 *butyric*, from Latin *būtyrum* BUTTER]

butyrin ('bjuːtɪrɪn) *n* a colourless liquid ester or oil found in butter. It is formed from butyric acid and glycerine [c20 from BUTYR(IC ACID + GLYCER)IN(E)]

buxom ('bʌksəm) *adj* **1** (esp of a woman) healthily plump, attractive, and vigorous **2** (of a woman) full-bosomed [c12 *buhsum* compliant, pliant, from Old English *būgan* to bend, BOW¹; related to Middle Dutch *būchsam* pliant, German *biegsam*] > 'buxomly *adv* > 'buxomness *n*

Buxton ('bʌkstən) *n* a town in N England, in NW Derbyshire in the Peak District: thermal springs. Pop: 20 836 (2001)

buy (baɪ) *vb* **buys, buying, bought** (mainly *tr*) **1** to acquire by paying or promising to pay a sum of money or the equivalent; purchase **2** to be capable of purchasing: *money can't buy love* **3** to acquire by any exchange or sacrifice: *to buy time by equivocation* **4** (*intr*) to act as a buyer **5** to bribe or corrupt; hire by or as by bribery **6** *slang* to accept as true, practical, etc **7** (*intr*; foll by *into*) to purchase shares of (a company): *we bought into General Motors* **8** (*tr*) *theol* (esp of Christ) to ransom or redeem (a Christian or the soul of a Christian) **9** have bought it *slang* to be killed ▷ *n* **10** a

purchase (often in the phrases **good** or **bad buy**) ▷ See also **buy in, buy into, buy off, buy out, buy up** [Old English *bycgan*; related to Old Norse *byggja* to let out, lend, Gothic *bugjan* to buy]

  USAGE The use of *off* after *buy* as in *I bought this off my neighbour* was formerly considered incorrect, but is now acceptable in informal contexts

buy-back ('baɪˌbæk) *n* *commerce* the repurchase by a company of some or all of its shares from an investor, who acquired them by putting venture capital into the company when it was formed

buyer ('baɪə) *n* **1** a person who buys; purchaser; customer **2** a person employed to buy merchandise, materials, etc, as for a shop or factory

buyers' market *n* a market in which supply exceeds demand and buyers can influence prices

buy in *vb* (*adverb*) **1** (*tr*) to buy back for the owner (an item in an auction) at or below the reserve price **2** (*intr*) to purchase shares in a company **3** (*intr*) to buy goods or securities on the open market against a defaulting seller, charging this seller with any market differences **4** (*tr*) Also: **buy into** *US informal* to pay money to secure a position or place for (someone, esp oneself) in some organization, esp a business or club **5** to purchase (goods, etc) in large quantities: *to buy in for the winter* ▷ *n* **buy-in 6** the purchase of a company by a manager or group who does not work for that company

buy into *vb* (*intr, preposition*) **1** to agree with or accept as valid (an argument, theory, etc) **2** *Austral and NZ informal* to get involved in (an argument, fight, etc)

buy off *vb* (*tr, adverb*) to pay (a person or group) to drop a charge, end opposition, relinquish a claim, etc

buy out *vb* (*tr, adverb*) **1** to purchase the ownership, controlling interest, shares, etc, of (a company, etc) **2** to gain the release of (a person) from the armed forces by payment of money **3** to pay (a person) once and for all to give up (property, interest, etc) ▷ *n* **buyout 4** the purchase of a company, esp by its former management or staff. See also **leveraged buyout, management buyout**

Buys Ballot's Law (baɪs bəˈlɒts, bɔɪs) *n* a law stating that if an observer stands with his back to the wind in the N hemisphere, atmospheric pressure is lower on his left, and vice versa in the S hemisphere [named after C. H. D. *Buys Ballot* (1817–90), Dutch meteorologist]

buy-to-let *n* (*modifier*) of or relating to the practice of buying a property to let to tenants rather than to live in onself: *the buy-to-let boom*

buy up *vb* (*tr, adverb*) **1** to purchase all, or all that is available, of (something) **2** *commerce* to purchase a controlling interest in (a company, etc), as by the acquisition of shares

buzkashi (ˌbuzˈkæʃɪ) *n* a game played in Afghanistan, in which opposing teams of horsemen strive for possession of the headless carcass of a goat

buzz (bʌz) *n* **1** a rapidly vibrating humming sound, as that of a prolonged *z* or of a bee in flight **2** a low sound, as of many voices in conversation **3** a rumour; report; gossip **4** *informal* a telephone call: *I'll give you a buzz* **5** *slang* **a** a pleasant sensation, as from a drug such as cannabis **b** a sense of excitement; kick ▷ *vb* **6** (*intr*) to make a vibrating sound like that of a prolonged *z* **7** (*intr*) to talk or gossip with an air of excitement or urgency: *the town buzzed with the news* **8** (*tr*) to utter or spread (a rumour) **9** (*intr*; often foll by *about*) to move around quickly and busily; bustle **10** (*tr*) to signal or summon with a buzzer **11** (*tr*) *informal* to call by telephone **12** (*tr*) *informal* **a** to fly an aircraft very low over (an object): *to buzz a ship* **b** to fly an aircraft at high speed very close to or across the path of (another aircraft), esp to warn or intimidate **13** (*tr*) (esp of insects) to make a buzzing sound with (wings, etc) ▷ See also **buzz in**

[c16 of imitative origin] > 'buzzing *n, adj*

buzzard ('bʌzəd) *n* **1** any diurnal bird of prey of the genus *Buteo*, typically having broad wings and tail and a soaring flight: family *Accipitridae* (hawks, etc). See **honey buzzard**. Compare **turkey buzzard 2** a mean or cantankerous person [c13 from Old French *buisard*, variant of *buison* buzzard, from Latin *būteō* hawk, falcon]

buzz bomb *n* another name for the **V-1** [c20 from the sound of its engine]

buzzer ('bʌzə) *n* **1** a person or thing that buzzes **2** a device that produces a buzzing sound, esp one similar to an electric bell without a hammer or gong **3** NZ a wood planing machine

buzz in *vb* (*tr, adverb*) *informal* to admit (someone) to a building by activating an electronically-controlled door

buzz off *vb* (*intr, adverb; often imperative*) *informal, chiefly Brit* to go away; leave; depart

buzz phrase *n* *informal* a phrase that comes into vogue in the same way as a buzz word

buzz saw *n* *US and Canadian* a power-operated circular saw

buzz word *n* *informal* a word, often originating in a particular jargon, that becomes a vogue word in the community as a whole or among a particular group

bv *the internet domain name for* Bouvet Island

BV *abbreviation for* **1** Beata Virgo **2** bene vale [(for sense 1) Latin: Blessed Virgin; (for sense 2) Latin: farewell]

BVA *abbreviation for* British Veterinary Association

BVM *abbreviation for* Beata Virgo Maria [Latin: Blessed Virgin Mary]

bw *the internet domain name for* Botswana

BW *abbreviation for* biological warfare

B/W *photog abbreviation for* black and white

bwana ('bwɑːnə) *n* (in E Africa) a master, often used as a respectful form of address corresponding to *sir* [Swahili, from Arabic *abūna* our father]

BWD *text messaging abbreviation for* backward

BWG *abbreviation for* Birmingham Wire Gauge: a notation for the diameters of metal rods, ranging from 0 (0.340 inch) to 36 (0.004 inch)

BWR *abbreviation for* boiling-water reactor

BWV (*preceding a number*) *music abbreviation for* Bach Werke-Verzeichnis: indicating the serial number in the catalogue of the works of J. S. Bach made by Wolfgang Schmieder (born 1901), published in 1950

bx *abbreviation for* box

by (baɪ) *prep* **1** used to indicate the agent after a passive verb: *seeds eaten by the birds* **2** used to indicate the person responsible for a creative work: *this song is by Schubert* **3** via; through: *enter by the back door* **4** followed by a gerund to indicate a means used: *he frightened her by hiding behind the door* **5** beside; next to; near: *a tree by the house* **6** passing the position of; past: *he drove by the cottage* **7** not later than; before: *return the books by Tuesday* **8** used to indicate extent, after a comparative: *it is hotter by five degrees than it was yesterday* **9** (esp in oaths) invoking the name of: *I swear by all the gods* **10** multiplied by: *four by three equals twelve* **11** (in habitual sentences) during the passing of (esp in the phrases **by day, by night**) **12** placed between measurements of the various dimensions of something: *a plank fourteen inches by seven* ▷ *adv* **13** near: *the house is close by* **14** away; aside: *he put some money by each week for savings* **15** passing a point near something; past: *he drove by* **16** *Scot* past; over and done with: *that's a' by now* **17** *Scot* aside; behind one: *you must put that by you* ▷ *n*, *pl* **byes 18** a variant spelling of **bye** [Old English *bī*; related to Gothic *bi*, Old High German *bī*, Sanskrit *abhi* to, towards]

by *the internet domain name for* Belarus

by- or **bye-** *prefix* **1** near: *bystander* **2** secondary or incidental: *by-effect; by-election; by-path; by-product* [from BY]

by and by *adv* **1** presently or eventually ▷ *n*

by-and-by 2 *US and Canadian* a future time or occasion

by and large *adv* in general; on the whole [c17 originally nautical (meaning: to the wind and off it)]

by-bidder *n* a bidder at an auction who bids up the price of an item for the benefit of a seller

by-blow *n* **1** a passing or incidental blow **2** an archaic word for a **bastard**

by-catch *n* unwanted fish and other sea animals caught in a fishing net along with the desired kind of fish

byde (baɪd) *vb Scot* a variant spelling of **bide**

Bydgoszcz (*Polish* ˈbɪdɡɔʃtʃ) *n* an industrial city and port in N Poland: under Prussian rule from 1772 to 1919. Pop: 579 000 (2005 est). German name: **Bromberg**

bye¹ (baɪ) *n* **1** *sport* the situation in which a player or team in an eliminatory contest wins a preliminary round by virtue of having no opponent **2** *golf* one or more holes of a stipulated course that are left unplayed after the match has been decided **3** *cricket* a run scored off a ball not struck by the batsman: allotted to the team as an extra and not to the individual batsman. See also **leg bye 4** something incidental or secondary **5 by the bye** incidentally; by the way: used as a sentence connector [c16 a variant of **by**]

bye² *or* **bye-bye** *sentence substitute Brit informal* goodbye

bye-byes *n* (*functioning as singular*) an informal word for **sleep**, used esp in addressing children (as in the phrase **go to bye-byes**)

by-election *or* **bye-election** *n* **1** (in the United Kingdom and other countries of the Commonwealth) an election held during the life of a parliament to fill a vacant seat in the lower chamber **2** (in the US) a special election to fill a vacant elective position with an unexpired term

Byelgorod-Dnestrovski *n* a variant spelling of **Belgorod-Dnestrovski**

Byelorussia *n* a variant spelling of **Belarus**

Byelorussian *adj, n* a variant spelling of **Belarussian**

Byelostok (bjɪlaˈstɔk) *n* a Russian name for **Białystok**

Byelovo *or* **Belovo** (*Russian* ˈbjɛləvə) *n* a city in W central Russia. Pop: 65 000 (2005 est)

by-form *n* a subsidiary or variant form

bygone (ˈbaɪˌɡɒn) *adj* **1** (*usually prenominal*) past; former ▷ *n* **2** (*often plural*) a past occurrence **3** (*often plural*) an artefact, implement, etc, of former domestic or industrial use, now often collected for interest **4 let bygones be bygones** to agree to forget past quarrels

byke (bəɪk, baɪk) *n Scot* a variant spelling of **bike²**

bylane (ˈbaɪˌleɪn) *n* a side lane or alley off a road

bylaw *or* **bye-law** (ˈbaɪˌlɔː) *n* **1** a rule made by a local authority for the regulation of its affairs or management of the area it governs **2** a regulation of a company, society, etc **3** a subsidiary law [c13 probably of Scandinavian origin; compare Old Norse *bȳr* dwelling, town; see **BOWER¹, LAW¹**]

by-line *n* **1** *journalism* a line under the title of a newspaper or magazine article giving the author's name **2** *soccer* another word for **touchline**

by-numbers *adj informal* done in an uninspired, simplistic, or formulaic way [c20 from *painting by numbers*, a method of painting a picture in which the colours to be used are indicated by numbers]

BYO *n Austral and NZ* an unlicensed restaurant at which diners may drink their own wine, etc [c20 from the phrase *bring your own*]

BYOB *abbreviation for* **1** bring your own beer **2** bring your own booze **3** bring your own bottle

bypass (ˈbaɪˌpɑːs) *n* **1** a main road built to avoid a city or other congested area **2** any system of pipes or conduits for redirecting the flow of a liquid **3** a means of redirecting the flow of a substance around an appliance through which it would otherwise pass **4** *surgery* **a** the redirection of blood flow, either to avoid a diseased blood vessel or in order to perform heart surgery. See **coronary bypass b** (*as modifier*): *bypass surgery* **5** *electronics* **a** an electrical circuit, esp one containing a capacitor, connected in parallel around one or more components, providing an alternative path for certain frequencies **b** (*as modifier*): *a bypass capacitor* ▷ *vb* **-passes, -passing, -passed** *or* **-past** (*tr*) **6** to go around or avoid (a city, obstruction, problem, etc) **7** to cause (traffic, fluid, etc) to go through a bypass **8** to proceed without reference to (regulations, a superior, etc); get round; avoid

bypass engine *n* a gas turbine in which a part of the compressor delivery bypasses the combustion zone, flowing directly into or around the main exhaust gas flow to provide additional thrust. Compare **turbofan**

bypass ratio *n aeronautics* the ratio of the amount of air that bypasses the combustion chambers of an aircraft gas turbine to that passing through them

bypath (ˈbaɪˌpɑːθ) *n* a little-used path or track, esp in the country

by-play *n* secondary action or talking carried on apart while the main action proceeds, esp in a play

by-product *n* **1** a secondary or incidental product of a manufacturing process **2** a side effect

Byrd Land *n* a part of Antarctica, east of the Ross Ice Shelf and the Ross Sea: claimed for the US by Admiral Richard E. Byrd in 1929, though all claims are suspended under the Antarctic Treaty of 1959. Former name: **Marie Byrd Land**

byre (baɪə) *n Brit* a shelter for cows [Old English *bȳre*; related to *būr* hut, cottage; see **BOWER¹**]

byrnie (ˈbɜːnɪ) *n* an archaic word for **coat of mail** [Old English *byrne*; related to Old Norse *brynja*, Gothic *brunjō*, Old High German *brunnia* coat of mail, Old Irish *bruinne* breast]

byroad (ˈbaɪˌrəʊd) *n* a secondary or side road

Byronic (baɪˈrɒnɪk) *adj* **1** of or relating to **George Gordon**, 6th Baron Byron, the British Romantic poet (1788–1824) **2** dark and romantically brooding ▷ **By'ronically** *adv* ▷ **'Byron,ism** *n*

byssinosis (ˌbɪsɪˈnəʊsɪs) *n* a lung disease caused by prolonged inhalation of fibre dust in textile factories [c19 from New Latin, from Greek *bussinos* of linen (see **BYSSUS**) + **-OSIS**]

byssus (ˈbɪsəs) *n, pl* **byssuses** *or* **byssi** (ˈbɪsaɪ) a mass of strong threads secreted by a sea mussel or similar mollusc that attaches the animal to a hard fixed surface [c17 from Latin, from Greek *bussos* linen, flax, ultimately of Egyptian origin]

bystander (ˈbaɪˌstændə) *n* a person present but not involved; onlooker; spectator

bystreet (ˈbaɪˌstriːt) *n* an obscure or secondary street

byte (baɪt) *n computing* **1** a group of bits, usually eight, processed as a single unit of data **2** the storage space in a memory or other storage device that is allocated to such a group of bits **3** a subdivision of a word [c20 probably a blend of **BIT⁴** + **BITE**]

Bytom (*Polish* ˈbɪtɔm) *n* an industrial city in SW Poland, in Upper Silesia: under Prussian and German rule from 1742 to 1945. Pop: 205 560 (1999 est). German name: **Beuthen**

byway (ˈbaɪˌweɪ) *n* **1** a secondary or side road, esp in the country **2** an area, field of study, etc, that is very obscure or of secondary importance

byword (ˈbaɪˌwɜːd) *n* **1** a person, place, or thing regarded as a perfect or proverbial example of something: *their name is a byword for good service* **2** an object of scorn or derision **3** a common saying; proverb [Old English *bȳwyrde*; see **BY, WORD**; compare Old High German *pīwurti*, from Latin *prōverbium* proverb]

by-your-leave *n* a request for permission (esp in the phrase **without so much as a by-your-leave**)

Byzantine (bɪˈzænˌtaɪn, -ˌtiːn, baɪ-, ˈbɪzənˌtiːn, -ˌtaɪn) *adj* **1** of, characteristic of, or relating to Byzantium or the Byzantine Empire **2** of, relating to, or characterizing the Orthodox Church or its rites and liturgy **3** of or relating to the highly coloured stylized form of religious art developed in the Byzantine Empire **4** of or relating to the style of architecture developed in the Byzantine Empire, characterized by massive domes with square bases, rounded arches, spires and minarets, and the extensive use of mosaics **5** denoting the Medieval Greek spoken in the Byzantine Empire **6** (of attitudes, etc) inflexible or complicated ▷ *n* **7** an inhabitant of Byzantium ▷ **Byzantinism** (bɪˈzæntaɪˌnɪzəm, -ti-, baɪ-, ˈbɪzəntɪˌnɪzəm, -taɪ-) *n*

Byzantine Church *n* another name for the **Orthodox Church**

Byzantine Empire *n* the continuation of the Roman Empire in the East, esp after the deposition of the last emperor in Rome (476 AD). It was finally extinguished by the fall of Constantinople, its capital, in 1453. See also **Eastern Roman Empire**

Byzantium (bɪˈzæntɪəm, baɪ-) *n* an ancient Greek city on the Bosporus: founded about 660 BC; rebuilt by Constantine I in 330 AD and called Constantinople; present-day Istanbul

bz *the internet domain name for* Belize

Bz *or* **Bz.** *abbreviation for* benzene

Cc

c or **C** (siː) *n, pl* **c's, C's** or **Cs 1** the third letter and second consonant of the modern English alphabet **2** a speech sound represented by this letter, in English usually either a voiceless alveolar fricative, as in *cigar,* or a voiceless velar stop, as in *case* **3** the third in a series, esp the third highest grade in an examination **4 a** something shaped like a C **b** (*in combination*): *a C-spring*

c *symbol for* **1** centi- **2** cubic **3** cycle **4** *maths* constant **5** specific heat capacity **6** the speed of light and other types of electromagnetic radiation in a vacuum **7** *chess* See **algebraic notation**

C *symbol for* **1** *music* **a** a note having a frequency of 261.63 hertz (**middle C**) or this value multiplied or divided by any power of 2; the first degree of a major scale containing no sharps or flats (**C major**) **b** a key, string, or pipe producing this note **c** the major or minor key having this note as its tonic **d** a time signature denoting four crotchet beats to the bar. See also **alla breve** (sense 2), **common time 2** *chem* carbon **3** *biochem* cytosine **4** capacitance **5** heat capacity **6** cold (water) **7** *physics* compliance **8** Celsius **9** centigrade **10** century: *C20* **11** coulomb **12** *the Roman numeral for* 100. See **Roman numerals 13** *international car registration for* Cuba ▷ *n* **14** a computer programming language combining the advantages of a high-level language with the ability to address the computer at a level comparable with that of an assembly language

c. *abbreviation for* **1** carat **2** *cricket* caught **3** cent(s) **4** century or centuries **5** (used esp preceding a date) circa: *c. 1800* [(for sense 5) Latin: *about*]

C. *abbreviation for* **1** (on maps as part of name) Cape **2** Catholic **3** Celtic **4** Conservative **5** Corps

c/- *Austral* (in addresses) *abbreviation for* care of

C- (of US military aircraft) *abbreviation for* cargo transport: *C-5*

(c) *symbol for* copyright

C1 *n* **a** a person whose job is supervisory or clerical, or who works in junior management **b** (*as adjective*): *C1 worker* ▷ See also **occupation groupings**

C2 *n* **a** a skilled manual worker, or a manual worker with responsibility for other people **b** (*as adjective*): *C2 worker* ▷ See also **occupation groupings**

C3 or **C-3** *adj* **1** in poor health or having a poor physique **2** *informal* inferior; worthless. ▷ Compare **A1**

C4 *n US* a type of plastic explosive [C20 from *C(omposition)* 4]

ca *the internet domain name for* Canada

Ca *the chemical symbol for* calcium

CA *abbreviation for* **1** California **2** Central America **3** chartered accountant **4** chief accountant **5** consular agent **6** (in Britain) Consumers' Association

ca. *abbreviation for* circa [Latin: *about*]

C/A *abbreviation for* **1** capital account **2** credit account **3** current account

caa¹ or **ca'** (kɔː) *vb, n* a Scot word for **call**

caa² or **ca'** (kɔː) *vb Scot* **1** to drive or propel **2** to knock **3** caa *or* ca' canny to proceed cautiously; go slow **4** caa *or* ca' the feet frae to send (a person) sprawling [see CAA¹]

CAA (in Britain) *abbreviation for* Civil Aviation Authority

Caaba (ˈkɑːbə) *n* a variant spelling of **Kaaba**

cab¹ (kæb) *n* **1 a** a taxi **b** (*as modifier*): *a cab rank* **2** the enclosed compartment of a lorry, locomotive, crane, etc, from which it is driven or operated **3** (formerly) a light horse-drawn vehicle used for public hire **4** first cab off the rank *Austral informal* the first person, etc, to do or take advantage of something [C19 shortened from CABRIOLET]

cab² or **kab** (kæb) *n* an ancient Hebrew measure equal to about 2.3 litres (4 pints) [C16 from Hebrew *qabh* container, something hollowed out]

CAB *abbreviation for* **1** (in Britain) Citizens' Advice Bureau **2** (in the US) Civil Aeronautics Board

cabal (kəˈbæl) *n* **1** a small group of intriguers, esp one formed for political purposes **2** a secret plot, esp a political one; conspiracy; intrigue **3** a secret or exclusive set of people; clique ▷ *vb* -bals, -balling, -balled (*intr*) **4** to form a cabal; conspire; plot [C17 from French *cabale,* from Medieval Latin *cabala;* see CABBALA]

Cabal (kəˈbæl) *n* the *English history* a group of ministers of Charles II that governed from 1667–73: consisting of Clifford, Ashley, Buckingham, Arlington, and Lauderdale [see CABBALA; by a coincidence, the initials of Charles II's ministers can be arranged to form this word]

cabala (kəˈbɑːlə) *n* a variant spelling of **kabbalah** ▷ cabalism (ˈkæbəˌlɪzəm) *n* ▷ 'cabalist *n* ▷ ˌcaba'listic *adj*

caballero (ˌkæbəˈljɛərəʊ; *Spanish* kaβaˈʎero) *n, pl* -ros (-rəʊz; *Spanish* -ros) **1** a Spanish gentleman **2** a southwestern US word for **horseman** [C19 from Spanish: gentleman, horseman, from Late Latin *caballārius* rider, groom, from *caballus* horse; compare CAVALIER]

cabana (kəˈbɑːnə) *n chiefly US* a tent used as a dressing room by the sea [from Spanish *cabaña:* CABIN]

cabaret (ˈkæbəˌreɪ) *n* **1** a floor show of dancing, singing, or other light entertainment at a nightclub or restaurant **2** *chiefly US* a nightclub or restaurant providing such entertainment [C17 from Norman French: tavern, probably from Late Latin *camera* an arched roof, CHAMBER]

cabbage¹ (ˈkæbɪdʒ) *n* **1** Also called: **cole** any of various cultivated varieties of the plant *Brassica oleracea capitata,* typically having a short thick stalk and a large head of green or reddish edible leaves: family *Brassicaceae* (*crucifers*). See also **brassica, savoy.** Compare **skunk cabbage, Chinese cabbage 2** wild cabbage a European plant, *Brassica oleracea,* with broad leaves and a long spike of yellow flowers: the plant from which the cabbages, cauliflower, broccoli, and Brussels sprout have been bred **3 a** the head of a cabbage **b** the edible

leaf bud of the cabbage palm **4** *informal* a dull or unimaginative person **5** *informal* a person who has no mental faculties and is dependent on others for his or her subsistence [C14 from Norman French *caboche* head; perhaps related to Old French *boce* hump, bump, Latin *caput* head]

cabbage² (ˈkæbɪdʒ) *Brit slang* ▷ *n* **1** snippets of cloth appropriated by a tailor from a customer's material ▷ *vb* **2** to steal; pilfer [C17 of uncertain origin; perhaps related to Old French *cabas* theft]

cabbage bug *n* another name for the **harlequin bug**

cabbage lettuce *n* any of several varieties of lettuce that have roundish flattened heads resembling cabbages

cabbage moth *n* a common brownish noctuid moth, *Mamestra brassicae,* the larva of which is destructive of cabbages and other plants

cabbage palm or **tree** *n* **1** a West Indian palm, *Roystonea* (or *Oreodoxa*) *oleracea,* whose leaf buds are eaten like cabbage **2** a similar Brazilian palm, *Euterpe oleracea* **3** an Australian palm tree, *Livistona australis* **4** any of several plants of the genus *Cordyline,* grown as ornamentals: family *Agavaceae*

cabbage palmetto *n* a tropical American fan palm, *Sabal palmetto,* with edible leaf buds and leaves used in thatching

cabbage root fly *n* a dipterous fly, *Erioischia brassicae,* whose larvae feed on the roots and stems of cabbages and other brassicas: family *Muscidae* (houseflies, etc)

cabbage rose *n* a rose, *Rosa centifolia,* with a round compact full-petalled head

Cabbagetown (ˈkæbɪdʒˌtaʊn) *n* a former slum area of Toronto, now known for its Victorian architecture and thriving arts community

cabbage tree *n* **1** Also called: **ti** a tree, *Cordyline australis,* of New Zealand having a tall branchless trunk and a palmlike top **2** any of several other similar trees of the genus *Cordyline*

cabbage white *n* any large white butterfly of the genus *Pieris,* esp the Eurasian species *P. brassicae,* the larvae of which feed on the leaves of cabbages and related vegetables: family *Pieridae*

cabbageworm (ˈkæbɪdʒˌwɜːm) *n US* any caterpillar that feeds on cabbages, esp that of the cabbage white

cabbala (kəˈbɑːlə) *n* a variant spelling of **kabbalah.** ▷ cabbalism (ˈkæbəˌlɪzəm) *n* ▷ 'cabbalist *n* ▷ ˌcabba'listic *adj*

cabbie or **cabby** (ˈkæbɪ) *n, pl* -bies *informal* a cab driver

CABE (in Britain) *abbreviation for* Commission for Architecture and the Built Environment

caber (ˈkeɪbə, *Scot* ˈkebər) *n Scot* a heavy section of trimmed tree trunk thrown in competition at Highland games (**tossing the caber**) [C16 from Gaelic *cabar* pole]

Cabernet Sauvignon (ˈkæbəneɪ ˈsəʊvɪnjɒn; *French* kabɛrnɛ soviɲɔ̃) *n* (*sometimes not capitals*) **1** a black grape originally grown in the Bordeaux area of

France, and now throughout the wine-producing world **2** any of various red wines made from this grape [French]

cabezon ('kæbɪzɒn) *or* **cabezone** ('kæbɪˌzəʊn) *n* a large food fish, *Scorpaenichthys marmoratus*, of North American Pacific coastal waters, having greenish flesh: family *Cottidae* (bullheads and sea scorpions) [Spanish, from *cabeza* head, ultimately from Latin *caput*]

Cabimas (*Spanish* kaˈβimas) *n* a town in NW Venezuela, on the NE shore of Lake Maracaibo. Pop: 284 000 (2005 est)

cabin ('kæbɪn) *n* **1** a small simple dwelling; hut **2** a simple house providing accommodation for travellers or holiday-makers at a motel or holiday camp **3** a room used as an office or living quarters in a ship **4** a covered compartment used for shelter or living quarters in a small boat **5** (in a warship) the compartment or room reserved for the commanding officer **6** *Brit* another name for **signal box 7 a** the enclosed part of a light aircraft in which the pilot and passengers sit **b** the part of an airliner in which the passengers are carried **c** the section of an aircraft used for cargo ▷ *vb* **8** to confine in a small space [c14 from Old French *cabane*, from Old Provençal *cabana*, from Late Latin *capanna* hut]

cabin boy *n* a boy who waits on the officers and passengers of a ship

cabin class *n* a class of accommodation on a passenger ship between first class and tourist class

cabin cruiser *n* a power boat fitted with a cabin and comforts for pleasure cruising or racing

Cabinda (kəˈbiːndə) *n* an exclave of Angola, separated from the rest of the country by part of the Democratic Republic of Congo (formerly Zaïre). Pop: 174 000 (1993 est). Area: 7270 sq km (2807 sq miles)

cabinet ('kæbɪnɪt) *n* **1 a** a piece of furniture containing shelves, cupboards, or drawers for storage or display **b** (*as modifier*): *cabinet teak* **2** the outer case of a television, radio, etc **3 a** (*often capital*) the executive and policy-making body of a country, consisting of all government ministers or just the senior ministers **b** (*sometimes capital*) an advisory council to a president, sovereign, governor, etc **c** (*as modifier*): *a cabinet reshuffle; a cabinet minister* **4 a** a standard size of paper, 6 × 4 inches (15 × 10 cm) or 6½ × 4¼ inches (16.5 × 10.5 cm), for mounted photographs **b** (*as modifier*): *a cabinet photograph* **5** *printing* an enclosed rack for holding cases of type, etc **6** *archaic* a private room **7** (*modifier*) suitable in size, value, decoration, etc, for a display cabinet: *a cabinet edition of Shakespeare* **8** (*modifier*) (of a drawing or projection of a three-dimensional object) constructed with true horizontal and vertical representation of scale but with oblique distances reduced to about half scale to avoid the appearance of distortion **9** (*modifier*) (of a wine) specially selected and usually rare [c16 from Old French, diminutive of *cabine*, of uncertain origin]

cabinet beetle *n* See dermestid

cabinet-maker *n* a craftsman specializing in the making of fine furniture > **cabinet-ˌmaking** *n*

cabinet pudding *n* a steamed suet pudding containing dried fruit

cabinetwork ('kæbɪnɪtˌwɜːk) *n* **1** the making of furniture, esp of fine quality **2** an article made by a cabinet-maker

cabin fever *n* *chiefly Canadian* acute depression resulting from being isolated or sharing cramped quarters in the wilderness, esp during the long northern winter

cable ('keɪbəl) *n* **1** a strong thick rope, usually of twisted hemp or steel wire **2** *nautical* an anchor chain or rope **3 a** a unit of distance in navigation, equal to one tenth of a sea mile (about 600 feet) **b** Also called: **cable length, cable's length** a unit of length in nautical use that has various values, including 100 fathoms (600 feet)

4 a wire or bundle of wires that conducts electricity: *a submarine cable*. See also **coaxial cable 5** Also called: **overseas** *or* **international telegram cablegram** a telegram sent abroad by submarine cable, radio, communications satellite, or by telephone line **6** See **cable stitch 7** short for **cable television** ▷ *vb* **8** to send (a message) to (someone) by cable **9** (*tr*) to fasten or provide with a cable or cables **10** (*tr*) to supply (a place) with or link (a place) to cable television [c13 from Old Norman French, from Late Latin *capulum* halter]

cable car *n* **1** a cabin suspended from and moved by an overhead cable in a mountain area **2** a cableway **3** a passenger car on a cable railway

cablegram ('keɪbəlˌgræm) *n* a more formal name for **cable** (sense 5)

cable-laid *adj* (of a rope) made of three plain-laid ropes twisted together in a left-handed direction

cable railway *n* a railway on which individual cars are drawn along by a strong cable or metal chain operated by a stationary motor

cable release *n* a short length of flexible cable, used to operate the shutter of a camera without shaking it

cable-stayed bridge *n* a type of suspension bridge in which the supporting cables are connected directly to the bridge deck without the use of suspenders

cable stitch *n* **a** a pattern or series of knitting stitches producing a design like a twisted rope **b** (*as modifier*): *a cable-stitch sweater*. Sometimes shortened to: **cable**

cablet ('keɪblɪt) *n* a small cable, esp a cable-laid rope that has a circumference of less than 25 centimetres (ten inches)

cable television *n* a television service in which programmes are distributed to subscribers' televisions by cable rather than by broadcast transmission

cableway ('keɪbəlˌweɪ) *n* a system for moving people or bulk materials in which suspended cars, buckets, etc, run on cables that extend between terminal towers

cabman ('kæbmən) *n*, *pl* -men the driver of a cab

cabob (kəˈbɒb) *n* a variant of **kebab**

cabochon ('kæbəˌʃɒn; *French* kabɔʃɔ̃) *n* a smooth domed gem, polished but unfaceted [c16 from Old French, from Old Norman French *caboche* head; see CABBAGE¹]

caboodle (kəˈbuːdəl) *n* *informal* a lot, bunch, or group (esp in the phrases **the whole caboodle, the whole kit and caboodle**) [c19 probably contraction of KIT¹ and BOODLE]

caboose (kəˈbuːs) *n* **1** *US informal* short for **calaboose 2** *railways, US and Canadian* a guard's van, esp one with sleeping and eating facilities for the train crew **3** *nautical* **a** a deckhouse for a galley aboard ship or formerly in Canada, on a lumber raft **b** *chiefly Brit* the galley itself **4** *Canadian* **a** a mobile bunkhouse used by lumbermen, etc **b** an insulated cabin on runners, equipped with a stove [c18 from Dutch *cabūse*, of unknown origin]

Cabora Bassa (kəˈbɔːrə ˈbæsə) *n* the site on the Zambezi River in N Mozambique of the largest dam in southern Africa

cabotage ('kæbəˌtɑːʒ) *n* **1** *nautical* coastal navigation or shipping, esp within the borders of one country **2** reservation to a country's carriers of its internal traffic, esp air traffic [c19 from French, from *caboter* to sail near the coast, apparently from Spanish *cabo* CAPE²]

cabover ('kæbˌəʊvə) *adj* of or denoting a truck or lorry in which the cab is over the engine

cab rank rule *n* *Brit* the rule that obliges barristers to take on any client in strict rotation [c20 from the idea of a queue of taxis, each taking the first customer who comes along]

cabretta (kəˈbrɛtə) *n* *chiefly US* a soft leather obtained from the skins of certain South American or African sheep [from Spanish *cabra* she-goat]

cabrilla (kəˈbrɪlə) *n* any of various serranid food fishes, esp *Epinephelus analogus*, occurring in warm seas around Florida and the Caribbean [Spanish, literally: little goat]

cabrio ('kæbrɪˌəʊ) *n* short for **cabriolet**

cabriole ('kæbrɪˌəʊl) *n* **1** Also called: **cabriole leg** a type of furniture leg, popular in the first half of the 18th century, in which an upper convex curve descends tapering to a concave curve **2** *ballet* a leap in the air with one leg outstretched and the other beating against it [c18 from French, from *cabrioler* to caper; from its being based on the leg of a capering animal; see CABRIOLET]

cabriolet (ˌkæbrɪəʊˈleɪ) *n* **1** a small two-wheeled horse-drawn carriage with two seats and a folding hood **2** a former name for a **drophead coupé** [c18 from French, literally: a little skip, from *cabriole*, from Latin *capreolus* wild goat, from *caper* goat; referring to the lightness of movement]

ca'canny (ˌkɔːˈkænɪ) *n* *Scot* **1** moderation or wariness **2 a** a policy of restricting the output of work; a go-slow **b** (*as modifier*): *a ca'canny policy*. ▷ See also **caa²** [c19 literally, *call canny* to drive gently]

cacao (kəˈkɑːəʊ, -ˈkeɪəʊ) *n* **1** a small tropical American evergreen tree, *Theobroma cacao*, having yellowish flowers and reddish-brown seed pods from which cocoa and chocolate are prepared: family *Sterculiaceae* **2** **cacao bean** another name for **cocoa bean 3** **cacao butter** another name for **cocoa butter** [c16 from Spanish, from Nahuatl *cacauatl* cacao beans]

cacciatore (ˌkɑːtʃəˈtɔːrɪ, ˌkætʃ-) *or* **cacciatora** *adj* (*immediately postpositive*) prepared with tomatoes, mushrooms, herbs, and other seasonings [Italian, literally: hunter]

Cáceres (*Spanish* ˈkaθeres) *n* a city in W Spain: held by the Moors (1142–1229). Pop: 87 088 (2003 est)

cachalot ('kæfəˌlɒt) *n* another name for **sperm whale** [c18 from French, from Portuguese *cachalote*, of unknown origin]

cache (kæʃ) *n* **1** a hidden store of provisions, weapons, treasure, etc **2** the place where such a store is hidden **3** *computing* a small high-speed memory that improves computer performance ▷ *vb* **4** (*tr*) to store in a cache [c19 from French, from *cacher* to hide]

cache memory *n* *computing* a small area of memory in a computer that can be accessed very quickly

cachepot ('kæʃˌpɒt, ˌkæʃˈpəʊ) *n* an ornamental container for a flowerpot [French: pot-hider]

cachet ('kæʃeɪ) *n* **1** an official seal on a document, letter, etc **2** a distinguishing mark; stamp **3** prestige; distinction **4** *philately* **a** a mark stamped by hand on mail for commemorative purposes **b** a small mark made by dealers and experts on the back of postage stamps. Compare **overprint** (sense 3), **surcharge** (sense 5) **5** a hollow wafer, formerly used for enclosing an unpleasant-tasting medicine [c17 from Old French, from *cacher* to hide]

cachexia (kəˈkɛksɪə) *or* **cachexy** *n* a generally weakened condition of body or mind resulting from any debilitating chronic disease [c16 from Late Latin from Greek *kakhexia*, from *kakos* bad + *hexis* condition, habit] > **cachectic** (kəˈkɛktɪk) *adj*

cachinnate ('kækɪˌneɪt) *vb* (*intr*) to laugh loudly [c19 from Latin *cacchināre*, probably of imitative origin] > ˌcachin'natory *adj*

cachinnation (ˌkækɪˈneɪʃən) *n* **1** raucous laughter **2** *psychiatry* inappropriate laughter, sometimes found in schizophrenia

cachou ('kæʃuː, kæˈʃuː) *n* **1** a lozenge eaten to sweeten the breath **2** another name for **catechu** [c18 via French from Portuguese, from Malay *kāchu*]

cachucha (kəˈtʃuːtʃə) *n* **1** a graceful Spanish solo dance in triple time **2** music composed for this dance [c19 from Spanish]

cacique (kəˈsiːk) *or* **cazique** (kəˈziːk) *n* **1** Native

American chief in a Spanish-speaking region **2** (esp in Spanish America) a local political boss **3** any of various tropical American songbirds of the genus *Cacicus* and related genera: family *Icteridae* (American orioles) [c16 from Spanish, of Arawak origin; compare Taino *cacique* chief]

caciquism (kə'siːkˌɪzəm) *n* (esp in Spanish America) government by local political bosses

cackermander ('kækəˌmɑːndə) *n Southeast English dialect* a friend

cack-handed (ˌkæk'hændɪd) *adj informal* **1** left-handed **2** clumsy [from dialect *cack* excrement, from the fact that clumsy people usually make a mess; via Middle Low German or Middle Dutch from Latin *cacāre* to defecate]

cackle ('kækəl) *vb* **1** (*intr*) (esp of a hen) to squawk with shrill notes **2** (*intr*) to laugh or chatter raucously **3** (*tr*) to utter in a cackling manner ▷ *n* **4** the noise or act of cackling **5** noisy chatter **6** cut the cackle *informal* to stop chattering; be quiet [c13 probably from Middle Low German *kākelen*, of imitative origin] > 'cackler *n*

cackleberry ('kækəlˌbɛrɪ) *n, pl* -ries a slang word for **egg**

cacky ('kækɪ) *adj informal* cackier, cackiest **1** of or like excrement **2** dirty, worthless, or contemptible [from dialect *cack* excrement]

caco- *combining form* bad, unpleasant, or incorrect: *cacophony* [from Greek *kakos* bad]

cacodemon or **cacodaemon** (ˌkækə'diːmən) *n* an evil spirit or devil [c16 from Greek *kakodaimōn* evil genius]

cacodyl ('kækədaɪl) *n* an oily poisonous liquid with a strong garlic smell; tetramethyldiarsine. Formula: [(CH₃)₂As]₂ [c19 from Greek *kakōdēs* evil-smelling (from *kakos* CACO- + *ozein* to smell) + -YL] > cacodylic (ˌkækə'dɪlɪk) *adj*

cacoepy (kə'kəʊɪpɪ) *n* bad or mistaken pronunciation [c19 from Greek *kakoepeia*] > cacoepistic (kəˌkəʊɪ'pɪstɪk) *adj*

cacoethes (ˌkækəʊ'iːθiːz) *n* an uncontrollable urge or desire, esp for something harmful; mania: *a cacoethes for smoking* [c16 from Latin *cacoēthes* malignant disease, from Greek *kakoēthēs* of an evil disposition, from *kakos* CACO- + *ēthos* character] > cacoethic (ˌkækəʊ'ɛθɪk) *adj*

cacogenics (ˌkækəʊ'dʒɛnɪks) *n* another name for **dysgenics** [c20 from CACO- + EUGENICS] > ˌcaco'genic *adj*

cacography (kæ'kɒɡrəfɪ) *n* **1** bad handwriting. Compare **calligraphy 2** incorrect spelling. Compare **orthography.** > ca'cographer *n* > cacographic (ˌkækə'ɡræfɪk) or ˌcaco'graphical *adj*

cacology (kə'kɒlədʒɪ) *n* a bad choice of words; faulty speech [c17 (in the sense: ill report): from Greek *kakologia*]

cacomistle ('kækəˌmɪsəl) or **cacomixle** ('kækəˌmɪksəl) *n* **1** a catlike omnivorous mammal, *Bassariscus astutus*, of S North America, related to but smaller than the raccoons: family *Procyonidae*, order *Carnivora* (carnivores). It has yellowish-grey fur and a long bushy tail banded in black and white **2** a related smaller animal, *Jentinkia* (or *Bassariscus*) *sumichrasti*, of Central America [c19 from Mexican Spanish, from Nahuatl *tlacomiztli*, from *tlaco* half + *miztli* cougar]

cacophonous (kə'kɒfənəs) or **cacophonic** (ˌkækə'fɒnɪk) *adj* jarring in sound; discordant; harsh > ca'cophonously or ˌcaco'phonically *adv*

cacophony (kə'kɒfənɪ) *n, pl* -nies **1** harsh discordant sound; dissonance **2** the use of unharmonious or dissonant speech sounds in language. ▷ Compare **euphony**

cactoblastis (ˌkæktəʊ'blæstɪs) *n* a moth, *Cactoblastis cactorum*, that was introduced into Australia to act as a biological control on the prickly pear

cactus ('kæktəs) *n, pl* -tuses or -ti (-taɪ) **1** any spiny succulent plant of the family *Cactaceae* of the arid regions of America. Cactuses have swollen tough stems, leaves reduced to spines or scales, and often large brightly coloured flowers **2**

cactus dahlia a double-flowered variety of dahlia [c17 from Latin: prickly plant, from Greek *kaktos* cardoon] > cactaceous (kæk'teɪʃəs) *adj*

cacuminal (kæ'kjuːmɪnəl) *phonetics* ▷ *adj* **1** Also called: **cerebral** relating to or denoting a consonant articulated with the tip of the tongue turned back towards the hard palate ▷ *n* **2** a consonant articulated in this manner [c19 from Latin *cacūmen* point, top]

cad (kæd) *n Brit informal, old-fashioned* a man who does not behave in a gentlemanly manner towards others [c18 shortened from CADDIE] > 'caddish *adj*

CAD *acronym for* computer-aided design

cadaga (kə'dɑːɡə) or **cadagi** (kə'dɑːdʒɪ) *n* a eucalyptus tree, *E. torelliana*, of tropical and subtropical Australia, having a smooth green trunk [of uncertain origin]

cadaster or **cadastre** (kə'dæstə) *n* an official register showing details of ownership, boundaries, and value of real property in a district, made for taxation purposes [c19 from French, from Provençal *cadastro*, from Italian *catastro*, from Late Greek *katastikhon* register, from *kata stikhon* line by line, from *kata* (see CATA-) + *stikhos* line, STICH] > ca'dastral *adj*

cadaver (kə'deɪvə, -'dɑːv-) *n med* a corpse [c16 from Latin, from *cadere* to fall] > ca'daveric *adj*

cadaverine (kə'dævəˌriːn) *n* a toxic diamine with an unpleasant smell, produced by protein hydrolysis during putrefaction of animal tissue. Formula: NH₂(CH₂)₅NH₂

cadaverous (kə'dævərəs) *adj* **1** of or like a corpse, esp in being deathly pale; ghastly **2** thin and haggard; gaunt > ca'daverously *adv* > ca'daverousness *n*

CADCAM ('kædˌkæm) *n acronym for* computer-aided design and manufacture

caddie or **caddy** ('kædɪ) *n, pl* -dies **1** *golf* an attendant who carries clubs, etc, for a player ▷ *vb* -dies, -dying, -died **2** (*intr*) to act as a caddie [c17 (originally: a gentleman learning the military profession by serving in the army without a commission, hence c18 (Scottish): a person looking for employment, an errand-boy): from French CADET]

caddie car or **caddie cart** *n golf* a small light two-wheeled trolley for carrying clubs

caddis or **caddice** ('kædɪs) *n* a type of coarse woollen yarn, braid, or fabric

caddis fly *n* any small mothlike insect of the order *Trichoptera*, having two pairs of hairy wings and aquatic larvae (caddis worms) [c17 of unknown origin]

caddis worm or **caddis** *n* the aquatic larva of a caddis fly, which constructs a protective case around itself made of silk, sand, stones, etc. Also called: **caseworm, strawworm**

Caddoan ('kædəʊən) *n* a family of Native American languages, including Pawnee, formerly spoken in a wide area of the Midwest, and probably distantly related to Siouan

caddy¹ ('kædɪ) *n, pl* -dies *chiefly Brit* a small container, esp for tea [c18 from Malay *kati*; see CATTY²]

caddy² ('kædɪ) *n, pl* -dies, *vb* -dies, -dying, -died a variant spelling of **caddie**

cade¹ (keɪd) *n* a juniper tree, *Juniperus oxycedrus* of the Mediterranean region, the wood of which yields an oily brown liquid (**oil of cade**) used to treat skin ailments [c16 via Old French from Old Provençal, from Medieval Latin *catanus*]

cade² (keɪd) *adj* (of a young animal) left by its mother and reared by humans, usually as a pet [c15 of unknown origin]

-cade *n combining form* indicating a procession of a specified kind: *motorcade* [abstracted from CAVALCADE]

cadelle (kə'dɛl) *n* a widely distributed beetle, *Tenebroides mauritanicus*, that feeds on flour, grain, and other stored foods, as well as on other insects: family *Trogositidae* [French, from Provençal *cadello*,

from Latin *catellus* a little dog]

cadence ('keɪdəns) or **cadency** *n, pl* -dences or -dencies **1** the beat or measure of something rhythmic **2** a fall in the pitch of the voice, as at the end of a sentence **3** modulation of the voice; intonation **4** a rhythm or rhythmic construction in verse or prose; measure **5** the close of a musical phrase or section [c14 from Old French, from Old Italian *cadenza*, literally: a falling, from Latin *cadere* to fall]

cadency ('keɪdənsɪ) *n, pl* -cies **1** the line of descent from a younger member of a family **2** another word for **cadence**

cadent ('keɪdənt) *adj* **1** having cadence; rhythmic **2** *archaic* falling; descending [c16 from Latin *cadēns* falling, from *cadere* to fall]

cadenza (kə'dɛnzə) *n* **1** a virtuoso solo passage occurring near the end of a piece of music, formerly improvised by the soloist but now usually specially composed **2** *South African informal* a fit or convulsion [c19 from Italian; see CADENCE]

cadet (kə'dɛt) *n* **1** a young person undergoing preliminary training, usually before full entry to the uniformed services, police, etc, esp for officer status **2** a school pupil receiving elementary military training in a school corps **3** (in England and in France before 1789) a gentleman, usually a younger son, who entered the army to prepare for a commission **4** a younger son or brother **5** cadet branch the family or family branch of a younger son **6** (in New Zealand) a person learning sheep farming on a sheep station [c17 from French, from dialect (Gascon) *capdet* captain, ultimately from Latin *caput* head] > ca'detship *n*

cadge (kædʒ) *vb* **1** to get (food, money, etc) by sponging or begging ▷ *n* **2** *Brit* a person who cadges **3** on the cadge *Brit informal* engaged in cadging [c17 of unknown origin]

cadger *n* **1** ('kædʒə) *Brit* a person who cadges **2** ('kædʒər) *Scot* a pedlar or carrier

cadi or **kadi** ('kɑːdɪ, 'keɪdɪ) *n, pl* -dis a judge in a Muslim community [c16 from Arabic *qāḍī* judge]

Cádiz (kə'dɪz; *Spanish* 'kaðiθ) *n* a port in SW Spain, on a narrow peninsula that forms the **Bay of Cádiz** at the E end of the **Gulf of Cádiz** founded about 1100 BC as a Phoenician trading colony; centre of trade with America from the 16th to 18th centuries. Pop: 134 989 (2003 est)

Cadmean victory ('kædmɪən) *n* another name for **Pyrrhic victory**

cadmium ('kædmɪəm) *n* a malleable ductile toxic bluish-white metallic element that occurs in association with zinc ores. It is used in electroplating, alloys, and as a neutron absorber in the control of nuclear fission. Symbol: Cd; atomic no.: 48; atomic wt.: 112.411; valency: 2; relative density: 8.65; melting pt.: 321.1°C; boiling pt.: 767°C [c19 from New Latin, from Latin *cadmīa* zinc ore, CALAMINE, referring to the fact that both calamine and cadmium are found in the ore]

cadmium cell *n* **1** a photocell with a cadmium electrode that is especially sensitive to ultraviolet radiation **2** a former name for **Weston standard cell**

cadmium sulphide *n* an orange or yellow insoluble solid used as a pigment in paints, etc (**cadmium yellow**). Formula: CdS

Cadmus ('kædməs) *n Greek myth* a Phoenician prince who killed a dragon and planted its teeth, from which sprang a multitude of warriors who fought among themselves until only five remained, who joined Cadmus to found Thebes > 'Cadmean *adj*

cadre ('kɑːdə) *n* **1** the nucleus of trained professional servicemen forming the basis for the training of new units or other military expansion **2** a basic unit or structure, esp of specialists or experts; nucleus; core **3** a group of revolutionaries or other political activists, esp when taking part in military or terrorist activities **4** a member of a cadre [c19 from French, from Italian *quadro*, from Latin *quadrum* square]

C

caduceus (kə'dju:sɪəs) *n, pl* **-cei** (-sɪ,aɪ) **1** *classical myth* a staff entwined with two serpents and bearing a pair of wings at the top, carried by Hermes (Mercury) as messenger of the gods **2** an insignia resembling this staff used as an emblem of the medical profession. Compare **staff of Aesculapius** [c16 from Latin, from Doric Greek *karukeion*, from *karux* herald]

caducibranchiate (kə,dju:sɪ'bræŋkɪ,eɪt) *adj* (of many amphibians, such as frogs) having gills during one stage of the life cycle only [from Latin *cadūcus* CADUCOUS + BRANCHIA]

caducity (kə'dju:sɪtɪ) *n* **1** perishableness **2** senility [c18 from French, from Latin *cadūcus* CADUCOUS]

caducous (kə'dju:kəs) *adj biology* (of parts of a plant or animal) shed during the life of the organism [c17 from Latin *cadūcus* falling, from *cadere* to fall]

CAE *abbreviation for* **computer-aided engineering**

caecilian (si:'sɪlɪən) *n* any tropical limbless cylindrical amphibian of the order *Apoda* (or *Gymnophiona*), resembling earthworms and inhabiting moist soil [c19 from Latin *caecilia* a kind of lizard, from *caecus* blind]

caecum *or US* **cecum** ('si:kəm) *n, pl* **-ca** (-kə) *anatomy* any structure or part that ends in a blind sac or pouch, esp the pouch that marks the beginning of the large intestine [c18 short for Latin *intestinum caecum* blind intestine, translation of Greek *tuphlon enteron*] ▷ **'caecal** *or US* **'cecal** *adj*

Caelian ('si:lɪən) *n* the southeasternmost of the Seven Hills of Rome

Caelum ('si:ləm) *n, Latin genitive* **Caeli** ('si:laɪ) a small faint constellation in the S hemisphere close to Eridanus [Latin: the sky, heaven]

Caen (kɒŋ; *French* kɑ̃) *n* an industrial city in NW France. Pop: 113 987 (1999)

caenogenesis (,si:nəʊ'dʒɛnɪsɪs), **cainogenesis**, **kainogenesis** *or US* **cenogenesis**, **kenogenesis** *n* the development of structures and organs in an embryo or larva that are adaptations to its way of life and are not retained in the adult form. Compare **recapitulation** (sense 2) ▷ **caenogenetic** (,si:nəʊdʒɪ'nɛtɪk) *or* ,caino'genetic, ,kainoge'netic *or US* ,cenoge'netic, ,kenoge'netic *adj* ▷ ,caenoge'netically, ,cainoge'netically, ,kainoge'netically *or US* ,cenoge'netically *or* ,kenoge'netically *adv*

Caenozoic (,si:nə'zəʊɪk) *adj* a variant spelling of **Cenozoic**

caeoma (si:'əʊmə) *n* an aecium in some rust fungi that has no surrounding membrane [New Latin, from Greek *kaiein* to burn; referring to its glowing colour]

Caerleon (kɑ:'lɪən) *n* a town in SE Wales, in Newport county borough on the River Usk: traditionally the seat of King Arthur's court. Pop: 9392 (2001)

Caernarfon, Caernarvon *or* **Carnarvon** (kɑ:'nɑ:vªn) *n* a port and resort in NW Wales, in Gwynedd on the Menai Strait: 13th-century castle. Pop: 9726 (2001)

Caernarvonshire (kɑ:'nɑ:vªnʃɪə, -ʃə) *n* (until 1974) a county of NW Wales, now part of Gwynedd

Caerphilly (kɛə'fɪlɪ) *n* **1** a market town in SE Wales, in Caerphilly county borough: site of the largest castle in Wales (13th–14th centuries). Pop: 31 060 (2001) **2** a county borough in SE Wales, created in 1996 from parts of Mid Glamorgan and Gwent. Pop: 170 200 (2003 est). Area: 275 sq km (106 sq miles) **3** a creamy white mild-flavoured cheese

caesalpinoid (sɛz'ælpɪn,ɔɪd) *or* **caesalpiniaceous** (,sɛzæl,pɪnɪ'eɪʃəs) *adj* of, relating to, or belonging to the *Caesalpinoideae*, a mainly tropical subfamily of leguminous plants that have irregular flowers: includes carob, senna, brazil, cassia, and poinciana [from New Latin *Caesalpinia* type genus, named after Andrea *Cesalpino* (1519–1603), Italian botanist]

Caesar ('si:zə) *n* **1** any Roman emperor **2** (*sometimes not capital*) any emperor, autocrat, dictator, or other powerful ruler **3** a title of the Roman emperors from Augustus to Hadrian **4** (in the Roman Empire) **a** a title borne by the imperial heir from the reign of Hadrian **b** the heir, deputy, and subordinate ruler to either of the two emperors under Diocletian's system of government [from Gaius Julius Caesar (100–44 BC), Roman general and statesman] **5** short for **Caesar salad**

Caesaraugusta (,si:zərɔ:'ɡʌstə) *n* the Latin name for **Zaragoza**

Caesarea (,si:zə'rɪə) *n* an ancient port in NW Israel, capital of Roman Palestine: founded by Herod the Great

Caesarea Mazaca ('mæzəkə) *n* the ancient name of **Kayseri**

Caesarean, Caesarian *or US* **Cesarean, Cesarian** (sɪ'zɛərɪən) *adj* **1** of or relating to any of the Caesars, esp Julius Caesar (100–44 BC), Roman general, statesman, and historian ▷ *n* **2** (*sometimes not capital*) *surgery* **a** short for **Caesarean section b** (*as modifier*): *Caesarean birth; Caesarean operation*

Caesarean section *n* surgical incision through the abdominal and uterine walls in order to deliver a baby [c17 from the belief that Julius Caesar was so delivered, the name allegedly being derived from *caesus*, past participle of *caedere* to cut]

Caesarism ('si:zə,rɪzəm) *n* an autocratic system of government. See also **Bonapartism**. ▷ **'Caesarist** *n* ▷ ,Caesar'istic *adj*

Caesar salad *n* a salad of lettuce, cheese, and croutons with a dressing of olive oil, garlic, and lemon juice [c20 named after *Caesar* Cardini (1896–1956), Mexican restaurateur who invented it]

caesious *or US* **cesious** ('si:zɪəs) *adj botany* having a waxy bluish-grey coating [c19 from Latin *caesius* bluish grey]

caesium *or US* **cesium** ('si:zɪəm) *n* a ductile silvery-white element of the alkali metal group that is the most electropositive metal. It occurs in pollucite and lepidolite and is used in photocells. The radioisotope **caesium-137**, with a half-life of 30.2 years, is used in radiotherapy. Symbol: Cs; atomic no.: 55; atomic wt.: 132.90543; valency: 1; relative density: 1.873; melting pt.: 28.39±0.01°C; boiling pt.: 671°C

caesium clock *n* a type of atomic clock that uses the frequency of radiation absorbed in changing the spin of electrons in caesium atoms. See also **second²**

caespitose *or US* **cespitose** ('sɛspɪ,təʊs) *adj botany* growing in dense tufts [c19 from New Latin *caespitōsus*, from *caespitem* turf] ▷ **'caespi,tosely** *or US* **'cespi,tosely** *adv*

caesura (sɪ'zjʊərə) *n, pl* **-ras** *or* **-rae** (-ri:) **1** (in modern prosody) a pause, esp for sense, usually near the middle of a verse line. Usual symbol: ‖ **2** (in classical prosody) a break between words within a metrical foot, usually in the third or fourth foot of the line [c16 from Latin, literally: a cutting, from *caedere* to cut] ▷ **cae'sural** *adj*

CAF *abbreviation for* cost and freight

cafard (*French* kafar) *n* a feeling of severe depression [c20 from French, literally: cockroach, hypocrite]

café ('kæfeɪ, 'kæfɪ) *n* **1** a small or inexpensive restaurant or coffee bar, serving light meals and refreshments **2** *South African* a corner shop or grocer [c19 from French: COFFEE]

café au lait *French* (kafe o lɛ) *n* **1** coffee with milk **2** a light brown colour

café-au-lait spot *n* a brown patch on the skin that can occur normally in small numbers or in neurofibromatosis, when they are more numerous

café noir *French* (kafe nwar) *n* black coffee

cafeteria (,kæfɪ'tɪərɪə) *n* a self-service restaurant [c20 from American Spanish: coffee shop]

cafetiere (,kæfə'tjɛə, ,kæfɪ'tɪə) *n* a kind of coffeepot in which boiling water is poured onto ground coffee and a plunger fitted with a metal filter is pressed down, forcing the grounds to the bottom [c20 from French *cafetière* coffeepot]

caff (kæf) *n* a slang word for **café**

caffeinated ('kæfɪ,neɪtəd) *adj* **1 a** with no natural caffeine removed **b** with added caffeine **2** highly stimulated by caffeine

caffeine *or* **caffein** ('kæfi:n, 'kæfɪ,i:n) *n* a white crystalline bitter alkaloid responsible for the stimulant action of tea, coffee, and cocoa: a constituent of many tonics and analgesics. Formula: $C_8H_{10}N_4O_2$. See also **xanthine** (sense 2) [c19 from German *Kaffein*, from *Kaffee* COFFEE]

caftan ('kæf,tæn, -,tɑ:n) *n* a variant spelling of **kaftan**

cag (kæg) *n mountaineering* short for **cagoule**

caganer (*Catalan* kaga'ne) *n* a figure of a squatting defecating person, a traditional character in Catalan Christmas crèche scenes [c20 from Catalan *cagar* shit]

cage (keɪdʒ) *n* **1 a** an enclosure, usually made with bars or wire, for keeping birds, monkeys, mice, etc **b** (*as modifier*): *cagebird* **2** a thing or place that confines or imprisons **3** something resembling a cage in function or structure: *the rib cage* **4** the enclosed platform of a lift, esp as used in a mine **5** *engineering* a skeleton ring device that ensures that the correct amount of space is maintained between the individual rollers or balls in a rolling bearing **6** *informal* the basket used in basketball **7** *informal* the goal in ice hockey **8** *US* a steel framework on which guns are supported **9** **rattle someone's cage** *informal* to upset or anger someone ▷ *vb* **10** (*tr*) to confine in or as in a cage [c13 from Old French, from Latin *cavea* enclosure, from *cavus* hollow]

cageling ('keɪdʒlɪŋ) *n* a bird kept in a cage

cagey *or* **cagy** ('keɪdʒɪ) *adj* **-ier, -iest** *informal* not open or frank; cautious; wary [c20 of unknown origin] ▷ **'cagily** *adv* ▷ **'caginess** *n*

cag-handed (,kæɡ'hændɪd) *adj dialect* a variant of **cack-handed**

Cagliari (kæl'jɑ:rɪ; *Italian* kaʎ'ʎari) *n* a port in Italy, the capital of Sardinia, on the S coast. Pop: 164 249 (2001)

cagmag ('kæɡ,mæɡ) *Midland English dialect* ▷ *adj* **1** done shoddily; left incomplete ▷ *vb* **-mags, -magging, -magged** (*intr*) **2** to chat idly; gossip [c18 of uncertain origin]

cagoule (kə'ɡu:l) *n* a lightweight usually knee-length type of anorak. Also spelt: **kagoul, kagoule**. Sometimes shortened to: **cag** [c20 from French]

cahier *French* (kaje) *n* **1** a notebook **2** a written or printed report, esp of the proceedings of a meeting

Cahokia Mounds (kə'həʊkɪə) *pl n* the largest group of prehistoric Indian earthworks in the US, located northeast of East St Louis

cahoots (kə'hu:ts) *pl n* (*sometimes singular*) *informal* **1** *US* partnership; league (esp in the phrases **go in cahoots with, go cahoot**) **2 in cahoots** in collusion [c19 of uncertain origin]

CAI *abbreviation for* computer-aided instruction

Caiaphas ('kaɪə,fæs) *n New Testament* the high priest at the beginning of John the Baptist's preaching and during the trial of Jesus (Luke 3:2; Matthew 26)

Caicos Islands ('keɪkəs) *pl n* a group of islands in the Caribbean: part of the British dependency of the **Turks and Caicos Islands**

cailleach ('kæljəx) *n Scot* an old woman [Gaelic]

caiman ('keɪmən) *n, pl* **-mans** a variant spelling of **cayman**

cain *or* **kain** (keɪn) *n history* (in Scotland and Ireland) payment in kind, usually farm produce paid as rent [c12 from Scottish Gaelic *cāin* rent, perhaps ultimately from Late Latin *canōn* tribute (see CANON); compare Middle Irish *cāin* law]

Cain (keɪn) *n* **raise Cain a** to cause a commotion **b** to react or protest heatedly [from Cain, the first son of Adam and Eve, who killed his brother Abel

(Genesis 4:1–16), used as a euphemism for hell or the devil]

cainogenesis (ˌkaɪnəʊˈdʒɛnɪsɪs) *n* a variant spelling of **caenogenesis**. ▷ cainogenetic (ˌkaɪnəʊdʒɪˈnɛtɪk) *adj* ▷ ˌcainogeˈnetically *adv*

Cainozoic (ˌkaɪnəʊˈzəʊɪk, ˌkeɪ-) *adj* a variant of **Cenozoic**

caïque (kaɪˈiːk) *n* **1** a long narrow light rowing skiff used on the Bosporus **2** a sailing vessel of the E Mediterranean with a sprit mainsail, square topsail, and two or more jibs or other sails [C17 from French, from Italian *caicco*, from Turkish *kayik*]

caird (kɛəd; *Scot* kerd) *n* *Scot obsolete* a travelling tinker; vagrant [C17 from Scottish Gaelic; related to Welsh *cerdd* craft]

Caird Coast (kɛəd) *n* a region of Antarctica: a part of Coats Land on the SE coast of the Weddell Sea; now included in the British Antarctic Territory (claim suspended under the Antarctic Treaty of 1959)

Cairene (ˈkaɪriːn) *adj* **1** of or relating to Cairo or its inhabitants ▷ *n* **2** a native or inhabitant of Cairo

cairn (kɛən) *n* **1** a mound of stones erected as a memorial or marker **2** Also called: **cairn terrier** a small rough-haired breed of terrier originally from Scotland [C15 from Gaelic *carn*]

cairngorm (ˈkɛənˌɡɔːm, ˌkɛənˈɡɔːm) *n* a smoky yellow, grey, or brown variety of quartz, used as a gemstone. Also called: **smoky quartz** [C18 from *Cairn Gorm* (literally: blue cairn), mountain in Scotland where it is found]

Cairngorm Mountains *pl n* a mountain range of NE Scotland: part of the Grampians. Highest peak: Ben Macdui, 1309 m (4296 ft); designated a national park in 2003. Also called: **the Cairngorms**

Cairns (kænz, kɛənz) *n* a port in NE Australia, in Queensland. Pop: 98 981 (2001)

Cairo (ˈkaɪrəʊ) *n* the capital of Egypt, on the Nile: the largest city in Africa and in the Middle East; industrial centre; site of the university and mosque of Al Azhar (founded in 972). Pop: 11 146 000 (2005 est). Arabic name: El Qahira (ɛl ˈkahiːrɔ) ▷ ˈCairene *n, adj*

caisson (kəˈsuːn, ˈkeɪsən) *n* **1** a watertight chamber open at the bottom and containing air under pressure, used to carry out construction work under water **2** a similar unpressurized chamber **3** a watertight float filled with air, used to raise sunken ships. See also **camel** (sense 2) **4** a watertight structure placed across the entrance of a basin, dry dock, etc, to exclude water from it **5 a** a box containing explosives, formerly used as a mine **b** an ammunition chest **c** a two-wheeled vehicle containing an ammunition chest **6** another name for **coffer** (sense 3) [C18 from French, assimilated to *caisse* CASE²]

caisson disease *n* another name for **decompression sickness**

Caithness (keɪθˈnɛs, ˈkeɪθnɛs) *n* (until 1975) a county of NE Scotland, now part of Highland

caitiff (ˈkeɪtɪf) *archaic or poetic* ▷ *n* **1** a cowardly or base person ▷ *adj* **2** cowardly; base [C13 from Old French *caitif* prisoner, from Latin *captīvus* CAPTIVE]

cajeput (ˈkædʒəˌpʊt) *n* a variant spelling of **cajuput**

cajole (kəˈdʒəʊl) *vb* to persuade (someone) by flattery or pleasing talk to do what one wants; wheedle; coax [C17 from French *cajoler* to coax, of uncertain origin] ▷ caˈjolement *n* ▷ caˈjoler *n* ▷ caˈjolery *n* ▷ caˈjolingly *adv*

Cajun (ˈkeɪdʒən) *n* **1** a native of Louisiana descended from 18th-century Acadian immigrants **2** the dialect of French spoken by such people **3** the music of this ethnic group, combining blues and European folk music ▷ *adj* **4** denoting, relating to, or characteristic of such people, their language, or their music [C19 alteration of ACADIAN; compare *Injun* for *Indian*]

cajuput or **cajeput** (ˈkædʒəˌpʊt) *n* **1** a small myrtaceous tree or shrub, *Melaleuca leucadendron,*

native to the East Indies and Australia, with whitish flowers and leaves **2** a green aromatic oil derived from this tree, used to treat skin diseases **3** a lauraceous tree, *Umbellularia californica,* whose aromatic leaves are used in medicine [C18 from Malay *kayu puteh,* from *kayu* wood + *puteh* white]

cake (keɪk) *n* **1** a baked food, usually in loaf or layer form, typically made from a mixture of flour, sugar, and eggs **2** a flat thin mass of bread, esp unleavened bread **3** a shaped mass of dough or other food of similar consistency: *a fish cake* **4** a mass, slab, or crust of a solidified or compressed substance, as of soap or ice **5** have one's cake and eat it to enjoy both of two desirable but incompatible alternatives **6** go or sell like hot cakes *informal* to be sold very quickly or in large quantities **7** piece of cake *informal* something that is easily achieved or obtained **8** take the cake *informal* to surpass all others, esp in stupidity, folly, etc **9** *informal* the whole or total of something that is to be shared or divided: *the miners are demanding a larger slice of the cake; that is a fair method of sharing the cake* ▷ *vb* **10** (*tr*) to cover with a hard layer; encrust: *the hull was caked with salt* **11** to form or be formed into a hardened mass [C13 from Old Norse *kaka;* related to Danish *kage,* German *Kuchen*] ▷ **cakey** or **caky** *adj*

cakewalk (ˈkeɪkˌwɔːk) *n* **1** a dance based on a march with intricate steps, originally performed by African-Americans with the prize of a cake for the best performers **2** a piece of music composed for this dance **3** *informal* an easily accomplished task ▷ *vb* (*intr*) to perform the cakewalk ▷ ˈcakeˌwalker *n*

CAL *abbreviation for* computer-aided (or -assisted) learning

cal. *abbreviation for* **1** calibre **2** calorie (small)

Cal. *abbreviation for* **1** Calorie (large) **2** California

Calabar (ˈkæləˌbɑː) *n* a port in SE Nigeria, capital of Cross River state. Pop: 418 000 (2005 est)

Calabar bean (ˌkæləˈbɑː, ˈkæləˌbɑː) *n* the dark brown very poisonous seed of a leguminous woody climbing plant, *Physostigma venenosum* of tropical Africa, used as a source of the drug physostigmine

calabash (ˈkæləˌbæʃ) *n* **1** Also called: **calabash tree** a tropical American evergreen tree, *Crescentia cujete,* that produces large round gourds: family *Bignoniaceae* **2** another name for the **bottle gourd 3** the gourd of either of these plants **4** the dried hollow shell of a gourd used as the bowl of a tobacco pipe, a bottle, rattle, etc **5** calabash nutmeg a tropical African shrub, *Monodora myristica,* whose oily aromatic seeds can be used as nutmegs: family *Annonaceae* [C17 from obsolete French *calabasse,* from Spanish *calabaza,* perhaps from Arabic *qar'ah yābisah* dry gourd, from *qar'ah* gourd + *yābisah* dry]

calabogus (ˌkæləˈbəʊɡəs) *n* *Canadian* a mixed drink containing rum, spruce beer, and molasses [C18 of unknown origin]

calaboose (ˈkæləˌbuːs) *n* *US informal* a prison; jail [C18 from Creole French, from Spanish *calabozo* dungeon, of unknown origin]

calabrese (ˌkæləˈbreɪzɪ) *n* a variety of green sprouting broccoli [C20 from Italian: Calabrian]

Calabria (kəˈlæbrɪə) *n* **1** a region of SW Italy: mostly mountainous and subject to earthquakes. Chief town: Reggio di Calabria. Pop: 2 007 392 (2003 est). Area: 15 080 sq km (5822 sq miles) **2** an ancient region of extreme SE Italy (3rd century BC to about 668 AD); now part of Apulia

Calabrian (kəˈlæbrɪən) *adj* **1** of or relating to Calabria or its inhabitants ▷ *n* **2** a native or inhabitant of Calabria

caladium (kəˈleɪdɪəm) *n* any of various tropical plants of the aroid genus *Caladium,* which are widely cultivated as potted plants for their colourful variegated foliage [C19 from New Latin, from Malay *kĕladi* araceous plant]

Calais (ˈkæleɪ; *French* kalɛ) *n* a port in N France, on the Strait of Dover: the nearest French port to

England; belonged to England 1347–1558. Pop: 77 333 (1999)

calalu or **calaloo** (ˈkæluː) *n* *Caribbean* the edible leaves of various plants, used as greens or in making thick soups [probably of African origin]

calamanco (ˌkæləˈmæŋkəʊ) *n* a glossy woollen fabric woven with a checked design that shows on one side only [C16 of unknown origin]

calamander (ˈkæləˌmændə) *n* the hard black-and-brown striped wood of several trees of the genus *Diospyros,* esp *D. quaesita* of India and Sri Lanka, used in making furniture: family *Ebenaceae.* See also **ebony** (sense 2) [C19 metathetic variant of *coromandel* in COROMANDEL COAST]

calamari (ˌkæləˈmɑːrɪ) *n* squid cooked for eating, esp cut into rings and fried in batter [C20 from Italian, pl of *calamaro* squid, from Latin *calamarium* pen-case, referring to the squid's internal shell, from Greek *kalamos* reed]

calamata olive (ˌkæləˈmɑːtə) *n* a variant spelling of **kalamata olive**

calamine (ˈkæləˌmaɪn) *n* **1** a pink powder consisting of zinc oxide and ferric oxide, (iron(III) oxide), used medicinally in the form of soothing lotions or ointments **2** *US* another name for **smithsonite** or **hemimorphite** [C17 from Old French, from Medieval Latin *calamīna,* from Latin *cadmia;* see CADMIUM]

calamint (ˈkæləˌmɪnt) *n* any aromatic Eurasian plant of the genus *Satureja* (or *Calamintha*), having clusters of purple or pink flowers: family *Lamiaceae* (labiates) [C14 from Old French *calament* (but influenced by English MINT¹), from Medieval Latin *calamentum,* from Greek *kalaminthē*]

calamite (ˈkæləˌmaɪt) *n* any extinct treelike plant of the genus *Calamites,* of Carboniferous times, related to the horsetails [C19 from New Latin *Calamītes* type genus, from Greek *kalamitēs* reedlike, from *kalamos* reed]

calamitous (kəˈlæmɪtəs) *adj* causing, involving, or resulting in a calamity; disastrous ▷ caˈlamitously *adv* ▷ caˈlamitousness *n*

calamity (kəˈlæmɪtɪ) *n, pl* **-ties 1** a disaster or misfortune, esp one causing extreme havoc, distress, or misery **2** a state or feeling of deep distress or misery [C15 from French *calamité,* from Latin *calamitās;* related to Latin *incolumis* uninjured]

calamondin (ˈkæləˌmʌndɪn) or **calamondin orange** *n* **1** a small citrus tree, *Citrus mitis,* of the Philippines **2** the acid-tasting fruit of this tree, resembling a small orange [from Tagalog *kalamunding*]

calamus (ˈkæləməs) *n, pl* **-mi** (-ˌmaɪ) **1** any tropical Asian palm of the genus *Calamus,* some species of which are a source of rattan and canes **2** another name for **sweet flag 3** the aromatic root of the sweet flag **4** *ornithol* the basal hollow shaft of a feather; quill [C14 from Latin, from Greek *kalamos* reed, cane, stem]

calando (kəˈlændəʊ) *adj, adv* *music* (to be performed) with gradually decreasing tone and speed [Italian: dropping, from *calare* to lower, to drop]

calandria (kəˈlændrɪə) *n* a cylindrical vessel through which vertical tubes pass, esp one forming part of an evaporator, heat exchanger, or nuclear reactor [C20 arbitrarily named, from Spanish, literally: lark]

calash (kəˈlæʃ) or **calèche** *n* **1** a horse-drawn carriage with low wheels and a folding top **2** the folding top of such a carriage **3** a woman's folding hooped hood worn in the 18th century [C17 from French *calèche,* from German *Kalesche,* from Czech *kolesa* wheels]

calathea (ˌkæləˈθɪə) *n* any plant of the S. American perennial genus *Calathea,* many species of which are grown as greenhouse or house plants for their decorative variegated leaves, esp the zebra plant (*C. zebrina*), the leaves of which are purplish below and dark green with lighter stripes above: family *Marantaceae* [New Latin, from Greek *kalathos* a basket]

calathus ('kæləθəs) *n, pl* -thi (-,θaɪ) a vase-shaped basket represented in ancient Greek art, used as a symbol of fruitfulness [c18 from Latin, from Greek *kalathos*]

calaverite (kə'lævə,raɪt) *n* a metallic pale yellow mineral consisting of a telluride of gold in the form of elongated striated crystals. It is a source of gold in Australia and North America. Formula: $AuTe_2$ [c19 named after *Calaveras*, county in California where it was discovered]

calc- *combining form* a variant of **calci-** before a vowel

calcaneus (kæl'keɪnɪəs) *or* **calcaneum** *n, pl* -nei (-nɪ,aɪ) *or* -nea (-nɪə) **1** the largest tarsal bone, forming the heel in man. Nontechnical name: **heel bone 2** the corresponding bone in other vertebrates [c19 from Late Latin: heel, from Latin *calx* heel] > cal'caneal *or* cal'canean *adj*

calcar ('kæl,kɑː) *n, pl* calcaria (kæl'kɛərɪə) a spur or spurlike process, as on the leg of a bird or the corolla of a flower [c19 from Latin, from *calx* heel]

calcareous (kæl'kɛərɪəs) *adj* of, containing, or resembling calcium carbonate; chalky [c17 from Latin *calcārius*, from *calx* lime]

calcariferous (,kælkə'rɪfərəs) *adj biology* having a spur or spurs

calceiform ('kælsɪɪ,fɔːm, kæl'siː-) *or* **calceolate** ('kælsɪə,leɪt) *adj botany* shaped like a shoe or slipper [c19 from Latin *calceus* shoe]

calceolaria (,kælsɪə'lɛərɪə) *n* any tropical American scrophulariaceous plant of the genus *Calceolaria*: cultivated for its speckled slipper-shaped flowers. Also called: **slipperwort** [c18 from Latin *calceolus* small shoe, from *calceus*]

calces ('kælsiːz) *n* a plural of **calx**

Calchas ('kælkæs) *n Greek myth* a soothsayer who assisted the Greeks in the Trojan War

calci- *or before a vowel* **calc-** *combining form* indicating lime or calcium: *calcify* [from Latin *calx, calc-* limestone]

calcic ('kælsɪk) *adj* of, containing, or concerned with lime or calcium [c19 from Latin *calx* lime]

calcicole ('kælsɪ,kəʊl) *n* any plant that thrives in lime-rich soils [c20 from CALCI- + *-cole*, from Latin *colere* to dwell] > **calcicolous** (kæl'sɪkələs) *adj*

calciferol (kæl'sɪfərɒl) *n* a fat-soluble steroid, found esp in fish-liver oils, produced by the action of ultraviolet radiation on ergosterol. It increases the absorption of calcium from the intestine and is used in the treatment of rickets. Formula: $C_{28}H_{43}OH$. Also called: **vitamin D₂** [c20 from CALCIF(EROUS + ERGOST)EROL]

calciferous (kæl'sɪfərəs) *adj* forming or producing salts of calcium, esp calcium carbonate

calcific (kæl'sɪfɪk) *adj* forming or causing to form lime or chalk

calcification (,kælsɪfɪ'keɪʃən) *n* **1** the process of calcifying or becoming calcified **2** *pathol* a tissue hardened by deposition of lime salts **3** any calcified object or formation

calcifuge ('kælsɪ,fjuːdʒ) *n* any plant that thrives in acid soils but not in lime-rich soils > **calcifugal** (,kælsɪ'fjuːgᵊl) *adj* > **calcifugous** (kæl'sɪfjəgəs) *adj*

calcify ('kælsɪ,faɪ) *vb* -fies, -fying, -fied **1** to convert or be converted into lime **2** to harden or become hardened by impregnation with calcium salts

calcimine ('kælsɪ,maɪn, -mɪn) *or* **kalsomine** *n* **1** a white or pale tinted wash for walls ▷ *vb* **2** (*tr*) to cover with calcimine [c19 changed from *Kalsomine*, a trademark]

calcine ('kælsaɪn, -sɪn) *vb* **1** (*tr*) to heat (a substance) so that it is oxidized, reduced, or loses water **2** (*intr*) to oxidize as a result of heating [c14 from Medieval Latin *calcināre* to heat, from Latin *calx* lime] > **calcination** (,kælsɪ'neɪʃən) *n*

calcinosis (,kælsɪ'nəʊsɪs) *n* the abnormal deposition of calcium salts in the tissues of the body

calcite ('kælsaɪt) *n* a colourless or white mineral (occasionally tinged with impurities), found in sedimentary and metamorphic rocks, in veins, in

limestone, and in stalagmites and stalactites. It is used in the manufacture of cement, plaster, paint, glass, and fertilizer. Composition: calcium carbonate. Formula: $CaCO_3$. Crystal structure: hexagonal (rhombohedral) > **calcitic** (kæl'sɪtɪk) *adj*

calcitonin (,kælsɪ'təʊnɪn) *n* a hormone secreted by the thyroid that inhibits the release of calcium from the skeleton and prevents a build-up of calcium in the blood. Also called: **thyrocalcitonin**. Compare **parathyroid hormone** [c20 from CALCI- + TON(IC) + -IN]

calcium ('kælsɪəm) *n* a malleable silvery-white metallic element of the alkaline earth group; the fifth most abundant element in the earth's crust (3.6 per cent), occurring esp as forms of calcium carbonate. It is an essential constituent of bones and teeth and is used as a deoxidizer in steel. Symbol: Ca; atomic no.: 20; atomic wt.: 40.078; valency: 2; relative density: 1.55; melting pt.: 842±2°C; boiling pt.: 1494°C [c19 from New Latin, from Latin *calx* lime]

calcium antagonist *n* another name for **calcium channel blocker**

calcium carbide *n* a grey salt of calcium used in the production of acetylene (by its reaction with water) and calcium cyanamide. Formula: CaC_2. Sometimes shortened to: **carbide**

calcium carbonate *n* a white crystalline salt occurring in limestone, chalk, marble, calcite, coral, and pearl: used in the production of lime and cement. Formula: $CaCO_3$

calcium channel blocker *n* any drug that prevents the influx of calcium ions into cardiac and smooth muscle: used to treat high blood pressure and angina. Also called **calcium antagonist**

calcium chloride *n* a white deliquescent salt occurring naturally in seawater and used in the de-icing of roads and as a drying agent. Formula: $CaCl_2$

calcium cyanamide *n* a white crystalline compound formed by heating calcium carbide with nitrogen. It is important in the fixation of nitrogen and can be hydrolysed to ammonia or used as a fertilizer. Formula: $CaCN_2$

calcium hydroxide *n* a white crystalline slightly soluble alkali with many uses, esp in cement, water softening, and the neutralization of acid soils. Formula: $Ca(OH)_2$. Also called: **lime, slaked lime, hydrated lime, calcium hydrate, caustic lime, lime hydrate**

calcium light *n* another name for **limelight**

calcium oxide *n* a white crystalline base used in the production of calcium hydroxide and bleaching powder and in the manufacture of glass, paper, and steel. Formula: CaO. Also called: **lime, quicklime, calx, burnt lime, calcined lime, fluxing lime**

calcium phosphate *n* **1** the insoluble nonacid calcium salt of orthophosphoric acid (phosphoric(V) acid): it occurs in bones and is the main constituent of bone ash. Formula: $Ca_3(PO_4)_2$ **2** any calcium salt of a phosphoric acid. Calcium phosphates are found in many rocks and used esp in fertilizers

calcrete ('kælkriːt) *n* another name for **caliche** (sense 1)

calcsinter ('kælk,sɪntə) *n* another name for **travertine** [c19 from German *Kalksinter*, from *Kalk* lime + *sinter* dross; see CHALK, SINTER]

calcspar ('kælk,spɑː) *n* another name for **calcite** [c19 partial translation of Swedish *kalkspat*, from *kalk* lime (ultimately from Latin *calx*) + *spat* SPAR³]

calc-tufa ('kælk,tuː:fə) *or* **calc-tuff** ('kælk,tʌf) *n* another name for **tufa**

calculable ('kælkjʊləbᵊl) *adj* **1** that may be computed or estimated **2** predictable; dependable > ,calcula'bility *n* > 'calculably *adv*

calculate ('kælkjʊ,leɪt) *vb* **1** to solve (one or more problems) by a mathematical procedure; compute **2** (*tr; may take a clause as object*) to determine beforehand by judgment, reasoning, etc; estimate

3 (*tr; usually passive*) to design specifically; aim: *the car was calculated to appeal to women* **4** (*intr; foll by on* or *upon*) to depend; rely **5** (*tr; may take a clause as object*) *US dialect* **a** to suppose; think **b** to intend (to do something) [c16 from Late Latin *calculāre*, from *calculus* pebble used as a counter; see CALCULUS] > **calculative** ('kælkjʊlətɪv) *adj*

calculated ('kælkjʊ,leɪtɪd) *adj* (*usually prenominal*) **1** undertaken after considering the likelihood of success or failure: *a calculated risk* **2** deliberately planned; premeditated: *a calculated insult*

calculating ('kælkjʊ,leɪtɪŋ) *adj* **1** selfishly scheming **2** shrewd; cautious > 'calcu,latingly *adv*

calculation (,kælkjʊ'leɪʃən) *n* **1** the act, process, or result of calculating **2** an estimation of probability; forecast **3** careful planning or forethought, esp for selfish motives

calculator ('kælkjʊ,leɪtə) *n* **1** a device for performing mathematical calculations, esp an electronic device that can be held in the hand **2** a person or thing that calculates **3** a set of tables used as an aid to calculations

calculous ('kælkjʊləs) *adj pathol* of or suffering from a calculus

calculus ('kælkjʊləs) *n, pl* -luses **1** a branch of mathematics, developed independently by Newton and Leibniz. Both **differential calculus** and **integral calculus** are concerned with the effect on a function of an infinitesimal change in the independent variable as it tends to zero **2** any mathematical system of calculation involving the use of symbols **3** *logic* an uninterpreted formal system. Compare **formal language** (sense 2) **4** *pl* -li (-,laɪ) *pathol* a stonelike concretion of minerals and salts found in ducts or hollow organs of the body [c17 from Latin: pebble, stone used in reckoning, from *calx* small stone, counter]

calculus of variations *n* a branch of calculus concerned with maxima and minima of definite integrals

Calcutta (kæl'kʌtə) *n* a port in E India, capital of West Bengal state, on the Hooghly River: former capital of the country (1833–1912); major commercial and industrial centre; three universities. Pop: 4 580 544 (2001). Official name: **Kolkata**

Calcutta Cup *n rugby Union* a trophy competed for annually by England and Scotland since 1879 [after the CALCUTTA Rugby and Cricket Club, who donated the trophy to the Rugby Football Union in 1878]

caldarium (kæl'dɛərɪəm) *n, pl* -daria (-'dɛərɪə) (in ancient Rome) a room for taking hot baths [c18 from Latin, from *calidus* warm, from *calēre* to be warm]

caldera (kæl'dɛərə, 'kɔːldərə) *n* a large basin-shaped crater at the top of a volcano, formed by the collapse or explosion of the cone. See **cirque** [c19 from Spanish *Caldera* (literally: CAULDRON), name of a crater in the Canary Islands]

Calderdale ('kɔːldə,deɪl) *n* a unitary authority in N England, in West Yorkshire. Pop: 193 200 (2003 est). Area: 364 sq km (140 sq miles)

caldron ('kɔːldrən) *n* a variant spelling of **cauldron**

calèche (French kalɛʃ) *n* a variant of **calash**

Caledonia (,kælɪ'dəʊnɪə) *n* the Roman name for Scotland: used poetically in later times

Caledonian (,kælɪ'dəʊnɪən) *adj* **1** of or relating to Scotland **2** of or denoting a period of mountain building in NW Europe in the Palaeozoic era ▷ *n* **3** *literary* a native or inhabitant of Scotland

Caledonian Canal *n* a canal in N Scotland, linking the Atlantic with the North Sea through the Great Glen: built 1803 47; now used mostly for leisure boating

calefacient (,kælɪ'feɪʃənt) *adj* **1** causing warmth ▷ *n* **2** *med obsolete* an agent that warms, such as a mustard plaster [c17 from Latin *calefaciēns*, from *calefacere* to heat] > **calefaction** (,kælɪ'fækʃən) *n*

calefactory (,kælɪ'fæktərɪ, -trɪ) *adj* **1** giving warmth ▷ *n, pl* -ries **2** a heated sitting room in a monastery [c16 from Latin *calefactōrius*, from *calefactus* made warm; see CALEFACIENT]

calendar ('kælɪndə) *n* **1** a system for determining the beginning, length, and order of years and their divisions. See also **Gregorian calendar, Jewish calendar, Julian calendar, Revolutionary calendar, Roman calendar** **2** a table showing any such arrangement, esp as applied to one or more successive years **3** a list, register, or schedule of social events, pending court cases, appointments, etc ▷ *vb* **4** (*tr*) to enter in a calendar; schedule; register [c13 via Norman French from Medieval Latin *kalendārium* account book, from *Kalendae* the CALENDS, when interest on debts became due] > calendrical (kæ'lɛndrɪk(ə)l) *or* ca'lendric *adj*

calendar day *n* See **day** (sense 1)

calendar month *n* See **month** (sense 1)

calendar year *n* See **year** (sense 1)

calender[1] ('kælɪndə) *n* **1** a machine in which paper or cloth is glazed or smoothed by passing between rollers ▷ *vb* **2** (*tr*) to subject (material) to such a process [c17 from French *calandre*, of unknown origin]

calender[2] ('kælɪndə) *n* a member of a mendicant order of dervishes in Turkey, Iran, and India [from Persian *kalandar*]

calends *or* **kalends** ('kælɪndz) *pl n* the first day of each month in the ancient Roman calendar [c14 from Latin *kalendae*; related to Latin *calāre* to proclaim]

calendula (kæ'lɛndjʊlə) *n* **1** any Eurasian plant of the genus *Calendula*, esp the pot marigold, having orange-and-yellow rayed flowers: family *Asteraceae* (composites) **2** the dried flowers of the pot marigold, formerly used medicinally and for seasoning [c19 from Medieval Latin, from Latin *kalendae* CALENDS; perhaps from its supposed efficacy in curing menstrual disorders]

calenture ('kælən,tjʊə) *n* a mild fever of tropical climates, similar in its symptoms to sunstroke [c16 from Spanish *calentura* fever, ultimately from Latin *calēre* to be warm]

calf[1] (kɑːf) *n, pl* **calves** **1** the young of cattle, esp domestic cattle. Related adj: **vituline** **2** the young of certain other mammals, such as the buffalo, elephant, giraffe, and whale **3** a large piece of floating ice detached from an iceberg, etc **4** **kill the fatted calf** to celebrate lavishly, esp as a welcome **5** another name for **calfskin** [Old English *cealf*; related to Old Norse *kālfr*, Gothic *kalbō*, Old High German *kalba*]

calf[2] (kɑːf) *n, pl* **calves** the thick fleshy part of the back of the leg between the ankle and the knee. Related adj: **sural** [c14 from Old Norse *kalfi*]

calf diphtheria *n vet science* a disease of the throat in young calves caused by *Fusobacterium necrophorum*, resulting in breathing difficulty and a painful cough

calf love *n* temporary infatuation or love of an adolescent for a member of the opposite sex. Also called: **puppy love**

calf's-foot jelly *n* a jelly made from the stock of boiled calves' feet and flavourings, formerly often served to invalids

calfskin ('kɑːf,skɪn) *n* **1** the skin or hide of a calf **2** Also called: **calf** **a** fine leather made from this skin **b** (*as modifier*): *calfskin boots*

Calgary ('kælgərɪ) *n* a city in Canada, in S Alberta: centre of a large agricultural region; oilfields. Pop: 879 277 (2001)

Calgon ('kælgɒn) *n trademark* a chemical compound, sodium hexametaphosphate, with water-softening properties, used in detergents

Cali (*Spanish* 'kali) *n* a city in SW Colombia: commercial centre in a rich agricultural region. Pop: 2 583 000 (2005 est)

Caliban ('kælɪ,bæn) *n* a brutish or brutalized man [c19 after a character in Shakespeare's *The Tempest* (1611)]

calibrate ('kælɪ,breɪt) *vb* (*tr*) **1** to measure the calibre of (a gun, mortar, etc) **2** to mark (the scale of a measuring instrument) so that readings can be made in appropriate units **3** to determine the accuracy of (a measuring instrument, etc) **4** to determine or check the range and accuracy of (a piece of artillery) > ,cali'bration *n* > 'cali,brator *or* 'cali,brater *n*

calibre *or US* **caliber** ('kælɪbə) *n* **1** the diameter of a cylindrical body, esp the internal diameter of a tube or the bore of a firearm **2** the diameter of a shell or bullet **3** ability; distinction: *a musician of high calibre* **4** personal character: *a man of high calibre* [c16 from Old French, from Italian *calibro*, from Arabic *qālib* shoemaker's last, mould] > 'calibred *or US* 'calibered *adj*

calices ('kælɪ,siːz) *n* the plural of **calix**

caliche (kæ'liːtʃɪ) *n* **1** Also called: **calcrete** a bed of sand or clay in arid regions cemented by calcium carbonate, sodium chloride, and other soluble minerals **2** a surface layer of soil encrusted with calcium carbonate, occurring in arid regions. Also called: **duricrust** [c20 from American Spanish, from Latin *calx* lime]

calicle ('kælɪk(ə)l) *n* a variant spelling of **calycle** > calicular (kə'lɪkjʊlə) *adj*

calico ('kælɪ,kəʊ) *n, pl* **-coes** *or* **-cos** **1** a white or unbleached cotton fabric with no printed design **2** *chiefly US* a coarse printed cotton fabric **3** (*modifier*) made of calico [c16 based on *Calicut*, town in India]

calico bush *n* another name for **mountain laurel**

Calicut ('kælɪ,kʌt) *n* the former name for **Kozhikode**

calif ('keɪlɪf, 'kæl-) *n* a variant spelling of **caliph**

Calif. *abbreviation for* California

califate ('keɪlɪ,feɪt, -fɪt, 'kæl-) *n* a variant spelling of **caliphate**

califont ('kælɪ,fɒnt) *n NZ* a gas water heater [from a trade name]

California (,kælɪ'fɔːnɪə) *n* **1** a state on the W coast of the US: the third largest state in area and the largest in population; consists of a narrow, warm coastal plain rising to the Coast Range, deserts in the south, the fertile central valleys of the Sacramento and San Joaquin Rivers, and the mountains of the Sierra Nevada in the east; major industries include the growing of citrus fruits and grapes, fishing, oil production, electronics, information technology, and films. Capital: Sacramento. Pop: 35 484 453 (2003 est). Area: 411 015 sq km (158 693 sq miles). Abbreviations: **Cal., Calif.**, (with zip code) **CA** **2** **Gulf of** an arm of the Pacific Ocean, between Sonora and Lower California

Californian (,kælɪ'fɔːnɪən) *adj* **1** of or relating to California or its inhabitants ▷ *n* **2** a native or inhabitant of California

Californian spangled cat *n* a breed of short-haired cat with a spotted coat, bred in California to resemble a leopard in appearance

California poppy *n* a papaveraceous plant, *Eschscholtzia californica*, of the Pacific coast of North America, having yellow or orange flowers and finely divided bluish-green leaves

californium (,kælɪ'fɔːnɪəm) *n* a metallic transuranic element artificially produced from curium. Symbol: Cf; atomic no.: 98; half-life of most stable isotope, ^{251}Cf: 800 years (approx.) [c20 New Latin; discovered at the University of *California*]

caliginous (kə'lɪdʒɪnəs) *adj archaic* dark; dim [c16 from Latin *cālīginōsus*, from *cālīgō* darkness] > caliginosity (kə,lɪdʒɪ'nɒsɪtɪ) *n*

Calimere ('kælɪmɪə) *n* **Point** a cape on the SE coast of India, on the Palk Strait

calipash *or* **callipash** ('kælɪ,pæʃ) *n* the greenish glutinous edible part of the turtle found next to the upper shell, considered a delicacy [c17 perhaps changed from Spanish *carapacho* CARAPACE]

calipee ('kælɪ,piː) *n* the yellow glutinous edible part of the turtle found next to the lower shell, considered a delicacy [c17 perhaps a variant of CALIPASH]

caliper ('kælɪpə) *n* the usual US spelling of **calliper**

caliph, calif, kalif *or* **khalif** ('keɪlɪf, 'kæl-) *n Islam* the title of the successors of Mohammed as rulers of the Islamic world, later assumed by the Sultans of Turkey [c14 from Old French, from Arabic *khalīfa* successor]

caliphate, califate *or* **kalifate** ('keɪlɪ,feɪt, -fɪt, 'kæl-) *n* the office, jurisdiction, or reign of a caliph

calisaya (,kælɪ'seɪə) *n* the bark of any of several tropical trees of the rubiaceous genus *Cinchona*, esp *C. calisaya*, from which quinine is extracted. Also called: **calisaya bark, yellowbark, cinchona** [c19 from Spanish, from the name of a Bolivian Indian who taught the uses of quinine to the Spanish]

calisthenics (,kælɪs'θɛnɪks) *n* a variant spelling (esp US) of **callisthenics**. > ,calis'thenic *adj*

calix ('keɪlɪks, 'kæ-) *n, pl* **calices** ('kælɪ,siːz) a cup; chalice [c18 from Latin: CHALICE]

calk[1] (kɔːk) *vb* a variant spelling of **caulk**

calk[2] (kɔːk), **calkin** ('kɔːkɪn, 'kæl-) *n* **1** a metal projection on a horse's shoe to prevent slipping **2** *chiefly US and Canadian* a set of spikes or a spiked plate attached to the sole of a boot, esp by loggers, to prevent slipping ▷ *vb* (*tr*) **3** to provide with calks **4** to wound with a calk [c17 from Latin *calx* heel]

calk[3] (kɔːk) *vb* (*tr*) to transfer (a design) by tracing it with a blunt point from one sheet backed with loosely fixed colouring matter onto another placed underneath [c17 from French *calquer* to trace; see CALQUE]

call (kɔːl) *vb* **1** (often foll by *out*) to speak or utter (words, sounds, etc) loudly so as to attract attention: *he called out her name* **2** (*tr*) to ask or order to come: *to call a policeman* **3** (*intr*; sometimes foll by *on*) to make a visit (to): *she called on him* **4** (often foll by *up*) to telephone (a person): *he called back at nine* **5** (*tr*) to summon to a specific office, profession, etc: *he was called to the ministry* **6** (of animals or birds) to utter (a characteristic sound or cry) **7** (*tr*) to summon (a bird or animal) by imitating its cry **8** (*tr*) to name or style: *they called the dog Rover* **9** (*tr*) to designate: *they called him a coward* **10** (*tr*) *Brit dialect* to speak ill of or scold **11** (*tr*) to regard in a specific way: *I call it a foolish waste of time* **12** (*tr*) to attract (attention) **13** (*tr*) to read (a list, register, etc) aloud to check for omissions or absentees **14** (when *tr*, usually foll by *for*) to give an order (for): *to call a strike* **15** (*intr*) to try to predict the result of tossing a coin **16** (*tr*) to awaken: *I was called early this morning* **17** (*tr*) to cause to assemble: *to call a meeting* **18** (*tr*) *sport* (of an umpire, referee, etc) to pass judgment upon (a shot, player, etc) with a call **19** (*tr*) *Austral and NZ* to broadcast a commentary on (a horse race or other sporting event) **20** (*tr*) to demand repayment of (a loan, redeemable bond, security, etc) **21** (*tr*; often foll by *up*) *accounting* to demand payment of (a portion of a share issue not yet paid by subscribers) **22** (*tr*) *Brit* to award (a student at an Inn of Court) the degree of barrister (esp in the phrase **call to the bar**) **23** (*tr*) *computing* to transfer control to (a named subprogram) **24** (*tr*) *poker* to demand that (a player) expose his hand, after equalling his bet **25** (*intr*) *bridge* to make a bid **26** (in square-dancing) to call out (instructions) to the dancers **27** *billiards* to ask (a player) to say what kind of shot he will play or (of a player) to name his shot **28** (*intr*; foll by *for*) **a** to require: *this problem calls for study* **b** to come or go (for) in order to fetch: *I will call for my book later* **29** (*intr*; foll by *on* or *upon*) to make an appeal or request (to): *they called upon him to reply* **30** (*tr*) to predict the outcome of an event: *we don't know yet if the plan has succeeded because it's too soon to call* **31** **call into being** to create **32** **call into play** to begin to operate **33** **call in** *or* **into question** See **question** (sense 12) **34** **call it a day** to stop work or other activity **35** **too close to call** (of the outcome of a competition, election, match, etc) unable to be predicted **36** **call to mind** to remember or cause to be remembered ▷ *n* **37** a cry or shout **38** the characteristic cry of a bird or animal **39** a device, such as a whistle, intended to imitate the cry of a bird or animal **40** a summons or invitation **41** a summons or signal sounded on a horn, bugle, etc **42** *hunting* any of several notes or patterns of notes, blown on a hunting horn as a signal **43** *hunting* **a** an imitation of the characteristic cry of a wild animal or bird to lure it to the hunter **b** an instrument for producing such an imitation **44** a short visit: *the doctor made six calls this morning* **45** an inner urge to some task or profession; vocation **46** allure or fascination, esp of a place: *the call of the forest* **47** *Brit* the summons to the bar of a student member of an Inn of Court **48** need, demand, or occasion: *there is no call to shout; we don't get much call for stockings these days* **49** demand or claim (esp in the phrase **the call of duty**) **50** *theatre* a notice to actors informing them of times of rehearsals **51** (in square dancing) an instruction to execute new figures **52** a conversation or a request for a connection by telephone **53** *commerce* **a** a demand for repayment of a loan **b** (*as modifier*): *call money* **54** *finance* **a** a demand for redeemable bonds or shares to be presented for repayment **b** a demand for an instalment payment on the issue price of bonds or shares **55** *billiards* a demand to an opponent to say what kind of shot he will play **56** *poker* a demand for a hand or hands to be exposed **57** *bridge* a bid, or a player's turn to bid **58** a decision or judgment: *it's your call* **59** *sport* a decision of an umpire or referee regarding a shot, pitch, etc **60** *Austral* a broadcast commentary on a horse race or other sporting event **61** Also called: **call option** *stock exchange* an option to buy a stated amount of securities at a specified price during a specified period. Compare **put** (sense 20) **62** See **roll call** **63** **call for margin** *stock exchange* a demand made by a stockbroker for partial payment of a client's debt due to decreasing value of the collateral **64** **call of nature** See **nature** (sense 16) **65** **on call** **a** (of a loan, etc) repayable on demand **b** available to be called for work outside normal working hours **66** **within call** within range; accessible ▷ See also **call down, call forth, call in, call off, call out, call up** [Old English *ceallian;* related to Old Norse *kalla,* Old High German *kallōn,* Old Slavonic *glasŭ* voice]

calla (ˈkælə) *n* **1** Also called: **calla lily, arum lily** any southern African plant of the aroid genus *Zantedeschia,* esp *Z. aethiopica,* which has a white funnel-shaped spathe enclosing a yellow spadix **2** an aroid plant, *Calla palustris,* that grows in wet places and has a white spathe enclosing a greenish spadix, and red berries [C19 from New Latin, probably from Greek *kalleia* wattles on a cock, probably from *kallos* beauty]

callable (ˈkɔːləbᵊl) *adj* **1** (of a security) subject to redemption before maturity **2** (of money loaned) repayable on demand

callais (kəˈleɪɪs) *n* a green stone found as beads and ornaments in the late Neolithic and early Bronze Age of W Europe [C19 from Greek *kallais*]

call alarm *n* **a** an electronic device that sends an alarm signal, usually to a distant monitoring centre **b** (*as modifier*): *a call-alarm system*

call-and-response *n* a form of interaction between a speaker and one or more listeners, in which every utterance of the speaker elicits a verbal or non-verbal response from the listener or listeners

Callanetics (ˌkæləˈnɛtɪks) *n* (*functioning as singular*) *trademark* a system of exercise involving frequent repetition of small muscular movements and squeezes, designed to improve muscle tone [C20 named after *Callan Pinckney* (born 1939), its US inventor]

callant (ˈkælənt) *or* **callan** (ˈkælən) *n Scot* a youth; lad [C16 from Dutch or Flemish *kalant* customer, fellow]

Callao (*Spanish* kaˈʎao) *n* a port in W Peru, near Lima, on **Callao Bay**: chief import centre of Peru. Pop: 407 904 (1998 est)

call box *n* a soundproof enclosure for a public telephone. Also called: **telephone box, telephone kiosk**

callboy (ˈkɔːlˌbɔɪ) *n* a person who notifies actors when it is time to go on stage

call centre *n* an office where staff carry out an organization's telephone transactions

call down *vb* (*tr, adverb*) to request or invoke: *to call down God's anger*

caller[1] (ˈkɔːlə) *n* a person or thing that calls, esp a person who makes a brief visit

caller[2] (ˈkælə; *Scot* ˈkælər, ˈkɒlər) *adj Scot* **1** (of food, esp fish) fresh **2** cool: *a caller breeze* [C14 perhaps a Scottish variant of *calver* to prepare fresh salmon or trout in a certain way; perhaps from Old English *calwer* curds, from a fancied resemblance with the flaked flesh of the fish]

call forth *vb* (*tr, adverb*) to cause (something) to come into action or existence: *she called forth all her courage*

call girl *n* a prostitute with whom appointments are made by telephone

calli- *combining form* beautiful: *calligraphy* [from Greek *kalli-,* from *kallos* beauty]

calligraphy (kəˈlɪɡrəfɪ) *n* handwriting, esp beautiful handwriting considered as an art. Also called: **chirography** > **calˈligrapher** *or* **calˈligraphist** *n* > **calligraphic** (ˌkælɪˈɡræfɪk) *adj* > **ˌcalliˈgraphically** *adv*

call in *vb* (*adverb*) **1** (*intr;* often foll by *on*) to pay a visit, esp a brief or informal one: *call in if you are in the neighbourhood* **2** (*tr*) to demand payment of: *to call in a loan* **3** (*tr*) to take (something) out of circulation, because it is defective or no longer useful **4** (*tr*) to summon to one's assistance: *they had to call in a specialist*

calling (ˈkɔːlɪŋ) *n* **1** a strong inner urge to follow an occupation, etc; vocation **2** an occupation, profession, or trade

calling card *n* a small card bearing the name and usually the address of a person, esp for giving to business or social acquaintances. Also called: **visiting card**

calliope (kəˈlaɪəpɪ) *n US and Canadian* a steam organ [C19 after Calliope (literally: beautiful-voiced)]

Calliope (kəˈlaɪəpɪ) *n Greek myth* the Muse of epic poetry

calliopsis (ˌkælɪˈɒpsɪs) *n* another name for **coreopsis**

callipash (ˈkælɪˌpæʃ) *n* a variant spelling of **calipash**

calliper *or US* **caliper** (ˈkælɪpə) *n* **1** (*often plural*) Also called: **calliper compasses** an instrument for measuring internal or external dimensions, consisting of two steel legs hinged together **2** Also called: **calliper splint** *med* a splint consisting of two metal rods with straps attached, for supporting or exerting tension on the leg ▷ *vb* **3** (*tr*) to measure the dimensions of (an object) with callipers [C16 variant of calibre]

calliper rule *n* a measuring instrument having two parallel jaws, one fixed at right angles to the end of a calibrated scale and the other sliding along it

callipygian (ˌkælɪˈpɪdʒɪən) *or* **callipygous** (ˌkælɪˈpaɪɡəs) *adj* having beautifully shaped buttocks [C19 from Greek *kallipugos,* epithet of a statue of Aphrodite, from calli- + *pugē* buttocks]

callistemon (kəˈlɪstəmən) *n* another name for **bottlebrush** (sense 2)

callisthenics *or* **calisthenics** (ˌkælɪsˈθɛnɪks) *n* **1** (*functioning as plural*) light exercises designed to promote general fitness, develop muscle tone, etc **2** (*functioning as singular*) the practice of callisthenic exercises [C19 from calli- + Greek *sthenos* strength] > **ˌcallisˈthenic** *or* **ˌcalisˈthenic** *adj*

Callisto[1] (kəˈlɪstəʊ) *n Greek myth* a nymph who attracted the love of Zeus and was changed into a bear by Hera. Zeus then set her in the sky as the constellation Ursa Major

Callisto[2] (kəˈlɪstəʊ) *n* the second largest (but faintest) of the four Galilean satellites of Jupiter, discovered in 1610 by Galileo. Approximate diameter: 4800 km; orbital radius: 1 883 000 km. See also **Galilean satellite**

call letters *pl n* the call sign of an American or Canadian radio station, esp that of a commercial broadcasting station

call loan *n* a loan that is repayable on demand. Also called: **demand loan.** Compare **time loan**

call money *n* money loaned by banks and recallable on demand

call number *n* the number given to a book in a library, indicating its shelf location. Also called: **call mark**

call off *vb* (*tr, adverb*) **1** to cancel or abandon: *the game was called off because of rain* **2** to order (an animal or person) to desist or summon away: *the man called off his dog* **3** to stop (something) or give the order to stop

callop (ˈkæləp) *n* an edible freshwater fish, *Plectroplites ambiguus,* of Australia, often golden or pale yellow in colour [from a native Australian language]

callose (ˈkæləʊz) *n* a carbohydrate, a polymer of glucose, found in plants, esp in the sieve tubes

callosity (kəˈlɒsɪtɪ) *n, pl* **-ties** **1** hardheartedness **2** another name for **callus** (sense 1)

callous (ˈkæləs) *adj* **1** unfeeling; insensitive **2** (of skin) hardened and thickened ▷ *vb* **3** *pathol* to make or become callous [C16 from Latin *callōsus;* see callus] > **ˈcallously** *adv* > **ˈcallousness** *n*

call out *vb* (*adverb*) **1** to utter aloud, esp loudly **2** (*tr*) to summon **3** (*tr*) to order (workers) to strike **4** (*tr*) to summon (an employee) to work at a time outside his normal working hours, usually in an emergency

callow (ˈkæləʊ) *adj* **1** lacking experience of life; immature **2** *rare* (of a young bird) unfledged and usually lacking feathers [Old English *calu;* related to Old High German *kalo,* Old Slavonic *golŭ* bare, naked, Lithuanian *galva* head, Latin *calvus* bald] > **ˈcallowness** *n*

call rate *n* the interest rate on a call loan

call sign *n* a group of letters and numbers identifying a radio transmitting station, esp an amateur radio station. Compare **call letters**

call slip *n* a form for requesting a library book by title and call number. Also called: **call card, requisition form**

call up *vb* (*adverb*) **1** to summon to report for active military service, as in time of war **2** (*tr*) to recall (something); evoke: *his words called up old memories* **3** (*tr*) to bring or summon (people, etc) into action: *to call up reinforcements* ▷ *n* **call-up** **4** **a** a general order to report for military service **b** the number of men so summoned

callus (ˈkæləs) *n, pl* **luses** **1** Also called: **callosity** an area of skin that is hard or thick, esp on the palm of the hand or sole of the foot, as from continual friction or pressure **2** an area of bony tissue formed during the healing of a fractured bone **3** *botany* **a** a mass of hard protective tissue produced in woody plants at the site of an injury **b** an accumulation of callose in the sieve tubes **4** *biotechnology* a mass of undifferentiated cells produced as the first stage in tissue culture ▷ *vb* **5** to produce or cause to produce a callus [C16 from Latin, variant of *callum* hardened skin]

calm (kɑːm) *adj* **1** almost without motion; still: *a calm sea* **2** *meteorol* of force 0 on the Beaufort scale; without wind **3** not disturbed, agitated, or excited; under control: *he stayed calm throughout the confusion* **4** tranquil; serene: *a calm voice* ▷ *n* **5** an absence of disturbance or rough motion; stillness **6** absence of wind **7** tranquillity ▷ *vb* **8** (often foll by *down*) to make or become calm [C14 from Old French *calme,* from Old Italian *calma,* from Late Latin *cauma* heat, hence a rest during the heat of the day, from Greek *kauma* heat, from *kaiein* to burn] > **ˈcalmly** *adv* > **ˈcalmness** *n*

calmative (ˈkælmətɪv, ˈkɑːmə-) *adj* **1** (of a remedy or agent) sedative ▷ *n* **2** a sedative remedy or drug

calmodulin (kəlˈmɒdjʊlɪn) *n biochem* a protein found in most living cells; it regulates many enzymic processes that are dependent on calcium [from CAL(CIUM) + MODUL(ATE) + -IN]

calomel (ˈkæləˌmɛl, -məl) *n* a colourless tasteless powder consisting chiefly of mercurous chloride, used medicinally, esp as a cathartic. Formula: Hg₂Cl₂ [C17 perhaps from New Latin *calomelas* (unattested), literally: beautiful black (perhaps so named because it was originally sublimed from a black mixture of mercury and mercuric chloride), from Greek *kalos* beautiful + *melas* black]

calorescence (ˌkæləˈrɛsəns) *n physics* the absorption of radiation by a body, subsequently re-emitted at a higher frequency (lower wavelength) > ˌcaloˈrescent *adj*

Calor Gas (ˈkælə) *n trademark* butane gas liquefied under pressure in portable containers for domestic use

caloric (kəˈlɒrɪk, ˈkælərɪk) *adj* **1** of or concerned with heat or calories ▷ **2** *obsolete* a hypothetical elastic fluid formerly postulated as the embodiment of heat > caloricity (ˌkæləˈrɪsɪtɪ) *n*

calorie *or* **calory** (ˈkælərɪ) *n, pl* -ries a unit of heat, equal to 4.1868 joules (**International Table calorie**): formerly defined as the quantity of heat required to raise the temperature of 1 gram of water by 1°C under standard conditions. It has now largely been replaced by the joule for scientific purposes. Abbreviation: cal. Also called: gram calorie, small calorie. Compare **Calorie** [C19 from French, from Latin *calor* heat]

Calorie (ˈkælərɪ) *n* **1** Also called: kilogram calorie, kilocalorie, large calorie a unit of heat, equal to one thousand calories, often used to express the heat output of an organism or the energy value of food. Abbreviation: Cal **2** the amount of a specific food capable of producing one thousand calories of energy

calorific (ˌkæləˈrɪfɪk) *adj* of, concerning, or generating heat > ˌcaloˈrifically *adv*

calorific value *n* the quantity of heat produced by the complete combustion of a given mass of a fuel, usually expressed in joules per kilogram

calorimeter (ˌkæləˈrɪmɪtə) *n* an apparatus for measuring amounts of heat, esp to find specific heat capacities, calorific values, etc > calorimetric (ˌkælərɪˈmɛtrɪk) *or* ˌcaloriˈmetrical *adj* > ˌcaloriˈmetrically *adv* > ˌcaloˈrimetry *n*

calorize (ˈkæləˌraɪz) *vb* (*tr*) to coat (a ferrous metal) by spraying with aluminium powder and then heating

calotte (kəˈlɒt) *n* **1** a skullcap worn by Roman Catholic clergy **2** *architect* a concavity in the form of a niche or cup, serving to reduce the apparent height of an alcove or chapel [C17 from French, from Provençal *calota*, perhaps from Greek *kaluptra* hood]

calotype (ˈkæləʊˌtaɪp) *n* **1** an early photographic process invented by W. H. Fox Talbot, in which the image was produced on paper treated with silver iodide and developed by sodium thiosulphite **2** a photograph made by this process [C19 from Greek *kalos* beautiful + -TYPE]

caloyer (ˈkælɔɪə) *n* a monk of the Greek Orthodox Church, esp of the Basilian Order [C17 from French, from Medieval Greek *kalogēros* venerable, from Greek *kalos* beautiful + *gēras* old age]

calpac, calpack *or* **kalpak** (ˈkælpæk) *n* a large black brimless hat made of sheepskin or felt, worn by men in parts of the Near East [C16 from Turkish *kalpāk*]

Calpe (ˈkælpɪ) *n* the ancient name for (the Rock of) Gibraltar

calque (kælk) *n* **1** another word for **loan translation** ▷ *vb* calques, calquing, calqued **2** (*tr*) another word for **calk³** [C20 from French: a tracing, from *calquer*, from Latin *calcāre* to tread]

Caltanissetta (*Italian* kaltanisˈsetta) *n* a city in central Sicily: sulphur mines. Pop: 61 438 (2001)

Caltech (ˈkælˌtɛk) *n* the California Institute of Technology

caltrop, caltrap (ˈkæltrəp) *or* **calthrop** (ˈkælθrəp) *n* **1** any tropical or subtropical plant of the zygophyllaceous genera *Tribulus* and *Kallstroemia* that have spiny burs or bracts **2** water caltrop another name for **water chestnut** (sense 1) **3** another name for the **star thistle 4** *military* a four-spiked iron ball or four joined spikes laid upon the ground as a device to lame cavalry horses, puncture tyres, etc [Old English *calcatrippe* (the plant), from Medieval Latin *calcatrippa*, probably from Latin *calx* heel + *trippa* TRAP¹]

calumet (ˈkæljʊˌmɛt) *n* a less common name for **peace pipe** [C18 from Canadian French, from French (Normandy dialect): straw, from Late Latin *calamellus* a little reed, from Latin: CALAMUS]

calumniate (kəˈlʌmnɪˌeɪt) *vb* (*tr*) to slander > caˈlumniable *adj* > caˌlumniˈation *n* > caˈlumniˌator *n*

calumnious (kəˈlʌmnɪəs) *or* **calumniatory** (kəˈlʌmnɪətərɪ, -trɪ) *adj* **1** of or using calumny **2** (of a person) given to calumny

calumny (ˈkæləmnɪ) *n, pl* -nies **1** the malicious utterance of false charges or misrepresentation; slander; defamation **2** such a false charge or misrepresentation [C15 from Latin *calumnia* deception, slander]

calutron (ˈkæljʊˌtrɒn) *n* a device used for the separation of isotopes [C20 from Cal(ifornia) U(niversity) + -TRON]

Calvados (ˈkælvəˌdɒs) *n* **1** a department of N France in the Basse-Normandie region. Capital: Caen. Pop: 659 893 (2003 est). Area: 5693 sq km (2198 sq miles) **2** an apple brandy distilled from cider in this region

calvaria (kælˈvɛərɪə) *n* the top part of the skull of vertebrates. Nontechnical name: skullcap [C14 from Late Latin: (human) skull, from Latin *calvus* bald]

calvary (ˈkælvərɪ) *n, pl* -ries **1** (*often capital*) a representation of Christ's crucifixion, usually sculptured and in the open air **2** any experience involving great suffering

Calvary (ˈkælvərɪ) *n* the place just outside the walls of Jerusalem where Jesus was crucified. Also called: Golgotha [from Late Latin *Calvāria*, translation of Greek *kranion* skull, translation of Aramaic *gulgulta* Golgotha]

Calvary cross *n* a Latin cross with a representation of three steps beneath it

calve (kɑːv) *vb* **1** to give birth to (a calf) **2** (of a glacier or iceberg) to release (masses of ice) in breaking up

calves (kɑːvz) *n* the plural of **calf¹** and **calf²**

Calvin cycle *n botany* a series of reactions, occurring during photosynthesis, in which glucose is synthesized from carbon dioxide [C20 named after Melvin *Calvin* (1911–97), US chemist, who elucidated it]

Calvinism (ˈkælvɪˌnɪzəm) *n* the theological system of John Calvin (original name *Jean Cauvin, Caulvin,* or *Chauvin.*; 1509–64), the French theologian and leader of the Protestant Reformation, and his followers, characterized by emphasis on the doctrines of predestination, the irresistibility of grace, and justification by faith > ˈCalvinist *n, adj* > ˌCalvinˈistic *or* ˌCalvinˈistical *adj*

calvities (kælˈvɪʃɪˌiːz) *n* baldness [C17 from Late Latin, from Latin *calvus* bald]

calx (kælks) *n, pl* calxes *or* calces (ˈkælsiːz) **1** the powdery metallic oxide formed when an ore or mineral is roasted **2** another name for **calcium oxide 3** *anatomy* the heel [C15 from Latin: lime, from Greek *khalix* pebble]

calyces (ˈkælɪˌsiːz, ˈkeɪlɪ-) *n* a plural of **calyx**

calycine (ˈkælɪˌsaɪn) *or* **calycinal** (kəˈlɪsɪnˀl) *adj* relating to, belonging to, or resembling a calyx

calycle, calicle (ˈkælɪkˀl) *or* **calyculus** (kəˈlɪkjʊləs) *n* **1** *zoology* a small cup-shaped structure, as in the coral skeleton **2** *botany* another name for **epicalyx** [C18 from Latin, diminutive of CALYX] > calycular (kəˈlɪkjʊlə) *adj*

Calydonian boar (ˌkælɪˈdəʊnɪən) *n Greek myth* a savage boar sent by Artemis to destroy Calydon, a city in Aetolia, because its king had neglected to sacrifice to her. It was killed by Meleager, the king's son

calypso¹ (kəˈlɪpsəʊ) *n, pl* -sos **1** a popular type of satirical, usually topical, West Indian ballad, esp from Trinidad, usually extemporized to a percussive syncopated accompaniment **2** a dance done to the rhythm of this song [C20 probably from CALYPSO]

calypso² (kəˈlɪpsəʊ) *n, pl* -sos a rare N temperate orchid, *Calypso* (or *Cytherea*) *bulbosa*, whose flower is pink or white with purple and yellow markings [C19 named after CALYPSO]

Calypso (kəˈlɪpsəʊ) *n Greek myth* (in Homer's *Odyssey*) a sea nymph who detained Odysseus on the island of Ogygia for seven years

calypsonian (ˌkælɪpˈsəʊnɪən) *n* a performer or writer of calypsos

calyptra (kəˈlɪptrə) *n botany* **1** a membranous hood covering the spore-bearing capsule of mosses and liverworts **2** any hoodlike structure, such as a root cap [C18 from New Latin, from Greek *kaluptra* hood, from *kaluptein* to cover] > calyptrate (kəˈlɪpˌtreɪt) *adj*

calyptrogen (kəˈlɪptrədʒən) *n* a layer of rapidly dividing cells at the tip of a plant root, from which the root cap is formed. It occurs in grasses and many other plants [C19 from CALYPTRA + -GEN]

calyx (ˈkeɪlɪks, ˈkælɪks) *n, pl* calyxes *or* calyces (ˈkælɪˌsiːz, ˈkeɪlɪ-) **1** the sepals of a flower collectively, forming the outer floral envelope that protects the developing flower bud. Compare **corolla 2** any cup-shaped cavity or structure, esp any of the divisions of the human kidney (**renal calyx**) that form the renal pelvis [C17 from Latin, from Greek *kalux* shell, from *kaluptein* to cover, hide] > calycate (ˈkælɪˌkeɪt) *adj*

calzone (kælˈtsəʊnɪ) *n* a dish of Italian origin consisting of pizza dough folded over a filling of cheese and tomatoes, herbs, ham, etc [C20 Italian, literally: trouser leg, from *calzoni* trousers]

cam (kæm) *n* a slider or roller attached to a rotating shaft to give a particular type of reciprocating motion to a part in contact with its profile [C18 from Dutch *kam* comb]

-cam *n combining form* camera: *webcam*

Cam (kæm) *n* a river in E England, in Cambridgeshire, flowing through Cambridge to the River Ouse. Length: about 64 km (40 miles)

CAM *abbreviation for* **1** computer-aided manufacture **2** *botany* **a** crassulacean acid metabolism: a form of photosynthesis, first described in crassulacean plants, in which carbon dioxide is taken up only at night **b** (*as modifier*): *a CAM plant* **3** complementary and alternative medicine **4** *international car registration for* Cameroon

cama (ˈkɑːmə) *n* the hybrid offspring of a camel and a llama

Camagüey (ˈkæməˌgweɪ; *Spanish* kamaˈɣwej) *n* a city in E central Cuba. Pop: 320 000 (2005 est)

camail (ˈkæmeɪl) *n armour* a neck and shoulders covering of mail worn with and laced to the basinet

caman (ˈkæmən) *n shinty* the wooden stick used to hit the ball [C19 from Gaelic]

camaraderie (ˌkæməˈrɑːdərɪ) *n* a spirit of familiarity and trust existing between friends [C19 from French, from COMRADE]

Camargue (kæˈmɑːg) *n* **la** (la) a delta region in S France, between the channels of the Grand and Petit Rhône: cattle, esp bulls for the Spanish bullrings, and horses are reared

camarilla (ˌkæməˈrɪlə; *Spanish* kamaˈriʎa) *n* a group of confidential advisers, esp formerly, to the Spanish kings; cabal [C19 from Spanish: literally: a little room]

camass *or* **camas** (ˈkæməs) *n* **1** Also called: quamash any of several North American plants of the liliaceous genus *Camassia*, esp *C. quamash*, which has a cluster of blue or white flowers and a

C

sweet edible bulb **2 death camass** any liliaceous plant of the genus *Zygadenus* (or *Zigadenus*), of the western US, that is poisonous to livestock, esp sheep [C19 from Chinook Jargon *kamass*, from Nootka *chamas* sweet]

Camb. abbreviation for Cambridge

Cambay (kæm'beɪ) *n* **Gulf of** an inlet of the Arabian Sea on the W coast of India, southeast of the Kathiawar Peninsula

camber ('kæmbə) *n* **1** a slight upward curve to the centre of the surface of a road, ship's deck, etc **2** another name for **bank²** (sense 7) **3** an outward inclination of the front wheels of a road vehicle so that they are slightly closer together at the bottom than at the top **4** Also called: **hog** a small arching curve of a beam or girder provided to lessen deflection and improve appearance **5** aerofoil curvature expressed by the ratio of the maximum height of the aerofoil mean line to its chord ▷ *vb* **6** to form or be formed with a surface that curves upwards to its centre [C17 from Old French (northern dialect) *cambre* curved, from Latin *camurus*; related to *camera* CHAMBER]

Camberwell beauty ('kæmbə,wɛl, -wəl) *n* a nymphalid butterfly, *Nymphalis antiopa*, of temperate regions, having dark purple wings with cream-yellow borders. US name: **mourning cloak** [C19 named after *Camberwell*, a district of S London]

Camberwell carrot *n* informal a large, almost conical, marijuana cigarette

cambist ('kæmbɪst) *n* finance **1** a dealer or expert in foreign exchange **2** a manual of currency exchange rates and similar equivalents of weights and measures [C19 from French *cambiste*, from Italian *cambista*, from *cambio* (money) exchange] > 'cambistry *n*

cambium ('kæmbɪəm) *n*, *pl* **-biums** or **-bia** (-bɪə) botany a meristem that increases the girth of stems and roots by producing additional xylem and phloem. See also **cork cambium** [C17 from Medieval Latin: exchange, from Late Latin *cambiāre* to exchange, barter] > 'cambial *adj*

Cambodia (kæm'bəʊdɪə) *n* a country in SE Asia: became part of French Indochina in 1887; achieved self-government in 1949 and independence in 1953; civil war (1970–74) ended in victory for the Khmer Rouge, who renamed the country Kampuchea (1975) and carried out extreme-radical political and economic reforms resulting in a considerable reduction of the population; Vietnamese forces ousted the Khmer Rouge in 1979 and set up a pro-Vietnamese government who reverted (1981) to the name Cambodia; after Vietnamese withdrawal in 1989 a peace settlement with exiled factions was followed in 1993 by the adoption of a democratic monarchist constitution restoring Prince Sihanouk to the throne. The country contains the central plains of the Mekong River and the Cardamom Mountains in the SW. Official language: Khmer; French is also widely spoken. Currency: riel. Capital: Phnom Penh. Pop: 14 482 000 (2004 est.). Area: 181 000 sq km (69 895 sq miles)

Cambodian (kæm'bəʊdɪən) *adj* **1** of or relating to Cambodia or its inhabitants ▷ *n* **2** a native or inhabitant of Cambodia

cambogia (kæm'bəʊdʒɪə) *n* another name for **gamboge** (senses 1, 2)

camboose (kæm'buːs) *n* (formerly, in Canada) **1** a cabin built as living quarters for a gang of lumbermen **2** an open fireplace in such a cabin [C19 from Canadian French, from French *cambuse* hut, store, from Dutch *kambuis*]

Camborne-Redruth ('kæmbɔːn'rɛd,ruːθ) *n* a former (until 1974) urban district in SW England, in Cornwall: formed in 1934 by the amalgamation of the neighbouring towns of Camborne and Redruth. Pop: 39 936 (2001)

Cambrai (French kɑ̃brɛ) *n* a town in NE France: textile industry: scene of a battle in which massed tanks were first used and broke through

the German line (November, 1917). Pop: 33 738 (1999)

cambrel ('kæmbrəl) *n* a variant of **gambrel**

Cambria ('kæmbrɪə) *n* the Medieval Latin name for **Wales**

Cambrian ('kæmbrɪən) *adj* **1** of, denoting, or formed in the first 65 million years of the Palaeozoic era, during which marine invertebrates, esp trilobites, flourished **2** of or relating to Wales ▷ *n* **3 the** the Cambrian period or rock system **4** a Welsh person

Cambrian Mountains *pl n* a mountain range in Wales, extending from Carmarthenshire in the S to Denbighshire in the N. Highest peak: Aran Fawddwy, 891 m (2970 ft)

cambric ('keɪmbrɪk) *n* a fine white linen or cotton fabric [C16 from Flemish *Kamerijk* CAMBRAI]

Cambridge ('keɪmbrɪdʒ) *n* **1** a city in E England, administrative centre of Cambridgeshire, on the River Cam: centred around the university, founded in the 12th century: electronics, biotechnology. Pop: 117 717 (2001). Medieval Latin name: Cantabrigia **2** short for **Cambridgeshire 3** a city in the US, in E Massachusetts: educational centre, with Harvard University (1636) and the Massachusetts Institute of Technology. Pop: 101 587 (2003 est.). Related adj: **Cantabrigian**

Cambridge blue *n* **1 a** a lightish blue colour **b** (*as adjective*): *a Cambridge-blue scarf* **2** a person who has been awarded a blue from Cambridge University

Cambridgeshire ('keɪmbrɪdʒ,ʃɪə, -ʃə) *n* a county of E England, in East Anglia: includes the former counties of the Isle of Ely and Huntingdon and lies largely in the Fens: Peterborough became an independent unitary authority in 1998. Administrative centre: Cambridge. Pop (excluding Peterborough): 571 000 (2003 est.). Area (excluding Peterborough): 3068 sq km (184 sq miles)

Cambs abbreviation for Cambridgeshire

camcorder ('kæm,kɔːdə) *n* a video camera and recorder combined in a portable unit

Camden ('kæmdən) *n* a borough of N Greater London. Pop: 210 700 (2003 est.). Area: 21 sq km (8 sq miles)

came¹ (keɪm) *vb* the past tense of **come**

came² (keɪm) *n* a grooved strip of lead used to join pieces of glass in a stained-glass window or a leaded light [C17 of unknown origin]

camel ('kæməl) *n* **1** either of two cud-chewing artiodactyl mammals of the genus *Camelus* (see **Arabian camel, Bactrian camel**): family *Camelidae*. They are adapted for surviving long periods without food or water in desert regions, esp by using humps on the back for storing fat **2** a float attached to a vessel to increase its buoyancy. See also **caisson** (sense 3) **3** a raft or float used as a fender between a vessel and a wharf **4 a** a fawn colour **b** (*as adjective*): *a camel dress* [Old English, from Latin *camēlus*, from Greek *kamēlos*, of Semitic origin; related to Arabic *jamal*]

cameleer (,kæmɪ'lɪə) *n* a camel-driver

camel hair or **camel's hair** *n* **1** the hair of the camel or dromedary, used in clothing, rugs, etc **2 a** soft cloth made of or containing this hair as a substitute, usually tan in colour **b** (*as modifier*): *a camelhair coat* **3 a** the hair of the squirrel's tail, used for paintbrushes **b** (*as modifier*): *a camelhair brush*

camelid (kə'mɛlɪd) *adj* **1** of or relating to camels **2** belonging to the camel family, *Camelidae* ▷ *n* **3** any animal of the camel family

camellia (kə'miːlɪə) *n* any ornamental shrub of the Asian genus *Camellia*, esp *C. japonica*, having glossy evergreen leaves and showy roselike flowers, usually white, pink or red: family *Theaceae*. Also called: **japonica** [C18 New Latin, named after Georg Josef *Kamel* (1661–1706), Moravian Jesuit missionary, who introduced it to Europe]

camelopard ('kæmɪlə,pɑːd, kə'mɛl-) *n* an obsolete word for **giraffe** [C14 from Medieval Latin *camēlopardus*, from Greek *kamēlopardalis*, from

kamēlos CAMEL + *pardalis* LEOPARD, because the giraffe was thought to have a head like a camel's and spots like a leopard's]

Camelopardus (kə,mɛlə'pɑːdəs) or **Camelopardalis** (kə,mɛlə'pɑːdəlɪs) *n*, Latin genitive **Cameolopardi** (kə,mɛlə'pɑːdaɪ) or **Cameolopardalis** (kə,mɛlə'pɑːdəlɪs) a faint extensive constellation in the N hemisphere close to Ursa Major and Cassiopeia

Camelot ('kæmɪ,lɒt) *n* **1** (in Arthurian legend) the English town where King Arthur's palace and court were situated **2** (in the US) the supposedly golden age of the presidency of John F. Kennedy, 1961–63

camel's hair *n* See **camel hair**

Camembert ('kæməm,bɛə; French kamɑ̃bɛr) *n* a rich soft creamy cheese [French, from *Camembert*, a village in Normandy where it originated]

Camenae (kə'miːniː) *pl n* Roman myth a group of nymphs originally associated with a sacred spring in Rome, later identified with the Greek Muses

cameo ('kæmɪ,əʊ) *n*, *pl* **cameos 1 a** a medallion, as on a brooch or ring, with a profile head carved in relief **b** (*as modifier*): *a cameo necklace* **2** an engraving upon a gem or other stone of at least two differently coloured layers, such as sardonyx, so carved that the background is of a different colour from the raised design **3** a stone with such an engraving **4 a** a single and often brief dramatic scene played by a well-known actor or actress in a film or television play **b** (*as modifier*): *a cameo role* **5 a** a short literary work or dramatic sketch **b** (*as modifier*): *a cameo sketch* [C15 from Italian *cammeo*, of uncertain origin]

cameo ware *n* jasper ware with applied decoration of classical motifs, resembling a cameo

camera ('kæmərə, 'kæmrə) *n* **1** an optical device consisting of a lens system set in a light-proof construction inside which a light-sensitive film or plate can be positioned. See also **cine camera, digital camera 2** television the equipment used to convert the optical image of a scene into the corresponding electrical signals **3** See **camera obscura 4** *pl* **-erae** (-ə,riː) a judge's private room **5** in camera **a** law relating to a hearing from which members of the public are excluded **b** in private **6** off camera not within an area being filmed **7** on camera (esp of an actor) being filmed [C18 from Latin: vault, from Greek *kamara*]

cameral ('kæmərəl) *adj* of or relating to a judicial or legislative chamber [C18 from Medieval Latin *camerālis*; see CAMERA]

camera lucida ('luːsɪdə) *n* an instrument attached to a microscope, etc to enable an observer to view simultaneously the image and a drawing surface to facilitate the sketching of the image [New Latin: light chamber]

cameraman ('kæmərə,mæn, 'kæmrə-) *n*, *pl* **-men** a person who operates a film or television camera

camera obscura (ɒb'skjʊərə) *n* a darkened chamber or small building in which images of outside objects are projected onto a flat surface by a convex lens in an aperture. Sometimes shortened to: **camera** [New Latin: dark chamber]

camera phone *n* a mobile phone incorporating a camera

camera-ready copy *n* printing type matter ready to be photographed for plate-making without further alteration. Also called: **mechanical**

camera-shy *adj* having an aversion to being photographed or filmed

caméra stylo (French kamera stilo) *n* films the use of the camera as a means of personal expression, especially as practised by some directors of the New Wave [French, literally: camera stylograph]

camera tube *n* the part of a television camera that converts an optical image into an electrical signal. See also **image orthicon, vidicon, Plumbicon, iconoscope**

camerlengo (,kæmə'lɛŋɡəʊ) or **camerlingo** (,kæmə'lɪŋɡəʊ) *n*, *pl* **-gos** RC Church a cardinal who acts as the pope's financial secretary and the papal treasurer [c17 from Italian *camerlingo*, of Germanic origin; compare CHAMBERLAIN]

Cameroon (ˌkæməˈruːn, ˈkæməˌruːn) *n* **1** a republic in West Africa, on the Gulf of Guinea: became a German colony in 1884; divided in 1919 into the **Cameroons** (administered by Britain) and **Cameroun** (administered by France); Cameroun and the S part of the Cameroons formed a republic in 1961 (the N part joined Nigeria); became a member of the Commonwealth in 1995. Official languages: French and English. Religions: Christian, Muslim, and animist. Currency: franc. Capital: Yaoundé. Pop: 16 296 000 (2004 est). Area: 475 500 sq km (183 591 sq miles). French name: Cameroun German name: Kamerun **2** an active volcano in W Cameroon: the highest peak on the West African coast. Height: 4070 m (13 352 ft)

Cameroun (kamrun) *n* the French name for **Cameroon**

cam follower *n engineering* the slider or roller in contact with the cam that transmits the movement dictated by the cam profile

camiknickers (ˈkæmɪˌnɪkəz) *pl n* women's knickers attached to a camisole top. Often shortened to: camiknicks

camion (ˈkæmɪən; *French* kamjɔ̃) *n* a lorry, or, esp formerly, a large dray [c19 from French, of obscure origin]

camisado (ˌkæmɪˈsɑːdəʊ) *or* **camisade** (ˌkæmɪˈseɪd) *n, pl* -sados *or* -sades (formerly) an attack made under cover of darkness [c16 from obsolete Spanish *camisada*, literally: an attack in one's shirt (worn over the armour as identification), from *camisa* shirt]

camise (kəˈmiːz) *n* a loose light shirt, smock, or tunic originally worn in the Middle Ages [c19 from Arabic *qamīs*, from Late Latin *camīsia*]

camisole (ˈkæmɪˌsəʊl) *n* **1** a woman's underbodice with shoulder straps, originally designed as a cover for a corset **2** a woman's dressing jacket or short negligée **3** (*modifier*) resembling a camisole (the underbodice), as in fitting snugly around the bust and having a straight neckline: *a camisole slip; a camisole top* [c19 from French, from Provençal *camisola*, from *camisa* shirt, from Late Latin *camīsia*]

camlet (ˈkæmlɪt) *n* **1** a tough waterproof cloth **2** a garment or garments made from such cloth **3** a soft woollen fabric used in medieval Asia [c14 from Old French *camelot*, perhaps from Arabic *hamlat* plush fabric]

camo (ˈkæməʊ) *n informal* short for **camouflage** (sense 2) *camo fatigues*

camogie (ka'mo:gi:) *n Irish* a form of hurling played by women [from Irish Gaelic *camógaíocht*, from *camóg* crooked stick]

camomile *or* **chamomile** (ˈkæməˌmaɪl) *n* **1** any aromatic plant of the Eurasian genus *Anthemis*, esp *A. nobilis*, whose finely dissected leaves and daisy-like flowers are used medicinally: family *Asteraceae* (composites) **2** any plant of the related genus *Matricaria*, esp *M. chamomilla* (**German** *or* **wild camomile**) **3** camomile tea a medicinal beverage made from the fragrant leaves and flowers of any of these plants [c14 from Old French *camomille*, from Medieval Latin *chamomilla*, from Greek *khamaimēlon*, literally: earth-apple (referring to the apple scent of the flowers)]

camoodi (kæˈmuːdɪ) *n* a Caribbean name for **anaconda** [c19 from an American Indian language of Guyana]

Camorra (kəˈmɒrə) *n* **1** a secret society organized in about 1820 in Naples, which thrives on blackmail and extortion **2** any similar clandestine group [c19 from Italian, probably from Spanish *quarrel*]

camouflage (ˈkæməˌflɑːʒ) *n* **1** the exploitation of natural surroundings or artificial aids to conceal or disguise the presence of military units, equipment, etc **2** (*modifier*) (of fabric or clothing) having a design of irregular patches of dull colours (such as browns and greens), as used in military camouflage **3** the means by which animals escape the notice of predators, usually because of a resemblance to their surroundings: includes cryptic and apatetic coloration **4** a device or expedient designed to conceal or deceive ▷ *vb* **5** (*tr*) to conceal by camouflage [c20 from French, from *camoufler*, from Italian *camuffare* to disguise, deceive, of uncertain origin]

camp¹ (kæmp) *n* **1** a place where tents, cabins, or other temporary structures are erected for the use of military troops, for training soldiers, etc **2** the military life **3** tents, cabins, etc, used as temporary lodgings by a group of travellers, holiday-makers, Scouts, etc **4** the group of people living in such lodgings **5** *South African* a field or paddock fenced off as pasture **6** a group supporting a given doctrine or theory: *the socialist camp* **7** (*modifier*) suitable for use in temporary quarters, on holiday, etc, esp by being portable and easy to set up: *a camp bed; a camp chair* ▷ *vb* **8** (*intr; often foll by down*) to establish or set up a camp **9** (*intr; often foll by out*) to live temporarily in or as if in a tent **10** (*tr*) to put in a camp [c16 from Old French, ultimately from Latin *campus* field] > ˈcamping *n*

camp² (kæmp) *informal* ▷ *adj* **1** effeminate; affected in mannerisms, dress, etc **2** homosexual **3** consciously artificial, exaggerated, vulgar, or mannered; self-parodying, esp when in dubious taste ▷ *vb* **4** (*tr*) to perform or invest with a camp quality **5** camp it up **a** to seek to focus attention on oneself by making an ostentatious display, overacting, etc **b** to flaunt one's homosexuality ▷ *n* **6** a camp quality, style, etc [c20 of uncertain origin]

campagna (kæmˈpɑːnjə) *n* another word for **champaign** (sense 1)

Campagna (kæmˈpɑːnjə) *n* a low-lying plain surrounding Rome, Italy: once fertile, it deteriorated to malarial marshes; recently reclaimed. Area: about 2000 sq km (800 sq miles). Also called: Campagna di Roma (dɪ ˈrəʊma)

campaign (kæmˈpeɪn) *n* **1** a series of coordinated activities, such as public speaking and demonstrating, designed to achieve a social, political, or commercial goal: *a presidential campaign; an advertising campaign* **2** *military* a number of complementary operations aimed at achieving a single objective, usually constrained by time or geographic area ▷ *vb* **3** (*intr; often foll by for*) to conduct, serve in, or go on a campaign [c17 from French *campagne* open country, from Italian *campagna*, from Late Latin *campānia*, from Latin *campus* field] > camˈpaigner *n*

Campania (kæmˈpeɪnɪə; *Italian* kamˈpaɲɲa) *n* a region of SW Italy: includes the islands of Capri and Ischia. Chief town: Naples. op.: 5 725 098 (2003 est). Area: 13 595 sq km (5248 sq miles)

campanile (ˌkæmpəˈniːlɪ) *n* (esp in Italy) a bell tower, not usually attached to another building. Compare **belfry** [c17 from Italian, from *campana* bell]

campanology (ˌkæmpəˈnɒlədʒɪ) *n* the art or skill of ringing bells musically [c19 from New Latin *campānologia*, from Late Latin *campāna* bell] > campanological (ˌkæmpənəˈlɒdʒɪkəl) *adj* > ˌcampaˈnologist *or* ˌcampaˈnologer *n*

campanula (kæmˈpænjʊlə) *n* any N temperate plant of the campanulaceous genus *Campanula*, typically having blue or white bell-shaped flowers. Also called: bellflower. See also **Canterbury bell, harebell** [c17 from New Latin: a little bell, from Late Latin *campāna* bell; see CAMPANILE]

campanulaceous (kəmˌpænjʊˈleɪʃəs) *adj* of, relating to, or belonging to the *Campanulaceae*, a family of temperate and subtropical plants, including the campanulas, having bell-shaped nodding flowers

campanulate (kæmˈpænjʊlɪt, -ˌleɪt) *adj* (esp of flower corollas) shaped like a bell [c17 from New Latin *campanulātus*; see CAMPANULA]

Campbell-Stokes recorder (ˌkæmbəlˈstəʊks) *n* an instrument for recording hours of sunshine per day, consisting of a solid glass sphere that focuses rays of sunlight onto a light-sensitive card on which a line is burnt

Camp David (ˈdeɪvɪd) *n* the US president's retreat in the Appalachian Mountains, Maryland: scene of the **Camp David Agreement** (Sept, 1978) between Anwar Sadat of Egypt and Menachem Begin of Israel, mediated by Jimmy Carter, which outlined a framework for establishing peace in the Middle East. This agreement was the basis of the peace treaty between Israel and Egypt signed in Washington (March, 1979)

camp-drafting *n Austral* a competitive test, esp at an agricultural show, of horsemen's skill in drafting cattle

Campeche (*Spanish* kamˈpetʃe) *n* **1** a state of SE Mexico, on the SW of the Yucatán peninsula: forestry and fishing. Capital: Campeche. Pop: 205 000 (2005 est). Area: 56 114 sq km (21 666 sq miles) **2** a port in SE Mexico, capital of Campeche state. Pop: 195 000 (2000 est) **3** Bay of Also called: Gulf of Campeche the SW part of the Gulf of Mexico

camper (ˈkæmpə) *n* **1** a person who lives or temporarily stays in a tent, cabin, etc **2** a vehicle equipped for camping out

camper van *n* a motor caravan

campestral (kæmˈpɛstrəl) *adj* of or relating to open fields or country [c18 from Latin *campester*, from *campus* field]

campfire (ˈkæmpˌfaɪə) *n* an outdoor fire in a camp, esp one used for cooking or as a focal point for community events

camp follower *n* **1** any civilian, esp a prostitute, who unofficially provides services to military personnel **2** a nonmember who is sympathetic to a particular group, theory, etc

camphene (ˈkæmfiːn) *n* a colourless crystalline insoluble optically active terpene derived from pinene and present in many essential oils. Formula: $C_{10}H_{16}$ [c19 from CAMPH(OR) + -ENE]

camphire (ˈkæmfaɪə) *n* an archaic name for **henna** (senses 1, 2)

camphor (ˈkæmfə) *n* a whitish crystalline aromatic terpene ketone obtained from the wood of the camphor tree or made from pinene: used in the manufacture of celluloid and in medicine as a liniment and treatment for colds. Formula: $C_{10}H_{16}O$ [c15 from Old French *camphre*, from Medieval Latin *camphora*, from Arabic *kāfūr*, from Malay *kāpūr* chalk; related to Khmer *kāpōr* camphor] > camphoric (kæmˈfɒrɪk) *adj*

camphorate (ˈkæmfəˌreɪt) *vb* (*tr*) to apply, treat with, or impregnate with camphor

camphorated oil *n* a liniment consisting of camphor and peanut oil, used as a counterirritant

camphor ball *n* another name for **mothball** (sense 1)

camphor ice *n* an ointment consisting of camphor, white wax, spermaceti, and castor oil, used to treat skin ailments, esp chapped skin

camphor laurel *n* an Australian name for the camphor tree, now occurring in the wild in parts of Australia

camphor tree *n* **1** a lauraceous evergreen E Asian tree, *Cinnamomum camphora*, whose aromatic wood yields camphor **2** any similar tree, such as the dipterocarpaceous tree *Dryobalanops aromatica* of Borneo

campimetry (kæmˈpɪmɪtrɪ) *n* a technique for assessing the central part of the visual field [c20 from New Latin, from Latin *campus* field + -*metry*; see -METER]

Campina Grande (*Portuguese* kɔmˈpiːnɐ ˈɡrɐ̃ndɐ) *n* a city in NE Brazil, in E Paraíba state. Pop: 366 000 (2005 est)

Campinas (kæmˈpiːnəs; *Portuguese* kəmˈpiːnɐʃ) *n* a city in SE Brazil, in São Paulo state: centre of a rich agricultural region, producing esp coffee. Pop: 2 640 000 (2005 est)

camping ground *n* another word for **camp site**

campion ('kæmpɪən) *n* any of various caryophyllaceous plants of the genera *Silene* and *Lychnis*, having red, pink, or white flowers. See also **bladder campion** [c16 probably from *campion*, obsolete variant of CHAMPION, perhaps so called because originally applied to *Lychnis coronaria*, the leaves of which were used to crown athletic champions]

CAM plant (kæm) *n* any plant that undergoes a form of photosynthesis known as crassulacean acid metabolism, in which carbon dioxide is taken up only at night [C(*rassulacean*) A(*cid*) M(*etabolism*) *plant*]

camp meeting *n* chiefly US a religious meeting held in a large tent or outdoors, often lasting several days

campo ('kæmpəʊ) *n, pl* **-pos** (*often plural*) level or undulating savanna country, esp in the uplands of Brazil [American Spanish, from Latin *campus*]

Campobello (,kæmpə'beləʊ) *n* an island in the Bay of Fundy, off the coast of SE Canada: part of New Brunswick province. Area: about 52 sq km (20 sq miles). Pop: 1195 (2001)

Campo Formio (*Italian* 'kampo 'fɔrmjo) *n* a village in NE Italy, in Friuli-Venezia Giulia: scene of the signing of a treaty in 1797 that ended the war between revolutionary France and Austria. Modern name: **Campoformido** (kampo'fɔrmido)

Campo Grande (*Portuguese* 'kɐ:mpu 'grɐ:ndɐ) *n* a city in SW Brazil, capital of Mato Grosso do Sul state on the São Paulo–Corumbá railway: market centre. Pop: 746 000 (2005 est)

camporee (,kæmpə'ri:) *n* a local meeting or assembly of Scouts [c20 from CAMP¹ + (JAMB)OREE]

Campos (*Portuguese* 'kɐ:mpuʃ) *n* a city in E Brazil, in E Rio de Janeiro state on the Paraíba River. Pop: 388 000 (2005 est)

camp oven *n* Austral and NZ a metal pot or box with a heavy lid, used for baking over an open fire

camp pie *n* Austral history tinned meat

camp site *n* an area on which holiday-makers may pitch a tent, etc. Also called: **camping site**

campus ('kæmpəs) *n, pl* **-puses 1** the grounds and buildings of a university **2** chiefly US the outside area of a college, university, etc [c18 from Latin: field]

campus university *n* Brit a university in which the buildings, often including shops and cafés, are all on one site. Compare **redbrick**

campy ('kæmpɪ) *adj* **campier, campiest** informal **1** effeminate; affected in mannerisms, dress, etc **2** relating to or considered characteristic of homosexuals **3** consciously artificial, exaggerated, vulgar, or mannered; self-parodying, esp when in dubious taste

campylobacter (,kæmpɪləʊ'bæktə) *n* a rod-shaped bacterium that causes infections in cattle and man. Unpasteurized milk infected with campylobacter is a common cause of gastroenteritis [from Greek *kampulos* bent + BACTER(IUM)]

CAMRA ('kæmrə) *n acronym for* Campaign for Real Ale

Cam Ranh ('kæm 'ræn) *n* a port in SE Vietnam: large natural harbour, in recent years used as a naval base by French, Japanese, US, and Russian forces successively. Pop: 114 041 (1992 est)

camshaft ('kæm,ʃɑ:ft) *n* a shaft having one or more cams attached to it, esp one used to operate the valves of an internal-combustion engine

camwood ('kæm,wʊd) *n* **1** a W African leguminous tree, *Baphia nitida*, whose hard wood was formerly used in making a red dye **2** the wood of this tree [c20 perhaps from Temne]

can¹ (kæn; *unstressed* kən) *vb, past* **could** (takes an infinitive without *to* or an implied infinitive) (*intr*) **1** used as an auxiliary to indicate ability, skill, or fitness to perform a task: *I can run a mile in under four minutes* **2** used as an auxiliary to indicate permission or the right to something: *can I have a drink?* **3** used as an auxiliary to indicate

knowledge of how to do something: *he can speak three languages fluently* **4** used as an auxiliary to indicate the possibility, opportunity, or likelihood: *my trainer says I can win the race if I really work hard* [Old English *cunnan*; related to Old Norse *kunna*, Old High German *kunnan*, Latin *cognōscere* to know, Sanskrit *jānāti* he knows; see KEN, UNCOUTH]

▦ USAGE See at **may**

can² (kæn) *n* **1** a container, esp for liquids, usually of thin sheet metal: *a petrol can; beer can* **2** another name (esp US) for **tin** (metal container) **3** Also called: **canful** the contents of a can or the amount a can will hold **4** a slang word for **prison 5** US and Canadian a slang word for **toilet** or **buttocks 6** US navy a slang word for **destroyer 7** naval slang a depth charge **8** a shallow cylindrical metal container of varying size used for storing and handling film **9** can of worms informal a complicated problem **10** carry the can See **carry** (sense 37) **11** in the can **a** (of a film, piece of music, etc) having been recorded, processed, edited, etc **b** informal arranged or agreed: *the contract is almost in the can* ▷ *vb* **cans, canning, canned 12** to put (food, etc) into a can or cans; preserve in a can **13** (*tr*) US slang to dismiss from a job **14** (*tr*) US informal to stop (doing something annoying or making an annoying noise) (esp in the phrase **can it!**) **15** (*tr*) informal to reject or discard [Old English *canne*; related to Old Norse, Old High German *kanna*, Irish *gann*, Swedish *kana* sled]

Can. *abbreviation for* **1** Canada **2** Canadian

Cana ('keɪnə) *n* New Testament the town in Galilee, north of Nazareth, where Jesus performed his first miracle by changing water into wine (John 2:1, 11)

Canaan ('keɪnən) *n* an ancient region between the River Jordan and the Mediterranean, corresponding roughly to Israel: the Promised Land of the Israelites

Canaan dog *n* a strongly-built medium-sized dog of a breed with erect ears, a dense coat, and a bushy tail carried curled over its back

Canaanite ('keɪnə,naɪt) *n* **1** a member of an ancient Semitic people who occupied the land of Canaan before the Israelite conquest **2** the extinct language of this people, belonging to the Canaanitic branch of the Semitic subfamily of the Afro-Asiatic family **3** (in later books of the Old Testament) a merchant or trader (Job 40:30; Proverbs 31:24)

Canaanitic (,keɪnə'nɪtɪk) *n* **1** a group of ancient languages belonging to the Semitic subfamily of the Afro-Asiatic family and including Canaanite, Phoenician, Ugaritic, and Hebrew ▷ *adj* **2** denoting, relating to, or belonging to this group of languages

Canada ('kænədə) *n* a country in North America: the second largest country in the world; first permanent settlements by Europeans were made by the French from 1605; ceded to Britain in 1763 after a series of colonial wars; established as the Dominion of Canada in 1867; a member of the Commonwealth. It consists generally of sparsely inhabited tundra regions, rich in natural resources, in the north, the Rocky Mountains in the west, the Canadian Shield in the east, and vast central prairies; the bulk of the population is concentrated along the US border and the Great Lakes in the south. Languages: English and French. Religion: Christian majority. Currency: Canadian dollar. Capital: Ottawa. Pop: 31 743 000 (2004 est). Area: 9 976 185 sq km (3 851 809 sq miles)

Canada balsam *n* **1** a yellow transparent resin obtained from the balsam fir. Because its refractive index is similar to that of glass, it is used as an adhesive in optical devices and as a mounting medium for microscope specimens **2** another name for **balsam fir**

Canada Day *n* (in Canada) July 1, the anniversary of the day in 1867 when Canada became the first British colony to receive dominion status: a bank

holiday. Former name: Dominion Day

Canada goose *n* a large common greyish-brown North American goose, *Branta canadensis*, with a black neck and head and a white throat patch

Canada jay *n* a large common jay of North America, *Perisoreus canadensis*, with a grey body, and a white-and-black crestless head

Canada lily *n* a lily, *Lilium canadense*, of NE North America, with small orange funnel-shaped nodding flowers. Also called: **meadow lily**

Canadarm ('kænəd,ɑ:m) *n* a type of robotic arm, developed in Canada, used on space vehicles

Canada thistle *n* the US and Canadian name for **creeping thistle**

Canadian (kə'neɪdɪən) *adj* **1** of or relating to Canada or its people ▷ *n* **2** a native, citizen, or inhabitant of Canada

Canadian Alliance *n* a Canadian right-wing federal political party, founded in 2000

Canadian bacon *n* the US name for **back bacon**

Canadian English *n* the English language as spoken in Canada

Canadian football *n* a game resembling American football, played on a grass pitch between two teams of 12 players

Canadian Forces *pl n* the official name for the military forces of Canada

Canadian French *n* **1** the French language as spoken in Canada, esp in Quebec ▷ *adj* **2** denoting this language or a French-speaking Canadian

Canadianism (kə'neɪdɪə,nɪzəm) *n* **1** the Canadian national character or spirit **2** loyalty to Canada, its political independence, culture, etc **3** a linguistic usage, custom, or other feature peculiar to or characteristic of Canada, its people, or their culture

Canadian pondweed *n* a North American aquatic plant, *Elodea* (or *Anacharis*) *canadensis*, naturalized in Europe, having crowded dark green leaves: family *Hydrocharitaceae*. It is used in aquariums

Canadian River *n* a river in the southern US, rising in NE New Mexico and flowing east to the Arkansas River in E Oklahoma. Length: 1458 km (906 miles)

Canadian Shield *n* (in Canada) the wide area of Precambrian rock extending west from the Labrador coast to the basin of the Mackenzie and north from the Great Lakes to the Arctic: rich in minerals. Also called: Laurentian Shield, Laurentian Plateau See **shield** (sense 7)

canaigre (kə'naɪgə) *n* a dock, *Rumex hymenosepalus*, of the southern US, the root of which yields a substance used in tanning [c19 from Mexican Spanish]

canaille *French* (kanaj) *n* the masses; mob; rabble [c17 from French, from Italian *canaglia* pack of dogs]

canakin ('kænɪkɪn) *n* a variant spelling of **cannikin**

canal (kə'næl) *n* **1** an artificial waterway constructed for navigation, irrigation, water power, etc **2** any of various tubular passages or ducts: *the alimentary canal* **3** any of various elongated intercellular spaces in plants **4** astronomy any of the indistinct surface features of Mars originally thought to be a network of channels but not seen on close-range photographs. They are caused by an optical illusion in which faint geological features appear to have a geometric structure ▷ *vb* **-nals, -nalling, -nalled** or US **-nals, -naling, -naled** (*tr*) **5** to dig a canal through **6** to provide with a canal or canals [c15 (in the sense: pipe, tube); from Latin *canālis* channel, water pipe, from *canna* reed, CANE¹]

canal boat *n* a long narrow boat used on canals, esp for carrying freight

canaliculus (,kænə'lɪkjʊləs) *n, pl* **-li** (-,laɪ) a small channel, furrow, or groove, as in some bones and parts of plants [c16 from Latin: a little channel, from *canālis* CANAL] ▷ ,cana'licular, canaliculate

(ˌkænəˈlɪkjʊlɪt, -ˌleɪt) *or* ˌcanaˈlicuˌlated *adj*

canalize *or* **canalise** (ˈkænəˌlaɪz) *vb (tr)* **1** to provide with or convert into a canal or canals **2** to give a particular direction to or provide an outlet for; channel **3** to divide a channel into separate reaches controlled by dams and weirs to aid navigation, control water levels, generate power, etc > ˌcanaliˈzation *or* ˌcanaliˈsation *n*

canal ray *n physics* a stream of positive ions produced in a discharge tube by allowing them to pass through holes in the cathode

Canal Zone *n* a former administrative region of the US, on the Isthmus of Panama around the Panama Canal: bordered on each side by the Republic of Panama, into which it was incorporated in 1979. Also called: **Panama Canal Zone**

canapé (ˈkænəpɪ, -ˌpeɪ; *French* kanape) *n* **1** a small piece of bread, toast, etc, spread with a savoury topping **2** (in French cabinetwork) a sofa [c19 from French: sofa]

Canara (kəˈnɑːrə) *n* a variant spelling of **Kanara**

canard (kæˈnɑːd; *French* kanar) *n* **1** a false report; rumour or hoax **2** an aircraft in which the tailplane is mounted in front of the wing [c19 from French: a duck, hoax, from Old French *caner* to quack, of imitative origin]

Canarese (ˌkænəˈriːz) *n, pl* **-rese,** *adj* a variant spelling of **Kanarese**

canary (kəˈnɛərɪ) *n, pl* **-naries 1** a small finch, *Serinus canaria,* of the Canary Islands and Azores: a popular cagebird noted for its singing. Wild canaries are streaked yellow and brown, but most domestic breeds are pure yellow **2** See **canary yellow 3** *Austral history* a convict **4** *archaic* a sweet wine from the Canary Islands similar to Madeira [c16 from Old Spanish *canario* of or from the Canary Islands]

canary creeper *n* a climbing plant, *Tropaeolum peregrinum,* similar to the nasturtium but with smaller yellow flowers and lobed leaves

canary grass *n* **1** any of various grasses of the genus *Phalaris,* esp *P. canariensis,* that is native to Europe and N Africa and has straw-coloured seeds used as birdseed **2 reed canary grass** a related plant, *Phalaris arundinacea,* used as fodder throughout the N hemisphere

Canary Islands *or* **Canaries** *pl n* a group of mountainous islands in the Atlantic off the NW coast of Africa, forming an Autonomous Community of Spain. Pop: 1 944 700 (2003 est)

canary seed *n* another name for **birdseed**

canary yellow *n* **a** a moderate yellow colour, sometimes with a greenish tinge **b** (*as adjective*): *a canary-yellow car.* Sometimes shortened to: canary

canasta (kəˈnæstə) *n* **1** a card game for two to six players who seek to amass points by declaring sets of cards **2** Also called: **meld** a declared set in this game, containing seven or more like cards, worth 500 points if the canasta is pure or 300 if wild (containing up to three jokers) [c20 from Spanish: basket (because two packs, or a basketful, of cards are required), variant of *canastro,* from Latin *canistrum;* see CANISTER]

canaster (ˈkænəstə) *n* coarsely broken dried tobacco leaves [c19 (meaning: rush basket in which tobacco was packed): from Spanish *canastro;* see CANISTER]

Canaveral (kəˈnævərəl) *n* **Cape** a cape on the E coast of Florida: site of the US Air Force Missile Test Centre, from which the majority of US space missions have been launched. Former name (1963–73): Cape **Kennedy**

Canberra (ˈkænbərə, -brə) *n* the capital of Australia, in Australian Capital Territory: founded in 1913 as a planned capital. Pop: 309 799 (2001)

can buoy *n nautical* a buoy with a flat-topped cylindrical shape above water, marking the left side of a channel leading into a harbour: red in British waters but green (occasionally black) in US waters. Compare **nun buoy**

cancan (ˈkænˌkæn) *n* a high-kicking dance performed by a female chorus, originating in the music halls of 19th-century Paris [c19 from French, of uncertain origin]

cancel (ˈkænsᵊl) *vb* **-cels, -celling, -celled** *or US* **-cels, -celing, -celed** (*mainly tr*) **1** to order (something already arranged, such as a meeting or event) to be postponed indefinitely; call off **2** to revoke or annul: *the order for the new television set was cancelled* **3** to delete (writing, numbers, etc); cross out: *he cancelled his name and substituted hers* **4** to mark (a cheque, postage stamp, ticket, etc) with an official stamp or by a perforation to prevent further use **5** (*also intr;* usually foll by *out*) to counterbalance; make up for (a deficiency, etc): *his generosity cancelled out his past unkindness* **6 a** to close (an account) by discharging any outstanding debts **b** (sometimes foll by *out*) *accounting* to eliminate (a debit or credit) by making an offsetting entry on the opposite side of the account **7** *maths* **a** to eliminate (numbers, quantities, or terms) as common factors from both the numerator and denominator of a fraction or as equal terms from opposite sides of an equation **b** (*intr*) to be able to be eliminated in this way ▷ *n* **8** a new leaf or section of a book replacing a defective one, one containing errors, or one that has been omitted **9** a less common word for **cancellation 10** *music* a US word for **natural** (sense 19a) [c14 from Old French *canceller,* from Medieval Latin *cancellāre,* from Late Latin: to strike out, make like a lattice, from Latin *cancellī* lattice, grating] > ˈ**canceller** *or US* ˈ**canceler** *n*

cancellate (ˈkænsɪˌleɪt), **cancellous** (ˈkænsɪləs) *or* **cancellated** *adj* **1** *anatomy* having a spongy or porous internal structure: *cancellate bones* **2** *botany* forming a network; reticulate: *a cancellate venation* [c17 from Latin *cancellāre* to make like a lattice; see CANCEL]

cancellation (ˌkænsɪˈleɪʃən) *n* **1** the fact or an instance of cancelling **2** something that has been cancelled, such as a theatre ticket, esp when it is available for another person to take: *we have a cancellation in the stalls* **3** the marks or perforation made by cancelling

cancer (ˈkænsə) *n* **1** any type of malignant growth or tumour, caused by abnormal and uncontrolled cell division: it may spread through the lymphatic system or blood stream to other parts of the body **2** the condition resulting from this **3** an evil influence that spreads dangerously ▷ Related prefix: **carcino-** [c14 from Latin: crab, a creeping tumour; related to Greek *karkinos* crab, Sanskrit *karkata*] > ˈ**cancerous** *adj* > ˈ**cancerously** *adv*

Cancer (ˈkænsə) *n, Latin genitive* **Cancri** (ˈkæŋkriː) **1** *astronomy* a small faint zodiacal constellation in the N hemisphere, lying between Gemini and Leo on the ecliptic and containing the star cluster Praesepe **2** *astrology* **a** Also called: **the Crab** the fourth sign of the zodiac, symbol ♋, having a cardinal water classification and ruled by the moon. The sun is in this sign between about June 21 and July 22 **b** Also called: **Moonchild** a person born during a period when the sun is in this sign **3 tropic of Cancer** See **tropic** (sense 1) ▷ *adj* **4** *astrology* born under or characteristic of Cancer ▷ Also (for senses 2b, 4): **Cancerian** (kænˈsɪərɪən)

cancerophobia (ˌkænsərəʊˈfəʊbɪə) *n* a morbid dread of being afflicted by cancer

cancer stick *n* a slang name for **cigarette**

cancrizans (ˈkænkrɪˌzæns, ˈkæŋ-) *adj* See **crab canon** [Medieval Latin: moving backwards, from *cancrizāre* to move crabwise]

cancroid (ˈkæŋkrɔɪd) *adj* **1** resembling a cancerous growth **2** resembling a crab ▷ *n* **3** a skin cancer, esp one of only moderate malignancy

Cancún (kaːnˈkuːn) *n* a coastal resort in SE Mexico on the Yucatán Peninsula. Pop: 457 000 (2004 est)

c & b *cricket abbreviation for* caught and bowled (by)

candela (kænˈdiːlə, -ˈdeɪlə) *n* the basic SI unit of luminous intensity; the luminous intensity in a given direction of a source that emits monochromatic radiation of frequency 540×10^{12} hertz and that has a radiant intensity in that direction of (1/683) watt per steradian. Symbol: cd. Also called: **candle, standard candle** [c20 from Latin: CANDLE]

candelabrum (ˌkændɪˈlɑːbrəm) *or* **candelabra** *n, pl* **-bra** (-brə) **-brums** *or* **-bras** a large branched candleholder or holder for overhead lights [c19 from Latin, from *candēla* CANDLE]

candent (ˈkændənt) *adj* an archaic word for **incandescent** [c16 from Latin *candēre* to shine]

candescent (kænˈdɛsᵊnt) *adj rare* glowing or starting to glow with heat [c19 from Latin *candescere,* from *candēre* to be white, shine] > canˈ**descence** *n* > canˈ**descently** *adv*

c & f *abbreviation for* cost and freight

C & G *abbreviation for* City and Guilds

Candia (ˈkandja) *n* the Italian name for **Iráklion**

candid (ˈkændɪd) *adj* **1** frank and outspoken: *he was candid about his dislike of our friends* **2** without partiality; unbiased **3** unposed or informal: *a candid photograph* **4** *obsolete* **a** white **b** clear or pure [c17 from Latin *candidus* white, from *candēre* to be white] > ˈ**candidly** *adv* > ˈ**candidness** *n*

candida (ˈkændɪdə) *n* any yeastlike parasitic fungus of the genus *Candida,* esp *C. albicans,* which causes thrush (**candidiasis**) [New Latin, feminine of *candidus* white]

candidate (ˈkændɪˌdeɪt, -dɪt) *n* **1** a person seeking or nominated for election to a position of authority or honour or selection for a job, promotion, etc **2** a person taking an examination or test **3** a person or thing regarded as suitable or likely for a particular fate or position: *this wine is a candidate for his cellar* [c17 from Latin *candidātus* clothed in white (because the candidate wore a white toga), from *candidus* white] > **candidacy** (ˈkændɪdəsɪ) *or* **candidature** (ˈkændɪdətʃə) *n*

candid camera *n* **a** a small camera that may be used to take informal photographs of people, usually without their knowledge **b** (*as modifier*): *a candid-camera photograph*

candied (ˈkændɪd) *adj* **1** impregnated or encrusted with or as if with sugar or syrup: *candied peel* **2** (of sugar, honey, etc) crystallized

Candiot (ˈkændɪˌɒt) *or* **Candiote** (ˈkændɪˌəʊt) *adj* **1** of or relating to Candia (Iráklion) or Crete; Cretan ▷ *n* **2** a native or inhabitant of Crete; a Cretan

candle (ˈkændᵊl) *n* **1** a cylindrical piece of wax, tallow, or other fatty substance surrounding a wick, which is burned to produce light **2** *physics* **a** See **international candle b** another name for **candela 3 burn the candle at both ends** to exhaust oneself, esp by being up late and getting up early to work **4 not hold a candle to** *informal* to be inferior or contemptible in comparison with: *your dog doesn't hold a candle to mine* **5 not worth the candle** *informal* not worth the price or trouble entailed (esp in the phrase **the game's not worth the candle**) ▷ *vb* **6** (*tr*) to examine (eggs) for freshness or the likelihood of being hatched by viewing them against a bright light [Old English *candel,* from Latin *candēla,* from *candēre* to be white, glitter] > ˈ**candler** *n*

candleberry (ˈkændᵊlbərɪ) *n, pl* **-ries** another name for **wax myrtle**

candlefish (ˈkændᵊlˌfɪʃ) *n, pl* **-fish** *or* **-fishes** a salmonoid food fish, *Thaleichthys pacificus,* that occurs in the N Pacific and has oily flesh. Also called: **eulachon**

candlelight (ˈkændᵊlˌlaɪt) *n* **1 a** the light from a candle or candles: *they ate by candlelight* **b** (*as modifier*): *a candlelight dinner* **2** dusk; evening

Candlemas (ˈkændᵊlməs) *n Christianity* Feb 2, the Feast of the Purification of the Virgin Mary and the presentation of Christ in the Temple: the day on which the church candles are blessed. In Scotland it is one of the four quarter days

candlenut (ˈkændᵊlˌnʌt) *n* **1** a euphorbiaceous tree, *Aleurites moluccana,* of tropical Asia and

C

Polynesia **2** the nut of this tree, which yields an oil used in paints and varnishes. In their native regions the nuts are strung together and burned as candles

candlepin ('kænd[?]l,pɪn) *n* a bowling pin, as used in skittles, tenpin bowling, candlepins, etc

candlepins ('kænd[?]l,pɪnz) *n* (*functioning as singular*) a type of bowling game, employing a smaller ball than tenpins, in which three balls are allowed to a frame and fallen pins are not removed from the alley

candlepower ('kænd[?]l,paʊə) *n* the luminous intensity of a source of light in a given direction: now expressed in candelas but formerly in terms of the international candle

candlestick ('kænd[?]l,stɪk) *or* **candleholder** ('kænd[?]l,həʊldə) *n* a holder, usually ornamental, with a spike or socket for a candle

candle-tree *n* another name for **wax myrtle**

candlewick ('kænd[?]l,wɪk) *n* **1** unbleached cotton or muslin into which loops of yarn are hooked and then cut to give a tufted pattern. It is used for bedspreads, dressing gowns, etc **2** the wick of a candle **3** (*modifier*) being or made of candlewick fabric

candlewood ('kænd[?]l,wʊd) *n* **1** the resinous wood of any of several trees, used for torches and candle substitutes **2** any tree or shrub, such as ocotillo, that produces this wood

C & M *abbreviation for* **1** care and maintenance **2** clicks and mortar (company)

can-do *adj* confident and resourceful in the face of challenges: *a can-do attitude*

Candomblé (*Portuguese* kæn'dɔmbleɪ, kændɒm'blɛɪ) *n* any of a number of similar religious cults in Brazil that combine elements of Roman Catholicism with elements of West African, especially Yoruba, and South American Indian religions

candour *or US* **candor** ('kændə) *n* **1** the quality of being open and honest; frankness **2** fairness; impartiality **3** *obsolete* purity or brightness [c17 from Latin *candor,* from *candēre* to be white, shine]

C & W *abbreviation for* country and western

candy ('kændɪ) *n, pl* **-dies 1** *chiefly US and Canadian* confectionery in general; sweets, chocolate, etc **2** a person or thing that is regarded as being attractive but superficial: *arm candy* **3 like taking candy from a baby** *informal* very easy to accomplish ▷ *vb* **-dies, -dying, -died 4** to cause (sugar, etc) to become crystalline, esp by boiling or (of sugar) to become crystalline through boiling **5** to preserve (fruit peel, ginger, etc) by boiling in sugar **6** to cover with any crystalline substance, such as ice or sugar [c18 from Old French *sucre candi* candied sugar, from Arabic *qandi* candied, from *qand* cane sugar, of Dravidian origin]

candyfloss ('kændɪ,flɒs) *n Brit* a very light fluffy confection made from coloured spun sugar, usually held on a stick. US and Canadian name: **cotton candy.** Austral name: **fairyfloss**

candy store *n US and Canadian* a shop solely or largely selling confectionery. Also called (in Britain and certain other countries): **sweet shop**

candy-striped *adj* (esp of clothing fabric) having narrow coloured stripes on a white background ▷ **candy stripe** *n*

candytuft ('kændɪ,tʌft) *n* either of two species of *Iberis* grown as annual garden plants for their umbels ("tufts") of white, red, or purplish flowers. See **iberis** [c17 from *Candy,* obsolete variant of CANDIA (Crete) + TUFT]

cane[1] (keɪn) *n* **1 a** the long jointed pithy or hollow flexible stem of the bamboo, rattan, or any similar plant **b** any plant having such a stem **2 a** strips of such stems, woven or interlaced to make wickerwork, the seats and backs of chairs, etc **b** (*as modifier*): *a cane chair* **3** the woody stem of a reed, young grapevine, blackberry, raspberry, or loganberry **4** any of several grasses with long stiff stems, esp *Arundinaria gigantea* of the southeastern US **5** a flexible rod with which to administer a beating as a punishment, as to schoolboys **6** a slender rod, usually wooden and often ornamental, used for support when walking; walking stick **7** See **sugar cane 8** a slender rod or cylinder, as of glass ▷ *vb* (*tr*) **9** to whip or beat with or as if with a cane **10** to make or repair with cane **11** *informal* to defeat: *we got well caned in the match* **12 cane it** *slang* to do something with great power, force, or speed or consume something such as alcohol in large quantities: *you can do it in ten minutes if you really cane it* [c14 from Old French, from Latin *canna,* from Greek *kanna,* of Semitic origin; related to Arabic *qanāh* reed] ▷ '**caner** *n*

cane[2] (keɪn) *n dialect* a female weasel [c18 of unknown origin]

Canea (kæ'nɪə) *or* **Chania** ('haːnɪə) *n* the chief port of Crete, on the NW coast. Pop: 50 000 (latest est). Greek name: Khaniá

canebrake ('keɪn,breɪk) *n US* a thicket of canes

cane grass *n Austral* any of several tall perennial hard-stemmed grasses, esp *Eragrostis australasica,* of inland swamps

canella (kə'nɛlə) *n* the fragrant cinnamon-like inner bark of a West Indian tree, *Canella winterana* (family *Canellaceae*) used as a spice and in medicine [c17 from Medieval Latin: cinnamon, from Latin *canna* cane, reed]

cane piece *n* (in the Caribbean) a field of sugar cane, esp a peasant's isolated field

cane rat *n* **1** Also called (in W Africa): **cutting grass** a tropical African cavy-like hystricomorph rodent, *Thryonomys swinderianus,* that lives in swampy regions: family *Thryonomyidae* **2** a similar but smaller species, *T. gregorianus*

canescent (kə'nɛs[?]nt) *adj* **1** *biology* white or greyish due to the presence of numerous short white hairs **2** becoming hoary, white, or greyish [c19 from Latin *cānescere* to grow white, become hoary, from *cānēre* to be white] ▷ **ca'nescence** *n*

cane sugar *n* **1** the sucrose obtained from sugar cane, which is identical to that obtained from sugar beet. See also **beet sugar 2** another name for **sucrose**

Canes Venatici ('kɑːniːz vɪ'nætɪ,saɪ) *n, Latin genitive* Canum Venaticorum ('kɑːnəm vɪ,nætɪ'kɔːrəm) a small faint constellation in the N hemisphere near Ursa Major that contains the globular cluster M3 and the spiral whirlpool galaxy M51 [Latin: hunting dogs]

cane toad *n* a large toad, *Bufo marinus,* native to Central and South America but introduced into many countries to control insects and other pests of sugar-cane plantations. Also called: **giant toad, marine toad**

canfield ('kæn,fiːld) *n cards* a gambling game adapted from a type of patience [c20 named after R. A. *Canfield* (1855–1914), US gambler]

cangue *or* **cang** (kæŋ) *n* (formerly in China) a large wooden collar worn by petty criminals as a punishment [c18 from French, from Portuguese *canga* yoke]

Canicula (kə'nɪkjʊlə) *n* another name for **Sirius** [Latin, literally: little dog, from *canis* dog]

canicular (kə'nɪkjʊlə) *adj* of or relating to the star Sirius or its rising

canikin ('kænɪkɪn) *n* a variant spelling of **cannikin**

canine ('keɪnaɪn, 'kæn-) *adj* **1** of or resembling a dog; doglike **2** of, relating to, or belonging to the *Canidae,* a family of mammals, including dogs, jackals, wolves, and foxes, typically having a bushy tail, erect ears, and a long muzzle: order *Carnivora* (carnivores) **3** of or relating to any of the four teeth, two in each jaw, situated between the incisors and the premolars ▷ *n also* **canid** ('keɪnɪd) **4** any animal of the family *Canidae* **5** a canine tooth [c17 from Latin *canīnus,* from *canis* dog]

canine distemper *n* See **distemper[1]**

canine parvovirus *n vet science* a highly contagious viral disease of dogs characterized by vomiting, haemorrhagic diarrhoea, depression, and, in severe cases, death

caning ('keɪnɪŋ) *n* **1** a beating with a cane as a punishment **2** *informal* a severe defeat

Canis Major ('keɪnɪs) *n, Latin genitive* Canis Majoris (mə'dʒɔːrɪs) a constellation in the S hemisphere close to Orion, containing Sirius, the brightest star in the sky. Also called: **the Great Dog** [Latin: the greater dog]

Canis Minor *n, Latin genitive* Canis Minoris (maɪ'nɔːrɪs) a small constellation in the N hemisphere close to Orion, containing the first magnitude star Procyon. Also called: **the Little Dog** [Latin: the lesser dog]

canister ('kænɪstə) *n* **1** a container, usually made of metal, in which dry food, such as tea or coffee, is stored **2** (formerly) **a** a type of shrapnel shell for firing from a cannon **b** Also called: **canister shot, case shot** the shot or shrapnel packed inside this [c17 from Latin *canistrum* basket woven from reeds, from Greek *kanastron,* from *kanna* reed, CANE[1]]

canker ('kæŋkə) *n* **1** an ulceration, esp of the lips or lining of the oral cavity **2** *vet science* **a** a disease of horses in which the horn of the hoofs becomes soft and spongy **b** an inflammation of the lining of the external ear, esp in dogs and cats, resulting in a discharge and sometimes ulceration **c** ulceration or abscess of the mouth, eyelids, ears, or cloaca of birds **3** an open wound in the stem of a tree or shrub, caused by injury or parasites **4** something evil that spreads and corrupts ▷ *vb* **5** to infect or become infected with or as if with canker [Old English *cancer,* from Latin *cancer* crab, cancerous sore]

cankerous ('kæŋkərəs) *adj* **1** having cankers **2** infectious; corrupting

cankerworm ('kæŋkə,wɜːm) *n* the larva of either of two geometrid moths, *Paleacrita vernata* or *Alsophila pometaria,* which feed on and destroy fruit and shade trees in North America

CanLit (,kæn'lɪt) *n acronym for* Canadian Literature

canna ('kænə) *n* any of various tropical plants constituting the genus *Canna,* having broad leaves and red or yellow showy flowers for which they are cultivated: family *Cannaceae* [c17 from New Latin CANE[1]]

cannabin ('kænəbɪn) *n* a greenish-black poisonous resin obtained from the Indian hemp plant. Also called: **cannabis resin**

cannabinoid ('kænəbɪ,nɔɪd) *n* any of the narcotic chemical substances found in cannabin

cannabis ('kænəbɪs) *n* **1** another name for **hemp** (the plant), esp Indian hemp (*Cannabis indica*) **2** the drug obtained from the dried leaves and flowers of the hemp plant, which is smoked or chewed for its psychoactive properties. It produces euphoria and relaxation; repeated use may lead to psychological dependence. See also **cannabin, hashish, marijuana, bhang** [c18 from Latin, from Greek *kannabis;* see HEMP] ▷ '**cannabic** *adj*

Cannae ('kæniː) *n* an ancient city in SE Italy: scene of a victory by Hannibal over the Romans (216 BC)

canned (kænd) *adj* **1** preserved and stored in airtight cans or tins: *canned meat* **2** *informal* prepared or recorded in advance; artificial; not spontaneous: *canned music* **3** a slang word for **drunk** (sense 1)

cannel coal *or* **cannel** ('kæn[?]l) *n* a dull coal having a high volatile content and burning with a smoky luminous flame [c16 from northern English dialect *cannel* candle: so called from its bright flame]

cannellini bean (,kænɪ'liːnɪ) *n* a cream-coloured, kidney-shaped bean with a mild flavour [Italian: small tubes]

cannelloni *or* **cannelloni** (,kænɪ'ləʊnɪ) *pl n* tubular pieces of pasta filled with meat or cheese [Italian, plural of *cannellone,* from *cannello* stalk, from *canna* CANE[1]]

cannelure ('kænə,lʊə) *n* a groove or fluting, esp one around the cylindrical part of a bullet [c18 from French, ultimately from Latin *canālis* CANAL]

canner ('kænə) *n* a person or organization whose job is to can foods

cannery ('kænərɪ) *n*, *pl* -neries a place where foods are canned

Cannes (kæn, kænz; *French* kan) *n* a port and resort in SE France: developed in the 19th century from a fishing village; annual film festival. Pop: 67 304 (1999)

cannibal ('kænɪbᵊl) *n* **1 a** a person who eats the flesh of other human beings **b** (*as modifier*): *cannibal tribes* **2** an animal that feeds on the flesh of others of its kind [c16 from Spanish *Canibales,* name used by Columbus to designate the Caribs of Cuba and Haiti, from Arawak *caniba,* variant of CARIB]

cannibalism ('kænɪbə,lɪzəm) *n* **1** the act of eating human flesh or the flesh of one's own kind **2** savage and inhuman cruelty ▷ ,cannibal'istic *adj* ▷ ,cannibal'istically *adv*

cannibalize or **cannibalise** ('kænɪbə,laɪz) *vb* (*tr*) to use (serviceable parts from one machine or vehicle) to repair another, esp as an alternative to using new parts ▷ ,cannibali'zation or ,cannibali'sation *n*

cannikin, canakin or **canikin** ('kænɪkɪn) *n* a small can, esp one used as a drinking vessel [c16 from Middle Dutch *kanneken;* see CAN², -KIN]

canning ('kænɪŋ) *n* the process or business of sealing food in cans or tins to preserve it

Canning Basin *n* an arid basin in NW Western Australia, largely unexplored. Area: 400 000 sq km (150 000 sq miles)

Cannock ('kænək) *n* a town in W central England, in S Staffordshire: **Cannock Chase** (a public area of heathland, once a royal preserve) is just to the east. Pop: 65 022 (2001)

cannon ('kænən) *n*, *pl* -nons or -non **1** an automatic aircraft gun of large calibre **2** *history* a heavy artillery piece consisting of a metal tube mounted on a carriage **3** a heavy tube or drum, esp one that can rotate freely on the shaft by which it is supported **4** the metal loop at the top of a bell, from which it is suspended **5** See **cannon bone 6** *billiards* **a** a shot in which the cue ball is caused to contact one object ball after another **b** the points scored by this. Usual US and Canadian word: **carom 7** a rebound or bouncing back, as of a ball off a wall **8** either of the two parts of a vambrace ▷ *vb* **9** (*intr; often foll by into*) to collide (with) **10** short for **cannonade 11** (*intr*) *billiards* to make a cannon [c16 from Old French *canon,* from Italian *cannone* cannon, large tube, from *canna* tube, CANE¹]

cannonade (,kænə'neɪd) *n* **1** an intense and continuous artillery bombardment ▷ *vb* **2** to attack (a target) with cannon

cannonball ('kænən,bɔːl) *n* **1** a projectile fired from a cannon: usually a solid round metal shot **2** *tennis* **a** a very fast low serve **b** (*as modifier*): *a cannonball serve* **3** a jump into water by a person who has his arms tucked into the body to form a ball ▷ *vb* (*intr*) **4** (*often foll by along,* etc) to rush along, like a cannonball **5** to execute a cannonball jump ▷ *adj* **6** very fast or powerful

cannon bone *n* a bone in the legs of horses and other hoofed animals consisting of greatly elongated fused metatarsals or metacarpals

cannoneer (,kænə'nɪə) *n* (formerly) a soldier who served and fired a cannon; artilleryman

cannon fodder *n* men regarded as expendable because they are part of a huge army

cannonry ('kænənrɪ) *n*, *pl* -ries *rare* **1** a volley of artillery fire **2** artillery in general

cannot ('kænɒt, kæ'nɒt) *vb* an auxiliary verb expressing incapacity, inability, withholding permission, etc; can not

cannula or **canula** ('kænjʊlə) *n*, *pl* -las or -lae (-,liː) *surgery* a narrow tube for insertion into a bodily cavity, as for draining off fluid, introducing medication, etc [c17 from Latin: a small reed, from *canna* a reed]

cannulate or **canulate** *vb* ('kænjʊ,leɪt) **1** to insert a cannula into ▷ *adj* ('kænjʊ,leɪt, -,lɪt) *also* **cannular** or **canular 2** shaped like a cannula ▷ ,cannu'lation or ,canu'lation *n*

canny ('kænɪ) *adj* -nier, -niest **1** shrewd, esp in business; astute or wary; knowing **2** *Scot and Northeast English dialect* good or nice: used as a general term of approval **3** *Scot* lucky or fortunate ▷ *adv* **4** *Scot and Northeast English dialect* quite; rather: *a canny long while* [c16 from CAN¹ (in the sense: to know how) + -Y¹] ▷ 'cannily *adv* ▷ 'canniness *n*

canoe (kə'nuː) *n* **1** a light narrow open boat, propelled by one or more paddles **2** *NZ* another word for **waka** (sense 1) **3** **in the same canoe** *NZ* of the same tribe ▷ *vb* -noes, -noeing, -noed **4** to go in a canoe or transport by canoe [c16 from Spanish *canoa,* of Carib origin] ▷ ca'noeing *n* ▷ ca'noeist *n*

canoewood (kə'nuː,wʊd) *n* another name for the **tulip tree**

canola (kə'nəʊlə) *n* a cooking oil extracted from a variety of rapeseed developed in Canada [c20 from CAN(ADA) + -*ola*, from OLEUM]

canon¹ ('kænən) *n* **1** *Christianity* a Church decree enacted to regulate morals or religious practices **2** (*often plural*) a general rule or standard, as of judgment, morals, etc **3** (*often plural*) a principle or accepted criterion applied in a branch of learning or art **4** *RC Church* the complete list of the canonized saints **5** *RC Church* the prayer in the Mass in which the Host is consecrated **6** a list of writings, esp sacred writings, officially recognized as genuine **7** a piece of music in which an extended melody in one part is imitated successively in one or more other parts. See also **round** (sense 31), **catch** (sense 33) **8** a list of the works of an author that are accepted as authentic **9** (*formerly*) a size of printer's type equal to 48 point [Old English, from Latin, from Greek *kanōn* rule, rod for measuring, standard; related to *kanna* reed, CANE¹]

canon² ('kænən) *n* **1** one of several priests on the permanent staff of a cathedral, who are responsible for organizing services, maintaining the fabric, etc **2** *RC Church* Also called: **canon regular** a member of either of two religious orders, the Augustinian or Premonstratensian Canons, living communally as monks but performing clerical duties [c13 from Anglo-French *canunie,* from Late Latin *canonicus* one living under a rule, from CANON¹]

cañon ('kænjən) *n* a variant spelling of **canyon**

canoness ('kænənɪs) *n* *RC Church* a woman belonging to any one of several religious orders and living under a rule but not under a vow

canonical (kə'nɒnɪkᵊl) or **canonic** *adj* **1** belonging to or included in a canon of sacred or other officially recognized writings **2** belonging to or in conformity with canon law **3** according to recognized law; accepted **4** *music* in the form of a canon **5** of or relating to a cathedral chapter **6** of or relating to a canon (clergyman) ▷ ca'nonically *adv*

canonical hour *n* **1** *RC Church* **a** one of the seven prayer times appointed for each day by canon law **b** the services prescribed for these times, namely matins, prime, terce, sext, nones, vespers, and compline **2** *Church of England* any time between 8:00 am and 6:00 pm at which marriages may lawfully be celebrated

canonicals (kə'nɒnɪkᵊlz) *pl n* the vestments worn by clergy when officiating

canonicate (kə'nɒnɪ,keɪt, -kɪt) *n* the office or rank of a canon; canonry

canonicity (,kænə'nɪsɪtɪ) *n* the fact or quality of being canonical

canonist ('kænənɪst) *n* a specialist in canon law

canonize or **canonise** ('kænə,naɪz) *vb* (*tr*) **1** *RC Church* to declare (a person) to be a saint and thus admit to the canon of saints **2** to regard as holy or as a saint **3** to sanction by canon law; pronounce valid ▷ ,canoni'zation or ,canoni'sation *n*

canon law *n* the law governing the affairs of a Christian Church, esp the law created or recognized by papal authority in the Roman Catholic Church. See **Corpus Juris Canonici, Codex Juris Canonici**

canonry ('kænənrɪ) *n*, *pl* -ries **1** the office, benefice, or status of a canon **2** canons collectively [c15 from CANON² + -RY]

canoodle (kə'nuːdᵊl) *vb* (*intr; often foll by with*) *slang* to kiss and cuddle; pet; fondle [c19 of unknown origin] ▷ ca'noodler *n*

can-opener *n* another name for **tin-opener**

Canopic jar, urn or **vase** (kə'nəʊpɪk) *n* (in ancient Egypt) one of four containers with tops in the form of animal heads of the gods, for holding the entrails of a mummy

Canopus¹ (kə'nəʊpəs) *n* the brightest star in the constellation Carina and the second brightest star in the sky. Visual magnitude: -0.7; spectral type: FoII; distance: 313 light years

Canopus² (kə'nəʊpəs) *n* a port in ancient Egypt east of Alexandria where granite monuments have been found inscribed with the name of Rameses II and written in languages similar to those of the Rosetta stone ▷ Ca'nopic *adj*

canopy ('kænəpɪ) *n*, *pl* -pies **1** an ornamental awning above a throne or bed or held over a person of importance on ceremonial occasions **2** a rooflike covering over an altar, niche, etc **3** a roofed structure serving as a sheltered passageway or area **4** a large or wide covering, esp one high above: *the sky was a grey canopy* **5** the nylon or silk hemisphere that forms the supporting surface of a parachute **6** the transparent cover of an aircraft cockpit **7** the highest level of branches and foliage in a forest, formed by the crowns of the trees ▷ *vb* -pies, -pying, -pied **8** (*tr*) to cover with or as if with a canopy [c14 from Medieval Latin *canōpeum* mosquito net, from Latin *cōnōpeum* gauze net, from Greek *kōnōpeion* bed with protective net, from *kōnōps* mosquito]

canorous (kə'nɔːrəs) *adj rare* tuneful; melodious [c17 from Latin *canōrus,* from *canere* to sing] ▷ ca'norously *adv* ▷ ca'norousness *n*

Canossa (kə'nɒsə; *Italian* ka'nossa) *n* a ruined castle in N Italy, in Emilia near Reggio nell'Emilia: scene of the penance done by the Holy Roman Emperor Henry IV before Pope Gregory VII

cans (kænz) *pl n* an informal name for **headphones**

Canso ('kænsəʊ) *n* **1** a cape in Canada, at the NE tip of Nova Scotia **2 Strait of Canso** Also called: **Gut of Canso** a channel in Canada, between the Nova Scotia mainland and S Cape Breton Island

canst (kænst) *vb archaic* the form of **can¹** used with the pronoun *thou* or its relative form

cant¹ (kænt) *n* **1** insincere talk, esp concerning religion or morals; pious platitudes **2** stock phrases that have become meaningless through repetition **3** specialized vocabulary of a particular group, such as thieves, journalists, or lawyers; jargon **4** singsong whining speech, as used by beggars ▷ *vb* **5** (*intr*) to speak in or use cant [c16 probably via Norman French *canter* to sing, from Latin *cantāre;* used disparagingly, from the 12th century, of chanting in religious services] ▷ 'canter *n* ▷ 'cantingly *adv*

cant² (kænt) *n* **1** inclination from a vertical or horizontal plane; slope; slant **2** a sudden movement that tilts or turns something **3** the angle or tilt thus caused **4** a corner or outer angle, esp of a building **5** an oblique or slanting surface, edge, or line ▷ *vb* (*tr*) **6** to tip, tilt, or overturn, esp with a sudden jerk **7** to set in an oblique position **8** another word for **bevel** (sense 1) ▷ *adj* **9** oblique; slanting **10** having flat

C

surfaces and without curves [c14 (in the sense: edge, corner): perhaps from Latin *canthus* iron hoop round a wheel, of obscure origin] > 'cantic *adj*

cant³ (kænt) *adj Scot and Northern English dialect* lusty; merry; hearty [c14 related to Low German *kant* bold, merry]

Cant. *abbreviation for* **1** Canterbury **2** *Bible* Canticles

can't (kɑːnt) *vb contraction of* cannot

Cantab. (kæn'tæb) *abbreviation for* Cantabrigiensis [Latin: of Cambridge]

cantabile (kæn'tɑːbɪlɪ) *music* ▷ *adj, adv* **1** (to be performed) in a singing style, i.e. flowingly and melodiously ▷ *n* **2** a piece or passage performed in this way [Italian, from Late Latin *cantābilis*, from Latin *cantāre* to sing]

Cantabrian Mountains (kæn'teɪbrɪən) *pl n* a mountain chain along the N coast of Spain, consisting of a series of high ridges that rise over 2400 m (8000 ft): rich in minerals (esp coal and iron)

Cantabrigian (,kæntə'brɪdʒɪən) *adj* **1** of, relating to, or characteristic of Cambridge or Cambridge University, or of Cambridge, Massachusetts, or Harvard University ▷ *n* **2** a member or graduate of Cambridge University or Harvard University **3** an inhabitant or native of Cambridge [c17 from Medieval Latin *Cantabrigia*]

Cantal (*French* kɑ̃tal) *n* **1** a department of S central France, in the Auvergne region. Capital: Aurillac. Pop: 148 359 (2003 est). Area: 5779 sq km (2254 sq miles) **2** a hard strong cheese made in this area

cantala (kæn'tɑːlə) *n* **1** a tropical American plant, *Agave cantala*, similar to the century plant: family *Agavaceae* (agaves) **2** the coarse tough fibre of this plant, used in making twine [of unknown origin]

cantaloupe *or* **cantaloup** ('kæntə,luːp) *n* **1** a cultivated variety of muskmelon, *Cucumis melo cantalupensis*, with ribbed warty rind and orange flesh **2** any of several other muskmelons [c18 from French, from *Cantaluppi*, former papal villa near Rome, where it was first cultivated in Europe]

cantankerous (kæn'tæŋkərəs) *adj* quarrelsome; irascible [c18 perhaps from c14 (obsolete) *conteckour* a contentious person, from *conteck* strife, from Anglo-French *contek*, of obscure origin] > can'tankerously *adv* > can'tankerousness *n*

cantata (kæn'tɑːtə) *n* a musical setting of a text, esp a religious text, consisting of arias, duets, and choruses interspersed with recitatives [c18 from Italian, from *cantare* to sing, from Latin]

cantatrice (*French* kɑ̃tatris) *n* a female singer, esp a professional soloist

canteen (kæn'tiːn) *n* **1** a restaurant attached to a factory, school, etc, providing meals for large numbers of people **2 a** a small shop that provides a limited range of items, such as toilet requisites, to a military unit **b** a recreation centre for military personnel **3** a soldier's eating and drinking utensils **4** a temporary or mobile stand at which food is provided **5 a** a box in which a set of cutlery is laid out **b** the cutlery itself **6** a flask or canister for carrying water or other liquids, as used by soldiers or travellers [c18 from French *cantine*, from Italian *cantina* wine cellar, from *canto* corner, from Latin *canthus* iron hoop encircling chariot wheel; see CANT²]

canteen culture *n* the alleged clannishness of the police force, whereby the prevalent attitudes inhibit officers from reporting or speaking out against malpractice, racism, etc

canter ('kæntə) *n* **1** an easy three-beat gait of horses, etc, between a trot and a gallop in speed **2** at a canter easily; without effort: *he won at a canter* ▷ *vb* **3** to move or cause to move at a canter [c18 short for *Canterbury trot*, the supposed pace at which pilgrims rode to Canterbury]

canterbury ('kæntəbərɪ, -brɪ) *n, pl* -buries *antiques* **1** a late 18th-century low wooden stand with partitions for holding cutlery and plates: often mounted on casters **2** a similar 19th-century

stand used for holding sheet music, music books, or magazines

Canterbury ('kæntəbərɪ, -brɪ) *n* **1** a city in SE England, in E Kent: starting point for St Augustine's mission to England (597 AD); cathedral where St Thomas à Becket was martyred (1170); seat of the archbishop and primate of England; seat of the University of Kent (1965). Pop: 43 552 (2001). Latin name: Durovernum (,duːrəʊ'vɜːnəm, ,djʊə-) **2** a regional council area of New Zealand, on E central South Island on **Canterbury Bight**: mountainous with coastal lowlands; agricultural. Chief town: Christchurch. Pop: 520 500 (2004 est). Area: 43 371 sq km (16 742 sq miles)

Canterbury bell *n* a campanulaceous biennial European plant, *Campanula medium*, widely cultivated for its blue, violet, or white flowers

Canterbury lamb *n* New Zealand lamb exported chilled or frozen to the United Kingdom

Canterbury Pilgrims *pl n* **1** the pilgrims whose stories are told in Chaucer's *Canterbury Tales* **2** NZ the early settlers in Christchurch, Canterbury region

cantharid ('kænθərɪd) *n* any beetle of the family *Cantharidae*, having a soft elongated body; though found frequenting flowers, they are carnivorous

cantharides (kæn'θærɪ,diːz) *pl n, sing* cantharis ('kænθərɪs) a diuretic and urogenital stimulant or irritant prepared from the dried bodies of Spanish fly (family *Meloidae*, not *Cantharidae*), once thought to be an aphrodisiac. Also called: Spanish fly [c15 from Latin, plural of *cantharis*, from Greek *kantharis* Spanish fly]

Can Tho ('kʌn 'təʊ, 'kæn) *n* a town in S Vietnam, on the River Mekong. Pop: 368 000 (2005 est)

cant hook *or* **dog** *n forestry* a wooden pole with a blunt steel tip and an adjustable hook at one end, used for handling logs

canthus ('kænθəs) *n, pl* -thi (-,θaɪ) the inner or outer corner or angle of the eye, formed by the natural junction of the eyelids [c17 from New Latin, from Latin: iron tyre] > 'canthal *adj*

canticle ('kæntɪk³l) *n* **1** a nonmetrical hymn, derived from the Bible and used in the liturgy of certain Christian churches **2** a song, poem, or hymn, esp one that is religious in character [c13 from Latin *canticulum*, diminutive of *canticus* a song, from *canere* to sing]

Canticle of Canticles *n* another name for the **Song of Solomon**, used in the Douay Bible

cantilena (,kæntɪ'leɪnə) *n* a smooth flowing style in the writing of vocal music [c18 Italian, from Latin *cantilēna* a song]

cantilever ('kæntɪ,liːvə) *n* **1 a** a beam, girder, or structural framework that is fixed at one end and is free at the other **b** (*as modifier*): *a cantilever wing* **2** a wing or tailplane of an aircraft that has no external bracing or support **3** a part of a beam or a structure projecting outwards beyond its support ▷ *vb* **4** (*tr*) to construct (a building member, beam, etc) so that it is fixed at one end only **5** (*intr*) to project like a cantilever [c17 perhaps from CANT² + LEVER]

cantilever bridge *n* a bridge having spans that are constructed as cantilevers and often a suspended span or spans, each end of which rests on one end of a cantilever span

cantillate ('kæntɪ,leɪt) *vb* **1** to chant (passages of the Hebrew Scriptures) according to the traditional Jewish melody **2** to intone or chant [c19 from Late Latin *cantillāre* to sing softly, from Latin *cantāre* to sing]

cantillation (,kæntɪ'leɪʃən) *n* **1** the traditional notation representing the various traditional Jewish melodies to which scriptural passages are chanted **2** chanting or intonation

cantina (kæn'tiːnə) *n* a bar or wine shop, esp in a Spanish-speaking country [from Spanish]

canting arms *pl n heraldry* a coat of arms making visual reference to the surname of its owner

cantle ('kænt³l) *n* **1** the back part of a saddle that

slopes upwards **2** a slice; a broken-off piece [c14 from Old Northern French *cantel*, from *cant* corner; see CANT²]

canto ('kæntəʊ) *n, pl* -tos **1** *music* another word for **cantus** (sense 2) **2** a main division of a long poem [c16 from Italian: song, from Latin *cantus*, from *canere* to sing]

canto fermo ('kæntəʊ 'fɜːməʊ) *or* **cantus firmus** ('kæntəs 'fɜːməs) *n* **1** a melody that is the basis to which other parts are added in polyphonic music **2** the traditional plainchant as prescribed by use and regulation in the Christian Church [Italian, from Medieval Latin, literally: fixed song]

canton *n* **1** ('kæntɒn, kæn'tɒn) **1** any of the 23 political divisions of Switzerland **2** a subdivision of a French arrondissement **3** ('kæntɒn) *heraldry* a small square or oblong charge on a shield, usually in the top left corner ▷ *vb* **4** (kæn'tɒn) (*tr*) to divide into cantons **5** (kæn'tuːn) (esp formerly) to allocate accommodation to (military personnel) [c16 from Old French: corner, division, from Italian *cantone*, from *canto* corner, from Latin *canthus* iron rim; see CANT²] > 'cantonal *adj*

Canton *n* **1** (kæn'tɒn) a port in SE China, capital of Guangdong province, on the Zhu Jiang (Pearl River): the first Chinese port open to European trade. Pop: 3 881 000 (2005 est). Chinese names: Guangzhou, Kwangchow **2** ('kæntɒn) a city in the US, in NE Ohio. Pop: 80 806 (2000)

Canton crepe ('kæntɒn, -tən) *n* a fine crinkled silk or rayon crepe fabric, slightly heavier than crepe de Chine [c19 named after *Canton*, China, where it was originally made]

Cantonese (,kæntə'niːz) *n* **1** the Chinese language spoken in the city of Canton, Guangdong and Guanxi provinces, Hong Kong, and elsewhere outside China **2** (*pl* -ese) a native or inhabitant of the city of Canton or Guangdong province ▷ *adj* **3** of or relating to the city of Canton, Guangdong province, or the Chinese language spoken there

Canton flannel ('kæntɒn, -tən) *n* another name for **cotton flannel** [c19 named after *Canton*, China]

cantonment (kən'tuːnmənt) *n military* (esp formerly) **1** a large training camp **2** living accommodation, esp the winter quarters of a campaigning army **3** *history* a permanent military camp in British India

Canton River (kæn'tɒn) *n* another name for the **Zhu Jiang**

cantor ('kæntɔː) *n* **1** *Judaism* Also called: chazan a man employed to lead synagogue services, esp to traditional modes and melodies **2** *Christianity* the leader of the singing in a church choir [c16 from Latin: singer, from *canere* to sing]

cantorial (kæn'tɔːrɪəl) *adj* **1** of or relating to a precentor **2** (of part of a choir) on the same side of a cathedral, etc, as the precentor; on the N side of the choir. Compare **decanal**

cantoris (kæn'tɔːrɪs) *adj* (in antiphonal music) to be sung by the cantorial side of a choir. Compare **decani** [Latin: genitive of *cantor* precentor]

Cantor's paradox ('kæntɔːz) *n logic* the paradox derived from the supposition of an all-inclusive universal set, since every set has more subsets than members while every subset of such a universal set would be a member of it [named after Georg Cantor (1845-1918), German mathematician, born in Russia]

cantrip ('kæntrɪp) *Scot* ▷ *n* **1** a magic spell **2** (*often plural*) a mischievous trick ▷ *adj* **3** (of an effect) produced by black magic [c18 Scottish, of unknown origin]

Cantuar. ('kæntjʊ,ɑː) *abbreviation for* Cantuariensis [Latin: (Archbishop) of Canterbury]

cantus ('kæntəs) *n, pl* -tus **1** a medieval form of church singing; chant **2** Also called: **canto** the highest part in a piece of choral music **3** (in 15th- or 16th-century music) a piece of choral music, usually secular, in polyphonic style [Latin: song, from *canere* to sing]

canty ('kæntɪ, 'kɑːn-) *adj* cantier, cantiest *Scot and*

Northern English dialect lively; brisk; in good spirits [C18 see CANT³] > 'cantily *adv* > 'cantiness *n*
Canuck (kə'nʌk) *n US and Canadian informal* **a** a Canadian **b** (formerly) esp a French Canadian [C19 of uncertain origin]
canula ('kænjʊlə) *n, pl* **-las** *or* **-lae** (-ˌliː) *surgery* a variant spelling of **cannula**
canvas ('kænvəs) *n* **1 a** a heavy durable cloth made of cotton, hemp, or jute, used for sails, tents, etc **b** (*as modifier*): *a canvas bag* **2 a** a piece of canvas or a similar material on which a painting is done, usually in oils **b** a painting on this material, esp in oils **3** a tent or tents collectively **4** *nautical* any cloth of which sails are made **5** *nautical* the sails of a vessel collectively **6** any coarse loosely woven cloth on which embroidery, tapestry, etc, is done **7** (preceded by *the*) the floor of a boxing or wrestling ring **8** *rowing* the tapering covered part at either end of a racing boat, sometimes referred to as a unit of length: *to win by a canvas* **9 under canvas a** in tents **b** *nautical* with sails unfurled [C14 from Norman French *canevas*, ultimately from Latin *cannabis* hemp]
canvasback ('kænvəsˌbæk) *n, pl* **-backs** *or* **-back** a North American diving duck, *Aythya valisineria*, the male of which has a white body and reddish-brown head
canvass ('kænvəs) *vb* **1** to solicit votes, orders, advertising, etc, from **2** to determine the feelings and opinions of (voters before an election, etc), esp by conducting a survey **3** to investigate (something) thoroughly, esp by discussion or debate **4** *chiefly US* to inspect (votes) officially to determine their validity ▷ *n* **5** a solicitation of opinions, votes, sales orders, etc **6** close inspection; scrutiny [C16 probably from obsolete sense of CANVAS (to toss someone in a canvas sheet, hence, to harass, criticize); the development of current senses is unexplained] > 'canvasser *n* > 'canvassing *n*
canyon *or* **cañon** ('kænjən) *n* a gorge or ravine, esp in North America, usually formed by the down-cutting of a river in a dry area where there is insufficient rainfall to erode the sides of the valley [C19 from Spanish *cañon*, from *caña* tube, from Latin *canna* cane]
canyoning ('kænjənɪŋ) *n* the sport of travelling down a river situated in a canyon by a variety of means including scrambling, floating, swimming, and abseiling
canzona (kæn'zəʊnə) *n* a type of 16th- or 17th-century contrapuntal music, usually for keyboard, lute, or instrumental ensemble [C19 from Italian, from Latin *cantiō* song, from *canere* to sing]
canzone (kæn'zəʊnɪ) *n, pl* **-ni** (-nɪ) **1** a Provençal or Italian lyric, often in praise of love or beauty **2 a** a song, usually of a lyrical nature **b** (in 16th-century choral music) a polyphonic song from which the madrigal developed [C16 from Italian: song, from Latin *cantiō*, from *canere* to sing]
canzonetta (ˌkænzə'nɛtə) *or* **canzonet** (ˌkænzə'nɛt) *n* a short cheerful or lively song, typically of the 16th to 18th centuries [C16 Italian *canzonetta*, diminutive of CANZONE]
caoutchouc ('kaʊtʃuːk, -tʃʊk, kaʊ'tʃuːk, -'tʃʊk) *n* another name for **rubber¹** (sense 1) [C18 from French, from obsolete Spanish *cauchuc*, from Quechua]
cap (kæp) *n* **1** a covering for the head, esp a small close-fitting one made of cloth or knitted **2** such a covering serving to identify the wearer's rank, occupation, etc: *a nurse's cap* **3** something that protects or covers, esp a small lid or cover: *lens cap* **4** an uppermost surface or part: *the cap of a wave* **5 a** See **percussion cap b** a small amount of explosive enclosed in paper and used in a toy gun **6** *sport, chiefly Brit* **a** an emblematic hat or beret given to someone chosen for a representative team: *he has won three England caps* **b** a player chosen for such a team **7** the upper part of a pedestal in a classical order **8** the roof of a windmill, sometimes in the form of a dome **9** *botany* the pileus of a mushroom or toadstool **10** *hunting* **a** money contributed to the funds of a hunt by a follower who is neither a subscriber nor a farmer, in return for a day's hunting **b** a collection taken at a meet of hounds, esp for a charity **11** *anatomy* **a** the natural enamel covering a tooth **b** an artificial protective covering for a tooth **12** See **Dutch cap** (sense 2) **13** an upper financial limit **14** a mortarboard when worn with a gown at an academic ceremony (esp in the phrase **cap and gown**) **15** *meteorol* **a** the cloud covering the peak of a mountain **b** the transient top of detached clouds above an increasing cumulus **16 cap in hand** humbly, as when asking a favour **17 if the cap fits** *Brit* the allusion or criticism seems to be appropriate to a particular person **18 set one's cap for** *or* **at** (of a woman) to be determined to win as a husband or lover ▷ *vb* **caps, capping, capped** (*tr*) **19** to cover, as with a cap: *snow capped the mountain tops* **20** *informal* to outdo; excel: *your story caps them all; to cap an anecdote* **21 to cap it all** to provide the finishing touch: *we had sun, surf, cheap wine, and to cap it all a free car* **22** *sport, Brit* to select (a player) for a representative team: *he was capped 30 times by Scotland* **23** to seal off (an oil or gas well) **24** to impose an upper limit on the level of increase of (a tax, such as the council tax): *rate-capping* **25** *hunting* to ask (hunt followers) for a cap **26** *chiefly Scot and NZ* to award a degree to [Old English *cæppe*, from Late Latin *cappa* hood, perhaps from Latin *caput* head] > 'capper *n*
CAP *abbreviation for* Common Agricultural Policy: (in the EU) the system for supporting farm incomes by maintaining agricultural prices at agreed levels
cap. *abbreviation for* **1** capital **2** capitalize **3** capitalization **4** capital letter [Latin: chapter]
capability (ˌkeɪpə'bɪlɪtɪ) *n, pl* **-ties 1** the quality of being capable; ability **2** the quality of being susceptible to the use or treatment indicated: *the capability of a metal to be fused* **3** (*usually plural*) a characteristic that may be developed; potential aptitude
capable ('keɪpəbᵊl) *adj* **1** having ability, esp in many different fields; competent **2** (*postpositive*; foll by *of*) able or having the skill (to do something): *she is capable of hard work* **3** (*postpositive*; foll by *of*) having the temperament or inclination (to do something): *he seemed capable of murder* [C16 from French, from Late Latin *capābilis* able to take in, from Latin *capere* to take] > 'capableness *n* > 'capably *adv*
capacious (kə'peɪʃəs) *adj* capable of holding much; roomy; spacious [C17 from Latin *capāx*, from Latin *capere* to take] > ca'paciously *adv* > ca'paciousness *n*
capacitance (kə'pæsɪtəns) *n* **1** the property of a system that enables it to store electric charge **2** a measure of this, equal to the charge that must be added to such a system to raise its electrical potential by one unit. Symbol: C. Former name: capacity [C20 from CAPACIT(Y) + -ANCE] > ca'pacitive *adj* > ca'pacitively *adv*
capacitate (kə'pæsɪˌteɪt) *vb* (*tr*) **1** to make legally competent **2** *rare* to make capable > caˌpaci'tation *n*
capacitor (kə'pæsɪtə) *n* a device for accumulating electric charge, usually consisting of two conducting surfaces separated by a dielectric. Former name: **condenser**
capacity (kə'pæsɪtɪ) *n, pl* **-ties 1** the ability or power to contain, absorb, or hold **2** the amount that can be contained; volume: *a capacity of six gallons* **3 a** the maximum amount something can contain or absorb (esp in the phrase **filled to capacity**) **b** (*as modifier*): *a capacity crowd* **4** the ability to understand or learn; aptitude; capability: *he has a great capacity for Greek* **5** the ability to do or produce (often in the phrase **at capacity**): *the factory's output was not at capacity* **6** a specified position or function: *he was employed in the capacity of manager* **7** a measure of the electrical output of a piece of apparatus such as a motor, generator, or accumulator **8** *electronics* a former name for **capacitance 9** *computing* **a** the number of words or characters that can be stored in a particular storage device **b** the range of numbers that can be processed in a register **10** the bit rate that a communication channel or other system can carry **11** legal competence: *the capacity to make a will* [C15 from Old French *capacite*, from Latin *capācitās*, from *capāx* spacious, from *capere* to take]
cap and bells *n* the traditional garb of a court jester, including a cap with bells attached to it
cap-a-pie (ˌkæpə'piː) *adv* (dressed, armed, etc) from head to foot [C16 from Old French]
caparison (kə'pærɪsᵊn) *n* **1** a decorated covering for a horse or other animal, esp (formerly) for a warhorse **2** rich or elaborate clothing and ornaments ▷ *vb* **3** (*tr*) to put a caparison on [C16 via obsolete French from Old Spanish *caparazón* saddlecloth, probably from *capa* CAPE¹]
cape¹ (keɪp) *n* **1** a sleeveless garment like a cloak but usually shorter **2** a strip of material attached to a coat or other garment so as to fall freely, usually from the shoulders [C16 from French, from Provençal *capa*, from Late Latin *cappa*; see CAP]
cape² (keɪp) *n* a headland or promontory [C14 from Old French *cap*, from Old Provençal, from Latin *caput* head]
Cape (keɪp) *n* **the 1** the SW region of South Africa, in Western Cape province **2** See **Cape of Good Hope**
Cape Barren goose *n* a greyish Australian goose, *Cereopsis novaehollandiae*, having a black bill with a greenish cere [C19 named after *Cape Barren* Island in the Bass Strait]
Cape Breton Island *n* an island off SE Canada, in NE Nova Scotia, separated from the mainland by the Strait of Canso: its easternmost point is **Cape Breton**. Pop: 120 098 (1991). Area: 10 280 sq km (3970 sq miles)
Cape buffalo *n* another name for **buffalo** (sense 1)
Cape cart *n South African* a two-wheeled horse-drawn vehicle sometimes with a canvas hood
Cape Cod *n* **1** a long sandy peninsula in SE Massachusetts, between **Cape Cod Bay** and the Atlantic **2** Also called: **Cape Cod cottage** a one-storey cottage of timber construction with a simple gable roof and a large central chimney: originated on Cape Cod in the 18th century
Cape Colony *n* the name from 1652 until 1910 of the former **Cape Province** of South Africa
Cape Coloured *n* (in South Africa) another name for a **Coloured** (sense 2)
Cape doctor *n South African informal* a strong fresh SE wind blowing in the vicinity of Cape Town, esp in the summer
Cape Dutch *n* **1** an obsolete name for **Afrikaans 2** (in South Africa) a distinctive style of furniture or architecture
Cape Flats *pl n* the strip of low-lying land in South Africa joining the Cape Peninsula proper to the African mainland
cape gooseberry *n* another name for **strawberry tomato**
Cape Horn *n* a rocky headland on an island at the extreme S tip of South America, belonging to Chile. It is notorious for gales and heavy seas; until the building of the Panama Canal it lay on the only sea route between the Atlantic and the Pacific. Also called: **the Horn**
Cape jasmine *n* a widely cultivated gardenia shrub, *Gardenia jasminoides*. See **gardenia**
capelin ('kæpəlɪn) *or* **caplin** *n* a small marine food fish, *Mallotus villosus*, occurring in northern and Arctic seas: family *Osmeridae* (smelts) [C17 from French *capelan*, from Old Provençal, literally: CHAPLAIN]
Capella (kə'pɛlə) *n* the brightest star in the constellation Auriga; it is a yellow giant and a spectroscopic binary. Visual magnitude: 0.08;

C

spectral type: G6III and G2III; distance: 42 light years [C17 New Latin, from Latin, diminutive of *capra* she-goat, from *caper* goat]

capellmeister *or* **kapellmeister** (kæˈpɛlˌmaɪstə) *n* a person in charge of an orchestra, esp in an 18th-century princely household. See also **maestro di cappella** [from German, from *Kapelle* chapel + *Meister* MASTER]

Cape of Good Hope *n* a cape in SW South Africa south of Cape Town

Cape Peninsula *n* (in South Africa) the peninsula and the part of the mainland on which Cape Town and most of its suburbs are located

Cape pigeon *n* a species of seagoing petrel, *Daption capensis,* with characteristic white wing patches: a common winter visitor off the coasts of southern Africa: family *Diomedeidae.* Also called: pintado petrel

Cape primrose *n* See **streptocarpus**

Cape Province *n* a former province of S South Africa; replaced in 1994 by the new provinces of Northern Cape, Western Cape, Eastern Cape and part of North-West. Capital: Cape Town. Official name: **Cape of Good Hope Province** Former name (1652–1910): Cape Colony

caper¹ (ˈkeɪpə) *n* **1** a playful skip or leap **2** a high-spirited escapade **3** *cut a* **caper** *or* **capers a** to skip or jump playfully **b** to act or behave playfully; frolic **4** *slang* a crime, esp an organized robbery **5** *Austral informal* a job or occupation **6** *Austral informal* a person's behaviour ▷ *vb* **7** (*intr*) to leap or dance about in a light-hearted manner [C16 probably from CAPRIOLE] > ˈcaperer *n* > ˈcaperingly *adv*

caper² (ˈkeɪpə) *n* **1** a spiny trailing Mediterranean capparidaceous shrub, *Capparis spinosa,* with edible flower buds **2** any of various similar plants or their edible parts. See also **bean caper, capers** [C15 from earlier *capers, capres* (assumed to be plural), from Latin *capparis,* from Greek *kapparis*]

capercaillie (ˌkæpəˈkeɪljɪ) *or* **capercailzie** (ˌkæpəˈkeɪljɪ, -ˈkeɪlzɪ) *n* a large European woodland grouse, *Tetrao urogallus,* having a black plumage and fan-shaped tail in the male [C16 from Scottish Gaelic *capull coille* horse of the woods]

Capernaum (kəˈpɜːnɪəm) *n* a ruined town in N Israel, on the NW shore of the Sea of Galilee: closely associated with Jesus Christ during his ministry

capers (ˈkeɪpəz) *pl n* the flower buds of the caper plant, which are pickled and used as a condiment

capeskin (ˈkeɪpˌskɪn) *n* **1** a soft leather obtained from the skins of a type of lamb or sheep having hairlike wool ▷ *adj* **2** made of this leather [C19 named after the *Cape of Good Hope*]

Cape smoke *n* South African *informal* South African brandy

Cape sparrow *n* a sparrow, *Passer melanurus,* very common in southern Africa: family *Ploceidae.* Also called (esp South African): mossie

Capetian (kəˈpiːʃən) *n* **1** a member of the dynasty founded by Hugh Capet (?938–996 AD), king of France (987–96), which ruled France from 987–1328 A.D ▷ *adj* **2** of, or relating to, the Capetian kings or their rule

Cape Town *n* the legislative capital of South Africa and capital of Western Cape province, situated in the southwest on Table Bay: founded in 1652, the first White settlement in southern Africa; important port. Pop: 827 219 (2001)

Cape Verde (vɜːd) *n* a republic in the Atlantic off the coast of West Africa, consisting of a group of ten islands and five islets: an overseas territory of Portugal until 1975, when the islands became independent. Official language: Portuguese. Religion: Christian (Roman Catholic) majority; animist minority. Currency: Cape Verdean escudo. Capital: Praia. Pop: 472 000 (2004 est). Area: 4033 sq km (1557 sq miles)

Cape Verdean (ˈvɜːdɪən) *adj* **1** of or relating to Cape Verde or its inhabitants ▷ *n* **2** a native or

inhabitant of Cape Verde

Cape York *n* the northernmost point of the Australian mainland, in N Queensland on the Torres Strait at the tip of **Cape York Peninsula** (a peninsula between the Coral Sea and the Gulf of Carpentaria)

Cap-Haitien (*French* kapaisjɛ̃, -tjɛ̃) *n* a port in N Haiti: capital during the French colonial period. Pop: 134 000 (2005 est). Also called: **le Cap** (lə kap)

capias (ˈkeɪpɪˌæs, ˈkæp-) *n law* (formerly) a writ directing a sheriff or other officer to arrest a named person [C15 from Latin, literally: you must take, from *capere*]

capillaceous (ˌkæpɪˈleɪʃəs) *adj* **1** having numerous filaments resembling hairs or threads **2** resembling a hair; capillary [C18 from Latin *capillāceus* hairy, from *capillus* hair]

capillarity (ˌkæpɪˈlærɪtɪ) *n* a phenomenon caused by surface tension and resulting in the distortion, elevation, or depression of the surface of a liquid in contact with a solid. Also called: capillary action

capillary (kəˈpɪlərɪ) *adj* **1** resembling a hair; slender **2** (of tubes) having a fine bore **3** *anatomy* of or relating to any of the delicate thin-walled blood vessels that form an interconnecting network between the arterioles and the venules **4** *physics* of or relating to capillarity ▷ *n, pl* **-laries 5** *anatomy* any of the capillary blood vessels **6** a fine hole or narrow passage in any substance [C17 from Latin *capillāris,* from *capillus* hair]

capillary tube *n* a glass tube with a fine bore and thick walls, used in thermometers, etc

capita (ˈkæpɪtə) *n* **1** See **per capita 2** *anatomy* the plural of **caput**

capital¹ (ˈkæpɪtəl) *n* **1 a** the seat of government of a country or other political unit **b** (*as modifier*): *a capital city* **2** material wealth owned by an individual or business enterprise **3** wealth available for or capable of use in the production of further wealth, as by industrial investment **4** *make capital (out) of* to get advantage from **5** (*sometimes capital*) the capitalist class or their interests: *capital versus labour* **6** *accounting* **a** the ownership interests of a business as represented by the excess of assets over liabilities **b** the nominal value of the authorized or issued shares **c** (*as modifier*): *capital issues* **7** any assets or resources, esp when used to gain profit or advantage **8 a** capital letter. Abbreviations: **cap, cap b** (*as modifier*): *capital B* **9** *with a capital A,* B, etc (used to give emphasis to a statement): *he is mean with a capital M* ▷ *adj* **10** (*prenominal*) *law* involving or punishable by death: *a capital offence* **11** very serious; fatal: *a capital error* **12** primary, chief, or principal: *our capital concern is that everyone be fed* **13** of, relating to, or designating the large modern majuscule letter used chiefly as the initial letter in personal names and place names and other uniquely specificatory nouns, and often for abbreviations and acronyms. Compare **small** (sense 9) See also **upper case 14** *chiefly Brit* excellent; first-rate: *a capital idea* [C13 from Latin *capitālis* concerning the head, chief, from *caput* head; compare Medieval Latin *capitāle* (n) wealth, from *capitālis* (adj)]

capital² (ˈkæpɪtəl) *n* the upper part of a column or pier that supports the entablature. Also called: chapiter, cap [C14 from Old French *capitel,* from Late Latin *capitellum,* diminutive of *caput* head]

capital account *n* **1** *economics* that part of a balance of payments composed of movements of capital and international loans and grants. Compare **current account** (sense 2) **2** *accounting* a financial statement showing the net value of a company at a specified date. It is defined as total assets minus total liabilities and represents ownership interests **3** *US* an account of fixed assets

capital allowance *n* the practice of allowing a certain amount of money spent by a company on fixed assets to be taken off the profits of the

company before tax is imposed

capital assets *pl n* another name for **fixed assets**

capital expenditure *n* expenditure on acquisitions of or improvements to fixed assets

capital gain *n* the amount by which the selling price of a financial asset exceeds its cost

capital gains tax *n* a tax on the profit made from the sale of an asset. Abbreviation: CGT

capital goods *pl n economics* goods that are themselves utilized in the production of other goods rather than being sold to consumers. Also called: producer goods. Compare **consumer goods**

capitalism (ˈkæpɪtəˌlɪzəm) *n* an economic system based on the private ownership of the means of production, distribution, and exchange, characterized by the freedom of capitalists to operate or manage their property for profit in competitive conditions. Also called: free enterprise, private enterprise. Compare **socialism** (sense 1)

capitalist (ˈkæpɪtəlɪst) *n* **1** a person who owns capital, esp capital invested in a business **2** *politics* a supporter of capitalism **3** *informal, usually derogatory* a rich person ▷ *adj* **4** of or relating to capital, capitalists, or capitalism > ˌcapitalˈistic *adj*

capitalization *or* **capitalisation** (ˌkæpɪtəlaɪˈzeɪʃən) *n* **1 a** the act of capitalizing **b** the sum so derived **2** *accounting* the par value of the total share capital issued by a company, including the loan capital and sometimes reserves **3** the act of estimating the present value of future payments, earnings, etc **4** the act of writing or printing in capital letters

capitalization issue *n* another name for **rights issue**

capitalize *or* **capitalise** (ˈkæpɪtəˌlaɪz) *vb* (*mainly tr*) **1** (*intr*; foll by *on*) to take advantage (of); profit (by) **2** to write or print (text) in capital letters or with the first letter of (a word or words) in capital letters **3** to convert (debt or retained earnings) into capital stock **4** to authorize (a business enterprise) to issue a specified amount of capital stock **5** to provide with capital **6** *accounting* to treat (expenditures) as assets **7 a** to estimate the present value of (a periodical income) **b** to compute the present value of (a business) from actual or potential earnings

capital levy *n* a tax on capital or property as contrasted with a tax on income

capitally (ˈkæpɪtəlɪ) *adv chiefly Brit* in an excellent manner; admirably

capital market *n* the financial institutions collectively that deal with medium-term and long-term capital and loans. Compare **money market**

capital punishment *n* the punishment of death for a crime; death penalty

capital ship *n* one of the largest and most heavily armed ships in a naval fleet

capital stock *n* **1** the par value of the total share capital that a company is authorized to issue **2** the total physical capital existing in an economy at any moment of time

capital surplus *n* another name (esp US) for **share premium**

capital transfer tax *n* (in Britain) a tax payable from 1974 to 1986 at progressive rates on the cumulative total of gifts of money or property made during the donor's lifetime or after his death. It was replaced by inheritance tax

capitate (ˈkæpɪˌteɪt) *adj* **1** *botany* shaped like a head, as certain flowers or inflorescences **2** *zoology* having an enlarged headlike end: *a capitate bone* [C17 from Latin *capitātus* having a (large) head, from *caput* head]

capitation (ˌkæpɪˈteɪʃən) *n* **1** a tax levied on the basis of a fixed amount per head **2** *capitation grant* a grant of money given to every person who qualifies under certain conditions **3** the process of assessing or numbering by counting heads [C17 from Late Latin *capitātiō,* from Latin *caput* head] > ˈcapitative *adj*

capitellum (ˌkæpɪ'tɛləm) n, pl -la (-lə) anatomy an enlarged knoblike structure at the end of a bone that forms an articulation with another bone; capitulum [C19 from Latin, diminutive of CAPITULUM]

Capitol ('kæpɪtᵊl) n 1 a another name for the Capitoline b the temple on the Capitoline 2 the the main building of the US Congress 3 (sometimes not capital) Also called: statehouse (in the US) the building housing any state legislature [C14 from Latin Capitōlium, from caput head]

Capitoline ('kæpɪtᵊˌlaɪn, kə'pɪtəʊ-) n 1 the the most important of the Seven Hills of Rome. The temple of Jupiter was on the southern summit and the ancient citadel on the northern summit ▷ adj 2 of or relating to the Capitoline or the temple of Jupiter

capitular (kə'pɪtjʊlə) adj 1 of or associated with a cathedral chapter 2 of or relating to a capitulum [C17 from Medieval Latin capitulāris, from capitulum CHAPTER] > ca'pitularly adv

capitulary (kə'pɪtjʊlərɪ) n, pl -laries any of the collections of ordinances promulgated by the Frankish kings (8th–10th centuries AD) [C17 from Medieval Latin capitulāris; see CAPITULAR]

capitulate (kə'pɪtjʊˌleɪt) vb (intr) to surrender, esp under agreed conditions [C16 (meaning: to arrange under heads, draw up in order; hence, to make terms of surrender): from Medieval Latin capitulare to draw up under heads, from capitulum CHAPTER] > ca'pitu,lator n

capitulation (kəˌpɪtjʊ'leɪʃən) n 1 the act of capitulating 2 a document containing terms of surrender 3 a statement summarizing the main divisions of a subject > ca'pitulatory adj

capitulum (kə'pɪtjʊləm) n, pl -la (-lə) 1 a racemose inflorescence in the form of a disc of sessile flowers, the youngest at the centre. It occurs in the daisy and related plants 2 anatomy, zoology a headlike part, esp the enlarged knoblike terminal part of a long bone, antenna, etc [C18 from Latin, literally: a little head, from caput head]

capiz ('kæpɪz) n the bivalve shell of a mollusc (Placuna placenta) found esp in the Philippines and having a smooth translucent shiny interior: used in jewellery, ornaments, lampshades, etc. Also called: jingle shell, window shell [from the native name in the Philippines]

caplet ('kæplɪt) n a medicinal tablet, usually oval in shape, coated in a soluble substance [C20 CAP(SULE) + (TAB)LET]

caplin ('kæplɪn) n a variant of capelin

capo¹ ('keɪpəʊ, 'kæpəʊ) n, pl -pos a device fitted across all the strings of a guitar, banjo, etc, so as to raise the pitch of each string simultaneously. Compare barré. Also called: capo tasto ('kæpəʊ 'tæstəʊ) [from Italian capo tasto head stop]

capo² ('kæpəʊ; Italian 'kapo) n, pl -pos the presumed head of a Mafia family [Italian: head]

capoeira (ˌkæpʊ'eɪrə) n a movement discipline combining martial art and dance, which originated among African slaves in 19th-century Brazil [C20 from Portuguese]

cap of maintenance n a ceremonial cap or hat worn or carried as a symbol of office, rank, etc

capon ('keɪpən) n a castrated cock fowl fattened for eating [Old English capun, from Latin cāpō capon; related to Greek koptein to cut off]

caponize or **caponise** ('keɪpəˌnaɪz) vb (tr) to make (a cock) into a capon

caporal (ˌkæpə'rɑːl) n a strong coarse dark tobacco [C19 from French tabac du caporal corporal's tobacco, denoting its superiority to tabac du soldat soldier's tobacco]

Caporetto (kapo'rɛtto) n the Italian name for Kobarid

capot (kə'pɒt) n piquet the winning of all the tricks by one player [C17 from French]

capote (kə'pəʊt; French kapɔt) n a long cloak or soldier's coat, usually with a hood [C19 from French: cloak, from cape; see CAPE¹]

Cappadocia (ˌkæpə'dəʊsɪə) n an ancient region of E Asia Minor famous for its horses

Cappadocian (ˌkæpə'dəʊsɪən) adj 1 of or relating to Cappadocia (an ancient region of E Asia Minor) or its inhabitants ▷ n 2 a native or inhabitant of Cappadocia

capparidaceous (ˌkæpərɪ'deɪʃəs) adj of, relating to, or belonging to the Capparidaceae (or (Capparaceae), a family of plants, mostly shrubs including the caper, of warm tropical regions [C19 from New Latin Capparidaceae, from Latin capparis caper]

cappelletti (ˌkæpə'lɛtɪ) n small squares of pasta containing a savoury mixture of meat, cheese, or vegetables [C19 Italian, plural of cappelletto, literally: little hat]

cappuccino (ˌkæpʊ'tʃiːnəʊ) n, pl -nos coffee with steamed milk, sometimes served with whipped cream or sprinkled with powdered chocolate [Italian: CAPUCHIN]

capreolate ('kæprɪəˌleɪt, kə'priː-) adj biology possessing or resembling tendrils [C18 from Latin capreolus tendril]

Capri (kə'priː; Italian 'kapri) n an island off W Italy, in the Bay of Naples: resort since Roman times. Pop: 8000 (latest est). Area: about 13 sq km (5 sq miles)

capric acid ('kæprɪk) n another name for decanoic acid [C19 from Latin caper goat, so named from its smell]

capriccio (kə'prɪtʃɪˌəʊ) or **caprice** n, pl -priccios, -pricci (-'prɪtʃɪ) or -prices music a lively piece composed freely and without adhering to the rules for any specific musical form [C17 from Italian: CAPRICE]

capriccioso (kəˌprɪtʃɪ'əʊzəʊ) adv music to be played in a free and lively style [Italian: from capriccio CAPRICE]

caprice (kə'priːs) n 1 a sudden or unpredictable change of attitude, behaviour, etc; whim 2 a tendency to such changes 3 another word for capriccio [C17 from French, from Italian capriccio a shiver, caprice, from capo head + riccio hedgehog, suggesting a convulsive shudder in which the hair stood on end like a hedgehog's spines; meaning also influenced by Italian capra goat, by folk etymology]

capricious (kə'prɪʃəs) adj characterized by or liable to sudden unpredictable changes in attitude or behaviour; impulsive; fickle > ca'priciously adv > ca'priciousness n

Capricorn ('kæprɪˌkɔːn) n 1 astrology a Also called: the Goat, Capricornus the tenth sign of the zodiac, symbol ♑, having a cardinal earth classification and ruled by the planet Saturn. The sun is in this sign between about Dec 22 and Jan 19 b a person born during the period when the sun is in this sign 2 astronomy another name for Capricornus 3 tropic of Capricorn See tropic (sense 1) ▷ adj 4 astrology born under or characteristic of Capricorn ▷ Also (for senses 1b, 4): Capricornean (ˌkæprɪ'kɔːnɪən) [C14 from Latin Capricornus (translating Greek aigokerōs goat-horned), from caper goat + cornū horn]

Capricornia (ˌkæprɪ'kɔːnɪə) n the regions of Australia in the tropic of Capricorn

Capricornus (ˌkæprɪ'kɔːnəs) n, Latin genitive -ni (-naɪ) a faint zodiacal constellation in the S hemisphere, lying between Sagittarius and Aquarius

caprification (ˌkæprɪfɪ'keɪʃən) n a method of pollinating the edible fig by hanging branches of caprifig flowers in edible fig trees. Parasitic wasps in the caprifig flowers transfer pollen to the edible fig flowers [C17 from Latin caprificātiō, from caprificāre to pollinate figs by this method, from caprificus CAPRIFIG]

caprifig ('kæprɪˌfɪg) n a wild variety of fig, Ficus carica sylvestris, of S Europe and SW Asia, used in the caprification of the edible fig [C15 from Latin caprificus literally: goat fig, from caper goat + ficus FIG¹]

caprifoliaceous (ˌkæprɪˌfəʊlɪ'eɪʃəs) adj of, relating to, or belonging to the Caprifoliaceae, a family of N temperate shrubs, small trees, and climbers including honeysuckle, elder, and guelder-rose [C19 from New Latin caprifoliāceae, from caprifolium type genus, from Medieval Latin: honeysuckle, from Latin caper goat + folium leaf]

caprine ('kæpraɪn) adj of or resembling a goat [C17 from Latin caprīnus, from caper goat]

capriole ('kæprɪˌəʊl) n 1 dressage a high upward but not forward leap made by a horse with all four feet off the ground 2 dancing a leap from bent knees ▷ vb 3 (intr) to perform a capriole [C16 from French, from Old Italian capriola, from capriolo roebuck, from Latin capreolus, from caper goat]

Capri pants or **Capris** pl n women's tight-fitting trousers

cap rock n 1 a layer of rock that overlies a salt dome and consists of limestone, gypsum, etc 2 a layer of relatively impervious rock overlying an oil- or gas-bearing rock

caproic acid (kə'prəʊɪk) n another name for hexanoic acid [C19 caproic, from Latin caper goat, alluding to its smell]

caprolactam (ˌkæprəʊ'læktæm) n a white crystalline cyclic imine used in the manufacture of nylon. Formula: $C_5H_{10}NHCO$ [C20 from CAPRO(IC ACID) + LACTAM]

caps. abbreviation for capital letters

capsaicin (kæp'seɪɪsɪn) n a colourless crystalline bitter alkaloid found in capsicums and used as a flavouring in vinegar and pickles. Formula: $C_{18}H_{27}O_3N$ [C19 capsicine, from CAPSICUM + -INE²; modern form refashioned from Latin capsa box, case + -IN]

cap screw n a screwed bolt with a cylindrical head having a hexagonal recess. The bolt is turned using a wrench of hexagonal cross section

Capsian ('kæpsɪən) n 1 a late Palaeolithic culture, dating from about 12 000 BC, found mainly around the salt lakes of Tunisia. The culture is characterized by the presence of microliths, backed blades, and engraved limestone slabs ▷ adj 2 of or relating to this culture [C20 from French capsien, from Capsa, Latinized form of Gafsa, Tunisia]

capsicum ('kæpsɪkəm) n 1 any tropical American plant of the solanaceous genus Capsicum, such as C. frutescens, having mild or pungent seeds enclosed in a pod-shaped or bell-shaped fruit 2 the fruit of any of these plants, used as a vegetable or ground to produce a condiment ▷ See also pepper (sense 4) [C18 from New Latin, from Latin capsa box, CASE²]

capsid¹ ('kæpsɪd) n any heteropterous bug of the family Miridae (formerly Capsidae), most of which feed on plant tissues, causing damage to crops [C19 from New Latin Capsus (genus)]

capsid² ('kæpsɪd) n the outer protein coat of a mature virus [C20 from French capside, from Latin capsa box]

capsize (kæp'saɪz) vb to overturn accidentally; upset [C18 of uncertain origin] > cap'sizal n

capsomere ('kæpsəˌmɪə) n any of the protein units that together form the capsid of a virus

capstan ('kæpstən) n 1 a machine with a drum that rotates round a vertical spindle and is turned by a motor or lever, used for hauling in heavy ropes, etc 2 any similar device, such as the rotating shaft in a tape recorder that pulls the tape past the head [C14 from Old Provençal cabestan, from Latin capistrum a halter, from capere to seize]

capstan bar n a lever, often wooden, for turning a capstan

capstan lathe n a lathe for repetitive work, having a rotatable turret resembling a capstan to hold tools for successive operations. Also called: turret lathe

capstone ('kæpˌstəʊn) or **copestone** ('kəʊpˌstəʊn) n 1 one of a set of slabs on the top of a wall, building, etc 2 mountaineering a chockstone occurring at the top of a gully or chimney 3 a crowning achievement; peak: *the capstone of his career*

capsulate ('kæpsjʊˌleɪt, -lɪt) *or* **capsulated** *adj* within or formed into a capsule ▷ ˌcapsu'lation *n*

capsule ('kæpsjuːl) *n* **1** a soluble case of gelatine enclosing a dose of medicine **2** a thin metal cap, seal, or cover, such as the foil covering the cork of a wine bottle **3** *botany* **a** a dry fruit that liberates its seeds by splitting, as in the violet, or through pores, as in the poppy **b** the spore-producing organ of mosses and liverworts **4** *bacteriol* a gelatinous layer of polysaccharide or protein surrounding the cell wall of some bacteria: thought to be responsible for the virulence in pathogens **5** *anatomy* **a** a cartilaginous, fibrous, or membranous envelope surrounding any of certain organs or parts **b** a broad band of white fibres (**internal capsule**) near the thalamus in each cerebral hemisphere **6** See **space capsule 7** an aeroplane cockpit that can be ejected in a flight emergency, complete with crew, instruments, etc **8** (*modifier*) in a highly concise form: *a capsule summary* **9** (*modifier*) (in the fashion industry) consisting of a few important representative items: *a capsule collection* [c17 from French, from Latin *capsula*, diminutive of *capsa* box]

capsule range *n* a small range of clothes by a particular designer, intended to be representative of the full range

capsule wardrobe *n* a collection of clothes and accessories that includes only items considered essential

capsulize *or* **capsulise** ('kæpsjʊˌlaɪz) *vb* (*tr*) **1** to state (information) in a highly condensed form **2** to enclose in a capsule

Capt. *abbreviation for* Captain

captain ('kæptɪn) *n* **1** the person in charge of and responsible for a vessel **2** an officer of the navy who holds a rank junior to a rear admiral but senior to a commander **3** an officer of the army, certain air forces, and the marine corps who holds a rank junior to a major but senior to a lieutenant **4** the officer in command of a civil aircraft, usually the senior pilot **5** the leader of a team in games **6** a person in command over a group, organization, etc; leader: *a captain of industry* **7** *US* a police officer in charge of a precinct **8** *US and Canadian* (formerly) a head waiter **9** Also called: **bell captain** *US and Canadian* a supervisor of bellboys in a hotel **10** *Austral informal* a person who is buying drinks for people in a bar ▷ *vb* **11** (*tr*) to be captain of [c14 from Old French *capitaine*, from Late Latin *capitāneus* chief, from Latin *caput* head] > 'captaincy *or* 'captainˌship *n*

Captain Cooker ('kʊkə) *n NZ* a wild pig [from Captain James Cook (1728–79), British navigator and explorer, who first released pigs in the New Zealand bush]

captain's biscuit *n* a type of hard fancy biscuit

caption ('kæpʃən) *n* **1** a title, brief explanation, or comment accompanying an illustration; legend **2** a heading, title, or headline of a chapter, article, etc **3** graphic material, usually containing lettering, used in television presentation **4** another name for **subtitle** (sense 2) **5** the formal heading of a legal document stating when, where, and on what authority it was taken or made ▷ *vb* **6** to provide with a caption or captions [c14 (meaning: seizure, an arrest; later, heading of a legal document): from Latin *captiō* a seizing, from *capere* to take]

captious ('kæpʃəs) *adj* apt to make trivial criticisms; fault-finding; carping [c14 (meaning: catching in error): from Latin *captiōsus*, from *captiō* a seizing; see CAPTION] > 'captiously *adv* > 'captiousness *n*

captivate ('kæptɪˌveɪt) *vb* (*tr*) **1** to hold the attention of by fascinating; enchant **2** an obsolete word for **capture** [c16 from Late Latin *captivāre*, from *captivus* CAPTIVE] > 'captiˌvatingly *adv* > ˌcapti'vation *n* > 'captiˌvator *n*

captive ('kæptɪv) *n* **1** a person or animal that is confined or restrained, esp a prisoner of war **2** a person whose behaviour is dominated by some emotion: *a captive of love* ▷ *adj* **3** held as prisoner **4** held under restriction or control; confined: *captive water held behind a dam* **5** captivated; enraptured **6** unable by circumstances to avoid speeches, advertisements, etc (esp in the phrase **captive audience**) [c14 from Latin *captivus*, from *capere* to take]

captive market *n* a group of consumers who are obliged through lack of choice to buy a particular product, thus giving the supplier a monopoly

captivity (kæp'tɪvɪtɪ) *n*, *pl* **-ties 1** the condition of being captive; imprisonment **2** the period of imprisonment

captopril ('kæptəprɪl) *n* an ACE inhibitor used to treat high blood pressure and congestive heart failure

captor ('kæptə) *n* a person or animal that holds another captive [c17 from Latin, from *capere* to take]

capture ('kæptʃə) *vb* (*tr*) **1** to take prisoner or gain control over: *to capture an enemy; to capture a town* **2** (in a game or contest) to win control or possession of: *to capture a pawn in chess* **3** to succeed in representing or describing (something elusive): *the artist captured her likeness* **4** *physics* (of an atom, molecule, ion, or nucleus) to acquire (an additional particle) **5** to insert or transfer (data) into a computer ▷ *n* **6** the act of taking by force; seizure **7** the person or thing captured; booty **8** *physics* a process by which an atom, molecule, ion, or nucleus acquires an additional particle **9** Also called: **piracy** *geography* the process by which the headwaters of one river are diverted into another through erosion caused by the second river's tributaries **10** the act or process of inserting or transferring data into a computer [c16 from Latin *captūra* a catching, that which is caught, from *capere* to take] > 'capturer *n*

Capua ('kæpjʊə; *Italian* 'kapua) *n* a town in S Italy, in NW Campania: strategically important in ancient times, situated on the Appian Way. Pop: 19 041 (2001)

capuche *or* **capouch** (kə'puːʃ) *n* a large hood or cowl, esp that worn by Capuchin friars [c17 from French, from Italian *cappuccio* hood, from Late Latin *cappa* cloak]

capuchin ('kæpjʊtʃɪn, -ʃɪn) *n* **1** any agile intelligent New World monkey of the genus *Cebus*, inhabiting forests in South America, typically having a cowl of thick hair on the top of the head **2** a woman's hooded cloak **3** (*sometimes capital*) a rare variety of domestic fancy pigeon [c16 from French, from Italian *cappuccino*, from *cappuccio* hood; see CAPUCHE]

Capuchin ('kæpjʊtʃɪn, 'kæpjʊʃɪn) *n* **a** a friar belonging to a strict and autonomous branch of the Franciscan order founded in 1525 **b** (*as modifier*): *a Capuchin friar* [c16 from French; see CAPUCHE]

caput ('keɪpət, 'kæp-) *n*, *pl* **capita** ('kæpɪtə) **1** *anatomy* a technical name for the **head 2** the main or most prominent part of an organ or structure [c18 from Latin]

capybara (ˌkæpɪ'bɑːrə) *n* the largest rodent: a pig-sized amphibious hystricomorph, *Hydrochoerus hydrochaeris*, resembling a guinea pig and inhabiting river banks in Central and South America: family *Hydrochoeridae* [c18 from Portuguese *capibara*, from Tupi]

Caquetá (*Spanish* kake'ta) *n* the Japurá River from its source in Colombia to the border with Brazil

car (kɑː) *n* **1 a** Also called: **motorcar, automobile** a self-propelled road vehicle designed to carry passengers, esp one with four wheels that is powered by an internal-combustion engine **b** (*as modifier*): *car coat* **2** a conveyance for passengers, freight, etc, such as a cable car or the carrier of an airship or balloon **3** *Brit* a railway vehicle for passengers only, such as a sleeping car or buffet

car **4** *chiefly US and Canadian* a railway carriage or van **5** *chiefly US* the enclosed platform of a lift **6** a poetic word for **chariot** [c14 from Anglo-French *carre*, ultimately related to Latin *carra, carrum* two-wheeled wagon, probably of Celtic origin; compare Old Irish *carr*]

CAR *abbreviation for* compound annual return

carabao (ˌkærə'beɪəʊ) *n*, *pl* **-os** another name for **water buffalo** [from Visayan *karabáw*; compare Malay *karbaw*]

carabid ('kærəbɪd) *n* **1** any typically dark-coloured beetle of the family *Carabidae*, including the bombardier and other ground beetles ▷ *adj* **2** of, relating to, or belonging to the *Carabidae* [c19 from New Latin, from Latin *cārabus* a kind of crab (name applied to these beetles)]

carabin ('kærəbɪn) *or* **carabine** ('kærəˌbaɪn) *n* variants of **carbine** (sense 2)

carabineer *or* **carabinier** (ˌkærəbɪ'nɪə) *n* variants of **carbineer**

carabiner (ˌkærə'biːnə) *n* a variant spelling of **karabiner**

carabiniere *Italian* (karabi'njɛːre) *n*, *pl* **-ri** (-ri) an Italian national policeman

caracal ('kærəˌkæl) *n* **1** Also called: **desert lynx** a lynxlike feline mammal, *Lynx caracal*, inhabiting deserts of N Africa and S Asia, having long legs, a smooth coat of reddish fur, and black-tufted ears **2** the fur of this animal [c18 from French, from Turkish *kara kūlāk*, literally: black ear]

caracara (ˌkɑːrə'kɑːrə) *n* any of various large carrion-eating diurnal birds of prey of the genera *Caracara, Polyborus*, etc, of S North, Central, and South America, having long legs and naked faces: family *Falconidae* (falcons) [c19 from Spanish or Portuguese, from Tupi; of imitative origin]

Caracas (kə'rækəs, -'rɑː-; *Spanish* ka'rakas) *n* the capital of Venezuela, in the north: founded in 1567; major industrial and commercial centre, notably for oil companies. Pop: 3 276 000 (2005 est)

caracole ('kærəˌkəʊl) *or* **caracol** ('kærəˌkɒl) *n* **1** *dressage* a half turn to the right or left **2** a spiral staircase ▷ *vb* (*intr*) **3** *dressage* to execute a half turn to the right or left [c17 from French, from Spanish *caracol* snail, spiral staircase, turn]

caracul ('kærəˌkʌl) *n* **1** Also called: **Persian lamb** the black loosely curled fur obtained from the skins of newly born lambs of the karakul sheep **2** a variant spelling of **karakul**

carafe (kə'ræf, -'rɑːf) *n* **a** an open-topped glass container for serving water or wine at table **b** (*as modifier*): *a carafe wine* [c18 from French, from Italian *caraffa*, from Spanish *garrafa*, from Arabic *gharrāfah* vessel]

carageen ('kærəˌgiːn) *n* a variant spelling of **carrageen**

carambola (ˌkærəm'bəʊlə) *n* **1** a tree, *Averrhoa carambola*, probably native to Brazil but cultivated in the tropics, esp SE Asia, for its edible fruit **2** Also called: **star fruit** the smooth-skinned yellow fruit of this tree, which is star-shaped on cross section [c18 Spanish *carambola* a sour greenish fruit, from Portuguese, from Marathi *karambal*]

caramel ('kærəməl, -ˌmɛl) *n* **1** burnt sugar, used for colouring and flavouring food **2** a chewy sweet made from sugar, butter, milk, etc ▷ See also **crème caramel** [c18 from French, from Spanish *caramelo*, of uncertain origin]

caramelize *or* **caramelise** ('kærəməˌlaɪz) *vb* to convert or be converted into caramel

carangid (kə'rændʒɪd, -'ræŋgɪd) *or* **carangoid** (kə'ræŋgɔɪd) *n* **1** any marine percoid fish of the family *Carangidae*, having a compressed body and deeply forked tail. The group includes the jacks, horse mackerel, pompano, and pilot fish ▷ *adj* **2** of, relating to, or belonging to the *Carangidae* [c19 from New Latin *Carangidae*, from *Caranx* type genus, from French *carangue* shad, from Spanish *caranga*, of obscure origin]

carapace ('kærəˌpeɪs) *n* the thick hard shield, made of chitin or bone, that covers part of the body of crabs, lobsters, tortoises, etc [c19 from

French, from Spanish *carapacho,* of unknown origin]

carat ('kærət) *n* **1** a measure of the weight of precious stones, esp diamonds. It was formerly defined as 3.17 grains, but the international carat is now standardized as 0.20 grams **2** Usual US spelling: **karat** a measure of the proportion of gold in an alloy, expressed as the number of parts of gold in 24 parts of the alloy [c16 from Old French, from Medieval Latin *carratus,* from Arabic *qīrāt* weight of four grains, carat, from Greek *keration* a little horn, from *keras* horn]

caravan (,kærə'væn) *n* **1 a** a large enclosed vehicle capable of being pulled by a car or lorry and equipped to be lived in. US and Canadian name: **trailer b** (*as modifier*): *a caravan site* **2** (esp in some parts of Asia and Africa) a company of traders or other travellers journeying together, often with a train of camels, through the desert **3** a group of wagons, pack mules, camels, etc, esp travelling in single file **4** a large covered vehicle, esp a gaily coloured one used by Gypsies, circuses, etc ▷ *vb* **-vans, -vanning, -vanned 5** (*intr*) *Brit* to travel or have a holiday in a caravan [c16 from Italian *caravana,* from Persian *kārwān*]
> 'cara,vanning *n*

caravanserai (,kærə'vænsə,raɪ, -,reɪ) or **caravansary** (,kærə'vænsərɪ) *n, pl* -rais or -ries (in some Eastern countries esp formerly) a large inn enclosing a courtyard providing accommodation for caravans [c16 from Persian *kārwānsarāī* caravan inn]

caravel ('kærə,vɛl) or **carvel** *n* a two- or three-masted sailing ship, esp one with a broad beam, high poop deck, and lateen rig that was used by the Spanish and Portuguese in the 15th and 16th centuries [c16 from Portuguese *caravela,* diminutive of *caravo* ship, ultimately from Greek *karabos* crab, horned beetle]

caraway ('kærə,weɪ) *n* **1** an umbelliferous Eurasian plant, *Carum carvi,* having finely divided leaves and clusters of small whitish flowers **2 caraway seed** the pungent aromatic one-seeded fruit of this plant, used in cooking and in medicine [c14 probably from Medieval Latin *carvi,* from Arabic *karawyā,* from Greek *karon*]

carb (kɑːb) *n informal* **1** short for **carbohydrate 2** short for **carburettor**

carb (kɑːb) *n* **1** short for **carburettor 2** short for **carbohydrate**

carbamate ('kɑːbə,meɪt) *n* a salt or ester of carbamic acid. The salts contain the monovalent ion NH_2COO^-, and the esters contain the group NH_2COO-

carbamazepine (,kɑːbə'mæzə,piːn) *n* an anticonvulsant drug used in the management of epilepsy

carbamic acid (kɑː'bæmɪk) *n* a hypothetical compound known only in the form of carbamate salts and esters. Formula: NH_2COOH

carbamide ('kɑːbə,maɪd) *n* another name for **urea**

carbamidine (kɑː'bæmɪ,daɪn) *n* another name for **guanidine**

carbanion (kɑː'bænaɪən) *n chem* a negatively charged organic ion in which most of the negative charge is localized on a carbon atom. Compare **carbonium ion**

carbaryl ('kɑːbərɪl) *n* an organic compound of the carbamate group: used as an insecticide, esp to treat head lice

carbazole ('kɑːbə,zəʊl) *n* a colourless insoluble solid obtained from coal tar and used in the production of some dyes. Formula: $C_{12}H_9N$. Also called: **diphenylenimine** (daɪ,fiːnaɪ'lɛnɪmɪːn)

carbeen ('kɑːbiːn) *n* an Australian eucalyptus tree, *E. tessellaris,* having drooping branches and grey bark. Also called: **Moreton Bay ash** [from a native Australian language]

carbene ('kɑːbiːn) *n chem* a neutral divalent free radical, such as methylene: CH_2

carbide ('kɑːbaɪd) *n* **1** a binary compound of carbon with a more electropositive element. See

also **acetylide 2** See **calcium carbide**

carbimazole (kɑː'bɪmə,zəʊl) *n* a drug that inhibits the synthesis of the hormone thyroxine, used in the management of hyperthyroidism

carbine ('kɑːbaɪn) *n* **1** a light automatic or semiautomatic rifle of limited range **2** Also called: **carabin, carabine** a light short-barrelled shoulder rifle formerly used by cavalry [c17 from French *carabine,* from Old French *carabin* carabineer, perhaps variant of *escarrabin* one who prepares corpses for burial, from *scarabée,* from Latin *scarabaeus* SCARAB]

carbineer (,kɑːbɪ'nɪə) or **carabineer, carabinier** (,kærəbɪ'nɪə) *n* (formerly) a soldier equipped with a carbine

carbo- or before a vowel **carb-** *combining form* carbon: *carbohydrate; carbonate*

carbocyclic (,kɑːbəʊ'saɪklɪk) *adj* (of a chemical compound) containing a closed ring of carbon atoms

carbohydrate (,kɑːbəʊ'haɪdreɪt) *n* any of a large group of organic compounds, including sugars, such as sucrose, and polysaccharides, such as cellulose, glycogen, and starch, that contain carbon, hydrogen, and oxygen, with the general formula $C_m(H_2O)_n$: an important source of food and energy for animals. Informal term: **carb**

carbolated ('kɑːbə,leɪtɪd) *adj* containing carbolic acid

carbolic acid (kɑː'bɒlɪk) *n* another name for **phenol,** esp when it is used as an antiseptic or disinfectant [c19 *carbolic,* from CARBO- + -OL^1 + -IC]

carbolize or **carbolise** ('kɑːbə,laɪz) *vb* (*tr*) another word for **phenolate**

carbon ('kɑːbᵊn) *n* **1 a** a nonmetallic element existing in the three crystalline forms: graphite, diamond, and buckminsterfullerene: occurring in carbon dioxide, coal, oil, and all organic compounds. The isotope **carbon-12** has been adopted as the standard for atomic wt.; **carbon-14,** a radioisotope with a half-life of 5700 years, is used in radiocarbon dating and as a tracer. Symbol: C; atomic no.: 6; atomic wt.: 12.011; valency: 2, 3, or 4; relative density: 1.8–2.1 (amorphous), 1.9–2.3 (graphite), 3.15–3.53 (diamond); sublimes at 3367±25°C; boiling pt.: 4827°C **b** (*as modifier*): *a carbon compound* **2** short for **carbon paper** or **carbon copy 3** a carbon electrode used in a carbon-arc light or in carbon-arc welding **4** a rod or plate, made of carbon, used in some types of battery [c18 from French *carbone,* from Latin *carbō* charcoal, dead or glowing coal]
> 'carbonous *adj*

carbonaceous (,kɑːbə'neɪʃəs) *adj* of, resembling, or containing carbon

carbonade (,kɑːbə'neɪd, -'nɑːd) *n* a stew of beef and onions cooked in beer [c20 from French]

carbonado^1 (,kɑːbə'neɪdəʊ, -'nɑːdəʊ) *n, pl* -does or -dos **1** a piece of meat, fish, etc, scored and grilled ▷ *vb* -dos, -doing, -doed (*tr*) **2** to score and grill (meat, fish, etc) **3** *archaic* to hack or slash [c16 from Spanish *carbonada,* from *carbón* charcoal; see CARBON]

carbonado^2 (,kɑːbə'neɪdəʊ, -'nɑːdəʊ) *n, pl* -dos or -does an inferior dark massive variety of diamond used in industry for polishing and drilling. Also called: **black diamond** [Portuguese, literally: carbonated]

carbon arc *n* **1 a** an electric arc produced between two carbon electrodes, formerly used as a light source **b** (*as modifier*): *carbon-arc light* **2 a** an electric arc produced between a carbon electrode and material to be welded **b** (*as modifier*): *carbon-arc welding*

Carbonari (,kɑːbə'nɑːrɪ) *pl n, sing* -naro (-'nɑːrəʊ) members of a secret political society with liberal republican aims, originating in S Italy about 1811 and particularly engaged in the struggle for Italian unification [c19 from Italian, plural of *carbonaro* seller or burner of charcoal, name adopted by the society]

carbonate *n* ('kɑːbə,neɪt, -nɪt) **1** a salt or ester of

carbonic acid. Carbonate salts contain the divalent ion CO_3^{2-} ▷ *vb* ('kɑːbə,neɪt) **2** to form or turn into a carbonate **3** (*tr*) to treat with carbon dioxide or carbonic acid, as in the manufacture of soft drinks [c18 from French, from *carbone* CARBON]

carbonation (,kɑːbə'neɪʃən) *n* **1** absorption of or reaction with carbon dioxide **2** another word for **carbonization**

carbon bisulphide *n* (not in technical usage) another name for **carbon disulphide**

carbon black *n* a black finely divided form of amorphous carbon produced by incomplete combustion of natural gas or petroleum: used to reinforce rubber and in the manufacture of pigments and ink

carbon brush *n* a small block of carbon used to convey current between the stationary and moving parts of an electric generator, motor, etc

carbon copy *n* **1** a duplicate copy of writing, typewriting, or drawing obtained by using carbon paper. Often shortened to: **carbon 2** *informal* a person or thing that is identical or very similar to another

carbon credit *n* a certificate showing that a government or company has paid to have a certain amount of carbon dioxide removed from the environment

carbon cycle *n* **1** the circulation of carbon between living organisms and their surroundings. Carbon dioxide from the atmosphere is synthesized by plants into plant tissue, which is ingested and metabolized by animals and converted to carbon dioxide again during respiration and decay **2** four thermonuclear reactions believed to be the source of energy in many stars. Carbon nuclei function as catalysts in the fusion of protons to form helium nuclei

carbon dating *n* short for **radiocarbon dating**

carbon dioxide *n* a colourless odourless incombustible gas present in the atmosphere and formed during respiration, the decomposition and combustion of organic compounds, and in the reaction of acids with carbonates: used in carbonated drinks, fire extinguishers, and as dry ice for refrigeration. Formula: CO_2. Also called: **carbonic-acid gas**

carbon dioxide snow *n* solid carbon dioxide, used as a refrigerant

carbon disulphide *n* a colourless slightly soluble volatile flammable poisonous liquid commonly having a disagreeable odour due to the presence of impurities: used as an organic solvent and in the manufacture of rayon and carbon tetrachloride. Formula: CS_2. Also called (not in technical usage): **carbon bisulphide**

carbonette (,kɑːbə'nɛt) *n NZ* a ball of compressed coal dust used as fuel

carbon fibre *n* a black silky thread of pure carbon made by heating and stretching textile fibres and used because of its lightness and strength at high temperatures for reinforcing resins, ceramics, and metals, esp in turbine blades and for fishing rods

carbon fixation *n* the process by which plants assimilate carbon from carbon dioxide in the atmosphere to form metabolically active compounds

carbon-14 dating *n* another name for **radiocarbon dating**

carbonic (kɑː'bɒnɪk) *adj* (of a compound) containing carbon, esp tetravalent carbon

carbonic acid *n* a weak acid formed when carbon dioxide combines with water: obtained only in aqueous solutions, never in the pure state. Formula: H_2CO_3

carbonic-acid gas *n* another name for **carbon dioxide**

carbonic anhydrase *n* an enzyme in blood cells that catalyses the decomposition of carbonic acid into carbon dioxide and water, facilitating the transport of carbon dioxide from the tissues to the lungs

C

carboniferous (ˌkɑːbəˈnɪfərəs) *adj* yielding coal or carbon

Carboniferous (ˌkɑːbəˈnɪfərəs) *adj* **1** of, denoting, or formed in the fifth period of the Palaeozoic era, between the Devonian and Permian periods, lasting for nearly 64 million years during which coal measures were formed ▷ *n* **2 the** the Carboniferous period or rock system

carbonium ion (kɑːˈbəʊnɪəm) *n chem* a positively charged organic ion in which most of the positive charge is localized on a carbon atom. Compare **carbanion**

carbonize *or* **carbonise** (ˈkɑːbəˌnaɪz) *vb* **1** to turn or be turned into carbon as a result of heating, fossilization, chemical treatment, etc **2** (*tr*) to enrich or coat (a substance) with carbon **3** (*intr*) to react or unite with carbon ▷ Also (for senses 2, 3): carburize > ˌcarboniˈzation *or* ˌcarboniˈsation *n* > ˈcarbonˌizer *or* ˈcarbonˌiser *n*

carbonless paper *n* a sheet of paper impregnated with dye which transfers writing or typing onto the copying surface below without the necessity for carbon pigment. See **carbon paper**

carbon microphone *n* a microphone in which a diaphragm, vibrated by sound waves, applies a varying pressure to a container packed with carbon granules, altering the resistance of the carbon. A current flowing through the carbon is thus modulated at the frequency of the sound waves

carbon monoxide *n* a colourless odourless poisonous flammable gas formed when carbon compounds burn in insufficient air and produced by the action of steam on hot carbon: used as a reducing agent in metallurgy and as a fuel. Formula: CO

carbon paper *n* **1** a thin sheet of paper coated on one side with a dark waxy pigment, often containing carbon, that is transferred by the pressure of writing or of typewriter keys onto the copying surface below. Often shortened to: carbon **2** another name for **carbon tissue**

carbon process *or* **printing** *n* a photographic process for producing positive prints by exposing sensitized carbon tissue to light passing through a negative. Washing removes the unexposed gelatine leaving the pigmented image in the exposed insoluble gelatine

carbon sequestration *n* the prevention of greenhouse gas build-up in the earth's atmosphere by methods such as planting trees to absorb carbon dioxide or pumping carbon dioxide into underground reservoirs

carbon sink *or* **carbon well** *n* areas of vegetation, especially forests, and the phytoplankton-rich seas that absorb the carbon dioxide produced by the burning of fossil fuels

carbon steel *n* steel whose characteristics are determined by the amount of carbon it contains

carbon tax *n* a tax on the emissions caused by the burning of coal, gas, and oil, aimed at reducing the production of greenhouse gases

carbon tetrachloride *n* a colourless volatile nonflammable sparingly soluble liquid made from chlorine and carbon disulphide; tetrachloromethane. It is used as a solvent, cleaning fluid, and insecticide. Formula: CCl₄

carbon tissue *n* a sheet of paper coated with pigmented gelatine, used in the carbon process. Also called: carbon paper

carbon trading *n* the trading by a country with a relatively low level of carbon dioxide emission of part of its emission entitlement to a country that has a higher level of emission

carbon value *n chem* an empirical measurement of the tendency of a lubricant to form carbon when in use

carbon well *n* another name for **carbon sink**

carbonyl (ˈkɑːbəˌnaɪl, -nɪl) *n chem* **1** (*modifier*) of, consisting of, or containing the divalent group =CO: *a carbonyl group or radical* **2** any one of a class of inorganic complexes in which carbonyl groups are bound directly to metal atoms > carbonylic (ˌkɑːbəˈnɪlɪk) *adj*

carbonyl chloride *n* (not in technical usage) another name for **phosgene**

car-boot sale *n* a sale of goods from car boots in a site hired for the occasion

Carborundum (ˌkɑːbəˈrʌndəm) *n trademark* **a** any of various abrasive materials, esp one consisting of silicon carbide **b** (*as modifier*): *a Carborundum wheel*

carboxyhaemoglobin *or US* **carboxyhemoglobin** (kɑːˌbɒksɪˌhiːməʊˈgləʊbɪn, -ˌhɛm-) *n* haemoglobin coordinated with carbon monoxide, formed as a result of carbon monoxide poisoning. As carbon monoxide is bound in preference to oxygen, tissues are deprived of oxygen

carboxylase (kɑːˈbɒksɪˌleɪz) *n* any enzyme that catalyses the release of carbon dioxide from certain acids

carboxylate (kɑːˈbɒksɪˌleɪt) *n* any salt or ester of a carboxylic acid having a formula of the type M(RCOO)ₓ, where M is a metal and R an organic group, or R¹COOR², where R¹ and R² are organic groups

carboxyl group *or* **radical** (kɑːˈbɒksaɪl, -sɪl) *n* the monovalent group –COOH, consisting of a carbonyl group bound to a hydroxyl group: the functional group in organic acids [c19 *carboxyl,* from CARBO- + OXY-² + -YL]

carboxylic acid (ˌkɑːbɒkˈsɪlɪk) *n* any of a class of organic acids containing the carboxyl group. See also **fatty acid**

carboy (ˈkɑːˌbɔɪ) *n* a large glass or plastic bottle, usually protected by a basket or box, used for containing corrosive liquids such as acids [c18 from Persian *qarāba*]

carbuncle (ˈkɑːˌbʌŋkᵊl) *n* **1** an extensive skin eruption, similar to but larger than a boil, with several openings: caused by staphylococcal infection **2** a rounded gemstone, esp a garnet cut without facets **3** a dark reddish-greyish-brown colour [c13 from Latin *carbunculus* diminutive of *carbō* coal] > ˈcarˌbuncled *adj* > carbuncular (kɑːˈbʌŋkjʊlə) *adj*

carburation (ˌkɑːbjʊˈreɪʃən) *n* the process of mixing a hydrocarbon fuel with a correct amount of air to make an explosive mixture for an internal-combustion engine

carburet (ˈkɑːbjʊˌrɛt, ˌkɑːbjʊˈrɛt, -bə-) *vb* -rets, -retting, -retted *or US* -rets, -reting, -reted (*tr*) to combine or mix (a gas) with carbon or carbon compounds [c18 from CARB(ON) + -URET]

carburettor, carburetter (ˌkɑːbjʊˈrɛtə, ˈkɑːbjʊˌrɛtə, -bə-) *or US,* **carburetor** (ˈkɑːbjʊˌreɪtə, -bə-) *n* a device used in petrol engines for atomizing the petrol, controlling its mixture with air, and regulating the intake of the air-petrol mixture into the engine. Informal term: carb. Compare **fuel injection**

carburize *or* **carburise** (ˈkɑːbjʊˌraɪz, -bə-) *vb* **1** another word for **carbonize** (senses 2, 3) **2** (*tr*) to increase the carbon content of (the surface of a low-carbon steel) so that the surface can be hardened by heat treatment > ˌcarburiˈzation *or* ˌcarburiˈsation *n*

carby (ˈkɑːbɪ) *n, pl* -bies *Austral informal* short for **carburettor**

carbylamine (ˌkɑːbɪləˈmiːn, -ˈæmɪn) *n* another name for **isocyanide**

carcajou (ˈkɑːkəˌdʒuː, -ˌʒuː) *n* a North American name for **wolverine** [c18 from Canadian French, from Algonquian *karkajou*]

carcanet (ˈkɑːkəˌnɛt, -nɪt) *n archaic* a jewelled collar or necklace [c16 from French *carcan,* of Germanic origin; compare Old Norse *kverkband* chin strap]

carcass *or* **carcase** (ˈkɑːkəs) *n* **1** the dead body of an animal, esp one that has been slaughtered for food, with the head, limbs, and entrails removed **2** *informal, usually facetious or derogatory* a person's body **3** the skeleton or framework of a structure **4** the remains of anything when its life or vitality is gone; shell [c14 from Old French *carcasse,* of obscure origin]

Carcassonne (*French* karkasɔn) *n* a city in SW France: extensive remains of medieval fortifications. Pop: 43 950 (1999)

Carchemish (ˈkɑːkəmɪʃ, kɑːˈkiː-) *n* an ancient city in Syria on the Euphrates, lying on major trade routes; site of a victory of the Babylonians over the Egyptians (605 BC)

carcinogen (kɑːˈsɪnədʒən, ˈkɑːˌsɪnəˌdʒɛn) *n pathol* any substance that produces cancer [c20 from Greek *karkinos* CANCER + -GEN] > ˌcarcinoˈgenic *adj* > ˌcarcinogenˈicity *n*

carcinogenesis (ˌkɑːsɪnəʊˈdʒɛnɪsɪs) *n pathol* the development of cancerous cells from normal ones

carcinoma (ˌkɑːsɪˈnəʊmə) *n, pl* -mas *or* -mata (-mətə) *pathol* **1** any malignant tumour derived from epithelial tissue **2** another name for **cancer** (sense 1) [c18 from Latin, from Greek *karkinōma,* from *karkinos* CANCER] > ˌcarciˈnomaˌtoid *or* ˌcarciˈnomatous *adj*

carcinomatosis (ˌkɑːsɪˌnəʊməˈtəʊsɪs) *n pathol* a condition characterized by widespread dissemination of carcinomas or by a carcinoma that affects a large area. Also called: carcinosis (ˌkɑːsɪˈnəʊsɪs)

car-crash TV *n* television programmes that show deliberately controversial, disturbing, or horrific material [c20 from their eliciting in the viewer a similar horrified fascination to that experienced by people watching scenes of cars crashing]

card[1] (kɑːd) *n* **1** a piece of stiff paper or thin cardboard, usually rectangular, with varied uses, as for filing information in an index, bearing a written notice for display, entering scores in a game, etc **2** such a card used for identification, reference, proof of membership, etc: *library card; identity card; visiting card* **3** such a card used for sending greetings, messages, or invitations, often bearing an illustration, printed greetings, etc: *Christmas card; birthday card* **4** one of a set of small pieces of cardboard, variously marked with significant figures, symbols, etc, used for playing games or for fortune-telling **5 a** short for **playing card b** (*as modifier*): *a card game* **c** (*in combination*): *cardsharp* **6** *informal* a witty, entertaining, or eccentric person **7** short for **cheque card** *or* **credit card 8** See **compass card 9** Also called: race card *horse racing* a daily programme of all the races at a meeting, listing the runners, riders, weights to be carried, distances to be run, and conditions of each race **10** a thing or action used in order to gain an advantage, esp one that is concealed and kept in reserve until needed (esp in the phrase **a card up one's sleeve**) **11** short for **printed circuit card** See **printed circuit** ▷ See also **cards** [c15 from Old French *carte,* from Latin *charta* leaf of papyrus, from Greek *khartēs,* probably of Egyptian origin]

card[2] (kɑːd) *vb* **1** (*tr*) to comb out and clean fibres of wool or cotton before spinning ▷ *n* **2** (formerly) a machine or comblike tool for carding fabrics or for raising the nap on cloth [c15 from Old French *carde* card, teasel, from Latin *carduus* thistle] > ˈcarding *n* > ˈcarder *n*

Card. *abbreviation for* Cardinal

cardamom, cardamum (ˈkɑːdəməm) *or* **cardamon** *n* **1** a tropical Asian zingiberaceous plant, *Elettaria cardamomum,* that has large hairy leaves **2** the seeds of this plant, used esp as a spice or condiment **3** a related East Indian plant, *Amomum cardamomum,* whose seeds are used as a substitute for cardamom seeds [c15 from Latin *cardamōmum,* from Greek *kardamomon,* from *kardamon* cress + *amōmon* an Indian spice]

cardan joint (ˈkɑːdæn) *n engineering* a type of universal joint in a shaft that enables it to rotate when out of alignment [c20 named after Geronimo *Cardan* (1501–76), Italian mathematician]

cardboard (ˈkɑːdˌbɔːd) *n* **1 a** a thin stiff board

made from paper pulp and used esp for making cartons **b** (*as modifier*): *cardboard boxes* ▷ *adj* **2** (*prenominal*) without substance: *a cardboard smile; a cardboard general*

cardboard city *n informal* an area of a city in which homeless people sleep rough, often in cardboard boxes

cardboardy ('kɑːdˌbɔːdɪ) *adj* like cardboard, esp in stiffness, texture, or taste: *it becomes cardboardy if cooked too long*

card-carrying *adj* being an official member of a specified organization: *a card-carrying union member; a card-carrying Communist*

card catalogue *n* a catalogue of books, papers, etc, filed on cards

card file *n* another term for **card index**

cardholder ('kɑːdˌhəʊldə) *n* a person who owns a credit or debit card

cardiac ('kɑːdɪˌæk) *adj* **1** of or relating to the heart **2** of or relating to the portion of the stomach connected to the oesophagus ▷ *n* **3** a person with a heart disorder **4** *obsolete* a drug that stimulates the heart muscle [c17 from Latin *cardiacus*, from Greek, from *kardia* heart]

cardiac arrest *n* failure of the pumping action of the heart, resulting in loss of consciousness and absence of pulse and breathing: a medical emergency requiring immediate resuscitative treatment

cardialgia (ˌkɑːdɪˈældʒɪə, -dʒə) *n* **1** *obsolete* pain in or near the heart **2** a technical name for **heartburn**. ▷ ˌcardiˈalgic *adj*

cardie *or* **cardy** ('kɑːdɪ) *n informal* short for **cardigan**

Cardiff ('kɑːdɪf) *n* **1** the capital of Wales, situated in the southeast, in Cardiff county borough: formerly an important port; seat of the Welsh assembly (1999); university (1883). Pop: 292 150 (2001) **2** a county borough in SE Wales, created in 1996 from part of South Glamorgan. Pop: 315 100 (2003 est). Area: 139 sq km (54 sq miles)

cardigan ('kɑːdɪgən) *n* a knitted jacket or sweater with buttons up the front [c19 named after James Thomas Brudenell, 7th Earl of Cardigan (1797–1868), British cavalry officer]

Cardigan ('kɑːdɪgən) *n* the larger variety of corgi, having a long tail

Cardigan Bay *n* an inlet of St George's Channel, on the W coast of Wales

Cardiganshire ('kɑːdɪgənˌʃɪə, -ʃə) *n* a former county of W Wales: became part of Dyfed in 1974; reinstated as **Ceredigion** in 1996

cardinal ('kɑːdɪnəl) *n* **1** *RC Church* any of the members of the Sacred College, ranking next after the pope, who elect the pope and act as his chief counsellors **2** Also called: **cardinal red** a deep vivid red colour **3** See **cardinal number 4** Also called: **cardinal grosbeak**, (US) **redbird** a crested North American bunting, *Richmondena* (or *Pyrrhuloxia*) *cardinalis*, the male of which has a bright red plumage and the female a brown one **5** a fritillary butterfly, *Pandoriana pandora*, found in meadows of southern Europe **6** a woman's hooded shoulder cape worn in the 17th and 18th centuries ▷ *adj* **7** (*usually prenominal*) fundamentally important; principal: *cardinal sin* **8** of a deep vivid red colour **9** *astrology* of or relating to the signs Aries, Cancer, Libra, and Capricorn. Compare **mutable** (sense 2), **fixed** (sense 10) [c13 from Latin *cardinālis*, literally: relating to a hinge, hence, that on which something depends, principal, from *cardō* hinge] ▷ ˈcardinally *adv*

cardinalate ('kɑːdɪnəˌleɪt) *or* **cardinalship** *n* **1** the rank, office, or term of office of a cardinal **2** the cardinals collectively

cardinal beetle *n* any of various large N temperate beetles of the family *Pyrochroidae*, such as *Pyrochroa serraticornis*, typically scarlet or partly scarlet in colour

cardinal flower *n* a campanulaceous plant, *Lobelia cardinalis* of E North America, that has brilliant scarlet, pink, or white flowers

cardinality (ˌkɑːdɪˈnælɪtɪ) *n* **1** *maths* the property of possessing a cardinal number **2** *maths, logic* (of a class) the cardinal number associated with the given class. Two classes have the same cardinality if they can be put in one-to-one correspondence

cardinal number *or* **numeral** *n* **1** a number denoting quantity but not order in a set. Sometimes shortened to: **cardinal 2** *maths, logic* **a** a measure of the size of a set that does not take account of the order of its members. Compare **natural number b** a particular number having this function ▷ Compare **ordinal number**

cardinal points *pl n* the four main points of the compass: north, south, east, and west

cardinal sin *n* **1** *theol* any of the seven deadly sins **2** *informal* an unforgivable error or misjudgment: *lack of impartiality is considered a cardinal sin in broadcasting circles*

cardinal spider *n* a large house spider, *Tegenaria parietina*

cardinal virtues *pl n* the most important moral qualities, traditionally justice, prudence, temperance, and fortitude

cardinal vowels *pl n* a set of theoretical vowel sounds, based on the shape of the mouth needed to articulate them, that can be used to classify the vowel sounds of any speaker in any language

card index *or* **file** *n* **1** an index in which each item is separately listed on systematically arranged cards ▷ *vb* **card-index** (*tr*) **2** to make such an index of (a book)

carding ('kɑːdɪŋ) *n* the process of preparing the fibres of cotton, wool, etc, for spinning

cardio- *or before a vowel* **cardi-** *combining form* heart: *cardiogram* [from Greek *kardia* heart]

cardiocentesis (ˌkɑːdɪəʊsɛnˈtiːsɪs) *n med* surgical puncture of the heart

cardiogram ('kɑːdɪəʊˌgræm) *n* short for **electrocardiogram**

cardiograph ('kɑːdɪəʊˌɡrɑːf, -ˌgræf) *n* **1** an instrument for recording the mechanical force and form of heart movements **2** short for **electrocardiograph**. ▷ cardiographer (ˌkɑːdɪˈɒgrəfə) *n* ▷ cardiographic (ˌkɑːdɪəʊˈgræfɪk) *or* ˌcardioˈgraphical *adj* ▷ ˌcardioˈgraphically *adv* ▷ ˌcardiˈography *n*

cardioid ('kɑːdɪˌɔɪd) *n* a heart-shaped curve generated by a fixed point on a circle as it rolls around another fixed circle of equal radius, *a*. Equation: $r = a(1 - \cos \varphi)$, where r is the radius vector and φ is the polar angle

cardiology (ˌkɑːdɪˈɒlədʒɪ) *n* the branch of medical science concerned with the heart and its diseases ▷ cardiological (ˌkɑːdɪəˈlɒdʒɪkəl) *adj* ▷ ˌcardiˈologist *n*

cardiomegaly (ˌkɑːdɪəʊˈmɛgəlɪ) *n pathol* another name for **megalocardia**

cardiomyopathy (ˌkɑːdɪəʊmaɪˈɒpəθɪ) *n pathol* a disease of the heart muscle usually caused by a biochemical defect or a toxin such as alcohol

cardioplegia (ˌkɑːdɪəʊˈpliːdʒɪə) *n med* deliberate arrest of the action of the heart, as by hypothermia or the injection of chemicals, to enable complex heart surgery to be carried out

cardiopulmonary (ˌkɑːdɪəʊˈpʌlmənərɪ, -mənrɪ, -ˈpʊl-) *adj* of, relating to, or affecting the heart and lungs

cardiopulmonary resuscitation *n* an emergency measure to revive a patient whose heart has stopped beating, in which compressions applied with the hands to the patient's chest are alternated with mouth-to-mouth respiration. Abbreviation: **CPR**

cardiothoracic (ˌkɑːdɪəʊθɔːˈræsɪk) *adj* of or relating to the heart and the chest

cardiovascular (ˌkɑːdɪəʊˈvæskjʊlə) *adj* of or relating to the heart and the blood vessels

carditis (kɑːˈdaɪtɪs) *n* inflammation of the heart

cardoon (kɑːˈduːn) *n* a thistle-like S European plant, *Cynara cardunculus*, closely related to the artichoke, with spiny leaves, purple flowers, and a leafstalk that may be blanched and eaten: family

Asteraceae (composites) [c17 from French *cardon*, ultimately from Latin *carduus* thistle, artichoke]

cardphone ('kɑːdfəʊn) *n* a public telephone operated by the insertion of a phonecard instead of coins

card punch *n* **1** a device, no longer widely used, controlled by a computer, for transferring information from the central processing unit onto punched cards. Compare **card reader 2** another name for **key punch**

card reader *n* a device, no longer widely used, for reading information on a punched card and transferring it to a computer. Compare **card punch**

cards (kɑːdz) *n* **1** (*usually functioning as singular*) **a** any game or games played with cards, esp playing cards **b** the playing of such a game **2** an employee's national insurance and other documents held by the employer **3** get one's cards to be told to leave one's employment **4** on the cards possible or likely. US equivalent: in the cards **5** play one's cards to carry out one's plans; take action (esp in the phrase **play one's cards right**) **6** put *or* lay one's cards on the table Also: show one's cards to declare one's intentions, resources, etc

cardsharp ('kɑːdˌʃɑːp) *or* **cardsharper** *n* a professional card player who cheats ▷ ˈcardˌsharping *n*

card surfing *n slang* a form of cash-card fraud in which one person watches another using a cash dispenser, notes his or her personal identification number, and, after an accomplice has stolen the card, uses the card to withdraw cash

carduaceous (ˌkɑːdjʊˈeɪʃəs) *adj* of, relating to, or belonging to the *Carduaceae*, a subfamily of composite plants that includes the thistle [c19 from New Latin *Carduāceae*, from *Carduus* type genus, from Latin: thistle]

card vote *n Brit* a vote by delegates, esp at a trade-union conference, in which each delegate's vote counts as a vote by all his constituents

cardy ('kɑːdɪ) *n, pl* **-dies** *informal* a variant spelling of **cardie**

care (kɛə) *vb* **1** (when *tr*, may take a clause as object) to be troubled or concerned; be affected emotionally: *he is dying, and she doesn't care* **2** (*intr*; foll by *for* or *about*) to have regard, affection, or consideration (for): *he cares more for his hobby than his job* **3** (*intr*; foll by *for*) to have a desire or taste (for): *would you care for some tea?* **4** (*intr*; foll by *for*) to provide physical needs, help, or comfort (for): *the nurse cared for her patients* **5** (*tr*) to agree or like (to do something): *would you care to sit down, please?* **6** for all I care *or* I couldn't care less I am completely indifferent ▷ *n* **7** careful or serious attention: *under her care the plant flourished; he does his work with care* **8** protective or supervisory control: *in the care of a doctor* **9** (*often plural*) trouble; anxiety; worry **10** an object of or cause for concern: *the baby's illness was her only care* **11** caution: *handle with care* **12** care of at the address of: written on envelopes. Usual abbreviation: **c/o 13** in (*or* into) care *social welfare* made the legal responsibility of a local authority by order of a court [Old English *cearu* (n), *cearian* (vb), of Germanic origin; compare Old High German *chara* lament, Latin *garrīre* to gossip]

CARE (kɛə) *n acronym for* **1** Cooperative for American Relief Everywhere, Inc.; a federation of US charities, giving financial and technical assistance to many regions of the world **2** communicated authenticity, regard, empathy: the three qualities believed to be essential in the therapist practising client-centred therapy

care and maintenance *n commerce* the state of a building, ship, machinery, etc, that is not in current use although it is kept in good condition to enable it to be quickly brought into service if there is demand for it. Abbreviation: **C & M**

care attendant *n social welfare* (in Britain) a person who is paid to look after one or more severely handicapped people by visiting them

C

frequently and staying when needed, but who does not live in

careen (kə'ri:n) *vb* **1** to sway or cause to sway dangerously over to one side **2** (*tr*) *nautical* to cause (a vessel) to keel over to one side, esp in order to clean or repair its bottom **3** (*intr*) *nautical* (of a vessel) to keel over to one side [c17 from French *carène* keel, from Italian *carena*, from Latin *carīna* keel] > ca'reenage *n* > ca'reener *n*

career (kə'rɪə) *n* **1** a path or progress through life or history **2** a profession or occupation chosen as one's life's work **3** (*modifier*) having or following a career as specified: *a career diplomat* **4** a course or path, esp a swift or headlong one **5** (*intr*) to move swiftly along; rush in an uncontrolled way [c16 from French *carrière*, from Late Latin *carrāria* carriage road, from Latin *carrus* two-wheeled wagon, CAR]

career girl *or* **woman** *n* a girl or woman, often unmarried, who follows a career or profession

careerist (kə'rɪərɪst) *n* a person who values success in his career above all else and seeks to advance it by any possible means > ca'reerism *n*

careers adviser *or* **advisor** *n* a person trained in giving vocational advice, esp in secondary, further, or higher education

careers master *n* a male teacher who gives pupils advice and information about careers

careers mistress *n* a female teacher who gives pupils advice and information about careers

Careers Officer *n* a person trained in giving vocational advice, esp to school leavers

carefree ('kɛə,fri:) *adj* without worry or responsibility > 'care,freeness *n*

careful ('kɛəfʊl) *adj* **1** cautious in attitude or action; prudent **2** painstaking in one's work; thorough: *he wrote very careful script* **3** (*usually postpositive*; foll by *of*, *in*, or *about*) solicitous; protective: *careful of one's reputation* **4** *archaic* full of care; anxious **5** *Brit* mean or miserly > 'carefully *adv* > 'carefulness *n*

caregiver ('kɛə,gɪvə) *n US and Canadian* a person who has accepted responsibility for looking after a vulnerable neighbour or relative. Also called: carer

careless ('kɛəlɪs) *adj* **1** done with or acting with insufficient attention; negligent **2** (often foll by *in*, *of*, or *about*) unconcerned in attitude or action; heedless; indifferent (to): *she's very careless about her clothes* **3** (*usually prenominal*) carefree **4** (*usually prenominal*) unstudied; artless: *an impression of careless elegance* > 'carelessly *adv* > 'carelessness *n*

careline ('kɛəlaɪn) *n* a telephone service set up by a company or other organization to provide its customers or clients with information about its products or services

care plan *n* a plan for the medical care of a particular patient or the welfare of a child in care

carer ('kɛərə) *n social welfare* a person who has accepted responsibility for looking after a vulnerable neighbour or relative. See also caretaker (sense 3). Usual US and Canadian term: caregiver

caress (kə'rɛs) *n* **1** a gentle touch or embrace, esp one given to show affection ▷ *vb* **2** (*tr*) to touch or stroke gently with affection or as with affection: *the wind caressed her face* [c17 from French *caresse*, from Italian *carezza*, from Latin *cārus* dear] > ca'resser *n* > ca'ressingly *adv*

caret ('kærɪt) *n* a symbol (ʌ) used to indicate the place in written or printed matter at which something is to be inserted [c17 from Latin, literally: there is missing, from *carēre* to lack]

caretaker ('kɛə,teɪkə) *n* **1** a person who is in charge of a place or thing, esp in the owner's absence: *the caretaker of a school* **2** (*modifier*) holding office temporarily; interim: *a caretaker government* **3** *social welfare* a person who takes care of a vulnerable person, often a close relative. See also carer. > 'care,taking *n*

careworn ('kɛə,wɔ:n) *adj* showing signs of care, stress, worry etc

Carey Street ('kɛərɪ) *n* **1** (formerly) the street in which the London bankruptcy court was situated **2** the state of bankruptcy

carfare ('ka:,fɛə) *n US and Canadian* the fare that a passenger is charged for a ride on a bus, etc

carfax ('ka:fæks) *n* a place where principal roads or streets intersect, esp a place in a town where four roads meet [c14 from Anglo-French *carfuks*, from Old French *carrefures*, from Latin *quadrifurcus* four-forked]

carfuffle (kə'fʌfᵊl) *n informal, chiefly Brit* a variant spelling of kerfuffle [c20 of unknown origin]

cargo ('ka:gəʊ) *n, pl* -goes *or* -gos **1 a** goods carried by a ship, aircraft, or other vehicle; freight **b** (*as modifier*): *a cargo vessel* **2** any load: *the train pulled in with its cargo of new arrivals* [c17 from Spanish: from *cargar* to load, from Late Latin *carricāre* to load a vehicle, from *carrus* CAR]

cargo cult *n* a religious movement of the SW Pacific, characterized by expectation of the return of spirits in ships or aircraft carrying goods that will provide for the needs of the followers

cargo pants *or* **trousers** *pl n* loose trousers with a large external pocket on the side of each leg

carhop ('ka:,hɒp) *n US and Canadian informal* a waiter or waitress at a drive-in restaurant

Caria ('kɛərɪə) *n* an ancient region of SW Asia Minor, on the Aegean Sea: chief cities were Halicarnassus and Cnidus: corresponds to the present-day Turkish districts of S Aydin and W Muğla

Carib ('kærɪb) *n* **1** (*pl* -ibs *or* -ib) a member of a group of American Indian peoples of NE South America and the Lesser Antilles **2** the family of languages spoken by these peoples [c16 from Spanish *Caribe*, from Arawak] > 'Cariban *adj*

Caribbean (,kærɪ'bi:ən; *US* kə'rɪbɪən) *adj* **1** of, or relating to, the Caribbean Sea and its islands **2** of, or relating to, the Carib or any of their languages ▷ *n* **3** the the states and islands of the Caribbean Sea, including the West Indies, when considered as a geopolitical region **4** short for the Caribbean Sea **5** a member of any of the peoples inhabiting the islands of the Caribbean Sea, such as a West Indian or a Carib

Caribbean Sea *n* an almost landlocked sea, part of the Atlantic Ocean, bounded by the Caribbean islands, Central America, and the N coast of South America. Area: 2 718 200 sq km (1 049 500 sq miles)

Caribbee bark ('kærɪ,bi:) *n* the bark of any of various tropical American and Caribbean rubiaceous trees of the genus *Exostema*, used as a substitute for cinchona bark

Caribbees ('kærɪ,bi:z) *pl n* the a former name for the Lesser Antilles

Cariboo ('kærɪ,bu:) *n* the *Canadian* a region in the W foothills of the Cariboo Mountains, scene of a gold rush beginning in 1860

Cariboo Mountains *pl n* a mountain range in SW Canada, in SE British Columbia. Highest peak: Mount Sir Wilfrid Laurier, 3520 m (11 549 ft)

caribou ('kærɪ,bu:) *n, pl* -bou *or* -bous a large deer, *Rangifer tarandus*, of Arctic regions of North America, having large branched antlers in the male and female: also occurs in Europe and Asia, where it is called a reindeer. Also called (Canadian): tuktu [c18 from Canadian French, of Algonquian origin; compare Micmac *khalibu* literally: scratcher]

Caribou ('kærɪ,bu:) *n Canadian* a mixed drink containing wine and grain alcohol

Caribou Inuit *n* a member of any of the Inuit peoples who formerly inhabited the Barren Lands of N Canada

caricature ('kærɪkə,tjʊə) *n* **1** a pictorial, written, or acted representation of a person, which exaggerates his characteristic traits for comic effect **2** a ludicrously inadequate or inaccurate imitation: *he is a caricature of a statesman* ▷ *vb* **3** (*tr*) to represent in caricature or produce a caricature of [c18 from Italian *caricatura* a distortion, exaggeration, from *caricare* to load, exaggerate; see

CARGO] > 'carica,tural *adj* > 'carica,turist *n*

CARICOM ('kærɪ,kɒm) *n acronym for* Caribbean Community and Common Market

caries ('kɛəri:z) *n, pl* -ies progressive decay of a bone or a tooth [c17 from Latin: decay; related to Greek *kēr* death]

CARIFTA (kæ'rɪftə) *n acronym for* Caribbean Free Trade Area

carillon (kə'rɪljən) *n music* **1** a set of bells usually hung in a tower and played either by keys and pedals or mechanically **2** a tune played on such bells **3** an organ stop giving the effect of a bell **4** a form of celesta or keyboard glockenspiel ▷ *vb* -lons, -lonning, -lonned **5** (*intr*) to play a carillon [c18 from French: set of bells, from Old French *quarregnon*, ultimately from Latin *quattuor* four]

carillonneur (kə,rɪljə'nɜ:) *n* a person who plays a carillon

carina (kə'ri:nə, -'raɪ-) *n, pl* -nae (-ni:) *or* -nas a keel-like part or ridge, as in the breastbone of birds or the fused lower petals of a leguminous flower [c18 from Latin: keel]

Carina (kə'ri:nə, -'raɪ-) *n, Latin genitive* Carinae (kə'ri:ni:, -'raɪ-) a large conspicuous constellation in the S hemisphere close to the Southern Cross that contains Canopus, the second brightest star in the sky. It was originally considered part of Argo

carinate ('kærɪ,neɪt) *or* **carinated** *adj biology* having a keel or ridge; shaped like a keel [c17 from Latin *carīnāre* to furnish with a keel or shell, from *carīna* keel]

caring ('kɛərɪŋ) *adj* **1** feeling or showing care and compassion: *a caring attitude* **2** of or relating to professional social or medical care: *nursing is a caring job* ▷ *n* **3** the practice or profession of providing social or medical care

Carinthia (kə'rɪnθɪə) *n* a state of S Austria: an independent duchy from 976 to 1276; mainly mountainous, with many lakes and resorts. Capital: Klagenfurt. Pop: 559 440 (2003 est). Area: 9533 sq km (3681 sq miles). German name: Kärnten

carioca (,kærɪ'əʊkə) *n* **1** a Brazilian dance similar to the samba **2** a piece of music composed for this dance [c19 from Brazilian Portuguese]

Cariocan (,kærɪ'əʊkən) *or* **Carioca** *n* a native of Rio de Janeiro, Brazil

cariogenic (,kɛərɪəʊ'dʒɛnɪk) *adj* (of a substance) producing caries, esp in the teeth

cariole *or* **carriole** ('kærɪ,əʊl) *n* **1** a small open two-wheeled horse-drawn vehicle **2** a covered cart [c19 from French *carriole*, ultimately from Latin *carrus*; see CAR]

carious ('kɛərɪəs) *or* **cariose** ('kɛərɪ,əʊz) *adj* (of teeth or bone) affected with caries; decayed > cariosity (,kɛərɪ'ɒsɪtɪ, ,kɛərɪ-) *or* 'cariousness *n*

Carisbrooke Castle ('kærɪz,brʊk) *n* a castle near Newport on the Isle of Wight: Charles I was held prisoner here from 1647 until his execution in 1649

carjack ('ka:,dʒæk) *vb* (*tr*) to attack (a driver in a car) in order to rob the driver or to steal the car for another crime [c20 CAR + (HI)JACK] > 'car,jacker *n*

cark¹ (ka:k) *vb* an archaic word for worry (senses 1, 2, 11, 13) [c13 *carken* to burden, from Old Northern French *carquier*, from Late Latin *carricāre* to load]

cark² (ka:k) *vb* (*intr*) *Austral slang* to break down; die [perhaps from the cry of the crow, as a carrion feeding bird]

carl *or* **carle** (ka:l) *n archaic* another word for churl [Old English, from Old Norse *karl*]

carlin ('ka:lɪn) *n* another word for pug¹ [c18 named after a French actor who played Harlequin, because of the resemblance of the dog's face to the black mask of the Harlequin]

carline¹ ('ka:lɪn) *n* a Eurasian thistle-like plant, *Carlina vulgaris*, having spiny leaves and flower heads surrounded by raylike whitish bracts: family *Asteraceae* (composites). Also called: carline thistle [c16 from French, probably from Latin *cardō* thistle]

carline² *or* **carlin** ('kɑːlɪn) *n* **1** *chiefly Scot* an old woman, hag, or witch **2** a variant of **carling** [c14 from Old Norse *kerling* old woman, diminutive of *karl* man, CHURL]

carling ('kɑːlɪn) *or* **carline** *n* a fore-and-aft beam in a vessel, used for supporting the deck, esp around a hatchway or other opening [c14 from Old Norse *kerling* old woman, CARLINE²]

Carlisle (kɑːˈlaɪl, ˈkɑːlaɪl) *n* a city in NW England, administrative centre of Cumbria: railway and industrial centre. Pop: 71 773 (2001). Latin name: **Luguvalium** (ˌluːguːˈvælləm)

Carlist ('kɑːlɪst) *n* **1** (in Spain) a supporter of Don Carlos or his descendants as the rightful kings of Spain **2** (in France) a supporter of Charles X or his descendants > **ˈCarlism** *n*

Carlovingian (ˌkɑːləʊˈvɪndʒɪən) *adj, n history* a variant of **Carolingian**

Carlow ('kɑːləʊ) *n* **1** a county of SE Republic of Ireland, in Leinster: mostly flat, with barren mountains in the southeast. County town: Carlow. Pop: 46 014 (2002). Area: 896 sq km (346 sq miles) **2** a town in SE Republic of Ireland, county town of Co Carlow. Pop: 18 487 (2002)

Carlsbad ('kɑːlsbɑːt) *n* a variant spelling of the German name for **Karlovy Vary**

Carlton ('kɑːltən) *n* a town in N central England, in S Nottinghamshire. Pop: 48 493 (2001)

carmagnole (ˌkɑːmənˈjəʊl; *French* karmaɲɔl) *n* **1** a dance and song popular during the French Revolution **2** the costume worn by many French Revolutionaries, consisting of a short jacket with wide lapels, black trousers, a red liberty cap, and a tricoloured sash [c18 from French, probably named after *Carmagnola*, Italy, taken by French Revolutionaries in 1792]

carman ('kɑːmən) *n, pl* -men **1** a man who drives a car or cart; carter **2** a man whose business is the transport of goods; haulier **3** *US and Canadian* a tram driver

Carmarthen (kɑːˈmɑːðən) *n* a market town in S Wales, the administrative centre of Carmarthenshire: Norman castle. Pop: 14 648 (2001)

Carmarthenshire (kɑːˈmɑːðənˌʃɪə, -ʃə) *n* a county of S Wales, formerly part of Dyfed (1974–96): on Carmarthen Bay, with the Cambrian Mountains in the N: generally agricultural (esp dairying). Administrative centre: Carmarthen. Pop: 176 000 (2003 est). Area: 2398 sq km (926 sq miles)

Carme¹ ('kɑːmɪ) *n Greek myth* a nymph who was one of Diana's attendants and mother of Britomaris by Jupiter

Carme² ('kɑːmɪ) *n* a small outer satellite of the planet Jupiter with a retrograde orbit

Carmel ('kɑːməl) *n* **Mount** a mountain ridge in NW Israel, extending from the Samarian Hills to the Mediterranean. Highest point: about 540 m (1800 ft)

Carmelite ('kɑːməˌlaɪt) *n* **1** *RC Church* a member of an order of mendicant friars founded about 1154; a White Friar **2** a member of a corresponding order of nuns founded in 1452, noted for its austere rule **3** (*modifier*) of or relating to the Carmelite friars or nuns [c14 from French; named after Mount CARMEL, where the order was founded]

carminative ('kɑːmɪnətɪv) *adj* **1** able to relieve flatulence ▷ *n* **2** a carminative drug [c15 from French *carminatif*, from Latin *carminare* to card wool, remove impurities, from *cārere* to card]

carmine ('kɑːmaɪn) *n* **1** a vivid red colour, sometimes with a purplish tinge **b** (*as adjective*): *carmine paint* **2** a pigment of this colour obtained from cochineal [c18 from Medieval Latin *carmīnus*, from Arabic *qirmiz* KERMES]

Carnac ('kɑːnæk) *n* a village in NW France: noted for its many megalithic monuments, including alignments of stone menhirs

carnage ('kɑːnɪdʒ) *n* extensive slaughter, esp of human beings in battle [c16 from French, from Italian *carnaggio*, from Medieval Latin *carnāticum*, from Latin *carō* flesh]

carnal ('kɑːnᵊl) *adj* relating to the appetites and passions of the body; sensual; fleshly [c15 from Late Latin: relating to flesh, from Latin *carō* flesh] > **ˈcarnalist** *n* > **carˈnality** *n* > **ˈcarnally** *adv*

carnal knowledge *n chiefly law* **1** sexual intercourse **2 have carnal knowledge of** to have sexual intercourse with

carnallite ('kɑːnəˌlaɪt) *n* a white or sometimes coloured mineral consisting of a hydrated chloride of potassium and magnesium in orthorhombic crystalline form: a source of potassium and also used as a fertilizer. Formula: $KCl.MgCl_2.6H_2O$ [c19 named after Rudolf von Carnall (1804–74), German mining engineer; see -ITE¹]

carnaroli (ˌkɑːnəˈrəʊlɪ) *n* a variety of short-grain rice used for risotto [Italian]

Carnarvon (kɑːˈnɑːvᵊn) *n* a variant spelling of **Caernarfon**

carnassial (kɑːˈnæsɪəl) *adj* **1** *zoology* of, relating to, or designating the last upper premolar and first lower molar teeth of carnivores, which have sharp edges for tearing flesh ▷ *n* **2** a carnassial tooth [c19 from French *carnassier* meat-eating, from Provençal, from *carnasso* abundance of meat, from *carn* meat, flesh, from Latin *carō*]

Carnatic (kɑːˈnætɪk) *n* a region of S India, between the Eastern Ghats and the Coromandel Coast: originally the country of the Kanarese; historically important as a rich and powerful trading centre; now part of Madras state

carnation (kɑːˈneɪʃən) *n* **1** Also called: **clove pink** a Eurasian caryophyllaceous plant, *Dianthus caryophyllus*, cultivated in many varieties for its white, pink, or red flowers, which have a fragrant scent of cloves **2** the flower of this plant **3 a** a pink or reddish-pink colour **b** (*as adjective*): *a carnation dress* **4** (*often plural*) a flesh tint in painting [c16 from French: flesh colour, from Late Latin *carnātiō* fleshiness, from Latin *carō* flesh]

carnauba (kɑːˈnaʊbə) *n* **1** Also called: **wax palm** a Brazilian fan palm, *Copernicia cerifera* **2** Also called: **carnauba wax** the wax obtained from the young leaves of this tree, used esp as a polish [from Brazilian Portuguese, probably of Tupi origin]

Carnegie Hall (kɑːˈnəɡɪ) *n* a famous concert hall in New York (opened 1891); endowed by Andrew Carnegie (1835–1919), Scots-born US steel manufacturer and philanthropist

carnelian (kɑːˈniːljən) *n* a red or reddish-yellow translucent variety of chalcedony, used as a gemstone [c17 variant of *cornelian*, from Old French *corneline*, of uncertain origin; *car*- spelling influenced by Latin *carneus* flesh-coloured]

carnet ('kɑːneɪ) *n* **1 a** a customs licence authorizing the temporary importation of a motor vehicle **b** an official document permitting motorists to cross certain frontiers **2** a book of tickets, travel coupons, etc [French: notebook, from Old French *quernet*, ultimately from Latin *quaternī* four at a time; see QUIRE¹]

carnify ('kɑːnɪˌfaɪ) *vb* -fies, -fying, -fied (*intr*) *pathol* (esp of lung tissue, as the result of pneumonia) to be altered so as to resemble skeletal muscle [c17 from Latin *carō* flesh + *facere* to make] > **carnification** (ˌkɑːnɪfɪˈkeɪʃən) *n*

Carniola (ˌkɑːnɪˈəʊlə) *n* a region of N Slovenia: a former duchy and crownland of Austria (1335–1919); divided between Yugoslavia and Italy in 1919; part of Yugoslavia (1947–92). German name: **Krain** (kraɪn) Slovene name: **Kranj**

carnival ('kɑːnɪvᵊl) *n* **1 a** a festive occasion or period marked by merrymaking, processions, etc: esp in some Roman Catholic countries, the period just before Lent **b** (*as modifier*): *a carnival atmosphere* **2** a travelling fair having merry go rounds, etc **3** a show or display arranged as an amusement **4** *Austral* a sports meeting [c16 from Italian *carnevale*, from Old Italian *carnelevare* a removing of meat (referring to the Lenten fast)]

carnivalesque (ˌkɑːnɪvᵊˈlɛsk) *adj* characteristic of, suitable for, or like a carnival

carnivore (ˈkɑːnɪˌvɔː) *n* **1** any placental mammal of the order *Carnivora*, typically having large pointed canine teeth and sharp molars and premolars, specialized for eating flesh. The order includes cats, dogs, bears, raccoons, hyenas, civets, and weasels **2** any other animal or any plant that feeds on animals **3** *informal* an aggressively ambitious person [c19 probably back formation from CARNIVOROUS]

carnivorous (kɑːˈnɪvərəs) *adj* **1** (esp of animals) feeding on flesh **2** (of plants such as the pitcher plant and sundew) able to trap and digest insects and other small animals **3** of or relating to the *Carnivora* **4** *informal* aggressively ambitious or reactionary [c17 from Latin *carnivorus*, from *carō* flesh + *vorāre* to consume] > **carˈnivorously** *adv* > **carˈnivorousness** *n*

Carnot cycle *n* an idealized reversible heat-engine cycle giving maximum efficiency and consisting of an isothermal expansion, an adiabatic expansion, an isothermal compression, and an adiabatic compression back to the initial state

carnotite (ˈkɑːnəˌtaɪt) *n* a radioactive yellow mineral consisting of hydrated uranium potassium vanadate: occurs in sedimentary rocks and is a source of uranium, radium, and vanadium. Formula: $K_2(UO_2)_2(VO_4)_2.3H_2O$ [c20 named after A. *Carnot* (died 1920), French inspector general of mines]

Carnot principle *n* the principle that no heat engine can be more efficient than one operating on a Carnot cycle of reversible changes

carny¹ *or* **carney** (ˈkɑːnɪ) *vb* -nies, -nying, -nied *or* -neys, -neying, -neyed *Brit informal* to coax or cajole or act in a wheedling manner [c19 of unknown origin]

carny², **carney** *or* **carnie** (ˈkɑːnɪ) *n, pl* -nies *US and Canadian slang* **1** short for **carnival 2** a person who works in a carnival

carob (ˈkærəb) *n* **1** Also called: **algarroba** an evergreen leguminous Mediterranean tree, *Ceratonia siliqua*, with compound leaves and edible pods **2** Also called: **algarroba, Saint John's bread** the long blackish sugary pod of this tree, used as a substitute for chocolate and for animal fodder [c16 from Old French *carobe*, from Medieval Latin *carrūbium*, from Arabic *al kharrūbah*]

caroche (kəˈrɒʃ) *n* a stately ceremonial carriage used in the 16th and 17th centuries [c16 from French, ultimately from Latin *carrus* CAR]

carol (ˈkærəl) *n* **1** a joyful hymn or religious song, esp one (a **Christmas carol**) celebrating the birth of Christ **2** *archaic* an old English circular dance ▷ *vb* -ols, -olling, -olled *or US* -ols, -oling, -oled **3** (*intr*) to sing carols at Christmas **4** to sing (something) in a joyful manner [c13 from Old French, of uncertain origin] > **ˈcaroler** *or* **ˈcaroller** *n* > **ˈcaroling** *or* **ˈcarolling** *n*

Carolina (ˌkærəˈlaɪnə) *n* a former English colony on the E coast of North America, first established in 1663: divided in 1729 into North and South Carolina, which are often referred to as **the Carolinas**

Caroline (ˈkærəˌlaɪn) *or* **Carolean** (ˌkærəˈliːən) *adj* **1** Also called: **Carolinian** characteristic of or relating to Charles I (1600–49) or Charles II (1630–85), Stuart kings of England, Scotland, and Ireland, the society over which they ruled, or their government **2** of or relating to any other king called Charles

Caroline Islands *pl n* an archipelago of over 500 islands and islets in the W Pacific Ocean east of the Philippines, all are now part of the Federated States of Micronesia, except for the Palau group: formerly part of the US Trust Territory of the Pacific Islands; centre of a typhoon zone. Area: (land) 1183 sq km (457 sq miles)

Carolingian (ˌkærəˈlɪndʒɪən) *adj* **1** of or relating to the Frankish dynasty founded by Pepin the Short (died 768 AD), son of Charles Martel (?688–741 AD), which ruled in France from 751–987 AD and in

Germany until 911 A.D ▷ *n* **2** a member of the dynasty of the Carolingian Franks ▷ Also: Carlovingian, Carolinian

Carolinian¹ (ˌkærəˈlɪnɪən) *adj, n* a variant of **Caroline** *or* **Carolingian**

Carolinian² (ˌkærəˈlɪnɪən) *adj* **1** of or relating to North or South Carolina ▷ *n* **2** a native or inhabitant of North or South Carolina

carolus (ˈkærələs) *n, pl* **-luses** *or* **-li** (-ˌlaɪ) any of several coins struck in the reign of a king called Charles, esp an English gold coin from the reign of Charles I

carom (ˈkærəm) *n billiards, US and Canadian* **a** a shot in which the cue ball is caused to contact one object ball after another **b** the points scored by this. Also called (in Britain and certain other countries): cannon [c18 from earlier *carambole* (taken as *carom ball*), from Spanish CARAMBOLA]

Caro's acid (ˈkærəʊz, ˈkɑː-) *n* another name for **peroxysulphuric acid** [c19 named after Heinrich Caro (died 1910), German chemist]

carotene (ˈkærəˌtiːn) *or* **carotin** (ˈkærətɪn) *n* any of four orange-red isomers of an unsaturated hydrocarbon present in many plants (β-carotene is the orange pigment of carrots) and converted to vitamin A in the liver. Formula: $C_{40}H_{56}$ [c19 carotin, from Latin *carōta* CARROT; see -ENE]

carotenoid *or* **carotinoid** (kəˈrɒtɪˌnɔɪd) *n* **1** any of a group of red or yellow pigments, including carotenes, found in plants and certain animal tissues ▷ *adj* **2** of or resembling carotene or a carotenoid

carotid (kəˈrɒtɪd) *n* **1** either one of the two principal arteries that supply blood to the head and neck ▷ *adj* **2** of or relating to either of these arteries [c17 from French, from Greek *karōtides*, from *karoun* to stupefy; so named by Galen, because pressure on them produced unconsciousness] ▷ **caˈrotidal** *adj*

carousal (kəˈraʊzəl) *n* a merry drinking party

carouse (kəˈraʊz) *vb* **1** (*intr*) to have a merry drinking spree; drink freely ▷ *n* **2** another word for **carousal** [c16 via French *carrousser* from German (*trinken*) *gar aus* (to drink) right out] ▷ **caˈrouser** *n*

carousel (ˌkærəˈsɛl, -ˈzɛl) *n* **1** a circular magazine in which slides for a projector are held: it moves round as each slide is shown **2** a rotating conveyor belt for luggage, as at an airport **3** *US and Canadian* a revolving circular platform provided with wooden animals, seats, etc, on which people ride for amusement. Also called (in Britain and certain other countries): merry-go-round, roundabout **4** *history* a tournament in which horsemen took part in races and various manoeuvres in formation [c17 from French *carrousel*, from Italian *carosello*, of uncertain origin]

carp¹ (kɑːp) *n, pl* **carp** *or* **carps 1** a freshwater teleost food fish, *Cyprinus carpio*, having a body covered with cycloid scales, a naked head, one long dorsal fin, and two barbels on each side of the mouth: family *Cyprinidae* **2** any other fish of the family *Cyprinidae*; a cyprinid. Related adjs: **cyprinid, cyprinoid** [c14 from Old French *carpe*, of Germanic origin; compare Old High German *karpfo*, Old Norse *karfi*]

carp² (kɑːp) *vb* (*intr*; often foll by *at*) to complain or find fault; nag pettily [c13 from Old Norse *karpa* to boast; related to Latin *carpere* to pluck] ▷ **ˈcarper** *n*

-carp *n combining form* (in botany) fruit or a reproductive structure that develops into a particular part of the fruit: *epicarp* [from New Latin *-carpium*, from Greek *-karpion*, from *karpos* fruit]

carpaccio (ˌkɑːˈpætʃɪəʊ; *Italian* karˈpattʃo) *n, pl* **-os** an Italian dish of thin slices of raw meat or fish [possibly after the Italian painter Vittore Carpaccio (?1460–?1525)]

carpal (ˈkɑːpᵊl) *n* **a** any bone of the wrist **b** (*as modifier*): *carpal bones*. Also: **carpale** (kɑːˈpeɪlɪ) [c18 from New Latin *carpālis*, from Greek *karpos* wrist]

carpal tunnel syndrome *n* a condition characterized by pain and tingling in the fingers, caused by pressure on a nerve as it passes under

the ligament situated across the front of the wrist

car park *n* an area or building reserved for parking cars. Usual US and Canadian term: parking lot

Carpathian Mountains (kɑːˈpeɪθɪən) *or* **Carpathians** *pl n* a mountain system of central and E Europe, extending from Slovakia to central Romania: mainly forested, with rich iron ore resources. Highest peak: Gerlachovka, 2663 m (8788 ft)

Carpatho-Ukraine (kɑːˈpeɪθəʊjuːˈkreɪn) *n* another name for **Ruthenia**

carpe diem Latin (ˈkɑːpɪ ˈdiːɛm) enjoy the pleasures of the moment, without concern for the future [literally: seize the day!]

carpel (ˈkɑːpᵊl) *n* the female reproductive organ of flowering plants, consisting of an ovary, style (sometimes absent), and stigma. The carpels are separate or fused to form a single pistil [c19 from New Latin *carpellum*, from Greek *karpos* fruit] ▷ **ˈcarpellary** *adj* ▷ **carpellate** (ˈkɑːpɪˌleɪt) *adj*

Carpentaria (ˌkɑːpᵊnˈtɛərɪə) *n* **Gulf of** a shallow inlet of the Arafura Sea, in N Australia between Arnhem Land and Cape York Peninsula

carpenter (ˈkɑːpɪntə) *n* **1** a person skilled in woodwork, esp in buildings, ships, etc ▷ *vb* **2** (*intr*) to do the work of a carpenter **3** (*tr*) to make or fit together by or as if by carpentry [c14 from Anglo-French, from Latin *carpentārius* wagon-maker, from *carpentum* wagon; of Celtic origin]

carpenter bee *n* any large solitary bee of the genus *Xylocopa* and related genera that lays its eggs in tunnels bored into wood or in plant stems: family *Apidae*

carpenter moth *n* any of various large moths of the family *Cossidae*, the larvae of which bore beneath and cause damage to tree bark

carpentry (ˈkɑːpɪntrɪ) *n* **1** the art or technique of working wood **2** the work produced by a carpenter; woodwork

carpet (ˈkɑːpɪt) *n* **1 a** a heavy fabric for covering floors **b** (*as modifier*): *a carpet sale* **2** a covering like a carpet: *a carpet of leaves* **3** **on the carpet** *informal* **a** before authority to be reproved for misconduct or error **b** under consideration ▷ *vb* (*tr*) **-pets, -peting, -peted 4** to cover with or as if with a carpet **5** *informal* to reprimand [c14 from Old French *carpite*, from Old Italian *carpita*, from Late Latin *carpeta*, literally: (wool) that has been carded, from Latin *carpere* to pluck, card]

carpetbag (ˈkɑːpɪtˌbæg) *n* a travelling bag originally made of carpeting

carpetbagger (ˈkɑːpɪtˌbægə) *n* **1** a politician who seeks public office in a locality where he has no real connections **2** *Brit* a person who makes a short-term investment in a mutual savings or life-assurance organization in order to benefit from free shares issued following the organization's conversion to a public limited company **3** *US* a Northern White who went to the South after the Civil War to profit from Reconstruction

carpet beetle *or US* **carpet bug** *n* any of various beetles of the genus *Anthrenus*, the larvae of which feed on carpets, furnishing fabrics, etc: family *Dermestidae*

carpet bombing *n* systematic intensive bombing of an area

carpet bowling *n* a form of bowls played indoors on a strip of carpet, at the centre of which lies an obstacle round which the bowl has to pass

carpeting (ˈkɑːpɪtɪŋ) *n* carpet material or carpets in general

carpet knight *n disparaging* a soldier who spends his life away from battle; idler

carpet moth *n* any of several geometrid moths with black- (or brown-)and-white mottled wings [c19 so named from the patterns on their wings]

carpet plot *n maths* the graphed values of a function of more than one variable, read from an ordinate at points located by the intersection of curves of constant values of each of the variables

[c20 from the shape of the graph, thought to resemble a flying carpet]

carpet shark *n* any of various sharks of the family *Orectolobidae*, having two dorsal fins and a patterned back, typically marked with white and brown

carpet slipper *n* one of a pair of slippers, originally one made with woollen uppers resembling carpeting

carpet snake *or* **python** *n* a large nonvenomous Australian snake, *Morelia variegata*, having a carpetlike pattern on its back

carpet-sweeper *n* a household device with a revolving brush for sweeping carpets

carpet tiles *pl n* small pieces of carpeting laid as tiles to cover a floor

car phone *n* a telephone that operates by cellular radio for use in a car

carpi (ˈkɑːpaɪ) *n* the plural of **carpus**

-carpic *adj combining form* a variant of **-carpous**

carping (ˈkɑːpɪŋ) *adj* tending to make petty complaints; fault-finding ▷ **ˈcarpingly** *adv*

carpo-¹ *combining form* (in botany) indicating fruit or a reproductive structure that develops into part of the fruit: *carpophore; carpogonium* [from Greek *karpos* fruit]

carpo-² *combining form* carpus or carpal bones: *carpometacarpus*

carpogonium (ˌkɑːpəˈgəʊnɪəm) *n, pl* **-nia** (-nɪə) the female sex organ of red algae, consisting of a swollen base containing the ovum and a long neck down which the male gametes pass ▷ **ˌcarpoˈgonial** *adj*

carpology (kɑːˈpɒlədʒɪ) *n* the branch of botany concerned with the study of fruits and seeds ▷ **carpological** (ˌkɑːpəˈlɒdʒɪkᵊl) *adj* ▷ **carˈpologist** *n*

carpometacarpus (ˌkɑːpəʊˌmɛtəˈkɑːpəs) *n* a bone in the wing of a bird that consists of the metacarpal bones and some of the carpal bones fused together

carpophagous (kɑːˈpɒfəgəs) *adj zoology* feeding on fruit: *carpophagous bats*

carpophore (ˈkɑːpəˌfɔː) *n* **1** the central column surrounded by carpels in such flowers as the geranium **2** a spore-bearing structure in some of the higher fungi

carport (ˈkɑːˌpɔːt) *n* a shelter for a car usually consisting of a roof built out from the side of a building and supported by posts

carpospore (ˈkɑːpəˌspɔː) *n* a sexual spore produced by red algae after fertilization of the carpogonium

-carpous *or* **-carpic** *adj combining form* (in botany) indicating a certain kind or number of fruit: *apocarpous* [from New Latin *-carpus*, from Greek *karpos* fruit]

carpus (ˈkɑːpəs) *n, pl* **-pi** (-paɪ) **1** the technical name for **wrist 2** the eight small bones of the human wrist that form the joint between the arm and the hand **3** the corresponding joint in other tetrapod vertebrates [c17 New Latin, from Greek *karpos*]

carr (kɑː) *n Brit* an area of bog or fen in which scrub, esp willow, has become established [c15 from Old Norse]

carrack (ˈkærək) *n* a galleon sailed in the Mediterranean as a merchantman in the 15th and 16th centuries [c14 from Old French *caraque*, from Old Spanish *carraca*, from Arabic *qarāqīr* merchant ships]

carrageen, carragheen *or* **carageen** (ˈkærəˌgiːn) *n* an edible red seaweed, *Chondrus crispus*, of North America and N Europe. Also called: **Irish moss** [c19 from *Carragheen*, near Waterford, Ireland, where it is plentiful]

carrageenan, carragheenan *or* **carageenan** (ˌkærəˈgiːnən) *n* a carbohydrate extracted from carrageen, used to make a beverage, medicine, and jelly, and as an emulsifying and gelling agent (**E407**) in various processed desserts and drinks

Carrantuohill *or* **Carrauntoohill** (ˌkærənˈtuːl) *n* a mountain in SW Republic of Ireland, in

Macgillicuddy's Reeks in Kerry: the highest peak in Ireland. Height: 1041 m (3414 ft)

Carrara (kəˈrɑːrə; *Italian* karˈraːra) *n* a town in NW Italy, in NW Tuscany: famous for its marble. Pop: 65 034 (2001)

carrefour ('kærəˌfɔː) *n* **1** a rare word for **crossroads 2** a public square, esp one at the intersection of several roads [C15 from Old French *quarrefour*, ultimately from Latin *quadrifurcus* having four forks]

carrel or **carrell** ('kærəl) *n* a small individual study room or private desk, often in a library, where a student or researcher can work undisturbed [C16 a variant of CAROL]

carriage ('kærɪdʒ) *n* **1** *Brit* a railway coach for passengers **2** the manner in which a person holds and moves his head and body; bearing **3** a four-wheeled horse-drawn vehicle for persons **4** the moving part of a machine that bears another part: *a typewriter carriage; a lathe carriage* **5** ('kærɪdʒ, 'kærɪɪdʒ) **a** the act of conveying; carrying **b** the charge made for conveying (esp in the phrases **carriage forward**, when the charge is to be paid by the receiver, and **carriage paid**) [C14 from Old Northern French *cariage*, from *carier* to CARRY]

carriage bolt *n* *chiefly US and Canadian* another name for **coach bolt**

carriage clock *n* a portable clock, usually in a rectangular case with a handle on the top, of a type originally used by travellers

carriage dog *n* a former name for **Dalmatian**

carriage line *n* another term for **coach line**

carriage trade *n* trade from the wealthy part of society

carriageway ('kærɪdʒˌweɪ) *n* *Brit* the part of a road along which traffic passes in a single line moving in one direction only: *a dual carriageway*

carrick bend ('kærɪk) *n* a knot used for joining two ropes or cables together [C19 perhaps variant of CARRACK]

carrick bitt *n* *nautical* either of a pair of strong posts used for supporting a windlass

Carrickfergus (ˌkærɪkˈfɜːgəs) *n* **1** a town in E Northern Ireland, in Carrickfergus district, Co Antrim; historic settlement of Scottish Protestants on Belfast Lough; Norman castle. Pop: 27 201 (2001) **2** a district of E Northern Ireland, in Co Antrim. Pop: 37 659 (2001). Area: 83 sq km (32 sq miles)

carrier ('kærɪə) *n* **1** a person, thing, or organization employed to carry goods, passengers, etc **2** a mechanism by which something is carried or moved, such as a device for transmitting rotation from the faceplate of a lathe to the workpiece **3** *pathol* another name for **vector** (sense 3) **4** *pathol* a person or animal that, without having any symptoms of a disease, is capable of transmitting it to others **5** Also called: **charge carrier** *physics* an electron, ion, or hole that carries the charge in a conductor or semiconductor **6** short for **carrier wave 7** *chem* **a** the inert solid on which a dyestuff is adsorbed in forming a lake **b** a substance, such as kieselguhr or asbestos, used to support a catalyst **c** an inactive substance containing a radioisotope used in radioactive tracing **d** an inert gas used to transport the sample through a gas-chromatography column **e** a catalyst that effects the transfer of an atom or group from one molecule to another **8** See **aircraft carrier 9** a breed of domestic fancy pigeon having a large walnut-shaped wattle over the beak; a distinct variety of pigeon from the homing or carrier pigeon. See also **carrier pigeon 10** a US name for **roof rack**

Carrier ('kærɪə) *n* a member of an Athapaskan Native North American people of British Columbia

carrier bag *n* *Brit* a large paper or plastic bag for carrying shopping

carrier pigeon *n* any homing pigeon, esp one used for carrying messages

carrier wave *n* *radio* a wave of fixed amplitude and frequency that is modulated in amplitude, frequency, or phase in order to carry a signal in radio transmission, etc. See **amplitude modulation, frequency modulation**

carriole (ˈkærɪˌəʊl) *n* a variant spelling of **cariole**

carrion ('kærɪən) *n* **1** dead and rotting flesh **2** (*modifier*) eating carrion: *carrion beetles* **3** something rotten or repulsive [C13 from Anglo-French *caroine*, ultimately from Latin *carō* flesh]

carrion beetle *n* any beetle of the family *Silphidae* that track carrion by a keen sense of smell: best known are the **burying** or **sexton beetles**

carrion crow *n* a common predatory and scavenging European crow, *Corvus corone*, similar to the rook but having a pure black bill. See also **hooded crow**

carrion flower *n* **1** a liliaceous climbing plant, *Smilax herbacea* of E North America, whose small green flowers smell like decaying flesh **2** any of several other plants, esp any of the genus *Stapelia*, whose flowers have an unpleasant odour

carronade (ˌkærəˈneɪd) *n* an obsolete naval gun of short barrel and large bore [C18 named after *Carron*, Scotland, where it was first cast; see -ADE]

carron oil ('kærən) *n* an ointment of limewater and linseed oil, formerly used to treat burns [C19 named after *Carron*, Scotland, where it was used among the ironworkers]

carrot ('kærət) *n* **1** an umbelliferous plant, *Daucus carota sativa*, with finely divided leaves and flat clusters of small white flowers. See also **wild carrot 2** the long tapering orange root of this plant, eaten as a vegetable **3 a** something offered as a lure or incentive **b** **carrot and stick** reward and punishment as methods of persuasion [C16 from Old French *carotte*, from Late Latin *carōta*, from Greek *karōton*; perhaps related to Greek *karē* head]

carrot fly *n* a dipterous insect, *Psila rosae*, that is a serious pest of carrots. The larvae tunnel into the root to feed

carroty ('kærətɪ) *adj* **1** of a reddish or yellowish-orange colour **2** having red hair

carrousel (ˌkærəˈsɛl, -ˈzɛl) *n* a variant spelling of **carousel**

carry ('kærɪ) *vb* -ries, -rying, -ried (*mainly tr*) **1** (*also intr*) to take or bear (something) from one place to another: *to carry a baby in one's arms* **2** to transfer for consideration; take: *he carried his complaints to her superior* **3** to have on one's person: *he always carries a watch* **4** (*also intr*) to be transmitted or serve as a medium for transmitting: *sound carries best over water* **5** to contain or be capable of containing: *the jug carries water* **6** to bear or be able to bear the weight, pressure, or responsibility of: *her efforts carry the whole production* **7** to have as an attribute or result: *this crime carries a heavy penalty* **8** to bring or communicate: *to carry news* **9** (*also intr*) to be pregnant with (young): *she is carrying her third child* **10** to bear (the head, body, etc) in a specified manner: *she carried her head high* **11** to conduct or bear (oneself) in a specified manner: *she carried herself well in a difficult situation* **12** to continue or extend: *the war was carried into enemy territory* **13** to cause to move or go: *desire for riches carried him to the city* **14** to influence, esp by emotional appeal: *his words carried the crowd* **15** to secure the passage of (a bill, motion, etc) **16** to win (an election) **17** to obtain victory for (a candidate or measure) in an election **18** *chiefly US* to win a plurality or majority of votes in (a district, legislative body, etc): *the candidate carried 40 states* **19** to capture: *our troops carried the town* **20** (of communications media) to include as the content: *this newspaper carries no book reviews* **21** Also (*esp US*): **carry over** *book-keeping* to transfer (an item) to another account, esp to transfer to the following year's account instead of writing off against profit and loss: *to carry a loss* **22** *maths* to transfer (a number) from one column of figures to the next, as from units to tens in multiplication and addition **23**

(of a shop, trader, etc) to keep in stock: *to carry confectionery* **24** to support (a musical part or melody) against the other parts **25** to sustain (livestock): *this land will carry twelve ewes to the acre* **26** to maintain (livestock) in good health but without increasing their weight or obtaining any products from them **27** (*intr*) (of a ball, projectile, etc) to travel through the air or reach a specified point: *his first drive carried to the green* **28** *sport*, *esp golf* (of a ball) to travel beyond: *the drive carried the trees* **29** (*intr*) (of a gun) to have a range as specified: *this rifle carries for 1200 yards* **30** to retain contact with and pursue (a line of scent) **31** (*intr*) (of ground) to be in such a condition that scent lies well upon it **32** *ice hockey* to move (the puck) forwards, keeping it against the blade of the stick **33** *informal* to imbibe (alcoholic drink) without showing ill effects **34** (*intr*) *slang* to have drugs on one's person **35** **carry all before (one)** to win unanimous support or approval for (oneself) **36** **carry a tune** to be able to sing in tune **37** **carry the can (for)** *informal* to take the responsibility for some misdemeanour, etc (on behalf of) **38** **carry the day** to win a contest or competition; succeed ▷ *n*, *pl* -ries **39** the act of carrying **40** *US and Canadian* a portion of land over which a boat must be portaged **41** the range of a firearm or its projectile **42** the distance travelled by a ball, etc, esp (in golf) the distance from where the ball is struck to where it first touches the ground [C14 *carien*, from Old Northern French *carier* to move by vehicle, from *car*, from Latin *carrum* transport wagon; see CAR]

carryall[1] ('kærɪˌɔːl) *n* a light four-wheeled horse-drawn carriage usually designed to carry four passengers

carryall[2] ('kærɪˌɔːl) *n* *US and Canadian* a large strong bag with handles. Also called (in Britain and certain other countries): **holdall**

carry away *vb* (*tr*, *adverb*) **1** to remove forcefully **2** (*usually passive*) to cause (a person) to lose self-control **3** (*usually passive*) to delight or enrapture: *he was carried away by the music*

carry back *tax accounting* ▷ *vb* **1** (*tr*, *adverb*) to apply (a legally permitted credit, esp an operating loss) to the taxable income of previous years in order to ease the overall tax burden ▷ *n* **carry-back 2** an amount carried back

carrycot ('kærɪˌkɒt) *n* a light cot with handles, similar to but smaller than the body of a pram and often attachable to an unsprung wheeled frame

carry forward *vb* (*tr*, *adverb*) **1** *book-keeping* to transfer (a balance) to the next page, column, etc **2** *tax accounting* to apply (a legally permitted credit, esp an operating loss) to the taxable income of following years to ease the overall tax burden ▷ Also: **carry over** ▷ *n* **carry-forward 3** Also called: **carry-over** *tax accounting* an amount carried forward

carry-in *adj* of or relating to a type of after-sales service in which the customer must take the product to the service provider for repair: *carry-in warranty*

carrying capacity *n* *ecology* the maximum number of individuals that an area of land can support, usually determined by their food requirements

carrying charge *n* the opportunity cost of unproductive assets, such as goods stored in a warehouse

carrying-on *n*, *pl* carryings-on *informal* **1** unconventional or questionable behaviour **2** excited or flirtatious behaviour, esp when regarded as foolish

carrying place *n* *Canadian* another name for **portage**

carry off *vb* (*tr*, *adverb*) **1** to remove forcefully **2** to win: *he carried off all the prizes* **3** to manage or handle (a situation) successfully: *he carried off the introductions well* **4** to cause to die: *he was carried off by pneumonia*

C

carry on *vb* (*adverb*) **1** (*intr*) to continue or persevere: *we must carry on in spite of our difficulties* **2** (*tr*) to manage or conduct: *to carry on a business* **3** (*intr; often foll by* *with*) *informal* to have an affair **4** (*intr*) *informal* to cause a fuss or commotion ▷ *n* carry-on **5** *informal, chiefly Brit* a fuss or commotion

carry out *vb* (*tr, adverb*) **1** to perform or cause to be implemented: *I wish he could afford to carry out his plan* **2** to bring to completion; accomplish ▷ *n* carry-out *chiefly Scot* **3** alcohol bought at a pub or off-licence for consumption elsewhere **4 a** hot cooked food bought at a shop or restaurant for consumption elsewhere **b** a shop or restaurant that sells such food: *we'll get something from the Chinese carry-out* **c** (*as modifier*): *a carry-out shop*

carry over *vb* (*tr, adverb*) **1** to postpone or defer **2** *book-keeping, tax accounting* another term for **carry forward** **3** (on the London Stock Exchange) to postpone (payment or settlement) until the next account day ▷ *n* carry-over **4** something left over for future use, esp goods to be sold **5** *book-keeping* a sum or balance carried forward **6** another name for **contango 7** *tax accounting* another name for **carry-forward**

carry through *vb* (*tr, adverb*) **1** to bring to completion **2** to enable to endure (hardship, trouble, etc); support

carse (kɑːs; *Scot* kærs) *n Scot* a riverside area of flat fertile alluvium [C14 of uncertain origin; perhaps from a plural form of CARR]

carsick (ˈkɑːˌsɪk) *adj* nauseated from riding in a car or other vehicle > ˈcar͵sickness *n*

Carson City (ˈkɑːsᵊn) *n* a city in W Nevada, capital of the state. Pop: 55 311 (2003 est)

Carstensz (ˈkɑːstənz) *n* **Mount** a former name of (Mount) **Jaya**

cart[1] (kɑːt) *n* **1** a heavy open vehicle, usually having two wheels and drawn by horses, used in farming and to transport goods **2** a light open horse-drawn vehicle having two wheels and springs, for business or pleasure **3** any small vehicle drawn or pushed by hand, such as a trolley **4 put the cart before the horse** to reverse the usual or natural order of things ▷ *vb* **5** (*usually tr*) to use or draw a cart to convey (goods, etc): *to cart groceries* **6** (*tr*) to carry (with effort); haul: *to cart wood home* [C13 from Old Norse *kartr*; related to Old English *cræt* carriage, Old French *carete*; see CAR] > ˈcartable *adj* > ˈcarter *n*

cart[2] (kɑːt) *n radio, television* short for **cartridge** (sense 4)

CART *abbreviation for* Championship Auto Racing Teams

cartage (ˈkɑːtɪdʒ) *n* the process or cost of carting

Cartagena (ˌkɑːtəˈdʒiːnə; *Spanish* kartaˈxena) *n* **1** a port in NW Colombia, on the Caribbean: centre for the Inquisition and the slave trade in the 16th century; chief oil port of Colombia. Pop: 1 002 000 (2005 est) **2** a port in SE Spain, on the Mediterranean: important since Carthaginian and Roman times for its minerals. Pop: 194 203 (2003 est)

carte (kɑːt) *n* a variant spelling of **quarte** (in fencing)

carte blanche (ˈkɑːt ˈblɑːntʃ; *French* kart blɑ̃ʃ) *n, pl* **cartes blanches** (ˈkɑːts ˈblɑːntʃ; *French* kart blɑ̃ʃ) **1** complete discretion or authority: *the government gave their negotiator carte blanche* **2** *cards* a piquet hand containing no court cards: scoring ten points [C18 from French: blank paper]

carte du jour (ˈkɑːt də ˈʒʊə, duː; *French* kart dy ʒur) *n, pl* **cartes du jour** (ˈkɑːts də ˈʒʊə, duː; *French* kart dy ʒur) a menu listing dishes available on a particular day [French, literally: card of the day]

cartel (kɑːˈtɛl) *n* **1** Also called: **trust** a collusive international association of independent enterprises formed to monopolize production and distribution of a product or service, control prices, etc **2** *politics* an alliance of parties or interests to further common aims [C20 from German *Kartell*, from French, from Italian *cartello* a written

challenge, public notice, diminutive of *carta* CARD[1]]

cartelize *or* **cartelise** (ˈkɑːtəlaɪz) *vb* to form or be formed into a cartel > ˌcarteliˈzation *or* ˌcarteliˈsation *n*

Cartesian (kɑːˈtiːzɪən, -ʒən) *adj* **1** of or relating to the works of René Descartes (1596–1650), the French philosopher and mathematician **2** of, relating to, or used in Descartes' mathematical system: *Cartesian coordinates* **3** of, relating to, or derived from Descartes' philosophy, esp his contentions that personal identity consists in the continued existence of a unique mind and that the mind and body are connected causally. See also **dualism** (sense 2) ▷ *n* **4** a follower of the teachings and methods of Descartes > Carˈtesianˌism *n*

Cartesian coordinates *pl n* a system of representing points in space in terms of their distance from a given origin measured along a set of mutually perpendicular axes. Written (x, y, z) with reference to three axes

Cartesian product *n maths, logic* the set of all ordered pairs of members of two given sets. The product $A \times B$ is the set of all pairs $< a, b >$ where a is a member of A and b is a member of B. Also called: **cross product**

cartful (ˈkɑːtfʊl) *n* the amount a cart can hold

Carthage (ˈkɑːθɪdʒ) *n* an ancient city state, on the N African coast near present-day Tunis. Founded about 800 BC by Phoenician traders, it grew into an empire dominating N Africa and the Mediterranean. Destroyed and then rebuilt by Rome, it was finally razed by the Arabs in 697 AD See also **Punic Wars**

Carthaginian (ˌkɑːθəˈdʒɪnɪən) *adj* **1** of or relating to Carthage (an ancient N African city state) or its inhabitants ▷ *n* **2** a native or inhabitant of Carthage

carthorse (ˈkɑːtˌhɔːs) *n* a large heavily built horse kept for pulling carts or carriages

Carthusian (kɑːˈθjuːzɪən) *n RC Church* **a** a member of an austere monastic order founded by Saint Bruno in 1084 near Grenoble, France **b** (*as modifier*): *a Carthusian monastery* [C14 from Medieval Latin *Carthusianus*, from Latin *Carthusia* Chartreuse, near Grenoble]

cartilage (ˈkɑːtɪlɪdʒ, ˈkɑːtlɪdʒ) *n* a tough elastic tissue composing most of the embryonic skeleton of vertebrates. In the adults of higher vertebrates it is mostly converted into bone, remaining only on the articulating ends of bones, in the thorax, trachea, nose, and ears. Nontechnical name: gristle [C16 from Latin *cartilāgō*] > cartilaginous (ˌkɑːtɪˈlædʒɪnəs) *adj*

cartilage bone *n* any bone that develops within cartilage rather than in a fibrous tissue membrane. Compare **membrane bone**

cartilaginous fish *n* any fish of the class *Chondrichthyes*, including the sharks, skates, and rays, having a skeleton composed entirely of cartilage

cartload (ˈkɑːtˌləʊd) *n* **1** the amount a cart can hold **2** a quantity of rubble, ballast, etc, of between one quarter and one half of a cubic yard

cart off, away *or* **out** *vb* (*tr, adverb*) *informal* to carry or remove brusquely or by force

cartogram (ˈkɑːtəˌɡræm) *n* a map showing statistical information in diagrammatic form [C20 from French *cartogramme*, from *carte* map, CHART; see -GRAM]

cartography *or* **chartography** (kɑːˈtɒɡrəfɪ) *n* the art, technique, or practice of compiling or drawing maps or charts [C19 from French *cartographie*, from *carte* map, CHART] > carˈtographer *or* charˈtographer *n* > cartographic (ˌkɑːtəˈɡræfɪk), ˌcartoˈgraphical, ˌchartoˈgraphic *or* ˌchartoˈgraphical *adj* > ˌcartoˈgraphically *or* ˌchartoˈgraphically *adv*

cartomancy (ˈkɑːtəˌmænsɪ) *n* the telling of fortunes with playing cards [C19 from French *carte* card + -MANCY]

carton (ˈkɑːtᵊn) *n* **1** a cardboard box for containing goods **2** a container of waxed paper or plastic in which liquids, such as milk, are sold **3** *shooting* **a** a white disc at the centre of a target **b** a shot that hits this disc ▷ *vb* (*tr*) **4** to enclose (goods) in a carton [C19 from French, from Italian *cartone* pasteboard, from *carta* CARD[1]]

cartoon (kɑːˈtuːn) *n* **1** a humorous or satirical drawing, esp one in a newspaper or magazine, concerning a topical event **2** Also called: **comic strip** a sequence of drawings in a newspaper, magazine, etc, relating a comic or adventurous situation **3** See **animated cartoon 4** a full-size preparatory sketch for a fresco, tapestry, mosaic, etc, from which the final work is traced or copied [C17 from Italian *cartone* pasteboard, sketch on stiff paper; see CARTON] > carˈtoonist *n*

cartoonish (ˌkɑːˈtuːnɪʃ) *adj* like a cartoon, esp in being one-dimensional, brightly coloured, or exaggerated

cartophily (kɑːˈtɒfɪlɪ) *n* the hobby of collecting cigarette cards [C20 from French *carte* card + -o- + -phily from Greek *philos* loving] > carˈtophilist *n*

cartouche *or* **cartouch** (kɑːˈtuːʃ) *n* **1** a carved or cast ornamental tablet or panel in the form of a scroll, sometimes having an inscription **2** an oblong figure enclosing characters expressing royal or divine names in Egyptian hieroglyphics **3** the paper case holding combustible materials in certain fireworks **4** *now rare* a cartridge or a box for cartridges [C17 from French: scroll, cartridge, from Italian *cartoccio*, from *carta* paper; see CARD[1]]

cartridge (ˈkɑːtrɪdʒ) *n* **1** a cylindrical, usually metal casing containing an explosive charge and often a bullet, for a rifle or other small arms **2** a case for an explosive, such as a blasting charge **3** an electromechanical transducer in the pick-up of a record player, usually either containing a piezoelectric crystal (**crystal cartridge**) or an electromagnet (**magnetic cartridge**) **4** a container for magnetic tape that is inserted into a tape deck in audio or video systems. It is about four times the size of a cassette **5** Also called: **cassette, magazine** *photog* a light-tight film container that enables a camera to be loaded and unloaded in normal light **6** *computing* a removable unit in a computer, such as an integrated circuit, containing software [C16 from earlier *cartage*, variant of CARTOUCHE (cartridge)]

cartridge belt *n* a belt with pockets for cartridge clips or loops for cartridges

cartridge clip *n* a metallic container holding cartridges for an automatic firearm

cartridge paper *n* **1** an uncoated type of drawing or printing paper, usually made from bleached sulphate wood pulp with an addition of esparto grass **2** a heavy paper used in making cartridges or as drawing or printing paper

cartridge pen *n* a pen having a removable ink reservoir that is replaced when empty

cart track *n* a rough track or road in a rural area. Also called: **cart road**

cartulary (ˈkɑːtjʊlərɪ) *or* **chartulary** (ˈtʃɑːtjʊlərɪ) *n, pl* **-laries** *law* **a** a collection of charters or records, esp relating to the title to an estate or monastery **b** any place where records are kept [C16 from Medieval Latin *cartulārium*, from Latin *chartula* a little paper, from *charta* paper; see CARD[1]]

cartwheel (ˈkɑːtˌwiːl) *n* **1** the wheel of a cart, usually having wooden spokes and metal tyres **2** an acrobatic movement in which the body makes a sideways revolution supported on the hands with arms and legs outstretched **3** *US slang* a large coin, esp the silver dollar

cartwheel flower *n* another name for **giant hogweed**

cartwright (ˈkɑːtˌraɪt) *n* a person who makes carts

caruncle (ˈkærəŋkᵊl, kəˈrʌŋ-) *n* **1** a fleshy outgrowth on the heads of certain birds, such as a cock's comb **2** an outgrowth near the hilum on the seeds of some plants **3** any small fleshy mass in or on the body, either natural or abnormal [C17 from obsolete French *caruncule*, from Latin *caruncula* a small piece of flesh, from *carō* flesh] > **caruncular** (kəˈrʌŋkjʊlə) *or* **caˈrunculous** *adj* > **carunculate** (kəˈrʌŋkjʊlɪt, -ˌleɪt) *or* **caˈruncuˌlated** *adj*

carve (kɑːv) *vb* **1** (*tr*) to cut or chip in order to form something: *to carve wood* **2** to decorate or form (something) by cutting or chipping: *to carve statues* **3** to slice (meat) into pieces: *to carve a turkey* [Old English *ceorfan*; related to Old Frisian *kerva*, Middle High German *kerben* to notch]

carvel (ˈkɑːvᵊl) *n* another word for **caravel**

carvel-built *adj* (of a vessel) having a hull with planks made flush at the seams. Compare **clinker-built**

carven (ˈkɑːvᵊn) *vb* an archaic or literary past participle of **carve**

carve out *vb* (*tr, adverb*) to make or create (a career): *he carved out his own future*

carver (ˈkɑːvə) *n* **1** a carving knife **2** (*plural*) a large matched knife and fork for carving meat **3** *Brit* a chair having arms that forms part of a set of dining chairs

carvery (ˈkɑːvərɪ) *n, pl* **-veries** an eating establishment at which customers pay a set price and may then have unrestricted helpings of food from a variety of meats, salads, and other vegetables

carve up *vb* (*tr, adverb*) **1** to cut (something) into pieces **2** to divide or dismember (a country, land, etc) ▷ *n* **carve-up 3** *informal* an act or instance of dishonestly prearranging the result of a competition **4** *slang* the distribution of something, as of booty

carving (ˈkɑːvɪŋ) *n* a figure or design produced by carving stone, wood, etc. Related adj: **glyptic**

carving knife *n* a long-bladed knife for carving cooked meat for serving

caryatid (ˌkærɪˈætɪd) *n, pl* **-ids** *or* **-ides** (-ɪˌdiːz) a column, used to support an entablature, in the form of a draped female figure. Compare **telamon** [C16 from Latin *Caryātides*, from Greek *Karuatides* priestesses of Artemis at *Karuai* (Caryae), village in Laconia] > ˌ**caryˈatidal**, ˌ**caryˌatiˈdean**, ˌ**caryˈatic** *or* **caryatidic** (ˌkærɪəˈtɪdɪk) *adj*

caryo- *combining form* a variant of **karyo-**

caryophyllaceous (ˌkærɪəʊfɪˈleɪʃəs) *adj* of, relating to, or belonging to the *Caryophyllaceae*, a family of flowering plants including the pink, carnation, sweet william, and chickweed [C19 from New Latin *Caryophyllāceae*, from *Caryophyllus* former type genus, from Greek *karuophullon* clove tree, from *karuon* nut + *phullon* leaf]

caryopsis (ˌkærɪˈɒpsɪs) *n, pl* **-ses** (-siːz) *or* **-sides** (-sɪˌdiːz) a dry seedlike fruit having the pericarp fused to the seed coat of the single seed: produced by the grasses [C19 New Latin; see KARYO-, -OPSIS]

CAS (in Canada) *abbreviation for* Children's Aid Society

casaba *or* **cassaba** (kəˈsɑːbə) *n* a kind of winter muskmelon having a yellow rind and sweet juicy flesh [from *Kassaba*, former name of Turgutlu, Turkey]

Casablanca (ˌkæsəˈblæŋkə) *n* a port in NW Morocco, on the Atlantic: largest city in the country; industrial centre. Pop: 3 523 000 (2003)

Casanova (ˌkæsəˈnəʊvə) *n* any man noted for his amorous adventures; a rake [from Giovanni Jacopo *Casanova* (1725–98), Italian adventurer]

casbah (ˈkæzbɑː) *n* (*sometimes capital*) a variant spelling of **kasbah**

cascabel (ˈkæskəˌbɛl) *n* **1** a knoblike protrusion on the rear part of the breech of an obsolete muzzle-loading cannon **2** the rear part itself [C17 from Spanish: small bell, rattle, of uncertain origin]

cascade (kæsˈkeɪd) *n* **1** a waterfall or series of waterfalls over rocks **2** something resembling this, such as folds of lace **3 a** a consecutive sequence of chemical or physical processes **b** (*as modifier*): *cascade liquefaction* **4 a** a series of stages in the processing chain of an electrical signal where each operates the next in turn **b** (*as modifier*): *a cascade amplifier* **5** the cumulative process responsible for the formation of an electrical discharge, cosmic-ray shower, or Geiger counter avalanche in a gas **6** the sequence of spontaneous decays by an excited atom or ion ▷ *vb* **7** (*intr*) to flow or fall in or like a cascade [C17 from French, from Italian *cascata*, from *cascare* to fall, ultimately from Latin *cadere* to fall]

Cascade Range *n* a chain of mountains in the US and Canada: a continuation of the Sierra Nevada range from N California through Oregon and Washington to British Columbia. Highest peak: Mount Rainier, 4392 m (14 408 ft)

cascading style sheet *n computing* a file recording style details, such as fonts, colours, etc, that is read by browsers so that style is consistent over multiple web pages. Abbreviation: CSS

cascara (kæsˈkɑːrə) *n* **1** See **cascara sagrada 2** Also called: **cascara buckthorn, bearwood** a shrub or small tree, *Rhamnus purshiana* of NW North America, whose bark is a source of cascara sagrada: family *Rhamnaceae* [C19 from Spanish: bark, from *cascar* to break, from Vulgar Latin *quassicāre* (unattested) to shake violently, shatter, from Latin *quassāre* to dash to pieces]

cascara sagrada (səˈgrɑːdə) *n* the dried bark of the cascara buckthorn, used as a stimulant and laxative. Often shortened to: **cascara** [Spanish, literally: sacred bark]

cascarilla (ˌkæskəˈrɪlə) *n* **1** a West Indian euphorbiaceous shrub, *Croton eluteria*, whose bitter aromatic bark is used as a tonic **2** the bark of this shrub [C17 from Spanish, diminutive of *cáscara* bark; see CASCARA]

case[1] (keɪs) *n* **1** a single instance, occurrence, or example of something **2** an instance of disease, injury, hardship, etc **3** a question or matter for discussion: *the case before the committee* **4** a specific condition or state of affairs; situation **5** a set of arguments supporting a particular action, cause, etc **6 a** a person attended or served by a doctor, social worker, solicitor, etc; patient or client **b** (*as modifier*): *a case study* **7 a** an action or suit at law or something that forms sufficient grounds for bringing an action: *he has a good case* **b** the evidence offered in court to support a claim **8** *grammar* **a** a set of grammatical categories of nouns, pronouns, and adjectives, marked by inflection in some languages, indicating the relation of the noun, adjective, or pronoun to other words in the sentence **b** any one of these categories: *the nominative case* **9** *informal* a person in or regarded as being in a specified condition: *the accident victim was a hospital case; he's a mental case* **10** *informal* a person of a specified character (esp in the phrase **a hard case**) **11** *informal* an odd person; eccentric **12** *US informal* love or infatuation **13** short for **case shot** See **canister** (sense 2b) **14 as the case may be** according to the circumstances **15 in any case** (*adverb*) no matter what; anyhow: *we will go in any case* **16 in case** (*adverb*) **a** in order to allow for eventualities **b** (*as conjunction*) in order to allow for the possibility that: *take your coat in case it rains* **c** *US* if **17 in case of** (*preposition*) in the event of **18 in no case** (*adverb*) under no circumstances: *in no case should you fight back* [Old English *casus* (grammatical) case, associated also with Old French *cas* a happening; both from Latin *cāsus*, a befalling, occurrence, from *cadere* to fall]

case[2] (keɪs) *n* **1 a** a container, such as a box or chest **b** (*in combination*): *suitcase; briefcase* **2** an outer cover or sheath, esp for a watch **3** a receptacle and its contents: *a case of ammunition* **4** a pair or brace, esp of pistols **5** *architect* another word for **casing** (sense 3) **6** a completed cover ready to be fastened to a book to form its binding **7** *printing* a tray divided into many compartments in which a compositor keeps individual metal types of a particular size and style. Cases were originally used in pairs, one (the **upper case**) for capitals, the other (the **lower case**) for small letters **8** *metallurgy* the surface of a piece of steel that has been case-hardened ▷ *vb* (*tr*) **9** to put into or cover with a case: *to case the machinery* **10** *slang* to inspect carefully (esp a place to be robbed) [C13 from Old French *casse*, from Latin *capsa*, from *capere* to take, hold]

casease (ˈkeɪsɪˌeɪz) *n* a proteolytic enzyme formed by certain bacteria that activates the solution of albumin and casein in milk and cheese [C20 from CASE(IN) + -ASE]

caseate (ˈkeɪsɪˌeɪt) *vb* (*intr*) *pathol* to undergo caseation [C19 from Latin *cāseus* CHEESE[1]]

caseation (ˌkeɪsɪˈeɪʃən) *n* **1** the formation of cheese from casein during the coagulation of milk **2** *pathol* the degeneration of dead tissue into a soft cheeselike mass

casebook (ˈkeɪsˌbʊk) *n* a book in which records of legal or medical cases are kept

casebound (ˈkeɪsˌbaʊnd) *adj* another word for **hardback**

casefy (ˈkeɪsɪˌfaɪ) *vb* **-fies, -fying, -fied** to make or become similar to cheese [C20 from Latin *cāseus* CHEESE[1] + -FY]

case grammar *n linguistics* a system of grammatical description based on the functional relations that noun groups have to the main verb of a sentence. Compare **systemic grammar, transformational grammar**

case-harden *vb* (*tr*) **1** *metallurgy* to form a hard surface layer of high carbon content on (a steel component) by heating in a carburizing environment with subsequent quenching or heat treatment **2** to harden the spirit or disposition of; make callous: *experience had case-hardened the judge*

case history *n* a record of a person's background, medical history, etc, esp one used for determining medical treatment

casein (ˈkeɪsɪɪn, -siːn) *n* a phosphoprotein, precipitated from milk by the action of rennin, forming the basis of cheese: used in the manufacture of plastics and adhesives. Also called (US): **paracasein** [C19 from Latin *cāseus* cheese + -IN]

caseinogen (ˌkeɪsɪˈɪnədʒən, keɪˈsiːnə-) *n* the principal protein of milk, converted to casein by rennin. Sometimes called (US): **casein**

case knife *n* another name for **sheath knife**

case law *n* law established by following judicial decisions given in earlier cases. Compare **statute law.** See also **precedent** (sense 1)

caseload (ˈkeɪsləʊd) *n* the number of cases constituting the work of a doctor, solicitor, social worker, etc over a specified period

casemate (ˈkeɪsˌmeɪt) *n* an armoured compartment in a ship or fortification in which guns are mounted [C16 from French, from Italian *casamatta*, perhaps from Greek *khasmata* apertures, plural of *khasma* CHASM] > ˈ**caseˌmated** *adj*

casement (ˈkeɪsmənt) *n* **1** a window frame that is hinged on one side **2** a window containing frames hinged at the side or at the top or bottom **3** a poetic word for **window** [C15 probably from Old Northern French *encassement* frame, from *encasser* to frame, encase, from *casse* framework, crate, CASE[2]]

caseose (ˈkeɪsɪˌəʊz, -ˌəʊs) *n* a peptide produced by the peptic digestion of casein [C20 from Latin *cāseus* cheese + -OSE[2]]

caseous (ˈkeɪsɪəs) *adj* of or like cheese [C17 from Latin *cāseus* CHEESE[1]]

casern *or* **caserne** (kəˈzɜːn) *n* (formerly) a billet or accommodation for soldiers in a town [C17 from French *caserne*, from Old Provençal *cazerna* group of four men, ultimately from Latin *quattuor* four]

Caserta (*Italian* kaˈzɛrta) *n* a town in S Italy, in Campania: centre of Garibaldi's campaigns for the unification of Italy (1860); Allied headquarters in World War II. Pop: 75 208 (2001)

case-sensitive *adj* distinguishing between upper-case and lower-case letters: *users can now perform case-sensitive searches*

case shot *n* another name for **canister** (sense 2b)

C

case stated *n law* a statement of the facts of a case prepared by one court for the opinion or judgment of another court. Also called: **stated case**

case study *n* the act or an instance of analysing one or more particular cases or case histories with a view to making generalizations

casework ('keɪsˌwɜːk) *n* social work based on close study of the personal histories and circumstances of individuals and families ▷ 'case,worker *n*

caseworm ('keɪsˌwɜːm) *n* another name for a **caddis worm**

cash¹ (kæʃ) *n* **1** banknotes and coins, esp in hand or readily available; money or ready money **2** immediate payment, in full or part, for goods or services (esp in the phrase **cash down**) **3** (*modifier*) of, for, or paid by cash: *a cash basis* **4** (usually preceded by *the*) *Canadian* a checkout counter ▷ *vb* **5** (*tr*) to obtain or pay ready money for: *to cash a cheque* ▷ See also **cash in**, **cash up** [c16 from Old Italian *cassa* money box, from Latin *capsa* CASE²] ▷ 'cashable *adj*

cash² (kæʃ) *n, pl* **cash** any of various Chinese, Indonesian, or Indian coins of low value [c16 from Portuguese *caixa*, from Tamil *kāsu*, from Sanskrit *karsa* weight of gold or silver]

cash-and-carry *adj* ▷ *adv* **1** sold or operated on a basis of cash payment for merchandise that is not delivered but removed by the purchaser ▷ *n* **2** a wholesale store, esp for groceries, that operates on this basis **3** an operation on a commodities futures market in which spot goods are purchased and sold at a profit on a futures contract

cashback ('kæʃˌbæk) *n* **1 a** a discount offered in return for immediate payment **b** (*as modifier*): *cashback price £519.99 — save £30!* **2 a** a service provided by some supermarkets in which customers paying by debit card can draw cash **b** the cash so drawn

cash-book *n book-keeping* a journal in which all cash or cheque receipts and disbursements are recorded

cash card *n* an embossed plastic card bearing the name and account details of a bank or building-society customer, used with a personal identification number to obtain money from a cash dispenser: may also function as a cheque card or debit card or both. Also called: **cash-point card**

cash cow *n* a product, acquisition, etc, that produces a steady flow of cash, esp one with a well-known brand name commanding a high market share

cash crop *n* a crop grown for sale rather than for subsistence

cash desk *n* a counter or till in a shop where purchases are paid for

cash discount *n* a discount granted to a purchaser who pays before a stipulated date

cash dispenser *n* a computerized device outside a bank that supplies cash or account information when the user inserts his cash card and keys in his identification number. Also called: **automated teller machine**

cashed up *adj Austral informal* having plenty of money

cashew ('kæʃuː, kæˈʃuː) *n* **1** a tropical American anacardiaceous evergreen tree, *Anacardium occidentale*, bearing kidney-shaped nuts that protrude from a fleshy receptacle **2** Also called: **cashew nut** the edible nut of this tree [c18 from Portuguese *cajú*, from Tupi *acajú*]

cash flow *n* **1** the movement of money into and out of a business **2** a prediction of such movement over a given period

cash-for-questions *adj Brit* of, involved in, or relating to a scandal in which some MPs were accused of accepting bribes to ask particular questions in Parliament

cashier¹ (kæˈʃɪə) *n* **1** a person responsible for receiving payments for goods, services, etc, as in a shop **2** Also called: **teller** an employee of a bank responsible for receiving deposits, cashing cheques, and other financial transactions; bank clerk **3** any person responsible for handling cash or maintaining records of its receipt and disbursement [c16 from Dutch *cassier* or French *caissier*, from *casse* money chest; see CASE²]

cashier² (kæˈʃɪə) *vb* (*tr*) **1** to dismiss with dishonour, esp from the armed forces **2** *rare* to put away or discard; reject [c16 from Middle Dutch *kasseren*, from Old French *casser*, from Latin *quassāre* to QUASH]

cash in *vb* (*adverb*) **1** (*tr*) to give (something) in exchange, esp for money **2** (*intr*; often foll by *on*) *informal* **a** to profit (from) **b** to take advantage (of) **3** (*intr*) a slang expression for **die¹**

cashless ('kæʃlɪs) *adj* functioning, operated, or performed without using coins or banknotes for money transactions but instead using credit cards or electronic transfer of funds: *cashless shopping*

cash limit *n* (*often plural*) a limit imposed as a method of curtailing overall expenditure without specifying the precise means of budgetary control

cashmere *or* **kashmir** ('kæʃmɪə) *n* **1** a fine soft wool from goats of the Kashmir area **2 a** a cloth or knitted material made from this or similar wool **b** (*as modifier*): *a cashmere sweater*

Cashmere ('kæʃmɪə) *n* a variant spelling of **Kashmir**

cash on delivery *n* a service entailing cash payment to the carrier on delivery of merchandise. Abbreviation: **COD**

cashpoint ('kæʃˌpɔɪnt) *n* a cash dispenser

cash ratio *n* the ratio of cash on hand to total deposits that by law or custom commercial banks must maintain. Also called: **liquidity ratio**

cash register *n* a till with a keyboard that operates a mechanism for displaying and adding the amounts of cash received in individual sales

cash-strapped *adj* short of money; impoverished: *cash-strapped local authorities*

cash up *vb* (*intr, adverb*) *Brit* (of cashiers, shopkeepers, etc) to add up the money taken, esp at the end of a working day

casimere ('kæsɪˌmɪə) *n* a variant spelling of **casimere**

casing ('keɪsɪŋ) *n* **1** a protective case or cover **2** material for a case or cover **3** Also called: **case** a frame containing a door, window, or staircase **4** the intestines of cattle, pigs, etc, or a synthetic substitute, used as a container for sausage meat **5** the outer cover of a pneumatic tyre **6** a pipe or tube used to line a hole or shaft **7** the outer shell of a steam or gas turbine

casino (kəˈsiːnəʊ) *n, pl* -nos **1** a public building or room in which gaming takes place, esp roulette and card games such as baccarat and chemin de fer **2** a variant spelling of **cassino** [c18 from Italian, diminutive of *casa* house, from Latin]

cask (kɑːsk) *n* **1** a strong wooden barrel used mainly to hold alcoholic drink: *a wine cask* **2** any barrel **3** the quantity contained in a cask **4** *Austral* a lightweight cardboard container with plastic lining and a small tap, used to hold and serve wine **5** *engineering* another name for **flask** (sense 6) [c15 from Spanish *casco* helmet, perhaps from *cascar* to break]

casket ('kɑːskɪt) *n* **1** a small box or chest for valuables, esp jewels **2** *chiefly US* another name for **coffin** (sense 1) [c15 probably from Old French *cassette* little box; see CASE²]

Caslon ('kæzlən) *n* a style of type designed by William Caslon, English type founder (1692–1766)

Caspar ('kæspə, ˈkæspɑː) *or* **Gaspar** *n* (in Christian tradition) one of the Magi, the other two being Melchior and Balthazar

Casparian strip (kæˈspɛərɪən) *n botany* a band of suberized material around the radial walls of endodermal cells: impervious to gases and liquids [c20 named after Robert *Caspary*, 19th-century German botanist]

Caspian Sea ('kæspɪən) *n* a salt lake between SE Europe and Asia: the largest inland sea in the world; fed mainly by the River Volga. Area: 394 299 sq km (152 239 sq miles)

casque (kæsk) *n zoology* a helmet or a helmet-like process or structure, as on the bill of most hornbills [c17 from French, from Spanish *casco*; see CASK] ▷ **casqued** *adj*

cassaba (kəˈsɑːbə) *n* a variant spelling of **casaba**

Cassandra (kəˈsændrə) *n Greek myth* **1** a daughter of Priam and Hecuba, endowed with the gift of prophecy but fated never to be believed **2** anyone whose prophecies of doom are unheeded

cassareep ('kæsəˌriːp) *n* the juice of the bitter cassava root, boiled down to a syrup and used as a flavouring, esp in West Indian cookery [c19 of Carib origin]

cassata (kəˈsɑːtə) *n* an ice cream, originating in Italy, usually containing nuts and candied fruit [from Italian]

cassation (kæˈseɪʃən) *n chiefly law* (esp in France) annulment, as of a judicial decision by a higher court [c15 from Old French, from Medieval Latin *cassātiō*, from Late Latin *cassāre* to cancel, from Latin *quassāre* to QUASH]

cassava (kəˈsɑːvə) *n* **1** Also called: **manioc** any tropical euphorbiaceous plant of the genus *Manihot*, esp the widely cultivated American species *M. esculenta* (or *utilissima*) (**bitter cassava**) and *M. dulcis* (**sweet cassava**) **2** a starch derived from the root of this plant: an important food in the tropics and a source of tapioca [c16 from Spanish *cazabe* cassava bread, from Taino *caçábi*]

Cassegrain telescope ('kæsɪˌgreɪn) *n* an astronomical reflecting telescope in which incident light is reflected from a large concave paraboloid mirror onto a smaller convex hyperboloid mirror and then back through a hole in the concave mirror to form the image [c19 named after N. *Cassegrain*, 17th-century French scientist who invented it]

Cassel (*German* ˈkasəl) *n* a variant spelling of **Kassel**

casserole ('kæsəˌrəʊl) *n* **1** a covered dish of earthenware, glass, etc, in which food is cooked and served **2** any food cooked and served in such a dish: *chicken casserole* ▷ *vb* **3** to cook or be cooked in a casserole [c18 from French, from Old French *casse* ladle, pan for dripping, from Old Provençal *cassa*, from Late Latin *cattia* dipper, from Greek *kuathion*, diminutive of *kuathos* cup]

cassette (kæˈsɛt) *n* **1 a** a plastic container for magnetic tape, as one inserted into a tape deck **b** (*as modifier*): *a cassette recorder* **2** *photog* another term for **cartridge** (sense 5) **3** *films* a container for film used to facilitate the loading of a camera or projector, esp when the film is used in the form of a loop **4** the injection of genes from one species into the fertilized egg of another species [c18 from French: little box; see CASE²]

cassia ('kæsɪə) *n* **1** any plant of the mainly tropical leguminous genus *Cassia*, esp *C. fistula*, whose pods yield **cassia pulp**, a mild laxative. See also **senna 2** a lauraceous tree, *Cinnamomum cassia*, of tropical Asia **3 cassia bark** the cinnamon-like bark of this tree, used as a spice [Old English, from Latin *casia*, from Greek *kasia*, of Semitic origin; related to Hebrew *qeṣī'āh* cassia]

cassimere *or* **casimere** ('kæsɪˌmɪə) *n* a woollen suiting cloth of plain or twill weave [c18 variant of *cashmere*, from KASHMIR]

Cassini's division (kæˈsiːnɪz) *n* the gap that divides Saturn's rings into two parts, discovered by Giovanni Domenico Cassini (1625–1712) in 1675

cassino *or* **casino** (kəˈsiːnəʊ) *n* a card game for two to four players in which players pair cards from their hands with others exposed on the table

Cassino (*Italian* kasˈsiːno) *n* a town in central Italy, in Latium at the foot of Monte Cassino: an ancient Volscian (and later Roman) town and citadel. Pop: 32 762 (2001). Latin name: **Casinum**

Cassiopeia¹ (ˌkæsɪəˈpiːə) *n Greek myth* the wife of

Cepheus and mother of Andromeda

Cassiopeia² (ˌkæsɪəˈpiːə) n, Latin genitive Cassiopeiae (ˌkæsɪˈpiːiː) a very conspicuous W-shaped constellation near the Pole Star. **Cassiopeia A** is a very strong radio and X-ray source, identified as the remnant of a supernova thought to have occurred in the late 17th century > ˌCassioˈpeian adj

cassis (kæˈsiːs) n a blackcurrant cordial [c19 from French]

cassiterite (kəˈsɪtəˌraɪt) n a black or brown mineral, found in igneous rocks and hydrothermal veins. It is a source of tin. Composition: tin oxide. Formula: SnO_2. Crystal structure: tetragonal. Also called: **tinstone** [c19 from Greek kassiteros tin]

cassock (ˈkæsək) n Christianity an ankle-length garment, usually black, worn by priests and choristers [c16 from Old French casaque, from Italian casacca a long coat, of uncertain origin] > ˈcassocked adj

cassoulet (ˌkæsəˈleɪ) n a stew originating from France, made from haricot beans and goose, duck, pork, etc [French, related to casse saucepan, bowl]

cassowary (ˈkæsəˌwɛərɪ) n, pl -waries any large flightless bird of the genus Casuarius, inhabiting forests in NE Australia, New Guinea, and adjacent islands, having a horny head crest, black plumage, and brightly coloured neck and wattles: order Casuariiformes (see **ratite**) [c17 from Malay kĕsuari]

casspir (ˈkæspɜː) n South African an armoured military vehicle [c20 coined from an anagram of CSIR (Council for Scientific and Industrial Research) and SAP (South African Police)]

cast (kɑːst) vb casts, casting, cast (mainly tr) **1** to throw or expel with violence or force **2** to throw off or away: she cast her clothes to the ground **3** to reject or dismiss: he cast the idea from his mind **4** to shed or drop: the snake cast its skin; the horse cast a shoe; the ship cast anchor **5** be cast NZ (of a sheep) to have fallen and been unable to rise **6** to cause to appear: to cast a shadow **7** to express (doubts, suspicions, etc) or cause (them) to be felt **8** to direct (a glance, attention, etc): cast your eye over this **9** to place, esp in a violent manner: he was cast into prison **10** (also intr) angling to throw (a line) into the water **11** to draw or choose (lots) **12** to give or deposit (a vote) **13** to select (actors) to play parts in (a play, film, etc) **14 a** to shape (molten metal, glass, etc) by pouring or pressing it into a mould **b** to make (an object) by such a process **15** (also intr; often foll by up) to compute (figures or a total) **16** to predict: the old woman cast my fortune **17** astrology to draw on (a horoscope) details concerning the positions of the planets in the signs of the zodiac at a particular time for interpretation in terms of human characteristics, behaviour, **18** to contrive (esp in the phrase **cast a spell**) **19** to formulate: he cast his work in the form of a chart **20** (also intr) to twist or cause to twist **21** (also intr) nautical to turn the head of (a sailing vessel) or (of a sailing vessel) to be turned away from the wind in getting under way **22** hunting to direct (a pack of hounds) over (ground) where their quarry may recently have passed **23** (intr) (of birds of prey) to eject from the crop and bill a pellet consisting of the indigestible parts of birds or animals previously eaten **24** falconry to hold the body of a hawk between the hands so as to perform some operation upon it **25** printing to stereotype or electrotype **26** cast or throw in one's lot with to share in the activities or fortunes of (someone else) ▷ n **27** the act of casting or throwing **28 a** Also called: **casting** something that is shed, dropped, or egested, such as the coil of earth left by an earthworm **b** another name for **pellet** (sense 4) **29** an object that is thrown **30** the distance an object is or may be thrown **31 a** a throw at dice **b** the resulting number shown **32** angling **a** a trace with a fly or flies attached **b** the act or an instance of casting **33** the wide sweep

made by a sheepdog to get behind a flock of sheep or by a hunting dog in search of a scent **34 a** the actors in a play collectively **b** (as modifier): a cast list **35 a** an object made of metal, glass, etc, that has been shaped in a molten state by being poured or pressed into a mould **b** the mould used to shape such an object **36** form or appearance **37** sort, kind, or style **38** a fixed twist or defect, esp in the eye **39** a distortion of shape **40** surgery a rigid encircling casing, often made of plaster of Paris, for immobilizing broken bones while they heal **41** pathol a mass of fatty, waxy, cellular, or other material formed in a diseased body cavity, passage, etc **42** the act of casting a pack of hounds **43** falconry a pair of falcons working in combination to pursue the same quarry **44** archery the speed imparted to an arrow by a particular bow **45** a slight tinge or trace, as of colour **46** a computation or calculation **47** a forecast or conjecture **48** fortune or a stroke of fate **49** palaeontol a replica of an organic object made of nonorganic material, esp a lump of sediment that indicates the internal or external surface of a shell or skeleton **50** palaeontol a sedimentary structure representing the infilling of a mark or depression in a soft layer of sediment (or bed) ▷ See also **cast about, castaway, cast back, cast down, cast-off, cast on, cast out, cast up** [c13 from Old Norse kasta]

castable (ˈkɑːstəbəl) adj **1** able to be cast; suitable for casting **2** (of an actor) able or likely to be selected to play a part in a play, film, etc

cast about or **around** vb (intr, adverb) to make a mental or visual search: to cast about for an idea for a book

Castalia (kæˈsteɪlɪə) n a spring on Mount Parnassus: in ancient Greece sacred to Apollo and the Muses and believed to be a source of inspiration > Casˈtalian adj

castanets (ˌkæstəˈnɛts) pl n curved pieces of hollow wood, usually held between the fingers and thumb and made to click together: used esp by Spanish dancers [c17 castanet, from Spanish castañeta, diminutive of castaña CHESTNUT]

castaway (ˈkɑːstəˌweɪ) n **1** a person who has been shipwrecked **2** something thrown off or away; castoff ▷ adj (prenominal) **3** shipwrecked or put adrift **4** thrown away or rejected ▷ vb **cast away** **5** (tr, adverb; often passive) to cause (a ship, person, etc) to be shipwrecked or abandoned

cast back vb (adverb) to turn (the mind) to the past

cast down vb (tr, adverb) to make (a person) discouraged or dejected

caste (kɑːst) n **1 a** any of the four major hereditary classes, namely the **Brahman**, **Kshatriya**, **Vaisya**, and **Sudra** into which Hindu society is divided **b** Also called: **caste system** the system or basis of such classes **c** the social position or rank conferred by this system **2** any social class or system based on such distinctions as heredity, rank, wealth, profession, etc **3** the position conferred by such a system **4** entomol any of various types of specialized individual, such as the worker, in social insects (hive bees, ants, etc) [c16 from Portuguese casta race, breed, ancestry, from casto pure, chaste, from Latin castus]

Castellammare di Stabia (Italian kastɛllamˈmaːre di ˈstabja) n a port and resort in SW Italy, in Campania on the Bay of Naples: site of the Roman resort of Stabiae, which was destroyed by the eruption of Vesuvius in 79 AD Pop: 66 929 (2001)

castellan (ˈkæstɪlən) n rare a keeper or governor of a castle. Also called: **chatelain** [c14 from Latin castellānus, from castellum CASTLE]

castellated (ˈkæstɪˌleɪtɪd) adj **1** having turrets and battlements, like a castle **2** having indentations like to battlements: a castellated nut; a castellated filament [c17 from Medieval Latin castellātus, from castellāre to fortify as a CASTLE] > ˌcastelˈlation n

Castellón de la Plana (Spanish kasteˈʎon de la ˈplana) n a port in E Spain. Pop: 160 714 (2003 est)

caster (ˈkɑːstə) n **1** a person or thing that casts **2** Also: **castor** a bottle with a perforated top for sprinkling sugar, etc, or a stand containing such bottles **3** Also: **castor** a small wheel mounted on a swivel so that the wheel tends to turn into its plane of rotation

caster action n the tendency, caused by the design of the mounting, of a wheel to turn into its plane of rotation

caster sugar (ˈkɑːstə) n finely ground white sugar

castigate (ˈkæstɪˌgeɪt) vb (tr) to rebuke or criticize in a severe manner; chastise [c17 from Latin castīgāre to correct, punish, from castum pure + agere to compel (to be)] > ˌcastiˈgation n > ˈcastiˌgator n > ˌcastiˈgatory adj

Castile (kæˈstiːl) or **Castilla** (Spanish kasˈtiʎa) n a former kingdom comprising most of modern Spain: originally part of León, it became an independent kingdom in the 10th century and united with Aragon (1469), the first step in the formation of the Spanish state

Castile soap n a hard soap made from olive oil and sodium hydroxide

Castilian (kæˈstɪljən) n **1** the Spanish dialect of Castile; the standard form of European Spanish **2** a native or inhabitant of Castile ▷ adj **3** denoting, relating to, or characteristic of Castile, its inhabitants, or the standard form of European Spanish

Castilla la Vieja (kasˈtiʎa la ˈbjexa) n the Spanish name for **Old Castile**

casting (ˈkɑːstɪŋ) n **1** an object or figure that has been cast, esp in metal from a mould **2** the process of transferring molten steel to a mould **3** the choosing of actors for a production **4** hunting the act of directing a pack of hounds over ground where their quarry may recently have passed so that they can quest for, discover, or recapture its scent **5** zoology another word for **cast** (sense 28) or **pellet** (sense 4)

casting couch n informal a couch on which a casting director is said to seduce women seeking a part in a film or play

casting vote n the deciding vote used by the presiding officer of an assembly when votes cast on both sides are equal in number

cast iron n **1** iron containing so much carbon (1.7 to 4.5 per cent) that it cannot be wrought and must be cast into shape ▷ adj **cast-iron 2** made of cast iron **3** rigid, strong, or unyielding: a cast-iron decision

castle (ˈkɑːsəl) n **1** a fortified building or set of buildings, usually permanently garrisoned, as in medieval Europe **2** any fortified place or structure **3** a large magnificent house, esp when the present or former home of a nobleman or prince **4** the citadel and strongest part of the fortifications of a medieval town **5** chess another name for **rook²** ▷ vb **6** chess to move (the king) two squares laterally on the first rank and place the nearest rook on the square passed over by the king, either towards the king's side (**castling short**) or the queen's side (**castling long**) [c11 from Latin castellum, diminutive of castrum fort]

Castlebar (ˌkɑːsəlˈbɑː) n the county town of Co Mayo, Republic of Ireland; site of the battle (1798) between the French and British known as Castlebar Races. Pop: 11 371 (2002)

castled (ˈkɑːsəld) adj **1** like a castle in construction; castellated: a castled mansion **2** (of an area) having many castles

Castleford (ˈkɑːsəlfəd) n a town in N England, in Wakefield unitary authority, West Yorkshire on the River Aire. Pop: 37 525 (2001)

Castle Howard (ˈhaʊəd) n a mansion near York in Yorkshire: designed in 1700 by Sir John Vanbrugh and Nicholas Hawksmoor; the grounds include the Temple of the Four Winds and a mausoleum

castle in the air or **in Spain** n a hope or desire

C

unlikely to be realized; daydream

castle nut *n* a hexagonal nut with six slots in the head, two of which take a locking pin to hold it firmly in position

Castlereagh ('kɑ:sᵊl,reɪ) *n* a district of E Northern Ireland, in Co Down. Pop: 66 076 (2003 est). Area.: 85 sq km (33 sq miles)

Castner process ('kæstnə) *n* a process for extracting sodium from sodium hydroxide, devised by Hamilton Young Castner (1858–98)

cast-off *adj* 1 (*prenominal*) thrown away; abandoned: *cast-off shoes* ▷ *n* **castoff** 2 a person or thing that has been discarded or abandoned 3 *printing* an estimate of the amount of space that a piece of copy will occupy when printed in a particular size and style of type ▷ *vb* **cast off** (*adverb*) 4 to remove (mooring lines) that hold (a vessel) to a dock 5 to knot (a row of stitches, esp the final row) in finishing off knitted or woven material 6 *printing* to estimate the amount of space that will be taken up by (a book, piece of copy, etc) when it is printed in a particular size and style of type 7 (*intr*) (in Scottish country dancing) to perform a progressive movement during which each partner of a couple dances separately behind one line of the set and then reunites with the other in their original position in the set or in a new position

cast on *vb* (*adverb*) to form (the first row of) stitches in knitting and weaving

castor[1] ('kɑ:stə) *n* 1 the brownish aromatic secretion of the anal glands of a beaver, used in perfumery and medicine 2 the fur of the beaver 3 a hat made of beaver or similar fur 4 a less common name for **beaver**[1] (sense 1) [c14 from Latin, from Greek *kastōr* beaver]

castor[2] ('kɑ:stə) *n* a variant spelling of **caster** (senses 2, 3)

Castor ('kɑ:stə) *n* 1 the second brightest star, Alpha Geminorum, in the constellation Gemini: a multiple star with six components lying close to the star Pollux. Distance: 52 light years 2 *classical myth* See **Castor and Pollux**

Castor and Pollux *n classical myth* the twin sons of Leda: Pollux was fathered by Zeus, Castor by the mortal Tyndareus. After Castor's death, Pollux spent half his days with his half-brother in Hades and half with the gods in Olympus

castor bean *n US and Canadian* 1 another name for **castor-oil plant** 2 the seed of this plant

castor oil *n* a colourless or yellow glutinous oil obtained from the seeds of the castor-oil plant and used as a fine lubricant and as a cathartic

castor-oil plant *n* a tall euphorbiaceous Indian plant, *Ricinus communis,* cultivated in tropical regions for ornament and for its poisonous seeds, from which castor oil is extracted. Also called (US and Canadian): **castor bean**

cast out *vb* (*intr, adverb*) *Scot* to quarrel; be no longer friends

castrate (kæ'streɪt) *vb* (*tr*) 1 to remove the testicles of; emasculate; geld 2 to deprive of vigour, masculinity, etc 3 to remove the ovaries of; spay 4 to expurgate or censor (a book, play, etc) [c17 from Latin *castrāre* to emasculate, geld] > **cas'tration** *n* > **cas'trator** *n*

castration complex *n psychoanal* an unconscious fear of having one's genitals removed, as a punishment for wishing to have sex with a parent

castrato (kæ'strɑ:təʊ) *n, pl* **-ti** (-tɪ) *or* **-tos** (in 17th- and 18th-century opera) a male singer whose testicles were removed before puberty, allowing the retention of a soprano or alto voice [c18 from Italian, from Latin *castrātus* castrated]

Castries (kæs'tri:s) *n* the capital and chief port of St Lucia. Pop: 14 000 (2005 est)

Castrop-Rauxel *or* **Kastrop-Rauxel** (German 'kastrop'rauksəl) *n* an industrial city in W Germany, in North Rhine-Westphalia. Pop: 78 208 (2003 est)

cast steel *n* steel containing varying amounts of

carbon, manganese, phosphorus, silicon, and sulphur that is cast into shape rather than wrought

cast stone *n building trades* a building component, such as a block or lintel, made from cast concrete with a facing that resembles natural stone

cast up *vb* (*tr, adverb*) 1 (of the sea) to cast ashore 2 to compute (figures or a total) 3 to bring up as a reproach against a person

casual ('kæʒjʊəl) *adj* 1 happening by accident or chance: *a casual meeting* 2 offhand; not premeditated: *a casual remark* 3 shallow or superficial: *a casual affair* 4 being or seeming unconcerned or apathetic: *he assumed a casual attitude* 5 (esp of dress) for informal wear: *a casual coat* 6 occasional or irregular: *casual visits; a casual labourer* 7 *biology* another term for **adventive** ▷ *n* 8 (*usually plural*) an informal article of clothing or footwear 9 an occasional worker 10 *biology* another term for an **adventive** 11 (*usually plural*) a young man dressed in expensive casual clothes who goes to football matches in order to start fights [c14 from Late Latin *cāsuālis* happening by chance, from Latin *cāsus* event, from *cadere* to fall; see CASE¹] > **'casually** *adv* > **'casualness** *n*

casual Friday *n* another name for **dress-down Friday**

casualization *or* **casualisation** (,kæʒjʊəlaɪ'zeɪʃən) *n* the altering of working practices so that regular workers are re-employed on a casual or short-term basis

casualty ('kæʒjʊəltɪ) *n, pl* **-ties** 1 a serviceman who is killed, wounded, captured, or missing as a result of enemy action 2 a person who is injured or killed in an accident 3 a hospital department in which victims of accidents, violence, etc, are treated 4 anything that is lost, damaged, or destroyed as the result of an accident, etc

casuarina (,kæsjʊə'ri:nə) *n* any tree of the genus *Casuarina,* of Australia and the East Indies, having jointed leafless branchlets: family *Casuarinaceae.* See also **beefwood, she-oak** [c19 from New Latin, from Malay *kĕsuari* CASSOWARY, referring to the resemblance of the branches to the feathers of the cassowary]

casuist ('kæzjʊɪst) *n* 1 a person, esp a theologian, who attempts to resolve moral dilemmas by the application of general rules and the careful distinction of special cases 2 a person who is oversubtle in his or her analysis of fine distinctions; sophist [c17 from French *casuiste,* from Spanish *casuista,* from Latin *cāsus* CASE¹] > **,casu'istic** *or* **,casu'istical** *adj* > **,casu'istically** *adv*

casuistry ('kæzjʊɪstrɪ) *n, pl* **-ries** 1 *philosophy* the resolution of particular moral dilemmas, esp those arising from conflicting general moral rules, by careful distinction of the cases to which these rules apply 2 reasoning that is specious, misleading, or oversubtle

casus belli *Latin* ('kɑ:sʊs 'beli:) *n, pl casus belli* ('kɑ:sʊs 'beli:) 1 an event or act used to justify a war 2 the immediate cause of a quarrel [literally: occasion of war]

cat[1] (kæt) *n* 1 Also called: **domestic cat** a small domesticated feline mammal, *Felis catus* (or *domesticus*), having thick soft fur and occurring in many breeds in which the colour of the fur varies greatly: kept as a pet or to catch rats and mice 2 Also called: **big cat** any of the larger felines, such as a lion or tiger 3 any wild feline mammal of the genus *Felis,* such as the lynx or serval, resembling the domestic cat ▷ Related adjective: **feline** 4 *informal* a woman who gossips maliciously 5 *slang* a man; guy 6 *nautical* a heavy tackle for hoisting an anchor to the cathead 7 a short sharp-ended piece of wood used in the game of tipcat 8 short for **catboat** 9 *informal* short for **Caterpillar** 10 short for **cat-o'-nine-tails** 11 **a bag of cats** *Irish informal* a bad-tempered person: *she's a real bag of cats this morning* 12 **fight like Kilkenny cats** to fight until both parties are destroyed 13 **let the cat out of the bag** to disclose a secret, often by mistake

14 **like a cat on a hot tin roof** *or* **on hot bricks** in an uneasy or agitated state 15 **like cat and dog** quarrelling savagely 16 **look like something the cat brought in** to appear dishevelled or bedraggled 17 **not a cat in hell's chance** no chance at all 18 **not have room to swing a cat** to have very little space 19 **play cat and mouse** to play with a person or animal in a cruel or teasing way, esp before a final act of cruelty or unkindness 20 **put, set, etc, the cat among the pigeons** to introduce some violently disturbing new element 21 **rain cats and dogs** to rain very heavily ▷ *vb* **cats, catting, catted** 22 (*tr*) to flog with a cat-o'-nine-tails 23 (*tr*) *nautical* to hoist (an anchor) to the cathead 24 (*intr*) a slang word for **vomit** [Old English *catte,* from Latin *cattus;* related to Old Norse *köttr,* Old High German *kazza,* Old French *chat,* Russian *kot*] > **'cat ,like** *adj* > **'cattish** *adj*

cat[2] (kæt) *n informal* short for **catamaran** (sense 1)

cat[3] (kæt) *n* 1 **a** short for **catalytic converter b** (*as modifier*): *a cat car* ▷ *adj* 2 short for **catalytic** *a cat cracker*

CAT *abbreviation for* 1 computer-aided teaching 2 computer-assisted trading

cat. *abbreviation for* 1 catalogue 2 catamaran

cata-, kata-, *before an aspirate* **cath-** *or before a vowel* **cat-** *prefix* 1 down; downwards; lower in position: *catadromous; cataphyll* 2 indicating reversal, opposition, degeneration, etc: *cataplasia; catatonia* [from Greek *kata-,* from *kata.* In compound words borrowed from Greek, *kata-* means: down (*catabolism*), away, off (*catalectic*), against (*category*), according to (*catholic*), and thoroughly (*catalogue*)]

catabasis (kə'tæbəsɪs) *n, pl* **-ses** (-,si:z) 1 a descent or downward movement 2 the decline of a disease > **catabatic** (,kætə'bætɪk) *adj*

catabolism *or* **katabolism** (kə'tæbə,lɪzəm) *n* a metabolic process in which complex molecules are broken down into simple ones with the release of energy; destructive metabolism. Compare **anabolism** [c19 *katabolism,* from Greek *katabolē* a throwing down, from *kataballein,* from *kata-* down + *ballein* to throw] > **catabolic** *or* **katabolic** (,kætə'bɒlɪk) *adj* > **,cata'bolically** *or* **,kata'bolically** *adv*

catabolite (kə'tæbə,laɪt) *n* a substance produced as a result of catabolism

catacaustic (,kætə'kɔ:stɪk, -'kɒs-) *physics* ▷ *adj* 1 (of a caustic curve or surface) formed by reflected light rays. Compare **diacaustic** ▷ *n* 2 a catacaustic curve or surface

catachresis (,kætə'kri:sɪs) *n* the incorrect use of words, as *luxuriant* for *luxurious* [c16 from Latin, from Greek *katakhrēsis* a misusing, from *katakhrēsthai,* from *khrēsthai* to use] > **catachrestic** (,kætə'krestɪk) *or* **,cata'chrestical** *adj* > **,cata'chrestically** *adv*

cataclasis (,kætə'kleɪsɪs) *n, pl* **-ses** (-si:z) *geology* the deformation of rocks by crushing and shearing [c19 New Latin, from Greek, from CATA- + *klasis* a breaking] > **cataclastic** (,kætə'klæstɪk) *adj*

cataclinal (,kætə'klaɪnᵊl) *adj* (of streams, valleys, etc) running in the direction of the dip of the surrounding rock strata

cataclysm ('kætə,klɪzəm) *n* 1 a violent upheaval, esp of a political, military, or social nature 2 a disastrous flood; deluge 3 *geology* another name for **catastrophe** (sense 4) [c17 via French from Latin, from Greek *kataklusmos* deluge, from *katakluzein* to flood, from *kluzein* to wash] > **,cata'clysmic** *or* **,cata'clysmal** *adj* > **,cata'clysmically** *adv*

catacomb ('kætə,kəʊm, -,ku:m) *n* 1 (*usually plural*) an underground burial place, esp the galleries at Rome, consisting of tunnels with vaults or niches leading off them for tombs 2 a series of interconnected underground tunnels or caves [Old English *catacumbe,* from Late Latin *catacumbas* (singular), name of the cemetery under the Basilica of St Sebastian, near Rome; origin unknown]

catadioptric (,kætədaɪ'ɒptrɪk) *adj* involving a

combination of reflecting and refracting components: *a catadioptric telescope* [c18 from CATA- + DIOPTRIC]

catadromous (kə'tædrəməs) *adj* (of fishes such as the eel) migrating down rivers to the sea in order to breed. Compare **anadromous** [c19 from Greek *katadromos*, from *kata-* down + *dromos*, from *dremein* to run]

catafalque ('kætə,fælk) *n* a temporary raised platform on which a body lies in state before or during a funeral [c17 from French, from Italian *catafalco*, of uncertain origin; compare SCAFFOLD]

Catalan ('kætə,læn, -lən) *n* 1 a language of Catalonia, quite closely related to Spanish and Provençal, belonging to the Romance group of the Indo-European family 2 a native or inhabitant of Catalonia ▷ *adj* 3 denoting, relating to, or characteristic of Catalonia, its inhabitants, or their language

catalase ('kætə,leɪs) *n* an enzyme that catalyses the decomposition of hydrogen peroxide

catalectic (,kætə'lɛktɪk) *adj prosody* (of a line of verse) having an incomplete final foot [c16 via Late Latin from Greek *katalēktikos* incomplete, from *katalēgein*, from *kata-* off + *lēgein* to stop]

catalepsy ('kætə,lɛpsɪ) *n* a state of prolonged rigid posture, occurring for example in schizophrenia or in hypnotic trances [c16 from Medieval Latin *catalēpsia*, variant of Late Latin *catalēpsis*, from Greek *katalēpsis*, literally: a seizing, from *katalambanein* to hold down, from *kata-* down + *lambanein* to grasp] > ,cata'leptic *adj*

Catalina Island (,kætə'liːnə) *n* another name for **Santa Catalina**

catalo ('kætə,ləʊ) *n, pl* -loes *or* -los a variant spelling of **cattalo**

catalogue *or US* **catalog** ('kætə,lɒg) *n* 1 a complete, usually alphabetical list of items, often with notes giving details 2 a book, usually illustrated, containing details of items for sale, esp as used by mail-order companies 3 a list of all the books or resources of a library 4 *US and Canadian* a publication issued by a university, college, etc, listing courses offered, regulations, services, etc 5 *NZ* a list of wool lots prepared for auction ▷ *vb* -logues, -loguing, -logued *or US* -logs, -loging, -loged 6 to compile a catalogue of (a library) 7 to add (books, items, etc) to an existing catalogue [c15 from Late Latin *catalogus*, from Greek *katalogos*, from *katalegein* to list, from *kata-* completely + *legein* to collect] > 'cata,loguer *or* 'cata,loguist *n*

catalogue raisonné *French* (katalɔg rɛzɔne) *n* a descriptive catalogue, esp one covering works of art in an exhibition or collection

Catalonia (,kætə'ləʊnɪə) *n* a region of NE Spain, with a strong separatist tradition: became an autonomous region with its own parliament in 1979; an important agricultural and industrial region, with many resorts. Pop: 7 012 600 (2003 est). Area: 31 929 sq km (12 328 sq miles). Catalan name: Catalunya (,katə'luːnjə) Spanish name: Cataluña (kata'luɲa)

catalpa (kə'tælpə) *n* any bignoniaceous tree of the genus *Catalpa* of North America and Asia, having large leaves, bell-shaped whitish flowers, and long slender pods [c18 New Latin, from Carolina Creek *kutuhlpa*, literally: winged head, referring to the appearance of the flowers]

catalyse *or US* **catalyze** ('kætə,laɪz) *vb* (*tr*) to influence (a chemical reaction) by catalysis > 'cata,lyser *or US* 'cata,lyzer *n*

catalysis (kə'tælɪsɪs) *n, pl* -ses (-,siːz) acceleration of a chemical reaction by the action of a catalyst [c17 from New Latin, from Greek *katalusis*, from *kataluein* to dissolve]

catalyst ('kætəlɪst) *n* 1 a substance that increases the rate of a chemical reaction without itself suffering any permanent chemical change. Compare **inhibitor** (sense 2) 2 a person or thing that causes a change

catalytic (,kætə'lɪtɪk) *adj* of or relating to

catalysis; involving a catalyst > ,cata'lytically *adv*

catalytic converter *n* a device using three-way catalysts to reduce the obnoxious and poisonous components of the products of combustion (mainly oxides of nitrogen, carbon monoxide, and unburnt hydrocarbons) from the exhausts of motor vehicles

catalytic cracker *n* a unit in an oil refinery in which mineral oils with high boiling points are converted to fuels with lower boiling points by a catalytic process. Often shortened to: **cat cracker**

catamaran (,kætəmə'ræn) *n* 1 a sailing, or sometimes motored, vessel with twin hulls held parallel by a rigid framework 2 a primitive raft made of logs lashed together 3 *informal* a quarrelsome woman [c17 from Tamil *kattumaram* tied timber]

catamenia (,kætə'miːnɪə) *pl n physiol* another word for **menses** [c18 from New Latin, from Greek *katamēnia* menses] > ,cata'menial *adj*

catamite ('kætə,maɪt) *n* a boy kept for homosexual purposes [c16 from Latin *Catamītus*, variant of *Ganymēdēs* GANYMEDE[1]]

catamount ('kætə,maʊnt) *or* **catamountain** *n* any of various medium-sized felines, such as the puma or lynx [c17 short for *cat of the mountain*]

catananche (,kætə'næŋkɪ) *n* any of the hardy perennial genus *Catananche*, from S Europe; some, esp *C. caerulea*, are grown for their blue-and-white flowers that can be dried as winter decoration: family *Asteraceae*. Also called: **cupid's dart** [from Greek *katanankē* a spell (from their use in love potions)]

Catania (*Italian* ka'taːnja) *n* a port in E Sicily, near Mount Etna. Pop: 313 110 (2001)

Catanzaro (*Italian* katan'dzaːro) *n* a city in S Italy, in Calabria. Pop: 95 251 (2001)

cataphora (kə'tæfərə) *n grammar* the use of a word such as a pronoun that has the same reference as a word used subsequently in the same discourse. Compare **anaphora** [from CATA- + Greek *pherein* to bear] > **cataphoric** (,kætə'fɒrɪk) *adj*

cataphoresis (,kætəfə'riːsɪs) *n* another name for **electrophoresis**. > **cataphoretic** (,kætəfə'rɛtɪk) *adj* > ,catapho'retically *adv*

cataphyll ('kætə,fɪl) *n* a simplified form of plant leaf, such as a scale leaf or cotyledon

cataplasia (,kætə'pleɪzɪə) *n* the degeneration of cells and tissues to a less highly developed form > **cataplastic** (,kætə'plæstɪk) *adj*

cataplasm ('kætə,plæzəm) *n med* another name for **poultice** [c16 from Latin *cataplasma*, from Greek, from *kataplassein* to cover with a plaster, from *plassein* to shape]

cataplexy ('kætə,plɛksɪ) *n* 1 sudden temporary paralysis, brought on by severe shock 2 a state of complete absence of movement assumed by animals while shamming death [c19 from Greek *kataplēxis* amazement, from *kataplēssein* to strike down (with amazement), confound, from *kata-* down + *plēssein* to strike] > ,cata'plectic *adj*

catapult ('kætə,pʌlt) *n* 1 a Y-shaped implement with a loop of elastic fastened to the ends of the two prongs, used mainly by children for shooting small stones, etc. US and Canadian name: **slingshot** 2 a heavy war engine used formerly for hurling stones, etc 3 a device installed in warships to launch aircraft ▷ *vb* 4 (*tr*) to shoot forth from or as if from a catapult 5 (foll by *over, into*, etc) to move precipitately: *she was catapulted to stardom overnight* [c16 from Latin *catapulta*, from Greek *katapeltēs*, from *kata-* down + *pallein* to hurl]

cataract ('kætə,rækt) *n* 1 a large waterfall or rapids 2 a deluge; downpour 3 *pathol* a partial or total opacity of the crystalline lens of the eye b the opaque area [c15 from Latin *cataracta*, from Greek *katarrhaktēs*, from *katarassein* to dash down, from *arassein* to strike]

catarrh (kə'tɑː) *n* 1 inflammation of a mucous membrane with increased production of mucus, esp affecting the nose and throat in the common cold 2 the mucus so formed [c16 via French from

Late Latin *catarrhus*, from Greek *katarrous*, from *katarrhein* to flow down, from *kata-* down + *rhein* to flow] > **ca'tarrhal** *or* **ca'tarrhous** *adj*

catarrhine ('kætə,raɪn) *adj* 1 (of apes and Old World monkeys) having the nostrils set close together and opening to the front of the face 2 Also: **leptorrhine** (of humans) having a thin or narrow nose ▷ *n* 3 an animal or person with this characteristic ▷ Compare **platyrrhine** [c19 from New Latin *Catarrhina* (for sense 1), all ultimately from Greek *katarrhin* having a hooked nose, from *kata-* down + *rhis* nose]

catastrophe (kə'tæstrəfɪ) *n* 1 a sudden, extensive, or notable disaster or misfortune 2 the denouement of a play, esp a classical tragedy 3 a final decisive event, usually causing a disastrous end 4 Also called: **cataclysm** any sudden and violent change in the earth's surface caused by flooding, earthquake, or some other rapid process [c16 from Greek *katastrophē*, from *katastrephein* to overturn, from *strephein* to turn] > **catastrophic** (,kætə'strɒfɪk) *adj* > ,cata'strophically *adv*

catastrophe theory *n* a a mathematical theory that classifies surfaces according to their form b the popular application of this theory to the explanation of abruptly changing phenomena, as by the discontinuity of a line on the topmost fold of a folded surface

catastrophism (kə'tæstrə,fɪzəm) *n* 1 an old doctrine, now discarded, that the earth was created and has subsequently been shaped by sudden divine acts which have no logical connection with each other rather than by gradual evolutionary processes 2 Also called: **neo-catastrophism** a modern doctrine that the gradual evolutionary processes shaping the earth have been supplemented in the past by the effects of huge natural catastrophes. See **uniformitarianism**. Compare **gradualism** (sense 2) > **ca'tastrophist** *n*

catatonia (,kætə'təʊnɪə) *n* a state of muscular rigidity and stupor, sometimes found in schizophrenia [c20 New Latin, from German *Katatonie*, from CATA- + *-tonia*, from Greek *tonos* tension] > **catatonic** (,kætə'tɒnɪk) *adj, n*

Catawba (kə'tɔːbə) *n 1* (*pl* -ba *or* -bas) a member of a North American Indian people, formerly of South Carolina, now almost extinct 2 their language, belonging to the Siouan family 3 a cultivated variety of red North American grape, widely grown in the eastern US 4 the wine made from these grapes

catbird ('kæt,bɜːd) *n* 1 any of several North American songbirds of the family *Mimidae* (mockingbirds), esp *Dumetella carolinensis*, whose call resembles the mewing of a cat 2 any of several Australian bowerbirds of the genera *Ailuroedus* and *Scenopoeetes*, having a catlike call

catboat ('kæt,bəʊt) *n* a sailing vessel with a single mast, set well forward and often unstayed, and a large sail, usually rigged with a gaff. Shortened form: **cat**

cat brier *n* another name for **greenbrier**

cat burglar *n* a burglar who enters buildings by climbing through upper windows, skylights, etc

catcall ('kæt,kɔːl) *n* 1 a shrill whistle or cry expressing disapproval, as at a public meeting, etc ▷ *vb* 2 to utter such a call (at); deride with catcalls > 'cat,caller *n*

catch (kætʃ) *vb* catches, catching, caught 1 (*tr*) to take hold of so as to retain or restrain: *he caught the ball* 2 (*tr*) to take, seize, or capture, esp after pursuit 3 (*tr*) to ensnare or deceive, as by trickery 4 (*tr*) to surprise or detect in an act: *he caught the dog rifling the larder* 5 (*tr*) to reach with a blow: *the stone caught him on the side of the head* 6 (*tr*) to overtake or reach in time to board: *if we hurry we should catch the next bus* 7 (*tr*) to see or hear; attend: *I didn't catch the Ibsen play* 8 (*tr*) to be infected with: *to catch a cold* 9 to hook or entangle or become hooked or entangled: *her dress caught on a nail* 10 to fasten or be fastened with or as if with a latch or other device **11** (*tr*) to attract or arrest: *she tried to catch his eye* **12** (*tr*) to comprehend: *I didn't catch his meaning* **13** (*tr*) to hear accurately: *I didn't catch what you said* **14** (*tr*) to captivate or charm **15** (*tr*) to perceive and reproduce accurately: *the painter managed to catch his model's beauty* **16** (*tr*) to hold back or restrain: *he caught his breath in surprise* **17** (*intr*) to become alight: *the fire won't catch* **18** (*tr*) *cricket* to dismiss (a batsman) by intercepting and holding a ball struck by him before it touches the ground **19** (*intr; often foll by at*) **a** to grasp or attempt to grasp **b** to take advantage (of), esp eagerly: *he caught at the chance* **20** (*intr; used passively*) *informal* to make pregnant **21 catch it** *informal* to be scolded or reprimanded **22 catch oneself on** *slang* to realize that one's actions are mistaken ▷ *n* **23** the act of catching or grasping **24** a device that catches and fastens, such as a latch **25** anything that is caught, esp something worth catching **26** the amount or number caught **27** *informal* a person regarded as an eligible matrimonial prospect **28** a check or break in the voice **29** a break in a mechanism **30** *informal* **a** a concealed, unexpected, or unforeseen drawback or handicap **b** (*as modifier*): *a catch question* **31** a game in which a ball is thrown from one player to another **32** *cricket* the catching of a ball struck by a batsman before it touches the ground, resulting in him being out **33** *music* a type of round popular in the 17th, 18th, and 19th centuries, having a humorous text that is often indecent or bawdy and hard to articulate. See **round** (sense 31), **canon¹** (sense 7) ▷ See also **catch on**, **catch out**, **catch up** [c13 *cacchen* to pursue, from Old Northern French *cachier*, from Latin *captāre* to snatch, from *capere* to seize] > **'catchable** *adj*

catch-all *n* **a** something designed to cover a variety of situations or possibilities **b** (*as modifier*): *a catch-all clause*

catch-as-catch-can *n* **1** a style of wrestling in which trips, holds below the waist, etc, are allowed ▷ *adj, adv* **2** *chiefly US and Canadian* using any method or opportunity that comes to hand

catch basin *n US and Canadian* a pit in a drainage system in which matter that might otherwise block a sewer is collected so that it may periodically be removed. Also called (in Britain and certain other countries): **catch pit**

catch crop *n* a quick-growing crop planted between two regular crops grown in consecutive seasons, or between two rows of regular crops in the same season

catchcry ('kætʃ,kraɪ) *n, pl* **-cries** *Austral* a well-known, frequently used phrase, esp one associated with a particular group, etc

catcher ('kætʃə) *n* **1** a person or thing that catches, esp in a game or sport **2** *baseball* a fielder who stands behind home plate and catches pitched balls not hit by the batter

catchfly ('kætʃ,flaɪ) *n, pl* **-flies** any of several caryophyllaceous plants of the genus *Silene* that have sticky calyxes and stems on which insects are sometimes trapped

catching ('kætʃɪŋ) *adj* **1** infectious **2** attractive; captivating

catching pen *n Austral and NZ* a pen adjacent to a shearer's stand containing the sheep ready for shearing

catchment ('kætʃmənt) *n* **1** the act of catching or collecting water **2** a structure in which water is collected **3** the water so collected **4** *Brit* the intake of a school from one catchment area

catchment area *n* **1** the area of land bounded by watersheds draining into a river, basin, or reservoir. Also called: **catchment basin**, **drainage area**, **drainage basin 2** the area from which people are allocated to a particular school, hospital, etc

Catchment board *n NZ* a public body concerned with the conservation and organization of water supply from a catchment area

catch on *vb* (*intr, adverb*) *informal* **1** to become

popular or fashionable **2** to grasp mentally; understand

catch out *vb* (*tr, adverb*) *informal, chiefly Brit* to trap (a person), esp in an error or doing something reprehensible

catchpenny ('kætʃ,pɛnɪ) *adj* **1** (*prenominal*) designed to have instant appeal, esp in order to sell quickly and easily without regard for quality: *catchpenny ornaments* ▷ *n, pl* **-nies 2** an item or commodity that is cheap and showy

catch phrase *n* a well-known frequently used phrase, esp one associated with a particular group, etc

catch pit *n* a pit in a drainage system in which matter that might otherwise block a sewer is collected so that it may periodically be removed. US and Canadian name: **catch basin**

catch points *pl n* railway points designed to derail a train running back in the wrong direction to prevent collision with a following train

catchpole or **catchpoll** ('kætʃ,pəʊl) *n* (in medieval England) a sheriff's officer who arrested debtors [Old English *cæcepol*, from Medieval Latin *cacepollus* tax-gatherer, literally: chicken-chaser, from *cace-* CATCH + *pollus* (from Latin *pullus* chick)]

catch-22 *n* **1** a situation in which a person is frustrated by a paradoxical rule or set of circumstances that preclude any attempt to escape from them **2** a situation in which any move that a person can make will lead to trouble [c20 from the title of a novel (1961) by J. Heller]

catchup ('kætʃəp, 'kɛtʃ-) *n* a variant spelling (esp US) of **ketchup**

catch up *vb* (*adverb*) **1** (*tr*) to seize and take up (something) quickly **2** (*when intr, often foll by with*) to reach or pass (someone or something), after following: *he soon caught him up* **3** (*intr; usually foll by on or with*) to make up for lost ground or deal with a backlog (in some specified task or activity) **4** (*tr; often passive*) to absorb or involve: *she was caught up in her reading* **5** (*tr*) to raise by or as if by fastening: *the hem of her dress was caught up with ribbons*

catchwater drain ('kætʃ,wɔ:tə) *n* a channel cut along the edge of high ground to catch surface water from it and divert it away from low-lying ground

catchweight ('kætʃ,weɪt) *adj wrestling* of or relating to a contest in which normal weight categories have been waived by agreement

catchword ('kætʃ,wɜ:d) *n* **1** a word or phrase made temporarily popular, esp by a political campaign; slogan **2** a word printed as a running head in a reference book **3** *theatre* an actor's cue to speak or enter **4** the first word of a printed or typewritten page repeated at the bottom of the page preceding

catchy ('kætʃɪ) *adj* **catchier, catchiest 1** (of a tune, etc) pleasant and easily remembered or imitated **2** tricky or deceptive: *a catchy question* **3** irregular: *a catchy breeze* > **'catchiness** *n*

cat cracker *n* an informal name for **catalytic cracker**

cat door *n* a small door or flap in a larger door through which a cat can pass

catechetical (,kætɪ'kɛtɪkəl) or **catechetic** *adj* of or relating to teaching by question and answer > ,cate'chetically *adv*

catechin ('kætəkɪn) *n* a soluble yellow solid substance found in catechu and mahogany wood and used in tanning and dyeing. Formula: $C_{15}H_{14}O_6$ [c19 from CATECHU + -IN]

catechism ('kætɪ,kɪzəm) *n* **1** instruction by a series of questions and answers, esp a book containing such instruction on the religious doctrine of a Christian Church **2** rigorous and persistent questioning, as in a test or interview [c16 from Late Latin *catēchismus*, ultimately from Greek *katēkhizein* (see CATECHIZE) > ,cate'chismal *adj*

catechize or **catechise** ('kætɪ,kaɪz) *vb* (*tr*) **1** to teach or examine by means of questions and answers **2** to give oral instruction in Christianity,

esp by using a catechism **3** to put questions to (someone) [c15 from Late Latin *catēchizāre*, from Greek *katēkhizein*, from *katēkhein* to instruct orally, literally: to shout down, from *kata-* down + *ēkhein* to sound] > 'catechist, 'cate,chizer or 'cate,chiser *n* > ,cate'chistic or ,cate'chistical *adj* > ,cate'chistically *adv* > ,catechi'zation or ,catechi'sation *n*

catechol ('kætɪ,tʃɒl, -,kɒl) *n* a colourless crystalline phenol found in resins and lignins; 1,2-dihydroxybenzene. It is used as a photographic developer. Formula: $C_6H_4(OH)_2$. Also called: **pyrocatechol** [c20 from CATECHU + -OL¹]

catecholamine (,kætə'kɒlə,mi:n) *n* any of a group of hormones that are catechol derivatives, esp adrenaline and noradrenaline [c20 from CATECHU + -OL¹ + AMINE]

catechu ('kætɪ,tʃu:), **cachou** or **cutch** *n* a water-soluble astringent resinous substance obtained from any of certain tropical plants, esp the leguminous tree *Acacia catechu* of S Asia, and used in medicine, tanning, and dyeing. See also **gambier** [c17 probably from Malay *kachu*, of Dravidian origin]

catechumen (,kætɪ'kju:mɛn) *n Christianity* a person, esp in the early Church, undergoing instruction prior to baptism [c15 via Old French, from Late Latin, from Greek *katēkhoumenos* one being instructed verbally, from *katēkhein*; see CATECHIZE] > ,cate'chumenal or catechumenical (,kætəkjʊ'mɛnɪkəl) *adj* > ,cate'chumenate *n* > ,cate'chumenism *n*

categorial (,kætɪ'gɔ:rɪəl) *adj* **1** of or relating to a category **2** *logic* (of a statement) consisting of a subject, S, and a predicate, P, each of which denotes a class, and having one of the following forms: *all S are P* (universal affirmative); *some S are P* (particular affirmative); *some S are not P* (particular negative); *no S are P* (universal negative). See **syllogism**

categorial grammar *n* a theory that characterizes syntactic categories in terms of functions between classes of expressions. The basic classes are names (N) and sentences (S). Intransitive verbs are symbols for functions which take a name and yield a sentence (written S/N), adverbs form compound verbs from verbs (for example, *run fast*) and so are (S/N)/(S/N), etc

categorical (,kætɪ'gɒrɪkəl) or **categoric** *adj* **1** unqualified; positive; unconditional: *a categorical statement* **2** relating to or included in a category **3** *logic* another word for **categorial**. > ,cate'gorically *adv* > ,cate'goricalness *n*

categorical imperative *n* (in the ethics of Kant) the unconditional moral principle that one's behaviour should accord with universalizable maxims which respect persons as ends in themselves; the obligation to do one's duty for its own sake and not in pursuit of further ends. Compare **hypothetical imperative**

categorize or **categorise** ('kætɪgə,raɪz) *vb* (*tr*) to place in a category; classify > ,categori'zation or ,categori'sation *n*

category ('kætɪgərɪ) *n, pl* **-ries 1** a class or group of things, people, etc, possessing some quality or qualities in common; a division in a system of classification **2** *metaphysics* any one of the most basic classes into which objects and concepts can be analysed **3 a** (in the philosophy of Aristotle) any one of ten most fundamental modes of being, such as quantity, quality, and substance **b** (in the philosophy of Kant) one of twelve concepts required by human beings to interpret the empirical world **c** any set of objects, concepts, or expressions distinguished from others within some logical or linguistic theory by the intelligibility of a specific set of statements concerning them. See also **category mistake** [c15 from Late Latin *catēgoria*, from Greek *katēgoria* to accuse, assert]

Category A *Brit* ▷ *adj* **1** (of a prisoner) regarded as highly dangerous and therefore requiring constant observation and maximum security **2** (of a prison or prison unit) designed for such prisoners

Category D *adj Brit* **1** (of a prisoner) regarded as sufficiently trustworthy to be kept under open prison conditions **2** (of a prison or prison unit) designed for such prisoners

category killer *n* a person, product, or business that dominates a particular market

category management *n marketing* the management of a range of related products in a way designed to increase sales of all of the products

category mistake *n philosophy, logic* a sentence that says of something in one category what can only intelligibly be said of something in another, as when speaking of the mind located in space

catena (kəˈtiːnə) *n, pl* **-nae** (-niː) a connected series, esp of patristic comments on the Bible [c17 from Latin: chain]

catenaccio *Italian* (kateˈnattʃo) *n football* an extremely defensive style of play [c20 from Latin *catena* chain]

catenane (ˈkætɪˌneɪn) *n* a type of chemical compound in which the molecules have two or more rings that are interlocked like the links of a chain [c20 from Latin *catena* chain + -ANE]

catenary (kəˈtiːnərɪ) *n, pl* **-ries 1** the curve assumed by a heavy uniform flexible cord hanging freely from two points. When symmetrical about the *y*-axis and intersecting it at *y* = *a*, the equation is $y = a \cosh x/a$ **2** the hanging cable between pylons along a railway track, from which the trolley wire is suspended ▷ *adj also* **catenarian** (ˌkætɪˈnɛərɪən) **3** of, resembling, relating to, or constructed using a catenary or suspended chain [c18 from Latin *catēnārius* relating to a chain]

catenate (ˈkætɪˌneɪt) *vb* **1** *biology* to arrange or be arranged in a series of chains or rings ▷ *adj* **2** another word for **catenulate** [c17 from Latin *catēnāre* to bind with chains] > ˌcateˈnation *n*

catenoid (ˈkætəˌnɔɪd) *n* the geometrical surface generated by rotating a catenary about its axis

catenulate (kəˈtɛnjuˌleɪt, -lɪt) *adj* (of certain spores) formed in a row or chain [c19 from Latin *catēnula*, diminutive of *catēna* chain]

cater (ˈkeɪtə) *vb* **1** (*intr*; foll by *for* or *to*) to provide what is required or desired (for): *to cater for a need; cater to your tastes* **2** (when *intr*, foll by *for*) to provide food, services, etc (for): *we cater for parties; to cater a banquet* [c16 from earlier *catour* purchaser, variant of *acatour*, from Anglo-Norman *acater* to buy, ultimately related to Latin *acceptāre* to ACCEPT]

cateran (ˈkætərən) *n* (formerly) a member of a band of brigands and marauders in the Scottish highlands [c14 probably from Scottish Gaelic *ceathairneach* robber, plunderer]

cater-cornered (ˈkeɪtəˌkɔːnəd) *adj, adv US and Canadian informal* diagonally placed; diagonal. Also: **catty-cornered, kitty-cornered** [c16 *cater*, from dialect *cater* (adv) diagonally, from obsolete *cater* (n) four-spot of dice, from Old French *quatre* four, from Latin *quattuor*]

cater-cousin (ˈkeɪtəˌkʌzªn) *n archaic* a close friend [c16 perhaps from obsolete *cater* caterer; for sense, compare FOSTER, as in *foster brother*, etc]

caterer (ˈkeɪtərə) *n* a person who caters, esp one who as a profession provides food for large social events, etc

catering (ˈkeɪtərɪŋ) *n* **1** the trade of a professional caterer **2** the food, etc, provided at a function by a caterer

caterpillar (ˈkætəˌpɪlə) *n* the wormlike larva of butterflies and moths, having numerous pairs of legs and powerful biting jaws. It may be brightly coloured, hairy, or spiny [c15 *catyrpel*, probably from Old Northern French *catepelose*, literally: hairy cat]

Caterpillar (ˈkætəˌpɪlə) *n trademark* **1** an endless track, driven by sprockets or wheels, used to propel a heavy vehicle and enable it to cross soft

or uneven ground **2** a vehicle, such as a tractor, tank, bulldozer, etc, driven by such tracks

caterpillar hunter *n* any of various carabid beetles of the genus *Calosoma*, of Europe and North America, which prey on the larvae of moths and butterflies

caterwaul (ˈkætəˌwɔːl) *vb* (*intr*) **1** to make a yowling noise, as a cat on heat ▷ *n* **2** a shriek or yell made by or sounding like a cat on heat [c14 of imitative origin] > ˈcaterˌwauler *n*

cates (keɪts) *pl n* (*sometimes singular*) *archaic* choice dainty food; delicacies [c15 variant of *acates* purchases, from Old Northern French *acater* to buy, from Vulgar Latin *acceptāre* (unattested); ultimately related to Latin *acceptāre* to ACCEPT]

catfall (ˈkætˌfɔːl) *n nautical* the line used in a cat

catfight (ˈkætˌfaɪt) *n informal* a fight between two women

catfish (ˈkætˌfɪʃ) *n, pl* **-fish** or **-fishes 1** any of numerous mainly freshwater teleost fishes having whisker-like barbels around the mouth, esp the silurids of Europe and Asia and the horned pouts of North America **2** another name for **wolffish**

cat flu *n vet science* an upper respiratory-tract infection in cats, resulting in sneezing, ocular and nasal discharges, and coughs

catgut (ˈkætˌgʌt) *n* a strong cord made from the dried intestines of sheep and other animals that is used for stringing certain musical instruments and sports rackets, and, when sterilized, as surgical ligatures. Often shortened to: **gut**

cath- *prefix* a variant of **cata-** before an aspirate: *cathode*

Cathar (ˈkæθə) or **Catharist** (ˈkæθərɪst) *n, pl* **-ars, -ari** (-ərɪ) or **-arists** a member of a Christian sect in Provence in the 12th and 13th centuries who believed the material world was evil and only the spiritual was good [from Medieval Latin *Cathari*, from Greek *katharoi* the pure] > ˈCatharˌism *n*

catharsis (kəˈθɑːsɪs) *n, pl* **-ses 1** (in Aristotelian literary criticism) the purging or purification of the emotions through the evocation of pity and fear, as in tragedy **2** *psychoanal* the bringing of repressed ideas or experiences into consciousness, thus relieving tensions. See also **abreaction 3** purgation, esp of the bowels [c19 New Latin, from Greek *katharsis*, from *kathairein* to purge, purify]

cathartic (kəˈθɑːtɪk) *adj* **1** purgative **2** effecting catharsis ▷ *n* **3** a purgative drug or agent > caˈthartically *adv*

Cathay (kæˈθeɪ) *n* a literary or archaic name for **China** [c14 from Medieval Latin *Cataya*, of Turkic origin]

cathead (ˈkætˌhed) *n* a fitting at the bow of a vessel for securing the anchor when raised

cathectic (kəˈθɛktɪk) *adj* of or relating to cathexis

cathedra (kəˈθiːdrə) *n* **1** a bishop's throne **2** the office or rank of a bishop **3** See **ex cathedra** [from Latin: chair]

cathedral (kəˈθiːdrəl) *n* **a** the principal church of a diocese, containing the bishop's official throne **b** (*as modifier*): *a cathedral city; cathedral clergy* [c13 from Late Latin (*ecclesia*) *cathedrālis* cathedral (church), from *cathedra* bishop's throne, from Greek *kathedra* seat]

cathepsin (kəˈθɛpsɪn) *n* a proteolytic enzyme responsible for the autolysis of cells after death [c20 from Greek *kathepsein* to boil down, soften]

Catherine wheel *n* **1** Also called: **pinwheel** a type of firework consisting of a powder-filled spiral tube, mounted with a pin through its centre. When lit it rotates quickly, producing a display of sparks and coloured flame **2** a circular window having ribs radiating from the centre [c16 named after St Catherine of Alexandria (died 307 AD), legendary Christian martyr who was tortured on a spiked wheel and beheaded]

catheter (ˈkæθɪtə) *n med* a long slender flexible tube for inserting into a natural bodily cavity or passage for introducing or withdrawing fluid, such as urine or blood [c17 from Late Latin, from

Greek *kathetēr*, from *kathienai* to send down, insert]

catheterize or **catheterise** (ˈkæθɪtəˌraɪz) *vb* (*tr*) to insert a catheter into > ˌcatheteriˈzation or ˌcatheteriˈsation *n*

cathexis (kəˈθɛksɪs) *n, pl* **-thexes** (-ˈθɛksiːz) *psychoanal* concentration of psychic energy on a single goal [c20 from New Latin, from Greek *kathexis*, from *katekhein* to hold fast, intended to render German *Besetzung* a taking possession of]

Catho (ˈkæθəʊ) *n, pl* **Cathos** *Austral slang* a member of the Catholic Church

cathode (ˈkæθəʊd) *n* **1** the negative electrode in an electrolytic cell; the electrode by which electrons enter a device from an external circuit **2** the negatively charged electron source in an electronic valve **3** the positive terminal of a primary cell ▷ Compare **anode** [c19 from Greek *kathodos* a descent, from *kata-* down + *hodos* way] > **cathodal** (kæˈθəʊdªl), **cathodic** (kæˈθɒdɪk, -ˈθəʊ-) or **caˈthodical** *adj*

cathode rays *pl n* a stream of electrons emitted from the surface of a cathode in a valve

cathode-ray tube *n* a valve in which a beam of high-energy electrons is focused onto a fluorescent screen to give a visible spot of light. The device, with appropriate deflection equipment, is used in television receivers, visual display units, oscilloscopes, etc. Abbreviation: CRT

cathodic protection *n metallurgy* a technique for protecting metal structures, such as steel ships and pipelines, from electrolytic corrosion by making the structure the cathode in a cell, either by applying an electromotive force directly or by putting it into contact with a more electropositive metal. See also **sacrificial anode**

cathodoluminescence (ˌkæθədəʊˌluːmɪˈnɛsəns) *n physics* luminescence caused by irradiation with electrons (cathode rays)

cat hole *n* one of a pair of holes in the after part of a ship through which hawsers are passed for steadying the ship or heaving astern

catholic (ˈkæθəlɪk, ˈkæθlɪk) *adj* **1** universal; relating to all men; all-inclusive **2** comprehensive in interests, tastes, etc; broad-minded; liberal [c14 from Latin *catholicus*, from Greek *katholikos* universal, from *katholou* in general, from *kata-* according to + *holos* whole] > **catholically** or **catholicly** (kəˈθɒlɪklɪ) *adv*

Catholic (ˈkæθəlɪk, ˈkæθlɪk) *adj Christianity* **1** denoting or relating to the entire body of Christians, esp to the Church before separation into the Greek or Eastern and Latin or Western Churches **2** denoting or relating to the Latin or Western Church after this separation **3** denoting or relating to the Roman Catholic Church **4** denoting or relating to any church, belief, or sect, that claims continuity with or originates in the ancient undivided Church ▷ *n* **5** a member of any of the Churches regarded as Catholic, esp the Roman Catholic Church

Catholic Church *n* **1** short for **Roman Catholic Church 2** any of several Churches claiming to have maintained continuity with the ancient and undivided Church

Catholic Epistles *pl n New Testament* the epistles of James, I and II Peter, I John, and Jude, which were addressed to the universal Church rather than to an individual or a particular church

Catholicism (kəˈθɒlɪˌsɪzəm) *n* **1** short for **Roman Catholicism 2** the beliefs, practices, etc, of any Catholic Church

catholicity (ˌkæθəˈlɪsɪtɪ) *n* **1** a wide range of interests, tastes, etc; liberality **2** universality; comprehensiveness

Catholicity (ˌkæθəˈlɪsɪtɪ) *n* the beliefs, etc, of the Catholic Church

catholicize or **catholicise** (kəˈθɒlɪˌsaɪz) *vb* **1** to make or become catholic **2** (*often capital*) to convert to or become converted to Catholicism > caˌtholiciˈzation or caˌtholiciˈsation *n*

catholicon (kəˈθɒlɪkən) *n* a remedy for all ills; panacea [c15 from Medieval Latin; see CATHOLIC]

C

Catholicos (kəˈθɒlɪkɒs) *n* the patriarch of the Armenian Church [c17 from Greek *katholikos*; see CATHOLIC]

cathouse (ˈkætˌhaʊs) *n US and Canadian* a slang word for **brothel**

cation (ˈkætaɪən) *n* a positively charged ion; an ion that is attracted to the cathode during electrolysis. Compare **anion** [c19 from CATA- + ION] > **cationic** (ˌkætaɪˈɒnɪk) *adj*

cationic detergent *n* a type of detergent in which the active part of the molecule is a positive ion (cation). Cationic detergents are usually quaternary ammonium salts and often also have bactericidal properties

catkin (ˈkætkɪn) *n* an inflorescence consisting of a spike, usually hanging, of much reduced flowers of either sex: occurs in birch, hazel, etc. Also called: **ament** [c16 from obsolete Dutch *katteken* kitten, identical in meaning with French *chaton*, German *Kätzchen*]

catling (ˈkætlɪŋ) *n* **1** a long double-edged surgical knife for amputations **2** *rare* catgut or a string made from it **3** an archaic word for **kitten** [c17 from CAT¹ + -LING¹]

cat litter *n* absorbent material, often in a granular form, that is used to line a receptacle in which a domestic cat can urinate and defecate indoors

catmint (ˈkætˌmɪnt) *n* a Eurasian plant, *Nepeta cataria*, having spikes of purple-spotted white flowers and scented leaves of which cats are fond: family *Lamiaeae* (labiates). Also called: **catnip**

catnap (ˈkætˌnæp) *n* **1** a short sleep or doze ▷ *vb* -naps, -napping, -napped **2** (*intr*) to sleep or doze for a short time or intermittently

catnip (ˈkætˌnɪp) *n* another name for **catmint**

catolyte (ˈkætəʊˌlaɪt) or **catholyte** (ˈkæθəʊˌlaɪt) *n electronics* the part of the electrolyte that surrounds the cathode in an electrolytic cell

cat-o'-mountain *n* another name for **catamount**

cat-o'-nine-tails *n*, *pl* -tails a rope whip consisting of nine knotted thongs, used formerly to flog prisoners. Often shortened to: **cat**

catoptrics (kəˈtɒptrɪks) *n* (*functioning as singular*) the branch of optics concerned with reflection, esp the formation of images by mirrors [c18 from Greek *katoptrikos*, from *katoptron* mirror] > **ca'toptric** or **ca'toptrical** *adj*

cat rig *n* the rig of a catboat > **'cat,rigged** *adj*

CATS (kæts) *n acronym for* credit accumulation transfer scheme: a scheme enabling school-leavers and others to acquire transferable certificates for relevant work experience and study towards a recognized qualification

CAT scanner (kæt) *n* former name for **CT scanner** [c20 (C)*omputerized* (A)*xial* (T)*omography*]

cat's cradle *n* a game played by making intricate patterns with a loop of string between the fingers

cat-scratch fever *n* a disease of humans caused by an organism, *Bartonella henselae*, usually resulting from a scratch by a cat and characterized by lymph node enlargement

cat's-ear *n* any of various European plants of the genus *Hypochoeris*, esp *H. radicata*, having dandelion-like heads of yellow flowers: family *Asteraceae* (composites)

Catseye (ˈkætsˌaɪ) *n trademark Brit* a glass reflector set into a small fixture, placed at intervals along roads to indicate traffic lanes at night

cat's-eye *n* **1** any of a group of gemstones, esp a greenish-yellow variety of chrysoberyl, that reflect a streak of light when cut in a rounded unfaceted shape **2** Also called: **ataata** a grazing marine gastropod, *Turbo smaragdus*, of New Zealand waters

cat's-foot *n*, *pl* -feet a European plant, *Antennaria dioica*, with whitish woolly leaves and heads of typically white flowers: family *Asteraceae* (composites). Also called: **mountain everlasting**

Catskill Mountains (ˈkætskɪl) *pl n* a mountain range in SE New York State: resort. Highest peak:

Slide Mountain, 1261 m (4204 ft). Also called: **Catskills**

cat's-paw *n* **1** a person used by another as a tool; dupe **2** *nautical* a hitch in the form of two loops, or eyes, in the bight of a line, used for attaching it to a hook **3** a pattern of ripples on the surface of water caused by a light wind [(sense 1) c18 so called from the tale of the monkey who used a cat's paw to draw chestnuts out of a fire]

cat's-tail *n* **1** another name for **reed mace** (sense 1) **2** another name for **catkin**

CAT standard *n* (in Britain) a standard accepted voluntarily by building societies relating to charges, access, etc, against which Individual Savings Accounts can be judged [c20 C(*harges*) A(*ccess*) T(*erms*)]

catsuit (ˈkætˌsuːt) *n* a one-piece usually close-fitting trouser suit

catsup (ˈkætsəp) *n* a variant (esp US) of **ketchup**

cat's whisker *n* **1** a pointed wire used to make contact with the crystal in a crystal radio receiver **2** any wire used to make contact with a semiconductor

cat's whiskers or **cat's pyjamas** *n* the *slang* a person or thing that is excellent or superior

cattalo or **catalo** (ˈkætəˌləʊ) *n*, *pl* -loes or -los a hardy breed of cattle developed by crossing the American bison with domestic cattle [c20 from CATT(LE + BUFF)ALO]

Cattegat (ˈkætɪˌɡæt) *n* a former spelling of **Kattegat**

Catterick (ˈkætərɪk) *n* a village in N England, in North Yorkshire on the River Swale: site of an important army garrison and a racecourse

cattery (ˈkætərɪ) *n*, *pl* -teries a place where cats are bred or looked after

cattle (ˈkætʰl) *n* (*functioning as plural*) **1** bovid mammals of the tribe *Bovini* (bovines), esp those of the genus *Bos* **2** Also called: **domestic cattle** any domesticated bovine mammals, esp those of the species *Bos taurus* (domestic ox) ▷ Related adjective: **bovine** [c13 from Old Northern French *catel*, Old French *chatel* CHATTEL]

cattle-cake *n* concentrated food for cattle in the form of cakes

cattle dog *n Austral informal* a catalogue [supposedly imitative of CATALOGUE]

cattle-grid *n* a grid of metal bars covering a hollow or hole dug in a roadway, intended to prevent the passage of livestock while allowing vehicles, etc, to pass unhindered

cattleman (ˈkætʰlmən) *n*, *pl* -men **1** a person who breeds, rears, or tends cattle **2** *chiefly US and Canadian* a person who owns or rears cattle on a large scale, usually for beef, esp the owner of a cattle ranch

cattle market *n Brit slang* a situation or place, such as a beauty contest or nightclub, in which women are felt to be, or feel themselves to be, on display and judged solely by their appearance

cattle plague *n* another name for **rinderpest**

cattle prod *n* a hand-held electrified rod with low voltage used to control cattle

cattle-stop *n NZ* a grid of metal bars covering a hollow or hole dug in a roadway, intended to prevent the passage of livestock while allowing vehicles, etc, to pass unhindered. Also called (in Britain and other countries): **cattle-grid**

cattle truck *n* a railway wagon designed for carrying livestock. US and Canadian equivalent: **stock car**

cattleya (ˈkætlɪə) *n* any tropical American orchid of the genus *Cattleya*, cultivated for their purplish-pink or white showy flowers [c19 New Latin, named after William *Cattley* (died 1832), English botanist]

cat-train or **cat-swing** *n Canadian* a train of sleds, cabooses, etc, pulled by a caterpillar tractor, used chiefly in the north during winter to transport freight

catty¹ (ˈkætɪ) or **cattish** *adj* -tier, -tiest **1** *informal* spiteful: *a catty remark* **2** of or resembling a cat

> **'cattily** or **'cattishly** *adv* > **'cattiness** or **'cattishness** *n*

catty² or **cattie** (ˈkætɪ) *n*, *pl* -ties a unit of weight, used esp in China, equal to about one and a half pounds or about 0.67 kilogram [c16 from Malay *kati*]

catty-cornered *adj* a variant of **cater-cornered**

CATV *abbreviation for* community antenna television

catwalk (ˈkætˌwɔːk) *n* **1** a narrow ramp extending from the stage into the audience in a theatre, nightclub, etc, esp as used by models in a fashion show **2** a narrow pathway over the stage of a theatre, along a bridge, etc

catworm (ˈkætˌwɜːm) *n* an active carnivorous polychaete worm, *Nephthys hombergi*, that is about 10cm (4in) long, having a pearly sheen to its body: often dug for bait. Also called: **white worm**, **white cat**

Cauca (*Spanish* ˈkauka) *n* a river in W Colombia, rising in the northwest and flowing north to the Magdalena River. Length: about 1350 km (840 miles)

Caucasia (kɔːˈkeɪzɪə, -ʒə) *n* a region in SW Russia, Georgia, Armenia, and Azerbaijan, between the Caspian Sea and the Black Sea: contains the Caucasus Mountains, dividing it into Ciscaucasia in the north and Transcaucasia in the south; one of the most complex ethnic areas in the world, with over 50 different peoples. Also called: **the Caucasus**

Caucasian (kɔːˈkeɪzɪən, -ʒən) or **Caucasic** (kɔːˈkeɪzɪk) *adj* **1** another word for **Caucasoid 2** of or relating to the Caucasus ▷ *n* **3** a member of the Caucasoid race; a white man **4** a native or inhabitant of Caucasia **5** any of three possibly related families of languages spoken in the Caucasus: **North-West Caucasian,** including Circassian and Abkhaz, **North-East Caucasian,** including Avar, and **South Caucasian** including Georgian

Caucasoid (ˈkɔːkəˌzɔɪd) *adj* **1** denoting, relating to, or belonging to the light-complexioned racial group of mankind, which includes the peoples indigenous to Europe, N Africa, SW Asia, and the Indian subcontinent and their descendants in other parts of the world ▷ *n* **2** a member of this racial group

Caucasus (ˈkɔːkəsəs) *n* the **1** a mountain range in SW Russia, running along the N borders of Georgia and Azerbaijan, between the Black Sea and the Caspian Sea: mostly over 2700 m (9000 ft). Highest peak: Mount Elbrus, 5642 m (18 510 ft). Also called: **Caucasus Mountains 2** another name for **Caucasia**

caucus (ˈkɔːkəs) *n*, *pl* -cuses **1** *chiefly US and Canadian* **a** a closed meeting of the members of one party in a legislative chamber, etc, to coordinate policy, choose candidates, etc **b** such a bloc of politicians: *the Democratic caucus in Congress* **2** *chiefly US* **a** a group of leading politicians of one party **b** a meeting of such a group **3** *chiefly US* a local meeting of party members **4** *Brit* a group or faction within a larger group, esp a political party, who discuss tactics, choose candidates, etc **5** *Austral* a meeting of the members of the Federal parliamentary Labor Party **6** *NZ* a formal meeting of all Members of Parliament belonging to one political party ▷ *vb* **7** (*intr*) to hold a caucus [c18 probably of Algonquian origin; related to *caucauasu* adviser]

cauda (ˈkɔːdə) *n* **1** *zoology* the area behind the anus of an animal; tail **2** *anatomy* **a** any tail-like structure **b** the posterior part of an organ [Latin: tail]

caudad (ˈkɔːdæd) *adv anatomy* towards the tail or posterior part. Compare **cephalad** [c19 from CAUDA + -AD²]

caudal (ˈkɔːdᵊl) *adj* **1** *anatomy* of or towards the posterior part of the body **2** *zoology* relating to, resembling, or in the position of the tail [c17 from New Latin *caudālis*, from CAUDA] > **'caudally** *adv*

caudal fin *n* the tail fin of fishes and some other aquatic vertebrates, used for propulsion during locomotion

caudate ('kɔːdeɪt) *or* **caudated** *adj* having a tail or a tail-like appendage [c17 from New Latin *caudātus*, from CAUDA] > cau'dation *n*

caudex ('kɔːdɛks) *n, pl* -dices (-dɪˌsiːz) *or* -dexes **1** the thickened persistent stem base of some herbaceous perennial plants **2** the woody stem of palms and tree ferns [c19 from Latin]

caudillo (kɔːˈdiːljəʊ; *Spanish* kauˈðiʎo) *n, pl* -los (-jəʊz; *Spanish* -ʎos) (in Spanish-speaking countries) a military or political leader [Spanish, from Late Latin *capitellum*, diminutive of Latin *caput* head]

Caudine Forks ('kɔːdaɪn) *pl n* a narrow pass in the Apennines, in S Italy, between Capua and Benevento: scene of the defeat of the Romans by the Samnites (321 BC)

caudle ('kɔːdᵊl) *n* a hot spiced wine drink made with gruel, formerly used medicinally [c13 from Old Northern French *caudel*, from Medieval Latin *caldellum*, from Latin *calidus* warm]

caught (kɔːt) *vb* the past tense and past participle of **catch**

caul (kɔːl) *n anatomy* **1** a portion of the amniotic sac sometimes covering a child's head at birth **2** a large fold of peritoneum hanging from the stomach across the intestines; the large omentum [c13 from Old French *cale*, back formation from *calotte* close-fitting cap, of Germanic origin]

cauld (kɔːld) *adj, n* a Scot word for **cold**

cauldrife ('kɔːldrɪf) *adj Scot* **1** susceptible to cold; chilly **2** lifeless [c18 from CAULD + RIFE]

cauldron *or* **caldron** ('kɔːldrən) *n* a large pot used for boiling, esp one with handles [c13 from earlier *cauderon*, from Anglo-French, from Latin *caldārium* hot bath, from *calidus* warm]

caulescent (kɔːˈlɛsᵊnt) *adj* having a stem clearly visible above the ground [c18 from Latin *caulis* stalk]

caulicle ('kɔːlɪkᵊl) *n botany* a small stalk or stem [c17 from Latin *cauliculus*, from *caulis* stem]

cauliflory ('kɔːlɪˌflɔːrɪ) *n botany* the production of flowers on the trunk, branches, etc, of a woody plant, as opposed to the ends of the twigs [c20 from Latin *caulis* stem + -*flory*, from *flōs* flower] > ˌcauli'florous *adj*

cauliflower ('kɒlɪˌflaʊə) *n* **1** a variety of cabbage, *Brassica oleracea botrytis*, having a large edible head of crowded white flowers on a very short thick stem **2** the flower head of this plant, used as a vegetable [c16 from Italian *caoli fiori*, literally: cabbage flowers, from *cavolo* cabbage (from Latin *caulis*) + *fiore* flower (from Latin *flōs*)]

cauliflower cheese *n* a dish of cauliflower with a cheese sauce, eaten hot

cauliflower ear *n* permanent swelling and distortion of the external ear as the result of ruptures of the blood vessels: usually caused by blows received in boxing. Also called: **boxer's ear** Technical name: **aural haematoma**

cauline ('kɔːlɪn, -laɪn) *adj* relating to or growing from a plant stem [c18 from New Latin *caulīnus*, from Latin *caulis* stem]

caulis ('kɔːlɪs) *n, pl* -les (-liːz) *rare* the main stem of a plant [c16 from Latin]

caulk *or* **calk** (kɔːk) *vb* **1** to stop up (cracks, crevices, etc) with a filler **2** *nautical* to pack (the seams) between the planks of the bottom of (a vessel) with waterproof material to prevent leakage [c15 from Old Northern French *cauquer* to press down, from Latin *calcāre* to trample, from *calx* heel] > 'caulker *or* 'calker *n*

causal ('kɔːzᵊl) *adj* **1** acting as or being a cause **2** stating, involving, or implying a cause: *the causal part of the argument* **3** *philosophy* (of a theory) explaining a phenomenon or analysing a concept in terms of some causal relation > 'causally *adv*

causalgia (kɔːˈzældʒɪə) *n pathol* a burning sensation along the course of a peripheral nerve

together with local changes in the appearance of the skin [c19 from New Latin, from Greek *kausos* fever + -ALGIA]

causality (kɔːˈzælɪtɪ) *n, pl* -ties **1 a** the relationship of cause and effect **b** the principle that nothing can happen without being caused **2** causal agency or quality

causation (kɔːˈzeɪʃən) *n* **1** the act or fact of causing; the production of an effect by a cause **2** the relationship of cause and effect > cau'sational *adj*

causative ('kɔːzətɪv) *adj* **1** *grammar* relating to a form or class of verbs, such as *persuade*, that express causation **2** (*often postpositive and foll by of*) producing an effect ▷ *n* **3** the causative form or class of verbs > 'causatively *adv* > 'causativeness *n*

cause (kɔːz) *n* **1** a person, thing, event, state, or action that produces an effect **2** grounds for action; motive; justification: *she had good cause to shout like that* **3** the ideals, etc, of a group or movement: *the Communist cause* **4** the welfare or interests of a person or group in a dispute: *they fought for the miners' cause* **5** a matter of widespread concern or importance: *the cause of public health* **6 a** a ground for legal action; matter giving rise to a lawsuit **b** the lawsuit itself **7** (in the philosophy of Aristotle) any of four requirements for a thing's coming to be, namely material (material cause), its nature (formal cause), an agent (efficient cause), and a purpose (final cause) **8 make common cause with** to join with (a person, group, etc) for a common objective ▷ *vb* **9** (*tr*) to be the cause of; bring about; precipitate; be the reason for [c13 from Latin *causa* cause, reason, motive] > 'causable *adj* > ˌcausa'bility *n* > 'causeless *adj* > 'causer *n*

cause célèbre ('kɔːz səˈlɛbrə, -ˈlɛb; *French* koz selɛbrə) *n, pl* **causes célèbres** ('kɔːz səˈlɛbrəz, -ˈlɛb, 'kɔːzɪz səˈlɛbrə, -ˈlɛbz; *French* koz selɛbrə) a famous lawsuit, trial, or controversy [c19 from French: famous case]

cause list *n Brit* a list of cases awaiting a hearing

causerie ('kəʊzərɪ; *French* kozri) *n* an informal talk or conversational piece of writing [c19 from French, from *causer* to chat]

causeway ('kɔːzˌweɪ) *n* **1** a raised path or road crossing water, marshland, sand, etc **2** a paved footpath **3** a road surfaced with setts [c15 *cauciwey* (from *cauci* + WAY); *cauci* paved road, from Medieval Latin (*via*) *calciāta, calciātus* paved with limestone, from Latin *calx* limestone]

causey ('kɔːzɪ) *n* **1** an archaic or dialect word for **causeway 2** *Scot* a cobbled street **3** *Scot* a cobblestone

caustic ('kɔːstɪk) *adj* **1** capable of burning or corroding by chemical action: *caustic soda* **2** sarcastic; cutting: *a caustic reply* **3** of, relating to, or denoting light that is reflected or refracted by a curved surface ▷ *n* **4** Also called: **caustic surface** a surface that envelopes the light rays reflected or refracted by a curved surface **5** Also called: **caustic curve** a curve formed by the intersection of a caustic surface with a plane **6** *chem* a caustic substance, esp an alkali [c14 from Latin *causticus*, from Greek *kaustikos*, from *kaiein* to burn] > 'caustical *adj* > 'caustically *adv* > 'causticness *or* causticity (kɔːˈstɪsɪtɪ) *n*

caustic potash *n* another name for **potassium hydroxide**

caustic soda *n* another name for **sodium hydroxide**

cauterant ('kɔːtərənt) *adj* **1** caustic; cauterizing ▷ *n* **2** another name for **cautery** (sense 2)

cauterize *or* **cauterise** ('kɔːtəˌraɪz) *vb* (*tr*) (esp in the treatment of a wound) to burn or sear (body tissue) with a hot iron or caustic agent [c14 from Old French *cauteriser*, from Late Latin *cautērizāre*, from *cautērium* branding iron, from Greek *kautērion*, from *kaiein* to burn] > ˌcauteri'zation *or* ˌcauteri'sation *n*

cautery ('kɔːtərɪ) *n, pl* -teries **1** the coagulation of blood or destruction of body tissue by cauterizing

2 Also called: **cauterant** an instrument or chemical agent for cauterizing [c14 from Old French *cautère*, from Latin *cautērium*; see CAUTERIZE]

caution ('kɔːʃən) *n* **1** care, forethought, or prudence, esp in the face of danger; wariness **2** something intended or serving as a warning; admonition **3** *law, chiefly Brit* a formal warning given to a person suspected or accused of an offence that his words will be taken down and may be used in evidence **4** a notice entered on the register of title to land that prevents a proprietor from disposing of his or her land without a notice to the person who entered the caution **5** *informal* an amusing or surprising person or thing: *she's a real caution* ▷ *vb* **6** (*tr*) to urge or warn (a person) to be careful **7** (*tr*) *law, chiefly Brit* to give a caution to (a person) **8** (*intr*) to warn, urge, or advise: *he cautioned against optimism* [c13 from Old French, from Latin *cautiō*, from *cavēre* to beware] > 'cautioner *n*

cautionary ('kɔːʃənərɪ) *adj* serving as a warning; intended to warn: *a cautionary tale*

caution money *n chiefly Brit* a sum of money deposited as security for good conduct, against possible debts, etc

cautious ('kɔːʃəs) *adj* showing or having caution; wary; prudent > 'cautiously *adv* > 'cautiousness *n*

Cauvery *or* **Kaveri** ('kɔːvərɪ) *n* a river in S India, rising in the Western Ghats and flowing southeast to the Bay of Bengal. Length: 765 km (475 miles)

CAV *or* **Cur. adv. vult** *law abbreviation for* Curia advisari vult: used in English law to indicate that a court has decided to consider a case privately before giving judgment, as when time is needed to consider arguments or submissions made to it. Compare **avizandum** [Medieval Latin: the court wishes to consider]

cava ('kɑːvə) *n* a Spanish sparkling wine produced by a method similar to that used for champagne [from Spanish]

cavalcade (ˌkævəlˈkeɪd) *n* **1** a procession of people on horseback, in cars, etc **2** any procession: *a cavalcade of guests* [c16 from French, from Italian *cavalcata*, from *cavalcare* to ride on horseback, from Late Latin *caballicāre*, from *caballus* horse]

cavalier (ˌkævəˈlɪə) *adj* **1** showing haughty disregard; offhand ▷ *n* **2** a gallant or courtly gentleman, esp one acting as a lady's escort **3** *archaic* a horseman, esp one who is armed [c16 from Italian *cavaliere*, from Old Provençal *cavalier*, from Late Latin *caballārius* rider, from *caballus* horse, of obscure origin] > ˌcava'lierly *adv*

Cavalier (ˌkævəˈlɪə) *n* a supporter of Charles I during the English Civil War. Compare **Roundhead**

cavalier King Charles spaniel *n* See **King Charles spaniel**

Cavalier poets *pl n* a group of mid-17th-century English lyric poets, mostly courtiers of Charles I. Chief among them were Robert Herrick, Thomas Carew, Sir John Suckling, and Richard Lovelace

cavalla (kəˈvælə) *or* **cavally** *n, pl* -la, -las *or* -lies any of various tropical carangid fishes, such as *Gnathanodon speciosus* (golden cavalla) [c19 from Spanish *caballa*, from Late Latin, feminine of *caballus* horse]

cavalry ('kævəlrɪ) *n, pl* -ries **1** (esp formerly) the part of an army composed of mounted troops **2** the armoured element of a modern army **3** (*as modifier*): *a cavalry unit; a cavalry charge* [c16 from French *cavallerie*, from Italian *cavalleria*, from *cavaliere* horseman; see CAVALIER] > 'cavalryman *n*

cavalry twill *n* a strong woollen twill fabric used for trousers, etc

Cavan ('kævᵊn) *n* **1** a county of N Republic of Ireland: hilly, with many small lakes and bogs. County town: Cavan. Pop: 56 546 (2002). Area: 1890 sq km (730 sq miles) **2** a market town in N Republic of Ireland, county town of Co Cavan. Pop: 6098 (2002)

cavatina (ˌkævəˈtiːnə) *n, pl* -ne (-nɪ) **1** a solo song resembling a simple aria **2** an instrumental composition reminiscent of this [c19 from Italian]

cave¹ (keɪv) *n* **1** an underground hollow with access from the ground surface or from the sea, often found in limestone areas and on rocky coastlines **2** *Brit history* a secession or a group seceding from a political party on some issue. See **Adullamite 3** (*modifier*) living in caves ▷ *vb* **4** (*tr*) to hollow out ▷ See also **cave in, caving** [c13 from Old French, from Latin *cava*, plural of *cavum* cavity, from *cavus* hollow]

cave² ('keɪvɪ) *Brit school slang* ▷ *n* **1** guard or lookout (esp in the phrase **keep cave**) ▷ *sentence substitute* **2** watch out! [from Latin *cavē!* beware!]

caveat ('keɪvɪˌæt, 'kæv-) *n* **1** *law* a formal notice requesting the court or officer to refrain from taking some specified action without giving prior notice to the person lodging the caveat **2** a warning; caution [c16 from Latin, literally: let him beware]

caveat emptor ('ɛmptɔː) *n* the principle that the buyer must bear the risk for the quality of goods purchased unless they are covered by the seller's warranty [Latin: let the buyer beware]

caveator ('keɪvɪˌeɪtə, 'kæv-) *n law* a person who enters a caveat

cavefish ('keɪvˌfɪʃ) *n, pl* -fish *or* -fishes any of various small freshwater cyprinodont fishes of the genera *Amblyopsis, Chologaster,* etc, living in subterranean and other waters in S North America. See also **blindfish**

cave in *vb* (*intr, adverb*) **1** to collapse; subside **2** *informal* to yield completely, esp under pressure ▷ *n* **cave-in 3** the sudden collapse of a roof, piece of ground, etc, into a hollow beneath it; subsidence **4** the site of such a collapse, as at a mine or tunnel **5** *informal* an instance of yielding completely, esp under pressure

cavel ('keɪvᵊl) *n* NZ a drawing of lots among miners for an easy and profitable place at the coalface [c19 from English dialect *cavel* to cast lots, apportion]

caveman ('keɪvˌmæn) *n, pl* -men **1** a man of the Palaeolithic age; cave dweller **2** *informal and facetious* a man who is primitive or brutal in behaviour, etc

cavendish ('kævəndɪʃ) *n* tobacco that has been sweetened and pressed into moulds to form bars [c19 perhaps from the name of the first maker]

cavern ('kævᵊn) *n* **1** a cave, esp when large and formed by underground water, or a large chamber in a cave ▷ *vb* (*tr*) **2** to shut in or as if in a cavern **3** to hollow out [c14 from Old French *caverne*, from Latin *caverna*, from *cavus* hollow; see CAVE¹]

cavernous ('kævənəs) *adj* **1** suggestive of a cavern in vastness, darkness, etc: *cavernous hungry eyes* **2** filled with small cavities; porous **3** (of rocks) containing caverns or cavities > '**cavernously** *adv*

cavesson ('kævɪsən) *n* a kind of hard noseband, used (esp formerly) in breaking a horse in [c16 via French from Italian *cavezzone*, from *cavezza* halter, ultimately related to Latin *caput* head]

cavetto (kə'vɛtəʊ; *Italian* ka'vetto) *n, pl* -ti (-tɪ; *Italian* -ti) *architect* a concave moulding, shaped to a quarter circle in cross section [c17 from Italian, from *cavo* hollow, from Latin *cavus*]

cave tubing *n* NZ another name for **blackwater rafting**

caviar *or* **caviare** ('kævɪˌɑː, ˌkævɪ'ɑː) *n* the salted roe of sturgeon, esp the beluga, usually served as an hors d'oeuvre [c16 from earlier *cavery*, from Old Italian *caviari*, plural of *caviaro* caviar, from Turkish *havyār*]

CAVIAR ('kævɪˌɑː) *n acronym for* Cinema and Video Industry Audience Research

cavicorn ('kævɪˌkɔːn) *adj* (of sheep, goats, etc) having hollow horns as distinct from the solid antlers of deer [c19 from Latin *cavus* hollow + *cornū* horn]

cavie ('keɪvɪ) *n Scot* a hen coop [c18 via Dutch or Flemish *kavie*, from Latin *cavea* cavity]

cavil ('kævɪl) *vb* -ils, -illing, -illed *or US* -ils, -iling,

-iled **1** (*intr*; foll by *at* or *about*) to raise annoying petty objections; quibble; carp ▷ *n* **2** a captious trifling objection [c16 from Old French *caviller,* from Latin *cavillārī* to jeer, from *cavilla* raillery] > '**caviller** *adj*

caving ('keɪvɪŋ) *n* the sport of climbing in and exploring caves > '**caver** *n*

cavitation (ˌkævɪ'teɪʃən) *n* **1** the formation of vapour- or gas-filled cavities in a flowing liquid when tensile stress is superimposed on the ambient pressure **2** the formation of cavities in a structure

Cavite (kə'viːtɪ, -teɪ) *n* a port in the N Philippines, in S Luzon on Manila Bay: a former US naval base. Pop: 109 000 (2005 est)

cavity ('kævɪtɪ) *n, pl* -ties **1** a hollow space; hole **2** *dentistry* a soft decayed area on a tooth. See **caries 3** any empty or hollow space within the body: *the oral cavity* **4** *electronics* See **cavity resonator** [c16 from French *cavité,* from Late Latin *cavitās,* from Latin *cavus* hollow]

cavity block *n* a precast concrete block that contains a cavity or cavities

cavity resonator *n electronics* a conducting surface enclosing a space in which an oscillating electromagnetic field can be maintained, the dimensions of the cavity determining the resonant frequency of the oscillations. It is used in microwave devices for frequencies exceeding 300 megahertz. Also called: **resonant cavity, rhumbatron**

cavity wall *n* a wall that consists of two separate walls, joined by wall-ties, with an airspace between them

cavolo nero ('kɑːvəˌləʊ 'nɛrəʊ) *n* an Italian variety of cabbage with dark green leaves [from Italian, black cabbage]

cavo-relievo *or* **cavo-rilievo** (ˌkɑːvəʊrɪ'liːvəʊ, ˌkeɪ-) *n, pl* -vos *or* -vi (-vɪ) a relief sculpture in which the highest point in the carving is below the level of the original surface [Italian, literally: hollow relief]

cavort (kə'vɔːt) *vb* (*intr*) to prance; caper [c19 perhaps from CURVET] > ca'**vorter** *n*

cavy ('keɪvɪ) *n, pl* -vies any small South American hystricomorph rodent of the family *Caviidae,* esp any of the genus *Cavia,* having a thickset body and very small tail. See also **guinea pig** [c18 from New Latin *Cavia,* from Galibi *cabiai*]

caw (kɔː) *n* **1** the cry of a crow, rook, or raven ▷ *vb* **2** (*intr*) to make this cry [c16 of imitative origin]

CAW *abbreviation for* Canadian Auto Workers (trade union)

Cawnpore (ˌkɔːn'pɔː) *or* **Cawnpur** (ˌkɔːn'pʊə) *n* the former name of **Kanpur**

Caxton ('kækstən) *n* **1** a book printed by William Caxton **2** a style of type, imitating the Gothic, that Caxton used in his books

cay (keɪ, kiː) *n* a small low island or bank composed of sand and coral fragments, esp in the Caribbean area. Also called: **key** [c18 from Spanish *cayo,* probably from Old French *quai* QUAY]

Cayenne (keɪ'ɛn) *n* the capital of French Guiana, on an island at the mouth of the Cayenne River: French penal settlement from 1854 to 1938. Pop: 50 594 (1999)

cayenne pepper (keɪ'ɛn) *n* a very hot condiment, bright red in colour, made from the dried seeds and pods of various capsicums. Often shortened to: **cayenne**. Also called: **red pepper** [c18 ultimately from Tupi *quiynha*]

Cayes (keɪ; *French* kaj) *n* short for **Les Cayes**

cayman *or* **caiman** ('keɪmən) *n, pl* -mans any tropical American crocodilian of the genus *Caiman* and related genera, similar to alligators but with a more heavily armoured belly: family *Alligatoridae* (alligators, etc) [c16 from Spanish *caiman,* from Carib *cayman,* probably of African origin]

Cayman Islands ('keɪmən) *pl n* three coral islands in the Caribbean Sea northwest of Jamaica: a dependency of Jamaica until 1962, now a UK Overseas Territory. Capital: Georgetown. Pop:

40 000 (2003 est). Area: about 260 sq km (100 sq miles)

Cayuga (keɪ'juːgə, kaɪ-) *n* (*pl* -gas *or* -ga) a member of a Native American people (one of the Iroquois peoples) formerly living around Cayuga Lake **2** the language of this people, belonging to the Iroquoian family

cayuse ('kaɪuːs) *n Western US and Canadian* a small Native American pony used by cowboys [c19 from a Chinookan language]

caz (kæz) *adj slang* short for **casual**

cb *abbreviation for* centre of buoyancy (of a boat, etc)

Cb *the chemical symbol for* columbium

CB *abbreviation for* **1** Citizens' Band **2** Companion of the (Order of the) Bath (an English title) **3** County Borough **4** (in Canada) Cape Breton Island

CBC *abbreviation for* Canadian Broadcasting Corporation

CBD *or* **cbd** *abbreviation for* **1** cash before delivery **2** central business district

CBE *abbreviation for* Commander of the (Order of the) British Empire

CBI *abbreviation for* Confederation of British Industry

CBR (of weapons or warfare) *abbreviation for* chemical, bacteriological, or radiological

CBRN (of weapons or warfare) *abbreviation for* chemical, bacteriological, radiological, or nuclear

CBS *abbreviation for* Columbia Broadcasting System

CBSO *abbreviation for* City of Birmingham Symphony Orchestra

CBT *abbreviation for* **1** computer-based training **2** Cognitive Behavioural Therapy

CBW *abbreviation for* chemical or biological weapon

cc¹ *or* **c.c.** *abbreviation for* **1** carbon copy *or* copies **2** South African close corporation **3** cubic centimetre(s)

cc² *the internet domain name for* Cocos Islands

CC *abbreviation for* **1** City Council **2** (in Britain) Competition Commission **3** County Council **4** Cricket Club **5** Companion of the Order of Canada

cc. *abbreviation for* chapters

CCANZ *abbreviation for* Council of Churches in Aotearoa/New Zealand

c.c.c. *abbreviation for* cwmni cyfyngedig cyhoeddus; a public limited company in Wales

CCD *electronics abbreviation for* **charge-coupled device**

CCEA *abbreviation for* Northern Ireland Council for the Curriculum, Examinations and Assessment

CCF (in Britain) *abbreviation for* Combined Cadet Force

CCJ (in England) *abbreviation for* county court judgment

C clef *n music* a symbol (𝄡), placed at the beginning of the staff, establishing middle C as being on its centre line. See **alto clef, soprano clef, tenor clef**

CCMA (in South Africa) *abbreviation for* Council for Conciliation, Mediation and Arbitration

CCRC *abbreviation for* Criminal Cases Review Commission: a British government body established in 1997 to investigate alleged miscarriages of justice

CCTA (in Britain) *abbreviation for* Central Computer and Telecommunications Agency

CCTV *abbreviation for* **closed-circuit television**

cd¹ *abbreviation for* **1** cash discount **2** *symbol for* candela

cd² *the internet domain name for* Democratic Republic of Congo

Cd 1 (in Britain) *abbreviation for* command (paper) **2** ▷ *the chemical symbol for* cadmium

CD *abbreviation for* **1** compact disc **2** Civil Defence (Corps) **3** Corps Diplomatique (Diplomatic Corps) **4** Conference on Disarmament: a United Nations standing conference, held in Geneva, to negotiate a global ban on chemical weapons **5** (in the US and Canada) certificate of deposit. Also **C.D.**

c/d *book-keeping abbreviation for* carried down

CDC *abbreviation for* **1** (in the US) Center for Disease

Control **2** Commonwealth Development Corporation

CDE *abbreviation for* compact disc erasable: a compact disc that can be used to record and rerecord. Compare **CDR**

cdf *statistics abbreviation for* cumulative distribution function

Cdn *abbreviation for* Canadian

CDN *international car registration for* Canada

cDNA *abbreviation for* complementary DNA; a form of DNA artificially synthesized from a messenger RNA template and used in genetic engineering to produce gene clones

CD player *n* a device for playing compact discs. In full: **compact-disc player**

Cdr *military abbreviation for* Commander

CDR *abbreviation for* compact disc recordable: a compact disc that can be used to record only once. Compare **CDE**

Cdre *abbreviation for* Commodore

CD-ROM (-'rɒm) *n* compact disc read-only memory; a compact disc used with a computer system as a read-only optical disk

CD-RW *n* compact disc rewritable; a compact disc that can be used to record and rerecord

CDT *abbreviation for* **1** US and Canadian Central Daylight Time **2** Craft, Design, and Technology: a subject on the GCSE syllabus, related to the National Curriculum

CDU *abbreviation for* Christlich-Demokratische Union: a German (until 1990 West German) political party [German: Christian Democratic Union]

CDV *abbreviation for* **1** CD-video **2** compact video disc

CD-video *n* a compact-disc player that, when connected to a television and hi-fi, produces high-quality stereo sound and synchronized pictures from a disc resembling a large compact audio disc. In full: **compact-disc video**

CD writer *n computing* a device on a computer for writing CDs

Ce *the chemical symbol for* cerium

CE *abbreviation for* **1** chief engineer **2** Church of England **3** civil engineer **4** Common Entrance **5** Common Era **6** Communauté Européenne (European Union)

ceanothus (ˌsiːə'nəʊθəs) *n* any shrub of the North American rhamnaceous genus *Ceanothus*: grown for their ornamental, often blue, flower clusters [c19 New Latin, from Greek *keanōthos* a kind of thistle]

Ceará (*Portuguese* siaˈra) *n* **1** a state of NE Brazil: sandy coastal plain, rising to a high plateau. Capital: Fortaleza. Pop: 7 654 535 (2002). Area: 150 630 sq km (58 746 sq miles) **2** another name for **Fortaleza**

cease (siːs) *vb* **1** (when *tr*, may take a gerund or an infinitive as object) to bring or come to an end; desist from; stop ▷ *n* **2** without cease without stopping; incessantly [c14 from Old French *cesser*, from Latin *cessāre*, frequentative of *cēdere* to yield, CEDE]

cease-fire *chiefly military* ▷ *n* **1** a period of truce, esp one that is temporary and a preliminary step to establishing a more permanent peace on agreed terms ▷ *interj* ▷ *n* **2** the order to stop firing

ceaseless ('siːslɪs) *adj* without stop or pause; incessant > 'ceaselessly *adv*

Cebu (sɪ'buː) *n* **1** an island in the central Philippines. Pop: 2 091 602 (latest est). Area: 4422 sq km (1707 sq miles) **2** a port in the Philippines, on E Cebu island. Pop: 796 000 (2005 est)

Čechy ('tʃɛxi) *n* the Czech name for **Bohemia**

cecity ('siːsɪtɪ) *n* a rare word for **blindness** [c16 from Latin *caecitās*, from *caecus* blind]

cecropia moth (sɪ'krəʊpɪə) *n* a large North American saturniid moth, *Hyalophora* (or *Samia*) *cecropia*, with brightly coloured wings and feathery antennae [c19 New Latin, from Latin *Cecropius* belonging to CECROPS]

Cecrops ('siːkrɒps) *n* (in ancient Greek tradition) the first king of Attica, represented as half-human, half-dragon

cecum ('siːkəm) *n*, *pl* **-ca** (-kə) US a variant spelling of **caecum**. > 'cecal *adj*

cedar ('siːdə) *n* **1** any Old World coniferous tree of the genus *Cedrus*, having spreading branches, needle-like evergreen leaves, and erect barrel-shaped cones: family Pinaceae. See also **cedar of Lebanon, deodar 2** any of various other conifers, such as the red cedars and white cedars **3** the wood of any of these trees **4** any of certain other plants, such as thr Spanish cedar ▷ *adj* **5** made of the wood of a cedar tree [c13 from Old French *cedre*, from Latin *cedrus*, from Greek *kedros*]

cedar of Lebanon *n* a cedar, *Cedrus libani*, of SW Asia with level spreading branches and fragrant wood

Cedar Rapids *n* a city in the US, in E Iowa. Pop: 122 542 (2003 est)

cede (siːd) *vb* **1** (when *intr*, often foll by *to*) to transfer, make over, or surrender (something, esp territory or legal rights): *the lands were ceded by treaty* **2** (*tr*) to allow or concede (a point in an argument, etc) [c17 from Latin *cēdere* to yield, give way] > 'ceder *n*

cedi ('seɪdɪ) *n*, *pl* **-di** the standard monetary unit of Ghana, divided into 100 pesewas

cedilla (sɪ'dɪlə) *n* a character (¸) placed underneath a *c* before *a*, *o*, or *u*, esp in French, Portuguese, or Catalan, denoting that it is to be pronounced (s), not (k). The same character is used in the scripts of other languages, as in Turkish under *s* [c16 from Spanish: little *z*, from *ceda* zed, from Late Latin *zeta*; a small *z* was originally written after *c* in Spanish, to indicate a sibilant]

Ceefax ('siːˌfæks) *n trademark* the BBC Teletext service. See **Teletext**

CEGB *Brit* ▷ *abbreviation for* (the former) Central Electricity Generating Board

ceiba ('seɪbə) *n* **1** any bombacaceous tropical tree of the genus *Ceiba*, such as the silk-cotton tree **2** silk cotton; kapok [c19 from New Latin, from Spanish, of Arawak origin]

ceil (siːl) *vb* (*tr*) **1** to line (a ceiling) with plaster, boarding, etc **2** to provide with a ceiling [c15 *celen*, perhaps back formation from CEILING]

ceilidh ('keɪlɪ) *n* (esp in Scotland and Ireland) an informal social gathering with folk music, singing, dancing, and storytelling [c19 from Gaelic]

ceiling ('siːlɪŋ) *n* **1** the inner upper surface of a room **2 a** an upper limit, such as one set by regulation on prices or wages **b** (*as modifier*): *ceiling prices* **3** the upper altitude to which an aircraft can climb measured under specified conditions. See also **service ceiling, absolute ceiling 4** *meteorol* the highest level in the atmosphere from which the earth's surface is visible at a particular time, usually the base of a cloud layer **5** a wooden or metal surface fixed to the interior frames of a vessel for rigidity [c14 of uncertain origin]

ceilometer (siː'lɒmɪtə) *n* a device for determining the cloud ceiling, esp by means of a reflected light beam [c20 from CEILING + -METER]

cel *or* **cell** (sɛl) *n* short for **celluloid** (senses 2b, 2c)

celadon ('sɛləˌdɒn) *n* **1** a type of porcelain having a greyish-green glaze: mainly Chinese **2** a pale greyish-green colour, sometimes somewhat yellow [c18 from French, from the name of the shepherd hero of *L'Astrée* (1610), a romance by Honoré d'Urfé]

Celaeno (sɛ'liːnəʊ) *n Greek myth* one of the Pleiades

celandine ('sɛlənˌdaɪn) *n* either of two unrelated plants, *Chelidonium majus* (see **greater celandine**) or *Ranunculus ficaria* (see **lesser celandine**) [c13 earlier *celydon*, from Latin *chelīdonia* (the plant), from *chelīdonius* of the swallow, from Greek *khelīdōn* swallow; the plant's season was believed to parallel the migration of swallows]

Celaya (*Spanish* θe'laja) *n* a city in central Mexico, in Guanajuato state: market town, famous for its sweetmeats; textile-manufacturing. Pop: 727 000 (2005 est)

-cele *n combining form* tumour or hernia: *hydrocele* [from Greek *kēlē* tumour]

celeb (sɪ'lɛb) *n informal* a celebrity

Celebes ('sɛlɪbiːz, sɛ'liːbɪz) *n* the English name for **Sulawesi**

Celebes Sea *n* the part of the Pacific Ocean between Sulawesi, Borneo, and Mindanao

celebrant ('sɛlɪbrənt) *n* **1** a person participating in a religious ceremony **2** *Christianity* an officiating priest, esp at the Eucharist

celebrate ('sɛlɪˌbreɪt) *vb* **1** to rejoice in or have special festivities to mark (a happy day, event, etc) **2** (*tr*) to observe (a birthday, anniversary, etc): *she celebrates her ninetieth birthday next month* **3** (*tr*) to perform (a solemn or religious ceremony), esp to officiate at (Mass) **4** (*tr*) to praise publicly; proclaim [c15 from Latin *celebrāre*, from *celeber* numerous, thronged, renowned] > ˌcele'bration *n* > 'celebrative *adj* > 'cele,brator *n* > 'cele,bratory *adj*

celebrated ('sɛlɪˌbreɪtɪd) *adj* (*usually prenominal*) famous: *a celebrated pianist; a celebrated trial*

celebrity (sɪ'lɛbrɪtɪ) *n*, *pl* **-ties 1** a famous person: *a show-business celebrity* **2** fame or notoriety

celeriac (sɪ'lɛrɪˌæk) *n* a variety of celery, *Apium graveolens rapaceum*, with a large turnip-like root, used as a vegetable [c18 from CELERY + -ac, of unexplained origin]

celerity (sɪ'lɛrɪtɪ) *n* rapidity; swiftness; speed [c15 from Old French *celerite*, from Latin *celeritās*, from *celer* swift]

celery ('sɛlərɪ) *n* **1** an umbelliferous Eurasian plant, *Apium graveolens dulce*, whose blanched leafstalks are used in salads or cooked as a vegetable. See also **celeriac 2 wild celery** a related and similar plant, *Apium graveolens* [c17 from French *céleri*, from Italian (Lombardy) dialect *selleri* (plural), from Greek *selinon* parsley]

celery pine *n* a New Zealand gymnosperm tree, *Phyllocladus trichomanoides*, with celerylike shoots and useful wood: family Phyllocladaceae

celesta (sɪ'lɛstə) *or* **celeste** (sɪ'lɛst) *n music* a keyboard percussion instrument consisting of a set of steel plates of graduated length that are struck with key-operated hammers. The tone is an ethereal tinkling sound. Range: four octaves upwards from middle C [c19 from French, Latinized variant of *céleste* heavenly]

celestial (sɪ'lɛstɪəl) *adj* **1** heavenly; divine; spiritual: *celestial peace* **2** of or relating to the sky: *celestial bodies* [c14 from Medieval Latin *cēlestiālis*, from Latin *caelestis*, from *caelum* heaven] > ce'lestially *adv*

Celestial Empire *n* an archaic or literary name for the **Chinese Empire**

celestial equator *n* the great circle lying on the celestial sphere the plane of which is perpendicular to the line joining the north and south celestial poles. Also called: **equinoctial, equinoctial circle**

celestial globe *n* a spherical model of the celestial sphere showing the relative positions of stars, constellations, etc

celestial guidance *n* the guidance of a spacecraft or missile by reference to the position of one or more celestial bodies

celestial horizon *n* See **horizon** (sense 2b)

celestial latitude *n* the angular distance of a celestial body north or south from the ecliptic. Also called: **ecliptic latitude**

celestial longitude *n* the angular distance measured eastwards from the vernal equinox to the intersection of the ecliptic with the great circle passing through a celestial body and the poles of the ecliptic. Also called: **ecliptic longitude**

celestial mechanics *n* the study of the motion of celestial bodies under the influence of gravitational fields

celestial navigation *n* navigation by observation

C

of the positions of the stars. Also called: astronavigation

celestial pole *n* either of the two points at which the earth's axis, extended to infinity, would intersect the celestial sphere. Sometimes shortened to: **pole**

celestial sphere *n* an imaginary sphere of infinitely large radius enclosing the universe so that all celestial bodies appear to be projected onto its surface

celestite ('sɛlɪˌstaɪt) *or* **celestine** ('sɛlɪstɪn, -ˌstaɪn) *n* a white, red, or blue mineral consisting of strontium sulphate in orthorhombic crystalline form: a source of strontium compounds. Formula: $SrSO_4$ [C19 from German *Zölestin*, from Latin *caelestis* CELESTIAL (referring to the blue colour) + -ITE[1]]

celiac ('siːlɪˌæk) *adj anatomy* the usual US spelling of **coeliac**

celibate ('sɛlɪbɪt) *n* **1** a person who is unmarried, esp one who has taken a religious vow of chastity ▷ *adj* **2** unmarried, esp by vow **3** abstaining from sexual intercourse [C17 from Latin *caelibātus*, from *caelebs* unmarried, of obscure origin] > **'celibacy** *n*

cell[1] (sɛl) *n* **1** a small simple room, as in a prison, convent, monastery, or asylum; cubicle **2** any small compartment: *the cells of a honeycomb* **3** *biology* the basic structural and functional unit of living organisms. It consists of a nucleus, containing the genetic material, surrounded by the cytoplasm in which are mitochondria, lysosomes, ribosomes, and other organelles. All cells are bounded by a cell membrane; plant cells have an outer cell wall in addition **4** *biology* any small cavity or area, such as the cavity containing pollen in an anther **5** a device for converting chemical energy into electrical energy, usually consisting of a container with two electrodes immersed in an electrolyte. See also **primary cell, secondary cell, dry cell, wet cell, fuel cell 6** short for **electrolytic cell 7** a small religious house dependent upon a larger one **8** a small group of persons operating as a nucleus of a larger political, religious, or other organization: *Communist cell* **9** *maths* a small unit of volume in a mathematical coordinate system **10** *zoology* one of the areas on an insect wing bounded by veins **11** the geographical area served by an individual transmitter in a cellular radio network [C12 from Medieval Latin *cella* monk's cell, from Latin: room, storeroom; related to Latin *cēlāre* to hide] > **'cell-ˌlike** *adj*

cell[2] (sɛl) *n* a variant spelling of **cel**

cella ('sɛlə) *n, pl* **-lae** (-liː) the inner room of a classical temple, esp the room housing the statue of a deity. Also called: **naos** [C17 from Latin: room, shrine; see CELL[1]]

cellar ('sɛlə) *n* **1** an underground room, rooms, or storey of a building, usually used for storage. Compare **basement 2** a place where wine is stored **3** a stock of bottled wines ▷ *vb* **4** (*tr*) to store in a cellar [C13 from Anglo-French, from Latin *cellārium* food store, from *cella* CELLA]

cellarage ('sɛlərɪdʒ) *n* **1** an area of a cellar **2** a charge for storing goods in a cellar, etc

cellar dwellers *pl n Austral slang* the team at the bottom of a sports league

cellarer ('sɛlərə) *n* a monastic official responsible for food, drink, etc

cellaret (ˌsɛlə'rɛt) *n* a case, cabinet, or sideboard with compartments for holding wine bottles

cell cycle *n* the growth cycle of eukaryotic cells. It is divided into five stages, known as G_0, in which the cell is quiescent, G_1 and G_2, in which it increases in size, S, in which it duplicates its DNA, and M, in which it undergoes mitosis and divides

cell division *n cytology* the division of a cell into two new cells during growth or reproduction. See **amitosis, meiosis, mitosis**

Celle (German 'tsɛlə) *n* a city in N Germany, on the Aller River in Lower Saxony: from 1378 to 1705 the

residence of the Dukes of Brunswick-Lüneburg. Pop: 71 319 (2003 est)

cellentani (ˌtʃɛlən'taːnɪ) *n* pasta in the form of corkscrews [Italian]

cell line *n biology* a clone of animal or plant cells that can be grown in a suitable nutrient culture medium in the laboratory

cell lineage *n biology* the developmental history of a tissue or part of an organism from particular cells in the fertilized egg or embryo through to their fully differentiated state

cell membrane *n* a very thin membrane, composed of lipids and protein, that surrounds the cytoplasm of a cell and controls the passage of substances into and out of the cell. Also called: plasmalemma, plasma membrane

cello ('tʃɛləʊ) *n, pl* **-los** *music* a bowed stringed instrument of the violin family. Range: more than four octaves upwards from C below the bass staff. It has four strings, is held between the knees, and has an extendible metal spike at the lower end, which acts as a support. Full name: violoncello > **'cellist** *n*

cellobiose (ˌsɛləʊ'baɪəʊz) *or* **cellose** ('sɛləʊz) *n* a disaccharide obtained by the hydrolysis of cellulose by cellulase. Formula: $C_{12}H_{22}O_{11}$ [C20 from CELLULOSE + BI-[1] + -OSE[2]]

celloidin (sə'lɔɪdɪn) *n* a nitrocellulose compound derived from pyroxylin, used in a solution of alcohol and ether for embedding specimens before cutting sections for microscopy [C20 from CELLULOSE + -OID + -IN]

Cellophane ('sɛləˌfeɪn) *n trademark* a flexible thin transparent sheeting made from wood pulp and used as a moisture-proof wrapping [C20 from CELLULOSE + -PHANE]

Cellosolve ('sɛləʊˌsɒlv) *n trademark* an organic compound used as a solvent in the plastics industry; 2-ethoxyethan-1-ol. Formula: $C_2H_5OCH_2CH_2OH$

cellphone ('sɛlˌfəʊn) *n* a portable telephone operated by cellular radio. In full: **cellular telephone**

cellular ('sɛljʊlə) *adj* **1** of, relating to, resembling, or composed of a cell or cells **2** having cells or small cavities; porous **3** divided into a network of cells **4** *textiles* woven with an open texture: *a cellular blanket* **5** designed for or involving cellular radio > **cellularity** (ˌsɛljʊ'lærɪtɪ) *n*

cellular radio *n* radio communication based on a network of transmitters each serving a small area known as a cell: used in personal communications systems in which the mobile receiver switches frequencies automatically as it passes from one cell to another

cellulase ('sɛljʊˌleɪz) *n* any enzyme that converts cellulose to the disaccharide cellobiose [C20 from CELLULOSE + -ASE]

cellule ('sɛljuːl) *n* a very small cell [C17 from Latin *cellula*, diminutive of *cella* CELL[1]]

cellulite ('sɛljʊˌlaɪt) *n* a name sometimes given to subcutaneous fat alleged to resist dieting [C20 from French, from *cellule* cell]

cellulitis (ˌsɛljʊ'laɪtɪs) *n* inflammation of any of the tissues of the body, characterized by fever, pain, swelling, and redness of the affected area [C19 from Latin *cellula* CELLULE + -ITIS]

celluloid ('sɛljʊˌlɔɪd) *n* **1** a flammable thermoplastic material consisting of cellulose nitrate mixed with a plasticizer, usually camphor: used in sheets, rods, and tubes for making a wide range of articles **2 a** a cellulose derivative used for coating film **b** one of the transparent sheets on which the constituent drawings of an animated film are prepared **c** a transparent sheet used as an overlay in artwork **d** cinema film

cellulose ('sɛljʊˌləʊz, -ˌləʊs) *n* a polysaccharide consisting of long unbranched chains of linked glucose units: the main constituent of plant cell walls and used in making paper, rayon, and film [C18 from French *cellule* cell (see CELLULE) + -OSE[2]] > ˌcellu'losic *adj, n*

cellulose acetate *n* nonflammable material made by acetylating cellulose: used in the manufacture of film, dopes, lacquers, and artificial fibres

cellulose nitrate *n* a compound made by treating cellulose with nitric and sulphuric acids, used in plastics, lacquers, and explosives: a nitrogen-containing ester of cellulose. Also called (not in chemical usage): nitrocellulose. See also **guncotton**

cell wall *n* the outer layer of a cell, esp the structure in plant cells that consists of cellulose, lignin, etc, and gives mechanical support to the cell

celom ('siːləm) *n* a less frequent US spelling of **coelom**

celosia (sə'ləʊsɪə) *n* See **cockscomb** (sense 2) [New Latin, from Greek *kēlos* dry, burnt (from the appearance of the flowers of some species)]

Celsius ('sɛlsɪəs) *adj* denoting a measurement on the Celsius scale. Symbol: C [C18 named after Anders *Celsius* (1701–44), Swedish astronomer who invented it]

Celsius scale *n* a scale of temperature in which 0° represents the melting point of ice and 100° represents the boiling point of water. See also **centigrade**. Compare **Fahrenheit scale**

celt (sɛlt) *n archaeol* a stone or metal axelike instrument with a bevelled edge [C18 from Late Latin *celtes* chisel, of obscure origin]

Celt (kɛlt, sɛlt) *or* **Kelt** *n* **1** a person who speaks a Celtic language **2** a member of an Indo-European people who in pre-Roman times inhabited Britain, Gaul, Spain, and other parts of W and central Europe

Celtiberian (ˌkɛltɪ'bɪərɪən, -taɪ-, ˌsɛl-) *n* **1** a member of a Celtic people (**Celtiberi**) who inhabited the Iberian peninsula during classical times **2** the extinct language of this people, possibly belonging to the Celtic branch of the Indo-European family, recorded in a number of inscriptions

Celtic ('kɛltɪk, 'sɛl-) *or* **Keltic** *n* **1** a branch of the Indo-European family of languages that includes Gaelic, Welsh, and Breton, still spoken in parts of Scotland, Ireland, Wales, and Brittany. Modern Celtic is divided into the Brythonic (southern) and Goidelic (northern) groups ▷ *adj* **2** of, relating to, or characteristic of the Celts or the Celtic languages > **'Celtically** *or* **'Keltically** *adv* > **Celticism** ('kɛltɪˌsɪzəm, 'sɛl-) *or* **'Kelticism** *n* > **'Celticist, 'Celtist, 'Kelticist** *or* **'Keltist** *n*

Celtic cross *n* a Latin cross with a broad ring surrounding the point of intersection

Celtic Sea *n* the relatively shallow part of the Atlantic Ocean lying between S Ireland, SW Wales, Cornwall, and W Brittany

cembalo ('tʃɛmbələʊ) *n, pl* **-li** (-lɪ) *or* **-los** another word for **harpsichord** [C19 shortened from CLAVICEMBALO] > **'cembalist** *n*

cement (sɪ'mɛnt) *n* **1** a fine grey powder made of a mixture of calcined limestone and clay, used with water and sand to make mortar, or with water, sand, and aggregate, to make concrete **2** a binder, glue, or adhesive **3** something that unites or joins; bond **4** *dentistry* any of various materials used in filling teeth **5** mineral matter, such as silica and calcite, that binds together particles of rock, bones, etc, to form a solid mass of sedimentary rock **6** another word for **cementum** ▷ *vb* **7** to reinforce or consolidate: *once a friendship is cemented it will last for life* **8** to join, bind, or glue together with or as if with cement **9** to coat or cover with cement [C13 from Old French *ciment*, from Latin *caementum* stone from the quarry, from *caedere* to hew] > **ce'menter** *n*

cementation (ˌsiːmɛn'teɪʃən) *n* **1** the process of heating a solid with a powdered material to modify the properties of the solid, esp the heating of wrought iron, surrounded with charcoal, to 750–900°C to produce steel **2** the process of cementing or being cemented **3** *civil engineering* the injection of cement grout into fissured rocks to make them watertight

cementite (sɪ'mɛntaɪt) *n* the hard brittle compound of iron and carbon that forms in carbon steels and some cast irons. Formula: Fe₃C

cementum (sɪ'mɛntəm) *n* a thin bonelike tissue that covers the dentine in the root of a tooth [c19 New Latin, from Latin: CEMENT]

cemetery ('sɛmɪtrɪ) *n, pl* **-teries** a place where the dead are buried, esp one not attached to a church [c14 from Late Latin *coemētērium*, from Greek *koimētērion* room for sleeping, from *koiman* to put to sleep]

cenacle or **coenacle** ('sɛnəkəl) *n* **1** a supper room, esp one on an upper floor **2** (*capital*) the room in which the Last Supper took place [c14 from Old French, from Late Latin *cēnāculum*, from *cēna* supper]

-cene *n and adj combining form* denoting a recent geological period: *Miocene* [from Greek *kainos* new]

CENELEC ('sɛnə,lɛk) *n acronym for* Commission Européenne de Normalisation Électrique: the EU standards organization for electrical goods. Also called: CEN

cenesthesia (,si:nɪs'θi:zɪə) *n psychol* a variant spelling (esp US) of **coenesthesia**

CEng *abbreviation for* chartered engineer

Cenis (*French* sənɪ) *n* **Mont** a pass over the Graian Alps in SE France, between Lanslebourg (France) and Susa (Italy): nearby tunnel, opened in 1871. Highest point: 2082 m (6831 ft). Italian name: Monte Cenisio ('monte tʃe'ni:zjo)

cenobite ('si:nəʊ,baɪt) *n* a variant spelling of **coenobite**

cenogenesis (,si:nəʊ'dʒɛnɪsɪs) *n* a US spelling of **caenogenesis**

cenospecies ('si:nə,spi:ʃi:z) *n, pl* **-species** a species related to another by the ability to interbreed: *dogs and wolves are cenospecies* [c20 from Greek *koinos* common + SPECIES]

cenotaph ('sɛnə,tɑ:f) *n* a monument honouring a dead person or persons buried elsewhere [c17 from Latin *cenotaphium*, from Greek *kenotaphion*, from *kenos* empty + *taphos* tomb] > ,ceno'taphic *adj*

Cenotaph ('sɛnə,tɑ:f) *n* **the** the monument in Whitehall, London, honouring the dead of both World Wars: designed by Sir Edwin Lutyens: erected in 1920

cenote (sɪ'nəʊteɪ) *n* (esp in the Yucatán peninsula) a natural well formed by the collapse of an overlying limestone crust: often used as a sacrificial site by the Mayas [c19 via Mexican Spanish from Maya *conot*]

Cenozoic, Caenozoic (,si:nəʊ'zəʊɪk) or **Cainozoic** *adj* **1** of, denoting, or relating to the most recent geological era, which began 65 000 000 years ago: characterized by the development and increase of the mammals ▷ *n* **2** **the** the Cenozoic era [c19 from Greek *kainos* new, recent + *zōikos*, from *zōion* animal]

cense (sɛns) *vb* (*tr*) to burn incense near or before (an altar, shrine, etc) [c14 from Old French *encenser*; see INCENSE¹]

censer ('sɛnsə) *n* a container for burning incense, esp one swung at religious ceremonies. Also called: thurible

censor ('sɛnsə) *n* **1** a person authorized to examine publications, theatrical presentations, films, letters, etc, in order to suppress in whole or part those considered obscene, politically unacceptable, etc **2** any person who controls or suppresses the behaviour of others, usually on moral grounds **3** (in republican Rome) either of two senior magistrates elected to keep the list of citizens up to date, control aspects of public finance, and supervise public morals **4** *psychoanal* the postulated factor responsible for regulating the translation of ideas and desires from the unconscious to the conscious mind. See also **superego** ▷ *vb* (*tr*) **5** to ban or cut portions of (a publication, film, letter, etc) **6** to act as a censor of (behaviour, etc) [c16 from Latin, from *cēnsēre* to

consider, assess] > 'censorable *adj* > censorial (sɛn'sɔːrɪəl) *adj*

censorious (sɛn'sɔːrɪəs) *adj* harshly critical; fault-finding > cen'soriously *adv* > cen'soriousness *n*

censorship ('sɛnsəʃɪp) *n* **1** a policy or programme of censoring **2** the act or system of censoring **3** *psychoanal* the activity of the mind in regulating impulses, etc, from the unconscious so that they are modified before reaching the conscious mind

censurable ('sɛnʃərəbəl) *adj* deserving censure, condemnation, or blame > 'censurableness or ,censura'bility *n* > 'censurably *adv*

censure ('sɛnʃə) *n* **1** severe disapproval; harsh criticism ▷ *vb* **2** to criticize (someone or something) severely; condemn [c14 from Latin *cēnsūra*, from *cēnsēre* to consider, assess] > 'censurer *n*

census ('sɛnsəs) *n, pl* **-suses 1** an official periodic count of a population including such information as sex, age, occupation, etc **2** any offical count: *a traffic census* **3** (in ancient Rome) a registration of the population and a property evaluation for purposes of taxation [c17 from Latin, from *cēnsēre* to assess] > 'censual *adj*

cent (sɛnt) *n* **1** a monetary unit of American Samoa, Andorra, Antigua and Barbuda, Aruba, Australia, Austria, the Bahamas, Barbados, Belgium, Belize, Bermuda, Bosnia and Hercegovina, Brunei, Canada, the Cayman Islands, Cyprus, Dominica, East Timor, Ecuador, El Salvador, Ethiopia, Fiji, Finland, France, French Guiana, Germany, Greece, Grenada, Guadeloupe, Guam, Guyana, Hong Kong, Ireland, Jamaica, Kenya, Kiribati, Kosovo, Liberia, Luxembourg, Malaysia, Malta, the Marshall Islands, Martinique, Mauritius, Mayotte, Micronesia, Monaco, Montenegro, Namibia, Nauru, the Netherlands, the Netherlands Antilles, New Zealand, the Northern Mariana Islands, Palau, Portugal, Puerto Rico, Réunion, Saint Kitts and Nevis, Saint Lucia, Saint Vincent and the Grenadines, San Marino, the Seychelles, Sierra Leone, Singapore, the Solomon Islands, Somalia, South Africa, Spain, Sri Lanka, Surinam, Swaziland, Taiwan, Tanzania, Trinidad and Tobago, Tuvalu, Uganda, the United States, the Vatican City, the Virgin Islands, and Zimbabwe. It is worth one hundredth of their respective standard units **2** an interval of pitch between two frequencies f_2 and f_1 equal to 3986.31 log (f_2/f_1); one twelve-hundredth of the interval between two frequencies having the ratio 1:2 (an octave) [c16 from Latin *centēsimus* hundredth, from *centum* hundred]

cental ('sɛntəl) *n* a unit of weight equal to 100 pounds (45.3 kilograms) [c19 from Latin *centum* hundred]

centas ('tsæntæs) *n, pl* **centai** ('tsæntaɪ) a monetary unit of Lithuania, worth one hundredth of a litas

centaur ('sɛntɔː) *n Greek myth* one of a race of creatures with the head, arms, and torso of a man, and the lower body and legs of a horse [c14 from Latin, from Greek *kentauros*, of unknown origin]

centaurea (,sɛntɔː'rɪə, sɛn'tɔːrɪə) *n* any plant of the genus *Centaurea*, which includes the cornflower and knapweed [c19 ultimately from Greek *Kentauros* the Centaur; see CENTAURY]

Centaurus (sɛn'tɔːrəs) *n, Latin genitive* **Centauri** (sɛn'tɔːraɪ) a conspicuous extensive constellation in the S hemisphere, close to the Southern Cross, that contains two first magnitude stars, Alpha Centauri and Beta Centauri, and the globular cluster Omega Centauri. Also called: The Centaur

centaury ('sɛntɔːrɪ) *n, pl* **-ries** any Eurasian plant of the genus *Centaurium*, esp *C. erythraea*, having purplish pink flowers and formerly believed to have medicinal properties: family *Gentianaceae* **2** any plant of the genus *Centaurea*, which includes the cornflower and knapweed: family *Compositae* (composites) [c14 ultimately from Greek *Kentauros*

the Centaur; from the legend that Chiron the Centaur divulged its healing properties]

centavo (sɛn'tɑːvəʊ) *n, pl* **-vos 1** a monetary unit of Argentina, Bolivia, Brazil, Cape Verde, Chile, Colombia, Cuba, the Dominican Republic, Guatemala, Guinea-Bissau, Honduras, Mexico, Mozambique, Nicaragua, and the Philippines. It is worth one hundredth of their respective standard units **2** a former monetary unit of Ecuador, El Salvador, and Portugal, worth one hundredth of their former standard units [Spanish: one hundredth part]

centenarian (,sɛntɪ'nɛərɪən) *n* **1** a person who is at least 100 years old ▷ *adj* **2** being at least 100 years old **3** of or relating to a centenarian

centenary (sɛn'tiːnərɪ) *adj* **1** of or relating to a period of 100 years **2** occurring once every 100 years ▷ *n, pl* **-naries 3** a 100th anniversary or its celebration [c17 from Latin *centēnārius* of a hundred, from *centēnī* a hundred each, from *centum* hundred]

centennial (sɛn'tɛnɪəl) *adj* **1** relating to, lasting for, or completing a period of 100 years **2** occurring every 100 years ▷ *n* **3** *chiefly US and Canadian* another name for **centenary** [c18 from Latin *centum* hundred, on the model of BIENNIAL] > cen'tennially *adv*

center ('sɛntə) *n, vb* the US spelling of **centre**

centered ('sɛntəd) *adj* the US spelling of **centred**

centering ('sɛntərɪŋ) *n* a US spelling of **centring**

centesimal (sɛn'tɛsɪməl) *n* **1** hundredth ▷ *adj* **2** relating to division into hundredths [c17 from Latin *centēsimus*, from *centum* hundred] > cen'tesimally *adv*

centesimo (sɛn'tɛsɪ,məʊ) *n, pl* **-mos, -mi** a former monetary unit of Italy, San Marino, and the Vatican City worth one hundredth of a lira [c19 from Italian, from Latin *centēsimus* hundredth, from *centum* hundred]

centésimo (sɛn'tɛsɪ,məʊ) *n, pl* **-mos** or **-mi** a monetary unit of Panama and Uruguay. It is worth one hundredth of their respective standard units [c19 from Spanish; see CENTESIMO]

centi- or before a vowel **cent-** *prefix* **1** denoting one hundredth: *centimetre*. Symbol: c **2** *rare* denoting a hundred: *centipede* [from French, from Latin *centum* hundred]

centiare ('sɛntɪ,ɛə; *French* sɑ̃tjar) or **centare** ('sɛntɛə; *French* sɑ̃tar) *n* a unit of area equal to one square metre [French, from CENTI- + *are* from Latin *ārea*; see ARE², AREA]

centigrade ('sɛntɪ,greɪd) *adj* **1** a former name for **Celsius** ▷ *n* **2** a unit of angle equal to one hundredth of a grade

> **USAGE** Although still used in meteorology, *centigrade*, when indicating the Celsius scale of temperature, is now usually avoided because of its possible confusion with the hundredth part of a grade

centigram or **centigramme** ('sɛntɪ,græm) *n* one hundredth of a gram

centile ('sɛntaɪl) *n* another word for **percentile**

centilitre or US **centiliter** ('sɛntɪ,liːtə) *n* one hundredth of a litre

centillion (sɛn'tɪljən) *n, pl* **-lions** or **-lion 1** (in Britain and Germany) the number represented as one followed by 600 zeros (10^{600}) **2** (in the US, Canada, and France) the number represented as one followed by 303 zeros (10^{303})

centime ('sɒn,tiːm; *French* sɑ̃tim) *n* **1** a monetary unit of Algeria, Benin, Burkina-Faso, Burundi, Cameroon, the Central African Republic, Chad, Comoros, Democratic Republic of Congo, Congo-Brazzaville, Côte d'Ivoire, Djibouti, Equatorial Guinea, French Polynesia, Gabon, Guinea, Guinea-Bissau, Haiti, Liechtenstein, Madagascar, Mali, Mayotte, Morocco, New Caledonia, Niger, Rwanda, Senegal, Switzerland, and Togo. It is worth one hundredth of their respective standard units **2** a former monetary unit of Andorra, Belgium, France, French Guiana, Guadeloupe,

Luxembourg, Martinique, Monaco, and Réunion, worth one hundredth of a franc [c18 from French, from Old French *centiesme* from Latin *centēsimus* hundredth, from *centum* hundred]

centimetre *or US* **centimeter** ('sɛntɪ,miːtə) *n* one hundredth of a metre

centimetre-gram-second *n* See cgs units

céntimo ('sɛntɪ,məʊ) *n, pl* **-mos 1** a monetary unit of Costa Rica, Paraguay, Peru, and Venezuela. It is worth one hundredth of their respective standard currency units **2** a former monetary unit of Andorra and Spain, worth one hundredth of a peseta [from Spanish; see CENTIME]

cêntimo ('sɛntɪ,məʊ) *n, pl* **-mos** a monetary unit of Sao Tomé e Principe, worth one hundredth of a dobra

centimorgan ('sɛntɪ,mɔːgən) *n genetics* a unit of chromosome length, used in genetic mapping, equal to the length of chromosome over which crossing over occurs with 1 per cent frequency [c20 named after Thomas Hunt *Morgan* (1866–1945), US biologist]

centipede ('sɛntɪ,piːd) *n* any carnivorous arthropod of the genera *Lithobius, Scutigera,* etc, having a body of between 15 and 190 segments, each bearing one pair of legs: class *Chilopoda.* See also myriapod

centipoise ('sɛntɪ,pɔɪz) *n* one hundredth of a poise. 1 centipoise is equal to 0.001 newton second per square metre

centner ('sɛntnə) *n* **1** Also called (*esp US*): short hundredweight a unit of weight equivalent to 100 pounds (45.3 kilograms) **2** (in some European countries) a unit of weight equivalent to 50 kilograms (110.23 pounds) **3** a unit of weight equivalent to 100 kilograms [c17 from German *Zentner,* ultimately from Latin *centēnārius* of a hundred; see CENTENARY]

cento ('sɛntəʊ) *n, pl* **-tos** a piece of writing, esp a poem, composed of quotations from other authors [c17 from Latin: literally: patchwork garment]

CENTO ('sɛntəʊ) *n acronym for* Central Treaty Organization; an organization for military and economic cooperation formed in 1959 by the UK, Iran, Pakistan, and Turkey as a successor to the Baghdad Pact: disbanded 1979

centra ('sɛntrə) *n* a plural of centrum

central ('sɛntrəl) *adj* **1** in, at, of, from, containing, or forming the centre of something: *the central street in a city; the central material of a golf ball* **2** main, principal, or chief; most important: *the central cause of a problem* **3 a** of or relating to the central nervous system **b** of or relating to the centrum of a vertebra **4** of, relating to, or denoting a vowel articulated with the tongue held in an intermediate position halfway between the positions for back and front vowels, as for the *a* of English *soda* **5** (of a force) directed from or towards a point **6** *informal* (*immediately postpositive*) used to describe a place where a specified thing, quality, etc is to be found in abundance: *nostalgia central* > 'centrally *adv*

Central African Federation *n* another name for the Federation of Rhodesia and Nyasaland

Central African Republic *n* a landlocked country of central Africa: joined with Chad as a territory of French Equatorial Africa in 1910; became an independent republic in 1960; a parliamentary monarchy (1976–79); consists of a huge plateau, mostly savanna, with dense forests in the south; drained chiefly by the Shari and Ubangi Rivers. Official language: French; Sango is the national language. Religion: Christian and animist. Currency: franc. Capital: Bangui. Pop: 3 912 000 (2004 est). Area: 622 577 sq km (240 376 sq miles). Former names: **Ubangi-Shari** (until 1958), **Central African Empire** (1976–79). French name: **République Centrafricaine** (repyblik sãtrafriken)

Central America *n* an isthmus joining the continents of North and South America, extending from the S border of Mexico to the NW border of Colombia and consisting of Belize,

Guatemala, Honduras, El Salvador, Nicaragua, Costa Rica, and Panama. Area: about 518 000 sq km (200 000 sq miles)

Central American *adj* **1** of or relating to Central America or its inhabitants ▷ *n* **2** a native or inhabitant of Central America

central angle *n* an angle whose vertex is at the centre of a circle

central bank *n* a national bank that does business mainly with a government and with other banks: it regulates the volume and cost of credit

Central Committee *n* (in Communist parties) the body responsible for party policy between meetings of the party congress: in practice, it is in charge of day-to-day operations of the party bureaucracy

Central European Time *n* the standard time adopted by Western European countries one hour ahead of Greenwich Mean Time, corresponding to British Summer Time. Abbreviation: CET

central heating *n* a system for heating the rooms of a building by means of radiators or air vents connected by pipes or ducts to a central source of heat

Central India Agency *n* a former group of 89 states in India, under the supervision of a British political agent until 1947: most important were Indore, Bhopal, and Rewa

Central Intelligence Agency *n* See CIA

centralism ('sɛntrə,lɪzəm) *n* the principle or act of bringing something under central control; centralization > 'centralist *n, adj* > ,central'istic *adj*

centrality (sɛn'trælɪtɪ) *n, pl* **-ties** the state or condition of being central

centralize *or* **centralise** ('sɛntrə,laɪz) *vb* **1** to draw or move (something) to or towards a centre **2** to bring or come under central control, esp governmental control > ,centrali'zation *or* ,centrali'sation > 'central,izer *or* 'central,iser *n*

Central Karoo (kə'ruː) *n* an arid plateau of S central South Africa, in Cape Province, separated from the Little Karoo to the southwest by the Swartberg range. Average height: 750 m (2500 ft)

central limit theorem *n statistics* the fundamental result that the sum (or mean) of independent identically distributed random variables with finite variance approaches a normally distributed random variable as their number increases, whence in particular if enough samples are repeatedly drawn from any population, the sum of the sample values can be thought of, approximately, as an outcome from a normally distributed random variable

central locking *n* a system by which all the doors of a motor vehicle can be locked simultaneously when the driver's door is locked

central nervous system *n* the mass of nerve tissue that controls and coordinates the activities of an animal. In vertebrates it consists of the brain and spinal cord. Abbreviation: CNS Compare autonomic nervous system

Central Powers *pl n European history* **a** (before World War I) Germany, Italy, and Austria-Hungary after they were linked by the Triple Alliance in 1882 **b** (during World War I) Germany and Austria-Hungary, together with their allies Turkey and Bulgaria

central processing unit *n* the part of a computer that performs logical and arithmetical operations on the data as specified in the instructions. Abbreviation: CPU

Central Provinces *pl n* the Canadian provinces of Ontario and Quebec

Central Provinces and Berar (bɛ'rɑː) *n* a former province of central India: renamed Madhya Pradesh in 1950, Berar being transferred to Maharashtra in 1956

Central Region *n* a former local government region in central Scotland, formed in 1975 from Clackmannanshire, most of Stirlingshire, and parts of Perthshire, West Lothian, Fife, and

Kinross-shire; in 1996 it was replaced by the council areas of Stirling, Clackmannanshire, and Falkirk

central reserve *or* **reservation** *n Brit* the strip, often covered with grass, that separates the two sides of a motorway or dual carriageway. US and Austral name: median strip. Canadian name: median

Central Standard Time *n* **1** one of the standard times used in North America, based on the local time of the 90° meridian, six hours behind Greenwich Mean Time **2** one of the standard times used in Australia. Abbreviation: CST

central sulcus *n* a deep cleft in each hemisphere of the brain separating the frontal lobe from the parietal lobe

central tendency *n statistics* the tendency of the values of a random variable to cluster around the mean, median, and mode

centre *or US* **center** ('sɛntə) *n* **1** *geometry* **a** the midpoint of any line or figure, esp the point within a circle or sphere that is equidistant from any point on the circumference or surface **b** the point within a body through which a specified force may be considered to act, such as the centre of gravity **2** the point, axis, or pivot about which a body rotates **3** a point, area, or part that is approximately in the middle of a larger area or volume **4** a place at which some specified activity is concentrated: *a shopping centre* **5** a person or thing that is a focus of interest **6** a place of activity or influence: *a centre of power* **7** a person, group, policy, or thing in the middle **8** (*usually capital*) *politics* **a** a political party or group favouring moderation, esp the moderate members of a legislative assembly **b** (*as modifier*): *a Centre-Left alliance* **9** *physiol* any part of the central nervous system that regulates a specific function: *respiratory centre* **10** a bar with a conical point upon which a workpiece or part may be turned or ground **11** a punch mark or small conical hole in a part to be drilled, which enables the point of the drill to be located accurately **12** *sport* **a** a player who plays in the middle of the forward line **b** the act or an instance of passing the ball from a wing to the middle of the field, court, etc **13** *basketball* **a** the position of a player who jumps for the ball at the start of play **b** the player in this position **14** *archery* **a** the ring around the bull's eye **b** a shot that hits this ring ▷ *vb* **15** to move towards, mark, put, or be at a centre **16** (*tr*) to focus or bring together: *to centre one's thoughts* **17** (*intr*; often foll by *on*) to have as a main point of view or theme: *the novel centred on crime* **18** (*tr*) to adjust or locate (a workpiece or part) using a centre **19** (*intr*; foll by *on* or *round*) to have as a centre **20** (*tr*) *sport* to pass (the ball) into the middle of the field or court [c14 from Latin *centrum* the stationary point of a compass, from Greek *kentron* needle, from *kentein* to prick]

Centre *n* **1** ('sɛntə) **the** the sparsely inhabited central region of Australia **2** (*French* sãtrə) a region of central France: generally low-lying; drained chiefly by the Rivers Loire, Loir, and Cher

centre bit *n* a drilling bit with a central projecting point and two side cutters

centreboard ('sɛntə,bɔːd) *n* a supplementary keel for a sailing vessel, which may be adjusted by raising and lowering. Compare daggerboard

centred ('sɛntəd) *or US* **centered** *adj* mentally and emotionally confident, focused, and well-balanced

centred dot *n printing* **1** Also called (esp US and Canadian): bullet a heavy dot (•) used to draw attention to a particular paragraph **2** a dot placed at a central level in a line of type or writing

centre-fire *adj* **1** (of a cartridge) having the primer in the centre of the base **2** (of a firearm) adapted for such cartridges ▷ Compare rim-fire

centrefold *or US* **centerfold** ('sɛntə,fəʊld) *n* **1** a large coloured illustration folded so that it forms the central spread of a magazine **2** a photograph of a nude or nearly nude woman (or man) in a magazine on such a spread

centre forward *n sport* the central forward in the attack

centre half *or* **centre back** *n soccer* a defender who plays in the middle of the defence

centre of curvature *n* the point on the normal at a given point on a curve on the concave side of the curve whose distance from the point on the curve is equal to the radius of curvature

centre of gravity *n* the point through which the resultant of the gravitational forces on a body always acts

centre of mass *n* the point at which the mass of a system could be concentrated without affecting the behaviour of the system under the action of external linear forces

centre of pressure *n* **1** *physics* the point in a body at which the resultant pressure acts when the body is immersed in a fluid **2** *aeronautics* the point at which the resultant aerodynamic forces intersect the chord line of the aerofoil

centre pass *n hockey* a push or hit made in any direction to start the game or to restart the game after a goal has been scored

centrepiece ('sentə,pi:s) *n* an object used as the centre of something, esp for decoration

centre punch *n* a small steel tool with a conical tip used to punch a small indentation at the location of the centre of a hole to be drilled

centre spread *n* **1** the pair of two facing pages in the middle of a magazine, newspaper, etc, often illustrated **2** a photograph of a nude or nearly nude woman (or man) in a magazine on such pages

centre stage *n* **1** the centre point on a stage **2** the main focus of attention

centre three-quarter *n rugby* either of two middle players on the three-quarter line

centri- *combining form* a variant of **centro-**

centric ('sentrɪk) *or* **centrical** *adj* **1** being central or having a centre **2** relating to or originating at a nerve centre **3** *botany* **a** Also: **concentric** (of vascular bundles) having one type of tissue completely surrounding the other **b** (of leaves, such as those of the onion) cylindrical > **'centrically** *adv* > **centricity** (sen'trɪsɪtɪ) *n*

-centric *suffix forming adjectives* having a centre as specified: *heliocentric* [abstracted from ECCENTRIC, CONCENTRIC, etc]

centrifugal (sen'trɪfjʊgəl, 'sentrɪ,fju:gəl) *adj* **1** acting, moving, or tending to move away from a centre. Compare **centripetal 2** of, concerned with, or operated by centrifugal force: *centrifugal pump* **3** *botany* (esp of certain inflorescences) developing outwards from a centre **4** *physiol* another word for **efferent** ▷ *n* **5** any device that uses centrifugal force for its action **6** the rotating perforated drum in a centrifuge [c18 from New Latin *centrifugus*, from CENTRI- + Latin *fugere* to flee] > **cen'trifugally** *adv*

centrifugal brake *n* a safety mechanism on a hoist, crane, etc, that consists of revolving brake shoes that are driven outwards by centrifugal force into contact with a fixed brake drum when the rope drum revolves at excessive speed

centrifugal clutch *n engineering* an automatic clutch in which the friction surfaces are engaged by weighted levers acting under centrifugal force at a certain speed of rotation

centrifugal force *n* a fictitious force that can be thought of as acting outwards on any body that rotates or moves along a curved path

centrifugal pump *n* a pump having a high-speed rotating impeller whose blades throw the water outwards

centrifuge ('sentrɪ,fju:dʒ) *n* **1** any of various rotating machines that separate liquids from solids or dispersions of one liquid in another, by the action of centrifugal force **2** any of various rotating devices for subjecting human beings or animals to varying accelerations for experimental

purposes ▷ *vb* **3** (*tr*) to subject to the action of a centrifuge > **centrifugation** (,sentrɪfjʊ'geɪʃən) *n*

centring ('sentrɪŋ) *or US* **centering** *n* a temporary structure, esp one made of timber, used to support an arch during construction

centriole ('sentrɪ,əʊl) *n* either of two rodlike bodies in most animal cells that form the poles of the spindle during mitosis [c19 from New Latin *centriolum*, diminutive of Latin *centrum* CENTRE]

centripetal (sen'trɪpɪtəl, 'sentrɪ,pi:təl) *adj* **1** acting, moving, or tending to move towards a centre. Compare **centrifugal 2** of, concerned with, or operated by centripetal force **3** *botany* (esp of certain inflorescences) developing from the outside towards the centre **4** *physiol* another word for **afferent** [c17 from New Latin *centripetus* seeking the centre; see CENTRI-, -PETAL] > **cen'tripetally** *adv*

centripetal force *n* a force that acts inwards on any body that rotates or moves along a curved path and is directed towards the centre of curvature of the path or the axis of rotation. Compare **centrifugal force**

centrist ('sentrɪst) *n* a person holding moderate political views > **'centrism** *n*

centro-, centri- *or before a vowel* **centr-** *combining form* denoting a centre: *centroclinal; centromere; centrosome; centrosphere; centrist* [from Greek *kentron* CENTRE]

centrobaric (,sentrəʊ'bærɪk) *adj* of or concerned with a centre of gravity [c18 from Late Greek *kentrobarikos*, from Greek *kentron bareos* centre of gravity]

centroclinal (,sentrəʊ'klaɪnəl) *adj geology* of, relating to, or designating a rock formation in which the strata slope down and in towards a central point or area

centroid ('sentrɔɪd) *n* **a** the centre of mass of an object of uniform density, esp of a geometric figure **b** (of a finite set) the point whose coordinates are the mean values of the coordinates of the points of the set

centrolecithal (,sentrəʊ'lesɪθəl) *adj zoology* (of animal eggs) having a centrally located yolk

centromere ('sentrə,mɪə) *n* the dense nonstaining region of a chromosome that attaches it to the spindle during mitosis > **centromeric** (,sentrə'merɪk, -'mɪərɪk) *adj*

centrosome ('sentrə,səʊm) *n* a small body in a cell where microtubules are produced. In animal cells it surrounds the centriole. Also called: **centrosphere** > **centrosomic** (,sentrə'sɒmɪk) *adj*

centrosphere ('sentrə,sfɪə) *n* **1** a former name for **core** (sense 4) **2** another name for **centrosome**

centrum ('sentrəm) *n, pl* **-trums** *or* **-tra** (-trə) the main part or body of a vertebra [c19 from Latin: CENTRE]

centum ('sentəm) *adj* denoting or belonging to the Indo-European languages in which original velar stops (k) were not palatalized, namely languages of the Hellenic, Italic, Celtic, Germanic, Anatolian, and Tocharian branches. Compare **satem** [Latin: HUNDRED, chosen because the *c* represents the Indo-European k]

centuplicate *vb* (sen'tju:plɪ,keɪt) **1** (*tr*) to increase 100 times ▷ *adj* (sen'tju:plɪkɪt, -,keɪt) **2** increased a hundredfold ▷ *n* (sen'tju:plɪkɪt, -,keɪt) **3** one hundredfold ▷ Also: **centuple** ('sentjʊpəl) [c17 from Late Latin *centuplicāre*, from *centuplex* hundredfold, from Latin *centum* hundred + *-plex* -fold] > **cen,tupli'cation** *n*

centurial (sen'tjʊərɪəl) *adj* **1** of or relating to a Roman century **2** *rare* involving a period of 100 years

centurion (sen'tjʊərɪən) *n* the officer commanding a Roman century [c14 from Latin *centuriō*, from *centuria* CENTURY]

century ('sentʃərɪ) *n, pl* **-ries 1** a period of 100 years **2** one of the successive periods of 100 years dated before or after an epoch or event, esp the birth of Christ **3 a** a score or grouping of 100: *to score a century in cricket* **b** *chiefly US* (*as modifier*): *the*

basketball team passed the century mark in their last game **4** (in ancient Rome) a unit of foot soldiers, originally 100 strong, later consisting of 60 to 80 men. See also **maniple 5** (in ancient Rome) a division of the people for purposes of voting **6** (*often capital*) a style of type [c16 from Latin *centuria*, from *centum* hundred]

century plant *n* an agave, *Agave americana*, native to tropical America but naturalized elsewhere, having very large spiny greyish leaves and greenish flowers on a tall fleshy stalk. It blooms only once in its life, after 10 to 30 years (formerly thought to flower after a century). Also called: **American aloe**

ceorl (tʃɛəl) *n* a freeman of the lowest class in Anglo-Saxon England [Old English; see CHURL] > **'ceorlish** *adj*

cep (sep) *n* another name for **porcino** [c19 from French *cèpe*, from Gascon dialect *cep*, from Latin *cippus* stake]

cepaceous (sɪ'peɪʃəs) *adj botany* having an onion-like smell or taste [from Latin *caepa* onion + -ACEOUS]

cephalad ('sefə,læd) *adv anatomy* towards the head or anterior part. Compare **caudad**

cephalalgia (,sefə'lældʒɪə, -dʒə) *n* a technical name for **headache**

cephalic (sɪ'fælɪk) *adj* **1** of or relating to the head **2** situated in, on, or near the head

-cephalic *or* **-cephalous** *adj combining form* indicating skull or head; -headed: *brachycephalic* [from Greek *-kephalos*] > **-cephaly** *or* **-cephalism** *n combining form*

cephalic index *n* the ratio of the greatest width of the human head to its greatest length, multiplied by 100

cephalic version *n* another name for **version** (sense 5)

cephalin ('sefəlɪn, 'kef-) *or* **kephalin** ('kefəlɪn) *n* a phospholipid, similar to lecithin, that occurs in the nerve tissue and brain. Systematic name: **phosphatidylethanolamine**

cephalization *or* **cephalisation** (,sefəlaɪ'zeɪʃən) *n* (in the evolution of animals) development of a head by the concentration of feeding and sensory organs and nervous tissue at the anterior end

cephalo- *or before a vowel* **cephal-** *combining form* indicating the head: *cephalopod* [via Latin from Greek *kephalo-*, from *kephale* head]

cephalochordate (,sefələʊ'kɔ:deɪt) *n* **1** any chordate animal of the subphylum *Cephalochordata*, having a fishlike body and no vertebral column; a lancelet ▷ *adj* **2** of, relating to, or belonging to the *Cephalochordata*

cephalometer (,sefə'lɒmɪtə) *n* an instrument for positioning the human head for X-ray examination in cephalometry

cephalometry (,sefə'lɒmɪtrɪ) *n* **1** measurement of the dimensions of the human head by radiography: used mainly in orthodontics **2** measurement of the dimensions of the fetal head by radiography or ultrasound > **cephalometric** (,sefələʊ'metrɪk) *adj*

Cephalonia (,sefə'ləʊnɪə) *n* a mountainous island in the Ionian Sea, the largest of the Ionian Islands, off the W coast of Greece. Pop: 36 404 (2001). Area: 935 sq km (365 sq miles). Modern Greek name: Kephallinía

cephalopod ('sefələ,pɒd) *n* **1** any marine mollusc of the class *Cephalopoda.*, characterized by well-developed head and eyes and a ring of sucker-bearing tentacles. The group also includes the octopuses, squids, cuttlefish, and pearly nautilus ▷ *adj* also **cephalopodic** *or* **cephalopodous** (,sefə'lɒpədəs) **2** of, relating to, or belonging to the *Cephalopoda* > ,cepha'lopodan *adj, n*

cephalosporin (,sefələʊ'spɔ:rɪn) *n* any of a group of broad-spectrum antibiotics obtained from fungi of the genus *Cephalosporium*

cephalothorax (,sefələʊ'θɔ:ræks) *n, pl* **-raxes** *or* **-races** (-rə,si:z) the anterior part of many crustaceans and some other arthropods

C

consisting of a united head and thorax
> **cephalothoracic** (ˌsɛfələʊθə'ræsɪk) *adj*

-cephalus *n combining form* denoting a cephalic abnormality: *hydrocephalus* [New Latin *-cephalus*; see -CEPHALIC]

Cepheid variable ('siːfɪɪd) *n astronomy* any of a class of variable stars with regular cycles of variations in luminosity (most ranging from three to fifty days). There is a relationship between the periods of variation and the absolute magnitudes, which is used for measuring the distance of such stars

Cepheus[1] ('siːfjuːs) *n, Latin genitive* **Cephei** ('siːfɪˌaɪ) a faint constellation in the N hemisphere near Cassiopeia and the Pole Star. See also **Cepheid variable** [from Latin *Cēpheus* named after the mythical king]

Cepheus[2] ('siːfjuːs) *n Greek myth* a king of Ethiopia, father of Andromeda and husband of Cassiopeia

CER *abbreviation for* Closer Economic Relations: a trade agreement between Australia and New Zealand signed in 1983

ceraceous (sɪ'reɪʃəs) *adj* waxlike or waxy [c18 from Latin *cēra* wax]

Ceram (sɪ'ræm) *n* a variant spelling of **Seram**

ceramal (sə'reɪməl) *n* another name for **cermet** [c20 from CERAM(IC) + AL(LOY)]

ceramic (sɪ'ræmɪk) *n* **1** a hard brittle material made by firing clay and similar substances **2** an object made from such a material ▷ *adj* **3** of, relating to, or made from a ceramic: *this vase is ceramic* **4** of or relating to ceramics: *ceramic arts and crafts* [c19 from Greek *keramikos*, from *keramos* potter's clay, pottery]

ceramic hob *n* (on an electric cooker) a flat ceramic cooking surface having heating elements fitted on the underside, usually patterned to show the areas where heat is produced

ceramic oxide *n* a compound of oxygen with nonorganic material: recently discovered to act as a high-temperature superconductor

ceramics (sɪ'ræmɪks) *n* (*functioning as singular*) the art and techniques of producing articles of clay, porcelain, etc > **ceramist** ('sɛrəmɪst) *or* **ce'ramicist** *n*

ceramide ('sɛrəˌmaɪd) *n* any of a class of biologically important compounds used as moisturizers in skin-care preparations

cerargyrite (sɪ'rɑːdʒɪˌraɪt) *n* another name for **chloroargyrite** [c19 from Greek *keras* horn + *arguros* silver + -ITE[1]]

cerastes (sə'ræstiːz) *n, pl* **-tes** any venomous snake of the genus *Cerastes*, esp the horned viper [c16 from Latin: horned serpent, from Greek *kerastēs* horned, from *keras* horn]

cerate ('sɪərɪt, -reɪt) *n* a hard ointment or medicated paste consisting of lard or oil mixed with wax or resin [c16 from Latin *cērātum*, from *cēra* wax]

cerated ('sɪəreɪtɪd) *adj* (of certain birds, such as the falcon) having a cere

cerato- *or before a vowel* **cerat-** *combining form* **1** denoting horn or a hornlike part: *ceratodus* **2** *anatomy* denoting the cornea ▷ Also: **kerato-** [from Greek *kerat-*, *keras* horn]

ceratodus (sɪ'rætədəs, ˌsɛrə'təʊdəs) *n, pl* **-duses** any of various extinct lungfish constituting the genus *Ceratodus*, common in Cretaceous and Triassic times. Compare **barramunda** [c19 New Latin, from CERATO- + Greek *odous* tooth]

ceratoid ('sɛrəˌtɔɪd) *adj* having the shape or texture of animal horn

Cerberus ('sɜːbərəs) *n* **1** *Greek myth* a dog, usually represented as having three heads, that guarded the entrance to Hades **2** a sop to Cerberus a bribe or something given to propitiate a potential source of danger or problems > **Cerberean** (sə'bɪərɪən) *adj*

cercal ('sɜːk°l) *adj zoology* **1** of or relating to a tail **2** of or relating to the cerci

cercaria (sə'kɛərɪə) *n, pl* **-iae** (-ɪˌiː) one of the larval forms of trematode worms. It has a short forked

tail and resembles an immature adult [c19 New Latin, literally: tailed creature, from Greek *kerkos* tail] > **cer'carial** *adj* > **cer'carian** *adj, n*

cercis ('sɜːsɪs) *n* any tree or shrub of the leguminous genus *Cercis*, which includes the redbud and Judas tree [c19 New Latin, from Greek *kerkis* weaver's shuttle, Judas tree]

cercopithecoid (ˌsɜːkəʊpɪ'θiːkɔɪd) *adj* **1** of, relating to, or belonging to the primate superfamily *Cercopithecoidea* (Old World monkeys) ▷ *n also* **cercopithecid** (ˌsɜːkəʊpɪ'θiːsɪd) **2** an Old World monkey [c19 from Latin *cercopithēcus* monkey with a tail (from Greek *kerkopithēkos*, from *kerkos* tail + *pithēkos* ape) + -OID]

cercus ('sɜːkəs) *n, pl* **-ci** (-siː) one of a pair of sensory appendages at the tip of the abdomen of some insects and other arthropods [c19 from New Latin, from Greek *kerkos* tail]

cere[1] (sɪə) *n* a soft waxy swelling, containing the nostrils, at the base of the upper beak in such birds as the parrot [c15 from Old French *cire* wax, from Latin *cēra*]

cere[2] (sɪə) *vb* (*tr*) to wrap (a corpse) in a cerecloth [c15 from Latin *cērāre*, from *cēra* wax]

cereal ('sɪərɪəl) *n* **1** any grass that produces an edible grain, such as oat, rye, wheat, rice, maize, sorghum, and millet **2** the grain produced by such a plant **3** any food made from this grain, esp breakfast food **4** (*modifier*) of or relating to any of these plants or their products: *cereal farming* [c19 from Latin *cereālis* concerning agriculture, of CERES[1]]

cerebellar syndrome *n* a disease of the cerebellum characterized by unsteady movements and mispronunciation of words. Also called: **Nonne's syndrome**

cerebellum (ˌsɛrɪ'bɛləm) *n, pl* **-lums** *or* **-la** (-lə) one of the major divisions of the vertebrate brain, situated in man above the medulla oblongata and beneath the cerebrum, whose function is coordination of voluntary movements and maintenance of bodily equilibrium [c16 from Latin, diminutive of CEREBRUM] > ˌcere'bellar *adj*

cerebral ('sɛrɪbrəl; *US also* sə'riːbrəl) *adj* **1** of or relating to the cerebrum or to the entire brain **2** involving intelligence rather than emotions or instinct **3** *phonetics* another word for **cacuminal** ▷ *n* **4** *phonetics* a consonant articulated in the manner of a cacuminal consonant > 'cerebrally *adv*

cerebral dominance *n* the normal tendency for one half of the brain, usually the left cerebral hemisphere in right-handed people, to exercise more control over certain functions (eg handedness and language) than the other

cerebral haemorrhage *n* bleeding from an artery in the brain, which in severe cases causes a stroke

cerebral hemisphere *n* either half of the cerebrum

cerebral palsy *n* a nonprogressive impairment of muscular function and weakness of the limbs, caused by lack of oxygen to the brain immediately after birth, brain injury during birth, or viral infection

cerebrate ('sɛrɪˌbreɪt) *vb* (*intr*) *usually facetious* to use the mind; think; ponder; consider

cerebration (ˌsɛrɪ'breɪʃən) *n* the act of thinking; consideration; thought [c19 from Latin *cerebrum* brain]

cerebro- *or before a vowel* **cerebr-** *combining form* indicating the brain: *cerebrospinal* [from CEREBRUM]

cerebroside ('sɛrɪbrəʊˌsaɪd) *n biochem* any glycolipid in which N-acyl sphingosine is combined with glucose or galactose: occurs in the myelin sheaths of nerves

cerebrospinal (ˌsɛrɪbrəʊ'spaɪn°l) *adj* of or relating to the brain and spinal cord

cerebrospinal fluid *n* the clear colourless fluid in the spaces inside and around the spinal cord and brain. Abbreviation: **CSF**

cerebrospinal meningitis *or* **fever** *n* an acute infectious form of meningitis caused by the

bacterium *Neisseria meningitidis*, characterized by high fever, skin rash, delirium, stupor, and sometimes coma. Also called: **epidemic meningitis**

cerebrotonia (ˌsɛrɪbrəʊ'təʊnɪə) *n* a personality type characterized by restraint, alertness, and an intellectual approach to life: said to be correlated with an ectomorph body type. Compare **somatotonia, viscerotonia**

cerebrovascular (ˌsɛrɪbrəʊ'væskjʊlə) *adj* of or relating to the blood vessels and the blood supply of the brain

cerebrovascular accident *or* **cerebral vascular accident** *n* a sudden interruption of the blood supply to the brain caused by rupture of an artery in the brain (**cerebral haemorrhage**) or the blocking of a blood vessel, as by a clot of blood (**cerebral occlusion**). See apoplexy, stroke (sense 4)

cerebrum ('sɛrɪbrəm) *n, pl* **-brums** *or* **-bra** (-brə) **1** the anterior portion of the brain of vertebrates, consisting of two lateral hemispheres joined by a thick band of fibres: the dominant part of the brain in man, associated with intellectual function, emotion, and personality. See **telencephalon 2** the brain considered as a whole **3** the main neural bundle or ganglion of certain invertebrates [c17 from Latin: the brain] > 'cere,broid *adj* > **cerebric** ('sɛrɪbrɪk) *adj*

cerecloth ('sɪəˌklɒθ) *n* waxed waterproof cloth of a kind formerly used as a shroud [c15 from earlier *cered cloth*, from Latin *cērāre* to wax; see CERE[2]]

Ceredigion (ˌkɛrə'dɪgj°n) *n* a county of W Wales, on Cardigan Bay: created in 1996 from part of Dyfed; corresponds to the former Cardiganshire (abolished 1974): mainly agricultural, with the Cambrian Mountains in the E and N. Administrative centre: Aberaeron. Pop: 77 200 (2003 est). Area: 1793 sq km (692 sq miles)

cerement ('sɪəmənt) *n* **1** another name for **cerecloth 2** any burial clothes [c17 from French *cirement*, from *cirer* to wax; see CERE[2]]

ceremonial (ˌsɛrɪ'məʊnɪəl) *adj* **1** involving or relating to ceremony or ritual ▷ *n* **2** the observance of formality, esp in etiquette **3** a plan for formal observances on a particular occasion; ritual **4** *Christianity* **a** the prescribed order of rites and ceremonies **b** a book containing this > ˌcere'monialism *n* > ˌcere'monialist *n* > ˌcere'monially *adv*

ceremonious (ˌsɛrɪ'məʊnɪəs) *adj* **1** especially or excessively polite or formal **2** observing ceremony; involving formalities > ˌcere'moniously *adv* > ˌcere'moniousness *n*

ceremony ('sɛrɪmənɪ) *n, pl* **-nies 1** a formal act or ritual, often set by custom or tradition, performed in observation of an event or anniversary: *a ceremony commemorating Shakespeare's birth* **2** a religious rite or series of rites **3** a courteous gesture or act: *the ceremony of toasting the Queen* **4** ceremonial observances or gestures collectively: *the ceremony of a monarchy* **5** stand on ceremony to insist on or act with excessive formality **6** without ceremony in a casual or informal manner [c14 from Medieval Latin *cēremōnia*, from Latin *caerimōnia* what is sacred, a religious rite]

Ceres[1] ('sɪəriːz) *n* the Roman goddess of agriculture. Greek counterpart: **Demeter**

Ceres[2] ('sɪəriːz) *n* the largest asteroid and the first to be discovered. It has a diameter of 930 kilometres

ceresin ('sɛrɪsɪn) *n* a white wax extracted from ozocerite [c19 irregularly from Latin *cēra* wax]

cereus ('sɪərɪəs) *n* **1** any tropical American cactus of the genus *Cereus*, esp *C. jamacaru* of N Brazil, which grows to a height of 13 metres (40 feet) **2** any of several similar and related cacti, such as the night-blooming cereus [c18 from New Latin, from Latin *cēreus* a wax taper, from *cēra* wax]

ceria ('sɪərɪə) *n* another name (not in technical usage) for **ceric oxide** [New Latin, from CERIUM]

ceric ('sɪərɪk) *adj* of or containing cerium in the tetravalent state

ceric oxide *n* a white or yellow solid used in

ceramics, enamels, and radiation shields. Formula: CeO$_2$. Also called: cerium dioxide, ceria

ceriferous (sɪˈrɪfərəs) *adj biology* producing or bearing wax

cerise (səˈriːz, -ˈriːs) *n* **a** a moderate to dark red colour **b** (*as adjective*): *a cerise scarf* [C19 from French: CHERRY]

cerium (ˈsɪərɪəm) *n* a malleable ductile steel-grey element of the lanthanide series of metals, used in lighter flints and as a reducing agent in metallurgy. Symbol: Ce; atomic no.: 58; atomic wt.: 140.115; valency: 3 or 4; relative density: 6.770; melting pt.: 798°C; boiling pt.: 3443°C [C19 New Latin, from CERES (the asteroid) + -IUM]

cerium metals *pl n* the metals lanthanum, cerium, praseodymium, neodymium, promethium, and samarium, forming a sub-group of the lanthanides

Cerlox (ˈsɜːlɒks) *n trademark US and Canadian* a type of plastic binding used in strips to curl through the perforations in separate sheets of paper to bind them together

cermet (ˈsɜːmɪt) *n* any of several materials consisting of a metal matrix with ceramic particles disseminated through it. They are hard and resistant to high temperatures. Also called: ceramal [C20 from CER(AMIC) + MET(AL)]

CERN (sɜːn) *n acronym for* Conseil Européen pour la Recherche Nucléaire; an organization of European states with a centre in Geneva for research in high-energy particle physics, now called the European Laboratory for Particle Physics

Cernăuți (tʃernəˈutsj) *n* the Romanian name for **Chernovtsy**

cernuous (ˈsɜːnjʊəs) *adj botany* (of some flowers or buds) drooping [C17 from Latin *cernuus* leaning forwards, of obscure origin]

cero (ˈsɪərəʊ, ˈsɪərəʊ) *n, pl* **-ro** *or* **-ros** **1** a large spiny-finned food fish, *Scomberomorus regalis*, of warm American coastal regions of the Atlantic: family *Scombridae* (mackerels, tunnies, etc) **2** any similar or related fish [C19 from Spanish: saw, sawfish, altered spelling of SIERRA]

cero- *combining form* indicating the use of wax: *ceroplastic* [from Greek *kēros* wax]

Ceroc (səˈrɒk) *n trademark* a form of dance combining elements of jive and salsa [C20 from French *C'est le Roc* It's Rock]

cerography (sɪəˈrɒɡrəfɪ) *n* the art of engraving on a waxed plate on which a printing surface is created by electrotyping > **cerographic** (ˌsɪərəʊˈɡræfɪk) *or* ˌcero'graphical *adj* > ce'rographist *n*

ceroplastic (ˌsɪərəʊˈplæstɪk) *adj* **1** relating to wax modelling **2** modelled in wax

ceroplastics (ˌsɪərəʊˈplæstɪks) *n* (*functioning as singular*) the art of wax modelling

cerotic acid (sɪˈrɒtɪk) *n* another name (not in technical usage) for **hexacosanoic acid**

cerotype (ˈsɪərətaɪp) *n* a process for preparing a printing plate by engraving a wax-coated copper plate and then using this as a mould for an electrotype

cerous (ˈsɪərəs) *adj* of or containing cerium in the trivalent state [C19 from CERIUM + -OUS]

Cerro de Pasco (*Spanish* ˈθɛrrɔ ðe ˈpasko) *n* a town in central Peru, in the Andes: one of the highest towns in the world, 4400 m (14 436 ft) above sea level; mining centre. Pop: 62 749 (1993)

Cerro Gordo (*Spanish* ˈθɛrrɔ ˈɡorðo) *n* a mountain pass in E Mexico, between Veracruz and Jalapa: site of a battle in the Mexican War (1847) in which American forces under General Scott decisively defeated the Mexicans

cert (sɜːt) *n informal* something that is a certainty, esp a horse that is certain to win a race (esp in the phrase **a dead cert**)

certain (ˈsɜːtən) *adj* **1** (*postpositive*) positive and confident about the truth of something; convinced: *I am certain that he wrote a book* **2** (*usually postpositive*) definitely known: *it is certain that they were on the bus* **3** (*usually postpositive*) sure; bound;

destined: *he was certain to fail* **4** decided or settled upon; fixed: *the date is already certain for the invasion* **5** unfailing; reliable: *his judgment is certain* **6** moderate or minimum: *to a certain extent* **7** make certain of to ensure (that one will get something); confirm ▷ *adv* **8** for certain definitely; without a doubt: *he will win for certain* ▷ *determiner* **9 a** known but not specified or named: *certain people may doubt this* **b** (*as pronoun; functioning as plural*): *certain of the members have not paid their subscriptions* **10** named but not known: *he had written to a certain Mrs Smith* [C13 from Old French, from Latin *certus* sure, fixed, from *cernere* to discern, decide]

certainly (ˈsɜːtənlɪ) *adv* **1** with certainty; without doubt: *he certainly rides very well* ▷ *sentence substitute* **2** by all means; definitely: used in answer to questions

certainty (ˈsɜːtəntɪ) *n, pl* **-ties** **1** the condition of being certain **2** something established as certain or inevitable **3** for a certainty without doubt

CertEd (*in Britain*) *abbreviation for* Certificate in Education

certes (ˈsɜːtɪz) *adv archaic* with certainty; truly [C13 from Old French, ultimately from Latin *certus* CERTAIN]

certifiable (ˈsɜːtɪˌfaɪəbᵊl) *adj* **1** capable of being certified **2** fit to be certified as insane > 'certiˌfiably *adv*

certificate *n* (səˈtɪfɪkɪt) **1** an official document attesting the truth of the facts stated, as of birth, marital status, death, health, completion of an academic course, ability to practise a profession, etc **2** short for **share certificate** ▷ *vb* (səˈtɪfɪˌkeɪt) **3** (*tr*) to authorize by or present with an official document [C15 from Old French *certificat*, from *certifier* CERTIFY] > cer'tificatory *adj*

certificate of deposit *n* a negotiable certificate issued by a bank in return for a deposit of money for a term of up to five years. Abbreviation: **CD**

certificate of incorporation *n company law* a signed statement by the Registrar of Companies that a company is duly incorporated

certificate of origin *n* a document stating the name of the country that produced a specified shipment of goods: often required before importation of goods

Certificate of Secondary Education *n* See **CSE**

certificate of unruliness *n* (*in Britain*) the decision of a juvenile court that a young person on remand is too unmanageable for local-authority care and should be taken into custody

certification (ˌsɜːtɪfɪˈkeɪʃən) *n* **1** the act of certifying or state of being certified **2** *law* a document attesting the truth of a fact or statement

certified (ˈsɜːtɪˌfaɪd) *adj* **1** holding or guaranteed by a certificate **2** endorsed or guaranteed: *a certified cheque* **3** (of a person) declared legally insane

certified accountant *n* (*in Britain*) a member of the Chartered Association of Certified Accountants, who is authorized to audit company accounts. Compare **chartered accountant**, **certified public accountant**

certified public accountant *n* (*in the US*) a public accountant certified to have met state legal requirements. Compare **certified accountant**

certify (ˈsɜːtɪˌfaɪ) *vb* **-fies, -fying, -fied 1** to confirm or attest (to); usually in writing: *the letter certified her age* **2** (*tr*) to endorse or guarantee (that certain required standards have been met) **3** to give reliable information or assurances: *he certified that it was Walter's handwriting* **4** (*tr*) to declare legally insane **5** (*tr*) *US and Canadian* (of a bank) to state in writing on (a cheque) that payment is guaranteed [C14 from Old French *certifier*, from Medieval Latin *certificāre* to make certain, from Latin *certus* CERTAIN + *facere* to make] > 'certiˌfier *n*

certiorari (ˌsɜːtɪɔːˈreəraɪ) *n law* an order of a superior court directing that a record of proceedings in a lower court be sent up for review.

See also **mandamus, prohibition** [C15 from legal Latin: to be informed]

certitude (ˈsɜːtɪˌtjuːd) *n* confidence; certainty [C15 from Church Latin *certitūdō*, from Latin *certus* CERTAIN]

cerulean (sɪˈruːlɪən) *n* **a** a deep blue colour; azure **b** (*as adjective*): *a cerulean sea* [C17 from Latin *caeruleus*, probably from *caelum* sky]

cerumen (sɪˈruːmɛn) *n* the soft brownish-yellow wax secreted by glands in the auditory canal of the external ear. Nontechnical name: earwax [C18 from New Latin, from Latin *cēra* wax + ALBUMEN] > ce'ruminous *adj*

ceruse (səˈruːs) *n* another name for **white lead** (sense 1) [C14 from Old French *céruse*, from Latin *cērussa*, perhaps ultimately from Greek *kēros* wax]

cerussite *or* **cerusite** (ˈsɪərəˌsaɪt) *n* a usually white mineral, found in veins. It is a source of lead. Composition: lead carbonate. Formula: PbCO$_3$. Crystal structure: orthorhombic. Also called: white lead ore [C19 from Latin *cērussa* (see CERUSE) + -ITE^1]

cervelat (ˈsɜːvəˌlæt, -ˌlɑː) *n* a smoked sausage made from pork and beef [C17 via obsolete French from Italian *cervellata*]

cervena (ˌsɜːˈvɛnə) *n trademark NZ* farm-produced venison

cervical (ˈsɜːvɪkᵊl, səˈvaɪ-) *adj* of or relating to the neck or cervix [C17 from New Latin *cervīcālis*, from Latin *cervīx* neck]

cervical smear *n med* a smear of cellular material taken from the neck (cervix) of the uterus for detection of cancer. Also called: Pap test *or* smear

cervicitis (ˌsɜːvɪˈsaɪtɪs) *n* inflammation of the neck of the uterus

cervicography (ˌsɜːvɪˈkɒɡrəfɪ) *n med* a method of cervical screening in which the neck of the uterus is photographed to facilitate the early detection of cancer

cervicum (ˈsɜːvɪkəm, səˈvaɪ-) *n zoology* the flexible region between the prothorax and head in insects

cervid (ˈsɜːvɪd) *n* **1** any ruminant mammal of the family *Cervidae*, including the deer, characterized by the presence of antlers ▷ *adj* **2** of, relating to, or belonging to the *Cervidae* [C19 from New Latin *Cervidae*, from Latin *cervus* deer]

Cervin (sɛrvɛ̃) *n* **Mont** the French name for the **Matterhorn**

cervine (ˈsɜːvaɪn) *adj* **1** resembling or relating to a deer **2** of a dark yellowish-brown colour [C19 from Latin *cervīnus*, from *cervus* a deer]

cervix (ˈsɜːvɪks) *n, pl* **cervixes** *or* **cervices** (səˈvaɪsiːz) **1** the technical name for **neck 2** any necklike part of an organ, esp the lower part of the uterus that extends into the vagina [C18 from Latin]

Cesarean *or* **Cesarian** (sɪˈzɛərɪən) *adj US* variant spellings of **Caesarean**

Cesena (*Italian* tʃeˈzeːna) *n* a city in N Italy, in Emilia-Romagna. Pop: 90 948 (2001)

cesium (ˈsiːzɪəm) *n* the usual US spelling of **caesium**

České Budějovice (*Czech* ˈtʃeskɛ ˈbudjɛjɔvitsɛ) *n* a city in the S Czech Republic, on the Vltava (Moldau) River. Pop: 175 000 (1993). German name: Budweis

Československo (ˈtʃeskɔslɔvɛnskɔ) *n* the Czech name for Czechoslovakia

Cesky terrier (ˈtʃeskɪ) *n* a sturdy long-bodied short-legged variety of terrier with a wavy grey or light brown coat

cespitose (ˈsɛspɪˌtəʊs) *adj* a variant spelling (esp US) of **caespitose**. > 'cespiˌtosely *adv*

cess^1 (sɛs) *n* **1** *Brit* any of several special taxes, such as a land tax in Scotland **2** (*formerly, in* Ireland) **a** the obligation to provide the soldiers and household of the lord deputy with supplies at fixed prices **b** any military exaction **3** (*tr*) *Brit* to tax or assess for taxation **4** (*tr*) (*formerly in* Ireland) to impose (soldiers) upon a population, to be supported by them [C16 short for ASSESSMENT]

C

cess² (sɛs) *n* an Irish slang word for **luck** (esp in the phrase **bad cess to you!**) [c19 probably from CESS¹ (sense 2)]

cess³ (sɛs) *n* short for **cesspool**

cessation (sɛ'seɪʃən) *n* a ceasing or stopping; discontinuance; pause: *temporary cessation of hostilities* [c14 from Latin *cessātiō* a delaying, inactivity, from *cessāre* to be idle, desist from, from *cēdere* to yield, CEDE]

cesser ('sɛsə) *n law* the coming to an end of a term interest or annuity

cession ('sɛʃən) *n* **1** the act of ceding, esp of ceding rights, property, or territory **2** something that is ceded, esp land or territory [c14 from Latin *cessiō*, from *cēdere* to yield]

cessionary ('sɛʃənərɪ) *n, pl* **-aries** *law* a person to whom something is transferred; assignee; grantee

cesspool ('sɛs,puːl) *or* **cesspit** ('sɛs,pɪt) *n* **1** Also called: **sink, sump** a covered cistern, etc, for collecting and storing sewage or waste water **2** a filthy or corrupt place: *a cesspool of iniquity* [c17 changed (through influence of POOL¹) from earlier *cesperalle*, from Old French *souspirail* vent, air, from *soupirer* to sigh; see SUSPIRE]

c'est la vie *French* (sɛ la vi) that's life

cestode ('sɛstəʊd) *n* any parasitic flatworm of the class *Cestoda*, which includes the tapeworms [c19 from New Latin *Cestoidea* ribbon-shaped creatures, from Latin *cestus* belt, girdle; see CESTUS¹]

cestoid ('sɛstɔɪd) *adj* (esp of tapeworms and similar animals) ribbon-like in form

cestus¹ ('sɛstəs), **cestos** ('sɛstɒs) *n classical myth* the girdle of Aphrodite (Venus) decorated to cause amorousness [c16 from Latin, from Greek *kestos* belt, from *kentein* to stitch]

cestus² *or* **caestus** ('sɛstəs) *n, pl* **-tus** *or* **-tuses** (in classical Roman boxing) a pugilist's gauntlet of bull's hide loaded or studded with metal [c18 from Latin *caestus*, probably from *caedere* to strike, slay]

cesura (sɪ'zjʊərə) *n, pl* **-ras** *or* **-rae** (-riː) *prosody* a variant spelling of **caesura**. ▷ **ce'sural** *adj*

CET *abbreviation for* **1** Central European Time **2** Common External Tariff

cetacean (sɪ'teɪʃən) *adj also* **cetaceous** **1** of, relating to, or belonging to the *Cetacea*, an order of aquatic placental mammals having no hind limbs and a blowhole for breathing: includes toothed whales (dolphins, porpoises, etc) and whalebone whales (rorquals, right whales, etc) ▷ *n* **2** a whale [c19 from New Latin *Cētācea*, ultimately from Latin *cētus* whale, from Greek *kētos*]

cetane ('siːteɪn) *n* a colourless insoluble liquid alkane hydrocarbon used in the determination of the cetane number of diesel fuel. Formula: $C_{16}H_{34}$. Also called: **hexadecane** [c19 from Latin *cētus* whale + -ANE, so called because related compounds are found in sperm whale oil]

cetane number *n* a measure of the quality of a diesel fuel expressed as the percentage of cetane in a mixture of cetane and 1-methylnapthalene of the same quality as the given fuel. Also called: **cetane rating** Compare **octane number**

Cetatea Albă (tʃe'tatea 'albə) *n* the Romanian name for **Belgorod-Dnestrovski**

cete (siːt) *n* a group of badgers [c15 perhaps from Latin *coetus* assembly, from *coīre* to come together]

ceteris paribus ('kɛtərɪs 'pɑːrɪbʊs) other things being equal [c17 Latin]

Cetinje (*Serbo-Croat* 'tsɛtɪɲɛ) *n* a city in Serbia and Montenegro, in SW Montenegro: former capital of Montenegro (until 1945); palace and fortified monastery, residences of Montenegrin prince-bishops. Pop: 15 924 (1991)

Cetnik ('tʃɛtnɪk, tʃɛt'niːk) *n* a variant spelling of **Chetnik**

cetology (siː'tɒlədʒɪ) *n* the branch of zoology concerned with the study of whales (cetaceans) [c19 from Latin *cētus* whale] ▷ **cetological** (,siːtə'lɒdʒɪkᵊl) *adj* ▷ **ce'tologist** *n*

cetrimide ('sɛtrɪ,maɪd) *n* a quaternary ammonium compound used as a detergent and,

having powerful antiseptic properties, for sterilizing surgical instruments, cleaning wounds, etc

Cetti's warbler ('tʃɛtɪz) *n* a reddish-brown Eurasian warbler, *Cettia cetti*, with a distinctive song [c19 after F. Cetti, 18th-century Italian ornithologist]

Cetus ('siːtəs) *n, Latin genitive* **Ceti** ('siːtaɪ) a large constellation on the celestial equator near Pisces and Aquarius. It contains the variable star Mira Ceti [Latin: whale]

Ceuta (*Spanish* 'θeuta) *n* an enclave in Morocco on the Strait of Gibraltar, consisting of a port and military station: held by Spain since 1580. Pop: 74 931 (2003 est)

Cévennes (*French* sevɛn) *n* a mountain range in S central France, on the SE edge of the Massif Central. Highest peak: 1754 m (5755 ft)

Ceylon (sɪ'lɒn) *n* **1** the former name (until 1972) of **Sri Lanka** **2** an island in the Indian Ocean, off the SE coast of India: consists politically of the republic of Sri Lanka. Area: 64 644 sq km (24 959 sq miles)

Ceylonese (,selə'niːz, ,siːlə-) *adj* of or relating to Ceylon or its inhabitants

Ceylon moss *n* a red East Indian seaweed, *Gracilaria lichenoides*, from which agar is made

Ceyx ('siːɪks) *n Greek myth* a king of Trachis in Thessaly and the husband of Alcyone. He died in a shipwreck and his wife drowned herself in grief. Compare **Alcyone¹** (sense 1)

cf *or* **CF** *abbreviation for* cost and freight. Also: **c & f**

cf² *the internet domain name for* Central African Republic

Cf *the chemical symbol for* californium

CF *chiefly Brit abbreviation for* Chaplain to the Forces

cf. *abbreviation for* confer [Latin: compare]

c/f *book-keeping abbreviation for* carried forward

CFB (in Canada) *abbreviation for* Canadian Forces Base

CFC *abbreviation for* chlorofluorocarbon

CFD *abbreviation for* computational fluid dynamics

CFE *abbreviation for* **1** College of Further Education **2** Conventional Forces in Europe: negotiations between NATO and the Warsaw Pact to reduce conventional forces located between the Atlantic and the Urals

cfi *or* **CFI** *abbreviation for* cost, freight, and insurance (included in the price quoted). Also: **c.i.f**

CFL *abbreviation for* Canadian Football League

CFS *abbreviation for* chronic fatigue syndrome

cg¹ **1** *abbreviation for* centre of gravity **2** *symbol for* centigram

cg² *the internet domain name for* Republic of Congo

CG *abbreviation for* **1** captain general **2** coastguard **3** Coldstream Guards **4** computer-generated **5** consul general

CGBR *abbreviation for* Central Government Borrowing Requirement

CGI *abbreviation for* **1** computer-generated image *or* imagery **2** common gateway interface

CGM *chiefly Brit abbreviation for* Conspicuous Gallantry Medal

CGS (in Britain) *abbreviation for* Chief of General Staff

cgs units *pl n* a metric system of units based on the centimetre, gram, and second. For scientific and technical purposes these units have been replaced by SI units

CGT *abbreviation for* capital gains tax

ch **1** *abbreviation for* custom house **2** *the internet domain name for* Switzerland

CH **1** *abbreviation for* Companion of Honour (a Brit title) **2** *international car registration for* Switzerland [from French *Confédération Helvétique*]

ch. *abbreviation for* **1** chain (unit of measure) **2** chapter **3** *chess* check **4** chief **5** church

chabazite ('kæbə,zaɪt) *n* a pink, white, or colourless zeolite mineral consisting of a hydrated silicate of calcium, sodium, potassium, and aluminium in hexagonal crystalline form.

Formula: $Ca_2Al_2Si_4O_{12}.6H_2O$ [c19 from French *chabazie* from Late Greek *khabazios*, erroneous for *khalazios* stone similar to a hailstone, from Greek *khalazios* of hail, from *khalaza* hailstone + -ITE¹]

Chablis ('ʃæblɪ; *French* ʃablɪ) *n* (*sometimes not capitals*) a dry white burgundy wine made around Chablis, in central France

cha-cha-cha (,tʃɑːtʃɑːˈtʃɑː) *or* **cha-cha** *n* **1** a Latin-American ballroom dance with small steps and swaying hip movements **2** a piece of music composed for this dance ▷ *vb* (*intr*) **3** to perform this dance [c20 from American (Cuban) Spanish]

chacma ('tʃækmə) *n* a baboon, *Papio* (or *Chaeropithecus*) *ursinus*, having coarse greyish hair and occurring in southern and eastern Africa [c19 from Khoikhoi]

Chaco (*Spanish* 'tʃako) *n* See **Gran Chaco**

chaconne (ʃə'kɒn; *French* ʃakɔn) *n* **1** a musical form consisting of a set of continuous variations upon a ground bass. See also **passacaglia 2** *archaic* a dance in slow triple time probably originating in Spain [c17 from French, from Spanish *chacona*, probably imitative of the castanet accompaniment]

chacun à son goût *French* (ʃakœn a sɔ̃ gu) each to his own taste

chad (tʃæd) *n* the small pieces of cardboard or paper removed during the punching of holes in computer printer paper, paper tape, etc [c20 perhaps based on CHAFF¹]

Chad (tʃæd) *n* **1** a republic in N central Africa: made a territory of French Equatorial Africa in 1910; became independent in 1960; contains much desert and the Tibesti Mountains, with Lake Chad in the west; produces chiefly cotton and livestock; suffered intermittent civil war from 1963 and prolonged drought. Official languages: Arabic; French. Religion: Muslim majority, also Christian and animist. Currency: franc. Capital: Ndjamena. Pop: 8 854 000 (2004 est). Area: 1 284 000 sq km (495 750 sq miles). French name: **Tchad 2 Lake** a lake in N central Africa: fed chiefly by the Shari River, it has no apparent outlet. Area: at fullest extent 10 000 to 26 000 sq km (4000 to 10 000 sq miles), varying seasonally; it has shrunk considerably in recent years

Chadderton ('tʃædətᵊn) *n* a town in NW England, in Oldham unitary authority, in Greater Manchester. Pop: 33 001 (2001)

Chadic ('tʃædɪk) *n* **1** a subfamily of the Afro-Asiatic family of languages, spoken in an area west and south of Lake Chad, the chief member of which is Hausa ▷ *adj* **2** denoting, relating to, or belonging to this group of languages

chado ('tʃɑːdəʊ), **sado** ('sɑːdəʊ) *or* **chanoyu** (,tʃɑːnɔː'yuː) *n* the Japanese tea ceremony [from Japanese *cha* or *sa* tea (from Chinese *cha*) + *dō* way (from Chinese *tao*); *chanoyu* literally: tea's hot water]

chador ('tʃʌdə) *n* a variant spelling of **chuddar**

chadri ('tʃædriː) *n* a shroud which covers the body from heat to foot, usually worn by females in Islamic countries

chaebol ('tʃeɪbɒl) *n* a large, usually family-owned, business group in South Korea [c20 from Korean, literally: money clan]

Chaeronea (,kerə'niːə) *n* an ancient Greek town in W Boeotia: site of the victory of Philip of Macedon over the Athenians and Thebans (338 BC) and of Sulla over Mithridates (86 BC)

chaeta ('kiːtə) *n, pl* **-tae** (-tiː) any of the chitinous bristles on the body of such annelids as the earthworm and the lugworm: used in locomotion; a seta [c19 New Latin, from Greek *khaitē* long hair]

chaetiferous (kiː'tɪfərəs) *adj zoology* having bristles

chaetognath ('kiːtɒg,næθ) *n* any small wormlike marine invertebrate of the phylum *Chaetognatha*, including the arrowworms, having a coelom and a ring of bristles around the mouth [c19 New Latin *Chaetognatha*, literally: hair-jaw, from CHAETA + Greek *gnathos* jaw]

chaetopod (ˈkiːtəˌpɒd) *n* any annelid worm of the classes *Oligochaeta* or *Polychaeta*. See **oligochaete, polychaete** [C19 from New Latin *Chaetopoda*; see CHAETA, -POD]

chafe (tʃeɪf) *vb* **1** to make or become sore or worn by rubbing **2** (*tr*) to warm (the hands, etc) by rubbing **3** to irritate or be irritated or impatient: *he was chafed because he was not allowed out* **4** (*intr*; often foll by *on, against*, etc) to cause friction; rub **5** **chafe at the bit** See **champ¹** (sense 3) ▷ *n* **6** a soreness or irritation caused by friction [C14 from Old French *chaufer* to warm, ultimately from Latin *calefacere*, from *calēre* to be warm + *facere* to make]

chafer (ˈtʃeɪfə) *n* any of various scarabaeid beetles, such as the cockchafer and rose chafer [Old English *ceafor*; related to Old Saxon *kevera*, Old High German *chevar*]

chaff¹ (tʃɑːf) *n* **1** the mass of husks, etc, separated from the seeds during threshing **2** finely cut straw and hay used to feed cattle **3** something of little worth; rubbish (esp in the phrase **separate the wheat from the chaff**) **4** the dry membranous bracts enclosing the flowers of certain composite plants **5** thin strips of metallic foil released into the earth's atmosphere to confuse radar signals and prevent detection [Old English *ceaf*; related to Old High German *keva* husk] > **'chaffy** *adj*

chaff² (tʃɑːf) *n* **1** light-hearted teasing or joking; banter ▷ *vb* **2** to tease good-naturedly; banter [C19 probably slang variant of CHAFE, perhaps influenced by CHAFF¹] > **'chaffer** *n*

chaffer (ˈtʃæfə) *vb* **1** (*intr*) to haggle or bargain **2** to chatter, talk, or say idly; bandy (words) **3** (*tr*) *obsolete* to deal in; barter ▷ *n* **4** haggling or bargaining [C13 *chaffare*, from *chep* bargain + *fare* journey; see CHEAP, FARE] > **'chafferer** *n*

chaffinch (ˈtʃæfɪntʃ) *n* a common European finch, *Fringilla coelebs*, with black and white wings and, in the male, a reddish body and blue-grey head [Old English *ceaffinc*, from *ceaf* CHAFF¹ + *finc* FINCH]

chafing dish (ˈtʃeɪfɪŋ) *n* a vessel with a heating apparatus beneath it, for cooking or keeping food warm at the table

Chagas' disease (ˈʃɑːgəs) *n* a form of trypanosomiasis found in South America, caused by the protozoan *Trypanosoma cruzi*, characterized by fever and, often, inflammation of the heart muscles. Also called: (South) American trypanosomiasis Compare **sleeping sickness** [C20 named after Carlos *Chagas* (1879–1934), Brazilian physician who first described it]

Chagres (*Spanish* ˈtʃaɣres) *n* a river in Panama, flowing southwest through Gatún Lake, then northwest to the Caribbean Sea

chagrin (ˈʃægrɪn) *n* **1** a feeling of annoyance or mortification ▷ *vb* (*tr*) **2** to embarrass and annoy; mortify [C17 from French *chagrin, chagriner*, of unknown origin] > **'chagrined** *adj*

chai (tʃaɪ) *n* tea, esp as made in India with added spices [C20 Indian]

chain (tʃeɪn) *n* **1** a flexible length of metal links, used for confining, connecting, pulling, etc, or in jewellery **2** (*usually plural*) anything that confines, fetters, or restrains: *the chains of poverty* **3** (*usually plural*) Also called: **snow chains** a set of metal links that fit over the tyre of a motor vehicle to increase traction and reduce skidding on an icy surface **4 a** a number of establishments such as hotels, shops, etc, having the same owner or management **b** (*as modifier*): *a chain store* **5** a series of related or connected facts, events, etc **6** a series of deals in which each depends on a purchaser selling before being able to buy **7** (*of reasoning*) a sequence of arguments each of which takes the conclusion of the preceding as a premise. See (as an example) **sorites 8** Also called: **Gunter's chain** a unit of length equal to 22 yards **9** Also called: **engineer's chain** a unit of length equal to 100 feet **10** *chem* two or more atoms or groups bonded together so that the configuration of the resulting molecule, ion, or radical resembles a chain. See also **open chain,**

ring¹ (sense 18) **11** *geography* a series of natural features, esp approximately parallel mountain ranges **12 off the chain** *Austral and NZ informal* free from responsibility **13 jerk** or **yank (someone's) chain** *informal* to tease, mislead, or harass (someone) ▷ *vb* **14** *surveying* to measure with a chain or tape **15** (*tr; often foll by up*) to confine, tie, or make fast with or as if with a chain **16** short for **chain stitch** [C13 from Old French *chaine*, ultimately from Latin; see CATENA]

chain drive *n engineering* a chain of links passing over sprockets that transmits rotation from one shaft to another

chain gang *n US* a group of convicted prisoners chained together, usually while doing hard labour

chain grate *n* a type of mechanical stoker for a furnace, in which the grate consists of an endless chain that draws the solid fuel into the furnace as it rotates

chain letter *n* a letter, often with a request for and promise of money, that is sent to many people who add to or recopy it and send it on to others: illegal in many countries

chain lightning *n* another name for **forked lightning**

chain mail *n* another term for **mail²** (sense 1)

chainman (ˈtʃeɪnmən) *n, pl* -men *surveying* a person who does the chaining in a survey

chainplate (ˈtʃeɪnˌpleɪt) *n* a metal plate on the side of a vessel, to which the shrouds are attached

chain printer *n* a line printer in which the type is on a continuous chain, used to print computer output

chain-react *vb* (*intr*) to undergo a chain reaction

chain reaction *n* **1** a process in which a neutron colliding with an atomic nucleus causes fission and the ejection of one or more other neutrons, which induce other nuclei to split **2** a chemical reaction in which the product of one step is a reactant in the following step **3** a series of rapidly occurring events, each of which precipitates the next

chain rule *n maths* a theorem that may be used in the differentiation of the function of a function. It states that $du/dx = (du/dy)(dy/dx)$, where y is a function of x and u a function of y

chain saw *n* a motor-driven saw, usually portable, in which the cutting teeth form links in a continuous chain

chain shot *n* cannon shot comprising two balls or half balls joined by a chain, much used formerly, esp in naval warfare to destroy rigging

chain-smoke *vb* to smoke (cigarettes, etc) continually, esp lighting one from the preceding one > **chain smoker** *n*

chain stitch *n* **1** an ornamental looped embroidery stitch resembling the links of a chain ▷ *vb* **chain-stitch 2** to sew (something) with this stitch

chain store *n* one of several retail enterprises under the same ownership and management. Also called: **multiple store**

chain wheel *n engineering* a toothed wheel that meshes with a roller chain to transmit motion

chair (tʃeə) *n* **1** a seat with a back on which one person sits, typically having four legs and often having arms **2** an official position of authority: *a chair on the board of directors* **3** the chairman of a debate or meeting: *the speaker addressed the chair* **4** a professorship: *the chair of German* **5** *railways* an iron or steel cradle bolted to a sleeper in which the rail sits and is locked in position **6** short for **sedan chair 7 in the chair** chairing a debate or meeting **8 take the chair** to preside as chairman for a meeting, etc **9 the chair** an informal name for **electric chair** ▷ *vb* (*tr*) **10** to preside over (a meeting) **11** *Brit* to carry aloft in a sitting position after a triumph or great achievement **12** to provide with a chair of office **13** to install in a chair [C13 from Old French *chaiere*, from Latin *cathedra*, from Greek *kathedra*, from *kata-* down +

hedra seat; compare CATHEDRAL]

chairborne (ˈtʃeəˌbɔːn) *adj informal* having an administrative or desk job rather than a more active one

chairbound (ˈtʃeəˌbaʊnd) *adj social welfare* unable to walk; dependent on a wheelchair for mobility

chairlift (ˈtʃeəˌlɪft) *n* a series of chairs suspended from a power-driven cable for conveying people, esp skiers, up a mountain

chairman (ˈtʃeəmən) *n, pl* -men **1** Also called: **chairperson**, (*fem*) **chairwoman** a person who presides over a company's board of directors, a committee, a debate, an administrative department, etc **2** *history* someone who carries a sedan chair > **'chairmanˌship** *n*

> USAGE *Chairman* can seem inappropriate when applied to a woman, while *chairwoman* can be offensive. *Chair* and *chairperson* can be applied to either a man or a woman; *chair* is generally preferred to *chairperson*

chairperson (ˈtʃeəˌpɜːsᵊn) *n* another word for **chairman** (sense 1)

> USAGE See at **chairman**

chaise (ʃeɪz) *n* **1** a light open horse-drawn carriage, esp one with two wheels designed for two passengers **2** short for **post chaise** and **chaise longue 3** a gold coin first issued in France in the 14th century, depicting the king seated on a throne [C18 from French, variant of Old French *chaiere* CHAIR]

chaise longue (ˈʃeɪz ˈlɒŋ; *French* ʃɛz lɔ̃g) *n, pl* **chaise longues** or **chaises longues** (ˈʃeɪz ˈlɒŋ; *French* ʃɛz lɔ̃g) a long low chair for reclining, with a back and single armrest [C19 from French: long chair]

chakalaka (ˌʃakaˈlaka) *n South African* a relish made from tomatoes, onions, and spices [of unknown origin]

chakra (ˈtʃækrə, ˈtʃʌkrə) *n* (in yoga) any of the seven major energy centres in the body [C19 from Sanskrit *cakra* wheel, circle]

chalaza (kəˈleɪzə) *n, pl* -zas or -zae (-ziː) **1** one of a pair of spiral threads of albumen holding the yolk of a bird's egg in position **2** the basal part of a plant ovule, where the integuments and nucellus are joined [C18 New Latin, from Greek: hailstone] > **chaˈlazal** *adj*

chalazion (kəˈleɪzɪən) *n* a small cyst on the eyelid resulting from chronic inflammation of a meibomian gland. Also called: **meibomian cyst** [C18 from Greek: a small CHALAZA]

chalcanthite (kælˈkænθaɪt) *n* a blue secondary mineral consisting of hydrated copper sulphate in triclinic crystalline form. Formula: $CuSO_4.5H_2O$ [C19 via German from Latin *chalcanthum* copper sulphate solution, from Greek *khalkanthon*, from *khalkos* copper + *anthos* flower; see -ITE¹]

chalcedony (kælˈsedənɪ) *n, pl* -nies a microcrystalline often greyish form of quartz with crystals arranged in parallel fibres: a gemstone. Formula: SiO_2 [C15 from Late Latin *chalcēdōnius*, from Greek *khalkēdōn* a precious stone (Revelation 21:19), perhaps named after *Khalkēdōn* Chalcedon, town in Asia Minor] > **chalcedonic** (ˌkælsɪˈdɒnɪk) *adj*

chalcid or **chalcid fly** (ˈkælsɪd) *n* any tiny hymenopterous insect of the family *Chalcididae* and related families, whose larvae are parasites of other insects [C19 from New Latin *Chalcis* type genus, from Greek *khalkos* copper, referring to its metallic sheen]

Chalcidice (kælˈsɪdɪsɪ) *n* a peninsula of N central Greece, in Macedonia Central, ending in the three promontories of Kassandra, Sithonia, and Akti. Area: 2945 sq km (1149 sq miles). Modern Greek name: Khalkidíki

Chalcis (ˈkælsɪs) *n* a city in the island of Euboea in SE Greece, at the narrowest point of the Euripus strait: important since the 7th century BC, founding many colonies in ancient times. Pop: 47 600 (1995 est). Modern Greek name: Khalkís

C

Medieval English name: **Negropont**

chalco- *or before a vowel* **chalc-** *combining form* indicating copper or a copper alloy: *chalcopyrite; chalcolithic* [from Greek *khalkos* copper]

chalcocite ('kælkə,saɪt) *n* a lead-grey or black mineral, found as a copper ore or in veins. It is a source of copper. Composition: copper sulphide. Formula: Cu$_2$S. Crystal structure: orthorhombic [C19 changed from earlier *chalcosine,* from Greek *khalkos* copper + -ITE^1]

chalcogen ('kælkə,dʒɛn) *n* any of the elements oxygen, sulphur, selenium, tellurium, or polonium, of group 6A of the periodic table [C20 from CHALCO(PYRITE) + -GEN]

chalcography (kæl'kɒgrəfɪ) *n* the art of engraving on copper or brass ▷ **chal'cographer** *or* **chal'cographist** *n* ▷ **chalcographic** (,kælkə'græfɪk) *or* ,chalco'graphical *adj*

chalcolithic (,kælkə'lɪθɪk) *adj archaeol* of or relating to a period characterized by the use of both stone and bronze implements

chalcopyrite (,kælkə'paɪraɪt, -'paɪə-) *n* a widely distributed yellow mineral consisting of a sulphide of copper and iron in tetragonal crystalline form: the principal ore of copper. Formula: CuFeS$_2$. Also called: **copper pyrites**

Chaldea *or* **Chaldaea** (kæl'diːə) *n* **1** an ancient region of Babylonia; the land lying between the Euphrates delta, the Persian Gulf, and the Arabian desert **2** another name for **Babylonia**

Chaldean *or* **Chaldaean** (kæl'diːən) *n* **1** a member of an ancient Semitic people who controlled S Babylonia from the late 8th to the late 7th century BC **2** the dialect of Babylonian spoken by this people ▷ *adj* **3** of or relating to the ancient Chaldeans or their language

Chaldee (kæl'diː) *n* **1** a nontechnical term for **Biblical Aramaic,** once believed to be the language of the ancient Chaldeans **2** the actual language of the ancient Chaldeans. See also **Chaldean** (sense 2) **3** an inhabitant of ancient Chaldea; a Chaldean ▷ Also (for senses 1, 2): **Chaldaic** (kæl'deɪɪk)

chaldron ('tʃɔːldrən) *n* a unit of capacity equal to 36 bushels. Formerly used in the US for the measurement of solids, being equivalent to 1.268 cubic metres. Used in Britain for both solids and liquids, it is equivalent to 1.309 cubic metres [C17 from Old French *chauderon* CAULDRON]

chalet ('ʃæleɪ; *French* ʃalɛ) *n* **1** a type of wooden house of Swiss origin, typically low, with wide projecting eaves **2** a similar house used esp as a ski lodge, garden house, etc [C19 from French (Swiss dialect)]

chalice ('tʃælɪs) *n* **1** *poetic* a drinking cup; goblet **2** *Christianity* a gold or silver cup containing the wine at Mass **3** the calyx of a flower, esp a cup-shaped calyx [C13 from Old French, from Latin *calix* cup; related to Greek *kalux* calyx]

chaliced ('tʃælɪst) *adj* (of plants) having cup-shaped flowers

chalicothere ('kælɪkəʊ,θɪə) *n* any of various very large extinct Tertiary horselike perissodactyl mammals that had clawed feet but otherwise resembled titanotheres [C19 from New Latin *Chalicotherium* type genus, from Greek *khalix* gravel + Greek *thērion* a little beast, from *thēr* wild animal]

chalk (tʃɔːk) *n* **1** a soft fine-grained white sedimentary rock consisting of nearly pure calcium carbonate, containing minute fossil fragments of marine organisms, usually without a cementing material **2** a piece of chalk or a substance like chalk, often coloured, used for writing and drawing on a blackboard **3** a line, mark, etc made with chalk **4** *billiards, snooker* a small cube of prepared chalk or similar substance for rubbing the tip of a cue **5** *Brit* a score, tally, or record **6** as alike (*or* different) as chalk and cheese *informal* totally different in essentials **7** by a long chalk *Brit informal* by far **8** can't tell (*or* doesn't know) chalk from cheese to be unable to judge or appreciate important differences **9** not by a long

chalk *Brit informal* by no means; not possibly **10** (*modifier*) made of chalk ▷ *vb* **11** to draw or mark (something) with chalk **12** (*tr*) to mark, rub, or whiten with or as if with chalk **13** (*intr*) (of paint) to become chalky; powder **14** (*tr*) to spread chalk on (land) as a fertilizer ▷ See also **chalk out, chalk up** [Old English *cealc,* from Latin *calx* limestone, from Greek *khalix* pebble] ▷ 'chalk,like *adj* ▷ 'chalky *adj* ▷ 'chalkiness *n*

chalk and talk *n sometimes derogatory* a formal method of teaching, in which the focal points are the blackboard and the teacher's voice, as contrasted with more informal child-centred activities

chalkboard ('tʃɔːk,bɔːd) *n US and Canadian* a hard or rigid surface made of a smooth usually dark substance, used for writing or drawing on with chalk, esp in teaching. Also called (in Britain and certain other countries): **blackboard**

chalkface ('tʃɔːk,feɪs) *n Brit informal* **a** the work or art of teaching in a school, esp classroom teaching as distinct from organizational responsibilities (esp in the phrase **at the chalkface**) **b** (*as modifier*): *chalkface experience*

chalk out *vb* (*tr, adverb*) to outline (a plan, scheme, etc); sketch

chalkpit ('tʃɔːk,pɪt) *n* a quarry for chalk

chalkstone ('tʃɔːk,stəʊn) *n pathol* another name for **tophus**

chalk talk *n US and Canadian* an informal lecture with pertinent points, explanatory diagrams, etc, shown on a blackboard

chalk up *vb* (*tr, adverb*) *informal* **1** to score or register (something): *we chalked up 100 in the game* **2** to credit (money) to an account etc (esp in the phrase **chalk it up**)

challah *or* **hallah** ('hɑːlə; *Hebrew* xa'la) *n, pl* **-lahs** *or* **-loth** (*Hebrew* -'lɔt) bread, usually in the form of a plaited loaf, traditionally eaten by Jews to celebrate the Sabbath [from Hebrew *hallāh*]

challenge ('tʃælɪndʒ) *vb* (*mainly tr*) **1** to invite or summon (someone to do something, esp to take part in a contest) **2** (*also intr*) to call (something) into question; dispute **3** to make demands on; stimulate: *the job challenges his ingenuity* **4** to order (a person) to halt and be identified or to give a password **5** *law* to make formal objection to (a juror or jury) **6** to lay claim to (attention, etc) **7** (*intr*) *hunting* (of a hound) to cry out on first encountering the scent of a quarry **8** to inject (an experimental animal immunized with a test substance) with disease microorganisms to test for immunity to the disease ▷ *n* **9** a call to engage in a fight, argument, or contest **10** a questioning of a statement or fact; a demand for justification or explanation **11** a demanding or stimulating situation, career, object, etc **12** a demand by a sentry, watchman, etc, for identification or a password **13** *US* an assertion that a person is not entitled to vote or that a vote is invalid **14** *law* a formal objection to a person selected to serve on a jury (**challenge to the polls**) or to the whole body of jurors (**challenge to the array**) [C13 from Old French *chalenge,* from Latin *calumnia* CALUMNY] ▷ 'challengeable *adj* ▷ 'challenger *n*

challenged ('tʃælɪndʒd) *adj* (*in combination*) disabled or disadvantaged in some way: *physically challenged performers*

challenging ('tʃælɪndʒɪŋ) *adj* demanding or stimulating: *a challenging new job*

challis ('ʃælɪ, -lɪs) *or* **challie** ('ʃælɪ) *n* a lightweight plain-weave fabric of wool, cotton, etc, usually with a printed design [C19 probably from a surname]

chalone ('kæləʊn) *n* any internal secretion that inhibits a physiological process or function [C20 from Greek *khalōn,* from *khalan* to slacken]

Châlons-en-Champagne (*French* ʃalɔ̃zɑ̃ʃapaɲ) *n* a city in NE France, on the River Marne: scene of Attila's defeat by the Romans (451 AD). Pop: 47 339 (1999). Former name: **Châlons-sur-Marne**

(ʃalɔ̃syrmarn) Shortened form: **Châlons**

Chalon-sur-Saône (*French* ʃalɔ̃syrson) *n* an industrial city in E central France, on the Saône River. Pop: 50 124 (1999). Shortened form: **Chalon**

chalutz *or* **halutz** *Hebrew* (xa'luts; *English* hɑ:'luts) *n, pl* **-lutzim** (-lu:'tsi:m; *English* -'lu:tsɪm) a member of an organization of immigrants to Israeli agricultural settlements [literally: pioneer, fighter]

chalybeate (kə'lɪbiɪt) *adj* **1** containing or impregnated with iron salts ▷ *n* **2** any drug containing or tasting of iron [C17 from New Latin *chalybēatus,* ultimately from *khalups* iron]

chalybite ('kælɪ,baɪt) *n* another name for **siderite** (sense 1)

cham (kæm) *n* an archaic word for **khan**^{1} (sense 1) [C16 from French, from Persian *khān;* see KHAN^1]

Cham (tʃæm) *n* **1** (*pl* **Cham** *or* **Chams**) a member of a people of Indonesian stock living in Cambodia and central Vietnam **2** the language of this people, belonging to the Malayo-Polynesian family

chamade (ʃə'mɑːd) *n military* (formerly) a signal by drum or trumpet inviting an enemy to a parley [C17 from French, from Portuguese *chamada,* from *chamar* to call, from Latin *clamāre*]

Chamaeleon (kə'miːlɪən) *n, Latin genitive* **Chamaeleontis** (kə,miːlɪ'ɒntɪs) a faint constellation lying between Volans and the South celestial pole

chamaephyte ('kæmə,faɪt) *n* a plant whose buds are close to the ground [C20 from Greek *khamai* on the ground + -PHYTE]

chamber ('tʃeɪmbə) *n* **1** a meeting hall, esp one used for a legislative or judicial assembly **2** a reception room or audience room in an official residence, palace, etc **3** *archaic or poetic* a room in a private house, esp a bedroom **4 a** a legislative, deliberative, judicial, or administrative assembly **b** any of the houses of a legislature **5** an enclosed space; compartment; cavity: *the smallest chamber in the caves* **6** the space between two gates of the locks of a canal, dry dock, etc **7** an enclosure for a cartridge in the cylinder of a revolver or for a shell in the breech of a cannon **8** *obsolete* a place where the money of a government, corporation, etc, was stored; treasury **9** short for **chamber pot 10** *NZ* the freezing room in an abattoir **11** (*modifier*) of, relating to, or suitable for chamber music: *a chamber concert* ▷ *vb* **12** (*tr*) to put in or provide with a chamber ▷ See also **chambers** [C13 from Old French *chambre,* from Late Latin *camera* room, Latin: vault, from Greek *kamara*]

chamber counsel *or* **counsellor** *n* a counsel who advises in private and does not plead in court

chambered nautilus *n* another name for the **pearly nautilus**

chamberhand ('tʃeɪmbə,hænd) *n NZ* a worker in the cold storage area of a slaughterhouse

chamberlain ('tʃeɪmbəlɪn) *n* **1** an officer who manages the household of a king **2** the steward of a nobleman or landowner **3** the treasurer of a municipal corporation [C13 from Old French *chamberlayn,* of Frankish origin; related to Old High German *chamarling* chamberlain, Latin *camera* CHAMBER] ▷ 'chamberlain,ship *n*

chambermaid ('tʃeɪmbə,meɪd) *n* a woman or girl employed to clean and tidy bedrooms, now chiefly in hotels

chamber music *n* music for performance by a small group of instrumentalists

chamber of commerce *n* (*sometimes capitals*) an organization composed mainly of local businessmen to promote, regulate, and protect their interests

chamber of trade *n* (*sometimes capitals*) a national organization representing local chambers of commerce

chamber orchestra *n* a small orchestra consisting of about 25 players, used for the authentic performance of baroque and early classical music as well as modern music written specifically for a small orchestra

chamber organ *n music* a small compact organ used esp for the authentic performance of preclassical music

chamber pot *n* a vessel for urine, used in bedrooms

chambers ('tʃeɪmbəz) *pl n* **1** a judge's room for hearing cases not taken in open court **2** (in England) the set of rooms occupied by barristers where clients are interviewed (in London, mostly in the Inns of Court) **3** *Brit archaic* a suite of rooms; apartments **4** (in the US) the private office of a judge **5** in chambers *law* **a** in the privacy of a judge's chambers **b** in a court not open to the public. Former name for sense 5 **in camera**

Chambertin (*French* ʃãbɛrtɛ̃) *n* a dry red burgundy wine produced in Gevrey-Chambertin in E France

Chambéry (*French* ʃãberi) *n* a city in SE France, in the Alps: skiing centre; former capital of the duchy of Savoy. Pop: 55 786 (1999)

Chambord (*French* ʃãbɔr) *n* a village in N central France: site of a famous Renaissance chateau

chambray ('ʃæmbreɪ) *n* a smooth light fabric of cotton, linen, etc, with white weft and a coloured warp [c19 after *Cambrai*; see CAMBRIC]

chambré ('ʃãbreɪ) *adj* (of wine) at room temperature [from French, from *chambrer* to bring (wine) to room temperature, from *chambre* room]

chameleon (kə'miːlɪən) *n* **1** any lizard of the family *Chamaeleontidae* of Africa and Madagascar, having long slender legs, a prehensile tail and tongue, and the ability to change colour **2** a changeable or fickle person [c14 from Latin *chamaeleon*, from Greek *khamaileōn*, from *khamai* on the ground + *leōn* LION] > **chameleonic** (kə,miːlɪ'ɒnɪk) *adj* > **cha'meleon-like** *adj*

chametz *or* **chometz** *Hebrew* (xa'mɛtʒ; *Yiddish* 'xomətʒ) *n Judaism* leavened food which may not be eaten during Passover

chamfer ('tʃæmfə) *n* **1** a narrow flat surface at the corner of a beam, post, etc, esp one at an angle of 45°. Compare **bevel** (sense 1) ▷ *vb* **2** to cut such a surface on (a beam, etc) **3** another word for **chase²** (sense 4) [c16 back formation from *chamfering*,from Old French *chamfrein*, from *chant* edge (see CANT²) + *fraindre* to break, from Latin *frangere*] > '**chamferer** *n*

chamfron, chamfrain ('tʃæmfrən) *or* **chanfron** *n* a piece of armour for a horse's head [c14 from Old French *chanfrein*, from *chafresner* to harness, from *chief* head + *frener* to bridle]

chamois ('ʃæmɪ; *French* ʃamwa) *n, pl* -**ois 1** ('ʃæmwɑ:) a sure-footed goat antelope, *Rupicapra rupicapra*, inhabiting mountains of Europe and SW Asia, having vertical horns with backward-pointing tips **2** a soft suede leather formerly made from the hide of this animal, now obtained from the skins of sheep and goats **3** Also called: **chamois leather, shammy (leather), chammy (leather)** ('ʃæmɪ) a piece of such leather or similar material used for polishing, etc **4** ('ʃæmwɑ:) a yellow to greyish-yellow colour ▷ *vb* (*tr*) **5** to dress (leather or skin) like chamois **6** to polish with a chamois [c16 from Old French, from Late Latin *camox* of uncertain origin]

chamomile ('kæmə,maɪl) *n* a variant spelling of **camomile**

Chamonix ('ʃæmənɪ; *French* ʃamɔni) *n* a town in SE France, in the Alps at the foot of Mont Blanc: skiing and tourist centre. Pop: 9830 (1999)

champ¹ (tʃæmp) *vb* **1** to munch (food) noisily like a horse **2** (when *intr*, often foll by *on*, *at*, etc) to bite (something) nervously or impatiently; gnaw **3 champ** (*or* **chafe**) **at the bit** *informal* to be impatient to start work, a journey, etc ▷ *n* **4** the act or noise of champing **5** *Ulster dialect* a dish, originating in Ireland, of mashed potatoes and spring onions or leeks [c16 probably of imitative origin] > '**champer** *n*

champ² (tʃæmp) *n informal* short for **champion** (sense 1)

champac *or* **champak** ('tʃæmpæk, 'tʃʌmpʌk) *n* a magnoliaceous tree, *Michelia champaca*, of India and the East Indies. Its fragrant yellow flowers yield an oil used in perfumes and its wood is used for furniture [c18 from Hindi *campak*, from Sanskrit *campaka*, of Dravidian origin]

champagne (ʃæm'peɪn) *n* **1** (*sometimes capital*) a white sparkling wine produced around Reims and Epernay, France **2** (*loosely*) any effervescent white wine **3 a** a colour varying from a pale orange-yellow to a greyish-yellow **b** (*as adjective*): *a champagne carpet* **4** (*modifier*) denoting a luxurious lifestyle: *a champagne capitalist*

Champagne-Ardenne (ʃæm'peɪnɑː'dɛn; *French* ʃãpanardɛn) *n* a region of NE France: a countship and commercial centre in medieval times; it consists of a great plain, with sheep and dairy farms and many vineyards

champagne socialist *n* a professed socialist who enjoys an extravagant lifestyle

champaign (ʃæm'peɪn) *n* **1** Also called: **campagna** an expanse of open level or gently undulating country **2** an obsolete word for **battlefield** [c14 from Old French *champaigne*, from Late Latin *campānia*; see CAMPAIGN]

champers ('ʃæmpəz) *n* a slang name for **champagne**

champerty ('tʃæmpətɪ) *n, pl* -**ties** *law* (formerly) an illegal bargain between a party to litigation and an outsider whereby the latter agrees to pay for the action and thereby share in any proceeds recovered. See also **maintenance** [c14 from Anglo-French *champartie*, from Old French *champart* share of produce, from *champ* field + *part* share (a feudal lord's)] > '**champertous** *adj*

champignon (tʃæm'pɪnjən) *n* any of various agaricaceous edible mushrooms, esp *Marasmius oreades* (**fairy ring champignon**) and the meadow mushroom [c16 from French, perhaps from Vulgar Latin *campīnus* (unattested) of the field, from Latin *campus* plain, field]

Champigny-sur-Marne (*French* ʃãpiɲisyrmarn) *n* a suburb of Paris, on the River Marne. Pop: 74 237 (1999)

champion ('tʃæmpɪən) *n* **1 a** a person who has defeated all others in a competition: *a chess champion* **b** (*as modifier*): *a champion team* **2 a** a plant or animal that wins first place in a show, etc **b** (*as modifier*): *a champion marrow* **3** a person who defends a person or cause: *champion of the underprivileged* **4** (formerly) a warrior or knight who did battle for another, esp a king or queen, to defend their rights or honour ▷ *adj* **5** *Northern English dialect* first rate; excellent ▷ *adv* **6** *Northern English dialect* very well; excellently ▷ *vb* (*tr*) **7** to support; defend: *we champion the cause of liberty* [c13 from Old French, from Late Latin *campiō*, from Latin *campus* field, battlefield]

championship ('tʃæmpɪənʃɪp) *n* **1** (*sometimes plural*) any of various contests held to determine a champion **2** the title or status of being a champion **3** support for or defence of a cause, person, etc

Champlain (ʃæm'pleɪn) *n* **Lake** a lake in the northeastern US, between the Green Mountains and the Adirondack Mountains: linked by the **Champlain Canal** to the Hudson River and by the Richelieu River to the St Lawrence; a major communications route in colonial times

champlevé *French* (ʃãlve; *English* ʃæmplə'veɪ) *adj* **1** of or relating to a process of enamelling by which grooves are cut into a metal base and filled with enamel colours ▷ *n* **2** an object enamelled by this process [c19 from *champ* field (level surface) + *levé* raised]

Champs-Elysées (ʃɒnz el'iːzeɪ; *French* ʃãz elize) *n* a major boulevard in Paris, leading from the Arc de Triomphe to the Elysée Palace and government offices

chance (tʃɑːns) *n* **1 a** the unknown and unpredictable element that causes an event to result in a certain way rather than another,

spoken of as a real force **b** (*as modifier*): *a chance meeting*. Related adj: **fortuitous 2** fortune; luck; fate **3** an opportunity or occasion **4** a risk; gamble: *you take a chance with his driving* **5** the extent to which an event is likely to occur; probability **6** an unpredicted event, esp a fortunate one: *that was quite a chance, finding him here* **7** *archaic* an unlucky event; mishap **8 by chance a** you slipped by chance **b** perhaps: *do you by chance have a room?* **9 (the) chances are...** it is likely (that) ... **10 on the chance** acting on the possibility; in case **11 the main chance** the opportunity for personal gain (esp in the phrase **an eye to the main chance**) ▷ *vb* **12** (*tr*) to risk; hazard: *I'll chance the worst happening* **13** to happen by chance; be the case by chance: *I chanced to catch sight of her as she passed* **14 chance on** (*or* **upon**) to come upon by accident: *he chanced on the solution to his problem* **15 chance one's arm** to attempt to do something although the chance of success may be slight [c13 from Old French *cheance*, from *cheoir* to fall, occur, from Latin *cadere*] > '**chanceful** *adj* > '**chanceless** *adj*

chancel ('tʃɑːnsəl) *n* the part of a church containing the altar, sanctuary, and choir, usually separated from the nave and transepts by a screen [c14 from Old French, from Latin *cancellī* (plural) lattice]

chancellery *or* **chancellory** ('tʃɑːnsələrɪ, -slərɪ) *n, pl* -**leries** *or* -**lories 1** the building or room occupied by a chancellor's office **2** the position, rank, or office of a chancellor **3** *US* **a** the residence or office of an embassy or legation **b** the office of a consulate **4** *Brit* another name for a diplomatic **chancery** [c14 from Anglo-French *chancellerie*, from Old French *chancelier* CHANCELLOR]

chancellor ('tʃɑːnsələ, -slə) *n* **1** the head of the government in several European countries **2** *US* the president of a university or, in some colleges, the chief administrative officer **3** *Brit and Canadian* the honorary head of a university. Compare **vice chancellor** (sense 1) **4** *US* (in some states) the presiding judge of a court of chancery or equity **5** *Brit* the chief secretary of an embassy **6** *Christianity* a clergyman acting as the law officer of a bishop **7** *archaic* the chief secretary of a prince, nobleman, etc [c11 from Anglo-French *chanceler*, from Late Latin *cancellārius* porter, secretary, from Latin *cancellī* lattice; see CHANCEL] > '**chancellor,ship** *n*

Chancellor of the Duchy of Lancaster *n Brit* a minister of the crown, nominally appointed as representative of the Queen (who is the Duke, not Duchess, of Lancaster), but in practice chiefly employed on parliamentary work determined by the prime minister

Chancellor of the Exchequer *n Brit* the cabinet minister responsible for finance

chance-medley *n law* a sudden quarrel in which one party kills another; unintentional but not blameless killing [c15 from Anglo-French *chance medlee* mixed chance]

chancer ('tʃɑːnsə) *n slang* an unscrupulous or dishonest opportunist who is prepared to try any dubious scheme for making money or furthering his or her own ends [c19 from CHANCE + -ER¹]

chancery ('tʃɑːnsərɪ) *n, pl* -**ceries 1** Also called: **Chancery Division** (in England) the Lord Chancellor's court, now a division of the High Court of Justice **2** Also called: **court of chancery** (in the US) a court of equity **3** *Brit* the political section or offices of an embassy or legation **4** another name for **chancellery 5** a court of public records; archives **6** *Christianity* a diocesan office under the supervision of a bishop's chancellor, having custody of archives, issuing official enactments, etc **7 in chancery a** *law* (of a suit) pending in a court of equity **b** *wrestling, boxing* (of a competitor's head) locked under an opponent's arm **c** in an awkward or helpless situation [c14 shortened from CHANCELLERY]

chancre ('ʃæŋkə) *n pathol* a small hard nodular

C

growth, which is the first diagnostic sign of acquired syphilis [C16 from French, from Latin: CANCER] > ˈchancrous *adj*

chancroid (ˈʃæŋkrɔɪd) *n* **1** a soft venereal ulcer, esp of the male genitals, caused by infection with the bacillus *Haemophilus ducreyi* ▷ *adj* **2** relating to or resembling a chancroid or chancre > chanˈcroidal *adj*

chancy *or* **chancey** (ˈtʃɑːnsɪ) *adj* chancier, chanciest *informal* of uncertain outcome or temperament; risky > ˈchancily *adv* > ˈchanciness *n*

chandelier (ˌʃændɪˈlɪə) *n* an ornamental hanging light with branches and holders for several candles or bulbs [C17 from French: candleholder, from Latin CANDELABRUM]

chandelle (ʃænˈdɛl; *French* ʃɑ̃dɛl) *n* **1** aeronautics an abrupt climbing turn almost to the point of stalling, in which an aircraft's momentum is used to increase its rate of climb ▷ *vb* **2** (*intr*) to carry out a chandelle [French, literally: CANDLE]

Chandernagore (ˌtʃʌndənəˈɡɔː) *n* a port in E India, in S West Bengal on the Hooghly River: a former French settlement (1686–1950). Pop: 162 166 (2001)

Chandigarh (ˌtʃʌndɪˈɡɑː) *n* a city and Union Territory of N India, joint capital of the Punjab and Haryana: modern city planned in the 1950s by Le Corbusier. Pop: Pop: 808 796 (2001), of city; 900 414 (2001), of union territory. Area (of union territory): 114 sq km (44 sq miles)

chandler (ˈtʃɑːndlə) *n* **1** a dealer in a specified trade or merchandise: *corn chandler; ship's chandler* **2** a person who makes or sells candles **3** *Brit obsolete* a retailer of grocery provisions; shopkeeper [C14 from Old French *chandelier* one who makes or deals in candles, from *chandelle* CANDLE]

chandlery (ˈtʃɑːndlərɪ) *n, pl* -dleries **1** the business, warehouse, or merchandise of a chandler **2** a place where candles are kept

Chandrasekhar limit (ˌtʃændrəˈsiːkə) *n astronomy* the upper limit to the mass of a white dwarf, equal to 1.44 solar masses. A star having a mass above this limit will continue to collapse to form a neutron star [C20 named after Subrahmanyan Chandrasekhar (1910–95), Indian-born US astronomer, who calculated it]

Chang (tʃæŋ) *n* another name for the **Yangtze**

changa (ˈtʃʌŋˌɡɑː) *interj Indian* an expression of approval or agreement [C21 Punjabi]

Changan (ˈtʃæŋˈɑːn) *n* a former name for **Xi'an**

Changchiakow *or* **Changchiak'ou** (ˈtʃæŋˈtʃɑːˈkəʊ) *n* a variant transliteration of the Chinese name for **Zhangjiakou**

Changchow *or* **Ch'ang-chou** (ˈtʃæŋˈtʃaʊ) *n* a variant transliteration of the Chinese name for **Zhangzhou**

Changchun *or* **Ch'ang Ch'un** (ˈtʃæŋˈtʃʊn) *n* a city in NE China, capital of Jilin province: as **Hsinking**, capital of the Japanese state of Manchukuo (1932–45). Pop: 3 092 000 (2005 est)

Changde (ˈtʃæŋˈdeɪ), **Changteh** *or* **Ch'ang-te** *n* a port in SE central China, in N Hunan province, near the mouth of the Yuan River: severely damaged by the Japanese in World War II. Pop: 1 483 000 (2005 est)

change (tʃeɪndʒ) *vb* **1** to make or become different; alter **2** (*tr*) to replace with or exchange for another: *to change one's name* **3** (sometimes foll by *to* or *into*) to transform or convert or be transformed or converted **4** to give and receive (something) in return; interchange: *to change places with someone* **5** (*tr*) to give or receive (money) in exchange for the equivalent sum in a smaller denomination or different currency **6** (*tr*) to remove or replace the coverings of: *to change a baby* **7** (when *intr*, may be foll by *into* or *out of*) to put on other clothes **8** (*intr*) (of the moon) to pass from one phase to the following one **9** to operate (the gear lever of a motor vehicle) in order to change the gear ratio: *to change gear* **10** to alight from (one bus, train, etc) and board another **11 change face** to rotate the telescope of a surveying instrument

through 180° horizontally and vertically, taking a second sighting of the same object in order to reduce error **12 change feet** *informal* to put on different shoes, boots, etc **13 change front a** *military* to redeploy (a force in the field) so that its main weight of weapons points in another direction **b** to alter one's attitude, opinion, etc **14 change hands** to pass from one owner to another **15 change one's mind** to alter one's decision or opinion **16 change one's tune** to alter one's attitude or tone of speech ▷ *n* **17** the act or fact of changing or being changed **18** a variation, deviation, or modification **19** the substitution of one thing for another; exchange **20** anything that is or may be substituted for something else **21** variety or novelty (esp in the phrase **for a change**): *I want to go to France for a change* **22** a different or fresh set, esp of clothes **23** money given or received in return for its equivalent in a larger denomination or in a different currency **24** the balance of money given or received when the amount tendered is larger than the amount due **25** coins of a small denomination regarded collectively **26** (*often capital*) *archaic* a place where merchants meet to transact business; an exchange **27** the act of passing from one state or phase to another **28** the transition from one phase of the moon to the next **29** the order in which a peal of bells may be rung **30** *sport* short for **changeover** (sense 3b) **31** *slang* desirable or useful information **32** *obsolete* fickleness or caprice **33 change of heart** a profound change of outlook, opinion, etc **34 get no change out of (someone)** *slang* not to be successful in attempts to exploit or extract information from (someone) **35 ring the changes** to vary the manner or performance of an action that is often repeated ▷ See also **change down, changeover, change round, change up** [C13 from Old French *changier*, from Latin *cambīre* to exchange, barter] > ˈchangeless *adj* > ˈchangelessly *adv* > ˈchangelessness *n* > ˈchanger *n*

changeable (ˈtʃeɪndʒəbəl) *adj* **1** able to change or be changed; fickle: *changeable weather* **2** varying in colour when viewed from different angles or in different lights > ˌchangeaˈbility *or* ˈchangeableness *n* > ˈchangeably *adv*

change down *vb* (*intr, adverb*) to select a lower gear when driving

changeful (ˈtʃeɪndʒfʊl) *adj* often changing; inconstant; variable > ˈchangefully *adv* > ˈchangefulness *n*

changeling (ˈtʃeɪndʒlɪŋ) *n* **1** a child believed to have been exchanged by fairies for the parents' true child **2** *archaic* **a** an idiot **b** a fickle or changeable person

change of life *n* a nontechnical name for **menopause**

change of venue *n law* the removal of a trial out of one jurisdiction into another

changeover (ˈtʃeɪndʒ,əʊvə) *n* **1** an alteration or complete reversal from one method, system, or product to another: *a changeover to decimal currency* **2** a reversal of a situation, attitude, etc **3** *sport* **a** the act of transferring to or being relieved by a team-mate in a relay race, as by handing over a baton, etc **b** Also called: **change, takeover** the point in a relay race at which the transfer is made **4** *sport, chiefly Brit* the exchange of ends by two teams, esp at half time ▷ *vb* **change over** (*adverb*) **5** to adopt (a completely different position or attitude): *the driver and navigator changed over after four hours* **6** (*intr*) *sport, chiefly Brit* (of two teams) to exchange ends of a playing field, etc, as after half time

change point *n surveying* a point to which a foresight and backsight are taken in levelling; turning point

change-ringing *n* **1** the art of bell-ringing in which a set of bells is rung in an established order which is then changed **2** variations on a topic or theme

change round *vb* (*adverb*) **1** to place in or adopt a different or opposite position ▷ *n* **changeround 2** the act of changing to a different position

change up *vb* **1** (*intr, adverb*) to select a higher gear when driving ▷ *n* **change-up 2** *baseball* an unexpectedly slow ball thrown in order to surprise the batter

Changsha *or* **Ch'ang-sha** (ˈtʃæŋˈʃɑː) *n* a port in SE China, capital of Hunan province, on the Xiang River. Pop: 2 051 000 (2005 est)

Changteh *or* **Ch'ang-te** (ˈtʃæŋˈteɪ) *n* a variant transliteration of the Chinese name for **Changde**

Chania *or* **Hania** (ˈhɑːnɪə) *n* the chief port of Crete, on the NW coast. Pop: 82 000 (2005 est). Greek name: Khaniá

channel¹ (ˈtʃænəl) *n* **1** a broad strait connecting two areas of sea **2** the bed or course of a river, stream, or canal **3** a navigable course through a body of water **4** (*often plural*) a means or agency of access, communication, etc: *to go through official channels* **5** a course into which something can be directed or moved: *a new channel of thought* **6** *electronics* **a** a band of radio frequencies assigned for a particular purpose, esp the broadcasting of a television signal **b** a path for an electromagnetic signal: *a stereo set has two channels* **c** a thin semiconductor layer between the source and drain of a field-effect transistor, the conductance of which is controlled by the gate voltage **7** a tubular or trough-shaped passage for fluids **8** a groove or flute, as in the shaft of a column **9** *computing* **a** a path along which data can be transmitted between a central processing unit and one or more peripheral devices **b** one of the lines along the length of a paper tape on which information can be stored in the form of punched holes **10** short for **channel iron** ▷ *vb* -nels, -nelling, -nelled *or US* -nels, -neling, -neled **11** to provide or be provided with a channel or channels; make or cut channels in (something) **12** (*tr*) to guide into or convey through a channel or channels: *information was channelled through to them* **13** to serve as a medium through whom the spirit of (a person of a former age) allegedly communicates with the living **14** (*tr*) to form a groove or flute in (a column, etc) [C13 from Old French *chanel*, from Latin *canālis* pipe, groove, conduit; see CANAL] > ˈchanneller *n*

channel² (ˈtʃænəl) *n nautical* a flat timber or metal ledge projecting from the hull of a vessel above the chainplates to increase the angle of the shrouds [C18 variant of earlier *chainwale*; see CHAIN, WALE¹ (planking)]

Channel (ˈtʃænəl) *n* **the** short for **English Channel**

channel captain *n marketing* the most powerful member, and often the one that decides specifications, in a channel for distributing goods (which usually consists of a manufacturer, wholesaler, and retailer). The channel captain is sometimes the manufacturer but in the case of a chain store it may be the retailer

Channel Country *n* **the** an area of E central Australia, in SW Queensland: crossed by intermittent rivers and subject to both flooding and long periods of drought

channel-hop *vb* -hops, -hopping, -hopped (*intr*) to change television channels repeatedly using a remote control device

channel iron *or* **bar** *n* a rolled-steel bar with a U-shaped cross section. Sometimes shortened to: **channel**

Channel Islands *pl n* a group of islands in the English Channel, off the NW coast of France, consisting of Jersey, Guernsey, Alderney, Brechou or Brecqhou, Sark, Herm, Jethou, and Lihou (all between them representing the United Kingdom Crown Dependencies of the Bailiwick of Jersey and the Bailiwick of Guernsey) - the only part of the duchy of Normandy remaining to Britain - and the Roches Douvres and the Îles Chausey (which belong to France). Pop: 149 878 (2001). Area: 194 sq km (75 sq miles)

channelize or **channelise** ('tʃænəlaɪz) vb (tr) to guide through or as if through a channel; provide a channel for

Channel Tunnel n the Anglo-French railway tunnel that runs beneath the English Channel, between Folkestone and Coquelles, near Calais; opened in 1994. Also called: **Chunnel, Eurotunnel**

chanoyo (,tʃɑːnɔːˈyuː) n a variant of **chado**

chanson de geste French (ʃɑ̃sɔ̃ də ʒɛst) n one of a genre of Old French epic poems celebrating heroic deeds, the most famous of which is the *Chanson de Roland* [literally: song of exploits]

chant (tʃɑːnt) n **1** a simple song or melody **2** a short simple melody in which several words or syllables are assigned to one note, as in the recitation of psalms **3** a psalm or canticle performed by using such a melody **4** a rhythmic or repetitious slogan, usually spoken or sung, as by sports supporters, etc **5** monotonous or singsong intonation in speech ▷ vb **6** to sing or recite (a psalm, prayer, etc) as a chant **7** to intone (a slogan) rhythmically or repetitiously **8** to speak or say monotonously as if intoning a chant [c14 from Old French *chanter* to sing, from Latin *cantāre*, frequentative of *canere* to sing] > 'chantingly adv

chanter ('tʃɑːntə) n **1** a person who chants **2** the pipe on a set of bagpipes that is provided with finger holes and on which the melody is played

chanterelle (,tʃæntəˈrɛl) n any saprotrophic basidiomycetous fungus of the genus *Cantharellus*, esp *C. cibarius*, having an edible yellow funnel-shaped mushroom: family Cantharellaceae [c18 from French, from New Latin *cantharella*, diminutive of Latin *cantharus* drinking vessel, from Greek *kantharos*]

chanteuse (French ʃɑ̃tøz) n a female singer, esp in a nightclub or cabaret [French: singer]

chantey ('ʃæntɪ, 'tʃæn-) n, pl **-teys** the usual US spelling of **shanty²**

chanticleer (,tʃæntɪˈklɪə) or **chantecler** (,tʃæntɪˈkleə) n a name for a cock, used esp in fables [c13 from Old French *Chantecler*, from *chanter cler* to sing clearly]

Chantilly (ʃæn'tɪlɪ; French ʃɑ̃tiji) n **1** a town in N France, near the **Forest of Chantilly** formerly famous for lace and porcelain. Pop: 10 902 (1999) **2** Also called: **Tiffany** a breed of medium-sized cat with silky semi-long hair ▷ adj **3** (of cream) lightly sweetened and whipped

Chantilly lace n (sometimes not capital) a delicate ornamental lace

chantry ('tʃɑːntrɪ) n, pl **-tries** Christianity **1** an endowment for the singing of Masses for the soul of the founder or others designated by him **2** a chapel or altar so endowed **3** (as modifier): *a chantry priest* [c14 from Old French *chanterie*, from *chanter* to sing; see CHANT]

chanty ('ʃæntɪ, 'tʃæn-) n, pl **-ties** a variant of **shanty²**

Chanukah ('hɑːnəkə, -nʊˌkɑː; Hebrew xanuˈka) n a variant spelling of **Hanukkah**

chanukiah ('hɑːnʊkɪə'; Hebrew xanuˈkiːə) n a variant spelling of **hanukiah**

Chaoan ('tʃaʊˈɑːn) n the former name of Chaozhou

Chaochow ('tʃaʊˈtʃəʊ) n a former spelling of Chaozhou

chaology (keɪˈɒlədʒɪ) n the study of chaos theory > chaˈologist n

Chao Phraya ('tʃaʊ prəˈjɑː) n a river in N Thailand, rising in the N highlands and flowing south to the Gulf of Siam. Length: (including the headstreams Nan and Ping) 1200 km (750 miles). Also called: **Menam**

chaordic (keɪˈɔːdɪk) adj (of a system, organization, or natural process) governed by or combining elements of both chaos and order [c20 blend of CHAOTIC + ORDER]

chaos ('keɪɒs) n **1** complete disorder; utter confusion **2** (usually capital) the disordered formless matter supposed to have existed before the ordered universe **3** an obsolete word for **abyss** [c15 from Latin, from Greek *khaos*; compare CHASM, yawn] > chaotic (keɪˈɒtɪk) adj > chaˈotically adv

chaos theory n a theory, applied in various branches of science, that apparently random phenomena have underlying order

Chaozhou ('tʃaʊˈtʃəʊ) n a city in SE China, in E Guangdong province, on the Han River: river port. Pop. 480 000 (2005 est.). Also called: **Chaochow.** Former name: **Chaoan**

chap¹ (tʃæp) vb **chaps, chapping, chapped 1** (of the skin) to make or become raw and cracked, esp by exposure to cold **2** Scot (of a clock) to strike (the hour) **3** Scot to knock (at a door, window, etc) ▷ n **4** (usually plural) a cracked or sore patch on the skin caused by chapping **5** Scot a knock [c14 probably of Germanic origin; compare Middle Dutch, German *kappen* to chop off]

chap² (tʃæp) n informal a man or boy; fellow [c16 (in the sense: buyer): shortened from CHAPMAN]

chap³ (tʃɒp, tʃæp) n a less common word for **chop³**

chap. abbreviation for **1** chaplain **2** chapter

chaparejos (ʃæpəˈreɪɒs; Spanish tʃapaˈrexos) or **chaparajos** (ʃæpəˈreɪɒs; Spanish tʃapaˈraxos) pl n another name for **chaps** [from Mexican Spanish]

chaparral (,tʃæpəˈræl, ʃæp-) n (in the southwestern US) a dense growth of shrubs and trees, esp evergreen oaks [c19 from Spanish, from *chaparra* evergreen oak]

chaparral cock n another name for **roadrunner**

chaparral pea n a thorny leguminous Californian shrub, *Pickeringia montana*, with reddish-purple showy flowers

chapati or **chapatti** (tʃəˈpætɪ, -ˈpʌtɪ, -ˈpɑːtɪ) n, pl **-ti, -tis** or **-ties** (in Indian cookery) a flat coarse unleavened bread resembling a pancake [from Hindi]

chapbook ('tʃæpˌbʊk) n a book of popular ballads, stories, etc, formerly sold by chapmen or pedlars

chape (tʃeɪp) n **1** a metal tip or trimming for a scabbard **2** the metal tongue of a buckle [c14 from Old French: hood, metal cover, from Late Latin *cappa* CAP] > 'chapeless adj

chapeau ('ʃæpəʊ; French ʃapo) n, pl **-peaux** (-pəʊ, -pəʊz; French -po) or **-peaus** a hat [c16 from French, from Late Latin *cappellus* hood, from *cappa* CAP]

chapel ('tʃæpəl) n **1** a place of Christian worship in a larger building, esp a place set apart, with a separate altar, in a church or cathedral **2** a similar place of worship in or attached to a large house or institution, such as a college, hospital or prison **3** a church subordinate to a parish church **4** (in Britain) **a** a Nonconformist place of worship **b** Nonconformist religious practices or doctrine **c** (as adjective): *he is chapel, but his wife is church.* Compare **church** (sense 8) **5** (in Scotland) a Roman Catholic church **6** the members of a trade union in a particular newspaper office, printing house, etc **7** a printing office [c13 from Old French *chapele*, from Late Latin *cappella*, diminutive of *cappa* cloak (see CAP); originally denoting the sanctuary where the cloak of St Martin of Tours was kept as a relic]

chapel of ease n a church built to accommodate those living at a distance from the parish church

chapelry n, pl **-ries** the district legally assigned to and served by an Anglican chapel

chaperon or **chaperone** ('ʃæpəˌrəʊn) n **1** (esp formerly) an older or married woman who accompanies or supervises a young unmarried woman on social occasions **2** someone who accompanies and supervises a group, esp of young people, usually when in public places ▷ vb **3** to act as a chaperon to [c14 from Old French, from *chape* hood, protective covering; see CAP] > chaperonage ('ʃæpərənɪdʒ) n

chapess (tʃæpˈɛs) n Brit informal, humorous a woman

chapfallen ('tʃæpˌfɔːlən) or **chopfallen** adj dejected; downhearted; crestfallen [c16 from CHOPS + FALLEN]

chapiter ('tʃæpɪtə) n architect another name for

capital² [c15 from Old French *chapitre*, from Latin *capitellum* CAPITAL²]

chaplain ('tʃæplɪn) n a Christian clergyman attached to a private chapel of a prominent person or institution or ministering to a military body, professional group, etc: *a military chaplain; a prison chaplain* [c12 from Old French *chapelain*, from Late Latin *cappellānus*, from *cappella* CHAPEL] > 'chaplaincy, 'chaplainˌship or 'chaplainry n

chaplet ('tʃæplɪt) n **1** an ornamental wreath of flowers, beads, etc, worn on the head **2** a string of beads or something similar **3** RC Church **a** a string of prayer beads constituting one third of the rosary **b** the prayers counted on this string **4** a narrow convex moulding in the form of a string of beads; astragal **5** a metal support for the core in a casting mould, esp for the core of a cylindrical pipe [c14 from Old French *chapelet* garland of roses, from *chapel* hat; see CHAPEAU] > 'chapleted adj

Chaplinesque (,tʃæplɪnˈɛsk) adj of or relating to Sir **Charles Spencer Chaplin**, known as *Charlie Chaplin*, the English comedian, film actor, and director (1889–1977), or his style of film comedy

chapman ('tʃæpmən) n, pl **-men** archaic a trader, esp an itinerant pedlar [Old English *cēapman*, from *cēap* buying and selling (see CHEAP)] > 'chapmanˌship n

Chapman Stick ('tʃæpmən) n an electronically amplified musical instrument with ten or twelve strings and a fretted neck, which is played by striking the strings against the frets with the fingers. Often shortened to: **Stick** [c20 named after its inventor, Emmett H. *Chapman* (born 1936), US guitarist]

chappal ('tʃʌpəl) n one of a pair of sandals, usually of leather, worn in India [from Hindi]

chappie ('tʃæpɪ) n informal another word for **chap** (sense 2)

chaps (tʃæps, ʃæps) pl n leather overalls without a seat, worn by cowboys. Also called: **chaparejos, chaparajos** [c19 shortened from CHAPAREJOS]

chapstick ('tʃæpˌstɪk) n chiefly US and Canadian a cylinder of a substance for preventing or soothing chapped lips [c20 from a trademark]

chaptalize or **chaptalise** ('tʃæptəˌlaɪz) vb (tr) to add sugar to (a fermenting wine) to increase the alcohol content [c19 after J. A. Chaptal (1756–1832), French chemist who originated the process] > ˌchaptaliˈzation or ˌchaptaliˈsation n

chapter ('tʃæptə) n **1** a division of a written work, esp narrative, usually titled or numbered **2** a sequence of events having a common attribute: *a chapter of disasters* **3 chapter of accidents a** a series of misfortunes **b** the unforeseeable course of events **4** an episode or period in a life, history, etc **5** a numbered reference to that part of a Parliamentary session which relates to a specified Act of Parliament **6** a branch of some societies, clubs, etc, esp of a secret society **7** the collective body or a meeting of the canons of a cathedral or collegiate church or of the members of a monastic or knightly order. Related adj: **capitular 8** a general assembly of some organization **9 chapter and verse** exact authority for an action or statement ▷ vb **10** (tr) to divide into chapters [c13 from Old French *chapitre*, from Latin *capitulum*, literally: little head, hence, section of writing, from *caput* head; in Medieval Latin: chapter of scripture or of a religious rule, a gathering for the reading of this, hence, assemblage of clergy]

chapter 7 n US the statute regarding liquidation proceedings that empowers a court to appoint a trustee to operate a failing business to prevent further loss [c20 from *chapter 7* of the Bankruptcy Reform Act (1978)]

chapter 11 n US the statute regarding the reorganization of a failing business empowering a court to allow the debtors to remain in control of the business to attempt to save it: *they are in chapter 11* [c20 from *chapter 11* of the Bankruptcy Reform Act (1978)]

C

chapterhouse ('tʃæptə,haʊs) n 1 the building attached to a cathedral, collegiate church, or religious house in which the chapter meets 2 US the meeting place of a college fraternity or sorority

chapter stop n any of several markers placed at intervals on a DVD film, enabling the viewer to find and select particular scenes

char¹ (tʃɑː) vb **chars, charring, charred** 1 to burn or be burned partially, esp so as to blacken the surface; scorch 2 (tr) to reduce (wood) to charcoal by partial combustion [C17 short for CHARCOAL]

char² or **charr** (tʃɑː) n, pl **char, chars** or **charr, charrs** any of various troutlike fishes of the genus Salvelinus, esp S. alpinus, occurring in cold lakes and northern seas: family Salmonidae (salmon) [C17 of unknown origin]

char³ (tʃɑː) n 1 informal short for **charwoman** ▷ vb **chars, charring, charred** 2 Brit informal to do housework, cleaning, etc, as a job [C18 from Old English cerr]

char⁴ (tʃɑː) n Brit a slang word for **tea** [from Chinese ch'a]

charabanc ('ʃærə,bæŋ; French ʃarabɑ̃) n Brit obsolete a motor coach, esp one used for sightseeing tours [C19 from French char-à-bancs, wagon with seats]

characin ('kærəsɪn) or **characid** n any small carnivorous freshwater cyprinoid fish of the family Characidae, of Central and South America and Africa. They are similar to the carps but more brightly coloured [C19 from New Latin Characinidae, from characinus, from Greek kharax a fish, probably the sea bream]

character ('kærɪktə) n 1 the combination of traits and qualities distinguishing the individual nature of a person or thing 2 one such distinguishing quality; characteristic 3 moral force; integrity: a man of character 4 a reputation, esp a good reputation b (as modifier): character assassination 5 a summary or account of a person's qualities and achievements; testimonial: my last employer gave me a good character 6 capacity, position, or status: he spoke in the character of a friend rather than a father 7 a person represented in a play, film, story, etc; role 8 an outstanding person: one of the great characters of the century 9 informal an odd, eccentric, or unusual person: he's quite a character 10 an informal word for **person**: a shady character 11 a symbol used in a writing system, such as a letter of the alphabet 12 Also called: **sort** printing any single letter, numeral, punctuation mark, or symbol cast as a type 13 computing any letter, numeral, etc, which is a unit of information and can be represented uniquely by a binary pattern 14 a style of writing or printing 15 genetics any structure, function, attribute, etc, in an organism, which may or may not be determined by a gene or group of genes 16 a short prose sketch of a distinctive type of person, usually representing a vice or virtue 17 in (or out of) character typical (or not typical) of the apparent character of a person or thing ▷ vb (tr) 18 to write, print, inscribe, or engrave 19 rare to portray or represent [C14 from Latin: distinguishing mark, from kharaktēr engraver's tool, from kharassein to engrave, stamp] > 'characterful adj > 'characterless adj

character actor n an actor who specializes in playing odd or eccentric characters

character armour n psychol the defence an individual exhibits to others and to himself to disguise his underlying weaknesses: a term coined by William Reich (1897–1957)

character assassination n the act of deliberately attempting to destroy a person's reputation by defamatory remarks

character code n computing a machine-readable code that identifies a specified character or a set of such codes

characteristic (,kærɪktə'rɪstɪk) n 1 a distinguishing quality, attribute, or trait 2 maths a the integral part of a common logarithm,

indicating the order of magnitude of the associated number: the characteristic of 2.4771 is 2. Compare **mantissa** b another name for **exponent** (sense 4), esp in number representation in computing ▷ adj 3 indicative of a distinctive quality, etc; typical > ,character'istically adv

characteristic curve n photog a graph of the density of a particular photographic material plotted against the logarithm of the exposure producing this density

characteristic function n 1 maths a function that assigns the value 1 to the members of a given set and the value 0 to its nonmembers 2 statistics a function derived from the probability distribution function that enables the distribution of the sum of given random variables to be analysed

characterization or **characterisation** (,kærɪktəraɪ'zeɪʃən) n 1 description of character, traits, etc 2 the act of characterizing

characterize or **characterise** ('kærɪktə,raɪz) vb (tr) 1 to be a characteristic of: loneliness characterized the place 2 to distinguish or mark as a characteristic 3 to describe or portray the character of > 'character,izable or 'character,isable adj > 'character,izer or 'character,iser n

character recognition n computing a magnetic or optical process used to detect the shape of individual characters printed or written on paper

character sketch n a brief description or portrayal of a person's character, qualities, etc

character type n psychol a cluster of personality traits commonly occurring together in an individual

charactery ('kærɪktərɪ, -trɪ) n, pl **-teries** archaic 1 the use of symbols to express thoughts 2 the group of symbols so used

charade (ʃə'rɑːd) n 1 an episode or act in the game of charades 2 chiefly Brit an absurd act; travesty

charades (ʃə'rɑːdz) n (functioning as singular) a parlour game in which one team acts out each syllable of a word, the other team having to guess the word [C18 from French charade entertainment, from Provençal charrado chat, from charra chatter, of imitative origin]

charanga (,tʃæ'ræŋgə) n a type of orchestra used in performing traditional Cuban music [Spanish]

charas ('tʃɑːrəs) n another name for **hashish** [C19 from Hindi]

charcoal ('tʃɑː,kəʊl) n 1 a black amorphous form of carbon made by heating wood or other organic matter in the absence of air: used as a fuel, in smelting metal ores, in explosives, and as an absorbent. See **activated charcoal** 2 a stick or pencil of this for drawing 3 a drawing done in charcoal 4 short for **charcoal grey** ▷ vb 5 (tr) to write, draw, or blacken with charcoal [C14 from char (origin obscure) + COAL]

charcoal-burner n (formerly) a person whose work was making charcoal by burning wood

charcoal grey n a a very dark grey colour b (as adjective): charcoal-grey trousers

charcuterie (ʃɑː'kuːtərɪ) n 1 cooked cold meats 2 a shop selling cooked cold meats [French]

chard (tʃɑːd) n a variety of beet, Beta vulgaris cicla, with large succulent leaves and thick stalks, used as a vegetable. Also called: **Swiss chard, leaf beet, seakale beet** [C17 probably from French carde edible leafstalk of the artichoke, but associated also with French chardon thistle, both ultimately from Latin carduus thistle; see CARDOON]

Chardonnay ('ʃɑːdə,neɪ) n (sometimes not capital) 1 a white grape originally grown in the Burgundy region of France, and now throughout the wine-producing world 2 any of various white wines made from this grape [French]

Charente (French ʃarɑ̃t) n 1 a department of W central France, in Poitou-Charentes region. Capital: Angoulême. Pop: 341 275 (2003 est). Area: 5972 sq km (2329 sq miles) 2 a river in W France, rising in the Massif Central and flowing west to

the Bay of Biscay. Length: 362 km (225 miles)

Charente-Maritime (French ʃarɑ̃tmaritim) n a department of W France, in Poitou-Charentes region. Capital: La Rochelle. Pop: 576 855 (2003 est). Area: 7232 sq km (2820 sq miles)

charge (tʃɑːdʒ) vb 1 to set or demand (a price): he charges too much for his services 2 (tr) to hold financially liable; enter a debit against 3 (tr) to enter or record as an obligation against a person or his account 4 (tr) to accuse or impute a fault to (a person, etc), as formally in a court of law 5 (tr) to command; place a burden upon or assign responsibility to: I was charged to take the message to headquarters 6 to make a rush at or sudden attack upon (a person or thing) 7 (tr) to fill (a receptacle) with the proper or appropriate quantity 8 (often foll by up) to cause (an accumulator, capacitor, etc) to take or store electricity or (of an accumulator) to have electricity fed into it 9 to fill or suffuse or to be filled or suffused with matter by dispersion, solution, or absorption: to charge water with carbon dioxide 10 (tr) to fill or suffuse with feeling, emotion, etc: the atmosphere was charged with excitement 11 (tr) law (of a judge) to address (a jury) authoritatively 12 (tr) to load (a firearm) 13 (tr) to aim (a weapon) in position ready for use 14 (tr) heraldry to paint (a shield, banner, etc) with a charge 15 (intr) (of hunting dogs) to lie down at command ▷ n 16 a price charged for some article or service; cost 17 a financial liability, such as a tax 18 a debt or a book entry recording it 19 an accusation or allegation, such as a formal accusation of a crime in law 20 a an onrush, attack, or assault b the call to such an attack in battle 21 custody or guardianship 22 a person or thing committed to someone's care 23 a a cartridge or shell b the explosive required to discharge a firearm or other weapon c an amount of explosive material to be detonated at any one time 24 the quantity of anything that a receptacle is intended to hold 25 physics a the attribute of matter by which it responds to electromagnetic forces responsible for all electrical phenomena, existing in two forms to which the signs negative and positive are arbitrarily assigned b a similar property of a body or system determined by the extent to which it contains an excess or deficiency of electrons c a quantity of electricity determined by the product of an electric current and the time for which it flows, measured in coulombs d the total amount of electricity stored in a capacitor e the total amount of electricity held in an accumulator, usually measured in ampere-hours. Symbol: q or Q 26 a load or burden 27 a duty or responsibility; control 28 a command, injunction, or order 29 slang a thrill 30 law the address made by a judge to the jury at the conclusion of the evidence 31 heraldry a design, device, or image depicted on heraldic arms: a charge of three lions 32 the solid propellant used in rockets, sometimes including the inhibitor 33 in charge in command 34 in charge of a having responsibility for b US under the care of [C13 from Old French chargier to load, from Late Latin carricāre; see CARRY]

chargeable ('tʃɑːdʒəbəl) adj 1 charged or liable to be charged 2 liable to result in a legal charge > 'chargeableness or ,chargea'bility n > 'chargeably adv

chargeable asset n any asset that can give rise to assessment for capital gains tax on its disposal. Exempt assets include principal private residences, cars, investments held in a personal equity plan, and government securities

chargeable transfer n a transfer of value made as a gift during a person's lifetime that is not covered by a specific exemption and therefore gives rise to liability under inheritance tax

charge account n another term for **credit account**

charge-cap ('tʃɑːdʒ,kæp) vb (tr) **-caps, -capping, -capped** (in Britain) to impose on (a local authority) an upper limit on the community charge it may levy > 'charge-,capping n

charge card n a card issued by a chain store, shop, or organization, that enables customers to obtain goods and services for which they pay at a later date

charge carrier n an electron, hole, or ion that transports the electric charge in an electric current

charge-coupled device n computing an electronic device, used in imaging and signal processing, in which information is represented as packets of electric charge that are stored in an array of tiny closely spaced capacitors and can be moved from one capacitor to another in a controlled way. Abbreviation: **CCD**

chargé d'affaires ('ʃaːʒeɪ dæˈfeə; French ʃarʒe dafɛr) n, pl chargés d'affaires ('ʃaːʒeɪ, -ʒeɪ; French ʃarʒe) **1** the temporary head of a diplomatic mission in the absence of the ambassador or minister **2** the head of a diplomatic mission of the lowest level [c18 from French: (one) charged with affairs]

charge density n the electric charge per unit volume of a medium or body or per unit area of a surface

charge hand n Brit a workman whose grade of responsibility is just below that of a foreman

charge nurse n Brit a nurse in charge of a ward in a hospital: the male equivalent of **sister**

charge of quarters n US a member of the armed forces who handles administration in his unit, esp after duty hours

charger¹ ('tʃaːdʒə) n **1** a person or thing that charges **2** a large strong horse formerly ridden into battle **3** a device for charging or recharging an accumulator or rechargeable battery

charger² ('tʃaːdʒə) n antiques a large dish for serving at table or for display [C14 chargeour something to bear a load, from chargen to CHARGE]

charge sheet n Brit a document on which a police officer enters details of the charge against a prisoner and the court in which he will appear

char-grilled adj (of food) grilled over charcoal

Chari ('tʃaːrɪ) or **Shari** n a river in N central Africa, rising in the N Central African Republic and flowing north to Lake Chad. Length: about 2250 km (1400 miles)

charidee ('tʃærɪdiː) n informal a jocular spelling of charity, as pronounced in a mid-Atlantic accent

charily ('tʃɛərɪlɪ) adv **1** cautiously; carefully **2** sparingly

chariness ('tʃɛərɪnɪs) n the state of being chary

Charing Cross ('tʃærɪŋ) n a district of London, in the city of Westminster: the modern cross (1863) in front of Charing Cross railway station replaces the one erected by Edward I (1290), the last of twelve marking the route of the funeral procession of his queen, Eleanor

Chari-Nile ('tʃaːrɪ'naɪl) n **1** a group of languages of E Africa, now generally regarded as a branch of the Nilo-Saharan family, spoken in parts of the Sudan, the Democratic Republic of Congo (formerly Zaïre), Uganda, Kenya, Tanzania, and adjacent countries ▷ adj **2** relating to or belonging to this group of languages

chariot ('tʃærɪət) n **1** a two-wheeled horse-drawn vehicle used in ancient Egypt, Greece, Rome, etc, in war, races, and processions **2** a light four-wheeled horse-drawn ceremonial carriage **3** poetic any stately vehicle [c14 from Old French, augmentative of char CAR]

charioteer (,tʃærɪə'tɪə) n the driver of a chariot

charisma (kə'rɪzmə) or **charism** ('kærɪzəm) n **1** a special personal quality or power of an individual making him capable of influencing or inspiring large numbers of people **2** a quality inherent in a thing which inspires great enthusiasm and devotion **3** Christianity a divinely bestowed power or talent [c17 from Church Latin, from Greek kharisma, from kharis grace, favour] > charismatic (,kærɪz'mætɪk) adj

charismatic movement n Christianity any of

various groups, within existing denominations, that emphasize communal prayer and the charismatic gifts of speaking in tongues, healing, etc

charitable ('tʃærɪtəbªl) adj **1** generous in giving to the needy **2** kind or lenient in one's attitude towards others **3** concerned with or involving charity > 'charitableness n > 'charitably adv

charitable trust n a trust set up for the benefit of a charity that complies with the regulations of the Charity Commissioners to enable it to be exempt from paying income tax

charity ('tʃærɪtɪ) n, pl -ties **1 a** the giving of help, money, food, etc, to those in need **b** (as modifier): a charity show **2 a** an institution or organization set up to provide help, money, etc, to those in need **b** (as modifier): charity funds **3** the help, money, etc, given to the needy; alms **4** a kindly and lenient attitude towards people **5** love of one's fellow men [c13 from Old French charite, from Latin cāritās affection, love, from cārus dear]

Charity Commissioners pl n (in Britain) members of a commission constituted to keep a register of charities and control charitable trusts

charivari (,ʃaːrɪ'vaːrɪ), **shivaree** or esp US **chivaree** n **1** a discordant mock serenade to newlyweds, made with pans, kettles, etc **2** a confused noise; din [c17 from French, from Late Latin caribaria headache, from Greek karēbaria, from karē head + barus heavy]

charkha or **charka** ('tʃaːkə) n (in India) a spinning wheel, esp for cotton [from Hindi]

charlady ('tʃaː,leɪdɪ) n, pl -dies another name for **charwoman**

charlatan ('ʃaːlətªn) n someone who professes knowledge or expertise, esp in medicine, that he or she does not have; quack [c17 from French, from Italian ciarlatano, from ciarlare to chatter] > 'charlatan,ism or 'charlatanry n > ,charlatan'istic adj

Charleroi (French ʃarlərwa) n a town in SW Belgium, in Hainaut province: centre of an industrial region. Pop: 200 608 (2004 est)

Charles' law ('tʃaːlzɪz) n the principle that all gases expand equally for the same rise of temperature if they are held at constant pressure: also that the pressures of all gases increase equally for the same rise of temperature if they are held at constant volume. The law is now known to be only true for ideal gases. Also called: Gay-Lussac's law [c18 named after Jacques A. C. Charles (1746–1823), French physicist who first formulated it]

Charles's Wain (weɪn) n another name for the **Plough** [Old English Carles wægn, from Carl Charlemagne (?742–814 AD), king of the Franks and Holy Roman Emperor + wægn WAIN]

charleston ('tʃaːlstən) n a fast rhythmic dance of the 1920s, characterized by kicking and by twisting of the legs from the knee down [c20 named after CHARLESTON, South Carolina]

Charleston ('tʃaːlstən) n **1** a city in central West Virginia: the state capital. Pop: 51 394 (2003 est) **2** a port in SE South Carolina, on the Atlantic: scene of the first action in the Civil War. Pop: 101 024 (2003 est)

Charleville-Mézières (French ʃarləvilmezjɛr) n twin towns on opposite sides of the River Meuse in NE France. Pop: 55 490 (1999). See **Mézières**

charley horse ('tʃaːlɪ) n US and Canadian informal muscle stiffness or cramp following strenuous athletic exercise [c19 of uncertain origin]

charlie ('tʃaːlɪ) n **1** Brit informal a silly person; fool **2** Austral informal a girl or woman [c20 for sense 1: shortened from Charlie Hunt, rhyming slang for CUNT; sense 2 is shortened from Charlie Wheeler, rhyming slang for SHEILA]

Charlie¹ ('tʃaːlɪ) n communications a code word for the letter c

Charlie² or **Charley** ('tʃaːlɪ) n US and Austral military slang a member of the Vietcong or the Vietcong collectively: Charlie hit us with rockets

[shortened from Victor Charlie, communications code for VC, abbreviation of Vietcong]

Charlie³ ('tʃaːlɪ) n slang cocaine

charlier shoe ('tʃaːlɪə) n a special light type of horseshoe that does not have a toe clip; it is applied by a farrier before a horse is turned out

charlock ('tʃaːlɒk) n **1** Also called: wild mustard a weedy Eurasian plant, Sinapis arvensis (or Brassica kaber), with hairy stems and foliage and yellow flowers: family: Brassicaceae (crucifers) **2** white charlock Also called: wild radish, runch (rʌntʃ) a related plant, Raphanus raphanistrum, with yellow, mauve, or white flowers and podlike fruits [Old English cerlic, of obscure origin]

charlotte ('ʃaːlət) n **1** a baked dessert served hot or cold, commonly made with fruit and layers or a casing of bread or cake crumbs, sponge cake, etc: apple charlotte **2** short for **charlotte russe** [c19 from French, from the name Charlotte]

Charlotte ('ʃaːlət) n a city in S North Carolina: the largest city in the state. Pop: 584 658 (2003 est)

Charlotte Amalie ('ʃaːlət ə'maːlɪə) n the capital of the Virgin Islands of the United States, a port on St Thomas Island. Pop: 18 914 (2000). Former name (1921–37): Saint Thomas

Charlottenburg (German ʃar'lɔtənburk) n a district of Berlin (of West Berlin until 1990), formerly an independent city. Pop: 145 564 (latest est)

charlotte russe (ruːs) n a cold dessert made in a mould with sponge fingers enclosing a mixture of whipped cream, custard, etc [French: Russian charlotte]

Charlottetown ('ʃaːlət,taʊn) n a port in SE Canada, capital of the province of Prince Edward Island. Pop: 38 114 (2001)

charm¹ (tʃaːm) n **1** the quality of pleasing, fascinating, or attracting people **2** a pleasing or attractive feature **3** a small object worn or kept for supposed magical powers of protection; amulet; talisman **4** a trinket worn on a bracelet **5** a magic spell; enchantment **6** a formula or action used in casting such a spell **7** physics an internal quantum number of certain elementary particles, used to explain some scattering experiments **8** like a charm perfectly; successfully ▷ vb **9** to attract or fascinate; delight greatly **10** to cast a magic spell on **11** to protect, influence, or heal, supposedly by magic **12** (tr) to influence or obtain by personal charm: he charmed them into believing him [c13 from Old French charme, from Latin carmen song, incantation, from canere to sing]

charm² (tʃaːm) n Southwest English dialect a loud noise, as of a number of people chattering or of birds singing [c16 variant of CHIRM]

charmed (tʃaːmd) adj **1** delighted or fascinated: a charmed audience **2** seemingly protected by a magic spell: he bears a charmed life **3** physics possessing charm: a charmed quark

charmer ('tʃaːmə) n **1** an attractive person **2** a person claiming or seeming to have magical powers

Charmeuse (ʃaː'muːz; French ʃarmøz) n trademark a lightweight fabric with a satin-like finish

Charminar (,tʃaːmɪ'naː) n a 16th-century monument with four minarets at Hyderabad, India

charming ('tʃaːmɪŋ) adj delightful; pleasant; attractive > 'charmingly adv

charm offensive n a concentrated attempt to gain favour or respectability by conspicuously cooperative or obliging behaviour

charmonium (tʃaː'məʊnɪəm) n, pl -nia physics an elementary particle that contains an antiquark and a charm quark [c20 from CHARM (sense 7)]

charnel ('tʃaːnªl) n **1** short for **charnel house** ▷ adj **2** ghastly; sepulchral; deathly [c14 from Old French: burial place, from Latin carnālis fleshly, CARNAL]

charnel house n (esp formerly) a building or vault where corpses or bones are deposited

Charolais ('ʃærəˌleɪ) n a breed of large white beef cattle that originated in France [C19 from French: named after Monts du *Charollais*, E France]

Charon[1] ('kɛərən) n *Greek myth* the ferryman who brought the dead across the rivers Styx or Acheron to Hades

Charon[2] ('kɛərən) n the only known satellite of Pluto, discovered in 1978

charpoy ('tʃɑːpɔɪ) or **charpai** ('tʃɑːpaɪ) n a bedstead of woven webbing or hemp stretched on a wooden frame on four legs, common in India [C19 from Urdu *cārpāī*]

charqui ('tʃɑːkɪ) n meat, esp beef, cut into strips and dried [C18 from Spanish, from Quechuan] ▷ **charquid** ('tʃɑːkɪd) adj

charr (tʃɑː) n, pl **charr** or **charrs** a variant spelling of **char** (the fish)

char siu (ˌtʃɑː 'sjuː) or **char sui** ('suːɪ) n barbecued marinated pork [C20 from Cantonese]

chart (tʃɑːt) n 1 a map designed to aid navigation by sea or air 2 an outline map, esp one on which weather information is plotted 3 a sheet giving graphical, tabular, or diagrammatical information 4 another name for **graph** (sense 1) 5 *astrology* another word for **horoscope** (sense 3) 6 **the charts** *informal* the lists produced weekly from various sources of the bestselling pop singles and albums or the most popular videos ▷ vb 7 (tr) to make a chart of 8 (tr) to make a detailed plan of 9 (tr) to plot or outline the course of 10 (intr) (of a record or video) to appear in the charts (sense 6) [C16 from Latin, from Greek *khartēs* papyrus, literally: something on which to make marks; related to Greek *kharattein* to engrave] ▷ **'chartable** adj

charter ('tʃɑːtə) n 1 a formal document from the sovereign or state incorporating a city, bank, college, etc, and specifying its purposes and rights 2 (*sometimes capital*) a formal document granting or demanding from the sovereign power of a state certain rights or liberties 3 a document issued by a society or an organization authorizing the establishment of a local branch or chapter 4 a special privilege or exemption 5 (*often capital*) the fundamental principles of an organization; constitution: *the Charter of the United Nations* 6 a the hire or lease of transportation b the agreement or contract regulating this c (*as modifier*): *a charter flight* 7 a law, policy, or decision containing a loophole which allows a specified group to engage more easily in an activity considered undesirable: *a beggars' charter* 8 *maritime law* another word for **charterparty** ▷ vb (tr) 9 to lease or hire by charterparty 10 to hire (a vehicle, etc) 11 to grant a charter of incorporation or liberties to (a group or person) [C13 from Old French *chartre*, from Latin *chartula* a little paper, from *charta* leaf of papyrus; see CHART] ▷ **'charterer** n

charter colony n *US history* a colony, such as Virginia or Massachusetts, created by royal charter under the control of an individual, trading company, etc, and exempt from interference by the Crown

chartered ('tʃɑːtəd) adj (of a professional person) having attained certain professional qualifications or standards and acquired membership of a particular professional body

chartered accountant n (in Britain) an accountant who has passed the professional examinations of the Institute of Chartered Accountants in England and Wales, the Institute of Chartered Accountants of Scotland, or the Institute of Chartered Accountants in Ireland. Abbreviation: **CA**

chartered club n NZ a private club licensed to serve alcohol to members

chartered engineer n (in Britain) an engineer who is registered with the Engineering Council as having the scientific and technical knowledge and practical experience to satisfy its professional requirements. Abbreviation: **CEng**

chartered librarian n (in Britain) a librarian who has obtained a qualification from the Library Association in addition to a degree or diploma in librarianship

chartered surveyor n (in Britain) a surveyor who is registered with the Royal Institution of Chartered Surveyors as having the qualifications, training, and experience to satisfy their professional requirements

chartered teacher n (in Scotland) a teacher with extensive qualifications and experience paid at a higher rate to remain as a classroom teacher rather than seek promotion to an administrative post

Charterhouse ('tʃɑːtəˌhaʊs) n a Carthusian monastery [C16 changed by folk etymology from Anglo-French *chartrouse*, after *Chartosse* (now Saint-Pierre-de-Chartreuse), village near Grenoble, France, the original home of the Carthusian order]

charter member n an original or founder member of a society or organization

charterparty ('tʃɑːtəˌpɑːtɪ) n, pl **-parties** 1 *maritime law* an agreement for the hire of all or part of a ship for a specified voyage or period of time 2 an individual or group that charters a ship, etc

Chartism ('tʃɑːˌtɪzəm) n *British history* the principles of the reform movement in Britain from 1838 to 1848, which included manhood suffrage, payment of Members of Parliament, equal electoral districts, annual parliaments, voting by ballot, and the abolition of property qualifications for MPs [named after the *People's Charter*, a document which stated their aims] ▷ **'Chartist** n, adj

chartist ('tʃɑːtɪst) n a stock market specialist who analyses and predicts market trends from graphs of recent price and volume movements of selected securities

chartless ('tʃɑːtlɪs) adj not mapped; uncharted

chartography (kɑː'tɒɡrəfɪ) n *rare* a variant spelling of **cartography**. ▷ **char'tographer** n ▷ **chartographic** (ˌkɑːtə'ɡræfɪk) or **ˌcharto'graphical** adj ▷ **ˌcharto'graphically** adv

Chartres (ʃɑːtrə, ʃɑːt; French ʃartrə) n a city in NW France: Gothic cathedral; market town. Pop: 40 361 (1999)

chartreuse (ʃɑː'trɜːz; French ʃartrøz) n 1 either of two liqueurs, green or yellow, made from herbs and flowers 2 a a colour varying from a clear yellowish-green to a strong greenish-yellow b (*as adjective*): *a chartreuse dress* [C19 from French, after *La Grande Chartreuse*, monastery near Grenoble, where the liqueur is produced]

Chartreux (ʃɑː'trɜː; French ʃartrø) n, pl **-treux** (-'trɜː; French -trø) a breed of sturdy cat with short dense woolly fur

chartulary ('tʃɑːtjʊlərɪ) n, pl **-laries** a variant of cartulary

Chartwell ('tʃɑːtˌwɛl) n a house near Westerham in Kent: home for 40 years of Sir Winston Churchill

charver ('ʃɑːvə) n *Northern English dialect derogatory* 1 a young woman 2 a young working-class person who dresses in casual sports clothes

charwoman ('tʃɑːˌwʊmən) n, pl **-women** *Brit* a woman who is hired to clean, tidy, etc, in a house or office

chary ('tʃɛərɪ) adj **charier**, **chariest** 1 wary; careful 2 choosy; finicky 3 shy 4 sparing; mean [Old English *cearig*; related to *caru* CARE, Old High German *charag* sorrowful]

Charybdis (kə'rɪbdɪs) n a ship-devouring monster in classical mythology, identified with a whirlpool off the north coast of Sicily, lying opposite Scylla on the Italian coast. Compare **Scylla**. ▷ **Cha'rybdian** adj

chase[1] (tʃeɪs) vb 1 to follow or run after (a person, animal, or goal) persistently or quickly 2 (tr; often foll by *out, away,* or *off*) to force to run (away); drive (out) 3 (tr) *informal* to court (a member of the

opposite sex) in an unsubtle manner 4 (tr; often foll by *up*) *informal* to pursue persistently and energetically in order to obtain results, information, etc: *chase up the builders and get a delivery date* 5 (intr) *informal* to hurry; rush ▷ n 6 the act of chasing; pursuit 7 any quarry that is pursued 8 *Brit* an unenclosed area of land where wild animals are preserved to be hunted 9 *Brit* the right to hunt a particular quarry over the land of others 10 **the chase** the act or sport of hunting 11 short for **steeplechase** 12 *real Tennis* a ball that bounces twice, requiring the point to be played again 13 **cut to the chase** *informal, chiefly US* to start talking about the important aspects of something 14 **give chase** to pursue (a person, animal, or thing) actively [C13 from Old French *chacier*, from Vulgar Latin *captiāre* (unattested), from Latin *captāre* to pursue eagerly, from *capere* to take; see CATCH] ▷ **'chaseable** adj

chase[2] (tʃeɪs) n 1 *printing* a rectangular steel or cast-iron frame into which metal type and blocks making up pages are locked for printing or plate-making 2 the part of a gun barrel from the front of the trunnions to the muzzle 3 a groove or channel, esp one that is cut in a wall to take a pipe, cable, etc ▷ vb (tr) 4 Also: **chamfer** to cut a groove, furrow, or flute in (a surface, column, etc) [C17 (in the sense: frame for letterpress matter): probably from French *châsse* frame (in the sense: bore of a cannon, etc): from Old French *chas* enclosure, from Late Latin *capsus* pen for animals; both from Latin *capsa* CASE[2]]

chase[3] (tʃeɪs) vb (tr) 1 Also: **enchase** to ornament (metal) by engraving or embossing 2 to form or finish (a screw thread) with a chaser [C14 from Old French *enchasser* ENCHASE]

chaser[1] (tʃeɪsə) n 1 a person or thing that chases 2 a drink drunk after another of a different kind, as beer after spirits 3 a cannon on a vessel situated either at the bow (**bow chaser**) or the stern (**stern chaser**) and used during pursuit by or of another vessel

chaser[2] ('tʃeɪsə) n 1 a person who engraves 2 a lathe cutting tool for accurately finishing a screw thread, having a cutting edge consisting of several repetitions of the thread form

chasm ('kæzəm) n 1 a deep cleft in the ground; abyss 2 a break in continuity; gap 3 a wide difference in interests, feelings, etc [C17 from Latin *chasma*, from Greek *khasma*; related to Greek *khainein* to gape] ▷ **chasmal** ('kæzməl) or **'chasmic** adj

chasmogamy (kæz'mɒɡəmɪ) n *botany* the production of flowers that open, so as to expose the reproductive organs and allow cross-pollination. Compare **cleistogamy** [C20 from New Latin (*flores*) *chasmogami* from Greek *khasma* CHASM + -GAMY] ▷ **chas'mogamous** adj

chassé ('ʃæseɪ) n 1 one of a series of gliding steps in ballet in which the same foot always leads 2 three consecutive dance steps, two fast and one slow, to four beats of music ▷ vb **-sés**, **-séing**, **-séd** 3 (intr) to perform either of these steps [C19 from French: a chasing]

chassepot ('ʃæspəʊ; French ʃaspo) n a breech-loading bolt-action rifle formerly used by the French Army [C19 named after A. A. *Chassepot* (1833–1905), French gunsmith who invented it]

chasseur (ʃæ'sɜː; French ʃasœr) n 1 *French army* a member of a unit specially trained and equipped for swift deployment 2 (in some parts of Europe, esp formerly) a uniformed attendant, esp one in the livery of a huntsman ▷ adj 3 (*often postpositive*) designating or cooked in a sauce consisting of white wine and mushrooms [C18 from French: huntsman]

Chassid, Chasid, Hassid or **Hasid** ('hæsɪd; *Hebrew* xa'sid) n, pl **Chassidim, Chasidim, Hassidim** or **Hasidim** ('hæsɪˌdiːm, -dɪm; *Hebrew* xasɪ'dim) 1 a sect of Jewish mystics founded in Poland about 1750, characterized by religious zeal and a spirit of prayer, joy, and charity 2 a Jewish sect of the 2nd century BC, formed to combat Hellenistic influences > **Chassidic, Chasidic, Hassidic** or **Hasidic** (həˈsɪdɪk) *adj* > **'Chassid,ism, 'Chasid,ism, 'Hassid,ism** or **'Hasid,ism** *n*

chassis (ˈʃæsɪ) *n, pl* **-sis** (-sɪz) **1** the steel frame, wheels, engine, and mechanical parts of a motor vehicle, to which the body is attached **2** *electronics* a mounting for the circuit components of an electrical or electronic device, such as a radio or television **3** the landing gear of an aircraft **4** *obsolete* a wooden framework for a window, screen, etc **5** the frame on which a cannon carriage moves backwards and forwards **6** *slang* the body of a person, esp a woman [C17 (meaning: window frame): from French *châssis* frame, from Vulgar Latin *capsicum* (unattested), ultimately from Latin *capsa* CASE²]

chaste (tʃeɪst) *adj* **1** not having experienced sexual intercourse; virginal **2** abstaining from unlawful or immoral sexual intercourse **3** (of conduct, speech, etc) pure; decent; modest **4** (of style or taste) free from embellishment; simple; restrained [C13 from Old French, from Latin *castus* pure; compare CASTE] > **'chastely** *adv* > **'chasteness** *n*

chasten (ˈtʃeɪsᵊn) *vb* (*tr*) **1** to bring to a state of submission; subdue; tame **2** to discipline or correct by punishment **3** to moderate; restrain; temper [C16 from Old French *chastier*, from Latin *castigāre*; see CASTIGATE] > **'chastener** *n* > **'chasteningly** *adv*

chaste tree *n* a small ornamental verbenaceous tree, *Vitex agnus-castus*, of S Europe and SW Asia, with spikes of pale blue flowers

chastise (tʃæsˈtaɪz) *vb* (*tr*) **1** to discipline or punish, esp by beating **2** to scold severely [C14 *chastisen*, irregularly from *chastien* to CHASTEN] > **chas'tisable** *adj* > **chastisement** (ˈtʃæstɪzmənt, tʃæsˈtaɪz-) *n* > **chas'tiser** *n*

chastity (ˈtʃæstɪtɪ) *n* **1** the state of being chaste; purity **2** abstention from sexual intercourse; virginity or celibacy: *a vow of chastity* [C13 from Old French *chasteté*, from Latin *castitās*, from *castus* CHASTE]

chastity belt *n* a locking beltlike device with a loop designed to go between a woman's legs in order to prevent her from having sexual intercourse

chasuble (ˈtʃæzjʊbᵊl) *n Christianity* a long sleeveless outer vestment worn by a priest when celebrating Mass [C13 from French, from Late Latin *casubla* garment with a hood, apparently from *casula* cloak, literally: little house, from Latin *casa* cottage]

chat¹ (tʃæt) *n* **1** informal conversation or talk conducted in an easy familiar manner **2** any Old World songbird of the subfamily *Turdinae* (thrushes, etc) having a harsh chattering cry. See also **stonechat, whinchat 3** any of various North American warblers, such as *Icteria virens* (**yellow-breasted chat**) **4** any of various Australian wrens (family *Muscicapidae*) of the genus *Ephthianura* and other genera ▷ *vb* **chats, chatting, chatted** (*intr*) **5** to talk in an easy familiar way ▷ See also **chat up** [C16 short for CHATTER]

chat² (tʃæt) *n archaic* or *dialect* a catkin, esp a willow catkin [C15 from French *chat* cat, referring to the furry appearance]

chatbot (ˈtʃæt,bɒt) *n* a computer program in the form of a virtual email correspondent that can reply to messages from computer users [C20 from CHAT¹ + (RO)BOT]

chateau or **château** (ˈʃætəʊ; *French* ʃato) *n, pl* **-teaux** (-təʊ, -təʊz; *French* -to) or **-teaus 1** a country house, castle, or manor house, esp in France **2** (in Quebec) the residence of a seigneur or (formerly) a governor **3** (in the name of a wine) estate or vineyard [C18 from French, from Old French *chastel*, from Latin *castellum* fortress, CASTLE]

Chateaubriand (*French* ʃatobrijã) *n* a thick steak cut from the fillet of beef [C19 named after François René, Vicomte de Chateaubriand

(1768–1848), French writer and statesman]

chateau cardboard *n NZ informal* wine sold in a winebox

Châteauroux (*French* ʃatoru) *n* a city in central France: 10th-century castle (**Château-Raoul**). Pop: 49 632 (1999)

Château-Thierry (ˈʃætəʊˈtɪərɪ; *French* ʃatotjeri) *n* a town in N central France, on the River Marne: scene of the second battle of the Marne (1918) during World War I. Pop: 14 967 (1999)

chateau wine *n* a wine produced from any of certain vineyards in the Bordeaux region of France

chatelain (ˈʃætᵊ,leɪn; *French* ʃatlɛ̃) *n* the keeper or governor of a castle [C16 from French, from Latin *castellānus* occupant of a CASTLE]

chatelaine (ˈʃætᵊ,leɪn; *French* ʃatlɛn) *n* **1** (esp formerly) the mistress of a castle or fashionable household **2** a chain or clasp worn at the waist by women in the 16th to the 19th centuries, with handkerchief, keys, etc, attached **3** a decorative pendant worn on the lapel

Chatham (ˈtʃætəm) *n* **1** a town in SE England, in N Kent on the River Medway: formerly royal naval dockyard. Pop: 73 468 (2001) **2** a city in SE Canada, in SE Ontario on the Thames River. Pop: 44 156 (2001)

Chatham Island *n* another name for **San Cristóbal** (sense 1)

Chatham Islands *pl n* a group of islands in the S Pacific Ocean, forming a county of South Island, New Zealand: consists of the main islands of Chatham, Pitt, and several rocky islets. Chief settlement: Waitangi. Pop: 750 (2004 est). Area: 963 sq km (372 sq miles)

chatline (ˈtʃæt,laɪn) *n* a telephone service enabling callers to join in general conversation with each other

chatoyant (ʃəˈtɔɪənt) *adj* **1** having changeable lustre; twinkling **2** (of a gem, esp a cabochon) displaying a band of light reflected off inclusions of other minerals ▷ *n* **3** a gemstone with a changeable lustre, such as a **cat's eye** [C18 from French, from *chatoyer* to gleam like a cat's eyes, from *chat* CAT¹] > **cha'toyancy** *n*

chatroom (ˈtʃæt,ruːm, -,rʊm) *n* a site on the internet, or another computer network, where users have group discussions by electronic mail, typically about one subject

chat show *n Brit* a television or radio show in which guests, esp celebrities, are interviewed informally. US name: **talk show**

Chatsworth House (ˈtʃætswɜːθ) *n* a mansion near Bakewell in Derbyshire: seat of the Dukes of Devonshire; built (1687–1707) in the classical style

Chattagam (ˈtʃatagam) *n* the official name for **Chittagong**

Chattanooga (,tʃætᵊˈnuːgə) *n* a city in SE Tennessee, on the Tennessee River: scene of two battles during the Civil War, in which the North defeated the Confederates, cleared Tennessee, and opened the way to Georgia (1863). Pop: 154 887 (2003 est)

chattel (ˈtʃætᵊl) *n* **1** (*often plural*) *property law* **a** chattel personal an item of movable personal property, such as furniture, domestic animals, etc **b** chattel real an interest in land less than a freehold, such as a lease **2** goods and chattels personal property [C13 from Old French *chatel* personal property, from Medieval Latin *capitāle* wealth; see CAPITAL¹]

chattel house *n* (esp in Barbados) a movable wooden dwelling, usually set on a foundation of loose stones on rented land

chattel mortgage *n US and Canadian* a mortgage on movable personal property

chatter (ˈtʃætə) *vb* **1** to speak (about unimportant matters) rapidly and incessantly; prattle **2** (*intr*) (of birds, monkeys, etc) to make rapid repetitive high-pitched noises resembling human speech **3** (*intr*) (of the teeth) to click together rapidly through cold or fear **4** (*intr*) to make rapid

intermittent contact with a component, as in machining, causing irregular cutting ▷ *n* **5** idle or foolish talk; gossip **6** the high-pitched repetitive noise made by a bird, monkey, etc **7** the rattling of objects, such as parts of a machine **8** the undulating pattern of marks in a machined surface from the vibration of the tool or workpiece. Also called: **chatter mark** [C13 of imitative origin] > **'chattery** *adj*

chatterati (,tʃætəˈrɑːtiː) *n informal* another word for **chattering classes** [C20 from CHATTER + *-ati* as in LITERATI]

chatterbox (ˈtʃætə,bɒks) *n informal* a person who talks constantly, esp about trivial matters

chatterer (ˈtʃætərə) *n* **1** someone or something that chatters **2** another name for **cotinga**

chattering classes *pl n informal often derogatory* (usually preceded by *the*) the educated sections of society, considered as enjoying discussion of political, social, and cultural issues

chatter mark *n* **1** any of a series of grooves, pits, and scratches on the surface of a rock, usually made by the movement of a glacier **2** another name for **chatter** (sense 8)

chatty (ˈtʃætɪ) *adj* **-tier, -tiest 1** full of trivial conversation; talkative **2** informal and friendly; gossipy: *a chatty letter* > **'chattily** *adv* > **'chattiness** *n*

chat up *vb* (*tr, adverb*) *Brit informal* **1** to talk flirtatiously to (a person), esp with the intention of seducing him or her **2** to talk persuasively to (a person), esp with an ulterior motive

Chaucerian (tʃɔːˈsɪərɪən) *adj* **1** of, relating to, or characteristic of the writings of Geoffrey Chaucer (?1340–1400), the English poet ▷ *n* **2** an imitator of Chaucer, esp one of a group of 15th-century Scottish writers who took him as a model **3 a** an admirer of Chaucer's works **b** a specialist in the study or teaching of Chaucer

chaudfroid *French* (ʃofrwa) *n* a sweet or savoury jellied sauce used to coat cold meat, chicken, etc [literally: hot-cold (because prepared as hot dish, but served cold)]

chauffer or **chaufer** (ˈtʃɔːfə) *n* a small portable heater or stove [C19 from French *chauffoir*, from *chauffer* to heat]

chauffeur (ˈʃəʊfə, ʃəʊˈfɜː) *n* **1** a person employed to drive a car ▷ *vb* **2** to act as driver for (a person): *he chauffeured me to the stadium; he chauffeurs for the Duke* [C20 from French, literally: stoker, from *chauffer* to heat] > **chauffeuse** (ʃəʊˈfɜːz) *fem n*

chaulmoogra (tʃɔːlˈmuːɡrə) *n* **1** a tropical Asian tree, *Taraktogenos* (or *Hydnocarpus*) *kurzii*: family *Flacourtiaceae* **2** oil from the seed of this tree, used in treating leprosy **3** any of several similar or related trees [from Bengali *cāulmugrā*, from *cāul* rice + *mugrā* hemp]

chaunt (tʃɔːnt) *n, vb* a less common variant of **chant**. > **'chaunter** *n*

chausses (ʃəʊs) *n* (*functioning as singular*) a tight-fitting medieval garment covering the feet and legs, usually made of chain mail [C15 from Old French *chauces*, plural of *chauce* leg-covering, from Medieval Latin *calcea*, from Latin *calceus* shoe, from *calx* heel]

chautauqua (ʃəˈtɔːkwə) *n* (in the US, formerly) a summer school or educational meeting held in the summer [C19 named after *Chautauqua*, a lake in New York near which such a school was first held]

chauvinism (ˈʃəʊvɪ,nɪzəm) *n* **1** aggressive or fanatical patriotism; jingoism **2** enthusiastic devotion to a cause **3** smug irrational belief in the superiority of one's own race, party, sex, etc: *male chauvinism* [C19 from French *chauvinisme*, after Nicolas Chauvin, legendary French soldier under Napoleon, noted for his vociferous and unthinking patriotism] > **'chauvinist** *n* > **,chauvin'istic** *adj* > **,chauvin'istically** *adv*

chav (tʃæv) *n Southern English informal derogatory* a young working-class person who dresses in casual sports clothes [perhaps from Romany *chavi* a child] > **'chavish** *adj*

chavette (tʃæˈvɛt) *n Southern English informal*

C

derogatory a young working-class woman who dresses in casual sports clothes [from CHAV + -ETTE (sense 2)]

chavtastic (ˌtʃævˈtæstɪk) adj informal **1** suitable for or designed for chavs **2** relating to or characteristic of a chav

chaw (tʃɔ:) dialect ▷ vb **1** to chew (tobacco), esp without swallowing it ▷ n **2** something chewed, esp a plug of tobacco > ˈchawer n

chawk (tʃɔ:k) n Southwest English dialect a jackdaw

chayote (tʃɑːˈjəʊteɪ, tʃaɪˈəʊtɪ) n **1** a tropical American cucurbitaceous climbing plant, Sechium edule, that has edible pear-shaped fruit enclosing a single enormous seed **2** the fruit of this plant, which is cooked and eaten as a vegetable [from Spanish, from Nahuatl chayotli]

chazan or **hazan, hazzan** Hebrew (xaˈzan; English ˈhɑːz‘n), n, pl chazanim (xazaˈnim; English hɑːˈzɔːniːm) or English chazans a person who leads synagogue services, esp as a profession; cantor

ChB abbreviation for Bachelor of Surgery [Latin: Chirurgiae Baccalaureus]

ChE abbreviation for Chemical Engineer

CHE (tʃiː) n (in New Zealand, formerly) ▷ acronym for Crown Health Enterprise: an agency supervising health expenditure in a district

cheap (tʃiːp) adj **1** costing relatively little; inexpensive; good value **2** charging low prices: a cheap hairdresser **3** of poor quality; shoddy: cheap furniture; cheap and nasty **4** worth relatively little: promises are cheap **5** not worthy of respect; vulgar **6** ashamed; embarrassed: to feel cheap **7** stingy; miserly **8** informal mean; despicable: a cheap liar **9** cheap as chips See chip (sense 11) **10** dirt cheap informal extremely inexpensive ▷ n **11** on the cheap Brit informal at a low cost ▷ adv **12** at very little cost [Old English ceap barter, bargain, price, property; related to Old Norse kaup bargain, Old High German kouf trade, Latin caupō innkeeper] > ˈcheapish adj > ˈcheaply adv > ˈcheapness n

cheapen (ˈtʃiːpᵊn) vb **1** to make or become lower in reputation, quality, etc; degrade or be degraded **2** to make or become cheap or cheaper > ˈcheapener n

cheap-jack informal ▷ n **1** a person who sells cheap and shoddy goods ▷ adj **2** shoddy or inferior [C19 from CHEAP + Jack (name used to typify a person)]

cheapo (ˈtʃiːpəʊ) adj, n, pl cheapos. informal very cheap and possibly shoddy

cheap out vb (intr, adverb) US and Canadian informal to take the cheapest option; try to do something as cheaply as possible

cheapskate (ˈtʃiːpˌskeɪt) n informal a miserly person

cheat (tʃiːt) vb **1** to deceive or practise deceit, esp for one's own gain; trick or swindle (someone) **2** (intr) to obtain unfair advantage by trickery, as in a game of cards **3** (tr) to escape or avoid (something unpleasant) by luck or cunning: to cheat death **4** (when intr, usually foll by on) informal to be sexually unfaithful to (one's wife, husband, or lover) ▷ n **5** a person who cheats **6** a deliberately dishonest transaction, esp for gain; fraud **7** informal sham **8** law the obtaining of another's property by fraudulent means **9** the usual US name for rye-brome [C14 short for ESCHEAT] > ˈcheatable adj > ˈcheater n > ˈcheatingly adv

Cheb (Czech xɛp) n a town in the W Czech Republic, in W Bohemia on the Ohře River: 12th-century castle where Wallenstein was murdered (1634); a centre of the Sudeten-German movement after World War I. Pop: 31 847 (1991). German name: Eger

Cheboksary (Russian tʃɪbakˈsari) n a port in W central Russia on the River Volga: capital of the Chuvash Republic. Pop: 446 000 (2005 est)

Chebyshev's inequality (ˈtʃɛbɪˌʃɒfs) n statistics the fundamental theorem that the probability that a random variable differs from its mean by more than k standard deviations is less than or equal to $1/k^2$ [named after P. L. Chebyshev (1821–94),

Russian mathematician]

Chechen (ˈtʃɛtʃɛn) n, pl -chens or -chen a member of a people of Russia, speaking a Circassian language and chiefly inhabiting the Chechen Republic

Chechen Republic n a constituent republic of S Russia, on the N slopes of the Caucasus Mountains: major oil and natural gas resources; formed an Autonomous Republic with Ingushetia from 1936 until 1944 and from 1957 until 1991; declared independence from Ingushetia in 1992; fighting between Chechen separatists and Russian forces (1994–96) led to de facto independence: reoccupied by Russia in 1999–2000. Capital: Grozny. Pop: 1 100 300 (2002). Area: 15 700 sq km (6010 sq miles). Also called: Chechenia (tʃɛˈtʃɛnɪə), Chechnya (tʃɛˈtʃnɪə)

check (tʃɛk) vb **1** to pause or cause to pause, esp abruptly **2** (tr) to restrain or control: to check one's tears **3** (tr) to slow the growth or progress of; retard **4** (tr) to rebuke or rebuff **5** (when intr, often foll by on or up on) to examine, investigate, or make an inquiry into (facts, a product, etc) for accuracy, quality, or progress, esp rapidly or informally **6** (tr) chiefly US and Canadian to mark off so as to indicate approval, correctness, or preference. Usual Brit word: tick **7** (intr; often foll by with) chiefly US and Canadian to correspond or agree: this report checks with the other **8** (tr) chiefly US, Canadian, and NZ to leave in or accept (clothing or property) for temporary custody **9** chess to place (an opponent's king) in check **10** (tr) to mark with a pattern of squares or crossed lines **11** to crack or cause to crack **12** agriculture short for checkrow **13** (tr) ice hockey to impede (an opponent) **14** (intr) hunting (of hounds) to pause in the pursuit of quarry while relocating a lost scent **15** (intr; foll by at) falconry to change from one quarry to another while in flight **16** (intr) to decline the option of opening the betting in a round of poker **17** check the helm nautical to swing back the helm of a vessel to prevent it from turning too quickly or too far ▷ n **18** a break in progress; stoppage **19** a restraint or rebuff **20 a** a person or thing that restrains, halts, etc **b** (as modifier): a check line **21 a** a control, esp a rapid or informal one, designed to ensure accuracy, progress, etc **b** (as modifier): a check list **22** a means or standard to ensure against fraud or error **23** the US word for tick¹ **24** the US spelling of cheque **25** chiefly US the bill in a restaurant **26** chiefly US and Canadian a ticket or tag used to identify clothing or property deposited for custody **27** a pattern of squares or crossed lines **28** a single square in such a pattern **29 a** a fabric with a pattern of squares or crossed lines **b** (as modifier): a check suit **30** chess the state or position of a king under direct attack, from which it must be moved or protected by another piece **31** a small crack, as one in veneer or one that occurs in timber during seasoning **32** part of the action of a piano that arrests the backward motion of a hammer after it has struck a string and holds it until the key is released **33** a chip or counter used in some card and gambling games **34** hunting a pause by the hounds in the pursuit of their quarry owing to loss of its scent **35** angling a ratchet fitted to a fishing reel to check the free running of the line **36** ice hockey the act of impeding an opponent with one's body or stick **37** in check under control or restraint ▷ interj **38** chess a call made to an opponent indicating that his king is in check **39** chiefly US and Canadian an expression of agreement ▷ See also check in, check off, check out, checkup [C14 from Old French eschec a check at chess, hence, a pause (to verify something), via Arabic from Persian shāh the king! (in chess)] > ˈcheckable adj

check digit n computing a digit derived from and appended to a string of data digits, used to detect corruption of the data string during transmission or transcription

checked (tʃɛkt) adj **1** having a pattern of small squares **2** phonetics (of a syllable) ending in a consonant

checker¹ (ˈtʃɛkə) n, vb **1** the usual US spelling of chequer ▷ n **2** textiles a variant spelling of chequer (sense 2) **3** US and Canadian any one of the 12 flat thick discs used by each player in the game of checkers. Also called (in Britain and certain other countries): draughtsman

checker² (ˈtʃɛkə) n chiefly US and Canadian **1** a cashier, esp in a supermarket **2** an attendant in a cloakroom, left-luggage office, etc

checkerberry (ˈtʃɛkəbərɪ, -brɪ) n, pl -ries **1** the fruit of any of various plants, esp the wintergreen (Gaultheria procumbens) **2** any plant bearing this fruit

checkerbloom (ˈtʃɛkəˌbluːm) n a Californian malvaceous plant, Sidalcea malvaeflora, with pink or purple flowers

checkerboard (ˈtʃɛkəˌbɔːd) n US and Canadian a square board divided into 64 squares of alternating colours, used for playing checkers or chess. Also called (in Britain and certain other countries): draughtsboard

checkers (ˈtʃɛkəz) n (functioning as singular) US and Canadian a game for two players using a checkerboard and 12 checkers each. The object is to jump over and capture the opponent's pieces

check in vb (adverb) **1** (intr) to record one's arrival, as at a hotel or for work; sign in or report **2** (tr) to register the arrival of (passengers, etc) ▷ n check-in **3 a** the formal registration of arrival, as at an airport or a hotel **b** (as modifier): check-in time **4** the place where one registers arrival at an airport, etc

checking account n the US name for current account

check list n a list of items, facts, names, etc, to be checked or referred to for comparison, identification, or verification

checkmate (ˈtʃɛkˌmeɪt) n **1** chess **a** the winning position in which an opponent's king is under attack and unable to escape **b** the move by which this position is achieved **2** utter defeat ▷ vb (tr) **3** chess to place (an opponent's king) in checkmate **4** to thwart or render powerless ▷ interj **5** chess a call made when placing an opponent's king in checkmate [C14 from Old French eschec mat, from Arabic shāh māt, the king is dead; see CHECK]

check off vb (tr, adverb) **1** to mark with a tick **2** to deduct (union contributions) from an employee's pay ▷ n check-off **3** a procedure whereby an employer deducts union contributions directly from an employee's pay and pays the money to the union

check out vb (adverb) **1** (intr) to pay the bill and depart, esp from a hotel **2** (intr) to depart from a place; record one's departure from work **3** to investigate or prove to be in order after investigation: the police checked out all the statements; their credentials checked out **4** (tr) informal to have a look at; inspect: check out the wally in the pink shirt ▷ n checkout **5 a** the latest time for vacating a room in a hotel, etc **b** (as modifier): checkout time **6** a counter, esp in a supermarket, where customers pay

checkpoint (ˈtʃɛkˌpɔɪnt) n a place, as at a frontier or in a motor rally, where vehicles or travellers are stopped for official identification, inspection, etc

checkrail (ˈtʃɛkˌreɪl) n Brit another word for guardrail (sense 2)

checkrein (ˈtʃɛkˌreɪn) n the usual US word for bearing rein

checkroom (ˈtʃɛkˌruːm, -ˌrʊm) n US and Canadian a place at a railway station, airport, etc, where luggage may be left for a small charge with an attendant for safekeeping. Also called (in Britain and certain other countries): left-luggage office

checkrow (ˈtʃɛkˌrəʊ) US agriculture ▷ n **1** a row of plants, esp corn, in which the spaces between adjacent plants are equal to those between adjacent rows to facilitate cultivation ▷ vb **2** (tr) to plant in checkrows

checks and balances *pl n* *government, chiefly US* competition and mutual restraint among the various branches of government

checkup ('tʃɛk,ʌp) *n* **1** an examination to see if something is in order **2** *med* a medical examination, esp one taken at regular intervals to verify a normal state of health or discover a disease in its early stages ▷ *vb* **check up** **3** (*intr, adverb*; sometimes foll by *on*) to investigate or make an inquiry into (a person's character, evidence, etc), esp when suspicions have been aroused

check valve *n* a valve that closes by fluid pressure to prevent return flow. Also called: **nonreturn valve**

checky ('tʃɛkɪ) *adj* (*usually postpositive*) *heraldry* having squares of alternating tinctures or furs; checked

Cheddar ('tʃɛdə) *n* **1** (*sometimes not capital*) any of several types of smooth hard yellow or whitish cheese **2** a village in SW England, in N Somerset: situated near **Cheddar Gorge**, a pass through the Mendip Hills renowned for its stalactitic caverns and rare limestone flora. Pop: 4796 (2001)

cheddite ('tʃɛdaɪt, 'ʃɛd-) *n* an explosive made by mixing a powdered chlorate or perchlorate with a fatty substance, such as castor oil [c20 from *Chedde* town in Savoy, France, where it was first made]

cheder or **heder** *Hebrew* ('xɛdər; *English* 'heɪdə) *n, pl* **chadarim** (xada'riːm) or *English* **cheders** *Judaism* **1** (in Western countries) elementary religious education classes, usually outside normal school hours **2** more traditionally, a full-time elementary religious school **3** *informal* a place of corrective instruction; prison [literally: room]

chee-chee ('tʃiː,tʃiː) *n* a less common spelling of **chichi²**

cheek (tʃiːk) *n* **1 a** either side of the face, esp that part below the eye **b** either side of the oral cavity; side of the mouth. Related adjs: **buccal, genal, malar 2** *informal* impudence; effrontery **3** (*often plural*) *informal* either side of the buttocks **4** (*often plural*) a side of a door jamb **5** *nautical* one of the two fore-and-aft supports for the trestletrees on a mast of a sailing vessel, forming part of the hounds **6** one of the jaws of a vice **7 cheek by jowl** close together; intimately linked **8 turn the other cheek** to be submissive and refuse to retaliate even when provoked or treated badly **9 with (one's) tongue in (one's) cheek** See **tongue** (sense 19) ▷ *vb* **10** (*tr*) *informal* to speak or behave disrespectfully to; act impudently towards [Old English *ceace;* related to Middle Low German *kāke*, Dutch *kaak*] > **'cheekless** *adj*

cheekbone ('tʃiːk,bəʊn) *n* the nontechnical name for **zygomatic bone** Related adj: **malar**

cheekpiece ('tʃiːk,piːs) *n* either of the two straps of a bridle that join the bit to the crownpiece

cheek pouch *n* a membranous pouch inside the mouth of many rodents and some other mammals: used for holding food

cheeky ('tʃiːkɪ) *adj* **cheekier, cheekiest** disrespectful in speech or behaviour; impudent: *a cheeky child* > **'cheekily** *adv* > **'cheekiness** *n*

cheep (tʃiːp) *n* **1** the short weak high-pitched cry of a young bird; chirp ▷ *vb* **2** (*intr*) (of young birds) to utter characteristic shrill sounds > **'cheeper** *n*

cheer (tʃɪə) *vb* **1** (usually foll by *up*) to make or become happy or hopeful; comfort or be comforted **2** to applaud with shouts **3** (when *tr*, sometimes foll by *on*) to encourage (a team, person, etc) with shouts, esp in contests ▷ *n* **4** a shout or cry of approval, encouragement, etc, often using such words as **hurrah!** or **rah! rah! rah!** **5 three cheers** three shouts of hurrah given in unison by a group to honour someone or celebrate something **6** happiness; good spirits **7** state of mind; spirits (archaic, except in the phrases **be of good cheer, with good cheer**) **8** *archaic* provisions for a feast; fare ▷ See also **cheers** [c13 (in the sense: face, welcoming aspect): from Old French *chere*, from Late Latin *cara* face, from Greek *kara* head] > **'cheerer** *n* > **'cheeringly** *adv*

cheerful ('tʃɪəfʊl) *adj* **1** having a happy disposition; in good spirits **2** pleasantly bright; gladdening: *a cheerful room* **3** hearty; ungrudging; enthusiastic: *cheerful help* > **'cheerfully** *adv* > **'cheerfulness** *n*

cheerio (,tʃɪərɪ'əʊ) *sentence substitute informal, chiefly Brit* **1** a farewell greeting **2** a drinking toast ▷ *n* **3** *NZ* a type of small sausage

cheerleader ('tʃɪə,liːdə) *n* a person who leads a crowd in formal cheers, esp at sports events

cheerless ('tʃɪəlɪs) *adj* dreary, gloomy, or pessimistic > **'cheerlessly** *adv* > **'cheerlessness** *n*

cheerly ('tʃɪəlɪ) *adj, adv archaic* cheerful or cheerfully

cheers (tʃɪəz) *sentence substitute informal, chiefly Brit* **1** a drinking toast **2** goodbye! cheerio! **3** thanks!

cheery ('tʃɪərɪ) *adj* **cheerier, cheeriest** showing or inspiring cheerfulness > **'cheerily** *adv* > **'cheeriness** *n*

cheese¹ (tʃiːz) *n* **1** the curd of milk separated from the whey and variously prepared as a food **2** a mass or complete cake of this substance **3** any of various substances of similar consistency, etc: *lemon cheese* **4 big cheese** *slang* an important person **5 as alike** (or **different**) **as chalk and cheese** See **chalk** (sense 6) [Old English *cēse*, from Latin *cāseus* cheese; related to Old Saxon *kāsi*]

cheese² (tʃiːz) *vb slang* **1** (*tr*) to stop; desist **2** (*intr*) *prison slang* to act in a grovelling manner [c19 of unknown origin]

cheeseboard ('tʃiːz,bɔːd) *n* a board from which cheese is served at a meal

cheeseburger ('tʃiːz,bɜːgə) *n* a hamburger cooked with a slice of cheese on top of it

cheesecake ('tʃiːz,keɪk) *n* **1** a rich tart with a biscuit base, filled with a mixture of cream cheese, cream, sugar, and often sultanas, sometimes having a fruit topping **2** *slang* women displayed for their sex appeal, as in photographs in magazines, newspapers, or films. Compare **beefcake**

cheesecloth ('tʃiːz,klɒθ) *n* a loosely woven cotton cloth formerly used only for wrapping cheese

cheese cutter *n* **1** a board with a wire attached for cutting cheese **2** *nautical* a keel that may be drawn up into the boat when not in use **3** a nautical peaked cap worn without a badge

cheesed off *adj* (*usually postpositive*) *Brit slang* bored, disgusted, or angry [c20 from CHEESE²]

cheese-head *adj* denoting or relating to a screw or bolt with a cylindrical slotted head

cheese mite *n* a white soft-bodied free-living mite, *Tyrophagus* (or *Tyroglyphus*) *longior*, sometimes found in decaying cheese

cheesemonger ('tʃiːz,mʌŋgə) *n* a person dealing in cheese, butter, etc

cheeseparing ('tʃiːz,pɛərɪŋ) *adj* **1** penny-pinching; stingy ▷ *n* **2 a** a paring of cheese rind **b** anything similarly worthless **3** stinginess

cheese skipper *n* a dipterous fly, *Piophila casei*, whose larvae feed on cheese and move by jumping: family *Piophilidae*

cheese straw *n* a long thin cheese-flavoured strip of pastry

cheesewood ('tʃiːz,wʊd) *n* *Austral rare* the tough yellowish wood of Australian trees of the genus *Pittosporum*: family *Pittosporaceae*

cheesy ('tʃiːzɪ) *adj* **cheesier, cheesiest 1** like cheese in flavour, smell, or consistency **2** *informal* (of a smile) broad but possibly insincere: *a big cheesy grin* **3** *informal* banal or trite; in poor taste > **'cheesiness** *n*

cheetah or **chetah** ('tʃiːtə) *n* a large feline mammal, *Acinonyx jubatus*, of Africa and SW Asia: the swiftest mammal, having very long legs, nonretractile claws, and a black-spotted light-brown coat [c18 from Hindi *cītā*, from Sanskrit *citrakāya* tiger, from *citra* bright, speckled + *kāya* body]

chef (ʃɛf) *n* a cook, esp the principal cook in a restaurant [c19 from French, from Old French *chief* head, CHIEF]

chef-d'oeuvre *French* (ʃɛdœvrə) *n, pl* **chefs-d'oeuvre** (ʃɛdœvrə) a masterpiece

Chefoo ('tʃiː'fuː) *n* another name for **Yantai**

cheiro- *combining form* a variant spelling of **chiro-**

Cheiron ('kaɪrɒn, -rən) *n* a variant spelling of **Chiron**

Cheju ('tʃɛ'dʒuː) *n* a volcanic island in the N East China Sea, southwest of Korea: constitutes a province (Cheju-do) of South Korea. Capital: Cheju. Pop: 302 000 (2005 est). Area: 1792 sq km (692 sq miles). Formerly called: Quelpart

Cheka *Russian* ('tʃɛka) *n* *Russian history* the secret police set up in 1917 by the Bolshevik government: reorganized in the Soviet Union in Dec 1922 as the GPU [c20 from Russian, acronym of *Chrezvychainaya Komissiya* Extraordinary Commission (to combat Counter-Revolution)]

Chekhovian or **Chekovian** (tʃɛ'kəʊvɪən) *adj* of or relating to Anton Pavlovich Chekhov, the Russian dramatist and short-story writer (1860–1904)

Chekiang ('tʃɛ'kjæŋ, -kɑ'æŋ) *n* a variant transliteration of the Chinese name for **Zhejiang**

chela¹ ('kiːlə) *n, pl* **lae** (-liː) a large pincer-like claw of such arthropods as the crab and scorpion [c17 New Latin, from Greek *khēlē* claw] > **cheliferous** (kɪ'lɪfərəs) *adj*

chela² ('tʃeɪlə) *n* *Hinduism* a disciple of a religious teacher [c19 from Hindi *celā*, from Sanskrit *ceta* servant, slave] > **'chela,ship** *n*

chelate ('kiːleɪt) *n* **1** *chem* a coordination compound in which a metal atom or ion is bound to a ligand at two or more points on the ligand, so as to form a heterocyclic ring containing a metal atom ▷ *adj* **2** *zoology* of or possessing chelae **3** *chem* of or denoting a chelate ▷ *vb* **4** (*intr*) *chem* to form a chelate [c20 from CHELA¹]

chelating agent *n* a chemical compound that coordinates with a metal to form a chelate, often used to trap or remove heavy metal ions

chelation ('kiːleɪʃən) *n* **1** *chem* the process by which a chelate is formed **2** *animal Husbandry* the process by which trace elements in an animal's feed are bonded to amino acids, ensuring their absorption into the animal's body **3** *geol* the chemical removal of metallic ions in a mineral or rock by weathering

chelicera (kɪ'lɪsərə) *n, pl* **-erae** (-ə,riː) one of a pair of appendages on the head of spiders and other arachnids: often modified as food-catching claws [c19 New Latin, from French *chélicère*, from *chél-* see CHELA¹ + *-cère* from Greek *keras* horn] > **che'liceral** *adj*

chelicerate (kɪ'lɪsə,reɪt) *adj* **1** of, relating to, or belonging to the *Chelicerata*, a subphylum of arthropods, including arachnids and the horseshoe crab, in which the first pair of limbs are modified as chelicerae ▷ *n* **2** any arthropod belonging to the *Chelicerata*

cheliform ('kiːlɪ,fɔːm) *adj* shaped like a chela; pincer-like

Chellean ('ʃɛlɪən) *n, adj* *archaeol* (no longer in technical usage) another word for **Abbevillian** [c19 from French *chelléen*, from *Chelles*, France, where various items were found]

chellup ('tʃɛləp) *n* *Northern and Midland English dialect* noise

Chelmsford ('tʃɛlmzfəd) *n* a city in SE England, administrative centre of Essex: electronics, retail; university (1992). Pop: 99 962 (2001)

cheloid ('kiːlɔɪd) *n* *pathol* a variant spelling of **keloid** > **che'loidal** *adj*

chelone (kə'ləʊnɪ) *n* any plant of the hardy N American genus *Chelone*, grown for its white, rose, or purple flower spikes: family *Scrophulariaceae* [New Latin, from Greek *chelōnē* a tortoise, from a fancied resemblance between a tortoise's head and the shape of the flower]

chelonian (kɪ'ləʊnɪən) *n* **1** any reptile of the order *Chelonia*, including the tortoises and turtles, in which most of the body is enclosed in a protective bony capsule ▷ *adj* **2** of, relating to, belonging to, or characteristic of the *Chelonia* [c19 from New

C

Latin *Chelōnia*, from Greek *khelōnē* tortoise]

chelp (tʃɛlp) *vb* (*intr*) *Northern and Midland English dialect* **1** (*esp of women or children*) to chatter or speak out of turn: *she's always chelping at the teacher* **2** (of birds) to squeak or chirp [c19 perhaps from *ch*(*irp*) + (*y*)*elp*]

Chelsea (ˈtʃɛlsɪ) *n* a residential district of SW London, in the Royal Borough of Kensington and Chelsea: site of the Chelsea Royal Hospital for old and invalid soldiers (**Chelsea Pensioners**)

Chelsea bun *n* a rolled yeast currant bun decorated with sugar

Chelsea tractor *n informal* a four-by-four [c21 from the idea of vehicles designed for rough terrain being popular among urban dwellers]

Cheltenham (ˈtʃɛltᵊnəm) *n* **1** a town in W England, in central Gloucestershire: famous for its schools, racecourse, and saline springs (discovered in 1716). Pop: 98 875 (2001) **2** a style of type

Chelyabinsk (*Russian* tʃɪˈljabinsk) *n* an industrial city in SW Russia. Pop: 1 067 000 (2005 est)

Chelyuskin (*Russian* tʃɪˈljuskin) *n* **Cape** a cape in N central Russia, in N Siberia at the end of the Taimyr Peninsula: the northernmost point of Asia

chem. *abbreviation for* **1** chemical **2** chemist **3** chemistry

chem- *combining form* variant of **chemo-** before a vowel

chemautotroph (ˌkiːməʊˈɔːtətrəʊf) *or* **chemoautotroph** (ˌkiːməʊˈɔːtrəʊf, ˌkɛm-) *n biology* an organism, such as a bacterium, that obtains its energy from inorganic reactions using simple compounds, such as ammonia or hydrogen sulphide. Also called: **chemolithotroph** > **chemautotrophic** (ˌkiːməʊˌɔːtəˈtrɒfɪk, ˌkɛm-) *adj*

chemical (ˈkɛmɪkᵊl) *n* **1** any substance used in or resulting from a reaction involving changes to atoms or molecules, especially one derived artificially for practical use ▷ *adj* **2** of or used in chemistry: *chemical balance* **3** of, made from, or using chemicals: *chemical fertilizer* > ˈ**chemically** *adv*

chemical bond *n* a mutual attraction between two atoms resulting from a redistribution of their outer electrons. See also **covalent bond, electrovalent bond, coordinate bond**

chemical engineering *n* the branch of engineering concerned with the design, operation, maintenance, and manufacture of the plant and machinery used in industrial chemical processes > **chemical engineer** *n*

chemical equation *n* a representation of a chemical reaction using symbols of the elements to indicate the amount of substance, usually in moles, of each reactant and product

chemical machining *n* the shaping of a metal part by controlled removal of unwanted metal by a flow of chemical solutions

chemical peeling *n* a cosmetic process in which a substance containing a chemical (*esp* alpha-hydroxy acids) is applied to the skin of the face and peeled away to remove a layer of dead cells

chemical potential *n* a thermodynamic function of a substance in a system that is the partial differential of the Gibbs function of the system with respect to the number of moles of the substance. Symbol: μ

chemical reaction *n* a process that involves changes in the structure and energy content of atoms, molecules, or ions but not their nuclei. Compare **nuclear reaction**

chemical warfare *n* warfare in which chemicals other than explosives are used as weapons, esp warfare using asphyxiating or nerve gases, poisons, defoliants, etc

chemico- *combining form* chemical: *chemicophysical*

chemiluminescence (ˌkɛmɪˌluːmɪˈnɛsəns) *n* the phenomenon in which a chemical reaction leads to the emission of light without incandescence > ˌchemiˌlumiˈnescent *adj*

chemin de fer (ʃəˈmæn də ˈfɛə; *French* ʃəmɛ̃dfɛr) *n* a gambling game, a variation of baccarat [French:

railway, referring to the fast tempo of the game]

chemiosmosis (ˌkɛmɪɒzˈməʊsɪs) *or* **chemosmosis** *n biochem* the mechanism by which the synthesis and utilization of the biochemical energy source ATP is regulated: the energy generated by oxidative phosphorylation generates a proton gradient across the membrane of the mitochondrion that drives the enzymic resynthesis of ATP **2** a chemical reaction between two compounds after osmosis through an intervening semipermeable membrane

chemise (ʃəˈmiːz) *n* **1** an unwaisted loose-fitting dress hanging straight from the shoulders **2** a loose shirtlike undergarment ▷ Also called: **shift** [c14 from Old French: shirt, from Late Latin *camisa*, perhaps of Celtic origin]

chemisette (ˌʃɛmɪˈzɛt) *n* an underbodice of lawn, lace, etc, worn to fill in a low-cut dress [c19 from French, diminutive of CHEMISE]

chemism (ˈkɛmɪzəm) *n obsolete* chemical action

chemisorb (ˌkɛmɪˈsɔːb) *or* **chemosorb** *vb* (*tr*) to take up (a substance) by chemisorption

chemisorption (ˌkɛmɪˈsɔːpʃən) *n* an adsorption process in which an adsorbate is held on the surface of an adsorbent by chemical bonds

chemist (ˈkɛmɪst) *n* **1** *Brit* a shop selling medicines, cosmetics, etc **2** *Brit* a qualified dispenser of prescribed medicines **3** a person studying, trained in, or engaged in chemistry **4** an obsolete word for **alchemist** [c16 from earlier *chimist*, from New Latin *chimista*, shortened from Medieval Latin *alchimista* ALCHEMIST]

chemistry (ˈkɛmɪstrɪ) *n, pl* **-tries 1** the branch of physical science concerned with the composition, properties, and reactions of substances. See also **inorganic chemistry, organic chemistry, physical chemistry 2** the composition, properties, and reactions of a particular substance **3** the nature and effects of any complex phenomenon: *the chemistry of humour* **4** *informal* a reaction, taken to be instinctual, between two persons [c17 from earlier *chimistrie*, from *chimist* CHEMIST]

chemmy (ˈʃɛmɪ) *n cards* short for **chemin de fer**

Chemnitz (*German* ˈkɛmnɪts) *n* a city in E Germany, in Saxony, at the foot of the Erzgebirge: textiles, engineering. Pop: 249 922 (2003 est). Also called (1953–90): **Karl-Marx-Stadt**

chemo (ˈkiːməʊ) *n informal* short for **chemotherapy**

chemo-, chemi- *or before a vowel* **chem-** *combining form* indicating that chemicals or chemical reactions are involved: *chemotherapy* [New Latin, from Late Greek *khēmeia*; see ALCHEMY]

chemoattractant (ˌkɛməʊəˈtræktənt) *n* a chemical substance that provokes chemotaxis, esp one that causes a bacterium to move in the direction in which its concentration is increasing

chemoautroph (ˌkiːməʊˈɔːtrəʊf) *n* a variant of chemautotroph

chemoheterotroph (ˌkiːməʊˈhɛtərəʊtrəʊf, ˌkɛm-) *n biology* an organism that obtains its energy from the oxidation of organic compounds. Also called: **chemo-organotroph** > **chemoheterotrophic** (ˌkiːməʊˌhɛtərəʊˈtrɒfɪk, ˌkɛm-) *adj*

chemokinesis (ˌkɛməʊkaɪˈniːsɪs) *n immunol* the random movement of cells, such as leucocytes, stimulated by substances in their environment

chemolithotroph (ˌkiːməʊˈlɪθətrəʊf, ˌkɛm-) *n* another name for **chemoautotroph**

chemonasty (ˈkɛməʊˌnæstɪ) *n botany* the nastic movement of a plant in response to a chemical stimulus

chemo-organotroph (ˌkiːməʊˈɔːgænətrəʊf, ˌkɛm-) *n* another name for **chemoheterotroph**

chemoprophylaxis (ˌkɛməʊˌprəʊfɪˈlæksɪs, -ˌprɒfə-) *n* the prevention of disease using chemical drugs > ˌchemoˌprophyˈlactic *adj*

chemoreceptor (ˌkɛməʊrɪˈsɛptə) *or* **chemoceptor** *n* a sensory receptor in a biological cell membrane to which an external molecule binds to generate a smell or taste sensation

chemosmosis (ˌkɛmɒzˈməʊsɪs) *n* a variant spelling of chemiosmosis. > chemosmotic (ˌkɛmɒzˈmɒtɪk) *adj*

chemosphere (ˈkɛməˌsfɪə) *n meteorol* a rare name for **thermosphere**. > chemospheric (ˌkɛməˈsfɛrɪk) *adj*

chemostat (ˈkiːməʊˌstæt, ˈkɛm-) *n* an apparatus for growing bacterial cultures at a constant rate by controlling the supply of nutrient medium

chemosynthesis (ˌkɛməʊˈsɪnθɪsɪs) *n* the formation of organic material by certain bacteria using energy derived from simple chemical reactions > **chemosynthetic** (ˌkɛməʊsɪnˈθɛtɪk) *adj* > ˌchemosynˈthetically *adv*

chemotaxis (ˌkɛməʊˈtæksɪs) *n* the movement of a microorganism or cell in response to a chemical stimulus > **chemoˈtactic** *adj* > ˌchemoˈtactically *adv*

chemotherapy (ˌkiːməʊˈθɛrəpɪ, kiːmə-) *n* treatment of disease, esp cancer, by means of chemical agents. Compare **radiotherapy** > ˌchemoˈtherapist *n*

chemotropism (ˌkɛməʊˈtrəʊˌpɪzəm) *n* the growth response of an organism, esp a plant, to a chemical stimulus > **chemotropic** (ˌkɛməʊˈtrɒpɪk) *adj* > ˌchemoˈtropically *adv*

chempaduk (ˈtʃɛmpəˌdʌk) *n* **1** an evergreen moraceous tree, *Artocarpus champeden* (or *A. integer*), of Malaysia, similar to the jackfruit **2** the fruit of this tree, edible when cooked, having yellow starchy flesh and a leathery rind [from Malay]

Chemulpo (ˌtʃɛmʊlˈpəʊ) *n* a former name of **Inchon**

chemurgy (ˈkɛmɜːdʒɪ) *n* the branch of chemistry concerned with the industrial use of organic raw materials, esp materials of agricultural origin > chemˈurgic *or* chemˈurgical *adj*

Chenab (tʃɪˈnæb) *n* a river rising in the Himalayas and flowing southwest to the Sutlej River in Pakistan. Length: 1087 km (675 miles)

Cheng-chiang (ˈtʃɛŋˈtʃæn) *n* a variant transliteration of the Chinese name for **Jinjiang**

Chengchow *or* **Cheng-chou** (ˈtʃɛŋˈtʃəʊ) *n* a variant transliteration of the Chinese name for **Zhengzhou**

Chengde, Chengteh *or* **Ch'eng-te** (ˈtʃɛŋˈteɪ) *n* a city in NE China, in Hebei on the Luan River: summer residence of the Manchu emperors. Pop: 470 000 (2005 est)

Chengdu, Chengtu *or* **Ch'eng-tu** (ˈtʃɛŋˈtuː) *n* a city in S central China, capital of Sichuan province. Pop: 3 478 000 (2005 est)

chenille (ʃəˈniːl) *n* **1** a thick soft tufty silk or worsted velvet cord or yarn used in embroidery and for trimmings, etc **2** a fabric of such yarn **3** a rich and hard-wearing carpet of such fabric [c18 from French, literally: hairy caterpillar, from Latin *canicula*, diminutive of *canis* dog]

Chenin Blanc (ʃəˌnɛ̃ ˈblɒŋk) *n* **1** a white grape grown in the Loire region of France and in South Africa, California, New Zealand, and elsewhere, used for making wine **2** any of various light dry white wines made from this grape

Chennai (tʃɪˈnaɪ) *n* the official name for **Madras**

chenopod (ˈkiːnəˌpɒd, ˈkɛn-) *n* any flowering plant of the family *Chenopodiaceae*, which includes the beet, mangel-wurzel, spinach, and goosefoot [c16 from Greek *khēn* goose + *pous* foot] > **chenopodiaceous** (ˌkiːnəˌpəʊdɪˈeɪʃəs, ˌkɛn-) *adj*

cheongsam (ˈtʃɒŋˈsæm) *n* a straight dress, usually of silk or cotton, with a stand-up collar and a slit in one side of the skirt, worn by Chinese women [from Chinese (Cantonese), variant of Mandarin *ch'ang shan* long jacket]

Chepstow (ˈtʃɛpstəʊ) *n* a town in S Wales, in Monmouthshire on the River Wye: tourism, light industry. Pop: 10 821 (2001)

cheque *or US* **check** (tʃɛk) *n* **1** a bill of exchange drawn on a bank by the holder of a current account; payable into a bank account, if crossed, or on demand, if uncrossed **2** *Austral and NZ* the total sum of money received for contract work or a crop **3** *Austral* and NZ wages [C18 from CHECK, in the sense: a means of verification]

cheque account *n* an account at a bank or a building society upon which cheques can be drawn

chequebook *or US* **checkbook** ('tʃɛk,bʊk) *n* a book containing detachable blank cheques and issued by a bank or building society to holders of cheque accounts

chequebook journalism *n* the practice of securing exclusive rights to material for newspaper stories by paying a high price for it, regardless of any moral implications such as paying people to boast of criminal or morally reprehensible activities

cheque card *n* a card issued by a bank or building society, guaranteeing payment of a customer's cheques up to a stated value: may also function as a cash card or debit card or both

chequer *or US* **checker** ('tʃɛkə) *n* **1** any of the marbles, pegs, or other pieces used in the game of Chinese chequers **2 a** a pattern consisting of squares of different colours, textures, or materials **b** one of the squares in such a pattern ▷ *vb* (*tr*) **3** to make irregular in colour or character; variegate **4** to mark off with alternating squares of colour ▷ See also **chequers** [C13 chessboard, from Anglo-French *escheker,* from *eschec* CHECK]

chequerboard ('tʃɛkə,bɔːd) *n* another name for a **draughtboard**

chequered *or esp US* **checkered** ('tʃɛkəd) *adj* marked by fluctuations of fortune (esp in the phrase **a chequered career**)

chequered flag *n* the black-and-white checked flag traditionally shown to the winner and all finishers at the end of a motor race by a senior race official

chequers ('tʃɛkəz) *n* (*functioning as singular*) another name for **draughts**

Chequers ('tʃɛkəz) *n* an estate and country house in S England, in central Buckinghamshire: the official country residence of the British prime minister

chequing account ('tʃɛkɪŋ) *n Canadian* an account at a bank or building society against which cheques may be drawn at any time. Also called (in Britain and certain other countries): **current account**

Cher (*French* ʃɛr) *n* **1** a department of central France, in E Centre region. Capital: Bourges. Pop: 312 277 (2003 est). Area: 7304 sq km (2849 sq miles) **2** a river in central France, rising in the Massif Central and flowing northwest to the Loire. Length: 354 km (220 miles)

Cherbourg (ʃɛəbʊəg; *French* ʃɛrbur) *n* a port in NW France, on the English Channel. Pop: 25 370 (1999)

Cheremiss *or* **Cheremis** (,tʃɛərə'mɪs, -'miːs, 'tʃɛərə,mɪs, -,miːs) *n* **1** (*pl* -**miss** *or* -**mis**) a member of an Ugrian people of the Volga region, esp of the Mari El Republic **2** Also called: **Mari** the language of this people, belonging to the Finno-Ugric family

Cherenkov radiation (tʃɪ'rɛnkɒf) *n* the electromagnetic radiation produced when a charged particle moves through a medium at a greater velocity than the velocity of light in that medium [C20 named after Pavel Alekseyevich Cherenkov (1904–90), Soviet physicist]

Cheribon ('tʃɪərə,bɒn) *n* a variant spelling of **Tjirebon**

cherish ('tʃɛrɪʃ) *vb* (*tr*) **1** to show great tenderness for; treasure **2** to cling fondly to (a hope, idea, etc); nurse: *to cherish ambitions* [C14 from Old French *cherir,* from *cher* dear, from Latin *cārus*] ▷ 'cherishable *adj* ▷ 'cherisher *n* ▷ 'cherishingly *adv*

Chernigov (tʃɜː'niɡɒf) *n* a city in N central Ukraine, on the River Desna: tyres, pianos, consumer goods. Pop: 308 000 (2005 est)

Chernobyl (tʃɜː'nəʊbəl, -'nɒbəl) *n* a town in N Ukraine; site of a nuclear power station accident in 1986

Chernovtsy (*Russian* tʃɪrnaf'tsi) *n* a city in

Ukraine on the Prut River: formerly under Polish, Austro-Hungarian, and Romanian rule; part of the Soviet Union (1947–91). Pop: 237 000 (2005 est). German name: **Czernowitz**. Romanian name: **Cernăuţi**

chernozem *or* **tschernosem** (tʃɜː'nəʊ,zɛm) *n* a black soil, rich in humus and carbonates, in cool or temperate semiarid regions, as the grasslands of Russia [from Russian, contraction of *chernaya zemlya* black earth]

Cherokee ('tʃɛrə,kiː, ,tʃɛrə'kiː) *n* **1** (*pl* -**kees** *or* -**kee**) a member of a Native American people formerly living in and around the Appalachian Mountains, now chiefly in Oklahoma; one of the Iroquois peoples **2** the language of this people, belonging to the Iroquoian family

Cherokee rose *n* an evergreen climbing Chinese rose, *Rosa laevigata*, that now grows wild in the southern US, having large white fragrant flowers

cheroot (ʃə'ruːt) *n* a cigar with both ends cut off squarely [C17 from Tamil *curuttu* curl, roll]

cherry ('tʃɛrɪ) *n, pl* -ries **1** any of several trees of the rosaceous genus *Prunus,* such as *P. avium* (**sweet cherry**), having a small fleshy rounded fruit containing a hard stone. See also **bird cherry 2** the fruit or wood of any of these trees **3** any of various unrelated plants, such as the ground cherry and Jerusalem cherry **4 a** a bright red colour; cerise **b** (*as adjective*): *a cherry coat* **5** *slang* virginity or the hymen as its symbol **6** (*modifier*) of or relating to the cherry fruit or wood: *cherry tart* [C14 back formation from Old English *ciris* (mistakenly thought to be plural), ultimately from Late Latin *ceresia,* perhaps from Latin *cerasus* cherry tree, from Greek *kerasios*] ▷ 'cherry-,like *adj*

cherry brandy *n* a red liqueur made of brandy flavoured with cherries

cherry laurel *n* a Eurasian rosaceous evergreen shrub, *Prunus laurocerasus,* having glossy aromatic leaves, white flowers, and purplish-black fruits

cherry-pick *vb* (*tr*) to choose or take the best or most profitable of (a number of things), esp for one's own benefit or gain: *cherry-pick the best routes*

cherry picker *n* a hydraulic crane, esp one mounted on a lorry, that has an elbow joint or telescopic arm supporting a basket-like platform enabling a person to service high power lines or to carry out similar operations above the ground

cherry-pie *n* a widely planted garden heliotrope, *Heliotropium peruvianum*

cherry plum *n* a small widely planted Asian rosaceous tree, *Prunus cerasifera,* with white flowers and red or yellow cherry-like fruit. Also called: **myrobalan**

cherry tomato *n* a miniature tomato not much bigger than a cherry

chersonese ('kɜːsə,niːs) *n* **a** a poetic or rhetorical word for **peninsula b** (*capital when part of a name*): *Thracian Chersonese* [C17 from Latin, from Greek *khersonēsos,* from *khersos* dry (land) + *nēsos* island]

chert (tʃɜːt) *n* a microcrystalline form of silica usually occurring as bands or layers of pebbles in sedimentary rock. Formula: SiO₂. Varieties include flint, lyddite (Lydian stone). Also called: **hornstone** [C17 of obscure origin] ▷ 'cherty *adj*

Chertsey ('tʃɜːtsɪ) *n* a town in S England, in N Surrey on the River Thames. Pop: 10 323 (2001)

cherub ('tʃɛrəb) *n, pl* **cherubs** *or* **cherubim** ('tʃɛrəbɪm, -,ʊbɪm) **1** *theol* a member of the second order of angels, whose distinctive gift is knowledge, often represented as a winged child or winged head of a child **2** an innocent or sweet child [Old English, from Hebrew *kĕrūbh*] ▷ **cherubic** (tʃə'ruːbɪk) *or* **che'rubical** *adj* ▷ **che'rubically** *adv*

chervil ('tʃɜːvɪl) *n* **1** an aromatic umbelliferous Eurasian plant, *Anthriscus cerefolium,* with small white flowers and aniseed-flavoured leaves used as herbs in soups and salads **2** *bur chervil* a similar and related plant, *Anthriscus caucalis* **3** a related plant, *Chaerophyllum temulentum,* having a hairy purple-spotted stem [Old English *cerfelle,* from Latin *caerephylla,* plural of *caerephyllum* chervil,

---

from Greek *khairephullon,* from *khairein* to enjoy + *phullon* leaf]

chervonets (tʃə'vɔːnɛts) *n* (*formerly*) a Soviet monetary unit and gold coin worth ten roubles [from Old Russian *červonyi,* from Old Polish *czerwony* golden, purple]

Ches. *abbreviation for* Cheshire

Chesapeake Bay ('tʃɛsə,piːk) *n* the largest inlet of the Atlantic in the coast of the US: bordered by Maryland and Virginia

Chesapeake Bay retriever *n* a strongly built variety of retriever with a short thick, slightly wavy coat in straw colour, reddish gold, or brown

Cheshire ('tʃɛʃə, 'tʃɛʃɪə) *n* a county of NW England: low-lying and undulating, bordering on the Pennines in the east; mainly agricultural: the geographic and ceremonial county includes Warrington and Halton, which became independent unitary authorities in 1998. Administrative centre: Chester. Pop (excluding unitary authorities): 678 700 (2003 est). Area (excluding unitary authorites): 2077 sq km (802 sq miles). Abbreviation: **Ches**

Cheshire cheese *n* a mild-flavoured cheese with a crumbly texture, originally made in Cheshire

Cheshunt ('tʃɛʃənt) *n* a town in SE England, in SE Hertfordshire: a dormitory town of London. Pop: 55 275 (2001)

Cheshvan *or* **Heshvan** (xɛʃ'van) *n* (in the Jewish calendar) the eighth month of the year according to biblical reckoning and the second month of the civil year, usually falling within October and November. Also called: **Marcheshvan** [from Hebrew]

chess¹ (tʃɛs) *n* a game of skill for two players using a chessboard on which chessmen are moved. Initially each player has one king, one queen, two rooks, two bishops, two knights, and eight pawns, which have different types of moves according to kind. The object is to checkmate the opponent's king [C13 from Old French *esches,* plural of *eschec* check (at chess); see CHECK]

chess² (tʃɛs) *n US* a less common name for **rye-brome** [C18 of unknown origin]

chess³ (tʃɛs) *n, pl* **chess** *or* **chesses** a floorboard of the deck of a pontoon bridge [C15 (in the sense: layer, tier): from Old French *chasse* frame, from Latin *capsa* box]

chessboard ('tʃɛs,bɔːd) *n* a square board divided into 64 squares of two alternating colours, used for playing chess or draughts

chessel ('tʃɛsəl) *n* a mould used in cheese-making [C18 probably from CHEESE¹ + WELL²]

chessman ('tʃɛs,mæn, -mən) *n, pl* -**men** any of the eight pieces and eight pawns used by each player in a game of chess [C17 back formation from *chessmen,* from Middle English *chessemeyne* chess company, from *meynie, menye* company, body of men, from Old French *meyné*]

chesspiece ('tʃɛs,piːs) *n* any of the eight pieces (excluding the pawns) used by each player in a game of chess

chest (tʃɛst) *n* **1 a** the front part of the trunk from the neck to the belly. Related adj: **pectoral b** (*as modifier*): *a chest cold* **2** **get (something) off one's chest** *informal* to unburden oneself of troubles, worries, etc, by talking about them **3** a box, usually large and sturdy, used for storage or shipping: *a tea chest* **4** Also: **chestful** the quantity a chest holds **5** *rare* **a** the place in which a public or charitable institution deposits its funds **b** the funds so deposited **6** a sealed container or reservoir for a gas: *a wind chest; a steam chest* [Old English *cest,* from Latin *cista* wooden box, basket, from Greek *kistē* box] ▷ 'chested *adj*

Chester ('tʃɛstə) *n* a city in NW England, administrative centre of Cheshire, on the River Dee: intact surrounding walls; 16th- and 17th-century double-tier shops. Pop: 80 121 (2001). Latin name: **Deva**

chesterfield ('tʃɛstə,fiːld) *n* **1** a man's knee-length overcoat, usually with a fly front to conceal the buttons and having a velvet collar **2** a large tightly stuffed sofa, often upholstered in leather, with straight upholstered arms of the same height as the back [c19 named after a 19th-century Earl of *Chesterfield*]

Chesterfield (ˈtʃɛstəˌfiːld) *n* an industrial town in N central England, in Derbyshire: famous 14th-century church with twisted spire. Pop: 70 260 (2001)

Chesterfieldian (ˌtʃɛstəˈfiːldɪən) *adj* of or like Lord Chesterfield; suave; elegant; polished

chestnut (ˈtʃɛsˌnʌt) *n* **1** any N temperate fagaceous tree of the genus *Castanea*, such as *C. sativa* (**sweet** or **Spanish chestnut**), which produce flowers in long catkins and nuts in a prickly bur. Compare **horse chestnut, water chestnut, dwarf chestnut 2** the edible nut of any of these trees **3** the hard wood of any of these trees, used in making furniture, etc **4 a** a reddish-brown to brown colour **b** (*as adjective*): *chestnut hair* **5** a horse of a yellow-brown or golden-brown colour **6** a small horny callus on the inner surface of a horse's leg **7** *informal* an old or stale joke [c16 from earlier *chesten nut*: *chesten*, from Old French *chastaigne*, from Latin *castanea*, from Greek *kastanea*]

chest of drawers *n* a piece of furniture consisting of a frame, often on short legs, containing a set of drawers

chest of viols *n* a set of viols of different sizes, usually six in number, used in consorts

chest-on-chest *n* another term for **tallboy**

chest voice or **register** *n* a voice of the lowest speaking or singing register. Compare **head voice**

chesty (ˈtʃɛstɪ) *adj* **chestier, chestiest** *informal* **1** *Brit* suffering from or symptomatic of chest disease: *a chesty cough* **2** having a large well-developed chest or bosom > **ˈchestiness** *n*

chetah (ˈtʃiːtə) *n* a variant spelling of **cheetah**

Chetnik (ˈtʃɛtnɪk, tʃɛtˈniːk) *n* **1** a Serbian nationalist belonging to a group that fought against the Turks before World War I and engaged in guerrilla warfare during both World Wars **2** a member of a Serbian nationalist paramilitary group fighting to retain Serbian influence in the countries which formerly constituted Yugoslavia [from Serbian *četnik*, from *četa* troop]

cheval-de-frise (ʃəˌvældəˈfriːz) *n, pl* **chevaux-de-frise** (ʃəˌvəʊdəˈfriːz) **1** a portable barrier of spikes, sword blades, etc, used to obstruct the passage of cavalry **2** a row of spikes or broken glass set as an obstacle on top of a wall [c17 from French, literally: horse from Friesland (where it was first used)]

cheval glass (ʃəˈvæl) *n* a full-length mirror mounted so as to swivel within a frame [c19 from French *cheval* support (literally: horse)]

chevalier (ˌʃɛvəˈlɪə) *n* **1** a member of certain orders of merit, such as the French Legion of Honour **2** *French history* **a** a mounted soldier or knight, esp a military cadet **b** the lowest title of rank in the old French nobility **3** an archaic word for **knight 4** a chivalrous man; gallant [c14 from Old French, from Medieval Latin *caballārius* horseman, CAVALIER]

chevet (ʃəˈveɪ) *n* a semicircular or polygonal east end of a church, esp a French Gothic church, often with a number of attached apses [c19 from French: pillow, from Latin *capitium*, from *caput* head]

Cheviot (ˈtʃiːvɪət, ˈtʃɛv-) *n* **1** a large British breed of sheep reared for its wool **2** (*often not capital*) a rough twill-weave woollen suiting fabric

Cheviot Hills *pl n* a range of hills on the border between England and Scotland, mainly in Northumberland

Chevra Kadisha *Hebrew* (xɛvˈra kadɪˈʃa; *Yiddish* ˈxɛvrə kaˈdɪʃə) *n* a Jewish burial society, usually composed of unpaid volunteers who provide funerals for members of their congregation [literally: Holy Company]

chèvre (ˈʃɛvrə) *n* any cheese made from goats' milk [c20 from French, literally: goat]

chevrette (ʃəˈvrɛt) *n* **1** the skin of a young goat **2** the leather made from this skin [c18 from French: kid, from *chèvre* goat, from Latin *capra*]

chevron (ˈʃɛvrən) *n* **1** *military* a badge or insignia consisting of one or more V-shaped stripes to indicate a noncommissioned rank or length of service **2** *heraldry* an inverted V-shaped charge on a shield, one of the earliest ordinaries found in English arms **3** (*usually plural*) a pattern of horizontal black and white V-shapes on a road sign indicating a sharp bend **4** any V-shaped pattern or device **5** Also called: **dancette** an ornamental moulding having a zigzag pattern [c14 from Old French, ultimately from Latin *caper* goat; compare Latin *capreoli* two pieces of wood forming rafters (literally: little goats)]

chevrotain (ˈʃɛvrəˌteɪn, -tɪn) *n* any small timid ruminant artiodactyl mammal of the genera *Tragulus* and *Hyemoschus*, of S and SE Asia: family Tragulidae. They resemble rodents, and the males have long tusklike upper canines. Also called: **mouse deer** [c18 from French, from Old French *chevrot* kid, from *chèvre* goat, from Latin *capra*, feminine of *caper* goat]

chevy (ˈtʃɛvɪ) *n, vb* a variant of **chivy**

chew (tʃuː) *vb* **1** to work the jaws and teeth in order to grind (food); masticate **2** to bite repeatedly: *she chewed her nails anxiously* **3** (*intr*) to use chewing tobacco **4 chew the fat** or **rag** *slang* **a** to argue over a point **b** to talk idly; gossip > *n* **5** the act of chewing **6** something that is chewed: *a chew of tobacco* > See also **chew out, chew over, chew up** [Old English *ceowan*; related to Old High German *kiuwan*, Dutch *kauwen*, Latin *gingīva* a gum] > **ˈchewable** *adj* > **ˈchewer** *n*

Chewa (ˈtʃeɪwə) *n* (*pl* **-was** or **-wa**) a member of a Negroid people of Malawi, E Zambia, and N Zimbabwe, related to the Bemba **2** the language of this people. See **Chichewa**

chewie (ˈtʃuːɪ) *n* *Austral informal* chewing gum

chewing gum *n* a preparation for chewing, usually made of flavoured and sweetened chicle or such substitutes as polyvinyl acetate

chew-'n'-spew or **chew and spew** *n* *Austral slang* any fast-food restaurant considered to be serving poor quality food

chew out *vb* (*tr, adverb*) *informal, chiefly US and Canadian* to reprimand

chew over *vb* (*tr, adverb*) to consider carefully; ruminate on

chew up *vb* (*tr, adverb*) **1** to damage or destroy (something) by or as by chewing or grinding **2** (*usually passive*) *slang* to cause (a person) to be nervous or worried: *he was all chewed up about the interview*

chewy (ˈtʃuːɪ) *adj* **chewier, chewiest** of a consistency requiring chewing; somewhat firm and sticky

Cheyenne¹ (ʃaɪˈæn) *n* **1** (*pl* **-enne** or **-ennes**) a member of a Native American people of the western Plains, now living chiefly in Montana and Oklahoma **2** the language of this people, belonging to the Algonquian family [via Canadian French from Dakota *Shaiyena*, from *shaia* to speak incoherently, from *sha* red + *ya* to speak]

Cheyenne² (ʃaɪˈæn, -ˈɛn) *n* a city in SE Wyoming, capital of the state. Pop: 54 374 (2003 est)

Cheyne-Stokes breathing (ˈtʃeɪnˈstəʊks) *n* *pathol* alternating shallow and deep breathing, as in comatose patients [c19 named after John *Cheyne* (1777–1836), Scottish physician, and William *Stokes* (1804–78), Irish physician]

chez *French* (ʃe) *prep* **1** at the home of **2** with, among, or in the manner of

chg. *commerce, finance* abbreviation for **charge**

Chhattisgarh (ˌtʃʌtɪsˈgaː) *n* a state of E central India, created from the SE part of Madhya Pradesh in 2000: consists of a hilly plateau, with extensive forests; agricultural. Capital: Raipur. Pop: 20 795 956 (2001). Area: 135 194 sq km (52 199 sq miles). Abbreviation: **Ches**

chi¹ (kaɪ) *n* the 22nd letter of the Greek alphabet

(X, χ), a consonant, transliterated as *ch* or rarely *kh*

chi², **ch'i** (tʃiː) or **qi** *n* (*sometimes capital*) (in Oriental medicine, martial arts, etc) vital energy believed to circulate round the body in currents [Chinese, literally: energy]

chiack or **chyack** (ˈtʃaɪæk) *Austral informal* > *vb* (*tr*) **1** to tease or banter > *n* **2** good-humoured banter [c19 from *chi-hike*, a shout or greeting]

Chian (ˈkaɪən) *adj* **1** of or relating to Chios > *n* **2** a native or inhabitant of Chios

chianti (kɪˈæntɪ) *n* (*sometimes capital*) a dry red wine produced in the Chianti region of Italy

Chianti (*Italian* ˈkjanti) *pl n* a mountain range in central Italy, in Tuscany, rising over 870 m (2900 ft): part of the Apennines

Chiantishire (kɪˈæntɪˌʃɪə) *n* *Brit informal* a nickname for Tuscany [c20 from CHIANTI + SHIRE¹, alluding to the large numbers of British people living or holidaying in Tuscany]

Chiapas (*Spanish* ˈtʃjapas) *n* a state of S Mexico: mountainous and forested; Maya ruins in the northeast; rich mineral resources. Capital: Tuxtla Gutiérrez. Pop: 3 920 515 (2000). Area: 73 887 sq km (28 816 sq miles)

chiaroscuro (kɪˌɑːrəˈskʊərəʊ) *n, pl* **-ros 1** the artistic distribution of light and dark masses in a picture **2** monochrome painting using light and dark only, as in grisaille [c17 from Italian, from *chiaro* CLEAR + *oscuro* OBSCURE] > **chiˌaroˈscurist** *n* > **chiˌaroˈscurism** *n*

chiasma (kaɪˈæzmə) or **chiasm** (ˈkaɪæzəm) *n, pl* **-mas, -mata** (-mətə) or **-asms 1** *cytology* the cross-shaped connection produced by the crossing over of pairing chromosomes during meiosis **2** *anatomy* the crossing over of two parts or structures, such as the fibres of the optic nerves in the brain [c19 from Greek *khiasma* wooden crosspiece, from *khiazein* to mark with an X, from *khi* CHI¹] > **chiˈasmal** or **chiˈasmic** *adj*

chiasmus (kaɪˈæzməs) *n, pl* **-mi** (-maɪ) *rhetoric* reversal of the order of words in the second of two parallel phrases: *he came in triumph and in defeat departs* [c19 from New Latin, from Greek *khiasmos* crisscross arrangement; see CHIASMA] > **chiastic** (kaɪˈæstɪk) *adj*

chiastolite (kaɪˈæstəˌlaɪt) *n* a variety of andalusite containing carbon impurities. Also called: **macle** [c19 from German *Chiastolith*, from Greek *khiastos* crossed, marked with a chi + *lithos* stone]

chib (tʃɪb) *Scot slang* > *vb* **chibs, chibbing, chibbed 1** (*tr*) to stab or slash with a sharp weapon > *n* **2** a sharp weapon, such as a knife or razor [perhaps related to CHIV]

Chiba (ˈtʃiːba) *n* an industrial city in central Japan, in SE Honshu on Tokyo Bay. Pop: 880 164 (2002 est)

Chibchan (ˈtʃɪbtʃən) *n* **1** a family of Indian languages found in Colombia and elsewhere in South America > *adj* **2** belonging or relating to this family of languages

chibol (ˈtʃɪbˀl) *n* *English dialect* a spring onion [see SYBO]

chibouk or **chibouque** (tʃɪˈbuːk) *n* a Turkish tobacco pipe with an extremely long stem [c19 from French *chibouque*, from Turkish *çubuk* pipe]

chic (ʃiːk, ʃɪk) *adj* **1** (esp of fashionable clothes, women, etc) stylish or elegant > *n* **2** stylishness, esp in dress; modishness; fashionable good taste [c19 from French, of uncertain origin] > **ˈchicly** *adv*

Chicago (ʃɪˈkɑːgəʊ) *n* a port in NE Illinois, on Lake Michigan: the third largest city in the US; it is a major railway and air traffic centre. Pop: 2 869 121 (2003 est)

chicalote (ˌtʃiːkɑːˈləʊteɪ) *n* a poppy, *Argemone platyceras*, of the southwestern US and Mexico with prickly leaves and white or yellow flowers [from Spanish, from Nahuatl *chicalotl*]

chicane (ʃɪˈkeɪn) *n* **1** a bridge or whist hand without trumps **2** *motor racing* a short section of sharp narrow bends formed by barriers placed on a motor-racing circuit to provide an additional test of driving skill **3** a less common word for **chicanery** ▷ *vb* **4** (*tr*) to deceive or trick by chicanery **5** (*tr*) to quibble about; cavil over **6** (*intr*) to use tricks or chicanery [c17 from French *chicaner* to quibble, of obscure origin] > chi'caner *n*

chicanery (ʃɪ'keɪnərɪ) *n*, *pl* -eries **1** verbal deception or trickery, esp in legal quibbling; dishonest or sharp practice **2** a trick, deception, or quibble

chicano (tʃɪ'kɑːnəʊ) *n*, *pl* -nos an American citizen of Mexican origin [c20 from Spanish *mejicano* Mexican]

chiccory ('tʃɪkərɪ) *n*, *pl* -ries a variant spelling of **chicory**

Chichagof Island ('tʃɪtʃəˌgɔːf) *n* an island of Alaska, in the Alexander Archipelago. Area: 5439 sq km (2100 sq miles)

Chichen Itzá (*Spanish* tʃi'tʃen it'sa) *n* a village in Yucatán state in Mexico: site of important Mayan ruins

Chichester ('tʃɪtʃɪstə) *n* a city in S England, administrative centre of West Sussex: Roman ruins; 11th-century cathedral; Festival Theatre. Pop: 27 477 (2001)

Chichewa (tʃɪ'tʃeɪwə) *n* the language of the Chewa people of central Africa, widely used as a lingua franca in Malawi. It belongs to the Bantu group of the Niger-Congo family

chichi[1] (ʃiːʃiː) *adj* **1** affectedly pretty or stylish ▷ *n* **2** the quality of being affectedly pretty or stylish [c20 from French]

chichi[2] ('tʃiːtʃiː) *n*, *pl* chichis (formerly, in India) **a** a person of mixed British and Indian descent; Anglo-Indian **b** (*as modifier*): *a chichi accent* ▷ Also (less common): chee-chee [c18 perhaps from Hindi *chhī-chhī*, literally: dirt, or perhaps imitative of their supposed singsong speech]

Chichihaerh or **Ch'i-ch'i-haerh** ('tʃiːtʃiː'haː) *n* a variant transliteration of the Chinese name for **Qiqihar**

chick (tʃɪk) *n* **1** the young of a bird, esp a domestic fowl **2** *slang* a girl or young woman, esp an attractive one **3** a young child: used as a term of endearment [c14 short for CHICKEN]

chickabiddy ('tʃɪkəˌbɪdɪ) *n*, *pl* -dies a term of endearment, esp for a child [c18 from CHICK + BIDDY[1]]

chickadee ('tʃɪkəˌdiː) *n* any of various small North American songbirds of the genus *Parus*, such as *P. atricapillus* (**black-capped chickadee**), typically having grey-and-black plumage: family *Paridae* (titmice) [c19 imitative of its note]

chickaree ('tʃɪkəˌriː) *n* another name for **American red squirrel** (see **squirrel** (sense 1))

Chickasaw ('tʃɪkəˌsɔː) *n* **1** (*pl* -saws or -saw) a member of a Native American people of N Mississippi **2** the language of this people, belonging to the Muskogean family and closely related to Choctaw

chicken ('tʃɪkɪn) *n* **1** a domestic fowl bred for its flesh or eggs, esp a young one **2** the flesh of such a bird used for food **3** any of various similar birds, such as a prairie chicken **4** *slang* a cowardly person **5** *slang* a young inexperienced person **6** *slang* an underage boy or girl regarded as a potential target for sexual abuse **7** *informal* any of various, often dangerous, games or challenges in which the object is to make one's opponent lose his nerve **8** count one's chickens before they are hatched to be overoptimistic in acting on expectations which are not yet fulfilled **9** like a headless chicken *Brit informal* disorganized and uncontrolled **10** no (spring) chicken *slang* no longer young: *she's no chicken* ▷ *adj* **11** *slang* easily scared; cowardly; timid [Old English *cīecen*; related to Old Norse *kjūklingr* gosling, Middle Low German *küken* chicken]

chicken breast *n pathol* another name for **pigeon breast**. > ˌchicken-'breasted *adj*

chicken feed *n slang* a trifling amount of money

chicken fillet *n* **1** a fillet cut from a chicken **2** *informal* a gel-filled pad inserted under clothing to

enlarge the appearance of a woman's breast

chicken-hearted or **chicken-livered** *adj* easily frightened; cowardly > ˌchicken-'heartedly *adv* > ˌchicken-'heartedness *n*

chicken louse *n* a louse, *Menopon pallidum* (or *gallinae*); a parasite of poultry: order *Mallophaga* (bird lice)

chicken out *vb* (*intr, adverb*) *informal* to fail to do something through fear or lack of conviction

chickenpox ('tʃɪkɪnˌpɒks) *n* a highly communicable viral disease most commonly affecting children, characterized by slight fever and the eruption of a rash

chicken wire *n* wire netting with a hexagonal mesh

chick flick *n informal derogatory* a film aimed at or appealing to women [c20 from CHICK (sense 2) + FLICK[2]]

chick lit *n* **a** a genre of fiction concentrating on young working women and their emotional lives **b** (*as modifier*): *chick-lit romances*

chickpea ('tʃɪkˌpiː) *n* **1** a bushy leguminous plant, *Cicer arietinum*, cultivated for its edible pealike seeds in the Mediterranean region, central Asia, and Africa **2** Also called: garbanzo the seed of this plant [c16 *ciche peasen*, from *ciche* (from French *chiche*, from Latin *cicer* chickpea) + *peasen*; see PEA]

chickweed ('tʃɪkˌwiːd) *n* **1** any of various caryophyllaceous plants of the genus *Stellaria*, esp *S. media*, a common garden weed with small white flowers **2** mouse-ear chickweed any of various similar and related plants of the genus *Cerastium*

Chiclayo (*Spanish* tʃi'klajo) *n* a city in NW Peru. Pop: 434 000 (2005 est)

chicle ('tʃɪkᵊl) *n* a gumlike substance obtained from the sapodilla; the main ingredient of chewing gum. See also: chicle gum [from Spanish, from Nahuatl *chictli*]

chico ('tʃiːkəʊ) *n*, *pl* -cos another name for **greasewood** (sense 1)

chicory ('tʃɪkərɪ) *n*, *pl* -ries **1** Also called: succory a blue-flowered plant, *Cichorium intybus*, cultivated for its leaves, which are used in salads, and for its roots: family *Asteraceae* (composites) **2** the root of this plant, roasted, dried, and used as a coffee substitute ▷ Compare endive [c15 from Old French *chicorée*, from Latin *cichorium*, from Greek *kikhōrion*]

chide (tʃaɪd) *vb* chides, chiding, chided or chid; chided, chid or chidden **1** to rebuke or scold **2** (*tr*) to goad into action [Old English *cīdan*] > 'chider *n* > 'chidingly *adv*

chief (tʃiːf) *n* **1** the head, leader, or most important individual in a group or body of people **2** another word for **chieftain** (sense 1) **3** *heraldry* the upper third of a shield **4** in chief primarily; especially ▷ *adj* **5** (*prenominal*) **a** most important; principal **b** highest in rank or authority ▷ *adv* **6** *archaic* principally [c13 from Old French, from Latin *caput* head]

Chief Education Officer *n Brit* an official who is the chief administrative officer of a Local Education Authority. Also called: Director of Education

chief executive *n* the person with overall responsibility for the efficient running of a company, organization, etc

chief justice *n* **1** (in any of several Commonwealth countries) the judge presiding over a supreme court **2** (in the US) the presiding judge of a court composed of a number of members ▷ See also **Lord Chief Justice**. > chief justiceship *n*

chiefly ('tʃiːflɪ) *adv* **1** especially or essentially; above all **2** in general; mainly; mostly ▷ *adj* **3** of or relating to a chief or chieftain

Chief of Staff *n* **1** the senior staff officer under the commander of a major military formation or organization **2** the senior officer of each service of the armed forces. Abbreviations: C of S, COS

chief petty officer *n* the senior naval rank for personnel without commissioned or warrant rank. Abbreviation: CPO

Chief Rabbi *n* the chief religious minister of a national Jewish community

chieftain ('tʃiːftən, -tɪn) *n* **1** the head or leader of a tribe or clan **2** the chief of a group of people [c14 from Old French *chevetaine*, from Late Latin *capitāneus* commander; see CAPTAIN] > 'chieftaincy or 'chieftainˌship *n*

chief technician *n* a noncommissioned officer in the Royal Air Force junior to a flight sergeant

chiel (tʃiːl) *n Scot* a young man; lad [c14 a Scot variant of CHILD]

Chiengmai ('tʃɪeŋ'maɪ) or **Chiang Mai** *n* a town in NW Thailand: teak, silver, silk industries: university (1964). Pop: 182 000 (2005 est)

chiffchaff ('tʃɪfˌtʃæf) *n* a common European warbler, *Phylloscopus collybita*, with a yellowish-brown plumage [c18 imitative of its call]

chiffon (ʃɪ'fɒn, 'ʃɪfɒn) *n* **1** a fine transparent or almost transparent plain-weave fabric of silk, nylon, etc **2** (*often plural*) *now rare* feminine finery ▷ *adj* **3** made of chiffon **4** (of soufflés, pies, cakes, etc) having a very light fluffy texture [c18 from French, from *chiffe* rag; probably related to CHIP] > 'chiffony *adj*

chiffonade (ˌʃɪfə'nɑːd) *n* finely shredded leaf vegetables used as a base for a dish or as a garnish

chiffonier or **chiffonnier** (ˌʃɪfə'nɪə) *n* **1** a tall, elegant chest of drawers, originally intended for holding needlework **2** a wide low open-fronted cabinet, sometimes fitted with two grille doors and shelves [c19 from French, from *chiffon* rag; see CHIFFON]

chigetai (ˌtʃɪgɪ'taɪ) *n* a variety of the Asiatic wild ass, *Equus hemionus*, of Mongolia. Also spelt: dziggetai [from Mongolian *tchikhitei* long-eared, from *tchikhi* ear]

chigga ('tʃɪgə) *n Austral informal derogatory* a young working-class person from Hobart, Tasmania [c20 from *Chigwell*, a suburb of HOBART]

chigger ('tʃɪgə) *n* **1** Also called: chigoe, redbug *US and Canadian* the parasitic larva of any of various free-living mites of the family *Trombidiidae*, which causes intense itching of human skin **2** another name for the **chigoe** (sense 1)

chignon ('ʃiːnjɒn; *French* ʃiɲɔ̃) *n* an arrangement of long hair in a roll or knot at the back of the head [c18 from French, from Old French *chaignon* link, from *chaine* CHAIN; influenced also by Old French *tignon* coil of hair, from *tigne*, moth, from Latin *tinea* moth] > 'chignoned *adj*

chigoe ('tʃɪgəʊ) *n* **1** Also called: chigger, jigger, sand flea a tropical flea, *Tunga penetrans*, the female of which lives on or burrows into the skin of its host, which includes man **2** another name for **chigger** (sense 1) [c17 from Carib *chigo*]

Chigwell ('tʃɪgwəl) *n* a town in S England, in W Essex. Pop: 10 128 (2001)

Chihli ('tʃiːliː) *n* Gulf of another name for the **Bohai**

Chihuahua (tʃɪ'wɑːwɑː, -wə) *n* **1** a state of N Mexico: mostly high plateau; important mineral resources, with many silver mines. Capital: Chihuahua. Pop: 728 000 (2005 est). Area: 247 087 sq km (153 194 sq miles) **2** a city in N Mexico, capital of Chihuahua state. Pop: 650 000 (2000 est) **3** a breed of tiny dog originally from Mexico, having short smooth hair, large erect ears, and protruding eyes

chi kung ('tʃiː 'gʊŋ) *n* a variant spelling of **qigong**

chilblain ('tʃɪlˌbleɪn) *n pathol* (*usually plural*) an inflammation of the fingers, toes, or ears, caused by prolonged exposure to moisture and cold. Technical name: pernio [c16 from CHILL (n) + BLAIN] > 'chilˌblained *adj*

child (tʃaɪld) *n*, *pl* children **1 a** a boy or girl between birth and puberty **b** (*as modifier*): *child labour* **2** a baby or infant **3** an unborn baby. ▷ Related prefix (senses 1 to 3) paedo- **4** with child another term for **pregnant 5** a human offspring; a son or daughter. Related adj: filial **6** a childish or immature person **7** a member of a family or tribe; descendant: *a child of Israel* **8** a person or

C

thing regarded as the product of an influence or environment: *a child of nature* **9** *Midland and Western English dialect* a female infant [Old English *cild*; related to Gothic *kilthei* womb, Sanskrit *jathara* belly, *jartu* womb] > **'childless** *adj* > **'childlessness** *n* > **'childly** *adj*

child abuse *n* physical, sexual, or emotional ill-treatment or neglect of a child, esp by those responsible for its welfare. See also **nonaccidental injury**

child-abuse register *n social welfare* (in Britain) a list of children deemed to be at risk of abuse or injury from their parents or guardians, compiled and held by a local authority, area health authority, or NSPCC Special Unit. Also called: **NAI register**

child-bearing *n* **a** the act or process of carrying and giving birth to a child **b** (*as modifier*): *of child-bearing age*

childbed ('tʃaɪld,bɛd) *n* **a** (often preceded by *in*) the condition of giving birth to a child **b** (*as modifier*): *childbed fever*

child benefit *n* (in Britain and New Zealand) a regular government payment to the parents of children up to a certain age

childbirth ('tʃaɪld,bɜːθ) *n* the act of giving birth to a child. Related adj: **obstetric**

childcare ('tʃaɪld,kɛə) *n Brit* **1** care provided for children without homes (or with a seriously disturbed home life) by a local authority **2** care and supervision of children whose parents are working, provided by a childminder or local authority

childe (tʃaɪld) *n archaic* a young man of noble birth [C13 variant of CHILD]

childermas ('tʃɪldə,mæs) *n archaic* Holy Innocents Day, Dec 28 [Old English *cylda-mæsse*, from *cildra*, genitive plural of CHILD, + *mæsse* MASS]

child guidance *n* the counselling of emotionally disturbed children

childhood ('tʃaɪldhʊd) *n* the condition of being a child; the period of life before puberty

childish ('tʃaɪldɪʃ) *adj* **1** in the manner of, belonging to, or suitable to a child **2** foolish or petty; puerile: *childish fears* > **'childishly** *adv* > **'childishness** *n*

child labour *n* the full-time employment of children below a minimum age laid down by statute

childlike ('tʃaɪld,laɪk) *adj* like or befitting a child, as in being innocent, trustful, etc. Compare **childish** (sense 2)

child minder *n* a person who looks after children, esp those whose parents are working

children ('tʃɪldrən) *n* the plural of **child**

Children's Panel *n* (in Scotland) a group of representatives of relevant agencies, with the power to deal with a child under sixteen who is in criminal or family trouble. Its hearings are private and replace most of the functions of juvenile courts

child's play *n informal* something that is easy to do

chile ('tʃɪlɪ) *n* a variant spelling of **chilli**

Chile ('tʃɪlɪ) *n* a republic in South America, on the Pacific, with a total length of about 4090 km (2650 miles) and an average width of only 177 km (110 miles): gained independence from Spain in 1818; the government of President Allende (elected 1970) attempted the implementation of Marxist policies within a democratic system until overthrown by a military coup (1973); democracy restored 1988. Chile consists chiefly of the Andes in the east, the Atacama Desert in the north, a central fertile region, and a huge S region of almost uninhabitable mountains, glaciers, fjords, and islands; an important producer of copper, iron ore, nitrates, etc. Language: Spanish. Religion: Roman Catholic majority. Currency: peso. Capital: Santiago. Pop: 15 997 000 (2004 est). Area: 756 945 sq km (292 256 sq miles)

Chilean ('tʃɪlɪən) *adj* **1** of or relating to Chile or its

inhabitants ▷ *n* **2** a native or inhabitant of Chile

Chilean sea bass *n* another name for **Patagonian toothfish**

Chile pine *n* another name for the **monkey puzzle**

Chile saltpetre *or* **nitre** *n* a naturally occurring form of sodium nitrate: a soluble white or colourless mineral occurring in arid regions, esp in Chile and Peru. Also called: **soda nitre**

chiliad ('kɪlɪˌæd) *n* **1** a group of one thousand **2** one thousand years [C16 from Greek *khilias*, from *khilioi* a thousand] > **chili'adal** *or* **chili'adic** *adj*

chiliasm ('kɪlɪˌæzəm) *n christian theol* another term for **millenarianism** or the **millennium** [C17 from Greek *khiliasmos*, from *khilioi* a thousand] > **'chili,ast** *n* > **,chili'astic** *adj*

Chilkoot Pass ('tʃɪlkuːt) *n* a mountain pass in North America between SE Alaska and NW British Columbia, over the Coast Range

chill (tʃɪl) *n* **1** a moderate coldness **2** a sensation of coldness resulting from a cold or damp environment, or from a sudden emotional reaction **3** a feverish cold **4** a check on enthusiasm or joy **5** a metal plate placed in a sand mould to accelerate cooling and control local grain growth **6** another name for **bloom¹** (sense 9) ▷ *adj* **7** another word for **chilly** ▷ *vb* **8** to make or become cold **9** (*tr*) to cool or freeze (food, drinks, etc) **10** (*tr*) **a** to depress (enthusiasm, etc) **b** to discourage **11** (*tr*) to cool (a casting or metal object) rapidly in order to prevent the formation of large grains in the metal **12** (*intr*) *slang, chiefly US* to relax; calm oneself ▷ See also **chill out** [Old English *ciele*; related to *calan* to COOL, Latin *gelidus* icy] > **'chillingly** *adv* > **'chillness** *n*

Chillán (*Spanish* tʃi'ʎan) *n* a city in central Chile. Pop: 149 000 (2005 est)

chilled (tʃɪld) *adj* **1** (of a person) feeling cold **2** (of food or drink) kept cool **3** *informal* Also: **chilled-out** relaxed or easy-going in character or behaviour

chiller ('tʃɪlə) *n* **1** *informal* short for **spine-chiller 2** *NZ* a refrigerated storage area for meat

chiller cabinet *n* a cupboard or chest in a shop where chilled foods and drinks are displayed and kept cool

chilli *or* **chili** ('tʃɪlɪ) *n, pl* **chillies** *or* **chilies** the small red hot-tasting pod of a type of capsicum used for flavouring sauces, pickles, etc [C17 from Spanish *chile*, from Nahuatl *chilli*]

chilli con carne (kɒn 'kɑːnɪ) *n* a highly seasoned Mexican dish of meat, onions, beans, and chilli powder [from Spanish *chile con carne* chilli with meat]

chilli powder *n* ground chilli blended with other spices

chilli sauce *n* a highly seasoned sauce made of tomatoes cooked with chilli and other spices and seasonings

Chillon (ʃɪ'lɒn; *French* ʃijɔ̃) *n* a castle in W Switzerland, in Vaud at the E end of Lake Geneva

chill out *informal* ▷ *vb* **1** (*intr, adverb*) to relax, esp after energetic dancing or a spell of hard work ▷ *adj* **chill-out 2** suitable for relaxation after energetic dancing or hard work: *a chill-out area; chill-out music*

chill pill *n informal* an imaginary medicinal pill with a calming, relaxing effect: *take a chill pill*

chillum ('tʃɪləm) *n* a short pipe, usually of clay, used esp for smoking cannabis [C18 from Hindi *cilam*, from Persian *chilam*]

chilly ('tʃɪlɪ) *adj* **-lier, -liest 1** causing or feeling cool or moderately cold **2** without warmth; unfriendly **3** (of people) sensitive to cold > **'chilliness** *n*

chilly bin *n NZ informal* a portable insulated container with provision for packing food and drink in ice

Chiloé Island (,tʃɪləʊ'eɪ) *n* an island administered by Chile, off the W coast of South America in the Pacific Ocean: timber. Pop: 116 000 (latest est). Area: 8394 sq km (3240 sq miles)

chilopod ('kaɪlə,pɒd) *n* any arthropod of the class

Chilopoda, which includes the centipedes. See also **myriapod** [C19 from New Latin *Chilopoda*, from Greek *kheilos* lip + *pous* foot; referring to the modification of the first pair of legs into jawlike claws] > **chi'lopodan** (kaɪ'lɒpədⁿ) *n, adj* > **chi'lopodous** *adj*

Chilpancingo (*Spanish* tʃilpan'θiŋɡo) *n* a town in S Mexico, capital of Guerrero state, in the Sierra Madre del Sur. Pop: 166 000 (2005 est)

Chiltern Hills ('tʃɪltən) *pl n* a range of low chalk hills in SE England extending northwards from the Thames valley. Highest point: 260 m (852 ft)

Chiltern Hundreds *pl n* (in Britain) short for **Stewardship of the Chiltern Hundreds**; a nominal office that an MP applies for in order to resign his seat

Chilung *or* **Chi-lung** ('tʃi:'lʊŋ) *n* a port in N Taiwan: fishing and industrial centre. Pop: 406 000 (2005 est). Also called: **Keelung, Kilung**

chimaera (kaɪ'mɪərə, kɪ-) *n* **1** any tapering smooth-skinned cartilaginous deep-sea fish of the subclass *Holocephali* (or *Bradyodonti*), esp any of the genus *Chimaera*. They have a skull in which the upper jaw is fused to the cranium. See also **rabbitfish** (sense 1) **2** *Greek myth* a variant spelling of **chimera** (sense 1)

chimb (tʃaɪm) *n* a variant spelling of **chime²**

Chimborazo (,tʃɪmbə'rɑːzəʊ, -'reɪ-; *Spanish* tʃimbo'raθo) *n* an extinct volcano in central Ecuador, in the Andes: the highest peak in Ecuador. Height: 6267 m (20 561 ft)

Chimbote (*Spanish* tʃim'bote) *n* a port in N central Peru: contains Peru's first steelworks (1958), using hydroelectric power from the Santa River. Pop: 328 000 (2005 est)

chime¹ (tʃaɪm) *n* **1** an individual bell or the sound it makes when struck **2** (*often plural*) the machinery employed to sound a bell in this way **3** Also called: **bell** a percussion instrument consisting of a set of vertical metal tubes of graduated length, suspended in a frame and struck with a hammer **4** a harmonious or ringing sound: *the chimes of children's laughter* **5** agreement; concord ▷ *vb* **6 a** to sound (a bell) or (of a bell) to be sounded by a clapper or hammer **b** to produce (music or sounds) by chiming **7** (*tr*) to indicate or show (time or the hours) by chiming **8** (*tr*) to summon, announce, or welcome by ringing bells **9** (*intr; foll by with*) to agree or harmonize **10** to speak or recite in a musical or rhythmic manner [C13 probably shortened from earlier *chymbe* bell, ultimately from Latin *cymbalum* CYMBAL] > **'chimer** *n*

chime², **chimb** (tʃaɪm) *or* **chine** *n* the projecting edge or rim of a cask or barrel [Old English *cimb-*; related to Middle Low German *kimme* outer edge, Swedish *kimb*]

chime in *vb* (*intr, adverb*) *informal* **1** to join in or interrupt (a conversation), esp repeatedly and unwelcomely **2** to voice agreement

chimera *or* **chimaera** (kaɪ'mɪərə, kɪ-) *n* **1** (*often capital*) *Greek myth* a fire-breathing monster with the head of a lion, body of a goat, and tail of a serpent **2** a fabulous beast made up of parts taken from various animals **3** a wild and unrealistic dream or notion **4** *biology* an organism, esp a cultivated plant, consisting of at least two genetically different kinds of tissue as a result of mutation, grafting, etc [C16 from Latin *chimaera*, from Greek *khimaira* she-goat, from *khimaros* he-goat]

chimere (tʃɪ'mɪə, ʃɪ-) *or* **chimer, chimar** ('tʃɪmə, 'ʃɪm-) *n Anglican Church* a sleeveless red or black gown, part of a bishop's formal dress though not a vestment [C14 perhaps from Medieval Latin *chimēra* (see CHIMERA) and related to Spanish *zamarra* sheepskin coat]

chimerical (kaɪ'mɛrɪkⁿl, kɪ-) *or* **chimeric** *adj* **1** wildly fanciful; imaginary **2** given to or indulging in fantasies > **chi'merically** *adv* > **chi'mericalness** *n*

Chimkent (tʃɪm'kɛnt) *n* a city in S Kazakhstan; a

major railway junction. Pop: 469 000 (2005 est)

chimney ('tʃɪmnɪ) *n* **1** a vertical structure of brick, masonry, or steel that carries smoke or steam away from a fire, engine, etc **2** another name for **flue¹** (sense 1) **3** short for **chimney stack 4** an open-ended glass tube fitting around the flame of an oil or gas lamp in order to exclude draughts **5** *Brit* a fireplace, esp an old and large one **6** *geology* **a** a cylindrical body of an ore, which is usually oriented vertically **b** the vent of a volcano **7** *mountaineering* a vertical fissure large enough for a person's body to enter **8** anything resembling a chimney in shape or function [c14 from Old French *cheminée*, from Late Latin *camīnāta*, from Latin *camīnus* furnace, from Greek *kaminos* fireplace, oven]

chimney breast *n* the wall or walls that surround the base of a chimney or fireplace

chimney corner *n* a recess that contains a seat in a large open fireplace; inglenook

chimneypiece ('tʃɪmnɪˌpiːs) *n* another name (esp Brit) for **mantelpiece** (sense 1)

chimneypot ('tʃɪmnɪˌpɒt) *n* a short pipe on the top of a chimney, which increases the draught and directs the smoke upwards

chimney stack *n* the part of a chimney that rises above the roof of a building

chimney swallow *n* **1** another name for **common swallow** (see **swallow²**) **2** a less common name for **chimney swift**

chimney sweep or **sweeper** *n* a person whose job is the cleaning out of soot from chimneys

chimney swift *n* a North American swift, *Chaetura pelagica*, that nests in chimneys and similar hollows

chimp (tʃɪmp) *n informal* short for **chimpanzee**

chimpanzee (ˌtʃɪmpænˈziː) *n* a gregarious and intelligent anthropoid ape, *Pan troglodytes*, inhabiting forests in central W Africa [c18 from Kongo dialect]

chin (tʃɪn) *n* **1** the protruding part of the lower jaw **2** the front part of the face below the lips. Related adj: **genial 3** keep one's chin up to keep cheerful under difficult circumstances. Sometimes shortened to: **chin up! 4** take it on the chin *informal* to face squarely up to a defeat, adversity, etc ▷ *vb* chins, chinning, chinned **5** *gymnastics* to raise one's chin to (a horizontal bar, etc) when hanging by the arms **6** (*tr*) *informal* to punch or hit (someone) on the chin [Old English *cinn*; related to Old Norse *kinn*, Old High German *kinni*, Latin *gena* cheek, Old Irish *gin* mouth, Sanskrit *hanu*]

Chin. *abbreviation for* **1** China **2** Chinese

china¹ ('tʃaɪnə) *n* **1** ceramic ware of a type originally from China **2** any porcelain or similar ware **3** cups, saucers, etc, collectively **4** (*modifier*) made of china: *a china tea service* [c16 *chiny*, from Persian *chīnī*]

china² ('tʃaɪnə) *n Brit and South African informal* a friend or companion [c19 originally Cockney rhyming slang: *china plate, mate*]

China ('tʃaɪnə) *n* **1 People's Republic of** Also called: **Communist China, Red China.** a republic in E Asia: the third largest and the most populous country in the world; the oldest continuing civilization (beginning over 2000 years BC); republic established in 1911 after the overthrow of the Manchu dynasty by Sun Yat-sen; People's Republic formed in 1949; the 1980s and 1990s saw economic liberalization but a rejection of political reform; contains vast deserts, steppes, great mountain ranges (Himalayas, Kunlun, Tian Shan, and Nan Shan), a central rugged plateau, and intensively cultivated E plains. Language: Chinese in various dialects, the chief of which is Mandarin. Religion: nonreligious majority; Buddhist and Taoist minorities. Currency: yuan. Capital: Beijing. Pop: 1 300 000 000 (2005 est). Area: 9 560 990 sq km (3 691 502 sq miles) **2 Republic of** Also called: **Nationalist China, Taiwan.** a republic (recognized as independent by only 26

nations) in E Asia occupying the island of Taiwan, 13 nearby islands, and 64 islands of the Penghu (Pescadores) group: established in 1949 by the Nationalist government of China under Chiang Kai-shek after its expulsion by the Communists from the mainland; its territory claimed by the People's Republic of China since the political separation from the mainland; under US protection 1954–79; lost its seat at the U.N. to the People's Republic of China in 1971; state of war with the People's Republic of China formally ended in 1991, though tensions continue owing to the unresolved territorial claim. Language: Mandarin Chinese. Religion: nonreligious majority, Buddhist and Taoist minorities. Currency: New Taiwan dollar. Capital: Taipei. Pop: 22 610 000 (2003 est). Area: 35 981 sq km (13 892 sq miles). Former name: **Formosa** ▷ Related adj: **Sinitic**

China aster *n* a Chinese plant, *Callistephus chinensis*, widely cultivated for its aster-like flowers: family *Asteraceae* (composites)

china bark *n* another name for **cinchona** (sense 2)

chinaberry ('tʃaɪnəˌbɛrɪ) *n, pl* -ries **1** Also called: **China tree, azedarach** a spreading Asian meliaceous tree, *Melia azedarach*, widely grown in the US for its ornamental white or purple flowers and beadlike yellow fruits **2** another name for **soapberry 3** the fruit of any of these trees

china clay or **stone** *n* another name for **kaolin**

Chinagraph ('tʃaɪnəˌɡrɑːf, -ˌɡræf) *n trademark* **a** a coloured pencil used for writing on china, glass, etc **b** (*as modifier*): *a Chinagraph pencil*

China ink *n* another name for **Indian ink**

Chinaman ('tʃaɪnəmən) *n, pl* -men **1** *archaic or derogatory* a native or inhabitant of China **2** (*often not capital*) *cricket* a ball bowled by a left-handed bowler to a right-handed batsman that spins from off to leg

Chinan or **Chi-nan** (tʃiːˈnæn) *n* a variant transliteration of the Chinese name for **Jinan**

China rose *n* **1** a rosaceous shrub, *Rosa chinensis* (or *R. indica*), with red, pink, or white fragrant flowers: the ancestor of many cultivated roses **2** a related dwarf plant, *Rosa semperflorens*, having crimson flowers **3** another name for **hibiscus**

China Sea *n* part of the Pacific Ocean off the coast of China: divided by Taiwan into the East China Sea in the north and the South China Sea in the south

china stone *n* **1** a type of kaolinized granitic rock containing unaltered plagioclase **2** any of certain limestones having a very fine grain and smooth texture

Chinatown ('tʃaɪnəˌtaʊn) *n* a quarter of any city or town outside China with a predominantly Chinese population

China tree *n* another name for **chinaberry** (sense 1)

chinaware ('tʃaɪnəˌwɛə) *n* **1** articles made of china, esp those made for domestic use **2** (*modifier*) made of china

chin ball *n NZ* a device fastened under the chin of a bull to mark cows he has mounted

chincapin ('tʃɪŋkəpɪn) *n* a variant spelling of **chinquapin**

chinch (tʃɪntʃ) *n Southern US* another name for a **bedbug** [c17 from Spanish *chinche*, from Latin *cīmex* bug]

chinch bug *n* **1** a black-and-white tropical American heteropterous insect, *Blissus leucopterus*, that is very destructive to grasses and cereals in the US: family *Lygaeidae* **2** a related and similar European insect, *Ischnodemus sabuleti*

chincherinchee (ˌtʃɪntʃərɪnˈtʃiː, -ˈrɪntʃɪ) *n* a bulbous South African liliaceous plant, *Ornithogalum thyrsoides*, having long spikes of white or yellow long-lasting flowers [of unknown origin]

chinchilla (tʃɪnˈtʃɪlə) *n* **1** a small gregarious hystricomorph rodent, *Chinchilla laniger*, inhabiting mountainous regions of South America: family

Chinchillidae. It has a stocky body and is bred in captivity for its soft silvery grey fur **2** the highly valued fur of this animal **3** mountain chinchilla Also called: **mountain viscacha** any of several long-tailed rodents of the genus *Lagidium*, having coarse poor quality fur **4** a breed of rabbit with soft silver-grey fur **5** a thick napped woollen cloth used for coats [c17 from Spanish, perhaps from Aymara]

chin-chin *sentence substitute informal* a greeting, farewell, or toast [c18 from Chinese (Peking) *ch'ing-ch'ing* please-please]

Chin-Chou or **Chin-chow** ('tʃɪn'tʃaʊ) *n* a variant transliteration of the Chinese name for **Jinzhou**

chin cough *n* another name for **whooping cough** [c16 changed (through influence from CHINE¹ and CHIN) from earlier *chink-cough*, from CHINK² + COUGH]

Chindit ('tʃɪndɪt) *n* a member of the Allied forces commanded by Orde Wingate fighting behind the Japanese lines in Burma (1943–45) [c20 from Burmese *chinthé* a fabulous lion a symbol of which was their badge; adoption of title perhaps influenced by CHINDWIN]

Chindwin ('tʃɪn'dwɪn) *n* a river in N Myanmar, rising in the Kumôn Range and flowing northwest then south to the Irrawaddy, of which it is the main tributary. Length: about 966 km (600 miles)

chine¹ (tʃaɪn) *n* **1** the backbone **2** the backbone of an animal with adjoining meat, cut for cooking **3** a ridge or crest of land **4** (in some boats) a corner-like intersection where the bottom meets the side ▷ *vb* **5** (*tr*) to cut (meat) along or across the backbone [c14 from Old French *eschine*, of Germanic origin; compare Old High German *scina* needle, shinbone; see SHIN¹]

chine² (tʃaɪn) *n* another word for **chime²**

chine³ (tʃaɪn) *n Southern English dialect* a deep fissure in the wall of a cliff [Old English *cīnan* to crack]

chiné ('ʃiːneɪ) *adj textiles* having a mottled pattern [c19 from French *chiner* to make in the Chinese fashion, from *Chine* China]

Chinee (tʃaɪˈniː) *n informal* a Chinaman

Chinese (tʃaɪˈniːz) *adj* **1** of, relating to, or characteristic of China, its people, or their languages ▷ *n* **2** (*pl* -nese) a native or inhabitant of China or a descendant of one **3** any of the languages of China belonging to the Sino-Tibetan family, sometimes regarded as dialects of one language. They share a single writing system that is not phonetic but ideographic. A phonetic system using the Roman alphabet was officially adopted by the Chinese government in 1966. See also **Mandarin Chinese, Pekingese, Cantonese** Related prefix: **Sino-**

Chinese block *n* a percussion instrument consisting of a hollow wooden block played with a drumstick

Chinese burn *n* a minor torture inflicted by twisting the skin of a person's wrist or arm in two different directions simultaneously

Chinese cabbage *n* **1** Also called: **pe-tsai cabbage** a Chinese plant, *Brassica pekinensis*, that is related to the cabbage and has crisp edible leaves growing in a loose cylindrical head **2** another name for **bok choy**

Chinese chequers *n* (*functioning as singular*) a board game played with marbles or pegs

Chinese Chippendale *n* **a** a branch of Chippendale style in which Chinese styles and motifs are used **b** (*as modifier*): *a Chinese Chippendale cabinet*

Chinese copy *n* an exact copy of an original

Chinese crested *n* a small dog of a Chinese breed having long slender legs and a hairless body with hair only on the feet, head, and tail

Chinese eddo *n* another name for **taro**

Chinese Empire *n* China as ruled by the emperors until the establishment of the republic in 1911–12

C

Chinese gooseberry *n* another name for **kiwi fruit**

Chinese ink *n* another name for **Indian ink**

Chinese lantern *n* **1** a collapsible lantern made of thin coloured paper **2** an Asian solanaceous plant, *Physalis franchetii,* cultivated for its attractive orange-red inflated calyx. See also **winter cherry**

Chinese leaf *pl n* the edible leaves of a Chinese cabbage

Chinese medicine *n* a traditional system of medical treatment based on the principles of Yin and Yang, involving such treatments as acupuncture and the use of a range of drugs derived from animal and vegetable sources

Chinese puzzle *n* **1** an intricate puzzle, esp one consisting of boxes within boxes **2** a complicated problem

Chinese red *n* **a** a bright red colour **b** (*as adjective*): *a Chinese-red bag*

Chinese restaurant syndrome *n* a group of symptoms such as dizziness, headache, and flushing thought to be caused in some people by consuming large amounts of monosodium glutamate, esp as used in Chinese food

Chinese Revolution *n* **1** the overthrow of the last Manchu emperor and the establishment of a republic in China (1911–12) **2** the transformation of China (esp in the 1940s and 1950s) under the Chinese Communist Party

Chinese sacred lily *n* a Chinese amaryllidaceous plant, *Narcissus tazetta orientalis,* widely grown as a house plant for its fragrant yellow and white flowers. See also **polyanthus** (sense 2)

Chinese Turkestan *n* the E part of the central Asian region of Turkestan: corresponds generally to the present-day Xinjiang Uygur Autonomous Region of China

Chinese wall *n* **1** a notional barrier between the parts of a business, esp between the market makers and brokers of a stock-exchange business, across which no information should pass to the detriment of clients **2** an insurmountable obstacle

Chinese water deer *n* a small Chinese or Korean deer, *Hydropotes inermis,* having tusks and no antlers: introduced into England and France

Chinese water torture *n* a form of torture in which water is made to drip for a long period of time onto a victim's forehead to drive him insane

Chinese wax *or* **treewax** ('triː,wæks) *n* a yellowish wax secreted by an oriental scale insect, *Ceroplastes ceriferus,* and used commercially

Chinese whispers *n* (*functioning as singular*) **1** a game in which a message is passed on, in a whisper, by each of a number of people, so that the final version of the message is often radically changed from the original **2** any situation where information is passed on in turn by a number of people, often becoming distorted in the process

Chinese white *n* white zinc oxide, formerly used in paints. Also called: **zinc white**

Chinese windlass *n* another name for **differential windlass**

Chinese wood oil *n* another name for **tung oil**

Ching *or* **Ch'ing** (tʃɪŋ) *adj* of, relating to, or designating the Manchu dynasty (1644–1912) of China

Chinghai *or* **Ch'ing-hai** ('tʃɪŋ'haɪ) *n* a variant transliteration of the Chinese name for **Qinghai**

Chingtao *or* **Ch'ing-tao** ('tʃɪŋ'taʊ) *n* a variant transliteration of the Chinese name for **Qingdao**

Ch'ing-yüan ('tʃɪŋ'juːɑːn) *n* a former name of **Baoding**

Chin Hills (tʃɪn) *pl n* a mountainous region of W Myanmar; part of the Arakan Yoma system. Highest peak: Mount Victoria, 3053 m (10 075 ft)

Chin-Hsien ('tʃɪn'ʃjɛn) *n* the former name (1913–47) of **Jinzhou**

chink¹ (tʃɪŋk) *n* **1** a small narrow opening, such as a fissure or crack **2** chink in one's armour a small but fatal weakness ▷ *vb* **3** (*tr*) *chiefly US and Canadian* to fill up or make cracks in [c16 perhaps variant of earlier *chine,* from Old English *cine* crack; related to Middle Dutch *kene,* Danish *kin*] > 'chinky *adj*

chink² (tʃɪŋk) *vb* **1** to make or cause to make a light ringing sound, as by the striking of glasses or coins ▷ *n* **2** such a sound [c16 of imitative origin]

Chink (tʃɪŋk) *or* **Chinky** ('tʃɪŋkɪ) *n, pl* **Chinks** *or* **Chinkies,** *adj* a derogatory term for **Chinese** [c20 probably from *Chinese,* influenced by CHINK¹ (referring to the characteristic shape of the Chinese eye)]

chinkapin ('tʃɪŋkəpɪn) *n* a variant spelling of **chinquapin**

Chinkiang ('tʃɪn'kjæŋ, -kaɪ'æŋ) *n* a variant transliteration of the Chinese name for **Jinjiang**

chinless ('tʃɪnlɪs) *adj* **1** having a receding chin **2** weak or ineffectual

chinless wonder *n Brit informal* a person, esp an upper-class one, lacking strength of character

chin music *n informal* **1** *cricket, baseball* bowling or pitching aimed at the batsman or batter's head **2** *US* idle conversation

chino ('tʃiːnəʊ) *n, pl* **-nos** *US* a durable cotton twill cloth [c20 from American Spanish, of obscure origin]

Chino- *combining form* of or relating to China. See also **Sino-**

chinoiserie (ʃiːn,wɑːzəˈriː, -ˈwɑːzərɪ) *n* **1** a style of decorative or fine art based on imitations of Chinese motifs **2** an object or objects in this style [French, from *chinois* CHINESE; see -ERY]

chinook (tʃɪˈnuːk, -ˈnʊk) *n* **1** Also called: **snow eater** a warm dry southwesterly wind blowing down the eastern slopes of the Rocky Mountains **2** Also called: **wet chinook** a warm moist wind blowing onto the Washington and Oregon coasts from the sea [c19 from Salish *c'inuk*]

Chinook (tʃɪˈnuːk, -ˈnʊk) *n* (*pl* **-nook** *or* **-nooks**) a Native American people of the Pacific coast near the Columbia River **2** the language of this people, probably forming a separate branch of the Penutian phylum

Chinook Jargon *n* a pidgin language containing elements of Native American languages, English, and French: formerly used among fur traders and Indians on the NW coast of North America

Chinook salmon *n* a Pacific salmon, *Oncorhynchus tschawytscha,* valued as a food fish. Also called: **quinnat salmon, king salmon**

chinos ('tʃiːnəʊz) *pl n* trousers made of chino

chinquapin, chincapin *or* **chinkapin** ('tʃɪŋkəpɪn) *n* **1** a dwarf chestnut tree, *Castanea pumila,* of the eastern US, yielding edible nuts **2** Also called: **giant chinquapin** a large evergreen fagaceous tree, *Castanopsis chrysophylla,* of W North America **3** the nut of either of these trees ▷ Compare **water chinquapin** [c17 of Algonquian origin; compare Algonquian *chechinkamin* chestnut]

chintz (tʃɪnts) *n* **1** a printed, patterned cotton fabric, with glazed finish **2** a painted or stained Indian calico [c17 from Hindi *chīnt,* from Sanskrit *citra* gaily-coloured]

chintzy ('tʃɪntsɪ) *adj* chintzier, chintziest **1** of, resembling, or covered with chintz **2** *Brit informal* typical of the decor associated with the use of chintz soft furnishings, as in a country cottage

chinwag ('tʃɪn,wæg) *n Brit informal* a chat or gossipy conversation

chionodoxa (kaɪ,ɒnəˈdɒksə) *n* any plant of the liliaceous genus *Chionodoxa,* of S Europe and W Asia. See **glory-of-the-snow** [c19 New Latin, from Greek *khiōn* snow + *doxa* glory]

Chios ('kiːɒs, -əʊs) *n* **1** an island in the Aegean Sea, off the coast of Turkey: belongs to Greece. Capital: Chios. Pop: 51 936 (2001). Area: 904 sq km (353 sq miles) **2** a port on the island of Chios: in ancient times, one of the 12 Ionian city-states. Pop: 54 000 (1995 est.). Modern Greek name: Khíos

chip (tʃɪp) *n* **1** a small piece removed by chopping, cutting, or breaking **2** a mark left after a small piece has been chopped, cut, or broken off something **3** (in some games) a counter used to represent money **4** a thin strip of potato fried in deep fat **5** *US and Canadian* a very thin slice of potato fried and eaten cold as a snack. Also called (in Britain and certain other countries): **crisp 6** a small piece or thin slice of food **7** *sport* a shot, kick, etc, lofted into the air, esp over an obstacle or an opposing player's head, and travelling only a short distance **8** *electronics* a tiny wafer of semiconductor material, such as silicon, processed to form a type of integrated circuit or component such as a transistor **9** a thin strip of wood or straw used for making woven hats, baskets, etc **10** *NZ* a container for soft fruit, made of thin sheets of wood; punnet **11** cheap as chips *Brit informal* inexpensive; good value **12** chip off the old block *informal* a person who resembles one of his or her parents in behaviour **13** have a chip on one's shoulder *informal* to be aggressively sensitive about a particular thing or bear a grudge **14** have had one's chips *Brit informal* to be defeated, condemned to die, killed, etc **15** when the chips are down *informal* at a time of crisis or testing ▷ *vb* chips, chipping, chipped **16** to break small pieces from or become broken off in small pieces: *will the paint chip?* **17** (*tr*) to break or cut into small pieces: *to chip ice* **18** (*tr*) to shape by chipping **19** *sport* to strike or kick (a ball) in a high arc [Old English *cipp* (n), *cippian* (vb), of obscure origin] > 'chipper *n*

chip and PIN *n* **a** a system for processing credit cards requiring the customer to enter a unique identification number instead of a signature to authorize a payment **b** (*as modifier*): *chip and PIN transactions* [c21 CHIP (sense 8) + PIN]

chip-based ('tʃɪp,beɪst) *adj* (of electronic equipment or components) using or incorporating microchips

chip basket *n* **1** a wire basket for holding potato chips, etc, while frying in deep fat **2** a basket made of thin strips of wood, used esp for packing fruit

chipboard ('tʃɪp,bɔːd) *n* a thin rigid sheet made of compressed wood chips bound with a synthetic resin

chip in *vb* (*adverb*) *informal* **1** to contribute (money, time, etc) to a cause or fund **2** (*intr*) to interpose a remark or interrupt with a remark

chip log *n nautical* a log for determining a vessel's speed, consisting of a wooden chip tossed overboard at the end of a line that is marked off in lengths of 47 feet 3 inches; the speed is calculated by counting the number of such intervals that pass overboard in a 28-second interval

chipmunk ('tʃɪp,mʌŋk) *n* any burrowing sciurine rodent of the genera *Tamias* of E North America and *Eutamias* of W North America and Asia, typically having black-striped yellowish fur and cheek pouches for storing food [c19 of Algonquian origin; compare Ojibwa *atchitamon* squirrel, literally: headfirst, referring to its method of descent from trees]

chipolata (,tʃɪpəˈlɑːtə) *n chiefly Brit* a small sausage in a narrow casing [via French from Italian *cipollata* an onion-flavoured dish, from *cipolla* onion]

chip pan *n* a deep pan for frying potato chips, etc

Chippendale ('tʃɪpᵊn,deɪl) *adj* (of furniture) designed by, made by, or in the style of Thomas Chippendale (?1718–79) English cabinet-maker and furniture designer, characterized by the use of Chinese and Gothic motifs, cabriole legs, and massive carving

chipper¹ ('tʃɪpə) *adj informal* **1** cheerful; lively **2** smartly dressed

chipper² ('tʃɪpər) *n Irish and Scot informal* a fish-and-chip shop

Chippewa ('tʃɪpɪ,wɑː) *or* **Chippeway** ('tʃɪpɪ,weɪ) *n, pl* **-was, -wa** *or* **-ways, -way** another name for **Ojibwa**

chipping ('tʃɪpɪŋ) n another name for **chip** (sense 1)

chipping sparrow n a common North American sparrow, *Spizella passerina*, having brown-and-grey plumage and a white eye stripe

chippy[1] ('tʃɪpɪ) n, pl -pies 1 Brit informal a fish-and-chip shop 2 Brit and NZ a slang word for **carpenter** 3 NZ a potato crisp [C19 from CHIP (n)]

chippy[2] ('tʃɪpɪ) adj -pier, -piest informal resentful or oversensitive about being perceived as inferior: *a chippy miner's son* [C20 from CHIP (sense 12)] > **'chippiness** n

chippy[3] or **chippie** ('tʃɪpɪ) n, pl -pies an informal name for **chipmunk** or **chipping sparrow**

chippy[4] or **chippie** ('tʃɪpɪ) n, pl -pies informal, chiefly US and Canadian a promiscuous woman [C19 perhaps from CHIP (n)]

chippy[5] ('tʃɪpɪ) adj -pier, -piest belligerent or touchy [C19 from CHIP (n), sense probably developing from: as dry as a chip of wood, hence irritable, touchy]

chipset ('tʃɪpsɛt) n 1 a highly integrated circuit on the motherboard of a computer that controls many of its data transfer functions 2 computing the main processing circuitry on many video cards

chip shot n golf a short approach shot to the green, esp one that is lofted

chip wagon n Canadian a small van in which chips are cooked and sold

chirality (kaɪˈrælɪtɪ) n the configuration or handedness (left or right) of an asymmetric, optically active chemical compound. Also called: **dissymmetry** [C19 from Greek *kheir* hand + -AL[1] + -ITY] > **'chiral** adj

chirm (tʃɜːm) n 1 the chirping of birds ▷ vb 2 (intr) (esp of a bird) to chirp [Old English *cierm* noise; related to Old Saxon *karm*]

chiro ('kaɪrəʊ) n, pl chiros an informal name for **chiropractor**

chiro- or **cheiro-** combining form indicating the hand; of or by means of the hand: *chiromancy* [via Latin from Greek *kheir* hand]

chirography (kaɪˈrɒɡrəfɪ) n another name for **calligraphy**. > **chiˈrographer** n > **chirographic** (ˌkaɪrəˈɡræfɪk) or **ˌchiroˈgraphical** adj

chiromancy ('kaɪrəˌmænsɪ) n another word for **palmistry**. > **'chiroˌmancer** n

Chiron or **Cheiron** ('kaɪrɒn, -rən) n 1 Greek myth a wise and kind centaur who taught many great heroes in their youth, including Achilles, Actaeon, and Jason 2 a minor planet, discovered by Charles Kowal in 1977, revolving round the sun between the orbits of Saturn and Uranus

chironomid (kaɪˈrɒnəmɪd) n 1 a member of the Chironomidae, a family of nonbiting midges ▷ adj 2 of or relating to this family [C19 from New Latin *chironomus*, from Greek *kheironomos* a gesturer, from *kheir* hand + *nomos* manager + -ID[2]]

chiropody (kɪˈrɒpədɪ) n the treatment of the feet, esp the treatment of corns, verrucas, etc > **chiˈropodist** n > **chiropodial** (ˌkaɪrəʊˈpəʊdɪəl) adj

chiropractic (ˌkaɪrəˈpræktɪk) n a system of treating bodily disorders by manipulation of the spine and other parts, based on the belief that the cause is the abnormal functioning of a nerve [C20 from CHIRO- + -practic, from Greek *praktikos* effective, PRACTICAL] > **'chiroˌpractor** n

chiropteran (kaɪˈrɒptərən) adj 1 of, relating to, or belonging to the Chiroptera, an order of placental mammals comprising the bats ▷ n 2 Also called: **chiropter** (kaɪˈrɒptə) a bat

chirp (tʃɜːp) vb (intr) 1 (esp of some birds and insects) to make a short high-pitched sound 2 to speak in a lively fashion ▷ n 3 a chirping sound, esp that made by a bird [C15 (as *chirpinge*, gerund): of imitative origin] > **'chirper** n

CHIRP (tʃɜːp) n acronym for Confidential Human Incidents Reporting Programme: a system, run by the RAF Institute of Medicine, by which commercial pilots can comment on safety trends without the knowledge of their employers

chirpy ('tʃɜːpɪ) adj chirpier, chirpiest informal cheerful; lively > **'chirpily** adv > **'chirpiness** n

chirr, chirre or **churr** (tʃɜː) vb 1 (intr) (esp of certain insects, such as crickets) to make a shrill trilled sound ▷ n 2 the sound of chirring [C17 of imitative origin]

chirrup ('tʃɪrəp) vb (intr) 1 (esp of some birds) to chirp repeatedly 2 to make clucking sounds with the lips ▷ n 3 such a sound [C16 variant of CHIRP] > **'chirruper** n > **'chirrupy** adj

chiru ('tʃɪruː) n a Tibetan antelope, *Pantholops hodgsoni*, having a dense woolly pinkish-brown fleece prized as the source of shahtoosh wool: now close to extinction due to illegal slaughter for its fleece [C19 probably from Tibetan]

chirurgeon (kaɪˈrɜːdʒən) n an archaic word for **surgeon** [C13 from Old French *cirurgeon*] > **chiˈrurgery** n

chisel ('tʃɪzˀl) n 1 a a hand tool for working wood, consisting of a flat steel blade with a cutting edge attached to a handle of wood, plastic, etc It is either struck with a mallet or used by hand b a similar tool without a handle for working stone or metal ▷ vb -els, -elling, -elled or US -els, -eling, -eled 2 to carve (wood, stone, metal, etc) or form (an engraving, statue, etc) with or as with a chisel 3 slang to cheat or obtain by cheating [C14 via Old French, from Vulgar Latin *cisellus* (unattested), from Latin *caesus* cut, from *caedere* to cut]

chiselled or US **chiseled** ('tʃɪzˀld) adj 1 carved or formed with or as if with a chisel 2 clear-cut: *finely chiselled features*

chiseller ('tʃɪzˀlə) n 1 a person who uses a chisel 2 informal a cheat 3 Dublin slang a child

Chishima (ˌtʃiːˈʃiːˈma) n the Japanese name for the Kuril Islands

Chisimaio (ˌkiːzɪˈmaːjəʊ) n a port in S Somalia, on the Indian Ocean. Pop: 200 000 (latest est). Also called: **Kismayu**

Chişinău (kiʃiˈnəu) n the Romanian name for **Kishinev**

chi-square distribution ('kaɪˌskwɛə) n statistics a continuous single-parameter distribution derived as a special case of the gamma distribution and used esp to measure goodness of fit and to test hypotheses and obtain confidence intervals for the variance of a normally distributed variable

chi-square test n statistics a test derived from the chi-square distribution to compare the goodness of fit of theoretical and observed frequency distributions or to compare nominal data derived from unmatched groups of subjects

chit[1] (tʃɪt) n 1 a voucher for a sum of money owed, esp for food or drink Also called: **chitty** ('tʃɪtɪ) chiefly Brit a a note or memorandum b a requisition or receipt [C18 from earlier *chitty*, from Hindi *cittha* note, from Sanskrit *citra* brightly-coloured]

chit[2] (tʃɪt) n facetious or derogatory a pert, impudent, or self-confident girl or child: *a young chit of a thing* [C14 (in the sense: young of an animal, kitten): of obscure origin]

Chita (Russian tʃiˈta) n an industrial city in SE Russia, on the Trans-Siberian railway. Pop: 309 000 (2005 est)

chital ('tʃiːtˀl) n another name for **axis**[2] (the deer) [from Hindi]

chitarrone (ˌkɪtaːˈrəʊnɪ, ˌtʃiːt-) n, pl -ni (-nɪ) a large lute with a double neck in common use during the baroque period, esp in Italy [Italian, from *chitarra*, from Greek *kithara* lyre]

chitchat ('tʃɪtˌtʃæt) n 1 talk of a gossipy nature ▷ vb -chats, -chatting, -chatted 2 (intr) to gossip

chitin ('kaɪtɪn) n a polysaccharide that is the principal component of the exoskeletons of arthropods and of the bodies of fungi [C19 from French *chitine*, from Greek *khitōn* CHITON + -IN] > **'chitinous** adj > **'chitinˌoid** adj

chiton ('kaɪtˀn, -tɒn) n 1 (in ancient Greece and Rome) a loose woollen tunic worn knee length by men and full length by women 2 Also called: **coat-of-mail shell** any small primitive marine mollusc of the genus *Chiton* and related genera, having an elongated body covered with eight overlapping shell plates: class Amphineura [C19 from Greek *khitōn* coat of mail, of Semitic origin; related to Hebrew *kethōnet*]

Chittagong ('tʃɪtəˌɡɒŋ) n a port in E Bangladesh, on the Bay of Bengal: industrial centre. Pop: 4 171 000 (2005 est). Official name: **Chattagam**

chitter ('tʃɪtə) vb (intr) 1 chiefly US to twitter or chirp 2 a dialect word for **shiver**[1] or (of the teeth) **chatter** [C14 of imitative origin]

chitterlings ('tʃɪtəlɪŋz), **chitlins** ('tʃɪtlɪnz) or **chitlings** ('tʃɪtlɪŋz) pl n (sometimes singular) the intestines of a pig or other animal prepared as a dish [C13 of uncertain origin; perhaps related to Middle High German *kutel*]

chiv (tʃɪv, ʃɪv) or **shiv** (ʃɪv) slang ▷ n 1 a knife ▷ vb chivs, chivving, chivved or shivs, shivving, shivved 2 to stab (someone) [C17 perhaps from Romany *chiv* blade]

chivalrous ('ʃɪvəlrəs) adj 1 gallant; courteous 2 involving chivalry [C14 from Old French *chevalerous*, from CHEVALIER] > **'chivalrously** adv > **'chivalrousness** n

chivalry ('ʃɪvəlrɪ) n, pl -ries 1 the combination of qualities expected of an ideal knight, esp courage, honour, justice, and a readiness to help the weak 2 courteous behaviour, esp towards women 3 the medieval system and principles of knighthood 4 knights, noblemen, etc, collectively [C13 from Old French *chevalerie*, from CHEVALIER] > **'chivalric** adj

chivaree (ˌʃɪvəˈriː, ˈʃɪvəˌriː) n a US spelling of **charivari**

chive (tʃaɪv) n a small Eurasian purple-flowered alliaceous plant, *Allium schoenoprasum*, whose long slender hollow leaves are used to flavour soups, stews, etc. Also called: **chives** [C14 from Old French *cive*, ultimately from Latin *caepa* onion]

chivy, chivvy ('tʃɪvɪ) or **chevy** Brit ▷ vb chivies, chivying, chivied, chivvies, chivvying, chivvied or chevies, chevying, chevied 1 (tr) to harass or nag 2 (tr) to hunt 3 (intr) to run about ▷ n, pl chivies, chivvies or chevies 4 a hunt 5 obsolete a hunting cry [C19 variant of *chevy*, probably from *Chevy Chase*, title of a Scottish border ballad]

Chkalov (Russian 'tʃkaləf) n the former name (1938–57) of **Orenburg**

Chladni figure ('klɑːdnɪ) n physics a pattern formed by fine powder placed on a vibrating surface, used to display the positions of nodes and antinodes [C19 named after Ernst *Chladni* (1756–1827), German physicist]

chlamydate ('klæmɪˌdeɪt) adj (of some molluscs) possessing a mantle [C19 from Latin *chlamydātus* wearing a mantle, from Greek *khlamus* mantle]

chlamydeous (klæˈmɪdɪəs) adj (of plants) relating to or possessing sepals and petals

chlamydia (kləˈmɪdɪə) n any Gram-negative bacteria of the genus *Chlamydia*, which are obligate intracellular parasites and are responsible for such diseases as trachoma, psittacosis, and some sexually transmitted diseases [C20 New Latin, from Greek *khlamus* mantle + -IA]

chlamydial (kləˈmɪdɪəl) adj of or relating to infections caused by bacteria of the genus *Chlamydia*

chlamydospore (kləˈmɪdəˌspɔː) n a thick-walled asexual spore of many fungi: capable of surviving adverse conditions

chloanthite (kləʊˈænθaɪt) n a form of nickel arsenide having commercial importance as a nickel ore [C19 from Greek *khloanthēs* budding, sprouting + -ITE[1]]

chloasma (kləʊˈæzmə) n, pl chloasmata (kləʊˈæzmətə) med the appearance on a person's skin, esp of the face, of patches of darker colour: associated with hormonal changes caused by liver disease or the use of oral contraceptives [C19 from New Latin, from Greek *khloasma* greenness]

Chloe ('kləʊɪ) n See **Daphnis and Chloe**

chlor- combining form a variant of **chloro-** before a vowel

chloracne (klɔːˈræknɪ) *n* a disfiguring skin disease that results from contact with or ingestion or inhalation of certain chlorinated aromatic hydrocarbons [C20 from CHLORO- + ACNE]

chloral (ˈklɔːrəl) *n* **1** a colourless oily liquid with a pungent odour, made from chlorine and acetaldehyde and used in preparing chloral hydrate and DDT; trichloroacetaldehyde **2** short for **chloral hydrate**

chloral hydrate *n* a colourless crystalline soluble solid produced by the reaction of chloral with water and used as a sedative and hypnotic; 2,2,2-trichloro-1,1-ethanediol. Formula: $CCl_3CH(OH)_2$

chlorambucil (klɔːˈræmbjʊsɪl) *n* an alkylating drug derived from nitrogen mustard, administered orally in the treatment of leukaemia and other malignant diseases. Formula: $C_{14}H_{19}Cl_2NO_2$

chloramine (ˈklɔːrəˌmiːn) *n* **1** an unstable colourless liquid with a pungent odour, made by the reaction of sodium hypochlorite and ammonia. Formula: NH_2Cl **2** any compound produced by replacing hydrogen atoms in an azo or amine group with chlorine atoms

chloramphenicol (ˌklɔːræmˈfɛnɪˌkɒl) *n* a broad-spectrum antibiotic used esp in treating typhoid fever and rickettsial infections: obtained from the bacterium *Streptomyces venezuelae* or synthesized. Formula: $C_{11}H_{12}N_2O_5Cl_2$ [C20 from CHLORO- + AM(IDO)- + PHE(NO)- + NI(TRO)- + (GLY)COL]

chlorate (ˈklɔːˌreɪt, -rɪt) *n* any salt of chloric acid, containing the monovalent ion ClO_3^-

chlordane (ˈklɔːdeɪn) *or* **chlordan** (ˈklɔːdæn) *n* a white insoluble toxic solid existing in several isomeric forms and usually used, as an insecticide, in the form of a brown impure liquid. Formula: $C_{10}H_6Cl_8$ [C20 from CHLORO- + (IN)D(ENE) + -ANE]

chlordiazepoxide (ˌklɔːdaɪˌeɪzɪˈpɒksaɪd) *n* a chemical compound used as a tranquillizer and muscle relaxant and in the treatment of delirium tremens. Formula: $C_{16}H_{14}ClN_3O$

chlorella (klɔːˈrelə, klə-) *n* any microscopic unicellular green alga of the genus *Chlorella*: some species are used in the preparation of human food [C19 from New Latin, from CHLORO- + Latin -*ella*, diminutive suffix]

chlorenchyma (kləˈrɛŋkɪmə) *n* plant tissue consisting of parenchyma cells that contain chlorophyll [C19 from CHLOR(OPHYLL) + -ENCHYMA]

chlorhexidine (klɔːˈhɛksɪdiːn) *n* an antiseptic compound used in skin cleansers, mouthwashes, etc [C20 from CHLOR(O)- + HEX(ANE) + -I(DE) + (AM)INE]

chloric (ˈklɔːrɪk) *adj* of or containing chlorine in the pentavalent state

chloric acid *n* a strong acid with a pungent smell, known only in solution and in the form of chlorate salts. Formula: $HClO_3$

chloride (ˈklɔːraɪd) *n* **1** any salt of hydrochloric acid, containing the chloride ion Cl^- **2** any compound containing a chlorine atom, such as methyl chloride (chloromethane), CH_3Cl > **chloridic** (kləˈrɪdɪk) *adj*

chloride of lime *or* **chlorinated lime** *n* another name for **bleaching powder**

chlorinate (ˈklɔːrɪˌneɪt) *vb* (tr) **1** to combine or treat (a substance) with chlorine **2** to disinfect (water) with chlorine > ˌchlorinˈation *n* > ˈchlorinˌator *n*

chlorine (ˈklɔːriːn) *or* **chlorin** (ˈklɔːrɪn) *n* a toxic pungent greenish-yellow gas of the halogen group; the 15th most abundant element in the earth's crust, occurring only in the combined state, mainly in common salt: used in the manufacture of many organic chemicals, in water purification, and as a disinfectant and bleaching agent. Symbol: Cl; atomic no.: 17; atomic wt.: 35.4527; valency: 1, 3, 5, or 7; density: 3.214 kg/m³; relative density: 1.56; melting pt.: −101.03°C; boiling pt.: −33.9°C [C19 (coined by Sir Humphrey

Davy): from CHLORO- + -INE², referring to its colour]

chlorite¹ (ˈklɔːraɪt) *n* any of a group of green soft secondary minerals consisting of the hydrated silicates of aluminium, iron, and magnesium in monoclinic crystalline form: common in metamorphic rocks [C18 from Latin *chlōrītis* precious stone of a green colour, from Greek *khlōritis*, from *khlōros* greenish yellow] > **chloritic** (klɔːˈrɪtɪk) *adj*

chlorite² (ˈklɔːraɪt) *n* any salt of chlorous acid, containing the monovalent ion ClO_2^-

chloro- *or before a vowel* **chlor-** *combining form* **1** indicating the colour green: *chlorophyll* **2** chlorine: *chloroform*

chloroacetic acid (ˌklɔːrəʊəˈsiːtɪk) *or* **chloracetic acid** (ˌklɔːrəˈsiːtɪk) *n* a colourless crystalline soluble strong acid prepared by chlorinating acetic acid and used as an intermediate in the manufacture of many chemicals; monochloracetic acid. Formula: $CH_2ClCOOH$ **2** either of two related compounds: **dichloracetic acid**, $CHCl_2COOH$, or **trichloracetic acid** CCl_3COOH

chloroargyrite (ˌklɔːrəʊˈɑːdʒɪˌraɪt) *n* a greyish-yellow or colourless soft secondary mineral consisting of silver chloride in cubic crystalline form: a source of silver. Formula: AgCl. Also called: **cerargyrite, horn silver** [C19 from Greek *keras* horn + *arguros* silver + -ITE¹]

chlorobenzene (ˌklɔːrəʊˈbɛnziːn) *n* a colourless volatile flammable insoluble liquid with an almond-like odour, made from chlorine and benzene and used as a solvent and in the preparation of many organic compounds, esp phenol and DDT. Formula: C_6H_5Cl

chlorofluorocarbon (ˌklɔːrəˌflʊərəʊˈkɑːbᵊn) *n chem* any of various gaseous compounds of carbon, hydrogen, chlorine, and fluorine, used as refrigerants, aerosol propellants, solvents, and in foam: some cause a breakdown of ozone in the earth's atmosphere. Abbreviation: **CFC**

chloroform (ˈklɔːrəˌfɔːm) *n* a heavy volatile liquid with a sweet taste and odour, used as a solvent and cleansing agent and in refrigerants: formerly used as an inhalation anaesthetic. Formula: $CHCl_3$. Systematic name: **trichloromethane** [C19 from CHLORO- + FORM(YL) (in an obsolete sense that applied to a CH radical)]

chlorohydrin (ˌklɔːrəʊˈhaɪdrɪn) *n* **1** any of a class of organic compounds containing a hydroxyl group and a chlorine atom **2** a colourless unstable hygroscopic liquid that is used mainly as a solvent; 3-chloropropane-1,2-diol. Formula: $CH_2OHCHOHCH_2Cl$ [C20 from CHLORO- + HYDRO- + -IN]

Chloromycetin (ˌklɔːrəʊmaɪˈsiːtɪn) *n trademark* a brand of **chloramphenicol**

chlorophyll *or US* **chlorophyl** (ˈklɔːrəfɪl) *n* the green pigment of plants and photosynthetic algae and bacteria that traps the energy of sunlight for photosynthesis and exists in several forms, the most abundant being **chlorophyll a** ($C_{55}H_{72}O_5N_4Mg$): used as a colouring agent in medicines or food (**E140**) > ˈchloroˌphylloid *adj* > ˌchloroˈphyllous *adj*

chlorophytum (ˌklɔːrəˈfaɪtəm) *n* any plant of the genus *Chlorophytum*, esp *C. elatum variegatum*, grown as a pot plant for its long narrow leaves with a light central stripe, and characterized by the production of offsets at the end of long scapes: family Liliaceae. Also called: **spider plant** [New Latin, from Greek *chlōros* green + *phyton* plant]

chloropicrin (ˌklɔːrəʊˈpɪkrɪn) *or* **chlorpicrin** (klɔːˈpɪkrɪn) *n* a colourless insoluble toxic lachrymatory liquid used as a pesticide and a tear gas; nitrotrichloromethane. Formula: CCl_3NO_2 [C20 from CHLORO- + PICRO- + -IN]

chloroplast (ˈklɔːrəʊˌplæst) *n* a plastid containing chlorophyll and other pigments, occurring in plants and algae that carry out photosynthesis > ˌchloroˈplastic *adj*

chloroprene (ˈklɔːrəʊˌpriːn) *n* a colourless liquid

derivative of butadiene that is used in making neoprene rubbers; 2-chloro-1,2-butadiene. Formula: $CH_2{:}CHCCl{:}CH_2$ [C20 from CHLORO- + (ISO)PRENE]

chloroquine (ˈklɔːrəʊˌkwiːn) *n* a synthetic drug administered orally to treat malaria. Formula: $C_{18}H_{26}ClN_3$ [C20 from CHLORO- + QUIN(OLINE)]

chlorosis (klɔːˈrəʊsɪs) *n* **1** *Also called:* **greensickness** *pathol* a disorder, formerly common in adolescent girls, characterized by pale greenish-yellow skin, weakness, and palpitation and caused by insufficient iron in the body **2** *botany* a deficiency of chlorophyll in green plants caused by mineral deficiency, lack of light, disease, etc, the leaves appearing uncharacteristically pale [C17 from CHLORO- + -OSIS] > **chlorotic** (klɔːˈrɒtɪk) *adj*

chlorothiazide (ˌklɔːrəˈθaɪəˌzaɪd) *n* a diuretic drug administered orally in the treatment of chronic heart and kidney disease and hypertension. Formula: $C_7H_6ClN_3O_4S_2$ [C20 from CHLORO- + THI(O-) + (DI)AZ(INE + DIOX)IDE]

chlorous (ˈklɔːrəs) *adj* **1** of or containing chlorine in the trivalent state **2** of or containing chlorous acid

chlorous acid *n* an unstable acid that is a strong oxidizing agent. Formula: $HClO_2$

chlorpromazine (klɔːˈprɒməˌziːn) *n* a drug derived from phenothiazine, used as a tranquillizer and sedative, esp in psychotic disorders. Formula: $C_{17}H_{19}ClN_2S$ [C20 from CHLORO- + PRO(PYL + A)M(INE) + AZINE]

chlorpropamide (klɔːˈprəʊpəˌmaɪd) *n* a sulfonylurea drug that reduces blood glucose and is administered orally in the treatment of diabetes mellitus. Formula: $C_{10}H_{13}ClN_2O_3S$

chlortetracycline (klɔːˌtɛtrəˈsaɪkliːn) *n* an antibiotic used in treating many bacterial and rickettsial infections: obtained from the bacterium *Streptomyces aureofaciens*. Formula: $C_{22}H_{23}ClN_2O_8$

chlorthalidone (klɔːˈθælɪdəʊn) *n* a diuretic used in the treatment of congestive heart failure and hypertension [C20 from CHLOR(O)- + TH(IAZINE) + -AL³ + I(D(E) + -ONE]

ChM *abbreviation for* Master of Surgery [Latin *Chirurgiae Magister*]

choanocyte (ˈkəʊənəˌsaɪt) *n* any of the flagellated cells in sponges that maintain a flow of water through the body. A collar of protoplasm surrounds the base of the flagellum. Also called: **collar cell** [C19 from Greek *khoanē* funnel (from *khein* to pour) + -CYTE]

choccy (ˈtʃɒkɪ) *informal* ▷ *n, pl* -**cies 1** a chocolate ▷ *adj* **2** made of, tasting of, smelling of, or resembling chocolate: *a delicious choccy taste*

choc-ice (ˈtʃɒkˌaɪs) *n* an ice cream covered with a thin layer of chocolate

chock (tʃɒk) *n* **1** a block or wedge of wood used to prevent the sliding or rolling of a heavy object **2** *nautical* **a** a fairlead consisting of a ringlike device with an opening at the top through which a rope is placed **b** a cradle-like support for a boat, barrel, etc **3** *mountaineering* See **nut** (sense 10) ▷ *vb* (tr) **4** (usually foll by *up*) *Brit* to cram full **5** to fit with or secure by a chock **6** to support (a boat, barrel, etc) on chocks ▷ *adv* **7** as closely or tightly as possible: *chock against the wall* [C17 of uncertain origin; perhaps related to Old French *çoche* log; compare Provençal *soca* tree stump]

chock-a-block *adj, adv* **1** filled to capacity; in a crammed state **2** *nautical* with the blocks brought close together, as when a tackle is pulled as tight as possible

chocker (ˈtʃɒkə) *adj* **1** *informal* full up; packed **2** *Brit slang* irritated; fed up [C20 from CHOCK-A-BLOCK]

chock-full, choke-full *or* **chuck-full** *adj* (*postpositive*) completely full [C17 *choke-full*; see CHOKE, FULL]

chockstone (ˈtʃɒkˌstəʊn) *n mountaineering* **1** a stone securely jammed in a crack. It may vary in size from a pebble to a large boulder **2** another name for **chock** (sense 3)

choco or **chocko** ('tʃɒkəʊ) *n, pl* **chocos, chockos** *Austral slang* (in World War II) **a** a member of the citizen army; militiaman **b** a conscript [c20 shortened from *chocolate soldier*]

chocoholic or **chocaholic** (,tʃɒkə'hɒlɪk) *n informal* **a** someone who is very fond of eating chocolate **b** (*as modifier*): *the chocoholic British* [c20 from CHOCO(LATE) + -HOLIC]

chocolate ('tʃɒkəlɪt, 'tʃɒklɪt, -lət) *n* **1** a food preparation made from roasted ground cacao seeds, usually sweetened and flavoured **2** a drink or sweetmeat made from this **3 a** a moderate to deep brown colour **b** (*as adjective*): *a chocolate carpet* [c17 from Spanish, from Aztec *xocolatl*, from *xococ* sour, bitter + *atl* water] > **'chocolaty** *adj*

chocolate-box *n* (*modifier*) *informal* sentimentally pretty or appealing

chocolate soldier *n informal* a person who mistakenly believes that he or she is very powerful, important, or impressive

chocolatier (,tʃɒkə'lætɪə; *French* ʃɔkalatje) *n* a person or company that makes or sells chocolate [French]

choctaw ('tʃɒktɔ:) *n skating* a turn from the inside edge of one skate to the outside edge of the other or vice versa [c19 after CHOCTAW]

Choctaw ('tʃɒktɔ:) *n* **1** (*pl* **-taws** or **-taw**) a member of a Native American people of Alabama **2** the language of this people, belonging to the Muskogean family [c18 from Choctaw *Chahta*]

chog ('tʃɒg) *n Northern English dialect* the core of a piece of fruit: *an apple chog*

Chogyal ('tʃɒgjɑːl) *n* the title of the ruler of Sikkim

choice (tʃɔɪs) *n* **1** the act or an instance of choosing or selecting **2** the opportunity or power of choosing **3** a person or thing chosen or that may be chosen: *he was a possible choice* **4** an alternative action or possibility: *what choice did I have?* **5** a supply from which to select: *a poor choice of shoes* **6 of choice** preferred; favourite ▷ *adj* **7** of superior quality; excellent: *choice wine* **8** carefully chosen, appropriate: *a few choice words will do the trick* **9** vulgar or rude: *choice language* [c13 from Old French *chois*, from *choisir* to CHOOSE] > **'choicely** *adv* > **'choiceness** *n*

choir (kwaɪə) *n* **1** an organized group of singers, esp for singing in church services **2 a** the part of a cathedral, abbey, or church in front of the altar, lined on both sides with benches, and used by the choir and clergy. Compare **chancel b** (*as modifier*): *choir stalls* **3** a number of instruments of the same family playing together: *a brass choir* **4** Also called: **choir organ** one of the manuals on an organ controlling a set of soft sweet-toned pipes. Compare **great** (sense 21), **swell** (sense 16) **5** any of the nine orders of angels in medieval angelology. Archaic spelling: **quire** [c13 *quer*, from Old French *cuer*, from Latin CHORUS] > **'choir,like** *adj*

choirboy ('kwaɪə,bɔɪ) *n* one of a number of young boys who sing the treble part in a church choir

choir loft *n* a gallery in a cathedral, abbey, or church used by the choir

choirmaster ('kwaɪə,mɑːstə) *n* a person who trains, leads, or conducts a choir

choir school *n* (in Britain) a school, esp a preparatory school attached to a cathedral, college, etc, offering general education to boys whose singing ability is good

Choiseul (*French* ʃwazœl) *n* an island in the SW Pacific Ocean, in the Solomon Islands: hilly and densely forested. Area: 3885 sq km (1500 sq miles)

choke (tʃəʊk) *vb* **1** (*tr*) to hinder or stop the breathing of (a person or animal), esp by constricting the windpipe or by asphyxiation **2** (*intr*) to have trouble or fail in breathing, swallowing, or speaking **3** (*tr*) to block or clog up (a passage, pipe, street, etc) **4** (*tr*) to retard the growth or action of: *the weeds are choking my plants* **5** (*tr*) to suppress (emotion): *she choked her anger* **6**

(*intr*) *slang* to die **7** (*tr*) to enrich the petrol-air mixture by reducing the air supply to (a carburettor, petrol engine, etc) **8** (*intr*) (*esp in sport*) to be seized with tension and fail to perform well ▷ *n* **9** the act or sound of choking **10** a device in the carburettor of a petrol engine that enriches the petrol-air mixture by reducing the air supply **11** any constriction or mechanism for reducing the flow of a fluid in a pipe, tube, etc **12** Also called: **choke coil** *electronics* an inductor having a relatively high impedance, used to prevent the passage of high frequencies or to smooth the output of a rectifier **13** the inedible centre of the head of an artichoke ▷ See also **choke back, choke up** [Old English *ācēocian*, of Germanic origin; related to CHEEK] > **'chokeable** *adj*

choke back or **down** *vb* (*tr, adverb*) to suppress (anger, tears, etc)

chokeberry ('tʃəʊk,bərɪ, -brɪ) *n, pl* **-ries 1** any of various North American rosaceous shrubs of the genus *Aronia* **2** the red or purple bitter fruit of any of these shrubs

chokebore ('tʃəʊk,bɔ:) *n* **1** a shotgun bore that becomes narrower towards the muzzle so that the shot is not scattered **2** a shotgun having such a bore

choke chain *n* a collar and lead for a dog so designed that if the dog drags on the lead the collar tightens round its neck

chokecherry ('tʃəʊk,tʃerɪ) *n, pl* **-ries 1** any of several North American species of cherry, esp *Prunus virginiana*, having very astringent dark red or black fruit **2** the fruit of any of these trees

choke coil *n* another name for **choke** (sense 12)

choked ('tʃəʊkt) *adj Brit informal* annoyed or disappointed

chokedamp ('tʃəʊk,dæmp) *n* another word for **blackdamp**

choke-full *adj* a less common spelling of **chock-full**

chokehold ('tʃəʊk,həʊld) *n* **1** the act of holding a person's neck across the windpipe, esp from behind using one arm **2** complete power or control: *the chokehold the mob has had on the town*

choker ('tʃəʊkə) *n* **1** a woman's high collar, popular esp in the late 19th century **2** any neckband or necklace worn tightly around the throat **3** a high clerical collar; stock **4** a person who chokes **5** something that causes a person to choke

choke up *vb* (*tr, adverb*) **1** to block (a drain, pipe, etc) completely **2** *informal* (*usually passive*) to overcome (a person) with emotion, esp without due cause

chokey or **choky** ('tʃəʊkɪ) *n Brit* a slang word for **prison** [c17 from Anglo-Indian, from Hindi *caukī* a shed or lockup]

choko ('tʃəʊkəʊ) *n, pl* **-kos** the cucumber-like fruit of a tropical American cucurbitaceous vine, *Sechium edule*: eaten as a vegetable in the Caribbean, Australia, and New Zealand [c18 from a Brazilian Indian name]

choky or **chokey** ('tʃəʊkɪ) *adj* **chokier, chokiest** involving, caused by, or causing choking

cholagogue ('kɒləgɒg) *n* a drug or other substance that promotes the flow of bile from the gall bladder into the duodenum > **,chola'gogic** *adj*

cholangiography (kə,lændʒɪ'ɒgrəfɪ) *n* radiographic examination of the bile ducts after the introduction into them of a contrast medium

chole- or before a vowel **chol-** *combining form* indicating bile or gall: *cholesterol* [from Greek *kholē*]

cholecalciferol (,kəʊlɪkæl'sɪfə,rɒl) *n* a compound occurring naturally in fish-liver oils, used to treat rickets. Formula: $C_{27}H_{44}O$. Also called: **vitamin D₃** See also **calciferol**

cholecyst ('kɒlɪsɪst) *n rare* another name for **gall bladder**

cholecystectomy (,kəʊlɪsɪs'tektəmɪ) *n, pl* **-mies** surgical removal of the gall bladder

cholecystitis (,kɒlɪsɪs'taɪtɪs) *n* inflammation of the gall bladder, due to bacterial infection or the

presence of gallstones

cholecystography (,kɒlɪsɪs'tɒgrəfɪ) *n med* radiography of the gall bladder after administration of a contrast medium

cholecystokinin (,kɒlɪ,sɪstə'kaɪnɪn) *n* a hormone secreted by duodenal cells that stimulates the contraction of the gall bladder and secretion of pancreatic enzymes. Also called: **pancreozymin**

cholent ('tʃɒlənt) *n Judaism* a meal usually consisting of a stew of meat, potatoes, and pulses prepared before the Sabbath on Friday and left to cook until eaten for Sabbath lunch

choler ('kɒlə) *n* **1** anger or ill humour **2** *archaic* one of the four bodily humours; yellow bile. See **humour** (sense 8) **3** *obsolete* biliousness [c14 from Old French *colère*, from Medieval Latin *cholera*, from Latin: jaundice, CHOLERA]

cholera ('kɒlərə) *n* an acute intestinal infection characterized by severe diarrhoea, cramp, etc: caused by ingestion of water or food contaminated with the bacterium *Vibrio comma*. Also called: **Asiatic cholera, epidemic cholera, Indian cholera** [c14 from Latin, from Greek *kholera* jaundice, from *kholē* bile] > **'chole,roid** *adj*

choleric ('kɒlərɪk) *adj* **1** bad-tempered **2** bilious or causing biliousness > **'cholerically** or **'cholericly** *adv*

cholesterol (kə'lestə,rɒl) *n* a sterol found in all animal tissues, blood, bile, and animal fats: a precursor of other body steroids. A high level of cholesterol in the blood is implicated in some cases of atherosclerosis, leading to heart disease. Formula: $C_{27}H_{45}OH$. Former name: **cholesterin** (kə'lestərɪn) [c19 from CHOLE- + Greek *stereos* hard, solid, so called because first observed in gallstones]

cholesterolaemia or US **cholesterolemia** (kə,lestərə'li:mɪə) *n* the presence of abnormally high levels of cholesterol in the blood

Chol Hamoed *Hebrew* (xol ha'moed; *Yiddish* xɔʊl hə'mavəd) *n Judaism* the middle days of the festivals of Passover and Sukkoth, on which necessary work is permitted [literally: the weekdays of the festival]

choli ('tʃəʊlɪ) *n, pl* **-lis** a short-sleeved bodice, as worn by Indian women [from Hindi]

cholic acid ('kəʊlɪk) *n* a crystalline insoluble acid present in bile: used as an emulsifying agent and an intermediate in the synthesis of organic compounds. Formula: $C_{24}H_{40}O_5$ [c19 from Greek *kholikos*; see CHOLE-]

choline ('kəʊli:n, -ɪn, 'kɒl-) *n* a colourless viscous soluble alkaline substance present in animal tissues, esp as a constituent of lecithin: used as a supplement to the diet of poultry and in medicine for preventing the accumulation of fat in the liver. Formula: $[(CH_3)_3NCH_2CH_2OH]^+OH^-$ [c19 from CHOLE- + -INE², so called because of its action in the liver]

cholinergic (,kəʊlɪ'nɜːdʒɪk) *adj* **1** denoting nerve fibres that release acetylcholine when stimulated **2** of or relating to the type of chemical activity associated with acetylcholine and similar substances [c20 from (ACETYL)CHOLIN(E) + Greek *ergon* work]

cholinesterase (,kəʊlɪ'nestə,reɪs, ,kɒl-) *n* an enzyme that hydrolyses acetylcholine to choline and acetic acid

cholla ('tʃɒljɑ:; *Spanish* 'tʃoʎa) *n* any of several spiny cacti of the genus *Opuntia* that grow in the southwestern US and Mexico and have cylindrical stem segments. See also **prickly pear** [Mexican Spanish, from Spanish: head, perhaps from Old French (dialect) *cholle* ball, of Germanic origin]

chollers ('tʃɒləz) *pl n Northeast English dialect* the jowls or cheeks [c18 perhaps from Old English *ceolur* throat. See JOWL²]

Cholon (tʃə'lʌn; *French* ʃɔlɔ̃) *n* a city in S Vietnam: a suburb of Ho Chi Minh City

Cholula (*Spanish* tʃo'lula) *n* a town in S Mexico, in Puebla state: ancient ruins, notably a pyramid, 53 m (177 ft) high. Pop: 37 791 (1990)

C

chometz *Hebrew* (xaˈmɛtʒ; *Yiddish* ˈxomətʒ) *n* a variant spelling of **chametz**

chommie (ˈtʃɒmɪ) *n South African informal* a friend, used esp by Black males [probably from Afrikaans *tjommie*, from CHUM[1]]

Chomolangma (ˈtʃəʊməʊˌlɑːŋmə) *n* a Chinese name for (Mount) **Everest**

chomophyte (ˈkɒməʊˌfaɪt) *n* any plant that grows on rocky ledges or in fissures and crevices

chomp (tʃɒmp) *or* **chump** *vb* **1** to chew (food) noisily; champ ▷ *n* **2** the act or sound of chewing in this manner [variant of CHAMP[1]]

Chomskyan (ˈtʃɒmskɪən) *adj* of or relating to (Avram) Noam Chomsky, the US linguist and political critic (born 1928)

chon (tʃɒn) *n, pl* **chon** a North and South Korean monetary unit worth one hundredth of a won

chondral (ˈkɒndrəl) *adj* of or relating to cartilage

chondrichthyan (kɒnˈdrɪkθɪən) *n zoology* a technical name for a **cartilaginous fish** [New Latin, from Greek *khondros* grain, cartilage + *ikhthus* fish]

chondrify (ˈkɒndrɪˌfaɪ) *vb* **-fies, -fying, -fied** to become or convert into cartilage > ˌchondrifiˈcation *n*

chondrin (ˈkɒndrɪn) *n* a resilient translucent bluish-white substance that forms the matrix of cartilage

chondriosome (ˈkɒndrɪəˌsəʊm) *n* another name for **mitochondrion**. > ˌchondrioˈsomal *adj*

chondrite (ˈkɒndraɪt) *n* a stony meteorite consisting mainly of silicate minerals in the form of chondrules. Compare **achondrite**. > chondritic (kɒnˈdrɪtɪk) *adj*

chondro-, chondri- *or before a vowel* **chondr-** *combining form* **1** indicating cartilage: *chondroma* **2** grain or granular: *chondrule* [from Greek *khondros* grain, cartilage]

chondroma (kɒnˈdrəʊmə) *n, pl* **-mas** *or* **-mata** (-mətə) *pathol* a benign cartilaginous growth or neoplasm > chonˈdromatous *adj*

chondroskeleton (ˈkɒndrəʊˌskɛlɪtən) *n* the cartilaginous part of the skeleton of vertebrates

chondrule (ˈkɒndruːl) *n* one of the small spherical masses of mainly silicate minerals present in chondrites

Chǒngjin *or* **Chungjin** (ˈtʃʌŋˈdʒɪn) *n* a port in E North Korea, on the Sea of Japan. Pop: 603 000 (2005 est)

Chongqing (ˈtʃʊŋˈtʃɪŋ), **Chungking** *or* **Ch'ung-ch'ing** *n* a river port in SW China, in Sichuan province at the confluence of the Yangtze and Jialing rivers: site of a city since the 3rd millennium BC; wartime capital of China (1938–45); major trade centre for W China. Pop: 4 975 000 (2005 est). Also called: **Pahsien**

Chǒnju (ˈtʃʌnˈdʒuː) *n* a city in SW South Korea: centre of large rice-growing region. Pop: 643 000 (2005 est)

choo-choo (ˈtʃuːˌtʃuː) *n Brit* a child's name for a railway train [C20 of imitative origin]

choof off (tʃʊf) *vb* (*intr, adverb*) *Austral slang* to go away; make off

chook (tʃʊk) *vb* **1** See **jook** ▷ *n* **2** Also called: **chookie** *Austral informal* a hen or chicken **3** *Austral informal* a woman ▷ *interj* **4** *Austral* a exclamation used to attract chickens **5** **he couldn't raffle a chook in a pub** he is incapable of carrying out even the simplest of tasks

chook chaser *n Austral derogatory slang* **1** a small motorcycle, esp for off-road use **2** a person who rides such a motorcycle

choom (tʃʊm) *n* (*often capital*) *old-fashioned, Austral slang* an Englishman

choose (tʃuːz) *vb* **chooses, choosing, chose, chosen** **1** to select (a person, thing, course of action, etc) from a number of alternatives **2** (*tr; takes a clause as object or an infinitive*) to consider it desirable or proper: *I don't choose to read that book* **3** (*intr*) to like; please: *you may stand if you choose* **4** **cannot choose but** to be obliged to: *we cannot choose but vote for him* **5** **nothing** *or* **little to choose**

between (of two people or objects) almost equal [Old English *ceosan*; related to Old Norse *kjōsa*, Old High German *kiosan*] > ˈchooser *n*

choosy (ˈtʃuːzɪ) *adj* **choosier, choosiest** *informal* particular in making a choice; difficult to please

chop[1] (tʃɒp) *vb* **chops, chopping, chopped** **1** (*often foll by* down *or* off) to cut (something) with a blow from an axe or other sharp tool **2** (*tr*) to produce or make in this manner: *to chop firewood* **3** (*tr; often foll by* up) to cut into pieces **4** (*tr*) *Brit informal* to dispense with or reduce **5** (*intr*) to move quickly or violently **6** *sport* to hit (a ball) sharply downwards **7** *boxing, martial Arts* to punch or strike (an opponent) with a short sharp blow **8** *West African* an informal word for **eat** ▷ *n* **9** a cutting blow **10** the act or an instance of chopping **11** a piece chopped off **12** a slice of mutton, lamb, or pork, generally including a rib **13** *Austral and NZ slang* a share (esp in the phrase **get** *or* **hop in for one's chop**) **14** *West African* an informal word for **food** **15** *Austral and NZ* a competition of skill and speed in chopping logs **16** *sport* a sharp downward blow or stroke **17** **not much chop** *Austral and NZ informal* not much good; poor **18** **the chop** *slang* dismissal from employment [C16 variant of CHAP[1]]

chop[2] (tʃɒp) *vb* **chops, chopping, chopped** **1** (*intr*) to change direction suddenly; vacillate (esp in the phrase **chop and change**) **2** *obsolete* to barter **3** **chop logic** to use excessively subtle or involved logic or argument [Old English *ceapian* to barter; see CHEAP, CHAPMAN]

chop[3] (tʃɒp) *n* a design stamped on goods as a trademark, esp in the Far East [C17 from Hindi *chhāp*]

chop chop *adv* pidgin English for **quickly** [C19 from Chinese dialect; related to Cantonese *kap kap*]

chopfallen (ˈtʃɒpˌfɔːlən) *adj* a variant of **chapfallen**

chophouse[1] (ˈtʃɒpˌhaʊs) *n* a restaurant specializing in steaks, grills, chops, etc

chophouse[2] (ˈtʃɒpˌhaʊs) *n* (*formerly*) a customs house in China

chopine (tʃɒˈpiːn) *or* **chopin** (ˈtʃɒpɪn) *n* a sandal-like shoe on tall wooden or cork bases popular in the 18th century [C16 from Old Spanish *chapín*, probably imitative of the sound made by the shoe when walking]

chopper (ˈtʃɒpə) *n* **1** *chiefly Brit* a small hand axe **2** a butcher's cleaver **3** a person or thing that cuts or chops **4** an informal name for a **helicopter** **5** *chiefly Brit* a slang name for **penis** **6** a device for periodically interrupting an electric current or beam of radiation to produce a pulsed current or beam. See also **vibrator** (sense 2) **7** a type of bicycle or motorcycle with very high handlebars and an elongated saddle **8** *NZ* a child's bicycle **9** *obsolete slang, chiefly US* a sub-machine-gun

chopper tool *n* a core tool of flint or stone, with a transverse cutting edge, characteristic of cultures in Asia and parts of the Middle East and Europe

choppy (ˈtʃɒpɪ) *adj* **-pier, -piest** (of the sea, weather, etc) fairly rough > ˈchoppily *adv* > ˈchoppiness *n*

chops (tʃɒps) *pl n* **1** the jaws or cheeks; jowls **2** the mouth **3** *slang* a *music* embouchure b *jazz* skill **4** **lick one's chops** *informal* to anticipate with pleasure [C16 of uncertain origin]

chopsticks (ˈtʃɒpstɪks) *pl n* a pair of thin sticks, of ivory, wood, etc, used as eating utensils by the Chinese, Japanese, and other people of East Asia [C17 from pidgin English, from *chop* quick, of Chinese dialect origin + STICK[1]]

chop suey (ˈsuːɪ) *n* a Chinese-style dish originating in the US, consisting of meat or chicken, bean sprouts, etc, stewed and served with rice [C19 from Chinese (Cantonese) *tsap sui* odds and ends]

choragus (kɒˈreɪgəs) *n, pl* **-gi** (-dʒaɪ) *or* **-guses** **1** (in ancient Greek drama) a the leader of a chorus b a sponsor of a chorus **2** a conductor of a festival [C17 from Latin, from Greek *khoragos*, from *khoros*

CHORUS + *agein* to lead] > **choragic** (kɒˈrædʒɪk, -ˈreɪ-) *adj*

choral (ˈkɔːrəl) *adj* **1** relating to, sung by, or designed for a chorus or choir ▷ *n* (kɒˈrɑːl) **2** a variant spelling of **chorale**. > ˈchorally *adv*

chorale *or* **choral** (kɒˈrɑːl) *n* **1** a slow stately hymn tune, esp of the Lutheran Church **2** *chiefly US* a choir or chorus [C19 from German *Choralgesang*, translation of Latin *cantus chorālis* choral song]

chorale prelude *n* a composition for organ using a chorale as a cantus firmus or as the basis for variations

chord[1] (kɔːd) *n* **1** *maths* a straight line connecting two points on a curve or curved surface b the line segment lying between two points of intersection of a straight line and a curve or curved surface **2** *engineering* one of the principal members of a truss, esp one that lies along the top or the bottom **3** *anatomy* a variant spelling of **cord** **4** an emotional response, esp one of sympathy: *the story struck the right chord* **5** an imaginary straight line joining the leading edge and the trailing edge of an aerofoil **6** *archaic* the string of a musical instrument [C16 from Latin *chorda*, from Greek *khordē* gut, string; see CORD] > ˈchorded *adj*

chord[2] (kɔːd) *n* **1** the simultaneous sounding of a group of musical notes, usually three or more in number. See **concord** (sense 4), **discord** (sense 3) ▷ *vb* **2** (*tr*) to provide (a melodic line) with chords [C15 short for ACCORD; spelling influenced by CHORD[1]] > ˈchordal *adj*

chordate (ˈkɔːˌdeɪt) *n* **1** any animal of the phylum *Chordata*, including the vertebrates and protochordates, characterized by a notochord, dorsal tubular nerve cord, and pharyngeal gill slits ▷ *adj* **2** of, relating to, or belonging to the *Chordata* [C19 from Medieval Latin *chordata*; see CHORD[1] + -ATE[1]]

chording (ˈkɔːdɪŋ) *n music* **1** the distribution of chords throughout a piece of harmony **2** the intonation of a group of instruments or voices

chordophone (ˈkɔːdəˌfəʊn) *n* any musical instrument producing sounds through the vibration of strings, such as the piano, harp, violin, or guitar

chord symbol *n music* any of a series of letters and numerals, used as a shorthand indication of chords, esp in jazz, folk, or pop music: *B7 indicates the dominant seventh chord in the key of E*

chordwise (ˈkɔːdˌwaɪz) *adv* **1** in the direction of an aerofoil chord ▷ *adj* **2** moving in this direction: *chordwise force*

chore (tʃɔː) *n* **1** a small routine task, esp a domestic one **2** an unpleasant task [C19 variant of Middle English *chare*; related to CHAR[3]]

-chore *n combining form* (in botany) indicating a plant distributed by a certain means: *anemochore* [from Greek *khōrein* to move] > **-chorous** *or* **-choric** *adj combining form*

chorea (kɒˈrɪə) *n* a disorder of the central nervous system characterized by uncontrollable irregular brief jerky movements. See **Huntington's disease, Sydenham's chorea** [C19 from New Latin, from Latin: dance, from Greek *khoreia*, from *khoros* dance; see CHORUS] > choˈreal *or* choˈreic *adj*

choreo- *combining form* indicating the art of dancing or ballet: *choreodrama; choreography* [from Greek *khoreios*, from *khoros* dance]

choreodrama (ˌkɒrɪəʊˈdrɑːmə) *n dancing* dance drama performed by a group

choreograph (ˈkɒrɪəˌgrɑːf) *vb* (*tr*) to compose the steps and dances for (a piece of music or ballet)

choreography (ˌkɒrɪˈɒɡrəfɪ) *or* **choregraphy** (kɒˈrɛɡrəfɪ) *n* **1** the composition of dance steps and sequences for ballet and stage dancing **2** the steps and sequences of a ballet or dance **3** the notation representing such steps **4** the art of dancing [C18 from Greek *khoreia* dance + -GRAPHY] > ˌchoreˈographer *or* choˈregrapher *n* > **choreographic** (ˌkɒrɪəˈɡræfɪk) *or* choregraphic

(ˌkɒrəˈɡræfɪk) *adj* > ˌchoreoˈgraphically *or* ˌchoreˈgraphically *adv*

choriamb (ˈkɒrɪˌæmb) *or* **choriambus** (ˌkɒrɪˈæmbəs) *n, pl* **-ambs** *or* **-ambi** (-ˈæmbaɪ) *prosody* a metrical foot used in classical verse consisting of four syllables, two short ones between two long ones (----) [c19 from Late Latin *choriambus*, from Greek *khoriambos*, from *khoreios* trochee, of a chorus, from *khoros* CHORUS] > ˌchoriˈambic *adj*

choric (ˈkɒrɪk) *adj* of, like, for, or in the manner of a chorus, esp in singing, dancing, or the speaking of verse

chorion (ˈkɔːrɪən) *n* the outer of two membranes (see also **amnion**) that form a sac around the embryonic reptile, bird, or mammal: contributes to the placenta in mammals [c16 from Greek *khorion* afterbirth] > ˌchoriˈonic *or* ˈchorial *adj*

chorionic gonadotrophin *n* a hormone secreted by the chorionic villi of the placenta in mammals, esp **human chorionic gonadotrophin**. It promotes the secretion of progesterone by the corpus luteum and its presence in the urine is an indication of pregnancy

chorionic villus sampling *n* a method of diagnosing genetic disorders early in pregnancy by the removal by catheter through the cervix or abdomen of a tiny sample of tissue from the chorionic villi. Abbreviation: **CVS**

chorister (ˈkɒrɪstə) *n* a singer in a choir, esp a choirboy [c14 from Medieval Latin *chorista*]

chorizo (tʃɔːˈriːzəʊ) *n, pl* **-zos** a kind of highly seasoned pork sausage of Spain or Mexico [c19 Spanish]

C horizon *n* the layer of a soil profile immediately below the B horizon and above the bedrock, composed of weathered rock little affected by soil-forming processes

Chorley (ˈtʃɔːlɪ) *n* a town in NW England, in S Lancashire: cotton textiles. Pop: 33 424 (2001)

chorography (kɒˈrɒɡrəfɪ) *n geography* **1** the technique of mapping regions **2** *pl* **-phies** a description or map of a region, as opposed to a small area [c16 via Latin from Greek *khōrographia*, from *khōros* place, country + -GRAPHY] > choˈrographer *n* > chorographic (ˌkɒrəˈɡræfɪk) *or* ˌchoroˈgraphical *adj* > ˌchoroˈgraphically *adv*

choroid (ˈkɔːrɔɪd) *or* **chorioid** (ˈkɔːrɪˌɔɪd) *adj* **1** resembling the chorion, esp in being vascular ▷ *n* **2** the brownish vascular membrane of the eyeball between the sclera and the retina [c18 from Greek *khoroeidēs*, erroneously for *khorioeidēs*, from CHORION]

choroid plexus *n* a multilobed vascular membrane, projecting into the cerebral ventricles, that secretes cerebrospinal fluid

chorology (kəˈrɒlədʒɪ) *n* **1** the study of the causal relations between geographical phenomena occurring within a particular region **2** the study of the spatial distribution of organisms [c20 from German *Chorologie*, from Greek *khōros* place + -LOGY] > choˈrologist *n*

choropleth (ˈkɔːrəˌplɛθ) *n* **a** a symbol or marked and bounded area on a map denoting the distribution of some property **b** (*as modifier*): *a choropleth map* [c20 from Gk *khōra* place + *plēthos* multitude]

chorrie (ˈtʃɒrɪ) *n South African informal* a dilapidated old car [c20 from Afrikaans *tjor* a crock]

chortle (ˈtʃɔːtᵊl) *vb* **1** (*intr*) to chuckle gleefully ▷ *n* **2** a gleeful chuckle [c19 coined (1871) by Lewis Carroll in *Through the Looking-glass*; probably a blend of CHUCKLE + SNORT] > ˈchortler *n*

chorus (ˈkɔːrəs) *n, pl* **-ruses** **1** a large choir of singers or a piece of music composed for such a choir **2** a body of singers or dancers who perform together, in contrast to principals or soloists **3** a section of a song in which a soloist is joined by a group of singers, esp in a recurring refrain **4** an intermediate section of a pop song, blues, etc, as distinct from the verse **5** *jazz* any of a series of variations on a theme **6** (in ancient Greece) **a** a lyric poem sung by a group of dancers, originally as a religious rite **b** an ode or series of odes sung by a group of actors **7 a** (in classical Greek drama) the actors who sang the chorus and commented on the action of the play **b** actors playing a similar role in any drama **8 a** (esp in Elizabethan drama) the actor who spoke the prologue, etc **b** the part of the play spoken by this actor **9** a group of people or animals producing words or sounds simultaneously **10** any speech, song, or other utterance produced by a group of people or animals simultaneously: *a chorus of sighs; the dawn chorus* **11 in chorus** in unison ▷ *vb* **12** to speak, sing, or utter (words, etc) in unison [c16 from Latin, from Greek *khoros*]

chorus girl *n* a girl who dances or sings in the chorus of a musical comedy, revue, etc

chorusmaster (ˈkɔːrəsˌmɑːstə) *n* the conductor of a choir

chorus pedal *n music* an electronic device that creates the effect of more than one sound from a single source by combining a short delay with slight deviations in pitch

Chorzów (*Polish* ˈxɔʒuf) *n* an industrial city in SW Poland: under German administration from 1794 to 1921. Pop: 121 708 (1999 est). German name: **Königshütte**

chose[1] (tʃəʊz) *vb* the past tense of **choose**

chose[2] (ʃəʊz) *n law* an article of personal property [c17 from French: thing, from Latin *causa* cause, case, reason]

chosen (ˈtʃəʊzᵊn) *vb* **1** the past participle of **choose** ▷ *adj* **2** selected or picked out, esp for some special quality

Chosen (ˈtʃəʊˈsɛn) *n* the official name for **Korea** as a Japanese province (1910–45)

chosen people *pl n* any of various peoples believing themselves to be chosen by God, esp the Jews

Chosŏn (ˈtʃəʊˈsɒn) *n* the Korean name for **North Korea**

Chota Nagpur (ˈtʃəʊtə ˈnɑːɡpʊə) *n* a plateau in E India, mainly in Jharkhand state since 2000: forested, with rich mineral resources and much heavy industry; produces chiefly lac (world's leading supplier), coal (half India's total output), and mica

chott (ʃɒt) *n* a variant spelling of **shott**

chou (ʃuː) *n, pl* **choux** (ʃuː) **1** a type of cabbage **2** a rosette **3** a round cream bun [c18 (a bun): from French, from Latin *caulis* cabbage]

Chou (tʃəʊ) *or* **Zhou** *n* the imperial dynasty of China from about 1126 to 255 BC

chough (tʃʌf) *n* **1** a large black passerine bird, *Pyrrhocorax pyrrhocorax*, of parts of Europe, Asia, and Africa, with a long downward-curving red bill: family *Corvidae* (crows) **2 alpine chough** a smaller related bird, *Pyrrhocorax graculus*, with a shorter yellow bill [c14 of uncertain origin; probably related to Old French *cauwe*, Old English *cēo*]

choux pastry (ʃuː) *n* a very light pastry made with eggs, used for eclairs, etc [partial translation of French *pâte choux* cabbage dough (from its round shape)]

chow (tʃaʊ) *n* **1** *informal* food **2** short for **chow-chow** (sense 1) ▷ See also **chow down**

chow-chow *n* **1** a thick-coated breed of the spitz type of dog with a curled tail and a characteristic blue-black tongue; it came originally from China. Often shortened to: **chow 2** a Chinese preserve of ginger, orange peel, etc in syrup **3** a mixed vegetable pickle [c19 from pidgin English, probably based on Mandarin Chinese *cha* miscellaneous]

chowder (ˈtʃaʊdə) *n* a thick soup or stew containing clams or fish [c18 from French *chaudière* kettle, from Late Latin *caldāria*; see CAULDRON]

chow down *vb* (*intr, adverb;* foll by *on*) *informal* to eat heartily

chowk (tʃaʊk) *n* (in the Indian subcontinent) **1** (*often in place names*) a marketplace or market area: *Vijay Chowk* **2** a courtyard **3** a road junction or roundabout [from Hindi *cauk*]

chow mein (meɪn) *n* a Chinese-American dish, consisting of mushrooms, meat, shrimps, etc, served with fried noodles [from Chinese (Cantonese), variant of Mandarin *ch'ao mien* fried noodles]

chrematistic (ˌkriːməˈtɪstɪk) *adj* of, denoting, or relating to money-making [c18 from Greek, from *khrēmatizein* to make money, from *khrēma* money] > ˌchremaˈtistics *n*

chresard (ˈkrɛsəd) *n* the amount of water present in the soil that is available to plants [c20 from Greek *khrēsis* use (from *khrēsthai* to use) + *ardein* to water]

chrestomathy (krɛsˈtɒməθɪ) *n, pl* **-thies** *rare* a collection of literary passages, used in the study of language [c19 from Greek *khrēstomatheia*, from *khrēstos* useful + *mathein* to learn] > **chrestomathic** (ˌkrɛstəʊˈmæθɪk) *adj*

Chrimbo *or* **Crimbo** (ˈkrɪmbəʊ) *n Brit* an informal word for **Christmas**

chrism *or* **chrisom** (ˈkrɪzəm) *n* a mixture of olive oil and balsam used for sacramental anointing in the Greek Orthodox and Roman Catholic Churches [Old English *crisma*, from Medieval Latin, from Greek *khrisma* unction, from *khriein* to anoint] > **chrismal** (ˈkrɪzməl) *adj*

chrismation (ˌkrɪzˈmeɪʃən) *n Greek Orthodox Church* a rite of initiation involving anointing with chrism and taking place at the same time as baptism

chrismatory (ˈkrɪzmətərɪ, -trɪ) *n, pl* **-ries** *RC Church* a small receptacle containing the three kinds of consecrated oil used in the sacraments

chrisom (ˈkrɪzəm) *n* **1** *Christianity* a white robe put on an infant at baptism and formerly used as a burial shroud if the infant died soon afterwards **2** *archaic* an infant wearing such a robe **3** a variant spelling of **chrism**

Chrissie (ˈkrɪsɪ) *n chiefly Austral* a slang name for **Christmas**

Christ (kraɪst) *n* **1** Jesus of Nazareth (Jesus Christ), regarded by Christians as fulfilling Old Testament prophecies of the Messiah **2** the Messiah or anointed one of God as the subject of Old Testament prophecies **3** an image or picture of Christ ▷ *interj* **4** *taboo slang* an oath expressing annoyance, surprise, etc ▷ See also **Jesus** [Old English *Crīst*, from Latin *Chrīstus*, from Greek *khristos* anointed one, from *khriein* to anoint), translating Hebrew *māshīah* MESSIAH] > ˈChristly *adj*

Christadelphian (ˌkrɪstəˈdɛlfɪən) *n* **1** a member of a Christian millenarian sect founded in the US about 1848, holding that only the just will enter eternal life, that the wicked will be annihilated, and that the ignorant, the unconverted, and infants will not be raised from the dead ▷ *adj* **2** of or relating to this body or its beliefs and practices [c19 from Late Greek *khristadelphos*, from *khristos* CHRIST + *adelphos* brother]

Christchurch (ˈkraɪstˌtʃɜːtʃ) *n* **1** a city in New Zealand, on E South Island: manufacturing centre of a rich agricultural region. Pop: 344 100 (2004 est) **2** a town and resort in S England, in SE Dorset. Pop: 40 208 (2001)

christcross (ˈkrɪsˌkrɒs) *n archaic* **1 a** the mark of a cross formerly placed in front of the alphabet in hornbooks **b** the alphabet itself **2** a cross used in place of a signature by someone unable to sign his name

christen (ˈkrɪsᵊn) *vb* (*tr*) **1** to give a Christian name to in baptism as a sign of incorporation into a Christian Church **2** another word for **baptize 3** to give a name to (anything), esp with some ceremony **4** *informal* to use for the first time [Old English *cristnian*, from *Crīst* CHRIST] > ˈchristener *n*

Christendom (ˈkrɪsᵊndəm) *n* **1** the collective body of Christians throughout the world or throughout history **2** an obsolete word for **Christianity**

christening (ˈkrɪsᵊnɪŋ) *n* the Christian sacrament

of baptism or the ceremony in which this is conferred

Christhood ('kraɪsthʊd) *n* the state of being the Christ, the anointed one of God

Christian ('krɪstʃən) *n* 1 a a person who believes in and follows Jesus Christ b a member of a Christian Church or denomination 2 *informal* a person who possesses Christian virtues, esp practical ones ▷ *adj* 3 of, relating to, or derived from Jesus Christ, his teachings, example, or his followers 4 (*sometimes not capital*) exhibiting kindness or goodness > '**Christianly** *adj, adv*

Christian Action *n* an inter-Church movement formed in 1946 to promote Christian ideals in society at large

Christian Brothers *pl n RC Church* a religious congregation of laymen founded in France in 1684 for the education of the poor. Also called: **Brothers of the Christian Schools**

Christian Democracy *n* the beliefs, principles, practices, or programme of a Christian Democratic party > **Christian Democratic** *adj*

Christian Democrat *n* 1 a member or supporter of a Christian Democratic party ▷ *adj* 2 of or relating to a Christian Democratic party

Christian Democratic Party *n* any of various political parties in Europe and Latin America which combine moderate conservatism with historical links to the Christian Church

Christian Era *n* the period beginning with the year of Christ's birth. Dates in this era are labelled AD, those previous to it BC. Also called: **Common Era**

Christiania (ˌkrɪstɪ'ɑːnɪə) *n* a former name (1624–1877) of **Oslo**

Christianity (ˌkrɪstɪ'ænɪtɪ) *n* 1 the Christian religion 2 Christian beliefs, practices or attitudes 3 a less common word for **Christendom** (sense 1)

Christianize or **Christianise** ('krɪstʃəˌnaɪz) *vb* (*tr*) 1 to make Christian or convert to Christianity 2 to imbue with Christian principles, spirit, or outlook > ˌ**Christiani'zation** or ˌ**Christiani'sation** *n* > '**Christian,izer** or '**Christian,iser** *n*

Christian name *n* a personal name formally given to Christians at christening. The term is loosely used to mean any person's first name as distinct from his or her surname. Also called: **first name, forename, given name**

Christiansand ('krɪstʃənˌsænd; *Norwegian* kristian'san) *n* a variant spelling of **Kristiansand**

Christian Science *n* the religious system and teaching of the Church of Christ, Scientist. It was founded by Mary Baker Eddy (1866) and emphasizes spiritual healing and the unreality of matter > **Christian Scientist** *n*

Christingle (ˌkrɪs'tɪŋɡ°l) *n* (in Britain) a Christian service for children held shortly before Christmas, in which each child is given a decorated fruit with a lighted candle in it [C20 from CHRISTMAS + INGLE]

Christlike ('kraɪst,laɪk) *adj* resembling or showing the spirit of Jesus Christ > '**Christ,likeness** *n*

Christmas ('krɪsməs) *n* 1 a the annual commemoration by Christians of the birth of Jesus Christ on Dec 25 b Also called: **Christmas Day** Dec 25, observed as a day of secular celebrations when gifts and greetings are exchanged c (*as modifier*): *Christmas celebrations* 2 Also called: **Christmas Day** (in England, Wales and Ireland) Dec 25, one of the four quarter days. Compare **Lady Day, Midsummer's Day, Michaelmas** 3 Also called: **Christmastide** the season of Christmas extending from Dec 24 (Christmas Eve) to Jan 6 (the festival of the Epiphany or Twelfth Night) [Old English *Crīstes mæsse* MASS of CHRIST]

Christmas beetle *n* any of various greenish-gold Australian scarab beetles of the genus *Anoplognathus*, which are common in summer

Christmas box *n* a tip or present given at Christmas, esp to postmen, tradesmen, etc

Christmas cactus *n* a Brazilian cactus, *Schlumbergera* (formerly *Zygocactus*) *truncatus*, widely cultivated as an ornamental for its showy red flowers

Christmas card *n* a greeting card sent at Christmas

Christmas disease *n* a relatively mild type of haemophilia, caused by lack of a protein (**Christmas factor**) implicated in the process of blood clotting [C20 named after S. *Christmas*, the first patient suffering from the disease who was examined in detail]

Christmas Eve *n* the evening or the whole day before Christmas Day

Christmas Island *n* 1 the former name (until 1981) of **Kiritimati** 2 an island in the Indian Ocean, south of Java: administered by Singapore (1900–58), now by Australia; phosphate mining. Pop: 1500 (2004 est). Area: 135 sq km (52 sq miles)

Christmas pudding *n Brit* a rich steamed pudding containing suet, dried fruit, spices, brandy, etc, served at Christmas. Also called: **plum pudding**

Christmas rose *n* an evergreen ranunculaceous plant, *Helleborus niger*, of S Europe and W Asia, with white or pinkish winter-blooming flowers. Also called: **hellebore, winter rose**

Christmas stocking *n* a stocking hung up by children on Christmas Eve for Santa Claus to fill with presents

Christmassy ('krɪsməsɪ) *adj* of, relating to, or suitable for Christmas

Christmastide ('krɪsməsˌtaɪd) *n* another name for **Christmas** (sense 3)

Christmas tree *n* 1 an evergreen tree or an imitation of one, decorated as part of Christmas celebrations 2 Also called: **Christmas bush** *Austral* any of various trees or shrubs flowering at Christmas and used for decoration 3 another name for **pohutukawa**

Christo- *combining form* indicating or relating to Christ: *Christology*

Christology (krɪ'stɒlədʒɪ, kraɪ-) *n* the branch of theology concerned with the person, attributes, and deeds of Christ > **Christological** (ˌkrɪstə'lɒdʒɪk°l) *adj* > **Chris'tologist** *n*

Christ's-thorn *n* any of several rhamnaceous plants of SW Asia, such as *Paliurus spina-christi* or the jujube, that have thorny stems and are popularly believed to have been used for Christ's Crown of Thorns

Christy or **Christie** ('krɪstɪ) *n, pl* -**ties** (*sometimes not capital*) *skiing* a turn in which the body is swung sharply round with the skis parallel, originating in Norway and used for stopping, slowing down, or changing direction quickly [C20 shortened from CHRISTIANIA]

chroma ('krəʊmə) *n* 1 the attribute of a colour that enables an observer to judge how much chromatic colour it contains irrespective of achromatic colour present. See also **saturation** (sense 4) 2 (in colour television) the colour component in a composite coded signal [C19 from Greek *khrōma* colour]

chromakey ('krəʊməˌkiː) *n* (in colour television) a special effect in which a coloured background can be eliminated and a different background substituted. Also called: **colour separation overlay**

chromate ('krəʊˌmeɪt) *n* any salt or ester of chromic acid. Simple chromate salts contain the divalent ion, CrO_4^{2-}, and are orange

chromatic (krə'mætɪk) *adj* 1 of, relating to, or characterized by a colour or colours 2 *music* a involving the sharpening or flattening of notes or the use of such notes in chords and harmonic progressions b of or relating to the chromatic scale or an instrument capable of producing it: *a chromatic harmonica* c of or relating to chromaticism. Compare **diatonic** [C17 from Greek *khrōmatikos*, from *khrōma* colour] > **chro'matically** *adv* > **chro'maticism** *n*

chromatic aberration *n* a defect in a lens system in which different wavelengths of light are focused at different distances because they are refracted through different angles. It produces a blurred image with coloured fringes

chromatic adaptation *n botany* the alteration by photosynthesizing organisms of the proportions of their photosynthetic pigments in response to the intensity and colour of the available light, as shown by algae in the littoral zone, which change from green to red as the zone is descended

chromatic colour *n physics* a formal term for **colour** (sense 2)

chromaticity (ˌkrəʊmə'tɪsɪtɪ) *n* the quality of a colour or light with reference to its purity and its dominant wavelength

chromaticity coordinates *pl n physics* three numbers used to specify a colour, each of which is equal to one of the three tristimulus values divided by their sum. Symbols: x, y, z

chromaticity diagram *n physics* a diagram in which values of two chromaticity coordinates are marked on a pair of rectangular axes, a point in the plane of these axes representing the chromaticity of any colour

chromaticness (krəʊ'mætɪknɪs) *n physics* the attribute of colour that involves both hue and saturation

chromatics (krəʊ'mætɪks) or **chromatology** (ˌkrəʊmə'tɒlədʒɪ) *n* (*functioning as singular*) the science of colour > **chromatist** ('krəʊmətɪst) or ˌ**chroma'tologist** *n*

chromatic scale *n* a twelve-note scale including all the semitones of the octave

chromatid ('krəʊmətɪd) *n* either of the two strands into which a chromosome divides during mitosis. They separate to form daughter chromosomes at anaphase

chromatin ('krəʊmətɪn) *n cytology* the part of the nucleus that consists of DNA and proteins, forms the chromosomes, and stains with basic dyes. See also **euchromatin, heterochromatin** > ˌchroma'tinic *adj* > 'chroma,toid *adj*

chromato- or *before a vowel* **chromat-** *combining form* 1 indicating colour or coloured: *chromatophore* 2 indicating chromatin: *chromatolysis* [from Greek *khrōma, khrōmat-* colour]

chromatogram ('krəʊmətəˌɡræm, krəʊ'mæt-) *n* 1 a column or strip of material containing constituents of a mixture separated by chromatography 2 a graph showing the quantity of a substance leaving a chromatography column as a function of time

chromatography (ˌkrəʊmə'tɒɡrəfɪ) *n* the technique of separating and analysing the components of a mixture of liquids or gases by selective adsorption in, for example, a column of powder (**column chromatography**) or on a strip of paper (**paper chromatography**). See also **gas chromatography**. > ˌchroma'tographer *n* > **chromatographic** (ˌkrəʊmətə'ɡræfɪk) *adj* > ˌchroma'graphically *adv*

chromatology (ˌkrəʊmə'tɒlədʒɪ) *n* another name for **chromatics**

chromatolysis (ˌkrəʊmə'tɒlɪsɪs) *n cytology* the dissolution of stained material, such as chromatin in injured cells

chromatophore ('krəʊmətəˌfɔː) *n* 1 a cell in the skin of frogs, chameleons, etc, in which pigment is concentrated or dispersed, causing the animal to change colour 2 another name for **chromoplast**. > ˌchromato'phoric or **chromatophorous** (ˌkrəʊmə'tɒfərəs) *adj*

chrome (krəʊm) *n* 1 a another word for **chromium**, esp when present in a pigment or dye b (*as modifier*): *a chrome dye* 2 anything plated with chromium, such as fittings on a car body 3 a pigment or dye that contains chromium ▷ *vb* 4 to plate or be plated with chromium, usually by electroplating 5 to treat or be treated with a chromium compound, as in dyeing or tanning [C19 via French from Greek *khrōma* colour]

-chrome *n and adj combining form* colour, coloured, or pigment: *monochrome* [from Greek *khrōma* colour]

chrome alum *n* a violet-red crystalline substance, used as a mordant in dyeing. Formula: $KCr(SO_4)_2.12H_2O$

chrome dioxide *n* another name for **chromium dioxide**

chrome green *n* **1** any green pigment made by mixing lead chromate with Prussian blue **2** any green pigment containing chromic oxide

chromel ('krəʊmɛl) *n* a nickel-based alloy containing about 10 per cent chromium, used in heating elements [c20 from CHRO(MIUM) + ME(TA)L]

chrome red *n* any red pigment used in paints, consisting of a mixture of lead chromate and lead oxide; basic lead chromate

chrome steel *n* any of various hard rust-resistant steels containing chromium. Also called: chromium steel

chrome tape *n* magnetic recording tape coated with chrome dioxide

chrome yellow *n* any yellow pigment consisting of lead chromate mixed with lead sulphate

chromic ('krəʊmɪk) *adj* **1** of or containing chromium in the trivalent state **2** of or derived from chromic acid

chromic acid *n* an unstable dibasic oxidizing acid known only in solution and in the form of chromate salts. Formula: H_2CrO_4

chrominance ('krəʊmɪnəns) *n* **1** the quality of light that causes the sensation of colour. It is determined by comparison with a reference source of the same brightness and of known chromaticity **2** the information that defines the colour (hue and saturation) of a television image, but not the brightness [c20 from CHROMO- + LUMINANCE]

chromite ('krəʊmaɪt) *n* **1** a brownish-black mineral consisting of a ferrous chromic oxide in cubic crystalline form, occurring principally in basic igneous rocks: the only commercial source of chromium and its compounds. Formula: $FeCr_2O_4$ **2** a salt of chromous acid

chromium ('krəʊmɪəm) *n* a hard grey metallic element that takes a high polish, occurring principally in chromite: used in steel alloys and electroplating to increase hardness and corrosion-resistance. Symbol: Cr; atomic no.: 24; atomic wt.: 51.9961; valency: 2, 3, or 6; relative density: 7.18–7.20; melting pt.: 1863±20°C; boiling pt.: 2672°C [c19 from New Latin, from French: CHROME]

chromium dioxide *n* a chemical compound used as a magnetic coating on cassette tapes; chromium(IV) oxide. Formula: CrO_2. Also called (not in technical usage): chrome dioxide

chromium steel *n* another name for **chrome steel**

chromo ('krəʊməʊ) *n, pl* -mos short for **chromolithograph**

chromo- *or before a vowel* **chrom-** *combining form* **1** indicating colour, coloured, or pigment: *chromogen* **2** indicating chromium: *chromyl* [from Greek *khrōma* colour]

chromogen ('krəʊmədʒən) *n* **1** a compound that forms coloured compounds on oxidation **2** a substance that can be converted to a dye **3** a bacterium that produces a pigment

chromogenic (ˌkrəʊməʊ'dʒɛnɪk) *adj* **1** producing colour **2** of or relating to a chromogen **3** *photog* involving the use of chromogens rather than silver halide during processing to produce the image: *chromogenic film*

chromolithograph (ˌkrəʊməʊ'lɪθəˌɡrɑːf, -ˌɡræf) *n* a picture produced by chromolithography

chromolithography (ˌkrəʊməʊlɪ'θɒɡrəfɪ) *n* the process of making coloured prints by lithography > ˌchromoli'thographer *n* > chromolithographic (ˌkrəʊməʊˌlɪθə'ɡræfɪk) *adj*

chromomere ('krəʊməˌmɪə) *n cytology* any of the dense areas of chromatin along the length of a chromosome during the early stages of cell division

chromonema (ˌkrəʊmə'niːmə) *n, pl* -mata (-mətə) *cytology* **1** the coiled mass of threads visible within a nucleus at the start of cell division **2** a coiled chromatin thread within a single chromosome [c20 from CHROMO- + Greek *nēma* thread, yarn] > ˌchromo'nemal, chromonematic (ˌkrəʊməʊnɪ'mætɪk) *or* ˌchromo'nemic *adj*

chromophore ('krəʊməˌfɔː) *n* a group of atoms in a chemical compound that is responsible for the colour of the compound > ˌchromo'phoric *or* ˌchromo'phorous *adj*

chromoplast ('krəʊməˌplæst) *n* a coloured plastid in a plant cell, esp one containing carotenoids

chromoprotein (ˌkrəʊməʊ'prəʊtiːn) *n* any of a group of conjugated proteins, such as haemoglobin, in which the protein is joined to a coloured compound, such as a metal-containing porphyrin

chromosome ('krəʊməˌsəʊm) *n* any of the microscopic rod-shaped structures that appear in a cell nucleus during cell division, consisting of nucleoprotein arranged into units (genes) that are responsible for the transmission of hereditary characteristics. See also **homologous chromosomes**. > ˌchromo'somal *adj* > ˌchromo'somally *adv*

chromosome band *n* any of the transverse bands that appear on a chromosome after staining. The banding pattern is unique to each type of chromosome, allowing characterization

chromosome map *n* a graphic representation of the positions of genes on chromosomes, obtained by observation of chromosome bands or by determining the degree of linkage between genes. See also **genetic map**. > chromosome mapping *n*

chromosome number *n* the number of chromosomes present in each somatic cell, which is constant for any one species of plant or animal. In the reproductive cells this number is halved. See also **diploid** (sense 1), **haploid**

chromosphere ('krəʊməˌsfɪə) *n* a gaseous layer of the sun's atmosphere extending from the photosphere to the corona and visible during a total eclipse of the sun > chromospheric (ˌkrəʊmə'sferɪk) *adj*

chromous ('krəʊməs) *adj* of or containing chromium in the divalent state

chromyl ('krəʊmɪl) *n* (*modifier*) of, consisting of, or containing the divalent radical CrO_2

Chron. *Bible abbreviation for* Chronicles

chronaxie *or* **chronaxy** ('krəʊnæksɪ) *n physiol* the minimum time required for excitation of a nerve or muscle when the stimulus is double the minimum (threshold) necessary to elicit a basic response. Compare **rheobase** [c20 from French, from CHRONO- + Greek *axia* worth, from *axios* worthy, of equal weight]

chronic ('krɒnɪk) *adj* **1** continuing for a long time; constantly recurring **2** (of a disease) developing slowly, or of long duration. Compare **acute** (sense 7) **3** inveterate; habitual: *a chronic smoker* **4** *informal* **a** very bad: *the play was chronic* **b** very serious: *he left her in a chronic condition* [c15 from Latin *chronicus* relating to time, from Greek *khronikos*, from *khronos* time] > 'chronically *adv* > chronicity (krɒ'nɪsɪtɪ) *n*

chronic fatigue syndrome *n* another name for **myalgic encephalopathy** Abbreviation: CFS

chronicle ('krɒnɪkᵊl) *n* **1** a record or register of events in chronological order ▷ *vb* **2** (*tr*) to record in or as if in a chronicle [c14 from Anglo-French *cronicle*, via Latin *chronica* (pl) from Greek *khronika* annals, from *khronikos* relating to time; see CHRONIC] > 'chronicler *n*

chronicle play *n* a drama based on a historical subject

Chronicles ('krɒnɪkᵊlz) *n* (*functioning as singular*) either of two historical books (I and II Chronicles) of the Old Testament

chrono- *or before a vowel* **chron-** *combining form* indicating time: *chronology; chronometer* [from Greek *khronos* time]

chronobiology (ˌkrɒnəbaɪ'ɒlədʒɪ, ˌkrəʊnə-) *n* the branch of biology concerned with the periodicity occurring in living organisms. See also **biological clock, circadian**. > ˌchronobi'ologist *n*

chronogram ('krɒnəˌgræm, 'krəʊnə-) *n* **1** a phrase or inscription in which letters such as M, C, X, L and V can be read as Roman numerals giving a date **2** a record kept by a chronograph > chronogrammatic (ˌkrɒnəʊɡrə'mætɪk) *or* ˌchronogram'matical *adj* > ˌchronogram'matically *adv*

chronograph ('krɒnəˌɡrɑːf, -ˌɡræf, 'krəʊnə-) *n* **1** an accurate instrument for recording small intervals of time **2** any timepiece, esp a wristwatch designed for maximum accuracy > chronographer (krə'nɒɡrəfə) *n* > chronographic (ˌkrɒnə'ɡræfɪk) *adj* > ˌchrono'graphically *adv*

chronological (ˌkrɒnə'lɒdʒɪkᵊl, ˌkrəʊ-) *or* **chronologic** *adj* **1** (esp of a sequence of events) arranged in order of occurrence **2** relating to or in accordance with chronology > ˌchrono'logically *adv*

chronology (krə'nɒlədʒɪ) *n, pl* -gies **1** the determination of the proper sequence of past events **2** the arrangement of dates, events, etc, in order of occurrence **3** a table or list of events arranged in order of occurrence > chro'nologist *n*

chronometer (krə'nɒmɪtə) *n* a timepiece designed to be accurate in all conditions of temperature, pressure, etc, used esp at sea > chronometric (ˌkrɒnə'mɛtrɪk) *or* ˌchrono'metrical *adj* > ˌchrono'metrically *adv*

chronometry (krə'nɒmɪtrɪ) *n* the science or technique of measuring time with extreme accuracy

chronon ('krəʊnɒn) *n* a unit of time equal to the time that a photon would take to traverse the diameter of an electron: about 10^{-24} seconds

chronoscope ('krɒnəˌskəʊp, 'krəʊnə-) *n* an instrument that registers small intervals of time on a dial, cathode-ray tube, etc > chronoscopic (ˌkrɒnə'skɒpɪk, ˌkrəʊnə-) *adj* > ˌchrono'scopically *adv*

-chroous *or* **-chroic** *adj combining form* coloured in a specified way: *isochroous* [from Greek *khrōs* skin, complexion, colour]

chrysalid ('krɪsəlɪd) *n* **1** another name for **chrysalis** ▷ *adj* also **chrysalidal** (krɪ'sælɪdᵊl) **2** of or relating to a chrysalis

chrysalis ('krɪsəlɪs) *n, pl* chrysalises *or* chrysalides (krɪ'sælɪˌdiːz) **1** the object pupa of a moth or butterfly **2** anything in the process of developing [c17 from Latin *chrȳsallis*, from Greek *khrusallis*, from *khrusos* gold, of Semitic origin; compare Hebrew *harūz* gold]

chrysanthemum (krɪ'sænθəməm) *n* **1** any widely cultivated plant of the genus *Chrysanthemum*, esp *C. morifolium* of China, having brightly coloured showy flower heads: family *Asteraceae* (composites) **2** any other plant of the genus *Chrysanthemum*, such as oxeye daisy [c16 from Latin: marigold, from Greek *khrusanthemon*, from *khrusos* gold + *anthemon* flower]

chrysarobin (ˌkrɪsə'rəʊbɪn) *n* a tasteless odourless powder containing anthraquinone derivatives of araroba, formerly used medicinally to treat chronic skin conditions [c20 from CHRYSO- (referring to its golden colour) + ARAROBA + -IN]

chryselephantine (ˌkrɪsɛlɪ'fæntɪn) *adj* (of ancient Greek statues) made of or overlaid with gold and ivory [c19 from Greek *khruselephantinos*, from *khrusos* gold + *elephas* ivory; see ELEPHANT]

chryso- *or before a vowel* **chrys-** *combining form* indicating gold or the colour of gold: *chryselephantine; chrysolite* [from Greek *khrusos* gold]

chrysoberyl ('krɪsəˌbɛrɪl) *n* a rare very hard greenish-yellow mineral consisting of beryllium aluminate in orthorhombic crystalline form and occurring in coarse granite: used as a gemstone in the form of cat's eye and alexandrite. Formula: $BeAl_2O_4$

chrysolite ('krɪsəˌlaɪt) *n* another name for **olivine** > chrysolitic (ˌkrɪsə'lɪtɪk) *adj*

chrysoprase ('krɪsəˌpreɪz) *n* an apple-green

C

305

variety of chalcedony: a gemstone [C13 *crisopace,* from Old French, from Latin *chrȳsoprasus,* from Greek *khrusoprasos,* from CHRYSO- + *prason* leek]

chrysotile ('krɪsətɪl) *n* a green, grey, or white fibrous mineral, a variety of serpentine, that is an important source of commercial asbestos. Formula: $Mg_3Si_2O_5(OH)_4$ [C20 from CHRYSO- + Greek *tilos* something plucked, shred, thread, from *tillein* to pluck]

chthonian ('θəʊnɪən) or **chthonic** ('θɒnɪk) *adj* of or relating to the underworld [C19 from Greek *khthonios* in or under the earth, from *khthōn* earth]

chub (tʃʌb) *n,* pl chub or chubs **1** a common European freshwater cyprinid game fish, *Leuciscus* (or *Squalius*) *cephalus,* having a cylindrical dark greenish body **2** any of various North American fishes, esp certain whitefishes and minnows [C15 of unknown origin]

Chubb (tʃʌb) *n trademark* a type of patent lock containing a device that sets the bolt immovably if the lock is picked

chubby ('tʃʌbɪ) *adj* -bier, -biest (esp of the human form) plump and round [C17 perhaps from CHUB, with reference to the plump shape of the fish] > 'chubbiness *n*

Chu Chiang ('tʃuː 'kjæŋ, kaɪ'æn) *n* a variant transliteration of the Chinese name for the **Zhu Jiang**

chuck[1] (tʃʌk) *vb* (mainly tr) **1** *informal* to throw **2** to pat affectionately, esp under the chin **3** (sometimes foll by in or up) *informal* to give up; reject: *he chucked up his job; she chucked her boyfriend* **4** (intr; usually foll by up) *slang, chiefly US* to vomit **5** chuck off at *Austral and NZ informal* to abuse or make fun of ▷ *n* **6** a throw or toss **7** a playful pat under the chin **8** the chuck *informal* dismissal ▷ See also **chuck in, chuck out** [C16 of unknown origin]

chuck[2] (tʃʌk) *n* **1** Also called: **chuck steak** a cut of beef extending from the neck to the shoulder blade **2 a** Also called: **three jaw chuck** a device that holds a workpiece in a lathe or tool in a drill, having a number of adjustable jaws geared to move in unison to centralize the workpiece or tool **b** Also called: **four jaw chuck, independent jaw chuck** a similar device having independently adjustable jaws for holding an unsymmetrical workpiece [C17 variant of CHOCK]

chuck[3] (tʃʌk) *vb* **1** (intr) a less common word for **cluck** (sense 2) ▷ *n* **2** a clucking sound **3** a term of endearment [C14 *chukken* to cluck, of imitative origin]

chuck[4] (tʃʌk) *n Canadian W coast* **1** a large body of water **2** short for **saltchuck** (the sea) [C19 from Chinook Jargon, from Nootka *chauk*]

chucker ('tʃʌkə) *n* **1** a person who throws something **2** *cricket informal* a bowler whose arm action is illegal

chuck-full *adj* a less common spelling of **chock-full**

chuckie ('tʃʌkɪ) *n Scot and NZ* a small stone [probably from CHUCK[1]]

chuck in *vb (adverb) informal* **1** (tr) *Brit* to abandon or give up: *chuck in a hopeless attempt* **2** (intr) *Austral* to contribute to the cost of something

chuckle ('tʃʌkᵊl) *vb* (intr) **1** to laugh softly or to oneself **2** (of animals, esp hens) to make a clucking sound ▷ *n* **3** a partly suppressed laugh [C16 probably from CHUCK[3]] > 'chuckler *n* > 'chucklingly *adv*

chucklehead ('tʃʌkᵊl,hɛd) *n informal* a stupid person; blockhead; dolt > 'chuckle,headed *adj* > 'chuckle,headedness *n*

chuck out *vb* (tr, adverb; often foll by of) *informal* to eject forcibly (from); throw out (of): *he was chucked out of the lobby*

chuck wagon *n* a wagon carrying provisions and cooking utensils for men, such as cowboys, who work in the open [C19 perhaps from CHUCK[2] (beef, food)]

chuckwalla ('tʃʌk,wɒlə) *n* a lizard, *Sauromalus obesus,* that has an inflatable body and inhabits

desert regions of the southwestern US: family *Iguanidae* (iguanas) [from Mexican Spanish *chacahuala,* from Shoshonean *tcaxxwal*]

chuck-will's-widow *n* a large North American nightjar, *Caprimulgus carolinensis,* similar to the whippoorwill

chuddar, chudder, chuddah or **chador** ('tʃʌdə) *n* a large shawl or veil worn by Muslim or Hindu women that covers them from head to foot [from Hindi *caddar,* from Persian *chaddar*]

chuddies ('tʃʌdɪz) *pl n Indian informal* underpants [C20 possibly from CHUDDAR]

Chudskoye Ozero (*Russian* 'tʃutskəjɪ 'ɔzɪrə) *n* the Russian name for Lake **Peipus**

chufa ('tʃuːfə) *n* a sedge, *Cyperus esculentus,* of warm regions of the Old World, with nutlike edible tubers [C19 from Old Spanish: a morsel, joke, from *chufar* to joke, from *chuflar* to deride, ultimately from Latin *sībilāre* to whistle]

chuff[1] (tʃʌf) *n* **1** a puffing sound of or as if of a steam engine ▷ *vb* **2** (intr) to move while emitting such sounds: *the train chuffed on its way* [C20 of imitative origin]

chuff[2] (tʃʌf) *n dialect* a boor; churl; sullen fellow [C17 from obsolete *chuff* (n) fat cheek, of obscure origin]

chuff[3] (tʃʌf) *vb* (tr; usually passive) *Brit slang* to please or delight: *he was chuffed by his pay rise* [probably from *chuff* (adj) pleased, happy (earlier: chubby), from C16 *chuff* (obsolete n) a fat cheek, of unknown origin]

chuffed (tʃʌft) *adj Brit slang* pleased or delighted: *none too chuffed*

chuffing ('tʃʌfɪŋ) *adj* (prenominal), *adv Brit slang* (intensifier): *that is the chuffing noise we hear; chuffing marvellous* [C20 from N English *chuff,* a euphemism for *fuck*]

chug (tʃʌg) *n* **1** a short dull sound, esp one that is rapidly repeated, such as that made by an engine ▷ *vb* **chugs, chugging, chugged 2** (intr) (of an engine, etc) to operate while making such sounds [C19 of imitative origin]

chugger ('tʃʌgə) *n informal* a charity worker who approaches people in the street to ask for financial support for the charity, esp regular support by direct debit [C21 CH(ARITY) + (M)UGGER]

chukar (tʃʌ'kɑː) *n* a common Indian partridge, *Alectoris chukar* (or *graeca*), having red legs and bill and a black-barred sandy plumage [from Hindi *cakor,* from Sanskrit *cakora,* probably of imitative origin]

Chukchi or **Chukchee** ('tʃʊktʃɪ) *n* **1** (pl -chi, -chis or -chee, -chees) a member of a people of the Chukchi Peninsula **2** the language of this people, related only to some of the smaller aboriginal languages of Siberia

Chukchi Peninsula *n* a peninsula in the extreme NE of Russia, in NE Siberia: mainly tundra. Also called: Chukot Peninsula ('tʃʊkɒts)

Chukchi Sea *n* part of the Arctic Ocean, north of the Bering Strait between Russia and North America. Russian name: Chukotskoye More (tʃu'kɒtskəjɪ 'mɔrjɪ) Also called: Chukot Sea ('tʃʊkɒts)

Chu Kiang ('tʃuː 'kjæŋ, kaɪ'æn) *n* a variant transliteration of the Chinese name for the **Zhu Jiang**

chukka or *US* **chukker** ('tʃʌkə) *n polo* a period of continuous play, generally lasting 7½ minutes [C20 from Hindi *cakkar,* from Sanskrit *cakra* wheel, circle]

chukka boot or **chukka** *n* an ankle-high boot made of suede or rubber and worn for playing polo

chum[1] (tʃʌm) *n* **1** *informal* a close friend ▷ *vb* **chums, chumming, chummed 2** (intr; usually foll by up with) to be or become an intimate friend (of) **3** (tr) *Scot* to accompany: *I'll chum you home* [C17 (meaning: a person sharing rooms with another): probably shortened from *chamber fellow,* originally student slang (Oxford); compare CRONY]

chum[2] (tʃʌm) *n angling, chiefly US and Canadian*

chopped fish, meal, etc, used as groundbait [C19 origin uncertain]

chum[3] (tʃʌm) *n* a Pacific salmon, *Oncorhynchus keta* [from Chinook Jargon *tsum* spots, marks, from Chinook]

chumash *Hebrew* (xʊ'maʃ; *Yiddish* 'xʊməʃ) *n Judaism* a printed book containing one of the Five Books of Moses [literally: a fifth (part of the Torah)]

chummy ('tʃʌmɪ) *adj* -mier, -miest *informal* friendly > 'chummily *adv* > 'chumminess *n*

chump[1] (tʃʌmp) *n* **1** *informal* a stupid person **2** a thick heavy block of wood **3 a** the thick blunt end of anything, esp of a piece of meat **b** (as modifier): *a chump chop* **4** *Brit slang* the head (esp in the phrase **off one's chump**) [C18 perhaps a blend of CHUNK and LUMP[1]]

chump[2] (tʃʌmp) *vb* a less common word for **chomp**

chumping ('tʃʌmpɪŋ) *n Yorkshire dialect* collecting wood for bonfires on Guy Fawkes Day [from CHUMP[1] sense 2)]

chunder ('tʃʌndə) *slang, chiefly Austral* ▷ *vb* (intr) **1** to vomit ▷ *n* **2** vomit [C20 of uncertain origin]

chunderous ('tʃʌndərəs) *adj Austral slang* nauseating

Chungjin ('tʃʌn'dʒɪn) *n* a variant spelling of **Chŏngjin**

Chungking ('tʃʊŋ'kɪŋ, 'tʃʌŋ-) or **Ch'ung-ch'ing** ('tʃʊŋ'tʃɪŋ, 'tʃʌŋ-) *n* a variant transliteration of the Chinese name for **Chongqing**

chunk (tʃʌŋk) *n* **1** a thick solid piece, as of meat, wood, etc **2** a considerable amount [C17 variant of CHUCK[2]]

chunking ('tʃʌŋkɪŋ) *n psychol* the grouping together of a number of items by the mind, after which they can be remembered as a single item, such as a word or a musical phrase

chunky ('tʃʌŋkɪ) *adj* chunkier, chunkiest **1** thick and short **2** consisting of or containing thick pieces: *chunky dog food* **3** *chiefly Brit* (of clothes, esp knitwear) made of thick bulky material > 'chunkily *adv* > 'chunkiness *n*

Chunnel ('tʃʌnᵊl) *n informal* a rail tunnel beneath the English Channel, linking England and France, opened in 1994 [C20 from CH(ANNEL) + (T)UNNEL]

chunter ('tʃʌntə) or **chunner** ('tʃʌnə) *vb* (intr; often foll by on) *Brit informal* to mutter or grumble incessantly in a meaningless fashion [C16 probably of imitative origin]

chupatti or **chupatty** (tʃə'pætɪ, -'pʌtɪ, -'pɑːtɪ) *n,* pl -patti, -pattis, -patties variant spellings of **chapati**

chuppah or **huppah** ('hʊpə) *n Judaism* **1** the canopy under which a marriage is performed **2** the wedding ceremony as distinct from the celebration [from Hebrew]

Chuquisaca (Spanish tʃuki'saka) *n* the former name (until 1839) of **Sucre**[1]

Chur (German kuːr) *n* a city in E Switzerland, capital of Graubünden canton. Pop: 32 989 (2000). Ancient name: Curia Rhaetorum ('kuːrɪə riː'tɔːrəm, 'kjuː-) French name: Coire

Churban or **Hurban** *Hebrew* (xuːr'bɑn; *Yiddish* 'xuːrbᵊn) *n Judaism* **1** the destruction of the Temple in Jerusalem, first by the Babylonians in 587 BC and again by the Romans in 70 A.D **2** another name for **holocaust** (sense 2) [literally: destruction]

church (tʃɜːtʃ) *n* **1** a building designed for public forms of worship, esp Christian worship **2** an occasion of public worship **3** the clergy as distinguished from the laity **4** (*usually capital*) institutionalized forms of religion as a political or social force: *conflict between Church and State* **5** (*usually capital*) the collective body of all Christians **6** (*often capital*) a particular Christian denomination or group of Christian believers **7** (*often capital*) the Christian religion **8** (in Britain) the practices or doctrines of the Church of England and similar denominations. Compare **chapel** (sense 4b). Related adj: **ecclesiastical** ▷ *vb* (*tr*) **9** *Church of England* to bring (someone, esp a woman after childbirth) to church for special ceremonies **10** *US* to impose church discipline upon [Old English *cirice*, from Late Greek *kurikon*, from Greek *kuriakon* (*dōma*) the Lord's (house), from *kuriakos* of the master, from *kurios* master, from *kuros* power]

Church Army *n* a voluntary Anglican organization founded in 1882 to assist the parish clergy

Church Commissioners *pl n Brit* a group of representatives of Church and State that administers the endowments and property of the Church of England

churchgoer ('tʃɜːˌɡəʊə) *n* **1** a person who attends church regularly **2** an adherent of an established Church in contrast to a Nonconformist > 'church,going *n, adj*

Churchill ('tʃɜːtʃɪl) *n* **1** a river in E Canada, rising in SE Labrador and flowing north and southeast over Churchill Falls, then east to the Atlantic. Length: about 1000 km (600 miles). Former name: **Hamilton River 2** a river in central Canada, rising in NW Saskatchewan and flowing east through several lakes to Hudson Bay. Length: about 1600 km (1000 miles)

Churchill Falls *pl n* a waterfall in E Canada, in SW Labrador on the Churchill River: site of one of the largest hydroelectric power projects in the world. Height: 75 m (245 ft). Former name: **Grand Falls**

church key *n US* a device with a triangular point at one end for making holes in the tops of cans

churchly ('tʃɜːtʃlɪ) *adj* appropriate to, associated with, or suggestive of church life and customs > 'churchliness *n*

churchman ('tʃɜːtʃmən) *n, pl* -men **1** a clergyman **2** a male practising member of a church > 'churchmanly *adj* > 'churchman,ship *n*

church mode *n music* a less common name for **mode** (sense 3a)

Church of Christ, Scientist *n* the official name for the **Christian Scientists**

Church of England *n* the reformed established state Church in England, Catholic in order and basic doctrine, with the Sovereign as its temporal head

Church of Jesus Christ of Latter-Day Saints *n* the official name for the **Mormon Church**

Church of Rome *n* another name for the **Roman Catholic Church**

Church of Scotland *n* the established church in Scotland, Calvinist in doctrine and Presbyterian in constitution

church parade *n* a parade by servicemen or members of a uniformed organization for the purposes of attending religious services

Church Slavonic or **Slavic** *n* Old Church Slavonic, esp as preserved in the liturgical use of the Orthodox church

church text *n* a heavy typeface in Gothic style

churchwarden (ˌtʃɜːtʃ'wɔːdən) *n* **1** *Church of England, Episcopal Church* one of two assistants of a parish priest who administer the secular affairs of the church **2** a long-stemmed tobacco pipe made of clay

churchwoman ('tʃɜːtʃˌwʊmən) *n, pl* -women a female practising member of a church

churchy ('tʃɜːtʃɪ) *adj* churchier, churchiest **1** like a church, church service, etc **2** excessively religious

churchyard ('tʃɜːtʃˌjɑːd) *n* the grounds surrounding a church, usually used as a graveyard

churchyard beetle *n* a blackish nocturnal ground beetle, *Blaps mucronata*, found in cellars and similar places

churidars ('tʃʊrɪˌdɑːz) *pl n* long tight-fitting trousers, worn by Indian men and women. Also called: **churidar pyjamas** [from Hindi]

churinga (tʃə'rɪŋɡə) *n, pl* -ga or -gas a sacred amulet of the native Australians [from a native Australian language]

churl (tʃɜːl) *n* **1** a surly ill-bred person **2** *archaic* a farm labourer **3** a variant spelling of **ceorl** [Old

English *ceorl*; related to Old Norse *karl*, Middle Low German *kerle*, Greek *gerōn* old man]

churlish ('tʃɜːlɪʃ) *adj* **1** rude or surly **2** of or relating to peasants **3** miserly > 'churlishly *adv* > 'churlishness *n*

churn (tʃɜːn) *n* **1** *Brit* a large container for milk **2** a vessel or machine in which cream or whole milk is vigorously agitated to produce butter **3** any similar device ▷ *vb* **4** the number of customers who switch from one supplier to another **5 a** to stir or agitate (milk or cream) in order to make butter **b** to make (butter) by this process **6** (sometimes foll by *up*) to move or cause to move with agitation: *ideas churned in his head* **7** (of a bank, broker, etc) to encourage an investor or policyholder to change investments, endowment policies, etc, to increase commissions at the client's expense **8** (of a government) to pay benefits to a wide category of people and claw it back by taxation from the well off **9** to promote the turnover of existing subscribers leasing, and new subscribers joining, a cable television system or mobile phone company [Old English *ciern*; related to Old Norse *kjarni*, Middle Low German *kerne* churn, German dialect *Kern* cream] > 'churner *n*

churning ('tʃɜːnɪŋ) *n* **1** the quantity of butter churned at any one time **2** the act, process, or effect of someone or something that churns

churn out *vb* (*tr, adverb*) *informal* **1** to produce (something) at a rapid rate: *to churn out ideas* **2** to perform (something) mechanically: *to churn out a song*

churr (tʃɜː) *vb, n* a variant spelling of **chirr**

churrigueresque (ˌtʃʊərɪɡə'rɛsk) or **churrigueresco** *adj* of or relating to a style of baroque architecture of Spain in the late 17th and early 18th centuries [C19 from Spanish *churrigueresco* in the style of José Churriguera (1650–1725), Spanish architect and sculptor]

chute¹ (ʃuːt) *n* **1** an inclined channel or vertical passage down which water, parcels, coal, etc, may be dropped **2** a steep slope, used as a slide as for toboggans **3** a slide into a swimming pool **4** a narrow passageway through which animals file for branding, spraying, etc **5** a rapid or waterfall [C19 from Old French *cheoite*, feminine past participle of *cheoir* to fall, from Latin *cadere*; in some senses, a variant spelling of SHOOT]

chute² (ʃuːt) *n, vb informal* short for **parachute** > 'chutist *n*

chutney ('tʃʌtnɪ) *n* **1** a pickle of Indian origin, made from fruit, vinegar, spices, sugar, etc: *mango chutney* **2** a type of music popular in the Caribbean Asian community, much influenced by calypso [C19 from Hindi *catni*, of uncertain origin]

chutzpah or **hutzpah** ('xʊtspə) *n informal* shameless audacity; impudence [C20 from Yiddish]

Chuvash (tʃʊ'vɑːʃ) *n* **1** (*pl* -vash or -vashes) a member of a Mongoloid people of Russia, living chiefly in the middle Volga region **2** the language of this people, generally classed within the Turkic branch of the Altaic family

Chuvash Republic *n* a constituent republic of W central Russia, in the middle Volga valley: generally low-lying with undulating plains and large areas of forest. Capital: Cheboksary. Pop: 1 313 900 (2002). Area: 18 300 sq km (7064 sq miles). Also called: **Chuvashia** (tʃuː'vɑːʃɪə)

chyack ('tʃaɪæk) *vb* a variant spelling of **chiack**

chyle (kaɪl) *n* a milky fluid composed of lymph and emulsified fat globules, formed in the small intestine during digestion [C17 from Late Latin *chȳlus*, from Greek *khulos* juice pressed from a plant; related to Greek *khein* to pour] > **chylaceous** (kaɪ'leɪʃəs) or **chylous** *adj*

chylomicron (ˌkaɪləʊ'maɪkrɒn) *n biochem* a minute droplet of fat, found in blood and chyle, that is the form in which dietary fat is carried in these fluids

chyme (kaɪm) *n* the thick fluid mass of partially

digested food that leaves the stomach [C17 from Late Latin *chȳmus*, from Greek *khumos* juice; compare CHYLE] > 'chymous *adj*

chymosin ('kaɪməsɪn) *n* another name for **rennin** [C20 from CHYME + -OSE² + -IN]

chymotrypsin (ˌkaɪməʊ'trɪpsɪn) *n* a powerful proteolytic enzyme secreted from the pancreas in the form of chymotrypsinogen, being converted to the active form by trypsin [C20 from CHYME + TRYPSIN]

chymotrypsinogen (ˌkaɪməʊtrɪp'sɪnədʒɪn) *n* the inactive precursor of chymotrypsin [C20 from CHYMOTRYPSIN + -GEN]

chypre *French* (ʃiprə) *n* a perfume made from sandalwood [literally: Cyprus, where it perhaps originated]

ci the internet domain name for Côte d'Ivoire

Ci *symbol for* curie

CI 1 *abbreviation for* Channel Islands **2** collective intelligence: the ability of a group to solve more problems than its individual members **3** international car registration for Côte d'Ivoire

CIA *abbreviation for* Central Intelligence Agency; a federal US bureau created in 1947 to coordinate and conduct espionage and intelligence activities

ciabatta (tʃə'bætə) *n* a type of open-textured bread made with olive oil [C20 from Italian, literally: slipper]

ciao *Italian* (tʃau) *sentence substitute* an informal word for **hello** or **goodbye**

CIB (in New Zealand) *abbreviation for* Criminal Investigation Branch (of New Zealand police)

ciborium (sɪ'bɔːrɪəm) *n, pl* -ria (-rɪə) *Christianity* **1** a goblet-shaped lidded vessel used to hold consecrated wafers in Holy Communion **2** a freestanding canopy fixed over an altar and supported by four pillars [C17 from Medieval Latin, from Latin: drinking cup, from Greek *kibōrion* cup-shaped seed vessel of the Egyptian lotus, hence, a cup]

CICA (in Britain) *abbreviation for* Criminal Injuries Compensation Authority

cicada (sɪ'kɑːdə) or **cicala** *n, pl* -das, -dae (-diː) or -las, -le (-leɪ) any large broad insect of the homopterous family *Cicadidae*, most common in warm regions. Cicadas have membranous wings and the males produce a high-pitched drone by vibration of a pair of drumlike abdominal organs [C19 from Latin]

cicala (sɪ'kɑːlə; *Italian* tʃi'kala) *n, pl* -las or -le (-leɪ; *Italian* -le) another name for **cicada** [C19 from Italian, from Latin: CICADA]

cicatricle ('sɪkəˌtrɪkəl) *n* **1** *zoology* the blastoderm in the egg of a bird **2** *biology* any small scar or mark [C17 from Latin *cicātrīcula* a little scar, from CICATRIX]

cicatrix ('sɪkətrɪks) *n, pl* cicatrices (ˌsɪkə'traɪsiːz) **1** the tissue that forms in a wound during healing; scar **2** a scar on a plant indicating the former point of attachment of a part, esp a leaf [C17 from Latin: scar, of obscure origin] > **cicatricial** (ˌsɪkə'trɪʃəl) *adj* > **cicatricose** (sɪ'kætrɪˌkəʊs, 'sɪkə-) *adj*

cicatrize or **cicatrise** ('sɪkəˌtraɪz) *vb* (of a wound or defect in tissue) to close or be closed by scar formation; heal > **cica'trizant** or **cica'trisant** *adj* > ˌcicatri'zation or ˌcicatri'sation *n* > 'cica,trizer or 'cica,triser *n*

cicely ('sɪsəlɪ) *n, pl* -lies short for **sweet cicely** [C16 from Latin *seselis*, from Greek, of obscure origin; influenced in spelling by the English proper name *Cicely*]

cicero ('sɪsəˌrəʊ) *n, pl* -ros a measure for type that is somewhat larger than the pica [C19 from its first being used in a 15th-century edition of the writings of Marcus Tullius *Cicero* (106–43 BC), the Roman consul, orator, and writer]

cicerone (ˌsɪsə'rəʊnɪ, ˌtʃɪtʃ-) *n, pl* -nes or -ni (-nɪ) a person who conducts and informs sightseers; a tour guide [C18 from Italian: antiquarian scholar, guide, after Marcus Tullius Cicero (106–43 BC), Roman consul, orator, and writer, alluding to the

C

eloquence and erudition of these men]

Ciceronian (ˌsɪsəˈrəʊnɪən) *adj* **1** of or resembling Marcus Tullius Cicero (106–43 BC), Roman consul, orator, and writer, or his rhetorical style; eloquent **2** (of literary style) characterized by the use of antithesis and long periods

cichlid (ˈsɪklɪd) *n* **1** any tropical freshwater percoid fish of the family *Cichlidae*, which includes the mouthbrooders. Cichlids are popular aquarium fishes ▷ *adj* **2** of, relating to, or belonging to the *Cichlidae* [C19 from New Latin *Cichlidae*, ultimately from Greek *kikhlē* a sea fish] > ˈcichloid *adj*

cicisbeo *Italian* (tʃitʃiˈzˈbɛːo) *n, pl* -**bei** (-ˈbɛːi) the escort or lover of a married woman, esp in 18th-century Italy [C18 Italian, of uncertain origin]

ciclosporin or **cyclosporin** (ˌsaɪkləʊˈspɔːrɪn) *n* a drug extracted from a fungus and used after organ transplantation to suppress the body's immune mechanisms, and so prevent rejection of an organ

CID (in Britain) *abbreviation for* Criminal Investigation Department; the detective division of a police force

-cide *n combining form* **1** indicating a person or thing that kills: *insecticide* **2** indicating a killing; murder: *homicide* [from Latin -*cīda* (agent), -*cīdium* (act), from *caedere* to kill] > -**cidal** *adj combining form*

cider or **cyder** (ˈsaɪdə) *n* **1** Also called (US): **hard cider** an alcoholic drink made from the fermented juice of apples **2** Also called: **sweet cider** *US and Canadian* an unfermented drink made from apple juice [C14 from Old French *cisdre*, via Medieval Latin, from Late Greek *sikera* strong drink, from Hebrew *shēkhār*]

ci-devant *French* (sidəvɑ̃) *adj* (esp of an office-holder) former; recent [literally: heretofore]

Cie *abbreviation for* compagnie [French: company]

CIE *abbreviation for* **1** Commission Internationale de l'Éclairage **2** Companion of the Indian Empire **3** (in the Irish Republic) Coras Iompair Eireann [(for sense 2) French: International Lighting Commission; (for sense 3) Irish Gaelic: Transport Organization of Ireland]

Cienfuegos (*Spanish* θienˈfueɣɔs) *n* a port in S Cuba, on Cienfuegos Bay. Pop: 147 000 (2005 est)

c.i.f. or **CIF** *abbreviation for* cost, insurance, and freight (included in the price quoted)

c.i.f.c.i. *abbreviation for* cost, insurance, freight, commission, and interest (included in the price quoted)

CIFE (in Britain) *abbreviation for* Colleges and Institutes for Further Education

cig (sɪg) or **ciggy** (ˈsɪgɪ) *n, pl* **cigs** or **ciggies** *informal* a cigarette

cigar (sɪˈgɑː) *n* a cylindrical roll of cured tobacco leaves, for smoking [C18 from Spanish *cigarro*, perhaps from Mayan *sicar* to smoke]

cigarette or *sometimes US* **cigaret** (ˌsɪgəˈrɛt) *n* a short tightly rolled cylinder of tobacco, wrapped in thin paper and often having a filter tip, for smoking. Shortened forms: **cig, ciggy** [C19 from French, literally: a little CIGAR]

cigarette card *n* a small picture card, formerly given away with cigarettes, now collected as a hobby

cigarette end *n* the part of a cigarette that is held in the mouth and that remains unsmoked after it is finished

cigarette holder *n* a mouthpiece of wood, ivory, etc, used for holding a cigarette while it is smoked

cigarette lighter *n* See **lighter**[1]

cigarette paper *n* a piece of thin paper rolled around tobacco to form a cigarette

cigarillo (ˌsɪgəˈrɪləʊ) *n, pl* -**los** a small cigar often only slightly larger than a cigarette

CIGS (formerly, in Britain) *abbreviation for* Chief of the Imperial General Staff

cilantro (sɪˈlæntrəʊ) *n US and Canadian* a European umbelliferous plant, *Coriandrum sativum*, widely cultivated for its aromatic seeds and leaves, used

in flavouring food, etc. Also called (in Britain and certain other countries): **coriander** [C20 Spanish]

cilia (ˈsɪlɪə) *n* the plural of **cilium**

ciliary (ˈsɪlɪərɪ) *adj* **1** of or relating to cilia **2** of or relating to the ciliary body

ciliary body *n* the part of the vascular tunic of the eye that connects the choroid with the iris

ciliate (ˈsɪlɪɪt, -eit) *adj* **1** Also: **ˈciliated** possessing or relating to cilia: *a ciliate epithelium* **2** of or relating to protozoans of the phylum *Ciliophora*, which have an outer layer of cilia ▷ *n* **3** a protozoan of the phylum *Ciliophora* > ˌciliˈation *n*

cilice (ˈsɪlɪs) *n* a haircloth fabric or garment [Old English *cilic*, from Latin *cilicium* shirt made of Cilician goats' hair, from Greek *kilikion*, from *Kilikia* CILICIA]

Cilicia (sɪˈlɪʃɪə) *n* an ancient region and former kingdom of SE Asia Minor, between the Taurus Mountains and the Mediterranean: corresponds to the region around present-day Adana

Cilician (sɪˈlɪʃɪən) *adj* **1** of or relating to Cilicia (an ancient region of SE Asia Minor) or its inhabitants ▷ *n* **2** a native or inhabitant of Cilicia

Cilician Gates *pl n* a pass in S Turkey, over the Taurus Mountains. Turkish name: **Gülek Bogaz**

ciliolate (ˈsɪlɪəlɪt, -ˌleit) *adj* covered with minute hairs, as some plants [C19 from New Latin *ciliolum*, diminutive of CILIUM]

cilium (ˈsɪlɪəm) *n, pl* **cilia** (ˈsɪlɪə) **1** any of the short thread-like projections on the surface of a cell, organism, etc, whose rhythmic beating causes movement of the organism or of the surrounding fluid **2** the technical name for **eyelash** [C18 New Latin, from Latin: (lower) eyelid, eyelash]

cill (sɪl) *n Brit* a variant spelling (used in the building industry) for **sill** (senses 1–4)

CIM *abbreviation for* **1** computer input on microfilm **2** computer integrated manufacture

cimbalom or **cymbalom** (ˈtsɪmbələm) *n* a type of dulcimer, esp of Hungary. See **dulcimer** (sense 1) [C19 Hungarian, from Italian *cembalo*; see CEMBALO]

Cimbri (ˈsɪmbriː, ˈkɪm-) *pl n* a Germanic people from N Jutland who migrated southwards in the 2nd century BC: annihilated by Marius in the Po valley (101 BC) > **Cimbrian** (ˈsɪmbrɪən) *n, adj* > ˈCimbric *adj*

Ciment Fondu (ˈsiːmɒn fɒnˈduː; *French* simɑ̃ fɔ̃dy) *n trademark* a type of quick-hardening refractory cement having a high alumina content. Also called: **aluminous cement**

cimetidine (saɪˈmɛtɪdiːn) *n* a drug used to suppress the formation of acid by the stomach and so to encourage the healing of gastric and duodenal ulcers. Formula: $C_{10}H_{16}N_6S$

cimex (ˈsaɪmɛks) *n, pl* **cimices** (ˈsɪmɪˌsiːz) any of the heteropterous insects of the genus *Cimex*, esp the bedbug [C16 from Latin: bug]

Cimmerian (sɪˈmɪərɪən) *adj* **1** (*sometimes not capital*) very dark; gloomy ▷ *n* **2** *Greek myth* one of a people who lived in a land of darkness at the edge of the world

C in C or **C.-in-C.** *military abbreviation for* Commander in Chief

cinch[1] (sɪntʃ) *n* **1** *slang* an easy task **2** *slang* a certainty **3** *US and Canadian* a band around a horse's belly to keep the saddle in position. Also called (in Britain and certain other countries): **girth 4** *informal* a firm grip ▷ *vb* **5** (*often foll by up*) *US and Canadian* to fasten a girth around (a horse) **6** (*tr*) *informal* to make sure of **7** (*tr*) *informal* to get a firm grip on [C19 from Spanish *cincha* saddle girth, from Latin *cingula* girdle, from *cingere* to encircle]

cinch[2] (sɪntʃ) *n* a card game in which the five of trumps ranks highest [C19 probably from CINCH[1]]

cinchona (sɪŋˈkəʊnə) *n* **1** any tree or shrub of the South American rubiaceous genus *Cinchona*, esp *C. calisaya*, having medicinal bark **2** Also called: **cinchona bark, Peruvian bark, calisaya, china bark** the dried bark of any of these trees, which yields quinine and other medicinal alkaloids **3** any of

the drugs derived from cinchona bark [C18 New Latin, named after the Countess of *Chinchón* (1576–1639), vicereine of Peru] > **cinchonic** (sɪŋˈkɒnɪk) *adj*

cinchonidine (sɪŋˈkɒnɪˌdiːn) *n* an alkaloid that is a stereoisomer of cinchonine, with similar properties and uses

cinchonine (ˈsɪŋkəˌniːn) *n* an insoluble crystalline alkaloid isolated from cinchona bark, used to treat malaria. Formula: $C_{19}H_{22}N_2O$

cinchonism (ˈsɪŋkəˌnɪzəm) *n* a condition resulting from an excessive dose of cinchona bark or its alkaloids, characterized chiefly by headache, ringing in the ears, and vomiting

cinchonize or **cinchonise** (ˈsɪŋkəˌnaɪz) *vb* (*tr*) to treat (a patient) with cinchona or one of its alkaloids, esp quinine > ˌcinchoniˈzation or ˌcinchoniˈsation *n*

Cincinnati (ˌsɪnsɪˈnætɪ) *n* a city in SW Ohio, on the Ohio River. Pop: 317 361 (2003 est)

cincture (ˈsɪŋktʃə) *n* something that encircles or surrounds, esp a belt, girdle, or border [C16 from Latin *cinctūra*, from *cingere* to gird]

cinder (ˈsɪndə) *n* **1** a piece of incombustible material left after the combustion of coal, coke, etc; clinker **2** a piece of charred material that burns without flames; ember **3** Also called: **sinter** any solid waste from smelting or refining **4** (*plural*) fragments of volcanic lava; scoriae ▷ *vb* **5** (*tr*) *rare* to burn to cinders [Old English *sinder*; related to Old Norse *sindr*, Old High German *sintar*, Old Slavonic *sedra* stalactite] > ˈcindery *adj*

cinder block *n* the usual US name for **breeze block**

Cinderella (ˌsɪndəˈrɛlə) *n* **1** a girl who achieves fame after being obscure **2 a** a poor, neglected, or unsuccessful person or thing **b** (*as modifier*): *a Cinderella service within the NHS* **3** (*modifier*) relating to dramatic success: *a Cinderella story* [C19 after *Cinderella*, the heroine of a fairy tale who is aided by a fairy godmother]

cinder track *n* a racetrack covered with fine cinders

cine- *combining form* indicating motion picture or cinema: *cine camera; cinephotography*

cineaste (ˈsɪnɪˌæst) *n* an enthusiast for films [C20 French, from CINEMA + -*aste*, as -*ast* in *enthusiast*]

cine camera (ˈsɪnɪ) *n Brit* a camera in which a strip of film moves past the lens, usually to give 16 or 24 exposures per second, thus enabling moving pictures to be taken. US and Canadian term: **movie camera**

cine film *n Brit* photographic film, wound on a spool, usually 8, 16, or 35 millimetres wide, up to several hundred metres long, and having one or two lines of sprocket holes along its length enabling it to be used in a cine camera. US and Canadian term: **movie film**

cinema (ˈsɪnɪmə) *n* **1** *chiefly Brit* **a** a place designed for the exhibition of films **b** (*as modifier*): *a cinema seat* **2** **the cinema a** the art or business of making films **b** films collectively [C19 (earlier spelling *kinema*): shortened from CINEMATOGRAPH] > **cinematic** (ˌsɪnɪˈmætɪk) *adj* > ˌcineˈmatically *adv*

CinemaScope (ˈsɪnɪməˌskəʊp) *n trademark* an anamorphic process of wide-screen film projection in which an image of approximately twice the usual width is squeezed into a 35mm frame and then screened by a projector having complementary lenses

cinematheque (ˌsɪnɪməˈtɛk) *n* a small intimate cinema [C20 from French *cinémathèque* film library, from CINEMA + (*biblio*)*thèque* library]

cinematograph (ˌsɪnɪˈmætəˌɡrɑːf, -ˌɡræf) *chiefly Brit* ▷ *n* **1** a combined camera, printer, and projector ▷ *vb* **2** to take pictures (of) with a film camera [C19 (earlier spelling *kinematograph*): from Greek *kinēmat-*, *kinēma* motion + -GRAPH]

cinematography (ˌsɪnɪməˈtɒɡrəfɪ) *n* the art or science of film (motion-picture) photography > **cinematographer** (ˌsɪnɪməˈtɒɡrəfə) *n* > **cinematographic** (ˌsɪnɪˌmætəˈɡræfɪk) *adj*

> ˌcineˌmato'graphically *adv*

cinéma vérité (*French* sinema verite) *n* films characterized by subjects, actions, etc, that have the appearance of real life [French, literally: cinema truth]

cineol ('sɪnɪˌɒl) *or* **cineole** ('sɪnɪˌəʊl) *n* another name for **eucalyptol** [c19 changed from New Latin *oleum cinae*, literally: oil of wormseed]

cinephile ('sɪnɪˌfaɪl) *n* a person who loves films and cinema

Cinerama (ˌsɪnə'rɑːmə) *n trademark* wide-screen presentation of films using either three separate 35mm projectors or one 70mm projector to produce an image on a large deeply curved screen

cineraria (ˌsɪnə'rɛərɪə) *n* a plant, *Senecio cruentus*, of the Canary Islands, widely cultivated for its blue, purple, red, or variegated daisy-like flowers: family *Asteraceae* (composites) [c16 from New Latin, from Latin *cinerārius* of ashes, from *cinis* ashes; from its downy leaves]

cinerarium (ˌsɪnə'rɛərɪəm) *n, pl* **-raria** (-'rɛərɪə) a place for keeping the ashes of the dead after cremation [c19 from Latin, from *cinerārius* relating to ashes; see CINERARIA] > **cinerary** ('sɪnərərɪ) *adj*

cinerator ('sɪnəˌreɪtə) *n* another name (esp US) for **cremator** (sense 1) > ˌcine'ration *n*

cinereous (sɪ'nɪərɪəs) *or* **cineritious** (ˌsɪnə'rɪʃəs) *adj* 1 of a greyish colour 2 resembling or consisting of ashes [c17 from Latin *cinereus*, from *cinis* ashes]

cinerin ('sɪnərɪn) *n* either of two similar organic compounds found in pyrethrum and used as insecticides. Formulas: $C_{20}H_{28}O_3$ (**cinerin I**), $C_{21}H_{28}O_5$ (**cinerin II**) [c20 from Latin *ciner-, cinis* ashes + -IN]

cingulum ('sɪŋɡjʊləm) *n, pl* **-la** (-lə) *anatomy* a girdle-like part, such as the ridge round the base of a tooth or the band of fibres connecting parts of the cerebrum [c19 from Latin: belt, from *cingere* to gird] > **cingulate** ('sɪŋɡjʊlɪt, -ˌleɪt) *or* **cinguˌlated** *adj*

cinnabar ('sɪnəˌbɑː) *n* 1 a bright red or brownish-red mineral form of mercuric sulphide (mercury(II) sulphide), found close to areas of volcanic activity and hot springs. It is the main commercial source of mercury. Formula: HgS. Crystal structure: hexagonal 2 the red form of mercuric sulphide (mercury(II) sulphide), esp when used as a pigment 3 a bright red to reddish-orange; vermilion 4 a large red-and-black European moth, *Callimorpha jacobaeae*: family *Arctiidae* (tiger moths, etc) [c15 from Old French *cenobre*, from Latin *cinnābaris*, from Greek *kinnabari*, of Oriental origin]

cinnamic acid (sɪ'næmɪk) *n* a white crystalline water-insoluble weak organic acid existing in two isomeric forms; 3-phenylpropenoic acid. The *trans*-form occurs naturally and its esters are used in perfumery. Formula: $C_6H_5CH:CHCOOH$ [c19 from CINNAM(ON) + -IC; from its being found in cinnamon oil]

cinnamon ('sɪnəmən) *n* 1 a tropical Asian lauraceous tree, *Cinnamomum zeylanicum*, having aromatic yellowish-brown bark 2 the spice obtained from the bark of this tree, used for flavouring food and drink 3 Saigon cinnamon an E Asian lauraceous tree, *Cinnamomum loureirii*, the bark of which is used as a cordial and to relieve flatulence 4 any of several similar or related trees or their bark. See **cassia** (sense 2) 5 a light yellowish brown [c15 from Old French *cinnamome*, via Latin and Greek, from Hebrew *qinnamown*] > **cin'namic** *or* **cinnamonic** (ˌsɪnə'mɒnɪk) *adj*

cinnamon bear *n* a reddish-brown variety of the American black bear. See **black bear** (sense 1)

cinnamon sedge *n* an angler's name for a small caddis fly, *Limnephilus lunatus*, having pale hind wings, that frequents sluggish water

cinnamon stone *n* another name for **hessonite**

cinquain (sɪŋ'keɪn, 'sɪŋkeɪn) *n* a stanza of five lines [c18 (in the sense: a military company of five): from French *cinq* five, from Latin *quinque*; compare QUATRAIN]

cinque (sɪŋk) *n* the number five in cards, dice, etc [c14 from Old French *cinq* five]

cinquecento (ˌtʃɪŋkwɪ'tʃɛntəʊ) *n* the 16th century, esp in reference to Italian art, architecture, or literature [c18 Italian, shortened from *milcinquecento* 1500] > ˌcinque'centist *n*

cinquefoil ('sɪŋkˌfɔɪl) *n* 1 any plant of the N temperate rosaceous genus *Potentilla*, typically having five-lobed compound leaves 2 an ornamental carving in the form of five arcs arranged in a circle and separated by cusps 3 *heraldry* a charge representing a five-petalled flower [c13 *sink foil*, from Old French *cincfoille*, from Latin *quinquefolium* plant with five leaves, translating Greek *pentaphullon* from *pente* five + *phullon* leaf]

Cinque Ports (sɪŋk) *pl n* an association of ports on the SE coast of England, originally consisting of Hastings, Romney, Hythe, Dover, and Sandwich, which from late Anglo-Saxon times provided ships for the king's service in return for the profits of justice in their courts. The Cinque Ports declined with the growth of other ports and surrendered their charters in 1685

Cintra ('sɪntrə) *n* the former name for **Sintra**

Cinzano (tʃɪn'zɑːnəʊ) *n trademark* an Italian vermouth

CIO *US* ▷ *abbreviation for* **Congress of Industrial Organizations.** See also **AFL-CIO**

Cipango (sɪ'pæŋɡəʊ) *n* (in medieval legend) an island E of Asia: called Zipangu by Marco Polo and sought by Columbus; identified with Japan

cipher *or* **cypher** ('saɪfə) *n* 1 a method of secret writing using substitution or transposition of letters according to a key 2 a secret message 3 the key to a secret message 4 an obsolete name for **zero** (sense 1) 5 any of the Arabic numerals (0, 1, 2, 3, etc, to 9) or the Arabic system of numbering as a whole 6 a person or thing of no importance; nonentity 7 a design consisting of interwoven letters; monogram 8 *music* a defect in an organ resulting in the continuous sounding of a pipe, the key of which has not been depressed ▷ *vb* 9 to put (a message) into secret writing 10 (*intr*) (of an organ pipe) to sound without having the appropriate key depressed 11 *rare* to perform (a calculation) arithmetically [c14 from Old French *cifre* zero, from Medieval Latin *cifra*, from Arabic *sifr* zero, empty]

cipolin ('sɪpəlɪn) *n* an Italian marble with alternating white and green streaks [c18 from French, from Italian *cipollino* a little onion, from *cipolla* onion, from Late Latin *cēpulla*, diminutive of Latin *cēpa* onion; from its likeness to the layers of an onion]

ciprofloxacin (ˌsɪprəʊ'flɒksəsɪn) *n* a broad-spectrum antibiotic used against Gram-negative bacteria. It is effective against anthrax

cir. *or* **circ.** *abbreviation for* (preceding a date) circa

circa ('sɜːkə) *prep* (used with a date) at the approximate time of: *circa 1182 BC*. Abbreviations: *c.* or *ca.* [Latin: about; related to Latin *circus* circle, CIRCUS]

circadian (sɜː'keɪdɪən) *adj* of or relating to biological processes that occur regularly at about 24-hour intervals, even in the absence of periodicity in the environment. See also **biological clock** [c20 from Latin *circa* about + *diēs* day]

Circassia (sɜː'kæsɪə) *n* a region of S Russia, on the Black Sea north of the Caucasus Mountains

Circassian (sɜː'kæsɪən) *n* 1 a native of Circassia 2 a language or languages spoken in Circassia, belonging to the North-West Caucasian family. See also **Adygei, Kabardian** ▷ *adj* also **Circassic** 3 relating to Circassia, its people, or language

Circe ('sɜːsɪ) *n Greek myth* an enchantress who detained Odysseus on her island and turned his men into swine > **Circean** (sɜː'sɪən) *adj*

circinate ('sɜːsɪˌneɪt) *adj* 1 *botany* (of part of a plant, such as a young fern) coiled so that the tip is at the centre 2 *anatomy* resembling a ring or a circle [c19 from Latin *circināre* to make round, from

circinus pair of compasses, from *circus*, see CIRCUS] > 'circiˌnately *adv*

Circinus ('sɜːsɪnəs) *n, Latin genitive* Circini ('sɜːsɪˌnaɪ) a small faint constellation in the S hemisphere close to Centaurus and the Southern Cross [c19 from Latin, a pair of compasses]

circle ('sɜːkəl) *n* 1 *maths* a closed plane curve every point of which is equidistant from a given fixed point, the centre. Equation: $(x - h)^2 + (y - k)^2 = r^2$ where *r* is the radius and (*h, k*) are the coordinates of the centre; area πr^2; circumference: $2\pi r$ 2 the figure enclosed by such a curve 3 *theatre* the section of seats above the main level of the auditorium, usually comprising the dress circle and the upper circle 4 something formed or arranged in the shape of a circle 5 a group of people sharing an interest, activity, upbringing, etc; set: *golf circles; a family circle* 6 a domain or area of activity, interest, or influence 7 a circuit 8 a process or chain of events or parts that forms a connected whole; cycle 9 a parallel of latitude. See also **great circle, small circle** 10 the ring of a circus 11 one of a number of Neolithic or Bronze Age rings of standing stones, such as Stonehenge, found in Europe and thought to be associated with some form of ritual or astronomical measurement 12 *hockey* See **striking circle** 13 a circular argument. See **vicious circle** (sense 2) 14 **come full circle** to arrive back at one's starting point. See also **vicious circle** 15 **go** *or* **run round in circles** to engage in energetic but fruitless activity ▷ *vb* 16 to move in a circle (around): *we circled the city by car* 17 (*tr*) to enclose in a circle; encircle [c14 from Latin *circulus* a circular figure, from *circus* ring, circle] > 'circler *n*

circlet ('sɜːklɪt) *n* a small circle or ring, esp a circular ornament worn on the head [c15 from Old French *cerclet* a little CIRCLE]

circlip ('sɜːˌklɪp) *n engineering* a flat spring ring split at one point so that it can be sprung open, passed over a shaft or spindle, and allowed to close into a closely fitting annular recess to form a collar on the shaft. A similar design can be closed to pass into a bore and allowed to spring out into an annular recess to form a shoulder in the bore. Also called: **retaining ring**

Circlorama (ˌsɜːklə'rɑːmə) *n trademark* a system of film projection in which a number of projectors and screens are employed to produce a picture that surrounds the viewer

circs (sɜːks) *n Brit informal* short for **circumstances** (see **circumstance** (sense 1))

circuit ('sɜːkɪt) *n* 1 a a complete route or course, esp one that is curved or circular or that lies around an object b the area enclosed within such a route 2 the act of following such a route: *we made three circuits of the course* 3 a a complete path through which an electric current can flow b (*as modifier*): *a circuit diagram* 4 a a periodical journey around an area, as made by judges, salesmen, etc b the route traversed or places visited on such a journey c the persons making such a journey 5 an administrative division of the Methodist Church comprising a number of neighbouring churches 6 *English law* one of six areas into which England is divided for the administration of justice 7 a number of theatres, cinemas, etc, under one management or in which the same film is shown or in which a company of performers plays in turn 8 *sport* a a series of tournaments in which the same players regularly take part: *the international tennis circuit* b (usually preceded by *the*) the contestants who take part in such a series 9 *chiefly Brit* a motor racing track, usually of irregular shape ▷ *vb* 10 to make or travel in a circuit around (something) [c14 from Latin *circuitus* a going around, from *circumīre*, from *circum* around + *īre* to go] > **circuital** *adj*

circuit binding *n* a style of limp-leather binding, used esp for Bibles and prayer books, in which the edges of the cover bend over to protect the edges of the pages

C

circuit board *n* short for **printed circuit board** See **printed circuit**

circuit breaker *n* a device that under abnormal conditions, such as a short circuit, interrupts the flow of current in an electrical circuit. Sometimes shortened to: **breaker** Compare **fuse²** (sense 6)

circuit judge *n* Brit a judge presiding over a county court or crown court

circuitous (sə'kju:ɪtəs) *adj* indirect and lengthy; roundabout: *a circuitous route* > cir'cuitously *adv* > cir'cuitousness *n*

circuit rider *n* US and Canadian (formerly) a minister of religion who preached from place to place along an established circuit

circuitry ('sɜ:kɪtrɪ) *n* 1 the design of an electrical circuit 2 the system of circuits used in an electronic device

circuit training *n* a form of athletic training in which a number of exercises are performed in turn

circuity (sə'kju:ɪtɪ) *n, pl* -ties (of speech, reasoning, etc) a roundabout or devious quality

circular ('sɜ:kjʊlə) *adj* 1 of, involving, resembling, or shaped like a circle 2 circuitous 3 (of arguments) futile because the truth of the premises cannot be established independently of the conclusion 4 travelling or occurring in a cycle 5 (of letters, announcements, etc) intended for general distribution ▷ *n* 6 a printed or duplicated advertisement or notice for mass distribution > circularity (ˌsɜ:kjʊ'lærɪtɪ) *or* 'circularness *n* > 'circularly *adv*

circular breathing *n* a technique for sustaining a phrase on a wind instrument, using the cheeks to force air out of the mouth while breathing in through the nose

circular function *n* another name for **trigonometric function** (sense 1)

circularize *or* **circularise** ('sɜ:kjʊləˌraɪz) *vb* (tr) 1 to distribute circulars to 2 to canvass or petition (people), as for support, votes, etc, by distributing letters, etc 3 to make circular > ˌcirculari'zation *or* ˌcirculari'sation *n* > 'circular,izer *or* 'circular,iser *n*

circular measure *n* the measurement of an angle in radians

circular mil *n* a unit of area of cross section of wire, equal to the area of a circle whose diameter is one thousandth of an inch. 1 circular mil is equal to 0.785 × 10⁻⁶ square inch or 0.2 × 10⁻⁹ square metre

circular polarization *n* electromagnetic radiation (esp light) in which the electric field vector describes a circle about the direction of propagation at any point in the path of the radiation

circular saw *n* a power-driven saw in which a circular disc with a toothed edge is rotated at high speed

circular triangle *n* a triangle in which each side is the arc of a circle

circulate ('sɜ:kjʊˌleɪt) *vb* 1 to send, go, or pass from place to place or person to person: *don't circulate the news* 2 to distribute or be distributed over a wide area 3 to move or cause to move through a circuit, system, etc, returning to the starting point: *blood circulates through the body* 4 to move in a circle: *the earth circulates around the sun* [C15 from Latin *circulārī* to assemble in a circle, from *circulus* CIRCLE] > 'circu,lative *adj* > 'circu,lator *n* > 'circulatory *adj*

circulating decimal *n* another name for **recurring decimal**

circulating library *n* 1 another name (esp US) for **lending library** 2 a small library circulated in turn to a group of schools or other institutions 3 a rare name for **subscription library**

circulating medium *n* finance currency serving as a medium of exchange

circulation (ˌsɜ:kjʊ'leɪʃən) *n* 1 the transport of oxygenated blood through the arteries to the capillaries, where it nourishes the tissues, and the return of oxygen-depleted blood through the

veins to the heart, where the cycle is renewed 2 the flow of sap through a plant 3 any movement through a closed circuit 4 the spreading or transmission of something to a wider group of people or area 5 (of air and water) free movement within an area or volume 6 a the distribution of newspapers, magazines, etc b the number of copies of an issue of such a publication that are distributed 7 library science a a book loan, as from a library lending department b each loan transaction of a particular book c the total issue of library books over a specified period 8 a rare term for **circulating medium** 9 in circulation a (of currency) serving as a medium of exchange b (of people) active in a social or business context

circulatory system *n* anatomy, zoology the system concerned with the transport of blood and lymph, consisting of the heart, blood vessels, lymph vessels, etc

circum- *prefix* around; surrounding; on all sides: *circumlocution; circumrotate* [from Latin *circum* around, from *circus* circle]

circumambient (ˌsɜ:kəm'æmbɪənt) *adj* surrounding [C17 from Late Latin *circumambīre*, from CIRCUM- + *ambīre* to go round] > ˌcircum'ambience *or* ˌcircum'ambiency *n*

circumambulate (ˌsɜ:kəm'æmbjʊˌleɪt) *vb* 1 to walk around (something) 2 (intr) to avoid the point [C17 from Late Latin CIRCUM- + *ambulāre* to walk] > ˌcircum,ambu'lation *n* > ˌcircum'ambu,lator *n* > ˌcircum'ambulatory *adj*

circumbendibus (ˌsɜ:kəm'bɛndɪbəs) *n* humorous a circumlocution [C17 coined from CIRCUM- + BEND¹, with a pseudo-Latin ending]

circumcise ('sɜ:kəmˌsaɪz) *vb* (tr) 1 to remove the foreskin of (a male) 2 to incise surgically the skin over the clitoris of (a female) 3 to remove the clitoris of (a female) 4 to perform the religious rite of circumcision on (someone) [C13 from Latin *circumcīdere*, from CIRCUM- + *caedere* to cut] > 'circum,ciser *n*

circumcision (ˌsɜ:kəm'sɪʒən) *n* 1 a surgical removal of the foreskin of males b surgical incision into the skin covering the clitoris in females c removal of the clitoris 2 the act of circumcision, performed as a religious rite by Jews and Muslims 3 RC Church the festival celebrated on Jan 1 in commemoration of the circumcision of Jesus

circumference (sə'kʌmfərəns) *n* 1 the boundary of a specific area or geometric figure, esp of a circle 2 the length of a closed geometric curve, esp of a circle. The circumference of a circle is equal to the diameter multiplied by π [C14 from Old French *circonference*, from Latin *circumferre* to carry around, from CIRCUM- + *ferre* to bear] > circumferential (səˌkʌmfə'rɛnʃəl) *adj* > cirˌcumfer'entially *adv*

circumflex ('sɜ:kəmˌflɛks) *n* 1 a mark (ˆ) placed over a vowel to show that it is pronounced with rising and falling pitch, as in ancient Greek, as a long vowel rather than a short one, as in French, or with some other different quality ▷ *adj* 2 (of certain nerves, arteries, or veins) bending or curving around [C16 from Latin *circumflexus*, from *circumflectere* to bend around, from CIRCUM- + *flectere* to bend] > ˌcircum'flexion *n*

circumfluous (sə'kʌmflʊəs) *adj* 1 Also: circumfluent flowing all around 2 surrounded by or as if by water [C17 from Latin *circumfluere* to flow around, from CIRCUM- + *fluere* to flow] > cir'cumfluence *n*

circumfuse (ˌsɜ:kəm'fju:z) *vb* (tr) 1 to pour or spread (a liquid, powder, etc) around 2 to surround with a substance, such as a liquid [C16 from Latin *circumfūsus*, from *circumfundere* to pour around, from CIRCUM- + *fundere* to pour] > circumfusion (ˌsɜ:kəm'fju:ʒən) *n*

circumlocution (ˌsɜ:kəmlə'kju:ʃən) *n* 1 an indirect way of expressing something 2 an indirect expression > circumlocutory (ˌsɜ:kəm'lɒkjʊtərɪ, -trɪ) *adj*

circumlunar (ˌsɜ:kəm'lu:nə) *adj* around or revolving around the moon: *a circumlunar orbit*

circumnavigate (ˌsɜ:kəm'næviˌgeɪt) *vb* (tr) to sail or fly completely around > ˌcircum'navigable *adj* > ˌcircum,navi'gation *n* > ˌcircum'navi,gator *n*

circumnutation (ˌsɜ:kəmnju:'teɪʃən) *n* another name for **nutation** (sense 3) [C19 from CIRCUM- + -*nutate*, from Latin *nūtāre* to nod repeatedly, sway]

circumpolar (ˌsɜ:kəm'pəʊlə) *adj* 1 (of a star or constellation) visible above the horizon at all times at a specified locality on the earth's surface 2 surrounding or located at or near either of the earth's poles

circumscissile (ˌsɜ:kəm'sɪsaɪl) *adj* (of the dry dehiscent fruits of certain plants) opening completely by a transverse split [C19 from CIRCUM- + Latin *scissilis* capable of splitting, from *scindere* to split]

circumscribe (ˌsɜ:kəm'skraɪb, 'sɜ:kəmˌskraɪb) *vb* (tr) 1 to restrict within limits 2 to mark or set the bounds of 3 to draw a geometric construction around (another construction) so that the two are in contact but do not intersect. Compare **inscribe** (sense 4) 4 to draw a line round [C15 from Latin *circumscrībere*, from CIRCUM- + *scrībere* to write] > ˌcircum'scribable *adj* > ˌcircum'scriber *n*

circumscription (ˌsɜ:kəm'skrɪpʃən) *n* 1 the act of circumscribing or the state of being circumscribed 2 something that limits or encloses 3 a circumscribed space 4 an inscription around a coin or medal > ˌcircum'scriptive *adj* > ˌcircum'scriptively *adv*

circumsolar (ˌsɜ:kəm'səʊlə) *adj* surrounding or rotating around the sun

circumspect ('sɜ:kəmˌspɛkt) *adj* cautious, prudent, or discreet [C15 from Latin *circumspectus*, from CIRCUM- + *specere* to look] > ˌcircum'spection *n* > ˌcircum'spective *adj* > 'circum,spectly *adv*

circumstance ('sɜ:kəmstəns) *n* 1 (usually plural) a condition of time, place, etc, that accompanies or influences an event or condition 2 an incident or occurrence, esp a chance one 3 accessory information or detail 4 formal display or ceremony (archaic except in the phrase **pomp and circumstance**) 5 under *or* in no circumstances in no case; never 6 under the circumstances because of conditions; this being the case 7 in good (or bad) circumstances (of a person) in a good (or bad) financial situation ▷ *vb* (tr) 8 to place in a particular condition or situation 9 obsolete to give in detail [C13 from Old French *circonstance*, from Latin *circumstantia*, from *circumstāre* to stand around, from CIRCUM- + *stāre* to stand]

circumstantial (ˌsɜ:kəm'stænʃəl) *adj* 1 of or dependent on circumstances 2 fully detailed 3 incidental > ˌcircum'stanti'ality *n* > ˌcircum'stantially *adv*

circumstantial evidence *n* indirect evidence that tends to establish a conclusion by inference. Compare **direct evidence**

circumstantiate (ˌsɜ:kəm'stænʃɪ,eɪt) *vb* (tr) to support by giving particulars > ˌcircum,stanti'ation *n*

circumvallate (ˌsɜ:kəm'væleɪt) *vb* (tr) to surround with a defensive fortification [C19 from Latin *circumvallāre*, from CIRCUM- + *vallum* rampart] > ˌcircumval'lation *n*

circumvent (ˌsɜ:kəm'vɛnt) *vb* (tr) 1 to evade or go around 2 to outwit 3 to encircle (an enemy) so as to intercept or capture [C15 from Latin *circumvenīre*, from CIRCUM- + *venīre* to come] > ˌcircum'venter *or* ˌcircum'ventor *n* > ˌcircum'vention *n* > ˌcircum'ventive *adj*

circumvolution (ˌsɜ:kəmvə'lu:ʃən) *n* 1 the act of turning, winding, or folding around a central axis 2 a single complete turn, cycle, or fold 3 anything winding or sinuous 4 a roundabout course or procedure [C15 from Medieval Latin *circumvolūtiō*, from Latin *circumvolvere*, from CIRCUM- + *volvere* to roll] > ˌcircumvo'lutory *adj*

circus ('sɜ:kəs) *n, pl* -cuses 1 a travelling company of entertainers such as acrobats, clowns, trapeze artistes, and trained animals **2** a public performance given by such a company **3** an oval or circular arena, usually tented and surrounded by tiers of seats, in which such a performance is held **4** a travelling group of professional sportsmen: *a cricket circus* **5** (in ancient Rome) **a** an open-air stadium, usually oval or oblong, for chariot races or public games **b** the games themselves **6** *Brit* an open place, usually circular, in a town, where several streets converge **b** (*capital when part of a name*): *Piccadilly Circus* **7** *informal* noisy or rowdy behaviour **8** *informal* a person or group of people whose behaviour is wild, disorganized, or (*esp unintentionally*) comic [c16 from Latin, from Greek *kirkos* ring]

Circus Maximus (ˈmæksɪməs) *n* an amphitheatre in Rome, used in ancient times for chariot races, public games, etc

ciré (ˈsɪəreɪ) *adj* **1** (of fabric) treated with a heat or wax process to make it smooth ▷ *n* **2** such a surface on a fabric **3** a fabric having such a surface [c20 French, from *cirer* to wax, from *cire*, from Latin *cēra* wax]

Cirenaica (ˌsaɪrəˈneɪɪkə, ˌsɪrə-) *n* a variant spelling of **Cyrenaica**

Cirencester (ˈsaɪrənˌsɛstə) *n* a market town in S England, in Gloucestershire: Roman amphitheatre. Pop: 15 861 (2001). Latin name: **Corinium**

cire perdue *French* (sir pɛrdy) *n* a method of casting bronze, in which a mould is formed around a wax pattern, which is subsequently melted and drained away [literally: lost wax]

cirque (sɜːk) *n* **1** Also called: **corrie, cwm** a semicircular or crescent-shaped basin with steep sides and a gently sloping floor formed in mountainous regions by the erosive action of a glacier **2** *archaeol* an obsolete term for **circle** (sense 11) **3** *poetic* a circle, circlet, or ring [c17 from French, from Latin *circus* ring, circle, CIRCUS]

cirrate (ˈsɪreɪt), **cirrose** or **cirrous** *adj biology* bearing or resembling cirri [c19 from Latin *cirrātus* curled, from CIRRUS]

cirrhosis (sɪˈrəʊsɪs) *n* any of various progressive diseases of the liver, characterized by death of liver cells, irreversible fibrosis, etc: caused by inadequate diet, excessive alcohol, chronic infection, etc. Also called: **cirrhosis of the liver** [c19 New Latin, from Greek *kirrhos* orange-coloured + -OSIS; referring to the appearance of the diseased liver] > **cir'rhosed** *adj* > **cirrhotic** (sɪˈrɒtɪk) *adj*

cirri (ˈsɪraɪ) *n* the plural of **cirrus**

cirripede (ˈsɪrɪˌpiːd) or **cirriped** (ˈsɪrɪˌpɛd) *n* **1** any marine crustacean of the subclass Cirripedia, including the barnacles, the adults of which are sessile or parasitic ▷ *adj* **2** of, relating to, or belonging to the Cirripedia

cirro- or **cirri-** *combining form* indicating cirrus or cirri: *cirrocumulus; cirriped*

cirrocumulus (ˌsɪrəʊˈkjuːmjʊləs) *n, pl* **-li** (-ˌlaɪ) *meteorol* a high cloud of ice crystals grouped into small separate globular masses, usually occurring above 6000 metres (20 000 feet). See also **mackerel sky**

cirrose (ˈsɪrəʊs, sɪˈrəʊs) or **cirrous** (ˈsɪrəs) *adj* **1** *biology* another word for **cirrate 2** characteristic of cirrus clouds

cirrostratus (ˌsɪrəʊˈstrɑːtəs) *n, pl* **-ti** (-taɪ) a uniform layer of cloud above about 6000 metres (20 000 feet) > **cirro'strative** *adj*

cirrus (ˈsɪrəs) *n, pl* **-ri** (-raɪ) **1** *meteorol* a thin wispy fibrous cloud at high altitudes, composed of ice particles **2** a plant tendril or similar part **3** *zoology* **a** a slender tentacle or filament in barnacles and other marine invertebrates **b** a hairlike structure in other animals, such as a filament on the appendage of an insect or a barbel of a fish [c18 from Latin: curl, tuft, fringe]

cirsoid (ˈsɜːsɔɪd) *adj pathol* resembling a varix. Also: **varicoid** [c19 from Greek *kirsoeidēs*, from *kirsos* swollen vein + -OID]

CIS *abbreviation for* **Commonwealth of Independent States**

cis- *prefix* **1** on this or the near side of: *cisalpine* **2** (often in italics) indicating that two groups of atoms in an unsaturated compound lie on the same side of a double bond: *cis*-butadiene. Compare **trans-** (sense 5) [from Latin]

cisalpine (sɪsˈælpaɪn) *adj* **1** on this (the southern) side of the Alps, as viewed from Rome **2** relating to a movement in the Roman Catholic Church to minimize the authority of the pope and to emphasize the independence of branches of the Church. Compare **ultramontane** (sense 2)

Cisalpine Gaul *n* (in the ancient world) that part of Gaul between the Alps and the Apennines

Ciscaucasia (ˌsɪskɔːˈkeɪzɪə, -ʒə) *n* the part of Caucasia north of the Caucasus Mountains

cisco (ˈsɪskəʊ) *n, pl* **-coes** or **-cos** any of various whitefish, esp *Coregonus artedi* (also called **lake herring**), of cold deep lakes of North America [c19 short for Canadian French *ciscoette*, from Ojibwa *pemitewiskawet* fish with oily flesh]

Ciskei (ˈsɪskaɪ) *n* (formerly) a Bantustan in SE South Africa; granted independence in 1981 but this was not recognized outside South Africa; abolished in 1993. Capital: Bisho

cislunar (sɪsˈluːnə) *adj* of or relating to the space between the earth and the moon. Compare **translunar**

cismontane (sɪsˈmɒnteɪn) *adj* on this (the writer's or speaker's) side of the mountains, esp the Alps. Compare **ultramontane** (sense 1) [c18 from Latin *cis-* + *montānus* of the mountains, from *mōns* mountain]

cispadane (ˈsɪspəˌdeɪn, sɪsˈpeɪdeɪn) *adj* on this (the southern) side of the River Po, as viewed from Rome. Compare **transpadane** [from Latin *cis-* + *Padānus* of the Po]

cisplatin (sɪsˈplætɪn) *n* a cytotoxic drug that acts by preventing DNA replication and hence cell division, used in the treatment of tumours, esp of the ovary and testis [c20 from *cis-* + PLATIN(UM)]

cissing (ˈsɪsɪŋ) *n building trades* the appearance of pinholes, craters, etc, in paintwork due to poor adhesion of the paint to the surface

cissoid (ˈsɪsɔɪd) *n* **1** a geometric curve whose two branches meet in a cusp at the origin and are asymptotic to a line parallel to the *y*-axis. Its equation is $y^2(2a - x) = x^3$ where 2a is the distance between the *y*-axis and this line ▷ *adj* **2** contained between the concave sides of two intersecting curves. Compare **sistroid** [c17 from Greek *kissoeidēs*, literally: ivy-shaped, from *kissos* ivy]

cissus (ˈsɪsəs) *n* any plant of the climbing genus *Cissus*, some species of which, esp the kangaroo vine (*C. antarctica*) from Australia, are grown as greenhouse or house plants for their shiny green or mottled leaves: family Vitaceae [New Latin, from Greek *kissos* ivy]

cissy (ˈsɪsɪ) *n* a variant spelling of **sissy**

cist¹ (sɪst) *n* a wooden box for holding ritual objects used in ancient Rome and Greece [c19 from Latin *cista* box, chest, basket, from Greek *kistē*]

cist² (sɪst) or **kist** *n archaeol* a box-shaped burial chamber made from stone slabs or a hollowed tree trunk [c19 from Welsh: chest, from Latin *cista* box; see CIST¹]

cistaceous (sɪˈsteɪʃəs) *adj* of, relating to, or belonging to the Cistaceae, a family of shrubby or herbaceous plants that includes the rockroses [c19 from New Latin *Cistaceae*, from Greek *kistos* rockrose]

Cistercian (sɪˈstɜːʃən) *n* **a** a member of a Christian order of monks and nuns founded in 1098, which follows an especially strict form of the Benedictine rule. Also called: White Monk **b** (*as modifier*): *a Cistercian monk* [c17 from French *Cistercien*, from Medieval Latin *Cisterciānus*, from *Cistercium* (modern *Cîteaux*), original home of the order]

cistern (ˈsɪstən) *n* **1** a tank for the storage of water, esp on or within the roof of a house or connected to a WC **2** an underground reservoir for the storage of a liquid, esp rainwater **3** *anatomy* another name for **cisterna** [c13 from Old French *cisterne*, from Latin *cisterna* underground tank, from *cista* box] > **cisternal** (sɪˈstɜːn³l) *adj*

cisterna (sɪˈstɜːnə) *n, pl* **-nae** (-niː) a sac or partially closed space containing body fluid, esp lymph or cerebrospinal fluid [New Latin, from Latin; see CISTERN]

cis-trans test (ˈsɪsˈtrɑːnz) *n genetics* a test to define the unit of genetic function, based on whether two mutations of the same character occur in a single chromosome (the cis position) or in different cistrons in each chromosome of a homologous pair (the trans position) [c20 see CIS-, TRANS-]

cistron (ˈsɪstrən) *n genetics* the section of a chromosome that encodes a single polypeptide chain [c20 from *cis-trans*; see CIS-TRANS TEST]

cistus (ˈsɪstəs) *n* any plant of the genus *Cistus*. See **rockrose** [c19 New Latin, from Greek *kistos*]

CIT (in New Zealand) *abbreviation for* Central Institute of Technology

cit. *abbreviation for* **1** citation **2** cited

citadel (ˈsɪtəd³l, -ˌdɛl) *n* **1** a stronghold within or close to a city **2** any strongly fortified building or place of safety; refuge **3** a specially strengthened part of the hull of a warship **4** (*often capital*) the headquarters of the Salvation Army [c16 from Old French *citadelle*, from Old Italian *cittadella* a little city, from *cittade* city, from Latin *cīvitās*]

citation (saɪˈteɪʃən) *n* **1** the quoting of a book or author in support of a fact **2** a passage or source cited for this purpose **3** a listing or recounting, as of facts **4** an official commendation or award, esp for bravery or outstanding service, work, etc, usually in the form of a formal statement made in public **5** *law* **a** an official summons to appear in court **b** the document containing such a summons **6** *law* the quoting of decided cases to serve as guidance to a court > **citatory** (ˈsaɪtətərɪ, -trɪ) *adj*

cite (saɪt) *vb* (*tr*) **1** to quote or refer to (a passage, book, or author) in substantiation as an authority, proof, or example **2** to mention or commend (a soldier, etc) for outstanding bravery or meritorious action **3** to summon to appear before a court of law **4** to enumerate: *he cited the king's virtues* [c15 from Old French *citer* to summon, from Latin *citāre* to rouse, from *citus* quick, from *ciēre* to excite] > **'citable** or **'citeable** *adj* > **'citer** *n*

CITES *abbreviation for* Convention on International Trade in Endangered Species

cithara (ˈsɪθərə) or **kithara** *n* a stringed musical instrument of ancient Greece and elsewhere, similar to the lyre and played with a plectrum [c18 from Greek *kithara*]

cither (ˈsɪθə) or **cithern** (ˈsɪθən) *n* variants of **cittern** [c17 from Latin *cithara*, from Greek *kithara* lyre]

citified or **cityfied** (ˈsɪtɪˌfaɪd) *adj often derogatory* having the customs, manners, or dress of city people

citify or **cityfy** (ˈsɪtɪˌfaɪ) *vb* **-fies, -fying, -fied** (*tr*) **1** to cause to conform to or adopt the customs, habits, or dress of city people **2** to make urban > **citifi'cation** or **cityfi'cation** *n*

citizen (ˈsɪtɪzən) *n* **1** a native registered or naturalized member of a state, nation, or other political community. Compare **alien 2** an inhabitant of a city or town **3** a native or inhabitant of any place **4** a civilian, as opposed to a soldier, public official, etc. Related adj: **civil** [c14 from Anglo-French *citesein*, from Old French *citeien*, from *cité*, CITY] > **citizeness** (ˈsɪtɪzənɪs, -ˌnɛs) *fem n* > **'citizenly** *adj*

citizenry (ˈsɪtɪzənrɪ) *n, pl* **-ries** citizens collectively

citizen's arrest *n* an arrest carried out by an ordinary member of the public rather than an officer of the law

C

Citizens' Band n a range of radio frequencies assigned officially for use by the public for private communication. Abbreviation: **CB**

Citizen's Charter n (formerly, in Britain) a government document setting out standards of service for public and private sector bodies, such as schools, hospitals, railway companies, water and energy suppliers, etc

citizenship ('sɪtɪzənˌʃɪp) n **1** the condition or status of a citizen, with its rights and duties **2** a person's conduct as a citizen: *an award for good citizenship*

Citlaltépetl (ˌsiːtlaːlˈteɪpɛtˀl) n a volcano in SE Mexico, in central Veracruz state: the highest peak in the country. Height: 5699 m (18 698 ft). Spanish name: **Pico de Orizaba** (piko de oriˈsaba)

citole ('sɪtəʊl, sɪˈtəʊl) n a rare word for **cittern** [C14 from Old French, probably from Latin *cithara* CITHER]

citral ('sɪtrəl) n a yellow volatile liquid with a lemon-like odour, found in oils of lemon grass, orange, and lemon and used in perfumery: a terpene aldehyde consisting of the *cis*- isomer (**citral-a** or **geranial**) and the *trans*- isomer (**citral-b** or **neral**). Formula: $(CH_3)_2C:CH(CH_2)_2C(CH_3):CHCHO$ [C19 from CITR(US) + -AL³]

citrate ('sɪtreɪt, -rɪt, 'saɪtreɪt) n any salt or ester of citric acid. Salts of citric acid are used in beverages and pharmaceuticals [C18 from CITR(US) + -ATE¹]

citreous ('sɪtrɪəs) adj of a greenish-yellow colour; citron

citric ('sɪtrɪk) adj of or derived from citrus fruits or citric acid

citric acid n a water-soluble weak tribasic acid found in many fruits, esp citrus fruits, and used in pharmaceuticals and as a flavouring (**E330**). It is extracted from citrus fruits or made by fermenting molasses and is an intermediate in carbohydrate metabolism. Formula: $CH_2(COOH)C(OH)(COOH)CH_2COOH$

citric acid cycle n another name for **Krebs cycle**

citriculture ('sɪtrɪˌkʌltʃə) n the cultivation of citrus fruits > ˌcitri'culturist n

citrin ('sɪtrɪn) n another name for **vitamin P**

citrine ('sɪtrɪn) n **1** a brownish-yellow variety of quartz: a gemstone; false topaz **2** the yellow colour of a lemon

citron ('sɪtrən) n **1** a small Asian rutaceous tree, *Citrus medica*, having lemon-like fruit with a thick aromatic rind. See also **citron wood 2** the fruit of this tree **3** Also called: **citron melon** a variety of watermelon, *Citrullus vulgaris citroides*, that has an inedible fruit with a hard rind **4** the rind of either of these fruits, candied and used for decoration and flavouring of foods **5** a greenish-yellow colour [C16 from Old French, from Old Provençal, from Latin *citrus* citrus tree]

citronella (ˌsɪtrəˈnɛlə) n **1** Also called: **citronella grass** a tropical Asian grass, *Cymbopogon* (or *Andropogon*) *nardus*, with bluish-green lemon-scented leaves **2** Also called: **citronella oil** the yellow aromatic oil obtained from this grass, used in insect repellents, soaps, perfumes, etc [C19 New Latin, from French *citronnelle* lemon balm, from *citron* lemon]

citronellal (ˌsɪtrəˈnɛlæl) n a colourless slightly water-soluble liquid with a lemon-like odour, a terpene aldehyde found esp in citronella and certain eucalyptus oils: used as a flavouring and in soaps and perfumes. Formula: $(CH_3)_2C:CH(CH_2)_2CH(CH_3)CH_2CHO$. Also called: **rhodinal**

citron wood n **1** the wood of the citron tree **2** the wood of the sandarac

citrulline ('sɪtrʊˌliːn) n an amino acid that occurs in watermelons and is an intermediate in the formation of urea. Formula: $NH_2CONH(CH_2)_3CHNH_2COOH$ [C20 from Medieval Latin *citrullus* a kind of watermelon, from Latin *citron*, referring to its colour]

citrus ('sɪtrəs) n, pl **-ruses 1** any tree or shrub of the tropical and subtropical rutaceous genus *Citrus*, which includes the orange, lemon, lime, grapefruit, citron, and calamondin ▷ adj also **citrous 2** of, relating to, or belonging to the genus *Citrus* or to the fruits of plants of this genus [C19 from Latin: citrus tree, sandarac tree; related to Greek *kedros* cedar]

citrussy ('sɪtrəsɪ) adj having or resembling the taste or colour of a citrus fruit

Città del Vaticano (tʃitˈta del vatiˈkaːno) n the Italian name for **Vatican City**

cittern ('sɪtɜːn), **cither** or **cithern** n a medieval stringed instrument resembling a lute but having wire strings and a flat back. Compare **gittern** [C16 perhaps a blend of CITHER + GITTERN]

city ('sɪtɪ) n, pl **cities 1** any large town or populous place **2** (in Britain) a large town that has received this title from the Crown: usually the seat of a bishop **3** (in the US) an incorporated urban centre with its own government and administration established by state charter **4** (in Canada) a similar urban municipality incorporated by the provincial government **5** an ancient Greek city-state; polis **6** the people of a city collectively **7** (*modifier*) in or characteristic of a city: *a city girl; city habits* ▷ Related adjectives: **civic, urban, municipal** [C13 from Old French *cité*, from Latin *cīvitās* citizenship, state, from *cīvis* citizen]

City ('sɪtɪ) n **the 1** short for **City of London**: the original settlement of London on the N bank of the Thames; a municipality governed by the Lord Mayor and Corporation. Resident pop.: 7186 (2001) **2** the area in central London in which the United Kingdom's major financial business is transacted **3** the various financial institutions located in this area

City and Guilds of London Institute n (in Britain) an examining body for technical and craft skills, many of the examinations being at a lower standard than for a degree. Often shortened to: **City and Guilds**

city blues n (*functioning as singular*) jazz another name for **urban blues**

City Code n (in Britain) short for **City Code on Takeovers and Mergers**: a code laid down in 1968 (later modified) to control takeover bids and mergers

City Company n (in Britain) a corporation that represents one of the historic trade guilds of London

city desk n **1** Brit the department of a newspaper office dealing with financial and commercial news **2** US and Canadian the department of a newspaper office dealing with local news

city editor n (on a newspaper) **1** Brit the editor in charge of financial and commercial news **2** US and Canadian the editor in charge of local news

city father n a person who is active or prominent in the public affairs of a city, such as an alderman

city hall n **1** the building housing the administrative offices of a city or municipal government **2** chiefly US and Canadian **a** municipal government **b** the officials of a municipality collectively **3** US informal bureaucracy

city manager n (in the US) an administrator hired by a municipal council to manage its affairs. See also **council-manager plan**

City of God n **1** Christianity heaven conceived of as the New Jerusalem **2** the Church in contrast to the world, as described by St Augustine

city planning n the US term for **town planning** > **city planner** n

cityscape ('sɪtɪskeɪp) n an urban landscape; view of a city

city slicker n informal **1** a person with the sophistication often attributed to city people **2** a smooth tricky untrustworthy person

city-state n a state consisting of a sovereign city and its dependencies. Among the most famous are the great independent cities of the ancient world, such as Athens, Sparta, Carthage, Thebes, Corinth, and Rome

city technology college n (in Britain) a type of senior secondary school specializing in technological subjects, set up in inner-city areas with funding from industry as well as the government. Abbreviation: **CTC**

Ciudad Bolívar (*Spanish* θiuˈðað boˈliβar) n a port in E Venezuela, on the Orinoco River: accessible to ocean-going vessels. Pop: 344 000 (2005 est). Former name (1764–1846): **Angostura**

Ciudad Guayana (*Spanish* θiuˈðað gwaˈjana) n an industrial conurbation in E Venezuela, on the River Orinoco: iron and steel processing, gold mining. Pop: 807 000 (2005 est). Former name: **Santo Tomé de Guayana**

Ciudad Juárez (*Spanish* θiuˈðað ˈxwareθ) n a city in N Mexico, in Chihuahua state on the Río Grande, opposite El Paso, Texas. Pop: 1 469 000 (2005 est). Former name (until 1888): **El Paso del Norte** (ɛl ˈpaso del ˈnɔrte)

Ciudad Real (*Spanish* θiuˈðað reˈal) n a market town in S central Spain. Pop: 65 703 (2003 est)

Ciudad Trujillo (*Spanish* θiuˈðað truˈxiʎo) n the former name (1936–61) of **Santo Domingo**

Ciudad Victoria (*Spanish* θiuˈðað bikˈtorja) n a city in E central Mexico, capital of Tamaulipas state. Pop: 285 000 (2005 est)

civet ('sɪvɪt) n **1** any catlike viverrine mammal of the genus *Viverra* and related genera, of Africa and S Asia, typically having blotched or spotted fur and secreting a powerfully smelling fluid from anal glands **2** the yellowish fatty secretion of such an animal, used as a fixative in the manufacture of perfumes **3** the fur of such an animal **4** short for **palm civet** [C16 from Old French *civette*, from Italian *zibetto*, from Arabic *zabād* civet perfume]

civic ('sɪvɪk) adj of or relating to a city, citizens, or citizenship: *civic duties* [C16 from Latin *cīvicus*, from *cīvis* citizen] > 'civically adv

civic centre n Brit the public buildings of a town, including recreational facilities and offices of local administration

civics ('sɪvɪks) n (*functioning as singular*) **1** the study of the rights and responsibilities of citizenship **2** US and Canadian the study of government and its workings

civic university n (in Britain) a university originally instituted as a higher education college serving a particular city

civies ('sɪvɪz) pl n informal a variant spelling of **civvies**

civil ('sɪvˀl) adj **1** of the ordinary life of citizens as distinguished from military, legal, or ecclesiastical affairs **2** of or relating to the citizen as an individual: *civil rights* **3** of or occurring within the state or between citizens: *civil strife* **4** polite or courteous **5** a less common word for **civic 6** of or in accordance with Roman law **7** relating to the private rights of citizens [C14 from Old French, from Latin *cīvīlis*, from *cīvis* citizen] > 'civilly adv > 'civilness n

civil day n another name for **calendar day** See **day** (sense 1)

civil death n law (formerly) the loss of all civil rights because of a serious conviction. See also **attainder**

civil defence n the organizing of civilians to deal with enemy attacks

civil disobedience n a refusal to obey laws, pay taxes, etc: a nonviolent means of protesting or of attempting to achieve political goals

civil engineer n a person qualified to design, construct, and maintain public works, such as roads, bridges, harbours, etc > **civil engineering** n

civilian (sɪˈvɪljən) n **a** a person whose primary occupation is civil or nonmilitary **b** (*as modifier*): *civilian life* [C14 (originally: a practitioner of civil law): from *civile* (from the Latin phrase *jūs cīvīle* civil law) + -IAN]

civilianize or **civilianise** (sɪˈvɪljəˌnaɪz) vb (tr) to change the status of (an armed force, a base, etc) from military to nonmilitary

civility (sɪˈvɪlɪtɪ) n, pl **-ties 1** politeness or courtesy, esp when formal **2** (often plural) an act of politeness

civilization or **civilisation** (ˌsɪvɪlaɪˈzeɪʃən) n **1** a human society that has highly developed material and spiritual resources and a complex cultural, political, and legal organization; an advanced state in social development **2** the peoples or nations collectively who have achieved such a state **3** the total culture and way of life of a particular people, nation, region, or period: *classical civilization* **4** the process of bringing or achieving civilization **5** intellectual, cultural, and moral refinement **6** cities or populated areas, as contrasted with sparsely inhabited areas, deserts, etc

civilize or **civilise** (ˈsɪvɪˌlaɪz) vb (tr) **1** to bring out of savagery or barbarism into a state characteristic of civilization **2** to refine, educate, or enlighten > ˈciviˌlizable or ˈciviˌlisable adj > ˈciviˌlizer or ˈciviˌliser n

civilized or **civilised** (ˈsɪvɪˌlaɪzd) adj **1** having a high state of culture and social development **2** cultured; polite: *a civilized discussion*

civil law n **1** the law of a state relating to private and civilian affairs **2** the body of law in force in ancient Rome, esp the law applicable to private citizens **3** any system of law based on the Roman system as distinguished from the common law and canon law **4** the law of a state as distinguished from international law

civil liberty n the right of an individual to certain freedoms of speech and action

civil list n (in Britain) the annuities voted by Parliament for the support of the royal household and the royal family

civil marriage n law a marriage performed by some official other than a clergyman

civil partnership n a legal union or contract, similar to a marriage, between two people of the same sex

civil rights pl n **1** the personal rights of the individual citizen, in most countries upheld by law, as in the US **2** (modifier) of, relating to, or promoting equality in social, economic, and political rights

civil servant n a member of the civil service

civil service n **1** the service responsible for the public administration of the government of a country. It excludes the legislative, judicial, and military branches. Members of the civil service have no official political allegiance and are not generally affected by changes of governments **2** the members of the civil service collectively

civil society n the elements such as freedom of speech, an independent judiciary, etc, that make up a democratic society

civil war n war between parties, factions, or inhabitants of different regions within the same nation

Civil War n **1** English history the conflict between Charles I and the Parliamentarians resulting from disputes over their respective prerogatives. Parliament gained decisive victories at Marston Moor in 1644 and Naseby in 1645, and Charles was executed in 1649 **2** US history the war fought from 1861 to 1865 between the North and the South, sparked off by Lincoln's election as president but with deep-rooted political and economic causes, exacerbated by the slavery issue. The advantages of the North in terms of population, finance, and communications brought about the South's eventual surrender at Appomattox

civil year n another name for **calendar year** See **year** (sense 1)

civism (ˈsɪvɪzəm) n rare good citizenship [C18 from French *civisme*, from Latin *cīvis* citizen]

civvy (ˈsɪvɪ) n, pl **civvies** slang **1** a civilian **2** (plural) civilian dress as opposed to uniform **3 civvy street** civilian life

CJ abbreviation for Chief Justice

CJA (in Britain) abbreviation for Criminal Justice Act

CJD abbreviation for **Creutzfeldt-Jakob disease**

ck the internet domain name for Cook Islands

cl¹ symbol for centilitre

cl² the internet domain name for Chile

Cl the chemical symbol for chlorine

CL international car registration for Sri Lanka [from Ceylon]

clabby-doo (ˌklæbɪˈduː) n Scot a variant of **clappy-doo**

clachan (Gaelic ˈklaxən; English ˈklæ-) n Scot and Irish dialect a small village; hamlet [C15 from Scottish Gaelic: probably from *clach* stone]

clack (klæk) vb **1** to make or cause to make a sound like that of two pieces of wood hitting each other **2** (intr) to jabber **3** a less common word for **cluck** ⊳ n **4** a short sharp sound **5** a person or thing that produces this sound **6** chatter **7** Also called: **clack valve** a simple nonreturn valve using either a hinged flap or a ball [C13 probably from Old Norse *klaka* to twitter, of imitative origin]

clacker (ˈklækə) n **1** an object that makes a clacking sound **2** Northern English dialect the mouth

Clackmannan (klækˈmænən) n a town in E central Scotland, in Clackmannanshire. Pop: 3450 (2001)

Clackmannanshire (klækˈmænənˌʃɪə, -ʃə) n a council area and historical county of central Scotland; became part of the Central region in 1975 but reinstated as an independent unitary authority in 1996; mainly agricultural. Administrative centre: Alloa. Pop: 47 680 (2003 est). Area: 142 sq km (55 sq miles)

Clacton or **Clacton-on-Sea** (ˈklæktən) n a town and resort in SE England, in E Essex. Pop: 51 284 (2001)

Clactonian (klækˈtəʊnɪən) n **1** one of the Lower Palaeolithic cultures found in England, characterized by the use of chopper tools ⊳ adj **2** of, designating, or relating to this culture [after CLACTON, Essex, where the tools of this culture were first found]

clad¹ (klæd) vb a past participle of **clothe** [Old English *clāthode* clothed, from *clāthian* to CLOTHE]

clad² (klæd) vb **clads, cladding, clad** (tr) to bond a metal to (another metal), esp to form a protective coating [C14 (in the obsolete sense: to clothe): special use of CLAD¹]

Claddagh ring (ˈklædə) n Irish any of various elaborately designed rings, esp one in the shape of two hands embracing a heart, given as a token of lasting affection [from *Claddagh*, a small fishing village on the edge of Galway city]

claddie (ˈklædɪ) n another name for **korari**

cladding (ˈklædɪŋ) n **1** the process of protecting one metal by bonding a second metal to its surface **2** the protective coating so bonded to metal **3** the material used for the outside facing of a building, etc

clade (kleɪd) n biology a group of organisms considered as having evolved from a common ancestor [C20 from Greek *klados* branch, shoot]

cladistics (kləˈdɪstɪks) n (functioning as singular) biology a method of grouping animals that makes use of lines of descent rather than structural similarities [C20 New Latin, from Greek *klādos* branch, shoot] > **cladism** (ˈklædɪzəm) n > **cladist** (ˈklædɪst) n

cladoceran (kləˈdɒsərən) n **1** any minute freshwater crustacean of the order *Cladocera*, which includes the water fleas ⊳ adj **2** of, relating to, or belonging to the *Cladocera* [C19 from New Latin *Cladocera*, from Greek *klados* shoot + *keras* horn]

cladode (ˈklædəʊd) n botany a flattened stem resembling and functioning as a leaf, as in butcher's-broom. Also called: **cladophyll, phylloclade** [C19 from New Latin *cladōdium*, from Late Greek *kladōdēs* having many shoots]

cladogram (ˈkleɪdəʊˌgræm) n biology a treelike diagram illustrating the development of a clade

See **clade** [C20 from CLADE + -O- + -GRAM]

cladophyll (ˈklædəˌfɪl) n another name for **cladode** [C19 from Greek *klados* branch + *phullon* leaf]

claes (klez) pl n a Scot word for **clothes**

clag (klæg) dialect ⊳ n **1** sticky mud ⊳ vb (intr) **clags, clagged, clagging 2** to stick, as mud [C16 perhaps of Scandinavian origin, related to Danish *klag* sticky mud]

claggy (ˈklægɪ) adj **-gier, -giest** chiefly dialect stickily clinging, as mud

claim (kleɪm) vb (mainly tr) **1** to demand as being due or as one's property; assert one's title or right to: *he claimed the record* **2** (takes a clause as object or an infinitive) to assert as a fact; maintain against denial: *he claimed to be telling the truth* **3** to call for or need; deserve: *this problem claims our attention* **4** to take: *the accident claimed four lives* ⊳ n **5** an assertion of a right; a demand for something as due **6** an assertion of something as true, real, or factual: *he made claims for his innocence* **7** a right or just title to something; basis for demand: *a claim to fame* **8** lay claim to or stake a claim to assert one's possession of or right to **9** anything that is claimed, esp in a formal or legal manner, such as a piece of land staked out by a miner **10** law a document under seal, issued in the name of the Crown or a court, commanding the person to whom it is addressed to do or refrain from doing some specified act. former name **writ 11 a** a demand for payment in connection with an insurance policy, etc **b** the sum of money demanded [C13 from Old French *claimer* to call, appeal, from Latin *clāmāre* to shout] > ˈclaimable adj > ˈclaimer n

claimant (ˈkleɪmənt) n **1** a person who makes a claim **2** a person who brings a civil action in a court of law. Formerly called: **plaintiff** Compare **defendant** (sense 1)

claiming race n US and Canadian horse racing a race in which each owner declares beforehand the price at which his horse will be offered for sale after the race

clairaudience (ˌklɛərˈɔːdɪəns) n psychol the postulated ability to hear sounds beyond the range of normal hearing. Compare **clairvoyance** [C19 from French *clair* clear + AUDIENCE, after CLAIRVOYANCE] > ˌclairˈaudient adj, n

clair-obscure (ˌklɛərəbˈskjʊə) n another word for **chiaroscuro** [C18 from French, literally: clear-obscure]

clairvoyance (klɛəˈvɔɪəns) n **1** the alleged power of perceiving things beyond the natural range of the senses. See also **extrasensory perception 2** keen intuitive understanding [C19 from French: clear-seeing, from *clair* clear, from Latin *clārus* + *voyance*, from *voir* to see, from Latin *vidēre*]

clairvoyant (klɛəˈvɔɪənt) adj **1** of, possessing, or relating to clairvoyance **2** having great insight or second sight ⊳ n **3** a person claiming to have the power to foretell future events > clairˈvoyantly adv

clam¹ (klæm) n **1** any of various burrowing bivalve molluscs of the genera *Mya*, *Venus*, etc Many species, such as the quahog and soft-shell clam, are edible and *Tridacna gigas* is the largest known bivalve, nearly 1.5 metres long **2** the edible flesh of such a mollusc **3** informal a reticent person ⊳ vb **clams, clamming, clammed 4** (intr) chiefly US to gather clams ⊳ See also **clam up** [C16 from earlier *clamshell*, that is, shell that clamps; related to Old English *clamm* fetter, Old High German *klamma* constriction; see CLAMP¹]

clam² (klæm) vb **clams, clamming, clammed** a variant of **clem**

clamant (ˈkleɪmənt) adj **1** noisy **2** calling urgently [C17 from Latin *clāmāns*, from *clāmāre* to shout]

clamatorial (ˌklæməˈtɔːrɪəl) adj of or relating to the American flycatchers (family *Tyrannidae*). See **flycatcher** (sense 2) [C19 from New Latin *clāmātōres*, plural of Latin *clāmātor* one who shouts; see CLAMANT]

C

clambake ('klæm,beɪk) *n US and Canadian* **1** a picnic, often by the sea, at which clams, etc, are baked **2** an informal party

clamber ('klæmbə) *vb* **1** (usually foll by *up, over,* etc) to climb (something) awkwardly, esp by using both hands and feet ▷ *n* **2** a climb performed in this manner [c15 probably a variant of CLIMB] > 'clamberer *n*

clam-diggers *pl n* calf-length trousers

clammy ('klæmɪ) *adj* -mier, -miest **1** unpleasantly sticky; moist: *clammy hands* **2** (of the weather, atmosphere, etc) close; humid [c14 from Old English *clǣman* to smear; related to Old Norse *kleima,* Old High German *kleimen*] > 'clammily *adv* > 'clamminess *n*

clamour *or US* **clamor** ('klæmə) *n* **1** a loud persistent outcry, as from a large number of people **2** a vehement expression of collective feeling or outrage: *a clamour against higher prices* **3** a loud and persistent noise: *the clamour of traffic* ▷ *vb* **4** (*intr;* often foll by *for* or *against*) to make a loud noise or outcry; make a public demand: *they clamoured for attention* **5** (*tr*) to move, influence, or force by outcry: *the people clamoured him out of office* [c14 from Old French *clamour,* from Latin *clāmor,* from *clāmāre* to cry out] > 'clamourer *or US* 'clamorer *n* > 'clamorous *adj* > 'clamorously *adv* > 'clamorousness *n*

clamp¹ (klæmp) *n* **1** a mechanical device with movable jaws with which an object can be secured to a bench or with which two objects may be secured together **2** a means by which a fixed joint may be strengthened **3** *nautical* a horizontal beam fastened to the ribs for supporting the deck beams in a wooden vessel ▷ *vb* (*tr*) **4** to fix or fasten with or as if with a clamp **5** to immobilize (a car) by means of a wheel clamp **6** to inflict or impose forcefully: *they clamped a curfew on the town* [c14 from Dutch or Low German *klamp;* related to Old English *clamm* bond, fetter, Old Norse *kleppr* lump]

clamp² (klæmp) *Brit agriculture* ▷ *n* **1** a mound formed out of a harvested root crop, covered with straw and earth to protect it from winter weather **2** a pile of bricks ready for processing in a furnace ▷ *vb* **3** (*tr*) to enclose (a harvested root crop) in a mound [c16 from Middle Dutch *klamp* heap; related to CLUMP]

clamp down *vb* (*intr, adverb;* often foll by *on*) **1** to behave repressively; attempt to repress something regarded as undesirable ▷ *n* **clampdown 2** a sudden restrictive measure

clamper ('klæmpə) *n* a spiked metal frame fastened to the sole of a shoe to prevent slipping on ice

clamshell ('klæm,ʃɛl) *n* **1** *chiefly US* a dredging bucket that is hinged like the shell of a clam **2** *aeronautics* **a** an aircraft cockpit canopy hinged at the front and rear **b** the hinged door of a cargo aircraft **c** another name for **eyelid** (sense 2) **3** any of a variety of objects hinged like the shell of a clam, such as a container for takeaway food, a portable computer, etc

clam up *vb* (*intr, adverb*) *informal* to keep or become silent or withhold information

clamworm ('klæm,wɜːm) *n* the US name for the **ragworm**

clan (klæn) *n* **1** a group of people interrelated by ancestry or marriage **2** a group of families with a common surname and a common ancestor, acknowledging the same leader, esp among the Scots and the Irish **3** a group of people united by common characteristics, aims, or interests [c14 from Scottish Gaelic *clann* family, descendants, from Latin *planta* sprout, PLANT¹]

clandestine (klæn'dɛstɪn) *adj* secret and concealed, often for illicit reasons; furtive [c16 from Latin *clandestinus,* from *clam* secretly; related to Latin *celāre* to hide] > clan'destinely *adv* > clan'destineness *n*

clang (klæŋ) *vb* **1** to make or cause to make a loud resounding noise, as metal when struck **2** (*intr*) to move or operate making such a sound ▷ *n* **3** a resounding metallic noise **4** the harsh cry of certain birds [c16 from Latin *clangere*]

clang association *n psychol* the association made between two words because they sound similar; for example *cling* and *ring*

clanger ('klæŋə) *n* **1** *informal* a conspicuous mistake (esp in the phrase **drop a clanger**) **2** something that clangs or causes a clang [c20 from CLANG, referring to a mistake whose effects seem to clang]

clangour *or US* **clangor** ('klæŋɡə, 'klæŋə) *n* **1** a loud resonant often-repeated noise **2** an uproar ▷ *vb* **3** (*intr*) to make or produce a loud resonant noise [c16 from Latin *clangor* a noise, from *clangere* to CLANG] > 'clangorous *adj* > 'clangorously *adv*

clank (klæŋk) *n* **1** an abrupt harsh metallic sound ▷ *vb* **2** to make or cause to make such a sound **3** (*intr*) to move or operate making such a sound [c17 of imitative origin] > 'clankingly *adv*

clannish ('klænɪʃ) *adj* **1** of or characteristic of a clan **2** tending to associate closely within a limited group to the exclusion of outsiders; cliquish > 'clannishly *adv* > 'clannishness *n*

clansman ('klænzmən) *n, pl* -men a man belonging to a clan

clanswoman ('klænz,wʊmən) *n, pl* -women a woman belonging to a clan

clap¹ (klæp) *vb* **claps, clapping, clapped 1** to make or cause to make a sharp abrupt sound, as of two nonmetallic objects struck together **2** to applaud (someone or something) by striking the palms of the hands together sharply **3** (*tr*) to strike (a person) lightly with an open hand, in greeting, encouragement, etc **4** (*tr*) to place or put quickly or forcibly: *they clapped him into jail* **5** (of certain birds) to flap (the wings) noisily **6** (*tr;* foll by *up* or *together*) to contrive or put together hastily: *they soon clapped up a shed* **7** **clap eyes on** *informal* to catch sight of **8** **clap hold of** *informal* to grasp suddenly or forcibly ▷ *n* **9** the sharp abrupt sound produced by striking the hands together **10** the act of clapping, esp in applause: *he deserves a good clap* **11** a sudden sharp sound, esp of thunder **12** a light blow **13** *archaic* a sudden action or mishap [Old English *clæppan;* related to Old High German *klepfen,* Middle Dutch *klape* rattle, Dutch *klepel* clapper; all of imitative origin]

clap² (klæp) *n* (usually preceded by *the*) a slang word for **gonorrhoea** [c16 from Old French *clapoir* venereal sore, from *clapier* brothel, from Old Provençal *clap* heap of stones, of obscure origin]

clapboard ('klæp,bɔːd, 'klæbəd) *n* **1 a** a long thin timber board with one edge thicker than the other, used esp in the US and Canada in wood-frame construction by lapping each board over the one below **b** (*as modifier*): *a clapboard house* ▷ *vb* **2** (*tr*) to cover with such boards [c16 partial translation of Low German *klappholt,* from *klappen* to crack + *holt* wood; related to Dutch *claphout;* see BOARD]

Clapham Sect ('klæpəm) *n* a group of early 19th-century Church of England evangelicals advocating personal piety, the abolition of slavery, etc [c19 named after *Clapham,* a district of London]

clap-net *n* a net, used esp by entomologists, that can be closed instantly by pulling a string

clapometer (,klæ'pɒmɪtə) *n* a device that measures applause

clap on *vb* (*tr*) to don hastily: *they clapped on their armour*

clapped out *adj* (**clapped-out** *when prenominal*) *Brit, Austral, and NZ informal* (esp of machinery) worn out; dilapidated

clapper ('klæpə) *n* **1** a person or thing that claps **2** a contrivance for producing a sound of clapping, as for scaring birds **3** Also called: **tongue** a small piece of metal suspended within a bell that causes it to sound when made to strike against its side **4** a slang word for **tongue** (sense 1) **5** **go (run, move) like the clappers** *Brit informal* to move extremely fast

clapperboard ('klæpə,bɔːd) *n* a pair of boards clapped together during film shooting in order to aid sound synchronization

clapper bridge *n* a primitive type of bridge in which planks or slabs of stone rest on piles of stones

clapperclaw ('klæpə,klɔː) *vb* (*tr*) *archaic* **1** to claw or scratch with the hands and nails **2** to revile; abuse [c16 perhaps from CLAPPER + CLAW] > 'clapper,clawer *n*

clappy-doo (,klæpɪ'duː) *or* **clabby-doo** *n Scot* a large black mussel [c19 probably from Scottish Gaelic *clab* enormous mouth + *dubh* black]

claptrap ('klæp,træp) *n informal* **1** contrived but foolish talk **2** insincere and pretentious talk: *politicians' claptrap* [c18 (in the sense: something contrived to elicit applause): from CLAP¹ + TRAP¹]

claque (klæk) *n* **1** a group of people hired to applaud **2** a group of fawning admirers [c19 from French, from *claquer* to clap, of imitative origin]

clarabella *or* **claribella** (,klærə'bɛlə) *n* an eight-foot flute stop on an organ [c19 from Latin *clāra,* feminine of *clārus* clear + *bella,* feminine of *bellus* beautiful]

Clare (klɛə) *n* a county of W Republic of Ireland, in Munster between Galway Bay and the Shannon estuary. County town: Ennis. Pop: 103 277 (2002). Area: 3188 sq km (1231 sq miles)

clarence ('klærəns) *n* a closed four-wheeled horse-drawn carriage, having a glass front [c19 named after the Duke of *Clarence* (1765–1837)]

Clarenceux ('klærənsuː) *n heraldry* the second King-of-Arms in England

clarendon ('klærəndən) *n printing* a style of boldface roman type [c20 named after the Clarendon Press at Oxford University]

Clarendon ('klærəndən) *n* a village near Salisbury in S England: site of a council held by Henry II in 1164 that produced a code of laws (the **Constitutions of Clarendon**) defining relations between church and state

Clarendon Code *n English history* four acts passed by the Cavalier Parliament between 1661 and 1665 to deal with the religious problems of the Restoration [c17 named after Edward Hyde, first Earl of Clarendon (1609–74), English statesman and historian, who was not, however, a supporter of the code]

claret ('klærət) *n* **1** *chiefly Brit* a red wine, esp one from the Bordeaux district of France **2 a** a purplish-red colour **b** (*as adjective*): *a claret carpet* [c14 from Old French (*vin*) *claret* clear (wine), from Medieval Latin *clārātum,* from *clārāre* to make clear, from Latin *clārus* CLEAR]

claret cup *n* an iced drink made of claret, brandy, lemon, sugar, and sometimes sherry, Curaçao, etc

clarify ('klærɪ,faɪ) *vb* -fies, -fying, -fied **1** to make or become clear or easy to understand **2** to make or become free of impurities **3** to make (fat, butter, etc) clear by heating, etc, or (of fat, etc) to become clear as a result of such a process [c14 from Old French *clarifier,* from Late Latin *clārificāre,* from Latin *clārus* clear + *facere* to make] > ,clarifi'cation *n* > 'clari,fier *n*

clarinet (,klærɪ'nɛt) *n music* **1** a keyed woodwind instrument with a cylindrical bore and a single reed. It is a transposing instrument, most commonly pitched in A or B flat. Obsolete name: clarionet (,klærɪə'nɛt) **2** an orchestral musician who plays the clarinet [c18 from French *clarinette,* probably from Italian *clarinetto,* from *clarino* trumpet] > ,clari'nettist *or* ,clari'netist *n*

clarino (klæ'riːnəʊ) *adj* **1** of or relating to a high passage for the trumpet in 18th-century music ▷ *n, pl* -nos *or* -ni (-nɪ) **2** the high register of the trumpet **3** an organ stop similar to the high register of the trumpet **4** a trumpet or clarion

clarion ('klærɪən) *n* **1** a four-foot reed stop of trumpet quality on an organ **2** an obsolete, high-pitched, small-bore trumpet **3** the sound of such an instrument or any similar sound ▷ *adj* **4**

(*prenominal*) clear and ringing; inspiring: *a clarion call to action* ▷ *vb* **5** to proclaim loudly [C14 from Medieval Latin *clāriō* trumpet, from Latin *clārus* clear]

clarity ('klærɪtɪ) *n* **1** clearness, as of expression **2** clearness, as of water [C16 from Latin *clāritās*, from *clārus* CLEAR]

Clark cell (klɑːk) *n physics* a cell having a mercury cathode surrounded by a paste of mercuric sulphate and a zinc anode in a saturated solution of zinc sulphate. Formerly used as a standard, its emf is 1.4345 volts [C19 named after Hosiah *Clark* (died 1898), English scientist]

clarkia ('klɑːkɪə) *n* any North American onagraceous plant of the genus *Clarkia*: cultivated for their red, purple, or pink flowers [C19 New Latin, named after William Clark (1770–1838), US explorer and frontiersman, who discovered it]

claro ('klɑːrəʊ) *n, pl* **-ros** *or* **-roes** a mild light-coloured cigar [from Spanish: CLEAR]

clarsach ('klɑrsəx, 'klɑːsək) *n* the Celtic harp of Scotland and Ireland [C15 *clareschaw*, from Scottish Gaelic *clarsach*, Irish Gaelic *cláirsach* harp]

clarthead ('klɑːtˌhɛd) *n Northern English dialect* a slow-witted or stupid person

clarts (klɑːts; *Scot* klærts) *pl n Scot and Northern English dialect* lumps of mud, esp on shoes [of unknown origin]

clarty ('klɑːtɪ; *Scot* 'klærtɪ) *adj* **clartier, clartiest** *Scot and Northern English dialect* dirty, esp covered in mud; filthy

clary ('klɛərɪ) *n, pl* **claries** any of several European plants of the genus *Salvia*, having aromatic leaves and blue flowers: family *Lamiaceae* (labiates) [C14 from earlier *sclarreye*, from Medieval Latin *sclareia*, of obscure origin]

-clase *n combining form* (in mineralogy) indicating a particular type of cleavage: *plagioclase* [via French from Greek *klasis* a breaking, from *klan* to break]

clash (klæʃ) *vb* **1** to make or cause to make a loud harsh sound, esp by striking together **2** (*intr*) to be incompatible; conflict **3** (*intr*) to engage together in conflict or contest **4** (*intr*) (of dates or events) to coincide **5** (*intr*) (of colours) to look ugly or inharmonious together ▷ *n* **6** a loud harsh noise **7** a collision or conflict **8** *Scot* gossip; tattle [C16 of imitative origin] > **'clasher** *n* > **'clashingly** *adv*

clasp (klɑːsp) *n* **1** a fastening, such as a catch or hook, used for holding things together **2** a firm grasp, hold, or embrace **3** *military* a bar or insignia on a medal ribbon, to indicate either a second award or the battle, campaign, or reason for its award ▷ *vb* (*tr*) **4** to hold in a firm grasp **5** to grasp firmly with the hand **6** to fasten together with or as if with a clasp [C14 of uncertain origin; compare Old English *clyppan* to embrace] > **'clasper** *n*

claspers ('klɑːspəz) *pl n zoology* **1** a paired organ of male insects, used to clasp the female during copulation **2** a paired organ of male sharks and related fish, used to assist the transfer of spermatozoa into the body of the female during copulation

clasp knife *n* a large knife with one or more blades or other devices folding into the handle

class (klɑːs) *n* **1** a collection or division of people or things sharing a common characteristic, attribute, quality, or property **2** a group of persons sharing a similar social position and certain economic, political, and cultural characteristics **3** (in Marxist theory) a group of persons sharing the same relationship to the means of production **4 a** the pattern of divisions that exist within a society on the basis of rank, economic status, etc **b** (*as modifier*): *the class struggle; class distinctions* **5 a** a group of pupils or students who are taught and study together **b** a meeting of a group of students for tuition **6** *chiefly US* a group of students who graduated in a specified year: *the class of '53* **7** (*in combination and as modifier*) *Brit* a grade of attainment in a university honours degree: *second-class honours* **8** one of several standards of accommodation in public transport. See also **first class, second class, third class 9 a** *informal* excellence or elegance, esp in dress, design, or behaviour: *that girl's got class* **b** (*as modifier*): *a class act* **10 a** outstanding speed and stamina in a racehorse **b** (*as modifier*): *the class horse in the race* **11** *biology* any of the taxonomic groups into which a phylum is divided and which contains one or more orders. *Amphibia*, *Reptilia*, and *Mammalia* are three classes of phylum *Chordata* **12** *maths, logic* **a** another name for **set**[2] (sense 3) **b** **proper class** a class which cannot itself be a member of other classes **13 in a class of its own** *or* **in a class by oneself** unequalled; unparalleled ▷ *vb* **14** to have or assign a place within a group, grade, or class [C17 from Latin *classis* class, rank, fleet; related to Latin *calāre* to summon] > **'classable** *adj* > **'classer** *n*

class-A amplifier *n* an electronic amplifier in which the output current flows for the whole of the input signal cycle

class action *n US law* a legal action undertaken by one or more people representing the interests of a large group of people with the same grievance

class A drug *n law* (in Britain) any of the most dangerous group of controlled drugs, including heroin, cocaine, and MDMA. Compare **class B drug, class C drug**

class-B amplifier *n* an electronic amplifier in which the output flows for half of the input signal cycle

class B drug *n law* (in Britain) any of the second most dangerous group of controlled drugs, including amphetamine. Compare **class A drug, class C drug**

class-C amplifier *n* an electronic amplifier in which the output current flows for less than half of the input cycle

class C drug *n law* (in Britain) any of the least dangerous group of controlled drugs, including temazepam and cannabis. Compare **class A drug, class B drug**

class-conscious *adj* aware of belonging to a particular social rank or grade, esp in being hostile or proud because of class distinctions > **ˌclass-'consciousness** *n*

classic ('klæsɪk) *adj* **1** of the highest class, esp in art or literature **2** serving as a standard or model of its kind; definitive **3** adhering to an established set of rules or principles in the arts or sciences: *a classic proof* **4** characterized by simplicity, balance, regularity, and purity of form; classical **5** of lasting interest or significance **6** continuously in fashion because of its simple and basic style: *a classic day dress* ▷ *n* **7** an author, artist, or work of art of the highest excellence **8** a creation or work considered as definitive **9** *horse racing* **a** any of the five principal races for three-year-old horses in Britain, namely the One Thousand Guineas, Two Thousand Guineas, Derby, Oaks, and Saint Leger **b** a race equivalent to any of these in other countries ▷ See also **classics** [C17 from Latin *classicus* of the first rank, from *classis* division, rank, CLASS]

classical ('klæsɪkᵊl) *adj* **1** of, relating to, or characteristic of the ancient Greeks and Romans or their civilization, esp in the period of their ascendancy **2** designating, following, or influenced by the art or culture of ancient Greece or Rome: *classical architecture* **3** *music* **a** of, relating to, or denoting any music or its period of composition marked by stability of form, intellectualism, and restraint. Compare **romantic** (sense 5) **b** accepted as a standard: *the classical suite* **c** denoting serious art music in general. Compare **pop** (sense 2) **4** *music* of or relating to a style of music composed, esp at Vienna, during the late 18th and early 19th centuries. This period is marked by the establishment, esp by Haydn and Mozart, of sonata form **5** denoting or relating to a style in any of the arts characterized by emotional restraint and conservatism: *a classical style of painting*. See **classicism** (sense 1) **6** well versed in the art and literature of ancient Greece and Rome **7** (of an education) based on the humanities and the study of Latin and Greek **8** *physics* **a** not involving the quantum theory or the theory of relativity: *classical mechanics* **b** obeying the laws of Newtonian mechanics or 19th-century physics: *a classical gas* **9** another word for **classic** (senses 2, 4) **10** (of a logical or mathematical system) according with the law of excluded middle, so that every statement is known to be either true or false even if it is not known which > **ˌclassi'cality** *or* **'classicalness** *n* > **'classically** *adv*

classical college *n* (in Quebec) a college offering a programme that emphasizes the classics and leads to university entrance

classical conditioning *n psychol* the alteration in responding that occurs when two stimuli are regularly paired in close succession: the response originally given to the second stimulus comes to be given to the first. See also **conditioned response**

classical probability *n* another name for **mathematical probability**

Classical school *n* economic theory based on the works of Adam Smith and David Ricardo, which explains the creation of wealth and advocates free trade

classic blues *n* (*functioning as singular or plural*) *jazz* a type of city blues performed by a female singer accompanied by a small group

classic car *n chiefly Brit* a car that is more than twenty-five years old. Compare **veteran car, vintage car**

classicism ('klæsɪˌsɪzəm) *or* **classicalism** ('klæsɪkəˌlɪzəm) *n* **1** a style based on the study of Greek and Roman models, characterized by emotional restraint and regularity of form, associated esp with the 18th century in Europe; the antithesis of romanticism. Compare **neoclassicism** **2** knowledge or study of the culture of ancient Greece and Rome **3 a** a Greek or Latin form or expression **b** an expression in a modern language, such as English, that is modelled on a Greek or Latin form

classicist ('klæsɪsɪst) *or* **classicalist** ('klæsɪkəlɪst) *n* **1 a** a student of ancient Latin and Greek **b** a person who advocates the study of ancient Latin and Greek **2** an adherent of classicism in literature or art > **ˌclassi'cistic** *adj*

classicize *or* **classicise** ('klæsɪˌsaɪz) *vb* **1** (*tr*) to make classic **2** (*intr*) to imitate classical style

classics ('klæsɪks) *pl n* **1 the** a body of literature regarded as great or lasting, esp that of ancient Greece or Rome **2 the** the ancient Greek and Latin languages **3** (*functioning as singular*) ancient Greek and Roman culture considered as a subject for academic study

classification (ˌklæsɪfɪ'keɪʃən) *n* **1** systematic placement in categories **2** one of the divisions in a system of classifying **3** *biology* **a** the placing of animals and plants in a series of increasingly specialized groups because of similarities in structure, origin, molecular composition, etc, that indicate a common relationship. The major groups are domain or superkingdom, kingdom, phylum (in animals) or division (in plants), class, order, family, genus, and species **b** the study of the principles and practice of this process; taxonomy **4** *government* the designation of an item of information as being secret and not available to people outside a restricted group [C18 from French; see CLASS, -IFY, -ATION] > **ˌclassifi'cational** *adj* > **ˌclassifi'catory** *adj*

classification schedule *n library science* the printed scheme of a system of classification

classified ('klæsɪˌfaɪd) *adj* **1** arranged according to some system of classification **2** *government* (of information) not available to people outside a restricted group, esp for reasons of national security **3** (of information) closely concealed or secret **4** (of advertisements in newspapers, etc)

C

arranged according to type **5** *Brit* (of newspapers) containing sports results, esp football results **6** (of British roads) having a number in the national road system. If the number is preceded by an M the road is a motorway, if by an A it is a first-class road, and if by a B it is a secondary road

classify (ˈklæsɪˌfaɪ) *vb* **-fies, -fying, -fied** (*tr*) **1** to arrange or order by classes; categorize **2** *government* to declare (information, documents, etc) of possible aid to an enemy and therefore not available to people outside a restricted group [c18 back formation from CLASSIFICATION] > ˈ**classiˌfiable** *adj* > ˈ**classiˌfier** *n*

class interval *n* *statistics* one of the intervals into which the range of a variable of a distribution is divided, esp one of the divisions of the base line of a bar chart or histogram

classis (ˈklæsɪs) *n, pl* **classes** (ˈklæsiːz) (in some Reformed Churches) **1** a governing body of elders or pastors **2** the district or group of local churches directed by such a body [c16 from Latin; see CLASS]

classism (ˈklɑːsɪzəm) *n* the belief that people from certain social or economic classes are superior to others > ˈ**classist** *adj*

classless (ˈklɑːslɪs) *adj* **1** not belonging to or forming a class **2** characterized by the absence of economic and social distinctions > ˈ**classlessness** *n*

class list *n* (in Britain) a list categorizing students according to the class of honours they have obtained in their degree examination

class mark *n* **1** *statistics* a value within a class interval, esp its midpoint or the nearest integral value, used to represent the interval for computational convenience **2** Also called: **class number** *library science* a symbol on a book or other publication indicating its subject field, shelf position, etc

classmate (ˈklɑːsˌmeɪt) *n* a friend or contemporary of the same class in a school, college, etc

classroom (ˈklɑːsˌruːm, -ˌrʊm) *n* a room in which classes are conducted, esp in a school or college

classroom assistant *n* a person whose job is to help a schoolteacher in the classroom. Also called: **learning support assistant**

class struggle *n* **the** *marxism* the continual conflict between the capitalist and working classes for economic and political power. Also called: **class war**

classy (ˈklɑːsɪ) *adj* **classier, classiest** *informal* elegant; stylish > ˈ**classily** *adv* > ˈ**classiness** *n*

clastic (ˈklæstɪk) *adj* **1** (of sedimentary rock, etc) composed of fragments of pre-existing rock that have been transported some distance from their points of origin **2** *biology* dividing into parts: *a clastic cell* **3** able to be dismantled for study or observation: *a clastic model of the brain* [c19 from Greek *klastos* shattered, from *klan* to break]

clat (klæt) *n* *dialect* an irksome or troublesome task

clathrate (ˈklæθreɪt) *adj* **1** resembling a net or lattice ▷ *n* **2** *chem* a solid compound in which molecules of one substance are physically trapped in the crystal lattice of another [c17 from Latin *clāthrāre* to provide with a lattice, from Greek *klēthra*, from *klaithron* a bar]

clatter (ˈklætə) *vb* **1** to make or cause to make a rattling noise, esp as a result of movement **2** (*intr*) to chatter ▷ *n* **3** a rattling sound or noise **4** a noisy commotion, such as one caused by loud chatter [Old English *clatrung* clattering (gerund); related to Dutch *klateren* to rattle, German *klatschen* to smack, Norwegian *klattra* to knock] > ˈ**clatterer** *n* > ˈ**clatteringly** *adv* > ˈ**clattery** *adj*

claudication (ˌklɔːdɪˈkeɪʃən) *n* **1** limping; lameness **2** *pathol* short for **intermittent claudication** [c18 from Latin *claudicātiō*, from *claudicāre*, from *claudus* lame]

clause (klɔːz) *n* **1** *grammar* a group of words, consisting of a subject and a predicate including a finite verb, that does not necessarily constitute a sentence. See also **main clause, subordinate clause, coordinate clause** **2** a section of a legal document such as a contract, will, or draft statute [c13 from Old French, from Medieval Latin *clausa* a closing (of a rhetorical period), back formation from Latin *clausula*, from *claudere* to close] > ˈ**clausal** *adj*

claustral (ˈklɔːstrəl) *adj* a less common variant of **cloistral**

claustrophobia (ˌklɔːstrəˈfəʊbɪə, ˌklɒs-) *n* an abnormal fear of being closed in or of being in a confined space [c19 from *claustro-*, from Latin *claustrum* CLOISTER + -PHOBIA] > ˈ**claustroˌphobe** *n*

claustrophobic (ˌklɔːstrəˈfəʊbɪk, ˌklɒs-) *adj* **1** suffering from claustrophobia **2** unpleasantly cramped, confined, or closed in: *narrow claustrophobic spaces* > ˌ**claustroˈphobically** *adv*

clavate (ˈkleɪveɪt, -vɪt) *or* **claviform** *adj* shaped like a club with the thicker end uppermost [c19 from Latin *clāva* club] > ˈ**clavately** *adv*

clave[1] (kleɪv, klɑːv) *n* *music* one of a pair of hardwood sticks struck together to make a hollow sound, esp to mark the beat of Latin-American dance music [c20 from American Spanish, from Latin *clavis* key]

clave[2] (kleɪv) *vb* *archaic* a past tense of **cleave**

clave[3] (kleɪv) *n* *zoology* a clublike thickening at the upper end of an organ, esp of the antenna of an insect [c19 from Latin *clāva* club]

claver (ˈkleɪvə) *vb* (*intr*) **1** to talk idly; gossip ▷ *n* **2** (*often plural*) idle talk; gossip [c13 of uncertain origin]

clavicembalo (ˌklævɪˈtʃɛmbələʊ) *n, pl* **-los** another name for **harpsichord** [c18 from Italian, from Medieval Latin *clāvis* key + *cymbalum* CYMBAL]

clavichord (ˈklævɪˌkɔːd) *n* a keyboard instrument consisting of a number of thin wire strings struck from below by brass tangents. The instrument is noted for its delicate tones, since the tangents do not rebound from the string until the key is released [c15 from Medieval Latin *clāvichordium*, from Latin *clāvis* key + *chorda* string, CHORD[1]] > ˈ**claviˌchordist** *n*

clavicle (ˈklævɪkᵊl) *n* **1** either of the two bones connecting the shoulder blades with the upper part of the breastbone. Nontechnical name: **collarbone** **2** the corresponding structure in other vertebrates [c17 from Medieval Latin *clāvicula*, from Latin *clāvis* key] > **clavicular** (kləˈvɪkjʊlə) *adj* > **claviculate** (kləˈvɪkjʊˌleɪt) *adj*

clavicorn (ˈklævɪˌkɔːn) *n* **1** any beetle of the group *Clavicornia*, including the ladybirds, characterized by club-shaped antennae ▷ *adj* **2** of, relating to, or belonging to the *Clavicornia* [c19 from New Latin *Clavicornia*, from Latin *clāva* club + *cornū* horn]

clavier (kləˈvɪə, ˈklævɪə) *n* **a** any keyboard instrument **b** the keyboard itself [c18 from French: keyboard, from Old French (in the sense: key bearer), from Latin *clāvis* key]

claviform (ˈklævɪˌfɔːm) *adj* another word for **clavate** [c19 from Latin *clāva* club]

Clavius (ˈkleɪvɪəs) *n* one of the largest of the craters on the moon, about 230 kilometres (145 miles) in diameter, whose walls have peaks up to 5700 metres (19 000 feet) above the floor. It lies in the SE quadrant

claw (klɔː) *n* **1** a curved pointed horny process on the end of each digit in birds, some reptiles, and certain mammals **2** a corresponding structure in some invertebrates, such as the pincer of a crab **3** a part or member like a claw in function or appearance **4** *botany* the narrow basal part of certain petals and sepals ▷ *vb* **5** to scrape, tear, or dig (something or someone) with claws, etc **6** (*tr*) to create by scratching as with claws: *to claw an opening* [Old English *clawu*; related to Old High German *kluwi*, Sanskrit *glau-* ball, sphere] > ˈ**clawer** *n* > ˈ**clawless** *adj*

claw back *vb* (*tr, adverb*) **1** to get back (something) with difficulty **2** to recover (a sum of money), esp by taxation or a penalty ▷ *n* **clawback** **3** the recovery of a sum of money, esp by taxation or a penalty **4** the sum so recovered

claw hammer *n* a hammer with a cleft at one end of the head for extracting nails. Also called: **carpenter's hammer**

claw hatchet *n* a hatchet with a claw at one end of its head for extracting nails

claw off *vb* (*adverb, usually tr*) *nautical* to avoid the dangers of (a lee shore or other hazard) by beating

claw setting *n* *Brit* a jewellery setting with clawlike prongs. US equivalent: **Tiffany setting**

clay (kleɪ) *n* **1** a very fine-grained material that consists of hydrated aluminium silicate, quartz, and organic fragments and occurs as sedimentary rocks, soils, and other deposits. It becomes plastic when moist but hardens on heating and is used in the manufacture of bricks, cement, ceramics, etc. Related adj: **figuline** **2** earth or mud in general **3** *poetic* the material of the human body ▷ *vb* **4** (*tr*) to cover or mix with clay [Old English *clǣg*; related to Old High German *klīa*, Norwegian *kli*, Latin *glūs* glue, Greek *gloios* sticky oil] > ˈ**clayey**, ˈ**clayish** *or* ˈ**clayˌlike** *adj*

claybank (ˈkleɪˌbæŋk) *n* *US* **a** a dull brownish-orange colour **b** (*as adjective*): *a claybank horse*

clay court *n* a tennis court with a playing surface topped by a layer of crushed shale, brick, or stone

claymation (ˌkleɪˈmeɪʃən) *n* the techniques of animation applied to clay models [c20 from CLAY + (ANI)MATION]

clay mineral *n* any of a group of minerals consisting of hydrated aluminium silicates: the major constituents of clays

claymore (ˈkleɪˌmɔː; *Scot* ˌkleˈmor) *n* **1** a large two-edged broadsword used formerly by Scottish Highlanders **2** a US type of antipersonnel mine [c18 from Gaelic *claidheamh mōr* great sword]

claypan (ˈkleɪˌpæn) *n* a layer of stiff impervious clay situated just below the surface of the ground, which holds water after heavy rain

clay pigeon *n* **1** a disc of baked clay hurled into the air from a machine as a target to be shot at **2** *US slang* a person in a defenceless position; sitting duck

clay road *n* *NZ* an unsealed and unmetalled road in a rural area

claystone (ˈkleɪˌstəʊn) *n* a compact very fine-grained rock consisting of consolidated clay particles

claytonia (kleɪˈtəʊnɪə) *n* any low-growing North American succulent portulacaceous plant of the genus *Claytonia* [c18 named after John *Clayton* (1693–1773), American botanist]

CLC *abbreviation for* Canadian Labour Congress

-cle *suffix forming nouns* indicating smallness: *cubicle; particle* [via Old French from Latin *-culus*. See -CULE]

clean (kliːn) *adj* **1** without dirt or other impurities; unsoiled **2** without anything in it or on it: *a clean page* **3** without extraneous or foreign materials **4** without defect, difficulties, or problems: *a clean test flight* **5** **a** (of a nuclear weapon) producing little or no radioactive fallout or contamination **b** uncontaminated. Compare **dirty** (sense 11) **6** (of a wound, etc) having no pus or other sign of infection **7** pure; morally sound **8** without objectionable language or obscenity: *a clean joke* **9** (of printer's proofs, etc) relatively free from errors; easily readable: *clean copy* **10** thorough or complete: *a clean break* **11** dexterous or adroit: *a clean throw* **12** *sport* played fairly and without fouls **13** simple in design: *a ship's clean lines* **14** *aeronautics* causing little turbulence; streamlined **15** (of an aircraft) having no projections, such as rockets, flaps, etc, into the airstream **16** honourable or respectable **17** habitually neat **18** (esp of a driving licence) showing or having no record of offences **19** *slang* **a** innocent; not guilty **b** not carrying illegal drugs, weapons, etc **20** *nautical* (of a vessel) **a** having its bottom clean **b** having a satisfactory bill of health **21** *Old Testament* **a** (of persons) free from ceremonial defilement **b** (of animals, birds, and fish) lawful to eat **22** *New Testament* morally and spiritually pure **23** **clean sweep** See **sweep**

(sense 33) ▷ *vb* **24** to make or become free of dirt, filth, etc: *the stove cleans easily* **25** (*tr*) to remove in making clean: *to clean marks off the wall* **26** (*tr*) to prepare (fish, poultry, etc) for cooking: *to clean a chicken* ▷ *adv* **27** in a clean way; cleanly **28** *not standard* (intensifier): *clean forgotten; clean dead* **29** **clean bowled** *cricket* bowled by a ball that breaks the wicket without hitting the batsman or his bat **30** **come clean** *informal* to make a revelation or confession ▷ *n* **31** the act or an instance of cleaning: *he gave his shoes a clean* ▷ See also **clean out, clean up** [Old English *clǣne*; related to Old Frisian *klēne* small, neat, Old High German *kleini*] > ˈ**cleanable** *adj* > ˈ**cleanness** *n*

clean-cut *adj* **1** clearly outlined; neat: *clean-cut lines of a ship* **2** definite: *a clean-cut decision in boxing*

cleaner (ˈkliːnə) *n* **1** a person, device, chemical agent, etc, that removes dirt, as from clothes or carpets **2** (*usually plural*) a shop, etc that provides a dry-cleaning service **3** **take (a person) to the cleaners** *informal* to rob or defraud (a person) of all of his money

clean-limbed *adj* having well-proportioned limbs

cleanly *adv* (ˈkliːnlɪ) **1** in a fair manner **2** easily or smoothly: *the screw went into the wood cleanly* ▷ *adj* (ˈklɛnlɪ) **-lier, -liest** **3** habitually clean or neat > **cleanlily** (ˈklɛnlɪlɪ) *adv* > **cleanliness** (ˈklɛnlɪnɪs) *n*

clean out *vb* (*tr, adverb*) **1** (foll by *of* or *from*) to remove (something) (from or away from) **2** *slang* to leave (someone) with no money: *gambling had cleaned him out* **3** *informal* to exhaust (stocks, goods, etc) completely

cleanse (klɛnz) *vb* (*tr*) **1** to remove dirt, filth, etc, from **2** to remove guilt from **3** to remove a group of people from (an area) by means of ethnic cleansing [Old English *clǣnsian*; related to Middle Low German *klēnsen*; see CLEAN] > ˈ**cleansable** *adj*

cleanser (ˈklɛnzə) *n* a cleansing agent, such as a detergent

clean-shaven *adj* (of men) having the facial hair shaved off

clean sheet *n* *sport* an instance of conceding no goals or points in a match or competition (esp in the phrase **keep a clean sheet**)

cleanskin (ˈkliːnˌskɪn) *n* *Austral* **1** an unbranded animal **2** *slang* a person without a criminal record

clean up *vb* (*adverb*) **1** to rid (something) of dirt, filth, or other impurities **2** to make (someone or something) orderly or presentable **3** (*tr*) to rid (a place) of undesirable people or conditions: *the campaign against vice had cleaned up the city* **4** (*intr*) *informal* to make a great profit ▷ *n* **cleanup** **5** **a** the process of cleaning up or eliminating something **b** (*as modifier*): *a cleanup campaign* **6** *informal, chiefly US* a great profit

clean wool *n* wool that has been scoured to remove wax

clear (klɪə) *adj* **1** free from darkness or obscurity; bright **2** (of weather) free from dullness or clouds **3** transparent: *clear water* **4** even and pure in tone or colour: *clear blue* **5** without discoloration, blemish, or defect: *a clear skin* **6** easy to see or hear; distinct **7** free from doubt or confusion: *his instructions are not clear* **8** (*postpositive*) certain in the mind; sure: *are you clear?* **9** evident or obvious: *it is clear that he won't come now* **10** (of sounds or the voice) not harsh or hoarse **11** serene; calm **12** without qualification or limitation; complete: *a clear victory* **13** free of suspicion, guilt, or blame: *a clear conscience* **14** free of obstruction; open: *a clear passage* **15** free from debt or obligation **16** (of money, profits, etc) without deduction; net **17** emptied of freight or cargo **18** (of timber) having a smooth, unblemished surface **19** Also: **in clear** (of a message, etc) not in code **20** Also: **light** *phonetics* denoting an (l) in whose articulation the main part of the tongue is brought forward giving the sound of a front-vowel timbre **21** *showjumping* (of a round) ridden without any fences being knocked down or any points being lost ▷ *adv* **22** in a clear or distinct manner **23** completely or utterly **24** (*postpositive; often foll by of*) not in contact (with); free: *stand clear of the gates* ▷ *n* **25** a clear space **26** another word for **clearance** **27** **in the clear** **a** free of suspicion, guilt, or blame **b** *sport* able to receive a pass without being tackled ▷ *vb* **28** to make or become free from darkness, obscurity, etc **29** (*intr*) **a** (of the weather) to become free from dullness, fog, rain, etc **b** (of mist, fog, etc) to disappear **30** (*tr*) to free from impurity or blemish **31** (*tr*) to free from doubt or confusion: *to clear one's mind* **32** (*tr*) to rid of objects, obstructions, etc **33** (*tr*) to make or form (a path, way, etc) by removing obstructions **34** (*tr*) to free or remove (a person or thing) from something, such as suspicion, blame, or guilt **35** (*tr*) to move or pass by or over without contact or involvement: *he cleared the wall easily* **36** (*tr*) to rid (the throat) of phlegm or obstruction **37** (*tr*) to make or gain (money) as profit **38** (*tr; often foll by off*) to discharge or settle (a debt) **39** (*tr*) to free (a debtor) from obligation **40** (*intr*) (of a cheque) to pass through one's bank and be charged against one's account **41** *banking* to settle accounts by exchanging (commercial documents) in a clearing house **42** to permit (ships, aircraft, cargo, passengers, etc) to unload, disembark, depart, etc, after fulfilling the customs and other requirements, or (of ships, etc) to be permitted to unload, etc **43** to obtain or give (clearance) **44** (*tr*) to obtain clearance from **45** (*tr*) *microscopy* to make (specimens) transparent by immersion in a fluid such as xylene **46** (*tr*) to permit (a person, company, etc) to see or handle classified information **47** (*tr*) *military* **a** to achieve transmission of (a signalled message) and acknowledgment of its receipt at its destination **b** to decode (a message, etc) **48** (*tr*) *sport* to hit, kick, carry, or throw (the ball) out of the defence area **49** (*tr*) *computing* to remove data from a storage device and replace it with particular characters that usually indicate zero **50** (*tr*) *NZ* to remove (trees, scrub, etc) from land **51** **clear the air** See **air** (sense 11) **52** **clear the decks** to prepare for action, as by removing obstacles from a field of activity or combat ▷ See also **clear away, clear off, clear out, clear up** [C13 *clere*, from Old French *cler*, from Latin *clārus* clear, bright, brilliant, illustrious] > ˈ**clearable** *adj* > ˈ**clearer** *n* > ˈ**clearness** *n*

clearance (ˈklɪərəns) *n* **1** **a** the process or an instance of clearing: *slum clearance* **b** (*as modifier*): *a clearance order* **2** space between two parts in motion or in relative motion **3** permission for an aircraft, ship, passengers, etc, to proceed **4** *banking* the exchange of commercial documents drawn on the members of a clearing house **5** **a** the disposal of merchandise at reduced prices **b** (*as modifier*): *a clearance sale* **6** *sport* **a** the act of hitting or kicking a ball out of the defensive area, as in football **b** an instance of this **7** the act of clearing an area of land of its inhabitants by mass eviction. See **Highland Clearances** **8** *dentistry* the extraction of all of a person's teeth **9** a less common word for **clearing**

clear away *vb* (*adverb*) to remove (objects) from (the table) after a meal

clearcole (ˈklɪəkəʊl) *n* **1** a type of size containing whiting ▷ *vb* **2** (*tr*) to paint (a wall) with this size [C19 from French *claire colle* clear size]

clear-cut *adj* (**clear cut** *when postpositive*) **1** definite; not vague: *a clear-cut proposal* **2** clearly outlined ▷ *vb* **3** (*tr*) another term for **clear-fell**

clear-eyed *adj* **1** discerning; perceptive **2** having clear eyes or sharp vision

clear-fell *vb* (*tr*) to cut down all of the trees in (a wood, part of a wood, or throughout an area of land)

clear-headed *adj* mentally alert; sensible; judicious > ˌ**clear-ˈheadedly** *adv* > ˌ**clear-ˈheadedness** *n*

clearing (ˈklɪərɪŋ) *n* an area with few or no trees or shrubs in wooded or overgrown land

clearing bank *n* (in Britain) any bank that makes use of the central clearing house in London for the transfer of credits and cheques between banks

clearing house *n* **1** *banking* an institution where cheques and other commercial papers drawn on member banks are cancelled against each other so that only net balances are payable **2** a central agency for the collection and distribution of information or materials

clearing sale *n* *Austral* the auction of plant, stock, and effects of a country property, esp after the property has changed hands

clearly (ˈklɪəlɪ) *adv* **1** in a clear, distinct, or obvious manner: *I could see everything quite clearly* **2** (*sentence modifier*) it is obvious that; evidently: *clearly the social services must be flexible*

clear off *vb* (*intr, adverb*) *informal* to go away: often used imperatively

clear out *vb* (*adverb*) **1** (*intr*) *informal* to go away: often used imperatively **2** (*tr*) to remove and sort the contents of (a room, container, etc) **3** (*tr*) *slang* to leave (someone) with no money **4** (*tr*) *slang* to exhaust (stocks, goods, etc) completely

clear-sighted *adj* **1** involving accurate perception or judgment: *a clear-sighted compromise* **2** having clear vision > ˌ**clear-ˈsightedly** *adv* > ˌ**clear-ˈsightedness** *n*

clearstory (ˈklɪəˌstɔːrɪ) *n* a variant spelling of **clerestory**. > ˈ**clearˌstoried** *adj*

clear up *vb* (*adverb*) **1** (*tr*) to explain or solve (a mystery, misunderstanding, etc) **2** to put (a place or thing that is disordered) in order **3** (*intr*) (of the weather) to become brighter ▷ *n* **clear-up** (ˈklɪərˌʌp) **4** the act or an instance of clearing up

clearway (ˈklɪəˌweɪ) *n* **1** *Brit* a stretch of road on which motorists may stop only in an emergency **2** an area at the end of a runway over which an aircraft taking off makes its initial climb: it is under the control of the airport

clearwing *or* **clearwing moth** (ˈklɪəˌwɪŋ) *n* any moth of the family *Sesiidae* (or *Aegeriidae*), characterized by the absence of scales from the greater part of the wings. They are day-flying and some, such as the **hornet clearwing** (*Sesia apiformis*), resemble wasps and other hymenopterans

cleat (kliːt) *n* **1** a wedge-shaped block, usually of wood, attached to a structure to act as a support **2** a device consisting of two hornlike prongs projecting horizontally in opposite directions from a central base, used for securing lines on vessels, wharves, etc **3** a short length of angle iron used as a bracket **4** a piece of metal, leather, etc, attached to the sole of a shoe to prevent wear or slipping **5** a small triangular-shaped nail used in glazing **6** any of the main cleavage planes in a coal seam ▷ *vb* (*tr*) **7** to supply or support with a cleat or cleats **8** to secure (a line) on a cleat [C14 of Germanic origin, compare Old High German *chlōz* clod, lump, Dutch *kloot* ball]

cleavage (ˈkliːvɪdʒ) *n* **1** *informal* the separation between a woman's breasts, esp as revealed by a low-cut dress **2** a division or split **3** (of crystals) the act of splitting or the tendency to split along definite planes so as to yield smooth surfaces **4** Also called: **segmentation** *embryol* (in animals) the repeated division of a fertilized ovum into a solid ball of cells (a morula), which later becomes hollow (a blastula) **5** the breaking of a chemical bond in a molecule to give smaller molecules or radicals **6** *geology* the natural splitting of certain rocks, or minerals such as slates, or micas along the planes of weakness

cleave[1] (kliːv) *vb* **cleaves, cleaving; cleft, cleaved** *or* **clove; cleft, cleaved** *or* **cloven** **1** to split or cause to split, esp along a natural weakness **2** (*tr*) to make by or as if by cutting: *to cleave a path* **3** (*when intr, foll by through*) to penetrate or traverse [Old English *clēofan*; related to Old Norse *kljūfa*, Old High German *klioban*, Latin *glūbere* to peel] > ˈ**cleavable** *adj* > ˌ**cleavaˈbility** *n*

cleave[2] (kliːv) *vb* (*intr; foll by to*) to cling or adhere

C

[Old English *cleofian;* related to Old High German *klebēn* to stick]

cleaver ('kliːvə) *n* a heavy knife or long-bladed hatchet, esp one used by butchers

cleavers ('kliːvəz) *n* (*functioning as singular*) a Eurasian rubiaceous plant, *Galium aparine,* having small white flowers and prickly stems and fruits. Also called: **goosegrass, hairif, sticky willie** [Old English *clīfe;* related to *clīfan* to CLEAVE²]

cleck¹ (klɛk) *vb* (*tr*) *Scot* 1 (of birds) to hatch 2 to lay or hatch (a plot or scheme) [c15 from Old Norse *klekja*]

cleck² (klɛk) *South Wales dialect* ▷ *vb* 1 (*intr;* often foll by *on*) to gossip (about); tell (on) 2 (*often plural*) a piece of gossip [from Welsh, from *clecan* to gossip, and *clec* gossip] > **'clecky** *adj*

cleek *or* **cleik** (kliːk) *n* 1 *chiefly Scot* a large hook, such as one used to land fish 2 *golf* a former name for a club, corresponding to the modern No. 1 or No. 2 iron, used for long low shots [c15 of uncertain origin]

Cleethorpes ('kliːθɔːps) *n* a resort in E England, in North East Lincolnshire unitary authority, Lincolnshire. Pop: 31 853 (2001)

clef (klɛf) *n* one of several symbols placed on the left-hand side beginning of each stave indicating the pitch of the music written after it. See also **alto clef, bass clef, C clef, soprano clef, tenor clef, treble clef** [c16 from French: key, clef, from Latin *clāvis;* related to Latin *claudere* to close]

cleft (klɛft) *vb* 1 the past tense and a past participle of **cleave**¹ ▷ *n* 2 a fissure or crevice 3 an indentation or split in something, such as the chin, palate, etc ▷ *adj* 4 split; divided 5 (of leaves) having one or more incisions reaching nearly to the midrib [Old English *geclyft* (n); related to Old High German *kluft* tongs, German *Kluft* gap, fissure; see CLEAVE¹]

cleft palate *n* a congenital crack or fissure in the midline of the hard palate, often associated with a harelip

cleg (klɛg) *n* another name for a **horsefly,** esp one of the genus *Haematopota* [c15 from Old Norse *kleggi*]

cleidoic egg (klaɪˈdəʊɪk) *n* the egg of birds and insects, which is enclosed in a protective shell limiting the exchange of water, gases, etc [c20 from Greek *kleidoun* to lock up, from *kleid-, kleis* key]

cleistogamy (klaɪˈstɒgəmɪ) *n* self-pollination and fertilization of an unopened flower, as in the flowers of the violet produced in summer. Compare **chasmogamy.** > **cleis'togamous** *or* **cleistogamic** (ˌklaɪstəˈgæmɪk) *adj*

clem (klɛm) *or* **clam** *vb* **clems, clemming, clemmed** *or* **clams, clamming, clammed** (when *tr,* usually passive) *English dialect* to be hungry or cause to be hungry [c16 of Germanic origin; related to Dutch, German *klemmen* to pinch, cramp; compare Old English *beclemman* to shut in]

clematis ('klɛmətɪs, kləˈmeɪtɪs) *n* any N temperate ranunculaceous climbing plant or erect shrub of the genus *Clematis,* having plumelike fruits. Many species are cultivated for their large colourful flowers. See also **traveller's joy** [c16 from Latin, from Greek *klēmatis* climbing plant, brushwood, from *klēma* twig]

clemency ('klɛmənsɪ) *n, pl* -cies 1 mercy or leniency 2 mildness, esp of the weather [c15 from Latin *clēmentia,* from *clēmēns* gentle]

clement ('klɛmənt) *adj* 1 merciful 2 (of the weather) mild [c15 from Latin *clēmēns* mild; probably related to Greek *klinein* to lean] > **'clemently** *adv*

clementine ('klɛmənˌtiːn, -ˌtaɪn) *n* a citrus fruit thought to be either a variety of tangerine or a hybrid between a tangerine and sweet orange [c20 from French *clémentine,* perhaps from the female Christian name]

Clementines ('klɛmənˌtiːnz, -ˌtaɪnz) *pl n RC Church* an official compilation of decretals named after Clement V and issued in 1317 which forms part of the Corpus Juris Canonici

clench (klɛntʃ) *vb* (*tr*) 1 to close or squeeze together (the teeth, a fist, etc) tightly 2 to grasp or grip firmly ▷ *n* 3 a firm grasp or grip 4 a device that grasps or grips, such as a clamp ▷ *n, vb* 5 another word for **clinch** [Old English *beclencan,* related to Old High German *klenken* to tie, Middle High German *klank* noose, Dutch *klinken* rivet]

cleome (klɪˈəʊmɪ) *n* any herbaceous or shrubby plant of the mostly tropical capparidaceous genus *Cleome,* esp *C. spinosa,* cultivated for their clusters of white or purplish flowers with long stamens [c19 New Latin, of obscure origin]

cleopatra (ˌkliːəˈpætrə, -ˈpɑː-) *n* a yellow butterfly, *Gonepteryx cleopatra,* the male of which has its wings flushed with orange

Cleopatra's Needle (ˌkliːəˈpætrəz, -ˈpɑː-) *n* either of two Egyptian obelisks, originally set up at Heliopolis about 1500 BC: one was moved to the Thames Embankment, London, in 1878, the other to Central Park, New York, in 1880

clepe (kliːp) *vb* **clepes, cleping; cleped** (kliːpt, klɛpt) **clept, ycleped** *or* **yclept** (*tr*) *archaic* to call by the name of [Old English *cleopian;* related to Middle Low German *kleperen* to rattle]

clepsydra ('klɛpsɪdrə) *n, pl* -dras *or* -drae (-ˌdriː) an ancient device for measuring time by the flow of water or mercury through a small aperture. Also called: **water clock** [c17 from Latin, from Greek *klepsudra,* from *kleptein* to steal + *hudōr* water]

cleptocracy (ˌklɛpˈtɒkrəsɪ) *n, pl* -cies a variant spelling of **kleptocracy**

cleptomania (ˌklɛptəʊˈmeɪnɪə, -ˈmeɪnjə) *n* a variant spelling of **kleptomania.** > **ˌclepto'mani,ac** *n*

clerestory *or* **clearstory** ('klɪəˌstɔːrɪ) *n, pl* -ries 1 a row of windows in the upper part of the wall of a church that divides the nave from the aisle, set above the aisle roof 2 the part of the wall in which these windows are set. Compare **blindstorey** [c15 from CLEAR + STOREY] > **'clere,storied** *or* **'clear,storied** *adj*

clergy ('klɜːdʒɪ) *n, pl* -gies the collective body of men and women ordained as religious ministers, esp of the Christian Church. Related adjs: **clerical, pastoral** [c13 from Old French *clergie,* from *clerc* ecclesiastic, CLERK]

clergyman ('klɜːdʒɪmən) *n, pl* -men a member of the clergy

cleric ('klɛrɪk) *n* a member of the clergy [c17 from Church Latin *clēricus* priest, CLERK]

clerical ('klɛrɪkᵊl) *adj* 1 relating to or associated with the clergy: *clerical dress* 2 of or relating to office clerks or their work: *a clerical error* 3 supporting or advocating clericalism > **'clerically** *adv*

clerical collar *n* a stiff white collar with no opening at the front that buttons at the back of the neck; the distinctive mark of the clergy in certain Churches. Informal name: **dog collar**

clericalism ('klɛrɪkᵊˌlɪzəm) *n* 1 a policy of upholding the power of the clergy 2 the power of the clergy esp when excessively strong > **'clericalist** *n*

clericals ('klɛrɪkᵊlz) *pl n* the distinctive dress of a member of the clergy

clerihew ('klɛrɪˌhjuː) *n* a form of comic or satiric verse, consisting of two couplets of metrically irregular lines, containing the name of a well-known person [c20 named after Edmund *Clerihew* Bentley (1875–1956), English writer who invented it]

clerk (klɑːk; *US and Canadian* klɜːrk) *n* 1 a worker, esp in an office, who keeps records, files, etc 2 **clerk to the justices** (in England) a legally qualified person who sits in court with lay justices to advise them on points of law 3 an employee of a court, legislature, board, corporation, etc, who keeps records and accounts, etc: *a town clerk* 4 Also called: **clerk of the House** *Brit* a senior official of the House of Commons 5 Also called: **clerk in holy orders** a cleric 6 *US and Canadian* short for **salesclerk** 7 Also called: **desk clerk** *US and Canadian* a hotel receptionist 8

archaic a scholar ▷ *vb* 9 (*intr*) to serve as a clerk [Old English *clerc,* from Church Latin *clēricus,* from Greek *klērikos* cleric, relating to the heritage (alluding to the Biblical Levites, whose inheritance was the Lord), from *klēros* heritage] > **'clerkdom** *n* > **'clerkish** *adj* > **'clerkship** *n*

clerkess (klɑːˈkɛs) *n* a female office clerk

clerkly ('klɑːklɪ) *adj* -lier, -liest 1 of or like a clerk 2 *obsolete* learned ▷ *adv* 3 *obsolete* in the manner of a clerk > **'clerkliness** *n*

clerk of works *n* an employee who supervises building work in progress or the upkeep of existing buildings

Clermont-Ferrand (French klɛrmɔ̃fɛrɑ̃) *n* a city in S central France: capital of Puy-de-Dôme department; industrial centre. Pop: 137 140 (1999)

cleruchy ('klɛəˌrʊkɪ) *n, pl* -chies (in the ancient world) a special type of Athenian colony, in which settlers (**cleruchs**) retained their Athenian citizenship and the community remained a political dependency of Athens > **cleruchial** (klɪˈruːkɪəl) *adj*

cleveite ('kliːvaɪt) *n* a crystalline variety of the mineral uranitite [c19 named after P. T. *Cleve* (1840–1905), Swedish chemist; see -ITE¹]

Cleveland ('kliːvlənd) *n* 1 a former county of NE England formed in 1974 from parts of E Durham and N Yorkshire; replaced in 1996 by the unitary authorities of Hartlepool (Durham), Stockton-on-Tees (Durham), Middlesbrough (North Yorkshire) and Redcar and Cleveland (North Yorkshire) 2 a port in NE Ohio, on Lake Erie: major heavy industries. Pop: 461 324 (2003 est) 3 a hilly region of NE England, extending from the **Cleveland Hills** to the River Tees

Cleveland Bay *n* one of the oldest British breeds of clean-legged, light draught farm and carriage horse, originating from Yorkshire

clever ('klɛvə) *adj* 1 displaying sharp intelligence or mental alertness 2 adroit or dexterous, esp with the hands 3 smart in a superficial way 4 *Brit informal* sly; cunning 5 (predicative; used with a negative) *dialect* healthy; fit [c13 *cliver* (in the sense: quick to seize, adroit), of uncertain origin] > **'cleverish** *adj* > **'cleverly** *adv* > **'cleverness** *n*

clever-clever *adj informal* clever in a showy manner; artful; overclever

clever Dick *or* **cleverdick** ('klɛvəˌdɪk) *n informal* a person considered to have an unwarrantably high opinion of his own ability or knowledge

clevis ('klɛvɪs) *n* the U-shaped component of a shackle for attaching a drawbar to a plough or similar implement [c16 related to CLEAVE¹]

clew (kluː) *n* 1 a ball of thread, yarn, or twine 2 *nautical* either of the lower corners of a square sail or the after lower corner of a fore-and-aft sail 3 (*usually plural*) the rigging of a hammock 4 a rare variant of **clue** ▷ *vb* 5 (*tr*) to coil or roll into a ball [Old English *cliewen* (vb); related to Old High German *kliu* ball]

clew line *n nautical* any of several lines fastened to the clews of a square sail and used for furling it

clew up *vb* (*adverb*) *nautical* to furl (a square sail) by gathering its clews up to the yard by means of clew lines

clianthus (klɪˈænθəs) *n* any Australian or New Zealand plant of the leguminous genus *Clianthus,* with ornamental clusters of slender scarlet flowers ▷ See also **desert pea** [c19 New Latin, probably from Greek *klei-, kleos* glory + *anthos* flower]

cliché ('kliːʃeɪ) *n* 1 a word or expression that has lost much of its force through overexposure, as for example the phrase: *it's got to get worse before it gets better* 2 an idea, action, or habit that has become trite from overuse 3 *printing, chiefly Brit* a stereotype or electrotype plate [c19 from French, from *clicher* to stereotype; imitative of the sound made by the matrix when it is dropped into molten metal] > **'clichéd** *or* **'cliché'd** *adj*

Clichy (kliːˈʃiː) *n* an industrial suburb of NW Paris: residence of the Merovingian kings (7th century). Pop: 50 179 (1999). Official name: **Clichy-la-Garenne** (*French* kliʃilagarɛn)

click (klɪk) *n* **1** a short light often metallic sound **2 a** the locking member of a ratchet mechanism, such as a pawl or detent **b** the movement of such a mechanism between successive locking positions **3** *phonetics* any of various stop consonants, found in Khoisan and as borrowings in southern Bantu languages, that are produced by the suction of air into the mouth **4** *US and Canadian slang* a kilometre **5** *computing* an act of pressing and releasing a button on a mouse ▷ *vb* **6** to make or cause to make a clicking sound: *to click one's heels* **7** (usually foll by *on*) *computing* to press and release (a button on a mouse) or to select (a particular function) by pressing and releasing a button on a mouse **8** (*intr*) *slang* to be a great success: *that idea really clicked* **9** (*intr*) *informal* to become suddenly clear: *it finally clicked when her name was mentioned* **10** (*intr*) *slang* to go or fit together with ease: *they clicked from their first meeting* [C17 of imitative origin] > **'clicker** *n*

clickable ('klɪkəbᵊl) *adj* (of a website) having links that can be accessed by clicking a computer mouse: *a clickable map*

click beetle *n* any beetle of the family *Elateridae*, which have the ability to right themselves with a snapping movement when placed on their backs. Also called: **snapping beetle, skipjack** See also **wireworm**

clicker ('klɪkə) *n* **1** a person or thing that clicks **2** *informal* a foreman in a shoe factory or printing works

clicks and mortar *adj* making use of traditional trading methods in conjunction with internet trading. Abbreviation: **C & M** [C20 pun on *bricks and mortar*, with CLICK referring to the computing sense]

clickstream ('klɪkˌstri:m) *n* a record of the path taken by users through a website, enabling designers to access the use being made of their website

click through *vb* (*tr, adverb*) **1** to navigate around (a website) using the links provided to move onto different pages ▷ *adj* **click-through 2** (of a website) able to be navigated by means of links between different pages

client ('klaɪənt) *n* **1** a person, company, etc, that seeks the advice of a professional man or woman **2** a customer **3** a person who is registered with or receiving services or financial aid from a welfare agency **4** *computing* a program or work station that requests data or information from a server **5** a person depending on another's patronage [C14 from Latin *cliēns* retainer, dependant; related to Latin *clīnāre* to lean] > **cliental** (klaɪ'ɛntᵊl) *adj*

client-centred therapy *n psychol* a form of psychotherapy in which the therapist makes no attempt to interpret what the patient says but encourages him to develop his own attitudes and insights, often by questioning him

clientele (ˌkli:ɒn'tɛl) *or* **clientage** ('klaɪəntɪdʒ) *n* customers or clients collectively [C16 from Latin *clientēla*, from *cliēns* CLIENT]

Clifden nonpareil ('klɪftᵊn) *n* a handsome nocturnal moth, *Catocala fraxini*, that is brown with bluish patches on the hindwings: related to the red underwing

cliff (klɪf) *n* a steep high rock face, esp one that runs along the seashore and has the strata exposed [Old English *clif*; related to Old Norse *kleif*, Middle Low German *klēf*, Dutch *klif*; see CLEAVE²] > **'cliffy** *adj*

cliffhanger ('klɪfˌhæŋə) *n* **1 a** a situation of imminent disaster usually occurring at the end of each episode of a serialized film **b** the serialized film itself **2** a situation that is dramatic or uncertain > **'cliffˌhanging** *adj*

cliff swallow *n* an American swallow, *Petrochelidon pyrrhonota*, that has a square-tipped tail and builds nests of mud on cliffs, walls, etc

climacteric (klaɪ'mæktərɪk, ˌklaɪmæk'tɛrɪk) *n* **1** a critical event or period **2** another name for **menopause 3** the period in the life of a man corresponding to the menopause, chiefly characterized by diminished sexual activity **4** *botany* the period during which certain fruits, such as apples, ripen, marked by a rise in the rate of respiration ▷ *adj also* **climacterical** (ˌklaɪmæk'tɛrɪkᵊl) **5** involving a crucial event or period [C16 from Latin *clīmactēricus*, from Greek *klimaktērikos*, from *klimakter* rung of a ladder, from *klimax* ladder; see CLIMAX] > **ˌclimac'terically** *adv*

climactic (klaɪ'mæktɪk) *or* **climactical** *adj* consisting of, involving, or causing a climax > **cli'mactically** *adv*

USAGE See at **climate**

climate ('klaɪmɪt) *n* **1** the long-term prevalent weather conditions of an area, determined by latitude, position relative to oceans or continents, altitude, etc **2** an area having a particular kind of climate **3** a prevailing trend or current of feeling: *the political climate* [C14 from Late Latin *clima*, from Greek *klima* inclination, region; related to Greek *klinein* to lean] > **climatic** (klaɪ'mætɪk), **cli'matical** *or* **'climatal** *adj* > **cli'matically** *adv*

USAGE *Climatic* is sometimes wrongly used where *climactic* is meant. *Climatic* is properly used to talk about things relating to climate; *climactic* is used to describe something which forms a climax

climatic zone *n* any of the eight principal zones, roughly demarcated by lines of latitude, into which the earth can be divided on the basis of climate

climatology (ˌklaɪmə'tɒlədʒɪ) *n* the study of climate > **climatologic** (ˌklaɪmətə'lɒdʒɪk) *or* **ˌclimato'logical** *adj* > **ˌclimato'logically** *adv* > **ˌclima'tologist** *n*

climax ('klaɪmæks) *n* **1** the most intense or highest point of an experience or of a series of events: *the party was the climax of the week* **2** a decisive moment in a dramatic or other work **3** a rhetorical device by which a series of sentences, clauses, or phrases are arranged in order of increasing intensity **4** *ecology* the stage in the development of a community during which it remains stable under the prevailing environmental conditions **5** Also called: **sexual climax** (esp in referring to women) another word for **orgasm** ▷ *vb* **6** to reach or bring to a climax [C16 from Late Latin, from Greek *klimax* ladder]

climb (klaɪm) *vb* (*mainly intr*) **1** (*also tr*; often foll by *up*) to go up or ascend (stairs, a mountain, etc) **2** (often foll by *along*) to progress with difficulty: *to climb along a ledge* **3** to rise to a higher point or intensity: *the temperature climbed* **4** to incline or slope upwards: *the road began to climb* **5** to ascend in social position **6** (of plants) to grow upwards by twining, using tendrils or suckers, etc **7** *informal* (foll by *into*) to put (on) or get (into) **8** to be a climber or mountaineer ▷ *n* **9** the act or an instance of climbing **10** a place or thing to be climbed, esp a route in mountaineering ▷ Related adjective: **scansorial** [Old English *climban*; related to Old Norse *klembra* to squeeze, Old High German *climban* to clamber] > **'climbable** *adj*

climb down *vb* (*intr, adverb*) **1** to descend **2** (often foll by *from*) to retreat (from an opinion, position, etc) ▷ *n* **climb-down 3** a retreat from an opinion, etc

climber ('klaɪmə) *n* **1** a person or thing that climbs **2** a plant that lacks rigidity and grows upwards by twining, scrambling, or clinging with tendrils and suckers **3** *chiefly Brit* short for **social climber**

climbing fish *or* **perch** *n* an Asian labyrinth fish, *Anabas testudineus*, that resembles a perch and can travel over land on its spiny gill covers and pectoral fins

climbing frame *n* a structure of wood or metal tubing used by children for climbing

climbing irons *pl n* spiked steel frames worn on the feet to assist in climbing trees, ice slopes, etc

climbing wall *n mountaineering* a specially constructed wall with recessed and projecting holds to give practice in rock climbing; a feature of many sports centres

clime (klaɪm) *n poetic* a region or its climate [C16 from Late Latin *clima*; see CLIMATE]

clinandrium (klɪ'nændrɪəm) *n, pl* **-dria** (-drɪə) *botany* a cavity in the upper part of the column of an orchid flower that contains the anthers. Also called: **androclinium** [C19 from New Latin, literally: bed for stamen, from Greek *klinē* couch + *anēr* man + -IUM]

clinch (klɪntʃ) *vb* **1** (*tr*) to secure (a driven nail) by bending the protruding point over **2** (*tr*) to hold together in such a manner: *to clinch the corners of the frame* **3** (*tr*) to settle (something, such as an argument, bargain, etc) in a definite way **4** (*tr*) *nautical* to fasten by means of a clinch **5** (*intr*) to engage in a clinch, as in boxing or wrestling ▷ *n* **6** the act of clinching **7 a** a nail with its point bent over **b** the part of such a nail, etc, that has been bent over **8** *boxing, wrestling* an act or an instance in which one or both competitors hold on to the other to avoid punches, regain wind, etc **9** *slang* a lovers' embrace **10** *nautical* a loop or eye formed in a line by seizing the end to the standing part ▷ Also (for senses 1, 2, 4, 7, 8, 10): **clench** [C16 variant of CLENCH]

clincher ('klɪntʃə) *n* **1** *informal* something decisive, such as a fact, score, etc **2** a person or thing that clinches

cline (klaɪn) *n* a continuous variation in form between members of a species having a wide variable geographical or ecological range [C20 from Greek *klinein* to lean] > **'clinal** *adj* > **'clinally** *adv*

-cline *n combining form* indicating a slope: *anticline* [back formation from INCLINE] > **-clinal** *adj combining form*

cling (klɪŋ) *vb* **clings, clinging, clung** (*intr*) **1** (often foll by *to*) to hold fast or adhere closely (to something), as by gripping or sticking **2** (foll by *together*) to remain in contact (with each other) **3** to be or remain physically or emotionally close: *to cling to outmoded beliefs* ▷ *n* **4** *agriculture, chiefly US* the tendency of cotton fibres in a sample to stick to each other **5** *agriculture obsolete* diarrhoea or scouring in animals **6** short for **clingstone** [Old English *clingan*; related to CLENCH] > **'clinger** *n* > **'clingingly** *adv* > **'clingy** *adj* > **'clinginess** *or* **'clingingness** *n*

clingfilm ('klɪŋˌfɪlm) *n* a thin polythene material that clings closely to any surface around which it is placed: used for wrapping food

clingfish ('klɪŋˌfɪʃ) *n, pl* **-fish** *or* **-fishes** any small marine teleost fish of the family *Gobiesocidae*, having a flattened elongated body with a sucking disc beneath the head for clinging to rocks, etc

clinging vine *n US and Canadian informal* a woman who displays excessive emotional dependence on a man

clingstone ('klɪŋˌstəʊn) *n* **a** a fruit, such as certain peaches, in which the flesh tends to adhere to the stone **b** (*as modifier*): *a clingstone peach* ▷ Compare **freestone** (sense 2)

clinic ('klɪnɪk) *n* **1** a place in which outpatients are given medical treatment or advice, often connected to a hospital **2** a similar place staffed by physicians or surgeons specializing in one or more specific areas: *eye clinic* **3** *Brit* a private hospital or nursing home **4** *obsolete* the teaching of medicine to students at the bedside **5** *US* a place in which medical lectures are given **6** *US* a clinical lecture **7** *chiefly US and Canadian* a group or centre that offers advice or instruction: *a vocational clinic* [C17 from Latin *clīnicus* one on a sickbed, from Greek, from *klinē* bed]

clinical ('klɪnɪkᵊl) *adj* **1** of or relating to a clinic **2** of or relating to the bedside of a patient, the course of his disease, or the observation and treatment of patients directly: *a clinical lecture; clinical medicine* **3** scientifically detached; strictly objective: *a clinical attitude to life* **4** plain, simple, and usually unattractive: *clinical furniture* > ˈ**clinically** *adv* > ˈ**clinicalness** *n*

clinical governance *n* a systematic approach to raising standards of health care and tackling poor performance in hospitals

clinically dead *adj* having no respiration, no heartbeat, and with no contraction of the pupils when exposed to a strong light

clinically obese *adj* the state at which being overweight causes medical complications

clinical psychology *n* the branch of psychology that studies and treats mental illness and mental retardation

clinical thermometer *n* a finely calibrated thermometer for determining the temperature of the body, usually placed under the tongue, in the armpit, or in the rectum

clinician (klɪˈnɪʃən) *n* a physician, psychiatrist, etc, who specializes in clinical work as opposed to one engaged in laboratory or experimental studies

clink[1] (klɪŋk) *vb* **1** to make or cause to make a light and sharply ringing sound ▷ *n* **2** a light and sharply ringing sound **3** *Brit* a pointed steel tool used for breaking up the surface of a road before it is repaired [c14 perhaps from Middle Dutch *klinken;* related to Old Low German *chlanch,* German *Klang* sound]

clink[2] (klɪŋk) *n* a slang word for **prison** [c16 after *Clink,* name of a prison in Southwark, London]

clinker (ˈklɪŋkə) *n* **1** the ash and partially fused residues from a coal-fired furnace or fire **2** Also called: **clinker brick** a hard brick used as a paving stone **3** a partially vitrified brick or mass of brick **4** *slang, chiefly US* something of poor quality, such as a film **5** *US and Canadian slang* a mistake or fault, esp a wrong note in music ▷ *vb* **6** (*intr*) to form clinker during burning [c17 from Dutch *klinker* a type of brick, from obsolete *klinckaerd,* literally: something that clinks (referring to the sound produced when one was struck), from *klinken* to CLINK[1]]

clinker-built *or* **clincher-built** *adj* (of a boat or ship) having a hull constructed with each plank overlapping that below. Also called: **lapstrake** Compare **carvel-built** [c18 *clinker* a nailing together, probably from CLINCH]

clinkstone (ˈklɪŋkˌstəʊn) *n* a variety of phonolite that makes a metallic sound when struck

clino- *or before a vowel* **clin-** *combining form* indicating a slope or inclination: *clinometer* [from New Latin, from Greek *klinein* to slant, lean]

clinometer (klaɪˈnɒmɪtə) *n* an instrument used in surveying for measuring an angle of inclination > **clinometric** (ˌklaɪnəˈmɛtrɪk) *or* ˌ**clinoˈmetrical** *adj* > **cliˈnometry** *n*

clinopyroxene (ˌklaɪnəʊpaɪˈrɒksiːn) *n* a member of the pyroxene group of minerals having a monoclinic crystal structure, such as augite, diopside, or jadeite

clinostat (ˈklaɪnəʊˌstæt) *n* an apparatus for studying tropisms in plants, usually a rotating disc to which the plant is attached so that it receives an equal stimulus on all sides

clinquant (ˈklɪŋkənt) *adj* **1** glittering, esp with tinsel ▷ *n* **2** tinsel or imitation gold leaf [c16 from French, from *clinquer* to clink, from Dutch *klinken,* of imitative origin]

clint (klɪnt) *n physical geography* **1** a section of a limestone pavement separated from adjacent sections by solution fissures. See **grike 2** any small surface exposure of hard or flinty rock, as on a hillside or in a stream bed [c12 from Danish and Swedish *klint,* from Old Swedish *klinter,* related to Icelandic *klettr* rock]

clintonia (klɪnˈtəʊnɪə) *n* any temperate liliaceous plant of the genus *Clintonia,* having white, greenish-yellow, or purplish flowers, broad ribbed leaves, and blue berries [c19 named after De Witt Clinton (1769–1828), US politician and naturalist]

Clio (ˈklaɪəʊ) *n Greek myth* the Muse of history [c19

from Latin, from Greek *Kleiō,* from *kleein* to celebrate]

cliometrics (ˌklaɪəʊˈmɛtrɪks) *n* (*functioning as singular*) the study of economic history using statistics and computer analysis [c20 CLIO + (ECONO)METRICS] > ˌ**clioˈmetric** *or* ˌ**clioˈmetrical** *adj* > **cliometrician** (ˌklaɪəʊməˈtrɪʃən) *n*

clip[1] (klɪp) *vb* clips, clipping, clipped (*mainly tr*) **1** (*also intr*) to cut, snip, or trim with or as if with scissors or shears, esp in order to shorten or remove a part **2** *Brit* to punch (a hole) in something, esp a ticket **3** to curtail or cut short **4** to move a short section from (a film, etc) **5** to shorten (a word) **6** (*intr*) to trot or move rapidly, esp over a long distance: *a horse clipping along the road* **7** *informal* to strike with a sharp, often slanting, blow **8** *slang* to obtain (money) by deception or cheating **9** *US slang* to murder; execute **10** clip (someone's) wings **a** to restrict (someone's) freedom **b** to thwart (someone's) ambition ▷ *n* **11** the act or process of clipping **12** something clipped off **13** an extract from a film, newspaper, etc **14** *informal* a sharp, often slanting, blow **15** *informal* speed: *a rapid clip* **16** *Austral and NZ* the total quantity of wool shorn, as in one place, season, etc **17** another word for **clipped form** [c12 from Old Norse *klippa* to cut; related to Low German *klippen*] > ˈ**clippable** *adj*

clip[2] (klɪp) *n* **1** any of various small implements used to hold loose articles together or to attach one article to another **2** an article of jewellery that can be clipped onto a dress, hat, etc **3** short for **paperclip** *or* **cartridge clip 4** the pointed flange on a horseshoe that secures it to the front part of the hoof ▷ *vb* clips, clipping, clipped (*tr*) **5** to hold together tightly, as with a clip **6** *archaic or dialect* to embrace [Old English *clyppan* to embrace; related to Old Frisian *kleppa,* Lithuanian *glebiu*]

clip art *n* a large collection of simple drawings stored in a computer from which items can be selected for incorporation into documents

clipboard (ˈklɪpˌbɔːd) *n* **1** a portable writing board with a spring clip at the top for holding paper **2** a temporary storage area in desktop publishing where text or graphics are held after the cut command or the copy command

clip-clop *n* the sound made by a horse's hooves

clip-fed *adj* (of an automatic firearm) loaded from a cartridge clip

clip joint *n slang* a place, such as a nightclub or restaurant, in which customers are overcharged

clip on *vb* **1** (*tr*) to attach by means of a clip **2** (*intr*) to be attached by means of a clip: *this clips on here* ▷ *adj* **clip-on 3** designed to be attached by means of a clip: *a clip-on bow tie* ▷ *pl n* **clip-ons 4** sunglasses designed to be clipped on to a person's spectacles

clipped (klɪpt) *adj* (of speech or voice) abrupt and distinct

clipped form *n* a shortened form of a word, as for example *doc* for *doctor*

clipper (ˈklɪpə) *n* **1** any fast sailing ship **2** a person or thing that cuts or clips **3** something, such as a horse or sled, that moves quickly **4** *electronics* another word for **limiter**

clippers (ˈklɪpəz) *or* **clips** *pl n* **1** a hand tool with two cutting blades for clipping fingernails, hedges, etc **2** a hairdresser's tool, operated either by hand or electrically, with one fixed and one reciprocating set of teeth for cutting short hair

clippie (ˈklɪpɪ) *n Brit informal* a bus conductress

clipping (ˈklɪpɪŋ) *n* **1** something cut out or trimmed off, esp an article from a newspaper; cutting **2** the distortion of an audio or visual signal in which the tops of peaks with a high amplitude are cut off, caused by, for example, overloading of amplifier circuits ▷ *adj* **3** (*prenominal*) *informal* fast: *a clipping pace*

clipshears (ˈklɪpˌʃɪəz) *or* **clipshear** (ˈklɪpˌʃɪə) *n* a Scot dialect name for an **earwig** [from the resemblance of the forceps at the tip of its abdomen to shears]

clique (kliːk, klɪk) *n* a small, exclusive group of friends or associates [c18 from French, perhaps from Old French: latch, from *cliquer* to click; suggestive of the necessity to exclude nonmembers] > ˈ**cliquish** *adj* > ˈ**cliquishly** *adv* > ˈ**cliquishness** *n*

cliquey *or* **cliquy** (ˈkliːkɪ, ˈklɪkɪ) *adj* **-ier, -iest** exclusive, confined to a small group; forming cliques

clishmaclaver (ˌklɪʃməˈkleɪvə) *n Scot* idle talk; gossip [c16 from *clish-clash,* reduplication of CLASH + CLAVER]

clitellum (klɪˈtɛləm) *n, pl* **-la** (-lə) a thickened saddle-like region of epidermis in earthworms and leeches whose secretions bind copulating worms together and later form a cocoon around the eggs [c19 from New Latin, from Latin *clītellae* (plural) packsaddle]

clitic (ˈklɪtɪk) *adj* **1** (of a word) incapable of being stressed, usually pronounced as if part of the word that follows or precedes it: for example, in French, *me, te,* and *le* are clitic pronouns. See also **proclitic, enclitic** ▷ *n* **2** a clitic word [c20 back formation from ENCLITIC and PROCLITIC]

clitoridectomy (ˌklɪtərɪˈdɛktəmɪ) *n, pl* **-mies** surgical removal of the clitoris: a form of female circumcision, esp practised as a religious or ethnic rite

clitoris (ˈklɪtərɪs, ˈklaɪ-) *n* a part of the female genitalia consisting of a small elongated highly sensitive erectile organ at the front of the vulva: homologous with the penis [c17 from New Latin, from Greek *kleitoris;* related to Greek *kleiein* to close] > ˈ**clitoral** *adj*

Cliveden (ˈklɪvdən) *n* a mansion in Buckinghamshire, on the N bank of the Thames near Maidenhead: formerly the home of Nancy Astor and the scene of gatherings of politicians and others (known as the **Cliveden Set**); now a hotel

Cllr *abbreviation for* Councillor

cloaca (kləʊˈeɪkə) *n, pl* **-cae** (-kiː) **1** a cavity in the pelvic region of most vertebrates, except higher mammals, and certain invertebrates, into which the alimentary canal and the genital and urinary ducts open **2** a sewer [c18 from Latin: sewer; related to Greek *kluzein* to wash out] > **cloˈacal** *adj*

cloacitis (ˌkləʊəˈsaɪtɪs) *n vet science* inflammation of the cloaca in birds, including domestic fowl, and other animals with a common opening of the urinary and gastrointestinal tracts

cloak (kləʊk) *n* **1** a wraplike outer garment fastened at the throat and falling straight from the shoulders **2** something that covers or conceals ▷ *vb* (*tr*) **3** to cover with or as if with a cloak **4** to hide or disguise [c13 from Old French *cloque,* from Medieval Latin *clocca* cloak, bell; referring to the bell-like shape]

cloak-and-dagger *n* (*modifier*) characteristic of or concerned with intrigue and espionage

cloakroom (ˈkləʊkˌruːm, -ˌrʊm) *n* **1** a room in which hats, coats, luggage, etc, may be temporarily deposited **2** *Brit* a euphemistic word for **lavatory**

cloam (kləʊm) *Southwestern English dialect* ▷ *adj* **1** made of clay or earthenware ▷ *n* **2** clay or earthenware pots, dishes, etc, collectively [Old English *clām* mud]

clobber[1] (ˈklɒbə) *vb* (*tr*) *slang* **1** to beat or batter **2** to defeat utterly **3** to criticize severely [c20 of unknown origin]

clobber[2] (ˈklɒbə) *n Brit slang* personal belongings, such as clothes and accessories [c19 of unknown origin]

clobber[3] (ˈklɒbə) *vb* (*tr*) to paint over existing decoration on (pottery) [c19 (originally in the sense: to patch up): of uncertain origin; perhaps related to CLOBBER[2]]

clobbering machine *n NZ informal* pressure to conform with accepted standards

cloche (klɒʃ) *n* **1** a bell-shaped cover used to protect young plants **2** a woman's almost brimless close-fitting hat, typical of the 1920s and 1930s [c19 from French: bell, from Medieval Latin *clocca*]

clock[1] (klɒk) *n* **1** a timepiece, usually free-standing, hanging, or built into a tower, having mechanically or electrically driven pointers that move constantly over a dial showing the numbers of the hours. Compare **digital clock, watch** (sense 7) **2** any clocklike device for recording or measuring, such as a taximeter or pressure gauge **3** the downy head of a dandelion that has gone to seed **4** an electrical circuit that generates pulses at a predetermined rate **5** *computing* an electronic pulse generator that transmits streams of regular pulses to which various parts of the computer and its operations are synchronized **6** short for **time clock 7 around** *or* **round the clock** all day and all night **8** (usually preceded by *the*) an informal word for **speedometer** *or* **mileometer 9** *Brit* a slang word for **face 10 against the clock a** under pressure, as to meet a deadline **b** (in certain sports, such as show jumping) timed by a stop clock: *the last round will be against the clock* **11 put the clock back** to regress ▷ *vb* **12** (*tr*) *Brit, Austral, and NZ slang* to strike, esp on the face or head **13** (*tr*) *Brit slang* to see or notice **14** (*tr*) to record time as with a stopwatch, esp in the calculation of speed **15** *electronics* to feed a clock pulse to (a digital device) in order to cause it to switch to a new state ▷ See also **atomic clock, biological clock, clock off, clock on, clock up** [c14 from Middle Dutch *clocke* clock, from Medieval Latin *clocca* bell, ultimately of Celtic origin] > ˈ**clocker** *n* > ˈ**clock,like** *adj*

clock[2] (klɒk) *n* an ornamental design either woven in or embroidered on the side of a stocking [c16 from Middle Dutch *clocke*, from Medieval Latin *clocca* bell]

clock golf *n* a putting game played on a circular area on a lawn

clockmaker (ˈklɒkˌmeɪkə) *n* a person who makes or mends clocks, watches, etc

clock off *or* **out** *vb* (*intr, adverb*) to depart from work, esp when it involves registering the time of departure on a card

clock on *or* **in** *vb* (*intr, adverb*) to arrive at work, esp when it involves registering the time of arrival on a card

clock up *vb* (*tr, adverb*) to record or register: *this car has clocked up 80 000 miles*

clock-watcher *n* an employee who checks the time in anticipation of a break or of the end of the working day

clockwise (ˈklɒkˌwaɪz) *adv, adj* in the direction that the hands of a clock rotate; from top to bottom towards the right when seen from the front

clockwork (ˈklɒkˌwɜːk) *n* **1** the mechanism of a clock **2** any similar mechanism, as in a wind-up toy **3 like clockwork** with complete regularity and precision

clod (klɒd) *n* **1** a lump of earth or clay **2** earth, esp when heavy or in hard lumps **3** Also called: **clodpole, clod poll, clodpate** a dull or stupid person **4** a cut of beef taken from the shoulder [Old English *clod-* (occurring in compound words) lump; related to CLOUD] > ˈ**cloddy** *adj* > ˈ**cloddish** *adj* > ˈ**cloddishly** *adv* > ˈ**cloddishness** *n*

clodhopper (ˈklɒdˌhɒpə) *n informal* **1** a clumsy person; lout **2** (*usually plural*) a large heavy shoe or boot > ˈ**clod,hopping** *adj*

clog[1] (klɒg) *vb* **clogs, clogging, clogged 1** to obstruct or become obstructed with thick or sticky matter **2** (*tr*) to encumber; hinder; impede **3** (*tr*) to fasten a clog or impediment to (an animal, such as a horse) **4** (*intr*) to adhere or stick in a mass **5** *slang* (in soccer) to foul (an opponent) ▷ *n* **6 a** any of various wooden or wooden-soled shoes **b** (*as modifier*): *clog dance* **7** a heavy block, esp of wood, fastened to the leg of a person or animal to impede motion **8** something that impedes motion or action; hindrance **9 pop one's clogs** *slang* to die [c14 (in the sense: block of wood): of unknown origin] > ˈ**cloggy** *adj* > ˈ**clogginess** *n*

clog[2] (klɒg) *vb* **clogs, clogging, clogged** to use a photo-enabled mobile phone to take a photograph of (someone) and send it to a website without his or her knowledge or consent [c21 C(AMERA) + LOG] > ˈ**clogging** *n*

cloggy (ˈklɒgɪ) *adj* **-gier, -giest** thick and sticky; causing clogging

cloisonné (klwɑːˈzɒneɪ; *French* klwazɔne) *n* **1 a** a design made by filling in with coloured enamel an outline of flattened wire put on edge **b** the method of doing this ▷ *adj* **2** of, relating to, or made by cloisonné [c19 from French, from *cloisonner* to divide into compartments, from *cloison* partition, ultimately from Latin *claudere* to CLOSE[2]]

cloister (ˈklɔɪstə) *n* **1** a covered walk, usually around a quadrangle in a religious institution, having an open arcade or colonnade on the inside and a wall on the outside **2** (*sometimes plural*) a place of religious seclusion, such as a monastery **3** life in a monastery or convent ▷ *vb* **4** (*tr*) to confine or seclude in or as if in a monastery [c13 from Old French *cloistre*, from Medieval Latin *claustrum* monastic cell, from Latin: bolt, barrier, from *claudere* to close; influenced in form by Old French *cloison* partition] > ˈ**cloister-,like** *adj*

cloistered (ˈklɔɪstəd) *adj* **1** secluded or shut up from the world **2** living in a monastery or nunnery **3** (of a building, courtyard, etc) having or provided with a cloister

cloistral (ˈklɔɪstrəl) *or* **claustral** *adj* of, like, or characteristic of a cloister

clomb (kləʊm) *vb archaic* a past tense and past participle of **climb**

clomiphene (ˈkləʊmɪˌfiːn) *n* a drug that stimulates the production of egg cells in the ovary: used to treat infertility in women

clomp (klɒmp) *n, vb* a less common word for **clump** (senses 2, 7)

clone (kləʊn) *n* **1** a group of organisms or cells of the same genetic constitution that are descended from a common ancestor by asexual reproduction, as by cuttings, grafting, etc, in plants **2** Also called: **gene clone** a segment of DNA that has been isolated and replicated by laboratory manipulation: used to analyse genes and manufacture their products (proteins) **3** *informal* a person or thing bearing a very close resemblance to another person or thing **4** *slang* **a** a mobile phone that has been given the electronic identity of an existing mobile phone, so that calls made on the second phone are charged to the owner of the first phone **b** any similar object or device, such as a credit card, that has been given the electronic identity of another device usually in order to commit theft ▷ *vb* **5** to produce or cause to produce a clone **6** *informal* to produce near copies (of a person or thing) **7** (*tr*) *slang* to give (a mobile phone, etc) the electronic identity of an existing mobile phone (or other device), so that calls, purchases, etc made with the second device are charged to the owner of the first device [c20 from Greek *klōn* twig, shoot; related to *klan* to break] > ˈ**clonal** *adj* > ˈ**clonally** *adv*

clonk (klɒŋk) *vb* **1** (*intr*) to make a loud dull thud **2** (*tr*) *informal* to hit ▷ *n* **3** a loud thudding sound [c20 of imitative origin]

Clonmel (klɒnˈmɛl) *n* the county town of Co Tipperary, Republic of Ireland; birthplace of Laurence Sterne; meat processing and enamelware. Pop: 16 910 (2002)

Clontarf (klɒnˈtɑːf) *n* **Battle of** a battle fought in 1014, near Dublin, in the Republic of Ireland, in which the Danes were defeated by the Irish but the Irish king, Brian Boru, was killed

clonus (ˈkləʊnəs) *n* a type of convulsion characterized by rapid contraction and relaxation of a muscle [c19 from New Latin, from Greek *klonos* turmoil] > **clonic** (ˈklɒnɪk) *adj* > **clonicity** (klɒˈnɪsɪtɪ) *n*

clop (klɒp) *vb* **clops, clopping, clopped 1** (*intr*) to make or move along with a sound as of a horse's hooves striking the ground ▷ *n* **2** a sound of this nature [c20 of imitative origin]

cloqué (ˈklɒkeɪ) *n* **a** a fabric with an embossed surface **b** (*as modifier*): *a cloqué dress* [from French, literally: blistered]

close[1] (kləʊs) *adj* **1** near in space or time; in proximity **2** having the parts near together; dense: *a close formation* **3** down or near to the surface; short: *a close haircut* **4** near in relationship: *a close relative* **5** intimate or confidential: *a close friend* **6** almost equal or even: *a close contest* **7** not deviating or varying greatly from a model or standard: *a close resemblance; a close translation* **8** careful, strict, or searching: *a close study* **9** (of a style of play in football, hockey, etc) characterized by short passes **10** confined or enclosed **11** shut or shut tight **12** oppressive, heavy, or airless: *a close atmosphere* **13** strictly guarded: *a close prisoner* **14** neat or tight in fit: *a close cap* **15** secretive or reticent **16** miserly; not generous, esp with money **17** (of money or credit) hard to obtain; scarce **18** restricted as to public admission or membership **19** hidden or secluded **20** Also: **closed** restricted or prohibited as to the type of game or fish able to be taken **21** Also: **closed, narrow** *phonetics* denoting a vowel pronounced with the lips relatively close together ▷ *adv* **22** closely; tightly **23** near or in proximity **24 close to the wind** *nautical* sailing as nearly as possible towards the direction from which the wind is blowing. See also **wind**[1] (sense 26) [c13 from Old French *clos* close, enclosed, from Latin *clausus* shut up, from *claudere* to close] > ˈ**closely** *adv* > ˈ**closeness** *n*

close[2] (kləʊz) *vb* **1** to put or be put in such a position as to cover an opening; shut: *the door closed behind him* **2** (*tr*) to bar, obstruct, or fill up (an entrance, a hole, etc): *to close a road* **3** to bring the parts or edges of (a wound, etc) together or (of a wound, etc) to be brought together **4** (*intr*; foll by *on, over*, etc) to take hold: *his hand closed over the money* **5** to bring or be brought to an end; terminate **6** to complete (an agreement, a deal, etc) successfully or (of an agreement, deal, etc) to be completed successfully **7** to cease or cause to cease to render service: *the shop closed at six* **8** (*intr*) *stock exchange* to have a value at the end of a day's trading, as specified: *steels closed two points down* **9** to complete an electrical circuit **10** (*tr*) *nautical* to pass near **11** (*tr*) *archaic* to enclose or shut in **12 close one's eyes a** *euphemistic* to die **b** (often foll by *to*) to ignore ▷ *n* **13** the act of closing **14** the end or conclusion: *the close of the day* **15** a place of joining or meeting **16** (kləʊs) *law* private property, usually enclosed by a fence, hedge, or wall **17** (kləʊs) *Brit* a courtyard or quadrangle enclosed by buildings or an entry leading to such a courtyard **18** (kləʊs) *Brit* (*capital when part of a street name*) a small quiet residential road: *Hillside Close* **19** *Brit* a field **20** (kləʊs) the precincts of a cathedral or similar building **21** (kləʊs) *Scot* the entry from the street to a tenement building **22** *music* another word for **cadence.** A perfect cadence is called a **full close** an imperfect one a **half close 23** *archaic or rare* an encounter in battle; grapple ▷ See also **close down, close in, close out, close-up, close with.** > ˈ**closer** *n*

close call (kləʊs) *n* another expression for **close shave**

close company (kləʊs) *n Brit* a company under the control of its directors or fewer than five independent participants. Also called: **closed company**

close corporation (kləʊs) *n South African* a small private limited company. Abbreviation: c.c.

closed (kləʊzd) *adj* **1** blocked against entry; shut **2** restricted; exclusive **3** not open to question or debate **4** (of a hunting season, etc) close **5** *maths* **a** (of a curve or surface) completely enclosing an area or volume **b** (of a set) having members that can be produced by a specific operation on other members of the same set: *the integers are a closed set*

C

under multiplication **6** Also: **checked** *phonetics* **a** denoting a syllable that ends in a consonant **b** another word for **close¹** (sense 21) **7** not open to public entry or membership: *the closed society of publishing*

closed book *n* **1** something deemed unknown or incapable of being understood **2** a matter that has been finally concluded and admits of no further consideration

closed-captioned *adj* (of a video recording) having subtitles which appear on screen only if the cassette is played through a special decoder

closed chain *n chem* another name for **ring¹** (sense 18)

closed circuit *n* a complete electrical circuit through which current can flow when a voltage is applied. Compare **open circuit**

closed-circuit television *n* a television system in which signals are transmitted from a television camera to the receivers by cables or telephone links forming a closed circuit, as used in security systems, etc

closed community *n ecology* a plant community that does not allow for further colonization, all the available niches being occupied

closed corporation *n US* a corporation the stock of which is owned by a small number of persons and is rarely traded on the open market. Also: **close corporation**

closed cycle *n engineering* a heat engine in which the working substance is continuously circulated and does not need replenishment

closed-door *adj* private; barred to members of the public: *a closed-door meeting*

closed game *n chess* a relatively complex game involving closed ranks and files and permitting only nontactical positional manoeuvring. Compare **open game**

closed interval *n maths* an interval on the real line including its end points, as [0, 1], the set of reals between and including 0 and 1

close down (kləʊz) *vb (adverb)* **1** to cease or cause to cease operations: *the shop closed down* **2** *(tr) sport* to mark or move towards (an opposing player) in order to prevent him or her running with the ball or making or receiving a pass ▷ *n* **close-down** ('kləʊz,daʊn) **3** a closure or stoppage of operations, esp in a factory **4** *Brit radio, television* the end of a period of broadcasting, esp late at night

closed primary *n US government* a primary in which only members of a particular party may vote. Compare **open primary**

closed scholarship *n* a scholarship for which only certain people, such as those from a particular school or with a particular surname, are eligible

closed sentence *n logic* a formula that contains no free occurrence of any variable. Compare **open sentence**

closed set *n maths* **1** a set that includes all the values obtained by application of a given operation to its members **2** (in topological space) a set that contains all its own limit points

closed shop *n* (formerly) an industrial establishment in which there exists a contract between a trade union and the employer permitting the employment of the union's members only. Compare **open shop, union shop**

closed source *n* **a** intellectual property, esp computer source code, that is not made available to the general public by its creators **b** *(as modifier)*: *closed source software*. Compare **open source**

close-fisted (,kləʊs'fɪstɪd) *adj* very careful with money; mean ▷ ,**close-'fistedness** *n*

close-grained (,kləʊs'greɪnd) *adj* (of wood) dense or compact in texture

close harmony (kləʊs) *n* a type of singing in which all the parts except the bass lie close together and are confined to the compass of a tenth

close-hauled (,kləʊs'hɔːld) *adj nautical* with the

sails flat, so as to sail as close to the wind as possible

close in (kləʊz) *vb (intr, adverb)* **1** (of days) to become shorter with the approach of winter **2** (foll by *on* or *upon*) to advance (on) so as to encircle or surround

close-knit (,kləʊs'nɪt) *adj* closely united, esp by social ties

close-lipped (,kləʊs'lɪpt) *or* **close-mouthed** (,kləʊs'maʊðd, -'maʊθt) *adj* not talking or revealing much

close out (kləʊz) *vb (adverb)* to terminate (a client's or other account) on which the margin is inadequate or exhausted, usually by sale of securities to realize cash

close punctuation (kləʊs) *n* punctuation in which many commas, full stops, etc, are used. Compare **open punctuation**

close quarters (kləʊs) *pl n* **1** a narrow cramped space or position **2** **at close quarters a** engaged in hand-to-hand combat **b** in close proximity; very near together

close season (kləʊs) *or* **closed season** *n* **1** the period of the year when it is prohibited to kill certain game or fish **2** *sport* the period of the year when there is no domestic competition

close shave (kləʊs) *n informal* a narrow escape

close-stool ('kləʊs,stuːl) *n* a wooden stool containing a covered chamber pot

closet ('klɒzɪt) *n* **1** a small cupboard or recess **2** a small private room **3** short for **water closet 4** *(modifier)* private or secret **5** *(modifier)* suited or appropriate for use in private: *closet meditations* **6** *(modifier) US and Canadian* based on or devoted to theory; speculative: *a closet strategist* ▷ *vb* -ets, -eting, -eted **7** *(tr)* to shut up or confine in a small private room, esp for conference or meditation [c14 from Old French, from *clos* enclosure; see **CLOSE¹**]

closet drama *n chiefly US* **a** drama suitable for reading rather than performing **b** a play of this kind

closet queen *n informal* a man who is homosexual but does not admit the fact

close-up ('kləʊs,ʌp) *n* **1** a photograph or film or television shot taken at close range **2** a detailed or intimate view or examination: *a close-up of modern society* ▷ *vb* **close up** (kləʊz) *(adverb)* **3** to shut entirely **4** *(intr)* to draw together: *the ranks closed up* **5** *(intr)* (of wounds) to heal completely

close with (kləʊz) *vb (intr, preposition)* to engage in battle with (an enemy)

closing time ('kləʊzɪŋ) *n* the time at which pubs must legally stop selling alcoholic drinks

clostridium (klɒ'strɪdɪəm) *n, pl* -iums *or* -ia (-ɪə) any anaerobic typically rod-shaped bacterium of the genus *Clostridium*, occurring mainly in soil, but also in the intestines of humans and animals: family *Bacillaceae*. The genus includes the species causing botulism and tetanus [c20 from New Latin, literally: small spindle, from Greek *klōstēr* spindle, from *klōthein* to spin; see -IUM] ▷ **clos'tridial** *or* **clos'tridian** *adj*

closure ('kləʊʒə) *n* **1** the act of closing or the state of being closed **2** an end or conclusion **3** something that closes or shuts, such as a cap or seal for a container **4** (in a deliberative body) a procedure by which debate may be halted and an immediate vote taken. See also **cloture, guillotine, gag rule 5** *chiefly US* **a** the resolution of a significant event or relationship in a person's life **b** a sense of contentment experienced after such a resolution **6** *geology* the vertical distance between the crest of an anticline and the lowest contour that surrounds it **7** *phonetics* the obstruction of the breath stream at some point along the vocal tract, such as the complete occlusion preliminary to the articulation of a stop **8** *logic* **a** the closed sentence formed from a given open sentence by prefixing universal or existential quantifiers to bind all its free variables **b** the process of forming such a closed sentence **9**

maths **a** the smallest closed set containing a given set **b** the operation of forming such a set **10** *psychol* the tendency, first noted by Gestalt psychologists, to see an incomplete figure like a circle with a gap in it as more complete than it is ▷ *vb* **11** *(tr)* (in a deliberative body) to end (debate) by closure [c14 from Old French, from Late Latin *clausūra* bar, from Latin *claudere* to close]

clot (klɒt) *n* **1** a soft thick lump or mass: *a clot of blood* **2** *Brit informal* a stupid person; fool ▷ *vb* **clots, clotting, clotted 3** to form or cause to form into a soft thick lump or lumps [Old English *clott*, of Germanic origin; compare Middle Dutch *klotte* block, lump] ▷ '**clottish** *adj*

cloth (klɒθ) *n, pl* **cloths** (klɒθs, klɒðz) **1 a** a fabric formed by weaving, felting or knitting wool, cotton, etc **b** *(as modifier)*: *a cloth bag* **2** a piece of such fabric used for a particular purpose, as for a dishcloth **3** (usually preceded by *the*) **a** the clothes worn by a clergyman **b** the clergy **4** *obsolete* clothing **5** *nautical* any of the panels of a sail **6** *chiefly Brit* a piece of coloured fabric, used on the stage as scenery **7** *West African* a garment in a traditional non-European style [Old English *clāth*; related to Old Frisian *klēth*, Middle High German *kleit* cloth, clothing]

clothbound ('klɒθ,baʊnd) *adj* (of a book) bound in stiff boards covered in cloth

cloth cap *n Brit* **1** Also called: **flat cap** a flat woollen cap with a stiff peak **2** *informal* **a** a symbol of working-class ethos or origin **b** *(as modifier)*: *cloth-cap attitudes*

clothe (kləʊð) *vb* **clothes, clothing, clothed** *or* **clad** *(tr)* **1** to dress or attire (a person) **2** to provide with clothing or covering **3** to conceal or disguise **4** to endow or invest [Old English *clāthian*, from *clāth* CLOTH; related to Old Norse *klætha*]

cloth-eared *adj informal* **1** deaf **2** insensitive

clothes (kləʊðz) *pl n* **1 a** articles of dress **b** *(as modifier)*: *clothes brush*. Related adj: **vestiary 2** *chiefly Brit* short for **bedclothes** [Old English *clāthas*, plural of *clāth* CLOTH]

clotheshorse ('kləʊðz,hɔːs) *n* **1** a frame on which to hang laundry for drying or airing **2** *informal* a dandy

clothesline ('kləʊðz,laɪn) *n* a piece of rope, cord, or wire on which clean washing is hung to dry or air

clothes moth *n* any of various tineid moths, esp *Tineola bisselliella*, the larvae of which feed on wool or fur

clothes peg *n* a small wooden or plastic clip for attaching washing to a clothesline

clothes pole *n* **1** a post to which a clothesline is attached. Also called: **clothes post 2** *Scot, US* another term for **clothes prop**

clothes-press *n* a piece of furniture for storing clothes, usually containing wide drawers and a cabinet

clothes prop *n* a long wooden pole with a forked end, used to raise a line of washing to enable it to catch the breeze

clothier ('kləʊðɪə) *n* a person who makes, sells, or deals in clothes or cloth

clothing ('kləʊðɪŋ) *n* **1** garments collectively **2** something that covers or clothes

Clotho ('kləʊθəʊ) *n Greek myth* one of the three Fates, spinner of the thread of life [Latin, from Greek *Klōthō*, one who spins, from *klōthein* to spin]

cloth of gold *n* cloth woven from silk threads interspersed with gold

clotted cream *n Brit* a thick cream made from scalded milk, esp in SW England. Also called: Devonshire cream

clotting factor *n* any one of a group of substances, including factor VIII, the presence of which in the blood is essential for blood clotting to occur. Also called: **coagulation factor**

cloture ('kləʊtʃə) *n* **1** closure in the US Senate ▷ *vb* **2** *(tr)* to end (debate) in the US Senate by cloture [c19 from French *clôture*, from Old French **CLOSURE**]

cloud (klaʊd) *n* **1** a mass of water or ice particles visible in the sky, usually white or grey, from which rain or snow falls when the particles coagulate. See also **cirrus, cumulonimbus, cumulus, stratus 2** any collection of particles visible in the air, esp of smoke or dust **3** a large number of insects or other small animals in flight **4** something that darkens, threatens, or carries gloom **5** *jewellery* a cloudlike blemish in a transparent stone **6 in the clouds** not in contact with reality **7 under a cloud a** under reproach or suspicion **b** in a state of gloom or bad temper **8 on cloud nine** *informal* elated; very happy ▷ *vb* **9** (when *intr*, often foll by *over* or *up*) to make or become cloudy, overcast, or indistinct **10** (*tr*) to make obscure; darken **11** (*tr*) to confuse or impair: *emotion clouded his judgment* **12** to make or become gloomy or depressed **13** (*tr*) to place under or render liable to suspicion or disgrace **14** to render (liquids) milky or dull or (of liquids) to become milky or dull **15** to become or render mottled or variegated [c13 (in the sense: a mass of vapour): from Old English *clūd* rock, hill; probably related to CLOD] > 'cloudless *adj* > 'cloudlessly *adv* > 'cloudlessness *n* > 'cloud,like *adj*

cloudberry ('klaʊdbərɪ, -brɪ) *n, pl* -ries a creeping Eurasian herbaceous rosaceous plant, *Rubus chamaemorus*, with white flowers and orange berry-like fruits (drupelets).

cloudburst ('klaʊd,bɜːst) *n* a heavy downpour

cloud chamber *n physics* an apparatus for detecting high-energy particles by observing their tracks through a chamber containing a supersaturated vapour. Each particle ionizes molecules along its path and small droplets condense on them to produce a visible track. Also called: Wilson cloud chamber

cloud-cuckoo-land *or* **cloudland** ('klaʊd,lænd) *n* a realm of fantasy, dreams, or impractical notions

clouded yellow *n* See **yellow** (sense 6)

cloudlet ('klaʊdlɪt) *n* a small cloud

cloud rack *n* a group of moving clouds

cloudscape ('klaʊdskeɪp) *n* **1** a picturesque formation of clouds **2** a picture or photograph of such a formation

cloudy ('klaʊdɪ) *adj* cloudier, cloudiest **1** covered with cloud or clouds **2** of or like a cloud or clouds **3** streaked or mottled like a cloud **4** opaque or muddy **5** obscure or unclear **6** troubled by gloom or depression: *his face had a cloudy expression* > 'cloudily *adv* > 'cloudiness *n*

clough (klʌf) *n dialect* a gorge or narrow ravine [Old English *clōh*]

clout (klaʊt) *n* **1** *informal* a blow with the hand or a hard object **2** power or influence, esp in politics **3** *archery* **a** the target used in long-distance shooting **b** the centre of this target **c** a shot that hits the centre **4** Also called: clout nail a short, flat-headed nail used esp for attaching sheet metal to wood **5** *Brit dialect* **a** a piece of cloth: *a dish clout* **b** a garment **c** a patch ▷ *vb* (*tr*) **6** *informal* to give a hard blow to, esp with the hand **7** to patch with a piece of cloth or leather [Old English *clūt* piece of metal or cloth, *clūtian* to patch (c14 to strike with the hand); related to Dutch *kluit* a lump, and to CLOD] > 'clouter *n*

clove¹ (kləʊv) *n* **1** a tropical evergreen myrtaceous tree, *Syzygium aromaticum*, native to the East Indies but cultivated elsewhere, esp Zanzibar **2** the dried unopened flower buds of this tree, used as a pungent fragrant spice [c14 from Old French *clou de girofle*, literally: nail of clove, *clou* from Latin *clāvus* nail + *girofle* clove tree]

clove² (kləʊv) *n* any of the segments of a compound bulb that arise from the axils of the scales of a large bulb [Old English *clufu* bulb; related to Old High German *klovolouh* garlic, see CLEAVE¹]

clove³ (kləʊv) *vb* a past tense of **cleave¹**

clove hitch *n* a knot or hitch used for securing a rope to a spar, post, or larger rope

Clovelly (klə'velɪ) *n* a village in SW England, in Devon on the Bristol Channel: famous for its steep cobbled streets: tourism, fishing. Pop: 500 (latest est)

cloven ('kləʊvᵊn) *vb* **1** a past participle of **cleave¹** ▷ *adj* **2** split; cleft; divided

cloven hoof *or* **foot** *n* **1** the divided hoof of a pig, goat, cow, deer, or related animal, which consists of the two middle digits of the foot **2** the mark or symbol of Satan > ,cloven-'hoofed *or* ,cloven-'footed *adj*

clove oil *n* a volatile pale-yellow aromatic oil obtained from clove flowers, formerly much used in confectionery, dentistry, and microscopy. Also called: oil of cloves

clove pink *n* another name for **carnation** (sense 1)

clover ('kləʊvə) *n* **1** any plant of the leguminous genus *Trifolium*, having trifoliate leaves and dense flower heads. Many species, such as red clover, white clover, and alsike, are grown as forage plants **2** any of various similar or related plants **3** sweet clover another name for **melilot 4** pin clover another name for **alfilaria 5 in clover** *informal* in a state of ease or luxury [Old English *clāfre*; related to Old High German *klēo*, Middle Low German *klēver*, Dutch *klāver*]

cloverleaf ('kləʊvə,liːf) *n, pl* -leaves **1** an arrangement of connecting roads, resembling a four-leaf clover in form, that joins two intersecting main roads **2** (*modifier*) in the shape or pattern of a leaf of clover

cloverleaf aerial *n* a type of aerial, having three or four similar coplanar loops arranged symmetrically around an axis, to which in-phase signals are fed

clovis point ('kləʊvɪs) *n* a concave-based flint projectile dating from the 10th millennium BC, found throughout most of Central and North America

clown (klaʊn) *n* **1** a comic entertainer, usually grotesquely costumed and made up, appearing in the circus **2** any performer who elicits an amused response **3** someone who plays jokes or tricks **4** a person who acts in a comic or buffoon-like manner **5** a coarse clumsy rude person; boor **6** *archaic* a countryman or rustic ▷ *vb* (*intr*) **7** to perform as a clown **8** to play jokes or tricks **9** to act foolishly [c16 perhaps of Low German origin; compare Frisian *klönne*, Icelandic *klunni* clumsy fellow] > 'clownery *n* > 'clownish *adj* > 'clownishly *adv* > 'clownishness *n*

cloxacillin (,klɒksə'sɪlɪn) *n* a semisynthetic penicillin used to treat staphylococcal infections due to penicillin-resistant organisms

cloy (klɔɪ) *vb* to make weary or cause weariness through an excess of something initially pleasurable or sweet [c14 (originally: to nail, hence, to obstruct): from earlier *acloyen*, from Old French *encloer*, from Medieval Latin *inclavāre*, from Latin *clāvāre* to nail, from *clāvus* a nail]

cloying ('klɔɪɪŋ) *adj* initially pleasurable or sweet but wearying in excess > 'cloyingly *adv*

cloze test (kləʊz) *n* a test of the ability to comprehend text in which the reader has to supply the missing words that have been removed from the text at regular intervals [altered from *close* to suggest completing a pattern (in Gestalt theory)]

club (klʌb) *n* **1** a stout stick, usually with one end thicker than the other, esp one used as a weapon **2** a stick or bat used to strike the ball in various sports, esp golf. See **golf club** (sense 1) **3** short for **Indian club 4** a group or association of people with common aims or interests: *a wine club* **5 a** the room, building, or facilities used by such a group **b** (*in combination*): *clubhouse* **6** a building in which elected, fee-paying members go to meet, dine, read, etc **7** a commercial establishment in which people can drink and dance, disco. See also **nightclub 8** *chiefly Brit* an organization, esp in a shop, set up as a means of saving **9** *Brit* an informal word for **friendly society 10 a** the black trefoil symbol on a playing card **b** a card with one or more of these symbols or (*when pl.*) the suit of cards so marked **11** *nautical* **a** a spar used for extending the clew of a gaff topsail beyond the peak of the gaff **b** short for **club foot** (sense 3) **12 in the club** *Brit slang* pregnant **13 on the club** *Brit slang* away from work due to sickness, esp when receiving sickness benefit ▷ *vb* clubs, clubbing, clubbed **14** (*tr*) to beat with or as if with a club **15** (often foll by *together*) to gather or become gathered into a group **16** (often foll by *together*) to unite or combine (resources, efforts, etc) for a common purpose **17** (*tr*) to use (a rifle or similar firearm) as a weapon by holding the barrel and hitting with the butt **18** (*intr*) *nautical* to drift in a current, reducing speed by dragging anchor [c13 from Old Norse *klubba*, related to Middle High German *klumpe* group of trees, CLUMP, Old English *clympre* lump of metal] > 'clubbing *n*

clubbable *or* **clubable** ('klʌbəbᵊl) *adj* suitable to be a member of a club; sociable > ,clubba'bility *or* ,cluba'bility *n*

clubbed (klʌbd) *adj* having a thickened end, like a club

clubber ('klʌbə) *n* a person who regularly frequents nightclubs and similar establishments

clubbing ('klʌbɪŋ) *n* the activity of frequenting nightclubs and similar establishments

clubby ('klʌbɪ) *adj* -bier, -biest **1** sociable, esp effusively so **2** exclusive or cliquish > 'clubbily *adv*

club class *n* **1** a class of air travel which is less luxurious than first class but more luxurious than economy class ▷ *adj* **2** club-class of or relating to this class of travel

club culture *n* the practice of protecting the reputation of one's workforce in the face of criticism, above all other considerations

club foot *n* **1** a congenital deformity of the foot, esp one in which the foot is twisted so that most of the weight rests on the heel. Technical name: talipes **2** a foot so deformed **3** *nautical* a boom attached to the foot of a jib > ,club-'footed *adj*

club hand *n* **1** a deformity of the hand, analogous to club foot **2** a hand so deformed > ,club-'handed *adj*

clubhaul ('klʌb,hɔːl) *vb nautical* to force (a sailing vessel) onto a new tack, esp in an emergency, by fastening a lee anchor to the lee quarter, dropping the anchor as the vessel comes about, and hauling in the anchor cable to swing the stern to windward

clubhouse ('klʌb,haʊs) *n* the premises of a sports or other club, esp a golf club

clubhouse sandwich *n* another name for **club sandwich**

clubland ('klʌb,lænd) *n* (in Britain) the area of London around St James's, which contains most of the famous London clubs

club line *n printing* See **orphan** (sense 3)

clubman ('klʌbmən) *n, pl* -men a man who is an enthusiastic member of a club or clubs

club moss *n* any mosslike tracheophyte plant of the phylum *Lycopodophyta*, having erect or creeping stems covered with tiny overlapping leaves

club root *n* a disease of cabbages and related plants, caused by the fungus *Plasmodiophora brassicae*, in which the roots become thickened and distorted

club sandwich *n* a sandwich consisting of three or more slices of toast or bread with a filling

clubwoman ('klʌb,wʊmən) *n, pl* -women a woman who is an enthusiastic member of a club or clubs

cluck (klʌk) *n* **1** the low clicking sound made by a hen or any similar sound ▷ *vb* **2** (*intr*) (of a hen) to make a clicking sound **3** (*tr*) to call or express (a feeling) by making a similar sound [c17 of imitative origin]

clucky ('klʌkɪ) *adj Austral Informal* (of a woman) **1** wishing to have a baby **2** excessively protective towards her children

clue (kluː) *n* **1** something that helps to solve a problem or unravel a mystery **2 not to have a clue a** to be completely baffled **b** to be completely ignorant or incompetent ▷ *vb* clues, cluing, clued

3 (*tr; usually foll by* in *or* up) to provide with helpful information ▷ *n* ▷ *vb* **4** a variant spelling of **clew** [C15 variant of CLEW]

clued-up *adj informal* shrewd; well-informed

clueless ('klu:lɪs) *adj slang* helpless; stupid

Cluj (kluʃ, klu:ʒ) *n* an industrial city in NW Romania, on the Someşul-Mic River: former capital of Transylvania. Pop: 297 000 (2005 est). German name: **Klausenburg** Hungarian name: **Kolozsvár**

clumber spaniel ('klʌmbə) *n* a type of thickset spaniel having a broad heavy head. Often shortened to: **clumber** [C19 named after *Clumber*, stately home of the Dukes of Newcastle where the breed was developed]

clump (klʌmp) *n* **1** a cluster, as of trees or plants **2** a dull heavy tread or any similar sound **3** an irregular mass: *a clump of hair or earth* **4** an inactive mass of microorganisms, esp a mass of bacteria produced as a result of agglutination **5** an extra sole on a shoe **6** *slang* a blow ▷ *vb* **7** (*intr*) to walk or tread heavily **8** to gather or be gathered into clumps, clusters, clots, etc **9** to cause (bacteria, blood cells, etc) to collect together or (of bacteria, etc) to collect together **10** (*tr*) *slang* to punch (someone) [Old English *clympe*; related to Middle Dutch *klampe* heap of hay, Middle Low German *klampe* CLAMP², Swedish *klimp* small lump] > 'clumpy *adj* > 'clumpiness *n*

clumsy ('klʌmzɪ) *adj* **-sier, -siest** **1** lacking in skill or physical coordination **2** awkwardly constructed or contrived [C16 (in obsolete sense: benumbed with cold; hence, awkward): perhaps from C13 dialect *clumse* to benumb, probably from Scandinavian; compare Swedish dialect *klumsig* numb] > 'clumsily *adv* > 'clumsiness *n*

clung (klʌŋ) *vb* the past tense and past participle of **cling**

Cluniac ('klu:nɪˌæk) *adj* of or relating to a reformed Benedictine order founded at the French town of Cluny in 910

clunk (klʌŋk) *n* **1** a blow or the sound of a blow **2** a dull metallic sound **3** a dull or stupid person **4** *chiefly Scot* **a** the gurgling sound of a liquid **b** the sound of a cork being removed from a bottle ▷ *vb* **5** to make or cause to make such a sound [C19 of imitative origin]

clunker ('klʌŋkə) *n informal* **1** *chiefly US* a dilapidated old car or other machine **2** something that fails: *the novel's last line is a clunker*

clunky ('klʌŋkɪ) *adj* **clunkier, clunkiest 1** making a clunking noise **2** *informal* ponderously ungraceful or unsophisticated: *clunky boots* **3** awkward or unsophisticated: *then you guffaw at clunky dialogue*

Cluny ('klu:nɪ; *French* klyni) *n* a town in E central France: reformed Benedictine order founded here in 910; important religious and cultural centre in the Middle Ages. Pop: 4376 (1999)

Cluny lace *n* a strong heavy silk and cotton bobbin lace made at Cluny or elsewhere

clupeid ('klu:pɪɪd) *n* **1** any widely distributed soft-finned teleost fish of the family *Clupeidae*, typically having oily flesh, and including the herrings, sardines, shad, etc ▷ *adj* **2** of, relating to, or belonging to the family *Clupeidae* [C19 from New Latin *Clupeidae*, from Latin *clupea* small river fish]

clupeoid ('klu:pɪˌɔɪd) *adj* **1** of, relating to, or belonging to the *Isospondyli* (or *Clupeiformes*), a large order of soft-finned fishes, including the herrings, salmon, and tarpon ▷ *n* **2** any fish belonging to the order *Isospondyli* [C19 from Latin *clupea* small fish + -OID]

cluster ('klʌstə) *n* **1** a number of things growing, fastened, or occurring close together **2** a number of persons or things grouped together **3** *US military* a metal insignia worn on a medal ribbon to indicate a second award or a higher class of a decoration or order **4** *military* **a** a group of bombs dropped in one stick, esp fragmentation and incendiary bombs **b** the basic unit of mines used in laying a minefield **5** *astronomy* an aggregation

of stars or galaxies moving together through space **6** a group of two or more consecutive vowels or consonants **7** *statistics* a naturally occurring subgroup of a population used in stratified sampling **8** *chem* **a** a chemical compound or molecule containing groups of metal atoms joined by metal-to-metal bonds **b** the group of linked metal atoms present ▷ *vb* **9** to gather or be gathered in clusters [Old English *clyster*; related to Low German *Kluster*; see CLOD, CLOT] > 'clustered *adj* > 'clusteringly *adv* > 'clustery *adj*

cluster area *n* a place where a concentration of a particular phenomenon is found

cluster bomb *n* a bomb that throws out a number of smaller bombs or antipersonnel projectiles when it explodes

cluster fly *n* a dipterous fly, *Pollenia rudis*, that tends to gather in large numbers in attics in the autumn: family *Calliphoridae*. The larvae are parasitic in earthworms

clutch¹ (klʌtʃ) *vb* **1** (*tr*) to seize with or as if with hands or claws **2** (*tr*) to grasp or hold firmly **3** (*intr; usually foll by* at) to attempt to get hold or possession (of) ▷ *n* **4** a device that enables two revolving shafts to be joined or disconnected as required, esp one that transmits the drive from the engine to the gearbox in a vehicle **5** a device for holding fast **6** a firm grasp **7** a hand, claw, or talon in the act of clutching: *in the clutches of a bear* **8** (*often plural*) power or control: *in the clutches of the Mafia* **9** Also called: **clutch bag** a handbag without handles [Old English *clyccan*; related to Old Frisian *kletsie* spear, Swedish *klyka* clasp, fork]

clutch² (klʌtʃ) *n* **1** a hatch of eggs laid by a particular bird or laid in a single nest **2** a brood of chickens **3** *informal* a group, bunch, or cluster ▷ *vb* **4** (*tr*) to hatch (chickens) [C17 (Northern English dialect) *cletch*, from Old Norse *klekja* to hatch]

Clutha ('klu:θə) *n* a river in New Zealand, the longest river in South Island; rising in the Southern Alps it flows southeast to the Pacific. Length: 338 km (210 miles)

clutter ('klʌtə) *vb* **1** (*usually tr; often foll by* up) to strew or amass (objects) in a disorderly manner **2** (*intr*) to move about in a bustling manner **3** (*intr*) to chatter or babble ▷ *n* **4** a disordered heap or mass of objects **5** a state of disorder **6** unwanted echoes that confuse the observation of signals on a radar screen [C15 *clotter*, from *clotteren* to CLOT]

Clwyd ('klu:ɪd) *n* a former county in NE Wales, formed in 1974 from Flintshire, most of Denbighshire, and part of Merionethshire; replaced in 1996 by Flintshire, Denbighshire, Wrexham county borough, and part of Conwy county borough

Clyde (klaɪd) *n* **1** Firth of an inlet of the Atlantic in SW Scotland. Length: 103 km (64 miles) **2** a river in S Scotland, rising in South Lanarkshire and flowing northwest to the Firth of Clyde: formerly extensive shipyards. Length: 170 km (106 miles)

Clydebank (ˌklaɪd'bæŋk, 'klaɪdˌbæŋk) *n* a town in W Scotland, in West Dunbartonshire on the north bank of the River Clyde. Pop: 29 858 (2001)

Clydesdale ('klaɪdzˌdeɪl) *n* a heavy powerful breed of carthorse, originally from Scotland

clype (klaɪp) *Scot* ▷ *vb* (*intr*) **1** to tell tales; be an informer ▷ *n* **2** a person who tells tales [from Old English *clipian, cleopian*; see CLEPE]

clypeus ('klɪpɪəs) *n, pl* **clypei** ('klɪpɪˌaɪ) a cuticular plate on the head of some insects between the labrum and the frons [C19 from New Latin, from Latin *clipeus* round shield] > 'clypeal *adj* > 'clypeate ('klɪpɪˌeɪt) *adj*

clyster ('klɪstə) *n med* a former name for an **enema** [C14 from Greek *klustēr*, from *kluzein* to rinse]

Clytemnestra *or* **Clytaemnestra** (ˌklaɪtɪm'nɛstrə) *n Greek myth* the wife of Agamemnon, whom she killed on his return from the Trojan War

cm¹ *symbol for* centimetre

cm² *the internet domain name for* Cameroon

Cm *the chemical symbol for* curium

CM *abbreviation for* Member of the Order of Canada

Cmdr *military abbreviation for* Commander

CMEA *abbreviation for* Council for Mutual Economic Assistance. See **Comecon**

CMG *abbreviation for* Companion of St Michael and St George (a British title)

CMIIW *text messaging abbreviation for* correct me if I'm wrong

cml *abbreviation for* commercial

CMOS ('si:mɒs) *adj computing acronym for* complementary metal oxide silicon: *CMOS memory*

CMV *abbreviation for* cytomegalovirus

cn *the internet domain name for* China

C/N, c/n *or* **cn** *commerce abbreviation for* credit note

CNA (in South Africa) *abbreviation for* Central News Agency, a national stationery chain

CNAA (in Britain) *abbreviation for* the Council for National Academic Awards: a former degree-awarding body separate from the universities

CNAR *abbreviation for* compound net annual rate

CND (in Britain) *abbreviation for* Campaign for Nuclear Disarmament

cnemis ('ni:mɪs) *n anatomy, zoology* the shin or tibia [from Greek *knēmē* leg] > 'cnemial *adj*

CNG *abbreviation for* compressed natural gas

cnidarian (naɪ'dɛərɪən, knaɪ-) *n* **1** any invertebrate of the phylum *Cnidaria*, which comprises the coelenterates ▷ *adj* **2** of, relating to, or belonging to the *Cnidaria* [C20 from New Latin *Cnidaria*, from Greek *knidē* nettle]

cnidoblast ('naɪdəʊˌblɑːst, 'knaɪ-) *n zoology* any of the cells of a coelenterate that contain nematocysts [C19 from New Latin *cnida*, from Greek *knidē* nettle + -BLAST]

Cnidus ('naɪdəs, 'knaɪ-) *n* an ancient Greek city in SW Asia Minor: famous for its school of medicine

CNN *abbreviation for* Cable Network News

Cnossus ('nɒsəs, 'knɒs-) *n* a variant spelling of **Knossos**

CNR *abbreviation for* Canadian National Railways

CNS *abbreviation for* **central nervous system**

co 1 *an internet domain name for* a commercial company (used with a country domain name) **2** ▷ *the internet domain name for* Colombia

Co *the chemical symbol for* cobalt

CO *abbreviation for* **1** Commanding Officer **2** Commonwealth Office **3** conscientious objector **4** Colorado **5** *international car registration for* Colombia

Co *or* **co** *abbreviation for* **1** (*esp in names of business organizations*) Company **2** **and co** (kəʊ) *informal* and the rest of them: *Harold and co*

Co *abbreviation for* County

co- *prefix* **1** together; joint or jointly; mutual or mutually: *coproduction* **2** indicating partnership or equality: *cofounder; copilot* **3** to the same or a similar degree: *coextend* **4** (in mathematics and astronomy) of the complement of an angle: *cosecant; codeclination* [from Latin, reduced form of COM-]

c/o *abbreviation for* **1** care of **2** book-keeping carried over

CoA *abbreviation for* coenzyme A

coacervate (kəʊ'æsəvɪt, -ˌveɪt) *n* either of two liquid phases that may separate from a hydrophilic sol, each containing a different concentration of a dispersed solid [C17 from Latin *coacervāre* to heap up, from *acervus* a heap] > coˌacer'vation *n*

coach (kəʊtʃ) *n* **1** a vehicle for several passengers, used for transport over long distances, sightseeing, etc **2** a large four-wheeled enclosed carriage, usually horse-drawn **3** a railway carriage carrying passengers **4** a trainer or instructor: *a drama coach* **5** a tutor who prepares students for examinations ▷ *vb* **6** to give tuition or instruction to (a pupil) **7** (*tr*) to transport in a bus or coach [C16 from French *coche*, from Hungarian *kocsi szekér* wagon of Kocs, village in

Hungary where coaches were first made; in the sense: to teach, probably from the idea that the instructor carried his pupils] > 'coacher n

coach bolt n a large round-headed bolt used esp to secure wood to masonry. Also called (chiefly US and Canadian): carriage bolt

coach box n the seat of a coachman on a horse-drawn carriage or coach

coach-built adj (of a vehicle) having specially built bodywork > 'coach-,builder n

coach class n the US and Canad. name for economy class. See economy (sense 6)

coach dog n a former name for Dalmatian

coachee (ˌkəʊtʃiː) n a person who receives training from a coach, esp in business or office practice

coach house n 1 a building in which a coach is kept 2 Also called: coaching house, coaching inn history an inn along a coaching route at which horses were changed

coach line n a decorative line on the bodywork of a motor vehicle. Also called: carriage line

coachman (ˈkəʊtʃmən) n, pl -men 1 the driver of a coach or carriage 2 a fishing fly with white wings and a brown hackle

coach screw n a large screw with a square head used in timber work in buildings, etc

coachwood (ˈkəʊtʃˌwʊd) n an Australian tree, Ceratopetalum apetalum, yielding light aromatic wood used for furniture, turnery, etc

coachwork (ˈkəʊtʃˌwɜːk) n 1 the design and manufacture of car bodies 2 the body of a car

coaction¹ (kəʊˈækʃən) n 1 any relationship between organisms within a community 2 joint action [c17 co- + ACTION] > co'active adj > co'actively adv > ,coac'tivity n

coaction² (kəʊˈækʃən) n obsolete a force or compulsion, either to compel or restrain [c14 from Late Latin coāctiō, from Latin cōgere to constrain, compel]

coadjutant (kəʊˈædʒətənt) adj 1 cooperating ▷ n 2 a helper

coadjutor (kəʊˈædʒʊtə) n 1 a bishop appointed as assistant to a diocesan bishop 2 rare an assistant [c15 via Old French from Latin co- together + adjūtor helper, from adjūtāre to assist, from juvāre to help] > co'adjutress or co'adjutrix fem n

coadunate (kəʊˈædjʊnɪt, -ˌneɪt) adj biology another word for connate (sense 3) [c19 from Late Latin coadūnāre to join together, from Latin adūnāre to join to, from ūnus one] > co,adu'nation n > co'adu,native adj

coagulant (kəʊˈæɡjʊlənt) or **coagulator** (kəʊˈæɡjʊˌleɪtə) n a substance that aids or produces coagulation

coagulase (kəʊˈæɡjʊˌleɪz) n any enzyme that causes coagulation of blood

coagulate vb (kəʊˈæɡjʊˌleɪt) 1 to cause (a fluid, such as blood) to change into a soft semisolid mass or (of such a fluid) to change into such a mass; clot; curdle 2 chem to separate or cause to separate into distinct constituent phases ▷ n (kəʊˈæɡjʊlɪt, -ˌleɪt) 3 the solid or semisolid substance produced by coagulation [c16 from Latin coāgulāre to make (a liquid) curdle, from coāgulum rennet, from cōgere to drive together] > co'agulable adj > co,agula'bility n > co,agu'lation n > coagulative (kəʊˈæɡjʊlətɪv) adj

coagulation factor n med another name for clotting factor

coagulum (kəʊˈæɡjʊləm) n, pl -la (-lə) any coagulated mass; clot; curd [c17 from Latin: curdling agent; see COAGULATE]

Coahuila (Spanish koaˈwila) n a state of N Mexico: mainly plateau, crossed by several mountain ranges that contain rich mineral resources. Capital: Saltillo. Pop: 2 295 808 (2000). Area: 151 571 sq km (59 112 sq miles)

coal (kəʊl) n 1 a a combustible compact black or dark-brown carbonaceous rock formed from compaction of layers of partially decomposed vegetation: a fuel and a source of coke, coal gas, and coal tar. See also anthracite, bituminous coal, lignite, peat¹ b (as modifier): coal cellar; coal merchant; coal mine; coal dust 2 one or more lumps of coal 3 short for charcoal 4 coals to Newcastle something supplied where it is already plentiful 5 haul (someone) over the coals to reprimand (someone) ▷ vb 6 to take in, provide with, or turn into coal [Old English col; related to Old Norse kol, Old High German kolo, Old Irish gūal] > 'coaly adj

coaler (ˈkəʊlə) n 1 a ship, train, etc, used to carry or supply coal 2 a person who sells or supplies coal

coalesce (ˌkəʊəˈlɛs) vb (intr) to unite or come together in one body or mass; merge; fuse; blend [c16 from Latin coalēscere from co- + alēscere to increase, from alere to nourish] > ,coa'lescence n > ,coa'lescent adj

coalface (ˈkəʊlˌfeɪs) n the exposed seam of coal in a mine

coalfield (ˈkəʊlˌfiːld) n an area rich in deposits of coal

coalfish (ˈkəʊlˌfɪʃ) n, pl -fish or -fishes a dark-coloured gadoid food fish, Pollachius virens, occurring in northern seas. Also called (Brit): saithe, coley

coal gas n a mixture of gases produced by the distillation of bituminous coal and used for heating and lighting: consists mainly of hydrogen, methane, and carbon monoxide

coal heaver n a workman who moves coal

coal hole n Brit informal a small coal cellar

coalition (ˌkəʊəˈlɪʃən) n 1 a an alliance or union between groups, factions, or parties, esp for some temporary and specific reason b (as modifier): a coalition government 2 a fusion or merging into one body or mass [c17 from Medieval Latin coalitiō, from Latin coalēscere to COALESCE] > ,coa'litional adj > ,coa'litionist or ,coa'litioner n

Coal Measures pl n the a series of coal-bearing rocks formed in the upper Carboniferous period; the uppermost series of the Carboniferous system

coal miner's lung n an informal name for anthracosis

coal oil n 1 US and Canadian petroleum or a refined product from petroleum, esp kerosene 2 a crude oil produced, together with coal gas, during the distillation of bituminous coal

Coalport (ˈkəʊlˌpɔːt) n antiques a white translucent bone china having richly coloured moulded patterns, made in the 19th century at Coalport near Shrewsbury

coal pot n a cooking device using charcoal, consisting of a raised iron bowl and a central grid

Coal Sack n a dark nebula in the Milky Way close to the Southern Cross

coal scuttle n a domestic metal container for coal

coal tar n a black tar, produced by the distillation of bituminous coal, that can be further distilled to yield benzene, toluene, xylene, anthracene, phenol, etc

coal-tar pitch n a residue left by the distillation of coal tar: a mixture of hydrocarbons and finely divided carbon used as a binder for fuel briquettes, road surfaces, and carbon electrodes

coal tit n a small European songbird, Parus ater, having a black head with a white patch on the nape: family Paridae (tits)

coaming (ˈkəʊmɪŋ) n a raised frame around the cockpit or hatchway of a vessel for keeping out water [c17 of unknown origin]

coaptation (ˌkəʊæpˈteɪʃən) n the joining or reuniting of two surfaces, esp the ends of a broken bone or the edges of a wound [c16 from Late Latin coaptātiō a meticulous joining together, from Latin co- together + aptāre to fit]

coarctate (kəʊˈɑːkteɪt) adj 1 (of a pupa) enclosed in a hard barrel-shaped case (puparium), as in the housefly 2 crowded or pressed together; constricted ▷ vb (intr) 3 pathol (esp of the aorta) to become narrower; become constricted [c15 from Latin coarctāre, to press together, from artus tight] > ,coarc'tation n

coarse (kɔːs) adj 1 rough in texture, structure, etc; not fine: coarse sand 2 lacking refinement or taste; indelicate; vulgar: coarse jokes 3 of inferior quality; not pure or choice 4 (of a metal) not refined 5 (of a screw) having widely spaced threads [c14 of unknown origin] > 'coarsely adv > 'coarseness n

coarse fish n a freshwater fish that is not a member of the salmon family. Compare game fish > coarse fishing n

coarse-grained adj 1 having a large or coarse grain 2 (of a person) having a coarse nature; gross

coarsen (ˈkɔːsən) vb to make or become coarse

coast (kəʊst) n 1 a the line or zone where the land meets the sea or some other large expanse of water b (in combination): coastland. Related adj: littoral 2 Brit the seaside 3 US a a slope down which a sledge may slide b the act or an instance of sliding down a slope 4 obsolete borderland or frontier 5 the coast is clear informal the obstacles or dangers are gone ▷ vb 6 to move or cause to move by momentum or force of gravity 7 (intr) to proceed without great effort: to coast to victory 8 to sail along (a coast) [c13 from Old French coste coast, slope, from Latin costa side, rib] > 'coastal adj > 'coastally adv

coasteering (ˌkəʊˈstɪərɪŋ) n the sport of following a coastline by swimming, climbing, diving, and walking while wearing a wetsuit, a life jacket, and a helmet [c20 from COAST + (MOUNTAIN)EERING]

coaster (ˈkəʊstə) n 1 Brit a vessel or trader engaged in coastal commerce 2 a small tray, sometimes on wheels, for holding a decanter, wine bottle, etc 3 a person or thing that coasts 4 a protective disc or mat for glasses or bottles 5 US short for roller coaster 6 West African a European resident on the coast

Coaster (ˈkəʊstə) n NZ a person from the West Coast of the South Island, New Zealand

coastguard (ˈkəʊstˌɡɑːd) n 1 a maritime force which aids shipping, saves lives at sea, prevents smuggling, etc 2 Also called: coastguardsman a member of such a force

coastline (ˈkəʊstˌlaɪn) n the outline of a coast, esp when seen from the sea, or the land adjacent to it

Coast Mountains pl n a mountain range in Canada, on the Pacific coast of British Columbia. Highest peak: Mount Waddington, 4043 m (13 266 ft)

coat (kəʊt) n 1 an outdoor garment with sleeves, covering the body from the shoulder to waist, knee, or foot 2 any similar garment, esp one forming the top to a suit 3 a layer that covers or conceals a surface: a coat of dust 4 the hair, wool, or fur of an animal 5 short for coat of arms 6 on the coat Austral in disfavour ▷ vb 7 (tr; often foll by with) to cover (with) a layer or covering 8 (tr) to provide with a coat [c16 from Old French cote of Germanic origin; compare Old Saxon kotta, Old High German kozzo]

coat armour n heraldry 1 coat of arms 2 an emblazoned surcoat

Coatbridge (ˈkəʊtˌbrɪdʒ; Scot ˌkəʊtˈbrɪdʒ) n an industrial town in central Scotland, in North Lanarkshire. Pop: 41 170 (2001)

coat dress n 1 a lightweight button-through garment that can be worn either as a dress or as a coat 2 formerly, a dress tailored and styled like a coat

coated (ˈkəʊtɪd) adj 1 covered with an outer layer, film, etc 2 (of paper) having a coating of a mineral, esp china clay, to provide a very smooth surface 3 (of textiles) having been given a plastic or other surface 4 photog, optics another word for bloomed

coatee (kəʊˈtiː, ˈkəʊtiː) n chiefly Brit a short coat, esp for a baby

coat hanger n a curved piece of wood, wire, plastic, etc, fitted with a hook and used to hang up clothes

C

coati (kəʊˈɑːtɪ) *or* **coati-mondi, coati-mundi** (kəʊˌɑːtɪˈmʌndɪ) *n, pl* **-tis** *or* **-dis** any omnivorous mammal of the genera *Nasua* and *Nasuella*, of Central and South America: family *Procyonidae*, order *Carnivora* (carnivores). They are related to but larger than the raccoons, having a long flexible snout and a brindled coat [c17 from Portuguese *coatí*, from Tupi, literally: belt-nosed, from *cua* belt + *tim* nose]

coating (ˈkəʊtɪŋ) *n* **1** a layer or film spread over a surface for protection or decoration **2** a heavy fabric suitable for coats **3** *Midland English dialect* a severe rebuke; ticking-off

coat of arms *n* **1** the heraldic bearings of a person, family, or corporation **2** a surcoat decorated with family or personal bearings

coat of mail *n* a protective garment made of linked metal rings (mail) or of overlapping metal plates; hauberk

coat-of-mail shell *n* another name for **chiton** (sense 2)

coat-tail *n* **1** the long tapering tails at the back of a man's tailed coat **2** **on someone's coat-tails** thanks to the popularity or success of someone else

coauthor (kəʊˈɔːθə) *n* **1** a person who shares the writing of a book, article, etc, with another ▷ *vb* **2** (*tr*) to be the joint author of (a book, article, etc)

coax¹ (kəʊks) *vb* **1** to seek to manipulate or persuade (someone) by tenderness, flattery, pleading, etc **2** (*tr.*) to obtain by persistent coaxing **3** (*tr*) to work on or tend (something) carefully and patiently so as to make it function as one desires: *he coaxed the engine into starting* **4** (*tr*) *obsolete* to caress **5** (*tr*) *obsolete* to deceive [c16 verb formed from obsolete noun *cokes* fool, of unknown origin] ▷ **ˈcoaxer** *n* ▷ **ˈcoaxingly** *adv*

coax² (ˈkəʊæks) *n* short for **coaxial cable**

coaxial (kəʊˈæksɪəl) *or* **coaxal** (kəʊˈæksəl) *adj* **1** having or being mounted on a common axis **2** *geometry* (of a set of circles) having all the centres on a straight line **3** *electronics* formed from, using, or connected to a coaxial cable

coaxial cable *n* a cable consisting of an inner insulated core of stranded or solid wire surrounded by an outer insulated flexible wire braid, used esp as a transmission line for radio-frequency signals. Often shortened to: **coax**

cob¹ (kɒb) *n* **1** a male swan **2** a thickset short-legged type of riding and draught horse **3** short for **corncob, corncob pipe** *or* **cobnut 4** *Brit* another name for **hazel** (sense 1) **5** a small rounded lump or heap of coal, ore, etc **6** *Brit and NZ* a building material consisting of a mixture of clay and chopped straw **7** Also called: **cob loaf** *Brit* a round loaf of bread ▷ *vb* **cobs, cobbing, cobbed 8** (*tr*) *Brit informal* to beat, esp on the buttocks [c15 of uncertain origin; probably related to Icelandic *kobbi* seal; see CUB]

cob² *or* **cobb** (kɒb) *n* an archaic or dialect name for a **gull** esp the greater black-backed gull (*Larus marinus*) [c16 of Germanic origin; related to Dutch *kob, kobbe*]

cobaea (kəʊˈbiːə) *n* any climbing shrub of the tropical American genus *Cobaea*, esp *C. scandens*, grown for its large trumpet-shaped purple or white flowers: family *Polemoniaceae* [named after Bernabé *Cobo* (1572–1659), Jesuit missionary and naturalist]

cobalt (ˈkəʊbɔːlt) *n* a brittle hard silvery-white element that is a ferromagnetic metal: occurs principally in cobaltite and smaltite and is widely used in alloys. The radioisotope **cobalt-60**, with a half-life of 5.3 years, is used in radiotherapy and as a tracer. Symbol: Co; atomic no.: 27; atomic wt.: 58.93320; valency: 2 or 3; relative density: 8.9; melting pt.: 1495°C; boiling pt.: 2928°C [c17 German *Kobalt*, from Middle High German *kobolt* goblin; from the miners' belief that malicious goblins placed it in the silver ore]

cobalt bloom *n* another name for **erythrite** (sense 1)

cobalt blue *n* **1** Also called: **Thénard's blue** any greenish-blue pigment containing cobalt aluminate, usually made by heating cobaltous sulphate, aluminium oxide, and phosphoric acid together **2** a deep blue to greenish-blue colour **b** (*as adjective*): *a cobalt-blue car*

cobalt bomb *n* **1** a cobalt-60 device used in radiotherapy **2** a nuclear weapon consisting of a hydrogen bomb encased in cobalt, which releases large quantities of radioactive cobalt-60 into the atmosphere

cobaltic (kəʊˈbɔːltɪk) *adj* of or containing cobalt, esp in the trivalent state

cobaltite (kəʊˈbɔːltaɪt, ˈkəʊbɔːlˌtaɪt) *or* **cobaltine** (ˈkəʊbɒˌltiːn, -tɪn) *n* a rare silvery-white mineral consisting of cobalt arsenic sulphide in cubic crystalline form: a major ore of cobalt, used in ceramics. Formula: CoAsS

cobaltous (kəʊˈbɔːltəs) *adj* of or containing cobalt in the divalent state

cobber (ˈkɒbə) *n Austral and NZ informal* a friend; mate: used as a term of address to males [c19 from dialect *cob* to take a liking to someone]

cobble¹ (ˈkɒbəl) *n* **1** short for **cobblestone 2** *geology* a rock fragment, often rounded, with a diameter of 64–256 mm and thus smaller than a boulder but larger than a pebble ▷ *vb* **3** (*tr*) to pave (a road) with cobblestones ▷ See also **cobbles** [c15 (in *cobblestone*): from COB¹] ▷ **ˈcobbled** *adj*

cobble² (ˈkɒbəl) *vb* (*tr*) **1** to make or mend (shoes) **2** to put together clumsily [c15 back formation from COBBLER¹]

cobbler¹ (ˈkɒblə) *n* a person who makes or mends shoes [c13 (as surname): of unknown origin]

cobbler² (ˈkɒblə) *n* **1** a sweetened iced drink, usually made from fruit and wine or liqueur **2** *chiefly US* a hot dessert made of fruit covered with a rich cakelike crust [c19 (for sense 1) perhaps shortened from *cobbler's punch;* (for both senses) compare *cobble* (vb)]

cobblers (ˈkɒbləz) *Brit slang* ▷ *pl n* **1** rubbish; nonsense: *a load of old cobblers* **2** another word for **testicles** ▷ *interj* **3** an exclamation of strong disagreement [c20 from rhyming slang *cobblers' awls* balls]

> **USAGE** The use of *cobblers* meaning "nonsense" is so mild that hardly anyone these days is likely to be offended by it. Most people are probably unaware of its rhyming-slang association with "balls", and therefore take it at its face value as a more colourful synonym for "nonsense". The classic formulation "a load of (old) cobblers" seems to be particularly popular in the tabloid press

cobbler's pegs (pɛgz) *pl n* a common Australian weed, *Bidens pilosa*, with spiky peglike awns

cobbler's wax *n* a resin used for waxing thread

cobbles (ˈkɒbəlz) *pl n* **1** coal in small rounded lumps **2** cobblestones

cobblestone (ˈkɒbəlˌstəʊn) *n* a rounded stone used for paving. Sometimes shortened to: **cobble** Compare **sett**

cobelligerent (ˌkəʊbɪˈlɪdʒərənt) *n* a country fighting in a war on the side of another country

Cóbh (kəʊv) *n* a port in S Republic of Ireland, in SE Co Cork: port of call for Atlantic liners. Pop: 9811 (2002). Former name (1849–1922): Queenstown

cobia (ˈkəʊbɪə) *n* a large dark-striped percoid game fish, *Rachycentron canadum*, of tropical and subtropical seas: family *Rachycentridae* [of unknown origin]

coble (ˈkəʊbəl, ˈkɒbəl) *n Scot and northern English* a small single-masted flat-bottomed fishing boat [c13 probably of Celtic origin; compare Welsh *ceubal* skiff]

Coblenz (*German* ˈkoːblɛnts) *n* a variant spelling of **Koblenz**

cob money *n* crude silver coins issued in the

Spanish colonies of the New World from about 1600 until 1820

cobnut (ˈkɒbˌnʌt) *or* **cob** *n* other names for a **hazelnut** [c16 from earlier *cobylle nut;* see COBBLE¹, NUT]

COBOL *or* **Cobol** (ˈkəʊbɒl) *n* a high-level computer programming language designed for general commercial use [c20 *co(mmon) b(usiness) o(riented) l(anguage)*]

cobra (ˈkəʊbrə) *n* **1** any highly venomous elapid snake of the genus *Naja*, such as *N. naja* (**Indian cobra**), of tropical Africa and Asia. When alarmed they spread the skin of the neck region into a hood **2** any related snake, such as the king cobra [c19 from Portuguese *cobra (de capello)* snake (with a hood), from Latin *colubra* snake]

cobra de capello (di: kəˈpɛləʊ) *n, pl* **cobras de capello** a cobra, *Naja tripudians,* that has ringlike markings on the body and exists in many varieties in S and SE Asia

coburg (ˈkəʊˌbɜːg) *n* (*sometimes capital*) a rounded loaf with a cross cut on the top. Also called: **coburg loaf** [c19 apparently named in honour of Prince Albert (of *Saxe-Coburg-Gotha*), the name of the British royal family from 1901–1917]

Coburg (ˈkəʊbɜːg; *German* ˈkoːburk) *n* a city in E Germany, in N Bavaria. Pop: 42 257 (2003 est)

cobweb (ˈkɒbˌwɛb) *n* **1** a web spun by certain spiders, esp those of the family *Theridiidae,* often found in the corners of disused rooms **2** a single thread of such a web **3** something like a cobweb, as in its flimsiness or ability to trap [c14 *cob,* from *coppe,* from Old English (*āter)coppe* spider; related to Middle Dutch *koppe* spider, Swedish (dialect) *etterkoppa*] ▷ **ˈcobˌwebbed** *adj* ▷ **ˈcobˌwebby** *adj*

cobwebs (ˈkɒbˌwɛbz) *pl n* **1** mustiness, confusion, or obscurity **2** *informal* stickiness of the eyelids experienced upon first awakening

coca (ˈkəʊkə) *n* **1** either of two shrubs, *Erythroxylon coca* or *E. truxiuense,* native to the Andes: family *Erythroxylaceae* **2** the dried leaves of these shrubs and related plants, which contain cocaine and are chewed by the peoples of the Andes for their stimulating effects [c17 from Spanish, from Quechuan *kúka*]

Coca-Cola (ˌkəʊkəˈkəʊlə) *n* **1** *trademark* a carbonated soft drink flavoured with coca leaves, cola nuts, caramel, etc **2** (*modifier*) denoting the spread of American culture and values to other parts of the world: *Coca-Cola generation*

cocaine *or* **cocain** (kəˈkeɪn) *n* an addictive narcotic drug derived from coca leaves or synthesized, used medicinally as a topical anaesthetic. Formula: $C_{17}H_{21}NO_4$ [c19 from COCA + -INE¹]

cocainize *or* **cocainise** (kəˈkeɪˌnaɪz, ˈkəʊkəˌnaɪz) *vb* (*tr*) to anaesthetize with cocaine ▷ **ˌcocaiˈnization** *or* **coˌcainiˈsation** *n*

cocci (ˈkɒksaɪ) *n* the plural of **coccus**

coccid (ˈkɒksɪd) *n* any homopterous insect of the superfamily *Coccoidea,* esp any of the family *Coccidae,* which includes the scale insects [c19 from New Latin *Coccidae;* see COCCUS]

coccidioidomycosis (kɒkˌsɪdɪˌɔɪdəʊmaɪˈkəʊsɪs) *n* a disease of the skin or viscera, esp the lungs, caused by infection with the fungus *Coccidioides immitis* [c20 from New Latin *Coccidioides* + -o- + MYCOSIS]

coccidiosis (kɒkˌsɪdɪˈəʊsɪs) *n* any disease of domestic and other animals caused by introcellular parasitic protozoa of the order *Coccidia.* One species, *Isospora hominis,* can infect humans [c19 from New Latin; see COCCUS, -OSIS]

cocciferous (kɒkˈsɪfərəs) *adj* (of plants) *obsolete* (of plants) bearing berries

coccolith (ˈkɒkəlɪθ) *n* any of the round calcareous plates in chalk formations: formed the outer layer of unicellular plankton [c19 New Latin, from Greek *kokkos* berry + *lithos* stone]

coccus (ˈkɒkəs) *n, pl* **-ci** (-saɪ) **1** any spherical or nearly spherical bacterium, such as a staphylococcus. Compare **bacillus** (sense 1),

spirillum (sense 1) **2** the part of a fruit that contains one seed and separates from the whole fruit at maturity **3** any of the scale insects of the genus *Coccus* [C18 from New Latin, from Greek *kokkos* berry, grain] > **coccoid**, **'coccal** or **coccic** ('kɒksɪk) *adj* > **'coccous** *adj*

coccyx ('kɒksɪks) *n, pl* **coccyges** (kɒk'saɪdʒiːz) a small triangular bone at the end of the spinal column in man and some apes, representing a vestigial tail [C17 from New Latin, from Greek *kokkux* cuckoo, of imitative origin; from the likeness of the bone to a cuckoo's beak] > **coccygeal** (kɒk'sɪdʒɪəl) *adj*

Cochabamba (*Spanish* kotʃa'βamba) *n* a city in central Bolivia. Pop: 561 000 (2005 est)

co-channel ('kəʊˌtʃænəl) *adj* denoting or relating to a radio transmission that is on the same frequency channel as another: *co-channel interference*

Cochin ('kəʊtʃɪn, 'kɒtʃ-) *n* **1** a region and former state of SW India: part of Kerala state since 1956 **2** a port in SW India, on the Malabar Coast: the first European settlement in India, founded by Vasco da Gama in 1502: shipbuilding, engineering. Pop: 596 473 (2001). Also called: **Kochi 3** a large breed of domestic fowl, with dense plumage and feathered legs, that originated in Cochin China

Cochin China *n* a former French colony of Indochina (1862–1948): now the part of Vietnam that lies south of Phan Thiet

cochineal (ˌkɒtʃɪ'niːl, 'kɒtʃɪˌniːl) *n* **1** Also called: **cochineal insect** a Mexican homopterous insect, *Dactylopius coccus,* that feeds on cacti **2** a crimson substance obtained from the crushed bodies of these insects, used for colouring food and for dyeing **3 a** the colour of this dye **b** (*as adjective*): *cochineal shoes* [C16 from Old Spanish *cochinilla,* from Latin *coccineus* scarlet-coloured, from *coccum* cochineal kermes, from Greek *kokkos* kermes berry]

cochlea ('kɒklɪə) *n, pl* **-leae** (-lɪˌiː) the spiral tube, shaped like a snail's shell, that forms part of the internal ear, converting sound vibrations into nerve impulses [C16 from Latin: snail, spiral, from Greek *kokhlias;* probably related to Greek *konkhē* CONCH] > **'cochlear** *adj*

cochlear implant ('kɒklɪə) *n* a device that stimulates the acoustic nerve in the inner ear in order to produce some form of hearing in people who are deaf from inner ear disease

cochleate ('kɒklɪˌeɪt, -lɪɪt) or **cochleated** *adj biology* shaped like a snail's shell; spirally twisted

cock¹ (kɒk) *n* **1** the male of the domestic fowl **2 a** any other male bird **b** the male of certain other animals, such as the lobster **c** (*as modifier*): *a cock sparrow* **3** short for **stopcock** or **weathercock 4** a taboo slang word for **penis 5 a** the hammer of a firearm **b** its position when the firearm is ready to be discharged **6** *Brit informal* a friend, mate, or fellow **7** a jaunty or significant tilting or turning upwards: *a cock of the head* **8** *Brit informal* nonsense ▷ *vb* **9** (*tr*) to set the firing pin, hammer, or breech block of (a firearm) so that a pull on the trigger will release it and thus fire the weapon **10** (*tr*) to set the shutter mechanism of (a camera) so that the shutter can be tripped by pressing the shutter-release button **11** (*tr*; sometimes foll by *up*) to raise in an alert or jaunty manner **12** (*intr*) to stick or stand up conspicuously ▷ See also **cockup** [Old English *cocc* (referring to the male fowl; the development of C15 sense spout, tap, and other transferred senses is not clear), ultimately of imitative origin; related to Old Norse *kokkr,* French *coq,* Late Latin *coccus*]

cock² (kɒk) *n* **1** a small, cone-shaped heap of hay, straw, etc ▷ *vb* **2** (*tr*) to stack (hay, straw, etc) in such heaps [C14 (in Old English, *cocc* is attested in place names). perhaps of Scandinavian origin, compare Norwegian *kok,* Danish dialect *kok*]

cockabully (ˌkɒkə'bʊlɪ) *n, pl* **-lies** any of several small freshwater fish of New Zealand [from Māori *kokopu*]

cockade (kɒ'keɪd) *n* a feather or ribbon worn on military headwear [C18 changed from earlier

cockard, from French *cocarde,* feminine of *cocard* arrogant, strutting, from *coq* COCK¹] > **cock'aded** *adj*

cock-a-doodle-doo (ˌkɒkəˌduːdᵊl'duː) *interj* an imitation or representation of a cock crowing

cock-a-hoop *adj* (*usually postpositive*) **1** in very high spirits **2** boastful **3** askew; confused [C16 perhaps from the phrase *to set the cock a hoop* to live prodigally, literally: to put a cock on a *hoop,* a full measure of grain]

Cockaigne or **Cockayne** (kɒ'keɪn) *n medieval legend* an imaginary land of luxury and idleness [C14 from Old French *cocaigne,* from Middle Low German *kōkenje* small CAKE (of which the houses in the imaginary land are built); related to Spanish *cucaña,* Italian *cuccagna*]

cock-a-leekie (ˌkɒkə'liːkɪ) *n* a variant of **cockieleekie**

cockalorum (ˌkɒkə'lɔːrəm) *n* **1** a self-important little man **2** bragging talk; crowing [C16 from COCK¹ + *-alorum,* a variant of Latin genitive plural ending *-orum;* perhaps intended to suggest: the cock of all cocks]

cockamamie (ˌkɒkə'meɪmɪ) *adj slang, chiefly US* ridiculous or nonsensical: *a cockamamie story* [C20 in an earlier sense: a paper transfer, prob. a variant of DECALCOMANIA]

cock-and-bull story *n informal* an obviously improbable story, esp a boastful one or one used as an excuse

cockatiel or **cockateel** (ˌkɒkə'tiːl) *n* a crested Australian parrot, *Leptolophus hollandicus,* having a greyish-brown and yellow plumage [C19 from Dutch *kaketielje,* from Portuguese *cacatilha* a little cockatoo, from *cacatua* COCKATOO]

cockatoo (ˌkɒkə'tuː, 'kɒkəˌtuː) *n, pl* **-toos 1** any of various parrots of the genus *Kakatoe* and related genera, such as *K. galerita* (**sulphur-crested cockatoo**), of Australia and New Guinea. They have an erectile crest and most of them are light-coloured **2** *Austral and NZ* a small farmer or settler **3** *Austral informal* a lookout during some illegal activity [C17 from Dutch *kaketoe,* from Malay *kakatua*]

cockatrice ('kɒkətrɪs, -ˌtraɪs) *n* **1** a legendary monster, part snake and part cock, that could kill with a glance **2** another name for **basilisk** (sense 1) [C14 from Old French *cocatris,* from Medieval Latin *cocatrix,* from Late Latin *calcātrix* trampler, tracker (translating Greek *ikhneumon* ICHNEUMON), from Latin *calcāre* to tread, from *calx* heel]

Cockayne (kɒ'keɪn) *n* a variant spelling of **Cockaigne**

cockboat ('kɒkˌbəʊt) or **cockleboat** *n* any small boat [C15 *cokbote,* perhaps ultimately from Late Latin *caudica* dug-out canoe, from Latin *caudex* tree trunk]

cockchafer ('kɒkˌtʃeɪfə) *n* any of various Old World scarabaeid beetles, esp *Melolontha melolontha* of Europe, whose larvae feed on crops and grasses. Also called: **May beetle, May bug** [C18 from COCK¹ + CHAFER]

cockcrow ('kɒkˌkrəʊ) or **cockcrowing** *n* daybreak

cocked hat *n* **1** a hat with opposing brims turned up and caught together in order to give two points (bicorn) or three points (tricorn) **2** knock into a cocked hat *slang* to outdo or defeat

cocker¹ ('kɒkə) *n* **1** a devotee of cockfighting **2** short for **cocker spaniel**

cocker² ('kɒkə) *vb* **1** (*tr*) *rare* to pamper or spoil by indulgence ▷ *n* **2** *Brit informal* a mate (esp in the phrase *old cocker*) [C15 perhaps from COCK¹ with the sense: to make a cock (i.e. pet) of]

Cocker ('kɒkə) *n* **according to Cocker** reliable or reliably; correct or correctly [from Edward Cocker (1631–75), English arithmetician]

cockerel ('kɒkərəl, 'kɒkrəl) *n* a young domestic cock, usually less than a year old [C15 diminutive of COCK¹]

cocker spaniel *n* a small compact breed of spaniel having sleek silky fur, a domed head, and long fringed ears [C19 *cocker,* from *cocking* hunting woodcocks]

cockeye ('kɒkˌaɪ) *n informal* an eye affected with strabismus or one that squints

cockeye bob or **cockeyed bob** *n Austral slang* a sudden storm or cyclone

cockeyed ('kɒkˌaɪd) *adj informal* **1** afflicted with cross-eye, squint, or any other visible abnormality of the eyes **2** appearing to be physically or logically abnormal, absurd, etc; crooked; askew; *cockeyed ideas* **3** drunk

cock feather *n archery* the odd-coloured feather set on the shaft of an arrow at right angles to the nock. Compare **shaft feather**

cockfight ('kɒkˌfaɪt) *n* a fight between two gamecocks fitted with sharp metal spurs > **'cockˌfighting** *n*

cockhorse ('kɒk'hɔːs) *n* another name for **rocking horse** or **hobbyhorse**

cockieleekie, cockyleeky or **cock-a-leekie** ('kɒkə'liːkɪ) *n Scot* a soup made from a fowl boiled with leeks

cockiness ('kɒkɪnɪs) *n* conceited self-assurance

cockle¹ ('kɒkᵊl) *n* **1** any sand-burrowing bivalve mollusc of the family *Cardiidae,* esp *Cardium edule* (**edible cockle**) of Europe, typically having a rounded shell with radiating ribs **2** any of certain similar or related molluscs **3** short for **cockleshell** (sense 1) **4** a wrinkle or puckering, as in cloth or paper **5** a small furnace or stove **6** cockles of one's heart one's deepest feelings (esp in the phrase **warm the cockles of one's heart**) ▷ *vb* **7** to contract or cause to contract into wrinkles [C14 from Old French *coquille* shell, from Latin *conchȳlium* shellfish, from Greek *konkhulion,* diminutive of *konkhule* mussel; see CONCH]

cockle² ('kɒkᵊl) *n* any of several plants, esp the corn cockle, that grow as weeds in cornfields

cockleboat ('kɒkᵊlˌbəʊt) *n* another word for **cockboat**

cocklebur ('kɒkᵊlˌbɜː) *n* **1** any coarse weed of the genus *Xanthium,* having spiny burs: family *Asteraceae* (composites) **2** the bur of any of these plants

cockleert ('kɒklɪərt) *n* a Southwest English dialect variant of **cockcrow**

cockler ('kɒklə) *n* a person employed to gather cockles from the seashore

cockleshell ('kɒkᵊlˌʃel) *n* **1** the shell of the cockle **2** any of the valves of the shells of certain other bivalve molluscs, such as the scallop **3** any small light boat **4** a badge worn by pilgrims

cockloft ('kɒkˌlɒft) *n* a small loft, garret, or attic

cockney ('kɒknɪ) *n* **1** (*often capital*) a native of London, esp of the working class born in the East End, speaking a characteristic dialect of English. Traditionally defined as someone born within the sound of the bells of St Mary-le-Bow church **2** the urban dialect of London or its East End **3** *Austral* a young snapper fish ▷ *adj* **4** characteristic of cockneys or their dialect of English [C14 from *cokeney,* literally: cock's egg, later applied contemptuously to townsmen, from *cokene,* genitive plural of *cok* COCK¹ + *ey* EGG¹] > **'cockneyish** *adj*

cockney bream *n Austral* a young snapper fish

cockneyfy or **cocknify** ('kɒknɪˌfaɪ) *vb* **-fies, -fying, -fied** (*tr*) to cause (one's speech, manners, etc) to fit the stereotyped idea of a cockney > ˌcockneyfi'cation or ˌcockni'fication *n*

cockneyism ('kɒknɪˌɪzəm) *n* a characteristic of speech or custom peculiar to cockneys

cock-of-the-rock *n* either of two tropical South American birds, *Rupicola rupicola* or *R. peruviana,* having an erectile crest and (in the male) a brilliant red or orange plumage: family *Cotingidae* (cotingas)

cock of the walk *n informal* a person who asserts himself in a strutting pompous way

cockpit ('kɒkˌpɪt) *n* **1** the compartment in a small aircraft in which the pilot, crew, and sometimes the passengers sit. Compare **flight deck** (sense 1) **2** the driver's compartment in a racing car **3** *nautical* **a** an enclosed or recessed area towards the stern of a small vessel from which it is steered **b** (formerly) an apartment in a warship used as quarters for junior officers and as a first-aid station during combat **4** the site of numerous battles or campaigns **5** an enclosure used for cockfights

cockroach ('kɒk,rəʊtʃ) *n* any insect of the suborder *Blattodea* (or *Blattaria*), such as *Blatta orientalis* (**oriental cockroach** or **black beetle**): order *Dictyoptera* They have an oval flattened body with long antennae and biting mouthparts and are common household pests. See also **German cockroach, mantis** [C17 from Spanish *cucaracha*, of obscure origin]

cock rock *n* an aggressive style of rock music performed by male bands

cockscomb or **coxcomb** ('kɒks,kəʊm) *n* **1** the comb of a domestic cock **2** an amaranthaceous garden or pot plant, *Celosia cristata*, with yellow, crimson, or purple feathery plumelike flowers in a broad spike resembling the comb of a cock **3** any similar species of *Celosia* **4** *informal* a conceited dandy

cocksfoot ('kɒks,fʊt) *n*, *pl* -foots a perennial Eurasian grass, *Dactylis glomerata*, cultivated as a pasture grass in North America and South Africa

cockshot ('kɒk,ʃɒt) *n* another name for **cockshy**

cockshy ('kɒk,ʃaɪ) *n*, *pl* -shies *Brit* **1** a target aimed at in throwing games **2** the throw itself ▷ Often shortened to: **shy** [C18 from shying (throwing objects at) a cock, which was given as a prize to the person who hit it]

cockspur ('kɒk,spɜː) *n* **1** a spur on the leg of a cock **2** an annual grass, *Echinochloa crus-galli*, widely distributed in tropical and warm temperate regions **3** a small thorny North American hawthorn tree, *Crataegus crus-galli*

cocksure (,kɒk'ʃʊə, -'ʃɔː) *adj* overconfident; arrogant [C16 of uncertain origin] > ,cock'surely *adv* > ,cock'sureness *n*

cockswain ('kɒksən, -,sweɪn) *n* a variant spelling of **coxswain**

cocktail¹ ('kɒk,teɪl) *n* **1 a** any mixed drink with a spirit base, usually drunk before meals **b** (*as modifier*): *the cocktail hour* **2** an appetizer of seafood, mixed fruits, etc **3** any combination of diverse elements, esp one considered potent **4** (*modifier*) appropriate for formal occasions: *a cocktail dress* [C19 of unknown origin]

cocktail² ('kɒk,teɪl) *n* **1** a horse with a docked tail **2** an animal of unknown or mixed breeding **3** *archaic* a person of little breeding pretending to be a gentleman [C19 originally *cocktailed* (adj) having a tail like a cock's]

cocktail lounge *n* a room in a hotel, restaurant, etc, where cocktails or other alcoholic drinks are served

cocktail stick *n* a small pointed stick used for holding cherries, olives, etc, in cocktails, and for serving snacks, such as small sausages

cockup ('kɒk,ʌp) *n* **1** *Brit slang* something done badly ▷ *vb* **cock up** (*tr, adverb*) **2** (of an animal) to raise (its ears), esp in an alert manner **3** *Brit slang* to botch

cocky¹ ('kɒkɪ) *adj* cockier, cockiest excessively proud of oneself > 'cockily *adv*

cocky² ('kɒkɪ) *n*, *pl* cockies *Austral informal* **1** short for **cockatoo** (sense 2) **2** a farmer whose farm is regarded as small or of little account

cockyleeky ('kɒkə'liːkɪ) *n* a variant spelling of **cockieleekie**

cocky's joy *n* *Austral slang* golden syrup

coco ('kəʊkəʊ) *n*, *pl* -cos short for **coconut** or **coconut palm** [C16 from Portuguese *coco* grimace; from the likeness of the three holes of the nut to a face]

cocoa ('kəʊkəʊ) or **cacao** *n* **1** a powder made from cocoa beans after they have been roasted, ground, and freed from most of their fatty oil **2** a hot or cold drink made from cocoa and milk or water **3 a** a light to moderate brown colour **b** (*as adjective*): *cocoa paint* [C18 altered from CACAO]

cocoa bean *n* the seed of the cacao

cocoa butter *n* a yellowish-white waxy solid that is obtained from cocoa beans and used for confectionery, soap, etc

coco de mer (də 'mɛə) *n* **1** a palm tree, *Lodoicea maldivica*, of the Seychelles, producing a large fruit containing a two-lobed edible nut **2** the nut of this palm ▷ Also called: **double coconut** [French: coconut of the sea]

coconut or **cocoanut** ('kəʊkə,nʌt) *n* **1** the fruit of the coconut palm, consisting of a thick fibrous oval husk inside which is a thin hard shell enclosing edible white meat. The hollow centre is filled with a milky fluid (**coconut milk**) **2 a** the meat of the coconut, often shredded and used in cakes, curries, etc **b** (*as modifier*): *coconut cake* **3** *slang derogatory* a black or Asian person who conforms to white culture at the expense of his or her ancestral culture, the idea being that, like a coconut, he or she is dark on the outside and white on the inside [C18 see COCO]

coconut butter *n* a solid form of coconut oil

coconut ice *n* a sweetmeat made from desiccated coconut and sugar

coconut matting *n* a form of coarse matting made from the fibrous husk of the coconut

coconut oil *n* the fatty oil obtained from the meat of the coconut and used for making soap, cosmetics, etc

coconut palm *n* a tall palm tree, *Cocos nucifera*, widely planted throughout the tropics, having coconuts as fruits. Also called: **coco palm, coconut tree**

coconut shy *n* a fairground stall in which balls are thrown to knock coconuts off stands

cocoon (kə'kuːn) *n* **1 a** a silky protective envelope secreted by silkworms and certain other insect larvae, in which the pupae develop **b** a similar covering for the eggs of the spider, earthworm, etc **2** a protective spray covering used as a seal on machinery **3** a cosy warm covering ▷ *vb* **4** (*tr*) to wrap in a cocoon [C17 from French *cocon*, from Provençal *coucoun* eggshell, from *coco* shell, from Latin *coccum* kermes berry, from Greek *kokkos* grain, seed, berry; compare COCCUS]

cocopan ('kəʊkəʊ,pæn) *n* (in South Africa) a small wagon running on narrow-gauge railway lines used in mines. Also called: **hopper** [C20 from Zulu *'ngkumbana* short truck]

Cocos Islands ('kəʊkɒs, 'kəʊkəs) *pl n* a group of 27 coral islands in the Indian Ocean, southwest of Java: a Territory of Australia since 1955. Pop: 621 (2001). Area: 13 sq km (5 sq miles). Also called: **Keeling Islands**

cocotte (kəʊ'kɒt, kə-; *French* kɔkɔt) *n* **1** a small fireproof dish in which individual portions of food are cooked and served **2** a prostitute or promiscuous woman [C19 from French, from nursery word for a hen, feminine of *coq* COCK¹]

cocoyam ('kəʊkəʊ,jæm) *n* **1** either of two food plants of West Africa, the taro or the yantia, both of which have edible underground stems **2** the underground stem of either of these plants [C20 from COCOA + YAM]

cocuswood ('kəʊkəs,wʊd) *n* **1** wood from the tropical American leguminous tree *Brya ebenus*, used for inlaying, turnery, musical instruments, etc **2** the source of this wood, an important timber tree in parts of the Caribbean ▷ Also called: **Jamaican ebony, West Indian ebony**

cod¹ (kɒd) *n*, *pl* cod or cods **1** any of the gadoid food fishes of the genus *Gadus*, esp *G. morhua* (or *G. callarias*), which occurs in the North Atlantic and has a long body with three rounded dorsal fins: family *Gadidae* They are also a source of cod-liver oil **2** any other fish of the family *Gadidae* (see **gadid**) **3** *Austral* any of various unrelated Australian fish, such as the Murray cod [C13 probably of Germanic origin; compare Old High German *cutte*]

cod² (kɒd) *n* **1** *Brit and US dialect* a pod or husk **2** an obsolete word for **scrotum** **3** *obsolete* a bag or

envelope [Old English *codd* husk, bag; related to Old Norse *koddi*, Danish *kodde*]

cod³ (kɒd) *vb* cods, codding, codded (*tr*) **1** *Brit and Irish slang* to make fun of; tease **2** *Brit and Irish slang* to play a trick on; fool ▷ *n* **3** *Brit and Irish slang* a hoax or trick **4** *Irish slang* a fraud; hoaxer: *he's an old cod* ▷ *adj* (*prenominal*) **5** *Brit slang* mock; sham: *cod Latin* [C19 perhaps from earlier *cod* a fool, perhaps shortened from CODGER]

cod⁴ (kɒd) *n* *Northern English* dialect a fellow; chap: *he's a nice old cod* [of unknown origin]

Cod *n* Cape See **Cape Cod**

COD abbreviation for **1** cash on delivery **2** (in the US) collect on delivery

coda ('kəʊdə) *n* **1** *music* the final, sometimes inessential, part of a musical structure **2** a concluding part of a literary work, esp a summary at the end of a novel of further developments in the lives of the characters [C18 from Italian: tail, from Latin *cauda*]

cod-act *vb* (*intr*) *Irish informal* to play tricks; fool [from COD³ + ACT]

codder¹ ('kɒdə) *n* a cod fisherman or his boat

codder² ('kɒdə) *n* *Yorkshire dialect* the leader of a team of workers on a press at a steelworks [perhaps from COD⁴]

coddle ('kɒdəl) *vb* (*tr*) **1** to treat with indulgence **2** to cook (something, esp eggs) in water just below the boiling point ▷ *n* **3** *Irish dialect* stew made from ham and bacon scraps [C16 of obscure origin; perhaps related to CAUDLE] > 'coddler *n*

code (kəʊd) *n* **1** a system of letters or symbols, and rules for their association by means of which information can be represented or communicated for reasons of secrecy, brevity, etc: *binary code; Morse code*. See also **genetic code** **2** a message in code **3** a symbol used in a code **4** a conventionalized set of principles, rules, or expectations: *a code of behaviour* **5** a system of letters or digits used for identification or selection purposes ▷ *vb* (*tr*) **6** to translate, transmit, or arrange into a code [C14 from French, from Latin *cōdex* book, CODEX]

codec ('kəʊ,dɛk) *n* *electronics* a set of equipment that encodes an analogue speech or video signal into digital form for transmission purposes and at the receiving end decodes the digital signal into a form close to its original [C20 from CO(DE) + DEC(ODE)]

codeclination (,kəʊdɛklɪ'neɪʃən) *n* another name for **polar distance**

codeine ('kəʊdiːn) *n* a white crystalline alkaloid prepared mainly from morphine and having a similar but milder action. It is used as an analgesic, an antidiarrhoeal, and to relieve coughing. Formula: $C_{18}H_{21}NO_3$ [C19 from Greek *kōdeia* head of a poppy, from *kōos* hollow place + -INE²]

Code Napoléon *French* (kɔd napɔleɔ̃) *n* the civil code of France, promulgated between 1804 and 1810, comprising the main body of French civil law. English name: **Napoleonic Code**

cod end *n* *sea fishing* the narrow end of a tapered trawl net [from COD²]

co-dependency (,kəʊdɪ'pɛndənsɪ) *n* *psychol* a state of mutual dependence between two people, esp when one partner relies emotionally on supporting and caring for the other partner > ,co-de'pendent *adj*, *n*

coder ('kəʊdə) *n* **1** a person or thing that codes **2** *electronics* a device for transforming normal signals into a coded form

Co Derry *abbreviation for* County Londonderry

code-sharing *n* a commercial agreement between two airlines that allows passengers to use a ticket from one airline to travel on another

codetermination (,kəʊdɪtɜːmɪ'neɪʃən) *n* joint participation of management and employees or employees' trade union representatives in some decisions

codeword ('kəʊd,wɜːd) *n* (esp in military use) a word used to identify a classified plan, operation, etc. Also: **codename**

codex ('kəʊdɛks) *n, pl* codices ('kəʊdɪˌsiːz, 'kɒdɪ-) **1** a volume, in book form, of manuscripts of an ancient text **2** *obsolete* a legal code [c16 from Latin: tree trunk, wooden block, book]

Codex Juris Canonici ('kəʊdɛks 'dʒʊərɪs kəˈnɒnɪˌsaɪ) the official code of canon law in force in the Roman Catholic Church; introduced in 1918 and revised in 1983. See also **Corpus Juris Canonici** [Latin: book of canon law]

codfish ('kɒdˌfɪʃ) *n, pl* -fish or -fishes a cod, esp *Gadus morhua*

codger ('kɒdʒə) *n informal* a man, esp an old or eccentric one: a term of affection or mild derision (often in the phrase **old codger**) [c18 probably variant of CADGER]

codices ('kəʊdɪˌsiːz, 'kɒdɪ-) *n* the plural of **codex**

codicil ('kɒdɪsɪl) *n* **1** *law* a supplement modifying a will or revoking some provision of it **2** an additional provision; appendix [c15 from Late Latin *cōdicillus*, literally: a little book, diminutive of CODEX] > codicillary (ˌkɒdɪ'sɪlərɪ) *adj*

codicology (ˌkəʊdɪ'kɒlədʒɪ) *n* the study of manuscripts [c20 via French from Latin *codic-*, CODEX + -LOGY] > codicological (ˌkəʊdɪkə'lɒdʒɪkᵊl) *adj*

codification (ˌkəʊdɪfɪ'keɪʃən, ˌkɒ-) *n* **1** systematic organization of methods, rules, etc **2** *law* the collection into one body of the principles of a system of law

codify ('kəʊdɪˌfaɪ, 'kɒ-) *vb* -fies, -fying, -fied (*tr*) to organize or collect together (laws, rules, procedures, etc) into a system or code > 'codiˌfier *n*

codling[1] ('kɒdlɪŋ), **codlin** ('kɒdlɪn) *n* **1** any of several varieties of long tapering apples used for cooking **2** any unripe apple [c15 *querdlyng*, of uncertain origin]

codling[2] ('kɒdlɪŋ) *n* a codfish, esp a young one

codling moth or **codlin moth** *n* a tortricid moth, *Carpocapsa pomonella*, the larvae of which are a pest of apples

codlins-and-cream *n* an onagraceous plant, *Epilobium hirsutum*, native to Europe and Asia and introduced into North America, having purplish-red flowers and hairy stems and leaves. Also called: **hairy willowherb**

cod-liver oil *n* an oil extracted from the livers of cod and related fish, rich in vitamins A and D and used to treat deficiency of these vitamins

codology (kɒd'ɒlədʒɪ) *n Irish informal* the art or practice of bluffing or deception

codomain (ˌkəʊdəʊ'meɪn) *n maths* the set of values that a function is allowed to take

codominant (kəʊ'dɒmɪnənt) *adj genetics* (of genes) having both alleles expressed equally in the phenotype of the organism > co'dominance *n*

codon ('kəʊdɒn) *n genetics, biochem* a unit that consists of three adjacent bases on a DNA molecule and that determines the position of a specific amino acid in a protein molecule during protein synthesis [c20 from CODE + -ON]

codpiece ('kɒdˌpiːs) *n* a bag covering the male genitals, attached to hose or breeches by laces, etc, worn in the 15th and 16th centuries [c15 from COD[2] + PIECE]

co-driver *n* one of two drivers who take turns to drive a car, esp in a rally

codswallop ('kɒdzˌwɒləp) *n Brit slang* nonsense [c20 of unknown origin]

Co Durham *abbreviation for* County Durham

cod war *n* any of three disputes that occurred in 1958, 1972–73, and 1975–76 between Britain and Iceland, concerning Iceland's unilateral extension of her fishing limits

co-ed (ˌkəʊ'ɛd) *adj* **1** coeducational ▷ *n* **2** *US* a female student in a coeducational college or university **3** *Brit* a school or college providing coeducation

coedit (kəʊ'ɛdɪt) *vb* (*tr*) to edit (a book, newspaper, etc) jointly > co'editor *n*

coeducation (ˌkəʊɛdjʊ'keɪʃən) *n* instruction in schools, colleges, etc, attended by both sexes > ˌcoeduˈcational *adj* > ˌcoeduˈcationally *adv*

coefficient (ˌkəʊɪ'fɪʃənt) *n* **1** *maths* **a** a numerical or constant factor in an algebraic term: *the coefficient of the term 3xyz is 3* **b** the product of all the factors of a term excluding one or more specified variables: *the coefficient of x in 3xyz is 3ayz* **2** *physics* a value that relates one physical quantity to another [c17 from New Latin *coefficiēns*, from Latin *co-* together + *efficere* to EFFECT]

coefficient of expansion *n* the amount of expansion (or contraction) per unit length of a material resulting from one degree change in temperature. Also called: **expansivity**

coefficient of friction *n mechanical engineering* the force required to move two sliding surfaces over each other, divided by the force holding them together. It is reduced once the motion has started

coefficient of variation *n statistics* a measure of the relative variation of distribution independent of the units of measurement; the standard deviation divided by the mean, sometimes expressed as a percentage

coel- *prefix* indicating a cavity within a body or a hollow organ or part: *coelacanth; coelenterate; coelenteron* [New Latin, from Greek *koilos* hollow]

coelacanth ('siːləˌkænθ) *n* a primitive marine bony fish of the genus *Latimeria* (subclass *Crossopterygii*), having fleshy limblike pectoral fins and occurring off the coast of E Africa: thought to be extinct until a living specimen was discovered in 1938 [c19 from New Latin *coelacanthus*, literally: hollow spine, from COEL- + Greek *akanthos* spine]

coelenterate (sɪ'lɛntəˌreɪt, -rɪt) *n* **1** any invertebrate of the phylum *Cnidaria* (formerly *Coelenterata*), having a saclike body with a single opening (mouth), which occurs in polyp and medusa forms. Coelenterates include the hydra, jellyfishes, sea anemones, and corals ▷ *adj* **2** (loosely) any invertebrate of the phyla *Cnidaria* or *Ctenophora* **3** of or relating to coelenterates [c19 from New Latin *Coelenterata*, hollow-intestined (creatures); see COEL-, ENTERON] > coelenteric (ˌsiːlɛn'tɛrɪk) *adj*

coelenteron (sɪ'lɛntəˌrɒn) *n, pl* -tera (-tərə) the simple saclike body cavity of a coelenterate

coeliac or *US* **celiac** ('siːlɪˌæk) *adj* of or relating to the abdomen [c17 from Latin *coeliacus*, from Greek *koiliakos*, from *koilia* belly]

coeliac disease *n* a chronic intestinal disorder of young children caused by sensitivity to the protein gliadin contained in the gluten of cereals, characterized by distention of the abdomen and frothy and pale foul-smelling stools

coelom or *esp US* **celom** ('siːləʊm, -ləm) *n* the body cavity of many multicellular animals, situated in the mesoderm and containing the digestive tract and other visceral organs [c19 from Greek *koilōma* cavity, from *koilos* hollow; see COEL-] > coelomic or *esp US* celomic (sɪ'lɒmɪk) *adj*

coelostat ('siːləˌstæt) *n* an astronomical instrument consisting of a plane mirror mounted parallel to the earth's axis and rotated about this axis once every two days so that light from a celestial body, esp the sun, is reflected onto a second mirror, which reflects the beam into a telescope. Compare **siderostat** [c19 *coelo-*, from Latin *caelum* heaven, sky + -STAT]

coelurosaur (sɪ'ljʊərəˌsɔː) *n* any of various small to very large bipedal carnivorous saurischian dinosaurs belonging to the suborder *Theropoda*, active in the Triassic and Cretaceous periods; Tyrannosaurus was a coelurosaur, and birds are thought to have evolved from small coelurosaurs [c20 from New Latin, from Greek *koilos* hollow + *ouros* tail + -SAUR]

coemption (kəʊ'ɛmpʃən) *n* the buying up of the complete supply of a commodity [c14 from Latin *coemptiōnem* a buying together]

coenacle ('sɛnəkᵊl) *n* a variant spelling of **cenacle**

Coenesque (ˌkæfkə'ɛsk) *adj* reminiscent of the work US film-makers of Joel and Ethan Coen (born 1954 and 1957 respectively), featuring bizarre

and involved plots, use of irony and black humour, and allusions to film classics

coenesthesia, cenesthesia (ˌsiːnɪs'θiːzɪə) or **coenesthesis, cenesthesis** (ˌsiːnɪs'θiːsɪs) *n psychol* general awareness of one's own body > coenesthetic or cenesthetic (ˌsiːnɪs'θɛtɪk) *adj*

coeno- or before a vowel **coen-** *combining form* common: *coenocyte* [New Latin, from Greek *koinos* common]

coenobite or **cenobite** ('siːnəʊˌbaɪt) *n* a member of a religious order following a communal rule of life. Compare **eremite** [c17 from Old French or ecclesiastical Latin, from Greek *koinobion* convent, from *koinos* common + *bios* life] > coenobitic (ˌsiːnəʊ'bɪtɪk), ˌcoeno'bitical, ˌceno'bitic or ˌceno'bitical *adj*

coenocyte ('siːnəʊˌsaɪt) *n botany* a mass of protoplasm containing many nuclei and enclosed by a cell wall: occurs in many fungi and some algae > coenocytic (ˌsiːnə'sɪtɪk) *adj*

coenosarc ('siːnəʊˌsɑːk) *n* a system of protoplasmic branches connecting the polyps of colonial organisms such as corals [c19 from COENO- + Greek *sarx* flesh]

coenosteum (sɪ'nɒstɪəm) *n zoology* the calcareous skeleton of a hydrocoral or a coral colony

coenurus (siː'njʊərəs) *n, pl* -ri (-raɪ) an encysted larval form of the tapeworm *Multiceps*, containing many encapsulated heads. In sheep it can cause the gid, and when eaten by dogs it develops into several adult forms [c19 from New Latin, from COENO- + Greek *oura* tail, literally: common tail, referring to the single body with its many heads]

coenzyme (kəʊ'ɛnzaɪm) *n biochem* a nonprotein organic molecule that forms a complex with certain enzymes and is essential for their activity. See also **apoenzyme**

coenzyme A *n* a constituent of biological cells that functions as the agent of acylation in metabolic reactions. Abbreviation: CoA

coenzyme Q *n* a quinone derivative, present in biological cells, that functions as an electron carrier in the electron transport chain. Also called: **ubiquinone**

coequal (kəʊ'iːkwəl) *adj* **1** of the same size, rank, etc ▷ *n* **2** a person or thing equal with another > coequality (ˌkəʊɪ'kwɒlɪtɪ) or co'equalness *n* > co'equally *adv*

coerce (kəʊ'ɜːs) *vb* (*tr*) to compel or restrain by force or authority without regard to individual wishes or desires [c17 from Latin *coercēre* to confine, restrain, from *co-* together + *arcēre* to enclose] > co'ercer *n* > co'ercible *adj*

coercimeter (ˌkəʊə'sɪmɪtə) *n* an instrument used for measurement of coercive force

coercion (kəʊ'ɜːʃən) *n* **1** the act or power of coercing **2** government by force > co'ercionist *n* > coercive (kəʊ'ɜːsɪv) *adj* > co'ercively *adv* > co'erciveness *n*

coercive force *n* a measure of the magnetization of a ferromagnetic material as expressed by the external magnetic field strength necessary to demagnetize it. Measured in amperes per metre. Compare **coercivity**

coercivity (ˌkəʊɜː'sɪvɪtɪ) *n* the magnetic-field strength necessary to demagnetize a ferromagnetic material that is magnetized to saturation. It is measured in amperes per metre. Compare **coercive force**

coessential (ˌkəʊɪ'sɛnʃəl) *adj Christianity* being one in essence or nature: a term applied to the three persons of the Trinity > coessentiality (ˌkəʊɪˌsɛnʃɪ'ælɪtɪ) or ˌcoes'sentialness *n* > ˌcoes'sentially *adv*

coetaneous (ˌkəʊɪ'teɪnɪəs) *adj rare* of the same age or period [c17 from Latin *coetāneus*, from *co-* same + *aetās* age] > ˌcoe'taneously *adv* > ˌcoe'taneousness *n*

coeternal (ˌkəʊɪ'tɜːnᵊl) *adj* existing together eternally > ˌcoe'ternally *adv*

coeternity (ˌkəʊɪ'tɜːnɪtɪ) *n* existence for, from, or in eternity with another being

C

coeval (kəʊˈiːvəl) *adj* **1** of or belonging to the same age or generation ▷ *n* **2** a contemporary [c17 from Late Latin *coaevus* from Latin *co-* + *aevum* age] > **coevality** (ˌkəʊɪˈvælɪtɪ) *n* > co'**evally** *adv*

coevolution (ˌkəʊˌiːvəˈluːʃən) *n* the evolution of complementary adaptations in two or more species of organisms because of a special relationship that exists between them, as in insect-pollinated plants and their insect pollinators

coexecutor (ˌkəʊɪɡˈzɛkjʊtə) *n law* a person acting jointly with another or others as executor > ˌcoex'**ecutrix** *fem n*

coexist (ˌkəʊɪɡˈzɪst) *vb* (*intr*) **1** to exist together at the same time or in the same place **2** to exist together in peace > ˌcoex'**istence** *n* > ˌcoex'**istent** *adj*

coextend (ˌkəʊɪkˈstɛnd) *vb* to extend or cause to extend equally in space or time > ˌcoex'**tension** *n*

coextensive (ˌkəʊɪkˈstɛnsɪv) *adj* of the same limits or extent > ˌcoex'**tensively** *adv*

cofactor (ˈkəʊˌfæktə) *n* **1** *maths* a number associated with an element in a square matrix, equal to the determinant of the matrix formed by removing the row and column in which the element appears from the given determinant. See **minor 2** *biochem* a nonprotein substance that forms a complex with certain enzymes and is essential for their activity. It may be a metal ion or a coenzyme

C of E *abbreviation for* Church of England

coff (kɒf) *vb* **coffs, coffing, coffed** *or* **coft** *Scot* to buy; purchase [c15 from the past participle of obsolete *copen* to buy, of Low German origin; compare German *kaufen* to buy]

coffee (ˈkɒfɪ) *n* **1 a** a drink consisting of an infusion of the roasted and ground or crushed seeds of the coffee tree **b** (*as modifier*): *coffee grounds* **2** Also called: **coffee beans** the beanlike seeds of the coffee tree, used to make this beverage **3** short for **coffee tree 4 a** a medium to dark brown colour **b** (*as adjective*): *a coffee carpet* **5** **wake up and smell the coffee** See **wake¹** (sense 7) [c16 from Italian *caffè*, from Turkish *kahve*, from Arabic *qahwah* coffee, wine]

coffee bag *n* a small bag containing ground coffee beans, infused to make coffee

coffee bar *n* a café; snack bar

coffee cup *n* a cup from which coffee may be drunk, usually smaller than a teacup

coffee house *n* a place where coffee is served, esp one that was a fashionable meeting place in 18th-century London

coffee mill *n* a machine for grinding roasted coffee beans

coffee morning *n* a social event (often held in order to raise money) at which coffee is served

coffee nut *n* **1** the fruit of the Kentucky coffee tree **2** another name for **Kentucky coffee tree**

coffeepot (ˈkɒfɪˌpɒt) *n* a pot in which coffee is brewed or served

coffee shop *n* a shop where coffee is sold or drunk

coffee table *n* **1** a low table, on which newspapers, etc, may be placed and coffee served **2** (*modifier*) implying an emphasis on appearance and style over substance: *coffee-table music*

coffee-table book *n* a book designed to be looked at rather than read

coffee tree *n* **1** any of several rubiaceous trees of the genus *Coffea*, esp *C. arabica*, the seeds of which are used in the preparation of the beverage coffee **2** short for **Kentucky coffee tree**

coffer (ˈkɒfə) *n* **1** a chest, esp for storing valuables **2** (*usually plural*) a store of money **3** Also called: caisson, lacuna an ornamental sunken panel in a ceiling, dome, etc **4** a watertight box or chamber **5 a** short for **cofferdam b** a recessed panel in a concrete, metal, or timber soffit ▷ *vb* (*tr*) **6** to store, as in a coffer **7** to decorate (a ceiling, dome, etc) with coffers [c13 from Old French *coffre*, from Latin *cophinus* basket, from Greek *kophinos*]

cofferdam (ˈkɒfəˌdæm) *n* **1** a watertight structure, usually of sheet piling, that encloses an area under water, pumped dry to enable construction work to be carried out. Below a certain depth a caisson is required **2** (on a ship) a compartment separating two bulkheads or floors, as for insulation or to serve as a barrier against the escape of gas or oil ▷ Often shortened to: **coffer**

coffin (ˈkɒfɪn) *n* **1** a box in which a corpse is buried or cremated **2** the part of a horse's foot that contains the coffin bone ▷ *vb* **3** (*tr*) to place in or as in a coffin **4** *engineering* another name for **flask** (sense 6) [c14 from Old French *cofin*, from Latin *cophinus* basket; see COFFER]

coffin bone *n* the terminal phalangeal bone inside the hoof of the horse and similar animals

coffin nail *n* a slang term for **cigarette**

coffle (ˈkɒfl) *n* (*esp formerly*) a line of slaves, beasts, etc, fastened together [c18 from Arabic *qāfilah* caravan]

C of I *abbreviation for* Church of Ireland

C of S *abbreviation for* **1** Chief of Staff **2** Church of Scotland

cog¹ (kɒɡ) *n* **1** any of the teeth or projections on the rim of a gearwheel or sprocket **2** a gearwheel, esp a small one **3** a person or thing playing a small part in a large organization or process ▷ *vb* **cogs, cogging, cogged 4** (*tr*) *metallurgy* to roll (cast-steel ingots) to convert them into blooms [c13 of Scandinavian origin; compare Danish *kogge*, Swedish *kugge*, Norwegian *kug*]

cog² (kɒɡ) *vb* **cogs, cogging, cogged** *slang* to cheat (in a game, esp dice), as by loading a dice [c16 originally a dice-playing term, of unknown origin]

cog³ (kɒɡ) *n* **1** a tenon that projects from the end of a timber beam for fitting into a mortise ▷ *vb* **cogs, cogging, cogged 2** (*tr*) to join (pieces of wood) with cogs [c19 of uncertain origin]

cogent (ˈkəʊdʒənt) *adj* compelling belief or assent; forcefully convincing [c17 from Latin *cōgent-, cōgēns*, driving together, from *cōgere*, from *co-* together + *agere* to drive] > '**cogency** *n* > '**cogently** *adv*

coggle (ˈkɒɡl) *vb* (*intr*) *Scot* to wobble or rock; be unsteady [of uncertain origin] > '**coggly** *adj*

cogitable (ˈkɒdʒɪtəbl) *adj rare* conceivable

cogitate (ˈkɒdʒɪˌteɪt) *vb* to think deeply about (a problem, possibility, etc); ponder [c16 from Latin *cōgitāre*, from *co-* (intensive) + *agitāre* to turn over, AGITATE] > 'cogi,**tatingly** *adv* > ˌcogi'**tation** *n* > 'cogi,**tator** *n*

cogitative (ˈkɒdʒɪtətɪv) *adj* **1** capable of thinking **2** thoughtful > '**cogitatively** *adv* > '**cogitativeness** *n*

cogito, ergo sum *Latin* (ˈkɒɡɪˌtəʊ ˈɜːɡəʊ ˈsʊm) I think, therefore I am; the basis of the philosophy of René Descartes (1596–1650), French philosopher and mathematician

Cognac (ˈkɒnjæk; *French* kɔɲak) *n* **1** a town in SW France: centre of the district famed for its brandy. Pop: 19 534 (1999) **2** (*sometimes not capital*) a high-quality grape brandy

cognate (ˈkɒɡneɪt) *adj* **1** akin; related: *cognate languages* **2** related by blood or descended from a common maternal ancestor. Compare **agnate 3 cognate object** *grammar* a noun functioning as the object of a verb to which it is etymologically related, as in *think a thought* or *sing a song* ▷ *n* **4** something that is cognate with something else [c17 from Latin *cognātus*, from *co-* same + *gnātus* born, variant of *nātus*, past participle of *nāscī* to be born] > '**cognately** *adv* > '**cognateness** *n* > ˌcog'**nation** *n*

cognition (kɒɡˈnɪʃən) *n* **1** the mental act or process by which knowledge is acquired, including perception, intuition, and reasoning **2** the knowledge that results from such an act or process [c15 from Latin *cognitiō*, from *cognōscere* from *co-* (intensive) + *nōscere* to learn; see KNOW] > cog'**nitional** *adj*

cognitive (ˈkɒɡnɪtɪv) *adj* of or relating to cognition

Cognitive Behavioural Therapy *n* a form of therapy in which, having learnt to understand their anxiety, patients attempt to overcome their usual behavioural responses to it

cognitive dissonance *n psychol* an uncomfortable mental state resulting from conflicting cognitions; usually resolved by changing some of the cognitions

cognitive ethology *n* a branch of ethology concerned with the influence of conscious awareness and intention on the behaviour of an animal

cognitive map *n psychol* a mental map of one's environment

cognitive psychology *n* the psychological study of higher mental processes, including thinking and perception

cognitive radio *n* a radio that can automatically alter frequency, power, modulation, etc, according to where it is located

cognitive science *n* the scientific study of cognition, including elements of the traditional disciplines of philosophy, psychology, semantics, and linguistics, together with artificial intelligence and computer science

cognitive therapy *n psychol* a form of psychotherapy in which the patient is encouraged to change the way he sees the world and himself: used particularly to treat depression

cognitivism (ˈkɒɡnɪtɪˌvɪzəm) *n philosophy* the meta-ethical thesis that moral judgments state facts and so are either true or false. Compare **emotivism, prescriptivism**. See also **naturalism** (sense 4), **non-naturalism**

cognizable *or* **cognisable** (ˈkɒɡnɪzəbl, ˈkɒnɪ-) *adj* **1** perceptible **2** *law* susceptible to the jurisdiction of a court > '**cognizably** *or* '**cognisably** *adv*

cognizance *or* **cognisance** (ˈkɒɡnɪzəns, ˈkɒnɪ-) *n* **1** knowledge; acknowledgment **2** **take cognizance of** to take notice of; acknowledge, esp officially **3** the range or scope of knowledge or perception **4** *law* **a** the right of a court to hear and determine a cause or matter **b** knowledge of certain facts upon which the court must act without requiring proof **c** *chiefly US* confession **5** *heraldry* a distinguishing badge or bearing [c14 from Old French *conoissance*, from *conoistre* to know, from Latin *cognōscere* to learn; see COGNITION]

cognizant *or* **cognisant** (ˈkɒɡnɪzənt, ˈkɒnɪ-) *adj* (*usually foll by of*) aware; having knowledge

cognize *or* **cognise** (ˈkɒɡnaɪz, kɒɡˈnaɪz) *vb* (*tr*) to perceive, become aware of, or know

cognomen (kɒɡˈnəʊmɛn) *n, pl* -**nomens** *or* -**nomina** (-ˈnɒmɪnə, -ˈnəʊ-) (*originally*) an ancient Roman's third name or nickname, which later became his family name. See also **agnomen, nomen, praenomen** [c19 from Latin: additional name, from *co-* together + *nōmen* name; influenced in form by *cognōscere* to learn] > **cognominal** (kɒɡˈnɒmɪnᵊl, -ˈnəʊ-) *adj* > cog'**nominally** *adv*

cognoscenti (ˌkɒnjəʊˈʃɛntɪ, ˌkɒɡnəʊ-) *or* **conoscenti** *pl n, sing* -**te** (-tiː) (*sometimes singular*) people with informed appreciation of a particular field, esp in the fine arts; connoisseurs [c18 from obsolete Italian (modern *conoscente*), from Latin *cognōscere* to know, learn about]

cogon (ˈkəʊɡɒn) *n* any of the coarse tropical grasses of the genus *Imperata*, esp *I. cylindrica* and *I. exaltata* of the Philippines, which are used for thatching [from Spanish *cogón*, from Tagalog *kugon*]

cog railway *or* **cogway** (ˈkɒɡˌweɪ) *n chiefly US* other terms for **rack railway**

cogwheel (ˈkɒɡˌwiːl) *n* another name for **gearwheel**

cohabit (kəʊˈhæbɪt) *vb* (*intr*) to live together as husband and wife, esp without being married [c16 via Late Latin, from Latin *co-* together + *habitāre* to live] > cohabi'**tee**, co'**habitant** *or* co'**habiter** *n*

cohabitation (kəʊˌhæbɪˈteɪʃən) n 1 the state or condition of living together as husband and wife without being married 2 (of political parties) the state or condition of cooperating for specific purposes without forming a coalition

coheir (kəʊˈɛə) n a person who inherits jointly with others ▷ co'heiress fem n

Cohen (kɒˈhɛn, kɔɪn) n a variant spelling of Kohen

cohere (kəʊˈhɪə) vb (intr) 1 to hold or stick firmly together 2 to be connected logically; be consistent 3 physics to be held together by the action of molecular forces [c16 from Latin cohaerēre from co- together + haerēre to cling, adhere]

coherence (kəʊˈhɪərəns) or **coherency** n 1 logical or natural connection or consistency 2 another word for **cohesion** (sense 1)

coherent (kəʊˈhɪərənt) adj 1 capable of logical and consistent speech, thought, etc 2 logical; consistent and orderly 3 cohering or sticking together 4 physics (of two or more waves) having the same phase or a fixed phase difference: coherent light 5 (of a system of units) consisting only of units the quotient or product of any two of which yield the unit of the resultant quantity ▷ co'herently adv

coherer (kəʊˈhɪərə) n physics an electrical component formerly used to detect radio waves, consisting of a tube containing loosely packed metal particles. The waves caused the particles to cohere, thereby changing the current through the circuit

cohesion (kəʊˈhiːʒən) n 1 the act or state of cohering; tendency to unite 2 physics the force that holds together the atoms or molecules in a solid or liquid, as distinguished from adhesion 3 botany the fusion in some plants of flower parts, such as petals, that are usually separate [c17 from Latin cohaesus stuck together, past participle of cohaerēre to COHERE]

cohesionless soil (kəʊˈhiːʒənlɪs) n any free-running type of soil, such as sand or gravel, whose strength depends on friction between particles. Also called: frictional soil. Compare **cohesive soil**

cohesive (kəʊˈhiːsɪv) adj 1 characterized by or causing cohesion 2 tending to cohere or stick together ▷ co'hesively adv ▷ co'hesiveness n

cohesive soil n sticky soil such as clay or clayey silt whose strength depends on the surface tension of capillary water. Compare **cohesionless soil**

coho (ˈkəʊhəʊ) n, pl -ho or -hos a Pacific salmon, Oncorhynchus kisutch. Also called: silver salmon [origin unknown; probably from an American Indian language]

cohobate (ˈkəʊhəʊˌbeɪt) vb (tr) pharmacol to redistil (a distillate), esp by allowing it to mingle with the remaining matter [c17 from New Latin cohobāre, perhaps from Arabic ka'aba to repeat an action]

cohort (ˈkəʊhɔːt) n 1 one of the ten units of between 300 and 600 men in an ancient Roman Legion 2 any band of warriors or associates: the cohorts of Satan 3 chiefly US an associate or follower 4 biology a taxonomic group that is a subdivision of a subclass (usually of mammals) or subfamily (of plants) 5 statistics a group of people with a statistic in common, esp having been born in the same year [c15 from Latin cohors yard, company of soldiers; related to hortus garden]

cohosh (ˈkəʊhɒʃ, kəʊˈhɒʃ) n any of several North American plants, such as the blue cohosh (Caulophyllum thalictroides: family Leonticaceae) and black cohosh (Cimicifuga racemosa: family Ranunculaceae) [c18 probably of Algonquian origin]

COHSE (ˈkəʊzɪ) n (formerly, in Britain) ▷ acronym for Confederation of Health Service Employees

cohune (kəʊˈhuːn) n a tropical American feather palm, Attalea (or Orbignya) cohune, whose large oily nuts yield an oil similar to coconut oil. Also called: cohune palm See also **coquilla nut** [c19 from American Spanish, from South American Indian ókhún]

COI (in Britain) abbreviation for Central Office of Information

coif (kɔɪf) n 1 a close-fitting cap worn under a veil, worn in the Middle Ages by many women but now only by nuns 2 any similar cap, such as a leather cap worn under a chain-mail hood 3 (formerly in England) the white cap worn by a serjeant at law 4 a base for the elaborate women's headdresses of the 16th century 5 (kwɑːf) a less common word for **coiffure** (sense 1) ▷ vb coifs, coiffing, coiffed (tr) 6 to cover with or as if with a coif 7 (kwɑːf) to arrange (the hair) [c14 from Old French coiffe, from Late Latin cofea helmet, cap, of obscure origin]

coiffeur (kwɑːˈfɜː; French kwafœr) n a hairdresser ▷ coiffeuse (kwɑːˈfɜːz; French kwaføz) fem n

coiffure (kwɑːˈfjʊə; French kwafyr) n 1 a hairstyle 2 an obsolete word for headdress ▷ vb 3 (tr) to dress or arrange (the hair)

coign or **coigne** (kɔɪn) n variant spellings of **quoin**

coign of vantage n an advantageous position or stance for observation or action

coil¹ (kɔɪl) vb 1 to wind or gather (ropes, hair, etc) into loops or (of rope, hair, etc) to be formed in such loops 2 (intr) to move in a winding course ▷ n 3 something wound in a connected series of loops 4 a single loop of such a series 5 an arrangement of pipes in a spiral or loop, as in a condenser 6 an electrical conductor wound into the form of a spiral, sometimes with a soft iron core, to provide inductance or a magnetic field. See also **induction coil** 7 an intrauterine contraceptive device in the shape of a coil 8 the transformer in a petrol engine that supplies the high voltage to the sparking plugs [c16 from Old French coillir to collect together; see CULL] ▷ 'coiler n

coil² (kɔɪl) n the troubles and activities of the world in the Shakespearean phrase this mortal coil) [c16 of unknown origin]

coil spring n a helical spring formed from wire

Coimbatore (ˌkɔɪmbəˈtɔː) n an industrial city in SW India, in W Tamil Nadu. Pop: 923 085 (2001)

Coimbra (Portuguese ˈkuimbrə) n a city in central Portugal: capital of Portugal from 1190 to 1260; seat of the country's oldest university. Pop: 148 474 (2001)

coin (kɔɪn) n 1 a metal disc or piece used as money 2 metal currency, as opposed to securities, paper currency, etc. Related adj: nummary 3 architect a variant spelling of quoin 4 pay (a person) back in (his) own coin to treat (a person) in the way that he has treated others 5 the other side of the coin the opposite view of a matter ▷ vb 6 (tr) to make or stamp (coins) 7 (tr) to make into a coin 8 (tr) to fabricate or invent (words, etc) 9 (tr) informal to make (money) rapidly (esp in the phrase coin it in) 10 coin a phrase said ironically after one uses a cliché [c14 from Old French: stamping die, from Latin cuneus wedge] ▷ 'coinable adj ▷ 'coiner n

coinage (ˈkɔɪnɪdʒ) n 1 coins collectively 2 the act of striking coins 3 the currency of a country 4 the act of inventing something, esp a word or phrase 5 a newly invented word, phrase, usage, etc

coin box n the part of a coin-operated machine into which coins are placed

coincide (ˌkəʊɪnˈsaɪd) vb (intr) 1 to occur or exist simultaneously 2 to be identical in nature, character, etc 3 to agree [c18 from Medieval Latin coincidere, from Latin co- together + incidere to occur, befall, from cadere to fall]

coincidence (kəʊˈɪnsɪdəns) n 1 a chance occurrence of events remarkable either for being simultaneous or for apparently being connected 2 the fact, condition, or state of coinciding 3 (modifier) electronics of or relating to a circuit that produces an output pulse only when both its input terminals receive pulses within a specified interval: coincidence gate. Compare **anticoincidence**

coincident (kəʊˈɪnsɪdənt) adj 1 having the same position in space or time 2 (usually postpositive and foll by with) in exact agreement; consonant

coincidental (kəʊˌɪnsɪˈdɛntəl) adj of or happening by a coincidence; fortuitous

coincidentally (kəʊˌɪnsɪˈdɛntəlɪ) adv (sentence modifier) by a coincidence; fortuitously

coin-op (ˈkɔɪnˌɒp) n a launderette or other service installation in which the machines are operated by the insertion of coins

coinsurance (ˌkəʊɪnˈʃʊərəns, -ˈʃɔː-) n 1 a method of insurance by which property is insured for a certain percentage of its value by a commercial insurance policy while the owner assumes liability for the remainder 2 joint insurance held by two or more persons

coinsure (ˌkəʊɪnˈʃʊə, -ˈʃɔː) vb 1 (intr) to take out coinsurance 2 to insure (property) jointly with another ▷ ˌcoin'surer n

Cointreau (ˈkwɑːntrəʊ) n trademark a colourless liqueur with orange flavouring

coir (kɔɪə) n the fibre prepared from the husk of the coconut, used in making rope and matting [c16 from Malayalam kāyar rope, from kāyaru to be twisted]

Coire (kwar) n the French name for Chur

coit (kɔɪt) n Austral slang buttocks; backside. Also: quoit [c20 perhaps a variant and special use of QUOIT, referring to roundness]

coitus (ˈkəʊɪtəs) or **coition** (kəʊˈɪʃən) n technical terms for **sexual intercourse** [c18 coitus: from Latin: a uniting, from coīre to meet, from īre to go] ▷ 'coital adj

coitus interruptus (ˌɪntəˈrʌptəs) n the deliberate withdrawal of the penis from the vagina before ejaculation

coitus reservatus (ˌrɛzəˈvɑːtəs) n the deliberate delaying or avoidance of orgasm during intercourse

cojones Spanish (koˈxones) pl n 1 testicles 2 manly courage

coke¹ (kəʊk) n 1 a solid-fuel product containing about 80 per cent of carbon produced by distillation of coal to drive off its volatile constituents: used as a fuel and in metallurgy as a reducing agent for converting metal oxides into metals 2 any similar material, such as the layer formed in the cylinders of a car engine by incomplete combustion of the fuel ▷ vb 3 to become or convert into coke [c17 probably a variant of C14 northern English dialect colk core, of obscure origin]

coke² (kəʊk) n slang short for **cocaine**

Coke (kəʊk) n trademark short for **Coca-Cola**

coked-up (ˈkəʊkdʌp) adj slang showing the effects of having taken cocaine

cokuloris (ˌkɒkəˈlɔːrɪs) n films a palette with irregular holes, placed between lighting and camera to prevent glare [c20 of unknown origin]

col (kɒl; French kɔl) n 1 the lowest point of a ridge connecting two mountain peaks, often constituting a pass 2 meteorol a pressure region between two anticyclones and two depressions, associated with variable weather [c19 from French: neck, col, from Latin collum neck]

col. abbreviation for column

Col. abbreviation for 1 Colombia(n) 2 Colonel 3 Bible Colossians

col-¹ prefix a variant of com- before l: collateral

col-² prefix a variant of colo- before a vowel: colectomy

cola¹ or **kola** (ˈkəʊlə) n 1 either of two tropical sterculiaceous trees, Cola nitida or C. acuminata, widely cultivated in tropical regions for their seeds (see cola nut) 2 a sweet carbonated drink flavoured with cola nuts [c18 from kola, probably variant of Mandingo kolo nut]

cola² (ˈkəʊlə) n a plural of colon¹ (sense 3) or colon²

COLA abbreviation for US 1 cost of living adjustment: an increase in benefit payments according to the rate of inflation **2** cost of living allowance: extra money paid to workers in areas where the cost of living is more expensive

colander ('kɒləndə, 'kʌl-) *or* **cullender** *n* a pan with a perforated bottom for straining or rinsing foods [c14 *colyndore*, probably from Old Provençal *colador*, via Medieval Latin, from Late Latin *cōlāre* to filter, from Latin *cōlum* sieve]

cola nut *n* any of the seeds of the cola tree, which contain caffeine and theobromine and are used medicinally and in the manufacture of soft drinks

colatitude (kəʊˈlætɪˌtjuːd) *n astronomy, navigation* the complement of the celestial latitude

Colby ('kɒlbɪ) *n* (*sometimes not capital*) *NZ* a type of mild-tasting hard cheese

colcannon (kəlˈkænən, 'kɒlˌkænən) *n* a dish, originating in Ireland, of potatoes and cabbage or other greens boiled and mashed together [c18 from Irish Gaelic *cál ceannann*, literally: white-headed cabbage]

Colchester ('kəʊltʃɪstə) *n* a town in E England, in NE Essex; university (1964). Pop: 104 390 (2001). Latin name: Camulodunum (ˌkæmjʊləʊˈdjuːnəm, ˌkæmʊləʊˈduːnəm)

colchicine ('kɒltʃɪˌsiːn, -sɪn, 'kɒlkɪ-) *n* a pale-yellow crystalline alkaloid extracted from seeds or corms of the autumn crocus. It is used in the treatment of gout and to create polyploid plants by inhibiting chromosome separation during meiosis. Formula: $C_{22}H_{25}NO_6$ [c19 from COLCHICUM + -INE²]

colchicum ('kɒltʃɪkəm, 'kɒlkɪ-) *n* **1** any Eurasian liliaceous plant of the genus *Colchicum*, such as the autumn crocus **2** the dried seeds or corms of the autumn crocus: a source of colchicine [c16 from Latin, from Greek *kolkhikon*, from *kolkhikos* of COLCHIS]

Colchis ('kɒlkɪs) *n* an ancient country on the Black Sea south of the Caucasus; the land of Medea and the Golden Fleece in Greek mythology

colcothar ('kɒlkəˌθɑː) *n* a finely powdered form of ferric oxide produced by heating ferric sulphate and used as a pigment and as jewellers' rouge. Also called: **crocus** [c17 from French *colcotar*, from Spanish *colcótar*, from Arabic dialect *qulqutār*]

cold (kəʊld) *adj* **1** having relatively little warmth; of a rather low temperature: *cold weather; cold hands* **2** without sufficient or proper warmth: *this meal is cold* **3** lacking in affection, enthusiasm, or warmth of feeling: *a cold manner* **4** not affected by emotion; objective: *cold logic* **5** dead **6** sexually unresponsive or frigid **7** lacking in freshness: *a cold scent; cold news* **8** chilling to the spirit; depressing **9** (of a colour) having violet, blue, or green predominating; giving no sensation of warmth **10** *metallurgy* denoting or relating to a process in which work-hardening occurs as a result of the plastic deformation of a metal at too low a temperature for annealing to take place **11** (of a process) not involving heat, in contrast with traditional methods: *cold typesetting; cold technology* **12** *informal* (of a seeker) far from the object of a search **13** denoting the contacting of potential customers, voters, etc, without previously approaching them in order to establish their interest: *cold mailing* **14** **cold comfort** little or no comfort **15** **cold steel** the use of bayonets, knives, etc, in combat **16** **from cold** without advance notice; without giving preparatory information **17** **in cold blood** showing no passion; deliberately; ruthlessly **18** **leave (someone) cold** *informal* to fail to excite (someone): *the performance left me cold* **19** **throw** (*or* **pour**) **cold water on** *informal* to be unenthusiastic about or discourage ▷ *n* **20** the absence of heat regarded as a positive force: *the cold took away our breath* **21** the sensation caused by loss or lack of heat **22** (**out**) **in the cold** *informal* neglected; ignored **23** an acute viral infection of the upper respiratory passages characterized by discharge of watery mucus from the nose, sneezing, etc **24** **catch a cold** *slang* to make a loss; lose one's investment ▷ *adv* **25** *informal* without

preparation: *he played his part cold* **26** *informal, chiefly US and Canadian* thoroughly; absolutely: *she turned him down cold* [Old English *ceald*; related to Old Norse *kaldr*, Gothic *kalds*, Old High German *kalt*; see COOL] > 'coldish *adj* > 'coldly *adv* > 'coldness *n*

cold-blooded *adj* **1** having or showing a lack of feeling or pity: *a cold-blooded killing* **2** *informal* particularly sensitive to cold **3** (of all animals except birds and mammals) having a body temperature that varies with that of the surroundings. Technical term: poikilothermic > ˌcold-'bloodedly *adv* > ˌcold-'bloodedness *n*

cold call *n* **1** a call made by a salesman on a potential customer without making an appointment ▷ *vb* **cold-call** **2** to call on (a potential customer) without making an appointment > **cold caller** *n* > **cold calling** *n*

cold cathode *n electronics* a cathode from which electrons are emitted at ambient temperature, due to a high potential gradient at the surface

cold chisel *n* a toughened steel chisel

cold cream *n* an emulsion of water and fat used cosmetically for softening and cleansing the skin

cold cuts *pl n* cooked meats sliced and served cold

cold-drawn *adj* (of metal wire, bars, etc) having been drawn unheated through a die to reduce dimensions, toughen, and improve surface finish

cold duck *n* an alcoholic beverage made from equal parts of burgundy and champagne

cold feet *pl n informal* loss or lack of courage or confidence

cold fish *n* an unemotional and unfriendly person

cold frame *n* an unheated wooden frame with a glass top, used to protect young plants from the cold

cold front *n meteorol* **1** the boundary line between a warm air mass and the cold air pushing it from beneath and behind as it moves **2** the line on the earth's surface where the cold front meets it ▷ Compare **warm front**

cold-hearted *adj* lacking in feeling or warmth; unkind > ˌcold-'heartedly *adv* > ˌcold-'heartedness *n*

coldie ('kəʊldɪ) *n Austral slang* a cold can or bottle of beer

Colditz ('kəʊldɪts) *n* a town in E Germany, on the River Mulde: during World War II its castle was used as a top-security camp for Allied prisoners of war; many daring escape attempts, some successful, were made

cold light *n* light emitted at low temperatures from a source that is not incandescent, such as fluorescence, phosphorescence, bioluminescence, or triboluminescence

cold moulding *n* the production of moulded articles from resins that polymerize chemically

cold pack *n* **1 a** a method of lowering the body temperature by wrapping a person in a sheet soaked in cold water **b** the sheet so used **2** a tinning process in which raw food is packed in cans or jars and then heated

cold-pressed *adj* (of an unrefined oil such as olive oil) produced by pressing the parent seed, nut, or grain at the lowest possible temperature without any further pressing

cold-rolled *adj* (of metal sheets, etc) having been rolled without heating, producing a smooth surface finish

cold rubber *n* synthetic rubber made at low temperatures (about 5°C). It is stronger than that made at higher temperatures and is used for car tyres

cold shoulder *informal* ▷ *n* **1** (often preceded by *the*) a show of indifference; a slight ▷ *vb* **cold-shoulder** (*tr*) **2** to treat with indifference

cold snap *n* a sudden short spell of cold weather

cold sore *n* a cluster of blisters at the margin of the lips that sometimes accompanies the common cold, caused by a viral infection. Technical name: herpes labialis

cold spot *n* an area where house prices are stable

and properties are slow to sell

cold start *n computing* the reloading of a program or operating system

cold storage *n* **1** the storage of things in an artificially cooled place for preservation **2** *informal* a state of temporary suspension: *to put an idea into cold storage*

Coldstream ('kəʊldˌstriːm) *n* a town in SE Scotland, in Scottish Borders on the English border: the Coldstream Guards were formed here (1660). Pop: 1813 (2001)

cold sweat *n informal* a bodily reaction to fear or nervousness, characterized by chill and moist skin

cold turkey *n* **1** *slang* a method of curing drug addiction by abrupt withdrawal of all doses **2** the withdrawal symptoms, esp nausea and shivering, brought on by this method

cold war *n* a state of political hostility and military tension between two countries or power blocs, involving propaganda, subversion, threats, economic sanctions, and other measures short of open warfare, esp that between the American and Soviet blocs after World War II (**the Cold War**)

cold warrior *n* a person who engages in or promotes a cold war

cold wave *n* **1** *meteorol* a sudden spell of low temperatures over a wide area, often following the passage of a cold front **2** *hairdressing* a permanent wave made by chemical agents applied at normal temperatures

cold-weld *vb* (*tr*) to join (two metal surfaces) without heat by forcing them together so that the oxide films are broken and adhesion occurs > **cold welding** *n*

cold work *n* **1** the craft of shaping metal without heat ▷ *vb* **cold-work** (*tr*) **2** to shape (metal) in this way

cole (kəʊl) *n* any of various plants of the genus *Brassica*, such as the cabbage and rape. Also called: **colewort** [Old English *cāl*, from Latin *caulis* plant stalk, cabbage]

colectomy (kəˈlɛktəmɪ) *n, pl* **-mies** surgical removal of part or all of the colon

colemanite ('kəʊlməˌnaɪt) *n* a colourless or white glassy mineral consisting of hydrated calcium borate in monoclinic crystalline form. It occurs with and is a source of borax. Formula: $Ca_2B_6O_{11}.5H_2O$ [c19 named after William T. *Coleman* (1824–93), American pioneer, owner of the mine in which it was discovered]

coleopter (ˌkɒlɪ'ɒptə) *n aeronautics obsolete* an aircraft that has an annular wing with the fuselage and engine on the centre line

coleopteran (ˌkɒlɪ'ɒptərən) *n also* **coleopteron 1** any of the insects of the cosmopolitan order *Coleoptera*, in which the forewings are modified to form shell-like protective elytra. The order includes the beetles and weevils ▷ *adj also* **coleopterous 2** of, relating to, or belonging to the order *Coleoptera* [c18 from New Latin *Coleoptera*, from Greek *koleoptera*, from *koleopteros* sheath-winged, from *koleon* sheath + *pteron* wing]

coleoptile (ˌkɒlɪ'ɒptaɪl) *n* a protective sheath around the plumule in grasses [c19 from New Latin *coleoptilum*, from Greek *koleon* sheath + *ptilon* down, soft plumage]

coleorhiza (ˌkɒlɪə'raɪzə) *n, pl* **-zae** (-ziː) a protective sheath around the radicle in grasses [c19 from New Latin, from Greek *koleon* sheath + *rhiza* root]

Coleraine ('kəʊl'reɪn) *n* **1** a town in N Northern Ireland, in Coleraine district, Co Antrim, on the River Bann; light industries; university (1965). Pop: 24 089 (2001). **2** a district in N Northern Ireland, in Co Antrim and Co Londonderry. Pop: 56 024 (2003 est). Area: 485 sq km (187 sq miles)

coleslaw ('kəʊlˌslɔː) *n* a salad of shredded cabbage, mayonnaise, carrots, onions, etc [c19 from Dutch *koolsla*, from *koolsalade*, literally: cabbage salad]

colestipol (kəˈlɛstɪˌpɒl) *n* a drug that reduces the

concentration of cholesterol in the blood: used, together with dietary restriction of cholesterol, to treat selected patients with hypercholesterolaemia and so prevent atherosclerosis

coletit ('kəʊl,tɪt) n another name for **coal tit**

coleus ('kəʊlɪəs) n, pl -uses any plant of the Old World genus *Coleus* cultivated for their variegated leaves, typically marked with red, yellow, or white: family *Lamiaceae* (labiates) [c19 from New Latin, from Greek *koleos*, variant of *koleon* sheath; from the way in which the stamens are joined]

colewort ('kəʊl,wɜːt) n another name for **cole**

coley ('kəʊlɪ, 'kɒlɪ) n Brit any of various edible fishes, esp the coalfish

colic ('kɒlɪk) n a condition characterized by acute spasmodic abdominal pain, esp that caused by inflammation, distention, etc, of the gastrointestinal tract [c15 from Old French *colique*, from Late Latin *cōlicus* ill with colic, from Greek *kōlon*, variant of *kolon* COLON²]

colicky ('kɒlɪkɪ) adj relating to or suffering from colic

colicroot ('kɒlɪk,ruːt) n 1 either of two North American liliaceous plants, *Aletris farinosa* or *A. aurea*, having tubular white or yellow flowers and a bitter root formerly used to relieve colic 2 any of various other plants formerly used to relieve colic

colicweed ('kɒlɪk,wiːd) n any of several plants of the genera *Dicentra* or *Corydalis*, such as the squirrel corn and Dutchman's-breeches: family *Fumariaceae*

coliform bacteria ('kɒlɪfɔːm) pl n a large group of bacteria inhabiting the intestinal tract of humans and animals that may cause disease and whose presence in water is an indicator of faecal pollution

Colima (Spanish ko'lima) n 1 a state of SW Mexico, on the Pacific coast: mainly a coastal plain, rising to the foothills of the Sierra Madre, with important mineral resources. Capital: Colima. Pop: 238 000 (2005 est). Area: 5455 sq km (2106 sq miles) 2 a city in SW Mexico, capital of Colima state, on the Colima River. Pop: 106 967 (1990) 3 Nevado de a volcano in SW Mexico, in Jalisco state. Height: 4339 m (14 235 ft)

coliseum (,kɒlɪ'sɪəm) or **colosseum** n a large building, such as a stadium or theatre, used for entertainments, sports, etc [c18 from Medieval Latin *Colisseum*, variant of COLOSSEUM]

colitis (kɒ'laɪtɪs, kə-) or **colonitis** (,kɒlə'naɪtɪs) n inflammation of the colon > colitic (kɒ'lɪtɪk) adj

collaborate (kə'læbə,reɪt) vb (intr) 1 (often foll by on, with, etc) to work with another or others on a joint project 2 to cooperate as a traitor, esp with an enemy occupying one's own country [c19 from Late Latin *collabōrāre*, from Latin *com-* together + *labōrāre* to work] > col'labo,rative adj > col'labo,rator n

collaboration (kə,læbə'reɪʃən) n 1 (often foll by on, with, etc) the act of working with another or others on a joint project 2 something created by working jointly with another or others 3 the act of cooperating as a traitor, esp with an enemy occupying one's own country > col,labo'rationist n

collage (kə'lɑːʒ, kɒ-; French kɔlaʒ) n 1 an art form in which compositions are made out of pieces of paper, cloth, photographs, and other miscellaneous objects, juxtaposed and pasted on a dry ground 2 a composition made in this way 3 any work, such as a piece of music, created by combining unrelated styles [c20 French, from *coller* to stick, from *colle* glue, from Greek *kolla*] > col'lagist n

collagen ('kɒlədʒən) n a fibrous scleroprotein of connective tissue and bones that is rich in glycine and proline and yields gelatine on boiling [c19 from Greek *kolla* glue + -GEN] > collagenic (,kɒlə'dʒɛnɪk) or collagenous (kə'lædʒənəs) adj

collagen injection n an injection of collagen into the lip in order to give it a fuller appearance

collapsar (kɒ'læpsɑː) n astronomy a collapsed star, either a white dwarf, neutron star, or black hole

collapse (kə'læps) vb 1 (intr) to fall down or cave in suddenly: *the whole building collapsed* 2 (intr) to fail completely: *his story collapsed on investigation* 3 (intr) to break down or fall down from lack of strength 4 to fold (furniture, etc) compactly or (of furniture, etc) to be designed to fold compactly ▷ n 5 the act or instance of suddenly falling down, caving in, or crumbling 6 a sudden failure or breakdown [c18 from Latin *collāpsus*, from *collābī* to fall in ruins, from *lābī* to fall] > col'lapsible or col'lapsable adj > col,lapsi'bility or col,lapsability n

collar ('kɒlə) n 1 the part of a garment around the neck and shoulders, often detachable or folded over 2 any band, necklace, garland, etc, encircling the neck: *a collar of flowers* 3 a band or chain of leather, rope, or metal placed around an animal's neck to restrain, harness, or identify it 4 biology a marking or structure resembling a collar, such as that found around the necks of some birds or at the junction of a stem and a root 5 a section of a shaft or rod having a locally increased diameter to provide a bearing seat or a locating ring 6 a cut of meat, esp bacon, taken from around the neck of an animal 7 hot under the collar informal aroused with anger, annoyance, etc ▷ vb (tr) 8 to put a collar on; furnish with a collar 9 to seize by the collar 10 informal to seize; arrest; detain [c13 from Latin *collāre* neckband, neck chain, collar, from *collum* neck]

collarbone ('kɒlə,bəʊn) n the nontechnical name for **clavicle**

collar cell n another name for **choanocyte**

collard ('kɒləd) n 1 a variety of the cabbage, *Brassica oleracea acephala*, having a crown of edible leaves. See also **kale** 2 the leaves of this plant, eaten as a vegetable [c18 variant of COLEWORT]

collared dove n a European dove, *Streptopelia decaocto*, having a brownish-grey plumage with a black band on the back of the neck

collarette (,kɒlə'rɛt) n a woman's fur or lace collar

collate (kɒ'leɪt, kə-) vb (tr) 1 to examine and compare (texts, statements, etc) in order to note points of agreement and disagreement 2 (in library work) to check the number and order of (the pages of a book) 3 bookbinding a to check the sequence of (the sections of a book) after gathering b a nontechnical word for **gather** (sense 9) 4 (often foll by to) Christianity to appoint (an incumbent) to a benefice [c16 from Latin *collātus* brought together (past participle of *conferre* to gather), from *com-* together + *lātus*, past participle of *ferre* to bring]

collateral (kɒ'lætərəl, kə-) n 1 a a security pledged for the repayment of a loan b (as modifier): *a collateral loan* 2 a person, animal, or plant descended from the same ancestor as another but through a different line ▷ adj 3 situated or running side by side 4 descended from a common ancestor but through different lines 5 serving to support or corroborate 6 aside from the main issue 7 uniting in tendency [c14 from Medieval Latin *collaterālis*, from Latin *com-* together + *laterālis* of the side, from *latus* side] > col'laterally adv

collateral damage n military unintentional damage to civil property and civilian casualties, caused by military operations

collation (kɒ'leɪʃən, kə-) n 1 the act or process of collating 2 a description of the technical features of a book 3 RC Church a light meal permitted on fast days 4 any light informal meal 5 the appointment of a clergyman to a benefice

collative (kɒ'leɪtɪv, 'kɒlə-) adj 1 involving collation 2 (of benefices) presented or held by collation

collator (kɒ'leɪtə, kəʊ-, 'kɒleɪtə, 'kəʊ-) n 1 a person or machine that collates texts or manuscripts 2 computing a device for matching or checking punched cards in separate files and for merging two or more files sorted into the same ordered sequence

colleague ('kɒliːg) n a fellow worker or member of a staff, department, profession, etc [c16 from French *collègue*, from Latin *collēga* one selected at the same time as another, from *com-* together + *lēgāre* to choose]

collect¹ (kə'lɛkt) vb 1 to gather together or be gathered together 2 to accumulate (stamps, books, etc) as a hobby or for study 3 (tr) to call for or receive payment of (taxes, dues, etc) 4 (tr) to regain control of (oneself, one's emotions, etc) as after a shock or surprise: *he collected his wits* 5 (tr) to fetch; pick up: *collect your own post; he collected the children after school* 6 (intr; sometimes foll by on) slang to receive large sums of money, as from an investment: *he really collected when the will was read* 7 (tr) Austral and NZ informal to collide with; be hit by 8 collect on delivery the US term for **cash on delivery** ▷ adv, adj 9 US (of telephone calls) on a reverse-charge basis ▷ n 10 Austral informal a winning bet [c16 from Latin *collēctus* collected, from *colligere* to gather together, from *com-* together + *legere* to gather]

collect² ('kɒlɛkt) n Christianity a short Church prayer generally preceding the lesson or epistle in Communion and other services [c13 from Medieval Latin *collecta* (from the phrase *ōrātiō ad collēctam* prayer at the (people's) assembly), from Latin *colligere* to COLLECT¹]

collectable or **collectible** (kə'lɛktəb²l) adj 1 (of antiques, objets d'art, etc) of interest to a collector ▷ n 2 any object regarded as being of interest to a collector

collectanea (,kɒlɛk'teɪnɪə) pl n a collection of excerpts from one or more authors; miscellany; anthology [c18 from Latin, from *collectāneus* assembled, from *colligere* to COLLECT¹]

collected (kə'lɛktɪd) adj 1 in full control of one's faculties; composed 2 assembled in totality or brought together into one volume or a set of volumes: *the collected works of Dickens* 3 (of a horse or a horse's pace) controlled so that movement is in short restricted steps: *a collected canter* > col'lectedly adv > col'lectedness n

collection (kə'lɛkʃən) n 1 the act or process of collecting 2 a number of things collected or assembled together 3 a selection of clothes, esp as presented by a particular designer for a specified season 4 something gathered into a mass or pile; accumulation: *a collection of rubbish* 5 a sum of money collected or solicited, as in church 6 removal, esp regular removal of letters from a postbox 7 (often plural) (at Oxford University) a college examination or an oral report by a tutor

collective (kə'lɛktɪv) adj 1 formed or assembled by collection 2 forming a whole or aggregate 3 of, done by, or characteristic of individuals acting in cooperation ▷ n 4 a a cooperative enterprise or unit, such as a collective farm b the members of such a cooperative 5 short for **collective noun** > col'lectively adv > col'lectiveness n

collective agreement n a negotiated agreement, which is not enforceable at law, between an employer and employees' representatives, covering rates of pay or terms and conditions of employment, or both

collective bargaining n negotiation between one or more trade unions and one or more employers or an employers' organization on the incomes and working conditions of the employees

collective farm n (chiefly in Communist countries) a farm or group of farms managed and owned, through the state, by the community. Russian name: kolkhoz

collective fruit n another name for **multiple fruit**

collective memory n the shared memories of a group, family, race, etc

collective noun n a noun that is singular in form but that refers to a group of people or things

> USAGE Collective nouns are usually used with singular verbs: *the family is on holiday; General Motors is mounting a*

C

big sales campaign. In British usage, however, plural verbs are sometimes employed in this context, esp when reference is being made to a collection of individual objects or people rather than to the group as a unit: *the family are all on holiday*. Care should be taken that the same collective noun is not treated as both singular and plural in the same sentence: *the family is well and sends its best wishes* or *the family are all well and send their best wishes*, but not *the family is well and send their best wishes*

collective ownership *n* ownership by a group for the benefit of members of that group

collective pitch lever *n* a lever in a helicopter to change the angle of attack of all the rotor blades simultaneously, causing it to rise or descend. Compare **cyclic pitch lever**

collective security *n* a system of maintaining world peace and security by concerted action on the part of the nations of the world

collective unconscious *n psychol* (in Jungian psychological theory) a part of the unconscious mind incorporating patterns of memories, instincts, and experiences common to all mankind. These patterns are inherited, may be arranged into archetypes, and are observable through their effects on dreams, behaviour, etc

collectivism (kəˈlɛktɪˌvɪzəm) *n* **1** the principle of ownership of the means of production, by the state or the people **2** a social system based on this principle > **colˈlectivist** *n* > **colˌlectiˈvistic** *adj*

collectivity (ˌkɒlɛkˈtɪvɪtɪ) *n*, *pl* -ties **1** the quality or state of being collective **2** a collective whole or aggregate **3** people regarded as a whole

collectivize *or* **collectivise** (kəˈlɛktɪˌvaɪz) *vb* (*tr*) to organize according to the principles of collectivism > **colˌlectiviˈzation** *or* **colˌlectiviˈsation** *n*

collector (kəˈlɛktə) *n* **1** a person or thing that collects **2** a person employed to collect debts, rents, etc **3** the head of a district administration in India **4** a person who collects or amasses objects as a hobby **5** *electronics* the region in a transistor into which charge carriers flow from the base > **colˈlectorˌship** *n*

collectorate (kəˈlɛktərɪt) *n* the office of a collector in India

collector's item *or* **piece** *n* a thing regarded as being exquisite or rare and thus worthy of the interest of one who collects such things

colleen (ˈkɒliːn, kɒˈliːn) *n* **1** an Irish word for **girl** **2** an Irish girl [c19 from Irish Gaelic *cailín* a girl, a young unmarried woman]

college (ˈkɒlɪdʒ) *n* **1** an institution of higher education; part of a university **2** a school or an institution providing specialized courses or teaching: *a college of music* **3** the building or buildings in which a college is housed **4** the staff and students of a college **5** an organized body of persons with specific rights and duties: *an electoral college*. See also **Sacred College** **6** a body of clerics living in community and supported by endowment **7** *chiefly Brit* an obsolete slang word for **prison** [c14 from Latin *collēgium* company, society, band of associates, from *collēga*; see **COLLEAGUE**]

college of advanced technology *n Brit* (formerly) a college offering degree or equivalent courses in technology, with research facilities. In the mid-1960s these were granted university status. Abbreviation: **CAT**

college of arms *n* any of several institutions in the United Kingdom having a royal charter to deal with matters of heraldry, grant armorial bearings, record and trace genealogies, etc. Also called: **heralds' college**

College of Cardinals *n RC Church* the collective body of cardinals having the function of electing and advising the pope

college of education *n Brit* a professional training college for teachers

College of Justice *n* the official name for the Scottish Court of Session; the supreme court of Scotland

college pudding *n Brit* a baked or steamed suet pudding containing dried fruit and spice

collegial (kəˈliːdʒɪəl) *adj* **1** of or relating to a college **2** having authority or power shared among a number of people associated as colleagues > **colˈlegially** *adv* > **colˌlegiˈality** *n*

collegian (kəˈliːdʒɪən) *n* a current member of a college; student

collegiate (kəˈliːdʒɪt) *adj* **1** Also: **collegial** of or relating to a college or college students **2** (of a university) composed of various colleges of equal standing ▷ *n* **3** *Canadian* short for **collegiate institute**

collegiate church *n* **1** *RC Church, Church of England* a church that has an endowed chapter of canons and prebendaries attached to it but that is not a cathedral **2** *US Protestantism* one of a group of churches presided over by a body of pastors **3** *Scot Protestantism* a church served by two or more ministers **4** a large church endowed in the Middle Ages to become a school **5** a chapel either endowed by or connected with a college

collegiate institute *n Canadian* (in certain provinces) a large secondary school with an academic, rather than vocational, emphasis

collegium (kəˈliːdʒɪəm) *n*, *pl* -giums *or* -gia (-dʒɪə) **1** (in the former Soviet Union) a board in charge of a department **2** another term for **College of Cardinals** *or* **Sacred College** [Latin: COLLEGE]

col legno (ˈkɒl ˈlegnəʊ, ˈleɪnjəʊ) *adv music* to be played (on a stringed instrument) by striking the strings with the back of the bow [Italian: with the wood]

collembolan (kəˈlɛmbələn) *n* **1** any small primitive wingless insect of the order *Collembola*, which comprises the springtails ▷ *adj* **2** of, relating to, or belonging to the *Collembola* [c19 from New Latin *Collembola*, from Greek *kolla* glue + *embolon* peg, wedge]

collenchyma (kəˈlɛŋkɪmə) *n* a strengthening and supporting tissue in plants, consisting of elongated living cells whose walls are thickened with cellulose and pectins [c19 New Latin, from Greek *kolla* glue + *enkhuma* infusion] > **collenchymatous** (ˌkɒlənˈkɪmətəs) *adj*

Colles' fracture (ˈkɒlɪs) *n* a fracture of the radius just above the wrist, with backward and outward displacement of the hand [c19 named after Abraham *Colles* (died 1843), Irish surgeon]

collet (ˈkɒlɪt) *n* **1** (in a jewellery setting) a band or coronet-shaped claw that holds an individual stone **2** *mechanical engineering* an externally tapered sleeve made in two or more segments and used to grip a shaft passed through its centre when the sleeve is compressed by being inserted in a tapered hole **3** *horology* a small collar that supports the inner end of the hairspring ▷ *vb* **4** (*tr*) *jewellery* to mount in a collet [c16 from Old French: a little collar, from *col* neckband, neck, from Latin *collum* neck]

colleterial gland (ˌkɒlɪˈtɪərɪəl) *n zoology* a paired accessory reproductive gland, present in most female insects, secreting a sticky substance that forms either the egg cases or the cement that binds the eggs to a surface [c19 from New Latin *colleterium* glue-secreting organ, from Greek *kolla* glue + -AL[1]]

colliculus (kɒˈlɪkjʊləs) *n*, *pl* -li *anatomy* a small elevation, as on the surface of the optic lobe of the brain [c19 New Latin]

collide (kəˈlaɪd) *vb* (*intr*) **1** to crash together with a violent impact **2** to conflict in attitude, opinion, or desire; clash; disagree [c17 from Latin *collīdere* to clash together, from *com-* together + *laedere* to strike, wound]

collider (kəˈlaɪdə) *n physics* a particle accelerator in which beams of particles are made to collide

collie (ˈkɒlɪ) *n* any of several silky-coated breeds of dog developed for herding sheep and cattle. See **Border collie, rough collie, bearded collie** [c17 Scottish, probably from earlier *colie* black with coal dust, from *cole* COAL]

collier (ˈkɒlɪə) *n chiefly Brit* **1** a coal miner **2 a** a ship designed to transport coal **b** a member of its crew [c14 from COAL + -IER]

colliery (ˈkɒljərɪ) *n*, *pl* -lieries *chiefly Brit* a coal mine

colligate (ˈkɒlɪˌgeɪt) *vb* (*tr*) **1** to connect or link together; tie; join **2** to relate (isolated facts, observations, etc) by a general hypothesis [c16 from Latin *colligāre* to fasten together, from *com-* together + *ligāre* to bind] > **colliˈgation** *n*

colligative (kəˈlɪgətɪv) *adj* (of a physical property of a substance) depending on the concentrations of atoms, ions, and molecules that are present rather than on their nature

collimate (ˈkɒlɪˌmeɪt) *vb* (*tr*) **1** to adjust the line of sight of (an optical instrument) **2** to use a collimator on (a beam of radiation or particles) **3** to make parallel or bring into line [c17 from New Latin *collimāre*, erroneously for Latin *collīneāre* to aim, from *com-* (intensive) + *līneāre*, from *līnea* line] > **colliˈmation** *n*

collimator (ˈkɒlɪˌmeɪtə) *n* **1** a small telescope attached to a larger optical instrument as an aid in fixing its line of sight **2** an optical system of lenses and slits producing a nondivergent beam of light, usually for use in spectroscopes **3** any device for limiting the size and angle of spread of a beam of radiation or particles

collinear (kɒˈlɪnɪə) *adj* **1** lying on the same straight line **2** having a common line > **collinearity** (ˌkɒlɪnɪˈærɪtɪ) *n* > **colˈlinearly** *adv*

collins (ˈkɒlɪnz) *n* a tall fizzy iced drink made with gin, vodka, rum, etc, mixed with fruit juice, soda water, and sugar [c20 probably after the proper name *Collins*]

collinsia (kəˈlɪnsɪə, -zɪə) *n* a North American plant of the scrophulariaceous genus *Collinsia*, having blue, white, or purple flowers [c19 New Latin, named after Zaccheus *Collins* (1764–1831), American botanist]

Collins Street Farmer *n Austral slang* a businessman who invests in farms, land, etc. Also called: **Pitt Street Farmer** [c20 after a principal business street in Melbourne]

collision (kəˈlɪʒən) *n* **1** a violent impact of moving objects; crash **2** the conflict of opposed ideas, wishes, attitudes, etc: *a collision of interests* **3** *physics* an event in which two or more bodies or particles come together with a resulting change of direction and, normally, energy [c15 from Late Latin *collīsiō* from Latin *collīdere* to COLLIDE]

collocate (ˈkɒləˌkeɪt) *vb* (*tr*) to group or place together in some system or order [c16 from Latin *collocāre*, from *com-* together + *locāre* to place, from *locus* place]

collocation (ˌkɒləˈkeɪʃən) *n* a grouping together of things in a certain order, as of the words in a sentence

collocutor (ˈkɒləˌkjuːtə) *n* a person who talks or engages in conversation with another

collodion (kəˈləʊdɪən) *or* **collodium** (kəˈləʊdɪəm) *n* a colourless or yellow syrupy liquid that consists of a solution of pyroxylin in ether and alcohol: used in medicine and in the manufacture of photographic plates, lacquers, etc [c19 from New Latin *collōdium*, from Greek *kollōdēs* glutinous, from *kolla* glue]

collogue (kɒˈləʊg) *vb* collogues, colloguing, collogued (*intr*; usually foll by *with*) to confer confidentially; intrigue or conspire [c16 perhaps from obsolete *colleague* (vb) to be or act as a colleague, conspire, influenced by Latin *colloquī* to talk with; see COLLEAGUE]

colloid (ˈkɒlɔɪd) *n* **1** Also called: colloidal solution *or* suspension a mixture having particles of one component, with diameters between 10^{-7} and 10^{-9} metres, suspended in a continuous phase of another component. The mixture has properties between those of a solution and a fine suspension **2** the solid suspended phase in such a mixture **3** *obsolete* a substance that in solution does not penetrate a semipermeable membrane. Compare **crystalloid** (sense 2) **4** *physiol* a gelatinous substance of the thyroid follicles that holds the hormonal secretions of the thyroid gland ▷ *adj* **5** *pathol* of or relating to the gluelike translucent material found in certain degenerating tissues **6** of, denoting, or having the character of a colloid [C19 from Greek *kolla* glue + -OID]

colloidal (kɒˈlɔɪdəl) *adj* of, denoting, or having the character of a colloid > **colloidality** (ˌkɒlɔɪˈdælɪtɪ) *n*

collop (ˈkɒləp) *n dialect* **1** a slice of meat **2** a small piece of anything [C14 of Scandinavian origin; compare Swedish *kalops* meat stew]

colloq. *abbreviation for* colloquial(ly)

colloquial (kəˈləʊkwɪəl) *adj* **1** of or relating to conversation **2** denoting or characterized by informal or conversational idiom or vocabulary. Compare **informal**. > col'loquially *adv* > col'loquialness *n*

colloquialism (kəˈləʊkwɪəˌlɪzəm) *n* **1** a word or phrase appropriate to conversation and other informal situations **2** the use of colloquial words and phrases

colloquium (kəˈləʊkwɪəm) *n, pl* -quiums *or* -quia (-kwɪə) **1** an informal gathering for discussion **2** an academic seminar [C17 from Latin: conversation, conference, COLLOQUY]

colloquy (ˈkɒləkwɪ) *n, pl* -quies **1** a formal conversation or conference **2** a literary work in dialogue form **3** an informal conference on religious or theological matters [C16 from Latin *colloquium* from *colloquī* to talk with, from *com*-together + *loquī* to speak] > 'colloquist *n*

collotype (ˈkɒləʊˌtaɪp) *n* **1** Also called: **photogelatine process** a method of lithographic printing from a flat surface of hardened gelatine: used mainly for fine-detail reproduction in monochrome or colour **2** a print made using this process [C19 from Greek *kolla* glue + TYPE] > collotypic (ˌkɒləˈtɪpɪk) *adj*

collude (kəˈluːd) *vb* (*intr*) to conspire together, esp in planning a fraud; connive [C16 from Latin *collūdere*, literally: to play together, from *com*-together + *lūdere* to play] > col'luder *n*

collusion (kəˈluːʒən) *n* **1** secret agreement for a fraudulent purpose; connivance; conspiracy **2** a secret agreement between opponents at law in order to obtain a judicial decision for some wrongful or improper purpose [C14 from Latin *collūsiō*, from *collūdere* to COLLUDE] > col'lusive *adj*

colluvium (kəˈluːvɪəm) *n, pl* -via (-vɪə) *or* -viums a mixture of rock fragments from the bases of cliffs [Latin: collection of filth, from *colluere* to wash thoroughly, from *com*- (intensive) + *luere* to wash] > col'luvial *adj*

colly (ˈkɒlɪ) *archaic or dialect* ▷ *n, pl* -lies **1** soot or grime, such as coal dust ▷ *vb* collies, collying, collied **2** (*tr*) to begrime; besmirch [C16 ultimately from Old English *col* COAL]

collyrium (kɒˈlɪərɪəm) *n, pl* -lyria (-ˈlɪərɪə) *or* -lyriums a technical name for an **eyewash** (sense 1) [C16 from Latin, from Greek *kollurion* poultice, eye salve]

collywobbles (ˈkɒlɪˌwɒbəlz) *pl n* (usually preceded by *the*) *slang* **1** an upset stomach **2** acute diarrhoea **3** an intense feeling of nervousness [C19 probably from New Latin *cholera morbus* the disease cholera, influenced through folk etymology by COLIC and WOBBLE]

Colmar (*French* kɔlmar) *n* a city in NE France: annexed to Germany 1871–1919 and 1940–45; textile industry. Pop: 65 136 (1999). German name: Kolmar

Colo. *abbreviation for* Colorado

colo- *or before a vowel* **col-** *combining form* indicating the colon: *colostomy; colotomy*

coloboma (ˌkɒləˈbəʊmə) *n* a structural defect of the eye, esp in the choroid, retina, or iris [C19 New Latin, from Greek *kolobōma* a part taken away in mutilation, from *kolobos* cut short]

colobus (ˈkɒləbəs) *n* any leaf-eating arboreal Old World monkey of the genus *Colobus*, of W and central Africa, having a slender body, long silky fur, long tail, and reduced or absent thumbs [C19 New Latin, from Greek *kolobos* cut short; referring to its thumb]

colocynth (ˈkɒləsɪnθ) *n* **1** a cucurbitaceous climbing plant, *Citrullus colocynthis*, of the Mediterranean region and Asia, having bitter-tasting fruit **2** the dried fruit pulp of this plant, used as a strong purgative ▷ Also called: **bitter apple** [C17 from Latin *colocynthis*, from Greek *kolokunthis*, from *kolokunthē* gourd, of obscure origin]

cologarithm (kəʊˈlɒgəˌrɪðəm) *n* the logarithm of the reciprocal of a number; the negative value of the logarithm: *the cologarithm of 4 is log ¼.* Abbreviation: **colog**

cologne (kəˈləʊn) *n* a perfumed liquid or solid made of fragrant essential oils and alcohol. Also called: **Cologne water, eau de Cologne** [C18 *Cologne water*, from COLOGNE, where it was first manufactured (1709)]

Cologne (kəˈləʊn) *n* an industrial city and river port in W Germany, in North Rhine-Westphalia on the Rhine: important commercially since ancient times; university (1388). Pop: 965 954 (2003 est). German name: **Köln**

Colombard (ˈkɒləmˌbɑːd) *n* **1** a white grape grown in France, California, and Australia, used for making wine **2** any of various moderately dry, spicy white wines made from this grape

Colomb-Béchar (*French* kɔlɔ̃beʃar) *n* the former name of **Béchar**

Colombes (*French* kɔlɔ̃b) *n* an industrial and residential suburb of NW Paris. Pop: 76 757 (1999)

Colombia (kəˈlɒmbɪə) *n* a republic in NW South America: inhabited by Chibchas and other Indians before Spanish colonization in the 16th century; independence won by Bolívar in 1819; became the Republic of Colombia in 1886; violence and unrest have been endemic since the 1970s. It consists chiefly of a hot swampy coastal plain, separated by ranges of the Andes from the pampas and the equatorial forests of the Amazon basin in the east. Language: Spanish. Religion: Roman Catholic majority. Currency: peso. Capital: Bogotá. Pop: 44 914 000 (2004 est). Area: 1 138 908 sq km (439 735 sq miles)

Colombian (kəˈlɒmbɪən) *adj* **1** of or relating to Colombia or its inhabitants ▷ *n* **2** a native or inhabitant of Colombia

Colombo (kəˈlʌmbəʊ) *n* the capital and chief port of Sri Lanka, on the W coast, with one of the largest artificial harbours in the world. Pop: 653 000 (2005 est)

colon¹ (ˈkəʊlən) *n* **1** (*pl* -lons) the punctuation mark :, usually preceding an explanation or an example of what has gone before, a list, or an extended quotation **2** (*pl* -lons) this mark used for certain other purposes, such as expressions of time, as in *2:45 p.m.*, or when a ratio is given in figures, as in *5:3* **3** *pl* -la (-lə) (in classical prosody) a part of a rhythmic period with two to six feet and one principal accent or ictus [C16 from Latin, from Greek *kōlon* limb, hence part of a strophe, clause of a sentence]

colon² (ˈkəʊlən) *n, pl* -lons *or* -la (-lə) the part of the large intestine between the caecum and the rectum [C16 from Latin: large intestine, from Greek *kolon*]

colon³ (kəˈlɒn; *French* kɔlɔ̃) *n* a colonial farmer or plantation owner, esp in a French colony [French: colonist, from Latin *colōnus*, from *colere* to till, inhabit]

colón (kəˈləʊn; *Spanish* koˈlon) *n, pl* -lons *or* -lones (*Spanish* -ˈlones) **1** the standard monetary unit of Costa Rica, divided into 100 céntimos **2** the former standard monetary unit of El Salvador,

divided into 100 centavos; replaced by the US dollar in 2001 [C19 American Spanish, from Spanish, after Cristóbal *Colón* Christopher Columbus]

Colón (kɒˈlɒn; *Spanish* koˈlon) *n* **1** a port in Panama, at the Caribbean entrance to the Panama Canal. Chief Caribbean port. Pop: 157 000 (2005 est). Former name: Aspinwall **2** Archipiélago (ˌartʃiˈpjelaɣo ðe) the official name of the **Galápagos Islands**

colonel (ˈkɜːnəl) *n* an officer of land or air forces junior to a brigadier but senior to a lieutenant colonel [C16 via Old French, from Old Italian *colonnello* column of soldiers, from *colonna* COLUMN] > 'colonelcy *or* 'colonel,ship *n*

Colonel Blimp *n* See blimp²

colonial (kəˈləʊnɪəl) *adj* **1** of, characteristic of, relating to, possessing, or inhabiting a colony or colonies **2** (*often capital*) characteristic of or relating to the 13 British colonies that became the United States of America (1776) **3** (*often capital*) of or relating to the colonies of the British Empire **4** denoting, relating to, or having the style of Neoclassical architecture used in the British colonies in America in the 17th and 18th centuries **5** of or relating to the period of Australian history before Federation (1901) **6** (of organisms such as corals and bryozoans) existing as a colony of polyps **7** (of animals and plants) having become established in a community in a new environment ▷ *n* **8** a native of a colony > co'lonially *adv*

colonial experience *n Austral history* experience of farming, etc, gained by a young Englishman in colonial Australia > colonial experiencer *n*

colonial goose *n* NZ an old-fashioned name for stuffed roast mutton

colonialism (kəˈləʊnɪəˌlɪzəm) *n* the policy and practice of a power in extending control over weaker peoples or areas. Also called: **imperialism** > co'lonialist *n, adj*

colonic (kəˈlɒnɪk) *adj* **1 a** *anatomy* of or relating to the colon **b** *med* relating to irrigation of the colon for cleansing purposes ▷ *n* **2** *med* irrigation of the colon by injecting large amounts of fluid high into the colon: *a high colonic*

Colonies (ˈkɒlənɪz) *pl n* **the 1** *Brit* the subject territories formerly in the British Empire **2** *US history* the 13 states forming the original United States of America when they declared their independence (1776). These were Connecticut, North and South Carolina, Delaware, Georgia, New Hampshire, New York, Maryland, Massachusetts, Pennsylvania, Rhode Island, Virginia, and New Jersey

colonist (ˈkɒlənɪst) *n* **1** a person who settles or colonizes an area **2** an inhabitant or member of a colony

colonitis (ˌkɒləˈnaɪtɪs) *n pathol* another word for **colitis**

colonize *or* **colonise** (ˈkɒləˌnaɪz) *vb* **1** to send colonists to or establish a colony in (an area) **2** to settle in (an area) as colonists **3** (*tr*) to transform (a community) into a colony **4** (of plants and animals) to become established in (a new environment) > 'colo,nizable *or* 'colo,nisable *adj* > ,coloni'zation *or* ,coloni'sation *n* > 'colo,nizer *or* 'colo,niser *n*

colonnade (ˌkɒləˈneɪd) *n* **1** a set of evenly-spaced columns **2** a row of regularly spaced trees [C18 from French, from *colonne* COLUMN; on the model of Italian *colonnato*, from *colonna* column] > ,colon'naded *adj*

colonoscope (kəˈlɒnəˌskəʊp) *n* an instrument for examining the colon, consisting of a flexible lighted tube that is inserted in the colon to look for abnormalities and to remove them or take tissue samples [C20 from COLON² + -O- + -SCOPE] > colonoscopy (ˌkɒlənˈɒskəpɪ) *n*

Colonsay (ˈkɒlənseɪ, -zeɪ) *n* an island in W Scotland, in the Inner Hebrides. Area: about 41 sq km (16 sq miles)

C

colony ('kɒlənɪ) *n, pl* -nies **1** a body of people who settle in a country distant from their homeland but maintain ties with it **2** the community formed by such settlers **3** a subject territory occupied by a settlement from the ruling state **4 a** a community of people who form a national, racial, or cultural minority: *an artists' colony; the American colony in London* **b** the area itself **5** *zoology* **a** a group of the same type of animal or plant living or growing together, esp in large numbers **b** an interconnected group of polyps of a colonial organism **6** *bacteriol* a group of bacteria, fungi, etc, derived from one or a few spores, esp when grown on a culture medium [c16 from Latin *colōnia*, from *colere* to cultivate, inhabit]

colony-stimulating factor *n immunol* any of a number of substances, secreted by the bone marrow, that cause stem cells to proliferate and differentiate, forming colonies of specific blood cells. Synthetic forms are being tested for their ability to reduce the toxic effects of chemotherapy. Abbreviation: CSF

colophon ('kɒlə,fɒn, -fən) *n* **1** a publisher's emblem on a book **2** (formerly) an inscription at the end of a book showing the title, printer, date, etc [c17 via Late Latin, from Greek *kolophōn* a finishing stroke]

colophony (kɒ'lɒfənɪ) *n* another name for **rosin** (sense 1) [c14 from Latin *Colophōnia rēsina* resin from Colophon]

coloquintida (,kɒlə'kwɪntɪdə) *n* another name for **colocynth** [c14 from Medieval Latin, from *colocynthid-* COLOCYNTH]

color ('kʌlə) *n, vb* the US spelling of **colour** > 'colorable *adj* > 'colorer *n* > 'colorful *adj* > 'coloring *n* > 'colorist *n* > 'colorless *adj*

Colorado (,kɒlə'rɑːdəʊ) *n* **1** a state of the central US: consists of the Great Plains in the east and the Rockies in the west; drained chiefly by the Colorado, Arkansas, South Platte, and Rio Grande Rivers. Capital: Denver. Pop: 4 550 688 (2003 est). Area: 269 998 sq km (104 247 sq miles). Abbreviations: **Colo.**, (with zip code) **CO 2** a river in SW North America, rising in the Rocky Mountains and flowing southwest to the Gulf of California: famous for the 1600 km (1000 miles) of canyons along its course. Length: about 2320 km (1440 miles) **3** a river in central Texas, flowing southeast to the Gulf of Mexico. Length: about 1450 km (900 miles) **4** a river in central Argentina, flowing southeast to the Atlantic. Length: about 850 km (530 miles) [Spanish, literally: red, from Latin *colōrātus* coloured, tinted red; see COLOUR]

Colorado beetle *n* a black-and-yellow beetle, *Leptinotarsa decemlineata*, that is a serious pest of potatoes, feeding on the leaves: family *Chrysomelidae*. Also called: **potato beetle**

Colorado Desert *n* an arid region of SE California and NW Mexico, west of the Colorado River. Area: over 5000 sq km (2000 sq miles)

Colorado ruby *n* a fire-red form of garnet found in Colorado and other parts of North America

Colorado Springs *n* a city and resort in central Colorado. Pop: 370 448 (2003 est)

Colorado topaz *n* **1** a tawny-coloured form of topaz found in Colorado **2** quartz of a similar colour

colorant ('kʌlərənt) *n* any substance that imparts colour, such as a pigment, dye, or ink; colouring matter

coloration *or* **colouration** (,kʌlə'reɪʃən) *n* **1** arrangement of colour and tones; colouring **2** the colouring or markings of insects, birds, etc. See also **apatetic, aposematic, cryptic 3** unwanted extraneous variations in the frequency response of a loudspeaker or listening environment

coloratura (,kɒlərə'tʊərə) *or* **coloratore** ('kɒlərə,tjʊə) *n music* **1 a** (in 18th- and 19th-century arias) a florid virtuoso passage **b** (*as modifier*): *a coloratura aria* **2** Also called: **coloratura soprano** a lyric soprano who specializes in such

music [c19 from obsolete Italian, literally: colouring, from Latin *colōrāre* to COLOUR]

colorectal (,kəʊləʊ'rɛktəl) *adj* of or relating to the colon and rectum

colorific (,kʌlə'rɪfɪk) *adj* producing, imparting, or relating to colour

colorimeter (,kʌlə'rɪmɪtə) *n* **1** Also called: **tintometer** an apparatus for determining the concentration of a solution of a coloured substance by comparing the intensity of its colour with that of a standard solution or with standard colour slides **2** any apparatus for measuring the quality of a colour by comparison with standard colours or combinations of colours > colorimetric (,kʌlərɪ'mɛtrɪk) *or* ,colori'metrical *adj* > ,colori'metrically *adv* > ,color'imetry *n*

Colossae (kə'lɒsiː) *n* an ancient city in SW Phrygia in Asia Minor: seat of an early Christian Church

colossal (kə'lɒsəl) *adj* **1** of immense size; huge; gigantic **2** (in figure sculpture) approximately twice life-size. Compare **heroic** (sense 7) **3** Also: **giant** *architect* of or relating to the order of columns and pilasters that extend more than one storey in a façade > co'lossally *adv*

colosseum (,kɒlə'sɪəm) *n* a variant spelling of **coliseum**

Colosseum (,kɒlə'sɪəm) *n* an amphitheatre in Rome built about 75–80 AD

Colossian (kə'lɒʃən) *n* **1** a native or inhabitant of Colossae **2** *New Testament* any of the Christians of Colossae to whom St Paul's Epistle was addressed

Colossians (kə'lɒʃənz) *n* (functioning as singular) a book of the New Testament (in full **The Epistle of Paul the Apostle to the Colossians**)

colossus (kə'lɒsəs) *n, pl* -si (-saɪ) *or* -suses something very large, esp a statue [c14 from Latin, from Greek *kolossos*]

Colossus of Rhodes *n* a giant bronze statue of Apollo built on Rhodes in about 292–280 BC; destroyed by an earthquake in 225 BC; one of the Seven Wonders of the World

colostomy (kə'lɒstəmɪ) *n, pl* -mies the surgical formation of an opening from the colon onto the surface of the body, which functions as an anus

colostrum (kə'lɒstrəm) *n* the thin milky secretion from the nipples that precedes and follows true lactation. It consists largely of serum and white blood cells [c16 from Latin, of obscure origin] > co'lostral *adj*

colotomy (kə'lɒtəmɪ) *n, pl* -mies a colonic incision

colour *or US* **color** ('kʌlə) *n* **1 a** an attribute of things that results from the light they reflect, transmit, or emit in so far as this light causes a visual sensation that depends on its wavelengths **b** the aspect of visual perception by which an observer recognizes this attribute **c** the quality of the light producing this aspect of visual perception **d** (*as modifier*): *colour vision* **2** Also called: **chromatic colour a** a colour, such as red or green, that possesses hue, as opposed to achromatic colours such as white or black **b** (*as modifier*): *a colour television; a colour film*. Compare **black-and-white** (sense 2) **3** a substance, such as a dye, pigment, or paint, that imparts colour to something **4 a** the skin complexion of a person, esp as determined by his race **b** (*as modifier*): *colour prejudice; colour problem* **5** the use of all the hues in painting as distinct from composition, form, and light and shade **6** the quantity and quality of ink used in a printing process **7** the distinctive tone of a musical sound; timbre **8** vividness, authenticity, or individuality: *period colour* **9** semblance or pretext (esp in the phrases **take on a different colour, under colour of**) **10** *US* a precious mineral particle, esp gold, found in auriferous gravel **11** *physics* one of three characteristics of quarks, designated red, blue, or green, but having no relationship with the physical sensation ⊳ *vb* **12** to give or apply colour to (something) **13** (*tr*) to give a convincing or

plausible appearance to (something, esp to that which is spoken or recounted): *to colour an alibi* **14** (*tr*) to influence or distort (something, esp a report or opinion): *anger coloured her judgment* **15** (*intr*; often foll by *up*) to become red in the face, esp when embarrassed or annoyed **16** (*intr*) (esp of ripening fruit) to change hue ⊳ See also **colours** [c13 from Old French *colour* from Latin *color* tint, hue]

colourable ('kʌlərəbəl) *adj* **1** capable of being coloured **2** appearing to be true; plausible: *a colourable excuse* **3** pretended; feigned: *colourable affection* > ,coloura'bility *or* 'colourableness *n* > 'colourably *adv*

colour bar *n* discrimination against people of a different race, esp as practised by Whites against Blacks

colour-blind *adj* **1** of or relating to any defect in the normal ability to distinguish certain colours. See **deuteranopia, protanopia, tritanopia 2** not discriminating on grounds of skin colour or ethnic origin > **colour blindness** *n*

colour code *n* a system of easily distinguishable colours, as for the identification of electrical wires or resistors

colour commentator *n* a sports celebrity who works as part of a commentary team

colour contrast *n psychol* the change in the appearance of a colour surrounded by another colour; for example, grey looks bluish if surrounded by yellow

coloured ('kʌləd) *adj* **1** possessing colour **2** having a strong element of fiction or fantasy; distorted (esp in the phrase **highly coloured**)

Coloured ('kʌləd) *n, pl* Coloureds *or* Coloured **1** an individual who is not a White person, esp a Black person **2** Also called: **Cape Coloured** (in South Africa) a person of racially mixed parentage or descent ⊳ *adj* **3** designating or relating to a Coloured person or Coloured people: *a Coloured gentleman*

⊓ **USAGE** The use of *Coloured* to refer to a person who is not White can be offensive and should be avoided

colourfast ('kʌlə,fɑːst) *adj* (of a fabric) having a colour that does not run or change when washed or worn > 'colour,fastness *n*

colour filter *n photog* a thin layer of coloured gelatine, glass, etc, that transmits light of certain colours or wavelengths but considerably reduces the transmission of others

colourful ('kʌləfʊl) *adj* **1** having intense colour or richly varied colours **2** vivid, rich, or distinctive in character > 'colourfully *adv* > 'colourfulness *n*

colour guard *n* a military guard in a parade, ceremony, etc, that carries and escorts the flag or regimental colours

colour index *n* **1** *astronomy* the difference between the apparent magnitude of a star measured in one standard waveband and in a longer standard waveband, indicating its colour and temperature **2** *geology* the sum of the dark or coloured minerals of a rock, expressed as a percentage of the total minerals **3** *chem, physics* a systematic arrangement of colours according to their hue, saturation, and brightness

colouring ('kʌlərɪŋ) *n* **1** the process or art of applying colour **2** anything used to give colour, such as dye, paint, etc **3** appearance with regard to shade and colour **4** arrangements of colours and tones, as in the markings of birds and animals **5** the colour of a person's features or complexion **6** a false or misleading appearance

colourist ('kʌlərɪst) *n* **1** a person who uses colour, esp an artist **2** a person who colours photographs, esp black-and-white ones > ,colour'istic *adj*

colourize, colourise *or US* **colorize** ('kʌlə,raɪz) *vb* (*tr*) to add colour electronically to (an old black-and-white film) > ,colouri'zation, ,colouri'sation *or US* ,colori'zation *n*

colourless ('kʌləlɪs) *adj* **1** without colour **2** lacking in interest: *a colourless individual* **3** grey or pallid in tone or hue **4** without prejudice; neutral > ˈcolourlessly *adv* > ˈcolourlessness *n*

colour line *n* the social separation of racial groups within a community (esp in the phrase **to cross the colour line**)

colourman (ˈkʌləmən) *n, pl* **-men** a person who deals in paints

colour phase *n* **1** a seasonal change in the coloration of some animals **2** an abnormal variation in the coloration shown by a group of animals within a species

colourpoint cat (ˈkʌləˌpɔɪnt) *n* a cat with increased pigmentation of cooler points of the body, such as ears, feet, tail, nose, and scrotum (in males). US name: **Himalayan cat**

colour-reversal *n* (*modifier*) *photog* (of film or photographic paper) designed to produce a positive image directly from a positive subject

colours (ˈkʌləz) *pl n* **1 a** the flag that indicates nationality **b** *military* the ceremony of hoisting or lowering the colours **2** a pair of silk flags borne by a military unit, esp British, comprising the **Queen's Colour** showing the unit's crest, and the **Regimental Colour** showing the crest and battle honours **3** true nature or character (esp in the phrase **show one's colours**) **4** a distinguishing badge or flag, as of an academic institution **5** *sport, Brit* a badge or other symbol denoting membership of a team, esp at a school or college **6** *informal* a distinguishing embroidered patch denoting membership of a motorcycle gang **7** **nail one's colours to the mast a** to refuse to admit defeat **b** to declare openly one's opinions or allegiances

colour scheme *n* a planned combination or juxtaposition of colours, as in interior decorating

colour separation *n* *printing* the division of a coloured original into cyan, magenta, yellow, and black so that plates may be made for print reproduction. Separation may be achieved by electronic scanning or by photographic techniques using filters to isolate each colour

colour separation overlay *n* another term for **chromakey**

colour sergeant *n* a sergeant who carries the regimental, battalion, or national colours, as in a colour guard

colour subcarrier (ˈsʌbˌkærɪə) *n* a component of a colour television signal on which is modulated the colour or chrominance information

colour supplement *n* *Brit* an illustrated magazine accompanying a newspaper, esp a Sunday newspaper

colour temperature *n* *physics* the temperature of a black-body radiator at which it would emit radiation of the same chromaticity as the light under consideration

colourwash (ˈkʌləˌwɒʃ) *n* **1** a coloured distemper ▷ *vb* (*tr*) **2** to paint with colourwash

colourway (ˈkʌləˌweɪ) *n* one of several different combinations of colours in which a given pattern is printed on fabrics, wallpapers, etc

coloury *or* **colory** (ˈkʌlərɪ) *adj* possessing colour

-colous *adj combining form* inhabiting or living on: *arenicolous* [from Latin *-cola* inhabitant + -OUS; related to *colere* to inhabit]

colpitis (kɒlˈpaɪtɪs) *n* *pathol* another name for **vaginitis** [C19 from Greek *kolpos* bosom, womb, vagina + -ITIS]

colpo- *or before a vowel* **colp-** *combining form* indicating the vagina: *colpitis; colpotomy* [from Greek *kolpos* womb]

colporteur (ˈkɒlˌpɔːtə; *French* kɔlpɔrtœr) *n* a hawker of books, esp bibles [C18 from French, from *colporter*, probably from Old French *comporter* to carry (see COMPORT); influenced through folk etymology by *porter à col* to carry on one's neck] > ˈcolˌportage *n*

colposcope (ˈkɒlpəˌskəʊp) *n* an instrument for examining the uterine cervix, esp for early signs of cancer [C20 from COLPO- + -SCOPE]

colpotomy (kɒlˈpɒtəmɪ) *n, pl* **-mies** a surgical incision into the wall of the vagina [C20 from COLPO- + -TOMY]

colt (kəʊlt) *n* **1** a male horse or pony under the age of four **2** an awkward or inexperienced young person **3** *sport* **a** a young and inexperienced player **b** a member of a junior team [Old English *colt* young ass, of obscure origin; compare Swedish dialect *kult* young animal, boy]

Colt (kəʊlt) *n* *trademark* a type of revolver, pistol, etc [C19 named after Samuel Colt (1814–62), American inventor]

coltan (ˈkɒlˌtæn) *n* a metallic ore found esp in the E Congo, consisting of columbite and tantalite and used as a source of tantalum [C20 from COLUMBITE + TANTALITE]

colter (ˈkəʊltə) *n* a variant spelling (esp US) of **coulter**

coltish (ˈkəʊltɪʃ) *adj* **1** inexperienced; unruly **2** playful and lively > ˈcoltishly *adv* > ˈcoltishness *n*

coltsfoot (ˈkəʊltsˌfʊt) *n, pl* **-foots** a European plant, *Tussilago farfara*, with yellow daisy-like flowers and heart-shaped leaves: a common weed: family *Asteraceae* (composites)

colubrid (ˈkɒljʊbrɪd) *n* **1** any snake of the family *Colubridae*, including many harmless snakes, such as the grass snake and whip snakes, and some venomous types ▷ *adj* **2** of, relating to, or belonging to the *Colubridae* [C19 from New Latin *Colubridae*, from Latin *coluber* snake]

colubrine (ˈkɒljʊˌbraɪn, -brɪn) *adj* **1** of or resembling a snake **2** of, relating to, or belonging to the *Colubrinae*, a subfamily of harmless colubrid snakes [C16 from Latin *colubrīnus*, from *coluber* snake]

colugo (kəˈluːgəʊ) *n, pl* **-gos** another name for **flying lemur** [from a native word in Malaya]

Columba (kəˈlʌmbə) *n, Latin genitive* **Columbae** (kəˈlʌmbiː) *as in Alpha Columbae*. a small constellation in the S hemisphere south of Orion [Latin, literally: dove]

columbarium (ˌkɒləmˈbɛərɪəm) *n, pl* **-ia** (-ɪə) **1** another name for a **dovecote 2** a vault having niches for funeral urns **3** a hole in a wall into which a beam is inserted [C18 from Latin, from *columba* dove]

Columbia[1] (kəˈlʌmbɪə) *n* **1** a river in NW North America, rising in the Rocky Mountains and flowing through British Columbia, then west to the Pacific. Length: about 1930 km (1200 miles) **2** a city in central South Carolina, on the Congaree River: the state capital. Pop: 117 357 (2003 est)

Columbia[2] (kəˈlʌmbɪə) *n* the first test vehicle of the NASA space shuttle fleet to prove the possibility of routine access to space for scientific and commercial ventures

Columbian (kəˈlʌmbɪən) *adj* **1** of or relating to the United States **2** relating to Christopher Columbus (Spanish name *Cristóbal Colón*, Italian name *Cristoforo Colombo*.; 1451–1506), Italian navigator and explorer in the service of Spain, who discovered the New World (1492) ▷ *n* **3** a size of printer's type, approximately equal to 16 point; two-line Brevier

columbic (kəˈlʌmbɪk) *adj* another word for **niobic**

columbine[1] (ˈkɒləmˌbaɪn) *n* any plant of the ranunculaceous genus *Aquilegia*, having purple, blue, yellow, or red flowers with five spurred petals. Also called: **aquilegia** [C13 from Medieval Latin *columbīna herba* dovelike plant, from Latin *columbīnus* dovelike, from the resemblance of the flower to a group of doves]

columbine[2] (ˈkɒləmˌbaɪn) *adj* of, relating to, or resembling a dove [C14 from Old French *colombin*, from Latin *columbīnus* dovelike, from *columba* dove]

Columbine (ˈkɒləmˌbaɪn) *n* **1** (originally) the character of a servant girl in commedia dell'arte **2** (later) the sweetheart of Harlequin in English pantomime

columbite (kəˈlʌmbaɪt) *n* a black mineral consisting of a niobium oxide of iron and manganese in orthorhombic crystalline form: occurs in coarse granite, often with tantalite, and is an ore of niobium. Formula: $(Fe, Mn)(Nb)_2O_6$. Also called: **niobite** [C19 from COLUMBIUM + -ITE[1]]

columbium (kəˈlʌmbɪəm) *n* the former name of **niobium** [C19 from New Latin, from *Columbia*, the United States of America]

columbous (kəˈlʌmbəs) *adj* another word for **niobous**

Columbus (kəˈlʌmbəs) *n* **1** a city in central Ohio: the state capital. Pop: 728 432 (2003 est) **2** a city in W Georgia, on the Chattahoochee River. Pop: 185 702 (2003 est)

Columbus Day *n* Oct 12, a legal holiday in most states of the US: the date of Columbus' landing in the West Indies (Caribbean) in 1492

columella (ˌkɒljuˈmɛlə) *n, pl* **-lae** (-liː) **1** *biology* **a** the central part of the spore-producing body of some fungi and mosses **b** any similar columnar structure **2** Also called: **columella auris** (ˈɔːrɪs) a small rodlike bone in the middle ear of frogs, reptiles, and birds that transmits sound to the inner ear: homologous to the mammalian stapes [C16 from Latin: diminutive of *columna* COLUMN] > ˌcoluˈmellar *adj*

column (ˈkɒləm) *n* **1** an upright post or pillar usually having a cylindrical shaft, a base, and a capital **2 a** a form or structure in the shape of a column: *a column of air* **b** a monument **3** a row, line, or file, as of people in a queue **4** *military* a narrow formation in which individuals or units follow one behind the other **5** *journalism* **a** any of two or more vertical sections of type on a printed page, esp on a newspaper page **b** a regular article or feature in a paper: *the fashion column* **6** a vertical array of numbers or mathematical terms **7** *botany* a long structure in a flower, such as that of an orchid, consisting of the united stamens and style **8** *anatomy, zoology* any elongated structure, such as a tract of grey matter in the spinal cord or the stalk of a crinoid [C15 from Latin *columna*, from *columen* top, peak; related to Latin *collis* hill] > **columnar** (kəˈlʌmnə) *adj* > ˈcolumned *or* **columnated** (ˈkɒləmˌneɪtɪd) *adj*

columniation (kəˌlʌmnɪˈeɪʃən) *n* the arrangement of architectural columns

column inch *n* a unit of measurement for advertising space, one inch deep and one column wide

columnist (ˈkɒləmɪst, -əmnɪst) *n* a journalist who writes a regular feature in a newspaper: *a gossip columnist*

colure (kəˈlʊə, ˈkəʊlʊə) *n* either of two great circles on the celestial sphere, one of which passes through the celestial poles and the equinoxes and the other through the poles and the solstices [C16 from Late Latin *colūrī* (plural), from Greek *kolourai* cut short, dock-tailed, from *kolos* docked + *oura* tail; so called because the view of the lower part is curtailed]

Colwyn Bay (ˈkɒlwɪn) *n* a town and resort in N Wales, in Conwy county borough. Pop: 30 269 (2001)

coly (ˈkəʊlɪ) *n, pl* **-lies** any of the arboreal birds of the genus *Colius*, family *Coliidae*, and order *Coliiformes*, of southern Africa. They have a soft hairlike plumage, crested head, and very long tail. Also called: **mousebird** [C19 from New Latin *colius*, probably from Greek *kolios* woodpecker]

colza (ˈkɒlzə) *n* another name for **rape**[2] [C18 via French (Walloon) *kolzat* from Dutch *koolzaad*, from *kool* cabbage, COLE + *zaad* SEED]

colza oil *n* the oil obtained from the seeds of the rape plant and used in making lubricants and synthetic rubber

com *an internet domain name for* a commercial company

COM (kɒm) *n* **a** a process in which a computer output is converted direct to microfiche or film, esp 35 or 16 millimetre film **b** (*as modifier*): *a COM machine* [(C)omputer (O)utput on (M)icrofilm]

Com. *abbreviation for* **1** Commander **2** committee **3** Commodore

com- *or* **con-** ▷ *prefix* together; with; jointly:

commingle [from Latin *com-*; related to *cum* with. In compound words of Latin origin, *com-* becomes *col-* and *cor-* before *l* and *r*, *co-* before *gn*, *h*, and most vowels, and *con-* before consonants other than *b*, *p*, and *m*. Although its sense in compounds of Latin derivation is often obscured, it means: together, with, etc (*combine*, *compile*); similar (*conform*); extremely, completely (*consecrate*)]

coma[1] ('kəʊmə) *n, pl* **-mas** a state of unconsciousness from which a person cannot be aroused, caused by injury to the head, rupture of cerebral blood vessels, narcotics, poisons, etc [c17 from medical Latin, from Greek *kōma* heavy sleep; related to Greek *koitē* bed, perhaps to Middle Irish *cuma* grief]

coma[2] ('kəʊmə) *n, pl* **-mae** (-miː) **1** *astronomy* the luminous cloud surrounding the frozen solid nucleus in the head of a comet, formed by vaporization of part of the nucleus when the comet is close to the sun **2** *botany* **a** a tuft of hairs attached to the seed coat of some seeds **b** the terminal crown of leaves of palms and moss stems **3** *optics* a type of lens defect characterized by the formation of a diffuse pear-shaped image from a point object [c17 from Latin: hair of the head, from Greek *komē*] > **'comal** *adj*

Coma Berenices ('kəʊmə ˌberɪ'naɪsiːz) *n, Latin genitive* **Comae Berenices** ('kəʊmiː) a faint constellation in the N hemisphere between Ursa Major and Boötes containing the **Coma Cluster** a cluster of approximately 1000 galaxies, at a mean distance of 300 million light years [from Latin, literally: Berenice's hair, named after *Berenice* (died 221 BC), consort of Ptolemy III]

Comanche (kə'mæntʃɪ) *n* **1** (*pl* **-ches** *or* **-che**) a member of a Native American people, formerly ranging from the River Platte to the Mexican border, now living in Oklahoma **2** the language of this people, belonging to the Shoshonean subfamily of the Uto-Aztecan family

Comanchean (kə'mæntʃɪən) (in North America) *adj* **1** of or relating to the early part of the Cretaceous system and period ▷ *n* **2** the strata and time corresponding to the early Cretaceous

comate ('kəʊmeɪt) *adj botany* **1** having tufts of hair **2** having or relating to a coma [c17 from Latin *comātus*, from *coma* hair]

comatose ('kəʊməˌtəʊs, -ˌtəʊz) *adj* **1** in a state of coma **2** torpid; lethargic > **'comaˌtosely** *adv*

comatulid (kə'mætjʊlɪd) *or* **comatula** *n, pl* **-lids** *or* **-lae** (-liː) any of a group of crinoid echinoderms, including the feather stars, in which the adults are free-swimming [c19 from New Latin *Comatulidae*, from *Comatula* type genus, from Latin *comātus* hairy]

comb (kəʊm) *n* **1** a toothed device of metal, plastic, wood, etc, used for disentangling or arranging hair **2** a tool or machine that separates, cleans, and straightens wool, cotton, etc **3** *Austral and NZ* the fixed cutter on a sheep-shearing machine **4** anything resembling a toothed comb in form or function **5** the fleshy deeply serrated outgrowth on the top of the heads of certain birds, esp the domestic fowl **6** anything resembling the comb of a bird **7** a currycomb **8** a honeycomb **9** the row of fused cilia in a ctenophore **10** **go over** (*or* **through**) **with a fine-tooth(ed) comb** to examine very thoroughly ▷ *vb* **11** (*tr*) to use a comb on **12** (when *tr*, often foll by *through*) to search or inspect with great care: *the police combed the woods* ▷ See also **comb out** [Old English *camb*; related to Old Norse *kambr*, Old High German *camb*]

combat *n* ('kɒmbæt, -bət, 'kʌm-) **1** a fight, conflict, or struggle **2** **a** an action fought between two military forces **b** (*as modifier*): *a combat jacket* **3** **single combat** a fight between two individuals; duel **4** **close** *or* **hand-to-hand combat** fighting at close quarters ▷ *vb* (kəm'bæt, 'kɒmbæt, 'kʌm-) **-bats, -bating, -bated 5** (*tr*) to fight or defy **6** (*intr*; often foll by *with* or *against*) to struggle or strive (against); be in conflict (with): *to combat against disease* [c16 from French, from Old French *combattre*, from Vulgar Latin *combattere* (unattested), from Latin *com-* with + *battuere* to beat, hit] > **com'batable** *adj* > **com'bater** *n*

combatant ('kɒmbətᵊnt, 'kʌm-) *n* **1** a person or group engaged in or prepared for a fight, struggle, or dispute ▷ *adj* **2** engaged in or ready for combat

combat boot *n* a heavy army boot

combat fatigue *n* another term for **battle fatigue**

combative ('kɒmbətɪv, 'kʌm-) *adj* eager or ready to fight, argue, etc; aggressive > **'combatively** *adv* > **'combativeness** *n*

combat trousers *or* **combats** ('kɒmbæts, -bəts, 'kʌm-) *pl n* loose casual trousers with large pockets on the legs

combe *or* **comb** (kuːm) *n* variant spellings of **coomb**

comber ('kəʊmə) *n* **1** a person, tool, or machine that combs wool, flax, etc **2** a long curling wave; roller

combination (ˌkɒmbɪ'neɪʃən) *n* **1** the act of combining or state of being combined **2** a union of separate parts, qualities, etc **3** an alliance of people or parties; group having a common purpose **4** **a** the set of numbers that opens a combination lock **b** the mechanism of this type of lock **5** *Brit* a motorcycle with a sidecar attached **6** *maths* **a** an arrangement of the numbers, terms, etc, of a set into specified groups without regard to order in the group: *the combinations of a, b, and c, taken two at a time, are ab, bc, ac* **b** a group formed in this way. The number of combinations of *n* objects taken *r* at a time is $n!/[(n-r)!r!]$. Symbol: $_nC_r$. Compare **permutation** (sense 1) **7** the chemical reaction of two or more compounds, usually to form one other compound **8** *chess* a tactical manoeuvre involving a sequence of moves and more than one piece ▷ See also **combinations.** > **ˌcombi'national** *adj*

combination lock *n* a type of lock that can only be opened when a set of dials releasing the tumblers of the lock are turned to show a specific sequence of numbers

combination room *n Brit* (at Cambridge University) a common room

combinations (ˌkɒmbɪ'neɪʃənz) *pl n Brit* a one-piece woollen undergarment with long sleeves and legs. Often shortened to: **combs** *or* **coms**. US and Canadian term: **union suit**

combination tone *n* another term for **resultant tone**

combinative ('kɒmbɪˌneɪtɪv, -nətɪv), **combinatorial** (ˌkɒmbɪnə'tɔːrɪəl) *or* **combinatory** ('kɒmbɪnətərɪ, -trɪ) *adj* **1** resulting from being, tending to be, or able to be joined or mixed together **2** *linguistics* (of a sound change) occurring only in specific contexts or as a result of some other factor, such as change of stress within a word. Compare **isolative** (sense 1)

combinatorial analysis *n* the branch of mathematics concerned with the theory of enumeration, or combinations and permutations, in order to solve problems about the possibility of constructing arrangements of objects which satisfy specified conditions. Also called: combinatorics (ˌkɒmbɪnə'tɔːrɪks)

combine *vb* (kəm'baɪn) **1** to integrate or cause to be integrated; join together **2** to unite or cause to unite to form a chemical compound **3** *agriculture* to harvest (crops) with a combine harvester ▷ *n* ('kɒmbaɪn) **4** *agriculture* short for **combine harvester** **5** an association of enterprises, esp in order to gain a monopoly of a market **6** an association of business corporations, political parties, sporting clubs, etc, for a common purpose [c15 from Late Latin *combīnāre*, from Latin *com-* together + *bīnī* two by two] > **com'binable** *adj* > **comˌbina'bility** *n* > **com'biner** *n*

combine harvester ('kɒmbaɪn) *n* a machine that simultaneously cuts, threshes, and cleans a standing crop of grain

combings ('kəʊmɪŋz) *pl n* **1** the loose hair, wool, etc, removed by combing, esp that of animals **2** the unwanted loose short fibres removed in combing cotton, etc

combining form *n* a linguistic element that occurs only as part of a compound word, such as *anthropo-* in *anthropology*

comb jelly *n* another name for a **ctenophore**

combo ('kɒmbəʊ) *n, pl* **-bos 1** a small group of musicians, esp of jazz musicians **2** *informal* any combination

comb out *vb* (*tr, adverb*) **1** to remove (tangles or knots) from (the hair) with a comb **2** to isolate and remove for a purpose **3** to survey carefully; examine systematically ▷ *n* **comb-out 4** an act of combing out

comb-over *n* a hairstyle in which long strands of hair from the side of the head are swept over the scalp to cover a bald patch

combust (kəm'bʌst) *adj* **1** *astrology* (of a star or planet) invisible for a period between 24 and 30 days each year due to its proximity to the sun ▷ *vb* **2** *chem* to burn

combustible (kəm'bʌstəbᵊl) *adj* **1** capable of igniting and burning **2** easily annoyed; excitable ▷ *n* **3** a combustible substance > **comˌbusti'bility** *or* **com'bustibleness** *n* > **com'bustibly** *adv*

combustion (kəm'bʌstʃən) *n* **1** the process of burning **2** any process in which a substance reacts with oxygen to produce a significant rise in temperature and the emission of light **3** a chemical process in which two compounds, such as sodium and chlorine, react together to produce heat and light **4** a process in which a compound reacts slowly with oxygen to produce little heat and no light [c15 from Old French, from Latin *combūrere* to burn up, from *com-* (intensive) + *ūrere* to burn] > **com'bustive** *n, adj*

combustion chamber *n* an enclosed space in which combustion takes place, such as the space above the piston in the cylinder head of an internal-combustion engine or the chambers in a gas turbine or rocket engine in which fuel and oxidant burn

combustor (kəm'bʌstə) *n* the combustion system of a jet engine or ramjet, comprising the combustion chamber, the fuel injection apparatus, and the igniter

comdg *military abbreviation for* commanding

Comdr *military abbreviation for* Commander

Comdt *military abbreviation for* Commandant

come (kʌm) *vb* **comes, coming, came, come** (*mainly intr*) **1** to move towards a specified person or place: *come to my desk* **2** to arrive by movement or by making progress **3** to become perceptible: *light came into the sky* **4** to occur in the course of time: *Christmas comes but once a year* **5** to exist or occur at a specific point in a series: *your turn comes next* **6** to happen as a result: *no good will come of this* **7** to originate or be derived: *good may come of evil* **8** to occur to the mind: *the truth suddenly came to me* **9** to extend or reach: *she comes up to my shoulder* **10** to be produced or offered: *that dress comes in red only* **11** to arrive at or be brought into a particular state or condition: *you will soon come to grief; the new timetable comes into effect on Monday* **12** (foll by *from*) to be or have been a resident or native (of): *I come from London* **13** to become: *your wishes will come true* **14** (*tr*; *takes an infinitive*) to be given awareness: *I came to realize its enormous value* **15** (of grain) to germinate **16** *slang* to have an orgasm **17** (*tr*) *Brit informal* to play the part of: *don't come the fine gentleman with me* **18** (*tr*) *Brit informal* to cause or produce: *don't come that nonsense again* **19** (*subjunctive use*) when (a specified time or event has arrived or begun): *she'll be sixteen come Sunday; come the revolution, you'll be the first to go* **20** **as...as they come** the most characteristic example of a class or type **21** **come again?** *informal* what did you say? **22** **come and** (*imperative or dependent imperative*) to move towards a particular person or thing or accompany a person with some specified purpose: *come and see what I've* found **23** come clean *informal* to make a revelation or confession **24** come good *informal* to recover and perform well after a bad start or setback **25** come it *slang* **a** to pretend; act a part **b** to exaggerate **c** (often foll by *over*) to try to impose (upon) **d** to divulge a secret; inform the police **26** come to light to be revealed **27** come to light with *Austral and NZ informal* to find or produce **28** come to pass *archaic* to take place **29** how come? *informal* what is the reason that? ▷ *interj* **30** an exclamation expressing annoyance, irritation, etc: *come now!; come come!* ▷ *n* **31** *taboo slang* semen ▷ See also **come about, come across, come along, come at, come away, comeback, come between, come by, comedown, come forward, come from, come in, come into, come of, come off, come on, come out, come over, come round, come through, come to, come up, come upon** [Old English *cuman;* related to Old Norse *koma*, Gothic *qiman*, Old High German *queman* to come, Sanskrit *gámati* he goes]

come about *vb (intr, adverb)* **1** to take place; happen **2** *nautical* to change tacks

come across *vb (intr)* **1** *(preposition)* to meet or find by accident **2** *(adverb)* (of a person or his or her words) to communicate the intended meaning or impression **3** (often foll by *with*) to provide what is expected

come-all-ye (kəˈmɔːljə, -jiː) *n* a street ballad or folk song [C19 from the common opening words *come all ye (young maidens, loyal heroes, etc)...*]

come along *vb* **1** *(intr, adverb)* to progress: *how's your French coming along?* **2** come along! **a** hurry up! **b** make an effort! ▷ *n* **come-along 3** *US and Canadian informal* a hand tool consisting of a ratchet lever, cable, and pulleys, used for moving heavy loads by hand or for tightening wire

come at *vb (intr, preposition)* **1** to discover or reach (facts, the truth, etc) **2** to attack (a person): *he came at me with an axe* **3** *Austral slang* to agree to do (something) **4** *(usually used with a negative) Austral slang* to stomach, tolerate: *I couldn't come at it* **5** *Austral slang* to presume; impose: *what are you coming at?*

come-at-able *adj* an informal expression for **accessible**

come away *vb (intr, adverb)* **1** to become detached **2** (foll by *with*) to leave (with)

comeback (ˈkʌmˌbæk) *n informal* **1** a return to a former position, status, etc **2** a return or response, esp recriminatory **3** a quick reply; retort ▷ *vb* **come back** *(intr, adverb)* **4** to return **5** to become fashionable again **6** to reply after a period of consideration: *I'll come back to you on that next week* **7** *US and Canadian* to argue back; retort **8** come back to (someone) (of something forgotten) to return to (someone's) memory

come between *vb (intr, preposition)* to cause the estrangement or separation of (two people): *nothing could come between the two lovers*

come by *vb (intr, preposition)* to find or obtain (a thing), esp accidentally: *do you ever come by any old books?*

Comecon (ˈkɒmɪˌkɒn) *n* (formerly) an association of Soviet-oriented Communist nations, founded in 1949 to coordinate economic development, etc; it was disbanded in 1991 when free-market policies were adopted by its members. Also: **CMEA** [C20 *Co(uncil for) M(utual) Econ(omic Assistance)*]

comedian (kəˈmiːdɪən) *n* **1** an entertainer who specializes in jokes, comic skits, etc **2** an actor in comedy **3** an amusing or entertaining person: sometimes used ironically

comedic (kəˈmiːdɪk) *adj* of or relating to comedy

Comédie Française *French* (kɔmedi frɑ̃sɛz) *n* the French national theatre, founded in Paris in 1680

comedienne (kəˌmiːdɪˈɛn) *n* a female comedian

comedo (ˈkɒmɪˌdəʊ) *n, pl* comedos *or* comedones (ˌkɒmɪˈdəʊniːz) *pathol* the technical name for **blackhead** [C19 from New Latin, from Latin: glutton, from *comedere* to eat up, from *com-* (intensive) + *edere* to eat]

comedown (ˈkʌmˌdaʊn) *n* **1** a decline in position, status, or prosperity **2** *informal* a disappointment **3** *slang* a depressed or unexcited state ▷ *vb* **come down** *(intr, adverb)* **4** to come to a place regarded as lower **5** to lose status, wealth, etc (esp in the phrase **to come down in the world**) **6** to reach a decision: *the report came down in favour of a pay increase* **7** (often foll by *to*) to be handed down or acquired by tradition or inheritance **8** *Brit* to leave college or university **9** (foll by *with*) to succumb (to illness or disease) **10** (foll by *on*) to rebuke or criticize harshly **11** (foll by *to*) to amount in essence (to): *it comes down to two choices* **12** *slang* to lose the effects of a drug and return to a normal or more normal state **13** *Austral informal* (of a river) to flow in flood

comedy (ˈkɒmɪdɪ) *n, pl* -dies **1** a dramatic or other work of light and amusing character **2** the genre of drama represented by works of this type **3** (in classical literature) a play in which the main characters and motive triumph over adversity **4** the humorous aspect of life or of events **5** an amusing event or sequence of events **6** humour or comic style: *the comedy of Chaplin* [C14 from Old French *comédie*, from Latin *cōmoedia*, from Greek *kōmōidia*, from *kōmos* village festival + *aeidein* to sing]

comedy of manners *n* **1** a comedy dealing with the way of life and foibles of a social group **2** the genre represented by works of this type

come forward *vb (intr, adverb)* **1** to offer one's services; volunteer **2** to present oneself

come from *vb (intr, preposition)* **1** to be or have been a resident or native (of): *Ernst comes from Geneva* **2** to originate from or derive from: *chocolate comes from the cacao tree; the word filibuster comes from the Dutch word for pirate* **3** where is someone is coming from *informal* the reasons for someone's behaviour, opinions, or comments: *I can understand where you're coming from*

come-hither *adj (usually prenominal) informal* alluring; seductive: *a come-hither look*

come in *vb (intr, mainly adverb)* **1** to enter, used in the imperative when admitting a person **2** to prove to be: *it came in useful* **3** to become fashionable or seasonable **4** *cricket* to begin an innings **5** *sport* to finish a race (in a certain position) **6** (of a politician or political party) to win an election **7** *radio, television* to be received: *news is coming in of a big fire in Glasgow* **8** (of money) to be received as income **9** to play a role; advance one's interests: *where do I come in?* **10** (foll by *for*) to be the object of: *the Chancellor came in for a lot of criticism in the Commons*

come into *vb (intr, preposition)* **1** to enter **2** to inherit **3** come into one's own **a** to become fulfilled: *she really came into her own when she got divorced* **b** to receive what is due to one

comely (ˈkʌmlɪ) *adj* -lier, -liest good-looking; attractive [Old English *cȳmlīc* beautiful; related to Old High German *cūmi* frail, Middle High German *komlīche* suitably] > ˈ**comeliness** *n*

come of *vb (intr, preposition)* **1** to be descended from **2** to result from: *nothing came of his experiments*

come off *vb (intr, mainly adverb)* **1** *(also preposition)* to fall (from), losing one's balance **2** to become detached or be capable of being detached **3** *(preposition)* to be removed from (a price, tax, etc): *will anything come off income tax in the budget?* **4** *(copula)* to emerge from or as if from a trial or contest: *he came off the winner* **5** *informal* to take place or happen **6** *informal* to have the intended effect; succeed: *his jokes did not come off* **7** *slang* to have an orgasm **8** come off it! *informal* stop trying to fool me!

come on *vb (intr, mainly adverb)* **1** (of power, a water supply, etc) to become available; start running or functioning **2** to make or show progress; develop: *my plants are coming on nicely* **3** to advance, esp in battle **4** to begin: *she felt a cold coming on; a new bowler has come on* **5** *theatre* to make an entrance on stage **6** to be considered, esp in a court of law **7** *(preposition)* See **come upon 8** come on! **a** hurry up! **b** cheer up! pull yourself together! **c** make an effort! **d** don't exaggerate! stick to the facts! **9** to attempt to give a specified impression: *he came on like a hard man* **10** come on strong to make a forceful or exaggerated impression **11** come on to *informal* to make sexual advances to ▷ *n* **come-on 12** *informal* anything that serves as a lure or enticement

come out *vb (intr, adverb)* **1** to be made public or revealed: *the news of her death came out last week* **2** to make a debut in society or on stage **3** **a** Also: come out of the closet to declare openly that one is a homosexual **b** to reveal or declare any habit or practice formerly concealed **4** *chiefly Brit* to go on strike **5** to declare oneself: *the government came out in favour of scrapping the project* **6** to be shown visibly or clearly: *you came out very well in the photos* **7** to yield a satisfactory solution: *these sums just won't come out* **8** to be published: *the paper comes out on Fridays* **9** (foll by *in*) to become covered with: *you're coming out in spots* **10** (foll by *with*) to speak or declare openly: *you can rely on him to come out with the facts*

come over *vb (intr)* **1** *(adverb)* (of a person or his words) to communicate the intended meaning or impression: *he came over very well* **2** *(adverb)* to change allegiances: *some people came over to our side in the war* **3** *informal* to undergo or feel a particular sensation: *I came over funny* ▷ *n* **comeover 4** (in the Isle of Man) a person who has come over from the mainland of Britain to settle

comer (ˈkʌmə) *n* **1** *(in combination)* a person who comes: *all-comers; newcomers* **2** *informal* a potential success

come round *or* **around** *vb (intr, adverb)* **1** to be restored to life or consciousness **2** to change or modify one's mind or opinion

comestible (kəˈmɛstɪbᵊl) *n* **1** *(usually plural)* food ▷ *adj* **2** a rare word for **edible** [C15 from Late Latin *comestibilis*, from *comedere* to eat up; see COMEDO]

comet (ˈkɒmɪt) *n* a celestial body that travels around the sun, usually in a highly elliptical orbit: thought to consist of a solid frozen nucleus part of which vaporizes on approaching the sun to form a gaseous luminous coma and a long luminous tail [C13 from Old French *comète*, from Latin *comēta*, from Greek *komētēs* long-haired, from *komē* hair] > ˈ**cometary** *or* **cometic** (kɒˈmɛtɪk) *adj*

come through *vb (intr)* **1** *(adverb)* to emerge successfully **2** *(preposition)* to survive (an illness, setback, etc)

come to *vb (intr)* **1** *(adverb or prep. and reflexive)* to regain consciousness or return to one's normal state **2** *(adverb) nautical* to slow a vessel or bring her to a stop **3** *(preposition)* to amount to (a sum of money): *your bill comes to four pounds* **4** *(preposition)* to arrive at (a certain state): *what is the world coming to?*

come up *vb (intr, adverb)* **1** to come to a place regarded as higher **2** (of the sun) to rise **3** to begin: *a wind came up* **4** to be regurgitated or vomited **5** to present itself or be discussed: *that question will come up again* **6** *Brit* to begin a term, esp one's first term, at a college or university **7** to appear from out of the ground: *my beans have come up early this year* **8** *informal* to win: *have your premium bonds ever come up?* **9** come up against to be faced with; come into conflict or competition with **10** come up to to equal or meet a standard: *that just doesn't come up to scratch* **11** come up with to produce or find: *she always comes up with the right answer*

come upon *vb (intr, preposition)* to meet or encounter unexpectedly: *I came upon an old friend in the street today*

comeuppance (ˌkʌmˈʌpəns) *n informal* just retribution [C19 from *come up* (in the sense: to appear before a judge or court for judgment)]

comfit (ˈkʌmfɪt, ˈkɒm-) *n* a sugar-coated sweet containing a nut or seed [C15 from Old French, from Latin *confectum* something prepared, from *conficere* to produce; see CONFECT]

comfort (ˈkʌmfət) *n* **1** a state of ease or well-being **2** relief from affliction, grief, etc **3** a

C

person, thing, or event that brings solace or ease **4** *obsolete* support **5** (*usually plural*) something that affords physical ease and relaxation ▷ *vb* (*tr*) **6** to ease the pain of; soothe; cheer **7** to bring physical ease to [c13 from Old French *confort*, from Late Latin *confortāre* to strengthen very much, from Latin *con-* (intensive) + *fortis* strong] > 'comforting *adj* > 'comfortingly *adv* > 'comfortless *adj* > 'comfortlessly *adv* > 'comfortlessness *n*

comfortable ('kʌmftəbªl, 'kʌmfətəbªl) *adj* **1** giving comfort or physical relief **2** at ease **3** free from affliction or pain **4** (of a person or situation) relaxing **5** *informal* having adequate income **6** *informal* (of income) adequate to provide comfort > 'comfortableness *n* > 'comfortably *adv*

comforter ('kʌmfətə) *n* **1** a person or thing that comforts **2** *chiefly Brit* a woollen scarf **3** a baby's dummy **4** *US* a quilted bed covering

Comforter ('kʌmfətə) *n Christianity* an epithet of the Holy Spirit [c14 translation of Latin *consolātor*, representing Greek *paraklētos*; see PARACLETE]

comfort food *n* food that is enjoyable to eat and makes the eater feel better emotionally

comfort station *n US* a public lavatory and rest room

comfort stop *n informal* a short break on a journey to allow travellers to go to the toilet

comfort zone *n* a situation or position in which a person feels secure, comfortable, or in control: *encouraging people to work outside their comfort zone*

comfrey ('kʌmfrɪ) *n* any hairy Eurasian boraginaceous plant of the genus *Symphytum*, having blue, purplish-pink, or white flowers [c15 from Old French *cunfirie*, from Latin *conferva* water plant; see CONFERVA]

comfy ('kʌmfɪ) *adj* -fier, -fiest *informal* short for **comfortable**

comic ('kɒmɪk) *adj* **1** of, relating to, characterized by, or characteristic of comedy **2** (*prenominal*) acting in, writing, or composing comedy: *a comic writer* **3** humorous; funny ▷ *n* **4** a person who is comic, esp a comic actor; comedian **5** a book or magazine containing comic strips **6** (*usually plural*) *chiefly US and Canadian* comic strips in newspapers, etc [c16 from Latin *cōmicus*, from Greek *kōmikos* relating to COMEDY]

comical ('kɒmɪkªl) *adj* **1** causing laughter **2** ludicrous; laughable > 'comically *adv* > 'comicalness *n*

comic opera *n* a play largely set to music, employing comic effects or situations. See also **opéra bouffe, opera buffa**

comic strip *n* a sequence of drawings in a newspaper, magazine, etc, relating a humorous story or an adventure. Also called: **strip cartoon**

Cominform ('kɒmɪnˌfɔːm) *n* short for **Communist Information Bureau**: established 1947 to exchange information among nine European Communist parties and coordinate their activities; dissolved in 1956

coming ('kʌmɪŋ) *adj* **1** (*prenominal*) (of time, events, etc) approaching or next: *this coming Thursday* **2** promising (esp in the phrase **up and coming**) **3** of future importance: *this is the coming thing* **4** **coming up!** *informal* an expression used to announce that a meal is about to be served **5** **have it coming to one** *informal* to deserve what one is about to suffer **6** **not know whether one is coming or going** to be totally confused ▷ *n* **7** arrival or approach **8** (*often capital*) *Christianity* the return of Christ in glory. See also **Second Coming**

Comintern or **Komintern** ('kɒmɪnˌtɜːn) *n* short for **Communist International**: an international Communist organization founded by Lenin in Moscow in 1919 and dissolved in 1943; it degenerated under Stalin into an instrument of Soviet politics. Also called: **Third International**

comitia (kə'mɪʃɪə) *n* an ancient Roman assembly that elected officials and exercised judicial and legislative authority [c17 from Latin *comitium* assembly, from *com-* together + *īre* to go] > **comitial** (kə'mɪʃəl) *adj*

comity ('kɒmɪtɪ) *n, pl* -ties **1** mutual civility; courtesy **2** short for **comity of nations 3** the policy whereby one religious denomination refrains from proselytizing the members of another [c16 from Latin *cōmitās*, from *cōmis* affable, obliging, of uncertain origin]

comity of nations *n* the friendly recognition accorded by one nation to the laws and usages of another

comma ('kɒmə) *n* **1** the punctuation mark, indicating a slight pause in the spoken sentence and used where there is a listing of items or to separate a nonrestrictive clause or phrase from a main clause **2** *music* a minute interval **3** short for **comma butterfly** [c16 from Latin, from Greek *komma* clause, from *kopteinto* cut]

comma bacillus *n* a comma-shaped bacterium, *Vibrio comma*, that causes cholera in man: family *Spirillaceae*

comma butterfly *n* an orange-brown European vanessid butterfly, *Polygonia c-album*, with a white comma-shaped mark on the underside of each hind wing

command (kə'mɑːnd) *vb* **1** (when *tr*, may take a clause as object or an infinitive) to order, require, or compel **2** to have or be in control or authority over (a person, situation, etc) **3** (*tr*) to have knowledge or use of: *he commands the language* **4** (*tr*) to receive as due or because of merit: *his nature commands respect* **5** to dominate (a view, etc) as from a height ▷ *n* **6** an order; mandate **7** the act of commanding **8** the power or right to command **9** the exercise of the power to command **10** ability or knowledge; control: *a command of French* **11** *chiefly military* the jurisdiction of a commander **12** a military unit or units commanding a specific area or function, as in the RAF **13** *Brit* **a** an invitation from the monarch **b** (*as modifier*): *a command performance* **14** *computing* a word or phrase that can be selected from a menu or typed after a prompt in order to carry out an action [c13 from Old French *commander*, from Latin *com-* (intensive) + *mandāre* to entrust, enjoin, command]

Command (kə'mɑːnd) *n* any of the three main branches of the Canadian military forces: *Air Command*

commandant ('kɒmənˌdænt, -ˌdɑːnt) *n* an officer commanding a place, group, or establishment

command economy *n* an economy in which business activities and the allocation of resources are determined by government order rather than market forces. Also called: **planned economy**

commandeer (ˌkɒmən'dɪə) *vb* (*tr*) **1** to seize for public or military use **2** to seize arbitrarily [c19 from Afrikaans *kommandeer*, from French *commander* to COMMAND]

commander (kə'mɑːndə) *n* **1** an officer in command of a military formation or operation **2** a naval commissioned rank junior to captain but senior to lieutenant commander **3** the second in command of larger British warships **4** someone who holds authority **5** a high-ranking member of some knightly or fraternal orders **6** an officer responsible for a district of the Metropolitan Police in London **7** *history* the administrator of a house, priory, or landed estate of a medieval religious order > com'manderˌship *n*

commander in chief *n, pl* commanders in chief **1** the officer holding supreme command of the forces in an area or operation **2** the officer holding command of a major subdivision of one military service

command guidance *n* a method of controlling a missile during flight by transmitting information to it

commanding (kə'mɑːndɪŋ) *adj* (*usually prenominal*) **1** being in command **2** having the air of authority: *a commanding voice* **3** (of a position, situation, etc) exerting control **4** (of a height, viewpoint, etc) overlooking; advantageous > com'mandingly *adv*

commanding officer *n* an officer in command of a military unit

command language *n computing* the language used to access a computer system

commandment (kə'mɑːndmənt) *n* **1** a divine command, esp one of the Ten Commandments of the Old Testament **2** *literary* any command

command module *n* the cone-shaped module used as the living quarters in an Apollo spacecraft and functioning as the splashdown vehicle

commando (kə'mɑːndəʊ) *n, pl* -dos or -does **1 a** an amphibious military unit trained for raiding **b** a member of such a unit **2** the basic unit of the Royal Marine Corps **3** (originally) an armed force raised by Boers during the Boer War **4** (*modifier*) denoting or relating to a commando or force of commandos: *a commando raid; a commando unit* ▷ *adv* **5** **go commando** *informal* to wear no underpants [c19 from Afrikaans *kommando*, from Dutch *commando* command, from French *commander* to COMMAND]

commando operation *n surgery* a major operation for treatment of cancer of the head and neck, involving removal of many facial structures and subsequent surgical reconstruction

command paper *n* (in Britain) a government document that is presented to Parliament, in theory by royal command. See also **green paper, white paper**

command performance *n* a performance of a play, opera, etc, at the request of a ruler or of royalty

command post *n military* the position from which a unit commander and his staff exercise command

comm badge *n* a small combined radio transmitter and receiver, carried around by one person, esp military personnel, in the form of a badge worn on the chest [c21 from *communications*]

commeasure (kə'mɛʒə) *vb* (*tr*) to coincide with in degree, extent, quality, etc > com'measurable *adj*

commedia dell'arte (*Italian* kɔm'meːdia del'arte) *n* a form of popular comedy developed in Italy during the 16th to 18th centuries, with stock characters such as Punchinello, Harlequin, and Columbine, in situations improvised from a plot outline [Italian, literally: comedy of art]

comme il faut *French* (kɔm il fo) correct or correctly

commemorate (kə'mɛməˌreɪt) *vb* (*tr*) to honour or keep alive the memory of [c16 from Latin *commemorāre* be mindful of, from *com-* (intensive) + *memorāre* to remind, from *memor* mindful] > com'memorative or com'memoratory *adj* > com'memoratively *adv* > com'memoˌrator *n*

commemoration (kəˌmɛmə'reɪʃən) *n* **1** the act of or an instance of commemorating **2** a ceremony or service in memory of a person or event > comˌmemo'rational *adj*

commence (kə'mɛns) *vb* to start or begin; come or cause to come into being, appear, etc [c14 from Old French *comencer*, from Vulgar Latin *cominitiāre* (unattested), from Latin *com-* (intensive) + *initiāre* to begin, from *initium* a beginning] > com'mencer *n*

commencement (kə'mɛnsmənt) *n* **1** the beginning; start **2 a** *US and Canadian* a ceremony for the presentation of awards at secondary schools **b** *US* a ceremony for the conferment of academic degrees

commend (kə'mɛnd) *vb* (*tr*) **1** to present or represent as being worthy of regard, confidence, kindness, etc; recommend **2** to give in charge; entrust **3** to express a good opinion of; praise **4** to give the regards of: *commend me to your aunt* [c14 from Latin *commendāre* to commit to someone's care, from *com-* (intensive) + *mandāre* to entrust] > com'mendable *adj* > com'mendableness *n* > com'mendably *adv* > com'mendatory *adj*

commendam (kə'mɛndæm) *n* **1** the temporary holding of an ecclesiastical benefice **2** a benefice so held [c16 from Medieval Latin phrase *dare in commendam* to give in trust, from *commenda* trust, back formation from Latin *commendāre* to entrust, COMMEND]

commendation (ˌkɒmɛnˈdeɪʃən) *n* **1** the act or an instance of commending; praise **2** an award

commensal (kəˈmɛnsəl) *adj* **1** (of two different species of plant or animal) living in close association, such that one species benefits without harming the other **2** *rare* of or relating to eating together, esp at the same table: *commensal pleasures* ▷ *n* **3** a commensal plant or animal **4** *rare* a companion at table [c14 from Medieval Latin *commensālis*, from Latin *com-* together + *mensa* table] > comˈmensalism *n* > commensality (ˌkɒmɛnˈsælɪtɪ) *n* > comˈmensally *adv*

commensurable (kəˈmɛnsərəbəl, -ʃə-) *adj* **1** *maths* **a** having a common factor **b** having units of the same dimensions and being related by whole numbers: *hours and minutes are commensurable* **2** well-proportioned; proportionate > comˌmensuraˈbility *n* > comˈmensurably *adv*

commensurate (kəˈmɛnsərɪt, -ʃə-) *adj* **1** having the same extent or duration **2** corresponding in degree, amount, or size; proportionate **3** able to be measured by a common standard; commensurable [c17 from Late Latin *commēnsūrātus*, from Latin *com-* same + *mēnsūrāre* to MEASURE] > comˈmensurately *adv* > comˈmensurateness *n* > commensuration (kəˌmɛnsəˈreɪʃən, -ʃə-) *n*

comment (ˈkɒmɛnt) *n* **1** a remark, criticism, or observation **2** talk or gossip **3** a note explaining or criticizing a passage in a text **4** explanatory or critical matter added to a text ▷ *vb* **5** (when *intr*, often foll by *on*; when *tr*, takes a clause as object) to remark or express an opinion **6** (*intr*) to write notes explaining or criticizing a text [c15 from Latin *commentum* invention, from *comminiscī* to contrive, related to *mens* mind] > ˈcommenter *n*

commentariat (ˌkɒmənˈtɛərɪæt) *n* the journalists and broadcasters who analyse and comment on current affairs [c20 from COMMENTATOR + PROLETARIAT]

commentary (ˈkɒməntərɪ, -trɪ) *n, pl* -taries **1** an explanatory series of notes or comments **2** a spoken accompaniment to a broadcast, film, etc, esp of a sporting event **3** an explanatory essay or treatise on a text **4** (*usually plural*) a personal record of events or facts: *the commentaries of Caesar* > commentarial (ˌkɒmənˈtɛərɪəl) *adj*

commentate (ˈkɒmənˌteɪt) *vb* **1** (*intr*) to serve as a commentator **2** (*tr*) *US* to make a commentary on (a text, event, etc)

USAGE The verb *commentate*, derived from *commentator*, is sometimes used as a synonym for *comment on* or *provide a commentary for*. It is not yet fully accepted as standard, though widespread in sports reporting and journalism

commentator (ˈkɒmənˌteɪtə) *n* **1** a person who provides a spoken commentary for a broadcast, film, etc, esp of a sporting event **2** a person who writes notes on a text, event, etc

commerce (ˈkɒmɜːs) *n* **1** the activity embracing all forms of the purchase and sale of goods and services **2** social relations and exchange, esp of opinions, attitudes, etc [c16 from Latin *commercium* trade, from *commercārī*, from *mercārī* to trade, from *merx* merchandise]

commercial (kəˈmɜːʃəl) *adj* **1** of, connected with, or engaged in commerce; mercantile **2** sponsored or paid for by an advertiser: *commercial television* **3** having profit as the main aim: *commercial music* **4** (of goods, chemicals, etc) of unrefined quality or presentation and produced in bulk for use in industry ▷ *n* **5** a commercially sponsored advertisement on radio or television > commerciality (kəˌmɜːʃɪˈælɪtɪ) *n* > comˈmercially *adv*

commercial art *n* graphic art for commercial uses such as advertising, packaging, etc > commercial artist *n*

commercial bank *n* a bank primarily engaged in making short-term loans from funds deposited in current accounts

commercial break *n* an interruption in a radio or television programme for the broadcasting of advertisements

commercial college *n* a college providing tuition in commercial skills, such as shorthand and book-keeping

commercialism (kəˈmɜːʃəˌlɪzəm) *n* **1** the spirit, principles, or procedure of commerce **2** exclusive or inappropriate emphasis on profit > comˈmercialist *n* > comˌmerciaˈlistic *adj*

commercialize *or* **commercialise** (kəˈmɜːʃəˌlaɪz) *vb* (*tr*) **1** to make commercial in aim, methods, or character **2** to exploit for profit, esp at the expense of quality > comˌmercialiˈzation *or* comˌmercialiˈsation *n*

commercial paper *n* a short-term negotiable document, such as a bill of exchange, promissory note, etc, calling for the transference of a specified sum of money at a designated date

commercial traveller *n* another name for a **travelling salesman**

commercial vehicle *n* a vehicle for carrying goods or (less commonly) passengers

commère (ˈkɒmɛə; *French* kɔmɛr) *n* a female compere [French, literally: godmother, from COM- + *mère* mother; see COMPERE]

commie *or* **commy** (ˈkɒmɪ) *n, pl* -mies, *adj informal and derogatory* short for **communist**

commination (ˌkɒmɪˈneɪʃən) *n* **1** the act or an instance of threatening punishment or vengeance **2** *Church of England* a recital of prayers, including a list of God's judgments against sinners, in the office for Ash Wednesday [c15 from Latin *comminātiō*, from *comminārī* to menace, from *com-* (intensive) + *minārī* to threaten] > comminatory (ˈkɒmɪnətərɪ, -trɪ) *adj*

commingle (kɒˈmɪŋgəl) *vb* to mix or be mixed; blend

comminute (ˈkɒmɪˌnjuːt) *vb* **1** to break (a bone) into several small fragments **2** to divide (property) into small lots **3** (*tr*) to pulverize [c17 from Latin *comminuere*, from *com-* (intensive) + *minuere* to reduce; related to MINOR] > ˌcommiˈnution *n*

comminuted fracture *n* a fracture in which the bone is splintered or fragmented

commis (ˈkɒmɪs, ˈkɒmɪ) *n, pl* -mis **1** an agent or deputy ▷ *adj* **2** (of a waiter or chef) apprentice [C16 (meaning: deputy): from French, from *commettre* to employ, COMMIT]

commiserate (kəˈmɪzəˌreɪt) *vb* (when *intr*, usually foll by *with*) to feel or express sympathy or compassion (for) [c17 from Latin *commiserārī*, from *com-* together + *miserārī* to bewail, pity, from *miser* wretched] > comˈmiserable *adj* > comˌmiseˈration *n* > comˈmiserative *adj* > comˈmiseratively *adv* > comˈmiserˌator *n*

commissaire (ˌkɒmɪˈsɛə) *n* (in professional cycle racing) a referee who travels in an open-topped car with the riders to witness any infringement of the rules [from French: see COMMISSARY]

commissar (ˈkɒmɪˌsɑː, ˌkɒmɪˈsɑː) *n* (in the former Soviet Union) **1** Also called: **political commissar** an official of the Communist Party responsible for political education, esp in a military unit **2** Also called: **People's Commissar** (before 1946) the head of a government department. Now called: **minister** [c20 from Russian *kommissar*, from German, from Medieval Latin *commissārius* COMMISSARY]

commissariat (ˌkɒmɪˈsɛərɪət) *n* **1** (in the former Soviet Union) a government department before 1946. Now called: **ministry** **2 a** a military department in charge of food supplies, equipment, etc **b** the offices of such a department **3** food supplies [c17 from New Latin *commissāriātus*, from Medieval Latin *commissārius* COMMISSARY]

commissary (ˈkɒmɪsərɪ) *n, pl* -saries **1** *US* a shop

supplying food or equipment, as in a military camp **2** *US army* an officer responsible for supplies and food **3** *US* a snack bar or restaurant in a film studio **4** a representative or deputy, esp an official representative of a bishop [c14 from Medieval Latin *commissārius* official in charge, from Latin *committere* to entrust, COMMIT] > commissarial (ˌkɒmɪˈsɛərɪəl) *adj* > ˈcommissaryˌship *n*

commission (kəˈmɪʃən) *n* **1** a duty or task committed to a person or group to perform **2** authority to undertake or perform certain duties or functions **3** a document granting such authority **4** *military* **a** a document conferring a rank on an officer **b** the rank or authority thereby granted **5** a group of people charged with certain duties: *a commission of inquiry* **6** a government agency or board empowered to exercise administrative, judicial, or legislative authority. See also **Royal Commission 7 a** the authority given to a person or organization to act as an agent to a principal in commercial transactions **b** the fee allotted to an agent for services rendered **8** the state of being charged with specific duties or responsibilities **9** the act of committing a sin, crime, etc **10** something, esp a sin, crime, etc, that is committed **11** good working condition or (esp of a ship) active service (esp in the phrases **in** *or* **into commission, out of commission**) **12** *US* the head of a department of municipal government ▷ *vb* **13** (*tr*) to grant authority to; charge with a duty or task **14** (*tr*) *military* to confer a rank on or authorize an action by **15** (*tr*) to equip and test (a ship) for active service **16** to make or become operative or operable: *the plant is due to commission next year* **17** (*tr*) to place an order for (something): *to commission a portrait* [c14 from Old French, from Latin *commissiō* a bringing together, from *committere* to COMMIT] > comˈmissional *or* comˈmissionary *adj*

commissionaire (kəˌmɪʃəˈnɛə) *n chiefly Brit* a uniformed doorman at a hotel, theatre, etc [c18 from French, from COMMISSION]

commissioned officer *n* a military officer holding a commission, such as Second Lieutenant in the British Army, Acting Sub-Lieutenant in the Royal Navy, Pilot Officer in the Royal Air Force, and officers of all ranks senior to these

commissioner (kəˈmɪʃənə) *n* **1** a person authorized to perform certain tasks or endowed with certain powers **2** *government* **a** any of several types of civil servant **b** an ombudsman ▷ See also **Health Service Commissioner, Parliamentary Commissioner 3** a member of a commission > comˈmissionerˌship *n*

Commissioner for Local Administration *n* (in Britain) the official name for a local ombudsman who investigates personal complaints of maladministration by police, water, or local authorities, referred through a local-government councillor, and who can require the offending authority to state its intention to make redress

commissioner for oaths *n* a solicitor authorized to authenticate oaths on sworn statements

Commission for Racial Equality *n* (in Britain) a body of fourteen members appointed by the Home Secretary under the Race Relations Act 1976 to enforce the provisions of that Act. Abbreviation: **CRE**

commission plan *n* (in the US) a system of municipal government that combines legislative and executive authority in a commission of five or six elected members

commissure (ˈkɒmɪˌsjʊə) *n* **1** a band of tissue linking two parts or organs, such as the nervous tissue connecting the right and left sides of the brain in vertebrates **2** any of various joints between parts, as between the carpels, leaf lobes, etc, of a plant [c15 from Latin *commissūra* a joining together, from *committere* COMMIT] > commissural (kəˈmɪsjʊrəl, ˌkɒmɪˈsjʊərəl) *adj*

commit (kəˈmɪt) *vb* -mits, -mitting, -mitted (*tr*) **1**

to hand over, as for safekeeping; charge; entrust: *to commit a child to the care of its aunt* **2 commit to memory** to learn by heart; memorize **3** to confine officially or take into custody: *to commit someone to prison* **4** (*usually passive*) to pledge or align (oneself), as to a particular cause, action, or attitude: *a committed radical* **5** to order (forces) into action **6** to perform (a crime, error, etc); do; perpetrate **7** to surrender, esp for destruction: *she committed the letter to the fire* **8** to refer (a bill, etc) to a committee of a legislature [c14 from Latin *committere* to join, from *com-* together + *mittere* to put, send] > **com'mittable** *adj* > **com'mitter** *n*

commitment (kə'mɪtmənt) *n* **1** the act of committing or pledging **2** the state of being committed or pledged **3** an obligation, promise, etc that restricts one's freedom of action **4** the referral of a bill to a committee or legislature **5** Also called (esp formerly): **mittimus** *law* a written order of a court directing that a person be imprisoned **6** the official consignment of a person to a mental hospital or prison **7** commission or perpetration, esp of a crime **8** a future financial obligation or contingent liability ▷ Also called (esp for senses 5, 6): **committal** (kə'mɪtəl)

commitment fee *n* a charge made by a bank, in addition to interest, to make a loan available to a potential borrower

committed facility *n* an agreement by a bank to provide a customer with funds up to a specified limit at a specified rate of interest

committee *n* **1** (kə'mɪtɪ) a group of people chosen or appointed to perform a specified service or function **2** (,kɒmɪ'tiː) (formerly) a person to whom the care of a mentally incompetent person or his property was entrusted by a court. See also **receiver** (sense 2) [c15 from *committen* to entrust + -EE]

committeeman (kə'mɪtɪmən, -,mæn) *n, pl* **-men** *chiefly US* a member of one or more committees > **com'mittee,woman** *fem n*

Committee of the Whole House *n* (in Britain) an informal sitting of the House of Commons to discuss and amend a bill

commix (kɒ'mɪks) *vb* a rare word for **mix** [c15 back formation from *commixt* mixed together; see MIX] > **com'mixture** *n*

commo ('kɒməʊ) *n, pl* **-mos,** *adj Austral slang* short for **communist**

commode (kə'məʊd) *n* **1** a piece of furniture, usually highly ornamented, containing drawers or shelves **2** a bedside table with a cabinet below for a chamber pot or washbasin **3** a movable piece of furniture, sometimes in the form of a chair, with a hinged flap concealing a chamber pot **4** a woman's high-tiered headdress of lace, worn in the late 17th century [c17 from French, from Latin *commodus* COMMODIOUS]

commodify (kə'mɒdɪ,faɪ) *vb* **-fies, -fying, -fied** (*tr*) to treatment (something) inappropriately as if it can be acquired or marketed like other commodities: *you can't commodify art* > **com,modifi'cation** *n*

commodious (kə'məʊdɪəs) *adj* **1** (of buildings, rooms, etc) large and roomy; spacious **2** *archaic* suitable; convenient [c15 from Medieval Latin *commodiōsus*, from Latin *commodus* convenient, from *com-* with + *modus* measure] > **com'modiously** *adv* > **com'modiousness** *n*

commoditize *or* **commoditise** (kə'mɒdɪ,taɪz) *vb* (*tr*) another term for **commodify**

commodity (kə'mɒdɪtɪ) *n, pl* **-ties 1** an article of commerce **2** something of use, advantage, or profit **3** *economics* an exchangeable unit of economic wealth, esp a primary product or raw material **4** *obsolete* **a** a quantity of goods **b** convenience or expediency [c14 from Old French *commodité*, from Latin *commoditās* suitability, benefit; see COMMODIOUS]

commodore ('kɒmə,dɔː) *n* **1** *Brit* a naval rank junior to rear admiral and senior to captain **2** the

senior captain of a shipping line **3** the officer in command of a convoy of merchant ships **4** the senior flag office of a yacht or boat club [c17 probably from Dutch *commandeur*, from French, from Old French *commander* to COMMAND]

common ('kɒmən) *adj* **1** belonging to or shared by two or more people: *common property* **2** belonging to or shared by members of one or more nations or communities; public: *a common culture* **3** of ordinary standard; average: *common decency* **4** prevailing; widespread: *common opinion* **5** widely known or frequently encountered; ordinary: *a common brand of soap* **6** widely known and notorious: *a common nuisance* **7** *derogatory* considered by the speaker to be low-class, vulgar, or coarse: *a common accent* **8** (*prenominal*) having no special distinction, rank, or status: *the common man* **9** *maths* **a** having a specified relationship with a group of numbers or quantities: *common denominator* **b** (of a tangent) tangential to two or more circles **10** *prosody* (of a syllable) able to be long or short, or (in nonquantitative verse) stressed or unstressed **11** *grammar* (in certain languages) denoting or belonging to a gender of nouns, esp one that includes both masculine and feminine referents: *Latin* sacerdos *is common* **12** *anatomy* **a** having branches: *the common carotid artery* **b** serving more than one function: *the common bile duct* **13** *Christianity* of or relating to the common of the Mass or divine office **14 common or garden** *informal* ordinary; unexceptional ▷ *n* **15** (*sometimes plural*) a tract of open public land, esp one now used as a recreation area **16** *law* the right to go onto someone else's property and remove natural products, as by pasturing cattle or fishing (esp in the phrase **right of common**) **17** *Christianity* **a** a form of the proper of the Mass used on festivals that have no special proper of their own **b** the ordinary of the Mass **18** *archaic* the ordinary people; the public, esp those undistinguished by rank or title **19 in common** mutually held or used with another or others ▷ See also **commons** [c13 from Old French *commun*, from Latin *commūnis* general, universal] > **'commonness** *n*

commonable ('kɒmənəb²l) *adj* **1** (of land) held in common **2** *English history* (esp of sheep and cattle) entitled to be pastured on common land

commonage ('kɒmənɪdʒ) *n* **1** *chiefly law* **a** the use of something, esp a pasture, in common with others **b** the right to such use **2** the state of being held in common **3** something held in common, such as land **4** another word for **commonalty** (sense 1)

Common Agricultural Policy *n* the full name for **CAP**

commonality (,kɒmə'nælɪtɪ) *n, pl* **-ties 1** the fact of being common to more than one individual; commonness **2** another word for **commonalty** (sense 1)

commonalty ('kɒmənəltɪ) *n, pl* **-ties 1** the ordinary people as distinct from those with authority, rank, or title, esp when considered as a political and social unit or estate of the realm. Compare **third estate 2** the members of an incorporated society [c13 from Old French *comunalte*, from *comunal* communal]

common carrier *n* a person or firm engaged in the business of transporting goods or passengers

common chord *n music* a chord consisting of the keynote, a major or minor third, and a perfect fifth: *the notes G, B, and D form the common chord of G major*

common cold *n* a mild viral infection of the upper respiratory tract, characterized by sneezing, coughing, watery eyes, nasal congestion, sore throat, etc

common denominator *n* **1** an integer exactly divisible by each denominator of a group of fractions: 1/3, 1/4, and 1/6 have a common denominator of 12 **2** a belief, attribute, etc, held in common by members of a class or group

common divisor *n* another name for **common factor**

Common Entrance *n* (in Britain) an entrance examination for a public school, usually taken at the age of 13

commoner ('kɒmənə) *n* **1** a person who does not belong to the nobility **2** a person who has a right in or over common land jointly with another or others **3** *Brit* a student at a university or other institution who is not on a scholarship

Common Era *n* another name for **Christian Era**

common factor *n* a number or quantity that is a factor of each member of a group of numbers or quantities: *5 is a common factor of 15 and 20.* Also called: common divisor

common fee *n* (in Australia) the agreed usual charge for any medical service, which determines the amount of reimbursement under the federal health scheme

common fraction *n* another name for **simple fraction**

common good *n* the part of the property of a Scottish burgh, in the form of land or funds, that is at the disposal of the community

common ground *n* an agreed basis, accepted by both or all parties, for identifying issues in an argument

commonhold ('kɒmən,həʊld) *n* a form of property tenure in which each flat in a multi-occupancy building is individually wholly owned and common areas are jointly owned

common knowledge *n* something widely or generally known

common law *n* **1** the body of law based on judicial decisions and custom, as distinct from statute law **2** the law of a state that is of general application, as distinct from regional customs **3 common-law** (*modifier*) denoting a marriage deemed to exist after a couple have cohabited for several years: *common-law marriage; common-law wife*

common logarithm *n* a logarithm to the base ten. Usually written log or $\log_{10}$. Compare **natural logarithm**

commonly ('kɒmənlɪ) *adv* **1** usually; ordinarily: *he was commonly known as Joe* **2** *derogatory* in a coarse or vulgar way: *she dresses commonly*

Common Market *n* **the** an informal name for the **European Economic Community** (now the European Community, part of the wider European Community) and its politics of greater economic cooperation between member states

common measure *n* **1** another term for **common time 2** the usual stanza form of a ballad, consisting of four iambic lines rhyming a b c b or a b a b

common metre *n* a stanza form, used esp for hymns, consisting of four lines, two of eight syllables alternating with two of six

common multiple *n* an integer or polynomial that is a multiple of each integer or polynomial in a group: *20 is a common multiple of 2, 4, 5, 10*

common noun *n grammar* a noun that refers to each member of a whole class sharing the features connoted by the noun, as for example *planet, orange,* and *drum.* Compare **proper noun**

commonplace ('kɒmən,pleɪs) *adj* **1** ordinary; everyday: *commonplace duties* **2** dull and obvious; trite: *commonplace prose* ▷ *n* **3** something dull and trite, esp a remark; platitude; truism **4** a passage in a book marked for inclusion in a commonplace book, etc **5** an ordinary or common thing [c16 translation of Latin *locus commūnis* argument of wide application, translation of Greek *koinos topos*] > **'common,placeness** *n*

commonplace book *n* a notebook in which quotations, poems, remarks, etc, that catch the owner's attention are entered

common pleas *n* short for **Court of Common Pleas**

common prayer *n* the liturgy of public services of the Church of England, esp Morning and Evening Prayer

common room *n chiefly Brit* a sitting room in schools, colleges, etc, for the relaxation of students or staff

commons ('kɒmənz) *n* **1** (*functioning as plural*) people not of noble birth viewed as forming a political order **2** (*functioning as plural*) the lower classes as contrasted to the ruling classes of society; the commonalty **3** (*functioning as singular*) *Brit* a building or hall for dining, recreation, etc, usually attached to a college **4** (*usually functioning as plural*) *Brit* food or rations (esp in the phrase **short commons**)

Commons ('kɒmənz) *n* the See **House of Commons**

common seal *n* the official seal of a corporate body

common sense *n* **1** plain ordinary good judgment; sound practical sense ▷ *adj* **common-sense** *also* common-sensical **2** inspired by or displaying sound practical sense

common stock *n* the US name for **ordinary shares**

common time *n music* a time signature indicating four crotchet beats to the bar; four-four time. Symbol: C

commonweal ('kɒmən,wiːl) *n archaic* **1** the good of the community **2** another name for **commonwealth**

commonwealth ('kɒmən,wɛlθ) *n* **1** the people of a state or nation viewed politically; body politic **2** a state or nation in which the people possess sovereignty; republic **3** the body politic organized for the general good **4** a group of persons united by some common interest **5** *obsolete* the general good; public welfare

Commonwealth ('kɒmən,wɛlθ) *n* the **1** Official name: **the Commonwealth of Nations** an association of sovereign states, almost all of which were at some time dependencies of the UK. All member states recognize the reigning British sovereign as **Head of the Commonwealth 2 a** the republic that existed in Britain from 1649 to 1660 **b** the part of this period up to 1653, when Cromwell became Protector **3** the official designation of Australia, four states of the US (Kentucky, Massachusetts, Pennsylvania, and Virginia), and Puerto Rico

Commonwealth Day *n* the anniversary of Queen Victoria's birth, May 24, celebrated (now on the second Monday in March) as a holiday in many parts of the Commonwealth. Former name: **Empire Day**

Commonwealth of Independent States *n* a loose organization of former Soviet republics, excluding the Baltic States, formed in 1991. Abbreviation: **CIS**

commotion (kə'məʊʃən) *n* **1** violent disturbance; upheaval **2** political insurrection; disorder **3** a confused noise; din [c15 from Latin *commōtiō*, from *commovēre* to throw into disorder, from *com-* (intensive) + *movēre* to MOVE] > com'motional *adj*

commove (kə'muːv) *vb* (*tr*) *rare* **1** to disturb; stir up **2** to agitate or excite emotionally

comms (kɒmz) *pl n informal* communications

communal ('kɒmjʊnˀl) *adj* **1** belonging or relating to a community as a whole **2** relating to different groups within a society: *communal strife* **3** of or relating to a commune or a religious community > communality (,kɒmjʊ'nælɪtɪ) *n* > 'communally *adv*

communal aerial *or* **antenna** *n* a television or radio receiving aerial from which received signals are distributed by cable to several outlets

communalism ('kɒmjʊnə,lɪzəm) *n* **1** a system or theory of government in which the state is seen as a loose federation of self-governing communities **2** an electoral system in which ethnic groups vote separately for their own representatives **3** loyalty to the interests of one's own ethnic group rather than to society as a whole **4** the practice or advocacy of communal living or ownership > 'communalist *n*

> ,communa'listic *adj*

communalize *or* **communalise** ('kɒmjʊnə,laɪz) *vb* (*tr*) to render (something) the property of a commune or community > ,communali'zation *or* ,communali'sation *n* > 'communal,izer *or* 'communal,iser *n*

communard ('kɒmjʊ,nɑːd) *n* a member of a commune

Communard ('kɒmjʊ,nɑːd) *n* any person who participated in or supported the Paris Commune formed after the Franco-Prussian War in 1871 [c19 from French]

communautaire *French* (kɔmynotɛr) *adj* supporting the principles of the European Community (now the European Union) [literally: community (as modifier)]

commune[1] *vb* (kə'mjuːn) (*intr*; usually foll by *with*) **1** to talk or converse intimately **2** to experience strong emotion or spiritual feelings (for): *to commune with nature* ▷ *n* ('kɒmjuːn) **3** intimate conversation; exchange of thoughts; communion [c13 from Old French *comuner* to hold in common, from *comun* COMMON]

commune[2] (kə'mjuːn) *vb* (*intr*) *Christianity, chiefly US* to partake of Communion [c16 back formation from COMMUNION]

commune[3] ('kɒmjuːn) *n* **1** a group of families or individuals living together and sharing possessions and responsibilities **2** any small group of people having common interests or responsibilities **3** the smallest administrative unit in Belgium, France, Italy, and Switzerland, governed by a mayor and council **4** the government or inhabitants of a commune **5** a medieval town enjoying a large degree of autonomy [c18 from French, from Medieval Latin *commūnia*, from Latin: things held in common, from *commūnis* COMMON]

Commune ('kɒmjuːn) *n French history* **1** See **Paris Commune 2** a committee that governed Paris during the French Revolution and played a leading role in the Reign of Terror: suppressed 1794

communicable (kə'mjuːnɪkəbˀl) *adj* **1** capable of being communicated **2** (of a disease or its causative agent) capable of being passed on readily > com,munica'bility *or* com'municableness *n* > com'municably *adv*

communicant (kə'mjuːnɪkənt) *n* **1** *Christianity* a person who receives Communion **2** a person who communicates or informs ▷ *adj* **3** communicating

communicate (kə'mjuːnɪ,keɪt) *vb* **1** to impart (knowledge) or exchange (thoughts, feelings, or ideas) by speech, writing, gestures, etc **2** (*tr*; usually foll by *to*) to allow (a feeling, emotion, etc) to be sensed (by), willingly or unwillingly; transmit (to): *the dog communicated his fear to the other animals* **3** (*intr*) to have a sympathetic mutual understanding **4** (*intr*; usually foll by *with*) to make or have a connecting passage or route; connect **5** (*tr*) to transmit (a disease); infect **6** (*intr*) *Christianity* to receive or administer Communion [c16 from Latin *commūnicāre* to share, from *commūnis* COMMON] > com'muni,cator *n* > com'municatory *adj*

communicating (kə'mjuːnɪ,keɪtɪŋ) *adj* making or having a direct connection from one room to another: *the suite is made up of three communicating rooms*

communication (kə,mjuːnɪ'keɪʃən) *n* **1** the act or an instance of communicating; the imparting or exchange of information, ideas, or feelings **2** something communicated, such as a message, letter, or telephone call **3 a** (*usually plural; sometimes functioning as singular*) the study of ways in which human beings communicate, including speech, gesture, telecommunication systems, publishing and broadcasting media, etc **b** (*as modifier*): *communication theory* **4** a connecting route, passage, or link **5** (*plural*) *military* the system of routes and facilities by which forces, supplies, etc,

are moved up to or within an area of operations

communication cord *n Brit* a cord or chain in a train which may be pulled by a passenger to stop the train in an emergency

communication interface *n* an electronic circuit, usually designed to a specific standard, that enables one machine to telecommunicate with another machine

communications satellite *n* an artificial satellite used to relay radio, television, and telephone signals around the earth, usually in geostationary orbit

communicative (kə'mjuːnɪkətɪv) *adj* **1** inclined or able to communicate readily; talkative **2** of or relating to communication > com'municatively *adv* > com'municativeness *n*

communion (kə'mjuːnjən) *n* **1** an exchange of thoughts, emotions, etc **2** possession or sharing in common; participation **3** (foll by *with*) strong emotional or spiritual feelings (for): *communion with nature* **4** a religious group or denomination having a common body of beliefs, doctrines, and practices **5** the spiritual union held by Christians to exist between individual Christians and Christ, their Church, or their fellow Christians [c14 from Latin *commūniō* general participation, from *commūnis* COMMON] > com'munional *adj* > com'munionally *adv*

Communion (kə'mjuːnjən) *n Christianity* **1** the act of participating in the Eucharist **2** the celebration of the Eucharist, esp the part of the service during which the consecrated elements are received **3 a** the consecrated elements of the Eucharist **b** (*as modifier*): *Communion cup* ▷ Also called: **Holy Communion**

communion of saints *n Christianity* the spiritual fellowship of all true Christians, living and dead

communiqué (kə'mjuːnɪ,keɪ) *n* an official communication or announcement, esp to the press or public [c19 from French, from *communiquer* to COMMUNICATE]

communism ('kɒmjʊ,nɪzəm) *n* **1** advocacy of a classless society in which private ownership has been abolished and the means of production and subsistence belong to the community **2** any social, economic, or political movement or doctrine aimed at achieving such a society **3** (*usually capital*) a political movement based upon the writings of Karl Marx, the German political philosopher (1818–83), that considers history in terms of class conflict and revolutionary struggle, resulting eventually in the victory of the proletariat and the establishment of a socialist order based on public ownership of the means of production. See also **Marxism, Marxism-Leninism, socialism 4** (*usually capital*) a social order or system of government established by a ruling Communist Party, esp in the former Soviet Union **5** (*often capital*) *chiefly US* any leftist political activity or thought, esp when considered to be subversive **6** communal living; communalism [c19 from French *communisme*, from *commun* COMMON]

communist ('kɒmjʊnɪst) *n* **1** a supporter of any form of communism **2** (*often capital*) a supporter of Communism or a Communist movement or state **3** (*often capital*) a member of a Communist party **4** a person who practises communal living; communalist **5** another name for **Communard** ▷ *adj* **6** of, characterized by, favouring, or relating to communism; communistic

Communist China *n* another name for (the People's Republic of) **China**

communistic (,kɒmjʊ'nɪstɪk) *adj* of, characteristic of, or relating to communism > ,commu'nistically *adv*

Communist Manifesto *n* a political pamphlet written by Marx and Engels in 1848: a fundamental statement of Marxist principles

Communist Party *n* **1** (in non-Communist countries) a political party advocating Communism **2** (in Communist countries) the

C

single official party of the state, composed of those who officially espouse Communism

communitarian (kəˌmjuːnɪˈtɛərɪən) *n* **1** a member of a communist community **2** an advocate of communalism

community (kəˈmjuːnɪtɪ) *n, pl* **-ties 1 a** the people living in one locality **b** the locality in which they live **c** (*as modifier*): *community spirit* **2** a group of people having cultural, religious, ethnic, or other characteristics in common: *the Protestant community* **3** a group of nations having certain interests in common **4** the public in general; society **5** common ownership or participation **6** similarity or agreement: *community of interests* **7** (in Wales since 1974 and Scotland since 1975) the smallest unit of local government; a subdivision of a district **8** *ecology* a group of interdependent plants and animals inhabiting the same region and interacting with each other through food and other relationships [C14 from Latin *commūnitās*, from *commūnis* COMMON]

community association *n* (in Britain) an organization of people and groups working for the common good of a neighbourhood, usually operating under a written constitution registered with the Charity Commissioners

community care *n social welfare* **1** help available to persons living in their own homes, rather than services provided in residential institutions **2** the policy of transferring responsibility for people in need from large, often isolated, state institutions to their relatives and local welfare agencies

community centre *n* a building used by members of a community for social gatherings, educational activities, etc

community charge *n* (formerly in Britain) a flat-rate charge paid by each adult in a community to their local authority in place of rates. Also called: **poll tax**

community chest *n US* a fund raised by voluntary contribution for local welfare activities

community college *n* **1** *Brit* another term for **village college 2** *chiefly US and Canadian* a nonresidential college offering two-year courses of study **3** *NZ* an adult education college with trade classes

community council *n* (in Scotland and Wales) an independent voluntary local body set up to attend to local interests and organize community activities

community education *n* the provision of a wide range of educational and special interest courses and activities by a local authority

community home *n* (in Britain) **1** a home provided by a local authority for children who cannot remain with parents or relatives, or be placed with foster parents **2** a boarding school for young offenders. Former name: **approved school**. Formal name: **community home with education on the premises**. Abbreviation: **CHE**

community language *pl n* a language spoken by members of a minority group or community within a majority language context

Community of Sovereign Republics *n* a political and economic union formed in 1996 by Russia and Belarus

community policing *n* the assigning of the same one or two policemen to a particular area so that they become familiar with the residents and the residents with them, as a way of reducing crime

Community Programme *n* (in Britain) a former government scheme to provide temporary work for people unemployed for over a year. Abbreviation: **CP**

community relations *pl n* **1** the particular state of affairs in an area where potentially conflicting ethnic, religious, cultural, political, or linguistic groups live together: *community relations in this neighbourhood were strained before the riots* **2 a** social engineering or mediating work with conflicting groups: *he spent ten years in community relations* **b** (*as*

modifier): *a community-relations officer*

community school *n Brit* a school offering some nonacademic activities related to life in a particular community and often serving as a community centre

community service *n* **1** voluntary work, intended to be for the common good, usually done as part of an organized scheme **2** See **community-service order**

community-service order *n* (in Britain) a court order requiring an offender over seventeen years old to do unpaid socially beneficial work under supervision instead of going to prison

community singing *n* singing, esp of hymns, by a large gathering of people

communize or **communise** (ˈkɒmjʊˌnaɪz) *vb* (*tr; sometimes capital*) **1** to make (property) public; nationalize **2** to make (a person or country) communist > ˌcommuniˈzation or ˌcommuniˈsation *n*

commutable (kəˈmjuːtəbˀl) *adj* **1** *law* (of a punishment) capable of being reduced in severity **2** able to be exchanged > comˌmutaˈbility or comˈmutableness *n*

commutate (ˈkɒmjʊˌteɪt) *vb* (*tr*) **1** to reverse the direction of (an electric current) **2** to convert (an alternating current) into a direct current

commutation (ˌkɒmjʊˈteɪʃən) *n* **1** a substitution or exchange **2 a** the replacement of one method of payment by another **b** the payment substituted **3** the reduction in severity of a penalty imposed by law **4** the process of commutating an electric current **5** *US* the travelling done by a commuter

commutation ticket *n* a US name for **season ticket**

commutative (kəˈmjuːtətɪv, ˈkɒmjʊˌteɪtɪv) *adj* **1** relating to or involving substitution **2** *maths, logic* **a** (of an operator) giving the same result irrespective of the order of the arguments; thus disjunction and addition are commutative but implication and subtraction are not **b** relating to this property: *the commutative law of addition* > comˈmutatively *adv*

commutator (ˈkɒmjʊˌteɪtə) *n* **1** a device used to reverse the direction of flow of an electric current **2** the segmented metal cylinder or disc mounted on the armature shaft of an electric motor, generator, etc, used to make electrical contact with the rotating coils and ensure unidirectional current flow

commute (kəˈmjuːt) *vb* **1** (*intr*) to travel some distance regularly between one's home and one's place of work **2** (*tr*) to substitute; exchange **3** (*tr*) *law* to reduce (a sentence) to one less severe **4** to pay (an annuity) at one time, esp with a discount, instead of in instalments **5** (*tr*) to transform; change: *to commute base metal into gold* **6** (*intr*) to act as or be a substitute **7** (*intr*) to make a substitution > *n* **8** a journey made by commuting [C17 from Latin *commutāre* to replace, from *com-* mutually + *mutāre* to change] > comˈmutable *adj* > comˈmutableness or comˌmutaˈbility *n*

commuter (kəˈmjuːtə) *n* **a** a person who travels to work over an appreciable distance, usually from the suburbs to the centre of a city **b** (*as modifier*): *the commuter belt*

commuter marriage *n* a marriage in which the partners live some distance apart most of the time, usually because of separate work commitments

Comnenus (kɒmˈniːnəs) *n* an important Byzantine family from which the imperial dynasties of Constantinople (1057–59; 1081–1185) and Trebizond (1204–1461) derived

Como (ˈkəʊməʊ; *Italian* ˈkɔːmo) *n* a city in N Italy, in Lombardy at the SW end of **Lake Como**: tourist centre. Pop: 78 680 (2001). Latin name: Comum (ˈkəʊmʊm)

comodo or **commodo** (kəˈməʊdəʊ) *adj, adv music* (to be performed) at a convenient relaxed speed

[Italian: comfortable, from Latin *commodus*, convenient; see COMMODIOUS]

Comorin (ˈkɒmərɪn) *n* **Cape** a headland at the southernmost point of India, in Tamil Nadu state

Comoros (ˈkɒməˌrəʊz, kəˈmɔːrəʊz) *pl n* a republic consisting of three volcanic islands in the Indian Ocean, off the NW coast of Madagascar; a French territory from 1947; became independent in 1976 except for Mayotte, the fourth island in the group, which chose to remain French. Official languages: Comorian, French, and Arabic; Swahili is used commercially. Religion: Muslim. Currency: franc. Capital: Moroni. Pop: 790 000 (2004 est.). Area: 1862 sq km (719 sq miles). Official name: Union of the Comoros

comose (ˈkəʊməʊs, kəʊˈməʊs) *adj botany* another word for **comate** [C18 from Latin *comōsus* hairy, from *coma* long hair; see COMA[2]]

Comox (ˈkəʊmɒks) *n* a member of a Salishan Native Canadian people living on Vancouver Island

comp (kɒmp) *informal* > *n* **1** a compositor **2** an accompanist **3** an accompaniment **4** a competition > *vb* **5** (*intr*) to work as a compositor in the printing industry **6** to play an accompaniment (to)

compact[1] *adj* (kəmˈpækt, ˈkɒmpækt) **1** closely packed together; dense **2** neatly fitted into a restricted space **3** concise; brief **4** well constructed; solid; firm **5** (foll by *of*) composed or made up (of) **6** denoting a tabloid-sized version of a newspaper that has traditionally been published in broadsheet form **7** *logic* (of a relation) having the property that for any pair of elements such that *a* is related to *b*, there is some element *c* such that *a* is related to *c* and *c* to *b*, as *less than* on the rational numbers **8** *US and Canadian* (of a car) small and economical > *vb* (kəmˈpækt) (*tr*) **9** to pack or join closely together; compress; condense **10** (foll by *of*) to create or form by pressing together: *sediment compacted of three types of clay* **11** *metallurgy* to compress (a metal powder) to form a stable product suitable for sintering > *n* (ˈkɒmpækt) **12** a small flat case containing a mirror, face powder, etc, designed to be carried in a woman's handbag **13** *US and Canadian* a comparatively small and economical car **14** *metallurgy* a mass of metal prepared for sintering by cold-pressing a metal powder **15** a tabloid-sized version of a newspaper that has traditionally been publis hed in broadsheet form [C16 from Latin *compactus*, from *compingere* to put together, from *com-* together + *pangere* to fasten] > comˈpacter *n* > comˈpaction *n* > comˈpactly *adv* > comˈpactness *n*

compact[2] (ˈkɒmpækt) *n* an official contract or agreement [C16 from Latin *compactum*, from *compaciscī* to agree, from *com-* together + *paciscī* to contract; see PACT]

compact camera (ˈkɒmpækt) *n* a simple 35 mm snapshot camera not having interchangeable lenses or through-the-lens focusing but sometimes having automatic focusing, exposure, and winding. Sometimes shortened to: **compact**

compact disc (ˈkɒmpækt) *n* a small digital audio disc on which sound is recorded as a series of metallic pits enclosed in PVC; the disc is spun by the compact disc player and read by an optical laser system. Also called: **compact audio disc**. Abbreviations: CD, CAD

compact disc erasable *n* the full name for CDE

compact disc player *n* a machine for playing compact discs

compact disc recordable *n* the full name for CDR

compactify (kəmˈpæktɪˌfaɪ) *vb* **-fies, -fying, -fied** to make or become compact; esp of higher dimensions in space-time, to become tightly curved so as to be unobservable under normal circumstances > comˌpactifiˈcation *n*

compact video disc *n* a compact laser disc that plays both pictures and sound. Abbreviation: CDV

compadre (kɒmˈpɑːdreɪ, kəm-) *n Southwestern US* a masculine friend [from Spanish: godfather, from Medieval Latin *compater*, from Latin *com-* with + *pater* father]

compages (kəmˈpeɪdʒiːz) *n (functioning as singular)* a structure or framework [c17 from Latin, from *com-* together + *pag-*, from *pangēre* to fasten]

compander (kəmˈpændə) *n* a system for improving the signal-to-noise ratio of a signal at a transmitter or recorder by first compressing the volume range of the signal and then restoring it to its original amplitude level at the receiving or reproducing apparatus [c20 from COM(PRESSOR) + (EX)PANDER]

companion[1] (kəmˈpænjən) *n* **1** a person who is an associate of another or others; comrade **2** (esp formerly) an employee, usually a woman, who provides company for an employer, esp an elderly woman **3 a** one of a pair; match **b** (as modifier): *a companion volume* **4** a guidebook or handbook **5** a member of the lowest rank of any of certain orders of knighthood **6** *astronomy* the fainter of the two components of a double star ▷ *vb* **7** (*tr*) to accompany or be a companion to [c13 from Late Latin *compāniō*, literally: one who eats bread with another, from Latin *com-* with + *pānis* bread] > com'panionless *adj*

companion[2] (kəmˈpænjən) *n nautical* **a** a raised frame on an upper deck with windows to give light to the deck below **b** (as modifier): *a companion ladder* [c18 from Dutch *kompanje* quarterdeck, from Old French *compagne*, from Old Italian *compagna* pantry, perhaps ultimately from Latin *pānis* bread]

companionable (kəmˈpænjənəbᵊl) *adj* suited to be a companion; sociable > com'panionableness or com,paniona'bility *n* > com'panionably *adv*

companion animal *n* an animal kept as a pet

companionate (kəmˈpænjənɪt) *adj* **1** resembling, appropriate to, or acting as a companion **2** harmoniously suited

companion set *n* a set of fire irons on a stand

companionship (kəmˈpænjənˌʃɪp) *n* the relationship of friends or companions; fellowship

companionway (kəmˈpænjənˌweɪ) *n* a stairway or ladder leading from one deck to another in a boat or ship

company (ˈkʌmpənɪ) *n, pl* -nies **1** a number of people gathered together; assembly **2** the fact of being with someone; companionship: *I enjoy her company* **3** a social visitor or visitors; guest or guests **4** a business enterprise **5** the members of an enterprise not specifically mentioned in the enterprise's title. Abbreviations: Co, co **6** a group of actors, usually including business and technical personnel **7** a unit of around 100 troops, usually comprising two or more platoons **8** the officers and crew of a ship **9** a unit of Girl Guides **10** *English history* a medieval guild **11 keep** *or* **bear company a** to accompany (someone) **b** (esp of lovers) to associate with each other; spend time together **12 part company a** to end a friendship or association, esp as a result of a quarrel; separate **b** (foll by *with*) to leave; go away (from); be separated (from) ▷ *vb* -nies, -nying, -nied **13** *archaic* to keep company or associate (with someone) [c13 from Old French *compaignie*, from *compain* companion, fellow, from Late Latin *compāniō*; see COMPANION[1]]

company doctor *n* **1** a businessman or accountant who specializes in turning ailing companies into profitable enterprises **2** a physician employed by a company to look after its staff and to advise on health matters

company man *n* an employee who puts allegiance to the company for which he works above personal opinion or friendship

company secretary *n Brit* an officer of an incorporated company who has certain legal obligations

company sergeant major *n military* the senior Warrant Officer II in a British or Commonwealth regiment or battalion, responsible under the company second in command for all aspects of duty and discipline of the NCOs and men in that subunit. Abbreviation: CSM. Compare **regimental sergeant major**. See also **warrant officer**

company town *n US and Canadian* a town built by a company for its employees

company union *n chiefly US and Canadian* an unaffiliated union of workers usually restricted to a single business enterprise

comparable (ˈkɒmpərəbᵊl) *adj* **1** worthy of comparison **2** able to be compared (with) > ,compara'bility *or* 'comparableness *n* > 'comparably *adv*

comparative (kəmˈpærətɪv) *adj* **1** denoting or involving comparison: *comparative literature* **2** judged by comparison; relative: *a comparative loss of prestige* **3** *grammar* denoting the form of an adjective that indicates that the quality denoted is possessed to a greater extent. In English the comparative form of an adjective is usually marked by the suffix *-er* or the word *more*. Compare **positive** (sense 10), **superlative** (sense 2) ▷ *n* **4** the comparative form of an adjective > com'paratively *adv* > com'parativeness *n*

comparative advertising *n* a form of advertising in which a product is compared favourably with similar products on the market

comparative judgment *n psychol* any judgment about whether there is a difference between two or more stimuli. Compare **absolute judgment**

comparative psychology *n* the study of the similarities and differences in the behaviour of different species

comparator (kəmˈpærətə) *n* **1** any instrument used to measure a property of a system by comparing it with a standard system **2** an electric circuit that compares two signals and gives an indication of the extent of their dissimilarity

compare (kəmˈpɛə) *vb* **1** (*tr*; usually foll by *to*) to regard or represent as analogous or similar; liken: *the general has been compared to Napoleon* **2** (*tr*; usually foll by *with*) to examine in order to observe resemblances or differences: *to compare rum with gin* **3** (*intr*; usually foll by *with*) to be of the same or similar quality or value: *gin compares with rum in alcoholic content* **4** (*intr*) to bear a specified relation of quality or value when examined: *this car compares badly with the other* **5** (*intr*; usually foll by *with*) to correspond to: *profits were £3.2 million. This compares with £2.6 million last year* **6** (*tr*) *grammar* to give the positive, comparative, and superlative forms of (an adjective) **7** (*intr*) *archaic* to compete or vie **8 compare notes** to exchange opinions ▷ *n* **9** comparison or analogy (esp in the phrase **beyond compare**) [c15 from Old French *comparer*, from Latin *comparāre* to couple together, match, from *compar* equal to one another, from *com-* together + *par* equal; see PAR] > com'parer *n*

comparison (kəmˈpærɪsᵊn) *n* **1** the act or process of comparing **2** the state of being compared **3** comparable quality or qualities; likeness: *there was no comparison between them* **4** a rhetorical device involving comparison, such as a simile **5** Also called: **degrees of comparison** *grammar* the listing of the positive, comparative, and superlative forms of an adjective or adverb **6 bear** *or* **stand comparison (with)** to be sufficiently similar in class or range to be compared with (something else), esp favourably

compartment (kəmˈpɑːtmənt) *n* **1** one of the sections into which an area, esp an enclosed space, is divided or partitioned **2** any separate part or section: *a compartment of the mind* **3** a small storage space; locker [c16 from French *compartiment*, ultimately from Late Latin *compartīrī* to share, from Latin *com-* with + *partīrī* to apportion, from *pars* PART] > compartmental (,kɒmpɑːˈtmɛntᵊl) *adj* > ,compart'mentally *adv*

compartmentalize *or* **compartmentalise** (,kɒmpɑːˈtmɛntᵊˌlaɪz) *vb* (*usually tr*) to put or divide into (compartments, categories, etc), esp to an excessive degree > ,compart,mentali'zation *or* ,compart,mentali'sation *n*

compass (ˈkʌmpəs) *n* **1** an instrument for finding direction, usually having a magnetized needle which points to magnetic north swinging freely on a pivot **2** (*often plural*) Also called: **pair of compasses** an instrument used for drawing circles, measuring distances, etc, that consists of two arms, joined at one end, one arm of which serves as a pivot or stationary reference point, while the other is extended or describes a circle **3** limits or range: *within the compass of education* **4** *music* the interval between the lowest and highest note attainable by a voice or musical instrument **5** *archaic* a circular course ▷ *vb* (*tr*) **6** to encircle or surround; hem in **7** to comprehend or grasp mentally **8** to achieve; attain; accomplish **9** *obsolete* to plot [c13 from Old French *compas*, from *compasser* to measure, from Vulgar Latin *compassāre* (unattested) to pace out, ultimately from Latin *passus* step] > 'compassable *adj*

compass card *n* a compass in the form of a card that rotates so that "0°" or "North" points to magnetic north

compassion (kəmˈpæʃən) *n* a feeling of distress and pity for the suffering or misfortune of another, often including the desire to alleviate it [c14 from Old French, from Late Latin *compassiō* fellow feeling, from *compati* to suffer with, from Latin *com-* with + *patī* to bear, suffer]

compassionate (kəmˈpæʃənət) *adj* **1** showing or having compassion **2 compassionate leave** leave granted, esp to a serviceman, on the grounds of bereavement, family illness, etc > com'passionately *adv* > com'passionateness *n*

Compassion Club *n* the (in Canada) a nonprofit organization that provides uncontaminated cannabis for medical purposes and natural therapies in a safe environment

compassion fatigue *n* the inability to react sympathetically to a crisis, disaster, etc, because of overexposure to previous crises, disasters, etc

compass plant *n* **1** Also called: **rosinweed** a tall plant, *Silphium laciniatum*, of central North America, that has yellow flowers and lower leaves that tend to align themselves at right angles to the strongest light, esp in a north-south plane: family *Asteraceae* (composites) **2** any of several similar plants

compass rose *n* a circle or decorative device printed on a map or chart showing the points of the compass measured from true north and usually magnetic north

compass saw *n* a hand saw with a narrow tapered blade for making a curved cut

compass window *n architect* a bay window having a semicircular shape

compatible (kəmˈpætəbᵊl) *adj* **1** (usually foll by *with*) able to exist together harmoniously **2** (usually foll by *with*) consistent or congruous: *her deeds were not compatible with her ideology* **3** (of plants) **a** capable of forming successful grafts **b** capable of successful self-fertilization ▷ See **self-compatible, self-incompatible 4** (of pieces of machinery, computer equipment, etc) capable of being used together without special modification or adaptation: *a PC-compatible disc* [c15 from Medieval Latin *compatibilis*, from Late Latin *compatī* to be in sympathy with; see COMPASSION] > com,pati'bility *or* com'patibleness *n* > com'patibly *adv*

compatriot (kəmˈpætrɪət) *n* a fellow countryman [c17 from French *compatriote*, from Late Latin *compatriōta*; see PATRIOT] > com,patri'otic *adj* > com'patriotism *n*

compeer (ˈkɒmpɪə) *n* **1** a person of equal rank, status, or ability; peer **2** a companion or comrade [c13 from Old French *comper*, from Medieval Latin *compater* godfather; see COMPADRE]

compel (kəmˈpɛl) *vb* -pels, -pelling, -pelled (*tr*) **1** to cause (someone) by force (to be or do something) **2** to obtain by force; exact: *to compel* obedience **3** to overpower or subdue **4** *archaic* to herd or drive together [C14 from Latin *compellere* to drive together, from *com-* together + *pellere* to drive] > com'pellable *adj* > com'pellably *adv* > com'peller *n*

compellation (ˌkɒmpɛ'leɪʃən) *n* a rare word for **appellation** [C17 from Latin *compellātiō,* from *compellāre* to accost, from *appellāre* to call]

compelling (kəm'pɛlɪŋ) *adj* **1** arousing or denoting strong interest, esp admiring interest **2** (of an argument, evidence, etc) convincing

compendious (kəm'pɛndɪəs) *adj* containing or stating the essentials of a subject in a concise form; succinct > com'pendiously *adv* > com'pendiousness *n*

compendium (kəm'pɛndɪəm) *n, pl* -diums *or* -dia (-dɪə) **1** *Brit* a book containing a collection of useful hints **2** *Brit* a selection, esp of different games or other objects in one container **3** a concise but comprehensive summary of a larger work [C16 from Latin: a saving, literally: something weighed, from *pendere* to weigh]

compensable (kəm'pɛnsəbʰl) *adj chiefly US* entitled to compensation or capable of being compensated

compensate ('kɒmpɛnˌseɪt) *vb* **1** to make amends to (someone), esp for loss or injury **2** (*tr*) to serve as compensation or damages for (injury, loss, etc) **3** to offset or counterbalance the effects of (a force, weight, movement, etc) so as to nullify the effects of an undesirable influence and produce equilibrium **4** (*intr*) to attempt to conceal or offset one's shortcomings by the exaggerated exhibition of qualities regarded as desirable [C17 from Latin *compēnsāre,* from *pēnsāre,* from *pendere* to weigh] > compensatory ('kɒmpɛnˌseɪtərɪ, kəm'pɛnsətərɪ, -trɪ) *or* compensative ('kɒmpɛnˌseɪtɪv, kəm'pɛnsə-) *adj* > 'compenˌsator *n*

compensated semiconductor *n physics* a semiconductor in which donors and acceptors are related in such a way that their opposing electrical effects are partially cancelled

compensation (ˌkɒmpɛn'seɪʃən) *n* **1** the act or process of making amends for something **2** something given as reparation for loss, injury, etc; indemnity **3** the automatic movements made by the body to maintain balance **4** the attempt to conceal or offset one's shortcomings by the exaggerated exhibition of qualities regarded as desirable **5** *biology* abnormal growth and increase in size in one organ in response to the removal or inactivation of another > ˌcompen'sational *adj*

compensation culture *n* a culture in which people are very ready to go to law over even relatively minor incidents in the hope of gaining compensation

compensation order *n* (in Britain) the requirement of a court that an offender pay compensation for injury, loss, or damage resulting from an offence, either in preference to or as well as a fine

compensation point *n botany* the concentration of atmospheric carbon dioxide at which the rate of carbon dioxide uptake by a photosynthesizing plant is exactly balanced by its rate of carbon dioxide release in respiration and photorespiration

compensatory finance *n* another name for **deficit financing**

comper ('kɒmpə) *n informal* a person who regularly enters competitions in newspapers, magazines, etc, esp competitions offering consumer goods as prizes [C20 COMP(ETITION) + -ER¹] > 'comping *n*

compere ('kɒmpɛə) *Brit* ⊳ *n* **1** a master of ceremonies who introduces cabaret, television acts, etc ⊳ *vb* **2** to act as a compere (for) [C20 from French, literally: godfather; see COMPEER, COMPADRE]

compete (kəm'piːt) *vb* (*intr*; often foll by *with*) to contend (against) for profit, an award, athletic supremacy, etc; engage in a contest (with) [C17

from Late Latin *competere* to strive together, from Latin: to meet, come together, agree, from *com-* together + *petere* to seek]

competence ('kɒmpɪtəns) *n* **1** the condition of being capable; ability **2** a sufficient income to live on **3** the state of being legally competent or qualified **4** *embryol* the ability of embryonic tissues to react to external conditions in a way that influences subsequent development **5** *linguistics* (in transformational grammar) the form of the human language faculty, independent of its psychological embodiment in actual human beings. Compare **performance** (sense 7), **langue, parole** (sense 5)

competency ('kɒmpɪtənsɪ) *n, pl* -cies **1** *law* capacity to testify in a court of law; eligibility to be sworn **2** a less common word for **competence** (senses 1, 2)

competent ('kɒmpɪtənt) *adj* **1** having sufficient skill, knowledge, etc; capable **2** suitable or sufficient for the purpose: *a competent answer* **3** *law* (of a witness) having legal capacity; qualified to testify, etc **4** (*postpositive*; foll by *to*) belonging as a right; appropriate [C14 from Latin *competēns,* from *competere* to be competent; see COMPETE] > 'competently *adv* > 'competentness *n*

competition (ˌkɒmpɪ'tɪʃən) *n* **1** the act of competing; rivalry **2** a contest in which a winner is selected from among two or more entrants **3** a series of games, sports events, etc **4** the opposition offered by a competitor or competitors **5** a competitor or competitors offering opposition **6** *ecology* the struggle between individuals of the same or different species for food, space, light, etc, when these are inadequate to supply the needs of all

competitive (kəm'pɛtɪtɪv) *adj* **1** involving or determined by rivalry: *competitive sports* **2** sufficiently low in price or high in quality to be successful against commercial rivals **3** relating to or characterized by an urge to compete: *a competitive personality* > com'petitively *adv* > com'petitiveness *n*

competitive exclusion *n ecology* the dominance of one species over another when both are competing for the same resources, etc

competitor (kəm'pɛtɪtə) *n* a person, group, team, firm, etc, that vies or competes; rival

Compiègne (French kɔ̃pjɛn) *n* a city in N France, on the Oise River: scene of the armistice at the end of World War I (1918) and of the Franco-German armistice of 1940. Pop: 41 254 (1999)

compilation (ˌkɒmpɪ'leɪʃən) *n* **1** something collected or compiled, such as a list, report, etc **2** the act or process of collecting or compiling

compilation film *n* film from an archive used in a film or documentary to give a feeling of the relevant period

compile (kəm'paɪl) *vb* (*tr*) **1** to make or compose from other materials or sources: *to compile a list of names* **2** to collect or gather for a book, hobby, etc **3** *computing* to create (a set of machine instructions) from a high-level programming language, using a compiler [C14 from Latin *compīlāre* to pile together, plunder, from *com-* together + *pīlāre* to thrust down, pack]

compiler (kəm'paɪlə) *n* **1** a person who collects or compiles something **2** a computer program by which a high-level programming language, such as COBOL or FORTRAN, is converted into machine language that can be acted upon by a computer. Compare **assembler**

complacency (kəm'pleɪsənsɪ) *or* **complacence** *n, pl* -cencies *or* -cences **1** a feeling of satisfaction, esp extreme self-satisfaction; smugness **2** an obsolete word for **complaisance**

complacent (kəm'pleɪsʰnt) *adj* **1** pleased or satisfied, esp extremely self-satisfied **2** an obsolete word for **complaisant** [C17 from Latin *complacēns* very pleasing, from *complacēre* to be most agreeable to, from *com-* (intensive) + *placēre* to please] > com'placently *adv*

complain (kəm'pleɪn) *vb* (*intr*) **1** to express resentment, displeasure, etc, esp habitually; grumble **2** (foll by *of*) to state the presence of pain, illness, etc, esp in the hope of sympathy: *she complained of a headache* [C14 from Old French *complaindre,* from Vulgar Latin *complangere* (unattested), from Latin *com-* (intensive) + *plangere* to bewail] > com'plainer *n* > com'plainingly *adv*

complainant (kəm'pleɪnənt) *n law* a person who makes a complaint, usually before justices; plaintiff

complaint (kəm'pleɪnt) *n* **1** the act of complaining; an expression of grievance **2** a cause for complaining; grievance **3** a mild ailment **4** *English law* a statement by which a civil proceeding in a magistrates' court is commenced

complaisance (kəm'pleɪzəns) *n* **1** deference to the wishes of others; willing compliance **2** an act of willing compliance

complaisant (kəm'pleɪzʰnt) *adj* showing a desire to comply or oblige; polite [C17 from French *complaire,* from Latin *complacēre* to please greatly; compare COMPLACENT] > com'plaisantly *adv*

complanate (kəm'pleɪneɪt) *adj botany* having a flattened or compressed aspect

compleat (kəm'pliːt) *adj* an archaic spelling of **complete**, used in the titles of handbooks, in imitation of *The Compleat Angler* by Izaak Walton

complect (kəm'plɛkt) *vb* (*tr*) *archaic* to interweave or entwine [C16 from Latin *complectī*; see COMPLEX]

complected (kəm'plɛktɪd) *adj* (in combination) a US dialect word for **complexioned**

complement *n* ('kɒmplɪmənt) **1** a person or thing that completes something **2** one of two parts that make up a whole or complete each other **3** a complete amount, number, etc (often in the phrase **full complement**) **4** the officers and crew needed to man a ship **5** *grammar* **a** a noun phrase that follows a copula or similar verb, as for example *an idiot* in the sentence *He is an idiot* **b** a clause that serves as the subject or direct object of a verb or the direct object of a preposition, as for example *that he would be early* in the sentence *I hoped that he would be early* **6** *maths* the angle that when added to a specified angle produces a right angle **7** *logic, maths* the class of all things, or of all members of a given universe of discourse, that are not members of a given set **8** *music* the inverted form of an interval that, when added to the interval, completes the octave: *the sixth is the complement of the third* **9** *immunol* a group of proteins in the blood serum that, when activated by antibodies, causes destruction of alien cells, such as bacteria ⊳ *vb* ('kɒmplɪˌmɛnt) **10** (*tr*) to add to, make complete, or form a complement to [C14 from Latin *complēmentum,* from *complēre* to fill up, from *com-* (intensive) + *plēre* to fill]

▮ USAGE Avoid confusion with **compliment**

complementarity (ˌkɒmplɪmən'tærɪtɪ) *n, pl* -ties **1** a state or system that involves complementary components **2** *physics* the principle that the complete description of a phenomenon in microphysics requires the use of two distinct theories that are complementary to each other. See also **duality** (sense 2)

complementary (ˌkɒmplɪ'mɛntərɪ, -trɪ) *or* **complemental** *adj* **1** acting as or forming a complement; completing **2** forming a satisfactory or balanced whole **3** forming a mathematical complement: *sine and cosine are complementary functions* **4** *maths, logic* (of a pair of sets, etc) mutually exclusive and exhaustive, each being the complement of the other **5** (of genes) producing an effect in association with other genes **6** involving or using the treatments and techniques of complementary medicine > ˌcomple'mentarily *or* ˌcomple'mentally *adv* > ˌcomple'mentariness *n*

complementary angle *n* either of two angles whose sum is 90°. Compare **supplementary angle**

complementary colour *n* one of any pair of

colours, such as yellow and blue, that give white or grey when mixed in the correct proportions

complementary DNA *n* a form of DNA artificially synthesized from a messenger RNA template and used in genetic engineering to produce gene clones. Abbreviation: **cDNA**

complementary gene *n* one of a pair of genes, each from different loci, that together are required for the expression of a certain characteristic

complementary medicine *n* the treatment, alleviation, or prevention of disease by such techniques as osteopathy, homeopathy, aromatherapy, and acupuncture, allied with attention to such factors as diet and emotional stability, which can affect a person's wellbeing. Also called: **alternative medicine** ▷ See also **holism** (sense 2)

complementary wavelength *n physics* the wavelength of monochromatic light that could be mixed in suitable proportions with a given coloured light so as to produce some specified achromatic light

complementation (ˌkɒmplɪmɛnˈteɪʃən) *n* **1** the act or process of forming a complement **2** *genetics* the combination of two homologous chromosomes, each with a different recessive mutant gene, in a single cell to produce a normal phenotype. The deficiency of one homologue is supplied by the normal allele of the other

complement fixation test *n med* a serological test for detecting the presence of a specific antibody or antigen, used in the diagnosis of syphilis, etc

complementizer (ˈkɒmplɪmənˌtaɪzə) *n generative grammar* a word or morpheme that serves to introduce a complement clause or a reduced form of such a clause, as *that* in *I wish that he would leave*

complete (kəmˈpliːt) *adj* **1** having every necessary part or element; entire **2** ended; finished **3** (*prenominal*) thorough; absolute: *he is a complete rogue* **4** perfect in quality or kind: *he is a complete scholar* **5** (of a logical system) constituted such that a contradiction arises on the addition of any proposition that cannot be deduced from the axioms of the system. Compare **consistent** (sense 5) **6** (of flowers) having sepals, petals, stamens, and carpels **7** *archaic* expert or skilled; accomplished ▷ *vb* (*tr*) **8** to make whole or perfect **9** to end; finish **10** (in land law) to pay any outstanding balance on a contract for the conveyance of land in exchange for the title deeds, so that the ownership of the land changes hands **11** *American football* (of a quarterback) to make a forward pass successfully [C14 from Latin *complētus*, past participle of *complēre* to fill up; see COMPLEMENT] > comˈpletely *adv* > comˈpleteness *n* > comˈpleter *n* > comˈpletion *n* > comˈpletive *adj*

completist (kəmˈpliːtɪst) *n* a person who collects objects or memorabilia obsessively: *ardent John Wayne completists*

complex (ˈkɒmplɛks) *adj* **1** made up of various interconnected parts; composite **2** (of thoughts, writing, etc) intricate or involved **3** *grammar* **a** (of a word) containing at least one bound form **b** (of a noun phrase) containing both a lexical noun and an embedded clause, as for example the italicized parts of the following sentence: *I didn't know the man who served me* **c** (of a sentence) formed by subordination of one clause to another **4** *maths* of or involving one or more complex numbers ▷ *n* **5** a whole made up of interconnected or related parts: *a building complex* **6** *psychoanal* a group of emotional ideas or impulses that have been banished from the conscious mind but that continue to influence a person's behaviour **7** *informal* an obsession or excessive fear: *he's got a complex about cats* **8** Also called: **coordination compound** a chemical compound in which molecules, groups, or ions are attached to a central metal atom, esp a transition metal atom, by coordinate bonds **9** any chemical compound in which one molecule is linked to another by a coordinate bond [C17 from Latin *complexus*, from *complectī* to entwine, from *com-* together + *plectere* to braid] > ˈcomplexly *adv* > ˈcomplexness *n*

▎ **USAGE** *Complex* is sometimes wrongly used where *complicated* is meant. *Complex* is properly used to say only that something consists of several parts. It should not be used to say that, because something consists of many parts, it is difficult to understand or analyse

complex conjugate *n maths* the complex number whose imaginary part is the negative of that of a given complex number, the real parts of both numbers being equal: *a – ib is the complex conjugate of a + ib*

complex fraction *n maths* a fraction in which the numerator or denominator or both contain fractions. Also called: **compound fraction**

complexion (kəmˈplɛkʃən) *n* **1** the colour and general appearance of a person's skin, esp of the face **2** aspect, character, or nature: *the general complexion of a nation's finances* **3** *obsolete* **a** the temperament of a person **b** the temperature and general appearance of the body [C14 from medical Latin *complexiō* one's bodily characteristics, from Latin: a combination, from *complectī* to embrace; see COMPLEX] > comˈplexional *adj*

complexioned (kəmˈplɛkʃənd) *adj* (*in combination*) of a specified complexion: *light-complexioned*

complexity (kəmˈplɛksɪtɪ) *n, pl* -ties **1** the state or quality of being intricate or complex **2** something intricate or complex; complication

complexity theory *n* **1** *mathematics* the study of complex systems, including subjects such as chaos theory and genetic algorithms **2** *computing* a field in theoretical computer science dealing with the resources required during computation to solve a given problem

complex number *n* any number of the form $a + ib$, where a and b are real numbers and $i = \sqrt{-1}$. See **number** (sense 1)

complexometric titration (kəmˌplɛksəʊˈmɛtrɪk) *n chem* a titration in which a coloured complex is formed, usually by the use of a chelating agent, such as EDTA, the end point being marked by a sharp decrease in the concentration of free metal ions

complexone (kəmˈplɛksəʊn) *n chem* any chelating agent, such as EDTA, used for the analytical determination of metals

complex salt *n* a salt that contains one or more complex ions. Compare **double salt**

complex sentence *n grammar* a sentence containing at least one main clause and one subordinate clause

complex wave *n physics* a waveform consisting of a fundamental frequency with superimposed harmonics

compliance (kəmˈplaɪəns) *or* **compliancy** *n* **1** the act of complying; acquiescence **2** a disposition to yield to or comply with others **3** a measure of the ability of a mechanical system to respond to an applied vibrating force, expressed as the reciprocal of the system's stiffness. Symbol: C

compliance officer *n* a specialist, usually a lawyer, employed by a financial group operating in a variety of fields and for multiple clients to ensure that no conflict of interest arises and that all obligations and regulations are complied with

compliant (kəmˈplaɪənt) *or* **compliable** *adj* complying, obliging, or yielding > comˈpliantly *or* comˈpliably *adv* > comˈpliantness *or* comˈpliableness *n*

complicacy (ˈkɒmplɪkəsɪ) *n, pl* -cies a less common word for **complexity**

complicate *vb* (ˈkɒmplɪˌkeɪt) **1** to make or become complex ▷ *adj* (ˈkɒmplɪkɪt) **2** *biology* folded on itself: *a complicate leaf* **3** a less common word for **complicated** [C17 from Latin *complicāre* to fold together, from *plicāre* to fold]

complicated (ˈkɒmplɪˌkeɪtɪd) *adj* made up of intricate parts or aspects that are difficult to understand or analyse > ˈcompliˌcatedly *adv* > ˈcompliˌcatedness *n*

complication (ˌkɒmplɪˈkeɪʃən) *n* **1** a condition, event, etc, that is complex or confused **2** the act or process of complicating **3** a situation, event, or condition that complicates or frustrates: *her coming was a serious complication* **4** a disease or disorder arising as a consequence of another disease

complice (ˈkɒmplɪs, ˈkʌm-) *n obsolete* an associate or accomplice [C15 from Old French, from Late Latin *complex* partner, associate, from Latin *complicāre* to fold together; see COMPLICATE]

complicity (kəmˈplɪsɪtɪ) *n, pl* -ties **1** the fact or condition of being an accomplice, esp in a criminal act **2** a less common word for **complexity**

compliment *n* (ˈkɒmplɪmənt) **1** a remark or act expressing respect, admiration, etc **2** (*usually plural*) a greeting of respect or regard ▷ *vb* (ˈkɒmplɪˌmɛnt) (*tr*) **3** to express admiration of; congratulate or commend **4** to express or show respect or regard for, esp by a gift [C17 from French, from Italian *complimento*, from Spanish *cumplimiento*, from *cumplir* to complete, do what is fitting, be polite]

▎ **USAGE** Avoid confusion with **complement**

complimentary (ˌkɒmplɪˈmɛntərɪ, -trɪ) *adj* **1** conveying, containing, or resembling a compliment **2** expressing praise; flattering **3** given free, esp as a courtesy or for publicity purposes > ˌcompliˈmentarily *adv*

compline (ˈkɒmplɪn, -plaɪn) *or* **complin** (ˈkɒmplɪn) *n RC Church* the last of the seven canonical hours of the divine office [C13 from Old French *complie*, from Medieval Latin *hōra complēta*, literally: the completed hour, from Latin *complēre* to fill up, COMPLETE]

complot *archaic* ▷ *n* (ˈkɒmplɒt) **1** a plot or conspiracy ▷ *vb* (kəmˈplɒt) -plots, -plotting, -plotted **2** to plot together; conspire [C16 from Old French, of unknown origin] > comˈplotter *n*

comply (kəmˈplaɪ) *vb* -plies, -plying, -plied (*intr*) **1** (usually foll by *with*) to act in accordance with rules, wishes, etc; be obedient (to) **2** *obsolete* to be obedient or complaisant [C17 from Italian *complire*, from Spanish *cumplir* to complete; see COMPLIMENT] > comˈplier *n*

compo (ˈkɒmpəʊ) *n, pl* -pos **1** a mixture of materials, such as mortar, plaster, etc **2** *Austral and NZ informal* compensation, esp for injury or loss of work ▷ *adj* **3** *military* intended to last for several days: *compo rations; a compo pack* [short for *composition, compensation, composite*]

component (kəmˈpəʊnənt) *n* **1** a constituent part or aspect of something more complex: *a component of a car* **2** Also called: **element** any electrical device, such as a resistor, that has distinct electrical characteristics and that may be connected to other electrical devices to form a circuit **3** *maths* **a** one of a set of two or more vectors whose resultant is a given vector **b** the projection of this given vector onto a specified line **4** one of the minimum number of chemically distinct constituents necessary to describe fully the composition of each phase in a system. See **phase rule** ▷ *adj* **5** forming or functioning as a part or aspect; constituent [C17 from Latin *compōnere* to put together, from *pōnere* to place, put] > componential (ˌkɒmpəˈnɛnʃəl) *adj*

compony (kəmˈpəʊnɪ) *or* **componé** (kəmˈpəʊneɪ) *adj* (*usually postpositive*) *heraldry* made up of alternating metal and colour, colour and fur, or fur and metal [C16 from Old French *componé*, from *copon* piece, COUPON]

comport (kəmˈpɔːt) *vb* **1** (*tr*) to conduct or bear (oneself) in a specified way **2** (*intr*; foll by *with*) to agree (with); correspond (to) [C16 from Latin *comportāre* to bear, collect, from *com-* together + *portāre* to carry]

C

comportment (kəmˈpɔːtmənt) *n* conduct; bearing

compose (kəmˈpəʊz) *vb (mainly tr)* **1** to put together or make up by combining; put in proper order **2** to be the component elements of **3** to produce or create (a musical or literary work) **4** (*intr*) to write music **5** to calm (someone, esp oneself); make quiet **6** to adjust or settle (a quarrel, etc) **7** to order the elements of (a painting, sculpture, etc); design **8** *printing* to set up (type) [c15 from Old French *composer*, from Latin *compōnere* to put in place; see COMPONENT]

composed (kəmˈpəʊzd) *adj* (of people) calm; tranquil; serene > **composedly** (kəmˈpəʊzɪdlɪ) *adv* > com'**posedness** *n*

composer (kəmˈpəʊzə) *n* **1** a person who composes music **2** a person or machine that composes anything, esp type for printing

composing room *n* the room in a printing establishment in which type is set

composing stick *n printing* a metal holder of adjustable width in which a compositor sets a line of type at a time by hand; now rarely used

composite (ˈkɒmpəzɪt) *adj* **1** composed of separate parts; compound **2** of, relating to, or belonging to the plant family *Asteraceae* **3** *maths* capable of being factorized or decomposed: *a composite function* **4** (*sometimes capital*) denoting or relating to one of the five classical orders of architecture: characterized by a combination of the Ionic and Corinthian styles. See also **Doric, Tuscan** ▷ *n* **5** something composed of separate parts; compound **6** any plant of the family *Asteraceae* (formerly *Compositae*), typically having flower heads composed of ray flowers (eg dandelion), disc flowers (eg thistle), or both (eg daisy) **7** a material, such as reinforced concrete, made of two or more distinct materials **8** a proposal that has been composited ▷ *vb* (ˈkɒmpəˌzaɪt) **9** (*tr*) to merge related motions from local branches of (a political party, trade union, etc) so as to produce a manageable number of proposals for discussion at national level [c16 from Latin *compositus* well arranged, from *compōnere* to collect, arrange; see COMPONENT] > 'compositely *adv* > 'compositeness *n*

composite colour signal *n* a colour television signal in which luminance and two chrominance components are encoded into a single signal

composite number *n* a positive integer that can be factorized into two or more other positive integers. Compare **prime number**

composite photograph *n* a photograph formed by superimposing two or more separate photographs

composite school *n Eastern Canadian* a secondary school offering both academic and nonacademic courses

composition (ˌkɒmpəˈzɪʃən) *n* **1** the act of putting together or making up by combining parts or ingredients **2** something formed in this manner or the resulting state or quality; a mixture **3** the parts of which something is composed or made up; constitution **4** a work of music, art, or literature **5** the harmonious arrangement of the parts of a work of art in relation to each other and to the whole **6** a piece of writing undertaken as an academic exercise in grammatically acceptable writing; an essay **7** *printing* the act or technique of setting up type **8** *linguistics* the formation of compound words **9** *logic* the fallacy of inferring that the properties of the part are also true of the whole, as *every member of the team has won a prize, so the team will win a prize* **10 a** a settlement by mutual consent, esp a legal agreement whereby the creditors agree to accept partial payment of a debt in full settlement **b** the sum so agreed **11** *chem* the nature and proportions of the elements comprising a chemical compound [c14 from Old French, from Latin *compositus*; see COMPOSITE, -ION] > ˌcompo'sitional *adj*

composition of forces *n* the combination, by vector algebra, of two or more forces into a single equivalent force (the resultant)

compositor (kəmˈpɒzɪtə) *n printing* a person who sets and corrects type and generally assembles text and illustrations for printing. Sometimes shortened to: **comp** > **compositorial** (kəmˌpɒzɪˈtɔːrɪəl) *adj*

compos mentis *Latin* (ˈkɒmpɒs ˈmɛntɪs) *adj* (*postpositive*) of sound mind; sane

compossible (kɒmˈpɒsɪbəl) *adj rare* possible in coexistence with something else

compost (ˈkɒmpɒst) *n* **1** a mixture of organic residues such as decomposed vegetation, manure, etc, used as a fertilizer **2** a mixture, normally of plant remains, peat, charcoal, etc, in which plants are grown, esp in pots **3** *rare* a compound or mixture ▷ *vb* (*tr*) **4** to make (vegetable matter) into compost **5** to fertilize with compost [c14 from Old French *compost*, from Latin *compositus* put together; see COMPOSITE]

compostable (kɒmˈpɒstəbəl) *adj* capable of being used as compost: *compostable waste*

Compostela (*Spanish* kɔmpɔsˈtela) *n* See **Santiago de Compostela**

composure (kəmˈpəʊʒə) *n* calmness, esp of the mind; tranquillity; serenity

compotation (ˌkɒmpəˈteɪʃən) *n rare* the act of drinking together in a company [c16 from Latin *compōtātiō*, translation of Greek SYMPOSIUM] > 'compoˌtator *n*

compote (ˈkɒmpəʊt; *French* kɔ̃pɔt) *n* a dish of fruit stewed with sugar or in a syrup and served hot or cold [c17 from French *composte*, from Latin *composita*, feminine of *compositus* put in place; see COMPOSITE]

compound¹ *n* (ˈkɒmpaʊnd) **1** a substance that contains atoms of two or more chemical elements held together by chemical bonds **2** any combination of two or more parts, aspects, etc **3** a word formed from two existing words or combining forms ▷ *vb* (kəmˈpaʊnd) (*mainly tr*) **4** to mix or combine so as to create a compound or other product **5** to make by combining parts, elements, aspects, etc: *to compound a new plastic* **6** to intensify by an added element: *his anxiety was compounded by her crying* **7** *finance* to calculate or pay (interest) on both the principal and its accrued interest **8** (*also intr*) to come to an agreement in (a quarrel, dispute, etc) **9** (*also intr*) to settle (a debt, promise, etc) for less than what is owed; compromise **10** *law* to agree not to prosecute in return for a consideration: *to compound a crime* **11** *electrical engineering* to place duplex windings on the field coil of (a motor or generator), one acting as a shunt, the other being in series with the main circuit, thus making the machine self-regulating ▷ *adj* (ˈkɒmpaʊnd) **12** composed of or created by the combination of two or more parts, elements, etc **13** (of a word) consisting of elements that are also words or productive combining forms **14** (of a sentence) formed by coordination of two or more sentences **15** (of a verb or the tense, mood, etc, of a verb) formed by using an auxiliary verb in addition to the main verb: *the future in English is a compound tense involving the use of such auxiliary verbs as "shall" and "will"* **16** *music* **a** denoting a time in which the number of beats per bar is a multiple of three: *six-four is an example of compound time* **b** (of an interval) greater than an octave **17** *zoology* another word for **colonial** (sense 6) **18** (of a steam engine, turbine, etc) having multiple stages in which the steam or working fluid from one stage is used in a subsequent stage **19** (of a piston engine) having a turbocharger powered by a turbine in the exhaust stream [c14 from earlier *compounen*, from Old French *compōnere*] > com'**poundable** *adj* > com'**pounder** *n*

compound² (ˈkɒmpaʊnd) *n* **1** (esp formerly in South Africa) an enclosure, esp on the mines, containing the living quarters for Black workers **2** any similar enclosure, such as a camp for prisoners of war **3** (formerly in India, China, etc) the enclosure in which a European's house or factory stood [c17 by folk etymology (influenced by COMPOUND¹) from Malay *kampong* village]

compound annual return *n* the total return available from an investment, deposit, etc, when the interest earned is used to augment the capital. Abbreviation: CAR

compound engine *n* **1** a steam engine in which the steam is expanded in more than one stage, first in a high-pressure cylinder and then in one or more low-pressure cylinders **2** a reciprocating engine in which the exhaust gases are expanded in a turbine to drive a turbocharger

compound eye *n* the convex eye of insects and some crustaceans, consisting of numerous separate light-sensitive units (ommatidia). See also **ocellus**

compound fault *n geology* a series of closely spaced faults

compound flower *n* a flower head made up of many small flowers appearing as a single bloom, as in the daisy

compound fraction *n* another name for **complex fraction**

compound fracture *n* a fracture in which the broken bone either pierces the skin or communicates with an open wound

compound interest *n* interest calculated on both the principal and its accrued interest. Compare **simple interest**

compound leaf *n* a leaf consisting of two or more leaflets borne on the same leafstalk

compound lens *n* a lens consisting of more than one component lens

compound microscope *n* an instrument for magnifying small objects, consisting of a lens of short focal length for forming an image that is further magnified by a second lens of longer focal length. Compare **simple microscope**

compound number *n* a quantity expressed in two or more different but related units: *3 hours 10 seconds is a compound number*

compound sentence *n* a sentence containing at least two coordinate clauses

compound time *n* See **compound** (sense 16)

comprador or **compradore** (ˌkɒmprəˈdɔː) *n* (formerly in China and some other Asian countries) a native agent of a foreign enterprise [c17 from Portuguese: buyer, from Late Latin *comparātor*, from Latin *comparāre* to purchase, from *parāre* to prepare]

comprehend (ˌkɒmprɪˈhɛnd) *vb* **1** to perceive or understand **2** (*tr*) to comprise or embrace; include [c14 from Latin *comprehendere*, from *prehendere* to seize]

comprehensible (ˌkɒmprɪˈhɛnsəbəl) *adj* capable of being comprehended > ˌcompreˌhensi'bility or ˌcompre'hensibleness *n* > ˌcompre'hensibly *adv*

comprehension (ˌkɒmprɪˈhɛnʃən) *n* **1** the act or capacity of understanding **2** the state of including or comprising something; comprehensiveness **3** *education* an exercise consisting of a previously unseen passage of text with related questions, designed to test a student's understanding esp of a foreign language **4** *logic obsolete* the attributes implied by a given concept or term; connotation

comprehensive (ˌkɒmprɪˈhɛnsɪv) *adj* **1** of broad scope or content; including all or much **2** (of a car insurance policy) providing protection against most risks, including third-party liability, fire, theft, and damage **3** having the ability to understand **4** of, relating to, or being a comprehensive school ▷ *n* **5** short for **comprehensive school**. > ˌcompre'hensively *adv* > ˌcompre'hensiveness *n*

comprehensive school *n* **1** *chiefly Brit* a secondary school for children of all abilities from the same district **2** *Eastern Canadian* another name for **composite school**

compress *vb* (kəmˈprɛs) **1** (*tr*) to squeeze together or compact into less space; condense **2** *computing* to apply a compression program to (electronic data) so that it takes up less space ▷ *n* ('kɒmprɛs) **3** a wet or dry cloth or gauze pad with or without medication, applied firmly to some part of the body to relieve discomfort, reduce fever, drain a wound, etc **4** a machine for packing material, esp cotton, under pressure [C14 from Late Latin *compressāre*, from Latin *comprimere*, from *premere* to press] > com'pressible *adj* > com'pressibleness *n* > com'pressibly *adv*

compressed (kəm'prɛst) *adj* **1** squeezed together or condensed **2** (of the form of flatfishes, certain plant parts, etc) flattened laterally along the whole length

compressed air *n* air at a higher pressure than atmospheric pressure: used esp as a source of power for machines

compressibility (kəm,prɛsɪ'bɪlɪtɪ) *n* **1** the ability to be compressed **2** *physics* the reciprocal of the bulk modulus; the ratio of volume strain to stress at constant temperature. Symbol: k

compression (kəm'prɛʃən) *n* **1** Also called: **compressure** (kəm'prɛʃə) the act of compressing or the condition of being compressed **2** an increase in pressure of the charge in an engine or compressor obtained by reducing its volume

compression-ignition engine *n* a type of internal-combustion engine, such as a diesel, in which ignition occurs as a result of the rise in temperature caused by compression of the mixture in the cylinder

compression ratio *n* the ratio of the volume enclosed by the cylinder of an internal-combustion engine at the beginning of the compression stroke to the volume enclosed at the end of it

compressive (kəm'prɛsɪv) *adj* compressing or having the power or capacity to compress > com'pressively *adv*

compressor (kəm'prɛsə) *n* **1** any reciprocating or rotating device that compresses a gas **2** the part of a gas turbine that compresses the air before it enters the combustion chambers **3** any muscle that causes compression of any part or structure **4** a medical instrument for holding down a part of the body **5** an electronic device for reducing the variation in signal amplitude in a transmission system. Compare **expander, compander**

comprise (kəm'praɪz) *vb* (*tr*) **1** to include; contain **2** to constitute the whole of; consist of: *her singing comprised the entertainment* [C15 from French *compris* included, understood, from *comprendre* to COMPREHEND] > com'prisable *adj* > com'prisal *n*

▌ USAGE The use of *of* after *comprise* should be avoided: *the library comprises* (not *comprises of*) *500 000 books and manuscripts*

compromise ('kɒmprə,maɪz) *n* **1** settlement of a dispute by concessions on both or all sides **2** the terms of such a settlement **3** something midway between two or more different things **4** an exposure of one's good name, reputation, etc, to injury ▷ *vb* **5** to settle (a dispute) by making concessions **6** (*tr*) to expose (a person or persons) to disrepute **7** (*tr*) to prejudice unfavourably; weaken: *his behaviour compromised his chances* **8** (*tr*) *obsolete* to pledge mutually [C15 from Old French *compromis*, from Latin *comprōmissum* mutual agreement to accept the decision of an arbiter, from *comprōmittere*, from *prōmittere* to promise] > 'compro,miser *n* > 'compro,misingly *adv*

compte rendu French (kɔ̃t rɑ̃dy) *n, pl* **comptes rendus** (kɔ̃t rɑ̃dy) **1** a short review or notice, esp of a book **2** a statement of account [literally: account rendered]

Comptometer (kɒmp'tɒmɪtə) *n trademark* a high-speed calculating machine: superseded by electronic calculators

Compton effect ('kɒmptən) *n* a phenomenon in which a collision between a photon and a particle results in an increase in the kinetic energy of the particle and a corresponding increase in the wavelength of the photon [C20 named after Arthur Holly *Compton* (1892–1962), US physicist]

comptroller (kən'trəʊlə) *n* a variant spelling of **controller** (sense 2), esp as a title of any of various financial executives > comp'troller,ship *n*

compulsion (kəm'pʌlʃən) *n* **1** the act of compelling or the state of being compelled **2** something that compels **3** *psychiatry* an inner drive that causes a person to perform actions, often of a trivial and repetitive nature, against his or her will. See also **obsession** [C15 from Old French, from Latin *compellere* to COMPEL]

compulsive (kəm'pʌlsɪv) *adj* **1** relating to or involving compulsion ▷ *n* **2** *psychiatry* an individual who is subject to a psychological compulsion > com'pulsively *adv* > com'pulsiveness *n*

compulsory (kəm'pʌlsərɪ) *adj* **1** required by regulations or laws; obligatory: *compulsory education* **2** involving or employing compulsion; compelling; necessary; essential > com'pulsorily *adv* > com'pulsoriness *n*

compulsory purchase *n* purchase of a house or other property by a local authority or government department for public use or to make way for development, regardless of whether or not the owner wishes to sell

compunction (kəm'pʌŋkʃən) *n* a feeling of remorse, guilt, or regret [C14 from Church Latin *compūnctiō*, from Latin *compungere* to sting, from *com-* (intensive) + *pungere* to puncture; see POINT] > com'punctious *adj* > com'punctiously *adv*

compurgation (,kɒmpɜ:'geɪʃən) *n law* (formerly) a method of trial whereby a defendant might be acquitted if a sufficient number of persons swore to his innocence [C17 from Medieval Latin *compurgātiō*, from Latin *compurgāre* to purify entirely, from *com-* (intensive) + *purgāre* to PURGE] > 'compur,gator *n* > com'purgatory or com,purga'torial *adj*

computation (,kɒmpjʊ'teɪʃən) *n* a calculation involving numbers or quantities > ,compu'tational *adj*

computational fluid dynamics *n* (*functioning as singular*) the prediction of the behaviour of fluids and of the effects of fluid motion past objects by numerical methods rather than model experiments

compute (kəm'pju:t) *vb* **1** to calculate (an answer, result, etc), often with the aid of a computer ▷ *n* **2** calculation; computation (esp in the phrase **beyond compute**) [C17 from Latin *computāre*, from *putāre* to think] > com'putable *adj* > com,puta'bility *n*

computed tomography *n med* another name for **computerized tomography** (esp US)

computer (kəm'pju:tə) *n* **1 a** a device, usually electronic, that processes data according to a set of instructions. The **digital computer** stores data in discrete units and performs arithmetical and logical operations at very high speed. The **analog computer** has no memory and is slower than the digital computer but has a continuous rather than a discrete input. The **hybrid computer** combines some of the advantages of digital and analog computers **b** (*as modifier*): *computer technology*. Related prefix: **cyber- 2** a person who computes or calculates

computer-aided design *n* the use of computer techniques in designing products, esp involving the use of computer graphics. Abbreviation: CAD

computer-aided engineering *n* the use of computers to automate manufacturing processes. Abbreviation: CAE

computer architecture *n* the structure, behaviour, and design of computers

computerate (kəm'pju:tərɪt) *adj* able to use computers [C20 COMPUTER + -ATE[1], by analogy with *literate*]

computer conferencing *n* the conduct of meetings through the use of computer-based telecommunications

computer dating *n* the use of computers by dating agencies to match their clients

computer game *n* any of various games, recorded on cassette or disc for use in a home computer, that are played by manipulating a mouse, joystick, or the keys on the keyboard of a computer in response to the graphics on the screen

computer graphics *n* (*functioning as singular*) the use of a computer to produce and manipulate pictorial images on a video screen, as in animation techniques or the production of audiovisual aids

computerize or **computerise** (kəm'pju:tə,raɪz) *vb* **1** (*tr*) to cause (certain operations) to be performed by a computer, esp as a replacement for human labour **2** (*intr*) to install a computer **3** (*tr*) to control or perform (operations within a system) by means of a computer **4** (*tr*) to process or store (information) by means of or in a computer > com,puteri'zation or com,puteri'sation *n*

computerized tomography *n med* a radiological technique that produces images of cross sections through a patient's body using low levels of radiation. Also called (esp US): **computed tomography**. Abbreviation: CT. See also **CT scanner**

computer language *n* another term for **programming language**

computer literate *adj* able to use computers > computer literacy *n*

computer science *n* the study of computers and their application

computer typesetting *n* a system for the high-speed composition of type by a device driven by punched paper tape or magnetic tape that has been processed by a computer

computing (kəm'pju:tɪŋ) *n* **1** the activity of using computers and writing programs for them **2** the study of computers and their implications ▷ *adj* **3** of or relating to computers: *computing skills*

Comr *abbreviation for* Commissioner

comrade ('kɒmreɪd, -rɪd) *n* **1** an associate or companion **2** a fellow member of a political party, esp a fellow Communist or socialist [C16 from French *camarade*, from Spanish *camarada* group of soldiers sharing a billet, from *cámara* room, from Latin; see CAMERA, CHAMBER] > 'comradely *adj* > 'comrade,ship *n*

Comrades Marathon *n* the *South African* an annual long-distance race run every year on the 16th of June from Durban to Pietermaritzburg, a distance of approximately 90 kilometres (56 miles). Often shortened to: **the Comrades** [C20 first run after WWI by returning servicemen to commemorate their fallen comrades]

Comsat ('kɒmsæt) *n trademark* short for **communications satellite**

comstockery ('kʌm,stɒkərɪ, 'kɒm-) *n US* immoderate censorship on grounds of immorality [C20 coined by G. B. Shaw (1905) after Anthony *Comstock* (1844–1915), US moral crusader, who founded the Society for the Suppression of Vice]

Comstock Lode ('kʌm,stɒk, 'kɒm-) *n* an extensive gold and silver vein in W Nevada, near Virginia City [C19 named after T. P. *Comstock* (1820–70), American prospector]

Comus ('kəʊməs) *n* (in late Roman mythology) a god of revelry [C17 from Latin, from Greek *kōmos* a revel]

Com. Ver. *abbreviation for* Common Version (of the Bible)

con[1] (kɒn) *informal* ▷ *n* **1 a** short for **confidence trick b** (*as modifier*): con man ▷ *vb* **cons, conning, conned 2** (*tr*) to swindle or defraud [C19 from CONFIDENCE]

con[2] (kɒn) *n* (*usually plural*) **1** an argument or vote against a proposal, motion, etc **2** a person who argues or votes against a proposal, motion, etc ▷ Compare **pro[1]**. See also **pros and cons** [from Latin *contrā* against, opposed to]

C

con³ (kɒn) *n slang* short for **convict**

con⁴ *or esp US* **conn** (kɒn) *nautical* ▷ *vb* cons *or* conns, conning, conned **1** (*tr*) to direct the steering of (a vessel) ▷ *n* **2** the place where a person who cons a vessel is stationed [C17 *cun*, from earlier *condien* to guide, from Old French *conduire*, from Latin *condūcere*; see CONDUCT]

con⁵ (kɒn) *vb* cons, conning, conned (*tr*) *archaic* to study attentively or learn (esp in the phrase **con by rote**) [C15 variant of CAN¹ in the sense: to come to know]

con⁶ (kɒn) *prep music* with [Italian]

Con. *abbreviation for* Conservative

con- *prefix* a variant of **com-**

conacre (kʌˈneːkər) *n Irish* farming land let for a season or for eleven months [C19 from CORN¹ + ACRE]

Conakry *or* **Konakri** (*French* kɔnakri) *n* the capital of Guinea, a port on the island of Tombo. Pop: 1 465 000 (2005 est)

con amore (kɒn æˈmɔːrɪ) *adj, adv music* (to be performed) lovingly [C19 from Italian: with love]

conation (kəʊˈneɪʃən) *n* the element in psychological processes that tends towards activity or change and appears as desire, volition, and striving [C19 from Latin *cōnātiō* an attempting, from *cōnārī* to try] > co'national *adj*

conative (ˈkɒnətɪv, ˈkəʊ-) *adj* **1** *grammar* denoting an aspect of verbs in some languages used to indicate the effort of the agent in performing the activity described by the verb **2** of or relating to conation

conatus (kəʊˈneɪtəs) *n, pl* -tus **1** an effort or striving of natural impulse **2** (esp in the philosophy of Spinoza) the tendency of all things to persist in their own being [C17 from Latin: effort, from *cōnārī* to try]

con brio (kɒn ˈbriːəʊ) *adj, adv music* (to be performed) with liveliness or spirit, as in the phrase **allegro con brio** [Italian: with energy]

conc. *abbreviation for* concentrated

concatenate (kɒnˈkætɪˌneɪt) *vb* **1** (*tr*) to link or join together, esp in a chain or series ▷ *adj* **2** linked or joined together [C16 from Late Latin *concatēnāre* from Latin *com-* together + *catēna* CHAIN]

concatenation (kɒnˌkætɪˈneɪʃən) *n* **1** a series of interconnected events, concepts, etc **2** the act of linking together or the state of being joined **3** *logic* a function that forms a single string of symbols from two given strings by placing the second after the first

concave (ˈkɒnkeɪv, kɒnˈkeɪv) *adj* **1** curving inwards **2** *physics* having one or two surfaces curved or ground in the shape of a section of the interior of a sphere, paraboloid, etc: *a concave lens* **3** *maths* (of a polygon) containing an interior angle greater than 180° **4** an obsolete word for **hollow** ▷ *vb* **5** (*tr*) to make concave ▷ Compare **convex** [C15 from Latin *concavus* arched, from *cavus* hollow] > con'cavely *adv* > 'concaveness *n*

concavity (kɒnˈkævɪtɪ) *n, pl* -ties **1** the state or quality of being concave **2** a concave surface or thing; cavity

concavo-concave (kɒnˌkeɪvəʊkɒnˈkeɪv) *adj* (esp of a lens) having both sides concave; biconcave

concavo-convex *adj* **1** having one side concave and the other side convex **2** (of a lens) having a concave face with greater curvature than the convex face. Compare **convexo-concave** (sense 2)

conceal (kənˈsiːl) *vb* (*tr*) **1** to keep from discovery; hide **2** to keep secret [C14 from Old French *conceler*, from Latin *concēlāre*, from *com-* (intensive) + *cēlāre* to hide] > con'cealable *adj* > con'cealer *n* > con'cealment *n*

concede (kənˈsiːd) *vb* **1** (when *tr*, may take a clause as object) to admit or acknowledge (something) as true or correct **2** to yield or allow (something, such as a right) **3** (*tr*) to admit as certain in outcome: *to concede an election* [C17 from Latin *concēdere*, from *cēdere* to give way, CEDE] > con'cededly *adv* > con'ceder *n*

conceit (kənˈsiːt) *n* **1** a high, often exaggerated, opinion of oneself or one's accomplishments; vanity **2** *literary* an elaborate image or far-fetched comparison, esp as used by the English Metaphysical poets **3** *archaic* **a** a witty expression **b** fancy; imagination **c** an idea **4** *obsolete* a small ornament ▷ *vb* (*tr*) **5** *Northern English dialect* to like or be able to bear (something, such as food or drink) **6** *obsolete* to think or imagine [C14 from CONCEIVE]

conceited (kənˈsiːtɪd) *adj* **1** having a high or exaggerated opinion of oneself or one's accomplishments **2** *archaic* fanciful **3** *obsolete* witty or intelligent > con'ceitedly *adv* > con'ceitedness *n*

conceivable (kənˈsiːvəbəl) *adj* capable of being understood, believed, or imagined; possible > con,ceiva'bility *or* con'ceivableness *n* > con'ceivably *adv*

conceive (kənˈsiːv) *vb* **1** (when *intr*, folly by *of*; when *tr*, often takes a clause as object) to have an idea (of); imagine; think **2** (*tr*; takes a clause as object or an infinitive) to hold as an opinion; believe **3** (*tr*) to develop or form, esp in the mind: *she conceived a passion for music* **4** to become pregnant with (young) **5** (*tr*) *rare* to express in words [C13 from Old French *conceivre*, from Latin *concipere* to take in, from *capere* to take] > con'ceiver *n*

concelebrate (kɒnˈsɛlɪˌbreɪt) *vb Christianity* to celebrate (the Eucharist or Mass) jointly with one or more other priests [C16 from Latin *concelebrāre*] > con,cele'bration *n*

concent (kənˈsɛnt) *n archaic* a concord, as of sounds, voices, etc [C16 from Latin *concentus* harmonious sounds, from *concinere* to sing together, from *canere* to sing]

concentrate (ˈkɒnsənˌtreɪt) *vb* **1** to come or cause to come to a single purpose or aim: *to concentrate one's hopes on winning* **2** to make or become denser or purer by the removal of certain elements, esp the solvent of a solution **3** (*tr*) to remove rock or sand from (an ore) to make it purer **4** (*intr*; often foll by *on*) to bring one's faculties to bear (on); think intensely (about) ▷ *n* **5** a concentrated material or solution: *tomato concentrate* [C17 back formation from CONCENTRATION, ultimately from Latin *com-* same + *centrum* CENTRE] > 'concen,trator *n*

concentration (ˌkɒnsənˈtreɪʃən) *n* **1** intense mental application; complete attention **2** the act or process of concentrating **3** something that is concentrated **4** the strength of a solution, esp the amount of dissolved substance in a given volume of solvent, usually expressed in moles per cubic metre or cubic decimetre (litre). Symbol: *c* **5** the process of increasing the concentration of a solution **6** *military* **a** the act of bringing together military forces **b** the application of fire from a number of weapons against a target **7** *economics* the degree to which the output or employment in an industry is accounted for by only a few firms **8** another name (esp US) for **Pelmanism**

concentration camp *n* a guarded prison camp in which nonmilitary prisoners are held, esp one of those in Nazi Germany in which millions were exterminated

concentrative (ˈkɒnsənˌtreɪtɪv) *adj* tending to concentrate; characterized by concentration > 'concen,tratively *adv* > 'concen,trativeness *n*

concentre (kɒnˈsɛntə) *or US* **concenter** *vb* to converge or cause to converge on a common centre; concentrate [C16 from French *concentrer*; see CONCENTRATE]

concentric (kənˈsɛntrɪk) *adj* having a common centre: *concentric circles*. Compare **eccentric** (sense 3) [C14 from Medieval Latin *concentricus*, from Latin *com-* same + *centrum* CENTRE] > con'centrically *adv* > con,cen'tricity (ˌkɒnsənˈtrɪsɪtɪ) *n*

Concepción (*Spanish* konθepˈθjon) *n* an industrial city in S central Chile. Pop: 378 000 (2005 est)

concept (ˈkɒnsɛpt) *n* **1** an idea, esp an abstract idea: *the concepts of biology* **2** *philosophy* a general idea or notion that corresponds to some class of entities and that consists of the characteristic or essential features of the class **3** *philosophy* **a** the conjunction of all the characteristic features of something **b** a theoretical construct within some theory **c** a directly intuited object of thought **d** the meaning of a predicate **4** (*modifier*) (of a product, esp a car) created as an exercise to demonstrate the technical skills and imagination of the designers, and not intended for mass production or sale [C16 from Latin *conceptum* something received or conceived, from *concipere* to take in, CONCEIVE]

conceptacle (kənˈsɛptəkəl) *n* a flask-shaped cavity containing the reproductive organs in some algae and fungi [C17 from Latin *conceptāculum* receptacle, from *concipere* to receive, CONCEIVE]

conception (kənˈsɛpʃən) *n* **1** something conceived; notion, idea, design, or plan **2** the description under which someone considers something: *her conception of freedom is wrong* **3** the fertilization of an ovum by a sperm in the Fallopian tube followed by implantation in the womb **4** origin or beginning: *from its conception the plan was a failure* **5** the act or power of forming notions; invention [C13 from Latin *conceptiō*, from *concipere* to CONCEIVE] > con'ceptional *or* con'ceptive *adj*

conception rate *n vet science* the success rate of artificial insemination in agricultural animals, usually expressed as a percentage

conceptual (kənˈsɛptjʊəl) *adj* **1** relating to or concerned with concepts; abstract **2** concerned with the definitions or relations of the concepts of some field of enquiry rather than with the facts > con'ceptually *adv*

conceptual art *n* art in which the idea behind a particular work, and the means of producing it, are more important than the finished work

conceptualism (kənˈsɛptjʊəˌlɪzəm) *n* **1** the philosophical theory that the application of general words to a variety of objects reflects the existence of some mental entity through which the application is mediated and which constitutes the meaning of the term. Compare **nominalism, realism, Platonism 2** the philosophical view that there is no reality independent of our conception of it, or (as in the philosophy of Immanuel Kant, the German philosopher (1724–1804)) that the intellect is not a merely passive recipient of experience but rather imposes a structure on it > con'ceptualist *n* > con,ceptual'istic *adj*

conceptualize *or* **conceptualise** (kənˈsɛptjʊəˌlaɪz) *vb* to form (a concept or concepts) out of observations, experience, data, etc > con,ceptuali'zation *or* con,ceptuali'sation *n*

concern (kənˈsɜːn) *vb* (*tr*) **1** to relate to; be of importance or interest to; affect **2** (usually foll by *with* or *in*) to involve or interest (oneself): *he concerns himself with other people's affairs* ▷ *n* **3** something that affects or is of importance to a person; affair; business **4** regard for or interest in a person or a thing: *he felt a strong concern for her* **5** anxiety, worry, or solicitude **6** important bearing or relation: *his news has great concern for us* **7** a commercial company or enterprise **8** *informal* a material thing, esp one of which one has a low opinion [C15 from Late Latin *concernere* to mingle together, from Latin *com-* together + *cernere* to sift, distinguish]

concerned (kənˈsɜːnd) *adj* **1** (*postpositive*) interested, guilty, involved, or appropriate: *I shall find the boy concerned and punish him* **2** worried, troubled, or solicitous > concernedly (kənˈsɜːnɪdlɪ) *adv* > con'cernedness *n*

concerning (kənˈsɜːnɪŋ) *prep* **1** about; regarding; on the subject of ▷ *adj* **2** worrying or troublesome

concernment (kənˈsɜːnmənt) *n* **1** *rare* affair or business; concern **2** *archaic* a matter of importance

concert *n* (ˈkɒnsɜːt, -sət) **1 a** a performance of music by players or singers that does not involve theatrical staging. Compare **recital** (sense 1) **b** (*as modifier*): *a concert version of an opera* **2** agreement in design, plan, or action **3** **in concert a** acting in a co-ordinated fashion with a common purpose **b** (of musicians, esp rock musicians) performing live ▷ *vb* (kən'sɜːt) **4** to arrange or contrive (a plan) by mutual agreement [C16 from French *concerter* to bring into agreement, from Italian *concertare*, from Late Latin *concertāre* to work together, from Latin: to dispute, debate, from *certāre* to contend]

concertante (ˌkɒntʃəˈtæntɪ) *music* ▷ *adj* **1** characterized by contrasting alternating tutti and solo passages ▷ *n, pl* **-ti** (-tɪ) **2** a composition characterized by such contrasts [C18 from Italian, from *concertare* to perform a concert, from *concerto* CONCERT]

concerted (kən'sɜːtɪd) *adj* **1** mutually contrived, planned, or arranged; combined (esp in the phrases **concerted action, concerted effort**) **2** *music* arranged in parts for a group of singers or players > con'certedly *adv*

Concertgebouw (*Dutch* kɔn'sɛrtxəbɔu) *n* a concert hall in Amsterdam, inaugurated in 1888: the **Concertgebouw Orchestra** established in 1888, has been independent of the hall since World War II

concertgoer ('kɒnsɜːtˌɡəʊə) *n* a person who attends concerts of music

concert grand *n* a full-size grand piano, usually around 7 feet in length. Compare **baby grand, boudoir grand**

concertina (ˌkɒnsəˈtiːnə) *n* **1** a small hexagonal musical instrument of the reed organ family in which metallic reeds are vibrated by air from a set of bellows operated by the player's hands. Notes are produced by pressing buttons ▷ *vb* **-nas, -naing, -naed 2** (*intr*) to collapse or fold up like a concertina [C19 CONCERT + -*ina*] > ˌconcer'tinist *n*

concertino (ˌkɒntʃəˈtiːnəʊ) *n, pl* **-ni** (-nɪ) **1** the small group of soloists in a concerto grosso. Compare **ripieno 2** a short concerto [C19 from Italian: a little CONCERTO]

concertize *or* **concertise** ('kɒnsəˌtaɪz) *vb* (*intr*) (esp of a soloist or conductor) to give concerts

concertmaster ('kɒnsətˌmɑːstə) *n* a US and Canadian word for **leader** (of an orchestra)

concerto (kən'tʃɛətəʊ) *n, pl* **-tos** *or* **-ti** (-tɪ) **1** a composition for an orchestra and one or more soloists. The classical concerto usually consisted of several movements, and often a cadenza. See also **sonata** (sense 1), **symphony** (sense 1) **2** another word for **ripieno** [C18 from Italian: CONCERT]

concerto grosso ('ɡrɒsəʊ) *n, pl* **concerti grossi** ('ɡrɒsɪ) *or* **concerto grossos** a composition for an orchestra and a group of soloists, chiefly of the baroque period [Italian, literally: big concerto]

concert overture *n* See **overture** (sense 1c)

concert party *n* **1** a musical entertainment popular in the early 20th century, esp one at a British seaside resort **2** *stock exchange informal* a group of individuals or companies who secretly agree to purchase shares separately in a particular company, which they plan to amalgamate later into a single holding: a malpractice that is illegal in some countries

concert pitch *n* **1** the frequency of 440 hertz assigned to the A above middle C. See **pitch¹** (sense 28b), **international pitch 2** *informal* a state of extreme readiness

concertstück (kən'sɜːtʃtuːk) *n music* **1** a composition in concerto style but shorter than a full concerto **2** (loosely) a piece suitable for concert performance [from German *Konzertstück* a concertino]

concert tuning *n music* the standard tuning for a guitar: E A D G B E

concession (kən'sɛʃən) *n* **1** the act of yielding or conceding, as to a demand or argument **2** something conceded **3** *Brit* a reduction in the usual price of a ticket granted to a special group of

customers: *a student concession* **4** any grant of rights, land, or property by a government, local authority, corporation, or individual **5** the right, esp an exclusive right, to market a particular product in a given area **6** *US and Canadian* **a** the right to maintain a subsidiary business on a lessor's premises **b** the premises so granted or the business so maintained **c** a free rental period for such premises **7** *Canadian* (chiefly in Ontario and Quebec) **a** a land subdivision in a township survey **b** another name for a **concession road** [C16 from Latin *concessiō* an allowing, from *concēdere* to CONCEDE] > con'cessible *adj*

concessionaire (kənˌsɛʃəˈnɛə), **concessioner** (kən'sɛʃənə) *or* **concessionary** *n* someone who holds or operates a concession

concessionary (kən'sɛʃənərɪ) *adj* **1** of, granted, or obtained by a concession ▷ *n, pl* **-aries 2** another word for **concessionaire**

concession road *n Canadian* (esp in Ontario) one of a series of roads separating concessions in a township

concessive (kən'sɛsɪv) *adj* **1** implying or involving concession; tending to concede **2** *grammar* a conjunction, preposition, phrase, or clause describing a state of affairs that might have been expected to rule out what is described in the main clause but in fact does not: *"Although" in the sentence "Although they had been warned, they refused to take care" is a concessive conjunction* [C18 from Late Latin *concessīvus*, from Latin *concēdere* to CONCEDE]

conch (kɒŋk, kɒntʃ) *n, pl* **conchs** (kɒŋks) *or* **conches** ('kɒntʃɪz) **1** any of various tropical marine gastropod molluscs of the genus *Strombus* and related genera, esp *S. gigas* (giant conch), characterized by a large brightly coloured spiral shell **2** the shell of such a mollusc, used as a trumpet **3** *architect* another name for **concha** (sense 2) [C16 from Latin *concha*, from Greek *konkhē* shellfish]

concha ('kɒŋkə) *n, pl* **-chae** (-kiː) **1** any bodily organ or part resembling a shell in shape, such as the external ear **2** *Also called:* **conch** *architect* the half dome of an apse > 'conchal *adj*

conchie *or* **conchy** ('kɒntʃɪ) *n, pl* **-chies** *informal* short for **conscientious objector**

conchiferous (kɒŋ'kɪfərəs) *adj* **1** (esp of molluscs) having or producing a shell **2** (of rocks) containing shells

conchiglie (kɒn'kiːljeɪ) *n* pasta in the form of shells [C20 Italian, literally: little shells, from Latin *concha* shell; see CONCH]

conchiolin (kɒŋ'kaɪəlɪn) *n* a fibrous insoluble protein that forms the basic structure of the shells of molluscs. Formula: $C_{30}H_{48}O_{11}N_9$ [C19 from CONCH; see -IN]

Conchobar ('kɒŋkəʊwə, 'kɒnʊə) *n* (in Irish legend) a king of Ulster at about the beginning of the Christian era. See also **Deirdre**

conchoid ('kɒŋkɔɪd) *n geometry* a plane curve consisting of two branches situated about a line to which they are asymptotic, so that a line from a fixed point (the pole) intersecting both branches is of constant length between asymptote and either branch. Equation: $(x − a)^2(x^2 + y^2) = b^2x^2$ where *a* is the distance between the pole and a vertical asymptote and *b* is the length of the constant segment

conchoidal (kɒŋ'kɔɪdᵊl) *adj* **1** (of the fracture of minerals and rocks) having smooth shell-shaped convex and concave surfaces **2** (of minerals and rocks, such as flint) having such a fracture > con'choidally *adv*

conchology (kɒŋ'kɒlədʒɪ) *n* the study and collection of mollusc shells > conchological (ˌkɒŋkə'lɒdʒɪkᵊl) *adj* > con'chologist *n*

concierge (ˌkɒnsɪ'ɛəʒ; *French* kɔ̃sjɛrʒ) *n* (esp in France) a caretaker of a block of flats, hotel, etc, esp one who lives on the premises [C17 from French, ultimately from Latin *conservus*, from *servus* slave]

conciliar (kən'sɪlɪə) *adj* of, from, or by means of a council, esp an ecclesiastical one > con'ciliarly *adv*

conciliate (kən'sɪlɪˌeɪt) *vb* (*tr*) **1** to overcome the hostility of; placate; win over **2** to win or gain (favour, regard, etc), esp by making friendly overtures **3** *archaic* to make compatible; reconcile [C16 from Latin *conciliāre* to bring together, from *concilium* COUNCIL] > con'ciliable *adj* > con'ciliˌator *n*

conciliation (kənˌsɪlɪ'eɪʃən) *n* **1** the act or process of conciliating **2** a method of helping the parties in a dispute to reach agreement, esp divorcing or separating couples to part amicably

conciliatory (kən'sɪljətərɪ, -trɪ) *or* **conciliative** (kən'sɪljətɪv) *adj* intended to placate or reconcile > con'ciliatorily *adv* > con'ciliatoriness *n*

concinnity (kən'sɪnɪtɪ) *n, pl* **-ties** a harmonious arrangement of parts, esp in literary works, speeches, etc [C16 from Latin *concinnitās* a skilful combining of various things, from *concinnāre* to adjust, of obscure origin] > con'cinnous *adj*

concise (kən'saɪs) *adj* expressing much in few words; brief and to the point [C16 from Latin *concīsus* cut up, cut short, from *concīdere* to cut to pieces, from *caedere* to cut, strike down] > con'cisely *adv* > con'ciseness *n*

concision (kən'sɪʒən) *n* the quality of being concise; brevity; terseness

conclave ('kɒnkleɪv, 'kɒŋ-) *n* **1** a confidential or secret meeting **2** *RC Church* **a** the closed apartments where the college of cardinals elects a new pope **b** a meeting of the college of cardinals for this purpose [C14 from Medieval Latin *conclāve*, from Latin: cage, place that may be locked, from *clāvis* key] > 'conclavist *n*

conclude (kən'kluːd) *vb* (*mainly tr*) **1** (*also intr*) to come or cause to come to an end or conclusion **2** (*takes a clause as object*) to decide by reasoning; deduce: *the judge concluded that the witness had told the truth* **3** to arrange finally; settle: *to conclude a treaty; it was concluded that he should go* **4** *obsolete* to confine [C14 from Latin *conclūdere* to enclose, end, from *claudere* to close] > con'cluder *n*

conclusion (kən'kluːʒən) *n* **1** end or termination **2** the last main division of a speech, lecture, essay, etc **3** the outcome or result of an act, process, event, etc (esp in the phrase a **foregone conclusion**) **4** a final decision or judgment; resolution (esp in the phrase **come to a conclusion**) **5** *logic* **a** a statement that purports to follow from another or others (the **premises**) by means of an argument **b** a statement that does validly follow from given premises **6** *law* **a** an admission or statement binding on the party making it; estoppel **b** the close of a pleading or of a conveyance **7** **in conclusion** lastly; to sum up **8** **jump to conclusions** to come to a conclusion prematurely, without sufficient thought or on incomplete evidence [C14 via Old French from Latin; see CONCLUDE, -ION]

conclusive (kən'kluːsɪv) *adj* **1** putting an end to doubt; decisive; final **2** approaching or involving an end or conclusion > con'clusively *adv* > con'clusiveness *n*

concoct (kən'kɒkt) *vb* (*tr*) **1** to make by combining different ingredients **2** to invent; make up; contrive [C16 from Latin *concoctus* cooked together, from *concoquere*, from *coquere* to cook] > con'cocter *or* con'coctor *n* > con'coctive *adj*

concoction (kən'kɒkʃən) *n* **1** the act or process of concocting **2** something concocted **3** an untruth; lie

concomitance (kən'kɒmɪtəns) *n* **1** existence or occurrence together or in connection with another **2** a thing that exists in connection with another **3** *Christian theol* the doctrine that the body and blood of Christ are present in the Eucharist

concomitant (kən'kɒmɪtənt) *adj* **1** existing or occurring together; associative ▷ *n* **2** a concomitant act, person, etc [C17 from Late Latin *concomitārī* to accompany, from *com-* with + *comes* companion, fellow] > con'comitantly *adv*

C

concord ('kɒnkɔːd, 'kɒŋ-) n 1 agreement or harmony between people or nations; amity 2 a treaty establishing peaceful relations between nations 3 agreement or harmony between things, ideas, etc 4 *music* a combination of musical notes, esp one containing a series of consonant intervals. Compare **discord** (sense 3) 5 *grammar* another word for **agreement** (sense 6) [c13 from Old French *concorde*, from Latin *concordia*, from *concors* of the same mind, harmonious, from *com-* same + *cor* heart]

Concord ('kɒŋkəd) n 1 a town in NE Massachusetts: scene of one of the opening military actions (1775) of the War of American Independence. Pop: 16 937 (2003 est) 2 a city in New Hampshire, the state capital: printing, publishing. Pop: 41 823 (2003 est)

concordance (kən'kɔːdᵊns) n 1 a state or condition of agreement or harmony 2 a book that indexes the principal words in a literary work, often with the immediate context and an account of the meaning 3 an index produced by computer or machine, alphabetically listing every word in a text 4 an alphabetical list of subjects or topics

concordant (kən'kɔːdᵊnt) adj being in agreement: harmonious > **con'cordantly** adv

concordat (kən'kɔːdæt) n a pact or treaty, esp one between the Vatican and another state concerning the interests of religion in that state [c17 via French, from Medieval Latin *concordātum*, from Latin: something agreed, from *concordāre* to be of one mind; see CONCORD]

Concorde ('kɒnkɔːd, 'kɒŋ-) n the first commercial supersonic airliner. Of Anglo-French construction, it is capable of cruising at over 2160 km per hr (1200 mph)

Concord grape ('kɒŋkəd, 'kɒnkɔːd) n a variety of grape with purple-black fruit covered with a bluish bloom [c19 discovered at CONCORD, Mass.]

concours d'élégance French (kɔ̃kur delegɑ̃s) n a parade of cars or other vehicles, prizes being awarded to the most elegant, best designed, or best turned-out

concourse ('kɒnkɔːs, 'kɒŋ-) n 1 a crowd; throng 2 a coming together; confluence: *a concourse of events* 3 a large open space for the gathering of people in a public place 4 *chiefly US* a ground for sports, racing, athletics, etc [c14 from Old French *concours*, ultimately from Latin *concurrere* to run together, from *currere* to run]

concrescence (kən'krɛsᵊns) n *biology* a growing together of initially separate parts or organs [c17 from Latin *concrēscentia*, from *concrēscere* to grow together, from *crēscere* to grow; see CRESCENT] > **con'crescent** adj

concrete ('kɒnkriːt) n 1 a a construction material made of a mixture of cement, sand, stone, and water that hardens to a stonelike mass b (*as modifier*): *a concrete slab* 2 *physics* a rigid mass formed by the coalescence of separate particles ▷ adj 3 relating to a particular instance or object; specific as opposed to general: *a concrete example* 4 a relating to or characteristic of things capable of being perceived by the senses, as opposed to abstractions b (*as noun*): *the concrete* 5 formed by the coalescence of particles; condensed; solid ▷ vb 6 (tr) to construct in or cover with concrete 7 (kən'kriːt) to become or cause to become solid; coalesce [c14 from Latin *concrētus* grown together, hardened, from *concrēscere*; see CONCRESCENCE] > **'concretely** adv > **'concreteness** n > **con'cretive** adj > **con'cretively** adv

concrete music n music consisting of an electronically modified montage of tape-recorded sounds

concrete noun n a noun that refers to a material object, as for example *horse*. Compare **abstract noun**

concrete number n a number referring to a particular object or objects, as in *three dogs, ten men*

concrete poetry n poetry in which the visual form of the poem is used to convey meaning

concretion (kən'kriːʃən) n 1 the act or process of coming or growing together; coalescence 2 a solid or solidified mass 3 something made real, tangible, or specific 4 any of various rounded or irregular mineral masses formed by chemical precipitation around a nucleus, such as a bone or shell, that is different in composition from the sedimentary rock that surrounds it 5 *pathol* another word for **calculus**. > **con'cretionary** adj

concretize or **concretise** ('kɒnkrɪˌtaɪz, 'kɒn-) vb (tr) to render concrete; make real or specific; give tangible form to > ˌconcreti'zation or ˌconcreti'sation n

concubinage (kɒn'kjuːbɪnɪdʒ) n 1 cohabitation without legal marriage 2 the state of living as a concubine

concubine ('kɒŋkjʊˌbaɪn, 'kɒn-) n 1 (in polygamous societies) a secondary wife, usually of lower social rank 2 a woman who cohabits with a man [c13 from Old French, from Latin *concubīna*, from *concumbere* to lie together, from *cubare* to lie] > **concubinary** (kɒn'kjuːbɪnərɪ) n, adj

concupiscence (kən'kjuːpɪsəns) n strong desire, esp sexual desire [c14 from Church Latin *concupiscentia*, from Latin *concupiscere* to covet ardently, from *cupere* to wish, desire] > **con'cupiscent** adj

concur (kən'kɜː) vb -curs, -curring, -curred (intr) 1 to agree; be of the same mind; be in accord 2 to combine, act together, or cooperate 3 to occur simultaneously; coincide 4 *rare* to converge [c15 from Latin *concurrere* to run together, from *currere* to run] > **con'curringly** adv

concurrence (kən'kʌrəns) n 1 the act of concurring 2 agreement in opinion; accord; assent 3 cooperation or combination 4 simultaneous occurrence; coincidence 5 *geometry* a point at which three or more lines intersect ▷ Also (for senses 1–4): **concurrency**

concurrent (kən'kʌrənt) adj 1 taking place at the same time or in the same location 2 cooperating 3 meeting at, approaching, or having a common point: *concurrent lines* 4 having equal authority or jurisdiction 5 in accordance or agreement; harmonious ▷ n 6 something joint or contributory; a concurrent circumstance or cause > **con'currently** adv

concurrent engineering n a method of designing and marketing new products in which development stages are run in parallel rather than in series, to reduce lead times and costs. Also called: **interactive engineering**

concurrent processing n the ability of a computer to process two or more programs in parallel

concurrent versions system n *computing* a system that allows more than one person to work on the same file at the same time, merging their changes but keeping records of the different versions

concuss (kən'kʌs) vb (tr) 1 to injure (the brain) by a violent blow, fall, etc 2 to shake violently; agitate; disturb [c16 from Latin *concussus* violently shaken, from *concutere* to disturb greatly, from *quatere* to shake]

concussion (kən'kʌʃən) n 1 a jarring of the brain, caused by a blow or a fall, usually resulting in loss of consciousness 2 any violent shaking; jarring > **con'cussive** adj

condemn (kən'dɛm) vb (tr) 1 to express strong disapproval of; censure 2 to pronounce judicial sentence on 3 to demonstrate the guilt of: *his secretive behaviour condemned him* 4 to judge or pronounce unfit for use: *that food has been condemned* 5 to compel or force into a particular state or activity: *his disposition condemned him to boredom* [c13 from Old French *condempner*, from Latin *condemnāre*, from *damnāre* to condemn; see DAMN] > **condemnable** (kən'dɛməbᵊl) adj > **con'demnably** adv > ˌcondem'nation n > **con'demner** n > **con'demningly** adv

condemnatory (ˌkɒndɛm'neɪtərɪ, kən'dɛmnətərɪ, -trɪ) adj expressing strong disapproval or censure

condemned cell n a prison cell in which a person condemned to death awaits execution

condensate (kən'dɛnseɪt) n a substance formed by condensation, such as a liquid from a vapour

condensation (ˌkɒndɛn'seɪʃən) n 1 the act or process of condensing, or the state of being condensed 2 anything that has condensed from a vapour, esp on a window 3 *chem* a type of reaction in which two organic molecules combine to form a larger molecule as well as a simple molecule such as water, methanol, etc 4 anything that has been shortened, esp an abridged version of a book 5 *psychoanal* a the fusion of two or more ideas, etc, into one symbol, occurring esp in dreams b the reduction of many experiences into one word or action, as in a phobia > ˌconden'sational adj

condensation trail n another name for **vapour trail**

condense (kən'dɛns) vb 1 (tr) to increase the density of; compress 2 to reduce or be reduced in volume or size; make or become more compact 3 to change or cause to change from a gaseous to a liquid or solid state 4 *chem* to undergo or cause to undergo condensation [c15 from Latin *condēnsāre*, from *dēnsāre* to make thick, from *dēnsus* DENSE] > **con'densable** or **con'densible** adj > conˌdensa'bility or conˌdensi'bility n

condensed (kən'dɛnst) adj 1 (of printers' type) narrower than usual for a particular height. Compare **expanded** (sense 1) 2 *botany* designating an inflorescence in which the flowers are crowded together and are almost or completely sessile 3 *chem* designating a polycyclic ring system in a molecule in which two rings share two or more common atoms, as in naphthalene. Also called: **fused**

condensed matter n *physics* a crystalline and amorphous solids and liquids, including liquid crystals, glasses, polymers, and gels b (*as modifier*): *condensed-matter physics*

condensed milk n milk reduced by evaporation to a thick concentration, with sugar added. Compare **evaporated milk**

condenser (kən'dɛnsə) n 1 a an apparatus for reducing gases to their liquid or solid form by the abstraction of heat b a device for abstracting heat, as in a refrigeration unit 2 a lens that concentrates light into a small area 3 another name for **capacitor** 4 a person or device that condenses

condescend (ˌkɒndɪ'sɛnd) vb (intr) 1 to act graciously towards another or others regarded as being on a lower level; behave patronizingly 2 to do something that one regards as below one's dignity [c14 from Church Latin *condēscendere* to stoop, condescend, from Latin *dēscendere* to DESCEND]

condescendence (ˌkɒndɪ'sɛndəns) n 1 *Scots law* a statement of facts presented by the plaintiff in a cause 2 a less common word for **condescension**

condescending (ˌkɒndɪ'sɛndɪŋ) adj showing or implying condescension by stooping to the level of one's inferiors, esp in a patronizing way > ˌconde'scendingly adv

condescension (ˌkɒndɪ'sɛnʃən) n the act or an instance of behaving in a patronizing way

condign (kən'daɪn) adj (esp of a punishment) fitting; deserved [c15 from Old French *condigne*, from Latin *condignus*, from *dignus* worthy] > **con'dignly** adv

condiment ('kɒndɪmənt) n any spice or sauce such as salt, pepper, mustard, etc [c15 from Latin *condīmentum* seasoning, from *condīre* to pickle]

condition (kən'dɪʃən) n 1 a particular state of being or existence; situation with respect to circumstances: *the human condition* 2 something that limits or restricts something else; a qualification: *you may enter only under certain conditions* 3 (*plural*) external or existing circumstances: *conditions were right for a takeover* 4 state of health or physical fitness, esp good health (esp in the phrases **in condition, out of condition**) **5** an ailment or physical disability: *a heart condition* **6** something indispensable to the existence of something else: *your happiness is a condition of mine* **7** something required as part of an agreement or pact; terms: *the conditions of the lease are set out* **8** *law* **a** a declaration or provision in a will, contract, etc, that makes some right or liability contingent upon the happening of some event **b** the event itself **9** *logic* a statement whose truth is either required for the truth of a given statement (a **necessary condition**) or sufficient to guarantee the truth of the given statement (a **sufficient condition**). See **sufficient** (sense 2), **necessary** (sense 3e) **10** *maths, logic* a presupposition, esp a restriction on the domain of quantification, indispensable to the proof of a theorem and stated as part of it **11** *statistics* short for **experimental condition 12** rank, status, or position in life **13** **on** (*or* **upon**) **condition that** (*conjunction*) provided that ▷ *vb* (*mainly tr*) **14** *psychol* **a** to alter the response of (a person or animal) to a particular stimulus or situation **b** to establish a conditioned response in (a person or animal) **15** to put into a fit condition or state **16** to improve the condition of (one's hair) by use of special cosmetics **17** to accustom or inure **18** to subject to a condition **19** (*intr*) *archaic* to make conditions [C14 from Latin *conditiō*, from *condīcere* to discuss, agree together, from *con-* together + *dīcere* to say]

conditional (kənˈdɪʃənəl) *adj* **1** depending on other factors; not certain **2** *grammar* (of a clause, conjunction, form of a verb, or whole sentence) expressing a condition on which something else is contingent: *"If he comes" is a conditional clause in the sentence "If he comes I shall go"* **3 a** (of an equation or inequality) true for only certain values of the variable: $x^2 - 1 = x + 1$ *is a conditional equation, only true for* $x = 2$ *or* -1 **b** (of an infinite series) divergent when the absolute values of the terms are considered **4** Also: **hypothetical** *logic* (of a proposition) consisting of two component propositions associated by the words *if...then* so that the proposition is false only when the antecedent is true and the consequent false. Usually written: *p→q* or *p⊃q*, where *p* is the antecedent, *q* the consequent, and → or ⊃ symbolizes *implies* ▷ *n* **5** *grammar* **a** a conditional form of a verb **b** a conditional clause or sentence **6** *logic* a conditional proposition > conˌditionˈality *n* > conˈditionally *adv*

conditional access *n* the encryption of television programme transmissions so that only authorized subscribers with suitable decoding apparatus may have access to them

conditionalization *or* **conditionalisation** (kənˌdɪʃənəlaɪˈzeɪʃən) *n logic* the derivation from an argument of a conditional statement with the conjunction of the premises as antecedent and the conclusion as consequent. If the argument is valid conditionalization yields a truth

conditional probability *n statistics* the probability of one event, *A*, occurring given that another, *B*, is already known to have occurred: written *P(A|B)* and equal to *P(A and B)|P(B)*

condition code register *n computing* a hardware register used for storing the current values of the condition codes

condition codes *pl n* a set of single bits that indicate specific conditions within a computer. The values of the condition codes are often determined by the outcome of a prior software operation and their principal use is to govern choices between alternative instruction sequences

conditioned (kənˈdɪʃənd) *adj* **1** *psychol* of or denoting a response that has been learned. Compare **unconditioned 2** (foll by *to*) accustomed; inured; prepared by training

conditioned response *n psychol* a response that is transferred from the second to the first of a pair of stimuli. See **classical conditioning**. A well-

known Pavlovian example is salivation by a dog when it hears a bell ring, because food has always been presented when the bell has been rung previously. Also called (esp formerly): **conditioned reflex**. See also **unconditioned response**

conditioned stimulus *n psychol* a stimulus to which an organism has learned to make a response by classical conditioning. Compare **unconditioned stimulus**

conditioned suppression *n psychol* the reduction in the frequency of a learned response, eg pressing a bar for water, that occurs when a stimulus previously associated with pain is present

conditioner (kənˈdɪʃənə) *n* **1** a person or thing that conditions **2** a substance, esp a cosmetic, applied to something to improve its condition: *hair conditioner*

conditioning (kənˈdɪʃənɪŋ) *n* **1** *psychol* the learning process by which the behaviour of an organism becomes dependent on an event occurring in its environment. See also **classical conditioning, instrumental learning** ▷ *adj* **2** (of a shampoo, cosmetic, etc) intended to improve the condition of something: *a conditioning rinse*

condo (ˈkɒndəʊ) *n, pl* -**dos**, *informal* a condominium building or apartment

condole (kənˈdəʊl) *vb* (*intr*; foll by *with*) to express sympathy with someone in grief, pain, etc [C16 from Church Latin *condolēre* to suffer pain (with another), from Latin *com-* together + *dolēre* to grieve, feel pain] > conˈdolatory *adj* > conˈdoler *n* > conˈdolingly *adv*

condolence (kənˈdəʊləns) *or* **condolement** *n* (*often plural*) an expression of sympathy with someone in grief, pain

con dolore (kɒn dʊˈlɔːrɪ) *adj, adv music* (to be performed) in a sad manner [Italian: with sorrow]

condom (ˈkɒndɒm, ˈkɒndəm) *n* a sheathlike covering of thin rubber worn on the penis or in the vagina during sexual intercourse to prevent conception or infection [C18 of unknown origin]

condominium (ˌkɒndəˈmɪnɪəm) *n, pl* -**ums 1** joint rule or sovereignty **2** a country ruled by two or more foreign powers **3** *US and Canadian* **a** an apartment building in which each apartment is individually wholly owned and the common areas are jointly owned **b** the title under which an apartment in such a building is owned. Sometimes shortened to: **condo**. Compare **cooperative** (sense 5) [C18 from New Latin, from Latin *com-* together + *dominium* ownership; see DOMINION]

condone (kənˈdəʊn) *vb* (*tr*) **1** to overlook or forgive (an offence) **2** *law* (esp of a spouse) to pardon or overlook (an offence, usually adultery) [C19 from Latin *condōnāre* to remit a debt, from *com-* (intensive) + *dōnāre* to DONATE] > conˈdonable *adj* > condonation (ˌkɒndəʊˈneɪʃən) *n* > conˈdoner *n*

condor (ˈkɒndɔː) *n* either of two very large rare New World vultures, *Vultur gryphus* (**Andean condor**), which has black plumage with white around the neck, and *Gymnogyps californianus* (**California condor**), which is similar but nearly extinct [C17 from Spanish *cóndor,* from Quechuan *kuntur*]

condottiere (ˌkɒndɒˈtjɛərɪ) *n, pl* -**ri** (-ˈriː) a commander or soldier in a professional mercenary company in Europe from the 13th to the 16th centuries [C18 from Italian, from *condotto* leadership, from *condurre* to lead, from Latin *condūcere*; see CONDUCT]

conduce (kənˈdjuːs) *vb* (*intr*; foll by *to*) to lead or contribute (to a result) [C15 from Latin *condūcere* to lead together, from *com-* together + *dūcere* to lead] > conˈducer *n* > conˈducible *adj* > conˈducingly *adv*

conducive (kənˈdjuːsɪv) *adj* (when *postpositive*, foll by *to*) contributing, leading, or tending > conˈduciveness *n*

conduct *n* (ˈkɒndʌkt) **1** the manner in which a person behaves; behaviour **2** the way of managing a business, affair, etc; handling **3** *rare*

the act of guiding or leading **4** *rare* a guide or leader ▷ *vb* (kənˈdʌkt) **5** (*tr*) to accompany and guide (people, a party, etc) (esp in the phrase **conducted tour**) **6** (*tr*) to lead or direct (affairs, business, etc); control **7** (*tr*) to do or carry out: *conduct a survey* **8** (*tr*) to behave or manage (oneself): *the child conducted himself well* **9** Also (esp US): **direct** to control or guide (an orchestra, choir, etc) by the movements of the hands or a baton **10** to transmit (heat, electricity, etc): *metals conduct heat* [C15 from Medieval Latin *conductus* escorted, from Latin: drawn together, from *condūcere* to CONDUCE] > conˈductible *adj* > conˌductiˈbility *n*

conductance (kənˈdʌktəns) *n* the ability of a system to conduct electricity, measured by the ratio of the current flowing through the system to the potential difference across it; the reciprocal of resistance. It is measured in reciprocal ohms, mhos, or siemens. Symbol: G

conducting tissue *n botany* another name for **vascular tissue**

conductometric titration (kənˌdʌktɪəʊˈmɛtrɪk) *n chem* a titration technique in which the end-point is determined by measuring the conductance of the solution

conduction (kənˈdʌkʃən) *n* **1** the transfer of energy by a medium without bulk movement of the medium itself: *heat conduction,; electrical conduction,; sound conduction*. Compare **convection** (sense 1) **2** the transmission of an electrical or chemical impulse along a nerve fibre **3** the act of conveying or conducting, as through a pipe **4** *physics* another name for **conductivity** (sense 1) > conˈductional *adj*

conduction band *n* See **energy band**

conductive (kənˈdʌktɪv) *adj* of, denoting, or having the property of conduction > conˈductively *adv*

conductive education *n* an educational system, developed in Hungary by András Petö, in which teachers (**conductors**) teach children and adults with motor disorders to function independently, by guiding them to attain their own goals in their own way

conductivity (ˌkɒndʌkˈtɪvɪtɪ) *n, pl* -**ties 1** Also called: **conduction** the property of transmitting heat, electricity, or sound **2 a** a measure of the ability of a substance to conduct electricity; the reciprocal of resistivity **b** in the case of a solution, the electrolytic conductivity is the current density divided by the electric field strength, measured in siemens per metre. Symbol: κ Formerly called: **specific conductance 3** See **thermal conductivity**

conductivity water *n* water that has a conductivity of less than 0.043×10^{-6} S cm^{-1}

conductor (kənˈdʌktə) *n* **1** an official on a bus who collects fares, checks tickets, etc **2** Also called (esp US): **director** a person who conducts an orchestra, choir, etc **3** a person who leads or guides **4** *US and Canadian* a railway official in charge of a train **5** a substance, body, or system that conducts electricity, heat, etc **6** See **lightning conductor**. > conˈductorˌship *n* > conductress (kənˈdʌktrɪs) *fem n*

conduit (ˈkɒndɪt, -djʊɪt) *n* **1** a pipe or channel for carrying a fluid **2** a rigid tube or duct for carrying and protecting electrical wires or cables **3** an agency or means of access, communication, etc **4** *botany* a water-transporting element in a plant; a xylem vessel or a tracheid **5** a rare word for **fountain** [C14 from Old French, from Medieval Latin *conductus* channel, aqueduct, from *condūcere* to lead, CONDUCE]

conduplicate (kɒnˈdjuːplɪkɪt) *adj botany* folded lengthways on itself: *conduplicate leaves in the bud* [C18 from Latin *conduplicāre* to double; see DUPLICATE] > conˌdupliˈcation *n*

condyle (ˈkɒndɪl) *n* the rounded projection on the articulating end of a bone, such as the ball portion of a ball-and-socket joint [C17 from Latin

C

condylus knuckle, joint, from Greek *kondulos*]
> ˈcondylar *adj*

condyloid (ˈkɒndɪˌlɔɪd) *adj* of or resembling a condyle

condyloma (ˌkɒndɪˈləʊmə) *n, pl* -mas or -mata (-mətə) a skin tumour near the anus or genital organs, esp as a result of syphilis [c17 from New Latin, from Greek *kondulōma*, from *kondulos* CONDYLE + -OMA] > **condylomatous** (ˌkɒndɪˈlɒmətəs, -ˈləʊ-)

cone (kəʊn) *n* **1 a** a geometric solid consisting of a plane base bounded by a closed curve, often a circle or an ellipse, every point of which is joined to a fixed point, the vertex, lying outside the plane of the base. A **right circular cone** has a vertex perpendicularly above or below the centre of a circular base. Volume of a cone: $\frac{1}{3}\pi r^2 h$, where *r* is the radius of the base and *h* is the height of the cone **b** a geometric surface formed by a line rotating about the vertex and connecting the peripheries of two closed plane bases, usually circular or elliptical, above and below the vertex. See also **conic section 2** anything that tapers from a circular section to a point, such as a wafer shell used to contain ice cream **3 a** the reproductive body of conifers and related plants, made up of overlapping scales, esp the mature **female cone**, whose scales each bear a seed **b** a similar structure in horsetails, club mosses, etc. Technical name: **strobilus 4** a small cone-shaped bollard used as a temporary traffic marker on roads **5** Also called: **retinal cone** any one of the cone-shaped cells in the retina of the eye, sensitive to colour and bright light ▷ *vb* **6** (*tr*) to shape like a cone or part of a cone [c16 from Latin *cōnus*, from Greek *kōnus* pine cone, geometrical cone]

coneflower (ˈkəʊnˌflaʊə) *n* any North American plant of the genera *Rudbeckia, Ratibida,* and *Echinacea,* which have rayed flowers with a conelike centre: family *Asteraceae* (composites). See also **black-eyed Susan**

cone off *vb* (*tr, adverb*) Brit to close (one carriageway of a motorway) by placing warning cones across it

cone penetration test *n* a method of testing soils by pressing a cone of standard dimensions into the soil under a known load and measuring the penetration

cone shell *n* any of various tropical marine gastropod molluscs of the genus *Conus* and related genera, having a smooth conical shell. Sometimes shortened to: **cone**

con espressione (*Italian* kɒn ˌespresˈsjone) *adj, adv music* (to be performed) with feeling; expressively [Italian, literally: with expression]

Conestoga wagon (ˌkɒnɪˈstəʊgə) *n US and Canadian* a large heavy horse-drawn covered wagon used in the 19th century [c19 after *Conestoga,* Pennsylvania, where it was first made]

coney (ˈkəʊnɪ) *n* a variant spelling of **cony**

Coney Island (ˈkəʊnɪ) *n* an island off the S shore of Long Island, New York: site of a large amusement park

confab (ˈkɒnfæb) *informal* ▷ *n* **1** a conversation or chat ▷ *vb* -fabs, -fabbing, -fabbed **2** (*intr*) to converse

confabulate (kənˈfæbjʊˌleɪt) *vb* (*intr*) **1** to talk together; converse; chat **2** *psychiatry* to replace the gaps left by a disorder of the memory with imaginary remembered experiences consistently believed to be true. See also **paramnesia** [c17 from Latin *confābulārī,* from *fābulārī* to talk, from *fābula* a story; see FABLE] > conˌfabuˈlation *n* > conˈfabuˌlator *n* > conˈfabulatory *adj*

confect (kənˈfɛkt) *vb* (*tr*) **1** to prepare by combining ingredients **2** to make; construct [c16 from Latin *confectus* prepared, from *conficere* to accomplish, from *com-* (intensive) + *facere* to make]

confection (kənˈfɛkʃən) *n* **1** the act or process of compounding or mixing **2** any sweet preparation of fruit, nuts, etc, such as a preserve or a sweet **3**

old-fashioned an elaborate article of clothing, esp for women **4** *informal* anything regarded as overelaborate or frivolous: *the play was merely an ingenious confection* **5** a medicinal drug sweetened with sugar, honey, etc [c14 from Old French, from Latin *confectiō* a preparing, from *conficere* to produce; see CONFECT]

confectionary (kənˈfɛkʃənərɪ) *n, pl* -aries **1** a place where confections are kept or made **2** a rare word for **confection** ▷ *adj* **3** of or characteristic of confections

confectioner (kənˈfɛkʃənə) *n* a person who makes or sells sweets or confections

confectioners' sugar *n* the US term for **icing sugar**

confectionery (kənˈfɛkʃənərɪ) *n, pl* -eries **1** sweets and other confections collectively **2** the art or business of a confectioner

Confed. *abbreviation for* **1** Confederate **2** Confederation

confederacy (kənˈfɛdərəsɪ, -ˈfɛdrəsɪ) *n, pl* -cies **1** a union or combination of peoples, states, etc; alliance; league **2** a combination of groups or individuals for unlawful purposes [c14 from Anglo-French *confederacie,* from Late Latin *confoederātiō* agreement, CONFEDERATION] > conˈfederal *adj*

Confederacy (kənˈfɛdərəsɪ, -ˈfɛdrəsɪ) *n* **the** another name for the **Confederate States of America**

confederate *n* (kənˈfɛdərɪt, -ˈfɛdrɪt) **1** a nation, state, or individual that is part of a confederacy **2** someone who is part of a conspiracy; accomplice ▷ *adj* (kənˈfɛdərɪt, -ˈfɛdrɪt) **3** united in a confederacy; allied ▷ *vb* (kənˈfɛdəˌreɪt) **4** to form into or become part of a confederacy [c14 from Late Latin *confoederātus,* from *confoederāre* to unite by a league, from Latin *com-* together + *foedus* treaty]

Confederate (kənˈfɛdərɪt, -ˈfɛdrɪt) *adj* **1** of, supporting, or relating to the Confederate States of America ▷ *n* **2** a supporter of the Confederate States of America

Confederate States of America *pl n US history* the 11 Southern states (Alabama, Arkansas, Florida, Georgia, North Carolina, South Carolina, Texas, Virginia, Tennessee, Louisiana, and Mississippi) that seceded from the Union in 1861, precipitating a civil war with the North. The Confederacy was defeated in 1865 and the South reincorporated into the US

confederation (kənˌfɛdəˈreɪʃən) *n* **1** the act or process of confederating or the state of being confederated **2** a loose alliance of political units. The union of the Swiss cantons is the oldest surviving confederation. Compare **federation 3** (esp in Canada) another name for a **federation** > conˌfederˈation.ism *n* > conˌfederˈationist *n* > conˈfederative *adj*

Confederation (kənˌfɛdəˈreɪʃən) *n* **1** the US history the original 13 states of the United States of America constituted under the Articles of Confederation and superseded by the more formal union established in 1789 **2** the federation of Canada, formed with four original provinces in 1867 and since joined by eight more

confer (kənˈfɜː) *vb* -fers, -ferring, -ferred **1** (*tr*; foll by *on* or *upon*) to grant or bestow (an honour, gift, etc) **2** (*intr*) to hold or take part in a conference or consult together **3** (*tr*) an obsolete word for **compare** [c16 from Latin *conferre* to gather together, compare, from *com-* together + *ferre* to bring] > conˈferment *or* conˈferral *n* > conˈferrable *adj* > conˈferrer *n*

conferee *or* **conferree** (ˌkɒnfɔːˈriː) *n* **1** a person who takes part in a conference **2** a person on whom an honour or gift is conferred

conference (ˈkɒnfərəns, -frəns) *n* **1** a meeting for consultation, exchange of information, or discussion, esp one with a formal agenda **2** a formal meeting of two or more states, political groups, etc, esp to discuss differences or

formulate common policy **3** an assembly of the clergy or of clergy and laity of any of certain Protestant Christian Churches acting as representatives of their denomination: *the Methodist conference* **4** *sport* a league or division of clubs or teams **5** *rare* an act of bestowal [c16 from Medieval Latin *conferentia,* from Latin *conferre* to bring together; see CONFER] > conferential (ˌkɒnfəˈrenʃəl) *adj*

conference call *n* a special telephone facility by which three or more people using conventional or cellular phones can be linked up to speak to one another

Conference pear (ˈkɒnfərəns, -frəns) *n* a variety of pear that has sweet and juicy fruit

conferva (kɒnˈfɜːvə) *n, pl* -vae (-viː) *or* -vas any of various threadlike green algae, esp any of the genus *Tribonema,* typically occurring in fresh water [c18 from Latin: a water plant, from *confervēre* to grow together, heal, literally: to seethe, from *fervēre* to boil; named with reference to its reputed healing properties] > conˈferval *adj* > conˈfervoid *n, adj*

confess (kənˈfɛs) *vb* (when *tr,* may take a clause as object) **1** (when *intr,* often foll by *to*) to make an acknowledgment or admission (of faults, misdeeds, crimes, etc) **2** (*tr*) to admit or grant to be true; concede **3** *Christianity, chiefly RC Church* to declare (one's sins) to God or to a priest as his representative, so as to obtain pardon and absolution [c14 from Old French *confesser,* from Late Latin *confessāre,* from Latin *confessus* confessed, from *confitērī* to admit, from *fatērī* to acknowledge; related to Latin *fārī* to speak] > conˈfessable *adj*

confessant (kənˈfɛsˀnt) *n Christianity, chiefly RC Church* a person who makes a confession

confessedly (kənˈfɛsɪdlɪ) *adv* (*sentence modifier*) by admission or confession; avowedly

confession (kənˈfɛʃən) *n* **1** the act of confessing **2** something confessed **3** an acknowledgment or declaration, esp of one's faults, misdeeds, or crimes **4** *Christianity, chiefly RC Church* the act of a penitent accusing himself or herself of his or her sins **5** confession of faith a formal public avowal of religious beliefs **6** a religious denomination or sect united by a common system of beliefs > conˈfessionary *adj*

confessional (kənˈfɛʃənˀl) *adj* **1** of, like, or suited to a confession ▷ *n* **2** *Christianity, chiefly RC Church* a small stall, usually enclosed and divided by a screen or curtain, where a priest hears confessions **3** a book of penitential prayers

confessional television *n* television programmes, esp talk shows, in which members of the public reveal their private lives, personal problems, etc

confessor (kənˈfɛsə) *n* **1** *Christianity, chiefly RC Church* a priest who hears confessions and sometimes acts as a spiritual counsellor **2** *history* a person who bears witness to his Christian religious faith by the holiness of his life, esp in resisting threats or danger, but does not suffer martyrdom **3** a person who makes a confession

confetti (kənˈfɛtɪ) *n* small pieces of coloured paper thrown on festive occasions, esp at the bride and groom at weddings [c19 from Italian, plural of *confetto,* originally a bonbon; see COMFIT]

confidant (ˌkɒnfɪˈdænt, ˈkɒnfɪˌdænt) *n* a person, esp a man, to whom private matters are confided [c17 from French *confident,* from Italian *confidente,* n use of adj: trustworthy, from Latin *confidens* CONFIDENT]

confidante (ˌkɒnfɪˈdænt, ˈkɒnfɪˌdænt) *n* a person, esp a woman, to whom private matters are confided

confide (kənˈfaɪd) *vb* **1** (usually foll by *in;* when *tr,* may take a clause as object) to disclose (secret or personal matters) in confidence (to); reveal in private (to) **2** (*intr;* foll by *in*) to have complete trust **3** (*tr*) to entrust into another's keeping [c15 from Latin *confidere,* from *fidere* to trust; related to Latin *foedus* treaty] > conˈfider *n*

confidence ('kɒnfɪdəns) *n* **1** a feeling of trust in a person or thing: *I have confidence in his abilities* **2** belief in one's own abilities; self-assurance **3** trust or a trustful relationship: *take me into your confidence* **4** something confided or entrusted; secret **5 in confidence** as a secret

confidence interval *n statistics* an interval of values bounded by **confidence limits** within which the true value of a population parameter is stated to lie with a specified probability

confidence level *n statistics* a measure of the reliability of a result. A confidence level of 95 per cent or 0.95 means that there is a probability of at least 95 per cent that the result is reliable. Compare **significance** (sense 4)

confidence man *or* **trickster** *n* another name for **con man**

confidence trick *or US and Canadian* **confidence game** *n* a swindle involving money, goods, etc, in which the victim's trust is won by the swindler. Informal shortened forms: **con trick**, (US and Canadian) **con game**

confident ('kɒnfɪdənt) *adj* **1** (*postpositive;* foll by *of*) having or showing confidence or certainty; sure: *confident of success* **2** sure of oneself; bold **3** presumptuous; excessively bold [c16 from Latin *confidens* trusting, having self-confidence, from *confidere* to have complete trust in; see CONFIDE] > 'confidently *adv*

confidential (ˌkɒnfɪ'dɛnʃəl) *adj* **1** spoken, written, or given in confidence; secret; private **2** entrusted with another's confidence or secret affairs: *a confidential secretary* **3** suggestive of or denoting intimacy: *a confidential approach* > ˌconfiˌdentiˈality *or* ˌconfiˈdentialness *n* > ˌconfiˈdentially *adv*

confiding (kən'faɪdɪŋ) *adj* unsuspicious; trustful > con'fidingly *adv* > con'fidingness *n*

configuration (kənˌfɪɡjʊ'reɪʃən) *n* **1** the arrangement of the parts of something **2** the external form or outline achieved by such an arrangement **3** *physics, chem* **a** Also called: **conformation** the shape of a molecule as determined by the arrangement of its atoms **b** the structure of an atom or molecule as determined by the arrangement of its electrons and nucleons **4** *psychol* the unit or pattern in perception studied by Gestalt psychologists **5** *computing* the particular choice of hardware items and their interconnection that make up a particular computer system [c16 from Late Latin *configūrātiō* a similar formation, from *configūrāre* to model on something, from *figūrāre* to shape, fashion] > conˌfiguˈrational *or* conˈfigurative *adj* > conˌfiguˈrationally *adv*

configure (ˌkən'fɪɡə) *vb* (*tr*) **1** to arrange or organize **2** *computing* to set up (a piece of hardware or software) as required

confine *vb* (kən'faɪn) (*tr*) **1** to keep or close within bounds; limit; restrict **2** to keep shut in; restrict the free movement of: *arthritis confined him to bed* ▷ *n* ('kɒnfaɪn) **3** (*often plural*) a limit; boundary [c16 from Medieval Latin *confināre* from Latin *confinis* adjacent, from *finis* end, boundary] > con'finable *or* con'fineable *adj* > 'confineless *adj* > con'finer *n*

confined (kən'faɪnd) *adj* **1** enclosed or restricted; limited **2** in childbed; undergoing childbirth > confinedly (kən'faɪnɪdlɪ) *adv* > con'finedness *n*

confinement (kən'faɪnmənt) *n* **1** the act of confining or the state of being confined **2** the period from the onset of labour to the birth of a child **3** *physics* another name for **containment** (sense 3)

confirm (kən'fɜːm) *vb* (*tr*) **1** (*may take a clause as object*) to prove to be true or valid; corroborate; verify **2** (*may take a clause as object*) to assert for a second or further time, so as to make more definite: *he confirmed that he would appear in court* **3** to strengthen or make more firm: *his story confirmed my doubts* **4** to make valid by a formal act or agreement; ratify **5** to administer the rite of confirmation to [c13 from Old French *confermer,* from Latin *confirmāre,* from *firmus* FIRM¹]

> con'firmable *adj* > con'firmatory *or* con'firmative *adj* > con'firmer *n*

confirmand ('kɒnfəˌmænd) *n* a candidate for confirmation

confirmation (ˌkɒnfə'meɪʃən) *n* **1** the act of confirming **2** something that confirms; verification **3** a rite in several Christian churches that confirms a baptized person in his or her faith and admits him or her to full participation in the church **4** (in the philosophy of science) the relationship between an observation and the theory which it supposedly renders more probable. Compare **hypothetico-deductive**

confirmed (kən'fɜːmd) *adj* **1** (*prenominal*) long-established in a habit, way of life, etc: *a confirmed bachelor* **2** having received the rite of confirmation **3** (of a disease) another word for **chronic** > confirmedly (kən'fɜːmɪdlɪ) *adv* > confirmedness (kən'fɜːmɪdnɪs, -'fɜːmd-) *n*

confiscable (kən'fɪskəbᵊl) *adj* subject or liable to confiscation or seizure

confiscate ('kɒnfɪˌskeɪt) *vb* (*tr*) **1** to seize (property), esp for public use and esp by way of a penalty ▷ *adj* **2** seized or confiscated; forfeit **3** having lost or been deprived of property through confiscation [c16 from Latin *confiscāre* to seize for the public treasury, from *fiscus* basket, treasury] > ˌconfis'cation *n* > 'confisˌcator *n*

confiscatory (kən'fɪskətərɪ, -trɪ) *adj* involving confiscation

confit *French* (kɔ̃fi) *n cookery* a preserve: *a confit of duck* [literally: preserve]

Confiteor (kən'fɪtɪˌɔː) *n RC Church* a prayer consisting of a general confession of sinfulness and an entreaty for forgiveness [c13 from Latin: I confess; from the beginning of the Latin prayer of confession]

confiture ('kɒnfɪˌtjʊə) *n* a confection, preserve of fruit, etc [c19 from French, from Old French *confire* to prepare, from Latin *conficere* to produce; see CONFECT]

conflagrant (kən'fleɪɡrənt) *adj rare* burning fiercely

conflagration (ˌkɒnflə'ɡreɪʃən) *n* a large destructive fire [c16 from Latin *conflagrātiō,* from *conflagrāre* to be burnt up, from *com-* (intensive) + *flagrāre* to burn; related to Latin *fulgur* lightning] > 'conflaˌgrative *adj*

conflate (kən'fleɪt) *vb* (*tr*) to combine or blend (two things, esp two versions of a text) so as to form a whole [c16 from Latin *conflāre* to blow together, from *flāre* to blow] > con'flation *n*

conflict *n* ('kɒnflɪkt) **1** a struggle or clash between opposing forces; battle **2** a state of opposition between ideas, interests, etc; disagreement or controversy **3** a clash, as between two appointments made for the same time **4** *psychol* opposition between two simultaneous but incompatible wishes or drives, sometimes leading to a state of emotional tension and thought to be responsible for neuroses ▷ *vb* (kən'flɪkt) (*intr*) **5** to come into opposition; clash **6** to fight [c15 from Latin *conflictus,* from *conflīgere* to combat, from *flīgere* to strike] > con'fliction *n* > con'flictive *or* con'flictory *adj*

conflicting (kən'flɪktɪŋ) *adj* clashing; contradictory: *conflicting rumours* > con'flictingly *adv*

confluence ('kɒnfluəns) *or* **conflux** ('kɒnflʌks) *n* **1** a merging or flowing together, esp of rivers **2** a gathering together, esp of people

confluent ('kɒnfluənt) *adj* **1** flowing together or merging ▷ *n* **2** a stream that flows into another, usually of approximately equal size [c17 from Latin *confluēns,* from *confluere* to flow together, from *fluere* to flow]

confocal (kɒn'fəʊkᵊl) *adj* having a common focus or common foci: *confocal ellipses*

confocal microscope *n* a light microscope with an optical system designed to reject background from matter outside the focal plane and therefore allowing images of different sections of a specimen to be obtained

conform (kən'fɔːm) *vb* **1** (*intr*; usually foll by *to*) to comply in actions, behaviour, etc, with accepted standards or norms **2** (*intr*; usually foll by *with*) to be in accordance; fit in: *he conforms with my idea of a teacher* **3** to make or become similar in character or form **4** (*intr*) to comply with the practices of an established church, esp the Church of England **5** (*tr*) to bring (oneself, ideas, etc) into harmony or agreement [c14 from Old French *conformer,* from Latin *confirmāre* to establish, strengthen, from *firmāre* to make firm, from *firmus* FIRM¹] > con'former *n* > con'formingly *adv*

conformable (kən'fɔːməbᵊl) *adj* **1** corresponding in character; similar **2** obedient; submissive **3** (foll by *to*) in agreement or harmony (with); consistent (with) **4** (of rock strata) lying in a parallel arrangement so that their original relative positions have remained undisturbed **5** *maths* (of two matrices) related so that the number of columns in one is equal to the number of rows in the other > conˌforma'bility *or* con'formableness *n* > con'formably *adv*

conformal (kən'fɔːməl) *adj maths* **a** (of a transformation) preserving the angles of the depicted surface **b** (of a parameter) relating to such a transformation **2** Also called: **orthomorphic** (of a map projection) maintaining true shape over a small area and scale in every direction [c17 from Late Latin *conformālis* having the same shape, from Latin *com-* same + *forma* shape]

conformation (ˌkɒnfɔː'meɪʃən) *n* **1** the general shape or outline of an object; configuration **2** the arrangement of the parts of an object **3** the act or state of conforming **4** *chem* **a** another name for **configuration** (sense 3a) **b** one of the configurations of a molecule that can easily change its shape and can consequently exist in equilibrium with molecules of different configuration > ˌconfor'mational *adj*

conformational analysis *n chem* the study of the spatial arrangement of atoms or groups of atoms in a molecule and the way in which this influences chemical behaviour

conformist (kən'fɔːmɪst) *n* **1** a person who adopts the attitudes, behaviour, dress, etc of the group to which he belongs **2** a person who complies with the practices of an established church, esp the Church of England ▷ *adj* **3** of a conforming nature or character

conformity (kən'fɔːmɪtɪ) *or* **conformance** *n, pl* **-ities** *or* **-ances** **1** compliance in actions, behaviour, etc, with certain accepted standards or norms **2** correspondence or likeness in form or appearance; congruity; agreement **3** compliance with the practices of an established church

confound (kən'faʊnd) *vb* (*tr*) **1** to astound or perplex; bewilder **2** to mix up; confuse **3** to treat mistakenly as similar to or identical with (one or more other things) **4** (kɒn'faʊnd) to curse or damn (usually as an expletive in the phrase **confound it!**) **5** to contradict or refute (an argument, etc) **6** to rout or defeat (an enemy) **7** *obsolete* to waste [c13 from Old French *confondre,* from Latin *confundere* to mingle, pour together, from *fundere* to pour] > con'foundable *adj* > con'founder *n*

confounded (kən'faʊndɪd) *adj* **1** bewildered; confused **2** (*prenominal*) *informal* execrable; damned > con'foundedly *adv* > con'foundedness *n*

confraternity (ˌkɒnfrə'tɜːnɪtɪ) *n, pl* **-ties** a group of men united for some particular purpose, esp Christian laymen organized for religious or charitable service; brotherhood [c15 from Medieval Latin *confrāternitās;* see CONFRÈRE, FRATERNITY] > confra'ternal *adj*

confrère ('kɒnfreə) *n* a fellow member of a profession, fraternity, etc [c15 from Old French, from Medieval Latin *confrāter* fellow member, from Latin *frāter* brother]

confront (kən'frʌnt) *vb* (*tr*) **1** (usually foll by *with*) to present or face (with something), esp in order

C

to accuse or criticize **2** to face boldly; oppose in hostility **3** to be face to face with; be in front of **4** to bring together for comparison [C16 from Medieval Latin *confrontārī* to stand face to face with, from *frons* forehead] > con'fronter *n*

confrontation (ˌkɒnfrʌn'teɪʃən) *or archaic* **confrontment** (kən'frʌntmənt) *n* **1** the act or an instance of confronting **2** a situation of mutual hostility between two powers or nations without open warfare **3** a state of conflict between two antagonistic forces, creeds, or ideas etc > ˌconfron'tational *adj*

Confucian (kən'fjuːʃən) *adj* **1** of or relating to the doctrines of Confucius (Chinese name *Kong Zi* or *K'ung Fu-tse.*; 551–479 BC), the Chinese philosopher and teacher of ethics ▷ *n* **2** a follower of Confucius

Confucianism (kən'fjuːʃəˌnɪzəm) *n* the ethical system of Confucius, the Chinese philosopher and teacher of ethics (551–479 BC), emphasizing moral order, the humanity and virtue of China's ancient rulers, and gentlemanly education > Con'fucianist *n*

con fuoco (kɒn fuˈəʊkəʊ) *adj, adv music* (to be performed) in a fiery manner [Italian: with fire]

confuse (kən'fjuːz) *vb* (*tr*) **1** to bewilder; perplex **2** to mix up (things, ideas, etc); jumble **3** to make unclear: *he confused his talk with irrelevant details* **4** to fail to recognize the difference between; mistake (one thing) for another **5** to disconcert; embarrass **6** to cause to become disordered: *the enemy ranks were confused by gas* [C18 back formation from *confused*, from Latin *confūsus* mingled together, from *confundere* to pour together; see CONFOUND] > con'fusable *adj* > conˌfusa'bility *n*

confused (kən'fjuːzd) *adj* **1** feeling or exhibiting an inability to understand; bewildered; perplexed **2** in a disordered state; mixed up; jumbled **3** lacking sufficient mental abilities for independent living, esp through old age > confusedly (kən'fjuːzɪdlɪ, -'fjuːzd-) *adv* > con'fusedness *n*

confused elderly *adj social welfare* **a** old and no longer having mental abilities sufficient for independent living **b** (*as collective noun*; preceded by *the*): *the confused elderly*

confusing (kən'fjuːzɪŋ) *adj* causing bewilderment; difficult to follow; puzzling > con'fusingly *adv*

confusion (kən'fjuːʒən) *n* **1** the act of confusing or the state of being confused **2** disorder; jumble **3** bewilderment; perplexity **4** lack of clarity; indistinctness **5** embarrassment; abashment > con'fusional *adj*

confute (kən'fjuːt) *vb* (*tr*) **1** to prove (a person or thing) wrong, invalid, or mistaken; disprove **2** *obsolete* to put an end to [C16 from Latin *confūtāre* to check, silence] > con'futable *adj* > confutation (ˌkɒnfjʊ'teɪʃən) *n* > con'futative *adj* > con'futer *n*

cong. *abbreviation for* **1** *pharmacol obsolete* congius **2** congregation [(for sense 1) Latin: gallon]

Cong. *abbreviation for* **1** Congregational **2** Congress **3** Congressional

conga ('kɒŋɡə) *n* **1** a Latin American dance of three steps and a kick to each bar, usually performed by a number of people in single file **2** *Also called:* conga drum a large tubular bass drum, used chiefly in Latin American and funk music and played with the hands ▷ *vb* -gas, -gaing, -gaed **3** (*intr*) to dance the conga [C20 from American Spanish, feminine of *congo* belonging to the CONGO]

congé ('kɒnʒeɪ) *n* **1** permission to depart or dismissal, esp when formal **2** a farewell **3** *architect* a concave moulding. See also **cavetto** [C16 from Old French *congié*, from Latin *commeātus* leave of absence, from *meātus* movement, from *meāre* to go, pass]

congeal (kən'dʒiːl) *vb* **1** to change or cause to change from a soft or fluid state to a firm or solid state **2** to form or cause to form into a coagulated mass; curdle; jell **3** (*intr*) (of ideas) to take shape or become fixed in form [C14 from Old French *congeler*, from Latin *congelāre*, from *com-* together + *gelāre* to freeze] > con'gealable *adj* > con'gealer *n* > con'gealment *n*

congelation (ˌkɒndʒɪ'leɪʃən) *n* **1** the process of congealing **2** something formed by this process

congener (kən'dʒiːnə, 'kɒndʒɪnə) *n* **1** a member of a class, group, or other category, esp any animal of a specified genus **2** a by-product formed in alcoholic drinks during the fermentation process, which largely determines the flavour and colour of the drink [C18 from Latin, from *com-* same + *genus* kind]

congeneric (ˌkɒndʒɪ'nɛrɪk) *or* **congenerous** (kɒn'dʒɛnərəs) *adj* belonging to the same group, esp (of animals or plants) belonging to the same genus

congenial (kən'dʒiːnjəl, -nɪəl) *adj* **1** friendly, pleasant, or agreeable: *a congenial atmosphere to work in* **2** having a similar disposition, tastes, etc; compatible; sympathetic [C17 from CON- (same) + GENIAL[1]] > congeniality (kənˌdʒiːnɪ'ælɪtɪ) *or* con'genialness *n* > con'genially *adv*

congenic (kən'dʒɛnɪk) *adj genetics* (of inbred animal cells) genetically identical except for a single gene locus

congenital (kən'dʒɛnɪtəl) *adj* **1** denoting or relating to any nonhereditary condition, esp an abnormal condition, existing at birth: *congenital blindness* **2** *informal* complete, as if from birth: *a congenital idiot* [C18 from Latin *congenitus* born together with, from *genitus* born, from *gignere* to bear, beget] > con'genitally *adv* > con'genitalness *n*

conger ('kɒŋɡə) *n* any large marine eel of the family *Congridae*, esp *Conger conger*, occurring in temperate and tropical coastal waters [C14 from Old French *congre*, from Latin *conger*, from Greek *gongros* sea eel]

congeries (kɒn'dʒɪərɪːz) *n* (*functioning as singular or plural*) a collection of objects or ideas; mass; heap [C17 from Latin, from *congerere* to pile up, from *gerere* to carry]

congest (kən'dʒɛst) *vb* **1** to crowd or become crowded to excess; overfill **2** to overload or clog (an organ or part) with blood or (of an organ or part) to become overloaded or clogged with blood **3** (*tr*; *usually passive*) to block (the nose) with mucus [C16 from Latin *congestus* pressed together, from *congerere* to assemble; see CONGERIES] > con'gestible *adj* > con'gestive *adj*

congested (kən'dʒɛstɪd) *adj* **1** crowded to excess; overfull **2** (of an organ or part) loaded or clogged with blood **3** (of the nose) blocked with mucus

congestion (kən'dʒɛstʃən) *n* **1** the state of being overcrowded, esp with with traffic or people **2** the state of being overloaded or clogged with blood **3** the state of being blocked with mucus

congestion charging *n* the practice of charging motorists for the right to drive on busy roads, esp at busy times > congestion charge *n*

congius ('kɒndʒɪəs) *n*, *pl* -gii (-dʒɪ,aɪ) **1** *pharmacol* a unit of liquid measure equal to 1 Imperial gallon **2** an ancient Roman unit of liquid measure equal to about 0.7 Imperial gallon or 0.84 US gallon [C14 from Latin, probably from Greek *konkhos* liquid measure, CONCH]

conglobate ('kɒnɡləʊˌbeɪt) *vb* **1** to form into a globe or ball ▷ *adj* **2** a rare word for **globular** [C17 from Latin *conglobāre* to gather into a ball, from *globāre* to make round, from *globus* a sphere] > ˌconglo'bation *n*

conglomerate *n* (kən'ɡlɒmərɪt) **1** a thing composed of heterogeneous elements; mass **2** any coarse-grained sedimentary rock consisting of rounded fragments of rock embedded in a finer matrix. Compare **agglomerate** (sense 3) **3** a large corporation consisting of a group of companies dealing in widely diversified goods, services, etc ▷ *vb* (kən'ɡlɒməˌreɪt) **4** to form into a cluster or mass ▷ *adj* (kən'ɡlɒmərɪt) **5** made up of heterogeneous elements; massed **6** (of sedimentary rocks) consisting of rounded fragments within a finer matrix [C16 from Latin *conglomerāre* to roll up, from *glomerāre* to wind into a ball, from *glomus* ball of thread]

conglomeration (kənˌɡlɒmə'reɪʃən) *n* **1** a conglomerate mass **2** a mass of miscellaneous things **3** the act of conglomerating or the state of being conglomerated

conglutinant (kən'ɡluːtɪnənt) *adj obsolete* (of the edges of a wound or fracture) promoting union; adhesive

conglutinate (kən'ɡluːtɪˌneɪt) *vb* **1** *obsolete* to cause (the edges of a wound or fracture) to join during the process of healing or (of the edges of a wound or fracture) to join during this process **2** to stick or become stuck together [C16 from Latin *conglūtināre* to glue together, from *glūtināre* to glue, from *glūten* GLUE] > conˌgluti'nation *n* > con'glutinative *adj*

Congo ('kɒŋɡəʊ) *n* **1** Democratic Republic of a republic in S central Africa, with a narrow strip of land along the Congo estuary leading to the Atlantic in the west: Congo Free State established in 1885, with Leopold II of Belgium as absolute monarch; became the Belgian Congo colony in 1908; gained independence in 1960, followed by civil war and the secession of Katanga (until 1963); President Mobutu Sese Seko seized power in 1965; declared a one-party state in 1978, and was overthrown by rebels in 1997. The country consists chiefly of the Congo basin, with large areas of dense tropical forest and marshes, and the Mitumba highlands reaching over 5000 m (16 000 ft) in the east. Official language: French. Religion: Christian majority, animist minority. Currency: Congolese franc. Capital: Kinshasa. Pop: 54 417 000 (2004 est). Area: 2 344 116 sq km (905 063 sq miles). Former names: Congo Free State (1885–1908), Belgian Congo (1908–60), Congo-Kinshasa (1960–71), Zaïre (1971–97) **2** Republic of the short name of Congo-Brazzaville **3** the second longest river in Africa, rising as the Lualaba on the Katanga plateau in the Democratic Republic of Congo and flowing in a wide northerly curve to the Atlantic: forms the border between Congo-Brazzaville and the Democratic Republic of Congo Length: about 4800 km (3000 miles). Area of basin: about 3 000 000 sq km (1 425 000 sq miles). Former Zaïrese name (1971–97): Zaïre **4** a variant spelling of **Kongo** (the people and language)

Congo-Brazzaville, Congo *or* **Republic of Congo** *n* a republic in W Central Africa: formerly the French colony of Middle Congo, part of French Equatorial Africa, it became independent in 1960; consists mostly of equatorial forest, with savanna and extensive swamps; drained chiefly by the Rivers Congo and Ubangi. Official language: French. Religion: Christian majority. Currency: franc. Capital: Brazzaville. Pop: 3 818 000 (2004 est). Area: 342 000 sq km (132 018 sq miles). Former names: Middle Congo (until 1958)

congo eel *or* **snake** *n* an aquatic salamander, *Amphiuma means*, having an eel-like body with gill slits and rudimentary limbs and inhabiting still muddy waters in the southern US: family *Amphiumidae*

Congo Free State *n* a former name (1885–1908) of (Democratic Republic of) Congo (sense 2)

Congolese (ˌkɒŋɡə'liːz) *adj* **1** of or relating to the People's Republic of the Congo or the Democratic Republic of the Congo or their inhabitants ▷ *n* **2** a native or inhabitant of the People's Republic of the Congo or the Democratic Republic of the Congo

Congo red *n* a brownish-red soluble powder, used as a dye, a diagnostic indicator, a biological stain, and a chemical indicator. Formula: $C_{32}H_{22}N_6O_6S_2Na_2$

congou ('kɒŋuː) *or* **congo** ('kɒŋɡəʊ) *n* a kind of black tea from China [C18 from Chinese (Amoy) *kong hu tē* tea prepared with care]

congrats (kən'ɡræts) *or chiefly Brit* **congratters**

(kən'grætəz) *pl n, sentence substitute* informal shortened forms of **congratulations**

congratulate (kən'grætjʊˌleɪt) *vb* (*tr*) **1** (usually foll by *on*) to communicate pleasure, approval, or praise to (a person or persons); compliment **2** (often foll by *on*) to consider (oneself) clever or fortunate (as a result of): *she congratulated herself on her tact* **3** *obsolete* to greet [c16 from Latin *congratulārī*, from *grātulārī* to rejoice, from *grātus* pleasing] > con,gratu'lation *n* > con'gratuˌlator *n* > con'gratulatory *or* con'gratulative *adj*

congratulations (kənˌgrætjʊ'leɪʃənz) *pl n, sentence substitute* expressions of pleasure or joy; felicitations

congregant ('kɒŋgrɪgənt) *n* a member of a congregation, esp a Jewish congregation

congregate *vb* ('kɒŋgrɪˌgeɪt) **1** to collect together in a body or crowd; assemble ▷ *adj* ('kɒŋgrɪgɪt, -ˌgeɪt) **2** collected together; assembled **3** relating to collecting; collective [c15 from Latin *congregāre* to collect into a flock, from *grex* flock] > 'congreˌgative *adj* > 'congreˌgativeness *n* > 'congreˌgator *n*

congregation (ˌkɒŋgrɪ'geɪʃən) *n* **1** a group of persons gathered for worship, prayer, etc, esp in a church or chapel **2** the act of congregating or collecting together **3** a group of people, objects, etc, collected together; assemblage **4** the group of persons habitually attending a given church, chapel, etc **5** *RC Church* **a** a society of persons who follow a common rule of life but who are bound only by simple vows **b** Also called: **dicastery** an administrative subdivision of the papal curia **c** an administrative committee of bishops for arranging the business of a general council **6** *chiefly Brit* an assembly of senior members of a university

congregational (ˌkɒŋgrɪ'geɪʃənᵊl) *adj* **1** of or relating to a congregation **2** (*usually capital*) of, relating to, or denoting the Congregational Church, its members, or its beliefs > 'congreˈgationally *adv*

Congregational Church *n* any evangelical Protestant Christian Church that is governed according to the principles of Congregationalism. In 1972 the majority of churches in the Congregational Church in England and Wales voted to become part of the United Reformed Church

Congregationalism (ˌkɒŋgrɪ'geɪʃənəˌlɪzəm) *n* a system of Christian doctrines and ecclesiastical government in which each congregation is self-governing and maintains bonds of faith with other similar local congregations > ,Congre'gationalist *adj, n*

congress ('kɒŋgrɛs) *n* **1** a meeting or conference, esp of representatives of a number of sovereign states **2** a national legislative assembly **3** a society or association **4** sexual intercourse [c16 from Latin *congressus* to meet with, from *congredī* to meet with, from *com-* together + *gradī* to walk, step]

Congress ('kɒŋgrɛs) *n* **1** the bicameral federal legislature of the US, consisting of the House of Representatives and the Senate **2** this body during any two-year term > Also called: **Congress Party** (in India) a major political party, which controlled the Union government from 1947 to 1977. Official name: **Indian National Congress** > Con'gressional *adj*

congressional (kən'grɛʃənᵊl) *adj* of or relating to a congress > con'gressionalist *n* > con'gressionally *adv*

Congressional district *n* (in the US) an electoral division of a state, entitled to send one member to the US House of Representatives

Congressional Medal of Honor *n* See **Medal of Honor**

Congressional Record *n* (in the US) the government journal that publishes all proceedings of Congress

Congressman ('kɒŋgrɛsmən) *n, pl* -men (in the US) a male member of Congress

Congress of Industrial Organizations *n* (in the US) a federation of industrial unions formed in 1935. It united with the AFL in 1955 to form the AFL-CIO. Abbreviation: **CIO**

Congress of Vienna *n* the European conference held at Vienna from 1814–15 to settle the territorial problems left by the Napoleonic Wars

Congresswoman ('kɒŋgrɛswʊmən) *n, pl* -women (in the US) a female member of Congress, esp of the House of Representatives

congruence ('kɒŋgrʊəns) *or* **congruency** *n* **1** the quality or state of corresponding, agreeing, or being congruent **2** *maths* the relationship between two integers, *x* and *y*, such that their difference, with respect to another positive integer called the modulus, *n*, is a multiple of the modulus. Usually written $x \equiv y \pmod{n}$, as in $25 \equiv 11 \pmod 7$

congruent ('kɒŋgrʊənt) *adj* **1** agreeing; corresponding; congruous **2** having identical shapes so that all parts correspond: *congruent triangles*. Compare **similar** (sense 2) **3** of or concerning two integers related by a congruence [c15 from Latin *congruere* to meet together, agree] > 'congruently *adv*

congruous ('kɒŋgrʊəs) *adj* **1** corresponding or agreeing **2** suitable; appropriate [c16 from Latin *congruus* suitable, harmonious; see CONGRUENT] > congruity (kən'gru:ɪtɪ) *or* 'congruousness *n* > 'congruously *adv*

conic ('kɒnɪk) *adj* *also* **conical 1 a** having the shape of a cone **b** of or relating to a cone ▷ *n* **2** another name for **conic section** ▷ See also **conics** [c16 from New Latin, from Greek *kōnikos*, from *kōnos* CONE] > 'conically *adv*

conic projection *or* **conical projection** *n* a map projection on which the earth is shown as projected onto a cone with its apex over one of the poles and with parallels of latitude radiating from this apex

conics ('kɒnɪks) *n* (*functioning as singular*) the branch of geometry concerned with the parabola, ellipse, and hyperbola

conic section *n* one of a group of curves formed by the intersection of a plane and a right circular cone. It is either a circle, ellipse, parabola, or hyperbola, depending on the eccentricity, *e*, which is constant for a particular curve $e = 0$ for a circle; $e < 1$ for an ellipse; $e = 1$ for a parabola; $e > 1$ for a hyperbola. Often shortened to: **conic**

conidiophore (kəʊ'nɪdɪəˌfɔː) *n* a simple or branched hypha that bears spores (conidia) in such fungi as *Penicillium* [c19 from CONIDIUM + -PHORE] > conidiophorous (kəʊˌnɪdɪ'ɒfərəs, kə-) *adj*

conidium (kəʊ'nɪdɪəm) *n, pl* -nidia (-'nɪdɪə) an asexual spore formed at the tip of a specialized hypha (conidiophore) in fungi such as *Penicillium* [c19 from New Latin, from Greek *konis* dust + IUM] > co'nidial *or* co'nidian *adj*

conifer ('kəʊnɪfə, 'kɒn-) *n* any gymnosperm tree or shrub of the phylum *Coniferophyta*, typically bearing cones and evergreen leaves. The group includes the pines, spruces, firs, larches, yews, junipers, cedars, cypresses, and sequoias [c19 from Latin, from *cōnus* CONE + *ferre* to bear]

coniferous (kə'nɪfərəs, kɒ-) *adj* of, relating to, or belonging to the plant phylum *Coniferophyta*. See **conifer**

coniine ('kəʊnɪˌiːn, -nɪɪn, -nɪɪn), **conin** ('kəʊnɪn) *or* **conine** ('kəʊniːn, -nɪn) *n* a colourless poisonous soluble liquid alkaloid found in hemlock; 2-propylpiperidine. Formula: $C_5H_{10}NC_3H_7$. Also called: cicutine ('sɪkjʊtiːn), conicine ('kɒnɪsiːn) [c19 from CONIUM + INE²]

coniology (ˌkəʊnɪ'ɒlədʒɪ) *n* a variant spelling of **koniology**

Coniston Water ('kɒnɪstən) *n* a lake in NW England, in Cumbria: scene of the establishment of world water speed records by Sir Malcolm Campbell (1939) and his son Donald Campbell (1959). Length: 8 km (5 miles)

conium ('kəʊnɪəm) *n* **1** either of the two N

temperate plants of the umbelliferous genus *Conium*, esp hemlock **2** an extract of either of these plants, formerly used to treat spasmodic disorders [c19 from Late Latin: hemlock, from Greek *kōneion*; perhaps related to Greek *kōnos* CONE]

conj. *grammar abbreviation for* conjugation, conjunction, *or* conjunctive

conjectural (kən'dʒɛktʃərəl) *adj* involving or inclined to conjecture > con'jecturally *adv*

conjecture (kən'dʒɛktʃə) *n* **1** the formation of conclusions from incomplete evidence; guess **2** the inference or conclusion so formed **3** *obsolete* interpretation of occult signs ▷ *vb* **4** to infer or arrive at (an opinion, conclusion, etc) from incomplete evidence [c14 from Latin *conjectūra* an assembling of facts, from *conicere* to throw together, from *jacere* to throw] > con'jecturable *adj* > con'jecturably *adv* > con'jecturer *n*

conjoin (kən'dʒɔɪn) *vb* to join or become joined [c14 from Old French *conjoindre*, from Latin *conjungere*, from *jungere* to JOIN] > con'joiner *n*

conjoined twins *pl n* twin babies born joined together at some point, such as at the hips. Some have lived for many years without being surgically separated. Non-technical name **Siamese twins**

conjoint (kən'dʒɔɪnt) *adj* united, joint, or associated > con'jointly *adv*

conjugal ('kɒndʒʊgᵊl) *adj* of or relating to marriage or the relationship between husband and wife: *conjugal rights* [c16 from Latin *conjugālis*, from *conjunx* wife or husband, from *conjungere* to unite; see CONJOIN] > conjugality (ˌkɒndʒʊ'gælɪtɪ) *n* > 'conjugally *adv*

conjugant ('kɒndʒʊgənt) *n* either of a pair of organisms or gametes undergoing conjugation

conjugate *vb* ('kɒndʒʊˌgeɪt) **1** (*tr*) *grammar* to inflect (a verb) systematically; state or set out the conjugation of (a verb) **2** (*intr*) (of a verb) to undergo inflection according to a specific set of rules **3** (*tr*) to join (two or more substances) together, esp in such a way that the resulting substance may easily be turned back into its original components **4** (*intr*) *biology* to undergo conjugation **5** (*tr*) *obsolete* to join together, esp in marriage ▷ *adj* ('kɒndʒʊgɪt, -ˌgeɪt) **6** joined together in pairs; coupled **7** (*Maths*) **a** (of two angles) having a sum of 360° **b** (of two complex numbers) differing only in the sign of the imaginary part as $4 + 3i$ and $4 - 3i$ **c** (of two algebraic numbers) being roots of the same irreducible algebraic equation with rational coefficients: *3 n 2 √2 are conjugate algebraic numbers, being roots of $x^2 - 6x + 1$* **d** (of two elements of a square matrix) interchanged when the rows and columns are interchanged **e** (of two arcs) forming a complete circle or other closed curved figure **8** *chem* of, denoting, or concerning the state of equilibrium in which two liquids can exist as two separate phases that are both solutions. The liquid that is the solute in one phase is the solvent in the other **9** another word for **conjugated 10** *chem* (of acids and bases) related by loss or gain of a proton: Cl^- is the *conjugate base of HCl; HCl is the conjugate acid of* Cl^- **11** *physics* **a** joined by a reciprocal relationship, such as in the case of two quantities, points, etc, that are interchangeable with respect to the properties of each of them **b** (of points connected with a lens) having the property that an object placed at one point will produce an image at the other point **12** (of a compound leaf) having one pair of leaflets **13** (of words) cognate; related in origin ▷ *n* ('kɒndʒʊgɪt) **14** one of a pair or set of conjugate substances, values, quantities, words, etc [c15 from Latin *conjugāre* to join together, from *com-* together + *jugāre* to marry, connect, from *jugum* a yoke] > 'conjugable *adj* > 'conjugately *adv* > 'conjugateness *n* > 'conju,gative *adj* > 'conju,gator *n*

conjugated ('kɒndʒʊˌgeɪtɪd) *adj* **1** *chem* **a** (of a molecule, compound, or substance) containing

C

two or more double bonds alternating with single bonds **b** (of a double bond) separated from another double bond by one single bond **2** *chem* formed by the union of two compounds: *a conjugated protein* ▷ Also: conjugate

conjugated protein *n* a biochemical compound consisting of a sequence of amino acids making up a simple protein to which another nonprotein group (a prosthetic group), such as a carbohydrate or lipid group, is attached

conjugation (ˌkɒndʒʊˈɡeɪʃən) *n* **1** *grammar* **a** inflection of a verb for person, number, tense, voice, mood, etc **b** the complete set of the inflections of a given verb **2** a joining, union, or conjunction **3** a type of sexual reproduction in ciliate protozoans involving the temporary union of two individuals and the subsequent migration and fusion of the gametic nuclei **4** (in bacteria) the direct transfer of DNA between two cells that are temporarily joined **5** the union of gametes, esp isogametes, as in some algae and fungi **6** the pairing of chromosomes in the early phase of a meiotic division **7** *chem* the existence of alternating double or triple bonds in a chemical compound, with consequent electron delocalization over part of the molecule > ˌconjuˈgational *adj* > ˌconjuˈgationally *adv*

conjunct (kənˈdʒʌŋkt, ˈkɒndʒʌŋkt) *adj* **1** joined; united **2** *music* relating to or denoting two adjacent degrees of a scale ▷ *n* **3** *logic* one of the propositions or formulas in a conjunction [c15 from Latin *conjunctus*, from *conjugere* to unite; see CONJOIN] > conˈjunctly *adv*

conjunction (kənˈdʒʌŋkʃən) *n* **1** the act of joining together; combination; union **2** simultaneous occurrence of events; coincidence **3** any word or group of words, other than a relative pronoun, that connects words, phrases, or clauses; for example *and* and *while*. Abbreviation: conj. See also **coordinating conjunction, subordinating conjunction 4** *astronomy* **a** the position of any two bodies that appear to meet, such as two celestial bodies on the celestial sphere **b** Also called: **solar conjunction** the position of a planet or the moon when it is in line with the sun as seen from the earth. The inner planets are in **inferior conjunction** when the planet is between the earth and the sun and in **superior conjunction** when the sun lies between the earth and the planet. Compare **opposition** (sense 8a) **5** *astrology* an exact aspect of 0° between two planets, etc, an orb of 8° being allowed. Compare **opposition** (sense 9), **square** (sense 10) **6** *logic* **a** the operator that forms a compound sentence from two given sentences, and corresponds to the English *and* **b** a sentence so formed. Usually written *p*&*q*, *p*∧*q*, or *p.q.*, where *p,q* are the component sentences, it is true only when both these are true **c** the relation between such sentences > conˈjunctional *adj* > conˈjunctionally *adv*

conjunction-reduction *n transformational grammar* a rule that reduces coordinate sentences, applied, for example, to convert *John lives in Ireland and Brian lives in Ireland* into *John and Brian live in Ireland*

conjunctiva (ˌkɒndʒʌŋkˈtaɪvə) *n, pl* -vas *or* -vae (-viː) the delicate mucous membrane that covers the eyeball and the under surface of the eyelid [c16 from New Latin *membrāna conjunctīva* the conjunctive membrane, from Late Latin *conjunctīvus* CONJUNCTIVE] > ˌconjuncˈtival *adj*

conjunctive (kənˈdʒʌŋktɪv) *adj* **1** joining; connective **2** joined **3** of or relating to conjunctions or their use **4** *logic* relating to, characterized by, or containing a conjunction ▷ *n* **5** a less common word for **conjunction** (*sense 3*) [c15 from Late Latin *conjunctīvus*, from Latin *conjungere* to CONJOIN] > conˈjunctively *adv*

conjunctive eye movement *n* any movement of both eyes in the same direction

conjunctivitis (kənˌdʒʌŋktɪˈvaɪtɪs) *n* inflammation of the conjunctiva

conjuncture (kənˈdʒʌŋktʃə) *n* **1** a combination of

events, esp a critical one **2** *rare* a union; conjunction > conˈjunctural *adj*

conjuration (ˌkɒndʒʊˈreɪʃən) *n* **1** a magic spell; incantation **2** a less common word for **conjuring 3** *archaic* supplication; entreaty

conjure (ˈkʌndʒə) *vb* **1** (*intr*) to practise conjuring or be a conjuror **2** (*intr*) to call upon supposed supernatural forces by spells and incantations **3** (kənˈdʒʊə) (*tr*) to appeal earnestly or strongly to: *I conjure you to help me* **4 a** to conjure with **a** a person thought to have great power or influence **b** any name that excites the imagination [c13 from Old French *conjurer* to plot, from Latin *conjūrāre* to swear together, form a conspiracy, from *jūrāre* to swear]

conjure up *vb* (*tr, adverb*) **1** to present to the mind; evoke or imagine: *he conjured up a picture of his childhood* **2** to call up or command (a spirit or devil) by an incantation

conjuring (ˈkʌndʒərɪŋ) *n* **1** the performance of tricks that appear to defy natural laws ▷ *adj* **2** denoting or relating to such tricks or entertainment

conjuror *or* **conjurer** (ˈkʌndʒərə) *n* **1** a person who practises conjuring, esp for people's entertainment **2** a person who practises magic; sorcerer

conk (kɒŋk) *slang* ▷ *vb* **1** to strike (someone) a blow, esp on the head or nose ▷ *n* **2** a punch or blow, esp on the head or nose **3** the head or (esp Brit and NZ) the nose [c19 probably changed from CONCH]

conker (ˈkɒŋkə) *n* an informal name for **horse chestnut** (sense 2)

conkers (ˈkɒŋkəz) *n* (*functioning as singular*) *Brit* a game in which a player swings a horse chestnut (conker), threaded onto a string, against that of another player to try to break it [c19 from dialect *conker* snail shell, originally used in the game]

conk out *vb* (*intr, adverb*) *informal* **1** (of machines, cars, etc) to fail suddenly **2** to tire suddenly or collapse, as from exhaustion [c20 of uncertain origin]

con man *n informal* a person who swindles another by means of a confidence trick. More formal term: confidence man

con moto (kɒn ˈməʊtəʊ) *adj, adv music* (to be performed) in a brisk or lively manner [Italian, literally: with movement]

conn (kɒn) *vb, n* a variant spelling (esp US) of **con⁴**

Conn. *abbreviation for* Connecticut

Connacht (ˈkɒnət) *or* **Connaught** *n* a province and ancient kingdom of NW Republic of Ireland: consists of the counties of Galway, Leitrim, Mayo, Roscommon, and Sligo. Pop: 464 296 (2002). Area: 17 122 sq km (6611 sq miles)

connate (ˈkɒneɪt) *adj* **1** existing in a person or thing from birth; congenital or innate **2** allied or associated in nature or origin; cognate: *connate qualities* **3** Also called: **coadunate** *biology* (of similar parts or organs) closely joined or united together by growth **4** *geology* (of fluids) produced or originating at the same time as the rocks surrounding them: *connate water* [c17 from Late Latin *connātus* born at the same time, from Latin *nātus*, from *nāscī* to be born] > ˈconnately *adv* > ˈconnateness *n*

connatural (kəˈnætʃərəl) *adj* **1** having a similar nature or origin **2** congenital or innate; connate > conˈnaturally *adv*

Connaught (ˈkɒnɔːt) *n* another name for **Connacht**

connect (kəˈnɛkt) *vb* **1** to link or be linked together; join; fasten **2** (*tr*) to relate or associate: *I connect him with my childhood* **3** (*tr*) to establish telephone communications with or between **4** (*intr*) to be meaningful or meaningfully related **5** (*intr*) (of two public vehicles, such as trains or buses) to have the arrival of one timed to occur just before the departure of the other, for the convenient transfer of passengers **6** (*intr*) *informal* to hit, punch, kick, etc, solidly **7** (*intr*) *US and*

Canadian informal to be successful **8** (*intr*) *slang* to find a source of drugs, esp illegal drugs [c17 from Latin *connectere* to bind together, from *nectere* to bind, tie] > conˈnectible *or* conˈnectable *adj* > conˈnector *or* conˈnecter *n*

connected (kəˈnɛktɪd) *adj* **1** joined or linked together **2** (of speech) coherent and intelligible **3** *logic, maths* (of a relation) such that either it or its converse holds between any two members of its domain > conˈnectedly *adv*

Connecticut (kəˈnɛtɪkət) *n* **1** a state of the northeastern US, in New England. Capital: Hartford. Pop: 3 483 372 (2003 est). Area: 12 973 sq km (5009 sq miles). Abbreviations: **Conn.**, (with zip code) **CT 2** a river in the northeastern US, rising in N New Hampshire and flowing south to Long Island Sound. Length: 651 km (407 miles)

connecting rod *n* **1** a rod or bar for transmitting motion, esp one that connects a rotating part to a reciprocating part **2** such a rod that connects the piston to the crankshaft in an internal-combustion engine or reciprocating pump. See also **big end, little end 3** a similar rod that connects the crosshead of a steam engine to the crank ▷ Often shortened to: **con rod**

connection *or* **connexion** (kəˈnɛkʃən) *n* **1** the act or state of connecting; union **2** something that connects, joins, or relates; link or bond **3** a relationship or association **4** logical sequence in thought or expression; coherence **5** the relation of a word or phrase to its context: *in this connection the word has no political significance* **6** (*often plural*) an acquaintance, esp one who is influential or has prestige **7** a relative, esp if distant and related by marriage **8 a** an opportunity to transfer from one train, bus, aircraft, ship, etc, to another **b** the vehicle, aircraft, etc, scheduled to provide such an opportunity **9** (*plural*) NZ the persons owning or controlling a racehorse **10** a link, usually a wire or metallic strip, between two components in an electric circuit or system **11** a communications link between two points, esp by telephone **12** *slang* a supplier of illegal drugs, such as heroin **13** *rare* sexual intercourse **14** *rare* a small sect or religious group united by a body of distinct beliefs or practices > conˈnectional *or* conˈnexional *adj*

connectionism (kəˈnɛkʃənɪzəm) *n psychol* the theory that the connections between brain cells mediate thought and govern behaviour

connective (kəˈnɛktɪv) *adj* **1** serving to connect or capable of connecting ▷ *n* **2** a thing that connects **3** *grammar, logic* **a** a less common word for **conjunction** (sense 3) **b** any word that connects phrases, clauses, or individual words **c** a symbol used in a formal language in the construction of compound sentences from simpler sentences, corresponding to terms such as *or, and, not,* etc, in ordinary speech **4** *botany* the tissue of a stamen that connects the two lobes of the anther **5** *anatomy* a nerve-fibre bundle connecting two nerve centres > conˈnectively *adv* > connectivity (ˌkɒnɛkˈtɪvɪtɪ) *n*

connective tissue *n* an animal tissue developed from the embryonic mesoderm that consists of collagen or elastic fibres, fibroblasts, fatty cells, etc, within a jelly-like matrix. It supports organs, fills the spaces between them, and forms tendons and ligaments

connectivity (ˌkɒnɛkˈtɪvɪtɪ) *n* **1** the state of being or being able to be connected **2** *computing* the state of being connected to the internet **3** *computing* the capacity of a machine or appliance to be connected to other machines, appliances, or facilities

Connemara (ˌkɒnɪˈmɑːrə) *n* a barren coastal region of W Republic of Ireland, in Co Galway: consists of quartzite mountains, peat bogs, and many lakes; noted for its breed of pony originating from the hilly regions

conning tower (ˈkɒnɪŋ) *n* **1** Also called: **sail** a superstructure of a submarine, used as the bridge when the vessel is on the surface **2** the armoured pilot house of a warship [C19 see CON[4]]

conniption (kəˈnɪpʃən) *n* (*often plural*) *US and Canadian slang* a fit of rage or tantrums [C19 arbitrary pseudo-Latin coinage]

connivance (kəˈnaɪvəns) *n* **1** the act or fact of conniving **2** *law* the tacit encouragement of or assent to another's wrongdoing, esp (formerly) of the petitioner in a divorce suit to the respondent's adultery

connive (kəˈnaɪv) *vb* (*intr*) **1** to plot together, esp secretly; conspire **2** (foll by *at*) *law* to give assent or encouragement (to the commission of a wrong) [C17 from French *conniver*, from Latin *connīvēre* to blink, hence, leave uncensured; *-nīvēre* related to *nictāre* to wink] > **conˈniver** *n* > **conˈnivingly** *adv*

connivent (kəˈnaɪvənt) *adj* (of parts of plants and animals) touching without being fused, as some petals, insect wings, etc [C17 from Latin *connīvēns*, from *connīvēre* to shut the eyes, CONNIVE] > **conˈnivently** *adv*

connoisseur (ˌkɒnɪˈsɜː) *n* a person with special knowledge or appreciation of a field, esp in the arts [C18 from French, from Old French *conoiseor*, from *connoistre* to know, from Latin *cognōscere*] > **ˌconnoisˈseurship** *n*

connotation (ˌkɒnəˈteɪʃən) *n* **1** an association or idea suggested by a word or phrase; implication **2** the act or fact of connoting **3** *logic* another name for **intension** (sense 1) > **connotative** (ˈkɒnəˌteɪtɪv, kəˈnəʊtə-) *or* **conˈnotive** *adj* > **ˈconnoˌtatively** *or* **conˈnotively** *adv*

connote (kɒˈnəʊt) *vb* (*tr; often takes a clause as object*) **1** (of a word, phrase, etc) to imply or suggest (associations or ideas) other than the literal meaning: *the word "maiden" connotes modesty* **2** to involve as a consequence or condition [C17 from Medieval Latin *connotāre*, from *notāre* to mark, make a note, from *nota* mark, sign, note]

connubial (kəˈnjuːbɪəl) *adj* of or relating to marriage; conjugal: *connubial bliss* [C17 from Latin *cōnūbiālis* from *cōnūbium* marriage, from *com-* together + *nūbere* to marry] > **conˌnubiˈality** *n* > **conˈnubially** *adv*

conodont (ˈkəʊnədɒnt, ˈkɒn-) *n* any of various small Palaeozoic toothlike fossils derived from an extinct eel-like marine animal [C19 from Greek *kōnos* CONE + ODONT]

conoid (ˈkəʊnɔɪd) *n* **1** a geometric surface formed by rotating a parabola, ellipse, or hyperbola about one axis ▷ *adj also* **conoidal** (kəʊˈnɔɪdəl) **2** conical, cone-shaped [C17 from Greek *kōnoeidēs*, from *kōnos* CONE] > **coˈnoidally** *adv*

conoscenti (ˌkɒnəʊˈʃɛntɪ) *pl n, sing* **-te** (-tiː) a variant spelling of **cognoscenti**

conquer (ˈkɒŋkə) *vb* **1** to overcome (an enemy, army, etc); defeat **2** to overcome (an obstacle, feeling, desire, etc); surmount **3** (*tr*) to gain possession or control of by or as if by force or war; win **4** (*tr*) to gain the love, sympathy, etc, of (someone) by seduction or force of personality [C13 from Old French *conquerre*, from Vulgar Latin *conquærere* (unattested) to obtain, from Latin *conquīrere* to search for, collect, from *quaerere* to seek] > **ˈconquerable** *adj* > **ˈconquerableness** *n* > **ˈconquering** *adj* > **ˈconqueror** *n*

conquest (ˈkɒnkwɛst, ˈkɒŋ-) *n* **1** the act or an instance of conquering or the state of having been conquered; victory **2** a person, thing, etc, that has been conquered or won **3** the act or art of gaining a person's compliance, love, etc, by seduction or force of personality **4** a person, whose compliance, love, etc, has been won over by seduction or force of personality [C13 from Old French *conqueste*, from Vulgar Latin *conquēsta* (unattested), from Latin *conquīsīta*, feminine past participle of *conquīrere* to seek out, procure; see CONQUER]

Conquest (ˈkɒnkwɛst, ˈkɒŋ-) *n* **1** the See **Norman Conquest** **2** the *Canadian* the conquest by the United Kingdom of French North America, ending in 1763

conquian (ˈkɒŋkɪən) *n* another word for **cooncan**

conquistador (kɒnˈkwɪstəˌdɔː; *Spanish* konkistaˈðor) *n, pl* **-dors** *or* **-dores** (*Spanish* -ˈðores) an adventurer or conqueror, esp one of the Spanish conquerors of the New World in the 16th century [C19 from Spanish, from *conquistar* to conquer; see CONQUEST]

con rod *n* short for **connecting rod**

Cons. *or* **cons.** *abbreviation for* **1** Conservative **2** Constitution **3** Consul

consanguinity (ˌkɒnsænˈɡwɪnɪtɪ) *n* **1** relationship by blood; kinship **2** close affinity or connection **3** *geology* (of igneous rocks) similarity of origin, as shown by common mineral and chemical compositions and often texture [C14 see CON-, SANGUINE] > **ˌconsanˈguineous** *or* **conˈsanguine** *adj* > **ˌconsanˈguineously** *adv*

conscience (ˈkɒnʃəns) *n* **1** **a** the sense of right and wrong that governs a person's thoughts and actions **b** regulation of one's actions in conformity to this sense **c** a supposed universal faculty of moral insight **2** conscientiousness; diligence **3** a feeling of guilt or anxiety: *he has a conscience about his unkind action* **4** *obsolete* consciousness **5** **in (all) conscience** **a** with regard to truth and justice **b** certainly **6** **on one's conscience** causing feelings of guilt or remorse [C13 from Old French, from Latin *conscientia* knowledge, consciousness, from *conscīre* to know; see CONSCIOUS] > **ˈconscienceless** *adj*

conscience clause *n* a clause in a law or contract exempting persons with moral scruples

conscience money *n* money paid voluntarily to compensate for dishonesty, esp money paid voluntarily for taxes formerly evaded

conscience-stricken *adj* feeling anxious or guilty. Also: **conscience-smitten**

conscientious (ˌkɒnʃɪˈɛnʃəs) *adj* **1** involving or taking great care; painstaking; diligent **2** governed by or done according to conscience > **ˌconsciˈentiously** *adv* > **ˌconsciˈentiousness** *n*

conscientious objector *n* a person who refuses to serve in the armed forces on the grounds of conscience

conscionable (ˈkɒnʃənəbəl) *adj obsolete* acceptable to one's conscience [C16 from *conscions*, obsolete form of CONSCIENCE] > **ˈconscionableness** *n* > **ˈconscionably** *adv*

conscious (ˈkɒnʃəs) *adj* **1** **a** alert and awake; not sleeping or comatose **b** aware of one's surroundings, one's own thoughts and motivations, etc **2** **a** aware of and giving value or emphasis to a particular fact or phenomenon: *I am conscious of your great kindness to me* **b** (*in combination*): *clothes-conscious* **3** done with full awareness; deliberate: *a conscious effort; conscious rudeness* **4** **a** denoting or relating to a part of the human mind that is aware of a person's self, environment, and mental activity and that to a certain extent determines his choices of action **b** (*as noun*): *the conscious is only a small part of the mind* ▷ Compare **unconscious** [C17 from Latin *conscius* sharing knowledge, from *com-* with + *scīre* to know] > **ˈconsciously** *adv* > **ˈconsciousness** *n*

consciousness raising *n* **a** the process of developing awareness in a person or group of a situation regarded as wrong or unjust, with the aim of producing active participation in changing it **b** (*as modifier*): *a consciousness-raising group*

conscript *n* (ˈkɒnskrɪpt) **1** **a** a person who is enrolled for compulsory military service **b** (*as modifier*): *a conscript army* ▷ *vb* (kənˈskrɪpt) **2** (*tr*) to enrol (youths, civilians, etc) for compulsory military service [C15 from Latin *conscrīptus*, past participle of *conscrībere* to write together in a list, enrol, from *scrībere* to write]

conscript fathers *pl n literary* august legislators, esp Roman senators

conscription (kənˈskrɪpʃən) *n* compulsory military service

consecrate (ˈkɒnsɪˌkreɪt) *vb* (*tr*) **1** to make or declare sacred or holy; sanctify **2** to dedicate (one's life, time, etc) to a specific purpose **3** to ordain (a bishop) **4** *Christianity* to sanctify (bread and wine) for the Eucharist to be received as the body and blood of Christ **5** to cause to be respected or revered; venerate: *time has consecrated this custom* ▷ *adj* **6** *archaic* consecrated [C15 from Latin *consecrāre*, from *com-* (intensive) + *sacrāre* to devote, from *sacer* sacred] > **ˌconseˈcration** *n* > **ˈconseˌcrator** *n* > **consecratory** (ˌkɒnsɪˈkreɪtərɪ) *or* **ˈconseˌcrative** *adj*

Consecration (ˌkɒnsɪˈkreɪʃən) *n RC Church* the part of the Mass after the sermon during which the bread and wine are believed to change into the Body and Blood of Christ

consecution (ˌkɒnsɪˈkjuːʃən) *n* **1** a sequence or succession of events or things **2** a logical sequence of deductions; inference [C16 from Latin *consecūtiō*, from *consequī* to follow up, pursue]

consecutive (kənˈsɛkjʊtɪv) *adj* **1** (of a narrative, account, etc) following chronological sequence **2** following one another without interruption; successive **3** characterized by logical sequence **4** *music* another word for **parallel** (sense 3) **5** *grammar* expressing consequence or result: *consecutive clauses* [C17 from French *consécutif*, from Latin *consecūtus* having followed, from *consequī* to pursue] > **conˈsecutively** *adv* > **conˈsecutiveness** *n*

consensual (kənˈsɛnsjʊəl) *adj* **1** *law* (of a contract, agreement, etc) existing by consent **2** *law* (of a sexual activity) performed with the consent of all parties involved **3** (of certain reflex actions of a part of the body) responding to stimulation of another part > **conˈsensually** *adv* [from CONSENSUS + -AL[1]]

consensus (kənˈsɛnsəs) *n* general or widespread agreement (esp in the phrase **consensus of opinion**) [C19 from Latin, from *consentīre* to feel together, agree; see CONSENT]

> USAGE Since *consensus* refers to a collective opinion, the words *of opinion* in the phrase *consensus of opinion* are redundant and should therefore be avoided

C

consensus sequence *n biochem* a DNA sequence common to different organisms and having a similar function in each

consent (kənˈsɛnt) *vb* **1** to give assent or permission (to do something); agree; accede **2** (*intr*) *obsolete* to be in accord; agree in opinion, feelings, etc ▷ *n* **3** acquiescence to or acceptance of something done or planned by another; permission **4** accordance or harmony in opinion; agreement (esp in the phrase **with one consent**) **5** **age of consent** the lowest age at which the law recognizes the right of a person to consent to sexual intercourse [C13 from Old French *consentir*, from Latin *consentīre* to feel together, agree, from *sentīre* to feel] > **conˈsenter** *n* > **conˈsenting** *adj*

consentaneous (ˌkɒnsɛnˈteɪnɪəs) *adj rare* **1** (foll by *to*) accordant or consistent (with) **2** done by general consent [C17 from Latin *consentāneus*, from *consentīre* to CONSENT] > **ˌconsenˈtaneously** *adv* > **consentaneity** (kənˌsɛntəˈniːɪtɪ) *or* **ˌconsenˈtaneousness** *n*

consentient (kənˈsɛnʃənt) *adj* being in agreement; united in opinion > **conˈsentience** *n*

consenting adult *n Brit* a male person over the age of sixteen, who may legally engage in homosexual behaviour in private

consequence (ˈkɒnsɪkwəns) *n* **1** a result or effect of some previous occurrence **2** an unpleasant result (esp in the phrase **take the consequences**) **3** significance or importance: *it's of no consequence; a man of consequence* **4** *logic* **a** a conclusion reached by reasoning **b** the conclusion of an argument **c** the relations between the conclusion and the premises of a valid argument **5** the relation between an effect and its cause **6** **in consequence** as a result

consequences (ˈkɒnsɪkwənsɪz) *pl n* (*functioning as singular*) *Brit* a game in which each player writes down a part of a story, folds over the paper, and passes it on to another player who continues the story. After several stages, the resulting (nonsensical) stories are read out

consequent ('kɒnsɪkwənt) *adj* **1** following as an effect or result **2** following as a logical conclusion or by rational argument **3** (of a river) flowing in the direction of the original slope of the land or dip of the strata ▷ *n* **4** something that follows something else, esp as a result **5** *logic* the resultant clause in a conditional sentence **6** **affirming the consequent** *logic* the fallacy of inferring the antecedent of a conditional sentence, given the truth of the conditional and its consequent, as *if John is six feet tall, he's more than five feet: he's more than five feet so he's six feet* **7** an obsolete term for **denominator** (sense 1) [c15 from Latin *consequēns* following closely, from *consequī* to pursue]

■ USAGE See at **consequential**

consequential (ˌkɒnsɪ'kwɛnʃəl) *adj* **1** important or significant **2** self-important; conceited **3** following as a consequence; resultant, esp indirectly: *consequential loss* > ˌconse'quenti'ality or ˌconse'quentialness *n* > ˌconse'quentially *adv*

■ USAGE Although both *consequential* and *consequent* can refer to something which happens as the result of something else, *consequent* is more common in this sense in modern English: *the new measures were put into effect, and the consequent protest led to the dismissal of those responsible*

consequentialism (ˌkɒnsɪ'kwɛnʃəˌlɪzəm) *n ethics* the doctrine that an action is right or wrong according as its consequences are good or bad

consequently ('kɒnsɪkwəntlɪ) *adv, sentence connector* as a result or effect; therefore; hence

conservancy (kən'sɜːvənsɪ) *n, pl* **-cies** **1** (in Britain) a court or commission with jurisdiction over a river, port, area of countryside, etc **2** another word for **conservation** (sense 2)

conservation (ˌkɒnsə'veɪʃən) *n* **1** the act or an instance of conserving or keeping from change, loss, injury, etc **2 a** protection, preservation, and careful management of natural resources and of the environment **b** (*as modifier*): *a conservation area* > ˌconser'vational *adj*

conservation grade *adj* relating to food produced using traditional methods where possible, and following strict specifications regarding animal feeds and welfare, the use of chemical fertilizers, wildlife conservation, and land management

conservationist (ˌkɒnsə'veɪʃənɪst) *n* a person who advocates or strongly promotes preservation and careful management of natural resources and of the environment

conservation of charge *n* the principle that the total charge of any isolated system is constant and independent of changes that take place within the system

conservation of energy *n* the principle that the total energy of any isolated system is constant and independent of any changes occurring within the system

conservation of mass *n* the principle that the total mass of any isolated system is constant and is independent of any chemical and physical changes taking place within the system

conservation of momentum *n* the principle that the total linear or angular momentum in any isolated system is constant, provided that no external force is applied

conservation of parity *n* the principle that the parity of the total wave function describing a system of elementary particles is conserved. In fact it is not conserved in weak interactions

conservatism (kən'sɜːvəˌtɪzəm) *n* **1** opposition to change and innovation **2** a political philosophy advocating the preservation of the best of the established order in society and opposing radical change

Conservatism (kən'sɜːvəˌtɪzəm) *n* (in Britain, Canada, etc) **1** the form of conservatism advocated by the Conservative Party **2** the policies, doctrines, or practices of the Conservative Party

conservative (kən'sɜːvətɪv) *adj* **1** favouring the preservation of established customs, values, etc, and opposing innovation **2** of, characteristic of, or relating to conservatism **3** tending to be moderate or cautious: *a conservative estimate* **4** conventional in style or type: *a conservative suit* **5** *med* (of treatment) designed to alleviate symptoms. Compare **radical** (sense 4) **6** *physics* a field of force, system, etc, in which the work done moving a body from one point to another is independent of the path taken between them: *electrostatic fields of force are conservative* ▷ *n* **7** a person who is reluctant to change or consider new ideas; conformist **8** a supporter or advocate of conservatism ▷ *adj* ▷ *n* **9** a less common word for **preservative.** > con'servatively *adv* > con'servativeness *n*

Conservative (kən'sɜːvətɪv) *adj* (in Britain, Canada, and elsewhere) **1** of, supporting, or relating to a Conservative Party **2** of, relating to, or characterizing Conservative Judaism ▷ *n* **3** a supporter or member of a Conservative Party

Conservative Judaism *n* a movement reacting against the radicalism of Reform Judaism, rejecting extreme change and advocating moderate relaxations of traditional Jewish law, by an extension of the process by which its adherents claim traditional Orthodox Judaism evolved. Compare **Orthodox Judaism, Reform Judaism**

Conservative Party *n* **1** (in Britain) the major right-wing party, which developed from the Tories in the 1830s. It advocates a mixed economy, and encourages property owning and free enterprise. In full: **Conservative and Unionist Party 2** (in Canada) short for **Progressive Conservative Party 3** (in other countries) any of various political parties generally opposing change

conservatoire (kən'sɜːvəˌtwɑː) *n* an institution or school for instruction in music. Also called: **conservatory** [c18 from French: CONSERVATORY]

conservator ('kɒnsəˌveɪtə, kən'sɜːvə-) *n* a person who conserves or keeps safe; custodian, guardian, or protector

conservatorium (kənˌsɜːvə'tɔːrɪəm) *n Austral* the usual term for **conservatoire**

conservatory (kən'sɜːvətrɪ) *n, pl* **-tories 1** a greenhouse, esp one attached to a house **2** another word for **conservatoire** ▷ *adj* **3** preservative

conserve *vb* (kən'sɜːv) (*tr*) **1** to keep or protect from harm, decay, loss, etc **2** to preserve (a foodstuff, esp fruit) with sugar ▷ *n* ('kɒnsɜːv, kən'sɜːv) **3** a preparation of fruit in sugar, similar to jam but usually containing whole pieces of fruit [(vb) c14 from Latin *conservāre* to keep safe, from *servāre* to save, protect; (n) c14 from Medieval Latin *conserva*, from Latin *conservāre*] > con'servable *adj* > con'server *n*

Consett ('kɒnsɪt) *n* a town in N England, in N Durham. Pop: 20 659 (2001)

consider (kən'sɪdə) *vb* (*mainly tr*) **1** (*also intr*) to think carefully about or ponder on (a problem, decision, etc); contemplate **2** (*may take a clause as object*) to judge, deem, or have as an opinion: *I consider him a fool* **3** to have regard for; respect: *consider your mother's feelings* **4** to treat with regard; regard: *he considered her face* **5** (*may take a clause as object*) to bear in mind as possible or acceptable: *when buying a car consider this make* **6** to describe or discuss: *in this programme we consider the traffic problem* **7** (*may take a clause as object*) to keep in mind and make allowances (for): *consider his childhood* [c14 from Latin *consīderāre* to inspect closely, literally: to observe the stars, from *sīdus* star] > con'siderer *n*

considerable (kən'sɪdərəbᵊl) *adj* **1** large enough to reckon with: *a considerable quantity* **2** a lot of; much: *he had considerable courage* **3** worthy of respect: *a considerable man in the scientific world* > con'siderably *adv*

considerate (kən'sɪdərɪt) *adj* **1** thoughtful towards other people; kind **2** *rare* carefully thought out; considered > con'siderately *adv* > con'siderateness *n*

consideration (kənˌsɪdə'reɪʃən) *n* **1** the act or an instance of considering; deliberation; contemplation **2 take into consideration** to bear in mind; consider **3 under consideration** being currently discussed or deliberated **4** a fact or circumstance to be taken into account when making a judgment or decision **5 on no consideration** for no reason whatsoever; never **6** thoughtfulness for other people; kindness **7** payment for a service; recompense; fee **8** thought resulting from deliberation; opinion **9** *law* the promise, object, etc, given by one party to persuade another to enter into a contract **10** estimation; esteem **11 in consideration of a** because of **b** in return for

considered (kən'sɪdəd) *adj* **1** presented or thought out with care: *a considered opinion* **2** (*qualified by a preceding adverb*) esteemed: *highly considered*

considering (kən'sɪdərɪŋ) *prep* **1** in view of ▷ *adv* **2** *informal* all in all; taking into account the circumstances: *it's not bad considering* ▷ *conj* **3** (*subordinating*) in view of the fact that

consign (kən'saɪn) *vb* (*mainly tr*) **1** to hand over or give into the care or charge of another; entrust **2** to commit irrevocably: *he consigned the papers to the flames* **3** to commit for admittance: *to consign someone to jail* **4** to address or deliver (goods) for sale, disposal, etc: *it was consigned to his London address* **5** (*intr*) *obsolete* to assent; agree [c15 from Old French *consigner*, from Latin *consignāre* to put one's seal to, sign, from *signum* mark, SIGN] > con'signable *adj* > ˌconsig'nation *n*

consignee (ˌkɒnsaɪ'niː) *n* a person, agent, organization, etc, to which merchandise is consigned

consignment (kən'saɪnmənt) *n* **1** the act of consigning; commitment **2** a shipment of goods consigned **3 on consignment** for payment by the consignee after sale: *he made the last shipment on consignment*

consignor (kən'saɪnə, ˌkɒnsaɪ'nɔː) or **consigner** (kən'saɪnə) *n* a person, enterprise, etc, that consigns goods

consist (kən'sɪst) *vb* (*intr*) **1** (foll by *of*) to be composed (of); be formed (of): *syrup consists of sugar and water* **2** (foll by *in* or *of*) to have its existence (in); lie (in); be expressed (by): *his religion consists only in going to church* **3** to be compatible or consistent; accord [c16 from Latin *consistere* to halt, stand firm, from *sistere* to stand, cause to stand; related to *stāre* to STAND]

consistency (kən'sɪstənsɪ) or **consistence** *n, pl* **-encies** or **-ences 1** agreement or accordance with facts, form, or characteristics previously shown or stated **2** agreement or harmony between parts of something complex; compatibility **3** degree of viscosity or firmness **4** the state or quality of holding or sticking together and retaining shape **5** conformity with previous attitudes, behaviour, practice, etc

consistent (kən'sɪstənt) *adj* **1** showing consistency; not self-contradictory **2** (*postpositive*; foll by *with*) in agreement or harmony; accordant **3** steady; even: *consistent growth* **4** *maths* (of two or more equations) satisfied by at least one common set of values of the variables: $x + y = 4$ and $x - y = 2$ are consistent **5** *logic* **a** (of a set of statements) capable of all being true at the same time or under the same interpretation **b** Also **sound** (of a formal system) not permitting the deduction of a contradiction from the axioms. Compare **complete** (sense 5) **6** *obsolete* stuck together; cohering > con'sistently *adv*

consistory (kənˈsɪstəri) *n, pl* -ries **1** *Church of England* **a** the court of a diocese (other than Canterbury) administering ecclesiastical law **b** the area in a church where the consistory meets **2** *RC Church* an assembly of the cardinals and the pope **3** (in certain Reformed Churches) the governing body of a local congregation or church **4** *archaic* a council or assembly [C14 from Old French *consistorie*, from Medieval Latin *consistōrium* ecclesiastical tribunal, ultimately from Latin *consistere* to stand still] > **consistorial** (ˌkɒnsɪˈstɔːrɪəl) *or* ˌconsisˈtorian *adj*

consociate *vb* (kənˈsəʊʃɪˌeɪt) **1** to enter into or bring into friendly association ▷ *adj* (kənˈsəʊʃɪɪt, -ˌeɪt) **2** associated or united ▷ *n* (kənˈsəʊʃɪɪt, -ˌeɪt) **3** an associate or partner [C16 from Latin *consociāre*, from *socius* partner] > conˌsociˈation *n*

consocies (kənˈsəʊʃiːz) *n, pl* -cies *ecology* a natural community with a single dominant species [C20 from CONSOCIATE + SPECIES]

consolation (ˌkɒnsəˈleɪʃən) *n* **1** the act of consoling or state of being consoled; solace **2** a person or thing that is a source of comfort in a time of suffering, grief, disappointment, etc > **consolatory** (kənˈsɒlətəri, -trɪ) *adj*

consolation prize *n* a prize given to console a loser of a game

console[1] (kənˈsəʊl) *vb* to serve as a source of comfort to (someone) in disappointment, loss, sadness, etc [C17 from Latin *consōlārī*, from *sōlārī* to comfort; see SOLACE] > conˈsolable *adj* > conˈsoler *n* > conˈsolingly *adv*

console[2] (ˈkɒnsəʊl) *n* **1** an ornamental bracket, esp one used to support a wall fixture, bust, etc **2** the part of an organ comprising the manuals, pedals, stops, etc **3** a unit on which the controls of an electronic system are mounted **4** same as **games console 5** a cabinet for a television, gramophone, etc, designed to stand on the floor **6** See **console table** [C18 from French, shortened from Old French *consolateur* one that provides support, hence, supporting bracket, from Latin *consōlātor* a comforter; see CONSOLE[1]]

console game *n* a video game requiring the use of a games console

console table (ˈkɒnsəʊl) *n* a table with one or more curved legs of bracket-like construction, designed to stand against a wall

consolidate (kənˈsɒlɪˌdeɪt) *vb* **1** to form or cause to form into a solid mass or whole; unite or be united **2** to make or become stronger or more stable **3** *military* to strengthen or improve one's control over (a situation, force, newly captured area, etc) [C16 from Latin *consolidāre* to make firm, from *solidus* strong, SOLID]

Consolidated Fund *n Brit* a fund into which tax revenue is paid in order to meet standing charges, esp interest payments on the national debt

consolidation (kənˌsɒlɪˈdeɪʃən) *n* **1** the act of consolidating or state of being consolidated **2** something that is consolidated or integrated **3** *law* **a** the combining of two or more actions at law **b** the combination of a number of Acts of Parliament into one codifying statute **4** *geology* the process, including compression and cementation, by which a loose deposit is transformed into a hard rock **5** *psychol* the process in the brain that makes the memory for an event enduring; the process is thought to continue for some time after the event > conˈsoliˌdative *adj*

consolidation loan *n* a single loan which is taken out to pay off several separate existing loans

consolidator (kənˈsɒlɪˌdeɪtə) *n* **1** a person or thing that consolidates **2** a company that offers flight tickets for a variety of different airlines, usually at a reduced price

consols (ˈkɒnsɒlz, kənˈsɒlz) *pl n* irredeemable British government securities carrying annual interest rates of two and a half or four per cent. Also called: **bank annuities** [short for *consolidated stock*]

consolute (ˈkɒnsəˌluːt) *adj* **1** (of two or more liquids) mutually soluble in all proportions **2** (of a substance) soluble in each of two conjugate liquids **3** of or concerned with the particular state in which two partially miscible liquids become totally miscible [C20 from Late Latin *consolūtus*, from Latin *con-* together + *solvere* to dissolve]

consommé (kənˈsɒmeɪ, ˈkɒnsɒˌmeɪ; *French* kɔ̃sɔme) *n* a clear soup made from meat or chicken stock [C19 from French, from *consommer* to finish, use up, from Latin *consummāre*; so called because all the goodness of the meat goes into the liquid]

consonance (ˈkɒnsənəns) *or* **consonancy** *n, pl* -nances *or* -nancies **1** agreement, harmony, or accord **2** *prosody* similarity between consonants, but not between vowels, as between the *s* and *t* sounds in *sweet silent thought*. Compare **assonance** (sense 1) **3** *music* **a** an aesthetically pleasing sensation or perception associated with the interval of the octave, the perfect fourth and fifth, the major and minor third and sixth, and chords based on these intervals. Compare **dissonance** (sense 3) **b** an interval or chord producing this sensation

consonant (ˈkɒnsənənt) *n* **1** a speech sound or letter of the alphabet other than a vowel; a stop, fricative, or continuant ▷ *adj* **2** (*postpositive*; foll by *with* or *to*) consistent; in agreement **3** harmonious in tone or sound **4** *music* characterized by the presence of a consonance **5** being or relating to a consonant [C14 from Latin *consonāns*, from *consonāre* to sound at the same time, be in harmony, from *sonāre* to sound] > ˈconsonantly *adv*

consonantal (ˌkɒnsəˈnæntəl) *adj* **1** relating to, functioning as, or constituting a consonant, such as the semivowel *w* in English *work* **2** consisting of or characterized by consonants: *a consonantal cluster* > ˌconsoˈnantally *adv*

con sordino *adv music* See **sordino** (sense 3)

consort *vb* (kənˈsɔːt) **1** (*intr*; usually foll by *with*) to keep company (with undesirable people); associate **2** (*intr*) to agree or harmonize **3** (*tr*) *rare* to combine or unite ▷ *n* (ˈkɒnsɔːt) **4** (*esp formerly*) **a** a small group of instruments, either of the same type, such as viols, (a **whole consort**) or of different types (a **broken consort**) **b** (*as modifier*): *consort music* **5** the husband or wife of a reigning monarch **6** a partner or companion, esp a husband or wife **7** a ship that escorts another **8** *obsolete* **a** companionship or association **b** agreement or accord [C15 from Old French, from Latin *consors* sharer, partner, from *sors* lot, fate, portion] > conˈsortable *adj* > conˈsorter *n*

consortium (kənˈsɔːtɪəm) *n, pl* -tia (-tɪə) **1** an association of financiers, companies, etc, esp one formed for a particular purpose **2** *law* the right of husband or wife to the company, assistance, and affection of the other [C19 from Latin: community of goods, partnership; see CONSORT] > conˈsortial *adj*

conspecific (ˌkɒnspɪˈsɪfɪk) *adj* (of animals or plants) belonging to the same species

conspectus (kənˈspɛktəs) *n* **1** an overall view; survey **2** a summary; résumé [C19 from Latin: a viewing, from *conspicere* to observe, from *specere* to look]

conspicuous (kənˈspɪkjʊəs) *adj* **1** clearly visible; obvious or showy **2** attracting attention because of a striking quality or feature: *conspicuous stupidity* [C16 from Latin *conspicuus*, from *conspicere* to perceive; see CONSPECTUS] > conˈspicuously *adv* > conˈspicuousness *n*

conspicuous consumption *n* spending in a lavish or ostentatious way, esp to impress others with one's wealth

conspiracy (kənˈspɪrəsɪ) *n, pl* -cies **1** a secret plan or agreement to carry out an illegal or harmful act, esp with political motivation; plot **2** the act of making such plans in secret > conˈspirator *n* > **conspiratorial** (kənˌspɪrəˈtɔːrɪəl) *or* conˈspiratory *adj* > conˌspiraˈtorially *adv*

conspiracy theory *n* the belief that the government or a covert organization is responsible for an event that is unusual or unexplained, esp when any such involvement is denied

conspire (kənˈspaɪə) *vb* (when *intr*, sometimes foll by *against*) **1** to plan or agree on (a crime or harmful act) together in secret **2** (*intr*) to act together towards some end as if by design: *the elements conspired to spoil our picnic* [C14 from Old French *conspirer*, from Latin *conspīrāre* to plot together, literally: to breathe together, from *spīrāre* to breathe] > conˈspirer *n* > conˈspiringly *adv*

con spirito (kɒn ˈspɪrɪtəʊ) *adj, adv music* (to be performed) in a spirited or lively manner (also in the phrases **allegro con spirito, presto con spirito**) [Italian: with spirit]

const. *abbreviation for* **constable** (ˈkʌnstəbəl, kɒn-) *n* **1** (in Britain, Australia, Canada, New Zealand, etc) a police officer of the lowest rank **2** any of various officers of the peace, esp one who arrests offenders, serves writs, etc **3** the keeper or governor of a royal castle or fortress **4** (in medieval Europe) the chief military officer and functionary of a royal household, esp in France and England **5** an officer of a hundred in medieval England, originally responsible for the military levy but later assigned other administrative duties [C13 from Old French, from Late Latin *comes stabulī* officer in charge of the stable, from Latin *comes* comrade + *stabulum* dwelling, stable; see also COUNT[2]] > ˈconstableˌship *n*

constabulary (kənˈstæbjʊlərɪ) *chiefly Brit* ▷ *n, pl* -laries **1** the police force of a town or district ▷ *adj* **2** of or relating to constables, constabularies, or their duties

Constance (ˈkɒnstəns) *n* **1** a city in S Germany, in Baden-Württemberg on Lake Constance: tourist centre. Pop: 80 716 (2003 est). German name: Konstanz **2** **Lake** a lake in W Europe, bounded by S Germany, W Austria, and N Switzerland, through which the Rhine flows. Area: 536 sq km (207 sq miles). German name: Bodensee

constancy (ˈkɒnstənsɪ) *n* **1** the quality of having a resolute mind, purpose, or affection; steadfastness **2** freedom from change or variation; stability **3** *psychol* the perceptual phenomenon in which attributes of an object appear to remain the same in a variety of different presentations, eg, a given object looks roughly the same size regardless of its distance from the observer **4** *ecology* the frequency of occurrence of a particular species in sample plots from a plant community

constant (ˈkɒnstənt) *adj* **1** fixed and invariable; unchanging **2** continual or continuous; incessant: *constant interruptions* **3** resolute in mind, purpose, or affection; loyal ▷ *n* **4** something that is permanent or unchanging **5** a specific quantity that is always invariable: *the velocity of light is a constant* **6** **a** *maths* a symbol representing an unspecified number that remains invariable throughout a particular series of operations **b** *physics* a theoretical or experimental quantity or property that is considered invariable throughout a particular series of calculations or experiments **7** See **logical constant** [C14 from Old French, from Latin *constāns* standing firm, from *constāre* to be steadfast, from *stāre* to stand] > ˈconstantly *adv*

Constanţa (*Romanian* konˈstantsa) *n* a port and resort in SE Romania, on the Black Sea: founded by the Greeks in the 6th century BC and rebuilt by Constantine the Great (4th century); exports petroleum. Pop: 265 000 (2005 est)

constantan (ˈkɒnstənˌtæn) *n* an alloy of copper (60 per cent) and nickel (40 per cent). It has a high resistivity that does not vary significantly with temperature and is used in resistors and, with copper, in thermocouples [C20 formed from CONSTANT]

Constantia (kɒnˈstænʃɪə) *n South African* **1** a region of the Cape Peninsula **2** any of several red or white wines produced around Constantia

Constantine ('kɒnstən,taɪn; French kɔ̃stãtin) *n* a walled city in NE Algeria: built on an isolated rock; military and trading centre. Pop: 482 000 (2005 est)

Constantinople (,kɒnstæntɪ'nəʊpəl) *n* the former name (330–1926) of **Istanbul**

constatation (,kɒnstə'teɪʃən) *n* **1** the process of verification **2** a statement or assertion [C20 from French, from *constater* to verify, from Latin *constat* it is certain; see CONSTANT]

constellate ('kɒnstɪ,leɪt) *vb* to form into clusters in or as if in constellations

constellation (,kɒnstɪ'leɪʃən) *n* **1 a** any of the 88 groups of stars as seen from the earth and the solar system, many of which were named by the ancient Greeks after animals, objects, or mythological persons **b** an area on the celestial sphere containing such a group **2** a gathering of brilliant or famous people or things **3** *psychoanal* a group of ideas felt to be related [C14 from Late Latin *constellātiō*, from Latin *com*- together + *stella* star] > constel'lational *adj* > constellatory (kən'stɛlətərɪ, -trɪ) *adj*

consternate ('kɒnstə,neɪt) *vb* (*tr; usually passive*) to fill with anxiety, dismay, dread, or confusion [C17 from Latin *consternāre,* from *sternere* to lay low, spread out]

consternation (,kɒnstə'neɪʃən) *n* a feeling of anxiety, dismay, dread, or confusion

constipate ('kɒnstɪ,peɪt) *vb* (*tr*) to cause constipation in [C16 from Latin *constīpāre* to press closely together, from *stīpāre* to crowd together]

constipated ('kɒnstɪ,peɪtɪd) *adj* **1** suffering from constipation **2** subject to restriction or blockage in a flow of productive activity or creativity

constipation (,kɒnstɪ'peɪʃən) *n* infrequent or difficult evacuation of the bowels, with hard faeces, caused by functional or organic disorders or improper diet

constituency (kən'stɪtjʊənsɪ) *n, pl* -cies **1** the whole body of voters who elect one representative to a legislature or all the residents represented by one deputy **2 a** a district that sends one representative to a legislature **b** (*as modifier*): *constituency organization*

constituent (kən'stɪtjʊənt) *adj* (*prenominal*) **1** forming part of a whole; component **2** having the power to frame a constitution or to constitute a government (esp in the phrases **constituent assembly, constituent power**) **3** *becoming rare* electing or having the power to elect ▷ *n* **4** a component part; ingredient **5** a resident of a constituency, esp one entitled to vote **6** *chiefly law* a person who appoints another to act for him, as by power of attorney **7** *linguistics* a word, phrase, or clause forming a part of a larger construction. Compare **immediate constituent, ultimate constituent** [C17 from Latin *constituēns* setting up, from *constituere* to establish, CONSTITUTE] > con'stituently *adv*

constitute ('kɒnstɪ,tjuːt) *vb* (*tr*) **1** to make up; form; compose: *the people who constitute a jury* **2** to appoint to an office or function: *a legally constituted officer* **3** to set up (a school or other institution) formally; found **4** *law* to give legal form to (a court, assembly, etc) **5** *law obsolete* to set up or enact (a law) [C15 from Latin *constituere,* from *com*- (intensive) + *statuere* to place] > 'consti,tuter or 'consti,tutor *n*

constitution (,kɒnstɪ'tjuːʃən) *n* **1** the act of constituting or state of being constituted **2** the way in which a thing is composed; physical make-up; structure **3** the fundamental political principles on which a state is governed, esp when considered as embodying the rights of the subjects of that state **4** (*often capital*) (in certain countries, esp Australia and the US) a statute embodying such principles **5** a person's state of health **6** a person's disposition of mind; temperament

constitutional (,kɒnstɪ'tjuːʃənəl) *adj* **1** denoting,

characteristic of, or relating to a constitution **2** authorized by or subject to a constitution **3** of or inherent in the physical make-up or basic nature of a person or thing: *a constitutional weakness* **4** beneficial to one's general physical wellbeing ▷ *n* **5** a regular walk taken for the benefit of one's health > ,consti'tutionally *adv*

constitutionalism (,kɒnstɪ'tjuːʃənə,lɪzəm) *n* **1** the principles, spirit, or system of government in accord with a constitution, esp a written constitution **2** adherence to or advocacy of such a system or such principles > ,consti'tutionalist *n*

constitutionality (,kɒnstɪ,tjuːʃə'nælɪtɪ) *n* the quality or state of being in accord with a constitution

constitutional monarchy *n* a monarchy governed according to a constitution that limits and defines the powers of the sovereign. Also called: **limited monarchy**

constitutional psychology *n* a school of thought postulating that the personality of an individual is dependent on the type of his physique (somatotype)

constitutional strike *n* a stoppage of work by the workforce of an organization, with the approval of the trade union concerned, in accordance with the dispute procedure laid down in a collective agreement between the parties

constitutive ('kɒnstɪ,tjuːtɪv) *adj* **1** having power to enact, appoint, or establish **2** *chem* (of a physical property) determined by the arrangement of atoms in a molecule rather than by their nature **3** *biochem* (of an enzyme) formed continuously, irrespective of the cell's needs **4** another word for **constituent** (sense 1) > 'consti,tutively *adv*

constrain (kən'streɪn) *vb* (*tr*) **1** to compel or force, esp by persuasion, circumstances, etc; oblige **2** to restrain by or as if by force; confine [C14 from Old French *constreindre,* from Latin *constringere* to bind together, from *stringere* to bind] > con'strainer *n*

constrained (kən'streɪnd) *adj* embarrassed, unnatural, or forced: *a constrained smile* > constrainedly (kən'streɪnɪdlɪ) *adv*

constraint (kən'streɪnt) *n* **1** compulsion, force, or restraint **2** repression or control of natural feelings or impulses **3** a forced unnatural manner; inhibition **4** something that serves to constrain; restrictive condition: *social constraints kept him silent* **5** *linguistics* any very general restriction on a sentence formation rule

constrict (kən'strɪkt) *vb* (*tr*) **1** to make smaller or narrower, esp by contracting at one place **2** to hold in or inhibit; limit [C18 from Latin *constrictus* compressed, from *constringere* to tie up together; see CONSTRAIN]

constriction (kən'strɪkʃən) *n* **1** a feeling of tightness in some part of the body, such as the chest **2** the act of constricting or condition of being constricted **3** something that is constricted **4** *genetics* a localized narrow region of a chromosome, esp at the centromere > con'strictive *adj* > con'strictively *adv* > con'strictiveness *n*

constrictor (kən'strɪktə) *n* **1** any of various nonvenomous snakes, such as the pythons, boas, and anaconda, that coil around and squeeze their prey to kill it **2** any muscle that constricts or narrows a canal or passage; sphincter **3** a person or thing that constricts

constringe (kən'strɪndʒ) *vb* (*tr*) *rare* to shrink or contract [C17 from Latin *constringere* to bind together; see CONSTRAIN] > con'stringency *n* > con'stringent *adj*

constringence (kən'strɪndʒəns) *n physics* inverse of the dispersive power of a medium

construct *vb* (kən'strʌkt) (*tr*) **1** to put together substances or parts, esp systematically, in order to make or build (a building, bridge, etc); assemble **2** to compose or frame mentally (an argument, sentence, etc) **3** *geometry* to draw (a line, angle, or figure) so that certain requirements are satisfied ▷ *n* ('kɒnstrʌkt) **4** something formulated or built

systematically **5** a complex idea resulting from a synthesis of simpler ideas **6** *psychol* a model devised on the basis of observation, designed to relate what is observed to some theoretical framework [C17 from Latin *constructus* piled up, from *construere* to heap together, build, from *struere* to arrange, erect] > con'structible *adj* > con'structor or con'structer *n*

construction (kən'strʌkʃən) *n* **1** the process or act of constructing or manner in which a thing is constructed **2** the thing constructed; a structure **3 a** the business or work of building dwellings, offices, etc **b** (*as modifier*): *a construction site* **4** an interpretation or explanation of a law, text, action, etc: *they put a sympathetic construction on her behaviour* **5** *grammar* a group of words that together make up one of the constituents into which a sentence may be analysed; a phrase or clause **6** *geometry* a drawing of a line, angle, or figure satisfying certain conditions, used in solving a problem or proving a theorem **7** an abstract work of art in three dimensions or relief. See also **constructivism** (sense 1) > con'structional *adj* > con'structionally *adv*

constructionist (kən'strʌkʃənɪst) *n US* a person who interprets constitutional law in a certain way, esp strictly

constructive (kən'strʌktɪv) *adj* **1** serving to build or improve; positive: *constructive criticism* **2** *law* deduced by inference or construction; not expressed but inferred **3** *law* having a deemed legal effect: *constructive notice* **4** another word for **structural.** > con'structively *adv* > con'structiveness *n*

constructive dismissal *n* a course of action taken by an employer that is detrimental to an employee and designed to leave the employee with no option but to resign

constructivism (kən'strʌktɪ,vɪzəm) *n* **1** a movement in abstract art evolved in Russia after World War I, primarily by Naum Gabo, the Russian-born US sculptor (1890–1977), which explored the use of movement and machine-age materials in sculpture and had considerable influence on modern art and architecture **2** *philosophy* the theory that mathematical entities do not exist independently of our construction of them. Compare **intuitionism** (sense 4), **finitism** > con'structivist *adj, n*

construe (kən'struː) *vb* -strues, -struing, -strued (*mainly tr*) **1** to interpret the meaning of (something): *you can construe that in different ways* **2** (*may take a clause as object*) to discover by inference; deduce **3** to analyse the grammatical structure of; parse (esp a Latin or Greek text as a preliminary to translation) **4** to combine (words) syntactically **5** (*also intr*) *old-fashioned* to translate literally, esp aloud as an academic exercise ▷ *n* **6** *old-fashioned* something that is construed, such as a piece of translation [C14 from Latin *construere* to pile up; see CONSTRUCT] > con'struable *adj* > con,strua'bility *n* > con'struer *n*

consubstantial (,kɒnsəb'stænʃəl) *adj christian theol* (esp of the three persons of the Trinity) regarded as identical in substance or essence though different in aspect [C15 from Church Latin *consubstāntiālis,* from Latin *com*- + *substantia* SUBSTANCE] > ,consub'stanti'ality *n* > ,consub'stantially *adv*

consubstantiate (,kɒnsəb'stænʃɪ,eɪt) *vb* (*intr*) *christian theol* (of the Eucharistic bread and wine and Christ's body and blood) to undergo consubstantiation

consubstantiation (,kɒnsəb,stænʃɪ'eɪʃən) *n christian theol* (in the belief of High-Church Anglicans) **1** the doctrine that after the consecration of the Eucharist the substance of the body and blood of Christ coexists within the substance of the consecrated bread and wine **2** the mystical process by which this is believed to take place during consecration ▷ Compare **transubstantiation**

consuetude ('kɒnswɪˌtjuːd) *n* an established custom or usage, esp one having legal force [C14 from Latin *consuētūdō*, from *consuēscere* to accustom, from CON- + *suēscere* to be wont] > ˌconsueˈtudinary *adj*

consul ('kɒnsəl) *n* **1** an official appointed by a sovereign state to protect its commercial interests and aid its citizens in a foreign city **2** (in ancient Rome) either of two annually elected magistrates who jointly exercised the highest authority in the republic **3** (in France from 1799 to 1804) any of the three chief magistrates of the First Republic [C14 from Latin, from *consulere* to CONSULT] > consular ('kɒnsjʊlə) *adj* > 'consulˌship *n*

consular agent *n* a consul of one of the lower grades

consulate ('kɒnsjʊlɪt) *n* **1** the business premises or residence of a consul **2** government by consuls **3** the office or period of office of a consul or consuls **4** (*often capital*) **a** the government of France by the three consuls from 1799 to 1804 **b** this period of French history **5** (*often capital*) **a** the consular government of the Roman republic **b** the office or rank of a Roman consul

consul general *n, pl* consuls general a consul of the highest grade, usually stationed in a city of considerable commercial importance

consult (kən'sʌlt) *vb* **1** (when *intr*, often foll by *with*) to ask advice from (someone); confer with (someone) **2** (*tr*) to refer to for information: *to consult a map* **3** (*tr*) to have regard for (a person's feelings, interests, etc) in making decisions or plans; consider **4** (*intr*) to make oneself available to give professional advice, esp at scheduled times and for a fee [C17 from French *consulter*, from Latin *consultāre* to reflect, take counsel, from *consulere* to consult] > con'sultable *adj* > con'sulter or con'sultor *n*

consultant (kən'sʌltªnt) *n* **1 a** a senior physician, esp a specialist, who is asked to confirm a diagnosis or treatment or to provide an opinion **b** a physician or surgeon holding the highest appointment in a particular branch of medicine or surgery in a hospital **2** a specialist who gives expert advice or information **3** a person who asks advice in a consultation > con'sultancy *n*

consultant nurse *n* (in Britain) another name for **supernurse**

consultation (ˌkɒnsªl'teɪʃən) *n* **1** the act or procedure of consulting **2** a conference for discussion or the seeking of advice, esp from doctors or lawyers

consultative (kən'sʌltətɪv), **consultatory** (kən'sʌltətərɪ, -trɪ) or **consultive** *adj* available for, relating to, or involving consultation; advisory > con'sultatively *adv*

consulting (kən'sʌltɪŋ) *adj* (*prenominal*) acting in an advisory capacity on professional matters: *a consulting engineer*

consulting room *n* a room in which a doctor, esp a general practitioner, sees his patients

consumable (kən'sjuːməbªl) *adj* **1** capable of being consumed ▷ *n* **2** (*usually plural*) goods intended to be bought and used; consumer goods

consume (kən'sjuːm) *vb* **1** (*tr*) to eat or drink **2** (*tr; often passive*) to engross or obsess **3** (*tr*) to use up; expend: *my car consumes little oil* **4** to destroy or be destroyed by burning, decomposition, etc: *fire consumed the forest* **5** (*tr*) to waste or squander: *the time consumed on that project was excessive* **6** (*passive*) to waste away [C14 from Latin *consūmere* to devour, from *com-* (intensive) + *sūmere* to take up, from *emere* to take, purchase] > con'suming *adj* > con'sumingly *adv*

consumedly (kən'sjuːmɪdlɪ) *adv old-fashioned* (*intensifier*): *a consumedly fascinating performance*

consumer (kən'sjuːmə) *n* **1** a person who acquires goods and services for his or her own personal needs. Compare **producer** (sense 6) **2** a person or thing that consumes **3** (*usually plural*) *ecology* an organism, esp an animal, within a community that feeds upon plants or other

animals. See also **decomposer, producer** (sense 8)

consumer durable *n* a manufactured product that has a relatively long useful life, such as a car or a television

consumer goods *pl n* goods that satisfy personal needs rather than those required for the production of other goods or services. Compare **capital goods**

consumerism (kən'sjuːməˌrɪzəm) *n* **1** protection of the interests of consumers **2** advocacy of a high rate of consumption and spending as a basis for a sound economy > con'sumerist *n, adj*

consumer terrorism *n* the practice of introducing dangerous substances to foodstuffs or other consumer products, esp to extort money from the manufacturers

consummate *vb* ('kɒnsəˌmeɪt) (*tr*) **1** to bring to completion or perfection; fulfil **2** to complete (a marriage) legally by sexual intercourse ▷ *adj* (kən'sʌmɪt, 'kɒnsəmɪt) **3** accomplished or supremely skilled: *a consummate artist* **4** (*prenominal*) (*intensifier*): *a consummate fool* [C15 from Latin *consummāre* to complete, from *summus* highest, utmost] > con'summately *adv* > ˌconsum'mation *n* > 'consumˌmative or con'summatory *adj* > 'consumˌmator *n*

consummatory behaviour (kən'sʌmətərɪ) *n psychol* any behaviour that leads directly to the satisfaction of an innate drive, eg eating or drinking

consumption (kən'sʌmpʃən) *n* **1** the act of consuming or the state of being consumed, esp by eating, burning, etc **2** *economics* expenditure on goods and services for final personal use **3** the quantity consumed **4** *pathol* a condition characterized by a wasting away of the tissues of the body, esp as seen in tuberculosis of the lungs [C14 from Latin *consumptiō* a wasting, from *consūmere* to CONSUME]

consumptive (kən'sʌmptɪv) *adj* **1** causing consumption; wasteful; destructive **2** *pathol* relating to or affected with consumption, esp tuberculosis of the lungs ▷ *n* **3** *pathol* a person who suffers from consumption > con'sumptively *adv* > con'sumptiveness *n*

contact *n* ('kɒntækt) **1** the act or state of touching physically **2** the state or fact of close association or communication (esp in the phrases **in contact, make contact**) **3 a** a junction of two or more electrical conductors **b** the part of the conductors that makes the junction **c** the part of an electrical device to which such connections are made **4** an acquaintance, esp one who might be useful in business, as a means of introduction, etc **5** any person who has been exposed to a contagious disease **6** *photog* See **contact print 7** (*usually plural*) an informal name for **contact lens 8** (*modifier*) of or relating to irritation or inflammation of the skin caused by touching the causative agent: *contact dermatitis* **9** (*modifier*) denoting an insecticide or herbicide that kills on contact, rather than after ingestion or absorption **10** (*modifier*) of or maintaining contact **11** (*modifier*) requiring or involving (physical) contact: *the contact sport of boxing* ▷ *vb* ('kɒntækt, kən'tækt) **12** (when *intr*, often foll by *with*) to put, come, or be in association, touch, or communication ▷ *interj* **13** *aeronautics* (formerly) a call made by the pilot to indicate that an aircraft's ignition is switched on and that the engine is ready for starting by swinging the propeller [C17 from Latin *contactus*, from *contingere* to touch on all sides, pollute, from *tangere* to touch] > contactual (kɒn'tæktjʊəl) *adj* > con'tactually *adv*

contactable (kɒn'tæktəbªl) *adj* able to be communicated with: *the manager is not contactable at the moment*

contact centre *n* another name for **call centre**

contact flight *n* **1** a flight in which the pilot remains in sight of land or water **2** air navigation by observation of prominent landmarks, beacons, etc

contact high *n* a state of altered consciousness caused by inhaling the drugs other people are smoking

contact lens *n* a thin convex lens, usually of plastic, which floats on the layer of tears in front of the cornea to correct defects of vision

contact magazine *n* a magazine in which to place adverts to make contacts, esp sexual ones

contact man *n* an intermediary or go-between

contactor (kɒn'tæktə) *n* a type of switch for repeatedly opening and closing an electric circuit. Its operation can be mechanical, electromagnetic, or pneumatic

contact print *n* a photographic print made by exposing the printing paper through a negative placed directly onto it

contagion (kən'teɪdʒən) *n* **1** the transmission of disease from one person to another by direct or indirect contact **2** a contagious disease **3** another name for **contagium 4** a corrupting or harmful influence that tends to spread; pollutant **5** the spreading of an emotional or mental state among a number of people: *the contagion of mirth* [C14 from Latin *contāgiō* a touching, infection, from *contingere; see* CONTACT]

contagious (kən'teɪdʒəs) *adj* **1** (of a disease) capable of being passed on by direct contact with a diseased individual or by handling clothing, etc, contaminated with the causative agent. Compare **infectious 2** (of an organism) harbouring or spreading the causative agent of a transmissible disease **3** causing or likely to cause the same reaction or emotion in several people; catching; infectious: *her laughter was contagious* > con'tagiously *adv* > con'tagiousness *n*

contagious abortion *n* another name for **brucellosis**

contagious ecthyma *n* the technical name for **orf**

contagious stomatitis *n* another name for **foot-and-mouth disease**

contagium (kən'teɪdʒɪəm) *n, pl* -gia (-dʒɪə) *pathol* the specific virus or other direct cause of any infectious disease [C17 from Latin, variant of *contāgiō* CONTAGION]

contain (kən'teɪn) *vb* (*tr*) **1** to hold or be capable of holding or including within a fixed limit or area: *this contains five pints* **2** to keep (one's feelings, behaviour, etc) within bounds; restrain **3** to consist of; comprise: *the book contains three different sections* **4** *military* to prevent (enemy forces) from operating beyond a certain level or area **5** *maths* **a** to be a multiple of, leaving no remainder: *6 contains 2 and 3* **b** to have as a subset [C13 from Old French *contenir*, from Latin *continēre*, from *com-* together + *tenēre* to hold] > con'tainable *adj*

container (kən'teɪnə) *n* **1** an object used for or capable of holding, esp for transport or storage, such as a carton, box, etc **2 a** a large cargo-carrying standard-sized container that can be loaded from one mode of transport to another **b** (*as modifier*): *a container port; a container ship*

container garden *n* a collection of pots or other receptacles containing soil for growing plants out of doors > container gardening *n*

containerize or **containerise** (kən'teɪnəˌraɪz) *vb* (*tr*) **1** to convey (cargo) in standard-sized containers **2** to adapt (a port or transportation system) to the use of standard-sized containers > conˌtaineri'zation or conˌtaineri'sation *n*

containment (kən'teɪnmənt) *n* **1** the act or condition of containing, esp of restraining the ideological or political power of a hostile country or the operations of a hostile military force **2** (from 1947 to the mid-1970s) a principle of US foreign policy that sought to prevent the expansion of Communist power **3** Also called: confinement *physics* the process of preventing the plasma in a controlled thermonuclear reactor from reaching the walls of the reaction vessel, usually by confining it within a configuration of magnetic fields. See **magnetic bottle**

C

contaminate vb (kən'tæmɪˌneɪt) (tr) **1** to make impure, esp by touching or mixing; pollute **2** to make radioactive by the addition of radioactive material ▷ adj (kən'tæmɪnɪt, -ˌneɪt) **3** archaic contaminated [c15 from Latin contamināre to defile; related to Latin contingere to touch] > con'taminable adj > con'taminant n > con'taminative adj > con'tamiˌnator n

contamination (kənˌtæmɪ'neɪʃən) n **1** the act or process of contaminating or the state of being contaminated **2** something that contaminates **3** linguistics the process by which one word or phrase is altered because of mistaken associations with another word or phrase; for example, the substitution of irregardless for regardless by association with such words as irrespective

contango (kən'tæŋgəʊ) n, pl -gos **1** (formerly, on the London Stock Exchange) postponement of payment for and delivery of stock from one account day to the next **2** the fee paid for such a postponement ▷ Also called: carry-over, continuation. Compare **backwardation** ▷ vb -goes, -going, -goed **3** (tr) to arrange such a postponement of payment (for): my brokers will contango these shares [c19 apparently an arbitrary coinage based on CONTINUE]

contd abbreviation for continued

conte French (kɔ̃t) n a tale or short story, esp of adventure

Conté ('kɒnteɪ; French kɔte) n trademark a hard crayon used by artists, etc, made of clay and graphite and often coloured a reddish-brown. Also called: conté-crayon [c19 named after N.J. Conté, 18th-century French chemist]

contemn (kən'tɛm) vb (tr) formal to treat or regard with contempt; scorn [c15 from Latin contemnere, from temnere to slight] > contemner (kən'tɛmnə, -'tɛmə) n > contemnible (kən'tɛmnɪbəl) adj > con'temnibly adv

contemplate ('kɒntɛmˌpleɪt, -təm-) vb (mainly tr) **1** to think about intently and at length; consider calmly **2** (intr) to think intently and at length, esp for spiritual reasons; meditate **3** to look at thoughtfully; observe pensively **4** to have in mind as a possibility: to contemplate changing jobs [c16 from Latin contemplāre, from templum TEMPLE[1]] > 'contemˌplator n

contemplation (ˌkɒntɛm'pleɪʃən, -təm-) n **1** thoughtful or long consideration or observation **2** spiritual meditation esp (in Christian religious practice) concentration of the mind and soul upon God. Compare **meditation 3** purpose or intention

contemplative ('kɒntɛmˌpleɪtɪv, -təm-, kən'tɛmplə-) adj **1** denoting, concerned with, or inclined to contemplation; meditative ▷ n **2** a person dedicated to religious contemplation or to a way of life conducive to this > 'contemˌplatively adv > 'contemˌplativeness n

contemporaneous (kənˌtɛmpə'reɪnɪəs) adj existing, beginning, or occurring in the same period of time > contemporaneity (kənˌtɛmpərə'niːɪtɪ) or conˌtempo'raneousness n > conˌtempo'raneously adv

contemporary (kən'tɛmprərɪ) adj **1** belonging to the same age; living or occurring in the same period of time **2** existing or occurring at the present time **3** conforming to modern or current ideas in style, fashion, design, etc **4** having approximately the same age as one another ▷ n, pl -raries **5** a person living at the same time or of approximately the same age as another **6** something that is contemporary **7** journalism a rival newspaper [c17 from Medieval Latin contemporārius, from Latin com- together + temporārius relating to time, from tempus time] > con'temporarily adv > con'temporariness n

USAGE Since contemporary can mean either of the same period or of the present period, it is best to avoid this word where ambiguity might arise, as in a production of Othello in contemporary dress. Modern dress or Elizabethan dress should be used in this example to avoid ambiguity

contemporize or **contemporise** (kən'tɛmpəˌraɪz) vb to be or make contemporary; synchronize

contempt (kən'tɛmpt) n **1** the attitude or feeling of a person towards a person or thing that he considers worthless or despicable; scorn **2** the state of being scorned; disgrace (esp in the phrase **hold in contempt**) **3** wilful disregard of or disrespect for the authority of a court of law or legislative body: contempt of court [c14 from Latin contemptus a despising, from contemnere to CONTEMN]

contemptible (kən'tɛmptəbəl) adj deserving or worthy of contempt; despicable > conˌtempti'bility or con'temptibleness n > con'temptibly adv

contemptuous (kən'tɛmptjʊəs) adj (when predicative, often foll by of) showing or feeling contempt; disdainful > con'temptuously adv > con'temptuousness n

contend (kən'tɛnd) vb **1** (intr; often foll by with) to struggle in rivalry, battle, etc; vie **2** to argue earnestly; debate **3** (tr; may take a clause as object) to assert or maintain [c15 from Latin contendere to strive, from com- with + tendere to stretch, aim] > con'tender n > con'tendingly adv

content[1] ('kɒntɛnt) n **1** (often plural) everything that is inside a container: the contents of a box **2** (usually plural) **a** the chapters or divisions of a book **b** a list, printed at the front of a book, of chapters or divisions together with the number of the first page of each **3** the meaning or significance of a poem, painting, or other work of art, as distinguished from its style or form **4** all that is contained or dealt with in a discussion, piece of writing, etc; substance **5** the capacity or size of a thing **6** the proportion of a substance contained in an alloy, mixture, etc: the lead content of petrol [c15 from Latin contentus contained, from continēre to CONTAIN]

content[2] (kən'tɛnt) adj (postpositive) **1** mentally or emotionally satisfied with things as they are **2** assenting to or willing to accept circumstances, a proposed course of action, etc ▷ vb **3** (tr) to make (oneself or another person) content or satisfied: to content oneself with property ▷ n **4** peace of mind; mental or emotional satisfaction ▷ interj **5** Brit (in the House of Lords) a formal expression of assent, as opposed to the expression **not content** [c14 from Old French, from Latin contentus contented, that is, having restrained desires, from continēre to restrain] > con'tently adv > con'tentment n

content-addressable storage n computing another name for **associative storage**

contented (kən'tɛntɪd) adj accepting one's situation or life with equanimity and satisfaction > con'tentedly adv > con'tentedness n

contention (kən'tɛnʃən) n **1** a struggling between opponents; competition **2** dispute in an argument (esp in the phrase **bone of contention**) **3** a point asserted in argument [c14 from Latin contentiō exertion, from contendere to CONTEND]

contentious (kən'tɛnʃəs) adj **1** tending to argue or quarrel **2** causing or characterized by dispute; controversial **3** law relating to a cause or legal business that is contested, esp a probate matter > con'tentiously adv > con'tentiousness n

content word ('kɒntɛnt) n a word to which an independent meaning can be given by reference to a world outside any sentence in which the word may occur. Compare **function word, lexical meaning**

conterminous (kən'tɜːmɪnəs) or **conterminal, coterminous** (kəʊ'tɜːmɪnəs) adj **1** enclosed within a common boundary **2** meeting at the ends; without a break or interruption [c17 from Latin conterminus, from CON- + terminus end, boundary] > con'terminously, con'terminally or co'terminously adv

contest n ('kɒntɛst) **1** a formal game or match in which two or more people, teams, etc, compete and attempt to win **2** a struggle for victory between opposing forces or interests ▷ vb (kən'tɛst) **3** (tr) to try to disprove; call in question **4** (when intr, foll by with or against) to fight, dispute, or contend (with): contest an election [c16 from Latin contestārī to introduce a lawsuit, from testis witness] > con'testable adj > con'testableness or conˌtesta'bility n > con'testably adv > con'testation n > con'tester n > con'testingly adv

contestant (kən'tɛstənt) n a person who takes part in a contest; competitor

context ('kɒntɛkst) n **1** the parts of a piece of writing, speech, etc, that precede and follow a word or passage and contribute to its full meaning: it is unfair to quote out of context **2** the conditions and circumstances that are relevant to an event, fact, etc [c15 from Latin contextus a putting together, from contexere to interweave, from com- together + texere to weave, braid]

contextual (kən'tɛkstjʊəl) adj relating to, dependent on, or using context: contextual criticism of a book > con'textually adv

contextualize or **contextualise** (kən'tɛkstjʊəˌlaɪz) vb (tr) to state the social, grammatical, or other context of; put into context

contexture (kən'tɛkstʃə) n **1** the fact, process, or manner of weaving or of being woven together **2** the arrangement of assembled parts; structure **3** an interwoven structure; fabric > con'textural adj

contiguous (kən'tɪgjʊəs) adj **1** touching along the side or boundary; in contact **2** physically adjacent; neighbouring **3** preceding or following in time [c17 from Latin contiguus, from contingere to touch; see CONTACT] > contiguity (ˌkɒntɪ'gjuːɪtɪ) or con'tiguousness n > con'tiguously adv

continent[1] ('kɒntɪnənt) n **1** one of the earth's large land masses (Asia, Australia, Africa, Europe, North and South America, and Antarctica) **2** that part of the earth's crust that rises above the oceans and is composed of sialic rocks. Including the continental shelves, the continents occupy 30 per cent of the earth's surface **3** obsolete **a** a mainland as opposed to islands **b** a continuous extent of land [c16 from the Latin phrase terra continens continuous land, from continēre; see CONTAIN] > continental (ˌkɒntɪ'nɛntəl) adj > ˌconti'nentally adv

continent[2] ('kɒntɪnənt) adj **1** able to control urination and defecation **2** exercising self-restraint, esp from sexual activity; chaste [c14 from Latin continent-, present participle of continēre; see CONTAIN] > 'continence or 'continency n > 'continently adv

Continent ('kɒntɪnənt) n **the** the mainland of Europe as distinguished from the British Isles

Continental (ˌkɒntɪ'nɛntəl) adj **1** of or characteristic of Europe, excluding the British Isles **2** of or relating to the 13 original British North American colonies during and immediately after the War of American Independence ▷ n **3** (sometimes not capital) an inhabitant of Europe, excluding the British Isles **4** a regular soldier of the rebel army during the War of American Independence **5** US history a currency note issued by the Continental Congress > ˌConti'nentalˌism n > ˌConti'nentalist n

continental breakfast n a light breakfast of coffee and rolls

continental climate n a climate characterized by hot summers, cold winters, and little rainfall, typical of the interior of a continent

Continental Congress n the assembly of delegates from the North American rebel colonies held during and after the War of American Independence. It issued the Declaration of Independence (1776) and framed the Articles of Confederation (1777)

continental crust n geology that part of the earth's crust that underlies the continents and continental shelves

continental divide n the watershed of a

continent, esp (often caps.) the principal watershed of North America, formed by the Rocky Mountains

continental drift n geology the theory that the earth's continents move gradually over the surface of the planet on a substratum of magma. The present-day configuration of the continents is thought to be the result of the fragmentation of a single landmass, Pangaea, that existed 200 million years ago. See also **plate tectonics**

continental quilt n Brit a quilt, stuffed with down or a synthetic material and containing pockets of air, used as a bed cover in place of the top sheet and blankets. Also called: duvet, (Austral) doona

continental shelf n the sea bed surrounding a continent at depths of up to about 200 metres (100 fathoms), at the edge of which the **continental slope** drops steeply to the ocean floor

Continental System n the Napoleon's plan in 1806 to blockade Britain by excluding her ships from ports on the mainland of Europe

contingence (kən'tɪndʒəns) n 1 the state of touching or being in contact 2 another word for **contingency**

contingency (kən'tɪndʒənsɪ) n, pl -cies 1 a a possible but not very likely future event or condition; eventuality b (as modifier): a contingency plan 2 something dependent on a possible future event 3 a fact, event, etc, incidental to or dependent on something else 4 (in systemic grammar) a modification of the meaning of a main clause by use of a bound clause introduced by a binder such as if, when, though, or since. Compare **adding** (sense 3) b (as modifier): a contingency clause 5 logic a the state of being contingent b a contingent statement 6 dependence on chance; uncertainty 7 statistics a the degree of association between theoretical and observed common frequencies of two graded or classified variables. It is measured by the chi-square test b (as modifier): a contingency table; the contingency coefficient

contingency fee n a lawyer's fee that only becomes payable if the case is successful

contingency table n statistics an array having the frequency of occurrence of certain events in each of a number of samples

contingent (kən'tɪndʒənt) adj 1 (when postpositive, often foll by on or upon) dependent on events, conditions, etc, not yet known; conditional 2 logic (of a proposition) true under certain conditions, false under others; not necessary 3 (in systemic grammar) denoting contingency (sense 4) 4 metaphysics (of some being) existing only as a matter of fact; not necessarily existing 5 happening by chance or without known cause; accidental 6 that may or may not happen; uncertain ▷ n 7 a part of a military force, parade, etc 8 a representative group distinguished by common origin, interests, etc, that is part of a larger group or gathering 9 a possible or chance occurrence [c14 from Latin contingere to touch, fall to one's lot, befall; see also CONTACT] > con'tingently adv

continual (kən'tɪnjʊəl) adj 1 recurring frequently, esp at regular intervals 2 occurring without interruption; continuous in time [c14 from Old French continuel, from Latin continuus uninterrupted, from continēre to hold together, CONTAIN] > con,tinu'ality or con'tinualness n > con'tinually adv

USAGE See at **continuous**

continuance (kən'tɪnjʊəns) n 1 the act or state of continuing 2 the duration of an action, condition, etc 3 US the postponement or adjournment of a legal proceeding

continuant (kən'tɪnjʊənt) phonetics ▷ n 1 a speech sound, such as (l), (r), (f), or (s), in which the closure of the vocal tract is incomplete, allowing the continuous passage of the breath ▷ adj 2 relating to or denoting a continuant

continuation (kən,tɪnjʊ'eɪʃən) n 1 a part or thing added, esp to a book or play, that serves to continue or extend; sequel 2 a renewal of an interrupted action, process, etc; resumption 3 the act or fact of continuing without interruption; prolongation 4 another word for **contango** (senses 1, 2)

continuative (kən'tɪnjʊətɪv) adj 1 serving or tending to continue 2 grammar a (of any word, phrase, or clause) expressing continuation b (of verbs) another word for **progressive** (sense 8) ▷ n 3 a continuative word, phrase, or clause > con'tinuatively adv

continuator (kən'tɪnjʊ,eɪtə) n a person who continues something, esp the work of someone else

continue (kən'tɪnju:) vb -ues, -uing, -ued 1 (when tr, may take an infinitive) to remain or cause to remain in a particular condition, capacity, or place 2 (when tr, may take an infinitive) to carry on uninterruptedly (a course of action); persist in (something): he continued running 3 (when tr, may take an infinitive) to resume after an interruption: we'll continue after lunch 4 to draw out or be drawn out; prolong or be prolonged: continue the chord until it meets the tangent 5 (tr) law, chiefly Scots to postpone or adjourn (legal proceedings) [c14 from Old French continuer, from Latin continuāre to join together, from continuus CONTINUOUS] > con'tinuable adj > con'tinuer n > con'tinuingly adv

continued fraction n a number plus a fraction whose denominator contains a number and a fraction whose denominator contains a number and a fraction, and so on

continuity (,kɒntɪ'nju:ɪtɪ) n, pl -ties 1 logical sequence, cohesion, or connection 2 a continuous or connected whole 3 the comprehensive script or scenario of detail and movement in a film or broadcast 4 the continuous projection of a film, using automatic rewind

continuity announcer n a person on radio or television who makes linking announcements betweeen programmes

continuity girl or **man** n a girl or man whose job is to ensure continuity and consistency, esp in matters of dress, make-up, etc, in successive shots of a film, esp when these shots are filmed on different days

continuo (kən'tɪnjʊ,əʊ) n, pl -os 1 music a a shortened form of **basso continuo** (see thorough bass) b (as modifier): a continuo accompaniment 2 the thorough-bass part as played on a keyboard instrument, often supported by a cello, bassoon, etc [Italian, literally: continuous]

continuous (kən'tɪnjʊəs) adj 1 prolonged without interruption; unceasing: a continuous noise 2 in an unbroken series or pattern 3 maths (of a function or curve) changing gradually in value as the variable changes in value. A function f is continuous if at every value a of the independent variable the difference between f(x) and f(a) approaches zero as x approaches a. Compare **discontinuous** (sense 2). See also **limit** (sense 5) 4 statistics (of a variable) having a continuum of possible values so that its distribution requires integration rather than summation to determine its cumulative probability. Compare **discrete** (sense 3) 5 grammar another word for **progressive** (sense 8) [c17 from Latin continuus, from continēre to hold together, CONTAIN] > con'tinuously adv > con'tinuousness n

USAGE Both continual and continuous can be used to say that something continues without interruption, but only continual can correctly be used to say that something keeps happening repeatedly

continuous assessment n the assessment of a pupil's progress throughout a course of study rather than exclusively by examination at the end of it

continuous creation n 1 the theory that matter is being created continuously in the universe. See **steady-state theory** 2 the theory that animate matter is being continuously created from inanimate matter

continuous processing n the systems in a plant or factory for the manufacturing of products, treating of materials, etc, that have been designed to run continuously and are often computer-controlled. Compare **batch processing**

continuous spectrum n a spectrum that contains or appears to contain all wavelengths but not spectrum lines over a wide portion of its range. The emission spectrum of incandescent solids is continuous; bremsstrahlung spectra consisting of a large number of lines may appear continuous

continuous stationery n computing paper that is perforated between pages and folded concertina fashion, used in dot-matrix, line, and daisywheel printers

continuous waves pl n radio waves generated as a continuous train of oscillations having a constant frequency and amplitude. Abbreviation: CW

continuum (kən'tɪnjʊəm) n, pl -tinua (-'tɪnjʊə) or -tinuums a continuous series or whole, no part of which is perceptibly different from the adjacent parts [c17 from Latin, neuter of continuus CONTINUOUS]

continuum hypothesis n maths the assertion that there is no set whose cardinality is greater than that of the integers and smaller than that of the reals

conto ('kɒntəʊ; Portuguese 'kõ:tu) n, pl -tos (-təʊz; Portuguese -tuʃ) 1 a former Portuguese monetary unit worth 1000 escudos 2 an unofficial Brazilian monetary unit worth 1000 cruzeiros (now replaced by the real) [c17 from Portuguese, from Late Latin computus calculation, from computāre to reckon, COMPUTE; see COUNT¹]

contort (kən'tɔ:t) vb to twist or bend severely out of place or shape, esp in a strained manner [c15 from Latin contortus intricate, obscure, from contorquēre to whirl around, from torquēre to twist, wrench] > con'tortive adj

contorted (kən'tɔ:tɪd) adj 1 twisted out of shape 2 (esp of petals and sepals in a bud) twisted so that they overlap on one side > con'tortedly adv > con'tortedness n

contortion (kən'tɔ:ʃən) n 1 the act or process of contorting or the state of being contorted 2 a twisted shape or position 3 something twisted or out of the ordinary in character, meaning, etc: mental contortions > con'tortional adj > con'tortioned adj

contortionist (kən'tɔ:ʃənɪst) n 1 a performer who contorts his body for the entertainment of others 2 a person who twists or warps meaning or thoughts: a verbal contortionist > con,tortion'istic adj

contour ('kɒntʊə) n 1 the outline of a mass of land, figure, or body; a defining line 2 a See **contour line** b (as modifier): a contour map 3 (often plural) the shape or surface, esp of a curving form: the contours of her body were full and round 4 (modifier) shaped to fit the form of something: a contour chair 5 a rising and falling variation pattern, as in music and intonation ▷ vb (tr) 6 to shape so as to form the contour of something 7 to mark contour lines on 8 to construct (a road, railway, etc) to follow the outline of the land [c17 from French, from Italian contorno, from contornare to sketch, from tornare to TURN]

contour feather n any of the feathers that cover the body of an adult bird, apart from the wings and tail, and determine its shape

contour interval n the difference in altitude represented by the space between two contour lines on a map

contour line n a line on a map or chart joining points of equal height or depth. Often shortened to: contour

C

contour ploughing *n* ploughing following the contours of the land, to minimize the effects of erosion

contra- *prefix* **1** against; contrary; opposing; contrasting: *contraceptive; contradistinction* **2** (in music) pitched below: *contrabass* [from Latin, from *contrā* against]

contraband ('kɒntrə,bænd) *n* **1 a** goods that are prohibited by law from being exported or imported **b** illegally imported or exported goods **2** illegal traffic in such goods; smuggling **3** Also called: **contraband of war** *international law* goods that a neutral country may not supply to a belligerent **4** (during the American Civil War) a Black slave captured by the Union forces or one who escaped to the Union lines ▷ *adj* **5** (of goods) **a** forbidden by law from being imported or exported **b** illegally imported or exported [c16 from Spanish *contrabanda*, from Italian *contrabando* (modern *contrabbando*), from Medieval Latin *contrabannum,* from CONTRA- + *bannum* ban, of Germanic origin] > 'contra,bandist *n*

contrabass (,kɒntrə'beɪs) *n* **1** a member of any of various families of musical instruments that is lower in pitch than the bass **2** another name for **double bass** ▷ *adj* **3** of or denoting the instrument of a family that is lower than the bass > contrabassist (,kɒntrə'beɪsɪst, -'bæs-) *n*

contrabassoon (,kɒntrəbə'su:n) *n* the largest instrument in the oboe family, pitched an octave below the bassoon; double bassoon > ,contrabas'soonist *n*

contraception (,kɒntrə'sepʃən) *n* the intentional prevention of conception by artificial or natural means. Artificial methods in common use include preventing the sperm from reaching the ovum (using condoms, diaphragms, etc), inhibiting ovulation (using oral contraceptive pills), preventing implantation (using intrauterine devices), killing the sperm (using spermicides), and preventing the sperm from entering the seminal fluid (by vasectomy). Natural methods include the rhythm method and coitus interruptus. Compare **birth control, family planning** [c19 from CONTRA- + CONCEPTION]

contraceptive (,kɒntrə'septɪv) *adj* **1** relating to or used for contraception; able or tending to prevent impregnation ▷ *n* **2** any device that prevents or tends to prevent conception

contract *vb* (kən'trækt) **1** to make or become smaller, narrower, shorter, etc: *metals contract as the temperature is reduced* **2** ('kɒntrækt) (when *intr,* sometimes foll by *for*; when *tr,* may take an infinitive) to enter into an agreement with (a person, company, etc) to deliver (goods or services) or to do (something) on mutually agreed and binding terms, often in writing **3** to draw or be drawn together; coalesce or cause to coalesce **4** (*tr*) to acquire, incur, or become affected by (a disease, liability, debt, etc) **5** (*tr*) to shorten (a word or phrase) by the omission of letters or syllables, usually indicated in writing by an apostrophe **6** *phonetics* to unite (two vowels) or (of two vowels) to be united within a word or at a word boundary so that a new long vowel or diphthong is formed **7** (*tr*) to wrinkle or draw together (the brow or a muscle) **8** (*tr*) to arrange (a marriage) for; betroth ▷ *n* ('kɒntrækt) **9** a formal agreement between two or more parties **10** a document that states the terms of such an agreement **11** the branch of law treating of contracts **12** marriage considered as a formal agreement **13** See **contract bridge 14** *bridge* **a** (in the bidding sequence before play) the highest bid, which determines trumps and the number of tricks one side must try to make **b** the number and suit of these tricks **15** *slang* **a** a criminal agreement to kill a particular person in return for an agreed sum of money **b** (*as modifier*): *a contract killing* [c16 from Latin *contractus* agreement, something drawn up, from *contrahere* to draw together, from *trahere* to draw] > con'tractible *adj* > con'tractibly *adv*

contract bridge ('kɒntrækt) *n* the most common variety of bridge, in which the declarer receives points counting towards game and rubber only for tricks he bids as well as makes, any overtricks receiving bonus points. Compare **auction bridge**

contractile (kən'træktaɪl) *adj* having the power to contract or to cause contraction > **contractility** (,kɒntræk'tɪlɪtɪ) *n*

contraction (kən'trækʃən) *n* **1** an instance of contracting or the state of being contracted **2** *physiol* any normal shortening or tensing of an organ or part, esp of a muscle, eg during childbirth **3** *pathol* any abnormal tightening or shrinking of an organ or part **4** a shortening of a word or group of words, often marked in written English by an apostrophe: *I've come* for *I have come* > con'tractive *adj* > con'tractively *adv* > con'tractiveness *n*

contract of employment *n* a written agreement between an employer and an employee, that, taken together with the rights of each under statute and common law, determines the employment relations between them

contractor ('kɒntræktə, kən'træk-) *n* **1** a person or firm that contracts to supply materials or labour, esp for building **2** something that contracts, esp a muscle **3** *law* a person who is a party to a contract **4** the declarer in bridge

contract out *vb* (*intr, adverb*) *Brit* to agree not to participate in something, esp the state pension scheme

contractual (kən'træktjʊəl) *adj* of the nature of or assured by a contract > con'tractually *adv*

contracture (kən'træktʃə) *n* a disorder in which a skeletal muscle is permanently tightened (contracted), most often caused by spasm or paralysis of the antagonist muscle that maintains normal muscle tension

contradance ('kɒntrə,dɑːns) *n* a variant spelling of **contredanse**

contradict (,kɒntrə'dɪkt) *vb* **1** (*tr*) to affirm the opposite of (a proposition, statement, etc) **2** (*tr*) to declare (a proposition, statement, etc) to be false or incorrect; deny gainsay **3** (*intr*) to be argumentative or contrary **4** (*tr*) to be inconsistent with (a proposition, theory, etc): *the facts contradicted his theory* **5** (*intr*) (of two or more facts, principles, etc) to be at variance; be in contradiction [c16 from Latin *contrādīcere,* from CONTRA- + *dīcere* to speak, say] > ,contra'dictable *adj* > ,contra'dicter *or* ,contra'dictor *n* > ,contra'dictive *or* ,contra'dictious *adj* > ,contra'dictively *or* ,contra'dictiously *adv* > ,contra'dictiveness *or* ,contra'dictiousness *n*

contradiction (,kɒntrə'dɪkʃən) *n* **1** the act of going against; opposition; denial **2** a declaration of the opposite or contrary **3** a statement that is at variance with itself (often in the phrase **a contradiction in terms**) **4** conflict or inconsistency, as between events, qualities, etc **5** a person or thing containing conflicting qualities **6** *logic* a statement that is false under all circumstances; necessary falsehood

contradictory (,kɒntrə'dɪktərɪ) *adj* **1** inconsistent; incompatible **2** given to argument and contention: *a contradictory person* **3** *logic* (of a pair of statements) unable both to be true or both to be false under the same circumstances. Compare **contrary** (sense 5), **subcontrary** (sense 1) ▷ *n, pl* -ries **4** *logic* a statement that cannot be true when a given statement is true or false when it is false > ,contra'dictorily *adv* > ,contra'dictoriness *n*

contradistinction (,kɒntrədɪ'stɪŋkʃən) *n* a distinction made by contrasting different qualities > ,contradis'tinctive *adj* > ,contradis'tinctively *adv*

contradistinguish (,kɒntrədɪ'stɪŋgwɪʃ) *vb* (*tr*) to differentiate by means of contrasting or opposing qualities

contraflow ('kɒntrə,fləʊ) *n Brit* two-way traffic on one carriageway of a motorway, esp to allow maintenance work to be carried out or an accident to be cleared

contrail ('kɒntreɪl) *n* another name for **vapour trail** [c20 from CON(DENSATION) + TRAIL]

contraindicate (,kɒntrə'ɪndɪ,keɪt) *vb* (*tr; usually passive*) *med* to advise against or indicate the possible danger of (a drug, treatment, etc) > ,contra'indicant *n* > ,contra,indi'cation *n*

contralateral (,kɒntrə'lætərəl) *adj anatomy, zoology* relating to or denoting the opposite side of a body, structure, etc

contralto (kən'træltəʊ, -'trɑː-) *n, pl* -tos *or* -ti (-tɪ) **1** the lowest female voice, usually having a range of approximately from F a fifth below middle C to D a ninth above it. In the context of a choir often shortened to: **alto 2** a singer with such a voice ▷ *adj* **3** of or denoting a contralto: *the contralto part* [c18 from Italian; see CONTRA-, ALTO]

contraposition (,kɒntrəpə'zɪʃən) *n* **1** the act of placing opposite or against, esp in contrast or antithesis **2** *logic* the derivation of the contrapositive of a given categorial proposition

contrapositive (,kɒntrə'pɒzɪtɪv) *adj* **1** placed opposite or against ▷ *n* **2 a** a conditional statement derived from another by negating and interchanging antecedent and consequent **b** a categorial proposition obtained from another, esp validly, by any of a number of operations including negation, transferring the terms, changing their quality, and also possibly weakening from universal to particular

contrapposto (,kɒntrə'pɒstəʊ) *n, pl* -tos (in the visual arts) a curving or asymmetrical arrangement of the human figure with the shoulders, hips, and legs in different planes [c20 from Italian, from the past participle of *contrapporre,* from Latin *contra* CONTRA- + *pōnere* to place]

contraption (kən'træpʃən) *n informal, often facetious or derogatory* a device or contrivance, esp one considered strange, unnecessarily intricate, or improvised [c19 perhaps from CON(TRIVANCE) + TRAP[1] + (INVEN)TION]

contrapuntal (,kɒntrə'pʌnt[ə]l) *adj music* characterized by counterpoint [c19 from Italian *contrappunto* COUNTERPOINT + AL[1]] > ,contra'puntally *adv*

contrapuntist (,kɒntrə'pʌntɪst) *or* **contrapuntalist** *n music* a composer skilled in counterpoint

contrarian (kən'treərɪən) *n* a contrary or obstinate person

contrariety (,kɒntrə'raɪətɪ) *n, pl* -ties **1** opposition between one thing and another; disagreement **2** an instance of such opposition; inconsistency; discrepancy **3** *logic* the relationship between two contraries

contrarily *adv* **1** (kən'treərɪlɪ) in a perverse or obstinate manner **2** ('kɒntrərɪlɪ) on the other hand; from the opposite point of view **3** ('kɒntrərɪlɪ) in an opposite, adverse, or unexpected way

contrarious (kən'treərɪəs) *adj rare* **1** (of people or animals) perverse or obstinate **2** (of conditions) unfavourable > con'trariously *adv* > con'trariousness *n*

contrariwise ('kɒntrərɪ,waɪz) *adv* **1** from a contrasting point of view; on the other hand **2** in the reverse way or direction **3** (kən'treərɪ,waɪz) in a contrary manner

contrary ('kɒntrərɪ) *adj* **1** opposed in nature, position, etc: *contrary ideas* **2** (kən'treərɪ) perverse; obstinate **3** (esp of wind) adverse; unfavourable **4** (of plant parts) situated at right angles to each other **5** *logic* (of a pair of propositions) related so that they cannot both be true at once, although they may both be false together. Compare **subcontrary** (sense 1), **contradictory** (sense 3) ▷ *n, pl* -ries **6** the exact opposite (esp in the phrase **to the contrary**) **7** on the contrary quite the reverse; not at all **8** either of two exactly opposite objects, facts, or qualities **9** *logic* a statement that cannot be true when a given statement is true ▷ *adv* (usually foll by *to*) **10** in an opposite or unexpected way: *contrary to usual belief* **11** in conflict (with) or contravention (of): *contrary to nature* [c14 from Latin *contrārius* opposite, from *contrā* against] > con'trariness *n*

contrasexual (ˌkɒntrəˈsɛksjʊəl) *adj* **1** (of a woman) appearing to defy the female sexual stereotype by being content to be single and childless while being sexually active and financially independent ▷ *n* **2** a contrasexual woman

contrast *vb* (kənˈtrɑːst) **1** (often foll by *with*) to distinguish or be distinguished by comparison of unlike or opposite qualities ▷ *n* (ˈkɒntrɑːst) **2** distinction or emphasis of difference by comparison of opposite or dissimilar things, qualities, etc (esp in the phrases **by contrast, in contrast to** *or* **with**) **3** a person or thing showing notable differences when compared with another **4** (in painting) the effect of the juxtaposition of different colours, tones, etc **5 a** (of a photographic emulsion) the degree of density measured against exposure used **b** the extent to which adjacent areas of an optical image, esp on a television screen or in a photographic negative or print, differ in brightness **6** *psychol* the phenomenon that when two different but related stimuli are presented close together in space and/ or time they are perceived as being more different than they really are [c16 (n): via French from Italian, from *contrastare* (vb), from Latin *contra*-against + *stare* to stand] > con'trastable *adj* > con'trastably *adv* > con'trasting *adj* > con'trastive *adj* > con'trastively *adv*

contrast medium *n med* a radiopaque substance, such as barium sulphate, used to increase the contrast of an image in radiography

contrasty (kənˈtrɑːstɪ) *adj* (of a photograph or subject) having sharp gradations in tone, esp between light and dark areas

contrasuggestible (ˌkɒntrəsəˈdʒɛstɪbᵊl) *adj psychol* responding or tending to respond to a suggestion by doing or believing the opposite > ˌcontrasugˌgesti'bility *n* > ˌcontrasug'gestion *n*

contravallation (ˌkɒntrəvəˈleɪʃən) *n* fortifications built by besiegers around the place besieged [c17 from CONTRA- + Latin *vallātiō* entrenchment; compare French *contrevallation*]

contravene (ˌkɒntrəˈviːn) *vb* (*tr*) **1** to come into conflict with or infringe (rules, laws, etc) **2** to dispute or contradict (a statement, proposition, etc) [c16 from Late Latin *contrāvenīre*, from Latin CONTRA- + *venīre* to come] > ˌcontra'vener *n* > ˌcontra'vention (ˌkɒntrəˈvɛnʃən) *n*

contrayerva (ˌkɒntrəˈjɜːvə) *n* the root of any of several tropical American moraceous plants of the genus *Dorstenia*, esp *D. contrayerva*, used as a stimulant and tonic [c17 from Spanish *contrayerba*, from CONTRA- + *yerba* grass, (poisonous) plant, from Latin *herba*; referring to the belief that it was an antidote to poisons]

contredanse *or* **contradance** (ˈkɒntrəˌdɑːns) *n* **1** a courtly Continental version of the English country dance, similar to the quadrille **2** music written for or in the rhythm of this dance [c19 from French, changed from English *country dance*; *country* altered to French *contre* (opposite) by folk etymology (because the dancers face each other)]

contre-jour (ˈkɒntrəˌʒʊə) *n photog* **a** the technique of taking photographs into the light, with the light source behind the subject **b** (*as modifier*): *a contre-jour shot* [c20 from French, literally: against day(light)]

contretemps (ˈkɒntrəˌtɑːn; French kɔ̃trətɑ̃) *n, pl* **-temps 1** an awkward or difficult situation or mishap **2** *fencing* a feint made with the purpose of producing a counterthrust from one's opponent **3** a small disagreement that is rather embarrassing [c17 from French, from *contre* against + *temps* time, from Latin *tempus*]

contrib. *abbreviation for* contributor

contribute (kənˈtrɪbjuːt) *vb* (often foll by *to*) **1** to give (support, money, etc) for a common purpose or fund **2** to supply (ideas, opinions, etc) as part of a debate or discussion **3** (*intr*) to be partly instrumental (in) or responsible (for): *drink contributed to the accident* **4** to write (articles) for a publication [c16 from Latin *contribuere* to collect, from *tribuere* to grant, bestow] > con'tributable *adj* > con'tributive *adj* > con'tributively *adv* > con'tributiveness *n*

contribution (ˌkɒntrɪˈbjuːʃən) *n* **1** the act of contributing **2** something contributed, such as money or ideas **3** an article, story, etc, contributed to a newspaper or other publication **4** *insurance* a portion of the total liability incumbent on each of two or more companies for a risk with respect to which all of them have issued policies **5** *archaic* a levy, esp towards the cost of a war

contributor (kənˈtrɪbjʊtə) *n* **1** a person who contributes, esp one who writes for a newspaper or one who makes a donation to a cause, etc **2** something that is a factor in or is partly responsible for something: *alcohol was a contributor to his death*

contributory (kənˈtrɪbjʊtərɪ, -trɪ) *adj* **1** (often foll by *to*) sharing in or being partly responsible (for the cause of something): *a contributory factor* **2** giving or donating to a common purpose or fund **3** of, relating to, or designating an insurance or pension scheme in which the premiums are paid partly by the employer and partly by the employees who benefit from it **4** liable or subject to a tax or levy ▷ *n, pl* **-ries 5** a person or thing that contributes **6** *company law* a member or former member of a company liable to contribute to the assets on the winding-up of the company

contributory negligence *n law* failure by an injured person to have taken proper precautions to prevent an accident

con trick *n informal* a shortened form of **confidence trick**

contrite (kənˈtraɪt, ˈkɒntraɪt) *adj* **1** full of guilt or regret; remorseful **2** arising from a sense of shame or guilt: *contrite promises* **3** *theol* remorseful for past sin and resolved to avoid future sin [c14 from Latin *contrītus* worn out, from *conterere* to bruise, from *terere* to grind] > con'tritely *adv* > con'triteness *n*

contrition (kənˈtrɪʃən) *n* **1** deeply felt remorse; penitence **2** *Christianity* detestation of past sins and a resolve to make amends, either from love of God (**perfect contrition**) or from hope of heaven (**imperfect contrition**)

contrivance (kənˈtraɪvəns) *n* **1** something contrived, esp an ingenious device; contraption **2** the act or faculty of devising or adapting; inventive skill or ability **3** an artificial rather than natural selection or arrangement of details, parts, etc **4** an elaborate or deceitful plan or expedient; stratagem

contrive (kənˈtraɪv) *vb* **1** (*tr*) to manage (something or to do something), esp by means of a trick; engineer: *he contrived to make them meet* **2** (*tr*) to think up or adapt ingeniously or elaborately: *he contrived a new mast for the boat* **3** to plot or scheme (treachery, evil, etc) [c14 from Old French *controver*, from Late Latin *contropāre* to represent by figures of speech, compare, from Latin *com-* together + *tropus* figure of speech, TROPE] > con'trivable *adj* > con'triver *n*

contrived (kənˈtraɪvd) *adj* obviously planned, artificial, or lacking in spontaneity; forced; unnatural

control (kənˈtrəʊl) *vb* **-trols, -trolling, -trolled** (*tr*) **1** to command, direct, or rule: *to control a country* **2** to check, limit, curb, or regulate; restrain: *to control one's emotions; to control a fire* **3** to regulate or operate (a machine) **4** to verify (a scientific experiment) by conducting a parallel experiment in which the variable being investigated is held constant or is compared with a standard **5 a** to regulate (financial affairs) **b** to examine and verify (financial accounts) **6** to restrict or regulate the authorized supply of (certain substances, such as drugs) ▷ *n* **7** power to direct or determine: *under control; out of control* **8** a means of regulation or restraint; curb; check: *a frontier control* **9** (*often plural*) a device or mechanism for operating a car, aircraft, etc **10** a standard of comparison used in a statistical analysis or scientific experiment **11 a** a device that regulates the operation of a machine. A **dynamic control** is one that incorporates a governor so that it responds to the output of the machine it regulates **b** (*as modifier*): *control panel; control room* **12** *spiritualism* an agency believed to assist the medium in a séance **13** Also called: **control mark** a letter, or letter and number, printed on a sheet of postage stamps, indicating authenticity, date, and series of issue **14** one of a number of checkpoints on a car rally, orienteering course, etc, where competitors check in and their time, performance, etc, is recorded [c15 from Old French *conteroller* to regulate, from *contrerolle* duplicate register, system of checking, from *contre*-COUNTER- + *rolle* ROLL] > con'trollable *adj* > conˌtrolla'bility *or* con'trollableness *n* > con'trollably *adv*

control account *n accounting* an account to which are posted the debit and credit totals of other accounts, usually in preparation of financial statements

control chart *n statistics* a chart on which observed values of a variable are plotted, usually against the expected value of the variable and its allowable deviation, so that excessive variations in the quality, quantity, etc, of the variable can be detected

control column *n* a lever or pillar, usually fitted with a handwheel, used to control the movements of an aircraft. Also called: **control stick, joy stick**

control commands *pl n* keyed instructions conveyed to a computer by using the control key in conjunction with the standard keys

control experiment *n* an experiment designed to check or correct the results of another experiment by removing the variable or variables operating in that other experiment. The comparison obtained is an indication or measurement of the effect of the variables concerned

control freak *n* a person with an obsessive need to be in control of what is happening

control freakery *n* an obsessive need to be in control of what is happening

control grid *n electronics* another name for **grid** (sense 6), in a tetrode, pentode and similar devices

control group *n* any group used as a control in a statistical experiment, esp a group of patients who receive either a placebo or a standard drug during an investigation of the effects of another drug on other patients

control key *n* a key on the keyboard of a computer that is used in conjunction with the standard keys in order to initiate a specific function, such as editing

controlled explosion *n* the deliberate detonation of an explosive device under strictly controlled circumstances

controller (kənˈtrəʊlə) *n* **1** a person who directs, regulates, or restrains **2** Also called: **comptroller** a business executive or government officer who is responsible for financial planning, control, etc **3** the equipment concerned with controlling the operation of an electrical device > con'trollerˌship *n*

controlling interest *n* a quantity of shares in a business that is sufficient to ensure control over its direction

control rod *n* one of a number of rods or tubes containing a neutron absorber, such as boron, that can be inserted into or retracted from the core of a nuclear reactor in order to control its rate of reaction

C

control stick *n* the lever by which a pilot controls the lateral and longitudinal movements of an aircraft. Also called: control column, joy stick

control surface *n* a movable surface, such as a rudder, elevator, aileron, etc, that controls an aircraft or rocket

control tower *n* a tower at an airport from which air traffic is controlled

controversy (ˈkɒntrəˌvɜːsɪ, kənˈtrɒvəsɪ) *n, pl* -sies dispute, argument, or debate, esp one concerning a matter about which there is strong disagreement and esp one carried on in public or in the press [C14 from Latin *contrōversia*, from *contrōversus* turned in an opposite direction, from CONTRA- + *vertere* to turn] > controversial (ˌkɒntrəˈvɜːʃəl) *adj* > ˌcontroˈversialˌism *n* > ˌcontroˈversialist *n* > ˌcontroˈversially *adv*

controvert (ˈkɒntrəˌvɜːt, ˌkɒntrəˈvɜːt) *vb* (*tr*) **1** to deny, refute, or oppose (some argument or opinion) **2** to argue or wrangle about [C17 from Latin *contrōversus*; see CONTROVERSY] > ˈcontroˌverter *n* > ˌcontroˈvertible *adj* > ˌcontroˈvertibly *adv*

contumacious (ˌkɒntjʊˈmeɪʃəs) *adj* stubbornly resistant to authority; wilfully obstinate > ˌcontuˈmaciously *adv* > ˌcontuˈmaciousness *n*

contumacy (ˈkɒntjʊməsɪ) *n, pl* -cies **1** obstinate and wilful rebelliousness or resistance to authority; insubordination; disobedience **2** the wilful refusal of a person to appear before a court or to comply with a court order [C14 from Latin *contumācia*, from *contumāx* obstinate; related to *tumēre* to swell, be proud]

contumely (ˈkɒntjʊmɪlɪ) *n, pl* -lies **1** scornful or insulting language or behaviour **2** a humiliating or scornful insult [C14 from Latin *contumēlia* invective, from *tumēre* to swell, as with wrath] > contumelious (ˌkɒntjʊˈmiːlɪəs) *adj* > ˌcontuˈmeliously *adv* > ˌcontuˈmeliousness *n*

contuse (kənˈtjuːz) *vb* (*tr*) to injure (the body) without breaking the skin; bruise [C15 from Latin *contūsus* bruised, from *contundere* to grind, from *tundere* to beat, batter] > conˈtusive *adj*

contusion (kənˈtjuːʒən) *n* an injury in which the skin is not broken; bruise > conˈtusioned *adj*

conundrum (kəˈnʌndrəm) *n* **1** a riddle, esp one whose answer makes a play on words **2** a puzzling question or problem [C16 of unknown origin]

conurbation (ˌkɒnɜːˈbeɪʃən) *n* a large densely populated urban sprawl formed by the growth and coalescence of individual towns or cities [C20 from CON- + -*urbation*, from Latin *urbs* city; see URBAN]

conure (ˈkɒnjʊə) *n* any of various small American parrots of the genus *Aratinga* and related genera [C19 from New Latin *conurus*, from Greek *kōnos* CONE + *oura* tail]

conus (ˈkəʊnəs) *n, pl* -ni anatomy, zoology any of several cone-shaped structures, such as the conus medullaris, the lower end of the spinal cord

convalesce (ˌkɒnvəˈlɛs) *vb* (*intr*) to recover from illness, injury, or the aftereffects of a surgical operation, esp by resting [C15 from Latin *convalēscere*, from *com-* (intensive) + *valēscere* to grow strong, from *valēre* to be strong]

convalescence (ˌkɒnvəˈlɛsəns) *n* **1** gradual return to health after illness, injury, or an operation, esp through rest **2** the period during which such recovery occurs > ˌconvaˈlescent *n, adj* > ˌconvaˈlescently *adv*

convection (kənˈvɛkʃən) *n* **1** a process of heat transfer through a gas or liquid by bulk motion of hotter material into a cooler region. Compare conduction (sense 1) **2** meteorol the process by which masses of relatively warm air are raised into the atmosphere, often cooling and forming clouds, with compensatory downward movements of cooler air **3** geology the slow circulation of subcrustal material, thought to be the mechanism by which tectonic plates are moved [C19 from Late Latin *convectiō* a bringing

together, from Latin *convehere* to bring together, gather, from *vehere* to bear, carry] > conˈvectional *adj* > conˈvective *adj*

convector (kənˈvɛktə) *n* a space-heating device from which heat is transferred to the surrounding air by convection

convenance French (kɔ̃vnɑ̃s) *n* suitable behaviour; propriety [from *convenir* to be suitable, from Latin *convenīre*; see CONVENIENT]

convene (kənˈviːn) *vb* **1** to gather, call together, or summon, esp for a formal meeting **2** (*tr*) to order to appear before a court of law, judge, tribunal, etc [C15 from Latin *convenīre* to assemble, from *venīre* to come]

convener or **convenor** (kənˈviːnə) *n* **1** a person who convenes or chairs a meeting, committee, etc, esp one who is specifically elected to do so: *a convener of shop stewards* **2** the chairman and civic head of certain Scottish councils. Compare provost (sense 3) > conˈvenership or conˈvenorship *n*

convenience (kənˈviːnɪəns) *n* **1** the state or quality of being suitable or opportune: *the convenience of the hour* **2** a convenient time or situation **3** at your convenience at a time suitable to you **4** at your earliest convenience formal as soon as possible **5** usefulness, comfort, or facility **6** an object that is particularly useful, esp a labour-saving device **7** euphemistic, chiefly Brit a lavatory, esp a public one **8** make a convenience of to take advantage of; impose upon

convenience food *n* food that needs little preparation, especially food that has been pre-prepared and preserved for long-term storage

convenience store *n* a shop that has long opening hours, caters to local tastes, and is conveniently situated

convenient (kənˈviːnɪənt) *adj* **1** suitable for one's purpose or needs; opportune **2** easy to use **3** close by or easily accessible; handy [C14 from Latin *conveniēns* appropriate, fitting, from *convenīre* to come together, be in accord with, from *venīre* to come] > conˈveniently *adv*

convent (ˈkɒnvənt) *n* **1** a building inhabited by a religious community, usually of nuns **2** the religious community inhabiting such a building **3** Also called: convent school a school in which the teachers are nuns [C13 from Old French *covent*, from Latin *conventus* meeting, from *convenīre* to come together; see CONVENE]

conventicle (kənˈvɛntɪkəl) *n* **1** a secret or unauthorized assembly for worship **2** a small meeting house or chapel for a religious assembly, esp of Nonconformists or Dissenters [C14 from Latin *conventiculum* a meeting, from *conventus*; see CONVENT] > conˈventicler *n*

convention (kənˈvɛnʃən) *n* **1 a** a large formal assembly of a group with common interests, such as a political party or trade union **b** the persons attending such an assembly **2** US politics an assembly of delegates of one party to select candidates for office **3** diplomacy an international agreement second only to a treaty in formality: *a telecommunications convention* **4** any agreement, compact, or contract **5** the most widely accepted or established view of what is thought to be proper behaviour, good taste, etc **6** an accepted rule, usage, etc: *a convention used by printers* **7** bridge Also called: conventional a bid or play not to be taken at its face value, which one's partner can interpret according to a prearranged bidding system [C15 from Latin *conventiō* an assembling, agreeing]

conventional (kənˈvɛnʃənəl) *adj* **1** following the accepted customs and proprieties, esp in a way that lacks originality: *conventional habits* **2** established by accepted usage or general agreement **3** of or relating to a convention or assembly **4** law based upon the agreement or consent of parties **5** arts represented in a simplified or generalized way; conventionalized **6** (of weapons, warfare, etc) not nuclear ▷ *n* **7** bridge

another word for **convention** (sense 7) > conˈventionally *adv*

conventionalism (kənˈvɛnʃənəˌlɪzəm) *n* **1** advocacy of or conformity to that which is established **2** something conventional **3** philosophy a theory that moral principles are not enshrined in the nature of things but merely reflect customary practice **4** philosophy the theory that meaning is a matter of convention and thus that scientific laws merely reflect such general linguistic agreement > conˈventionalist *n*

conventionality (kənˌvɛnʃəˈnælɪtɪ) *n, pl* -ties **1** the quality or characteristic of being conventional, esp in behaviour, thinking, etc **2** (often plural) something conventional, esp a normal or accepted rule of behaviour; propriety

conventionalize or **conventionalise** (kənˈvɛnʃənəˌlaɪz) *vb* (*tr*) **1** to make conventional **2** to simplify or stylize (a design, decorative device, etc) > conˌventionaliˈzation or conˌventionaliˈsation *n*

conventual (kənˈvɛntjʊəl) *adj* **1** of, belonging to, or characteristic of a convent ▷ *n* **2** a member of a convent > conˈventually *adv*

converge (kənˈvɜːdʒ) *vb* **1** to move or cause to move towards the same point: *crowds converged on the city* **2** to meet or cause to meet; join **3** (*intr*) (of opinions, effects, etc) to tend towards a common conclusion or result **4** (*intr*) maths (of an infinite series or sequence) to approach a finite limit as the number of terms increases **5** (*intr*) (of animals and plants during evolutionary development) to undergo convergence [C17 from Late Latin *convergere*, from Latin *com-* together + *vergere* to incline]

convergence (kənˈvɜːdʒəns) *n* **1** Also called: convergency the act, degree, or a point of converging **2** concurrence of opinions, results, etc **3** maths the property or manner of approaching a finite limit, esp of an infinite series: *conditional convergence* **4** the combining of different forms of electronic technology, such as data processing and word processing converging into information processing **5** Also called: convergent evolution the evolutionary development of a superficial resemblance between unrelated animals that occupy a similar environment, as in the evolution of wings in birds and bats **6** meteorol an accumulation of air in a region that has a greater inflow than outflow of air, often giving rise to vertical air currents. See also Intertropical Convergence Zone **7** the turning of the eyes inwards in order to fixate an object nearer than that previously being fixated. Compare divergence (sense 6)

convergence zone *n* geology a zone where tectonic plates collide, typified by earthquakes, mountain formation, and volcanic activity

convergent (kənˈvɜːdʒənt) *adj* **1** (of two or more lines, paths, etc) moving towards or meeting at some common point **2** (of forces, ideas, etc) tending towards the same result; merging **3** maths (of an infinite series) having a finite limit

convergent thinking *n* psychol analytical, usually deductive, thinking in which ideas are examined for their logical validity or in which a set of rules is followed, eg in arithmetic

conversable (kənˈvɜːsəbəl) *adj* **1** easy or pleasant to talk to **2** able or inclined to talk > conˈversableness *n* > conˈversably *adv*

conversant (kənˈvɜːsənt) *adj* (usually postpositive and foll by with) experienced (in), familiar (with), or acquainted (with) > conˈversance or conˈversancy *n* > conˈversantly *adv*

conversation (ˌkɒnvəˈseɪʃən) *n* **1** the interchange through speech of information, ideas, etc; spoken communication **2** make conversation to talk in an artificial way. Related adj: colloquial

conversational (ˌkɒnvəˈseɪʃənəl) *adj* **1** of, using, or in the manner of conversation **2** inclined to or skilled in conversation; conversable > ˌconverˈsationally *adv*

conversational implicature *n logic, philosophy* another term for **implicature**
conversationalist (ˌkɒnvəˈseɪʃənəlɪst) *or* **conversationist** *n* a person who enjoys or excels in conversation
conversation piece *n* **1** something, esp an unusual object, that provokes conversation **2** (esp in 18th-century Britain) a group portrait in a landscape or domestic setting **3** a play emphasizing dialogue
conversazione *Italian* (konversatˈtsjone; *English* ˌkɒnvəˌsætsɪˈəʊnɪ) *n, pl* **-zioni** (*Italian* -ˈtsjoni) **-ziones** (*English* -tsɪˈəʊniːz) a social gathering for discussion of the arts, literature, etc [C18 literally: conversation]
converse[1] *vb* (kənˈvɜːs) (*intr; often foll by with*) **1** to engage in conversation (with) **2** to commune spiritually (with) **3** *obsolete* **a** to associate; consort **b** to have sexual intercourse ▷ *n* (ˈkɒnvɜːs) **4** conversation (often in the phrase **hold converse with**) **5** *obsolete* **a** fellowship or acquaintance **b** sexual intercourse [C16 from Old French *converser*, from Latin *conversārī* to keep company with, from *conversāre* to turn constantly, from *vertere* to turn] > **conˈverser** *n*
converse[2] (ˈkɒnvɜːs) *adj* **1** (*prenominal*) reversed; opposite; contrary ▷ *n* **2** something that is opposite or contrary **3** *logic* **a** a categorical proposition obtained from another by the transposition of subject and predicate, as *no bad man is bald* from *no bald man is bad* **b** a proposition so derived, possibly by weakening a universal proposition to the corresponding particular, as *some socialists are rich* from *all rich men are socialists* **4** *logic, maths* a relation that holds between two relata only when a given relation holds between them in reverse order: thus *father of* is the converse of *son of* [C16 from Latin *conversus* turned around; see CONVERSE[1]]
conversely (ˈkɒnvɜːslɪ) *adv* (*sentence modifier*) in a contrary or opposite way; on the other hand
conversion (kənˈvɜːʃən) *n* **1** **a** a change or adaptation in form, character, or function **b** something changed in one of these respects **2** a change to another attitude or belief, as in a change of religion **3** *maths* a change in the units or form of a number or expression: *the conversion of miles to kilometres involves multiplying by 1.61* **4** *logic* a form of inference by which one proposition is obtained as the converse of another proposition **5** *law* **a** unauthorized dealing with or the assumption of rights of ownership to another's personal property **b** the changing of real property into personalty or personalty into realty **6** *rugby* a score made after a try by kicking the ball over the crossbar from a place kick **7** *physics* a change of fertile material to fissile material in a reactor **8** **a** an alteration to a car engine to improve its performance **b** (*as modifier*): *a conversion kit* **9** material alteration to the structure or fittings of a building undergoing a change in function or legal status **10** *NZ* the unauthorized appropriation of a motor vehicle [C14 from Latin *conversiō* a turning around; see CONVERT] > **conˈversional** *or* **conˈversionary** *adj*
conversion disorder *n* a psychological disorder in which severe physical symptoms like blindness or paralysis appear with no apparent physical cause
convert *vb* (kənˈvɜːt) (*mainly tr*) **1** to change or adapt the form, character, or function of; transform **2** to cause (someone) to change in opinion, belief, etc **3** to change (a person or his way of life, etc) for the better **4** (*intr*) to admit of being changed (into): *the table converts into a tray* **5** (*also intr*) to change or be changed into another chemical compound or physical state: *to convert water into ice* **6** *law* **a** to assume unlawful proprietary rights over (personal property) **b** to change (property) from realty into personalty or vice versa **7** (*also intr*) *rugby* to make a conversion after (a try) **8** *logic* to transpose the subject and predicate of (a proposition) by conversion **9** to change (a value or measurement) from one system of units to another **10** to exchange (a security or bond) for something of equivalent value ▷ *n* (ˈkɒnvɜːt) **11** a person who has been converted to another belief, religion, etc [C13 from Old French *convertir*, from Latin *convertere* to turn around, alter, transform, from *vertere* to turn] > **conˈvertive** *adj*
converter *or* **convertor** (kənˈvɜːtə) *n* **1** a person or thing that converts **2** *physics* **a** a device for converting alternating current to direct current or vice versa **b** a device for converting a signal from one frequency to another or from analogue to digital forms **3** a vessel in which molten metal is refined, using a blast of air or oxygen. See also **Bessemer converter, L-D converter** **4** short for **converter reactor** **5** *computing* a device for converting one form of coded information to another, such as an analogue-to-digital converter
converter reactor *n* a nuclear reactor for converting one fuel into another, esp one that transforms fertile material into fissionable material. Compare **breeder reactor**
convertible (kənˈvɜːtəb°l) *adj* **1** capable of being converted **2** (of a car) having a folding or removable roof **3** *finance* **a** a bond or debenture that can be converted to ordinary or preference shares on a fixed date at a fixed price **b** (of a paper currency) exchangeable on demand for precious metal to an equivalent value ▷ *n* **4** a car with a folding or removable roof > **conˌvertiˈbility** *or* **conˈvertibleness** *n* > **conˈvertibly** *adv*
convertiplane, convertaplane *or* **convertoplane** (kənˈvɜːtəˌpleɪn) *n* an aircraft that can land and take off vertically by temporarily directing its propulsive thrust downwards
convertite (ˈkɒnvəˌtaɪt) *n archaic* a convert, esp a reformed prostitute
convex (ˈkɒnvɛks, kɒnˈvɛks) *adj* **1** curving or bulging outwards **2** *physics* having one or two surfaces curved or ground in the shape of a section of the exterior of a sphere, paraboloid, ellipsoid, etc: *a convex lens* **3** *maths* (of a polygon) containing no interior angle greater than 180° ▷ *vb* **4** (*tr*) to make convex ▷ Compare **concave** [C16 from Latin *convexus* vaulted, rounded] > ˈ**convexly** *adv*
convexity (kənˈvɛksɪtɪ) *n, pl* **-ties** **1** the state or quality of being convex **2** a convex surface, object, etc; bulge
convexo-concave (kənˌvɛksəʊkɒnˈkeɪv) *adj* **1** having one side convex and the other side concave **2** (of a lens) having a convex face with greater curvature than the concave face. Compare **concavo-convex** (sense 2)
convexo-convex *adj* (esp of a lens) having both sides convex; biconvex
convex sole *n* another name for **dropped sole**
convey (kənˈveɪ) *vb* (*tr*) **1** to take, carry, or transport from one place to another **2** to communicate (a message, information, etc) **3** (of a channel, path, etc) to conduct, transmit, or transfer **4** *law* to transmit or transfer (the title to property) **5** *archaic* to steal [C13 from Old French *conveier*, from Medieval Latin *conviāre* to escort, from Latin *com-* with + *via* way] > **conˈveyable** *adj*
conveyance (kənˈveɪəns) *n* **1** the act of conveying **2** a means of transport **3** *law* **a** a transfer of the legal title to property **b** the document effecting such a transfer > **conˈveyancer** *n*
conveyancing (kənˈveɪənsɪŋ) *n* the branch of law dealing with the transfer of ownership of property
conveyor *or* **conveyer** (kənˈveɪə) *n* **1** a person or thing that conveys **2** short for **conveyor belt**
conveyor belt *n* a flexible endless strip of fabric or linked plates driven by rollers and used to transport objects, esp in a factory
convict *vb* (kənˈvɪkt) (*tr*) **1** to pronounce (someone) guilty of an offence ▷ *n* (ˈkɒnvɪkt) **2** a person found guilty of an offence against the law, esp one who is sentenced to imprisonment **3** a person serving a prison sentence ▷ *adj* (kənˈvɪkt) **4** *obsolete* convicted [C14 from Latin *convictus* convicted of crime, from *convincere* to prove guilty, CONVINCE] > **conˈvictable** *or* **conˈvictible** *adj*
conviction (kənˈvɪkʃən) *n* **1** the state or appearance of being convinced **2** a fixed or firmly held belief, opinion, etc **3** the act of convincing **4** the act or an instance of convicting or the state of being convicted **5** **carry conviction** to be convincing > **conˈvictional** *adj*
convictive (kənˈvɪktɪv) *adj* able or serving to convince or convict > **conˈvictively** *adv*
convince (kənˈvɪns) *vb* (*tr*) **1** (*may take a clause as object*) to make (someone) agree, understand, or realize the truth or validity of something; persuade **2** *chiefly US* to persuade (someone) to do something **3** *obsolete* **a** to overcome **b** to prove guilty [C16 from Latin *convincere* to demonstrate incontrovertibly, from *com-* (intensive) + *vincere* to overcome, conquer] > **conˈvincement** *n* > **conˈvincer** *n* > **conˈvincible** *adj*

USAGE The use of *convince* to talk about persuading someone to do something is considered by many British speakers to be wrong or unacceptable

convincing (kənˈvɪnsɪŋ) *adj* **1** credible or plausible **2** *chiefly law* persuading by evidence or argument > **conˈvincingly** *adv* > **conˈvincingness** *n*
convivial (kənˈvɪvɪəl) *adj* sociable; jovial or festive: *a convivial atmosphere* [C17 from Late Latin *convīviālis* pertaining to a feast, from Latin *convīvium*, a living together, banquet, from *vīvere* to live] > **conˈvivialist** *n* > **conˌviviˈality** *n* > **conˈvivially** *adv*
convocation (ˌkɒnvəˈkeɪʃən) *n* **1** a large formal assembly, esp one specifically convened **2** the act of convoking or state of being convoked **3** *Church of England* either of the synods of the provinces of Canterbury or York **4** *Episcopal Church* **a** an assembly of the clergy and part of the laity of a diocese **b** a district represented at such an assembly **5** (*sometimes capital*) (in some British universities) a legislative assembly composed mainly of graduates **6** (in India) a degree-awarding ceremony **7** (in Australia and New Zealand) the graduate membership of a university > ˌ**convoˈcational** *adj* > ˈ**convoˌcator** *n*
convoke (kənˈvəʊk) *vb* (*tr*) to call (a meeting, assembly, etc) together; summon [C16 from Latin *convocāre*, from *vocāre* to call] > **convocative** (kənˈvɒkətɪv) *adj* > **conˈvoker** *n*
convolute (ˈkɒnvəˌluːt) *vb* (*tr*) **1** to form into a twisted, coiled, or rolled shape ▷ *adj* **2** *botany* rolled longitudinally upon itself: *a convolute petal* **3** another word for **convoluted** (sense 2) [C18 from Latin *convolūtus* rolled up, from *convolvere* to roll together, from *volvere* to turn] > ˈ**convoˌlutely** *adv*
convoluted (ˈkɒnvəˌluːtɪd) *adj* **1** (esp of meaning, style, etc) difficult to comprehend; involved **2** wound together; coiled > ˈ**convoˌlutedly** *adv* > ˈ**convoˌlutedness** *n*
convolution (ˌkɒnvəˈluːʃən) *n* **1** a twisting together; a turn, twist, or coil **2** an intricate, involved, or confused matter or condition **3** Also called: **gyrus** any of the numerous convex folds or ridges of the surface of the brain > ˌ**convoˈlutional** *or* ˌ**convoˈlutionary** *adj*
convolve (kənˈvɒlv) *vb* to wind or roll together; coil; twist [C16 from Latin *convolvere*; see CONVOLUTE]
convolvulaceous (kənˌvɒlvjʊˈleɪʃəs) *adj* of, relating to, or belonging to the *Convolvulaceae*, a family of plants having trumpet-shaped flowers and typically a climbing, twining, or prostrate habit: includes bindweed, morning-glory, and sweet potato
convolvulus (kənˈvɒlvjʊləs) *n, pl* **-luses** *or* **-li** (-ˌlaɪ) any typically twining herbaceous convolvulaceous plant of the genus *Convolvulus*, having funnel-shaped flowers and triangular leaves. See also

C

bindweed [C16 from Latin: bindweed; see CONVOLUTE]

convoy ('kɒnvɔɪ) *n* **1** a group of merchant ships with an escort of warships **2** a group of land vehicles assembled to travel together **3** the act of travelling or escorting by convoy (esp in the phrase **in convoy**) ▷ *vb* **4** (*tr*) to escort while in transit [C14 from Old French *convoier* to CONVEY]

convulsant (kən'vʌlsənt) *adj* **1** producing convulsions ▷ *n* **2** a drug that produces convulsions [C19 from French, from *convulser* to CONVULSE]

convulse (kən'vʌls) *vb* **1** (*tr*) to shake or agitate violently **2** (*tr*) to cause (muscles) to undergo violent spasms or contractions **3** (*intr; often foll by with*) *informal* to shake or be overcome (with violent emotion, esp laughter) **4** (*tr*) to disrupt the normal running of (a country, etc): *student riots have convulsed India* [C17 from Latin *convulsus*, from *convellere* to tear up, from *vellere* to pluck, pull] > con'vulsive *adj* > con'vulsively *adv* > con'vulsiveness *n*

convulsion (kən'vʌlʃən) *n* **1** a violent involuntary contraction of a muscle or muscles **2** a violent upheaval, disturbance, or agitation, esp a social one **3** (*usually plural*) *informal* uncontrollable laughter: *I was in convulsions* > con'vulsionary *adj*

Conwy ('kɒnwɪ) *n* **1** a market town and resort in N Wales, in Conwy county borough on the estuary of the River Conwy: medieval town walls, 13th-century castle. Pop: 3847 (2001). Former name: Conway **2** a county borough in N Wales, created in 1996 from parts of Gwynedd and Clwyd. Pop: 110 900 (2003 est). Area: 1130 sq km (436 sq miles)

cony *or* **coney** ('kəʊnɪ) *n, pl* **-nies** *or* **-neys** **1** a rabbit or fur made from the skin of a rabbit **2** (in the Bible) another name for the **hyrax,** esp the Syrian rock hyrax **3** another name for the **pika** **4** *archaic* a fool or dupe [C13 back formation from *conies*, from Old French *conis*, plural of *conil*, from Latin *cunīculus* rabbit]

coo (ku:) *vb* **coos, cooing, cooed** **1** (*intr*) (of doves, pigeons, etc) to make a characteristic soft throaty call **2** (*tr*) to speak in a soft murmur **3** (*intr*) to murmur lovingly (esp in the phrase **bill and coo**) ▷ *n* **4** the sound of cooing ▷ *interj* **5** *Brit slang* an exclamation of surprise, awe, etc > 'cooer *n* > 'cooingly *adv*

CoO *abbreviation for* cost of ownership

COO *abbreviation for* chief operating officer

Cooch Behar *or* **Kuch Bihar** (ku:tʃ bɪ'hɑ:) *n* **1** a former state of NE India: part of West Bengal since 1950 **2** a city in India, in NE West Bengal: capital of the former state of Cooch Behar. Pop: 76 812 (2001)

cooee *or* **cooey** ('ku:i:) *interj* **1** a call used to attract attention, esp (originally) a long loud high-pitched call on two notes used in the Australian bush ▷ *vb* **cooees, cooeeing, cooeed** *or* **cooeys, cooeying, cooeyed** **2** (*intr*) to utter this call ▷ *n* **3** *Austral and NZ informal* calling distance (esp in the phrase **within** (**a**) **cooee** (**of**)) [C19 from a native Australian language]

cook (kʊk) *vb* **1** to prepare (food) by the action of heat, as by boiling, baking, etc, or (of food) to become ready for eating through such a process. Related adj: **culinary** **2** to subject or be subjected to the action of intense heat: *the town cooked in the sun* **3** (*tr*) *slang* to alter or falsify (something, esp figures, accounts, etc): *to cook the books* **4** (*tr*) *slang* to spoil or ruin (something) **5** (*intr*) *slang* to happen (esp in the phrase **what's cooking?**) **6** (*tr*) *slang* to prepare (any of several drugs) by heating **7** (*intr*) *music slang* to play vigorously: *the band was cooking* **8** **cook someone's goose** *informal* **a** to spoil a person's plans **b** to bring about someone's ruin, downfall, etc ▷ *n* **9** a person who prepares food for eating, esp as an occupation ▷ See also **cook up** [Old English *cōc* (n), from Latin *coquus* a cook, from *coquere* to cook] > 'cookable *adj*

Cook (kʊk) *n* **Mount** **1** Official name: **Aorangi-Mount Cook** a mountain in New Zealand, in the South Island, in the Southern Alps: the highest peak in New Zealand. Height: reduced in 1991 by a rockfall from 3764 m (12 349 ft) to 3754 m (12 316 ft) **2** a mountain in SE Alaska, in the St Elias Mountains. Height: 4194 m (13 760 ft)

cook-chill *n* a method of food preparation used by caterers, in which cooked dishes are chilled rapidly and reheated as required

cooker ('kʊkə) *n* **1** an apparatus, usually of metal and heated by gas, electricity, oil, or solid fuel, for cooking food; stove **2** *Brit* any large sour apple used in cooking

cookery ('kʊkərɪ) *n* **1** the art, study, or practice of cooking **2** *US* a place for cooking **3** *Canadian* a cookhouse at a mining or lumber camp

cookery book *or* **cookbook** ('kʊk,bʊk) *n* a book containing recipes and instructions for cooking

cook-general *n, pl* **cooks-general** *Brit* (formerly, esp in the 1920s and '30s) a domestic servant who did cooking and housework

cookhouse ('kʊk,haʊs) *n* a place for cooking, esp a camp kitchen

cookie *or* **cooky** ('kʊkɪ) *n, pl* **-ies** **1** *US and Canadian* a small flat dry sweet or plain cake of many varieties, baked from a dough. Also called (in Britain and certain other countries): **biscuit** **2** a Scot word for **bun** **3** *informal* a person: *smart cookie* **4** *computing* a piece of data downloaded to a computer by a website, containing details of the preferences of that computer's user which identify the user when revisiting that website **5** **that's the way the cookie crumbles** *informal* matters are inevitably or unalterably so [C18 from Dutch *koekje*, diminutive of *koek* cake]

cookie-cutter *n* **1** a shape with a sharp edge for cutting individual biscuits from a sheet of dough ▷ *adj* **2** resembling many others of the same kind: *a row of cookie-cutter houses*

Cook Inlet *n* an inlet of the Pacific on the coast of S Alaska: part of the Gulf of Alaska

Cook Island Māori *n NZ* a dialect of Māori spoken in the Cook Islands

Cook Islands *pl n* a group of islands in the SW Pacific, an overseas territory of New Zealand: consists of the **Lower Cooks** and the **Northern Cooks** Capital: Avarua, on Rarotonga. Pop: 18 000 (2003 est). Area: 234 sq km (90 sq miles)

cookout ('kʊk,aʊt) *n US and Canadian* a party where a meal is cooked and eaten out of doors

cook shop *n* **1** *Brit* a shop that sells cookery equipment **2** *US* a restaurant

Cook's tour *n informal* a rapid but extensive tour or survey of anything [C19 after Thomas Cook (1808–92), British travel agent]

Cookstown ('kʊkstaʊn) *n* a district of central Northern Ireland, in Co Tyrone. Pop: 33 387 (2003 est). Area: 622 sq km (240 sq miles)

Cook Strait *n* the strait between North and South Islands, New Zealand. Width: 26 km (16 miles)

cooktop ('kʊk,tɒp) *n US* a flat unit for cooking in saucepans or the top part of a stove

Cooktown orchid ('kʊktaʊn) *n* a purple Australian orchid, *Dendrobium bigibbum*, found in Queensland, of which it is the floral emblem [named after *Cooktown*, a coastal town in NE Queensland]

cook up *vb* (*tr, adverb*) **1** *informal* to concoct or invent (a story, alibi, etc) **2** to prepare (a meal), esp quickly **3** *slang* to prepare (a drug) for use by heating, as by dissolving heroin in a spoon ▷ *n* **cook-up** **4** (in the Caribbean) a dish consisting of mixed meats, rice, shrimps, and sometimes vegetables

cool (ku:l) *adj* **1** moderately cold: *a cool day* **2** comfortably free of heat: *a cool room* **3** producing a pleasant feeling of coldness: *a cool shirt* **4** able to conceal emotion; calm: *a cool head* **5** lacking in enthusiasm, affection, cordiality, etc: *a cool welcome* **6** calmly audacious or impudent **7** *informal* (esp of numbers, sums of money, etc) without exaggeration; actual: *a cool ten thousand* **8** (of a colour) having violet, blue, or green predominating; cold **9** (of jazz) characteristic of the late 1940s and early 1950s, economical and rhythmically relaxed **10** *informal* sophisticated or elegant, esp in an unruffled way **11** *informal* excellent; marvellous ▷ *adv* **12** *not standard* in a cool manner; coolly ▷ *n* **13** coolness: *the cool of the evening* **14** *slang* calmness; composure (esp in the phrases **keep** *or* **lose one's cool**) **15** *slang* unruffled elegance or sophistication ▷ *vb* **16** (usually foll by *down* or *off*) to make or become cooler **17** (usually foll by *down* or *off*) to lessen the intensity of (anger or excitement) or (of anger or excitement) to become less intense; calm down **18** **cool it** (*usually imperative*) *slang* to calm down; take it easy **19** **cool one's heels** to wait or be kept waiting ▷ See also **cool out** [Old English *cōl*; related to Old Norse *kōlna*, Old High German *kuoli*; see COLD, CHILL] > 'coolingly *adv* > 'coolingness *n* > 'coolish *adj* > 'coolly *adv* > 'coolness *n*

coolabah *or* **coolibah** ('ku:lə,bɑ:) *n* an Australian myrtaceous tree, *Eucalyptus microtheca*, that grows along rivers and has smooth bark and long narrow leaves [from a native Australian language]

coolamon ('ku:ləmɒn) *n Austral* a shallow dish of wood or bark, used for carrying water [C19 from a native Australian language]

coolant ('ku:lənt) *n* **1** a fluid used to cool a system or to transfer heat from one part of it to another **2** a liquid, such as an emulsion of oil, water, and soft soap, used to lubricate and cool the workpiece and cutting tool during machining

cool bag *or* **box** *n* an insulated container used to keep food cool on picnics, to carry frozen food, etc

cool drink *n South African* any soft drink

cooler ('ku:lə) *n* **1** a container, vessel, or apparatus for cooling, such as a heat exchanger **2** a slang word for **prison** **3** a drink consisting of wine, fruit juice, and carbonated water

Cooley's anaemia ('ku:lɪz) *n* another name for **thalassaemia** [named after Thomas B. *Cooley* (1871–1945), US paediatrician who reported on it in children in the Mediterranean area]

Coolgardie safe (ku:l'gɑ:dɪ) *n* a cupboard with wetted hessian walls for keeping food cool: used esp in Australia. Sometimes shortened to: **Coolgardie** [named after *Coolgardie*, Western Australia, perhaps because of resemblance to COOL and GUARD]

cool hunter *n informal* a person who is employed to identify future trends, esp in fashion or the media

coolie *or* **cooly** ('ku:lɪ) *n, pl* **-ies** **1** a cheaply hired unskilled Oriental labourer **2** *derogatory* an Indian living in South Africa [C17 from Hindi *kulī*, probably of Dravidian origin; related to Tamil *kūli* hire, hireling]

cooling-off period *n* **1** a period during which the contending sides to a dispute reconsider their options before taking further action **2** a statutory period, often 14 days, that begins when a sale contract or life-assurance policy is received by a member of the public, during which the contract or policy can be cancelled without loss

cooling tower *n* a tall hollow structure in which steam is condensed or water that is used as a coolant in some industrial process is allowed to cool for reuse by trickling down a surface

cool out *vb* (*intr, adverb*) *Caribbean* to relax and cool down

cool school *n NZ* a school where the students resolve conflict without the involvement of teachers

coolth (ku:lθ) *n* coolness [C16 originally dialect, from COOL + -TH[1]]

coom *or* **coomb** (ku:m) *n dialect, chiefly Scot and Northern English* waste material, such as dust from coal, grease from axles, etc [C16 (meaning: soot): probably a variant of CULM[1]]

coomb, combe, coombe *or* **comb** (ku:m) *n* **1** *chiefly Southern English* a short valley or deep hollow, esp in chalk areas **2** *chiefly Northern English* another name for a **cirque** [Old English *cumb* (in place names), probably of Celtic origin; compare Old French *combe* small valley and Welsh *cwm* valley]

coon (kuːn) *n* **1** *informal* short for **raccoon 2** *offensive slang* a Black or a native Australian **3** *South African offensive* a person of mixed race

cooncan ('kuːnˌkæn) *or* **conquian** *n* a card game for two players, similar to rummy [c19 from (Mexican) Spanish *con quién* with whom?, apparently with reference to the forming and declaring of sequences and sets of cards]

coonhound ('kuːnˌhaʊnd) *n* another name for **raccoon dog** (sense 2)

coon's age *n US slang* a long time

coonskin ('kuːnˌskɪn) *n* **1** the pelt of a raccoon **2** a raccoon cap with the tail hanging at the back **3** *US* an overcoat made of raccoon

coontie ('kuːntɪ) *n* **1** an evergreen plant, *Zamia floridana* of S Florida, related to the cycads and having large dark green leathery leaves: family *Zamiaceae* **2** a starch derived from the underground stems of this plant [c19 from Seminole *kunti* flour from this plant]

coop¹ (kuːp) *n* **1** a cage or small enclosure for poultry or small animals **2** a small narrow place of confinement, esp a prison cell **3** a wicker basket for catching fish ▷ *vb* **4** (*tr*; often foll by *up* or *in*) to confine in a restricted area [c15 probably from Middle Low German *kūpe* basket, tub; related to Latin *cūpa* cask, vat]

coop² *or* **co-op** ('kəʊˌɒp) *n* a cooperative, cooperative society, or shop run by a cooperative society

coop³ *an internet domain name for* a cooperative

coop. *or* **co-op.** *abbreviation for* cooperative

cooper ('kuːpə) *n* **1** Also called: hooper a person skilled in making and repairing barrels, casks, etc ▷ *vb* **2** (*tr*) to make or mend (barrels, casks, etc) **3** (*intr*) to work as a cooper [c13 from Middle Dutch *cūper* or Middle Low German *kūper*; see COOP¹]

cooperage ('kuːpərɪdʒ) *n* **1** Also called: coopery the craft, place of work, or products of a cooper **2** the labour fee charged by a cooper

cooperate *or* **co-operate** (kəʊˈɒpəˌreɪt) *vb* (*intr*) **1** to work or act together **2** to be of assistance or be willing to assist **3** *economics* (of firms, workers, consumers, etc) to engage in economic cooperation [c17 from Late Latin *cooperārī* to work with, combine, from Latin *operārī* to work] ▷ coˈoperˌator *or* co-ˈoperˌator *n*

cooperation *or* **co-operation** (kəʊˌɒpəˈreɪʃən) *n* **1** joint operation or action **2** assistance or willingness to assist **3** *economics* the combination of consumers, workers, farmers, etc, in activities usually embracing production, distribution, or trade **4** *ecology* beneficial but inessential interaction between two species in a community ▷ coˌoperˈationist *or* co-ˌoperˈationist *n*

cooperative *or* **co-operative** (kəʊˈɒpərətɪv, -ˈɒprə-) *adj* **1** willing to cooperate; helpful **2** acting in conjunction with others; cooperating **3 a** (of an enterprise, farm, etc) owned collectively and managed for joint economic benefit **b** (of an economy or economic activity) based on collective ownership and cooperative use of the means of production and distribution ▷ *n* **4** a cooperative organization **5** Also called: cooperative apartment *US* a block of flats belonging to a corporation in which shares are owned in proportion to the relative value of the flat occupied. Sometimes shortened to: coop. Compare **condominium** (sense 3) ▷ coˈoperatively *or* co-ˈoperatively *adv* ▷ coˈoperativeness *or* co-ˈoperativeness *n*

cooperative bank *n* a US name for **building society**

cooperative farm *n* **1** a farm that is run in cooperation with others in the purchasing and using of machinery, stock, etc, and in the marketing of produce through its own institutions (**farmers' cooperatives**) **2** a farm that is owned by a cooperative society **3** a farm run on a communal basis, such as a kibbutz **4** another

name for **collective farm**

Cooperative Party *n* (in Great Britain) a political party supporting the cooperative movement and linked with the Labour Party: founded in 1917

cooperative society *n* a commercial enterprise owned and managed by and for the benefit of customers or workers. Often shortened to: coop, co-op

cooperativity (kəʊˌɒpərəˈtɪvɪtɪ) *n biochem, chem* an interaction between structural units within a molecule or between molecules in an assemblage that enables the system to respond more sharply to an external change than would isolated units

Cooper Creek ('kuːpə) *n* an intermittent river in E central Australia, in the Channel Country: rises in central Queensland and flows generally southwest, reaching Lake Eyre only during wet-year floods; scene of the death of the explorers Burke and Wills in 1861; the surrounding basin provides cattle pastures after the floods subside. Total length: 1420 km (880 miles)

Cooper pair *n physics* a pair of weakly bound electrons responsible for the transfer of charge in a superconducting material [c20 named after Leon Neil Cooper (born 1930), US physicist]

Cooper's hawk *n* a small North American hawk, *Accipiter cooperii*, having a bluish-grey back and wings and a reddish-brown breast [c19 named after William *Cooper* (died 1864), American naturalist]

coopery ('kuːpərɪ) *n*, *pl* -eries another word for **cooperage** (sense 1)

co-opetition (ˌkəʊɒpəˈtɪʃən) *n* cooperation between competitors in business, esp in the computer industry

coopt *or* **co-opt** (kəʊˈɒpt) *vb* (*tr*) **1** to add (someone) to a committee, board, etc, by the agreement of the existing members **2** to appoint summarily; commandeer [c17 from Latin *cooptāre* to elect, from *optāre* to choose] ▷ coˈoption, co-ˈoption, ˌcoopˈtation *or* ˌco-opˈtation *n* ▷ coˈoptative *or* co-ˈoptative *adj*

Coopworth ('kuːpˌwɜːθ) *n* a New Zealand and Australian breed of sheep derived from the Romney Marsh

coordinal *or* **co-ordinal** (kəʊˈɔːdɪnəl) *adj* (of animals or plants) belonging to the same order

coordinate *or* **co-ordinate** *vb* (kəʊˈɔːdɪˌneɪt) **1** (*tr*) to organize or integrate (diverse elements) in a harmonious operation **2** to place (things) in the same class or order, or (of things) to be placed in the same class or order **3** to work together, esp harmoniously **4** (*intr*) to take or be in the form of a harmonious order **5** *chem* to form or cause to form a coordinate bond ▷ *n* (kəʊˈɔːdɪnɪt, -ˌneɪt) **6** *maths* any of a set of numbers that defines the location of a point in space. See **Cartesian coordinates, polar coordinates 7** a person or thing equal in rank, type, etc ▷ *adj* (kəʊˈɔːdɪnɪt, -ˌneɪt) **8** of, concerned with, or involving coordination **9** of the same rank, type, etc **10** of or involving the use of coordinates: *coordinate geometry* ▷ See also **coordinates**. ▷ coˈordinately *or* co-ˈordinately *adv* ▷ coˈordinateness *or* co-ˈordinateness *n* ▷ coˈordinative *or* co-ˈordinative *adj* ▷ coˈordiˌnator *or* co-ˈordiˌnator *n*

coordinate bond *n* a type of covalent chemical bond in which both the shared electrons are provided by one of the atoms. Also called: dative bond, semipolar bond

coordinate clause *n* one of two or more clauses in a sentence having the same status and introduced by coordinating conjunctions. Compare **subordinate clause**

coordinate geometry *n* another term for **analytical geometry**

coordinates (kəʊˈɔːdɪnɪts, -ˌneɪts) *pl n* clothes of matching or harmonious colours and design, suitable for wearing together. Compare **separates**

coordinating conjunction *n* a conjunction that introduces coordinate clauses, such as *and, but,* and *or*. Compare **subordinating conjunction**

coordination *or* **co-ordination** (kəʊˌɔːdɪˈneɪʃən) *n* balanced and effective interaction of movement, actions, etc [c17 from Late Latin *coordinātiō*, from Latin *ordinātiō* an arranging; see ORDINATE]

coordination compound *n* another name for **complex** (sense 8)

coordination number *n chem* the number of coordinated species surrounding the central atom in a complex or crystal

Coorg (kʊəg) *n* a former province of SW India: since 1956 part of Karnataka state

coorie ('kʊːrɪ) *vb* (*intr*) *Scot* a variant spelling of **courie**

coot (kuːt) *n* **1** any aquatic bird of the genus *Fulica*, esp *F. atra* of Europe and Asia, having lobed toes, dark plumage, and a white bill with a frontal shield: family *Rallidae* (rails, crakes, etc) **2** a foolish person, esp an old man (often in the phrase **old coot**) [c14 probably from Low German; compare Dutch *koet*]

cootch *or* **cwtch** (kʊtʃ) *South Wales dialect* ▷ *n* **1** a hiding place **2** a room, shed, etc, used for storage: *a coal cootch* ▷ *vb* **3** (*tr*) to hide **4** (often foll by *up*) to cuddle or be cuddled **5** (*tr*) to clasp (someone or something) to oneself [from French *couche* COUCH, probably influenced by Welsh *cwt* hut]

cootie ('kuːtɪ) *n US and NZ* a slang name for the **body louse** See **louse** (sense 1) Also called (NZ): kutu [c20 perhaps from Malay or Māori *kutu* louse]

cooze (kuːz) *n taboo slang, chiefly US and Canadian* **1** the female genitals **2** a girl or woman considered sexually [c20 of unknown origin]

cop¹ (kɒp) *slang* ▷ *n* **1** another name for **policeman 2** *Brit* an arrest (esp in the phrase **a fair cop**) **3** an instance of plagiarism ▷ *vb* cops, copping, copped (*tr*) **4** to seize or catch **5** to steal **6** to buy, steal, or otherwise obtain (illegal drugs). Compare **score** (sense 26) **7** Also: cop it to suffer (a punishment): *you'll cop a clout if you do that!* **8** cop it sweet *Austral slang* **a** to accept a penalty without complaint **b** to have good fortune ▷ See also **cop off, cop out** [c18 (vb) perhaps from obsolete *cap* to arrest, from Old French *caper* to seize; sense 1, back formation from COPPER²]

cop² (kɒp) *n* **1** a conical roll of thread wound on a spindle **2** *now chiefly dialect* the top or crest, as of a hill [Old English *cop, copp* top, summit, of uncertain origin; perhaps related to Old English *copp* CUP]

cop³ (kɒp) *n Brit slang* (usually used with a negative) worth or value: *that work is not much cop* [c19 n use of COP¹ (in the sense: to catch, hence something caught, something of value)]

COP (in New Zealand) *abbreviation for* Certificate of Proficiency: a pass in a university subject

copacetic, copasetic, copesetic *or* **copesettic** (ˌkəʊpəˈsɛtɪk) *adj US and Canadian slang* very good; excellent; completely satisfactory [c20 of unknown origin]

copaiba (kəʊˈpaɪbə) *or* **copaiva** (kəʊˈpaɪvə) *n* a transparent yellowish viscous oleoresin obtained from certain tropical South American trees of the leguminous genus *Copaifera*: used in varnishes and ointments. Also called: copaiba balsam, copaiba resin [c18 via Spanish via Portuguese from Tupi]

copal ('kəʊpəl, -pæl) *n* a hard aromatic resin, yellow, orange, or red in colour, obtained from various tropical trees and used in making varnishes and lacquers [c16 from Spanish, from Nahuatl *copalli* resin]

copalm ('kəʊˌpɑːm) *n* **1** the aromatic brown resin obtained from the sweet gum tree **2** another name for the **sweet gum** [c19 from Louisiana French, from Mexican Spanish *copalme*; see COPAL, PALMATE]

Copán (Spanish koˈpan) *n* a town in W Honduras: site of a ruined Mayan city. Pop: 21 200 (1991)

coparcenary (kəʊˈpɑːsənərɪ) *or* **coparceny** (kəʊˈpɑːsɪnɪ) *n law* a form of joint ownership of property, esp joint heirship. Also called: parcenary

coparcener (kəʊˈpɑːsɪnə) *n law* a person who

inherits an estate as coheir with others. Also called: **parcener**

copartner (kəʊˈpɑːtnə) *n* a partner or associate, esp an equal partner in business

copartnership (kəʊˈpɑːtnəʃɪp) *n* **1** a partnership or association between two equals, esp in a business enterprise **2** a form of industrial democracy in which the employees of an organization are partners in the company and share in part of its profits

cope[1] (kəʊp) *vb* **1** (*intr*; foll by *with*) to contend (against) **2** (*intr*) to deal successfully with or handle a situation; manage: *she coped well with the problem* **3** (*tr*) *archaic* **a** to deal with **b** to meet in battle [c14 from Old French *coper* to strike, cut, from *coup* blow; see COUP[1]]

cope[2] (kəʊp) *n* **1** a large ceremonial cloak worn at solemn liturgical functions by priests of certain Christian sects **2** any covering shaped like a cope ▷ *vb* **3** (*tr*) to dress (someone) in a cope [Old English *cāp*, from Medieval Latin *cāpa*, from Late Latin *cappa* hooded cloak; see CAP]

cope[3] (kəʊp) *vb* (*tr*) **1** to provide (a wall) with a coping **2** to join (two moulded timber members) ▷ *n* **3** another name for **coping** [c17 probably from French *couper* to cut; see COPE[1]]

copeck (ˈkəʊpɛk) *n* a variant spelling of **kopeck**

Copenhagen (ˌkəʊpənˈheɪɡən, -ˈhɑː-, ˈkəʊpənˌheɪ-, -ˌhɑː-) *n* the capital of Denmark, a port on Zealand and Amager Islands on a site inhabited for some 6000 years: exports chiefly agricultural products; iron and steel works; university (1479). Pop: 501 664 (2004 est). Danish name: **København**

Copenhagen blue *n* **a** a greyish-blue colour **b** (*as adjective*): *Copenhagen-blue markings*

Copenhagen interpretation *n* an interpretation of quantum mechanics developed by Niels Bohr and his colleagues at the University of Copenhagen, based on the concept of wave–particle duality and the idea that the observation influences the result of an experiment

copepod (ˈkəʊpɪˌpɒd) *n* **1** any minute free-living or parasitic crustacean of the subclass *Copepoda* of marine and fresh waters: an important constituent of plankton ▷ *adj* **2** of, relating to, or belonging to the *Copepoda* [from New Latin *Copepoda*, from Greek *kōpē* oar + *pous* foot]

coper (ˈkəʊpə) *n* a horse-dealer [c17 (a dealer, chapman): from dialect *cope* to buy, barter, from Low German; related to Dutch *koopen* to buy]

Copernican (kəˈpɜːnɪkən) *adj* of or relating to Nicolaus Copernicus, the Polish astronomer (1473–1543)

Copernican system *n* the theory published in 1543 by Copernicus (1473–1543) which stated that the earth and the planets rotated around the sun and which opposed the Ptolemaic system

Copernicus (kəˈpɜːnɪkəs) *n* a conspicuous crater on the moon, over 4000 metres deep and 90 kilometres in diameter, from which a system of rays emanates

copestone (ˈkəʊpˌstəʊn) *n* **1** Also called: **coping stone** a stone used to form a coping **2** Also called: **capstone** the stone at the top of a building, wall, etc

copier (ˈkɒpɪə) *n* **1** a person or device that copies **2** another word for **copyist**

copilot (ˈkəʊˌpaɪlət) *n* a second or relief pilot of an aircraft

coping (ˈkəʊpɪŋ) *n* the sloping top course of a wall, usually made of masonry or brick. Also called: **cope**

coping saw *n* a handsaw with a U-shaped frame used for cutting curves in a material too thick for a fret saw

coping stone *n* another word for **copestone** (sense 1)

copious (ˈkəʊpɪəs) *adj* **1** abundant; extensive in quantity **2** having or providing an abundant supply **3** full of words, ideas, etc; profuse [c14 from Latin *cōpiōsus* well supplied, from *cōpia*

abundance, from *ops* wealth] > **ˈcopiously** *adv* > **ˈcopiousness** *n*

copita (Spanish koˈpita; English kəˈpiːtə) *n* **1** a tulip-shaped sherry glass **2** a glass of sherry [diminutive of *copa* cup]

coplanar (kəʊˈpleɪnə) *adj* lying in the same plane: *coplanar lines* > ˌcoplaˈnarity *n*

cop off *vb* (*intr, adverb*) **cop off with** *Brit informal* to establish an amorous or sexual relationship with

copolymer (kəʊˈpɒlɪmə) *n* a chemical compound of high molecular weight formed by uniting the molecules of two or more different compounds (monomers). Compare **polymer, oligomer**

copolymerize *or* **copolymerise** (kəʊˈpɒlɪməˌraɪz) *vb* to react (two compounds) together to produce a copolymer > coˌpolymeriˈzation *or* coˌpolymeriˈsation *n*

cop out *slang* ▷ *vb* **1** (*intr, adverb*) to fail to assume responsibility or to commit oneself ▷ *n* **cop-out 2** an instance of avoiding responsibility or commitment **3** a person who acts in this way [c20 probably from COP[1]]

copper[1] (ˈkɒpə) *n* **1 a** a malleable ductile reddish metallic element occurring as the free metal, copper glance, and copper pyrites: used as an electrical and thermal conductor and in such alloys as brass and bronze. Symbol: Cu; atomic no.: 29; atomic wt.: 63.546; valency: 1 or 2; relative density: 8.96; melting pt.: 1084.87±0.2°C; boiling pt.: 2563°C. Related adjs: **cupric, cuprous**. Related prefix: **cupro- b** (*as modifier*): *a copper coin* **2 a** the reddish-brown colour of copper **b** (*as adjective*): *copper hair* **3** *informal* any copper or bronze coin **4** *chiefly Brit* a large vessel, formerly of copper, used for boiling or washing **5** any of various small widely distributed butterflies of the genera *Lycaena, Heodes*, etc, typically having reddish-brown wings: family *Lycaenidae* ▷ *vb* **6** (*tr*) to coat or cover with copper [Old English *coper*, from Latin *Cyprium aes* Cyprian metal, from Greek *Kupris* Cyprus] > ˈcoppery *adj*

copper[2] (ˈkɒpə) *n* a slang word for **policeman** Often shortened to: **cop** [c19 from COP[1] (vb) + -ER[1]]

copperas (ˈkɒpərəs) *n* a less common name for **ferrous sulphate** [c14 *coperose*, via Old French from Medieval Latin *cuperosa*, perhaps originally in the phrase *aqua cuprosa* copper water]

copper beech *n* a cultivated variety of European beech that has dark purple leaves

Copper Belt *n* a region of Central Africa, along the border between Zambia and the Democratic Republic of Congo: rich deposits of copper

copper-bottomed *adj* reliable, esp financially reliable [from the former practice of coating the bottoms of ships with copper to prevent the timbers rotting]

copper-fasten *vb* (*tr*) *Irish* to make (a bargain or agreement) binding

copperhead (ˈkɒpəˌhɛd) *n* **1** a venomous reddish-brown snake, *Agkistrodon contortrix*, of the eastern US: family *Crotalidae* (pit vipers) **2** a venomous reddish-brown Australian elapid snake, *Denisonia superba* **3** *US informal* a Yankee supporter of the South during the Civil War

copperplate (ˈkɒpəˌpleɪt) *n* **1** a polished copper plate on which a design has been etched or engraved **2** a print taken from such a plate **3** a fine handwriting based upon that used on copperplate engravings

copper pyrites (ˈpaɪraɪts) *n* (*functioning as singular*) another name for **chalcopyrite**

coppersmith (ˈkɒpəˌsmɪθ) *n* **1** a person who works copper or copper alloys **2** an Asian barbet (a bird), *Megalaima haemacephala*, the call of which has a ringing metallic note

copper sulphate *n* a copper salt found naturally as chalcanthite and made by the action of sulphuric acid on copper oxide. It usually exists as blue crystals of the pentahydrate that form a white anhydrous powder when heated: used as a mordant, in electroplating, and in plant sprays. Formula: $CuSO_4$

coppice (ˈkɒpɪs) *n* **1** a thicket or dense growth of small trees or bushes, esp one regularly trimmed back to stumps so that a continual supply of small poles and firewood is obtained ▷ *vb* **2** (*tr*) to trim back (trees or bushes) to form a coppice **3** (*intr*) to form a coppice [c14 from Old French *copeiz*, from *couper* to cut] > **ˈcoppiced** *adj* > **ˈcoppicing** *n*

copra (ˈkɒprə) *n* the dried, oil-yielding kernel of the coconut [c16 from Portuguese, from Malayalam *koppara*, probably from Hindi *khoprā* coconut]

copro- *or before a vowel* **copr-** *combining form* indicating dung or obscenity: *coprology* [from Greek *kopros* dung]

coprocessor (ˌkəʊˈprəʊsɛsə) *n* *computing* a microprocessor circuit that operates alongside and supplements the capabilities of the main processor, providing, for example, high-speed arithmetic

coprolalia (ˌkɒprəˈleɪlɪə) *n* obsessive use of obscene or foul language

coprolite (ˈkɒprəˌlaɪt) *n* any of various rounded stony nodules thought to be the fossilized faeces of Palaeozic-Cenozoic vertebrates > coprolitic (ˌkɒprəˈlɪtɪk) *adj*

coprology (kɒpˈrɒlədʒɪ) *n* preoccupation with excrement. Also called: **scatology**

coprophagous (kɒˈprɒfəɡəs) *adj* (esp of certain beetles) feeding on dung > copˈrophagy *n*

coprophilia (ˌkɒprəʊˈfɪlɪə) *n* an abnormal interest in faeces and their evacuation

coprophilous (kəˈprɒfɪləs) *or* **coprophilic** (ˌkɒprəʊˈfɪlɪk) *adj* growing in or on dung

coprosma (kəˈprɒzmə) *n* any shrub of the Australasian rubiaceous genus *Coprosma*: sometimes planted for ornament [c19 New Latin, from Greek *kopros* excrement + *osmē* smell]

coprozoic (ˌkɒprəʊˈzəʊɪk) *adj* (of animals) living in dung

copse (kɒps) *n* another word for **coppice** (sense 1) [c16 by shortening from COPPICE]

cop shop *n* *slang* a police station

Copt (kɒpt) *n* **1** a member of the Coptic Church **2** an Egyptian descended from the ancient Egyptians [c17 from Arabic *qubt* Copts, from Coptic *kyptios* Egyptian, from Greek *Aiguptios*, from *Aiguptos* Egypt]

copter *or* **'copter** (ˈkɒptə) *n* *informal* short for **helicopter**

Coptic (ˈkɒptɪk) *n* **1** an Afro-Asiatic language, written in the Greek alphabet but descended from ancient Egyptian. It was extinct as a spoken language by about 1600 AD but survives in the Coptic Church ▷ *adj* **2** of or relating to this language **3** of or relating to the Copts

Coptic Church *n* the ancient Christian Church of Egypt

copula (ˈkɒpjʊlə) *n, pl* **-las** *or* **-lae** (-ˌliː) **1** a verb, such as *be, seem*, or *taste*, that is used merely to identify or link the subject with the complement of a sentence. Copulas may serve to link nouns (or pronouns), as in *he became king*, nouns (or pronouns) and adjectival complements, as in *sugar tastes sweet*, or nouns (or pronouns) and adverbial complements, as in *John is in jail* **2** anything that serves as a link **3** *logic* the often unexpressed link between the subject and predicate terms of a categorial proposition, as *are* in *all men are mortal* [c17 from Latin: bond, connection, from *co-* together + *apere* to fasten] > **ˈcopular** *adj*

copulate (ˈkɒpjʊˌleɪt) *vb* (*intr*) to perform sexual intercourse [c17 from Latin *copulāre* to join together; see COPULA] > ˌcopuˈlation *n* > **ˈcopulatory** *adj*

copulative (ˈkɒpjʊlətɪv) *adj* **1** serving to join or unite **2** of or characteristic of copulation **3** *grammar* (of a verb) having the nature of a copula > **ˈcopulatively** *adv*

copy (ˈkɒpɪ) *n, pl* **copies 1** an imitation or reproduction of an original **2** a single specimen of something that occurs in a multiple edition, such as a book, article, etc **3 a** a matter to be reproduced in print **b** written matter or text as distinct from graphic material in books, newspapers, etc **4** the words used to present a promotional message in an advertisement **5** *journalism informal* suitable material for an article or story: *disasters are always good copy* **6** *archaic* a model to be copied, esp an example of penmanship ▷ *vb* **copies, copying, copied 7** (when *tr*, often foll by *out*) to make a copy or reproduction of (an original) **8** (*tr*) to imitate as a model **9** (*intr*) to imitate unfairly [c14 from Medieval Latin *cōpia* an imitation, something copied, from Latin: abundance, riches; see COPIOUS]

copybook ('kɒpɪ,bʊk) *n* **1** a book of specimens, esp of penmanship, for imitation **2** *chiefly US* a book for or containing documents **3 blot one's copybook** *informal* to spoil one's reputation by making a mistake, offending against social customs, etc **4** (*modifier*) trite or unoriginal: *copybook sentiments*

copycat ('kɒpɪ,kæt) *n informal* **a** a person, esp a child, who imitates or copies another **b** (*as modifier*): *copycat murders*

copy desk *n journalism* a desk where copy is edited

copy-edit *vb journalism* to prepare (copy) for printing by styling, correcting, etc ▷ **copy editor** *n*

copygraph ('kɒpɪ,grɑːf, -,græf) *n* another name for **hectograph**

copyhold ('kɒpɪ,həʊld) *n law* (formerly) **a** a tenure less than freehold of land in England evidenced by a copy of the Court roll **b** land held in this way

copyholder ('kɒpɪ,həʊldə) *n* **1** *printing* one who reads aloud from the copy as the proof corrector follows the reading in the proof **2** *printing* a device that holds copy in place for the compositor **3** *law* (formerly) a person who held land by copyhold tenure

copyist ('kɒpɪɪst) *n* **1** a person who makes written copies; transcriber **2** a person who imitates or copies

copyread ('kɒpɪ,riːd) *vb* **-reads, -reading, -read** *US* to subedit

copyreader ('kɒpɪ,riːdə) *n US* a person who edits and prepares newspaper copy for publication; subeditor

copyright ('kɒpɪ,raɪt) *n* **1** the exclusive right to produce copies and to control an original literary, musical, or artistic work, granted by law for a specified number of years (in Britain, usually 70 years from the death of the author, composer, etc, or from the date of publication if later). Symbol: (c) ▷ *adj* **2** (of a work, etc) subject to or controlled by copyright ▷ *vb* **3** (*tr*) to take out a copyright on ▷ '**copy,rightable** *adj* ▷ '**copy,righter** *n*

copyright deposit library *n* one of six libraries legally entitled to receive a gratis copy of every book published in the United Kingdom: the British Library, Bodleian, Cambridge University, Trinity College in Dublin, Scottish National Library, and National Library of Wales

copytaker ('kɒpɪ,teɪkə) *n* (esp in a newspaper office) a person employed to type reports as journalists dictate them over the telephone

copy taster *n* a person who selects or approves text for publication, esp in a periodical

copy typist *n* a typist whose job is to type from written or typed drafts rather than dictation

copywriter ('kɒpɪ,raɪtə) *n* a person employed to write advertising copy ▷ 'copy,writing *n*

coq au vin *French* (kɔk o vɛ̃) *n* chicken stewed with red wine, onions, etc [literally: cock with wine]

coquelicot ('kəʊklɪ,kəʊ) *n* another name for **corn poppy** [c18 from French: crow of a cock, from its resemblance to a cock's comb]

coquet (kəʊ'kɛt, kɒ-) *vb* **-quets, -quetting, -quetted** (*intr*) **1** to behave flirtatiously **2** to dally or trifle [c17 from French: a gallant, literally: a little cock, from *coq* cock]

coquetry ('kəʊkɪtrɪ, 'kɒk-) *n, pl* **-ries** flirtation

coquette (kəʊ'kɛt, kɒ'kɛt) *n* **1** a woman who flirts

2 any hummingbird of the genus *Lophornis,* esp the crested Brazilian species *L. magnifica* [c17 from French, feminine of COQUET] ▷ co'quettish *adj* ▷ co'quettishly *adv* ▷ co'quettishness *n*

coquilla nut (kɒ'kiːljə) *n* the nut of a South American palm tree, *Attalea funifera,* having a hard brown shell used for carving. See also **cohune** [c19 from Portuguese *coquilho,* diminutive of *côco* coconut; see COCO]

coquille (*French* kɔkij) *n* **1** any dish, esp seafood, served in a scallop shell: *Coquilles St Jacques* **2** a scallop shell, or dish resembling a shell **3** *fencing* a bell-shaped hand guard on a foil [French, literally: shell, from Latin *conchȳlium* mussel; see COCKLE¹]

coquimbite (kɒ'kɪmbaɪt) *n mineralogy* hydrated ferric sulphate found in certain rocks and in volcanic fumaroles [c19 from *Coquimbo,* Chilean province where it was originally found, + -ITE¹]

coquina (kɒ'kiːnə) *n* a soft limestone consisting of shells, corals, etc, that occurs in parts of the US [c19 from Spanish: shellfish, probably from *concha* shell, CONCH]

coquito (kɒ'kiːtəʊ) *n, pl* **-tos** a Chilean palm tree, *Jubaea spectabilis,* yielding edible nuts and a syrup [c19 from Spanish: a little coco palm, from *coco* coco palm]

cor (kɔː) *interj Brit slang* an exclamation of surprise, amazement, or admiration [c20 corruption of *God*]

Cor. *Bible abbreviation for* Corinthians

coraciiform (,kɒrə'saɪɪ,fɔːm) *adj* of, relating to, or belonging to the *Coraciiformes,* an order of birds including the kingfishers, bee-eaters, hoopoes, and hornbills [c20 from New Latin *Coracias* name of genus, from Greek *korakias* a chough + -I- + -FORM; related to Greek *korax* raven]

coracle ('kɒrək²l) *n* a small roundish boat made of waterproofed hides stretched over a wicker frame [c16 from Welsh *corwgl;* related to Irish *curach* boat]

coracoid ('kɒrə,kɔɪd) *n* a paired ventral bone of the pectoral girdle in vertebrates. In mammals it is reduced to a peg (the **coracoid process**) on the scapula [c18 from New Latin *coracoīdēs,* from Greek *korakoeidēs* like a raven, curved like a raven's beak, from *korax* raven]

coral ('kɒrəl) *n* **1** any marine mostly colonial coelenterate of the class *Anthozoa* having a calcareous, horny, or soft skeleton. See also **stony coral, sea fan 2 a** the calcareous or horny material forming the skeleton of certain of these animals **b** (*as modifier*): *a coral reef.* See also **red coral 3 a** a rocklike aggregation of certain of these animals or their skeletons, forming an island or reef **b** (*as modifier*): *a coral island* **4 a** an object made of coral, esp a piece of jewellery **b** (*as modifier*): *a coral necklace* **5 a** deep-pink to yellowish-pink colour **b** (*as adjective*): *coral lipstick* **6** the roe of a lobster or crab, which becomes pink when cooked [c14 from Old French, from Latin *corāllium,* from Greek *korallion,* probably of Semitic origin]

coral fern *n Austral* a scrambling fern of the genus *Gleichenia,* having repeatedly forked fronds

coralline ('kɒrə,laɪn) *adj* **1** Also: **coralloid** of, relating to, or resembling coral **2** of the colour of coral ▷ *n* **3** any of various red algae impregnated with calcium carbonate, esp any of the genus *Corallina* **4** any of various animals that resemble coral, such as certain sponges [c16 from Late Latin *corallīnus* coral red, from Latin *corāllium* CORAL]

corallite ('kɒrə,laɪt) *n* the skeleton of a coral polyp

coralloid ('kɒrə,lɔɪd) *adj* of or resembling coral

coral reef *n* a marine ridge or reef consisting of coral and other organic material consolidated into limestone

coralroot ('kɒrəl,ruːt) *n* any N temperate leafless orchid of the genus *Corallorhiza,* with small yellow-green or purple flowers and branched roots resembling coral

Coral Sea *n* the SW arm of the Pacific, between

Australia, New Guinea, and Vanuatu

coral snake *n* **1** any venomous elapid snake of the genus *Micrurus* and related genera, of tropical and subtropical America, marked with red, black, yellow, and white transverse bands **2** any of various other brightly coloured elapid snakes of Africa and SE Asia

coral tree *n Austral* any of various thorny trees of the leguminous genus *Erythrina,* having bright red flowers and reddish shiny seeds

coral trout *n* an Australian fish, *Plectropomus maculatus,* of the Great Barrier Reef which is an important food fish

coram populo Latin ('kɔːræm 'pɒpʊ,ləʊ) *adv* in the presence of the people; publicly

cor anglais ('kɔːr 'ɑːŋgleɪ) *n, pl* **cors anglais** ('kɔːz 'ɑːŋgleɪ) *music* a woodwind instrument, the alto of the oboe family. It is a transposing instrument in F. Range: two and a half octaves upwards from E on the third space of the bass staff. Also called: English horn [c19 from French: English horn]

Corantijn ('kɒrən,teɪn) *n* the Dutch name of **Courantyne**

coranto (kɒ'ræntəʊ) *n, pl* **-tos** a variant of **courante**

corban ('kɔːbən; *Hebrew* kɔr'ban) *n* **1** *Old Testament* a gift to God **2** *New Testament, Judaism* the Temple treasury or a consecration or gift to it (Matthew 27:6; Mark 7:11) [c14 from Late Latin, from Greek *korban,* from Hebrew *qorbān* offering, literally: a drawing near]

corbeil *or* **corbeille** ('kɔːb²l; *French* kɔrbɛj) *n architect* a carved ornament in the form of a basket of fruit, flowers, etc [c18 from French *corbeille* basket, from Late Latin *corbicula* a little basket, from Latin *corbis* basket]

corbel ('kɔːb²l) *architect* ▷ *n* **1** Also called: **truss** a bracket, usually of stone or brick ▷ *vb* **-bels, -belling, -belled** *or US* **-bels, -beling, -beled 2** (*tr*) to lay (a stone or brick) so that it forms a corbel [c15 from Old French, literally: a little raven, from Medieval Latin *corvellus,* from Latin *corvus* raven]

corbelling *or US* **corbeling** ('kɔːbəlɪŋ) *n* a set of corbels stepped outwards, one above another

corbel out *or* **off** *vb* (*tr, adverb*) to support on corbels

Corbett ('kɔːbət) *n mountaineering* any separate mountain peak between 2500 feet and 3000 feet high: originally used of Scotland only, but now sometimes extended to other parts of the British Isles

corbicula (kɔː'bɪkjʊlə) *n, pl* **-lae** (-,liː) the technical name for **pollen basket** [c19 from Late Latin, diminutive of Latin *corbis* basket]

corbie ('kɔːbɪ; *Scot* 'kɔːrbɪ) *n* a Scot name for **raven¹** *or* **crow¹** [c15 from Old French *corbin,* from Latin *corvīnus* CORVINE]

corbie gable *n architect* a gable having corbie-steps

corbie-step *or* **corbel step** *n architect* any of a set of steps on the top of a gable. Also called: **crow step**

cor blimey ('kɔː 'blaɪmɪ) *or* **gorblimey** *interj Brit slang* an exclamation of surprise or annoyance [c20 corruption of *God blind me*]

Corby ('kɔːbɪ) *n* a town in central England, in N Northamptonshire: designated a new town in 1950. Pop: 49 222 (2001)

Corcovado *n* **1** (*Spanish* korko'βaðo) a volcano in S Chile, in the Andes. Height: 2300 m (7546 ft) **2** (*Portuguese* korku'va:du) a mountain in SE Brazil, in SW Rio de Janeiro city, famous for a massive statue of Christ the Redeemer. Height: 704 m (2310 ft)

Corcyra (kɔː'saɪərə) *n* the ancient name for **Corfu**

cord (kɔːd) *n* **1** string or thin rope made of several twisted strands **2** a length of woven or twisted strands of silk, etc, sewn on clothing or used as a belt **3** a ribbed fabric, esp corduroy **4** any influence that binds or restrains **5** *US and Canadian* a flexible insulated electric cable, used esp to connect appliances to mains. Also called (in

C

Britain and certain other countries): **flex 6** *anatomy* any part resembling a string or rope: *the spinal cord* **7** a unit of volume for measuring cut wood, equal to 128 cubic feet ▷ *vb* (*tr*) **8** to bind or furnish with a cord or cords **9** to stack (wood) in cords [c13 from Old French *corde,* from Latin *chorda* cord, from Greek *khordē;* see CHORD¹] › 'cord,like *adj*

cordage ('kɔːdɪdʒ) *n* **1** *nautical* the lines and rigging of a vessel **2** an amount of wood measured in cords

cordate ('kɔːdeɪt) *adj* heart-shaped: *a cordate leaf; cordate shells* › 'cordately *adv*

corded ('kɔːdɪd) *adj* **1** bound or fastened with cord **2** (of a fabric) ribbed **3** (of muscles) standing out like cords

Cordelier (,kɔːdɪ'lɪə) *n* RC Church a Franciscan friar of the order of the Friars Minor [c19 from Old French *cordelle,* literally: a little cord, from the knotted cord girdles that they wear]

Cordeliers (,kɔːdɪ'lɪəz) *n* **the** a political club founded in 1790 and meeting at an old Cordelier convent in Paris

cord grass *n* a coarse perennial grass of the genus *Spartina,* characteristically growing in mud or marsh. Also called: **rice grass**

cordial ('kɔːdɪəl) *adj* **1** warm and friendly: *a cordial greeting* **2** giving heart; stimulating ▷ *n* **3** a drink with a fruit base, usually in concentrated form and diluted with water before being drunk: *lime cordial* **4** another word for **liqueur** [c14 from Medieval Latin *cordiālis,* from Latin *cor* heart] › 'cordially *adv* › 'cordialness *n*

cordiality (,kɔːdɪ'ælɪtɪ) *n, pl* **-ties** warmth of feeling

cordierite ('kɔːdɪə,raɪt) *n* a grey or violet-blue dichroic mineral that consists of magnesium aluminium iron silicate in orthorhombic crystalline form and is found in metamorphic rocks. Formula: $(Mg,Fe)_2AL_4Si_5O_{18}.nH_2O$. Also called: **dichroite, iolite** [c19 named after Pierre L. A. *Cordier* (1777–1861), French geologist who described it]

cordiform ('kɔːdɪ,fɔːm) *adj* heart-shaped [c19 from Latin *cor* heart]

cordillera (,kɔːdɪ'ljɛərə) *n* a series of parallel ranges of mountains, esp in the northwestern US [c18 from Spanish, from *cordilla,* literally: a little cord, from *cuerda* mountain range, CORD] › ,cordil'leran *adj*

Cordilleras (,kɔːdɪ'ljɛərəz; *Spanish* korði'ʎeras) *pl n* **the** the complex of mountain ranges on the W side of the Americas, extending from Alaska to Cape Horn and including the Andes and the Rocky Mountains

cordite ('kɔːdaɪt) *n* any of various explosive materials used for propelling bullets, shells, etc, containing cellulose nitrate, sometimes mixed with nitroglycerine, plasticizers, and stabilizers [c19 from CORD + -ITE¹, referring to its stringy appearance]

cordless ('kɔːdlɪs) *adj* (of an electrical device) operated by an internal battery so that no connection to mains supply or other apparatus is needed

cordless telephone *n* a portable battery-powered telephone with a short-range radio link to a fixed base unit

córdoba ('kɔːdəbə) *n* the standard monetary unit of Nicaragua, divided into 100 centavos [named in honour of Francisco Fernández de *Córdoba* (died 1518), Spanish explorer]

Córdoba (*Spanish* 'kɔrðoβa) *n* **1** a city in central Argentina: university (1613). Pop: 1 592 000 (2005 est) **2** a city in S Spain, on the Guadalquivir River: centre of Moorish Spain (711–1236). Pop: 318 628 (2003 est). English name: **Cordova**

cordon ('kɔːdᵊn) *n* **1** a chain of police, soldiers, ships, etc, stationed around an area **2** a ribbon worn as insignia of honour or rank **3** a cord or ribbon worn as an ornament or fastening **4** Also called: **string course, belt course, table** *architect*

an ornamental projecting band or continuous moulding along a wall **5** *horticulture* a form of fruit tree consisting of a single stem bearing fruiting spurs, produced by cutting back all lateral branches ▷ *vb* **6** (*tr;* often foll by *off*) to put or form a cordon (around); close (off) [c16 from Old French, literally: a little cord, from *corde* string, CORD]

cordon bleu (*French* kɔrdɔ̃ blø) *n* **1** *French history* **a** the sky-blue ribbon worn by members of the highest order of knighthood under the Bourbon monarchy **b** a knight entitled to wear the cordon bleu **2** any very high distinction ▷ *adj* **3** of or denoting food prepared to a very high standard [French, literally: blue ribbon]

cordon sanitaire *French* (kɔrdɔ̃ saniter) *n* **1** a guarded line serving to cut off an infected area **2** a line of buffer states, esp when protecting a nation from infiltration or attack [c19 literally: sanitary line]

Cordova ('kɔːdəvə) *n* the English name for **Córdoba** (sense 2)

cordovan ('kɔːdəvᵊn) *n* a fine leather now made principally from horsehide, isolated from the skin layers above and below it and tanned [c16 from Spanish *cordobán* (n), from *cordobán* (adj) of CÓRDOBA]

Cordovan ('kɔːdəvᵊn) *n* **1** a native or inhabitant of Córdoba, Spain ▷ *adj* **2** of or relating to Córdoba, Spain

cords (kɔːdz) *pl n* trousers, esp jeans, made of corduroy

corduroy ('kɔːdə,rɔɪ, ,kɔːdə'rɔɪ) *n* **a** a heavy cotton pile fabric with lengthways ribs **b** (*as modifier*): *a corduroy coat* ▷ See also **corduroys** [c18 perhaps from the proper name *Corderoy*]

corduroy road *n* a road across swampy ground, made of logs laid transversely

corduroys (,kɔːdə'rɔɪz, 'kɔːdə,rɔɪz) *pl n* trousers or breeches of corduroy

cordwain ('kɔːd,weɪn) *n* an archaic name for **cordovan** [c12 *cordewan,* from Old French *cordoan,* from Old Spanish *cordovan* CORDOVAN]

cordwainer ('kɔːd,weɪnə) *n* archaic a shoemaker or worker in cordovan leather › 'cord,wainery *n*

cordwood ('kɔːd,wʊd) *n* wood that has been cut into lengths of four feet so that it can be stacked in cords

core (kɔː) *n* **1** the central part of certain fleshy fruits, such as the apple or pear, consisting of the seeds and supporting parts **2 a** the central, innermost, or most essential part of something: *the core of the argument* **b** (*as modifier*): *the core meaning* **3** a piece of magnetic material, such as soft iron, placed inside the windings of an electromagnet or transformer to intensify and direct the magnetic field **4** *geology* the central part of the earth, beneath the mantle, consisting mainly of iron and nickel, which has an inner solid part surrounded by an outer liquid part **5** a cylindrical sample of rock, soil, etc, obtained by the use of a hollow drill **6** shaped body of material (in metal casting usually of sand) supported inside a mould to form a cavity of predetermined shape in the finished casting **7** *physics* the region of a nuclear reactor in which the reaction takes place **8** a layer of wood serving as a backing for a veneer **9** *computing* **a** a ferrite ring formerly used in a computer memory to store one bit of information **b** short for **core store c** (*as modifier*): *core memory* **10** *archaeol* a lump of stone or flint from which flakes or blades have been removed **11** *physics* the nucleus together with all complete electron shells of an atom ▷ *vb* **12** (*tr*) to remove the core from (fruit) [c14 of uncertain origin] › 'coreless *adj*

CORE (kɔː) *n* (in the US) *acronym for* Congress of Racial Equality

-core *n combining form* indicating a type of popular music: *dancecore*

coreferential (,kəʊrɛfə'rɛnʃəl) *adj philosophy* (of more than one linguistic expression) designating the same individual or class

coreligionist (,kəʊrɪ'lɪdʒənɪst) *n* an adherent of the same religion as another

corella (kə'rɛlə) *n* any of certain white Australian cockatoos of the genus *Kakatoe* [c19 probably from native Australian *carall*]

coreopsis (,kɒrɪ'ɒpsɪs) *n* any plant of the genus *Coreopsis,* of America and tropical Africa, cultivated for their yellow, brown, or yellow-and-red daisy-like flowers: family *Asteraceae* (composites). Also called: **calliopsis** Compare **caryopsis** [c18 from New Latin, from Greek *koris* bedbug + -OPSIS; so called from the appearance of the seed]

co-respondent (,kəʊrɪ'spɒndənt) *n law* a person cited in divorce proceedings, who is alleged to have committed adultery with the respondent › ,co-re'spondency *n*

co-respondent shoes *pl n* men's two-coloured shoes, usually black and white or brown and white. Also called: **co-respondents**

core store *n* an obsolete type of computer memory made up of a matrix of cores

core subjects *pl n* Brit education three foundation subjects (English, mathematics, and science) that are compulsory throughout each key stage in the National Curriculum

core time *n* See flexitime

corf (kɔːf) *n, pl* **corves** Brit a wagon or basket used formerly in mines [c14 from Middle Dutch *corf* or Middle Low German *korf,* probably from Latin *corbis* basket]

Corfam ('kɔːfæm) *n trademark* a synthetic water-repellent material used as a substitute for shoe leather

Corfu (kɔː'fuː) *n* **1** an island in the Ionian Sea, in the Ionian Islands: forms, with neighbouring islands, a department of Greece. Pop: 107 879 (2001). Area: 641 sq km (247 sq miles) **2** a port on E Corfu island. Pop: 107 879 (1995 est). Modern Greek name: **Kérkyra** Ancient name: **Corcyra**

corgi ('kɔːgɪ) *n* either of two long-bodied short-legged sturdy breeds of dog, the Cardigan and the Pembroke. Also called: **Welsh corgi** [c20 from Welsh, from *cor* dwarf + *ci* dog]

coriaceous (,kɔːrɪ'eɪʃəs) *or* **corious** *adj* of or resembling leather [c17 from Late Latin *coriāceus* from *corium* leather]

coriander (,kɒrɪ'ændə) *n* a European umbelliferous plant, *Coriandrum sativum,* widely cultivated for its aromatic seeds and leaves, used in flavouring food, etc. US and Canadian name: **cilantro** [c14 from Old French *coriandre,* from Latin *coriandrum,* from Greek *koriannon,* of uncertain origin]

Corinth ('kɒrɪnθ) *n* **1** a port in S Greece, in the NE Peloponnese: the modern town is near the site of the ancient city, the largest and richest of the city-states after Athens. Pop: 29 600 (1995 est). Modern Greek name: **Kórinthos 2** a region of ancient Greece, occupying most of the Isthmus of Corinth and part of the NE Peloponnese **3 Gulf of** Also called: **Gulf of Lepanto** an inlet of the Ionian Sea between the Peloponnese and central Greece **4 Isthmus of** a narrow strip of land between the Gulf of Corinth and the Saronic Gulf: crossed by the **Corinth Canal** making navigation possible between the gulfs

Corinthian (kə'rɪnθɪən) *adj* **1** of, characteristic of, or relating to Corinth **2** of, denoting, or relating to one of the five classical orders of architecture: characterized by a bell-shaped capital having carved ornaments based on acanthus leaves. See also **Ionic, Doric, Composite, Tuscan 3** given to luxury; dissolute **4** ornate and elaborate ▷ *n* **5** a native or inhabitant of Corinth **6** an amateur sportsman **7** *rare* a man about town, esp one who is dissolute

Corinthians (kə'rɪnθɪənz) *n* (*functioning as singular*) either of two books of the New Testament (in full **The First and Second Epistles of Paul the Apostle to the Corinthians**)

Coriolis force (,kɒrɪ'əʊlɪs) *n* a fictitious force used to explain a deflection in the path of a body moving in latitude relative to the earth when observed from the earth. The deflection (**Coriolis effect**) is due to the earth's rotation and is to the east when the motion is towards a pole [c19 named after Gaspard G. *Coriolis* (1792–1843), French civil engineer]

corious ('kɔːrɪəs) *adj* a variant of **coriaceous**

corium ('kɔːrɪəm) *n, pl* -ria (-rɪə) **1** Also called: **derma, dermis** the deep inner layer of the skin, beneath the epidermis, containing connective tissue, blood vessels, and fat **2** *entomol* the leathery basal part of the forewing of hemipterous insects [c19 from Latin: rind, skin, leather]

corixid (kə'rɪksɪd) *n* **1** any heteropterous water bug of the vegetarian family *Corixidae*, typified by *Corixa punctata*, common in sluggish waters. The forelegs have become modified and are used in stridulation, as by the **water singer** (*Micronecta poweri*). See also **water boatman** ▷ *adj* **2** of or relating to the Corixidae [from New Latin *corixa*, from Greek *koris* bedbug]

cork (kɔːk) *n* **1** the thick light porous outer bark of the cork oak, used widely as an insulator and for stoppers for bottles, casks, etc **2** a piece of cork or other material used as a stopper **3** an angling float **4** Also called: **phellem** *botany* a protective layer of dead impermeable cells on the outside of the stems and roots of woody plants, produced by the outer layer of the cork cambium ▷ *adj* **5** made of cork. Related adj: **suberose** ▷ *vb* (*tr*) **6** to stop up (a bottle, cask, etc) with or as if with a cork; fit with a cork **7** (often foll by *up*) to restrain: *to cork up the emotions* **8** to black (the face, hands, etc) with burnt cork [c14 probably from Arabic *qurq*, from Latin *cortex* bark, especially of the cork oak] ▷ 'cork,like *adj*

Cork (kɔːk) *n* **1** a county of SW Republic of Ireland, in Munster province: crossed by ridges of low mountains; scenic coastline. County town: Cork. Pop: 447 829 (2002). Area: 7459 sq km (2880 sq miles) **2** a city and port in S Republic of Ireland, county town of Co Cork, at the mouth of the River Lee: seat of the University College of Cork (1849). Pop: 186 239 (2002). Gaelic name: **Corcaigh**

corkage ('kɔːkɪdʒ) *n* a charge made at a restaurant for serving wine, etc, bought off the premises

corkboard ('kɔːk,bɔːd) *n* a thin slab made of granules of cork, used as a floor or wall finish and as an insulator

cork cambium *n* a layer of meristematic cells in the cortex of the stems and roots of woody plants, the outside of which gives rise to cork cells and the inside to secondary cortical cells (phelloderm). Also called: **phellogen**

corked (kɔːkt) *adj* **1** Also: **corky** (of a wine) tainted through having a cork containing excess tannin **2** (*postpositive*) *Brit* a slang word for **drunk**

corker ('kɔːkə) *n* **1** *slang* **a** something or somebody striking or outstanding: *that was a corker of a joke* **b** an irrefutable remark that puts an end to discussion **2** a person or machine that inserts corks

corking ('kɔːkɪŋ) *adj* (*prenominal*) *Brit slang* excellent

cork oak *n* an evergreen Mediterranean oak tree, *Quercus suber*, with a porous outer bark from which cork is obtained. Also called: **cork tree**

Corkonian (kɔː'kəʊnɪən, kə'kəʊnɪən) *n* a native or inhabitant of the city of Cork

corkscrew ('kɔːk,skruː) *n* **1** a device for drawing corks from bottles, typically consisting of a pointed metal spiral attached to a handle or screw mechanism **2** *boxing slang* a blow that ends with a twist of the fist, esp one intended to cut the opponent **3** (*modifier*) resembling a corkscrew in shape ▷ *vb* **4** to move or cause to move in a spiral or zigzag course

cork-tipped ('kɔːk,tɪpt) *adj* (of a cigarette) having a filter of cork or some material resembling cork

corkwing ('kɔːk,wɪŋ) *n* a greenish or bluish European fish of the wrasse family, *Ctenolabrus melops* [of uncertain origin]

corkwood ('kɔːk,wʊd) *n* **1** a small tree, *Leitneria floridana*, of the southeastern US, having very lightweight porous wood: family *Leitneriaceae* **2** any other tree with light porous wood **3** the wood of any of these trees

corm (kɔːm) *n* an organ of vegetative reproduction in plants such as the crocus, consisting of a globular stem base swollen with food and surrounded by papery scale leaves. Compare **bulb** (sense 1) [c19 from New Latin *cormus*, from Greek *kormos* tree trunk from which the branches have been lopped] ▷ 'cormous *adj*

cormel ('kɔːmel) *n* a new small corm arising from the base of a fully developed one

cormophyte ('kɔːmə,faɪt) *n* any of the *Cormophyta*, a major division (now obsolete) of plants having a stem, root, and leaves: includes the mosses, ferns, and seed plants [c19 from Greek *kormos* tree trunk + -PHYTE] ▷ cormophytic (,kɔːmə'fɪtɪk) *adj*

cormorant ('kɔːmərənt) *n* any aquatic bird of the family *Phalacrocoracidae*, of coastal and inland waters, having a dark plumage, a long neck and body, and a slender hooked beak: order *Pelecaniformes* (pelicans, etc) [c13 from Old French *cormareng*, from *corp* raven, from Latin *corvus* + -*mareng* of the sea, from Latin *mare* sea]

corn¹ (kɔːn) *n* **1** *Brit* **a** any of various cereal plants, esp the predominant crop of a region, such as wheat in England and oats in Scotland and Ireland **b** the seeds of such plants, esp after harvesting **c** a single seed of such plants; a grain **2** Also called: **Indian corn** British equivalent: **maize a** a tall annual grass, *Zea mays*, cultivated for its yellow edible grains, which develop on a spike **b** the grain of this plant, used for food, fodder, and as a source of oil. See also **sweet corn** (sense 1), **popcorn** (sense 1) **3 a** the plants producing these kinds of grain considered as a growing crop: *spring corn* **b** (*in combination*): *a cornfield* **4** short for **corn whisky 5** *slang* an idea, song, etc, regarded as banal or sentimental **6** *archaic or dialect* any hard particle or grain ▷ *vb* (*tr*) **7** to feed (animals) with corn, esp oats **8 a** to preserve in brine **b** to salt **9** to plant corn on [Old English *corn*; related to Old Norse, Old High German *corn*, Gothic *kaúrn*, Latin *grānum*, Sanskrit *jīrná* fragile]

corn² (kɔːn) *n* **1** a hardening or thickening of the skin around a central point in the foot, caused by pressure or friction **2 tread on (someone's) corns** *Brit informal* to offend or hurt (someone) by touching on a sensitive subject or encroaching on his privileges [c15 from Old French *corne* horn, from Latin *cornū*]

cornaceous (kɔː'neɪʃəs) *adj* of, relating to, or belonging to the *Cornaceae*, a family of temperate plants, mostly trees and shrubs, including dogwood, cornel, and spotted laurel (see **laurel**(sense 5)) [c19 from New Latin *Cornaceae*, from *Cornus* genus name, from Latin: CORNEL]

cornball ('kɔːn,bɔːl) *chiefly US* ▷ *n* **1** a person given to mawkish or unsophisticated behaviour ▷ *adj* **2** another word for **corny** [c20 from *corn ball* a sweet consisting of a ball of popcorn and molasses]

corn borer *n* the larva of the pyralid moth *Pyrausta nubilalis*, native to S and Central Europe: in E North America a serious pest of maize

corn bread *n* a kind of bread made from maize meal. Also called: **Indian bread**

corn bunting *n* a heavily built European songbird, *Emberiza calandra*, with a streaked brown plumage: family *Emberizidae* (buntings)

corn circle *n* another name for **crop circle**

corncob ('kɔːn,kɒb) *n* **1** the core of an ear of maize, to which kernels are attached **2** short for **corncob pipe**

corncob pipe *n* a pipe made from a dried corncob

corncockle ('kɔːn,kɒkᵊl) *n* a European caryophyllaceous plant, *Agrostemma githago*, that has reddish-purple flowers and grows in cornfields and by roadsides

corncrake ('kɔːn,kreɪk) *n* a common Eurasian rail, *Crex crex*, of fields and meadows, with a buff speckled plumage and reddish wings

corncrib ('kɔːn,krɪb) *n chiefly US and Canadian* a ventilated building for the storage of unhusked maize

corn dolly *n* a decorative figure made by plaiting straw

cornea ('kɔːnɪə) *n, pl* -neas (-nɪəz) *or* -neae (-nɪ,iː) the convex transparent membrane that forms the anterior covering of the eyeball and is continuous with the sclera [c14 from Medieval Latin *cornea tēla* horny web, from Latin *cornū* HORN] ▷ 'corneal *adj*

corn earworm *n US* the larva of the noctuid moth *Heliothis armigera*, which feeds on maize and many other crop plants. See also **bollworm**

corned (kɔːnd) *adj* (esp of beef) cooked and then preserved or pickled in salt or brine, now often canned

cornel ('kɔːnᵊl) *n* any cornaceous plant of the genus *Cornus*, such as the dogwood and dwarf cornel [c16 probably from Middle Low German *kornelle*, from Old French *cornelle*, from Vulgar Latin *cornicula* (unattested), from Latin *cornum* cornel cherry, from *cornus* cornel tree]

cornelian (kɔː'niːlɪən) *n* a variant spelling of **carnelian**

corneous ('kɔːnɪəs) *adj* horny; hornlike [c17 from Latin *corneus* horny, from *cornū* HORN]

corner ('kɔːnə) *n* **1** the place, position, or angle formed by the meeting of two converging lines or surfaces **2** a projecting angle of a solid object or figure **3** the place where two streets meet **4** any small, secluded, secret, or private place **5** a dangerous or awkward position, esp from which escape is difficult: *a tight corner* **6** any part, region or place, esp a remote place **7** something used to protect or mark a corner, as of the hard cover of a book **8** *commerce* a monopoly over the supply of a commodity so that its market price can be controlled **9** *soccer, hockey* a free kick or shot from the corner of the field, taken against a defending team when the ball goes out of play over their goal line after last touching one of their players **10** either of two opposite angles of a boxing ring in which the opponents take their rests **11** *mountaineering* a junction between two rock faces forming an angle of between 60° and 120°. US name: **dihedral 12 cut corners** to do something in the easiest and shortest way, esp at the expense of high standards **13 (just) round the corner** close at hand **14 turn the corner** to pass the critical point (in an illness, etc) **15** (*modifier*) located on a corner: *a corner shop* **16** (*modifier*) suitable or designed for a corner: *a corner table* **17** *logic* either of a pair of symbols used in the same way as ordinary quotation marks to indicate quasi quotation. See **quasi-quotation** ▷ *vb* **18** (*tr*) to manoeuvre (a person or animal) into a position from which escape is difficult or impossible: *finally they cornered the fox* **19** (*tr*) to furnish or provide with corners **20** (*tr*) to place in or move into a corner **21** (*tr*) **a** to acquire enough of (a commodity) to attain control of the market **b** Also: **engross** to attain control of (a market) in such a manner. Compare **forestall** (sense 3) **22** (*intr*) (of vehicles, etc) to turn a corner **23** (*intr*) *US* to be situated on a corner **24** (*intr*) (in soccer, etc) to take a corner [c13 from Old French *corniere*, from Latin *cornū* point, extremity, HORN]

Corner *n* **the** *informal* an area in central Australia, at the junction of the borders of Queensland and South Australia

cornerback ('kɔːnə,bæk) *n American football* a defensive back

cornerstone ('kɔːnə,stəʊn) *n* **1** a stone at the corner of a wall, uniting two intersecting walls; quoin **2** a stone placed at the corner of a building during a ceremony to mark the start of construction **3** a person or thing of prime importance; basis: *the cornerstone of the whole*

C

argument; he is the cornerstone of the team

cornerwise ('kɔːnəˌwaɪz) *or* **cornerways** ('kɔːnəˌweɪz) *adv, adj* with a corner in front; diagonally

cornet ('kɔːnɪt) *n* **1** Also called: **cornet à pistons** ('kɔːnɪt ə 'pɪstənz; *French* kɔrne a pistɔ̃) a three-valved brass instrument of the trumpet family. Written range: about two and a half octaves upwards from E below middle C. It is a transposing instrument in B flat or A **2** a person who plays the cornet **3** a variant spelling of **cornett 4** a cone-shaped paper container for sweets, etc **5** *Brit* a cone-shaped wafer container for ice cream **6** (formerly) the lowest rank of commissioned cavalry officer in the British army **7** *South African* short for **field cornet 8** a starched and wired muslin or lace cap worn by women from the 12th to the 15th centuries **9** the large white headdress of some nuns [c14 from Old French, from *corn*, from Latin *cornū* HORN]

cornetcy ('kɔːnɪtsɪ) *n, pl* **-cies** *obsolete* the commission or rank of a cornet

cornetist *or* **cornettist** (kɔːˈnɛtɪst) *n* a person who plays the cornet

cornett (kɔːˈnɛt) *or* **cornet** *n* a musical instrument consisting of a straight or curved tube of wood or ivory having finger holes like a recorder and a cup-shaped mouthpiece like a trumpet [from Old French *cornet* a little horn, from *corn* horn, from Latin *cornū*]

corn exchange *n* a building where corn is bought and sold

corn factor *n* a person who deals in corn

cornfield ('kɔːnˌfiːld) *n* a field planted with cereal crops

cornflakes ('kɔːnˌfleɪks) *pl n* a breakfast cereal made from toasted maize, eaten with milk, sugar, etc

cornflour ('kɔːnˌflaʊə) *n* **1** a fine starchy maize flour, used esp for thickening sauces. US and Canadian name: **cornstarch 2** *NZ* a fine wheat flour

cornflower ('kɔːnˌflaʊə) *n* a Eurasian herbaceous plant, *Centaurea cyanus*, with blue, purple, pink, or white flowers, formerly a common weed in cornfields: family *Asteraceae* (composites). Also called: **bluebottle**. See also **bachelor's-buttons**

cornhusk ('kɔːnˌhʌsk) *n US and Canadian* the outer protective covering of an ear of maize; the chaff

cornice ('kɔːnɪs) *n* **1** *architect* **a** the top projecting mouldings of an entablature **b** a continuous horizontal projecting course or moulding at the top of a wall, building, etc **2** an overhanging ledge of snow formed by the wind on the edge of a mountain ridge, cliff, or corrie ▷ *vb* **3** (*tr*) *architect* to furnish or decorate with or as if with a cornice [c16 from Old French, from Italian, perhaps from Latin *cornix* crow, but influenced also by Latin *corōnis* decorative flourish used by scribes, from Greek *korōnis*, from *korōnē* curved object, CROWN]

corniche ('kɔːnɪʃ) *n* a coastal road, esp one built into the face of a cliff [c19 from *corniche road*, originally the coastal road between Nice and Monte Carlo; see CORNICE]

cornichon ('kɔːnɪˌʃɒn) *n* a type of small gherkin [French: gherkin]

corniculate (kɔːˈnɪkjʊˌleɪt, -lɪt) *adj* **1** having horns or hornlike projections **2** relating to or resembling a horn [c17 from Latin *corniculātus* horned, from *corniculum* a little horn, from *cornū* HORN]

Cornish ('kɔːnɪʃ) *adj* **1** of, relating to, or characteristic of Cornwall, its inhabitants, their former language, or their present-day dialect of English ▷ *n* **2** a former language of Cornwall, belonging to the S Celtic branch of the Indo-European family and closely related to Breton: extinct by 1800 **3** the (*functioning as plural*) the natives or inhabitants of Cornwall

Cornishman ('kɔːnɪʃmən) *n, pl* **-men** a man who is a native or inhabitant of Cornwall

Cornish pasty ('pæstɪ) *n cookery* a pastry case

with a filling of meat and vegetables

Cornish Rex *n* a breed of cat with a very soft wavy coat, a small head, large eyes, and very large ears

Cornish split *n* another term for **Devonshire split**

Corn Laws *pl n* the laws introduced in Britain in 1804 to protect domestic farmers against foreign competition by the imposition of a heavy duty on foreign corn: repealed in 1846. See also **Anti-Corn Law League**

corn lily *n* any of several South African iridaceous plants of the genus *Ixia*, which have coloured lily-like flowers

corn marigold *n* an annual plant, *Chrysanthemum segetum*, with yellow daisy-like flower heads: a common weed of cultivated land: family *Asteraceae* (composites)

corn meal *n* meal made from maize. Also called: **Indian meal**

Corno (*Italian* 'kɔrno) *n* **Monte** ('monte). a mountain in central Italy: the highest peak in the Apennines. Height: 2912 m (9554 ft)

corn oil *n* an oil prepared from maize, used in cooking and in making soaps, lubricants, etc

corn on the cob *n* a cob of maize, boiled and eaten as a vegetable

corn-picker *n chiefly US and Canadian* a machine for removing ears of maize from the standing stalks, often also equipped to separate the corn from the husk and shell

corn pone *n Southern US* corn bread, esp a plain type made with water. Sometimes shortened to: **pone**

corn poppy *n* a poppy, *Papaver rhoeas*, that has bright red flowers and grows in cornfields. Since World War I it has been the symbol of fallen soldiers. Also called: **coquelicot, Flanders poppy, field poppy**

corn rose *n Brit archaic* any of several red-flowered weeds of cornfields, such as the corn poppy

corn row (rəʊ) *n* a Black, originally African, hair-style in which the hair is plaited in close parallel rows, resembling furrows in a ploughed field

corn salad *n* any valerianaceous plant of the genus *Valerianella*, esp the European species *V. locusta*, which often grows in cornfields and whose leaves are sometimes used in salads. Also called: **lamb's lettuce**

corn shock *n* a stack or bundle of bound or unbound corn piled upright for curing or drying

corn shuck *n US and Canadian* the husk of an ear of maize

corn silk *n US and Canadian* the silky tuft of styles and stigmas at the tip of an ear of maize, formerly used as a diuretic

corn smut *n* **1** an ascomycetous parasitic fungus, *Ustilago zeae*, that causes gall-like deformations on maize grain **2** the condition produced by this fungus

corn snow *n skiing, US and Canadian* granular snow formed by alternate freezing and thawing

cornstalk ('kɔːnˌstɔːk) *n* **1** a stalk or stem of corn **2** *Austral slang* a tall thin man

cornstarch ('kɔːnˌstɑːtʃ) *n US and Canadian* a fine starchy maize flour, used esp for thickening sauces. Also called (in Britain and certain other countries): **cornflour**

cornstone ('kɔːnˌstəʊn) *n* a mottled green and red limestone

corn syrup *n* syrup prepared from maize

cornu ('kɔːnjuː) *n, pl* **-nua** (-njʊə) *anatomy* a part or structure resembling a horn or having a hornlike pattern, such as a cross section of the grey matter of the spinal cord [c17 from Latin: a horn] ▷ **'cornual** *adj*

cornucopia (ˌkɔːnjʊˈkəʊpɪə) *n* **1** *Greek myth* the horn of Amalthea, the goat that suckled Zeus **2** a representation of such a horn in painting, sculpture, etc, overflowing with fruit, vegetables, etc; horn of plenty **3** a great abundance; overflowing supply **4** a horn-shaped container

[c16 from Late Latin, from Latin *cornūcōpiae* horn of plenty] ▷ ˌcornu'copian *adj*

cornute (kɔːˈnjuːt) *or* **cornuted** *adj biology* having or resembling cornua; hornlike: *the cornute process of a bone* [c17 from Latin *cornūtus* horned, from *cornū* HORN]

Cornwall ('kɔːnˌwɔːl, -wəl) *n* a county of SW England: hilly, with a deeply indented coastline. Administrative centre: Truro. Pop: 513 500 (2003 est). Area: 3564 sq km (1376 sq miles)

corn whisky *n* whisky made from maize

corny ('kɔːnɪ) *adj* **cornier, corniest** *slang* **1** trite or banal **2** sentimental or mawkish **3** abounding in corn [c16 (c20 in the sense rustic, banal): from CORN[1] + -Y[1]]

corody *or* **corrody** ('kɒrədɪ) *n, pl* **-dies** *history* **1** (originally) the right of a lord to receive free quarters from his vassal **2** an allowance for maintenance [c15 from Medieval Latin *corrōdium* something provided, from Old French *corroyer* to provide, of Germanic origin]

corolla (kəˈrɒlə) *n* the petals of a flower collectively, forming an inner floral envelope. Compare **calyx**

corollaceous (ˌkɒrəˈleɪʃəs) *adj* of, relating to, resembling, or having a corolla

corollary (kəˈrɒlərɪ) *n, pl* **-laries 1** a proposition that follows directly from the proof of another proposition **2** an obvious deduction **3** a natural consequence or result ▷ *adj* **4** consequent or resultant [c14 from Latin *corollārium* money paid for a garland, from Latin *corolla* garland, from *corōna* CROWN]

Coromandel Coast (ˌkɒrəˈmændəl) *n* the SE coast of India, along the Bay of Bengal, extending from Point Calimere to the mouth of the Krishna River

corona (kəˈrəʊnə) *n, pl* **-nas** *or* **-nae** (-niː) **1** a circle of light around a luminous body, usually the moon **2** Also called: **aureole** the outermost region of the sun's atmosphere, visible as a faint halo during a solar eclipse **3** *architect* the flat vertical face of a cornice just above the soffit **4** something resembling a corona or halo **5** a circular chandelier suspended from the roof of a church **6** *botany* **a** the trumpet-shaped part of the corolla of daffodils and similar plants; the crown **b** a crown of leafy outgrowths from inside the petals of some flowers **7** *anatomy* a crownlike structure, such as the top of the head **8** *zoology* the head or upper surface of an animal, such as the body of an echinoid or the disc and arms of a crinoid **9** a long cigar with blunt ends **10** *physics* short for **corona discharge** [c16 from Latin: crown, from Greek *korōne* anything curved; related to Greek *korōnis* wreath, *korax* crow, Latin *curvus* curved]

Corona Australis (ɒˈstreɪlɪs) *n, Latin genitive* **Coronae Australis** (kəˈrəʊniː:) a small faint constellation in the S hemisphere between Ara and Pavo [literally: Southern crown]

Corona Borealis (ˌbɔːrɪˈeɪlɪs) *n, Latin genitive* **Coronae Borealis** (kəˈrəʊniː:) a small compact constellation in the N hemisphere lying between Boötes and Hercules [literally: Northern crown]

coronach ('kɒrənəx, -nək) *n Scot or Irish* a dirge or lamentation for the dead [c16 from Scottish Gaelic *corranach*; related to Irish *rānadh* a crying]

corona discharge *n* an electrical discharge appearing on and around the surface of a charged conductor, caused by ionization of the surrounding gas. Also called: **corona**. See also **Saint Elmo's fire**

coronagraph *or* **coronograph** (kəˈrəʊnəˌɡrɑːf, -ˌɡræf) *n* an optical instrument used to simulate an eclipse of the sun so that the faint solar corona can be studied

coronal *n* ('kɒrənəl) **1** *poetic* a circlet for the head; crown **2** a wreath or garland **3** *anatomy* short for **coronal suture** ▷ *adj* (kəˈrəʊnəl) **4** of or relating to a corona or coronal **5** *phonetics* a less common word for **retroflex** [c16 from Late Latin *corōnālis* belonging to a CROWN]

coronal suture *n* the serrated line across the skull between the frontal bone and the parietal bones

coronary ('kɒrənərɪ) *adj* **1** *anatomy* designating blood vessels, nerves, ligaments, etc, that encircle a part or structure ▷ *n, pl* -naries **2** short for **coronary thrombosis** [c17 from Latin *corōnārius* belonging to a wreath or crown; see CORONA]

coronary artery *n* either of two arteries branching from the aorta and supplying blood to the heart

coronary bypass *n* the surgical bypass of a narrowed or blocked coronary artery by grafting a section of a healthy blood vessel taken from another part of the patient's body

coronary heart disease *n* any heart disorder caused by disease of the coronary arteries

coronary insufficiency *n* inadequate circulation of blood through the coronary arteries, characterized by attacks of angina pectoris

coronary thrombosis *n* a condition of interrupted blood flow to the heart due to a blood clot in a coronary artery, usually as a consequence of atherosclerosis: characterized by intense pain. Sometimes shortened to: coronary. Compare **myocardial infarction**

coronation (,kɒrə'neɪʃən) *n* the act or ceremony of crowning a monarch [c14 from Old French, from *coroner* to crown, from Latin *corōnāre*]

coronation chicken *n* (*sometimes capital*) a dish of cold cooked chicken in a mild creamy curry sauce [c20 so-called because it was served at the coronation lunch of Elizabeth II (born 1926), queen of Great Britain and Northern Ireland from 1952]

coronavirus (kə'rəʊnə,vaɪrəs) *n* a type of airborne virus accounting for 10-30% of all colds [c20 so-called because of their corona-like appearance in electron micrographs]

coroner ('kɒrənə) *n* a public official responsible for the investigation of violent, sudden, or suspicious deaths and inquiries into treasure trove. The investigation (**coroner's inquest**) is held in the presence of a jury (**coroner's jury**). See also **procurator fiscal**. Compare **medical examiner** [c14 from Anglo-French *corouner* officer in charge of the pleas of the Crown, from Old French *corone* CROWN] > 'coroner,ship *n*

coronet ('kɒrənɪt) *n* **1** any small crown, esp one worn by princes or peers as a mark of rank **2** a woman's jewelled circlet for the head **3** the margin between the skin of a horse's pastern and the horn of the hoof **4** the knob at the base of a deer's antler **5** *heraldry* a support for a crest shaped like a crown [c15 from Old French *coronete* a little crown, from *corone* CROWN]

coroneted (,kɒrə'nɛtɪd) *adj* **1** wearing a coronet **2** belonging to the peerage

co-routine ('kəʊruː,tiːn) *n* *computing* a section of a computer program similar to but differing from a subroutine in that it can be left and re-entered at any point

corozo (kə'rəʊzəʊ) *n, pl* -zos a tropical American palm, *Corozo oleifera*, whose seeds yield a useful oil [c18 via Spanish from an Indian name]

corp. *abbreviation for* **1** corporation **2** corporal

corpora ('kɔːpərə) *n* the plural of **corpus**

corporal[1] ('kɔːpərəl, -prəl) *adj* **1** of or relating to the body; bodily **2** an obsolete word for **corporeal** [c14 from Latin *corpōrālis* of the body, from *corpus* body] > ,corpo'rality *n* > 'corporally *adv*

corporal[2] ('kɔːpərəl, -prəl) *n* **1** a noncommissioned officer junior to a sergeant in the army, air force, or marines **2** (in the Royal Navy) a petty officer who assists the master-at-arms [c16 from Old French, via Italian, from Latin *caput* head; perhaps also influenced in Old French by *corps* body (of men)] > 'corporal,ship *n*

corporal[3] ('kɔːpərəl, -prəl) *or* **corporale** (,kɔːpə'reɪlɪ) *n* a white linen cloth on which the bread and wine are placed during the Eucharist [c14 from Medieval Latin *corporāle pallium* eucharistic altar cloth, from Latin *corporālis* belonging to the body, from *corpus* body (of Christ)]

Corporal of Horse *n* a noncommissioned rank in the British Household Cavalry above that of sergeant and below that of staff sergeant

corporal punishment *n* punishment of a physical nature, such as caning, flogging, or beating

corporate ('kɔːpərɪt, -prɪt) *adj* **1** forming a corporation; incorporated **2** of or belonging to a corporation or corporations: *corporate finance* **3** of or belonging to a united group; joint [c15 from Latin *corporātus* made into a body, from *corporāre*, from *corpus* body] > 'corporately *adv*

corporate anorexia *n* a malaise of a business organization resulting from making too many creative people redundant in a cost-cutting exercise

corporate culture *n* the distinctive ethos of an organization that influences the level of formality, loyalty, and general behaviour of its employees

corporate governance *n* the balance of control between the stakeholders, managers, and directors of an organization

corporate identity *or* **image** *n* the way an organization is presented to or perceived by its members and the public

corporate manslaughter *n* *law* the death of someone caused by an act of corporate negligence

corporate raider *n* *finance* a person or organization that acquires a substantial holding of the shares of a company in order to take it over or to force its management to act in a desired way

corporate restructuring *n* a change in the business strategy of an organization resulting in diversification, closing parts of the business, etc, to increase its long-term profitability

corporate venturing *n* *finance* the provision of venture capital by one company for another in order to obtain information about the company requiring capital or as a step towards acquiring it

corporate village *n* an area close to the workplace where many everyday facilities are provided for a company's workers

corporation (,kɔːpə'reɪʃən) *n* **1** a group of people authorized by law to act as a legal personality and having its own powers, duties, and liabilities **2** Also called: **municipal corporation** the municipal authorities of a city or town **3** a group of people acting as one body **4** See **public corporation** **5** *informal* a large paunch or belly

corporation tax *n* a British tax on the profits of a company or other incorporated body

corporatism ('kɔːpərɪtɪzəm, -prɪtɪzəm) *n* the organization of a state on a corporative basis > 'corporatist *n, adj*

corporative ('kɔːpərətɪv, -prətɪv) *adj* **1** of or characteristic of a corporation **2** (of a state) organized into and governed by corporations of individuals involved in any given profession, industry, etc

corporatize *or* **corporatise** ('kɔːpərətaɪz, -prə-) *vb* **1** (*tr*) to convert (a government-controlled industry or enterprise) into an independent company **2** (*intr*) to be influenced by or take on the features of a large commercial business, esp in being bureaucratic and uncaring

corporator ('kɔːpə,reɪtə) *n* a member of a corporation

corporeal (kɔː'pɔːrɪəl) *adj* **1** of the nature of the physical body; not spiritual **2** of a material nature; physical [c17 from Latin *corporeus*, from *corpus* body] > cor,pore'ality *or* cor'porealness *n* > cor'poreally *adv*

corporeity (,kɔːpɔ'riːɪtɪ) *n* bodily or material nature or substance; physical existence; corporeality

corposant ('kɔːpə,zænt) *n* another name for **Saint Elmo's fire** [c17 from Portuguese *corpo-santo*, literally: holy body, from Latin *corpus sanctum*]

corps (kɔː) *n, pl* **corps** (kɔːz) **1** a military

formation that comprises two or more divisions and additional support arms **2** a military body with a specific function: *intelligence corps; medical corps* **3** a body of people associated together: *the diplomatic corps* [c18 from French, from Latin *corpus* body]

corps de ballet ('kɔː də 'bæleɪ; *French* kɔr də balɛ) *n* the members of a ballet company who dance together in a group

corps diplomatique (,dɪpləʊmæ'tiːk) *n* another name for **diplomatic corps**. Abbreviation: CD

corpse (kɔːps) *n* **1** a dead body, esp of a human being; cadaver ▷ *vb* **2** *theatre slang* to laugh or cause to laugh involuntarily or inopportunely while on stage [c14 from Old French *corps* body, from Latin *corpus* body]

corpsman ('kɔːmən) *n, pl* -men *US military* a medical orderly or stretcher-bearer

corpulent ('kɔːpjʊlənt) *adj* physically bulky; fat [c14 from Latin *corpulentus* fleshy] > 'corpulence *or* 'corpulency *n* > 'corpulently *adv*

cor pulmonale (kɔː pʌlmə'nɑːlɪ) *n* pulmonary heart disease: a serious heart condition in which there is enlargement and failure of the right ventricle resulting from lung disease [New Latin]

corpus ('kɔːpəs) *n, pl* -pora (-pərə) **1** a collection or body of writings, esp by a single author or on a specific topic: *the corpus of Dickens's works* **2** the main body, section, or substance of something **3** *anatomy* **a** any distinct mass or body **b** the main part of an organ or structure **4** the inner layer or layers of cells of the meristem at a shoot tip, which produces the vascular tissue and pith ▷ Compare **tunica** (sense 2) **5** *linguistics* a body of data, esp the finite collection of grammatical sentences of a language that a linguistic theory seeks to describe by means of an algorithm **6** a capital or principal sum, as contrasted with a derived income **7** *obsolete* a human or animal body, esp a dead one [c14 from Latin: body]

corpus callosum (kə'ləʊsəm) *n, pl* corpora callosa (kə'ləʊsə) the band of white fibres that connects the cerebral hemispheres in mammals [New Latin, literally: callous body]

corpus cavernosum (,kævə'nəʊsəm) *n, pl* corpora cavernosa either of two masses of erectile tissue in the penis of mammals [New Latin, literally: cavernous body]

Corpus Christi[1] ('krɪstɪ) *n chiefly RC Church* a festival in honour of the Eucharist, observed on the Thursday after Trinity Sunday [c14 from Latin: body of Christ]

Corpus Christi[2] ('krɪstɪ) *n* a port in S Texas, on **Corpus Christi Bay**, an inlet of the Gulf of Mexico. Pop: 279 208 (2003 est)

corpuscle ('kɔːpʌsᵊl) *n* **1** any cell or similar minute body that is suspended in a fluid, esp any of the **red blood corpuscles** (see **erythrocyte**) or **white blood corpuscles** (see **leucocyte**) **2** *anatomy* the encapsulated ending of a sensory nerve **3** *physics* a discrete particle such as an electron, photon, ion, or atom **4** Also called: corpuscule (kɔː'pʌskjuːl) any minute particle [c17 from Latin *corpusculum* a little body, from *corpus* body] > corpuscular (kɔː'pʌskjʊlə)

corpuscular theory *n* the theory, originally proposed by Newton, and revived with the development of the quantum theory, that light consists of a stream of particles. See **photon**. Compare **wave theory**

corpus delicti (dɪ'lɪktaɪ) *n law* the body of facts that constitute an offence [New Latin, literally: the body of the crime]

corpus juris ('dʒʊərɪs) *n* a body of law, esp the laws of a nation or state [from Late Latin, literally: a body of law]

Corpus Juris Canonici (kə'nɒnɪ,saɪ) *n RC Church* the official compilation of canon law published by authority of Gregory XIII in 1582, superseded by the Codex Juris Canonici in 1918. See also **Clementines, Decretals, Decretum, Extravagantes, Sext, Codex Juris Canonici**

C

[Medieval Latin, literally: body of canon law]

Corpus Juris Civilis (sɪˈvaɪlɪs) *n law* the body of Roman or civil law consolidated by Justinian in the 6th century AD. It consists of four parts, the Institutes, Digest, Code, and Novels [New Latin, literally: body of civil law]

corpus luteum (ˈluːtɪəm) *n, pl* **corpora lutea** (ˈluːtɪə) a yellow glandular mass of tissue that forms in a Graafian follicle following release of an ovum. It secretes progesterone, a hormone necessary to maintain pregnancy [New Latin, literally: yellow body]

corpus luteum hormone *n* another name for **progesterone**

corpus spongiosum (ˌspʌndʒɪˈəʊsəm) *n* a mass of tissue that, with the corpora cavernosa, forms the erectile tissue of the penis of mammals [New Latin, literally: spongy body]

corpus striatum (straɪˈeɪtəm) *n, pl* **corpora striata** (straɪˈeɪtə) a striped mass of white and grey matter situated in front of the thalamus in each cerebral hemisphere [New Latin, literally: striated body]

corpus vile Latin (ˈkɔːpəs ˈvaɪlɪ) *n, pl* **corpora vilia** (ˈkɔːpərə ˈvɪlɪə) a person or thing fit only to be the object of an experiment [literally: worthless body]

corrade (kɒˈreɪd) *vb* (of rivers, streams, etc) to erode (land) by the abrasive action of rock particles [c17 from Latin *corrādere* to scrape together, from *rādere* to scrape]

corral (kɒˈrɑːl) *n* **1** *chiefly US and Canadian* an enclosure for confining cattle or horses **2** *chiefly US* (formerly) a defensive enclosure formed by a ring of covered wagons ▷ *vb* **-rals, -ralling, -ralled** (*tr*) *US and Canadian* **3** to drive into and confine in or as in a corral **4** *informal* to capture [c16 from Spanish, from Vulgar Latin *currāle* (unattested) area for vehicles, from Latin *currus* wagon, from *currere* to run]

corrasion (kəˈreɪʒən) *n* erosion of a rock surface by rock fragments transported over it by water, wind, or ice. Compare **abrasion** (sense 3), **attrition** (sense 4) > **corrasive** (kəˈreɪsɪv) *adj*

correa (ˈkɒrɪə, kəˈriːə) *n* an Australian evergreen shrub of the genus *Correa*, with large showy tubular flowers [c19 after Jose Francesco Correa da Serra (1750–1823), Portuguese botanist]

correct (kəˈrɛkt) *vb* (*tr*) **1** to make free from errors **2** to indicate the errors in **3** to rebuke or punish in order to set right or improve: *to correct a child; to stand corrected* **4** to counteract or rectify (a malfunction, ailment, etc): *these glasses will correct your sight* **5** to adjust or make conform, esp to a standard ▷ *adj* **6** free from error; true; accurate: *the correct version* **7** in conformity with accepted standards: *correct behaviour* [c14 from Latin *corrigere* to make straight, put in order, from *com*- (intensive) + *regere* to rule] > **corˈrectable** or **corˈrectible** *adj* > **corˈrectly** *adv* > **corˈrectness** *n* > **corˈrector** *n*

correction (kəˈrɛkʃən) *n* **1** the act or process of correcting **2** something offered or substituted for an error; an improvement **3** the act or process of punishing; reproof **4** a number or quantity added to or subtracted from a scientific or mathematical calculation or observation to increase its accuracy

correctional (kəˈrɛkʃənəl) *adj chiefly US* of or relating to the punishment and rehabilitation of criminals: *a correctional facility*

correctitude (kəˈrɛktɪˌtjuːd) *n* the quality of correctness, esp conscious correctness in behaviour

corrective (kəˈrɛktɪv) *adj* **1** tending or intended to correct ▷ *n* **2** something that tends or is intended to correct > **corˈrectively** *adv*

Corregidor (kəˈrɛgɪˌdɔː) *n* an island at the entrance to Manila Bay, in the Philippines: site of the defeat of American forces by the Japanese (1942) in World War II

correlate (ˈkɒrɪˌleɪt) *vb* **1** to place or be placed in a mutual, complementary, or reciprocal relationship **2** (*tr*) to establish or show a

correlation ▷ *adj* **3** having a mutual, complementary, or reciprocal relationship ▷ *n* **4** either of two things mutually or reciprocally related > **ˈcorreˌlatable** *adj*

correlation (ˌkɒrɪˈleɪʃən) *n* **1** a mutual or reciprocal relationship between two or more things **2** the act or process of correlating or the state of being correlated **3** *statistics* the extent of correspondence between the ordering of two variables. Correlation is positive or direct when two variables move in the same direction and negative or inverse when they move in opposite directions [c16 from Medieval Latin *correlātiō*, from *com*- together + *relātiō*, RELATION] > ˌcorreˈlational *adj*

correlation coefficient *n statistics* a statistic measuring the degree of correlation between two variables as by dividing their covariance by the square root of the product of their variances. The closer the correlation coefficient is to 1 or –1 the greater the correlation; if it is random, the coefficient is zero. See also **Pearson's correlation coefficient, Spearman's rank-order coefficient**

correlative (kɒˈrɛlətɪv) *adj* **1** in mutual, complementary, or reciprocal relationship; corresponding **2** denoting words, usually conjunctions, occurring together though not adjacently in certain grammatical constructions, as for example *neither* and *nor* in such sentences as *he neither ate nor drank* ▷ *n* **3** either of two things that are correlative **4** a correlative word > **corˈrelatively** *adv* > **corˈrelativeness** or **corˌrelaˈtivity** *n*

correspond (ˌkɒrɪˈspɒnd) *vb* (*intr*) **1** (usually foll by *with* or *to*) to conform, be in agreement, or be consistent or compatible (with); tally (with) **2** (usually foll by *to*) to be similar or analogous in character or function **3** (usually foll by *with*) to communicate by letter [c16 from Medieval Latin *corrēspondēre*, from Latin *respondēre* to RESPOND] > ˌcorreˈspondingly *adv*

correspondence (ˌkɒrɪˈspɒndəns) *n* **1** the act or condition of agreeing or corresponding **2** similarity or analogy **3** agreement or conformity **4 a** communication by the exchange of letters **b** the letters so exchanged

correspondence column *n* a section of a newspaper or magazine in which are printed readers' letters to the editor

correspondence school *n* an educational institution that offers tuition (**correspondence courses**) by post

correspondent (ˌkɒrɪˈspɒndənt) *n* **1** a person who communicates by letter or by letters **2** a person employed by a newspaper, etc, to report on a special subject or to send reports from a foreign country **3** a person or firm that has regular business relations with another, esp one in a different part of the country or abroad **4** something that corresponds to another ▷ *adj* **5** similar or analogous

Corrèze (French kɔrɛz) *n* a department of central France, in Limousin region. Capital: Tulle. Pop: 234 144 (2003 est). Area: 5888 sq km (2296 sq miles)

corrida (koˈrriða) *n* the Spanish word for **bullfight** [Spanish, from the phrase *corrida de toros*, literally: a running of bulls, from *correr* to run, from Latin *currere*]

corridor (ˈkɒrɪˌdɔː) *n* **1** a hallway or passage connecting parts of a building **2** a strip of land or airspace along the route of a road or river: *the M1 corridor* **3** a strip of land or airspace that affords access, either from a landlocked country to the sea (such as the **Polish corridor**, 1919-39, which divided Germany) or from a state to an exclave (such as the **Berlin corridor**, 1945–90, which passed through the former East Germany) **4** a passageway connecting the compartments of a railway coach **5 corridors of power** the higher echelons of government, the Civil Service, etc, considered as the location of power and influence **6** a flight path that affords safe access for

intruding aircraft **7** the path that a spacecraft must follow when re-entering the atmosphere, above which lift is insufficient and below which heating effects are excessive [c16 from Old French, from Old Italian *corridore*, literally: place for running, from *correre* to run, from Latin *currere*]

corrie (ˈkɒrɪ) *n geology* another name for **cirque** (sense 1) [c18 from Gaelic *coire* cauldron, kettle]

Corriedale (ˈkɒrɪˌdeɪl) *n* a breed of sheep reared for both wool and meat, originally developed in New Zealand and Australia

corrie-fisted (ˌkɒrɪˈfɪstɪd) *adj Scot dialect* left-handed [c20 from earlier *car, ker* left hand or side, from Gaelic *cearr* left or wrong hand]

Corrientes (Spanish koˈrrjentes) *n* a port in NE Argentina, on the Paraná River. Pop: 340 000 (2005 est)

corrigendum (ˌkɒrɪˈdʒɛndəm) *n, pl* **-da** (-də) **1** an error to be corrected **2** (*sometimes plural*) Also called: **erratum** a slip of paper inserted into a book after printing, listing errors and corrections [c19 from Latin: that which is to be corrected, from *corrigere* to CORRECT]

corrigible (ˈkɒrɪdʒɪbəl) *adj* **1** capable of being corrected **2** submissive or submitting to correction [c15 from Old French, from Medieval Latin *corrigibilis*, from Latin *corrigere* to set right, CORRECT] > ˌcorrigiˈbility *n*

corrival (kɒˈraɪvəl) *n, vb* a rare word for **rival** [c16 from Old French, from Late Latin *corrīvālis*, from Latin *com*- together, mutually + *rīvālis* RIVAL] > **corˈrivalry** *n*

corroborant (kəˈrɒbərənt) *adj archaic* **1** serving to corroborate **2** strengthening

corroborate *vb* (kəˈrɒbəˌreɪt) **1** (*tr*) to confirm or support (facts, opinions, etc), esp by providing fresh evidence: *the witness corroborated the accused's statement* ▷ *adj* (kəˈrɒbərɪt) *archaic* **2** serving to corroborate a fact, an opinion, etc **3** (of a fact) corroborated [c16 from Latin *corrōborāre* to invigorate, from *rōborāre* to make strong, from *rōbur* strength, literally: oak] > corˈroboˈration *n* > **corroborative** (kəˈrɒbərətɪv) or **corˈroboˌratory** *adj* > corˈroboratively *adv* > corˈroboˌrator *n*

corroboree (kəˈrɒbərɪ) *n Austral* **1** a native assembly of sacred, festive, or warlike character **2** *informal* any noisy gathering [c19 from a native Australian language]

corrode (kəˈrəʊd) *vb* **1** to eat away or be eaten away, esp by chemical action as in the oxidation or rusting of a metal **2** (*tr*) to destroy gradually; consume: *his jealousy corroded his happiness* [c14 from Latin *corrōdere* to gnaw to pieces, from *rōdere* to gnaw; see RODENT, RAT] > **corˈrodant** or **corˈrodent** *n* > **corˈroder** *n* > **corˈrodible** *adj* > corˌrodiˈbility *n*

corrody (ˈkɒrədɪ) *n, pl* **-dies** a variant spelling of **corody**

corrosion (kəˈrəʊʒən) *n* **1** a process in which a solid, esp a metal, is eaten away and changed by a chemical action, as in the oxidation of iron in the presence of water by an electrolytic process **2** slow deterioration by being eaten or worn away **3** the condition produced by or the product of corrosion

corrosive (kəˈrəʊsɪv) *adj* **1** (esp of acids or alkalis) capable of destroying solid materials **2** tending to eat away or consume **3** cutting; sarcastic: *a corrosive remark* ▷ *n* **4** a corrosive substance, such as a strong acid or alkali > **corˈrosively** *adv* > **corˈrosiveness** *n*

corrosive sublimate *n* another name for **mercuric chloride**

corrugate *vb* (ˈkɒrʊˌgeɪt) **1** (*usually tr*) to fold or be folded into alternate furrows and ridges ▷ *adj* (ˈkɒrʊgɪt, -ˌgeɪt) **2** folded into furrows and ridges; wrinkled [c18 from Latin *corrūgāre*, from *rūga* a wrinkle] > ˌcorruˈgation *n*

corrugated iron *n* a thin structural sheet made of iron or steel, formed with alternating ridges and troughs

corrugated paper *n* a packaging material made from layers of heavy paper, the top layer of which is grooved and ridged

corrugator ('kɒrʊˌɡeɪtə) *n* a muscle whose contraction causes wrinkling of the brow

corrupt (kə'rʌpt) *adj* **1** lacking in integrity; open to or involving bribery or other dishonest practices: *a corrupt official; corrupt practices in an election* **2** morally depraved **3** putrid or rotten **4** contaminated; unclean **5** (of a text or manuscript) made meaningless or different in meaning from the original by scribal errors or alterations **6** (of computer programs or data) containing errors ▷ *vb* **7** to become or cause to become dishonest or disloyal **8** to debase or become debased morally; deprave **9** (*tr*) to infect or contaminate; taint **10** (*tr*) to cause to become rotten **11** (*tr*) to alter (a text, manuscript, etc) from the original **12** (*tr*) *computing* to introduce errors into (data or a program) [c14 from Latin *corruptus* spoiled, from *corrumpere* to ruin, literally: break to pieces, from *rumpere* to break] > cor'rupter *or* cor'ruptor *n* > cor'ruptive *adj* > cor'ruptively *adv* > cor'ruptly *adv* > cor'ruptness *n*

corruptible (kə'rʌptəbəl) *adj* susceptible to corruption; capable of being corrupted > corˌrupti'bility *or* cor'ruptibleness *n* > cor'ruptibly *adv*

corruption (kə'rʌpʃən) *n* **1** the act of corrupting or state of being corrupt **2** moral perversion; depravity **3** dishonesty, esp bribery **4** putrefaction or decay **5** alteration, as of a manuscript **6** an altered form of a word > cor'ruptionist *n*

corsac ('kɔːsæk) *n* a fox, *Vulpes corsac*, of central Asia [c19 from a Turkic language]

corsage (kɔː'sɑːʒ) *n* **1** a flower or small bunch of flowers worn pinned to the lapel, bosom, etc, or sometimes carried by women **2** the bodice of a dress [c15 from Old French, from *cors* body, from Latin *corpus*]

corsair ('kɔːsɛə) *n* **1** a pirate **2** a privateer, esp of the Barbary Coast [c15 from Old French *corsaire* pirate, from Medieval Latin *cursārius*, from Latin *cursus* a running, COURSE]

corse (kɔːs) *n* an archaic word for **corpse**

Corse (kɔrs) *n* the French name for **Corsica**

corselet ('kɔːslɪt) *n* **1** Also spelt: **corslet** a piece of armour for the top part of the body **2** a one-piece foundation garment, usually combining a brassiere and a corset [c15 from Old French, from *cors* bodice of a garment, from Latin *corpus* body]

corset ('kɔːsɪt) *n* **1 a** a stiffened, elasticated, or laced foundation garment, worn esp by women, that usually extends from below the chest to the hips, providing support for the spine and stomach and shaping the figure **b** a similar garment worn because of injury, weakness, etc, by either sex **2** *informal* a restriction or limitation, esp government control of bank lending **3** a stiffened outer bodice worn by either sex, esp in the 16th century ▷ *vb* **4** (*tr*) to dress or enclose in, or as in, a corset [c14 from Old French, literally: a little bodice; see CORSELET]

corsetier (ˌkɔːsɪ'tɪə) *n* a man who makes and fits corsets

corsetière (ˌkɔːsɛtɪ'ɛə, kɔːˌsɛt-) *n* a woman who makes and fits corsets

corsetry ('kɔːsɪtrɪ) *n* **1** the making of or dealing in corsets **2** corsets considered collectively

corsey ('kɔːsɪ) *n Northern English dialect* a pavement or pathway

Corsica ('kɔːsɪkə) *n* an island in the Mediterranean, west of N Italy: forms, with 43 islets, a region of France; mountainous; settled by Greeks in about 560 BC; sold by Genoa to France in 1768. Capital: Ajaccio. Pop: 265 999 (2003 est). Area: 8682 sq km (3367 sq miles). French name: Corse

Corsican ('kɔːsɪkən) *adj* **1** of or relating to Corsica or its inhabitants ▷ *n* **2** a native or inhabitant of Corsica

CORSO ('kɔːsəʊ) *n* (in New Zealand) ▷ *acronym for* Council of Organizations for Relief Services Overseas

cortege *or* **cortège** (kɔː'teɪʒ) *n* **1** a formal procession, esp a funeral procession **2** a train of attendants; retinue [c17 from French, from Italian *corteggio*, from *corteggiare* to attend, from *corte* COURT]

Cortes ('kɔːtɛz; *Spanish* 'kortes) *n* the national assembly of Spain and (until 1910) Portugal [c17 from Spanish, literally: courts, plural of *corte* court, from Latin *cohors* COHORT]

cortex ('kɔːtɛks) *n, pl* **-tices** (-tɪˌsiːz) **1** *anatomy* the outer layer of any organ or part, such as the grey matter in the brain that covers the cerebrum (**cerebral cortex**) or the outer part of the kidney (**renal cortex**) **2** *botany* **a** the unspecialized tissue in plant stems and roots between the vascular bundles and the epidermis **b** the outer layer of a part such as the bark of a stem [c17 from Latin: bark, outer layer] > cortical ('kɔːtɪkəl) *adj* > 'cortically *adv*

corticate ('kɔːtɪkɪt, -ˌkeɪt) *or* **corticated** *adj* (of plants, seeds, etc) having a bark, husk, or rind [c19 from Latin *corticātus* covered with bark] > ˌcorti'cation *n*

cortico- *or before a vowel* **cortic-** *combining form* indicating the cortex: *corticotrophin*

corticolous (kɔː'tɪkələs) *adj biology* living or growing on the surface of bark

corticosteroid (ˌkɔːtɪkəʊ'stɪərɔɪd) *or* **corticoid** *n* **1** any steroid hormone produced by the adrenal cortex that affects carbohydrate, protein, and electrolyte metabolism, gonad function, and immune response **2** any similar synthetic substance, used in treating inflammatory and allergic diseases ▷ See also **glucocorticoid, mineralocorticoid**

corticosterone (ˌkɔːtɪ'kɒstəˌrəʊn) *n* a glucocorticoid hormone secreted by the adrenal cortex. Formula: $C_{21}H_{30}O_4$. See also **corticosteroid** [c20 from CORTICO- + STER(OL) + -ONE]

corticotrophic (ˌkɔːtɪkəʊ'trəʊfɪk) *or* **corticotropic** (ˌkɔːtɪkəʊ'trɒpɪk) *adj* stimulating the adrenal cortex; adrenocorticotrophic

corticotrophin (ˌkɔːtɪkəʊ'trəʊfɪn) *n* another name for **adrenocorticotrophic hormone**. See ACTH

cortisol ('kɔːtɪˌsɒl) *n* another name for **hydrocortisone** [c20 from CORTIS(ONE) + -OL²]

cortisone ('kɔːtɪˌsəʊn, -ˌzəʊn) *n* a glucocorticoid hormone, the synthetic form of which has been used in treating rheumatoid arthritis, allergic and skin diseases, leukaemia, etc; 17-hydroxy-11-dehydrocorticosterone. Formula: $C_{21}H_{28}O_5$ [c20 shortened from CORTICOSTERONE]

Cortona (kɔː'təʊnə; *Italian* kɔr'tona) *n* a town in central Italy, in Tuscany: Roman and Etruscan remains, 15th-century cathedral. Pop: 22 048 (2001)

corundum (kə'rʌndəm) *n* a white, grey, blue, green, red, yellow, or brown mineral, found in metamorphosed shales and limestones, in veins, and in some igneous rocks. It is used as an abrasive and as gemstone; the red variety is ruby, the blue is sapphire. Composition: aluminium oxide. Formula: Al_2O_3. Crystal structure: hexagonal (rhombohedral) [c18 from Tamil *kuruntam*; related to Sanskrit *kuruvinda* ruby]

Corunna (kə'rʌnə) *n* the English name for **La Coruña**

coruscate ('kɒrəˌskeɪt) *vb* (*intr*) to emit flashes of light; sparkle [c18 from Latin *coruscāre* to flash, vibrate]

coruscation (ˌkɒrə'skeɪʃən) *n* **1** a gleam or flash of light **2** a sudden or striking display of brilliance, wit, etc

corvée ('kɔːveɪ) *n* **1** *European history* a day's unpaid labour owed by a feudal vassal to his lord **2** the practice or an instance of forced labour [c14 from Old French, from Late Latin *corrogāta* contribution, from Latin *corrogāre* to collect, from *rogāre* to ask]

corves (kɔːvz) *n* the plural of **corf**

corvette (kɔː'vɛt) *n* a lightly armed escort warship [c17 from Old French, perhaps from

Middle Dutch *corf* basket, small ship, from Latin *corbis* basket]

corvina (kɔː'viːnə) *n* **1** a marine food fish, *Menticirrhus undulatus*, found in Pacific waters off Mexico and California **2** any of several related marine fishes of the family *Sciaenidae* [from Spanish *corbina, corvina*, from feminine of *corvino* ravenlike, from Latin *corvus* raven]

corvine ('kɔːvaɪn) *adj* **1** of, relating to, or resembling a crow **2** of, relating to, or belonging to the passerine bird family *Corvidae*, which includes the crows, raven, rook, jackdaw, magpies, and jays [c17 from Latin *corvīnus* ravenlike, from *corvus* a raven]

Corvus ('kɔːvəs) *n, Latin genitive* Corvi ('kɔːvaɪ) a small quadrilateral-shaped constellation in the S hemisphere, lying between Virgo and Hydra [Latin: raven]

Corybant ('kɒrɪˌbænt) *n, pl* Corybants *or* Corybantes (ˌkɒrɪ'bæntiːz) *classical myth* a wild attendant of the goddess Cybele [c14 from Latin *Corybās*, from Greek *Korubas*, probably of Phrygian origin] > ˌCory'bantian, ˌCory'bantic *or* ˌCory'bantine *adj*

corydalis (kə'rɪdəlɪs) *n* any erect or climbing plant of the N temperate genus *Corydalis*, having finely-lobed leaves and spurred yellow or pinkish flowers: family *Fumariaceae*. Also called: fumitory [c19 from New Latin, from Greek *korudallis* variant of *korudos* crested lark, from *korus* helmet, crest; alluding to the appearance of the flowers]

Corydon ('kɒrɪdən, -ˌdɒn) *n* (in pastoral literature) a shepherd or rustic

corymb ('kɒrɪmb, -rɪm) *n* an inflorescence in the form of a flat-topped flower cluster with the oldest flowers at the periphery. This type of raceme occurs in the candytuft [c18 from Latin *corymbus*, from Greek *korumbos* cluster] > 'corymbed *adj* > co'rymbose *or* co'rymbous *adj* > co'rymbosely *adv*

coryphaeus (ˌkɒrɪ'fiːəs) *n, pl* **-phaei** (-'fiːaɪ) **1** (in ancient Greek drama) the leader of the chorus **2** *archaic or literary* a leader of a group [c17 from Latin, from Greek *koruphaios* leader, from *koruphē* summit]

coryphée (ˌkɒrɪ'feɪ) *n* a leading dancer of a corps de ballet [c19 from French, from Latin *coryphaeus* CORYPHAEUS]

coryza (kə'raɪzə) *n* acute inflammation of the mucous membrane of the nose, with discharge of mucus; a head cold [c17 from Late Latin: catarrh, from Greek *koruza*]

cos¹ *or* **cos lettuce** (kɒs) *n* a variety of lettuce with a long slender head and crisp leaves. Compare **cabbage lettuce** Usual US and Canadian name: romaine [c17 named after *Kos*, the Aegean island of its origin]

cos² (kɒz) *abbreviation for* cosine

Cos (kɒs) *n* a variant spelling of **Kos**

COS *abbreviation for* Chief of Staff

Cosa Nostra ('kəʊsə 'nɒstrə) *n* the branch of the Mafia that operates in the US [Italian, literally: our thing]

COSAS ('kəʊˌzæs) *n acronym for* Congress of South African Students

COSATU (ˌkəʊ'zɑːtuː) *n acronym for* Congress of South Africa Trade Unions

cosec ('kəʊsɛk) *abbreviation for* cosecant

cosecant (kəʊ'siːkənt) *n* (of an angle) a trigonometric function that in a right-angled triangle is the ratio of the length of the hypotenuse to that of the opposite side; the reciprocal of sine. Abbreviation: cosec

cosech ('kəʊsɛtʃ, -sɛk) *n* hyperbolic cosecant; a hyperbolic function that is the reciprocal of sinh

coseismal (kəʊ'saɪzməl) *or* **coseismic** *adj* **1** of or designating points at which earthquake waves are felt at the same time **2** (of a line on a map) connecting such points ▷ *n* **3** such a line on a map

Cosenza (*Italian* ko'zɛntsa) *n* a city in S Italy, in Calabria. Pop: 72 998 (2001)

cosh¹ (kɒʃ) *Brit* ▷ *n* **1** a blunt weapon, often made of hard rubber; bludgeon **2** an attack with such a weapon ▷ *vb* (*tr*) **3** to hit with such a weapon, esp on the head [C19 from Romany *kosh,* from *koshter* skewer, stick]

cosh² (kɒʃ, ˈkɒsˈeɪtʃ) *n* hyperbolic cosine; a hyperbolic function, cosh $z = \frac{1}{2}(e^z + e^{-z})$, related to cosine by the expression cosh iz = cos z, where i = $\sqrt{-1}$ [C19 from COS(INE) + H(YPERBOLIC)]

cosher (ˈkɒʃə) *vb Irish* **1** (*tr*) to pamper or coddle **2** (*intr*) to live or be entertained at the expense of another

cosignatory (kəʊˈsɪɡnətərɪ, -trɪ) *n, pl* -**ries 1** a person, country, etc, that signs a document jointly with others ▷ *adj* **2** signing jointly with another or others

cosine (ˈkəʊˌsaɪn) *n* (of an angle) a trigonometric function that in a right-angled triangle is the ratio of the length of the adjacent side to that of the hypotenuse; the sine of the complement ▷ *Abbreviation:* **cos** [C17 from New Latin *cosinus;* see CO-, SINE¹]

COSLA (ˈkɒzlə) *n acronym for* Convention of Scottish Local Authorities

cosmetic (kɒzˈmɛtɪk) *n* **1** any preparation applied to the body, esp the face, with the intention of beautifying it ▷ *adj* **2** serving or designed to beautify the body, esp the face **3** having no other function than to beautify: *cosmetic illustrations in a book* **4** *slightly derogatory* designed to cover up a greater flaw or deficiency; superficial: *their resignation is a cosmetic exercise* [C17 from Greek *kosmētikos,* from *kosmein* to arrange, from *kosmos* order] > **cos'metically** *adv* > **cos,meti'cology** *n*

cosmetician (ˌkɒzmɪˈtɪʃən) *n* a person who makes, sells, or applies cosmetics

cosmetic surgery *n* surgery performed to improve the appearance, rather than for medical reasons

cosmetologist (ˌkɒzmɪˈtɒlədʒɪst) *n* a person skilled or trained in the use of cosmetics and beauty treatments [C20 a blend of COSMETICS + -OLOGIST]

cosmetology (ˌkɒzmɛˈtɒlədʒɪ) *n* the work of beauty therapists, including hairdressing, facials, manicures, etc

cosmic (ˈkɒzmɪk) *adj* **1** of or relating to the whole universe: *cosmic laws* **2** occurring or originating in outer space, esp as opposed to the vicinity of the earth, the solar system, or the local galaxy: *cosmic rays* **3** immeasurably extended in space or time; vast **4** *rare* harmonious > **'cosmically** *adv*

cosmic dust *n* fine particles of solid matter occurring throughout interstellar space and often collecting into clouds of extremely low density. See also **nebula** (sense 1)

cosmic rays *pl n* radiation consisting of particles, esp protons, of very high energy that reach the earth from outer space. Also called: **cosmic radiation**

cosmic string *n* a one-dimensional defect in space-time postulated in certain theories of cosmology to exist in the universe as a consequence of the big bang: See also **string** (sense 11)

cosmine (ˈkɒzmiːn) *or* **cosmin** *n zoology* a substance resembling dentine, forming the outer layer of cosmoid scales [C20 from Greek *kosmos* arrangement + -INE¹]

cosmo- *or before a vowel* **cosm-** *combining form* indicating the world or universe: *cosmology; cosmonaut; cosmography* [from Greek: COSMOS]

cosmodrome (ˈkɒzməˌdrəʊm) *n* a site, esp one in the former Soviet Union, from which spacecraft are launched

cosmogony (kɒzˈmɒɡənɪ) *n, pl* -**nies 1** the study of the origin and development of the universe or of a particular system in the universe, such as the solar system **2** a theory of such an origin or evolution [C17 from Greek *kosmogonia,* from COSMO- + *gonos* creation] > **cos'mogonal** *adj* > **cosmogonic** (ˌkɒzməˈɡɒnɪk) *or* ˌcosmo'gonical *adj* > **cos'mogonist** *n*

cosmography (kɒzˈmɒɡrəfɪ) *n* **1** a representation of the world or the universe **2** the science dealing with the whole order of nature > **cos'mographer** *or* **cos'mographist** *n* > **cosmographic** (ˌkɒzməˈɡræfɪk) *or* ˌcosmo'graphical *adj* > ˌcosmo'graphically *adv*

cosmoid (ˈkɒzmɔɪd) *adj* (of the scales of coelacanths and lungfish) consisting of two inner bony layers and an outer layer of cosmine [C20 from COSM(INE) + -OID]

cosmological argument *n philosophy* one of the arguments that purport to prove the existence of God from empirical facts about the universe, esp the argument to the existence of a first cause. Compare **ontological argument** (sense 1), **teleological argument**

cosmological principle *n astronomy* the theory that the universe is uniform, homogenous, and isotropic, and therefore appears the same from any position

cosmology (kɒzˈmɒlədʒɪ) *n* **1** the philosophical study of the origin and nature of the universe **2** the branch of astronomy concerned with the evolution and structure of the universe **3** a particular account of the origin or structure of the universe: *Ptolemaic cosmology* > **cosmological** (ˌkɒzməˈlɒdʒɪkəl) *or* ˌcosmo'logic *adj* > ˌcosmo'logically *adv* > **cos'mologist** *n*

cosmonaut (ˈkɒzməˌnɔːt) *n* an astronaut, esp in the former Soviet Union [C20 from Russian *kosmonavt,* from COSMO- + Greek *nautēs* sailor; compare ARGONAUT]

cosmopolis (kɒzˈmɒpəlɪs) *n* an international city [C19 see COSMO-, POLIS¹]

cosmopolitan (ˌkɒzməˈpɒlɪtən) *n* **1** a person who has lived and travelled in many countries, esp one who is free of national prejudices ▷ *adj* **2** having interest in or familiar with many parts of the world **3** sophisticated or urbane **4** composed of people or elements from all parts of the world or from many different spheres **5** (of plants or animals) widely distributed [C17 from French, ultimately from Greek *kosmopolitēs,* from *kosmo-* COSMO- + *politēs* citizen] > ˌcosmo'politanism *n*

cosmopolite (kɒzˈmɒpəˌlaɪt) *n* **1** a less common word for **cosmopolitan** (sense 1) **2** an animal or plant that occurs in most parts of the world > **cos'mopolit,ism** *n*

cosmos (ˈkɒzmɒs) *n* **1** the world or universe considered as an ordered system **2** any ordered system **3** harmony; order **4** (*pl* -**mos** *or* -**moses**) any tropical American plant of the genus *Cosmos,* cultivated as garden plants for their brightly coloured flowers: family *Asteraceae* (composites) [C17 from Greek *kosmos* order, world, universe]

Cosmos (ˈkɒzmɒs) *n astronautics* any of various types of Soviet satellite, including Cosmos 1 (launched 1962) and nearly 2000 subsequent satellites

Cosmotron (ˈkɒzməˌtrɒn) *n* a large synchrotron which was used for accelerating protons to high energies (of the order of 1 GeV) [C20 from COSM(IC RAY) + -TRON]

coss (kɒs) *n* another name for **kos**

Cossack (ˈkɒsæk) *n* **1** (formerly) any of the free warrior-peasants of chiefly East Slavonic descent who lived in communes, esp in Ukraine, and served as cavalry under the tsars ▷ *adj* **2** of, relating to, or characteristic of the Cossacks: *a Cossack dance* [C16 from Russian *kazak* vagabond, of Turkic origin]

cossack hat *n* a warm brimless hat of fur or sheepskin

cosset (ˈkɒsɪt) *vb* (*tr*) -**sets,** -**seting,** -**seted 1** to pamper; coddle; pet ▷ *n* **2** any pet animal, esp a lamb [C16 of unknown origin]

cossie (ˈkɒzɪ) *n* an informal name for a swimming costume

cost (kɒst) *n* **1** the price paid or required for acquiring, producing, or maintaining something, usually measured in money, time, or energy; expense or expenditure; outlay **2** suffering or sacrifice; loss; penalty: *count the cost to your health; I*

know to my cost **3** **a** the amount paid for a commodity by its seller: *to sell at cost* **b** (*as modifier*): *the cost price* **4** (*plural*) *law* the expenses of judicial proceedings **5** **at any cost** *or* **at all costs** regardless of cost or sacrifice involved **6** **at the cost of** at the expense of losing ▷ *vb* **costs, costing, cost 7** (*tr*) to be obtained or obtainable in exchange for (money or something equivalent); be priced at: *the ride cost one pound* **8** to cause or require the expenditure, loss, or sacrifice (of): *the accident cost him dearly* **9** to estimate the cost of (a product, process, etc) for the purposes of pricing, budgeting, control, etc [C13 from Old French (n), from *coster* to cost, from Latin *constāre* to stand at, cost, from *stāre* to stand] > **costless** *adj*

costa (ˈkɒstə) *n, pl* -**tae** (-tiː) **1** the technical name for **rib¹** (sense 1) **2** a riblike part, such as the midrib of a plant leaf [C19 from Latin: rib, side, wall] > **'costal** *adj*

Costa Brava (ˈkɒstə ˈbrɑːvə) *n* a coastal region of NE Spain along the Mediterranean, extending from Barcelona to the French border: many resorts

cost accounting *n* the recording and controlling of all the expenditures of an enterprise in order to facilitate control of separate activities. Also called: **management accounting** > **cost accountant** *n*

co-star *n* **1** an actor who shares star billing with another ▷ *vb* -**stars,** -**starring,** -**starred 2** (*intr; often foll by with*) to share star billing (with another actor) **3** (*tr*) to present as sharing top billing: *the film co-starred Mae West and W. C. Fields*

costard (ˈkɒstəd) *n* **1** an English variety of apple tree **2** the large ribbed apple of this tree **3** *archaic, humorous* a slang word for **head** [C14 from Anglo-Norman, from Old French *coste* rib]

Costa Rica (ˈkɒstə ˈriːkə) *n* a republic in Central America: gained independence from Spain in 1821; mostly mountainous and volcanic, with extensive forests. Official language: Spanish. Official religion: Roman Catholic. Currency: colón. Capital: San José. Pop: 4 250 000 (2004 est). Area: 50 900 sq km (19 652 sq miles)

Costa Rican (ˈkɒstə ˈriːkən) *adj* **1** of or relating to Costa Rica or its inhabitants ▷ *n* **2** a native or inhabitant of Costa Rica

costate (ˈkɒsteɪt) *adj* **1** *anatomy* having ribs **2** (of leaves) having veins or ridges, esp parallel ones [C19 from Late Latin *costātus,* from Latin *costa* rib]

cost-benefit *adj* denoting or relating to a method of assessing a project that takes into account its costs and its benefits to society as well as the revenue it generates: *a cost-benefit analysis; the project was assessed on a cost-benefit basis*

cost centre *n* a unit, such as a department of a company, to which costs may be allocated for cost accounting purposes

cost-effective *adj* providing adequate financial return in relation to outlay > **cost-effectiveness** *n*

Costermansville (ˈkɒstəmənsˌvɪl) *n* the former name (until 1966) of **Bukavu**

costermonger (ˈkɒstəˌmʌŋɡə) *or* **coster** *n Brit rare* a person who sells fruit, vegetables, etc, from a barrow [C16 *coster-,* from COSTARD + MONGER]

costive (ˈkɒstɪv) *adj* **1** having constipation; constipated **2** sluggish **3** niggardly [C14 from Old French *costivé,* from Latin *constipātus;* see CONSTIPATE] > **'costively** *adv* > **'costiveness** *n*

costly (ˈkɒstlɪ) *adj* -**lier,** -**liest 1** of great price or value; expensive **2** entailing great loss or sacrifice: *a costly victory* **3** splendid; lavish > **'costliness** *n*

costmary (ˈkɒstˌmɛərɪ) *n, pl* -**maries** a herbaceous plant, *Chrysanthemum balsamita,* native to Asia. Its fragrant leaves were used as a seasoning and to flavour ale: family *Asteraceae* (composites). Also called: **alecost** [C15 *costmarie,* from Latin *costum* aromatic plant + *Marie* (the Virgin) Mary]

cost of living *n* **1** **a** the basic cost of the food, clothing, shelter, and fuel necessary to maintain life, esp at a standard regarded as basic or minimal **b** (*as modifier*): *the cost-of-living index* **2** the average expenditure of a person or family in a given period

costotomy (kɒˈstɒtəmɪ) *n, pl* -mies surgical incision into a rib

cost-plus *n* **a** a method of establishing a selling price in which an agreed percentage is added to the cost price to cover profit **b** (*as modifier*): *cost-plus pricing*

cost-push inflation *n* See **inflation**

costrel (ˈkɒstrəl) *n obsolete* a flask, usually of earthenware or leather [C14 from Old French *costerel,* from *coste* side, rib, from Latin *costa*]

cost rent *n* (in Britain) the rent of a dwelling calculated on the cost of providing and maintaining the property without allowing for a profit

costume (ˈkɒstjuːm) *n* **1** a complete style of dressing, including all the clothes, accessories, etc, worn at one time, as in a particular country or period; dress: *national costume* **2** old-fashioned a woman's suit **3** a set of clothes, esp unusual or period clothes, worn in a play by an actor or at a fancy dress ball: *a jester's costume* **4** short for **swimming costume** ▷ *vb* (*tr*) **5** to furnish the costumes for (a show, film, etc) **6** to dress (someone) in a costume [C18 from French, from Italian: dress, habit, CUSTOM]

costume jewellery *n* jewellery that is decorative but has little intrinsic value

costume piece *n* any theatrical production, film, television presentation, etc, in which the performers wear the costumes of a former age. Also called: **costume drama**

costumier (kɒˈstjuːmɪə) *or* **costumer** (kɒˈstjuːmə) *n* a person or firm that makes or supplies theatrical or fancy costumes

cosy *or US* **cozy** (ˈkəʊzɪ) *adj* -sier, -siest *or US* -zier, -ziest **1** warm and snug **2** intimate; friendly **3** convenient, esp for devious purposes: *a cosy deal* ▷ *n, pl* -sies *or US* -zies **4** a cover for keeping things warm: *egg cosy* [C18 from Scots, of unknown origin] > ˈcosily *or US* ˈcozily *adv* > ˈcosiness *or US* ˈcoziness *n*

cosy along *vb* -sies, -sying, -sied (*tr, adverb*) to reassure (someone), esp with false assurances

cosy up *or US* **cozy up** *vb* (*intr*, often foll by *to*) *chiefly US and Canadian* **1** to seek to become intimate or to ingratiate oneself (with someone) **2** to draw close to (somebody or something) for warmth or for affection; snuggle up

cot¹ (kɒt) *n* **1** a child's boxlike bed, usually incorporating vertical bars **2** a collapsible or portable bed **3** a light bedstead **4** *nautical* a hammock-like bed with a stiff frame [C17 from Hindi *khāt* bedstead, from Sanskrit *khátvā,* of Dravidian origin; related to Tamil *kattil* bedstead]

cot² (kɒt) *n* **1** *literary or archaic* a small cottage **2** Also called: **cote a** a small shelter, esp one for pigeons, sheep, etc **b** (*in combination*): *dovecot* **3** another name for **fingerstall** [Old English *cot;* related to Old Norse *kot* little hut, Middle Low German *cot*]

cot³ (kɒt) *abbreviation for* cotangent

cot⁴ (kɒt) *vb* cots, cotting, cotted *Midland English dialect* to entangle or become entangled

cotan (ˈkəʊˌtæn) *abbreviation for* cotangent

cotangent (kəʊˈtændʒənt) *n* (of an angle) a trigonometric function that in a right-angled triangle is the ratio of the length of the adjacent side to that of the opposite side; the reciprocal of tangent. Abbreviations: **cot, cotan, ctn** > **cotangential** (ˌkəʊtænˈdʒɛnʃəl) *adj*

cot case *n Austral and NZ* **1** a person confined to bed through illness **2** *humorous* a person who is incapacitated by drink

cot death *n* the unexplained sudden death of an infant during sleep. Technical name: **sudden infant death syndrome.** Also called (US and Canadian): **crib death**

cote¹ (kəʊt) *or* **cot** *n* **1 a** a small shelter for pigeons, sheep, etc **b** (*in combination*): *dovecote* **2** *dialect, chiefly Brit* a small cottage [Old English *cote;*

related to Low German *Kote;* see COT²]

cote² (kəʊt) *vb* (*tr*) *archaic* to pass by, outstrip, or surpass [C16 perhaps from Old French *costoier* to run alongside, from *coste* side; see COAST]

Côte d'Azur (French kot dazyr) *n* the Mediterranean coast of France, including the French Riviera: forms an administrative region with Provence

Côte d'Ivoire (French kot divwar) *n* a republic in West Africa, on the Gulf of Guinea: Portuguese trading for ivory and slaves began in the 16th century; made a French protectorate in 1842 and became independent in 1960; major producer of coffee and cocoa. Official language: French. Religion: Muslim majority, with animist, atheist, and Roman Catholic minorities. Currency: franc. Capital: Yamoussoukro (administrative); Abidjan (legislative). Pop: 16 897 000 (2004 est). Area: 319 820 sq km (123 483 sq miles). Former name (until 1986): **the Ivory Coast**

Côte-d'Or (French kotdɔr) *n* a department of E central France, in NE Burgundy. Capital: Dijon. Pop: 510 334 (2003 est). Area: 8787 sq km (3427 sq miles)

cotemporary (kəʊˈtɛmpərərɪ) *adj* a variant of **contemporary**

cotenant (kəʊˈtɛnənt) *n* a person who holds property jointly or in common with others > co'tenancy *n*

coterie (ˈkəʊtərɪ) *n* a small exclusive group of friends or people with common interests; clique [C18 from French, from Old French: association of tenants, from *cotier* (unattested) cottager, from Medieval Latin *cotārius* COTTER²; see COT²]

coterminous (kəʊˈtɜːmɪnəs) *or* **conterminous** *adj* **1** having a common boundary; bordering; contiguous **2** coextensive or coincident in range, time, scope, etc

Côtes-d'Armor (French kotdarmɔr) *n* a department of W France, on the N coast of Brittany. Capital: St Brieuc. Pop: 553 969 (2003 est). Area: 6878 sq km (2656 sq miles). Former name: **Côtes-du-Nord**

Côtes-du-Nord (French kotdynɔr) *n* the former name of **Côtes-d'Armor**

coth (kɒθ) *n* hyperbolic cotangent; a hyperbolic function that is the ratio of cosh to sinh, being the reciprocal of tanh [C20 from COT(ANGENT) + H(YPERBOLIC)]

cothurnus (kəʊˈθɜːnəs) *or* **cothurn** (ˈkəʊθɜːn, kəʊˈθɜːn) *n, pl* -thurni (-ˈθɜːnaɪ) *or* -thurns the buskin worn in ancient Greek tragedy [C18 from Latin, from Greek *kothornos*]

cotidal (kəʊˈtaɪdəl) *adj* (of a line on a tidal chart) joining points at which high tide occurs simultaneously

cotillion *or* **cotillon** (kəˈtɪljən, kəʊ-) *n* **1** a French formation dance of the 18th century **2** *US* a quadrille **3** *US* a complicated dance with frequent changes of partners **4** *US and Canadian* a formal ball, esp one at which debutantes are presented [C18 from French *cotillon* dance, from Old French: petticoat, from *cote* COAT]

cotinga (kəˈtɪŋɡə) *n* any tropical American passerine bird of the family *Cotingidae,* such as the umbrella bird and the cock-of-the-rock, having a broad slightly hooked bill. Also called: **chatterer**

cotoneaster (kəˌtəʊnɪˈæstə) *n* any Old World shrub of the rosaceous genus *Cotoneaster:* cultivated for their small ornamental white or pinkish flowers and red or black berries [C18 from New Latin, from Latin *cotōneum* QUINCE]

Cotonou (ˌkəʊtəˈnuː) *n* the chief port and official capital of Benin, on the Bight of Benin. Pop: 891 000 (2005 est)

Cotopaxi (Spanish koto'paksi) *n* a volcano in central Ecuador, in the Andes: the world's highest active volcano. Height: 5896 m (19 344 ft)

cotquean (ˈkɒtˌkwiːn) *n archaic* **1** a coarse woman **2** a man who does housework [C16 see COT², QUEAN]

cotransport (kəʊˈtrænsˌpɔːt) *n biochem* the

transport of one solute across a membrane from a region of low concentration of another solute to a region of high concentration of that solute. See **active transport**

co-trimoxazole (ˌkəʊtrɪˈmɒksəzəʊl) *n* an antibiotic consisting of a mixture of trimethoprim and sulfamethoxazole (a sulfa drug): used esp to treat infections of the urinary tract and lungs (as in AIDS)

Cotswold (ˈkɒtsˌwəʊld, -wəld) *n* a breed of sheep with long wool that originated in the Cotswolds. It is believed to be one of the oldest breeds in the world

Cotswolds (ˈkɒtsˌwəʊldz, -wəldz) *pl n* a range of low hills in SW England, mainly in Gloucestershire: formerly a centre of the wool industry

cotta (ˈkɒtə) *n RC Church* a short form of surplice [C19 from Italian: tunic, from Medieval Latin; see COAT]

cottage (ˈkɒtɪdʒ) *n* **1** a small simple house, esp in a rural area **2** *US and Canadian* a small house in the country or at a resort, used for holiday purposes **3** *US* one of several housing units, as at a hospital, for accommodating people in groups **4** *slang* a public lavatory [C14 from COT²]

cottage cheese *n* a mild loose soft white cheese made from skimmed milk curds

cottage country *n Canadian* any lakeside region where many country cottages are located

cottage flat *n Brit* any of the flats in a two-storey house that is divided into four flats, two on each floor

cottage hospital *n Brit* a small rural hospital

cottage industry *n* an industry in which employees work in their own homes, often using their own equipment

cottage loaf *n Brit* a loaf consisting of two round pieces, the smaller of which sits on top of the larger

cottage piano *n* a small upright piano

cottage pie *n Brit* another term for **shepherd's pie**

cottager (ˈkɒtɪdʒə) *n* **1** a person who lives in a cottage **2** a rural labourer **3** *chiefly Canadian* a person holidaying in a cottage, esp an owner and seasonal resident of a cottage in a resort area **4** *history* another name for **cotter²**

cottaging (ˈkɒtɪdʒɪŋ) *n Brit* homosexual activity between men in a public lavatory [C20 from COTTAGE (sense 4)]

Cottbus (German 'kɔtbʊs) *n* an industrial city in E Germany, in Brandenburg on the Spree River. Pop: 107 549 (2003 est)

cotter¹ (ˈkɒtə) *machinery* ▷ *n* **1** any part, such as a pin, wedge, key, etc, that is used to secure two other parts so that relative motion between them is prevented **2** short for **cotter pin** ▷ *vb* **3** (*tr*) to secure (two parts) with a cotter [C14 shortened from *cotterel,* of unknown origin]

cotter² (ˈkɒtə) *n* **1** Also called: **cottier** *English history* a villein in late Anglo-Saxon and early Norman times occupying a cottage and land in return for labour **2** Also called: **cottar** a peasant occupying a cottage and land in the Scottish Highlands under the same tenure as an Irish cottier ▷ See also **cottier** (sense 2), **cottager** (sense 1) [C14 from Medieval Latin *cotārius,* from Middle English *cote* COT²]

cotter pin *n machinery* **1** a split pin secured, after passing through holes in the parts to be attached, by spreading the ends **2** a tapered pin threaded at the smaller end and secured by a nut after insertion

Cottian Alps (ˈkɒtɪən) *pl n* a mountain range in SW Europe, between NW Italy and SE France: part of the Alps. Highest peak: Monte Viso, 3841 m (12 600 ft)

cottid (ˈkɒtɪd) *n* any fish of the scorpaenoid family *Cottidae,* typically possessing a large head, tapering body, and spiny fins, including the pogge, sea scorpion, bullhead, father lasher, and

cottus [from New Latin *Cottidae*, from *cottus*, from Greek *kottos*, the name of an unidentified river fish]

cottier ('kɒtɪə) *n* **1** another name for **cotter²** (sense 1) **2** (in Ireland) a peasant farming a smallholding under **cottier tenure** (the holding of not more than half an acre at a rent of not more than five pounds a year) **3** another name for **cottager** (sense 1) [C14 from Old French *cotier*; see COTE¹, COTERIE]

cotton ('kɒt³n) *n* **1** any of various herbaceous plants and shrubs of the malvaceous genus *Gossypium*, such as **sea-island cotton**, cultivated in warm climates for the fibre surrounding the seeds and the oil within the seeds **2** the soft white downy fibre of these plants: used to manufacture textiles **3** cotton plants collectively, as a cultivated crop **4 a** a cloth or thread made from cotton fibres **b** (*as modifier*): *a cotton dress* **5** any substance, such as kapok (**silk cotton**), resembling cotton but obtained from other plants ▷ See also **cotton on, cotton to** [C14 from Old French *coton*, from Arabic dialect *qutun*, from Arabic *qutn*] > **'cottony** *adj*

cottonade (,kɒt³'neɪd) *n* a coarse fabric of cotton or mixed fibres, used for work clothes, etc [C19 from French *cotonnade*, from *coton* COTTON + -ADE]

cotton belt *n* a belt of land in the southeastern US that specializes in the production of cotton

cotton bush *n Austral* any of various downy chenopodiaceous shrubs, esp *Kochia aphylla*, which is used to feed livestock

cotton cake *n* cottonseed meal compressed into nuts or cubes of various sizes for feeding to animals

cotton candy *n US and Canadian* a very light fluffy confection made from coloured spun sugar, usually held on a stick. Also called (in Britain and certain other countries): **candyfloss**. Austral name: **fairyfloss**

cotton flannel *n* a plain-weave or twill-weave fabric with nap on one side only. Also called: **Canton flannel**

cotton grass *n* any of various N temperate and arctic grasslike bog plants of the cyperaceous genus *Eriophorum*, whose clusters of long silky hairs resemble cotton tufts. Also called: **bog cotton**

cottonmouth ('kɒt³n,maʊθ) *n* another name for the **water moccasin**

cotton on *vb* (*intr, adverb; often foll by to*) *informal* **1** to perceive the meaning (of) **2** to make use (of)

cotton picker *n* **1** a machine for harvesting cotton fibre **2** a person who picks ripe cotton fibre from the plants

cotton-picking *adj US and Canadian slang* (intensifier qualifying something undesirable): *you cotton-picking layabout!*

cotton sedge *n Canadian* another name for **cotton grass**

cottonseed ('kɒt³n,siːd) *n, pl* **-seeds** *or* **-seed** the seed of the cotton plant: a source of oil and fodder

cottonseed meal *n* the residue of cottonseed kernels from which oil has been extracted, used as fodder or fertilizer

cottonseed oil *n* a yellowish or dark red oil with a nutlike smell, extracted or expelled from cottonseed, used in cooking and in the manufacture of paints, soaps, etc

cotton stainer *n* any of various heteropterous insects of the genus *Dysdercus*: serious pests of cotton, piercing and staining the cotton bolls: family *Pyrrhocoridae*

cottontail ('kɒt³n,teɪl) *n* any of several common rabbits of the genus *Sylvilagus*, such as *S. floridanus* (**eastern cottontail**), of American woodlands

cotton to *vb* (*intr, preposition*) *US and Canadian informal* **1** to become friendly with **2** to approve of

cotton waste *n* refuse cotton yarn, esp when used as a cleaning material

cottonweed ('kɒt³n,wiːd) *n* **1** a downy perennial plant, *Otanthus maritimus*, of European coastal

regions, having small yellow flowers surrounded by large hairy bracts: family *Asteraceae* (composites) **2** any of various similar plants

cottonwood ('kɒt³n,wʊd) *n* **1** any of several North American poplars, esp *Populus deltoides*, whose seeds are covered with cottony hairs **2** a native New Zealand shrub, *Cassinia leptophylla*, with daisy-like flowers. Also called: **tauhinu**

cotton wool *n* **1** Also called: **purified cotton** *chiefly Brit* bleached and sterilized cotton from which the gross impurities, such as the seeds and waxy matter, have been removed: used for surgical dressings, tampons, etc. Usual US term: **absorbent cotton 2** cotton in the natural state **3** *Brit informal* **a** a state of pampered comfort and protection **b** (*as modifier*) *a cotton-wool existence*

cottony-cushion scale *n* a small scale insect, *Icerya purchasi*, that is a pest of citrus trees in California: it is controlled by introducing an Australian ladybird, *Rodolia cardinalis*, into affected areas

cottus ('kɒtəs) *n* a scorpaenoid fish of the family *Cottidae*; the type genus, having four yellowish knobs on its head. See also **cottid**

cotyledon (,kɒtɪ'liːd³n) *n* **1** a simple embryonic leaf in seed-bearing plants, which, in some species, forms the first green leaf after germination **2** a tuft of villi on the mammalian placenta [C16 from Latin: a plant, navelwort, from Greek *kotulēdōn*, from *kotulē* cup, hollow] > ,coty'ledonous *or* ,coty'ledo,noid *adj* > ,coty'ledonal *adj* > ,coty'ledonary *adj*

cotyloid ('kɒtɪ,lɔɪd) *or* **cotyloidal** *anatomy* ▷ *adj* **1 a** shaped like a cup **b** of or relating to the acetabulum ▷ *n* **2** a small bone forming part of the acetabular cavity in some mammals [C18 from Greek *kotuloeidēs* cup-shaped, from *kotulē* a cup]

cotype ('kəʊ,taɪp) *n biology* an additional type specimen from the same brood as the original type specimen

coucal ('kuːkæl, -k³l) *n* any ground-living bird of the genus *Centropus*, of Africa, S Asia, and Australia, having long strong legs: family *Cuculidae* (cuckoos) [C19 from French, perhaps from *couc(ou)* cuckoo + *al(ouette)* lark]

couch (kaʊtʃ) *n* **1** a piece of upholstered furniture, usually having a back and armrests, for seating more than one person **2** a bed, esp one used in the daytime by the patients of a doctor or a psychoanalyst **3** a frame upon which barley is malted **4** a priming layer of paint or varnish, esp in a painting **5** *papermaking* **a** a board on which sheets of handmade paper are dried by pressing **b** a felt blanket onto which sheets of partly dried paper are transferred for further drying **c** a roll on a papermaking machine from which the wet web of paper on the wire is transferred to the next section **6** *archaic* the lair of a wild animal ▷ *vb* **7** (*tr*) to express in a particular style of language: *couched in an archaic style* **8** (when *tr*, usually reflexive or passive) to lie down or cause to lie down for or as for sleep **9** (*intr*) *archaic* to lie in ambush; lurk **10** (*tr*) to spread (barley) on a frame for malting **11** (*intr*) (of decomposing leaves) to lie in a heap or bed **12** (*tr*) to embroider or depict by couching **13** (*tr*) to lift (sheets of handmade paper) onto the board on which they will be dried **14** (*tr*) *surgery* to remove (a cataract) by downward displacement of the lens of the eye **15** (*tr*) *archaic* to lower (a lance) into a horizontal position [C14 from Old French *couche* a bed, lair, from *coucher* to lay down, from Latin *collocāre* to arrange, from *locāre* to place; see LOCATE] > **'coucher** *n*

couchant ('kaʊtʃənt) *adj* (*usually postpositive*) *heraldry* in a lying position: *a lion couchant* [C15 from French: lying, from Old French *coucher* to lay down; see COUCH]

couchette (kuː'ʃet) *n* a bed in a railway carriage, esp one converted from seats [C20 from French, diminutive of *couche* bed]

couch grass (kaʊtʃ, kuːtʃ) *n* a grass, *Agropyron repens*, with a yellowish-white creeping

underground stem by which it spreads quickly: a troublesome weed. Sometimes shortened to: **couch**. Also called: **scutch grass, twitch grass, quitch grass**

couching ('kaʊtʃɪŋ) *n* **a** a method of embroidery in which the thread is caught down at intervals by another thread passed through the material from beneath **b** a pattern or work done by this method

couch potato *n slang* a lazy person whose recreation consists chiefly of watching television and videos

cou-cou ('kuːkuː, 'kʊkuː) *n* a preparation of boiled corn meal and okras, stirred to a stiff consistency with a **cou-cou stick**, eaten in the Caribbean [of uncertain origin]

coudé (kuː'deɪ) *adj* (of a reflecting telescope) having plane mirrors positioned to reflect light from the primary mirror along the axis onto a detector [French, literally: bent in the shape of an elbow, from *coude* an elbow]

cougan ('kuːgən) *n Austral slang* a rowdy person, esp one who drinks large quantities of alcohol

cougar ('kuːgə) *n* another name for **puma** [C18 from French *couguar*, from Portuguese *cuguardo*, from Tupi *suasuarana*, literally: deerlike, from *suasú* deer + *rana* similar to]

cough (kɒf) *vb* **1** (*intr*) to expel air or solid matter from the lungs abruptly and explosively through the partially closed vocal chords **2** (*intr*) to make a sound similar to this **3** (*tr*) to utter or express with a cough or coughs **4** (*intr*) *slang* to confess to a crime ▷ *n* **5** an act, instance, or sound of coughing **6** a condition of the lungs or throat that causes frequent coughing [Old English *cohhetten*; related to Middle Dutch *kochen*, Middle High German *kūchen* to wheeze; probably of imitative origin] > **'cougher** *n*

cough drop *n* a lozenge to relieve a cough

cough mixture *n* any medicine that relieves coughing

cough up *vb* (*adverb*) **1** *informal* to surrender (money, information, etc), esp reluctantly **2** (*tr*) to bring into the mouth or eject (phlegm, food, etc) by coughing

could (kʊd) *vb* (takes an infinitive without *to* or an implied infinitive) **1** used as an auxiliary to make the past tense of **can¹ 2** used as an auxiliary to make the subjunctive mood of **can¹**, esp used in polite requests or in conditional sentences: *could I see you tonight?; she'd telephone if she could* **3** used as an auxiliary to indicate suggestion of a course of action: *you could take the car tomorrow if it's raining* **4** (often foll by *well*) used as an auxiliary to indicate a possibility: *he could well be a spy* [Old English *cūthe*; influenced by WOULD, should; see CAN¹]

couldn't ('kʊd³nt) *contraction of* could not

couldst (kʊdst) *vb archaic* the form of **could** used with the pronoun *thou* or its relative form

coulee ('kuːleɪ, -lɪ) *n* **1 a** a flow of molten lava **b** such lava when solidified **2** *Western US and Canadian* a dry stream valley, especially a long steep-sided gorge or ravine that once carried melt water from a glacier **3** a small intermittent stream in such a ravine [C19 from Canadian French *coulée* a flow, from French, from *couler* to flow, from Latin *cōlāre* to sift, purify; see COLANDER]

coulibiaca (,kuːlɪ'bjɑːkə) *n* a variant spelling of **koulibiaca**

coulis ('kuːliː) *n* a thin purée of vegetables, fruit, etc, usually served as a sauce surrounding a dish [C20 French, literally: purée]

coulisse (kuː'liːs) *n* **1** Also called: **cullis** a timber member grooved to take a sliding panel, such as a sluicegate, portcullis, or stage flat **2 a** a flat piece of scenery situated in the wings of a theatre; wing flat **b** a space between wing flats **3** part of the Paris Bourse where unofficial securities are traded. Compare **parquet** (sense 4) [C19 from French: groove, from Old French *couleïce* PORTCULLIS]

couloir ('ku:lwɑ:; *French* kulwar) *n* a deep gully on a mountain side, esp in the French Alps [C19 from French: corridor, from *couler* to pour; see COULEE]

coulomb ('ku:lɒm) *n* the derived SI unit of electric charge; the quantity of electricity transported in one second by a current of 1 ampere. Symbol: C [C19 named after Charles Augustin de Coulomb (1736–1806), French physicist]

Coulomb field *n* the electrostatic field around an electrically charged body or particle

Coulomb's law *n* the principle that the force of attraction or repulsion between two point electric charges is directly proportional to the product of the charges and inversely proportional to the square of the distance between them. A similar law holds for particles with mass

coulometer (ku:'lɒmɪtə) *or* **coulombmeter** ('ku:lɒm,mi:tə) *n* an electrolytic cell for measuring the magnitude of an electric charge by determining the total amount of decomposition resulting from the passage of the charge through the cell. Also called: voltameter [C19 from COULOMB + METER[3]] > **coulometric** (,ku:lə'mɛtrɪk) *adj* > **cou'lometry** *n*

coulter ('kəʊltə) *n* a blade or sharp-edged disc attached to a plough so that it cuts through the soil vertically in advance of the ploughshare. Also (esp US): colter [Old English *culter*, from Latin: ploughshare, knife]

coumarin *or* **cumarin** ('ku:mərɪn) *n* a white vanilla-scented crystalline ester, used in perfumes and flavourings and as an anticoagulant. Formula: $C_9H_6O_2$ [C19 from French *coumarine*, from *coumarou* tonka-bean tree, from Spanish *cumarú*, from Tupi] > **coumaric** *or* **cumaric** *adj*

coumarone ('ku:mə,rəʊn) *n* another name for **benzofuran** [C19 from COUMAR(IN) + -ONE]

council ('kaʊnsəl) *n* **1** an assembly of people meeting for discussion, consultation, etc: *an emergency council* **2** a body of people elected or appointed to serve in an administrative, legislative, or advisory capacity: *a student council* **3** *Brit* (*sometimes capital; often preceded by the*) the local governing authority of a town, county, etc **4** a meeting or the deliberation of a council **5** (*modifier*) of, relating to, provided for, or used by a local council: *a council chamber; council offices* **6** (*modifier*) *Brit* provided by a local council, esp (of housing) at a subsidized rent: *a council house; a council estate* **7** *Austral* an administrative or legislative assembly, esp the upper house of a state parliament in Australia **8** *Christianity* an assembly of bishops, theologians, and other representatives of several churches or dioceses, convened for regulating matters of doctrine or discipline [C12 from Old French *concile*, from Latin *concilium* assembly, from *com-* together + *calāre* to call; influenced also by Latin *consilium* advice, COUNSEL]

　　■ USAGE Avoid confusion with **counsel**

council area *n* any of the 32 unitary authorities into which Scotland has been divided for administrative purposes since April 1996

councillor *or US* **councilor** ('kaʊnsələ) *n* a member of a council > 'councillor,ship *or US* 'councilor,ship *n*

　　■ USAGE Avoid confusion with **counsellor**

councilman ('kaʊnsəlmən) *n, pl* -men *chiefly US* a member of a council, esp of a town or city; councillor

council-manager plan *n* (in the US) a system of local government with an elected legislative council and an appointed administrative manager. See also city manager

Council of Europe *n* an association of European states, established in 1949 to promote unity between its members, defend human rights, and increase social and economic progress

Council of States *n* another name for **Rajya Sabha**

Council of Trent *n* the council of the Roman Catholic Church that met between 1545 and 1563 at Trent in S Tyrol. Reacting against the Protestants, it reaffirmed traditional Catholic beliefs and formulated the ideals of the Counter-Reformation

council of war *n* **1** an assembly of military leaders in wartime **2** an emergency meeting to formulate a plan

councilor ('kaʊnsələ) *n* **1** a variant US spelling of **councillor** **2** an archaic spelling of **counsellor** > 'councilor,ship *n*

council school *n* *Brit* (esp formerly) any school maintained by the state

council tax *n* (in Britain) a tax, based on the relative value of property, levied to fund local council services

counsel ('kaʊnsəl) *n* **1** advice or guidance on conduct, behaviour, etc **2** discussion, esp on future procedure; consultation: *to take counsel with a friend* **3** a person whose advice or guidance is or has been sought **4** a barrister or group of barristers engaged in conducting cases in court and advising on legal matters: *counsel for the prosecution* **5** a policy or plan **6** *Christianity* any of the **counsels of perfection** or **evangelical counsels**, namely poverty, chastity, and obedience **7** **counsel of perfection** excellent but unrealizable advice **8** private opinions or plans (esp in the phrase **keep one's own counsel**) **9** *archaic* wisdom; prudence ▷ *vb* -sels, -selling, -selled *or US* -sels, -seling, -seled **10** (*tr*) to give advice or guidance to **11** (*tr; often takes a clause as object*) to recommend the acceptance of (a plan, idea, etc); urge **12** (*intr*) *archaic* to take counsel; consult [C13 from Old French *counseil*, from Latin *consilium* deliberating body; related to CONSUL, CONSULT] > 'counsellable *or US* 'counselable *adj*

　　■ USAGE Avoid confusion with **council**

counselling *or US* **counseling** ('kaʊnsəlɪŋ) *n* guidance offered by social workers, doctors, etc, to help a person resolve social or personal problems

counsellor *or US* **counselor** ('kaʊnsələ) *n* **1** a person who gives counsel; adviser **2** a person, such as a social worker, who is involved in counselling **3** Also called: counselor-at-law *US* a lawyer, esp one who conducts cases in court; attorney **4** a senior British diplomatic officer **5** a US diplomatic officer ranking just below an ambassador or minister **6** a person who advises students or others on personal problems or academic and occupational choice > 'counsellor,ship *or US* 'counselor,ship *n*

　　■ USAGE Avoid confusion with **councillor**

count[1] (kaʊnt) *vb* **1** to add up or check (each unit in a collection) in order to ascertain the sum; enumerate: *count your change* **2** (*tr*) to recite numbers in ascending order up to and including **3** (*tr; often foll by in*) to take into account or include: *we must count him in* **4** not counting excluding **5** (*tr*) to believe to be; consider; think; deem: *count yourself lucky* **6** (*intr*) to recite or list numbers in ascending order either in units or groups: *to count in tens* **7** (*intr*) to have value, importance, or influence: *this picture counts as a rarity* **8** (*intr; often foll by for*) to have a certain specified value or importance: *the job counts for a lot* **9** (*intr*) *music* to keep time by counting beats ▷ *n* **10** the act of counting or reckoning **11** the number reached by counting; sum **12** *law* a paragraph in an indictment containing a distinct and separate charge **13** *physics* the total number of photons or ionized particles detected by a counter **14** keep count to keep a record of items, events, etc **15** lose count to fail to keep an accurate record of items, events, etc **16** *boxing, wrestling* the act of telling off a number of seconds by the referee, as when a boxer has been knocked down or a wrestler pinned by his opponent **17** out for the count *boxing* knocked out and unable to continue after a count of ten by the referee **18** take the

count *boxing* to be unable to continue after a count of ten **19** *archaic* notice; regard; account ▷ See also **count against, countdown, count on, count out** [C14 from Anglo-French *counter*, from Old French *conter*, from Latin *computāre* to calculate, COMPUTE]

count[2] (kaʊnt) *n* **1** a nobleman in any of various European countries having a rank corresponding to that of a British earl **2** any of various officials in the late Roman Empire and under various Germanic kings in the early Middle Ages **3** a man who has received an honour (**papal knighthood**) from the Pope in recognition of good deeds, achievements, etc [C16 from Old French *conte*, from Late Latin *comes* occupant of a state office, from Latin: overseer, associate, literally: one who goes with, from COM- with + *īre* to go] > 'count,ship *n*

countable ('kaʊntəb⁹l) *adj* **1** capable of being counted **2** *maths, logic* able to be counted using the natural numbers; finite or denumerable **3** *linguistics* denoting a count noun

count against *vb* (*intr, preposition*) to have influence to the disadvantage of: *your bad timekeeping will count against you*

countback ('kaʊnt,bæk) *n* a system of deciding the winner of a tied competition by comparing earlier points or scores

countdown ('kaʊnt,daʊn) *n* **1** the act of counting backwards to time a critical operation exactly, such as the launching of a rocket or the detonation of explosives ▷ *vb* count down (*intr, adverb*) **2** to count numbers backwards towards zero, esp in timing such a critical operation

countenance ('kaʊntɪnəns) *n* **1** the face, esp when considered as expressing a person's character or mood: *a pleasant countenance* **2** support or encouragement; sanction **3** composure; self-control (esp in the phrases **keep** *or* **lose one's countenance; out of countenance**) ▷ *vb* (*tr*) **4** to support or encourage; sanction **5** to tolerate; endure [C13 from Old French *contenance* mien, behaviour, from Latin *continentia* restraint, control; see CONTAIN] > 'countenancer *n*

counter[1] ('kaʊntə) *n* **1** a horizontal surface, as in a shop or bank, over which business is transacted **2** (in some cafeterias) a long table on which food is served to customers **3** **a** a small flat disc of wood, metal, or plastic, used in various board games **b** a similar disc or token used as an imitation coin **4** a person or thing that may be used or manipulated **5** a skating figure consisting of three circles **6** under the counter (**under-the-counter** *when prenominal*) (of the sale of goods, esp goods in short supply) clandestine, surreptitious, or illegal; not in an open manner **7** over the counter (**over-the-counter** *when prenominal*) (of security transactions) through a broker rather than on a stock exchange [C14 from Old French *comptouer*, ultimately from Latin *computāre* to COMPUTE]

counter[2] ('kaʊntə) *n* **1** a person who counts **2** an apparatus that records the number of occurrences of events **3** any instrument for detecting or counting ionizing particles or photons. See **Geiger counter, scintillation counter, crystal counter** **4** *electronics* another name for **scaler** (sense 2) [C14 from Old French *conteor*, from Latin *computātor*; see COUNT[1]]

counter[3] ('kaʊntə) *adv* **1** in a contrary direction or manner **2** in a wrong or reverse direction **3** run counter to to have a contrary effect or action to ▷ *adj* **4** opposing; opposite; contrary ▷ *n* **5** something that is contrary or opposite to some other thing **6** an act, effect, or force that opposes another **7** a return attack, such as a blow in boxing **8** *fencing* a parry in which the foils move in a circular fashion **9** the portion of the stern of a boat or ship that overhangs the water aft of the rudder **10** Also called: void *printing* the inside area of a typeface that is not type high, such as the centre of an "o", and therefore does not print

C

11 the part of a horse's breast under the neck and between the shoulders **12** a piece of leather forming the back of a shoe ▷ *vb* **13** to say or do (something) in retaliation or response **14** (*tr*) to move, act, or perform in a manner or direction opposite to (a person or thing) **15** to return the attack of (an opponent) [c15 from Old French *contre,* from Latin *contrā* against]

counter- *prefix* **1** against; opposite; contrary: *counterattack* **2** complementary; corresponding: *counterfoil* **3** duplicate or substitute: *counterfeit* [via Norman French from Latin *contrā* against, opposite; see CONTRA-]

counteract (ˌkaʊntərˈækt) *vb* (*tr*) to oppose, neutralize, or mitigate the effects of by contrary action; check ▷ ˌcounterˈaction *n* ▷ ˌcounterˈactive *adj* ▷ ˌcounterˈactively *adv*

counterattack (ˈkaʊntərəˌtæk) *n* **1** an attack in response to an attack ▷ *vb* **2** to make a counterattack (against)

counterattraction (ˈkaʊntərəˌtrækʃən) *n* a rival attraction

counterbalance *n* (ˈkaʊntəˌbæləns) **1** a weight or force that balances or offsets another ▷ *vb* (ˌkaʊntəˈbæləns) (*tr*) **2** to act as a counterbalance ▷ Also: **counterpoise**

counterblast (ˈkaʊntəˌblɑːst) *n* **1** an aggressive response to a verbal attack **2** a blast that counteracts another

counterchange (ˌkaʊntəˈtʃeɪndʒ) *vb* (*tr*) **1** to change parts, qualities, etc **2** *poetic* to chequer, as with contrasting colours

countercharge (ˈkaʊntəˌtʃɑːdʒ) *n* **1** a charge brought by an accused person against the accuser **2** *military* a retaliatory charge ▷ *vb* **3** (*tr*) to make a countercharge against

countercheck *n* (ˈkaʊntəˌtʃɛk) **1** a check or restraint, esp one that acts in opposition to another **2** a restraint that reinforces another restraint **3** a double check, as for accuracy ▷ *vb* (ˌkaʊntəˈtʃɛk) (*tr*) **4** to oppose by counteraction **5** to control or restrain by a second check **6** to double-check

counterclaim (ˈkaʊntəˌkleɪm) *chiefly law* ▷ *n* **1** a claim set up in opposition to another, esp by the defendant in a civil action against the plaintiff ▷ *vb* **2** to set up (a claim) in opposition to another claim ▷ ˌcounterˈclaimant *n*

counterclockwise (ˌkaʊntəˈklɒkˌwaɪz) or **contraclockwise** *adv, adj US and Canadian* in the opposite direction to the rotation of the hands of a clock. Also called (in Britain and certain other countries): **anticlockwise**

counterconditioning (ˌkaʊntəkənˈdɪʃənɪŋ) *n psychol* the conditioning of a response that is incompatible with some previously learned response; for example, in psychotherapy an anxious person might be taught relaxation, which is incompatible with anxiety

counterculture (ˈkaʊntəˌkʌltʃə) *n* an alternative culture, deliberately at variance with the social norm

counterespionage (ˌkaʊntərˈɛspɪəˌnɑːʒ) *n* activities designed to detect and counteract enemy espionage

counterexample (ˈkaʊntərɪɡˌzɑːmpəl) *n* an example or fact that is inconsistent with a hypothesis and may be used in argument against it

counterfactual (ˌkaʊntəˈfæktʃʊəl) *logic* ▷ *adj* **1** expressing what has not happened but could, would, or might under differing conditions ▷ *n* **2** a conditional statement in which the first clause is a past tense subjunctive statement expressing something contrary to fact, as in: *if she had hurried she would have caught the bus*

counterfeit (ˈkaʊntəfɪt) *adj* **1** made in imitation of something genuine with the intent to deceive or defraud; forged **2** simulated; sham: *counterfeit affection* ▷ *n* **3** an imitation designed to deceive or defraud **4** *archaic* an impostor; cheat ▷ *vb* **5** (*tr*) to make a fraudulent imitation of **6** (*intr*) to make

counterfeits **7** to feign; simulate **8** (*tr*) to imitate; copy [c13 from Old French *contrefait,* from *contrefaire* to copy, from *contre-* COUNTER- + *faire* to make, from Latin *facere*] > ˈcounterfeiter *n*

counterfoil (ˈkaʊntəˌfɔɪl) *n Brit* the part of a cheque, postal order, receipt, etc, detached and retained as a record of the transaction. Also called (esp US and Canadian): **stub**

counterfort (ˈkaʊntəˌfɔːt) *n civil engineering* a strengthening buttress at right angles to a retaining wall, bonded to it to prevent overturning or to increase its bending strength [from a partial translation of French *contrefort,* from *contre* counter + *fort* strength; see FORT]

counterglow (ˈkaʊntəˌɡləʊ) *n* another name for **gegenschein**

counterinsurgency (ˌkaʊntərɪnˈsɜːdʒənsɪ) *n* action taken by a government to counter the activities of rebels, guerrillas, etc

counterintelligence (ˌkaʊntərɪnˈtɛlɪdʒəns) *n* **1** activities designed to frustrate enemy espionage **2** intelligence collected about enemy espionage

counterirritant (ˌkaʊntərˈɪrɪtᵊnt) *n* **1** an agent that causes a superficial irritation of the skin and thereby relieves inflammation of deep structures ▷ *adj* **2** producing a counterirritation > ˌcounterˌirriˈtation *n*

counter jumper *n old-fashioned derogatory* a sales assistant in a shop

countermand *vb* (ˌkaʊntəˈmɑːnd) (*tr*) **1** to revoke or cancel (a command, order, etc) **2** to order (forces, etc) to return or retreat; recall ▷ *n* (ˈkaʊntəˌmɑːnd) **3** a command revoking another [c15 from Old French *contremander,* from *contre-* COUNTER- + *mander* to command, from Latin *mandāre;* see MANDATE]

countermarch (ˈkaʊntəˌmɑːtʃ) *vb* **1** *chiefly military* **a** to march or cause to march back along the same route **b** to change the order of soldiers during a march ▷ *n* **2** the act or instance of countermarching **3** a reversal of method, conduct, etc

countermeasure (ˈkaʊntəˌmɛʒə) *n* action taken to oppose, neutralize, or retaliate against some other action

countermine *n* (ˈkaʊntəˌmaɪn) **1** *military* a tunnel dug to defeat similar activities by an enemy **2** a plot to frustrate another plot ▷ *vb* (ˌkaʊntəˈmaɪn) **3** to frustrate by countermeasures **4** *military* to take measures to defeat the underground operations of (an enemy) **5** *military* to destroy enemy mines in (an area) with mines of one's own

countermove (ˈkaʊntəˌmuːv) *n* **1** an opposing move ▷ *vb* **2** to make or do (something) as an opposing move > ˈcounterˌmovement *n*

counteroffensive (ˈkaʊntərəˌfɛnsɪv) *n* a series of attacks by a defending force against an attacking enemy

counteroffer (ˈkaʊntərˌɒfə) *n* a response to a bid in which a seller amends his original offer, making it more favourable to the buyer

counterpane (ˈkaʊntəˌpeɪn) *n* another word for **bedspread** [c17 from obsolete *counterpoint* (influenced by *pane* coverlet), changed from Old French *coutepointe* quilt, from Medieval Latin *culcita puncta* quilted mattress]

counterpart (ˈkaʊntəˌpɑːt) *n* **1** a person or thing identical to or closely resembling another **2** one of two parts that complement or correspond to each other **3** a person acting opposite another in a play **4** a duplicate, esp of a legal document; copy

counterparty (ˈkaʊntəˌpɑːtɪ) *n, pl* **-parties** a person who is a party to a contract

counterparty risk *n* the risk that a person who is a party to a contract will default on their obligations under that contract

counterplot (ˈkaʊntəˌplɒt) *n* **1** a plot designed to frustrate another plot ▷ *vb* **-plots, -plotting, -plotted 2** (*tr*) to oppose with a counterplot **3** (*intr*) to devise or carry out a counterplot

counterpoint (ˈkaʊntəˌpɔɪnt) *n* **1** the technique involving the simultaneous sounding of two or more parts or melodies **2** a melody or part combined with another melody or part. See also **descant** (sense 1) **3** the musical texture resulting from the simultaneous sounding of two or more melodies or parts **4** strict counterpoint the application of the rules of counterpoint as an academic exercise **5** a contrasting or interacting element, theme, or item; foil **6** *prosody* the use of a stress or stresses at variance with the regular metrical stress ▷ *vb* **7** (*tr*) to set in contrast ▷ Related adjective: **contrapuntal** [c15 from Old French *contrepoint,* from *contre-* COUNTER- + *point* dot, note in musical notation, that is, an accompaniment set against the notes of a melody]

counterpoise (ˈkaʊntəˌpɔɪz) *n* **1** a force, influence, etc, that counterbalances another **2** a state of balance; equilibrium **3** a weight that balances another **4** a radial array of metallic wires, rods, or tubes arranged horizontally around the base of a vertical aerial to increase its transmitting efficiency ▷ *vb* **5** to oppose with something of equal effect, weight, or force; offset **6** to bring into equilibrium **7** *archaic* to consider (one thing) carefully in relation to another

counterpoise bridge *n* another name for **bascule bridge** (see **bascule**, sense 1)

counterproductive (ˌkaʊntəprəˈdʌktɪv) *adj* tending to hinder or act against the achievement of an aim

counterproof (ˈkaʊntəˌpruːf) *n printing* a reverse impression of a newly printed proof of an engraving made by laying it while wet upon plain paper and passing it through the press

counterproposal (ˈkaʊntəprəˌpəʊzᵊl) *n* a proposal offered as an alternative to a previous proposal

counterpunch (ˈkaʊntəˌpʌntʃ) *boxing* ▷ *vb* (*intr*) **1** to punch an attacking opponent; return an attack ▷ *n* **2** a return punch

Counter-Reformation (ˌkaʊntəˌrɛfəˈmeɪʃən) *n* the reform movement of the Roman Catholic Church in the 16th and early 17th centuries considered as a reaction to the Protestant Reformation

counter-revolution (ˌkaʊntəˌrɛvəˈluːʃən) *n* a revolution opposed to a previous revolution and aimed at reversing its effects > ˌcounter-ˌrevoˈlutionist *n*

counter-revolutionary (ˌkaʊntəˌrɛvəˈluːʃənərɪ, -nrɪ) *n, pl* **-aries 1** a person opposed to revolution **2** a person who opposes a specific revolution or revolutionary government ▷ *adj* **3** characterized by opposition to a revolution or revolutions in general

counterscarp (ˈkaʊntəˌskɑːp) *n fortifications* the outer side of the ditch of a fort. Compare **escarp** (sense 1)

countershading (ˌkaʊntəˈʃeɪdɪŋ) *n* (in the coloration of certain animals) a pattern, serving as camouflage, in which dark colours occur on parts of the body exposed to the light and pale colours on parts in the shade

countershaft (ˈkaʊntəˌʃɑːft) *n* an intermediate shaft that is driven by, but rotates in the opposite direction to, a main shaft, esp in a gear train

countersign *vb* (ˈkaʊntəˌsaɪn, ˌkaʊntəˈsaɪn) **1** (*tr*) to sign (a document already signed by another) ▷ *n* (ˈkaʊntəˌsaɪn) **2** Also called: **countersignature** the signature so written **3** a secret sign given in response to another sign **4** *chiefly military* a password

countersink (ˈkaʊntəˌsɪŋk) *vb* **-sinks, -sinking, -sank, -sunk** (*tr*) **1** to enlarge the upper part of (a hole) in timber, metal, etc, so that the head of a bolt or screw can be sunk below the surface **2** to drive (a screw) or sink (a bolt) into such an enlarged hole ▷ *n* **3** Also called: **countersink bit** a tool for countersinking **4** a countersunk depression or hole

counterspy (ˈkaʊntəˌspaɪ) *n, pl* **-spies** a spy working against or investigating enemy espionage

counterstain (ˈkaʊntəˌsteɪn) *vb microscopy* **1** to apply two or more stains in sequence to (a specimen to be examined), each of which colours a different tissue **2** (*tr; usually passive*) to apply (one of a series of stains) to a specimen to be examined: *haematoxylin is counterstained with eosin*

countersubject (ˈkaʊntəˌsʌbdʒɪkt) *n music* (in a fugue) the theme in one voice that accompanies the statement of the subject in another

countersuit (ˈkaʊntəˌsuːt) *n law* a legal claim made as a reaction to a claim made against one

countertenor (ˌkaʊntəˈtɛnə) *n* **1** an adult male voice with an alto range **2** a singer with such a voice

counterterrorism (ˌkaʊntəˈtɛrəˌrɪzəm) *n* activities that are intended to prevent terrorist acts or to eradicate terrorist groups > ˌcounterˈterrorist *adj*

countertrade (ˈkaʊntəˌtreɪd) *n* **1** international trade in which payment is made in goods rather than currency ▷ *vb* (*tr*) **2** to buy or sell goods by countertrade: *countertrading weapons for coffee beans*

countertype (ˈkaʊntəˌtaɪp) *n* **1** an opposite type **2** a corresponding type

countervail (ˌkaʊntəˈveɪl, ˈkaʊntəˌveɪl) *vb* **1** (when *intr*, usually foll by *against*) to act or act against with equal power or force **2** (*tr*) to make up for; compensate; offset [c14 from Old French *contrevaloir*, from Latin *contrā valēre*, from *contrā* against + *valēre* to be strong]

countervailing duty *n* an extra import duty imposed by a country on certain imports, esp to prevent dumping or to counteract subsidies in the exporting country

counterweigh (ˌkaʊntəˈweɪ) *vb* another word for **counterbalance**

counterweight (ˈkaʊntəˌweɪt) *n* a counterbalancing weight, influence, or force > ˈcounterˌweighted *adj*

counterword (ˈkaʊntəˌwɜːd) *n* a word widely used in a sense much looser than its original meaning, such as *tremendous* or *awful*

counterwork (ˈkaʊntəˌwɜːk) *n* **1** work done in opposition to other work **2** defensive fortifications put up against attack > ˈcounterˌworker *n*

countess (ˈkaʊntɪs) *n* **1** the wife or widow of a count or earl **2** a woman of the rank of count or earl

counting house *n rare, chiefly Brit* a room or building used by the accountants of a business

countless (ˈkaʊntlɪs) *adj* innumerable; myriad

count noun *n linguistics, logic* a noun that can be qualified by the indefinite article, and may be used in the plural, as *telephone* and *thing* but not *airs and graces* or *bravery*. Compare **mass noun, sortal**

count on *vb* (*intr, preposition*) to rely or depend on

count out *vb* (*tr, adverb*) **1** *informal* to leave out; exclude: *count me out!* **2** (of a boxing referee) to judge (a floored boxer) to have failed to recover within the specified time. See **count¹** (sense 16) **3** to count (something) aloud

count palatine *n, pl* **counts palatine** *history* **1** (in the Holy Roman Empire) **a** originally an official who administered the king's domains or his justice **b** later, a count who exercised royal authority in his own domains **2** (in England and Ireland) an earl or other lord of a county palatine **3** (in the late Roman Empire) a palace official who exercised judicial authority

countrified *or* **countryfied** (ˈkʌntrɪˌfaɪd) *adj* in the style, manners, etc, of the country; rural

country (ˈkʌntrɪ) *n, pl* **-tries 1** a territory distinguished by its people, culture, language, geography, etc **2** an area of land distinguished by its political autonomy; state **3** the people of a territory or state: *the whole country rebelled* **4** an area associated with a particular person: *Burns country* **5 a** the part of the land that is away from cities or industrial areas; rural districts **b** (*as modifier*): *country cottage* **c** (*in combination*): *a countryman*. Related adj: **pastoral, rural 6** short for **country music 7** *archaic* a particular locality or district **8** up country away from the coast or the capital **9** one's native land or nation of citizenship **10** (usually preceded by *the*) *Brit informal* the outlying area or area furthest from the finish of a sports ground or racecourse **11** (*modifier*) rough, uncouth; rustic: *country manners* **12** across country not keeping to roads, etc **13** go *or* appeal to the country *chiefly Brit* to dissolve Parliament and hold an election **14** unknown country an unfamiliar topic, place, matter, etc [c13 from Old French *contrée*, from Medieval Latin *contrāta*, literally: that which lies opposite, from Latin *contrā* opposite]

country and western *n* **1** another name for **country music 2** a fusion of cowboy songs and Appalachian music **3** (*as modifier*): *country-and-western music*. Abbreviation: **C & W**

country blues *n* (*sometimes functioning as singular*) acoustic folk blues with a guitar accompaniment. Compare **urban blues**

country club *n* a club in the country, having sporting and social facilities

country code *n* (in Britain) a code of good practice recommended to those who use the countryside for recreational purposes

country cousin *n* an unsophisticated person from the country, esp one regarded as an object of amusement

country dance *n* a type of folk dance in which couples are arranged in sets and perform a series of movements, esp facing one another in a line > country dancing *n*

country gentleman *n* a rich man with an estate in the country

country house *n* a large house in the country, esp a mansion belonging to a wealthy family

countryman (ˈkʌntrɪmən) *n, pl* **-men 1** a person who lives in the country **2** a person from a particular country or from one's own country (esp in the phrase **fellow countryman**) > ˈcountryˌwoman *fem n*

country music *n* a type of 20th-century popular music based on White folk music of the southeastern US. Sometimes shortened to: country

country park *n Brit* an area of countryside, usually not less than 10 hectares, set aside for public recreation: often funded by a Countryside Commission grant

country rock¹ *n* the rock surrounding a mineral vein or igneous intrusion

country rock² *n* a style of rock music influenced by country and western

country seat *n* a large estate or property in the country

countryside (ˈkʌntrɪˌsaɪd) *n* a rural area or its population

Countryside Agency *n* (in England) a government agency that promotes the conservation and enjoyment of the countryside and aims to stimulate employment in rural areas

county (ˈkaʊntɪ) *n, pl* **-ties 1 a** any of the administrative or geographic subdivisions of certain states, esp any of the major units into which England and Wales are or have been divided for purposes of local government **b** (*as modifier*): *county cricket* **2** *NZ* an electoral division in a rural area **3** *obsolete* the lands under the jurisdiction of a count or earl ▷ *adj* **4** *Brit informal* having the characteristics and habits of the inhabitants of country houses and estates, esp an upper-class accent and an interest in horses, dogs, etc [c14 from Old French *conté* land belonging to a count, from Late Latin *comitātus* office of a count, from *comes* COUNT²]

county borough *n* **1** (in England and Wales from 1888 to 1974 and in Wales from 1996) a borough administered independently of any higher tier of local government **2** (in the Republic of Ireland) any of the four largest boroughs, governed independently of the administrative county around it by an elected council that constitutes an all-purpose authority

county court *n* (in England) a local court exercising limited jurisdiction in civil matters

county palatine *n, pl* **counties palatine 1** the lands of a count palatine **2** (in England and Ireland) a county in which the earl or other lord exercised many royal powers, esp judicial authority

county seat *n chiefly US* another term for **county town**

county town *n* the town in which a county's affairs are or were administered

coup¹ (kuː) *n* **1** a brilliant and successful stroke or action **2** short for **coup d'état** [c18 from French: blow, from Latin *colaphus* blow with the fist, from Greek *kolaphos*]

coup² *or* **cowp** (kaʊp) *Scot* ▷ *vb* **1** to turn or fall over ▷ *n* **2** a rubbish tip [c15 perhaps identical with obsolete *cope* to strike; see COPE¹]

coup³ (kaʊp) *vb Scot* to barter; traffic; deal [c14 from Old Norse *kaupa* to buy]

coup de foudre *French* (ku də fudrə) *n, pl* **coups de foudre** (ku də fudrə) a sudden and amazing action or event [literally: lightning flash]

coup de grâce *French* (ku də grɑs) *n, pl* **coups de grâce** (ku də grɑs) **1** a mortal or finishing blow, esp one delivered as an act of mercy to a sufferer **2** a final or decisive stroke [literally: blow of mercy]

coup de main *French* (ku də mɛ̃) *n, pl* **coups de main** (ku də mɛ̃) *chiefly military* an attack that achieves complete surprise [literally: blow with the hand]

coup d'état (ˈkuː deɪˈtɑː; *French* ku deta) *n, pl* **coups d'état** (ˈkuːz deɪˈtɑː; *French* ku deta) a sudden violent or illegal seizure of government [French, literally: stroke of state]

coup de théâtre *French* (ku də teɑtrə) *n, pl* **coups de théâtre** (ku də teɑtrə) **1** a dramatic turn of events, esp in a play **2** a sensational device of stagecraft **3** a stage success [literally: stroke of the theatre]

coup d'oeil *French* (ku dœj) *n, pl* **coups d'oeil** (ku dœj) a quick glance [literally: stroke of the eye]

coupe (kuːp) *n* **1** a dessert of fruit and ice cream, usually served in a glass goblet **2** a dish or stemmed glass bowl designed for this dessert [c19 from French: goblet, CUP]

coupé (ˈkuːpeɪ) *n* **1** Also called: **fixed-head coupé** a four-seater car with a fixed roof, a sloping back, and usually two doors. Compare **drophead coupé 2** a four-wheeled horse-drawn carriage with two seats inside and one outside for the driver **3** an end compartment in a European railway carriage with seats on one side only [c19 from French, short for *carosse coupé*, literally: cut-off carriage, from *couper* to cut, from *coup* blow, stroke]

couple (ˈkʌpəl) *n* **1** two people who regularly associate with each other or live together: *an engaged couple* **2** (*functioning as singular or plural*) two people considered as a pair, for or as if for dancing, games, etc **3** *chiefly hunting or coursing* **a** a pair of collars joined by a leash, used to attach hounds to one another **b** two hounds joined in this way **c** the unit of reckoning for hounds in a pack: *twenty and a half couple* **4** a pair of equal and opposite parallel forces that have a tendency to produce rotation with a torque or turning moment equal to the product of either force and the perpendicular distance between them **5** *physics* **a** two dissimilar metals, alloys, or semiconductors in electrical contact, across which a voltage develops. See **thermocouple b** Also called: **galvanic couple** two dissimilar metals or alloys in electrical contact that when immersed in an electrolyte act as the electrodes of an electrolytic cell **6** a connector or link between two members, such as a tie connecting a pair of rafters in a roof **7** a **couple of** (*functioning as singular or plural*) **a** a combination of two; a pair of: *a couple of men* **b** *informal* a small number of; a few: *a couple*

C

of days ▷ *pron* **8** (usually preceded by *a; functioning as singular or plural*) two; a pair: *give him a couple* ▷ *vb* **9** (*tr*) to connect (two things) together or to connect (one thing) to (another): *to couple railway carriages* **10** (*tr*) to do (two things) simultaneously or alternately: *he couples studying with teaching* **11** to form or be formed into a pair or pairs **12** to associate, put, or connect together: *history is coupled with sociology* **13** to link (two circuits) by electromagnetic induction **14** (*intr*) to have sexual intercourse **15** to join or be joined in marriage; marry **16** (*tr*) to attach (two hounds to each other) [C13 from Old French: a pair, from Latin *cōpula* a bond; see COPULA]

coupled ('kʌpᵊld) *adj* being one of the partners in a permanent sexual relationship

coupledom ('kʌpᵊldəm) *n* the state of living as a couple, esp when regarded as being interested in each other to the exclusion of the outside world

coupler ('kʌplə) *n* **1** a link or rod transmitting power between two rotating mechanisms or a rotating part and a reciprocating part **2** *music* a device on an organ or harpsichord connecting two keys, two manuals, etc, so that both may be played at once **3** *electronics* a device, such as a transformer, used to couple two or more electrical circuits **4** *US and Canadian* a device for connecting railway cars or trucks together. Also called (in eg Britain): **coupling**

couplet ('kʌplɪt) *n* two successive lines of verse, usually rhymed and of the same metre [C16 from French, literally: a little pair; see COUPLE]

coupling ('kʌplɪŋ) *n* **1** a mechanical device that connects two things **2** a device for connecting railway cars or trucks together **3** the part of the body of a horse, dog, or other quadruped that lies between the forequarters and the hindquarters **4** *electronics* the act or process of linking two or more circuits so that power can be transferred between them usually by mutual induction, as in a transformer, or by means of a capacitor or inductor common to both circuits. See also **direct coupling** **5** *physics* an interaction between different properties of a system, such as a group of atoms or nuclei, or between two or more systems **6** *genetics* the occurrence of two specified nonallelic genes from the same parent on the same chromosome

coupon ('kuːpɒn) *n* **1** **a** a detachable part of a ticket or advertisement entitling the holder to a discount, free gift, etc **b** a detachable slip usable as a commercial order form **c** a voucher given away with certain goods, a certain number of which are exchangeable for goods offered by the manufacturers **2** one of a number of detachable certificates attached to a bond, esp a bearer bond, the surrender of which entitles the bearer to receive interest payments **3** one of several detachable cards used for making hire-purchase payments **4** a ticket issued to facilitate rationing **5** *Brit* a detachable entry form for any of certain competitions, esp football pools [C19 from French, from Old French *colpon* piece cut off, from *colper* to cut, variant of *couper*; see COPE[1]]

courage ('kʌrɪdʒ) *n* **1** the power or quality of dealing with or facing danger, fear, pain, etc **2** **the courage of one's convictions** the confidence to act in accordance with one's beliefs **3** **take one's courage in both hands** to nerve oneself to perform an action **4** *obsolete* mind; disposition; spirit [C13 from Old French *corage*, from *cuer* heart, from Latin *cor*]

courageous (kə'reɪdʒəs) *adj* possessing or expressing courage > **cou'rageously** *adv* > **cou'rageousness** *n*

courante (kʊ'rɑːnt) *n* *music* **1** an old dance in quick triple time **2** a movement of a (mostly) 16th- to 18th-century suite based on this ▷ Also called (esp for the dance): **coranto** [C16 from French, literally: running, feminine of *courant*, present participle of *courir* to run, from Latin *currere*]

Courantyne ('kɜːrənˌtaɪn) *n* a river in N South America, rising in S Guyana and flowing north to the Atlantic, forming the boundary between Guyana and Surinam. Length: 765 km (475 miles). Dutch name: **Corantijn**

courbaril ('kʊəbərɪl) *n* a tropical American leguminous tree, *Hymenaea courbaril*. Its wood is a useful timber and its gum is a source of copal. Also called: **West Indian locust** [C18 from a native American name]

Courbevoie (*French* kurbəvwa) *n* an industrial suburb of Paris, on the Seine. Pop: 69 694 (1999)

coureur de bois (*French* kurœr də bwa) *n, pl* **coureurs de bois** (kurœr də bwa) *Canadian history* a French Canadian woodsman or Métis who traded with Indians for furs [Canadian French: trapper (literally: wood-runner)]

courgette (kʊə'ʒɛt) *n* *chiefly Brit* a small variety of vegetable marrow, cooked and eaten as a vegetable. Also called: **zucchini** [from French, diminutive of *courge* marrow, gourd]

courie *or* **coorie** ('kuːrɪ) *vb* (*intr*) *Scot* (often foll by *doun*) to nestle or snuggle [C19 from *coor* a Scot word for COWER]

courier ('kʊərɪə) *n* **1** a special messenger, esp one carrying diplomatic correspondence **2** a person who makes arrangements for or accompanies a group of travellers on a journey or tour ▷ *vb* **3** (*tr*) to send (a parcel, letter, etc) by courier [C16 from Old French *courrier*, from Old Latin *corriere*, from *correre* to run, from Latin *currere*]

courlan ('kʊələn) *n* another name for **limpkin** [C19 from French, variant of *courliri*, from Galibi *kurliri*]

Courland *or* **Kurland** ('kʊələnd) *n* a region of Latvia, between the Gulf of Riga and the Lithuanian border. Latvian name: **Kurzeme**

course (kɔːs) *n* **1** a continuous progression from one point to the next in time or space; onward movement: *the course of his life* **2** a route or direction followed: *they kept on a southerly course* **3** **a** the path or channel along which something moves: *the course of a river* **b** (*in combination*): *a watercourse* **4** an area or stretch of land or water on which a sport is played or a race is run: *a golf course* **5** a period of time; duration: *in the course of the next hour* **6** the usual order of and time required for a sequence of events; regular procedure: *the illness ran its course* **7** a mode of conduct or action: *if you follow that course, you will certainly fail* **8** a connected series of events, actions, etc **9** **a** a prescribed number of lessons, lectures, etc, in an educational curriculum **b** the material covered in such a curriculum **10** a prescribed regimen to be followed for a specific period of time: *a course of treatment* **11** a part of a meal served at one time: *the fish course* **12** a continuous, usually horizontal, layer of building material, such as a row of bricks, tiles, etc **13** *nautical* any of the sails on the lowest yards of a square-rigged ship **14** *knitting* the horizontal rows of stitches. Compare **wale**[1] (sense 2b) **15** (in medieval Europe) a charge by knights in a tournament **16** **a** a hunt by hounds relying on sight rather than scent **b** a match in which two greyhounds compete in chasing a hare **17** the part or function assigned to an individual bell in a set of changes **18** *archaic* a running race **19** **as a matter of course** as a natural or normal consequence, mode of action, or event **20** **the course of nature** the ordinary course of events **21** **in course of** in the process of: *the ship was in course of construction* **22** **in due course** at some future time, esp the natural or appropriate time **23** **of course** **a** (*adverb*) as expected; naturally **b** (*sentence substitute*) certainly; definitely **24** **run** (*or* **take**) **its course** (of something) to complete its development or action ▷ *vb* **25** (*intr*) to run, race, or flow, esp swiftly and without interruption **26** to cause (hounds) to hunt by sight rather than scent or (of hounds) to hunt (a quarry) thus **27** (*tr*) to run through or over; traverse **28** (*intr*) to take a direction; proceed on a course ▷ See also **courses** [C13 from Old French *cours*, from Latin *cursus* a running, from *currere* to run]

courser[1] ('kɔːsə) *n* **1** a person who courses hounds or dogs, esp greyhounds **2** a hound or dog trained for coursing

courser[2] ('kɔːsə) *n* *literary* a swift horse; steed [C13 from Old French *coursier*, from *cours* COURSE]

courser[3] ('kɔːsə) *n* a terrestrial plover-like shore bird, such as *Cursorius cursor* (cream-coloured courser), of the subfamily *Cursoriinae* of desert and semidesert regions of the Old World: family *Glareolidae*, order *Charadriiformes* [C18 from Latin *cursōrius* suited for running, from *cursus* COURSE]

courses ('kɔːsɪz) *pl n* (*sometimes singular*) *physiol* another word for **menses**

coursework ('kɔːsˌwɜːk) *n* written or oral work completed by a student within a given period, which is assessed as an integral part of an educational course

coursing ('kɔːsɪŋ) *n* **1** hunting with hounds or dogs that follow their quarry by sight **2** a sport in which hounds are matched against one another in pairs for the hunting of hares by sight

court (kɔːt) *n* **1** an area of ground wholly or partly surrounded by walls or buildings **2** *Brit* (*capital when part of a name*) **a** a block of flats: *Selwyn Court* **b** a mansion or country house **c** a short street, sometimes closed at one end **3** a space inside a building, sometimes surrounded with galleries **4** **a** the residence, retinues, or household of a sovereign or nobleman **b** (*as modifier*): *a court ball* **5** a sovereign or prince and his retinue, advisers, etc **6** any formal assembly, reception, etc, held by a sovereign or nobleman with his courtiers **7** homage, flattering attention, or amorous approaches (esp in the phrase **pay court to someone**) **8** *law* **a** an authority having power to adjudicate in civil, criminal, military, or ecclesiastical matters **b** the regular sitting of such a judicial authority **c** the room or building in which such a tribunal sits **9** **a** a marked outdoor or enclosed area used for any of various ball games, such as tennis, squash, etc **b** a marked section of such an area: *the service court* **10** **a** the board of directors or council of a corporation, company, etc **b** *chiefly Brit* the supreme council of some universities **11** a branch of any of several friendly societies **12** **go to court** to take legal action **13** **hold court** to preside over admirers, attendants, etc **14** **out of court** **a** without a trial or legal case: *the case was settled out of court* **b** too unimportant for consideration **c** *Brit* so as to ridicule completely (in the phrase **laugh out of court**) **15** **the ball is in your court** you are obliged to make the next move ▷ *vb* **16** to attempt to gain the love of (someone); woo **17** (*tr*) to pay attention to (someone) in order to gain favour **18** (*tr*) to try to obtain (fame, honour, etc) **19** (*tr*) to invite, usually foolishly, as by taking risks: *to court disaster* **20** *old-fashioned* to be conducting a serious emotional relationship usually leading to marriage [C12 from Old French, from Latin *cohors* COHORT]

court-bouillon ('kʊət'buːjɒn; *French* kurbujɔ̃) *n* a stock made from root vegetables, water, and wine or vinegar, used primarily for poaching fish [from French, from *court* short, from Latin *curtus* + *bouillon* broth, from *bouillir* to BOIL[1]]

court card *n* (in a pack of playing cards) a king, queen, or jack of any suit. US equivalent: **face card** [C17 altered from earlier *coat-card*, from the decorative coats worn by the figures depicted]

court circular *n* (in countries having a monarchy) a daily report of the activities, engagements, etc, of the sovereign, published in a national newspaper

court cupboard *n* a wooden stand with two or three tiers, used in the 16th and 17th centuries to display pewter, silver, etc

court dress *n* the formal clothing worn at court

Courtelle (kɔː'tɛl) *n* *trademark* a synthetic acrylic fibre resembling wool

courteous ('kɜːtɪəs) *adj* polite and considerate in

manner [C13 *corteis*, literally: with courtly manners, from Old French; see COURT]
> 'courteously *adv* > 'courteousness *n*

courtesan *or* **courtezan** (ˌkɔːtɪˈzæn) *n* (esp formerly) a prostitute, or the mistress of a man of rank [C16 from Old French *courtisane*, from Italian *cortigiana* female courtier, from *cortigiano* courtier, from *corte* COURT]

courtesy ('kɔːtɪsɪ) *n, pl* -sies **1** politeness; good manners **2** a courteous gesture or remark **3** favour or consent (esp in the phrase **by courtesy of**) **4** common consent as opposed to right (esp in the phrase **by courtesy**). See also **courtesy title 5** ('kɜːtɪsɪ) an archaic spelling of **curtsy** [C13 *curteisie*, from Old French, from *corteis* COURTEOUS]

courtesy light *n* the interior light in a motor vehicle

courtesy title *n* any of several titles having no legal significance, such as those borne by the children of peers

court hand *n* a style of handwriting formerly used in English law courts

courthouse ('kɔːtˌhaʊs) *n* a public building in which courts of law are held

courtier ('kɔːtɪə) *n* **1** an attendant at a court **2** a person who seeks favour in an ingratiating manner [C13 from Anglo-French *courteour* (unattested), from Old French *corteier* to attend at court]

court-leet *n* the full name for **leet¹** (sense 1)

courtly ('kɔːtlɪ) *adj* -lier, -liest **1** of or suitable for a royal court **2** refined in manner **3** ingratiating > 'courtliness *n*

courtly love *n* a tradition represented in Western European literature between the 12th and the 14th centuries, idealizing love between a knight and a revered (usually married) lady

court martial *n, pl* court martials *or* courts martial **1** a military court that tries persons subject to military law ▷ *vb* court-martial, -tials, -tialling, -tialled *or US* -tials, -tialing, -tialed **2** (*tr*) to try by court martial

Court of Appeal *n* a branch of the Supreme Court of Judicature that hears appeals from the High Court in both criminal and civil matters and from the county and crown courts

Court of Common Pleas *n* **1** *English law* (formerly) a superior court exercising jurisdiction in civil actions between private citizens **2** *US law* (in some states) a court exercising original and general jurisdiction

Court of Exchequer *n* (formerly) an English civil court where Crown revenue cases were tried. Also called: **Exchequer**

court of first instance *n* a court in which legal proceedings are begun or first heard

court of honour *n* a military court that is instituted to investigate matters involving personal honour

court of inquiry *n* **1** *Brit* a group of people appointed to investigate the causes of a disaster, accident, etc **2** a military court set up to inquire into a military matter such as a failure of equipment or procedure

Court of Justiciary *n* short for **High Court of Justiciary**

Court of Session *n* the supreme civil court in Scotland

Court of St James's *n* the official name of the royal court of Britain

court plaster *n* a plaster, composed of isinglass on silk, formerly used to cover superficial wounds [C18 so called because formerly used by court ladies for beauty spots]

Courtrai (*French* kurtrɛ) *n* a town in W Belgium, in West Flanders on the Lys River: the largest producer of linen in W Europe. Pop: 73 984 (2004 est). Flemish name: **Kortrijk**

court roll *n* *history* the register of land holdings, etc, in a manorial court

courtroom ('kɔːtˌruːm, -ˌrʊm) *n* a room in which the sittings of a law court are held

courtship ('kɔːtʃɪp) *n* **1** the act, period, or art of seeking the love of someone with intent to marry **2** the seeking or soliciting of favours **3** *obsolete* courtly behaviour

court shoe *n* a low-cut shoe for women, having no laces or straps

court tennis *n* the US term for **real tennis**

courtyard ('kɔːtˌjɑːd) *n* an open area of ground surrounded by walls or buildings; court

couscous ('kuːskuːs) *n* **1** a type of semolina originating from North Africa, consisting of granules of crushed durum wheat **2** a spicy North African dish consisting of steamed semolina with meat, vegetables, or fruit C17: via French from Arabic *kouskous*, from *kaskasa* to pound until fine

cousin ('kʌzʳn) *n* **1** Also called: first cousin, cousin-german, full cousin the child of one's aunt or uncle **2** a relative who has descended from one of one's common ancestors. A person's **second cousin** is the child of one of his parents' first cousins. A person's **third cousin** is the child of one of his parents' second cousins. A **first cousin once removed** (or loosely **second cousin**) is the child of one's first cousin **3** a member of a group related by race, ancestry, interests, etc: *our Australian cousins* **4** a title used by a sovereign when addressing another sovereign or a nobleman [C13 from Old French *cosin*, from Latin *consōbrīnus* cousin, from *sōbrīnus* cousin on the mother's side; related to *soror* sister] > 'cousin,hood *or* 'cousin,ship *n* > 'cousinly *adj, adv*

couteau (kuːˈtəʊ) *n, pl* -teaux (-ˈtəʊz) a large two-edged knife used formerly as a weapon [C17 from Old French *coutel*, from Latin *cultellus* a little knife, from *culter* knife, ploughshare]

couth (kuːθ) *adj* **1** *facetious* refined **2** *archaic* familiar; known [Old English *cūth* known, past participle of *cunnan* to know; sense 1, back formation from UNCOUTH]

couthie *or* **couthy** ('kuːθɪ) *adj Scot* **1** sociable; friendly; congenial **2** comfortable; snug **3** plain; homely; unsophisticated: *a couthie saying* [C13 see COUTH, UNCOUTH]

couture (kuːˈtʊə; *French* kutyr) *n* **a** high-fashion designing and dressmaking **b** (*as modifier*): *couture clothes* [from French: sewing, dressmaking, from Old French *cousture* seam, from Latin *consuere* to stitch together, from *suere* to sew]

couturier (kuːˈtʊərɪˌeɪ; *French* kutyrje) *n* a person who designs, makes, and sells fashion clothes for women [from French: dressmaker; see COUTURE] > couturière (kuːˌtʊərɪˈɛə; *French* kutyrjɛr) *fem n*

couvade (kuːˈvɑːd; *French* kuvad) *n anthropol* a custom in certain cultures of treating the husband of a woman giving birth as if he were bearing the child [C19 from French, from *couver* to hatch, from Latin *cubāre* to lie down]

couvade syndrome *n* a psychosomatic condition in which the husband or partner of a pregnant woman experiences symptoms of childbirth or pregnancy [C20 see COUVADE]

couvert (kʊˈvɛə) *n* another word for **cover** (sense 32) [C18 from French]

couzin ('kʌzʳn) *n South African* a friend

COV *abbreviation for* **1** *statistics* covariance **2** *genetics* crossover value

covalency (kəʊˈveɪlənsɪ) *or US* **covalence** *n* **1** the formation and nature of covalent bonds **2** the number of covalent bonds that a particular atom can make with other atoms in forming a molecule > co'valent *adj* > co'valently *adv*

covalent bond *n* a type of chemical bond involving the sharing of electrons between atoms in a molecule, esp the sharing of a pair of electrons by two adjacent atoms

covariance (kəʊˈvɛərɪəns) *n statistics* a measure of the association between two random variables, equal to the expected value of the product of the deviations from the mean of the two variables, and estimated by the sum of products of deviations from the sample mean for associated values of the two variables, divided by the

number of sample points. Written as *Cov (X, Y)*

cove¹ (kəʊv) *n* **1** a small bay or inlet, usually between rocky headlands **2** a narrow cavern formed in the sides of cliffs, mountains, etc, usually by erosion **3** a sheltered place **4** Also called: coving *architect* a concave curved surface between the wall and ceiling of a room ▷ *vb* **5** (*tr*) to form an architectural cove in [Old English *cofa*; related to Old Norse *kofi*, Old High German *kubisi* tent]

cove² (kəʊv) *n* **1** *old-fashioned slang, Brit and Austral* a fellow; chap **2** *Austral history* an overseer of convict labourers [C16 probably from Romany *kova* thing, person]

coven ('kʌvʳn) *n* **1** a meeting of witches **2** a company of 13 witches [C16 probably from Old French *covin* group, ultimately from Latin *convenīre* to come together; compare CONVENT]

covenant ('kʌvənənt) *n* **1** a binding agreement; contract **2** *law* **a** an agreement in writing under seal, as to pay a stated annual sum to a charity **b** a particular clause in such an agreement, esp in a lease **3** (in early English law) an action in which damages were sought for breach of a sealed agreement **4** *Bible* God's promise to the Israelites and their commitment to worship him alone ▷ *vb* **5** to agree to a covenant (concerning) [C13 from Old French, from *covenir* to agree, from Latin *convenīre* to come together, make an agreement; see CONVENE] > covenantal (ˌkʌvəˈnæntʳl) *adj* > ˌcove'nantally *adv*

Covenant ('kʌvənənt) *n Scot history* any of the bonds entered into by Scottish Presbyterians to defend their religion, esp one in 1638 (**National Covenant**) and one of 1643 (**Solemn League and Covenant**)

covenantee (ˌkʌvənənˈtiː) *n* the person to whom the promise in a covenant is made

Covenanter ('kʌvənəntə, ˌkʌvəˈnæntə) *n* a person upholding the National Covenant of 1638 or the Solemn League and Covenant of 1643 between Scotland and England to establish and defend Presbyterianism

covenantor *or* **covenanter** ('kʌvənəntə) *n* a party who makes a promise and who is to perform the obligation expressed in a covenant

Covent Garden ('kʌvənt, 'kɒv-) *n* **1** a district of central London: famous for its former fruit, vegetable, and flower market, now a shopping precinct **2** the Royal Opera House (built 1858) in Covent Garden

Coventry ('kɒvəntrɪ) *n* **1** a city in central England, in Coventry unitary authority, West Midlands: devastated in World War II; modern cathedral (1954–62); industrial centre, esp for motor vehicles; two universities (1965, 1992). Pop: 303 475 (2001) **2** a unitary authority in central England, in West Midlands. Pop: 305 000 (2003 est). Area: 97 sq km (37 sq miles) **3** send to Coventry to ostracize or ignore

cover ('kʌvə) *vb* (*mainly tr*) **1** to place or spread something over so as to protect or conceal **2** to provide with a covering; clothe **3** to put a garment, esp a hat, on (the body or head) **4** to extend over or lie thickly on the surface of; spread: *snow covered the fields* **5** to bring upon (oneself); invest (oneself) as if with a covering: *covered with shame* **6** (sometimes foll by *up*) to act as a screen or concealment for; hide from view **7** *military* to protect (an individual, formation, or place) by taking up a position from which fire may be returned if those being protected are fired upon **8** (*also intr, often foll by for*) to assume responsibility for (a person or thing): *to cover for a colleague in his absence* **9** (*intr; foll by for or up for*) to provide an alibi (for) **10** to have as one's territory: *this salesman covers your area* **11** to travel over: *to cover three miles a day* **12** (*tr*) to have or place in the aim and within the range of (a firearm) **13** to include or deal with: *his talk covered all aspects of the subject* **14** (of an asset or income) to be sufficient to meet (a liability or expense) **15 a** to insure against loss, risk, etc **b** to provide for (loss, risk, etc) by insurance **16** (*also intr*) *finance* to purchase (securities, etc) in order to meet contracts, esp short sales **17** to deposit (an equivalent stake) in a bet or wager **18** (*also intr*) to play a card higher in rank than (one played beforehand by another player) **19** to act as reporter or photographer on (a news event, etc) for a newspaper or magazine: *to cover sports events* **20** *sport* to guard or protect (an opponent, team-mate, or area) **21** *music* to record a cover version of **22** (of a male animal, esp a horse) to copulate with (a female animal) **23** (of a bird) to brood (eggs) ▷ *n* **24** anything that covers, spreads over, protects, or conceals **25** woods or bushes providing shelter or a habitat for wild creatures **26 a** a blanket used on a bed for warmth **b** another word for **bedspread 27** *finance* liquid assets, reserves, or guaranteed income sufficient to discharge a liability, meet an expenditure, etc **28** a pretext, disguise, or false identity: *the thief sold brushes as a cover* **29** *insurance* another word for **coverage** (sense 3) **30** an envelope or package for sending through the post: *under plain cover* **31** *philately* **a** an entire envelope that has been postmarked **b** on cover (of a postage stamp) kept in this form by collectors **32** an individual table setting, esp in a restaurant **33** *sport* the guarding or protection of an opponent, team-mate, or area **34** Also called: **cover version** a version by a different artist of a previously recorded musical item **35** *cricket* **a** (*often plural*) the area more or less at right angles to the pitch on the off side and usually about halfway to the boundary: *to field in the covers* **b** (*as modifier*): *a cover drive by a batsman* **c** Also called: **cover point** a fielder in such a position **36** *ecology* the percentage of the ground surface covered by a given species of plant **37 break cover** (esp of game animals) to come out from a shelter or hiding place **38 take cover** to make for a place of safety or shelter **39 under cover** protected, concealed, or in secret: *under cover of night* ▷ See also **cover-up** [c13 from Old French *covrir*, from Latin *cooperīre* to cover completely, from *operīre* to cover over] > 'coverable *adj* > 'coverer *n* > 'coverless *adj*

coverage ('kʌvərɪdʒ) *n* **1** the amount or extent to which something is covered **2** *journalism* the amount and quality of reporting or analysis given to a particular subject or event **3** the extent of the protection provided by insurance **4** *finance* **a** the value of liquid assets reserved to meet liabilities **b** the ratio of liquid assets to specific liabilities **c** the ratio of total net profit to distributed profit in a company **5** the section of the public reached by a medium of communication

coverall ('kʌvər,ɔːl) *n* **1** a thing that covers something entirely **2** (*usually plural*) protective outer garments for the body

cover charge *n* a sum of money charged in a restaurant for each individual customer in addition to the cost of food and drink

cover crop *n* a crop planted between main crops to prevent leaching or soil erosion or to provide green manure

covered wagon *n* *US and Canadian* a large wagon with an arched canvas top, used formerly for prairie travel

cover girl *n* a girl, esp a glamorous one, whose picture appears on the cover of a newspaper or magazine

cover glass *n* a thin square of mounted glass used to protect a photographic slide

covering ('kʌvərɪŋ) *n* another word for **cover** (sense 24)

covering fire *n* *military* firing intended to protect an individual or formation making a movement by forcing the enemy to take cover

covering letter *n* an accompanying letter sent as an explanation, introduction, or record

coverlet ('kʌvəlɪt) *n* another word for **bedspread**

Coverley ('kʌvəlɪ) *n* See **Sir Roger de Coverley**

covermount ('kʌvə,maʊnt) *marketing* ▷ *n* **1** an

item attached to the front of a magazine as a gift ▷ *vb* **2** (*tr*) to attach (an item) to the front of a magazine as a gift

cover note *n* *Brit* a certificate issued by an insurance company stating that a policy is operative: used as a temporary measure between the commencement of cover and the issue of the policy

cover point *n* *cricket* **a** a fielding position in the covers **b** a fielder in this position

covers ('kəʊvɜːs) *abbreviation for* coversed sine

coversed sine ('kəʊvɜːst) *n* *obsolete* a trigonometric function equal to one minus the sine of the specified angle. Abbreviation: **covers**

cover-shoulder *n* a type of blouse worn in Ghana

cover slip *n* a very thin piece of glass placed over a specimen on a glass slide that is to be examined under a microscope

covert ('kʌvət) *adj* **1** concealed or secret: *covert jealousy* **2** *law* See **feme covert**. Compare **discovert** ▷ *n* **3** a shelter or disguise **4** a thicket or woodland providing shelter for game **5** short for **covert cloth 6** *ornithol* any of the small feathers on the wings and tail of a bird that surround the bases of the larger feathers **7** a flock of coots [c14 from Old French: covered, from *covrir* to COVER] > 'covertly *adv* > 'covertness *n*

covert cloth *n* a twill-weave cotton or worsted suiting fabric. Sometimes shortened to: **covert**

covert coat *n* *Brit* a short topcoat worn for hunting

coverture ('kʌvətʃə) *n* **1** *law* the condition or status of a married woman considered as being under the protection and influence of her husband **2** *rare* shelter, concealment, or disguise [c13 from Old French, from *covert* covered; see COVERT]

cover-up *n* **1** concealment or attempted concealment of a mistake, crime, etc ▷ *vb* **cover up** (*adverb*) **2** (*tr*) to cover completely **3** (when *intr*, often foll by *for*) to attempt to conceal (a mistake or crime): *she tried to cover up for her friend* **4** (*intr*) *boxing* to defend the body and head with the arms

cover version *n* another name for **cover** (sense 34)

cove stripe *n* *nautical* a decorative stripe painted along the sheer strake of a vessel, esp a sailing boat

covet ('kʌvɪt) *vb* (*tr*) **-vets, -veting, -veted** to wish, long, or crave for (something, esp the property of another person) [c13 from Old French *coveitier*, from *coveitié* eager desire, ultimately from Latin *cupiditā* CUPIDITY] > 'covetable *adj* > 'coveter *n*

covetous ('kʌvɪtəs) *adj* (*usually postpositive* and foll by *of*) jealously eager for the possession of something (esp the property of another person) > 'covetously *adv* > 'covetousness *n*

covey ('kʌvɪ) *n* **1** a small flock of grouse or partridge **2** a small group, as of people [c14 from Old French *covee*, from *cover* to sit on, hatch; see COUVADE]

covin ('kʌvɪn) *n* *law* a conspiracy between two or more persons to act to the detriment or injury of another [c14 from Old French; see COVEN, CONVENE]

cow¹ (kaʊ) *n* **1** the mature female of any species of cattle, esp domesticated cattle **2** the mature female of various other mammals, such as the elephant, whale, and seal **3** (*not in technical use*) any domestic species of cattle **4** *informal* a disagreeable woman **5** *Austral and NZ* *slang* something objectionable (esp in the phrase **a fair cow**) **6** **till the cows come home** *informal* for a very long time; effectively for ever [Old English *cū*; related to Old Norse *kȳr*, Old High German *kuo*, Latin *bōs*, Greek *boûs*, Sanskrit *gāūs*]

cow² (kaʊ) *vb* (*tr*) to frighten or overawe, as with threats [c17 from Old Norse *kūga* to oppress, related to Norwegian *kue*, Swedish *kuva*]

cowage or **cowhage** ('kaʊɪdʒ) *n* **1** a tropical climbing leguminous plant, *Stizolobium* (or *Mucuna*) *pruriens*, whose bristly pods cause severe itching

and stinging **2** the pods of this plant or the stinging hairs covering them [c17 from Hindi *kavāch*, of obscure origin]

cowal ('kaʊəl) *n* *Austral* a shallow lake or swampy depression supporting vegetation [from a native Australian language]

coward ('kaʊəd) *n* a person who shrinks from or avoids danger, pain, or difficulty [c13 from Old French *cuard*, from *coue* tail, from Latin *cauda*; perhaps suggestive of a frightened animal with its tail between its legs]

cowardice ('kaʊədɪs) *n* lack of courage in facing danger, pain, or difficulty

cowardly ('kaʊədlɪ) *adj* of or characteristic of a coward; lacking courage > 'cowardliness *n*

cow bail *n* See **bail³** (sense 3)

cowbane ('kaʊ,beɪn) *n* **1** Also called: **water hemlock** any of several N temperate poisonous umbelliferous marsh plants of the genus *Cicuta*, esp *C. virosa*, having clusters of small white flowers **2** a similar and related plant, *Oxypolis rigidior* of the southeastern and central US **3** any umbelliferous plant reputed to be poisonous to cattle

cowbell ('kaʊ,bel) *n* **1** a bell hung around a cow's neck so that the cow can be easily located **2** a metal percussion instrument usually mounted on the bass drum or hand-held and struck with a drumstick **3** *US* another name for **bladder campion**

cowberry ('kaʊbərɪ, -brɪ) *n*, *pl* **-ries 1** a creeping ericaceous evergreen shrub, *Vaccinium vitis-idaea*, of N temperate and arctic regions, with pink or red flowers and edible slightly acid berries **2** the berry of this plant ▷ Also called: **red whortleberry**

cowbind ('kaʊ,baɪnd) *n* any of various bryony plants, esp the white bryony

cowbird ('kaʊ,bɜːd) *n* any of various American orioles of the genera *Molothrus, Tangavius*, etc, esp *M. ater* (common or brown-headed cowbird). They have a dark plumage and short bill

cowboy ('kaʊ,bɔɪ) *n* **1** Also called: **cowhand** a hired man who herds and tends cattle, usually on horseback, esp in the western US **2** a conventional character of Wild West folklore, films, etc, esp one involved in fighting Indians **3** *informal* **a** a person who is an irresponsible or unscrupulous operator in business **b** (*as modifier*): *cowboy contractors; cowboy shop steward* **4** *Austral* a man or boy who tends cattle > 'cow,girl *fem n*

cowcatcher ('kaʊ,kætʃə) *n* *US and Canadian* a metal frame on the front of a locomotive to clear the track of animals or other obstructions

cow cocky *n*, *pl* **cow cockies** *Austral and NZ* a one-man dairy farmer

cower ('kaʊə) *vb* (*intr*) to crouch or cringe, as in fear [c13 from Middle Low German *kūren* to lie in wait; related to Swedish *kura* to lie in wait, Danish *kure* to squat]

Cowes (kaʊz) *n* a town in S England, on the Isle of Wight: famous for its annual regatta. Pop: 19 110 (2001)

cowfeteria (,kaʊfɪ'tɪərɪə) *n* *NZ* *informal* a calf feeder with multiple teats [from a blend of *cow* and *cafeteria*]

cowfish ('kaʊ,fɪʃ) *n*, *pl* **-fish** or **-fishes 1** any trunkfish, such as *Lactophrys quadricornis*, having hornlike spines over the eyes **2** (*loosely*) any of various large aquatic animals, such as a sea cow

cowflop ('kaʊ,flɒp) *n* *Southwest English* *dialect* a foxglove

Cow Gum *n* *trademark* a colourless adhesive based on a natural rubber solution

cowherb ('kaʊ,hɜːb) *n* a European caryophyllaceous plant, *Saponaria vaccaria*, having clusters of pink flowers: a weed in the US. See also **soapwort**

cowherd ('kaʊ,hɜːd) *n* a person employed to tend cattle

cowhide ('kaʊ,haɪd) *n* **1** the hide of a cow **2** the leather made from such a hide ▷ Also called: **cowskin**

Cowichan sweater ('kaʊɪtʃən) *n* *Canadian* a

heavy sweater of grey, unbleached wool with distinctive designs that were originally black-and-white but are now sometimes coloured: knitted originally by Cowichan Indians in British Columbia. Also called: Cowichan Indian sweater, siwash, siwash sweater

cowitch ('kaʊɪtʃ) *n* another name for **cowage** [c17 alteration of COWAGE by folk etymology]

cowk (kaʊk) *vb* (*intr*) *Northeast Scot dialect* to retch or feel nauseated [of obscure origin]

cowl (kaʊl) *n* **1** a hood, esp a loose one **2** the hooded habit of a monk **3** a cover fitted to a chimney to increase ventilation and prevent draughts **4** the part of a car body that supports the windscreen and the bonnet **5** *aeronautics* another word for **cowling** ▷ *vb* (*tr*) **6** to cover or provide with a cowl **7** to make a monk of [Old English *cugele*, from Late Latin *cuculla* cowl, from Latin *cucullus* covering, cap, hood]

cowlick ('kaʊ,lɪk) *n* a tuft of hair over the forehead

cowling ('kaʊlɪŋ) *n* a streamlined metal covering, esp one fitted around an aircraft engine. Also called: cowl. Compare **fairing¹**

cowl neckline *n* a neckline of women's clothes loosely folded over and sometimes resembling a folded hood

cowman ('kaʊmən) *n*, *pl* -men **1** *Brit* another name for **cowherd 2** *US and Canadian* a man who owns cattle; rancher

co-worker *n* a fellow worker; associate

cow parsley *n* a common Eurasian umbelliferous hedgerow plant, *Anthriscus sylvestris,* having umbrella-shaped clusters of white flowers. Also called: keck, Queen Anne's lace

cow parsnip *n* any tall coarse umbelliferous plant of the genus *Heracleum,* such as *H. sphondylium* of Europe and Asia, having thick stems and flattened clusters of white or purple flowers. Also called: hogweed, keck

cowpat ('kaʊ,pæt) *n* a single dropping of cow dung

cowpea ('kaʊ,piː) *n* **1** a leguminous tropical climbing plant, *Vigna sinensis,* producing long pods containing edible pealike seeds: grown for animal fodder and sometimes as human food **2** Also called: black-eyed pea the seed of this plant

Cowper's glands ('kuː,pəz) *pl n* two small yellowish glands near the prostate that secrete a mucous substance into the urethra during sexual stimulation in males. Compare **Bartholin's glands** [c18 named after William Cowper (1666–1709), English anatomist who discovered them]

cow pillow *n* (in India) a large cylindrical pillow stuffed with cotton and used for reclining rather than sleeping

cow pony *n* a horse used by cowboys when herding

cowpox ('kaʊ,pɒks) *n* a contagious viral disease of cows characterized by vesicles on the skin, esp on the teats and udder. Inoculation of humans with this virus provides temporary immunity to smallpox. It can be transmitted to other species, esp cats

cowpuncher ('kaʊ,pʌntʃə) or **cowpoke** ('kaʊ,pəʊk) *n* *US and Canadian informal* words for **cowboy**

cowrie or **cowry** ('kaʊrɪ) *n*, *pl* -ries **1** any marine gastropod mollusc of the mostly tropical family *Cypraeidae,* having a glossy brightly marked shell with an elongated opening **2** the shell of any of these molluscs, esp the shell of *Cypraea moneta* (**money cowry**), used as money in parts of Africa and S Asia [c17 from Hindi *kaurī,* from Sanskrit *kaparda,* of Dravidian origin; related to Tamil *kōtu* shell]

cow shark *n* any large primitive shark, esp *Hexanchus griseum,* of the family *Hexanchidae* of warm and temperate waters. Also called: six-gilled shark

cowskin ('kaʊ,skɪn) *n* another word for **cowhide**

cowslip ('kaʊ,slɪp) *n* **1** Also called: paigle a

primrose, *Primula veris,* native to temperate regions of the Old World, having fragrant yellow flowers **2** *US and Canadian* another name for **marsh marigold** [Old English *cūslyppe*; see COW¹, SLIP³]

cow-spanker *n* *NZ informal* a dairy farmer

cow tree *n* a South American moraceous tree, *Brosimum galactodendron,* producing latex used as a substitute for milk

cox (kɒks) *n* **1** a coxswain, esp of a racing eight or four ▷ *vb* **2** to act as coxswain of (a boat) ▷ 'coxless *adj*

coxa ('kɒksə) *n*, *pl* coxae ('kɒksiː) **1** a technical name for the hipbone or hip joint **2** the basal segment of the leg of an insect [c18 from Latin: hip] > 'coxal *adj*

coxalgia (kɒk'sældʒɪə) *n* **1** pain in the hip joint **2** disease of the hip joint causing pain [c19 from COXA + -ALGIA] > cox'algic *adj*

coxcomb ('kɒks,kəʊm) *n* **1** a variant spelling of **cockscomb 2** *archaic* a foppish man **3** *obsolete* the cap, resembling a cock's comb, worn by a jester

coxcombry ('kɒks,kəʊmrɪ) *n*, *pl* -ries conceited arrogance or foppishness

Coxsackie virus (kʊk'sɑː,kɪ) *n* any of various viruses that occur in the intestinal tract of man and cause diseases, some of which resemble poliomyelitis [c20 after *Coxsackie,* a town in New York state, where the virus was first found]

Cox's Orange Pippin ('kɒksɪz) *n* a variety of eating apple with sweet flesh and a red-tinged green skin. Often shortened to: Cox [c19 named after R. *Cox,* its English propagator]

coxswain ('kɒksən, -,sweɪn) *n* the helmsman of a lifeboat, racing shell, etc. Also called: cockswain [c15 from *cock* a ship's boat + SWAIN]

coy (kɔɪ) *adj* **1** (usually of a woman) affectedly demure, esp in a playful or provocative manner **2** shy; modest **3** evasive, esp in an annoying way [c14 from Old French *coi* reserved, from Latin *quiētus* QUIET] > 'coyish *adj* · 'coyly *adv* · 'coyness *n*

Coy. *military abbreviation for* company

coyote ('kɔɪəʊt, kɔɪ'əʊt, kɔɪ'əʊtɪ) *n*, *pl* -otes or -ote **1** Also called: prairie wolf a predatory canine mammal, *Canis latrans,* related to but smaller than the wolf, roaming the deserts and prairies of North America **2** (in Native American legends of the West) a trickster and culture hero represented as a man or as an animal [c19 from Mexican Spanish, from Nahuatl *coyotl*]

coyotillo (,kəʊjəʊ'tiːljəʊ) *n*, *pl* -los a thorny poisonous rhamnaceous shrub, *Karwinskia humboldtiana* of Mexico and the southwestern US, the berries of which cause paralysis [Mexican Spanish, literally: a little COYOTE]

coypu ('kɔɪpuː) *n*, *pl* -pus or -pu **1** an aquatic South American hystricomorph rodent, *Myocastor coypus,* introduced into Europe: family *Capromyidae.* It resembles a small beaver with a ratlike tail and is bred in captivity for its soft grey underfur **2** the fur of this animal ▷ Also called: nutria [c18 from American Spanish *coipú,* from Araucanian *kóypu*]

coz (kʌz) *n* an archaic word for **cousin**: used chiefly as a term of address

cozen ('kʌzᵊn) *vb* to cheat or trick (someone) [c16 cant perhaps related to COUSIN] > 'cozenage *n* · 'cozener *n*

cozy ('kəʊzɪ) *adj* -zier, -ziest, *n*, *pl* -zies the usual US spelling of **cosy**. > 'cozily *adv* · 'coziness *n*

cp *abbreviation for* **1** candlepower **2** chemically pure

CP *abbreviation for* **1** Canadian Press **2** *military* Command Post **3** Common Prayer **4** Communist Party **5** (formerly in Britain) Community Programme **6** Court of Probate

cp. *abbreviation for* compare

CPA (in the US) *abbreviation for* certified public accountant

CPAG (in Britain) *abbreviation for* Child Poverty Action Group

cpd *zoology, botany, chem abbreviation for* compound

CPD *abbreviation for* continuing professional development

cpi *abbreviation for* characters per inch

CPI *abbreviation for* consumer price index

Cpl *abbreviation for* Corporal

CP/M *n* an operating system widely used on microcomputers to enable a wide range of software from many suppliers to be run on them

CPO *abbreviation for* Chief Petty Officer

CPR *abbreviation for* **cardiopulmonary resuscitation**

CPRE *abbreviation for* Council for the Protection of Rural England

cps *abbreviation for* **1** *physics* cycles per second **2** *computing* characters per second

CPS (in England and Wales) *abbreviation for* **Crown Prosecution Service**

CPSA (in Britain) *abbreviation for* Civil and Public Services Association

CPSU *abbreviation for* (formerly) Communist Party of the Soviet Union

CPU *computing abbreviation for* **central processing unit**

CPVE (in Britain) *abbreviation for* Certificate of Pre-vocational Education: a certificate awarded for completion of a broad-based course of study offered as a less advanced alternative to traditional school-leaving qualifications

CQ *n* **1** *telegraphy, telephony* a symbol transmitted by an amateur radio operator requesting two-way communication with any other amateur radio operator listening **2** *military abbreviation for* **charge of quarters**

CQB *military abbreviation for* close-quarter battle

CQSW (in Britain) *abbreviation for* Certificate of Qualification in Social Work

cr *the internet domain name for* Costa Rica

Cr **1** *abbreviation for* Councillor **2** *the chemical symbol for* chromium

CR *abbreviation for* **1** Community of the Resurrection **2** Costa Rica **3** *international car registration for* Costa Rica

cr. *abbreviation for* **1** credit **2** creditor

crab¹ (kræb) *n* **1** any chiefly marine decapod crustacean of the genus *Cancer* and related genera (section *Brachyura*), having a broad flattened carapace covering the cephalothorax, beneath which is folded the abdomen. The first pair of limbs are modified as pincers. See also **fiddler crab, soft-shell crab, pea crab, oyster crab.** Related adj: **cancroid 2** any of various similar or related arthropods, such as the hermit crab and horseshoe crab **3** short for **crab louse 4** a manoeuvre in which an aircraft flies slightly into the crosswind to compensate for drift **5** a mechanical lifting device, esp the travelling hoist of a gantry crane **6** *wrestling* See **Boston crab 7** **catch a crab** *rowing* to make a stroke in which the oar either misses the water or digs too deeply, causing the rower to fall backwards ▷ *vb* crabs, crabbing, crabbed **8** (*intr*) to hunt or catch crabs **9** (*tr*) to fly (an aircraft) slightly into a crosswind to compensate for drift **10** (*intr*) *nautical* to move forwards with a slight sideways motion, as to overcome an offsetting current **11** (*intr*) to move sideways ▷ See also **crabs** [Old English *crabba*; related to Old Norse *krabbi,* Old High German *krebiz* crab, Dutch *krabben* to scratch]

crab² (kræb) *informal* ▷ *vb* crabs, crabbing, crabbed **1** (*intr*) to find fault; grumble **2** (*tr*) *chiefly US* to spoil (esp in the phrase **crab someone's act**) ▷ *n* **3** an irritable person **4** **draw the crabs** *Austral* to attract unwelcome attention [c16 probably back formation from CRABBED]

crab³ (kræb) *n* short for **crab apple** [c15 perhaps of Scandinavian origin; compare Swedish *skrabbe* crab apple]

Crab (kræb) *n* **the** the constellation Cancer, the fourth sign of the zodiac

crab apple *n* **1** any of several rosaceous trees of the genus *Malus* that have white, pink, or red flowers and small sour apple-like fruits **2** the fruit of any of these trees, used to make jam

crabbed ('kræbɪd) *adj* **1** surly; irritable; perverse **2** (esp of handwriting) cramped and hard to

C

decipher [C13 probably from CRAB¹ (from its wayward gait), influenced by CRAB(APPLE) (from its tartness)] > 'crabbedly adv > 'crabbedness n

crabber ('kræbə) n **1** a crab fisherman **2** a boat used for crab-fishing

crabby ('kræbɪ) adj **-bier, -biest** bad-tempered

crab canon n music a canon in which the imitating voice repeats the notes of the theme in reverse order. Also called: **retrograde canon, canon cancrizans** [from the mistaken medieval notion that crabs move backwards]

crab grass n any of several coarse weedy grasses of the genus Digitaria, which grow in warm regions and tend to displace other grasses in lawns

crab louse n a parasitic louse, Pthirus (or Phthirus) pubis, that infests the pubic region in man

Crab Nebula n the expanding remnant of the supernova observed in 1054 AD, lying in the constellation Taurus at an approximate distance of 6500 light years

crabs (kræbz) n (sometimes functioning as singular) the lowest throw in a game of chance, esp two aces in dice [plural of CRAB¹]

crabstick ('kræb,stɪk) n **1** a stick, cane, or cudgel made of crab-apple wood **2** informal a bad-tempered person

crabwise ('kræb,waɪz) adj, adv (of motion) sideways; like a crab

crabwood ('kræb,wʊd) n **1** a tropical American meliaceous tree, Carapa guianensis **2** the wood of this tree, used for construction

CRAC abbreviation for Careers Research and Advisory Centre

crack (kræk) vb **1** to break or cause to break without complete separation of the parts: the vase was cracked but unbroken **2** to break or cause to break with a sudden sharp sound; snap: to crack a nut **3** to make or cause to make a sudden sharp sound: to crack a whip **4** to cause (the voice) to change tone or become harsh or (of the voice) to change tone, esp to a higher register; break **5** informal to fail or cause to fail **6** to yield or cause to yield: to crack under torture **7** (tr) to hit with a forceful or resounding blow **8** (tr) to break into or force open: to crack a safe **9** (tr) to solve or decipher (a code, problem, etc) **10** (tr) informal to tell (a joke, etc) **11** to break (a molecule) into smaller molecules or radicals by the action of heat, as in the distillation of petroleum **12** (tr) to open (esp a bottle) for drinking: let's crack another bottle **13** (intr) Scot and Northern English dialect to chat; gossip **14** (tr) informal to achieve (esp in the phrase **crack it**) **15** (tr) Austral informal to find or catch: to crack a wave in surfing **16** **crack a smile** informal to break into a smile **17** **crack hardy** or **hearty** Austral and NZ informal to disguise one's discomfort, etc; put on a bold front ▷ n **18** **crack the whip** informal to assert one's authority, esp to put people under pressure to work harder **19** a sudden sharp noise **20** a break or fracture without complete separation of the two parts: a crack in the window **21** a narrow opening or fissure **22** informal a resounding blow **23** a physical or mental defect; flaw **24** a moment or specific instant: the crack of day **25** a broken or cracked tone of voice, as a boy's during puberty **26** (often foll by at) informal an attempt; opportunity to try: he had a crack at the problem **27** slang a gibe; wisecrack; joke **28** slang a person that excels **29** Scot and Northern English dialect a talk; chat **30** slang a processed form of cocaine hydrochloride used as a stimulant. It is highly addictive **31** Also: **craic** informal, chiefly Irish fun; informal entertainment: the crack was great in here last night **32** obsolete slang a burglar or burglary **33** **crack of dawn** **a** the very instant that the sun rises **b** very early in the morning **34** **a fair crack of the whip** informal a fair chance or opportunity **35** **crack of doom** doomsday; the end of the world; the Day of Judgment ▷ adj **36** (prenominal) slang first-class; excellent: a crack shot ▷ See also **crack down, crack on, crack up** [Old English

cracian; related to Old High German krahhōn, Dutch kraken, Sanskrit gárjati he roars]

cracka ('krækə) n US derogatory another word for **poor White**

crackberry ('kræk,bərɪ) n, pl **-ries** informal nickname for a BlackBerry handheld device that functions as a telephone, PDA, and emailer and appears to have an addictive hold on its users [C21 from CRACK (sense 30) + BLACKBERRY]

crackbrain ('kræk,breɪn) n a person who is insane

crackbrained ('kræk,breɪnd) adj insane, idiotic, or crazy

crack down vb (intr, adverb; often foll by on) **1** to take severe measures (against); become stricter (with) ▷ n **crackdown 2** severe or repressive measures

cracked (krækt) adj **1** damaged by cracking **2** informal crazy

cracked heels pl n another name for **scratches**

cracked wheat n whole wheat cracked between rollers so that it will cook more quickly

cracker ('krækə) n **1** a decorated cardboard tube that emits a bang when pulled apart, releasing a toy, a joke, or a paper hat **2** short for **firecracker 3** a thin crisp biscuit, usually unsweetened **4** a person or thing that cracks **5** US another word for **poor White 6** Brit slang a thing or person of notable qualities or abilities **7** **not worth a cracker** Austral and NZ informal worthless; useless

cracker-barrel adj US rural; rustic; homespun: a cracker-barrel philosopher

crackerjack ('krækə,dʒæk) informal ▷ adj **1** excellent ▷ n **2** a person or thing of exceptional quality or ability [C20 changed from CRACK (first-class) + JACK¹ (man)]

crackers ('krækəz) adj (postpositive) Brit a slang word for **insane**

cracket ('krækɪt) n dialect **1** a low stool, often one with three legs **2** a box for a miner to kneel on when working a low seam [variant of CRICKET³]

crackhead ('kræk,hed) n slang a person addicted to the drug crack

cracking ('krækɪŋ) adj **1** (prenominal) informal fast; vigorous (esp in the phrase **a cracking pace**) **2** **get cracking** informal to start doing something quickly or do something with increased speed ▷ adv, adj **3** Brit informal first-class; excellent: a cracking good match ▷ n **4** the process in which molecules are cracked, esp the oil-refining process in which heavy oils are broken down into hydrocarbons of lower molecular weight by heat or catalysis. See also **catalytic cracker**

crackjaw ('kræk,dʒɔː) informal ▷ adj **1** difficult to pronounce ▷ n **2** a word or phrase that is difficult to pronounce

crackle ('krækəl) vb **1** to make or cause to make a series of slight sharp noises, as of paper being crushed or of a wood fire burning **2** (tr) to decorate (porcelain or pottery) by causing a fine network of cracks to appear in the glaze **3** (intr) to abound in vivacity or energy ▷ n **4** the act or sound of crackling **5** intentional crazing in the glaze of a piece of porcelain or pottery **6** Also called: **crackleware** porcelain or pottery so decorated

crackling ('kræklɪŋ) n the crisp browned skin of roast pork

cracknel ('kræknəl) n **1** a type of hard plain biscuit **2** (often plural) US and Canadian crisply fried bits of fat pork [C15 perhaps from Old French craquelin, from Middle Dutch krākelinc, from krāken to CRACK]

crack on vb (intr; often foll by with) informal to continue to do something as quickly as possible

crackpot ('kræk,pɒt) informal ▷ n **1** an eccentric person; crank ▷ adj **2** (usually prenominal) eccentric; crazy

cracksman ('kræksmən) n, pl **-men** slang a burglar, esp a safe-breaker

crack up vb (adverb) **1** (intr) to break into pieces **2** (intr) informal to undergo a physical or mental breakdown **3** (tr) informal to present or report, esp

in glowing terms: it's not all it's cracked up to be **4** informal, chiefly US and Canadian to laugh or cause to laugh uproariously or uncontrollably ▷ n **crackup 5** informal a physical or mental breakdown

crack willow n **1** a species of commonly grown willow, Salix fragilis, with branches that snap easily **2** any of various related willows

Cracow ('krækaʊ, -əʊ, -ɒf) n an industrial city in S Poland, on the River Vistula: former capital of the country (1320–1609); university (1364). Pop: 822 000 (2005 est). Polish name: **Kraków** German name: **Krakau**

-cracy n combining form indicating a type of government or rule: plutocracy; mobocracy. See also **-crat** [from Greek -kratia, from kratos power]

cradle ('kreɪdəl) n **1** a baby's bed with enclosed sides, often with a hood and rockers **2** a place where something originates or is nurtured during its early life: the cradle of civilization **3** the earliest period of life: they knew each other from the cradle **4** a frame, rest, or trolley made to support or transport a piece of equipment, aircraft, ship, etc **5** a platform, cage, or trolley, in which workmen are suspended on the side of a building or ship **6** the part of a telephone on which the handset rests when not in use **7** a holder connected to a computer allowing data to be transferred from a PDA, digital camera, etc **8** another name for **creeper** (sense 5) **9** agriculture **a** a framework of several wooden fingers attached to a scythe to gather the grain into bunches as it is cut **b** a scythe equipped with such a cradle; cradle scythe **c** a collar of wooden fingers that prevents a horse or cow from turning its head and biting itself **10** Also called: **rocker** a boxlike apparatus for washing rocks, sand, etc, containing gold or gem stones **11** engraving a tool that produces the pitted surface of a copper mezzotint plate before the design is engraved upon it **12** a framework used to prevent the bedclothes from touching a sensitive part of an injured person **13** **from the cradle to the grave** throughout life ▷ vb **14** (tr) to rock or place in or as if in a cradle; hold tenderly **15** (tr) to nurture in or bring up from infancy **16** (tr) to replace (the handset of a telephone) on the cradle **17** to reap (grain) with a cradle scythe **18** (tr) to wash (soil bearing gold, etc) in a cradle **19** lacrosse to keep (the ball) in the net of the stick, esp while running with it [Old English cradol; related to Old High German kratto basket] > 'cradler n

cradle cap n a form of seborrhoea of the scalp common in young babies. Technical name: **crusta lactea**

cradle snatcher n informal someone who marries or has an affair with a much younger person

cradlesong ('kreɪdəl,sɒŋ) n another word for **lullaby**

cradling ('kreɪdlɪŋ) n architect a framework of iron or wood, esp as used in the construction of a ceiling

craft (krɑːft) n **1** skill or ability, esp in handiwork **2** skill in deception and trickery; guile; cunning **3** an occupation or trade requiring special skill, esp manual dexterity **4 a** the members of such a trade, regarded collectively **b** (as modifier): a craft guild **5** a single vessel, aircraft, or spacecraft **6** (functioning as plural) ships, boats, aircraft, or spacecraft collectively ▷ vb **7** (tr) to make or fashion with skill, esp by hand [Old English cræft skill, strength; related to Old Norse kraptr power, skill, Old High German kraft]

craft apprenticeship n a period of training for a skilled trade in industry, such as for a plumber or electrician

craftsman ('krɑːftsmən) n, pl **-men 1** a member of a skilled trade; someone who practises a craft; artisan **2** Also called (fem): **craftswoman** an artist skilled in the techniques of an art or craft > 'craftsmanly adj > 'craftsman,ship n

craft union n a labour organization membership of which is restricted to workers in a specified trade or craft. Compare **industrial union**

crafty ('krɑːftɪ) *adj* craftier, craftiest **1** skilled in deception; shrewd; cunning **2** *archaic* skilful > 'craftily *adv* > 'craftiness *n*

crag (kræg) *n* a steep rugged rock or peak [c13 of Celtic origin; related to Old Welsh *creik* rock]

Crag (kræg) *n* a formation of shelly sandstone in E England, deposited during the Pliocene and Pleistocene epochs

craggy ('krægɪ) *or US* **cragged** ('krægɪd) *adj* -gier, -giest **1** having many crags **2** (of the face) rugged; rocklike > 'craggily *adv* > 'cragginess *n*

cragsman ('krægzmən) *n, pl* -men a rock climber

craic (kræk) *n* an Irish spelling of **crack** (sense 30)

craig (kreg, kreɪg) *n* a Scot word for **crag**

Craigavon (ˌkreɪgˈævˀn) *n* a district in central Northern Ireland, in Co Armagh. Pop: 57 685 (2001). Area: 279 sq km (108 sq miles)

Craiova (*Romanian* kraˈjova) *n* a city in SW Romania, on the Jiul River. Pop: 285 000 (2005 est)

crake (kreɪk) *n zoology* any of several rails that occur in the Old World, such as the corncrake and the spotted crake [c14 from Old Norse *krāka* crow or *krākr* raven, of imitative origin]

cram (kræm) *vb* crams, cramming, crammed **1** (*tr*) to force (people, material, etc) into (a room, container, etc) with more than it can hold; stuff **2** to eat or cause to eat more than necessary **3** *informal* to study or cause to study (facts, etc), esp for an examination, by hastily memorizing ⊳ *n* **4** the act or condition of cramming **5** a crush [Old English *crammian*; related to Old Norse *kremja* to press]

crambo ('kræmbəʊ) *n* a word game in which one team says a rhyme or rhyming line for a word or line given by the other team [c17 from earlier *crambe*, probably from Latin *crambē repetīta* cabbage repeated, hence an old story, a rhyming game, from Greek *krambē*]

cram-full *adj* stuffed full

crammer ('kræmə) *n* a person or school that prepares pupils for an examination, esp pupils who have already failed that examination

cramoisy *or* **cramoisie** ('kræmɔɪzɪ, -əzɪ) *archaic* ⊳ *adj* **1** of a crimson colour ⊳ *n* **2** crimson cloth [c15 from Old French *cramoisi*, from Arabic *qirmizī* red obtained from kermes; see CRIMSON, KERMES]

cramp¹ (kræmp) *n* **1** a painful involuntary contraction of a muscle, typically caused by overexertion, heat, or chill **2** temporary partial paralysis of a muscle group: *writer's cramp* **3** (*usually plural in the US and Canada*) severe abdominal pain ⊳ *vb* **4** (*tr*) to affect with or as if with a cramp [c14 from Old French *crampe*, of Germanic origin; compare Old High German *krampho*]

cramp² (kræmp) *n* **1** Also called: cramp iron a strip of metal with its ends bent at right angles, used to bind masonry **2** a device for holding pieces of wood while they are glued; clamp **3** something that confines or restricts **4** a confined state or position ⊳ *vb* (*tr*) **5** to secure or hold with a cramp **6** to confine, hamper, or restrict **7** cramp (someone's) style *informal* to prevent (a person) from using his abilities or acting freely and confidently [c15 from Middle Dutch *crampe* cramp, hook, of Germanic origin; compare Old High German *khramph* bent; see CRAMP¹]

cramp ball *n* a hard round blackish ascomycetous fungus, *Daldinia concentrica*, characteristically found on the bark of ash trees and formerly carried to ward off cramp. The specific name refers to the concentric rings revealed if the fungus is sliced

cramped (kræmpt) *adj* **1** closed in; restricted **2** (esp of handwriting) small and irregular; difficult to read

cramper ('kræmpə) *n curling* a spiked metal plate used as a brace for the feet in throwing the stone

crampon ('kræmpən) *n* **1** one of a pair of pivoted steel levers used to lift heavy objects; grappling iron **2** (*often plural*) one of a pair of frames each with 10 or 12 metal spikes, strapped to boots for climbing or walking on ice or snow ⊳ *vb* **3** to climb using crampons [c15 from French, from Middle Dutch *crampe* hook; see CRAMP²]

cran (kræn) *n* a unit of capacity used for measuring fresh herring, equal to 37.5 gallons [c18 of uncertain origin]

cranage ('kreɪnɪdʒ) *n* **1** the use of a crane **2** a fee charged for such use

cranberry ('krænbərɪ, -brɪ) *n, pl* -ries **1** any of several trailing ericaceous shrubs of the genus *Vaccinium*, such as the European *V. oxycoccus*, that bear sour edible red berries **2** the berry of this plant, used to make sauce or jelly [c17 from Low German *kraanbere*, from *kraan* CRANE + *bere* BERRY]

cranberry bush *or* **tree** *n* a North American caprifoliaceous shrub or small tree, *Viburnum trilobum*, producing acid red fruit

Cranborne money ('krænbɔːn) *n* (in Britain) the annual payment made to Opposition parties in the House of Lords to help them pay for certain services necessary to the carrying out of their parliamentary duties; established in 1996. Compare **Short money** [named after Viscount Cranborne, Leader of the House of Lords in 1996]

crane (kreɪn) *n* **1** any large long-necked long-legged wading bird of the family *Gruidae*, inhabiting marshes and plains in most parts of the world except South America, New Zealand, and Indonesia: order *Gruiformes*. See also **demoiselle** (sense 1), **whooping crane 2** (*not in ornithological use*) any similar bird, such as a heron **3** a device for lifting and moving heavy objects, typically consisting of a moving boom, beam, or gantry from which lifting gear is suspended. See also **gantry 4** *films* a large trolley carrying a boom, on the end of which is mounted a camera ⊳ *vb* **5** (*tr*) to lift or move (an object) by or as if by a crane **6** to stretch out (esp the neck), as to see over other people's heads **7** (*intr*) (of a horse) to pull up short before a jump [Old English *cran*; related to Middle High German *krane*, Latin *grūs*, Greek *géranos*]

crane fly *n* any dipterous fly of the family *Tipulidae*, having long legs, slender wings, and a narrow body. Also called (Brit): **daddy-longlegs**

cranesbill ('kreɪnzˌbɪl) *n* any of various plants of the genus *Geranium*, having pink or purple flowers and long slender beaked fruits: family *Geraniaceae*. See also **herb Robert, storksbill**

cranial ('kreɪnɪəl) *adj* of or relating to the skull > 'cranially *adv*

cranial index *n* the ratio of the greatest length to the greatest width of the cranium, multiplied by 100: used in comparative anthropology. Compare **cephalic index**

cranial nerve *n* any of the 12 paired nerves that have their origin in the brain and reach the periphery through natural openings in the skull

craniate ('kreɪnɪɪt, -ˌeɪt) *adj* **1** having a skull or cranium ⊳ *adj* ⊳ *n* **2** another word for **vertebrate**

cranio- *or before a vowel* **crani-** *combining form* indicating the cranium or cranial: *craniotomy*

craniology (ˌkreɪnɪˈɒlədʒɪ) *n* the branch of science concerned with the shape and size of the human skull, esp with reference to variations between different races > craniological (ˌkreɪnɪəˈlɒdʒɪkˀl) *adj* > ˌcranioˈlogically *adv* > ˌcraniˈologist *n*

craniometer (ˌkreɪnɪˈɒmɪtə) *n* an instrument for measuring the cranium or skull

craniometry (ˌkreɪnɪˈɒmɪtrɪ) *n* the study and measurement of skulls > craniometric (ˌkreɪnɪəˈmɛtrɪk) *or* ˌcranioˈmetrical *adj* > ˌcranioˈmetrically *adv* > ˌcraniˈometrist *n*

craniopagus (ˌkreɪnɪˈɒpəgəs) *n* the condition of Siamese twins joined at the head

craniosacral therapy (ˌkreɪnɪəˈseɪkrəl) *n* a form of therapy for various disorders in which the therapist manipulates the bones of the skull

craniotomy (ˌkreɪnɪˈɒtəmɪ) *n, pl* -mies **1** any surgical incision into the skull, esp to expose the brain for neurosurgery **2** the surgical crushing of a fetal skull to extract a dead fetus

cranium ('kreɪnɪəm) *n, pl* -niums *or* -nia (-nɪə) **1** the skull of a vertebrate **2** the part of the skull that encloses the brain. Nontechnical name: brainpan [c16 from Medieval Latin *crānium* skull, from Greek *kranion*]

crank¹ (kræŋk) *n* **1** a device for communicating motion or for converting reciprocating motion into rotary motion or vice versa. It consists of an arm projecting from a shaft, often with a second member attached to it parallel to the shaft **2** Also called: crank handle, starting handle a handle incorporating a crank, used to start an engine or motor **3** *informal* **a** an eccentric or odd person, esp someone who stubbornly maintains unusual views **b** *US and Canadian* a bad-tempered person ⊳ *vb* **4** (*tr*) to rotate (a shaft) by means of a crank **5** (*tr*) to start (an engine, motor, etc) by means of a crank handle **6** (*tr*) to bend, twist, or make into the shape of a crank **7** (*intr*) *obsolete* to twist or wind ⊳ See also **crank up** [Old English *cranc*; related to Middle Low German *krunke* wrinkle, Dutch *krinkel* CRINKLE]

crank² (kræŋk) *or* **cranky** *adj* (of a sailing vessel) easily keeled over by the wind; tender [c17 of uncertain origin; perhaps related to CRANK¹]

crankcase ('kræŋkˌkeɪs) *n* the metal housing that encloses the crankshaft, connecting rods, etc, in an internal-combustion engine, reciprocating pump, etc

crankpin ('kræŋkˌpɪn) *n* a short cylindrical bearing surface fitted between two arms of a crank and set parallel to the main shaft of the crankshaft

crankshaft ('kræŋkˌʃɑːft) *n* a shaft having one or more cranks, esp the main shaft of an internal-combustion engine to which the connecting rods are attached

crank up *vb* (*tr*) *slang* **1** to increase (loudness, output, etc): *he cranked up his pace* **2** to set in motion or invigorate: *news editors have to crank up tired reporters* **3** (*intr, adverb*) to inject a narcotic drug

cranky¹ ('kræŋkɪ) *adj* crankier, crankiest **1** *informal* eccentric **2** *chiefly US, Canadian, and Irish informal* fussy and bad-tempered **3** shaky; out of order **4** full of bends and turns **5** *dialect* unwell > 'crankily *adv* > 'crankiness *n*

cranky² ('kræŋkɪ) *adj* crankier, crankiest *nautical* another word for **crank²**

crannog ('krænəg) *or* **crannoge** ('krænədʒ) *n* an ancient Celtic lake or bog dwelling dating from the late Bronze Age to the 16th century AD, often fortified and used as a refuge [c19 from Irish Gaelic *crannóg*, from Old Irish *crann* tree]

cranny ('krænɪ) *n, pl* -nies a narrow opening, as in a wall or rock face; chink; crevice (esp in the phrase **every nook and cranny**) [c15 from Old French *cran* notch, fissure; compare CRENEL] > 'crannied *adj*

Cranwell ('krænwəl) *n* a village in E England, in Lincolnshire: Royal Air Force College (1920)

crap¹ (kræp) *n* **1** a losing throw in the game of craps **2** another name for **craps** [c20 back formation from CRAPS]

crap² (kræp) *slang* ⊳ *n* **1** nonsense **2** rubbish **3** another word for **faeces** ⊳ *vb* craps, crapping, crapped **4** (*intr*) another word for **defecate** [C15 *crappe* chaff, from Middle Dutch, probably from *crappen* to break off]

USAGE This word was formerly considered to be taboo, and it was labelled as such in previous editions of *Collins English Dictionary*. However, it has now become acceptable in speech, although some older or more conservative people may object to its use

crapaud ('kræpəʊ, 'krɑ-) *n Caribbean* a frog or toad [from French: toad]

crape (kreɪp) *n* **1** a variant spelling of **crepe 2** crepe, esp when used for mourning clothes **3** a band of black crepe worn in mourning > 'crapy *adj*

C

crape myrtle or **crepe myrtle** n an oriental lythraceous shrub, *Lagerstroemia indica*, cultivated in warm climates for its pink, red, or white flowers

crapola (kræ'pəʊlə) n *informal* rubbish; nonsense

crap out vb (intr, adverb) **1** *US slang* to make a losing throw in craps **2** *US slang* to fail; withdraw **3** *US slang* to rest **4** *slang* to fail to do or attempt something through fear

crappie ('kræpɪ) n either of two North American freshwater percoid food and game fishes, *Pomoxis nigromaculatus* (**black crappie**) or *P. annularis* (**white crappie**): family *Centrarchidae* (sunfishes, etc) [c19 from Canadian French *crapet*]

craps (kræps) n (usually functioning as singular) **1** a gambling game using two dice, in which a player wins the bet if 7 or 11 is thrown first, and loses if 2, 3, or 12 is thrown **2** **shoot craps** to play this game [c19 probably from *crabs* lowest throw at dice, plural of CRAB[1]]

crapshooter ('kræpˌʃuːtə) n *US* a person who plays the game of craps

crapulent ('kræpjʊlənt) or **crapulous** ('kræpjʊləs) adj **1** given to or resulting from intemperance **2** suffering from intemperance; drunken [c18 from Late Latin *crāpulentus* drunk, from Latin *crāpula*, from Greek *kraipalē* drunkenness, headache resulting therefrom] > 'crapulence n > 'crapulently or 'crapulously adv > 'crapulousness n

craquelure ('krækəlʊə) n a network of fine cracks on old paintings caused by the deterioration of pigment or varnish [c20 from French, from *craqueler* to crackle, from *craquer* to crack, of imitative origin]

crash[1] (kræʃ) vb **1** to make or cause to make a loud noise as of solid objects smashing or clattering **2** to fall or cause to fall with force, breaking in pieces with a loud noise as of solid objects smashing **3** (intr) to break or smash in pieces with a loud noise **4** (intr) to collapse or fail suddenly: *this business is sure to crash* **5** to cause (an aircraft) to hit land or water violently resulting in severe damage or (of an aircraft) to hit land or water in this way **6** to cause (a car, etc) to collide with another car or other object or (of two or more cars) to be involved in a collision **7** to move or cause to move violently or noisily: *to crash through a barrier* **8** *Brit informal* short for **gate-crash** **9** (intr) (of a computer system or program) to fail suddenly and completely because of a malfunction **10** (intr) *slang* another term for **crash out 11** **crash and burn** *informal* to fail; be unsuccessful ▷ n **12** an act or instance of breaking and falling to pieces **13** a sudden loud noise: *the crash of thunder* **14** a collision, as between vehicles **15** a sudden descent of an aircraft as a result of which it hits land or water **16** the sudden collapse of a business, stock exchange, etc, esp one causing further financial failure **17** (modifier) **a** requiring or using intensive effort and all possible resources in order to accomplish something quickly: *a crash programme* **b** sudden or vigorous: *a crash halt; a crash tackle* **18** **crash-and-burn** *informal* a complete failure ▷ See also **crash out** [c14 probably from *crasen* to smash, shatter + *dasshen* to strike violently, DASH[1]; see CRAZE] > 'crasher n

crash[2] (kræʃ) n a coarse cotton or linen cloth used for towelling, curtains, etc [c19 from Russian *krashenina* coloured linen]

crash barrier n a barrier erected along the centre of a motorway, around a racetrack, etc, for safety purposes

crash dive n **1** a sudden steep dive from the surface by a submarine ▷ vb **crash-dive 2** (usually of an aircraft) to descend steeply and rapidly, before hitting the ground **3** to perform or cause to perform a crash dive

crash helmet n a padded helmet worn for motorcycling, flying, bobsleighing, etc, to protect the head in a crash

crashing ('kræʃɪŋ) adj (prenominal) *informal* (intensifier) (esp in the phrase **a crashing bore**)

crash-land vb to land (an aircraft) in an emergency causing damage or (of an aircraft) to land in this way > 'crash-ˌlanding n

crash out vb (intr, adverb) *slang* **1 a** to go to sleep **b** to spend the night (in a place): *we crashed out at John's place* **2** to pass out

crash pad n *slang* a place to sleep or live temporarily

crash team n a medical team with special equipment able to be mobilized quickly to treat cardiac arrest

crash-test vb (tr) to test (a new product) for safety and reliability by finding out its breaking point under pressure, heat, etc

crashworthiness ('kræʃˌwɜːðɪnɪs) n the ability of a vehicle structure to withstand a crash > 'crash,worthy adj

crasis ('kreɪsɪs) n, pl -ses (-siːz) the fusion or contraction of two adjacent vowels into one. Also called: **syneresis** [c17 from Greek *krasis* a mingling, from *kerannunai* to mix]

crass (kræs) adj stupid; gross [c16 from Latin *crassus* thick, dense, gross] > 'crassly adv > 'crassness or 'crassi,tude n

crassulacean acid metabolism (ˌkræsjʊ'leɪʃən) n the full name for CAM (sense 2)

crassulaceous (ˌkræsjʊ'leɪʃəs) adj of, relating to, or belonging to the *Crassulaceae*, a family of herbaceous or shrubby flowering plants with fleshy succulent leaves, including the houseleeks and stonecrops [c19 from New Latin *Crassula* name of genus, from Medieval Latin: stonecrop, from Latin *crassus* thick]

-crat n combining form indicating a person who takes part in or is a member of a form of government or class: *democrat; technocrat.* See also **-cracy** [from Greek *-kratēs*, from *-kratia* -CRACY] > **-cratic** or **-cratical** adj combining form

cratch (krætʃ) n a rack for holding fodder for cattle, etc [c14 from Old French: CRÈCHE]

crate (kreɪt) n **1** a fairly large container, usually made of wooden slats or wickerwork, used for packing, storing, or transporting goods **2** *slang* an old car, aeroplane, etc ▷ vb **3** (tr) to pack or place in a crate [c16 from Latin *crātis* wickerwork, hurdle] > 'crater n > 'crateful n

crater ('kreɪtə) n **1** the bowl-shaped opening at the top or side of a volcano or top of a geyser through which lava and gases are emitted **2** a similarly shaped depression formed by the impact of a meteorite or exploding bomb **3** any of the circular or polygonal walled formations covering the surface of the moon and some other planets, formed probably either by volcanic action or by the impact of meteorites. They can have a diameter of up to 240 kilometres (150 miles) and a depth of 8900 metres (29 000 feet) **4** a pit in an otherwise smooth surface **5** a large open bowl with two handles, used for mixing wines, esp in ancient Greece ▷ vb **6** to make or form craters in (a surface, such as the ground) **7** *slang* to fail; collapse; crash [c17 from Latin: mixing bowl, crater, from Greek *kratēr*, from *kerannunai* to mix] > 'cratered adj > 'craterless adj > 'crater-,like adj

Crater ('kreɪtə) n, Latin genitive Crateris ('kreɪtərɪs) a small faint constellation in the S hemisphere lying between Virgo and Hydra

C rations or **C-rations** pl n tinned food formerly issued in packs to US soldiers [c20 C(ombat) *rations*]

craton ('kreɪtən) n *geology* a stable part of the earth's continental crust or lithosphere that has not been deformed significantly for many millions, even hundreds of millions, of years. See **shield** (sense 7) [c20 from Greek *kratos* strength] > **cratonic** adj

cratur ('kreɪtər) n *Irish and Scot* **1** the whisky or whiskey: *a drop of the cratur* **2** a person [from CREATURE]

craunch (krɔːntʃ) vb a dialect word for **crunch** > 'craunchable adj > 'craunchy adj > 'craunchiness n

cravat (krə'væt) n a scarf of silk or fine wool, worn round the neck, esp by men [c17 from French *cravate*, from Serbo-Croat *Hrvat* Croat; so called because worn by Croats in the French army during the Thirty Years' War]

crave (kreɪv) vb **1** (when intr, foll by for or after) to desire intensely; long (for) **2** (tr) to need greatly or urgently **3** (tr) to beg or plead for [Old English *crafian*; related to Old Norse *krefja* to demand, *kræfr* strong; see CRAFT] > 'craver n

craven ('kreɪvᵊn) adj **1** cowardly; mean-spirited ▷ n **2** a coward [c13 *cravant*, probably from Old French *crevant* bursting, from *crever* to burst, die, from Latin *crepāre* to burst, crack] > 'cravenly adv > 'cravenness n

craving ('kreɪvɪŋ) n an intense desire or longing

craw (krɔː) n **1** a less common word for **crop** (sense 6) **2** the stomach of an animal **3** **stick in one's craw** or **throat** *informal* to be difficult, or against one's conscience, for one to accept, utter, or believe [c14 related to Middle High German *krage*, Middle Dutch *crāghe* neck, Icelandic *kragi* collar]

crawfish ('krɔːˌfɪʃ) n, pl -fish or -fishes a variant (esp US) of **crayfish** (esp sense 2)

crawl[1] (krɔːl) vb (intr) **1** to move slowly, either by dragging the body along the ground or on the hands and knees **2** to proceed or move along very slowly or laboriously: *the traffic crawled along the road* **3** to act or behave in a servile manner; fawn; cringe **4** to be or feel as if overrun by something unpleasant, esp crawling creatures: *the pile of refuse crawled with insects* **5** (of insects, worms, snakes, etc) to move with the body close to the ground **6** to swim the crawl ▷ n **7** a slow creeping pace or motion **8** Also called: **Australian crawl, front crawl** *swimming* a stroke in which the feet are kicked like paddles while the arms reach forward and pull back through the water [c14 probably from Old Norse *krafla* to creep; compare Swedish *kravla*, Middle Low German *krabbelen* to crawl, Old Norse *krabbi* CRAB[1]] > 'crawlingly adv

crawl[2] (krɔːl) n an enclosure in shallow, coastal water for fish, lobsters, etc [c17 from Dutch *kraal* KRAAL]

crawler ('krɔːlə) n **1** *slang* a servile flatterer **2** a person or animal that crawls **3** *US* an informal name for an **earthworm 4** a computer program that is capable of performing recursive searches on the World Wide Web **5** (plural) a baby's overalls; rompers

crawler lane n a lane on an uphill section of a motorway reserved for slow vehicles

crawler track n **1** another name for **crawler lane 2** another name for **Caterpillar** (sense 2)

Crawley ('krɔːlɪ) n a town in S England, in NE West Sussex: designated a new town in 1956. Pop: 100 547 (2001)

crawling ('krɔːlɪŋ) n a defect in freshly applied paint or varnish characterized by bare patches and ridging

crawling peg n a method of stabilizing exchange rates, prices, etc, by maintaining a fixed level for a specified period or until the level has persisted at an upper or lower limit for a specified period and then permitting a predetermined incremental rise or fall

crawly ('krɔːlɪ) adj crawlier, crawliest *informal* feeling or causing a sensation like creatures crawling on one's skin

craw-thumper n *Irish informal* an ostentatiously pious person [c18 in the sense: breast-beater, from CRAW]

cray (kreɪ) n *Austral and NZ informal* a crayfish

crayfish ('kreɪˌfɪʃ) or esp US **crawfish** n, pl -fish or -fishes **1** any freshwater decapod crustacean of the genera *Astacus* and *Cambarus*, resembling a small lobster **2** any of various similar crustaceans, esp the spiny lobster [c14 *cray*, by folk etymology, from Old French *crevice* crab, from Old High German *krebiz* + FISH]

crayon ('kreɪən, -ɒn) n **1** a small stick or pencil of charcoal, wax, clay, or chalk mixed with coloured pigment **2** a drawing made with crayons ▷ *vb* **3** to draw or colour with crayons [c17 from French, from *craie*, from Latin *crēta* chalk] > ˈcrayonist *n*

craythur *n Irish* **1** (ˈkreːθər) **the** a variant of **cratur** (sense 1) **2** (ˈkreːtʃər) a variant of **cratur** (sense 2) [from Irish Gaelic *Créatur* creature]

craze (kreɪz) *n* **1** a short-lived current fashion **2** a wild or exaggerated enthusiasm: *a craze for chestnuts* **3** mental disturbance; insanity ▷ *vb* **4** to make or become mad **5** *ceramics, metallurgy* to develop or cause to develop a fine network of cracks **6** (*tr*) *Brit dialect or obsolete* to break **7** (*tr*) *archaic* to weaken [c14 (in the sense: to break, shatter): probably of Scandinavian origin; compare Swedish *krasa* to shatter, ultimately of imitative origin]

crazed (kreɪzd) *adj* **1** driven insane **2** (of porcelain or pottery) having a fine network of cracks in the glaze

crazy (ˈkreɪzɪ) *adj* -zier, -ziest **1** *informal* insane **2** fantastic; strange; ridiculous: *a crazy dream* **3** (*postpositive; foll by about or over*) *informal* extremely fond (of) **4** *slang* very good or excellent ▷ *n, pl* crazies **5** *informal* a crazy person > ˈcrazily *adv* > ˈcraziness *n*

crazy bone *n* a US name for **funny bone**

crazy golf *n* a putting game in which the ball has to be played via various obstacles

crazy paving *n Brit* a form of paving, as for a path, made of slabs of stone of irregular shape fitted together

crazy quilt *n* a patchwork quilt made from assorted pieces of material of irregular shape, size, and colour

CRE (in Britain) *abbreviation for* **Commission for Racial Equality**

creak (kriːk) *vb* **1** to make or cause to make a harsh squeaking sound **2** (*intr*) to make such sounds while moving: *the old car creaked along* ▷ *n* **3** a harsh squeaking sound [c14 variant of CROAK, of imitative origin] > ˈcreaky *adj* > ˈcreakily *adv* > ˈcreakiness *n*

cream (kriːm) *n* **1 a** the fatty part of milk, which rises to the top if the milk is allowed to stand **b** (*as modifier*): *cream buns* **2** anything resembling cream in consistency: *shoe cream; beauty cream* **3** the best one or most essential part of something; pick: *the cream of the bunch; the cream of the joke* **4** a soup containing cream or milk: *cream of chicken soup* **5** any of various dishes, cakes, biscuits, etc, resembling or containing cream **6** a confection made of fondant or soft fudge, often covered in chocolate **7 cream sherry** a full-bodied sweet sherry **8 a** a yellowish-white colour **b** (*as adjective*): *cream wallpaper* ▷ *vb* **9** (*tr*) to skim or otherwise separate the cream from (milk) **10** (*tr*) to beat (foodstuffs, esp butter and sugar) to a light creamy consistency **11** (*intr*) to form cream **12** (*tr*) to add or apply cream or any creamlike substance to: *to cream one's face; to cream coffee* **13** (*tr; sometimes foll by off*) to take away the best part of **14** (*tr*) to prepare or cook (vegetables, chicken, etc) with cream or milk **15** to allow (milk) to form a layer of cream on its surface or (of milk) to form such a layer **16** (*tr*) *slang, chiefly US, Canadian, and Austral* to beat thoroughly **17** (*intr*) *slang* (of a man) to ejaculate during orgasm [c14 from Old French *cresme*, from Late Latin *crāmum* cream, of Celtic origin; influenced by Church Latin *chrisma* unction, CHRISM] > ˈcreamˌlike *adj*

cream cheese *n* a smooth soft white cheese made from soured cream or milk

cream cracker *n Brit* a crisp unsweetened biscuit, often eaten with cheese

cream-crackered *adj Brit slang* exhausted [c20 rhyming slang for *knackered*]

creamcups (ˈkriːmˌkʌps) *n* (*functioning as singular or plural*) a Californian papaveraceous plant, *Platystemon californicus*, with small cream-coloured or yellow flowers on long flower stalks

creamer (ˈkriːmə) *n* **1** a vessel or device for separating cream from milk **2** a powdered substitute for cream, used in coffee **3** *chiefly US and Canadian* a small jug or pitcher for serving cream

creamery (ˈkriːmərɪ) *n, pl* -eries **1** an establishment where milk and cream are made into butter and cheese **2** a place where dairy products are sold **3** a place where milk is left to stand until the cream rises to the top

creamlaid (ˈkriːmˌleɪd) *adj* (of laid paper) cream-coloured and of a ribbed appearance

cream of tartar *n* another name for **potassium hydrogen tartrate**, esp when used in baking powders

cream puff *n* **1** a shell of light pastry with a custard or cream filling **2** *informal* an effeminate man

cream sauce *n* a white sauce made from cream, butter, etc

cream soda *n* a carbonated soft drink flavoured with vanilla

cream tea *n* afternoon tea including bread or scones served with clotted cream and jam

creamware (ˈkriːmˌwɛə) *n* a type of earthenware with a deep cream body developed about 1720 and widely produced. See also **Queensware**

creamwove (ˈkriːmˌwəʊv) *adj* (of wove paper) cream-coloured and even-surfaced

creamy (ˈkriːmɪ) *adj* creamier, creamiest **1** resembling cream in colour, taste, or consistency **2** containing cream > ˈcreamily *adv* > ˈcreaminess *n*

crease[1] (kriːs) *n* **1** a line or mark produced by folding, pressing, or wrinkling **2** a wrinkle or furrow, esp on the face **3** *cricket* any three lines near each wicket marking positions for the bowler or batsman. See also **bowling crease, popping crease, return crease** **4** *ice hockey* the small rectangular area in front of each goal cage **5** Also called: **goal crease** *lacrosse* the circular area surrounding the goal ▷ *vb* **6** to make or become wrinkled or furrowed **7** (*tr*) to graze with a bullet, causing superficial injury **8** (*often foll by up*) *slang* to be or cause to be greatly amused [c15 from earlier *crēst*; probably related to Old French *cresté* wrinkled] > ˈcreaseless *adj* > ˈcreaser *n* > ˈcreasy *adj*

crease[2] (kriːs) *n* a rare spelling of **kris**

crease-resistant *adj* (of a fabric, garment, etc) designed to remain uncreased when subjected to wear or use

create (kriːˈeɪt) *vb* **1** (*tr*) to cause to come into existence **2** (*tr*) to invest with a new honour, office, or title; appoint **3** (*tr*) to be the cause of: *these circumstances created the revolution* **4** (*tr*) to act (a role) in the first production of a play **5** (*intr*) to be engaged in creative work **6** (*intr*) *Brit slang* to make a fuss or uproar [c14 from Latin *creātus*, from *creāre* to produce, make] > creˈatable *adj*

creatine (ˈkriːəˌtiːn, -tɪn) *or* **creatin** (ˈkriːətɪn) *n* an important metabolite involved in many biochemical reactions and present in many types of living cells [c19 *creat*- from Greek *kreas* flesh + -INE[2]]

creatinine (kriːˈætəˌniːn) *n* an anhydride of creatine that is abundant in muscle and excreted in the urine [c19 from German *Kreatinin*, from *Kreatin* CREATINE + *-in* -INE[2]]

creation (kriːˈeɪʃən) *n* **1** the act or process of creating **2** the fact of being created or produced **3** something that has been brought into existence or created, esp a product of human intelligence or imagination **4** the whole universe, including the world and all the things in it **5** an unusual or striking garment or hat > creˈational *adj*

Creation (kriːˈeɪʃən) *n theol* **1** (often preceded by *the*) God's act of bringing the universe into being **2** the universe as thus brought into being by God

creationism (kriːˈeɪʃəˌnɪzəm) *n* **1** the belief that God brings individual human souls into existence at conception or birth. Compare **traducianism 2** the doctrine that ascribes the origins of all things to God's acts of creation rather than to evolution > creˈationist *n* > creˌationˈistic *adj*

creative (kriːˈeɪtɪv) *adj* **1** having the ability to create **2** characterized by originality of thought; having or showing imagination: *a creative mind* **3** designed to stimulate the imagination: *creative toys* **4** characterized by sophisticated bending of the rules or conventions: *creative accounting* ▷ *n* **5** a creative person, esp one who devises advertising campaigns > creˈatively *adv* > creˈativeness *n* > ˌcreaˈtivity *n*

creative tension *n* a situation where disagreement or discord ultimately gives rise to better ideas or outcomes

creator (kriːˈeɪtə) *n* a person or thing that creates; originator > creˈatorˌship *n* > creˈatress *or* creˈatrix *fem n*

Creator (kriːˈeɪtə) *n* (usually preceded by *the*) an epithet of God

creature (ˈkriːtʃə) *n* **1** a living being, esp an animal **2** something that has been created, whether animate or inanimate: *a creature of the imagination* **3** a human being; person: used as a term of scorn, pity, or endearment **4** a person who is dependent upon another; tool or puppet [c13 from Church Latin *crēātūra*, from Latin *crēare* to create] > ˈcreatural *or* ˈcreaturely *adj* > ˈcreatureliness *n*

creature comforts *pl n* material things or luxuries that help to provide for one's bodily comfort

creature feature *n* a horror film featuring a monster

CREB *n* cyclic amp-response element binding protein; a protein involved in the long-term memory process

crèche (krɛʃ, kreɪʃ; *French* krɛʃ) *n* **1** *chiefly Brit* **a** a day nursery for very young children **b** a supervised play area provided for young children for short periods **2** a tableau of Christ's Nativity **3** a foundling home or hospital [c19 from Old French: manger, crib, ultimately of Germanic origin; compare Old High German *kripja* crib]

Crécy (ˈkrɛsɪ; *French* kresi) *n* a village in N France: scene of the first decisive battle of the Hundred Years' War when the English defeated the French (1346). Official name: **Crécy-en-Ponthieu** (-ɑ̃pɔ̃tjø) former English name: **Cressy**

cred (krɛd) *n slang* short for **credibility** (esp in the phrase **street cred**)

credence (ˈkriːdəns) *n* **1** acceptance or belief, esp with regard to the truth of the evidence of others: *I cannot give credence to his account* **2** something supporting a claim to belief; recommendation; credential (esp in the phrase **letters of credence**) **3** short for **credence table** [c14 from Medieval Latin *crēdentia* trust, credit, from Latin *crēdere* to believe]

credence table *n* **1** a small sideboard, originally one at which food was tasted for poison before serving **2** *Christianity* a small table or ledge on which the bread, wine, etc, are placed before being consecrated in the Eucharist

credendum (krɪˈdɛndəm) *n, pl* -da (-də) (*often plural*) *Christianity* an article of faith [Latin: a thing to be believed, from *crēdere* to believe]

credent (ˈkriːdənt) *adj obsolete* believing or believable [c17 from Latin *crēdēns* believing]

credential (krɪˈdɛnʃəl) *n* **1** something that entitles a person to confidence, authority, etc **2** (*plural*) a letter or certificate giving evidence of the bearer's identity or competence ▷ *adj* **3** entitling one to confidence, authority, etc [c16 from Medieval Latin *crēdentia* credit, trust; see CREDENCE] > creˈdentialed *adj*

credenza (krɪˈdɛnzə) *n* another name for **credence table** [Italian: see CREDENCE]

credibility (ˌkrɛdɪˈbɪlɪtɪ) *n* the quality of being believed or trusted

credibility gap *n* a disparity between claims or statements made and the evident facts of the situation or circumstances to which they relate

credible (ˈkrɛdɪbəl) *adj* **1** capable of being believed **2** trustworthy or reliable: *the latest claim is the only*

C

one to involve a credible witness [C14 from Latin *crēdibilis,* from Latin *crēdere* to believe] > 'credibleness *n* > 'credibly *adv*

credit ('krɛdɪt) *n* **1** commendation or approval, as for an act or quality: *she was given credit for her work* **2** a person or thing serving as a source of good influence, repute, ability, etc: *a credit to the team* **3** the quality of being believable or trustworthy: *that statement had credit* **4** influence or reputation coming from the approval or good opinion of others: *he acquired credit within the community* **5** belief in the truth, reliability, quality, etc, of someone or something: *I would give credit to that philosophy* **6** a sum of money or equivalent purchasing power, as at a shop, available for a person's use **7 a** the positive balance in a person's bank account **b** the sum of money that a bank makes available to a client in excess of any deposit **8 a** the practice of permitting a buyer to receive goods or services before payment **b** the time permitted for paying for such goods or services **9** reputation for solvency and commercial or financial probity, inducing confidence among creditors **10** *accounting* **a** acknowledgment of an income, liability, or capital item by entry on the right-hand side of an account **b** the right-hand side of an account **c** an entry on this side **d** the total of such entries **e** (*as modifier*): *credit entries.* Compare **debit** (sense 1) **11** short for **tax credit 12** *education* **a** a distinction awarded to an examination candidate obtaining good marks **b** a section of an examination syllabus satisfactorily completed, as in higher and professional education **13** **letter of credit** an order authorizing a named person to draw money from correspondents of the issuer **14** **on credit** with payment to be made at a future date ▷ *vb* (*tr*) **-its, -iting, -ited 15** (foll by *with*) to ascribe (to); give credit (for): *they credited him with the discovery* **16** to accept as true; believe **17** to do credit to **18** *accounting* **a** to enter (an item) as a credit in an account **b** to acknowledge (a payer) by making such an entry. Compare **debit** (sense 2) **19** to award a credit to (a student) ▷ See also **credits** [C16 from Old French *crédit,* from Italian *credito,* from Latin *crēditum* loan, from *crēdere* to believe] > 'creditless *adj*

creditable ('krɛdɪtəbəl) *adj* **1** deserving credit, honour, etc; praiseworthy **2** *obsolete* credible > 'creditableness *or* ˌcredita'bility *n* > 'creditably *adv*

credit account *n Brit* a credit system by means of which customers may obtain goods and services before payment. Also called: **charge account**

credit card *n* a card issued by banks, businesses, etc, enabling the holder to obtain goods and services on credit

credit line *n* **1** an acknowledgment of origin or authorship, as in a newspaper or film **2** Also called: **line of credit** *US and Canadian* the maximum credit that a customer is allowed

creditor ('krɛdɪtə) *n* a person or commercial enterprise to whom money is owed. Compare **debtor**

credit rating *n* an evaluation of the creditworthiness of an individual or business enterprise

credit-reference agency *n* an agency, other than a bank, that specializes in providing credit ratings of people or organizations

credits ('krɛdɪts) *pl n* a list of those responsible for the production of a film or television programme

credit squeeze *n* the control of credit facilities as an instrument of economic policy, associated with restrictions on bank loans and overdrafts, raised interest rates, etc

credit standing *n* reputation for discharging financial obligations

credit transfer *n* a method of settling a debt by transferring money through a bank or post office, esp for those who do not have cheque accounts

credit union *n* a cooperative association whose members can obtain low-interest loans out of their combined savings

creditworthy ('krɛdɪtˌwɜːðɪ) *adj* (of an individual or business enterprise) adjudged as meriting credit on the basis of such factors as earning power, previous record of debt repayment, etc > 'credit,worthiness *n*

credo ('kriːdəʊ, 'kreɪ-) *n, pl* **-dos** any formal or authorized statement of beliefs, principles, or opinions

Credo ('kriːdəʊ, 'kreɪ-) *n, pl* **-dos 1** the Apostles' Creed or the Nicene Creed **2** a musical setting of the Creed [C12 from Latin, literally: I believe; first word of the Apostles' and Nicene Creeds]

credulity (krɪ'djuːlɪtɪ) *n* disposition to believe something on little evidence; gullibility

credulous ('krɛdjʊləs) *adj* **1** tending to believe something on little evidence **2** arising from or characterized by credulity: *credulous beliefs* [C16 from Latin *crēdulus,* from *crēdere* to believe] > 'credulously *adv* > 'credulousness *n*

cree (kriː) *n South Wales and southwest English dialect* temporary immunity from the rules of a game: said by children [of unknown origin]

Cree (kriː) *n* **1** (*pl* **Cree** *or* **Crees**) a member of a Native American people living in Ontario, Saskatchewan, and Manitoba **2** the language of this people, belonging to the Algonquian family **3** a syllabic writing system of this and certain other languages [from first syllable of Canadian French *Christianaux,* probably based on Ojibwa *Kenistenoag* (tribal name)]

creed (kriːd) *n* **1** a concise, formal statement of the essential articles of Christian belief, such as the Apostles' Creed or the Nicene Creed **2** any statement or system of beliefs or principles [Old English *crēda,* from Latin *crēdo* I believe] > 'creedal *or* 'credal *adj*

creek (kriːk) *n* **1** *chiefly Brit* a narrow inlet or bay, esp of the sea **2** *US, Canadian, Austral and NZ* a small stream or tributary **3** **up the creek** *slang* in trouble; in a difficult position [C13 from Old Norse *kriki* nook; related to Middle Dutch *krēke* creek, inlet]

Creek (kriːk) *n* **1** (*pl* **Creek** *or* **Creeks**) a member of a confederacy of Native American peoples formerly living in Georgia and Alabama, now chiefly in Oklahoma **2** any of the languages of these peoples, belonging to the Muskhogean family

creel (kriːl) *n* **1** a wickerwork basket, esp one used to hold fish **2** a wickerwork trap for catching lobsters, etc **3** the framework on a spinning machine that holds the bobbins **4** *West Yorkshire dialect* a wooden frame suspended from a ceiling, used for drying clothes [C15 from Scottish, of obscure origin]

creep (kriːp) *vb* **creeps, creeping, crept** (*intr*) **1** to crawl with the body near to or touching the ground **2** to move slowly, quietly, or cautiously **3** to act in a servile way; fawn; cringe **4** to move or slip out of place, as from pressure or wear **5** (of plants) to grow along the ground or over rocks, producing roots, suckers, or tendrils at intervals **6** (of a body or substance) to become permanently deformed as a result of an applied stress, often when combined with heating **7** to develop gradually: *creeping unrest* **8** to have the sensation of something crawling over the skin **9** (of metals) to undergo slow plastic deformation ▷ *n* **10** the act of creeping or a creeping movement **11** *slang* a person considered to be obnoxious or servile **12** the continuous permanent deformation of a body or substance as a result of stress or heat **13** *geology* the gradual downwards movement of loose rock material, soil, etc, on a slope **14** a slow relative movement of two adjacent parts, structural components, etc **15** slow plastic deformation of metals ▷ See also **creeps** [Old English *crēopan;* related to Old Frisian *kriāpa,* Old Norse *krjūpa,* Middle Low German *krūpen*]

creeper ('kriːpə) *n* **1** a person or animal that creeps **2** a plant, such as the ivy or periwinkle, that grows by creeping **3** *US and Canadian* any

small songbird of the family *Certhiidae* of the N hemisphere, having a brown-and-white plumage and slender downward-curving bill. They creep up trees to feed on insects. Also called: **tree creeper 4** a hooked instrument for dragging deep water **5** Also called: **cradle** a flat board or framework mounted on casters, used to lie on when working under cars **6** Also called: **daisycutter** *cricket* a bowled ball that keeps low or travels along the ground **7** either of a pair of low iron supports for logs in a hearth **8** *informal* a shoe with a soft sole

creep-feeding *n* the practice of feeding young farm animals (esp piglets, calves, and lambs) in a sectioned-off part of their indoor environment, in order to prevent the mother from gaining access to the food

creep-grazing *n* a method of pasture management that allows young farm animals (esp lambs) to graze part of the pasture before the adults in the group

creepie ('kriːpɪ, 'krɪp-) *n chiefly Scot* a low stool

creeping bent grass *n* a grass, *Agrostis stolonifera,* grown as a pasture grass in Europe and North America: roots readily from the stem

creeping Jennie ('dʒɛnɪ) *or US and Canadian* **creeping Charlie** *n* other names for **moneywort**

creeping Jesus *n derogatory slang* **1** an obsequious or servile person **2** a hypocritically religious person

creeping thistle *n* a weedy Eurasian thistle, *Cirsium arvense,* common as a fast-spreading weed in the US and Canadian name: **Canada thistle**

creeps (kriːps) *pl n* (preceded by *the*) *informal* a feeling of fear, repulsion, disgust, etc

creepy ('kriːpɪ) *adj* **creepier, creepiest 1** *informal* having or causing a sensation of repulsion, horror, or fear, as of creatures crawling on the skin **2** creeping; slow-moving > 'creepily *adv* > 'creepiness *n*

creepy-crawly *Brit informal* ▷ *n, pl* **-crawlies 1** a small crawling creature ▷ *adj* **2** feeling or causing a sensation as of creatures crawling on one's skin

creese (kriːs) *n* a rare spelling of **kris**

crem (krɛm) *n informal* short for **crematorium**

crémant (*French* kremã) *adj* (of a wine) moderately sparkling [C21 French, literally: creaming]

cremate (krɪ'meɪt) *vb* (*tr*) to burn up (something, esp a corpse) and reduce to ash [C19 from Latin *cremāre*] > cre'mation *n* > cre'mationism *n* > cre'mationist *n*

cremator (krɪ'meɪtə) *n* **1** Also called (esp US): **cinerator** *Brit* a furnace for cremating corpses **2** a person who operates such a furnace

crematorium (ˌkrɛmə'tɔːrɪəm) *n, pl* **-riums** *or* **-ria** (-rɪə) *Brit* a building in which corpses are cremated

crematory ('krɛmətərɪ, -trɪ) *adj* **1** of or relating to cremation or crematoriums ▷ *n, pl* **-ries 2** another word (esp US) for **crematorium**

crème (krɛm, kriːm, kreɪm) *n* **1** cream **2** any of various sweet liqueurs: *crème de moka* ▷ *adj* **3** (of a liqueur) rich and sweet

crème brûlée *French* (krɛm bryle) *n* a cream or custard dessert covered with caramelized sugar [literally, burnt cream]

crème caramel *n* a dessert made of eggs, sugar, milk, etc, topped with caramel. Also called: **caramel cream**

crème de cacao ('krɛm də kɑː'kɑːəʊ, 'kəʊkəʊ 'kriːm, 'kreɪm) *n* a sweet liqueur with a chocolate flavour [French, literally: cream of cacao]

crème de la crème *French* (krɛm də la krɛm) *n* the very best [literally: cream of the cream]

crème de menthe ('krɛm də 'mɛnθ, 'mɪnt, 'kriːm, 'kreɪm) *n* a liqueur flavoured with peppermint, usually bright green in colour [French, literally: cream of mint]

crème fraîche ('krɛm 'frɛʃ) *n* thickened and slightly fermented cream [French, literally: fresh cream]

Cremona (*Italian* kre'moːna) *n* a city in N Italy, in

Lombardy on the River Po: noted for the manufacture of fine violins in the 16th–18th centuries. Pop: 70 887 (2001)

crenate ('kri:neɪt) or **crenated** adj having a scalloped margin, as certain leaves [c18 from New Latin crēnātus, from Medieval Latin, probably from Late Latin crēna a notch] > **'crenately** adv

crenation (krɪ'neɪʃən) or **crenature** ('krɛnə,tjʊə, 'kri:-) n 1 any of the rounded teeth or the notches between them on a crenate structure 2 a crenate formation or condition

crenel ('krɛnəl) or **crenelle** (krɪ'nɛl) n 1 any of a set of openings formed in the top of a wall or parapet and having slanting sides, as in a battlement 2 another name for **crenation** [c15 from Old French, literally: a little notch, from cren notch, from Late Latin crēna]

crenellate or US **crenelate** ('krɛnɪ,leɪt) vb (tr) 1 to supply with battlements 2 to form square indentations in (a moulding, etc) [c19 from Old French creneler, from CRENEL] > ,crenel'lation or US ,crenel'ation n

crenellated or US **crenelated** ('krɛnɪ,leɪtɪd) adj 1 having battlements 2 (of a moulding, etc) having square indentations

crenulate ('krɛnjʊ,leɪt, -lɪt) or **crenulated** adj having a margin very finely notched with rounded projections, as certain leaves [c18 from New Latin crēnulātus, from crēnula, literally: a little notch; see CRENEL]

crenulation (,krɛnjʊ'leɪʃən) n 1 any of the teeth or notches of a crenulate structure 2 a crenulate formation

creodont ('kri:ə,dɒnt) n any of a group of extinct Tertiary mammals some of which are thought to have been the ancestors of modern carnivores: order Carnivora [c19 from New Latin Creodonta, from Greek kreas flesh + odōn tooth]

creole ('kri:əʊl) n 1 a language that has its origin in extended contact between two language communities, one of which is generally European. It incorporates features from each and constitutes the mother tongue of a community. Compare **pidgin** ▷ adj 2 denoting, relating to, or characteristic of creole 3 (of a sauce or dish) containing or cooked with tomatoes, green peppers, onions, etc [c17 via French and Spanish probably from Portuguese crioulo slave born in one's household, person of European ancestry born in the colonies, probably from criar to bring up, from Latin creāre to CREATE]

Creole ('kri:əʊl) n 1 (sometimes not capital) (in the Caribbean and Latin America) a a native-born person of European, esp Spanish, ancestry b a native-born person of mixed European and African ancestry who speaks a French or Spanish creole c a native-born Black person as distinguished from one brought from Africa 2 (in Louisiana and other Gulf States of the US) a native-born person of French ancestry 3 the creolized French spoken in Louisiana, esp in New Orleans ▷ adj 4 of, relating to, or characteristic of any of these peoples

creolized or **creolised** ('kri:ə,laɪzd) adj (of a language) incorporating a considerable range of features from one or more unrelated languages, as the result of contact between language communities

Creon ('kri:ɒn) n Greek myth the successor to Oedipus as king of Thebes; the brother of Jocasta. See also **Antigone**

creophagous (krɪ'ɒfəgəs) adj flesh-eating or carnivorous [c19 from Greek kreophagos, from kreas flesh + -phagein to consume] > **creophagy** (krɪ'ɒfədʒɪ) n

creosol ('kri:ə,sɒl) n a colourless or pale yellow insoluble oily liquid with a smoky odour and a burning taste; 2-methoxy-4-methylphenol: an active principle of creosote. Formula: $CH_3O(CH_3)C_6H_3OH$ [c19 from CREOS(OTE) + -OL[1]]

creosote ('kri:ə,səʊt) n 1 a colourless or pale yellow liquid mixture with a burning taste and

penetrating odour distilled from wood tar, esp from beechwood, contains creosol and other phenols, and is used as an antiseptic 2 Also called: **coal-tar creosote** a thick dark liquid mixture prepared from coal tar, containing phenols: used as a preservative for wood ▷ vb 3 to treat (wood) with creosote [c19 from Greek kreas flesh + sōtēr preserver, from sōzein to keep safe] > **creo'sotic** (,kri:ə'sɒtɪk) adj

creosote bush n a shrub, Larrea (or Covillea) tridentata of the western US and Mexico, that has resinous leaves with an odour resembling creosote: family Zygophyllaceae. Also called: **greasewood**

crepe or **crape** (kreɪp) n 1 a a light cotton, silk, or other fabric with a fine ridged or crinkled surface b (as modifier): a crepe dress 2 a black armband originally made of this, worn as a sign of mourning 3 a very thin pancake, often rolled or folded around a filling 4 short for **crepe paper** or **crepe rubber** ▷ vb 5 (tr) to cover or drape with crepe [c19 from French crêpe, from Latin crispus curled, uneven, wrinkled]

crepe de Chine (kreɪp də 'ʃiːn) n a a very thin crepe of silk or a similar light fabric b (as modifier): a crepe-de-Chine blouse [c19 from French: Chinese crepe]

crepe hair n artificial hair, usually plaited and made of wool or vegetable fibre, used in theatrical make-up

crepe paper n thin crinkled coloured paper, resembling crepe and used for decorations

creperie ('krɛpərɪ, 'kreɪp-) n an eating establishment that specializes in pancakes; pancake house

crepe rubber n 1 a type of crude natural rubber in the form of colourless or pale yellow crinkled sheets, prepared by pressing bleached coagulated latex through corrugated rollers: used for the soles of shoes and in making certain surgical and medical goods. Sometimes shortened to: **crepe**. Compare **smoked rubber** 2 a similar synthetic rubber

crêpe suzette (kreɪp su:'zɛt) n, pl crêpes suzettes (sometimes plural) an orange-flavoured pancake flambéed in a liqueur or brandy

crepitate ('krɛpɪ,teɪt) vb (intr) to make a rattling or crackling sound; rattle or crackle [c17 from Latin crepitāre] > **'crepitant** adj

crepitation (,krɛpɪ'teɪʃən) n 1 the act of crepitating 2 zoology the sudden expulsion of an acrid fluid by some beetles as a means of self-defence 3 another name for **crepitus**

crepitus ('krɛpɪtəs) n 1 a crackling chest sound heard in pneumonia and other lung diseases 2 the grating sound of two ends of a broken bone rubbing together ▷ Also called: crepitation [c19 from Latin, from crepāre to crack, creak]

crept (krɛpt) vb the past tense and past participle of **creep**

crepuscular (krɪ'pʌskjʊlə) adj 1 of or like twilight; dim 2 (of certain insects, birds, and other animals) active at twilight or just before dawn [c17 from Latin crepusculum dusk, from creper dark]

crepy or **crepey** ('kreɪpɪ) adj (esp of the skin) having a dry wrinkled appearance like crepe

Cres. abbreviation for Crescent

crescendo (krɪ'ʃɛndəʊ) n, pl -dos or -di (-dɪ) 1 music a a gradual increase in loudness or the musical direction or symbol indicating this. Abbreviation: cresc. Symbol: < (written over the music affected) b (as modifier): a crescendo passage 2 a gradual increase in loudness or intensity: the rising crescendo of a song 3 a peak of noise or intensity: the cheers reached a crescendo ▷ vb -does, -doing, -doed 4 (intr) to increase in loudness or force ▷ adv 5 with a crescendo [c18 from Italian, literally: increasing, from crescere to grow, from Latin]

crescent ('krɛsənt, -zənt) n 1 the biconcave shape of the moon in its first or last quarters 2 any shape or object resembling this 3 chiefly Brit a a

crescent-shaped street, often lined with houses of the same style b (capital when part of a name): Pelham Crescent 4 heraldry a crescent moon, used as the cadency mark of a second son 5 (often capital and preceded by the) a the emblem of Islam or Turkey b Islamic or Turkish power ▷ adj 6 archaic or poetic increasing or growing [c14 from Latin crescēns increasing, from crescere to grow] > **crescentic** (krɪ'sɛntɪk) adj

cresol ('kri:sɒl) n an aromatic compound derived from phenol, existing in three isomeric forms: found in coal tar and creosote and used in making synthetic resins and as an antiseptic and disinfectant; hydroxytoluene. Formula: $C_6H_4(CH_3)OH$. Also called: **cresylic acid**. Systematic name: **methylphenol**

cress (krɛs) n any of various plants of the genera Lepidium, Cardamine, Arabis, etc, having pungent leaves often used in salads and as a garnish: family Brassicaceae (crucifers). See also **watercress, garden cress** [Old English cressa; related to Old High German cresso cress, kresan to crawl]

cresset ('krɛsɪt) n history a metal basket mounted on a pole in which oil or pitch was burned for illumination [c14 from Old French craisset, from craisse GREASE]

Cressida ('krɛsɪdə), **Criseyde** or **Cressid** n (in medieval adaptations of the story of Troy) a lady who deserts her Trojan lover Troilus for the Greek Diomedes

Cressy ('krɛsɪ) n rare the former English name for **Crécy**

crest (krɛst) n 1 a tuft or growth of feathers, fur, or skin along the top of the heads of some birds, reptiles, and other animals 2 something resembling or suggesting this 3 the top, highest point, or highest stage of something 4 a ridge on the neck of a horse, dog, lion, etc 5 the mane or hair growing from this ridge 6 an ornamental piece, such as a plume, on top of a helmet 7 heraldry a symbol of a family or office, usually representing a beast or bird, borne in addition to a coat of arms and used in medieval times to decorate the helmet 8 a ridge along the top of a roof, wall, etc 9 a ridge along the surface of a bone 10 Also called: cresting archery identifying rings painted around an arrow shaft ▷ vb 11 (intr) to come or rise to a high point 12 (tr) to lie at the top of; cap 13 (tr) to go to or reach the top of (a hill, wave, etc) [c14 from Old French creste, from Latin crista] > **'crested** adj > **'crestless** adj

CREST (krɛst) n an electronic share-settlement system, created by the Bank of England and owned by 69 firms, that began operations in 1996 [c20 from CrestCo, the name of the operating company]

cresta run ('krɛstə) n a an activity involving travelling at high speed in a toboggan down a steep narrow passage of compacted snow and ice b the passage itself

crested dog's-tail n a common wiry perennial grass, Cynosurus cristatus, of meadows and pasture [c19 named from the fancied resemblance between its one-sided flower spike and a dog's feathery tail]

crested tit n a small European songbird, Parus cristatus, that has a greyish-brown plumage with a prominent speckled black-and-white crest: family Paridae (tits)

crestfallen ('krɛst,fɔ:lən) adj dejected, depressed, or disheartened > **'crest,fallenly** adv

cresting ('krɛstɪŋ) n 1 an ornamental ridge along the top of a roof, wall, etc 2 furniture a shaped decorative toprail or horizontal carved ornament surmounting a chair, mirror, etc

cresylic (krɪ'sɪlɪk) adj of, concerned with, or containing creosote or cresol [c19 from CRE(O)S(OTE) + -YL + -IC]

cretaceous (krɪ'teɪʃəs) adj consisting of or resembling chalk [c17 from Latin crētāceus, from crēta, literally: Cretan earth, that is, chalk] > **cre'taceously** adv

Cretaceous (krɪ'teɪʃəs) *adj* **1** of, denoting, or formed in the last period of the Mesozoic era, between the Jurassic and Tertiary periods, lasting 80 million years during which chalk deposits were formed and flowering plants first appeared ▷ *n* **2 the** the Cretaceous period or rock system

Cretan ('kri:tən) *adj* **1** of or relating to Crete or its inhabitants ▷ *n* **2** a native or inhabitant of Crete

Crete (kri:t) *n* a mountainous island in the E Mediterranean, the largest island of Greece: of archaeological importance for the ruins of Minoan civilization. Pop: 601 131 (2001). Area: 8331 sq km (3216 sq miles). Modern Greek name: Κρίτι

cretic ('kri:tɪk) *n prosody* a metrical foot consisting of three syllables, the first long, the second short, and the third long (-∪-). Also called: **amphimacer.** Compare **amphibrach** [C16 from Latin *crēticus* consisting of the amphimacer, literally: Cretan, from Greek *krētikos*, from *Krētē* CRETE]

cretin ('kretɪn) *n* **1** a person afflicted with cretinism **2** a person considered to be extremely stupid [C18 from French *crétin*, from Swiss French *crestin*, from Latin *Chrīstiānus* CHRISTIAN, alluding to the humanity of such people, despite their handicaps] > 'cretin,oid *adj* > 'cretinous *adj*

cretinism ('kretɪ,nɪzəm) *n* a condition arising from a deficiency of thyroid hormone, present from birth, characterized by dwarfism and mental retardation. See also **myxoedema**

cretonne (krɛ'tɒn, 'krɛtɒn) *n* **a** a heavy cotton or linen fabric with a printed design, used for furnishing **b** (*as modifier*): *cretonne chair covers* [C19 from French, from *Creton* Norman village where it originated]

Creuse (*French* krøz) *n* a department of central France, in Limousin region. Capital: Guéret. Pop: 122 713 (2003 est.). Area: 5606 sq km (2186 sq miles)

Creutzfeldt-Jakob disease ('krɔɪtsfɛlt 'jɑːkɒp) *n pathol* a fatal slow-developing disease that affects the central nervous system, characterized by mental deterioration and loss of coordination of the limbs. It is thought to be caused by an abnormal prion protein in the brain [C20 named after Hans G. *Creutzfeldt* (1885–1964) and Alfons *Jakob* (1884–1931), German physicians]

crevasse (krɪ'væs) *n* **1** a deep crack or fissure, esp in the ice of a glacier **2** *US* a break in a river embankment ▷ *vb* **3** (*tr*) *US* to make a break or fissure in (a dyke, wall, etc) [C19 from French: CREVICE]

crevice ('krɛvɪs) *n* a narrow fissure or crack; split; cleft [C14 from Old French *crevace*, from *crever* to burst, from Latin *crepāre* to crack]

crew[1] (kru:) *n* (*sometimes functioning as plural*) **1** the men who man a ship, boat, aircraft, etc **2** *nautical* a group of people assigned to a particular job or type of work **3** *informal* a gang, company, or crowd ▷ *vb* **4** to serve on (a ship) as a member of the crew [C15 *crue* (military) reinforcement, from Old French *creue* augmentation, from Old French *creistre* to increase, from Latin *crescere*]

crew[2] (kru:) *vb* a past tense of **crow**[2]

crew cut *n* a closely cropped haircut for men, originating in the US [C20 from the style of haircut worn by the boat crews at Harvard and Yale Universities]

Crewe (kru:) *n* a town in NW England, in Cheshire: major railway junction. Pop: 67 683 (2001)

crewel ('kru:ɪl) *n* a loosely twisted worsted yarn, used in fancy work and embroidery [C15 of unknown origin] > 'crewelist *n* > 'crewel,work *n*

crewmate ('kru:,meɪt) *n* a colleague on the crew of a boat or ship

crew neck *n* a plain round neckline in sweaters > 'crew-,neck *or* 'crew-,necked *adj*

CRI (in New Zealand) *abbreviation for* Crown Research Institutes

crib (krɪb) *n* **1** a child's bed with slatted wooden sides; cot **2** a cattle stall or pen **3** a fodder rack or manger **4** a bin or granary for storing grain, etc **5** a small crude cottage or room **6** *US informal* a

house or residence **7** *NZ* a weekend cottage: term is South Island usage only **8** any small confined space **9** *informal* a brothel **10** a wicker basket **11** a representation of the manger in which the infant Jesus was laid at birth **12** *informal* a theft, esp of another's writing or thoughts **13** Also called (esp US): **pony** *informal, chiefly Brit* a translation of a foreign text or a list of answers used by students, often illicitly, as an aid in lessons, examinations, etc **14** short for **cribbage** **15** *cribbage* the discard pile **16** Also called: **cribwork** a framework of heavy timbers laid in layers at right angles to one another, used in the construction of foundations, mines, etc **17** a storage area for floating logs contained by booms **18** *Austral and NZ* a packed lunch taken to work ▷ *vb* **cribs, cribbing, cribbed** **19** (*tr*) to put or enclose in or as if in a crib; furnish with a crib **20** (*tr*) *informal* to steal (another's writings or thoughts) **21** (*intr*) *informal* to copy either from a crib or from someone else during a lesson or examination **22** (*tr*) to line (a construction hole) with timber beams, logs, or planks **23** (*intr*) *informal* to grumble [Old English *cribb*; related to Old Saxon *kribbia*, Old High German *krippa*; compare Middle High German *krēbe* basket] > 'cribber *n*

cribbage ('krɪbɪdʒ) *n* a game of cards for two to four, in which players try to win a set number of points before their opponents. Often shortened to: **crib** [C17 of uncertain origin]

cribbage board *n* a board, with pegs and holes, used for scoring at cribbage

crib-biting *n* a harmful habit of horses in which the animal leans on the manger or seizes it with the teeth and swallows a gulp of air > 'crib-,biter *n*

crib death *n US and Canadian* the unexplained sudden death of an infant during sleep. Technical name: **sudden infant death syndrome.** Also called (in Britain and certain other countries): **cot death**

cribellum (krɪ'bɛləm) *n, pl* **-la** (-lə) a sievelike spinning organ in certain spiders that occurs between the spinnerets [C19 New Latin, from Late Latin *cribellum*, diminutive of Latin *cribrum* a sieve]

cribriform ('krɪbrɪ,fɔːm), **cribrous** ('krɪbrəs) *or* **cribrose** ('kraɪ,brəʊs) *adj* pierced with holes; sievelike [C18 from New Latin *crībriformis*, from Latin *crībrum* a sieve + -FORM]

crib-wall *n NZ* a supporting wall constructed by laying cribs at right angles to each other, as in cribwork

cribwork ('krɪb,wɜːk) *n* another name for **crib** (sense 16)

crick[1] (krɪk) *informal* ▷ *n* **1** a painful muscle spasm or cramp, esp in the neck or back ▷ *vb* **2** (*tr*) to cause a crick in (the neck, back, etc) [C15 of uncertain origin]

crick[2] (krɪk) *n US and Canadian* a dialect word for **creek** (sense 2)

cricket[1] ('krɪkɪt) *n* **1** any insect of the orthopterous family *Gryllidae*, having long antennae and, in the males, the ability to produce a chirping sound (stridulation) by rubbing together the leathery forewings **2** any of various related insects, such as the mole cricket [C14 from Old French *criquet*, from *criquer* to creak, of imitative origin]

cricket[2] ('krɪkɪt) *n* **1 a** a game played by two teams of eleven players on a field with a wicket at either end of a 22-yard pitch, the object being for one side to score runs by hitting a hard leather-covered ball with a bat while the other side tries to dismiss them by bowling, catching, running them out, etc **b** (*as modifier*): *a cricket bat* **2 not cricket** *informal* not fair play ▷ *vb* **3** to play cricket [C16 from Old French *criquet* goalpost, wicket, of uncertain origin] > 'cricketer *n*

cricket[3] ('krɪkɪt) *n* a small low stool [C17 of unknown origin]

cricoid ('kraɪkɔɪd) *adj* **1** of or relating to the ring-shaped lowermost cartilage of the larynx ▷ *n* **2** this cartilage [C18 from New Latin *cricoīdes*, from Greek *krikoeidēs* ring-shaped, from *krikos* ring]

cri de coeur (,kri: də 'kɜ:) *n, pl* **cris de coeur** a cry from the heart; heartfelt or sincere appeal [C20 altered from French *cri du coeur*]

crier ('kraɪə) *n* **1** a person or animal that cries **2** (*formerly*) an official who made public announcements, esp in a town or court **3** a person who shouts advertisements about the goods he is selling

crikey ('kraɪkɪ) *interj slang* an expression of surprise [C19 euphemistic for *Christ*!]

crim (krɪm) *n, adj slang* short for **criminal**

crim. *abbreviation for* criminal

crime (kraɪm) *n* **1** an act or omission prohibited and punished by law **2 a** unlawful acts in general: *a wave of crime* **b** (*as modifier*): *crime wave* **3** an evil act **4** *informal* something to be regretted: *it is a crime that he died young* [C14 from Old French, from Latin *crīmen* verdict, accusation, crime]

Crimea (kraɪ'mɪə) *n* a peninsula and autonomous region in Ukraine between the Black Sea and the Sea of Azov: a former autonomous republic of the Soviet Union (1921–45), part of the Ukrainian SSR from 1945 until 1991. Russian name: **Krym**

Crimean (kraɪ'mɪən) *adj* **1** of or relating to the Crimea or its inhabitants ▷ *n* **2** a native or inhabitant of the Crimea

Crimean War *n* the war fought mainly in the Crimea between Russia on one side and Turkey, France, Sardinia, and Britain on the other (1853-56)

crimen injuria ('kraɪmən ɪn'dʒʊərɪə) *n South African law* an action that injures the dignity of another person, esp use of racially offensive language

crime passionnel (*French* krim pasjɒnɛl) *n, pl* **crimes passionnels** a crime committed from passion, esp sexual passion. Also called: **crime of passion** [from French]

crime sheet *n military* a record of an individual's offences against regulations

crimewave ('kraɪm,weɪv) *n* a period of increased criminal activity

criminal ('krɪmɪn'l) *n* **1** a person charged with and convicted of crime **2** a person who commits crimes for a living ▷ *adj* **3** of, involving, or guilty of crime **4** (*prenominal*) of or relating to crime or its punishment: *criminal court; criminal lawyer* **5** *informal* senseless or deplorable: *a criminal waste of money* [C15 from Late Latin *crīminālis*; see CRIME, -AL[1]] > 'criminally *adv*

criminal conversation *n* **1** (*formerly*) a common law action brought by a husband by which he claimed damages against an adulterer **2** another term for **adultery**

Criminal Investigation Department *n* the full name for **CID**

criminality (,krɪmɪ'nælɪtɪ) *n, pl* **-ties 1** the state or quality of being criminal **2** (*often plural*) *now rare* a criminal act or practice

criminalize *or* **criminalise** ('krɪmɪnə,laɪz) *vb* (*tr*) **1** to make (an action or activity) criminal **2** to treat (a person) as a criminal > ,criminali'zation *or* ,criminali'sation *n*

criminal law *n* the body of law dealing with the constitution of offences and the punishment of offenders

Criminal Records Bureau *n* (in England and Wales) a service offering employers and voluntary organizations access to police, health, and education records

criminate ('krɪmɪ,neɪt) *vb* (*tr*) *rare* **1** to charge with a crime; accuse **2** to condemn or censure (an action, event, etc) **3** short for **incriminate** [C17 from Latin *crīminārī* to accuse] > ,crimi'nation *n* > 'criminative *or* criminatory ('krɪmɪnətərɪ, -trɪ) *adj* > 'crimi,nator *n*

criminology (,krɪmɪ'nɒlədʒɪ) *n* the scientific study of crime, criminal behaviour, law enforcement, etc. See also **penology** [C19 from Latin *crimin-* CRIME, -LOGY] > criminological (,krɪmɪnə'lɒdʒɪk³l) *or* ,crimino'logic *adj* > ,crimino'logically *adv* > ,crimi'nologist *n*

crimmer ('krɪmə) *n* a variant spelling of **krimmer**

crimp[1] (krɪmp) *vb (tr)* **1** to fold or press into ridges **2** to fold and pinch together (something, such as the edges of two pieces of metal) **3** to curl or wave (the hair) tightly, esp with curling tongs **4** to decorate (the edge of pastry) by pinching with the fingers to give a fluted effect **5** to gash (fish or meat) with a knife to make the flesh firmer and crisper when cooked **6** to bend or mould (leather) into shape, as for shoes **7** *metallurgy* to bend the edges of (a metal plate) before forming into a cylinder **8** *informal, chiefly US* to hinder ▷ *n* **9** the act or result of folding or pressing together or into ridges **10** a tight wave or curl in the hair **11** a crease or fold in a metal sheet **12** the natural wave of wool fibres [Old English *crympan*; related to *crump* bent, Old Norse *kreppa* to contract, Old High German *crumpf*, Old Swedish *crumb* crooked; see CRAMP[1]] > **'crimper** *n* > **'crimpy** *adj*

crimp[2] (krɪmp) *n* **1** (formerly) a person who swindled or pressganged men into naval or military service ▷ *vb* **2** to recruit by coercion or under false pretences [C17 of unknown origin]

crimple ('krɪmpᵊl) *vb* to crumple, wrinkle, or curl

Crimplene ('krɪmpliːn) *n trademark* a synthetic material similar to Terylene, characterized by its crease-resistance

crimson ('krɪmzən) *n* **1 a** a deep or vivid red colour **b** (*as adjective*): *a crimson rose* ▷ *vb* **2** to make or become crimson **3** (*intr*) to blush [C14 from Old Spanish *cremesin*, from Arabic *qirmizi* red of the kermes, from *qirmiz* KERMES] > **'crimsonness** *n*

cringe (krɪndʒ) *vb (intr)* **1** to shrink or flinch, esp in fear or servility **2** to behave in a servile or timid way **3** *informal* **a** to wince in embarrassment or distaste **b** to experience a sudden feeling of embarrassment or distaste ▷ *n* **4** the act of cringing **5 the cultural cringe** *Austral* subservience to overseas cultural standards [Old English *cringan* to yield in battle; related to Old Norse *krangr* weak, Middle High German *krenken* to weaken] > **'cringer** *n* > **'cringingly** *adv*

cringe-making *or* **cringeworthy** ('krɪndʒˌwɜːðɪ) *adj Brit informal* causing feelings of acute embarrassment or distaste

cringle ('krɪŋgᵊl) *n* an eye at the edge of a sail, usually formed from a thimble or grommet [C17 from Low German *Kringel* small RING[1]; see CRANK[1], CRINKLE]

crinite[1] ('kraɪnaɪt) *adj biology* covered with soft hairs or tufts [C16 from Latin *crīnītus* hairy, from *crīnis* hair]

crinite[2] ('kraɪnaɪt, 'krɪn-) *n* short for **encrinite** [C19 from Greek *krinon* lily + -ITE[1]]

crinkle ('krɪŋkᵊl) *vb* **1** to form or cause to form wrinkles, twists, or folds **2** to make or cause to make a rustling noise ▷ *n* **3** a wrinkle, twist, or fold **4** a rustling noise [Old English *crincan* to bend, give way; related to Middle Dutch *krinkelen* to crinkle, Middle High German *krank* weak, ill, *krenken* to weaken]

crinkleroot ('krɪŋkᵊlˌruːt) *n* any of several species of the toothwort *Dentaria*, esp *D. diphylla* of E North America, which has a fleshy pungent rhizome and clusters of white or pinkish flowers: family *Brassicaceae* (crucifers)

crinkly ('krɪŋklɪ) *adj* **1** wrinkled; crinkled ▷ *n, pl* **-lies 2** *slang* an old person

crinkum-crankum ('krɪŋkəm'kræŋkəm) *n* a fanciful name for any object that is full of twists and turns [C18 coinage based on CRANK[1]]

crinoid ('kraɪnɔɪd, 'krɪn-) *n* **1** any primitive echinoderm of the class *Crinoidea*, having delicate feathery arms radiating from a central disc. The group includes the free-swimming feather stars, the sessile sea lilies, and many stemmed fossil forms ▷ *adj* **2** of, relating to, or belonging to the *Crinoidea* **3** shaped like a lily [C19 from Greek *krinoeidēs* lily-like] > **cri'noidal** *adj*

crinoline ('krɪnᵊlɪn) *n* **1** a stiff fabric, originally of horsehair and linen used in lining garments **2** a petticoat stiffened with this, worn to distend skirts, esp in the mid-19th century **3** a framework of steel hoops worn for the same purpose [C19 from French, from Italian *crinolino*, from *crino* horsehair, from Latin *crīnis* hair + *lino* flax, from Latin *līnum*]

crinum ('kraɪnəm) *n* any plant of the mostly tropical amaryllidaceous genus *Crinum*, having straplike leaves and clusters of lily-like flowers. Also called: **crinum lily** [Latin: lily, from Greek *krinon*]

criollo (kriː'əʊləʊ; *Spanish* 'krjoʎo) *n, pl* **-los** (-ləʊz; *Spanish* -ʎos) **1** a native or inhabitant of Latin America of European descent, esp of Spanish descent **2 a** any of various South American breeds of domestic animal **b** (*as modifier*): *a criollo pony* **3** a high-quality variety of cocoa ▷ *adj* **4** of, relating to, or characteristic of a criollo or criollos [Spanish: native; see CREOLE]

crios (krɪs) *n Irish* a multicoloured woven woollen belt traditionally worn by men in the Aran Islands [Irish Gaelic]

cripes (kraɪps) *interj old-fashioned slang* an expression of surprise [C20 euphemistic for *Christ!*]

cripple ('krɪpᵊl) *n* **1** *offensive* a person who is lame **2** *offensive* a person who is or seems disabled or deficient in some way: *a mental cripple* **3** *US dialect* a dense thicket, usually in marshy land ▷ *vb* **4** (*tr*) to make a cripple of; disable [Old English *crypel*; related to *crēopan* to CREEP, Old Frisian *kreppel* a cripple, Middle Low German *kröpel*] > **'crippler** *n*

Cripple Creek *n* a village in central Colorado: gold-mining centre since 1891, once the richest in the world

crippling ('krɪplɪŋ) *adj* damaging or injurious > **'cripplingly** *adv*

Criseyde (krɪ'seɪdə) *n* a variant of **Cressida**

crisis ('kraɪsɪs) *n, pl* **-ses** (-siːz) **1** a crucial stage or turning point in the course of something, esp in a sequence of events or a disease **2** an unstable period, esp one of extreme trouble or danger in politics, economics, etc **3** *pathol* a sudden change, for better or worse, in the course of a disease [C15 from Latin: decision, from Greek *krisis*, from *krinein* to decide]

crisp (krɪsp) *adj* **1** dry and brittle **2** fresh and firm: *crisp lettuce* **3** invigorating or bracing: *a crisp breeze* **4** clear; sharp: *crisp reasoning* **5** lively or stimulating: *crisp conversation* **6** clean and orderly; neat: *a crisp appearance* **7** concise and pithy; terse: *a crisp reply* **8** wrinkled or curly: *crisp hair* ▷ *vb* **9** to make or become crisp ▷ *n* **10** *Brit* a very thin slice of potato fried and eaten cold as a snack **11** something that is crisp [Old English, from Latin *crispus* curled, uneven, wrinkled] > **'crisply** *adv* > **'crispness** *n*

crispate ('krɪspeɪt, -pɪt), **crispated** *or* **crisped** *adj* having a curled or waved appearance [C19 from Latin *crispāre* to curl]

crispation (krɪ'speɪʃən) *n* **1** the act of curling or state of being curled **2** any slight muscular spasm or contraction that gives a creeping sensation **3** a slight undulation, such as a ripple on the surface of water

crispbread ('krɪspˌbrɛd) *n* a thin dry biscuit made of wheat or rye

crisper ('krɪspə) *n* a compartment in a refrigerator for storing salads, vegetables, etc, in order to keep them fresh

crispy ('krɪspɪ) *adj* **crispier, crispiest 1** crisp **2** having waves or curls > **'crispily** *adv* > **'crispiness** *n*

crisscross ('krɪsˌkrɒs) *vb* **1** to move or cause to move in a crosswise pattern **2** to mark with or consist of a pattern of crossing lines ▷ *adj* **3** (esp of a number of lines) crossing one another in different directions ▷ *n* **4** a pattern made of crossing lines **5** a US term for **noughts and crosses** ▷ *adv* **6** in a crosswise manner or pattern

crissum ('krɪsəm) *n, pl* **-sa** (-sə) the area or feathers surrounding the cloaca of a bird [C19 from New Latin, from Latin *crissāre* to move the haunches] > **'crissal** *adj*

crista ('krɪstə) *n, pl* **-tae** (-tiː) *biology* a structure resembling a ridge or crest, such as that formed by folding of the inner membrane of a mitochondrion [C20 from Latin: CREST]

cristate ('krɪsteɪt) *or* **cristated** *adj* **1** having a crest **2** forming a crest [C17 from Latin *cristātus*, from *crista* CREST]

cristobalite (krɪs'təʊbəˌlaɪt) *n* a white microcrystalline mineral consisting of silica and occurring in volcanic rocks. Formula: SiO_2 [C19 from German, named after Cerro San *Cristóbal*, Mexico, where it was discovered]

crit. *abbreviation for* **1** critic **2** criticism

criterion (kraɪ'tɪərɪən) *n, pl* **-ria** (-rɪə) *or* **-rions 1** a standard by which something can be judged or decided **2** *philosophy* a defining characteristic of something [C17 from Greek *kritērion* from *kritēs* judge, from *krinein* to decide]

> USAGE *Criteria*, the plural of *criterion*, is not acceptable as a singular noun: *this criterion is not valid; these criteria are not valid*

critic ('krɪtɪk) *n* **1** a person who judges something **2** a professional judge of art, music, literature, etc **3** a person who often finds fault and criticizes [C16 from Latin *criticus*, from Greek *kritikos* capable of judging, from *kritēs* judge; see CRITERION]

critical ('krɪtɪkᵊl) *adj* **1** containing or making severe or negative judgments **2** containing careful or analytical evaluations: *a critical dissertation* **3** of or involving a critic or criticism **4** of or forming a crisis; crucial; decisive: *a critical operation* **5** urgently needed: *critical medical supplies* **6** *informal* so seriously injured or ill as to be in danger of dying **7** *physics* of, denoting, or concerned with a state in which the properties of a system undergo an abrupt change: *a critical temperature* **8 go critical** (of a nuclear power station or reactor) to reach a state in which a nuclear-fission chain reaction becomes self-sustaining > **'critically** *adv* > **'criticalness** *n*

critical angle *n* **1** the smallest possible angle of incidence for which light rays are totally reflected at an interface between substances of different refractive index **2** another name for **stalling angle**

critical apparatus *n* the variant readings, footnotes, etc found in a scholarly work or a critical edition of a text. Also called: **apparatus criticus**

critical constants *pl n* the physical constants that express the properties of a substance in its critical state. See **critical pressure, critical temperature**

critical damping *n physics* the minimum amount of viscous damping that results in a displaced system returning to its original position without oscillation. Symbol: C_c

critical density *n* the density of matter that would be required to halt the expansion of the universe

criticality (ˌkrɪtɪ'kælɪtɪ) *n* **1** the state of being critical **2** *physics* the condition in a nuclear reactor when the fissionable material can sustain a chain reaction by itself

critical mass *n* **1** the minimum mass of fissionable material that can sustain a nuclear chain reaction **2** the minimum amount of money or number of people required to start or sustain an operation, business, process, etc: *the critical mass for a subscription digital sports channel*

critical path analysis *n* a technique for planning complex projects by analysing alternative systems with reference to the critical path, which is the sequence of stages requiring the longest time. Compare **programme evaluation and review technique**

critical period *n psychol* a period in a lifetime during which a specific stage of development usually occurs. If it fails to do so, it cannot readily occur afterwards

critical point *n* **1** *physics* **a** the point on a phase diagram that represents the critical state of a

C

substance **b** another name for **critical state 2** *maths* the US name for **stationary point**

critical pressure *n* the pressure of a gas or the saturated vapour pressure of a substance in its critical state

critical region *n* that part of a statistical distribution in which the probability of a given hypothesis is less than the chosen significance level, so that the hypothesis would be rejected

critical state *n* the state of a substance in which two of its phases have the same temperature, pressure, and volume. Also called: **critical point**

critical temperature *n* the temperature of a substance in its critical state. A gas can only be liquefied by pressure alone at temperatures below its critical temperature

critical volume *n* the volume occupied by one mole or unit mass of a substance in its critical state

criticism ('krɪtɪˌsɪzəm) *n* **1** the act or an instance of making an unfavourable or severe judgment, comment, etc **2** the analysis or evaluation of a work of art, literature, etc **3** the occupation of a critic **4** a work that sets out to evaluate or analyse **5** Also called: **textual criticism** the investigation of a particular text, with related material, in order to establish an authentic text

criticize or **criticise** ('krɪtɪˌsaɪz) *vb* **1** to judge (something) with disapproval; censure **2** to evaluate or analyse (something) > **'criti,cizable** or **'criti,cisable** *adj* > **'criti,cizer** or **'criti,ciser** *n* > **'criti,cizingly** or **'criti,cisingly** *adv*

critique (krɪ'ti:k) *n* **1** a critical essay or commentary, esp on artistic work **2** the act or art of criticizing [c17 from French, from Greek *kritikē*, from *kritikos* able to discern]

critter ('krɪtə) *n US and Canadian* a dialect word for **creature**

CRM *abbreviation for* customer relationship management

CRO *abbreviation for* **1** cathode-ray oscilloscope **2** (in Britain) Community Relations Officer **3** Criminal Records Office

Croagh Patrick (krɔːx) *n* a mountain in NW Republic of Ireland, in Mayo: a place of pilgrimage as Saint Patrick is said to have prayed and fasted there. Height: 765 m (2510 ft)

croak (krəʊk) *vb* **1** (intr) (of frogs, crows, etc) to make a low, hoarse cry **2** to utter (something) in this manner: *he croaked out the news* **3** (intr) to grumble or be pessimistic **4** *slang* **a** (intr) to die **b** (tr) to kill ▷ *n* **5** a low hoarse utterance or sound [Old English *crācettan;* related to Old Norse *krāka* a crow; see CREAK] > **croaky** *adj* > **'croakily** *adv* > **'croakiness** *n*

croaker ('krəʊkə) *n* **1** an animal, bird, etc, that croaks **2** any of various mainly tropical marine sciaenid fishes, such as *Umbrina roncador* (**yellowfin croaker**), that utter croaking noises **3** a grumbling person

Croat ('krəʊæt) *n* **1 a** a native or inhabitant of Croatia **b** a speaker of Croatian ▷ *n* ▷ *adj* **2** another word for **Croatian**

Croatia (krəʊ'eɪʃə) *n* a republic in SE Europe: settled by Croats in the 7th century; belonged successively to Hungary, Turkey, and Austria; formed part of Yugoslavia (1918–91); became independent in 1991 but was invaded by Serbia and fighting continued until 1995; involved in the civil war in Bosnia-Herzegovina (1991–95). Language: Croatian. Religion: Roman Catholic majority. Currency: kuna. Capital: Zagreb. Pop: 4 416 000 (2004 est). Area: 55 322 sq km (21 359 sq miles). Croatian name: **Hrvatska**

Croatian (krəʊ'eɪʃən) *adj* **1** of, relating to, or characteristic of Croatia, its people, or their language ▷ *n* **2** the language that is spoken in Croatia, a dialect of Serbo-Croat (Croato-Serb) **3 a** a native or inhabitant of Croatia **b** a speaker of Croatian

Croato-Serb (krəʊˌeɪtəʊ'sɜːb) *n adj* another name for **Serbo-Croat**

croc (krɒk) *n* short for **crocodile** (senses 1–3)

crocein ('krəʊsɪɪn) *n* any one of a group of red or orange acid azo dyes [c20 from Latin *croceus* yellow + -IN]

crochet ('krəʊʃeɪ, -ʃɪ) *vb* -chets (-ʃeɪz, -ʃɪz) -cheting (-ʃeɪɪŋ, -ʃɪɪŋ) -cheted (-ʃeɪd, -ʃɪd) **1** to make (a piece of needlework, a garment, etc) by looping and intertwining thread with a hooked needle (**crochet hook**) ▷ *n* **2** work made by crocheting **3** *architect* another name for **cricket 4** *zoology* a hooklike structure of insect larvae that aids locomotion [c19 from French *crochet,* diminutive of *croc* hook, probably of Scandinavian origin] > **'crocheter** *n*

crocidolite (krəʊ'sɪdəˌlaɪt) *n* a blue fibrous amphibole mineral consisting of sodium iron silicate: a variety of asbestos used in cement products and pressure piping [c19 from Greek *krokis* nap on woollen cloth + -LITE]

crock[1] (krɒk) *n* **1** an earthen pot, jar, etc **2** a piece of broken earthenware **3** Also: **crock of shit** *US and Canadian informal* a quantity or source of lies or nonsense [Old English *crocc* pot; related to Old Norse *krukka* jug, Middle Low German *krūke* pot]

crock[2] (krɒk) *n* **1** *slang, chiefly Brit* a person or thing, such as a car, that is old or decrepit (esp in the phrase **old crock**) **2** an old broken-down horse or ewe ▷ *vb* **3** *slang, chiefly Brit* to become or cause to become weak or disabled [c15 originally Scottish; related to Norwegian *krake* unhealthy animal, Dutch *kraak* decrepit person or animal]

crock[3] (krɒk) *n* **1** *dialect, chiefly Brit* soot or smut **2** colour that rubs off fabric ▷ *vb* **3** (tr) *dialect, chiefly Brit* to soil with or as if with soot **4** (intr) (of a dyed fabric) to release colour when rubbed, as a result of imperfect dyeing [c17 probably from CROCK[1]]

crocked (krɒkt) *adj slang* **1** *Brit* injured **2** *US and Canadian* drunk

crockery ('krɒkərɪ) *n* china dishes, earthen vessels, etc, collectively

crocket ('krɒkɪt) *n* a carved ornament in the form of a curled leaf or cusp, used in Gothic architecture. Also called: **crochet** [c17 from Anglo-French *croket* a little hook, from *croc* hook, of Scandinavian origin]

Crockford ('krɒkfəd) *n* short for *Crockford's Clerical Directory,* the standard directory of living Anglican clergy [c19 named after John Crockford (1823–65), clerk to Edward William Cox (1809–79), a lawyer who devised the directory]

crocodile ('krɒkəˌdaɪl) *n* **1** any large tropical reptile, such as *C. niloticus* (**African crocodile**), of the family *Crocodylidae:* order *Crocodilia* (crocodilians). They have a broad head, tapering snout, massive jaws, and a thick outer covering of bony plates **2** any other reptile of the order *Crocodilia;* a crocodilian **3 a** leather made from the skin of any of these animals **b** (*as modifier*): *crocodile shoes* **4** *Brit informal* a line of people, esp schoolchildren, walking two by two [c13 via Old French, from Latin *crocodīlus,* from Greek *krokodeilos* lizard, ultimately from *krokē* pebble + *drilos* worm; referring to its fondness for basking on shingle]

crocodile bird *n* an African courser, *Pluvianus aegyptius,* that lives close to rivers and is thought to feed on insects parasitic on crocodiles

crocodile clip *n* a clasp with serrated interlocking edges used for making electrical connections

Crocodile River *n* **1** a river in N South Africa, rising north of Johannesburg and flowing north-westerly into the Marico River on the Botswanan border; a tributary of the Limpopo **2** a river that rises in NE South Africa, in the Kruger National Park, and flows south-easterly into Mozambique

crocodile tears *pl n* an insincere show of grief; false tears [from the belief that crocodiles wept over their prey to allure further victims]

crocodilian (ˌkrɒkə'dɪlɪən) *n* **1** any large predatory reptile of the order *Crocodilia,* which includes the crocodiles, alligators, and caymans. They live in or

near water and have a long broad snout, powerful jaws, a four-chambered heart, and socketed teeth ▷ *adj* **2** of, relating to, or belonging to the *Crocodilia* **3** of, relating to, or resembling a crocodile

crocoite ('krɒkəʊˌaɪt) or **crocoisite** (krəʊ'kəʊɪˌsaɪt, 'krəʊkwəˌsaɪt) *n* a rare orange secondary mineral consisting of lead chromate in monoclinic crystalline form. Formula: $PbCrO_4$. Also called: **red-lead ore** [c19 from Greek *krokoeis* saffron-coloured, golden + -ITE[1]]

crocosmia (krə'kɒzmɪə) *n* any plant of the cormous S. African genus *Crocosmia,* including the plant known to gardeners as montbretia: family *Iridaceae* [New Latin, from Greek *krokos* saffron + *osmē* smell, from the odour of the dried flowers when wetted]

crocus ('krəʊkəs) *n, pl* **-cuses 1** any plant of the iridaceous genus *Crocus,* widely cultivated in gardens, having white, yellow, or purple flowers. See also **autumn crocus 2** another name for **jeweller's rouge** ▷ *adj* **3** of a saffron yellow colour [c17 from New Latin, from Latin *crocus,* from Greek *krokos* saffron, of Semitic origin]

Croesus ('kri:səs) *n* any very rich man [from Croesus, the last king of Lydia (560–546), noted for his great wealth]

croft (krɒft) *n Brit* **1** a small enclosed plot of land, adjoining a house, worked by the occupier and his family, esp in Scotland **2** *Lancashire dialect* a patch of wasteland, formerly one used for bleaching fabric in the sun [Old English *croft;* related to Middle Dutch *krocht* hill, field, Old English *creopan* to CREEP]

crofter ('krɒftə) *n Brit* an owner or tenant of a small farm, esp in Scotland or northern England

crofting ('krɒftɪŋ) *n Brit* the system or occupation of working land in crofts

crog (krɒg) *vb* (intr) *Northern and Midland English dialect* to ride on a bicycle as a passenger

croggy ('krɒgɪ) *n, pl* **croggies** *Northern and Midland English dialect* a ride on a bicycle as a passenger: *give us a croggy!*

Crohn's disease (krəʊnz) *n* inflammation, thickening, and ulceration of any of various parts of the intestine, esp the ileum. Also called: regional enteritis. See also **Johne's disease** [c20 named after B B Crohn (1884–1983), US physician]

croissant ('krwʌsɒŋ; *French* krwasā) *n* a flaky crescent-shaped bread roll made of a yeast dough similar to puff pastry [French, literally: crescent]

Croix de Guerre *French* (krwa də gɛr) *n* a French military decoration awarded for gallantry in battle: established 1915 [literally: cross of war]

crokinole ('krɒkəˌnəʊl) *n* a board game popular in Canada in which players flick wooden discs [c20 from French *croquignole* a flick]

Cro-Magnon man ('krəʊ'mænjɒn, -'mægnɒn) *n* an early type of modern man, *Homo sapiens,* who lived in Europe during late Palaeolithic times, having tall stature, long head, and a relatively large cranial capacity [c19 named after the cave (Cro-Magnon), Dordogne, France, where the remains were first found]

crombec ('krɒmbɛk) *n* any African Old World warbler of the genus *Sylvietta,* having colourful plumage [c19 via French from Dutch *krom* crooked + *bek* BEAK[1]]

Cromer ('krəʊmə) *n* a resort in E England, on the Norfolk coast: fishing. Pop: 8836 (2001)

cromlech ('krɒmlɛk) *n* **1** a circle of prehistoric standing stones **2** (no longer in technical usage) a megalithic chamber tomb or dolmen [c17 from Welsh, from *crom,* feminine of *crwm* bent, arched + *llech* flat stone]

Cromwell Current ('krɒmwɛl, -wəl) *n* an equatorial Pacific current, flowing eastward from the Hawaiian Islands to the Galápagos Islands [c20 named after T. Cromwell (1922–58), US oceanographer]

Cromwellian (krɒm'wɛlɪən) *adj* **1** of or relating to Oliver Cromwell, the English general (1599-1658) ▷ *n* **2** a follower or admirer of Oliver Cromwell

crone (krəʊn) *n* a witchlike old woman [c14 from Old Northern French *carogne* carrion, ultimately from Latin *caro* flesh]

cronk (krɒŋk) *adj Austral* unfit; unsound [c19 compare CRANK²]

Cronus (ˈkrəʊnəs) *or* **Cronos, Kronos** (ˈkrəʊnɒs) *n Greek myth* a Titan, son of Uranus (sky) and Gaea (earth), who ruled the world until his son Zeus dethroned him. Roman counterpart: **Saturn**

crony (ˈkrəʊnɪ) *n, pl* **-nies** a friend or companion [c17 student slang (Cambridge), from Greek *khronios* of long duration, from *khronos* time]

cronyism (ˈkrəʊnɪˌɪzəm) *n* the practice of appointing friends to high-level, esp political, posts regardless of their suitability

crook (krʊk) *n* **1** a curved or hooked thing **2** a staff with a hooked end, such as a bishop's crosier or shepherd's staff **3** a turn or curve; bend **4** *informal* a dishonest person, esp a swindler or thief **5** the act or an instance of crooking or bending **6** Also called: **shank** a piece of tubing added to a brass instrument in order to obtain a lower harmonic series ▷ *vb* **7** to bend or curve or cause to bend or curve ▷ *adj* **8** *Austral and NZ informal* **a** ill **b** of poor quality **c** unpleasant; bad **9** **go (off) crook** *Austral and NZ informal* to lose one's temper **10** **go crook at** *or* **on** *Austral and NZ informal* to rebuke or upbraid [c12 from Old Norse *krokr* hook; related to Swedish *krok*, Danish *krog* hook, Old High German *krācho* hooked tool]

crookback (ˈkrʊkˌbæk) *n* a rare word for **hunchback**. > ˈ**crookˌbacked** *adj*

crooked (ˈkrʊkɪd) *adj* **1** bent, angled or winding **2** set at an angle; not straight **3** deformed or contorted **4** *informal* dishonest or illegal **5** **crooked on** (*also* krʊkt) *Austral informal* hostile or averse to > ˈ**crookedly** *adv* > ˈ**crookedness** *n*

Crookes lens (krʊks) *n* a type of lens, used in sunglasses, that is made from glass containing cerium. It reduces the transmission of ultraviolet radiation

Crookes radiometer *n physics* a type of radiometer consisting of an evacuated glass bulb containing a set of lightweight vanes, each blackened on one side. The vanes are mounted on a vertical axis and revolve when light, or other radiant energy, falls on them

Crookes space *n* a dark region near the cathode in some low-pressure gas-discharge tubes. Also called: **Crookes dark space**

Crookes tube *n* a type of cathode-ray tube in which the electrons are produced by a glow discharge in a low-pressure gas

crool (kru:l) *vb Austral slang* **1** (*tr*) to spoil: *don't crool your chances* **2** **crool someone's pitch** to spoil an opportunity for someone

croon (kru:n) *vb* **1** to sing or speak in a soft low tone ▷ *n* **2** a soft low singing or humming [c14 via Middle Dutch *crōnen* to groan; compare Old High German *chrōnan* to chatter, Latin *gingrīre* to cackle (of geese)] > ˈ**crooner** *n*

crop (krɒp) *n* **1** the produce of cultivated plants, esp cereals, vegetables, and fruit **2** **a** the amount of such produce in any particular season **b** the yield of some other farm produce: *the lamb crop* **3** a group of products, thoughts, people, etc, appearing at one time or in one season: *a crop of new publications* **4** the stock of a thonged whip **5** short for **riding crop** **6** **a** a pouchlike expanded part of the oesophagus of birds, in which food is stored or partially digested before passing on to the gizzard **b** a similar structure in insects, earthworms, and other invertebrates **7** the entire tanned hide of an animal **8** a short cropped hairstyle. See also **Eton crop** **9** a notch in or a piece cut out of the ear of an animal **10** the act of cropping ▷ *vb* **crops, cropping, cropped** (*mainly tr*) **11** to cut (hair, grass, etc) very short **12** to cut and collect (mature produce) from the land or plant on which it has been grown **13** to clip part of (the ear or ears) of (an animal), esp as a means of identification **14** (*also intr*) to cause (land) to bear or (of land) to bear or yield a crop: *the land cropped well* **15** (of herbivorous animals) to graze on (grass or similar vegetation) **16** *photog* to cut off or mask unwanted edges or areas of (a negative or print) ▷ See also **crop out, crop up** [Old English *cropp*; related to Old Norse *kroppr* rump, body, Old High German *kropf* goitre, Norwegian *kröypa* to bend]

crop circle *n* any of various patterns, usually wholly or partly consisting of ring shapes, formed by the unexplained flattening of cereals growing in a field

crop-dusting *n* the spreading of fungicide, etc on crops in the form of dust, often from an aircraft

crop-eared *adj* having the ears or hair cut short

crop out *vb* (*intr, adverb*) (of a formation of rock strata) to appear or be exposed at the surface of the ground; outcrop

cropper (ˈkrɒpə) *n* **1** a person who cultivates or harvests a crop **2** **a** a cutting machine for removing the heads from castings and ingots **b** a guillotine for cutting lengths of bar or strip **3** a machine for shearing the nap from cloth **4** a plant or breed of plant that will produce a certain kind of crop under specified conditions: *a poor cropper on light land* **5** (*often capital*) a variety of domestic pigeon with a puffed-out crop **6** **come a cropper** *informal* **a** to fall heavily **b** to fail completely

crop rotation *n* the system of growing a sequence of different crops on the same ground so as to maintain or increase its fertility

crop top *n* a short T-shirt or vest that reveals the wearer's midriff

crop up *vb* (*intr, adverb*) *informal* to occur or appear, esp unexpectedly

croquet (ˈkrəʊkeɪ, -kɪ) *n* **1** a game for two to four players who hit a wooden ball through iron hoops with mallets in order to hit a peg **2** the act of croqueting ▷ *vb* **-quets** (-keɪz, -kɪz) **-queting** (-keɪɪŋ, -kɪɪŋ) **-queted** (-keɪd, -kɪd) **3** to drive away (another player's ball) by hitting one's own ball when the two are in contact [c19 perhaps from French dialect, variant of CROCHET (little hook)]

croquette (krəʊˈkɛt, krɒ-) *n* a savoury cake of minced meat, fish, etc, fried in breadcrumbs [c18 from French, from *croquer* to crunch, of imitative origin]

crore (krɔ:) *n* (in Indian English) ten million [c17 from Hindi *karōr*, from Prakrit *krodi*]

Crosby (ˈkrɒzbɪ) *n* a town in NW England, in Sefton unitary authority, Merseyside. Pop: 51 789 (2001)

crosier *or* **crozier** (ˈkrəʊʒə) *n* **1** a staff surmounted by a crook or cross, carried by bishops as a symbol of pastoral office **2** the tip of a young plant, esp a fern frond, that is coiled into a hook [c14 from Old French *crossier* staff bearer, from *crosse* pastoral staff, literally: hooked stick, of Germanic origin]

cross (krɒs) *n* **1** a structure or symbol consisting essentially of two intersecting lines or pieces at right angles to one another **2** a wooden structure used as a means of execution, consisting of an upright post with a transverse piece to which people were nailed or tied **3** a representation of the Cross used as an emblem of Christianity or as a reminder of Christ's death **4** any mark or shape consisting of two intersecting lines, esp such a symbol (×) used as a signature, point of intersection, error mark, etc **5** a sign representing the Cross made either by tracing a figure in the air or by touching the forehead, breast, and either shoulder in turn **6** any conventional variation of the Christian symbol, used emblematically, decoratively, or heraldically, such as a Maltese, tau, or Greek cross **7** *heraldry* any of several charges in which one line crosses or joins another at right angles **8** a cruciform emblem awarded to indicate membership of an order or as a decoration for distinguished service **9** (*sometimes capital*) Christianity or Christendom, esp as contrasted with non-Christian religions: *Cross and Crescent* **10** the place in a town or village where a cross has been set up **11** a pipe fitting, in the form of a cross, for connecting four pipes **12** *biology* **a** the process of crossing; hybridization **b** an individual produced as a result of this process **13** a mixture of two qualities or types: *he's a cross between a dictator and a saint* **14** an opposition, hindrance, or misfortune; affliction (esp in the phrase **bear one's cross**) **15** *slang* a match or game in which the outcome has been rigged **16** *slang* a fraud or swindle **17** *boxing* a straight punch delivered from the side, esp with the right hand **18** *football* the act or an instance of kicking or passing the ball from a wing to the middle of the field **19** **on the cross** **a** diagonally **b** *slang* dishonestly ▷ *vb* **20** (sometimes foll by *over*) to move or go across (something); traverse or intersect: *we crossed the road* **21** **a** to meet and pass: *the two trains crossed* **b** (of each of two letters in the post) to be dispatched before receipt of the other **22** (*tr*; usually foll by *out, off,* or *through*) to cancel with a cross or with lines; delete **23** (*tr*) to place or put in a form resembling a cross: *to cross one's legs* **24** (*tr*) to mark with a cross or crosses **25** (*tr*) *Brit* to draw two parallel lines across the face of (a cheque) and so make it payable only into a bank account **26** (*tr*) **a** to trace the form of the Cross, usually with the thumb or index finger upon (someone or something) in token of blessing **b** to make the sign of the Cross upon (oneself) **27** (*intr*) (of telephone lines) to interfere with each other so that three or perhaps four callers are connected together at one time **28** to cause fertilization between (plants or animals of different breeds, races, varieties, etc) **29** (*tr*) to oppose the wishes or plans of; thwart: *his opponent crosses him at every turn* **30** *football* to kick or pass (the ball) from a wing to the middle of the field **31** (*tr*) *nautical* to set (the yard of a square sail) athwartships **32** **cross a bridge when one comes to it** to deal with matters, problems, etc, as they arise; not to anticipate difficulties **33** **cross one's fingers** to fold one finger across another in the hope of bringing good luck: *keep your fingers crossed* **34** **cross one's heart** to promise or pledge, esp by making the sign of a cross over one's heart **35** **cross one's mind** to occur to one briefly or suddenly **36** **cross someone's palm** to give someone money **37** **cross the path (of)** to meet or thwart (someone) **38** **cross swords** to argue or fight ▷ *adj* **39** angry; ill-humoured; vexed **40** lying or placed across; transverse: *a cross timber* **41** involving interchange; reciprocal **42** contrary or unfavourable **43** another word for **crossbred** (sense 1) **44** a Brit slang word for **dishonest** [Old English *cros*, from Old Irish *cross* (unattested), from Latin *crux*; see CRUX] > ˈ**crosser** *n* > ˈ**crossly** *adv* > ˈ**crossness** *n*

C

Cross (krɒs) *n* **the 1** the cross on which Jesus Christ was crucified **2** the Crucifixion of Jesus

cross- *combining form* **1** indicating action from one individual, group, etc, to another: *cross-cultural; cross-fertilize; cross-refer* **2** indicating movement, position, etc, across something (sometimes implying interference, opposition, or contrary action): *crosscurrent; crosstalk* **3** indicating a crosslike figure or intersection: *crossbones* [from CROSS (in various senses)]

crossandra (krɒˈsɑːndrə) *n* any shrub of the free-flowering mostly African genus *Crossandra*, grown in greenhouses for their large yellow, lilac, or orange flowers: family *Acanthaceae* [New Latin, from Greek *krossos* fringed + *andros*, genitive of *anēr* man, male (from the fringed anthers)]

cross assembler *n* an assembler that runs on a computer other than the one for which it assembles programs

crossbar (ˈkrɒsˌbɑː) *n* **1** a horizontal bar, line, stripe, etc **2** a horizontal beam across a pair of goalposts **3** a horizontal bar mounted on vertical posts used in athletics or show-jumping **4** the horizontal bar on a man's bicycle that joins the handlebar and saddle supports

crossbeam ('krɒs,biːm) *n* a beam that spans from one support to another

cross bedding *n geology* layering within one or more beds in a series of rock strata that does not run parallel to the plane of stratification. Also called: **false bedding**

cross-bench *n* (*usually plural*) *Brit* a seat in Parliament occupied by a neutral or independent member > 'cross-ˌbencher *n*

crossbill ('krɒs,bɪl) *n* any of various widely distributed finches of the genus *Loxia*, such as *L. curvirostra*, that occur in coniferous woods and have a bill with crossed mandible tips for feeding on conifer seeds

crossbones ('krɒs,bəʊnz) *pl n* See **skull and crossbones**

crossbow ('krɒs,bəʊ) *n* a type of medieval bow fixed transversely on a wooden stock grooved to direct a square-headed arrow (quarrel) > 'cross,bowman *n*

crossbred ('krɒs,brɛd) *adj* **1** (of plants or animals) produced as a result of crossbreeding ▷ *n* **2** a crossbred plant or animal, esp an animal resulting from a cross between two pure breeds. Compare **grade** (sense 9), **purebred** (sense 2)

crossbreed ('krɒs,briːd) *vb* -breeds, -breeding, -bred **1** Also: **interbreed** to breed (animals or plants) using parents of different races, varieties, breeds, etc ▷ *n* **2** the offspring produced by such a breeding

cross-buttock *n* a wrestling throw in which the hips are used as a fulcrum to throw an opponent

crosscheck (ˌkrɒs'tʃɛk) *vb* **1** to verify (a fact, report, etc) by considering conflicting opinions or consulting other sources **2** (in ice hockey) to check illegally, as by chopping at an opponent's arms or stick ▷ *n* **3** the act or an instance of crosschecking

cross colour *n* distortion in a colour television receiver in which high-frequency luminance detail is interpreted as colour information and reproduced as flashes of spurious colour

cross-correlation *n statistics* the correlation between two sequences of random variables in a time series

cross-country *adj* ▷ *adv* **1** by way of fields, woods, etc, as opposed to roads: *cross-country running* **2** across a country: *a cross-country railway* ▷ *n* **3** a long race held over open ground

cross-cultural *adj* involving or bridging the differences between cultures

crosscurrent ('krɒs,kʌrənt) *n* **1** a current in a river or sea flowing across another current **2** a conflicting tendency moving counter to the usual trend

cross-curricular *adj Brit education* denoting or relating to an approach to a topic that includes contributions from several different disciplines and viewpoints

crosscut ('krɒs,kʌt) *adj* **1** cut at right angles or obliquely to the major axis ▷ *n* **2** a transverse cut or course **3** a less common word for **short cut 4** *mining* a tunnel through a vein of ore or from the shaft to a vein ▷ *vb* -cuts, -cutting, -cut **5** to cut across **6** Also: **intercut** *films* to link (two sequences or two shots) so that they appear to be taking place at the same time

crosscut file *n* a file having two intersecting rows of teeth

crosscut saw *n* a saw for cutting timber across the grain

cross-cutting *adj* linking traditionally separate or independent parties or interests: *a multi-agency, cross-cutting approach on drugs*

cross-dating *n archaeol* a method of dating objects, remains, etc, by comparison and correlation with other sites and levels

cross-dressing *n* **1** transvestism. See **transvestite 2** the wearing of clothes normally associated with the opposite sex > 'cross-'dresser *n*

crosse (krɒs) *n* a light staff with a triangular frame to which a network is attached, used in playing lacrosse [French, from Old French *croce* CROSIER]

cross-examine *vb* (*tr*) **1** *law* to examine (a witness for the opposing side), as in attempting to discredit his testimony. Compare **examine-in-chief 2** to examine closely or relentlessly > 'cross-exˌami'nation *n* > ˌcross-ex'aminer *n*

cross-eye *n* a turning inwards towards the nose of one or both eyes, caused by abnormal alignment. See also **strabismus**

cross-eyed *adj* having one or both eyes turning inwards towards the nose

cross-fade *vb radio, television* to fade in (one sound or picture source) as another is being faded out

cross-fertilization *n* fertilization by the fusion of male and female gametes from different individuals of the same species. Compare **self-fertilization**. > ˌcross-'fertile *adj*

cross-fertilize *vb* to subject or be subjected to cross-fertilization

crossfire ('krɒs,faɪə) *n* **1** *military* converging fire from one or more positions **2** a lively exchange of ideas, opinions, etc

cross-garnet *n* a hinge with a long horizontal strap fixed to the face of a door and a short vertical leaf fixed to the door frame

cross-grained *adj* **1** (of timber) having the fibres arranged irregularly or in a direction that deviates from the axis of the piece **2** perverse, cantankerous, or stubborn: *he's nothing but a cross-grained old miser*

cross hairs *pl n* two fine mutually perpendicular lines or wires that cross in the focal plane of a theodolite, gunsight, or other optical instrument and are used to define the line of sight. Also called: **cross wires**

crosshatch ('krɒs,hætʃ) *vb drawing* to shade or hatch (forms, figures, etc) with two or more sets of parallel lines that cross one another > 'cross,hatching *n*

crosshead ('krɒs,hɛd) *n* **1** *printing* a subsection or paragraph heading printed within the body of the text **2** a block or beam, usually restrained by sliding bearings in a reciprocating mechanism, esp the junction piece between the piston rod and connecting rod of an engine **3** *nautical* a bar fixed across the top of the rudder post to which the tiller is attached **4** a block, rod, or beam fixed at the head of any part of a mechanism

cross-index *n* **1** a note or notes referring the reader to other material ▷ *vb* **2** (*intr*) (of a note in a book) to refer to related material **3** to provide or be provided with cross-indexes

crossing ('krɒsɪŋ) *n* **1** the place where one thing crosses another **2** a place, often shown by markings, lights, or poles, where a street, railway, etc, may be crossed **3** the intersection of the nave and transept in a church **4** the act or instance of travelling across something, esp the sea **5** the act or process of crossbreeding

crossing over *n biology* the interchange of sections between pairing homologous chromosomes during the diplotene stage of meiosis. It results in the rearrangement of genes and produces variation in the inherited characteristics of the offspring. See also **linkage** (sense 4)

crossjack ('krɒs,dʒæk; *Nautical* 'krɔːdʒɪk, 'krɒdʒ-) *n nautical* a square sail on a ship's mizzenmast

cross-legged ('krɒs'lɛgɪd, -'lɛgd) *adj* **1** sitting with the legs bent and the knees pointing outwards **2** standing or sitting with one leg crossed over the other

crosslet or **cross crosslet** ('krɒslɪt) *n heraldry* a cross having a smaller cross near the end of each arm [C16 *croslet* a little CROSS]

cross-link or **cross-linkage** *n* a chemical bond, atom, or group of atoms that connects two adjacent chains of atoms in a large molecule such as a polymer or protein

cross-match *vb immunol* to test the compatibility of (a donor's and recipient's blood) by checking that the red cells of each do not agglutinate in the other's serum

cross-nodal *adj* having to do with interaction between the senses

cross of Lorraine *n* a cross with two horizontal bars above and below the midpoint of the vertical bar, the lower longer than the upper

Cross of Valour *n* the highest Canadian award for bravery. Abbreviation: **CV**

crossopterygian (krɒˌsɒptə'rɪdʒɪən) *n* **1** any bony fish of the subclass *Crossopterygii*, having fleshy limblike pectoral fins. The group, now mostly extinct, contains the ancestors of the amphibians. See also **coelacanth** ▷ *adj* **2** of, relating to, or belonging to the *Crossopterygii* [C19 from New Latin *Crossopterygii*, from Greek *krossoi* fringe, tassels + *pterugion* a little wing, from *pterux* wing]

crossover ('krɒs,əʊvə) *n* **1** a place at which a crossing is made **2** *genetics* **a** another term for **crossing over b** a chromosomal structure or character resulting from crossing over **3** *railways* a point of transfer between two main lines **4** short for **crossover network 5** a recording, book, or other product that becomes popular in a genre other than its own ▷ *adj* **6** (of music, fashion, art, etc) combining two distinct styles **7** (of a performer, writer, recording, book, etc) having become popular in more than one genre

crossover network *n* an electronic network in a loudspeaker system that separates the signal into two or more frequency bands, the lower frequencies being fed to a woofer, the higher frequencies to a tweeter

crossover value *n genetics* the percentage of offspring showing recombination among the total offspring of a given cross. It indicates the amount of crossing over that has occurred and therefore the relative positions of the genes on the chromosomes. Abbreviation: **COV**

crosspatch ('krɒs,pætʃ) *n informal* a peevish bad-tempered person [C18 from CROSS + obsolete *patch* fool]

crosspiece ('krɒs,piːs) *n* a transverse beam, joist, etc

cross-ply *adj* (of a motor tyre) having the fabric cords in the outer casing running diagonally to stiffen the sidewalls. Compare **radial-ply**

cross-pollinate *vb* to subject or be subjected to cross-pollination

cross-pollination *n* the transfer of pollen from the anthers of one flower to the stigma of another flower by the action of wind, insects, etc. Compare **self-pollination**

cross press *n* a fall in wrestling using the weight of the body to pin an opponent's shoulders to the floor

cross product *n maths* **1** another name for **vector product 2** another name for **Cartesian product**

cross protection *n botany* the protection against a viral infection given to a plant by its prior inoculation with a related but milder virus

cross-purpose *n* **1** a contrary aim or purpose **2** at cross-purposes conflicting; opposed; disagreeing

cross-question *vb* (*tr*) **1** to cross-examine ▷ *n* **2** a question asked in cross-examination > 'cross-'questioning *n*

cross-refer *vb* to refer from one part of something, esp a book, to another

cross-reference *n* **1** a reference within a text to another part of the text ▷ *vb* **2** to cross-refer

cross relation *n* another term (esp US) for **false relation**

Cross River *n* a state of SE Nigeria, on the Gulf of Guinea. Capital: Calabar. Pop: 2 085 926 (1995 est). Area: 20 156 sq km (7782 sq miles). Former name (until 1976): **South-Eastern State**

crossroad ('krɒs,rəʊd) *n US and Canadian* **1** a road that crosses another road **2** Also called: **crossway** a road that crosses from one main road to another

crossroads ('krɒs,rəʊdz) *n* (*functioning as singular*) **1**

an area or the point at which two or more roads cross each other **2** the point at which an important choice has to be made (esp in the phrase **at the crossroads**)

Crossroads care attendant scheme *n social welfare* (in Britain) a service providing paid attendants for disabled people who need continuous supervision [so named because the idea arose out of criticism of the plight of a disabled character in the TV serial *Crossroads*]

crossruff ('krɒsˌrʌf) *bridge, whist* ▷ *n* **1** the alternate trumping of each other's leads by two partners, or by declarer and dummy ▷ *vb* **2** (*intr*) to trump alternately in two hands of a partnership

cross section *n* **1** *maths* a plane surface formed by cutting across a solid, esp perpendicular to its longest axis **2** a section cut off in this way **3** the act of cutting anything in this way **4** a random selection or sample, esp one regarded as representative: *a cross section of the public* **5** *surveying* a vertical section of a line of ground at right angles to a survey line **6** *physics* a measure of the probability that a collision process will result in a particular reaction. It is expressed by the effective area that one participant presents as a target for the other ▷ ˌcross-'sectional *adj*

cross-slide *n* the part of a lathe or planing machine on which the tool post is mounted and across which it slides at right angles to the bed of the lathe

cross-stitch *n* **1** an embroidery stitch made by two stitches forming a cross **2** embroidery worked with this stitch ▷ *vb* **3** to embroider (a piece of needlework) with cross-stitch

crosstalk ('krɒsˌtɔːk) *n* **1** unwanted signals in one channel of a communications system as a result of a transfer of energy from one or more other channels **2** *Brit* rapid or witty talk or conversation

cross-town *adj US and Canadian* going across or following a route across a town: *a cross-town bus*

cross training *n* training in two or more sports to improve performance, esp on one's main sport

crosstree ('krɒsˌtriː) *n nautical* either of a pair of wooden or metal braces on the head of a mast to support the topmast, etc

cross vine *n* a woody bignoniaceous vine, *Bignonia capreolata,* of the southeastern US, having large trumpet-shaped reddish flowers

crosswalk ('krɒsˌwɔːk) *n US and Canadian* a path across a road marked as a crossing for pedestrians. Also called (in Britain and certain other countries): **pedestrian crossing**. See also **zebra crossing, pelican crossing**

crosswind ('krɒsˌwɪnd) *n* a wind that blows at right angles to the direction of travel

cross wires *pl n* another name for **cross hairs**

crosswise ('krɒsˌwaɪz) or **crossways** ('krɒsˌweɪz) *adj, adv* **1** across; transversely **2** in the shape of a cross

crossword puzzle ('krɒsˌwɜːd) *n* a puzzle in which the solver deduces words suggested by numbered clues and writes them into corresponding boxes in a grid to form a vertical and horizontal pattern. Sometimes shortened to: **crossword**

crosswort ('krɒsˌwɜːt) *n* a herbaceous perennial Eurasian rubiaceous plant, *Galium cruciata,* with pale yellow flowers and whorls of hairy leaves. Also called: **mugwort**

crostini (krɒ'stiːnɪ) *pl n* pieces of toasted bread served with a savoury topping [Italian: literally, little crusts]

crotal or **crottle** ('krɒt³l) *n Scot* any of various lichens used in dyeing wool, esp for the manufacture of tweeds [Gaelic *crotal*]

crotch (krɒtʃ) *n* **1** Also called (Brit): **crutch a** the angle formed by the inner sides of the legs where they join the human trunk **b** the human external genitals or the genital area **c** the corresponding part of a pair of trousers, pants, etc

2 a forked region formed by the junction of two members **3** a forked pole or stick [c16 probably variant of CRUTCH] > **crotched** *adj*

crotchet ('krɒtʃɪt) *n* **1** *music* a note having the time value of a quarter of a semibreve. Usual US and Canadian name: **quarter note 2** a small hook or hooklike device **3** a perverse notion **4** *zoology* a small notched or hooked process, as in an insect [c14 from Old French *crochet,* literally: little hook, from *croche* hook; see CROCKET]

crotchety ('krɒtʃɪtɪ) *adj* **1** *informal* cross; irritable; contrary **2** full of crotchets > **'crotchetiness** *n*

croton ('krəʊt³n) *n* **1** any shrub or tree of the chiefly tropical euphorbiaceous genus *Croton,* esp *C. tiglium,* the seeds of which yield croton oil **2** any of various tropical plants of the related genus *Codiaeum,* esp *C. variegatum pictum,* a house plant with variegated foliage [c18 from New Latin, from Greek *krotōn* tick, castor-oil plant (whose berries resemble ticks)]

Croton bug *n US* another name for the **German cockroach** [c19 named after the *Croton* river, whose water was piped to New York City in 1842]

Crotone (*Italian* kro'to:ne) *n* a town in S Italy, on the coast of Calabria: founded in about 700 BC by the Achaeans; chemical works and zinc-smelting. Pop: 60 010 (2001)

crotonic acid (krəʊ'tɒnɪk) *n* a colourless crystalline insoluble unsaturated carboxylic acid produced by oxidation of crotonaldehyde and used in organic synthesis; trans-2-butenoic acid. Formula: $CH_3CH:CHCOOH$

croton oil *n* a yellowish-brown oil obtained from the plant *Croton tiglium,* formerly used as a drastic purgative. See also **croton** (sense 1)

crottle ('krɒt³l) *n* a variant spelling of **crotal**

crouch (kraʊtʃ) *vb* **1** (*intr*) to bend low with the limbs pulled up close together, esp (of an animal) in readiness to pounce **2** (*intr*) to cringe, as in humility or fear **3** (*tr*) to bend (parts of the body), as in humility or fear ▷ *n* **4** the act of stooping or bending [c14 perhaps from Old French *crochir* to become bent like a hook, from *croche* hook]

croup¹ (kruːp) *n* a throat condition, occurring usually in children, characterized by a hoarse cough and laboured breathing, resulting from inflammation and partial obstruction of the larynx [c16 *croup* to cry hoarsely, probably of imitative origin] > **'croupous** or **'croupy** *adj*

croup² or **croupe** (kruːp) *n* the hindquarters of a quadruped, esp a horse [c13 from Old French *croupe*; related to German *Kruppe*]

croupier ('kruːpɪə; *French* krupje) *n* a person who deals cards, collects bets, etc, at a gaming table [c18 literally: one who rides behind another, from French *croupe* CROUP²]

crouse (kruːs) *adj Scot and Northern English dialect* lively, confident, or saucy [c14 (Scottish and Northern) English: from Middle Low German *krūs* twisted, curled, confused]

croute (kruːt) *n* a small round of toasted bread on which a savoury mixture is served [from French *croûte* CRUST]

crouton ('kruːtɒn) *n* a small piece of fried or toasted bread, usually served in soup [French: diminutive of *croûte* CRUST]

crow¹ (krəʊ) *n* **1** any large gregarious songbird of the genus *Corvus,* esp *C. corone* (**carrion crow**) of Europe and Asia: family *Corvidae.* Other species are the raven, rook, and jackdaw and all have a heavy bill, glossy black plumage, and rounded wings. Related adj: **corvine 2** any of various other corvine birds, such as the jay, magpie, and nutcracker **3** any of various similar birds of other families **4** short for **crowbar 5 as the crow flies** as directly as possible **6 eat crow** *US and Canadian informal* to be forced to do something humiliating **7 stone the crows** (*interjection*) *Brit and Austral slang* an expression of surprise, dismay, etc [Old English *crāwa*; related to Old Norse *krāka,* Old High German *krāia,* Dutch *kraai*]

crow² (krəʊ) *vb* (*intr*) **1** (past tense **crowed** or **crew**)

to utter a shrill squawking sound, as a cock **2** (often foll by *over*) to boast one's superiority **3** (esp of babies) to utter cries of pleasure ▷ *n* **4** the act or an instance of crowing [Old English *crāwan*; related to Old High German *krāen,* Dutch *kraaien*] > **'crower** *n* > **'crowingly** *adv*

Crow (krəʊ) *n* **1** (*pl* **Crows** or **Crow**) a member of a Native American people living in E Montana **2** the language of this people, belonging to the Siouan family

crowbar ('krəʊˌbɑː) *n* a heavy iron lever with one pointed end, and one forged into a wedge shape

crowberry ('krəʊbərɪ, -brɪ) *n, pl* **-ries 1** a low-growing N temperate evergreen shrub, *Empetrum nigrum,* with small purplish flowers and black berry-like fruit: family *Empetraceae* **2** any of several similar or related plants **3** the fruit of any of these plants

crow-bill *n* a type of forceps used to extract bullets, etc, from wounds

crow blackbird *n* another name for **grackle**

crowboot ('krəʊˌbuːt) *n* a type of Inuit boot made of fur and leather

crowd¹ (kraʊd) *n* **1** a large number of things or people gathered or considered together **2** a particular group of people, esp considered as a social or business set: *the crowd from the office* **3 a** (preceded by *the*) the common people; the masses **b** (*as modifier*): *crowd ideas* **4 follow the crowd** to conform with the majority ▷ *vb* **5** (*intr*) to gather together in large numbers; throng **6** (*tr*) to press together into a confined space **7** (*tr*) to fill to excess; fill by pushing into **8** (*tr*) *informal* to urge or harass by urging **9 crowd on sail** *nautical* to hoist as much sail as possible [Old English *crūdan*; related to Middle Low German *krūden* to molest, Middle Dutch *crūden* to push, Norwegian *kryda* to swarm] > **'crowded** *adj* > **'crowdedly** *adv* > **'crowdedness** *n* > **'crowder** *n*

crowd² (kraʊd) *n music* an ancient bowed stringed instrument; crwth [c13 from Welsh *crwth*]

crowdie ('kraʊdɪ) *n Scot* **1** a porridge of meal and water; brose **2** a cheese-like dish made by straining the whey from soured milk and beating up the remaining curd with salt [c17 of unknown origin]

crowd puller *n informal* a person, object, event, etc, that attracts a large audience

crowd surfing *n* the practice of being passed over the top of a crowd of people such as an audience at a pop concert

crowea ('krəʊɪə) *n* an Australian shrub of the genus *Crowea,* having pink flowers [named after James Crowe (1750–1807), British surgeon and botanist]

crowfoot ('krəʊˌfʊt) *n, pl* **-foots 1** any of several plants of the genus *Ranunculus,* such as *R. sceleratus* and *R. aquatilis* (**water crowfoot**) that have yellow or white flowers and divided leaves resembling the foot of a crow. See also **buttercup 2** any of various other plants that have leaves or other parts resembling a bird's foot **3** *pl* **-feet** *nautical* a bridle-like arrangement of lines rove through a wooden block or attached to a ring for supporting an awning from above **4** *pl* **-feet** *military* another name for **caltrop**

crown (kraʊn) *n* **1** an ornamental headdress denoting sovereignty, usually made of gold embedded with precious stones **2** a wreath or garland for the head, awarded as a sign of victory, success, honour, etc **3** (*sometimes capital*) monarchy or kingship **4** an award, distinction, or title, given as an honour to reward merit, victory, etc **5** anything resembling or symbolizing a crown, such as a sergeant major's badge or a heraldic bearing **6 a** *history* a coin worth 25 pence (five shillings) **b** any of several continental coins, such as the krona or krone, with a name meaning *crown* **7** the top or summit of something, esp of a rounded object: *crown of a hill; crown of the head* **8** the centre part of a road, esp when it is cambered **9** *botany* **a** the leaves and upper branches of a tree

C

b the junction of root and stem, usually at the level of the ground **c** another name for **corona** (sense 6) **10** *zoology* **a** the cup and arms of a crinoid, as distinct from the stem **b** the crest of a bird **11** the outstanding quality, achievement, state, etc: *the crown of his achievements* **12 a** the enamel-covered part of a tooth above the gum **b** artificial crown a substitute crown, usually of gold, porcelain, or acrylic resin, fitted over a decayed or broken tooth **13** the part of a cut gem above the girdle **14** *horology* a knurled knob for winding a watch **15** the part of an anchor where the arms are joined to the shank **16** the highest part of an arch or vault **17** a standard size of printing paper, 15 by 20 inches ▷ *vb* (*tr*) **18** to put a crown on the head of, symbolically vesting with royal title, powers, etc **19** to place a crown, wreath, garland, etc, on the head of **20** to place something on or over the head or top of: *he crowned the pie with cream* **21** to confer a title, dignity, or reward upon: *he crowned her best cook* **22** to form the summit or topmost part of: *the steeple crowned the tower* **23** to cap or put the finishing touch to a series of events: *to crown it all it rained, too* **24** *draughts* to promote (a draught) to a king by placing another draught on top of it, as after reaching the end of the board **25** to attach a crown to (a tooth) **26** *slang* to hit over the head [c12 from Old French *corone*, from Latin *corōna* wreath, crown, from Greek *korōnē* crown, something curved] > 'crownless *adj*

Crown (kraʊn) *n* (*sometimes not capital*; usually preceded by *the*) **1** the sovereignty or realm of a monarch **2 a** the government of a constitutional monarchy **b** (*as modifier*): *Crown property*

Crown Agent *n* **1** a member of a board appointed by the Minister for Overseas Development to provide financial, commercial, and professional services for a number of overseas governments and international bodies **2** *Scot* (*not capitals*) a solicitor dealing with criminal prosecutions

crown and anchor *n* a game played with dice marked with crowns and anchors

Crown attorney *n Canadian* a lawyer who acts for the Crown, esp as prosecutor in a criminal court

crown cap *n Brit* an airtight metal seal crimped on the top of most bottled beers, ciders, mineral waters, etc

crown colony *n* a British colony whose administration and legislature is controlled by the Crown

crown court *n English law* a court of criminal jurisdiction holding sessions in towns throughout England and Wales at which circuit judges hear and determine cases

Crown Derby *n* a type of porcelain manufactured at Derby from 1784–1848

crowned head *n* a monarch: *the crowned heads of Europe*

crowner ('kraʊnə) *n* a promotional label consisting of a shaped printed piece of card or paper attached to a product on display

crown ether *n chem* a type of cyclic ether consisting of a ring of carbon and oxygen atoms, with two or more carbon atoms between each oxygen atom

crown glass *n* **1** another name for **optical crown** **2** an old form of window glass made by blowing a globe and spinning it until it formed a flat disc

crown graft *n horticulture* a type of graft in which the scion is inserted at the crown of the stock

crown green *n* a type of bowling green in which the sides are lower than the middle

crown imperial *n* a liliaceous garden plant, *Fritillaria imperialis*, with a cluster of leaves and orange bell-shaped flowers at the top of the stem

crowning ('kraʊnɪŋ) *n obstetrics* the stage of labour when the infant's head is passing through the vaginal opening

crown-jewel option *n informal* an option given by a company subjected to an unwelcome takeover bid to a friendly firm, allowing this firm to buy one or more of its best businesses if the bid succeeds

crown jewels *pl n* the jewellery, including the regalia, used by a sovereign on a state occasion

crownland ('kraʊn,lænd) *n* a large administrative division of the former empire of Austria-Hungary

crown land *n* **1** (in the United Kingdom) land belonging to the Crown **2** public land in some dominions of the Commonwealth

crown lens *n* a lens made of optical crown, esp the optical-crown part of a compound achromatic lens

Crown Office *n* (in England) an office of the Queen's Bench Division of the High Court that is responsible for administration and where actions are entered for trial

crown-of-thorns *n* **1** a starfish, *Acanthaster planci*, that has a spiny test and feeds on living coral in coral reefs **2** Also called: **Christ's thorn** a thorny euphorbiaceous Madagascan shrub, *Euphorbia milii* var. *splendens*, cultivated as a hedging shrub or pot plant, having flowers with scarlet bracts

crownpiece ('kraʊn,piːs) *n* **1** the piece forming or fitting the top of something **2** the strap of a bridle that goes over a horse's head behind the ears

crown prince *n* the male heir to a sovereign throne

crown princess *n* **1** the wife of a crown prince **2** the female heir to a sovereign throne

Crown Prosecution Service *n* (in England and Wales) an independent prosecuting body, established in 1986, that decides whether cases brought by the police should go to the courts: headed by the Director of Public Prosecutions. Compare **procurator fiscal**. Abbreviation: **CPS**

Crown prosecutor *n Canadian* another name for **Crown attorney**

crown roast *n* a roast consisting of ribs of lamb or pork arranged in a crown shape

crown saw *n* a hollow cylinder with cutting teeth forming a rotary saw for trepanning

crown vetch *n* a trailing leguminous European plant, *Coronilla varia*, with clusters of white or pink flowers: cultivated in North America as a border plant. Also called (US): **axseed** ('æks,iːd)

crown wheel *n* **1** *horology* the wheel next to the winding knob that has one set of teeth at right angles to the other **2** the larger of the two gears in a bevel gear

crownwork ('kraʊn,wɜːk) *n* **1 a** the manufacture of artificial crowns for teeth **b** such an artificial crown or crowns **2** *fortifications* a covering or protective outwork

crow's-foot *n, pl* -feet **1** (*often plural*) a wrinkle at the outer corner of the eye **2** an embroidery stitch with three points, used esp as a finishing at the end of a seam **3** a system of diverging short ropes to distribute the pull of a single rope, used esp in balloon and airship riggings

crow's-nest *n* a lookout platform high up on a ship's mast

crow step *n* another term for **corbie-step**

Croydon ('krɔɪdən) *n* a borough in S Greater London (since 1965): formerly important for its airport (1915–59). Pop: 336 700 (2003 est). Area: 87 sq km (33 sq miles)

croze (krəʊz) *n* **1** the recess cut at the end of a barrel or cask to receive the head **2** a tool for cutting this recess [c17 probably from Old French *crues* a hollow]

crozier ('krəʊzə) *n* a variant spelling of **crosier**

crozzled ('krɒzəld) *adj Northern English dialect* blackened or burnt at the edges: *that bacon is crozzled*

CRP (in India) *abbreviation for* Central Reserve Police

CRP² *abbreviation for* C-reactive protein; a chemical in the blood that can be measured to indicate inflammation in the body and a person's risk of suffering a heart attack

CRT *abbreviation for* **1 cathode-ray tube 2** (in Britain) composite rate tax: a system of paying interest to savers by which a rate of tax for a period, such as one financial year, is determined in advance, and interest is paid net of tax which is deducted at source

cru (kruː; *French* kry) *n winemaking* (in France) a vineyard, group of vineyards, or wine-producing region [from French: production, from *crû*, past participle of *croître* to grow]

cruces ('kruːsiːz) *n* a plural of **crux**

crucial ('kruːʃəl) *adj* **1** involving a final or supremely important decision or event; decisive; critical **2** *informal* very important **3** *slang* very good [c18 from French, from Latin *crux* CROSS] > 'crucially *adv*

crucian ('kruːʃən) *n* a European cyprinid fish, *Carassius carassius*, with a dark-green back, a golden-yellow undersurface, and reddish dorsal and tail fins: an aquarium fish [c18 from Low German *Karusse*]

cruciate ('kruːʃɪɪt, -,eɪt) *adj* shaped or arranged like a cross: *cruciate petals* [c17 from New Latin *cruciātus*, from Latin *crux* CROSS] > 'cruciately *adv*

cruciate ligament *n anatomy* either of a pair of ligaments that cross each other in the knee, connecting the tibia and the femur

crucible ('kruːsɪbəl) *n* **1** a vessel in which substances are heated to high temperatures **2** the hearth at the bottom of a metallurgical furnace in which the metal collects **3** a severe trial or test [c15 *corusible*, from Medieval Latin *crūcibulum* night lamp, crucible, of uncertain origin]

Crucible ('kruːsɪbəl) *n* **the a** Sheffield theatre, venue of the annual world professional snooker championship

crucible steel *n* a high-quality steel made by melting wrought iron, charcoal, and other additives in a crucible

crucifer ('kruːsɪfə) *n* **1** any plant of the family *Brassicaceae* (formerly *Cruciferae*), having a corolla of four petals arranged like a cross and a fruit called a siliqua. The family includes the brassicas, mustard, cress, and wallflower **2** a person who carries a cross [c16 from Late Latin, from Latin *crux* cross + *ferre* to carry] > cruciferous (kruː'sɪfərəs) *adj*

cruciferous (kruː'sɪfərəs) *adj* of, relating to, or belonging to the plant family *Cruciferae*. See **crucifer** (sense 1)

crucifix ('kruːsɪfɪks) *n* a cross or image of a cross with a figure of Christ upon it [c13 from Church Latin *crucifixus* the crucified Christ, from *crucifigere* to CRUCIFY]

crucifixion (,kruːsɪ'fɪkʃən) *n* a method of putting to death by nailing or binding to a cross, normally by the hands and feet, which was widespread in the ancient world

Crucifixion (,kruːsɪ'fɪkʃən) *n* **1** (usually preceded by *the*) the crucifying of Christ at Calvary, regarded by Christians as the culminating redemptive act of his ministry **2** a picture or representation of this

cruciform ('kruːsɪ,fɔːm) *adj* **1** shaped like a cross ▷ *n* **2** a geometric curve, shaped like a cross, that has four similar branches asymptotic to two mutually perpendicular pairs of lines. Equation: $x^2y^2 - a^2x^2 - a^2y^2 = 0$, where $x = y = \pm a$ are the four lines [c17 from Latin *crux* cross + -FORM] > 'cruci,formly *adv*

crucify ('kruːsɪ,faɪ) *vb* -fies, -fying, -fied (*tr*) **1** to put to death by crucifixion **2** *slang* to defeat, ridicule, etc, totally: *the critics crucified his performance* **3** to treat very cruelly; torment **4** to subdue (passion, lust, etc); mortify [c13 from Old French *crucifier*, from Late Latin *crucifigere* to crucify, to fasten to a cross, from Latin *crux* cross + *figere* to fasten] > 'cruci,fier *n*

cruciverbalist (,kruːsɪ'vɜːbəlɪst) *n* a crossword puzzle enthusiast [c20 from Latin *crux* cross + *verbum* word]

cruck (krʌk) *n* one of a pair of curved wooden timbers supporting the end of the roof in certain types of building [c19 variant of CROOK (n)]

crud (krʌd) *slang* ▷ *n* **1** a sticky substance, esp when dirty and encrusted **2** an undesirable residue from a process, esp one inside a nuclear reactor **3** something or someone that is worthless, disgusting, or contemptible **4** (sometimes preceded by *the*) a disease; rot ▷ *interj* **5** an expression of disgust, disappointment, etc [C14 earlier form of CURD]

cruddy (ˈkrʌdɪ) *adj* **cruddier, cruddiest** *slang* **1** dirty or unpleasant **2** of poor quality; contemptible

crude (kruːd) *adj* **1** lacking taste, tact, or refinement; vulgar: *a crude joke* **2** in a natural or unrefined state **3** lacking care, knowledge, or skill: *a crude sketch* **4** (*prenominal*) stark; blunt: *the crude facts* **5** (of statistical data) unclassified or unanalysed **6** *archaic* unripe ▷ *n* **7** short for **crude oil** [C14 from Latin *crūdus* bloody, raw; related to Latin *cruor* blood] > ˈ**crudely** *adv* > ˈ**crudity** *or* ˈ**crudeness** *n*

crude oil *n* petroleum before it has been refined

crudités (ˌkruːdɪˈteɪ) *pl n* a selection of raw vegetables, usually cut into strips or small chunks and served, with a dip, as an hors d'oeuvre [C20 from French, plural of *crudité*, literally: rawness]

cruel (ˈkruːəl) *adj* **1** causing or inflicting pain without pity: *a cruel teacher* **2** causing pain or suffering: *a cruel accident* [C13 from Old French, from Latin *crūdēlis*, from *crūdus* raw, bloody] > ˈ**cruelly** *adv* > ˈ**cruelness** *n*

cruels *n* another name for **actinobacillosis** (in sheep)

cruelty (ˈkruːəltɪ) *n, pl* **-ties** **1** deliberate infliction of pain or suffering **2** the quality or characteristic of being cruel **3** a cruel action **4** *law* conduct that causes danger to life or limb or a threat to bodily or mental health, on proof of which a decree of divorce may be granted

cruelty-free *adj* (of a cosmetic or other product) developed without being tested on animals

cruet (ˈkruːɪt) *n* **1** a small container for holding pepper, salt, vinegar, oil, etc, at table **2** a set of such containers, esp on a stand **3** *Christianity* either of a pair of small containers for the wine and water used in the Eucharist **4** *Austral* a slang word for **head** (sense 1) **5** **do one's cruet** *Austral slang* to be extremely angry; go into a rage ▷ *pl n* **6** *Austral slang* the testicles [C13 from Anglo-French, diminutive of Old French *crue* flask, of Germanic origin; compare Old Saxon *krūka*, Old English *crūce* pot]

cruise (kruːz) *vb* **1** (*intr*) to make a trip by sea in a liner for pleasure, usually calling at a number of ports **2** to sail or travel over (a body of water) for pleasure in a yacht, cruiser, etc **3** (*intr*) to search for enemy vessels in a warship **4** (*intr*) (of a vehicle, aircraft, or vessel) to travel at a moderate and efficient speed **5** (*intr*) *informal* to search the streets or other public places for a sexual partner ▷ *n* **6** an act or instance of cruising, esp a trip by sea [C17 from Dutch *kruisen* to cross, from *cruis* CROSS; related to French *croiser* to cross, cruise, Spanish *cruzar*, German *kreuzen*]

cruise control *n* a system in a road vehicle that automatically maintains a selected speed until cancelled

cruise missile *n* an air-breathing low-flying subsonic missile that is continuously powered and guided throughout its flight and carries a warhead

cruiser (ˈkruːzə) *n* **1** a high-speed, long-range warship of medium displacement, armed with medium calibre weapons or missiles **2** Also called: **cabin cruiser** a pleasure boat, esp one that is power-driven and has a cabin **3** any person or thing that cruises **4** *boxing* short for **cruiserweight** (see **light heavyweight**)

cruiserweight (ˈkruːzəˌweɪt) *n boxing* another term (esp Brit) for **light heavyweight**

cruiseway (ˈkruːzˌweɪ) *n* a canal used for recreational purposes

cruizie, cruzie *or* **crusie** (ˈkruːzɪ) *n Scot* an oil lamp [C18 perhaps from *cruset* crucible, from French *creuset*]

cruller *or* **kruller** (ˈkrʌlə) *n US and Canadian* a light sweet ring-shaped cake, fried in deep fat [C19 from Dutch *krulle*, from *krullen* to CURL]

crumb (krʌm) *n* **1** a small fragment of bread, cake, or other baked foods **2** a small piece or bit: *crumbs of information* **3** the soft inner part of bread **4** *slang* a contemptible person ▷ *vb* **5** (*tr*) to prepare or cover (food) with breadcrumbs **6** to break into small fragments ▷ *adj* **7** (esp of pie crusts) made with a mixture of biscuit crumbs, sugar, etc [Old English *cruma*; related to Middle Dutch *krome*, Middle High German *krüme*, Latin *grūmus* heap of earth] > ˈ**crumber** *n*

crumble (ˈkrʌmbᵊl) *vb* **1** to break or be broken into crumbs or fragments **2** (*intr*) to fall apart or away: *his resolution crumbled* ▷ *n* **3** *Brit* a baked pudding consisting of a crumbly mixture of flour, fat, and sugar over stewed fruit: *apple crumble* [C16 variant of *crimble*, of Germanic origin; compare Low German *krömeln*, Dutch *kruimelen*]

crumbly (ˈkrʌmblɪ) *adj* **-blier, -bliest** easily crumbled or crumbling > ˈ**crumbliness** *n*

crumbs (krʌmz) *interj slang* an expression of dismay or surprise [C20 euphemistic for *Christ!*]

crumby (ˈkrʌmɪ) *adj* **crumbier, crumbiest** **1** full of or littered with crumbs **2** soft, like the inside of bread **3** a variant spelling of **crummy**[1]

crumhorn *or* **krummhorn** (ˈkrʌmˌhɔːn) *n* a medieval woodwind instrument of bass pitch, consisting of an almost cylindrical tube curving upwards and blown through a double reed covered by a pierced cap [C17 *cromorne*, *krumhorn*, from German *Krummhorn* curved horn]

Crummock Water (ˈkrʌmək) *n* a lake in NW England, in Cumbria in the Lake District. Length: 4 km (2.5 miles)

crummy[1] (ˈkrʌmɪ) *adj* **-mier, -miest** *slang* **1** of little value; inferior; contemptible **2** unwell or depressed: *to feel crummy* [C19 variant spelling of CRUMBY]

crummy[2] (ˈkrʌmɪ) *n, pl* **-mies** *Canadian* a lorry that carries loggers to work from their camp [probably originally meaning: makeshift camp, from CRUMMY[1]]

crump (krʌmp) *vb* **1** (*intr*) to thud or explode with a loud dull sound **2** (*tr*) to bombard with heavy shells ▷ *n* **3** a crunching, thudding, or exploding noise [C17 of imitative origin]

crumpet (ˈkrʌmpɪt) *n chiefly Brit* **1** a light soft yeast cake full of small holes on the top side, eaten toasted and buttered **2** (in Scotland) a large flat sweetened cake made of batter **3** *slang* women collectively **4** **a piece of crumpet** *slang* a sexually desirable woman **5** **not worth a crumpet** *Austral slang* utterly worthless [C17 of uncertain origin]

crumple (ˈkrʌmpᵊl) *vb* **1** (when *intr*, often foll by *up*) to collapse or cause to collapse: *his courage crumpled* **2** (when *tr*, often foll by *up*) to crush or cause to be crushed so as to form wrinkles or creases **3** (*intr*) to shrink; shrivel ▷ *n* **4** a loose crease or wrinkle [C16 from obsolete *crump* to bend; related to Old High German *krimpfan* to wrinkle, Old Norse *kreppa* to contract] > ˈ**crumply** *adj*

crumple zones *pl n* parts of a motor vehicle, at the front and the rear, that are designed to crumple in a collision, thereby absorbing the impact

crunch (krʌntʃ) *vb* **1** to bite or chew (crisp foods) with a crushing or crackling sound **2** to make or cause to make a crisp or brittle sound: *the snow crunched beneath his feet* ▷ *n* **3** the sound or act of crunching **4** short for **abdominal crunch** **5** **the crunch** *informal* the critical moment or situation ▷ *adj* **6** *informal* critical; decisive: *crunch time* ▷ Also: **craunch** [C19 changed (through influence of MUNCH) from earlier *craunch*, of imitative origin] > ˈ**crunchable** *adj* > ˈ**crunchy** *adj* > ˈ**crunchily** *adv* > ˈ**crunchiness** *n*

crunchie (ˈkrʌntʃɪ) *n South African derogatory slang* another name for an **Afrikaner**

crunode (ˈkruːnəʊd) *n* a point at which two branches of a curve intersect, each branch having a distinct tangent; node [C19 *cru-* from Latin *crux* cross + NODE]

cruor (ˈkrʊɔː) *n, pl* **cruores** (ˈkrʊɔːriːz) *med* a blood clot

crupper (ˈkrʌpə) *n* **1** a strap from the back of a saddle that passes under the horse's tail to prevent the saddle from slipping forwards **2** the part of the horse's rump behind the saddle [C13 from Old French *crupiere*, from *crupe* CROUP[2]]

crura (ˈkrʊərə) *n* the plural of **crus**

crural (ˈkrʊərəl) *adj* of or relating to the leg or thigh [C16 from Latin *crūrālis*, from *crūs* leg, shin]

crus (krʌs) *n, pl* **crura** (ˈkrʊərə) **1** *anatomy* the leg, esp from the knee to the foot **2** (*usually plural*) leglike parts or structures [C17 from Latin: leg]

crusade (kruːˈseɪd) *n* **1** (*often capital*) any of the military expeditions undertaken in the 11th, 12th, and 13th centuries by the Christian powers of Europe to recapture the Holy Land from the Muslims **2** (formerly) any holy war undertaken on behalf of a religious cause **3** a vigorous and dedicated action or movement in favour of a cause ▷ *vb* (*intr*) **4** to campaign vigorously for something **5** to go on a crusade [C16 from earlier *croisade*, from Old French *crois* cross, from Latin *crux*; influenced also by Spanish *cruzada*, from *cruzar* to take up the cross] > **cruˈsader** *n*

crusado (kruːˈseɪdəʊ) *or* **cruzado** (kruːˈzeɪdəʊ; *Portuguese* kruˈzaːdu) *n, pl* **-does** *or* **-dos** (-dəʊz; *Portuguese* -duʃ) a former gold or silver coin of Portugal bearing on its reverse the figure of a cross [C16 literally, marked with a cross, from *cruzar* to bear a cross; see CRUSADE]

cruse (kruːz) *n* a small earthenware container used, esp formerly, for liquids [Old English *crūse*; related to Middle High German *krūse*, Dutch *kroes* jug]

crush[1] (krʌʃ) *vb* (*mainly tr*) **1** to press, mash, or squeeze so as to injure, break, crease, etc **2** to break or grind (rock, ore, etc) into small particles **3** to put down or subdue, esp by force: *to crush a rebellion* **4** to extract (juice, water, etc) by pressing: *to crush the juice from a lemon* **5** to oppress harshly **6** to hug or clasp tightly: *he crushed her to him* **7** to defeat or humiliate utterly, as in argument or by a cruel remark **8** (*intr*) to crowd; throng **9** (*intr*) to become injured, broken, or distorted by pressure ▷ *n* **10** a dense crowd, esp at a social occasion **11** the act of crushing; pressure **12** a drink or pulp prepared by or as if by crushing fruit: *orange crush* **13** *informal* **a** an infatuation: *she had a crush on him* **b** the person with whom one is infatuated [C14 from Old French *croissir*, of Germanic origin; compare Gothic *kriustan* to gnash; see CRUNCH] > ˈ**crushable** *adj* > ˌ**crushaˈbility** *n* > ˈ**crusher** *n*

C

crush[2] (krʌʃ) *n vet science* a construction designed to confine and limit the movement of an animal, esp a large or dangerous animal, for examination or to perform a procedure on it

crush bar *n* a bar at a theatre for serving drinks during the intervals of a play

crush barrier *n* a barrier erected to separate sections of large crowds in order to prevent crushing

crush-resistant *adj* not being easily creased

crusie (ˈkruːzɪ) *n* a variant spelling of **cruizie**

Crusoe (ˈkruːsəʊ, -zəʊ) *n* **Robinson**. See **Robinson Crusoe**

crust (krʌst) *n* **1** **a** the hard outer part of bread **b** a piece of bread consisting mainly of this **2** the baked shell of a pie, tart, etc **3** any hard or stiff outer covering or surface: *a crust of ice* **4** the solid outer shell of the earth, with an average thickness of 30–35 km in continental regions and 5 km beneath the oceans, forming the upper part of the lithosphere and lying immediately above the mantle, from which it is separated by the Mohorovičić discontinuity. See also **sial, sima** **5** the dry covering of a skin sore or lesion; scab **6** a layer of acid potassium tartrate deposited by some wine, esp port, on the inside of the bottle **7** the hard outer layer of such organisms as lichens and crustaceans **8** *slang* impertinence **9** *Brit, Austral and NZ slang* a living (esp in the phrase **earn a crust**) ▷ *vb* **10** to cover with or acquire a crust **11** to form or be formed into a crust [c14 from Latin *crusta* hard surface, rind, shell]

crustacean (krʌˈsteɪʃən) *n* **1** any arthropod of the mainly aquatic class *Crustacea*, typically having a carapace hardened with lime and including the lobsters, crabs, shrimps, woodlice, barnacles, copepods, and water fleas ▷ *adj also* **crustaceous 2** of, relating to, or belonging to the *Crustacea* [c19 from New Latin *crustaceus* hard-shelled, from Latin *crusta* shell, CRUST]

crustaceous (krʌˈsteɪʃəs) *adj* **1** forming, resembling, or possessing a surrounding crust or shell **2** *zoology* another word for **crustacean** (sense 2)

crustal (ˈkrʌstəl) *adj* of or relating to the earth's crust

crustose (ˈkrʌstəʊs) *adj biology* having a crustlike appearance: *crustose lichens*

crusty (ˈkrʌstɪ) *adj* **crustier, crustiest 1** having or characterized by a crust, esp having a thick crust **2** having a rude or harsh character or exterior; surly; curt: *a crusty remark* ▷ *n, pl* **crusties 3** *slang* a dirty type of punk or hippy whose lifestyle involves travelling and squatting > ˈcrustily *adv* > ˈcrustiness *n*

crutch (krʌtʃ) *n* **1** a long staff of wood or metal having a rest for the armpit, for supporting the weight of the body **2** something that supports or sustains: *a crutch to the economy* **3** *Brit* another word for **crotch** (sense 1) **4** *nautical* **a** a forked support for a boom or oar, etc **b** a brace for reinforcing the frames at the stern of a wooden vessel ▷ *vb* **5** (*tr*) to support or sustain (a person or thing) as with a crutch **6** *Austral and NZ slang* to clip (wool) from the hindquarters of a sheep [Old English *crycc*; related to Old High German *krucka*, Old Norse *krykkja*; see CROSIER, CROOK]

Crutched Friar (krʌtʃt, ˈkrʌtʃɪd) *n* a member of a mendicant order, suppressed in 1656 [c16 *crutched*, variant of *crouched*, literally: crossed, referring to the cross worn on their habits]

crutchings (ˈkrʌtʃɪŋz) *pl n Austral and NZ* the wool clipped from a sheep's hindquarters

crux (krʌks) *n, pl* **cruxes** *or* **cruces** (ˈkruːsiːz) **1** a vital or decisive stage, point, etc (often in the phrase **the crux of the matter**) **2** a baffling problem or difficulty **3** *mountaineering* the most difficult and often decisive part of a climb or pitch **4** a rare word for **cross** [c18 from Latin: cross]

Crux (krʌks) *n, Latin genitive* Crucis (ˈkruːsɪs) the more formal name for the **Southern Cross**

crux ansata (ænˈseɪtə) *n, pl* **cruces ansatae** (ænˈseɪtiː) another term for **ankh** [New Latin, literally: cross with a handle]

cruzado (kruːˈzeɪdəʊ; *Portuguese* kruˈzaːdu) *n, pl* **-does** *or* **-dos** (-dəʊz; *Portuguese* -duʃ) **1** a former standard monetary unit of Brazil, replaced by the cruzeiro **2** another name for **crusado** [c16 literally marked with a cross, from *cruzar* to bear a cross; see CRUSADE]

cruzeiro (kruːˈzɛərəʊ; *Portuguese* kruˈzeiru) *n, pl* **-ros** (-rəʊz; *Portuguese* -ruʃ) a former monetary unit of Brazil, replaced by the cruzeiro real [Portuguese: from *cruz* CROSS]

cruzeiro real *n* a former monetary unit of Brazil, replaced by the **real**[3] (sense 1)

cruzie (ˈkruːzɪ) *n* a variant spelling of **cruizie**

crwth (kruːθ) *n* an ancient stringed instrument of Celtic origin similar to the cithara but bowed in later types [Welsh; compare Middle Irish *crott* harp]

cry (kraɪ) *vb* **cries, crying, cried 1** (*intr*) to utter inarticulate sounds, esp when weeping; sob **2** (*intr*) to shed tears; weep **3** (*intr*; usually foll by *out*) to scream or shout in pain, terror, etc **4** (*tr*; often foll by *out*) to utter or shout (words of appeal, exclamation, fear, etc) **5** (*intr*; often foll by *out*) (of animals, birds, etc) to utter loud characteristic sounds **6** (*tr*) to hawk or sell by public announcement: *to cry newspapers* **7** to announce (something) publicly or in the streets **8** (*intr*; foll by *for*) to clamour or beg **9** *Scot* to call **10** **cry for the moon** to desire the unattainable **11** **cry one's eyes** *or* **heart out** to weep bitterly **12** **cry quits** *or* **mercy** to give up a task, fight, etc ▷ *n, pl* **cries 13** the act or sound of crying; a shout, exclamation, scream, or wail **14** the characteristic utterance of an animal or bird: *the cry of gulls* **15** *Scot* a call **16** *archaic* an oral announcement, esp one made by town criers **17** a fit of weeping **18** *hunting* the baying of a pack of hounds hunting their quarry by scent **19** a pack of hounds **20** **a far cry a** a long way **b** something very different **21** **in full cry** (esp of a pack of hounds) in hot pursuit of a quarry ▷ See also **cry down, cry off, cry out, cry up** [c13 from Old French *crier*, from Latin *quiritare* to call for help]

crybaby (ˈkraɪˌbeɪbɪ) *n, pl* **-bies** a person, esp a child, given to frequent crying or complaint

cry down *vb* (*tr, adverb*) **1** to belittle; disparage **2** to silence by making a greater noise: *to cry down opposition*

crying (ˈkraɪɪŋ) *adj* (*prenominal*) notorious; lamentable (esp in the phrase **crying shame**)

cryo- *combining form* indicating low temperature; frost, cold, or freezing: *cryogenics; cryosurgery* [from Greek *kruos* icy cold, frost]

cryobiology (ˌkraɪəʊbaɪˈɒlədʒɪ) *n* the branch of biology concerned with the study of the effects of very low temperatures on organisms > ˌcryobiˈologist *n*

cryocable (ˌkraɪəʊˈkeɪbəl) *n* a highly conducting electrical cable cooled with a refrigerant such as liquid nitrogen

cry off *vb* (*intr*) *informal* to withdraw from or cancel (an agreement or arrangement)

cryogen (ˈkraɪədʒən) *n* a substance used to produce low temperatures; a freezing mixture

cryogenics (ˌkraɪəˈdʒɛnɪks) *n* (*functioning as singular*) the branch of physics concerned with the production of very low temperatures and the phenomena occurring at these temperatures > ˌcryoˈgenic *adj*

cryoglobulin (ˌkraɪəʊˈɡlɒbjʊlɪn) *n med* an abnormal immunoglobulin, present in the blood in certain diseases, that precipitates below about 10°C, obstructing small blood vessels in the fingers and toes

cryohydrate (ˌkraɪəʊˈhaɪdreɪt) *n* a crystalline substance containing water and a salt in definite proportions at low temperatures: a eutectic crystallizing below the freezing point of water

cryolite (ˈkraɪəˌlaɪt) *n* a white or colourless mineral consisting of a fluoride of sodium and aluminium in monoclinic crystalline form: used in the production of aluminium, glass, and enamel. Formula: Na_3AlF_6

cryometer (kraɪˈɒmɪtə) *n* a thermometer for measuring low temperatures > cryˈometry *n*

cryonics (kraɪˈɒnɪks) *n* (*functioning as singular*) the practice of freezing a human corpse in the hope of restoring it to life in the future

cryophilic (ˌkraɪəˈfɪlɪk) *adj biology* able to thrive at low temperatures

cryophyte (ˈkraɪəˌfaɪt) *n* an organism, esp an alga or moss, that grows on snow or ice

cryoplankton (ˌkraɪəʊˈplæŋktən) *n* minute organisms, esp algae, living in ice, snow, or icy water

cryoprecipitate (ˌkraɪəʊprɪˈsɪpɪteɪt) *n* a precipitate obtained by controlled thawing of a previously frozen substance. Factor VIII, for treating haemophilia, is often obtained as a cryoprecipitate from frozen blood

cryoscope (ˈkraɪəˌskəʊp) *n* any instrument used to determine the freezing point of a substance

cryoscopy (kraɪˈɒskəpɪ) *n, pl* **-pies** the determination of freezing points, esp for the determination of molecular weights by measuring the lowering of the freezing point of a solvent when a known quantity of solute is added > cryoscopic (ˌkraɪəˈskɒpɪk) *adj*

cryostat (ˈkraɪəˌstæt) *n* an apparatus for maintaining a constant low temperature or a vessel in which a substance is stored at a low temperature

cryosurgery (ˌkraɪəʊˈsɜːdʒərɪ) *n* surgery involving the local destruction of tissues by quick freezing for therapeutic benefit

cryotherapy (ˌkraɪəʊˈθɛrəpɪ) *or* **crymotherapy** (ˌkraɪməʊˈθɛrəpɪ) *n* medical treatment in which all or part of the body is subjected to cold temperatures, as by means of ice packs

cryotron (ˈkraɪəˌtrɒn) *n* a miniature switch working at the temperature of liquid helium and depending for its action on the production and destruction of superconducting properties in the conductor

cry out *vb* (*intr, adverb*) **1** to scream or shout aloud, esp in pain, terror, etc **2** (often foll by *for*) *informal* to demand in an obvious manner: *our inner cities are crying out for redevelopment* **3** **for crying out loud** *informal* an exclamation of anger or dismay

crypt (krɪpt) *n* **1** a cellar, vault, or underground chamber, esp beneath a church, where it is often used as a chapel, burial place, etc **2** *anatomy* any pitlike recess or depression [c18 from Latin *crypta*, from Greek *kruptē* vault, secret place, from *kruptos* hidden, from *kruptein* to hide] > ˈcryptal *adj*

cryptaesthesia *or US* **cryptesthesia** (ˌkrɪptəsˈθiːzɪə) *n psychol* another term for **extrasensory perception**

cryptanalysis (ˌkrɪptəˈnælɪsɪs) *n* the study of codes and ciphers; cryptography [c20 from CRYPTOGRAPH + ANALYSIS] > cryptanalytic (ˌkrɪptænəˈlɪtɪk) *adj* > crypt'analyst *n*

cryptic (ˈkrɪptɪk) *or* **cryptical** *adj* **1** hidden; secret; occult **2** (esp of comments, sayings, etc) obscure in meaning **3** (of the coloration of animals) tending to conceal by disguising or camouflaging the shape [c17 from Late Latin *crypticus*, from Greek *kruptikos*, from *kruptos* concealed; see CRYPT] > ˈcryptically *adv*

crypto- *or before a vowel* **crypt-** *combining form* secret, hidden, or concealed: *cryptography; crypto-fascist* [New Latin, from Greek *kruptos* hidden, from *kruptein* to hide]

cryptobiont (ˌkrɪptəʊˈbaɪɒnt) *n* any organism that exhibits cryptobiosis

cryptobiosis (ˌkrɪptəʊbaɪˈəʊsɪs) *n zoology* a temporary state in an organism in which metabolic activity is absent or undetectable

cryptoclastic (ˌkrɪptəʊˈklæstɪk) *adj* (of minerals and rocks) composed of microscopic fragments

cryptocrystalline (ˌkrɪptəʊˈkrɪstəlaɪn) *adj* (of rocks) composed of crystals that can be distinguished individually only by the use of a polarizing microscope

cryptogam (ˈkrɪptəʊˌɡæm) *n* (in former plant classification schemes) any organism that does not produce seeds, including algae, fungi, mosses, and ferns. Compare **phanerogam** [c19 from New Latin *Cryptogamia*, from CRYPTO- + Greek *gamos* marriage] > ˌcryptoˈgamic *or* cryptogamous (krɪpˈtɒɡəməs) *adj*

cryptogenic (ˌkrɪptəʊˈdʒɛnɪk) *adj* (esp of diseases) of unknown or obscure origin

cryptograph (ˈkrɪptəʊˌɡrɑːf, -ˌɡrɑːf) *n* **1** something written in code or cipher **2** a code using secret symbols (**cryptograms**) **3** a device for translating text into cipher, or vice versa

cryptography (krɪpˈtɒɡrəfɪ) *n* the science or study of analysing and deciphering codes, ciphers, etc; cryptanalysis > cryp'tographer, cryp'tographist *or* cryp'tologist *n* > cryptographic (ˌkrɪptəˈɡræfɪk) *or* ˌcryptoˈgraphical *adj* > ˌcryptoˈgraphically *adv*

cryptomeria (ˌkrɪptəʊˈmɪərɪə) *n* a coniferous tree, *Cryptomeria japonica*, of China and Japan, with curved needle-like leaves and small round cones:

family *Taxodiaceae* [C19 from New Latin, from CRYPTO- + Greek *meros* part; so called because the seeds are hidden by scales]

cryptometer (krɪpˈtɒmɪtə) *n* an instrument used to determine the opacity of pigments and paints

cryptophyte (ˈkrɪptəˌfaɪt) *n* any perennial plant that bears its buds below the soil or water surface > **cryptophytic** (ˌkrɪptəˈfɪtɪk) *adj*

cryptorchid (krɪpˈtɔːkɪd) *n* **1** an animal or human in which the testes fail to descend into the scrotum ▷ *adj* **2** denoting or relating to such an individual [from CRYPTO- + *orchid*, from Greek *orkhis* testicle] > **cryp'torchid,ism** *n*

cryptosporidium (ˌkrɪptəʊspɒˈrɪdɪəm) *n* any parasitic sporozoan protozoan of the genus *Cryptosporidium*, species of which are parasites of birds and animals and can be transmitted to humans, causing severe abdominal pain and diarrhoea (**cryptosporidiosis**)

cryptozoic (ˌkrɪptəʊˈzəʊɪk) *adj* (of animals) living in dark places, such as holes, caves, and beneath stones

Cryptozoic (ˌkrɪptəʊˈzəʊɪk) *adj* **1** of or relating to that part of geological time represented by rocks in which the evidence of life is slight and the life forms are primitive; pre-Phanerozoic ▷ *n* **2** the the Cryptozoic era ▷ See also **Precambrian** Compare **Phanerozoic**

cryptozoite (ˌkrɪptəʊˈzəʊaɪt) *n* a malarial parasite at the stage of development in its host before it enters the red blood cells

cryptozoology (ˌkrɪptəʊzəʊˈɒlədʒɪ, -zuː-) *n* the study of creatures, such as the Loch Ness monster, whose existence has not been scientifically proved

cryst. *abbreviation for* **1** crystalline **2** *Also:* **crystall** crystallography

crystal (ˈkrɪstəl) *n* **1** a piece of solid substance, such as quartz, with a regular shape in which plane faces intersect at definite angles, due to the regular internal structure of its atoms, ions, or molecules **2** a single grain of a crystalline substance **3** anything resembling a crystal, such as a piece of cut glass **4 a** a highly transparent and brilliant type of glass, often used in cut-glass tableware, ornaments, etc **b** (*as modifier*): *a crystal chandelier* **5** something made of or resembling crystal **6** crystal glass articles collectively **7** *electronics* **a** a crystalline element used in certain electronic devices as a detector, oscillator, transducer, etc **b** (*as modifier*): *crystal pick-up; crystal detector* **8** a transparent cover for the face of a watch, usually of glass or plastic **9** (*modifier*) of or relating to a crystal or the regular atomic arrangement of crystals: *crystal structure; crystal lattice* ▷ *adj* **10** resembling crystal; transparent: *crystal water* [Old English *cristalla*, from Latin *crystallum*, from Greek *krustallos* ice, crystal, from *krustainein* to freeze]

crystal ball *n* the glass globe used in crystal gazing

crystal class *n crystallog* any of 32 possible types of crystals, classified according to their rotational symmetry about axes through a point. *Also called:* point group

crystal counter *n* an instrument for detecting and measuring the intensity of high-energy radiation, in which particles collide with a crystal and momentarily increase its conductivity

crystal detector *n electronics* a demodulator, used esp in microwave circuits and in early radio receivers, consisting of a thin metal wire in point contact with a semiconductor crystal

crystal form *n crystallog* a symmetrical set of planes in space, associated with a crystal, having the same symmetry as the crystal class. Compare **crystal habit**

crystal gazing *n* **1** the act of staring into a crystal globe (**crystal ball**) supposedly in order to arouse visual perceptions of the future, etc **2** the act of trying to predict something > **crystal gazer** *n*

crystal habit *n crystallog* the external shape of a crystal. Compare **crystal form**

crystal healing *n* (in alternative therapy) the use of the supposed power of crystals to affect the human energy field

crystal lattice *n* the regular array of points about which the atoms, ions, or molecules composing a crystal are centred

crystalline (ˈkrɪstəˌlaɪn) *adj* **1** having the characteristics or structure of crystals **2** consisting of or containing crystals **3** made of or like crystal; transparent; clear > **crystallinity** (ˌkrɪstəˈlɪnɪtɪ) *n*

crystalline lens *n* a biconvex transparent elastic structure in the eye situated behind the iris, serving to focus images on the retina

crystallite (ˈkrɪstəˌlaɪt) *n* any of the minute rudimentary or imperfect crystals occurring in many glassy rocks > **crystallitic** (ˌkrɪstəˈlɪtɪk) *adj*

crystallize, crystalize, crystallise or **crystalise** (ˈkrɪstəˌlaɪz) *vb* **1** to form or cause to form crystals; assume or cause to assume a crystalline form or structure **2** to coat or become coated with sugar: *crystallized fruit* **3** to give a definite form or expression to (an idea, argument, etc) or (of an idea, argument, etc) to assume a recognizable or definite form > **'crystal,lizable, 'crystal,izable, 'crystal,lisable** or **'crystal,isable** *adj* > **,crystal,liza'bility, ,crystal,iza'bility, ,crystal,lisa'bility** or **,crystal,isa'bility** *n* > **,crystalli'zation, ,crystali'zation, ,crystalli'sation** or **,crystali'sation** *n* > **'crystal,lizer, 'crystal,izer, 'crystal,liser** or **'crystal,iser** *n*

crystallo- or *before a vowel* **crystall-** *combining form* crystal: *crystallography*

crystallog. *abbreviation for* crystallography

crystallography (ˌkrɪstəˈlɒɡrəfɪ) *n* the science concerned with the formation, properties, and structure of crystals > **,crystal'lographer** *n* > **,crystallo'graphic** (ˌkrɪstələʊˈɡræfɪk) *adj* > **,crystallo'graphically** *adv*

crystalloid (ˈkrɪstəˌlɔɪd) *adj* **1** resembling or having the appearance or properties of a crystal or crystalloid ▷ *n* **2** a substance that in solution can pass through a semipermeable membrane. Compare **colloid** (sense 3) **3** *botany* any of numerous crystals of protein occurring in certain seeds and other storage organs > **,crystal'loidal** *adj*

crystal microphone *n* a microphone that uses a piezoelectric crystal to convert sound energy into electrical energy

crystal nucleus *n chem* the tiny crystal that forms at the onset of crystallization

Crystal Palace *n* a building of glass and iron designed by Joseph Paxton to house the Great Exhibition of 1851. Erected in Hyde Park, London, it was moved to Sydenham (1852–53): destroyed by fire in 1936

crystal pick-up *n* a record-player pick-up in which the current is generated by the deformation of a piezoelectric crystal caused by the movements of the stylus

crystal set *n* an early form of radio receiver having a crystal detector to demodulate the radio signals but no amplifier, therefore requiring earphones

crystal system *n crystallog* any of six, or sometimes seven, classifications of crystals depending on their symmetry. The classes are cubic, tetragonal, hexagonal, orthorhombic, monoclinic, and triclinic. Sometimes an additional system, trigonal, is distinguished, although this is usually included in the hexagonal system. See also **crystal class**

crystal violet *n* another name for **gentian violet**

cry up *vb* (*tr, adverb*) to praise highly, extol

Cs *the chemical symbol for* caesium

CS *abbreviation for* **1** *Also:* **cs** capital stock **2** chartered surveyor **3** Christian Science **4** Christian Scientist **5** Civil Service **6** *Also:* **cs** Court of Session **7** (formerly) *international car registration for* Czechoslovakia

CSA (in Britain) *abbreviation for* Child Support Agency

CSB *abbreviation for* chemical stimulation of the brain

csc *abbreviation for* cosecant

CSC *abbreviation for* Civil Service Commission

CSCE *abbreviation for* (formerly) Conference for Security and Cooperation in Europe

csch *n* a US form of cosech

CSE (in Britain, formerly) *abbreviation for* Certificate of Secondary Education

CSF *abbreviation for* **1** *physiol* cerebrospinal fluid **2** *immunol* colony-stimulating factor

CS gas *n* a gas causing tears, salivation, and painful breathing, used in civil disturbances; *ortho*-chlorobenzal malononitrile. Formula: $C_6H_4ClCH:C(CN)_2$ [C20 from the surname initials of its US inventors, Ben Carson and Roger Staughton]

CSIRO (in Australia) *abbreviation for* Commonwealth Scientific and Industrial Research Organization

CSM (in Britain) *abbreviation for* **company sergeant-major**

C-spanner *n* a sickle-shaped spanner having a projection at the end of the curve, used for turning large narrow nuts that have an indentation into which the projection on the spanner fits

CSR (in Australia) *abbreviation for* Colonial Sugar Refining Company

CSS (in Britain) *abbreviation for* Certificate in Social Service

CSS² *abbreviation for computing* cascading style sheet

CST *abbreviation for* **Central Standard Time**

CSV *abbreviation for* Community Service Volunteer

CSYS (in Scotland) *abbreviation for* Certificate of Sixth Year Studies

ct *abbreviation for* **1** cent **2** court

CT *abbreviation for* **1** central time **2** Connecticut **3** computerized tomography (see also **CT scanner**)

CTC (in Britain) *abbreviation for* **city technology college**

ctenidium (tɪˈnɪdɪəm) *n, pl* **-ia** (-ɪə) one of the comblike respiratory gills of molluscs [C19 New Latin, from Greek *ktenidion*, diminutive of *kteis* comb]

ctenoid (ˈtiːnɔɪd, ˈtɛn-) *adj biology* toothed like a comb, as the scales of perches [C19 from Greek *ktenoeidēs*, from *kteis* comb + *-oeidēs* -OID]

ctenophore (ˈtɛnəˌfɔː, ˈtiːnə-) *n* any marine invertebrate of the phylum *Ctenophora*, including the sea gooseberry and Venus's-girdle, whose body bears eight rows of fused cilia, for locomotion. *Also called:* **comb jelly** [C19 from New Latin *ctenophorus*, from Greek *kteno-, kteis* comb + -PHORE] > **ctenophoran** (tɪˈnɒfərən) *adj, n*

Ctesiphon (ˈtɛsɪˌfɒn) *n* an ancient city on the River Tigris about 100 km (60 miles) above Babylon. First mentioned in 221 BC, it was destroyed in the 7th and 8th centuries A.D

ctn *abbreviation for* cotangent

CTO *philately abbreviation for* cancelled to order (of postage stamps); postmarked in sheets for private sale

CTR *abbreviation for* Control Traffic Zone: an area established around an airport to afford protection to aircraft entering or leaving the terminal area

cts *abbreviation for* cents

CT scanner *n* computerized tomography scanner: an X-ray machine that can produce stereographic images. Former name: **CAT scanner**

CTU (in New Zealand) *abbreviation for* Conference of Trade Unions

CTV *abbreviation for* Canadian Television Network Limited

cu *the internet domain name for* Cuba

Cu *the chemical symbol for* copper [from Late Latin *cuprum*]

CU¹ *text messaging abbreviation for* see you

CU² *international car registration for* Cuba

cu. *abbreviation for* cubic

C

cub (kʌb) *n* **1** the young of certain animals, such as the lion, bear, etc **2** a young or inexperienced person ▷ *vb* **cubs, cubbing, cubbed 3** to give birth to (cubs) [c16 perhaps from Old Norse *kubbi* young seal; see COB¹] > 'cubbish *adj* > 'cubbishly *adv*

Cub *n* short for **Cub Scout**

Cuba ('kjuːbə) *n* a republic and the largest island in the Caribbean, at the entrance to the Gulf of Mexico: became a Spanish colony after its discovery by Columbus in 1492; gained independence after the Spanish-American War of 1898 but remained subject to US influence until declared a people's republic under Castro in 1960; subject of an international crisis in 1962, when the US blockaded the island in order to compel the Soviet Union to dismantle its nuclear missile base. Sugar comprises about 80 per cent of total exports; the economy was badly affected by loss of trade following the collapse of the Soviet Union and by the continuing US trade embargo. Language: Spanish. Religion: nonreligious majority. Currency: peso. Capital: Havana. Pop: 11 328 000 (2004 est). Area: 110 922 sq km (42 827 sq miles)

cubage ('kjuːbɪdʒ) *n* another word for **cubature** (sense 2)

Cuba libre ('kjuːbə 'liːbrə) *n* chiefly US a drink of rum, cola, lime juice, and ice [Spanish, literally: free Cuba, a toast during the Cuban War of Independence]

Cuban ('kjuːbən) *adj* **1** of or relating to Cuba or its inhabitants ▷ *n* **2** a native or inhabitant of Cuba

cubane ('kjuːbeɪn) *n* a rare octahedral hydrocarbon formed by eight CH groups, each of which is situated at the corner of a cube. Formula: C_8H_8 **b** (*as modifier*): *cubane chemistry* [c20 from CUBE¹ + -ANE]

Cuban heel *n* a moderately high heel for a shoe or boot

cubature ('kjuːbətʃə) *n* **1** the determination of the cubic contents of something **2** Also called: **cubage** cubic contents [c17 from CUBE¹ + -ature, on the model of *quadrature*]

cubby ('kʌbɪ) *adj Midland English dialect* short and plump; squat

cubbyhole ('kʌbɪˌhəʊl) *n* **1** a small enclosed space or room **2** any small compartment, such as a pigeonhole Often shortened to: **cubby** ('kʌbɪ) [c19 from dialect *cub* cattle pen; see COVE¹]

cube¹ (kjuːb) *n* **1** a solid having six plane square faces in which the angle between two adjacent sides is a right angle **2** the product of three equal factors: the cube of 2 is 2 × 2 × 2 (usually written 2³) **3** something in the form of a cube: *a bath cube* ▷ *vb* **4** to raise (a number or quantity) to the third power **5** (*tr*) to measure the cubic contents of **6** (*tr*) to make, shape, or cut (something, esp food) into cubes **7** (*tr*) *US and Canadian* to tenderize (meat) by scoring into squares or by pounding with a device which has a surface of metal cubes [c16 from Latin *cubus* die, cube, from Greek *kubos*] > 'cuber *n*

cube² ('kjuːbeɪ) *n* **1** any of various tropical American plants, esp any of the leguminous genus *Lonchocarpus*, the roots of which yield rotenone **2** an extract from the roots of these plants: a fish poison and insecticide [American Spanish *cubé*, of unknown origin]

cubeb ('kjuːbɛb) *n* **1** a SE Asian treelike piperaceous woody climbing plant, *Piper cubeba*, with brownish berries **2** the unripe spicy fruit of this plant, dried and used as a stimulant and diuretic and sometimes smoked in cigarettes [c14 from Old French *cubebe*, from Medieval Latin *cubeba*, from Arabic *kubabah*]

cube farm *n US and Canadian informal* an office which is divided up by mid-height partitions to create separate work spaces

cube root *n* the number or quantity whose cube is a given number or quantity: 2 is the cube root of 8 (usually written ³√ 8 or 8⅓)

cube van *n Canadian* a van with a cube-shaped

storage compartment that is wider and taller than the front of the vehicle

cubic ('kjuːbɪk) *adj* **1** having the shape of a cube **2 a** having three dimensions **b** denoting or relating to a linear measure that is raised to the third power: *a cubic metre*. Abbreviations: **cu.**, **c 3** *maths* of, relating to, or containing a variable to the third power or a term in which the sum of the exponents of the variables is three **4** Also: **isometric, regular** *crystallog* relating to or belonging to the crystal system characterized by three equal perpendicular axes. The unit cell of cubic crystals is a cube with a lattice point at each corner (**simple cubic**) and one in the cube's centre (**body-centred cubic**), or a lattice point at each corner and one at the centre of each face (**face-centred cubic**) ▷ *n* **5** *maths* **a** a cubic equation, such as $x^3 + x + 2 = 0$ **b** a cubic term or expression

cubical ('kjuːbɪkəl) *adj* **1** of or related to volume: *cubical expansion* **2** shaped like a cube **3** of or involving the third power > 'cubically *adv* > 'cubicalness *n*

cubicle ('kjuːbɪkəl) *n* **1** a partially or totally enclosed section of a room, as in a dormitory **2** an indoor construction designed to house individual cattle while allowing them free access to silage [c15 from Latin *cubiculum*, from *cubāre* to lie down, lie asleep]

cubic measure *n* a system of units for the measurement of volumes, based on the cubic inch, the cubic centimetre, etc

cubiculum (kjuːˈbɪkjʊləm) *n, pl* **-la** (-lə) an underground burial chamber in Imperial Rome, such as those found in the catacombs [c19 from Latin: CUBICLE]

cubiform ('kjuːbɪˌfɔːm) *adj* having the shape of a cube

cubism ('kjuːbɪzəm) *n* (*often capital*) a French school of painting, collage, relief, and sculpture initiated in 1907 by Pablo Picasso, the Spanish painter and sculptor (1881–1973) and Georges Braque, the French painter (1882–1963), which amalgamated viewpoints of natural forms into a multifaceted surface of geometrical planes > 'cubist *adj, n* > cu'bistic *adj* > cu'bistically *adv*

cubit ('kjuːbɪt) *n* an ancient measure of length based on the length of the forearm [c14 from Latin *cubitum* elbow, cubit]

cubital ('kjuːbɪtəl) *adj* of or relating to the forearm

cuboid ('kjuːbɔɪd) *adj also* **cuboidal** (kjuːˈbɔɪdəl) **1** shaped like a cube; cubic **2** of or denoting the cuboid bone ▷ *n* **3** the cubelike bone of the foot; the outer distal bone of the tarsus **4** *maths* a geometric solid whose six faces are rectangles; rectangular parallelepiped

Cu-bop ('kjuːˌbɒp) *n jazz* music of the 1940s in which Cuban rhythms are combined with bop. Compare **Afro-Cuban**

cub reporter *n* a trainee reporter on a newspaper

Cub Scout *or* **Cub** *n* a member of a junior branch (for those aged 8–11 years) of the Scout Association

Cuchulain, Cuchulainn *or* **Cuchullain** (kuːˈkʌlɪn, kʊˈxʊlɪn) *n Celtic myth* a legendary hero of Ulster

cucking stool ('kʌkɪŋ) *n history* a stool to which suspected witches, scolds, etc, were tied and pelted or ducked into water as a punishment. Compare **ducking stool** [c13 *cucking stol*, literally: defecating chair, from *cukken* to defecate; compare Old Norse *kúkr* excrement]

cuckold ('kʌkəld) *n* **1** a man whose wife has committed adultery, often regarded as an object of scorn ▷ *vb* **2** (*tr*) to make a cuckold of [c13 *cukeweld*, from Old French *cucuault*, from *cucu* CUCKOO; perhaps an allusion to the parasitic cuckoos that lay their eggs in the nests of other birds] > 'cuckoldry *n*

cuckoo ('kʊkuː) *n, pl* **-oos 1** any bird of the family Cuculidae, having medium-long wings, a long tail, and zygodactyl feet: order Cuculiformes. Many species, including the **European cuckoo** (*Cuculus canorus*), lay their eggs in the nests of other birds and have

a two-note call **2** *informal* an insane or foolish person ▷ *adj* **3** *informal* insane or foolish ▷ *interj* **4** an imitation or representation of the call of a cuckoo ▷ *vb* **-oos, -ooing, -ooed 5** (*tr*) to repeat over and over **6** (*intr*) to make the sound imitated by the word *cuckoo* [c13 from Old French *cucu*, of imitative origin; related to German *kuckuck*, Latin *cucūlus*, Greek *kokkux*]

cuckoo bee *n* any of several species of parasitic or inquiline bee the queen of which lays her eggs in the nest of the bumblebee or other species, sometimes killing the host queen, leaving her eggs to be raised by the workers of the nest

cuckoo clock *n* a clock in which a mechanical cuckoo pops out with a sound like a cuckoo's call when the clock strikes

cuckooflower ('kʊkuːˌflaʊə) *n* another name for **lady's-smock** and **ragged robin**

cuckoopint ('kʊkuːˌpaɪnt) *n* a European aroid plant, *Arum maculatum*, with arrow-shaped leaves, a spathe marked with purple, a pale purple spadix, and scarlet berries. Also called: **lords-and-ladies**, (chiefly US) **wake-robin**

cuckoo shrike *n* any Old World tropical songbird of the family *Campephagidae*, typically having a strong notched bill, long rounded tail, and pointed wings. See also **minivet**

cuckoo spit *n* a white frothy mass on the stems and leaves of many plants, produced by froghopper larvae (**cuckoo spit insects**) which feed on the plant juices. Also called: **frog spit**

cuculiform (kjʊˈkjuːlɪˌfɔːm) *adj* of, relating to, or belonging to the order *Cuculiformes*, which includes the cuckoos [from Latin *cucūlus* cuckoo + -FORM]

cucullate ('kjuːkəˌleɪt, -lɪt) *adj* shaped like a hood or having a hoodlike part: *cucullate sepals* [c18 from Late Latin *cucullātus*, from Latin *cucullus* hood, cap] > 'cucul,lately *adv*

cucumber ('kjuːˌkʌmbə) *n* **1** a creeping cucurbitaceous plant, *Cucumis sativus*, cultivated in many forms for its edible fruit. Compare **squirting cucumber 2** the cylindrical fruit of this plant, which has hard thin green rind and white crisp flesh **3** any of various similar or related plants or their fruits **4 cool as a cucumber** very calm; self-possessed [c14 from Latin *cucumis*, of unknown origin]

cucumber tree *n* **1** any of several American trees or shrubs of the genus *Magnolia*, esp *M. acuminata*, of E and central North America, having cup-shaped greenish flowers and cucumber-shaped fruits **2** an E Asian tree, *Averrhoa bilimbi*, with edible fruits resembling small cucumbers: family *Averrhoaceae*. See also **carambola**

cucurbit (kjuːˈkɜːbɪt) *n* any creeping flowering plant of the mainly tropical and subtropical family Cucurbitaceae, which includes the pumpkin, cucumber, squashes, and gourds [c14 from Old French, from Latin *cucurbita* gourd, cup] > cu,curbi'taceous *adj*

Cúcuta (*Spanish* 'kukuta) *n* a city in E Colombia: commercial centre of a coffee-producing region. Pop: 883 000 (2005 est). Official name: San José de Cúcuta (san xo'se ðe)

cud (kʌd) *n* **1** partially digested food regurgitated from the first stomach of cattle and other ruminants to the mouth for a second chewing **2 chew the cud** to reflect or think over something [Old English *cudu*, from *cwidu* what has been chewed; related to Old Norse *kvātha* resin (for chewing), Old High German *quiti* glue, Sanskrit *jatu* rubber]

cudbear ('kʌdˌbɛə) *n* another name for **orchil** [c18 whimsical alteration of *Cuthbert*, the Christian name of Dr Gordon, 18th-century Scot who patented the dye. See CUDDY²]

cuddle ('kʌdəl) *vb* **1** to hold (another person or thing) close or (of two people, etc) to hold each other close, as for affection, comfort, or warmth; embrace; hug **2** (*intr; foll by up*) to curl or snuggle up into a comfortable or warm position ▷ *n* **3** a close embrace, esp when prolonged [c18 of uncertain origin] > 'cuddlesome *adj* > 'cuddly *adj*

cuddy¹ ('kʌdɪ) *n, pl* **-dies 1** a small cabin in a boat **2** a small room, cupboard, etc [C17 perhaps from Dutch *kajute*; compare Old French *cahute*]

cuddy² *or* **cuddie** ('kʌdɪ) *n, pl* **-dies** *dialect, chiefly Scot* a donkey or horse [C18 probably from *Cuddy*, nickname for *Cuthbert*]

cuddy³ ('kʌdɪ) *n, pl* **-dies** a young coalfish [C18 of unknown origin]

cudgel ('kʌdʒəl) *n* **1** a short stout stick used as a weapon **2 take up the cudgels** (often foll by *for* or *on behalf of*) to join in a dispute, esp to defend oneself or another ▷ *vb* **-els, -elling, -elled** *or US* **-els, -eling, -eled 3** (*tr*) to strike with a cudgel or similar weapon **4 cudgel one's brains** to think hard about a problem [Old English *cycgel*; related to Middle Dutch *koghele* stick with knob] > 'cudgeller *n*

cudgerie ('kʌdʒərɪ) *n Austral* **1** a large tropical rutaceous tree, *Flindersia schottina*, having light-coloured wood **2** Also called: **pink poplar** an anacardiaceous rainforest tree, *Euroschinus falcatus*

cudweed ('kʌd,wiːd) *n* **1** any of various temperate woolly plants of the genus *Gnaphalium*, having clusters of whitish or yellow button-like flowers: family *Asteraceae* (composites) **2** any of several similar and related plants of the genus *Filago*, esp *F. germanica*

cue¹ (kjuː) *n* **1 a** (in the theatre, films, music, etc) anything spoken or done that serves as a signal to an actor, musician, etc, to follow with specific lines or action **b on cue** at the right moment **2** a signal or reminder to do something **3** *psychol* the part of any sensory pattern that is identified as the signal for a response **4** the part, function, or action assigned to or expected of a person ▷ *vb* **cues, cueing, cued 5** (*tr*) to give a cue or cues to (an actor) **6** (usually foll by *in* or *into*) to signal (to something or somebody) at a specific moment in a musical or dramatic performance: *to cue in a flourish of trumpets* **7** (*tr*) to give information or a reminder to (someone) **8** (*intr*) to signal the commencement of filming, as with the word "Action!" [C16 probably from name of the letter *q*, used in an actor's script to represent Latin *quando* when]

cue² (kjuː) *n* **1** *billiards, snooker* a long tapered shaft with a leather tip, used to drive the balls **2** hair caught at the back forming a tail or braid **3** *US* a variant spelling of **queue** ▷ *vb* **cues, cueing, cued 4** to drive (a ball) with a cue **5** (*tr*) to twist or tie (the hair) into a cue [C18 variant of **queue**]

cue ball *n billiards, snooker* the ball struck by the cue, as distinguished from the object balls

cue bid *n contract bridge* a bid in a suit made to show an ace or a void in that suit

cueing ('kjuːɪŋ) *n* another name for **foldback**

Cuenca (*Spanish* 'kweŋka) *n* **1** a city in SW Ecuador: university (1868). Pop: 311 000 (2005 est) **2** a town in central Spain: prosperous in the Middle Ages for its silver and textile industries. Pop: 47 201 (2003 est)

Cuernavaca (*Spanish* kwerna'βaka) *n* a city in S central Mexico, capital of Morelos state: resort with nearby Cacahuamilpa Caverns. Pop: 723 000 (2005 est)

cuesta ('kwɛstə) *n* a long low ridge with a steep scarp slope and a gentle back slope, formed by the differential erosion of strata of differing hardness [Spanish: shoulder, from Latin *costa* side, rib]

cuff¹ (kʌf) *n* **1** the part of a sleeve nearest the hand, sometimes turned back and decorative **2** the part of a gauntlet or glove that extends past the wrist **3** *US, Canadian, and Austral* the turned-up fold at the bottom of some trouser legs. Also called (in eg Britain): **turn-up 4 off the cuff** *informal* improvised; extemporary ▷ See also **cuffs** [C14 *cuffe* glove, of obscure origin]

cuff² (kʌf) *vb* **1** (*tr*) to strike with an open hand ▷ *n* **2** a blow of this kind [C16 of obscure origin]

cuff link *n* one of a pair of linked buttons, used to join the buttonholes on the cuffs of a shirt

cuffs (kʌfs) *pl n informal* short for **handcuffs**

Cufic ('kuːfɪk, 'kjuː-) *n, adj* a variant spelling of **Kufic**

Cuiabá *or* **Cuyabá** (*Portuguese* kuia'ba) *n* **1** a port in W Brazil, capital of Mato Grosso state, on the Cuiabá River. Pop: 777 000 (2005 est) **2** a river in SW Brazil, rising on the Mato Grosso plateau and flowing southwest into the São Lourenço River. Length: 483 km (300 miles)

cui bono *Latin* (kwiː 'bəʊnəʊ) for whose benefit? for what purpose?

cuirass (kwɪ'ræs) *n* **1** a piece of armour, of leather or metal covering the chest and back **2** a hard outer protective covering of some animals, consisting of shell, plate, or scales **3** any similar protective covering, as on a ship ▷ *vb* **4** (*tr*) to equip with a cuirass [C15 from French *cuirasse*, from Late Latin *coriacea*, from *coriaceus* made of leather, from Latin *corium* leather]

cuirassier (,kwɪərə'sɪə) *n* a mounted soldier, esp of the 16th century, who wore a cuirass

cuir-bouilli (,kwiːəbuː'jiː) *n* a type of leather hardened by soaking in wax, used for armour before the 14th century [French, literally: boiled leather]

Cuisenaire rod (,kwiːzə'nɛə) *n trademark* one of a set of rods of various colours and lengths representing different numbers, used to teach arithmetic to young children [C20 named after Emil-Georges *Cuisenaire* (?1891–1976), Belgian educationalist]

cuisine (kwɪ'ziːn) *n* **1** a style or manner of cooking: *French cuisine* **2** the food prepared by a restaurant, household, etc [C18 from French, literally: kitchen, from Late Latin *coquīna*, from Latin *coquere* to cook]

cuisine minceur *French* (kɥizin mɛ̃sœr) *n* a style of cooking, originating in France, that limits the use of starch, sugar, butter, and cream traditionally used in French cookery [literally: slimness cooking]

cuisse (kwɪs) *or* **cuish** (kwɪʃ) *n* a piece of armour for the thigh [C15 back formation from *cuisses* (plural), from Old French *cuisseaux* thigh guards, from *cuisse* thigh, from Latin *coxa* hipbone]

culch *or* **cultch** (kʌltʃ) *n* **1** a mass of broken stones, shells, and gravel that forms the basis of an oyster bed **2** the oyster spawn attached to such a structure **3** *dialect* refuse; rubbish [C17 perhaps ultimately from Old French *culche* bed, **couch**]

culchie ('kʌltʃiː) *n Irish informal* a rough or unsophisticated country-dweller from outside Dublin [from a local pronunciation of the Mayo town of Kiltimagh]

cul-de-sac ('kʌldə,sæk, 'kʊl-) *n, pl* **culs-de-sac** *or* **cul-de-sacs 1** a road with one end blocked off; dead end **2** an inescapable position **3** any tube-shaped bodily cavity or pouch closed at one end, such as the caecum [C18 from French, literally: bottom of the bag]

-cule *suffix forming nouns* indicating smallness: *animalcule* [from Latin *-culus*, diminutive suffix; compare **-CLE**]

Culebra Cut (kuː'lɛbrə) *n* the former name of the **Gaillard Cut**

culet ('kjuːlɪt) *n* **1** *jewellery* the flat face at the bottom of a gem **2** either of the plates of armour worn at the small of the back [C17 from obsolete French, diminutive of *cul*, from Latin *cūlus* bottom]

culex ('kjuːlɛks) *n, pl* **-lices** (-lɪ,siːz) any mosquito of the genus *Culex*, such as *C. pipiens*, the common mosquito [C15 from Latin: midge, gnat; related to Old Irish *cuil* gnat]

Culham ('kʌləm) *n* a village in S central England, in Oxfordshire: site of the UK centre for thermonuclear reactor research and of the Joint European Torus (JET) programme

Culiacán (*Spanish* kulja'kan) *n* a city in NW Mexico, capital of Sinaloa state. Pop: 799 000 (2005 est)

culicid (kjuː'lɪsɪd) *n* **1** any dipterous insect of the family *Culicidae*, which comprises the mosquitos ▷ *adj* **2** of, relating to, or belonging to the *Culicidae* [C19 from New Latin *Culicidae*, from Latin *culex* gnat, **CULEX**]

culinary ('kʌlɪnərɪ) *adj* of, relating to, or used in the kitchen or in cookery [C17 from Latin *culīna* kitchen] > 'culinarily *adv*

cull (kʌl) *vb* (*tr*) **1** to choose or gather the best or required examples **2** to take out (an animal, esp an inferior one) from a herd **3** to reduce the size of (a herd or flock) by killing a proportion of its members **4** to gather (flowers, fruit, etc) **5** to cease to employ; get rid of ▷ *n* **6** the act or product of culling **7** an inferior animal taken from a herd or group [C15 from Old French *coillir* to pick, from Latin *colligere*; see **COLLECT**¹]

cullender ('kʌlɪndə) *n* a variant of **colander**

culler ('kʌlə) *n* **1** a person employed to cull animals **2** *Austral and NZ* an animal, esp a sheep, designated for culling

cullet ('kʌlɪt) *n* waste glass for melting down to be reused [C17 perhaps variant of **COLLET** (literally: little neck, referring to the glass neck of newly blown bottles, etc)]

cullis ('kʌlɪs) *n* **1** a gutter in or at the eaves of a roof **2** another word for **coulisse** (sense 1) [C19 from French *coulisse* channel, groove; see **COULISSE**]

Culloden (kə'lɒdən) *n* a moor near Inverness in N Scotland: site of a battle in 1746 in which government troops under the Duke of Cumberland defeated the Jacobites under Prince Charles Edward Stuart

cully ('kʌlɪ) *n, pl* **-lies** *slang* pal; mate [C17 of unknown origin]

culm¹ (kʌlm) *n mining* **1** coal-mine waste **2** inferior anthracite [C14 probably related to **COAL**]

culm² (kʌlm) *n* the hollow jointed stem of a grass or sedge [C17 from Latin *culmus* stalk; see **HAULM**]

Culm *or* **Culm Measures** *n* a formation consisting mainly of shales and sandstone deposited during the Carboniferous period in parts of Europe [C19 from **CULM**¹]

culmiferous (kʌl'mɪfərəs) *adj* (of grasses) having a hollow jointed stem

culminant ('kʌlmɪnənt) *adj* highest or culminating

culminate ('kʌlmɪ,neɪt) *vb* **1** (when *intr*, usually foll by *in*) to end or cause to end, esp to reach or bring to a final or climactic stage **2** (*intr*) (of a celestial body) to cross the meridian of the observer [C17 from Late Latin *culmināre* to reach the highest point, from Latin *culmen* top]

culmination (,kʌlmɪ'neɪʃən) *n* **1** the final, highest, or decisive point **2** the act of culminating **3** *astronomy* the highest or lowest altitude attained by a heavenly body as it crosses the meridian

culottes (kjuː'lɒts) *pl n* women's flared trousers cut to look like a skirt [C20 from French, literally: breeches, from *cul* bottom; see **CULET**]

culpa ('kʊlpɑː) *n, pl* **-pae** (-piː) **1** *civil law* an act of neglect; a fault; sin; guilt [Latin: fault]

culpable ('kʌlpəb°l) *adj* deserving censure; blameworthy [C14 from Old French *coupable*, from Latin *culpābilis*, from *culpāre* to blame, from *culpa* fault] > ,culpa'bility *or* 'culpableness *n* > 'culpably *adv*

culpable homicide *n Scots law* manslaughter

culprit ('kʌlprɪt) *n* **1** *law* a person awaiting trial, esp one who has pleaded not guilty **2** the person responsible for a particular offence, misdeed, etc [C17 from Anglo-French *cul-*, short for *culpable* guilty + *prit* ready, indicating that the prosecution was ready to prove the guilt of the one charged]

CUL8R *text messaging abbreviation for* see you later

cult (kʌlt) *n* **1** a specific system of religious worship, esp with reference to its rites and deity **2** a sect devoted to such a system **3** a quasi-religious organization using devious psychological techniques to gain and control adherents **4** *sociol* a group having an exclusive ideology and ritual practices centred on sacred

C

symbols, esp one characterized by lack of organizational structure **5** intense interest in and devotion to a person, idea, or activity: *the cult of yoga* **6** the person, idea, etc, arousing such devotion **7 a** something regarded as fashionable or significant by a particular group **b** (*as modifier*): *a cult show* **8** (*modifier*) of, relating to, or characteristic of a cult or cults: *a cult figure* [c17 from Latin *cultus* cultivation, refinement, from *colere* to till] > **'cultism** *n* > **'cultist** *n*

cultch (kʌltʃ) *n* a variant spelling of **culch**

cultic ('kʌltɪk) *adj* of or relating to a religious cult

cultigen ('kʌltɪdʒən) *n* a species of plant that is known only as a cultivated form and did not originate from a wild type [c20 from CULTI(VATED) + -GEN]

cultish ('kʌltɪʃ) *or* **culty** ('kʌltɪ) *adj* intended to appeal to a small group of fashionable people > **'cultishly** *adv*

cultivable ('kʌltɪvəbᵊl) *or* **cultivatable** ('kʌltɪˌveɪtəbᵊl) *adj* (of land) capable of being cultivated [c17 from French, from Old French *cultiver* to CULTIVATE] > ˌcultiva'bility *n*

cultivar ('kʌltɪˌvɑː) *n* a variety of a plant that was produced from a natural species and is maintained by cultivation [c20 from CULTI(VATED) + VAR(IETY)]

cultivate ('kʌltɪˌveɪt) *vb* (*tr*) **1** to till and prepare (land or soil) for the growth of crops **2** to plant, tend, harvest, or improve (plants) by labour and skill **3** to break up (land or soil) with a cultivator or hoe **4** to improve or foster (the mind, body, etc) as by study, education, or labour **5** to give special attention to: *to cultivate a friendship; to cultivate a hobby* **6** to give or bring culture to (a person, society, etc); civilize [c17 from Medieval Latin *cultivāre* to till, from Old French *cultiver,* from Medieval Latin *cultīvus* cultivable, from Latin *cultus* cultivated, from *colere* to till, toil over]

cultivated ('kʌltɪˌveɪtɪd) *adj* **1** cultured, refined, or educated **2** (of land or soil) **a** subjected to tillage or cultivation **b** tilled and broken up **3** (of plants) specially bred or improved by cultivation

cultivation (ˌkʌltɪ'veɪʃən) *n* **1** *agriculture* **a** the planting, tending, improving, or harvesting of crops or plants **b** the preparation of ground to promote their growth **2** development, esp through education, training, etc **3** culture or sophistication, esp social refinement

cultivator ('kʌltɪˌveɪtə) *n* **1** a farm implement equipped with shovels, blades, etc, used to break up soil and remove weeds **2** a person or thing that cultivates **3** a person who grows, tends, or improves plants or crops

cultrate ('kʌltreɪt) *or* **cultrated** *adj* shaped like a knife blade: *cultrate leaves* [c19 from Latin *cultrātus,* from *culter* knife]

cultural ('kʌltʃərəl) *adj* **1** of or relating to artistic or social pursuits or events considered to be valuable or enlightened **2** of or relating to a culture or civilization **3** (of certain varieties of plant) obtained by specialized breeding > **'culturally** *adv*

cultural anthropology *n* the branch of anthropology dealing with cultural as opposed to biological and racial features > **cultural anthropologist** *n*

cultural lag *or* **culture lag** *n* the difference in the rate of change between two parts of a culture

Cultural Revolution *n* (in China) a mass movement (1965–68), in which the youthful Red Guard played a prominent part. It was initiated by Mao Tse-tung to destroy the power of the bureaucrats and to revolutionize the attitudes and behaviour of the people. Also called: **Great Proletarian Cultural Revolution**

culture ('kʌltʃə) *n* **1** the total of the inherited ideas, beliefs, values, and knowledge, which constitute the shared bases of social action **2** the total range of activities and ideas of a group of people with shared traditions, which are transmitted and reinforced by members of the group: *the Mayan culture* **3** a particular civilization at a particular period **4** the artistic and social pursuits, expression, and tastes valued by a society or class, as in the arts, manners, dress, etc **5** the enlightenment or refinement resulting from these pursuits **6** the attitudes, feelings, values, and behaviour that characterize and inform society as a whole or any social group within it: *yob culture* **7** the cultivation of plants, esp by scientific methods designed to improve stock or to produce new ones **8** *stockbreeding* the rearing and breeding of animals, esp with a view to improving the strain **9** the act or practice of tilling or cultivating the soil **10** *biology* **a** the experimental growth of microorganisms, such as bacteria and fungi, in a nutrient substance (see **culture medium**), usually under controlled conditions **b** a group of microorganisms grown in this way ▷ *vb* (*tr*) **11** to cultivate (plants or animals) **12** to grow (microorganisms) in a culture medium [c15 from Old French, from Latin *cultūra* a cultivating, from *colere* to till; see CULT] > **'culturist** *n* > **'cultureless** *adj*

cultured ('kʌltʃəd) *adj* **1** showing or having good taste, manners, upbringing, and education **2** artificially grown or synthesized: *cultured pearls*

cultured pearl *n* a pearl induced to grow in the shell of an oyster or clam, by the insertion of a small object around which layers of nacre are deposited

culture-free test *n* a test (usually for intelligence) that does not put anyone taking it at a disadvantage, for instance, as regards material or cultural background

culture jamming *n* a form of political and social activism which, by means of fake adverts, hoax news stories, pastiches of company logos and product labels, computer hacking, etc, draws attention to and at the same time subverts the power of the media, governments, and large corporations to control and distort the information that they give to the public in order to promote consumerism, militarism, etc

culture medium *n* a nutritive substance, such as an agar gel or liquid medium, in which cultures of bacteria, fungi, animal cells, or plant cells are grown

culture shock *n* *sociol* the feelings of isolation, rejection, etc, experienced when one culture is brought into sudden contact with another, as when a primitive tribe is confronted by modern civilization

culture vulture *n* *informal* a person considered to be excessively, and often pretentiously, interested in the arts

cultus ('kʌltəs) *n, pl* **-tuses** *or* **-ti** (-taɪ) *chiefly RC Church* another word for **cult** (sense 1) [c17 from Latin: a toiling over something, refinement, CULT]

culver ('kʌlvə) *n* an archaic or poetic name for **pigeon¹** *or* **dove¹** [Old English *culfre,* from Latin *columbula* a little dove, from *columba* dove]

culverin ('kʌlvərɪn) *n* **1** a long-range medium to heavy cannon used during the 15th, 16th, and 17th centuries **2** a medieval musket [c15 from Old French *couleuvrine,* from *couleuvre,* from Latin *coluber* serpent]

Culver's root *or* **physic** ('kʌlvəz) *n* **1** a tall North American scrophulariaceous plant, *Veronicastrum virginicum,* having spikes of small white or purple flowers **2** the dried roots of this plant, formerly used as a cathartic and emetic [c19 named after a Dr Culver, 18th-century American physician]

culvert ('kʌlvət) *n* **1** a drain or covered channel that crosses under a road, railway, etc **2** a channel for an electric cable **3** a tunnel through which water is pumped into or out of a dry dock [c18 of unknown origin]

Culzean Castle (kə'leɪn) *n* a Gothic Revival castle near Ayr in South Ayrshire, in SW Scotland: designed by Robert Adam (1772–92); includes a room dedicated to General Eisenhower

cum (kʌm) *prep* used between two nouns to designate an object of a combined nature: *a kitchen-cum-dining room* [Latin: with, together with, along with]

cumacean (kjʊ'meɪʃᵊn) *n* **1** any small malacostracan marine crustacean of the *Cumacea* family, mostly dwelling on the sea bed but sometimes found among the plankton ▷ *adj* **2** of, relating to, or belonging to the *Cumacea* [c19 from New Latin *cuma,* from Greek *kuma* (see CYMA) + -EAN]

Cumae ('kjuːmiː) *n* the oldest Greek colony in Italy, founded about 750 BC near Naples > **Cu'maean** *adj*

Cumaná (*Spanish* kuma'na) *n* a city in NE Venezuela: founded in 1523; the oldest European settlement in South America. Pop: 271 000 (2005 est)

cumber ('kʌmbə) *vb* (*tr*) **1** to obstruct or hinder **2** *obsolete* to inconvenience ▷ *n* **3** a hindrance or burden [c13 probably from Old French *combrer* to impede, prevent, from *combre* barrier; see ENCUMBER] > **'cumberer** *n*

Cumberland ('kʌmbələnd) *n* (until 1974) a county of NW England, now part of Cumbria

Cumberland sauce *n* *Brit* a cold sauce made from orange and lemon juice, port, and redcurrant jelly, served with ham, game, or other meat

Cumbernauld (ˌkʌmbə'nɔːld) *n* a town in central Scotland, in North Lanarkshire, northeast of Glasgow: developed as a new town since 1956. Pop: 49 664 (2001)

cumbersome ('kʌmbəsəm) *or* **cumbrous** ('kʌmbrəs) *adj* **1** awkward because of size, weight, or shape: *cumbersome baggage* **2** difficult because of extent or complexity: *cumbersome accounts* [c14 *cumber,* short for ENCUMBER + -SOME¹] > **'cumbersomely** *or* **'cumbrously** *adv* > **'cumbersomeness** *or* **'cumbrousness** *n*

cumbrance ('kʌmbrəns) *n* **1** a burden, obstacle, or hindrance **2** trouble or bother

Cumbria ('kʌmbrɪə) *n* (since 1974) a county of NW England comprising the former counties of Westmorland and Cumberland together with N Lancashire: includes the Lake District mountain area and surrounding coastal lowlands with the Pennine uplands in the extreme east. Administrative centre: Carlisle. Pop: 489 800 (2003 est). Area: 6810 sq km (2629 sq miles)

Cumbrian ('kʌmbrɪən) *adj* **1** of or relating to Cumbria or its inhabitants ▷ *n* **2** a native or inhabitant of Cumbria

Cumbrian Mountains ('kʌmbrɪən) *pl n* a mountain range in NW England, in Cumbria. Highest peak: Scafell Pike, 977 m (3206 ft)

cumbungi (kʌm'bʌŋgɪ) *n* any of various tall Australian marsh plants of the genus *Typha* [from a native Australian language]

cum dividend *adv* (of shares, etc) with the right to current dividend. Compare **ex dividend** [*cum,* from Latin: with]

cum grano salis *Latin* (kʊm 'grɑːnəʊ 'sɑːlɪs) *adv* with a grain of salt; not too literally

cumin *or* **cummin** ('kʌmɪn) *n* **1** an umbelliferous Mediterranean plant, *Cuminum cyminum,* with finely divided leaves and small white or pink flowers **2** the aromatic seeds (collectively) of this plant, used as a condiment and a flavouring [c12 from Old French, from Latin *cumīnum,* from Greek *kuminon,* of Semitic origin; compare Hebrew *kammōn*]

cum laude (kʌm 'lɔːdɪ, kʊm 'laʊdeɪ) *adv chiefly US* with praise: the lowest of three designations for above-average achievement in examinations. Compare **magna cum laude, summa cum laude** [Latin]

cummerbund *or* **kummerbund** ('kʌməˌbʌnd) *n* a wide sash, worn with a dinner jacket [c17 from Hindi *kamarband,* from Persian, from *kamar* loins, waist + *band* band]

cum new *adv, adj* (of shares, etc) with rights to take up any scrip or rights issue. Compare **ex new**

cumquat ('kʌmkwɒt) *n* a variant spelling of **kumquat**

cumshaw ('kʌmʃɔː) *n* (used, esp formerly, by beggars in Chinese ports) a present or tip [C19 from pidgin English, from Chinese (Amoy) *kam siā*, from Mandarin *kan hsieh* grateful thanks]

cumulate *vb* ('kjuːmjʊ,leɪt) **1** to accumulate **2** (*tr*) to combine (two or more sequences) into one ▷ *adj* ('kjuːmjʊlɪt, -,leɪt) **3** heaped up [C16 from Latin *cumulāre* from *cumulus* heap] > **'cumu'lation** *n*

cumulative ('kjuːmjʊlətɪv) *adj* **1** growing in quantity, strength, or effect by successive additions or gradual steps: *cumulative pollution* **2** gained by or resulting from a gradual building up: *cumulative benefits* **3** *finance* **a** (of preference shares) entitling the holder to receive any arrears of dividend before any dividend is distributed to ordinary shareholders **b** (of dividends or interest) intended to be accumulated if not paid when due **4** *statistics* **a** (of a frequency) including all values of a variable either below or above a specified value **b** (of error) tending to increase as the sample size is increased > **'cumulatively** *adv* > **'cumulativeness** *n*

cumulative distribution function *n statistics* a function defined on the sample space of a distribution and taking as its value at each point the probability that the random variable has that value or less. The function $F(x) = P(X \leq x)$ where X is the random variable, which is the sum or integral of the probability density function of the distribution. Sometimes shortened to: **distribution function**

cumulative evidence *n law* additional evidence reinforcing testimony previously given

cumulative voting *n* a system of voting in which each elector has as many votes as there are candidates in his constituency. Votes may all be cast for one candidate or distributed among several

cumulet ('kjuːmjʊlɪt) *n* (*sometimes capital*) a variety of domestic fancy pigeon, pure white or white with light red markings [C19 from CUMULUS]

cumuliform ('kjuːmjʊlɪ,fɔːm) *adj* resembling a cumulus cloud

cumulonimbus (,kjuːmjʊləʊ'nɪmbəs) *n, pl* **-bi** (-baɪ) *or* **-buses** *meteorol* a cumulus cloud of great vertical extent, the top often forming an anvil shape and the bottom being dark coloured, indicating rain or hail: associated with thunderstorms

cumulostratus (,kjuːmjʊləʊ'streɪtəs) *n, pl* **-ti** (-taɪ) *meteorol* another name for **stratocumulus**

cumulous ('kjuːmjʊləs) *adj* resembling or consisting of cumulus clouds

cumulus ('kjuːmjʊləs) *n, pl* **-li** (-,laɪ) **1** a bulbous or billowing white or dark grey cloud associated with rising air currents. Compare **cirrus** (sense 1), **stratus 2** *histology* the mass of cells surrounding a recently ovulated egg cell in a Graafian follicle [C17 from Latin: mass]

Cunaxa (kjuː'næksə) *n* the site near the lower Euphrates where Artaxerxes II defeated Cyrus the Younger in 401 BC

cunctation (kʌŋk'teɪʃən) *n rare* delay [C16 from Latin *cunctātiō* a hesitation, from *cunctārī* to delay] > **cunctative** ('kʌŋktətɪv) *adj* > **cunc'tator** *n*

cuneal ('kjuːnɪəl) *adj* wedge-shaped; cuneiform [C16 from Latin *cuneālis*, from *cuneus* wedge]

cuneate ('kjuːnɪɪt, -,eɪt) *adj* wedge-shaped: *cuneate leaves are attached at the narrow end* [C19 from Latin *cuneāre* to make wedge-shaped, from *cuneus* a wedge] > **'cuneately** *adv*

cuneiform ('kjuːnɪ,fɔːm) *adj* **1** Also: **cuneal wedge-shaped 2** of, relating to, or denoting the wedge-shaped characters employed in the writing of several ancient languages of Mesopotamia and Persia, esp Sumerian, Babylonian, etc **3** of or relating to a tablet in which this script is employed **4** of or relating to any of the three tarsal bones ▷ *n* **5** cuneiform characters or

writing **6** any one of the three tarsal bones [C17 probably from Old French *cunéiforme*, from Latin *cuneus* wedge]

Cuneo (*Italian* 'kuːneo) *n* a city in NW Italy, in Piedmont. Pop: 52 334 (2001)

cuneus ('kjuːnɪəs) *n* a small wedge-shaped area of the cerebral cortex [C19 from Latin *cuneus* wedge]

cunjevoi ('kʌndʒɪ,vɔɪ) *n Austral* **1** an aroid plant, *Alocasia macrorrhiza*, of tropical Asia and Australia, cultivated for its edible rhizome **2** a sea squirt [C19 from a native Australian language]

cunnilingus (,kʌnɪ'lɪŋgəs) *or* **cunnilinctus** (,kʌnɪ'lɪŋktəs) *n* a sexual activity in which the female genitalia are stimulated by the partner's lips and tongue. Compare **fellatio** [C19 from New Latin, from Latin *cunnus* vulva + *lingere* to lick]

cunning ('kʌnɪŋ) *adj* **1** crafty and shrewd, esp in deception; sly: *cunning as a fox* **2** made with or showing skill or cleverness; ingenious ▷ *n* **3** craftiness, esp in deceiving; slyness **4** cleverness, skill, or ingenuity [Old English *cunnende*; related to *cunnan* to know (see CAN¹), *cunnian* to test, experience, Old Norse *kunna* to know] > **'cunningly** *adv* > **'cunningness** *n*

cunt (kʌnt) *n taboo* **1** the female genitals **2** *offensive slang* a woman considered sexually **3** *offensive slang* a mean or obnoxious person [C13 of Germanic origin; related to Old Norse *kunta*, Middle Low German *kunte*]

USAGE Although there has been some relaxation of the taboo against using words such as *fuck* in conversation and print, the use of *cunt* is still not considered acceptable by most people outside very limited social contexts. Though originally a racily descriptive word in Middle English, it has been taboo for many centuries and continues to be so

cup (kʌp) *n* **1** a small open container, usually having one handle, used for drinking from **2** the contents of such a container: *that cup was too sweet* **3** Also called: **teacup, cupful** a unit of capacity used in cooking equal to approximately half a pint, 8 fluid ounces, or about one quarter of a litre **4** something resembling a cup in shape or function, such as the flower base of some plants of the rose family or a cuplike bodily organ **5** either of two cup-shaped parts of a brassiere, designed to support the breasts **6** a cup-shaped trophy awarded as a prize **7** *Brit* **a** a sporting contest in which a cup is awarded to the winner **b** (*as modifier*): *a cup competition* **8** a mixed drink with one ingredient as a base, usually served from a bowl: *claret cup* **9** *golf* the hole or metal container in the hole on a green **10** the chalice or the consecrated wine used in the Eucharist **11** one's lot in life **12** *in one's cups* drunk **13** *one's cup of tea informal* one's chosen or preferred thing, task, company, etc: *she's not my cup of tea* ▷ *vb* **cups, cupping, cupped** (*tr*) **14** to form (something, such as the hands) into the shape of a cup **15** to put into or as if into a cup **16** *archaic* to draw blood to the surface of the body of (a person) by using a cupping glass [Old English *cuppe*, from Late Latin *cuppa* cup, alteration of Latin *cūpa* cask] > **'cup,like** *adj*

cupbearer ('kʌp,bɛərə) *n* an attendant who fills and serves wine cups, as in a royal household

cupboard ('kʌbəd) *n* a piece of furniture or a recessed area of a room, with a door concealing storage space

cupboard love *n* a show of love inspired only by some selfish or greedy motive

cupcake ('kʌp,keɪk) *n* a small cake baked in a cup-shaped foil or paper case

CUPE ('kjuːpɪ) *n acronym for* Canadian Union of Public Employees

cupel ('kjuːpəl, kjʊ'pɛl) *n* **1** a refractory pot in which gold or silver is refined **2** a small porous bowl made of bone ash in which gold and silver are recovered from a lead button during assaying

▷ *vb* **-pels, -pelling, -pelled** *or US* **-pels, -peling, -peled 3** (*tr*) to refine (gold or silver) by means of cupellation [C17 from French *coupelle*, diminutive of *coupe* CUP] > **'cupeller** *n*

cupellation (,kjuːpɪ'leɪʃən) *n* **1** the process of recovering precious metals from lead by melting the alloy in a cupel and oxidizing the lead by means of an air blast **2** the manufacture of lead oxide by melting and oxidizing lead

Cup Final *n* **1** (often preceded by *the*) the annual final of the FA Cup soccer competition, played at Wembley, or the Scottish Cup, played at Hampden Park **2** (*often not capitals*) the final of any cup competition

cup-holder *n* **1** a device for holding a cup upright, esp in a motor vehicle **2** the reigning champion or champions in a cup competition

Cupid ('kjuːpɪd) *n* **1** the Roman god of love, represented as a winged boy with a bow and arrow. Greek counterpart: **Eros 2** (*not capital*) any similar figure, esp as represented in Baroque art [C14 from Latin *Cupīdō*, from *cupīdō* desire, from *cupidus* desirous; see CUPIDITY]

cupidity (kjuː'pɪdɪtɪ) *n* strong desire, esp for possessions or money; greed [C15 from Latin *cupiditās*, from *cupidus* eagerly desiring, from *cupere* to long for]

Cupid's bow *n* a shape of the upper lip considered to resemble Cupid's double-curved bow

cupid's dart *n* another name for **catananche**

cupola ('kjuːpələ) *n* **1** a roof or ceiling in the form of a dome **2** a small structure, usually domed, on the top of a roof or dome **3** a protective dome for a gun on a warship **4** a vertical air-blown coke-fired cylindrical furnace in which iron is remelted for casting [C16 from Italian, from Late Latin *cūpula* a small cask, from Latin *cūpa* tub] > **cupolated** ('kjuːpə,leɪtɪd) *adj*

cuppa *or* **cupper** ('kʌpə) *n Brit informal* a cup of tea

cupped (kʌpt) *adj* hollowed like a cup; concave

cupping ('kʌpɪŋ) *n med archaic* the process of applying a cupping glass to the skin

cupping glass *n med archaic* a glass vessel from which air can be removed by suction or heat to create a partial vacuum: formerly used in drawing blood to the surface of the skin for slow bloodletting. Also called: **artificial leech**

cupreous ('kjuːprɪəs) *adj* **1** of, consisting of, containing, or resembling copper; coppery **2** of the reddish-brown colour of copper [C17 from Late Latin *cupreus*, from *cuprum* COPPER¹]

cupressus (kjʊ'presəs) *n* any tree of the genus *Cupressus*. See **cypress¹**

cupric ('kjuːprɪk) *adj* of or containing copper in the divalent state [C18 from Late Latin *cuprum* copper]

cupriferous (kjuː'prɪfərəs) *adj* (of a substance such as an ore) containing or yielding copper

cuprite ('kjuːpraɪt) *n* a red secondary mineral consisting of cuprous oxide in cubic crystalline form: a source of copper. Formula: Cu_2O

cupro-, cupri- *or before a vowel* **cupr-** *combining form* indicating copper: *cupronickel; cuprite* [from Latin *cuprum*]

cupronickel (,kjuːprəʊ'nɪk³l) *n* any ductile corrosion-resistant copper alloy containing up to 40 per cent nickel: used in coins, condenser tubes, turbine blades, etc

cuprous ('kjuːprəs) *adj* of or containing copper in the monovalent state

cuprum ('kjuːprəm) *n* an obsolete name for **copper** [Latin: COPPER¹]

cup tie *n sport* an eliminating match or round between two teams in a cup competition

cup-tied *adj sport* **1** (of a team) unable to play another fixture because of involvement in a cup tie **2** (of a player) unable to play in a cup tie because of some disallowance

cupula ('kʌpjʊlə) *n, pl* **-lae** (-liː) *anatomy, zoology* a dome-shaped structure, esp the sensory structure

within the semicircular canals of the ear
cupulate ('kju:pjʊ,leɪt) *or* **cupular** ('kju:pjʊlə) *adj* 1 shaped like a small cup 2 (of plants or animals) having cupules
cupule ('kju:pju:l) *n biology* a cup-shaped part or structure, such as the cup around the base of an acorn [C19 from Late Latin *cūpula;* see CUPOLA]
cur (kɜ:) *n* 1 any vicious dog, esp a mongrel 2 a despicable or cowardly person [C13 shortened from *kurdogge;* probably related to Old Norse *kurra* to growl]
curable ('kjʊərəbᵊl) *adj* capable of being cured > ,**cura'bility** *or* '**curableness** *n* > '**curably** *adv*
Curaçao (,kjʊərə'səʊ) *n* 1 an island in the Caribbean, the largest in the Netherlands Antilles. Capital: Willemstad. Pop: 133 644 (2004 est). Area: 444 sq km (171 sq miles) 2 an orange-flavoured liqueur originally made there
curacy ('kjʊərəsɪ) *n, pl* **-cies** the office or position of curate
Cur. adv. vult *abbreviation for* See **CAV**
curagh *Gaelic* ('kʌrəx, 'kʌrə) *n* a variant spelling of ***currach***
curare *or* **curari** (kjʊ'rɑ:rɪ) *n* 1 black resin obtained from certain tropical South American trees, esp *Chondrodendron tomentosum,* acting on the motor nerves to cause muscular paralysis: used medicinally as a muscle relaxant and by South American Indians as an arrow poison 2 any of various trees of the genera *Chondrodendron* (family *Menispermaceae*) and *Strychnos* (family *Loganiaceae*) from which this resin is obtained [C18 from Portuguese and Spanish, from Carib *kurari*]
curarine ('kjʊərə,ri:n) *n* an alkaloid extracted from curare, used as a muscle relaxant in surgery. Formula: $C_{19}H_{26}ON_2$
curarize *or* **curarise** ('kjʊərə,raɪz) *vb (tr)* to paralyse or treat with curare > ,**curari'zation** *or* ,**curari'sation** *n*
curassow ('kjʊərə,səʊ) *n* any gallinaceous ground-nesting bird of the family *Cracidae,* of S North, Central, and South America. Curassows have long legs and tails and, typically, a distinctive crest of curled feathers. See also **guan** [C17 anglicized variant of CURAÇAO (island)]
curate[1] ('kjʊərɪt) *n* 1 a clergyman appointed to assist a parish priest 2 a clergyman who has the charge of a parish (**curate-in-charge**) 3 *Irish* an assistant barman [C14 from Medieval Latin *cūrātus,* from *cūra* spiritual oversight, CURE]
curate[2] (kjʊə'reɪt) *vb (tr)* to be in charge of (an art exhibition or museum) [C20 back formation from CURATOR]
curate's egg *n* something that has both good and bad parts [C20 derived from a cartoon in *Punch* (November, 1895) in which a timid curate, who has been served a bad egg while breakfasting with his bishop, says that parts of the egg are excellent]
curative ('kjʊərətɪv) *adj* 1 able or tending to cure ▷ *n* 2 anything able to heal or cure > '**curatively** *adv* > '**curativeness** *n*
curator (kjʊə'reɪtə) *n* 1 the administrative head of a museum, art gallery, or similar institution 2 *law, chiefly Scots* a guardian of a minor, mentally ill person, etc [C14 from Latin: one who cares, from *cūrāre* to care for, from *cūra* care] > **curatorial** (,kjʊərə'tɔ:rɪəl) *adj* > **cu'rator,ship** *n*
curb[1] (kɜ:b) *n* 1 something that restrains or holds back 2 any enclosing framework, such as a wall of stones around the top of a well 3 a Also called: **curb bit** a horse's bit with an attached chain or strap, which checks the horse b Also called: **curb chain** the chain or strap itself 4 a hard swelling on the hock of a horse ▷ *vb (tr)* 5 to control with or as if with a curb; restrain ▷ See also **kerb** [C15 from Old French *courbe* curved piece of wood or metal, from Latin *curvus* curved]
curb[2] *n vet science* a swelling on the leg of a horse, below the point of the hock, usually caused by a sprain
curbing ('kɜ:bɪŋ) *n* the US spelling of **kerbing**
curb roof *n* a roof having two or more slopes on each side of the ridge. See also **mansard** (sense 1), **gambrel roof** (sense 2)
curbstone ('kɜ:b,stəʊn) *n* the US spelling of **kerbstone**
curch (kɜ:tʃ) *n* a woman's plain cap or kerchief. Also called: **curchef** [C15 probably back formation from *courcheis* (plural), from Old French *couvrechies,* plural of *couvrechef* KERCHIEF]
curculio (kɜ:'kju:lɪ,əʊ) *n, pl* **-lios** any of various American weevils, esp *Conotrachelus nenuphar* (**plum curculio**), a pest of fruit trees [C18 from Latin: grain weevil]
curcuma ('kɜ:kjʊmə) *n* any tropical Asian tuberous plant of the genus *Curcuma,* such as *C. longa,* which is the source of turmeric, and *C. zedoaria,* which is the source of zedoary: family *Zingiberaceae* [C17 from New Latin, from Arabic *kurkum* turmeric]
curcumin ('kɜ:kjʊmɪn) *n* a yellow pigment, derived from the rhizome of *Curcuma longa,* and the main active ingrediant of turmeric. It is an antioxidant and has anti-inflammatory properties [C20 from CURCUMA]
curd (kɜ:d) *n* 1 *(often plural)* a substance formed from the coagulation of milk by acid or rennet, used in making cheese or eaten as a food 2 something similar in consistency ▷ *vb* 3 to turn into or become curd [C15 from earlier *crud,* of unknown origin] > '**curdy** *adj* > '**curdiness** *n*
curd cheese *n* a mild white cheese made from skimmed milk curds, smoother and fattier than cottage cheese
curdle ('kɜ:dᵊl) *vb* 1 to turn or cause to turn into curd 2 **curdle someone's blood** to fill someone with fear [C16 (*crudled,* past participle): from CURD] > '**curdler** *n*
cure (kjʊə) *vb* 1 *(tr)* to get rid of (an ailment, fault, or problem); heal 2 *(tr)* to restore to health or good condition 3 *(intr)* to bring about a cure 4 *(tr)* to preserve (meat, fish, etc) by salting, smoking, etc 5 *(tr)* a to treat or finish (a substance) by chemical or physical means b to vulcanize (rubber) c to allow (a polymer) to set often using heat or pressure 6 *(tr)* to assist the hardening of (concrete, mortar, etc) by keeping it moist ▷ *n* 7 a return to health, esp after specific treatment 8 any course of medical therapy, esp one proved effective in combating a disease 9 a means of restoring health or improving a condition, situation, etc 10 the spiritual and pastoral charge of a parish: *the cure of souls* 11 a process or method of preserving meat, fish, etc, by salting, pickling, or smoking [(n) C13 from Old French, from Latin *cūra* care; in ecclesiastical sense, from Medieval Latin *cūra* spiritual charge; (vb) C14 from Old French *curer,* from Latin *cūrāre* to attend to, heal, from *cūra* care] > '**cureless** *adj* > '**curer** *n*
curé ('kjʊəreɪ) *n* a parish priest in France [French, from Medieval Latin *cūrātus;* see CURATE[1]]
cure-all *n* something reputed to cure all ailments
curettage (,kjʊərɪ'tɑ:ʒ, kjʊə'rɛtɪdʒ) *or* **curettement** (kjʊə'rɛtmənt) *n* the process of using a curette. See also **D and C**
curette *or* **curet** (kjʊə'rɛt) *n* 1 a surgical instrument for removing dead tissue, growths, etc, from the walls of certain body cavities ▷ *vb* **-rettes** *or* **-rets, -retting, -retted** 2 *(tr)* to scrape or clean with such an instrument [C18 from French, from *curer* to heal, make clean; see CURE]
curfew ('kɜ:fju:) *n* 1 an official regulation setting restrictions on movement, esp after a specific time at night 2 the time set as a deadline by such a regulation 3 (in medieval Europe) a the ringing of a bell to prompt people to extinguish fires and lights b the time at which the curfew bell was rung c the bell itself [C13 from Old French *cuevrefeu,* literally: cover the fire]
curia ('kjʊərɪə) *n, pl* **-riae** (-rɪ,i:) 1 *(sometimes capital)* the papal court and government of the Roman Catholic Church 2 (in ancient Rome) a any of the ten subdivisions of the Latin, Sabine, or Etruscan tribes b a meeting place of such a subdivision c the senate house of Rome d the senate of an Italian town under Roman administration 3 (in the Middle Ages) a court held in the king's name. See also **Curia Regis** [C16 from Latin, from Old Latin *coviria*(unattested), from co- + *vir* man] > '**curial** *adj*
Curia Regis ('ri:dʒɪs) *n, pl* **Curiae Regis** (in Norman England) the king's court, which performed all functions of government [Latin, literally: council of the king]
curie ('kjʊərɪ, -ri:) *n* a unit of radioactivity that is equal to 3.7×10^{10} disintegrations per second. Symbol: Ci [C20 named after Pierre Curie (1859–1906), French physicist and chemist]
Curie point *or* **temperature** *n* the temperature above which a ferromagnetic substance loses its ferromagnetism and becomes paramagnetic [C20 named after Pierre Curie (1859–1906), French physicist and chemist]
Curie's law *n* the principle that the magnetic susceptibility of a paramagnetic substance is inversely proportional to its thermodynamic temperature. See also **Curie-Weiss law**
Curie-Weiss law ('kjʊərɪ'waɪs, -'vaɪs) *n* the principle that the magnetic susceptibility of a paramagnetic substance is inversely proportional to the difference between its temperature and its Curie point [C20 named after Pierre Curie (1859–1906), French physicist and chemist and Pierre-Ernest *Weiss* (died 1940), French physicist]
curio ('kjʊərɪ,əʊ) *n, pl* **-rios** a small article valued as a collector's item, esp something fascinating or unusual [C19 shortened from CURIOSITY]
curiosa (,kjʊərɪ'əʊsə) *n (functioning as plural)* 1 curiosities 2 books on strange subjects, esp erotica [New Latin: from Latin *cūriōsus* CURIOUS]
curiosity (,kjʊərɪ'ɒsɪtɪ) *n, pl* **-ties** 1 an eager desire to know; inquisitiveness 2 a the quality of being curious; strangeness b *(as modifier): the ring had curiosity value only* 3 something strange or fascinating 4 a rare or strange object; curio 5 *obsolete* fastidiousness
curious ('kjʊərɪəs) *adj* 1 eager to learn; inquisitive 2 over inquisitive; prying 3 interesting because of oddness or novelty; strange; unexpected 4 *rare* (of workmanship, etc) highly detailed, intricate, or subtle 5 *obsolete* fastidious or hard to please [C14 from Latin *cūriōsus* taking pains over something, from *cūra* care] > '**curiously** *adv* > '**curiousness** *n*
Curitiba (,kʊərɪ'ti:bə) *n* a city in SE Brazil, capital of Paraná state: seat of the University of Paraná (1946). Pop: 2 871 000 (2005 est)
curium ('kjʊərɪəm) *n* a silvery-white metallic transuranic element artificially produced from plutonium. Symbol: Cm; atomic no.: 96; half-life of most stable isotope, ^{247}Cm: 1.6×10^7 years; valency: 3 and 4; relative density: 13.51 (calculated); melting pt.: 1345±400°C [C20 New Latin, named after Pierre Curie (1859–1906), French physicist and chemist, and his wife Marie Curie (1867–1934), Polish-born French physicist and chemist]
curl (kɜ:l) *vb* 1 *(intr)* (esp of hair) to grow into curves or ringlets 2 *(tr; sometimes foll by up)* to twist or roll (something, esp hair) into coils or ringlets 3 (often foll by *up*) to become or cause to become spiral-shaped or curved; coil: *the heat made the leaves curl up* 4 *(intr)* to move in a curving or twisting manner 5 *(intr)* to play the game of curling 6 **curl one's lip** to show contempt, as by raising a corner of the lip ▷ *n* 7 a curve or coil of hair 8 a curved or spiral shape or mark, as in wood 9 the act of curling or state of being curled 10 any of various plant diseases characterized by curling of the leaves 11 Also called: **rot, rotation** *maths* a vector quantity associated with a vector field that is the vector product of the operator ∇ and a vector function ***A***, where $\nabla = \mathbf{i}\partial/\partial x + \mathbf{j}\partial/\partial y + \mathbf{k}\partial/\partial z$, ***i, j,*** and ***k*** being unit vectors. Usually written curl ***A***, rot ***A***. Compare **divergence** (sense 4),

gradient (sense 4) ▷ See also **curl up** [C14 probably from Middle Dutch *crullen* to curl; related to Middle High German *krol* curly, Middle Low German *krūs* curly]

curled paperwork *n* another name for **rolled paperwork**

curler ('kɜːlə) *n* **1** any of various pins, clasps, or rollers used to curl or wave hair **2** a person or thing that curls **3** a person who plays curling

curlew ('kɜːljuː) *n* any large shore bird of the genus *Numenius*, such as *N. arquata* of Europe and Asia: family *Scolopacidae* (sandpipers, etc), order *Charadriiformes*. They have a long downward-curving bill and occur in northern and arctic regions. Compare **stone curlew** [C14 from Old French *corlieu*, perhaps of imitative origin]

curlew sandpiper *n* a common Eurasian sandpiper, *Calidris ferruginea*, having a brick-red breeding plumage and a greyish winter plumage

curli ('kɜːlɪ) *pl n bacteriol* curled hairlike processes on the surface of the bacterium *Escherichia coli* by means of which the bacterium adheres to and infects wounds [C20 from *curl(ed)* (PIL)I]

curlicue ('kɜːlɪˌkjuː) *n* an intricate ornamental curl or twist [C19 from CURLY + CUE²]

curling ('kɜːlɪŋ) *n* a game played on ice, esp in Scotland and Canada, in which heavy stones with handles (**curling stones**) are slid towards a target (**tee**)

curling tongs *pl n* a metal scissor-like device that is heated, so that strands of hair may be twined around it in order to form curls. Also called: **curling iron, curling irons, curling pins**

curlpaper ('kɜːlˌpeɪpə) *n* a strip of paper used to roll up and set a section of hair, usually wetted, into a curl

curl up *vb (adverb)* **1** *(intr)* to adopt a reclining position with the legs close to the body and the back rounded **2** to become or cause to become spiral-shaped or curved **3** *(intr)* to retire to a quiet cosy setting: *to curl up with a good novel* **4** *Brit informal* to be or cause to be embarrassed or disgusted (esp in the phrase **curl up and die**)

curly ('kɜːlɪ) *adj* **curlier, curliest 1** tending to curl; curling **2** having curls **3** (of timber) having irregular curves or waves in the grain **4** *Austral and NZ* difficult to counter or answer: *a curly question* > '**curliness** *n*

curly-coated retriever *n* a strongly built variety of retriever with a tightly curled black or liver-coloured coat

curmudgeon (kɜː'mʌdʒən) *n* a surly or miserly person [C16 of unknown origin] > **cur'mudgeonly** *adj*

currach, curagh *or* ***curragh*** *Gaelic* ('kʌrəx, 'kʌrə) *n* a Scot or Irish name for **coracle** [C15 from Irish Gaelic *currach*; compare CORACLE]

currajong ('kʌrəˌdʒɒŋ) *n* a variant spelling of **kurrajong**

currant ('kʌrənt) *n* **1** a small dried seedless grape of the Mediterranean region, used in cooking **2** any of several mainly N temperate shrubs of the genus *Ribes*, esp *R. rubrum* (redcurrant) and *R. nigrum* (blackcurrant): family *Grossulariaceae*. See also **gooseberry** (sense 1) **3** the small acid fruit of any of these plants [C16 shortened from *rayson of Corannte* raisin of Corinth]

currant bun *n* **1** *Brit* a sweet bun containing currants **2** *Scot* another name for **black bun 3** *Cockney rhyming slang* son

currawong ('kʌrəˌwɒŋ) *n* any Australian crowlike songbird of the genus *Strepera*, having black, grey, and white plumage: family *Cracticidae*. Also called: **bell magpie** [from a native Australian name]

currency ('kʌrənsɪ) *n, pl* **-cies 1** a metal or paper medium of exchange that is in current use in a particular country **2** general acceptance or circulation; prevalence: *the currency of ideas* **3** the period of time during which something is valid, accepted, or in force **4** the act of being passed from person to person **5** *Austral* (formerly) the local medium of exchange, esp in the colonies, as distinct from sterling **6** *Austral slang* (formerly) the native-born Australians, as distinct from the British immigrants [C17 from Medieval Latin *currentia*, literally: a flowing, from Latin *currere* to run, flow]

currency bar *n* **1** a long narrow iron bar, often sword-like or spear-like in shape, dating from the pre-Roman and Roman period in Britain; the purpose of currency bars is not certain, and while they may have been used in trade, they may have had a ritual significance **2** a metal bar of any of various shapes, used as a form of currency

currency note *n* another name for **treasury note** (sense b)

current ('kʌrənt) *adj* **1** of the immediate present; in progress: *current events* **2** most recent; up-to-date **3** commonly known, practised, or accepted; widespread: *a current rumour* **4** circulating and valid at present: *current coins* ▷ *n* **5** (esp of water or air) a steady usually natural flow **6** a mass of air, body of water, etc, that has a steady flow in a particular direction **7** the rate of flow of such a mass **8** Also called: **electric current** *physics* **a** a flow of electric charge through a conductor **b** the rate of flow of this charge. It is measured in amperes. Symbol: **I 9** a general trend or drift: *currents of opinion* [C13 from Old French *corant*, literally: running, from *corre* to run, from Latin *currere*] > '**currently** *adv* > '**currentness** *n*

current account *n* **1** an account at a bank or building society against which cheques may be drawn at any time. US name: **checking account.** Canadian name: **chequing account 2** *economics* that part of the balance of payments composed of the balance of trade and the invisible balance. Compare **capital account** (sense 1)

current assets *pl n* cash and operating assets that are convertible into cash within a year. Also called: **floating assets.** Compare **fixed assets**

current-cost accounting *n* a method of accounting that values assets at their current replacement cost rather than their original cost. Compare **historical-cost accounting**

current density *n* the ratio of the electric current flowing at a particular point in a conductor to the cross-sectional area of the conductor taken perpendicular to the current flow at that point. It is measured in amperes per square metre. Symbol: **J**

current efficiency *n physics* the ratio of the actual mass of a substance liberated from an electrolyte by the passage of current to the theoretical mass liberated according to Faraday's law

current expenses *pl n* noncapital and usually recurrent expenditures necessary for the operation of a business

current liabilities *pl n* business liabilities maturing within a year

curricle ('kʌrɪkᵊl) *n* a two-wheeled open carriage drawn by two horses side by side [C18 from Latin *curriculum* from *currus* chariot, from *currere* to run]

curriculum (kə'rɪkjʊləm) *n, pl* **-la** (-lə) *or* **-lums 1** a course of study in one subject at a school or college **2** a list of all the courses of study offered by a school or college **3** any programme or plan of activities [C19 from Latin: course, from *currere* to run] > **cur'ricular** *adj*

curriculum vitae ('viːtaɪ, 'vaɪtiː) *n, pl* **curricula vitae** an outline of a person's educational and professional history, usually prepared for job applications. Abbreviation: **CV** [Latin, literally: the course of one's life]

currier ('kʌrɪə) *n* a person who curries leather [C14 from Old French *corier*, from Latin *coriārius* a tanner, from *corium* leather]

curriery ('kʌrɪərɪ) *n, pl* **-eries** the trade, work, or place of occupation of a currier

currish ('kɜːrɪʃ) *adj* of or like a cur; rude or bad-tempered > '**currishly** *adv* > '**currishness** *n*

curry¹ ('kʌrɪ) *n, pl* **-ries 1** a spicy dish of oriental, esp Indian, origin that is made in many ways but usually consists of meat or fish prepared in a hot piquant sauce **2** curry seasoning or sauce **3 give someone curry** *Austral slang* to assault (a person) verbally or physically ▷ *vb* **-ries, -rying, -ried 4** *(tr)* to prepare (food) with curry powder or sauce [C16 from Tamil *kari* sauce, relish]

curry² ('kʌrɪ) *vb* **-ries, -rying, -ried** *(tr)* **1** to beat vigorously, as in order to clean **2** to dress and finish (leather) after it has been tanned to make it strong, flexible, and waterproof **3** to groom (a horse) **4 curry favour** to ingratiate oneself, esp with superiors [C13 from Old French *correer* to make ready, from Vulgar Latin *conrēdāre* (unattested), from *rēdāre* (unattested) to provide, of Germanic origin]

currycomb ('kʌrɪˌkəʊm) *n* a square comb consisting of rows of small teeth, used for grooming horses

curry powder *n* a mixture of finely ground pungent spices, such as turmeric, cumin, coriander, ginger, etc, used in making curries

curry puff *n* (in eastern cookery) a type of pie or pasty consisting of a pastry case containing curried meat and vegetables

curse (kɜːs) *n* **1** a profane or obscene expression of anger, disgust, surprise, etc; oath **2** an appeal to a supernatural power for harm to come to a specific person, group, etc **3** harm resulting from an appeal to a supernatural power: *to be under a curse* **4** something that brings or causes great trouble or harm **5** a saying, charm, effigy, etc, used to invoke a curse **6** an ecclesiastical censure of excommunication **7** (preceded by *the*) *informal* menstruation or a menstrual period ▷ *vb* **curses, cursing, cursed** *or archaic* **curst 8** *(intr)* to utter obscenities or oaths **9** *(tr)* to abuse (someone) with obscenities or oaths **10** *(tr)* to invoke supernatural powers to bring harm to (someone or something) **11** *(tr)* to bring harm upon **12** *(tr)* another word for **excommunicate** [Old English *cursian* to curse, from *curs* a curse] > '**curser** *n*

cursed ('kɜːsɪd, kɜːst) *or* **curst** *adj* **1** under a curse **2** deserving to be cursed; detestable; hateful > '**cursedly** *adv* > '**cursedness** *n*

curses ('kɜːsɪz) *interj often facetious* an expression of disappointment or dismay

cursive ('kɜːsɪv) *adj* **1** of or relating to handwriting in which letters are formed and joined in a rapid flowing style **2** *printing* of or relating to typefaces that resemble handwriting ▷ *n* **3** a cursive letter or printing type **4** a manuscript written in cursive letters [C18 from Medieval Latin *cursīvus* running, ultimately from Latin *currere* to run] > '**cursively** *adv*

cursor ('kɜːsə) *n* **1** the sliding part of a measuring instrument, esp a transparent sliding square on a slide rule **2** any of various means, typically a flashing bar or underline, of identifying a particular position on a computer screen, such as the insertion point for text

cursorial (kɜː'sɔːrɪəl) *adj zoology* adapted for running: *a cursorial skeleton; cursorial birds*

cursory ('kɜːsərɪ) *adj* hasty and usually superficial; quick: *a cursory check* [C17 from Late Latin *cursōrius* of running, from Latin *cursus* a course, from *currere* to run] > '**cursorily** *adv* > '**cursoriness** *n*

curst (kɜːst) *vb* **1** *archaic* a past tense and past participle of **curse** ▷ *adj* **2** a variant of **cursed**

curt (kɜːt) *adj* **1** rudely blunt and brief; abrupt: *a curt reply* **2** short or concise [C17 from Latin *curtus* cut short, mutilated] > '**curtly** *adv* > '**curtness** *n*

curtail (kɜː'teɪl) *vb (tr)* to cut short; abridge [C16 changed (through influence of TAIL¹) from obsolete *curtal* to dock; see CURTAL] > **cur'tailer** *n* > **cur'tailment** *n*

curtail step ('kɜːteɪl) *n* the step or steps at the foot of a flight of stairs, widened at one or both ends and terminated with a scroll

curtain ('kɜːtᵊn) *n* **1** a piece of material that can be drawn across an opening or window, to shut out light or to provide privacy **2** a barrier to

C

vision, access, or communication: *a curtain of secrecy* **3** a hanging cloth or similar barrier for concealing all or part of a theatre stage from the audience **4** (often preceded by *the*) the end of a scene of a play, opera, etc, marked by the fall or closing of the curtain **5** the rise or opening of the curtain at the start of a performance ▷ *vb* **6** (*tr*; sometimes foll by *off*) to shut off or conceal with or as if with a curtain **7** (*tr*) to provide (a window, etc) with curtains ▷ See also **curtains** [c13 from Old French *courtine*, from Late Latin *cortīna* enclosed place, curtain, probably from Latin *cohors* courtyard]

curtain call *n* the appearance of performers at the end of a theatrical performance to acknowledge applause

curtain lecture *n* a scolding or rebuke given in private, esp by a wife to her husband [alluding to the curtained beds where such rebukes were once given]

curtain-raiser *n* **1** *theatre* a short dramatic piece presented before the main play **2** any preliminary event: *the debate was a curtain-raiser to the election*

curtains ('kɜːtᵊnz) *pl n* **1** *informal* death or ruin; the end: *if the enemy see us it will be curtains for us* **2** a hairstyle in which the hair is parted in the centre of the forehead and curved out over the temples

curtain speech *n* **1** a talk given in front of the curtain after a stage performance, often by the author or an actor **2** the final speech of an act or a play

curtain-twitcher *n informal* a person who likes to watch what other people are doing, while remaining unobserved themselves

curtain wall *n* **1** a non-load-bearing external wall attached to a framed structure, often one that is prefabricated **2** a low wall outside the outer wall of a castle, serving as a first line of defence

curtal ('kɜːtᵊl) *obsolete* ▷ *adj* **1** cut short **2** (of friars) wearing a short frock ▷ *n* **3** an animal whose tail has been docked **4** something that is cut short [c16 from Old French *courtault* animal whose tail has been docked, from *court* short, from Latin *curtus*; see CURT]

curtal axe *n* an obsolete term for **cutlass** [c16 alteration by folk etymology of Old French *coutelas* CUTLASS; see CURTAL]

curtana (kɜːˈtɑːnə) *n* the unpointed sword carried before an English sovereign at a coronation as an emblem of mercy [c15 from Anglo-Latin, from Old French *cortain*, the name of Roland's sword, which was broken at the point, ultimately from Latin *curtus* short]

curtate ('kɜːteɪt) *adj* shortened [c17 from Late Latin *curtāre* to shorten, from *curtus* cut short; see CURT]

curtilage ('kɜːtɪlɪdʒ) *n* the enclosed area of land adjacent to a dwelling house [c14 from Old French *cortillage*, from *cortil* a little yard, from *cort* COURT]

curtsy or **curtsey** ('kɜːtsɪ) *n, pl* **-sies** or **-seys 1** a formal gesture of greeting and respect made by women in which the knees are bent, the head slightly bowed, and the skirt held outwards ▷ *vb* **-sies, -sying, -sied** or **-seys, -seying, -seyed 2** (*intr*) to make a curtsy [c16 variant of COURTESY]

curule ('kjʊəruːl) *adj* (in ancient Rome) of the highest rank, esp one entitled to use a curule chair [c16 from Latin *curūlis* of a chariot, from *currus* chariot, from *currere* to run]

curule chair *n* an upholstered folding seat with curved legs used by the highest civil officials of ancient Rome

curvaceous (kɜːˈveɪʃəs) *adj informal* (esp of a woman) having shapely curves or a well-rounded body ▷ **cur'vaceously** *adv*

curvature ('kɜːvətʃə) *n* **1** something curved or a curved part of a thing **2** any normal or abnormal curving of a bodily part: *curvature of the spine* **3** *geometry* the change in inclination of a tangent to a curve over unit length of arc. For a circle or sphere it is the reciprocal of the radius. See also **radius of curvature, centre of curvature 4** the act

of curving or the state or degree of being curved

curve (kɜːv) *n* **1** a continuously bending line that has no straight parts **2** something that curves or is curved, such as a bend in a road or the contour of a woman's body **3** the act or extent of curving; curvature **4** *maths* **a** a system of points whose coordinates satisfy a given equation; a locus of points **b** the graph of a function with one independent variable **5** a line representing data, esp statistical data, on a graph: *an unemployment curve* **6 ahead of** or **behind the curve** ahead of or behind the times; ahead of or behind schedule **7** short for **French curve** ▷ *vb* **8** to take or cause to take the shape or path of a curve; bend ▷ Related adjective: **sinuous** [c15 from Latin *curvāre* to bend, from *curvus* crooked] ▷ **curvedly** ('kɜːvɪdlɪ) *adv* ▷ **'curvedness** *n* ▷ **'curvy** *adj*

curve ball *n* **1** *baseball* a ball pitched in a curving path so as to make it more difficult to hit **2** *informal* something deceptive: *his wholesome image was a curve ball thrown to deceive the public*

curvet (kɜːˈvɛt) *n* **1** *dressage* a low leap with all four feet off the ground ▷ *vb* **-vets, -vetting, -vetted** or **-vets, -veting, -veted 2** *dressage* to make or cause to make such a leap **3** (*intr*) to prance or frisk about [c16 from Old Italian *corvetta*, from French *courbette*, from *courber* to bend, from Latin *curvāre*]

curvilinear (ˌkɜːvɪˈlɪnɪə) or **curvilineal** *adj* **1** consisting of, bounded by, or characterized by a curved line **2** along a curved line: *curvilinear motion* **3** *maths* (of a set of coordinates) determined by or determining a system of three orthogonal surfaces ▷ **ˌcurvi'linearity** *n* ▷ **ˌcurvi'linearly** *adv*

Cusco (*Spanish* 'kusko) *n* a variant of **Cuzco**

cuscus ('kʌskʌs) *n, pl* **-cuses** any of several large nocturnal phalangers of the genus *Phalanger*, of N Australia, New Guinea, and adjacent islands, having dense fur, prehensile tails, large eyes, and a yellow nose [c17 New Latin, probably from a native name in New Guinea]

cusec ('kjuːsɛk) *n* a unit of flow equal to 1 cubic foot per second. 1 cusec is equivalent to 0.028 317 cubic metre per second [c20 from *cu(bic foot per) sec(ond)*]

Cush or **Kush** (kʌʃ, kʊʃ) *n Old Testament* **1** the son of Ham and brother of Canaan (Genesis 10:6) **2** the country of the supposed descendants of Cush (ancient Ethiopia), comprising approximately Nubia and the modern Sudan, and the territory of southern (or Upper) Egypt

cushat ('kʌʃət) *n* another name for **wood pigeon** [Old English *cūscote*; perhaps related to *scēotan* to shoot]

cushie-doo (ˌkʊʃɪˈduː) *n* a Scot name for a **wood pigeon** Often shortened to: **cushie** [from CUSHAT + DOO]

Cushing's disease or **syndrome** ('kʊʃɪŋz) *n* a rare condition caused by excess corticosteroid hormones in the body, characterized chiefly by obesity of the trunk and face, high blood pressure, fatigue, and loss of calcium from the bones [c20 named after Harvey Williams *Cushing* (1869–1939), US neurosurgeon]

cushion ('kʊʃən) *n* **1** a bag made of cloth, leather, plastic, etc, filled with feathers, air, or other yielding substance, used for sitting on, leaning against, etc **2** something resembling a cushion in function or appearance, esp one to support or pad or to absorb shock **3** the resilient felt-covered rim of a billiard table **4** another name for **pillow** (sense 2) **5** short for **air cushion 6** a capital, used in Byzantine, Romanesque, and Norman architecture, in the form of a bowl with a square top ▷ *vb* (*tr*) **7** to place on or as on a cushion **8** to provide with cushions **9** to protect, esp against hardship or change **10 a** to check the motion of (a mechanism) gently, esp by the compression of trapped fluid in a cylinder **b** to provide with a means of absorbing shock [from Latin *culcita* mattress] ▷ **'cushiony** *adj*

cushion plant *n* a type of low-growing plant

having many closely spaced short upright shoots, typical of alpine and arctic habitats

Cushitic (kʊˈʃɪtɪk) *n* **1** a group of languages of Somalia, Ethiopia, NE Kenya, and adjacent regions: a subfamily within the Afro-Asiatic family of languages ▷ *adj* **2** denoting, relating to, or belonging to this group of languages

cushty ('kʊʃtɪ) *interj Brit informal* an exclamation of pleasure, agreement, approval, etc

cushy ('kʊʃɪ) *adj* **cushier, cushiest** *informal* easy; comfortable: *a cushy job* [c20 from Hindi *khush* pleasant, from Persian *khōsh*]

cusk (kʌsk) *n, pl* **cusks** or **cusk** *US and Canadian* a gadoid food fish, *Brosmius brosme*, of northern coastal waters, having a single long dorsal fin. aslo called: **torsk** [c17 probably alteration of *tusk* of Scandinavian origin; compare Old Norse *thorskr* codfish]

CUSO ('kjuːsəʊ) *n acronym for* Canadian University Services Overseas; an organization that sends students to work as volunteers in developing countries

cusp (kʌsp) *n* **1** any of the small elevations on the grinding or chewing surface of a tooth **2** any of the triangular flaps of a heart valve **3** a point or pointed end **4** Also called: **spinode** *geometry* a point at which two arcs of a curve intersect and at which the two tangents are coincident **5** *architect* a carving at the meeting place of two arcs **6** *astronomy* either of the points of a crescent moon or of a satellite or inferior planet in a similar phase **7** *astrology* any division between houses or signs of the zodiac [c16 from Latin *cuspis* point, pointed end]

cuspate ('kʌspɪt, -peɪt) or **cuspated, cusped** (kʌspt) *adj* **1** having a cusp or cusps **2** shaped like a cusp; cusplike

cuspid ('kʌspɪd) *n* a tooth having one point; canine tooth

cuspidate ('kʌspɪˌdeɪt) or **cuspidated, cuspidal** ('kʌspɪdᵊl) *adj* **1** having a cusp or cusps **2** (esp of leaves) narrowing to a point **5** [c17 from Latin *cuspidāre* to make pointed, from *cuspis* a point]

cuspidation (ˌkʌspɪˈdeɪʃən) *n architect* decoration using cusps

cuspidor ('kʌspɪˌdɔː) *n* another word (esp US) for **spittoon** [c18 from Portuguese, from *cuspir* to spit, from Latin *conspuere*, from *spuere* to spit]

cuss (kʌs) *informal* ▷ *n* **1** a curse; oath **2** a person or animal, esp an annoying one ▷ *vb* **3** another word for **curse** (senses 8, 9)

cussed ('kʌsɪd) *adj informal* **1** another word for **cursed 2** obstinate **3** annoying: *a cussed nuisance* ▷ **'cussedly** *adv* ▷ **'cussedness** *n*

custard ('kʌstəd) *n* **1** a baked sweetened mixture of eggs and milk **2** a sauce made of milk and sugar and thickened with cornflour [c15 alteration of Middle English *crustade* kind of pie, probably from Old Provençal *croustado*, from *crosta* CRUST]

custard apple *n* **1** a West Indian tree, *Annona reticulata*: family Annonaceae **2** the large heart-shaped fruit of this tree, which has a fleshy edible pulp **3** any of several related trees or fruits, esp the papaw and sweetsop ▷ Also called (for senses 1, 2): **bullock's heart**

custard pie *n* **a** a flat, open pie filled with real or artificial custard, as thrown in slapstick comedy **b** (*as modifier*): *custard-pie humour*

custard powder *n* a powder containing cornflour, sugar, etc, for thickening milk to make a yellow sauce. See **custard** (sense 2)

custodian (kʌˈstəʊdɪən) *n* **1** a person who has custody, as of a prisoner, ward, etc **2** a guardian or keeper, as of an art collection, etc

custodianship (kʌˈstəʊdɪənʃɪp) *n* **1** the condition of being a custodian **2** (in Britain) a legal basis for the care of children under the Children's Act 1975, midway between fostering and adoption, devised for children settled in long-term foster care or living permanently with relatives or a step-parent

custody ('kʌstədɪ) *n, pl* **-dies 1** the act of keeping safe or guarding, esp the right of guardianship of a minor **2** the state of being held by the police; arrest (esp in the phrases **in custody, take into custody**) [C15 from Latin *custōdia*, from *custōs* guard, defender] > **custodial** (kʌ'stəʊdɪəl) *adj*

custom ('kʌstəm) *n* **1** a usual or habitual practice; typical mode of behaviour **2** the long-established habits or traditions of a society collectively; convention: *custom dictates good manners* **3 a** a practice which by long-established usage has come to have the force of law **b** such practices collectively (esp in the phrase **custom and practice**) **4** habitual patronage, esp of a shop or business **5** the customers of a shop or business collectively **6** (in feudal Europe) a tribute paid by a vassal to his lord ▷ *adj* **7** made to the specifications of an individual customer (often in the combinations **custom-built, custom-made**) **8** specializing in goods so made ▷ See also **customs** [C12 from Old French *costume*, from Latin *consuētūdō*, from *consuēscere* to grow accustomed to, from *suēscere* to be used to]

customable ('kʌstəməbᵊl) *adj* subject to customs

customary ('kʌstəmərɪ, -təmrɪ) *adj* **1** in accordance with custom or habitual practice; usual; habitual **2** *law* **a** founded upon long continued practices and usage rather than law **b** (of land, esp a feudal estate) held by custom ▷ *n, pl* **-aries 3 a** a statement in writing of customary laws and practices **b** a body of such laws and customs > **'customarily** *adv* > **'customariness** *n*

custom-built *adj* (of cars, houses, etc) made according to the specifications of an individual buyer

customer ('kʌstəmə) *n* **1** a person who buys **2** *informal* a person with whom one has dealings: *a cool customer*

customer-facing *adj* interacting or communicating directly with customers: *good customer-facing skills*

customer relationship management *n* the practice of building a strong relationship between a business and its customers and potential customers. Abbreviation: **CRM**

custom house *or* **customs house** *n* a government office, esp at a port, where customs are collected and ships cleared for entry

customize *or* **customise** ('kʌstəˌmaɪz) *vb* (*tr*) to modify (something) according to a customer's individual requirements > **ˌcustomi'zation** *or* **ˌcustomi'sation** *n*

custom-made *adj* (of suits, dresses, etc) made according to the specifications of an individual buyer

customs ('kʌstəmz) *n* (*functioning as singular or plural*) **1** duty on imports or exports **2** the government department responsible for the collection of these duties **3** the part of a port, airport, frontier station, etc, where baggage and freight are examined for dutiable goods and contraband **4** the procedure for examining baggage and freight, paying duty, etc **5** (*as modifier*): *customs officer*

customs union *n* an association of nations which promotes free trade within the union and establishes common tariffs on trade with nonmember nations

custos ('kʌstɒs) *n, pl* **custodes** (kʌ'stəʊdiːz) a superior in the Franciscan religious order. Also called (in England): **guardian** [C15 from Latin: keeper, guard]

custumal ('kʌstjʊməl) *n, adj* another word for **customary** (senses 2, 3) [C16 from Medieval Latin *custumālis* relating to CUSTOM]

cut (kʌt) *vb* **cuts, cutting, cut 1** to open up or incise (a person or thing) with a sharp edge or instrument; gash **2** (of a sharp instrument) to penetrate or incise (a person or thing) **3** to divide or be divided with or as if with a sharp instrument: *cut a slice of bread* **4** (*intr*) to use a sharp-edged instrument or an instrument that cuts **5** (*tr*) to trim or prune by or as if by clipping: *to cut hair* **6** (*tr*) to reap or mow (a crop, grass, etc) **7** (*tr*) to geld or castrate **8** (*tr; sometimes foll by out*) to make, form, or shape by cutting: *to cut a suit* **9** (*tr*) to hollow or dig out; excavate: *to cut a tunnel through the mountain* **10** to strike (an object) sharply **11** (*tr*) *sport* to hit (a ball) with a downward slicing stroke so as to impart spin or cause it to fall short **12** *cricket* to hit (the ball) to the off side, usually between cover and third man, with a roughly horizontal bat **13** to hurt or wound the feelings of (a person), esp by malicious speech or action **14** (*tr*) *informal* to refuse to recognize; snub **15** (*tr*) *informal* to absent oneself from (an activity, location, etc), esp without permission or in haste: *to cut class* **16** (*tr*) to abridge, shorten, or edit by excising a part or parts **17** (*tr; often foll by down*) to lower, reduce, or curtail: *to cut losses* **18** (*tr*) to dilute or weaken: *heroin that was cut with nontoxic elements* **19** (*tr*) to dissolve or break up: *to cut fat* **20** (when *intr*, foll by *across* or *through*) to cross or traverse: *the footpath cuts through the field* **21** (*intr*) to make a sharp or sudden change in direction; veer **22** to grow (teeth) through the gums or (of teeth) to appear through the gums **23** (*intr*) *films* **a** to call a halt to a shooting sequence **b** (foll by *to*) to move quickly to another scene **24** *films* to edit (film) **25** (*tr*) to switch off (a light, car engine, etc) **26** (*tr*) (of a performer, recording company, etc) to make (a record or tape of a song, concert, performance, etc) **27** *cards* **a** to divide (the pack) at random into two parts after shuffling **b** (*intr*) to pick cards from a spread pack to decide dealer, partners, etc **28** (*tr*) to remove (material) from an object by means of a chisel, lathe, etc **29** (*tr*) (of a tool) to bite into (an object) **30** (*intr*) (of a horse) to injure the leg just above the hoof by a blow from the opposite foot **31** **cut a caper** *or* **capers a** to skip or jump playfully **b** to act or behave playfully; frolic **32** **cut both ways a** to have both good and bad effects **b** to affect both sides of something, as two parties in an argument, etc **33** **cut a dash** to behave or dress showily or strikingly; make a stylish impression **34** **cut (a person) dead** *informal* to ignore (a person) completely **35** **cut a (good, poor, etc) figure** to appear or behave in a specified manner **36** **cut and run** *informal* to make a rapid escape **37** **cut it** *slang* be successful in doing something **38** **cut it fine** *informal* to allow little margin of time, space, etc **39** **cut corners** to do something in the easiest or shortest way, esp at the expense of high standards: *we could finish this project early only if we cut corners* **40** **cut loose** to free or become freed from restraint, custody, anchorage, etc **41** **cut no ice** *informal* to fail to make an impression **42** **cut one's losses** to give up spending time, money, or energy on an unprofitable or unsuccessful activity **43** **cut one's teeth on** *informal* **a** to use at an early age or stage **b** to practise on ▷ *adj* **44** detached, divided, or separated by cutting **45** *botany* incised or divided: *cut leaves* **46** made, shaped, or fashioned by cutting **47** reduced or diminished by or as if by cutting: *cut prices* **48** gelded or castrated **49** weakened or diluted **50** *Brit* a slang word for **drunk** **51** hurt; resentful **52** **cut and dried** *informal* settled or arranged in advance **53** **cut lunch** *Austral and NZ* a sandwich lunch carried from home to work, school, etc ▷ *n* **54** the act of cutting **55** a stroke or incision made by cutting; gash **56** a piece or part cut off, esp a section of food cut from the whole: *a cut of meat* **57** the edge of anything cut or sliced **58** a passage, channel, path, etc, cut or hollowed out **59** an omission or deletion, esp in a text, film, or play **60** a reduction in price, salary, etc **61** a decrease in government finance in a particular department or area, usually leading to a reduction of services, staff numbers, etc **62** short for **power cut** **63** *chiefly US and Canadian* a quantity of timber cut during a specific time or operation **64** *informal* a portion or share **65** *informal* a straw, slip of paper, etc, used in drawing lots **66** the manner or style in which a thing, esp a garment, is cut; fashion **67 a** *Irish informal* a person's general appearance: *I didn't like the cut of him* **b** *Irish derogatory* a dirty or untidy condition: *look at the cut of your shoes* **68** a direct route; short cut **69** the US name for **block** (sense 15) **70** *sport* the spin of a cut ball **71** *cricket* a stroke made with the bat in a roughly horizontal position **72** *films* an immediate transition from one shot to the next, brought about by splicing the two shots together **73** *informal* an individual piece of music on a record; track **74** words or an action that hurt another person's feelings **75** a refusal to recognize an acquaintance; snub **76** *informal, chiefly US* an unauthorized absence, esp from a school class **77** *chem* a fraction obtained in distillation, as in oil refining **78** the metal removed in a single pass of a machine tool **79 a** the shape of the teeth of a file **b** their coarseness or fineness **80** *Brit* a stretch of water, esp a canal **81** **a cut above** *informal* superior (to); better (than) **82** **make the cut** *golf* to better or equal the required score after two rounds in a strokeplay tournament, thus avoiding elimination from the final two rounds **83** **miss the cut** *golf* to achieve a greater score after the first two rounds of a strokeplay tournament than that required to play in the remaining two rounds ▷ See also **cut across, cut along, cutback, cut down, cut in, cut off, cut out, cut up** [C13 probably of Scandinavian origin; compare Norwegian *kutte* to cut, Icelandic *kuti* small knife]

cut across *vb* (*preposition*) **1** (*intr*) to be contrary to ordinary procedure or limitations: *opinion on European integration still cuts clean across party lines* **2** to cross or traverse, making a shorter route: *she cut across the field quickly*

cut along *vb* (*intr, adverb*) *Brit informal* to hurry off

cut-and-cover *adj* designating a method of constructing a tunnel by excavating a cutting to the required depth and then backfilling the excavation over the tunnel roof

cut and paste *n* a technique used in word processing by which a section of text can be moved within a document

cut and thrust *n* **1** *fencing* using both the blade and the point of a sword **2** (in argument, debate, etc) a lively and spirited exchange of ideas or opinions

cutaneous (kjuː'teɪnɪəs) *adj* of, relating to, or affecting the skin [C16 from New Latin *cutāneus*, from Latin *cutis* skin; see HIDE²] > **cu'taneously** *adv*

cutaway ('kʌtəˌweɪ) *n* **1** a man's coat cut diagonally from the front waist to the back of the knees **2 a** a drawing or model of a machine, engine, etc, in which part of the casing is omitted to reveal the workings **b** (*as modifier*): *a cutaway model* **3** *films, television* a shot separate from the main action of a scene, to emphasize something or to show simultaneous events

cutback ('kʌtˌbæk) *n* **1** a decrease or reduction **2** another word (esp US) for **flashback** ▷ *vb* **cut back** (*adverb*) **3** (*tr*) to shorten by cutting off the end; prune **4** (when *intr*, foll by *on*) to reduce or make a reduction (in) **5** (*intr*) *chiefly US* (in films) to show an event that took place earlier in the narrative; flash back

cutch (kʌtʃ) *n* another name for **catechu**

Cutch (kʌtʃ) *n* a variant spelling of **Kutch**

cutcherry *or* **cutchery** ('kʌtʃərɪ) *n, pl* **-cherries** *or* **-cheries** (formerly, in India) government offices and law courts collectively [C17 from Hindi *Kachahrī*]

cut down *vb* (*adverb*) **1** (*tr*) to fell **2** (when *intr*, often foll by *on*) to reduce or make a reduction (in): *to cut down on drink* **3** (*tr*) to remake (an old garment) in order to make a smaller one **4** (*tr*) to kill: *he was cut down in battle* **5** **cut (a person) down to size** to reduce in importance or decrease the conceit of

cute (kjuːt) *adj* **1** appealing or attractive, esp in a pretty way **2** *informal* affecting cleverness or

C

prettiness **3** clever; shrewd [C18 (in the sense: clever): shortened from ACUTE] ▷ ˈcutely adv ▷ ˈcuteness n

cutesy (ˈkjuːtsɪ) adj cutesier, cutesiest informal, chiefly US affectedly cute or coy

cut glass n **1 a** glass, esp bowls, vases, etc, decorated by facet-cutting or grinding **b** (as modifier): a cut-glass vase **2** (modifier) (of an accent) upper-class; refined

cuticle (ˈkjuːtɪkəl) n **1** dead skin, esp that round the base of a fingernail or toenail **2** another name for **epidermis 3** any covering layer or membrane **4** the protective layer, containing cutin, that covers the epidermis of higher plants **5** the hard protective layer covering the epidermis of many invertebrates [C17 from Latin cutĭcula diminutive of cutis skin] ▷ cuticular (kjuːˈtɪkjʊlə) adj

cuticula (kjuːˈtɪkjʊlə) n, pl -lae (-liː) anatomy cuticle (sense 1); see CUTICLE]

cutie or **cutey** (ˈkjuːtɪ) n slang a person regarded as appealing or attractive, esp a girl or woman

cut in vb (adverb) **1** (intr; often foll by on) Also: **cut into** to break in or interrupt **2** (intr) to interrupt a dancing couple to dance with one of them **3** (intr) (of a driver, motor vehicle, etc) to draw in front of another vehicle leaving too little space **4** (tr) informal to allow to have a share **5** (intr) to take the place of a person in a card game ▷ n **cut-in 6** Also called: **insert** films a separate shot or scene inserted at a relevant point

cutin (ˈkjuːtɪn) n a waxy waterproof substance, consisting of derivatives of fatty acids, that is the main constituent of the plant cuticle [C19 from Latin cutis skin + -IN]

cutinize or **cutinise** (ˈkjuːtɪˌnaɪz) vb to become or cause to become covered or impregnated with cutin ▷ ˌcutiniˈzation or ˌcutiniˈsation n

cutis (ˈkjuːtɪs) n, pl -tes (-tiːz) or -tises zoology a technical name for the **skin** [C17 from Latin: skin]

cutlass (ˈkʌtləs) n a curved, one-edged sword formerly used by sailors [C16 from French coutelas, from coutel knife, from Latin cultellus a small knife, from culter knife; see COULTER]

cutlass fish n US another name for the **hairtail** (the fish)

cutler (ˈkʌtlə) n a person who makes or sells cutlery [C14 from French coutelier, ultimately from Latin culter knife; see CUTLASS]

cutlery (ˈkʌtlərɪ) n **1** implements used for eating, such as knives, forks, and spoons **2** instruments used for cutting **3** the art or business of a cutler

cutlet (ˈkʌtlɪt) n **1** a piece of meat taken esp from the best end of neck of lamb, pork, etc **2** a flat croquette of minced chicken, lobster, etc [C18 from Old French costelette, literally: a little rib, from coste rib, from Latin costa]

cutline (ˈkʌtˌlaɪn) n **1** US and Canadian a caption accompanying an illustration **2** US and Canadian a line marked on a piece of wood, metal, etc, to show where it is to be cut

cut off vb (tr, adverb) **1** to remove by cutting **2** to intercept or interrupt something, esp a telephone conversation **3** to discontinue the supply of: to cut off the water **4** to bring to an end **5** to deprive of rights; disinherit: she was cut off without a penny **6** to sever or separate: she was cut off from her family **7** to occupy a position so as to prevent or obstruct (a retreat or escape) ▷ n **cutoff 8 a** the act of cutting off; limit or termination **b** (as modifier): the cutoff point **9** chiefly US a route or way that is shorter than the usual one; short cut **10** a device to terminate the flow of a fluid in a pipe or duct **11** the remnant of metal, plastic, etc, left after parts have been machined or trimmed. Also called: **offcut 12** electronics **a** the value of voltage, frequency, etc, below or above which an electronic device cannot function efficiently **b** (as modifier): cutoff voltage **13** a channel cutting across the neck of a meander, which leaves an oxbow lake **14** another name for **oxbow** (the lake)

cut-offs (ˈkʌtɒfs) pl n trousers that have been

shortened to calf length or to make shorts

cut out vb (adverb) **1** (tr) to delete or remove **2** (tr) to shape or form by cutting: to cut out a dress **3** (tr; usually passive) to suit or equip for: you're not cut out for this job **4** (intr) (of an engine, etc) to cease to operate suddenly **5** (tr) printing to remove the background from a photograph or drawing to make the outline of the subject stand out **6** (intr) (of an electrical device) to switch off, usually automatically **7** (tr) informal to oust and supplant (a rival) **8** (intr) (of a person) to be excluded from a card game **9** (tr) informal to cease doing something, esp something undesirable (esp in the phrase **cut it out**) **10** (tr) soccer to intercept (a pass) **11** (tr) to separate (cattle) from a herd **12** (intr) Austral and NZ to end or finish: the road cuts out at the creek **13 have one's work cut out** to have as much work as one can manage ▷ n **cutout 14** something that has been or is intended to be cut out from something else **15** a photograph or drawing from which the background has been cut away **16** a device that switches off or interrupts an electric circuit, esp a switch acting as a safety device **17** an impressed stamp cut out from an envelope for collecting purposes **18** Austral slang the end of shearing

cut-price or esp US **cut-rate** adj **1** available at prices or rates below the standard price or rate **2** (prenominal) offering goods or services at prices below the standard price: a cut-price shop

cutpurse (ˈkʌtˌpɜːs) n an archaic word for **pickpocket**

CUTS (kʌts) n acronym for Computer Users' Tape System

cut sheet feed n computing the automatic movement of single sheets of paper through the platen of the printer

cut string n another name for **bridgeboard**

Cuttack (kʌˈtæk) n a city in NE India, in E Orissa near the mouth of the Mahanadi River: former state capital until 1948. Pop: 535 139 (2001)

cutter (ˈkʌtə) n **1** a person or thing that cuts, esp a person who cuts cloth for clothing **2** a sailing boat with its mast stepped further aft so as to have a larger foretriangle than that of a sloop **3** a ship's boat, powered by oars or sail, for carrying passengers or light cargo **4** a small lightly armed boat, as used in the enforcement of customs regulations **5** a pig weighing between 68 and 82 kg, from which fillets and larger joints are cut

cut-throat n **1** a person who cuts throats; murderer **2** Also called: **cut-throat razor** Brit a razor with a long blade that usually folds into the handle. US name: **straight razor** ▷ adj **3** bloodthirsty or murderous; cruel **4** fierce or relentless in competition: cut-throat prices **5** (of some games) played by three people: cut-throat poker

cutting (ˈkʌtɪŋ) n **1** a piece cut off from the main part of something **2** horticulture **a** a method of vegetative propagation in which a part of a plant, such as a stem or leaf, is induced to form its own roots **b** a part separated for this purpose **3** Also called (esp US and Canadian): **clipping** an article, photograph, etc, cut from a newspaper or other publication **4** the editing process by which a film is cut and made **5** an excavation in a piece of high land for a road, railway, etc, enabling it to remain at approximately the same level **6** Irish informal sharp-wittedness: there is no cutting in him **7** (modifier) designed for or adapted to cutting; edged; sharp: a cutting tool ▷ adj **8** keen; piercing: a cutting wind **9** tending to hurt the feelings: a cutting remark ▷ ˈcuttingly adv

cutting compound n engineering a mixture, such as oil, water, and soap, used for cooling drills and other cutting tools

cutting edge n **1** the leading position in any field; forefront: on the cutting edge of space technology ▷ adj **cutting-edge 2** at the forefront of people or things in a field of activity; leading: cutting-edge technology

cutting grass n a W African name for **cane rat** (sense 1)

cutting horse n US and Canadian a saddle horse trained for use in separating an individual animal, such as a cow, from a herd

cuttle (ˈkʌtəl) n **1** short for **cuttlefish** or **cuttlebone 2** little cuttle a small cuttlefish, Sepiola atlantica, often found on beaches [Old English cudele; related to Old High German kiot bag, Norwegian dialect kaule cuttle, Old English codd bag]

cuttlebone (ˈkʌtəlˌbəʊn) n the internal calcareous shell of the cuttlefish, used as a mineral supplement to the diet of cage-birds and as a polishing agent

cuttlefish (ˈkʌtəlˌfɪʃ) n, pl -fish or -fishes any cephalopod mollusc of the genus Sepia and related genera, which occur near the bottom of inshore waters and have a broad flattened body: order Decapoda (decapods). Sometimes shortened to: **cuttle**. See also **squid**

cutty (ˈkʌtɪ) Scot and Northern English dialect ▷ adj **1** short or cut short ▷ n, pl -ties **2** something cut short, such as a spoon or short-stemmed tobacco pipe **3** an immoral girl or woman (in Scotland used as a general term of abuse for a woman) **4** a short thickset girl [C18 (Scottish and northern English): from CUT (vb)]

cutty grass n a species of sedge, Cyperus ustulatus, of New Zealand with sharp leaves

Cutty Sark n a three-masted merchant clipper built in 1869: now kept at Greenwich, London [named after the witch in Robert Burns' poem Tam O'Shanter, who wore only a cutty sark (short shirt)]

cutty stool n (formerly, in Scotland) the church seat on which an unchaste person sat while being harangued by the minister

cut up vb (tr, adverb) **1** to cut into pieces **2** to inflict injuries on **3** (usually passive) informal to affect the feelings of deeply **4** informal to subject to severe criticism **5** informal (of a driver) to overtake or pull in front of (another driver) in a dangerous manner **6 cut up rough** Brit informal to become angry or bad-tempered ▷ n **cut-up 7** informal, chiefly US a joker or prankster

cut-up technique n a technique of writing involving cutting up lines or pages of prose and rearranging these fragments, popularized by the novelist William Burroughs (1914–97)

cutwater (ˈkʌtˌwɔːtə) n the forward part of the stem of a vessel, which cuts through the water

cutwork (ˈkʌtˌwɜːk) n openwork embroidery in which the pattern is cut away from the background

cutworm (ˈkʌtˌwɜːm) n the caterpillar of various noctuid moths, esp those of the genus Argrotis, which is a pest of young crop plants in North America

cuvée (kuːˈveɪ) n an individual batch or blend of wine [C19 from French, literally: put in a cask, from cuve cask]

cuvette (kjuːˈvɛt) n a shallow dish or vessel for holding liquid [C17 from French, diminutive of cuve cask, from Latin cupa]

Cuxhaven (ˈkʊksˌhɑːvən; German kʊksˈhɑːfən) n a port in NW Germany, at the mouth of the River Elbe. Pop: 52 876 (2003 est)

Cuyabá (Portuguese kujaˈba) n a variant spelling of **Cuiabá**

Cuzco (Spanish ˈkuθko) or **Cusco** n a city in S central Peru: former capital of the Inca Empire, with extensive Inca remains; university (1692). Pop: 307 000 (2005 est)

cv the internet domain name for Cape Verde

CV abbreviation for **1 curriculum vitae 2** (in Canada) Cross of Valour

CVA abbreviation for **cerebrovascular accident**

CVO abbreviation for Commander of the Royal Victorian Order

CVS abbreviation for **1** (in Britain) Council of Voluntary Service **2 chorionic villus sampling 3** computing concurrent versions system

CW 1 *radio abbreviation for* **continuous waves** ▷ *n* **2 a** an informal term for **Morse code b** (*as modifier*): *his CW speed is 30 words per minute* **3** *abbreviation for* chemical weapons *or* chemical warfare

CWA (*in Australia*) *abbreviation for* Country Women's Association

Cwlth *abbreviation for* Commonwealth

cwm (kuːm) *n* **1** (*in Wales*) a valley **2** *geology* another name for **cirque** (sense 1)

Cwmbran (ˌkuːmˈbrɑːn) *n* a new town in SE Wales, in Torfaen county borough, developed in the 1950s. Pop: 47 254 (2001)

c.w.o. *or* **CWO** *abbreviation for* cash with order

c-word *n* (*sometimes capital; preceded by the*) a euphemistic way of referring to the word **cunt**

CWS *abbreviation for* Cooperative Wholesale Society

cwt *abbreviation for* hundredweight [*c*, from the Latin numeral C one hundred (*centum*)]

CWU (*in Britain*) *abbreviation for* Communications Workers Union

cx *the internet domain name for* Christmas Island

CY *international car registration for* Cyprus

-cy *suffix* **1** (*forming nouns from adjectives ending in -t, -tic, -te, and -nt*) indicating state, quality, or condition: *plutocracy; lunacy; intimacy; infancy* **2** (*forming abstract nouns from other nouns*) rank or office: *captaincy* [via Old French from Latin *-cia, -tia*, Greek *-kia, -tia*, abstract noun suffixes]

CYA *text messaging abbreviation for* see you: used as a farewell in text messages, emails, etc [C20]

cyan (ˈsaɪæn, ˈsaɪən) *n* **1** a highly saturated green-blue that is the complementary colour of red and forms, with magenta and yellow, a set of primary colours ▷ *adj* **2** of this colour: *a cyan filter* [C19 from Greek *kuanos* dark blue]

cyan- *combining form* a variant of **cyano-** before a vowel: *cyanamide; cyanide*

cyanamide (saɪˈænəˌmaɪd, -mɪd) *or* **cyanamid** (saɪˈænəmɪd) *n* **1** Also called: **cyanogenamide** (ˌsaɪənəʊˈdʒɛnəˌmaɪd, -mɪd) a white or colourless crystalline soluble weak dibasic acid, which can be hydrolysed to urea. Formula: H_2NCN **2** a salt or ester of cyanamide **3** short for **calcium cyanamide**

cyanate (ˈsaɪəˌneɪt) *n* any salt or ester of cyanic acid, containing the ion ^-OCN or the group $-OCN$

cyanic acid (saɪˈænɪk) *n* a colourless poisonous volatile liquid acid that hydrolyses readily to ammonia and carbon dioxide. Formula: HOCN. Compare **isocyanic acid, fulminic acid**

cyanide (ˈsaɪəˌnaɪd) *or* **cyanid** (ˈsaɪənɪd) *n* **1** any salt or ester of hydrocyanic acid. Cyanides contain the ion CN^- and are extremely poisonous **2** another name (*not in technical usage*) for **nitrile** ▷ ˌcyaniˈdation *n*

cyanide process *n* a process for recovering gold and silver from ores by treatment with a weak solution of sodium cyanide. Also called: **cyaniding**

cyanine (ˈsaɪəˌniːn) *or* **cyanin** (ˈsaɪənɪn) *n* **1** a blue dye used to extend the sensitivity of photographic emulsions to colours other than blue and ultraviolet **2** any of a class of chemically related dyes, used for the same purpose

cyanite (ˈsaɪəˌnaɪt) *n* a variant spelling of **kyanite** ▷ **cyanitic** (ˌsaɪəˈnɪtɪk) *adj*

cyano- *or before a vowel* **cyan-** *combining form* **1** blue or dark blue: *cyanotype* **2** indicating cyanogen: *cyanohydrin* **3** indicating cyanide [from Greek *kuanos* (adj) dark blue, (n) dark blue enamel, lapis lazuli]

cyanoacrylate (ˌsaɪənəʊˈækrɪleɪt) *n* a substance with an acrylate base, usually sold in the form of a quick-setting highly adhesive glue

cyanobacteria (ˌsaɪənəʊbækˈtɪərɪə) *pl n, sing* **-rium** (-rɪəm) a group of photosynthetic bacteria (phylum *Cyanobacteria*) containing a blue photosynthetic pigment. Former name: **blue-green algae**

cyanocobalamin (ˌsaɪənəʊkəʊˈbæləmɪn) *n* a complex red crystalline compound, containing cyanide and cobalt and occurring in liver: lack of it in the tissues leads to pernicious anaemia.

Formula: $C_{63}H_{88}O_{14}N_{14}PCo$. Also called: **vitamin B$_{12}$** [C20 from CYANO- + COBAL(T) + (VIT)AMIN]

cyanogen (saɪˈænədʒɪn) *n* an extremely poisonous colourless flammable gas with an almond-like odour: has been used in chemical warfare. Formula: $(CN)_2$ [C19 from French *cyanogène*; see CYANO-, -GEN; so named because it is one of the constituents of Prussian blue]

cyanogenesis (ˌsaɪənəʊˈdʒɛnɪsɪs) *n botany* the release by certain plants, such as cherry laurel, of hydrogen cyanide, esp after wounding or invasion by pathogens

cyanohydrin (ˌsaɪənəʊˈhaɪdrɪn) *n* any of a class of organic compounds containing a cyanide group and a hydroxyl group bound to the same carbon atom

cyanophyte (saɪˈænəfaɪt) *n* a former name for a cyanobacterium. See **cyanobacteria**

cyanosis (ˌsaɪəˈnəʊsɪs) *n pathol* a bluish-purple discoloration of skin and mucous membranes usually resulting from a deficiency of oxygen in the blood ▷ **cyanotic** (ˌsaɪəˈnɒtɪk) *adj*

cyanotype (saɪˈænəˌtaɪp) *n* another name for **blueprint** (sense 1)

Cybele (ˈsɪbɪlɪ) *n classical myth* the Phrygian goddess of nature, mother of all living things and consort of Attis; identified with the Greek Rhea or Demeter

cyber- *combining form* indicating computers: *cyberphobia* [C20 back formation from CYBERNETICS]

cyberathlete (ˈsaɪbəˌæθliːt) *n* a professional player of computer games ▷ ˌcyberathˈletics *n*

cybercafé (ˈsaɪbəˌkæfeɪ, -ˌkæfɪ) *n* a café with computer equipment that gives public access to the internet

cybercrime (ˈsaɪbəˌkraɪm) *n* **1** the illegal use of computers and the internet **2** crime committed by means of computers or the internet ▷ ˌcyberˈcriminal *n*

cybernate (ˈsaɪbəˌneɪt) *vb* to control (a manufacturing process) with a servomechanism or (of a process) to be controlled by a servomechanism [C20 from CYBER(NETICS) + -ATE¹] ▷ ˌcyberˈnation *n*

cybernetics (ˌsaɪbəˈnɛtɪks) *n* (*functioning as singular*) the branch of science concerned with control systems in electronic and mechanical devices and the extent to which useful comparisons can be made between man-made and biological systems. See also **feedback** (sense 1) [C20 from Greek *kubernētēs* steersman, from *kubernan* to steer, control] ▷ ˌcyberˈnetic *adj* ▷ ˌcyberˈneticist *n*

cyberpet (ˈsaɪbəˌpɛt) *n* an electronic toy that simulates the activities of a pet, requiring the owner to feed, discipline, and entertain it

cyberphobia (ˌsaɪbəˈfəʊbɪə) *n* an irrational fear of computers ▷ ˌcyberˈphobic *adj*

cyberpunk (ˈsaɪbəˌpʌŋk) *n* **1** a genre of science fiction that features rebellious computer hackers and is set in a dystopian society integrated by computer networks **2** a writer of cyberpunk

cybersecurity (ˌsaɪbəsɪˈkjʊərɪtɪ) *n computing* the state of being safe from electronic crime and the measures taken to achieve this

cybersex (ˈsaɪbəˌsɛks) *n* **1** the exchanging of sexual messages or information via the internet **2** sexual activity performed remotely by means of virtual reality equipment

cyberspace (ˈsaɪbəˌspeɪs) *n* all of the data stored in a large computer or network represented as a three-dimensional model through which a virtual-reality user can move

cybersquatting (ˈsaɪbəˌskwɒtɪŋ) *n* the practice of registering an internet domain name that is likely to be wanted by another person, business, or organization in the hope that it can be sold to them for a profit ▷ ˈcyberˌsquatter *n*

cyberterrorism (ˈsaɪbəˌtɛrərɪzəm) *n* the illegal use of computers and the internet to achieve some goal ▷ ˈcyberˌterrorist *n*

cyberwar (ˈsaɪbəˌwɔː) *n* another term for **information warfare**

cyborg (ˈsaɪˌbɔːg) *n* (in science fiction) a living being whose powers are enhanced by computer implants or mechanical body parts [C20 from *cyb(ernetic) org(anism)*]

cycad (ˈsaɪkæd) *n* any tropical or subtropical gymnosperm plant of the phylum *Cycadophyta*, having an unbranched stem with fernlike leaves crowded at the top. See also **sago palm** (sense 2) [C19 from New Latin *Cycas* name of genus, from Greek *kukas*, scribe's error for *koïkas*, from *koïx* a kind of palm, probably of Egyptian origin] ▷ ˌcycaˈdaceous *adj*

Cyclades (ˈsɪkləˌdiːz) *pl n* a group of over 200 islands in the S Aegean Sea, forming a department of Greece. Capital: Hermoupolis (Siros). Pop: 112 615 (2001). Area: 2572 sq km (993 sq miles). Modern Greek name: *Kikládhes*

Cycladic (sɪˈklædɪk) *adj* of or relating to the Cyclades or their inhabitants

cyclamate (ˈsaɪkləˌmeɪt, ˈsɪkləˌmeɪt) *n* a salt or ester of cyclamic acid. Certain of the salts have a very sweet taste and were formerly used as food additives and sugar substitutes [C20 *cycl(ohexyl-sulph)amate*]

cyclamen (ˈsɪkləmən, -ˌmɛn) *n* **1** any Old World plant of the primulaceous genus *Cyclamen*, having nodding white, pink, or red flowers, with reflexed petals. See also **sowbread** ▷ *adj* **2** of a dark reddish-purple colour [C16 from Medieval Latin, from Latin *cyclamīnos*, from Greek *kuklaminos*, probably from *kuklos* circle, referring to the bulb-like roots]

cycle (ˈsaɪkəl) *n* **1** a recurring period of time in which certain events or phenomena occur and reach completion or repeat themselves in a regular sequence **2** a completed series of events that follows or is followed by another series of similar events occurring in the same sequence **3** the time taken or needed for one such series **4** a vast period of time; age; aeon **5** a group of poems or prose narratives forming a continuous story about a central figure or event: *the Arthurian cycle* **6** a series of miracle plays: *the Chester cycle* **7** a group or sequence of songs (see **song cycle**) **8** short for **bicycle, tricycle, motorcycle,** etc **9** *astronomy* the orbit of a celestial body **10** a recurrent series of events or processes in plants and animals: *a life cycle; a growth cycle; a metabolic cycle* **11** *physics* a continuous change or a sequence of changes in the state of a system that leads to the restoration of the system to its original state after a finite period of time **12** one of a series of repeated changes in the magnitude of a periodically varying quantity, such as current or voltage **13** *computing* **a** a set of operations that can be both treated and repeated as a unit **b** the time required to complete a set of operations **c** one oscillation of the regular voltage waveform used to synchronize processes in a digital computer **14** (in generative grammar) the set of cyclic rules ▷ *vb* **15** (*tr*) to process through a cycle or system **16** (*intr*) to move in or pass through cycles **17** to travel by or ride a bicycle or tricycle [C14 from Late Latin *cyclus*, from Greek *kuklos* cycle, circle, ring, wheel; see WHEEL] ▷ ˈcycling *n, adj*

cycle of erosion *n* the hypothetical sequence of modifications to the earth's surface by erosion, from the original uplift of the land to the ultimate low plain, usually divided into the youthful, mature, and old stages

cyclic (ˈsaɪklɪk, ˈsɪklɪk) *or* **cyclical** (ˈsaɪklɪkəl, ˈsɪklɪkəl) *adj* **1** recurring or revolving in cycles **2** (of an organic compound) containing a closed saturated or unsaturated ring of atoms. See also **heterocyclic** and **homocyclic 3** *botany* arranged in whorls: *cyclic petals* **b** having parts arranged in this way: *cyclic flowers* **4** *music* of or relating to a musical form consisting of several movements sharing thematic material **5** *geometry* (of a polygon) having vertices that lie on a circle **6** (in generative grammar) denoting one of a set of transformational rules all of which must apply to

C

a clause before any one of them applies to any clause in which the first clause is embedded > 'cyclically adv

cyclical unemployment n unemployment caused by fluctuations in the level of economic activity inherent in trade cycles

cyclic AMP n cyclic adenosine monophosphate: a constituent of biological cells, responsible for triggering processes that are dependent on hormones

cyclic pitch lever n a lever in a helicopter to change the angle of attack of individual rotor blades, causing the helicopter to move forwards, backwards, or sideways. Compare **collective pitch lever**

cycling shorts pl n tight-fitting shorts reaching partway to the knee for cycling, sport, etc

cyclist ('saɪklɪst) or US **cycler** n a person who rides or travels by bicycle, motorcycle, etc

cyclo- or before a vowel **cycl-** combining form **1** indicating a circle or ring: cyclotron **2** denoting a cyclic compound: cyclohexane [from Greek kuklos CYCLE]

cycloalkane (ˌsaɪkləʊ'ælkeɪn) n any saturated hydrocarbon similar to an alkane but having a cyclic molecular structure and the general formula C_nH_{2n}. Also called: cycloparaffin

cyclo-cross n a form of cycle race held over rough ground b this sport

cyclogiro ('saɪkləʊˌdʒaɪrəʊ) n aeronautics obsolete an aircraft lifted and propelled by pivoted blades rotating parallel to roughly horizontal transverse axes

cyclograph ('saɪkləʊˌɡrɑːf, -ˌɡræf) n another name for **arcograph**

cyclohexane (ˌsaɪkləʊ'hɛkseɪn, ˌsɪk-) n a colourless insoluble flammable liquid cycloalkane with a pungent odour, made by hydrogenation of benzene and used as a paint remover and solvent. Formula: C_6H_{12}

cyclohexanone (ˌsaɪkləʊ'hɛksəˌnəʊn) n a colourless liquid used as a solvent for cellulose lacquers. Formula: $C_6H_{10}O$

cycloid ('saɪklɔɪd) adj **1** resembling a circle **2** (of fish scales) rounded, thin, and smooth-edged, as those of the salmon **3** psychiatry (of a type of personality) characterized by exaggerated swings of mood between elation and depression. See also **cyclothymia** ▷ n **4** geometry the curve described by a point on the circumference of a circle as the circle rolls along a straight line. Compare **trochoid** (sense 1) **5** a fish that has cycloid scales > cy'cloidal adj > cy'cloidally adv

cyclometer (saɪ'klɒmɪtə) n a device that records the number of revolutions made by a wheel and hence the distance travelled > cy'clometry n

cyclone ('saɪkləʊn) n **1** another name for **depression** (sense 6) **2** a violent tropical storm; hurricane [c19 from Greek kuklōn a turning around, from kukloein to revolve, from kuklos wheel] > cyclonic (saɪ'klɒnɪk), cy'clonical or 'cyclonal adj > cy'clonically adv

Cyclone ('saɪkləʊn) adj trademark Austral and NZ (of fencing) made of interlaced wire and metal

cyclonite ('saɪkləˌnaɪt) n a white crystalline insoluble explosive prepared by the action of nitric acid on hexamethylenetetramine; cyclotrimethylenetrinitramine: used in bombs and shells. Formula: $C_3H_6N_6O_6$ [c20 from CYCLO- + (trimethylene-tri)nit(ramin)e]

cycloparaffin (ˌsaɪkləʊ'pærəfɪn, ˌsɪk-) n another name for **cycloalkane**

Cyclopean (ˌsaɪkləʊ'piːən, saɪ'kləʊpɪən) adj **1** of, relating to, or resembling the Cyclops **2** denoting, relating to, or having the kind of masonry used in preclassical Greek architecture, characterized by large dry undressed blocks of stone

cyclopedia or **cyclopaedia** (ˌsaɪkləʊ'piːdɪə) n a less common word for **encyclopedia**. > ˌcyclo'pedic or ˌcyclo'paedic adj > ˌcyclo'pedist or ˌcyclo'paedist n

cyclopentadiene (ˌsaɪkləʊˌpɛntə'daɪiːn) n a colourless liquid unsaturated cyclic hydrocarbon

obtained in the cracking of petroleum hydrocarbons and the distillation of coal tar: used in the manufacture of plastics and insecticides. Formula: C_5H_6

cyclopentane (ˌsaɪkləʊ'pɛnteɪn, ˌsɪk-) n a colourless insoluble cycloalkane found in petroleum and used mainly as a solvent. Formula: C_5H_{10}

cyclophosphamide (ˌsaɪkləʊ'fɒsfəˌmaɪd) n an alkylating agent used in the treatment of leukaemia and lymphomas [c20 from CYCLO- + PHOSPH(ORUS) + AMIDE]

cycloplegia (ˌsaɪkləʊ'pliːdʒɪə, ˌsɪk-) n paralysis of the muscles that adjust the shape of the lens of the eye, resulting in loss of ability to focus > ˌcyclo'plegic adj

cyclopropane (ˌsaɪkləʊ'prəʊpeɪn, ˌsɪk-) n a colourless flammable gaseous hydrocarbon, used in medicine as an anaesthetic; trimethylene. It is a cycloalkane with molecules containing rings of three carbon atoms. Formula: C_3H_6; boiling pt.: −34°C

cyclops ('saɪklɒps) n, pl cyclops or cyclopes (saɪ'kləʊpiːz) any copepod of the genus Cyclops, characterized by having one eye

Cyclops ('saɪklɒps) n, pl Cyclopes (saɪ'kləʊpiːz) or Cyclopses classical myth one of a race of giants having a single eye in the middle of the forehead, encountered by Odysseus in the Odyssey See also **Polyphemus** [c15 from Latin Cyclōps, from Greek Kuklōps, literally: round eye, from kuklos circle + ōps eye]

cyclorama (ˌsaɪkləʊ'rɑːmə) n **1** Also called: panorama a large picture, such as a battle scene, on the interior wall of a cylindrical room, designed to appear in natural perspective to a spectator in the centre **2** theatre **a** a curtain or wall curving along the back of a stage, usually painted to represent the sky and serving to enhance certain lighting effects **b** any set of curtains that enclose the back and sides of a stage setting [c19 CYCLO- + Greek horama view, sight, on the model of panorama] > cycloramic (ˌsaɪkləʊ'ræmɪk) adj

cyclosis (saɪ'kləʊsɪs) n, pl -ses (-siːz) biology the circulation of cytoplasm or cell organelles, such as food vacuoles in some protozoans [c19 from Greek kuklōsis an encircling, from kukloun to surround, from kuklos circle]

cyclosporin (ˌsaɪkləʊ'spɔːrɪn) n a variant spelling of **ciclosporin**

cyclostome ('saɪkləˌstəʊm, 'sɪk-) n **1** any primitive aquatic jawless vertebrate of the class Cyclostomata, such as the lamprey and hagfish, having a round sucking mouth and pouchlike gills ▷ adj **2** of, relating to, or belonging to the class Cyclostomata ▷ Also: marsipobranch > cyclostomate (saɪ'klɒstəmɪt, -ˌmeɪt) or cyclostomatous (ˌsaɪkləʊ'stɒmətəs, -'stəʊmə-, ˌsɪk-) adj

cyclostyle ('saɪkləˌstaɪl) n **1** a kind of pen with a small toothed wheel, used for cutting minute holes in a specially prepared stencil. Copies of the design so formed can be printed on a duplicator by forcing ink through the holes **2** an office duplicator using a stencil prepared in this way ▷ vb **3** (tr) to print on a duplicator using such a stencil > 'cycloˌstyled adj

cyclothymia (ˌsaɪkləʊ'θaɪmɪə, ˌsɪk-) n psychiatry a condition characterized by periodical swings of mood between excitement and depression, activity and inactivity. See also **manic-depressive** > ˌcyclo'thymic or ˌcyclo'thymiˌac adj, n

cyclotron ('saɪkləˌtrɒn) n a type of particle accelerator in which the particles spiral inside two D-shaped hollow metal electrodes placed facing each other under the effect of a strong vertical magnetic field, gaining energy by a high-frequency voltage applied between these electrodes

cyder ('saɪdə) n a variant spelling (esp Brit) of **cider**

Cydnus ('sɪdnəs) n the ancient name for the (River) Tarsus

cyesis (saɪ'iːsɪs) n, pl -ses (-siːz) med the technical name for **pregnancy** [from Greek kuēsis]

CYF (in New Zealand) abbreviation for Child, Youth, and Family: a section of the Ministry of Social Development

cygnet ('sɪɡnɪt) n a young swan [c15 sygnett, from Old French cygne swan, from Latin cygnus, from Greek kuknos]

Cygnus ('sɪɡnəs) n, Latin genitive Cygni ('sɪɡnaɪ) a constellation in the N hemisphere lying between Pegasus and Draco in the Milky Way. The constellation contains the **Cygnus Loop** supernova remnant, the intense radio galaxy Cygnus A, and the intense galactic X-ray source Cygnus X-1, which is probably a black hole [Latin: swan; see CYGNET]

cylinder ('sɪlɪndə) n **1** a solid consisting of two parallel planes bounded by identical closed curves, usually circles, that are interconnected at every point by a set of parallel lines, usually perpendicular to the planes. Volume base area × length **2** a surface formed by a line moving round a closed plane curve at a fixed angle to it **3** any object shaped like a cylinder **4** the chamber in a reciprocating internal-combustion engine, pump, or compressor within which the piston moves. See also **cylinder block 5** the rotating mechanism of a revolver, situated behind the barrel and containing cartridge chambers **6** printing any of the rotating drums on a printing press **7** Also called: cylinder seal a cylindrical seal of stone, clay, or precious stone decorated with linear designs, found in the Middle East and Balkans: dating from about 6000 BC **8** Also called: hot-water cylinder Brit a vertical cylindrical tank for storing hot water, esp an insulated one made of copper used in a domestic hot-water system **9** firing on all cylinders working or performing at full capability ▷ vb **10** (tr) to provide (a system) with cylinders [c16 from Latin cylindrus, from Greek kulindros a roller, from kulindein to roll] > 'cylinder-ˌlike adj

cylinder barrel n engineering the metal casting containing a cylinder of a reciprocating internal-combustion engine

cylinder block n the metal casting containing the cylinders and cooling channels or fins of a reciprocating internal-combustion engine. Sometimes shortened to: **block**

cylinder head n the detachable metal casting that fits onto the top of a cylinder block. In an engine it contains part of the combustion chamber and in an overhead-valve four-stroke engine it houses the valves and their operating mechanisms. Sometimes shortened to: **head**

cylinder press n printing another name for **flat-bed press**

cylindrical (sɪ'lɪndrɪkᵊl) or **cylindric** adj of, shaped like, or characteristic of a cylinder > cyˌlindri'cality or cy'lindricalness n > cy'lindrically adv

cylindrical coordinates pl n three coordinates defining the location of a point in three-dimensional space in terms of its polar coordinates (r, θ) in one plane, usually the (x, y) plane, and its perpendicular distance, z, measured from this plane

cylindroid ('sɪlɪnˌdrɔɪd) n **1** a cylinder with an elliptical cross section ▷ adj **2** resembling a cylinder

cylix ('saɪlɪks, 'sɪl-) n, pl -lices (-lɪˌsiːz) a variant of **kylix**

cyma ('saɪmə) n, pl -mae (-miː) or -mas **1** either of two mouldings having a double curve, part concave and part convex. **Cyma recta** has the convex part nearer the wall and **cyma reversa** has the concave part nearer the wall **2** botany a rare variant of **cyme** [c16 from New Latin, from Greek kuma something swollen, from kuein to be pregnant]

cymar (sɪˈmɑː) *n* a woman's short fur-trimmed jacket, popular in the 17th and 18th centuries [C17 variant of *simar*, from French *simarre*, perhaps ultimately from Basque *zamar* sheepskin]

cymatium (sɪˈmeɪtɪəm, -ʃɪəm) *n, pl* **-tia** (-tɪə, -ʃɪə) *architect* the top moulding of a classical cornice or entablature [C16 see CYMA]

cymbal (ˈsɪmbᵊl) *n* a percussion instrument of indefinite pitch consisting of a thin circular piece of brass, which vibrates when clashed together with another cymbal or struck with a stick [Old English *cymbala*, from Medieval Latin, from Latin *cymbalum*, from Greek *kumbalon*, from *kumbē* something hollow] > **ˈcymbaler**, ˌcymbalˈeer or ˈcymbalist *n* > ˈcymbalˌlike *adj*

cymbalo (ˈsɪmbəˌləʊ) *n, pl* **-los** another name for **dulcimer** [from Italian; see CYMBAL]

cymbidium (sɪmˈbɪdɪəm) *n, pl* **-diums** a genus, *Cymbidium*, of subtropical and tropical orchids native to Australia and Asia, having boat-shaped showy flowers [C19 from Latin *cymba* boat]

cyme (saɪm) *n* an inflorescence in which the first flower is the terminal bud of the main stem and subsequent flowers develop as terminal buds of lateral stems [C18 from Latin *cȳma* cabbage sprout, from Greek *kuma* anything swollen; see CYMA] > **cymiferous** (saɪˈmɪfərəs) *adj*

cymene (ˈsaɪmiːn) *n* a colourless insoluble liquid with an aromatic odour that exists in three isomeric forms; methylpropylbenzene: used as solvents and for making synthetic resins. The *para-* isomer is present in several essential oils. Formula: $CH_3C_6H_4CH(CH_3)_2$ [C19 *cym-* from Greek *kuminon* CUMIN + -ENE]

cymogene (ˈsaɪməˌdʒiːn) *n US* a mixture of volatile flammable hydrocarbons, mainly butane, obtained in the distillation of petroleum [C19 from CYMENE + -GENE]

cymograph (ˈsaɪməˌɡrɑːf, -ˌɡræf) *n* **1** a variant of **kymograph** **2** an instrument for tracing the outline of an architectural moulding > **cymographic** (ˌsaɪməˈɡræfɪk) *adj*

cymoid (ˈsaɪmɔɪd) *adj architect, botany* resembling a cyme or cyma

cymophane (ˈsaɪməˌfeɪn) *n* a yellow or green opalescent variety of chrysoberyl [C19 from Greek *kuma* wave, undulation + -PHANE]

cymose (ˈsaɪməʊs, -məʊz, saɪˈməʊs) *adj* having the characteristics of a cyme > ˈcymosely *adv*

Cymric or **Kymric** (ˈkɪmrɪk) *n* **1** the Welsh language **2** the Brythonic group of Celtic languages **3** a breed of medium-sized cat with soft semi-long hair ▷ *adj* **4** of or relating to the Cymry, any of their languages, Wales, or the Welsh

Cymru (*Welsh* kumˈriː) *n* the Welsh name for **Wales**

Cymry or **Kymry** (ˈkɪmrɪ) *n* the (*functioning as plural*) **1** the Brythonic branch of the Celtic people, comprising the present-day Welsh, Cornish, and Bretons. See **Brythonic** **2** the Welsh people [Welsh: the Welsh]

cynghanedd (kʌŋˈhaneð) *n* a complex system of rhyme and alliteration used in Welsh verse [from Welsh]

cynic (ˈsɪnɪk) *n* **1** a person who believes the worst about people or the outcome of events ▷ *adj* **2** a less common word for **cynical** **3** *astronomy* of or relating to Sirius, the Dog Star [C16 via Latin from Greek *Kunikos*, from *kuōn* dog]

Cynic (ˈsɪnɪk) *n* a member of a sect founded by Antisthenes that scorned worldly things and held that self-control was the key to the only good

cynical (ˈsɪnɪkᵊl) *adj* **1** distrustful or contemptuous of virtue, esp selflessness in others; believing the worst of others, esp that all acts are selfish **2** sarcastic; mocking **3** showing contempt for accepted standards of behaviour, esp of honesty or morality: *the politician betrayed his promises in a cynical way* > ˈcynically *adv* > ˈcynicalness *n*

cynicism (ˈsɪnɪˌsɪzəm) *n* **1** the attitude or beliefs

of a cynic **2** a cynical action, remark, idea, etc

Cynicism (ˈsɪnɪˌsɪzəm) *n* the doctrines of the Cynics

cyno- *combining form* indicating a dog: *cynopodous; cynophobia* [from Greek *kuōn* dog]

cynodont (ˈsaɪnəˌdɒnt) *n* a carnivorous mammal-like reptile of the late Permian and Triassic periods, whose specialized teeth were well developed

cynophobia (ˌsaɪnəˈfəʊbɪə) *n* an irrational fear of dogs

cynopodous (saɪˈnɒpədəs) *adj* (of some mammals, such as dogs) having claws that do not retract [from New Latin, from CYNO- + -PODOUS]

cynosure (ˈsɪnəˌzjʊə, -ʃʊə) *n* **1** a person or thing that attracts notice, esp because of its brilliance or beauty **2** something that serves as a guide [C16 from Latin *Cynosūra* the constellation of Ursa Minor, from Greek *Kunosoura*, from CYNO- + *oura* tail] > ˌcynoˈsural *adj*

Cynthia (ˈsɪnθɪə) *n* another name for **Artemis** (Diana)

cyperaceous (ˌsaɪpəˈreɪʃəs) *adj* of, relating to, or belonging to the *Cyperaceae*, a family of grasslike flowering plants with solid triangular stems, including the sedges, bulrush, cotton grass, and certain rushes. Some are grown as water plants or as ornamental grasses; *Cyperus papyrus* is the papyrus plant. Compare **juncaceous** [C19 from New Latin *Cyperus* type genus, from Latin *cypēros* a kind of rush, from Greek *kupeiros* marsh plant, probably of Semitic origin]

cypher (ˈsaɪfə) *n, vb* a variant spelling of **cipher**

cy pres (siː ˈpreɪ) *n law* the doctrine that the intention of a donor or testator should be carried out as closely as practicable when literal compliance is impossible [C15 from Anglo-French, literally: as near (as possible, etc)]

cypress¹ (ˈsaɪprəs) *n* **1** any coniferous tree of the N temperate genus *Cupressus*, having dark green scalelike leaves and rounded cones: family *Cupressaceae*. See also **Leyland cypress** **2** any of several similar and related trees, such as the widely cultivated *Chamaecyparis lawsoniana* (**Lawson's cypress**), of the western US **3** any of various other coniferous trees, esp the swamp cypress **4** the wood of any of these trees [Old English *cypresse*, from Latin *cyparissus*, from Greek *kuparissos*; related to Latin *cupressus*]

cypress² or **cyprus** (ˈsaɪprəs) *n* a fabric, esp a fine silk, lawn, or crepelike material, often black and worn as mourning [C14 *cyprus* from the island of CYPRUS]

cypress pine *n* any coniferous tree of the Australian genus *Callitris*, having leaves in whorls and yielding valuable timber: family *Cupressaceae*

cypress vine *n* a tropical American convolvulaceous climbing plant, *Ipomoea pennata*, having finely divided compound leaves and scarlet or white tubular flowers

Cyprian (ˈsɪprɪən) *adj* **1** of or relating to Cyprus **2** of or resembling the ancient orgiastic worship of Aphrodite on Cyprus ▷ *n* **3** (*often not capital*) obsolete a licentious person, esp a prostitute or dancer ▷ *n* ▷ *adj* **4** another word for **Cypriot**

cyprinid (sɪˈpraɪnɪd, ˈsɪprɪnɪd) *n* **1** any teleost fish of the mainly freshwater family *Cyprinidae*, typically having toothless jaws and cycloid scales and including such food and game fishes as the carp, tench, roach, rudd, and dace ▷ *adj* **2** of, relating to, or belonging to the *Cyprinidae* **3** resembling a carp; cyprinoid [C19 from New Latin *Cyprīnidae*, from Latin *cyprīnus* carp, from Greek *kuprinos*]

cyprinodont (sɪˈprɪnəˌdɒnt, sɪˈpraɪ-) *n* **1** any small tropical or subtropical soft-finned fish of the mostly marine family *Cyprinodontidae*, resembling carp but having toothed jaws. The group includes the guppy, killifish, swordtail, and topminnow ▷ *adj* **2** of, relating to, or belonging to the *Cyprinodontidae* [C19 from Latin *cyprīnus* carp (see CYPRINID) + -ODONT]

cyprinoid (ˈsɪprɪˌnɔɪd, sɪˈpraɪnɔɪd) *adj* **1** of, relating to, or belonging to the *Cyprinoidea*, a large suborder of teleost fishes including the cyprinids, characins, electric eels, and loaches **2** of, relating to, or resembling the carp ▷ *n* **3** any fish belonging to the *Cyprinoidea* [C19 from Latin *cyprīnus* carp]

Cypriot (ˈsɪprɪət) or **Cypriote** (ˈsɪprɪˌəʊt) *n* **1** a native, citizen, or inhabitant of Cyprus **2** the dialect of Ancient or Modern Greek spoken in Cyprus ▷ *adj* **3** denoting or relating to Cyprus, its inhabitants, or dialects

cypripedium (ˌsɪprɪˈpiːdɪəm) *n* **1** any orchid of the genus *Cypripedium*, having large flowers with an inflated pouchlike lip. See also **lady's-slipper 2** any cultivated tropical orchid of the genus *Paphiopedilum*, having yellow, green, or brownish-purple waxy flowers [C18 from New Latin, from Latin *Cypria* the Cyprian, that is, Venus + *pēs* foot (that is, Venus' slipper)]

Cyprus (ˈsaɪprəs) *n* an island in the E Mediterranean: ceded to Britain by Turkey in 1878 and made a colony in 1925; became an independent republic in 1960 as a member of the Commonwealth; invaded by Turkey in 1974 following a Greek-supported military coup, leading to the partition of the island. In 1983 the Turkish-controlled northern sector declared itself to be an independent state as the Turkish Republic of Northern Cyprus but failed to receive international recognition. Attempts by the U.N. to broker a reunification agreement have failed. Cyprus joined the EU in 2004. The UK maintains two enclaves as military bases (Akrotiri and Dhekelia Sovereign Base Areas), which are not included in Cyprus politically. Languages: Greek and Turkish. Religions: Greek Orthodox and Muslim. Currency: pound and Turkish lira. Capital: Nicosia. Pop (Greek): 675 000 (2001 est); (Turkish): 198 000 (2001 est). Area: 9251 sq km (3571 sq miles)

cypsela (ˈsɪpsɪlə) *n, pl* **-lae** (-ˌliː) the dry one-seeded fruit of the daisy and related plants, which resembles an achene but is surrounded by a calyx sheath [C19 from New Latin, from Greek *kupselē* chest, hollow vessel]

Cyrenaic (ˌsaɪrəˈneɪɪk, ˌsɪrə-) *adj* **1** (in the ancient world) of or relating to the city of Cyrene or the territory of Cyrenaica **2** of or relating to the philosophical school founded by the Greek philosopher Aristippus (?435–?356 BC) in Cyrene that held pleasure to be the highest good ▷ *n* **3** an inhabitant of Cyrene or Cyrenaica **4** a follower of the Cyrenaic school of philosophy

Cyrenaica or **Cirenaica** (ˌsaɪrəˈneɪkə, ˌsɪrə-) *n* a region and former province (1951–63) of E Libya: largely desert; settled by the Greeks in about 630 BC; ruled successively by the Egyptians, Romans, Arabs, Turks, and Italians. Area: 855 370 sq km (330 258 sq miles)

Cyrene (saɪˈriːnɪ) *n* an ancient Greek city of N Africa, near the coast of Cyrenaica: famous for its medical school

Cyrillic (sɪˈrɪlɪk) *adj* **1** denoting or relating to the alphabet derived from that of the Greeks, supposedly by Saint Cyril, for the writing of Slavonic languages: now used primarily for Russian, Bulgarian, and the Serbian dialect of Serbo-Croat ▷ *n* **2** this alphabet

cyst (sɪst) *n* **1** *pathol* any abnormal membranous sac or blisterlike pouch containing fluid or semisolid material **2** *anatomy* any normal sac or vesicle in the body **3** a thick-walled protective membrane enclosing a cell, larva, or organism [C18 from New Latin *cystis*, from Greek *kustis* pouch, bag, bladder]

-cyst *n combining form* indicating a bladder or sac: *otocyst* [from Greek *kustis* bladder]

cystectomy (sɪˈstɛktəmɪ) *n, pl* **-mies** **1** surgical removal of the gall bladder or of part of the urinary bladder **2** surgical removal of any abnormal cyst

cysteine ('sɪstɪ,iːn, -ɪn) *n* a sulphur-containing amino acid, present in proteins, that oxidizes on exposure to air to form cystine. Formula: HSCH₂CH(NH₂)COOH [C19 variant of CYSTINE] > ˌcyste'inic *adj*

cystic ('sɪstɪk) *adj* **1** of, relating to, or resembling a cyst **2** having or enclosed within a cyst; encysted **3** relating to the gall bladder or urinary bladder

cysticercoid (ˌsɪstɪ'sɜːkɔɪd) *n* the larva of any of certain tapeworms, which resembles a cysticercus but has a smaller bladder

cysticercus (ˌsɪstɪ'sɜːkəs) *n, pl* **-ci** (-saɪ) an encysted larval form of many tapeworms, consisting of a head (scolex) inverted in a fluid-filled bladder. See also **hydatid** (sense 1), **coenurus** [C19 from New Latin, from Greek *kustis* pouch, bladder + *kerkos* tail]

cystic fibrosis *n* an inheritable disease of the exocrine glands, controlled by a recessive gene: affected children inherit defective alleles from both parents. It is characterized by chronic infection of the respiratory tract and by pancreatic insufficiency

cystine ('sɪstiːn, -tɪn) *n* a sulphur-containing amino acid present in proteins: yields two molecules of cysteine on reduction. Formula: HOOCCH(NH₂)CH₂SSCH₂CH(NH₂)COOH [C19 see CYSTO- (bladder), -INE²; named from its being discovered in a type of urinary calculus]

cystitis (sɪ'staɪtɪs) *n* inflammation of the urinary bladder

cysto- *or before a vowel* **cyst-** *combining form* indicating a cyst or bladder: *cystocarp; cystoscope*

cystocarp ('sɪstə,kɑːp) *n* a reproductive body in red algae, developed after fertilization and consisting of filaments bearing carpospores > ˌcysto'carpic *adj*

cystocele ('sɪstə,siːl) *n pathol* a hernia of the urinary bladder, esp one protruding into the vagina

cystogenous (sɪs'tɒdʒɪnəs) *adj biology* forming or secreting cysts

cystography (sɪs'tɒɡrəfɪ) *n* radiography of the urinary bladder using a contrast medium

cystoid ('sɪstɔɪd) *adj* **1** resembling a cyst or bladder ▷ *n* **2** a tissue mass, such as a tumour, that resembles a cyst but lacks an outer membrane

cystolith ('sɪstəlɪθ) *n* **1** a knoblike deposit of calcium carbonate in the epidermal cells of such plants as the stinging nettle **2** *pathol* a urinary calculus

cystoscope ('sɪstə,skəʊp) *n* a slender tubular medical instrument for examining the interior of the urethra and urinary bladder > cystoscopic (ˌsɪstə'skɒpɪk) *adj* > cystoscopy (sɪs'tɒskəpɪ) *n*

cystotomy (sɪs'tɒtəmɪ) *n, pl* **-mies 1** surgical incision into the gall bladder or urinary bladder **2** surgical incision into the capsule of the lens of the eye

cytaster (saɪ'tæstə, 'saɪtæs-) *n cytology* another word for **aster** (sense 3) [C19 from CYTO- + ASTER]

-cyte *n combining form* indicating a cell: *spermatocyte* [from New Latin *-cyta*, from Greek *kutos* container, body, hollow vessel]

Cythera (sɪ'θɪərə) *n* **1** a Greek island off the SE coast of the Peloponnese: in ancient times a centre of the worship of Aphrodite. Pop: 3354 (2001). Area: about 285 sq km (110 sq miles) **2** the chief town of this island, on the S coast. Pop: 300 (latest est) ▷ Modern Greek name: Kíthira

Cytherea (ˌsɪθə'riːə) *n* another name for **Aphrodite** (Venus) > ˌCyther'ean *adj*

cytidine ('sɪtɪ,daɪn) *n biochem* a nucleoside formed by the condensation of cytosine and ribose [C20 from CYTO- + -IDE + -INE²]

cytidylic acid (ˌsɪtɪ'dɪlɪk) *n* a nucleotide

consisting of cytosine, ribose or deoxyribose, and a phosphate group. It is a constituent of DNA or RNA. Also called: cytidine monophosphate

cyto- *combining form* indicating a cell: *cytolysis; cytoplasm* [from Greek *kutos* vessel, container; related to *kuein* to contain]

cytochemistry (ˌsaɪtəʊ'kɛmɪstrɪ) *n* the chemistry of living cells > ˌcyto'chemical *adj*

cytochrome ('saɪtəʊ,krəʊm) *n* any of a group of naturally occurring compounds, consisting of iron, a protein, and a porphyrin, that are important in cell oxidation-reduction reactions

cytochrome reductase *n* another name for flavoprotein

cytogenesis (ˌsaɪtəʊ'dʒɛnɪsɪs) or **cytogeny** (saɪ'tɒdʒənɪ) *n* the origin and development of plant and animal cells

cytogenetics (ˌsaɪtəʊdʒɪ'nɛtɪks) *n* (*functioning as singular*) the branch of genetics that correlates the structure, number, and behaviour of chromosomes with heredity and variation > ˌcytoge'netic *adj* > ˌcytoge'netically *adv* > ˌcytoge'neticist *n*

cytokine ('saɪtəʊ,kaɪn) *n* any of various proteins, secreted by cells, that carry signals to neighbouring cells. Cytokines include interferon

cytokinesis (ˌsaɪtəʊkɪ'niːsɪs, -kaɪ-) *n* division of the cytoplasm of a cell, occurring at the end of mitosis or meiosis

cytokinin (ˌsaɪtəʊ'kaɪnɪn) *n* any of a group of plant hormones that promote cell division and retard ageing in plants. Also called: kinin

cytology (saɪ'tɒlədʒɪ) *n* **1** the study of plant and animal cells, including their structure, function, and formation **2** the detailed structure of a tissue, as revealed by microscopic examination > cytological (ˌsaɪtə'lɒdʒɪkᵊl) *adj* > ˌcyto'logically *adv* > cy'tologist *n*

cytolysin (saɪ'tɒlɪsɪn) *n* a substance that can partially or completely destroy animal cells

cytolysis (saɪ'tɒlɪsɪs) *n cytology* the dissolution of cells, esp by the destruction of their membranes > cytolytic (ˌsaɪtə'lɪtɪk) *adj*

cytomegalovirus (ˌsaɪtəʊ'mɛɡələʊ,vaɪrəs) *n* a virus of the herpes virus family that may cause serious disease in patients whose immune systems are compromised. Abbreviation: CMV

cytoplasm ('saɪtəʊ,plæzəm) *n* the protoplasm of a cell contained within the cell membrane but excluding the nucleus: contains organelles, vesicles, and other inclusions > ˌcyto'plasmic *adj*

cytoplast ('saɪtəʊ,plɑːst, -,plæst) *n* the intact cytoplasm of a single cell > cytoplastic (ˌsaɪtəʊ'plæstɪk) *adj*

cytosine ('saɪtəsɪn) *n* a white crystalline pyrimidine occurring in nucleic acids; 6-amino-2-hydroxy pyrimidine. Formula: C₄H₅N₃O. See also **DNA, RNA**

cytoskeleton ('saɪtəʊ,skɛlɪtən) *n* a network of fibrous proteins that governs the shape and movement of a biological cell

cytosol ('saɪtəʊ,sɒl) *n* the solution of proteins and metabolites inside a biological cell, in which the organelles are suspended

cytotaxis (ˌsaɪtəʊ'tæksɪs) *n biology* movement of cells due to external stimulation

cytotaxonomy (ˌsaɪtəʊtæk'sɒnəmɪ) *n* classification of organisms based on cell structure, esp the number, shape, etc, of the chromosomes > ˌcyto,taxo'nomic *adj* > ˌcytotax'onomist *n*

cytotoxic (ˌsaɪtəʊ'tɒksɪk) *adj* poisonous to living cells: denoting certain drugs used in the treatment of leukaemia and other cancers > cytotoxicity (ˌsaɪtəʊtɒk'sɪsɪtɪ) *n*

cytotoxin (ˌsaɪtəʊ'tɒksɪn) *n* any substance that is poisonous to living cells

Cyzicus ('sɪzɪkəs) *n* an ancient Greek colony in NW Asia Minor on the S shore of the Sea of Marmara: site of Alcibiades' naval victory over the Peloponnesians (410 BC)

cz *the internet domain name for* Czech Republic

CZ *international car registration for* the Czech Republic

czar (zɑː) *n* a variant spelling (esp US) of **tsar** > 'czardom *n*

czardas ('tʃɑː,dæʃ) *n* **1** a Hungarian national dance of alternating slow and fast sections **2** a piece of music composed for or in the rhythm of this dance [from Hungarian *csárdás*]

czarevitch ('zɑː,rɪvɪtʃ) *n* a variant spelling (esp US) of **tsarevitch**

czarevna (zɑː'rɛvnə) *n* a variant spelling (esp US) of **tsarevna**

czarina (zɑː'riːnə) or **czaritza** (zɑː'rɪtsə) *n* variant spellings (esp US) of **tsarina** or **tsaritsa**

czarism ('zɑːrɪzəm) *n* a variant spelling (esp US) of **tsarism**

czarist ('zɑːrɪst) *adj, n* a variant spelling (esp US) of **tsarist**

Czech (tʃɛk) *adj* **1 a** of, relating to, or characteristic of the Czech Republic, its people, or its language **b** of, relating to, or characteristic of Bohemia and Moravia, their people, or their language **c** (loosely) of, relating to, or characteristic of the former Czechoslovakia or its people ▷ *n* **2** the official language of the Czech Republic, belonging to the West Slavonic branch of the Indo-European family; also spoken in Slovakia. Czech and Slovak are closely related and mutually intelligible **3 a** a native or inhabitant of the Czech Republic **b** a native or inhabitant of Bohemia or Moravia **c** (loosely) a native, inhabitant, or citizen of the former Czechoslovakia [C19 from Polish, from Czech *Čech*]

Czechoslovak (ˌtʃɛkəʊ'sləʊvæk) *adj* **1** of, relating to, or characteristic of the former Czechoslovakia, its peoples, or their languages ▷ *n* **2** (loosely) either of the two mutually intelligible languages of the former Czechoslovakia; Czech or Slovak

Czechoslovakia (ˌtʃɛkəʊsləʊ'vækɪə) *n* a former republic in central Europe: formed after the defeat of Austria-Hungary (1918) as a nation of Czechs in Bohemia and Moravia and Slovaks in Slovakia; occupied by Germany from 1939 until its liberation by the Soviet Union in 1945; became a people's republic under the Communists in 1948; invaded by Warsaw Pact troops in 1968, ending Dubček's attempt to liberalize communism; in 1989 popular unrest led to the resignation of the politburo and the formation of a non-Communist government. It consisted of two federal republics, the **Czech Republic** and the **Slovak Republic**, which became independent in 1993. Czech name: Československo

Czechoslovakian (ˌtʃɛkəʊsləʊ'vækɪən) *adj* **1** of, relating to, or characteristic of the former republic of Czechoslovakia, its peoples, or their languages ▷ *n* **2** a native or inhabitant of the former republic of Czechoslovakia

Czech Republic *n* a country in central Europe; formed part of Czechoslovakia until 1993; mostly wooded, with lowlands surrounding the River Morava, rising to the Bohemian plateau in the W and to highlands in the N; joined the EU in 2004. Language: Czech. Religion: Christian majority. Currency: koruna. Capital Prague. Pop: 10 226 000 (2004 est). Area: 78 864 sq km (30 450 sq miles)

Czernowitz ('tʃɛrnəvɪts) *n* the German name for **Chernovtsy**

Częstochowa (Polish tʃɛ̃stɔ'xɔva) *n* an industrial city in S Poland, on the River Warta: pilgrimage centre. Pop: 293 000 (2005 est)

D d

d *or* **D** (di:) *n, pl* **d's, D's** *or* **Ds 1** the fourth letter and third consonant of the modern English alphabet **2** a speech sound represented by this letter, usually a voiced alveolar stop, as in *dagger* **3** the semicircle on a billiards table having a radius of 11½ inches and its straight edge in the middle of the baulk line

d *symbol for* **1** *physics* density or relative density **2** *maths* a small increment in a given variable or function: used to indicate a derivative of one variable with respect to another, as in d*y*/d*x* **3** *chess* See **algebraic notation**

D *symbol for* **1** *music* **a** a note having a frequency of 293.66 hertz (**D above middle C**) or this value multiplied or divided by any power of 2; the second note of the scale of C major **b** a key, string, or pipe producing this note **c** the major or minor key having this note as its tonic **2** *chem* deuterium **3** *maths* the first derivative of a function, as in D($x^3 + x^2$) = $3x^2 + 2x$ **4** *physics* **a** dispersion **b** electric displacement **5** *aeronautics* drag **6 a** a semiskilled or unskilled manual worker, or a trainee or apprentice to a skilled worker **b** (*as modifier*): D worker ▷ See also **occupation groupings** ▷ *abbreviation for* **7** *Austral informal* defence: *I'm playing D in the match this afternoon* **8** *Austral informal* defensive play **9** ▷ *the Roman numeral for* 500. See **Roman numerals 10** ▷ *international car registration for* Germany [(for sense 10) from German *Deutschland*]

D *or* **D.** *abbreviation for* Deutsch: indicating the serial number in the catalogue (1951) of the musical compositions of Schubert made by Otto Deutsch (1883–1967)

2,4-D *n* a synthetic auxin widely used as a weedkiller; 2,4-dichlorophenoxyacetic acid

d. *abbreviation for* **1** (in animal pedigrees) dam **2** daughter **3** *Brit currency before decimalization* penny or pennies [Latin *denarius*] **4** diameter **5** died **6** dinar(s) **7** dollar(s) **8** drachma(s)

D. *abbreviation for* **1** *US politics* Democrat(ic) **2** *government* Department [Latin: God] **3** dinar(s) [Latin: Lord] **4** Don (a Spanish title) **5** Duchess **6** Duke **7** (in the US and Canada) Doctor

'd *contraction of* would *or* had: *I'd; you'd*

DA *abbreviation for* **1** (in the US) District Attorney **2** Diploma of Art **3** duck's arse (hairstyle)

D/A *or* **d.a.** *abbreviation for* **1** deposit account **2** *commerce* documents against acceptance

dab¹ (dæb) *vb* **dabs, dabbing, dabbed 1** to touch lightly and quickly **2** (*tr*) to daub with short tapping strokes: *to dab the wall with paint* **3** (*tr*) to apply (paint, cream, etc) with short tapping strokes ▷ *n* **4** a small amount, esp of something soft or moist: *a dab of ink* **5** a small light stroke or tap, as with the hand **6** (*often plural*) *chiefly Brit* a slang word for **fingerprint** [c14 of imitative origin]

dab² (dæb) *n* **1** a small common European brown flatfish, *Limanda limanda,* covered with rough toothed scales: family *Pleuronectidae*: a food fish **2** (*often plural*) any of various other small flatfish, esp flounders ▷ Compare **sand dab 3** Also called: patiki a sand flounder, *Rhombosolea plebia*, common around New Zealand's South Island [c15 from Anglo-French *dabbe*, of uncertain origin]

dab³ (dæb) *n Brit informal* See **dab hand** [c17 perhaps from DAB¹ (vb)]

DAB *abbreviation for* digital audio broadcasting

dabba ('dæbə) *n* (in Indian cookery) a round metal box used to transport hot food, either from home or from a restaurant, to a person's place of work [c20 from Hindi: lunchbox]

dabber ('dæbə) *n* **1** a pad used by printers for applying ink by hand **2** a felt-tip pen with a very broad writing point, used especially by bingo players to cancel numbers on their cards

dabble ('dæbᵊl) *vb* **1** to dip, move, or splash (the fingers, feet, etc) in a liquid **2** (*intr; usually foll by in, with,* or *at*) to deal (with) or work (at) frivolously or superficially; play (at) **3** (*tr*) to daub, mottle, splash, or smear: *his face was dabbled with paint* [c16 probably from Dutch *dabbelen*; see DAB¹] > **'dabbler** *n*

dabchick ('dæb,tʃɪk) *n* any of several small grebes of the genera *Podiceps* and *Podilymbus,* such as *Podiceps ruficollis* of the Old World [c16 probably from Old English *dop* to dive + CHICK; see DEEP, DIP]

dab hand *n Brit informal* a person who is particularly skilled at something; expert: *a dab hand at chess*

dabster ('dæbstə) *n* **1** *Brit* a dialect word for **dab hand 2** *US informal* an incompetent or amateurish worker; bungler [c18 from DAB¹ + -STER]

da capo (dɑː 'kɑːpəʊ) *adj, adv music* to be repeated (in whole or part) from the beginning. Abbreviation: DC See also **fine³** [c18 from Italian, literally: from the head]

Dacca ('dækə) *n* the former name (until 1982) of **Dhaka**

dace (deɪs) *n, pl* **dace** *or* **daces 1** a European freshwater cyprinid fish, *Leuciscus leuciscus,* with a slender bluish-green body **2** any of various similar fishes [c15 from Old French *dars* DART, probably referring to its swiftness]

dacha *or* **datcha** ('dætʃə) *n* a country house or cottage in Russia [from Russian: a giving, gift]

Dachau (*German* 'daxau) *n* a town in S Germany, in Bavaria: site of a Nazi concentration camp. Pop: 39 474 (2003 est)

dachshund ('dæks,hʊnd; *German* 'dakshʊnt) *n* a long-bodied short-legged breed of dog [c19 from German, from *Dachs* badger + *Hund* dog, HOUND¹]

Dacia ('deɪsɪə) *n* an ancient region bounded by the Carpathians, the Tisza, and the Danube, roughly corresponding to modern Romania. United under kings from about 60 BC, it later contained the Roman province of the same name (about 105 to 270 AD) > **'Dacian** *adj, n*

dack (dæk) *vb* (*tr*) *Austral informal* to remove the trousers from (someone) by force

dacks (dæks) *pl n Austral* another word for **daks**

dacoit (də'kɔɪt) *n* (in India and Myanmar) a member of a gang of armed robbers [c19 from Hindi *dakait,* from *dākā* robbery]

dacoity (də'kɔɪtɪ) *n, pl* **-coities** (in India and Myanmar) robbery by an armed gang

Dacron ('deɪkrɒn, 'dæk-) *n* the US name (trademark) for **Terylene**

dactyl ('dæktɪl) *n* **1** Also called: dactylic *prosody* a metrical foot of three syllables, one long followed by two short (–ᴗᴗ). Compare **bacchius 2** *zoology* any digit of a vertebrate [c14 via Latin from Greek *daktulos* finger, dactyl, comparing the finger's three joints to the three syllables]

dactylic (dæk'tɪlɪk) *adj* **1** of, relating to, or having a dactyl: *dactylic verse* ▷ *n* **2** a variant of **dactyl** (sense 1) > **dac'tylically** *adv*

dactylo- *or before a vowel* **dactyl-** *combining form* finger or toe: *dactylogram* [from Greek *daktulos* finger]

dactylogram (dæk'tɪlə,græm) *n chiefly US* a technical term for **fingerprint**

dactylography (,dæktɪ'lɒgrəfɪ) *n chiefly US* the scientific study of fingerprints for purposes of identification > **,dacty'lographer** *n* > **dactylographic** (dæk,tɪlə'græfɪk) *adj*

dactylology (,dæktɪ'lɒlədʒɪ) *n, pl* **-gies** the method of using manual sign language, as in communicating with deaf people

dad (dæd) *n* an informal word for **father** [c16 childish word; compare Greek *tata*]

Dada ('dɑː:dɑː:) *or* **Dadaism** ('dɑː:dɑː:,ɪzəm) *n* a nihilistic artistic movement of the early 20th century in W Europe and the US, founded on principles of irrationality, incongruity, and irreverence towards accepted aesthetic criteria [c20 from French, from a children's word for hobbyhorse, the name being arbitrarily chosen] > **'Dadaist** *n, adj* > **,Dada'istic** *adj*

dadah ('dɑː:dɑː:) *n Austral slang* illegal drugs [Malay: medicinal herb]

Dad and Dave (dæd ən deɪv) *n Austral* stereotypes of the unsophisticated rural dweller before World War II [from characters in the stories of Steele Rudd, pen name of Arthur Hoey Davis (1868–1935), Australian author]

daddy ('dædɪ) *n, pl* **-dies 1** an informal word for **father 2** the daddy *slang, chiefly US, Canadian, and Austral* the supreme or finest example: *the daddy of them all* **3** *slang* the dominant male in a group; boss; top man

daddy-longlegs *n* **1** *Brit* an informal name for a **crane fly 2** *Austral, US, and Canadian* an informal name for **harvestman** (sense 2)

dado ('deɪdəʊ) *n, pl* **does** *or* **-dos 1** the lower part of an interior wall that is decorated differently from the upper part **2** *architect* the part of a pedestal between the base and the cornice ▷ *vb* **3** (*tr*) to provide with a dado [c17 from Italian: die, die-shaped pedestal, perhaps from Arabic *dad* game]

Dadra and Nagar Haveli (dəˈdrɑː ˈnʌɡə əˈvɛlɪ) *n* a union territory of W India, on the Gulf of Cambay: until 1961 administratively part of Portuguese Damão. Capital: Silvassa. Pop: 220 451 (2001). Area: 489 sq km (191 sq miles)

Dad rock *n often disparaging* a type of classic rock music that tends to appeal to adults, often played by middle-aged musicians

dae (de) *vb* a Scot word for **do¹**

daedal *or* **dedal** (ˈdiːd²l) *adj literary* skilful or intricate [C16 via Latin from Greek *daidalos*; see DAEDALUS]

Daedalus (ˈdiːdələs) *n Greek myth* an Athenian architect and inventor who built the labyrinth for Minos on Crete and fashioned wings for himself and his son Icarus to flee the island ▷ Daedalian, Daedalean (dɪˈdeɪlɪən) *or* Daedalic (dɪˈdælɪk) *adj*

daemon (ˈdiːmən) *or* **daimon** *n* 1 a demigod 2 the guardian spirit of a place or person 3 a variant spelling of **demon** (sense 3) ▷ daemonic (diːˈmɒnɪk) *adj*

daff¹ (dæf) *n informal* short for **daffodil**

daff² (dɑːf) *vb* (*intr*) *chiefly Scot* to frolic; play the fool [C16 from obsolete *daff* fool, of uncertain origin]

daffodil (ˈdæfədɪl) *n* 1 Also called: Lent lily a widely cultivated Eurasian amaryllidaceous plant, *Narcissus pseudonarcissus*, having spring-blooming yellow flowers 2 any other plant of the genus *Narcissus* 3 a a brilliant yellow colour b (*as adjective*): *daffodil paint* 4 a daffodil, or a representation of one, as a national emblem of Wales [C14 from Dutch *de affodil* the asphodel, from Medieval Latin *affodillus*, variant of Latin *asphodelus* ASPHODEL]

daffy (ˈdæfɪ) *adj* daffier, daffiest *informal* another word for **daft** (senses 1, 2) [C19 from obsolete *daff* fool; see DAFT]

daft (dɑːft) *adj chiefly Brit* 1 *informal* foolish, simple, or stupid 2 a slang word for **insane** 3 *informal* (*postpositive*; foll by *about*) extremely fond (of) 4 *slang* frivolous; giddy [Old English *gedæfte* gentle, foolish; related to Middle Low German *ondaft* incapable] ▷ ˈdaftly *adv* ▷ ˈdaftness *n*

dag¹ (dæg) *n* 1 short for **daglock** 2 NZ *informal* an amusing person 3 rattle one's dags NZ *informal* to hurry up ▷ *vb* dags, dagging, dagged 4 to cut the daglock away from (a sheep) [C18 of obscure origin] ▷ ˈdagger *n*

dag² (dæg) *n Austral and NZ informal* 1 a character; eccentric 2 a person who is untidily dressed 3 a person with a good sense of humour [back formation from DAGGY]

Dagan (ˈdɑːɡən) *n* an earth god of the Babylonians and Assyrians

Dagenham (ˈdæɡənəm) *n* part of the Greater London borough of Barking and Dagenham: engineering and chemicals

Dagestan Republic (ˌdɑːɡɪˈstɑːn) *n* a constituent republic of S Russia, on the Caspian Sea: annexed from Persia in 1813; rich mineral resources. Capital: Makhachkala. Pop: 2 584 200 (2002). Area: 50 278 sq km (19 416 sq miles). Also called: Dagestan *or* Daghestan

dagga (ˈdaxə, ˈdaːɡə) *n South African informal* a local name for marijuana [C19 from Afrikaans, from Khoikhoi *dagab*]

dagger (ˈdæɡə) *n* 1 a short stabbing weapon with a pointed blade 2 Also called: obelisk a character (†) used in printing to indicate a cross reference, esp to a footnote 3 at daggers drawn in a state of open hostility 4 look daggers to glare with hostility; scowl ▷ *vb* (*tr*) 5 to mark with a dagger 6 *archaic* to stab with a dagger [C14 of uncertain origin]

daggerboard (ˈdæɡəˌbɔːd) *n* a light bladelike board inserted into the water through a slot in the keel of a boat to reduce keeling and leeway. Compare **centreboard**

daggy (ˈdæɡɪ) *Austral and NZ informal* ▷ *adj* 1 untidy; dishevelled 2 eccentric [from DAG¹]

daglock (ˈdæɡˌlɒk) *n* a dung-caked lock of wool around the hindquarters of a sheep [C17 see DAG¹, LOCK²]

dago (ˈdeɪɡəʊ) *n, pl* -gos *or* -goes *derogatory* a member of a Latin race, esp a Spaniard or Portuguese [C19 alteration of *Diego*, a common Spanish name]

dagoba (ˈdɑːɡəbə) *n* a dome-shaped shrine containing relics of the Buddha or a Buddhist saint [C19 from Sinhalese *dāgoba*, from Sanskrit *dhātugarbha* containing relics]

Dagon (ˈdeɪɡɒn) *n Bible* a god worshipped by the Philistines, represented as half man and half fish [C14 via Latin and Greek from Hebrew *Dāgōn*, literally: little fish]

daguerreotype (dəˈɡɛrəˌtaɪp) *n* 1 one of the earliest photographic processes, in which the image was produced on iodine-sensitized silver and developed in mercury vapour 2 a photograph formed by this process ▷ daˈguerreoˌtyper *or* daˈguerreoˌtypist *n* ▷ daˈguerreoˌtypy *n*

dah (dɑː) *n* the long sound used in combination with the short sound *dit*, in the spoken representation of Morse and other telegraphic codes. Compare **dash¹** (sense 14)

dahabeah, dahabeeyah *or* **dahabiah** (ˌdɑːhəˈbiːə) *n* a houseboat used on the Nile [from Arabic *dhahabiyah*, literally: the golden one (that is, gilded barge)]

dahlia (ˈdeɪljə) *n* 1 any herbaceous perennial plant of the Mexican genus *Dahlia*, having showy flowers and tuberous roots, esp any horticultural variety derived from *D. pinnata*: family *Asteraceae* (composites) 2 the flower or root of any of these plants [C19 named after Anders *Dahl*, 18th-century Swedish botanist; see -IA]

Dahna (ˈdɑːxnɑː) *n* another name for **Rub' al Khali**

Dahomey (dəˈhəʊmɪ) *n* the former name (until 1975) of **Benin**

daikon (ˈdaɪkɒn) *n* another name for **mooli** [C20 Japanese, from *dai* big + *kon* root]

Dáil Éireann (dɑːl ˈɛrɪn) *or* **Dáil** *n* (in the Republic of Ireland) the lower chamber of parliament. See also **Oireachtas** [from Irish *dáil* assembly (from Old Irish *dāl*) + *Éireann* of Eire]

dailies (ˈdeɪlɪz) *pl n films* another word for **rushes**

daily (ˈdeɪlɪ) *adj* 1 of or occurring every day or every weekday: *a daily paper* 2 earn one's daily bread to earn one's living 3 the daily round the usual activities of one's day ▷ *n, pl* -lies 4 a daily publication, esp a newspaper 5 Also called: daily help *Brit* another name for a **charwoman** ▷ *adv* 6 every day 7 constantly; often [Old English *dæglīc*; see DAY, -LY¹]

daily double *n horse racing* a single bet on the winners of two named races in any one day's racing

Daimoku *or* **daimoku** (ˈdaɪməʊkuː) *n* a (in Nichiren Buddhism) the words *nam myoho renge kyo* ('devotion to the Lotus Sutra') chanted to the Gohonzon b the act of chanting these words [from Japanese, literally: title]

daimon (ˈdaɪmɒn) *n* a variant of **daemon** *or* **demon** (sense 3) ▷ daiˈmonic *adj*

daimyo *or* **daimio** (ˈdaɪmjəʊ) *n, pl* -myo, -myos *or* -mio, -mios (in Japan) one of the territorial magnates who dominated much of the country from about the 11th to the 19th century [from Japanese, from Ancient Chinese *d'âi miäng* great name]

daimyo bond *n* a bearer bond issued in Japan and the eurobond market by the World Bank

dainty (ˈdeɪntɪ) *adj* -tier, -tiest 1 delicate or elegant: *a dainty teacup* 2 pleasing to the taste; choice; delicious: *a dainty morsel* 3 refined, esp excessively genteel; fastidious ▷ *n, pl* -ties 4 a choice piece of food, esp a small cake or sweet; delicacy [C13 from Old French *deintié*, from Latin *dignitās* DIGNITY] ▷ ˈdaintily *adv* ▷ ˈdaintiness *n*

daiquiri (ˈdaɪkɪrɪ, ˈdæk-) *n, pl* -ris an iced drink containing rum, lime juice, and syrup or sugar [C20 named after *Daiquiri*, rum-producing town in Cuba]

Dairen (daɪˈrɛn) *n* a former name of **Dalian**

dairy (ˈdɛərɪ) *n, pl* dairies 1 a company that supplies milk and milk products 2 a a shop that sells provisions, esp milk and milk products b NZ a shop that remains open outside normal trading hours 3 a room or building where milk and cream are stored or made into butter and cheese 4 a (*modifier*) of or relating to the production of milk and milk products: *dairy cattle* b (*in combination*): *a dairymaid*; *a dairyman* 5 (*modifier*) containing milk or milk products: *dairy produce* [C13 *daierie*, from Old English *dæge* servant girl, one who kneads bread; see DOUGH, LADY]

dairy factory *n* NZ a factory making butter, cheese, lactose, etc from milk collected from surrounding farming areas

dairying (ˈdɛərɪɪŋ) *n* the business of producing, processing, and selling dairy products

dairymaid (ˈdɛərɪˌmeɪd) *n* (esp formerly) a girl or woman who works in a dairy, esp one who milks cows and makes butter and cheese on a farm

dairyman (ˈdɛərɪmən) *n, pl* -men a man who works in a dairy or deals in dairy products

dais (ˈdeɪɪs, deɪs) *n* a raised platform, usually at one end of a hall, used by speakers, etc [C13 from Old French *deis*, from Latin *discus* DISCUS]

daisy (ˈdeɪzɪ) *n, pl* -sies 1 a small low-growing European plant, *Bellis perennis*, having a rosette of leaves and flower heads of yellow central disc flowers and pinkish-white outer ray flowers: family *Asteraceae* (composites) 2 Also called: oxeye daisy, marguerite, moon daisy a Eurasian composite plant, *Leucanthemum vulgare* having flower heads with a yellow centre and white outer rays 3 any of various other composite plants having conspicuous ray flowers, such as the Michaelmas daisy and Shasta daisy 4 *slang* an excellent person or thing 5 pushing up the daisies dead and buried [Old English *dægesēge* day's eye] ▷ ˈdaisied *adj*

daisy bush *n* any of various shrubs of the genus *Olearia*, of Australia and New Zealand, with daisy-like flowers: family *Asteraceae* (composites)

daisy chain *n* a garland made, esp by children, by threading daisies together

daisy cutter *n* 1 *soccer* a powerful shot that moves close to the ground 2 a powerful bomb with a huge blast effect

daisywheel (ˈdeɪzɪˌwiːl) *n computing* a component of a computer printer in the shape of a wheel with many spokes that prints characters using a disk with characters around the circumference as the print element. Also called: printwheel

dak (dɑːk) *or* **dawk** (dɔːk) *n* (formerly, in India) a a system of mail delivery or passenger transport by relays of bearers or horses stationed at intervals along a route b (*as modifier*): *dak bearers* [C18 from Hindi *dāk*, from Sanskrit *drāk* quickly]

Dak. *abbreviation for* Dakota

Dakar (ˈdækə) *n* the capital and chief port of Senegal, on the SE side of Cape Verde peninsula. Pop: 2 313 000 (2005 est)

dak bungalow *n* (in India, formerly) a house where travellers on a dak route could be accommodated

Dakin's solution (ˈdeɪkɪnz) *n* a dilute solution containing sodium hypochlorite and boric acid, used as an antiseptic in the treatment of wounds [C20 named after Henry D. *Dakin* (1880–1952), English chemist]

Dakota (dəˈkəʊtə) *n* a former territory of the US: divided into the states of North Dakota and South Dakota in 1889

Dakotan (dəˈkəʊtən) *adj* 1 of or relating to Dakota or its inhabitants ▷ *n* 2 a native or inhabitant of Dakota

daks *or* **dacks** (dæks) *pl n Austral* an informal name for **trousers** [from a brand name]

dal¹ (dɑːl) *n* 1 split grain, a common foodstuff in India; pulse 2 a variant spelling of **dhal**

dal² *symbol for* decalitre(s)

Dalai Lama (ˈdælaɪ ˈlɑːmə) *n* (until 1959) the chief

lama and ruler of Tibet [from Mongolian *dalai* ocean; see LAMA]

dalasi (dəˈlɑːsɪ) *n* the standard monetary unit of The Gambia, divided into 100 bututs [from a Gambian native name]

dale (deɪl) *n* an open valley, usually in an area of low hills [Old English *dæl*; related to Old Frisian *del*, Old Norse *dalr*, Old High German *tal* valley]

Dalek (ˈdɑːlɛk) *n* any of a set of fictional robot-like creations that are aggressive, mobile, and produce rasping staccato speech [c20 from a children's television series, *Dr Who*]

d'Alembert's principle (French dalɑ̃bɛr) *n physics* the principle that for a moving body the external forces are in equilibrium with the inertial forces; a generalization of Newton's third law of motion [c18 named after Jean Le Rond *d'Alembert* (1717–83), French mathematician, physicist, and rationalist philosopher]

Dales[1] (deɪlz) *pl n* (*sometimes not capital*) **the**. short for the **Yorkshire Dales**

Dales[2] (deɪlz) *n* a strong working breed of pony, originating from Yorkshire and Durham

dalesman (ˈdeɪlzmən) *n, pl* -men a person living in a dale, esp in the dales of N England

daleth *or* **daled** (ˈdɑːlɪd; *Hebrew* ˈdalet) *n* the fourth letter of the Hebrew alphabet (ד), transliterated as *d* or, when final, *dh* [Hebrew]

dalgyte (ˈdælgaɪt) *n Austral* another name for **bilby**

Dalian (dɑːˈljɛn) *or* **Talien** (tɑːˈljɛn) *n* a city in NE China, at the end of the Liaodong Peninsula: with the adjoining city of Lüshun comprises the port complex of Lüda. Pop: 2 709 000 (2005 est). Former name: Dairen

Dalit (ˈdɑːlɪt) *n* a member of the lowest class in India, whom those of the four main castes were formerly forbidden to touch. formerly called (*offensive*): **untouchable** [from Hindi, from Sanskrit *dalita*, literally: oppressed]

Dallas (ˈdæləs) *n* a city in NE Texas, on the Trinity River: scene of the assassination of President John F. Kennedy (1963). Pop: 1 208 318 (2003 est)

dalles (ˈdæləs, dælz) *pl n Canadian* a stretch of a river between high rock walls, with rapids and dangerous currents [from Canadian French, from French (Normandy dialect): sink; compare DALE]

dalliance (ˈdælɪəns) *n* **1** waste of time in frivolous action or in dawdling **2** an archaic word for **flirtation**

dally (ˈdælɪ) *vb* -lies, -lying, -lied (*intr*) **1** to waste time idly; dawdle **2** (*usually foll by with*) to deal frivolously or lightly with; trifle; toy: *to dally with someone's affections* [c14 from Anglo-French *dalier* to gossip, of uncertain origin] > **ˈdallier** *n*

Dalmatia (dælˈmeɪʃə) *n* a region of W Croatia along the Adriatic: mountainous, with many offshore islands

Dalmatian (dælˈmeɪʃən) *n* **1** Also called (esp formerly): **carriage dog, coach dog** a large breed of dog having a short smooth white coat with black or (in liver-spotted dalmatians) brown spots **2** a native or inhabitant of Dalmatia ▷ *adj* **3** of or relating to Dalmatia or its inhabitants

dalmatic (dælˈmætɪk) *n* **1** a wide-sleeved tunic-like vestment open at the sides, worn by deacons and bishops **2** a similar robe worn by a king at his coronation [c15 from Late Latin *dalmatica* (*vestis*) Dalmatian (robe) (originally made of Dalmatian wool)]

Dalriada (dælˈrɪədə) *n* a former Gaelic kingdom (5th century AD–9th century AD) comprising Argyll, parts of the Inner Hebrides, and parts of modern Antrim [named after the *Dalriada* family, its founders]

dal segno (dæl ˈsɛnjəʊ) *adj, adv music* (of a piece of music) to be repeated from the point marked with a sign to the word *fine*. Abbreviation: DS See also **fine**[3] [Italian, literally: from the sign]

dalton (ˈdɔːltən) *n* another name for **atomic mass unit** [c20 named after John *Dalton* (1766–1844), English chemist and physicist]

daltonism (ˈdɔːltəˌnɪzəm) *n* colour blindness, esp the confusion of red and green [c19 from French *daltonisme*, after John *Dalton* (1766–1844), English chemist and physicist, who gave the first accurate description of colour blindness, from which he suffered] > **daltonic** (dɔːlˈtɒnɪk) *adj*

Dalton plan *or* **system** (ˈdɔːltən) *n* a system devised to encourage pupils to learn and develop at their own speed, using libraries and other sources to complete long assignments [c20 named after *Dalton*, Massachusetts, where the plan was used in schools]

Dalton's atomic theory (ˈdɔːltənz) *n chem* the theory that matter consists of indivisible particles called atoms and that atoms of a given element are all identical and can neither be created nor destroyed. Compounds are formed by combination of atoms in simple ratios to give compound atoms (molecules). The theory was the basis of modern chemistry [c19 named after John *Dalton* (1766–1844), English chemist and physicist]

Dalton's law (ˈdɔːltənz) *n* the principle that the pressure exerted by a mixture of gases in a fixed volume is equal to the sum of the pressures that each gas would exert if it occupied the whole volume. Also called: **Dalton's law of partial pressures** [c19 named after John *Dalton* (1766–1844), English chemist and physicist]

dam[1] (dæm) *n* **1** a barrier of concrete, earth, etc, built across a river to create a body of water for a hydroelectric power station, domestic water supply, etc **2** a reservoir of water created by such a barrier **3** something that resembles or functions as a dam ▷ *vb* dams, damming, dammed **4** (*tr; often foll by up*) to obstruct or restrict by or as if by a dam [c12 probably from Middle Low German; compare Old Icelandic *damma* to block up]

dam[2] (dæm) *n* the female parent of an animal, esp of domestic livestock [c13 variant of DAME]

dam[3] (dæm) *interj, adv, adj* a variant spelling of **damn** (sense 1–4); often used in combination, as in **damfool, damme, dammit**

dam[4] *symbol for* decametre(s)

damage (ˈdæmɪdʒ) *n* **1** injury or harm impairing the function or condition of a person or thing **2** loss of something desirable **3** *informal* cost; expense (esp in the phrase **what's the damage?**) ▷ *vb* **4** (*tr*) to cause damage to **5** (*intr*) to suffer damage [c14 from Old French, from Latin *damnum* injury, loss, fine] > **ˈdamageable** *adj* > ˌdamageaˈbility *n* > **ˈdamager** *n* > **ˈdamaging** *adj* > **ˈdamagingly** *adv*

damaged goods *n informal* **1** a person considered to be less than perfect psychologically, as a result of a traumatic experience **2** a person, esp a public figure, whose reputation has been damaged

damages (ˈdæmɪdʒɪz) *pl n law* money to be paid as compensation to a person for injury, loss, etc

daman (ˈdæmən) *n* a rare name for the **hyrax** esp the Syrian rock hyrax. See also **cony** (sense 2) [from Arabic *damān Isrā'īl* sheep of Israel]

Daman (dɑːˈmɑːn) *n* a coastal town in W India, the chief town of Daman and Diu. Pop: 35 743 (2001). Portuguese name: Damão

Daman and Diu (dɑːˈmɑːn ɛn ˈdiːuː) *n* a union territory in W India: formerly a district of Portuguese India (1559–1961) then part of the union territory of Goa, Daman, and Diu (1961–87). Area: 112 sq km (43 sq miles). Pop: 158 059 (2001)

Damanhûr (ˌdɑːmənˈhʊə) *n* a city in NE Egypt, in the Nile delta. Pop: 229 000 (2005 est)

Damão (dəˈm[~ə]u) *n* the Portuguese name for **Daman**, a former Portuguese settlement now in **Daman and Diu**

damar (ˈdæmə) *n* a variant spelling of **dammar**

Damara (dəˈmɑːrə) *n, pl* -ras *or* -ra Also called: **Bergdama** a member of a Negroid people of South West Africa **2** the language of this people, a dialect of Nama

Damaraland (dəˈmɑːrəˌlænd) *n* a plateau region of central Namibia, the traditional homeland of the Damara people

damascene (ˈdæməˌsiːn, ˌdæməˈsiːn) *vb* **1** (*tr*) to ornament (metal, esp steel) by etching or by inlaying, usually with gold or silver ▷ *n* **2** a design or article produced by this process ▷ *adj* **3** of or relating to this process [c14 from Latin *damascēnus* of Damascus]

Damascene (ˈdæməˌsiːn, ˌdæməˈsiːn) *adj* **1** of or relating to Damascus ▷ *n* **2** a native or inhabitant of Damascus **3** a variety of domestic fancy pigeon with silvery plumage

Damascus (dəˈmɑːskəs, -ˈmæs-) *n* the capital of Syria, in the southwest: reputedly the oldest city in the world, having been inhabited continuously since before 2000 BC Pop: 2 317 000 (2005 est). Arabic names: Dimashq, Esh Sham (ɛʃ ʃæm)

Damascus steel *or* **damask steel** *n history* a hard flexible steel with wavy markings caused by forging the metal in strips: used for sword blades

damask (ˈdæməsk) *n* **1 a** a reversible fabric, usually silk or linen, with a pattern woven into it. It is used for table linen, curtains, etc **b** table linen made from this **c** (*as modifier*): *a damask tablecloth* **2** short for **Damascus steel 3** the wavy markings on such steel **4 a** the greyish-pink colour of the damask rose **b** (*as adjective*): *damask wallpaper* ▷ *vb* **5** (*tr*) another word for **damascene** (sense 1) [c14 from Medieval Latin *damascus*, from Damascus, where this fabric was originally made]

damask rose *n* a rose, *Rosa damascena*, native to Asia and cultivated for its pink or red fragrant flowers, which are used to make the perfume attar [c16 from Medieval Latin *rosa damascēna* rose of Damascus]

dame (deɪm) *n* **1** (*formerly*) a woman of rank or dignity; lady **2** a nun who has taken the vows of her order, esp a Benedictine **3** *archaic, chiefly Brit* a matronly or elderly woman **4** *slang, chiefly US and Canadian* a woman **5** Also called: **pantomime dame** *Brit* the role of a comic old woman in a pantomime, usually played by a man [c13 from Old French, from Latin *domina* lady, mistress of a household]

Dame (deɪm) *n* (*in Britain*) **1** the title of a woman who has been awarded the Order of the British Empire or any of certain other orders of chivalry **2** the legal title of the wife or widow of a knight or baronet, placed before her name: *Dame Judith*. Compare **Lady**

dame school *n* (*formerly*) a small school, often in a village, usually run by an elderly woman in her own home to teach young children to read and write

dame's violet, dame's rocket *or* **damewort** (ˈdeɪmˌwɜːt) *n* a Eurasian hairy perennial plant, *Hesperis matronalis*, cultivated in gardens for its mauve or white fragrant flowers: family Brassicaceae (crucifers)

Damietta (ˌdæmɪˈɛtə) *n* a town in NE Egypt, in the Nile delta: important medieval commercial centre. Pop: 113 000 (1991). Arabic name: Dumyat

dammar, damar *or* **dammer** (ˈdæmə) *n* any of various resins obtained from SE Asian trees, esp of the genera *Agathis* (conifers) and *Shorea* (family Dipterocarpaceae): used for varnishes, lacquers, bases for oil paints, etc [c17 from Malay *damar* resin]

dammit (ˈdæmɪt) *interj* a contracted form of *damn it*

damn (dæm) *interj* **1** *slang* an exclamation of annoyance (often in exclamatory phrases such as **damn it! damn you!** etc) **2** *informal* an exclamation of surprise or pleasure (esp in the exclamatory phrase **damn me!**) ▷ *adj* **3** (*prenominal*) *slang* deserving damnation; detestable ▷ *adv, adj* (*prenominal*) **4** *slang* (intensifier): *damn fool; a damn good pianist* ▷ *adv* **5** **damn all** *slang* absolutely nothing ▷ *vb* (*mainly tr*) **6** to condemn as bad, worthless, etc **7** to condemn to eternal damnation **8** (*often passive*) to doom to ruin; cause to fail: *the venture was damned from the start* **10** (*also intr*) to prove (someone) guilty: *damning evidence* **11** to swear (at) using the word *damn* **12** as near as damn it *Brit informal* as near as possible; very near **13 damn with faint praise** to praise so unenthusiastically that the effect is condemnation ▷ *n* **14** *slang* something of negligible value; jot (esp in the phrase **not worth a damn**) **15** not give a damn *informal* to be unconcerned; not care [c13 from Old French *dampner*, from Latin *damnāre* to injure, condemn, from *damnum* loss, injury, penalty]

damnable ('dæmnəb³l) *adj* **1** execrable; detestable **2** liable to or deserving damnation > 'damnableness *or* ,damna'bility *n*

damnably ('dæmnəblɪ) *adv* **1** in a detestable manner **2** (intensifier): *it was damnably unfair*

damnation (dæm'neɪʃən) *n* **1** the act of damning or state of being damned **2** a cause or instance of being damned ▷ *interj* **3** an exclamation of anger, disappointment, etc

damnatory ('dæmnətərɪ, -trɪ) *adj* threatening or occasioning condemnation

damned (dæmd) *adj* **1 a** condemned to hell **b** (*as noun*): *the damned* ▷ *adv, adj slang* **2** (intensifier): *a damned good try; a damned liar; I should damned well think so!* **3** used to indicate amazement, disavowal, or refusal (in such phrases as **I'll be damned** and **damned if I care**)

damnedest ('dæmdɪst) *n informal* utmost; best (esp in the phrase **do** *or* **try one's damnedest**)

damnify ('dæmnɪ,faɪ) *vb* -fies, -fying, -fied (*tr*) *law* to cause loss or damage to (a person); injure [c16 from Old French *damnifier*, ultimately from Latin *damnum* harm, + *facere* to make] > ,damnifi'cation *n*

Damocles ('dæmə,kliːz) *n classical legend* a sycophant forced by Dionysius, tyrant of Syracuse, to sit under a sword suspended by a hair to demonstrate that being a king was not the happy state Damocles had said it was. See also **Sword of Damocles.** > ,Damo'clean *adj*

Damodar ('dæmə,dɑː) *n* a river in NE India, rising in Jharkhand and flowing east through West Bengal to the Hooghly River: the **Damodar Valley** is an important centre of heavy industry

damoiselle, damosel *or* **damozel** (,dæmə'zɛl) *n* archaic variants of **damsel**

Damon and Pythias ('deɪmən) *n classical legend* two friends noted for their mutual loyalty. Damon offered himself as a hostage for Pythias, who was to be executed for treason by Dionysius of Syracuse. When Pythias returned to save his friend's life, he was pardoned

damp (dæmp) *adj* **1** slightly wet, as from dew, steam, etc **2** *archaic* dejected ▷ *n* **3** slight wetness; moisture; humidity **4** rank air or poisonous gas, esp in a mine. See also **firedamp 5** a discouragement; damper **6** *archaic* dejection ▷ *vb* (*tr*) **7** to make slightly wet **8** (often foll by *down*) to stifle or deaden: *to damp one's ardour* **9** (often foll by *down*) to reduce the flow of air to (a fire) to make it burn more slowly or to extinguish it **10** *physics* to reduce the amplitude of (an oscillation or wave) **11** *music* to muffle (the sound of an instrument) ▷ See also **damp off** [c14 from Middle Low German *damp* steam; related to Old High German *demphen* to cause to steam] > 'dampish *adj* > 'damply *adv* > 'dampness *n*

dampcourse ('dæmp,kɔːs) *n* a horizontal layer of impervious material in a brick wall, fairly close to the ground, to stop moisture rising. Also called: **damp-proof course**

dampen ('dæmpən) *vb* **1** to make or become damp **2** (*tr*) to stifle; deaden > 'dampener *n*

damper ('dæmpə) *n* **1** a person, event, or circumstance that depresses or discourages **2** **put a damper on:** *the bad news put a damper on the party* to produce a depressing or inhibiting effect on **3** a movable plate to regulate the draught in a stove or furnace flue **4** a device to reduce electronic, mechanical, acoustic, or aerodynamic oscillations in a system **5** *music* the pad in a piano or harpsichord that deadens the vibration of each string as its key is released **6** *chiefly Austral and NZ* any of various unleavened loaves and scones,

typically cooked on an open fire

damping ('dæmpɪŋ) *n* **1** moistening or wetting **2** stifling, as of spirits **3** *electronics* the introduction of resistance into a resonant circuit with the result that the sharpness of response at the peak of a frequency is reduced **4** *engineering* any method of dispersing energy in a vibrating system

damping off *n* any of various diseases of plants, esp the collapse and death of seedlings caused by the parasitic fungus *Pythium debaryanum* and related fungi in conditions of excessive moisture

damp off *vb* (*intr, adverb*) (of plants, seedlings, shoots, etc) to be affected by damping off

damp-proof *vb building trades* **1** to protect against the incursion of damp by adding a dampcourse or by coating with a moisture-resistant preparation ▷ *adj* **2** protected against damp or causing protection against damp: *a damp-proof course*

damsel ('dæmz³l) *n archaic or poetic* a young unmarried woman; maiden [c13 from Old French *damoisele*, from Vulgar Latin *domnicella* (unattested) young lady, from Latin *domina* mistress; see DAME]

damsel bug *n* any of various bugs of the carnivorous family *Nabiidae*, related to the bedbugs but feeding on other insects. The larvae of some species mimic and associate with ants

damselfish ('dæmz³l,fɪʃ) *n, pl* -fish *or* -fishes any small tropical percoid fish of the family *Pomacentridae*, having a brightly coloured deep compressed body. See also **anemone fish**

damselfly ('dæmz³l,flaɪ) *n, pl* -flies any insect of the suborder *Zygoptera* similar to but smaller than dragonflies and usually resting with the wings closed over the back: order *Odonata*

damson ('dæmzən) *n* **1** a small rosaceous tree, *Prunus domestica institita* (or *P. institita*), cultivated for its blue-black edible plumlike fruit and probably derived from the bullace. See also **plum¹** (sense 1) **2** the fruit of this tree [c14 from Latin *prūnum Damascēnum* Damascus plum]

damson cheese *n* thick damson jam

dan¹ (dæn) *n* a small buoy used as a marker at sea. Also called: **dan buoy** [c17 of unknown origin]

dan² (dæn) *n martial Arts* **1** any one of the 10 black-belt grades of proficiency **2** a competitor entitled to dan grading ▷ Compare **kyu** [Japanese]

Dan¹ (dæn) *n* an archaic title of honour, equivalent to *Master* or *Sir*: *Dan Chaucer*

Dan² (dæn) *n Old Testament* **1 a** the fourth son of Jacob (Genesis 30:1–6) **b** the tribe descended from him **2** a city in the northern territory of Canaan

Dan. *abbreviation for* **1** *Bible* Daniel **2** Danish

Danaë ('dæneɪ,iː) *n Greek myth* the mother of Perseus by Zeus, who came to her in prison as a shower of gold

Danaides (də'neɪɪ,diːz) *pl n, sing* Danaid *Greek myth* the fifty daughters of Danaüs. All but Hypermnestra murdered their bridegrooms and were punished in Hades by having to pour water perpetually into a jar with a hole in the bottom > Danaidean (,dænɪ'ɪdɪən, ,dænɪə'diːən) *adj*

Da Nang ('dɑː 'næŋ) *n* a port in central Vietnam, on the South China Sea. Pop: 448 000 (2005 est). Former name: Tourane

Danaüs ('dænɪəs) *n Greek myth* a king of Argos who told his fifty daughters, the Danaides, to kill their bridegrooms on their wedding night

dance (dɑːns) *vb* **1** (*intr*) to move the feet and body rhythmically, esp in time to music **2** (*tr*) to perform (a particular dance) **3** (*intr*) to skip or leap, as in joy, etc **4** to move or cause to move in a light rhythmic way **5 dance attendance on** (someone) to attend (someone) solicitously or obsequiously ▷ *n* **6** a series of rhythmic steps and movements, usually in time to music. Related adj: **Terpsichorean 7** an act of dancing **8 a** a social meeting arranged for dancing; ball **b** (*as modifier*): *a dance hall* **9** a piece of music in the rhythm of a particular dance form, such as a waltz **10** short for **dance music** (sense 2) **11** dancelike movements made by some insects and birds, esp as part of a

behaviour pattern **12 lead** (someone) a dance *Brit informal* to cause (someone) continued worry and exasperation; play up [c13 from Old French *dancier*] > 'danceable *adj* > 'dancer *n* > 'dancing *n, adj*

dancehall ('dɑːns,hɔːl) *n* a style of dance-oriented reggae, originating in the late 1980s

dance music *n* **1** music that is suitable for dancing **2** Also called: **dance** pop music with a strong electronic rhythm

dance of death *n* a pictorial, literary, or musical representation, current esp in the Middle Ages, of a dance in which living people, in order of social precedence, are led off to their graves, by a personification of death. Also called (French): **danse macabre**

dancette (dɑːn'sɛt) *n* another name for **chevron** (sense 5)

dancey (,dɑːnsɪ) *adj* dancier, danciest, of, relating to, or resembling dance music: *a cool dancey track*

dancing girl *n* a professional female dancer who dances to entertain customers at a club, theatre, etc

D and C *n med* dilation and curettage; a therapeutic or diagnostic procedure in obstetrics and gynaecology involving dilation of the cervix and curettage of the cavity of the uterus, as for abortion

dandelion ('dændɪ,laɪən) *n* **1** a plant, *Taraxacum officinale*, native to Europe and Asia and naturalized as a weed in North America, having yellow rayed flowers and deeply notched basal leaves, which are used for salad or wine: family *Asteraceae* (composites) **2** any of several similar related plants [c15 from Old French *dent de lion*, literally: tooth of a lion, referring to its leaves]

dander¹ ('dændə) *n* **1** small particles or scales of hair or feathers **2 get one's** (*or* someone's) **dander up** *informal* to become or cause to become annoyed or angry [c19 changed from DANDRUFF]

dander² ('dændə; *Scot* 'dændər) *Scot and northern English dialect* ▷ *n* **1** a stroll ▷ *vb* **2** (*intr*) to stroll [c19 of unknown origin]

Dandie Dinmont ('dændɪ 'dɪnmɒnt) *n* a breed of small terrier with a long coat and drooping ears. Also called: Dandie Dinmont terrier [c19 named after a character who owned two terriers in *Guy Mannering* (1815), a novel by Sir Walter Scott]

dandify ('dændɪ,faɪ) *vb* -fies, -fying, -fied (*tr*) to dress like or cause to resemble a dandy > ,dandifi'cation *n*

dandiprat ('dændɪ,præt) *n* **1** a small English coin minted in the 16th century **2** *archaic* **a** a small boy **b** an insignificant person [c16 of unknown origin]

dandle ('dænd³l) *vb* (*tr*) **1** to move (a young child, etc) up and down (on the knee or in the arms) **2** to pet; fondle [c16 of uncertain origin] > 'dandler *n*

Dandong ('dæn'dʊŋ) *n* another name for **Andong** Former spelling: Tan-tung

dandruff ('dændrəf) *n* loose scales of dry dead skin shed from the scalp. Also called (now rarely): dandriff [c16 dand-, of unknown origin + -ruff, probably from Middle English *roufe* scab, from Old Norse *hrūfa*] > 'dandruffy *adj*

dandy¹ ('dændɪ) *n, pl* -dies **1** a man greatly concerned with smartness of dress; beau **2** a yawl or ketch ▷ *adj* -dier, -diest **3** *informal* very good or fine [c18 perhaps short for *jack-a-dandy*] > 'dandily *adv* > 'dandyish *adj* > 'dandyism *n*

dandy² ('dændɪ) *n* another name for **dengue**

dandy-brush *n* a stiff brush used for grooming a horse

dandy roll *or* **roller** *n* a light roller used in the manufacture of certain papers to produce watermarks

Dane (deɪn) *n* **1** a native, citizen, or inhabitant of Denmark **2** any of the Vikings who invaded England from the late 8th to the 11th century AD

Danegeld ('deɪn,gɛld) *or* **Danegelt** ('deɪn,gɛlt) *n* the tax first levied in the late 9th century in Anglo-Saxon England to provide protection money for or to finance forces to oppose Viking invaders [C11 from *Dan* Dane + *geld* tribute; see YIELD]

Danelaw *or* **Danelagh** ('deɪnˌlɔː) *n* the northern, central and eastern parts of Anglo-Saxon England in which Danish law and custom were observed [Old English *Dena lagu* Danes' law; term revived in the 19th century]

danewort ('deɪnˌwɜːt) *n* a caprifoliaceous shrub, *Sambucus ebulus*, native to Europe and Asia and having serrated leaves and white flowers. See also **elder²**

dang (dæŋ) *interj, adv, adj* a euphemistic word for **damn** (senses 1–4)

danger ('deɪndʒə) *n* **1** the state of being vulnerable to injury, loss, or evil; risk **2** a person or thing that may cause injury, pain, etc **3** *obsolete* power **4** **in danger of** liable to **5** **on the danger list** critically ill in hospital [C13 *daunger* power, hence power to inflict injury, from Old French *dongier* (from Latin *dominium* ownership) blended with Old French *dam* injury, from Latin *damnum*] > 'dangerless *adj*

danger money *n* extra money paid to compensate for the risks involved in certain dangerous jobs

dangerous ('deɪndʒərəs) *adj* causing danger; perilous > 'dangerously *adv* > 'dangerousness *n*

dangerous offender *n* *US and Canadian* an offender who is deemed by a court of law to be likely to engage in further violent conduct, and who thus becomes eligible for an indefinite prison sentence

dangle ('dæŋgəl) *vb* **1** to hang or cause to hang freely: *his legs dangled over the wall* **2** (*tr*) to display as an enticement: *the hope of a legacy was dangled before her* ▷ *n* **3** the act of dangling or something that dangles [C16 perhaps from Danish *dangle*, probably of imitative origin] > 'dangler *n* > 'danglingly *adv*

dangling participle *n grammar* a participle intended to modify a noun but having the wrong grammatical relationship to it as for example *having left* in the sentence *Having left Europe for good, Peter's future seemed bleak indeed*. Also called: **misplaced modifier**

Dani ('dɑːnɪ) *n* **1** *pl* Dani ('dɑːnɪ) a member of a New Guinea people living in the central highlands of West Irian **2** the language of this people, probably related to other languages of New Guinea

Daniel ('dænjəl) *n* **1** *Old Testament* **a** a youth who was taken into the household of Nebuchadnezzar, received guidance and apocalyptic visions from God, and was given divine protection when thrown into the lions' den **b** the book that recounts these experiences and visions (in full **The Book of the Prophet Daniel**) **2** (often preceded by *a*) a wise upright person [sense 2: referring to Daniel in the Apocryphal *Book of Susanna*]

Daniell cell ('dænjəl) *n physics* a type of cell having a zinc anode in dilute sulphuric acid separated by a porous barrier from a copper cathode in copper sulphate solution. It has an emf of 1.1 volts [C19 named after John *Daniell* (1790–1845), English scientist]

danio ('deɪnɪˌəʊ) *n, pl* -os any brightly coloured tropical freshwater cyprinid fish of the genus *Danio* and related genera: popular aquarium fishes [C19 from New Latin, of obscure origin]

Danish ('deɪnɪʃ) *adj* **1** of, relating to, or characteristic of Denmark, its people, or their language ▷ *n* **2** the official language of Denmark, belonging to the North Germanic branch of the Indo-European family

Danish blue *n* a strong-tasting white cheese with blue veins

Danish loaf *n Brit* a large white loaf with a centre split having the top crust dusted with flour, esp one baked on the sole of the oven

Danish pastry *n* a rich puff pastry filled with apple, almond paste, icing, etc

Danish West Indies *pl n* the former possession of Denmark in the W Lesser Antilles, sold to the US

in 1917 and since then named the **Virgin Islands of the United States**

dank (dæŋk) *adj* (esp of cellars, caves, etc) unpleasantly damp and chilly [C14 probably of Scandinavian origin; compare Swedish *dank* marshy spot] > 'dankly *adv* > 'dankness *n*

Danmark ('danmarg) *n* the Danish name for **Denmark**

danny ('dænɪ) *or* **donny** *n, pl* -nies *dialect* the hand (used esp when addressing children) [probably from *dandy*, childish pronunciation of HAND]

Dano-Norwegian (ˌdeɪnəʊnɔːˈwiːdʒən) *n* another name for **Bokmål**

danse macabre French (dãs makabrə) *n* another name for **dance of death**

danseur French (dãsœr) *n* a male ballet dancer

danseuse French (dãsøz) *n* a female ballet dancer

Dantean ('dæntɪən, dænˈtiːən) *or* **Dantesque** (dænˈtɛsk) *adj* of or relating to Dante (Alighieri), the Italian poet (1265–1321), or reminiscent of his allegorical account of a journey through Hell in *La Divina Commedia*

danthonia (dænˈθəʊnɪə) *n* any of various grasses of the genus *Danthonia*, of N temperate regions and South America [named after E. *Danthoine*, French botanist]

Danube ('dænjuːb) *n* a river in central and SE Europe, rising in the Black Forest in Germany and flowing to the Black Sea. Length: 2859 km (1776 miles). German name: Donau Czech name: Dunaj Hungarian name: Duna Serbo-Croat name: Dunav ('dunaf) Romanian name: Dunărea

Danubian (dænˈjuːbɪən) *adj* of or relating to the river Danube

Danzig ('dænsɪɡ; *German* 'dantsɪç) *n* **1** the German name for **Gdańsk** **2** a rare variety of domestic fancy pigeon originating in this area

dap¹ (dæp) *vb* daps, dapping, dapped **1** *angling* to fish with a natural or artificial fly on a floss silk line so that the wind makes the fly bob on and off the surface of the water **2** (*intr*) (as of a bird) to dip lightly into water **3** to bounce or cause to bounce [C17 of imitative origin]

dap² (dæp) *n Southwest Brit dialect* another word for **plimsoll** [C20 probably special use of DAP¹ (in the sense: to bounce, skip)]

DAP *computing abbreviation for* **distributed array processor**

daphne ('dæfnɪ) *n* any shrub of the Eurasian thymelaeaceous genus *Daphne*, such as the mezereon and spurge laurel: ornamentals with shiny evergreen leaves and clusters of small bell-shaped flowers. See also **laurel** (sense 4) [via Latin from Greek: laurel]

Daphne ('dæfnɪ) *n Greek myth* a nymph who was saved from the amorous attentions of Apollo by being changed into a laurel tree

daphnia ('dæfnɪə) *n* any water flea of the genus *Daphnia*, having a rounded body enclosed in a transparent shell and bearing branched swimming antennae [C19 from New Latin, probably from DAPHNE]

Daphnis ('dæfnɪs) *n Greek myth* a Sicilian shepherd, the son of Hermes and a nymph, who was regarded as the inventor of pastoral poetry

Daphnis and Chloe *n* two lovers in pastoral literature, esp in a prose idyll attributed to the Greek writer Longus

dapper ('dæpə) *adj* **1** neat and spruce in dress and bearing; trim **2** small and nimble [C15 from Middle Dutch: active, nimble] > 'dapperly *adv* > 'dapperness *n*

dapple ('dæpəl) *vb* **1** to mark or become marked with spots or patches of a different colour; mottle ▷ *n* **2** mottled or spotted markings **3** a dappled horse, etc ▷ *adj* **4** marked with dapples or spots [C14 of unknown origin]

dapple-grey *n* a horse with a grey coat having spots of darker colour

Dapsang (dʌpˈsʌn) *n* another name for **K2**

dapsone ('dæpˌsəʊn) *n* an antimicrobial drug

used to treat leprosy and certain types of dermatitis. Formula: $C_{12}H_{12}N_2O_2S$ [C20 from *d(i)a(minodi)p(henyl) s(ulph)one*]

DAR *abbreviation for* **Daughters of the American Revolution**

daraf ('dærəf) *n physics* a unit of elastance equal to a reciprocal farad [C20 reverse spelling of FARAD]

darbies ('dɑːbɪz) *pl n Brit* a slang term for **handcuffs** (sense 2) [C16 perhaps from the phrase *Father Derby's* or *Father Darby's bonds*, a rigid agreement between a usurer and his client]

Darby and Joan ('dɑːbɪ) *n* **1** an ideal elderly married couple living in domestic harmony **2** Darby and Joan Club a club for elderly people [C18 a couple in an 18th-century English ballad]

darcy ('dɑːsɪ) *n geology* a unit expressing the permeability coefficient of rock. Symbol: D [named after Henri-Philibert-Gaspard *Darcy* (1803–58), French hydraulic engineer]

Dard (dɑːd) *n* a member of any of the Indo-European peoples speaking a Dardic language

Dardan ('dɑːdən) *or* **Dardanian** (dɑːˈdeɪnɪən) *n* another name for a **Trojan**

Dardanelles (ˌdɑːdəˈnɛlz) *n* the strait between the Aegean and the Sea of Marmara, separating European from Asian Turkey. Ancient name: Hellespont

Dardanus ('dɑːdənəs) *n classical myth* the son of Zeus and Electra who founded the royal house of Troy

Dardic ('dɑːdɪk) *adj* **1** belonging or relating to a group of languages spoken in Kashmir, N Pakistan, and E Afghanistan, regarded as a subbranch of the Indic branch of the Indo-European family but showing certain Iranian characteristics ▷ *n* **2** this group of languages

dare (dɛə) *vb* **1** (*tr*) to challenge (a person to do something) as proof of courage **2** (can take an infinitive with or without *to*) to be courageous enough to try (to do something): *she dares to dress differently from the others; you wouldn't dare!* **3** (*tr*) *rare* to oppose without fear; defy **4** **I dare say** Also: **I daresay** **a** (it is) quite possible (that) **b** probably: used as sentence substitute ▷ *n* **5** a challenge to do something as proof of courage **6** something done in response to such a challenge [Old English *durran*; related to Old High German *turran* to venture] > 'darer *n*

d

USAGE When used negatively or interrogatively, *dare* does not usually add *-s: he dare not come; dare she come?* When used negatively in the past tense, however, *dare* usually adds *-d: he dared not come*

daredevil ('dɛəˌdɛvəl) *n* **1** a recklessly bold person ▷ *adj* **2** reckless; daring; bold > 'dare,devilry *or* 'dare,deviltry *n*

Dar es Salaam ('dɑːr ɛs səˈlɑːm) *n* the chief port of Tanzania, on the Indian Ocean: capital of German East Africa (1891–1916); capital of Tanzania until 1983 when it was replaced by Dodoma; university (1963). Pop: 2 683 000 (2005 est)

Darfur (dɑːˈfʊə) *n* a region of the W Sudan; an independent kingdom until conquered by Egypt in 1874

darg (dɑːɡ) *n Scot and northern English dialect* a day's work [C15 formed by syncope from *day-work*]

dargah *or* **durgah** ('dɜːɡɑː) *n* the tomb of a Muslim saint; a Muslim shrine [Persian]

Dari ('dɑːrɪ) *n* the local name for the dialect of the Persian language spoken in Afghanistan

daric ('dærɪk) *n* a gold coin of ancient Persia. Compare **siglos** [C16 from Greek *Dareikos*, probably after *Darius I* of Persia]

Darien ('dɛərɪən, 'dæ-) *n* **1** the E part of the Isthmus of Panama, between the **Gulf of Darien** on the Caribbean coast and the Gulf of San Miguel on the Pacific coast; chiefly within the republic of Panama but extending also into Colombia: site of a disastrous attempt to establish a Scottish colony in 1698 **2 Isthmus of** the former name of the Isthmus of **Panama** ▷ Spanish name: Darién (da'rjen)

daring ('dɛərɪŋ) *adj* **1** adventurous; reckless ▷ *n* **2** courage in taking risks > 'daringly *adv*

dariole ('dærɪˌəʊl) *n* **1** Also called: dariole mould a small cup-shaped mould used for making individual sweet or savoury dishes **2** a dish prepared in such a mould [c14 from Old French]

Darjeeling (dɑː'dʒiːlɪŋ) *n* **1** a town in NE India, in West Bengal in the Himalayas, at an altitude of about 2250 m (7500 ft). Pop: 107 530 (2001). Official name: Darjiling **2** a high-quality black tea grown in the mountains around Darjeeling

dark (dɑːk) *adj* **1** having little or no light: *a dark street* **2** (of a colour) reflecting or transmitting little light: *dark brown*. Compare **light¹** (sense 29), **medium** (sense 2) **3 a** (of complexion, hair colour, etc) not fair or blond; swarthy; brunette **b** (*in combination*): *dark-eyed* **4** gloomy or dismal **5** sinister; evil: *a dark purpose* **6** sullen or angry: *a dark scowl* **7** ignorant or unenlightened: *a dark period in our history* **8** secret or mysterious: *keep it dark* **9** *phonetics* denoting an (l) pronounced with a velar articulation giving back vowel resonance. In English, *l* is usually dark when final or preconsonantal. Compare **light¹** (sense 30) ▷ *n* **10** absence of light; darkness **11** night or nightfall **12** a dark place, patch, or shadow **13** a state of ignorance (esp in the phrase **in the dark**) ▷ *vb* **14** an archaic word for **darken** [Old English *deorc*; related to Old High German *terchennen* to hide] > 'darkish *adj* > 'darkly *adv* > 'darkness *n*

Dark Ages *pl n* the *European history* **1** the period from about the late 5th century AD to about 1000 AD, once considered an unenlightened period **2** (occasionally) the whole medieval period

Dark Continent *n* **the** a term for Africa when it was relatively unexplored

dark current *n* the residual current produced by a photoelectric device when not illuminated

darken ('dɑːkən) *vb* **1** to make or become dark or darker **2** to make or become gloomy, angry, or sad: *his mood darkened* **3 darken (someone's) door** (*usually used with a negative*) to visit someone: *never darken my door again!* > 'darkener *n*

dark-field illumination *n* illumination of the field of a microscope from the side so that the specimen is viewed against a dark background

dark-field microscope *n* another name for an **ultramicroscope**

dark glasses *pl n* spectacles with lenses tinted to reduce transmitted light

dark horse *n* **1** a competitor in a race or contest about whom little is known; an unknown **2** a person who reveals little about himself or his activities, esp one who has unexpected talents or abilities **3** *US politics* a candidate who is unexpectedly nominated or elected

dark lantern *n* a lantern having a sliding shutter or panel to dim or hide the light

darkle ('dɑːkəl) *vb archaic or literary* **1** to grow dark; darken **2** (*intr*) to appear dark or indistinct [c19 back formation from DARKLING]

darkling ('dɑːklɪŋ) *poetic* ▷ *adv, adj* **1** in the dark or night ▷ *adj* **2** darkening or almost dark; obscure [c15 from DARK + -LING²]

dark matter *n astronomy* matter known to make up perhaps 90% of the mass of the universe, but not detectable by its absorption or emission of electromagnetic radiation

dark nebula *n* a type of nebula that is observed by its blocking of radiation from other sources. See **nebula**

dark reaction *n botany* the stage of photosynthesis involving the reduction of carbon dioxide and the dissociation of water, using chemical energy stored in ATP: does not require the presence of light. Compare **light reaction**

darkroom ('dɑːkˌruːm, -ˌrʊm) *n* a room in which photographs are processed in darkness or safe light

darksome ('dɑːksəm) *adj literary* dark or darkish

dark star *n* an invisible star known to exist only from observation of its radio, infrared, or other spectrum or of its gravitational effect, such as an invisible component of a binary or multiple star

darky, darkie *or* **darkey** ('dɑːkɪ) *n, pl* darkies *or* darkeys *informal* **1** an offensive word for a Black **2** *Austral* an offensive word for a native Australian

darling ('dɑːlɪŋ) *n* **1** a person very much loved: often used as a term of address **2** a favourite: *the teacher's darling* ▷ *adj* (*prenominal*) **3** beloved **4** much admired; pleasing: *a darling hat* [Old English *dēorling*; see DEAR, -LING¹]

Darling Downs *pl n* a plateau in NE Australia, in SE Queensland: a vast agricultural and stock-raising area

Darling Range *n* a ridge in SW Western Australia, parallel to the coast. Highest point: about 582 m (1669 ft)

Darling River *n* a river in SE Australia, rising in the Eastern Highlands and flowing southwest to the Murray River. Length: 2740 km (1702 miles)

Darlington ('dɑːlɪŋtən) *n* **1** an industrial town in NE England in Darlington unitary authority, S Durham: developed mainly with the opening of the Stockton-Darlington railway (1825). Pop: 86 082 (2001) **2** a unitary authority in NE England, in Durham. Pop: 98 200 (2003 est). Area: 198 sq km (77 sq miles)

Darmstadt ('dɑːmstæt; German 'darmʃtat) *n* an industrial city in central Germany, in Hesse: former capital of the grand duchy of Hesse-Darmstadt (1567–1945). Pop: 139 698 (2003 est)

darn¹ (dɑːn) *vb* **1** to mend (a hole or a garment) with a series of crossing or interwoven stitches ▷ *n* **2** a patch of darned work on a garment **3** the process or act of darning [c16 probably from French (Channel Islands dialect) *darner*; compare Welsh, Breton *darn* piece] > 'darner *n* > 'darning *n*

darn² (dɑːn) *interj, adj, adv, n* a euphemistic word for **damn** (senses 1–4, 15)

darned (dɑːnd) *adv, adj slang* **1** (intensifier): *this darned car won't start; a darned good shot* ▷ *adj* **2** another word for **damned** (senses 2, 3)

darnedest (ˌdɑːndɪst) *n* a euphemistic word for **damnedest**

darnel (dɑːnªl) *n* any of several grasses of the genus *Lolium*, esp *L. temulentum*, that grow as weeds in grain fields in Europe and Asia [c14 probably related to French (Walloon dialect) *darnelle*, of obscure origin]

darning egg *or* **mushroom** *n* a rounded piece of wood or plastic used in darning to support the fabric around the hole

darning needle *n* **1** a long needle with a large eye used for darning **2** *US and Canadian* a dialect name for a **dragonfly**

darogha (dɑː'rəʊɡɑː) *n* (in India and Pakistan) **1** a manager **2** an inspector [Urdu]

dart¹ (dɑːt) *n* **1** a small narrow pointed missile that is thrown or shot, as in the game of darts **2** a sudden quick movement **3** *zoology* a slender pointed structure, as in snails for aiding copulation or in nematodes for penetrating the host's tissues **4** a tapered tuck made in dressmaking ▷ *vb* **5** to move or throw swiftly and suddenly; shoot: *she darted across the room* ▷ See also **darts** [c14 from Old French, of Germanic origin; related to Old English *daroth* spear, Old High German *tart*] *adj* > 'darting *adj* > 'dartingly *adv*

dart² (dɑːt) *n* any of various tropical and semitropical marine fish [from Middle English *darce*, from Late Latin *dardus*, dart, javelin]

dartboard ('dɑːtˌbɔːd) *n* a circular piece of wood, cork, etc, used as the target in the game of **darts**. It is divided into numbered sectors with central inner and outer bull's-eyes

darter ('dɑːtə) *n* **1** Also called: anhinga, snakebird any aquatic bird of the genus *Anhinga* and family *Anhingidae*, of tropical and subtropical inland waters, having a long slender neck and bill: order *Pelecaniformes* (pelicans, cormorants, etc) **2** any

small brightly coloured North American freshwater fish of the genus *Etheostoma* and related genera: family *Percidae* (perches)

Dartford ('dɑːtfəd) *n* a town in SE England, in NW Kent. Pop: 56 818 (2001)

Dartmoor ('dɑːtˌmʊə) *n* **1** a moorland plateau in SW England, in SW Devon: a national park since 1951. Area: 945 sq km (365 sq miles) **2** a prison in SW England, on Dartmoor: England's main prison for long-term convicts **3** a small strong breed of pony, originally from Dartmoor **4** a hardy coarse-woolled breed of sheep originally from Dartmoor

Dartmouth ('dɑːtməθ) *n* **1** a port in SW England, in S Devon: Royal Naval College (1905). Pop: 5512 (2001) **2** a city in SE Canada, in S Nova Scotia, on Halifax Harbour: oil refineries and shipyards. Pop: 65 741 (2001)

darts (dɑːts) *n* (*functioning as singular*) any of various competitive games in which darts are thrown at a dartboard

Darwin ('dɑːwɪn) *n* a port in N Australia, capital of the Northern Territory: destroyed by a cyclone in 1974 but rebuilt on the same site. Pop: 71 347 (2001). Former name (1869–1911): Palmerston

Darwinian (dɑː'wɪnɪən) *adj* **1** of or relating to Charles Darwin (1809–82), the English naturalist who formulated the theory of evolution by natural selection, or his theory ▷ *n* **2** a person who accepts, supports, or uses this theory

Darwinism ('dɑːwɪˌnɪzəm) *or* **Darwinian theory** *n* the theory of the origin of animal and plant species by evolution through a process of natural selection. Compare **Lamarckism** See also **Neo-Darwinism**. > 'Darwinist *or* 'Darwinite *n, adj* > ˌDarwin'istic *adj*

Darwin's finches *pl n* the finches of the subfamily *Geospizinae* of the Galapagos Islands, showing great variation in bill structure and feeding habits: provided Darwin with evidence to support his theory of evolution

dash¹ (dæʃ) *vb* (*mainly tr*) **1** to hurl; crash: *he dashed the cup to the floor; the waves dashed against the rocks* **2** to mix: *white paint dashed with blue* **3** (*intr*) to move hastily or recklessly; rush: *he dashed to her rescue* **4** (usually foll by *off* or *down*) to write (down) or finish (off) hastily **5** to destroy; frustrate: *his hopes were dashed* **6** to daunt (someone); cast down; discourage: *he was dashed by her refusal* ▷ *n* **7** a sudden quick movement; dart **8** a small admixture: *coffee with a dash of cream* **9** a violent stroke or blow **10** the sound of splashing or smashing: *the dash of the waves* **11** panache; style: *he rides with dash* **12 cut a dash** See **cut** (sense 33) **13** the punctuation mark —, used singly in place of a colon, esp to indicate a sudden change of subject or grammatical anacoluthon, or in pairs to enclose a parenthetical remark **14** the symbol (–) used, in combination with the symbol **dot** (•), in the written representation of Morse and other telegraphic codes. Compare **dah 15** *athletics* another word (esp US and Canadian) for **sprint 16** *informal* short for **dashboard** [Middle English *dasche, dasse*]

dash² (dæʃ) *interj informal* a euphemistic word for **damn** (senses 1, 2)

dash³ (dæʃ) *W African* ▷ *n* **1** a gift, commission, tip, or bribe ▷ *vb* **2** to give (a dash) to someone [c16 perhaps from Fanti]

dashboard ('dæʃˌbɔːd) *n* **1** Also called (Brit): **fascia** the instrument panel in a car, boat, or aircraft. Sometimes shortened to: **dash 2** *obsolete* a board at the side of a carriage or boat to protect against splashing

dasheen (dæ'ʃiːn) *n* another name for **taro** [c19 perhaps changed from French (*chou*) *de Chine* (cabbage) of China]

dasher ('dæʃə) *n* the plunger in a churn, often with paddles attached

dashi (dæʃɪ) *n* a clear stock made from dried fish and kelp [c20 Japanese]

dashiki (dɑː'ʃiːkɪ) *n* a large loose-fitting buttonless upper garment worn esp by Blacks in the US, Africa, and the Caribbean [c20 of W African origin]

dashing ('dæʃɪŋ) *adj* **1** spirited; lively: *a dashing young man* **2** stylish; showy: *a dashing hat* > 'dashingly *adv*

Dashing White Sergeant *n* a lively Scottish dance for sets of six people

dashpot ('dæʃ,pɒt) *n* a device for damping vibrations; the vibrating part is attached to a piston moving in a liquid-filled cylinder [c20 from DASH + POT¹]

Dasht-i-Kavir or **Dasht-e-Kavir** (,dæʃti:kæ'vɪə) *n* a salt waste on the central plateau of Iran: a treacherous marsh beneath a salt crust. Also called: Kavir Desert

Dasht-i-Lut or **Dasht-e-Lut** (,dæʃti:'lʊt) *n* a desert plateau in central and E central Iran

Dassehra ('dæsɛræ) *n* an annual Hindu festival celebrated on the 10th lunar day of Navaratri; images of the goddess Durga are immersed in water

dassie ('dæsɪ) *n* another name for a **hyrax**, esp the rock hyrax [c19 from Afrikaans]

dastard ('dæstəd) *n archaic* a contemptible sneaking coward [c15 (in the sense: dullard): probably from Old Norse *dæstr* exhausted, out of breath]

dastardly ('dæstədlɪ) *adj* mean and cowardly > 'dastardliness *n*

dasypaedal (,dæsɪ'piːdəl) *adj* (of the young of some species of birds after hatching) having a covering of down [from Greek *dasus* shaggy + *pais, paid-* child]

dasyure ('dæsɪ,jʊə) *n* any small carnivorous marsupial, such as *Dasyurus quoll* (**eastern dasyure**), of the subfamily *Dasyurinae*, of Australia, New Guinea, and adjacent islands. See also **Tasmanian devil** [c19 from New Latin *Dasyūrus*, from Greek *dasus* shaggy + *oura* tail; see DENSE]

DAT *abbreviation for* **digital audio tape**

dat. *abbreviation for* **dative**

data ('deɪtə, 'dɑːtə) *pl n* **1** a series of observations, measurements, or facts; information **2** Also called: **information** *computing* the information operated on by a computer program [c17 from Latin, literally: (things) given, from *dare* to give]

> USAGE Although now often used as a singular noun, *data* is properly a plural

data bank *n* a store of a large amount of information, esp in a form that can be handled by a computer

database ('deɪtə,beɪs) *n* **1** a systematized collection of data that can be accessed immediately and manipulated by a data-processing system for a specific purpose **2** *informal* any large store of information: *a database of knowledge*

database management *n* the maintenance of information stored in a computer system

data capture *n* any process for converting information into a form that can be handled by a computer

datacard ('deɪtə,kɑːd) *n* a credit card-sized electronic device containing an electronic memory, and sometimes an embedded microchip; smart card

data dictionary *n computing* an index of data held in a database and used to assist in the access to data. Also called: data directory

dataflow architecture ('deɪtə,fləʊ, 'dɑːtə-) *n* a means of arranging computer data processing in which operations are governed by the data present and the processing it requires rather than by a prewritten program that awaits data to be processed

datal ('deɪtəl) *adj Northern English dialect* slow-witted

data mining *n* the gathering of information from pre-existing data stored in a database, such as one held by a supermarket about customers' shopping habits

data pen *n* a device for reading or scanning magnetically coded data on labels, packets, etc

data processing *n* **a** a sequence of operations performed on data, esp by a computer, in order to extract information, reorder files, etc **b** (*as modifier*): *a data-processing centre*. See also **automatic data processing**

data protection *n* (in Britain) safeguards for individuals relating to personal data stored on a computer

datary ('deɪtərɪ) *n, pl* -ries *RC Church* the head of the **dataria** (deɪ'tɛərɪə), the papal office that assesses candidates for benefices reserved to the Holy See [c16 from Medieval Latin *datārius* official who dated papal letters, from Late Latin *data* DATE¹]

data set *n computing* another name for **file¹** (sense 7)

data structure *n* an organized form, such as an array list or string, in which connected data items are held in a computer

datcha ('dætʃə) *n* a variant spelling of **dacha**

date¹ (deɪt) *n* **1** a specified day of the month: *today's date is October 27* **2** the particular day or year of an event: *the date of the Norman Conquest was 1066* **3** (*plural*) the years of a person's birth and death or of the beginning and end of an event or period **4** an inscription on a coin, letter, etc, stating when it was made or written **5 a** an appointment for a particular time, esp with a person to whom one is sexually or romantically attached: *she has a dinner date* **b** the person with whom the appointment is made **6** the present moment; now (esp in the phrases **to date, up to date**) ▷ *vb* **7** (*tr*) to mark (a letter, coin, etc) with the day, month, or year **8** (*tr*) to assign a date of occurrence or creation to **9** (*intr*) foll by *from* or *back to*) to have originated (at a specified time): *his decline dates from last summer* **10** (*tr*) to reveal the age of: *that dress dates her* **11** to make or become old-fashioned: *some good films hardly date at all* **12** *informal, chiefly US and Canadian* **a** to be a boyfriend or girlfriend of (someone of the opposite sex) **b** to accompany (a member of the opposite sex) on a date [c14 from Old French, from Latin *dare* to give, as in the phrase *epistula data Romae* letter handed over at Rome] > 'datable or 'dateable *adj* > 'dateless *adj*

> USAGE See at **year**

date² (deɪt) *n* **1** the fruit of the date palm, having sweet edible flesh and a single large woody seed **2** short for **date palm** [c13 from Old French, from Latin, from Greek *daktulos* finger]

dated ('deɪtɪd) *adj* **1** unfashionable; outmoded: *dated clothes* **2** (of a security) having a fixed date for redemption

Datel ('deɪ,tɛl) *n trademark* a British Telecom service providing for the direct transmission of data from one computer to another [c20 from DA(TA) + TEL(EX)]

dateless ('deɪtlɪs) *adj* **1** likely to remain fashionable, relevant, or interesting regardless of age; timeless **2** having no date or limit

dateline ('deɪt,laɪn) *n journalism* the date and location of a story, placed at the top of an article

date line *n* (*often capitals*) short for **International Date Line**

date palm *n* a feather palm, *Phoenix dactylifera*, probably native to N Africa and SW Asia and widely grown in other warm temperate and subtropical regions for its edible fruit (dates)

date rape *n* **1** the act or an instance of a man raping a woman while they are on a date together **2** an act of sexual intercourse regarded as tantamount to rape, esp if the woman was encouraged to drink excessively or was subjected to undue pressure

date stamp *n* **1** an adjustable rubber stamp for recording the date **2** an inked impression made by this

dating ('deɪtɪŋ) *n* any of several techniques, such as radioactive dating, dendrochronology, or varve dating, for establishing the age of rocks,

palaeontological or archaeological specimens, etc

dating agency *n* an agency that provides introductions to people seeking a companion with similar interests

dative ('deɪtɪv) *grammar* ▷ *adj* **1** denoting a case of nouns, pronouns, and adjectives used to express the indirect object, to identify the recipients, and for other purposes ▷ *n* **2 a** the dative case **b** a word or speech element in this case [c15 from Latin *datīvus*, from *dare* to give; translation of Greek *dotikos*] > dival (deɪ'taɪvəl) *adj* > 'datively *adv*

dative bond *n chem* another name for **coordinate bond**

dato ('dɑːtəʊ) *n, pl* -tos the chief of any of certain Muslim tribes in the Philippine Islands [c19 from Spanish, ultimately from Malay *dato'* grandfather]

datolite ('deɪtə,laɪt) *n* a colourless mineral consisting of a hydrated silicate of calcium and boron in monoclinic crystalline form, occurring in cavities in igneous rocks. Formula: CaBSiO₄(OH) [c19 *dato-* from Greek *dateisthai* to divide + -LITE]

Datuk ('dæ'tʊk) *n* (in Malaysia) a title denoting membership of a high order of chivalry [from Malay *datu* chief] > Datin (dæ'tiːn) *fem n*

datum ('deɪtəm, 'dɑːtəm) *n, pl* -ta (-tə) **1** a single piece of information; fact **2** a proposition taken for granted, often in order to construct some theoretical framework upon it; a given. See also **sense datum** [c17 from Latin: something given; see DATA]

datum plane, level or **line** *n surveying* the horizontal plane from which heights and depths are calculated

datura (də'tjʊərə) *n* any of various chiefly Indian solanaceous plants of the genus *Datura*, such as the moonflower and thorn apple, having large trumpet-shaped flowers, prickly pods, and narcotic properties [c16 from New Latin, from Hindi *dhatūra* jimson weed, from Sanskrit *dhattūra*]

DATV *abbreviation for* **digitally assisted television**: a technique in which special digital signals are transmitted with an analogue picture signal to assist the receiver to display the picture to the best advantage

daub (dɔːb) *vb* **1** (*tr*) to smear or spread (paint, mud, etc), esp carelessly **2** (*tr*) to cover or coat (with paint, plaster, etc) carelessly **3** to paint (a picture) clumsily or badly ▷ *n* **4** an unskilful or crude painting **5** something daubed on, esp as a wall covering. See also **wattle and daub 6** a smear (of paint, mud, etc) **7** the act of daubing [c14 from Old French *dauber* to paint, whitewash, from Latin *dealbāre*, from *albāre* to whiten, from *albus* white] > 'dauber *n* > 'dauby *adj*

daube (dəʊb) *n* a braised meat stew [from French]

daubery ('dɔːbərɪ) *n* **1** the act or an instance of daubing **2** an unskilful painting

daud (dɔːd, dɒd) *n Scot* a lump or chunk of something [c18 from earlier *dad* to strike, of unknown origin]

Daugava ('daʊɡə,va) *n* the Latvian name for the Western **Dvina**

Daugavpils (*Latvian* 'daʊɡəf,pils) *n* a city in SE Latvia on the Western Dvina River: founded in 1274 by Teutonic Knights; ruled by Poland (1559–1772) and Russia (1772–1915); retaken by the Russians in 1940. Pop: 112 609 (2002 est). German name (until 1893): Dünaburg Former Russian name (1893–1920): Dvinsk

daughter ('dɔːtə) *n* **1** a female offspring; a girl or woman in relation to her parents **2** a female descendant **3** a female from a certain country, etc, or one closely connected with a certain environment, etc: *a daughter of the church* ▷ Related adjective: filial **4** (*often capital*) *archaic* a form of address for a girl or woman ▷ *modifier* **5** *biology* denoting a cell or unicellular organism produced by the division of one of its own kind **6** *physics* (of a nuclide) formed from another nuclide by radioactive decay [Old English *dohtor*; related to Old High German *tohter* daughter, Greek *thugatēr*,

d

Sanskrit *duhitá*] > ˈdaughterhood *n* > ˈdaughterless *adj* > ˈdaughter-ˌlike *adj* > ˈdaughterliness *n* > ˈdaughterly *adj*

daughter-in-law *n, pl* daughters-in-law the wife of one's son

Daughters of the American Revolution *n* the an organization of women descended from patriots of the period of the War of Independence. Abbreviation: DAR

daunt (dɔːnt) *vb* (*tr; often passive*) **1** to intimidate **2** to dishearten [c13 from Old French *danter,* changed from *donter* to conquer, from Latin *domitāre* to tame] > ˈdaunter *n*

daunting (ˈdɔːntɪŋ) *adj* causing fear or discouragement; intimidating > ˈdauntingly *adv*

dauntless (ˈdɔːntlɪs) *adj* bold; fearless; intrepid > ˈdauntlessly *adv* > ˈdauntlessness *n*

dauphin (ˈdɔːfɪn, dɔːˈfɪn; *French* dofɛ̃) *n* (1349–1830) the title of the direct heir to the French throne; the eldest son of the king of France [c15 from Old French: originally a family name; adopted as a title by the Counts of Vienne and later by the French crown princes]

dauphine (ˈdɔːfiːn, dɔːˈfiːn; *French* dofin) or **dauphiness** (ˈdɔːfɪnɪs) *n French history* the wife of a dauphin

Dauphiné (*French* dofine) *n* a former province of SE France: its rulers, the Counts of Vienne, assumed the title of *dauphin;* annexed to France in 1457

daur (dɔːr) *vb* a Scot word for **dare**

Davao (daˈvaːo) *n* a port in the S Philippines, in SE Mindanao. Pop: 1 326 000 (2005 est)

daven (ˈdavən) *vb* (*intr*) *Judaism* **1** to pray **2** to lead prayers [from Yiddish]

davenport (ˈdævənˌpɔːt) *n* **1** *chiefly Brit* a tall narrow desk with a slanted writing surface and drawers at the side **2** *US and Canadian* a large sofa, esp one convertible into a bed [c19 sense 1 said to be named after Captain *Davenport* who commissioned the first ones]

Daventry (ˈdævəntrɪ) *n* a town in central England, in Northamptonshire: light industries, site of an important international radio transmitter. Pop: 21 731 (2001)

Davis Cup (ˈdeɪvɪs) *n* **1** an annual international lawn tennis championship for men's teams **2** the trophy awarded for this [c20 after Dwight F. *Davis* (1879–1945), American civic leader who donated the cup]

Davis Strait (ˈdeɪvɪs) *n* a strait between Baffin Island, in Canada, and Greenland [named after John *Davis* (??1550–1605), English navigator]

davit (ˈdævɪt, ˈdeɪ-) *n* a cranelike device, usually one of a pair, fitted with a tackle for suspending or lowering equipment, esp a lifeboat [c14 from Anglo-French *daviot,* diminutive of *Davi* David]

Davos (ˈdævɒs) *n* a mountain resort in Switzerland: winter sports, site of the Parsenn ski run. Pop: 11 417 (2000). Height: about 1560 m (5118 ft). Romansch name: Tarau

Davy Jones (ˈdeɪvɪ) *n* **1** Also called: Davy Jones's locker the ocean's bottom, esp when regarded as the grave of those lost or buried at sea **2** the spirit or devil of the sea [c18 of unknown origin]

Davy lamp *n* See **safety lamp** [c19 named after its inventor Sir Humphry *Davy* (1778–1829), English chemist]

daw (dɔː) *n* an archaic, dialect, or poetic name for a **jackdaw** [c15 related to Old High German *taha*]

dawah (ˈdaːwə) *n Islam* the practice or policy of conveying the message of Islam to non-Muslims [c21 from Arabic]

dawbake (ˈdɔːbeɪk) *n Southwest English dialect* a foolish or slow witted person

dawdle (ˈdɔːdəl) *vb* **1** (*intr*) to be slow or lag behind **2** (when *tr,* often foll by *away*) to waste (time); trifle [c17 of uncertain origin] > ˈdawdler *n* > ˈdawdlingly *adv*

dawk¹ (dɔːk) *n* a variant spelling of **dak**

dawk² (dɔːk) *n dialect* a Northern English dialect word for **hand**

dawn (dɔːn) *n* **1** daybreak; sunrise. Related adj: **auroral 2** the sky when light first appears in the morning **3** the beginning of something ▷ *vb* (*intr*) **4** to begin to grow light after the night **5** to begin to develop, appear, or expand **6** (usually foll by *on* or *upon*) to begin to become apparent (to) [Old English *dagian* to dawn; see DAY] > ˈdawnˌlike *adj*

dawn chorus *n* the singing of large numbers of birds at dawn

dawney (ˈdɑːnɪ) *adj Irish* (of a person) dull or slow; listless [of unknown origin]

dawn raid *n stock exchange* an unexpected attempt to acquire a substantial proportion of a company's shares at the start of a day's trading as a preliminary to a takeover bid

dawn redwood *n* a deciduous conifer, *Metasequoia glyptostroboides,* native to China but planted in other regions as an ornamental tree: family *Taxodiaceae.* Until the 1940s it was known only as a fossil

Dawson (ˈdɔːsən) *n* a town in NW Canada, in the Yukon on the Yukon River: a boom town during the Klondike gold rush (at its height in 1899). Pop: 1251 (2001)

Dawson Creek *n* a town in W Canada, in NE British Columbia: SE terminus of the Alaska Highway. Pop: 10 754 (2001)

day (deɪ) *n* **1** Also called: civil day the period of time, the **calendar day,** of 24 hours' duration reckoned from one midnight to the next **2** the period of light between sunrise and sunset, as distinguished from the night **3** the part of a day occupied with regular activity, esp work: *he took a day off* **4** (*sometimes plural*) a period or point in time: *he was a good singer in his day; in days gone by; any day now* **5** the period of time, the **sidereal day** during which the earth makes one complete revolution on its axis relative to a particular star. The **mean sidereal day** lasts 23 hours 56 minutes 4.1 seconds of the mean solar day **6** the period of time, the **solar day** during which the earth makes one complete revolution on its axis relative to the sun. The **mean solar day** is the average length of the apparent solar day and is some four minutes (3 minutes 56.5 seconds of sidereal time) longer than the sidereal day **7** the period of time taken by a specified planet to make one complete rotation on its axis: *the Martian day* **8** (*often capital*) a day designated for a special observance, esp a holiday: *Christmas Day* **9** all in a day's work part of one's normal activity; no trouble **10** at the end of the day in the final reckoning **11** day of rest the Sabbath; Sunday **12** end one's days to pass the end of one's life **13** every dog has his day one's luck will come **14** in this day and age nowadays **15** it's early days it's too early to tell how things will turn out **16** late in the day **a** very late (in a particular situation) **b** too late **17** that will be the day **a** I look forward to that **b** that is most unlikely to happen **18** a time of success, recognition, power, etc: *his day will soon come* **19** a struggle or issue at hand: *the day is lost* **20** **a** the ground surface over a mine **b** (*as modifier*): *the day level* **21** from day to day without thinking of the future **22** call it a day to stop work or other activity **23** day after day without respite; relentlessly **24** day by day gradually or progressively; daily: *he weakened day by day* **25** day in, day out every day and all day long **26** from Day 1 or Day One from the very beginning **27** one of these days at some future time **28** (*modifier*) of, relating to, or occurring in the day: *the day shift* ▷ Related adjective: **diurnal** See also **days** [Old English *dæg;* related to Old High German *tag,* Old Norse *dagr*]

Dayak (ˈdaɪæk) *n, pl* -aks or -ak a variant spelling of **Dyak**

dayan (daˈjɑn, ˈdajən) *n Judaism* a senior rabbi, esp one who sits in a religious court [from Hebrew, literally: judge]

day bed *n* a narrow bed, with a head piece and sometimes a foot piece and back, on which to recline during the day

day blindness *n* a nontechnical name for **hemeralopia**

daybook (ˈdeɪˌbʊk) *n book-keeping* a book in which the transactions of each day are recorded as they occur

dayboy (ˈdeɪˌbɔɪ) *n Brit* a boy who attends a boarding school daily, but returns home each evening

daybreak (ˈdeɪˌbreɪk) *n* the time in the morning when light first appears; dawn; sunrise

daycare (ˈdeɪˌkeə) *n social welfare* **1** *Brit* occupation, treatment, or supervision during the working day for people who might be at risk if left on their own, or whose usual carers need daytime relief **2** *Brit* welfare services provided by a local authority, health service, or voluntary body during the day. Compare **residential care 3** *NZ* short for **daycare centre**

daycare centre *n US, Canadian, Austral, and NZ* an establishment offering daycare to preschool children, enabling their parents to work full time or have extended relief if child care is a problem. Also called (esp in Britain): day nursery

daycentre (ˈdeɪˌsɛntə) or **day centre** *n social welfare* (in Britain) **1** a building used for daycare or other welfare services. See also **drop-in centre 2** the enterprise itself, including staff, users, and organization

daych (deɪtʃ) *vb Southwest English dialect* to thatch

day-clean *n Caribbean and West African informal* the time after first dawn when the sun begins to shine; clear daybreak

daydream (ˈdeɪˌdriːm) *n* **1** a pleasant dreamlike fantasy indulged in while awake; idle reverie **2** a pleasant scheme or wish that is unlikely to be fulfilled; pipe dream ▷ *vb* **3** (*intr*) to have daydreams; indulge in idle fantasy > ˈdayˌdreamer *n* > ˈdayˌdreamy *adj*

dayflower (ˈdeɪˌflaʊə) *n* any of various tropical and subtropical plants of the genus *Commelina,* having jointed creeping stems, narrow pointed leaves, and blue or purplish flowers which wilt quickly: family *Commelinaceae*

dayfly (ˈdeɪˌflaɪ) *n, pl* -flies another name for a **mayfly**

Day-Glo *n trademark* **a** a brand of fluorescent colouring materials, as of paint **b** (*as modifier*): *Day-Glo colours*

day hospital *n Brit* part of a hospital that offers therapeutic services, where patients usually attend all day but go home or to a hospital ward at night

day labourer *n* an unskilled worker hired and paid by the day

daylight (ˈdeɪˌlaɪt) *n* **1** **a** light from the sun **b** (*as modifier*): *daylight film* **2** the period when it is light; daytime **3** daybreak **4** see daylight **a** to understand something previously obscure **b** to realize that the end of a difficult task is approaching ▷ See also **daylights**

daylight lamp *n physics* a lamp whose light has a range of wavelengths similar to that of natural sunlight

daylight robbery *n informal* blatant overcharging

daylights (ˈdeɪˌlaɪts) *pl n* consciousness or wits (esp in the phrases **scare, knock,** or **beat the (living) daylights out of someone**)

daylight-saving time *n* time set usually one hour ahead of the local standard time, widely adopted in the summer to provide extra daylight in the evening. Also called (in the US): daylight time See also **British Summer Time**

day lily *n* **1** any widely cultivated Eurasian liliaceous plant of the genus *Hemerocallis,* having large yellow, orange, or red lily-like flowers, which typically last for only one day and are immediately succeeded by others **2** the flower of any of these plants

daylong (ˈdeɪˌlɒŋ) *adj, adv* lasting the entire day; all day

day name *n W African* a name indicating a person's day of birth

day-neutral *adj* (of plants) having an ability to mature and bloom that is not affected by day length

day nursery *n social welfare, Brit and NZ* an establishment offering daycare to preschool children, enabling their parents to work full time or have extended relief if child care is a problem. Also called (US, Canadian, Austral, and NZ): daycare centre

Day of Atonement *n* another name for **Yom Kippur**

Day of Judgment *n* another name for **Judgment Day**

day of reckoning *n* a time when the effects of one's past mistakes or misdeeds catch up with one

day release *n Brit* a system whereby workers are released for part-time education without loss of pay

day return *n* a reduced fare for a journey (by train, etc) travelling both ways in one day

day room *n* a communal living room in a residential institution such as a hospital

days (deɪz) *adv informal* during the day, esp regularly: *he works days*

day school *n* 1 a private school taking day students only. Compare **boarding school** 2 a school giving instruction during the daytime. Compare **night school**

dayshell ('deɪʃɛl) *n Southwest English dialect* a thistle

day shift *n* 1 a group of workers who work a shift during the daytime in an industry or occupation where a night shift or a back shift is also worked 2 the period worked ▷ See also **back shift**

Days of Awe *pl n Judaism* another name for **High Holidays** [a literal translation of YAMIM NORA'IM]

days of grace *pl n* days permitted by custom for payment of a promissory note, bill of exchange, etc, after it falls due

dayspring ('deɪˌsprɪŋ) *n* a poetic word for **dawn**

daystar ('deɪˌstɑː) *n* 1 a poetic word for the **sun** 2 another word for the **morning star**

daytime ('deɪˌtaɪm) *n* the time between dawn and dusk; the day as distinct from evening or night

day-to-day *adj* routine; everyday: *day-to-day chores*

Dayton ('deɪtªn) *n* an industrial city in SW Ohio: aviation research centre. Pop: 161 696 (2003 est)

Daytona Beach (deɪ'təʊnə) *n* a city in NE Florida, on the Atlantic: a resort with a beach of hard white sand, used since 1903 for motor speed trials. Pop: 64 581 (2003 est)

day trading *n* the practice of buying and selling shares on the same day, often via the internet, in order to make a quick profit ▷ **day trader** *n*

day trip *n* a journey made to and from a place within one day ▷ **day-ˌtripper** *n*

Da Yunhe ('dæ 'juːnhə) *n* the Pinyin transliteration of the Chinese name for the **Grand Canal** (sense 1)

daze (deɪz) *vb (tr)* 1 to stun or stupefy, esp by a blow or shock 2 to bewilder, amaze, or dazzle ▷ *n* 3 a state of stunned confusion or shock (esp in the phrase **in a daze**) [c14 from Old Norse *dasa-*, as in *dasask* to grow weary] ▷ **dazedly** ('deɪzɪdlɪ) *adv*

dazzle ('dæzªl) *vb* 1 (*usually tr*) to blind or be blinded partially and temporarily by sudden excessive light 2 to amaze, as with brilliance: *she was dazzled by his wit; she dazzles in this film* ▷ *n* 3 bright light that dazzles 4 bewilderment caused by glamour, brilliance, etc: *the dazzle of fame* [c15 from DAZE]

dazzling ('dæzlɪŋ) *adj* 1 so bright as to blind someone temporarily 2 extremely clever, attractive, or impressive; brilliant; amazing ▷ **'dazzlingly** *adv*

dB *or* **db** *symbol for* decibel *or* decibels

DB *abbreviation for* **defined-benefit**

DBE *abbreviation for* Dame (Commander of the Order) of the British Empire (a Brit title)

Dbh *or* **DBH** *forestry abbreviation for* diameter at breast height

DBib *abbreviation for* **Douay Bible**

DBMS *abbreviation for* database management system

DBS *abbreviation for* 1 direct broadcasting by satellite 2 direct broadcasting satellite

dbx *or* **DBX** *n trademark electronics* a noise-reduction system that works as a compander across the full frequency spectrum

DC *abbreviation for* 1 *music* da capo 2 Detective Constable 3 direct current. Compare **AC** 4 district commissioner 5 Also: D.C. District of Columbia 6 **defined-contribution**

D.C. (in the US and Canada) *abbreviation for* Doctor of Chiropractic

DCB *abbreviation for* Dame Commander of the Order of the Bath (a Brit title)

DCC *abbreviation for* **digital compact cassette**

DCF *accounting abbreviation for* **discounted cash flow**

DCIS *abbreviation for* ductal carcinoma in situ

DCL *abbreviation for* Doctor of Civil Law

DCM *Brit military abbreviation for* Distinguished Conduct Medal

DCMG *abbreviation for* Dame Commander of the Order of St Michael and St George (a Brit title)

DCMS (in Britain) *abbreviation for* Department for Culture, Media, and Sport

DCVO *abbreviation for* Dame Commander of the Royal Victorian Order (a Brit title)

DD *abbreviation for* 1 Also: dd direct debit 2 Doctor of Divinity

D-day *n* 1 the day, June 6, 1944, on which the Allied invasion of Europe began 2 the day on which any large-scale operation is planned to start [c20 from D(*ay*)-day; compare H-HOUR]

DDoS *abbreviation for* distributed denial of service: a method of attacking a computer system by flooding it with so many messages that it is obliged to shut down

DDR *abbreviation for* Deutsche Demokratische Republik (the former East Germany; GDR)

DDS *abbreviation for* 1 **Dewey Decimal System** 2 Doctor of Dental Surgery

DDSc *abbreviation for* Doctor of Dental Science

DDT *n* dichlorodiphenyltrichloroethane; a colourless odourless substance used as an insecticide. It is toxic to animals and is known to accumulate in the tissues. It is now banned in the UK

de¹, De *or before a vowel* **d', D'** (də) of; from: occurring as part of some personal names and originally indicating place of origin: *Simon de Montfort; D'Arcy; de la Mare* (*ˌdē*; see DE-]

de² the internet domain name for Germany

DE *abbreviation for* 1 (formerly in Britain) Department of Employment 2 Delaware

de- *prefix forming verbs and verbal derivatives* 1 removal of or from something specified: *deforest; dethrone* 2 reversal of something: *decode; decompose; desegregate* 3 departure from: *decamp* [from Latin, from *dē* (prep) from, away from, out of, etc. In compound words of Latin origin, *de-* also means away, away from (*decease*); down (*degrade*); reversal (*detect*); removal (*defoliate*); and is used intensively (*devote*) and pejoratively (*detest*)]

deacon ('diːkən) *n Christianity* 1 (in the Roman Catholic and other episcopal churches) an ordained minister ranking immediately below a priest 2 (in Protestant churches) a lay official appointed or elected to assist the minister, esp in secular affairs 3 *Scot* the president of an incorporated trade or body of craftsmen in a burgh ▷ Related adjective: **diaconal** [Old English, ultimately from Greek *diakonos* servant] ▷ **'deaconˌship** *n*

deaconess ('diːkənɪs) *n Christianity* (in the early church and in some modern Churches) a female member of the laity with duties similar to those of a deacon

deaconry ('diːkənrɪ) *n, pl* -ries 1 the office or

status of a deacon 2 deacons collectively

deactivate (diː'æktɪˌveɪt) *vb* 1 (*tr*) to make (a bomb, etc) harmless or inoperative 2 (*intr*) to become less radioactive 3 (*tr*) US to end the active status of (a military unit) 4 *chem* to return or cause to return from an activated state to a normal or ground state ▷ de,acti'vation *n* ▷ de'acti,vator *n*

dead (dɛd) *adj* 1 a no longer alive b (*as noun*): *the dead* 2 not endowed with life; inanimate 3 no longer in use, valid, effective, or relevant: *a dead issue; a dead language* 4 unresponsive or unaware; insensible: *he is dead to my strongest pleas* 5 lacking in freshness, interest, or vitality: *a dead handshake* 6 devoid of physical sensation; numb: *his gums were dead from the anaesthetic* 7 resembling death; deathlike: *a dead sleep* 8 no longer burning or hot: *dead coals* 9 (of flowers or foliage) withered; faded 10 (*prenominal*) (intensifier): *a dead stop; a dead loss* 11 *informal* very tired 12 *electronics* a drained of electric charge; fully discharged: *the battery was dead* b not connected to a source of potential difference or electric charge 13 lacking acoustic reverberation: *a dead sound; a dead surface* 14 *sport* (of a ball, etc) out of play 15 unerring; accurate; precise (esp in the phrase **a dead shot**) 16 lacking resilience or bounce: *a dead ball* 17 *printing* a (of type) set but no longer needed for use. Compare **standing** (sense 7) b (of copy) already composed 18 not yielding a return; idle: *dead capital* 19 *informal* certain to suffer a terrible fate; doomed: *you're dead if your mother catches you at that* 20 (of colours) not glossy or bright; lacklustre 21 stagnant: *dead air* 22 *military* shielded from view, as by a geographic feature or environmental condition: *a dead zone; dead space* 23 dead as a doornail informal completely dead 24 dead from the neck up *informal* stupid or unintelligent 25 dead in the water *informal* unsuccessful, and with little or no hope of future success: *the talks are now dead in the water* 26 dead to the world *informal* unaware of one's surroundings, esp fast asleep or very drunk 27 leave for dead a to abandon b *informal* to surpass or outdistance by far 28 wouldn't be seen dead (in, at, etc) *informal* to refuse to wear, to go (to), etc ▷ *n* 29 a period during which coldness, darkness, or some other quality associated with death is at its most intense: *the dead of winter* ▷ *adv* 30 (intensifier): *dead easy; stop dead; dead level* 31 dead on exactly right [Old English *dēad*; related to Old High German *tōt*, Old Norse *dauthr*; see DIE¹] ▷ **'deadness** *n*

dead-and-alive *adj Brit* (of a place, activity, or person) dull; uninteresting

dead arm *n informal* temporary loss of sensation in the arm, caused by a blow to a muscle

dead-ball line *n rugby* a line not more than 22 metres behind the goal line at each end of the field beyond which the ball is out of play

deadbeat ('dɛd,biːt) *n* 1 *informal* a lazy or socially undesirable person 2 *chiefly US* a a person who makes a habit of avoiding or evading his or her responsibilities or debts b (*as modifier*): *a deadbeat dad* 3 a high grade escapement used in pendulum clocks 4 (*modifier*) (of a clock escapement) having a beat without any recoil 5 (*modifier*) *physics* a (of a system) returning to an equilibrium position with little or no oscillation b (of an instrument or indicator) indicating a true reading without oscillation

dead beat *adj informal* tired out; exhausted

deadboy ('dɛd,bɔɪ) *n* See **deadman** (sense 2)

dead-cat bounce *n stock exchange informal* a temporary recovery in prices following a substantial fall as a result of speculators buying stocks they have already sold rather than as a result of a genuine reversal of the downward trend

dead centre *n* 1 the exact top (**top dead centre**) or bottom (**bottom dead centre**) of the piston stroke in a reciprocating engine or pump 2 a pointed rod mounted in the tailstock of a lathe to support

d

a workpiece ▷ Also called: dead point

dead data n computing data that is no longer relevant

dead duck n slang a person or thing doomed to death, failure, etc, esp because of a mistake or misjudgment

deaden ('dɛdᵊn) vb 1 to make or become less sensitive, intense, lively, etc; damp or be damped down; dull 2 (tr) to make acoustically less resonant: he deadened the room with heavy curtains > 'deadener n > 'deadening adj

dead end n 1 another name for cul-de-sac 2 a situation in which further progress is impossible 3 (as modifier): a dead-end street; a dead-end job dead-end ▷ vb 4 (intr) chiefly US and Canadian to come to a dead end

deadeye ('dɛd,aɪ) n 1 nautical either of a pair of disclike wooden blocks, supported by straps in grooves around them, between which a line is rove so as to draw them together to tighten a shroud. Compare bull's-eye (sense 9) 2 chiefly US informal an expert marksman

deadfall ('dɛd,fɔːl) n a type of trap, used esp for catching large animals, in which a heavy weight falls to crush the prey. Also called: downfall

dead fingers n (functioning as singular) med a disease of users of pneumatic drills, characterized by anaesthesia of the fingertips and cyanosis

dead hand n 1 an oppressive or discouraging influence or factor: the dead hand of centralized control 2 law a less common word for mortmain

deadhead ('dɛd,hɛd) n 1 a dull unenterprising person 2 a person who uses a free ticket, as for a train, the theatre, etc 3 US and Canadian a train, etc, travelling empty 4 US and Canadian a totally or partially submerged log floating in a lake, etc ▷ vb 5 (tr) to cut off withered flowers from (a plant) 6 (intr) US and Canadian to drive an empty bus, train, etc

Dead Heart n (usually preceded by the) Austral the remote interior of Australia [c20 from the title The Dead Heart of Australia (1906) by J. W. Gregory (1864–1932), British geologist]

dead heat n a a race or contest in which two or more participants tie for first place b a tie between two or more contestants in any position

dead key n a key on the keyboard of a typewriter which does not automatically advance the carriage when depressed

dead leg n informal temporary loss of sensation in the leg, caused by a blow to a muscle

dead letter n 1 a letter that cannot be delivered or returned because it lacks adequate directions 2 a law or ordinance that is no longer enforced but has not been formally repealed 3 informal anything considered no longer worthy of consideration

dead letter box or **drop** n a place where messages and other material can be left and collected secretly without the sender and the recipient meeting

deadlight ('dɛd,laɪt) n 1 nautical a a bull's-eye let into the deck or hull of a vessel to admit light to a cabin b a shutter of wood or metal for sealing off a porthole or cabin window 2 a skylight designed not to be opened

deadline ('dɛd,laɪn) n a time limit for any activity

dead load n the intrinsic invariable weight of a structure, such as a bridge. It may also include any permanent loads attached to the structure. Also called: dead weight Compare live load

deadlock ('dɛd,lɒk) n 1 a state of affairs in which further action between two opposing forces is impossible; stalemate 2 a tie between opposite sides in a contest 3 a lock having a bolt that can be opened only with a key ▷ vb 4 to bring or come to a deadlock

dead loss n 1 informal a person, thing, or situation that is completely useless or unprofitable 2 a complete loss for which no compensation is received

deadly ('dɛdlɪ) adj -lier, -liest 1 likely to cause

death: deadly poison; deadly combat 2 informal extremely boring ▷ adv, adj 3 like death in appearance or certainty: deadly pale; a deadly sleep > 'deadliness n

deadly nightshade n a poisonous Eurasian solanaceous plant, Atropa belladonna, having dull purple bell-shaped flowers and small very poisonous black berries. Also called: belladonna, dwale

deadly sins pl n theol the sins of pride, covetousness, lust, envy, gluttony, anger, and sloth

deadman ('dɛd,mæn) n, pl -men 1 civil engineering a heavy plate, wall, or block buried in the ground that acts as an anchor for a retaining wall, sheet pile, etc, by a tie connecting the two 2 mountaineering a metal plate with a wire loop attached for thrusting into firm snow to serve as a belay point, a smaller version being known as a deadboy

dead man's fingers n (functioning as singular) a soft coral, Alcyonium digitatum, with long finger-like polyps

dead man's handle or **pedal** n a safety switch on a piece of machinery, such as a train, that allows operation only while depressed by the operator

dead march n a piece of solemn funeral music played to accompany a procession, esp at military funerals

dead-nettle n any Eurasian plant of the genus Lamium, such as L. alba (white dead-nettle), having leaves resembling nettles but lacking stinging hairs: family Lamiaceae (labiates)

deadpan ('dɛd,pæn) adj, adv with a deliberately emotionless face or manner: deadpan humour

dead point n another name for dead centre

dead president n US informal a banknote [c20 from the pictures of various dead presidents that appear on US banknotes]

dead reckoning n a method of establishing one's position using the distance and direction travelled rather than astronomical observations

Dead Sea n a lake between Israel, Jordan, and the West Bank, 417 m (1373 ft) below sea level; originally 390 m (1285 ft): the lowest lake in the world, with no outlet and very high salinity; outline, esp at the southern end, reduced considerably in recent years. Area: originally about 950 sq km (365 sq miles); by 2003 about 625 sq km (240 sq miles)

Dead Sea Scrolls pl n a collection of manuscripts in Hebrew and Aramaic discovered in caves near the Dead Sea between 1947 and 1956. They are widely held to have been written between about 100 BC and 68 AD and provide important biblical evidence

dead set adv 1 absolutely: he is dead set against going to Spain ▷ n 2 the motionless position of a dog when pointing with its muzzle towards game ▷ adj 3 (of a hunting dog) in this position ▷ interj 4 Austral slang an expression of affirmation: dead set, I worked from dawn to dusk

dead-smooth file n engineering the smoothest grade of file commonly used

dead soldier or **marine** n informal an empty beer or spirit bottle

dead stock n farm equipment. Compare livestock

dead time n electronics the interval of time immediately following a stimulus, during which an electrical device, component, etc, is insensitive to a further stimulus

dead-tree adj informal printed on paper: a dead-tree edition of her book

dead weight n 1 a heavy weight or load 2 an oppressive burden; encumbrance 3 the difference between the loaded and the unloaded weights of a ship 4 another name for dead load 5 (in shipping) freight chargeable by weight rather than by bulk

Dead White European Male or **Dead White Male** n a man whose importance and talents

may have been exaggerated because he belonged to a historically dominant gender and ethnic group

deadwood ('dɛd,wʊd) n 1 dead trees or branches 2 informal a useless person; encumbrance 3 nautical a filler piece between the keel and the stern of a wooden vessel

deaf (dɛf) adj 1 a partially or totally unable to hear b (as collective noun; preceded by the): the deaf ▷ See also tone-deaf 2 refusing to heed: deaf to the cries of the hungry [Old English dēaf; related to Old Norse daufr] > 'deafly adv > 'deafness n

USAGE See at disabled

deaf aid n another name for hearing aid

deaf-and-dumb offensive ▷ adj 1 unable to hear or speak ▷ n 2 a deaf-mute person

deafblind ('dɛf'blaɪnd) adj a unable to hear or see b (as collective noun; preceded by the): the deafblind

deafen ('dɛfᵊn) vb (tr) to make deaf, esp momentarily, as by a loud noise

deafening ('dɛfᵊnɪŋ) n excessively loud: deafening music

deaf-mute n 1 a person who is unable to hear or speak. See also mute¹ (sense 7), mutism (sense 2b) ▷ adj 2 unable to hear or speak [c19 translation of French sourd-muet] > 'deaf-,muteness or 'deaf-,mutism n

deaf without speech adj a (usually of a prelingually deaf person) able to utter sounds but not speak b (as collective noun; preceded by the): the deaf without speech

deal¹ (diːl) vb deals, dealing, dealt (dɛlt) 1 (intr; foll by in) to engage (in) commercially: to deal in upholstery 2 (often foll by out) to apportion (something, such as cards) to a number of people; distribute 3 (tr) to give (a blow) to (someone); inflict 4 (intr) slang to sell any illegal drug ▷ n 5 informal a bargain, transaction, or agreement 6 a particular type of treatment received, esp as the result of an agreement: a fair deal 7 an indefinite amount, extent, or degree (esp in the phrases good or great deal) 8 cards a the process of distributing the cards b a player's turn to do this c a single round in a card game 9 See big deal 10 cut a deal informal, chiefly US to come to an arrangement; make a deal ▷ See also deal with 11 the real deal informal a person or thing seen as being authentic and not inferior in any way [Old English dǣlan, from dǣl a part; compare Old High German teil a part, Old Norse deild a share]

deal² (diːl) n 1 a plank of softwood timber, such as fir or pine, or such planks collectively 2 the sawn wood of various coniferous trees, such as that from the Scots pine (red deal) or from the Norway Spruce (white deal) ▷ adj 3 of fir or pine [c14 from Middle Low German dele plank; see THILL]

Deal (diːl) n a town in SE England, in Kent, on the English Channel: two 16th-century castles; tourism, light industries. Pop: 96 670 (2003 est)

dealate ('diːeɪ,leɪt, -lɪt) or **dealated** ('diːeɪ,leɪtɪd) adj (of ants and other insects) having lost their wings, esp by biting or rubbing them off after mating [from DE- + ALATE] > ,dea'lation n

dealer ('diːlə) n 1 a person or firm engaged in commercial purchase and sale; trader: a car dealer 2 cards the person who distributes the cards 3 slang a person who sells illegal drugs > 'dealer,ship n

dealfish ('diːl,fɪʃ) n, pl -fish or -fishes any deep-sea teleost fish of the genus Trachipterus, esp T. arcticus, related to the ribbonfishes and having a very long tapelike body and a fan-shaped tail fin

dealings ('diːlɪŋz) pl n (sometimes singular) transactions or business relations

dealt (dɛlt) vb the past tense and past participle of deal¹

deal with vb (tr, adverb) 1 to take action on: to deal with each problem in turn 2 to punish: the headmaster will deal with the culprit 3 to be concerned with: the book deals with Dutch art 4 to conduct oneself (towards others), esp with regard to fairness: he can be relied on to deal fairly with everyone 5 to do business with: *the firm deals with many overseas suppliers*

deaminate (di:ˈæmɪˌneɪt), **deaminize** *or* **deaminise** *vb* (*tr*) to remove one or more amino groups from (a molecule) > deˌamiˈnation, deˌaminiˈzation *or* deˌaminiˈsation *n*

dean (di:n) *n* **1** the chief administrative official of a college or university faculty **2** (at Oxford and Cambridge universities) a college fellow with responsibility for undergraduate discipline **3** *chiefly Church of England* the head of a chapter of canons and administrator of a cathedral or collegiate church **4** *RC Church* the cardinal bishop senior by consecration and head of the college of cardinals ▷ Related adjective: **decanal** See also **rural dean** [C14 from Old French *deien,* from Late Latin *decānus* one set over ten persons, from Latin *decem*] > ˈdeanˌship *n*

Dean (di:n) *n* **Forest of** a forest in W England, in Gloucestershire, between the Rivers Severn and Wye: formerly a royal hunting ground

deanery (ˈdi:nərɪ) *n, pl* **-eries 1** the office or residence of dean **2** the group of parishes presided over by a rural dean

de-anglicization *or* **de-anglicisation** *n* (in Ireland) the elimination of English influence, language, customs, etc

Dean of Faculty *n* the president of the Faculty of Advocates in Scotland

dean of guild *n* the titular head of the guild or merchant company in a Scots burgh, who formerly exercised jurisdiction over all building in the burgh in the **Dean of Guild Court**

dear (dɪə) *adj* **1** beloved; precious **2** used in conventional forms of address preceding a title or name, as in *Dear Sir* or *my dear Mr Smith* **3** (*postpositive;* foll by *to*) important; close: *a wish dear to her heart* **4 a** highly priced **b** charging high prices **5** appealing or pretty: *what a dear little ring!* **6 for dear life** urgently or with extreme vigour or desperation ▷ *interj* **7** used in exclamations of surprise or dismay, such as *Oh dear!* and *dear me!* ▷ *n* **8** (*often used in direct address*) someone regarded with affection and tenderness; darling ▷ *adv* **9** dearly: *his errors have cost him dear* [Old English *dēore;* related to Old Norse *dȳrr*] > ˈdearness *n*

Dearborn (ˈdɪəbən, -ˌbɔːn) *n* a city in SE Michigan, near Detroit: automobile industry. Pop: 96 670 (2003 est)

Dear John letter *n informal* a letter from someone (esp to a man) breaking off a love affair

dearly (ˈdɪəlɪ) *adv* **1** very much: *I would dearly like you to go* **2** affectionately **3** at a great cost

dearth (dɜ:θ) *n* an inadequate amount, esp of food; scarcity [C13 *derthe,* from *dēr* DEAR]

deary *or* **dearie** (ˈdɪərɪ) *n, pl* **dearies** *informal* **1** a term of affection: now often sarcastic or facetious **2 deary** *or* **dearie me!** an exclamation of surprise or dismay

deasil (ˈdiːzʲəl, ˈdiːʃʲəl) *Scot* ▷ *adv* **1** in the direction of the apparent course of the sun; clockwise ▷ *n* **2** motion in this direction ▷ Compare **withershins** [C18 Scot Gaelic *deiseil*]

death (dɛθ) *n* **1** the permanent end of all functions of life in an organism or some of its cellular components **2** an instance of this: *his death ended an era* **3** a murder or killing: *he had five deaths on his conscience* **4** termination or destruction: *the death of colonialism* **5** a state of affairs or an experience considered as terrible as death: *your constant nagging will be the death of me* **6** a cause or source of death **7** (*usually capital*) a personification of death, usually a skeleton or an old man holding a scythe **8 a** to death *or* to the death until dead: *bleed to death; a fight to the death* **b** to death excessively: *bored to death* **9 at death's door** likely to die soon **10 catch one's death (of cold)** *informal* to contract a severe cold **11 to death a** to kill or to overuse (a joke, etc) so that it no longer has any effect **12 in at the death a** present when an animal that is being hunted is caught and killed **b** present at the finish or

climax **13 like death warmed up** *informal* very ill **14 like grim death** as if afraid of one's life **15 put to death** to kill deliberately or execute ▷ Related adjectives: **fatal, lethal, mortal** ▷ Related prefixes: **necro-, thanato-** [Old English *dēath;* related to Old High German *tōd* death, Gothic *dauthus*]

death adder *n* a venomous Australian elapid snake, *Acanthophis antarcticus,* resembling an adder

deathbed (ˈdɛθˌbɛd) *n* **1 a** the bed in which a person is about to die **b** (*as modifier*): *a deathbed conversion* **2 on one's deathbed** about to die

deathblow (ˈdɛθˌbləʊ) *n* a thing or event that destroys life or hope, esp suddenly

death camp *n* a concentration camp in which the conditions are so brutal that few prisoners survive, or one to which prisoners are sent for execution

death cap *or* **angel** *n* a poisonous woodland saprotrophic basidiomycetous fungus, *Amanita phalloides,* differing from the edible mushroom (*Agaricus*) only in its white gills (pinkish-brown in *Agaricus*) and the presence of a volva. See also **amanita**

death cell *n* a prison cell for criminals sentenced to death

death certificate *n* a legal document issued by a qualified medical practitioner certifying the death of a person and stating the cause if known

death-dealing *adj* fatal; lethal

death duty *n* a tax on property inheritances: in Britain, replaced in 1975 by capital transfer tax and since 1986 by inheritance tax. Also called: **estate duty**

death futures *pl n* life insurance policies of terminally ill people that are bought speculatively for a lump sum by a company, enabling it to collect the proceeds of the policies when the sufferers die

death grant *n* (in the British National Insurance scheme) a grant payable to a relative, executor, etc, after the death of a person

death knell *or* **bell** *n* **1** something that heralds death or destruction **2** a bell rung to announce a death

deathless (ˈdɛθlɪs) *adj* immortal, esp because of greatness; everlasting > ˈdeathlessly *adv* > ˈdeathlessness *n*

deathly (ˈdɛθlɪ) *adj* **1** deadly **2** resembling death: *a deathly quiet* > ˈdeathliness *n*

death mask *n* a cast of a person's face taken shortly after death. Compare **life mask**

death metal *n* **a** a type of heavy-metal music characterized by extreme speed and lyrics dealing with violence, satanism, etc **b** (*as modifier*): *a death-metal band*

death penalty *n* (often preceded by *the*) capital punishment

death rate *n* the ratio of deaths in a specified area, group, etc, to the population of that area, group, etc. Also called (esp US): **mortality rate**

death rattle *n* a low-pitched gurgling sound sometimes made by a dying person, caused by air passing through an accumulation of mucus in the trachea

death ray *n* an imaginary ray capable of killing

death row *or* **house** *n US* the part of a prison where those sentenced to death are confined

death seat *n US and Austral slang* the seat beside the driver of a vehicle

death's-head *n* a human skull or a representation of one

death's-head moth *n* a European hawk moth, *Acherontia atropos,* having markings resembling a human skull on its upper thorax

death tourist *n informal* a seriously ill person who seeks to terminate his or her own life by travelling to a country where medically assisted suicide is legal

death trap *n* a building, vehicle, etc, that is considered very unsafe

Death Valley *n* a desert valley in E California and W Nevada: the lowest, hottest, and driest area of

the US. Lowest point: 86 m (282 ft) below sea level. Area: about 3885 sq km (1500 sq miles)

death-valley curve *n* a curve on a graph showing how the capital of a new company plotted against time declines sharply as the venture capital is used up before income reaches predicted levels

death warrant *n* **1** the official authorization for carrying out a sentence of death **2 sign one's (own) death warrant** to cause one's own destruction

deathwatch (ˈdɛθˌwɒtʃ) *n* **1** a vigil held beside a dying or dead person **2 deathwatch beetle** a beetle, *Xestobium rufovillosum,* whose woodboring larvae are a serious pest. The adult produces a rapid tapping sound with its head that was once popularly supposed to presage death. See also **anobiid**

death wish *n* (in Freudian psychology) the desire for self-annihilation. See also **Thanatos**

Deauville (ˈdəʊviːl; *French* dovil) *n* a town and resort in NW France: casino. Pop: 4364 (1999)

deave (di:v) *vb* (*tr*) *Scot* **1** to deafen **2** to bewilder or weary (a person) with noise [Old English *dēafian*]

deb (dɛb) *n informal* short for **debutante**

deb. *abbreviation for* debenture

debacle (deɪˈbɑːkʲl, dɪ-) *n* **1** a sudden disastrous collapse or defeat, esp one involving a disorderly retreat; rout **2** the breaking up of ice in a river during spring or summer, often causing flooding **3** a violent rush of water carrying along debris [C19 from French *débâcle,* from French *desbacler* to unbolt, ultimately from Latin *baculum* rod, staff]

debag (diːˈbæg) *vb* **-bags, -bagging, -bagged** (*tr*) *Brit slang* to remove the trousers from (someone) by force

debar (dɪˈbɑː) *vb* **-bars, -barring, -barred** (*tr;* usually foll by *from*) to exclude from a place, a right, etc; bar > deˈbarment *n*

■ USAGE See at **disbar**

debark[1] (diːˈbɑːk) *vb* a less common word for **disembark** [C17 from French *débarquer,* from *dé-* DIS[1] + *barque* BARQUE] > debarkation (ˌdiːbɑːˈkeɪʃən) *n*

debark[2] (diːˈbɑːk) *vb* (*tr*) to remove the bark from (a tree)

debase (dɪˈbeɪs) *vb* (*tr*) to lower in quality, character, or value, as by adding cheaper metal to coins; adulterate [C16 see DE-, BASE[2]] > deˈbasedness (dɪˈbeɪsɪdnɪs) *n* > deˈbasement *n* > deˈbaser *n* > deˈbasingly *adv*

debatable *or* **debateable** (dɪˈbeɪtəbʲl) *adj* **1** open to question; disputable **2** *law* in dispute, as land or territory to which two parties lay claim

debate (dɪˈbeɪt) *n* **1** a formal discussion, as in a legislative body, in which opposing arguments are put forward **2** discussion or dispute **3** the formal presentation and opposition of a specific motion, followed by a vote ▷ *vb* **4** to discuss (a motion), esp in a formal assembly **5** to deliberate upon (something): *he debated with himself whether to go* [C13 from Old French *debatre* to discuss, argue, from Latin *battuere*] > deˈbater *n*

debauch (dɪˈbɔːtʃ) *vb* **1** (when *tr,* usually *passive*) to lead into a life of depraved self-indulgence **2** (*tr*) to seduce (a woman) ▷ *n* **3** an instance or period of extreme dissipation [C16 from Old French *desbaucher* to corrupt, literally: to shape (timber) roughly, from *bauch* beam, of Germanic origin] > deˈbauchedly *adv* > deˈbauchedness *n* > deˈbaucher *n* > deˈbauchery *or* deˈbauchment *n*

debauchee (ˌdɛbɔːˈtʃiː, -ːˈʃiː) *n* a man who leads a life of reckless drinking, promiscuity, and self-indulgence

debe (ˈdɛbɛ) *n E African* a tin [C20 from Swahili]

debeak *vb* (*tr*) to remove part of the beak of poultry to reduce the risk of such habits as feather-picking or cannibalism

debenture (dɪˈbɛntʃə) *n* **1** Also called: **debenture bond** a long-term bond, bearing fixed interest and usually unsecured, issued by a company or governmental agency **2** a certificate

d

acknowledging the debt of a stated sum of money to a specified person **3** a customs certificate providing for a refund of excise or import duty [c15 from Latin *dēbentur mihi* there are owed to me, from *dēbēre* to owe] > de'bentured *adj*

debilitate (dɪ'bɪlɪˌteɪt) *vb* (*tr*) to make feeble; weaken [c16 from Latin *dēbilitāre*, from *dēbilis* weak] > deˌbili'tation *n*

debilitating (dɪ'bɪlɪteɪtɪŋ) *adj* tending to weaken or enfeeble

debility (dɪ'bɪlɪtɪ) *n*, *pl* **-ties** weakness or infirmity

debit ('dɛbɪt) *accounting* ▷ *n* **1 a** acknowledgment of a sum owing by entry on the left side of an account **b** the left side of an account **c** an entry on this side **d** the total of such entries **e** (*as modifier*): *a debit balance.* Compare **credit** (sense 10) ▷ *vb* **-its, -iting, -ited 2** (*tr*) **a** to record (an item) as a debit in an account **b** to charge (a person or his account) with a debt. Compare **credit** (sense 17) [c15 from Latin *dēbitum* DEBT]

debit card *n* an embossed plastic card issued by a bank or building society to enable its customers to pay for goods or services by inserting it into a computer-controlled device at the place of sale, which is connected through the telephone network to the bank or building society. It may also function as a cash card, a cheque card, or both

debonair *or* **debonnaire** (ˌdɛbə'nɛə) *adj* (esp of a man or his manner) **1** suave and refined **2** carefree; light-hearted **3** courteous and cheerful; affable [c13 from Old French *debonaire*, from *de bon aire* having a good disposition] > ˌdebo'nairly *adv* > ˌdebo'nairness *n*

Deborah ('dɛbərə, -brə) *n Old Testament* **1** a prophetess and judge of Israel who fought the Canaanites (Judges 4, 5) **2** Rebecca's nurse (Genesis 35:8)

debouch (dɪ'baʊtʃ) *vb* **1** (*intr*) (esp of troops) to move into a more open space, as from a narrow or concealed place **2** (*intr*) (of a river, glacier, etc) to flow from a valley into a larger area or body ▷ *n* **3** Also called: débouché (*French* debyʃe) *fortifications* an outlet or passage, as for the exit of troops [c18 from French *déboucher*, from *dé-* DIS¹ + *bouche* mouth, from Latin *bucca* cheek]

debouchment (dɪ'baʊtʃmənt) *n* **1** the act or an instance of debouching **2** Also called: debouchure (ˌdeɪbuː'ʃʊə) an outlet, mouth, or opening

Debrecen ('dɛbrɛtsɛn) *n* a city in E Hungary: seat of the revolutionary government of 1849. Pop: 205 881 (2003 est)

Debrett (də'brɛt) *n* a list of the British aristocracy. In full: **Debrett's Peerage** [c19 after J. *Debrett* (c. 1750–1822), London publisher who first issued it]

débridement (dɪ'briːdmənt, deɪ-) *n* the surgical removal of dead tissue or cellular debris from the surface of a wound [c19 from French, from Old French *desbrider* to unbridle, from *des-* DE- + *bride* BRIDLE]

debrief (diː'briːf) *vb* (of a soldier, astronaut, diplomat, etc) to make or (of his superiors) to elicit a report after a mission or event. Compare **brief** (sense 13)

debris *or* **débris** ('deɪbriː, 'dɛbriː) *n* **1** fragments or remnants of something destroyed or broken; rubble **2** a collection of loose material derived from rocks, or an accumulation of animal or vegetable matter [c18 from French, from obsolete *debrisier* to break into pieces, from *bruisier* to shatter, of Celtic origin]

debris bug *n* a bug of the family *Cimicidae* found where vegetable debris accumulates and feeding on small arthropods like springtails: related to the bedbugs

de Broglie waves (də 'brɔɡlɪ) *pl n physics* the set of waves that represent the behaviour of an elementary particle, or some atoms and molecules, under certain conditions. The **de Broglie wavelength**, λ, is given by $\lambda = h/mv$, where *h* is the Planck constant, *m* the mass, and *v* the

velocity of the particle. Also called: matter waves [c20 named after Prince Louis Victor *de Broglie* (1892–1987), French physicist]

debt (dɛt) *n* **1** something that is owed, such as money, goods, or services **2** bad debt a debt that has little or no prospect of being paid **3** an obligation to pay or perform something; liability **4** the state of owing something, esp money, or of being under an obligation (esp in the phrases **in debt, in** (someone's) **debt**) [c13 from Old French *dette*, from Latin *dēbitum*, from *dēbēre* to owe, from DE- + *habēre* to have; English spelling influenced by the Latin etymon] > 'debtless *adj*

debt of honour *n* a debt that is morally but not legally binding, such as one contracted in gambling

debtor ('dɛtə) *n* a person or commercial enterprise that owes a financial obligation. Compare **creditor**

debt swap *n* See **swap** (sense 4)

debud (diː'bʌd) *vb* **-buds, -budding, -budded** another word for **disbud**

debug (diː'bʌɡ) *informal* ▷ *vb* **-bugs, -bugging, -bugged** (*tr*) **1** to locate and remove concealed microphones from (a room, etc) **2** to locate and remove defects in (a device, system, plan, etc) **3** to remove insects from ▷ *n* **4 a** something, esp a computer program, that locates and removes defects in (a device, system, etc) **b** (*as modifier*): *a debug program* [c20 from DE- + BUG¹]

debunk (diː'bʌŋk) *vb* (*tr*) *informal* to expose the pretensions or falseness of, esp by ridicule [c20 from DE- + BUNK²] > de'bunker *n*

deburr (diː'bɜː) *vb* (*tr*) **1** to remove burrs from (a workpiece) **2** *textiles* to remove dirt and debris from (raw wool)

debus (diː'bʌs) *vb* **debuses, debusing, debused** *or* **debusses, debussing, debussed** to unload (goods) or (esp of troops) to alight from a motor vehicle

debut ('deɪbjuː, 'dɛbjuː) *n* **1 a** the first public appearance of an actor, musician, etc, or the first public presentation of a show **b** (*as modifier*): *debut album* **2** the presentation of a debutante ▷ *vb* (*intr*) **3** to make a debut [c18 from French *début*, from Old French *desbuter* to play first (hence: make one's first appearance), from *des-* DE- + *but* goal, target; see BUTT²]

debutant ('dɛbjuˌtɑːnt, -ˌtænt) *n* a person who is making a first appearance in a particular capacity, such as a sportsperson playing in a first game for a team

debutante ('dɛbjuˌtɑːnt, -ˌtænt) *n* **1** a young woman of upper-class background who is presented to society, usually at a formal ball **2** a girl or young woman regarded as being upper-class, wealthy, and of a frivolous or snobbish social set [c19 from French, from *débuter* to lead off in a game, make one's first appearance; see DEBUT]

Dec *abbreviation for* December

dec. *abbreviation for* **1** deceased **2** *music* decrescendo

deca-, deka- *or before a vowel* **dec-, dek-** *prefix* denoting ten: *decagon*. In conjunction with scientific units the symbol **da** is used [from Greek *deka*]

decade ('dɛkeɪd, dɪ'keɪd) *n* **1** a period of ten consecutive years **2** a group or series of ten [c15 from Old French, from Late Latin *decad-, decas*, from Greek *dekas*, from *deka* ten] > de'cadal *adj*

decadence ('dɛkədəns) *or* **decadency** *n* **1** deterioration, esp of morality or culture; decay; degeneration **2** the state reached through such a process [c16 from French, from Medieval Latin *dēcadentia*, literally: a falling away; see DECAY]

decadent ('dɛkədənt) *adj* **1** characterized by decay or decline, as in being self-indulgent or morally corrupt **2** belonging to a period of decline in artistic standards ▷ *n* **3** a decadent person **4** (*often capital*) one of a group of French and English writers of the late 19th century whose works were characterized by refinement of style and a

tendency toward the artificial and abnormal > 'decadently *adv*

decaf ('diːkæf) *informal* ▷ *n* **1** decaffeinated coffee ▷ *adj* **2** decaffeinated

decaffeinate (dɪ'kæfɪˌneɪt) *vb* (*tr*) to remove all or part of the caffeine from (coffee, tea, etc)

decagon ('dɛkəˌɡɒn) *n* a polygon having ten sides > decagonal (dɪ'kæɡənəl) *adj* > de'cagonally *adv*

decahedron (ˌdɛkə'hiːdrən) *n* a solid figure having ten plane faces. See also **polyhedron** > ˌdeca'hedral *adj*

decal (dɪ'kæl, 'diːkæl) *n* **1** short for **decalcomania** ▷ *vb* **2** to transfer (a design) by decalcomania

decalcify (diː'kælsɪˌfaɪ) *vb* **-fies, -fying, -fied** (*tr*) to remove calcium or lime from (bones, teeth, etc) > decalcification (diːˌkælsɪfɪ'keɪʃən) *n* > de'calciˌfier *n*

decalcomania (dɪˌkælkə'meɪnɪə) *n* **1** the art or process of transferring a design from prepared paper onto another surface, such as china, glass or paper **2** a design so transferred [c19 from French *décalcomanie*, from *décalquer* to transfer by tracing, from *dé-* DE- + *calquer* to trace + *-manie* -MANIA]

decalescence (ˌdiːkə'lɛsᵊns) *n* the absorption of heat when a metal is heated through a particular temperature range, caused by a change in internal crystal structure [c19 from Late Latin *dēcalescere* to become warm, from Latin DE- + *calescere*, from *calēre* to be warm] > ˌdeca'lescent *adj*

decalitre *or US* **decaliter** ('dɛkəˌliːtə) *n* ten litres. One decalitre is equal to about 2.2 imperial gallons. Symbol: dal

Decalogue ('dɛkəˌlɒɡ) *n* another name for the **Ten Commandments** [c14 from Church Latin *decalogus*, from Greek, from *deka* ten + *logos* word]

decametre *or US* **decameter** ('dɛkəˌmiːtə) *n* ten metres. Symbol: dam

decamp (dɪ'kæmp) *vb* (*intr*) **1** to leave a camp; break camp **2** to depart secretly or suddenly; abscond > de'campment *n*

decanal (dɪ'keɪnᵊl) *adj* **1** of or relating to a dean or deanery **2** (of part of a choir) on the same side of a cathedral, etc, as the dean; on the S side of the choir ▷ Compare **cantorial** [c18 from Medieval Latin *decānālis, decānus* DEAN] > de'canally *or* decanically (dɪ'kænɪkəlɪ) *adv*

decane ('dɛkeɪn) *n* a liquid alkane hydrocarbon existing in several isomeric forms. Formula: $C_{10}H_{22}$ [c19 from DECA- + -ANE]

decanedioic acid (ˌdɛkeɪndaɪ'əʊɪk) *n* a white crystalline carboxylic acid obtained by heating castor oil with sodium hydroxide, used in the manufacture of polyester resins and rubbers and plasticizers. Formula: $HOOC(CH_2)_8COOH$. Also called: sebacic acid

decani (dɪ'keɪnaɪ) *adj, adv music* to be sung by the decanal side of a choir. Compare **cantoris** [Latin: genitive of *decānus*]

decanoic acid (ˌdɛkə'nəʊɪk) *n* a white crystalline insoluble carboxylic acid with an unpleasant odour, used in perfumes and for making fruit flavours. Formula: $C_9H_{19}COOH$. Also called: capric acid

decant (dɪ'kænt) *vb* **1** to pour (a liquid, such as wine) from one container to another, esp without disturbing any sediment **2** (*tr*) to rehouse (people) while their homes are being rebuilt or refurbished [c17 from Medieval Latin *dēcanthāre*, from *canthus* spout, rim; see CANTHUS]

decanter (dɪ'kæntə) *n* a stoppered bottle, usually of glass, into which a drink, such as wine, is poured for serving

decapitate (dɪ'kæpɪˌteɪt) *vb* (*tr*) to behead [c17 from Late Latin *dēcapitāre*, from Latin DE- + *caput* head] > deˌcapi'tation *n* > de'capiˌtator *n*

decapod ('dɛkəˌpɒd) *n* **1** any crustacean of the mostly marine order *Decapoda*, having five pairs of walking limbs: includes the crabs, lobsters, shrimps, prawns, and crayfish **2** any cephalopod mollusc of the order *Decapoda*, having a ring of eight short tentacles and two longer ones:

includes the squids and cuttlefish ▷ *adj* **3** of, relating to, or belonging to either of these orders **4** (of any other animal) having ten limbs > **decapodal** (dɪˈkæpədᵊl), **deˈcapodan** *or* **deˈcapodous** *adj*

Decapolis (dɪˈkæpəlɪs) *n* a league of ten cities, including Damascus, in the northeast of ancient Palestine: established in 63 BC by Pompey and governed by Rome

decapsulate (diːˈkæpsjʊˌleɪt) *vb* (*tr*) *med* to remove a capsule from (a part or organ, esp the kidney) > **deˌcapsuˈlation** *n*

decarbonate (diːˈkɑːbəˌneɪt) *vb* (*tr*) to remove carbon dioxide from (a solution, substance, etc) > **deˌcarbonˈation** *n* > **deˈcarbonˌator** *n*

decarbonize *or* **decarbonise** (diːˈkɑːbəˌnaɪz) *vb* (*tr*) to remove carbon from (the walls of the combustion chamber of an internal-combustion engine). Also: **decoke, decarburize** > **deˌcarboniˈzation** *or* **deˌcarboniˈsation** *n* > **deˈcarbonˌizer** *or* **deˈcarbonˌiser** *n*

decarboxylase (ˌdiːkɑːˈbɒksɪˌleɪs) *n* an enzyme that catalyses the removal of carbon dioxide from a compound

decarboxylation (ˌdiːkɑːˌbɒksəˈleɪʃən) *n* the removal or loss of a carboxyl group from an organic compound

decarburize *or* **decarburise** (diːˈkɑːbjʊˌraɪz) *vb* another word for **decarbonize**. > **deˌcarburiˈzation, deˌcarburiˈsation** *or* **deˌcarbuˈration** *n*

decare (ˈdɛkɛə, dɛˈkɛə) *n* ten ares or 1000 square metres [C19 from French *décare*; see DECA-, ARE[2]]

decastyle (ˈdɛkəˌstaɪl) *n* *architect* a portico consisting of ten columns

decasyllable (ˈdɛkəˌsɪləbᵊl) *n* a word or line of verse consisting of ten syllables > **decasyllabic** (ˌdɛkəsɪˈlæbɪk) *adj*

decathlon (dɪˈkæθlɒn) *n* an athletic contest for men in which each athlete competes in ten different events. Compare **pentathlon** [C20 from DECA- + Greek *athlon* contest, prize; see ATHLETE] > **deˈcathlete** *n*

decay (dɪˈkeɪ) *vb* **1** to decline or cause to decline gradually in health, prosperity, excellence, etc; deteriorate; waste away **2** to rot or cause to rot as a result of bacterial, fungal, or chemical action; decompose **3** (*intr*) *Also*: **disintegrate** *physics* **a** (of an atomic nucleus) to undergo radioactive disintegration **b** (of an elementary particle) to transform into two or more different elementary particles **4** (*intr*) *physics* (of a stored charge, magnetic flux, etc) to decrease gradually when the source of energy has been removed ▷ *n* **5** the process of decline, as in health, mentality, beauty, etc **6** the state brought about by this process **7** decomposition, as of vegetable matter **8** rotten or decayed matter: *the dentist drilled out the decay* **9** *physics* **a** See **radioactive decay** **b** a spontaneous transformation of an elementary particle into two or more different particles **c** of an excited atom or molecule, losing energy by the spontaneous emission of photons **10** *physics* a gradual decrease of a stored charge, magnetic flux, current, etc, when the source of energy has been removed. See also **time constant** **11** *music* the fading away of a note [C15 from Old Northern French *decaïr*, from Late Latin *dēcadere*, literally: to fall away, from Latin *cadere* to fall] > **deˈcayable** *adj*

Deccan (ˈdɛkən) *n* the **1** a plateau in S India, between the Eastern Ghats, the Western Ghats, and the Narmada River **2** the whole Indian peninsula south of the Narmada River

decd *abbreviation for* deceased

decease (dɪˈsiːs) *n* **1** a more formal word for **death** ▷ *vb* **2** (*intr*) a more formal word for **die**[1] [C14 (n): from Old French *deces*, from Latin *dēcēdere* to depart]

deceased (dɪˈsiːst) *adj* **a** a more formal word for **dead** (sense 1) **b** (*as noun*): *the deceased*

decedent (dɪˈsiːdᵊnt) *n* *law, chiefly US* a deceased person [C16 from Latin *dēcēdēns* departing; see DECEASE]

deceit (dɪˈsiːt) *n* **1** the act or practice of deceiving **2** a statement, act, or device intended to mislead; fraud; trick **3** a tendency to deceive [C13 from Old French *deceite*, from *deceivre* to DECEIVE]

deceitful (dɪˈsiːtfʊl) *adj* full of deceit > **deˈceitfully** *adv* > **deˈceitfulness** *n*

deceive (dɪˈsiːv) *vb* (*tr*) **1** to mislead by deliberate misrepresentation or lies **2** to delude (oneself) **3** to be unfaithful to (one's sexual partner) **4** *archaic* to disappoint: *his hopes were deceived* [C13 from Old French *deceivre*, from Latin *dēcipere* to ensnare, cheat, from *capere* to take] > **deˈceivable** *adj* > **deˈceivably** *adv* > **deˈceivableness** *or* **deˌceivaˈbility** *n* > **deˈceiver** *n* > **deˈceiving** *n, adj* > **deˈceivingly** *adv*

decelerate (diːˈsɛləˌreɪt) *vb* to slow down or cause to slow down [C19 from DE- + ACCELERATE] > **deˌcelerˈation** *n* > **deˈcelerˌator** *n*

decelerometer (dɪˌsɛləˈrɒmɪtə) *n* an instrument for measuring deceleration

December (dɪˈsɛmbə) *n* the twelfth and last month of the year, consisting of 31 days [C13 from Old French *decembre*, from Latin *december* the tenth month (the Roman year originally began with March), from *decem* ten]

Decembrist (dɪˈsɛmbrɪst) *n* *Russian history* a participant in the unsuccessful revolt against Tsar Nicolas I in Dec 1825 [C19 translation of Russian *dekabrist*]

decemvir (dɪˈsɛmvə) *n, pl* **-virs** *or* **-viri** (-vɪˌriː) **1** (in ancient Rome) a member of a board of ten magistrates, esp either of the two commissions established in 451 and 450 BC to revise the laws **2** a member of any governing body composed of ten men [C17 from Latin, from *decem* ten + *virī* men] > **deˈcemviral** *adj*

decemvirate (dɪˈsɛmvɪrɪt, -ˌreɪt) *n* **1** a board of decemvirs **2** the rule or rank of decemvirs

decenary *or* **decennary** (dɪˈsɛnərɪ) *adj* *history* of or relating to a tithing [C13 from Medieval Latin *decēna* a tithing, from *decem* ten]

decencies (ˈdiːsᵊnsɪz) *pl n* **1** **the** those things that are considered necessary for a decent life **2** another word for **proprieties**

decency (ˈdiːsᵊnsɪ) *n, pl* **-cies** **1** conformity to the prevailing standards of propriety, morality, modesty, etc **2** the quality of being decent

decennial (dɪˈsɛnɪəl) *adj* **1** lasting for ten years **2** occurring every ten years ▷ *n* **3** a tenth anniversary or its celebration > **deˈcennially** *adv*

decennium (dɪˈsɛnɪəm) *or* **decennary** (dɪˈsɛnərɪ) *n, pl* **-niums, -nia** (-nɪə) *or* **-naries** a less common word for **decade** (sense 1) [C17 from Latin, from *decem* ten + *annus* year]

decent (ˈdiːsᵊnt) *adj* **1** polite or respectable: *a decent family* **2** proper and suitable; fitting: *a decent burial* **3** conforming to conventions of sexual behaviour; not indecent **4** free of oaths, blasphemy, etc: *decent language* **5** good or adequate: *a decent wage* **6** *informal* kind; generous: *he was pretty decent to me* **7** *informal* sufficiently clothed to be seen by other people: *are you decent?* [C16 from Latin *decēns* suitable, from *decēre* to be fitting] > **ˈdecently** *adv* > **ˈdecentness** *n*

decentralize *or* **decentralise** (diːˈsɛntrəˌlaɪz) *vb* **1** to reorganize (a government, industry, etc) into smaller more autonomous units **2** to disperse (a concentration, as of industry or population) > **deˈcentralist** *n, adj* > **deˌcentraliˈzation** *or* **deˌcentraliˈsation** *n*

decentralized processing *n* *computing* the use of word processing or data processing units in stand-alone or localized situations

deception (dɪˈsɛpʃən) *n* **1** the act of deceiving or the state of being deceived **2** something that deceives; trick

deceptive (dɪˈsɛptɪv) *adj* **1** likely or designed to deceive; misleading: *appearances can be deceptive* **2** *music* (of a cadence) another word for **interrupted** (sense 3) > **deˈceptively** *adv* > **deˈceptiveness** *n*

decerebrate *vb* (diːˈsɛrɪˌbreɪt) **1** (*tr*) to remove the brain or a large section of the brain or to cut the spinal cord at the level of the brain stem of (a person or animal) ▷ *n* (diːˈsɛrɪbrɪt) **2** a decerebrated individual [C19 from DE- + CEREBRO- + -ATE[1]] > **deˌcereˈbration** *n*

decern (dɪˈsɜːn) *vb* (*tr*) **1** *Scots law* to decree or adjudge **2** an archaic spelling of **discern** [C15 from Old French *decerner*, from Latin *dēcernere* to judge, from *cernere* to discern]

decertify (diːˈsɜːtɪˌfaɪ) *vb* **-fies, -fying, -fied** (*tr*) to withdraw or remove a certificate or certification from (a person, organization, or country) > **deˌcertifiˈcation** *n*

deci- *prefix* denoting one tenth; 10^{-1}: *decimetre*. Symbol: **d** [from French *déci-*, from Latin *decimus* tenth]

deciare (ˈdɛsɪˌɛə) *n* one tenth of an are or 10 square metres [C19 from French *déciare*; see DECI-, ARE[2]]

decibel (ˈdɛsɪˌbɛl) *n* **1** a unit for comparing two currents, voltages, or power levels, equal to one tenth of a bel **2** a similar unit for measuring the intensity of a sound. It is equal to ten times the logarithm to the base ten of the ratio of the intensity of the sound to be measured to the intensity of some reference sound, usually the lowest audible note of the same frequency. Abbreviation: **dB** See also **perceived noise decibel**

decidable (dɪˈsaɪdəbᵊl) *adj* **1** able to be decided **2** *logic* (of a formal theory) having the property that it is possible by a mechanistic procedure to determine whether or not any well-formed formula is a theorem

decide (dɪˈsaɪd) *vb* **1** (*may take a clause or an infinitive as object*; when *intr*, sometimes foll by *on* or *about*) to reach a decision: *decide what you want; he decided to go* **2** (*tr*) to cause (a person) to reach a decision: *the weather decided me against going* **3** (*tr*) to determine or settle (a contest or question): *he decided his future plans* **4** (*tr*) to influence decisively the outcome of (a contest or question): *Borg's stamina decided the match* **5** (*intr*; foll by *for* or *against*) to pronounce a formal verdict [C14 from Old French *decider*, from Latin *dēcīdere*, literally: to cut off, from *caedere* to cut]

decided (dɪˈsaɪdɪd) *adj* (*prenominal*) **1** unmistakable: *a decided improvement* **2** determined; resolute: *a girl of decided character* > **deˈcidedly** *adv* > **deˈcidedness** *n*

decider (dɪˈsaɪdə) *n* the point, goal, game, etc, that determines who wins a match or championship

decidua (dɪˈsɪdjʊə) *n, pl* **-ciduas** *or* **-ciduae** (-ˈsɪdjʊˌiː) the specialized mucous membrane that lines the uterus of some mammals during pregnancy: is shed, with the placenta, at parturition [C18 from New Latin, from Latin *dēciduus* falling down; see DECIDUOUS] > **deˈcidual** *or* **deˈciduate** *adj*

deciduous (dɪˈsɪdjʊəs) *adj* **1** (of trees and shrubs) shedding all leaves annually at the end of the growing season and then having a dormant period without leaves. Compare **evergreen** (sense 1) **2** (of antlers, wings, teeth, etc) being shed at the end of a period of growth **3** *rare* impermanent; transitory. Compare **evergreen** (sense 2) [C17 from Latin *dēciduus* falling off, from *dēcidere* to fall down, from *cadere* to fall] > **deˈciduously** *adv* > **deˈciduousness** *n*

decile (ˈdɛsɪl, -aɪl) *n* *statistics* **a** one of nine actual or notional values of a variable dividing its distribution into ten groups with equal frequencies: the ninth decile is the value below which 90% of the population lie. See also **percentile** **b** a tenth part of a distribution [C17 from DECA- + -ILE]

decilitre *or US* **deciliter** (ˈdɛsɪˌliːtə) *n* one tenth of a litre. Symbol: **dl**

decillion (dɪˈsɪljən) *n* **1** (in Britain, France, and Germany) the number represented as one followed by 60 zeros (10^{60}) **2** (in the US and Canada) the number represented as one followed by 33 zeros (10^{33}) [C19 from Latin *decem* ten + *-illion* as in *million*] > de'cillionth *adj*

decimal ('dɛsɪməl) *n* **1** Also called: **decimal fraction** a fraction that has a denominator of a power of ten, the power depending on or deciding the decimal place. It is indicated by a decimal point to the left of the numerator, the denominator being omitted. Zeros are inserted between the point and the numerator, if necessary, to obtain the correct decimal place **2** any number used in the decimal system ▷ *adj* **3 a** relating to or using powers of ten **b** of the base ten **4** (*prenominal*) expressed as a decimal [c17 from Medieval Latin *decimālis* of tithes, from Latin *decima* a tenth, from *decem* ten] > 'decimally *adv*

decimal classification *n* another term for **Dewey Decimal System**

decimal currency *n* a system of currency in which the monetary units are parts or powers of ten

decimal fraction *n* another name for **decimal** (sense 1)

decimalize *or* **decimalise** ('dɛsɪmə,laɪz) *vb* to change (a system, number, etc) to the decimal system: *Britain has decimalized her currency* > ,decimali'zation *or* ,decimali'sation *n*

decimal place *n* **1** the position of a digit after the decimal point, each successive decimal to the right having a denominator of an increased power of ten: *in 0.025, 5 is in the third decimal place* **2** the number of digits to the right of the decimal point: *3.142 is a number given to three decimal places*. Compare **significant figures** (sense 2)

decimal point *n* a full stop or a raised full stop placed between the integral and fractional parts of a number in the decimal system

USAGE Conventions relating to the use of the decimal point are confused. The IX General Conference on Weights and Measures resolved in 1948 that the decimal point should be a point on the line or a comma, but not a centre dot. It also resolved that figures could be grouped in threes about the decimal point, but that no point or comma should be used for this purpose. These conventions are adopted in this dictionary. However, the Decimal Currency Board recommended that for sums of money the centre dot should be used as the decimal point and that the comma should be used as the thousand marker. Moreover, in some countries the position is reversed, the comma being used as the decimal point and the dot as the thousand marker

decimal system *n* **1** the number system in general use, having a base of ten, in which numbers are expressed by combinations of the ten digits 0 to 9 **2** a system of measurement, such as the metric system, in which the multiple and submultiple units are related to a basic unit by powers of ten

decimate ('dɛsɪ,meɪt) *vb* (*tr*) **1** to destroy or kill a large proportion of: *a plague decimated the population* **2** (esp in the ancient Roman army) to kill every tenth man of (a mutinous section) [c17 from Latin *decimāre*, from *decimus* tenth, from *decem* ten] > ,deci'mation *n* > 'deci,mator *n*

USAGE One talks about the whole of something being *decimated*, not a part: *disease decimated the population*, not *disease decimated most of the population*

decimetre *or US* **decimeter** ('dɛsɪ,miːtə) *n* one tenth of a metre. Symbol: dm > decimetric (,dɛsɪ'mɛtrɪk) *adj*

decipher (dɪ'saɪfə) *vb* (*tr*) **1** to determine the meaning of (something obscure or illegible) **2** to convert from code into plain text; decode > de'cipherable *adj* > de,ciphera'bility *n* > de'cipherer *n* > de'cipherment *n*

decision (dɪ'sɪʒən) *n* **1** a judgment, conclusion, or resolution reached or given; verdict **2** the act of making up one's mind **3** firmness of purpose or character; determination [c15 from Old French, from Latin *dēcīsiō*, literally: a cutting off; see DECIDE] > de'cisional *adj*

decision support system *n* a system in which one or more computers and computer programs assist in decision-making by providing information

decision table *n* a table within a computer program that specifies the actions to be taken when certain conditions arise

decision theory *n statistics* the study of strategies for decision-making under conditions of uncertainty in such a way as to maximize the expected utility. See also **game theory**

decision tree *n* a treelike diagram illustrating the choices available to a decision maker, each possible decision and its estimated outcome being shown as a separate branch of the tree

decisive (dɪ'saɪsɪv) *adj* **1** influential; conclusive: *a decisive argument* **2** characterized by the ability to make decisions, esp quickly; resolute > de'cisively *adv* > de'cisiveness *n*

deck (dɛk) *n* **1** *nautical* any of various platforms built into a vessel: *a promenade deck; the poop deck* **2** a similar floor or platform, as in a bus **3 a** the horizontal platform that supports the turntable and pick-up of a record player **b** See **tape deck** **4** *chiefly US* a pack of playing cards **5** Also called: **pack** *computing, obsolete* a collection of punched cards relevant to a particular program **6** a raised wooden platform built in a garden to provide a seating area **7 clear the decks** *informal* to prepare for action, as by removing obstacles from a field of activity or combat **8 hit the deck** *informal* **a** to fall to the floor or ground, esp in order to avoid injury **b** to prepare for action **c** to get out of bed ▷ *vb* (*tr*) **9** (often foll by *out*) to dress or decorate **10** to build a deck on (a vessel) **11** *slang* to knock (a person) to the floor or ground ▷ See also **deck over** [c15 from Middle Dutch *dec* a covering; related to THATCH] > 'decker *n*

deck-access *adj* (of a block of flats) having a continuous inset balcony at each level onto which the front door of each flat on that level opens

deck beam *n nautical* a stiffening deck member supported at its extremities by knee connections to frames or bulkheads

deck bridge *n civil engineering* a bridge with an upper horizontal beam that carries the roadway. Compare **through bridge**

deckchair ('dɛk,tʃɛə) *n* **1** a folding chair for use out of doors, consisting of a wooden frame suspending a length of canvas **2** rearranging the deckchairs on the Titanic *humorous* engaged in futile or ineffectual actions

deck crane *n nautical* a deck-mounted crane used for loading and unloading cargo

deck department *n* the part of a ship's crew, from the captain down, concerned with running the ship but not with heavy machinery or catering

decked (dɛkt) *adj* having a wooden deck or platform: *a decked terrace*

-decker *adj* (*in combination:*) having a certain specified number of levels or layers: *a double-decker bus*

deck hand *n* **1** a seaman assigned various duties, such as mooring and cargo handling, on the deck of a ship **2** (in Britain) a seaman over 17 years of age who has seen sea duty for at least one year **3** a helper aboard a yacht

deckhouse ('dɛk,haʊs) *n* a houselike cabin on the deck of a ship

decking ('dɛkɪŋ) *n* a wooden deck or platform, esp one in a garden for deckchairs, etc

deckle *or* **deckel** ('dɛkəl) *n* **1** a frame used to contain pulp on the mould in the making of handmade paper **2** Also called: **deckle strap** a strap on each edge of the moving web of paper on

a paper-making machine that fixes the width of the paper **3** See **deckle edge** [c19 from German *Deckel* lid, from *decken* to cover]

deckle edge *n* **1** the rough edge of handmade paper, caused by pulp seeping between the mould and the deckle: often left as ornamentation in fine books and writing papers **2** a trimmed edge imitating this > 'deckle-'edged *adj*

deck officer *n* a ship's officer who is part of the deck crew

deck over *vb* (*tr*) to complete the construction of the upper deck between the bulwarks of (a vessel)

deck shoe *n* **1** a rubber-soled leather shoe worn when boating **2** a casual cloth or soft leather shoe resembling this

deck tennis *n* a game played on board ship in which a quoit is tossed to and fro across a high net on a small court resembling a tennis court

declaim (dɪ'kleɪm) *vb* **1** to make a (speech, statement, etc) loudly and in a rhetorical manner **2** to speak lines from (a play, poem, etc) with studied eloquence; recite **3** (*intr*; foll by *against*) to protest (against) loudly and publicly [c14 from Latin *dēclāmāre*, from *clāmāre* to call out] > de'claimer *n*

declamation (,dɛklə'meɪʃən) *n* **1** a rhetorical or emotional speech, made esp in order to protest or condemn; tirade **2** a speech, verse, etc, that is or can be spoken **3** the act or art of declaiming **4** *music* the artistry or technique involved in singing recitative passages

declamatory (dɪ'klæmətərɪ, -trɪ) *adj* **1** relating to or having the characteristics of a declamation **2** merely rhetorical; empty and bombastic > de'clamatorily *adv*

declarant (dɪ'klɛərənt) *n chiefly law* a person who makes a declaration

declaration (,dɛklə'reɪʃən) *n* **1** an explicit or emphatic statement **2** a formal statement or announcement; proclamation **3** the act of declaring **4** the ruling of a judge or court on a question of law, esp in the chancery division of the High Court **5** *law* an unsworn statement of a witness admissible in evidence under certain conditions. See also **statutory declaration** **6** *cricket* the voluntary closure of an innings before all ten wickets have fallen **7** *contract bridge* the final contract **8** a statement or inventory of goods, etc, submitted for tax assessment: *a customs declaration* **9** *cards* an announcement of points made after taking a trick, as in bezique

Declaration of Independence *n* **1** the proclamation made by the second American Continental Congress on July 4, 1776, which asserted the freedom and independence of the 13 Colonies from Great Britain **2** the document formally recording this proclamation

declarative (dɪ'klærətɪv) *adj* making or having the nature of a declaration > de'claratively *adv*

declarator (dɪ'klærətə) *n Scots law* an action seeking to have some right, status, etc, judicially ascertained

declaratory (dɪ'klærətərɪ, -trɪ) *adj* **1** another word for **declarative** **2** *law* **a** (of a statute) stating the existing law on a particular subject; explanatory **b** (of a decree or judgment) stating the rights of the parties without specifying the action to be taken > de'claratorily *adv*

declare (dɪ'klɛə) *vb* (*mainly tr*) **1** (may take a clause as object) to make clearly known or announce officially: *to declare one's interests; war was declared* **2** to state officially that (a person, fact, etc) is as specified: *he declared him fit* **3** (may take a clause as object) to state emphatically; assert **4** to show, reveal, or manifest: *the heavens declare the glory of God* **5** (*intr*; often foll by *for* or *against*) to make known one's choice or opinion **6** to make a complete statement of (dutiable goods, etc) **7** (*also intr*) *cards* **a** to display (a card or series of) on the table so as to add to one's score **b** to decide (the trump suit) by making the final bid **8** (*intr*) *cricket* to close an innings voluntarily before all ten wickets have fallen **9** to authorize the payment of (a dividend) from corporate net profit [C14 from Latin *dēclārāre* to make clear, from *clārus* bright, clear] > de'clarable *adj*

declarer (dɪ'klɛərə) *n* **1** a person who declares **2** *bridge* the player who, as first bidder of the suit of the final contract, plays both hands of the partnership

declass (diː'klɑːs) *vb* (*tr*) to lower in social status or position; degrade

déclassé (French deklɑse) *adj* having lost social standing or status [C19 from French *déclasser* to DECLASS] > **déclassée** *fem adj*

declassify (diː'klæsɪˌfaɪ) *vb* -fies, -fying, -fied (*tr*) to release (a document or information) from the security list > de'classiˌfiable *adj* > deˌclassifi'cation *n*

declension (dɪ'klɛnʃən) *n* **1** *grammar* **a** inflection of nouns, pronouns, or adjectives for case, number, and gender **b** the complete set of the inflections of such a word: *"puella" is a first-declension noun in Latin* **2** a decline or deviation from a standard, belief, etc **3** a downward slope or bend [C15 from Latin *dēclīnātiō*, literally: a bending aside, hence variation, inflection; see DECLINE] > de'clensional *adj* > de'clensionally *adv*

declinate ('dɛklɪˌneɪt, -nɪt) *adj* (esp plant parts) descending from the horizontal in a curve; drooping

declination (ˌdɛklɪ'neɪʃən) *n* **1** *astronomy* the angular distance, esp in degrees, of a star, planet, etc, from the celestial equator measured north (positive) or south (negative) along the great circle passing through the celestial poles and the body. Symbol: δ Compare **right ascension 2** See **magnetic declination 3** a refusal, esp a courteous or formal one > ˌdecli'national *adj*

decline (dɪ'klaɪn) *vb* **1** to refuse to do or accept (something), esp politely **2** (*intr*) to grow smaller; diminish: *demand has declined over the years* **3** to slope or cause to slope downwards **4** (*intr*) to deteriorate gradually, as in quality, health, or character **5** *grammar* to state or list the inflections of (a noun, adjective, or pronoun), or (of a noun, adjective, or pronoun) to be inflected for number, case, or gender. Compare **conjugate** (sense 1) ▷ *n* **6** gradual deterioration or loss **7** a movement downward or towards something smaller; diminution **8** a downward slope; declivity **9** *archaic* any slowly progressive disease, such as tuberculosis [C14 from Old French *decliner* to inflect, turn away, sink, from Latin *dēclīnāre* to bend away, inflect grammatically] > de'clinable *adj* > de'cliner *n*

declinometer (ˌdɛklɪ'nɒmɪtə) *n* an instrument for measuring magnetic declination

declivity (dɪ'klɪvɪtɪ) *n, pl* -ties a downward slope, esp of the ground. Compare **acclivity** [C17 from Latin *dēclīvitās*, from DE- + *clīvus* a slope, hill] > de'clivitous *adj*

declutch (dɪ'klʌtʃ) *vb* (*intr*) to disengage the clutch of a motor vehicle

declutter (diː'klʌtə) *vb* to simplify or get rid of mess, disorder, complications, etc: *declutter your life*

decoct (dɪ'kɒkt) *vb* to extract the essence or active principle from (a medicinal or similar substance) by boiling [C15 see DECOCTION]

decoction (dɪ'kɒkʃən) *n* **1** *pharmacol* the extraction of the water-soluble substances of a drug or medicinal plants by boiling **2** the essence or liquor resulting from this [C14 from Old French, from Late Latin *dēcoctiō*, from *dēcoquere* to boil down, from *coquere* to COOK]

decode (diː'kəʊd) *vb* **1** to convert (a message, text, etc) from code into ordinary language **2** *computing* to convert (coded characters) from one form to another, as from binary-coded decimals to decimal numbers. Compare **encode** (sense 2) **3** *electronics* to convert (a coded electrical signal) into normal analogue components **4** to analyse and understand the construction of words and phrases, esp in a foreign language > de'coder *n*

decoherence (ˌdiːkəʊ'hɪərəns) *n physics* the process in which a system's behaviour changes from that which can be explained by quantum mechanics to that which can be explained by classical mechanics

decoke (diː'kəʊk) *vb* (*tr*) another word for **decarbonize**

decollate (dɪ'kɒleɪt, 'dɛkəˌleɪt, diː'kəˈleɪt) *vb* **1** to separate (continuous stationery, etc) into individual forms **2** an archaic word for **decapitate** [C16 from Latin *dēcollāre* to behead, from DE- + *collum* neck] > decol'lation *n* > 'decolˌlator *n*

décolletage (ˌdeɪkɒl'tɑːʒ; French dekɔltaʒ) *n* a low-cut neckline or a woman's garment with a low neck [C19 from French; see DÉCOLLETÉ]

décolleté (deɪ'kɒlteɪ; French dekɔlte) *adj* **1** (of a woman's garment) low-cut **2** wearing a low-cut garment ▷ *n* **3** a low-cut neckline [C19 from French *décolleter* to cut out the neck (of a dress), from *collet* collar]

decolonize or **decolonise** (diː'kɒləˌnaɪz) *vb* (*tr*) to grant independence to (a colony) > deˌcoloni'zation or deˌcoloni'sation *n*

decolorant (diː'kʌlərənt) *adj* **1** able to decolour or bleach ▷ *n* **2** a substance that decolours

decolour (diː'kʌlə), **decolorize** or **decolorise** *vb* (*tr*) to deprive of colour, as by bleaching > deˌcolor'ation *n* > deˌcolori'zation or deˌcolori'sation *n*

decommission (ˌdiːkə'mɪʃən) *vb* (*tr*) to dismantle or remove from service (a nuclear reactor, weapon, ship, etc which is no longer required)

decommit (ˌdiːkə'mɪt) *vb* -mits, -mitting, -mitted (*intr*) to withdraw from a commitment or agreed course of action

decompensation (diːˌkɒmpɛn'seɪʃən) *n pathol* inability of an organ, esp the heart, to maintain its function due to overload caused by a disease

decompose (ˌdiːkəm'pəʊz) *vb* **1** to break down (organic matter) or (of organic matter) to be broken down physically and chemically by bacterial or fungal action; rot **2** *chem* to break down or cause to break down into simpler chemical compounds **3** to break up or separate into constituent parts **4** (*tr*) *maths* to express in terms of a number of independent simpler components, as a set as a canonical union of disjoint subsets, or a vector into orthogonal components > ˌdecom'posable *adj* > ˌdecomˌposa'bility *n* > decomposition (ˌdiːkɒmpə'zɪʃən) *n*

decomposer (ˌdiːkəm'pəʊzə) *n ecology* any organism in a community, such as a bacterium or fungus, that breaks down dead tissue enabling the constituents to be recycled to the environment. See also **consumer** (sense 3), **producer** (sense 8)

decompound (ˌdiːkəm'paʊnd) *adj* **1** (of a compound leaf) having leaflets consisting of several distinct parts **2** made up of one or more compounds ▷ *vb* **3** a less common word for **decompose 4** *obsolete* to mix with or form from one or more compounds

decompress (ˌdiːkəm'prɛs) *vb* **1** to relieve (a substance) of pressure or (of a substance) to be relieved of pressure **2** to return (a diver, caisson worker, etc) to a condition of normal atmospheric pressure gradually from a condition of increased pressure or (of a diver, etc) to be returned to such a condition > ˌdecom'pression *n* > ˌdecom'pressive *adj*

decompression chamber *n* a chamber in which the pressure of air can be varied slowly for returning people from abnormal pressures to atmospheric pressure without inducing decompression sickness

decompression sickness or **illness** *n* a disorder characterized by severe pain in muscles and joints, cramp, and difficulty in breathing, caused by a sudden and sustained decrease in air pressure, resulting in the deposition of nitrogen

bubbles in the tissues. Also called: caisson disease, aeroembolism Nontechnical name: the bends

decongestant (ˌdiːkən'dʒɛstənt) *adj* **1** relieving congestion, esp nasal congestion ▷ *n* **2** a decongestant drug

deconsecrate (diː'kɒnsɪˌkreɪt) *vb* (*tr*) to transfer (a church) to secular use > deˌconse'cration *n*

deconstruct (ˌdiːkən'strʌkt) *vb* (*tr*) **1** to apply the theories of deconstruction to (a text, film, etc) **2** to expose or dismantle the existing structure in (a system, organization, etc)

deconstructed (ˌdiːkən'strʌktɪd) *adj* having no formal structure: *a deconstructed jacket*

deconstruction (ˌdiːkən'strʌkʃən) *n* a technique of literary analysis that regards meaning as resulting from the differences between words rather than their reference to the things they stand for. Different meanings are discovered by taking apart the structure of the language used and exposing the assumption that words have a fixed reference point beyond themselves

decontaminate (ˌdiːkən'tæmɪˌneɪt) *vb* (*tr*) to render (an area, building, object, etc) harmless by the removal, distribution, or neutralization of poisons, radioactivity, etc > ˌdecon'taminant *n* > ˌdeconˌtami'nation *n* > ˌdecon'taminative *adj* > ˌdeconˌtami'nator *n*

decontrol (ˌdiːkən'trəʊl) *vb* -trols, -trolling, -trolled (*tr*) to free of restraints or controls, esp government controls: *to decontrol prices*

décor or **decor** ('deɪkɔː) *n* **1** a style or scheme of interior decoration, furnishings, etc, as in a room or house **2** stage decoration; scenery [C19 from French, from *décorer* to DECORATE]

decorate ('dɛkəˌreɪt) *vb* **1** (*tr*) to make more attractive by adding ornament, colour, etc **2** to paint or wallpaper (a room, house, etc) **3** (*tr*) to confer a mark of distinction, esp a military medal, upon **4** (*tr*) to evaporate a metal film onto (a crystal) in order to display dislocations in structure [C16 from Latin *decorāre*, from *decus* adornment; see DECENT]

Decorated style or **architecture** *n* a 14th-century style of English architecture characterized by the ogee arch, geometrical tracery, and floral decoration

decoration (ˌdɛkə'reɪʃən) *n* **1** an addition that renders something more attractive or ornate; adornment **2** the act, process, or art of decorating **3** a medal, badge, etc, conferred as a mark of honour

decorative ('dɛkərətɪv, 'dɛkrətɪv) *adj* serving to decorate or adorn; ornamental > 'decoratively *adv* > 'decorativeness *n*

decorator ('dɛkəˌreɪtə) *n* **1** *Brit* a person whose profession is the painting and wallpapering of buildings **2** a person who decorates **3** See **interior decorator** (sense 1)

decorous ('dɛkərəs) *adj* characterized by propriety in manners, conduct, etc [C17 from Latin *decōrus*, from *decor* elegance] > 'decorously *adv* > 'decorousness *n*

decorticate (diː'kɔːtɪˌkeɪt) *vb* **1** (*tr*) to remove the bark or some other outer layer from **2** *surgery* to remove the cortex of (an organ or part) [C17 from Latin *dēcorticāre*, from DE- + *-corticāre*, from *cortex* bark] > deˌcorti'cation *n* > de'cortiˌcator *n*

decorum (dɪ'kɔːrəm) *n* **1** propriety, esp in behaviour or conduct **2** a requirement of correct behaviour in polite society [C16 from Latin: propriety]

decoupage (ˌdeɪkuː'pɑːʒ) *n* **1** the art or process of decorating a surface with shapes or illustrations cut from paper, card, etc **2** anything produced by this technique [C20 from French, from *découper* to cut out, from DE- + *couper* to cut]

decouple (ˌdiː'kʌpəl) *vb* (*tr*) to separate (joined or coupled subsystems) thereby enabling them to exist and operate separately

decoupling (diː'kʌplɪŋ) *n* **1** the separation of previously linked systems so that they may operate independently **2** *electronics* the reduction or avoidance of undesired distortion or oscillations in a circuit, caused by unwanted common coupling between two or more circuits

decoy *n* ('diːkɔɪ, dɪ'kɔɪ) **1** a person or thing used to beguile or lead someone into danger; lure **2** *military* something designed to deceive an enemy or divert his attention **3** a bird or animal, or an image of one, used to lure game into a trap or within shooting range **4** an enclosed space or large trap, often with a wide funnelled entrance, into which game can be lured for capture ▷ *vb* (dɪ'kɔɪ) **5** to lure or be lured by or as if by means of a decoy [C17 probably from Dutch *de kooi*, literally: the cage, from Latin *cavea* CAGE] > de'coyer *n*

decrease *vb* (dɪ'kriːs) **1** to diminish or cause to diminish in size, number, strength, etc ▷ *n* ('diːkriːs, dɪ'kriːs) **2** the act or process of diminishing; reduction **3** the amount by which something has been diminished [C14 from Old French *descreistre*, from Latin *dēcrescere* to grow less, from DE- + *crescere* to grow] > de'creasingly *adv*

decree (dɪ'kriː) *n* **1** an edict, law, etc, made by someone in authority **2** an order or judgment of a court made after hearing a suit, esp in matrimonial proceedings. See **decree nisi, decree absolute** ▷ *vb* decrees, decreeing, decreed **3** to order, adjudge, or ordain by decree [C14 from Old French *decre*, from Latin *dēcrētum* ordinance, from *dēcrētus* decided, past participle of *dēcernere* to determine; see DECERN] > de'creeable *adj* > de'creer *n*

decree absolute *n* the final decree in divorce proceedings, which leaves the parties free to remarry. Compare **decree nisi**

decree nisi ('naɪsaɪ) *n* a provisional decree, esp in divorce proceedings, which will later be made absolute unless cause is shown why it should not. Compare **decree absolute**

decreet (dɪ'kriːt) *n* *Scots law* the final judgment or sentence of a court [C14 *decret*: from Old French, from Latin *dēcrētum* DECREE]

decrement ('dɛkrɪmənt) *n* **1** the act of decreasing; diminution **2** *maths* a negative increment **3** *physics* a measure of the damping of an oscillator, expressed by the ratio of the amplitude of a cycle to its amplitude after one period **4** of spectra, a sequence of related spectrum lines decaying in intensity, eg Balmer decay [C17 from Latin *dēcrēmentum*, from *dēcrescere* to DECREASE]

decrepit (dɪ'krɛpɪt) *adj* **1** enfeebled by old age; infirm **2** broken down or worn out by hard or long use; dilapidated [C15 from Latin *dēcrepitus*, from *crepāre* to creak] > de'crepi,tude *n*

decrepitate (dɪ'krɛpɪ,teɪt) *vb* **1** (tr) to heat (a substance, such as a salt) until it emits a crackling sound or until this sound stops **2** (intr) (esp of a salt) to crackle, as while being heated [C17 from New Latin *dēcrepitāre*, from *crepitāre* to crackle, from *crepāre* to creak] > de,crepi'tation *n*

decresc. *music* abbreviation for decrescendo

decrescendo (,diːkrɪ'ʃɛndəʊ) *n, adj* another word for **diminuendo** [Italian, from *decrescere* to DECREASE]

decrescent (dɪ'krɛsənt) *adj* (esp of the moon) decreasing; waning [C17 from Latin *dēcrescēns* growing less; see DECREASE] > de'crescence *n*

decretal (dɪ'kriːtəl) *n* **1** *RC Church* a papal edict on doctrine or church law ▷ *adj* **2** of or relating to a decretal or a decree [C15 from Old French, from Late Latin *dēcrētālis*; see DECREE] > de'cretalist *n*

Decretals (dɪ'kriːtəlz) *pl n* *RC Church* a compilation of decretals, esp the authoritative compilation (**Liber Extra**) of Gregory IX (1234) which forms part of the Corpus Juris Canonici

Decretum (dɪ'kriːtəm) *n* *RC Church* the name given to various collections of canon law, esp that made by the monk Gratian in the 12th century, which forms the first part of the Corpus Juris Canonici

decriminalize or **decriminalise** (diː'krɪmənə,laɪz) *vb* (tr) to remove (an action) from the legal category of criminal offence: *to decriminalize the possession of marijuana* > ,decriminali'zation or ,decriminali'sation *n*

decry (dɪ'kraɪ) *vb* -cries, -crying, -cried (tr) **1** to express open disapproval of; disparage **2** to depreciate by proclamation: *to decry obsolete coinage* [C17 from Old French *descrier*, from *des-* DIS[1] + *crier* to CRY] > de'crial *n* > de'crier *n*

decrypt (diː'krɪpt) *vb* (tr) **1** to decode (a message) with or without previous knowledge of its key **2** to make intelligible (a television or other signal) that has been deliberately distorted for transmission [C20 from DE- + *crypt*, as in CRYPTIC] > de'crypted *adj* > de'cryption *n*

decubitus (dɪ'kjuːbɪtəs) *n* *med* the posture adopted when lying down [C19 Latin, past participle of *decumbere* to lie down] > de'cubital *adj*

decubitus ulcer *n* a chronic ulcer of the skin and underlying tissues caused by prolonged pressure on the body surface of bedridden patients. Nontechnical names: bedsore, pressure sore

decumbent (dɪ'kʌmbənt) *adj* **1** lying down or lying flat **2** *botany* (of certain stems) lying flat with the tip growing upwards [C17 from Latin *dēcumbēns*, present participle of *dēcumbere* to lie down] > de'cumbence or de'cumbency *n* > de'cumbently *adv*

decuple ('dɛkjʊpəl) *vb* **1** (tr) to increase by ten times ▷ *n* **2** an amount ten times as large as a given reference ▷ *adj* **3** increasing tenfold [C15 from Old French, from Late Latin *decuplus* tenfold, from Latin *decem* ten]

decurion (dɪ'kjʊərɪən) *n* (in the Roman Empire) **1** a local councillor **2** the commander of a troop of ten cavalrymen [C14 from Latin *decuriō*, from *decuria* company of ten, from *decem* ten]

decurrent (dɪ'kʌrənt) *adj* *botany* extending down the stem, esp (of a leaf) having the base of the blade extending down the stem as two wings [C15 from Latin *dēcurrere* to run down, from *currere* to run] > de'currently *adv*

decurved (diː'kɜːvd) *adj* bent or curved downwards: *a decurved bill; decurved petals*

decury ('dɛkjʊərɪ) *n, pl* -ries (in ancient Rome) a body of ten men [C16 from Latin *decuria*; see DECURION]

decussate *vb* (dɪ'kʌseɪt) **1** to cross or cause to cross in the form of the letter X; intersect ▷ *adj* (dɪ'kʌseɪt, dɪ'kʌsɪt) **2** in the form of the letter X; crossed; intersected **3** *botany* (esp of leaves) arranged in opposite pairs, with each pair at right angles to the one above and below it [C17 from Latin *decussāre*, from *decussis* the number ten, from *decem* ten] > de'cussately *adv* > ,decus'sation *n*

Ded (dɛd) *n* (in the Russian army) a soldier who has served two or three years [Russian *ded* grandfather]

dedal ('diːdəl) *adj* a variant spelling of **daedal**

dedans *French* (dədã) *n* *real tennis* the open gallery at the server's end of the court [literally: interior]

Dedéagach, Dedeagatch or **Dedeağaç** ('dɛdeɪə'gɑːtʃ) *n* a former name (until the end of World War I) of Alexandroúpolis

Dedekind cut (German 'deːdə,kɪnt) *n* a method of according the same status to irrational and rational numbers, devised by Julius Wilhelm *Dedekind* (1831–1916)

dedicate ('dɛdɪ,keɪt) *vb* (tr) **1** (often foll by *to*) to devote (oneself, one's time, etc) wholly to a special purpose or cause; commit wholeheartedly or unreservedly **2** (foll by *to*) to address or inscribe (a book, artistic performance, etc) to a person, cause, etc as a token of affection or respect **3** (foll by *to*) to request or play (a record) on radio for another person as a greeting **4** to assign or allocate to a particular project, function, etc **5** to set apart for a deity or for sacred uses; consecrate ▷ *adj* **6** an archaic word for **dedicated** [C15 from Latin *dēdicāre* to announce, from *dicāre* to make known, variant of *dīcere* to say] > 'dedica,tee *n* > 'dedi,cator *n*

> **dedicatory** ('dɛdɪ,keɪtərɪ, 'dɛdɪkətərɪ, -trɪ) or 'dedi,cative *adj*

dedicated ('dɛdɪ,keɪtɪd) *adj* **1** devoted to a particular purpose or cause: *a dedicated man* **2** assigned or allocated to a particular project, function, etc: *a dedicated transmission line; dedicated parking space* **3** *computing* designed to fulfil one function: *a dedicated microprocessor*

dedication (,dɛdɪ'keɪʃən) *n* **1** the act of dedicating or the state of being dedicated **2** an inscription or announcement prefixed to a book, piece of music, etc, dedicating it to a person or thing **3** complete and wholehearted devotion, esp to a career, ideal, etc **4** a ceremony in which something, such as a church, is dedicated > ,dedi'cational *adj*

de dicto *Latin* ('deɪ'dɪktəʊ) *adj* *logic, philosophy* relating to the expression of a belief, possibility, etc, rather than to the individuals mentioned, as in *the number of the planets is the number of satellites of the sun*, the truth of which is independent of what number that is. Compare **de re** See also **Electra paradox** [literally: about the saying]

dedifferentiation (diː,dɪfə,rɛnʃɪ'eɪʃən) *n* the reversion of the cells of differentiated tissue to a less specialized form

deduce (dɪ'djuːs) *vb* (tr) **1** (may take a clause as object) to reach (a conclusion about something) by reasoning; conclude (that); infer **2** *archaic* to trace the origin, course, or derivation of [C15 from Latin *dēdūcere* to lead away, derive, from DE- + *dūcere* to lead] > de'ducible *adj* > de,duci'bility or de'ducibleness *n*

deduct (dɪ'dʌkt) *vb* (tr) to take away or subtract (a number, quantity, part, etc): *income tax is deducted from one's wages* [C15 from Latin *dēductus*, past participle of *dēdūcere* to DEDUCE]

deductible (dɪ'dʌktəbəl) *adj* **1** capable of being deducted **2** *US and Canadian* short for **tax-deductible** ▷ *n* **3** *insurance, US and Canadian* a specified contribution towards the cost of a claim, stipulated on certain insurance policies as being payable by the policyholder. Also called (in Britain and certain other countries): excess > de,ducti'bility *n*

deduction (dɪ'dʌkʃən) *n* **1** the act or process of deducting or subtracting **2** something, esp a sum of money, that is or may be deducted **3 a** the process of reasoning typical of mathematics and logic, whose conclusions follow necessarily from their premises **b** an argument of this type **c** the conclusion of such an argument **4** *logic* **a** a systematic method of deriving conclusions that cannot be false when the premises are true, esp one amenable to formalization and study by the science of logic **b** an argument of this type. Compare **induction** (sense 4)

deduction theorem *n* *logic* the property of many formal systems that the conditional derived from a valid argument by taking the conjunction of the premises as antecedent and the conclusion as consequent is true

deductive (dɪ'dʌktɪv) *adj* of or relating to deduction: *deductive reasoning* > de'ductively *adv*

dee (diː) *vb* a Scot word for **die**[1]

Dee (diː) *n* **1** a river in N Wales and NW England, rising in S Gwynedd and flowing east and north to the Irish Sea. Length: about 112 km (70 miles) **2** a river in NE Scotland, rising in the Cairngorms and flowing east to the North Sea. Length: about 140 km (87 miles) **3** a river in S Scotland, flowing south to the Solway Firth. Length: about 80 km (50 miles)

deed (diːd) *n* **1** something that is done or performed; act **2** a notable achievement; feat; exploit **3** action or performance, as opposed to words **4** *law* a formal legal document signed, witnessed, and delivered to effect a conveyance or transfer of property or to create a legal obligation or contract ▷ *vb* **5** (tr) *US and Canadian* to convey or transfer (property) by deed [Old English *dēd*; related to Old High German *tāt*, Gothic *gadeths*; see DO[1]]

deed box *n* a lockable metal box for storing documents
deed poll *n law* a deed made by one party only, esp one by which a person changes his name
deejay ('diːˌdʒeɪ) *n* an informal name for **disc jockey** [c20 from the initials DJ]
deek (diːk) *vb (tr; imperative) Edinburgh and Northumbrian dialect* to look at: *deek that!* [perhaps of Romany origin]
deely boppers ('diːlɪˌbɒpəz) *pl n* a hairband with two balls on springs attached, resembling antennae
deem (diːm) *vb (tr)* to judge or consider: *I do not deem him worthy of this honour* [Old English *dēman;* related to Old High German *tuomen* to judge, Gothic *domjan;* see DOOM]
de-emphasize *or* **de-emphasise** (diːˈɛmfəˌsaɪz) *vb (tr)* to remove emphasis from
deemster ('diːmstə) *n* the title of one of the two justices in the Isle of Man. Also called: **dempster** > **'deemsterˌship** *n*
de-energize *or* **de-energise** (diːˈɛnədʒaɪz) *vb (tr) electrical engineering* to disconnect (an electrical circuit) from its source > **de-ˌenergiˈzation** *or* **de-ˌenergiˈsation** *n*
deep (diːp) *adj* **1** extending or situated relatively far down from a surface: *a deep pool* **2** extending or situated relatively far inwards, backwards, or sideways: *a deep border of trees* **3** *cricket* relatively far from the pitch: *the deep field; deep third man* **4** **a** *(postpositive)* of a specified dimension downwards, inwards, or backwards: *six feet deep* **b** *(in combination)*: *a six-foot-deep trench* **5** coming from or penetrating to a great depth: *a deep breath* **6** difficult to understand and penetrate; abstruse **7** learned or intellectually demanding: *a deep discussion* **8** of great intensity; extreme: *deep happiness; deep trouble* **9** *(postpositive;* foll by *in)* absorbed or enveloped (by); engrossed or immersed (in): *deep in study; deep in debt* **10** very cunning or crafty; devious: *a deep plot* **11** mysterious or obscure: *a deep secret* **12** (of a colour) having an intense or dark hue **13** low in pitch or tone: *a deep voice* **14** **go off the deep end** *informal* **a** to lose one's temper; react angrily **b** *chiefly US* to act rashly **15** **in deep water** in a tricky position or in trouble **16** **throw (someone) in at the deep end** See **end** (sense 28) ▷ *n* **17** any deep place on land or under water, esp below 6000 metres (3000 fathoms) **18** **the deep** **a** a poetic term for the **ocean** **b** *cricket* the area of the field relatively far from the pitch **19** the most profound, intense, or central part: *the deep of winter* **20** a vast extent, as of space or time **21** *nautical* one of the intervals on a sounding lead, one fathom apart ▷ *adv* **22** far on in time; late: *they worked deep into the night* **23** profoundly or intensely **24** **deep down** *informal* in reality, esp as opposed to appearance: *she is a very kind person deep down* **25** **deep in the past** long ago [Old English *dēop;* related to Old High German *tiof* deep, Old Norse *djupr*] > **'deeply** *adv* > **'deepness** *n*
deep design *n (often capitals)* **a** a design process used in architecture, town planning, engineering, interior design, etc, the goal of which is to appeal not only to the thoughts and feelings of the conscious mind but also the visual imagery of the unconscious, while also aiming for sustainability **b** *(as modifier)*: *deep-design thinking* > **deep designer** *n*
deep-discount bond *n* a fixed-interest security that pays little or no interest but is issued at a substantial discount to its redemption value, thus largely substituting capital gain for income
deep-dish pie *n chiefly US and Canadian* a pie baked in a deep dish and having only a top crust
deep-dyed *adj usually derogatory* thoroughgoing; absolute; complete
deepen ('diːpᵊn) *vb* to make or become deep, deeper, or more intense > **'deepener** *n*
deepfreeze (ˌdiːpˈfriːz) *n* **1** a type of refrigerator in which food, etc, is stored for long periods at temperatures below freezing **2** storage in or as if in a deepfreeze **3** *informal* a state of suspended activity ▷ *vb* **deep-freeze** **-freezes, -freezing, -froze, -frozen** **4** *(tr)* to freeze or keep in or as if in a deepfreeze
deep-fry *vb* **-fries, -frying, -fried** to cook (fish, potatoes, etc) in sufficient hot fat to cover the food entirely
deep green *n* **1** a person, esp a politician, who is in favour of taking extreme measures to tackle environmentalist issues ▷ *adj* **2** in favour of or relating to extreme measures to tackle environmentalist issues: *deep green environmentalists*
deep kiss *n* another name for **French kiss**
deep-laid *adj* (of a plot or plan) carefully worked out and kept secret
deep-litter *n (modifier) poultry farming* **1** denoting a system in which a number of hens are housed in one covered enclosure, within which they can move about freely, on a layer of straw or wood shavings several centimetres deep: *deep-litter system* **2** kept in or produced by the deep-litter method: *deep-litter eggs*
deep-rooted *or* **deep-seated** *adj* (of ideas, beliefs, prejudices, etc) firmly fixed, implanted, or held; ingrained
deep-sea *n (modifier)* of, found in, or characteristic of the deep parts of the sea: *deep-sea fishing*
deep-set *adj* (of the eyes) deeply set into the face
deep-six *vb (tr) US slang* to dispose of (something, such as documents) completely; destroy [c20 from *six feet deep,* the traditional depth for a grave]
Deep South *n* the SE part of the US, esp South Carolina, Georgia, Alabama, Mississippi, and Louisiana
deep space *n* any region of outer space beyond the system of the earth and moon
deep structure *n generative grammar* a representation of a sentence at a level where logical or grammatical relations are made explicit, before transformational rules have been applied. Compare **surface structure**
deep therapy *n* radiotherapy with very penetrating short-wave radiation
deep throat *n* an anonymous source of secret information [c20 from the code name of such a source in the Watergate scandal; a reference to the title of a pornographic film]
deep-vein thrombosis *n, pl* **-ses** (-siːz) a blood clot in one of the major veins, usually in the legs or pelvis; can be caused by prolonged sitting in the same position, as on long-haul air flights. Abbreviation: **DVT**
deer (dɪə) *n, pl* **deer** *or* **deers** **1** any ruminant artiodactyl mammal of the family *Cervidae,* including reindeer, elk, muntjacs, and roe deer, typically having antlers in the male. Related adj: **cervine** **2** (in N Canada) another name for **caribou** [Old English *dēor* beast; related to Old High German *tior* wild beast, Old Norse *dȳr*]
deergrass ('dɪəˌgrɑːs) *n* a perennial cyperaceous plant, *Trichophorum caespitosum,* that grows in dense tufts in peat bogs of temperate regions
deerhound ('dɪəˌhaʊnd) *n* a very large rough-coated breed of dog of the greyhound type
deer lick *n* a naturally or artificially salty area of ground where deer come to lick the salt
deer mouse *n* any of various mice of the genus *Peromyscus,* esp *P. maniculatus,* of North and Central America, having brownish fur with white underparts: family *Cricetidae*. See also **white-footed mouse** [so named because of its agility]
deerskin ('dɪəˌskɪn) *n* **a** the hide of a deer **b** *(as modifier)*: *a deerskin jacket*
deerstalker ('dɪəˌstɔːkə) *n* **1** Also called: **stalker** a person who stalks deer, esp in order to shoot them **2** a hat, peaked in front and behind, with earflaps usually turned up and tied together on the top > **'deerˌstalking** *adj, n*
de-escalate (diːˈɛskəˌleɪt) *vb* to reduce the level or intensity of (a crisis, etc) > **de-ˌescaˈlation** *n*
DEET (diːt) *n acronym for* diethyl(meta)toluamide; an insect repellent
def (dɛf) *adj slang* very good, esp of hip-hop [c20 perhaps from *definitive*]
def. *abbreviation for* definition
deface (dɪˈfeɪs) *vb (tr)* to spoil or mar the surface, legibility, or appearance of; disfigure > **deˈfaceable** *adj* > **deˈfacement** *n* > **deˈfacer** *n*
de facto (deɪ ˈfæktəʊ) *adv* **1** in fact ▷ *adj* **2** existing in fact, whether legally recognized or not: *a de facto regime*. Compare **de jure** ▷ *n, pl* **tos** **3** *Austral and NZ* a de facto husband or wife [c17 Latin]
defaecate ('dɛfɪˌkeɪt) *vb* a variant spelling of **defecate**
defalcate ('diːfælˌkeɪt) *vb (intr) law* to misuse or misappropriate property or funds entrusted to one [c15 from Medieval Latin *dēfalcāre* to cut off, from Latin DE- + *falx* sickle] > **ˌdefalˈcation** *n* > **ˈdefalˌcator** *n*
defamation (ˌdɛfəˈmeɪʃən) *n* **1** *law* the injuring of a person's good name or reputation. Compare **libel, slander** **2** the act of defaming or state of being defamed
defamatory (dɪˈfæmətərɪ, -trɪ) *adj* injurious to someone's name or reputation > **deˈfamatorily** *adv*
defame (dɪˈfeɪm) *vb (tr)* **1** to attack the good name or reputation of; slander; libel **2** *archaic* to indict or accuse [c14 from Old French *defamer,* from Latin *dēfāmāre,* from *diffāmāre* to spread by unfavourable report, from *fāma* FAME] > **deˈfamer** *n*
default (dɪˈfɔːlt) *n* **1** a failure to act, esp a failure to meet a financial obligation or to appear in a court of law at a time specified **2** absence: *he lost the chess game by default* **3** **in default of** through or in the lack or absence of **4** **judgment by default** *law* a judgment in the plaintiff's favour when the defendant fails to plead or to appear **5** lack, want, or need **6** *(also* ˈdiːfɔːlt) *computing* **a** the preset selection of an option offered by a system, which will always be followed except when explicitly altered **b** *(as modifier)*: *default setting* ▷ *vb* **7** *(intr;* often foll by *on* or *in)* to fail to make payment when due **8** *(intr)* to fail to fulfil or perform an obligation, engagement, etc: *to default in a sporting contest* **9** *law* to lose (a case) by failure to appear in court **10** *(tr)* to declare that (someone) is in default [c13 from Old French *defaute,* from *defaillir* to fail, from Vulgar Latin *dēfallīre* (unattested) to be lacking]
defaulter (dɪˈfɔːltə) *n* **1** a person who defaults **2** *chiefly Brit* a person, esp a soldier, who has broken the disciplinary code of his service
defeasance (dɪˈfiːzᵊns) *n chiefly law* **1** the act or process of rendering null and void; annulment **2** **a** a condition, the fulfilment of which renders a deed void **b** the document containing such a condition [c14 from Old French, from *desfaire* to DEFEAT]
defeasible (dɪˈfiːzəbᵊl) *adj* **1** *law* (of an estate or interest in land) capable of being defeated or rendered void **2** *philosophy* (of a judgment, opinion, etc) having a presupposition in its favour but open to revision if countervailing evidence becomes known. Compare **incorrigible** (sense 3) > **deˈfeasibleness** *or* **deˌfeasiˈbility** *n*
defeat (dɪˈfiːt) *vb (tr)* **1** to overcome in a contest or competition; win a victory over **2** to thwart or frustrate: *this accident has defeated all his hopes of winning* **3** *law* to render null and void; annul ▷ *n* **4** the act of defeating or state of being defeated **5** an instance of defeat **6** overthrow or destruction **7** *law* an annulment [c14 from Old French *desfait,* from *desfaire* to undo, ruin, from *des-* DIS-[1] + *faire* to do, from Latin *facere*] > **deˈfeater** *n*
defeatism (dɪˈfiːtɪzəm) *n* a ready acceptance or expectation of defeat > **deˈfeatist** *n, adj*
defecate *or* **defaecate** ('dɛfɪˌkeɪt) *vb* **1** *(intr)* to discharge waste from the body through the anus **2** *(tr)* to clarify or remove impurities from (a solution, esp of sugar) [c16 from Latin *dēfaecāre* to cleanse from dregs, from DE- + *faex* sediment, dregs] > **ˌdefeˈcation** *or* **ˌdefaeˈcation** *n* > **ˈdefeˌcator** *or* **ˈdefaeˌcator** *n*

d

defect *n* (dɪˈfɛkt, ˈdiːfɛkt) **1** a lack of something necessary for completeness or perfection; shortcoming; deficiency **2** an imperfection, failing, or blemish **3** *crystallog* a local deviation from regularity in the crystal lattice of a solid. See also **point defect, dislocation** (sense 3) ▷ *vb* (dɪˈfɛkt) **4** (*intr*) to desert one's country, cause, allegiance, etc, esp in order to join the opposing forces [c15 from Latin *dēfectus*, from *dēficere* to forsake, fail; see DEFICIENT] > deˈfector *n*

defection (dɪˈfɛkʃən) *n* **1** the act or an instance of defecting **2** abandonment of duty, allegiance, principles, etc; backsliding **3** another word for **defect** (senses 1, 2)

defective (dɪˈfɛktɪv) *adj* **1** having a defect or flaw; imperfect; faulty **2** (of a person) below the usual standard or level, esp in intelligence **3** *grammar* (of a word) lacking the full range of inflections characteristic of its form class, as for example *must,* which has no past tense > deˈfectively *adv* > deˈfectiveness *n*

defence *or US* **defense** (dɪˈfɛns) *n* **1** resistance against danger, attack, or harm; protection **2** a person or thing that provides such resistance **3** a plea, essay, speech, etc, in support of something; vindication; justification **4 a** a country's military measures or resources **b** (*as modifier*): *defence spending* **5** *law* a defendant's denial of the truth of the allegations or charge against him **6** *law* the defendant and his legal advisers collectively. Compare **prosecution 7** *sport* **a** the action of protecting oneself, one's goal, or one's allotted part of the playing area against an opponent's attacks **b** the method of doing this **c** (usually preceded by *the*) the players in a team whose function is to do this **8** *American football* (usually preceded by *the*) **a** the team that does not have possession of the ball **b** the members of a team that play in such circumstances **9** *psychoanal* See **defence mechanism 10** (*plural*) fortifications [c13 from Old French, from Late Latin *dēfensum,* past participle of *dēfendere* to DEFEND]
> deˈfenceless *or US* deˈfenseless *adj*
> deˈfencelessly *or US* deˈfenselessly *adv*
> deˈfencelessness *or US* deˈfenselessness *n*

defence in depth *n military* the act or practice of positioning successive mutually supporting lines of defence in a given area

defence mechanism *n* **1** *psychoanal* a usually unconscious mental process designed to reduce the anxiety, shame, etc, associated with instinctive desires **2** *physiol* the protective response of the body against disease organisms

defend (dɪˈfɛnd) *vb* **1** to protect (a person, place, etc) from harm or danger; ward off an attack on **2** (*tr*) to support in the face of criticism, esp by argument or evidence **3** to represent (a defendant) in court in a civil or criminal action **4** *sport* to guard or protect (oneself, one's goal, etc) against attack **5** (*tr*) to protect (a championship or title) against a challenge [c13 from Old French *defendre,* from Latin *dēfendere* to ward off, from DE- + *-fendere* to strike] > deˈfendable *adj* > deˈfender *n*

defendant (dɪˈfɛndənt) *n* **1** a person against whom an action or claim is brought in a court of law. Compare **plaintiff** ▷ *adj* **2** making a defence; defending

Defender of the Faith *n* the title conferred upon Henry VIII by Pope Leo X in 1521 in recognition of the King's pamphlet attacking Luther's doctrines and retained by subsequent monarchs of England. Latin term: *Fidei Defensor*

defenestration (diːˌfɛnɪˈstreɪʃən) *n* the act of throwing someone out of a window [c17 from New Latin *dēfenestrātiō,* from Latin DE- + *fenestra* window]

defensible (dɪˈfɛnsɪbəl) *adj* capable of being defended, as in war, an argument, etc
> deˌfensiˈbility *or* deˈfensibleness *n*
> deˈfensibly *adv*

defensive (dɪˈfɛnsɪv) *adj* **1** intended, suitable, or done for defence, as opposed to offence **2**

rejecting criticisms of oneself or covering up one's failings ▷ *n* **3** a position of defence **4 on the defensive** in an attitude or position of defence, as in being ready to reject criticism > deˈfensively *adv* > deˈfensiveness *n*

defensive medicine *n* the practice by a doctor of ordering extensive, often unnecessary tests in order to minimize liability if accused of negligence

defer[1] (dɪˈfɜː) *vb* **-fers, -ferring, -ferred** (*tr*) to delay or cause to be delayed until a future time; postpone [c14 from Old French *differer* to be different, postpone; see DIFFER] > deˈferrable *or* deˈferable *adj* > deˈferrer *n*

defer[2] (dɪˈfɜː) *vb* **-fers, -ferring, -ferred** (*intr*; foll by *to*) to yield (to) or comply (with) the wishes or judgments of another: *I defer to your superior knowledge* [c15 from Latin *dēferre,* literally: to bear down, from DE- + *ferre* to bear]

deference (ˈdɛfərəns) *n* **1** submission to or compliance with the will, wishes, etc, of another **2** courteous regard; respect [c17 from French *déférence;* see DEFER[2]]

deferent[1] (ˈdɛfərənt) *adj* another word for **deferential**

deferent[2] (ˈdɛfərənt) *adj* **1** (esp of a bodily nerve, vessel, or duct) conveying an impulse, fluid, etc, outwards, down, or away; efferent ▷ *n* **2** *astronomy* (in the Ptolemaic system) a circle centred on the earth around which the centre of the epicycle was thought to move [c17 from Latin *dēferre;* see DEFER[2]]

deferential (ˌdɛfəˈrɛnʃəl) *adj* marked by or showing deference or respect; respectful
> ˌdeferˈentially *adv*

deferment (dɪˈfɜːmənt) *or* **deferral** (dɪˈfɜːrəl) *n* the act of deferring or putting off until another time; postponement

deferred (dɪˈfɜːd) *adj* **1** withheld over a certain period; postponed: *a deferred payment* **2** (of shares) ranking behind other types of shares for dividend

deferred annuity *n* an annuity that commences not less than one year after the final purchase premium. Compare **immediate annuity**

deferred sentence *n law* a sentence that is postponed for a specific period to allow a court to examine the conduct of the offender during the deferment. Compare **suspended sentence**

defervescence (ˌdɛfəˈvɛsəns) *n med* **1** the abatement of a fever **2** the period during which this occurs

deffo (ˈdɛfəʊ) *interj Brit informal* definitely: an expression of agreement or consent

defiance (dɪˈfaɪəns) *n* **1** open or bold resistance to or disregard for authority, opposition, or power **2** a challenging attitude or behaviour; challenge

defiant (dɪˈfaɪənt) *adj* marked by resistance or bold opposition, as to authority; challenging > deˈfiantly *adv*

defibrillation (diːˌfaɪbrɪˈleɪʃən, -fɪb-) *n med* the application of an electric current to the heart to restore normal rhythmic contractions after the onset of atrial or ventricular fibrillation

defibrillator (dɪˈfaɪbrɪˌleɪtə, -ˈfɪb-) *n med* an apparatus for stopping fibrillation of the heart by application of an electric current to the chest wall or directly to the heart

deficiency (dɪˈfɪʃənsɪ) *n, pl* **-cies 1** the state or quality of being deficient **2** a lack or insufficiency; shortage **3** another word for **deficit 4** *biology* the absence of a gene or a region of a chromosome normally present

deficiency disease *n med* any condition, such as pellagra, beriberi, or scurvy, produced by a lack of vitamins or other essential substances. Compare **avitaminosis 2** *botany* any disease caused by lack of essential minerals

deficient (dɪˈfɪʃənt) *adj* **1** lacking some essential; incomplete; defective **2** inadequate in quantity or supply; insufficient [c16 from Latin *dēficiēns* lacking, from *dēficere* to fall short; see DEFECT] > deˈficiently *adv*

deficit (ˈdɛfɪsɪt, dɪˈfɪsɪt) *n* **1** the amount by which an actual sum is lower than that expected or required **2 a** an excess of liabilities over assets **b** an excess of expenditures over revenues during a certain period **c** an excess of payments over receipts on the balance of payments [c18 from Latin, literally: there is lacking, from *dēficere* to be lacking]

deficit financing *n* government spending in excess of revenues so that a budget deficit is incurred, which is financed by borrowing: recommended by Keynesian economists in order to increase economic activity and reduce unemployment. Also called: **compensatory finance, pump priming**

de fide (Latin diː ˈfaɪdɪ) *adj RC Church* (of a doctrine) belonging to the essentials of the faith, esp by virtue of a papal ruling [literally: from faith]

defilade (ˌdɛfɪˈleɪd) *military* ▷ *n* **1** protection provided by obstacles against enemy crossfire from the rear, or observation **2** the disposition of defensive fortifications to produce this protection ▷ *vb* (*tr*) **3** to provide protection for by defilade [c19 see DE-, ENFILADE]

defile[1] (dɪˈfaɪl) *vb* (*tr*) **1** to make foul or dirty; pollute **2** to tarnish or sully the brightness of; taint; corrupt **3** to damage or sully (someone's good name, reputation, etc) **4** to make unfit for ceremonial use; desecrate **5** to violate the chastity of [c14 from earlier *defoilen* (influenced by *filen* to FILE[3]), from Old French *defouler* to trample underfoot, abuse, from DE- + *fouler* to tread upon; see FULL[2]] > deˈfilement *n* > deˈfiler *n*

defile[2] (ˈdiːfaɪl, dɪˈfaɪl) *n* **1** a narrow pass or gorge, esp one between two mountains **2** a single file of soldiers, etc ▷ *vb* **3** *chiefly military* to march or cause to march in single file [c17 from French *défilé,* from *défiler* to file off, from *filer* to march in a column, from Old French: to spin, from *fil* thread, from Latin *fīlum*]

define (dɪˈfaɪn) *vb* (*tr*) **1** to state precisely the meaning of (words, terms, etc) **2** to describe the nature, properties, or essential qualities of **3** to determine the boundary or extent of **4** (*often passive*) to delineate the form or outline of: *the shape of the tree was clearly defined by the light behind it* **5** to fix with precision; specify [c14 from Old French *definer* to determine, from Latin *dēfinīre* to set bounds to, from *finīre* to FINISH] > deˈfinable *adj* > deˈfinably *adv* > deˈfiner *n*

defined-benefit *adj* denoting an occupational pension scheme that guarantees a specified payout, usually based on an employee's final salary and years of service. Abbreviation: DB Also called: **final-salary**

definiendum (dɪˌfɪnɪˈɛndəm) *n, pl* **-da** (-də) something to be defined, esp the term or phrase to be accounted for in a dictionary entry. Compare **definiens** [Latin]

definiens (dɪˈfɪnɪænz) *n, pl* **definientia** (dɪˌfɪnɪˈɛnʃə) the word or words used to define or give an account of the meaning of another word, as in a dictionary entry. Compare **definiendum** [Latin: defining]

definite (ˈdɛfɪnɪt) *adj* **1** clearly defined; exact; explicit **2** having precise limits or boundaries **3** known for certain; sure: *it is definite that they have won* **4** *botany* **a** denoting a type of growth in which the main stem ends in a flower, as in a cymose inflorescence; determinate **b** (esp of flower parts) limited or fixed in number in a given species [c15 from Latin *dēfinītus* limited, distinct; see DEFINE] > **definiteness** *n* > **definitude** (dɪˈfɪnɪˌtjuːd) *n*

definite article *n grammar* a determiner that expresses specificity of reference, such as *the* in English. Compare **indefinite article**

definite description *n* **1** a description that is modified by the definite article or a possessive, such as *the woman in white* or *Rosemary's baby* **2** a similar plural expression, such as *the kings of Scotland*

definite integral *n maths* **a** the evaluation of the indefinite integral between two limits, representing the area between the given function and the *x*-axis between these two values of *x* **b** the expression for that function, $\int_a^b f(x)dx$, where $f(x)$ is the given function and $x = a$ and $x = b$ are the limits of integration. Where $F(x) = \int f(x)dx$, the indefinite integral, $\int_a^b f(x)dx = F(b)-F(a)$

definitely (ˈdɛfɪnɪtlɪ) *adv* **1** in a definite manner **2** (*sentence modifier*) certainly: *he said he was coming, definitely* ▷ *sentence substitute* **3** unquestionably: used to confirm an assumption by a questioner

definition (ˌdɛfɪˈnɪʃən) *n* **1** a formal and concise statement of the meaning of a word, phrase, etc **2** the act of defining a word, phrase, etc **3** specification of the essential properties of something, or of the criteria which uniquely identify it **4** the act of making clear or definite **5** the state or condition of being clearly defined or definite **6** a measure of the clarity of an optical, photographic, or television image as characterized by its sharpness and contrast > ˌ**defiˈnitional** *adj*

definitive (dɪˈfɪnɪtɪv) *adj* **1** serving to decide or settle finally; conclusive **2** most reliable, complete, or authoritative: *the definitive reading of a text* **3** serving to define or outline **4** *zoology* fully developed; complete: *the definitive form of a parasite* **5** **a** (of postage stamps) permanently on sale **b** (*as noun*) a definitive postage stamp ▷ *n* **6** *grammar* a word indicating specificity of reference, such as the definite article or a demonstrative adjective or pronoun > **deˈfinitively** *adv* > **deˈfinitiveness** *n*

deflagrate (ˈdɛfləˌgreɪt, ˈdiː-) *vb* to burn or cause to burn with great heat and light [C18 from Latin *dēflagrāre*, from DE- + *flagrāre* to burn] > ˌ**deflaˈgration** *n*

deflate (dɪˈfleɪt) *vb* **1** to collapse or cause to collapse through the release of gas **2** (*tr*) to take away the self-esteem or conceit from **3** *economics* to cause deflation of (an economy, the money supply, etc) [C19 from DE- + (IN)FLATE] > **deˈflator** *n*

deflation (dɪˈfleɪʃən) *n* **1** the act of deflating or state of being deflated **2** *economics* a reduction in the level of total spending and economic activity resulting in lower levels of output, employment, investment, trade, profits, and prices. Compare **disinflation** **3** *geology* the removal of loose rock material, sand, and dust by the wind > **deˈflationary** *adj* > **deˈflationist** *n, adj*

deflationary gap *n economics* a situation in which total spending in an economy is insufficient to buy all the output that can be produced with full employment

deflect (dɪˈflɛkt) *vb* to turn or cause to turn aside from a course; swerve [C17 from Latin *dēflectere*, from *flectere* to bend] > **deˈflector** *n*

deflection *or* **deflexion** (dɪˈflɛkʃən) *n* **1** the act of deflecting or the state of being deflected **2** the amount of deviation **3** the change in direction of a light beam as it crosses a boundary between two media with different refractive indexes **4** a deviation of the indicator of a measuring instrument from its zero position **5** the movement of a structure or structural member when subjected to a load > **deˈflective** *adj*

deflexed (dɪˈflɛkst, ˈdiːflɛkst) *adj* (of leaves, petals, etc) bent sharply outwards and downwards

deflocculate (dɪˈflɒkjʊˌleɪt) *vb* (*tr*) **1** to disperse, forming a colloid or suspension **2** to prevent flocculation of (a colloid or suspension) > **deˌfloccuˈlation** *n* > **deˈfloccuˌlant** *n*

defloration (ˌdiːflɔːˈreɪʃən) *n* the act of deflowering [C15 from Late Latin *dēflōrātiō*; see DE-, FLOWER]

deflower (diːˈflaʊə) *vb* (*tr*) **1** to deprive of virginity, esp by rupturing the hymen through sexual intercourse **2** to despoil of beauty, innocence, etc; mar; violate **3** to rob or despoil of flowers > **deˈflowerer** *n*

defoliant (diːˈfəʊlɪənt) *n* a chemical sprayed or dusted onto trees to cause their leaves to fall, esp to remove cover from an enemy in warfare

defoliate *vb* (diːˈfəʊlɪˌeɪt) **1** to deprive (a plant) of its leaves, as by the use of a herbicide, or (of a plant) to shed its leaves ▷ *adj* (diːˈfəʊlɪɪt) **2** (of a plant) having shed its leaves [C18 from Medieval Latin *dēfoliāre*, from Latin DE- + *folium* leaf] > **deˌfoliˈation** *n* > **deˈfoliˌator** *n*

deforce (dɪˈfɔːs) *vb* (*tr*) *property law* **1** to withhold (property, esp land) wrongfully or by force from the rightful owner **2** to eject or keep forcibly from possession of property [C13 from Anglo-French, from *deforcer*] > **deˈforcement** *n*

deforest (diːˈfɒrɪst) *vb* (*tr*) to clear of trees. Also: **disforest** > **deˌforesˈtation** *n* > **deˈforester** *n*

deform (dɪˈfɔːm) *vb* **1** to make or become misshapen or distorted **2** (*tr*) to mar the beauty of; disfigure **3** (*tr*) to subject or be subjected to a stress that causes a change of dimensions [C15 from Latin *dēfōrmāre*, from DE- + *forma* shape, beauty] > **deˈformable** *adj* > **deˌformaˈbility** *n* > **deˈformer** *n*

deformation (ˌdiːfɔːˈmeɪʃən) *n* **1** the act of deforming; distortion **2** the result of deforming; a change in form, esp for the worse **3** a change in the dimensions of an object resulting from a stress

deformed (dɪˈfɔːmd) *adj* **1** disfigured or misshapen **2** morally perverted; warped > **deformedly** (dɪˈfɔːmɪdlɪ) *adv* > **deˈformedness** *n*

deformity (dɪˈfɔːmɪtɪ) *n, pl* **-ties** **1** a deformed condition; disfigurement **2** *pathol* an acquired or congenital distortion of an organ or part **3** a deformed person or thing **4** a defect, esp of the mind or morals; depravity

Defra (ˈdɛfrə) (in Britain) *n acronym for* Department for Environment, Food and Rural Affairs

defraud (dɪˈfrɔːd) *vb* (*tr*) to take away or withhold money, rights, property, etc, from (a person) by fraud; cheat; swindle > **defraudation** (ˌdiːfrɔːˈdeɪʃən) *or* **deˈfraudment** *n* > **deˈfrauder** *n*

defray (dɪˈfreɪ) *vb* (*tr*) to furnish or provide money for (costs, expenses, etc); pay [C16 from Old French *deffroier* to pay expenses, from *de-* DIS-¹ + *frai* expenditure, originally: cost incurred through breaking something, from Latin *frangere* to break] > **deˈfrayable** *adj* > **deˈfrayal** *or* **deˈfrayment** *n* > **deˈfrayer** *n*

defrock (diːˈfrɒk) *vb* (*tr*) to deprive (a person in holy orders) of ecclesiastical status; unfrock

defrost (diːˈfrɒst) *vb* **1** to make or become free of frost or ice **2** to thaw, esp through removal from a refrigerator

defroster (diːˈfrɒstə) *n* a device by which the de-icing process of a refrigerator is accelerated, usually by circulating the refrigerant without the expansion process

deft (dɛft) *adj* quick and neat in movement; nimble; dexterous [C13 (in the sense: gentle): see DAFT] > ˈ**deftly** *adv* > ˈ**deftness** *n*

defunct (dɪˈfʌŋkt) *adj* **1** no longer living; dead or extinct **2** no longer operative or valid [C16 from Latin *dēfungī* to discharge (one's obligations), die; see DE-, FUNCTION] > **deˈfunctive** *adj* > **deˈfunctness** *n*

defuse *or sometimes US* **defuze** (diːˈfjuːz) *vb* (*tr*) **1** to remove the triggering device of (a bomb, etc) **2** to remove the cause of tension from (a crisis, etc)

USAGE Avoid confusion with **diffuse**

defy (dɪˈfaɪ) *vb* **-fies, -fying, -fied** (*tr*) **1** to resist (a powerful person, authority, etc) openly and boldly **2** to elude, esp in a baffling way: *his actions defy explanation* **3** *formal* to challenge or provoke (someone to do something judged to be impossible); dare: *I defy you to climb that cliff* **4** *archaic* to invite to do battle or combat [C14 from Old French *desfier*, from *des-* DE- + *fier* to trust, from Latin *fidere*] > **deˈfier** *n*

deg (dɛg) *vb* **degs, degging, degged** (*tr*) *Northern English dialect* to water (a plant, etc)

deg. *abbreviation for* degree

dégagé *French* (degaʒe) *adj* **1** unconstrained in manner; casual; relaxed **2** uninvolved; detached

degas (diːˈgæs) *vb* **-gases** *or* **-gasses, -gassing, -gassed** **1** (*tr*) to remove gas from (a container, vacuum tube, liquid, adsorbent, etc) **2** (*intr*) to lose adsorbed or absorbed gas by desorption > **deˈgasser** *n*

degauss (diːˈgaʊs, -ˈgɔːs) *vb* (*tr*) **1** to neutralize the magnetic field of a ship's hull (as a protection against magnetic mines) using equipment producing an opposing magnetic field **2** another word for **demagnetize**

degearing (diːˈgɪərɪŋ) *n finance* the process in which a company replaces some or all of its fixed-interest loan stock with ordinary shares

degeneracy (dɪˈdʒɛnərəsɪ) *n, pl* **-cies** **1** the act or state of being degenerate **2** the process of becoming degenerate **3** *physics* the number of degenerate quantum states of a particular orbital, degree of freedom, energy level, etc

degenerate *vb* (dɪˈdʒɛnəˌreɪt) (*intr*) **1** to become degenerate **2** *biology* (of organisms or their parts) to become less specialized or functionally useless ▷ *adj* (dɪˈdʒɛnərɪt) **3** having declined or deteriorated to a lower mental, moral, or physical level; debased; degraded; corrupt **4** *physics* **a** (of the constituents of a system) having the same energy but different wave functions **b** (of a semiconductor) containing a similar number of electrons in the conduction band to the number of electrons in the conduction band of metals **c** (of a resonant device) having two or more modes of equal frequency **5** (of a code) containing symbols that represent more than one letter, figure, etc **6** (of a plant or animal) having undergone degeneration ▷ *n* (dɪˈdʒɛnərɪt) **7** a degenerate person [C15 from Latin *dēgenerāre*, from *dēgener* departing from its kind, ignoble, from DE- + *genus* origin, race] > **deˈgenerately** *adv* > **deˈgenerateness** *n*

degenerate matter *n astronomy* the highly compressed state of matter, esp in white dwarfs and neutron stars, supported against gravitational collapse by quantum mechanical effects

degeneration (dɪˌdʒɛnəˈreɪʃən) *n* **1** the process of degenerating **2** the state of being degenerate **3** *biology* the loss of specialization, function, or structure by organisms and their parts, as in the development of vestigial organs **4** **a** impairment or loss of the function and structure of cells or tissues, as by disease or injury, often leading to death (necrosis) of the involved part **b** the resulting condition **5** *electronics* negative feedback of a signal

degenerative (dɪˈdʒɛnəˌreɪtɪv) *adj* (of a disease or condition) getting steadily worse

degenerative joint disease *n* another name for **osteoarthritis**

deglaze (diːˈgleɪz) *vb* (*tr*) to dilute meat sediments in (a pan) in order to make a sauce or gravy

deglutinate (diːˈgluːtɪˌneɪt) *vb* (*tr*) to extract the gluten from (a cereal, esp wheat) [C17 from Latin *dēglūtināre* to unglue, from DE- + *glūtināre*, from *glūten* GLUE] > **deˌglutiˈnation** *n*

deglutition (ˌdiːgluːˈtɪʃən) *n* the act of swallowing [C17 from French *déglutition*, from Late Latin *dēglūtīre* to swallow down, from DE- + *glutīre* to swallow]

degradable (dɪˈgreɪdəbᵊl) *adj* **1** (of waste products, packaging materials, etc) capable of being decomposed chemically or biologically. See also **biodegradable** **2** capable of being degraded > **deˌgradaˈbility** *n*

degradation (ˌdɛgrəˈdeɪʃən) *n* **1** the act of degrading or the state of being degraded **2** a state of degeneration, squalor, or poverty **3** some act, constraint, etc, that is degrading **4** the wearing down of the surface of rocks, cliffs, etc, by erosion, weathering, or some other process **5** *chem* a breakdown of a molecule into atoms or smaller molecules **6** *physics* an irreversible process in which the energy available to do work is decreased **7** *RC Church* the permanent unfrocking of a priest

degrade (dɪ'greɪd) *vb* **1** (*tr*) to reduce in worth, character, etc; disgrace; dishonour **2** (dɪ'greɪd) (*tr*) to reduce in rank, status, or degree; remove from office; demote **3** (*tr*) to reduce in strength, quality, intensity, etc **4** to reduce or be reduced by erosion or down-cutting, as a land surface or bed of a river. Compare **aggrade 5** *chem* to decompose or be decomposed into atoms or smaller molecules [c14 from Late Latin *dēgradāre*, from Latin DE- + *gradus* rank, degree] > de'grader *n*

degrading (dɪ'greɪdɪŋ) *adj* causing humiliation; debasing > de'gradingly *adv* > de'gradingness *n*

degrease (di:'gri:s) *vb* (*tr*) to remove grease from

degree (dɪ'gri:) *n* **1** a stage in a scale of relative amount or intensity: *a high degree of competence* **2** an academic award conferred by a university or college on successful completion of a course or as an honorary distinction (**honorary degree**) **3** any of three categories of seriousness of a burn. See **burn¹** (sense 22) **4** (in the US) any of the categories into which a crime is divided according to its seriousness: *first-degree murder* **5** *genealogy* a step in a line of descent, used as a measure of the closeness of a blood relationship **6** *grammar* any of the forms of an adjective used to indicate relative amount or intensity: in English they are *positive, comparative,* and *superlative* **7** *music* any note of a diatonic scale relative to the other notes in that scale: *D is the second degree of the scale of C major* **8** a unit of temperature on a specified scale: *the normal body temperature of man is 36.8 degrees Celsius.* Symbol: ° See also **Celsius scale, Fahrenheit scale 9** a measure of angle equal to one three-hundred-and-sixtieth of the angle traced by one complete revolution of a line about one of its ends. Symbol: ° See also **minute¹** (sense 2), **second²** (sense 2) Compare **radian 10 a** a unit of latitude or longitude, divided into 60 minutes, used to define points on the earth's surface or on the celestial sphere **b** a point or line defined by units of latitude and/or longitude. Symbol: ° **11** a unit on any of several scales of measurement, as for alcohol content or specific gravity. Symbol: ° **12** *maths* **a** the highest power or the sum of the powers of any term in a polynomial or by itself: $x^4 + x + 3$ *and* xyz^2 *are of the fourth degree* **b** the greatest power of the highest order derivative in a differential equation **13** *obsolete* a step; rung **14** *archaic* a stage in social status or rank **15** **by degrees** little by little; gradually **16 to a degree** somewhat; rather **17 degrees of frost** See **frost** (sense 3) [c13 from Old French *degre*, from Latin DE- + *gradus* step, GRADE] > de'greeless *adj*

degree day *n* a day on which university degrees are conferred

degree-day *n* a unit used in estimating fuel requirements in heating buildings. It is equal to a fall of temperature of 1 degree below the mean outside temperature (usually taken as 18°C) for one day

degree of difficulty *n* a rating which reflects the difficulty of the manoeuvre or action an athlete is attempting to perform in sports such as gymnastics and diving, and which is factored into the final score

degree of freedom *n* **1** *physics* one of the minimum number of parameters necessary to describe a state or property of a system **2** one of the independent components of motion (translation, vibration, and rotation) of an atom or molecule **3** *chem* one of a number of intensive properties that can be independently varied without changing the number of phases in a system. See also **phase rule 4** *statistics* one of the independent unrestricted random variables constituting a statistic

degression (dɪ'greʃən) *n* **1** a decrease by stages **2** a gradual decrease in the tax rate on amounts below a specified sum [c15 from Medieval Latin *dēgressiō* descent, from Latin *dēgredī* to go down,

from DE- + *gradī* to take steps, go]

degust (dɪ'gʌst) *or* **degustate** (dɪ'gʌsteɪt) *vb* (*tr*) *rare* to taste, esp with care or relish; savour [c17 from Latin *dēgustāre*, from *gustāre*, from *gustus* a tasting, taste] > degustation (ˌdi:gʌ'steɪʃən) *n*

dehisce (dɪ'hɪs) *vb* (*intr*) (of fruits, anthers, etc) to burst open spontaneously, releasing seeds, pollen, etc [c17 from Latin *dēhiscere* to split open, from DE- + *hiscere* to yawn, gape]

dehiscent (dɪ'hɪsənt) *adj* (of fruits, anthers, etc) opening spontaneously to release seeds or pollen > de'hiscence *n*

dehorn (di:'hɔ:n) *vb* (*tr*) **1** to remove or prevent the growth of the horns of (cattle, sheep, or goats) **2** to cut back (the larger limbs of a tree) drastically > de'horner *n*

Dehra Dun ('deərə 'du:n) *n* a city in N India, the capital of Uttaranchal: Indian military academy (1932). Pop: 447 808 (2001)

dehumanize *or* **dehumanise** (di:'hju:mə,naɪz) *vb* (*tr*) **1** to deprive of human qualities **2** to render mechanical, artificial, or routine > de,humani'zation *or* de,humani'sation *n*

dehumidifier (ˌdi:hju:'mɪdɪ,faɪə) *n* a device for reducing the moisture content of the atmosphere

dehumidify (ˌdi:hju:'mɪdɪ,faɪ) *vb* -fies, -fying, -fied (*tr*) to remove water from (something, esp the air) > dehu,midifi'cation *n*

dehydrate (di:'haɪdreɪt, ˌdi:haɪ'dreɪt) *vb* **1** to lose or cause to lose water; make or become anhydrous **2** to lose or cause to lose hydrogen atoms and oxygen atoms in the proportions in which they occur in water, as in a chemical reaction **3** to lose or deprive of water, as the body or tissues > ,dehy'dration *n* > de'hydrator *n*

dehydroepiandrosterone (di:,haɪdrəʊ,ɛpiæn'drɒstə,rəʊn) *n* the most abundant steroid in the human body, that is involved in the manufacture of testosterone, oestrogen, progesterone, and corticosteroine

dehydrogenase (di:'haɪdrədʒə,neɪz) *n* an enzyme, such as any of the respiratory enzymes, that activates oxidation-reduction reactions by transferring hydrogen from substrate to acceptor

dehydrogenate (di:'haɪdrədʒə,neɪt) *or* **dehydrogenize, dehydrogenise** (di:'haɪdrədʒə,naɪz) *vb* (*tr*) to remove hydrogen from > de,hydroge'nation, de,hydrogeni'zation *or* de,hydrogeni'sation *n*

dehydroretinol (di:,haɪdrəʊ'rɛtɪnɒl) *n* another name for **vitamin A₂**

dehypnotize *or* **dehypnotise** (di:'hɪpnə,taɪz) *vb* (*tr*) to bring out of the hypnotic state > de,hypnoti'zation *or* de,hypnoti'sation *n*

Deianira (ˌdi:ə'naɪərə, -deɪə-) *n* *Greek myth* a sister of Meleager and wife of Hercules. She unintentionally killed Hercules by dipping his tunic in the poisonous blood of the Centaur Nessus, thinking it to be a love charm

de-ice (di:'aɪs) *vb* to free or be freed of ice

de-icer (di:'aɪsə) *n* **1** a mechanical or thermal device designed to melt or stop the formation of ice on an aircraft, usually fitted to the aerofoil surfaces. Compare **anti-icer 2** a chemical or other substance used for this purpose, esp an aerosol that can be sprayed on car windscreens to remove ice or frost

deicide (di:ɪ,saɪd) *n* **1** the act of killing a god **2** a person who kills a god [c17 from ecclesiastical Latin *deicida*, from Latin *deus* god; see -CIDE] > ,dei'cidal *adj*

deictic ('daɪktɪk) *adj* **1** *logic* proving by direct argument. Compare **elenctic** ⊳ *n* **2** another word for **indexical** (sense 2) [c17 from Greek *deiktikos* concerning proof, from *deiknunai* to show] > 'deictically *adv*

deid (di:d) *adj* a Scot word for **dead**

deif (di:f) *adj* a Scot word for **deaf**

deific (di:'ɪfɪk, deɪ-) *adj* **1** making divine or exalting to the position of a god **2** divine or godlike

deification (ˌdi:ɪfɪ'keɪʃən, ˌdeɪ-) *n* **1** the act or

process of exalting to the position of a god **2** the state or condition of being deified

deiform ('di:ɪ,fɔ:m) *adj* having the form or appearance of a god; sacred or divine

deify ('di:ɪ,faɪ, 'deɪɪ-) *vb* -fies, -fying, -fied (*tr*) **1** to exalt to the position of a god or personify as a god **2** to accord divine honour or worship to **3** to exalt in an extreme way; idealize [c14 from Old French *deifier*, from Late Latin *deificāre*, from Latin *deus* god + *facere* to make] > 'dei,fier *n*

deign (deɪn) *vb* **1** (*intr*) to think it fit or worthy of oneself (to do something); condescend: *he will not deign to speak to us* **2** (*tr*) *archaic* to vouchsafe: *he deigned no reply* [c13 from Old French *deignier*, from Latin *dignārī* to consider worthy, from *dignus* worthy]

Dei gratia (Latin 'di:ɪ 'greɪʃɪə, 'deɪɪ 'grɑ:tɪə) *adv* by the grace of God

deil (di:l) *n* a Scot word for **devil**

Deimos ('deɪmɒs) *n* the smaller of the two satellites of Mars and the more distant from the planet. Approximate diameter: 13 km. Compare **Phobos**

deindex (di:'ɪndɛks) *vb* (*tr*) to cause to become no longer index-linked

deindividuation (di:,ɪndɪvɪdjʊ'eɪʃən) *n* *psychol* the loss of a person's sense of individuality and personal responsibility

deindustrialization *or* **deindustrialisation** (ˌdi:ɪn,dʌstrɪəlaɪ'zeɪʃən) *n* the decline in importance of manufacturing industry in the economy of a nation or area

deindustrialize *or* **deindustrialise** (ˌdi:ɪn,dʌstrɪəl,aɪz) *vb* **1** (*tr*) to reduce the importance of manufacturing industry in the economy of (a nation or area) **2** (*intr*) (of a nation or area) to undergo reduction in the importance of manufacturing industry in the economy

de-ionize *or* **de-ionise** (di:'aɪə,naɪz) *vb* (*tr*) to remove ions from (water, etc), esp by ion exchange > de,ioni'zation *or* de,ioni'sation *n*

deipnosophist (daɪp'nɒsəfɪst) *n* *rare* a person who is a master of dinner-table conversation [c17 from Greek *deipnosophistai*, title of a Greek work by Athenaeus (3rd century), describing learned discussions at a banquet, from *deipnon* meal + *sophistai* wise men; see SOPHIST]

Deirdre ('dɪədrɪ) *n* *Irish myth* a beautiful girl who was raised by Conchobar to be his wife but eloped with Naoise. When Conchobar treacherously killed Naoise she took her own life: often used to symbolize Ireland. See also **Naoise**

deism ('di:ɪzəm, 'deɪ-) *n* belief in the existence of God based solely on natural reason, without reference to revelation. Compare **theism** [c17 from French *déisme*, from Latin *deus* god] > 'deist *n, adj* > de'istic *or* de'istical *adj* > de'istically *adv*

deity ('deɪtɪ, 'di:ɪ-) *n, pl* -ties **1** a god or goddess **2** the state of being divine; godhead **3** the rank, status, or position of a god **4** the nature or character of God [c14 from Old French, from Late Latin *deitās*, from Latin *deus* god]

Deity ('deɪtɪ, 'di:ɪ-) *n* **the** the Supreme Being; God

deixis ('daɪksɪs) *n* *grammar* the use or reference of a deictic word [c20 from Greek, from *deiknunai* to show]

déjà vu ('deɪʒæ 'vu:; *French* deʒa vy) *n* the experience of perceiving a new situation as if it had occurred before. It is sometimes associated with exhaustion or certain types of mental disorder [from French, literally: already seen]

deject (dɪ'dʒɛkt) *vb* **1** (*tr*) to have a depressing effect on; dispirit; dishearten ⊳ *adj* **2** *archaic* downcast; dejected [c15 from Latin *dēicere* to cast down, from DE- + *iacere* to throw]

dejecta (dɪ'dʒɛktə) *pl n* waste products excreted through the anus; faeces [c19 New Latin: things cast down; see DEJECT]

dejected (dɪ'dʒɛktɪd) *adj* miserable; despondent; downhearted > de'jectedly *adv* > de'jectedness *n*

dejection (dɪ'dʒɛkʃən) *n* **1** lowness of spirits; depression; melancholy **2 a** faecal matter evacuated from the bowels; excrement **b** the act of defecating; defecation

de jure (deɪ ˈdʒʊəreɪ) *adv* according to law; by right; legally. Compare **de facto** [Latin]

deka- *or* **dek-** *combining form* variants of **deca-**

deke (diːk) *US and Canadian* ▷ *n* **1** *sport* (esp in ice hockey) the act or an instance of feinting ▷ *vb* **2** *sport* (esp in ice hockey) to deceive (an opponent) by carrying out a feint [C20 shortened from DECOY]

dekko (ˈdɛkəʊ) *n, pl* **-kos** *Brit slang* a look; glance; view (esp in the phrase **take a dekko (at)**) [C19 from Hindi *dekho!* look! from *dekhnā* to see]

del (dɛl) *n maths* the differential operator **i**(∂/∂x) + **j**(∂/∂y) + **k**(∂/∂z), where **i**, **j**, and **k** are unit vectors in the *x*, *y*, and *z* directions. Symbol: ∇ Also called: **nabla**

del. *abbreviation for* delegate

Del. *abbreviation for* Delaware

Delagoa Bay (ˌdɛləˈɡəʊə) *n* an inlet of the Indian Ocean, in S Mozambique. Official name: **Baía de Lourenço Marques**

delaine (dəˈleɪn) *n* a sheer wool or wool and cotton fabric [C19 from French *mousseline de laine* muslin of wool]

delaminate (diːˈlæmɪˌneɪt) *vb* to divide or cause to divide into thin layers > **deˌlamiˈnation** *n*

delate (dɪˈleɪt) *vb* (*tr*) **1** (formerly) to bring a charge against; denounce; impeach **2** *rare* to report (an offence, etc) **3** *obsolete* to make known or public [C16 from Latin *dēlātus*, from *dēferre* to bring down, report, indict, from DE- + *ferre* to bear] > **deˈlation** *n* > **deˈlator** *n*

Delaware[1] (ˈdɛləˌwɛə) *n* **1** (*pl* **-wares** *or* **-ware**) a member of a North American Indian people formerly living near the Delaware River **2** the language of this people, belonging to the Algonquian family

Delaware[2] (ˈdɛləˌwɛə) *n* **1** a state of the northeastern US, on the Delmarva Peninsula: mostly flat and low-lying, with hills in the extreme north and cypress swamps in the extreme south. Capital: Dover. Pop: 817 491 (2003 est). Area: 5004 sq km (1932 sq miles). Abbreviations: **Del**, (with zip code) **DE** **2** a river in the northeastern US, rising in the Catskill Mountains and flowing south into **Delaware Bay**, an inlet of the Atlantic. Length 660 km (410 miles)

Delaware[3] (ˈdɛləˌwɛə) *n* an American variety of grape that has sweet light red fruit

Delawarean (ˌdɛləˈwɛərɪən) *adj* **1** of or relating to the state of Delaware or its inhabitants **2** of or relating to the Delaware river

delay (dɪˈleɪ) *vb* **1** (*tr*) to put off to a later time; defer **2** (*tr*) to slow up, hinder, or cause to be late; detain **3** (*intr*) to be irresolute or put off doing something; procrastinate **4** (*intr*) to linger; dawdle ▷ *n* **5** the act or an instance of delaying or being delayed **6** the interval between one event and another; lull; interlude [C13 from Old French *delaier*, from *des-* off + *laier*, variant of *laissier* to leave, from Latin *laxāre* to loosen, from *laxus* slack, LAX] > **deˈlayer** *n*

delayed action *or* **delay action** *n* **a** a device for operating a mechanism, such as a camera shutter, a short time after setting **b** (*as modifier*): *a delayed-action fuse*

delayed drop *n aeronautics* a parachute descent with the opening of the parachute delayed, usually for a predetermined period

delayed neutron *n* a neutron produced in a nuclear reactor by the breakdown of a fission product and released a short time after neutrons produced in the primary process

delayed opening *n aeronautics* the automatic opening of a parachute after a predetermined delay to allow the parachutist to reach a particular height

delayer (diːˈleɪə) *vb* (*tr*) to prune the administrative structure of (a large organization) by reducing the number of tiers in its hierarchy

delayering (diːˈleɪərɪŋ) *n* the process of pruning the administrative structure of a large organization by reducing the number of tiers in its hierarchy

delaying action *n* a measure or measures taken to gain time, as when weaker military forces harass the advance of a superior enemy without coming to a pitched battle

delay line *n* a device in which a known delay time is introduced in the transmission of a signal. An **acoustic delay line** delays a sound wave by circulating it through a liquid or solid medium

dele (ˈdiːlɪ) *n, pl* **deles** **1** a sign (₰) indicating that typeset matter is to be deleted. Compare **stet** ▷ *vb* **deles, deleing, deled** **2** (*tr*) to mark (matter to be deleted) with a dele [C18 from Latin: delete (imperative), from *dēlēre* to destroy, obliterate; see DELETE]

delectable (dɪˈlɛktəbᵊl) *adj* highly enjoyable, esp pleasing to the taste; delightful [C14 from Latin *dēlectābilis*, from *dēlectāre* to DELIGHT] > **deˈlectableness** *or* **deˌlectaˈbility** *n* > **deˈlectably** *adv*

delectation (ˌdiːlɛkˈteɪʃən) *n* pleasure; enjoyment

delegacy (ˈdɛlɪɡəsɪ) *n, pl* **-cies** **1** a less common word for **delegation** (senses 1, 2) **2** **a** an elected standing committee at some British universities **b** a department or institute of a university: *a delegacy of Education*

delegate *n* (ˈdɛlɪˌɡeɪt, -ɡɪt) **1** a person chosen or elected to act for or represent another or others, esp at a conference or meeting **2** *US government* a representative of a territory in the US House of Representatives ▷ *vb* (ˈdɛlɪˌɡeɪt) **3** to give or commit (duties, powers, etc) to another as agent or representative; depute **4** (*tr*) to send, authorize, or elect (a person) as agent or representative **5** (*tr*) *chiefly US* to assign (a person owing a debt to oneself) to one's creditor in substitution for oneself [C14 from Latin *dēlēgāre* to send on a mission, from *lēgāre* to send, depute; see LEGATE] > **delegable** (ˈdɛlɪɡəbᵊl) *adj*

delegation (ˌdɛlɪˈɡeɪʃən) *n* **1** a person or group chosen to represent another or others **2** the act of delegating or state of being delegated **3** *US politics* all the members of Congress from one state

delegitimize *or* **delegitimise** (ˌdiːlɪˈdʒɪtɪmaɪz) *vb* (*tr*) to make invalid, illegal, or unacceptable: *crushing and delegitimizing all dissent in Central Asia* > **ˌdelegitimiˈzation** *or* **ˌdelegitimiˈsation** *n*

delete (dɪˈliːt) *vb* (*tr*) to remove (something printed or written); erase; cancel; strike out [C17 from Latin *dēlēre* to destroy, obliterate]

deleterious (ˌdɛlɪˈtɪərɪəs) *adj* harmful; injurious; hurtful [C17 from New Latin *dēlētērius*, from Greek *dēlētērios* injurious, destructive, from *dēleisthai* to hurt] > **ˌdeleˈteriously** *adv* > **ˌdeleˈteriousness** *n*

deletion (dɪˈliːʃən) *n* **1** the act of deleting or fact of being deleted **2** a deleted passage, word, etc, in text **3** the loss or absence of a section of a chromosome

Delft (dɛlft) *n* **1** a town in the SW Netherlands, in South Holland province. Pop: 97 000 (2003 est) **2** Also called: **delftware** tin-glazed earthenware made in Delft since the 17th century, typically having blue decoration on a white ground **3** a similar earthenware made in England

Delgado (dɛlˈɡɑːdəʊ) *n* **Cape** a headland on the NE coast of Mozambique

Delhi (ˈdɛlɪ) *n* **1** the capital of India, in the N central part, on the Jumna river: consists of **Old Delhi** (a walled city reconstructed in 1639 on the site of former cities of Delhi, which date from the 15th century BC) and **New Delhi** to the south, chosen as the capital in 1912, replacing Calcutta; university (1922). Pop: 9 817 439 (2001) **2** an administrative division (National Capital Territory) of N India, formerly a Union Territory. Capital: Delhi. Area: 1483 sq km (572 sq miles). Pop: 13 782 976 (2001)

deli (ˈdɛlɪ) *n, pl* **delis** an informal word for **delicatessen**

Delia (ˈdiːlɪə) *n* **a** the recipes or style of cooking of British cookery writer Delia Smith (born 1941) **b** (*as modifier*): *a Delia dish*

Delian (ˈdiːlɪən) *n* **1** a native or inhabitant of Delos ▷ *adj* **2** of or relating to Delos **3** of or relating to Delius

Delian League *or* **Confederacy** *n* an alliance of ancient Greek states formed in 478–77 BC to fight Persia

deliberate *adj* (dɪˈlɪbərɪt) **1** carefully thought out in advance; planned; studied; intentional: *a deliberate insult* **2** careful or unhurried in speech or action: *a deliberate pace* ▷ *vb* (dɪˈlɪbəˌreɪt) **3** to consider (something) deeply; ponder; think over [C15 from Latin *dēlīberāre* to consider well, from *lībrāre* to weigh, from *lībra* scales] > **deˈliberately** *adv* > **deˈliberateness** *n* > **deˈliberˌator** *n*

deliberation (dɪˌlɪbəˈreɪʃən) *n* **1** thoughtful, careful, or lengthy consideration **2** (*often plural*) formal discussion and debate, as of a committee, jury, etc **3** care, thoughtfulness, or absence of hurry, esp in movement or speech

deliberative (dɪˈlɪbərətɪv) *adj* **1** involved in, organized for, or having the function of deliberating: *a deliberative assembly* **2** characterized by or resulting from deliberation: *a deliberative conclusion* > **deˈliberatively** *adv* > **deˈliberativeness** *n*

delicacy (ˈdɛlɪkəsɪ) *n, pl* **-cies** **1** fine or subtle quality, character, construction, etc: *delicacy of craftsmanship* **2** fragile, soft, or graceful beauty **3** something that is considered choice to eat, such as caviar **4** fragile construction or constitution; frailty **5** refinement of feeling, manner, or appreciation: *the delicacy of the orchestra's playing* **6** fussy or squeamish refinement, esp in matters of taste, propriety, etc **7** need for tactful or sensitive handling **8** accuracy or sensitivity of response or operation, as of an instrument **9** (in systemic grammar) the level of detail at which a linguistic description is made; the degree of fine distinction in a linguistic description **10** *obsolete* gratification, luxury, or voluptuousness

delicate (ˈdɛlɪkɪt) *adj* **1** exquisite, fine, or subtle in quality, character, construction, etc **2** having a soft or fragile beauty **3** (of colour, tone, taste, etc) pleasantly subtle, soft, or faint **4** easily damaged or injured; lacking robustness, esp in health; fragile **5** precise, skilled, or sensitive in action or operation: *a delicate mechanism* **6** requiring tact and diplomacy **7** sensitive in feeling or manner; showing regard for the feelings of others **8** excessively refined; squeamish ▷ *n* **9** *archaic* a delicacy; dainty [C14 from Latin *dēlicātus* affording pleasure, from *dēliciae* (pl) delight, pleasure; see DELICIOUS] > **ˈdelicately** *adv* > **ˈdelicateness** *n*

delicatessen (ˌdɛlɪkəˈtɛsᵊn) *n* **1** a shop selling various foods, esp unusual or imported foods, already cooked or prepared **2** such foods [C19 from German *Delikatessen*, literally: delicacies, pl of *Delikatesse* a delicacy, from French *délicatesse*]

delicious (dɪˈlɪʃəs) *adj* **1** very appealing to the senses, esp to the taste or smell **2** extremely enjoyable or entertaining: *a delicious joke* [C13 from Old French, from Late Latin *dēliciōsus*, from Latin *dēliciae* delights, charms, from *dēlicere* to entice; see DELIGHT] > **deˈliciously** *adv* > **deˈliciousness** *n*

delict (dɪˈlɪkt, ˈdiːlɪkt) *n* **1** *law, chiefly Scots* a wrongful act for which the person injured has the right to a civil remedy. See also **tort** **2** *Roman law* a civil wrong redressable by compensation or punitive damages [C16 from Latin *dēlictum* a fault, crime, from *dēlinquere* to fail, do wrong; see DELINQUENCY]

delight (dɪˈlaɪt) *vb* **1** (*tr*) to please greatly **2** (*intr*; foll by *in*) to take great pleasure (in) ▷ *n* **3** extreme pleasure or satisfaction; joy **4** something that causes this: *music was always his delight* [C13 from Old French *delit*, from *deleitier* to please, from Latin *dēlectāre*, from *dēlicere* to allure, from DE- + *lacere* to entice; see DELICIOUS; English spelling influenced by *light*] > **deˈlighter** *n*

delighted (dɪˈlaɪtɪd) *adj* **1** (often foll by an

infinitive) extremely pleased (to do something): *I'm delighted to hear it!* ▷ *sentence substitute* **2** I should be delighted to! > **deˈlightedly** *adv* > **deˈlightedness** *n*

delightful (dɪˈlaɪtfʊl) *adj* giving great delight; very pleasing, beautiful, charming, etc > **deˈlightfully** *adv* > **deˈlightfulness** *n*

Delilah (dɪˈlaɪlə) *n* **1** Samson's Philistine mistress, who deprived him of his strength by cutting off his hair (Judges 16:4–22) **2** a voluptuous and treacherous woman; temptress

delimit (diːˈlɪmɪt) *or* **delimitate** *vb* (*tr*) to mark or prescribe the limits or boundaries of; demarcate > **deˌlimiˈtation** *n* > **deˈlimitative** *adj*

delineate (dɪˈlɪnɪˌeɪt) *vb* (*tr*) **1** to trace the shape or outline of; sketch **2** to represent pictorially, as by making a chart or diagram; depict **3** to portray in words, esp with detail and precision; describe [C16 from Latin *dēlīneāre* to sketch out, from *līnea* LINE[1]] > **deˈlineable** *adj* > **deˌlineˈation** *n* > **deˈlineative** *adj*

delineator (dɪˈlɪnɪˌeɪtə) *n* a tailor's pattern, adjustable for different sizes

delinquency (dɪˈlɪŋkwənsɪ) *n, pl* **-cies 1** an offence or misdeed, usually of a minor nature, esp one committed by a young person. See **juvenile delinquency 2** failure or negligence in duty or obligation; dereliction **3** a delinquent nature or delinquent behaviour [C17 from Late Latin *dēlinquentia* a fault, offence, from Latin *dēlinquere* to transgress, from DE- + *linquere* to forsake]

delinquent (dɪˈlɪŋkwənt) *n* **1** someone, esp a young person, guilty of delinquency. See **juvenile delinquent 2** *archaic* a person who fails in an obligation or duty ▷ *adj* **3** guilty of an offence or misdeed, esp one of a minor nature **4** failing in or neglectful of duty or obligation [C17 from Latin *dēlinquēns* offending; see DELINQUENCY] > **deˈlinquently** *adv*

deliquesce (ˌdɛlɪˈkwɛs) *vb* (*intr*) **1** (esp of certain salts) to dissolve gradually in water absorbed from the air **2** (esp of certain fungi) to dissolve into liquid, usually at maturity **3** (of a plant stem) to form many branches [C18 from Latin *dēliquēscere* to melt away, become liquid, from DE- + *liquēscere* to melt, from *liquēre* to be liquid]

deliquescence (ˌdɛlɪˈkwɛsᵊns) *n* **1** the process of deliquescing **2** a solution formed when a solid or liquid deliquesces > ˌ**deliˈquescent** *adj*

delirious (dɪˈlɪrɪəs) *adj* **1** affected with delirium **2** wildly excited, esp with joy or enthusiasm > **deˈliriously** *adv* > **deˈliriousness** *n*

delirium (dɪˈlɪrɪəm) *n, pl* **-liriums, -liria** (-ˈlɪrɪə) **1** a state of excitement and mental confusion, often accompanied by hallucinations, caused by high fever, poisoning, brain injury, etc **2** violent excitement or emotion; frenzy [C16 from Latin: madness, from *dēlīrāre*, literally: to swerve from a furrow, hence be crazy, from DE- + *līra* ridge, furrow] > **deˈliriant** *adj*

delirium tremens (ˈtrɛmɛnz, ˈtriː-) *n* a severe psychotic condition occurring in some persons with chronic alcoholism, characterized by delirium, tremor, anxiety, and vivid hallucinations. Abbreviations: **dt,** (informal) **DT's** [C19 New Latin, literally: trembling delirium]

delist (ˌdiːˈlɪst) *vb* (*tr*) **1** to remove from a list **2** *stock exchange* to remove (a security) from the register of those that may be traded on the recognized market

delitescence (ˌdɛlɪˈtɛsᵊns) *n* the sudden disappearance of a lesion or of the signs and symptoms of a disease [C18 from Latin *dēlitēscens*, present participle of *dēlitēscere* to lurk, from *latēscere* to become hidden, from *latēre* to be hidden; see LATENT] > ˌ**deliˈtescent** *adj*

deliver (dɪˈlɪvə) *vb* (*mainly tr*) **1** to carry (goods, etc) to a destination, esp to carry and distribute (goods, mail, etc) to several places: *to deliver letters; our local butcher delivers* **2** (often foll by *over* or *up*) to hand over, transfer, or surrender **3** (often foll by *from*) to release or rescue (from captivity, harm, corruption, etc) **4** (*also intr*) **a** to aid in the birth of (offspring) **b** to give birth to (offspring) **c** (usually foll by *of*) to aid or assist (a female) in the birth of (offspring) **d** (*passive*; foll by *of*) to give birth (to offspring) **5** to utter or present (a speech, oration, idea, etc) **6** short for **deliver the goods**: see sense 11, below **7** to utter (an exclamation, noise, etc): *to deliver a cry of exultation* **8** to discharge or release (something, such as a blow or shot) suddenly **9** *chiefly US* to cause (voters, constituencies, etc) to support a given candidate, cause, etc: *can you deliver the Bronx?* **10 deliver oneself of** to speak with deliberation or at length: *to deliver oneself of a speech* **11 deliver the goods** *informal* to produce or perform something promised or expected [C13 from Old French *delivrer*, from Late Latin *dēlīberāre* to set free, from Latin DE- + *līberāre* to free] > **deˈliverable** *adj* > **deˌliveraˈbility** *n* > **deˈliverer** *n*

deliverance (dɪˈlɪvərəns) *n* **1** a formal pronouncement or expression of opinion **2** rescue from moral corruption or evil; salvation **3** another word for **delivery** (senses 3–5)

delivery (dɪˈlɪvərɪ) *n, pl* **-eries 1 a** the act of delivering or distributing goods, mail, etc **b** something that is delivered **c** (*as modifier*): *a delivery service* **2** the act of giving birth to a child: *she had an easy delivery* **3** manner or style of utterance, esp in public speaking or recitation: *the chairman had a clear delivery* **4** the act of giving or transferring or the state of being given or transferred **5** the act of rescuing or state of being rescued; liberation **6** *sport* **a** the act or manner of bowling or throwing a ball **b** the ball so delivered: *a fast delivery* **7** an actual or symbolic handing over of property, a deed, etc **8** the discharge rate of a compressor or pump **9** (in South Africa) the supply of basic services to communities deprived under apartheid

delivery van *n* a small van used esp for delivery rounds. US and Canadian name: **panel truck**

dell (dɛl) *n* a small, esp wooded hollow [Old English; related to Middle Low German *delle* valley; compare DALE]

Delmarva Peninsula (dɛlˈmɑːvə) *n* a peninsula of the northeast US, between Chesapeake Bay and the Atlantic

delo (ˈdɛləʊ) *n Austral* an informal word for **delegate**

delocalize *or* **delocalise** (diːˈləʊkᵊˌlaɪz) *vb* (*tr*) **1** to remove from the usual locality **2** to free from local influences > **deˌlocaliˈzation** *or* **deˌlocaliˈsation** *n*

Delors plan (dəlɔː) *n* a plan for closer European union, originated by Jacques *Delors*, President of the European Commission (1985–94)

Delos (ˈdiːlɒs) *n* a Greek island in the SW Aegean Sea, in the Cyclades: a commercial centre in ancient times; the legendary birthplace of Apollo and Artemis. Area: about 5 sq km (2 sq miles). Modern Greek name: **Dhílos**

delouse (diːˈlaʊs, -ˈlaʊz) *vb* (*tr*) to rid (a person or animal) of lice as a sanitary measure

Delphi (ˈdɛlfɪ) *n* an ancient Greek city on the S slopes of Mount Parnassus: site of the most famous oracle of Apollo

Delphic (ˈdɛlfɪk) *or* **Delphian** *adj* **1** of or relating to Delphi or its oracle or temple **2** obscure or ambiguous

Delphic oracle *n* the oracle of Apollo at Delphi that gave answers held by the ancient Greeks to be of great authority but also noted for their ambiguity. Related word: **Pythian**

delphinium (dɛlˈfɪnɪəm) *n, pl* **-iums** *or* **-ia** (-ɪə) any ranunculaceous plant of the genus *Delphinium*: many varieties are cultivated as garden plants for their spikes of blue, pink, or white spurred flowers. See also **larkspur** [C17 New Latin, from Greek *delphinion* larkspur, from *delphis* DOLPHIN, referring to the shape of the nectary]

Delphinus (dɛlˈfaɪnəs) *n, Latin genitive* **Delphini** (dɛlˈfaɪnaɪ) a small constellation in the N hemisphere, between Pegasus and Sagitta [C17 from Latin: DOLPHIN]

Delphi technique *n* a forecasting or decision-making technique that makes use of written questionnaires to eliminate the influence of personal relationships and the domination of committees by strong personalities

Delsarte system (ˈdɛlsɑːt) *n* a method of teaching drama and dancing based on the exercises of Alexandre Delsarte (1811–71), famous teacher at the Paris Conservatoire

delta (ˈdɛltə) *n* **1** the fourth letter in the Greek alphabet (Δ or δ), a consonant transliterated as *d* **2** an object resembling a capital delta in shape **3** (*capital when part of name*) the flat alluvial area at the mouth of some rivers where the mainstream splits up into several distributaries: *the Mississippi Delta* **4** *maths* a finite increment in a variable [C16 via Latin from Greek, of Semitic origin; compare Hebrew *dāleth*] > **deltaic** (dɛlˈteɪɪk) *or* ˈ**deltic** *adj*

Delta (ˈdɛltə) *n* **1** (*foll by the genitive case of a specified constellation*) usually the fourth brightest star in a constellation **2** any of a group of US launch vehicles used to put unmanned satellites into orbit **3** *communications* a code word for the letter *d*

delta connection *n* a connection used in a three-phase electrical system in which three elements in series form a triangle, the supply being input and output at the three junctions. Compare **star connection**

Delta Force *n* (in the US) an élite army unit involved in counterterrorist operations abroad

delta iron *n* an allotrope of iron that exists between 1400°C and the melting point of iron and has the same structure as alpha iron

delta particle *n physics* a very short-lived hyperon

delta ray *n* a particle, esp an electron, ejected from matter by ionizing radiation

delta rhythm *or* **wave** *n physiol* the normal electrical activity of the cerebral cortex during deep sleep, occurring at a frequency of 1 to 4 hertz and detectable with an electroencephalograph. See also **brain wave**

delta stock *n* any of the fourth rank of active securities on the Stock Exchange. Market makers need not display prices of these securities continuously and any prices displayed are taken only as an indication rather than an offer to buy or sell

delta wing *n* a triangular sweptback aircraft wing

deltiology (ˌdɛltɪˈɒlədʒɪ) *n* the collection and study of picture postcards [C20 from Greek *deltion*, diminutive of *deltos* a writing tablet + -LOGY] > ˌ**deltiˈologist** *n*

deltoid (ˈdɛltɔɪd) *n* **1** the thick muscle forming the rounded contour of the outer edge of the shoulder and acting to raise the arm ▷ *adj* **2** shaped like a Greek capital delta, Δ; triangular [C18 from Greek *deltoeidēs* triangular, from DELTA]

delude (dɪˈluːd) *vb* (*tr*) **1** to deceive the mind or judgment of; mislead; beguile **2** *rare* to frustrate (hopes, expectations, etc) [C15 from Latin *dēlūdere* to mock, play false, from DE- + *lūdere* to play] > **deˈludable** *adj* > **deˈluder** *n* > **deˈludingly** *adv*

deluge (ˈdɛljuːdʒ) *n* **1** a great flood of water **2** torrential rain; downpour **3** an overwhelming rush or number: *a deluge of requests* ▷ *vb* (*tr*) **4** to flood, as with water; soak, swamp, or drown **5** to overwhelm or overrun; inundate [C14 from Old French, from Latin *dīluvium* a washing away, flood, from *dīluere* to wash away, drench, from *di-* DIS-[1] + *-luere*, from *lavere* to wash]

Deluge (ˈdɛljuːdʒ) *n* **the** another name for the **Flood**

delusion (dɪˈluːʒən) *n* **1** a mistaken or misleading opinion, idea, belief, etc: *he has delusions of grandeur* **2** *psychiatry* a belief held in the face of evidence to the contrary, that is resistant to all reason. See also **illusion, hallucination 3** the act of deluding or state of being deluded > **deˈlusional** *adj* > **deˈlusive** *adj* > **deˈlusively** *adv* > **deˈlusiveness** *n* > **delusory** (dɪˈluːsərɪ) *adj*

de luxe (də ˈlʌks, ˈlʊks) *adj* **1** (esp of products,

articles for sale, etc) rich, elegant, or sumptuous; superior in quality, number of accessories, etc: *the de luxe model of a car* ▷ *adv* **2** *chiefly US* in a luxurious manner [C19 from French, literally: of luxury]

delve (dɛlv) *vb* (*mainly intr; often foll by in or into*) **1** to inquire or research deeply or intensively (for information, etc): *he delved in the Bible for quotations* **2** to search or rummage (in a drawer, the pockets, etc) **3** (*esp of an animal*) to dig or burrow deeply (into the ground, etc) **4** (*also tr*) *archaic or dialect* to dig or turn up (earth, a garden, etc), as with a spade [Old English *delfan*; related to Old High German *telban* to dig, Russian *dolbit* to hollow out with a chisel] > 'delver *n*

Dem. *US* ▷ *abbreviation for* Democrat(ic)

demagnetize *or* **demagnetise** (diː'mægnə,taɪz) *vb* to lose magnetic properties or remove magnetic properties from. Also: **degauss** > de,magneti'zation *or* de,magneti'sation *n* > de'magnet,izer *or* de'magnet,iser *n*

demagogic (,dɛmə'gɒgɪk) *or* **demagogical** *adj* of, characteristic of, relating to, or resembling a demagogue > ,dema'gogically *adv*

demagogue *or sometimes US* **demagog** ('dɛmə,gɒg) *n* **1** a political agitator who appeals with crude oratory to the prejudice and passions of the mob **2** (*esp in the ancient world*) any popular political leader or orator [C17 from Greek *dēmagōgos* people's leader, from *dēmos* people + *agein* to lead]

demagoguery (,dɛmə'gɒgərɪ) *or* **demagoguism** ('dɛmə,gɒgɪzəm) *n* the methods, practices, or rhetoric of a demagogue

demagogy ('dɛmə,gɒgɪ) *n, pl* **-gogies 1** demagoguery **2** rule by a demagogue or by demagogues **3** a group of demagogues

de-man *vb* (*tr*) **-mans, -manning, -manned** *Brit* to reduce the workforce of (a plant, industry, etc)

demand (dɪ'mɑːnd) *vb* (*tr; may take a clause as object or an infinitive*) **1** to request peremptorily or urgently **2** to require or need as just, urgent, etc: *the situation demands attention* **3** to claim as a right; exact: *his parents demanded obedience of him* **4** *law* to make a formal legal claim to (property, esp realty) ▷ *n* **5** an urgent or peremptory requirement or request **6** something that requires special effort or sacrifice: *a demand on one's time* **7** the act of demanding something or the thing demanded: *the kidnappers' demand was a million pounds* **8** an insistent question or query **9** *economics* **a** willingness and ability to purchase goods and services **b** the amount of a commodity that consumers are willing and able to purchase at a specified price. Compare **supply¹** (sense 9) **10** *law* a formal legal claim, esp to real property **11** in demand sought after; popular **12** on demand as soon as requested: *a draft payable on demand* [C13 from Anglo-French *demaunder*, from Medieval Latin *dēmandāre*, from Latin: to commit to, from DE- + *mandāre* to command, entrust; see MANDATE] > de'mandable *adj* > de'mander *n*

demandant (dɪ'mɑːndənt) *n law* (formerly) the plaintiff in an action relating to real property [C14 from Old French, from *demander* to DEMAND]

demand bill *or* **draft** *n* a bill of exchange that is payable on demand. Also called: **sight bill**

demand deposit *n* a bank deposit from which withdrawals may be made without notice. Compare **time deposit**

demand feeding *n* the practice of feeding a baby whenever it seems to be hungry, rather than at set intervals

demanding (dɪ'mɑːndɪŋ) *adj* requiring great patience, skill, etc: *a demanding job* > de'mandingly *adv*

demand loan *n* another name for **call loan**

demand management *n economics* the regulation of total spending in an economy to required levels, attempted by a government esp in order to avoid unemployment or inflation: a measure advocated by Keynesian economists

demand note *n* a promissory note payable on demand

demand-pull inflation *n* See **inflation** (sense 2)

demantoid (dɪ'mæntɔɪd) *n* a bright green variety of andradite garnet [C19 from German, from obsolete *Demant* diamond, from Old French *diamant* + -OID]

demarcate ('diːmɑː,keɪt) *vb* (*tr*) **1** to mark, fix, or draw the boundaries, limits, etc, of **2** to separate or distinguish between (areas with unclear boundaries) > 'demar,cator *n*

demarcation *or* **demarkation** (,diːmɑː'keɪʃən) *n* **1** the act of establishing limits or boundaries **2** a limit or boundary **3 a** a strict separation of the kinds of work performed by members of different trade unions **b** (*as modifier*): *demarcation dispute* **4** separation or distinction (often in the phrase **line of demarcation**) [C18 Latinized version of Spanish *demarcación,* from *demarcar* to appoint the boundaries of, from *marcar* to mark, from Italian *marcare*, of Germanic origin; see MARK¹]

démarche French (demarʃ) *n* **1** a move, step, or manoeuvre, esp in diplomatic affairs **2** a representation or statement of views, complaints, etc, to a public authority [C17 literally: walk, gait, from Old French *demarcher* to tread, trample; see DE-, MARCH¹]

demarket (diː'mɑːkɪt) *vb* to discourage consumers from buying (a particular product), either because it is faulty or because it could jeopardize the seller's reputation

dematerialize *or* **dematerialise** (diːmə'tɪərɪə,laɪz) *vb* (*intr*) **1** to cease to have material existence, as in science fiction or spiritualism **2** to disappear without trace; vanish > de,materiali'zation *or* de,materiali'sation *n*

Demavend ('dɛmə,vɛnd) *n* **Mount** a volcanic peak in N Iran, in the Elburz Mountains. Height: 5601 m (18 376 ft)

deme (diːm) *n* **1 a** (in preclassical Greece) the territory inhabited by a tribe **b** (in ancient Attica) a geographical unit of local government **2** *biology* a group of individuals within a species that possess particular characteristics of cytology, genetics, etc [C19 from Greek *dēmos* district in local government, the populace]

demean¹ (dɪ'miːn) *vb* (*tr*) to lower (oneself) in dignity, status, or character; humble; debase [C17 see DE-, MEAN²; on the model of *debase*]

demean² (dɪ'miːn) *vb* (*tr*) *rare* to behave or conduct (oneself) in a specified way [C13 from Old French *demener*, from DE- + *mener* to lead, drive, from Latin *mināre* to drive (animals), from *minārī* to use threats]

demeanour *or US* **demeanor** (dɪ'miːnə) *n* **1** the way a person behaves towards others; conduct **2** bearing, appearance, or mien [C15 see DEMEAN²]

dement (dɪ'mɛnt) *vb* **1** (*intr*) to deteriorate mentally, esp because of old age **2** (*tr*) *rare* to drive mad; make insane [C16 from Late Latin *dēmentāre* to drive mad, from Latin DE- + *mēns* mind]

demented (dɪ'mɛntɪd) *adj* mad; insane > de'mentedly *adv* > de'mentedness *n*

dementia (dɪ'mɛnʃə, -ʃɪə) *n* a state of serious emotional and mental deterioration, of organic or functional origin [C19 from Latin: madness; see DEMENT]

dementia praecox ('priːkɒks) *n* a former name for **schizophrenia** [C19 New Latin, literally: premature dementia]

demerara (,dɛmə'rɛərə, -'rɑːrə) *n* **1** brown crystallized cane sugar from the Caribbean and nearby countries **2** a highly flavoured rum used mainly for blending purposes [C19 named after *Demerara*, a region of Guyana]

Demerara (,dɛmə'rɛərə, -'rɑːrə) *n* **the** a river in Guyana, rising in the central forest area and flowing north to the Atlantic at Georgetown. Length: 346 km (215 miles)

demerge (diː'mɜːdʒ) *vb* **1** (*tr*) to separate a company from another with which it was previously merged **2** (*intr*) to carry out the separation of a company from another with which it was previously merged

demerger (diː'mɜːdʒə) *n* the separation of two or more companies which have previously been merged

demerit (diː'mɛrɪt, 'diː,mɛrɪt) *n* **1** something, esp conduct, that deserves censure **2** *US and Canadian* a mark given against a person for failure or misconduct, esp in schools or the armed forces **3** a fault or disadvantage [C14 (originally: worth, later specialized to mean: something worthy of blame): from Latin *dēmerērī* to deserve] > de,meri'torious *adj* > de,meri'toriously *adv*

demersal (dɪ'mɜːsᵊl) *adj* living or occurring on the bottom of a sea or a lake: *demersal fish* [C19 from Latin *dēmersus* submerged (from *dēmergere* to plunge into, from *mergere* to dip) + -AL¹]

demesne (dɪ'meɪn, -'miːn) *n* **1** land, esp surrounding a house or manor, retained by the owner for his own use **2** *property law* the possession and use of one's own property or land **3** the territory ruled by a state or a sovereign; realm; domain **4** a region or district; domain [C14 from Old French *demeine*; see DOMAIN]

Demeter (dɪ'miːtə) *n Greek myth* the goddess of agricultural fertility and protector of marriage and women. Roman counterpart: **Ceres**

demi- *prefix* **1** half: *demirelief.* Compare **hemi-, semi-** (sense 1) **2** of less than full size, status, or rank: *demigod* [via French from Medieval Latin *dīmedius,* from Latin *dīmīdius* half, from *dis-* apart + *medius* middle]

demibastion (,dɛmɪ'bæstɪən) *n fortifications* half a bastion, having only one flank, at right angles to the wall

demicanton (,dɛmɪ'kæntən, -kæn'tɒn) *n* either of the two parts of certain Swiss cantons

demigod ('dɛmɪ,gɒd) *n* **1 a** a mythological being who is part mortal, part god **b** a lesser deity **2** a person with outstanding or godlike attributes [C16 translation of Latin *sēmideus*] > 'demi,goddess *fem n*

demijohn ('dɛmɪ,dʒɒn) *n* a large bottle with a short narrow neck, often with small handles at the neck and encased in wickerwork [C18 probably by folk etymology from French *dame-jeanne,* from *dame* lady + *Jeanne* Jane]

demilitarize *or* **demilitarise** (diː'mɪlɪtə,raɪz) *vb* (*tr*) **1** to remove any military presence or function in (an area): *demilitarized zone* **2** to free of military character, purpose, etc: *11 regiments were demilitarized* > de,militari'zation *or* de,militari'sation *n*

demilune ('dɛmɪ,luːn, -,ljuːn) *n* **1** *fortifications* an outwork in front of a fort, shaped like a crescent moon **2** a crescent-shaped object or formation; half-moon [C18 from French, literally: half-moon]

demimondaine (,dɛmɪ'mɒndeɪn; *French* dəmimɔ̃dɛn) *n* a woman of the demimonde [C19 from French]

demimonde (,dɛmɪ'mɒnd; *French* dəmimɔ̃d) *n* **1** (esp in the 19th century) those women considered to be outside respectable society, esp on account of sexual promiscuity **2** any social group considered to be not wholly respectable [C19 from French, literally: half-world]

demineralize *or* **demineralise** (diː'mɪnərə,laɪz) *vb* (*tr*) to remove dissolved salts from (a liquid, esp water) > de,minerali'zation *or* de,minerali'sation *n*

de-mining *n* the process of removing landmines

demi-pension French (dəmipɑ̃sjɔ̃) *n* another name for **half board**

demirelief (,dɛmɪrɪ'liːf) *n* a less common term for **mezzo-relievo**

demirep ('dɛmɪ,rɛp) *n rare* a woman of bad repute, esp a prostitute [C18 from DEMI- + REP(UTATION)]

demise (dɪ'maɪz) *n* **1** failure or termination: *the demise of one's hopes* **2** a euphemistic or formal word for **death** **3** *property law* **a** a transfer of an estate by lease **b** the passing or transfer of an estate on the death of the owner **4** the immediate transfer of sovereignty to a successor upon the death, abdication, etc, of a ruler (esp in

d

the phrase **demise of the crown** ▷ *vb* **5** to transfer or be transferred by inheritance, will, or succession **6** (*tr*) *property law* to transfer (an estate, etc) for a limited period; lease **7** (*tr*) to transfer (sovereignty, a title, etc) by or as if by the death, deposition, etc, of a ruler [C16 from Old French, feminine of *demis* dismissed, from *demettre* to send away, from Latin *dīmittere*; see DISMISS] > de'misable *adj*

demi-sec (ˌdɛmɪ'sɛk) *adj* (of wine, esp champagne) medium-sweet [C20 from French, from *demi* half + *sec* dry]

demisemiquaver ('dɛmɪˌsɛmɪˌkweɪvə) *n music* a note having the time value of one thirty-second of a semibreve. Usual US and Canadian name: **thirty-second note**

demission (dɪ'mɪʃən) *n rare* relinquishment of or abdication from an office, responsibility, etc [C16 from Anglo-French *dimissioun*, from Latin *dīmissiō* a dismissing; see DISMISS]

demist (diː'mɪst) *vb* to free or become free of condensation through evaporation produced by a heater and/or blower

demister (diː'mɪstə) *n* a device incorporating a heater and/or blower used in a motor vehicle to free the windscreen of condensation

demit (dɪ'mɪt) *vb* -mits, -mitting, -mitted *Scot* **1** to resign (an office, position, etc) **2** (*tr*) to dismiss [C16 from Latin *dīmittere* to send forth, discharge, renounce, from DI-² + *mittere* to send]

demitasse ('dɛmɪˌtæs; *French* dəmitas) *n* a small cup used to serve coffee, esp after a meal [C19 French, literally: half-cup]

demiurge ('dɛmɪˌɜːdʒ, 'diː-) *n* **1 a** (in the philosophy of Plato) the creator of the universe **b** (in Gnostic and some other philosophies) the creator of the universe, supernatural but subordinate to the Supreme Being **2** (in ancient Greece) a magistrate with varying powers found in any of several states [C17 from Church Latin *dēmiūrgus*, from Greek *dēmiourgos* skilled workman, literally: one who works for the people, from *dēmos* people + *ergon* work] > ˌdemi'urgeous, ˌdemi'urgic or ˌdemi'urgical *adj* > ˌdemi'urgically *adv*

demiveg ('dɛmɪˌvɛdʒ) *informal* ▷ *n* **1** a person who eats poultry and fish, but no red meat ▷ *adj* **2** denoting a person who eats poultry and fish, but no red meat [C20 from DEMI- + VEG(ETARIAN)]

demivierge ('dɛmɪˌvjɛəʒ) *n* a woman who engages in promiscuous sexual activity but retains her virginity [C20 French, literally: half-virgin]

demivolt *or* **demivolte** ('dɛmɪˌvɒlt) *n dressage* a half turn on the hind legs

demo ('dɛməʊ) *n, pl* -os *informal* **1** short for **demonstration** (sense 4) **2 a** a demonstration record or tape, used for audition purposes **b** a demonstration of a prototype system **3** *US* short for **demonstrator** (sense 3)

demo- *or before a vowel* **dem-** *combining form* indicating people or population: *demography* [from Greek *dēmos*]

demob (diː'mɒb) *Brit informal* ▷ *vb* -mobs, -mobbing, -mobbed **1** short for **demobilize** ▷ *n* **2 a** short for **demobilization b** (*as modifier*): *a demob suit* **3** a soldier who has been demobilized

demobilize *or* **demobilise** (diː'məʊbɪˌlaɪz) *vb* to disband, as troops, etc > deˌmobili'zation *or* deˌmobili'sation *n*

demob suit *n Brit informal* a suit of civilian clothes issued to a demobilized soldier, esp at the end of World War II

democracy (dɪ'mɒkrəsɪ) *n, pl* -cies **1** government by the people or their elected representatives **2** a political or social unit governed ultimately by all its members **3** the practice or spirit of social equality **4** a social condition of classlessness and equality **5** the common people, esp as a political force [C16 from French *démocratie*, from Late Latin *dēmocratia*, from Greek *dēmokratia* government by the people; see DEMO-, -CRACY]

democrat ('dɛməˌkræt) *n* **1** an advocate of democracy; adherent of democratic principles **2** a member or supporter of a democratic party or movement

Democrat ('dɛməˌkræt) *n* (in the US) a member or supporter of the Democratic Party > ˌDemo'cratic *adj*

democratic (ˌdɛmə'krætɪk) *adj* **1** of, characterized by, derived from, or relating to the principles of democracy **2** upholding or favouring democracy or the interests of the common people **3** popular with or for the benefit of all: *democratic sports* > ˌdemo'cratically *adv*

democratic centralism *n* the Leninist principle that policy should be decided centrally by officials, who are nominally democratically elected

democratic deficit *n* any situation in which there is believed to be a lack of democratic accountability and control over the decision-making process

Democratic Party *n* **1** (in the US) the older and more liberal of the two major political parties, so named since 1840. Compare **Republican Party 2** (in South Africa) a multiracial political party of the centre-left, now the main opposition to the African National Congress. Abbreviation: **DP**

Democratic-Republican Party *n US history* the antifederalist party originally led by Thomas Jefferson, which developed into the modern Democratic Party

Democratic Republic of Congo *n* **the** See **Congo** (sense 2)

democratize *or* **democratise** (dɪ'mɒkrəˌtaɪz) *vb* (*tr*) to make democratic > deˌmocrati'zation *or* deˌmocrati'sation *n*

démodé *French* (demɔde) *adj* out of fashion; outmoded [French, from *dé-* out of + *mode* style, fashion]

demodulate (diː'mɒdjʊˌleɪt) *vb* to carry out demodulation on (a wave or signal) > de'moduˌlator *n*

demodulation (ˌdiːmɒdjʊ'leɪʃən) *n electronics* the act or process by which an output wave or signal is obtained having the characteristics of the original modulating wave or signal; the reverse of modulation

Demogorgon (ˌdiːmə'ɡɔːɡən) *n* a mysterious and awesome god in ancient mythology, often represented as ruling in the underworld [C16 via Late Latin from Greek]

demographic (ˌdɛmə'ɡræfɪk, ˌdiːmə-) *adj* of or relating to demography > ˌdemo'graphical *adj* > ˌdemo'graphically *adv*

demographics (ˌdɛmə'ɡræfɪks, ˌdiːmə-) *pl n* data resulting from the science of demography; population statistics

demographic timebomb *n chiefly Brit* a predicted shortage of school-leavers and consequently of available workers, caused by an earlier drop in the birth rate, resulting in an older workforce

demography (dɪ'mɒɡrəfɪ) *n* the scientific study of human populations, esp with reference to their size, structure, and distribution [C19 from French *démographie*, from Greek *dēmos* the populace; see -GRAPHY] > de'mographer *or* de'mographist *n* -

demoiselle (dəmwɑː'zɛl) *n* **1** Also called: **demoiselle crane, Numidian crane** a small crane, *Anthropoides virgo*, of central Asia, N Africa, and SE Europe, having grey plumage with long black breast feathers and white ear tufts **2** a less common name for a **damselfly 3** another name for **damselfish 4** a literary word for **damsel** [C16 from French: young woman; see DAMSEL]

demolish (dɪ'mɒlɪʃ) *vb* (*tr*) **1** to tear down or break up (buildings, etc) **2** to destroy; put an end to (an argument, etc) **3** *facetious* to eat up: *she demolished the whole cake!* [C16 from French *démolir*, from Latin *dēmōlīrī* to throw down, destroy, from DE- + *mōlīrī* to strive, toil, construct, from *mōles* mass, bulk] > de'molisher *n* > de'molishment *n*

demolition (ˌdɛmə'lɪʃən, ˌdiː-) *n* **1** the act of demolishing or state of being demolished **2** *chiefly military* **a** destruction by explosives **b** (*as modifier*): *a demolition charge* > ˌdemo'litionist *n, adj*

demolition derby *n chiefly US and Canadian* a competition in which contestants drive old cars into each other until there is only one car left running

demolitions (ˌdɛmə'lɪʃənz, ˌdiː-) *pl n chiefly military* **1 a** explosives, as when used to blow up bridges, etc **b** (*as modifier*): *a demolitions expert* **2** targets prepared for destruction by explosives

demon ('diːmən) *n* **1** an evil spirit or devil **2** a person, habit, obsession, etc, thought of as evil, cruel, or persistently tormenting **3** Also called: **daemon, daimon** an attendant or ministering spirit; genius: *the demon of inspiration* **4 a** a person who is extremely skilful in, energetic at, or devoted to a given activity, esp a sport: *a demon at cycling* **b** (*as modifier*): *a demon cyclist* **5** a variant spelling of **daemon** (sense 1) **6** *Austral and NZ informal archaic* a detective or policeman **7** *computing* a part of a computer program, such as a help facility, that can run in the background behind the current task or application, and which will only begin to work when certain conditions are met or when it is specifically invoked [C15 from Latin *daemōn* evil spirit, spirit, from Greek *daimōn* spirit, deity, fate; see DAEMON]

demonetarize *or* **demonetarise** (diː'mʌnətəˌraɪz) *vb* (*tr*) another word for **demonetize** (sense 1) > deˌmonetari'zation *or* deˌmonetari'sation *n*

demonetize *or* **demonetise** (diː'mʌnɪˌtaɪz) *vb* (*tr*) **1** to deprive (a metal) of its capacity as a monetary standard **2** to withdraw from use as currency > deˌmoneti'zation *or* deˌmoneti'sation *n*

demoniac (dɪ'məʊnɪˌæk) *adj also* **demoniacal** (ˌdiːmə'naɪək²l) **1** of, like, or suggestive of a demon; demonic **2** suggesting inner possession or inspiration: *the demoniac fire of genius* **3** frantic; frenzied; feverish: *demoniac activity* ▷ *n* **4** a person possessed by an evil spirit or demon > ˌdemo'niacally *adv*

demonic (dɪ'mɒnɪk) *adj* of, relating to, or characteristic of a demon; fiendish **2** inspired or possessed by a demon, or seemingly so: *demonic laughter* > de'monically *adv*

demonism ('diːməˌnɪzəm) *n* **1** a belief in the existence and power of demons **b** worship of demons **2** another word for **demonology** > 'demonist *n*

demonize *or* **demonise** ('diːməˌnaɪz) *vb* (*tr*) **1** to make into or like a demon **2** to subject to demonic influence **3** to mark out or describe as evil or culpable: *the technique of demonizing the enemy in the run-up to war*

demonolater (ˌdiːmə'nɒlətə) *n* a person who worships demons [C19 back formation from DEMONOLATRY]

demonolatry (ˌdiːmə'nɒlətrɪ) *n* the worship of demons [C17 see DEMON, -LATRY]

demonology (ˌdiːmə'nɒlədʒɪ) *n* **1** the study of demons or demonic beliefs. Also called: **demonism 2** a set of people or things that are disliked or held in low esteem: *the place occupied by Hitler in contemporary demonology* > demonological (ˌdiːmənə'lɒdʒɪk²l) *adj* > demon'ologist *n*

demonstrable ('dɛmənstrəb²l, dɪ'mɒn-) *adj* able to be demonstrated or proved > ˌdemonstra'bility *or* 'demonstrableness *n* > demonstrably ('dɛmənstrəblɪ, dɪ'mɒn-) *adv*

demonstrate ('dɛmənˌstreɪt) *vb* **1** (*tr*) to show, manifest, or prove, esp by reasoning, evidence, etc: *it is easy to demonstrate the truth of this proposition* **2** (*tr*) to evince; reveal the existence of: *the scheme later demonstrated a fatal flaw* **3** (*tr*) to explain or illustrate by experiment, example, etc **4** (*tr*) to display, operate, and explain the workings of (a machine, product, etc) **5** (*intr*) to manifest support, protest, etc, by public parades or rallies **6** (*intr*) to be employed as a demonstrator of machinery, etc **7** (*intr*) *military* to make a show of force, esp in order to deceive one's enemy [c16 from Latin *dēmonstrāre* to point out, from *monstrāre* to show]

demonstration (ˌdɛmənˈstreɪʃən) *n* **1** the act of demonstrating **2** proof or evidence leading to proof **3** an explanation, display, illustration, or experiment showing how something works **4** a manifestation of grievances, support, or protest by public rallies, parades, etc **5** a manifestation of emotion **6** a show of military force or preparedness **7** *maths* a logical presentation of the assumptions and equations used in solving a problem or proving a theorem > ˌdemonˈstrational *adj* > ˌdemonˈstrationist *n*

demonstration model *n* a nearly new product, such as a car or washing machine, that has been used only to demonstrate its performance for a dealer and is offered for sale at a discount

demonstrative (dɪˈmɒnstrətɪv) *adj* **1** tending to manifest or express one's feelings easily or unreservedly **2** (*postpositive*; foll by *of*) serving as proof; indicative **3** involving or characterized by demonstration: *a demonstrative lecture* **4** conclusive; indubitable: *demonstrative arguments* **5** *grammar* denoting or belonging to a class of determiners used to point out the individual referent or referents intended, such as *this, that, these,* and *those.* Compare **interrogative, relative** ▷ *n* **6** *grammar* a demonstrative word or construction > deˈmonstratively *adv* > deˈmonstrativeness *n*

demonstrator (ˈdɛmənˌstreɪtə) *n* **1** a person who demonstrates equipment, machines, products, etc **2** a person who takes part in a public demonstration **3** a piece of merchandise, such as a car that one test-drives, used to display merits or performance to prospective buyers

demoralize or **demoralise** (dɪˈmɒrəˌlaɪz) *vb* (*tr*) **1** to undermine the morale of; dishearten: *he was demoralized by his defeat* **2** to debase morally; corrupt **3** to throw into confusion > deˌmoraliˈzation or deˌmoraliˈsation *n* > deˈmoralˌizer or deˈmoralˌiser *n*

De Morgan's laws *pl n* (in formal logic and set theory) the principles that conjunction and disjunction, or union and intersection, are dual. Thus the negation of *P* & *Q* is equivalent to *not-P* or *not-Q* [named after Augustus *De Morgan* (1806–71), British mathematician]

demos (ˈdiːmɒs) *n* **1** the people of a nation regarded as a political unit **2** *rare* the common people; masses [c19 from Greek: the populace; see DEME]

demote (dɪˈməʊt) *vb* (*tr*) to lower in rank or position; relegate [c19 from DE- + (PRO)MOTE] > deˈmotion *n*

demotic (dɪˈmɒtɪk) *adj* **1** of or relating to the common people; popular **2** of or relating to a simplified form of hieroglyphics used in ancient Egypt by the ordinary literate class outside the priesthood. Compare **hieratic** ▷ *n* **3** the demotic script of ancient Egypt [c19 from Greek *dēmotikos* of the people, from *dēmotēs* a man of the people, commoner; see DEMOS] > deˈmotist *n*

Demotic (dɪˈmɒtɪk) *n* **1** the spoken form of Modern Greek, now increasingly used in literature. Compare **Katharevusa** ▷ *adj* **2** denoting or relating to this

demount (diːˈmaʊnt) *vb* (*tr*) to remove (a motor, gun, etc) from its mounting or setting > deˈmountable *adj*

dempster (ˈdɛmpstə) *n* a variant spelling of **deemster**

demulcent (dɪˈmʌlsənt) *adj* **1** soothing; mollifying ▷ *n* **2** a drug or agent that soothes the irritation of inflamed or injured skin surfaces [c18 from Latin *dēmulcēre* to caress soothingly, from DE- + *mulcēre* to stroke]

demulsify (diːˈmʌlsɪˌfaɪ) *vb* -fies, -fying, -fied to undergo or cause to undergo a process in which an emulsion is permanently broken down into its constituents [c20 from DE- + EMULSIFY] > deˌmulsifiˈcation *n* > deˈmulsiˌfier *n*

demur (dɪˈmɜː) *vb* -murs, -murring, -murred (*intr*)

1 to raise objections or show reluctance; object **2** *law* to raise an objection by entering a demurrer **3** *archaic* to hesitate; delay ▷ *n also* **demurral** (dɪˈmʌrəl) **4** the act of demurring **5** an objection raised **6** *archaic* hesitation [c13 from Old French *demorer*, from Latin *dēmorārī* to loiter, linger, from *morārī* to delay, from *mora* a delay] > deˈmurrable *adj*

demure (dɪˈmjʊə) *adj* **1** sedate; decorous; reserved **2** affectedly modest or prim; coy [c14 perhaps from Old French *demorer* to delay, linger; perhaps influenced by *meur* ripe, MATURE] > deˈmurely *adv* > deˈmureness *n*

demurrage (dɪˈmʌrɪdʒ) *n* **1** the delaying of a ship, railway wagon, etc, caused by the charterer's failure to load, unload, etc, before the time of scheduled departure **2** the extra charge required as compensation for such delay **3** a fee charged by the Bank of England for changing bullion into notes [c17 from Old French *demorage, demourage*; see DEMUR]

demurrer (dɪˈmʌrə) *n* **1** *law* a pleading that admits an opponent's point but denies that it is a relevant or valid argument **2** any objection raised

demutualize or **demutualise** (diːˈmjuːtʃuəˌlaɪz) *vb* to convert (a mutual society, such as a building society) to a public limited company or (of such a society) to be converted > ˌdemutualiˈzation or ˌdemutualiˈsation *n*

demy (dɪˈmaɪ) *n, pl* -mies **1 a** a size of printing paper, 17½ by 22½ inches (444.5 × 571.5 mm) **b** a size of writing paper, 15½ by 20 inches (Brit) (393.7 × 508 mm) or 16 by 21 inches (US) (406.4 × 533.4 mm) **2** either one of two book sizes, 8½ by 5½ inches (**demy octavo**) or (chiefly Brit) 11¾ by 8⅝ inches (**demy quarto**) [c16 see DEMI-]

demystify (diːˈmɪstɪˌfaɪ) *vb* -fies, -fying, -fied (*tr*) to remove the mystery from; make clear > deˌmystifiˈcation *n*

demythologize or **demythologise** (ˌdiːmɪˈθɒləˌdʒaɪz) *vb* (*tr*) **1** to eliminate all mythical elements from (a piece of writing, esp the Bible) so as to arrive at an essential meaning **2** to restate (a message, esp a religious one) in rational terms > ˌdemyˌthologiˈzation or ˌdemyˌthologiˈsation *n*

den (dɛn) *n* **1** the habitat or retreat of a lion or similar wild animal; lair **2** a small or secluded room in a home, often used for carrying on a hobby **3** a squalid or wretched room or retreat **4** a site or haunt: *a den of vice* **5** *Scot* a small wooded valley; dingle **6** *Scot and northern English dialect* a place of sanctuary in certain catching games; home or base ▷ *vb* dens, denning, denned **7** (*intr*) to live in or as if in a den [Old English *denn*; related to Old High German *tenni* threshing floor, early Dutch *denne* low ground, den, cave]

Den. *abbreviation for* Denmark

denar (ˈdiːnə) *n* the standard monetary unit of Macedonia, divided into 100 deni

denarius (dɪˈnɛərɪəs) *n, pl* -narii (-ˈnɛərɪˌaɪ) **1** a silver coin of ancient Rome, often called a penny in translation **2** a gold coin worth 25 silver denarii [c16 from Latin: coin originally equal to ten asses, from *dēnārius* (adj) containing ten, from *dēnī* ten each, from *decem* ten]

denary (ˈdiːnərɪ) *adj* **1** calculated by tens; based on ten; decimal **2** containing ten parts; tenfold [c16 from Latin *dēnārius* containing ten; see DENARIUS]

denationalize or **denationalise** (diːˈnæʃənəˌlaɪz) *vb* **1** to return or transfer (an industry, etc) from public to private ownership **2** to deprive (an individual, people, institution, etc) of national character or nationality > deˌnationaliˈzation or deˌnationaliˈsation *n*

denaturalize or **denaturalise** (diːˈnætʃrəˌlaɪz) *vb* (*tr*) **1** to deprive of nationality **2** to make unnatural > deˌnaturaliˈzation or deˌnaturaliˈsation *n*

denature (diːˈneɪtʃə) or **denaturize, denaturise** (diːˈneɪtʃəˌraɪz) *vb* (*tr*) **1** to change the nature of **2** to change (a protein) by chemical or physical

means, such as the action of acid or heat, to cause loss of solubility, biological activity, etc **3** to render (something, such as ethanol) unfit for consumption by adding nauseous substances **4** to render (fissile material) unfit for use in nuclear weapons by addition of an isotope > deˈnaturant *n* > deˌnaturˈation *n*

denatured alcohol *n chem* ethanol rendered unfit for human consumption by the addition of a noxious substance, as in methylated spirits

denazify (diːˈnɑːtsɪˌfaɪ) *vb* -fies, -fying, -fied (*tr*) to free or declare (people, institutions, etc) freed from Nazi influence or ideology > deˌnazifiˈcation *n*

Denbighshire (ˈdɛnbɪˌʃɪə, -ʃə) *n* a county of N Wales: split between Clwyd and Gwynedd in 1974; reinstated with different boundaries in 1996; borders the Irish Sea, with the Cambrian Mountains in the south: chiefly agricultural. Administrative centre: Ruthin. Pop: 94 900 (2003 est). Area: 844 sq km (327 sq miles)

Den Bosch (dən bɒs) *n* another name for **'s Hertogenbosch**

dendriform (ˈdɛndrɪˌfɔːm) *adj* branching or treelike in appearance

dendrite (ˈdɛndraɪt) *n* **1** Also called: dendron any of the short branched threadlike extensions of a nerve cell, which conduct impulses towards the cell body **2** a branching mosslike crystalline structure in some rocks and minerals **3** a crystal that has branched during growth and has a treelike form [c18 from Greek *dendritēs* relating to a tree] > dendritic (dɛnˈdrɪtɪk) or denˈdritical *adj* > denˈdritically *adv*

dendro-, dendri- or before a vowel **dendr-** *combining form* tree: *dendrochronology; dendrite* [New Latin, from Greek, from *dendron* tree]

dendrochronology (ˌdɛndrəʊkrəˈnɒlədʒɪ) *n* the study of the annual rings of trees, used esp to date past events > dendrochronological (ˌdɛndrəʊˌkrɒnəˈlɒdʒɪkəl) *adj* > ˌdendrochroˈnologist *n*

dendrogram (ˈdɛndrəʊˌgræm) *n* any branching diagram, such as a cladogram, showing the interconnections between treelike organisms

dendroid (ˈdɛndrɔɪd) or **dendroidal** (dɛnˈdrɔɪdəl) *adj* **1** freely branching; arborescent; treelike **2** (esp of tree ferns) having a tall trunklike stem [c19 from Greek *dendroeidēs* like a tree]

dendrology (dɛnˈdrɒlədʒɪ) *n* the branch of botany that is concerned with the natural history of trees and shrubs > dendrological (ˌdɛndrəˈlɒdʒɪkəl), ˌdendroˈlogic or denˈdrologous *adj* > denˈdrologist *n*

dendron (ˈdɛndrɒn) *n* another name for **dendrite** (sense 1)

dene¹ or **dean** (diːn) *n* *Brit* a valley, esp one that is narrow and wooded [Old English *denu* valley; see DEN]

dene² or **dean** (diːn) *n* *dialect, chiefly Southern English* a sandy stretch of land or dune near the sea [c13 probably related to Old English *dūn* hill; see DOWN³]

Dene (ˈdɛnɪ, ˈdɛneɪ) *pl n* the North American Indian peoples of Nunavut and the Northwest Territories in Canada. The official body representing them is called the Dene Nation [via French *déné*, from Athapascan *dene* people]

Deneb (ˈdɛnɛb) *n* the brightest star in the constellation Cygnus and one of the brightest but remotest stars in the night sky. Visual magnitude: 1.25; spectral type: A2I [c19 from Arabic *dhanab* a tail]

Denebola (dɪˈnɛbələ) *n* the second brightest star in the constellation Leo. Visual magnitude: 2.14; spectral type: A3V [from Arabic *dhanab al-(asad)* tail of the (lion)]

denegation (ˌdɛnɪˈgeɪʃən) *n* a denial, contradiction, or refusal [c17 from Late Latin *dēnegātiō*, from Latin *dēnegāre* to deny, refuse, from *negāre* to deny]

dene hole *n* a hole or shaft excavated in the chalk of southern England or northern France, of

d

uncertain origin and purpose [of uncertain origin: perhaps from DENE[1]]

denervate ('dɛnə,veɪt) *vb* (*tr*) to deprive (a tissue or organ) of its nerve supply > ,dener'vation *n*

DEng. *abbreviation for* Doctor of Engineering

Denglish ('dɛŋglɪʃ) *n* a variety of German containing a high proportion of English words [c20 from a blend of German *Deutsch* German + ENGLISH]

dengue ('dɛŋgɪ) *or* **dandy** ('dændɪ) *n* an acute viral disease transmitted by mosquitoes, characterized by headache, fever, pains in the joints, and skin rash. Also called: **breakbone fever** [c19 from Spanish, probably of African origin; compare Swahili *kidinga*]

Den Haag (dɛn 'ha:x) *n* a Dutch name for (The) Hague

Den Helder (*Dutch* dɛn 'hɛldər) *n* a port in the W Netherlands, in North Holland province: fortified by Napoleon in 1811; naval station. Pop: 60 000 (2003 est)

deni (dɪ'nɪ) *n* a monetary unit of the Former Yugoslav Republic of Macedonia, worth one hundredth of a denar

deniable (dɪ'naɪəb[ə]l) *adj* able to be denied; questionable > de'niably *adv*

denial (dɪ'naɪəl) *n* 1 a refusal to agree or comply with a statement; contradiction 2 the rejection of the truth of a proposition, doctrine, etc: *a denial of God's existence* 3 a negative reply; rejection of a request 4 a refusal to acknowledge; renunciation; disavowal: *a denial of one's leader* 5 a psychological process by which painful truths are not admitted into an individual's consciousness. See also **defence mechanism** 6 abstinence; self-denial

denier[1] *n* 1 ('dɛnɪ,eɪ, 'dɛnjə) a unit of weight used to measure the fineness of silk and man-made fibres, esp when woven into women's tights, etc. It is equal to 1 gram per 9000 metres 2 (də'njeɪ, -'nɪə) any of several former European coins of various denominations [c15 from Old French: coin, from Latin *dēnārius* DENARIUS]

denier[2] (dɪ'naɪə) *n* a person who denies

denigrate ('dɛnɪ,greɪt) *vb* 1 (*tr*) to belittle or disparage the character of; defame 2 a rare word for **blacken** [c16 from Latin *dēnigrāre* to make very black, defame, from *nigrāre* to blacken, from *niger* black] > ,deni'gration *n* > 'deni,grator *n*

denim ('dɛnɪm) *n textiles* 1 a a hard-wearing twill-weave cotton fabric used for trousers, work clothes, etc b (*as modifier*): *a denim jacket* 2 a a similar lighter fabric used in upholstery b (*as modifier*): *denim cushion covers* [c17 from French (*serge*) *de Nîmes* (serge) of NÎMES]

denims ('dɛnɪmz) *pl n* jeans or overalls made of denim

denitrate (di:'naɪtreɪt) *vb* to undergo or cause to undergo a process in which a compound loses a nitro or nitrate group, nitrogen dioxide, or nitric acid > ,deni'tration *n*

denitrify (di:'naɪtrɪ,faɪ) *vb* -fies, -fying, -fied to undergo or cause to undergo loss or removal of nitrogen compounds or nitrogen > de,nitrifi'cation *n*

denizen ('dɛnɪzən) *n* 1 an inhabitant; occupant; resident 2 *Brit* an individual permanently resident in a foreign country where he enjoys certain rights of citizenship 3 a plant or animal established in a place to which it is not native 4 a naturalized foreign word ▷ *vb* 5 (*tr*) to make a denizen [c15 from Anglo-French *denisein*, from Old French *denzein*, from *denz* within, from Latin *de intus* from within]

Denmark ('dɛnmɑ:k) *n* a kingdom in N Europe, between the Baltic and the North Sea: consists of the mainland of Jutland and about 100 inhabited islands (chiefly Zealand, Lolland, Funen, Falster, Langeland, and Bornholm); extended its territory throughout the Middle Ages, ruling Sweden until 1523 and Norway until 1814, and incorporating Greenland as a province from 1953 to 1979; joined the Common Market (now the EU) in 1973; an

important exporter of dairy produce. Language: Danish. Religion: Christian, Lutheran majority. Currency: krone. Capital: Copenhagen. Pop: 5 375 000 (2004 est). Area: 43 031 sq km (16 614 sq miles). Danish name: Danmark Related adj: **Danish**

Denmark Strait *n* a channel between SE Greenland and Iceland, linking the Arctic Ocean with the Atlantic

denom. *abbreviation for* (religious) denomination

denominate *vb* (dɪ'nɒmɪ,neɪt) 1 (*tr*) to give a specific name to; designate ▷ *adj* (dɪ'nɒmɪnɪt, -,neɪt) 2 *maths* (of a number) representing a multiple of a unit of measurement: *4 is the denominate number in 4 miles* [c16 from DE- + Latin *nōmināre* to call by name; see NOMINATE] > de'nominable *adj*

denomination (dɪ,nɒmɪ'neɪʃən) *n* 1 a group having a distinctive interpretation of a religious faith and usually its own organization 2 a grade or unit in a series of designations of value, weight, measure, etc: *coins of this denomination are being withdrawn* 3 a name given to a class or group; classification 4 the act of giving a name 5 a name; designation [c15 from Latin *dēnōminātiō* a calling by name; see DENOMINATE] > de,nomi'national *adj* > de,nomi'nationally *adv*

denominationalism (dɪ,nɒmɪ'neɪʃə,lɪzəm) *n* 1 adherence to particular principles, esp to the tenets of a religious denomination; sectarianism 2 the tendency to divide or cause to divide into sects or denominations 3 division into denominations > de,nomi'nationalist *n, adj*

denominative (dɪ'nɒmɪnətɪv) *adj* 1 giving or constituting a name; naming 2 *grammar* a (of a word other than a noun) formed from or having the same form as a noun b (*as noun*): *the verb "to mushroom" is a denominative* > de'nominatively *adv*

denominator (dɪ'nɒmɪ,neɪtə) *n* 1 the divisor of a fraction, as 8 in ⅞. Compare **numerator** (sense 1) 2 *archaic* a person or thing that denominates or designates

denotation (,di:nəʊ'teɪʃən) *n* 1 the act or process of denoting; indication 2 a particular meaning, esp one given explicitly rather than by suggestion 3 a something designated or referred to. See **referent** Compare **connotation** b another name for **extension** (sense 11)

denotative (dɪ'nəʊtətɪv) *adj* 1 able to denote; designative 2 explicit; overt > de'notatively *adv*

denote (dɪ'nəʊt) *vb* (*tr; may take a clause as object*) 1 to be a sign, symbol, or symptom of; indicate or designate 2 (of words, phrases, expressions, etc) to have as a literal or obvious meaning [c16 from Latin *dēnotāre* to mark, from *notāre* to mark, NOTE] > de'notable *adj* > de'notement *n*

denouement (deɪ'nu:mɒn) *or* **dénouement** (*French* denumɑ̃) *n* 1 a the final clarification or resolution of a plot in a play or other work b the point at which this occurs 2 final outcome; solution [c18 from French, literally: an untying, from *dénouer* to untie, from Old French *desnoer*, from *des*- DE- + *noer* to tie, knot, from Latin *nōdāre*, from *nōdus* a knot; see NODE]

denounce (dɪ'naʊns) *vb* (*tr*) 1 to deplore or condemn openly or vehemently 2 to give information against; accuse 3 to announce formally the termination of (a treaty, etc) 4 *obsolete* a to announce (something evil) b to portend [c13 from Old French *denoncier* to proclaim, from Latin *dēnuntiāre* to make an official proclamation, threaten, from DE- + *nuntiāre* to announce] > de'nouncement *n* > de'nouncer *n*

de novo (*Latin* di: 'nəʊvəʊ) *adv* from the beginning; anew

dense (dɛns) *adj* 1 thickly crowded or closely set: *a dense crowd* 2 thick; impenetrable: *a dense fog* 3 *physics* having a high density 4 stupid; dull; obtuse 5 (of a photographic negative) having many dark or exposed areas 6 (of an optical glass, colour, etc) transmitting little or no light [c15 from Latin *densus* thick; related to Greek *dasus*

thickly covered with hair or leaves] > 'densely *adv* > 'denseness *n*

densimeter (dɛn'sɪmɪtə) *n physics* any instrument for measuring density > **densimetric** (,dɛnsɪ'mɛtrɪk) *adj* > den'simetry *n*

densitometer (,dɛnsɪ'tɒmɪtə) *n* an instrument for measuring the optical density of a material by directing a beam of light onto the specimen and measuring its transmission or reflection > **densitometric** (,dɛnsɪtə'mɛtrɪk) *adj* > ,densi'tometry *n*

density ('dɛnsɪtɪ) *n, pl* -ties 1 the degree to which something is filled, crowded, or occupied: *high density of building in towns* 2 obtuseness; stupidity 3 a measure of the compactness of a substance, expressed as its mass per unit volume. It is measured in kilograms per cubic metre or pounds per cubic foot. Symbol: ρ See also **relative density** 4 a measure of a physical quantity per unit of length, area, or volume. See **charge density, current density** 5 *physics, photog* See **transmission density, reflection density**

density function *n statistics* short for **probability density function**

dent[1] (dɛnt) *n* 1 a hollow or dip in a surface, as one made by pressure or a blow 2 an appreciable effect, esp of lessening: *a dent in our resources* ▷ *vb* 3 to impress or be impressed with a dent or dents [c13 (in the sense: a stroke, blow): variant of DINT]

dent[2] (dɛnt) *n* 1 a toothlike protuberance, esp the tooth of a sprocket or gearwheel 2 *textiles* the space between two wires in a loom through which a warp thread is drawn [c16 from French: tooth]

dent. *abbreviation for* 1 dental 2 dentistry

dental ('dɛnt[ə]l) *adj* 1 of or relating to the teeth 2 of or relating to dentistry 3 *phonetics* a pronounced or articulated with the tip of the tongue touching the backs of the upper teeth, as for *t* in French *tout* b (esp in the phonology of some languages, such as English) another word for **alveolar** ▷ *n* 4 *phonetics* a dental consonant [c16 from Medieval Latin *dentālis*, from Latin *dens* tooth]

dental clinic *n* NZ a school clinic in which minor dental work is carried out by dental nurses

dental floss *n* a soft usually flattened often waxed thread for cleaning the teeth and the spaces between them

dental hygiene *n* the maintenance of the teeth and gums in healthy condition, esp by proper brushing, the removal of plaque, etc. Also called: **oral hygiene**

dental hygienist *n* a dentist's assistant skilled in dental hygiene. Also called: **oral hygienist**

dentalium (dɛn'teɪlɪəm) *n, pl* -liums *or* -lia (-lɪə) any scaphopod mollusc of the genus *Dentalium*. See **tusk shell** [c19 New Latin, from Medieval Latin *dentālis* DENTAL]

dental nurse *n* 1 a dentist's assistant, esp one who passes instruments, mixes fillings, etc 2 NZ a nurse trained to do fillings and carry out other minor dental work on schoolchildren

dental plaque *n* a filmy deposit on the surface of a tooth consisting of a mixture of mucus, bacteria, food, etc. Also called: **bacterial plaque**

dental surgeon *n* another name for **dentist**

dentate ('dɛnteɪt) *adj* 1 having teeth or toothlike processes 2 (of leaves) having a toothed margin [c19 from Latin *dentātus*] > 'dentately *adv*

dentation (dɛn'teɪʃən) *n* 1 the state or condition of being dentate 2 an angular projection or series of projections, as on the margin of a leaf

dentex ('dɛntɛks) *n* a large active predatory sparid fish, *Dentex dentex*, of Mediterranean and E Atlantic waters, having long sharp teeth and powerful jaws [c19 from Latin *dentix, dentex* from *dens* tooth]

denti- *or before a vowel* **dent-** *combining form* indicating a tooth: *dentiform; dentine* [from Latin *dēns, dent-*]

denticle ('dɛntɪk[ə]l) *n* a small tooth or toothlike

part, such as any of the placoid scales of sharks [c14 from Latin *denticulus*]

denticulate (dɛnˈtɪkjʊlɪt, -ˌleɪt) *adj* **1** *biology* very finely toothed: *denticulate leaves* **2** having denticles **3** *architect* having dentils [c17 from Latin *denticulātus* having small teeth] > den'ticulately *adv*

denticulation (dɛnˌtɪkjʊˈleɪʃən) *n* **1** a denticulate structure **2** a less common word for **denticle**

dentiform ('dɛntɪˌfɔːm) *adj* shaped like a tooth

dentifrice ('dɛntɪfrɪs) *n* any substance, esp paste or powder, for use in cleaning the teeth [c16 from Latin *dentifricium* tooth powder, from *dent-, dens* tooth + *fricāre* to rub]

dentil ('dɛntɪl) *n* one of a set of small square or rectangular blocks evenly spaced to form an ornamental row, usually under a classical cornice on a building, piece of furniture, etc [c17 from French, from obsolete *dentille* a little tooth, from *dent* tooth]

dentilabial (ˌdɛntɪˈleɪbɪəl) *adj* another word for **labiodental**

dentilingual (ˌdɛntɪˈlɪŋɡwəl) *adj* **1** *phonetics* pronounced or articulated with the tongue touching the upper teeth ▷ *n* **2** a consonant so pronounced

dentine ('dɛntiːn) or **dentin** ('dɛntɪn) *n* the calcified tissue surrounding the pulp cavity of a tooth and comprising the bulk of the tooth [c19 from DENTI- + -IN] > 'dentinal *adj*

dentist ('dɛntɪst) *n* a person qualified to practise dentistry [c18 from French *dentiste*, from *dent* tooth]

dentistry ('dɛntɪstrɪ) *n* the branch of medical science concerned with the diagnosis and treatment of diseases and disorders of the teeth and gums

dentition (dɛnˈtɪʃən) *n* **1** the arrangement, type, and number of the teeth in a particular species. Man has a **primary dentition** of deciduous teeth and a **secondary dentition** of permanent teeth **2** teething or the time or process of teething [c17 from Latin *dentītiō* a teething]

dentoid ('dɛntɔɪd) *adj* resembling a tooth

Denton ('dɛntən) *n* a town in NW England, in Tameside unitary authority, Greater Manchester. Pop: 26 866 (2001)

D'Entrecasteaux Islands (French dɑ̃trəkasto) *pl n* a group of volcanic islands in the Pacific, off the SE coast of New Guinea: part of Papua New Guinea. Pop: 49 167 (1990 est). Area: 3141 sq km (1213 sq miles)

denture ('dɛntʃə) *n* (usually plural) **1** Also called: **dental plate, false teeth** a partial or full set of artificial teeth **2** *rare* a set of natural teeth [c19 from French, from *dent* tooth + -URE]

denuclearize or **denuclearise** (diːˈnjuːklɪəˌraɪz) *vb* (*tr*) to deprive (a country, state, etc) of nuclear weapons > deˌnucleari'zation or deˌnucleari'sation *n*

denudate ('dɛnjʊˌdeɪt, dɪˈnjuːdeɪt) *vb* **1** a less common word for **denude** ▷ *adj* **2** denuded; bare

denude (dɪˈnjuːd) *vb* (*tr*) **1** to divest of covering; make bare; uncover; strip **2** to expose (rock) by the erosion of the layers above [c16 from Latin *dēnūdāre*; see NUDE] > denudation (ˌdɛnjʊˈdeɪʃən, ˌdiː-) *n* > de'nuder *n*

denumerable (dɪˈnjuːmərəbəl) *adj* *maths* capable of being put into a one-to-one correspondence with the positive integers; countable > de'numerably *adv*

denunciate (dɪˈnʌnsɪˌeɪt) *vb* (*tr*) to condemn; denounce [c16 from Latin *dēnuntiāre*; see DENOUNCE] > deˈnunciˌator *n* > deˈnunciatory *adj*

denunciation (dɪˌnʌnsɪˈeɪʃən) *n* **1** open condemnation; censure; denouncing **2** *law obsolete* a charge or accusation of crime made by an individual before a public prosecutor or tribunal **3** a formal announcement of the termination of a treaty **4** *archaic* an announcement in the form of an impending threat or warning

Denver ('dɛnvə) *n* a city in central Colorado: the

state capital. Pop: 557 478 (2003 est)

Denver boot *n* a slang name for **wheel clamp** [c20 from DENVER, Colorado, where the device was first used]

deny (dɪˈnaɪ) *vb* -nies, -nying, -nied (*tr*) **1** to declare (an assertion, statement, etc) to be untrue: *he denied that he had killed her* **2** to reject as false; refuse to accept or believe **3** to withhold; refuse to give **4** to refuse to fulfil the requests or expectations of: *it is hard to deny a child* **5** to refuse to acknowledge or recognize; disown; disavow: *the baron denied his wicked son* **6** to refuse (oneself) things desired [c13 from Old French *denier*, from Latin *dēnegāre*, from *negāre*]

deoch-an-doruis ('djɒxən'dɒrɪs, dɒx-) *n Scot* a parting drink or stirrup cup. Also: doch-an-doris [Scottish Gaelic: drink at the door]

deodand ('diːəʊˌdænd) *n English law* (formerly) a thing that had caused a person's death and was forfeited to the crown for a charitable purpose: abolished 1862 [c16 from Anglo-French *deodande*, from Medieval Latin *deōdandum*, from Latin *Deō dandum* (something) to be given to God, from *deus* god + *dare* to give]

deodar ('diːəʊˌdɑː) *n* **1** a Himalayan cedar, *Cedrus deodara*, with drooping branches **2** the durable fragrant highly valued wood of this tree [c19 from Hindi *deodār*, from Sanskrit *devadāru*, literally: wood of the gods, from *deva* god + *dāru* wood]

deodorant (diːˈəʊdərənt) *n* **1 a** a substance applied to the body to suppress or mask the odour of perspiration or other body odours **b** (*as modifier*): *a deodorant spray.* Compare **antiperspirant 2** any substance for destroying or masking odours, such as liquid sprayed into the air

deodorize or **deodorise** (diːˈəʊdəˌraɪz) *vb* (*tr*) to remove, disguise, or absorb the odour of, esp when unpleasant > deˌodori'zation or deˌodori'sation *n* > de'odorˌizer or de'odorˌiser *n*

Deo gratias (Latin 'deɪəʊ 'ɡrɑːtɪəs) thanks be to God. Abbreviation: DG

deontic (diːˈɒntɪk) *adj logic* **a** of or relating to such ethical concepts as obligation and permissibility **b** designating the branch of modal logic that deals with the formalization of these concepts [c19 from Greek *deon* duty, from impersonal *dei* it behoves, it is binding]

deontological (dɪˌɒntəˈlɒdʒɪkəl) *adj philosophy* (of an ethical theory) regarding obligation as deriving from reason or as residing primarily in certain specific rules of conduct rather than in the maximization of some good

deontology (ˌdiːɒnˈtɒlədʒɪ) *n* the branch of ethics dealing with duty, moral obligation, and moral commitment [c19 from Greek *deon* duty (see DEONTIC) + -LOGY] > ˌdeon'tologist *n*

Deo volente (Latin 'deɪəʊ vɒ'lɛntɪ) God willing. Abbreviation: DV

deoxidize or **deoxidise** (diːˈɒksɪˌdaɪz) *vb* **1** (*tr*) **a** to remove oxygen atoms from (a compound, molecule, etc) **b** another word for **deoxygenate 2** another word for **reduce** (sense 12) > deˌoxidi'zation or deˌoxidi'sation *n* > de'oxiˌdizer or de'oxiˌdiser *n*

deoxy- or **desoxy-** *combining form* indicating the presence of less oxygen than in a specified related compound: *deoxyribonucleic acid*

deoxycorticosterone (diːˌɒksɪˌkɔːtɪkəʊˈstɪərəʊn) or **deoxycortone** (diːˌɒksɪˈkɔːtəʊn) *n* a corticosteroid hormone important in maintaining sodium and water balance in the body

deoxygenate (diːˈɒksɪdʒɪˌneɪt) or **deoxygenize, deoxygenise** (diːˈɒksɪdʒɪˌnaɪz) *vb* (*tr*) to remove oxygen from (water, air, etc) > deˌoxygen'ation *n*

deoxyribonuclease (diːˌɒksɪˌraɪbəʊˈnjuːˌklɪeɪz) *n* the full name for **DNAase**

deoxyribonucleic acid (diːˌɒksɪˌraɪbəʊnjuːˈkleɪɪk) or **desoxyribonucleic acid** *n* the full name for **DNA**

deoxyribose (diːˌɒksɪˈraɪbəʊs, -bəʊz) or **desoxyribose** (dɛsˌɒksɪˈraɪbəʊs, -bəʊz) *n* a

pentose sugar obtained by the hydrolysis of DNA. Formula: $C_5H_{10}O_4$

dep. *abbreviation for* **1** departs **2** departure **3** deposit **4** depot **5** deputy

dépanneur (ˌdɛpəˈnɜː) *n Canadian* (in Quebec) a convenience store [from Canadian French]

depart (dɪˈpɑːt) *vb* (*mainly intr*) **1** to go away; leave **2** to start out; set forth **3** (usually foll by *from*) to deviate; differ; vary: *to depart from normal procedure* **4** (*tr*) to quit (archaic, except in the phrase **depart this life**) [c13 from Old French *departir*, from DE- + *partir* to go away, divide, from Latin *partīrī* to divide, distribute, from *pars* a part]

departed (dɪˈpɑːtɪd) *adj euphemistic* **a** dead; deceased **b** (*as sing or collective noun;* preceded by *the*): *the departed*

département (French departəmɑ̃) *n* (in France) a major subdivision or branch of the administration of the government [c18 from *départir* to divide; see DEPART]

department (dɪˈpɑːtmənt) *n* **1** a specialized division of a large concern, such as a business, store, or university: *the geography department* **2** a major subdivision or branch of the administration of a government **3** a branch or subdivision of learning: *physics is a department of science* **4** a territorial and administrative division in several countries, such as France **5** *informal* a specialized sphere of knowledge, skill, or activity: *wine-making is my wife's department* [c18 from French *département*, from *départir* to divide; see DEPART] > departmental (ˌdiːpɑːˈtmɛntˀl) *adj* > ˌdepart'mentally *adv*

departmentalism (ˌdiːpɑːˈtmɛntˀlɪzəm) *n* division into departments, esp when resulting in impaired efficiency

departmentalize or **departmentalise** (ˌdiːpɑːˈtmɛntˀlaɪz) *vb* (*tr*) to organize into departments, esp excessively > ˌdepartˌmentali'zation or ˌdepartˌmentali'sation *n*

department store *n* a large shop divided into departments selling a great many kinds of goods

departure (dɪˈpɑːtʃə) *n* **1** the act or an instance of departing **2** a deviation or variation from previous custom; divergence **3** a project, course of action, venture, etc: *selling is a new departure for him* **4** *nautical* **a** the net distance travelled due east or west by a vessel **b** Also called: point of departure the latitude and longitude of the point from which a vessel calculates dead reckoning **5** a euphemistic word for **death**

depasture (diːˈpɑːstʃə) *vb* **1** to graze or denude by grazing (a pasture, esp a meadow specially grown for the purpose) **2** (*tr*) to pasture (cattle or sheep)

depend (dɪˈpɛnd) *vb* (*intr*) **1** (foll by *on* or *upon*) to put trust (in); rely (on); be sure (of) **2** (usually foll by *on* or *upon*; often with *it* as subject) to be influenced or determined (by); be resultant (from): *whether you come or not depends on what father says; it all depends on you* **3** (foll by *on* or *upon*) to rely (on) for income, support, etc **4** (foll by *from*) *rare* to hang down; be suspended **5** to be undecided or pending [c15 from Old French *dependre*, from Latin *dēpendēre* to hang from, from DE- + *pendēre* to hang]

dependable (dɪˈpɛndəbəl) *adj* able to be depended on; reliable; trustworthy > deˌpenda'bility or de'pendableness *n* > de'pendably *adv*

dependant (dɪˈpɛndənt) *n* a person who depends on another person, organization, etc, for support, aid, or sustenance, esp financial support

USAGE Avoid confusion with **dependent**

dependence or *sometimes US* **dependance** (dɪˈpɛndəns) *n* **1** the state or fact of being dependent, esp for support or help **2** reliance; trust; confidence **3** *rare* an object or person relied upon

dependency or *sometimes US* **dependancy** (dɪˈpɛndənsɪ) *n, pl* -cies **1** a territory subject to a state on which it does not border **2** a dependent or subordinate person or thing **3** *psychol* overreliance by a person on another person or on a

d

drug, etc **4** another word for **dependence**

dependent *or sometimes US* **dependant** (dɪˈpɛndənt) *adj* **1** depending on a person or thing for aid, support, life, etc **2** (*postpositive*; foll by *on* or *upon*) influenced or conditioned (by); contingent (on) **3** subordinate; subject: *a dependent prince* **4** *obsolete* hanging down **5** *maths* **a** (of a variable) having a value depending on that assumed by a related independent variable **b** (of a linear equation) having every solution as a solution of one or more given linear equations ▷ *n* **6** *grammar* an element in a phrase or clause that is not the governor **7** a variant spelling (esp US) of **dependant**. > deˈpendently *adv*

> **USAGE** Avoid confusion with **dependant**

dependent clause *n grammar* another term for **subordinate clause**

dependent variable *n* **1** a variable in a mathematical equation or statement whose value depends on that taken on by the independent variable: *in "y = f(x)", "y" is the dependent variable* **2** *psychol, statistics* the variable measured by the experimenter. It is controlled by the value of the independent variable, of which it is an index

depersonalization *or* **depersonalisation** (dɪˌpɜːsnəlaɪˈzeɪʃən) *n* **1** the act or an instance of depersonalizing **2** *psychiatry* an abnormal state of consciousness in which the subject feels unreal and detached from himself and the world

depersonalize *or* **depersonalise** (dɪˈpɜːsnəˌlaɪz) *vb* (*tr*) **1** to deprive (a person, organization, system, etc) of individual or personal qualities; render impersonal **2** to cause (someone) to lose his sense of personal identity [c19 from DE- + PERSONAL + -IZE]

depict (dɪˈpɪkt) *vb* (*tr*) **1** to represent by or as by drawing, sculpture, painting, etc; delineate; portray **2** to represent in words; describe [c17 from Latin *dēpingere*, from *pingere* to paint] > deˈpicter *or* deˈpictor *n* > deˈpiction *n* > deˈpictive *adj*

depicture (dɪˈpɪktʃə) *vb* a less common word for **depict**

depilate (ˈdɛpɪˌleɪt) *vb* (*tr*) to remove the hair from [c16 from Latin *dēpilāre*, from *pilāre* to make bald, from *pilus* hair] > ˌdepiˈlation *n* > ˈdepiˌlator *n*

depilatory (dɪˈpɪlətərɪ, -trɪ) *adj* **1** able or serving to remove hair ▷ *n, pl* -ries **2** a chemical that is used to remove hair from the body

deplane (diːˈpleɪn) *vb* (*intr*) *chiefly US and Canadian* to disembark from an aeroplane [c20 from DE- + PLANE¹]

deplete (dɪˈpliːt) *vb* (*tr*) **1** to use up (supplies, money, energy, etc); reduce or exhaust **2** to empty entirely or partially **3** *med* to empty or reduce the fluid contents of (an organ or vessel) [c19 from Latin *dēplēre* to empty out, from DE- + *plēre* to fill] > deˈpletable *adj* > deˈpletion *n* > deˈpletive *or* deˈpletory *adj*

depleted uranium *n chem* uranium containing a smaller proportion of the isotope uranium–235 than is present in the natural form of uranium; used in anti-tank weapons and other armaments

depletion layer *n electronics* a region at the interface between dissimilar zones of conductivity in a semiconductor, in which there are few charge carriers

deplorable (dɪˈplɔːrəbəl) *adj* **1** lamentable: *a deplorable lack of taste* **2** worthy of censure or reproach; very bad: *deplorable behaviour* > deˈplorableness *or* deˌploraˈbility *n* > deˈplorably *adv*

deplore (dɪˈplɔː) *vb* (*tr*) **1** to express or feel sorrow about; lament; regret **2** to express or feel strong disapproval of; censure [c16 from Old French *deplorer*, from Latin *dēplōrāre* to weep bitterly, from *plōrāre* to weep, lament] > deˈploringly *adv*

deploy (dɪˈplɔɪ) *vb chiefly military* **1** to adopt or cause to adopt a battle formation, esp from a narrow front formation **2** (*tr*) to redistribute (forces) to or within a given area [c18 from French *déployer*, from Latin *displicāre* to unfold; see DISPLAY] > deˈployment *n*

deplume (diːˈpluːm) *vb* (*tr*) **1** to deprive of feathers; pluck **2** to deprive of honour, position, wealth, etc > ˌdepluˈmation *n*

depolarize *or* **depolarise** (diːˈpəʊləˌraɪz) *vb* to undergo or cause to undergo a loss of polarity or polarization > deˌpolariˈzation *or* deˌpolariˈsation *n* > deˈpolarˌizer *or* deˈpolarˌiser *n*

depoliticize *or* **depoliticise** (ˌdiːpəˈlɪtɪˌsaɪz) *vb* (*tr*) to deprive of a political nature; render apolitical: *two years on the committee totally depoliticized him*

depolymerize *or* **depolymerise** (diːˈpɒlɪməˌraɪz) *vb* to break (a polymer) into constituent monomers or (of a polymer) to decompose in this way > deˌpolymeriˈzation *or* deˌpolymeriˈsation *n*

depone (dɪˈpəʊn) *vb law, chiefly Scots* to declare (something) under oath; testify; depose [c16 from Latin *dēpōnere* to put down, from DE- + *pōnere* to put, place]

deponent (dɪˈpəʊnənt) *adj* **1** *grammar* (of a verb, esp in Latin) having the inflectional endings of a passive verb but the meaning of an active verb ▷ *n* **2** *grammar* a deponent verb **3** *law* **a** a person who makes an affidavit **b** a person, esp a witness, who makes a deposition [c16 from Latin *dēpōnēns* putting aside, putting down, from *dēpōnere* to put down, DEPONE]

depopulate (dɪˈpɒpjʊˌleɪt) *vb* to be or cause to be reduced in population > deˌpopuˈlation *n*

deport (dɪˈpɔːt) *vb* (*tr*) **1** to remove (an alien) forcibly from a country; expel **2** to carry (an inhabitant) forcibly away from his homeland; transport; exile; banish **3** to conduct, hold, or behave (oneself) in a specified manner [c15 from French *déporter*, from Latin *dēportāre* to carry away, banish, from DE- + *portāre* to carry] > deˈportable *adj*

deportation (ˌdiːpɔːˈteɪʃən) *n* **1** the act of expelling an alien from a country; expulsion **2** the act of transporting someone from his country; banishment

deportee (ˌdiːpɔːˈtiː) *n* a person deported or awaiting deportation

deportment (dɪˈpɔːtmənt) *n* the manner in which a person behaves, esp in physical bearing: *military deportment* [c17 from French *déportement*, from Old French *deporter* to conduct (oneself); see DEPORT]

deposal (dɪˈpəʊzəl) *n* another word for **deposition** (sense 2)

depose (dɪˈpəʊz) *vb* **1** (*tr*) to remove from an office or position, esp one of power or rank **2** *law* to testify or give (evidence, etc) on oath, esp when taken down in writing; make a deposition [c13 from Old French *deposer* to put away, put down, from Late Latin *dēpōnere* to depose from office, from Latin: to put aside; see DEPONE] > deˈposable *adj* > deˈposer *n*

deposit (dɪˈpɒzɪt) *vb* (*tr*) **1** to put or set down, esp carefully or in a proper place; place **2** to entrust for safekeeping; consign **3** to place (money) in a bank or similar institution in order to earn interest or for safekeeping **4** to give (money) in part payment or as security **5** to lay down naturally; cause to settle: *the river deposits silt* ▷ *n* **6** **a** an instance of entrusting money or valuables to a bank or similar institution **b** the money or valuables so entrusted **7** money given in part payment or as security, as when goods are bought on hire-purchase. See also **down payment** **8** a consideration, esp money, given temporarily as security against loss of or damage to something borrowed or hired **9** an accumulation of sediments, mineral ores, coal, etc **10** any deposited material, such as a sediment or a precipitate that has settled out of solution **11** a coating produced on a surface, esp a layer of metal formed by electrolysis **12** a depository or storehouse **13** **on deposit** payable as the first instalment, as when buying on hire-purchase [c17 from Medieval Latin *dēpositāre*, from Latin *dēpositus* put down]

deposit account *n Brit* a bank account that earns interest and usually requires notice of withdrawal

depositary (dɪˈpɒzɪtərɪ, -trɪ) *n, pl* -taries **1** a person or group to whom something is entrusted for safety or preservation **2** a variant spelling of **depository** (sense 1)

deposition (ˌdɛpəˈzɪʃən, ˌdiːpə-) *n* **1** *law* **a** the giving of testimony on oath **b** the testimony so given **c** the sworn statement of a witness used in court in his absence **2** the act or instance of deposing **3** the act or an instance of depositing **4** something that is deposited; deposit [c14 from Late Latin *dēpositiō* a laying down, disposal, burying, testimony]

Deposition (ˌdɛpəˈzɪʃən, ˌdiːpə-) *n* the taking down of Christ's body from the Cross or a representation of this

depositor (dɪˈpɒzɪtə) *n* a person who places or has money on deposit in a bank or similar organization

depository (dɪˈpɒzɪtərɪ, -trɪ) *n, pl* -ries **1** a store, such as a warehouse, for furniture, valuables, etc; repository **2** a variant spelling of **depositary** (sense 1) [c17 (in the sense: place of a deposit): from Medieval Latin *dēpositōrium*; c18 (in the sense: depositary): see DEPOSIT, -ORY¹]

depot (ˈdɛpəʊ; *US and Canadian* ˈdiːpəʊ) *n* **1** a storehouse or warehouse **2** *military* **a** a store for supplies **b** a training and holding centre for recruits and replacements **3** *chiefly Brit* a building used for the storage and servicing of buses or railway engines **4** *US and Canadian* **a** a bus or railway station **b** (*as modifier*): *a depot manager* ▷ *adj* **5** (of a drug or drug dose) designed for gradual release from the site of an injection so as to act over a long period [c18 from French *dépôt*, from Latin *dēpositum* a deposit, trust]

deprave (dɪˈpreɪv) *vb* (*tr*) **1** to make morally bad; corrupt; vitiate **2** *obsolete* to defame; slander [c14 from Latin *dēprāvāre* to distort, corrupt, from DE- + *prāvus* crooked] > depravation (ˌdɛprəˈveɪʃən) *n* > deˈpraver *n*

depraved (dɪˈpreɪvd) *adj* morally bad or debased; corrupt; perverted > depravedness > depravedness (dɪˈpreɪvɪdnɪs) *n*

depravity (dɪˈprævɪtɪ) *n, pl* -ties the state or an instance of moral corruption

deprecate (ˈdɛprɪˌkeɪt) *vb* (*tr*) **1** to express disapproval of; protest against **2** to depreciate (a person, someone's character, etc); belittle **3** *archaic* to try to ward off by prayer [c17 from Latin *dēprecārī* to avert, ward off by entreaty, from DE- + *precārī* to PRAY] > ˈdepreˌcating *adj* > ˈdepreˌcatingly *adv* > ˌdepreˈcation *n* > ˈdeprecative *adj* > ˈdeprecatively *adv* > ˈdepreˌcator *n*

> **USAGE** Avoid confusion with **depreciate**

deprecatory (ˈdɛprɪkətərɪ) *adj* **1** expressing disapproval; protesting **2** expressing apology; apologetic > ˈdeprecatorily *adv*

depreciable (dɪˈpriːʃəbəl) *adj* **1** *US* able to be depreciated for tax deduction **2** liable to depreciation

depreciate (dɪˈpriːʃɪˌeɪt) *vb* **1** to reduce or decline in value or price **2** (*tr*) to lessen the value of by derision, criticism, etc; disparage [c15 from Late Latin *dēpretiāre* to lower the price of, from Latin DE- + *pretium* PRICE] > deˈpreciatingly *adv* > deˈpreciˌator *n* > depreciatory (dɪˈpriːʃɪətərɪ, -trɪ) *or* deˈpreciative *adj*

> **USAGE** Avoid confusion with **deprecate**

depreciation (dɪˌpriːʃɪˈeɪʃən) *n* **1** *accounting* **a** the reduction in value of a fixed asset due to use, obsolescence, etc **b** the amount deducted from gross profit to allow for such reduction in value **2** *accounting* a modified amount permitted for purposes of tax deduction **3** the act or an instance of depreciating or belittling; disparagement **4** a decrease in the exchange value of currency against gold or other currencies brought about by excess supply of that currency under conditions of fluctuating exchange rates. Compare **devaluation** (sense 1)

depredate (ˈdɛprɪˌdeɪt) *vb* (*tr*) *rare* to plunder or destroy; pillage [c17 from Late Latin *dēpraedāri* to ravage, from Latin DE- + *praeda* booty; see PREY] ▷ ˈdepreˌdator *n* ▷ depredatory (ˈdɛprɪˌdeɪtərɪ, dɪˈprɛdɪtərɪ, ˌtrɪ) *adj*

depredation (ˌdɛprɪˈdeɪʃən) *n* the act or an instance of plundering; robbery; pillage

depress (dɪˈprɛs) *vb* (*tr*) **1** to lower in spirits; make gloomy; deject **2** to weaken or lower the force, vigour, or energy of **3** to lower prices of (securities or a security market) **4** to press or push down **5** to lower the pitch of (a musical sound) **6** *obsolete* to suppress or subjugate [c14 from Old French *depresser*, from Latin *dēprimere* from DE- + *premere* to PRESS¹] ▷ deˈpressible *adj*

depressant (dɪˈprɛsᵊnt) *adj* **1** *med* able to diminish or reduce nervous or functional activity **2** causing gloom or dejection; depressing ▷ *n* **3** a depressant drug

depressed (dɪˈprɛst) *adj* **1** low in spirits; downcast; despondent **2** lower than the surrounding surface **3** pressed down or flattened **4** Also: distressed characterized by relative economic hardship, such as unemployment: *a depressed area* **5** lowered in force, intensity, or amount **6** (of plant parts) flattened as though pressed from above **7** *zoology* flattened from top to bottom: *the depressed bill of the spoonbill*

depressing (dɪˈprɛsɪŋ) *adj* causing a feeling of dejection or low spirits ▷ deˈpressingly *adv*

depression (dɪˈprɛʃən) *n* **1** the act of depressing or state of being depressed **2** a depressed or sunken place or area **3** a mental disorder characterized by extreme gloom, feelings of inadequacy, and inability to concentrate **4** *pathol* an abnormal lowering of the rate of any physiological activity or function, such as respiration **5** an economic condition characterized by substantial and protracted unemployment, low output and investment, etc; slump **6** Also called: cyclone, low *meteorol* a large body of rotating and rising air below normal atmospheric pressure, which often brings rain **7** (esp in surveying and astronomy) the angular distance of an object, celestial body, etc, below the horizontal plane through the point of observation. Compare **elevation** (sense 11)

Depression (dɪˈprɛʃən) *n* (usually preceded by *the*) the worldwide economic depression of the early 1930s, when there was mass unemployment. Also called: the Great Depression, the Slump

depressive (dɪˈprɛsɪv) *adj* **1** tending to depress; causing depression **2** *psychol* tending to be subject to periods of depression. See also **manic-depressive.** ▷ deˈpressively *adv* ▷ deˈpressiveness *n*

depressomotor (dɪˌprɛsəʊˈməʊtə) *adj* **1** *physiol* retarding motor activity ▷ *n* **2** a depressomotor drug

depressor (dɪˈprɛsə) *n* **1** a person or thing that depresses **2** any muscle that draws down a part **3** *med* an instrument used to press down or aside an organ or part: *a tongue depressor* **4** Also called: depressor nerve any nerve that when stimulated produces a fall in blood pressure by dilating the arteries or lowering the heartbeat

depressurize or **depressurise** (dɪˈprɛʃəˌraɪz) *vb* (*tr*) to reduce the pressure of a gas inside (a container or enclosed space), as in an aircraft cabin ▷ deˌpressuriˈzation or deˌpressuriˈsation *n*

deprivation (ˌdɛprɪˈveɪʃən) *n* **1** an act or instance of depriving **2** the state of being deprived: *social deprivation; a cycle of deprivation and violence*

deprive (dɪˈpraɪv) *vb* (*tr*) **1** (foll by *of*) to prevent from possessing or enjoying; dispossess (of) **2** *archaic* to remove from rank or office; depose; demote [c14 from Old French *depriver*, from Medieval Latin *dēprīvāre*, from Latin DE- + *prīvāre* to deprive of, rob; see PRIVATE] ▷ deˈprivable *adj* ▷ deˈprival *n* ▷ deˈpriver *n*

deprived (dɪˈpraɪvd) *adj* lacking adequate food,

shelter, education, etc: *derived inner-city areas*

de profundis (*Latin* deɪ prɒˈfʊndɪs) *adv* out of the depths of misery or dejection [from the first words of Psalm 130]

deprogramme or **deprogram** (diːˈprəʊɡræm) *vb* to free (someone) from the effects of indoctrination, esp by a religious cult or political group

depside (ˈdɛpsaɪd, -sɪd) *n* any ester formed by the condensation of the carboxyl group of one phenolic carboxylic acid with the hydroxyl group of another, found in plant cells [c20 *deps-*, from Greek *depsein* to knead + -IDE]

dept *abbreviation for* department

Deptford (ˈdɛtfəd) *n* a district in the Greater London borough of Lewisham, on the S bank of the River Thames: formerly the site of the Royal Naval dockyard

depth (dɛpθ) *n* **1** the extent, measurement, or distance downwards, backwards, or inwards **2** the quality of being deep; deepness **3** intensity or profundity of emotion or feeling **4** profundity of moral character; penetration; sagacity; integrity **5** complexity or abstruseness, as of thought or objects of thought **6** intensity, as of silence, colour, etc **7** lowness of pitch **8** *nautical* the distance from the top of a ship's keel to the top of a particular deck **9** (*often plural*) a deep, far, inner, or remote part, such as an inaccessible region of a country **10** (*often plural*) the deepest, most intense, or most severe part: *the depths of winter* **11** (*usually plural*) a low moral state; demoralization: *how could you sink to such depths?* **12** (*often plural*) a vast space or abyss **13** beyond or out of one's depth **a** in water deeper than one is tall **b** beyond the range of one's competence or understanding **14** in depth thoroughly or comprehensively. See also **in-depth** [c14 from *dep* DEEP + -TH¹]

depth charge or **bomb** *n* a bomb used to attack submarines that explodes at a pre-set depth of water

depth gauge *n* a device attached to a drill bit to prevent the hole from exceeding a predetermined depth

depth of field *n* the range of distance in front of and behind an object focused by an optical instrument, such as a camera or microscope, within which other objects will also appear clear and sharply defined in the resulting image. Compare **depth of focus**

depth of focus *n* the amount by which the distance between the camera lens and the film can be altered without the resulting image appearing blurred. Compare **depth of field**

depth psychology *n* *psychol* the study of unconscious motives and attitudes

depurate (ˈdɛpjʊˌreɪt) *vb* **1** to cleanse or purify or to be cleansed or purified **2** *obsolete* to promote the elimination of waste products from (the body) [c17 from Medieval Latin *dēpūrāre*, from Latin DE- + *pūrāre* to purify; see PURE] ▷ ˌdepuˈration *n* ▷ ˈdepuˌrator *n*

depurative (ˈdɛpjʊˌreɪtɪv, -rətɪv) *adj* **1** used for or capable of depurating; purifying; purgative ▷ *n* **2** a depurative substance or agent

deputation (ˌdɛpjʊˈteɪʃən) *n* **1** the act of appointing a person or body of people to represent or act on behalf of others **2** a person or, more often, a body of people so appointed; delegation

depute *vb* (dɪˈpjuːt) (*tr*) **1** to appoint as an agent, substitute, or representative **2** to assign or transfer (authority, duties, etc) to a deputy; delegate ▷ *n* (ˈdɛpjuːt) **3** *Scot* a deputy **b** (*as modifier; usually postpositive*): *sheriff depute* [c15 from Old French *deputer*, from Late Latin *dēputāre* to assign, allot, from Latin DE- + *putāre* to think, consider]

deputize or **deputise** (ˈdɛpjʊˌtaɪz) *vb* to appoint or act as deputy

deputy (ˈdɛpjʊtɪ) *n, pl* -ties **1 a** a person appointed to act on behalf of or represent another **b** (*as modifier*): *the deputy chairman* **2** a member of

the legislative assembly or of the lower chamber of the legislature in various countries, such as France **3** *Brit mining* another word for **fireman** (sense 4) [c16 from Old French *depute*, from *deputer* to appoint; see DEPUTE]

deputy minister *n* (in Canada) the senior civil servant in a government department

deracinate (dɪˈræsɪˌneɪt) *vb* (*tr*) **1** to pull up by or as if by the roots; uproot; extirpate **2** to remove, as from a natural environment [c16 from Old French *desraciner*, from *des-* DIS-¹ + *racine* root, from Late Latin *rādīcīna* a little root, from Latin *rādīx* a root] ▷ deˌraciˈnation *n*

deraign or **darraign** (dəˈreɪn) *vb* (*tr*) *obsolete* **1** *law* to contest (a claim, suit, etc) **2** to arrange (soldiers) for battle [c13 from Old French *deraisnier* to defend, from Vulgar Latin *ratiōnāre* (unattested) to REASON] ▷ deˈraignment or darˈraignment *n*

derail (dɪˈreɪl) *vb* **1** to go or cause to go off the rails, as a train, tram, etc ▷ *n* **2** Also called: derailer *chiefly US* a device designed to make rolling stock or locomotives leave the rails to avoid a collision or accident ▷ deˈrailment *n*

derailleur (dəˈreɪljə) *n* a mechanism for changing gear on bicycles, consisting of a device that lifts the driving chain from one sprocket wheel to another of different size [French *dérailleur* derailer]

derange (dɪˈreɪndʒ) *vb* (*tr*) **1** to disturb the order or arrangement of; throw into disorder; disarrange **2** to disturb the action or operation of **3** to make insane; drive mad [c18 from Old French *desrengier*, from *des-* DIS-¹ + *reng* row, order]

derangement (dɪˈreɪndʒmənt) *n* **1** the act of deranging or state of being deranged **2** disorder or confusion **3** *psychiatry* a mental disorder or serious mental disturbance

derate (diːˈreɪt) *vb* (*tr*) *Brit* to assess the value of (some types of property, such as agricultural land) at a lower rate than others for local taxation ▷ deˈrating *n*

deration (diːˈræʃən) *vb* (*tr*) to end rationing of (food, petrol, etc)

Derbent (*Russian* dɪrˈbjɛnt) *n* a port in S Russia, in the Dagestan Republic on the Caspian Sea: founded by the Persians in the 6th century. Pop: 106 000 (2005 est)

derby (ˈdɜːbɪ) *n, pl* -bies *US and Canadian* a stiff felt hat with a rounded crown and narrow curved brim. Also called (in Britain and certain other countries): bowler

Derby¹ (ˈdɑːbɪ; *US* ˈdɜːbɪ) *n* **1 the** an annual horse race run at Epsom Downs, Surrey, since 1780: one of the English flat-racing classics **2** any of various other horse races **3** local Derby a football match between two teams from the same area [c18 named after the twelfth Earl of *Derby* (died 1834), who founded the horse race at Epsom Downs in 1780]

Derby² (ˈdɑːbɪ) *n* **1** a city in central England, in Derby unitary authority, Derbyshire: engineering industries (esp aircraft engines and railway rolling stock); university (1991). Pop: 229 407 (2001) **2** a unitary authority in central England, in Derbyshire. Pop: 233 200 (2003 est). Area: 78 sq km (30 sq miles) **3** a firm-textured pale-coloured type of cheese **4** sage Derby a green-and-white Derby cheese flavoured with sage

Derbyshire (ˈdɑːbɪʃɪə, -ʃə) *n* a county of N central England: contains the Peak District and several resorts with mineral springs: the geographical and ceremonial county includes the city of Derby, which became an independent unitary authority in 1997. Administrative centre: Matlock. Pop (excluding Derby city): 743 000 (2003 est). Area (excluding Derby city): 2551 sq km (985 sq miles)

de re *Latin* (ˈdeɪ ˈreɪ) *adj logic, philosophy* (of a belief, possibility, etc) relating to the individual rather than to an expression, as the necessity of *the number of wonders of the world is prime* since that number, seven, is necessarily prime. Compare **de dicto** [literally: about the thing]

derecognize or **derecognise** (diːˈrɛkəɡˌnaɪz) *vb*

d

(tr) **1** to cease to recognize a trade union as having special negotiating rights within a company or industry **2** to advise (a trade union) of such action > ˌderecog'nition n

deregister (diː'rɛdʒɪstə) vb to remove (oneself, a car, etc) from a register > ˌderegis'tration n

deregulate (diː'rɛgjʊˌleɪt) vb (tr) to remove regulations or controls from > deˌregu'lation n > de'regulator n > de'regulatory adj

derelict ('dɛrɪlɪkt) adj **1** deserted or abandoned, as by an owner, occupant, etc **2** falling into ruins; neglected; dilapidated **3** neglectful of duty or obligation; remiss ▷ n **4** a person abandoned or neglected by society; a social outcast or vagrant **5** property deserted or abandoned by an owner, occupant, etc **6** a vessel abandoned at sea **7** a person who is neglectful of duty or obligation [c17 from Latin dērelictus forsaken, from dērelinquere to abandon, from DE- + relinquere to leave]

dereliction (ˌderɪ'lɪkʃən) n **1** deliberate, conscious, or wilful neglect (esp in the phrase **dereliction of duty**) **2** the act of abandoning or deserting or the state of being abandoned or deserted **3** law **a** accretion of dry land gained by the gradual receding of the sea or by a river changing its course **b** the land thus left

derequisition (diːˌrɛkwɪ'zɪʃən) vb (tr) to release from military to civilian use

derestrict (ˌdiːrɪ'strɪkt) vb (tr) to render or leave free from restriction, esp a road from speed limits > ˌdere'striction n

Dergue (dɜːg) n **the** the socialist ruling body of Ethiopia, established in 1974 [c20 from Amharic, literally, committee]

deride (dɪ'raɪd) vb (tr) to speak of or treat with contempt, mockery, or ridicule; scoff or jeer at [c16 from Latin dērīdēre to laugh to scorn, from DE- + rīdēre to laugh, smile] > de'rider n > de'ridingly adv

de rigueur French (də rigœr; English də rɪ'gɜː) adj required by etiquette or fashion [literally: of strictness]

derisible (dɪ'rɪzɪbᵊl) adj subject to or deserving of derision; ridiculous

derision (dɪ'rɪʒən) n **1** the act of deriding; mockery; scorn **2** an object of mockery or scorn [c15 from Late Latin dērīsiō, from Latin dērīsus; see DERIDE]

derisive (dɪ'raɪsɪv, -zɪv) adj showing or characterized by derision; mocking; scornful > de'risively adv > de'risiveness n

derisory (dɪ'raɪsərɪ, -zərɪ) adj **1** subject to or worthy of derision, esp because of being ridiculously small or inadequate **2** another word for **derisive**

derivation (ˌderɪ'veɪʃən) n **1** the act of deriving or state of being derived **2** the source, origin, or descent of something, such as a word **3** something derived; a derivative **4 a** the process of deducing a mathematical theorem, formula, etc, as a necessary consequence of a set of accepted statements **b** this sequence of statements **c** the operation of finding a derivative > ˌderi'vational adj

derivative (dɪ'rɪvətɪv) adj **1** resulting from derivation; derived **2** based on or making use of other sources; not original or primary **3** copied from others, esp slavishly; plagiaristic ▷ n **4** a term, idea, etc, that is based on or derived from another in the same class **5** a word derived from another word **6** chem a compound that is formed from, or can be regarded as formed from, a structurally related compound: chloroform is a derivative of methane **7** maths **a** Also called: **differential coefficient, first derivative** the change of a function, f(x), with respect to an infinitesimally small change in the independent variable, x; the limit of [f(a + Δx)−f(a)]/Δx, at x = a, as the increment, Δx, tends to 0. Symbols: df(x)/dx, f'(x), Df(x): the derivative of x^n is nx^{n-1} **b** the rate of change of one quantity with respect to another: velocity is the derivative of distance with respect to time **8** finance a financial instrument, such as a futures

contract or option, the price of which is largely determined by the commodity, currency, share price, interest rate, etc, to which it is linked **9** psychoanal an activity that represents the expression of hidden impulses and desires by channelling them into socially acceptable forms > de'rivatively adv

derive (dɪ'raɪv) vb **1** (usually foll by from) to draw or be drawn (from) in source or origin; trace or be traced **2** (tr) to obtain by reasoning; deduce; infer **3** (tr) to trace the source or development of **4** (usually foll by from) to produce or be produced (from) by a chemical reaction **5** maths to obtain (a function) by differentiation [c14 from Old French deriver to spring from, from Latin dērīvāre to draw off, from DE- + rīvus a stream] > de'rivable adj > de'river n

derived fossil n another name for **reworked fossil**

derived unit n a unit of measurement obtained by multiplication or division of the base units of a system without the introduction of numerical factors

-derm n combining form indicating skin: endoderm [via French from Greek derma skin]

derma¹ ('dɜːmə) n another name for **corium** Also: **derm** (dɜːm) [c18 New Latin, from Greek: skin, from derein to skin]

derma² ('dɜːmə) n beef or fowl intestine used as a casing for certain dishes, esp kishke [from Yiddish derme, plural of darm intestine, from Old High German daram; related to Old English thearm gut, Old Norse tharmr]

dermabrasion (ˌdɜːmə'breɪʒən) n a procedure in cosmetic surgery in which rough facial skin is removed by scrubbing [c20 from Greek derma skin + ABRASION]

dermal ('dɜːmᵊl) adj of or relating to the skin

dermapteran (dɜː'mæptərən) n **1** any insect of the order Dermaptera, the earwigs ▷ adj **2** of, relating to, or belonging to this order [c19 from Greek derma (see DERMA¹) + pteron wing]

dermatitis (ˌdɜːmə'taɪtɪs) n inflammation of the skin

dermato-, derma- or before a vowel **dermat-, derm-** combining form indicating skin: dermatology; dermatome; dermal; dermatitis [from Greek derma skin]

dermatogen (də'mætədʒən, 'dɜːməˌtəʊdʒən) n botany a meristem at the apex of stems and roots that gives rise to the epidermis

dermatoglyphics (ˌdɜːmətəʊ'glɪfɪks) pl n **1** the lines forming a skin pattern, esp on the palms of the hands and soles of the feet **2** (functioning as singular) the study of such skin patterns [c20 from DERMATO- + Greek gluphē a carving; see GLYPH]

dermatoid ('dɜːməˌtɔɪd) adj resembling skin

dermatology (ˌdɜːmə'tɒlədʒɪ) n the branch of medicine concerned with the skin and its diseases > dermatological (ˌdɜːmətə'lɒdʒɪkᵊl) adj > ˌderma'tologist n

dermatome ('dɜːməˌtəʊm) n **1** a surgical instrument for cutting thin slices of skin, esp for grafting **2** the area of skin supplied by nerve fibres from a single posterior spinal root **3** embryol the part of a somite in a vertebrate embryo that gives rise to the dermis > dermatomic (ˌdɜːmə'tɒmɪk) adj

dermatophyte ('dɜːmətəʊˌfaɪt) n any parasitic fungus that affects the skin > dermatophytic (ˌdɜːmətəʊ'fɪtɪk) adj

dermatophytosis (ˌdɜːmətəʊfaɪ'təʊsɪs) n a fungal infection of the skin, esp the feet. See **athlete's foot**

dermatoplasty ('dɜːmətəʊˌplæstɪ) n any surgical operation on the skin, esp skin grafting > ˌdermato'plastic adj

dermatosis (ˌdɜːmə'təʊsɪs) n, pl -toses (-'təʊsiːz) any skin disease

dermestid ('dɜː'mɛstɪd) n any beetle of the family Dermestidae, whose members are destructive at both larval and adult stages to a wide range of stored organic materials such as wool, fur, feathers, and meat. They include the bacon (or

larder), cabinet, carpet, leather, and museum beetles [c19 from New Latin dermestida, from Greek dermēstēs, from derma skin + esthiein to eat]

dermis ('dɜːmɪs) n another name for **corium** [c19 New Latin, from EPIDERMIS] > 'dermic adj

dermoid ('dɜːmɔɪd) adj **1** of or resembling skin ▷ n **2** a congenital cystic tumour whose walls are lined with epithelium

dernier cri French (dɛrnje kri) n **le** (lə) the latest fashion; the last word [literally: last cry]

dero ('dɛrəʊ) n, pl deros a tramp or derelict [c20 shortened from DERELICT]

derogate vb ('dɛrəˌgeɪt) **1** (intr; foll by from) to cause to seem inferior or be in disrepute; detract **2** (intr; foll by from) to deviate in standard or quality; degenerate **3** (tr) to cause to seem inferior, etc; disparage **4** (tr) to curtail the application of (a law or regulation) ▷ adj ('dɛrəgɪt, -ˌgeɪt) **5** archaic debased or degraded [c15 from Latin dērogāre to repeal some part of a law, modify it, from DE- + rogāre to ask, propose a law] > 'derogately adv > ˌdero'gation n > derogative (dɪ'rɒgətɪv) adj > de'rogatively adv

derogatory (dɪ'rɒgətərɪ, -trɪ) adj tending or intended to detract, disparage, or belittle; intentionally offensive > de'rogatorily adv > de'rogatoriness n

derrick ('dɛrɪk) n **1** a simple crane having lifting tackle slung from a boom **2** the framework erected over an oil well to enable drill tubes to be raised and lowered ▷ vb **3** to raise or lower the jib of (a crane) [c17 (in the sense: gallows): from Derrick, name of a celebrated hangman at Tyburn]

derrière (ˌdɛrɪ'eə; French dɛrjɛr) n a euphemistic word for **buttocks** [c18 literally: behind (prep), from Old French deriere, from Latin dē retrō from the back]

derring-do ('dɛrɪŋ'duː) n archaic or literary a daring spirit or deed; boldness or bold action [c16 from Middle English durring don daring to do, from durren to dare + don to do]

derringer or **deringer** ('dɛrɪndʒə) n a short-barrelled pocket pistol of large calibre [c19 named after Henry Deringer, American gunsmith who invented it]

derris ('dɛrɪs) n any East Indian leguminous woody climbing plant of the genus Derris, esp D. elliptica, whose roots yield the compound rotenone [c19 New Latin, from Greek: covering, leather, from deros skin, hide, from derein to skin]

derro ('dɛrəʊ) n, pl derros Austral slang a vagrant [from DERELICT]

derry¹ ('dɛrɪ) n, pl -ries Austral and NZ **have a derry on** to have a prejudice or grudge against [c19 probably from derry down, a refrain in some folk songs, alluding to the phrase have a down on; see DOWN¹]

derry² ('dɛrɪ) n, pl -ries slang a derelict house, esp one used by tramps, drug addicts, etc [c20 shortened from DERELICT]

Derry ('dɛrɪ) n **1** a district in NW Northern Ireland, in Co Londonderry. Pop: 106 456 (2003 est). Area: 387 sq km (149 sq miles) **2** another name for **Londonderry**

derv (dɜːv) n a Brit name for **diesel oil** when used for road transport [c20 from d(iesel) e(ngine) r(oad) v(ehicle)]

dervish ('dɜːvɪʃ) n a member of any of various Muslim orders of ascetics, some of which (**whirling dervishes**) are noted for a frenzied, ecstatic, whirling dance [c16 from Turkish: beggar, from Persian darvīsh mendicant monk] > 'dervish-ˌlike adj

Derwent ('dɜːwənt) n **1** a river in S Australia, in S Tasmania, flowing southeast to the Tasman Sea. Length: 172 km (107 miles) **2** a river in N central England, in N Derbyshire, flowing southeast to the River Trent. Length: 96 km (60 miles) **3** a river in N England, in Yorkshire, rising on the North York Moors and flowing south to the River Ouse. Length: 92 km (57 miles) **4** a river in NW England, in Cumbria, rising on the Borrowdale

Fells and flowing north and west to the Irish Sea. Length: 54 km (34 miles)

Derwentwater ('dɜːwənt,wɔːtə) *n* a lake in NW England, in Cumbria in the Lake District. Area: about 8 sq km (3 sq miles)

DES (in Britain) *abbreviation for* (former) Department of Education and Science

desalinate (diː'sælɪ,neɪt), **desalinize** *or* **desalinise** *vb* (*tr*) to remove the salt from (esp from sea water). Also: desalt (diː'sɔːlt)

desalination (diː,sælɪ'neɪʃən), **desalinization** *or* **desalinisation** *n* the process of removing salt, esp from sea water so that it can be used for drinking or irrigation

desaturation (diː,sætʃə'reɪʃən) *n physics* the addition of white light to a pure colour to produce a paler less saturated colour

descale (,diː'skeɪl) *vb* (*tr*) to remove the hard deposit formed by chemicals in water from (a kettle, pipe, etc)

descant *n* ('dɛskænt, 'dɪs-) **1** Also called: discant a decorative counterpoint added above a basic melody **2** a comment, criticism, or discourse ▷ *adj* ('dɛskænt, 'dɪs-) **3** Also: discant of or pertaining to the highest member in common use of a family of musical instruments: *a descant recorder* ▷ *vb* (dɛs'kænt, dɪs-) (*intr*) **4** Also: discant (often foll by *on* or *upon*) to compose or perform a descant (for a piece of music) **5** (often foll by *on* or *upon*) to discourse at length or make varied comments [C14 from Old Northern French, from Medieval Latin *discantus*, from Latin DIS-¹ + *cantus* song; see CHANT] > des'canter *n*

descend (dɪ'sɛnd) *vb* (*mainly intr*) **1** (*also tr*) to move, pass, or go down (a hill, slope, staircase, etc) **2** (of a hill, slope, or path) to lead or extend down; slope; incline **3** to move to a lower level, pitch, etc; fall **4** (often foll by *from*) to be connected by a blood relationship (to a dead or extinct individual, race, species, etc) **5** to be passed on by parents or ancestors; be inherited **6** to sink or come down in morals or behaviour; lower oneself **7** (often foll by *on* or *upon*) to arrive or attack in a sudden or overwhelming way: *their relatives descended upon them last week* **8** (of the sun, moon, etc) to move towards the horizon [C13 from Old French *descendre*, from Latin *dēscendere*, from DE- + *scandere* to climb; see SCAN] > des'cendable *adj*

descendant (dɪ'sɛndənt) *n* **1** a person, animal, or plant when described as descended from an individual, race, species, etc **2** something that derives or is descended from an earlier form ▷ *adj* **3** a variant spelling of **descendent**

Descendant (dɪ'sɛndənt) *n astrology* the point on the ecliptic lying directly opposite the Ascendant

descendent (dɪ'sɛndənt) *adj* **1** coming or going downwards; descending **2** deriving by descent, as from an ancestor

descender (dɪ'sɛndə) *n* **1** a person or thing that descends **2** *printing* the portion of a letter, such as j, p, or y, below the level of the base of an x or n

descendeur (*French* dɛsɑ̃dœr) *n mountaineering* a shaped metal piece through which the rope can be fed: used to control the rate of descent in abseiling. Also called: descender [C20]

descendible *or* **descendable** (dɪ'sɛndəbᵊl) *adj law* capable of being inherited

descent (dɪ'sɛnt) *n* **1** the act of descending **2** a downward slope or inclination **3** a passage, path, or way leading downwards **4** derivation from an ancestor or ancestral group; lineage **5** (in genealogy) a generation in a particular lineage **6** a decline or degeneration **7** a movement or passage in degree or state from higher to lower **8** (often foll by *on*) a sudden and overwhelming arrival or attack **9** *property law* (formerly) the transmission of real property to the heir on an intestacy

deschool (,diː'skuːl) *vb* (*tr*) to separate education from the institution of school and operate through the pupil's life experience as opposed to a set curriculum

descramble (diː'skræmbᵊl) *vb* to restore (a scrambled signal) to an intelligible form, esp automatically by the use of electronic devices > ,de'scrambler *n*

describe (dɪ'skraɪb) *vb* (*tr*) **1** to give an account or representation of in words **2** to pronounce or label: *he has been described as a genius* **3** to draw a line or figure, such as a circle [C15 from Latin *dēscrībere* to copy off, write out, delineate, from DE- + *scrībere* to write] > de'scribable *adj* > de'scriber *n*

description (dɪ'skrɪpʃən) *n* **1** a statement or account that describes; representation in words **2** the act, process, or technique of describing **3** sort, kind, or variety: *reptiles of every description* **4** *geometry* the act of drawing a line or figure, such as an arc **5** *philosophy* a noun phrase containing a predicate that may replace a name as the subject of a sentence

descriptive (dɪ'skrɪptɪv) *adj* **1** characterized by or containing description; serving to describe **2** *grammar* (of an adjective) serving to describe the referent of the noun modified, as for example the adjective *brown* as contrasted with *my* and *former* **3** relating to or based upon description or classification rather than explanation or prescription: *descriptive linguistics* > de'scriptively *adv* > de'scriptiveness *n*

descriptive geometry *n* the study of the projection of three-dimensional figures onto a plane surface

descriptive linguistics *n* (*functioning as singular*) the study of the description of the internal phonological, grammatical, and semantic structures of languages at given points in time without reference to their histories or to one another. Also called: synchronic linguistics Compare **historical linguistics**

descriptive metaphysics *n* (*functioning as singular*) the philosophical study of the structure of how we think about the world

descriptive notation *n chess* a method of denoting the squares on the chessboard in which each player names the files from the pieces that stand on them at the opening and numbers the ranks away from himself. Compare **algebraic notation**

descriptive statistics *n* (*functioning as singular*) the use of statistics to describe a set of known data in a clear and concise manner, as in terms of its mean and variance, or diagramatically, as by a histogram. Compare **statistical inference**

descriptivism (dɪ'skrɪptɪ,vɪzəm) *n ethics* the theory that moral utterances have a truth value. Compare **prescriptivism, emotivism** > de'scripti,vist *adj*

descry (dɪ'skraɪ) *vb* -scries, -scrying, -scried (*tr*) **1** to discern or make out; catch sight of **2** to discover by looking carefully; detect [C14 from Old French *descrier* to proclaim, DECRY] > de'scrier *n*

desecrate ('dɛsɪ,kreɪt) *vb* (*tr*) **1** to violate or outrage the sacred character of (an object or place) by destructive, blasphemous, or sacrilegious action **2** to remove the consecration from (a person, object, building, etc); deconsecrate [C17 from DE- + CONSECRATE] > 'dese,crator *or* 'dese,crater *n* > ,dese'cration *n*

desegregate (diː'sɛgrɪ,geɪt) *vb* to end racial segregation in (a school or other public institution) > ,desegre'gation *n* > ,desegre'gationist *n, adj*

deselect (,diːsɪ'lɛkt) *vb* (*tr*) **1** *Brit politics* (of a constituency organization) to refuse to select (an existing MP) for re-election **2** *US* to discharge (a trainee) during the period of training **3** *computing* to cancel (a highlighted selection of data) on a computer screen **4** *computing* to remove (the check mark) at an option in a dialogue box > ,dese'lection *n*

desensitize *or* **desensitise** (diː'sɛnsɪ,taɪz) *vb* (*tr*) **1** to render insensitive or less sensitive: *the patient was desensitized to the allergen; to desensitize photographic film* **2** *psychol* to decrease the abnormal fear in (a person) of a situation or object, by exposing him to it either in reality or in his imagination > de,sensiti'zation *or* de,sensiti'sation *n* > de'sensi,tizer *or* de'sensi,tiser *n*

desert¹ ('dɛzət) *n* **1** a region that is devoid or almost devoid of vegetation, esp because of low rainfall **2** an uncultivated uninhabited region **3** a place which lacks some desirable feature or quality: *a cultural desert* **4** (*modifier*) of, relating to, or like a desert; infertile or desolate [C13 from Old French, from Church Latin *dēsertum*, from Latin *dēserere* to abandon, literally: to sever one's links with, from DE- + *serere* to bind together]

desert² (dɪ'zɜːt) *vb* **1** (*tr*) to leave or abandon (a person, place, etc) without intending to return, esp in violation of a duty, promise, or obligation **2** *military* to abscond from (a post or duty) with no intention of returning **3** (*tr*) to fail (someone) in time of need: *his good humour temporarily deserted him* **4** (*tr*) *Scots law* to give up or postpone (a case or charge) [C15 from French *déserter*, from Late Latin *dēsertāre*, from Latin *dēserere* to forsake; see DESERT¹] > de'serter *n* > de'serted *adj*

desert³ (dɪ'zɜːt) *n* **1** (*often plural*) something that is deserved or merited; just reward or punishment **2** the state of deserving a reward or punishment **3** virtue or merit [C13 from Old French *deserte*, from *deservir* to DESERVE]

desert boots *pl n* ankle-high suede boots with laces and soft soles, worn informally by men and women

desert cooler *n* (in India) a cooling device in which air is driven by an electric fan through wet grass

desertification (dɪ,zɜːtɪfɪ'keɪʃən) *n* a process by which fertile land turns into barren land or desert

desertion (dɪ'zɜːʃən) *n* **1** the act of deserting or abandoning or the state of being deserted or abandoned **2** *law* wilful abandonment, esp of one's spouse or children, without consent and in breach of obligations

desert island *n* a small remote tropical island

desert lynx *n* another name for **caracal**

desert oak *n* a tree, *Casuarina decaisneana*, of Central and NW Australia, the timber of which is resistant to termite attack

desert pea *n* an Australian trailing leguminous plant, *Clianthus formosus*, with scarlet flowers

desert rat *n* **1** a jerboa, *Jaculus orientalis*, inhabiting the deserts of N Africa **2** *Brit informal* a soldier who served in North Africa with the British 7th Armoured Division in 1941–42

desert rock *n* a type of heavy-metal music that has strong country-rock and folk influences

desert soil *n* a type of soil developed in arid climates, characterized by a lack of leaching and small humus content

deserve (dɪ'zɜːv) *vb* **1** (*tr*) to be entitled to or worthy of; merit **2** (*intr*; foll by *of*) *obsolete* to be worthy [C13 from Old French *deservir*, from Latin *dēservīre* to serve devotedly, from DE- + *servīre* to SERVE] > de'served *adj* > deservedness (dɪ'zɜːvɪdnɪs) *n* > de'server *n*

deservedly (dɪ'zɜːvɪdlɪ) *adv* according to merit; justly

deserving (dɪ'zɜːvɪŋ) *adj* **1** (often *postpositive* and foll by *of*) worthy, esp of praise or reward ▷ *n* **2** *rare* a merit or demerit; desert > de'servingly *adv* > de'servingness *n*

desexualize *or* **desexualise** (diː'sɛksjʊə,laɪz) *vb* (*tr*) to deprive of sexual characteristics by the surgical removal of the testicles or ovaries; castrate or spay. Often shortened to: desex (diː'sɛks) > de,sexuali'zation *or* de,sexuali'sation *n*

deshabille (,deɪzæ'biːl) *or* **dishabille** *n* **1** the state of being partly or carelessly dressed **2** *archaic* clothes worn in such a state [C17 from French *déshabillé* undressed, from *dés-* DIS-¹ + *habiller* to dress; see HABILIMENT]

desi *or* **deshi** ('deɪsiː) *adj Hinglish* **1** indigenous or local: *a desi buda* **2** authentic: *desi music* [C21 Hindi, from Sanskrit *deśa* a country]

d

desiccant ('dɛsɪkənt) *adj* **1** desiccating or drying ▷ *n* **2** a substance, such as calcium oxide, that absorbs water and is used to remove moisture; a drying agent [c17 from Latin *dēsiccāns* drying up; see DESICCATE]

desiccate ('dɛsɪ.keɪt) *vb* **1** (*tr*) to remove most of the water from (a substance or material); dehydrate **2** (*tr*) to preserve (food) by removing moisture; dry **3** (*intr*) to become dried up [c16 from Latin *dēsiccāre* to dry up, from DE- + *siccāre* to dry, from *siccus* dry] > desic'cation *n* > 'desiccative *adj*

desiccated ('dɛsɪ.keɪtɪd) *adj* **1** dehydrated and powdered: *desiccated coconut* **2** lacking in spirit or animation

desiccator ('dɛsɪ.keɪtə) *n* **1** any apparatus for drying milk, fruit, etc **2** an airtight box or jar containing a desiccant, used to dry chemicals and protect them from the water vapour in the atmosphere

desiderata (dɪ.zɪdə'rɑːtə) *n* the plural of **desideratum**

desiderate (dɪ'zɪdə.reɪt) *vb* (*tr*) to feel the lack of or need for; long for; miss [c17 from Latin *dēsīderāre*, from DE- + *sīdus* star; see DESIRE] > de.sider'ation *n*

desiderative (dɪ'zɪdərətɪv) *adj* **1** feeling or expressing desire **2** (in certain languages, of a verb) related in form to another verb and expressing the subject's desire or intention to perform the act denoted by the other verb ▷ *n* **3** a desiderative verb

desideratum (dɪ.zɪdə'rɑːtəm) *n, pl* **-ta** (-tə) something lacked and wanted [c17 from Latin; see DESIDERATE]

design (dɪ'zaɪn) *vb* **1** to work out the structure or form of (something), as by making a sketch, outline, pattern, or plans **2** to plan and make (something) artistically or skilfully **3** (*tr*) to form or conceive in the mind; invent **4** (*tr*) to intend, as for a specific purpose; plan **5** (*tr*) *obsolete* to mark out or designate ▷ *n* **6** a plan, sketch, or preliminary drawing **7** the arrangement or pattern of elements or features of an artistic or decorative work: *the design of the desk is Chippendale* **8** a finished artistic or decorative creation **9** the art of designing **10** a plan, scheme, or project **11** an end aimed at or planned for; intention; purpose **12** (*often plural; often foll by on or against*) a plot or hostile scheme, often to gain possession of (something) by illegitimate means **13** a coherent or purposeful pattern, as opposed to chaos: *God's design appears in nature* **14** argument from design *philosophy* another name for **teleological argument** [c16 from Latin *dēsignāre* to mark out, describe, from DE- + *signāre* to mark, from *signum* a mark, SIGN] > de'signable *adj*

designate *vb* ('dɛzɪg.neɪt) (*tr*) to indicate or specify **2** to give a name to; style; entitle **3** to select or name for an office or duty; appoint ▷ *adj* ('dɛzɪgnɪt, -.neɪt) **4** (*immediately postpositive*) appointed, but not yet in office: *a minister designate* [c15 from Latin *dēsignātus* marked out, defined; see DESIGN] > 'desig.native or 'desig.natory (.dɛzɪg'neɪtərɪ) *adj* > 'desig.nator *n*

designated *adj logic* (of a truth value) corresponding to truth in a two-valued logic, or having one of the analogous values in a many-valued logic

designated driver *n* a person who volunteers not to drink alcohol on a social occasion, so that he or she can safely drive other people who have been drinking

designated employment *n* (in Britain) any of certain kinds of jobs reserved for handicapped workers under the Disabled Persons (Employment) Act 1944

designation (.dɛzɪg'neɪʃən) *n* **1** something that designates, such as a name or distinctive mark **2** the act of designating or the fact of being designated

designedly (dɪ'zaɪnɪdlɪ) *adv* by intention or

design; on purpose; deliberately

designer (dɪ'zaɪnə) *n* **1** a person who devises and executes designs, as for works of art, clothes, machines, etc **2** (*modifier*) designed by and bearing the label or signature of a well-known fashion designer: *designer jeans* **3** (*modifier*) (of things, ideas, etc) having an appearance of fashionable trendiness: *designer pop songs; designer stubble* **4** (*modifier*) (of cells, chemicals, etc) designed (or produced) to perform a specific function or combat a specific problem: *designer insecticide* **5** a person who devises plots or schemes; intriguer

designer baby *n informal* a baby that is the product of genetic engineering

designer drug *n* **1** any of various narcotic or hallucinogenic substances manufactured illegally from a range of chemicals **2** *med* a drug designed to act on a specific molecular target

designing (dɪ'zaɪnɪŋ) *adj* artful and scheming; conniving; crafty > de'signingly *adv*

desinence ('dɛsɪnəns) *n grammar* an ending or termination, esp an inflectional ending of a word [c16 from French *désinence*, from Latin *dēsinēns* ending, from *dēsinere* to leave off, from DE- + *sinere* to leave, permit] > 'desinent or desinential (.dɛsɪ'nɛnʃəl) *adj*

desirable (dɪ'zaɪərəbəl) *adj* **1** worthy of desire or recommendation: *a desirable residence* **2** arousing desire, esp sexual desire; attractive ▷ *n* **3** a person or thing that is the object of desire > de.sira'bility or de'sirableness *n* > de'sirably *adv*

desire (dɪ'zaɪə) *vb* (*tr*) **1** to wish or long for; crave; want **2** to express a wish or make a request; ask for ▷ *n* **3** a wish or longing; craving **4** an expressed wish; request **5** sexual appetite; lust **6** a person or thing that is desired. Related *adj*: **orectic** [c13 from Old French *desirer*, from Latin *dēsīderāre* to desire earnestly; see DESIDERATE] > de'sirer *n*

desirous (dɪ'zaɪərəs) *adj* (*usually postpositive and foll by of*) having or expressing desire (for); having a wish or longing (for) > de'sirously *adv* > de'sirousness *n*

desist (dɪ'zɪst) *vb* (*intr; often foll by from*) to cease, as from an action; stop or abstain [c15 from Old French *desister*, from Latin *dēsistere* to leave off, stand apart, from DE- + *sistere* to stand, halt] > de'sistance or de'sistence *n*

desk (dɛsk) *n* **1** a piece of furniture with a writing surface and usually drawers or other compartments **2** a service counter or table in a public building, such as a hotel: *information desk* **3** a support, lectern, or book rest for the book from which services are read in a church **4** the editorial section of a newspaper, etc, responsible for a particular subject: *the news desk* **5 a** a music stand shared by two orchestral players **b** these two players **6** (*modifier*) **a** made for use at a desk: *a desk calendar* **b** done at a desk: *a desk job* [c14 from Medieval Latin *desca* table, from Latin *discus* disc, dish]

desk-bound *adj* engaged in or involving sedentary work, as at an office desk

desk clerk *n US and Canadian* a hotel receptionist. Also called: **clerk**

deskfast ('dɛskfəst) *n* breakfast eaten at one's desk at work [c20 from DESK + (BREAK)FAST]

deskill (diː'skɪl) *vb* (*tr*) **1** to mechanize or computerize (a job or process) to such an extent that little human skill is required to do it **2** to cause (skilled persons or a labour force) to work at a job that does not utilize their skills > de'skilling *n*

desknote or **desknote computer** ('dɛsk.nəʊt) *n* a computer that is similar in size to a notebook computer, but is designed to remain stationary, like a desktop computer

desktop ('dɛsk.tɒp) *n* (*modifier*) denoting a computer system, esp for word processing, that is small enough to use at a desk

desktop publishing *n* a means of publishing reports, advertising, etc, to typeset quality using a

desktop computer. Abbreviation: DTP

desman ('dɛsmən) *n, pl* **-mans** either of two molelike amphibious mammals *Desmana moschata* (**Russian desman**) or *Galemys pyrenaicus* (**Pyrenean desman**), having dense fur and webbed feet: family *Talpidae*, order *Insectivora* (insectivores) [c18 from Swedish *desmansråtta*, from *desman* musk (of Germanic origin) + *råtta* rat]

desmid ('dɛsmɪd) *n* any freshwater green alga of the mainly unicellular family *Desmidioideae*, typically constricted into two symmetrical halves [c19 from New Latin *Desmidium* (genus name), from Greek *desmos* bond, from *dein* to bind] > des'midian *adj*

desmoid ('dɛsmɔɪd) *adj* **1** *anatomy* resembling a tendon or ligament ▷ *n* **2** *pathol* a very firm tumour of connective tissue [c19 from Greek *desmos* band + -OID; see DESMID]

Des Moines (də'mɔɪn, 'mɔɪnz) *n* **1** a city in S central Iowa: state capital. Pop: 196 093 (2003 est) **2** a river in the N central US, rising in SW Minnesota and flowing southeast to join the Mississippi. Length: 861 km (535 miles)

Desmond Tutu (.dɛzmənd 'tuː.tuː) *n Brit informal* a university degree graded 2:2 (second class lower bracket). Often shortened to: **Desmond** [c20 from rhyming slang, after Desmond *Tutu* (born 1931), South African clergyman and anti-apartheid campaigner]

desmosome ('dɛsmə.səʊm) *n cytology* a structure in the cell membranes of adjacent cells that binds them together

desnood (diː'snuːd) *vb* (*tr*) to remove the snood of a turkey poult to reduce the risk of cannibalism

desolate *adj* ('dɛsəlɪt) **1** uninhabited; deserted **2** made uninhabitable; laid waste; devastated **3** without friends, hope, or encouragement; forlorn, wretched, or abandoned **4** gloomy or dismal; depressing ▷ *vb* ('dɛsə.leɪt) (*tr*) **5** to deprive of inhabitants; depopulate **6** to make barren or lay waste; devastate **7** to make wretched or forlorn **8** to forsake or abandon [c14 from Latin *dēsōlāre* to leave alone, from DE- + *sōlāre* to make lonely, lay waste, from *sōlus* alone] > 'deso.later or 'deso.lator *n* > 'desolately *adv* > 'desolateness *n*

desolation (.dɛsə'leɪʃən) *n* **1** the act of desolating or the state of being desolated; ruin or devastation **2** solitary misery; wretchedness **3** a desolate region; barren waste

desorb (dɪ'sɔːb, -'zɔːb) *vb chem* to change from an adsorbed state on a surface to a gaseous or liquid state

desorption (dɪ'sɔːpʃən, -'zɔːp-) *n* the action or process of desorbing

desoxy- *combining form* a variant of **deoxy-**

despair (dɪ'spɛə) *vb* **1** (*intr; often foll by of*) to lose or give up hope **2** (*tr*) *obsolete* to give up hope of; lose hope in ▷ *n* **3** total loss of hope **4** a person or thing that causes hopelessness or for which there is no hope [c14 from Old French *despoir* hopelessness, from *desperer* to despair, from Latin *dēspērāre*, from DE- + *spērāre* to hope]

despairing (dɪ'spɛərɪŋ) *adj* marked by or resulting from despair; hopeless or desperate > des'pairingly *adv*

despatch (dɪ'spætʃ) *vb* (*tr*) a less common spelling of **dispatch**. > des'patcher *n*

desperado (.dɛspə'rɑːdəʊ) *n, pl* **-does** or **-dos** a reckless or desperate person, esp one ready to commit any violent illegal act [c17 probably pseudo-Spanish variant of obsolete *desperate* (n) a reckless character]

desperate ('dɛspərɪt, -prɪt) *adj* **1** careless of danger, as from despair; utterly reckless **2** (of an act) reckless, risky **3** used or undertaken in desperation or as a last resort: *desperate measures* **4** critical; very grave: *in desperate need* **5** (*often postpositive and foll by for*) in distress and having a great need or desire **6** moved by or showing despair or hopelessness; despairing [c15 from Latin *dēspērāre* to have no hope; see DESPAIR] > 'desperately *adv* > 'desperateness *n*

desperation (ˌdɛspəˈreɪʃən) *n* **1** desperate recklessness **2** the act of despairing or the state of being desperate

despicable (dɪˈspɪkəb^{ə}l, ˈdɛspɪk-) *adj* worthy of being despised; contemptible; mean [C16 from Late Latin *dēspicābilis*, from *dēspicārī* to disdain; compare DESPISE] > **deˌspicaˈbility** *or* **deˈspicableness** *n* > **deˈspicably** *adv*

despise (dɪˈspaɪz) *vb* (*tr*) to look down on with contempt; scorn: *he despises flattery* [C13 from Old French *despire*, from Latin *dēspicere* to look down, from DE- + *specere* to look] > **deˈspiser** *n*

despite (dɪˈspaɪt) *prep* **1** in spite of; undeterred by ▷ *n* **2** *archaic* contempt; insult **3** **in despite of** (*preposition*) *rare* in spite of ▷ *vb* **4** (*tr*) an archaic word for **spite** [C13 from Old French *despit*, from Latin *dēspectus* contempt; see DESPISE]

despiteful (dɪˈspaɪtfʊl) *or* **despiteous** (dɪˈspɪtɪəs) *adj* an archaic word for **spiteful**. > **deˈspitefully** *adv* > **deˈspitefulness** *n*

despoil (dɪˈspɔɪl) *vb* (*tr*) to strip or deprive by force; plunder; rob; loot [C13 from Old French *despoillier*, from Latin *dēspoliāre*, from DE- + *spoliāre* to rob (esp of clothing); see SPOIL] > **deˈspoiler** *n* > **deˈspoilment** *n*

despoliation (dɪˌspəʊlɪˈeɪʃən) *n* **1** the act of despoiling; plunder or pillage **2** the state of being despoiled

despond *vb* (dɪˈspɒnd) **1** (*intr*) to lose heart or hope; become disheartened; despair ▷ *n* (ˈdɛspɒnd, dɪˈspɒnd) **2** an archaic word for **despondency** [C17 from Latin *dēspondēre* to promise, make over to, yield, lose heart, from DE- + *spondēre* to promise] > **deˈspondingly** *adv*

despondent (dɪˈspɒndənt) *adj* downcast or disheartened; lacking hope or courage; dejected > **deˈspondence** *n* > **deˈspondency** *n* > **deˈspondently** *adv*

despot (ˈdɛspɒt) *n* **1** an absolute or tyrannical ruler; autocrat or tyrant **2** any person in power who acts tyrannically **3** a title borne by numerous persons of rank in the later Roman, Byzantine, and Ottoman Empires: *the despot of Servia* [C16 from Medieval Latin *despota*, from Greek *despotēs* lord, master; related to Latin *domus* house] > **despotic** (dɛsˈpɒtɪk) *or* **desˈpotical** *adj* > **desˈpotically** *adv*

despotism (ˈdɛspəˌtɪzəm) *n* **1** the rule of a despot; arbitrary, absolute, or tyrannical government **2** arbitrary or tyrannical authority or behaviour

despumate (dɪˈspjuːmeɪt, ˈdɛspjʊˌmeɪt) *vb* **1** (*tr*) to clarify or purify (a liquid) by skimming a scum from its surface **2** (*intr*) (of a liquid) to form a scum or froth [C17 from Latin *dēspūmāre* to skim off, from DE- + *spūma* foam, froth] > ˌ**despuˈmation** *n*

desquamate (ˈdɛskwəˌmeɪt) *vb* (*intr*) (esp of the skin in certain diseases) to peel or come off in scales [C18 from Latin *dēsquāmāre* to scale off, from DE- + *squāma* a scale] > ˌ**desquaˈmation** *n*

des res (dɛz rɛz) *n* (in estate agents' jargon) a desirable residence

Dessau (*German* ˈdɛsau) *n* an industrial city in E Germany, in Saxony-Anhalt: capital of Anhalt state from 1340 to 1918. Pop: 78 380 (2003 est)

dessert (dɪˈzɜːt) *n* **1** the sweet, usually last course of a meal **2** *chiefly Brit* (esp formerly) fruit, dates, nuts, etc, served at the end of a meal [C17 from French, from *desservir* to clear a table, from *des-* DIS-[1] + *servir* to SERVE]

dessertspoon (dɪˈzɜːtˌspuːn) *n* a spoon intermediate in size between a tablespoon and a teaspoon

dessiatine (ˈdɛsjəˌtiːn) *n* a Russian unit of area equal to approximately 2.7 acres or 10 800 square metres [C18 from Russian *desyatina*, literally: tithe, from *desyat* ten]

destabilize *or* **destabilise** (diːˈsteɪbɪˌlaɪz) *vb* (*tr*) to undermine or subvert (a government, economy, etc) so as to cause unrest or collapse > ˌ**destabiliˈzation** *or* ˌ**destabiliˈsation** *n*

de-Stalinization *or* **de-Stalinisation** (diːˌstɑːlɪnaɪˈzeɪʃən) *n* the elimination of the influence of Stalin

De Stijl (də staɪl) *n* a group of artists and architects in the Netherlands in the 1920s, including Mondrian and van Doesburg, devoted to neoplasticism and then dada [Dutch, literally: the style, title of this group's own magazine]

destination (ˌdɛstɪˈneɪʃən) *n* **1** the predetermined end of a journey or voyage **2** the ultimate end or purpose for which something is created or a person is destined

destine (ˈdɛstɪn) *vb* (*tr*) to set apart or appoint (for a certain purpose or person, or to do something); intend; design [C14 from Old French *destiner*, from Latin *dēstināre* to appoint, from DE- + *-stināre*, from *stāre* to stand]

destined (ˈdɛstɪnd) *adj* (*postpositive*) **1** foreordained or certain; meant: *he is destined to be famous* **2** (usually foll by *for*) heading (towards a specific destination); directed: *a letter destined for Europe*

destiny (ˈdɛstɪnɪ) *n, pl* **-nies** **1** the future destined for a person or thing; fate; fortune; lot **2** the predetermined or inevitable course of events **3** the ultimate power or agency that predetermines the course of events [C14 from Old French *destinee*, from *destiner* to DESTINE]

Destiny (ˈdɛstɪnɪ) *n, pl* **-nies** the power that predetermines events, personified as a goddess

destitute (ˈdɛstɪˌtjuːt) *adj* **1** lacking the means of subsistence; totally impoverished **2** (*postpositive*; foll by *of*) completely lacking; deprived or bereft (of): *destitute of words* **3** *obsolete* abandoned or deserted [C14 from Latin *dēstitūtus* forsaken, from *dēstituere* to leave alone, from *statuere* to place] > ˈ**destiˌtuteness** *n*

destitution (ˌdɛstɪˈtjuːʃən) *n* **1** the state of being destitute; utter poverty **2** *rare* lack or deficiency

destock (diːˈstɒk) *vb* (of a retailer) to reduce the amount of stock held or cease to stock certain products

de-stress *vb* to become or cause to become less stressed or anxious

destrier (ˈdɛstrɪə) *n* an archaic word for **warhorse** (sense 1) [C13 from Old French, from *destre* right hand, from Latin *dextra*; from the fact that a squire led a knight's horse with his right hand]

destroy (dɪˈstrɔɪ) *vb* (*mainly tr*) **1** to ruin; spoil; render useless **2** to tear down or demolish; break up; raze **3** to put an end to; do away with; extinguish **4** to kill or annihilate **5** to crush, subdue, or defeat **6** (*intr*) to be destructive or cause destruction [C13 from Old French *destruire*, from Latin *dēstruere* to pull down, from DE- + *struere* to pile up, build] > **deˈstroyable** *adj*

destroyer (dɪˈstrɔɪə) *n* **1** a small fast lightly armoured but heavily armed warship **2** a person or thing that destroys

destroyer escort *n* a lightly armed warship smaller than a destroyer, designed to escort fleets or convoys

destroying angel *n* a white slender very poisonous basidiomycetous toadstool, *Amanita virosa*, having a pronounced volva, frilled, shaggy stalk, and sickly smell

destruct (dɪˈstrʌkt) *vb* **1** to destroy (one's own missile or rocket) for safety **2** (*intr*) (of a missile or rocket) to be destroyed, for safety, by those controlling it; self-destruct ▷ *n* **3** the act of destructing ▷ *adj* **4** designed to be capable of destroying itself or the object, system, or installation containing it: *destruct mechanism*

destructible (dɪˈstrʌktəb^{ə}l) *adj* capable of being or liable to be destroyed > **deˌstructiˈbility** *n*

destruction (dɪˈstrʌkʃən) *n* **1** the act of destroying or state of being destroyed; demolition **2** a cause of ruin or means of destroying [C14 from Latin *dēstructiō* a pulling down; see DESTROY]

destructionist (dɪˈstrʌkʃənɪst) *n* a person who believes in destruction, esp of social institutions

destructive (dɪˈstrʌktɪv) *adj* **1** (often *postpositive* and foll by *of* or *to*) causing or tending to cause the destruction (of) **2** intended to disprove or discredit, esp without positive suggestions or help; negative: *destructive criticism*. Compare **constructive** (sense 1) > **deˈstructively** *adv* > **deˈstructiveness** *or* **destructivity** (ˌdiːstrʌkˈtɪvɪtɪ) *n*

destructive distillation *n* the decomposition of a complex substance, such as wood or coal, by heating it in the absence of air and collecting the volatile products

destructo (dɪˈstrʌktəʊ) *n, pl* **-tos** *Austral informal* a person who causes havoc or destruction

destructor (dɪˈstrʌktə) *n* **1** a furnace or incinerator for the disposal of refuse, esp one that uses the resulting heat to generate power **2** a device used to blow up a dangerously defective missile or rocket after launching

desuetude (dɪˈsjuːɪˌtjuːd, ˈdɛswɪtjuːd) *n* *formal* the condition of not being in use or practice; disuse *those ceremonies had fallen into desuetude* [C15 from Latin *dēsuētūdō*, from *dēsuescere* to lay aside a habit, from DE- + *suescere* to grow accustomed]

desulphurize *or* **desulphurise** (diːˈsʌlfjʊˌraɪz) *vb* to free or become free from sulphur > **deˌsulphuriˈzation** *or* **deˌsulphuriˈsation** *n* > **deˈsulphurˌizer** *or* **deˈsulphurˌiser** *n*

desultory (ˈdɛsəltərɪ, -trɪ) *adj* **1** passing or jumping from one thing to another, esp in a fitful way; unmethodical; disconnected **2** occurring in a random or incidental way; haphazard: *a desultory thought* [C16 from Latin *dēsultōrius*, relating to one who vaults or jumps, hence superficial, from *dēsilīre* to jump down, from DE- + *salīre* to jump] > ˈ**desultorily** *adv* > ˈ**desultoriness** *n*

DET *abbreviation for* diethyltryptamine, a hallucinogenic drug

detach (dɪˈtætʃ) *vb* (*tr*) **1** to disengage and separate or remove, as by pulling; unfasten; disconnect **2** *military* to separate (a small unit) from a larger, esp for a special assignment [C17 from Old French *destachier*, from *des-* DIS-[1] + *attachier* to ATTACH] > **deˈtachable** *adj* > **deˌtachaˈbility** *n* > **deˈtacher** *n*

d

detached (dɪˈtætʃt) *adj* **1** disconnected or standing apart; not attached: *a detached house* **2** having or showing no bias or emotional involvement; disinterested **3** *social welfare* working at the clients' normal location rather than from an office; not dependent on premises for providing a service: *a detached youth worker*. Compare **outreach** (sense 7) **4** *ophthalmol* (of the retina) separated from the choroid layer of the eyeball to which it is normally attached, resulting in loss of vision in the affected part

detachment (dɪˈtætʃmənt) *n* **1** indifference to other people or to one's surroundings; aloofness **2** freedom from self-interest or bias; disinterest **3** the act of disengaging or separating something **4** the condition of being disengaged or separated; disconnection **5** *military* **a** the separation of a small unit from its main body, esp of ships or troops **b** the unit so detached **6** *logic* the rule whereby the consequent of a true conditional statement, given the truth of its antecedent, may be asserted on its own. See also **modus ponens**

detail (ˈdiːteɪl) *n* **1** an item or smaller part that is considered separately; particular **2** an item or circumstance that is insignificant or unimportant: *passengers' comfort was regarded as a detail* **3** treatment of or attention to items or particulars: *this essay includes too much detail* **4** items collectively; particulars **5** a small or accessory section or element in a painting, building, statue, etc, esp when considered in isolation **6** *military* **a** the act of assigning personnel for a specific duty, esp a fatigue **b** the personnel selected **c** the duty or assignment **7** **go into detail** to include all or most particulars **8** **in detail** including all or most particulars or items thoroughly ▷ *vb* (*tr*) **9** to list or relate fully **10** *military* to select (personnel) for a specific duty **11** to decorate or elaborate (carving, etc) with fine delicate drawing or designs [C17 from French *détail*, from Old French *detailler* to cut in pieces, from *de-* DIS-[1] + *tailler* to cut; see TAILOR]

detail drawing *n* a separate large-scale drawing of a small part or section of a building, machine, etc

detailed ('diːteɪld) *adj* having many details or giving careful attention to details: *a detailed list of the ingredients required*

detain (dɪ'teɪn) *vb* (tr) 1 to delay; hold back; stop 2 to confine or hold in custody; restrain 3 *archaic* to retain or withhold [c15 from Old French *detenir*, from Latin *dētinēre* to hold off, keep back, from DE- + *tenēre* to hold] > de'tainable *adj* > detainee (ˌdiːteɪˈniː) *n* > de'tainment *n*

detainer (dɪ'teɪnə) *n law* 1 the wrongful withholding of the property of another person 2 a the detention of a person in custody b a writ authorizing the further detention of a person already in custody [c17 from Anglo-French *detener* (n), from *detener* to DETAIN]

detect (dɪ'tɛkt) *vb* (tr) 1 to perceive or notice: *to detect a note of sarcasm* 2 to discover the existence or presence of (esp something likely to elude observation): *to detect alcohol in the blood* 3 to extract information from (an electromagnetic wave) 4 *obsolete* to reveal or expose (a crime, criminal, etc) [c15 from Latin *dētectus* uncovered, from *dētegere* to uncover, from DE- + *tegere* to cover] > de'tectable or de'tectible *adj* > de'tecter *n*

detection (dɪ'tɛkʃən) *n* 1 the act of discovering or the fact of being discovered: *detection of crime* 2 the act or process of extracting information, esp at audio or video frequencies, from an electromagnetic wave. See also **demodulation**

detective (dɪ'tɛktɪv) *n* 1 a a police officer who investigates crimes b See **private detective** c (as modifier): *a detective story* ▷ *adj* 2 used in or serving for detection 3 serving to detect

detector (dɪ'tɛktə) *n* 1 a person or thing that detects 2 any mechanical sensing device 3 *electronics* a device used in the detection of radio signals

detectorist (dɪ'tɛktərɪst) *n informal* a person whose hobby is using a metal detector

detent (dɪ'tɛnt) *n* the locking piece of a mechanism, often spring-loaded to check the movement of a wheel in one direction only. See also **pawl** [c17 from Old French *destente*, a loosening, trigger: see DÉTENTE]

détente (deɪ'tɑːnt; French detɑ̃t) *n* the relaxing or easing of tension, esp between nations [French, literally: a loosening, from Old French *destendre* to release, from *tendre* to stretch]

detention (dɪ'tɛnʃən) *n* 1 the act of detaining or state of being detained 2 a custody or confinement, esp of a suspect awaiting trial b (as modifier): *a detention order* 3 a form of punishment in which a pupil is detained after school 4 the withholding of something belonging to or claimed by another [c16 from Latin *dētentiō* a keeping back; see DETAIN]

detention centre *n* a place where persons (typically asylum seekers, illegal immigrants, or people awaiting trial) may be detained for short periods by order of a court

deter (dɪ'tɜː) *vb* -ters, -terring, -terred (tr) to discourage (from acting) or prevent (from occurring), usually by instilling fear, doubt, or anxiety [c16 from Latin *dēterrēre*, from DE- + *terrēre* to frighten] > de'terment *n*

deterge (dɪ'tɜːdʒ) *vb* (tr) to wash or wipe away; cleanse: *to deterge a wound* [c17 from Latin *dētergēre* to wipe away, from DE- + *tergēre* to wipe]

detergency (dɪ'tɜːdʒənsɪ) or **detergence** *n* cleansing power

detergent (dɪ'tɜːdʒənt) *n* 1 a cleansing agent, esp a surface-active chemical such as an alkyl sulphonate, widely used in industry, laundering, shampoos, etc ▷ *adj* also **detersive** (dɪ'tɜːsɪv) 2 having cleansing power [c17 from Latin *dētergēns* wiping off; see DETERGE]

deteriorate (dɪ'tɪərɪəˌreɪt) *vb* 1 to make or become worse or lower in quality, value, character, etc; depreciate 2 (intr) to wear away or disintegrate

[c16 from Late Latin *dēteriōrāre*, from Latin *dēterior* worse] > deˌterio'ration *n* > de'teriorative *adj*

determinable (dɪ'tɜːmɪnəbəl) *adj* 1 able to be decided, fixed, or found out 2 *law* liable to termination under certain conditions; terminable > de'terminably *adv*

determinant (dɪ'tɜːmɪnənt) *adj* 1 serving to determine or affect ▷ *n* 2 a factor, circumstance, etc, that influences or determines 3 *maths* a square array of elements that represents the sum of certain products of these elements, used to solve simultaneous equations, in vector studies, etc. Compare **matrix** (sense 9)

determinate (dɪ'tɜːmɪnɪt) *adj* 1 definitely limited, defined, or fixed; distinct 2 a less common word for **determined** 3 a able to be predicted or deduced b (of an effect) obeying the law of causality 4 *botany* (of an inflorescence) having the main and branch stems ending in flowers and unable to grow further; cymose 5 (of a structure, stress, etc) able to be fully analysed or determined > de'terminately *adv* > de'terminateness *n*

determination (dɪˌtɜːmɪ'neɪʃən) *n* 1 the act or an instance of making a decision 2 the condition of being determined; resoluteness 3 the act or an instance of ending an argument by the opinion or decision of an authority 4 the act or an instance of fixing or settling the quality, limit, position, etc, of something 5 a decision or opinion reached, rendered, or settled upon 6 a resolute movement towards some object or end 7 *law* the termination of an estate or interest 8 *law* the decision reached by a court of justice on a disputed matter 9 *logic* a the process of qualifying or limiting a proposition or concept b the qualifications or limitations used in this process 10 the condition of embryonic tissues of being able to develop into only one particular tissue or organ in the adult

determinative (dɪ'tɜːmɪnətɪv) *adj* 1 able to or serving to settle or determine; deciding ▷ *n* 2 a factor, circumstance, etc, that settles or determines 3 *grammar* a less common word for **determiner** 4 (in a logographic writing system) a logogram that bears a separate meaning, from which compounds and inflected forms are built up > de'terminatively *adv* > de'terminativeness *n*

determine (dɪ'tɜːmɪn) *vb* 1 to settle or decide (an argument, question, etc) conclusively, as by referring to an authority 2 (tr) to ascertain or conclude, esp after observation or consideration 3 (tr) to shape or influence; give direction to: *experience often determines ability* 4 (tr) to fix in scope, extent, variety, etc: *the river determined the edge of the property* 5 to make or cause to make a decision: *he determined never to marry* 6 (tr) *logic* to define or limit (a notion) by adding or requiring certain features or characteristics 7 (tr) *geometry* to fix or specify the position, form, or configuration of: *two points determine a line* 8 *chiefly law* to come or bring to an end, as an estate or interest in land 9 (tr) to decide (a legal action or dispute) [c14 from Old French *determiner*, from Latin *dētermināre* to set boundaries to, from DE- + *termināre* to limit; see TERMINATE]

determined (dɪ'tɜːmɪnd) *adj* of unwavering mind; resolute; firm > de'terminedly *adv* > de'terminedness *n*

determiner (dɪ'tɜːmɪnə) *n* 1 a word, such as a number, article, personal pronoun, that determines (limits) the meaning of a noun phrase, eg *their* in 'their black cat' 2 a person or thing that determines

determinism (dɪ'tɜːmɪˌnɪzəm) *n* 1 the philosophical doctrine that all events including human actions and choices are fully determined by preceding events and states of affairs, and so that freedom of choice is illusory. Also called: necessitarianism Compare **free will** (sense 1b) 2 the scientific doctrine that all occurrences in nature take place in accordance with natural laws

3 the principle in classical mechanics that the values of dynamic variables of a system and of the forces acting on the system at a given time, completely determine the values of the variables at any later time > de'terminist *n, adj* > deˌtermin'istic *adj*

deterrent (dɪ'tɛrənt) *n* 1 something that deters 2 a weapon or combination of weapons, esp nuclear, held by one state, etc, to deter attack by another ▷ *adj* 3 tending or used to deter; restraining [c19 from Latin *dēterrēns* hindering; see DETER] > de'terrence *n*

detest (dɪ'tɛst) *vb* (tr) to dislike intensely; loathe [c16 from Latin *dētestārī* to curse (while invoking a god as witness), from DE- + *testārī* to bear witness, from *testis* a witness] > de'tester *n*

detestable (dɪ'tɛstəbəl) *adj* being or deserving to be abhorred or detested; abominable; odious > deˌtesta'bility or de'testableness *n* > de'testably *adv*

detestation (ˌdiːtɛs'teɪʃən) *n* 1 intense hatred; abhorrence 2 a person or thing that is detested

dethrone (dɪ'θrəʊn) *vb* (tr) to remove from a throne or deprive of any high position or title; depose: *the champion was dethroned by a young boxer* > de'thronement *n* > de'throner *n*

detinue ('dɛtɪˌnjuː) *n law* an action brought by a plaintiff to recover goods wrongfully detained [c15 from Old French *detenue*, from *detenir* to DETAIN]

Detmold ('dɛtməʊld; German 'dɛtmɔlt) *n* a city in NW Germany, in North Rhine-Westphalia. Pop: 73 880 (2003 est)

detonate ('dɛtəˌneɪt) *vb* to cause (a bomb, mine, etc) to explode or (of a bomb, mine, etc) to explode; set off or be set off [c18 from Latin *dētonāre* to thunder down, from DE- + *tonāre* to THUNDER]

detonation (ˌdɛtə'neɪʃən) *n* 1 an explosion or the act of exploding 2 the spontaneous combustion in an internal-combustion engine of part of the mixture before it has been reached by the flame front, causing the engine to knock 3 *physics* rapid combustion, esp that occurring within a shock wave > 'detoˌnative *adj*

detonator ('dɛtəˌneɪtə) *n* 1 a small amount of explosive, as in a percussion cap, used to initiate a larger explosion 2 a device, such as an electrical generator, used to set off an explosion from a distance 3 a substance or object that explodes or is capable of exploding

detour ('diːtʊə) *n* 1 a deviation from a direct, usually shorter route or course of action ▷ *vb* 2 to deviate or cause to deviate from a direct route or course of action [c18 from French *détour*, from Old French *destorner* to divert, turn away, from *des-* DE- + *torner* to TURN]

detox ('diːtɒks) *informal* ▷ *n* 1 treatment designed to rid the body of poisonous substances, esp alcohol and drugs ▷ *vb* 2 to undergo treatment to rid the body of poisonous substances, esp alcohol and drugs [c20 from (for sense 1) DETOXIFICATION or (for sense 2) DETOXICATE]

detoxicate (diː'tɒksɪˌkeɪt) *vb* (tr) 1 to rid (a patient) of a poison or its effects 2 to counteract (a poison) [c19 DE- + *-toxicate*, from Latin *toxicum* poison; see TOXIC] > de'toxicant *adj, n* > deˌtoxi'cation *n*

detoxification centre *n* a place that specializes in the treatment of alcoholism or drug addiction

detoxify (diː'tɒksɪˌfaɪ) *vb* -fies, -fying, -fied (tr) to remove poison from; detoxicate > deˌtoxifi'cation *n*

DETR (in Britain) *abbreviation for* Department of the Environment, Transport, and the Regions

detract (dɪ'trækt) *vb* 1 (when *intr*, usually foll by *from*) to take away a part (of); diminish: *her anger detracts from her beauty* 2 (tr) to distract or divert 3 (tr) *obsolete* to belittle or disparage [c15 from Latin *dētractus* drawn away, from *dētrahere* to pull away, disparage, from DE- + *trahere* to drag] > de'tractingly *adv* > de'tractive or de'tractory *adj* > de'tractively *adv* > de'tractor *n*

■ USAGE *Detract* is sometimes wrongly

used where *distract* is meant: *a noise distracted (not detracted) my attention*

detraction (dɪˈtrækʃən) *n* **1** a person, thing, circumstance, etc, that detracts **2** the act of discrediting or detracting from another's reputation, esp by slander; disparagement

detrain (diːˈtreɪn) *vb* to leave or cause to leave a railway train, as passengers, etc > **deˈtrainment** *n*

detribalize *or* **detribalise** (diːˈtraɪbəˌlaɪz) *vb* (*tr*) **1** to cause members of a tribe to lose their characteristic customs or social, religious, or other organizational features **2** to cause tribal people to adopt urban ways of life > deˌtribaliˈzation *or* deˌtribaliˈsation *n*

detriment (ˈdɛtrɪmənt) *n* **1** disadvantage or damage; harm; loss **2** a cause of disadvantage or damage [c15 from Latin *dētrīmentum*, a rubbing off, hence damage, from *dēterere* to rub away, from DE- + *terere* to rub]

detrimental (ˌdɛtrɪˈmɛntəl) *adj* (when *postpositive*, foll by *to*) harmful; injurious; prejudicial: *smoking can be detrimental to health* > ˌdetriˈmentally *adv*

detrition (dɪˈtrɪʃən) *n* the act of rubbing or wearing away by friction [c17 from Medieval Latin *dētrītiō*, from Latin *dētrītus* worn away; see DETRIMENT]

detritovore (dɪˈtraɪtəˌvɔː) *n ecology* any organism that feeds on detritus

detritus (dɪˈtraɪtəs) *n* **1** a loose mass of stones, silt, etc, worn away from rocks **2** an accumulation of disintegrated material or debris **3** the organic debris formed from the decay of organisms [c18 from French *détritus*, from Latin *dētrītus* a rubbing away; see DETRIMENT] > deˈtrital *adj*

Detroit (dɪˈtrɔɪt) *n* **1** a city in SE Michigan, on the Detroit River: a major Great Lakes port; largest car-manufacturing centre in the world. Pop: 911 402 (2003 est) **2** a river in central North America, flowing along the US-Canadian border from Lake St Clair to Lake Erie

de trop French (də trɔ) *adj* (*postpositive*) not wanted; in the way; superfluous [literally: of too much]

detrude (dɪˈtruːd) *vb* (*tr*) to force down or thrust away or out [c16 from Latin *dētrūdere* to push away, from DE- + *trūdere* to thrust] > **detrusion** (dɪˈtruːʒən) *n*

detruncate (diːˈtrʌŋkeɪt) *vb* (*tr*) another word for **truncate**. > ˌdetrunˈcation *n*

detumescence (ˌdiːtjʊˈmɛsəns) *n* the subsidence of a swelling, esp the return of a swollen organ, such as the penis, to the flaccid state [c17 from Latin *dētumescere* to cease swelling, from DE- + *tumescere*, from *tumēre* to swell]

Deucalion (djuːˈkeɪlɪən) *n* the son of Prometheus and, with his wife Pyrrha, the only survivor on earth of a flood sent by Zeus (**Deucalion's flood**). Together, they were allowed to repopulate the world by throwing stones over their shoulders, which became men and women

deuce¹ (djuːs) *n* **1 a** a playing card or dice with two pips or spots; two **b** a throw of two in dice **2** *tennis* a tied score (in tennis 40-all) that requires one player to gain two successive points to win the game [c15 from Old French *deus* two, from Latin *duos*, accusative masculine of *duo* two]

deuce² (djuːs) *informal* ▷ *interj* **1** an expression of annoyance or frustration ▷ *n* **2** the deuce (intensifier) used in such phrases as **what the deuce, where the deuce**, etc [c17 probably special use of DEUCE¹ (in the sense: lowest throw at dice)]

deuced (ˈdjuːsɪd, djuːst) *Brit informal* ▷ *adj* **1** (intensifier, usually qualifying something undesirable) damned; confounded: *he's a deuced idiot* ▷ *adv* **2** (intensifier): *deuced good luck* > ˈdeucedly *adv*

Deurne (Flemish ˈdɜːrnə) *n* a town in N Belgium, a suburb of E Antwerp: site of Antwerp airport. Pop: 68 308 (2002 est)

Deus (Latin ˈdeɪʊs) *n* God [related to Greek *Zeus*]

deus ex machina (Latin ˈdeɪʊs ɛks ˈmækɪnə) *n* **1** (in ancient Greek and Roman drama) a god

introduced into a play to resolve the plot **2** any unlikely or artificial device serving this purpose [literally: god out of a machine, translating Greek *theos ek mēkhanēs*]

Deut. *Bible abbreviation for* Deuteronomy

deuteragonist (ˌdjuːtəˈrægənɪst) *n* (in ancient Greek drama) the character next in importance to the protagonist, esp the antagonist [c19 from Greek *deuteragōnistēs*, from DEUTERO- + *agōnistēs* contestant, actor]

deuteranopia (ˌdjuːtərəˈnəʊpɪə) *n* a form of colour blindness in which there is a tendency to confuse blues and greens, and greens and reds, and in which sensitivity to green is reduced [c20 New Latin, from DEUTERO- (referring to the theory in which green is the second primary colour) + AN- + Greek *-ops* eye] > deuteranopic (ˌdjuːtərəˈnɒpɪk) *adj*

deuterate (ˈdjuːtəˌreɪt) *vb* to treat or combine with deuterium

deuteride (ˈdjuːtəˌraɪd) *n* a compound of deuterium with some other element. It is analogous to a hydride

deuterium (djuːˈtɪərɪəm) *n* a stable isotope of hydrogen, occurring in natural hydrogen (156 parts per million) and in heavy water: used as a tracer in chemistry and biology. Symbol: D or ²H; atomic no.: 1; atomic wt.: 2.014; boiling pt.: –249.7°C [c20 New Latin; see DEUTERO-, -IUM; from the fact that it is the second heaviest hydrogen isotope]

deuterium oxide *n* another name for **heavy water**

deutero-, deuto- *or before a vowel* **deuter-, deut-** *combining form* **1** second or secondary: *deuterogamy; deuterium* **2** (in chemistry) indicating the presence of deuterium [from Greek *deuteros* second]

deuterogamy (ˌdjuːtəˈrɒgəmɪ) *n* another word for **digamy**. > ˌdeuterˈogamist *n*

deuteron (ˈdjuːtəˌrɒn) *n* the nucleus of a deuterium atom, consisting of one proton and one neutron

Deuteronomist (ˌdjuːtəˈrɒnəmɪst) *n* one of the writers of Deuteronomy

Deuteronomy (ˌdjuːtəˈrɒnəmɪ) *n* the fifth book of the Old Testament, containing a second statement of the Mosaic Law [from Late Latin *Deuteronomium*, from Greek *Deuteronomion*; see DEUTERO-, -NOMY] > Deuteronomic (ˌdjuːtərəˈnɒmɪk) *adj*

deuterotoky (ˌdjuːtəˈrɒtəkɪ) *n biology* parthenogenesis in which both males and females are produced [from DEUTERO- + *-toky* from Greek *tokos* bringing forth]

deutoplasm (ˈdjuːtəˌplæzəm) *or* **deuteroplasm** (ˈdjuːtərəʊˌplæzəm) *n now rare* nutritive material in a cell, esp the yolk in a developing ovum > ˌdeutoˈplasmic *or* ˌdeutoˈplastic *adj*

Deutschland (ˈdɔɪtʃlant) *n* the German name for **Germany**

Deutschmark (ˈdɔɪtʃˌmɑːk) *or* **Deutsche Mark** (ˈdɔɪtʃə) *n* the former standard monetary unit of Germany, divided into 100 pfennigs; replaced by the euro in 2002: until 1990 the standard monetary unit of West Germany. Abbreviation: DM

deutzia (ˈdjuːtsɪə) *n* any saxifragaceous shrub of the genus *Deutzia*: cultivated for their clusters of white or pink spring-blooming flowers [c19 New Latin, named after Jean *Deutz*, 18th-century Dutch patron of botany]

Deux-Sèvres (French døsɛvrə) *n* a department of W France, in Poitou-Charentes region. Capital: Niort. Pop: 347 652 (2003 est). Area: 6054 sq km (2337 sq miles)

deva (ˈdeɪvə) *n* (in Hinduism and Buddhism) a divine being or god [c19 from Sanskrit: god]

devaluation (diːˌvæljuːˈeɪʃən) *n* **1** a decrease in the exchange value of a currency against gold or other currencies, brought about by a government. Compare **depreciation** (sense 4) **2** a reduction in value, status, importance, etc

devalue (diːˈvæljuː) *or* **devaluate** (diːˈvæljuːˌeɪt) *vb* -values, -valuing, -valued *or* -valuates, -valuating, -valuated **1** to reduce (a currency) or (of a currency) be reduced in exchange value **2** (*tr*) to reduce the value or worth of (something)

Devanagari (ˌdeɪvəˈnɑːgərɪ) *n* a syllabic script in which Sanskrit, Hindi, and other modern languages of India are written [c18 from Sanskrit: alphabet of the gods, from *deva* god + *nagarī* an Indian alphabet]

devastate (ˈdɛvəˌsteɪt) *vb* (*tr*) **1** to lay waste or make desolate; ravage; destroy **2** to confound or overwhelm, as with grief or shock [c17 from Latin *dēvastāre*, from DE- + *vastāre* to ravage; related to *vastus* waste, empty] > ˌdevasˈtation *n* > ˈdevasˌtative *adj* > ˈdevasˌtator *n*

devastating (ˈdɛvəˌsteɪtɪŋ) *adj* extremely effective in a destructive way: *a devastating war; a devastating report on urban deprivation* > ˈdevasˌtatingly *adv*

develop (dɪˈvɛləp) *vb* **1** to come or bring to a later or more advanced or expanded stage; grow or cause to grow gradually **2** (*tr*) to elaborate or work out in detail **3** to disclose or unfold (thoughts, a plot, etc) gradually or (of thoughts, etc) to be gradually disclosed or unfolded **4** to come or bring into existence; generate or be generated: *he developed a new faith in God* **5** (*intr*; often foll by *from*) to follow as a result (of); ensue (from): *a row developed following the chairman's remarks* **6** (*tr*) to contract (a disease or illness) **7** (*tr*) to improve the value or change the use of (land), as by building **8** (*tr*) to exploit or make available the natural resources of (a country or region) **9** (*tr*) *photog* **a** to treat (film, plate, or paper previously exposed to light, or the latent image in such material) with chemical solutions in order to produce a visible image **b** to process (photographic material) in order to produce negatives and prints **10** *biology* to progress or cause to progress from simple to complex stages in the growth of an individual or the evolution of a species **11** (*tr*) to elaborate upon (a musical theme) by varying the melody, key, etc **12** (*tr*) *maths* to expand (a function or expression) in the form of a series **13** (*tr*) *geometry* to project or roll out (a surface) onto a plane without stretching or shrinking any element **14** *chess* to bring (a piece) into play from its initial position on the back rank **15** (*tr*) *obsolete* to disclose or reveal [c19 from Old French *desveloper* to unwrap, from des- DIS-¹ + *veloper* to wrap; see ENVELOP] > deˈvelopable *adj*

developer (dɪˈvɛləpə) *n* **1** a person or thing that develops something, esp a person who develops property **2** *photog* a solution of a chemical reducing agent that converts the latent image recorded in the emulsion of a film or paper into a visible image

developing agent *n* another name for **developer** (sense 2)

developing country *n* a nonindustrialized poor country that is seeking to develop its resources by industrialization

developing world *n* another name for **Third World**

development (dɪˈvɛləpmənt) *n* **1** the act or process of growing, progressing, or developing **2** the product or result of developing **3** a fact, event, or happening, esp one that changes a situation **4** an area or tract of land that has been developed **5** Also called: development section the section of a movement, usually in sonata form, in which the basic musical themes are developed **6** *chess* **a** the process of developing pieces **b** the manner in which they are developed **c** the position of the pieces in the early part of a game with reference to their attacking potential or defensive efficiency > deˌvelopˈmental *adj* > deˌvelopˈmentally *adv*

developmental disorder *n psychiatry* any condition, such as autism or dyslexia, that appears in childhood and is characterized by delay in the development of one or more psychological functions, such as language skill

development area *n* (in Britain) an area suffering from high unemployment and economic depression, because of the decline of its main industries, that is given government help to establish new industries

development education *n* *Brit* an area of study that aims to give pupils an understanding of their involvement in world affairs

development system *n* a computer system, including hardware and software, that is specifically designed to aid in the development of software and interfaces

development well *n* (in the oil industry) a well drilled for the production of oil or gas from a field already proven by appraisal drilling to be suitable for exploitation

Deventer ('deɪvəntə; *Dutch* 'de:vəntər) *n* an industrial city in the E Netherlands, in Overijssel province, on the River IJssel: medieval intellectual centre; early centre of Dutch printing. Pop: 88 000 (2003 est)

devest (dɪ'vɛst) *vb* (*tr*) a rare variant spelling of **divest**

Devi ('deɪviː) *n* a Hindu goddess and embodiment of the female energy of Siva [Sanskrit: goddess; see DEVA]

deviance ('diːvɪəns) *n* 1 Also called: **deviancy** the act or state of being deviant 2 *statistics* a measure of the degree of fit of a statistical model compared to that of a more complete model

deviant ('diːvɪənt) *adj* 1 deviating, as from what is considered acceptable behaviour ▷ *n* 2 a person whose behaviour, esp sexual behaviour, deviates from what is considered to be acceptable

deviate *vb* ('diːvɪˌeɪt) 1 (*usually intr*) to differ or diverge or cause to differ or diverge, as in belief or thought 2 (*usually intr*) to turn aside or cause to turn aside; diverge or cause to diverge 3 (*intr*) *psychol* to depart from an accepted standard or convention ▷ *n, adj* ('diːvɪɪt) 4 another word for **deviant** [c17 from Late Latin *dēviāre* to turn aside from the direct road, from DE- + *via* road] > 'devi,ator *n* > 'deviatory *adj*

deviation (ˌdiːvɪ'eɪʃən) *n* 1 an act or result of deviating 2 *statistics* the difference between an observed value in a series of such values and their arithmetic mean 3 the error of a compass due to local magnetic disturbances

deviationism (ˌdiːvɪ'eɪʃəˌnɪzəm) *n* ideological deviation (esp from orthodox Communism) > ˌdevi'ationist *n, adj*

device (dɪ'vaɪs) *n* 1 a machine or tool used for a specific task; contrivance 2 *euphemistic* a bomb 3 a plan or plot, esp a clever or evil one; scheme; trick 4 any ornamental pattern or picture, as in embroidery 5 computer hardware that is designed for a specific function 6 a written, printed, or painted design or figure, used as a heraldic sign, emblem, trademark, etc 7 a particular pattern of words, figures of speech, etc, used in literature to produce an effect on the reader 8 *archaic* the act or process of planning or devising 9 **leave** (someone) **to his own devices** to leave (someone) alone to do as he wishes [c13 from Old French *devis* purpose, contrivance and *devise* difference, intention, from *deviser* to divide, control; see DEVISE]

devil ('dɛvᵊl) *n* 1 *theol* (*often capital*) the chief spirit of evil and enemy of God, often represented as the ruler of hell and often depicted as a human figure with horns, cloven hoofs, and tail 2 *theol* one of the subordinate evil spirits of traditional Jewish and Christian belief 3 a person or animal regarded as cruel, wicked, or ill-natured 4 a person or animal regarded as unfortunate or wretched: *that poor devil was ill for months* 5 a person or animal regarded as clever, daring, mischievous, or energetic 6 *informal* something difficult or annoying 7 *Christian Science* the opposite of truth; an error, lie, or false belief in sin, sickness, and death 8 (in Malaysia) a ghost 9 a portable

furnace or brazier, esp one used in road-making or one used by plumbers. Compare **salamander** (sense 7) 10 any of various mechanical devices, usually with teeth, such as a machine for making wooden screws or a rag-tearing machine 11 See **printer's devil** 12 *law* (in England) a junior barrister who does work for another in order to gain experience, usually for a half fee 13 *meteorol* a small whirlwind in arid areas that raises dust or sand in a column 14 **between the devil and the deep blue sea** between equally undesirable alternatives 15 **devil of** *informal* (intensifier): *a devil of a fine horse* 16 **give the devil his due** to acknowledge the talent or the success of an opponent or unpleasant person 17 **go to the devil a** to fail or become dissipated **b** (*interjection*) used to express annoyance with the person causing it 18 **like the devil** with great speed, determination, etc 19 **play the devil with** *informal* to make much worse; upset considerably: *the damp plays the devil with my rheumatism* 20 **raise the devil a** to cause a commotion **b** to make a great protest 21 **talk** (*or* **speak**) **of the devil!** (*interjection*) used when an absent person who has been the subject of conversation appears 22 **the devil!** (*intensifier:*) **a** used in such phrases as **what the devil, where the devil**, etc **b** an exclamation of anger, surprise, disgust, etc 23 **the devil's own** a very difficult or problematic (thing) 24 (**let**) **the devil take the hindmost** look after oneself and leave others to their fate 25 **the devil to pay** problems or trouble to be faced as a consequence of an action 26 **the very devil** something very difficult or awkward ▷ *vb* -ils, -illing, -illed *or US* -ils, -iling, -iled 27 (*tr*) to prepare (esp meat, poultry, or fish) by coating with a highly flavoured spiced paste or mixture of condiments before cooking 28 (*tr*) to tear (rags) with a devil 29 (*intr*) to serve as a printer's devil 30 (*intr*) *chiefly Brit* to do hackwork, esp for a lawyer or author; perform arduous tasks, often without pay or recognition of one's services 31 (*tr*) *US informal* to harass, vex, torment, etc [Old English *dēofol*, from Latin *diabolus*, from Greek *diabolos* enemy, accuser, slanderer, from *diaballein*, literally: to throw across, hence, to slander]

devilfish ('dɛvᵊl,fɪʃ) *n, pl* -fish *or* -fishes 1 Also called: **devil ray** another name for **manta** (the fish) 2 another name for **octopus**

devilish ('dɛvəlɪʃ, 'dɛvlɪʃ) *adj* 1 of, resembling, or befitting a devil; diabolic; fiendish ▷ *adv, adj* *informal* 2 (intensifier): *devilish good food; this devilish heat* > 'devilishly *adv* > 'devilishness *n*

devil-may-care *adj* careless or reckless; happy-go-lucky: *a devil-may-care attitude*

devilment ('dɛvᵊlmənt) *n* devilish or mischievous conduct

devilry ('dɛvᵊlrɪ) *or* **deviltry** *n, pl* -ries *or* -tries 1 reckless or malicious fun or mischief 2 wickedness or cruelty 3 black magic or other forms of diabolism [c18 from French *diablerie*, from *diable* DEVIL]

devil's advocate *n* 1 a person who advocates an opposing or unpopular view, often for the sake of argument 2 *RC Church* the official appointed to put the case against the beatification or canonization of a candidate. Technical name: **promotor fidei** (prəʊ'məʊtɔː fɪ'deɪiː) [translation of New Latin *advocātus diabolī*]

devil's bit *n* short for **devil's bit scabious** (see **scabious²** (sense 3))

devil's coach-horse *n* a large black rove beetle, *Ocypus olens*, with large jaws and ferocious habits

devil's darning needle *n* a popular name for a **dragonfly**

devil's food cake *n* *chiefly US and Canadian* a rich chocolate cake

Devil's Island *n* one of the three Safety Islands, off the coast of French Guiana: formerly a leper colony, then a French penal colony from 1895 until 1938. Area: less than 2 sq km (1 sq mile). French name: Île du Diable

devils-on-horseback *n* (*functioning as singular or*

plural) a savoury of prunes wrapped in bacon slices and served on toast

devious ('diːvɪəs) *adj* 1 not sincere or candid; deceitful; underhand 2 (of a route or course of action) rambling; indirect; roundabout 3 going astray from a proper or accepted way; erring [c16 from Latin *dēvius* lying to one side of the road, from DE- + *via* road] > 'deviously *adv* > 'deviousness *n*

devisable (dɪ'vaɪzəbᵊl) *adj* 1 *law* (of property, esp realty) capable of being transferred by will 2 able to be invented, contrived, or devised

devisal (dɪ'vaɪzᵊl) *n* the act of inventing, contriving, or devising; contrivance

devise (dɪ'vaɪz) *vb* 1 to work out, contrive, or plan (something) in one's mind 2 (*tr*) *law* to dispose of (property, esp real property) by will 3 (*tr*) *obsolete* to imagine or guess ▷ *n* *law* 4 **a** a disposition of property by will **b** the property so transmitted. Compare **bequeath** (sense 1) 5 a will or clause in a will disposing of real property. Compare **bequest** (sense 2) [c15 from Old French *deviser* to divide, apportion, intend, from Latin *dīvidere* to DIVIDE] > de'viser *n*

devisee (dɪvaɪ'ziː, ˌdɛvɪ-) *n* *property law* a person to whom property, esp realty, is devised by will. Compare **legatee**

devisor (dɪ'vaɪzə) *n* *property law* a person who devises property, esp realty, by will

devitalize *or* **devitalise** (diː'vaɪtᵊˌlaɪz) *vb* (*tr*) to lower or destroy the vitality of; make weak or lifeless: *the war devitalized the economy* > deˌvitali'zation *or* deˌvitali'sation *n*

devitrify (diː'vɪtrɪˌfaɪ) *vb* -fies, -fying, -fied 1 to change from a vitreous state to a crystalline state 2 to lose or cause to lose the properties of a glass and become brittle and opaque > deˌvitrifi'cation *n*

Devizes (də'vaɪzəz) *n* a market town in S England, in Wiltshire: agricultural and dairy products. Pop: 14 379 (2001)

devoice (diː'vɔɪs) *or* **devocalize, devocalise** (diː'vəʊkəˌlaɪz) *vb* (*tr*) *phonetics* to make (a voiced speech sound) voiceless

devoid (dɪ'vɔɪd) *adj* (*postpositive; foll by of*) destitute or void (of); free (from) [c15 originally past participle of *devoid* (*vb*) to remove, from Old French *devoidier*, from *de-* DE- + *voider* to VOID]

devoirs (də'vwɑː; *French* dəvwar) *pl n* (*sometimes singular*) compliments or respects; courteous attentions [c13 from Old French: duty, from *devoir* to be obliged to, owe, from Latin *dēbēre*; see DEBT]

devolution (ˌdiːvə'luːʃən) *n* 1 the act, fact, or result of devolving 2 a passing onwards or downwards from one stage to another 3 another word for **degeneration** (sense 3) 4 a transfer or allocation of authority, esp from a central government to regional governments or particular interests [c16 from Medieval Latin *dēvolūtiō* a rolling down, from Latin *dēvolvere* to roll down, sink into; see DEVOLVE] > ˌdevo'lutionary *adj* > ˌdevo'lutionist *n, adj*

devolve (dɪ'vɒlv) *vb* 1 (foll by *on, upon, to*, etc) to pass or cause to pass to a successor or substitute, as duties, power, etc 2 (*intr; foll by on or upon*) *law* (of an estate, etc) to pass to another by operation of law, esp on intestacy or bankruptcy 3 (*intr; foll by on or upon*) to depend (on): *your argument devolves on how you interpret this clause* 4 *archaic* to roll down or cause to roll down [c15 from Latin *dēvolvere* to roll down, fall into, from DE- + *volvere* to roll] > de'volvement *n*

devon ('dɛvən) *n* *Austral* a bland processed meat in sausage form, eaten cold in slices [named after DEVON]

Devon ('dɛvᵊn) *n* 1 Also called: **Devonshire** a county of SW England, between the Bristol Channel and the English Channel, including the island of Lundy. The geographic and ceremonial county includes Plymouth and Torbay, which became independent unitary authorities in 1998; hilly, rising to the uplands of Exmoor and Dartmoor, with wooded river valleys and a rugged coastline. Administrative centre: Exeter. Pop (excluding unitary authorities): 714 900 (2003 est). Area (excluding unitary authorities): 6569 sq km (2536 sq miles) **2** a breed of large red beef cattle originally from Devon

Devonian (də'vəʊnɪən) *adj* **1** of, denoting, or formed in the fourth period of the Palaeozoic era, between the Silurian and Carboniferous periods, lasting 60–70 million years during which amphibians first appeared **2** of or relating to Devon ▷ *n* **3** **the** the Devonian period or rock system

Devon minnow *n angling* a spinning lure intended to imitate the swimming motion of a minnow. Often shortened to: **Devon**

Devon Rex *n* a breed of medium-sized curly-haired cat with large eyes and very large ears

Devonshire cream *n* another name for **clotted cream**

Devonshire split *n* a kind of yeast bun split open and served with whipped cream or butter and jam. Also called: **Cornish split, split**

devoré (də'vɔːreɪ) *n* a velvet fabric with a raised pattern created by disintegrating some of the pile with chemicals [from French, past participle of *dévorer* to devour]

devote (dɪ'vəʊt) *vb* (*tr*) **1** to apply or dedicate (oneself, time, money, etc) to some pursuit, cause, etc **2** *obsolete* to curse or doom [c16 from Latin *dēvōtus* devoted, solemnly promised, from *dēvovēre* to vow; see DE-, vow] > de'votement *n*

devoted (dɪ'vəʊtɪd) *adj* **1** feeling or demonstrating loyalty or devotion; ardent; devout **2** (*postpositive; foll by to*) set apart, dedicated, or consecrated > de'votedly *adv* > de'votedness *n*

devotee (ˌdɛvə'tiː) *n* **1** a person ardently enthusiastic about or devoted to something, such as a sport or pastime **2** a zealous follower of a religion

devotion (dɪ'vəʊʃən) *n* **1** (*often foll by to*) strong attachment (to) or affection (for a cause, person, etc) marked by dedicated loyalty **2** religious zeal; piety **3** (*often plural*) religious observance or prayers

devotional (dɪ'vəʊʃənəl) *adj* **1** relating to, characterized by, or conducive to devotion ▷ *n* **2** (*often plural*) a short religious or prayer service > de,votion'ality *or* de'votionalness *n* > de'votionally *adv*

devour (dɪ'vaʊə) *vb* (*tr*) **1** to swallow or eat up greedily or voraciously **2** to waste or destroy; consume: *the flames devoured the curtains* **3** to consume greedily or avidly with the senses or mind: *he devoured the manuscripts* **4** to engulf or absorb: *the flood devoured the land* [c14 from Old French *devourer*, from Latin *dēvorāre* to gulp down, from DE- + *vorāre* to consume greedily; see VORACIOUS] > de'vourer *n* > de'vouring *adj* > de'vouringly *adv*

devout (dɪ'vaʊt) *adj* **1** deeply religious; reverent **2** sincere; earnest; heartfelt: *a devout confession* [c13 from Old French *devot*, from Late Latin *dēvōtus*, from Latin: faithful; see DEVOTE] > de'voutly *adv* > de'voutness *n*

dew (djuː) *n* **1 a** drops of water condensed on a cool surface, esp at night, from vapour in the air **b** (*in combination*): *dewdrop* **2** something like or suggestive of this, esp in freshness: *the dew of youth* **3** small drops of moisture, such as tears ▷ *vb* **4** (*tr*) *poetic* to moisten with or as with dew [Old English *dēaw*; related to Old High German *tou* dew, Old Norse *dögg*]

dewan *or* **diwan** (dɪ'waːn) *n* (formerly in India) the chief minister or finance minister of a state ruled by an Indian prince [c17 from Hindi *dīwān*, from Persian *dēvān* register, book of accounts; see DIVAN]

Dewar flask ('djuːə) *n* a type of vacuum flask, esp one used in scientific experiments to keep liquid air, helium, etc; Thermos [c20 named after Sir James Dewar (1842–1923), Scottish chemist and physicist]

dewberry ('djuːbərɪ, -brɪ) *n, pl* -ries **1** any trailing bramble, such as *Rubus hispidus* of North America and *R. caesius* of Europe and NW Asia, having blue-black fruits **2** the fruit of any such plant

dewclaw ('djuːˌklɔː) *n* **1** a nonfunctional claw in dogs; the rudimentary first digit **2** an analogous rudimentary hoof in deer, goats, etc > 'dew,clawed *adj*

dewdrop ('djuːˌdrɒp) *n* **1** a drop of dew **2** *Brit euphemistic* a drop of mucus on the end of one's nose

Dewey Decimal System ('djuːɪ) *n* a frequently used system of library book classification and arrangement with ten main subject classes. Also called: **decimal classification** Abbreviation: **DDS** [c19 named after Melvil *Dewey* (1851–1931), US educator who invented the system]

dewlap ('djuːˌlæp) *n* **1** a loose fold of skin hanging from beneath the throat in cattle, dogs, etc **2** loose skin on an elderly person's throat [c14 *dewlappe,* from DEW (probably changed by folk etymology from an earlier form of different meaning) + LAP¹ (from Old English *læppa* hanging flap), perhaps of Scandinavian origin; compare Danish *doglæp*] > 'dew,lapped *adj*

DEW line (djuː) *n acronym for* distant early warning line, a network of radar stations situated mainly in Arctic regions to give early warning of aircraft or missile attack on North America

dew point *n* the temperature at which water vapour in the air becomes saturated and water droplets begin to form

dew pond *n* a shallow pond that is kept supplied with water by dew and condensation

Dewsbury ('djuːzbərɪ, -brɪ) *n* a town in N England, in Kirklees unitary authority, West Yorkshire: formerly a centre of the woollen industry. Pop: 54 341 (2001)

dew snail *n Southwest English dialect* a slug

dew-worm *n* any large earthworm that is found on the ground at night and is used as fishing bait

dewy ('djuːɪ) *adj* dewier, dewiest **1** moist with or as with dew: *a dewy complexion* **2** of or resembling dew **3** *poetic* suggesting, falling, or refreshing like dew: *dewy sleep* > 'dewily *adv* > 'dewiness *n*

dewy-eyed *adj* naive, innocent, or trusting, esp in a romantic or childlike way

Dexedrine ('dɛksɪˌdriːn) *n* a trademark for **dextroamphetamine**

dexiotropic (ˌdɛksɪəʊ'trɒpɪk) *adj embryol* (of cleavage) spiral; twisting in a spiral fashion from left to right [c19 from Greek *dexios* right + -TROPIC]

dexter¹ ('dɛkstə) *adj* **1** *archaic* of or located on the right side **2** (*usually postpositive*) *heraldry* of, on, or starting from the right side of a shield from the bearer's point of view and therefore on the spectator's left ▷ Compare **sinister** [c16 from Latin; compare Greek *dexios* on the right hand]

dexter² ('dɛkstə) *n* a small breed of red or black beef cattle, originally from Ireland [c19 perhaps from the surname of the original breeder]

dexterity (dɛk'stɛrɪtɪ) *n* **1** physical, esp manual, skill or nimbleness **2** mental skill or adroitness; cleverness **3** *rare* the characteristic of being right-handed [c16 from Latin *dexteritās* aptness, readiness, prosperity; see DEXTER¹]

dexterous *or* **dextrous** ('dɛkstrəs) *adj* **1** possessing or done with dexterity **2** a rare word for **right-handed.** > 'dexterously *or* 'dextrously *adv* > 'dexterousness *or* 'dextrousness *n*

dextral ('dɛkstrəl) *adj* **1** of, relating to, or located on the right side, esp of the body; right-hand **2** of or relating to a person who prefers to use his right foot, hand, or eye; right-handed **3** (of the shells of certain gastropod molluscs) coiling in an anticlockwise direction from the apex; dextrorse ▷ Compare **sinistral.** > dextrality (dɛk'strælɪtɪ) *n* > 'dextrally *adv*

dextran ('dɛkstrən) *n biochem* a polysaccharide produced by the action of bacteria on sucrose: used as a substitute for plasma in blood transfusions [c19 from DEXTRO- + -AN]

dextrin ('dɛkstrɪn) *or* **dextrine** ('dɛkstrɪn, -triːn) *n* any of a group of sticky substances that are intermediate products in the conversion of starch to maltose: used as thickening agents in foods and as gums [c19 from French *dextrine*; see DEXTRO-, -IN]

dextro ('dɛkstrəʊ) *adj* short for **dextrorotatory**

dextro- *or before a vowel* **dextr-** *combining form* **1** on or towards the right: *dextrorotation* **2** (in chemistry) indicating a dextrorotatory compound: *dextroglucose* [from Latin, from *dexter* on the right side]

dextroamphetamine (ˌdɛkstrəʊæm'fɛtəˌmiːn, -mɪn) *n* a dextrorotatory amphetamine, used to suppress appetite

dextrocardia (ˌdɛkstrəʊ'kɑːdɪə) *n med* the abnormal location of the heart in the right side of the chest

dextroglucose (ˌdɛkstrəʊ'gluːkəʊz, -kəʊs) *n* another name for **dextrose**

dextrogyrate (ˌdɛkstrəʊ'dʒaɪrɪt, -ˌreɪt) *or* **dextrogyre** ('dɛkstrəʊˌdʒaɪə) *adj* having dextrorotation

dextrorotation (ˌdɛkstrəʊrəʊ'teɪʃən) *n* a rotation to the right; clockwise rotation, esp of the plane of polarization of plane-polarized light passing through a crystal, liquid, or solution, as seen by an observer facing the oncoming light. Compare **laevorotation.** > dextrorotatory (ˌdɛkstrəʊ'rəʊtətərɪ, -trɪ) *or* ,dextro'rotary *adj*

dextrorse ('dɛkstrɔːs, dɛk'strɔːs) *or* **dextrorsal** (dɛk'strɔːsəl) *adj* (of some climbing plants) growing upwards in a helix from left to right or anticlockwise. Compare **sinistrorse** [c19 from Latin *dextrorsum* towards the right, from DEXTRO- + *vorsus* turned, variant of *versus*, from *vertere* to turn] > 'dextrorsely *adv*

dextrose ('dɛkstrəʊz, -trəʊs) *n* a white soluble sweet-tasting crystalline solid that is the dextrorotatory isomer of glucose, occurring widely in fruit, honey, and in the blood and tissue of animals. Formula: $C_6H_{12}O_6$. Also called: grape sugar, dextroglucose

dextrous ('dɛkstrəs) *adj* a variant spelling of **dexterous.** > 'dextrously *adv* > 'dextrousness *n*

dey (deɪ) *n* **1** the title given to commanders or (from 1710) governors of the Janissaries of Algiers (1671–1830) **2** a title applied by Western writers to various other Ottoman governors, such as the bey of Tunis [c17 from French, from Turkish *dayi*, literally: maternal uncle, hence title given to an older person]

Dezhnev (*Russian* dɪʒ'njɒf) *n* **Cape** a cape in NE Russia at the E end of Chukchi Peninsula: the northeasternmost point of Asia. Former name: East Cape

DF *abbreviation for* **Defender of the Faith**

D/F *or* **DF** *telecomm abbreviation for* **1** direction finder **2** direction finding

DFC *abbreviation for* **Distinguished Flying Cross**

DfEE (in Britain) *abbreviation for* **Department for Education and Employment**

DFID (in Britain) *abbreviation for* **Department for International Development**

DFM *abbreviation for* **Distinguished Flying Medal**

dg *or* **dg.** *abbreviation for* **decigram**

DG *abbreviation for* **1** Deo gratias **2** director-general

DHA (in Britain) *abbreviation for* **District Health Authority**

Dhahran (dɑː'rɑːn) *n* a town in E Saudi Arabia: site of the original discovery of oil in the country (1938)

dhak (dɑːk, dɔːk) *n* a tropical Asian leguminous tree, *Butea frondosa,* that has bright red flowers and yields a red resin, used as an astringent [c19 from Hindi]

Dhaka *or* **Dacca** ('dækə) *n* the capital of Bangladesh, in the E central part: capital of Bengal (1608–39; 1660–1704) and of East Pakistan (1949–71); jute and cotton mills; university (1921). Pop: 12 560 000 (2005 est)

dhal, dal *or* **dholl** (dɑːl) *n* **1** a tropical African

d

and Asian leguminous shrub, *Cajanus cajan,* cultivated in tropical regions for its nutritious pealike seeds **2** the seed of this shrub ▷ Also called: **pigeon pea 3** a curry made from lentils or other pulses [C17 from Hindi *dāl* split pulse, from Sanskrit *dal* to split]

dhamma ('dɑːmə, 'dʌmə) *n Buddhism* a variant of **dharma** [from Pali, from Sanskrit: see DHARMA]

dhansak ('dænzæk) *n* any of a variety of Indian dishes consisting of meat or vegetables braised with water or stock and lentils [C20 from Urdu]

dharma ('dɑːmə) *n* **1** *Hinduism* social custom regarded as a religious and moral duty **2** *Hinduism* **a** the essential principle of the cosmos; natural law **b** conduct that conforms with this **3** *Buddhism* ideal truth as set forth in the teaching of Buddha [Sanskrit: habit, usage, law, from *dhārayati* he holds]

dharna *or* **dhurna** ('dʌnə, 'dɑː-) *n* (in India) a method of obtaining justice, as the payment of a debt, by sitting, fasting, at the door of the person from whom reparation is sought [C18 from Hindi, literally: a placing]

Dhaulagiri (ˌdaʊləˈgɪərɪ) *n* a mountain in W central Nepal, in the Himalayas. Height: 8172 m (26 810 ft)

DHB (in New Zealand) *abbreviation for* District Health Board

DHEA *abbreviation for* dehydroisoandrosterone: the major androgen precursor in females, secreted by the adrenal cortex

DHEAS *abbreviation for* dehydroisoandrosterone sulfate: a weak androgen produced by the adrenal cortex in both males and females

Dhílos ('ðiːlɒs) *n* transliteration of the Modern Greek name for **Delos**

dhobi ('dəʊbɪ) *n, pl* -bis (in India, Malaya, East Africa, etc, esp formerly) a washerman [C19 from Hindi, from *dhōb* washing; related to Sanskrit *dhāvaka* washerman]

dhobi itch *n* a fungal disease of the skin: a type of ringworm chiefly affecting the groin. Also called: **tinea cruris**

Dhodhekánisos (ðɔðɛˈkanisɔs) *n* a transliteration of the Modern Greek name for the **Dodecanese**

dhole (dəʊl) *n* a fierce canine mammal, *Cuon alpinus,* of the forests of central and SE Asia, having a reddish-brown coat and rounded ears: hunts in packs [C19 of uncertain origin]

dholl (dɑːl) *n* a variant spelling of **dhal**

dhoti ('dəʊtɪ), **dhooti, dhootie** *or* **dhuti** ('duːtɪ) *n, pl* -tis a long loincloth worn by men in India [C17 from Hindi]

dhow (daʊ) *n* a lateen-rigged coastal Arab sailing vessel with one or two masts [C19 from Arabic *dāwa*]

DHS (in Canada) *abbreviation for* district high school

DHSS (formerly, in Britain) *abbreviation for* Department of Health and Social Security

Di *the chemical symbol for* didymium

DI *abbreviation for* **1** Defence Intelligence **2** Detective Inspector **3** Donor Insemination

di-¹ *prefix* **1** twice; two; double: *dicotyledon* **2 a** containing two specified atoms or groups of atoms: *dimethyl ether; carbon dioxide* **b** a nontechnical equivalent of **bi-¹** (sense 5c) [via Latin from Greek, from *dis* twice, double, related to *duo* two. Compare BI-¹]

di-² *combining form* variant of **dia-** before a vowel: *diopter*

dia- *or* **di-** *prefix* **1** through, throughout, or during: *diachronic* **2** across: *diactinic* **3** apart: *diacritic* **4** (in botany) at right angles: *diatropism* **5** in opposite or different directions: *diamagnetism* [from Greek *dia* through, between, across, by]

diabase ('daɪəˌbeɪs) *n* **1** *Brit* an altered dolerite **2** *US* another name for **dolerite** [C19 from French, from Greek *diabasis* a crossing over, from *diabainein* to cross over, from DIA- + *bainein* to go] > ˌdiaˈbasic *adj*

diabetes (ˌdaɪəˈbiːtɪs, -tiːz) *n* any of various disorders, esp diabetes mellitus, characterized by excretion of an abnormally large amount of urine [C16 from Latin: siphon, from Greek, literally: a passing through (referring to the excessive urination), from *diabainein* to pass through, cross over; see DIABASE]

diabetes insipidus (ɪnˈsɪpɪdəs) *n* a disorder of the pituitary gland causing excessive thirst and excretion of large quantities of dilute urine [C18 New Latin, literally: insipid diabetes]

diabetes mellitus (məˈlaɪtəs) *n* a disorder of carbohydrate metabolism characterized by excessive thirst and excretion of abnormally large quantities of urine containing an excess of sugar, caused by a deficiency of insulin ▷ See also **IDDM, NIDDM** [C18 New Latin, literally: honey-sweet diabetes]

diabetic (ˌdaɪəˈbɛtɪk) *adj* **1** of, relating to, or having diabetes **2** for the use of diabetics: *diabetic chocolate* ▷ *n* **3** a person who has diabetes

diablerie (dɪˈɑːblərɪ; *French* djɑbləri) *n* **1** magic or witchcraft connected with devils **2** demonic lore or esoteric knowledge of devils **3** the domain of devils **4** devilry; mischief [C18 from Old French, from *diable* devil, from Latin *diabolus;* see DEVIL]

diabolic (ˌdaɪəˈbɒlɪk) *adj* **1** of, relating to, or proceeding from the devil; satanic **2** befitting a devil; extremely cruel or wicked; fiendish **3** very difficult or unpleasant [C14 from Late Latin *diabolicus,* from Greek *diabolikos,* from *diabolos* DEVIL] > ˌdiaˈbolically *adv* > ˌdiaˈbolicalness *n*

diabolical (ˌdaɪəˈbɒlɪkəl) *adj informal* **1** excruciatingly bad; outrageous **2** (intensifier): *a diabolical liberty* > ˌdiaˈbolically *adv* > ˌdiaˈbolicalness *n*

diabolism (daɪˈæbəˌlɪzəm) *n* **1 a** activities designed to enlist the aid of devils, esp in witchcraft or sorcery **b** worship of devils or beliefs and teachings concerning them **c** the nature of devils **2** character or conduct that is devilish or fiendish; devilry > diˈabolist *n*

diabolize *or* **diabolise** (daɪˈæbəˌlaɪz) *vb* (tr) **1 a** to make (someone or something) diabolical **b** to subject to the influence of devils **2** to portray as diabolical

diabolo (dɪˈæbələʊ) *n, pl* -los **1** a game in which one throws and catches a spinning top on a cord fastened to two sticks held in the hands **2** the top used in this game

diacaustic (ˌdaɪəˈkɔːstɪk, -kɒs-) *adj* **1** (of a caustic curve or surface) formed by refracted light rays ▷ *n* **2** a diacaustic curve or surface ▷ Compare **catacaustic**

diacetylmorphine (daɪˌæsɪtɪlˈmɔːfiːn) *n* another name for **heroin**

diachronic (ˌdaɪəˈkrɒnɪk) *adj* of, relating to, or studying the development of a phenomenon through time; historical: *diachronic linguistics.* Compare **synchronic** [C19 from DIA- + Greek *khronos* time]

diachronism (daɪˈækrəˌnɪzəm) *n geology* the passage of a geological formation across time planes, as occurs when a marine sediment laid down by an advancing sea is noticeably younger in the direction of advancement > diˈachronous *adj*

diacid (daɪˈæsɪd) *adj* **1** another word for **diacidic 2** (of a salt or acid) containing two acidic hydrogen atoms: NaH_2PO_4 *is a diacid salt of phosphoric acid* ▷ *n* **3** an acid or salt that contains two acidic hydrogen atoms

diacidic (ˌdaɪəˈsɪdɪk) *adj* (of a base, such as calcium hydroxide $Ca(OH)_2$) capable of neutralizing two protons with one of its molecules. Also: diacid. Compare **dibasic**

diaconal (daɪˈækənəl) *adj* of or associated with a deacon or the diaconate [C17 from Late Latin *diāconālis,* from *diāconus* DEACON]

diaconate (daɪˈækənɪt, -ˌneɪt) *n* the office, sacramental status, or period of office of a deacon [C17 from Late Latin *diāconātus;* see DEACON]

diacritic (ˌdaɪəˈkrɪtɪk) *n* **1** Also called: diacritical mark a sign placed above or below a character or letter to indicate that it has a different phonetic value, is stressed, or for some other reason ▷ *adj* **2** another word for **diacritical** [C17 from Greek *diakritikos* serving to distinguish, from *diakrinein,* from DIA- + *krinein* to separate]

diacritical (ˌdaɪəˈkrɪtɪkəl) *adj* **1** of or relating to a diacritic **2** showing up a distinction > ˌdiaˈcritically *adv*

diactinic (ˌdaɪækˈtɪnɪk) *adj physics* able to transmit photochemically active radiation > diˈactinism *n*

diadelphous (ˌdaɪəˈdɛlfəs) *adj* **1** (of stamens) having united filaments so that they are arranged in two groups **2** (of flowers) having diadelphous stamens [C19 from DI-¹ + Greek *adelphos* brother]

diadem ('daɪəˌdɛm) *n* **1** a royal crown, esp a light jewelled circlet **2** royal dignity or power ▷ *vb* **3** (tr) to adorn or crown with or as with a diadem [C13 from Latin *diadēma,* from Greek: fillet, royal headdress, from *diadein* to bind around, from DIA- + *dein* to bind]

diadem spider *n* a common Eurasian spider, *Araneus diadematus,* that constructs orb webs: family *Argiopidae*

Diadochi (daɪˈædəkaɪ) *pl n* the six Macedonian generals who, after the death of Alexander the Great, fought for control of his empire in the **Wars of the Diadochi** (321–281 BC) [Greek: successors]

diadochy (daɪˈædəkɪ) *n geology* the replacement of one element in a crystal by another [C20 from Greek *diadochē* succession]

diadromous (daɪˈædrəməs) *adj* **1** *botany* of or possessing a leaf venation in the shape of a fan **2** (of some fishes) migrating between fresh and salt water. See also **anadromous, catadromous**

diaeresis *or* **dieresis** (daɪˈɛrɪsɪs) *n, pl* -ses (-ˌsiːz) **1** the mark ¨, in writing placed over the second of two adjacent vowels to indicate that it is to be pronounced separately rather than forming a diphthong with the first, as in some spellings of *coöperate, naïve,* etc **2** this mark used for any other purpose, such as to indicate that a special pronunciation is appropriate to a particular vowel. Compare **umlaut 3** a pause in a line of verse occurring when the end of a foot coincides with the end of a word [C17 from Latin *diarēsis,* from Greek *diairesis* a division, from *diairein,* from DIA- + *hairein* to take; compare HERESY] > diaeretic *or* dieretic (ˌdaɪəˈrɛtɪk) *adj*

diag. *abbreviation for* diagram

diagenesis (ˌdaɪəˈdʒɛnɪsɪs) *n* **1** the sum of the physical, chemical, and biological changes that take place in sediments as they become consolidated into rocks, including compaction and cementation, but excluding weathering and metamorphic changes **2** *chem* recrystallization of a solid to form large crystal grains from smaller ones > diagenetic (ˌdaɪədʒəˈnɛtɪk) *adj*

diageotropism (ˌdaɪədʒɪˈɒtrəˌpɪzəm) *n* a diatropic response of plant parts, such as rhizomes, to the stimulus of gravity > diageotropic (ˌdaɪəˌdʒiːəʊˈtropɪk) *adj*

diagnose ('daɪəgˌnəʊz) *vb* **1** to determine or distinguish by diagnosis **2** (tr) to examine (a person or thing), as for a disease > ˌdiagˈnosable *adj*

diagnosis (ˌdaɪəgˈnəʊsɪs) *n, pl* -ses (-siːz) **1 a** the identification of diseases by the examination of symptoms and signs and by other investigations **b** an opinion or conclusion so reached **2 a** a thorough analysis of facts or problems in order to gain understanding and aid future planning **b** an opinion or conclusion reached through such analysis **3** a detailed description of an organism, esp a plant, for the purpose of classification [C17 New Latin, from Greek: a distinguishing, from *diagignōskein* to distinguish, from *gignōskein* to perceive, KNOW]

diagnostic (ˌdaɪəgˈnɒstɪk) *adj* **1** of, relating to, or of value in diagnosis ▷ *n* **2** *med* any symptom that provides evidence for making a specific

diagnosis 3 a diagnosis > ˌdiagˈnostically *adv*
diagnostician (ˌdaɪəgnɒsˈtɪʃən) *n* a specialist or expert in making diagnoses
diagnostics (ˌdaɪəgˈnɒstɪks) *n* (*functioning as singular*) the art or practice of diagnosis, esp of diseases
diagonal (daɪˈægənəl) *adj* **1** *maths* connecting any two vertices that in a polygon are not adjacent and in a polyhedron are not in the same face **2** slanting; oblique **3** marked with slanting lines or patterns ▷ *n* **4** *maths* a diagonal line or plane **5** *chess* any oblique row of squares of the same colour **6** cloth marked or woven with slanting lines or patterns **7** something put, set, or drawn obliquely **8** another name for **solidus** (sense 1) **9** one front leg and the hind leg on the opposite side of a horse, which are on the ground together when the horse is trotting [c16 from Latin *diagōnālis*, from Greek *diagōnios*, from DIA- + *gōnia* angle] > diˈagonally *adv*
diagonal process *n maths, logic* a form of argument in which a new member of a set is constructed from a list of its known members by making the *n*th term of the new member differ from the *n*th term of the *n*th member. The new member is thus different from every member of the list
diagram (ˈdaɪəˌgræm) *n* **1** a sketch, outline, or plan demonstrating the form or workings of something **2** *maths* a pictorial representation of a quantity or of a relationship: *a Venn diagram* ▷ *vb* -grams, -gramming, -grammed *or US* -grams, -graming, -gramed **3** to show in or as if in a diagram [c17 from Latin *diagramma*, from Greek, from *diagraphein*, from *graphein* to write] > diagrammatic (ˌdaɪəgrəˈmætɪk) *adj* > ˌdiagramˈmatically *adv*
diagraph (ˈdaɪəˌgrɑːf, -ˌgræf) *n* **1** a device for enlarging or reducing maps, plans, etc **2** a protractor and scale used in drawing [c19 from French *diagraphe*, from Greek *diagraphein* to represent with lines; see DIAGRAM]
diakinesis (ˌdaɪəkɪˈniːsɪs, -kaɪ-) *n* the final stage of the prophase of meiosis, during which homologous chromosomes start to separate after crossing over [c20 from DIA- + Greek *kinēsis* movement]
dial (ˈdaɪəl, daɪl) *n* **1** the face of a watch, clock, chronometer, sundial, etc, marked with divisions representing units of time **2** the circular graduated disc of various measuring instruments **3 a** the control on a radio or television set used to change the station or channel **b** the panel on a radio on which the frequency, wavelength, or station is indicated by means of a pointer **4** a numbered disc on a telephone that is rotated a set distance for each digit of a number being called **5** a miner's compass for surveying in a mine **6** *Brit* a slang word for **face** (sense 1) ▷ *vb* dials, dialling, dialled *or US* dials, dialing, dialed **7** to establish or try to establish a telephone connection with (a subscriber or his number) by operating the dial on a telephone **8** (*tr*) to indicate, measure, or operate with a dial [c14 from Medieval Latin *diālis* daily, from Latin *diēs* day] > ˈdialler *n*
dial. *abbreviation for* dialect(al)
dialect (ˈdaɪəˌlekt) *n* **a** a form of a language spoken in a particular geographical area or by members of a particular social class or occupational group, distinguished by its vocabulary, grammar, and pronunciation **b** a form of a language that is considered inferior: *the farmer spoke dialect and was despised by the merchants* **c** (*as modifier*): *a dialect word* [c16 from Latin *dialectus*, from Greek *dialektos* speech, dialect, discourse, from *dialegesthai* to converse, from *legein* to talk, speak] > ˌdiaˈlectal *adj*
dialect atlas *n* another term for **linguistic atlas**
dialect geography *n* another term for **linguistic geography.** > dialect geographer *n*
dialectic (ˌdaɪəˈlektɪk) *n* **1** disputation or debate, esp intended to resolve differences between two

views rather than to establish one of them as true **2** *philosophy* **a** the conversational Socratic method of argument **b** (in Plato) the highest study, that of the Forms **3** (in the writings of Kant) the exposure of the contradictions implicit in applying empirical concepts beyond the limits of experience **4** *philosophy* the process of reconciliation of contradiction either of beliefs or in historical processes. See also **Hegelian dialectic, dialectical materialism** ▷ *adj* **5** of or relating to logical disputation [c17 from Latin *dialectica*, from Greek *dialektikē* (*tekhnē*) (the art) of argument; see DIALECT] > dialecˈtician *n*
dialectical (ˌdaɪəˈlektɪkəl) *adj* of or relating to dialectic or dialectics > ˌdiaˈlectically *adv*
dialectical materialism *n* the economic, political, and philosophical system of Karl Marx (1818-83) and Friedrich Engels (1820–95), the German political philosophers, that combines traditional materialism and Hegelian dialectic > dialectical materialist *n*
dialectics (ˌdaɪəˈlektɪks) *n* (*functioning as plural or* (*sometimes*) *singular*) **1** the study of reasoning or of argumentative methodology **2** a particular methodology or system; a logic **3** the application of the Hegelian dialectic or the rationale of dialectical materialism
dialectology (ˌdaɪəlekˈtɒlədʒɪ) *n* the study of dialects and dialectal variations > dialectological (ˌdaɪəˌlektəˈlɒdʒɪkəl) *adj* > ˌdiaˌlectoˈlogically *adv* > ˌdialecˈtologist *n*
dial gauge *n* another name for an **indicator** (sense 6)
diallage (ˈdaɪəlɪdʒ) *n* a green or brownish-black variety of the mineral augite in the form of layers of platelike crystals [c19 from Greek *diallagē* interchange]
dialling code *n* a sequence of numbers which are dialled for connection with another exchange before an individual subscriber's telephone number is dialled
dialling tone *or US and Canadian* **dial tone** *n* a continuous sound, either purring or high-pitched, heard over a telephone indicating that a number can be dialled. Compare **ringing tone, engaged tone**
dialogism (daɪˈæləˌdʒɪzəm) *n* **1** *logic* a deduction with one premise and a disjunctive conclusion **2** *rhetoric* a discussion in an imaginary dialogue or discourse
dialogist (daɪˈælədʒɪst) *n* a person who writes or takes part in a dialogue > ˌdialoˈgistic *or* ˌdialoˈgistical *adj*
dialogize *or* **dialogise** (daɪˈæləˌdʒaɪz) *vb* (*intr*) to carry on a dialogue
dialogue *or often US* **dialog** (ˈdaɪəˌlɒg) *n* **1** conversation between two or more people **2** an exchange of opinions on a particular subject; discussion **3** the lines spoken by characters in drama or fiction **4** a particular passage of conversation in a literary or dramatic work **5** a literary composition in the form of a dialogue **6** a political discussion between representatives of two nations or groups **7** (*tr*) *rare* to put into the form of a dialogue **8** (*intr*) to take part in a dialogue; converse [c13 from Old French *dialoge*, from Latin *dialogus*, from Greek *dialogos*, from *dialegesthai* to converse; see DIALECT] > dialogic (ˌdaɪəˈlɒdʒɪk) *adj* > ˈdiaˌloguer *n*
dialogue *or* **dialog box** *n computing* a window that may appear on a VDU display to prompt the user to enter further information or select an option
dialyse *or US* **dialyze** (ˈdaɪəˌlaɪz) *vb* (*tr*) to separate by dialysis > ˈdiaˌlysable *or US* ˈdiaˌlyzable *adj* > ˌdiaˌlysaˈbility *or US* ˌdiaˌlyzaˈbility *n* > ˌdialyˈsation *or US* ˌdialyˈzation *n*
dialyser *or US* **dialyzer** (ˈdaɪəˌlaɪzə) *n* a machine that performs dialysis, esp one that removes impurities from the blood of patients with malfunctioning kidneys; kidney machine
dialysis (daɪˈælɪsɪs) *n, pl* -ses (-ˌsiːz) **1** the

separation of small molecules from large molecules and colloids in a solution by the selective diffusion of the small molecules through a semipermeable membrane **2** *med* See **haemodialysis, peritoneal dialysis** [c16 from Late Latin: a separation, from Greek *dialusis* a dissolution, from *dialuein* to tear apart, dissolve, from *luein* to loosen] > dialytic (ˌdaɪəˈlɪtɪk) *adj* > ˌdiaˈlytically *adv*
diam. *abbreviation for* diameter
diamagnet (ˈdaɪəˌmægnɪt) *n* a substance exhibiting diamagnetism
diamagnetic (ˌdaɪəmægˈnetɪk) *adj* of, exhibiting, or concerned with diamagnetism > ˌdiamagˈnetically *adv*
diamagnetism (ˌdaɪəˈmægnɪˌtɪzəm) *n* the phenomenon exhibited by substances that have a relative permeability less than unity and a negative susceptibility. It is caused by the orbital motion of electrons in the atoms of the material and is unaffected by temperature. Compare **ferromagnetism, paramagnetism**
diamanté (ˌdaɪəˈmæntɪ, -ˌdɪə-) *adj* **1** decorated with glittering ornaments, such as artificial jewels or sequins ▷ *n* **2** a fabric so covered [c20 from French, from *diamanter* to adorn with diamonds, from *diamant* DIAMOND]
diamantine (ˌdaɪəˈmæntaɪn) *adj* of or resembling diamonds [c17 from French *diamantin*, from *diamant* DIAMOND]
diameter (daɪˈæmɪtə) *n* **1 a** a straight line connecting the centre of a geometric figure, esp a circle or sphere, with two points on the perimeter or surface **b** the length of such a line **2** the thickness of something, esp with circular cross section [c14 from Medieval Latin *diametrus*, variant of Latin *diametros*, from Greek: diameter, diagonal, from DIA- + *metron* measure]
diametral (daɪˈæmɪtrəl) *adj* **1** located on or forming a diameter: *diametral plane* **2** a less common word for **diametric.** > diˈametrally *adv*
diametric (ˌdaɪəˈmetrɪk) *or* **diametrical** *adj* **1** Also: **diametral** of, related to, or along a diameter **2** completely opposed
diametrically (ˌdaɪəˈmetrɪkəlɪ) *adv* completely; utterly (esp in the phrase **diametrically opposed**)
diamine (ˈdaɪəˌmiːn, -mɪn, ˌdaɪəˈmiːn) *n* any chemical compound containing two amino groups in its molecules
diamond (ˈdaɪəmənd) *n* **1 a** a colourless exceptionally hard mineral (but often tinted yellow, orange, blue, brown, or black by impurities), found in certain igneous rocks (esp the kimberlites of South Africa). It is used as a gemstone, as an abrasive, and on the working edges of cutting tools. Composition: carbon. Formula: C. Crystal structure: cubic **b** (*as modifier*): *a diamond ring*. Related adj: **diamantine 2** *geometry* **a** a figure having four sides of equal length forming two acute angles and two obtuse angles; rhombus **b** (*modifier*) rhombic **3 a** a red lozenge-shaped symbol on a playing card **b** a card with one or more of these symbols or (*when plural*) the suit of cards so marked **4** *baseball* **a** the whole playing field **b** the square formed by the four bases **5** (formerly) a size of printer's type approximately equal to 4½ point **6** black diamond a figurative name for **coal 7** rough diamond **a** an unpolished diamond **b** a person of fine character who lacks refinement and polish ▷ *vb* **8** (*tr*) to decorate with or as with diamonds [c13 from Old French *diamant*, from Medieval Latin *diamas*, modification of Latin *adamas* the hardest iron or steel, diamond; see ADAMANT] > ˈdiamond-ˌlike *adj*
diamond anniversary *n* a 60th, or occasionally 75th, anniversary
diamondback (ˈdaɪəməndˌbæk) *n* **1** Also called: **diamondback terrapin** *or* **turtle** any edible North American terrapin of the genus *Malaclemys*, esp *M. terrapin*, occurring in brackish and tidal waters and having diamond-shaped markings on the shell: family *Emydidae* **2** a large North American

d

rattlesnake, *Crotalus adamanteus,* having cream-and-grey diamond-shaped markings

diamond bird *n* any small insectivorous Australian songbird of the genus *Pardalotus,* having a diamond-patterned plumage. Also called: pardalote

diamond jubilee *n* the celebration of a 60th, or occasionally 75th, anniversary

diamond point *n* a diamond-tipped engraving tool

diamond snake *n* a python, *Morelia argus,* of Australia and New Guinea, with yellow diamond-shaped markings

diamond wedding *n* the 60th, or occasionally the 75th, anniversary of a marriage

diamond willow *n* *Canadian* wood that may come from any species of willow and has a diamond pattern in the grain, used for making walking sticks, table lamps, etc

diamorphine (ˌdaɪəˈmɔːfiːn) *n* a technical name for **heroin**

Diana (daɪˈænə) *n* the virginal Roman goddess of the hunt and the moon. Greek counterpart: Artemis

diandrous (daɪˈændrəs) *adj* (of some flowers or flowering plants) having two stamens

dianoetic (ˌdaɪənəʊˈɛtɪk) *adj* of or relating to thought, esp to discursive reasoning rather than intuition. Compare **discursive** (sense 2) [c17 from Greek *dianoētikos,* from *dianoia* the thinking process, an opinion, from DIA- + *noein* to think]

dianoia (ˌdaɪəˈnɔɪə) *n* *philosophy* 1 perception and experience regarded as lower modes of knowledge. Compare **noesis** 2 the faculty of discursive reasoning [from Greek; see DIANOETIC]

dianthus (daɪˈænθəs) *n, pl* **-thuses** any Eurasian caryophyllaceous plant of the widely cultivated genus *Dianthus,* such as the carnation, pink, and sweet william [c19 New Latin, from Greek DI-¹ + *anthos* flower]

diapason (ˌdaɪəˈpeɪzᵊn, -ˈpeɪsᵊn) *n* *music* 1 either of two stops (**open** and **stopped diapason**) usually found throughout the compass of a pipe organ that give it its characteristic tone colour 2 the compass of an instrument or voice 3 (chiefly in French usage) a a standard pitch used for tuning, esp the now largely obsolete one of A above middle C = 435 hertz, known as **diapason normal** (French djapazɔ̃ nɔrmal) b a tuning fork or pitch pipe 4 (in classical Greece) an octave [c14 from Latin: the whole octave, from Greek: (hē) dia pasōn (khordōn sumphōnia) (concord) through all (the notes), from *dia* through + *pas* all] > dia'pasonal or diapasonic (ˌdaɪəpeɪˈzɒnɪk, -ˈsɒn-) *adj*

diapause (ˈdaɪəˌpɔːz) *n* a period of suspended development and growth accompanied by decreased metabolism in insects and some other animals. It is correlated with seasonal changes [c19 from Greek *diapausis* pause, from *diapauein* to pause, bring to an end, from DIA- + *pauein* to stop]

diapedesis (ˌdaɪəpəˈdiːsɪs) *n* the passage of blood cells through the unruptured wall of a blood vessel into the surrounding tissues [c17 New Latin, from Greek: a leaping through, from *diapēdan* to spring through, from DIA- + *pēdan* to leap] > diapedetic (ˌdaɪəpəˈdɛtɪk) *adj*

diapente (ˌdaɪəˈpɛntɪ) *n* *music* (in classical Greece) the interval of a perfect fifth [c14 from Latin, from Greek *dia pente khordōn sumphōnia* concord through five notes, from *dia* through + *pente* five]

diaper (ˈdaɪəpə) *n* 1 *US and Canadian* a piece of soft material, esp towelling or a disposable material, wrapped around a baby in order to absorb its excrement. Also called (in Britain and certain other countries): nappy 2 a a woven pattern on fabric consisting of a small repeating design, esp diamonds b fabric having such a pattern c such a pattern, used as decoration ▷ *vb* 3 (tr) to decorate with such a pattern [c14 from Old French *diaspre,* from Medieval Latin *diasprus* made of diaper, from Medieval Greek *diaspros* pure white, from DIA- + *aspros* white, shining]

diaphanous (daɪˈæfənəs) *adj* (usually of fabrics such as silk) fine and translucent [c17 from Medieval Latin *diaphanus,* from Greek *diaphanēs* transparent, from *diaphainein* to show through, from DIA- + *phainein* to show] > di'aphanously *adv* > di'aphanousness or diaphaneity (ˌdaɪəfəˈniːɪtɪ) *n*

diaphone (ˈdaɪəˌfəʊn) *n* 1 a the set of all realizations of a given phoneme in a language b one of any number of corresponding sounds in different dialects of a language 2 a foghorn that emits a two-toned signal [c20 from DIA(LECT) + PHONE²]

diaphony (daɪˈæfənɪ) *n* *music* 1 a style of two-part polyphonic singing; organum or a freer form resembling it 2 (in classical Greece) another word for **dissonance** (sense 3) Compare **symphony** (sense 5a) [c17 from Late Latin *diaphōnia,* from Greek, from *diaphōnos* discordant, from DIA- + *phōnē* sound] > diaphonic (ˌdaɪəˈfɒnɪk) *adj*

diaphoresis (ˌdaɪəfəˈriːsɪs) *n* 1 a technical name for **sweating** 2 perceptible and excessive sweating; sweat [c17 via Late Latin from Greek, from *diaphorein* to disperse by perspiration, from DIA- + *phorein* to carry, variant of *pherein*]

diaphoretic (ˌdaɪəfəˈrɛtɪk) *adj* 1 relating to or causing sweat ▷ *n* 2 a diaphoretic drug or agent

diaphototropism (ˌdaɪəfəʊtəʊˈtrəʊpɪzəm) *n* growth of a plant or plant part in a direction transverse to that of the light [c20 from Greek, from DIA- + PHOTOTROPIC] > diaphototropic (ˌdaɪəfəʊtəʊˈtrɒpɪk) *adj*

diaphragm (ˈdaɪəˌfræm) *n* 1 *anatomy* any separating membrane, esp the dome-shaped muscular partition that separates the abdominal and thoracic cavities in mammals. Related adj: **phrenic** 2 a circular rubber or plastic contraceptive membrane placed over the mouth of the uterine cervix before copulation to prevent entrance of sperm 3 any thin dividing membrane 4 Also called: **stop** a disc with a fixed or adjustable aperture to control the amount of light or other radiation entering an optical instrument, such as a camera 5 a thin disc that vibrates when receiving or producing sound waves, used to convert sound signals to electrical signals or vice versa in telephones, etc 6 *chem* a a porous plate or cylinder dividing an electrolytic cell, used to permit the passage of ions and prevent the mixing of products formed at the electrodes b a semipermeable membrane used to separate two solutions in osmosis 7 *botany* a transverse plate of cells that occurs in the stems of certain aquatic plants [c17 from Late Latin *diaphragma,* from Greek, from DIA- + *phragma* fence] > diaphragmatic (ˌdaɪəfræɡˈmætɪk) *adj* > ˌdiaphrag'matically *adv*

diaphysis (daɪˈæfɪsɪs) *n, pl* **-ses** (-ˌsiːz) the shaft of a long bone. Compare **epiphysis** [c19 New Latin, from Greek *diaphusis,* from *diaphuesthai* to grow between, from DIA- + *phuein* to produce] > diaphysial (ˌdaɪəˈfɪzɪəl) *adj*

diapir (ˈdaɪəˌpɪə) *n* *geology* an anticlinal fold in which the brittle overlying rock has been pierced by material, such as salt, from beneath [c20 from Greek *diapeirainein* to make holes through, pierce]

diapophysis (ˌdaɪəˈpɒfɪsɪs) *n, pl* **-ses** (-ˌsiːz) *anatomy* the upper or articular surface of a transverse vertebral process [c19 New Latin, from DI-² + APOPHYSIS] > diapophysial (ˌdaɪəˈfɪzɪəl) *adj*

diapositive (ˌdaɪəˈpɒzɪtɪv) *n* a positive transparency; slide

diarch (ˈdaɪɑːk) *adj* *botany* (of a vascular bundle) having two strands of xylem [c19 from Greek DI-¹ + *archē* beginning, origin]

diarchy or **dyarchy** (ˈdaɪɑːkɪ) *n, pl* **-chies** government by two states, individuals, etc > di'archic, di'archical, di'archal, dy'archic, dy'archical or dy'archal *adj*

diarist (ˈdaɪərɪst) *n* a person who keeps or writes a diary, esp one that is subsequently published

diarize or **diarise** (ˈdaɪəraɪz) *vb* to make use of a diary to record past events or those planned for the future

diarrhoea or *esp US* **diarrhea** (ˌdaɪəˈrɪə) *n* frequent and copious discharge of abnormally liquid faeces [c16 from Late Latin, from Greek *diarrhoia,* from *diarrhein* to flow through, from DIA- + *rhein* to flow] > ˌdiar'rhoeal, ˌdiar'rhoeic or *esp US* ˌdiar'rheal, ˌdiar'rheic *adj*

diarthrosis (ˌdaɪɑːˈθrəʊsɪs) *n, pl* **-ses** (-siːz) *anatomy* any freely movable joint, such as the shoulder and hip joints [c16 New Latin, from DI-² + Greek *arthrōsis,* from *arthroun* to fasten by a joint, from *arthron* joint] > ˌdiar'throdial *adj*

diary (ˈdaɪərɪ) *n, pl* **-ries** 1 a personal record of daily events, appointments, observations, etc 2 a book for keeping such a record [c16 from Latin *diārium* daily allocation of food or money, journal, from *diēs* day]

diascope (ˈdaɪəˌskəʊp) *n* an optical projector used to display transparencies

Diaspora (daɪˈæspərə) *n* 1 a the dispersion of the Jews after the Babylonian and Roman conquests of Palestine b the Jewish communities outside Israel c the Jews living outside Israel d the extent of Jewish settlement outside Israel 2 (in the New Testament) the body of Christians living outside Palestine 3 (*often not capital*) a dispersion or spreading, as of people originally belonging to one nation or having a common culture [c19 from Greek: a scattering, from *diaspeirein* to disperse, from DIA- + *speirein* to scatter, sow; see SPORE]

diaspore (ˈdaɪəˌspɔː) *n* 1 a white, yellowish, or grey mineral consisting of hydrated aluminium oxide in orthorhombic crystalline form, found in bauxite and corundum. Formula: $AlO(OH)$ 2 any propagative part of a plant, esp one that is easily dispersed, such as a spore [c19 from Greek *diaspora* a scattering, dispersion; see DIASPORA: so named from its dispersion and crackling when highly heated]

diastalsis (ˌdaɪəˈstælsɪs) *n, pl* **-ses** (-siːz) *physiol* a downward wave of contraction occurring in the intestine during digestion. See also **peristalsis** [c20 New Latin, from DIA- + (PERI)STALSIS] > ˌdia'staltic *adj*

diastase (ˈdaɪəˌsteɪs, -ˌsteɪz) *n* any of a group of enzymes that hydrolyse starch to maltose. They are present in germinated barley and in the pancreas. See also **amylase** [c19 from French, from Greek *diastasis* a separation; see DIASTASIS] > ˌdia'stasic *adj*

diastasis (daɪˈæstəsɪs) *n, pl* **-ses** (-ˌsiːz) 1 *pathol* a the separation of an epiphysis from the long bone to which it is normally attached without fracture of the bone b the separation of any two parts normally joined 2 *physiol* the last part of the diastolic phase of the heartbeat [c18 New Latin, from Greek: a separation, from *diistanai* to separate, from DIA- + *histanai* to place, make stand] > diastatic (ˌdaɪəˈstætɪk) *adj*

diastema (ˌdaɪəˈstiːmə) *n, pl* **-mata** (-mətə) 1 an abnormal space, fissure, or cleft in a bodily organ or part 2 a gap between the teeth [c19 New Latin, from Greek: gap, from *diistanai* to separate; see DIASTASIS]

diaster (daɪˈæstə) *n* *cytology now rare* the stage in cell division at which the chromosomes are in two groups at the poles of the spindle before forming daughter nuclei [c19 from DI-¹ + Greek *astēr* star] > di'astral *adj*

diastereoisomer (ˌdaɪəˌstɛrɪəʊˈaɪsəmə) *n* *chem* a type of isomer that differs in the spatial arrangement of atoms in the molecule, but is not a mirror image; a stereoisomer that is not an enantiomer

diastole (daɪˈæstəlɪ) *n* the dilatation of the chambers of the heart that follows each contraction, during which they refill with blood. Compare **systole** [c16 via Late Latin from Greek: an expansion, from *diastellein* to expand, from DIA- + *stellein* to place, bring together, make ready] > diastolic (ˌdaɪəˈstɒlɪk) *adj*

diastrophism (daɪˈæstrəˌfɪzəm) *n* the process of movement and deformation of the earth's crust that gives rise to large-scale features such as continents, ocean basins, and mountains. See also **orogeny, epeirogeny** [C19 from Greek *diastrophē* a twisting; see DIA-, STROPHE] > diastrophic (ˌdaɪə'strɒfɪk) *adj*

diastyle ('daɪəˌstaɪl) *architect* ▷ *adj* **1** having columns about three diameters apart ▷ *n* **2** a diastyle building [C16 via Latin from Greek *diastȳlos* having spaced pillars]

diatessaron (ˌdaɪə'tɛsəˌrɒn) *n* **1** *music* (in classical Greece) the interval of a perfect fourth **2** a conflation of the four Gospels into a single continuous narrative [C14 from Late Latin, from Greek *dia tessarōn khordōn sumphōnia* concord through four notes, from *dia* through + *tessares* four]

diathermancy (ˌdaɪə'θɜːmənsɪ) *n, pl* **-cies** the property of transmitting infrared radiation [C19 from French *diathermansie*, from DIA- + Greek *thermansis* heating, from *thermainein* to heat, from *thermos* hot] > ˌdia'thermanous *adj*

diathermic (ˌdaɪə'θɜːmɪk) *adj* **1** of or relating to diathermy **2** able to conduct heat; passing heat freely

diathermy ('daɪəˌθɜːmɪ) *or* **diathermia** (ˌdaɪə'θɜːmɪə) *n* local heating of the body tissues with an electric current for medical or surgical purposes [C20 from New Latin *diathermia*, from DIA- + Greek *thermē* heat]

diathesis (daɪ'æθɪsɪs) *n, pl* **-ses** (-ˌsiːz) a hereditary or acquired susceptibility of the body to one or more diseases [C17 New Latin, from Greek: propensity, from *diatithenai* to dispose, from DIA- + *tithenai* to place] > diathetic (ˌdaɪə'θɛtɪk) *adj*

diatom ('daɪətəm, -ˌtɒm) *n* any microscopic unicellular alga of the phylum *Bacillariophyta*, occurring in marine or fresh water singly or in colonies, each cell having a cell wall made of two halves and impregnated with silica. See also **diatomite** [C19 from New Latin *Diatoma* (genus name), from Greek *diatomos* cut in two, from *diatemnein* to cut through, from DIA- + *temnein* to cut]

diatomaceous (ˌdaɪətə'meɪʃəs) *adj* of, relating to, consisting of, or containing diatoms or their fossil remains

diatomaceous earth *n* an unconsolidated form of diatomite. Also called: **kieselguhr**

diatomic (ˌdaɪə'tɒmɪk) *adj* (of a compound or molecule) **a** containing two atoms **b** containing two characteristic groups or atoms: *ethylene glycol is a diatomic alcohol* > diatomicity (ˌdaɪətə'mɪsɪtɪ) *n*

diatomite (daɪ'ætəˌmaɪt) *n* a soft very fine-grained whitish rock consisting of the siliceous remains of diatoms deposited in the ocean or in ponds or lakes. It is used as an absorbent, filtering medium, insulator, filler, etc. See also **diatomaceous earth**

diatonic (ˌdaɪə'tɒnɪk) *adj* **1** of, relating to, or based upon any scale of five tones and two semitones produced by playing the white keys of a keyboard instrument, esp the natural major or minor scales forming the basis of the key system in Western music. Compare **chromatic** (sense 2) **2** not involving the sharpening or flattening of the notes of the major or minor scale nor the use of such notes as modified by accidentals [C16 from Late Latin *diatonicus*, from Greek *diatonikos*, from *diatonos* extending, from *diateinein* to stretch out, from DIA- + *teinein* to stretch] > ˌdia'tonically *adv* > diatonicism (ˌdaɪə'tɒnɪˌsɪzəm) *n*

diatribe ('daɪəˌtraɪb) *n* a bitter or violent criticism or attack; denunciation [C16 from Latin *diatriba* learned debate, from Greek *diatribē* discourse, pastime, from *diatribein* to while away, from DIA- + *tribein* to rub]

diatropism (daɪ'ætrəˌpɪzəm) *n* a response of plants or parts of plants to an external stimulus by growing at right angles to the direction of the stimulus > diatropic (ˌdaɪə'trɒpɪk) *adj*

diazepam (daɪ'æzəˌpæm) *n* a chemical compound used as a minor tranquillizer and muscle relaxant and to treat acute epilepsy. Formula: $C_{16}H_{13}ClN_2O$ [C20 from DI-¹ + AZO- + EP(OXIDE) + -*am*]

diazine ('daɪəˌziːn, daɪ'æziːn, -ɪn) *or* **diazin** ('daɪəzɪn, daɪ'æzɪn) *n* any organic compound whose molecules contain a hexagonal ring of four carbon atoms and two nitrogen atoms, esp any of three isomers with the formula $C_4N_2H_4$. See also **pyrimidine**

diazo (daɪ'eɪzəʊ) *adj* **1** of, consisting of, or containing the divalent group, =N:N, or the divalent group, -N:N-: *diazo compound*. See also **azo 2** Also: **dyeline** of or relating to the reproduction of documents using the bleaching action of ultraviolet radiation on diazonium salts ▷ *n, pl* **-os** *or* **-oes** a document produced by this method

diazole (daɪ'eɪzəʊl) *n* any organic compound whose molecules contain a pentagonal ring of three carbon atoms and two nitrogen atoms, esp imidazole (**1,3-diazole**) or pyrazole (**1,1-diazole**)

diazomethane (daɪˌeɪzəʊ'miːθeɪn) *n* a yellow odourless explosive gas, used as a methylating agent. Formula: $CH_2:N:N$

diazonium (ˌdaɪə'zəʊnɪəm) *n* (*modifier*) of, consisting of, or containing the group, Ar-N:N-, where Ar is an aryl group: *diazonium group or radical; a diazonium compound* [C19 DIAZO + (AMM)ONIUM]

diazonium salt *n* any of a class of compounds with the general formula $ArN:N^-M^+$, where Ar is an aryl group and M is a metal atom; made by the action of nitrous acid on aromatic amines and used in dyeing

diazotize *or* **diazotise** (daɪ'eɪzəˌtaɪz) *vb* (*tr*) to cause (an aryl amine) to react with nitrous acid to produce a diazonium salt > diˌazoti'zation *or* diˌazoti'sation *n*

dib (dɪb) *vb* **dibs, dibbing, dibbed** (*intr*) to fish by allowing the bait to bob and dip on the surface [C17 perhaps alteration of DAB¹]

dibasic (daɪ'beɪsɪk) *adj* **1** (of an acid, such as sulphuric acid, H_2SO_4) containing two acidic hydrogen atoms. Compare **diacidic 2** (of a salt) derived by replacing two acidic hydrogen atoms: *dibasic sodium phosphate*, Na_2HPO_4 > dibasicity (ˌdaɪbeɪ'sɪsɪtɪ) *n*

dibble¹ ('dɪbᵊl) *n* **1** Also called (esp Brit): **dibber** ('dɪbə) a small hand tool used to make holes in the ground for planting or transplanting bulbs, seeds, or roots ▷ *vb* **2** to make a hole in (the ground) with a dibble **3** to plant (bulbs, seeds, etc) with a dibble [C15 of obscure origin] > 'dibbler *n*

dibble² ('dɪbᵊl) *vb* (*intr*) **1** a variant of **dib 2** a less common word for **dabble**

dibble³ ('dɪbᵊl) *n Brit slang* a policeman [C20 allusion to the police officer of that name in the childrens' animated cartoon *Top Cat*]

dibbuk ('dɪbək; *Hebrew* di'buk) *n, pl* **-buks** *or* **-bukkim** (*Hebrew* -bu'kim) a variant spelling of **dybbuk**

dibranchiate (daɪ'bræŋkɪɪt, -ˌeɪt) *adj* **1** of, relating to, or belonging to the *Dibranchiata*, a group or former order of cephalopod molluscs, including the octopuses, squids, and cuttlefish, having two gills ▷ *n* **2** any dibranchiate mollusc

dibromide (daɪ'brəʊmaɪd) *n* a chemical compound that contains two bromine atoms per molecule

dibs (dɪbz) *pl n* **1** another word for **jacks 2** a slang word for **money 3** (foll by *on*) *informal* rights (to) or claims (on): used mainly by children [C18 shortened from *dibstones* children's game played with knucklebones or pebbles, probably from *dib* to tap, dip, variant of DAB¹]

dicarboxylic acid (daɪˌkɑːbɒk'sɪlɪk) *n* any carboxylic acid that contains two carboxyl groups per molecule

dicast ('dɪkæst) *n* (in ancient Athens) a juror in the popular courts chosen by lot from a list of citizens [C19 from Greek *dikastēs*, from *dikazein* to judge, from *dikē* right, judgment, order] > di'castic *adj*

dicastery (dɪ'kæstərɪ) *n, pl* **-ries** *RC Church* another word for **congregation** (sense 5b) [C19 from DICAST]

dice (daɪs) *pl n* **1** cubes of wood, plastic, etc, each of whose sides has a different number of spots (1 to 6), used in games of chance and in gambling to give random numbers **2** (*functioning as singular*) Also called: **die** one of these cubes **3** small cubes as of vegetables, chopped meat, etc **4** **no dice** *slang, chiefly US and Canadian* an expression of refusal or rejection ▷ *vb* **5** to cut (food, etc) into small cubes **6** (*intr*) to gamble or play at a game involving dice **7** (*intr*) to take a chance or risk (esp in the phrase **dice with death**) **8** (*tr*) *Austral informal* to abandon or reject **9** (*tr*) to decorate or mark with dicelike shapes [C14 plural of DIE²] > 'dicer *n*

dicentra (daɪ'sɛntrə) *n* any Asian or North American plant of the genus *Dicentra*, such as bleeding heart and Dutchman's-breeches, having finely divided leaves and ornamental clusters of drooping flowers: family *Fumariaceae* [C19 New Latin, from Greek *dikentros* having two sharp points, from DI-¹ + *kentron* sharp point, from *kentein* to prick; see CENTRE]

dicephalous (daɪ'sɛfələs) *adj* having two heads > di'cephalism *n*

dicey ('daɪsɪ) *adj* **dicier, diciest** *informal, chiefly Brit* difficult or dangerous; risky; tricky

dichasium (daɪ'keɪzɪəm) *n, pl* **-sia** (-zɪə) a cymose inflorescence in which each branch bearing a flower gives rise to two other flowering branches, as in the stitchwort. Compare **monochasium** [C19 New Latin, from Greek *dikhasis* a dividing, from *dikhazein* to divide in two, from *dikha* in two] > di'chasial *adj* > di'chasially *adv*

dichlamydeous (ˌdaɪklə'mɪdɪəs) *adj* (of a flower) having a corolla and calyx [C19 from Greek, from DI-¹ + *khlamus* a cloak + -EOUS]

dichloride (daɪ'klɔːraɪd) *n* a compound in which two atoms of chlorine are combined with another atom or group. Also called: **bichloride**

dichlorodifluoromethane (daɪˌklɔːrəʊdaɪˌflʊərəʊ'miːθeɪn) *n* a colourless nonflammable gas easily liquefied by pressure: used as a propellant in aerosols and fire extinguishers and as a refrigerant. Formula: CCl_2F_2. See also **Freon**

dichlorodiphenyltrichloroethane (daɪˌklɔːrəʊdaɪˌfiːnaɪltraɪˌklɔːrəʊ'iːθeɪn, -nɪl-, -ˌfɛn-) *n* the full name for **DDT**

dichloromethane (daɪˌklɔːrəʊ'miːθeɪn) *n* a noxious colourless liquid widely used as a solvent, eg in paint strippers. Formula: CH_2Cl_2. Traditional name: **methylene dichloride**

dicho- *or before a vowel* **dich-** *combining form* in two parts; in pairs: *dichotomy* [from Greek *dikho-*, from *dikha* in two]

dichogamy (daɪ'kɒgəmɪ) *n* the maturation of male and female parts of a flower at different times, preventing automatic self-pollination. Compare **homogamy** (sense 2) > di'chogamous *or* dichogamic (ˌdaɪkəʊ'gæmɪk) *adj*

dichoptic (daɪ'kɒptɪk) *adj zoology* having the eyes distinctly separate

dichotic (daɪ'kɒtɪk) *adj* relating to or involving the stimulation of each ear simultaneously by different sounds [DICHO- + -IC]

dichotomize *or* **dichotomise** (daɪ'kɒtəˌmaɪz) *vb* to divide or become divided into two parts or classifications > di'chotomist *n* > diˌchotomi'zation *or* diˌchotomi'sation *n*

dichotomous key *n* a key used to identify a plant or animal in which each stage presents descriptions of two distinguishing characters, with a direction to another stage in the key, until the species is identified

dichotomous question *n* a question to which there can only be one of two answers, often "yes" or "no"

dichotomy (daɪ'kɒtəmɪ) *n, pl* **-mies 1** division into two parts or classifications, esp when they are sharply distinguished or opposed: *the dichotomy between eastern and western cultures* **2** *logic* the division of a class into two mutually exclusive

d

subclasses: *the dichotomy of married and single people* **3** *botany* a simple method of branching by repeated division into two equal parts **4** the phase of the moon, Venus, or Mercury when half of the disc is visible [C17 from Greek *dichotomia*; see DICHO-, -TOMY] > di'chotomous *or* dichotomic (ˌdaɪkəʊ'tɒmɪk) *adj* > di'chotomously *adv*

> USAGE *Dichotomy* should always refer to a division of some kind into two groups. It is sometimes used to refer to a puzzling situation which seems to involve a contradiction, but this use is generally thought to be incorrect

dichroic (daɪ'krəʊɪk) *or* **dichroitic** (ˌdaɪkrəʊ'ɪtɪk) *adj* **1** (of a solution or uniaxial crystal) exhibiting dichroism **2** another word for **dichromatic** [C19 from Greek *dikhroos* having two colours, from DI¹ + *khrōs* colour]

dichroic filter *n* an optical colour filter operating on the principle of wave interference between closely spaced reflecting surfaces, rather than by colour absorption

dichroism ('daɪkrəʊˌɪzəm) *n* **1** Also called: **dichromaticism** a property of a uniaxial crystal, such as tourmaline, of showing a perceptible difference in colour when viewed along two different axes in transmitted white light. See also **pleochroism 2** a property of certain solutions as a result of which the wavelength (colour) of the light transmitted depends on the concentration of the solution and the length of the path of the light within the solution

dichroite ('daɪkrəʊˌaɪt) *n* another name for **cordierite** [C19 from Greek *dikhroos* two-coloured + -ITE¹]

dichromate (daɪ'krəʊmeɪt) *n* any salt or ester of dichromic acid. Dichromate salts contain the ion $Cr_2O_7^{2-}$. Also called: **bichromate**

dichromatic (ˌdaɪkrəʊ'mætɪk) *adj* **1** Also: **dichroic** having or consisting of only two colours **2** (of animal species) having two different colour varieties that are independent of sex and age **3** able to perceive only two (instead of three) primary colours and the mixes of these colours > **dichromatism** (daɪ'krəʊməˌtɪzəm) *n*

dichromaticism (ˌdaɪkrəʊ'mætɪˌsɪzəm) *n* another name for **dichroism** (sense 1)

dichromic (daɪ'krəʊmɪk) *adj* of or involving only two colours; dichromatic

dichromic acid *n* an unstable dibasic oxidizing acid known only in solution and in the form of dichromate salts. Formula: $H_2Cr_2O_7$

dichroscope ('daɪkrəˌskəʊp) *n* an instrument for investigating the dichroism of solutions or crystals. Also called: dichroiscope, dichrooscope [C19 from Greek *dikhroos* two-coloured + -SCOPE] > dichroscopic (ˌdaɪkrə'skɒpɪk), ˌdichroi'scopic *or* ˌdichroo'scopic *adj*

dick¹ (dɪk) *n chiefly US* a slang word for **detective** [C20 by shortening and alteration from DETECTIVE; probably influenced by proper name *Dick*]

dick² (dɪk) *n slang* **1** *Brit* a fellow or person **2 clever dick** *Brit* a person who is obnoxiously opinionated or self-satisfied; know-all **3** a slang word for **penis** [C16 (meaning: fellow): from the name *Dick*, familiar form of *Richard*, applied generally (like *Jack*) to any fellow, lad, etc; hence, C19 penis]

> USAGE The third sense of this word was formerly considered to be taboo and it was labelled as such in previous editions of *Collins English Dictionary*. However, it has now become acceptable in speech, although some older or more conservative people may object to its use

dickens ('dɪkɪnz) *n informal* a euphemistic word for **devil** (used as intensifier in the interrogative phrase **what the dickens**) [C16 from the name *Dickens*]

Dickensian (dɪ'kɛnzɪən) *adj* **1** of Charles Dickens (1812–70), the English novelist, or his works **2** resembling or suggestive of conditions described in Dickens' novels, esp **a** squalid and poverty-stricken: *working conditions were truly Dickensian* **b** characterized by jollity and conviviality: *a Dickensian scene round the Christmas tree* **3** grotesquely comic, as some of the characters of Dickens

dicker ('dɪkə) *vb* **1** to trade (goods) by bargaining; barter **2** (*intr*) to negotiate a political deal ▷ *n* **3 a** a petty bargain or barter **b** the item or items bargained or bartered **4** a political deal or bargain [C12 ultimately from Latin *decuria* DECURY; related to Middle Low German *dēker* lot of ten hides]

dickhead ('dɪkˌhɛd) *n slang* a stupid or despicable man or boy [C20 from DICK² (in the sense: penis) + HEAD]

Dick test (dɪk) *n* a skin test for determining whether a person is immune or susceptible to scarlet fever [C20 named after George F. *Dick* (1881–1967), US physician who devised it]

dicky¹ *or* **dickey** ('dɪkɪ) *n, pl* dickies *or* dickeys **1** a woman's false blouse front, worn to fill in the neck of a jacket or low-cut dress **2** a man's false shirt front, esp one worn with full evening dress **3** Also called: **dicky bow** *Brit* a bow tie **4** *chiefly Brit* an informal name for **donkey**, esp a male one **5** Also called: dickybird, dickeybird a child's word for a **bird**, esp a small one **6** a folding outside seat at the rear of some early cars. US and Canadian name: **rumble seat 7** *Indian* an enclosed compartment of a car for holding luggage, etc, usually at the rear. Also called: **boot** [C18 (in the senses: donkey, shirt front): from *Dickey*, diminutive of *Dick* (name); the relationship of the various senses is obscure]

dicky² *or* **dickey** ('dɪkɪ) *adj* dickier, dickiest *Brit informal* in bad condition; shaky, unsteady, or unreliable: *I feel a bit dicky today* [C18 perhaps from the name *Dick* in the phrase *as queer as Dick's hatband* feeling ill]

dickybird *or* **dickeybird** ('dɪkɪˌbɜːd) *n* **1** See **dicky¹** (sense 5) **2 not a dickybird** *informal* not a word; nothing: *I haven't heard a dickybird from them*

diclinous ('daɪklɪnəs, daɪ'klaɪ-) *adj* **1** (of flowering plants) bearing unisexual flowers **2** (of flowers) unisexual. Compare **monoclinous**. > 'diclinism *n* > dicliny ('daɪklɪnɪ, daɪ'klaɪ-) *n*

Diconal ('daɪkənæl) *n trademark* a brand of dipanone, an opiate drug with potent analgesic properties: used to relieve severe pain

dicotyledon (ˌdaɪˌkɒtɪ'liːdᵊn, ˌdaɪkɒt-) *n* **1** any flowering plant of the class *Dicotyledonae*, normally having two embryonic seed leaves and leaves with netlike veins. The group includes many herbaceous plants and most families of trees and shrubs **2** primitive dicotyledon. any living relative of early angiosperms that branched off before the evolution of monocotyledons and eudicotyledons. The group comprises about 5 per cent of the world's plants. Often shortened to: dicot Compare **monocotyledon** > ˌdicoty'ledonous *adj*

dicrotic (daɪ'krɒtɪk) *or* **dicrotal** ('daɪkrətᵊl) *adj physiol* having or relating to a double pulse for each heartbeat [C19 from Greek *dikrotos* double-beating, from DI-¹ + *krotein* to beat] > dicrotism ('daɪkrəˌtɪzəm) *n*

dicta ('dɪktə) *n* a plural of **dictum**

Dictaphone ('dɪktəˌfəʊn) *n trademark* a tape recorder designed for recording dictation and later reproducing it for typing

dictate *vb* (dɪk'teɪt) **1** to say (messages, letters, speeches, etc) aloud for mechanical recording or verbatim transcription by another person **2** (*tr*) to prescribe (commands) authoritatively **3** (*intr*) to act in a tyrannical manner; seek to impose one's will on others ▷ *n* ('dɪkteɪt) **4** an authoritative command **5** a guiding principle or rule: *the dictates of reason* [C17 from Latin *dictāre* to say repeatedly, order, from *dīcere* to say]

dictation (dɪk'teɪʃən) *n* **1** the act of dictating material to be recorded or taken down in writing **2** the material dictated **3** authoritative commands or the act of giving them > dic'tational *adj*

dictator (dɪk'teɪtə) *n* **1 a** a ruler who is not effectively restricted by a constitution, laws, recognized opposition, etc **b** an absolute, esp tyrannical, ruler **2** (in ancient Rome) a person appointed during a crisis to exercise supreme authority **3** a person who makes pronouncements, as on conduct, fashion, etc, which are regarded as authoritative **4** a person who behaves in an authoritarian or tyrannical manner > dictatress (dɪk'teɪtrɪs) *or* dictatrix ('dɪktətrɪks) *fem n*

dictatorial (ˌdɪktə'tɔːrɪəl) *adj* **1** of or characteristic of a dictator **2** tending to dictate; tyrannical; overbearing > ˌdicta'torially *adv* > ˌdicta'torialness *n*

dictatorship (dɪk'teɪtəˌʃɪp) *n* **1** the rank, office, or period of rule of a dictator **2** government by a dictator or dictators **3** a country ruled by a dictator or dictators **4** absolute or supreme power or authority

diction ('dɪkʃən) *n* **1** the choice and use of words in writing or speech **2** the manner of uttering or enunciating words and sounds; elocution [C15 from Latin *dictiō* a saying, mode of expression, from *dīcere* to speak, say]

dictionary ('dɪkʃənərɪ, -ʃənrɪ) *n, pl* -aries **1 a** a reference book that consists of an alphabetical list of words with their meanings and parts of speech, and often a guide to accepted pronunciation and syllabification, irregular inflections of words, derived words of different parts of speech, and etymologies **b** a similar reference book giving equivalent words in two or more languages. Such dictionaries often consist of two or more parts, in each of which the alphabetical list is given in a different language: *a German-English dictionary* **c** (*as modifier*): *a dictionary definition*. See also **glossary, lexicon, thesaurus 2** a reference book listing words or terms of a particular subject or activity, giving information about their meanings and other attributes: *a dictionary of gardening* **3** a collection of information or examples with the entries alphabetically arranged: *a dictionary of quotations* [C16 from Medieval Latin *dictiōnārium* collection of words, from Late Latin *dictiō* word; see DICTION]

dictionary attack *n* an attempt to hack into a computer or network by submitting every word in a dictionary as a possible password

dictionary catalogue *n* a catalogue of the authors, titles and subjects of books in one alphabetical sequence

Dictograph ('dɪktəˌɡrɑːf, -ˌɡræf) *n trademark* a telephonic instrument for secretly monitoring or recording conversations by means of a small, sensitive, and often concealed microphone

dictum ('dɪktəm) *n, pl* -tums *or* -ta (-tə) **1** a formal or authoritative statement or assertion; pronouncement **2** a popular saying or maxim **3** *law* See **obiter dictum** [C16 from Latin, from *dīcere* to say]

dictyopteran (ˌdɪktɪ'ɒptərən) *n* any insect of the order *Dictyoptera*, which comprises the cockroaches and mantises [New Latin, from Greek *diktuon* a net, from *dikein* to cast + *pteron* a wing]

dicyclic (daɪ'saɪklɪk) *adj* **1** *botany* having the perianth arranged in two whorls; having separate petals and sepals **2** *chem* (of a molecule) containing only two rings of atoms

dicynodont (daɪ'sɪnəˌdɒnt) *n* any of various extinct Triassic mammal-like reptiles having a single pair of tusklike teeth [C19 from Greek, from DI-¹ + *kuōn* dog + -ODONT]

did (dɪd) *vb* the past tense of **do¹**

Didache ('dɪdəˌkiː) *n* a treatise, perhaps of the 1st or early 2nd century AD, on Christian morality and practices. Also called: the Teaching of the Twelve

Apostles [C19 from Greek, literally: a teaching, from *didaskein* to teach]

didactic (dɪˈdæktɪk) *adj* **1** intended to instruct, esp excessively **2** morally instructive; improving **3** (of works of art or literature) containing a political or moral message to which aesthetic considerations are subordinated [C17 from Greek *didaktikos* skilled in teaching, from *didaskein* to teach] > di'dactically *adv* > di'dacticism *n*

didactics (dɪˈdæktɪks) *n* (*functioning as singular*) the art or science of teaching

didactyl (daɪˈdæktɪl) *adj* (esp of many marsupials) having the hind toes separate > di'dactylism *n*

diddle¹ ('dɪdᵊl) *vb informal* **1** (*tr*) to cheat or swindle **2** (*intr*) an obsolete word for **dawdle** [C19 back formation from Jeremy *Diddler,* a scrounger in J. Kenney's farce *Raising the Wind* (1803)] > 'diddler *n*

diddle² ('dɪdᵊl) *vb dialect* to jerk (an object) up and down or back and forth; shake rapidly [C17 probably variant of *doderen* to tremble, totter; see DODDER¹]

diddly-squat ('dɪdlɪˌskwɒt) *pron US and Canadian informal* (*usually used with a negative*) anything: *that doesn't mean diddly-squat*

diddy ('dɪdɪ) *n, pl* -dies *dialect* a female breast or nipple [C18 from *titty,* diminutive of TIT²]

didgeridoo (ˌdɪdʒərɪˈduː) *n music* a deep-toned native Australian wind instrument made from a long hollowed-out piece of wood [C20 imitative of its sound]

didicoy, diddicoy ('dɪdɪˌkɔɪ) *or* **didakai** ('dɪdəˌkaɪ) *n, pl* -coys *or* -kais (in Britain) one of a group of caravan-dwelling roadside people who live like Gypsies but are not true Romanies [C19 from Romany]

didn't ('dɪdᵊnt) *contraction of* did not

dido ('daɪdəʊ) *n, pl* -dos *or* -does (*usually plural*) *informal* an antic; prank; trick [C19 originally US: of uncertain origin]

Dido ('daɪdəʊ) *n classical myth* a princess of Tyre who founded Carthage and became its queen. Virgil tells of her suicide when abandoned by her lover Aeneas

didst (dɪdst) *vb archaic* (used with the pronoun *thou* or its relative equivalent) a form of the past tense of **do¹**

didymium (daɪˈdɪmɪəm, dɪ-) *n* **1** a mixture of the metallic rare earths neodymium and praseodymium, once thought to be an element **2** a mixture of rare earths and their oxides used in colouring glass [C19 from New Latin, from Greek *didumos* twin + -IUM]

didymous ('dɪdɪməs) *adj biology* in pairs or in two parts [C18 from Greek *didumos* twin, from *duo* two]

didynamous (daɪˈdɪnəməs) *adj* (of plants) having four stamens arranged in two pairs of unequal length, as in the foxglove [C18 from New Latin *Didynamia* name of former class, from DI-¹ + Greek *dunamis* power, referring to the greater strength of the two long stamens]

die¹ (daɪ) *vb* dies, dying, died (*mainly intr*) **1** (of an organism or its cells, organs, etc) to cease all biological activity permanently: *she died of pneumonia* **2** (of something inanimate) to cease to exist; come to an end: *the memory of her will never die* **3** (often foll by *away, down,* or *out*) to lose strength, power, or energy, esp by degrees **4** (often foll by *away* or *down*) to become calm or quiet; subside: *the noise slowly died down* **5** to stop functioning: *the engine died* **6** to languish or pine, as with love, longing, etc **7** (usually foll by *of*) *informal* to be nearly overcome (with laughter, boredom, etc) **8** *theol* to lack spiritual life within the soul, thus separating it from God and leading to eternal punishment **9** (*tr*) to undergo or suffer (a death of a specified kind) (esp in phrase *such as* **die a saintly death**) **10** (foll by *to*) to become indifferent or apathetic (to): *to die to the world* **11** never say die *informal* never give up **12 die hard** to cease to exist after resistance or a struggle: *old habits die hard* **13 die in harness** to die while still working or active, prior to retirement **14 be dying** (foll by *for* or an

infinitive) to be eager or desperate (for something or to do something): *I'm dying to see the new house* **15 to die for** *informal* highly desirable: *a salary to die for* ▷ See also **dieback, die down, die out** [Old English *dīegan,* probably of Scandinavian origin; compare Old Norse *deyja,* Old High German *touwen*]

▪ USAGE It was formerly considered incorrect to use the preposition *from* after *die,* but *of* and *from* are now both acceptable: *he died of/from his injuries*

die² (daɪ) *n* **1 a** a shaped block of metal or other hard material used to cut or form metal in a drop forge, press, or similar device **b** a tool of metal, silicon carbide, or other hard material with a conical hole through which wires, rods, or tubes are drawn to reduce their diameter **2** an internally-threaded tool for cutting external threads. Compare **tap²** (sense 6) **3** a casting mould giving accurate dimensions and a good surface to the object cast. See also **die-cast 4** *architect* the dado of a pedestal, usually cubic **5** another name for **dice** (sense 2) **6 as straight as a die** perfectly honest **7 the die is cast** the decision that commits a person irrevocably to an action has been taken [C13 *dee,* from Old French *de,* perhaps from Vulgar Latin *datum* (unattested) a piece in games, noun use of past participle of Latin *dare* to play]

dieback ('daɪˌbæk) *n* **1** a disease of trees and shrubs characterized by death of the young shoots, which spreads to the larger branches: caused by injury to the roots or attack by bacteria or fungi **2** any similar condition of herbaceous plants ▷ *vb* **die back 3** (*intr, adverb*) (of plants) to suffer from dieback

die-cast *vb* -casts, -casting, -cast (*tr*) to shape or form (a metal or plastic object) by introducing molten metal or plastic into a reusable mould, esp under pressure, by gravity, or by centrifugal force > 'die-ˌcasting *n*

diecious (daɪˈiːʃəs) *adj* a variant spelling of **dioecious.** > di'eciously *adv*

die-cutting *adv, n printing* the cutting by machine of paper or card into shapes with sharp steel knives, such as in the manufacture of cardboard boxes

die down *vb* (*intr, adverb*) **1** (of some perennial plants) to wither and die above ground, leaving only the root alive during the winter **2** to lose strength or power, esp by degrees **3** to become calm or quiet

dièdre (French djɛdrə) *n mountaineering* a large shallow groove or corner in a rock face [C20 dihedral]

dieffenbachia (ˌdiːfᵊnˈbækɪə) *n* any plant of the tropical American evergreen perennial genus *Dieffenbachia,* some species of which are grown as pot plants for their handsome variegated foliage. The plants are poisonous and the sap is extremely acrid: family *Araceae* [named after Ernst *Dieffenbach* (died 1855), German horticulturist]

Diégo-Suarez (French djegosɥarɛs) *n* the former name of **Antseranana**

die-hard *n* **1** a person who resists change or who holds onto an untenable position or outdated attitude **2** (*modifier*) obstinately resistant to change > 'die-ˌhardism *n*

dieldrin ('diːldrɪn) *n* a crystalline insoluble substance, consisting of a chlorinated derivative of naphthalene: a contact insecticide the use of which is now restricted as it accumulates in the tissues of animals. Formula: $C_{12}H_8OCl_6$ [C20 from DIEL(S-AL)D(E)R (REACTION) + -IN]

dielectric (ˌdaɪɪˈlɛktrɪk) *n* **1** a substance or medium that can sustain a static electric field within it **2** a substance or body of very low electrical conductivity; insulator ▷ *adj* **3** of, concerned with, or having the properties of a dielectric [from DIA- + ELECTRIC] > ˌdie'lectrically *adv*

dielectric constant *n* another name for **relative permittivity**

dielectric heating *n* a technique in which an insulator is heated by the application of a high-frequency electric field

dielectric lens *n physics* a lens constructed of a material that converges or diverges a beam of electromagnetic radiation of radio frequency

Diels-Alder reaction ('diːlzˈɔːldə) *n chem* a type of chemical reaction in which one organic compound containing conjugated double bonds adds to another containing an ethylenic bond to form a product containing a ring [C20 named after Otto *Diels* (1876–1954) and Kurt *Alder* (1902–58), German chemists]

Dien Bien Phu (ˌdjɛn bjɛn 'fuː) *n* a village in NW Vietnam: French military post during the Indochina War; scene of a major defeat of French forces by the Vietminh (1954)

diencephalon (ˌdaɪɛnˈsɛfəˌlɒn) *n* the part of the brain that includes the basal ganglia, thalamus, hypothalamus, and associated areas > diencephalic (ˌdaɪɛnsɪˈfælɪk) *adj*

diene ('daɪiːn) *n chem* a hydrocarbon that contains two carbon-to-carbon double bonds in its molecules

-diene *n combining form* denoting an organic compound containing two double bonds between carbon atoms: *butadiene* [from DI-¹ + -ENE]

die out *or* **off** *vb* (*intr, adverb*) **1** (of a family, race, etc) to die one after another until few or none are left **2** to become extinct, esp after a period of gradual decline

Dieppe (dɪˈɛp; French djɛp) *n* a port and resort in N France, on the English Channel. Pop: 34 653 (1999)

dieresis (daɪˈɛrɪsɪs) *n, pl* -ses (-ˌsiːz) a variant spelling of **diaeresis.** > dieretic (ˌdaɪəˈrɛtɪk) *adj*

diesel ('diːzᵊl) *n* **1** See **diesel engine 2** a ship, locomotive, lorry, etc, driven by a diesel engine **3** *informal* short for **diesel oil** (*or* **fuel**) **4** *South African slang* any cola drink: *spook and diesel* **5** sucking diesel See **suck** (sense 10)

diesel cycle *n* a four-stroke cycle in which combustion takes place at constant pressure and heat is rejected at constant volume. Compare **Otto cycle**

diesel-electric *n* **1** a locomotive fitted with a diesel engine driving an electric generator that feeds electric traction motors ▷ *adj* **2** of or relating to such a locomotive or system

diesel engine *or* **motor** *n* a type of internal-combustion engine in which atomized fuel oil is sprayed into the cylinder and ignited by compression alone

diesel-hydraulic *n* **1** a locomotive driven by a diesel engine through hydraulic transmission and torque converters ▷ *adj* **2** of or relating to such a locomotive or system

diesel oil *or* **fuel** *n* a fuel obtained from petroleum distillation that is used in diesel engines. It has a relatively low ignition temperature (540°C) and is ignited by the heat of compression. Also called (Brit): **derv** See also **cetane number**

Dies Irae (Latin 'diːeɪz 'ɪəraɪ) *n* **1** *Christianity* a famous Latin hymn of the 13th century, describing the Last Judgment. It is used in the Mass for the dead **2** a musical setting of this hymn, usually part of a setting of the Requiem [literally: day of wrath]

diesis ('daɪɪsɪs) *n, pl* -ses (-ˌsiːz) **1** *printing* another name for **double dagger 2** *music* **a** (in ancient Greek theory) any interval smaller than a whole tone, esp a semitone in the Pythagorean scale **b** (in modern theory) the discrepancy of pitch in just intonation between an octave and either a succession of four ascending minor thirds (**great diesis**), or a succession of three ascending major thirds (**minor diesis**) [C16 via Latin from Greek: a quarter tone, literally: a sending through, from *diienai;* the double dagger was originally used in musical notation]

dies non ('daɪiːz nɒn) *n law* a day on which no legal business may be transacted. Also called: dies

d

non juridicus (dʒʊˈrɪdɪkəs) Compare **juridical days** [c19 shortened from Latin phrase *diēs nōn jūridicus* literally: day which is not juridical, that is, not reserved for legal affairs]

die stamping *n printing* the production of words or decoration on a surface by using a steel die so that the printed images stand in relief

diestock (ˈdaɪˌstɒk) *n* the device holding the dies used to cut an external screw thread

diestrus (daɪˈiːstrəs) *n* the US spelling of **dioestrus**

diet¹ (ˈdaɪət) *n* **1 a** a specific allowance or selection of food, esp prescribed to control weight or in disorders in which certain foods are contraindicated: *a salt-free diet; a 900-calorie diet* **b** (*as modifier*): *a diet bread* **2** the food and drink that a person or animal regularly consumes: *a diet of nuts and water* **3** regular activities or occupations ▷ *vb* **4** (*usually intr*) to follow or cause to follow a dietary regimen [c13 from Old French *diete,* from Latin *diaeta,* from Greek *diaita* mode of living, from *diaitan* to direct one's own life] > ˈdieter *n*

diet² (ˈdaɪət) *n* **1** (*sometimes capital*) a legislative assembly in various countries, such as Japan **2** (*sometimes capital*) Also called: Reichstag the assembly of the estates of the Holy Roman Empire **3** *Scots law* **a** the date fixed by a court for hearing a case **b** a single session of a court [c15 from Medieval Latin *diēta* public meeting, probably from Latin *diaeta* DIET¹ but associated with Latin *diēs* day]

dietary (ˈdaɪətərɪ, -trɪ) *adj* **1** of or relating to a diet ▷ *n, pl* **-taries 2** a regulated diet **3** a system of dieting

dietary fibre *n* fibrous substances in fruits and vegetables, such as the structural polymers of cell walls, consumption of which aids digestion and is believed to help prevent certain diseases. Also called: roughage

dietetic (ˌdaɪˈtɛtɪk) *or* **dietetical** *adj* **1** denoting or relating to diet or the regulation of food intake **2** prepared for special dietary requirements > ˌdieˈtetically *adv*

dietetics (ˌdaɪˈtɛtɪks) *n* (*functioning as singular*) the scientific study and regulation of food intake and preparation

diethylene glycol (daɪˈɛθɪˌliːn ˈɡlaɪkɒl) *n* a colourless soluble liquid used as an antifreeze and solvent. Formula: $(C_2H_4OH)_2O$

diethyl ether (daɪˈɛθɪl) *n* a formal name for **ether** (sense 1)

diethylstilbestrol *or* **diethylstilboestrol** (daɪˌɛθɪlstɪlˈbɛstrɒl, -ˌiːθəl-) *n* a synthetic hormone with oestrogenic properties, used to relieve menopausal symptoms. Formula: $OHC_6H_4CH:CHC_6H_4OH$. Also called: stilbestrol, stilboestrol

dietician *or* **dietitian** (ˌdaɪˈtɪʃən) *n* a person who specializes in dietetics

Dieu et mon droit French (djø e mɔ̃ drwa) God and my right: motto of the Royal Arms of Great Britain

differ (ˈdɪfə) *vb* (*intr*) **1** (*often foll by from*) to be dissimilar in quality, nature, or degree (to); vary (from) **2** (*often foll by from or with*) to be at variance (with); disagree (with) **3** *dialect* to quarrel or dispute **4 agree to differ** to end an argument amicably while maintaining differences of opinion [c14 from Latin *differre,* literally: to bear off in different directions, hence scatter, put off, be different, from *dis-* apart + *ferre* to bear]

difference (ˈdɪfərəns, ˈdɪfrəns) *n* **1** the state or quality of being unlike **2** a specific instance of being unlike **3** a distinguishing mark or feature **4** a significant change in a situation: *the difference in her is amazing* **5** a disagreement or argument: *he had a difference with his wife* **6** a degree of distinctness, as between two people or things **7 a** the result of the subtraction of one number, quantity, etc, from another **b** the single number that when added to the subtrahend gives the

minuend; remainder **8** *logic* another name for **differentia 9** *maths* (of two sets) **a** the set of members of the first that are not members of the second. Symbol: A – B **b symmetric difference** the set of members of one but not both of the given sets. Often symbolized: A + B **10** *heraldry* an addition to the arms of a family to represent a younger branch **11 make a difference a** to have an effect **b** to treat differently **12 split the difference a** to settle a dispute by a compromise **b** to divide a remainder equally **13 with a difference** with some peculiarly distinguishing quality, good or bad ▷ *vb* (*tr*) **14** *rare* to distinguish **15** *heraldry* to add a charge to (arms) to differentiate a branch of a family

difference threshold *n psychol* the minimum difference between two stimuli that is just detectable by a person

different (ˈdɪfərənt, ˈdɪfrənt) *adj* **1** partly or completely unlike **2** not identical or the same; other: *he always wears a different tie* **3** out of the ordinary; unusual > ˈdifferently *adv* > ˈdifferentness *n*

> USAGE The constructions *different from, different to,* and *different than* are all found in the works of writers of English during the past. Nowadays, however, the most widely acceptable preposition to use after *different* is *from. Different to* is common in British English, but is considered by some people to be incorrect, or less acceptable. *Different than* is a standard construction in American English, and has the advantage of conciseness when a clause or phrase follows, as in *this result is only slightly different than in the US.* As, however, this idiom is not regarded as totally acceptable in British usage, it is preferable either to use *different from: this result is only slightly different from that obtained in the US* or to rephrase the sentence: *this result differs only slightly from that in the US*

differentia (ˌdɪfəˈrɛnʃɪə) *n, pl* **-tiae** (-ʃɪˌiː) *logic* a feature by which two subclasses of the same class of named objects can be distinguished. Also called: **difference** [c19 from Latin: diversity, DIFFERENCE]

differentiable (ˌdɪfəˈrɛnʃɪəbᵊl) *adj* **1** capable of being differentiated **2** *maths* possessing a derivative > ˌdifferˌentiaˈbility *n*

differential (ˌdɪfəˈrɛnʃəl) *adj* **1** of, relating to, or using a difference **2** constituting a difference; distinguishing **3** *maths* of, containing, or involving one or more derivatives or differentials **4** *physics, engineering* relating to, operating on, or based on the difference between two effects, motions, forces, etc: *differential amplifier* ▷ *n* **5** a factor that differentiates between two comparable things **6** *maths* **a** an increment in a given function, expressed as the product of the derivative of that function and the corresponding increment in the independent variable **b** an increment in a given function of two or more variables, $f(x_1, x_2, ...x_n)$, expressed as the sum of the products of each partial derivative and the increment in the corresponding variable **7** an epicyclic gear train that permits two shafts to rotate at different speeds while being driven by a third shaft. See also **differential gear 8** *chiefly Brit* the difference between rates of pay for different types of labour, esp when forming a pay structure within an industry **9** (*in commerce*) a difference in rates, esp between comparable labour services or transportation routes > ˌdifferˈentially *adv*

differential calculus *n* the branch of calculus concerned with the study, evaluation, and use of derivatives and differentials. Compare **integral calculus**

differential coefficient *n maths* another name for **derivative**

differential equation *n* an equation containing differentials or derivatives of a function of one independent variable. A **partial differential equation** results from a function of more than one variable

differential gear *n* the epicyclic gear mounted in the driving axle of a road vehicle that permits one driving wheel to rotate faster than the other, as when cornering

differential geometry *n* the application of differential calculus to geometrical problems; the study of objects that remain unchanged by transformations that preserve derivatives

differential operator *n* any operator involving differentiation, such as the mathematical operator del ∇, used in vector analysis, where ∇ = $i\partial/\partial x + j\partial/\partial y + k\partial/\partial z$, *i, j,* and *k* being unit vectors and $\partial/\partial x, \partial/\partial y,$ and $\partial/\partial z$ the partial derivatives of a function in *x, y,* and *z*

differential windlass *n* a windlass employing the velocity ratio incurred in unwinding from a small drum while winding onto a larger drum rotating at a common speed. Also called: Chinese windlass

differentiate (ˌdɪfəˈrɛnʃɪˌeɪt) *vb* **1** (*tr*) to serve to distinguish between **2** (*when intr, often foll by between*) to perceive, show, or make a difference (in or between); discriminate **3** (*intr*) to become dissimilar or distinct **4** *maths* to perform a differentiation on (a quantity, expression, etc) **5** (*intr*) (of unspecialized cells, etc) to change during development to more specialized forms > ˈdifferˌentiˌator *n*

differentiation (ˌdɪfəˌrɛnʃɪˈeɪʃən) *n* **1** the act, process, or result of differentiating **2** *maths* an operation used in calculus in which the derivative of a function or variable is determined; the inverse of **integration** (sense 6) **3** any process in which a mixture of materials separates out partially or completely into its constituent parts, as in the cooling and solidification of a magma into two or more different rock types or in the gradual separation of an originally homogeneous earth into crust, mantle, and core

difficult (ˈdɪfɪkᵊlt) *adj* **1** not easy to do; requiring effort: *a difficult job* **2** not easy to understand or solve; intricate: *a difficult problem* **3** hard to deal with; troublesome: *a difficult child* **4** not easily convinced, pleased, or satisfied: *a difficult audience* **5** full of hardships or trials: *difficult times ahead* [c14 back formation from DIFFICULTY] > ˈdifficultly *adv*

difficulty (ˈdɪfɪkᵊltɪ) *n, pl* **-ties 1** the state or quality of being difficult **2** a task, problem, etc, that is hard to deal with **3** (*often plural*) a troublesome or embarrassing situation, esp a financial one **4** a dispute or disagreement **5** (*often plural*) an objection or obstacle: *he always makes difficulties* **6** a trouble or source of trouble; worry **7** lack of ease; awkwardness: *he could run only with difficulty* [c14 from Latin *difficultās,* from *difficilis* difficult, from *dis-* not + *facilis* easy, FACILE]

diffident (ˈdɪfɪdənt) *adj* lacking self-confidence; timid; shy [c15 from Latin *diffidere* to distrust, from *dis-* not + *fidere* to trust] > ˈdiffidence *n* > ˈdiffidently *adv*

diffract (dɪˈfrækt) *vb* to undergo or cause to undergo diffraction: *to diffract light; the light diffracts at a slit* > difˈfractive *adj* > difˈfractively *adv* > difˈfractiveness *n*

diffraction (dɪˈfrækʃən) *n* **1** *physics* a deviation in the direction of a wave at the edge of an obstacle in its path **2** any phenomenon caused by diffraction and interference of light, such as the formation of light and dark fringes by the passage of light through a small aperture **3** deflection of sound waves caused by an obstacle or by nonhomogeneity of a medium [c17 from New Latin *diffractiō* a breaking to pieces, from Latin *diffringere* to shatter, from *dis-* apart + *frangere* to break]

diffraction grating *n* a glass plate or a mirror

with a large number of equidistant parallel lines or grooves on its surface. It causes diffraction of transmitted or reflected light, ultraviolet radiation, or X-rays

diffraction pattern *n physics* the distinctive pattern of light and dark fringes, rings, etc, formed by diffraction

diffractometer (ˌdɪfræk'tɒmɪtə) *n physics* an instrument used in studying diffraction, as in the determination of crystal structure by diffraction of X-rays

diffuse *vb* (dɪ'fjuːz) **1** to spread or cause to spread in all directions **2** to undergo or cause to undergo diffusion **3** to scatter or cause to scatter; disseminate; disperse ▷ *adj* (dɪ'fjuːs) **4** spread out over a wide area **5** lacking conciseness **6** (esp of some creeping stems) spreading loosely over a large area **7** characterized by or exhibiting diffusion: *diffuse light; diffuse reflection* **8** *botany* (of plant growth) occurring throughout a tissue [C15 from Latin *diffūsus* spread abroad, from *diffundere* to pour forth, from *dis-* away + *fundere* to pour] > **diffusely** (dɪ'fjuːslɪ) *adv* > **dif'fuseness** *n* > **diffusible** (dɪ'fjuːzəbᵊl) *adj* > **difˌfusi'bility** *or* **dif'fusibleness** *n*

USAGE Avoid confusion with **defuse**

diffused junction *n* a semiconductor junction formed by diffusing acceptor or donor impurity atoms into semiconductor material to form regions of p-type or n-type conductivity. See also **photolithography** (sense 2) Compare **alloyed junction**

diffuser *or* **diffusor** (dɪ'fjuːzə) *n* **1** a person or thing that diffuses **2** a part of a lighting fixture consisting of a translucent or frosted covering or of a rough reflector: used to scatter the light and prevent glare **3** a cone, wedge, or baffle placed in front of the diaphragm of a loudspeaker to diffuse the sound waves **4** a duct, esp in a wind tunnel or jet engine, that widens gradually in the direction of flow to reduce the speed and increase the pressure of the air or fluid **5** *photog* a light-scattering medium, such as a screen of fine fabric, placed in the path of a source of light to reduce the sharpness of shadows and thus soften the lighting **6** a perforated plate or similar device for distributing compressed air in the aeration of sewage **7** a device, attached to a hairdryer, which diffuses the warm air as it comes out

diffusion (dɪ'fjuːʒən) *n* **1** the act or process of diffusing or being diffused; dispersion **2** verbosity **3** *physics* **a** the random thermal motion of atoms, molecules, clusters of atoms, etc, in gases, liquids, and some solids **b** the transfer of atoms or molecules by their random motion from one part of a medium to another **4** *physics* the transmission or reflection of electromagnetic radiation, esp light, in which the radiation is scattered in many directions and not directly reflected or refracted; scattering **5** Also called: **diffusivity** *physics* the degree to which the directions of propagation of reverberant sound waves differ from point to point in an enclosure **6** *anthropol* the transmission of social institutions, skills, and myths from one culture to another

diffusion coefficient *or* **constant** *n* the rate at which a diffusing substance is transported between opposite faces of a unit cube of a system when there is unit concentration difference between them. Symbol: *D* Also called: **diffusivity**

diffusion line *n* a range of clothes made by a top fashion designer for a high-street retailer

diffusive (dɪ'fjuːsɪv) *adj* characterized by diffusion > **dif'fusively** *adv* > **dif'fusiveness** *n*

diffusivity (ˌdɪfjuː'sɪvɪtɪ) *n* **1** a measure of the ability of a substance to transmit a difference in temperature; expressed as the thermal conductivity divided by the product of specific heat capacity and density **2** *physics* **a** the ability of a substance to permit or undergo diffusion **b** another name for **diffusion coefficient** **3** another name for **diffusion** (sense 5)

difunctional (daɪ'fʌŋkʃənᵊl) *chem* ▷ *adj* **1** (of a compound) having two sites in the molecule that are highly reactive ▷ *n* **2** a compound having two sites in the molecule that are highly reactive

dig (dɪg) *vb* digs, digging, dug **1** (when *tr*, often foll by *up*) to cut into, break up, and turn over or remove (earth, soil, etc), esp with a spade **2** to form or excavate (a hole, tunnel, passage, etc) by digging, usually with an implement or (of animals) with feet, claws, etc: *to dig a tunnel* **3** (often foll by *through*) to make or force (one's way), esp by removing obstructions: *he dug his way through the crowd* **4** (*tr*; often foll by *out* or *up*) to obtain by digging: *to dig potatoes; to dig up treasure* **5** (*tr*; often foll by *out* or *up*) to find or discover by effort or searching: *to dig out unexpected facts* **6** (*tr*; foll by *in* or *into*) to thrust or jab (a sharp instrument, weapon, etc); poke: *he dug his spurs into the horse's side* **7** (*tr*; foll by *in* or *into*) to mix (compost, etc) with soil by digging **8** (*tr*) *informal* to like, understand, or appreciate **9** (*intr*) *US slang* to work hard, esp for an examination **10** (*intr*) *Brit informal* to have lodgings: *I dig in South London* ▷ *n* **11** the act of digging **12** a thrust or poke, esp in the ribs **13** a cutting or sarcastic remark **14** *informal* an archaeological excavation ▷ See also **dig in, digs** [C13 *diggen*, of uncertain origin]

Dig (dɪg) *n NZ informal* short for **Digger** (sense 1)

digamma (daɪ'gæmə) *n* a letter of the Greek alphabet (Ϝ) that became obsolete before the classical period of the language. It represented a semivowel like English W and was used as a numeral in later stages of written Greek, and passed into the Roman alphabet as F [C17 via Latin from Greek, from DI-[1] + GAMMA; from its shape, which suggests one gamma upon another]

digamy ('dɪgəmɪ) *n, pl* -mies a second marriage contracted after the termination of the first by death or divorce. Also called: **deuterogamy** Compare **bigamy** [C17 from Late Latin *digamia*, from Greek, from DI[1] + *gamos* marriage] > **'digamist** *n* > **'digamous** *adj*

digastric (daɪ'gæstrɪk) *adj* **1** (of certain muscles) having two fleshy portions joined by a tendon ▷ *n* **2** a muscle of the mandible that assists in lowering the lower jaw [C17 from New Latin *digastricus* (with two bellies), from DI-[1] + *gastricus* gastric, from Greek *gastēr* belly]

Digby chicken *or* **chick** ('dɪgbɪ) *n Canadian informal* dried herring [after *Digby*, a town in Nova Scotia, Canada]

digenesis (daɪ'dʒɛnɪsɪs) *n zoology* another name for **alternation of generations**

digenetic (ˌdaɪdʒɪ'nɛtɪk) *adj zoology* **1** of or relating to digenesis **2** (of parasites) having two hosts

digerati (ˌdɪdʒə'rɑːtɪ) *pl n* the people who earn large amounts of money through internet-related business

digest *vb* (dɪ'dʒɛst, daɪ-) **1** to subject (food) to a process of digestion **2** (*tr*) to assimilate mentally **3** *chem* to soften or disintegrate or be softened or disintegrated by the action of heat, moisture, or chemicals; decompose **4** (*tr*) to arrange in a methodical or systematic order; classify **5** (*tr*) to reduce to a summary **6** (*tr*) *archaic* to tolerate ▷ *n* ('daɪdʒɛst) **7** a comprehensive and systematic compilation of information or material, often condensed **8** a magazine, periodical, etc, that summarizes news of current events **9** a compilation of rules of law based on decided cases [C14 from Late Latin *dīgesta* writings grouped under various heads, from Latin *dīgerere* to divide, from *di-* apart + *gerere* to bear]

Digest ('daɪdʒɛst) *n Roman law* an arrangement of excerpts from the writings and opinions of eminent lawyers, contained in 50 books compiled by order of Justinian in the sixth century A.D

digestant (dɪ'dʒɛstənt, daɪ-) *n* a substance, such as hydrochloric acid or a bile salt, that promotes or aids digestion

digester (dɪ'dʒɛstə, daɪ-) *n* **1** *chem* an apparatus or vessel, such as an autoclave, in which digestion is carried out **2** a less common word for **digestant** **3** a person or thing that digests

digestible (dɪ'dʒɛstəbᵊl, daɪ-) *adj* capable of being digested or easy to digest > **diˌgesti'bility** *or* **di'gestibleness** *n* > **di'gestibly** *adv*

digestif *French* (diʒɛstif) *n* something, esp a drink, taken as an aid to digestion, either before or after a meal

digestion (dɪ'dʒɛstʃən, daɪ-) *n* **1** the act or process in living organisms of breaking down ingested food material into easily absorbed and assimilated substances by the action of enzymes and other agents. Related adj: **peptic** **2** mental assimilation, esp of ideas **3** *bacteriol* the decomposition of sewage by the action of bacteria **4** *chem* the treatment of material with heat, solvents, chemicals, etc, to cause softening or decomposition [C14 from Old French, from Latin *digestiō* a dissolving, digestion] > **di'gestional** *adj*

digestive (dɪ'dʒɛstɪv, daɪ-) *or* **digestant** (daɪ'dʒɛstənt) *adj* **1** relating to, aiding, or subjecting to digestion: *a digestive enzyme* ▷ *n* **2** a less common word for **digestant** **3** short for **digestive biscuit**. > **di'gestively** *adv*

digestive biscuit *n* a round semisweet biscuit made from wholemeal flour

digged (dɪgd) *vb archaic* a past tense of **dig**

digger ('dɪgə) *n* **1** a person, animal, or machine that digs **2** a miner, esp one who digs for gold **3** a tool or part of a machine used for excavation, esp a mechanical digger fitted with a head for digging trenches

Digger ('dɪgə) *n* **1** (*sometimes not capital*) *archaic slang* **a** an Australian or New Zealander, esp a soldier: often used as a term of address **b** (*as modifier*): *a Digger accent* **2** one of a number of tribes of America whose diet was largely composed of roots dug out of the ground

Diggers ('dɪgəz) *pl n* **the** a radical English Puritan group, led by Gerrard Winstanley, which advocated communal ownership of land (1649–50)

digger wasp *n* any solitary wasp of the families *Sphecidae* and *Pamphilidae* that digs nest holes in the ground, rotten wood, or a hollow stem and stocks them with live insects for the larvae

diggings ('dɪgɪŋz) *pl n* **1** (*functioning as plural*) material that has been dug out **2** (*functioning as singular or plural*) a place where mining, esp gold mining, has taken place **3** (*functioning as plural*) *Brit informal* a less common name for **digs**

dight (daɪt) *vb* **dights, dighting, dight** *or* **dighted** (*tr*) *archaic* to adorn or equip, as for battle [Old English *dihtan* to compose, from Latin *dictāre* to DICTATE]

Digibox ('dɪdʒɪbɒks) *n trademark* a device which converts the signals from a digital television broadcast into a form which can be viewed on a standard television set [C20 from DIGI(TAL) (sense 3) + BOX[1]]

digicam ('dɪdʒɪˌkæm) *n* a digital camera

dig in *vb (adverb)* **1** *military* to create (a defensive position) by digging foxholes, trenches, etc **2** *informal* to entrench (oneself) firmly **3** (*intr*) *informal* to defend or maintain a position firmly, as in an argument **4** (*intr*) *informal* to begin vigorously to eat: *don't wait, just dig in* **5** **dig one's heels in** *informal* to refuse stubbornly to move or be persuaded

digit ('dɪdʒɪt) *n* **1** a finger or toe **2** Also called: **figure** any of the ten Arabic numerals from 0 to 9 **3** another name for **finger** (sense 4) **4** *astronomy* one twelfth of the diameter of the sun or moon, used to express the magnitude of an eclipse [C15 from Latin *digitus* toe, finger]

digital ('dɪdʒɪtᵊl) *adj* **1** of, relating to, resembling, or possessing a digit or digits **2** performed with the fingers **3** representing data as a series of numerical values **4** displaying information as numbers rather than by a pointer moving over a dial: *a digital voltmeter; digital read-out* **5** *electronics* responding to discrete values of input voltage and

d

producing discrete output voltage levels, as in a logic circuit: *digital circuit* **6** a less common word for **digitate** ▷ *n* **7** *music* one of the keys on the manuals of an organ or on a piano, harpsichord, etc > 'digitally *adv*

digital audio tape *n* magnetic tape on which sound is recorded digitally, giving high-fidelity reproduction. Abbreviation: DAT

digital camera *n* a camera that produces digital images that can be stored in a computer, displayed on a screen and printed

digital clock *or* **watch** *n* a clock or watch in which the hours, minutes, and sometimes seconds are indicated by digits, rather than by hands on a dial. Compare **analogue clock**

digital compact cassette *n* a magnetic tape cassette on which sound can be recorded in a digital format. Abbreviation: DCC

digital computer *n* an electronic computer in which the input is discrete rather than continuous, consisting of combinations of numbers, letters, and other characters written in an appropriate programming language and represented internally in binary notation. Compare **analog computer**

digital divide *n informal* the gap between those people who have internet access and those who do not

digital fount *n* a typeface of which the letter-shapes have been converted into digital form so that they can be used in computer-aided typesetting

digital immigrant *n informal* a person who has become used to using information technology as a young adult. Compare **digital native, analogue** (sense 3)

digitalin (ˌdɪdʒɪˈteɪlɪn) *n* a poisonous amorphous crystalline mixture of glycosides extracted from digitalis leaves and formerly used in treating heart disease [C19 from DIGITAL(IS) + -IN]

digitalis (ˌdɪdʒɪˈteɪlɪs) *n* **1** any Eurasian scrophulariaceous plant of the genus *Digitalis*, such as the foxglove, having bell-shaped flowers and a basal rosette of leaves **2 a** a drug prepared from the dried leaves or seeds of the foxglove: a mixture of glycosides used medicinally to treat heart failure and some abnormal heart rhythms **b** any cardiac glycoside, whatever its origin [C17 from New Latin, from Latin: relating to a finger (referring to the corollas of the flower); based on German *Fingerhut* foxglove, literally: finger-hat or thimble]

digitalism (ˈdɪdʒɪtəˌlɪzəm) *n* a serious condition resulting from digitalis poisoning, characterized by nausea, vomiting, and a disturbance in heart rhythm or rate

digitalize *or* **digitalise** (ˈdɪdʒɪtəˌlaɪz) *vb* (*tr*) to administer digitoxin or digoxin to (a patient) for the treatment of certain heart disorders > ˌdigitaliˈzation *or* ˌdigitaliˈsation *n*

digital mapping *n* a method of preparing maps in which the data is stored in a computer for ease of access and updating > **digital map** *n*

digital native *n informal* a person who has been familiar with information technology since childhood. Compare **digital immigrant, analogue** (sense 3)

digital radio *n* **1** radio in which the audio information is transmitted in digital form and decoded at the radio receiver **2** a radio that can receive and decode digital audio information

digital recording *n* a sound recording process that converts audio or analogue signals into a series of pulses that correspond to the voltage level. These can be stored on tape or on any other memory system

digital signature *n computing* electronic proof of a person's identity involving the use of encryption; used to authenticate documents

digital television *n* **1** television in which the picture information is transmitted in digital form and decoded at the television receiver **2** a

television set that can decode digital picture information and convert it into visible images

digital versatile disk *or* **digital video disk** *n* See DVD

digital video *n* video output based on digital rather than analogue signals

digitate (ˈdɪdʒɪˌteɪt) *or* **digitated** *adj* **1** (of compound leaves) having the leaflets in the form of a spread hand **2** (of animals) having digits or corresponding parts > ˈdigiˌtately *adv* > ˌdigiˈtation *n*

digitiform (ˈdɪdʒɪtɪˌfɔːm) *adj* shaped like a finger

digitigrade (ˈdɪdʒɪtɪˌɡreɪd) *adj* **1** (of dogs, cats, horses, etc) walking so that only the toes touch the ground ▷ *n* **2** a digitigrade animal

digitize *or* **digitise** (ˈdɪdʒɪˌtaɪz) *vb* (*tr*) to transcribe (data) into a digital form so that it can be directly processed by a computer > ˌdigitiˈzation *or* ˌdigitiˈsation *n* > ˈdigiˌtizer *or* ˈdigiˌtiser *n*

digitized *or* **digitised** (ˈdɪdʒɪˌtaɪzd) *adj computing* recorded or stored in digital form: *export your digitized colour photos*

digitoxin (ˌdɪdʒɪˈtɒksɪn) *n* a white toxic bitter-tasting glycoside, extracted from the leaves of the purple foxglove (*Digitalis purpurea*) and used in the treatment of heart failure and some abnormal heart rhythms. Formula: $C_{41}H_{64}O_{13}$ [from DIGI(TALIS) + TOXIN]

digitron (ˈdɪdʒɪˌtrɒn) *n electronics* a type of tube, for displaying information, having a common anode and several cathodes shaped in the form of characters, which can be lit by a glow discharge. Also called: Nixie tube [C20 from DIGIT + -TRON]

digitule (ˈdɪdʒɪtjuːl) *n zoology* any small finger-like process

diglossia (daɪˈɡlɒsɪə) *n linguistics* the existence in a language of a high, or socially prestigious, and a low, or everyday, form, as German and Swiss German in Switzerland [C20 New Latin, via French, from Greek *diglōssos* speaking two languages: see DIGLOT]

diglot (ˈdaɪɡlɒt) *adj* **1** a less common word for **bilingual** ▷ *n* **2** a bilingual book [C19 from Greek (Attic) *diglōttos*, from DI-¹ + *glōtta* tongue] > diˈglottic *adj*

dignified (ˈdɪɡnɪˌfaɪd) *adj* characterized by dignity of manner or appearance; stately > ˈdigniˌfiedly *adv* > ˈdigniˌfiedness *n*

dignify (ˈdɪɡnɪˌfaɪ) *vb* -fies, -fying, -fied (*tr*) **1** to invest with honour or dignity; ennoble **2** to add distinction to: *the meeting was dignified by the minister* **3** to add a semblance of dignity to, esp by the use of a pretentious name or title: *she dignifies every plant with its Latin name* [C15 from Old French *dignifier*, from Late Latin *dignificāre*, from Latin *dignus* worthy + *facere* to make]

dignitary (ˈdɪɡnɪtərɪ, -trɪ) *n, pl* -taries a person of high official position or rank, esp in government or the church

dignity (ˈdɪɡnɪtɪ) *n, pl* -ties **1** a formal, stately, or grave bearing: *he entered with dignity* **2** the state or quality of being worthy of honour: *the dignity of manual labour* **3** relative importance; rank: *he is next in dignity to the mayor* **4** sense of self-importance (often in the phrases **stand** (or **be**) **on one's dignity, beneath one's dignity**) **5** high rank, esp in government or the church **6** a person of high rank or such persons collectively [C13 from Old French *dignite*, from Latin *dignitās* merit, from *dignus* worthy]

digonal (daɪˈɡəʊnəl) *adj maths* of or relating to a symmetry operation in which the original figure is reconstructed after a 180° turn about an axis

digoneutic (ˌdaɪɡəˈnjuːtɪk) *adj zoology* producing offspring twice yearly [C19 from DI-¹ + Greek *goneuein* to beget] > ˌdigoˈneutism *n*

digoxin (daɪˈdʒɒksɪn) *n* a glycoside extracted from the leaves of the woolly foxglove (*Digitalis lanata*) and used in the treatment of heart failure. Formula: $C_{41}H_{64}O_{14}$

digraph (ˈdaɪɡrɑːf, -ɡræf) *n* a combination of two letters or characters used to represent a single

speech sound such as *gh* in English *tough*. Compare **ligature** (sense 5), **diphthong**. > digraphic (daɪˈɡræfɪk) *adj*

digress (daɪˈɡrɛs) *vb* (*intr*) **1** to depart from the main subject in speech or writing **2** to wander from one's path or main direction [C16 from Latin *dīgressus* turned aside, from *dīgredī*, from *dis-* apart + *gradī* to go] > diˈgresser *n*

digression (daɪˈɡrɛʃən) *n* an act or instance of digressing from a main subject in speech or writing > diˈgressional *adj*

digressive (daɪˈɡrɛsɪv) *adj* characterized by digression or tending to digress > diˈgressively *adv* > diˈgressiveness *n*

digs (dɪɡz) *pl n Brit informal* lodgings [C19 shortened from DIGGINGS, perhaps referring to where one *digs* or works, but see also DIG IN]

dihedral (daɪˈhiːdrəl) *adj* **1** having or formed by two intersecting planes; two-sided: *a dihedral angle* ▷ *n* **2** Also called: dihedron, dihedral angle the figure formed by two intersecting planes **3** the US name for **corner** (sense 11) **4** the upward inclination of an aircraft wing in relation to the lateral axis. Compare **anhedral**

dihedron (daɪˈhiːdrən) *n* another name for **dihedral** (sense 2)

dihybrid (daɪˈhaɪbrɪd) *n genetics* the offspring of two individuals that differ with respect to two pairs of genes; an individual heterozygous for two pairs of genes > diˈhybridism *n*

dihydric (daɪˈhaɪdrɪk) *adj* (of an alcohol) containing two hydroxyl groups per molecule

Dijon (French diʒɔ̃) *n* a city in E France: capital of the former duchy of Burgundy. Pop: 149 867 (1999)

dik-dik (ˈdɪkˌdɪk) *n* any small antelope of the genus *Madoqua*, inhabiting semiarid regions of Africa, having an elongated muzzle and, in the male, small stout horns [C19 an East African name, probably of imitative origin]

dike (daɪk) *n, vb* a variant spelling of **dyke**

dikkop (ˈdɪkəp) *n South African* any of several brownish shore birds of the family *Burhinidae*, esp *Burhinus oedicnemus*, having a large head and eyes: order *Charadriiformes*. Also called: stone curlew [from Afrikaans, from *dik* thick + *kop* head]

diktat (ˈdɪktɑːt) *n* **1** decree or settlement imposed, esp by a ruler or a victorious nation **2** a dogmatic statement [German: dictation, from Latin *dictātum*, from *dictāre* to DICTATE]

dilapidate (dɪˈlæpɪˌdeɪt) *vb* to fall or cause to fall into ruin or decay [C16 from Latin *dīlapidāre* to scatter, waste, from *dis-* apart + *lapidāre* to stone, throw stones, from *lapis* stone]

dilapidated (dɪˈlæpɪˌdeɪtɪd) *adj* falling to pieces or in a state of disrepair; shabby

dilapidation (dɪˌlæpɪˈdeɪʃən) *n* **1** the state of being or becoming dilapidated **2** (*often plural*) *property law* **a** the state of disrepair of premises at the end of a tenancy due to neglect **b** the extent of repairs necessary to such premises > diˈlapiˌdator *n*

dilatancy (daɪˈleɪtənsɪ, dɪ-) *n* a phenomenon caused by the nature of the stacking or fitting together of particles or granules in a heterogeneous system, such as the solidification of certain sols under pressure, and the thixotropy of certain gels

dilatant (daɪˈleɪtᵊnt, dɪ-) *adj* **1** tending to dilate; dilating **2** *physics* of, concerned with, or exhibiting dilatancy ▷ *n* **3** something, such as a catheter, that causes dilation

dilate (daɪˈleɪt, dɪ-) *vb* **1** to expand or cause to expand; make or become wider or larger: *the pupil of the eye dilates in the dark* **2** (*intr*; often foll by *on* or *upon*) to speak or write at length; expand or enlarge [C14 from Latin *dīlātāre* to spread out, amplify, from *dis-* apart + *lātus* wide] > diˈlatable *adj* > diˌlataˈbility *or* diˈlatableness *n* > diˈlation *or* dilatation (ˌdaɪləˈteɪʃən, dɪ-) *n* > dilatative *adj* > dilative (daɪˈleɪtɪv, dɪ-) *adj*

dilatometer (ˌdɪləˈtɒmɪtə) *n* any instrument for measuring changes in dimension: often a glass bulb fitted with a long stopper through which a capillary tube runs, used for measuring volume changes of liquids > dilatometric (ˌdɪlətə'mɛtrɪk) adj > ˌdilato'metrically adv > ˌdila'tometry n

dilator, dilater (daɪ'leɪtə, dɪ-) or **dilatator** (ˌdaɪlə'teɪtə, ˌdɪ-) n 1 something that dilates an object, esp a surgical instrument for dilating a bodily cavity 2 a muscle that expands an orifice or dilates an organ

dilatory ('dɪlətərɪ, -trɪ) adj 1 tending or inclined to delay or waste time 2 intended or designed to waste time or defer action [c15 from Late Latin dīlātōrius inclined to delay, from differre to postpone; see DIFFER] > 'dilatorily adv > 'dilatoriness n

dildo or **dildoe** ('dɪldəʊ) n, pl -dos or -does an object used as a substitute for an erect penis [c16 of unknown origin]

dilemma (dɪ'lɛmə, daɪ-) n 1 a situation necessitating a choice between two equal, esp equally undesirable, alternatives 2 a problem that seems incapable of a solution 3 logic a form of argument one of whose premises is the conjunction of two conditional statements and the other of which affirms the disjunction of their antecedents, and whose conclusion is the disjunction of their consequents. Its form is if p then q and if r then s; either p or r so either q or s 4 on the horns of a dilemma a faced with the choice between two equally unpalatable alternatives b in an awkward situation [c16 via Latin from Greek, from DI-[1] + lēmma assumption, proposition, from lambanein to take, grasp] > dilemmatic (ˌdɪlɪ'mætɪk, ˌdaɪlɪ-) or dil'emmic adj

USAGE The use of dilemma to refer to a problem that seems incapable of a solution is considered by some people to be incorrect

dilettante (ˌdɪlɪ'tɑːntɪ) n, pl -tantes or -tanti (-'tɑːntɪ) 1 a person whose interest in a subject is superficial rather than professional 2 a person who loves the arts ▷ adj 3 of or characteristic of a dilettante [c18 from Italian, from dilettare to delight, from Latin dēlectāre] > ˌdilet'tantish or ˌdilet'tanteish adj > ˌdilet'tantism or ˌdilet'tanteism n

Dili or **Dilli** ('diːliː) n the capital (from 2002) of independent East Timor: the former capital (until 1976) of Portuguese Timor. Pop: 50 000 (2005 est)

diligence[1] ('dɪlɪdʒəns) n 1 steady and careful application 2 proper attention or care 3 law the degree of care required in a given situation [c14 from Latin dīligentia care, attentiveness]

diligence[2] ('dɪlɪdʒəns; French diliʒɑ̃s) n history a stagecoach [c18 from French, shortened from carosse de diligence, literally: coach of speed]

diligent ('dɪlɪdʒənt) adj 1 careful and persevering in carrying out tasks or duties 2 carried out with care and perseverance: diligent work [c14 from Old French, from Latin dīligere to value, from dis- apart + legere to read] > 'diligently adv

dill (dɪl) n 1 an umbelliferous aromatic Eurasian plant, Anethum graveolens, with finely dissected leaves and umbrella-shaped clusters of yellow flowers 2 the leaves or seedlike fruits of this plant, used for flavouring in pickles, soups, etc, and in medicine 3 informal, chiefly Austral and NZ a fool; idiot [Old English dile; related to Old High German tilli] > 'dilly adj

dill pickle n a pickled cucumber flavoured with dill

dilly ('dɪlɪ) n, pl -lies slang, chiefly US and Canadian a person or thing that is remarkable [c20 perhaps from girl's proper name Dilly]

dilly bag n Austral a small bag, esp one made of plaited grass, etc, often used for carrying food. Sometimes shortened to: dilly [from native Australian dilly small bag or basket]

dilly-dally (ˌdɪlɪ'dælɪ) vb -lies, -lying, -lied (intr) informal to loiter or vacillate [c17 by reduplication from DALLY]

diluent ('dɪljʊənt) adj 1 causing dilution or serving to dilute ▷ n 2 a substance used for or

causing dilution [c18 from Latin dīluēns dissolving; see DILUTE]

dilute (daɪ'luːt) vb 1 to make or become less concentrated, esp by adding water or a thinner 2 to make or become weaker in force, effect, etc: he diluted his story ▷ adj 3 chem a (of a solution, suspension, mixture, etc) having a low concentration or a concentration that has been reduced by admixture b (of a substance) present in solution, esp a weak solution in water: dilute acetic acid [c16 from Latin dīluere, from dis- apart + -luere, from lavāre to wash] > dilu'tee n > di'luter n

dilution (daɪ'luːʃən) n 1 the act of diluting or state of being diluted 2 a diluted solution

diluvial (daɪ'luːvɪəl, dɪ-) or **diluvian** adj 1 of or connected with a deluge, esp with the great Flood described in Genesis 2 of or relating to diluvium [c17 from Late Latin dīluviālis; see DILUVIUM]

diluvialism (daɪ'luːvɪəlɪzm) n the theory, generally abandoned in the mid-19th century, that the earth's surface was shaped by the biblical flood

diluvium (daɪ'luːvɪəm, dɪ-) n, pl -via (-vɪə) geology a former name for **glacial drift**. See **drift** (sense 12) [c19 from Latin: flood, from dīluere to wash away; see DILUTE]

dim (dɪm) adj dimmer, dimmest 1 badly illuminated: a dim room 2 not clearly seen; indistinct; faint: a dim shape 3 having weak or indistinct vision: eyes dim with tears 4 lacking in understanding; mentally dull 5 not clear in the mind; obscure: a dim memory 6 lacking in brilliance, brightness, or lustre: a dim colour 7 tending to be unfavourable; gloomy or disapproving (esp in the phrase **take a dim view**) ▷ vb dims, dimming, dimmed 8 to become or cause to become dim 9 (tr) to cause to seem less bright, as by comparison 10 US and Canadian (tr) to switch (car headlights) from the main to the lower beam. Also called (in Britain and certain other countries): **dip** [Old English dimm; related to Old Norse dimmr gloomy, dark] > 'dimly adv > 'dimness n

Dimashq (diː'mæʃk) n an Arabic name for **Damascus**

dim bulb n informal a slow-witted unintelligent person

dime (daɪm) n 1 a coin of the US and Canada, worth one tenth of a dollar or ten cents 2 a dime a dozen very cheap or common [c14 from Old French disme, from Latin decimus tenth, from decem ten]

dimenhydrinate (ˌdaɪmen'haɪdrɪˌneɪt) n a white slightly soluble bitter-tasting crystalline substance: an antihistamine used in the prevention of nausea, esp in travel sickness. Formula: $C_{24}H_{28}ClN_5O_3$ [from dime(thyl + AMI)N(E) + (diphen)hydr(am)in(e) + -ATE[1]]

dime novel n US (formerly) a cheap melodramatic novel, usually in paperback. Also called (esp Brit): penny-dreadful

dimension (dɪ'mɛnʃən) n 1 (often plural) a measurement of the size of something in a particular direction, such as the length, width, height, or diameter 2 (often plural) scope; size; extent: a problem of enormous dimensions 3 aspect: a new dimension to politics 4 maths the number of coordinates required to locate a point in space 5 physics a the product or the quotient of the fundamental physical quantities (such as mass, length, or time) raised to the appropriate power in a derived physical quantity: the dimensions of velocity are length divided by time b the power to which such a fundamental quantity has to be raised in a derived quantity ▷ vb 6 (tr) chiefly US a to shape or cut to specified dimensions b to mark with specified dimensions [c14 from Old French, from Latin dīmensiō an extent, from dīmētīrī to measure out, from mētīrī] > di'mensional adj > diˌmensi'onality n > di'mensionally adv > di'mensionless adj

dimer ('daɪmə) n chem a a molecule composed of

two identical simpler molecules (monomers) b a compound consisting of dimers

dimercaprol (ˌdaɪmə'kæprɒl) n a colourless oily liquid with an offensive smell, used as an antidote to lewisite and similar toxic substances. Formula: CH₂(SH)CH(SH)CH₂OH. Also called: BAL [c20 by shortening and altering from dimercaptopropanol]

dimerize or **dimerise** ('daɪməˌraɪz) vb to react or cause to react to form a dimer > ˌdimeri'zation or ˌdimeri'sation n

dimerous ('dɪmərəs) adj 1 consisting of or divided into two segments, as the tarsi of some insects 2 (of flowers) having their floral parts arranged in whorls of two [c19 from New Latin dimerus, from Greek dimerēs, from DI-[1] + meros part] > 'dimerism n

dimeter ('dɪmɪtə) n prosody a line of verse consisting of two metrical feet or a verse written in this metre

dimethylformamide (daɪˌmiːθaɪl'fɔːməˌmaɪd, -ˌmɛθ-) n a colourless liquid widely used as a solvent and sometimes as a catalyst. Formula: (CH₃)₂NCHO. Abbreviation: DMF

dimethylsulphoxide or **dimethylsulfoxide** (daɪˌmiːθaɪlsʌl'fɒksaɪd, -ˌmɛθ-) n a colourless odourless liquid substance used as a solvent and in medicine as an agent to improve the penetration of drugs applied to the skin. Formula: (CH₃)₂SO. Abbreviation: DMSO

USAGE See at sulphur

dimethyltryptamine (daɪˌmiːθaɪl'trɪptəmɪn, -ˌmɛθ-) n a hallucinogenic agent that may trigger the onset of psychosis or emotional problems in predisposed individuals. Abbreviation: DMT

dimetric (daɪ'mɛtrɪk) adj crystallog another word for **tetragonal**

dimidiate adj (dɪ'mɪdɪɪt) 1 divided in halves 2 biology now rare having one of two sides or parts less developed than the other: dimidiate antlers ▷ vb (dɪ'mɪdɪˌeɪt) 3 (tr) heraldry to halve (two bearings) so that they can be represented on the same shield [c17 from Latin dīmidiāre to halve, from dīmidius half, from dis- apart + medius middle] > diˌmidi'ation n

diminish (dɪ'mɪnɪʃ) vb 1 to make or become smaller, fewer, or less 2 (tr) architect to cause (a column, etc) to taper 3 (tr) music to decrease (a minor or perfect interval) by a semitone 4 to belittle or be belittled; reduce in authority, status, etc; depreciate [c15 blend of diminuen to lessen (from Latin dēminuere to make smaller, from minuere to reduce) + archaic minish to lessen] > di'minishable adj > di'minishingly adv > di'minishment n

diminished (dɪ'mɪnɪʃt) adj 1 reduced or lessened; made smaller 2 music denoting any minor or perfect interval reduced by a semitone 3 music denoting a triad consisting of the root plus a minor third and a diminished fifth 4 music (postpositive) (esp in jazz or pop music) denoting a diminished seventh chord having as its root the note specified: B diminished

diminished responsibility n law a plea under which proof of an impairing abnormality of mind is submitted as demonstrating lack of premeditation and therefore criminal responsibility

diminished seventh chord n a chord often used in an enharmonic modulation and very common in modern music, esp jazz and pop music, consisting of a diminished triad with an added diminished seventh above the root. Often shortened to: diminished seventh

diminishing returns pl n economics 1 progressively smaller rises in output resulting from the increased application of a variable input, such as labour, to a fixed quantity, as of capital or land 2 the increase in the average cost of production that may arise beyond a certain point as a result of increasing the overall scale of production

d

diminuendo (dɪˌmɪnjʊˈɛndəʊ) *music* ▷ *n*, *pl* -dos **1 a** a gradual decrease in loudness or the musical direction indicating this. Abbreviation: dim Symbol: > (written over the music affected) **b** a musical passage affected by a diminuendo ▷ *adj* **2** gradually decreasing in loudness **3** with a diminuendo ▷ Also: decrescendo [C18 from Italian, from *diminuire* to DIMINISH]

diminution (ˌdɪmɪˈnjuːʃən) *n* **1** reduction; decrease **2** *music* the presentation of the subject of a fugue, etc, in which the note values are reduced in length. Compare **augmentation** (sense 3) [C14 from Latin *dēminūtiō*; see DIMINISH]

diminutive (dɪˈmɪnjʊtɪv) *adj* **1** very small; tiny **2** *grammar* **a** denoting an affix added to a word to convey the meaning *small* or *unimportant* or to express affection, as for example the suffix *-ette* in French **b** denoting a word formed by the addition of a diminutive affix ▷ *n* **3** *grammar* a diminutive word or affix **4** a tiny person or thing ▷ Compare (for senses 2, 3) **augmentative**. ▷ diminutival (dɪˌmɪnjʊˈtaɪvᵊl) *adj* ▷ diˈminutively *adv* ▷ diˈminutiveness *n*

dimissory (dɪˈmɪsərɪ) *adj* **1** granting permission to be ordained: *a bishop's dimissory letter* **2** granting permission to depart

Dimitrovo (*Bulgarian* diˈmitrovo) *n* the former name (1949–62) of Pernik

dimity (ˈdɪmɪtɪ) *n*, *pl* -ties **a** a light strong cotton fabric with woven stripes or squares **b** (*as modifier*): *a dimity bonnet* [C15 from Medieval Latin *dimitum*, from Greek *dimiton*, from DI-¹ + *mitos* thread of the warp]

dimmer (ˈdɪmə) *n* **1** a device, such as a rheostat, for varying the current through an electric light and thus changing the illumination **2** (*often plural*) *US* **a** a dipped headlight on a road vehicle **b** a parking light on a car

dimorph (ˈdaɪmɔːf) *n* either of two forms of a substance that exhibits dimorphism

dimorphism (daɪˈmɔːfɪzəm) *n* **1** the occurrence within a plant of two distinct forms of any part, such as the leaves of some aquatic plants **2** the occurrence in an animal or plant species of two distinct types of individual **3** a property of certain substances that enables them to exist in two distinct crystalline forms ▷ diˈmorphic *or* diˈmorphous *adj*

dimp (dɪmp) *n* *Northern English dialect* a cigarette butt

dimple (ˈdɪmpᵊl) *n* **1** a small natural dent or crease in the flesh, esp on the cheeks or chin **2** any slight depression in a surface **3** a bubble or dent in glass ▷ *vb* **4** to make or become dimpled **5** (*intr*) to produce dimples by smiling [C13 *dympull*; compare Old English *dyppan* to dip, German *Tümpel* pool] ▷ ˈdimply *adj*

dimpsy (ˈdɪmpsɪ) *n* *Southwest English dialect* twilight

dim sum (dɪm ˈsʌm) *n* a Chinese appetizer of steamed dumplings containing various fillings [Cantonese]

dimwit (ˈdɪmˌwɪt) *n* *informal* a stupid or silly person ▷ ˌdim-ˈwitted *adj* ▷ ˌdim-ˈwittedly *adv* ▷ ˌdim-ˈwittedness *n*

din¹ (dɪn) *n* **1** a loud discordant confused noise ▷ *vb* dins, dinning, dinned **2** (*tr*; usually foll by *into*) to instil (into a person) by constant repetition **3** (*tr*) to subject to a din **4** (*intr*) to make a din [Old English *dynn*; compare Old Norse *dynr*, Old High German *tuni*]

din² (dɪn) *n* *Judaism* **1** a particular religious law; the halacha about something **2** the ruling of a Beth Din or religious court [from Hebrew, literally: judgment]

din³ (diːn) *n* *Islam* religion in general, esp the beliefs and obligations of Islam [Arabic, related to *dain* debt]

DIN (dɪn) *n* **1** a formerly used logarithmic expression of the speed of a photographic film, plate, etc, given as −10log₁₀E, where E is the exposure of a point 0.1 density units above the fog level; high-speed films have high numbers. Compare **ISO rating 2** a system of standard plugs, sockets, and cables formerly used for interconnecting domestic audio and video equipment [C20 from German *D(eutsche) I(ndustrie) N(orm)* German Industry Standard]

Din. *abbreviation for* dinar

Dinah (ˈdaɪnə) *n* the daughter of Jacob and Leah (Genesis 30:21; 34)

Dinan (*French* dinã) *n* a town in NW France, in Brittany, on the estuary of the River Rance: medieval buildings, including town walls and castle: tourism, hosiery, cider: Pop: 10 907 (1999)

Dinant (*French* dinã) *n* a town in S Belgium, on the River Meuse below steep limestone cliffs: 11th-century citadel: famous in the Middle Ages for fine brassware, known as *dinanderie*: tourism, metalwork, biscuits. Pop: 12 719 (2004 est)

dinar (ˈdiːnɑː) *n* **1** the standard monetary unit of the following countries or territories. Algeria: divided into 100 centimes. Bahrain: divided into 1000 fils. Iraq: divided into 1000 fils. Jordan: divided into 1000 fils. Kuwait: divided into 1000 fils. Libya: divided into 1000 dirhams. Serbia: divided into 100 paras (formerly the standard monetary unit of Yugoslavia). Sudan, Tunisia: divided into 1000 millimes. Abbreviation: Din, D, d **2** a monetary unit of the United Arab Emirates worth one tenth of a dirham **3** a coin, esp one of gold, formerly used in the Middle East [C17 from Arabic, from Late Greek *dēnarion*, from Latin *dēnārius* DENARIUS]

Dinaric Alps (dɪˈnærɪk, daɪ-) *pl n* a mountain range in W Croatia, Bosnia-Herzegovina, and Serbia: connected with the main Alpine system by the Julian Alps. Highest peak: Troglav, 1913 m (6277 ft)

dine (daɪn) *vb* **1** (*intr*) to eat dinner **2** (*intr*; often foll by *on*, *off*, or *upon*) to make one's meal (of): *the guests dined upon roast beef* **3** (*tr*) *informal* to entertain to dinner (esp in the phrase **to wine and dine someone**) [C13 from Old French *disner*, contracted from Vulgar Latin *disjējūnāre* (unattested) to cease fasting, from *dis-* not + Late Latin *jējūnāre* to fast; see JEJUNE]

dine out *vb* (*intr*, *adverb*) **1** to dine away from home, esp in a restaurant **2** (*foll by on*) to have dinner at the expense of someone else mainly for the sake of one's knowledge or conversation about (a subject or story)

diner (ˈdaɪnə) *n* **1** a person eating a meal, esp in a restaurant **2** *chiefly US and Canadian* a small restaurant, often at the roadside **3** a fashionable bar, or a section of one, where food is served

dineric (dɪˈnerɪk) *adj* of or concerned with the interface between immiscible liquids [C20 from DI-¹ + Late Greek *nēron* water + -IC]

dinette (daɪˈnet) *n* an alcove or small area for use as a dining room

ding¹ (dɪŋ) *vb* **1** to ring or cause to ring, esp with tedious repetition **2** (*tr*) another word for **din¹** (sense 2) ▷ *n* **3** an imitation or representation of the sound of a bell **4** *Austral informal* a party or social event [C13 probably of imitative origin, but influenced by DIN¹ + RING²; compare Old Swedish *diunga* to beat]

ding² (dɪŋ) *vb Scot* **1** to strike; dash down **2** to surpass [Middle English *dingen*]

Ding an sich (dɪn æn sɪk; *German* dɪŋ an zɪç) *n philosophy* the thing in itself

dingbat (ˈdɪŋˌbæt) *n* *US slang* **1** any unnamed object, esp one used as a missile **2** a crazy or stupid person [C19 of unknown origin]

dingbats (ˈdɪŋˌbæts) *Austral and NZ* ▷ *pl n* **1** the *slang* delirium tremens **2** give someone the dingbats *informal* to make someone nervous ▷ *adj* **3** *informal* crazy or stupid

ding-dong *n* **1** the sound of a bell or bells, esp two bells tuned a fourth or fifth apart **2** an imitation or representation of the sound of a bell **3 a** a violent exchange of blows or words **b** (*as modifier*): *a ding-dong battle in the board room* ▷ *adj* **4** sounding or ringing repeatedly [C16 of imitative origin; see DING¹]

dinge¹ (dɪndʒ) *n* dinginess [C19 back formation from DINGY]

dinge² (dɪndʒ) *US derogatory slang* ▷ *n* **1** a Black person ▷ *adj* **2** of or relating to Black people

dinge³ (dɪndʒ) *dialect* ▷ *vb* (*tr*) **1** to make a dent in (something) ▷ *n* **2** a dent [of unknown origin]

dinger (ˈdɪŋə) *n* *US* an informal word for home run

dinges (ˈdɪŋəs) *n* *South African informal* a jocular word for something whose name is unknown or forgotten; thingumabob [from Afrikaans, from *ding* thing]

dinghy (ˈdɪŋɪ) *n*, *pl* -ghies any small boat, powered by sail, oars, or outboard motor. Also (esp formerly): dingy, dingey [C19 from Hindi or Bengali *dingi* a little boat, from *dingā* boat]

dingle (ˈdɪŋᵊl) *n* a small wooded dell [C13 of uncertain origin]

dingo (ˈdɪŋɡəʊ) *n*, *pl* -goes **1** a wild dog, *Canis dingo*, of Australia, having a yellowish-brown coat and resembling a wolf **2** *Austral slang* a cheat or coward ▷ *vb* -goes, -going, -goed (*intr*) *Austral slang* **3 a** to act in a cowardly manner **b** to drop out of something **4** (*foll by on*) to let (someone) down [C18 native Australian name]

dingy (ˈdɪndʒɪ) *adj* -gier, -giest **1** lacking light or brightness; drab **2** dirty; discoloured [C18 perhaps from an earlier dialect word related to Old English *dynge* dung] ▷ ˈdingily *adv* ▷ ˈdinginess *n*

dining car *n* a railway coach in which meals are served at tables. Also called: restaurant car

dining room *n* a room where meals are eaten

dinitrobenzene (daɪˌnaɪtrəʊˈbenziːn, -ˈbenˈziːn) *n* a yellow crystalline compound existing in three isomeric forms, obtained by reaction of benzene with nitric and sulphuric acids. The *meta*- form is used in the manufacture of dyes and plastics. Formula: $C_6H_4(No_2)_2$

dinitrogen tetroxide (daɪˈnaɪtrədʒən) *n* a colourless gaseous substance that exists in equilibrium with nitrogen dioxide. As the temperature is reduced the proportion of the tetroxide increases. Formula: N_2O_4

dink¹ (dɪŋk) *adj* **1** *Scot and northern English dialect* neat or neatly dressed ▷ *vb* **2** *Austral and NZ chiefly children's slang* **a** (*tr*) to carry (a second person) on a horse, bicycle, etc **b** (*intr*) (of two people) to travel together on a horse, bicycle, etc [C16 of unknown origin]

dink² (dɪŋk) *sport* ▷ *n* **1** a ball struck delicately ▷ *vb* **2** to hit or kick (a ball) delicately [C20 imitative of a delicate strike]

Dinka (ˈdɪŋkə) *n* **1** (*pl* -kas *or* -ka) a member of a Nilotic people of the S Sudan, noted for their height, which often reaches seven feet tall: chiefly herdsmen **2** the language of this people, belonging to the Nilotic group of the Nilo-Saharan family [from Dinka *jieng* people]

dinkie (ˈdɪŋkɪ) *n* **1** an affluent married childless person ▷ *adj* **2** designed for or appealing to dinkies [C20 from *d(ouble) i(ncome) n(o) k(ids)* + -IE]

dinkum (ˈdɪŋkəm) *adj* *Austral and NZ informal* **1** Also: dinky-di genuine or right (usually preceded by *fair* and used esp as an interjection): *a fair dinkum offer* **2** dinkum oil *archaic* the truth [C19 from English dialect: work, of unknown origin]

dinky (ˈdɪŋkɪ) *adj* dinkier, dinkiest *informal* **1** *Brit* small and neat; dainty **2** *US* inconsequential; insignificant [C18 (in the sense: dainty): from DINK]

dinna (ˈdɪnə) *vb Scot* do not

dinner (ˈdɪnə) *n* **1** a meal taken in the evening **2** a meal taken at midday, esp when it is the main meal of the day; lunch **3 a** a formal evening meal, as of a club, society, etc **b** a public banquet in honour of someone or something **4** a complete meal at a fixed price in a restaurant; table d'hôte **5** (*modifier*) of, relating to, or used at dinner: *dinner plate; dinner table; dinner hour* **6** do like a dinner (*usually passive*) *Austral informal* to do for, overpower, or outdo [C13 from Old French *disner*; see DINE]

dinner-dance *n* a formal dinner followed by dancing

dinner jacket *n* a man's semiformal evening jacket without tails, usually black with a silk facing over the collar and lapels. Abbreviations: DJ, dj US and Canadian name: tuxedo

dinner lady *n Brit* a female cook or canteen worker in a school

dinner service *n* a set of matching plates, dishes, etc, suitable for serving a meal to a certain number of people

dinoceras (daɪˈnɒsərəs) *n* another name for a **uintathere** [C19 New Latin, from Greek *deinos* fearful + *keras* horn]

dinoflagellate (ˌdaɪnəʊˈflædʒɪlɪt, -ˌleɪt) *n* **1** any of a group of unicellular biflagellate aquatic organisms forming a constituent of plankton: now usually classified as a phylum of protoctists (*Dinoflagellata*) ▷ *adj* **2** of or relating to dinoflagellates [C19 from New Latin *Dinoflagellata*, from Greek *dinos* whirling + FLAGELLUM + -ATE¹]

dinosaur (ˈdaɪnəˌsɔː) *n* **1** any extinct terrestrial reptile of the orders *Saurischia* and *Ornithischia*, many of which were of gigantic size and abundant in the Mesozoic era. See also **saurischian, ornithischian** Compare **pterosaur, plesiosaur 2** a person or thing that is considered to be out of date [C19 from New Latin *dinosaurus*, from Greek *deinos* fearful + *sauros* lizard] > ˌdinoˈsaurian *adj*

dinothere (ˈdaɪnəˌθɪə) *n* any extinct late Tertiary elephant-like mammal of the genus *Dinotherium* (or *Deinotherium*), having a down-turned jaw with tusks curving downwards and backwards [C19 from New Latin *dinotherium*, from Greek *deinos* fearful + *thērion*, diminutive of *thēr* beast]

dint (dɪnt) *n* **1 by dint of** by means or use of: *by dint of hard work* **2** *archaic* a blow or a mark made by a blow ▷ *vb* **3** (*tr*) to mark with dints ▷ *n, vb* **4** a variant of **dent¹** [Old English *dynt*; related to Old Norse *dyttr* blow] > ˈdintless *adj*

diocesan (daɪˈɒsɪsən) *adj* **1** of or relating to a diocese ▷ *n* **2** the bishop of a diocese

diocese (ˈdaɪəsɪs) *n* the district under the jurisdiction of a bishop [C14 from Old French, from Late Latin *diocēsis*, from Greek *dioikēsis* administration, from *dioikein* to manage a household, from *oikos* house]

diode (ˈdaɪəʊd) *n* **1** a semiconductor device containing one p-n junction, used in circuits for converting alternating current to direct current. More formal name: **semiconductor diode 2** the earliest and simplest type of electronic valve having two electrodes, an anode and a cathode, between which a current can flow only in one direction. It was formerly widely used as a rectifier and detector but has now been replaced in most electrical circuits by the more efficient and reliable semiconductor diode [C20 from DI-¹ + -ODE²]

dioecious, diecious (daɪˈiːʃəs) *or* **dioicous** (daɪˈɔɪkəs) *adj* (of some plants) having the male and female reproductive organs in separate flowers on separate plants. Compare **monoecious** [C18 from New Latin *Dioecia* name of class, from DI¹ + Greek *oikia* house, dwelling] > diˈoeciously, diˈeciously *or* diˈoicously *adv* > diˈoeciousness, diˈeciousness *or* diˈoicousness *n*

dioestrus *or US* **diestrus** (daɪˈiːstrəs) *n* a period of sexual inactivity between periods of oestrus in animals that have several oestrous cycles in one breeding season

diol (ˈdaɪɒl) *n chem* any of a class of alcohols that have two hydroxyl groups in each molecule. Also called: **glycol, dihydric alcohol** [from DI-¹ + (ALCOH)OL]

Diomede Islands (ˈdaɪəˌmiːd) *pl n* two small islands in the Bering Strait, separated by the international date line and by the boundary line between the US and Russia

Diomedes (ˌdaɪəˈmiːdiːz) *or* **Diomede, Diomed** (ˈdaɪəˌmed) *n Greek myth* **1** a king of Argos, and suitor of Helen, who fought with the Greeks at Troy **2** a king of the Bistones in Thrace whose savage horses were strangers

Dione¹ (daɪˈəʊnɪ) *n Greek myth* a Titaness; the earliest consort of Zeus and mother of Aphrodite

Dione² (daɪˈəʊnɪ) *n* one of the larger satellites of the planet Saturn

Dionysia (ˌdaɪəˈnɪzɪə) *pl n* (in ancient Greece) festivals of the god Dionysus: a source of Athenian drama

Dionysiac (ˌdaɪəˈnɪzɪˌæk) *adj* **1** of or relating to Dionysus or his worship **2** a less common word for **Dionysian**

Dionysian (ˌdaɪəˈnɪzɪən) *adj* **1** of or relating to Dionysus **2** (*sometimes not capital*) (in the philosophy of Nietzsche) of or relating to the set of creative qualities that encompasses spontaneity, irrationality, the rejection of discipline, etc **3** (*often not capital*) wild or orgiastic **4** of or relating to any of the historical characters named Dionysius ▷ Compare (for senses 2, 3) **Apollonian**

Dionysus *or* **Dionysos** (ˌdaɪəˈnaɪsəs) *n* the Greek god of wine, fruitfulness, and vegetation, worshipped in orgiastic rites. He was also known as the bestower of ecstasy and god of the drama, and identified with Bacchus

Diophantine equation (ˌdaɪəʊˈfæntaɪn) *n* (in number theory) an equation in more than one variable and with integral coefficients, for which integral solutions are sought [C18 after *Diophantus*, Greek mathematician of the 3rd century AD]

diopside (daɪˈɒpsaɪd, -sɪd) *n* a colourless or pale-green pyroxene mineral consisting of calcium magnesium silicate in monoclinic crystalline form: used as a gemstone. Formula: $CaMgSi_2O_6$ [C19 from DI-² + Greek *opsis* sight, appearance + -IDE]

dioptase (daɪˈɒpteɪs, -teɪz) *n* a green glassy mineral consisting of hydrated copper silicate in hexagonal crystalline form. Formula: $Cu_6Si_6O_{18}.6H_2O$ [C19 from French, from Greek *dia-* through + *optos* visible]

dioptometer (ˌdaɪɒpˈtɒmɪtə) *n* an instrument for measuring ocular refraction [from DI-² + OPT(IC) + METER] > ˌdiopˈtometry *n*

dioptre *or US* **diopter** (daɪˈɒptə) *n* a unit for measuring the refractive power of a lens: the reciprocal of the focal length of the lens expressed in metres [C16 from Latin *dioptra* optical instrument, from Greek, from *dia-* through + *opsesthai* to see] > diˈoptral *adj*

dioptric (daɪˈɒptrɪk) *or* **dioptrical** *adj* **1** of or concerned with dioptrics **2** of or denoting refraction or refracted light > diˈoptrically *adv*

dioptrics (daɪˈɒptrɪks) *n* (*functioning as singular*) the branch of geometrical optics concerned with the formation of images by lenses [C20 from DIOPTRE + -ICS]

diorama (ˌdaɪəˈrɑːmə) *n* **1** a miniature three-dimensional scene, in which models of figures are seen against a background **2** a picture made up of illuminated translucent curtains, viewed through an aperture **3** a museum display, as of an animal, of a specimen in its natural setting **4** *films* a scene produced by the rearrangement of lighting effects [C19 from French, from Greek *dia-* through + Greek *horama* view, from *horan* to see] > dioramic (ˌdaɪəˈræmɪk) *adj*

diorite (ˈdaɪəˌraɪt) *n* a dark coarse-grained igneous plutonic rock consisting of plagioclase feldspar and ferromagnesian minerals such as hornblende [C19 from French, from Greek *diorizein* to distinguish (from *dia-* apart + *horizein* to define) + -ITE¹] > dioritic (ˌdaɪəˈrɪtɪk) *adj*

Dioscuri (ˌdaɪɒsˈkjʊərɪ) *pl n* the Greek name for **Castor and Pollux**, when considered together

dioxan (daɪˈɒksən) *or* **dioxane** (daɪˈɒkseɪn) *n* a colourless insoluble toxic liquid made by heating ethanediol with sulphuric acid; 1,4-diethylene dioxide: used as a solvent, esp for waxes and

cellulose acetate resins. Formula: $(CH_2)_2O(CH_2)_2O$

dioxide (daɪˈɒksaɪd) *n* **1** any oxide containing two oxygen atoms per molecule, both of which are bonded to an atom of another element **2** another name for a **peroxide** (sense 4)

dioxin (daɪˈɒksɪn) *n* any of a number of mostly poisonous chemical by-products of the manufacture of certain herbicides and bactericides, esp the extremely toxic 2,3,7,8-tetrachlorodibenzo-para-dioxin

dip (dɪp) *vb* dips, dipping, dipped **1** to plunge or be plunged quickly or briefly into a liquid, esp to wet or coat **2** (*intr*) to undergo a slight decline, esp temporarily: *sales dipped in November* **3** (*intr*) to slope downwards: *the land dips towards the river* **4** (*intr*) to sink or appear to sink quickly: *the sun dipped below the horizon* **5** (*tr*) to switch (car headlights) from the main to the lower beam. US and Canadian word: **dim 6** (*tr*) **a** to immerse (poultry, sheep, etc) briefly in a liquid chemical to rid them of or prevent infestation by insects, etc **b** to immerse (grain, timber, or wood) in a preservative liquid **7** (*tr*) to stain or dye by immersing in a liquid **8** (*tr*) to baptize (someone) by immersion **9** (*tr*) to plate or galvanize (a metal, etc) by immersion in an electrolyte or electrolytic cell **10** (*tr*) to scoop up a liquid or something from a liquid in the hands or in a container **11** to lower or be lowered briefly: *she dipped her knee in a curtsy* **12** (*tr*) to make (a candle) by plunging the wick into melted wax **13** (*intr*) to plunge a container, the hands, etc, into something, esp to obtain or retrieve an object: *he dipped in his pocket for money* **14** (*intr; foll by in or into*) to dabble (in); play (at): *he dipped into black magic* **15** (*intr*) (of an aircraft) to drop suddenly and then regain height **16** (*intr*) (of a rock stratum or mineral vein) to slope downwards from the horizontal **17** (*intr; often foll by for*) (in children's games) to select (a leader, etc) by reciting any of various rhymes **18** (*tr*) *slang* to pick (a person's) pocket ▷ *n* **19** the act of dipping or state of being dipped **20** a brief swim in water **21 a** any liquid chemical preparation in which poultry, sheep, etc are dipped **b** any liquid preservative into which objects, esp of wood, are dipped **22** a preparation of dyeing agents into which fabric is immersed **23** a depression, esp in a landscape **24** something taken up by dipping **25** a container used for dipping; dipper **26** a momentary sinking down **27** the angle of slope of rock strata, fault planes, etc, from the horizontal plane **28** Also called: **angle of dip, magnetic dip, inclination** the angle between the direction of the earth's magnetic field and the plane of the horizon; the angle that a magnetic needle free to swing in a vertical plane makes with the horizontal **29** a creamy mixture into which pieces of food are dipped before being eaten **30** *surveying* the angular distance of the horizon below the plane of observation **31** a candle made by plunging a wick repeatedly into wax **32** a momentary loss of altitude when flying **33** (in gymnastics) a chinning exercise on the parallel bars **34** a slang word for **pickpocket** ▷ See also **dip into, dip out** [Old English *dyppan*; related to Old High German *tupfen* to wash, German *taufen* to baptize; see DEEP]

dip. *or* **Dip.** *abbreviation for* diploma

DipAD (in Britain) *abbreviation for* Diploma in Art and Design

dip-and-scarp *adj* (of topography) characterized by alternating steeper scarp slopes and gentler dip slopes

DipChemEng *abbreviation for* Diploma in Chemical Engineering

dip circle *n* an instrument for measuring dip, consisting of a dip needle with a vertical circular scale of angles. Also called: **inclinometer**

DipCom *abbreviation for* Diploma of Commerce

DipEd (in Britain) *abbreviation for* Diploma in Education

dipeptide (daɪˈpɛptaɪd) *n* a compound consisting

d

of two linked amino acids. See **peptide**

dipetalous (daɪˈpɛtələs) adj another word for **bipetalous**

dip fault n geology a fault that runs perpendicular to the strike of the affected rocks (i.e. parallel to the plane of the angle of dip of the rocks)

diphase (ˈdaɪˌfeɪz) or **diphasic** adj physics of, having, or concerned with two phases

diphasic (daɪˈfeɪzɪk) adj 1 zoology (of parasites) having a free active stage in the life cycle 2 physics another word for **diphase**

diphenyl (daɪˈfiːnaɪl, -nɪl, -ˈfɛnɪl) n another name for **biphenyl**

diphenylamine (daɪˌfiːnaɪləˈmiːn, -ˈæmɪn, -nɪl-, -ˌfɛn-) n a colourless insoluble crystalline derivative of benzene, used in the manufacture of dyes, as a stabilizer in plastics, etc Formula: $(C_6H_5)_2NH$

diphenylhydantoin sodium (daɪˌfiːnaɪlhaɪˈdæntəʊɪn, -nɪl-, -ˌfɛn-) n another name for **phenytoin**

diphosgene (daɪˈfɒzdʒiːn) n an oily liquid with an extremely poisonous vapour, made by treating methanol with phosgene and chlorinating the product: has been used in chemical warfare. Formula: $ClCOOCCl_3$

diphtheria (dɪpˈθɪərɪə, dɪf-) n an acute contagious disease caused by the bacillus Corynebacterium diphtheriae, producing fever, severe prostration, and difficulty in breathing and swallowing as the result of swelling of the throat and formation of a false membrane [c19 New Latin, from French diphthérie, from Greek diphthera leather; from the nature of the membrane] > diphˈtherial, diphtheritic (ˌdɪpθəˈrɪtɪk, dɪf-) or diphtheric (dɪpˈθɛrɪk, dɪf-) adj > diphtheˌroid adj

diphthong (ˈdɪfθɒŋ, ˈdɪp-) n 1 a vowel sound, occupying a single syllable, during the articulation of which the tongue moves from one position to another, causing a continual change in vowel quality, as in the pronunciation of a in English late, during which the tongue moves from the position of (e) towards (ɪ) 2 a digraph or ligature representing a composite vowel such as this, as ae in Caesar [c15 from Late Latin diphthongus, from Greek diphthongos, from DI-¹ + phthongos sound] > diphˈthongal adj

diphthongize or **diphthongise** (ˈdɪfθɒŋˌaɪz, -ˌgaɪz, ˈdɪp-) vb (often passive) to make (a simple vowel) into a diphthong > ˌdiphthongiˈzation or ˌdiphthongiˈsation n

diphycercal (ˌdɪfɪˈsɜːkəl) adj ichthyol of or possessing a symmetrical or pointed tail with the vertebral column extending to the tip, as in primitive fishes [c19 from Greek diphuēs twofold (from DI-¹ + phuē growth) + kerkos tail]

diphyletic (ˌdaɪfaɪˈlɛtɪk) adj relating to or characterized by descent from two ancestral groups of animals or plants

diphyllous (daɪˈfɪləs) adj (of certain plants) having two leaves

diphyodont (ˈdɪfɪəʊˌdɒnt) adj having two successive sets of teeth, as mammals (including man). Compare **polyphyodont** [c19 from Greek diphuēs double (see DIPHYCERCAL) + -ODONT]

dip into vb (intr, preposition) 1 to draw (upon): he dipped into his savings 2 to read (passages) at random or cursorily in a book, newspaper, etc)

diplegia (daɪˈpliːdʒə) n paralysis of corresponding parts on both sides of the body; bilateral paralysis > diˈplegic adj

diplo- or before a vowel **dipl-** combining form double: diplococcus [from Greek, from diploos, from DI-¹ + -ploos -fold]

diplobiont (ˌdɪpləʊˈbaɪɒnt) n biology an organism that has both haploid and diploid individuals in its life cycle > ˌdiploˈbiontic adj

diploblastic (ˌdɪpləʊˈblæstɪk) adj (of jellyfish, corals, and other coelenterates) having a body developed from only two germ layers (ectoderm and endoderm). Compare **triploblastic**

diplocardiac (ˌdɪpləʊˈkɑːdɪˌæk) adj (of birds and mammals) having a four-chambered heart, which enables two separate circulations and prevents mixing of the arterial and venous blood

Diplock court (ˈdɪplɒk) n in Northern Ireland, a court of law designed to try cases linked with terrorism. In order to prevent the intimidation of jurors, the court consists of a single judge and no jury [c20 named after Lord Diplock, who introduced the courts in 1972]

diplococcus (ˌdɪpləʊˈkɒkəs) n, pl -cocci (-ˈkɒksaɪ) any of various spherical Gram-positive bacteria that occur in pairs, esp any of the genus Diplococcus, such as D. pneumoniae, which causes pneumonia: family Lactobacillaceae > ˌdiploˈcoccal or diploˈcoccic (ˌdɪpləʊˈkɒksɪk, -ˈkɒkɪk) adj

diplodocus (dɪˈplɒdəkəs, ˌdɪpləʊˈdəʊkəs) n, pl -cuses any herbivorous quadrupedal late Jurassic dinosaur of the genus Diplodocus, characterized by a very long neck and tail and a total body length of 27 metres: suborder Sauropoda (sauropods) [c19 from New Latin, from DIPLO- + Greek dokos beam]

diploë (ˈdɪpləʊˌiː) n anatomy the spongy bone separating the two layers of compact bone of the skull [c17 via New Latin, from Greek: a fold, from diploos double]

diploid (ˈdɪplɔɪd) adj 1 biology (of cells or organisms) having pairs of homologous chromosomes so that twice the haploid number is present 2 double or twofold ▷ n 3 biology a diploid cell or organism > ˈdiploidic adj > ˈdiploidy n

diploma (dɪˈpləʊmə) n 1 a document conferring a qualification, recording success in examinations or successful completion of a course of study 2 an official document that confers an honour or privilege [c17 from Latin: official letter or document, literally: letter folded double, from Greek; see DIPLO-]

diplomacy (dɪˈpləʊməsɪ) n, pl -cies 1 the conduct of the relations of one state with another by peaceful means 2 skill in the management of international relations 3 tact, skill, or cunning in dealing with people [c18 from French diplomatie, from diplomatique DIPLOMATIC]

diplomat (ˈdɪpləˌmæt) n 1 an official, such as an ambassador or first secretary, engaged in diplomacy 2 a person who deals with people tactfully or skilfully

diplomate (ˈdɪpləˌmeɪt) n any person who has been granted a diploma, esp a physician certified as a specialist

diplomatic (ˌdɪpləˈmætɪk) adj 1 of or relating to diplomacy or diplomats 2 skilled in negotiating, esp between states or people 3 tactful in dealing with people 4 of or relating to diplomatics [c18 from French diplomatique concerning the documents of diplomacy, from New Latin diplōmaticus; see DIPLOMA] > ˌdiploˈmatically adv

diplomatic bag n a container or bag in which official mail is sent, free from customs inspection, to and from an embassy or consulate

diplomatic corps or **body** n the entire body of diplomats accredited to a given state

diplomatic immunity n the immunity from local jurisdiction and exemption from taxation in the country to which they are accredited afforded to diplomats

diplomatics (ˌdɪpləˈmætɪks) n (functioning as singular) 1 the critical study of historical documents 2 a less common word for **diplomacy**

Diplomatic Service n 1 (in Britain) the division of the Civil Service which provides diplomats to represent the U.K. abroad 2 (not capitals) the equivalent institution of any other country

diplomatist (dɪˈpləʊmətɪst) n a less common word for **diplomat**

diplonema (ˌdɪpləʊˈniːmə) n biology a less common name for **diplotene**

diplont (ˈdɪplɒnt) n an animal or plant that has the diploid number of chromosomes in its somatic cells [c20 DIPLO- + Greek ōn being, from einai to be] > dipˈlontic adj

diplopia (dɪˈpləʊpɪə) n a visual defect in which a single object is seen in duplicate; double vision. It can be caused by incorrect fixation or by an abnormality in the visual system [c19 New Latin, from DIPLO- + Greek ōps eye] > diplopic (dɪˈplɒpɪk) adj

diplopod (ˈdɪpləˌpɒd) n any arthropod of the class Diplopoda, which includes the millipedes

diplosis (dɪˈpləʊsɪs) n biology the doubling of the haploid number of chromosomes that occurs during fusion of gametes to form a diploid zygote [c20 from Greek diplōsis doubling, from diploun to double, from diploos double]

diplostemonous (ˌdɪpləʊˈstiːmənəs, -ˈstɛm-) adj (of plants) having twice as many stamens as petals, esp with the stamens arranged in two whorls [c19 from New Latin diplostemonus (unattested), from DIPLO- + -stemonus relating to a STAMEN]

diplotene (ˈdɪpləʊˌtiːn) n the fourth stage of the prophase of meiosis, during which the paired homologous chromosomes separate except at the places where genetic exchange has occurred. See also **chiasma** (sense 1), **crossing over** [c20 from DIPLO- + Greek tainia band]

diplozoic (ˌdɪpləˈzəʊɪk) adj (of certain animals) bilaterally symmetrical

DipMet abbreviation for Diploma in Metallurgy

dip needle n a magnetized needle pivoted through its centre of gravity able to rotate freely in a vertical plane, used to determine the inclination of the earth's magnetic field. See also **dip circle**

dipnoan (dɪpˈnəʊən) adj 1 of, relating to, or belonging to the Dipnoi, a subclass of bony fishes comprising the lungfishes ▷ n 2 any lungfish [c19 from New Latin Dipnoi, from Greek dipnoos, double-breathing, from DI-¹ + pnoē breathing, air, from pnein to breathe]

dipody (ˈdɪpədɪ) n, pl -dies prosody a metrical unit consisting of two feet [c19 from Late Latin dipodia, from Greek DI-¹ + pous foot]

dipole (ˈdaɪˌpəʊl) n 1 two electric charges or magnetic poles that have equal magnitudes but opposite signs and are separated by a small distance 2 a molecule in which the centre of positive charge does not coincide with the centre of negative charge 3 Also called: dipole aerial a directional radio or television aerial consisting of two equal lengths of metal wire or rods, with a connecting wire fixed between them in the form of a T > diˈpolar adj

dipole moment n chem a measure of the polarity in a chemical bond or molecule, equal to the product of one charge and the distance between the charges. Symbol: μ

dip out vb (intr, adverb) Austral and NZ informal (often foll by on) to miss out on or fail to participate in something: he dipped out on the examination

dipper (ˈdɪpə) n 1 a ladle used for dipping 2 Also called: water ouzel any aquatic songbird of the genus Cinclus and family Cinclidae, esp C. cinclus. They inhabit fast-flowing streams and resemble large wrens 3 a slang word for **pickpocket** 4 a person or thing that dips, such as the mechanism for directing car headlights downwards 5 a small metal cup clipped onto a painter's palette for holding diluent or medium 6 archaic an Anabaptist ▷ See also **big dipper**

dippy (ˈdɪpɪ) adj -pier, -piest slang odd, eccentric, or crazy [c20 of unknown origin]

dipropellant (ˌdaɪprəˈpɛlənt) n another name for **bipropellant**

diprotodon (daɪˈprəʊtəˌdɒn) n a large extinct marsupial of the Australian genus Diprotodon [c19 from Greek from DI-¹ + PROTO- + -ODONT, from its two prominent lower incisors]

diprotodont (daɪˈprəʊtəˌdɒnt) n any marsupial of the group or suborder Diprotodontia, including kangaroos, phalangers, and wombats, having fewer than three upper incisor teeth on each side of the jaw. Compare **polyprotodont** [c19 from

Greek from DI-¹ + PROTO- + -ODONT]

dip-slip fault n geology a fault on which the movement is in the direction of the dip of the fault

dipsomania (ˌdɪpsəʊˈmeɪnɪə) n a compulsive desire to drink alcoholic beverages [C19 New Latin, from Greek dipsa thirst + -MANIA]

dipsomaniac (ˌdɪpsəʊˈmeɪnɪˌæk) n 1 any person who has an uncontrollable and recurring urge to drink alcohol. Shortened form: dipso ▷ adj 2 relating to or affected with dipsomania > dipsomaniacal (ˌdɪpsəʊməˈnaɪəkəl) adj

dipstick (ˈdɪpˌstɪk) n a graduated rod or strip dipped into a container to indicate the fluid level

dip switch n a device for dipping car headlights

dipteral (ˈdɪptərəl) adj architect having a double row of columns

dipteran (ˈdɪptərən) or **dipteron** (ˈdɪptəˌrɒn) n 1 any dipterous insect ▷ adj 2 another word for **dipterous** (sense 1)

dipterocarpaceous (ˌdɪptərəʊkɑːˈpeɪʃəs) adj of, relating to, or belonging to the Dipterocarpaceae, a family of trees chiefly native to tropical SE Asia, having two-winged fruits. Many species yield useful timber and resins [C19 via New Latin from Greek dipteros two-winged + karpos fruit]

dipterous (ˈdɪptərəs) adj 1 Also: dipteran of, relating to, or belonging to the Diptera, a large order of insects having a single pair of wings and sucking or piercing mouthparts. The group includes flies, mosquitoes, craneflies, and midges 2 botany having two winglike parts: a dipterous seed [C18 from New Latin, from Greek dipteros, from di- two + pteros wing]

diptych (ˈdɪptɪk) n 1 a pair of hinged wooden tablets with waxed surfaces for writing 2 a painting or carving on two panels, usually hinged like a book [C17 from Greek diptukhos folded together, from DI¹ + ptukhos fold; compare TRIPTYCH]

diquark (ˈdaɪkwɑːk) n a low-energy configuration of two quarks attracted to one another by virtue of having antisymmetric colours and spins

dir. abbreviation for director

Dirac constant (dɪˈræk) n a constant used in quantum mechanics, equal to the Planck constant divided by 2π. It has a value of $1.054571596 \pm 0.000000078 \times 10^{-34}$ joule seconds. Symbol: ħ or ħ Also called: crossed-h, h-bar [C20 named after Paul Adrien Maurice Dirac (1902–84), English physicist]

dire (daɪə) adj (usually prenominal) 1 Also: direful disastrous; fearful 2 desperate; urgent: a dire need 3 foreboding disaster; ominous: a dire warning [C16 from Latin dīrus ominous, fearful; related to Greek deos fear] > ˈdirely adv > ˈdireness n

direct (dɪˈrɛkt, daɪ-) vb (mainly tr) 1 to regulate, conduct, or control the affairs of 2 (also intr) to give commands or orders with authority to (a person or group): he directed them to go away 3 to tell or show (someone) the way to a place 4 to aim, point, or cause to move towards a goal 5 to address (a letter, parcel, etc) 6 to address (remarks, words, etc): to direct comments at someone 7 (also intr) to provide guidance to (actors, cameramen, etc) in the rehearsal of a play or the filming of a motion picture 8 (also intr) a to conduct (a piece of music or musicians), usually while performing oneself b another word for (US) for conduct (sense 9) ▷ adj 9 without delay or evasion; straightforward: a direct approach 10 without turning aside; uninterrupted; shortest; straight: a direct route 11 without intervening persons or agencies; immediate: a direct link 12 honest; frank; candid: a direct answer 13 (usually prenominal) precise, exact: a direct quotation 14 diametrical: the direct opposite 15 in an unbroken line of descent, as from father to son over succeeding generations: a direct descendant 16 (of government, decisions, etc) by or from the electorate rather than through representatives 17 logic, maths (of a proof) progressing from the

premises to the conclusion, rather than eliminating the possibility of the falsehood of the conclusion. Compare **indirect proof** 18 astronomy moving from west to east on the celestial sphere. Compare **retrograde** (sense 4a) 19 a of or relating to direct current b (of a secondary induced current) having the same direction as the primary current 20 music a (of motion) in the same direction. See **motion** (sense 9) b (of an interval or chord) in root position; not inverted ▷ adv 21 directly; straight: he went direct to the office [C14 from Latin dīrectus; from dīrigere to guide, from dis- apart + regere to rule] > diˈrectness n

direct access n a method of reading data from a computer file without reading through the file from the beginning as on a disk or drum. Also called: random access Compare **sequential access**

direct action n action such as strikes or civil disobedience, employed by organized labour or other groups to obtain demands from an employer, government, etc

direct coupling n electronics conductive coupling between electronic circuits, as opposed to inductive or capacitive coupling. See also **coupling** (sense 4) > **direct coupled** adj

direct current n a continuous electric current that flows in one direction only, without substantial variation in magnitude. Abbreviation: DC Compare **alternating current**

direct debit n an order given to a bank or building society by a holder of an account, instructing it to pay to a specified person or organization any sum demanded by that person or organization. Compare **standing order**

direct distance dialing n US and Canadian a service by which telephone subscribers can obtain long-distance calls by dialling direct without the aid of an operator. British equivalent: subscriber trunk dialling

direct dye n any of a number of dyes that can be applied without the use of a mordant. They are usually azo dyes applied to cotton or rayon from a liquid bath containing an electrolyte such as sodium sulphate

directed (dɪˈrɛktɪd, daɪ-) adj maths (of a number, line, or angle) having either a positive or negative sign to distinguish measurement in one direction or orientation from that in the opposite direction or orientation

direct evidence n law evidence, usually the testimony of a witness, directly relating to the fact in dispute. Compare **circumstantial evidence**

direct-grant school n (in Britain, formerly) a school financed by endowment, fees, and a state grant conditional upon admittance of a percentage of nonpaying pupils nominated by the local education authority

direct injection n See **solid injection**

direct input n a device, such as a keyboard, used to insert data directly into a computerized system

direction (dɪˈrɛkʃən, daɪ-) n 1 the act of directing or the state of being directed 2 management, control, or guidance 3 the work of a stage or film director 4 the course or line along which a person or thing moves, points, or lies 5 the course along which a ship, aircraft, etc, is travelling, expressed as the angle between true or magnetic north and an imaginary line through the main fore-and-aft axis of the vessel 6 the place towards which a person or thing is directed 7 a line of action; course 8 the name and address on a letter, parcel, etc 9 music the process of conducting an orchestra, choir, etc 10 music an instruction in the form of a word or symbol heading or occurring in the body of a passage, movement, or piece to indicate tempo, dynamics, mood, etc 11 (modifier) maths a (of an angle) being any one of the three angles that a line in space makes with the three positive directions of the coordinate axes. Usually given as α, β, and γ with respect to the x-, y-, and z-axes b (of a cosine) being the cosine of any of the direction angles

▷ See also **directions**

directional (dɪˈrɛkʃənᵊl, daɪ-) adj 1 of or relating to a spatial direction 2 electronics a having or relating to an increased sensitivity to radio waves, sound waves, nuclear particles, etc, coming from a particular direction b (of an aerial) transmitting or receiving radio waves more effectively in some directions than in others 3 physics, electronics a concentrated in, following, or producing motion in a particular direction b indicating direction 4 indicating the direction something, such as a fashion trend, might take: directional fashion looks > diˌrectionˈality n

directional drilling n a method of drilling for oil in which the well is not drilled vertically, as when a number of wells are to be drilled from a single platform to reach different areas of an oil field. Also called: deviated drilling

direction finder n a highly directional aerial system that can be used to determine the direction of incoming radio signals, used esp as a navigation aid. Abbreviations: D/F or DF > direction finding n

directions (dɪˈrɛkʃənz, daɪ-) pl n (sometimes singular) instructions for doing something or for reaching a place

directive (dɪˈrɛktɪv, daɪ-) n 1 an instruction; order ▷ adj 2 tending to direct; directing 3 indicating direction

direct labour n commerce 1 work that is an essential part of a production process or the provision of a service. Compare **indirect labour** 2 Brit workers who are part of an employer's own labour force rather than hired through a contractor, such as building workers employed by a local authority

direct lighting n electrical engineering a lighting system in which a large proportion (at least 90 per cent) of the light is directed downwards

directly (dɪˈrɛktlɪ, daɪ-) adv 1 in a direct manner 2 at once; without delay 3 (foll by before or after) immediately; just ▷ conj 4 (subordinating) as soon as: we left directly the money arrived

direct-mail shot n marketing the posting of unsolicited sales literature to potential customers' homes or business addresses

direct marketing n selling goods directly to consumers rather than through retailers, usually by mail order, direct-mail shot, newspaper advertising, door-to-door selling, telephone selling, the internet, or television home-shopping channels. Also called: direct selling

direct memory access n a process in which data may be moved directly to or from the main memory of a computer system by operations not under the control of the central processing unit. Abbreviation: DMA

direct method n a method of teaching a foreign language with minimal use of the pupil's native language and of formal grammar

direct object n grammar a noun, pronoun, or noun phrase whose referent receives the direct action of a verb. For example, a book is the direct object in the sentence They bought Anne a book. Compare **indirect object**

Directoire French (direktwar) n 1 history the French Directory. See **Directory** ▷ adj 2 of, in, or relating to a decorative style of the end of the 18th century in France; a form of neoclassicism 3 characteristic of women's dress during the French Directory, typically an almost transparent dress with the waistline under the bust

director (dɪˈrɛktə, daɪ-) n 1 a person or thing that directs, controls, or regulates 2 a member of the governing board of a business concern who may or may not have an executive function 3 a person who directs the affairs of an institution, trust, educational programme, etc 4 the person responsible for the artistic and technical aspects of making a film or television programme. Compare **producer** (sense 4) 5 music another word (esp US) for **conductor** (sense 2) > ˌdirecˈtorial adj

d

> ˌdirec'torially *adv* > di'rectorˌship *n* > di'rectress *fem n*

directorate (dɪ'rɛktərɪt, daɪ-) *n* **1** a board of directors **2** Also: **directorship** the position of director

director-general *n, pl* directors-general the head of a large organization such as the CBI or BBC

Director of Education *n Brit* another term for **Chief Education Officer**

Director of Public Prosecutions *n* (in Britain) an official who, as head of the Crown Prosecution Service, is responsible for conducting all criminal prosecutions initiated by the police. Abbreviation: **DPP**

director's chair *n* a light wooden folding chair with arm rests and a canvas seat and back

director's cut *n films* a version of a film which realizes the artistic aims of the director more fully than the original version

directory (dɪ'rɛktərɪ, -trɪ, daɪ-) *n, pl* -ries **1** a book, arranged alphabetically or classified by trade listing names, addresses, telephone numbers, etc, of individuals or firms **2** a book or manual giving directions **3** a book containing the rules to be observed in the forms of worship used in churches **4** a less common word for **directorate** (sense 2) **5** *computing* an area of a disk, Winchester disk, or floppy disk that contains the names and locations of files currently held on that disk ▷ *adj* **6** directing

Directory (dɪ'rɛktərɪ, -trɪ, daɪ-) *n the history* the body of five directors in power in France from 1795 until their overthrow by Napoleon in 1799. Also called: **French Directory**

direct primary *n US government* a primary in which voters directly select the candidates who will run for office

direct question *n* a question asked in direct speech, such as *Why did you come?*. Compare **indirect question**

direct-reading *adj* (of an instrument) calibrated so that a given quantity to be measured can be read directly off the scale without the need of a multiplying constant

directrix (dɪ'rɛktrɪks, daɪ-) *n* **1** *geometry* a fixed reference line, situated on the convex side of a conic section, that is used when defining or calculating its eccentricity **2** a directress [c17 New Latin, feminine of DIRECTOR]

direct selling *n* another name for **direct marketing**

direct speech *or esp US* **direct discourse** *n* the reporting of what someone has said or written by quoting his exact words

direct tax *n* a tax paid by the person or organization on which it is levied. Compare **indirect tax**. > direct taxation *n*

dirge (dɜːdʒ) *n* **1** a chant of lamentation for the dead **2** the funeral service in its solemn or sung forms **3** any mourning song or melody [c13 changed from Latin *dīrigē* direct (imperative), opening word of the Latin antiphon used in the office of the dead] > 'dirgeful *adj*

dirham ('dɪəræm) *n* **1** the standard monetary unit of Morocco, divided into 100 centimes **2** the standard monetary unit of the United Arab Emirates, divided into 10 dinars and 100 fils **3 a** a Kuwaiti monetary unit worth one tenth of a dinar and 100 fils **b** a Tunisian monetary unit worth one tenth of a dinar and 100 millimes **c** a Qatari monetary unit worth one hundredth of a riyal **d** a Libyan monetary unit worth one thousandth of a dinar **4** any of various silver coins minted in North African countries at different periods [c18 from Arabic, from Latin DRACHMA]

dirigible (dɪ'rɪdʒɪbəl) *adj* **1** able to be steered or directed ▷ *n* **2** another name for **airship** [c16 from Latin *dīrigere* to DIRECT] > 'dirigi'bility *n*

dirigisme (diːriːˈʒiːzəm) *n* control by the state of economic and social matters [c20 from French] > dirig'iste *adj*

diriment ('dɪrɪmənt) *adj* **1** (of an impediment to

marriage in canon law) totally invalidating **2** *rare* nullifying [c19 from Latin *dirimēns* separating, from Latin *dirimere* to part, from DIS-¹ + *emere* to obtain]

dirk (dɜːk) *n* **1** a dagger esp as formerly worn by Scottish Highlanders ▷ *vb* (*tr*) **2** to stab with a dirk [c16 from Scottish *durk*, perhaps from German *Dolch* dagger]

dirndl ('dɜːndʰl) *n* **1** a woman's dress with a full gathered skirt and fitted bodice; originating from Tyrolean peasant wear **2** a gathered skirt of this kind [German (Bavarian and Austrian): shortened from *Dirndlkleid*, from *Dirndl* little girl + *Kleid* dress]

dirt (dɜːt) *n* **1** any unclean substance, such as mud, dust, excrement, etc; filth **2** loose earth; soil **3 a** packed earth, gravel, cinders, etc, used to make a racetrack **b** (*as modifier*): *a dirt track* **4** *mining* the gravel or soil from which minerals are extracted **5** a person or thing regarded as worthless **6** obscene or indecent speech or writing **7** *slang* gossip; scandalous information **8** moral corruption **9 do** (*someone*) **dirt** *slang* to do something vicious to (someone) **10 dish the dirt** *informal* to spread malicious gossip **11 eat dirt** *slang* to accept insult without complaining **12 treat someone like dirt** to have no respect or consideration for someone [from Old Norse *drit* excrement; related to Middle Dutch *drēte*]

dirt bike *n* a type of motorbike designed for use over rough ground

dirt-cheap *adj, adv informal* at an extremely low price

dirt-poor *adj chiefly US* extremely poor

dirt road *n* an unsealed country road

dirty ('dɜːtɪ) *adj* dirtier, dirtiest **1** covered or marked with dirt; filthy **2 a** obscene; salacious: *dirty books* **b** sexually clandestine: *a dirty weekend* **3** causing one to become grimy: *a dirty job* **4** (of a colour) not clear and bright; impure **5** unfair; dishonest; unscrupulous; unsporting **6** mean; nasty: *a dirty cheat* **7** scandalous; unkind: *a dirty rumour* **8** revealing dislike or anger: *a dirty look* **9** (of weather) rainy or squally; stormy **10** (of an aircraft) having projections into the airstream, such as lowered flaps **11** (of an explosive device) modified to cause radioactive contamination. Compare **clean** (sense 5) **12 be dirty on** *Austral slang* to be offended by or be hostile towards **13 dirty dog** a despicable person **14 dirty linen** *informal* intimate secrets, esp those that might give rise to gossip **15 dirty word a** an obscene word **b** something that is regarded with disapproval: *federalism is a dirty word* **16 dirty work** unpleasant or illicit activity **17 do the dirty on** *Brit informal* to behave meanly or unkindly towards ▷ *vb* dirties, dirtying, dirtied **18** to make or become dirty; stain; soil > 'dirtily *adv* > 'dirtiness *n*

dirty bomb *n informal* a bomb made from nuclear waste combined with conventional explosives that is capable of spreading radioactive material over a very wide area

dirty realism *n* a style of writing, originating in the US in the 1980s, which depicts in great detail the seamier or more mundane aspects of ordinary life > dirty realist *n*

dirty trick *n* **1** a malicious and contemptible action **2** (*plural*) **a** underhand activity and machinations in political or governmental affairs **b** (*as modifier*): *dirty-tricks operation*

dis (dɪs) *vb* a variant spelling of **diss**

Dis (dɪs) *n* **1** Also called: Orcus, Pluto the Roman god of the underworld **2** the abode of the dead; underworld ▷ Greek equivalent: Hades

dis-¹ *prefix* **1** indicating reversal: *disconnect; disembark* **2** indicating negation, lack, or deprivation: *dissimilar; distrust; disgrace* **3** indicating removal or release: *disembowel; disburden* **4** expressing intensive force: *dissever* [from Latin *dis-* apart; in some cases, via Old French *des-*. In compound words of Latin origin, *dis-* becomes *dif-* before *f* and *di-* before some consonants]

dis-² *combining form* variant of **di-¹** before *s: dissyllable*

disability (ˌdɪsə'bɪlɪtɪ) *n, pl* -ties **1** the condition of being unable to perform a task or function because of a physical or mental impairment **2** something that disables; handicap **3** lack of necessary intelligence, strength, etc **4** an incapacity in the eyes of the law to enter into certain transactions

disability clause *n* (in life assurance policies) a clause enabling a policyholder to cease payment of premiums without loss of coverage and often to receive a pension or indemnity if he becomes permanently disabled

Disability Rights Commission *n* (in Britain) a body appointed by the Government to enforce anti-discrimination law affecting people with disabilities

disable (dɪs'eɪbəl) *vb* (*tr*) **1** to make ineffective, unfit, or incapable, as by crippling **2** to make or pronounce legally incapable **3** to switch off (an electronic device) > dis'ablement *n*

disabled (dɪs'eɪbəld) *adj* **a** lacking one or more physical powers, such as the ability to walk or to coordinate one's movements, as from the effects of a disease or accident, or through mental impairment **b** (*as collective noun*; preceded by *the*): *the disabled*

▌ **USAGE** The use of *the disabled, the blind*, etc can be offensive and should be avoided. Instead one should talk about *disabled people, blind people*, etc

disabled list *n* the US term for **injury list**

disablement benefit *n* (in Britain) a noncontributory benefit payable to a person disabled through injury or disease caused by their work

disabuse (ˌdɪsə'bjuːz) *vb* (*tr*; usually foll by *of*) to rid (oneself, another person, etc) of a mistaken or misguided idea; set right > ˌdisa'busal *n*

disaccharide (daɪ'sækəˌraɪd, -rɪd) *or* **disaccharid** *n* any of a class of sugars, such as maltose, lactose, and sucrose, having two linked monosaccharide units per molecule

disaccord (ˌdɪsə'kɔːd) *n* **1** lack of agreement or harmony ▷ *vb* **2** (*intr*) to be out of agreement; disagree

disaccredit (ˌdɪsə'krɛdɪt) *vb* (*tr*) to take away the authorization or credentials of

disaccustom (ˌdɪsə'kʌstəm) *vb* (*tr*; usually foll by *to*) to cause to lose a habit

disadvantage (ˌdɪsəd'vɑːntɪdʒ) *n* **1** an unfavourable circumstance, state of affairs, thing, person, etc **2** injury, loss, or detriment **3** an unfavourable condition or situation (esp in the phrase **at a disadvantage**) ▷ *vb* **4** (*tr*) to put at a disadvantage; handicap

disadvantaged (ˌdɪsəd'vɑːntɪdʒd) *adj* socially or economically deprived or discriminated against

disadvantageous (dɪsˌædvən'teɪdʒəs, ˌdɪsəd-) *adj* unfavourable; detrimental > disˌadvan'tageously *adv* > disˌadvan'tageousness *n*

disaffect (ˌdɪsə'fɛkt) *vb* (*tr*; often passive) to cause to lose loyalty or affection; alienate > ˌdisaf'fectedly *adv* > ˌdisaf'fectedness *n*

disaffection (ˌdɪsə'fɛkʃən) *n* a state of dissatisfaction or alienation: *the growing disaffection between players*

disaffiliate (ˌdɪsə'fɪlɪˌeɪt) *vb* to sever an affiliation (with); dissociate > ˌdisafˌfili'ation *n*

disaffirm (ˌdɪsə'fɜːm) *vb* (*tr*) **1** to deny or contradict (a statement) **2** *law* **a** to annul or reverse (a decision) **b** to repudiate obligations > ˌdisaf'firmance *or* disaffirmation (ˌdɪsæfə'meɪʃən)

disafforest (ˌdɪsə'fɒrɪst) *vb* (*tr*) **1** *English law* to reduce (land) from the status of a forest to the state of ordinary ground **2** to remove forests from (land) > ˌdisafˌfores'tation *or* ˌdisaf'forestment *n*

disaggregate (dɪs'ægrɪˌgeɪt) *vb* **1** to separate from a group or mass **2** to divide into parts > ˌdisaggre'gation *n*

disagree (ˌdɪsə'griː) *vb* -grees, -greeing, -greed

(*intr; often foll by with*) **1** to dissent in opinion (from another person) or dispute (about an idea, fact, etc) **2** to fail to correspond; conflict **3** to be unacceptable (to) or unfavourable (for); be incompatible (with): *curry disagrees with me* **4** to be opposed (to) in principle

disagreeable (ˌdɪsəˈgriːəbᵊl) *adj* **1** not likable, esp bad-tempered, offensive, or disobliging: *disagreeable remarks* **2** not to one's liking; unpleasant: *a disagreeable task* > **ˌdisaˈgreeableness** *or* **ˌdisaˌgreeaˈbility** *n* > **ˌdisaˈgreeably** *adv*

disagreement (ˌdɪsəˈgriːmənt) *n* **1** refusal or failure to agree **2** a failure to correspond **3** an argument or dispute

disallow (ˌdɪsəˈlaʊ) *vb* (*tr*) **1** to reject as untrue or invalid **2** to cancel > **ˌdisalˈlowable** *adj* > **ˌdisalˈlowance** *n*

disambiguate (ˌdɪsæmˈbɪgjʊˌeɪt) *vb* (*tr*) to make (an ambiguous expression) unambiguous > **ˌdisamˌbiguˈation** *n*

disannul (ˌdɪsəˈnʌl) *vb* **-nuls, -nulling, -nulled** (*tr*) *chiefly law* to cancel; make void > **ˌdisanˈnulment** *n*

disappear (ˌdɪsəˈpɪə) *vb* **1** (*intr*) to cease to be visible; vanish **2** (*intr*) to go away or become lost, esp secretly or without explanation **3** (*intr*) to cease to exist, have effect, or be known; become extinct or lost: *the pain has disappeared* **4** (*tr*) (esp in South and Central America) to arrest secretly and presumably imprison or kill (a member of an opposing political group) > **ˌdisapˈpearance** *n*

disapplication (ˌdɪsæplɪˈkeɪʃən) *n Brit education* a provision for exempting schools or individuals from the requirements of the National Curriculum in special circumstances

disappoint (ˌdɪsəˈpɔɪnt) *vb* (*tr*) **1** to fail to meet the expectations, hopes, desires, or standards of; let down **2** to prevent the fulfilment of (a plan, intention, etc); frustrate; thwart [C15 (originally meaning: to remove from office): from Old French *desapointier*; see DIS-[1], APPOINT]

disappointed (ˌdɪsəˈpɔɪntɪd) *adj* saddened by the failure of an expectation, etc > **ˌdisapˈpointedly** *adv*

disappointing (ˌdɪsəˈpɔɪntɪŋ) *adj* failing to meet one's expectations, hopes, desires, or standards > **ˌdisapˈpointingly** *adv*

disappointment (ˌdɪsəˈpɔɪntmənt) *n* **1** the act of disappointing or the state of being disappointed **2** a person, thing, or state of affairs that disappoints

disapprobation (ˌdɪsæprəʊˈbeɪʃən) *n* moral or social disapproval

disapproval (ˌdɪsəˈpruːvᵊl) *n* the act or a state or feeling of disapproving; censure; condemnation

disapprove (ˌdɪsəˈpruːv) *vb* **1** (*intr; often foll by of*) to consider wrong, bad, etc **2** (*tr*) to withhold approval from > **ˌdisapˈproving** *adj* > **ˌdisapˈprovingly** *adv*

disarm (dɪsˈɑːm) *vb* **1** (*tr*) to remove defensive or offensive capability from (a country, army, etc) **2** (*tr*) to deprive of weapons **3** (*tr*) to remove the triggering device of (a bomb, shell, etc) **4** (*tr*) to win the confidence or affection of **5** (*intr*) (of a nation, etc) to decrease the size and capability of one's armed forces **6** (*intr*) to lay down weapons > **disˈarmer** *n*

disarmament (dɪsˈɑːməmənt) *n* **1** the reduction of offensive or defensive fighting capability, as by a nation **2** the act of disarming or state of being disarmed

disarming (dɪsˈɑːmɪŋ) *adj* tending to neutralize or counteract hostility, suspicion, etc > **disˈarmingly** *adv*

disarrange (ˌdɪsəˈreɪndʒ) *vb* (*tr*) to throw into disorder > **ˌdisarˈrangement** *n*

disarray (ˌdɪsəˈreɪ) *n* **1** confusion, dismay, and lack of discipline **2** (esp of clothing) disorderliness, untidiness ▷ *vb* (*tr*) **3** to throw into confusion **4** *archaic* to undress

disarticulate (ˌdɪsɑːˈtɪkjʊˌleɪt) *vb* to separate or cause to separate at the joints, esp those of bones > **ˌdisarˌticuˈlation** *n* > **ˌdisarˈticuˌlator** *n*

disassemble (ˌdɪsəˈsɛmbᵊl) *vb* (*tr*) to take apart (a piece of machinery, etc); dismantle > **ˌdisasˈsembly** *n*

disassembler (ˌdɪsəˈsɛmblə) *n computing* a computer program that translates machine code into assembly language

disassociate (ˌdɪsəˈsəʊʃɪˌeɪt) *vb* a less common word for **dissociate**. > **ˌdisasˌsociˈation** *n*

disaster (dɪˈzɑːstə) *n* **1** an occurrence that causes great distress or destruction **2** a thing, project, etc, that fails or has been ruined [C16 (originally in the sense: malevolent astral influence): from Italian *disastro*, from *dis-* (pejorative) + *astro* star, from Latin *astrum*, from Greek *astron*] > **disˈastrous** *adj*

disavow (ˌdɪsəˈvaʊ) *vb* (*tr*) to deny knowledge of, connection with, or responsibility for > **ˌdisaˈvowal** *n* > **ˌdisaˈvowedly** *adv* > **ˌdisaˈvower** *n*

disband (dɪsˈbænd) *vb* to cease to function or cause to stop functioning, as a unit, group, etc > **disˈbandment** *n*

disbar (dɪsˈbɑː) *vb* **-bars, -barring, -barred** (*tr*) *law* to deprive of the status of barrister; expel from the Bar > **disˈbarment** *n*

> USAGE *Disbar* is sometimes wrongly used where *debar* is meant: *he was debarred* (not *disbarred*) *from attending meetings*

disbelief (ˌdɪsbɪˈliːf) *n* refusal or reluctance to believe

disbelieve (ˌdɪsbɪˈliːv) *vb* **1** (*tr*) to reject as false or lying; refuse to accept as true or truthful **2** (*intr; usually foll by in*) to have no faith (in): *disbelieve in God* > **ˌdisbeˈliever** *n* > **ˌdisbeˈlieving** *adj* > **ˌdisbeˈlievingly** *adv*

disbranch (dɪsˈbrɑːntʃ) *vb* (*tr*) to remove or cut a branch or branches from (a tree)

disbud (dɪsˈbʌd) *or* **debud** (diːˈbʌd) *vb* **-buds, -budding, -budded** **1** to remove superfluous buds, flowers, or shoots from (a plant, esp a fruit tree) **2** *vet science* to remove the horn buds of (calves, lambs, and kids) to prevent horns growing

disburden (dɪsˈbɜːdᵊn) *vb* **1** to remove a load from (a person or animal) **2** (*tr*) to relieve (oneself, one's mind, etc) of a distressing worry or oppressive thought > **disˈburdenment** *n*

disburse (dɪsˈbɜːs) *vb* (*tr*) to pay out [C16 from Old French *desborser*, from *des-* DIS-[1] + *borser* to obtain money, from *borse* bag, from Late Latin *bursa*] > **disˈbursable** *adj* > **disˈbursement** *n* > **disˈburser** *n*

> USAGE *Disburse* is sometimes wrongly used where *disperse* is meant: *the police used a water cannon to disperse* (not *disburse*) *the crowd*

disc *or now esp US* **disk** (dɪsk) *n* **1** a flat circular plate **2** something resembling or appearing to resemble this: *the sun's disc* **3** another word for (gramophone) **record** **4** *anatomy* any approximately circular flat structure in the body, esp an intervertebral disc **5 a** the flat receptacle of composite flowers, such as the daisy **b** (*as modifier*): *a disc floret* **6** the middle part of the lip of an orchid **7 a** Also called: **parking disc** a marker or device for display in a parked vehicle showing the time of arrival or the latest permitted time of departure or both **b** (*as modifier*): *a disc zone; disc parking* **8** *computing* a variant spelling of **disk** (sense 2) ▷ *vb* **9** to work (land) with a disc harrow [C18 from Latin *discus*, from Greek *diskos* quoit]

discal (ˈdɪskᵊl) *adj biology, zoology* relating to or resembling a disc; disclike: *discal cells*

discalced (dɪsˈkælst) *adj* barefooted: used to denote friars and nuns who wear sandals [C17 from Latin *discalceātus*, from DIS-[1] + *calceātus* shod, from *calceāre* to provide with shoes, from *calceus* shoe, from *calx* heel]

discant *n* (ˈdɪskænt), *vb* (dɪsˈkænt) a variant of **descant** (senses 1, 3, 4) > **disˈcanter** *n*

discard *vb* (dɪsˈkɑːd) **1** (*tr*) to get rid of as useless or undesirable **2** *cards* to throw out (a card or cards) from one's hand **3** *cards* to play (a card not of the suit led nor a trump) when unable to follow suit ▷ *n* (ˈdɪskɑːd) **4** a person or thing that has been cast aside **5** *cards* a discarded card **6** the act of discarding > **disˈcarder** *n*

disc brake *n* a type of brake in which two calliper-operated pads rub against a flat disc attached to the wheel hub when the brake is applied

discern (dɪˈsɜːn) *vb* **1** (*tr*) to recognize or perceive clearly **2** to recognize or perceive (differences) [C14 from Old French *discerner*, from Latin *discernere* to divide, from DIS-[1] (apart) + *cernere* to separate] > **disˈcerner** *n*

discernible *or rarely* **discernable** (dɪˈsɜːnəbᵊl) *adj* able to be discerned; perceptible > **disˈcernibly** *or rarely* **disˈcernably** *adv*

discerning (dɪˈsɜːnɪŋ) *adj* having or showing good taste or judgment; discriminating > **disˈcerningly** *adv*

discernment (dɪˈsɜːnmənt) *n* keen perception or judgment

disc floret *or* **flower** *n* any of the small tubular flowers at the centre of the flower head of certain composite plants, such as the daisy. Compare **ray floret**

discharge *vb* (dɪsˈtʃɑːdʒ) **1** (*tr*) to release or allow to go: *the hospital discharged the patient* **2** (*tr*) to dismiss from or relieve of duty, office, employment, etc **3** to fire or be fired, as a gun **4** to pour forth or cause to pour forth: *the boil discharges pus* **5** (*tr*) to remove (the cargo) from (a boat, etc); unload **6** (*tr*) to perform (the duties of) or meet (the demands of an office, obligation, etc): *he discharged his responsibilities as mayor* **7** (*tr*) to relieve oneself of (a responsibility, debt, etc) **8** (*intr*) *physics* **a** to lose or remove electric charge **b** to form an arc, spark, or corona in a gas **c** to take or supply electrical current from a cell or battery **9** (*tr*) *law* to release (a prisoner from custody, etc) **10** (*tr*) to remove dye from (a fabric), as by bleaching **11** (*intr*) (of a dye or colour) to blur or run **12** (*tr*) *architect* **a** to spread (weight) evenly over a supporting member **b** to relieve a member of (excess weight) by distribution of pressure ▷ *n* (ˈdɪstʃɑːdʒ, dɪsˈtʃɑːdʒ) **13** a person or thing that is discharged **14 a** dismissal or release from an office, job, institution, etc **b** the document certifying such release **15** the fulfilment of an obligation or release from a responsibility or liability: *honourable discharge* **16** the act of removing a load, as of cargo **17** a pouring forth of a fluid; emission **18 a** the act of firing a projectile **b** the volley, bullet, missile, etc, fired **19** *law* **a** a release, as of a person held under legal restraint **b** an annulment, as of a court order **20** *physics* **a** the act or process of removing or losing charge or of equalizing a potential difference **b** a transient or continuous conduction of electricity through a gas by the formation and movement of electrons and ions in an applied electric field **21 a** the volume of fluid flowing along a pipe or a channel in unit time **b** the output rate of a plant or piece of machinery, such as a pump > **disˈchargeable** *adj* > **disˈcharger** *n*

discharge tube *n electronics* an electrical device in which current flow is by electrons and ions in an ionized gas, as in a fluorescent light or neon tube

disc harrow *n* a harrow with sharp-edged slightly concave discs mounted on horizontal shafts and used to cut clods or debris on the surface of the soil or to cover seed after planting

disciple (dɪˈsaɪpᵊl) *n* **1** a follower of the doctrines of a teacher or a school of thought **2** one of the personal followers of Christ (including his 12 apostles) during his earthly life [Old English *discipul*, from Latin *discipulus* pupil, from *discere* to learn] > **disˈcipleˌship** *n* > **discipular** (dɪˈsɪpjʊlə) *adj*

Disciples of Christ *pl n* a Christian denomination founded in the US in 1809 by Thomas and Alexander Campbell

disciplinant (ˈdɪsɪˌplɪnənt) *n* (*often capital*) *RC Church* a person belonging to a former order of flagellants in Spain

disciplinarian (ˌdɪsɪplɪˈnɛərɪən) *n* **1** a person who imposes or advocates discipline ▷ *adj* **2** a less common word for **disciplinary**

disciplinary ('dɪsɪˌplɪnərɪ) or **disciplinarian** adj 1 of, promoting, or used for discipline; corrective 2 relating to a branch of learning: *criticism that crosses disciplinary boundaries*

discipline ('dɪsɪplɪn) n 1 training or conditions imposed for the improvement of physical powers, self-control, etc 2 systematic training in obedience to regulations and authority 3 the state of improved behaviour, etc, resulting from such training or conditions 4 punishment or chastisement 5 a system of rules for behaviour, methods of practice, etc 6 a branch of learning or instruction 7 the laws governing members of a Church 8 a scourge of knotted cords ▷ vb (tr) 9 to improve or attempt to improve the behaviour, orderliness, etc, of by training, conditions, or rules 10 to punish or correct [c13 from Latin *disciplīna* teaching, from *discipulus* DISCIPLE] > 'disci,plinable adj > disciplinal (ˌdɪsɪ'plaɪn³l, 'dɪsɪplɪn³l) adj > 'disci,pliner n

discission (dɪs'sɪʒən) n med surgical incision, esp of a cataract

disc jockey n a person who announces and plays recorded music, esp pop music, on a radio programme, etc. Abbreviations: DJ, dj

disclaim (dɪs'kleɪm) vb 1 (tr) to deny or renounce (any claim, connection, etc) 2 (tr) to deny the validity or authority of 3 law to renounce or repudiate (a legal claim or right) > disclamation (ˌdɪsklə'meɪʃən) n

disclaimer (dɪs'kleɪmə) n a repudiation or denial

disclimax (dɪs'klaɪmæks) n ecology a climax community resulting from the activities of man or domestic animals in climatic and other conditions that would otherwise support a different type of community

disclose (dɪs'kləʊz) vb (tr) 1 to make (information) known 2 to allow to be seen; lay bare > dis'closer n

disclosing agent n dentistry a vegetable dye, administered as a liquid or in tablet form (**disclosing tablet**), that stains plaque, making it readily apparent on the teeth

disclosure (dɪs'kləʊʒə) n 1 something that is disclosed 2 the act of disclosing; revelation

Discman ('dɪskmən) n trademark a small portable CD player with light headphones

disco ('dɪskəʊ) n, pl -cos 1 a an occasion at which typically young people dance to amplified pop records, usually compered by a disc jockey and featuring special lighting effects b (as modifier): *disco dancing* 2 a nightclub or other public place where such dances take place 3 mobile equipment, usually accompanied by a disc jockey who operates it, for providing music for a disco 4 a a type of dance music designed to be played in discos, with a solid thump on each beat b (as modifier): *a disco record* [c20 shortened from DISCOTHEQUE]

discobolus or **discobolos** (dɪs'kɒbələs) n, pl -li (-ˌlaɪ) 1 (in classical Greece) a discus thrower 2 a statue of a discus thrower [c18 from Latin, from Greek *diskobolos*, from *diskos* DISCUS + -bolos, from *ballein* to throw]

discography (dɪs'kɒgrəfɪ) n 1 a classified reference list of gramophone records 2 another word for **discology**. > dis'cographer n

discoid ('dɪskɔɪd) adj also **discoidal** (dɪs'kɔɪd³l) 1 like a disc 2 (of a composite flower such as the tansy) consisting of disc florets only ▷ n 3 a disclike object

discology (dɪs'kɒlədʒɪ) n the study of gramophone records > dis'cologist n

discolour or US **discolor** (dɪs'kʌlə) vb to change or cause to change in colour; fade or stain > dis,color'ation or dis,colour'ation n > dis'colourment or US dis'colorment n

discombobulate (ˌdɪskəm'bɒbjʊˌleɪt) vb (tr) informal, chiefly US and Canadian to throw into confusion [c20 probably a whimsical alteration of DISCOMPOSE or DISCOMFIT]

discomfit (dɪs'kʌmfɪt) vb (tr) 1 to make uneasy, confused, or embarrassed 2 to frustrate the plans or purpose of 3 archaic to defeat in battle [c14 from Old French *desconfire* to destroy, from *des-* (indicating reversal) + *confire* to make, from Latin *conficere* to produce; see CONFECT] > dis'comfiter n > dis'comfiture n

discomfort (dɪs'kʌmfət) n 1 an inconvenience, distress, or mild pain 2 something that disturbs or deprives of ease ▷ vb 3 (tr) to make uncomfortable or uneasy

discomfortable (dɪs'kʌmfətəb³l, -'kʌmftə-) adj archaic tending to deprive of mental or physical ease or comfort

discommend (ˌdɪskə'mɛnd) vb (tr) 1 rare to express disapproval of 2 obsolete to bring into disfavour > ˌdiscom'mendable adj > ˌdiscommen'dation n

discommode (ˌdɪskə'məʊd) vb (tr) to cause inconvenience or annoyance to; disturb > ˌdiscom'modious adj > ˌdiscom'modiously adv

discommodity (ˌdɪskə'mɒdɪtɪ) n, pl -ties 1 economics a commodity without utility 2 archaic the state or a source of inconvenience

discommon (dɪs'kɒmən) vb (tr) law to deprive (land) of the character and status of common, as by enclosure

discompose (ˌdɪskəm'pəʊz) vb (tr) 1 to disturb the composure of; disconcert 2 now rare to disarrange > ˌdiscom'posedly adv > ˌdiscom'posingly adv > ˌdiscom'posure n

disconcert (ˌdɪskən'sɜːt) vb (tr) 1 to disturb the composure of 2 to frustrate or upset > ˌdiscon'certion or ˌdiscon'certment n

disconcerted (ˌdɪskən'sɜːtɪd) adj perturbed, embarrassed, or confused > ˌdiscon'certedly adv > ˌdiscon'certedness n

disconcerting (ˌdɪskən'sɜːtɪŋ) adj causing a feeling of disturbance, embarrassment, or confusion; perturbing; worrying > ˌdiscon'certingly adv

disconfirm (ˌdɪskən'fɜːm) vb (tr) (of a fact or argument) to suggest that a hypothesis is wrong or ill-formulated > ˌdisconfir'mation n

disconformity (ˌdɪskən'fɔːmɪtɪ) n, pl -ties 1 lack of conformity; discrepancy 2 the junction between two parallel series of stratified rocks, representing a considerable period of erosion of the much older underlying rocks before the more recent ones were deposited

disconnect (ˌdɪskə'nɛkt) vb 1 (tr) to undo or break the connection of or between (something, such as a plug and a socket) ▷ n 2 a lack of a connection; disconnection: *a disconnect between political discourse and the public* > ˌdiscon'necter n > ˌdiscon'nection or ˌdiscon'nexion n > ˌdiscon'nective adj

disconnected (ˌdɪskə'nɛktɪd) adj 1 not rationally connected; confused or incoherent 2 not connected or joined > ˌdiscon'nectedly adv > ˌdiscon'nectedness n

disconsolate (dɪs'kɒnsəlɪt) adj 1 sad beyond comfort; inconsolable 2 disappointed; dejected [c14 from Medieval Latin *disconsōlātus*, from DIS-¹ + *consōlātus* comforted; see CONSOLE¹] > dis'consolately adv > dis'consolateness or dis,conso'lation n

discontent (ˌdɪskən'tɛnt) n 1 Also called: **discontentment** lack of contentment, as with one's condition or lot in life 2 a discontented person ▷ adj 3 dissatisfied ▷ vb 4 (tr) to make dissatisfied > ˌdiscon'tented adj > ˌdiscon'tentedly adv > ˌdiscon'tentedness n

discontinue (ˌdɪskən'tɪnjuː) vb -ues, -uing, -ued 1 to come or bring to an end; interrupt or be interrupted; stop 2 (tr) law to terminate or abandon (an action, suit, etc) > ˌdiscon'tinuance n > ˌdiscon'tinu'ation n > ˌdiscon'tinuer n

discontinuity (ˌdɪskɒntɪ'njuːɪtɪ) n, pl -ties 1 lack of rational connection or cohesion 2 a break or interruption 3 maths a the property of being discontinuous b the point or the value of the variable at which a curve or function becomes

discontinuous 4 geology a a zone within the earth where a sudden change in physical properties, such as the velocity of earthquake waves, occurs. Such a zone marks the boundary between the different layers of the earth, as between the core and mantle. See also **Mohorovičić discontinuity** b a surface separating rocks that are not continuous with each other

discontinuous (ˌdɪskən'tɪnjʊəs) adj 1 characterized by interruptions or breaks; intermittent 2 maths (of a function or curve) changing suddenly in value for one or more values of the variable or at one or more points. Compare **continuous** (sense 3) > ˌdiscon'tinuously adv > ˌdiscon'tinuousness n

discord n ('dɪskɔːd) 1 lack of agreement of harmony; strife 2 harsh confused mingling of sounds 3 a combination of musical notes containing one or more dissonant intervals. See **dissonance** (sense 3), **concord** (sense 4) ▷ vb (dɪs'kɔːd) 4 (intr) to disagree; clash [c13 from Old French *descort*, from *descorder* to disagree, from Latin *discordāre*, from *discors* at variance, from DIS-¹ + *cor* heart]

discordance (dɪs'kɔːd³ns) or **discordancy** n 1 geology an arrangement of rock strata in which the older underlying ones dip at a different angle from the younger overlying ones; unconformity 2 lack of agreement or consonance 3 variants of **discord**

discordant (dɪs'kɔːd³nt) adj 1 at variance; disagreeing 2 harsh in sound; inharmonious > dis'cordantly adv

discotheque ('dɪskəˌtɛk) n the full name of **disco** [c20 from French *discothèque*, from Greek *diskos* disc + -o- + Greek *thēkē* case]

discount vb (dɪs'kaʊnt, 'dɪskaʊnt) (mainly tr) 1 to leave out of account as being unreliable, prejudiced, or irrelevant 2 to anticipate and make allowance for, often so as to diminish the effect of 3 a to deduct (a specified amount or percentage) from the usual price, cost, etc b to reduce (the regular price, cost, etc) by a stated percentage or amount 4 to sell or offer for sale at a reduced price 5 to buy or sell (a bill of exchange, etc) before maturity, with a deduction for interest determined by the time to maturity and also by risk 6 (also intr) to loan money on (a negotiable instrument that is not immediately payable) with a deduction for interest determined by risk and time to maturity ▷ n ('dɪskaʊnt) 7 a deduction from the full amount of a price or debt, as in return for prompt payment or to a special group of customers. See also **cash discount, trade discount** 8 Also called: discount rate a the amount of interest deducted in the purchase or sale of or the loan of money on unmatured negotiable instruments b the rate of interest deducted 9 a (in the issue of shares) a percentage deducted from the par value to give a reduced amount payable by subscribers b the amount by which the par value of something, esp shares, exceeds its market value. Compare **premium** (sense 3) 10 the act or an instance of discounting a negotiable instrument 11 at a discount a below the regular price b (of share values) below par c held in low regard; not sought after or valued 12 (modifier) offering or selling at reduced prices: *a discount shop* > dis'countable adj > dis'counter n

discounted cash flow n accounting a technique for appraising an investment that takes into account the different values of future returns according to when they will be received. Abbreviation: DCF

discountenance (dɪs'kaʊntɪnəns) vb (tr) 1 to make ashamed or confused 2 to disapprove of ▷ n 3 disapproval

discount house n 1 chiefly Brit a financial organization engaged in discounting bills of exchange, etc on a large scale primarily by borrowing call money from commercial banks 2 chiefly US another name for **discount store**

discount market *n* the part of the money market consisting of banks, discount houses, and brokers on which bills are discounted

discount store *n* a shop where goods are sold at a low price

discourage (dɪsˈkʌrɪdʒ) *vb* (*tr*) **1** to deprive of the will to persist in something **2** to inhibit; prevent: *this solution discourages rust* **3** to oppose by expressing disapproval ▷ disˈcouragement *n* ▷ disˈcourager *n* ▷ disˈcouragingly *adv*

discourse *n* (ˈdɪskɔːs, dɪsˈkɔːs) **1** verbal communication; talk; conversation **2** a formal treatment of a subject in speech or writing, such as a sermon or dissertation **3** a unit of text used by linguists for the analysis of linguistic phenomena that range over more than one sentence **4** *archaic* the ability to reason or the reasoning process ▷ *vb* (dɪsˈkɔːs) **5** (*intr*; often foll by *on* or *upon*) to speak or write (about) formally and extensively **6** (*intr*) to hold a discussion **7** (*tr*) *archaic* to give forth (music) [C14 from Medieval Latin *discursus* argument, from Latin: a running to and fro, from *discurrere* to run different ways, from DIS-¹ + *currere* to run] ▷ disˈcourser *n*

discourteous (dɪsˈkɜːtɪəs) *adj* showing bad manners; impolite; rude ▷ disˈcourteously *adv* ▷ disˈcourteousness *n*

discourtesy (dɪsˈkɜːtɪsɪ) *n, pl* -sies **1** bad manners; rudeness **2** a rude remark or act

discover (dɪˈskʌvə) *vb* (*tr; may take a clause as object*) **1** to be the first to find or find out about: *Fleming discovered penicillin* **2** to learn about or encounter for the first time; realize: *she discovered the pleasures of wine* **3** to find after study or search: *I discovered a leak in the tank* **4** to reveal or make known ▷ disˈcoverable *adj* ▷ disˈcoverer *n*

discovered check *n chess* check given by moving a man that has been masking a potential check from a bishop, rook, or queen

discovert (dɪsˈkʌvət) *adj law* (of a woman) not under the protection of a husband; being a widow, spinster, or divorcée [C14 from Old French *descovert*, past participle of *descouvrir* to DISCOVER] ▷ disˈcoverture *n*

discovery (dɪˈskʌvərɪ) *n, pl* -eries **1** the act, process, or an instance of discovering **2** a person, place, or thing that has been discovered **3** *law* the compulsory disclosure by a party to an action of relevant documents in his possession

Discovery Bay *n* an inlet of the Indian Ocean in SE Australia

disc plough *n* a plough that cuts by means of revolving steel discs

discredit (dɪsˈkrɛdɪt) *vb* (*tr*) **1** to damage the reputation of **2** to cause to be disbelieved or distrusted **3** to reject as untrue or of questionable accuracy ▷ *n* **4** a person, thing, or state of affairs that causes disgrace **5** damage to a reputation **6** lack of belief or confidence

discreditable (dɪsˈkrɛdɪtəbəl) *adj* tending to bring discredit; shameful or unworthy ▷ disˈcreditably *adv*

discreet (dɪˈskriːt) *adj* careful to avoid social embarrassment or distress, esp by keeping confidences secret; tactful [C14 from Old French *discret*, from Medieval Latin *discrētus*, from Latin *discernere* to DISCERN] ▷ disˈcreetly *adv* ▷ disˈcreetness *n*

▮ USAGE Avoid confusion with **discrete**

discrepancy (dɪsˈkrɛpənsɪ) *n, pl* -cies a conflict or variation, as between facts, figures, or claims

▮ USAGE *Discrepancy* is sometimes wrongly used where *disparity* is meant. A *discrepancy* exists between things which ought to be the same; it can be small but is usually significant. A *disparity* is a large difference between measurable things such as age, rank, or wages

discrepant (dɪsˈkrɛpənt) *adj* inconsistent; conflicting; at variance [C15 from Latin *discrepāns*, from *discrepāre* to differ in sound, from DIS-¹ +

crepāre to be noisy] ▷ disˈcrepantly *adv*

discrete (dɪsˈkriːt) *adj* **1** separate or distinct in form or concept **2** consisting of distinct or separate parts **3** *statistics* **a** (of a variable) having consecutive values that are not infinitesimally close, so that its analysis requires summation rather than integration **b** (of a distribution) relating to a discrete variable. Compare **continuous** (sense 4) [C14 from Latin *discrētus* separated, set apart; see DISCREET] ▷ disˈcretely *adv* ▷ disˈcreteness *n*

▮ USAGE Avoid confusion with **discreet**

discretion (dɪˈskrɛʃən) *n* **1** the quality of behaving or speaking in such a way as to avoid social embarrassment or distress **2** freedom or authority to make judgments and to act as one sees fit (esp in the phrases **at one's own discretion, at the discretion of**) **3** **age** or **years of discretion** the age at which a person is considered to be able to manage his own affairs

discretionary (dɪˈskrɛʃənərɪ, -ənrɪ) or **discretional** *adj* having or using the ability to decide at one's own discretion: *discretionary powers* ▷ disˈcretionarily or disˈcretionally *adv*

discretionary trust *n* a trust in which the beneficiaries' shares are not fixed in the trust deed but are left to the discretion of other persons, often the trustees

discriminant (dɪˈskrɪmɪnənt) *n* an algebraic expression related to the coefficients of a polynomial equation whose value gives information about the roots of the polynomial: $b^2 – 4ac$ is the discriminant of $ax^2 + bx + c = 0$

discriminate *vb* (dɪˈskrɪmɪˌneɪt) **1** (*intr*; usually foll by *in favour of* or *against*) to single out a particular person, group, etc, for special favour or, esp, disfavour, often because of a characteristic such as race, colour, sex, intelligence, etc **2** (when *intr*, foll by *between* or *among*) to recognize or understand the difference (between); distinguish: *to discriminate right and wrong; to discriminate between right and wrong* **3** (*intr*) to constitute or mark a difference **4** (*intr*) to be discerning in matters of taste ▷ *adj* (dɪˈskrɪmɪnɪt) **5** showing or marked by discrimination [C17 from Latin *discrīmināre* to divide, from *discrīmen* a separation, from *discernere* to DISCERN] ▷ disˈcriminately *adv* ▷ disˈcrimiˌnator *n*

discriminating (dɪˈskrɪmɪˌneɪtɪŋ) *adj* **1** able to see fine distinctions and differences **2** discerning in matters of taste **3** (of a tariff, import duty, etc) levied at differential rates in order to favour or discourage imports or exports ▷ disˈcrimiˌnatingly *adv*

discrimination (dɪˌskrɪmɪˈneɪʃən) *n* **1** unfair treatment of a person, racial group, minority, etc; action based on prejudice **2** subtle appreciation in matters of taste **3** the ability to see fine distinctions and differences **4** *electronics* the selection of a signal having a particular frequency, amplitude, phase, etc, effected by the elimination of other signals by means of a discriminator ▷ disˌcrimiˈnational *adj*

discrimination learning *n psychol* a learning process in which an organism learns to react differently to different stimuli. Compare **generalization** (sense 3)

discriminator (dɪˈskrɪmɪˌneɪtə) *n* **1** an electronic circuit that converts a frequency or phase modulation into an amplitude modulation for subsequent demodulation **2** an electronic circuit that has an output voltage only when the amplitude of the input pulses exceeds a predetermined value

discriminatory (dɪˈskrɪmɪnətərɪ, -trɪ) or **discriminative** (dɪˈskrɪmɪnətɪv) *adj* **1** based on or showing prejudice; biased **2** capable of making fine distinctions **3** (of a statistical test) unbiased ▷ disˈcriminatorily or disˈcriminatively *adv*

discursive (dɪsˈkɜːsɪv) *adj* **1** passing from one topic to another, usually in an unmethodical way; digressive **2** *philosophy* of or relating to knowledge obtained by reason and argument rather than

intuition. Compare **dianoetic** [C16 from Medieval Latin *discursīvus*, from Late Latin *discursus* DISCOURSE] ▷ disˈcursively *adv* ▷ disˈcursiveness *n*

discus (ˈdɪskəs) *n, pl* discuses or disci (ˈdɪskaɪ) **1** (originally) a circular stone or plate used in throwing competitions by the ancient Greeks **2** *athletics* **a** a similar disc-shaped object with a heavy middle thrown by athletes **b** (*as modifier*): *a discus thrower* **3** (preceded by *the*) the event or sport of throwing the discus **4** a South American cichlid fish, *Symphysodon discus*, that has a compressed coloured body and is a popular aquarium fish [C17 from Latin, from Greek *diskos* from *dikein* to throw]

discuss (dɪˈskʌs) *vb* (*tr*) **1** to have a conversation about; consider by talking over; debate **2** to treat (a subject) in speech or writing: *the first three volumes discuss basic principles* **3** *facetious, rare* to eat or drink with enthusiasm [C14 from Late Latin *discussus* examined, from *discutere* to investigate, from Latin: to dash to pieces, from DIS-¹ + *quatere* to shake, strike] ▷ disˈcussant or disˈcusser *n* ▷ disˈcussible or disˈcussable *adj*

discussion (dɪˈskʌʃən) *n* the examination or consideration of a matter in speech or writing ▷ disˈcussional *adj*

disc wheel *n* a road wheel of a motor vehicle that has a round pressed disc in place of spokes. Compare **wire wheel**

disdain (dɪsˈdeɪn) *n* **1** a feeling or show of superiority and dislike; contempt; scorn ▷ *vb* **2** (*tr, may take an infinitive*) to refuse or reject with disdain [C13 *dedeyne*, from Old French *desdeign*, from *desdeigner* to reject as unworthy, from Latin *dēdignārī*; see DIS-¹, DEIGN]

disdainful (dɪsˈdeɪnful) *adj* showing or feeling disdain ▷ disˈdainfully *adv* ▷ disˈdainfulness *n*

disease (dɪˈziːz) *n* **1** any impairment of normal physiological function affecting all or part of an organism, esp a specific pathological change caused by infection, stress, etc, producing characteristic symptoms; illness or sickness in general **2** a corresponding condition in plants **3** any situation or condition likened to this: *the disease of materialism*. Related adj: **pathological** [C14 from Old French *desaise*; see DIS-¹, EASE]

diseased (dɪˈziːzd) *adj* having or affected with disease

diseconomy (ˌdɪsɪˈkɒnəmɪ) *n, pl* -mies *economics* disadvantage, such as lower efficiency or higher average costs, resulting from the scale on which an enterprise produces goods or services

disembark (ˌdɪsɪmˈbɑːk) *vb* to land or cause to land from a ship, aircraft, etc: *several passengers disembarked; we will disembark the passengers* ▷ disembarkation (dɪsˌɛmbɑːˈkeɪʃən) or ˌdisemˈbarkment *n*

disembarrass (ˌdɪsɪmˈbærəs) *vb* (*tr*) **1** to free from embarrassment, entanglement, etc **2** to relieve or rid of something burdensome ▷ ˌdisemˈbarrassment *n*

disembodied (ˌdɪsɪmˈbɒdɪd) *adj* **1** lacking a body or freed from the body; incorporeal **2** lacking in substance, solidity, or any firm relation to reality

disembody (ˌdɪsɪmˈbɒdɪ) *vb* -bodies, -bodying, -bodied (*tr*) to free from the body or from physical form ▷ ˌdisemˈbodiment *n*

disembogue (ˌdɪsɪmˈbəʊg) *vb* -bogues, -boguing, -bogued **1** (of a river, stream, etc) to discharge (water) at the mouth **2** (*intr*) to flow out [C16 from Spanish *desembocar*, from *des-* DIS-¹ + *embocar* put into the mouth, from *em-* + *boca* mouth, from Latin *bucca* cheek] ▷ ˌdisemˈboguement *n*

disembowel (ˌdɪsɪmˈbaʊəl) *vb* -els, -elling, -elled *or US* -els, -eling, -eled (*tr*) to remove the entrails of ▷ ˌdisemˈbowelment *n*

disembroil (ˌdɪsɪmˈbrɔɪl) *vb* (*tr*) to free from entanglement or a confused situation

disempower (ˌdɪsɪmˈpaʊə) *vb* (*tr*) to deprive (a person) of power or authority ▷ ˌdisemˈpowerment *n*

disenable (ˌdɪsɪˈneɪbəl) *vb* (*tr*) to cause to become

d

incapable; prevent > ˌdisenˈablement n

disenchant (ˌdɪsɪnˈtʃɑːnt) vb (tr; when passive, foll by *with* or *by*) to make disappointed or disillusioned: *she is disenchanted with the marriage*

disenchanted (ˌdɪsɪnˈtʃɑːntɪd) adj disappointed or disillusioned

disenchantment (ˌdɪsɪnˈtʃɑːntmənt) n a state of disappointment or disillusionment

disencumber (ˌdɪsɪnˈkʌmbə) vb (tr) to free from encumbrances > ˌdisenˈcumberment n

disendow (ˌdɪsɪnˈdaʊ) vb (tr) to take away an endowment from > ˌdisenˈdower n > ˌdisenˈdowment n

disenfranchise (ˌdɪsɪnˈfræntʃaɪz) or **disfranchise** vb (tr) 1 to deprive (a person) of the right to vote or other rights of citizenship 2 to deprive (a place) of the right to send representatives to an elected body 3 to deprive (a business concern, etc) of some privilege or right 4 to deprive (a person, place, etc) of any franchise or right > disenfranchisement (ˌdɪsɪnˈfræntʃɪzmənt) or disˈfranchisement n

disengage (ˌdɪsɪnˈgeɪdʒ) vb 1 to release or become released from a connection, obligation, etc: *press the clutch to disengage the gears* 2 military to withdraw (forces) from close action 3 fencing to move (one's blade) from one side of an opponent's blade to another in a circular motion to bring the blade into an open line of attack

disengagement (ˌdɪsɪnˈgeɪdʒmənt) n 1 the act or process of disengaging or the state of being disengaged 2 leisure; ease > ˌdisenˈgaged adj

disentail (ˌdɪsɪnˈteɪl) property law ▷ vb 1 to free (an estate) from entail ▷ n 2 the act of disentailing; disentailment > ˌdisenˈtailment n

disentangle (ˌdɪsɪnˈtæŋgəl) vb 1 to release or become free from entanglement or confusion 2 (tr) to unravel or work out > ˌdisenˈtanglement n

disenthral or US **disenthrall** (ˌdɪsɪnˈθrɔːl) vb -thrals, -thralling, -thralled or US -thralls, -thralling, -thralled (tr) to set free > ˌdisenˈthralment or US ˌdisenˈthrallment n

disentitle (ˌdɪsɪnˈtaɪtəl) vb (tr) to deprive of a title, right, or claim

disentomb (ˌdɪsɪnˈtuːm) vb (tr) to disinter; unearth

disentwine (ˌdɪsɪnˈtwaɪn) vb to become or cause to become untwined; unwind

disepalous (daɪˈsɛpələs) adj (of flowers or plants) having two sepals

disequilibrium (ˌdɪsiːkwɪˈlɪbriəm) n a loss or absence of equilibrium, esp in an economy

disestablish (ˌdɪsɪˈstæblɪʃ) vb (tr) to deprive (a church, custom, institution, etc) of established status > ˌdisesˈtablishment n

disesteem (ˌdɪsɪˈstiːm) vb 1 (tr) to think little of ▷ n 2 lack of esteem

diseuse (French dizøz) n (esp formerly) an actress who presents dramatic recitals, usually sung accompanied by music. Male counterpart: diseur (French dizœr) [c19 from French, feminine of diseur speaker, from dire to speak, from Latin dīcere]

disfavour or US **disfavor** (dɪsˈfeɪvə) n 1 disapproval or dislike 2 the state of being disapproved of or disliked 3 an unkind act 4 a damaging or disadvantageous effect; detriment ▷ vb 5 (tr) to regard or treat with disapproval or dislike

disfeature (dɪsˈfiːtʃə) vb (tr) to mar the features or appearance of; deface > disˈfeaturement n

disfellowship (ˌdɪsˈfɛləʊʃɪp) vb -ships, -shipping, -shipped or US -ships, -shiping, -shiped (tr) to excommunicate

disfigure (dɪsˈfɪgə) vb (tr) 1 to spoil the appearance or shape of; deface 2 to mar the effect or quality of > disˈfigurer n

disfigurement (dɪsˈfɪgəmənt) or **disfiguration** (ˌdɪsfɪgəˈreɪʃən) n 1 something that disfigures 2 the act of disfiguring or the state of being disfigured

disforest (dɪsˈfɒrɪst) vb (tr) 1 another word for **deforest** 2 English law a less common word for

disafforest. > disˌforesˈtation n

disfranchise (dɪsˈfræntʃaɪz) vb another word for **disenfranchise**

disfrock (dɪsˈfrɒk) vb another word for **unfrock**

disgorge (dɪsˈgɔːdʒ) vb 1 to throw out (swallowed food, etc) from the throat or stomach; vomit 2 to discharge or empty of (contents) 3 (tr) to yield up unwillingly or under pressure 4 (tr) angling to remove (a hook) from the mouth or throat of (a fish) > disˈgorgement n

disgorger (dɪsˈgɔːdʒə) n angling a thin notched metal implement for removing hooks from a fish

disgrace (dɪsˈgreɪs) n 1 a condition of shame, loss of reputation, or dishonour 2 a shameful person, thing, or state of affairs 3 exclusion from confidence or trust: *he is in disgrace with his father* ▷ vb (tr) 4 to bring shame upon; be a discredit to 5 to treat or cause to be treated with disfavour > disˈgracer n

disgraceful (dɪsˈgreɪsfʊl) adj shameful; scandalous > disˈgracefully adv > disˈgracefulness n

disgruntle (dɪsˈgrʌntəl) vb (tr; usually passive) to make sulky or discontented [c17 DIS-¹ + obsolete gruntle to complain; see GRUNT] > disˈgruntlement n

disgruntled (dɪsˈgrʌntəld) adj feeling or expressing discontent or anger

disguise (dɪsˈgaɪz) vb 1 to modify the appearance or manner in order to conceal the identity of (oneself, someone, or something) 2 (tr) to misrepresent in order to obscure the actual nature or meaning: *to disguise the facts* ▷ n 3 a mask, costume, or manner that disguises 4 the act of disguising or the state of being disguised [c14 from Old French desguisier, from des- DIS-¹ + guise manner; see GUISE] > disˈguisable adj > disˈguised adj > disguisedly (dɪsˈgaɪzɪdlɪ) adv > disˈguiser n

disgust (dɪsˈgʌst) vb (tr) 1 to sicken or fill with loathing 2 to offend the moral sense, principles, or taste of ▷ n 3 a great loathing or distaste aroused by someone or something 4 in disgust as a result of disgust [c16 from Old French desgouster, from des- DIS-¹ + gouster to taste, from goust taste, from Latin gustus] > disˈgustedly adv > disˈgustedness n

disgusting (dɪsˈgʌstɪŋ) adj loathsome; repugnant. Also (rare): disgustful > disˈgustingly adv

dish (dɪʃ) n 1 a container used for holding or serving food, esp an open shallow container of pottery, glass, etc 2 the food that is served or contained in a dish 3 a particular article or preparation of food: *a local fish dish* 4 Also called: dishful the amount contained in a dish 5 something resembling a dish, esp in shape 6 a concavity or depression 7 short for **dish aerial** or **satellite dish aerial** 8 informal an attractive person 9 informal something that one particularly enjoys or excels in ▷ vb (tr) 10 to put into a dish 11 to make hollow or concave 12 Brit informal to ruin or spoil: *he dished his chances of getting the job* ▷ See also **dish out, dish up** [Old English disc, from Latin discus quoit, see DISC] > ˈdishˌlike adj

dishabille (ˌdɪsæˈbiːl) n a variant of **deshabille**

dish aerial n 1 a microwave aerial, used esp in radar, radio telescopes, and satellite broadcasting, consisting of a parabolic reflector. Formal name: parabolic aerial Often shortened to: dish 2 short for **satellite dish aerial** ▷ Also called: dish antenna

disharmony (dɪsˈhɑːmənɪ) n, pl -nies 1 lack of accord or harmony 2 a situation, circumstance, etc, that is inharmonious > disharmonious (ˌdɪshɑːˈməʊnɪəs) adj > ˌdisharˈmoniously adv

dishcloth (ˈdɪʃˌklɒθ) n a cloth or rag for washing or drying dishes. Also called (dialect): dishclout (ˈdɪʃˌkluːt)

dishcloth gourd n 1 any of several tropical climbing plants of the cucurbitaceous genus *Luffa*, esp L. *cylindrica*, which is cultivated for ornament and for the fibrous interior of its fruits (see **loofah**) 2 the fruit of any of these plants ▷ Also called: vegetable sponge

dishdasha (ˈdɪʃˌdæʃə) n a white long-sleeved collarless garment worn by Muslim men in the Arabian peninsula [Arabic]

dishearten (dɪsˈhɑːtən) vb (tr) to weaken or destroy the hope, courage, enthusiasm, etc, of > disˈhearteningly adv > disˈheartenment n

dished (dɪʃt) adj 1 shaped like a dish; concave 2 (of a pair of road wheels) arranged so that they are closer to one another at the bottom than at the top 3 informal exhausted or defeated

dishevel (dɪˈʃɛvəl) vb -els, -elling, -elled or US -els, -eling, -eled to disarrange (the hair or clothes) of (someone) [c15 back formation from DISHEVELLED] > diˈshevelment n

dishevelled (dɪˈʃɛvəld) adj 1 (esp of hair) hanging loosely 2 (of general appearance) unkempt; untidy [c15 dischevelee, from Old French deschevelé, from des- DIS-¹ + chevel hair, from Latin capillus]

dishonest (dɪsˈɒnɪst) adj not honest or fair; deceiving or fraudulent > disˈhonestly adv

dishonesty (dɪsˈɒnɪstɪ) n, pl -ties 1 lack of honesty or fairness; deceit 2 a deceiving act or statement; fraud

dishonour or US **dishonor** (dɪsˈɒnə) vb (tr) 1 to treat with disrespect 2 to fail or refuse to pay (a cheque, bill of exchange, etc) 3 to cause the disgrace of (a woman) by seduction or rape ▷ n 4 a lack of honour or respect 5 a state of shame or disgrace 6 a person or thing that causes a loss of honour: *he was a dishonour to his family* 7 an insult; affront: *we did him a dishonour by not including him* 8 refusal or failure to accept or pay a commercial paper > disˈhonourer or US disˈhonorer n

dishonourable or US **dishonorable** (dɪsˈɒnərəbəl, -ˈɒnrəbəl) adj 1 characterized by or causing dishonour or discredit 2 having little or no integrity; unprincipled > disˈhonourableness or US disˈhonorableness n > disˈhonourably or US disˈhonorably adv

dish out vb informal 1 (tr, adverb) to distribute 2 dish it out to inflict punishment: *he can't take it, but he can sure dish it out*

dishpan (ˈdɪʃˌpæn) n chiefly US and Canadian a large pan for washing dishes, pots, etc

dishtowel (ˈdɪʃˌtaʊəl) n chiefly US and Canadian a towel for drying dishes and kitchen utensils. Also called (in Britain and certain other countries): tea towel

dish up vb (adverb) 1 to serve (a meal, food, etc) 2 (tr) informal to prepare or present, esp in an attractive manner

dishwasher (ˈdɪʃˌwɒʃə) n 1 an electrically operated machine for washing, rinsing, and drying dishes, cutlery, etc 2 a person who washes dishes, etc

dishwater (ˈdɪʃˌwɔːtə) n 1 water in which dishes and kitchen utensils are or have been washed 2 something resembling this: *that was dishwater, not coffee*

dishy (ˈdɪʃɪ) adj dishier, dishiest informal, chiefly Brit good-looking or attractive

disillusion (ˌdɪsɪˈluːʒən) vb 1 (tr) to destroy the ideals, illusions, or false ideas of ▷ n also disillusionment 2 the act of disillusioning or the state of being disillusioned

disillusioned (ˌdɪsɪˈluːʒənd) adj having lost one's ideals, illusions, or false ideas about someone or something; disenchanted

disincentive (ˌdɪsɪnˈsɛntɪv) n 1 something that acts as a deterrent ▷ adj 2 acting as a deterrent: *a disincentive effect on productivity*

disincline (ˌdɪsɪnˈklaɪn) vb to make or be unwilling, reluctant, or averse > disinclination (ˌdɪsɪnklɪˈneɪʃən) n

disinfect (ˌdɪsɪnˈfɛkt) vb (tr) to rid of microorganisms potentially harmful to man, esp by chemical means > ˌdisinˈfection n > ˌdisinˈfector n

disinfectant (ˌdɪsɪnˈfɛktənt) n an agent that destroys or inhibits the activity of microorganisms that cause disease

disinfest (ˌdɪsɪnˈfɛst) vb (tr) to rid of vermin > disˌinfesˈtation n

disinflation (ˌdɪsɪnˈfleɪʃən) n economics a

reduction or stabilization of the general price level intended to improve the balance of payments without incurring reductions in output, employment, and investment. Compare **deflation** (sense 2)

disinformation (ˌdɪsɪnfəˈmeɪʃən) n false information intended to deceive or mislead

disingenuous (ˌdɪsɪnˈdʒɛnjʊəs) adj not sincere; lacking candour > ˌdisinˈgenuously adv > ˌdisinˈgenuousness n

disinherit (ˌdɪsɪnˈhɛrɪt) vb (tr) **1** law to deprive (an heir or next of kin) of inheritance or right to inherit **2** to deprive of a right or heritage > ˌdisinˈheritance n

disinhibition (ˌdɪsɪnɪˈbɪʃən, -ɪnhɪ-) n psychol a temporary loss of inhibition, caused by an outside stimulus such as alcohol or a drug

disintegrate (dɪsˈɪntɪˌɡreɪt) vb **1** to break or be broken into fragments or constituent parts; shatter **2** to lose or cause to lose cohesion or unity **3** (intr) to lose judgment or control; deteriorate **4** physics **a** to induce or undergo nuclear fission, as by bombardment with fast particles **b** another word for **decay** (sense 3) > disˈintegrable adj > disˌinteˈgration n > disˈintegrative adj > disˈinteˌgrator n

disinter (ˌdɪsɪnˈtɜː) vb -ters, -terring, -terred (tr) **1** to remove or dig up; exhume **2** to bring (a secret, hidden facts, etc) to light; expose > ˌdisinˈterment n

disinterest (dɪsˈɪntrɪst, -tərɪst) n **1** freedom from bias or involvement **2** lack of interest; indifference ▷ vb **3** (tr) to free from concern for personal interests

disinterested (dɪsˈɪntrɪstɪd, -tərɪs-) adj **1** free from bias or partiality; objective **2** not interested > disˈinterestedly adv > disˈinterestedness n

▎ USAGE Many people consider that the use of *disinterested* to mean not interested is incorrect and that *uninterested* should be used

disintermediation (dɪsˌɪntəˌmiːdɪˈeɪʃən) n finance the elimination of such financial intermediaries as banks and brokers in transactions between principals, often as a result of deregulation and the use of computers

disinvest (ˌdɪsɪnˈvɛst) vb economics **1** (usually foll by in) to remove investment (from) **2** (intr) to reduce the capital stock of an economy or enterprise, as by not replacing obsolete machinery > ˌdisinˈvestment n

disject (dɪsˈdʒɛkt) vb (tr) to break apart; scatter [c16 from Latin *disjectus*, from *disjicere* to scatter, from DIS-¹ + *jacere* to throw]

disjecta membra (Latin dɪsˈdʒɛktə ˈmɛmbrə) pl n scattered fragments, esp parts taken from a writing or writings

disjoin (dɪsˈdʒɔɪn) vb to disconnect or become disconnected; separate > disˈjoinable adj

disjoint (dɪsˈdʒɔɪnt) vb **1** to take apart or come apart at the joints **2** (tr) to disunite or disjoin **3** to dislocate or become dislocated **4** (tr; usually passive) to end the unity, sequence, or coherence of ▷ adj **5** maths (of two sets) having no members in common **6** obsolete disjointed

disjointed (dɪsˈdʒɔɪntɪd) adj **1** having no coherence; disconnected **2** separated at the joint **3** dislocated > disˈjointedly adv > disˈjointedness n

disjunct adj (dɪsˈdʒʌŋkt) **1** not united or joined **2** (of certain insects) having deep constrictions between the head, thorax, and abdomen **3** music denoting two notes the interval between which is greater than a second ▷ n (ˈdɪsdʒʌŋkt) **4** logic one of the propositions or formulas in a disjunction

disjunction (dɪsˈdʒʌŋkʃən) n **1** Also called: disjuncture the act of disconnecting or the state of being disconnected; separation **2** cytology the separation of the chromosomes of each homologous pair during the anaphase of meiosis **3** logic **a** the operator that forms a compound sentence from two given sentences and corresponds to the English *or* **b** a sentence so

formed. Usually written p∨q where p, q are the component sentences, it is true (inclusive sense) whenever either or both of the latter are true; the exclusive disjunction, for which there is no symbol, is true when either but not both disjuncts is **c** the relation between such sentences

disjunctive (dɪsˈdʒʌŋktɪv) adj **1** serving to disconnect or separate **2** grammar **a** denoting a word, esp a conjunction, that serves to express opposition or contrast: *but* in the sentence *She was poor but she was honest* **b** denoting an inflection of pronouns in some languages that is used alone or after a preposition, such as *moi* in French **3** Also: alternative logic relating to, characterized by, or containing disjunction ▷ n **4** grammar **a** a disjunctive word, esp a conjunction **b** a disjunctive pronoun **5** logic a disjunctive proposition; disjunction > disˈjunctively adv

disk (dɪsk) n **1** a variant spelling (esp US and Canadian) of **disc 2** Also called: **magnetic disk, hard disk** computing a direct-access storage device consisting of a stack of plates coated with a magnetic layer, the whole assembly rotating rapidly as a single unit. Each surface has a read-write head that can move radially to read or write data on concentric tracks. Compare **drum¹** (sense 9) See also **floppy disk**

disk crash n computing the failure of a disk storage system, usually resulting from the read/write head touching the moving disk surface and causing mechanical damage

disk drive n computing the controller and mechanism for reading and writing data on computer disks. See also **disk** (sense 2)

diskette (dɪsˈkɛt) n computing another name for **floppy disk**

Disko (ˈdɪskəʊ) n an island in Davis Strait, off the W coast of Greenland: extensive coal deposits

disk operating system n an operating system used on a computer system with one or more disk drives. Often shortened to: **DOS**

dislike (dɪsˈlaɪk) vb **1** (tr) to consider unpleasant or disagreeable ▷ n **2** a feeling of aversion or antipathy > disˈlikable or disˈlikeable adj

dislimn (dɪsˈlɪm) vb (tr) poetic to efface

dislocate (ˈdɪsləˌkeɪt) vb (tr) **1** to disrupt or shift out of place or position **2** to displace (an organ or part) from its normal position, esp a bone from its joint

dislocation (ˌdɪsləˈkeɪʃən) n **1** the act of displacing or the state of being displaced; disruption **2** (esp of the bones in a joint) the state or condition of being dislocated **3** a line, plane, or region in which there is a discontinuity in the regularity of a crystal lattice **4** geology a less common word for **fault** (sense 6)

dislodge (dɪsˈlɒdʒ) vb to remove from or leave a lodging place, hiding place, or previously fixed position > disˈlodgment or disˈlodgement n

disloyal (dɪsˈlɔɪəl) adj not loyal or faithful; deserting one's allegiance or duty > disˈloyally adv

disloyalty (dɪsˈlɔɪəltɪ) n, pl -ties the condition of or an instance of being unfaithful or disloyal

dismal (ˈdɪzməl) adj **1** causing gloom or depression **2** causing dismay or terror [c13 from *dismal* (noun) list of 24 unlucky days in the year, from Medieval Latin *diēs malī* bad days, from Latin *diēs* day + *malus* bad] > ˈdismally adv > ˈdismalness n

dismal science n the a name for economics coined by Thomas Carlyle, the Scottish essayist and historian (1795–1881)

Dismal Swamp or **Great Dismal Swamp** n a coastal marshland in SE Virginia and NE North Carolina: partly reclaimed. Area: about 1940 sq km (750 sq miles). Area before reclamation: 5200 sq km (2000 sq miles)

dismantle (dɪsˈmæntəl) vb (tr) **1** to take apart **2** to demolish or raze **3** to strip of covering [c17 from Old French *desmanteler* to remove a cloak from; see MANTLE] > disˈmantlement n > disˈmantler n

dismast (dɪsˈmɑːst) vb (tr) to break off the mast or

masts of (a sailing vessel) > disˈmastment n

dismay (dɪsˈmeɪ) vb (tr) **1** to fill with apprehension or alarm **2** to fill with depression or discouragement ▷ n **3** consternation or agitation [c13 from Old French *desmaiier* (unattested), from *des-* DIS-¹ + *esmayer* to frighten, ultimately of Germanic origin; see MAY¹] > disˈmaying adj

dismember (dɪsˈmɛmbə) vb (tr) **1** to remove the limbs or members of **2** to cut to pieces **3** to divide or partition (something, such as an empire) > disˈmemberer n > disˈmemberment n

dismiss (dɪsˈmɪs) vb (tr) **1** to remove or discharge from employment or service **2** to send away or allow to go or disperse **3** to dispel from one's mind; discard; reject **4** to cease to consider (a subject): *they dismissed the problem* to decline further hearing to (a claim or action): *the judge dismissed the case* **6** cricket to bowl out a side for a particular number of runs ▷ sentence substitute **7** military an order to end an activity or give permission to disperse [c15 from Medieval Latin *dismissus* sent away, variant of Latin *dīmissus*, from *dīmittere*, from *dī-* DIS-¹ + *mittere* to send] > disˈmissible adj > disˈmissive adj

dismissal (dɪsˈmɪsəl) n **1** an official notice of discharge from employment or service **2** the act of dismissing or the condition of being dismissed

dismount (dɪsˈmaʊnt) vb **1** to get off a horse, bicycle, etc **2** (tr) to disassemble or remove from a mounting ▷ n **3** the act of dismounting > disˈmountable adj

Disneyesque (ˌdɪznɪˈɛsk) adj reminiscent of the animated cartoons produced by Walt(er Elias) Disney, the US film producer (1901–66) or his studio

Disneyfy (ˈdɪznɪˌfaɪ) vb -fies, -fying, -fied (tr) to transform (historical places, local customs, etc) into trivial entertainment for tourists [c20 from the DISNEYLAND amusement park] > ˌDisneyfiˈcation n

Disneyland (ˈdɪznɪˌlænd) n an amusement park in Anaheim, California, founded by Walt Disney and opened in 1955. **Walt Disney World**, a second amusement park, opened in 1971 near Orlando, Florida. Further parks have opened in Tokyo and near Paris

disobedience (ˌdɪsəˈbiːdɪəns) n lack of obedience

disobedient (ˌdɪsəˈbiːdɪənt) adj not obedient; neglecting or refusing to obey > ˌdisoˈbediently adv

disobey (ˌdɪsəˈbeɪ) vb to neglect or refuse to obey (someone, an order, etc) > ˌdisoˈbeyer n

disoblige (ˌdɪsəˈblaɪdʒ) vb (tr) **1** to disregard the desires of **2** to slight; insult **3** informal to cause trouble or inconvenience to > ˌdisoˈbliging adj > ˌdisoˈbligingly adv > ˌdisoˈbligingness n

disomic (daɪˈsəʊmɪk) adj genetics having an extra chromosome in the haploid state that is homologous to an existing chromosome in this set > diˈsomy n

disoperation (dɪsˌɒpəˈreɪʃən) n ecology a relationship between two organisms in a community that is harmful to both

disorder (dɪsˈɔːdə) n **1** a lack of order; disarray; confusion **2** a disturbance of public order or peace **3** an upset of health; ailment **4** a deviation from the normal system or order ▷ vb (tr) **5** to upset the order of; disarrange; muddle **6** to disturb the health or mind of

disorderly (dɪsˈɔːdəlɪ) adj **1** untidy; irregular **2** uncontrolled; unruly **3** law violating public peace or order ▷ adv **4** in an irregular or confused manner > disˈorderliness n

disorderly conduct n law any of various minor offences tending to cause a disturbance of the peace

disorderly house n law an establishment in which unruly behaviour habitually occurs, esp a brothel or a gaming house

disorganize or **disorganise** (dɪsˈɔːgəˌnaɪz) vb (tr) to disrupt or destroy the arrangement, system, or unity of > disˌorganiˈzation or disˌorganiˈsation n

d

> dis'organ,izer or dis'organ,iser n

disorientate (dɪsˈɔːrɪɛnˌteɪt) or **disorient** vb (tr) **1** to cause (someone) to lose his bearings **2** to perplex; confuse > dis,orien'tation n

disown (dɪsˈəʊn) vb (tr) to deny any connection with; refuse to acknowledge > dis'owner n > dis'ownment n

disparage (dɪˈspærɪdʒ) vb (tr) **1** to speak contemptuously of; belittle **2** to damage the reputation of [c14 from Old French *desparagier*, from *des-* DIS-¹ + *parage* equality, from Latin *par* equal] > dis'paragement n > dis'parager n > dis'paraging adj > dis'paragingly adv

disparate ('dɪspərɪt) adj **1** utterly different or distinct in kind ⊳ n **2** (*plural*) unlike things or people [c16 from Latin *disparāre* to divide, from DIS-¹ + *parāre* to prepare; also influenced by Latin *dispar* unequal] > 'disparately adv > 'disparateness n

disparity (dɪˈspærɪtɪ) n, pl -ties **1** inequality or difference, as in age, rank, wages, etc **2** dissimilarity

■ USAGE See at **discrepancy**

dispassion (dɪsˈpæʃən) n detachment; objectivity

dispassionate (dɪsˈpæʃənɪt) adj devoid of or uninfluenced by emotion or prejudice; objective; impartial > dis'passionately adv > dis'passionateness n

dispatch or **despatch** (dɪˈspætʃ) vb (tr) **1** to send off promptly, as to a destination or to perform a task **2** to discharge or complete (a task, duty, etc) promptly **3** *informal* to eat up quickly **4** to murder or execute ⊳ n **5** the act of sending off a letter, messenger, etc **6** prompt action or speed (often in the phrase **with dispatch**) **7** an official communication or report, sent in haste **8** *journalism* a report sent to a newspaper, etc, by a correspondent **9** murder or execution [c16 from Italian *dispacciare*, from Provençal *despachar*, from Old French *despeechier* to set free, from *des-* DIS-¹ + *-peechier*, ultimately from Latin *pedica* a fetter] > dis'patcher n

dispatch box n a case or box used to hold valuables or documents, esp official state documents

dispatch case n a case used for carrying papers, documents, books, etc, usually flat and stiff

dispatch rider n a horseman or motorcyclist who carries dispatches

dispel (dɪˈspɛl) vb -pels, -pelling, -pelled (tr) to disperse or drive away [c17 from Latin *dispellere*, from DIS-¹ + *pellere* to drive] > dis'peller n

dispend (dɪˈspɛnd) vb (tr) *obsolete* to spend [c14 from Old French *despendre*, from Latin *dispendere* to distribute; see DISPENSE]

dispensable (dɪˈspɛnsəbəl) adj **1** not essential; expendable **2** capable of being distributed **3** (of a law, vow, etc) able to be relaxed > dis,pensa'bility or dis'pensableness n

dispensary (dɪˈspɛnsərɪ, -srɪ) n, pl -ries a place where medicine and medical supplies are dispensed

dispensation (ˌdɪspɛnˈseɪʃən) n **1** the act of distributing or dispensing **2** something distributed or dispensed **3** a system or plan of administering or dispensing **4** *chiefly RC Church* **a** permission to dispense with an obligation of church law **b** the document authorizing such permission **5** any exemption from a rule or obligation **6** *Christianity* **a** the ordering of life and events by God **b** a divine decree affecting an individual or group **c** a religious system or code of prescriptions for life and conduct regarded as of divine origin > ,dispen'sational adj

dispensatory (dɪˈspɛnsətərɪ, -trɪ) n, pl -ries **1** a book listing the composition, preparation, and application of various drugs ⊳ adj **2** of or involving dispensation

dispense (dɪˈspɛns) vb **1** (tr) to give out or issue in portions **2** (tr) to prepare and distribute (medicine), esp on prescription **3** (tr) to administer (the law, etc) **4** (intr; foll by *with*) to do away (with) or manage (without) **5** to grant a

dispensation to (someone) from (some obligation of church law) **6** to exempt or excuse from a rule or obligation [c14 from Medieval Latin *dispensāre* to pardon, from Latin *dispendere* to weigh out, from DIS-¹ + *pendere* to weigh]

■ USAGE *Dispense with* is sometimes wrongly used where *dispose of* is meant: *this task can be disposed of* (not *dispensed with*) *quickly and easily*

dispenser (dɪˈspɛnsə) n **1** a device, such as a vending machine, that automatically dispenses a single item or a measured quantity **2** a person or thing that dispenses

dispensing optician n See **optician**

dispermous (daɪˈspɜːməs) adj (of flowering plants) producing or having two seeds [c18 from DI-¹ + Greek *sperma* seed]

dispersal (dɪˈspɜːsəl) n **1** the act of dispersing or the condition of being dispersed **2** the spread of animals, plants, or seeds to new areas

dispersal prison n a prison organized and equipped to accommodate a proportion of the most dangerous and highest security risk prisoners

dispersant (dɪsˈpɜːsənt) n a liquid or gas used to disperse small particles or droplets, as in an aerosol

disperse (dɪˈspɜːs) vb **1** to scatter; distribute over a wide area **2** to dissipate or cause to dissipate **3** to leave or cause to leave a gathering, often in a random manner **4** to separate or be separated by dispersion **5** (tr) to diffuse or spread (news, information, etc) **6** to separate (particles) throughout a solid, liquid, or gas, as in the formation of a suspension or colloid ⊳ adj **7** of or consisting of the particles in a colloid or suspension: *disperse phase* [c14 from Latin *dispersus* scattered, from *dispergere* to scatter widely, from DI-² + *spargere* to strew] > dispersedly (dɪˈspɜːsɪdlɪ) adv > dis'perser n

■ USAGE See at **disburse**

dispersion (dɪˈspɜːʃən) n **1** another word for **dispersal 2** *physics* **a** the separation of electromagnetic radiation into constituents of different wavelengths **b** a measure of the ability of a substance to separate by refraction, expressed by the first differential of the refractive index with respect to wavelength at a given value of wavelength. Symbol: D **3** *statistics* the degree to which values of a frequency distribution are scattered around some central point, usually the arithmetic mean or median **4** *chem* a system containing particles dispersed in a solid, liquid, or gas **5** *military* the pattern of fire from a weapon system **6 a** the range of speeds of such objects as the stars in a galaxy **b** the frequency-dependent retardation of radio waves as they pass through the interstellar medium **c** the deviation of a rocket from its prescribed path **7** *ecology* the distribution pattern of an animal or a plant population

Dispersion (dɪˈspɜːʃən) n the another name for the **Diaspora**

dispersion hardening n the strengthening of an alloy as a result of the presence of fine particles in the lattice

dispersion relation n *physics* the relationship between the angular frequency (Gomega;) of a wave and the magnitude of its wave vector (k). Thus the wave's speed is ω/k

dispersive (dɪˈspɜːsɪv) adj tending or serving to disperse > dis'persively adv > dis'persiveness n

dispersive medium n *physics* a substance in which waves of different frequencies travel at different speeds

dispersoid (dɪˈspɜːsɔɪd) n *chem* a system, such as a colloid or suspension, in which one phase is dispersed in another

dispirit (dɪˈspɪrɪt) vb (tr) to lower the spirit or enthusiasm of; make downhearted or depressed; discourage

dispirited (dɪˈspɪrɪtɪd) adj low in spirit or

enthusiasm; downhearted or depressed; discouraged > dis'piritedly adv > dis'piritedness n

dispiriting (dɪˈspɪrɪtɪŋ) adj tending to lower the spirit or enthusiasm; depressing; discouraging > dis'piritingly adv

displace (dɪsˈpleɪs) vb (tr) **1** to move from the usual or correct location **2** to remove from office or employment **3** to occupy the place of; replace; supplant **4** to force (someone) to leave home or country, as during a war **5** *chem* to replace (an atom or group in a chemical compound) by another atom or group **6** *physics* to cause a displacement of (a quantity of liquid, usually water of a specified type and density) > dis'placeable adj > dis'placer n

displaced person n a person forced from his home or country, esp by war or revolution. Abbreviation: DP

displacement (dɪsˈpleɪsmənt) n **1** the act of displacing or the condition of being displaced **2** the weight or volume displaced by a floating or submerged body in a fluid **3** *chem* another name for **substitution 4** the volume displaced by the piston of a reciprocating pump or engine **5** *psychoanal* the transferring of emotional feelings from their original object to one that disguises their real nature **6** *geology* the distance any point on one side of a fault plane has moved in relation to a corresponding point on the opposite side **7** *astronomy* an apparent change in position of a body, such as a star **8** *maths* the distance measured in a particular direction from a reference point. Symbol: *s*

displacement activity n **1** *psychol* behaviour that occurs typically when there is a conflict between motives and that has no relevance to either motive: *eg head scratching* **2** *zoology* the substitution of a pattern of animal behaviour that is different from behaviour relevant to the situation: *eg preening at an apparently inappropriate time*

displacement ton n the full name for **ton¹** (sense 6)

displant (dɪsˈplɑːnt) vb (tr) *obsolete* **1** to displace **2** to transplant (a plant)

display (dɪˈspleɪ) vb **1** (tr) to show or make visible **2** (tr) to disclose or make evident; reveal: *to display anger* **3** (tr) to flaunt in an ostentatious way: *to display military might* **4** (tr) to spread or open out; unfurl or unfold **5** (tr) to give prominence to (headings, captions, etc) by the use of certain typefaces **6** (intr) *zoology* to engage in a display ⊳ n **7** the act of exhibiting or displaying; show: *a display of fear* **8** something exhibited or displayed **9** an ostentatious or pretentious exhibition: *a display of his accomplishments* **10 a** an arrangement of certain typefaces to give prominence to headings, captions, advertisements, etc **b** printed matter that is eye-catching **11** *electronics* **a** a device capable of representing information visually, as on a cathode-ray tube screen **b** the information so presented **12** *zoology* a pattern of behaviour in birds, fishes, etc, by which the animal attracts attention while it is courting the female, defending its territory, etc **13** (*modifier*) relating to or using typefaces that give prominence to the words they are used to set [c14 from Anglo-French *despleier* to unfold, from Late Latin *displicāre* to scatter, from DIS-¹ + *plicāre* to fold] > dis'player n

display advertisement or **display ad** n an advertisement designed to attract attention by using devices such as conspicuous or elegant typefaces, graphics, etc. See **small advertisement**

displease (dɪsˈpliːz) vb to annoy, offend, or cause displeasure to (someone) > dis'pleasing adj > dis'pleasingly adv

displeasure (dɪsˈplɛʒə) n **1** the condition of being displeased **2** *archaic* **a** pain **b** an act or cause of offence ⊳ vb **3** an archaic word for **displease**

displode (dɪsˈpləʊd) vb an obsolete word for **explode** [c17 from Latin *displōdere* from DIS-¹ +

plaudere to clap]

disport (dɪ'spɔːt) vb 1 (tr) to indulge (oneself) in pleasure 2 (intr) to frolic or gambol ▷ n 3 archaic amusement [C14 from Anglo-French desporter, from des- DIS-¹ + porter to carry]

disposable (dɪ'spəʊzəb³l) adj 1 designed for disposal after use: disposable cups 2 available for use if needed: disposable assets ▷ n 3 something, such as a baby's nappy, that is designed for disposal 4 (plural) short for **disposable goods** > dis,posa'bility or dis'posableness n

disposable goods pl n consumer goods that are used up a short time after purchase, including perishables, newspapers, clothes, etc. Compare **durable goods** Also called: disposables

disposable income n 1 the money a person has available to spend after paying taxes, pension contributions, etc 2 the total amount of money that the individuals in a community, country, etc, have available to buy consumer goods

disposal (dɪ'spəʊz³l) n 1 the act or means of getting rid of something 2 placement or arrangement in a particular order 3 a specific method of tending to matters, as in business 4 the act or process of transferring something to or providing something for another 5 the power or opportunity to make use of someone or something (esp in the phrase at one's disposal) 6 a means of destroying waste products, as by grinding into particles ▷ Also (for senses 2–5): disposition

dispose (dɪ'spəʊz) vb 1 (intr; foll by of) a to deal with or settle b to give, sell, or transfer to another c to throw out or away d to consume, esp hurriedly e to kill 2 to arrange or settle (matters) by placing into correct or final condition: man proposes, God disposes 3 (tr) to make willing or receptive 4 (tr) to adjust or place in a certain order or position 5 (tr; often foll by to) to accustom or condition ▷ n 6 an obsolete word for disposal or disposition [C14 from Old French disposer, from Latin disponere to set in different places, arrange, from DIS-¹ + ponere to place] > dis'poser n

disposed (dɪ'spəʊzd) adj a having an inclination as specified (towards something) b (in combination): well-disposed

disposition (,dɪspə'zɪʃən) n 1 a person's usual temperament or frame of mind 2 a natural or acquired tendency, inclination, or habit in a person or thing 3 another word for disposal (senses 2–5) 4 philosophy, logic a property that consists not in the present state of an object, but in its propensity to change in a certain way under certain conditions, as brittleness which consists in the propensity to break when struck. Compare occurrent 5 archaic manner of placing or arranging > ,dispo'sitional adj

dispossess (,dɪspə'zɛs) vb (tr) to take away possession of something, esp property; expel > ,dispos'session n > ,dispos'sessor n > ,dispos'sessory adj

disposure (dɪ'spəʊʒə) n a rare word for disposal or disposition

dispraise (dɪs'preɪz) vb 1 (tr) to express disapproval or condemnation of ▷ n 2 the disapproval, etc, expressed > dis'praiser n > dis'praisingly adv

disprize (dɪs'praɪz) vb (tr) archaic to scorn; disdain

disproof (dɪs'pruːf) n 1 facts that disprove something 2 the act of disproving

disproportion (,dɪsprə'pɔːʃən) n 1 lack of proportion or equality 2 an instance of disparity or inequality ▷ vb 3 (tr) to cause to become exaggerated or unequal > ,dispro'portionable adj > ,dispro'portionableness n > ,dispro'portionably adv

disproportionate adj (,dɪsprə'pɔːʃənɪt) 1 out of proportion; unequal ▷ vb (,dɪsprə'pɔːʃə,neɪt) 2 chem to undergo or cause to undergo disproportionation > ,dispro'portionately adv > ,dispro'portionateness n

disproportionation (,dɪsprə,pɔːʃə'neɪʃən) n a reaction between two identical molecules in which one is reduced and the other oxidized

disprove (dɪs'pruːv) vb (tr) to show (an assertion, claim, etc) to be incorrect > dis'provable adj > dis'proval n

disputable (dɪ'spjuːtəb³l, 'dɪspjʊtə-) adj capable of being argued; debatable > dis,puta'bility or dis'putableness n > dis'putably adv

disputant (dɪ'spjuːt³nt, 'dɪspjʊtənt) n 1 a person who argues; contestant ▷ adj 2 engaged in argument

disputation (,dɪspjʊ'teɪʃən) n 1 the act or an instance of arguing 2 a formal academic debate on a thesis 3 an obsolete word for conversation

disputatious (,dɪspjʊ'teɪʃəs) or **disputative** (dɪ'spjuːtətɪv) adj inclined to argument > dis'putatiously or dis'putatively adv > dis'putatiousness or dis'putativeness n

dispute vb (dɪ'spjuːt) 1 to argue, debate, or quarrel about (something) 2 (tr; may take a clause as object) to doubt the validity, etc, of 3 (tr) to seek to win; contest for 4 (tr) to struggle against; resist ▷ n (dɪ'spjuːt, 'dɪspjuːt) 5 an argument or quarrel [C13 from Late Latin disputāre to contend verbally, from Latin: to discuss, from DIS-¹ + putāre to think] > dis'puter n

disqualify (dɪs'kwɒlɪ,faɪ) vb -fies, -fying, -fied (tr) 1 to make unfit or unqualified 2 to make ineligible, as for entry to an examination 3 to debar (a player or team) from a sporting contest 4 to divest or deprive of rights, powers, or privileges: disqualified from driving > dis'quali,fiable adj > dis,qualifi'cation n > dis'quali,fier n

disquiet (dɪs'kwaɪət) n 1 a feeling or condition of anxiety or uneasiness ▷ vb 2 (tr) to make anxious or upset 3 archaic uneasy or anxious > dis'quietedly or dis'quietly adv > dis'quietedness or dis'quietness n > dis'quieting adj > dis'quietingly adv

disquietude (dɪs'kwaɪɪ,tjuːd) n a feeling or state of anxiety or uneasiness

disquisition (,dɪskwɪ'zɪʃən) n a formal written or oral examination of a subject [C17 from Latin disquīsītiō, from disquīrere to make an investigation, from DIS-¹ + quaerere to seek] > ,disqui'sitional adj

disrate (dɪs'reɪt) vb (tr) naval to punish (an officer) by lowering him in rank

disregard (,dɪsrɪ'gɑːd) vb (tr) 1 to give little or no attention to; ignore 2 to treat as unworthy of consideration or respect ▷ n 3 lack of attention or respect 4 (often plural) social welfare capital or income which is not counted in calculating the amount payable to a claimant for a means-tested benefit > disre'garder n > disre'gardful adj > disre'gardfully adv > disre'gardfulness n

disrelish (dɪs'relɪʃ) vb 1 (tr) to have a feeling of aversion for; dislike ▷ n 2 such a feeling

disremember (,dɪsrɪ'mɛmbə) vb informal, chiefly US to fail to recall (someone or something)

disrepair (,dɪsrɪ'pɛə) n the condition of being worn out or in poor working order; a condition requiring repairs

disreputable (dɪs'rɛpjʊtəb³l) adj 1 having or causing a lack of repute 2 disordered in appearance > dis,repu'tability or dis'reputableness n > dis'reputably adv

disrepute (,dɪsrɪ'pjuːt) n a loss or lack of credit or repute

disrespect (,dɪsrɪ'spɛkt) n 1 contempt; rudeness ▷ vb 2 (tr) to show lack of respect for > ,disre'spectful adj > ,disre'spectfully adv > ,disre'spectfulness n

disrespectable (,dɪsrɪ'spɛktəb³l) adj unworthy of respect; not respectable > ,disre,specta'bility n

disrobe (dɪs'rəʊb) vb 1 to remove the clothing of (a person) or (of a person) to undress 2 (tr) to divest of authority, etc > dis'robement n > dis'rober n

disrupt (dɪs'rʌpt) vb 1 (tr) to throw into turmoil or disorder 2 (tr) to interrupt the progress of (a movement, meeting, etc) 3 to break or split

(something) apart [C17 from Latin disruptus burst asunder, from dīrumpere to dash to pieces, from DIS-¹ + rumpere to burst] > dis'rupter or dis'ruptor n > dis'ruption n

disruptive (dɪs'rʌptɪv) adj involving, causing, or tending to cause disruption > dis'ruptively adv

disruptive discharge n a sudden large increase in current through an insulating medium resulting from failure of the medium to withstand an applied electric field

diss or **dis** (dɪs) vb slang, chiefly US to treat (someone) with contempt [C20 originally Black rap slang, short for DISRESPECT]

dissatisfaction (dɪs,sætɪs'fækʃən) n the state of being unsatisfied or disappointed > ,dissatis'factory adj

dissatisfied (dɪs'sætɪs,faɪd) adj having or showing dissatisfaction; discontented > dis'satis,fiedly adv

dissatisfy (dɪs'sætɪs,faɪ) vb -fies, -fying, -fied (tr) to fail to satisfy; disappoint

dissect (dɪ'sɛkt, daɪ-) vb 1 to cut open and examine the structure of (a dead animal or plant) 2 (tr) to examine critically and minutely [C17 from Latin dissecāre, from DIS-¹ + secāre to cut] > dis'sectible adj > dis'section n > dis'sector n

dissected (dɪ'sɛktɪd, daɪ-) adj 1 botany in the form of narrow lobes or segments: dissected leaves 2 geology (of plains) cut by erosion into hills and valleys, esp following tectonic movements

disseise or **disseize** (dɪs'siːz) vb (tr) property law to deprive of seisin; wrongfully dispossess of a freehold interest in land [C14 from Anglo-Norman desseisir, from DIS-¹ + SEIZE] > dis'seisor or dis'seizor n

disseisin or **disseizin** (dɪs'siːzɪn) n the act of disseising or state of being disseised [C14 from Old French dessaisine; see DIS-¹, SEISIN]

disselboom ('dɪsəl,bʊəm) n South African the main haulage shaft of a wagon or cart [from Afrikaans dissel shaft + boom beam]

dissemble (dɪ'sɛmb³l) vb 1 to conceal (one's real motives, emotions, etc) by pretence 2 (tr) to pretend; simulate 3 obsolete to ignore [C15 from earlier dissimulen, from Latin dissimulāre; probably influenced by obsolete semble to resemble] > dis'semblance n > dis'sembler n > dis'sembling, adj > dis'semblingly adv

disseminate (dɪ'sɛmɪ,neɪt) vb (tr) to distribute or scatter about; diffuse [C17 from Latin dissēmināre, from DIS-¹ + sēmināre to sow, from sēmen seed] > dis,semi'nation n > dis'seminative adj > dis'semi,nator n

disseminated sclerosis n another name for multiple sclerosis

disseminule (dɪ'sɛmɪ,njuːl) n any propagative part of a plant, such as a seed or spore, that helps to spread the species [C20 from DISSEMINATE + -ULE]

dissension (dɪ'sɛnʃən) n disagreement, esp when leading to a quarrel [C13 from Latin dissēnsiō, from dissentīre to dissent]

dissent (dɪ'sɛnt) vb (intr) 1 to have a disagreement or withhold assent 2 Christianity to refuse to conform to the doctrines, beliefs, or practices of an established church, and to adhere to a different system of beliefs and practices ▷ n 3 a difference of opinion 4 Christianity separation from an established church; Nonconformism 5 the voicing of a minority opinion in announcing the decision on a case at law; dissenting judgment [C16 from Latin dissentīre to disagree, from DIS-¹ + sentīre to perceive, feel] > dis'senter n > dis'senting adj > dis'sentingly adv

Dissenter (dɪ'sɛntə) n Christianity, chiefly Brit a Nonconformist or a person who refuses to conform to the established church

dissentient (dɪ'sɛnʃənt) adj 1 dissenting, esp from the opinion of the majority ▷ n 2 a dissenter > dis'sentience or dis'sentiency n > dis'sentiently adv

dissentious (dɪ'sɛnʃəs) adj argumentative

d

dissepiment (dɪˈsɛpɪmənt) n biology a dividing partition or membrane, such as that between the chambers of a syncarpous ovary [c18 from Late Latin dissaepimentum, from DIS-¹ + saepīmentum hedge, from saepīre to enclose] > disˌsepiˈmental adj

dissertate (ˈdɪsəˌteɪt) vb (intr) rare to give or make a dissertation [c18 from Latin dissertāre to debate, from disserere to examine, from DIS-¹ + serere to arrange] > ˈdisserˌtator n

dissertation (ˌdɪsəˈteɪʃən) n 1 a written thesis, often based on original research, usually required for a higher degree 2 a formal discourse > ˌdisserˈtational adj > ˌdisserˈtationist n

disserve (dɪsˈsɜːv) vb (tr) archaic to do a disservice to

disservice (dɪsˈsɜːvɪs) n an ill turn; wrong; injury, esp when trying to help > disˈserviceable adj

dissever (dɪˈsɛvə) vb 1 to break off or become broken off 2 (tr) to divide up into parts [c13 from Old French desseverer, from Late Latin DIS-¹ + sēparāre to SEPARATE] > disˈseverance, disˈseverment or disˌseverˈation n

dissident (ˈdɪsɪdənt) adj 1 disagreeing; dissenting ▷ n 2 a person who disagrees, esp one who disagrees with the government [c16 from Latin dissidēre to be remote from, from DIS-¹ + sedēre to sit] > ˈdissidence n > ˈdissidently adv

dissimilar (dɪˈsɪmɪlə) adj not alike; not similar; different > disˈsimilarly adv

dissimilarity (ˌdɪsɪmɪˈlærɪtɪ) n, pl -ties 1 difference; unlikeness 2 a point or instance of difference

dissimilate (dɪˈsɪmɪˌleɪt) vb 1 to make or become dissimilar 2 (usually foll by to) phonetics to change or displace (a consonant) or (of a consonant) to be changed to or displaced by (another consonant) so that its manner of articulation becomes less similar to a speech sound in the same word. Thus (r) in the final syllable of French marbre is dissimilated to (l) in its English form marble [c19 from DIS-¹ + ASSIMILATE] > disˈsimilative adj > disˈsimilatory adj

dissimilation (ˌdɪsɪmɪˈleɪʃən) n 1 the act or an instance of making dissimilar 2 phonetics the alteration or omission of a consonant as a result of being dissimilated 3 biology a less common word for catabolism

dissimilitude (ˌdɪsɪˈmɪlɪˌtjuːd) n 1 dissimilarity; difference 2 a point of difference

dissimulate (dɪˈsɪmjʊˌleɪt) vb to conceal (one's real feelings) by pretence > disˌsimuˈlation n > disˈsimulative adj > disˈsimuˌlator n

dissipate (ˈdɪsɪˌpeɪt) vb 1 to exhaust or be exhausted by dispersion 2 (tr) to scatter or break up 3 (intr) to indulge in the pursuit of pleasure [c15 from Latin dissipāre to disperse, from DIS-¹ + supāre to throw] > ˈdissiˌpater or ˈdissiˌpator n > ˈdissiˌpative adj

dissipated (ˈdɪsɪˌpeɪtɪd) adj 1 indulging without restraint in the pursuit of pleasure; debauched 2 wasted, scattered, or exhausted > ˈdissiˌpatedly adv > ˈdissiˌpatedness n

dissipation (ˌdɪsɪˈpeɪʃən) n 1 the act of dissipating or condition of being dissipated 2 unrestrained indulgence in physical pleasures, esp alcohol 3 excessive expenditure; wastefulness 4 amusement; diversion

dissociable (dɪˈsəʊʃɪəbəl, -ʃə-) adj 1 able to be dissociated; distinguishable 2 incongruous; irreconcilable 3 (dɪˈsəʊʃəbəl) Also: dissocial a less common word for unsociable. > disˌsociaˈbility or disˈsociableness n > disˈsociably adv

dissociate (dɪˈsəʊʃɪˌeɪt, -sɪ-) vb 1 to break or cause to break the association between (people, organizations, etc) 2 (tr) to regard or treat as separate or unconnected 3 to undergo or subject to dissociation > disˈsociative adj

dissociation (dɪˌsəʊsɪˈeɪʃən, -ʃɪ-) n 1 the act of dissociating or the state of being dissociated 2 chem a a reversible chemical change of the molecules of a single compound into two or more other molecules, atoms, ions, or radicals b any

decomposition of the molecules of a single compound into two or more other compounds, atoms, ions, or radicals 3 separation of molecules or atoms that occurs when a liquid or solid changes to a gas 4 psychiatry the separation of a group of mental processes or ideas from the rest of the personality, so that they lead an independent existence, as in cases of multiple personality

dissociative disorder n psychol an emotional disorder characterized by fugue states or multiple personality

dissoluble (dɪˈsɒljʊbəl) adj a less common word for soluble [c16 from Latin dissolūbilis, from dissolvere to DISSOLVE] > disˌsoluˈbility or disˈsolubleness n

dissolute (ˈdɪsəˌluːt) adj given to dissipation; debauched [c14 from Latin dissolūtus loose, from dissolvere to DISSOLVE] > ˈdissoˌlutely adv > ˈdissoˌluteness n

dissolution (ˌdɪsəˈluːʃən) n 1 the resolution or separation into component parts; disintegration 2 destruction by breaking up and dispersing 3 the termination of a meeting or assembly, such as Parliament 4 the termination of a formal or legal relationship, such as a business enterprise, marriage, etc 5 the state of being dissolute; dissipation 6 the act or process of dissolving > ˈdissoˌlutive adj

dissolve (dɪˈzɒlv) vb 1 to go or cause to go into solution: salt dissolves in water; water dissolves sugar 2 to become or cause to become liquid; melt 3 to disintegrate or disperse 4 to come or bring to an end 5 to dismiss (a meeting, parliament, etc) or (of a meeting, etc) to be dismissed 6 to collapse or cause to collapse emotionally: to dissolve into tears 7 to lose or cause to lose distinctness or clarity 8 (tr) to terminate legally, as a marriage, etc 9 (intr) films, television to fade out one scene and replace with another to make two scenes merge imperceptibly (**fast dissolve**) or slowly overlap (**slow dissolve**) over a period of about three or four seconds ▷ n 10 films, television a scene filmed or televised by dissolving [c14 from Latin dissolvere to make loose, from DIS-¹ + solvere to release] > disˈsolvable adj > disˌsolvaˈbility or disˈsolvableness n > disˈsolver n

dissolvent (dɪˈzɒlvənt) n 1 a rare word for solvent (sense 3) ▷ adj 2 able to dissolve

dissonance (ˈdɪsənəns) or **dissonancy** n 1 a discordant combination of sounds 2 lack of agreement or consistency 3 music a a sensation commonly associated with all intervals of the second and seventh, all diminished and augmented intervals, and all chords based on these intervals. Compare **consonance** (sense 3) b an interval or chord of this kind

dissonant (ˈdɪsənənt) adj 1 discordant; cacophonous 2 incongruous or discrepant 3 music characterized by dissonance [c15 from Latin dissonāre to be discordant, from DIS-¹ + sonāre to sound] > ˈdissonantly adv

dissuade (dɪˈsweɪd) vb (tr) 1 (often foll by from) to deter (someone) by persuasion from a course of action, policy, etc 2 to advise against (an action, etc) [c15 from Latin dissuādēre, from DIS-¹ + suādēre to persuade] > disˈsuadable adj > disˈsuader n > disˈsuasion n > disˈsuasive adj > disˈsuasively adv > disˈsuasiveness n

dissyllable (dɪˈsɪləbəl, ˈdɪsˌsɪl-, ˈdaɪsɪl-) or **disyllable** (ˈdaɪsɪləbəl, ˈdɪsɪl-) n grammar a word of two syllables > dissyllabic (ˌdɪsɪˈlæbɪk, ˌdɪsɪ-, ˌdaɪ-) or disyllabic (ˌdaɪsɪˈlæbɪk, ˌdɪ-) adj

dissymmetry (dɪˈsɪmɪtrɪ, dɪsˈsɪm-) n, pl -tries 1 lack of symmetry 2 the relationship between two objects when one is the mirror image of the other. See also **chirality** 3 another name for **chirality** > dissymmetric (ˌdɪsɪˈmɛtrɪk, ˌdɪssɪ-) or ˌdissymˈmetrical adj > ˌdissymˈmetrically adv

distaff (ˈdɪstɑːf) n 1 the rod on which flax is wound preparatory to spinning 2 figurative women's work [Old English distæf, from dis- bunch of flax + stæf STAFF¹; see DIZEN]

distaff side n the female side or branch of a family. Compare **spear side**

distal (ˈdɪstəl) adj anatomy (of a muscle, bone, limb, etc) situated farthest from the centre, median line, or point of attachment or origin. Compare **proximal** [c19 from DISTANT + -AL¹] > ˈdistally adv

distance (ˈdɪstəns) n 1 the intervening space between two points or things 2 the length of this gap 3 the state of being apart in space; remoteness 4 an interval between two points in time 5 the extent of progress; advance 6 a distant place or time: he lives at a distance from his work 7 a separation or remoteness in relationship; disparity 8 keep one's distance to maintain a proper or discreet reserve in respect of another person 9 geometry a the length of the shortest line segment joining two points b the length along a straight line or curve 10 (preceded by the) the most distant or a faraway part of the visible scene or landscape 11 horse racing a Brit a point on a racecourse 240 yards from the winning post b Brit any interval of more than 20 lengths between any two finishers in a race c US the part of a racecourse that a horse must reach in any heat before the winner passes the finishing line in order to qualify for later heats 12 go the distance a boxing to complete a bout without being knocked out b to be able to complete an assigned task or responsibility 13 the distant parts of a picture, such as a landscape 14 middle distance a (in a picture) halfway between the foreground and the horizon b (in a natural situation) halfway between the observer and the horizon 15 (modifier) athletics relating to or denoting the longer races, usually those longer than a mile: a distance runner ▷ vb (tr) 16 to hold or place at a distance 17 to separate (oneself) mentally or emotionally from something 18 to outdo; outstrip

distance learning n a teaching system consisting of video, audio, and written material designed for a person to use in studying a subject at home

distance modulus n astronomy a measure of the distance, r, of a celestial object too far away to show measurable parallax. It is given by $m–M = 5 \log(r/10)$, where m is its apparent magnitude (corrected for interstellar absorption) and M is its absolute magnitude

distant (ˈdɪstənt) adj 1 far away or apart in space or time 2 (postpositive) separated in space or time by a specified distance 3 apart in relevance, association, or relationship: a distant cousin 4 coming from or going to a faraway place: a distant journey 5 remote in manner; aloof 6 abstracted; absent: a distant look [c14 from Latin distāre to be distant, from DIS-¹ + stāre to stand] > ˈdistantly adv > ˈdistantness n

distant early warning n a US radar detection system to warn of missile attack. See also DEW line

distaste (dɪsˈteɪst) n 1 (often foll by for) an absence of pleasure (in); dislike (of); aversion (to): to look at someone with distaste ▷ vb 2 (tr) an archaic word for **dislike**

distasteful (dɪsˈteɪstfʊl) adj unpleasant or offensive > disˈtastefully adv > disˈtastefulness n

distemper¹ (dɪsˈtɛmpə) n 1 any of various infectious diseases of animals, esp **canine distemper**, a highly contagious viral disease of dogs, characterized initially by high fever and a discharge from the nose and eyes. See also **hard pad, strangles** 2 archaic a a disease or disorder b disturbance c discontent ▷ vb 3 (tr) archaic to disturb [c14 from Late Latin distemperāre to derange the health of, from Latin DIS-¹ + temperāre to mix in correct proportions]

distemper² (dɪsˈtɛmpə) n 1 a technique of painting in which the pigments are mixed with water, glue, size, etc, used for poster, mural, and scene painting 2 the paint used in this technique or any of various water-based paints, including, in Britain, whitewash ▷ *vb* **3** (*tr*) to mix (pigments) with water and size **4** to paint (something) with distemper [C14 from Medieval Latin *distemperāre* to soak, from Latin DIS-[1] + *temperāre* to mingle]

distend (dɪˈstɛnd) *vb* **1** to expand or be expanded by or as if by pressure from within; swell; inflate **2** (*tr*) to stretch out or extend **3** (*tr*) to magnify in importance; exaggerate [C14 from Latin *distendere*, from DIS-[1] + *tendere* to stretch] > **disˈtender** *n* > **disˈtensible** *adj* > **disˌtensiˈbility** *n* > **disˈtension** *or* **disˈtention** *n*

distich (ˈdɪstɪk) *n prosody* a unit of two verse lines, usually a couplet [C16 from Greek *distikhos* having two lines, from DI-[1] + *stikhos* STICH] > **ˈdistichal** *adj*

distichous (ˈdɪstɪkəs) *adj* (of leaves) arranged in two vertical rows on opposite sides of the stem > **ˈdistichously** *adv*

distil *or US* **distill** (dɪsˈtɪl) *vb* **-tils** *or* **-tills, -tilling, -tilled 1** to subject to or undergo distillation. See also **rectify** (sense 2) **2** (sometimes foll by *out* or *off*) to purify, separate, or concentrate, or be purified, separated, or concentrated by distillation **3** to obtain or be obtained by distillation: *to distil whisky* **4** to exude or give off (a substance) in drops or small quantities **5** (*tr*) to extract the essence of as if by distillation [C14 from Latin *dēstillāre* to distil, from DE- + *stillāre* to drip] > **disˈtillable** *adj*

distillate (ˈdɪstɪlɪt, -ˌleɪt) *n* **1** Also called: **distillation** the product of distillation **2** a concentrated essence

distillation (ˌdɪstɪˈleɪʃən) *n* **1** the act, process, or product of distilling **2** the process of evaporating or boiling a liquid and condensing its vapour **3** purification or separation of mixture by using different evaporation rates or boiling points of their components. See also **fractional distillation** **4** the process of obtaining the essence or an extract of a substance, usually by heating it in a solvent **5** another name for **distillate** (sense 1) **6** a concentrated essence > **disˈtillatory** *adj*

distiller (dɪˈstɪlə) *n* a person or organization that distils, esp a company that makes spirits

distillers' grain *n* a by-product of the distillation process for making whisky, used as an animal foodstuff

distillery (dɪˈstɪlərɪ) *n, pl* **-eries** a place where alcoholic drinks, etc, are made by distillation

distinct (dɪˈstɪŋkt) *adj* **1** easily sensed or understood; clear; precise **2** (when postpositive, foll by *from*) not the same (as); separate (from); distinguished (from) **3** not alike; different **4** sharp; clear **5** recognizable; definite: *a distinct improvement* **6** explicit; unequivocal **7** *maths, logic* (of a pair of entities) not identical **8** *botany* (of parts of a plant) not joined together; separate [C14 from Latin *distinctus*, from *distinguere* to DISTINGUISH] > **disˈtinctly** *adv* > **disˈtinctness** *n*

distinction (dɪˈstɪŋkʃən) *n* **1** the act or an instance of distinguishing or differentiating **2** a distinguishing feature **3** the state of being different or distinguishable **4** special honour, recognition, or fame **5** excellence of character; distinctive qualities: *a man of distinction* **6** distinguished appearance **7** a symbol of honour or rank

distinctive (dɪˈstɪŋktɪv) *adj* **1** serving or tending to distinguish **2** denoting one of a set of minimal features of a phoneme in a given language that serve to distinguish it from other phonemes. The distinctive features of /p/ in English are that it is voiceless, bilabial, non-nasal, and plosive; /b/ is voiced, bilabial, non-nasal, and plosive: the two differ by the distinctive feature of voice > **disˈtinctively** *adv* > **disˈtinctiveness** *n*

distinctiveness ratio *n statistics* the ratio of the relative frequency of some event in a given sample to that in the general population or another relevant sample

distingué *French* (distɛ̃ge) *adj* distinguished or noble

distinguish (dɪˈstɪŋgwɪʃ) *vb* (*mainly tr*) **1** (when *intr*, foll by *between* or *among*) to make, show, or recognize a difference or differences (between or among); differentiate (between) **2** to be a distinctive feature of; characterize **3** to make out; perceive **4** to mark for a special honour or title **5** to make (oneself) noteworthy: *he distinguished himself by his cowardice* **6** to classify; categorize: *we distinguished three species* [C16 from Latin *distinguere* to separate, discriminate] > **disˈtinguishable** *adj* > **disˈtinguishably** *adv* > **disˈtinguisher** *n* > **disˈtinguishing** *adj* > **disˈtinguishingly** *adv*

distinguished (dɪˈstɪŋgwɪʃt) *adj* **1** noble or dignified in appearance or behaviour **2** eminent; famous; celebrated

distort (dɪˈstɔːt) *vb* (*tr*) **1** (*often passive*) to twist or pull out of shape; make bent or misshapen; contort; deform **2** to alter or misrepresent (facts, motives, etc) **3** *electronics* to reproduce or amplify (a signal) inaccurately, changing the shape of the waveform [C16 from Latin *distortus* misshapen, from *distorquēre* to turn different ways, from DIS-[1] + *torquēre* to twist] > **disˈtorted** *adj* > **disˈtortedly** *adv* > **disˈtortedness** *n* > **disˈtorter** *n* > **disˈtortive** *adj*

distortion (dɪˈstɔːʃən) *n* **1** the act or an instance of distorting or the state of being distorted **2** something that is distorted **3** an aberration of a lens or optical system in which the magnification varies with the lateral distance from the axis **4** *electronics* **a** an undesired change in the shape of an electromagnetic wave or signal **b** the result of such a change in waveform, esp a loss of clarity in radio reception or sound reproduction **5** *psychol* a change in perception so that it does not correspond to reality **6** *psychoanal* the disguising of the meaning of unconscious thoughts so that they may appear in consciousness, eg in dreams > **disˈtortional** *adj*

distract (dɪˈstrækt) *vb* (*tr*) **1** (*often passive*) to draw the attention of (a person) away from something **2** to divide or confuse the attention of (a person) **3** to amuse or entertain **4** to trouble greatly **5** to make mad [C14 from Latin *distractus* perplexed, from *distrahere* to pull in different directions, from DIS-[1] + *trahere* to drag] > **disˈtracter** *n* > **disˈtractible** *adj* > **disˌtractiˈbility** *n* > **disˈtracting** *adj* > **disˈtractingly** *adv* > **disˈtractive** *adj* > **disˈtractively** *adv*

distracted (dɪˈstræktɪd) *adj* **1** bewildered; confused **2** mad > **disˈtractedly** *adv* > **disˈtractedness** *n*

distraction (dɪˈstrækʃən) *n* **1** the act or an instance of distracting or the state of being distracted **2** something that serves as a diversion or entertainment **3** an interruption; an obstacle to concentration **4** mental turmoil or madness

distrain (dɪˈstreɪn) *vb law* to seize (personal property) by way of distress [C13 from Old French *destreindre*, from Latin *distringere* to impede, from DIS-[1] + *stringere* to draw tight] > **disˈtrainable** *adj* > **disˈtrainment** *n* > **disˈtrainor** *or* **disˈtrainer** *n*

distrainee (ˌdɪstreɪˈniː) *n law* a person whose property has been seized by way of distraint

distraint (dɪˈstreɪnt) *n law* the act or process of distraining; distress

distrait (dɪˈstreɪ; *French* distrɛ) *adj* absent-minded; abstracted [C18 from French, from *distraire* to DISTRACT]

distraught (dɪˈstrɔːt) *adj* **1** distracted or agitated **2** *rare* mad [C14 changed from obsolete *distract* through influence of obsolete *straught*, past participle of STRETCH]

distress (dɪˈstrɛs) *vb* (*tr*) **1** to cause mental pain to; upset badly **2** (*usually passive*) to subject to financial or other trouble **3** to damage (esp furniture), as by scratching or denting it, in order to make it appear older than it is **4** *law* a less common word for **distrain** **5** *archaic* to compel ▷ *n* **6** mental pain; anguish **7** the act of distressing or the state of being distressed **8** physical or financial trouble **9** **in distress** (of a ship, aircraft, etc) in dire need of help **10** *law* **a** the seizure and holding of property as security for payment of or in satisfaction of a debt, claim, etc; distraint **b** the property thus seized **c** *US* (*as modifier*): *distress merchandise* [C13 from Old French *destresse* distress, via Vulgar Latin, from Latin *districtus* divided in mind; see DISTRAIN] > **disˈtressful** *adj* > **disˈtressfully** *adv* > **disˈtressfulness** *n* > **disˈtressing** *adj, n* > **disˈtressingly** *adv*

distressed (dɪˈstrɛst) *adj* **1** much troubled, upset, afflicted **2** in financial straits; poor **3** (of furniture, fabric, etc) having signs of ageing artificially applied **4** *economics* another word for **depressed** (sense 4)

distress merchandise *n US* goods sold at reduced prices in order to pay overdue debts, etc

distress signal *n* a signal by radio, Very light, etc from a ship or other vessel in need of immediate assistance

distributary (dɪˈstrɪbjʊtərɪ, -trɪ) *n, pl* **-taries** one of several outlet streams draining a river, esp on a delta

distribute (dɪˈstrɪbjuːt) *vb* (*tr*) **1** to give out in shares; dispense **2** to hand out or deliver: *to distribute handbills* **3** (*often passive*) to spread throughout a space or area: *gulls are distributed along the west coast* **4** (*often passive*) to divide into classes or categories; classify: *these books are distributed in four main categories* **5** *printing* to return (used type) to the correct positions in the type case **6** *logic* to incorporate in a distributed term of a categorial proposition **7** *maths, logic* to expand an expression containing two operators in such a way that the precedence of the operators is changed; for example, distributing multiplication over addition in $a(b + c)$ yields $ab + ac$ **8** *obsolete* to dispense (justice) [C15 from Latin *distribuere* from DIS-[1] + *tribuere* to give] > **disˈtributable** *adj*

distributed array processor *n* a type of computer system that uses a coordinated array of separate processors applied to a single problem. Abbreviation: DAP

distributed logic *n* a computer system in which remote terminals and electronic devices, distributed throughout the system, supplement the main computer by doing some of the computing or decision making

distributed practice *n psychol* learning with reasonably long intervals between separate occasions of learning. Compare **massed practice**

distributed systems *pl n* two or more computers linked by telecommunication, each of which can perform independently

distributed term *n logic* a term applying equally to every member of the class it designates, as *doctors* in *no doctors are overworked*

distributee (dɪˌstrɪbjʊˈtiː) *n law, chiefly US* a person entitled to share in the estate of an intestate

distribution (ˌdɪstrɪˈbjuːʃən) *n* **1** the act of distributing or the state or manner of being distributed **2** a thing or portion distributed **3** arrangement or location **4** *commerce* the process of physically satisfying the demand for goods and services **5** *economics* the division of the total income of a community among its members, esp between labour incomes (wages and salaries) and property incomes (rents, interest, and dividends) **6** *statistics* the set of possible values of a random variable, or points in a sample space, considered in terms of new theoretical or observed frequency: *a normal distribution* **7** *law* the apportioning of the estate of a deceased intestate among the persons entitled to share in it **8** *law* the lawful division of the assets of a bankrupt among his creditors **9** *finance* **a** the division of part of a company's profit as a dividend to its shareholders **b** the amount paid by dividend in a particular distribution **10** *engineering* the way in which the fuel-air mixture is supplied to each cylinder of a multicylinder internal-combustion engine > **ˌdistriˈbutional** *adj*

distribution channel *n marketing* the network of organizations, including manufacturers, wholesalers, and retailers, that distributes goods or services to consumers

distribution function *n* short for **cumulative distribution function**

distributive (dɪˈstrɪbjʊtɪv) *adj* **1** characterized by or relating to distribution **2** *grammar* referring separately to the individual people or items in a group, as the words *each* and *every* ▷ *n* **3** *grammar* a distributive word **4** *maths* able to be distributed:: *multiplication is distributive over addition* > **disˈtributively** *adv* > **disˈtributiveness** *n*

distributive bargaining *n industrial relations* a negotiation process aimed at reaching a compromise agreement over how resources may be allocated between the parties

distributive law *n maths, logic* a theorem asserting that one operator can validly be distributed over another. See **distribute** (sense 7)

distributor *or* **distributer** (dɪˈstrɪbjʊtə) *n* **1** a person or thing that distributes **2** a wholesaler or middleman engaged in the distribution of a category of goods, esp to retailers in a specific area **3** the device in a petrol engine that distributes the high-tension voltage to the sparking plugs in the sequence of the firing order

district (ˈdɪstrɪkt) *n* **1 a** an area of land marked off for administrative or other purposes **b** (*as modifier*): *district nurse* **2** a locality separated by geographical attributes; region **3** any subdivision of any territory, region, etc **4** (in England from 1974 and in Wales 1974–96) any of the subdivisions of the nonmetropolitan counties that elects a council responsible for local planning, housing, rates, etc. See also **metropolitan district** **5** (in Scotland until 1975) a landward division of a county **6** (in Scotland 1975–96) any of the subdivisions of the regions that elected a council responsible for environmental health services, housing, etc **7** any of the 26 areas into which Northern Ireland has been divided since 1973. Elected district councils are responsible for environmental health services, etc ▷ *vb* **8** (*tr*) to divide into districts [C17 from Medieval Latin *districtus* area of jurisdiction, from Latin *distringere* to stretch out; see DISTRAIN]

district attorney *n* (in the US) the state prosecuting officer in a specified judicial district

district court *n* **1** (in Scotland) a court of summary jurisdiction held by a stipendiary magistrate or one or more justices of the peace to deal with minor criminal offences **2** (in the US) **a** a federal trial court serving a federal judicial district **b** (in some states) a court having general jurisdiction in a state judicial district **3** (in Australia and New Zealand) a court lower than a high court. Former name: **magistrates' court**

district court judge *n Austral and NZ* a judge presiding over a lower court. Former name: **magistrate**

district high school *n NZ* a school in a rural area that includes primary and post-primary classes

district nurse *n* (in Britain) a nurse employed within the National Health Service to attend patients in a particular area, usually by visiting them in their own homes

District of Columbia *n* a federal district of the eastern US, coextensive with the federal capital, Washington. Pop: 564 326 (2003 est). Area: 178 sq km (69 sq miles). Abbreviations: **D.C.**, (with zip code) **DC**

District Six *n* an area of Cape Town that was inhabited by a racially mixed community until it was forcibly removed in 1966

distringas (dɪsˈtrɪŋgæs) *n law* (formerly) a writ directing a sheriff to distrain [from Latin: you shall distrain (the opening word of the writ)]

Distrito Federal (*Portuguese* disˈtritu fedeˈral) *n* a district in S central Brazil, containing Brasília: detached from Goiás state in 1960. Pop: 2 145 839 (2002). Area: 5815 sq km (2245 sq miles)

distrix (ˈdɪstrɪks) *n med* the splitting of the ends of hairs [from Greek DIS-² + *thrix* hair]

distrust (dɪsˈtrʌst) *vb* **1** to regard as untrustworthy or dishonest ▷ *n* **2** suspicion; doubt > **disˈtruster** *n* > **disˈtrustful** *adj* > **disˈtrustfully** *adv* > **disˈtrustfulness** *n*

disturb (dɪˈstɜːb) *vb* (*tr*) **1** to intrude on; interrupt **2** to destroy or interrupt the quietness or peace of **3** to disarrange; muddle **4** (*often passive*) to upset or agitate; trouble: *I am disturbed at your bad news* **5** to inconvenience; put out: *don't disturb yourself on my account* [C13 from Latin *disturbāre*, from DIS-¹ + *turbāre* to confuse] > **disˈturber** *n*

disturbance (dɪˈstɜːbəns) *n* **1** the act of disturbing or the state of being disturbed **2** an interruption or intrusion **3** an unruly outburst or tumult **4** *law* an interference with another's rights **5** *geology* **a** a minor movement of the earth causing a small earthquake **b** a minor mountain-building event **6** *meteorol* a small depression **7** *psychiatry* a mental or emotional disorder

disturbed (dɪˈstɜːbd) *adj psychiatry* emotionally upset, troubled, or maladjusted

disturbing (dɪˈstɜːbɪŋ) *adj* tending to upset or agitate; troubling; worrying > **disˈturbingly** *adv*

disulfiram (ˌdaɪsʌlˈfɪərəm) *n* a drug used in the treatment of alcoholism that acts by inducing nausea and other unpleasant effects following ingestion of alcohol [C20 from tetraethylthiu*ram disulfide*]

disulphate (daɪˈsʌlfeɪt) *n* another name for **pyrosulphate**

disulphide (daɪˈsʌlfaɪd) *n* any chemical compound containing two sulphur atoms per molecule. Also called (not in technical usage): **bisulphide**

disulphuric acid (ˌdaɪsʌlˈfjʊərɪk) *n* another name for **pyrosulphuric acid**

disunite (ˌdɪsjʊˈnaɪt) *vb* **1** to separate or become separate; disrupt **2** (*tr*) to set at variance; estrange > **disˈunion** *n* > ˌ**disuˈniter** *n*

disunity (dɪsˈjuːnɪtɪ) *n, pl* **-ties** dissension or disagreement

disuse (dɪsˈjuːs) *n* the condition of being unused; neglect (often in the phrases **in** *or* **into disuse**)

disused (dɪsˈjuːzd) *adj* no longer used: *a disused mine*

disutility (ˌdɪsjuːˈtɪlɪtɪ) *n, pl* **-ties** *economics* **a** the shortcomings of a commodity or activity in satisfying human wants **b** the degree to which a commodity or activity fails to satisfy human wants ▷ Compare **utility** (sense 4)

disyllable (ˈdaɪsɪləbᵊl, dɪˈsɪl-) *n* a variant of **dissyllable**. > **disyllabic** (ˌdaɪsɪˈlæbɪk, ˌdɪ-) *adj*

dit (dɪt) *n* the short sound used, in combination with the long sound *dah*, in the spoken representation of Morse and other telegraphic codes. Compare **dot¹** (sense 6)

dita (ˈdiːtə) *n* an apocynaceous shrub, *Alstonia scholaris*, of tropical Africa and Asia, having large shiny whorled leaves and medicinal bark [C19 from Tagalog]

ditch (dɪtʃ) *n* **1** a narrow channel dug in the earth, usually used for drainage, irrigation, or as a boundary marker **2** any small, natural waterway **3** *Irish* a bank made of earth excavated from and placed alongside a drain or stream **4** *informal* either of the gutters at the side of a tenpin bowling lane **5** **last ditch** a last resort or place of last defence ▷ *vb* **6** to make a ditch or ditches in (a piece of ground) **7** (*intr*) to edge with a ditch **8** *slang* to crash or be crashed, esp deliberately, as to avoid more unpleasant circumstances: *he had to ditch the car* **9** (*tr*) *slang* to abandon or discard: *to ditch a girlfriend* **10** *slang* to land (an aircraft) on water in an emergency **11** (*tr*) *US slang* to evade: *to ditch the police* [Old English *dīc*; related to Old Saxon *dīk*, Old Norse *dīki*, Middle High German *tīch* dyke, pond, Latin *fīgere* to stick, see DYKE¹] > **ˈditcher** *n* > **ˈditchless** *adj*

ditchwater (ˈdɪtʃˌwɔːtə) *n* **1** stagnant water **2** (as) **dull as ditchwater** extremely uninspiring

ditheism (ˈdaɪθiːˌɪzəm) *n theol* **1** the belief in two equal gods **2** the belief that two equal principles reign over the world, one good and one evil > **ˈditheist** *n* > ˌ**ditheˈistic** *adj*

dither (ˈdɪðə) *vb* (*intr*) **1** *chiefly Brit* to be uncertain or indecisive **2** *chiefly US* to be in an agitated state **3** to tremble, as with cold ▷ *n* **4** *chiefly Brit* a state of indecision **5** a state of agitation [C17 variant of C14 (northern English dialect) *didder*, of uncertain origin] > **ˈditherer** *n* > **ˈdithery** *adj*

dithionite (daɪˈθaɪəˌnaɪt) *n* any salt of dithionous acid. Also called: **hyposulphite, hydrosulphite**

dithionous acid (daɪˈθaɪənəs) *n* an unstable dibasic acid known only in solution and in the form of dithionite salts. It is a powerful reducing agent. Formula: $H_2S_2O_4$. Also called: **hyposulphurous acid, hydrosulphurous acid** [from DI-¹ + *thion-*, from Greek *theion* sulphur + -OUS]

dithyramb (ˈdɪθɪˌræm, -ˌræmb) *n* **1** (in ancient Greece) a passionate choral hymn in honour of Dionysus; the forerunner of Greek drama **2** any utterance or a piece of writing that resembles this [C17 from Latin *dīthyrambus*, from Greek *dithurambos*; related to *iambos* IAMB]

dithyrambic (ˌdɪθɪˈræmbɪk) *adj* **1** *prosody* of or relating to a dithyramb **2** passionately eloquent > ˌ**dithyˈrambically** *adv*

dittander (dɪˈtændə, ˈdɪtᵊn-) *n* a plant, *Lepidium latifolium*, of coastal regions of Europe, N Africa, and SW Asia, with clusters of small white flowers: family *Brassicaceae* (crucifers)

dittany (ˈdɪtənɪ) *n, pl* **-nies** **1** an aromatic Cretan plant, *Origanum dictamnus*, with pink drooping flowers: formerly credited with great medicinal properties: family *Lamiaceae* (labiates) **2** Also called: **stone mint** a North American labiate plant, *Cunila origanoides*, with clusters of purplish flowers **3** another name for **gas plant** [C14 from Old French *ditan*, from Latin *dictamnus*, from Greek *diktamnon*, perhaps from *Diktē*, mountain in Crete]

ditto (ˈdɪtəʊ) *n, pl* **-tos** **1** the aforementioned; the above; the same. Used in accounts, lists, etc, to avoid repetition and symbolized by two small marks (") known as **ditto marks**, placed under the thing repeated. Abbreviation: **do.** **2** *informal* **a** a duplicate **b** (*as modifier*): *a ditto copy* ▷ *adv* **3** in the same way **4** ▷ *sentence substitute informal* used to avoid repeating or to confirm agreement with an immediately preceding sentence ▷ *vb* **-tos, -toing, -toed** **5** (*tr*) to copy; repeat [C17 from Italian (Tuscan dialect), variant of *detto* said, from *dicere* to say, from Latin]

dittography (dɪˈtɒgrəfɪ) *n, pl* **-phies** **1** the unintentional repetition of letters or words **2** a passage of manuscript demonstrating dittography > **dittographic** (ˌdɪtəˈgræfɪk) *adj*

ditty (ˈdɪtɪ) *n, pl* **-ties** a short simple song or poem [C13 from Old French *ditie* poem, from *ditier* to compose, from Latin *dictāre* DICTATE]

ditty bag *n* a sailor's cloth bag for personal belongings or tools. A box used for these purposes is termed a **ditty box** [C19 perhaps from obsolete *dutty* calico, from Hindi *dhotī* loincloth, DHOTI]

ditz (dɪts) *n slang, chiefly US* a silly scatterbrained person [C20 back-formation from DITZY]

ditzy *or* **ditsy** (ˈdɪtzɪ) *adj* **-zier, -ziest** *or* **-sier, -siest** *slang* silly and scatterbrained [C20 perhaps from DOTTY + DIZZY]

Diu (ˈdiːuː) *n* a small island off the NW coast of India: together with a mainland area, it formed a district of Portuguese India (1535–1961); formerly part of the Indian Union Territory of Goa, Daman, and Diu (1962–87)

diuresis (ˌdaɪjʊˈriːsɪs) *n* excretion of an unusually large quantity of urine [C17 from New Latin, from Greek *diourein* to urinate]

diuretic (ˌdaɪjʊˈrɛtɪk) *adj* **1** acting to increase the flow of urine ▷ *n* **2** a drug or agent that increases the flow of urine > ˌ**diuˈretically** *adv* > ˌ**diuˈreticalness** *n*

diurnal (daɪˈɜːnᵊl) *adj* **1** happening during the day or daily **2** (of flowers) open during the day and closed at night **3** (of animals) active during the day ▷ Compare **nocturnal** ▷ *n* **4** a service book containing all the canonical hours except matins [C15 from Late Latin *diurnālis*, from Latin *diurnus*, from *diēs* day] > di'urnally *adv*

diurnal motion *n* motion that occurs during the day or night, such as the diurnal rotation of the celestial sphere

diurnal parallax *n* See **parallax** (sense 2)

div¹ (dɪv) *n maths* short for **divergence** (sense 4)

div² (dɪv) *n prison slang* a stupid or foolish person [C20 probably shortened and changed from DEVIANT]

diva ('di:və) *n, pl* -vas *or* -ve (-vɪ) a highly distinguished female singer; prima donna [C19 via Italian from Latin: a goddess, from *dīvus* DIVINE]

divagate ('daɪvəˌgeɪt) *vb* (*intr*) *rare* to digress or wander [C16 from Latin DI-² + *vagārī* to wander] > ˌdiva'gation *n*

divalent (daɪ'veɪlənt, 'daɪˌveɪ-) *adj chem* 1 having a valency of two 2 having two valencies ▷ Also: **bivalent** > di'valency *n*

divan (dɪ'væn) *n* 1 a a backless sofa or couch, designed to be set against a wall b a bed resembling such a couch 2 (*esp formerly*) a room for smoking and drinking, as in a coffee shop 3 a a Muslim law court, council chamber, or counting house b a Muslim council of state 4 a collection of poems 5 (in Muslim law) an account book ▷ Also called (for senses 2–5): diwan [C16 from Turkish *dīvān*, from Persian *dīwān*]

divaricate *vb* (daɪ'værɪˌkeɪt) 1 (*intr*) (*esp of branches*) to diverge at a wide angle ▷ *adj* (daɪ'værɪkɪt, -ˌkeɪt) 2 branching widely; forked [C17 from Latin *dīvāricāre* to stretch apart, from DI-² + *vāricāre* to stand astride] > di'varicately *adv* > di'variˌcatingly *adv* > diˌvari'cation *n*

divaricator (daɪ'værɪˌkeɪtə) *n zoology* a muscle in brachiopods that controls the opening of the shell

dive (daɪv) *vb* dives, diving, dived *or US* dove, dived (*mainly intr*) 1 to plunge headfirst into water 2 (of a submarine, swimmer, etc) to submerge under water 3 (*also tr*) to fly (an aircraft) in a steep nose-down descending path, or, (of an aircraft) to fly in such a path 4 to rush, go, or reach quickly, as in a headlong plunge: *he dived for the ball* 5 (*also tr;* foll by *in or into*) to dip or put (one's hand) quickly or forcefully (into): *to dive into one's pocket* 6 (*usually foll by in or into*) to involve oneself (in something), as in eating food 7 *soccer slang* (of a footballer) to pretend to have been tripped or impeded by an opposing player in order to win a free kick or penalty ▷ *n* 8 a headlong plunge into water, esp one of several formalized movements executed as a sport 9 an act or instance of diving 10 a steep nose-down descent of an aircraft 11 *slang* a disreputable or seedy bar or club 12 *boxing slang* the act of a boxer pretending to be knocked down or out: *he took a dive in the fourth round* 13 *soccer slang* the act of a player pretending to have been tripped or impeded [Old English *dȳfan* to dip; related to Old Norse *dȳfa* to dip, Frisian *dīvi;* see DEEP, DIP]

dive-bomb *vb* (*tr*) to bomb (a target) using or in the manner of a dive bomber

dive bomber *n* a military aircraft designed to release its bombs on a target during a steep dive

dive brake *n* 1 a flap or spoiler extended from the wings of a ground-attack aircraft for controlling a dive 2 another name for **air brake**

Divehi ('dɪveɪ) *n* the language of the Maldive Islands, belonging to the Indic branch of the Indo-European family

diver ('daɪvə) *n* 1 a person or thing that dives 2 a person who works or explores underwater 3 any aquatic bird of the genus *Gavia*, family *Gaviidae*, and order *Gaviiformes* of northern oceans, having a straight pointed bill, small wings, and a long body: noted for swiftness and skill in swimming and diving. US and Canadian name: loon 4 any of various other diving birds 5 *soccer slang* a player who pretends to have been tripped or impeded by an opposing player in order to win a free kick or penalty

diverge (daɪ'vɜːdʒ) *vb* 1 to separate or cause to

separate and go in different directions from a point 2 (*intr*) to be at variance; differ: *our opinions diverge* 3 (*intr*) to deviate from a prescribed course 4 (*intr*) *maths* (of a series or sequence) to have no limit [C17 from Medieval Latin *dīvergere*, from Latin DI-² + *vergere* to turn]

divergence (daɪ'vɜːdʒəns) *n* 1 the act or result of diverging or the amount by which something diverges 2 the condition of being divergent 3 *meteorol* the outflowing of airstreams from a particular area, caused by expanding air 4 *maths* a the scalar product of the operator, ∇, and a vector function, *A*, where ∇= *i∂/∂x* + *j∂/∂y*+ *k∂/∂z*, and *i, j,* and *k* are unit vectors. Usually written: div *A*, ∇*A*, or ∇*A*.. Compare **curl** (sense 11), **gradient** (sense 4) b the property of being divergent 5 the spreading of a stream of electrons as a result of their mutual electrostatic repulsion 6 the turning of the eyes outwards in order to fixate an object farther away than that previously being fixated. Compare **convergence** (sense 7) 7 Also called: divergent evolution the evolutionary development of structures or organisms that differ from each other in form and function but have evolved from the same basic structure or organism. Compare **convergence** (sense 5) ▷ Also called (for senses 1, 2): divergency

divergent (daɪ'vɜːdʒənt) *adj* 1 diverging or causing divergence 2 (of opinions, interests, etc) different 3 *maths* (of a series) having no limit; not convergent 4 *botany* (of plant organs) farther apart at their tops than at their bases > di'vergently *adv*

> USAGE The use of *divergent* to mean different as in *they hold widely divergent views* is considered by some people to be incorrect

divergent thinking *n psychol* thinking in an unusual and unstereotyped way, eg to generate several possible solutions to a problem. Compare **convergent thinking**

divers ('daɪvəz) *determiner archaic or literary* a various; sundry; some b (*as pronoun; functioning as plural*): *divers of them* [C13 from Old French, from Latin *dīversus* turned in different directions; see DIVERT]

diverse (daɪ'vɜːs, 'daɪvɜːs) *adj* 1 having variety; assorted 2 distinct in kind [C13 from Latin *dīversus;* see DIVERS] > di'versely *adv* > di'verseness *n*

diversification (daɪˌvɜːsɪfɪ'keɪʃən) *n* 1 *commerce* the practice of varying products, operations, etc, in order to spread risk, expand, exploit spare capacity, etc 2 (in regional planning policies) the attempt to provide regions with an adequate variety of industries 3 the act of diversifying

diversiform (daɪ'vɜːsɪˌfɔːm) *adj* having various forms

diversify (daɪ'vɜːsɪˌfaɪ) *vb* -fies, -fying, -fied 1 (*tr*) to create different forms of; variegate; vary 2 (of an enterprise) to vary (products, operations, etc) in order to spread risk, expand, etc 3 to distribute (investments) among several securities in order to spread risk [C15 from Old French *diversifier*, from Medieval Latin *diversificāre*, from Latin *dīversus* DIVERSE + *facere* to make] > di'versiˌfiable *adj* > diˌversifi'ability *n* > di'versiˌfier *n*

diversion (daɪ'vɜːʃən) *n* 1 the act of diverting from a specified course 2 *chiefly Brit* an official detour used by traffic when a main route is closed 3 something that distracts from business, etc; amusement 4 *military* a feint attack designed to draw an enemy away from the main attack > di'versional *or* di'versionary *adj*

diversity (daɪ'vɜːsɪtɪ) *n* 1 the state or quality of being different or varied 2 a point of difference 3 *logic* the relation that holds between two entities when and only when they are not identical; the property of being numerically distinct

divert (daɪ'vɜːt) *vb* 1 to turn (a person or thing) aside from a course; deflect 2 (*tr*) to entertain; amuse 3 (*tr*) to distract the attention of [C15 from French *divertir*, from Latin *dīvertere* to turn aside,

from DI-² + *vertere* to turn] > di'verter *n* > di'vertible *adj* > di'verting *adj* > di'vertingly *adv* > di'vertive *adj*

diverticulitis (ˌdaɪvəˌtɪkjʊ'laɪtɪs) *n* inflammation of one or more diverticula, esp of the colon

diverticulosis (ˌdaɪvəˌtɪkjʊ'ləʊsɪs) *n pathol* the presence of several diverticula, esp in the intestines [from New Latin, from DIVERTICULUM + -OSIS]

diverticulum (ˌdaɪvə'tɪkjʊləm) *n, pl* -la (-lə) any sac or pouch formed by herniation of the wall of a tubular organ or part, esp the intestines [C16 from New Latin, from Latin *dēverticulum* by-path, from *dēvertere* to turn aside, from *vertere* to turn] > ˌdiver'ticular *adj*

divertimento (dɪˌvɜːtɪ'mɛntəʊ) *n, pl* -ti (-tɪ) 1 a piece of entertaining music in several movements, often scored for a mixed ensemble and having no fixed form 2 an episode in a fugue ▷ See also **divertissement** [C18 from Italian]

divertissement (dɪ'vɜːtɪsmənt; *French* divɛrtismɑ̃) *n* 1 a brief entertainment or diversion, usually between the acts of a play 2 *music* a fantasia on popular melodies; potpourri b a piece or pieces written to be played during the intervals in a play, opera, etc c another word for **divertimento** [C18 from French: entertainment]

Dives ('daɪviːz) *n* 1 a rich man in the parable in Luke 16:19–31 2 a very rich man

divest (daɪ'vɛst) *vb* (*tr;* usually foll by *of*) 1 to strip (of clothes): *to divest oneself of one's coat* 2 to deprive or dispossess 3 *property law* to take away an estate or interest in property vested (in a person) [C17 changed from earlier DEVEST] > di'vestible *adj* > divestiture (daɪ'vɛstɪtʃə), divesture (daɪ'vɛstʃə) *or* di'vestment *n*

divi ('dɪvɪ) *n* an alternative spelling of **divvy¹**

divide (dɪ'vaɪd) *vb* 1 to separate or be separated into parts or groups; split up; part 2 to share or be shared out in parts; distribute 3 to diverge or cause to diverge in opinion or aim: *the issue divided the management* 4 (*tr*) to keep apart or be a boundary between: *the Rio Grande divides Mexico from the United States* 5 (*intr*) (in Parliament and similar legislatures) to vote by separating into two groups 6 to categorize; classify 7 to calculate the quotient of (one number or quantity) and (another number or quantity) by division: *to divide 50 by 10; to divide 10 into 50; to divide by 10* 8 (*intr*) to diverge: *the roads divide* 9 (*tr*) to mark increments of (length, angle, etc) as by use of an engraving machine ▷ *n* 10 *chiefly US and Canadian* an area of relatively high ground separating drainage basins; watershed. See also **continental divide** 11 a division; split [C14 from Latin *dīvidere* to force apart, from DI-² + *vid-* separate, from the source of *viduus* bereaved, *vidua* WIDOW] > di'vidable *adj*

divided (dɪ'vaɪdɪd) *adj* 1 *botany* another word for **dissected** (sense 1) 2 split; not united > di'videdly *adv* > di'videdness *n*

divided highway *n US and Canadian* a road on which traffic travelling in opposite directions is separated by a central strip of turf, etc. Also called (in Britain and certain other countries): dual carriageway

dividend ('dɪvɪˌdɛnd) *n* 1 *finance* a a distribution from the net profits of a company to its shareholders b a pro-rata portion of this distribution received by a shareholder 2 the share of a cooperative society's surplus allocated at the end of a period to members 3 *insurance* a sum of money distributed from a company's net profits to the holders of certain policies 4 something extra; bonus 5 a number or quantity to be divided by another number or quantity. Compare **divisor** 6 *law* the proportion of an insolvent estate payable to the creditors [C15 from Latin *dīvidendum* what is to be divided; see DIVIDE]

dividend cover *n* the number of times that a company's dividends to shareholders could be paid out of its annual profits after tax, used as an indication of the probability that dividends will

d

be maintained in subsequent years

divider (dɪ'vaɪdə) *n* **1** Also called: **room divider** a screen or piece of furniture placed so as to divide a room into separate areas **2** a person or thing that divides **3** *electronics* an electrical circuit with an output that is a well-defined fraction of the given input: *a voltage divider*

dividers (dɪ'vaɪdəz) *pl n* a type of compass with two pointed arms, used for measuring lines or dividing them

divi-divi (ˌdɪvɪ'dɪvɪ) *n, pl* -divis or -divi **1** a tropical American leguminous tree, *Caesalpinia coriaria* **2** the pods of this plant, which yield a substance used in tanning leather [c19 from Spanish, of Cariban origin]

divination (ˌdɪvɪ'neɪʃən) *n* **1** the art, practice, or gift of discerning or discovering future events or unknown things, as though by supernatural powers **2** a prophecy **3** a presentiment or guess > **divinatory** (dɪ'vɪnətərɪ, -trɪ) *adj*

divine (dɪ'vaɪn) *adj* **1** of, relating to, or characterizing God or a deity **2** godlike **3** of, relating to, or associated with religion or worship: *the divine liturgy* **4** of supreme excellence or worth **5** *informal* splendid; perfect ▷ *n* **6** (*often capital; preceded by the*) another term for **God 7** a priest, esp one learned in theology ▷ *vb* **8** to perceive or understand (something) by intuition or insight **9** to conjecture (something); guess **10** to discern (a hidden or future reality) as though by supernatural power **11** (*tr*) to search for (underground supplies of water, metal, etc) using a divining rod [c14 from Latin *dīvīnus*, from *dīvus* a god; related to *deus* a god] > di'**vinable** *adj* > di'**vinely** *adv* > di'**vineness** *n* > di'**viner** *n*

divine office *n* (*sometimes capitals*) the canonical prayers (in the Roman Catholic Church those of the breviary) recited daily by priests, those in religious orders, etc

divine right of kings *n history* the concept that the right to rule derives from God and that kings are answerable for their actions to God alone

divine service *n* a service of the Christian church, esp one at which no sacrament is given

diving beetle *n* any of the aquatic predatory beetles of the widely distributed family *Dytiscidae,* characterized by flattened hindlegs adapted for swimming and diving

diving bell *n* an early diving submersible having an open bottom and being supplied with compressed air

diving board *n* a platform or springboard from which swimmers may dive

diving duck *n* any of various ducks, such as the pochard, scaup, redhead, and canvasback, that inhabit bays, estuaries, lakes, etc, and can dive and swim beneath the surface of the water

diving suit *or* **dress** *n* a waterproof suit used by divers, having a heavy detachable helmet and an air supply

divining rod *n* a rod, usually a forked hazel twig, said to move or dip when held over ground in which water, metal, etc, is to be found. Also called: **dowsing rod**

divinity (dɪ'vɪnɪtɪ) *n, pl* -ties **1** the nature of a deity or the state of being divine **2** a god or other divine being **3** (*often capital; preceded by the*) another term for **God 4** another word for **theology**

divinize *or* **divinise** ('dɪvɪˌnaɪz) *vb* (*tr*) to make divine; deify > ˌdivini'**zation** *or* ˌdivini'**sation** *n*

divisibility (dɪˌvɪzɪ'bɪlɪtɪ) *n* the capacity of a dividend to be exactly divided by a given number

divisible (dɪ'vɪzəb³l) *adj* capable of being divided, usually with no remainder > di'**visibleness** *n* > di'**visibly** *adv*

division (dɪ'vɪʒən) *n* **1** the act of dividing or state of being divided **2** the act of sharing out; distribution **3** something that divides or keeps apart, such as a boundary **4** one of the parts, groups, etc, into which something is divided **5** a part of a government, business, country, etc, that

has been made into a unit for administrative, political, or other reasons **6** a formal vote in Parliament or a similar legislative body **7** a difference of opinion, esp one that causes separation **8** (in sports) a section, category, or class organized according to age, weight, skill, etc **9** a mathematical operation, the inverse of multiplication, in which the quotient of two numbers or quantities is calculated. Usually written: $a \div b$, $\frac{a}{b}$, a/b **10 a** *army* a major formation, larger than a regiment or brigade but smaller than a corps, containing the necessary arms to sustain independent combat **b** *navy* a group of ships of similar type or a tactical unit of naval aircraft **c** *air force* an organization normally comprising two or more wings with required support units **11** (*plural*) *navy* the assembly of all crew members for the captain's inspection **12** *biology* (in traditional classification systems) a major category of the plant kingdom that contains one or more related classes. Compare **phylum** (sense 1) **13** *horticulture* any type of propagation in plants in which a new plant grows from a separated part of the original **14** *logic* the fallacy of inferring that the properties of the whole are also true of the parts, as *Britain is in debt, so John Smith is in debt* **15** (esp in 17th-century English music) the art of breaking up a melody into quick phrases, esp over a ground bass [c14 from Latin *dīvīsiō*, from *dīvidere* to DIVIDE] > di'**visional** *or* di'**visionary** *adj* > di'**visionally** *adv*

divisionism (dɪ'vɪʒəˌnɪzəm) *n* the pointillism of Georges Seurat, the French neoimpressionist painter (1859–91), and his followers > di'**visionist** *n, adj*

division of labour *n* a system of organizing the manufacture of an article in a series of separate specialized operations, each of which is carried out by a different worker or group of workers

division sign *n* the symbol ÷, placed between the dividend and the divisor to indicate division, as in $12 \div 6 = 2$

divisive (dɪ'vaɪsɪv) *adj* **1** causing or tending to cause disagreement or dissension **2** *archaic* having the quality of distinguishing > di'**visively** *adv* > di'**visiveness** *n*

divisor (dɪ'vaɪzə) *n* **1** a number or quantity to be divided into another number or quantity (the **dividend**) **2** a number that is a factor of another number

divorce (dɪ'vɔːs) *n* **1** the dissolution of a marriage by judgment of a court or by accepted custom **2** a judicial decree declaring a marriage to be dissolved **3** a separation, esp one that is total or complete ▷ *vb* **4** to separate or be separated by divorce; give or obtain a divorce (to a couple or from one's spouse) **5** (*tr*) to remove or separate, esp completely [c14 from Old French, from Latin *dīvortium* from *dīvertere* to separate; see DIVERT] > di'**vorceable** *adj* > di'**vorcer** *n* > di'**vorcive** *adj*

divorcé (dɪ'vɔːseɪ) *n* a man who has been divorced

divorcée (dɪvɔː'siː) *n* a person, esp a woman, who has been divorced

divorcement (dɪ'vɔːsmənt) *n* a less common word for **divorce**

divot ('dɪvət) *n* a piece of turf dug out of a grass surface, esp by a golf club or by horses' hooves [c16 from Scottish, of obscure origin]

divulgate (dɪ'vʌlgeɪt) *vb* (*tr*) *archaic* to make publicly known [c16 from Latin *dīvulgāre*; see DIVULGE] > di'**vulgator** *or* di'**vulgater** *n* > ˌdivul'**gation** *n*

divulge (daɪ'vʌldʒ) *vb* (*tr; may take a clause as object*) to make known (something private or secret); disclose [c15 from Latin *dīvulgāre*, from DI-² + *vulgāre* to spread among the people, from *vulgus* the common people] > di'**vulgence** *or* di'**vulgement** *n* > di'**vulger** *n*

divulsion (daɪ'vʌlʃən) *n* a tearing or pulling apart [c17 from Latin *dīvulsiō*, from *dīvulsus* torn apart, from *dīvellere* to rend, from DI-² + *vellere* to pull] > di'**vulsive** *adj*

divvy¹ ('dɪvɪ) *informal* ▷ *n, pl* -vies **1** *Brit* short for **dividend,** esp (formerly) one paid by a cooperative society **2** *US and Canadian* a share; portion ▷ *vb* -vies, -vying, -vied **3** (*tr; usually foll by up*) to divide and share

divvy² ('dɪvɪ) *n, pl* -vies *dialect* a stupid or foolish person

Diwali (dɪ'wɑːlɪ) *n* a major Hindu religious festival, honouring Lakshmi, the goddess of wealth. Held over the New Year according to the Vikrama calendar, it is marked by feasting, gifts, and the lighting of lamps

diwan (dɪ'wɑːn) *n* a variant of **dewan** or **divan** (senses 2–5)

dixie¹ ('dɪksɪ) *n* **1** *chiefly military* a large metal pot for cooking, brewing tea, etc **2** a mess tin [c19 from Hindi *degcī*, diminutive of *degcā* pot]

dixie² ('dɪksɪ) *n* *Northern English dialect* a lookout

Dixie ('dɪksɪ) *n* **1** Also called: **Dixieland** the southern states of the US; the states that joined the Confederacy during the Civil War **2** a song adopted as a marching tune by the Confederate states during the American Civil War ▷ *adj* **3** of, relating to, or characteristic of the southern states of the US [c19 perhaps from the nickname of New Orleans, from *dixie* a ten-dollar bill printed there, from French *dix* ten]

Dixieland ('dɪksɪˌlænd) *n* **1** a form of jazz that originated in New Orleans, becoming popular esp with White musicians in the second decade of the 20th century **2** a revival of this style in the 1950s **3** See **Dixie** (sense 1)

DIY *or* **d.i.y.** (in Britain and Canada) *abbreviation for* do-it-yourself > DI'**Yer** *n*

Diyarbakir *or* **Diyarbekir** (diː'jɑːbɛkɪə) *n* a city in SE Turkey, on the River Tigris: ancient black basalt walls. Pop: 607 000 (2005 est). Ancient name: Amida (ə'miːdə)

dizen ('daɪz³n) *vb* an archaic word for **bedizen** [c16 from Middle Dutch *dīsen* to dress a distaff with flax; see DISTAFF] > '**dizenment** *n*

dizzy ('dɪzɪ) *adj* -zier, -ziest **1** affected with a whirling or reeling sensation; giddy **2** mentally confused or bewildered **3** causing or tending to cause vertigo or bewilderment **4** *informal* foolish or flighty ▷ *vb* -zies, -zying, -zied **5** (*tr*) to make dizzy [Old English *dysig* silly; related to Old High German *tusīg* weak, Old Norse *dos* quiet] > '**dizzily** *adv* > '**dizziness** *n*

dj *the internet domain name for* Djibouti

DJ *or* **dj** *abbreviation for* **1** disc jockey **2** dinner jacket

Djailolo *or* **Jilolo** (dʒaɪ'ləʊləʊ) *n* the Dutch name for Halmahera

Djaja ('dʒɑːdʒə) *n* a variant spelling of (Mount) Jaya

Djajapura (ˌdʒɑːdʒɑː'pʊərə) *n* a variant spelling of Jayapura

Djakarta (dʒə'kɑːtə) *n* a variant spelling of Jakarta

Djambi ('dʒæmbɪ) *n* a variant spelling of Jambi

djebel ('dʒɛb³l) *n* a variant spelling of jebel

djellabah, djellabah, jellaba *or* **jellabah** ('dʒɛləbə) *n* a kind of loose cloak with a hood, worn by men esp in North Africa and the Middle East [from Arabic *jallabah*]

djembe ('dʒɛmbɛ) *n* a W African drum played by beating with the hand

Djerba *or* **Jerba** (dʒɜː'bə) *n* an island off the SE coast of Tunisia, in the Gulf of Gabès: traditionally Homer's land of the lotus-eaters. Pop: 92 269 (latest est). Area: 510 sq km (197 sq miles). Ancient name: Meninx ('mɛnɪŋks)

Djibouti *or* **Jibouti** (dʒɪ'buːtɪ) *n* **1** a republic in E Africa, on the Gulf of Aden: a French overseas territory (1946–77); became independent in 1977; mainly desert. Official languages: Arabic and French. Religion: Muslim majority. Currency: Djibouti franc. Capital: Djibouti. Pop: 712 000 (2004 est). Area: 23 200 sq km (8950 sq miles). Former name (until 1977): (Territory of the) Afars and the Issas **2** the capital of Djibouti, a port on the Gulf of Aden: an outlet for Ethiopian goods. Pop: 523 000 (2005 est)

djinni or **djinny** (dʒɪˈniː, ˈdʒɪnɪ) *n, pl* **djinn** (dʒɪn) variant spellings of **jinni**

dk *the internet domain name for* Denmark

DK *international car registration for* Denmark

dl *symbol for* decilitre(s)

DLitt or **DLit** *abbreviation for* 1 Doctor of Letters 2 Doctor of Literature [Latin *Doctor Litterarum*]

DLL *abbreviation for* dynamic link library

dlr *abbreviation for* dealer

DLR (in Britain) *abbreviation for* Docklands Light Railway (in E London)

dm[1] *symbol for* decimetre

dm[2] *the internet domain name for* Dominica

DM *abbreviation for* 1 (in Canada) deputy minister 2 (the former) **Deutschmark**

DMA *computing abbreviation for* **direct memory access**

DMAC *abbreviation for* duobinary multiplexed analogue component: a transmission coding system using duobinary techniques for the digital sound and data components of colour television using satellite broadcasting

D-mark or **D-Mark** *n* short for (the former) **Deutschmark**

DMD *abbreviation for* Duchenne muscular dystrophy

DMF *abbreviation for* dimethylformamide

DMK (in India) *abbreviation for* Dravida Munnetra Kazgham: a political party in the state of Tamil Nadu

DMs *abbreviation for* **Doc Martens**

DMS (in Britain) *abbreviation for* Diploma in Management Studies

DMSO *abbreviation for* dimethylsulphoxide

DMT *abbreviation for* dimethyltryptamine, a hallucinogenic drug

DMus *abbreviation for* Doctor of Music

DMV (in the US and Canada) *abbreviation for* Department of Motor Vehicles

DMZ *abbreviation for* demilitarized zone

DNA *n* 1 deoxyribonucleic acid; a nucleic acid that is the main constituent of the chromosomes of all organisms (except some viruses). The DNA molecule consists of two polynucleotide chains in the form of a double helix, containing phosphate and the sugar deoxyribose and linked by hydrogen bonds between the complementary bases adenine and thymine or cytosine and guanine. DNA is self-replicating, plays a central role in protein synthesis, and is responsible for the transmission of hereditary characteristics from parents to offspring. See also **genetic code** 2 did not attend

DNAase (ˌdiːɛnˈeɪeɪz) or **DNase** (ˌdiːɛnˈeɪz) *n* deoxyribonuclease; any of a number of enzymes that hydrolyse DNA. See **endonuclease, exonuclease**

DNA fingerprint or **profile** *n* another name for **genetic fingerprint**

DNA sequencing *n* the procedure of determining the order of base pairs in a section of DNA

Dneprodzerzhinsk (Russian dnɪprədzɪrˈʒinsk) *n* an industrial city in E Ukraine on the Dnieper River. Pop: 250 000 (2005 est)

Dnepropetrovsk (Russian dnɪprəpɪˈtrɔfsk) *n* a city in E central Ukraine on the Dnieper River: a major centre of the metallurgical industry. Pop: 1 036 000 (2005 est). Former name (1787–1796, 1802–1926): **Yekaterinoslav**

DNF *motor Sport, athletics abbreviation for* did not finish

Dnieper (ˈdniːpə) *n* a river in NE Europe, rising in Russia, in the Valdai Hills NE of Smolensk and flowing south to the Black Sea: the third longest river in Europe; a major navigable waterway. Length: 2200 km (1370 miles). Russian name: Dnepr (ˈdnjɛpr)

Dniester (ˈdniːstə) *n* a river in E Europe, rising in Ukraine, in the Carpathian Mountains and flowing generally southeast to the Black Sea.

Length: 1411 km (877 miles). Russian name: Dnestr (ˈdnjɛstə)

D-notice *n Brit* an official notice sent to newspapers, prohibiting the publication of certain security information [c20 from their administrative classification letter]

DNR *abbreviation for* do not resuscitate

DNS *abbreviation for* 1 (formerly in Britain) Department for National Savings 2 *computing* domain name system

do[1] (duː; *unstressed* dʊ, də) *vb* does, doing, did, done 1 to perform or complete (a deed or action): *to do a portrait; the work is done* 2 (often *intr*; foll by *for*) to serve the needs of; be suitable for (a person, situation, etc); suffice: *there isn't much food, but it'll do for the two of us* 3 (*tr*) to arrange or fix: *you should do the garden now* 4 (*tr*) to prepare or provide; serve: *this restaurant doesn't do lunch on Sundays* 5 (*tr*) to make tidy, elegant, ready, etc, as by arranging or adorning: *to do one's hair* 6 (*tr*) to improve (esp in the phrase **do something to** or **for**) 7 (*tr*) to find an answer to (a problem or puzzle) 8 (*tr*) to translate or adapt the form or language of: *the book was done into a play* 9 (*intr*) to conduct oneself: *do as you please* 10 (*intr*) to fare or manage: *how are you doing these days?* 11 (*tr*) to cause or produce: *complaints do nothing to help* 12 (*tr*) to give or render: *your portrait doesn't do you justice; do me a favour* 13 (*tr*) to work at, esp as a course of study or a profession: *he is doing chemistry; what do you do for a living?* 14 (*tr*) to perform (a play, etc); act: *they are doing "Hamlet" next week* 15 (*tr*) to travel at a specified speed, esp as a maximum: *this car will do 120 mph* 16 (*tr*) to travel or traverse (a distance): *we did 15 miles on our walk* 17 (takes an infinitive without *to*) used as an auxiliary before the subject of an interrogative sentence as a way of forming a question: *do you agree?; when did John go out?* 18 (takes an infinitive without *to*) used as an auxiliary to intensify positive statements and commands: *I do like your new house; do hurry!* 19 (takes an infinitive without *to*) used as an auxiliary before a negative adverb to form negative statements or commands: *he does not like cheese; do not leave me here alone!* 20 (takes an infinitive without *to*) used as an auxiliary in inverted constructions: *little did he realize that; only rarely does he come in before ten o'clock* 21 used as an auxiliary to replace an earlier verb or verb phrase to avoid repetition: *he likes you as much as I do* 22 (*tr*) *informal* to visit or explore as a sightseer or tourist: *to do Westminster Abbey* 23 (*tr*) to wear out; exhaust 24 (*intr*) to happen (esp in the phrase **nothing doing**) 25 (*tr*) *slang* to serve (a period of time) as a prison sentence: *he's doing five years for burglary; he's doing time* 26 (*tr*) *informal* to cheat or swindle 27 (*tr*) *slang* to rob: *they did three shops last night* 28 (*tr*) *slang* a to arrest b to convict of a crime 29 (*tr*) *Austral informal* to lose or spend (money) completely 30 (*tr*) *slang, chiefly Brit* to treat violently; assault 31 (*tr*) *slang* to take or use (a drug) 32 (*tr*) *taboo slang* (of a male) to have sexual intercourse with 33 (*tr*) to partake in (a meal): *let's do lunch* 34 **do** (a) *informal* to act like; imitate: *he's a good mimic — he can do all his friends well* 35 **do or die** to make a final or supreme effort 36 **how do you do?** a conventional formula when being introduced 37 **make do** to manage with whatever is available ▷ *pl* **dos** or **do's** 38 *slang* an act or instance of cheating or swindling 39 *informal, chiefly Brit and NZ* a formal or festive gathering; party 40 **do's and don'ts** *informal* those things that should or should not be done; rules ▷ See also **do away with, do by, do down, do for, do in, done, do out, do over, do up, do with, do without** [Old English *dōn*; related to Old Frisian *duān*, Old High German *tuon*, Latin *abdere* to put away, Greek *tithenai* to place; see DEED, DOOM]

do[2] (dəʊ) *n, pl* **dos** a variant spelling of **doh**

do[3] *the internet domain name for* Dominican Republic

DO *abbreviation for* 1 Doctor of Optometry 2 Doctor of Osteopathy

do. *abbreviation for* ditto

D/O or **d.o.** *commerce abbreviation for* delivery order

DOA *abbreviation for* dead on arrival

doab (ˈdəʊɑːb) *n* the alluvial land between two converging rivers, esp the area between the Ganges and Jumna in N India [c20 from Persian *dōāb*, from *dō* two + *āb* water]

doable (ˈduːəbʰl) *adj* capable of being done; practical

doat (dəʊt) *vb* (*intr*) a variant (now rare) spelling of **dote**

do away with *vb* (*intr, adverb* + *preposition*) 1 to kill or destroy 2 to discard or abolish

dobber-in (ˌdɒbərˈɪn) *n Austral slang* an informant or traitor. Sometimes shortened to: **dobber**

dobbin (ˈdɒbɪn) *n* 1 a name for a horse, esp a workhorse, often used in children's tales, etc 2 NZ a trolley for moving loose wool in a woolshed or shearing shed [c16 from *Robin*, pet form of *Robert*]

dobby (ˈdɒbɪ) *n, pl* -bies an attachment to a loom, used in weaving small figures [c17 perhaps from *Dobby*, pet form of *Robert*]

Dobell's solution (ˈdəʊbəlz) *n* a solution of sodium borate, sodium bicarbonate, phenol, and glycerol, used as an astringent or antiseptic wash for the throat and nose [c19 named after Horace B. Dobell (1828–1917), British physician]

Doberman pinscher (ˈdəʊbəmən ˈpɪnʃə) or **Doberman** *n* a fairly large slender but muscular breed of dog, originally from Germany, with a glossy black-and-tan coat, a short tail, and erect ears. Also spelt: **Dobermann** [c19 probably named after L. *Dobermann*, 19th-century German dog breeder who bred it + *Pinscher*, a type of terrier, perhaps after *Pinzgau*, district in Austria]

dob in *vb* dobs, dobbing, dobbed (*adverb*) *Austral and NZ informal* 1 (*tr*) to inform against or report, esp to the police 2 to contribute to a fund for a specific purpose

dobla (ˈdəʊblə) *n* a medieval Spanish gold coin, probably worth 20 maravedis [Spanish, from Latin *dupla*, feminine of *duplus* twofold, DOUBLE]

doblón (dəˈbləʊn; Spanish doˈβlon) *n* a variant spelling of **doubloon** [Spanish; see DOUBLOON]

dobra (ˈdəʊbrə) *n* the standard monetary unit of São Tomé e Príncipe, divided into 100 cêntimos

Dobro (ˈdəʊbrəʊ) *n, pl* -bros *trademark* an acoustic guitar having a metal resonator built into the body

Dobruja (Bulgarian ˈdɔbrudʒa) *n* a region of E Europe, between the River Danube and the Black Sea: the north passed to Romania and the south to Bulgaria after the Berlin Congress (1878). Romanian name: **Dobrogea** (doˈbrodʒea)

dobsonfly (ˈdɒbsʰnˌflaɪ) *n, pl* -flies *US and Canadian* a large North American neuropterous insect, *Corydalis cornutus*: the male has elongated horn-like mouthparts and the larva (a **hellgrammite** or **dobson**) is used as bait by anglers: suborder *Megaloptera* [c20 origin uncertain, perhaps after the surname *Dobson*]

do by *vb* (*intr, preposition*) to treat in the manner specified: *employers do well by hard working employees*

doc (dɒk) *n informal* short for **doctor**, esp a medical doctor: often used as a term of address

DOC *abbreviation for* 1 Denominazione di Origine Controllata: used of wines [Italian, literally: name of origin controlled] 2 (in New Zealand) Department of Conservation

doc. *abbreviation for* document

docent (ˈdəʊsʰnt) *n* 1 a voluntary worker who acts as a guide in a museum, art gallery, etc 2 (dəʊˈsɛnt; German doˈtsɛnt) (in the US) a lecturer in some colleges or universities [c19 from German *Dozent*, from Latin *docēns* from *docēre* to teach] > ˈdocentˌship *n*

Docetism (ˈdəʊsɪˌtɪzəm) *n* (in the early Christian Church) a heresy that the humanity of Christ, his sufferings, and his death were apparent rather than real [c19 from Medieval Latin *Docētae*, from Greek *Dokētai*, from *dokein* to seem]

DOCG *abbreviation for* Denominazione di Origine

d

483

Controllata Garantita: used of wines [Italian, literally: name of origin guaranteed controlled]

doch-an-doris (ˌdɒxən'dɒrɪs) *n* a variant spelling of **deoch-an-doruis**

docile ('dəʊsaɪl) *adj* **1** easy to manage, control, or discipline; submissive **2** *rare* ready to learn; easy to teach [c15 from Latin *docilis* easily taught, from *docēre* to teach] > 'docilely *adv* > docility (dəʊ'sɪlɪtɪ) *n*

dock¹ (dɒk) *n* **1** a wharf or pier **2** a space between two wharves or piers for the mooring of ships **3** an area of water that can accommodate a ship and can be closed off to allow regulation of the water level **4** short for **dry dock 5** short for **scene dock 6** *chiefly US and Canadian* a platform from which lorries, goods trains, etc, are loaded and unloaded ▷ *vb* **7** to moor (a vessel) at a dock or (of a vessel) to be moored at a dock **8** to put (a vessel) into a dry dock for repairs or (of a vessel) to come into a dry dock **9** (of two spacecraft) to link together in space or link together (two spacecraft) in space [c14 from Middle Dutch *docke*; perhaps related to Latin *ducere* to lead]

dock² (dɒk) *n* **1** the bony part of the tail of an animal, esp a dog or sheep **2** the part of an animal's tail left after the major part of it has been cut off ▷ *vb* (*tr*) **3** to remove (the tail or part of the tail) of (an animal) by cutting through the bone: *to dock a tail; to dock a horse* **4** to deduct (an amount) from (a person's wages, pension, etc): *they docked a third of his wages* [c14 *dok*, of uncertain origin]

dock³ (dɒk) *n* an enclosed space in a court of law where the accused sits or stands during his trial [c16 from Flemish *dok* sty]

dock⁴ (dɒk) *n* **1** any of various temperate weedy plants of the polygonaceous genus *Rumex*, having greenish or reddish flowers and typically broad leaves **2** any of several similar or related plants [Old English *docce*; related to Middle Dutch, Old Danish *docke*, Gaelic *dogha*]

dockage¹ ('dɒkɪdʒ) *n* **1** a charge levied upon a vessel for using a dock **2** facilities for docking vessels **3** the practice of docking vessels

dockage² ('dɒkɪdʒ) *n* **1** a deduction, as from a price or wages **2** *agriculture* the seeds of weeds and other waste material in commercial seeds, removable by normal cleaning methods

docken ('dɒkᵊn) *n* *chiefly Scot* **1** another name for **dock⁴ 2** something of no value or importance: *not worth a docken* [c14 *doken*, from Old English *doccan*, pl of *docce* DOCK⁴]

docker¹ ('dɒkə) *n* *Brit* a man employed in the loading or unloading of ships. US and Canadian equivalent: **longshoreman** See also **stevedore**

docker² ('dɒkə) *n* a person or thing that docks something, such as the tail of a horse

docket ('dɒkɪt) *n* **1** *chiefly Brit* a piece of paper accompanying or referring to a package or other delivery, stating contents, delivery instructions, etc, sometimes serving as a receipt **2** *law* **a** an official summary of the proceedings in a court of justice **b** a register containing such a summary **3** *Brit* a customs certificate declaring that duty has been paid **b** certificate giving particulars of a shipment and allowing its holder to obtain a delivery order **4** a summary of contents, as in a document **5** *US* a list of things to be done **6** *US law* **a** a list of cases awaiting trial **b** the names of the parties to pending litigation ▷ *vb* (*tr*) **7** to fix a docket to (a package, etc) **8** *law* **a** to make a summary of (a document, judgment, etc) **b** to abstract and enter in a book or register **9** to endorse (a document, etc) with a summary [c15 of unknown origin]

docking station *n* a device used to connect one appliance to another, esp a portable computer and a desktop computer, to make use of its external power supply, monitor, and keyboard, esp to enable the transfer of data between the machines

dockland ('dɒkˌlænd) *n* the area around the docks

dockyard ('dɒkˌjɑːd) *n* a naval establishment with docks, workshops, etc, for the building, fitting out, and repair of vessels

Doc Martens (dɒk 'mɑːtənz) *pl n trademark* a brand of lace-up boots with thick lightweight resistant soles. In full: Doctor Martens Abbreviation: DMs

doco ('dɒkəʊ) *n, pl* docos *Austral informal* short for **documentary**

doctor ('dɒktə) *n* **1** a person licensed to practise medicine **2** a person who has been awarded a higher academic degree in any field of knowledge **3** *chiefly US and Canadian* a person licensed to practise dentistry or veterinary medicine **4** (*often capital*) Also called: Doctor of the Church a title given to any of several of the leading Fathers or theologians in the history of the Christian Church down to the late Middle Ages whose teachings have greatly influenced orthodox Christian thought **5** *angling* any of various gaudy artificial flies **6** *informal* a person who mends or repairs things **7** *slang* a cook on a ship or at a camp **8** *archaic* a man, esp a teacher, of learning **9** a device used for local repair of electroplated surfaces, consisting of an anode of the plating material embedded in an absorbent material containing the solution **10** (in a paper-making machine) a blade that is set to scrape the roller in order to regulate the thickness of pulp or ink on it **11** go for the doctor *Austral slang* to make a great effort or move very fast, esp in a horse race **12** what the doctor ordered something needed or desired ▷ *vb* **13** (*tr*) **a** to give medical treatment to **b** to prescribe for (a disease or disorder) **14** (*intr*) *informal* to practise medicine: *he doctored in Easter Island for six years* **15** (*tr*) to repair or mend, esp in a makeshift manner **16** (*tr*) to make different in order to deceive, tamper with, falsify, or adulterate **17** (*tr*) to adapt for a desired end, effect, etc **18** (*tr*) to castrate (a cat, dog, etc) [c14 from Latin: teacher, from *docēre* to teach] > 'doctoral *or* doctorial (dɒk'tɔːrɪəl) *adj*

doctorate ('dɒktərɪt, -trɪt) *n* the highest academic degree in any field of knowledge. Also called: doctor's degree

Doctor of Philosophy *n* a doctorate awarded for original research in any subject except law, medicine, or theology. Abbreviations: PhD, DPhil

Doctor's Commons *n informal* the London building of the College of Advocates and Doctors of Law between 1572 and 1867, in which the ecclesiastical and Admiralty courts were housed

doctrinaire (ˌdɒktrɪ'nɛə) *adj* **1** stubbornly insistent on the observation of the niceties of a theory, esp without regard to practicality, suitability, etc **2** theoretical; impractical ▷ *n* **3** a person who stubbornly attempts to apply a theory without regard to practical difficulties > ˌdoctri'nairism *or* ˌdoctri'narism *n* > ˌdoctri'narian *n*

doctrine ('dɒktrɪn) *n* **1** a creed or body of teachings of a religious, political, or philosophical group presented for acceptance or belief; dogma **2** a principle or body of principles that is taught or advocated [c14 from Old French, from Latin *doctrīna* teaching, from *doctor* see DOCTOR] > doctrinal (dɒk'traɪnᵊl) *adj* > doctrinality (ˌdɒktrɪ'nælɪtɪ) *n* > doc'trinally *adv* > 'doctrinism *n* > 'doctrinist *n*

doctrine of descent *n* the theory that animals and plants arose by descent from previously existing organisms; theory of evolution

docudrama ('dɒkjʊˌdrɑːmə) *n* a film or television programme based on true events, presented in a dramatized form

document *n* ('dɒkjʊmənt) **1** a piece of paper, booklet, etc, providing information, esp of an official or legal nature **2** a piece of text or text and graphics stored in a computer as a file for manipulation by document processing software **3** *archaic* evidence; proof ▷ *vb* ('dɒkjʊˌment) (*tr*) **4** to record or report in detail, as in the press, on television, etc: *the trial was well documented by the media* **5** to support (statements in a book) with citations, references, etc **6** to support (a claim, etc) with evidence or proof **7** to furnish (a vessel) with official documents specifying its ownership, registration, weight, dimensions, and function [c15 from Latin *documentum* a lesson, from *docēre* to teach]

documentarian (ˌdɒkjʊmən'tɛərɪən) *n* *chiefly US* a person who makes documentary films

documentary (ˌdɒkjʊ'mentərɪ, -trɪ) *adj* **1** Also: documental consisting of, derived from, or relating to documents **2** presenting factual material with little or no fictional additions: *the book gives a documentary account of the war* ▷ *n, pl* -ries **3** a factual film or television programme about an event, person, etc, presenting the facts with little or no fiction > ˌdocu'mentarily *adv*

documentation (ˌdɒkjʊmən'teɪʃən) *n* **1** the act of supplying with or using documents or references **2** the documents or references supplied **3** the furnishing and use of documentary evidence, as in a court of law **4** *computing* the written comments, graphical illustrations, flowcharts, manuals, etc, supplied with a program or software system

document reader *n computing* a device that reads and inputs into a computer marks and characters on a special form, as by optical or magnetic character recognition

docu-soap ('dɒkjʊˌsəʊp) *n* a television documentary series in which the lives of the people filmed are presented as entertainment or drama [c20 from DOCU(MENTARY) + SOAP (OPERA)]

DOD (in the US) *abbreviation for* Department of Defense

dodder¹ ('dɒdə) *vb* (*intr*) **1** to move unsteadily; totter **2** to shake or tremble, as from age [c17 variant of earlier *dadder*; related to Norwegian *dudra* to tremble] > 'dodderer *n* > 'doddery *adj*

dodder² ('dɒdə) *n* any rootless parasitic plant of the convolvulaceous genus *Cuscuta*, lacking chlorophyll and having slender twining stems with suckers for drawing nourishment from the host plant, scalelike leaves, and whitish flowers [c13 of Germanic origin; related to Middle Dutch, Middle Low German *dodder*, Middle High German *toter*]

doddering ('dɒdərɪŋ) *adj* shaky, feeble, or infirm, esp from old age

doddle ('dɒdᵊl) *n* *Brit informal* something easily accomplished

dodeca- *n combining form* indicating twelve: *dodecagon; dodecahedron; dodecaphonic* [from Greek *dōdeka* twelve]

dodecagon (dəʊ'dekəˌgɒn) *n* a polygon having twelve sides > dodecagonal (ˌdəʊdɛ'kægᵊnᵊl) *adj*

dodecahedron (ˌdəʊdɛkə'hiːdrən) *n* a solid figure having twelve plane faces. A **regular dodecahedron** has regular pentagons as faces. See also **polyhedron**. > ˌdodeca'hedral *adj*

Dodecanese (ˌdəʊdɪkə'niːz) *pl n* a group of islands in the SE Aegean Sea, forming a department of Greece: part of the Southern Sporades. Capital: Rhodes. Pop: 190 071 (2001). Area: 2663 sq km (1028 sq miles). Modern Greek name: Dhodhekánisos

dodecanoic acid (ˌdəʊdɛkə'nəʊɪk) *n* a crystalline fatty acid found as glycerides in many vegetable oils: used in making soaps, insecticides, and synthetic resins. Formula: $CH_3(CH_2)_{10}COOH$. Also called: lauric acid [c20 from *dodecane* (see DODECA-, -ANE)]

dodecaphonic (ˌdəʊdɛkə'fɒnɪk) *adj* of or relating to the twelve-tone system of serial music > ˌdodeca'phonism *n* > ˌdodeca'phony *n*

dodecasyllable (ˌdəʊdɛkə'sɪləbᵊl) *n prosody* a line of twelve syllables

dodge (dɒdʒ) *vb* **1** to avoid or attempt to avoid (a blow, discovery, etc), as by moving suddenly **2** to evade (questions, etc) by cleverness or trickery **3** (*intr*) *bell-ringing* to make a bell change places with its neighbour when sounding in successive changes **4** (*tr*) *photog* to lighten or darken (selected areas on a print) by manipulating the light from an enlarger ▷ *n* **5** a plan or expedient contrived to deceive **6** a sudden evasive or hiding movement **7** a clever contrivance **8** *bell-ringing* the act of dodging [C16 of unknown origin]

dodge ball *n* a game in which the players form a circle and try to hit opponents in the circle with a large ball

Dodge City *n* a city in SW Kansas, on the Arkansas River: famous as a frontier town on the Santa Fe Trail. Pop: 25 568 (2003 est)

Dodgem ('dɒdʒəm) *n trademark* another name for **bumper car**

dodger ('dɒdʒə) *n* **1** a person who evades or shirks **2** a shifty dishonest person **3** a canvas shelter, mounted on a ship's bridge or over the companionway of a sailing yacht to protect the helmsman from bad weather **4** *archaic, US and Austral* a handbill **5** *Austral informal* food, esp bread

dodgy ('dɒdʒɪ) *adj* dodgier, dodgiest *Brit, Austral, and NZ informal* **1** risky, difficult, or dangerous **2** uncertain or unreliable; tricky

dodo ('dəʊdəʊ) *n, pl* dodos *or* dodoes **1** any flightless bird, esp *Raphus cucullatus*, of the recently extinct family *Raphidae* of Mauritius and adjacent islands: order *Columbiformes* (pigeons, etc). They had a hooked bill, short stout legs, and greyish plumage. See also **ratite 2** *informal* an intensely conservative or reactionary person who is unaware of changing fashions, ideas, etc **3** (as) **dead as a dodo** (of a person or thing) irretrievably defunct or out of date [C17 from Portuguese *doudo*, from *doudo* stupid] > 'dodoism *n*

Dodoma ('dəʊdəmə) *n* a city in central Tanzania, the legislative capital of the country. Pop: 169 000 (2005 est)

Dodona (dəʊ'dəʊnə) *n* an ancient Greek town in Epirus: seat of an ancient sanctuary and oracle of Zeus and later the religious centre of Pyrrhus' kingdom > Dodonaean *or* Dodonean (,dəʊdəʊ'niːən) *adj*

do down *vb* (*tr, adverb*) **1** to belittle or humiliate **2** to deceive or cheat

doe (dəʊ) *n, pl* does *or* doe the female of the deer, hare, rabbit, and certain other animals [Old English *dā*; related to Old English *dēon* to suck, Sanskrit *dhēnā* cow]

Doe (dəʊ) *n* **1** *law* (formerly) the plaintiff in a fictitious action, Doe versus Roe, to test a point of law. See also **Roe 2** John *or* Jane *US* an unknown or unidentified male or female person

DOE *or* **DoE** *abbreviation for* **1** (in Canada and, formerly, in Britain) Department of the Environment **2** (in the US) Department of Energy

doek (dʊk) *n South African informal* a square of cloth worn mainly by African women to cover the head, esp to indicate married status [C18 from Afrikaans: cloth]

doer ('duːə) *n* **1** a person or thing that does something or acts in a specified manner: *a doer of good* **2** an active or energetic person **3** a thriving animal, esp a horse

doer and gone ('dʊə) *adj South African* far away: *Afrikaans*

does¹ (dʌz) *vb* (used with a singular noun or the pronouns he, she, or it) a form of the present tense (indicative mood) of **do¹**

does² (dʊəs) *n South African taboo slang* a foolish or despicable person [Afrikaans]

doeskin ('dəʊˌskɪn) *n* **1** the skin of a deer, lamb, or sheep **2** a very supple leather made from this skin and used esp for gloves **3** a heavy smooth satin-weave or twill-weave cloth **4** (*modifier*) made of doeskin

dof (dɒf) *adj South African informal* stupid: *Afrikaans*

doff (dɒf) *vb* (*tr*) **1** to take off or lift (one's hat) in salutation **2** to remove (clothing) [Old English *dōn of*; see **DO¹**, **OFF**; compare **DON¹**] > 'doffer *n*

do for *vb* (*preposition*) *informal* **1** (*tr*) to convict of a crime or offence: *they did him for manslaughter* **2** (*intr*) to cause the ruin, death, or defeat of: *the last punch did for him* **3** (*intr*) to do housework for **4** do well for oneself to thrive or succeed

dog (dɒg) *n* **1 a** a domesticated canine mammal, *Canis familiaris*, occurring in many breeds that show a great variety in size and form **b** (*as modifier*): *dog biscuit* **2 a** any other carnivore of the family *Canidae*, such as the dingo and coyote **b** (*as modifier*): *the dog family*. Related adj: **canine 3 a** the male of animals of the dog family **b** (*as modifier*): *a dog fox* **4** (*modifier*) **a** spurious, inferior, or useless: *dog Latin* **b** (*in combination*): *dogberry* **5** a mechanical device for gripping or holding, esp one of the axial slots by which gear wheels or shafts are engaged to transmit torque **6** *informal* a fellow; chap: *you lucky dog* **7** *informal* a man or boy regarded as unpleasant, contemptible, or wretched **8** *slang* an unattractive or boring girl or woman **9** *US and Canadian informal* something unsatisfactory or inferior **10** short for **firedog 11** any of various atmospheric phenomena. See **fogdog, seadog, sundog 12** a dog's chance no chance at all **13** a dog's dinner or breakfast *informal* something that is messy or bungled **14** a dog's life a wretched existence **15** dog eat dog ruthless competition or self-interest **16** like a dog's dinner *informal* dressed smartly or ostentatiously **17** put on the dog *US and Canadian informal* to behave or dress in an ostentatious or showy manner ▷ *vb* dogs, dogging, dogged (*tr*) **18** to pursue or follow after like a dog **19** to trouble; plague: *to be dogged by ill health* **20** to chase with a dog or dogs **21** to grip, hold, or secure by a mechanical device ▷ *adv* **22** (usually in combination) thoroughly; utterly: *dog-tired* ▷ See also **dogs** [Old English *docga*, of obscure origin] > 'dogˌlike *adj*

dog and bone *n Cockney rhyming slang* a telephone

dogbane ('dɒgˌbeɪn) *n* any of several North American apocynaceous plants of the genus *Apocynum*, esp *A. androsaemifolium*, having bell-shaped white or pink flowers: thought to be poisonous to dogs

dogberry¹ ('dɒgˌberɪ, -bərɪ, -brɪ) *n, pl* -ries **1** any of certain plants that have berry-like fruits, such as the European dogwood or the bearberry **2** the fruit of any of these plants

dogberry² ('dɒgˌberɪ, -bərɪ, -brɪ) *n, pl* -ries (*sometimes capital*) a foolish, meddling, and usually old official [after Dogberry, character in Shakespeare's *Much Ado about Nothing* (1598)] > 'dogberryˌism *n*

dog biscuit *n* a hard biscuit for dogs

dog box *n* **1** *Austral informal* a compartment in a railway carriage with no corridor **2** *NZ informal* disgrace; disfavour (in the phrase **in the dog box**)

dogcart ('dɒgˌkɑːt) *n* a light horse-drawn two-wheeled vehicle: originally, one containing a box or section for transporting gun dogs

dog-catcher *n Now chiefly US and Canadian* a local official whose job is to catch and impound stray dogs, cats, etc

dog collar *n* **1** a collar for a dog **2** an informal name for a **clerical collar 3** *informal* a tight-fitting necklace

dog days *pl n* **1** the hot period of the summer reckoned in ancient times from the heliacal rising of Sirius (the Dog Star) **2** a period marked by inactivity [C16 translation of Late Latin *diēs caniculārēs*, translation of Greek *hēmerai kunades*]

doge (dəʊdʒ) *n* (formerly) the chief magistrate in the republics of Venice (until 1797) and Genoa (until 1805) [C16 via French from Italian (Venetian dialect), from Latin *dux* leader] > 'dogeship *n*

dog-ear *vb* **1** (*tr*) to fold down the corner of (a page) **2** *computing* to bookmark (a website) ▷ *n* also **dog's-ear 3** a folded-down corner of a page **4** *computing* a bookmark

dog-eared *adj* **1** having dog-ears **2** shabby or worn

dog-end *n* an informal name for **cigarette end**

dog fennel *n* **1** another name for **mayweed 2** a weedy plant, *Eupatorium capillifolium*, of the southeastern US, having divided leaves and greenish rayless flower heads: family *Asteraceae* (composites)

dogfight ('dɒgˌfaɪt) *n* **1** close quarters combat between fighter aircraft **2** any rough violent fight

dogfish ('dɒgˌfɪʃ) *n, pl* -fish *or* -fishes **1** any of several small spotted European sharks, esp *Scyliorhinus caniculus* (**lesser spotted dogfish**): family *Scyliorhinidae* **2** any small shark of the family *Squalidae*, esp *Squalus acanthias* (**spiny dogfish**), typically having a spine on each dorsal fin **3** any small smooth-skinned shark of the family *Triakidae*, esp *Mustelus canis* (**smooth dogfish** or **smooth hound**) **4** a less common name for the **bowfin**

dog fouling *n* the offence of being in charge of a dog and failing to remove the faeces after it defecates in a public place

dogged ('dɒgɪd) *adj* obstinately determined; wilful or tenacious > 'doggedly *adv* > 'doggedness *n*

dogger¹ ('dɒgə) *n* a Dutch fishing vessel with two masts [C14 probably from Middle Dutch *dogge* trawler]

dogger² ('dɒgə) *n* a large concretion of consolidated material occurring in certain sedimentary rocks [C17 of uncertain origin]

dogger³ ('dɒgə) *n Austral* a hunter of dingoes [C20 from DOG (see sense 2a) + -ER¹]

Dogger ('dɒgə) *n geology* a formation of mid-Jurassic rocks in N England

Dogger Bank ('dɒgə) *n* an extensive submerged sandbank in the North Sea between N England and Denmark: fishing ground

doggerel ('dɒgərəl) *or* **dogrel** ('dɒgrəl) *n* **1 a** comic verse, usually irregular in measure **b** (*as modifier*): *a doggerel rhythm* **2** nonsense; drivel [C14 *dogerel* worthless, perhaps from *dogge* DOG]

doggery ('dɒgərɪ) *n, pl* -geries **1** surly behaviour **2** dogs collectively **3** a mob

Doggett's Coat and Badge race ('dɒgɪts) *n* an annual rowing race held on the River Thames to commemorate the accession of George I: the winner is presented with a coat bearing an embroidered badge [C18 after Thomas *Doggett* (1670–1721), British actor who initiated it]

dogging ('dɒgɪŋ) *n Brit slang* the practice of carrying out or watching sexual activities in semi-secluded locations such as parks or car parks, often arranged by e-mail or text messages

doggish ('dɒgɪʃ) *adj* **1** of or like a dog **2** surly; snappish > 'doggishly *adv* > 'doggishness *n*

doggo ('dɒgəʊ) *adv Brit informal* in hiding and keeping quiet (esp in the phrase **lie doggo**) [C19 probably from DOG]

doggone ('dɒgɒn) *US and Canadian informal* ▷ *interj* **1** an exclamation of annoyance, disappointment, etc ▷ *adj* (*prenominal*) ▷ *adv* **2** Also: **doggoned** another word for **damn** (senses 3, 4) [C19 euphemism for *God damn*]

doggy *or* **doggie** ('dɒgɪ) *n, pl* -gies **1** a children's word for a dog ▷ *adj* **2** of, like, or relating to a dog **3** fond of dogs

doggy bag *n* a bag into which leftovers from a meal may be put and taken away, supposedly for the diner's dog

doggy paddle *or* **doggie paddle** *n* **1** a swimming stroke in which the swimmer lies on his front, paddles his hands in imitation of a swimming dog, and beats his legs up and down ▷ *vb* doggy-paddle *or* doggie-paddle **2** (*intr*) to swim using the doggy paddle. Also called: **dog paddle**

dog handler *n* a member of the police force, security organization, etc, who works in collaboration with a specially trained dog

doghouse ('dɒgˌhaʊs) *n* **1** *US and Canadian* a hutlike shelter for a dog. Also called (in Britain and certain other countries): **kennel 2** *informal* disfavour (in the phrase **in the doghouse**)

dogie, dogy *or* **dogey** ('dəʊgɪ) *n, pl* -gies *or* -geys *Western US and Canadian* a motherless calf [C19 from

d

dough-guts, because they were fed on flour and water paste]

dog in the manger *n* **a** a person who prevents others from using something he has no use for **b** (*as modifier*): *a dog-in-the-manger attitude*

dog Latin *n* spurious or incorrect Latin

dogleg ('dɒg,lɛg) *n* **1 a** a sharp bend or angle **b** something with a sharp bend ▷ *vb* -**legs, -legging, -legged 2** (*intr*) to go off at an angle ▷ *adj* **3** of or with the shape of a dogleg > **doglegged** (,dɒg'lɛgɪd, 'dɒg,lɛgd) *adj*

dogleg fence *n Austral* a fence made of sloping poles supported by forked uprights

dogma ('dɒgmə) *n, pl* -**mas** *or* -**mata** (-mətə) **1** a religious doctrine or system of doctrines proclaimed by ecclesiastical authority as true **2** a belief, principle, or doctrine or a code of beliefs, principles, or doctrines: *Marxist dogma* [c17 via Latin from Greek: opinion, belief, from *dokein* to seem good]

dogman ('dɒgmən) *n, pl* -**men** *Austral* a person who directs the operation of a crane whilst riding on an object being lifted by it

dogmatic (dɒg'mætɪk) *or* **dogmatical** *adj* **1 a** (of a statement, opinion, etc) forcibly asserted as if authoritative and unchallengeable **b** (of a person) prone to making such statements **2** of, relating to, or constituting dogma: *dogmatic writings* **3** based on assumption rather than empirical observation > **dog'matically** *adv*

dogmatics (dɒg'mætɪks) *n* (*functioning as singular*) the study of religious dogmas and doctrines. Also called: **dogmatic** (*or* **doctrinal**) **theology**

dogmatist ('dɒgmətɪst) *n* **1** a dogmatic person **2** a person who formulates dogmas

dogmatize *or* **dogmatise** ('dɒgmə,taɪz) *vb* to say or state (something) in a dogmatic manner > '**dogmatism** *n* > ,**dogmati'zation** *or* ,**dogmati'sation** *n* > '**dogma,tizer** *or* '**dogma,tiser** *n*

Dogme ('dɒgmɪ) *n* a group of Danish film-makers, formed by Lars von Trier and Thomas Vinterberg, who have a set of strict rules, such as not using artificial lighting, always filming on location, and always using a hand-held camera [Danish: literally: dogma]

dognap ('dɒgnæp) *vb* -**naps, -napping, -napped** *or* US -**naps, -naping, -naped** (*tr*) to carry off and hold (a dog), usually for ransom [c20 from DOG + KIDNAP] > '**dognapper** *n* > '**dognapping** *or* US '**dognaping** *n*

do-gooder *n informal, usually disparaging* a well-intentioned person, esp a naive or impractical one > ,**do-'goodery** *n* > ,**do-'gooding** *n, adj*

dog paddle *n* another name for **doggy paddle**

Dogrib ('dɒg,rɪb) *n* **1** a member of a Dene Native Canadian people of northern Canada **2** the Athapascan language of this people [from Dogrib *Thlingchadinne*, dog's flank, referring to the people's belief that they are descended from a dog]

dog-roll *n NZ* a large sausage-shaped roll of processed meat used for dog food

dog rose *n* a prickly wild rose, *Rosa canina*, that is native to Europe and has pink or white delicate scentless flowers [translation of the Latin name, from Greek; from the belief that its root was effective against the bite of a mad dog]

dogs (dɒgz) *pl n* **1** the *Brit informal* greyhound racing **2** *slang* the feet **3** *marketing informal* goods with a low market share, which are unlikely to yield substantial profits **4 go to the dogs** *informal* to go to ruin physically or morally **5 let sleeping dogs lie** to leave things undisturbed **6 throw** (*someone*) **to the dogs** to abandon (someone) to criticism or attack

Dogs (dɒgz) *n* **Isle of** a district in the East End of London, bounded on three sides by the River Thames

dogsbody ('dɒgz,bɒdɪ) *n, pl* -**bodies 1** *informal* a person who carries out menial tasks for others; drudge ▷ *vb* -**bodies, -bodying, -bodied 2** (*intr*) to act as a dogsbody

dog-sitter *n* a person who looks after a dog while its owner is away

dogsled ('dɒg,slɛd) *n chiefly US and Canadian* a sleigh drawn by dogs. Also called (Brit): **dog sledge, dog sleigh**

dog's mercury *n* a hairy somewhat poisonous euphorbiaceous perennial, *Mercurialis perennis*, having broad lanceolate toothed leaves and small greenish male and female flowers, the males borne in catkins. It often carpets shady woodlands

dog's-tail *n* any of several grasses of the genus *Cynosurus*, esp *C. cristatus* (crested dog's-tail), that are native to Europe and have flowers clustered in a dense narrow spike

Dog Star *n* the another name for **Sirius**

dog's-tongue *n* another name for **hound's-tongue**

dog's-tooth check *or* **dog-tooth check** *n* other names for **hound's-tooth check**

dog tag *n US slang* a military personal-identification disc

dog-tired *adj* (*usually postpositive*) *informal* exhausted

dogtooth ('dɒg,tuːθ) *n, pl* -**teeth 1** another name for a **canine** (sense 3) **2** *architect* a carved ornament in the form of four leaflike projections radiating from a raised centre, used in England in the 13th century

dogtooth violet *n* a name for various plants of the liliaceous genus *Erythronium*, esp the North American *E. americanum*, with yellow nodding flowers, or the European *E. dens-canis*, with purple flowers. Also called: **adders-tongue, fawn lily**

dog train *n Canadian* a sleigh drawn by a team of dogs

dogtrot ('dɒg,trɒt) *n* a gently paced trot

dog tucker *n NZ* the meat of a sheep killed on a farm and used as dog food

dogvane ('dɒg,veɪn) *n nautical* a light windvane consisting of a feather or a piece of cloth or yarn mounted on the side of a vessel. Also called: **telltale**

dog violet *n* a violet, *Viola canina*, that grows in Europe and N Asia and has blue yellow-spurred flowers

dogwatch ('dɒg,wɒtʃ) *n* **1** either of two two-hour watches aboard ship, from four to six p.m. or from six to eight p.m **2** *NZ* a shift from midnight to six a.m. in a mine

dogwood ('dɒg,wʊd) *n* any of various cornaceous trees or shrubs of the genus *Cornus*, esp *C. sanguinea*, a European shrub with clusters of small white flowers and black berries: the shoots are red in winter

dogy ('dəʊgɪ) *n, pl* -**gies** a variant spelling of **dogie**

doh¹ (dəʊ) *n, pl* **dohs** *music* **1** (in tonic sol-fa) the first degree of any major scale **2** up to high doh *informal, chiefly Scot* extremely excited or keyed up [c18 from Italian; see GAMUT]

doh² (dəʊ) *interj informal* an exclamation of annoyance when something goes wrong

DoH (in Britain) *abbreviation for* Department of Health

Doha ('dəʊhaː, 'dəʊə) *n* the capital and chief port of Qatar, on the E coast of the peninsula. Pop: 370 000 (2002 est). Former name: Bida, El Beda

doily, doyley *or* **doyly** ('dɔɪlɪ) *n, pl* -**lies** *or* -**leys** a decorative mat of lace or lacelike paper, etc, laid on or under plates [c18 named after *Doily*, a London draper]

do in *vb* (*tr, adverb*) *slang* **1** to murder or kill **2** to exhaust

doing ('duːɪŋ) *n* **1** an action or the performance of an action: *whose doing is this?* **2** *informal* a beating or castigation

doings ('duːɪŋz) *pl n* **1** deeds, actions or events **2** *Brit and NZ informal* anything of which the name is not known, or euphemistically left unsaid, etc: *have you got the doings for starting the car?*

doit (dɔɪt) *n* **1** a former small copper coin of the Netherlands **2** a trifle [c16 from Middle Dutch *duit*]

doited ('dɔɪtɪd) *or* **doitit** ('dɔɪtɪt) *adj Scot* foolish or childish, as from senility [c15 probably from *doten* to DOTE]

do-it-yourself *n* **a** the hobby or process of constructing and repairing things oneself **b** (*as modifier*): *a do-it-yourself kit*

dojo ('dəʊdʒəʊ) *n, pl* -**jos** a room or hall for the practice of martial arts [c20 from Japanese *dōjō* Buddhist seminary, from Sanskrit *bodhi-manda* seat of wisdom]

dol (dɒl) *n* a unit of pain intensity, as measured by dolorimetry [c20 by shortening, from Latin *dolor* pain]

dol. *abbreviation for* **1** *music* dolce **2** (*pl* **dols**) dollar

dolabriform (dəʊ'læbrɪ,fɔːm) *or* **dolabrate** (dəʊ'læbreɪt) *adj biology* shaped like a hatchet or axe head [c18 from Latin *dolābra* pickaxe]

Dolby ('dɒlbɪ) *n trademark* any of various specialized electronic circuits, esp those used for noise reduction in tape recorders by functioning as companders on high-frequency signals [named after R. *Dolby* (born 1933), its US inventor]

dolce ('dɒltʃɪ; *Italian* 'dɒltʃe) *adj, adv music* (to be performed) gently and sweetly [Italian: sweet]

dolce far niente *Italian* ('dɒltʃe far 'njɛnte) *n* pleasant idleness [literally: sweet doing nothing]

Dolcelatte (,dɒltʃɪ'lɑːtɪ) *n* a soft creamy blue-veined cheese made in Italy [Italian, literally: sweet milk]

dolce vita ('dɒltʃɪ 'viːtə; *Italian* 'dɒltʃe 'vita) *n* a life of luxury [Italian, literally: sweet life]

doldrums ('dɒldrəmz) *n* **the 1** a depressed or bored state of mind **2** a state of inactivity or stagnation **3 a** a belt of light winds or calms along the equator **b** the weather conditions experienced in this belt, formerly a hazard to sailing vessels [c19 probably from Old English *dol* DULL, influenced by TANTRUM]

dole¹ (dəʊl) *n* **1** a small portion or share, as of money or food, given to a poor person **2** the act of giving or distributing such portions **3** (*usually preceded by the*) *Brit informal* money received from the state while out of work **4 on the dole** *Brit informal* receiving such money **5** *archaic* fate ▷ *vb* **6** (*tr; usually foll by out*) to distribute, esp in small portions [Old English *dāl* share; related to Old Saxon *dēl*, Old Norse *deild*, Gothic *dails*, Old High German *teil*; see DEAL¹]

dole² (dəʊl) *n archaic* grief or mourning [c13 from Old French, from Late Latin *dolus*, from Latin *dolēre* to lament]

dole bludger *n Austral slang, offensive* a person who draws unemployment benefit without making any attempt to find work

doleful ('dəʊlfʊl) *adj* dreary; mournful. Archaic word: dolesome ('dəʊlsəm) > '**dolefully** *adv* > '**dolefulness** *n*

dolente (dɒ'lɛntɪ) *adj, adv music* (to be performed) in a sorrowful manner

dolerite ('dɒlə,raɪt) *n* **1** a dark basic intrusive igneous rock consisting of plagioclase feldspar and a pyroxene, such as augite; often emplaced in dykes **2** any dark igneous rock whose composition cannot be determined with the naked eye [c19 from French *dolérite*, from Greek *doleros* deceitful; so called because of the difficulty of determining its composition] > doleritic (,dɒlə'rɪtɪk) *adj*

Dolgellau (dɒl'gɛθlaɪ; *Welsh* dɒl'gɛθlaɪn) *n* a market town and tourist centre in NW Wales, in Gwynedd. Pop: 2407 (2001). Former spelling: Dolgelley

dolichocephalic (,dɒlɪkəʊsɪ'fælɪk) *or* **dolichocephalous** (,dɒlɪkəʊ'sɛfələs) *adj* **1** having a head much longer than it is broad, esp one with a cephalic index under 75 ▷ *n* **2** an individual with such a head ▷ Compare **brachycephalic, mesocephalic, scaphocephalic** > ,**dolicho'cephalism** *or* ,**dolicho'cephaly** *n*

dolichosaurus (,dɒlɪkəʊ'sɔːrəs) *n* any of various extinct Cretaceous aquatic reptiles that had long necks and bodies and well-developed limbs [c20 from Greek, from *dolikhos* long + -SAUR]

doline *or* **dolina** (də'li:nə) *n* a shallow usually funnel-shaped depression of the ground surface formed by solution in limestone regions [C20 from Russian *dolina*, valley, plain; related to DALE]

doll (dɒl) *n* **1** a small model or dummy of a human being, used as a toy **2** *slang* a pretty girl or woman of little intelligence: sometimes used as a term of address [C16 probably from *Doll*, pet name for *Dorothy*] > **'dollish** *adj* > **'dollishly** *adv* > **'dollishness** *n*

dollar ('dɒlə) *n* **1** the standard monetary unit of the US and its dependencies, divided into 100 cents **2** the standard monetary unit, comprising 100 cents, of the following countries or territories: Antigua and Barbuda, Australia, the Bahamas, Barbados, Belize, Bermuda, the British Virgin Islands, Brunei, Canada, the Cayman Islands, Dominica, East Timor, Ecuador, El Salvador, Fiji, Grenada, Guatemala, Guyana, Hong Kong, Jamaica, Kiribati, Liberia, Malaysia, the Marshall Islands, Micronesia, Namibia, Nauru, New Zealand, Saint Kitts and Nevis, Saint Lucia, Saint Vincent and the Grenadines, Singapore, Solomon Islands, Taiwan, Trinidad and Tobago, Tuvalu, and Zimbabwe **3** *Brit informal* (formerly) five shillings or a coin of this value **4** **look** *or* **feel (like) a million dollars** *informal* to look *or* feel extremely well [C16 from Low German *daler*, from German *Taler, Thaler*, short for *Joachimsthaler* coin made from metal mined in *Joachimsthal* Jachymov, town now in the Czech Republic]

dollarbird ('dɒlə,bɜːd) *n* a bird, *Eurystomus orientalis*, of S and SE Asia and Australia, with a round white spot on each wing: family *Coraciidae* (rollers), order *Coraciiformes*

dollar diplomacy *n chiefly US* **1** a foreign policy that encourages and protects capital investment and commercial and financial involvement abroad **2** use of financial power as a diplomatic weapon

dollarfish ('dɒlə,fɪʃ) *n, pl* -fish *or* -fishes any of various fishes that have a rounded compressed silvery body, esp the moonfishes or the American butterfly

dollarization *or* **dollarisation** (,dɒləraɪ'zeɪʃən) *n* the process of converting a country's currency to US dollars

dollop ('dɒləp) *informal* ▷ *n* **1** a semisolid lump **2** a large serving, esp of food ▷ *vb* **3** (*tr;* foll by *out*) to serve out (food) [C16 of unknown origin]

doll up *vb* (*tr, adverb*) *slang* to adorn or dress (oneself or another, esp a child) in a stylish or showy manner

dolly ('dɒlɪ) *n, pl* -lies **1** a child's word for a **doll 2** *films, television* a wheeled support on which a camera may be mounted **3** a cup-shaped anvil held against the head of a rivet while the other end is being hammered **4** a shaped block of lead used to hammer dents out of sheet metal **5** a distance piece placed between the head of a pile and the pile-driver to form an extension to the length of the pile **6** *cricket* a simple catch **7** Also called: **dolly bird** *slang, chiefly Brit* an attractive and fashionable girl, esp one who is considered to be unintelligent ▷ *vb* -lies, -lying, -lied **8** *films, television* to wheel (a camera) backwards or forwards on a dolly

dolly-posh *adj Northern English dialect* left-handed

Dolly Varden ('dɒlɪ 'vɑːdən) *n* **1** a woman's large-brimmed hat trimmed with flowers **2** a red-spotted trout, *Salvelinus malma*, occurring in lakes in W North America [C19 from the name of a character in Dickens' *Barnaby Rudge* (1841)]

dolma ('dɒlmə, -mɑː) *n, pl* dolmas *or* dolmades (dɒl'mɑːdiːz) a vine leaf stuffed with a filling of meat and rice [C19 Turkish *dolma* literally something filled]

dolman ('dɒlmən) *n, pl* -mans **1** a long Turkish outer robe **2** Also called: **dolman jacket** a hussar's jacket worn slung over the shoulder **3** a woman's cloak with voluminous sleeves [C16 via

French from German *Dolman,* from Turkish *dolaman* a winding round, from *dolamak* to wind]

dolman sleeve *n* a sleeve that is very wide at the armhole and tapers to a tight wrist

dolmen ('dɒlmɛn) *n* **1** (in British archaeology) a Neolithic stone formation, consisting of a horizontal stone supported by several vertical stones, and thought to be a tomb **2** (in French archaeology) any megalithic tomb [C19 from French, probably from Old Breton *tol* table, from Latin *tabula* board + Breton *mēn* stone, of Celtic origin; see TABLE]

dolomite ('dɒlə,maɪt) *n* **1** a white mineral often tinted as impurities, found in sedimentary rocks and veins. It is used in the manufacture of cement and as a building stone (marble). Composition: calcium magnesium carbonate. Formula: $CaMg(CO_3)_2$. Crystal structure: hexagonal (rhombohedral) **2** a sedimentary rock resembling limestone but consisting principally of the mineral dolomite. It is an important source of magnesium and its compounds, and is used as a building material and refractory [C18 named after Déodat de *Dolomieu* (1750–1801), French mineralogist] > **dolomitic** (,dɒlə'mɪtɪk) *adj*

Dolomites ('dɒlə,maɪts) *pl n* a mountain range in NE Italy: part of the Alps; formed of dolomitic limestone. Highest peak: Marmolada, 3342 m (10 965 ft)

dolorimetry (,dɒlə'rɪmətrɪ) *n* a technique for measuring the level of pain perception by applying heat to the skin

doloroso (,dɒlə'rəʊsəʊ) *adj, adv music* (to be performed) in a sorrowful manner [Italian: dolorous]

dolorous ('dɒlərəs) *adj* causing or involving pain or sorrow > **'dolorously** *adv* > **'dolorousness** *n*

dolos ('dɒlɒs) *n, pl* -osse *South African* a knucklebone of a sheep, buck, etc, used esp by diviners [from Afrikaans, possibly from *dollen* play + *os* ox or from *dobbel* dice + *os* ox]

dolostone ('dɒlə,stəʊn) *n* rock composed of the mineral dolomite

dolour *or US* **dolor** ('dɒlə) *n poetic* grief or sorrow [C14 from Latin, from *dolēre* to grieve]

dolphin ('dɒlfɪn) *n* **1** any of various marine cetacean mammals of the family *Delphinidae*, esp *Delphinus delphis*, that are typically smaller than whales and larger than porpoises and have a beaklike snout **2** river dolphin any freshwater cetacean of the family *Platanistidae*, inhabiting rivers of North and South America and S Asia. They are smaller than marine dolphins and have a longer narrower snout **3** Also called: dorado either of two large marine percoid fishes, *Coryphaena hippurus* or *C. equisetis*, that resemble the cetacean dolphins and have an iridescent coloration **4** *nautical* a post or buoy for mooring a vessel [C13 via Old French *dauphin*, via Latin, from Greek *delphin-, delphis*]

dolphinarium (,dɒlfɪ'nɛərɪəm) *n* a pool or aquarium for dolphins, esp one in which they give public displays

dolphin striker *n nautical* a short vertical strut between the bowsprit and a rope or cable (martingale) from the end of the jib boom to the stem or bows, used for maintaining tension and preventing upward movement of the jib boom. Also called: martingale boom, martingale

dolt (dəʊlt) *n* a slow-witted or stupid person [C16 probably related to Old English *dol* stupid; see DULL] > **'doltish** *adj* > **'doltishly** *adv* > **'doltishness** *n*

dom (dɒm) *n* **1** (*sometimes capital*) *RC Church* a title given to Benedictine, Carthusian, and Cistercian monks and to certain of the canons regular **2** (formerly in Portugal and Brazil) a title borne by royalty, princes of the Church, and nobles [C18 (monastic title): from Latin *dominus* lord]

DOM *abbreviation for* **1** Deo Optimo Maximo [Latin: to God, the best, the Greatest] **2** *informal* Dirty Old Man **3** *international car registration for* Dominican Republic

Dom. *RC Church abbreviation for* Dominican

-dom *suffix forming nouns* **1** state or condition: *freedom; martyrdom* **2** rank or office: *earldom* **3** a collection of persons: *kingdom; Christendom* **4** a collection of persons: *officialdom* [Old English *-dōm*]

domain (də'meɪn) *n* **1** land governed by a ruler or government **2** land owned by one person or family **3** a field or scope of knowledge or activity **4** a region having specific characteristics or containing certain types of plants or animals **5** *Austral and NZ* a park or recreation reserve maintained by a public authority, often the government **6** *law* the absolute ownership and right to dispose of land. See also **demesne, eminent domain 7** *maths* **a** the set of values of the independent variable of a function for which the functional value exists: *the domain of sin x is all real numbers*. Compare **range** (sense 8a) **b** any open set containing at least one point **8** *logic* another term for **universe of discourse** (esp in the phrase **domain of quantification**) **9** *philosophy* range of significance (esp in the phrase **domain of definition**) **10** Also called: magnetic domain *physics* one of the regions in a ferromagnetic solid in which all the atoms have their magnetic moments aligned in the same direction **11** *computing* a group of computers that have the same suffix (**domain name**) in their names on the internet, specifying the country, type of institution, etc where they are located **12** Also called: superkingdom *biology* the highest level of classification of living organisms. Three domains are recognized: *Archaea* (see **archaean**), *Bacteria* (see **bacteria**), and *Eukarya* (see **eukaryote**) **13** *biochem* a structurally compact portion of a protein molecule [C17 from French *domaine*, from Latin *dominium* property, from *dominus* lord]

domain name *n computing* the suffix in a computer's internet name, specifying the country, type of institution, etc, where it is located

d

domatium (dɒ'meɪʃɪəm) *n, pl* -tia *botany* a plant cavity inhabited by commensal insects or mites or, occasionally, microorganisms

dome (dəʊm) *n* **1** a hemispherical roof or vault or a structure of similar form **2** something shaped like this **3** *crystallog* a crystal form in which two planes intersect along an edge parallel to a lateral axis **4** a slang word for the **head 5** *geology* **a** a structure in which rock layers slope away in all directions from a central point **b** another name for **pericline** (sense 2) ▷ *vb* (*tr*) **6** to cover with or as if with a dome **7** to shape like a dome [C16 from French, from Italian *duomo* cathedral, from Latin *domus* house] > **'dome,like** *adj* > **domical** ('dəʊmɪkəl, 'dɒm-) *adj*

dome fastener *n US and Canadian* a fastening device consisting of one part with a projecting knob that snaps into a hole on another like part, used esp in closures in clothing. Also called (in Britain and certain other countries): **press stud**

Dome of the Rock *n* the mosque in Jerusalem, Israel, built in 691 AD by caliph 'Abd al-Malik: the third most holy place of Islam; stands on the Temple Mount alongside the **al-Aqsa** mosque. Also called (not in Muslim usage): Mosque of Omar

domesday ('duːmz,deɪ) *n* a variant spelling of **doomsday**

Domesday Book *or* **Doomsday Book** *n history* the record of a survey of the land of England carried out by the commissioners of William I in 1086

domestic (də'mɛstɪk) *adj* **1** of or involving the home or family **2** enjoying or accustomed to home or family life **3** (of an animal) bred or kept by man as a pet or for purposes such as the supply of food **4** of, produced in, or involving one's own country or a specific country: *domestic and foreign affairs* ▷ *n* **5** a household servant **6** *informal* (esp in police use) an incident of violence in the home, esp between a man and a woman [C16 from Old

French *domestique,* from Latin *domesticus* belonging to the house, from *domus* house]
> do'**mestically** *adv*

domesticate (dəˈmɛstɪˌkeɪt) *or sometimes US*
domesticize (dəˈmɛstɪˌsaɪz) *vb* (*tr*) **1** to bring or keep (wild animals or plants) under control or cultivation **2** to accustom to home life **3** to adapt to an environment: *to domesticate foreign trees*
> do'**mesticable** *adj* > do,**mesti'cation** *n*
> do'**mesticative** *adj* > do'**mesti,cator** *n*

domestic court *n* (in England) a magistrates' court for domestic proceedings, such as matrimonial, guardianship, custodianship, affiliation, or adoption disputes

domestic fowl *n* a domesticated gallinaceous bird thought to be descended from the red jungle fowl (*Gallus gallus*) and occurring in many varieties. Often shortened to: **fowl**

domesticity (ˌdəʊmɛˈstɪsɪtɪ) *n, pl* -ties **1** home life **2** devotion to or familiarity with home life **3** (*usually plural*) a domestic duty, matter, or condition

domestic science *n* the study of cooking, needlework, and other subjects concerned with household skills

domicile (ˈdɒmɪˌsaɪl) *or* **domicil** (ˈdɒmɪsɪl) *formal*
▷ *n* **1** a dwelling place **2** a permanent legal residence **3** *commerce, Brit* the place where a bill of exchange is to be paid ▷ *vb also* **domiciliate** (ˌdɒmɪˈsɪlɪˌeɪt) **4** to establish or be established in a dwelling place [C15 from Latin *domicilium,* from *domus* house]

domiciliary (ˌdɒmɪˈsɪlɪərɪ) *adj* of, involving, or taking place in the home

domiciliary care *or* **services** *n* social welfare services, such as meals-on-wheels, health visiting, and home help, provided by a welfare agency for people in their own homes

dominance (ˈdɒmɪnəns) *n* control; ascendancy

dominant (ˈdɒmɪnənt) *adj* **1** having primary control, authority, or influence; governing; ruling **2** predominant or primary: *the dominant topic of the day* **3** occupying a commanding position **4** *genetics* **a** (of an allele) producing the same phenotype in the organism irrespective of whether the allele of the same gene is identical or dissimilar **b** (of a character) controlled by such a gene. Compare **recessive** (sense 2) **5** *music* of or relating to the fifth degree of a scale **6** *ecology* (of a plant or animal species within a community) more prevalent than any other species and determining the appearance and composition of the community ▷ *n* **7** *genetics* **a** a dominant allele or character **b** an organism having such an allele or character **8** *music* the fifth degree of a scale and the second in importance after the tonic **b** a key or chord based on this **9** *ecology* a dominant plant or animal in a community > '**dominantly** *adv*

dominant hemisphere *n* See **cerebral dominance**

dominant seventh chord *n* a chord consisting of the dominant and the major third, perfect fifth, and minor seventh above it. Its most natural resolution is to a chord on the tonic

dominant tenement *n* *property law* the land or tenement with the benefit of an easement over land belonging to another. Compare **servient tenement**

dominant wavelength *n* *physics* the wavelength of monochromatic light that would give the same visual sensation if combined in a suitable proportion with an achromatic light. See also **complementary wavelength**

dominate (ˈdɒmɪˌneɪt) *vb* **1** to control, rule, or govern (someone or something) **2** to tower above (surroundings, etc); overlook **3** (*tr; usually passive*) to predominate in (something or someone) [C17 from Latin *dominārī* to be lord over, from *dominus* lord] > '**domi,nating** *adj* > '**domi,natingly** *adv* > '**dominative** *adj* > '**domi,nator** *n*

domination (ˌdɒmɪˈneɪʃən) *n* **1** the act of dominating or state of being dominated **2** authority; rule; control

dominations (ˌdɒmɪˈneɪʃənz) *pl n* (*sometimes capital*) the fourth order of medieval angelology. Also called: **dominions**

dominatrix (ˌdɒmɪˈneɪtrɪks) *n, pl* dominatrices (ˌdɒmɪnəˈtraɪsiːz) **1** a woman who is the dominant sexual partner in a sadomasochistic relationship **2** a dominant woman [C16 from Latin, fem of *dominātor,* from *dominārī* to be lord over]

dominee (ˈduːmɪnɪ, 'dʊə-) *n* (in South Africa) a minister in any of the Afrikaner Churches. Also called: **predikant** [from Afrikaans, from Dutch; compare DOMINIE]

domineer (ˌdɒmɪˈnɪə) *vb* (*intr; often foll by over*) to act with arrogance or tyranny; behave imperiously [C16 from Dutch *domineren,* from French *dominer* to DOMINATE]

domineering (ˌdɒmɪˈnɪərɪŋ) *adj* acting with or showing arrogance or tyranny; imperious: *a domineering boss* > ,domi'**neeringly** *adv* > ,domi'**neeringness** *n*

Dominica (ˌdɒmɪˈniːkə, dəˈmɪnɪkə) *n* a republic in the E Caribbean, comprising a volcanic island in the Windward Islands group; a former British colony; became independent as a member of the Commonwealth in 1978. Official language: English. Religion: Roman Catholic majority. Currency: East Caribbean dollar. Capital: Roseau. Pop: 79 000 (2003 est). Area: 751 sq km (290 sq miles). Official name: **Commonwealth of Dominica**

dominical (dəˈmɪnɪkəl) *adj* **1** of, relating to, or emanating from Jesus Christ as Lord **2** of or relating to Sunday as the Lord's Day [C15 from Late Latin *dominicālis,* from Latin *dominus* lord]

dominical letter *n* *Christianity* any one of the letters A to G as used to denote Sundays in a given year in order to determine the church calendar

Dominican[1] (dəˈmɪnɪkən) *n* **1 a** a member of an order of preaching friars founded by Saint Dominic (original name *Domingo de Guzman;* ?1170–1221), the Spanish priest, in 1215; a Blackfriar **b** a nun of one of the orders founded under the patronage of Saint Dominic ▷ *adj* **2** of or relating to Saint Dominic or the Dominican order

Dominican[2] (dəˈmɪnɪkən) *adj* **1** of or relating to the Dominican Republic or Dominica ▷ *n* **2** a native or inhabitant of the Dominican Republic or Dominica

Dominican Republic *n* a republic in the Caribbean, occupying the eastern half of the island of Hispaniola: colonized by the Spanish after its discovery by Columbus in 1492; gained independence from Spain in 1821. It is generally mountainous, dominated by the Cordillera Central, which rises over 3000 m (10 000 ft), with fertile lowlands. Language: Spanish. Religion: Roman Catholic majority. Currency: peso. Capital: Santo Domingo. Pop: 8 873 000 (2004 est). Area: 48 441 sq km (18 703 sq miles). Former name (until 1844): **Santo Domingo**

dominie (ˈdɒmɪnɪ) *n* **1** a Scot word for **schoolmaster 2** a minister or clergyman: also used as a term of address [C17 from Latin *dominē,* vocative case of *dominus* lord]

dominion (dəˈmɪnjən) *n* **1** rule; authority **2** the land governed by one ruler or government **3** sphere of influence; area of control **4** a name formerly applied to self-governing divisions of the British Empire **5** (*capital*) **the** New Zealand **6** *law* a less common word for **dominium** [C15 from Old French, from Latin *dominium* ownership, from *dominus* master]

Dominion Day *n* the former name for **Canada Day**

dominions (dəˈmɪnjənz) *pl n* (*often capital*) another term for **dominations**

dominium (dəˈmɪnɪəm) *or rarely* **dominion** *property law* the ownership or right to possession of property, esp realty [C19 from Latin: property, ownership; see DOMINION]

domino[1] (ˈdɒmɪˌnəʊ) *n, pl* -noes **1** a small rectangular block used in dominoes, divided on one side into two equal areas, each of which is either blank or marked with from one to six dots **2** (*modifier*) exhibiting the domino effect: *a domino pattern of takeovers* ▷ See also **dominoes** [C19 from French, from Italian, perhaps from *domino!* master, said by the winner]

domino[2] (ˈdɒmɪˌnəʊ) *n, pl* -noes *or* -nos **1** a large hooded cloak worn with an eye mask at a masquerade **2** the eye mask worn with such a cloak [C18 from French or Italian, probably from Latin *dominus* lord, master]

domino effect *n* a series of similar or related events occurring as a direct and inevitable result of one initial event [C20 alluding to a row of dominoes, each standing on end, all of which fall when one is pushed: originally used with reference to possible Communist takeovers of countries in SE Asia]

dominoes (ˈdɒmɪˌnəʊz) *n* (*functioning as singular*) any of several games in which matching halves of dominoes are laid together

Dominus *Latin* (ˈdɒmɪnʊs) *n* God or Christ

Domrémy-la-Pucelle (French dɔremilapysɛl) *or* **Domrémy** *n* a village in NE France, in the Vosges: birthplace of Joan of Arc

don[1] (dɒn) *vb* dons, donning, donned (*tr*) to put on (clothing) [C14 from DO + ON; compare DOFF]

don[2] (dɒn) *n* **1** *Brit* a member of the teaching staff at a university or college, esp at Oxford or Cambridge **2** a Spanish gentleman or nobleman **3** (in the Mafia) the head of a family [C17 ultimately from Latin *dominus* lord]

Don[1] (dɒn; *Spanish* don) *n* a Spanish title equivalent to *Mr:* placed before a name to indicate respect [C16 via Spanish, from Latin *dominus* lord; see DON[2]]

Don[2] (dɒn) *n* **1** a river rising in W Russia, southeast of Tula and flowing generally south, to the Sea of Azov: linked by canal to the River Volga. Length: 1870 km (1162 miles) **2** a river in NE Scotland, rising in the Cairngorm Mountains and flowing east to the North Sea. Length: 100 km (62 miles) **3** a river in N central England, rising in S Yorkshire and flowing northeast to the Humber. Length: about 96 km (60 miles)

Dona (*Portuguese* ˈdõːnə) *n* a Portuguese title of address equivalent to *Mrs* or *Madam:* placed before a name to indicate respect [C19 from Latin *domina* lady, feminine of *dominus* master]

Doña (ˈdɒnjə; *Spanish* ˈdoɲa) *n* a Spanish title of address equivalent to *Mrs* or *Madam:* placed before a name to indicate respect [C17 via Spanish, from Latin *domina;* see DONA]

Donar (ˈdəʊnɑː; *German* ˈdoːnar) *n* the Germanic god of thunder, corresponding to Thor in Norse mythology

donate (dəʊˈneɪt) *vb* to give (money, time, etc), esp to a charity > do'**nator** *n*

donation (dəʊˈneɪʃən) *n* **1** the act of giving, esp to a charity **2** a contribution [C15 from Latin *dōnātiō* a presenting, from *dōnāre* to give, from *dōnum* gift]

Donatist (ˈdəʊnətɪst) *n* a member of a schismatic heretical Christian sect originating in N Africa in 311 AD, that maintained that it alone constituted the true church [C15 from Late Latin *Dōnātista* a follower of *Dōnātus,* bishop of Carthage] > 'Dona,**tism** *n*

donative (ˈdəʊnətɪv) *n* **1** a gift or donation **2** a benefice capable of being conferred as a gift ▷ *adj* **3** of or like a donation **4** being or relating to a benefice [C15 from Latin *dōnātīvum* donation made to soldiers by a Roman emperor, from *dōnāre* to present]

Donau (ˈdoːnau) *n* the German name for the **Danube**

Donbass *or* **Donbas** (dɒnˈbɑːs) *n* an industrial region in E Ukraine in the plain of the Rivers Donets and lower Dnieper: the site of a major coalfield. Also called: **Donets Basin**

Doncaster (ˈdɒŋkəstə) *n* **1** an industrial town in N England, in Doncaster unitary authority, South

Yorkshire, on the River Don. Pop: 67 977 (2001) **2** a unitary authority in N England, in South Yorkshire. Pop: 288 400 (2003 est). Area: 582 sq km (225 sq miles)

donder ('dɒndə) *South African slang* ▷ *vb* (*tr*) **1** to beat (someone) up ▷ *n* **2** a wretch; swine [c19 Afrikaans, from Dutch *donderen* to swear, bully]

done (dʌn) *vb* **1** the past participle of **do**[1] **2** *be* or *have done with* to end relations with **3** *have done* to be completely finished: *have you done?* **4** *that's done it* **a** an exclamation of frustration when something is ruined **b** an exclamation when something is completed ▷ *interj* **5** an expression of agreement, as on the settlement of a bargain between two parties ▷ *adj* **6** completed; finished **7** cooked enough: *done to a turn* **8** *used up: they had to surrender when the ammunition was done* **9** socially proper or acceptable: *that isn't done in higher circles* **10** *informal* cheated; tricked **11** *done for informal* **a** dead or almost dead **b** in serious difficulty **12** *done in* or *up informal* physically exhausted

donee (dəʊ'niː) *n law* **1** a person who receives a gift **2** a person to whom a power of appointment is given [c16 from DON(OR) + -EE]

Donegal ('dɒnɪˌgɔːl, ˌdɒnɪ'gɔːl, ˌdʌnɪ'gɔːl) *n* a county in NW Republic of Ireland, on the Atlantic: mountainous, with a rugged coastline and many offshore islands. County town: Lifford. Pop: 137 575 (2002). Area: 4830 sq km (1865 sq miles)

doner kebab ('dɒnə) *n* a fast-food dish comprising grilled meat and salad served in pitta bread with chilli sauce [from Turkish *döner* rotating + KEBAB]

Donets (*Russian* dɑ'njɛts) *n* a river rising in SW Russia, in the Kursk steppe and flowing southeast, through Ukraine, to the Don River. Length: about 1078 km (670 miles)

Donets Basin (də'nɛts) *n* another name for the **Donbass**

Donetsk (*Russian* dɑ'njɛtsk) *n* a city in E Ukraine: the chief industrial centre of the Donbass; first ironworks founded by a Welshman, John Hughes (1872), after whom the town was named **Yuzovka** (Hughesovka). Pop: 992 000 (2005 est). Former names (from 1924 until 1961): **Stalin** or **Stalino**

dong (dɒŋ) *n* **1** the deep reverberating sound of a large bell **2** *Austral and NZ informal* a heavy blow **3** a slang word for **penis** ▷ *vb* **4** (*intr*) (of a bell) to make a deep reverberating sound **5** (*tr*) *Austral and NZ informal* to strike or punch [c16 of imitative origin]

dông (dɒŋ) *n* the standard monetary unit of Vietnam, divided into 10 hào or 100 xu [from Vietnamese]

donga[1] ('dɒŋgə) *n South African, Austral, and NZ* a steep-sided gully created by soil erosion [c19 Afrikaans, from Nguni *donga* washed out gully]

donga[2] ('dɒŋgə) *n* (in Papua New Guinea) a house or shelter

dongle ('dɒŋgəl) *n computing* an electronic device that accompanies a software item to prevent the unauthorized copying of programs

Dongola ('dɒŋgələ) *n* a small town in the N Sudan, on the Nile: built on the site of Old Dongola, the capital of the Christian Kingdom of Nubia (6th to 14th centuries). Pop: 5937 (latest est)

Dongting ('dʊŋ'tɪŋ), **Tungting** or **Tung-t'ing** *n* a lake in S China, in NE Hunan province: main outlet flows to the Yangtze; rice-growing in winter. Area: (in winter) 3900 sq km (1500 sq miles)

donjon ('dʌndʒən, 'dɒn-) *n* the heavily fortified central tower or keep of a medieval castle. Also called: dungeon [c14 archaic variant of *dungeon*]

Don Juan ('dɒn 'dʒuːən; *Spanish* don xwan) *n* **1** a legendary Spanish nobleman and philanderer: hero of many poems, plays, and operas, including treatments by de Molina, Molière, Goldoni, Mozart, Byron, and Shaw **2** a successful seducer of women

donkey ('dɒŋkɪ) *n* **1** Also called: ass a long-eared

domesticated member of the horse family (*Equidae*), descended from the African wild ass (*Equus asinus*) **2** a stupid or stubborn person **3** *Brit slang, derogatory* a footballer known for his or her lack of skill: *the players are a bunch of overpriced and overrated donkeys* **4** *talk the hind leg(s) off a donkey* to talk endlessly [c18 perhaps from *dun* dark + -*key*, as in *monkey*]

donkey derby *n* a race in which contestants ride donkeys, esp at a rural fête

donkey engine *n* a small auxiliary engine, such as one used for pumping water into the boilers of a steamship

donkey jacket *n* a hip-length jacket usually made of a thick navy fabric with a waterproof panel across the shoulders

donkey-lick *vb Austral slang* to defeat decisively

donkey's years *n informal* a long time

donkey vote *n Austral* a vote on a preferential ballot on which the voter's order of preference follows the order in which the candidates are listed

donkey-work *n* **1** groundwork **2** drudgery. US equivalent: draft-mule work

donko ('dɒŋkəʊ) *n, pl* -kos *NZ informal* a tearoom or cafeteria in a factory, wharf area, etc [origin unknown]

Donna ('dɒnə; *Italian* 'dɔnna) *n* an Italian title of address equivalent to *Madam*, indicating respect [c17 from Italian, from Latin *domina* lady, feminine of *dominus* lord, master]

donnée or **donné** *French* (dɔne) *n* **1** a subject or theme **2** a basic assumption or fact [literally: (a) given]

donnert ('dɒnərt) or **donnard, donnered** ('dɒnərd) *adj Scot* stunned [c18 from Scottish dialect *donner* to astound, perhaps from Dutch *donderen* to thunder, from Middle Dutch *donder* thunder]

donnish ('dɒnɪʃ) *adj* of or resembling a university don > 'donnishly *adv* > 'donnishness *n*

donny ('dɒnɪ) *n* a variant of **danny**

donnybrook ('dɒnɪˌbrʊk) *n* a rowdy brawl [c19 after *Donnybrook Fair*, an annual event until 1855 near Dublin]

donor ('dəʊnə) *n* **1** a person who makes a donation **2** *med* any person who voluntarily gives blood, skin, a kidney etc, for use in the treatment of another person **3** *law* **a** a person who makes a gift of property **b** a person who bestows upon another a power of appointment over property **4** the atom supplying both electrons in a coordinate bond **5** an impurity, such as antimony or arsenic, that is added to a semiconductor material in order to increase its n-type conductivity by contributing free electrons. Compare **acceptor** (sense 2) [c15 from Old French *doneur*, from Latin *dōnātor*, from *dōnāre* to give] > 'donor,ship *n*

donor card *n* a card carried by a person to show that the bodily organs specified on it may be used for transplants after the person's death

Donostia-San Sebastián (*Spanish* donostja san seβas'tjan) *n* the official name (including the Basque name Donostia) for **San Sebastián**

Don Quixote ('dɒn kiː'həʊtiː, -'kwɪksət; *Spanish* don ki'xote) *n* an impractical idealist [after the hero of Cervantes' *Don Quixote de la Mancha*]

don't (dəʊnt) contraction of *do not*

don't know *n* a person who has not reached a definite opinion on a subject, esp as a response to a questionnaire

donut ('dəʊnʌt) *n* a variant spelling (esp US) of **doughnut**

doo (duː) *n* a Scot word for **dove**[1] or **pigeon**[1]

doob (duːb) *n US slang* a cannabis cigarette [c20 origin unknown]

dooced (duːst) **to get dooced** *chiefly US slang* to be dismissed from one's employment because of what one has written on a website or blog [c21 after the web address of the first person to experience this]

doodah ('duːˌdɑː) or *US and Canadian* **doodad**

('duːdæd) *n informal* **1** an unnamed thing, esp an object the name of which is unknown or forgotten **2** *all of a doodah* excited; agitated [c20 of uncertain origin]

doodle ('duːdəl) *informal* ▷ *vb* **1** to scribble or draw aimlessly **2** to play or improvise idly **3** (*intr*; often foll by *away*) US to dawdle or waste time ▷ *n* **4** a shape, picture, etc, drawn aimlessly [c20 perhaps from c17 *doodle* a foolish person, but influenced in meaning by DAWDLE; compare Low German *dudeltopf* simpleton] > 'doodler *n*

doodlebug ('duːdəlˌbʌg) *n* **1** another name for the **V-1 2** a diviner's rod **3** a US name for an **antlion** (the larva) **4** US any of certain insect larvae that resemble the antlion [c20 probably from DOODLE + BUG[1]]

doo-doo ('duːˌduː) *n US and Canadian informal* a child's word for **excrement**

doofus ('duːfəs) *n informal, chiefly US* a slow-witted or stupid person [c20 from Black slang]

doohickey ('duːˌhɪkɪ) *n US and Canadian informal* another name for **doodah** (sense 1)

dook[1] or **douk** (dʊk) *n Scot* a wooden plug driven into a wall to hold a nail, screw, etc [of unknown origin]

dook[2], **douk** (dʊk) *Scot* ▷ *vb* **1** to dip or plunge **2** to bathe ▷ *n* **3** an instance of dipping, plunging, or bathing [a Scot form of DUCK[2]]

dooket ('duːkɪt, 'dʊkɪt) *n Scot* **1** a dovecote **2** a small closet or cupboard

doolally (duː'lælɪ) *adj slang* out of one's mind; crazy. In full: **doolally tap** [c19 originally military slang, from *Deolali*, a town near Bombay, the location of a military sanatorium + Hindustani *tap* fever]

doolan ('duːlən) *n NZ informal* a Roman Catholic [probably from the Irish surname *Doolan*]

doom (duːm) *n* **1** death or a terrible fate **2** a judgment or decision **3** (*sometimes capital*) another term for the **Last Judgment** ▷ *vb* **4** (*tr*) to destine or condemn to death or a terrible fate [Old English *dōm*; related to Old Norse *dōmr* judgment, Gothic *dōms* sentence, Old High German *tuom* condition, Greek *thomos* crowd, Sanskrit *dhāman* custom; see DO[1], DEEM, DEED, -DOM]

doom-laden *adj* conveying a sense of disaster and tragedy

doom palm *n* a variant spelling of **doum palm**

doomsday or **domesday** ('duːmzˌdeɪ) *n* **1** (*sometimes capital*) the day on which the Last Judgment will occur **2** any day of reckoning **3** (*modifier*) characterized by predictions of disaster: *doomsday scenario* [Old English *dōmes dæg* Judgment Day; related to Old Norse *domsdagr*]

Doomsday Book *n* a variant spelling of **Domesday Book**

doomster ('duːmstə) *n informal* **1** a person habitually given to predictions of impending disaster or doom **2** *archaic* a judge

doomwatch ('duːmˌwɒtʃ) *n* **1** surveillance of the environment to warn of and prevent harm to it from human factors such as pollution or overpopulation **2** a watching for or prediction of impending disaster > 'doomwatcher *n*

doomy ('duːmɪ) *adj informal* **1** despondent or pessimistic **2** depressing, frightening, or chilling > 'doomily *adv*

doon or **doun** (duːn) *prep, adv, adj* a Scot word for **down**[1]

doona ('duːnə) *n Austral* a quilt, stuffed with down or a synthetic material and containing pockets of air, used as a bed cover in place of the top sheet and blankets. Also called: **duvet**, (Brit) **continental quilt** [from a trademark]

door (dɔː) *n* **1 a** a hinged or sliding panel for closing the entrance to a room, cupboard, etc **b** (*in combination*): *doorbell; doorknob* **2** a doorway or entrance to a room or building **3** a means of access or escape: *a door to success* **4** *lay at someone's door* to lay (the blame or responsibility) on someone **5** *out of doors* in or into the open air **6** *show someone the door* to

d

order someone to leave ▷ See also **next door** [Old English *duru*; related to Old Frisian *dure*, Old Norse *dyrr*, Old High German *turi*, Latin *forēs*, Greek *thura*]

do-or-die *adj* (*prenominal*) of or involving a determined and sometimes reckless effort to succeed

doorframe ('dɔːˌfreɪm) *n* a frame that supports a door. Also called: **doorcase**

door furniture *n* locks, handles, etc, designed for use on doors

doorjamb ('dɔːˌdʒæm) *n* one of the two vertical members forming the sides of a doorframe. Also called: **doorpost**

doorkeeper ('dɔːˌkiːpə) *n* **1** a person attending or guarding a door or gateway **2** *RC Church* (formerly) the lowest grade of holy orders

doorknock ('dɔːˌnɒk) *n* *Austral* a fund-raising campaign for charity conducted by seeking donations from door to door

doorman ('dɔːˌmæn, -mən) *n, pl* -men a man employed to attend the doors of certain buildings

doormat ('dɔːˌmæt) *n* **1** a mat, placed at the entrance to a building, for wiping dirt from shoes **2** *informal* a person who offers little resistance to ill-treatment by others

Doorn (*Dutch* dɔːrn) *n* a town in the central Netherlands, in Utrecht province: residence of Kaiser William II of Germany from his abdication (1919) until his death (1941)

doornail ('dɔːˌneɪl) *n* (as) **dead as a doornail** dead beyond any doubt

Doornik ('dɔːrnɪk) *n* the Flemish name for **Tournai**

doorpost ('dɔːˌpəʊst) *n* another name for **doorjamb**

doorsill ('dɔːˌsɪl) *n* a horizontal member of wood, stone, etc, forming the bottom of a doorframe

doorstep ('dɔːˌstɛp) *n* **1** a step in front of a door **2 on one's doorstep** very close or accessible **3** *informal* a thick slice of bread ▷ *vb* -steps, -stepping, -stepped (*tr*) **4** to canvass (a district) or interview (a member of the public) by or in the course of door-to-door visiting

doorstop ('dɔːˌstɒp) *n* **1** a heavy object, wedge, or other device which prevents an open door from moving **2** a projecting piece of rubber, etc, fixed to the floor to stop a door from striking a wall **3** *informal* a very thick book

door to door *adj* (**door-to-door** *when prenominal*) ▷ *adv* **1** (of selling, canvassing, etc) from one house to the next **2** (of journeys, deliveries, etc) direct

doorway ('dɔːˌweɪ) *n* **1** an opening into a building, room, etc, esp one that has a door **2** a means of access or escape: *a doorway to freedom*

dooryard ('dɔːˌjɑːd) *n* *US and Canadian* a yard in front of the front or back door of a house

doosra ('duːzrə) *n* a delivery, bowled by an off-spinner, that turns the opposite way from an off-break [c20 from Urdu, Hindi: second one, other one]

do out *vb* (*tr, adverb*) *informal* **1** to make tidy or clean; redecorate **2** (foll by *of*) to deprive (a person) of by swindling or cheating

do over *vb* (*tr, adverb*) **1** *informal* to renovate or redecorate **2** *Brit, Austral, and NZ slang* to beat up; thrash

doo-wop ('duːˌwɒp) *n* rhythm-and-blues harmony vocalizing developed by unaccompanied street-corner groups in the US in the 1950s [c20 of imitative origin]

doozy ('duːzɪ) *n, pl* -zies *slang* something excellent: *the plot's a doozy*

dop ('dɒp) *South African* ▷ *n* **1** *South African informal* a tot or small drink, usually alcoholic ▷ *vb* **2** to fail to reach the required standard in (an examination, course, etc) [Afrikaans]

dopa ('dəʊpə) *n* See **L-dopa**

dopamine ('dɒpəmɪn) *n* a chemical found in the brain that acts as a neurotransmitter and is an intermediate compound in the synthesis of noradrenaline. Formula: $(HO)_2C_6H_3(CH_2)_2NH_2$

[from *d(ihydr)o(xy)p(henylethyl)amine*]

dopant ('dəʊpənt) *n* an element or compound used to dope a semiconductor [c20 see DOPE, -ANT]

dope (dəʊp) *n* **1** any of a number of preparations made by dissolving cellulose derivatives in a volatile solvent, applied to fabric in order to improve strength, tautness, etc **2** an additive used to improve the properties of something, such as an antiknock compound added to petrol **3** a thick liquid, such as a lubricant, applied to a surface **4** a combustible absorbent material, such as sawdust or wood pulp, used to hold the nitroglycerine in dynamite **5** *slang* **a** any illegal drug, usually cannabis **b** (*as modifier*): *a dope fiend* **6** a drug administered to a racehorse or greyhound to affect its performance **7** *informal* a person considered to be stupid or slow-witted **8** *informal* news or facts, esp confidential information **9** *US and Canadian informal* a photographic developing solution ▷ *vb* (*tr*) **10** *electronics* to add impurities to (a semiconductor) in order to produce or modify its properties **11** to apply or add a dopant to **12** to administer a drug to (oneself or another) **13** (*intr*) to take dope ▷ *adj* **14** *slang, chiefly US* excellent [c19 from Dutch *doop* sauce, from *doopen* to DIP]

dope out *vb* (*tr, adverb*) *US slang* to devise, solve, or contrive: *to dope out a floor plan*

dope sheet *n* *horse racing slang* a publication giving information on horses running in races

dopester ('dəʊpstə) *n* *US and Canadian slang* a person who makes predictions, esp in sport or politics

dopey or **dopy** ('dəʊpɪ) *adj* dopier, dopiest **1** *slang* silly **2** *informal* half-asleep or in a state of semiconsciousness, as when under the influence of a drug ▷ '**dopily** *adv* ▷ '**dopiness** *n*

dopiaza ('dəʊpɪˌɑːzə) *n* (in Indian cookery) a dish of meat or fish cooked in an onion sauce: *lamb dopiaza* [c20 from Hindi: *do* two + *pyāz* onion]

doppelgänger ('dɒpˀlˌgɛŋə; *German* 'dɔpəlˌgɛŋər) *n* *legend* a ghostly duplicate of a living person [from German *Doppelgänger*, literally: double-goer]

Dopper ('dɒpə) *n* (in South Africa) a member of the most conservative Afrikaner Church, which practises a strict Calvinism [c19 from Afrikaans, of unknown origin]

doppio ('dɒpɪəʊ) *n* a double measure, esp of espresso coffee [c20 from Italian, literally: double]

Doppler effect ('dɒplə) *n* a phenomenon, observed for sound waves and electromagnetic radiation, characterized by a change in the apparent frequency of a wave as a result of relative motion between the observer and the source. Also called: **Doppler shift** [c19 named after C. J. Doppler (1803–53), Austrian physicist]

dor (dɔː) *n* any European dung beetle of the genus *Geotrupes* and related genera, esp *G. stercorarius*, having a droning flight [Old English *dora* bumblebee; related to Middle Low German *dorte* DRONE[1]]

dorado (dəˈrɑːdəʊ) *n* **1** another name for **dolphin** (sense 3) **2** a South American river fish of the genus *Salminus* that resembles a salmon

Dorado (dəˈrɑːdəʊ) *n, Latin genitive* Doradus (dəˈrɑːdəs) a constellation in the S hemisphere lying between Reticulum and Pictor and containing part of the Large Magellanic cloud [c17 from Spanish, from *dorar* to gild, from Latin DE- + -*aurāre*, from *aurum* gold]

dorba ('dɔːbə) *n* *Austral slang* a stupid, inept, or clumsy person. Also called: **dorb**

Dorcas ('dɔːkəs) *n* a charitable woman of Joppa (Acts 9:36–42)

Dorcas society *n* a Christian charitable society for women with the aim of providing clothes for the poor

Dorchester ('dɔːtʃɪstə) *n* a town in S England, administrative centre of Dorset: associated with Thomas Hardy, esp as the Casterbridge of his novels. Pop: 16 171 (2001). Latin name: Durnovaria (ˌdjɜːnəʊˈveɪrɪə)

Dordogne (*French* dɔrdɔɲ) *n* **1** a river in SW

France, rising in the Auvergne Mountains and flowing southwest and west to join the Garonne river and form the Gironde estuary. Length: 472 km (293 miles) **2** a department of SW France, in Aquitaine region. Capital: Périgueux. Pop: 392 291 (2003 est). Area: 9224 sq km (3597 sq miles)

Dordrecht (*Dutch* 'dɔrdrɛxt) *n* a port in the SW Netherlands, in South Holland province: chief port of the Netherlands until the 17th century. Pop: 120 000 (2003 est). Also called: **Dort**

doré ('dɔreɪ, -riː) *n* another name for **walleye** (the fish) [c18 from French, gilded; see DORY]

do-re-mi *n* *US slang* money [c20 pun on DOUGH (sense 3)]

Dorian ('dɔːrɪən) *n* **1** a member of a Hellenic people who invaded Greece around 1100 BC, overthrew the Mycenaean civilization, and settled chiefly in the Peloponnese ▷ *adj* **2** of or relating to this people or their dialect of Ancient Greek; Doric **3** *music* of or relating to a mode represented by the ascending natural diatonic scale from D to D. See also **Hypo-**

Doric ('dɒrɪk) *adj* **1** of or relating to the Dorians, esp the Spartans, or their dialect of Ancient Greek **2** of, denoting, or relating to one of the five classical orders of architecture: characterized by a column having no base, a heavy fluted shaft, and a capital consisting of an ovolo moulding beneath a square abacus. See also **Ionic, composite** (sense 4), **Corinthian, Tuscan 3** (*sometimes not capital*) rustic ▷ *n* **4** one of four chief dialects of Ancient Greek, spoken chiefly in the Peloponnese. Compare **Aeolic, Arcadic, Ionic.** See also **Attic** (sense 3) **5** any rural dialect, esp that spoken in the northeast of Scotland

doris ('dɒrɪs) *n* *slang* a woman [c20 from the girl's name *Doris*]

Doris[1] ('dɒrɪs) *n* (in ancient Greece) **1** a small landlocked area north of the Gulf of Corinth. Traditionally regarded as the home of the Dorians, it was perhaps settled by some of them during their southward migration **2** the coastal area of Caria in SW Asia Minor, settled by Dorians

Doris[2] ('dɒrɪs) *n* *Greek myth* a sea nymph

dork (dɔːk) *n* *slang* **1** a stupid or incompetent person **2** *US* a penis [c20 of unknown origin] ▷ '**dorky** *adj*

Dorking ('dɔːkɪŋ) *n* a heavy breed of domestic fowl [c19 after *Dorking*, town in Surrey]

Dorkland ('dɔːklənd) *n* *NZ informal* an offensive name for Auckland ▷ '**Dorklander** *n*

dorm (dɔːm) *n* *informal* short for **dormitory**

dormant ('dɔːmənt) *adj* **1** quiet and inactive, as during sleep **2** latent or inoperative **3** (of a volcano) neither extinct nor erupting **4** *biology* alive but in a resting torpid condition with suspended growth and reduced metabolism **5** (*usually postpositive*) *heraldry* (of a beast) in a sleeping position ▷ Compare **active, passive** [c14 from Old French *dormant*, from *dormir* to sleep, from Latin *dormīre*] ▷ '**dormancy** *n*

dormer ('dɔːmə) *n* a construction with a gable roof and a window at its outer end that projects from a sloping roof. Also called: **dormer window** [c16 from Old French *dormoir*, from Latin *dormītōrium* DORMITORY]

dormie or **dormy** ('dɔːmɪ) *adj golf* (of a player) as many holes ahead of an opponent as there are still to play: *dormie three* [c19 of unknown origin]

Dormition of the Blessed Virgin (dɔːˈmɪʃˀn) *n* another name for **Feast of the Assumption**: see **Assumption**

dormitory ('dɔːmɪtərɪ, -trɪ) *n, pl* -ries **1** a large room, esp at a school or institution, containing several beds **2** *US* a building, esp at a college or camp, providing living and sleeping accommodation **3** (*modifier*) *Brit* denoting or relating to an area from which most of the residents commute to work (esp in the phrase **dormitory suburb**) ▷ Often (for senses 1, 2) shortened to: **dorm** [c15 from Latin *dormītōrium*, from *dormīre* to sleep]

Dormobile ('dɔːməʊˌbiːl) *n trademark* a vanlike vehicle specially equipped for living in while travelling

dormouse ('dɔːˌmaʊs) *n, pl* -mice any small Old World rodent of the family *Gliridae*, esp the Eurasian *Muscardinus avellanarius*, resembling a mouse with a furry tail [c15 *dor*-, perhaps from Old French *dormir* to sleep, from Latin *dormīre* + MOUSE]

Dornbirn (*German* 'dɔrnbɪrn) *n* a city in W Austria, in Vorarlberg. Pop: 42 301 (2001)

dornick¹ ('dɔːnɪk) *or* **dorneck** *n* a heavy damask cloth, formerly used for vestments, curtains, etc [c15 from *Doornik* Tournai in Belgium where it was first manufactured]

dornick² ('dɔːnɪk) *n US* a small stone or pebble [c15 probably from Irish Gaelic *dornóg*, from *dorn* hand]

doronicum (dəˈrɒnɪkəm) *n* any plant of the Eurasian and N African genus *Doronicum*, such as leopard's-bane, having yellow daisy-like flower heads: family *Asteraceae* (composites) [c17 New Latin, from Arabic *dorūnaj*]

Dorothy Dixer (ˌdɒrəθɪ 'dɪksə) *n Austral informal* a parliamentary question asked by a member of the government so that the minister may give a prepared answer [from pen name *Dorothy Dix* of US journalist Elizabeth Meriwether (1870–1951), who wrote a column replying to correspondents' problems]

dorp (dɔːp) *n archaic except in South Africa* a small town or village [c16 from Dutch: village; related to THORP]

Dorpat ('dɔrpat) *n* the German name for **Tartu**

dorsad ('dɔːsæd) *adj anatomy* towards the back or dorsal aspect [c19 from Latin *dorsum* back + *ad* to, towards]

dorsal ('dɔːsəl) *adj* **1** *anatomy, zoology* relating to the back or spinal part of the body. Compare **ventral** (sense 1) **2** *botany* of, relating to, or situated on the side of an organ that is directed away from the axis **3** articulated with the back of the tongue, as the (k) sound in English *coot* [c15 from Medieval Latin *dorsālis*, from Latin *dorsum* back] > **'dorsally** *adv*

dorsal fin *n* any unpaired median fin on the backs of fishes and some other aquatic vertebrates: maintains balance during locomotion

Dorset ('dɔːsɪt) *n* a county in SW England, on the English Channel: mainly hilly but low-lying in the east: the geographical and ceremonial county includes Bournemouth and Poole, which became independent unitary authorities in 1997. Administrative centre: Dorchester. Pop (excluding unitary authorities): 398 200 (2003 est). Area (excluding unitary authorities): 2544 sq km (982 sq miles)

Dorset Down *n* a breed of stocky hornless sheep having a broad head, dark face, and a dense fleece: kept for lamb production

Dorset Horn *n* a breed of horned sheep with dense fine-textured wool

dorsiferous (dɔːˈsɪfərəs) *adj botany, zoology rare* bearing or carrying (young, spores, etc) on the back or dorsal surface

dorsiflexion (ˌdɔːsɪˈflɛkʃən) *n med* the bending back of a part, esp the hand or foot or their digits

dorsigrade ('dɔːsɪˌɡreɪd) *adj* (of animals such as certain armadillos) walking on the backs of the toes [c19 from Latin, from *dorsum* back + -GRADE]

dorsiventral (ˌdɔːsɪˈvɛntrəl) *adj* **1** (of leaves and similar flat parts) having distinct upper and lower faces **2** a variant spelling of **dorsoventral** > **dorsiventrality** (ˌdɔːsɪvɛnˈtrælɪtɪ) *n* > **ˌdorsiˈventrally** *adv*

dorso-, dorsi- *or before a vowel* **dors-** *combining form* indicating dorsum or dorsal: *dorsiventral*

dorsoventral (ˌdɔːsəʊˈvɛntrəl) *adj* **1** relating to both the dorsal and ventral sides; extending from the back to the belly **2** *botany* a variant spelling of **dorsiventral** > **dorsoˈventrally** *adv*

dorsum ('dɔːsəm) *n, pl* -sa (-sə) *anatomy* **1** a technical name for the **back 2** any analogous surface: *the dorsum of the hand* [c18 from Latin, literally: back]

Dort (Dutch dɔrt) *n* another name for **Dordrecht**

Dortmund ('dɔːtmənd; *German* 'dɔrtmʊnt) *n* an industrial city in W Germany, in North Rhine-Westphalia at the head of the **Dortmund–Ems Canal**: university (1966). Pop: 589 661 (2003 est)

dorty ('dɔːtɪ) *adj* dortier, dortiest *Scot* haughty, or sullen [c17 from Scottish *dort* peevishness] > **'dortiness** *n*

dory¹ ('dɔːrɪ) *n, pl* -ries **1** any spiny-finned marine teleost food fish of the family *Zeidae*, esp the John Dory, having a deep compressed body **2** another name for **walleye** (the fish) [c14 from French *dorée* gilded, from *dorer* to gild, from Late Latin *deaurāre*, ultimately from Latin *aurum* gold]

dory² ('dɔːrɪ) *n, pl* -ries *US and Canadian* a flat-bottomed rowing boat with a high bow, stern, and sides [c18 from Mosquito (an American Indian language of Honduras and Nicaragua) *dóri* dugout]

DOS (dɒs) *n trademark computing* acronym for disk-operating system, often prefixed, as in MS-DOS and PC-DOS; a computer operating system

dos-à-dos (ˌdəʊsɪˈdəʊ; *French* dozado) *n* **1** a seat on which the users sit back to back **2** an alternative spelling of **do-si-do** [literally: back to back]

dosage ('dəʊsɪdʒ) *n* **1** the administration of a drug or agent in prescribed amounts and at prescribed intervals **2** the optimum therapeutic dose and optimum interval between doses **3** another name for **dose** (senses 3, 4)

dose (dəʊs) *n* **1** *med* a specific quantity of a therapeutic drug or agent taken at any one time or at specified intervals **2** *informal* something unpleasant to experience: *a dose of influenza* **3** Also called: **dosage** the total energy of ionizing radiation absorbed by unit mass of material, esp of living tissue; usually measured in grays (SI unit) or rads **4** Also called: **dosage** a small amount of syrup added to wine, esp sparkling wine, when the sediment is removed and the bottle is corked **5** *slang* a venereal infection, esp gonorrhoea **6** like a dose of salts very quickly indeed ⊳ *vb* (*tr*) **7** to administer a dose or doses to (someone) **8** *med* to give (a therapeutic drug or agent) in appropriate quantities **9** (often foll by *up*) to give (someone, esp oneself) drugs, medicine, etc, esp in large quantities **10** to add syrup to (wine) during bottling [c15 from French, from Late Latin *dosis*, from Greek: a giving, from *didonai* to give] > **'doser** *n*

dose equivalent *n* a quantity that expresses the probability that exposure to ionizing radiation will cause biological effects. It is usually obtained by multiplying the dose by the quality factor of the radiation, but other factors may be considered. It is measured in sieverts (SI unit) or rems

dosh (dɒʃ) *n Brit* a slang word for **money** [c20 of unknown origin]

do-si-do (ˌdəʊsɪˈdəʊ) *n* **1** a square-dance figure in which dancers pass each other with right shoulders close or touching and circle back to back ⊳ *sentence substitute* **2** a call instructing dancers to perform such a figure ⊳ Also: dos-à-dos [c20 from DOS-À-DOS]

dosimeter (dəʊˈsɪmɪtə) *or* **dosemeter** ('dəʊsˌmiːtə) *n* an instrument for measuring the dose of X-rays or other radiation absorbed by matter or the intensity of a source of radiation > **dosimetric** (ˌdəʊsɪˈmɛtrɪk) *adj* > **dosimetrician** (ˌdəʊsɪmə'trɪʃən) *or* **do'simetrist** *n* > **do'simetry** *n*

dosing strip *n* (in New Zealand) an area set aside for treating dogs suspected of having hydatid disease

doss (dɒs) *Brit slang* ⊳ *vb* **1** (*intr*; often foll by *down*) to sleep, esp in a dosshouse **2** (*intr*; often foll by *around*) to pass time aimlessly ⊳ *n* **3** a bed, esp in a dosshouse **4** a slang word for **sleep 5** short for **dosshouse 6** a task or pastime requiring little effort: *making a film is a bit of a doss* [c18 of uncertain origin]

dossal *or* **dossel** ('dɒsəl) *n* an ornamental hanging, placed at the back of an altar or at the sides of a chancel [c17 from Medieval Latin *dossāle*, neuter of *dossālis*, variant of *dorsālis* DORSAL]

dosser¹ ('dɒsə) *n rare* a bag or basket for carrying objects on the back [c14 from Old French *dossier*, from Medieval Latin *dorsārium*, from Latin *dorsum* back]

dosser² ('dɒsə) *n* **1** *Brit slang* a person who sleeps in dosshouses **2** *Brit slang* another word for **dosshouse 3** *slang* a lazy person; idler

dosshouse ('dɒsˌhaʊs) *n Brit slang* a cheap lodging house, esp one used by tramps. US and Canadian name: flophouse

dossier ('dɒsɪˌeɪ, -sɪə; *French* dosje) *n* a collection of papers containing information on a particular subject or person [c19 from French: a file with a label on the back, from *dos* back, from Latin *dorsum*]

dost (dʌst) *vb archaic or dialect* (used with the pronoun *thou* or its relative equivalent) a singular form of the present tense (indicative mood) of **do¹**

dot¹ (dɒt) *n* **1** a small round mark made with or as with a pen, etc; spot; speck; point **2** anything resembling a dot; a small amount: *a dot of paint* **3** the mark (ˑ) that appears above the main stem of the letters *i, j* **4** *music* **a** the symbol (•) placed after a note or rest to increase its time value by half **b** this symbol written above or below a note indicating that it must be played or sung staccato **5** *maths, logic* **a** the symbol (.) indicating multiplication or logical conjunction **b** a decimal point **6** the symbol (•) used, in combination with the symbol for *dash* (–), in the written representation of Morse and other telegraphic codes. Compare **dit 7** the year dot *informal* as long ago as can be remembered **8** on the dot at exactly the arranged time ⊳ *vb* dots, dotting, dotted **9** (*tr*) to mark or form with a dot: *to dot a letter; a dotted crotchet* **10** (*tr*) to scatter or intersperse (with dots or something resembling dots): *bushes dotting the plain* **11** (*intr*) to make a dot or dots **12** dot one's i's and cross one's t's to pay meticulous attention to detail [Old English *dott* head of a boil; related to Old High German *tutta* nipple, Norwegian *dott*, Dutch *dott* lump] > **'dotter** *n*

dot² (dɒt) *n civil law* a woman's dowry [c19 from French, from Latin *dōs*; related to *dōtāre* to endow, *dāre* to give] > **dotal** ('dəʊtəl) *adj*

dotage ('dəʊtɪdʒ) *n* **1** feebleness of mind, esp as a result of old age **2** foolish infatuation [c14 from DOTE + -AGE]

dotard ('dəʊtəd) *n* a person who is weak-minded, esp through senility [c14 from DOTE + -ARD] > **'dotardly** *adj*

dotation (dəʊˈteɪʃən) *n law* the act of giving a dowry; endowment [c14 from Latin *dōtātiō*, from *dōtāre* to endow]

dot ball *n cricket* a ball from which a run is not scored [when no run is scored, the scorer places a dot in his or her record book]

dotcom *or* **dot.com** (ˌdɒt'kɒm) *n* **a** a company that conducts most of its business on the internet **b** (*as modifier*): *dotcom stocks* [c20 from .com, the domain name suffix of businesses trading on the internet]

dotcommer (dɒt'kɒmə) *n* a person who carries out business on the internet

dote *or now rarely* **doat** (dəʊt) *vb* (*intr*) **1** (foll by *on* or *upon*) to love to an excessive or foolish degree **2** to be foolish or weak-minded, esp as a result of old age [c13 related to Middle Dutch *doten* to be silly, Norwegian *dudra* to shake] > **'doter** *or now rarely* **'doater** *n*

doth (dʌθ) *vb archaic or dialect* (used with the pronouns *he, she, or it* or with a noun) a singular form of the present tense of **do¹**

dot-matrix printer *n computing* a printer in which each character is produced as an array of dots by a printhead

dot product *n* another name for **scalar product**

d

dotted ('dɒtɪd) *adj* **1** having dots, esp having a pattern of dots **2** *music* **a** (of a note) increased to one and a half times its original time value. See dot[1] (sense 4) **b** (of a musical rhythm) characterized by dotted notes. Compare **double-dotted**. See also **notes inégales**

dotted line *n* **1** a line of dots or dashes on a form or document **2 sign on the dotted line** to agree formally, esp by signing one's name on a document

dotterel *or* **dottrel** ('dɒtrəl) *n* **1** a rare Eurasian plover, *Eudromias morinellus*, with reddish-brown underparts and white bands around the head and neck **2** *Austral* any similar and related bird, esp of the genus *Charadrius* **3** *dialect* a person who is foolish or easily duped [C15 *dotterelle*; see DOTE]

dottle *or* **dottel** ('dɒt³l) *n* the plug of tobacco left in a pipe after smoking [C15 diminutive of *dot* lump; see DOT[1]]

dotty ('dɒtɪ) *adj* **-tier, -tiest 1** *slang, chiefly Brit* feeble-minded; slightly crazy **2** *Brit slang* (foll by *about*) extremely fond (of) **3** marked with dots [C19 from DOT[1]: sense development of 1 from meaning of "unsteady on one's feet"] > 'dottily *adv* > 'dottiness *n*

Douai ('du:eɪ; *French* dwɛ) *n* an industrial city in N France: the political and religious centre of exiled English Roman Catholics in the 16th and 17th centuries. Pop: 42 796 (1999)

Douala *or* **Duala** (duˈɑːlə) *n* the chief port and largest city in W Cameroon, on the Bight of Bonny: capital of the German colony of Kamerun (1901–16). Pop: 1 980 000 (2005 est)

Douay Bible *or* **Version** ('du:eɪ) *n* an English translation of the Bible from the Latin Vulgate text completed by Roman Catholic scholars at Douai in 1610

double ('dʌb³l) *adj* (*usually prenominal*) **1** as much again in size, strength, number, etc: *a double portion* **2** composed of two equal or similar parts; in a pair; twofold: *a double egg cup* **3** designed for two users: *a double room* **4** folded in two; composed of two layers: *double paper* **5** stooping; bent over **6** having two aspects or existing in two different ways; ambiguous: *a double meaning* **7** false, deceitful, or hypocritical: *a double life* **8** (of flowers) having more than the normal number of petals **9** *maths* **a** (of a root) being one of two equal roots of a polynomial equation **b** (of an integral) having an integrand containing two independent variables requiring two integrations, in each of which one variable is kept constant **10** *music* **a** (of an instrument) sounding an octave lower than the pitch indicated by the notation: *a double bass* **b** (of time) duple, usually accompanied by the direction *alla breve* ▷ *adv* **11** twice over; twofold **12** two together; two at a time (esp in the phrase **see double**) ▷ *n* **13** twice the number, amount, size, etc **14** a double measure of spirits, such as whisky or brandy **15** a duplicate or counterpart, esp a person who closely resembles another; understudy **16** a wraith or ghostly apparition that is the exact counterpart of a living person; doppelgänger **17** a sharp turn, esp a return on one's own tracks **18** an evasive shift or artifice; trick **19** an actor who plays two parts in one play **20** *bridge* a call that increases certain scoring points if the last preceding bid becomes the contract **21** *billiards, snooker* a strike in which the object ball is struck so as to make it rebound against the cushion to an opposite pocket **22** a bet on two horses in different races in which any winnings from the horse in the first race are placed on the horse in the later race **23** (*often capital*) *chiefly RC Church* one of the higher-ranking feasts on which the antiphons are recited both before and after the psalms **24** *music* an ornamented variation in 16th and 17th century music **25** Also called: **double time** a pace of twice the normal marching speed **26** *tennis* See **double fault 27 a** the narrow outermost ring on a dartboard **b** a hit on this ring **28 at** *or* **on the**

double **a** at twice normal marching speed **b** quickly or immediately ▷ *vb* **29** to make or become twice as much **30** to bend or fold (material, a bandage, etc) **31** (*tr*; sometimes foll by *up*) to clench (a fist) **32** (*tr*; often foll by *together* or *up*) to join or couple: *he doubled up the team* **33** (*tr*) to repeat exactly; copy **34** (*intr*) to play two parts or serve two roles **35** (*intr*) to turn sharply; follow a winding course **36** *nautical* to sail around (a headland or other point) **37** *music* **a** to duplicate (a voice or instrumental part) either in unison or at the octave above or below it **b** (*intr*; usually foll by *on*) to be capable of performing (upon an instrument additional to one's normal one): *the third trumpeter doubles on cornet* **38** *bridge* to make a call that will double certain scoring points if the preceding bid becomes the contract **39** *billiards, snooker* to cause (a ball) to rebound or (of a ball) to rebound from a cushion across or up or down the table **40** *chess* **a** to cause two pawns of the same colour to be on the same file **b** to place both rooks of the same colour on the same rank or the same file **41** (*intr*; foll by *for*) to act as substitute (for an actor or actress) **42** (*intr*) to go or march at twice the normal speed ▷ See also **double back, doubles, double up** [C13 from Old French, from Latin *duplus* twofold, from *duo* two + *-plus* -FOLD] > 'doubleness *n* > 'doubler *n*

double-acting *adj* **1** (of a reciprocating engine or pump) having a piston or pistons that are pressurized alternately on opposite sides. Compare **single-acting 2** (of a hinge, door, etc) having complementary actions in opposed directions

double agent *n* a spy employed by two mutually antagonistic countries, companies, etc

double-aspect theory *n philosophy* a monistic theory that holds that mind and body are not distinct substances but merely different aspects of a single substance

double back *vb* (*intr, adverb*) to go back in the opposite direction (esp in the phrase **to double back on one's tracks**)

double-bank *vb Austral and NZ informal* to carry a second person on (a horse, bicycle, etc). Also: **dub**

double bar *n music* a symbol, consisting of two ordinary bar lines or a single heavy one, that marks the end of a composition or a section within it

double-barrelled *or US* **double-barreled** *adj* **1** (of a gun) having two barrels **2** extremely forceful or vehement **3** *Brit* (of a surname) having hyphenated parts **4** serving two purposes; ambiguous: *a double-barrelled remark*

double bass (beɪs) *n* **1** Also called (US): **bass viol** a stringed instrument, the largest and lowest member of the violin family. Range: almost three octaves upwards from E in the space between the fourth and fifth leger lines below the bass staff. It is normally bowed in classical music, but it is very common in a jazz or dance band, where it is practically always played pizzicato. Informal name: **bass fiddle** ▷ *adj* **double-bass 2** of or relating to an instrument whose pitch lies below that regarded as the bass; contrabass

double bassoon *n music* the lowest and largest instrument in the oboe class; contrabassoon

double bill *n* a programme or event with two main items

double bind *n* a situation of conflict from which there is no escape; unresolvable dilemma

double-blind *adj* of or relating to an experiment to discover reactions to certain commodities, drugs, etc, in which neither the experimenters nor the subjects know the particulars of the test items during the experiments. Compare **single-blind**

double boiler *n US and Canadian* a cooking utensil consisting of two saucepans, one fitting inside the other. The bottom saucepan contains water that, while boiling, gently heats food in the upper pan. Also called (in Britain and certain other

countries): **double saucepan**

double bond *n* a type of chemical bond consisting of two covalent bonds linking two atoms in a molecule

double-breasted *adj* (of a garment) having overlapping fronts such as to give a double thickness of cloth

double bridle *n* a bridle with four reins coming from a bit with two rings on each side

double-check *vb* **1** to check twice or again; verify ▷ *n* **double check 2** a second examination or verification **3** *chess* a simultaneous check from two pieces brought about by moving one piece to give check and thereby revealing a second check from another piece

double chin *n* a fold of fat under the chin > ˌdouble-'chinned *adj*

double concerto *n* a concerto for two solo instruments

double cream *n* thick cream with a high fat-content

double cross *n* a technique for producing hybrid stock, esp seed for cereal crops, by crossing the hybrids between two different pairs of inbred lines

double-cross *vb* **1** (*tr*) to cheat or betray ▷ *n* **2** the act or an instance of double-crossing; betrayal > 'double-'crosser *n*

double dagger *n* a character (‡) used in printing to indicate a cross reference, esp to a footnote. Also called: **diesis, double obelisk**

double day *n* the dual responsibilities borne by working mothers, who when their paid work is over for the day must then work at looking after their family and home

double-dealing *n* **a** action characterized by treachery or deceit **b** (*as modifier*): *double-dealing treachery* > 'double-'dealer *n*

double-decker *n* **1** *chiefly Brit* a bus with two passenger decks **2** *informal* **a** a thing or structure having two decks, layers, etc **b** (*as modifier*): *a double-decker sandwich*

double-declutch *vb* (*intr*) *Brit* to change to a lower gear in a motor vehicle by first placing the gear lever into the neutral position before engaging the desired gear, at the same time releasing the clutch pedal and increasing the engine speed. US term: **double-clutch**

double decomposition *n* a chemical reaction between two compounds that results in the interchange of one part of each to form two different compounds, as in $AgNO_3 + KI \rightarrow AgI + KNO_3$. Also called: **metathesis**

double density *computing n* a disk with more than the normal capacity for storage

double digging *n Brit* a method of digging ground in a series of trenches two spits deep, mixing the soil of the bottom spit with manure, and then transferring the soil from the top spit of one trench to the top spit of the preceding one

double dip *n economics* **a** a recession in which a brief recovery in output is followed by another fall, because demand remains low **b** (*as modifier*): *a double-dip recession*

double-dotted *adj music* **1** (of a note) increased to one and three quarters of its original time value by the addition of two dots **2** (of a rhythm) characterized by pairs of notes in which the first one, lengthened by two dots, makes up seven eighths of the time value of the pair

double-double *n Canadian* a cup of coffee served with two helpings of cream and sugar

double drummer *n Austral informal* a type of cicada

double-dumped *adj NZ* (of a wool bale) compressed, with two bales occupying the volume-equivalent of one ordinary bale

double Dutch *n Brit informal* incomprehensible talk; gibberish

double-dyed *adj* **1** confirmed; inveterate: *a double-dyed villain* **2** dyed twice

double eagle *n* a former US gold coin, having a

nominal value of 20 dollars

double-edged *adj* **1** acting in two ways; having a dual effect: *a double-edged law* **2** (of a remark, argument, etc) having two possible interpretations, esp applicable both for and against or being really malicious though apparently innocuous **3** (of a sword, knife, etc) having a cutting edge on either side of the blade

double entendre ('dʌbᵊl dʌn'tʊ:ndrə, -'tɑ:nd; *French* dubl ɑ̃tɑ̃drə) *n* **1** a word, phrase, etc, that can be interpreted in two ways, esp one having one meaning that is indelicate **2** the type of humour that depends upon such ambiguity [c17 from obsolete French: double meaning]

double entry *n* **a** a book-keeping system in which any commercial transaction is entered as a debit in one account and as a credit in another. Compare **single entry b** (*as modifier*): *double-entry book-keeping*

double exposure *n* **1** the act or process of recording two superimposed images on a photographic medium, usually done intentionally to produce a special effect **2** the photograph resulting from such an act

double-faced *adj* **1** (of textiles) having a finished nap on each side; reversible **2** insincere or deceitful

double fault *tennis* ▷ *n* **1** the serving of two faults in succession, thereby losing a point ▷ *vb* **double-fault** **2** (*intr*) to serve a double fault

double feature *n films* a programme showing two full-length films. Informal name (US): twin bill

double first *n Brit* a first-class honours degree in two subjects

double flat *n* **1** *music* **a** an accidental that lowers the pitch of the following note two semitones. Usual symbol: ♭ **b** a note affected by this accidental ▷ *adj* **double-flat 2** (*postpositive*) denoting a note of a given letter name lowered in pitch by two semitones

double glazing *n* **1** two panes of glass in a window, fitted to reduce the transmission of heat, sound, etc **2** the fitting of glass in such a manner

double Gloucester *n* a type of smooth orange-red cheese of mild flavour

double-header *n* **1** a train drawn by two locomotives coupled together to provide extra power **2** Also called: twin bill *sport, US and Canadian* two games played consecutively by the same teams or by two different teams **3** *Austral and NZ informal* a coin with the impression of a head on each side **4** *Austral informal* a double ice-cream cone

double-helical gear *n* another name for herringbone gear

double helix *n biochem* the form of the molecular structure of DNA, consisting of two helical polynucleotide chains linked by hydrogen bonds and coiled around the same axis

double-hung *adj* (of a window) having two vertical sashes, the upper one sliding in grooves outside those of the lower

double indemnity *n US and Canadian* (in life assurance policies) a clause providing for the payment of double the policy's face value in the event of the policyholder's accidental death

double jeopardy *n* the act of prosecuting a defendant a second time for an offence for which he has already been tried

double-jointed *adj* having unusually flexible joints permitting an abnormal degree of motion of the parts

double knit *n* **a** a knitted material made on two sets of needles that produce a double thickness joined with interlocking stitches **b** (*as modifier*): *a double-knit fabric*

double knitting *n* **a** a widely used medium thickness of knitting wool **b** (*as modifier*): *double-knitting wool*

double-minded *adj rare* undecided; vacillating ▷ ˌdouble-ˈmindedness *n*

double negation *n logic* the principle that a statement is equivalent to the denial of its negation, as *it is not the case that John is not here* meaning *John is here*

double negative *n* a syntactic construction, often considered ungrammatical in standard Modern English, in which two negatives are used where one is needed, as in *I wouldn't never have believed it*

> **USAGE** There are two contexts where double negatives are used. An adjective with negative force is often used with a negative in order to express a nuance of meaning somewhere between the positive and the negative: *he was a not infrequent visitor; it is a not uncommon sight*. Two negatives are also found together where they reinforce each other rather than conflict: *he never went back, not even to collect his belongings*. These two uses of what is technically a double negative are acceptable. A third case, illustrated by *I shouldn't wonder if it didn't rain today*, has the force of a weak positive statement (*I expect it to rain today*) and is common in informal English

double obelisk *n* another name for **double dagger**

double or quits *n* a game, throw, toss, etc, to decide whether the stake due is to be doubled or cancelled

double-park *vb* to park (a car or other vehicle) alongside or directly opposite another already parked by the roadside, thereby causing an obstruction

double play *n baseball* a play in which two runners are put out

double pneumonia *n* pneumonia affecting both lungs

double printing *n photog* the exposure of the same positive photographic emulsion to two or more negatives, resulting in the superimposition of multiple images after development

double-quick *adj* **1** very quick; rapid ▷ *adv* **2** in a very quick or rapid manner

double-reed *adj* relating to or denoting a wind instrument in which the sounds are produced by air passing over two reeds that vibrate against each other

double refraction *n* the splitting of a ray of unpolarized light into two unequally refracted rays polarized in mutually perpendicular planes. Also called: birefringence

doubles ('dʌbᵊlz) *n* (*functioning as plural*) **a** a game between two pairs of players, as in tennis, badminton, etc **b** (*as modifier*): *a doubles player*

double salt *n* a solid solution of two simple salts formed by crystallizing a solution of the two salts. Compare **complex salt**

double saucepan *n Brit* a cooking utensil consisting of two saucepans, one fitting inside the other. The bottom saucepan contains water that, while boiling, gently heats food in the upper pan. US and Canadian name: double boiler

double scull *n rowing* a racing shell in which two scullers sit one behind the other and pull two oars each. Compare **pair-oar**

double sharp *n* **1** *music* **a** an accidental that raises the pitch of the following note by two semitones. Usual symbol: × **b** a note affected by this accidental ▷ *adj* **2** (*immediately postpositive*) denoting a note of a given letter name raised in pitch by two semitones

double-space *vb* to type (copy) with a full space between lines

doublespeak ('dʌbᵊlˌspi:k) *n* the practice of using ambiguous language regarding political, military, or corporate matters in a deliberate attempt to disguise the truth

double spread *n printing* two facing pages of a

publication treated as a single unit

double standard *n* a set of principles that allows greater freedom to one person or group than to another

double star *n* two stars, appearing close together when viewed through a telescope; either physically associated (see **binary star**) or not associated (**optical double star**)

double stop *vb* **stops, stopping, stopped** to play (two notes or parts) simultaneously on a violin or related instrument by drawing the bow over two strings

double-system sound recording *n films* a system in which picture and sound are taken simultaneously and the sound is recorded separately on magnetic tape

doublet ('dʌblɪt) *n* **1** (formerly) a man's close-fitting jacket, with or without sleeves (esp in the phrase **doublet and hose.**) **2 a** a pair of similar things, esp two words deriving ultimately from the same source, for example *reason* and *ratio* or *fragile* and *frail* **b** one of such a pair **3** *jewellery* a false gem made by welding a thin layer of a gemstone onto a coloured glass base or by fusing two small stones together to make a larger one **4** *physics* **a** a multiplet that has two members **b** a closely spaced pair of related spectral lines **5** (*plural*) two dice each showing the same number of spots on one throw **6** *physics* two simple lenses designed to be used together, the optical distortion in one being balanced by that in the other [c14 from Old French, from DOUBLE]

double tackle *n* a lifting or pulling tackle in which a rope is passed around the twin pulleys of a pair of pulley blocks in sequence

double take *n* (esp in comedy) a delayed reaction by a person to a remark, situation, etc

double talk *n* **1** rapid speech with a mixture of nonsense syllables and real words; gibberish **2** empty, deceptive, or ambiguous talk, esp by politicians

doublethink ('dʌbᵊlˌθɪŋk) *n* deliberate, perverse, or unconscious acceptance or promulgation of conflicting facts, principles, etc

double time *n* **1** a doubled wage rate, paid for working on public holidays, etc **2** *music* **a** a time twice as fast as an earlier section **b** two beats per bar **3** a slow running pace, keeping in step **4** *US army* a fast march of 180 paces to the minute ▷ *vb* **double-time 5** to move or cause to move in double time

doubleton ('dʌbᵊltən) *n bridge* an original holding of two cards only in a suit

double-tongue *vb* **-tongues, -tonguing, -tongued** *music* to play (fast staccato passages) on a wind instrument by rapid obstruction and uncovering of the air passage through the lips with the tongue. Compare **single-tongue, triple-tongue** ▷ double tonguing *n*

double-tongued *adj* deceitful or hypocritical in speech

double top *n darts* a score of double 20

doubletree ('dʌbᵊlˌtri:) *n* a horizontal pivoted bar on a vehicle to the ends of which swingletrees are attached for harnessing two horses side by side

double up *vb* (*adverb*) **1** to bend or cause to bend in two: *he doubled up with the pain* **2** (*intr*) to share a room or bed designed for one person, family, etc **3** (*intr*) *Brit* to use the winnings from one bet as the stake for another. US and Canadian term: parlay

doubloon (dʌ'blu:n) *or* **doblón** *n* **1** a former Spanish gold coin **2** (*plural*) *slang* money [c17 from Spanish *doblón*, from DOBLA]

doublure (də'blʊə; *French* dublyr) *n* a decorative lining of vellum or leather, etc, on the inside of a book cover [c19 from French: lining, from Old French *doubler* to make double]

doubly ('dʌblɪ) *adv* **1** to or in a double degree, quantity, or measure: *doubly careful* **2** in two ways: *doubly wrong*

Doubs (*French* du) *n* **1** a department of E France, in Franche-Comté region. Capital: Besançon. Pop:

d

505 557 (2003 est). Area: 5258 sq km (2030 sq miles) **2** a river in E France, rising in the Jura Mountains, becoming part of the border between France and Switzerland and flowing generally southwest to the Saône River. Length: 430 km (267 miles)

doubt (daʊt) *n* **1** uncertainty about the truth, fact, or existence of something (esp in the phrases **in doubt, without doubt, beyond a shadow of doubt,** etc) **2** (*often plural*) lack of belief in or conviction about something: *all his doubts about the project disappeared* **3** an unresolved difficulty, point, etc **4** *philosophy* the methodical device, esp in the philosophy of Descartes, of identifying certain knowledge as the residue after rejecting any proposition which might, however improbably, be false **5** *obsolete* fear **6 give (someone) the benefit of the doubt** to presume (someone suspected of guilt) innocent; judge leniently **7 no doubt** almost certainly ▷ *vb* **8** (*tr; may take a clause as object*) to be inclined to disbelieve: *I doubt we are late* **9** (*tr*) to distrust or be suspicious of: *he doubted their motives* **10** (*intr*) to feel uncertainty or be undecided **11** (*tr; may take a clause as object*) *Scot* to be inclined to believe **12** (*tr*) *archaic* to fear **13 I wouldn't doubt (someone)** *Irish* I would expect nothing else from (someone) [c13 from Old French *douter,* from Latin *dubitāre*] > 'doubtable *adj* > 'doubtably *adv* > 'doubter *n* > 'doubtingly *adv*

USAGE Where a clause follows *doubt* in a positive sentence, it was formerly considered correct to use *whether:* (I doubt whether he will come), but now *if* and *that* are also acceptable. In negative statements, *doubt* is followed by *that:* (*I do not doubt that he is telling the truth.* In such sentences, but (*I do not doubt but that he is telling the truth*) is redundant

doubtful ('daʊtfʊl) *adj* **1** unlikely; improbable **2** characterized by or causing doubt; uncertain: *a doubtful answer* **3** unsettled; unresolved **4** of questionable reputation or morality **5** having reservations or misgivings **6** (of a sportsperson) not likely to be fit enough to play or take part ▷ *n* **7** a person who is undecided or uncertain about an issue **8** a sportsperson who is not likely to be fit enough to play or take part > 'doubtfully *adv* > 'doubtfulness *n*

USAGE It was formerly considered correct to use *whether* after *doubtful* (it is doubtful whether he will come), but now *if* and *that* are also acceptable

doubting Thomas *n* a person who insists on proof before he will believe anything; sceptic [after THOMAS (the apostle), who did not believe that Jesus had been resurrected until he had proof]

doubtless ('daʊtlɪs) *adv also* doubtlessly (*sentence substitute or sentence modifier*) **1** certainly **2** probably ▷ *adj* **3** certain; assured > 'doubtlessness *n*

douc (duːk) *n* an Old World monkey, *Pygathrix nemaeus,* of SE Asia, with a bright yellow face surrounded by tufts of reddish-brown fur, a white tail, and white hindquarters: one of the langurs [c18 from French, from the native name]

douce (duːs) *adj Scot and northern English dialect* quiet; sober; sedate [c14 from Old French, feminine of *dous,* from Latin *dulcis* sweet] > 'doucely *adv*

douceur (duːˈsɜː; *French* dusœr) *n* **1** a gratuity, tip, or bribe **2** sweetness [c17 from French, from Late Latin *dulcor,* from Latin *dulcis* sweet]

douche (duːʃ) *n* **1** a stream of water or air directed onto the body surface or into a body cavity, for cleansing or medical purposes **2** the application of such a stream of water or air **3** an instrument, such as a special syringe, for applying a douche ▷ *vb* **4** to cleanse or treat or be cleansed or treated by means of a douche [c18 from French, from Italian *doccia,* pipe; related to Latin *ductus* DUCT]

douche bag *n* **1** the bag forming part of a douche

2 *slang* a contemptible person

dough (dəʊ) *n* **1** a thick mixture of flour or meal and water or milk, used for making bread, pastry, etc **2** any similar pasty mass **3** a slang word for **money** [Old English *dāg;* related to Old Norse *deig,* Gothic *daigs,* Old High German *teig* dough, Sanskrit *degdhi* he daubs; see DAIRY, DUFF¹, LADY]

doughboy ('dəʊˌbɔɪ) *n* **1** *US informal* an infantryman, esp in World War I **2** dough that is boiled or steamed as a dumpling

doughnut *or esp US* **donut** ('dəʊnʌt) *n* **1** a small cake of sweetened dough, often ring-shaped or spherical with a jam or cream filling, cooked in hot fat **2** anything shaped like a ring, such as the reaction vessel of a thermonuclear reactor ▷ *vb* -nuts, -nutting, -nutted **3** (*tr*) *informal* (of Members of Parliament) to surround (a speaker) during the televising of Parliament to give the impression that the chamber is crowded or the speaker is well supported

doughty ('daʊtɪ) *adj* -tier, -tiest hardy; resolute [Old English *dohtig;* related to Old High German *toht* worth, Middle Dutch *duchtich* strong, Greek *tukhē* luck] > 'doughtily *adv* > 'doughtiness *n*

doughy ('dəʊɪ) *adj* doughier, doughiest resembling dough in consistency, colour, etc; soft, pallid, or flabby

Douglas ('dʌɡləs) *n* a town and resort on the Isle of Man, capital of the island, on the E coast. Pop: 25 347 (2001)

Douglas fir, spruce *or* **hemlock** *n* a North American pyramidal coniferous tree, *Pseudotsuga menziesii,* widely planted for ornament and for timber, having needle-like leaves and hanging cones: family *Pinaceae.* Also called: **Oregon fir, Oregon pine** [c19 named after David *Douglas* (1798–1834), Scottish botanist]

Douglas Hurd (ˌdʌɡləs 'hɜːd) *n Brit informal* a third-class university degree. Often shortened to: **Douglas** [c20 from rhyming slang, after Douglas *Hurd* (born 1930), British Conservative politician]

Douglas scale *n* an international scale of sea disturbance and swell ranging from 0 to 9 with one figure for disturbance and one for swell [c20 named after Sir Henry *Douglas* (1876–1939), former director of the British Naval Meteorological Service]

douk (dʊk) *n* a variant spelling of **dook¹, dook²**

Doukhobor *or* **Dukhobor** ('duːkəʊˌbɔː) *n* a member of a Russian sect of Christians that originated in the 18th century. In the late 19th century a large minority emigrated to W Canada, where most Doukhobors now live [from Russian *dukhoborcy* spirit wrestler, from *dukh* spirit + *borcy* wrestler]

doula ('duːlə) *n* a woman who is trained to provide support to women and their families during pregnancy, childbirth, and the period of time following the birth [c20 from Greek *doule* female slave]

douma *Russian* ('duːmə) *n* a variant spelling of **duma**

doum palm *or* **doom palm** (duːm) *n* an Egyptian palm tree, *Hyphaene thebaica,* with a divided trunk and edible apple-sized fruits [c19 *doum,* via French from Arabic *dawm*]

doun (duːn) *prep, adv, adj* a variant spelling of **doon**

Dounreay (duːnˈreɪ) *n* the site in N Scotland of a nuclear power station, which contained the world's first fast-breeder reactor (1962–77). A prototype fast-breeder operated from 1974 until 1994: a nuclear fuel re-processing plant has also operated at the site

do up *vb* (*adverb; mainly tr*) **1** to wrap and make into a bundle: *to do up a parcel* **2** to cause the downfall of (a person) **3** to beautify or adorn **4** (*also intr*) to fasten or be fastened: *this skirt does up at the back* **5** *informal* to renovate or redecorate **6** *slang* to assault

dour (dʊə, 'daʊə) *adj* **1** sullen **2** hard or obstinate [c14 probably from Latin *dūrus* hard] > 'dourly *adv* > 'dourness *n*

doura ('dʊərə) *n* a variant of **durra**

dourine ('dʊəriːn) *n* an infectious venereal disease of horses characterized by swollen glands, inflamed genitals, and paralysis of the hindquarters, caused by the protozoan *Trypanosoma equiperdum* contracted during copulation [c19 from French, from Arabic *darina* to be dirty, scabby]

Douro ('dʊərəʊ; *Portuguese* 'doru) *n* a river in SW Europe, rising in N central Spain and flowing west to NE Portugal, then south as part of the border between the two countries and finally west to the Atlantic. Length: 895 km (556 miles). Spanish name: **Duero**

douroucouli (ˌdʊːruːˈkuːlɪ) *n* a nocturnal omnivorous New World monkey, *Aotus trivirgatus,* of Central and South America, with large eyes, thick fur, and a round head with pale and dark markings [from a South American Indian name]

douse¹ *or* **dowse** (daʊs) *vb* **1** to plunge or be plunged into water or some other liquid; duck **2** (*tr*) to drench with water, esp in order to wash or clean **3** (*tr*) to put out (a light, candle, etc) ▷ *n* **4** an immersion [c16 perhaps related to obsolete *douse* to strike, of obscure origin] > 'douser *or* 'dowser *n*

douse² (daʊs) *vb* (*tr*) **1** *nautical* to lower (sail) quickly **2** *archaic* to strike or beat ▷ *n* **3** *archaic* a blow [c16 of uncertain origin; perhaps related to DOUSE¹]

D out *vb* (*adverb*) *Austral slang* (in sport) to prevent an opponent from attacking by using successful defence techniques

douzepers ('duːzˌpɛəz) *pl n French history* the 12 great peers of the realm, seen as the symbolic heirs of Charlemagne's 12 chosen peers [c13 from Old French *douze pers;* see DOZEN, PEER¹]

DOVAP ('dəʊˌvæp) *n* a tracking system for determining the position and velocity of spacecraft, missiles, etc, based on the Doppler effect [c20 from *Do(ppler) v(elocity) a(nd) p(osition)*]

dove¹ (dʌv) *n* **1** any of various birds of the family *Columbidae,* having a heavy body, small head, short legs, and long pointed wings: order *Columbiformes.* They are typically smaller than pigeons. Related adj: **columbine 2** *politics* a person opposed to war. Compare **hawk¹** (sense 3) **3** a gentle or innocent person: used as a term of endearment **4 a** a greyish-brown colour **b** (*as adjective*): *dove walls* [Old English *dūfe* (unattested except as a feminine proper name); related to Old Saxon *dūbva,* Old High German *tūba*] > 'doveˌlike *adj* > 'dovish *adj*

dove² (dəʊv) *vb chiefly US* a past tense of **dive**

Dove (dʌv) *n Christianity* **the** a manifestation of the Holy Spirit (John 1:32)

dovecote ('dʌvˌkəʊt) *or* **dovecot** ('dʌvˌkɒt) *n* a structure for housing pigeons, often raised on a pole or set on a wall, containing compartments for the birds to roost and lay eggs

dovekie *or* **dovekey** ('dʌvkɪ) *n* another name for the **little auk** (see **auk**) [c19 Scottish diminutive of DOVE¹]

dove prion *n* a common petrel, *Pachyptila desolata,* of the southern seas, having a bluish back and white underparts. Also called: Antarctic prion, (NZ informal) blue billy

Dover ('dəʊvə) *n* **1** a port in SE England, in E Kent on the Strait of Dover: the only one of the Cinque Ports that is still important; a stronghold since ancient times and Caesar's first point of attack in the invasion of Britain (55 BC). Pop: 34 087 (2001) **2 Strait of** a strait between SE England and N France, linking the English Channel with the North Sea. Width: about 32 km (20 miles). French name: Pas de Calais **3** a city in the US, the capital of Delaware, founded in 1683: 18th-century buildings. Pop: 32 808 (2003 est)

Dover's powder *n* a preparation of opium and ipecacuanha, formerly used to relieve pain, induce sweating, and check spasms [c19 named after Thomas *Dover* (1660–1742), English physician]

dovetail ('dʌvˌteɪl) *n* **1** a wedge-shaped tenon **2** Also called: dovetail joint a joint containing such tenons ▷ *vb* **3** (*tr*) to join by means of dovetails **4** to fit or cause to fit together closely or neatly: *he dovetailed his arguments to the desired conclusion*

dovetail saw *n building trades* a saw similar to a tenon saw but of smaller size

dowable ('daʊəbᵊl) *adj law* **1** capable of being endowed **2** (of a person, esp a widow) entitled to dower

dowager ('daʊədʒə) *n* **1 a** a widow possessing property or a title obtained from her husband **b** (*as modifier*): *the dowager duchess* **2** a wealthy or dignified elderly woman [C16 from Old French *douagiere*, from *douage* DOWER]

dowdy ('daʊdɪ) *adj* -dier, -diest **1** (esp of a woman's dress) drab, unflattering, and old-fashioned ▷ *n, pl* -dies **2** a dowdy woman [C14 *dowd* slut, of unknown origin] > 'dowdily *adv* > 'dowdiness *n* > 'dowdyish *adj*

dowel ('daʊəl) *n* a wooden or metal peg that fits into two corresponding holes to join two adjacent parts. Also called: dowel pin [C14 from Middle Low German *dövel*, from Old High German *tubili*; related to Greek *thuphos* wedge]

doweling or **dowelling** ('daʊlɪŋ, -əlɪŋ) *n carpentry, cabinetmaking* **1** the joining of two pieces of wood using dowels **2** wood or other material in a long thin rod for cutting up into dowels

dower ('daʊə) *n* **1** the life interest in a part of her husband's estate allotted to a widow by law **2** an archaic word for **dowry** (sense 1) **3** a natural gift or talent ▷ *vb* **4** (*tr*) to endow [C14 from Old French *douaire*, from Medieval Latin *dōtārium*, from Latin *dōs* gift] > 'dowerless *adj*

dower house *n* a house set apart for the use of a widow, often on her deceased husband's estate

dowitcher ('daʊɪtʃə) *n* either of two snipelike shore birds, *Limnodromus griseus* or *L. scolopaceus*, of arctic and subarctic North America: family *Scolopacidae* (sandpipers, etc), order *Charadriiformes* [C19 of Iroquoian origin]

do with *vb* **1** could *or* can do with to find useful; benefit from: *she could do with a night's sleep* **2** have to do with to be involved in or connected with: *his illness has a lot to do with his failing the exam* **3** to do with concerning; related to **4** what...do with **a** to put or place: *what did you do with my coat?* **b** to handle or treat: *what are we going to do with these hooligans?* **c** to fill one's time usefully: *she didn't know what to do with herself when term ended*

do without *vb* (*intr, preposition*) **1** to forgo; manage without: *I can't do without cigarettes* **2** not to require (uncalled-for comments or advice): *we can do without your criticisms thank you*

Dow-Jones average *n US* a daily index of stock-exchange prices based on the average price of a selected number of securities [C20 named after Charles H. *Dow* (died 1902) and Edward D. *Jones* (died 1920), American financial statisticians]

dowly ('daʊlɪ) *adj Northern English dialect* dull; low-spirited; dismal [perhaps from Old English *dol* dull]

down¹ (daʊn) *prep* **1** used to indicate movement from a higher to a lower position: *they went down the mountain* **2** at a lower or further level or position on, in, or along: *he ran down the street* ▷ *adv* **3** downwards; at or to a lower level or position: *don't fall down* **4** (*particle*) used with many verbs when the result of the verb's action is to lower or destroy its object: *pull down; knock down; bring down* **5** (*particle*) used with several verbs to indicate intensity or completion: *calm down* **6** immediately; at once: *on paper: write this down* **7** put down: *cash down* **8** arranged; scheduled: *the meeting is down for next week* **9** in a helpless position: *they had him down on the ground* **10 a** away from a more important place: *down from London* **b** away from a more northerly place: *down from Scotland* **c** (of a member of some British universities) away from the university; on vacation **d** in a particular part of a country: *down south* **11** *nautical* (of a helm) having the rudder to windward **12** reduced to a state of

lack or want: *down to the last pound* **13** lacking a specified amount: *at the end of the day the cashier was ten pounds down* **14** lower in price: *bacon is down* **15** including all intermediate terms, grades, people, etc: *from managing director down to tea-lady* **16** from an earlier to a later time: *the heirloom was handed down* **17** to a finer or more concentrated state: *to grind down; boil down* **18** *sport* being a specified number of points, goals, etc behind another competitor, team, etc: *six goals down* **19** (of a person) being inactive, owing to illness: *down with flu* **20** (functioning as imperative) (to dogs): *down Rover!* **21** (functioning as imperative) down with wanting the end of somebody or something: *down with the king!* **22 get down on something** *Austral and NZ* to procure something, esp in advance of needs or in anticipation of someone else ▷ *adj* **23** (*postpositive*) depressed or miserable **24** (*prenominal*) of or relating to a train or trains from a more important place or one regarded as higher: *the down line* **25** (*postpositive*) (of a device, machine, etc, esp a computer) temporarily out of action **26** made in cash: *a down payment* **27** down to the responsibility or fault of: *this defeat was down to me* ▷ *vb* **28** (*tr*) to knock, push or pull down **29** (*intr*) to go or come down **30** (*tr*) *informal* to drink, esp quickly: *he downed three gins* **31** (*tr*) to bring (someone) down, esp by tackling ▷ *n* **32** *American football* one of a maximum of four consecutive attempts by one team to advance the ball a total of at least ten yards **33** a descent; downward movement **34** a lowering or a poor period (esp in the phrase **ups and downs**) **35 have a down on** *informal* to bear ill will towards (someone or something) [Old English *dūne*, short for *adūne*, variant of *of dūne*, literally: from the hill, from *of*, OFF + *dūn* hill; see DOWN³]

down² (daʊn) *n* **1** the soft fine feathers with free barbs that cover the body of a bird and prevent loss of heat. In the adult they lie beneath and between the contour feathers **2** another name for **eiderdown** (sense 1) **3** *botany* a fine coating of soft hairs, as on certain leaves, fruits, and seeds **4** any growth or coating of soft fine hair, such as that on the human face [C14 of Scandinavian origin; related to Old Norse *dūnn*]

down³ (daʊn) *n archaic* a hill, esp a sand dune ▷ See also **downs** (sense 1), **Downs** (sense 1) [Old English *dūn*; related to Old Frisian *dūne*, Old Saxon *dūna* hill, Old Irish *dūn* fortress, Greek *this* sandbank; see DUNE, TOWN]

Down¹ (daʊn) *n* **1** a district of SE Northern Ireland, in Co Down. Pop: 65 195 (2003 est). Area: 649 sq km (250 sq miles) **2** a historical county of SE Northern Ireland, on the Irish Sea: generally hilly, rising to the Mountains of Mourne: in 1973 it was replaced for administrative purposes by the districts of Ards, Banbridge, Castlereagh, Down, Newry and Mourne, North Down, and part of Lisburn. Area: 2466 sq km (952 sq miles)

Down² (daʊn) *n* **1** any of various lowland breeds of sheep, typically of stocky build and having dense close wool, originating from various parts of southern England, such as Oxford, Hampshire, etc. See also **Dorset Down 2** another name for **Hampshire Down**

down and dirty *adj* (**down-and-dirty** when prenominal) *informal, chiefly US* **1** ruthlessly competitive or underhand: *if Bush gets down and dirty the Governor will give as good as he gets* **2** uninhibited; frank

down-and-out *adj* **1** without any means of livelihood; impoverished and, often, socially outcast ▷ *n* **2** a person who is destitute and, often, homeless; a social outcast or derelict

downbeat ('daʊnˌbiːt) *n* **1** *music* the first beat of a bar or the downward gesture of a conductor's baton indicating this. Compare **upbeat 2** *informal* depressed; gloomy **3** *informal* relaxed; unemphatic

down-bow ('daʊnˌbəʊ) *n* a downward stroke of the bow from its nut to its tip across a stringed

instrument. Compare **up-bow**

downburst ('daʊnˌbɜːst) *n* a very high-speed downward movement of turbulent air in a limited area for a short time. Near the ground it spreads out from its centre with high horizontal velocities. Also called: microburst

downcast ('daʊnˌkɑːst) *adj* **1** dejected **2** (esp of the eyes) directed downwards ▷ *n* **3** *mining* a ventilation shaft **4** *geology* another word for **downthrow**

downcome ('daʊnˌkʌm) *n* **1** *archaic* downfall **2** another name for **downcomer**

downcomer ('daʊnˌkʌmə) *n* a pipe that connects a cistern to a WC, wash basin, etc. Also called: downcome

downdraught ('daʊnˌdrɑːft) *n* the large-scale downward movement of air in the lee of large objects, mountains, etc

downer ('daʊnə) *n slang* **1** Also called: down a barbiturate, tranquillizer, or narcotic. Compare **upper 2** a depressing experience **3** a state of depression: *he's on a downer today*

downfall ('daʊnˌfɔːl) *n* **1** a sudden loss of position, health, or reputation **2** a fall of rain, snow, etc, esp a sudden heavy one **3** another word for **deadfall**

downfallen ('daʊnˌfɔːlən) *adj* **1** (of a building, etc) decrepit **2** *chiefly US* (of a person) ruined; fallen

downforce ('daʊnˌfɔːs) *n* a force produced by air resistance plus gravity that increases the stability of an aircraft or motor vehicle by pressing it downwards

downgrade ('daʊnˌɡreɪd) *vb* (*tr*) **1** to reduce in importance, esteem, or value, esp to demote (a person) to a poorer job **2** to speak of disparagingly ▷ *n* **3** *chiefly US and Canadian* a downward slope, esp in a road **4 on the downgrade** waning in importance, popularity, health, etc

downhaul ('daʊnˌhɔːl) *n nautical* a line for hauling down a sail or for increasing the tension at its luff

downhearted (ˌdaʊnˈhɑːtɪd) *adj* discouraged; dejected > ˌdown'heartedly *adv* > ˌdown'heartedness *n*

downhill ('daʊnˈhɪl) *adj* **1** going or sloping down ▷ *adv* **2** towards the bottom of a hill; downwards **3 go downhill** *informal* to decline; deteriorate ▷ *n* **4** the downward slope of a hill; descent **5** a competitive event in which skiers are timed in a downhill run

downhole ('daʊnˌhəʊl) *adj* (in the oil industry) denoting any piece of equipment that is used in the well itself

down-home *adj slang, chiefly US* of, relating to, or reminiscent of rural life, esp in the southern US; unsophisticated

Downing Street ('daʊnɪŋ) *n* **1** a street in W central London, in Westminster: official residences of the British prime minister and the chancellor of the exchequer **2** *informal* the prime minister or the British Government [named after Sir George *Downing* (1623–84), English statesman]

download ('daʊnˌləʊd) *vb* (*tr*) **1** to copy or transfer (data or a program) into the memory of one's own computer from another computer or the internet **2** to broadcast specialist programmes, for such groups as doctors, outside normal broadcasting hours. They are often recorded on video tapes and viewed later. Compare **upload 3** to delegate or assign (work) to someone else; off-load ▷ *n* **4** a file transferred onto a computer from another computer or the internet

download ('daʊnˌləʊd) *vb* (*tr*) **1** to copy or transfer (data or a program) into the memory of one's own computer from another computer ▷ *n* **2** a file obtained in this way. Compare **upload**

down-market *adj* relating to commercial products, services, etc, that are cheap, have little prestige, or are poor in quality

Downpatrick (ˌdaʊnˈpætrɪk) *n* a market town in Northern Ireland: reputedly the burial place of

d

Saint Patrick. Pop: 10 316 (2001)

down payment *n* the deposit paid on an item purchased on hire-purchase, mortgage, etc

downpipe ('daʊnˌpaɪp) *n Brit and NZ* a pipe for carrying rainwater from a roof gutter to the ground or to a drain. Also called: rainwater pipe, drainpipe. Usual US and Canadian name: downspout

downplay ('daʊnˌpleɪ) *vb* (*tr*) to play down; make little of

downpour ('daʊnˌpɔː) *n* a heavy continuous fall of rain

downrange ('daʊnˈreɪndʒ) *adj, adv* in the direction of the intended flight path of a rocket or missile

downregulation ('daʊnˌrɛgjʊˈleɪʃən) *n* a decrease in sensitivity, through overexposure, to a drug or other chemical caused by a reduction in the number or density of receptors on cell surfaces

downright ('daʊnˌraɪt) *adj* **1** frank or straightforward; blunt: *downright speech* **2** *archaic* directed or pointing straight down ▷ *adv, adj* (*prenominal*) **3** (*intensifier*): *a downright certainty; downright rude* > 'down,rightly *adv* > 'down,rightness *n*

downs (daʊnz) *pl n* **1** Also called: downland rolling upland, esp in the chalk areas of S Britain, characterized by lack of trees and used mainly as pasture **2** *Austral and NZ* a flat grassy area, not necessarily of uplands

Downs (daʊnz) *n* **the 1** any of various ranges of low chalk hills in S England, esp the **South Downs** in Sussex **2** a roadstead off the SE coast of Kent, protected by the Goodwin Sands

downshifting ('daʊnˌʃɪftɪŋ) *n* the practice of simplifying one's lifestyle and becoming less materialistic > 'down,shifter *n*

downside ('daʊnˌsaɪd) *n* the disadvantageous aspect of a situation: *the downside of twentieth-century living*

downsize ('daʊnˌsaɪz) *vb* **-sizes, -sizing, -sized** (*tr*) **1** to reduce the operating costs of a company by reducing the number of people it employs **2** to reduce the size of or produce a smaller version of (something) **3** to upgrade (a computer system) by replacing a mainframe or minicomputer with a network of microcomputers. Compare **rightsize**

downspout ('daʊnˌspaʊt) *n US and Canadian* a pipe for carrying rainwater from a roof gutter to the ground or to a drain. Also called: drainpipe, (in Britain and certain other countries) downpipe

Down's syndrome *n* a *pathol* a chromosomal abnormality resulting in a flat face and nose, short stubby fingers, a vertical fold of skin at the inner edge of the eye, and mental retardation. Former name: mongolism **b** (*as modifier*): *a Down's syndrome baby* [c19 after John Langdon-Down (1828–96), English physician]

downstage ('daʊnˈsteɪdʒ) *theatre* ▷ *adv* **1** at or towards the front of the stage ▷ *adj* **2** of or relating to the front of the stage ▷ *n* **3** the front half of the stage

downstairs ('daʊnˈstɛəz) *adv* **1** down the stairs; to or on a lower floor ▷ *n* **2** a a lower or ground floor **b** (*as modifier*): *a downstairs room* **3** *Brit informal, old-fashioned* the servants of a household collectively. Compare **upstairs** (sense 6)

downstate ('daʊnˈsteɪt) *US* ▷ *adj* **1** in, or relating to the part of the state away from large cities, esp the southern part ▷ *adv* **2** towards the southern part of a state ▷ *n* **3** the southern part of a state

downstream ('daʊnˈstriːm) *adv, adj* **1** in or towards the lower part of a stream; with the current **2** (in the oil industry) of or for the refining, distribution, or marketing of oil or its derived products. Compare **upstream** (sense 2)

downswing ('daʊnˌswɪŋ) *n* **1** a statistical downward trend in business activity, the death rate, etc **2** *golf* the downward movement or line of a club when striking the ball

downthrow ('daʊnˌθrəʊ) *n* **1** the state of throwing down or being thrown down **2** *geology*

the sinking of rocks on one side of a fault plane

downtime ('daʊnˌtaɪm) *n* **1** *commerce* time during which a machine or plant is not working because it is incapable of production, as when under repair: the term is sometimes used to include all nonproductive time. Compare **idle time 2** *informal* time spent not working; spare time

down-to-earth *adj* sensible; practical; realistic

downtown ('daʊnˈtaʊn) *US, Canadian, and NZ* ▷ *n* **1** the central or lower part of a city, esp the main commercial area ▷ *adv* **2** towards, to, or into this area ▷ *adj* **3** of, relating to, or situated in the downtown area: *downtown Manhattan* > 'down'towner *n*

downtrodden ('daʊnˌtrɒdən) or **downtrod** *adj* **1** subjugated; oppressed **2** trodden down; trampled

downturn ('daʊnˌtɜːn) *n* a drop or reduction in the success of a business or economy

down under *informal* ▷ *n* **1** Australia or New Zealand ▷ *adv* **2** in or to Australia or New Zealand

downward ('daʊnwəd) *adj* **1** descending from a higher to a lower level, condition, position, etc **2** descending from a beginning ▷ *adv* **3** a variant of **downwards**. > 'downwardly *adv* > 'downwardness *n*

downward mobility *n sociol* the movement of an individual, social group, or class to a lower status. Compare **upward mobility** See also **horizontal mobility, vertical mobility**

downwards ('daʊnwədz) or **downward** *adv* **1** from a higher to a lower place, level, etc **2** from an earlier time or source to a later: *from the Tudors downwards*

downwash ('daʊnˌwɒʃ) *n* the downward deflection of an airflow, esp one caused by an aircraft wing

downwind ('daʊnˈwɪnd) *adv, adj* **1** in the same direction towards which the wind is blowing; with the wind from behind **2** towards or on the side away from the wind; leeward

downy ('daʊnɪ) *adj* **downier, downiest 1** covered with soft fine hair or feathers **2** light, soft, and fluffy **3** made from or filled with down **4** resembling downs; undulating **5** *Brit slang* sharp-witted; knowing > 'downiness *n*

downy mildew *n* **1** a serious plant disease, characterized by yellowish patches on the undersurface of the leaves, caused by the parasitic fungi of the family *Peronosporaceae*, such as *Peronospora destructor*: affects onions, cauliflower, lettuce, etc **2** any of the fungi causing this disease ▷ Compare **powdery mildew**

dowry ('daʊərɪ) *n, pl* **-ries 1** the money or property brought by a woman to her husband at marriage **2** (esp formerly) a gift made by a man to his bride or her parents **3** *Christianity* a sum of money required on entering certain orders of nuns **4** a natural talent or gift **5** *obsolete* a widow's dower [c14 from Anglo-French *douarie*, from Medieval Latin *dōtārium*; see **DOWER**]

dowsabel ('duːsəˌbɛl, 'daʊs-) *n* an obsolete word for **sweetheart** [c16 from Latin *Dulcibella* feminine given name, from *dulcis* sweet + *bellus* beautiful]

dowse¹ (daʊs) *vb, n* a variant spelling of **douse¹** > 'dowser *n*

dowse² (daʊz) *vb* (*intr*) to search for underground water, minerals, etc, using a divining rod; divine [c17 of unknown origin] > 'dowser *n*

dowsing rod ('daʊzɪŋ) *n* another name for **divining rod**

doxastic (dɒksˈæstɪk) *adj logic* **1** of or relating to belief **2** denoting the branch of modal logic that studies the concept of belief [c18 from Greek *doxastikos* having an opinion, ultimately from *doxazein* to conjecture]

doxographer (ˌdɒksˈɒgrəfə) *n rare* a person who collects the opinions and conjectures of ancient Greek philosophers [c19 from New Latin *doxographus*, from Greek *doxa* opinion, conjecture + *graphos* writer] > ˌdoxo'graphic *adj* > ˌdox'ography *n*

doxology (dɒkˈsɒlədʒɪ) *n, pl* **-gies** a hymn, verse, or form of words in Christian liturgy glorifying God [c17 from Medieval Latin *doxologia*, from Greek,

from *doxologos* uttering praise, from *doxa* praise; see -LOGY] > doxological (ˌdɒksəˈlɒdʒɪkəl) *adj* > ˌdoxo'logically *adv*

doxy¹ or **doxie** ('dɒksɪ) *n, pl* **doxies** opinion or doctrine, esp concerning religious matters [c18 independent use of -doxy as in *orthodoxy, heterodoxy*]

doxy² ('dɒksɪ) *n, pl* **doxies** *archaic slang* a prostitute or mistress [c16 probably from Middle Flemish *docke* doll; compare Middle Dutch *docke* doll]

doxycycline (ˌdɒksɪˈsaɪklɪn) *n* a tetracycline antibiotic used to treat conditions caused by a wide range of bacteria, including anthrax

doy ('dɔɪ) *n Northern English dialect* a beloved person: used esp as an endearment

doyen ('dɔɪən; French dwayɛ̃) *n* the senior member of a group, profession, or society [c17 from French, from Late Latin *decānus* leader of a group of ten; see DEAN] > doyenne (dɔɪˈɛn; French dwajɛn) *fem n*

doyley ('dɔɪlɪ) *n* a variant spelling of **doily**

doz. *abbreviation for* dozen

doze (dəʊz) *vb* (*intr*) **1** to sleep lightly or intermittently **2** (often foll by *off*) to fall into a light sleep ▷ *n* **3** a short sleep [c17 probably from Old Norse *dūs* lull; related to Danish *dose* to drowse, Swedish dialect *dusa* slumber] > 'dozer *n*

dozed (dɒzd, dəʊzd) *adj chiefly Irish* (of timber or rubber) rotten or decayed [from DOZE]

dozen ('dʌzən) *determiner* **1** (preceded by *a* or a numeral) **a** twelve or a group of twelve: *a dozen eggs; two dozen oranges* **b** (as pronoun; functioning as sing or plural): *give me a dozen; there are at least a dozen who haven't arrived yet* ▷ *n, pl* **dozens** or **dozen 2** by the dozen in large quantities **3** See **baker's dozen 4** talk nineteen to the dozen to talk without stopping ▷ See also **dozens** [c13 from Old French *douzaine*, from *douze* twelve, from Latin *duodecim*, from *duo* two + *decem* ten] > 'dozenth *adj*

dozens ('dʌzənz) *pl n* (usually foll by *of*) *informal* a lot: *I've got dozens of things to do*

dozer ('dəʊzə) *n chiefly US* short for **bulldozer**

dozy ('dəʊzɪ) *adj* **dozier, doziest 1** drowsy **2** *Brit informal* stupid > 'dozily *adv* > 'doziness *n*

DP *abbreviation for* **1** data processing **2** displaced person **3** (in South Africa) Democratic Party

D/P *commerce abbreviation for* documents against presentation

DPB (in New Zealand) *abbreviation for* domestic purposes benefit: an allowance paid to solo parents

DPH *abbreviation for* Diploma in Public Health

DPhil or **DPh** *abbreviation for* Doctor of Philosophy. Also: PhD

dpi *abbreviation for* dots per inch: a measure of the resolution of a typesetting machine, computer screen, etc

DPM *abbreviation for* Diploma in Psychological Medicine

DPN *n biochem* diphosphopyridine nucleotide; the former name for **NAD**

DPNH *n biochem* the reduced form of DPN; the former name for **NADH**

DPP (in Britain) *abbreviation for* **Director of Public Prosecutions**

dpt *abbreviation for* department

DPW (in Britain, formerly) *abbreviation for* Department of Public Works

dr *abbreviation for* **1** debtor **2** Also: dr dram **3** drawer

Dr *abbreviation for* **1** Doctor **2** (in street names) Drive

DR *abbreviation for* **dry riser**

dr. *abbreviation for* **1** debit **2** Also: dr dram **3** (the former) drachma

drab¹ (dræb) *adj* **drabber, drabbest 1** dull; dingy; shabby **2** cheerless; dreary: *a drab evening* **3** of the colour drab ▷ *n* **4** a light olive-brown colour **5** a fabric of a dull grey or brown colour [c16 from Old French *drap* cloth, from Late Latin *drappus*, perhaps of Celtic origin] > 'drably *adv* > 'drabness *n*

drab² (dræb) *archaic* ▷ *n* **1** a slatternly woman **2** a whore ▷ *vb* **drabs, drabbing, drabbed 3** (*intr*) to consort with prostitutes [c16 of Celtic origin;

compare Scottish Gaelic *drabag*]
drabbet (ˈdræbɪt) *n Brit* a yellowish-brown fabric of coarse linen [C19 see DRAB[1]]
drabble (ˈdræbᵊl) *vb* to make or become wet or dirty [C14 from Low German *drabbelen* to paddle in mud; related to DRAB[2]]
dracaena (drəˈsiːnə) *n* **1** any tropical plant of the genus *Dracaena*: some species are cultivated as house plants for their decorative foliage: family *Agavaceae*. See also **dragon's blood, dragon tree** **2** any of several similar plants of the related genus *Cordyline* [C19 from New Latin, from Latin: she-dragon, from Greek *drakaina*, feminine of *drakōn* DRAGON]
drachm (dræm) *n* **1** Also called: **fluid dram** *Brit* one eighth of a fluid ounce **2** *US* another name for **dram** (sense 2) **3** another name for **drachma** [C14 learned variant of DRAM]
drachma (ˈdrækmə) *n, pl* **-mas** *or* **-mae** (-miː) **1** the former standard monetary unit of Greece, divided into 100 lepta; replaced by the euro in 2002 **2** *US* another name for **dram** (sense 2) **3** a silver coin of ancient Greece **4** a unit of weight in ancient Greece [C16 from Latin, from Greek *drakhmē* a handful, from *drassesthai* to seize]
drack *or* **drac** (dræk) *adj Austral slang* (esp of a woman) unattractive [perhaps from *Dracula's Daughter*]
Draco (ˈdreɪkəʊ) *n, Latin genitive* **Draconis** (dreɪˈkəʊnɪs) a faint extensive constellation twisting around the N celestial pole and lying between Ursa Major and Cepheus [from Latin, from Greek *drakōn* DRAGON]
draco lizard (ˈdreɪkəʊ) *n* another name for **flying lizard**
dracone (ˈdrækəʊn) *n* a large flexible cylindrical container towed by a ship, used for transporting liquids [C20 from Latin: DRAGON]
draconian (dreɪˈkəʊnɪən) *or* **draconic** (dreɪˈkɒnɪk) *adj* (*sometimes capital*) **1** of or relating to Draco, 7th-century Athenian statesman and lawmaker, or his code of laws, which prescribed death for almost every offence **2** harsh: *draconian legislation* > draˈconianism *n*
draconic (dreɪˈkɒnɪk) *adj* of, like, or relating to a dragon [C17 from Latin *dracō* DRAGON] > draˈconically *adv*
draconic month *n astronomy* the mean time taken by the moon between successive passages through the ascending node of its orbit. It is about 2.5 hours shorter than the sidereal month. Also called: **nodical month**
draff (dræf) *n* the residue of husks after fermentation of the grain used in brewing, used as a food for cattle [C13 from Old Norse *draf*; related to Old High German *trebir*, Russian *drob* fragment; see DRIVEL] > ˈdraffy *adj*
draft (drɑːft) *n* **1** a plan, sketch, or drawing of something **2** a preliminary outline of a book, speech, etc **3** another word for **bill of exchange** **4** a demand or drain on something **5** the divergent duct leading from a water turbine to its tailrace **6** *US* selection for compulsory military service **7** detachment of military personnel from one unit to another **8** *commerce* an allowance on merchandise sold by weight **9** a line or narrow border that is chiselled on the surface of a stone to serve as a guide for levelling it **10** *Austral and NZ* a group of livestock separated from the rest of the herd or flock ▷ *vb* (*tr*) **11** to draw up an outline or sketch for something: *to draft a speech* **12** to prepare a plan or design of **13** to detach (military personnel) from one unit to another **14** *chiefly US* to select for compulsory military service **15** to chisel a draft on (stone, etc) **16** *Austral and NZ* **a** to select (cattle or sheep) from a herd or flock **b** to select (farm stock) for sale ▷ *n, vb* **17** the usual US spelling of **draught** (senses 1–8, 11) [C16 variant of DRAUGHT] > ˈdrafter *n*
draft board *n US* a tribunal responsible for the selection of personnel liable for compulsory military service
draft dodger *n US* one who evades compulsory military service
draftee (drɑːfˈtiː) *n US* a conscript
draft-mule work *n US and Canadian* drudgery. Also called (in Britain and certain other countries): **donkey-work**
draft-quality printing *n computing* low-quality, high-speed output in printed form from a printer linked to a word processor. Compare **letter-quality printing**
draftsman (ˈdrɑːftsmən) *n, pl* **-men** the usual US spelling of **draughtsman** (senses 1, 2) > ˈdraftsmanship *n*
drafty (ˈdrɑːftɪ) *adj* **draftier, draftiest** the usual US spelling of **draughty.** > ˈdraftily *adv* > ˈdraftiness *n*
drag (dræg) *vb* **drags, dragging, dragged** **1** to pull or be pulled with force, esp along the ground or other surface **2** (*tr; often foll by* away *or* from) to persuade to come away (from something attractive or interesting): *he couldn't drag himself away from the shop* **3** to trail or cause to trail on the ground **4** (*tr*) to move (oneself, one's feet, etc) with effort or difficulty: *he drags himself out of bed at dawn* **5** to linger behind **6** (*often foll by* on *or* out) to prolong or be prolonged tediously or unnecessarily: *his talk dragged on for hours* **7** (*tr; foll by* out) to pass (time) in discomfort, poverty, unhappiness, etc: *he dragged out his few remaining years* **8** (*when intr, usually foll by* for) to search (the bed of a river, canal, etc) with a dragnet or hook: *they dragged the river for the body* **9** (*tr foll by* out *or* from) to crush (clods) or level (a soil surface) by use of a drag **10** (of hounds) to follow (a fox or its trail) to the place where it has been lying **11** (*intr*) *slang* to draw (on a cigarette, pipe, etc) **12** *computing* to move (data) from one place to another on the screen by manipulating a mouse with its button held down **13** **drag anchor** (of a vessel) to move away from its mooring because the anchor has failed to hold **14** **drag one's feet** *or* **heels** *informal* to act with deliberate slowness **15** **drag (someone's) name in the mud** to disgrace or defame (someone) ▷ *n* **16** the act of dragging or the state of being dragged **17** an implement, such as a dragnet, dredge, etc, used for dragging **18** Also called: **drag harrow** a type of harrow consisting of heavy beams, often with spikes inserted, used to crush clods, level soil, or prepare seedbeds **19** a sporting coach with seats inside and out, usually drawn by four horses **20** a braking or retarding device, such as a metal piece fitted to the underside of the wheel of a horse-drawn vehicle **21** a person or thing that slows up progress **22** slow progress or movement **23** *aeronautics* the resistance to the motion of a body passing through a fluid, esp through air: applied to an aircraft in flight, it is the component of the resultant aerodynamic force measured parallel to the direction of air flow **24** the trail of scent left by a fox or other animal hunted with hounds **25** an artificial trail of a strong-smelling substance, sometimes including aniseed, drawn over the ground for hounds to follow **26** See **drag hunt** **27** *angling* unnatural movement imparted to a fly, esp a dry fly, by tension on the angler's line **28** *informal* a person or thing that is very tedious; bore: *exams are a drag* **29** *slang* a car **30** short for **drag race** **31** *slang* **a** women's clothes worn by a man, usually by a transvestite (esp in the phrase **in drag**) **b** (*as modifier*): *a drag club; drag show* **c** clothes collectively **32** *informal* a draw on a cigarette, pipe, etc **33** *US slang* influence or persuasive power **34** *chiefly US slang* a street or road ▷ See also **drag down, drag in, drag out of, drag up** [Old English *dragan* to DRAW; related to Swedish *dragga*]
drag down *vb* (*tr, adverb*) to depress or demoralize: *the flu really dragged her down*
dragée (dræˈʒeɪ) *n* **1** a sweet made of a nut, fruit, etc, coated with a hard sugar icing **2** a tiny beadlike sweet used for decorating cakes, etc **3** a medicinal formulation coated with sugar to disguise the taste [C19 from French; see DREDGE[2]]
dragging (ˈdrægɪŋ) *n* a decorating technique in which paint is applied with a specially modified brush to create a marbled or grainy effect
draggle (ˈdrægᵊl) *vb* **1** to make or become wet or dirty by trailing on the ground; bedraggle **2** (*intr*) to lag; dawdle [C16 probably frequentative of DRAG]
draggletailed (ˈdrægᵊlˌteɪld) *adj archaic* (esp of a woman) bedraggled; besmirched
draggy (ˈdrægɪ) *adj* **-gier, -giest** *slang* **1** slow or boring: *a draggy party* **2** dull and listless
draghound (ˈdrægˌhaʊnd) *n* a hound used to follow an artificial trail of scent in a drag hunt
drag hunt *n* **1** a hunt in which hounds follow an artificial trail of scent **2** a club that organizes such hunts ▷ *vb* **drag-hunt** **3** to follow draghounds, esp on horseback, or cause (draghounds) to follow an artificial trail of scent
drag in *vb* (*tr, adverb*) to introduce or mention (a topic, name, etc) with slight or no pretext
drag king *n* **1** a female who dresses as a man and impersonates male characteristics for public entertainment **2** *slang* a female transvestite
dragline (ˈdrægˌlaɪn) *n* **1** another word for **dragrope** (sense 2) **2** Also called: **dragline crane, dragline excavator** a power shovel that operates by being dragged by cables at the end of an arm or jib: used for quarrying, opencast mining, etc
drag link *n* a link for conveying motion between cranks on parallel shafts that are slightly offset. It is used in cars to connect the steering gear to the steering arm
dragnet (ˈdrægˌnɛt) *n* **1** a heavy or weighted net used to scour the bottom of a pond, river, etc, as when searching for something **2** any system of coordinated efforts by police forces to track down wanted persons
dragoman (ˈdrægəʊmən) *n, pl* **-mans** *or* **-men** (in some Middle Eastern countries, esp formerly) a professional interpreter or guide [C14 from French, from Italian *dragomano*, from Medieval Greek *dragoumanos*, from Arabic *targumān* an interpreter, from Aramaic *tūrgemānā*, of Akkadian origin]
dragon (ˈdrægən) *n* **1** a mythical monster usually represented as breathing fire and having a scaly reptilian body, wings, claws, and a long tail **2** *informal* a fierce or intractable person, esp a woman **3** any of various very large lizards, esp the Komodo dragon **4** any of various North American aroid plants, esp the green dragon **5** *Christianity* a manifestation of Satan or an attendant devil **6** a yacht of the International Dragon Class, 8.88m long (29.2 feet), used in racing **7** **chase the dragon** *slang* to smoke opium or heroin [C13 from Old French, from Latin *dracō*, from Greek *drakōn*; related to *drakos* eye] > ˈdragoness *fem n* > ˈdragonish *adj*
dragonet (ˈdrægənɪt) *n* any small spiny-finned fish of the family *Callionymidae*, having a flat head and a slender tapering brightly coloured body and living at the bottom of shallow seas [C14 (meaning: small dragon): from French; applied to fish C18]
dragonfly (ˈdrægənˌflaɪ) *n, pl* **-flies** **1** any predatory insect of the suborder *Anisoptera*, having a large head and eyes, a long slender body, two pairs of iridescent wings that are outspread at rest, and aquatic larvae: order *Odonata*. See also **damselfly** **2** any other insect of the order *Odonata*
dragon fruit *n* another name for **pitahaya**
dragonhead (ˈdrægənˌhɛd) *or* **dragon's-head** *n* **1** any plant of the genus *Dracocephalum*, of Europe, Asia, and North America, having dense spikes of white or bluish flowers: family *Lamiaceae* (labiates) **2** any North American plant of the related genus *Physostegia*, having pink or purplish flowers
dragon market *n informal* any of the emerging markets of the Pacific rim, esp Indonesia, Malaysia, Thailand, and the Philippines. Compare **tiger market**
dragonnade (ˌdrægəˈneɪd) *n* **1** *history* the

d

persecution of French Huguenots during the reign of Louis XIV by dragoons quartered in their villages and homes **2** subjection by military force ▷ *vb* **3** (*tr*) to subject to persecution by military troops [c18 from French, from *dragon* DRAGOON]

dragonroot ('dræɡən,ruːt) *n* **1** a North American aroid plant, *Arisaema dracontium*, having a greenish spathe and a long pointed spadix **2** the tuberous root of this plant, formerly used in medicine as an expectorant and diaphoretic

dragon's blood *n* **1** a red resinous substance obtained from the fruit of a Malaysian palm, *Daemonorops* (or *Calamus*) *draco*: formerly used medicinally and now used in varnishes and lacquers **2** any of several similar resins obtained from other trees, esp from the dragon tree and a related species, *Dracaena cinnabari* (Socotra dragon's blood dracaena)

dragon's teeth *pl n* **1** *informal* conical or wedge-shaped concrete antitank obstacles protruding from the ground in rows: used in World War II **2** sow dragon's teeth to take some action that is intended to prevent strife or trouble but that actually brings it about [sense 2 from the story of CADMUS]

dragon tree *n* a tree, *Dracaena draco*, of the Canary Islands, having clusters of sword-shaped leaves at the tips of its branches: family *Agavaceae*. It is a source of dragon's blood

dragoon (drə'ɡuːn) *n* **1** (originally) a mounted infantryman armed with a carbine **2** (*sometimes capital*) a domestic fancy pigeon **3 a** a type of cavalryman **b** (*pl*; *cap when part of a name*): *the Royal Dragoons* ▷ *vb* (*tr*) **4** to coerce; force: *he was dragooned into admitting it* **5** to persecute by military force [c17 from French *dragon* (special use of DRAGON), soldier armed with a carbine, perhaps suggesting that a carbine, like a dragon, breathed forth fire] > dra'goonage *n*

drag out of *vb* (*tr, adverb + preposition*) to obtain or extract (a confession, statement, etc), esp by force: *we dragged the name out of him*. Also: **drag from**

drag queen *n* **1** a male who dresses as a woman and impersonates female characteristics for public entertainment **2** *slang* a male transvestite

drag race *n* a type of motor race in which specially built or modified cars or motorcycles are timed over a measured course > **drag racer** *n* > drag racing *n*

dragrope ('dræɡ,rəʊp) *n* **1** a rope used to drag military equipment, esp artillery **2** Also called: dragline, guide rope a rope trailing from a balloon or airship for mooring or braking purposes

drag sail *n* another term for **sea anchor**

dragster ('dræɡstə) *n* a car specially built or modified for drag racing

drag up *vb* (*tr, adverb*) *informal* **1** to rear (a child) poorly and in an undisciplined manner **2** to introduce or revive (an unpleasant fact or story)

drail (dreɪl) *angling* ▷ *n* **1** a weighted hook used in trolling ▷ *vb* **2** (*intr*) to fish with a drail [c16 apparently from TRAIL, influenced by DRAW]

drain (dreɪn) *n* **1** a pipe or channel that carries off water, sewage, etc **2** an instance or cause of continuous diminution in resources or energy; depletion **3** *surgery* a device, such as a tube, for insertion into a wound, incision, or bodily cavity to drain off pus, etc **4** *electronics* the electrode region in a field-effect transistor into which majority carriers flow from the interelectrode conductivity channel **5** down the drain wasted ▷ *vb* **6** (*tr*; *often foll by off*) to draw off or remove (liquid) from: *to drain water from vegetables; to drain vegetables* **7** (*intr*; *often foll by away*) to flow (away) or filter (off) **8** (*intr*) to dry or be emptied as a result of liquid running off or flowing away: *leave the dishes to drain* **9** (*tr*) to drink the entire contents of (a glass, cup, etc) **10** (*tr*) to consume or make constant demands on (resources, energy, etc); exhaust; sap **11** (*intr*) to disappear or leave, esp gradually: *the colour drained from his face* **12** (*tr*) (of a

river, etc) to carry off the surface water from (an area) **13** (*intr*) (of an area) to discharge its surface water into rivers, streams, etc [Old English *drēahnian*; related to Old Norse *drangr* dry wood; see DRY] > 'drainable *adj*

drainage ('dreɪnɪdʒ) *n* **1** the process or a method of draining **2** a system of watercourses or drains **3** liquid, sewage, etc, that is drained away

drainage basin *or* **area** *n* another name for **catchment area**

drainer ('dreɪnə) *n* **1** a person or thing that drains **2** another name for **draining board 3** a rack near a sink on which washed dishes, etc are placed to drain

draining board *n* a sloping grooved surface at the side of a sink, used for draining washed dishes, etc. Also called: **drainer**

drainlayer ('dreɪn,leɪə) *n NZ* a person trained to build or repair drains

drainpipe ('dreɪn,paɪp) *n* a pipe for carrying off rainwater, sewage, etc; downpipe

drainpipes ('dreɪn,paɪps) *pl n* trousers with very narrow legs

drain rod *n* one of a series of flexible rods with threaded ends that screw together and can be pushed to and fro in a drain to clear a blockage

drake¹ (dreɪk) *n* the male of any duck [c13 perhaps from Low German; compare Middle Dutch *andrake*, Old High German *antrahho*]

drake² (dreɪk) *n* **1** *angling* an artificial fly resembling a mayfly **2** *history* a small cannon **3** an obsolete word for **dragon** [Old English *draca*, ultimately from Latin *dracō* DRAGON]

Drakensberg ('drɑːkənz,bɜːɡ) *n* a mountain range in southern Africa, extending through Lesotho, E South Africa, and Swaziland. Highest peak: Thabana Ntlenyana, 3482 m (11 425 ft). Sotho name: Quathlamba

Drake Passage *n* a strait between S South America and the South Shetland Islands, connecting the Atlantic and Pacific Oceans

Dralon ('dreɪlɒn) *n trademark* an acrylic fibre fabric used esp for upholstery

dram (dræm) *n* **1** one sixteenth of an ounce (avoirdupois). 1 dram is equivalent to 0.0018 kilogram **2** Also called: **drachm, drachma** *US* one eighth of an apothecaries' ounce; 60 grains. 1 dram is equivalent to 0.0039 kilogram **3** a small amount of an alcoholic drink, esp a spirit; tot **4** the standard monetary unit of Armenia, divided into 100 lumas [c15 from Old French *dragme*, from Late Latin *dragma*, from Greek *drakhmē*; see DRACHMA]

DRAM *or* **D-RAM** ('diːræm) *acronym for* **1** dynamic random access memory: a widely used type of random access memory. See RAM¹ ▷ *n* **2** a chip containing such a memory

drama ('drɑːmə) *n* **1** a work to be performed by actors on stage, radio, or television; play **2** the genre of literature represented by works intended for the stage **3** the art of the writing and production of plays **4** a situation or sequence of events that is highly emotional, tragic, or turbulent [c17 from Late Latin: a play, from Greek: something performed, from *drān* to do]

Dramamine ('dræmə,miːn) *n* a trademark for **dimenhydrinate**

drama queen *n* *informal* a person who tends to react to every situation in an overdramatic or exaggerated manner

dramatic (drə'mætɪk) *adj* **1** of or relating to drama **2** like a drama in suddenness, emotional impact, etc **3** striking; effective **4** acting or performed in a flamboyant way **5** *music* (of a voice) powerful and marked by histrionic quality > dra'matically *adv*

dramatic irony *n theatre* the irony occurring when the implications of a situation, speech, etc, are understood by the audience but not by the characters in the play

dramatics (drə'mætɪks) *n* **1** (*functioning as singular or plural*) **a** the art of acting or producing plays **b**

dramatic productions **2** (*usually functioning as plural*) histrionic behaviour

dramatis personae ('drɑːmətɪs pə'səʊnaɪ) *pl n* (*often functioning as singular*) **1** the characters or a list of characters in a play or story **2** the main personalities in any situation or event [c18 from New Latin]

dramatist ('dræmətɪst) *n* a writer of plays; playwright

dramatization *or* **dramatisation** (,dræmətaɪ'zeɪʃən) *n* **1** the reconstruction of an event, novel, story, etc in a form suitable for dramatic presentation **2** the art or act of dramatizing

dramatize *or* **dramatise** ('dræmə,taɪz) *vb* **1** (*tr*) to put into dramatic form **2** to express or represent (something) in a dramatic or exaggerated way: *he dramatizes his illness* > 'drama,tizable *or* 'drama,tisable *adj* > 'drama,tizer *or* 'drama,tiser *n*

dramaturge ('dræmə,tɜːdʒ) *n* **1** Also called: dramaturgist a dramatist, esp one associated with a particular company or theatre **2** Also called: dramaturg a literary adviser on the staff of a theatre, film corporation, etc, whose responsibilities may include selection and editing of texts, liaison with authors, preparation of printed programmes, and public relations work [c19 probably from French, from Greek *dramatourgos* playwright, from DRAMA + *ergon* work]

dramaturgy ('dræmə,tɜːdʒɪ) *n* the art and technique of the theatre; dramatics > ,drama'turgic *or* ,drama'turgical *adj* > ,drama'turgically *adv*

Drambuie (dræm'bjuːɪ) *n trademark* a liqueur based on Scotch whisky and made exclusively in Scotland from a recipe dating from the 18th century

dramedy ('drɑːmɪdɪ) *n, pl* **-dies** a television or film drama in which there are important elements of comedy [c20 from DRAM(A) + (COM)EDY]

Drammen (*Norwegian* 'drɑːmən) *n* a port in S Norway. Pop: 56 688 (2004 est)

Drancy (*French* drɑ̃si) *n* a residential suburb of NE Paris. Pop: 62 263 (1999)

drangway ('dræŋ,weɪ) *n Southwest English dialect* a narrow lane; passageway

drank (dræŋk) *vb* the past tense of **drink**

drap (dræp) *n, vb* a Scot word for **drop**

drape (dreɪp) *vb* **1** (*tr*) to hang or cover with flexible material or fabric, usually in folds; adorn **2** to hang or arrange or be hung or arranged, esp in folds **3** (*tr*) to place casually and loosely; hang: *she draped her arm over the back of the chair* ▷ *n* **4** (*often plural*) a cloth or hanging that covers something in folds; drapery **5** the way in which fabric hangs ▷ See also **drapes** [c15 from Old French *draper*, from *drap* piece of cloth; see DRAB¹] > 'drapable *or* 'drapeable *adj*

draper ('dreɪpə) *n Brit* a dealer in fabrics and sewing materials

drapery ('dreɪpərɪ) *n, pl* **-peries 1** fabric or clothing arranged and draped **2** (*often plural*) curtains or hangings that drape **3** *Brit* the occupation or shop of a draper **4** fabrics and cloth collectively > 'draperied *adj*

drapes (dreɪps) *or* **draperies** ('dreɪpərɪz) *pl n* *chiefly US and Canadian* curtains, esp ones of heavy fabric

drappie ('dræpɪ) *n Scot* a little drop, esp a small amount of spirits

drastic ('dræstɪk) *adj* extreme or forceful; severe [c17 from Greek *drastikos*, from *dran* to do, act] > 'drastically *adv*

drat (dræt) *interj slang* an exclamation of annoyance (also in the phrases **drat it! drat you!** etc) [c19 probably alteration of *God rot*]

dratted ('drætɪd) *adj* (*prenominal*) *informal* wretched; annoying

draught *or US* **draft** (drɑːft) *n* **1** a current of air, esp one intruding into an enclosed space **2 a** the act of pulling a load, as by a vehicle or animal **b**

(*as modifier*): *a draught horse* **3** the load or quantity drawn **4** a portion of liquid to be drunk, esp a dose of medicine **5** the act or an instance of drinking; a gulp or swallow **6** the act or process of drawing air, smoke, etc, into the lungs **7** the amount of air, smoke, etc, inhaled in one breath **8 a** beer, wine, etc, stored in bulk, esp in a cask, as opposed to being bottled **b** (*as modifier*): *draught beer* **c on draught** drawn from a cask or keg **9** Also called: **draughtsman** any one of the 12 flat thick discs used by each player in the game of draughts. US and Canadian equivalent: **checker** **10** the depth of a loaded vessel in the water, taken from the level of the waterline to the lowest point of the hull **11 feel the draught** to be short of money ▷ See also **draughts** [C14 probably from Old Norse *drahtr*, of Germanic origin; related to DRAW] > 'draughter *or US* 'drafter *n*

draughtboard ('drɑːftˌbɔːd) *n* a square board divided into 64 squares of alternating colours, used for playing draughts or chess

draughts (drɑːfts) *n* (*functioning as singular*) a game for two players using a draughtboard and 12 draughtsmen each. The object is to jump over and capture the opponent's pieces. US and Canadian name: **checkers** [C14 plural of DRAUGHT (in obsolete sense: a chess move)]

draughtsman *or US* **draftsman** ('drɑːftsmən) *n, pl* **-men** **1** Also called (feminine): **draughtswoman** a person who practises or is qualified in mechanical drawing, employed to prepare detailed scale drawings of machinery, buildings, devices, etc **2** Also called (feminine): **draughtswoman** a person skilled in drawing **3** *Brit* any of the 12 flat thick discs used by each player in the game of draughts. US and Canadian equivalent: **checker** > 'draughtsmanˌship *or US* 'draftsmanˌship *n*

draughty *or US* **drafty** ('drɑːftɪ) *adj* **draughtier, draughtiest** *or US* **draftier, draftiest** characterized by or exposed to draughts of air > 'draughtily *or US* 'draftily *adv* > 'draughtiness *or US* 'draftiness *n*

Drava *or* **Drave** ('drɑːvə) *n* a river in S central Europe, rising in N Italy and flowing east through Austria, then southeast along the southern Hungarian border to join the River Danube. Length: 725 km (450 miles). German name: **Drau** (drau)

Dravidian (drə'vɪdɪən) *n* **1** a family of languages spoken in S and central India and Sri Lanka, including Tamil, Malayalam, Telugu, Kannada, and Gondi **2** a member of one of the aboriginal races of India, pushed south by the Indo-Europeans and now mixed with them ▷ *adj* **3** denoting, belonging to, or relating to this family of languages or these peoples

draw (drɔː) *vb* **draws, drawing, drew, drawn** **1** to cause (a person or thing) to move towards or away by pulling **2** to bring, take, or pull (something) out, as from a drawer, holster, etc **3** (*tr*) to extract or pull or take out: *to draw teeth; to draw a card from a pack* **4** (*tr; often foll by* off) to take (liquid) out of a cask, keg, tank, etc, by means of a tap **5** (*intr*) to move, go, or proceed, esp in a specified direction: *to draw alongside* **6** (*tr*) to attract or elicit: *to draw a crowd; draw attention* **7** (*tr*) to cause to flow: *to draw blood* **8** to depict or sketch (a form, figure, picture, etc) in lines, as with a pencil or pen, esp without the use of colour; delineate **9** (*tr*) to make, formulate, or derive: *to draw conclusions, comparisons, parallels* **10** (*tr*) to write (a legal document) in proper form **11** (*tr; sometimes foll by* in) to suck or take in (air, liquid, etc): *to draw a breath* **12** (*intr*) to induce or allow a draught to carry off air, smoke, etc: *the flue draws well* **13** (*tr*) to take or receive from a source: *to draw money from the bank* **14** (*tr*) to earn: *draw interest* **15** (*tr*) *finance* to write out (a bill of exchange or promissory note): *to draw a cheque* **16** (*tr*) to choose at random: *to draw lots* **17** (*tr*) to reduce the diameter of (a wire or metal rod) by pulling it through a die **18** (*tr*) to shape (a sheet of metal or glass) by rolling, by pulling it through a die or by stretching **19** *archery* to bend (a bow) by pulling the string **20** to steep (tea) or (of tea) to steep in boiling water **21** (*tr*) to disembowel: *draw a chicken* **22** (*tr*) to cause (pus, blood, etc) to discharge from an abscess or wound **23** (*intr*) (of two teams, contestants, etc) to finish a game with an equal number of points, goals, etc; tie **24** (*tr*) *bridge, whist* to keep leading a suit in order to force out (all outstanding cards) **25 draw trumps** *bridge, whist* to play the trump suit until the opponents have none left **26** (*tr*) *billiards* to cause (the cue ball) to spin back after a direct impact with another ball by applying backspin when making the stroke **27** (*tr*) to search (a place) in order to find wild animals, game, etc, for hunting **28** *golf* to cause (a golf ball) to move with a controlled right-to-left trajectory or (of a golf ball) to veer gradually from right to left **29** (*tr*) *curling* to deliver (the stone) gently **30** (*tr*) *nautical* (of a vessel) to require (a certain depth) in which to float **31 draw (a) blank** to get no results from something **32 draw and quarter** to disembowel and dismember (a person) after hanging **33 draw stumps** *cricket* to close play, as by pulling out the stumps **34 draw the line (at)** See **line¹** (sense 51) **35 draw the short straw** See **short straw** **36 draw the shot** *bowls* to deliver the bowl in such a way that it approaches the jack ▷ *n* **37** the act of drawing **38** *US* a sum of money advanced to finance anticipated expenses **39** an event, occasion, act, etc, that attracts a large audience **40** a raffle or lottery **41** something taken or chosen at random, as a ticket in a raffle or lottery **42** a contest or game ending in a tie **43** *US and Canadian* a small natural drainage way or gully **44** a defect found in metal castings due to the contraction of the metal on solidification ▷ See also **drawback, draw in, draw off, draw on, draw out, draw up** [Old English *dragan*; related to Old Norse *draga*; Old Frisian *draga*, Old Saxon *dragan*, Old High German *tragan* to carry] > 'drawable *adj*

drawback ('drɔːˌbæk) *n* **1** a disadvantage or hindrance **2** a refund of customs or excise duty paid on goods that are being exported or used in the production of manufactured exports ▷ *vb* **draw back** (*intr, adverb; often foll by* from) **3** to retreat; move backwards **4** to turn aside from an undertaking

drawbar ('drɔːˌbɑː) *n* a strong metal bar on a tractor, locomotive, etc, bearing a hook or link and pin to attach a trailer, wagon, etc

drawbridge ('drɔːˌbrɪdʒ) *n* a bridge that may be raised to prevent access or to enable vessels to pass

drawdown ('drɔːˌdaʊn) *n* **1** a depletion or reduction, for example of supplies **2** a continuous decline in an investment or fund, usually expressed as a percentage between its highest and lowest levels **3** the intentional draining of a body of water such as a lake or reservoir, to a given depth

drawee (drɔː'iː) *n* the person or organization on which a cheque or other order for payment is drawn

drawer ('drɔːə) *n* **1** a person or thing that draws, esp a draughtsman **2** a person who draws a cheque. See **draw** (sense 15) **3** a person who draws up a commercial paper **4** *archaic* a person who draws beer, etc, in a bar **5** (drɔː) a boxlike container in a chest, table, etc, made for sliding in and out

drawers (drɔːz) *pl n* a legged undergarment for either sex, worn below the waist. Also called: **underdrawers**

draw-gate *n* the valve that controls a sluice

draw gear *n Brit* an apparatus for coupling railway cars

draw in *vb* (*intr, adverb*) **1** (of hours of daylight) to become shorter **2** (of a train) to arrive at a station

drawing ('drɔːɪŋ) *n* **1** a picture or plan made by means of lines on a surface, esp one made with a pencil or pen without the use of colour **2** a sketch, plan, or outline **3** the art of making drawings; draughtsmanship

drawing account *n US* an account out of which an employee, partner, or salesman may make withdrawals to meet expenses or as advances against expected income

drawing board *n* **1** a smooth flat rectangular board on which paper, canvas, etc, is placed for making drawings **2 back to the drawing board** return to an earlier stage in an enterprise because a planned undertaking has failed

drawing card *n US and Canadian theatre* a performer, act, etc, certain to attract a large audience

drawing pin *n Brit* a short tack with a broad smooth head for fastening papers to a drawing board, etc. US and Canadian name: **thumbtack**

drawing room *n* **1** a room where visitors are received and entertained; living room; sitting room **2** *archaic* a ceremonial or formal reception, esp at court

drawknife ('drɔːˌnaɪf) *or* **drawshave** *n, pl* **-knives** *or* **-shaves** a woodcutting tool with two handles at right angles to the blade, used to shave wood. US name: **spokeshave**

drawl (drɔːl) *vb* **1** to speak or utter (words) slowly, esp prolonging the vowel sounds ▷ *n* **2** the way of speech of someone who drawls [C16 probably frequentative of DRAW] > 'drawler *n* > 'drawling *adj* > 'drawly *adj*

drawn (drɔːn) *adj* haggard, tired, or tense in appearance

drawn butter *n* melted butter often with seasonings

drawn work *n* ornamental needlework done by drawing threads out of the fabric and using the remaining threads to form lacelike patterns. Also called: **drawn-thread work**

draw off *vb* (*adverb*) **1** (*tr*) to cause (a liquid) to flow from something **2** to withdraw (troops)

draw on *vb* **1** (*intr, preposition*) to use or exploit (a source, fund, etc): *to draw on one's experience* **2** (*intr, adverb*) to come near: *the time for his interview drew on* **3** (*tr, preposition*) to withdraw (money) from (an account) **4** (*tr, adverb*) to put on (clothes) **5** (*tr, adverb*) to lead further; entice or encourage: *the prospect of nearing his goal drew him on*

draw out *vb* (*adverb*) **1** to extend or cause to be extended: *he drew out his stay* **2** (*tr*) to cause (a person) to talk freely: *she's been quiet all evening — see if you can draw her out* **3** (*tr; foll by* of) Also: **draw from** to elicit (information) (from): *he managed to draw out of his son where he had been* **4** (*tr*) to withdraw (money) as from a bank account or a business **5** (*intr*) (of hours of daylight) to become longer **6** (*intr*) (of a train) to leave a station **7** (*tr*) to extend (troops) in line; lead from camp **8** (*intr*) (of troops) to proceed from camp

drawplate ('drɔːˌpleɪt) *n* a plate used to reduce the diameter of wire by drawing it through conical holes

drawstring ('drɔːˌstrɪŋ) *n* **a** a cord, ribbon, etc, run through a hem around an opening, as on the bottom of a sleeve or at the mouth of a bag, so that when it is pulled tighter, the opening closes **b** (*as modifier*): *a drawstring neckline*

drawtube ('drɔːˌtjuːb) *n* a tube, such as one of the component tubes of a telescope, fitting coaxially within another tube through which it can slide

draw up *vb* (*adverb*) **1** to come or cause to come to a halt **2** (*tr*) **a** to prepare a draft of (a legal document) **b** to formulate and write out in appropriate form: *to draw up a contract* **3** (*used reflexively*) to straighten oneself **4** to form or arrange (a body of soldiers, etc) in order or formation

dray¹ (dreɪ) *n* **1 a** a low cart without fixed sides, used for carrying heavy loads **b** (*in combination*): *a drayman* **2** any other vehicle or sledge used to carry a heavy load [Old English *dræge* dragnet; related to Old Norse *draga* load of timber carried on horseback and trailing on the ground; see DRAW]

d

dray² (dreɪ) *n* a variant spelling of **drey**

drayage ('dreɪɪdʒ) *n US* **a** the act of transporting something a short distance by lorry or other vehicle **b** the charge made for such a transport

drayhorse ('dreɪ,hɔːs) *n* a large powerful horse used for drawing a dray

DRE (in the US) *abbreviation for* direct recording electronic: a system of voting in elections in which voters enter choices using an electronic device such as a touch screen

dread (drɛd) *vb* (*tr*) **1** to anticipate with apprehension or terror **2** to fear greatly **3** *archaic* to be in awe of ▷ *n* **4** great fear; horror **5** an object of terror **6** *slang* a Rastafarian **7** *archaic* deep reverence ▷ *adj* **8** *literary* awesome; awe-inspiring [Old English *ondrǣdan*; related to Old Saxon *antdrādan*, Old High German *intrātan*]

dreadful ('drɛdfʊl) *adj* **1** extremely disagreeable, shocking, or bad: *what a dreadful play* **2** (intensifier): *this is a dreadful waste of time* **3** causing dread; terrifying **4** *archaic* inspiring awe > 'dreadfulness *n*

dreadfully ('drɛdfʊlɪ) *adv* **1** in a shocking, or disagreeable manner **2** (intensifier): *you're dreadfully kind*

dreadlocks ('drɛd,lɒks) *pl n* hair worn in the Rastafarian style of long matted or tightly curled strands

dreadnought *or* **dreadnaught** ('drɛd,nɔːt) *n* **1** a battleship armed with heavy guns of uniform calibre **2** an overcoat made of heavy cloth **3** *slang* a heavyweight boxer **4** a person who fears nothing

dream (driːm) *n* **1 a** mental activity, usually in the form of an imagined series of events, occurring during certain phases of sleep **b** (*as modifier*): *a dream sequence* **c** (*in combination*): *dreamland*. Related adj: **oneiric 2 a** a sequence of imaginative thoughts indulged in while awake; daydream; fantasy **b** (*as modifier*): *a dream world* **3** a person or thing seen or occurring in a dream **4** a cherished hope; ambition; aspiration **5** a vain hope **6** a person or thing that is as pleasant, or seemingly unreal as a dream **7 go like a dream** to move, develop, or work very well ▷ *vb* **dreams, dreaming, dreamed** *or* **dreamt** (drɛmt) **8** (*may take a clause as object*) to undergo or experience (a dream or dreams) **9** (*intr*) to indulge in daydreams **10** (*intr*) to suffer delusions; be unrealistic: *you're dreaming if you think you can win* **11** (when *intr*, foll by *of* or *about*) to have an image (of) or fantasy (about) in or as if in a dream **12** (*intr*; foll by *of*) to consider the possibility (of): *I wouldn't dream of troubling you* ▷ See also **dream up** ▷ *adj* **13** too good to be true; ideal: *dream kitchen* [Old English *drēam* song; related to Old High German *troum*, Old Norse *draumr*, Greek *thrulos* noise] > 'dreamful *adj* > 'dreamfully *adv* > 'dreaming *n*, *adj* > 'dreamingly *adv* > 'dreamless *adj* > 'dreamlessly *adv* > 'dreamlessness *n* > 'dream,like *adj*

dreamboat ('driːm,bəʊt) *n* old-fashioned slang an exceptionally attractive person or thing, esp a person of the opposite sex

dreamer ('driːmə) *n* **1** a person who dreams habitually **2** a person who lives in or escapes to a world of fantasy or illusion; escapist **3** *archaic* a prophet; visionary

dreamland ('driːm,lænd) *n* an ideal land existing in dreams or in the imagination

dreamt (drɛmt) *vb* a past tense and past participle of **dream**

dream team *n* informal a group of people regarded as having the prefect combination of talents

dream ticket *n* a combination of two people, usu. candidates in an election, that is considered to be ideal

Dreamtime ('driːm,taɪm) *n* **1** (in the mythology of Australian Aboriginal peoples) a mythical Golden Age of the past. Also called: **alchera** ('æltʃərə), **alcheringa 2** *Austral informal* any remote period, out of touch with the actualities of the present

dream up *vb* (*tr, adverb*) to invent by ingenuity and imagination: *to dream up an excuse for leaving*

dreamy ('driːmɪ) *adj* **dreamier, dreamiest 1** vague or impractical **2** resembling a dream in quality **3** relaxing; gentle: *dreamy music* **4** *informal* wonderful **5** having dreams, esp daydreams > 'dreamily *adv* > 'dreaminess *n*

dreary ('drɪərɪ) *adj* **drearier, dreariest 1** sad or dull; dismal **2** wearying; boring **3** *archaic* miserable ▷ Also (literary): **drear** [Old English *drēorig* gory; related to Old High German *trūreg* sad] > 'drearily *adv* > 'dreariness *n*

dreck (drɛk) *n slang, chiefly US* rubbish; trash [from Yiddish *drek* filth, dregs] > 'drecky *adj*

drecksill ('drɛk,sɪl) *n Southwest English dialect* a doorstep

dredge¹ (drɛdʒ) *n* **1** Also called: **dredger** a machine, in the form of a bucket ladder, grab, or suction device, used to remove material from a riverbed, channel, etc **2** another name for **dredger¹** (sense 1) ▷ *vb* **3** to remove (material) from a riverbed, channel, etc, by means of a dredge **4** (*tr*) to search for (a submerged object) with or as if with a dredge; drag [C16 perhaps ultimately from Old English *dragan* to DRAW; see DRAG]

dredge² (drɛdʒ) *vb* to sprinkle or coat (food) with flour, sugar, etc [C16 from Old French *dragie*, perhaps from Latin *tragēmata* spices, from Greek]

dredger¹ ('drɛdʒə) *n* **1** Also called: **dredge** a vessel used for dredging, often bargelike and sometimes equipped with retractable steel piles that are driven into the bottom for stability **2** another name for **dredge¹** (sense 1)

dredger² ('drɛdʒə) *n* a container with a perforated top for sprinkling flour, sugar, etc

dredge up *vb* (*tr, adverb*) **1** to bring to notice, esp with considerable effort and from an obscure, remote, or unlikely source: *to dredge up worthless ideas* **2** to raise with or as if with a dredge: *they dredged up the corpse from the lake*

dree (driː) *Scot literary* ▷ *vb* **drees, dreeing, dreed 1** (*tr*) to endure **2 dree one's weird** to endure one's fate ▷ *adj* **3** another word for **dreich** [Old English *drēogan*; related to Old Norse *drȳgja* to perpetrate]

dreg (drɛg) *n* a small quantity: *not a dreg of pity*. See also **dregs** [see DREGS]

dreggy ('drɛgɪ) *adj* **-gier, -giest** like or full of dregs

D region *or* **layer** *n* the lowest region of the ionosphere, extending from a height of about 60 kilometres to about 90 kilometres: contains a low concentration of free electrons and reflects low-frequency radio waves. See also **ionosphere**

dregs (drɛgz) *pl n* **1** solid particles that tend to settle at the bottom of some liquids, such as wine or coffee **2** residue or remains **3** *Brit slang* a despicable person [C14 *dreg*, from Old Norse *dregg*; compare Icelandic *dreggjar* dregs, Latin *fracēs* oil dregs]

Dreibund *German* ('draɪbʊnt) *n* a triple alliance, esp that formed between Germany, Austria-Hungary, and Italy (1882–1915) [from *drei* THREE + *Bund* union, alliance]

dreich *or* **dreigh** (driːx) *adj Scot dialect* dreary [Middle English *dreig, drih* enduring, from Old English *drēog* (unattested); see DREE]

dreikanter ('draɪkæntə) *n* a pebble, common in desert areas, typically having three curved faces shaped by wind-blown sand [C20 from German: three-edged thing]

drench (drɛntʃ) *vb* (*tr*) **1** to make completely wet; soak **2** to give liquid medicine to (an animal), esp by force ▷ *n* **3** the act or an instance of drenching **4** a dose of liquid medicine given to an animal [Old English *drencan* to cause to drink; related to Old High German *trenken*] > 'drencher *n* > 'drenching *n*, *adj*

Drenthe (*Dutch* 'drɛntə) *n* a province of the NE Netherlands: a low plateau, with many raised bogs, partially reclaimed; agricultural, with oil deposits. Capital: Assen. Pop: 481 000 (2003 est). Area: 2647 sq km (1032 sq miles)

drepanid ('drɛpənɪd) *n* any moth of the superfamily Drepanoidae (family Drepanidae): it comprises the hook-tip moths

Dresden ('drɛzdən) *n* **1** an industrial city in SE Germany, the capital of Saxony on the River Elbe: it was severely damaged in the Seven Years' War (1760); the baroque city was almost totally destroyed in World War II by Allied bombing (1945). Pop: 483 632 (2003 est) ▷ *adj* **2** relating to, designating, or made of Dresden china

Dresden china *n* porcelain ware, esp delicate and elegantly decorative objects and figures of high quality, made at Meissen, near Dresden, since 1710

dress (drɛs) *vb* **1** to put clothes on (oneself or another); attire **2** (*intr*) **a** to change one's clothes **b** to wear formal or evening clothes **3** (*tr*) to provide (someone) with clothing; clothe **4** (*tr*) to arrange merchandise in (a shop window) for effective display **5** (*tr*) to comb out or arrange (the hair) into position **6** (*tr*) to apply protective or therapeutic covering to (a wound, sore, etc) **7** (*tr*) to prepare (food, esp fowl and fish) for cooking or serving by cleaning, trimming, gutting, etc **8** (*tr*) to put a finish on (the surface of stone, metal, etc) **9** (*tr*) to till and cultivate (land), esp by applying manure, compost, or fertilizer **10** (*tr*) to prune and trim (trees, bushes, etc) **11** (*tr*) to groom (an animal, esp a horse) **12** (*tr*) to convert (tanned hides) into leather **13** (*tr*) *archaic* to spay or neuter (an animal) **14** *angling* to tie (a fly) **15** *military* to bring (troops) into line or (of troops) to come into line (esp in the phrase **dress ranks**) **16 dress ship** *nautical* to decorate a vessel by displaying all signal flags on lines run from the bow to the stern over the mast trucks ▷ *n* **17** a one-piece garment for a woman, consisting of a skirt and bodice **18** complete style of clothing; costume: *formal dress; military dress* **19** (*modifier*) suitable or required for a formal occasion: *a dress shirt* **20** the outer covering or appearance, esp of living things: *trees in their spring dress of leaves* ▷ See also **dress down, dress up** [C14 from Old French *drecier*, ultimately from Latin *dīrigere* to DIRECT]

dressage ('drɛsɑːʒ) *n* **1** the method of training a horse to perform manoeuvres in response to the rider's body signals **2** the manoeuvres performed by a horse trained in this method [French: preparation, from Old French *dresser* to prepare; see DRESS]

dress circle *n* a tier of seats in a theatre or other auditorium, usually the first gallery above the ground floor

dress coat *n* a man's formal tailcoat with a cutaway skirt

dress code *n* a set of rules or guidelines regarding the manner of dress acceptable in an office, restaurant, etc

dress down *vb* (*adverb*) **1** (*tr*) *informal* to reprimand severely or scold (a person) **2** (*intr*) to dress in a casual or informal manner, esp at work

dress-down Friday *n* a policy adopted by some business organizations of promoting a relaxed atmosphere by allowing employees to wear informal clothing on a Friday

dresser¹ ('drɛsə) *n* **1** a set of shelves, usually also with cupboards or drawers, for storing or displaying dishes, etc **2** *US* a chest of drawers for storing clothing in a bedroom or dressing room, often having a mirror on the top [C14 *dressour*, from Old French *dreceore*, from *drecier* to arrange; see DRESS]

dresser² ('drɛsə) *n* **1** a person who dresses in a specified way: *a fashionable dresser* **2** *theatre* a person employed to assist actors in putting on and taking off their costumes **3** a tool used for dressing stone or other materials **4** *Brit* a person who assists a surgeon during operations **5** *Brit* See **window-dresser**

dress form *n* an adjustable dummy used in dressmaking that can be made to conform to a person's figure

dressing ('drɛsɪŋ) *n* **1** a sauce for food, esp for

salad **2** *US and Canadian* a mixture of chopped and seasoned ingredients with which poultry, meat, etc, is stuffed before cooking. Also called (in Britain and certain other countries): **stuffing 3** a covering for a wound, sore, etc **4** manure or artificial fertilizer spread on land **5** size used for stiffening textiles **6** the processes in the conversion of certain rough tanned hides into leather ready for use ▷ See also **dressings**

dressing case *n* (esp formerly) a box or case fitted with all the toilet articles necessary for dressing oneself, arranging one's hair, etc

dressing-down *n informal* a severe scolding or thrashing

dressing gown *n* a full robe worn before dressing or for lounging

dressing room *n* **1** *theatre* a room backstage for an actor to change clothing and to make up **2** any room used for changing clothes, such as one at a sports ground or off a bedroom

dressings ('drɛsɪŋz) *pl n* dressed stonework, mouldings, and carved ornaments used to form quoins, keystones, sills, and similar features

dressing station *n military* a first-aid post close to a combat area

dressing table *n* a piece of bedroom furniture with a mirror and a set of drawers for clothes, cosmetics, etc

dressmaker ('drɛs,meɪkə) *n* a person whose occupation is making clothes, esp for women > '**dress,making** *n*

dress parade *n military* a formal parade of sufficient ceremonial importance for the wearing of dress uniform

dress rehearsal *n* **1** the last complete rehearsal of a play or other work, using costumes, scenery, lighting, etc, as for the first night **2** any full-scale practice

dress shield *n* a fabric pad worn under the armpits or attached to the armhole of a garment to prevent sweat from showing on or staining the clothing

dress shirt *n* a man's shirt, usually white, worn as part of formal evening dress, usually having a stiffened or decorative front

dress suit *n* an ensemble of matching formal evening wear

dress uniform *n military* formal ceremonial uniform

dress up *vb* (*adverb*) **1** to attire (oneself or another) in one's best clothes **2** to put fancy dress, disguise, etc, on (oneself or another), as in children's games: *let's dress up as ghosts!* **3** (*tr*) to improve the appearance or impression of: *it's no good trying to dress up the facts*

dressy ('drɛsɪ) *adj* **dressier, dressiest 1** (of clothes) elegant **2** (of persons) dressing stylishly **3** over-elegant > '**dressily** *adv* > '**dressiness** *n*

dressy casual *adj* (of clothes) informal yet expensive, smart, or stylish

drew (dru:) *vb* the past tense of **draw**

drey *or* **dray** (dreɪ) *n* a squirrel's nest [C17 of unknown origin]

dribble ('drɪbªl) *vb* **1** (*usually intr*) to flow or allow to flow in a thin stream or drops; trickle **2** (*intr*) to allow saliva to trickle from the mouth **3** (in soccer, basketball, hockey, etc) to propel (the ball) by repeatedly tapping it with the hand, foot, or stick ▷ *n* **4** a small quantity of liquid falling in drops or flowing in a thin stream **5** a small quantity or supply **6** an act or instance of dribbling [C16 frequentative of *drib,* variant of DRIP] > '**dribbler** *n* > '**dribbly** *adj*

driblet *or* **dribblet** ('drɪblɪt) *n* a small quantity or amount, as of liquid [C17 from obsolete *drib* to fall bit by bit + -LET]

dribs and drabs (drɪbz) *pl n* small sporadic amounts

dried (draɪd) *vb* the past tense and past participle of **dry**

drier¹ ('draɪə) *adj* a comparative of **dry**

drier² ('draɪə) *n* a variant spelling of **dryer¹**

driest ('draɪɪst) *adj* a superlative of **dry**

drift (drɪft) *vb* (*mainly intr*) **1** (*also tr*) to be carried along by or as if by currents of air or water or (of a current) to carry (a vessel, etc) along **2** to move aimlessly from place to place or from one activity to another **3** to wander or move gradually away from a fixed course or point; stray **4** (*also tr*) (of snow, sand, etc) to accumulate in heaps or banks or to drive (snow, sand, etc) into heaps or banks ▷ *n* **5** something piled up by the wind or current, such as a snowdrift **6** tendency, trend, meaning, or purport: *the drift of the argument* **7** a state of indecision or inaction **8** the extent to which a vessel, aircraft, projectile, etc is driven off its course by adverse winds, tide, or current **9** a general tendency of surface ocean water to flow in the direction of the prevailing winds: *North Atlantic Drift* **10** a driving movement, force, or influence; impulse **11** a controlled four-wheel skid, used by racing drivers to take bends at high speed **12** a loose unstratified deposit of sand, gravel, etc, esp one transported and deposited by a glacier or ice sheet **13** a horizontal passage in a mine that follows the mineral vein **14** something, esp a group of animals, driven along by human or natural agencies: *a drift of cattle* **15** Also called: **driftpin** a tapering steel tool driven into holes to enlarge or align them before bolting or riveting **16** an uncontrolled slow change in some operating characteristic of a piece of equipment, esp an electronic circuit or component **17** *linguistics* gradual change in a language, esp in so far as this is influenced by the internal structure of the language rather than by contact with other languages **18** *South African* a ford **19** *engineering* a copper or brass bar used as a punch [C13 from Old Norse: snowdrift; related to Old High German *trift* pasturage] > '**drifty** *adj*

driftage ('drɪftɪdʒ) *n* **1** the act of drifting **2** matter carried along or deposited by drifting **3** the amount by which an aircraft or vessel has drifted from its intended course

drift anchor *n* another term for **sea anchor**

drifter ('drɪftə) *n* **1** a person or thing that drifts **2** a person who moves aimlessly from place to place, usually without a regular job **3** a boat used for drift-net fishing **4** *nautical* a large jib of thin material used in light breezes

drift ice *n* masses of ice floating in the open sea

drift net *n* a large fishing net supported by floats or attached to a drifter that is allowed to drift with the tide or current

drift transistor *n* a transistor in which the impurity concentration in the base increases from the collector-base junction to the emitter-base junction, producing a resistivity gradient that greatly increases its high-frequency response

drift tube *n physics* a hollow cylindrical electrode to which a radio-frequency voltage is applied in a linear accelerator

driftwood ('drɪft,wʊd) *n* wood floating on or washed ashore by the sea or other body of water

drill¹ (drɪl) *n* **1** a rotating tool that is inserted into a drilling machine or tool for boring cylindrical holes **2** a hand tool, either manually or electrically operated, for drilling holes **3** *military* **a** training in procedures or movements, as for ceremonial parades or the use of weapons **b** (*as modifier*): *drill hall* **4** strict and often repetitious training or exercises used as a method of teaching **5** *informal* correct procedure or routine **6** a marine gastropod mollusc, *Urosalpinx cinera,* closely related to the whelk, that preys on oysters ▷ *vb* **7** to pierce, bore, or cut (a hole) in (material) with or as if with a drill: *to drill a hole; to drill metal* **8** to instruct or be instructed in military procedures or movements **9** (*tr*) to teach by rigorous exercises or training **10** (*tr*) *informal* to hit (a ball) in a straight line at great speed **11** (*tr*) *informal* to riddle with bullets ▷ See also **drill down** [C17 from Middle Dutch *drillen;* related to Old High German *drāen* to turn] > '**drillable** *adj* > '**driller** *n*

drill² (drɪl) *n* **1** a machine for planting seeds in rows or depositing fertilizer **2** a small furrow in which seeds are sown **3** a row of seeds planted using a drill ▷ *vb* **4** to plant (seeds) by means of a drill [C18 of uncertain origin; compare German *Rille* furrow] > '**driller** *n*

drill³ (drɪl) *or* **drilling** *n* a hard-wearing twill-weave cotton cloth, used for uniforms, etc [C18 variant of German *Drillich,* from Latin *trilīx,* from TRI- + *līcium* thread]

drill⁴ (drɪl) *n* an Old World monkey, *Mandrillus leucophaeus,* of W Africa, related to the mandrill but smaller and less brightly coloured [C17 from a West African word; compare MANDRILL]

drill down *vb* (*intr, adverb*) to look at or examine something in depth: *to drill down through financial data*

drilling mud *n* a mixture of clays, water, and chemicals pumped down the drill string while an oil well is being drilled to lubricate the mechanism, carry away rock cuttings, and maintain pressure so that oil or gas does not escape

drilling platform *n* a structure, either fixed to the sea bed or mobile, which supports the machinery and equipment (**drilling rig**), together with the stores, required for digging an offshore oil well

drilling rig *n* **1** the full name for **rig** (sense 6) **2** a mobile drilling platform used for exploratory offshore drilling

drillmaster ('drɪl,mɑ:stə) *n* **1** *obsolete* Also called: **drill sergeant** a military drill instructor **2** a person who instructs in a strict manner

drill press *n* a machine tool for boring holes, having a stand and work table with facilities for lowering the tool to the workpiece

drillstock ('drɪl,stɒk) *n* the part of a machine tool that holds the shank of a drill or bit; chuck

drill string *or* **pipe** *n* (in the oil industry) a pipe made of lengths of steel tubing that is attached to the drilling tool and rotates during drilling to form a bore

drily *or* **dryly** ('draɪlɪ) *adv* in a dry manner

Drin (drɪn) *n* a river in S Europe, rising in SW Macedonia and flowing north and west, through Albania, into the Adriatic Sea. Length: about 270 km (170 miles)

drink (drɪŋk) *vb* **drinks, drinking, drank** (dræŋk) **drunk** (drʌŋk) **1** to swallow (a liquid); imbibe **2** (*tr*) to take in or soak up (liquid); absorb: *this plant drinks a lot of water* **3** (*tr; usually foll by in*) to pay close attention (to); be fascinated (by): *he drank in the speaker's every word* **4** (*tr*) to bring (oneself into a certain condition) by consuming alcohol **5** (*tr; often foll by away*) to dispose of or ruin by excessive expenditure on alcohol: *he drank away his fortune* **6** (*intr*) to consume alcohol, esp to excess **7** (when *intr,* foll by *to*) to drink (a toast) in celebration, honour, or hope (of) **8** **drink (someone) under the table** to be able to drink more intoxicating beverage than (someone) **9** **drink the health of** to salute or celebrate with a toast **10** **drink with the flies** *Austral informal* to drink alone ▷ *n* **11** liquid suitable for drinking; any beverage **12** alcohol or its habitual or excessive consumption **13** a portion of liquid for drinking; draught **14** **the drink** *informal* the sea [Old English *drincan;* related to Old Frisian *drinka,* Gothic *drigkan,* Old High German *trinkan*] > '**drinkable** *adj*

drink-driving *n* (*modifier*) of or relating to driving a car after drinking alcohol: *drink-driving offences; drink-driving campaign*

drinker ('drɪŋkə) *n* **1** a person who drinks, esp a person who drinks alcohol habitually **2** short for **drinker moth**

drinker moth *n* a large yellowish-brown bombycid eggar moth, *Philudoria potatoria,* having a stout hairy body, the larvae of which drink dew and feed on grasses. Also called: **drinker**

drinking fountain *n* a device for providing a flow

d

or jet of drinking water, usually in public places

drinking-up time *n* (in Britain) a short time allowed for finishing drinks before closing time in a public house

drinking water *n* water reserved or suitable for drinking

drip (drɪp) *vb* **drips, dripping, dripped 1** to fall or let fall in drops ▷ *n* **2** the formation and falling of drops of liquid **3** the sound made by falling drops **4** *architect* a projection at the front lower edge of a sill or cornice designed to throw water clear of the wall below **5** *informal* an inane, insipid person **6** *med* **a** the usually intravenous drop-by-drop administration of a therapeutic solution, as of salt or sugar **b** the solution administered **c** the equipment used to administer a solution in this way [Old English *dryppan*, from *dropa* DROP]

drip-dry *adj* **1** designating clothing or a fabric that will dry relatively free of creases if hung up when wet ▷ *vb* **-dries, -drying, -dried 2** to dry or become dry thus

drip-feed *n* **1** another name for **drip** (sense 6) ▷ *vb* (*tr*) **drip feed 2** to administer a solution (to someone) by means of a drip-feed **3** to supply information constantly but in small amounts **4** *informal* to fund (a new company) in stages rather than by injecting a large sum at its inception ▷ *n* **5** a constant supply of small amounts of information

dripping ('drɪpɪŋ) *n* **1** the fat exuded by roasting meat **2** (*often plural*) liquid that falls in drops ▷ *adv* **3** (intensifier): *dripping wet*

dripping pan *or* **drip pan** *n* a shallow pan placed under roasting meat to catch the dripping

drippy ('drɪpɪ) *adj* **-pier, -piest 1** *informal* mawkish, insipid, or inane **2** tending to drip

dripstone ('drɪpˌstəʊn) *n* **1** the form of calcium carbonate existing in stalactites or stalagmites **2** Also called: **label, hood mould** *architect* a drip made of stone

drisheen (drɪ'ʃiːn) *n* *Irish* a pudding made of sheep's intestines filled with meal and sheep's blood [c20 from Irish Gaelic *drisín* an animal's intestines]

drive (draɪv) *vb* **drives, driving, drove** (drəʊv) **driven** ('drɪvən) **1** to push, propel, or be pushed or propelled **2** to control and guide the movement of (a vehicle, draught animal, etc): *to drive a car* **3** (*tr*) to compel or urge to work or act, esp excessively **4** (*tr*) to goad or force into a specified attitude or state: *work drove him to despair* **5** (*tr*) to cause (an object) to make or form (a hole, crack, etc): *his blow drove a hole in the wall* **6** to move or cause to move rapidly by striking or throwing with force **7** *sport* to hit (a ball) very hard and straight, as (in cricket) with the bat swinging more or less vertically **8** *golf* to strike (the ball) with a driver, as in teeing off **9** (*tr*) **a** to chase (game) from cover into more open ground **b** to search (an area) for game **10** to transport or be transported in a driven vehicle **11** (*intr*) to rush or dash violently, esp against an obstacle or solid object: *the waves drove against the rock* **12** (*tr*) to carry through or transact with vigour (esp in the phrase **drive a hard bargain**) **13** (*tr*) to force (a component) into or out of its location by means of blows or a press **14** (*tr*) *mining* to excavate horizontally **15** (*tr*) NZ to fell (a tree or trees) by the impact of another felled tree **16 drive home a** to cause to penetrate to the fullest extent **b** to make clear by special emphasis ▷ *n* **17** the act of driving **18** a trip or journey in a driven vehicle **19 a** a road for vehicles, esp a private road leading to a house **b** (*capital when part of a street name*): *Woodland Drive* **20** vigorous or urgent pressure, as in business **21** a united effort, esp directed towards a common goal: *a charity drive* **22** *Brit* a large gathering of persons to play cards, etc. See **beetle drive, whist drive 23** energy, ambition, or initiative **24** *psychol* a motive or interest, such as sex, hunger, or ambition, that actuates an organism to attain a goal **25** a sustained and powerful military offensive **26 a** the means by which force, torque, motion, or power is transmitted in a mechanism: *fluid drive* **b** (*as modifier*): *a drive shaft* **27** *sport* a hard straight shot or stroke **28** a search for and chasing of game towards waiting guns **29** *electronics* the signal applied to the input of an amplifier [Old English *drīfan*; related to Old Frisian *drīva*, Old Norse *drīfa*, Gothic *dreiban*, Old High German *trīban*] > '**drivable** *or* '**driveable** *adj* > ˌ**driva'bility** *or* ˌ**drivea'bility** *n*

drive at *vb* (*intr, preposition*) *informal* to intend or mean: *what are you driving at?*

drive-by download *n* an incidence of an unwanted program being automatically downloaded to a computer, often without the user's knowledge

drive-by shooting *n* an incident in which a person, building, or vehicle is shot at by someone in a moving vehicle. Sometimes shortened to: **drive-by**

drive-in *n* *chiefly US and Canadian* **a** a cinema designed to be used by patrons seated in their cars **b** (*modifier*) a public facility or service designed for use in such a manner: *a drive-in restaurant; a drive-in bank*

drivel ('drɪvəl) *vb* **-els, -elling, -elled** *or US* **-els, -eling, -eled 1** to allow (saliva) to flow from the mouth; dribble **2** (*intr*) to speak foolishly or childishly ▷ *n* **3** foolish or senseless talk **4** saliva flowing from the mouth; slaver [Old English *dreflian* to slaver; see DRAFF] > '**driveller** *n*

driven ('drɪvən) *vb* the past participle of **drive**

drive-off *n* *informal* **a** the act or an instance of leaving a filling station without paying for one's fuel **b** (*as modifier*): *a drive-off theft*

driver ('draɪvə) *n* **1** a person who drives a vehicle **2 in the driver's seat** in a position of control **3** a person who drives animals **4** a mechanical component that exerts a force on another to produce motion **5** *golf* a club, a No. 1 wood, with a large head and deep face for tee shots **6** *electronics* a circuit whose output provides the input of another circuit **7** *computing* a computer program that controls a device **8** something that creates and fuels activity, or gives force or impetus > '**driverless** *adj*

driver ant *n* any of various tropical African predatory ants of the subfamily *Dorylinae*, which live in temporary nests and travel in vast hordes preying on other animals. See also **army ant**

drive shaft *n* another name for **propeller shaft**

drive-thru *n* **a** a takeaway restaurant, bank, etc designed so that customers can use it without leaving their cars **b** (*as modifier*): *a drive-thru restaurant*

drive-time *n* **a** the time of day when many people are driving to or from work, regarded as a broadcasting slot **b** (*as modifier*): *the daily drive-time show*

driveway ('draɪvˌweɪ) *n* a private road for vehicles, often connecting a house or garage with a public road; drive

driving ('draɪvɪŋ) *adj* **1** having or moving with force and violence: *driving rain* **2** forceful or energetic **3** relating to the controlling of a motor vehicle in motion: *driving test*

driving chain *n* *engineering* a roller chain that transmits power from one toothed wheel to another. Also called: **drive chain**

driving licence *n* an official document or certificate authorizing a person to drive a motor vehicle

driving wheel *n* **1** a wheel, esp a gear wheel, that causes other wheels to rotate **2** any wheel of a vehicle that transforms torque into a tractive force

drizzle ('drɪzəl) *n* **1** very light rain, specifically consisting of droplets less than 0.5 mm in diameter ▷ *vb* **2** (*intr*) to rain lightly **3** (*tr*) to moisten with tiny droplets [Old English *drēosan* to fall; related to Old Saxon *driosan*, Gothic *driusan*, Norwegian *drjōsa*] > '**drizzly** *adj*

drizzle cake *n* a sponge cake that has syrup drizzled over it immediately after baking

Drogheda ('drɔɪɪdə) *n* a port in NE Republic of Ireland, in Co Louth near the mouth of the River Boyne: captured by Cromwell in 1649 and its inhabitants massacred. Pop: 31 020 (2002)

drogue (drəʊg) *n* **1** any funnel-like device, esp one of canvas, used as a sea anchor **2 a** a small parachute released behind a jet aircraft to reduce its landing speed **b** a small parachute released before a heavier main parachute during the landing of a spacecraft **3** a device towed behind an aircraft as a target for firing practice **4** a funnel-shaped device on the end of the refuelling hose of a tanker aircraft, to assist stability and the location of the probe of the receiving aircraft **5** another name for **windsock** [c18 probably based ultimately on Old English *dragan* to DRAW]

droit (drɔɪt; *French* drwa) *n, pl* **droits** (drɔɪts; *French* drwa) a legal or moral right or claim; due [c15 from French: legal right, from Medieval Latin *dīrēctum* law, from Latin: a straight line; see DIRECT]

droit de suite (*French* drwad sɥit) *n* a right recognized by the legislation of several member countries of the European Union whereby an artist, or his or her heirs, is entitled to a share of the price of a work of art if it is resold during the artist's lifetime or for 70 years after his or her death [from French, literally: the right of following]

droit du seigneur (*French* drwa dy sɛɲœr) *n* in feudal times, the right of a lord to have sexual intercourse with a vassal's bride on her wedding night [from French, literally: the right of the lord]

droll (drəʊl) *adj* amusing in a quaint or odd manner; comical [c17 from French *drôle* scamp, from Middle Dutch: imp] > '**drollness** *n* > '**drolly** *adv*

drollery ('drəʊlərɪ) *n, pl* **-eries 1** humour; comedy **2** *rare* a droll act, story, or remark

Drôme (*French* drom) *n* a department of SE France, in Rhône-Alpes region. Capital: Valence. Pop: 452 652 (2003 est. Area: 6561 sq km (2559 sq miles)

-drome *n combining form* **1** a course, racecourse: *hippodrome* **2** a large place for a special purpose: *aerodrome* [via Latin from Greek *dromos* race, course]

dromedary ('drʌmədərɪ, -drɪ, 'drɒm-) *n, pl* **-daries 1** a type of Arabian camel bred for racing and riding, having a single hump and long slender legs **2** another name for **Arabian camel** [c14 from Late Latin *dromedārius* (*camēlus*), from Greek *dromas* running]

dromond ('drɒmənd, 'drʌm-) *or* **dromon** ('drɒmən, 'drʌm-) *n* a large swift sailing vessel of the 12th to 15th centuries [c13 from Anglo-French *dromund*, ultimately from Late Greek *dromōn* light swift ship, from *dromos* a running]

-dromous *adj combining form* moving or running: *anadromous; catadromous* [via New Latin from Greek *-dromos*, from *dromos* a running]

drone[1] (drəʊn) *n* **1** a male bee in a colony of social bees, whose sole function is to mate with the queen **2** *Brit* a person who lives off the work of others **3** a pilotless radio-controlled aircraft [Old English *drān*; related to Old High German *treno* drone, Gothic *drunjus* noise, Greek *tenthrēnē* wasp; see DRONE[2]] > '**dronish** *adj*

drone[2] (drəʊn) *vb* **1** (*intr*) to make a monotonous low dull sound; buzz or hum **2** (when *intr*, often foll by *on*) to utter (words) in a monotonous tone, esp to talk without stopping ▷ *n* **3** a monotonous low dull sound **4** *music* **a** a sustained bass note or chord of unvarying pitch accompanying a melody **b** (*as modifier*): *a drone bass* **5** *music* one of the single-reed pipes in a set of bagpipes, used for accompanying the melody played on the chanter **6** a person who speaks in a low monotonous tone [c16 related to DRONE[1] and Middle Dutch *drōnen*, German *dröhnen*] > '**droning** *adj* > '**droningly** *adv*

drone aircraft *n* a pilotless radio-controlled aircraft used for reconnaissance or bombing

drongo ('drɒŋgəʊ) *n, pl* **-gos 1** Also called: **drongo**

shrike any insectivorous songbird of the family *Dicruridae*, of the Old World tropics, having a glossy black plumage, a forked tail, and a stout bill **2** *Austral and NZ slang* a slow-witted person **3** *Austral informal* a new recruit in the Royal Australian Air Force [C19 from Malagasy]

dronklap (ˈdrɒŋkˌlæp) *n South African* a drunkard

dronkverdriet (ˌdrɒŋkfəˈdriːt) *adj South African* drunk and maudlin [Afrikaans, literally: drunk and remorseful]

droob (druːb) *n Austral archaic slang* a pathetic person [C20 of unknown origin]

drook (drʊk) *vb* (*tr*) *Scot* a variant spelling of **drouk**

drookit (ˈdrʊkɪt) *adj Scot* a variant spelling of **droukit**

drool (druːl) *vb* **1** (*intr;* often foll by *over*) to show excessive enthusiasm (for) or pleasure (in); gloat (over) ▷ *vb, n* **2** another word for **drivel** (senses 1, 2, 4) [C19 probably alteration of DRIVEL]

droop (druːp) *vb* **1** to sag or allow to sag, as from weakness or exhaustion; hang down; sink **2** (*intr*) to be overcome by weariness; languish; flag **3** (*intr*) to lose courage; become dejected ▷ *n* **4** the act or state of drooping [C13 from Old Norse *drūpa;* see DROP] > ˈ**drooping** *adj* > ˈ**droopingly** *adv*

droopy (ˈdruːpɪ) *adj* hanging or sagging downwards: *a droopy moustache* > ˈ**droopily** *adv* > ˈ**droopiness** *n*

drop (drɒp) *n* **1** a small quantity of liquid that forms or falls in a spherical or pear-shaped mass; globule **2** a very small quantity of liquid **3** a very small quantity of anything **4** something resembling a drop in shape or size, such as a decorative pendant or small sweet **5** the act or an instance of falling; descent **6** a decrease in amount or value; slump: *a drop in prices* **7** the vertical distance that anything may fall **8** a steep or sheer incline or slope **9** short for **fruit drop** **10** the act of unloading troops, equipment, or supplies by parachute **11** (in cable television) a short spur from a trunk cable that feeds signals to an individual house **12** *theatre* See **drop curtain** **13** another word for **trap door** *or* **gallows** **14** *chiefly US and Canadian* a slot or aperture through which an object can be dropped to fall into a receptacle **15** *nautical* the midships height of a sail bent to a fixed yard. Compare **hoist** (sense 6a) **16** *Austral cricket slang* a fall of the wicket: *he came in at first drop* **17** See **drop shot** **18** **a drop in the bucket** (*or* **in the ocean**) an amount very small in relation to what is needed or desired **19** **at the drop of a hat** without hesitation or delay **20** **have had a drop too much** to be drunk **21** **have the drop on** (someone) *US and NZ* to have the advantage over (someone) ▷ *vb* **drops, dropping, dropped** **22** (of liquids) to fall or allow to fall in globules **23** to fall or allow to fall vertically **24** (*tr*) to allow to fall by letting go of **25** to sink or fall or cause to sink or fall to the ground, as from a blow, wound, shot, weariness, etc **26** (*intr;* foll by *back, behind,* etc) to fall, move, or go in a specified manner, direction, etc **27** (*intr;* foll by *in, by,* etc) *informal* to pay a casual visit (to) **28** to decrease or cause to decrease in amount or value: *the cost of living never drops* **29** to sink or cause to sink to a lower position, as on a scale **30** to make or become less in strength, volume, etc **31** (*intr*) to sink or decline in health or condition **32** (*intr;* sometimes foll by *into*) to pass easily into a state or condition: *to drop into a habit* **33** (*intr*) to move along gently as with a current of water or air **34** (*tr*) to allow to pass casually in conversation: *to drop a hint* **35** (*tr*) to leave out (a word or letter) **36** (*tr*) to set down or unload (passengers or goods) **37** (*tr*) to send or post: *drop me a line* **38** (*tr*) to discontinue; terminate: *let's drop the matter* **39** (*tr*) to cease to associate or have to do with **40** (*tr*) *slang, chiefly US* to cease to employ: *he was dropped from his job* **41** (*tr;* sometimes foll by *in, off,* etc) *informal* to leave or deposit, esp at a specified place **42** (of animals) to give birth to (offspring) **43** *slang, chiefly US and Canadian* to lose (money), esp when gambling **44** (*tr*) to lengthen (a hem, etc) **45** (*tr*) to unload (troops, equipment, or supplies) by parachute **46** (*tr*) *nautical* to leave behind; sail out of sight of **47** (*tr*) *sport* to omit (a player) from a team **48** (*tr*) to lose (a score, game, or contest): *the champion dropped his first service game* **49** (*tr*) *sport* to hit or throw (a ball) into a goal: *he dropped a 30 foot putt* **50** (*tr*) to hit (a ball) with a drop shot **51** **drop astern** *nautical* to fall back to the stern (of another vessel) **52** (*tr*) *motor racing slang* to spin (the car) and (usually) crash out of the race **53** (*tr*) *slang* to swallow (a drug, esp a barbiturate or LSD) **54** **drop dead!** *slang* an exclamation of contempt ▷ *n, vb* **55** *rugby* short for **drop kick** *or* **drop-kick** ▷ See also **drop away, drop in, drop off, dropout, drops** [Old English *dropian;* related to Old High German *triofan* to DRIP]

drop away *vb* (*intr, adverb*) to fall or go away gradually

drop cannon *n billiards* a shot in which the first object ball joins or gathers with the cue ball and the other object ball, esp at the top of the table

drop curtain *n theatre* a curtain that is suspended from the flies and can be raised and lowered onto the stage. Also called: **drop cloth, drop**

drop-dead *adv informal* outstandingly or exceptionally: *drop-dead gorgeous*

drop-dead date *n* an absolute deadline that cannot be missed

drop-dead fee *n* a fee paid to an organization lending money to a company that is hoping to use it to finance a takeover bid. The fee is only paid if the bid fails and interest charges are only incurred if the money is needed

drop-down menu *n* a menu that appears on a computer screen when its title is selected and remains on display until dismissed

drop forge *n* **1** Also called: **drop hammer** a device for forging metal between two dies, one of which is fixed, the other acting by gravity or by steam or hydraulic pressure ▷ *vb* **drop-forge** (*tr*) **2** to forge (metal) into (a component) by the use of a drop forge

drop goal *n rugby* a goal scored with a drop kick during the run of play

drop hammer *n* another name for **drop forge**

drophead coupé *n Brit* a two-door four-seater car with a folding roof and a sloping back

drop in *vb* (*intr, adverb*) *surfing* to intrude on a wave that another surfer is already riding

drop-in centre *n social welfare* (in Britain) a daycentre run by the social services or a charity that clients may attend on an informal basis

drop kick *n* **1** a kick in certain sports such as rugby, in which the ball is dropped and kicked as it bounces from the ground. Compare **punt²**, **place kick** **2** a wrestling attack, illegal in amateur wrestling, in which a wrestler leaps in the air and kicks his opponent in the face or body with both feet **3** *Austral slang* a stupid or worthless person ▷ *vb* **drop-kick** **4** to kick (a ball, etc) using a drop kick **5** to kick (an opponent in wrestling) by the use of a drop kick

drop leaf *n* **a** a hinged flap on a table that can be raised and supported by a bracket or additional pivoted leg to extend the surface **b** (*as modifier*): *a drop-leaf table*

droplet (ˈdrɒplɪt) *n* a tiny drop

droplight (ˈdrɒpˌlaɪt) *n* an electric light that may be raised or lowered by means of a pulley or other mechanism

drop lock *n finance* a variable-rate bank loan used on international markets that is automatically replaced by a fixed-rate long-term bond if the long-term interest rates fall to a specified level; it thus combines the advantages of a bank loan with those of a bond

drop off *vb* (*adverb*) **1** (*intr*) to grow smaller or less; decline **2** (*tr*) to allow to alight; set down **3** (*intr*) *informal* to fall asleep ▷ *n* **drop-off** **4** a steep or vertical descent **5** a sharp decrease

dropout (ˈdrɒpˌaʊt) *n* **1** a student who fails to complete a school or college course **2** a person who rejects conventional society **3** **drop-out** *rugby* a drop kick taken by the defending team to restart play, as after a touchdown **4** **drop-out** *electronics* a momentary loss of signal in a magnetic recording medium as a result of an imperfection in its magnetic coating ▷ *vb* **drop out** (*intr, adverb;* often foll by *of*) **5** to abandon or withdraw from (a school, social group, job, etc)

dropped sole *n vet science* a condition in which the foot of a horse is convex instead of concave. Also called: **convex sole**

dropper (ˈdrɒpə) *n* **1** a small tube having a rubber bulb at one end for drawing up and dispensing drops of liquid **2** a person or thing that drops **3** *angling* a short length of monofilament by which a fly is attached to the main trace or leader above the tail fly **4** *Austral and NZ* a batten attached to the top wire of a fence to keep the wires apart

droppings (ˈdrɒpɪŋz) *pl n* the dung of certain animals, such as rabbits, sheep, and birds

drops (drɒps) *pl n* any liquid medication applied by means of a dropper

drop scone *n* a flat spongy cake made by dropping a spoonful of batter on a griddle. Also called: **girdlecake, griddlecake, Scotch pancake,** (*Scot*) **pancake**

drop shipment *n* a consignment invoiced to a wholesaler or other middleman but sent directly to the retailer by a manufacturer

drop shot *n* **1** **a** *tennis* a softly-played return that drops abruptly after clearing the net, intended to give an opponent no chance of reaching the ball and usually achieved by imparting backspin **b** *squash* a similar shot that stops abruptly after hitting the front wall of the court **2** a type of shot made by permitting molten metal to percolate through a sieve and then dropping it into a tank of water

dropsonde (ˈdrɒpsɒnd) *n meteorol* a radiosonde dropped by parachute [C20 DROP + (RADIO)SONDE]

dropsy (ˈdrɒpsɪ) *n* **1** *pathol* a condition characterized by an accumulation of watery fluid in the tissues or in a body cavity **2** *slang* a tip or bribe [C13 shortened from *ydropesie,* from Latin *hydrōpisis,* from Greek *hudrōps,* from *hudōr* water] > **dropsical** (ˈdrɒpsɪkᵊl) *or* ˈ**dropsied** *adj* > ˈ**dropsically** *adv*

drop tank *n* an external aircraft tank, usually containing fuel, that can be detached and dropped in flight

dropwort (ˈdrɒpˌwɜːt) *n* **1** a Eurasian rosaceous plant, *Filipendula vulgaris,* with finely divided leaves and clusters of white or reddish flowers. See also **meadowsweet** (sense 1) **2** **water dropwort** any of several umbelliferous marsh plants of the genus *Oenanthe,* with umbrella-shaped clusters of white flowers

droshky (ˈdrɒʃkɪ) *or* **drosky** (ˈdrɒskɪ) *n, pl* **-kies** an open four-wheeled horse-drawn passenger carriage, formerly used in Russia [C19 from Russian *drozhki,* diminutive of *drogi* a wagon, from *droga* shaft]

drosometer (drɒˈsɒmɪtə) *n* an instrument that measures the amount of dew deposited [C19 from Greek *drosos* dew + -METER]

drosophila (drɒˈsɒfɪlə) *n, pl* **-las** *or* **-lae** (-ˌliː) any small dipterous fly of the genus *Drosophila,* esp *D. melanogaster,* a species widely used in laboratory genetics studies: family *Drosophilidae.* They feed on plant sap, decaying fruit, etc. Also called: **fruit fly, vinegar fly** [C19 New Latin, from Greek *drosos* dew, water + *-phila;* see -PHILE]

dross (drɒs) *n* **1** the scum formed, usually by oxidation, on the surfaces of molten metals **2** worthless matter; waste [Old English *drōs* dregs; related to Old High German *truosana*] > ˈ**drossy** *adj* > ˈ**drossiness** *n*

drought (draʊt) *n* **1** a prolonged period of scanty rainfall **2** a prolonged shortage **3** an archaic or dialect word for **thirst** Archaic and Scot form:

d

drouth (dru:θ) [Old English *drūgoth*; related to Dutch *droogte*; see DRY] > **'drouthy** *adj*

drouk *or* **drook** (druk) *vb* (*tr*) *Scot* to drench; soak [C16 of uncertain origin; compare Old Norse *drukna* to be drowned]

droukit *or* **drookit** ('drukɪt) *adj Scot* drenched; soaked [from DROUK]

drouthy ('druθɪ) *adj Scot* thirsty or dry

drove¹ (drəʊv) *vb* the past tense of **drive**

drove² (drəʊv) *n* **1** a herd of livestock being driven together **2** (*often plural*) a moving crowd of people **3** a narrow irrigation channel **4** Also called: **drove chisel** a chisel with a broad edge used for dressing stone ⊳ *vb* **5 a** (*tr*) to drive (a group of livestock), usually for a considerable distance **b** (*intr*) to be employed as a drover **6** to work (a stone surface) with a drove [Old English *drāf* herd; related to Middle Low German *drēfwech* cattle pasture; see DRIVE, DRIFT]

drover ('drəʊvə) *n* a person whose occupation is the driving of sheep or cattle, esp to and from market

drown (draʊn) *vb* **1** to die or kill by immersion in liquid **2** (*tr*) to destroy or get rid of as if by submerging: *he drowned his sorrows in drink* **3** (*tr*) to drench thoroughly; inundate; flood **4** (*tr; sometimes foll by out*) to render (a sound) inaudible by making a loud noise [C13 probably from Old English *druncnian*; related to Old Norse *drukna* to be drowned] > **'drowner** *n*

drowse (draʊz) *vb* **1** to be or cause to be sleepy, dull, or sluggish ⊳ *n* **2** the state of being drowsy [C16 probably from Old English *drūsian* to sink; related to *drēosan* to fall]

drowsy ('draʊzɪ) *adj* drowsier, drowsiest **1** heavy with sleepiness; sleepy **2** inducing sleep; soporific **3** sluggish or lethargic; dull > **'drowsily** *adv* > **'drowsiness** *n*

drub (drʌb) *vb* drubs, drubbing, drubbed (*tr*) **1** to beat as with a stick; cudgel; club **2** to defeat utterly, as in a contest **3** to drum or stamp (the feet) **4** to instil with force or repetition: *the master drubbed Latin into the boys* ⊳ *n* **5** a blow, as from a stick [C17 probably from Arabic *dáraba* to beat]

drubbing ('drʌbɪŋ) *n* **1** a beating, as with a stick, cudgel, etc **2** a comprehensive or heavy defeat, esp in a sporting competition

drudge (drʌdʒ) *n* **1** a person, such as a servant, who works hard at wearisome menial tasks ⊳ *vb* **2** (*intr*) to toil at such tasks [C16 perhaps from *druggen* to toil] > **'drudger** *n* > **'drudgingly** *adv*

drudgery ('drʌdʒərɪ) *n*, *pl* -eries hard, menial, and monotonous work

drug (drʌg) *n* **1** any synthetic, semisynthetic, or natural chemical substance used in the treatment, prevention, or diagnosis of disease, or for other medical reasons. Related adj: **pharmaceutical 2** a chemical substance, esp a narcotic, taken for the pleasant effects it produces **3** drug on the market a commodity available in excess of the demands of the market ⊳ *vb* **drugs, drugging, drugged** (*tr*) **4** to mix a drug with (food, drink, etc) **5** to administer a drug to **6** to stupefy or poison with or as if with a drug. Related prefix: **pharmaco-** [C14 from Old French *drogue*, probably of Germanic origin] > **'druggy** *adj*

drug addict *n* any person who is abnormally dependent on narcotic drugs. See **addiction**

drug baron *n* the head of an organization that deals in illegal drugs

drugget ('drʌgɪt) *n* a coarse fabric used as a protective floor-covering, etc [C16 from French *droguet* useless fabric, from *drogue* trash]

druggie ('drʌgɪ) *n informal* a drug addict

druggist ('drʌgɪst) *n US and Canadian* a person qualified to prepare and dispense drugs. Also called: **pharmacist**

druglord ('drʌg,lɔːd) *n* a criminal who controls the distribution and sale of large quantities of illegal drugs

drugstore ('drʌg,stɔː) *n US and Canadian* a shop where medical prescriptions are made up and a wide variety of goods and sometimes light meals are sold

druid ('druːɪd) *n* (*sometimes capital*) **1** a member of an ancient order of priests in Gaul, Britain, and Ireland in the pre-Christian era **2** a member of any of several modern movements attempting to revive druidism [C16 from Latin *druides*, of Gaulish origin; compare Old Irish *druid* wizards] > **druidess** ('druːɪdɪs) *fem n* > **dru'idic** *or* **dru'idical** *adj* > **'druid,ism** *or* **'druidry** *n*

drum¹ (drʌm) *n* **1** *music* a percussion instrument sounded by striking a membrane stretched across the opening of a hollow cylinder or hemisphere **2** beat the drum for *informal* to attempt to arouse interest in **3** the sound produced by a drum or any similar sound **4** an object that resembles a drum in shape, such as a large spool or a cylindrical container **5** *architect* **a** one of a number of cylindrical blocks of stone used to construct the shaft of a column **b** the wall or structure supporting a dome or cupola **6** short for **eardrum 7** Also called: **drumfish** any of various North American marine and freshwater sciaenid fishes, such as *Equetus pulcher* (**striped drum**), that utter a drumming sound **8** a type of hollow rotor for steam turbines or axial compressors **9** *computing* a rotating cylindrical device on which data may be stored for later retrieval: now mostly superseded by disks. See **disk** (sense 2) **10** *archaic* a drummer **11 the drum** *Austral informal* the necessary information (esp in the phrase **give** (someone) the drum) ⊳ *vb* **drums, drumming, drummed 12** to play (music) on or as if on a drum **13** to beat or tap (the fingers) rhythmically or regularly **14** (*intr*) (of birds) to produce a rhythmic sound, as by beating the bill against a tree, branch, etc **15** (*tr*; sometimes foll by *up*) to summon or call by drumming **16** (*tr*) to instil by constant repetition: *to drum an idea into someone's head* ⊳ See also **drum out**, **drum up** [C16 probably from Middle Dutch *tromme*, of imitative origin]

drum² (drʌm) *n Scot, Irish* a narrow ridge or hill [C18 from Scottish Gaelic *druim*]

drumbeat ('drʌm,biːt) *n* the sound made by beating a drum

drum brake *n* a type of brake used on the wheels of vehicles, consisting of two pivoted shoes that rub against the inside walls of the brake drum when the brake is applied

drumfire ('drʌm,faɪə) *n* heavy, rapid, and continuous gunfire, the sound of which resembles rapid drumbeats

drumfish ('drʌm,fɪʃ) *n*, *pl* -fish *or* -fishes another name for **drum¹** (sense 7)

drumhead ('drʌm,hɛd) *n* **1** *music* the part of a drum that is actually struck with a stick or the hand **2** the head of a capstan, pierced with holes for the capstan bars **3** another name for **eardrum**

drumhead court-martial *n* a military court convened to hear urgent charges of offences committed in action [C19 from the use of a drumhead as a table around which the court-martial was held]

drumhead service *n* a religious service attended by members of a military unit while in the field

drumlin ('drʌmlɪn) *n* a streamlined mound of glacial drift, rounded or elongated in the direction of the original flow of ice [C19 from Irish Gaelic *druim* ridge + -lin -LING¹]

drum machine *n* a synthesizer specially programmed to reproduce the sound of drums and other percussion instruments in variable rhythms and combinations selected by the musician; the resulting beat is produced continually until stopped or changed

drum major *n* the noncommissioned officer, usually of warrant officer's rank, who is appointed to command the corps of drums of a military band and who is in command of both the drums and the band when paraded together

drum majorette *n* a girl who marches at the head of a procession, twirling a baton

drummer ('drʌmə) *n* **1** a person who plays a drum or set of drums **2** *chiefly US* a salesman, esp a travelling salesman **3** *Austral and NZ slang* the slowest shearer in a team

drummy ('drʌmɪ) *n*, *pl* -mies (in South Africa) short for **drum majorette**

drum'n'bass *or* **drum and bass** *n* **a** a type of electronic dance music using mainly bass guitar and drum sounds **b** (*as modifier*): *a drum'n'bass backing*

drum out *vb* (*tr, adverb*; usually foll by *of*) **a** to expel from a club, association, etc **b** (*formerly*) to dismiss from military service to the beat of a drum

drumstick ('drʌm,stɪk) *n* **1** a stick used for playing a drum **2** the lower joint of the leg of a cooked fowl

drum up *vb* (*tr, adverb*) to evoke or obtain (support, business, etc) by solicitation or canvassing

drunk (drʌŋk) *adj* **1** intoxicated with alcohol to the extent of losing control over normal physical and mental functions **2** overwhelmed by strong influence or emotion: *drunk with joy* ⊳ *n* **3** a person who is drunk or drinks habitually to excess **4** *informal* a drinking bout [Old English *druncen*, past participle of *drincan* to drink; see DRINK]

drunkard ('drʌŋkəd) *n* a person who is frequently or habitually drunk

drunkathon ('drʌŋkə,θɒn) *n informal* a session in which excessive quantities of alcohol are consumed

drunken ('drʌŋkən) *adj* **1** intoxicated with or as if with alcohol **2** frequently or habitually drunk **3** (*prenominal*) caused by or relating to alcoholic intoxication: *a drunken brawl* > **'drunkenly** *adv* > **'drunkenness** *n*

drunk tank *n informal* a large police cell used for detaining drunks overnight

drupe (druːp) *n* an indehiscent fruit consisting of outer epicarp, fleshy or fibrous mesocarp, and stony endocarp enclosing a single seed, as in the peach, plum, and cherry [C18 from Latin *druppa* wrinkled overripe olive, from Greek: olive] > **drupaceous** (druː'peɪʃəs) *adj*

drupelet ('druːplɪt) *or* **drupel** ('druːpᵊl) *n* a small drupe, usually one of a number forming a compound fruit

Drury Lane ('drʊərɪ) *n* a street in the West End of London, formerly famous for its theatres

druse (druːz) *n* **1** an aggregate of small crystals within a cavity, esp those lining a cavity in a rock or mineral **2** *botany* a globular mass of calcium oxalate crystals formed around an organic core, found in some plant cells [C19 from German, from Old High German *druos* bump]

Druse *or* **Druze** (druːz) *n*, *pl* Druse *or* Druze **a** a member of a religious sect, mainly living in Syria, Lebanon, and Israel, having certain characteristics in common with Muslims **b** (*as modifier*): *Druse beliefs* [C18 from Arabic *Durūz* the Druses, after *Ismail al-Darazi* Ismail the tailor, 11th-century Muslim leader who founded the sect] > **'Drusean, 'Drusian, 'Druzean** *or* **'Druzian** *adj*

dry (draɪ) *adj* drier, driest *or* dryer, dryest **1** lacking moisture; not damp or wet **2** having little or no rainfall **3** not in or under water: *dry land* **4** having the water drained away or evaporated: *a dry river* **5** not providing milk: *a dry cow* **6** (of the eyes) free from tears **7 a** *informal* in need of a drink; thirsty **b** causing thirst: *dry work* **8** eaten without butter, jam, etc: *dry toast* **9** (of a wine, cider, etc) not sweet **10** *pathol* not accompanied by or producing a mucous or watery discharge: *a dry cough* **11** consisting of solid as opposed to liquid substances or commodities **12** without adornment; plain: *dry facts* **13** lacking interest or stimulation: *a dry book* **14** lacking warmth or emotion; cold: *a dry greeting* **15** (of wit or humour) shrewd and keen in an impersonal, sarcastic, or laconic way **16** opposed to or prohibiting the sale of alcoholic liquor for human consumption: *a dry area* **17** NZ (of a ewe) without a lamb after the mating season **18** *electronics* (of a soldered electrical joint) imperfect because the solder has not adhered to the metal, thus reducing conductance ▷ *vb* dries, drying, dried **19** (when *intr*, often foll by *off*) to make or become dry or free from moisture **20** (*tr*) to preserve (meat, vegetables, fruit, etc) by removing the moisture ▷ *n*, *pl* drys *or* dries **21** *Brit informal* a Conservative politician who is considered to be a hard-liner. Compare **wet** (sense 10) **22** the dry *Austral informal* the dry season **23** *US and Canadian* an informal word for **prohibitionist** ▷ See also **dry out, dry up** [Old English *drȳge*; related to Old High German *truckan*, Old Norse *draugr* dry wood] > ˈdryable *adj* > ˈdryness *n*

dryad (ˈdraɪəd, -æd) *n*, *pl* -ads *or* -ades (-əˌdiːz) *Greek myth* a nymph or divinity of the woods [c14 from Latin *Dryas*, from Greek *Druas*, from *drus* tree] > dryadic (draɪˈædɪk) *adj*

dry battery *n* an electric battery consisting of two or more dry cells

dry-bone ore *n* a mining term for **smithsonite**

dry-bulb thermometer *n* an ordinary thermometer used alongside a wet-bulb thermometer to obtain relative humidity. See also **psychrometer**

dry cell *n* a primary cell in which the electrolyte is in the form of a paste or is treated in some way to prevent it from spilling. Compare **wet cell**

dry-clean *vb* (*tr*) to clean (clothing, fabrics, etc) with a solvent other than water, such as trichloroethylene > ˌdry-ˈcleaner *n* > ˌdry-ˈcleaning *n*

dry distillation *n* another name for **destructive distillation**

dry dock *n* **1** a basin-like structure that is large enough to admit a ship and that can be pumped dry for work on the ship's bottom ▷ *vb* dry-dock **2** to put (a ship) into a dry dock, or (of a ship) to go into a dry dock

dry drunk *n* an alcoholic who is not currently drinking alcohol but is still following an irregular undisciplined lifestyle like that of a drunkard

dryer[1] (ˈdraɪə) *n* **1** a person or thing that dries **2** an apparatus for removing moisture by forced draught, heating, or centrifuging **3** any of certain chemicals added to oils such as linseed oil to accelerate their drying when used as bases in paints, etc

dryer[2] (ˈdraɪə) *adj* a variant spelling of **drier**[1]

dry farming *n* a system of growing crops in arid or semiarid regions without artificial irrigation, by reducing evaporation and by special methods of tillage > dry farmer *n*

dry fly *n angling* **a** an artificial fly designed and prepared to be floated or skimmed on the surface of the water **b** (*as modifier*): *dry-fly fishing* ▷ Compare **wet fly**

dry hole *n* (in the oil industry) a well that is drilled but does not produce oil or gas in commercially worthwhile amounts

dry ice *n* solid carbon dioxide, which sublimes at −78.5°C: used as a refrigerant, and to create billows of smoke in stage shows. Also called: **carbon dioxide snow**

drying (ˈdraɪɪŋ) *n* **1** the action or process of making or becoming dry **2** Also called (not now in technical usage): **seasoning** the processing of timber until it has a moisture content suitable for the purposes for which it is to be used ▷ *adj* **3** causing dryness: *a drying wind*

drying oil *n* one of a number of animal or vegetable oils, such as linseed oil, that harden by oxidation on exposure to air: used as a base for some paints and varnishes

dry kiln *n* an oven in which cut timber is dried and seasoned

dry law *n chiefly US* a law prohibiting the sale of alcoholic beverages

dry lightning *n US* lightning produced by a thunderstorm that is unaccompanied by rain

dryly (ˈdraɪlɪ) *adv* a variant spelling of **drily**

dry martini *n* a cocktail of between four and ten parts gin to one part dry vermouth

dry measure *n* a unit or a system of units for measuring dry goods, such as fruit, grains, etc

dry nurse *n* **1** a nurse who cares for a child without suckling it. Compare **wet nurse** ▷ *vb* dry-nurse **2** to care for (a baby or young child) without suckling

dryopithecine (ˌdraɪəʊˈpɪθəˌsiːn) *n* any extinct Old World ape of the genus *Dryopithecus*, common in Miocene and Pliocene times: thought to be the ancestors of modern apes [c20 from New Latin *Dryopithēcus*, from Greek *drus* tree + *pithēkos* ape]

dry out *vb* (*adverb*) **1** to make or become dry **2** to undergo or cause to undergo treatment for alcoholism or drug addiction

dry point *n* **1** a technique of intaglio engraving with a hard steel needle, without acid, on a copper plate **2** the sharp steel needle used in this process **3** an engraving or print produced by this method

dry riser *n* a vertical pipe, not containing water, having connections on different floors of a building for a fireman's hose to be attached. A fire tender can be connected at the lowest level to make water rise under pressure within the pipe. Abbreviation: DR

dry rot *n* **1** crumbling and drying of timber, bulbs, potatoes, or fruit, caused by saprotrophic basidiomycetous fungi **2** any fungus causing this decay, esp of the genus *Merulius* **3** moral degeneration or corrupt practices, esp when previously unsuspected

dry run *n* **1** *military* practice in weapon firing, a drill, or a manoeuvre without using live ammunition **2** *informal* a trial or practice, esp in simulated conditions; rehearsal

dry-salt *vb* to preserve (food) by salting and removing moisture

drysalter (ˈdraɪˌsɔːltə) *n obsolete* a dealer in certain chemical products, such as dyestuffs and gums, and in dried, tinned, or salted foods and edible oils

Drysdale (ˈdraɪzdeɪl) *n* a New Zealand breed of sheep with hair growing among its wool: bred for its coat which is used in making carpets

dry slope *n* an artificial ski slope used for tuition and practice. Also called: **dry-ski slope**

dry steam *n* steam that does not contain droplets of water

dry stock *n NZ* cattle that are raised for meat

dry-stone *adj* (of a wall) made without mortar

Dry Tortugas (tɔːˈtuːɡəz) *n* a group of eight coral islands at the entrance to the Gulf of Mexico: part of Florida

dry up *vb* (*adverb*) **1** (*intr*) to become barren or unproductive; fail: *in middle age his inspiration dried up* **2** to dry (dishes, cutlery, etc) with a tea towel after they have been washed **3** (*intr*) *informal* to stop talking or speaking: *when I got on the stage I just dried up; dry up!*

dry valley *n* a valley originally produced by running water but now waterless

DS *abbreviation for* **1** Also: ds *music* dal segno **2** Detective Sergeant

DSc *abbreviation for* Doctor of Science

DSC *military abbreviation for* Distinguished Service Cross

DSM *military abbreviation for* Distinguished Service Medal

DSO *Brit military abbreviation for* Distinguished Service Order

dsp *abbreviation for* decessit sine prole [Latin: died without issue]

DSS (in Britain) *abbreviation for* **1** Director of Social Services **2** Department of Social Security

DST *abbreviation for* Daylight Saving Time

DTI (in Britain) *abbreviation for* Department of Trade and Industry

DTL *electronics abbreviation for* diode transistor logic: a stage in the development of electronic logic circuits

DTLR (in Britain) *abbreviation for* Department of Transport, Local Government, and the Regions

DTP *abbreviation for* **desktop publishing**

DT's *informal abbreviation for* **delirium tremens**

DTT *abbreviation for* digital terrestrial television

DU *abbreviation for* depleted uranium

Du. *abbreviation for* **1** Duke **2** Dutch

duad (ˈdjuːæd) *n* a rare word for **pair**[1] [c17 from Greek *duas* two, a pair]

dual (ˈdjuːəl) *adj* **1** relating to or denoting two **2** twofold; double **3** (in the grammar of Old English, Ancient Greek, and certain other languages) denoting a form of a word indicating that exactly two referents are being referred to **4** *maths, logic* (of structures or expressions) having the property that the interchange of certain pairs of terms, and usually the distribution of negation, yields equivalent structures or expressions ▷ *n* **5** *grammar* **a** the dual number **b** a dual form of a word ▷ *vb* duals, dualling, dualled **6** (*tr*) *Brit* to make (a road) into a dual carriageway [c17 from Latin *duālis* concerning two, from *duo* two] > ˈdually *adv*

Duala (duˈɑːlə, -lɑː) *n* **1** (*pl* -la *or* -las) a member of a Negroid people of W Africa living chiefly in Cameroon **2** the language of this people, belonging to the Bantu group of the Niger-Congo family

Dual Alliance *n* **1** the alliance between France and Russia (1893–1917) **2** the secret Austro-German alliance against Russia (1879) later expanded to the Triple Alliance

dual carriageway *n Brit* a road on which traffic travelling in opposite directions is separated by a central strip of turf, etc. US and Canadian name: **divided highway**

dual heritage *n* **a** an upbringing in which one's parents are of different ethnic or religious backgrounds **b** (*as modifier*): *dual-heritage adoptive families*

dualism (ˈdjuːəˌlɪzəm) *n* **1** the state of being twofold or double **2** *philosophy* the doctrine, as opposed to idealism and materialism, that reality consists of two basic types of substance usually taken to be mind and matter or two basic types of entity, mental and physical. Compare **monism 3 a** the theory that the universe has been ruled from its origins by two conflicting powers, one good and one evil, both existing as equally ultimate first causes **b** the theory that there are two personalities, one human and one divine, in Christ > ˈdualist *n* > ˌdualˈistic *adj* > ˌdualˈistically *adv*

duality (djuːˈælɪtɪ) *n*, *pl* -ties **1** the state or quality of being two or in two parts; dichotomy **2** *physics* the principle that a wave-particle duality exists in microphysics in which wave theory and corpuscular theory are complementary. The propagation of electromagnetic radiation is analysed using wave theory but its interaction with matter is described in terms of photons. The condition of particles such as electrons, neutrons, and atoms is described in terms of de Broglie waves **3** *geometry* the interchangeability of the roles of the point and the plane in statements and theorems in projective geometry

Dual Monarchy *n* the monarchy of Austria-Hungary from 1867 to 1918

dual-purpose *adj* having or serving two functions

duathlon (djuːˈæθlɒn) *n* an athletic contest in which each athlete competes in running and cycling events [c20 from DUO- + Greek *athlon* contest]

dub[1] (dʌb) *vb* dubs, dubbing, dubbed **1** (*tr*) to invest (a person) with knighthood by the ritual of tapping on the shoulder with a sword **2** (*tr*) to invest with a title, name, or nickname **3** (*tr*) to dress (leather) by rubbing **4** *angling* to dress (a fly) ▷ *n* **5** the sound of a drum [Old English *dubbian*; related to Old Norse *dubba* to dub a knight, Old High German *tubili* plug, peg]

dub² (dʌb) vb dubs, dubbing, dubbed films, television **1** to alter the soundtrack of (an old recording, film, etc) **2** (tr) to substitute for the soundtrack of (a film) a new soundtrack, esp in a different language **3** (tr) to provide (a film or tape) with a soundtrack **4** (tr) to alter (a taped soundtrack) by removing some parts and exaggerating others ▷ n **5** films the new sounds added **6 a** music a style of record production associated with reggae, involving the removal or exaggeration of instrumental parts, extensive use of echo, etc **b** (as modifier): a dub mix [c20 shortened from DOUBLE]

dub³ (dʌb) vb dubs, dubbing, dubbed Austral and NZ informal short for **double-bank**

dub⁴ (dʌb) US and Canadian informal ▷ n **1** a clumsy or awkward person or player ▷ vb dubs, dubbing, dubbed **2** to bungle (a shot), as in golf [c19 of uncertain origin]

dub⁵ (dʌb) n Scot and northern English dialect a pool of water; puddle [c16 Scottish dialect dubbe; related to Middle Low German dobbe]

dub⁶ (dʌb) vb dubs, dubbing, dubbed (intr; foll by in, up, or out) slang to contribute to the cost of (something); pay [c19 of obscure origin]

Dubai (du:'baɪ) n a sheikhdom in the NE United Arab Emirates, consisting principally of the port of Dubai, on the Persian Gulf: oilfields. Pop: 1 026 000 (2005 est)

dubbin ('dʌbɪn) or **dubbing** n Brit a greasy mixture of tallow and oil applied to leather to soften it and make it waterproof [c18 from dub to dress leather; see DUB¹]

dubbing¹ ('dʌbɪŋ) n films **1** the replacement of a soundtrack in one language by one in another language **2** the combination of several soundtracks into a single track **3** the addition of a soundtrack to a film or broadcast

dubbing² ('dʌbɪŋ) n **1** angling hair or fur spun on waxed silk and added to the body of an artificial fly to give it shape **2** a variant of **dubbin**

dubbo ('dʌbəʊ) Austral slang ▷ adj **1** stupid ▷ n, pl -bos **2** a stupid person [from Dubbo, a town in New South Wales, Australia]

dubiety (dju:'baɪɪtɪ) or **dubiosity** (ˌdju:bɪ'ɒsɪtɪ) n, pl -ties **1** the state of being doubtful **2** a doubtful matter [c18 from Late Latin dubietās, from Latin dubius DUBIOUS]

dubious ('dju:bɪəs) adj **1** marked by or causing doubt: a dubious reply **2** unsettled in mind; uncertain; doubtful **3** of doubtful quality; untrustworthy: a dubious reputation **4** not certain in outcome [c16 from Latin dubius wavering] ▷ 'dubiously adv ▷ 'dubiousness n

dubitable ('dju:bɪtəbⁱl) adj open to doubt [c17 from Latin dubitāre to DOUBT] ▷ 'dubitably adv

dubitation (ˌdju:bɪ'teɪʃən) n another word for **doubt**

Dublin ('dʌblɪn) n **1** the capital of the Republic of Ireland, on Dublin Bay: under English rule from 1171 until 1922; commercial and cultural centre; contains one of the world's largest breweries and exports whiskey, stout, and agricultural produce. Pop: 1 004 614 (2002). Gaelic name: **Baile Átha Cliath 2** a county in E Republic of Ireland, in Leinster on the Irish Sea: mountainous in the south but low-lying in the north and centre. County seat: Dublin. Pop: 1 122 821 (2002). Area: 922 sq km (356 sq miles)

Dublin Bay prawn n a large prawn usually used in a dish of scampi

Dubliner ('dʌblɪnə) n a native or inhabitant of Dublin

Dubna ('dʌbnə) n a new town in W Russia, founded in 1956: site of the United Institute of Nuclear Research. Pop: 66 000 (1990 est)

dubnium ('dʌbnɪəm) n a synthetic transactinide element produced in minute quantities by bombarding plutonium with high-energy neon ions. Symbol: Du; atomic no. 105. compare **hahnium** [c20 after DUBNA where it was first reported]

dubonnet (dju:'bɒneɪ) n **a** a dark purplish-red colour **b** (as adjective): a dubonnet coat [from DUBONNET]

Dubonnet (dju:'bɒneɪ) n trademark a sweet usually red apéritif wine flavoured with quinine and cinchona

Dubrovnik (du'brɒvnɪk) n a port in W Croatia, on the Dalmatian coast: an important commercial centre in the Middle Ages; damaged in 1991 when it was shelled by Serbian artillery. Pop: 49 730 (1991). Former Italian name (until 1918): Ragusa

ducal ('dju:kⁱl) adj of or relating to a duke or duchy [c16 from French, from Late Latin ducālis of a leader, from dux leader] ▷ 'ducally adv

ducat ('dʌkət) n **1** any of various former European gold or silver coins, esp those used in Italy or the Netherlands **2** (often plural) any coin or money [c14 from Old French, from Old Italian ducato coin stamped with the doge's image, from duca doge, from Latin dux leader]

duce ('du:tʃɪ; Italian 'du:tʃe) n leader [c20 from Italian, from Latin dux]

Duce (Italian 'du:tʃe) n **Il** (il). the title assumed by Benito Mussolini as leader of Fascist Italy (1922–43)

Duchenne dystrophy (du:'ʃɛn) or **Duchenne muscular dystrophy** n the most common form of muscular dystrophy, usually affecting only boys. Abbreviation: DMD [named after Guillaume Duchenne (1806–75), French neurologist]

duchess ('dʌtʃɪs) n **1** the wife or widow of a duke **2** a woman who holds the rank of duke in her own right ▷ vb **3** Austral informal to overwhelm with flattering attention [c14 from Old French duchesse, feminine of duc DUKE]

duchy ('dʌtʃɪ) n, pl duchies the territory of a duke or duchess; dukedom [c14 from Old French duche, from duc DUKE]

duck¹ (dʌk) n, pl ducks or duck **1** any of various small aquatic birds of the family Anatidae, typically having short legs, webbed feet, and a broad blunt bill: order Anseriformes **2** the flesh of this bird, used as food **3** the female of such a bird, as opposed to the male (drake) **4** any other bird of the family Anatidae, including geese, and swans **5** Also: **ducks** Brit informal dear or darling: used as a term of endearment or of general address. See also **ducky 6** informal a person, esp one regarded as odd or endearing **7** cricket a score of nothing by a batsman **8 like water off a duck's back** informal without effect **9 take to something like a duck to water** informal to become adept at or attracted to something very quickly [Old English dūce duck, diver; related to DUCK²]

duck² (dʌk) vb **1** to move (the head or body) quickly downwards or away, esp so as to escape observation or evade a blow **2** to submerge or plunge suddenly and often briefly under water **3** (when intr, often foll by out) informal to dodge or escape (a person, duty, etc) **4** (intr) bridge to play a low card when possessing a higher one rather than try to win a trick ▷ n **5** the act or an instance of ducking [c14 related to Old High German tūhhan to dive, Middle Dutch dūken] ▷ 'ducker n

duck³ (dʌk) n a heavy cotton fabric of plain weave, used for clothing, tents, etc. See also **ducks** [c17 from Middle Dutch doek; related to Old High German tuoh cloth]

duck⁴ (dʌk) n an amphibious vehicle used in World War II [c20 from code name DUKW]

duck-billed dinosaur n another name for **hadrosaur**

duck-billed platypus n an amphibious egg-laying mammal, Ornithorhynchus anatinus, of E Australia, having dense fur, a broad bill and tail, and webbed feet: family Ornithorhynchidae. Sometimes shortened to: **duckbill, platypus** See also **monotreme**

duckboard ('dʌkˌbɔ:d) n a board or boards laid so as to form a floor or path over wet or muddy ground

duck-egg blue n **a** a pale greenish-blue colour **b** (as adjective): duck-egg blue walls

duckfoot quote ('dʌkfʊt) n printing a chevron-shaped quotation mark (« or ») used in Europe. Also called: **guillemet**

duck hawk n a variety of peregrine falcon, Falco peregrinus anatum, occurring in North America

ducking stool n history a chair or stool used for the punishment of offenders by plunging them into water

duckling ('dʌklɪŋ) n a young duck

ducks (dʌks) pl n clothing made of duck, esp white trousers for sports

ducks and drakes n (functioning as singular) **1** a game in which a flat stone is bounced across the surface of water **2 make ducks and drakes of** or **play (at) ducks and drakes with** to use recklessly; squander or waste

duck's arse n a hairstyle in which the hair is swept back to a point at the nape of the neck, resembling a duck's tail. Also called: **DA**

duck shove vb Austral and NZ informal to evade responsibility ▷ **duck shover** n ▷ **duck shoving** n

duck soup n US slang something that is easy to do

duckweed ('dʌkˌwi:d) n any of various small stemless aquatic plants of the family Lemnaceae, esp any of the genus Lemna, that have rounded leaves and occur floating on still water in temperate regions

ducky or **duckie** ('dʌkɪ) informal ▷ n, pl duckies **1** Brit darling or dear: used as a term of endearment among women, but now often used in imitation of the supposed usage of homosexual men ▷ adj **2** delightful; fine

duct (dʌkt) n **1** a tube, pipe, or canal by means of which a substance, esp a fluid or gas, is conveyed **2** any bodily passage, esp one conveying secretions or excretions **3** a narrow tubular cavity in plants, often containing resin or some other substance **4** Also called: **conduit** a channel or pipe carrying electric cable or wires **5** a passage through which air can flow, as in air conditioning **6** the ink reservoir in a printing press [c17 from Latin ductus a leading (in Medieval Latin: aqueduct), from dūcere to lead] ▷ 'ductless adj

ductal carcinoma in situ ('dʌktəl) n a form of breast cancer originating in the breast itself rather than spreading from another site. Abbreviation: DCIS

ductile ('dʌktaɪl) adj **1** (of a metal, such as gold or copper) able to be drawn out into wire **2** able to be moulded; pliant; plastic **3** easily led or influenced; tractable [c14 from Old French, from Latin ductilis, from dūcere to lead] ▷ 'ductilely adv ▷ ductility (dʌk'tɪlɪtɪ) or 'ductileness n

ductless gland n anatomy See **endocrine gland**

duct tape n a type of strong waterproof adhesive silver-coloured cloth tape used for repairs by plumbers, electricians, etc

ductule ('dʌktju:l) n anatomy, zoology a small duct

dud (dʌd) informal ▷ n **1** a person or thing that proves ineffectual or a failure **2** a shell, etc, that fails to explode **3** (plural) old-fashioned clothes or other personal belongings ▷ adj **4** failing in its purpose or function: a dud cheque [c15 (in the sense: an article of clothing, a thing, used disparagingly): of unknown origin]

dude (du:d, dju:d) n informal **1** Western US and Canadian a city dweller, esp one holidaying on a ranch **2** chiefly US and Canadian a dandy **3** US and Canadian a person: often used to any male in direct address [c19 of unknown origin] ▷ 'dudish adj ▷ 'dudishly adv

dudeen (du:'di:n) n a clay pipe with a short stem [c19 from Irish dúidín a little pipe, from dúd pipe]

dude ranch n US and Canadian a ranch used as a holiday resort offering activities such as riding and camping

dudgeon¹ ('dʌdʒən) n anger or resentment (archaic, except in the phrase in high dudgeon) [c16 of unknown origin]

dudgeon² (ˈdʌdʒən) *n* **1** *obsolete* a wood used in making the handles of knives, daggers, etc **2** *archaic* a dagger, knife, etc, with a dudgeon hilt [C15 from Anglo-Norman *digeon*, of obscure origin]

Dudley (ˈdʌdlɪ) *n* **1** a town in W central England, in Dudley unitary authority, West Midlands: wrought-iron industry. Pop: 194 919 (2001) **2** a unitary authority in W central England, in West Midlands. Pop: 304 800 (2003 est). Area: 98 sq km (38 sq miles)

due (djuː) *adj* **1** (*postpositive*) immediately payable **2** (*postpositive*) owed as a debt, irrespective of any date for payment **3** requisite; fitting; proper **4** (*prenominal*) adequate or sufficient; enough **5** (*postpositive*) expected or appointed to be present or arrive: *the train is now due* **6** **due to** attributable to or caused by ▷ *n* **7** something that is owed, required, or due **8** **give (a person) his due** to give or allow what is deserved or right ▷ *adv* **9** directly or exactly; straight: *a course due west* ▷ See also **dues** [C13 from Old French *deu*, from *devoir* to owe, from Latin *debēre*; see DEBT, DEBIT]

▎USAGE The use of *due to* as a compound preposition (*the performance has been cancelled due to bad weather*) was formerly considered incorrect, but is now acceptable

due bill *n* *chiefly US* a document acknowledging indebtedness, exchangeable for goods or services

duel (ˈdjuːəl) *n* **1** a prearranged combat with deadly weapons between two people following a formal procedure in the presence of seconds and traditionally fought until one party was wounded or killed, usually to settle a quarrel involving a point of honour **2** a contest or conflict between two persons or parties ▷ *vb* duels, duelling, duelled *or US* duels, dueling, dueled (*intr*) **3** to fight in a duel **4** to contest closely [C15 from Medieval Latin *duellum*, from Latin, poetical variant of *bellum* war; associated by folk etymology with Latin *duo* two] > ˈdueller *or* ˈduellist *n*

duello (djuːˈɛləʊ) *n*, *pl* -los **1** the art of duelling **2** the code of rules for duelling [C16 from Italian; see DUEL]

duende (duːˈɛndeɪ) *n* inspiration or passion, esp associated with flamenco [C20 Spanish, spirit]

duenna (djuːˈɛnə) *n* (in Spain and Portugal, etc) an elderly woman retained by a family to act as governess and chaperon to young girls [C17 from Spanish *dueña*, from Latin *domina* lady, feminine of *dominus* master]

due process of law *n* the administration of justice in accordance with established rules and principles

Duero (ˈduero) *n* the Spanish name for the **Douro**

dues (djuːz) *pl n* (*sometimes singular*) charges, as for membership of a club or organization; fees: *trade-union dues*

duet (djuːˈɛt) *n* **1** Also called (esp for instrumental compositions): **duo** a musical composition for two performers or voices **2** an action or activity performed by a pair of closely connected individuals ▷ *vb* duets, duetting, duetted **3** (*intr*) to perform a duet [C18 from Italian *duetto* a little duet, from *duo* duet, from Latin: two] > duˈettist *n*

duff¹ (dʌf) *n* **1** a thick flour pudding, often flavoured with currants, citron, etc, and boiled in a cloth bag: *plum duff* **2** **up the duff** *slang* pregnant [C19 Northern English variant of DOUGH]

duff² (dʌf) *vb* (*tr*) **1** *slang* to change the appearance of or give a false appearance to (old or stolen goods); fake **2** *Austral slang* to steal (cattle), altering the brand **3** *golf informal* to bungle (a shot) by hitting the ground behind the ball ▷ *adj* **4** *Brit informal* bad or useless, as by not working out or operating correctly; dud: *a duff idea; a duff engine* ▷ See also **duff up** [C19 probably back formation from DUFFER]

duff³ (dʌf) *n* *slang* the rump or buttocks [C20 special use of DUFF¹]

duffel *or* **duffle** (ˈdʌfʲl) *n* **1** a heavy woollen cloth with a thick nap **2** *chiefly US and Canadian*

equipment or supplies, esp those of a camper [C17 after *Duffel*, Belgian town]

duffel bag *n* a cylindrical drawstring canvas bag, originally used esp by sailors for carrying personal articles

duffel coat *n* a knee-length or short wool coat, usually with a hood and fastened with toggles

duffer (ˈdʌfə) *n* **1** *informal* a dull or incompetent person **2** *slang* something worthless **3** *dialect* a peddler or hawker **4** *Austral slang* **a** a mine that proves unproductive **b** a person who steals cattle [C19 of uncertain origin]

duff up *vb* (*tr, adverb*) *Brit slang* to beat or thrash (a person) severely

dug¹ (dʌg) *vb* the past tense and past participle of **dig**

dug² (dʌg) *n* **1** the nipple, teat, udder, or breast of a female mammal **2** a human breast, esp when old and withered [C16 of Scandinavian origin; compare Danish *dægge* to coddle, Gothic *daddjan* to give suck]

dug³ (dʌg) *n* a Scot word for **dog**

dugite (ˈduːɡaɪt) *n* a medium-sized venomous snake, *Pseudonaja affinis*, of Central and W Australia, having a small head and slender olive-coloured body with black specks

dugong (ˈduːɡɒŋ) *n* a whalelike sirenian mammal, *Dugong dugon*, occurring in shallow tropical waters from E Africa to Australia: family *Dugongidae* [C19 from Malay *duyong*]

dugout (ˈdʌɡˌaʊt) *n* **1** a canoe made by hollowing out a log **2** *military* a covered excavation dug to provide shelter **3** *slang* a retired officer, former civil servant, etc, recalled to employment **4** (at a sports ground) the covered bench where managers, trainers, etc sit and players wait when not on the field

duh (dɜː) *interj slang* an ironic response to a question or statement, implying that the speaker is stupid or that the reply is obvious: *how did you get in here? – through the door, duh*

duiker *or* **duyker** (ˈdaɪkə) *n*, *pl* -kers *or* -ker **1** Also called: **duikerbok** (ˈdaɪkəbɒk) any small antelope of the genera *Cephalophus* and *Sylvicapra*, occurring throughout Africa south of the Sahara, having short straight backward-pointing horns, pointed hooves, and an arched back **2** *South African* any of several cormorants, esp the long-tailed shag (*Phalacrocorax africanus*) [C18 via Afrikaans from Dutch *duiker* diver, from *duiken* to dive; see DUCK²]

Duisburg (*German* ˈdyːsbʊrk) *n* an industrial city in NW Germany, in North Rhine-Westphalia at the confluence of the Rivers Rhine and Ruhr: one of the world's largest and busiest inland ports; university (1972). Pop: 506 496 (2003 est)

du jour (duː ˈʒɔː; *French* dy ʒur) *adj* (*postpositive*) *informal* currently very fashionable or popular: *the young writer du jour* [C20 from French, literally: of the day (as used on restaurant menus of items that change daily)]

duka (ˈduːka) *n E African* a shop; store [C20 from Swahili]

duke (djuːk) *n* **1** a nobleman of high rank: in the British Isles standing above the other grades of the nobility **2** the prince or ruler of a small principality or duchy. Related adj: **ducal** [C12 from Old French *duc*, from Latin *dux* leader]

dukedom (ˈdjuːkdəm) *n* **1** another name for a **duchy** **2** the title, rank, or position of a duke

dukes (djuːks) *pl n slang* the fists (esp in the phrase **put your dukes up**) [C19 from *Duke of Yorks* rhyming slang for *forks* (fingers)]

Dukhobor (ˈduːkəʊˌbɔː) *pl n* a variant spelling of **Doukhobor**

dukka *or* **dukkah** (ˈdʊkə) *n* a mix of ground roast nuts and spices, originating in Egypt, and used for sprinkling on meat or as a dip

dukkha (ˈdʊkə) *n* (in Theravada Buddhism) the belief that all things are suffering, due to the desire to seek permanence or recognize the self when neither exist: one of the three basic characteristics of existence. Sanskrit word:

duhkha Compare **anata, anicca** [Pali, literally: suffering, illness]

dulcet (ˈdʌlsɪt) *adj* (of a sound) soothing or pleasant; sweet [C14 from Latin *dulcis* sweet] > ˈdulcetly *adv* > ˈdulcetness *n*

dulciana (ˌdʌlsɪˈɑːnə) *n* a sweet-toned organ stop, controlling metal pipes of narrow scale [C18 from Latin *dulcis* sweet]

dulcify (ˈdʌlsɪˌfaɪ) *vb* -fies, -fying, -fied (*tr*) **1** *rare* to make pleasant or agreeable **2** a rare word for **sweeten** [C16 from Late Latin *dulcificāre*, from Latin *dulcis* sweet + *facere* to make] > ˌdulcifiˈcation *n*

dulcimer (ˈdʌlsɪmə) *n* *music* **1** a tuned percussion instrument consisting of a set of strings of graduated length stretched over a sounding board and struck with a pair of hammers **2** an instrument used in US folk music, consisting of an elliptical body, a fretted fingerboard, and usually three strings plucked with a goose quill [C15 from Old French *doulcemer*, from Old Italian *dolcimelo*, from *dolce* sweet, from Latin *dulcis* + *-melo*, perhaps from Greek *melos* song]

dulcinea (ˌdʌlsɪˈnɪə) *n* a man's sweetheart [C18 from the name of Don Quixote's mistress Dulcinea del Toboso in Cervantes' novel; from Spanish *dulce* sweet]

dulia (ˈdjuːlɪə) *n* the veneration accorded to saints in the Roman Catholic and Eastern Churches, as contrasted with hyperdulia and latria [C17 from Medieval Latin: service, from Greek *douleia* slavery, from *doulos* slave]

dull (dʌl) *adj* **1** slow to think or understand; stupid **2** lacking in interest **3** lacking in perception or the ability to respond; insensitive **4** lacking sharpness; blunt **5** not acute, intense, or piercing **6** (of weather) not bright or clear; cloudy **7** not active, busy, or brisk **8** lacking in spirit or animation; listless **9** (of colour) lacking brilliance or brightness; sombre **10** not loud or clear; muffled **11** *med* (of sound elicited by percussion, esp of the chest) not resonant ▷ *vb* **12** to make or become dull [Old English *dol*; related to Old Norse *dul* conceit, Old High German *tol* foolish, Greek *tholeros* confused] > ˈdullish *adj* > ˈdullness *or* ˈdulness *n* > ˈdully *adv*

dullard (ˈdʌləd) *n* a dull or stupid person

dullsville (ˈdʌlzvɪl) *n slang* **1** a thing, place, or activity that is boring or dull **2** the state of being bored

dulosis (djuːˈləʊsɪs) *n* a practice of some ants, in which one species forces members of a different species to do the work of the colony. Also called: helotism [C20 from Greek: enslavement, from *doulos* slave] > dulotic (djuːˈlɒtɪk) *adj*

dulse (dʌls) *n* any of several seaweeds, esp *Rhodymenia palmata*, that occur on rocks and have large red edible fronds [C17 from Old Irish *duilesc* seaweed]

Duluth (dəˈluːθ) *n* a port in E Minnesota, at the W end of Lake Superior. Pop: 85 734 (2003 est)

Dulwich (ˈdʌlɪtʃ) *n* a residential district in the Greater London borough of Southwark: site of an art gallery and the public school, Dulwich College

duly (ˈdjuːlɪ) *adv* **1** in a proper or fitting manner **2** at the proper time; punctually [C14 see DUE, -LY²]

duma *or* **douma** *Russian* (ˈduːmə) *n Russian history* **1** (*usually capital*) the elective legislative assembly established by Tsar Nicholas II in 1905: overthrown by the Bolsheviks in 1917 **2** (before 1917) any official assembly or council **3** short for **State Duma,** the lower chamber of the Russian parliament [C20 from *duma* thought, of Germanic origin; related to Gothic *dōms* judgment]

dumb (dʌm) *adj* **1** lacking the power to speak, either because of defects in the vocal organs or because of hereditary deafness; mute **2** lacking the power of human speech: *dumb animals* **3** temporarily lacking or bereft of the power to speak: *struck dumb* **4** refraining from speech; uncommunicative **5** producing no sound; silent: *a dumb piano* **6** made, done, or performed without speech **7** *informal* **a** slow to understand; dim-

d

witted **b** foolish; stupid. See also **dumb down 8** (of a projectile or bomb) not guided to its target [Old English; related to Old Norse *dumbr*, Gothic *dumbs*, Old High German *tump*] > 'dumbly *adv* > 'dumbness *n*

dumb ague *n* an irregular form of malarial fever (ague) lacking the typically symptomatic chill

Dumbarton (dʌmˈbɑːtᵊn) *n* a town in W Scotland, in West Dunbartonshire near the confluence of the Rivers Leven and Clyde: centred around the **Rock of Dumbarton**, an important stronghold since ancient times; engineering and distilling. Pop: 20 527 (2001)

Dumbarton Oaks (ˈdʌmˌbɑːtᵊn) *n* an estate in the District of Columbia in the US: scene of conferences in 1944 concerned with creating the United Nations

dumb-ass *slang* ▷ *n* **1** a stupid person ▷ *adj* **2** extremely stupid

dumbbell (ˈdʌmˌbɛl) *n* **1** *gymnastics, weightlifting* an exercising weight consisting of a single bar with a heavy ball or disc at either end **2** a small wooden object shaped like this used in dog training for the dog to retrieve **3** *slang, chiefly US and Canadian* a fool

dumb-cane *n* a West Indian aroid plant, *Dieffenbachia seguine*, chewing the stem of which induces speechlessness by paralysing the throat muscles

dumb down *vb* (*tr*) to make or become less intellectually demanding or sophisticated

dumbfound *or* **dumfound** (dʌmˈfaʊnd) *vb* (*tr*) to strike dumb with astonishment; amaze [c17 from DUMB + (CON)FOUND]

dumbledore (ˈdʌmbᵊlˌdɔː) *n English dialect* a bumblebee. Also (Southwest English): drumbledrane [Old English *dumble*, variant of *drumble* to move sluggishly + *dor* humming insect]

dumbo (ˈdʌmbəʊ) *n, pl* **-bos** *slang* a slow-witted unintelligent person [c20 after the flying elephant in *Dumbo*, the Walt Disney cartoon released in 1941]

dumbshit (ˈdʌmˌʃɪt) *taboo slang* ▷ *n* **1** a stupid person ▷ *adj* **2** extremely stupid

dumb show *n* **1** a part of a play acted in pantomime, popular in early English drama **2** meaningful gestures; mime

dumbstruck (ˈdʌmˌstrʌk) *or* **dumbstricken** (ˈdʌmˌstrɪkᵊn) *adj* temporarily deprived of speech through shock or surprise

dumbwaiter (ˈdʌmˌweɪtə) *n* **1** *Brit* **a** a stand placed near a dining table to hold food **b** a revolving circular tray placed on a table to hold food. US and Canadian name: **lazy Susan 2** a lift for carrying food, rubbish, etc, between floors

dumdum (ˈdʌmˌdʌm) *n* a soft-nosed or hollow-nosed small-arms bullet that expands on impact and inflicts extensive laceration. Also called: **dumdum bullet** [c19 named after *Dum-Dum*, town near Calcutta where these bullets were made]

dumela (dʊˈmɛla) *sentence substitute South African* hello; good morning [Sotho]

Dumfries (dʌmˈfriːs) *n* a town in S Scotland on the River Nith, administrative centre of Dumfries and Galloway. Pop: 31 146 (2001)

Dumfries and Galloway *n* a council area in SW Scotland: created in 1975 from the counties of Dumfries, Kirkcudbright, and Wigtown; became a unitary authority in 1996; chiefly agricultural. Administrative centre: Dumfries. Pop: 147 210 (2003 est). Area: 6439 sq km (2486 sq miles)

Dumfriesshire (dʌmˈfriːsʃɪə, -ʃə) *n* (until 1975) a county in S Scotland, on the Solway Firth, now part of Dumfries and Galloway

dummelhead (ˈdʌmᵊlˌhɛd) *n Northern English dialect* a stupid or slow-witted person

dummy (ˈdʌmɪ) *n, pl* **-mies 1** a figure representing the human form, used for displaying clothes, in a ventriloquist's act, as a target, etc **2 a** a copy or imitation of an object, often lacking some essential feature of the original **b** (*as modifier*): *a dummy drawer* **3** *slang* a

stupid person; fool **4** *derogatory slang* a person without the power of speech; mute **5** *informal* a person who says or does nothing **6 a** a person who appears to act for himself while acting on behalf of another **b** (*as modifier*): *a dummy buyer* **7** *military* a weighted round without explosives, used in drill and training **8** *bridge* **a** the hand exposed on the table by the declarer's partner and played by the declarer **b** the declarer's partner **9 a** a prototype of a proposed book, indicating the general appearance and dimensions of the finished product **b** a designer's layout of a page indicating the positions for illustrations, etc **10** a feigned pass or move in a sport such as football or rugby **11** *Brit* a rubber teat for babies to suck or bite on. US and Canadian equivalent: **pacifier 12** (*modifier*) counterfeit; sham **13** (*modifier*) (of a card game) played with one hand exposed or unplayed ▷ *vb* **-mies, -mying, -mied 14** to prepare a dummy of (a proposed book, page, etc) **15** Also: **sell** (**someone**) **a dummy** *sport* to use a dummy pass in order to trick (an opponent) [c16 from DUMB, -Y³]

dummy head *n* a model of the human head with a microphone in each ear intended to receive sound in binaural and surround sound reproduction and transmission

dummy load *n* a resistive component that absorbs all the output power of an electrical generator or radio transmitter in order to simulate working conditions for test purposes

dummy run *n* a practice or rehearsal; trial run

dummy variable *n* a variable appearing in a mathematical expression that can be replaced by any arbitrary variable, not occurring in the expression, without affecting the value of the whole

dumortierite (djuːˈmɔːtɪəˌraɪt) *n* a hard fibrous blue or green mineral consisting of hydrated aluminium borosilicate. Formula: $Al_7O_3BO_3(SiO_4)_3$ [c19 named after Eugène *Dumortier*, 19th-century French palaeontologist who discovered it]

dump¹ (dʌmp) *vb* **1** to drop, fall, or let fall heavily or in a mass **2** (*tr*) to empty (objects or material) out of a container **3** to unload, empty, or make empty (a container), as by tilting or overturning **4** (*tr*) *informal* to dispose of **5** (*tr*) to dispose of (waste, esp radioactive nuclear waste) in the sea or on land **6** *commerce* **a** to market (goods) in bulk and at low prices **b** to offer for sale large quantities of (goods) on foreign markets at low prices in order to maintain a high price in the home market and obtain a share of the foreign markets **7** (*tr*) to store (supplies, arms, etc) temporarily **8** (*intr*) *slang, chiefly US* to defecate **9** (*tr*) *surfing* (of a wave) to hurl a swimmer or surfer down **10** (*tr*) *Austral and NZ* to compact (bales of wool) by hydraulic pressure **11** (*tr*) *computing* to record (the contents of part or all of the memory) on a storage device, such as magnetic tape, at a series of points during a computer run ▷ *n* **12 a** a place or area where waste materials are dumped **b** (*in combination*): *rubbish dump* **13** a pile or accumulation of rubbish **14** the act of dumping **15** *informal* a dirty or unkempt place **16** *military* a place where weapons, supplies, etc, are stored **17** *slang, chiefly US* an act of defecation ▷ See also **dump on** [c14 probably of Scandinavian origin; compare Norwegian *dumpa* to fall suddenly, Middle Low German *dumpeln* to duck] > 'dumper *n*

dump² (dʌmp) *n obsolete* a mournful song; lament [c16 see DAMP]

dump bin *n* **1** a free-standing unit in a bookshop in which the books of a particular publisher are displayed **2** a container in a shop in which goods are heaped, often in a disorderly fashion

dumpling (ˈdʌmplɪŋ) *n* **1** a small ball of dough cooked and served with stew **2** a pudding consisting of a round pastry case filled with fruit: *apple dumpling* **3** *informal* a short plump person [c16 *dump-*, perhaps variant of LUMP¹ + -LING¹]

dump on *vb* (*intr, preposition*) *informal, chiefly US* to abuse or criticize

dump orbit *n* an earth orbit into which communications satellites may be moved at the end of their operational lives, where there is no risk of their interference or collision with working satellites in the normal orbits. Also called: **graveyard orbit**

dumps (dʌmps) *pl n informal* a state of melancholy or depression (esp in the phrase **down in the dumps**) [c16 probably from Middle Dutch *domp* haze, mist; see DAMP]

dump truck *or* **dumper-truck** *n* a small truck used on building sites, having a load-bearing container at the front that can be tipped up to unload the contents

dumpy¹ (ˈdʌmpɪ) *adj* **dumpier, dumpiest** short and plump; squat [c18 perhaps related to DUMPLING] > 'dumpily *adv* > 'dumpiness *n*

dumpy² (ˈdʌmpɪ), *or* **dumpish** (ˈdʌmpɪʃ) *adj rare* in low spirits; depressed; morose [c17 from c16 *dump*; see DUMPS]

dumpy level *n surveying* a levelling instrument consisting of a horizontal telescope with various rotational arrangements and a spirit level

Dumyat (dʊmˈjæt) *n* the Arabic name for **Damietta**

dun¹ (dʌn) *vb* **duns, dunning, dunned 1** (*tr*) to press or importune (a debtor) for the payment of a debt ▷ *n* **2** a person, esp a hired agent, who importunes another for the payment of a debt **3** a demand for payment, esp one in writing [c17 of unknown origin]

dun² (dʌn) *n* **1** a brownish-grey colour **2** a horse of this colour **3** *angling* **a** an immature adult mayfly (the subimago), esp one of the genus *Ephemera* **b** an artificial fly imitating this or a similar fly ▷ *adj* **4** of a dun colour **5** dark and gloomy [Old English *dunn*; related to Old Norse *dunna* wild duck, Middle Irish *doun* dark; see DUSK]

Duna (ˈdunɔ) *n* the Hungarian name for the **Danube**

Dünaburg (ˈdyːnabʊrk) *n* the German name (until 1893) for **Daugavpils**

Dunaj (ˈdunaj) *n* the Czech name for the **Danube**

Dunărea (ˈdunərja) *n* the Romanian name for the **Danube**

Dunbar (dʌnˈbɑː) *n* a port and resort in SE Scotland, in East Lothian: scene of Cromwell's defeat of the Scots (1650). Pop: 6354 (2001)

Dunbartonshire (dʌnˈbɑːtᵊnʃɪə, -ʃə) *n* a historical county of W Scotland: became part of Strathclyde region in 1975; administered since 1996 by the council areas of East Dunbartonshire and West Dunbartonshire

Duncan Phyfe *or* **Fife** (faɪf) *n* (*modifier*) *US furniture* of or in the manner of Duncan Phyfe (?1768–1854), Scottish-born US cabinet-maker, esp in that which followed the Sheraton and Directoire styles

dunce (dʌns) *n* a person who is stupid or slow to learn [c16 from *Dunses* or *Dunsmen*, term of ridicule applied to the followers of John *Duns* Scotus (?1265–1308), Scottish scholastic theologian and Franciscan priest, especially by 16th-century humanists] > 'dunce,like *adj*

dunce cap *or* **dunce's cap** *n* a conical paper hat, formerly placed on the head of a dull child at school

Dundalk (dʌnˈdɔːk) *n* a town in NE Republic of Ireland, on **Dundalk Bay**: county town of Co Louth. Pop: 32 505 (2002)

Dundee (dʌnˈdiː) *n* **1** a port in E Scotland, in City of Dundee council area, on the Firth of Tay: centre of the former British jute industry; university (1967). Pop: 154 674 (2001) **2 City of** a council area in E Scotland. Pop: 143 090 (2003 est). Area: 65 sq km (25 sq miles)

Dundee cake *n chiefly Brit* a fairly rich fruit cake decorated with almonds

dunderhead (ˈdʌndəˌhɛd) *n* a stupid or slow-witted person; dunce. Also called: **dunderpate** [c17 probably from Dutch *donder* thunder + HEAD;

compare BLOCKHEAD] > 'dunder,headed *adj* > 'dunder,headedness *n*

Dundonian (dʌnˈdəʊnɪən) *n* **1** a native or inhabitant of Dundee ▷ *adj* **2** of or relating to Dundee or its inhabitants

dune (djuːn) *n* a mound or ridge of drifted sand, occurring on the sea coast and in deserts [c18 via Old French from Middle Dutch *dūne*; see DOWN³]

Dunedin (dʌnˈiːdɪn) *n* a port in New Zealand, on SE South Island: founded (1848) by Scottish settlers. Pop: 121 900 (2004 est)

Dunfermline (dʌnˈfɜːmlɪn) *n* a city in E Scotland, in SW Fife: ruined palace, a former residence of Scottish kings. Pop: 39 229 (2001)

dung (dʌŋ) *n* **1 a** excrement, esp of animals; manure **b** (*as modifier*): *dung cart* **2** something filthy ▷ *vb* **3** (*tr*) to cover (ground) with manure [Old English: prison; related to Old High German *tunc* cellar roofed with dung, Old Norse *dyngja* manure heap] > 'dungy *adj*

Dungannon (dʌnˈgænən) *n* a district of S Northern Ireland, in Co Tyrone. Pop: 48 695 (2003 est). Area: 783 sq km (302 sq miles)

dungaree (ˌdʌŋgəˈriː) *n* **1** a coarse cotton fabric used chiefly for work clothes, etc **2** (*plural*) **a** a suit of workman's overalls made of this material consisting of trousers with a bib attached **b** a casual garment resembling this, usually worn by women or children **3** *US* trousers [c17 from Hindi *dungrī*, after *Dungrī*, district of Bombay, where this fabric originated]

dung beetle *or* **chafer** *n* any of the various beetles of the family *Scarabaeidae* and related families that feed on or breed in dung

Dungeness (ˌdʌndʒəˈnɛs) *n* a low shingle headland on the S coast of England, in Kent: two nuclear power stations: automatic lighthouse

dungeon (ˈdʌndʒən) *n* **1** a close prison cell, often underground **2** a variant of **donjon** [c14 from Old French *donjon*; related to Latin *dominus* master]

dunger (ˈdʌŋə) *NZ informal* ▷ *n* **1** an old decrepit car **2** any old worn-out machine

dung fly *n* any of various muscid flies of the subfamily *Cordilurinae*, such as the predatory **yellow dung fly** (*Scatophaga stercoraria*), that frequents cowpats to feed and lay its eggs

dunghill (ˈdʌŋˌhɪl) *n* **1** a heap of dung **2** a foul place, condition, or person

dunite (ˈdʌnaɪt) *n* an ultrabasic igneous rock consisting mainly of olivine [c19 named after Dun Mountain, a mountain in New Zealand where it is abundant]

duniwassal (ˈduːnɪˌwɑːsˀl) *n* (in Scotland) a minor nobleman [c16 from Gaelic *duine* man + *uasal* noble]

dunk (dʌŋk) *vb* **1** to dip (bread, etc) in tea, soup, etc, before eating **2** to submerge or be submerged in liquid: *dunk new plants in water before planting* [c20 from Pennsylvania Dutch, from Middle High German *dunken*, from Old High German *dunkōn*; see DUCK², TINGE] > 'dunker *n*

Dunker (ˈdʌŋkə) *or* **Dunkard** (ˈdʌŋkəd) *n* a member of the German Baptist Brethren [c18 from German *Tunker* ducker]

Dunkerque (*French* dœ̃kɛrk) *n* a port in N France, on the Strait of Dover: scene of the evacuation of British and other Allied troops after the fall of France in 1940; industrial centre with an oil refinery and naval shipbuilding yards. Pop: 70 850 (1999). English name: Dunkirk (dʌnˈkɜːk)

Dún Laoghaire (duːn ˈlɪərɪ) *n* a port in E Republic of Ireland, on Dublin Bay. Pop: 24 447 (2002). Former names: Dunleary (until 1821), Kingstown (1821–1921)

dunlin (ˈdʌnlɪn) *n* a small sandpiper, *Calidris* (or *Erolia*) *alpina*, of northern and arctic regions, having a brown back and black breast in summer. Also called: **red-backed sandpiper** [c16 DUN⁴ + -LING]

dunnage (ˈdʌnɪdʒ) *n* loose material used for packing cargo [c14 of uncertain origin]

dunnakin (ˈdʌnəkɪn) *n dialect* a lavatory. Also

called: dunny [of obscure origin; but perhaps related to DUNG]

dunnart (ˈdʌnɑːt) *n* a mouselike insectivorous marsupial of the genus *Sminthopsis* of Australia and New Guinea [c20 from a native Australian language]

dunnite (ˈdʌnaɪt) *n* an explosive containing ammonium picrate [c20 named after Colonel B. W. Dunn (1860–1936), American army officer who invented it]

dunno (dʌˈnəʊ, dʊ-, də-) *slang contraction of* (I) do not know

dunnock (ˈdʌnək) *n* another name for **hedge sparrow** [from DUN² + -OCK]

dunny (ˈdʌnɪ) *n, pl* -nies **1** *Scot dialect* a cellar or basement **2** *dialect* another word for **dunnakin 3** *Austral and NZ informal* **a** an outside lavatory **b** (*as modifier*): *a dunny roll; a dunny seat* [c20 of obscure origin; but see DUNNAKIN]

Dunoon (dəˈnuːn) *n* a town and resort in W Scotland, in Argyll and Bute, on the Firth of Clyde. Pop: 8251 (2001)

Dunsinane (dʌnˈsɪnən) *n* a hill in central Scotland, in the Sidlaw Hills: the ruined fort at its summit is regarded as Macbeth's castle. Height: 308 m (1012 ft)

USAGE The pronunciation (ˈdʌnsɪˌneɪn) is used in Shakespeare's *Macbeth* for the purposes of rhyme

Dunstable (ˈdʌnstəbˀl) *n* an industrial town in SE central England, in Bedfordshire. Pop: 50 775 (2001)

dunt (dʌnt, dʊnt) *Scot and northern English dialect* ▷ *n* **1** a blow; thump **2** the injury caused by such a blow ▷ *vb* **3** to strike [c15 perhaps variant of DINT]

Duntroon (dʌnˈtruːn) *n* a suburb of Canberra: seat of the Royal Military College of Australia

duo (ˈdjuːəʊ) *n, pl* duos *or* dui (ˈdjuːiː) **1** *music* **a** a pair of performers **b** another word for **duet 2** a pair of actors, entertainers, etc **3** *informal* a pair of closely connected individuals [c16 via Italian from Latin: two]

duo- *combining form* indicating two: *duotone* [from Latin]

duobinary (ˌdjuːəʊˈbaɪnərɪ) *adj* denoting a communications system for coding digital data in which three data bands are used, 0, +1, –1. Compare **binary notation**

duodecimal (ˌdjuːəʊˈdɛsɪməl) *adj* **1** relating to twelve or twelfths ▷ *n* **2** a twelfth **3** one of the numbers used in a duodecimal number system > ˌduo'decimally *adv*

duodecimo (ˌdjuːəʊˈdɛsɪˌməʊ) *n, pl* -mos **1** a book size resulting from folding a sheet of paper into twelve leaves. Also called: **twelvemo**. Often written: 12mo, 12° **2** a book of this size [c17 from Latin phrase *in duodecimō* in twelfth, from *duodecim* twelve]

duodenary (ˌdjuːəˈdiːnərɪ) *adj* of or relating to the number 12; duodecimal [c17 from Latin *duodēnārius* containing twelve]

duodenitis (ˌdjuːəʊdɪˈnaɪtɪs) *n* inflammation of the duodenum

duodenum (ˌdjuːəʊˈdiːnəm) *n, pl* -na (-nə) *or* -nums the first part of the small intestine, between the stomach and the jejunum [c14 from Medieval Latin, shortened from *intestinum duodenum digitorum* intestine of twelve fingers' length, from Latin *duodēnī* twelve each] > ˌduo'denal *adj*

duologue *or sometimes US* **duolog** (ˈdjuːəˌlɒg) *n* **1** a part or all of a play in which the speaking roles are limited to two actors **2** a less common word for **dialogue**

duopoly (djʊˈɒpəlɪ) *n* a situation in which control of a commodity or service in a particular market is vested in just two producers or suppliers > duopolistic (ˌdjʊɒpəˈlɪstɪk) *adj*

Duo-Tang (ˈdjuːəˌtæŋ) *n trademark Canadian* a type of folder with flexible metal fasteners

duotone (ˈdjuːəˌtəʊn) *n printing* **1** a process for producing halftone illustrations using two shades

of a single colour or black and a colour **2** a picture produced by this process

dup (dʌp) *vb* dups, dupping, dupped (*tr*) *archaic or dialect* to open [c16 contraction of DO¹ + UP]

D up *vb* (*adverb*) *Austral sport* **a** to set up a defence **b** to mark an opponent

dupatta (dʊˈpʌtə) *n* a scarf worn in India

dupe (djuːp) *n* **1** a person who is easily deceived **2** a person who unwittingly serves as the tool of another person or power ▷ *vb* **3** (*tr*) to deceive, esp by trickery; make a dupe or tool of; cheat; fool [c17 from French, from Old French *duppe*, contraction of *de huppe* of (a) hoopoe (from Latin *upupa*); from the bird's reputation for extreme stupidity] > 'dupable *adj* > ˌdupa'bility *n* > 'duper *n* > 'dupery *n*

dupion (ˈdjuːpɪən, -ˈpɪɒn) *n* a silk fabric made from the threads of double cocoons [c19 from French *doupion*, from Italian *doppione* double]

duple (ˈdjuːpˀl) *adj* **1** a less common word for **double 2** *music* (of time or music) having two beats in a bar [c16 from Latin *duplus* twofold, double]

duplet (ˈdjuːplɪt) *n* **1** a pair of electrons shared between two atoms in a covalent bond **2** *music* a group of two notes played in the time of three

duple time *n* musical time with two beats in each bar

duplex (ˈdjuːplɛks) *n* **1** *US and Canadian* a duplex apartment or house **2** a double-stranded region in a nucleic acid molecule ▷ *adj* **3** having two parts **4** *machinery* having pairs of components of independent but identical function **5** permitting the transmission of simultaneous signals in both directions in a radio, telecommunications, or computer channel [c19 from Latin: twofold, from *duo* two + *-plex* -FOLD] > du'plexity *n*

duplex apartment *n US and Canadian* an apartment on two floors

duplex chain *n engineering* a roller chain having two sets of rollers linked together, used for heavy-duty applications

duplex house *n US and Canadian* a house divided into two separate dwellings. Also called (US): **semidetached**

duplicate *adj* (ˈdjuːplɪkɪt) **1** copied exactly from an original **2** identical **3** existing as a pair or in pairs; twofold ▷ *n* (ˈdjuːplɪkɪt) **4** an exact copy; double **5** something additional or supplementary of the same kind **6** two exact copies (esp in the phrase **in duplicate**) ▷ *vb* (ˈdjuːplɪˌkeɪt) **7** (*tr*) to make a replica of **8** (*tr*) to do or make again **9** (*tr*) to make in a pair; make double **10** (*intr*) *biology* to reproduce by dividing into two identical parts: *the chromosomes duplicated in mitosis* [c15 from Latin *duplicāre* to double, from *duo* two + *plicāre* to fold] > duplicable (ˈdjuːplɪkəbˀl) *adj* > ˌduplica'bility *n* > 'duplicately *adv* > 'duplicative *adj*

duplicate bridge *n* a form of contract bridge, esp at clubs and in competitions, in which the hands are kept as dealt and played by different players. The partners with the highest average score are the winners. Also called: **board bridge**. Compare **rubber bridge**

duplication (ˌdjuːplɪˈkeɪʃən) *n* **1** the act of duplicating or the state of being duplicated **2** a copy; duplicate **3** *genetics* a mutation in which there are two or more copies of a gene or of a segment of a chromosome

duplicator (ˈdjuːplɪˌkeɪtə) *n* an apparatus for making replicas of an original, such as a machine using a stencil wrapped on an ink-loaded drum

duplicident (djuːˈplɪsɪdənt) *adj* (of certain animals, such as rabbits) having two pairs of incisors in the upper jaw

duplicity (djuːˈplɪsɪtɪ) *n, pl* -ties deception; double dealing [c15 from Old French *duplicite*, from Late Latin *duplicitās* a being double, from Latin DUPLEX] > du'plicitous *adj*

dupondius (djuːˈpɒndɪəs) *n, pl* -dii (-dɪˌaɪ) a brass coin of ancient Rome worth half a sesterce [from Latin, from *duo* two + *pondus* weight]

duppy (ˈdʌpɪ) *n, pl* -pies *Caribbean* a spirit or ghost

d

[C18 probably of African origin]

Duque de Caxias (*Portuguese* 'duːke də kə'ʃiəʃ) *n* a city in SE Brazil, near Rio de Janeiro. Pop: 116 000 (2005 est)

Dur. *abbreviation for* Durham

durable ('djʊərəb°l) *adj* long-lasting; enduring: *a durable fabric* [C14 from Old French, from Latin *dūrābilis*, from *dūrāre* to last; see ENDURE]
> ˌdura'bility *or* 'durableness *n* > 'durably *adv*

durable goods *pl n* goods, such as most producer goods and some consumer goods, that require infrequent replacement. Compare **disposable goods, perishables** Also called: **durables**

durable press *n* **a** another term for **permanent press b** (*as modifier*): *durable-press skirts*

dural ('djʊərəl) *adj* relating to or affecting the dura mater

Duralumin (djʊ'ræljʊmɪn) *n trademark* a light strong aluminium alloy containing 3.5–4.5 per cent of copper with small quantities of silicon, magnesium, and manganese; used in aircraft manufacture

dura mater ('djʊərə 'meɪtə) *n* the outermost and toughest of the three membranes (see **meninges**) covering the brain and spinal cord. Often shortened to: **dura** [C15 from Medieval Latin, hard mother]

duramen (djʊ'reɪmɛn) *n* another name for **heartwood** [C19 from Latin: hardness, from *dūrāre* to harden]

durance ('djʊərəns) *n archaic or literary* **1** imprisonment **2** duration [C15 from Old French, from *durer* to last, from Latin *dūrāre*]

Durance (*French* dyrɑ̃s) *n* a river in S France, rising in the Alps and flowing generally southwest into the Rhône. Length: 304 km (189 miles)

Durango (djʊ'ræŋgəʊ; *Spanish* du'raŋgo) *n* **1** a state in N central Mexico: high plateau, with the Sierra Madre Occidental in the west; irrigated agriculture (esp cotton) and rich mineral resources. Capital: Durango. Pop: 1 448 661 (2000). Area: 119 648 sq km (46 662 sq miles) **2** a city in NW central Mexico, capital of Durango state: mining centre. Pop: 520 000 (2005 est). Official name: **Victoria de Durango**

duration (djʊ'reɪʃən) *n* the length of time that something lasts or continues [C14 from Medieval Latin *dūrātiō*, from Latin *dūrāre* to last]
> du'rational *adj*

durative ('djʊərətɪv) *grammar* ▷ *adj* **1** denoting an aspect of verbs that includes the imperfective and the progressive ▷ *n* **2 a** the durative aspect of a verb **b** a verb in this aspect

Durazzo (du'rattso) *n* the Italian name for **Durrës**

Durban ('dɜːb°n) *n* a port in E South Africa, in E KwaZulu/Natal province on the Indian Ocean: University of Natal (1909); resort and industrial centre, with oil refineries, shipbuilding yards, etc. Pop: 536 644 (2001)

Durban poison *n South African slang* a particularly potent variety of cannabis grown in Natal

durbar ('dɜːbɑː, ˌdɜː'bɑː) *n* **a** (formerly) the court of a native ruler or a governor in India and British Colonial West Africa **b** a levee at such a court [C17 from Hindi *darbār* court, from Persian, from *dar* door + *bār* entry, audience]

Düren (*German* 'dyːrən) *n* a city in W Germany, in North Rhine-Westphalia. Pop: 92 966 (2003 est)

duress (djʊ'rɛs, djʊə-) *n* **1** compulsion by use of force or threat; constraint; coercion (often in the phrase **under duress**) **2** *law* the illegal exercise of coercion **3** confinement; imprisonment [C14 from Old French *duresse*, from Latin *dūritia* hardness, from *dūrus* hard]

Durex ('djʊərɛks) *n, pl* -rex *trademark* **1** a brand of condom **2** *Austral* a brand of adhesive tape

Durga ('dʊəgæ) *n Hinduism* the goddess Parvati portrayed as a warrior: renowned for slaying the buffalo demon, Mahisha [from Sanskrit: the inaccessible one]

durgah ('dɜːgɑː) *n* a variant spelling of **dargah**

Durga Puja (ˌdʊəgæ 'puːdʒə) *n* another name for **Navaratri** [from Sanskrit DURGA + *puja* worship]

Durgapur ('dɜːgəˌpʊə) *n* a city in NE India, in West Bengal: heavy industry, including steelworks. Pop: 492 996 (2001)

Durham ('dʌrəm) *n* **1** a county of NE England, on the North Sea: rises to the N Pennines in the west: the geographical and ceremonial county includes the unitary authorities of Hartlepool and Stockton-on-Tees (both part of Cleveland until 1996) and Darlington (created in 1997). Administrative centre: Durham. Pop (excluding unitary authorities): 494 200 (2003 est). Area (excluding unitary authorities): 2434 sq km (940 sq miles). Abbreviation: **Dur 2** a city in NE England, administrative centre of Co Durham, on the River Wear: Norman cathedral; 11th-century castle (founded by William the Conqueror), now occupied by the University of Durham (1832). Pop: 42 939 (2001) **3** a rare variety of shorthorn cattle. See **shorthorn**

durian *or* **durion** ('djʊərɪən) *n* **1** a SE Asian bombacaceous tree, *Durio zibethinus*, having very large oval fruits with a hard spiny rind containing seeds surrounded by edible evil-smelling aril **2** the fruit of this tree, which has an offensive smell but a pleasant taste: supposedly an aphrodisiac [C16 from Malay, from *duri* thorn]

duricrust ('djʊərɪˌkrʌst) *n* another name for **caliche** (sense 2)

during ('djʊərɪŋ) *prep* **1** concurrently with (some other activity): *kindly don't sleep during my lectures!* **2** within the limit of (a period of time): *during the day* [C14 from *duren* to last, ultimately from Latin *dūrāre* to last]

durmast *or* **durmast oak** ('dɜːˌmɑːst) *n* **1** Also called: **sessile oak** a large Eurasian oak tree, *Quercus petraea*, with lobed leaves and sessile acorns. Compare **pedunculate oak 2** the heavy elastic wood of this tree, used in building and cabinetwork [C18 probably alteration of *dun mast*; see DUN², MAST²]

durn (dɜːn) *interj, adj, adv, n* a US variant of **darn²**

duro ('dʊərəʊ) *n, pl* -ros the silver peso of Spain or Spanish America [from Spanish, shortened from *peso duro* hard peso, ultimately from Latin *dūrus* hard]

Duroc ('djʊərɒk) *n* an American breed of red lard pig [C19 from *Duroc*, name of a stallion owned by the man who developed this breed]

durra ('dʌrə) *or* **doura, dourah** ('dʊərə) *n* an Old World variety of sorghum, *Sorghum vulgare durra*, with erect hairy flower spikes and round seeds: cultivated for grain and fodder. Also called: Guinea corn, Indian millet [C18 from Arabic *dhurah* grain]

Durrës ('dʊrəs) *n* a port in W Albania, on the Adriatic. Pop: 86 900 (1991 est). Ancient names: Epidamnus (ˌɛpɪ'dæmnəs); Dyrrachium (də'reɪkɪəm); Italian name: Durazzo

durrie ('dʌrɪ) *n* a cotton carpet made in India, often in rectangular pieces fringed at the ends: sometimes used as a sofa cover, wall hanging, etc [from Hindi *darī*]

durry ('dʌrɪ) *n, pl* -ries *Austral slang* a cigarette [from DURRIE]

durst (dɜːst) *vb* a past tense of **dare**

durum *or* **durum wheat** ('djʊərəm) *n* a variety of wheat, *Triticum durum*, with a high gluten content, cultivated mainly in the Mediterranean region, and used chiefly to make pastas [C20 short for New Latin *trīticum dūrum*, literally: hard wheat]

durzi ('dɜːzɪ) *n* an Indian tailor [C19 from Hindi, from Persian *darzī* from *darz* sewing]

Dushanbe (duː'ʃɑːnbɪ) *n* the capital of Tajikistan; a cultural centre. Pop: 551 000 (2005 est). Former name (1929–61): Stalinabad

dusk (dʌsk) *n* **1** twilight or the darker part of twilight **2** *poetic* gloom; shade ▷ *adj* **3** *poetic* shady; gloomy ▷ *vb* **4** *poetic* to make or become dark [Old English *dox*; related to Old Saxon *dosan*

brown, Old High German *tusin* yellow, Norwegian *dusmen* misty, Latin *fuscus* dark brown]

dusky ('dʌskɪ) *adj* duskier, duskiest **1** dark in colour; swarthy or dark-skinned **2** dim > 'duskily *adv* > 'duskiness *n*

Düsseldorf ('dʊsəlˌdɔːf; *German* 'dʏsəldɔrf) *n* an industrial city in W Germany, capital of North Rhine-Westphalia, on the Rhine: commercial centre of the Rhine-Ruhr industrial area. Pop: 572 511 (2003 est)

dust (dʌst) *n* **1** dry fine powdery material, such as particles of dirt, earth or pollen **2** a cloud of such fine particles **3** the powdery particles to which something is thought to be reduced by death, decay, or disintegration **4 a** the mortal body of man **b** the corpse of a dead person **5** the earth; ground **6** *informal* a disturbance; fuss (esp in the phrases **kick up a dust, raise a dust**) **7** something of little or no worth **8** *informal* (in mining parlance) silicosis or any similar respiratory disease **9** short for **gold dust 10** ashes or household refuse **11** **bite the dust a** to fail completely or cease to exist **b** to fall down dead **12** **dust and ashes** something that is very disappointing **13** **leave (someone *or* something) in the dust** to outdo comprehensively or with ease: *leaving their competitors in the dust* **14** **shake the dust off one's feet** to depart angrily or contemptuously **15** **throw dust in the eyes of** to confuse or mislead ▷ *vb* **16** (*tr*) to sprinkle or cover (something) with (dust or some other powdery substance): *to dust a cake with sugar; to dust sugar onto a cake* **17** to remove dust by wiping, sweeping, or brushing **18** *archaic* to make or become dirty with dust ▷ See also **dust down, dust-up** [Old English *dūst*; related to Danish *dyst* flour dust, Middle Dutch *dūst* dust, meal dust, Old High German *tunst* storm] > 'dustless *adj*

dust-bath *n* the action of a bird of driving dust into its feathers, which may dislodge parasites

dustbin ('dʌstˌbɪn) *n* a large, usually cylindrical container for rubbish, esp one used by a household. US and Canadian names: **garbage can, trash can**

dust bowl *n* a semiarid area in which the surface soil is exposed to wind erosion and dust storms occur

Dust Bowl *n* **the** the area of the south central US that became denuded of topsoil by wind erosion during the droughts of the mid-1930s

dust bunny *n* a small mass of fluff and dust

dustcart ('dʌstˌkɑːt) *n* a road vehicle for collecting domestic refuse. US and Canadian name: **garbage truck**

dust coat *n Brit* a loose lightweight coat worn for early open motor-car riding. US name: **duster**

dust cover *n* **1** another name for **dustsheet 2** another name for **dust jacket 3** a perspex cover for the turntable of a record player

dust devil *n* a strong miniature whirlwind that whips up dust, litter, leaves, etc into the air

dust down *vb* (*tr, adverb*) **1** to remove dust from by brushing or wiping **2** to reprimand severely > **dusting down** *n*

duster ('dʌstə) *n* **1** a cloth used for dusting furniture, etc. US name: **dust cloth 2** a machine for blowing out dust over trees or crops **3** a person or thing that dusts

duster coat *n* a woman's loose summer coat with wide sleeves and no buttons, popular in the mid-20th century

dust explosion *n* an explosion caused by the ignition of an inflammable dust, such as flour or sawdust, in the air

dusting-powder *n* fine powder (such as talcum powder) used to absorb moisture, etc

dust jacket *or* **cover** *n* a removable paper cover used to protect a bound book. Also called: **book jacket, jacket**

dustman ('dʌstmən) *n, pl* -men *Brit* a man whose job is to collect domestic refuse

dust mite *n* either of two mites, *Dermatophagoides farinae* or *D. pteronyssinus*, that feed on shed human skill cells. Their excrement is a household allergen associated with respiratory allergies and asthma

dustpan ('dʌst,pæn) *n* a short-handled hooded shovel into which dust is swept from floors, etc

dustsheet ('dʌst,ʃiːt) *n Brit* a large cloth or sheet used for covering furniture to protect it from dust. Also called: dust cover

dust shot *n* the smallest size of shot for a shotgun

dust storm *n* a windstorm that whips up clouds of dust

dust-up *informal* ▷ *n* **1** a quarrel, fight, or argument ▷ *vb* dust up **2** (*tr, adverb*) to attack or assault (someone)

dusty ('dʌstɪ) *adj* dustier, dustiest **1** covered with or involving dust **2** like dust in appearance or colour **3** (of a colour) tinged with grey; pale: *dusty pink* **4** a dusty answer an unhelpful or bad-tempered reply **5** not so dusty *informal* not too bad; fairly well: often in response to the greeting *how are you?* > 'dustily *adv* > 'dustiness *n*

dusty miller *n* **1** Also called: snow-in-summer a caryophyllaceous plant, *Cerastium tomentosum,* of SE Europe and Asia, having white flowers and downy stems and leaves: cultivated as a rock plant **2** a plant, *Artemisia stelleriana,* of NE Asia and E North America, having small yellow flower heads and downy stems and leaves: family *Asteraceae* (composites) **3** any of various other downy plants, such as the rose campion

dutch (dʌtʃ) *n Cockney slang* wife [c19 short for *duchess*]

Dutch (dʌtʃ) *n* **1** the language of the Netherlands, belonging to the West Germanic branch of the Indo-European family and quite closely related to German and English. See also **Flemish, Afrikaans** **2** the Dutch (*functioning as plural*) the natives, citizens, or inhabitants of the Netherlands **3** See **Pennsylvania Dutch 4** See double Dutch **5** in Dutch *slang* in trouble ▷ *adj* **6** of, relating to, or characteristic of the Netherlands, its inhabitants, or their language ▷ *adv* **7** go Dutch *informal* to share expenses equally

Dutch auction *n* an auction in which the price is lowered by stages until a buyer is found

Dutch barn *n Brit* a farm building consisting of a steel frame and a curved roof

Dutch cap *n* **1** a woman's lace cap with triangular flaps, characteristic of Dutch national dress **2** a contraceptive device for women. See diaphragm (sense 2)

Dutch courage *n* **1** false courage gained from drinking alcohol **2** alcoholic drink

Dutch disease *n* the deindustrialization of an economy as a result of the discovery of a natural resource, as that which occurred in Holland with the exploitation of North Sea Oil, which raised the value of the Dutch currency, making its exports uncompetitive and causing its industry to decline

Dutch doll *n* a jointed wooden doll

Dutch door *n US and Canadian* a door with an upper and lower leaf that may be opened separately. Also called (in Britain and certain other countries): stable door

Dutch East Indies *n* the a former name (1798–1945) of **Indonesia** Also called: Netherlands East Indies

Dutch elm *n* a widely planted hybrid elm tree, *Ulmus hollandica,* with spreading branches and a short trunk

Dutch elm disease *n* a disease of elm trees caused by the fungus *Ceratocystis ulmi* and characterized by withering of the foliage and stems and eventual death of the parts of the tree above ground

Dutch gold *n* another name for **Dutch metal**

Dutch Guiana or **Netherlands Guiana** *n* the former name of **Surinam**

Dutch guinea pig *n* a breed of two-tone short-haired guinea pig

Dutch hoe *n* a type of hoe in which the head consists of a two-edged cross-blade attached to two prongs or of a single pressing of this shape

Dutchman ('dʌtʃmən) *n, pl* -men **1** a native, citizen, or inhabitant of the Netherlands **2** a piece of wood, metal, etc, used to repair or patch faulty workmanship **3** *South African often derogatory* an Afrikaaner

Dutchman's-breeches *n* (*functioning as singular*) a North American plant, *Dicentra cucullaria,* with finely divided basal leaves and pink flowers: family *Fumariaceae.* Also called: colicweed

Dutchman's-pipe *n* a woody climbing plant, *Aristolochia sipho,* of the eastern US, cultivated for its greenish-brown mottled flowers, which are shaped like a curved pipe: family *Aristolochiaceae*

Dutch mattress *n* another name for **mattress** (sense 2)

Dutch medicine *n South African* patent medicine, esp made of herbs

Dutch metal or **gold** *n* a substitute for gold leaf, consisting of thin sheets of copper that have been turned yellow by exposure to the fumes of molten zinc

Dutch New Guinea *n* a former name (until 1963) of **Papua** (formerly **Irian Jaya**)

Dutch oven *n* **1** an iron or earthenware container with a cover used for stews, etc **2** a metal box, open in front, for cooking in front of an open fire

Dutch Reformed Church *n* any of the three Calvinist Churches to which most Afrikaans-speaking South Africans belong

Dutch rise *n NZ* an increase in wages that is of no benefit to the recipient

Dutch rush *n* (*sometimes not capital*) a horsetail, *Equisetum hyemale,* whose siliceous stems have been used for polishing and scouring pots and pans. Also called: scouring rush

Dutch treat *n informal* an entertainment, meal, etc, where each person pays for himself

Dutch uncle *n informal* a person who criticizes or reproves frankly and severely

Dutch West Indies *pl n* the a former name of the **Netherlands Antilles**

Dutch wife *n* a long hard bolster used, esp in the tropics, to support one's uppermost knee when sleeping on one's side

duteous ('djuːtɪəs) *adj formal or archaic* dutiful; obedient > 'duteously *adv* > 'duteousness *n*

dutiable ('djuːtɪəbəl) *adj* (of goods) liable to duty > ˌdutia'bility *n*

dutiful ('djuːtɪfʊl) *adj* **1** exhibiting or having a sense of duty **2** characterized by or resulting from a sense of duty > 'dutifully *adv* > 'dutifulness *n*

duty ('djuːtɪ) *n, pl* -ties **1** a task or action that a person is bound to perform for moral or legal reasons **2** respect or obedience due to a superior, older persons, etc: *filial duty* **3** the force that binds one morally or legally to one's obligations **4** a government tax, esp on imports **5** *Brit* **a** the quantity or intensity of work for which a machine is designed **b** a measure of the efficiency of a machine **6** the quantity of water necessary to irrigate an area of land to grow a particular crop **7 a** a job or service allocated **b** (*as modifier*): *duty rota* **8** do duty for to act as a substitute for **9** on (*or* off) duty at (*or* not at) work [c13 from Anglo French *duteé,* from Old French *deu* DUE]

duty-bound *adj* morally obliged as a matter of duty

duty-free *adj, adv* **1** with exemption from customs or excise duties ▷ *n* **2** goods sold in a duty-free shop

duty-free shop *n* a shop, esp one at an airport or on board a ship, that sells perfume, tobacco, etc, at duty-free prices

duty officer *n* an officer (in the armed forces, police, etc) on duty at a particular time

duumvir (djuːˈʌmvə) *n, pl* -virs or -viri (-vɪˌriː) **1** *Roman history* one of two coequal magistrates or officers **2** either of two men who exercise a joint authority [c16 from Latin, from *duo* two + *vir* man]

duumvirate (djuːˈʌmvɪrɪt) *n* the office of or government by duumvirs

duvet ('duːveɪ) *n* **1** another name for **continental quilt 2** Also called: duvet jacket a down-filled jacket used esp by mountaineers [c18 from French, from earlier *dumet,* from Old French *dum* DOWN²]

duvet day *n informal* a day of leave from work that an employee is allowed to take at short notice [c20 from the idea of staying in bed rather than going to work]

duvetyn, duvetine or **duvetyne** ('djuːvəˌtiːn) *n* a soft napped velvety fabric of cotton, silk, wool, or rayon [c20 from French *duvetine,* from *duvet* down + -INE²]

dux (dʌks) *n* (in Scottish and certain other schools) the top pupil in a class or school [Latin: leader]

duyker ('daɪkə) *n* a variant spelling of **duiker**

DV *abbreviation for* **1** Deo volente [Latin: God willing] **2** Douay Version (of the Bible) **3** digital video

dvandva ('dvɑːndvɑː) *n* **1** a class of compound words consisting of two elements having a coordinate relationship as if connected by *and* **2** a compound word of this type, such as *Austro-Hungarian, tragicomic* [from Sanskrit *dvamdva* a pair, from the reduplication of *dva* TWO]

DVD *abbreviation for* digital versatile *or* digital video disk: an optical disk used to store audio, video, or computer data, esp feature films for home viewing

DVD-A *abbreviation for* DVD-Audio

DVD writer *n computing* a device on a computer for writing DVDs

Dvina (Russian dviˈna) *n* **1** Northern a river in NW Russia, formed by the confluence of the Sukhona and Yug Rivers and flowing northwest to *Dvina Bay* in the White Sea. Length: 750 km (466 miles). Russian name: Severnaya Dvina **2** Western a river rising in W Russia, in the Valdai Hills and flowing south and southwest then northwest to the Gulf of Riga. Length: 1021 km (634 miles). Russian name: Zapadnaya Dvina ('zapədnəjə) Latvian name: Daugava

Dvina Bay or **Dvina Gulf** *n* an inlet of the White Sea, off the coast of NW Russia

Dvinsk (dvinsk) *n* transliteration of the former Russian name for **Daugavpils**

DVLA (in Britain) *abbreviation for* Driver and Vehicle Licensing Agency

DVM *abbreviation for* Doctor of Veterinary Medicine

DVT *abbreviation for* **deep vein thrombosis**

D/W *abbreviation for* dock warrant

dwaal (dwɑːl) *n South African* a state of befuddlement [Afrikaans]

dwale (dweɪl) *n* another name for **deadly nightshade** [c14 perhaps of Scandinavian origin]

dwam (dwɑːm) or **dwaum** (dwɔːm) *Scot* ▷ *n* **1** a stupor or daydream (esp in the phrase in a dwam) ▷ *vb* **2** (*intr*) to faint or fall ill [Old English *dwolma* confusion]

dwang (dwæŋ) *n Scot and NZ* another name for **nogging** (sense 1) [c19 Scot; compare Dutch *dwang* force, Middle Low German *dwanc*]

dwarf (dwɔːf) *n, pl* dwarfs or dwarves (dwɔːvz) **1** an abnormally undersized person, esp one with a large head and short arms and legs. Compare **midget 2 a** an animal or plant much below the average height for the species **b** (*as modifier*): *a dwarf tree* **3** (in folklore) a small ugly manlike creature, often possessing magical powers **4** *astronomy* short for **dwarf star** ▷ *vb* **5** to become or cause to become comparatively small in size, importance, etc **6** (*tr*) to stunt the growth of [Old English *dweorg;* related to Old Norse *dvorgr,* Old High German *twerc*] > 'dwarfish *adj* > 'dwarfishly *adv* > 'dwarfishness *n*

dwarf bean *n* another name for **French bean**

dwarf chestnut *n* **1** the edible nut of the chinquapin tree **2** another name for **chinquapin** (sense 1)

d

dwarf cornel *n* an arctic and subarctic cornaceous plant *Cornus suecica*, having small purple flowers surrounded by white petal-like bracts

dwarfism ('dwɔːfɪzəm) *n* the condition of being a dwarf

dwarf male *n* a male animal that is much smaller, and often internally simpler, than its female counterpart. Dwarf males are commonly carried by the female, as in species of angler fish

dwarf mallow *n* a European malvaceous plant, *Malva neglecta* (or *M. rotundifolia*), having rounded leaves and small pinkish-white flowers

dwarf star *n* any luminosity class V star, such as the sun, lying in the main sequence of the Hertzsprung-Russell diagram. Also called: main-sequence star See also **red dwarf**, **white dwarf**

dweeb (dwiːb) *n slang, chiefly US* a stupid or uninteresting person [c20 of unknown origin]

dweeby ('dwiːbɪ) *adj* dweebier, dweebiest *slang, chiefly US* like or typical of a dweeb

dwell (dwɛl) *vb* dwells, dwelling, dwelt (dwɛlt) *or* dwelled (intr) **1** *formal, literary* to live as a permanent resident **2** to live (in a specified state): *to dwell in poverty* ▷ *n* **3** a regular pause in the operation of a machine **4** a flat or constant-radius portion on a linear or rotary cam enabling the cam follower to remain static for a brief time [Old English *dwellan* to seduce, get lost; related to Old Saxon *bidwellian* to prevent, Old Norse *dvelja*, Old High German *twellen* to prevent] > **'dweller** *n*

dwelling ('dwɛlɪŋ) *n formal, literary* a place of residence

dwell on *or* **upon** *vb* (intr, preposition) to think, speak, or write at length: *it's no good dwelling on your misfortunes*

dwell time *n marketing* the amount of time a customer spends waiting in a queue

dwelt (dwɛlt) *vb* a past tense of **dwell**

Dwem (dwɛm) *n acronym for* Dead White European Male

dwindle ('dwɪndəl) *vb* to grow or cause to grow less in size, intensity, or number; diminish or shrink gradually [c16 from Old English *dwīnan* to waste away; related to Old Norse *dvīna* to pine away]

DWP (in Britain) *abbreviation for* Department for Work and Pensions

dwt *abbreviation for* **1** deadweight tonnage **2** Also: dwt *obsolete* pennyweight [*d*, from Latin *denarius* penny]

DX *telegraphy, telephony* **1** *symbol for* long distance **2** (of a radio station) indicating that it is far away

DX code *n photog* a code on a film cassette that automatically adjusts the film-speed setting on a suitably equipped camera to the correct ISO rating [c20 from *d(aylight) (e)x(posure)*]

Dy *the chemical symbol for* dysprosium

DY *international car registration for* Benin [from Dahomey]

dyad ('daɪæd) *n* **1** *maths* an operator that is the unspecified product of two vectors. It can operate on a vector to produce either a scalar or vector product **2** an atom or group that has a valency of two **3** a group of two; couple [c17 from Late Latin *dyas*, from Greek *duas* two, a pair]

dyadic (daɪˈædɪk) *adj* **1** of or relating to a dyad **2** relating to or based on two; twofold **3** *logic, maths* (of a relation, predicate, etc) relating two terms; binary. Compare **monadic, polyadic**

Dyak *or* **Dayak** ('daɪæk) *n, pl* -aks *or* -ak a member of a Malaysian people of the interior of Borneo: noted for their long houses [from Malay *Dayak* upcountry, from *darat* land]

dyarchy ('daɪɑːkɪ) *n, pl* -chies a variant spelling of **diarchy**. > dy'archic, dy'archical *or* dy'archal *adj*

dybbuk ('dɪbək; Hebrew diˈbuk) *n, pl* -buks *or* -bukkim (Hebrew -buˈkim) *Judaism* (in the folklore of the cabala) the soul of a dead sinner that has transmigrated into the body of a living person [from Yiddish *dibbūk* devil, from Hebrew *dibbūq*; related to *dābhaq* to hang on, cling]

dye (daɪ) *n* **1** a staining or colouring substance, such as a natural or synthetic pigment **2** a liquid that contains a colouring material and can be used to stain fabrics, skins, etc **3** the colour or shade produced by dyeing ▷ *vb* dyes, dyeing, dyed **4** (tr) to impart a colour or stain to (something, such as fabric or hair) by or as if by the application of a dye [Old English *dēagian*, from *dēag* a dye; related to Old High German *tugōn* to change, Lettish *dūkans* dark] > **'dyable** *or* **'dyeable** *adj* > **'dyer** *n*

dyed-in-the-wool *adj* **1** extreme or unchanging in attitude, opinion, etc **2** (of a fabric) made of dyed yarn

dyeing ('daɪɪŋ) *n* the process or industry of colouring yarns, fabric, etc

dyeline ('daɪˌlaɪn) *adj* another word for **diazo** (sense 2)

dyer's-greenweed *or esp US* **dyer's-broom** *n* a small Eurasian leguminous shrub, *Genista tinctoria*, whose yellow flowers yield a yellow dye, formerly mixed with woad to produce the colour Kendal green. Also called: woadwaxen, woadwax

dyer's rocket *n* a Eurasian resedaceous plant, *Reseda luteola*, with a spike of yellowish-green flowers and long narrow leaves: formerly cultivated as the source of a yellow dye, used with woad to make Lincoln green. Also called: weld

dyer's-weed *n* any of several plants that yield a dye, such as woad, dyer's rocket, and dyer's-greenweed

dyestuff ('daɪˌstʌf) *n* a substance that can be used as a dye or from which a dye can be obtained

dyewood ('daɪˌwʊd) *n* any wood, such as brazil, from which dyes and pigments can be obtained

Dyfed ('dʌvɛd) *n* a former county in SW Wales: created in 1974 from Cardiganshire, Pembrokeshire, and Carmarthenshire; in 1996 it was replaced by Pembrokeshire, Carmarthenshire, and Ceredigion

dying ('daɪɪŋ) *vb* **1** the present participle of **die¹** ▷ *adj* **2** relating to or occurring at the moment of death: *a dying wish*

dyke¹ *or* **dike** (daɪk) *n* **1** an embankment constructed to prevent flooding, keep out the sea, etc **2** a ditch or watercourse **3** a bank made of earth excavated for and placed alongside a ditch **4** *Scot* a wall, esp a dry-stone wall **5** a barrier or obstruction **6** a vertical or near-vertical wall-like body of igneous rock intruded into cracks in older rock **7** *Austral and NZ informal* **a** a lavatory **b** (as modifier): *a dyke roll* ▷ *vb* **8** *civil engineering* an embankment or wall built to confine a river to a particular course **9** (tr) to protect, enclose, or drain (land) with a dyke [c13 modification of Old English *dīc* ditch; compare Old Norse *dīki* ditch]

dyke² *or* **dike** (daɪk) *n slang* a lesbian [c20 of unknown origin]

dynameter (daɪˈnæmɪtə) *n* an instrument for determining the magnifying power of telescopes

dynamic (daɪˈnæmɪk) *adj* **1** of or concerned with energy or forces that produce motion, as opposed to *static* **2** of or concerned with dynamics **3** Also: dynamical characterized by force of personality, ambition, energy, new ideas, etc **4** *music* of, relating to, or indicating dynamics: *dynamic marks* **5** *computing* (of a memory) needing its contents refreshed periodically. Compare **static** (sense 8) [c19 from French *dynamique*, from Greek *dunamikos* powerful, from *dunamis* power, from *dunasthai* to be able] > dy'namically *adv*

dynamic link library *n computing* a set of programs that can be activated and then discarded by other programs. Abbreviation: DLL

dynamic pricing *n commerce* offering goods at a price that changes according to the level of demand, the type of customer, or the state of the weather

dynamic psychology *n psychol* any system of psychology that emphasizes the interaction between different motives, emotions, and drives

dynamic range *n* the range of signal amplitudes over which an electronic communications channel can operate within acceptable limits of distortion. The range is determined by system noise at the lower end and by the onset of overload at the upper end

dynamics (daɪˈnæmɪks) *n* **1** (*functioning as singular*) the branch of mechanics concerned with the forces that change or produce the motions of bodies. Compare **statics, kinematics 2** (*functioning as singular*) the branch of mechanics that includes statics and kinetics. See **statics, kinetics 3** (*functioning as singular*) the branch of any science concerned with forces **4** those forces that produce change in any field or system **5** *music* **a** the various degrees of loudness called for in performance **b** Also called: dynamic marks, dynamic markings directions and symbols used to indicate degrees of loudness

dynamism ('daɪnəˌmɪzəm) *n* **1** *philosophy* any of several theories that attempt to explain phenomena in terms of an immanent force or energy. Compare **mechanism** (sense 5), **vitalism 2** the forcefulness of an energetic personality > 'dynamist *n* > ˌdyna'mistic *adj*

dynamite ('daɪnəˌmaɪt) *n* **1** an explosive consisting of nitroglycerine or ammonium nitrate mixed with kieselguhr, sawdust, or wood pulp **2** *informal* a spectacular or potentially dangerous person or thing ▷ *vb* **3** (tr) to mine or blow up with dynamite [c19 (coined by Alfred Nobel): from DYNAMO- + -ITE¹] > 'dyna,miter *n*

dynamo ('daɪnəˌməʊ) *n, pl* -mos **1** a device for converting mechanical energy into electrical energy, esp one that produces direct current. Compare **generator** (sense 1) **2** *informal* an energetic hard-working person [c19 short for *dynamoelectric machine*]

dynamo- *or sometimes before a vowel* **dynam-** *combining form* indicating power: *dynamoelectric; dynamite* [from Greek, from *dunamis* power]

dynamoelectric (ˌdaɪnəməʊɪˈlɛktrɪk) *or* **dynamoelectrical** *adj* of or concerned with the interconversion of mechanical and electrical energy

dynamometer (ˌdaɪnəˈmɒmɪtə) *n* any of a number of instruments for measuring power or force

dynamometry (ˌdaɪnəˈmɒmɪtrɪ) *n* **1** the science of power measurement **2** the manufacture and use of dynamometers > dynamometric (ˌdaɪnəməʊˈmɛtrɪk) *or* ˌdynamo'metrical *adj*

dynamotor ('daɪnəˌməʊtə) *n* an electrical machine having a single magnetic field and two independent armature windings of which one acts as a motor and the other a generator: used to convert direct current from a battery into alternating current

dynast ('dɪnəst, -æst) *n* a ruler, esp a hereditary one [c17 from Latin *dynastēs*, from Greek *dunastēs*, from *dunasthai* to be powerful]

dynasty ('dɪnəstɪ) *n, pl* -ties **1** a sequence of hereditary rulers: *an Egyptian dynasty* **2** any sequence of powerful leaders of the same family: *the Kennedy dynasty* [c15 via Late Latin from Greek *dunasteia*, from *dunastēs* DYNAST] > dynastic (dɪˈnæstɪk) *or* dy'nastical *adj* > dy'nastically *adv*

dynatron oscillator ('daɪnəˌtrɒn) *n electronics* an oscillator containing a tetrode in which the screen grid is more positive than the anode, causing the anode current to decrease as its voltage increases [c20 from DYNA(MO-) + -TRON]

dyne (daɪn) *n* the cgs unit of force; the force that imparts an acceleration of 1 centimetre per second to a mass of 1 gram. 1 dyne is equivalent to 10^{-5} newton or 7.233×10^{-5} poundal [c19 from French, from Greek *dunamis* power, force]

dynode ('daɪnəʊd) *n* an electrode onto which a beam of electrons can fall, causing the emission of a greater number of electrons by secondary emission. They are used in photomultipliers to amplify the signal

dys- *prefix* **1** diseased, abnormal, or faulty: *dysentery; dyslexia* **2** difficult or painful: *dysuria* **3** unfavourable or bad: *dyslogistic* [via Latin from Greek *dus-*]

dysarthria (dɪsˈɑːθrɪə) *n* imperfect articulation of speech caused by damage to the nervous system [from DYS- + *arthria* from Greek *arthron* articulation]

dysbindin (dɪsˈbɪndɪn) *n* a gene associated with schizophrenia [C20 from dys(trobrevin-)bind(ing) (prote)in]

dyscalculia (ˌdɪskælˈkjuːlɪə) *n* severe difficulty in making simple mathematical calculations, due to cerebral disease or injury [C20 from DYS- + Latin *calculare* to calculate]

dyscrasia (dɪsˈkreɪzɪə) *n obsolete* any abnormal physiological condition, esp of the blood [C19 New Latin, from Medieval Latin: an imbalance of humours, from Greek, from DYS- + *-krasia*, from *krasis* a mixing]

dysentery (ˈdɪsəntrɪ) *n* infection of the intestine with bacteria or amoebae, marked chiefly by severe diarrhoea with the passage of mucus and blood [C14 via Latin from Greek *dusentería*, from *dusentera*, literally: bad bowels, from DYS- + *enteron* intestine] > dysenteric (ˌdɪsənˈtɛrɪk) *adj*

dysfunction (dɪsˈfʌŋkʃən) *n* **1** *med* any disturbance or abnormality in the function of an organ or part **2** (esp of a family) failure to show the characteristics or fulfil the purposes accepted as normal or beneficial

dysfunctional (dɪsˈfʌŋkʃənᵊl) *adj* **1** *med* (of an organ or part) not functioning normally **2** (esp of a family) characterized by a breakdown of normal or beneficial relationships between members of the group

dysgenic (dɪsˈdʒɛnɪk) *adj* **1** of, relating to, or contributing to a degeneration or deterioration in the fitness and quality of a race or strain **2** of or relating to dysgenics

dysgenics (dɪsˈdʒɛnɪks) *n* (*functioning as singular*) the study of factors capable of reducing the quality of a race or strain, esp the human race. Also called: cacogenics

dysgraphia (dɪsˈɡræfɪə) *n* inability to write correctly, caused by disease of part of the brain

dyskinesia (ˌdɪskɪˈniːzɪə) *n* involuntary repetitive movements, such as those occurring in chorea [DYS- + *-kinesia* from Greek *kinesis* movement]

dyslalia (dɪsˈleɪlɪə) *n* defective speech characteristic of those affected by aphasia

dyslexia (dɪsˈlɛksɪə) *n* a developmental disorder which can cause learning difficulty in one or more of the areas of reading, writing, and numeracy. Nontechnical name: word blindness [from DYS- + *-lexia* from Greek *lexis* word] > dyslectic (dɪsˈlɛktɪk) *adj, n* > dysˈlexic *adj*

dyslogistic (ˌdɪsləˈdʒɪstɪk) *adj rare* disapproving [C19 from DYS- + *-logistic*, as in *eulogistic*] > ˌdysloˈgistically *adv*

dysmenorrhoea *or esp US* **dysmenorrhea** (ˌdɪsmɛnəˈrɪə, dɪsˌmɛn-) *n* abnormally difficult or painful menstruation > ˌdysmenorˈrhoeal *or esp US* ˌdysmenorˈrheal *adj*

dysmorphophobia (dɪsˌmɔːfəʊˈfəʊbɪə) *n* an obsessive fear that one's body, or any part of it, is repulsive or may become so

dyspepsia (dɪsˈpɛpsɪə) *or* **dyspepsy** (dɪsˈpɛpsɪ) *n* indigestion or upset stomach [C18 from Latin, from Greek *duspepsia*, from DYS- + *pepsis* digestion]

dyspeptic (dɪsˈpɛptɪk) *adj also* dyspeptical **1** relating to or suffering from dyspepsia **2** irritable ▷ *n* **3** a person suffering from dyspepsia > dysˈpeptically *adv*

dysphagia (dɪsˈfeɪdʒɪə) *n* difficulty in swallowing, caused by obstruction or spasm of the oesophagus [C18 New Latin, from DYS- + Greek *-phagos*; see PHAGO-] > dysphagic (dɪsˈfædʒɪk) *adj*

dysphasia (dɪsˈfeɪzɪə) *n* a disorder of language caused by a brain lesion [see DYS- + -PHASIA] > dysˈphasic *adj, n*

dysphemism (ˈdɪsfɪˌmɪzəm) *n* **1** substitution of a derogatory or offensive word or phrase for an innocuous one **2** the word or phrase so substituted [C19 DYS- + EUPHEMISM] > ˌdyspheˈmistic *adj*

dysphonia (dɪsˈfəʊnɪə) *n* any impairment in the ability to speak normally, as from spasm or strain of the vocal cords [C18 New Latin, from Greek: harshness of sound, from DYS- + *-phōnia* -PHONY] > dysphonic (dɪsˈfɒnɪk) *adj*

dysphoria (dɪsˈfɔːrɪə) *n* a feeling of being ill at ease [C20 New Latin, from Greek DYS- + *-phoria*, from *pherein* to bear] > dysphoric (dɪsˈfɒrɪk) *adj*

dysplasia (dɪsˈpleɪzɪə) *n* abnormal development of an organ or part of the body, including congenital absence [C20 New Latin, from DYS- + *-plasia*, from Greek *plasis* a moulding] > dysplastic (dɪsˈplæstɪk) *adj*

dyspnoea *or US* **dyspnea** (dɪspˈniːə) *n* difficulty in breathing or in catching the breath. Compare **eupnoea** [C17 via Latin from Greek *duspnoia*, from DYS- + *pnoē* breath, from *pnein* to breathe] > dyspˈnoeal, dyspˈnoeic *or US* dyspˈneal, dyspˈneic *adj*

dyspraxia (dɪsˈpræksɪə) *n pathol* an impairment in the control of the motor system; it may be developmental or acquired, resulting from a cerebral lesion [DYS- + PRAX(IS) + -IA]

dysprosium (dɪsˈprəʊsɪəm) *n* a soft silvery-white metallic element of the lanthanide series: used in laser materials and as a neutron absorber in nuclear control rods. Symbol: Dy; atomic no.: 66; atomic wt.: 162.50; valency: 3; relative density: 8.551; melting pt.: 1412°C; boiling pt.: 2567°C [C20 New Latin, from Greek *dusprositos* difficult to get near + -IUM]

dyssynergia (ˌdɪsɪˈnɜːdʒɪə) *n* muscular incoordination caused by a brain disorder [from DYS- + Greek *synergia* cooperation]

dystaxia (dɪsˈtæksɪə) *n pathol* lack of muscular coordination resulting in shaky limb movements and unsteady gait [from DYS- + Greek *-taxia*, from *tassein* to put in order]

dysteleology (ˌdɪstɛlɪˈɒlədʒɪ, -tiːlɪ-) *n philosophy* the denial of purpose in life. Compare **teleology** > dysˌteleoˈlogical *adj* > ˌdysteleˈologist *n*

dysthymia (dɪsˈθaɪmɪə) *n psychiatry* **1** the characteristics of the neurotic and introverted, including anxiety, depression, and compulsive behaviour **2** *obsolete* a relatively mild depression [C19 New Latin, from Greek *dusthumia*, from DYS- + *thumos* mind] > dysˈthymic *adj*

dysthymic disorder *n* a psychiatric disorder characterized by generalized depression that lasts for at least a year

dystocia (dɪsˈtəʊʃə) *n med* abnormal, slow, or difficult childbirth, usually because of disordered or ineffective contractions of the uterus [New Latin, from Greek, from *dus-* (see DYS-) + *tokos* childbirth + -IA] > dysˈtocial *adj*

dystonia (dɪsˈtəʊnɪə) *n* a neurological disorder, caused by disease of the basal ganglia, in which the muscles of the trunk, shoulders, and neck go into spasm, so that the head and limbs are held in unnatural positions [from DYS- + *-tonia* from Greek *tonos* tension, from *teinen* to stretch]

dystopia (dɪsˈtəʊpɪə) *n* an imaginary place where everything is as bad as it can be [C19 (coined by John Stuart Mill (1806–73), English philosopher and economist): from DYS- + UTOPIA] > dysˈtopian *adj, n*

dystrophin (ˈdɪstrəfɪn) *n* a protein, the absence of which is believed to cause muscular dystrophy

dystrophy (ˈdɪstrəfɪ) *or* **dystrophia** (dɪˈstrəʊfɪə) *n* **1** any of various bodily disorders, characterized by wasting of tissues. See also **muscular dystrophy** **2** *ecology* a condition of lake water when it is too acidic and poor in oxygen to support life, resulting from excessive humus content [C19 New Latin *dystrophia*, from DYS- + Greek *trophē* food] > dystrophic (dɪsˈtrɒfɪk) *adj*

dysuria (dɪsˈjʊərɪə) *n* difficult or painful urination [C14 via Latin from Greek *dusouria*, from DYS- + -URIA] > dysˈuric *adj*

dytiscid (dɪˈtɪsɪd, daɪ-) *n* **1** any carnivorous aquatic beetle of the family *Dytiscidae*, having large flattened back legs used for swimming ▷ *adj* **2** of, relating to, or belonging to the *Dytiscidae* [C19 from New Latin *Dytiscus* genus name, changed from Greek *dutikos* able to dive, from *duein* to dive]

Dyula (diːˈuːlə, ˈdjuːlə) *n* **1** (*pl* **-la** *or* **-las**) a member of a negroid people of W Africa, living chiefly in the rain forests of the Ivory Coast, where they farm rice, etc **2** the language of this people, belonging to the Mande branch of the Niger-Congo family

dz *the internet domain name for* Algeria

DZ *international car registration for* Algeria [from Arabic *Djazïr*]

Dzaudzhikau (dzəʊdʒɪˈkaʊ) *n* the former name (1944–54) of **Vladikavkaz**

Dzerzhinsk (*Russian* dzɪrˈʒinsk) *n* an industrial city and port in central Russia. Pop: 257 000 (2005 est)

Dzhambul (*Russian* dʒamˈbul) *n* a former name of **Taraz**

dziggetai (ˈdʒɪɡɪˌtaɪ) *n* a variant of **chigetai**

dzo (zəʊ) *n, pl* dzos *or* dzo a variant spelling of **zo**

Dzongka *or* **Dzongkha** (ˈzɒŋkə) *n* the official language of Bhutan: a dialect of Tibetan

Dzungaria (dzʊŋˈɡɛərɪə, zʊŋ-) *n* another name for **Junggar Pendi**

d

E*e*

e *or* **E** (iː) *n, pl* **e's** *or* **E's** *or* **Es** **1** the fifth letter and second vowel of the modern English alphabet **2** any of several speech sounds represented by this letter, in English as in *he, bet,* or *below*

e *symbol for* **1** *maths* a transcendental number, fundamental to mathematics, that is the limit of $(1 + 1/n)^n$ as n increases to infinity: used as the base of natural logarithms. Approximate value: 2.718 282...; relation to π: $e^{\pi i} = -1$, where $i = \sqrt{-1}$ **2** electron **3** *chess* See **algebraic notation**

E *symbol for* **1** earth **2** East **3** English **4** Egypt(ian) **5** exa- **6** *music* **a** a note having a frequency of 329.63 hertz (**E above middle C**) or this value multiplied or divided by any power of 2; the third note of the scale of C major **b** a key, string, or pipe producing this note **c** the major or minor key having this note as its tonic **7** *physics* **a** energy **b** electric field strength **c** electromotive force **d** Young's modulus (of elasticity) **8** *logic* a universal negative categorical proposition, such as *no pigs can fly*: often symbolized as SeP. Compare **A, I², O¹** [from Latin *(n)e(go)* I deny] **9 a** a person without a regular income, or who is dependent on the state on a long-term basis because of unemployment, sickness, old age, etc **b** (*as modifier*): E worker ▷ See also **occupation groupings** **10** *international car registration for* Spain [(for sense 10) from Spanish *España*]

E. *abbreviation for* Earl

e-¹ *prefix forming verbs and verbal derivatives* **1** out: *eviscerate; egest* **2** away: *elapse; elongate* **3** outside: *evaginate* **4** completely: *evaporate* **5** without: *ebracteate* [from Latin *ē* away; related to EX-¹]

e-² *prefix* electronic, indicating the involvement of the internet: *e-business; e-money*

E- *prefix* used with numbers indicating a standardized system within the European Union, as of recognized food additives or standard pack sizes. See also **E number**

ea. *abbreviation for* each

each (iːtʃ) *determiner* **1 a** every (one) of two or more considered individually: *each day; each person* **b** (*as pronoun*): *each gave according to his ability* ▷ *adv* **2** for, to, or from each one; apiece: *four apples each* [Old English *ǣlc*; related to Old High German *ēogilīk*, Old Frisian *ellik*, Dutch *elk*]

> USAGE *Each* is a singular pronoun and should be used with a singular form of a verb: *each of the candidates was* (not *were*) *interviewed separately.* See also at **either**

each other *pron* used when the action, attribution, etc, is reciprocal: *furious with each other*

> USAGE *Each other* and *one another* are interchangeable in modern British usage

each way *adj, adv horse racing, chiefly Brit* (of a bet) made on the same runner or contestant to win or come second or third in a race. Also: **both ways** US term: **across-the-board**

EACSO (iːˈɑːksəʊ) *n acronym for* East African Common Services Organization

e-address *n* an e-mail address

eager¹ (ˈiːɡə) *adj* **1** (*postpositive; often foll by* to *or* for) impatiently desirous (of); anxious or avid (for): *he was eager to see her departure* **2** characterized by or feeling expectancy or great desire: *an eager look* **3** *archaic* tart or biting; sharp [c13 from Old French *egre*, from Latin *acer* sharp, keen] > ˈ**eagerly** *adv* > ˈ**eagerness** *n*

eager² (ˈeɪɡə) *n* a variant spelling of **eagre**

eager beaver *n informal* a person who displays conspicuous diligence, esp one who volunteers for extra work

eagle (ˈiːɡ°l) *n* **1** any of various birds of prey of the genera *Aquila, Harpia,* etc (see **golden eagle, harpy eagle**), having large broad wings and strong soaring flight: family *Accipitridae* (hawks, etc). See also **sea eagle** Related adj: **aquiline 2** a representation of an eagle used as an emblem, etc, esp representing power: *the Roman eagle* **3** a standard, seal, etc, bearing the figure of an eagle **4** *golf* a score of two strokes under par for a hole **5** a former US gold coin worth ten dollars: withdrawn from circulation in 1934 **6** the shoulder insignia worn by a US full colonel or equivalent rank ▷ *vb* **7** *golf* to score two strokes under par for a hole [c14 from Old French *aigle*, from Old Provençal *aigla*, from Latin *aquila*, perhaps from *aquilus* dark]

eagle-eyed *adj* having keen or piercing eyesight

eagle-hawk *n* a large aggressive Australian eagle, *Aquila audax.* Also called: **wedge-tailed eagle**

eagle owl *n* a large owl, *Bubo bubo,* of Europe and Asia. It has brownish speckled plumage and large ear tufts

eagle ray *n* any of various rays of the family *Myliobatidae,* related to the stingrays but having narrower pectoral fins and a projecting snout with heavily browed eyes

eaglestone (ˈiːɡ°lˌstəʊn) *n* a hollow oval nodule of clay ironstone, formerly thought to have magical properties

eaglet (ˈiːɡlɪt) *n* a young eagle

eaglewood (ˈiːɡ°lˌwʊd) *n* **1** an Asian thymelaeaceous tree, *Aquilaria agallocha,* having fragrant wood that yields a resin used as a perfume **2** the wood of this tree ▷ Also called: **aloes, aloes wood, agalloch, lignaloes**

eagre *or* **eager** (ˈeɪɡə) *n* a tidal bore, esp of the Humber or Severn estuaries [c17 perhaps from Old English *ēagor* flood; compare Old English *ēa* river, water]

EAK *international car registration for* (East Africa) Kenya

ealdorman (ˈɔːldəmən) *n, pl* **-men** an official of Anglo-Saxon England, appointed by the king, who was responsible for law, order, and justice in his shire and for leading his local fyrd in battle [Old English *ealdor* lord + MAN]

Ealing (ˈiːlɪŋ) *n* a borough of W Greater London, formed in 1965 from Acton, Ealing, and Southall.

Pop: 3 050 000 (2003 est). Area: 55 sq km (21 sq miles)

EAM *n* (in World War II) the leftist resistance in German-occupied Greece [c20 from Modern Greek *Ethniko Apeleutherotiko Metopo* National Liberation Front]

-ean *suffix forming adjectives* a variant of **-an**: *Caesarean*

E & OE *abbreviation for* errors and omissions excepted

ear¹ (ɪə) *n* **1** the organ of hearing and balance in higher vertebrates and of balance only in fishes. In man and other mammals it consists of three parts (see **external ear, middle ear, internal ear**). Related adjs: **aural, otic 2** the outermost cartilaginous part of the ear (pinna) in mammals, esp man **3** the sense of hearing **4** sensitivity to musical sounds, poetic diction, etc: *he has an ear for music* **5** attention, esp favourable attention; consideration; heed (esp in the phrases **give ear to, lend an ear**) **6** an object resembling the external ear in shape or position, such as a handle on a jug **7** Also called (esp Brit): **earpiece** a display box at the head of a newspaper page, esp the front page, for advertisements, etc **8 all ears** very attentive; listening carefully **9 by ear** without reading from written music **10 chew someone's ear** *slang* to reprimand severely **11 fall on deaf ears** to be ignored or pass unnoticed **12 have hard ears** *Caribbean* to be stubbornly disobedient **13 a flea in one's ear** *informal* a sharp rebuke **14 have the ear of** to be in a position to influence: *he has the ear of the president* **15 in one ear and out the other** heard but unheeded **16 keep** (*or* **have**) **one's ear to the ground** to be or try to be well informed about current trends and opinions **17 make a pig's ear of** *informal* to ruin disastrously **18 one's ears are burning** one is aware of being the topic of another's conversation **19 out on one's ear** *informal* dismissed unceremoniously **20 play by ear a** to act according to the demands of a situation rather than to a plan; improvise **b** to perform a musical piece on an instrument without written music **21 prick up one's ears** to start to listen attentively; become interested **22 set by the ears** to cause disagreement or commotion **23 a thick ear** *informal* a blow on the ear delivered as punishment, in anger, etc **24 turn a deaf ear** to be deliberately unresponsive **25 up to one's ears** *informal* deeply involved, as in work or debt **26 wet behind the ears** *informal* inexperienced; naive; immature [Old English *ēare*; related to Old Norse *eyra*, Old High German *ōra*, Gothic *ausō*, Greek *ous*, Latin *auris*] > ˈ**earless** *adj* > ˈ**earˌlike** *adj*

ear² (ɪə) *n* **1** the part of a cereal plant, such as wheat or barley, that contains the seeds, grains, or kernels ▷ *vb* **2** (*intr*) (of cereal plants) to develop such parts [Old English *ēar*; related to Old High German *ahar*, Old Norse *ax*, Gothic *ahs* ear, Latin *acus* chaff, Greek *akros* pointed]

earache ('ɪərˌeɪk) *n* pain in the middle or inner ear. Technical name: **otalgia** Compare **otitis**

earball ('ɪərˌbɔːl) *n* (in acupressure) a small ball kept in position in the ear and pressed when needed to relieve stress

earbash ('ɪəˌbæʃ) *vb* (intr) Austral and NZ slang to talk incessantly ▷ 'ear,basher *n* ▷ 'ear,bashing *n*

earbud ('ɪəˌbʌd) *n* a small earphone worn in the ear for use with a mobile phone

eardrop ('ɪəˌdrɒp) *n* a pendant earring

eardrops ('ɪəˌdrɒps) *pl n* liquid medication for inserting into the external ear

eardrum ('ɪəˌdrʌm) *n* the nontechnical name for **tympanic membrane**

eared (ɪəd) *adj* **a** having an ear or ears **b** (in combination): long-eared; two-eared

eared seal *n* any seal of the pinniped family Otariidae, typically having visible earflaps and conspicuous hind limbs that can be used for locomotion on land. Compare **earless seal**

earflap ('ɪəˌflæp) *n* **1** Also called: **earlap** either of two pieces of fabric or fur attached to a cap, which can be let down to keep the ears warm **2** zoology a small flap of skin forming the pinna of such animals as seals

earful ('ɪəfʊl) *n* informal **1** something heard or overheard **2** a rebuke or scolding, esp a lengthy or severe one

ear-grabbing *adj* informal (of music) immediately capturing and holding the attention of listeners

earing ('ɪərɪŋ) *n* nautical a line fastened to a corner of a sail for reefing [C17 from EAR¹ + -ING¹ or perhaps RING¹]

earl (ɜːl) *n* **1** (in the British Isles) a nobleman ranking below a marquess and above a viscount. Female equivalent: **countess 2** (in Anglo-Saxon England) a royal governor of any of the large divisions of the kingdom, such as Wessex [Old English eorl; related to Old Norse jarl chieftain, Old Saxon erl man]

earlap ('ɪəˌlæp) *n* **1** another word for **earflap** (sense 1) **2** rare **a** the external ear **b** the ear lobe [C16 from EAR¹ + LAP¹]

earldom ('ɜːldəm) *n* **1** the rank, title, or dignity of an earl or countess **2** the lands of an earl or countess

earless seal *n* any seal of the pinniped family Phocidae, typically having rudimentary hind limbs, no external earflaps, and a body covering of hair with no underfur. Also called: **hair seal** Compare **eared seal**

Earl Grey *n* a variety of China tea flavoured with oil of bergamot

Earl Marshal *n* an officer of the English peerage who presides over the College of Heralds and organizes royal processions and other important ceremonies

ear lobe *n* the fleshy lower part of the external ear

early ('ɜːlɪ) *adj* -lier, -liest, *adv* **1** before the expected or usual time **2** occurring in or characteristic of the first part of a period or sequence **3** occurring in or characteristic of a period far back in time **4** occurring in the near future **5 at the earliest** not before the time or date mentioned **6 early days** too soon to tell how things will turn out [Old English ǣrlīce, from ǣr ERE + -līce -LY²; related to Old Norse arliga] ▷ 'earliness *n*

early bird *n* informal a person who rises early or arrives in good time

Early Bird *n* one of a number of communications satellites, the first of which was launched in 1965 into a stationary orbit and provided telephone channels between Europe and the US. See also **Intelsat**

Early Christian *adj* denoting or relating to the style of architecture that started in Italy in the 3rd century AD and spread through the Roman empire until the 5th century

early closing *n* Brit **1 a** the shutting of most of the shops in a town one afternoon each week **b** (as adjective): early-closing day **2** the day on which this happens: Thursday is early closing in Aylesbury

Early English *n* a style of architecture used in England in the 12th and 13th centuries, characterized by lancet arches, narrow openings, and plate tracery

early music *n* **1** music of the Middle Ages and Renaissance, sometimes also including music of the baroque and early classical periods ▷ modifier **early-music 2** of or denoting an approach to musical performance emphasizing the use of period instruments and historically researched scores and playing techniques: the early-music movement

early purple orchid *n* a Eurasian orchid, Orchis mascula, with purplish-crimson flowers and stems marked with blackish-purple spots

Early Renaissance *n* the the period from about 1400 to 1500 in European, esp Italian, painting, sculpture, and architecture, when naturalistic styles and humanist theories were evolved from the study of classical sources, notably by Donatello, Masaccio, and Alberti

early-type star *n* astronomy any massive hot star of spectral type O, B, or A. Compare: **late-type star** [C20 from the mistaken belief that hot and old stars evolved into cool young stars]

early warning *n* advance notice of some impending event or development

early warning system *n* **1** a network of radar and communications units intended to detect at the earliest possible moment an attack by enemy aircraft or missiles **2** anything that gives advance notice of something

earmark ('ɪəˌmɑːk) *vb* (tr) **1** to set aside or mark out for a specific purpose **2** to make an identification mark on the ear of (a domestic animal) ▷ *n* **3** a mark of identification on the ear of a domestic animal **4** any distinguishing mark or characteristic

earmuff ('ɪəˌmʌf) *n* one of a pair of pads of fur or cloth, joined by a headband, for keeping the ears warm

earn (ɜːn) *vb* **1** to gain or be paid (money or other payment) in return for work or service **2** (tr) to acquire, merit, or deserve through behaviour or action: he has earned a name for duplicity **3** (tr) (of securities, investments, etc) to gain (interest, return, profit, etc) [Old English earnian; related to Old High German arnēn to reap, Old Saxon asna salary, tithe] ▷ 'earner *n*

earned income *n* income derived from paid employment and comprising mainly wages and salaries

earnest¹ ('ɜːnɪst) *adj* **1** serious in mind or intention: an earnest student **2** showing or characterized by sincerity of intention: an earnest promise **3** demanding or receiving serious attention ▷ *n* **4** seriousness **5 in earnest** with serious or sincere intentions [Old English eornost; related to Old High German ernust seriousness, Old Norse ern energetic, efficient, Gothic arniba secure] ▷ 'earnestly *adv* ▷ 'earnestness *n*

earnest² ('ɜːnɪst) *n* **1** a part or portion of something given in advance as a guarantee of the remainder **2** Also called: **earnest money** contract law something given, usually a nominal sum of money, to confirm a contract **3** any token of something to follow; pledge; assurance [C13 from Old French erres pledges, plural of erre earnest money, from Latin arrha, shortened from arrabō pledge, from Greek arrabon, from Hebrew 'ērābhôn pledge, from 'ārabh he pledged]

earnings ('ɜːnɪŋz) *pl n* **1** money or other payment earned **2** the profits of an enterprise

Earnings Related Supplement *or* **Benefit** *n* (formerly, in the British National Insurance scheme) a payment based on earnings in the previous tax year, payable (in addition to unemployment or sickness benefit) for about six months to a sick or unemployed person. Abbreviation: ERS

EAROM ('ɪərɒm) *n* computing acronym for electrically alterable read-only memory

earphone ('ɪəˌfəʊn) *n* a device for converting electric currents into sound waves, held close to or inserted into the ear

earpiece ('ɪəˌpiːs) *n* the earphone in a telephone receiver

ear piercing *n* **1** the making of a hole in the lobe of an ear, using a sterilized needle, so that an earring may be worn fastened in the hole ▷ *adj* **ear-piercing 2** so loud or shrill as to hurt the ears

earplug ('ɪəˌplʌg) *n* a small piece of soft material, such as wax, placed in the ear to keep out noise or water

earring ('ɪəˌrɪŋ) *n* an ornament for the ear, usually clipped onto the lobe or fastened through a hole pierced in the lobe

ear shell *n* another name for the **abalone**

earshot ('ɪəˌʃɒt) *n* the range or distance within which sound may be heard (esp in the phrases **within earshot, out of earshot**)

ear-splitting *adj* so loud or shrill as to hurt the ears

earth (ɜːθ) *n* **1** (sometimes capital) the third planet from the sun, the only planet on which life is known to exist. It is not quite spherical, being flattened at the poles, and consists of three geological zones, the core, mantle, and thin outer crust. The surface, covered with large areas of water, is enveloped by an atmosphere principally of nitrogen (78 per cent), oxygen (21 per cent), and some water vapour. The age is estimated at over four thousand million years. Distance from sun: 149.6 million km; equatorial diameter: 12 756 km; mass: 5.976×10^{24} kg; sidereal period of axial rotation: 23 hours 56 minutes 4 seconds; sidereal period of revolution about sun: 365.256 days. Related adjs: **terrestrial, tellurian, telluric, terrene 2** the inhabitants of this planet: the whole earth rejoiced **3** the dry surface of this planet as distinguished from sea or sky; land; ground **4** the loose soft material that makes up a large part of the surface of the ground and consists of disintegrated rock particles, mould, clay, etc; soil **5** worldly or temporal matters as opposed to the concerns of the spirit **6** the hole in which some species of burrowing animals, esp foxes, live **7** chem See **rare earth, alkaline earth 8 a** a connection between an electrical circuit or device and the earth, which is at zero potential **b** a terminal to which this connection is made. US and Canadian equivalent: **ground 9** Also called: **earth colour** any of various brown pigments composed chiefly of iron oxides **10** (modifier) astrology of or relating to a group of three signs of the zodiac, Taurus, Virgo, and Capricorn. Compare **air** (sense 20), **fire** (sense 24), **water** (sense 12) **11 cost the earth** informal to be very expensive **12 come back** or **down to earth** to return to reality from a fantasy or daydream **13 on earth** used as an intensifier in such phrases as **what on earth, who on earth**, etc **14 run to earth a** to hunt (an animal, esp a fox) to its earth and trap it there **b** to find (someone) after searching ▷ *vb* **15** (intr) (of a hunted fox) to go to ground **16** (tr) to connect (a circuit, device, etc) to earth ▷ See also **earth up** [Old English eorthe; related to Old Norse jorth, Old High German ertha, Gothic airtha, Greek erā]

earthborn ('ɜːθˌbɔːn) *adj* chiefly poetic **1** of earthly origin **2** human; mortal

earthbound ('ɜːθˌbaʊnd) *adj* **1** confined to the earth **2** lacking in imagination; pedestrian or dull **3** moving or heading towards the earth

earth closet *n* a type of lavatory in which earth is used to cover excreta

earthen ('ɜːθən) *adj* (prenominal) **1** made of baked clay: an earthen pot **2** made of earth

earthenware ('ɜːθənˌwɛə) *n* **a** vessels, etc, made of baked clay **b** (as adjective): an earthenware pot

earth-grazer *n* an asteroid in an orbit that takes it close to the earth. Also called: **near-earth asteroid**

earth inductor compass *n* a compass that depends on the current induced in a coil revolving in the earth's magnetic field. Also called: **inductor compass**

earthlight ('ɜːθ,laɪt) *n* another name for **earthshine**

earthling ('ɜːθlɪŋ) *n* (esp in poetry or science fiction) an inhabitant of the earth; human being [C16 from EARTH + LING[1]]

earthly ('ɜːθlɪ) *adj* -lier, -liest **1** of or characteristic of the earth as opposed to heaven; material or materialistic; worldly **2** (*usually used with a negative*) *informal* conceivable or possible; feasible (in such phrases as **not an earthly** (**chance**), etc) ▷ 'earthliness *n*

earthman ('ɜːθ,mæn) *n, pl* -men (esp in science fiction) an inhabitant or native of the earth

earth mother *n* **1** (in various mythologies) **a** a female goddess considered as the source of fertility and life **b** the earth personified **2** *informal* a sensual or fecund woman

earth mover *n* a machine, such as a bulldozer, that is used for excavating and moving large quantities of earth

earthnut ('ɜːθ,nʌt) *n* **1** Also called: **pignut** a perennial umbelliferous plant, *Conopodium majus*, of Europe and Asia, having edible dark brown tubers **2** any of various plants having an edible root, tuber, underground pod, or similar part, such as the peanut or truffle

earth pillar *n* a landform consisting of a column of clay or earth capped and protected from erosion by a boulder

earthquake ('ɜːθ,kweɪk) *n* a sudden release of energy in the earth's crust or upper mantle, usually caused by movement along a fault plane or by volcanic activity and resulting in the generation of seismic waves which can be destructive. Related adj: **seismic**

earth return *n* the return path for an electrical circuit made by connections to earth at each end

earthrise ('ɜːθ,raɪz) *n* the rising of the earth above the lunar horizon, as seen from a spacecraft emerging from the lunar farside

earth science *n* any of various sciences, such as geology, geography, and geomorphology, that are concerned with the structure, age, and other aspects of the earth

Earthshaker ('ɜːθ,ʃeɪkə) *n* the *classical myth* Poseidon (or Neptune) in his capacity as the bringer of earthquakes

earthshaking ('ɜːθ,ʃeɪkɪŋ) *adj informal* of enormous importance or consequence; momentous

earthshine ('ɜːθ,ʃaɪn) or **earthlight** *n* the ashen light reflected from the earth, which illuminates the new moon when it is not receiving light directly from the sun

earthstar ('ɜːθ,stɑː) *n* any of various basidiomycetous saprotrophic woodland fungi of the genus *Geastrum*, whose brown onion-shaped reproductive body splits into a star shape to release the spores

earth up *vb* (*tr, adverb*) to cover (part of a plant, esp the stem) with soil in order to protect from frost, light, etc

earthward ('ɜːθwəd) *adj* **1** directed towards the earth ▷ *adv* **2** a variant of **earthwards**

earthwards ('ɜːθwədz) or **earthward** *adv* towards the earth

earth wax *n* another name for **ozocerite**

earthwork ('ɜːθ,wɜːk) *n* **1** excavation of earth, as in engineering construction **2** a fortification made of earth

earthworm ('ɜːθ,wɜːm) *n* any of numerous oligochaete worms of the genera *Lumbricus*, *Allolobophora*, *Eisenia*, etc, which burrow in the soil and help aerate and break up the ground. Related adj: **lumbricoid**

earthy ('ɜːθɪ) *adj* earthier, earthiest **1** of, composed of, or characteristic of earth **2** robust, lusty, or uninhibited **3** unrefined, coarse, or

crude **4** an archaic word for **worldly** (sense 1) **5** *electrical engineering* on the earthed side of an electrical circuit, but not necessarily with a direct current connection to earth ▷ 'earthily *adv* ▷ 'earthiness *n*

ear trumpet *n* a trumpet-shaped instrument that amplifies sounds and is held to the ear: an old form of hearing aid

earwax ('ɪə,wæks) *n* the nontechnical name for **cerumen**

earwig ('ɪə,wɪg) *n* **1** any of various insects of the order *Dermaptera*, esp *Forficula auricularia* (**common European earwig**), which typically have an elongated body with small leathery forewings, semicircular membranous hindwings, and curved forceps at the tip of the abdomen ▷ *vb* -wigs, -wigging, -wigged **2** *informal* to eavesdrop **3** (*tr*) *archaic* to attempt to influence (a person) by private insinuation [Old English *ēarwicga*, from *ēare* EAR[1] + *wicga* beetle, insect; probably from a superstition that the insect crept into human ears]

earwigging ('ɪə,wɪgɪŋ) *n* *informal* a scolding or harangue: *I'll give him an earwigging about that*

earworm ('ɪə,wɜːm) *n* *informal* an irritatingly catchy tune [C20 from German *Ohrwurm* earwig]

EAS *aeronautics* abbreviation for **equivalent air speed**

ease (iːz) *n* **1** freedom from discomfort, worry, or anxiety **2** lack of difficulty, labour, or awkwardness; facility **3** rest, leisure, or relaxation **4** freedom from poverty or financial embarrassment; affluence: *a life of ease* **5** lack of restraint, embarrassment, or stiffness: *his ease of manner disarmed us* **6** *military* **at ease a** (of a standing soldier, etc) in a relaxed position with the feet apart and hands linked behind the back **b** a command to adopt such a position **c** in a relaxed attitude or frame of mind ▷ *vb* **7** to make or become less burdensome **8** (*tr*) to relieve (a person) of worry or care; comfort **9** (*tr*) to make comfortable or give rest to **10** (*tr*) to make less difficult; facilitate **11** to move or cause to move into, out of, etc, with careful manipulation: *to ease a car into a narrow space* **12** (when *intr*, often foll by *off* or *up*) to lessen or cause to lessen in severity, pressure, tension, or strain; slacken, loosen, or abate **13** **ease oneself** or **ease nature** *archaic, euphemistic* to urinate or defecate **14** **ease the helm** *nautical* to relieve the pressure on the rudder of a vessel, esp by bringing the bow into the wind [C13 from Old French *aise* ease, opportunity, from Latin *adjacēns* neighbouring (area); see ADJACENT] ▷ 'easer *n*

easeful ('iːzfʊl) *adj* characterized by or bringing ease; peaceful; tranquil ▷ 'easefully *adv* ▷ 'easefulness *n*

easel ('iːzəl) *n* a frame, usually in the form of an upright tripod, used for supporting or displaying an artist's canvas, blackboard, etc [C17 from Dutch *ezel* ASS[1]; related to Gothic *asilus*, German *Esel*, Latin *asinus* ass]

easement ('iːzmənt) *n* **1** *property law* the right enjoyed by a landowner of making limited use of his neighbour's land, as by crossing it to reach his own property **2** the act of easing or something that brings ease

easily ('iːzɪlɪ) *adv* **1** with ease; without difficulty or exertion **2** by far; beyond question; undoubtedly: *he is easily the best in the contest* **3** probably; almost certainly: *he may easily come first*

▮ USAGE See at **easy**

easiness ('iːzɪnɪs) *n* **1** the quality or condition of being easy to accomplish, do, obtain, etc **2** ease or relaxation of manner; nonchalance

east (iːst) *n* **1** one of the four cardinal points of the compass, 90° clockwise from north and 180° from west **2** the direction along a parallel towards the sunrise, at 90° to north; the direction of the earth's rotation **3** **the east** (*often capital*) any area lying in or towards the east. Related adj: **oriental 4** *cards* (*usually capital*) the player or position at the table corresponding to east on the

compass ▷ *adj* **5** situated in, moving towards, or facing the east **6** (esp of the wind) from the east ▷ *adv* **7** in, to, or towards the east **8** *archaic* (of the wind) from the east ▷ Symbol: E [Old English *ēast*; related to Old High German *ōstar* to the east, Old Norse *austr*, Latin *aurora* dawn, Greek *eōs*, Sanskrit *usās* dawn, morning]

East (iːst) *n* **the 1** the continent of Asia regarded as culturally distinct from Europe and the West; the Orient **2** the countries under Communist rule and formerly under Communist rule, lying mainly in the E hemisphere. Compare **West**[1] (sense 2) **3** (in the US) **a** the area north of the Ohio and east of the Mississippi **b** the area north of Maryland and east of the Alleghenies ▷ *adj* **4 a** of or denoting the eastern part of a specified country, area, etc **b** (*as part of a name*): *East Sussex* ▷ 'Eastern *adj*

East Africa *n* a region of Africa comprising Kenya, Uganda, and Tanzania

East African *adj* **1** of or relating to East Africa or its inhabitants ▷ *n* **2** a native or inhabitant of East Africa

East African Community *n* an association established in 1967 by Kenya, Uganda, and Tanzania to promote closer economic and social ties between member states: dissolved in 1977

East Anglia *n* **1** a region of E England south of the Wash: consists of Norfolk and Suffolk, and parts of Essex and Cambridgeshire **2** an Anglo-Saxon kingdom that consisted of Norfolk and Suffolk in the 6th century AD; became a dependency of Mercia in the 8th century

East Anglian *adj* **1** of or relating to East Anglia or its inhabitants ▷ *n* **2** a native or inhabitant of East Anglia

East Ayrshire *n* a council area of SW Scotland, comprising the E part of the historical county of Ayrshire: part of Strathclyde region from 1975 to 1996: chiefly agricultural. Administrative centre: Kilmarnock. Pop: 119 530 (2003 est). Area: 1252 sq km (483 sq miles)

East Bengal *n* the part of the former Indian province of Bengal assigned to Pakistan in 1947 (now Bangladesh)

East Bengali *adj* **1** of or relating to East Bengal (now Bangladesh) or its inhabitants ▷ *n* **2** a native or inhabitant of East Bengal

East Berlin *n* (formerly) the part of Berlin under East German control

East Berliner *n* a native or inhabitant of the former East Berlin

eastbound ('iːst,baʊnd) *adj* going or leading towards the east

Eastbourne ('iːst,bɔːn) *n* a resort in SE England, in East Sussex on the English Channel. Pop: 106 592 (2001)

east by north *n* **1** one point on the compass north of east, 78° 45′ clockwise from north ▷ *adj, adv* **2** in, from, or towards this direction

east by south *n* **1** one point on the compass south of east, 101° 15′ clockwise from north ▷ *adj, adv* **2** in, from, or towards this direction

East Cape *n* **1** the easternmost point of New Guinea, on Milne Bay **2** the easternmost point of New Zealand, on North Island **3** the former name for Cape **Dezhnev**

East China Sea *n* part of the N Pacific, between the E coast of China and the Ryukyu Islands

east coast fever *n* a disease of cattle, endemic in east and central Africa, caused by a parasite, *Theileria parva*, that is carried by ticks

East Dunbartonshire *n* a council area of central Scotland to the N of Glasgow: part of Strathclyde region from 1975 until 1996: mainly agricultural and residential. Administrative centre: Kirkintilloch. Pop: 106 970 (2003 est). Area: 172 sq km (66 sq miles)

East End *n* **the** a densely populated part of E London containing former industrial and dock areas

East Ender *n* a native or inhabitant of the East

End of London

Easter ('i:stə) *n* **1** the most important festival of the Christian Church, commemorating the Resurrection of Christ: falls on the Sunday following the first full moon after the vernal equinox **2** Also called: **Easter Sunday, Easter Day** the day on which this festival is celebrated **3** the period between Good Friday and Easter Monday. Related adj: **Paschal** [Old English *ēastre*, after a Germanic goddess *Eostre*; related to Old High German *ōstarūn* Easter, Old Norse *austr* to the EAST, Old Slavonic *ustru* like summer]

Easter cactus *n* a Brazilian cactus, *Rhipsalidopsis gaertneri*, widely cultivated as an ornamental for its showy red flowers

Easter egg *n* **1** an egg given to children at Easter, usually a chocolate egg or a hen's egg with its shell painted **2** a bonus or extra feature hidden inside a website, computer game, or DVD, that is only revealed after repeated or lengthy viewing or playing

Easter Island *n* an isolated volcanic island in the Pacific, 3700 km (2300 miles) west of Chile, of which it is a dependency: discovered on Easter Sunday, 1722; annexed by Chile in 1888; noted for the remains of an aboriginal culture, which includes gigantic stone figures. Pop: 3791 (2002). Area: 166 sq km (64 sq miles). Also called: **Rapa Nui** Spanish name: **Isla de Pascua**

Easter Islander *n* a native or inhabitant of Easter Island

Easter-ledges *n* **1** (*functioning as singular*) another name for **bistort** (sense 1) **2** *Northern English dialect* a pudding made from the young leaves of the bistort

Easter lily *n* any of various lilies, esp *Lilium longiflorum*, that have large showy white flowers

easterly ('i:stəlɪ) *adj* **1** of, relating to, or situated in the east ▷ *adv, adj* **2** towards or in the direction of the east **3** from the east: *an easterly wind* ▷ *n, pl* **-lies 4** a wind from the east

eastern ('i:stən) *adj* **1** situated in or towards the east **2** facing or moving towards the east

Eastern Cape *n* a province of S South Africa; formed in 1994 from the E part of the former Cape Province: service industries, agriculture, and mining. Capital: Bisho. Pop: 7 088 547 (2004 est). Area: 169 600 sq km (65 483 sq miles). Also called: **Eastern Province**

Eastern Church *n* **1** any of the Christian Churches of the former Byzantine Empire **2** any Church owing allegiance to the Orthodox Church and in communion with the Greek patriarchal see of Constantinople **3** any Church, including Uniat Churches, having Eastern forms of liturgy and institutions

Easterner ('i:stənə) *n* (*sometimes not capital*) a native or inhabitant of the east of any specified region, esp of the Orient or of the eastern states of the US

Eastern Ghats *pl n* a mountain range in S India, parallel to the Bay of Bengal: united with the Western Ghats by the Nilgiri Hills; forms the E margin of the Deccan plateau

eastern hemisphere *n* (*often capitals*) **1** that half of the globe containing Europe, Asia, Africa, and Australia, lying east of the Greenwich meridian **2** the lands in this, esp Asia

easternmost ('i:stən,məʊst) *adj* situated or occurring farthest east

Eastern Orthodox Church *n* another name for the **Orthodox Church**

Eastern Province *n* another name for **Eastern Cape**

Eastern rite *n* the rite and liturgy of an Eastern Church or of a Uniat Church

Eastern Roman Empire *n* the eastern of the two empires created by the division of the Roman Empire in 395 AD. See also **Byzantine Empire**

Eastern Standard Time *n* **1** one of the standard times used in North America, five hours behind Greenwich Mean Time **2** one of the standard times used in Australia. Abbreviation: EST

Eastern Townships *n* an area of central Canada, in S Quebec: consists of 11 townships south of the St Lawrence

Eastern tradition *n* any of the philosophies and teachings that derive from Hinduism, Buddhism, Taoism, and other spiritual traditions of the East

Easter Rising *n* an armed insurrection in Dublin in 1916 against British rule in Ireland: the insurgents proclaimed the establishment of an independent Irish republic before surrendering, 16 of the leaders later being executed

Easter term *n* the term at the Inns of Court following the Hilary term

Eastertide ('i:stə,taɪd) *n* the Easter season

East Flanders *n* a province of W Belgium: low-lying, with reclaimed land in the northeast: textile industries. Capital: Ghent. Pop: 1 373 720 (2004 est). Area: 2979 sq km (1150 sq miles)

East German *adj* **1** of or relating to the former republic of East Germany or its inhabitants ▷ *n* **2** a native or inhabitant of the former East Germany

East Germanic *n* a subbranch of the Germanic languages: now extinct. The only member of which records survive is Gothic

East Germany *n* a former republic in N central Europe: established in 1949 and declared a sovereign state by the Soviet Union in 1954; Communist regime replaced by a multiparty democracy in 1989; reunited with West Germany in 1990. Official name: **German Democratic Republic** Abbreviations: **DDR, GDR** See also **Germany**

East India Company *n* **1** the company chartered in 1600 by the British government to trade in the East Indies: after being driven out by the Dutch, it developed trade with India until the Indian Mutiny (1857), when the Crown took over the administration: the company was dissolved in 1874 **2** any similar trading company, such as any of those founded by the Dutch, French, and Danes in the 17th and 18th centuries

East Indian *n* **1** *Caribbean* an immigrant to the countries of the Caribbean (West Indies) who is of Indian origin; an Asian West Indian ▷ *adj* **2** *US and Canadian* of, relating to, or originating in the East Indies

East Indies *pl n* **the 1** the Malay Archipelago, including or excluding the Philippines **2** SE Asia in general

easting ('i:stɪŋ) *n* **1** *nautical* the net distance eastwards made by a vessel moving towards the east **2** *cartography* **a** the distance eastwards of a point from a given meridian indicated by the first half of a map grid reference **b** a longitudinal grid line. Compare **northing** (sense 3)

East Kilbride (kɪl'braɪd) *n* a town in W Scotland, in South Lanarkshire near Glasgow: designated a new town in 1947. Pop: 73 796 (2001)

Eastleigh ('i:st,li:) *n* a town in S England, in S Hampshire: railway engineering industry. Pop: 52 894 (2001)

East London *n* a port in S South Africa, in S Eastern Cape province. Pop: 135 560 (2001)

East Lothian *n* a council area and historical county of E central Scotland, on the Firth of Forth and the North Sea: part of Lothian region from 1975 to 1996: chiefly agricultural. Administrative centre: Haddington. Pop: 91 090 (2003 est). Area: 678 sq km (262 sq miles)

east-northeast *n* **1** the point on the compass or the direction midway between northeast and east, 67° 30′ clockwise from north ▷ *adj, adv* **2** in, from, or towards this direction ▷ Symbol: ENE

East Pakistan *n* the former name (until 1971) of Bangladesh

East Pakistani *adj* **1** of or relating to East Pakistan (now Bangladesh) or its inhabitants ▷ *n* **2** a native or inhabitant of the former East Pakistan

East Prussia *n* a former province of NE Germany on the Baltic Sea: separated in 1919 from the rest of Germany by the Polish Corridor and Danzig: in 1945 Poland received the south part, the Soviet Union the north. German name: Ostpreussen (ost'prɔysən)

East Prussian *adj* **1** of or relating to the former German province of East Prussia or its inhabitants ▷ *n* **2** a native or inhabitant of the former East Prussia

East Renfrewshire *n* a council area of W central Scotland, comprising part of the historical county of Renfrewshire; part of Strathclyde region from 1975 to 1996: chiefly agricultural and residential. Administrative centre: Giffnock. Pop: 89 680 (2003 est). Area: 173 sq km (67 sq miles)

East Riding of Yorkshire *n* a county of NE England, a historical division of Yorkshire on the North Sea and the Humber estuary: became part of Humberside in 1974; reinstated as an independent unitary authority in 1996, with a separate authority for Kingston upon Hull: chiefly agricultural and low-lying, with various industries in Hull. Administrative centre: Beverley. Pop (excluding Hull): 321 300 (2003 est). Area (excluding Hull): 748 sq km (675 sq miles)

east-southeast *n* **1** the point on the compass or the direction midway between east and southeast, 112° 30′ clockwise from north ▷ *adj, adv* **2** in, from, or towards this direction ▷ Symbol: ESE

East Sussex *n* a county of SE England comprising part of the former county of Sussex: mainly undulating agricultural land, with the South Downs and seaside resorts in the south: Brighton and Hove became an independent unitary authority in 1997 but is part of the geographical and ceremonial county. Administrative centre: Lewes. Pop (excluding Brighton and Hove): 496 100 (2003 est). Area (excluding Brighton and Hove): 1795 sq km (693 sq miles)

East Timor *n* a small country in SE Asia, comprising part of the island of Timor: colonized by Portugal in the 19th century; declared independence in 1975 but immediately invaded by Indonesia; under UN administration from 1999 and an independent state from 2002. It is mountainous with a monsoon climate; subsistence agriculture is the main occupation. Languages: Portuguese, Tetun (a lingua franca), and Bahasa Indonesia. Religion: Roman Catholic majority. Currency: US dollar. Capital: Dili. Pop: 820 000 (2004 est). Area: 14 874 sq km (5743 sq miles). Official name: **Timor-Leste**

East Timorese *adj* **1** of or relating to East Timor or its inhabitants ▷ *n* **2** a native or inhabitant of East Timor

eastward ('i:stwəd) *adj* **1** situated or directed towards the east ▷ *adv* **2** a variant of **eastwards** ▷ *n* **3** the eastward part, direction, etc > 'eastwardly *adv, adj*

eastwards *or* **eastward** ('i:stwədz) *adv* towards the east

easy ('i:zɪ) *adj* easier, easiest **1** not requiring much labour or effort; not difficult; simple: *an easy job* **2** free from pain, care, or anxiety: *easy in one's mind* **3** not harsh or restricting; lenient: *easy laws* **4** tolerant and undemanding; easy-going: *an easy disposition* **5** readily influenced or persuaded; pliant: *she was an easy victim of his wiles* **6** not tight or constricting; loose: *an easy fit* **7** not strained or extreme; moderate; gentle: *an easy pace; an easy ascent* **8** *economics* **a** readily obtainable **b** (of a market) characterized by low demand or excess supply with prices tending to fall. Compare **tight** (sense 10) **9** *informal* ready to fall in with any suggestion made; not predisposed: *he is easy about what to do* **10** *slang* sexually available **11** easy on the eye *informal* pleasant to look at; attractive, esp sexually **12** woman of easy virtue a sexually available woman, esp a prostitute ▷ *adv* **13** *informal* in an easy or relaxed manner **14** *informal* easy does it go slowly and carefully; be careful **15** go easy on **a** to use in moderation **b** to treat

e

leniently **16 stand easy** *military* a command to soldiers standing at ease that they may relax further **17 take it easy a** to avoid stress or undue hurry **b** to remain calm; not become agitated or angry ▷ *vb* **easies, easying, easied 18** (*usually imperative*) Also: **easy-oar** to stop rowing [c12 from Old French *aisié*, past participle of *aisier* to relieve, EASE]

▌ USAGE *Easy* is not used as an adverb by careful speakers and writers except in certain set phrases: *to take it easy; easy does it*. Where a fixed expression is not involved, the usual adverbial form of *easily* is preferred: *this polish goes on more easily* (not *easier*) *than the other*

easy-care *adj* (esp of a fabric or garment) hardwearing, practical, and requiring no special treatment during washing, cleaning, etc

easy chair *n* a comfortable upholstered armchair

easy game or **easy mark** *n informal* a person who is easily deceived or taken advantage of

easy-going ('iːzɪ'gəʊɪŋ) *adj* **1** relaxed in manner or attitude; inclined to be excessively tolerant **2** moving at a comfortable pace: *an easy-going horse*

easy meat *n informal* **1** someone easily seduced or deceived **2** something easy to get or do

easy money *n* **1** money made with little effort, sometimes dishonestly **2** *commerce* money that can be borrowed at a low interest rate

Easy Street *n* (*sometimes not capitals*) *informal* a state of financial security

eat (iːt) *vb* **eats, eating, ate, eaten 1** to take into the mouth and swallow (food, etc), esp after biting and chewing **2** (*tr; often foll by away or up*) to destroy as if by eating: *the damp had eaten away the woodwork* **3** (*often foll by into*) to use up or waste: *taxes ate into his inheritance* **4** (*often foll by into or through*) to make (a hole, passage, etc) by eating or gnawing: *rats ate through the floor* **5** to take or have (a meal or meals): *we always eat at six* **6** (*tr*) to include as part of one's diet: *he doesn't eat fish* **7** (*tr*) *informal* to cause to worry; make anxious: *what's eating you?* **8** (*tr*) *slang* to perform cunnilingus or fellatio upon **9 I'll eat my hat if** *informal* to be greatly surprised if (something happens that proves one wrong) **10 eat one's heart out** to brood or pine with grief or longing **11 eat one's words** to take back something said; recant; retract **12 eat out of (someone's) hand** to be entirely obedient to (someone) **13 eat** (someone) **out of house and home** to ruin (someone, esp one's parent or one's host) by consuming all his food. ▷ See also **eat out, eats, eat up** [Old English *etan*; related to Gothic *itan*, Old High German *ezzan*, Latin *edere*, Greek *edein*, Sanskrit *admi*] > **eater** *n*

EAT or **EAZ** *international car registration for* Tanzania [from E(ast) A(frica) T(anganyika) or E(ast) A(frica) Z(anzibar)]

eatable ('iːtəbəl) *adj* fit or suitable for eating; edible

eatables ('iːtəbəlz) *pl n* (*sometimes singular*) food

eatage ('iːtɪdʒ) *n Northern English dialect* grazing rights

eaten ('iːtᵊn) *vb* the past participle of **eat**

eatery ('iːtərɪ) or **eaterie** *n, pl* -eries (-ərɪz) *informal* a restaurant or eating house

eating ('iːtɪŋ) *n* **1** food, esp in relation to its quality or taste: *this fruit makes excellent eating* ▷ *adj* **2** relating to or suitable for eating, esp uncooked: *eating pears* **3** relating to or for eating: *an eating house*

eat out *vb* (*intr, adverb*) to eat away from home, esp in a restaurant

eats (iːts) *pl n informal* articles of food; provisions

eat up *vb* (*adverb, mainly tr*) **1** (*also intr*) to eat or consume entirely: often used as an exhortation to children **2** *informal* to listen with enthusiasm or appreciation: *the audience ate up the speaker's every word* **3** (*often passive*) *informal* to affect grossly: *she was eaten up by jealousy* **4** *informal* to travel (a distance) quickly: *we just ate up the miles*

EAU *international car registration for* (East Africa) Uganda

eau de Cologne (əʊ də kə'ləʊn) *n* See **cologne** [French, literally: water of Cologne]

eau de Javelle (əʊ də ʒæ'vɛl, ʒə-; *French* od ʒavɛl) *n* another name for **Javel water**

eau de nil (əʊ də niːl) *n, adj* **a** a pale yellowish-green colour **b** (*as adjective*): *eau-de-nil walls* [French, literally: water of the Nile]

eau de vie (əʊ də viː; *French* od vi) *n* brandy or other spirits [French, literally: water of life]

eaves (iːvz) *pl n* the edge of a roof that projects beyond the wall [Old English *efes*; related to Gothic *ubizwa* porch, Greek *hupsos* height]

eavesdrop ('iːvz,drɒp) *vb* -drops, -dropping, -dropped (*intr*) to listen secretly to the private conversation of others [c17 back formation from earlier *evesdropper*, from Old English *yfesdrype* water dripping from the eaves; see EAVES, DROP; compare Old Norse *upsardropi*] > **eaves,dropper** *n*

eavestrough ('iːvz,trɒf) *n Canadian* a gutter at the eaves of a building

eBayer or **ebayer** ('iː,beɪə) *n* any person who buys or sells using the internet auction site, eBay > **e,Baying** or **e,baying** *n*

ebb (ɛb) *vb* (*intr*) **1** (of tide water) to flow back or recede. Compare **flow** (sense 9) **2** to fall away or decline ▷ *n* **3 a** the flowing back of the tide from high to low water or the period in which this takes place **b** (*as modifier*): *the ebb tide.* Compare **flood** (sense 3) **4 at a low ebb** in a state or period of weakness, lack of vigour, or decline [Old English *ebba*; related to Old Norse *efja* river bend, Gothic *ibuks* moving backwards, Old High German *ippihōn* to roll backwards, Middle Dutch *ebbe* ebb]

Ebbw Vale ('ɛbuː veɪl) *n* a town in S Wales, in Blaenau Gwent county borough: a former coal mining centre. Pop: 18 558 (2001)

EBCDIC ('ɛbsɪ,dɪk) *n acronym for* extended binary-coded decimal-interchange code: a computer code for representing alphanumeric characters

EBITDA *abbreviation for* earnings before interest, tax, depreciation, and amortization

Eblis ('ɛblɪs) *n* the chief evil jinni in Islamic mythology [Arabic *Iblīs*, from Greek *diabolos* slanderer, DEVIL]

E-boat *n* (in World War II) a fast German boat carrying guns and torpedoes [c20 from *enemy boat*]

Ebola virus disease (iː'bəʊlə) *n* a severe infectious disease characterized by fever, vomiting, and internal bleeding. Compare **Marburg disease** [c20 named after the *Ebola* river, N Democratic Republic of Congo (formerly Zaïre), where an outbreak occurred in 1976]

ebon ('ɛbᵊn) *n, adj* a poetic word for **ebony** [c14 from Latin *hebenus*; see EBONY]

ebonics (ɪ'bɒnɪks) *n* (*functioning as singular*) *US* another name for **African-American Vernacular English** [c20 from EBONY + PHONICS]

ebonite ('ɛbə,naɪt) *n* another name for **vulcanite**

ebonize or **ebonise** ('ɛbə,naɪz) *vb* (*tr*) to stain or otherwise finish in imitation of ebony

ebony ('ɛbənɪ) *n, pl* -onies **1** any of various tropical and subtropical trees of the genus *Diospyros*, esp *D. ebenum* of S India, that have hard dark wood: family *Ebenaceae*. See also **persimmon 2** the wood of such a tree, much used for cabinetwork **3 a** a black colour, sometimes with a dark olive tinge **b** (*as adjective*): *an ebony skin* [c16 *hebeny*, from Late Latin *ebeninus* from Greek *ebeninos*, from *ebenos* ebony, of Egyptian origin]

e-book *n* **1** a book in electronic form ▷ *vb* **2** (*tr*) to book (hospital appointments, airline tickets, etc) through the internet [c20 *electronic book*] > **e-,booking** *n*

Ebor. ('iːbɔː) *abbreviation for* Eboracensis [Latin: (Archbishop) of York]

Eboracum (iː'bɒrəkəm, ,iːbɔː'rɑːkəm) *n* the Roman name for **York** (sense 1)

ebracteate (ɪ'bræktɪ,eɪt, -tɪt) *adj* (of plants) having no bracts [c19 from New Latin *ebracteātus*; see E-¹, BRACTEATE]

EBRD *abbreviation for* European Bank for Reconstruction and Development

Ebro ('iːbrəʊ; *Spanish* 'eβro) *n* the second largest river in Spain, rising in the Cantabrian Mountains and flowing southeast to the Mediterranean. Length: 910 km (565 miles)

EBS *abbreviation for* electronic braking system

EBU *abbreviation for* European Broadcasting Union

ebullient (ɪ'bʌljənt, ɪ'bʊl-) *adj* **1** overflowing with enthusiasm or excitement; exuberant **2** boiling [c16 from Latin *ēbullīre* to bubble forth, be boisterous, from *bullīre* to BOIL¹] > **e'bullience** or **e'bulliency** *n* > **e'bulliently** *adv*

ebulliometer (ɪ,bʌlɪ'ɒmɪtə) *n physics* a device used to determine the boiling point of a solution > **e,bulli'ometry** *n*

ebullioscopy (ɪ,bʌlɪ'ɒskəpɪ, ɪ,bʊl-) *n chem* a technique for finding molecular weights of substances by measuring the extent to which they change the boiling point of a solvent [c19 from *ebullioscope*, from Latin *ebullire* to boil over + -SCOPE] > **ebullioscopic** (ɪ,bʌlɪə'skɒpɪk, ɪ,bʊl-) *adj* > **e,bullio'scopically** *adv*

ebullition (,ɛbə'lɪʃən) *n* **1** the process of boiling **2** a sudden outburst, as of intense emotion [c16 from Late Latin *ēbullītiō*; see EBULLIENT]

eburnation (,iːbə'neɪʃən, ,ɛb-) *n* a degenerative condition of bone or cartilage characterized by unusual hardness and a polished appearance [c19 from Latin *eburnus* of ivory, from *ebur* ivory]

EBV *abbreviation for* **Epstein-Barr virus**

ec the internet domain name for Ecuador

EC *abbreviation for* **1** European Community (now subsumed within the European Union) **2** (in London postal code) East Central **3** *international car registration for* Ecuador

ec- *combining form* out from; away from: *ecbolic; eccentric; ecdysis* [from Greek *ek* (before a vowel *ex*) out of, away from; see EX-¹]

ecad ('iːkæd) *n* an organism whose form has been affected by its environment [c20 from EC(OLOGY) + -AD¹]

e-car *n* a car powered by electricity [c20 *electric car*]

ecarinate (iː'kærɪnɪt) *adj biology* having no carina or keel [E-¹ + CARINATE]

écarté (eɪ'kɑːteɪ; *French* ekarte) *n* **1** a card game for two, played with 32 cards and king high **2** *ballet* **a** a body position in which one arm and the same leg are extended at the side of the body **b** (*as adjective*): *the écarté position* [c19 from French, from *écarter* to discard, from *carte* CARD¹]

ECB *abbreviation for* **European Central Bank**

Ecbatana (ɛk'bætənə) *n* an ancient city in Iran, on the site of modern Hamadān; capital of Media and royal residence of the Persians and Parthians

ecbolic (ɛk'bɒlɪk) *adj* **1** hastening labour or abortion ▷ *n* **2** a drug or agent that hastens labour or abortion [c18 from Greek *ekbolē* a throwing out, from *ekballein* to throw out, from *ballein* to throw]

Ecce Homo ('ɛkeɪ 'həʊməʊ, 'ɛksɪ) *n* a picture or sculpture of Christ crowned with thorns [Latin: behold the man, the words of Pontius Pilate to his accusers (John 19:5)]

eccentric (ɪk'sɛntrɪk) *adj* **1** deviating or departing from convention, esp in a bizarre manner; irregular or odd **2** situated away from the centre or the axis **3** not having a common centre: *eccentric circles.* Compare **concentric 4** not precisely circular ▷ *n* **5** a person who deviates from normal forms of behaviour, esp in a bizarre manner **6** a device for converting rotary motion to reciprocating motion [c16 from Medieval Latin *eccentricus*, from Greek *ekkentros* out of centre, from *ek-* EX-¹ + *kentron* centre] > **ec'centrically** *adv*

eccentricity (,ɛksɛn'trɪsɪtɪ) *n, pl* -ties **1** unconventional or irregular behaviour **2** deviation from a circular path or orbit **3** a measure of the noncircularity of an elliptical orbit, the distance between the foci divided by the length of the major axis **4** *geometry* a number that expresses the shape of a conic section: the ratio of the distance of a point on the curve from a fixed point (the focus) to the distance of the point from a fixed line (the directrix) **5** the degree of displacement of the geometric centre of a rotating part from the true centre, esp of the axis of rotation of a wheel or shaft

ecchymosis (ˌɛkɪˈməʊsɪs) *n, pl* **-ses** (-siːz) discoloration of the skin through bruising [C16 from New Latin, from Greek *ekkhumōsis*, from *ekkhumousthai* to pour out, from *khumos* juice] ▷ **ecchymosed** (ˈɛkɪˌməʊzd, -ˌməʊst) *or* **ecchymotic** (ˌɛkɪˈmɒtɪk) *adj*

eccl. *or* **eccles.** *abbreviation for* ecclesiastic(al)

Eccles (ˈɛkºlz) *n* a town in NW England, in Salford unitary authority, Greater Manchester. Pop: 36 610 (2001)

Eccles. *or* **Eccl.** *Bible abbreviation for* Ecclesiastes

Eccles cake *n* *Brit* a pastry with a filling of dried fruit

ecclesia (ɪˈkliːzɪə) *n, pl* **-siae** (-zɪˌiː) **1** (in formal Church usage) a congregation **2** the assembly of citizens of an ancient Greek state [C16 from Medieval Latin, from Late Greek *ekklēsia* assembly, from *ekklētos* called, from *ekkalein* to call out, from *kalein* to call]

Ecclesiastes (ɪˌkliːzɪˈæstiːz) *n* (*functioning as singular*) a book of the Old Testament, probably written about 250 BC [via Late Latin, from Greek *ekklēsiastēs* member of the assembly; see ECCLESIA]

ecclesiastic (ɪˌkliːzɪˈæstɪk) *n* **1** a clergyman or other person in holy orders ▷ *adj* **2** of or associated with the Christian Church or clergy

ecclesiastical (ɪˌkliːzɪˈæstɪkºl) *adj* of or relating to the Christian Church ▷ ecˌclesiˈastically *adv*

Ecclesiastical Commissioners *pl n* the administrators of the properties of the Church of England from 1836 to 1948, when they were combined with Queen Anne's Bounty to form the Church Commissioners

ecclesiasticism (ɪˌkliːzɪˈæstɪˌsɪzəm) *n* exaggerated attachment to the practices or principles of the Christian Church

Ecclesiasticus (ɪˌkliːzɪˈæstɪkəs) *n* one of the books of the Apocrypha, written around 180 BC and also called **the Wisdom of Jesus, the son of Sirach**

ecclesiolatry (ɪˌkliːzɪˈɒlətrɪ) *n* obsessional devotion to ecclesiastical traditions ▷ ecˌclesiˈolater *n*

ecclesiology (ɪˌkliːzɪˈɒlədʒɪ) *n* **1** the study of the Christian Church **2** the study of Church architecture and decoration ▷ **ecclesiological** (ɪˌkliːzɪəˈlɒdʒɪkºl) *adj* ▷ ecˌclesioˈlogically *adv* ▷ ecˌclesiˈologist *n*

Ecclus. *Bible abbreviation for* Ecclesiasticus

eccremocarpus (ˌɛkrəməˈkɑːpəs) *n* any plant of the evergreen climbing genus *Eccremocarpus*, esp *E. scaber*, grown for its decorative pinnate foliage and bright orange-red bell flowers: family *Bignoniaceae* [New Latin, from Greek *ekkremēs* suspended + *karpos* fruit]

eccrine (ˈɛkrɪn) *adj* of or denoting glands that secrete externally, esp the numerous sweat glands on the human body. Compare **apocrine** [from Greek *ekkrinein* to secrete, from *ek-* EC- + *krinein* to separate]

eccrinology (ˌɛkrɪˈnɒlədʒɪ) *n* the branch of medical science concerned with secretions of the eccrine glands

ecdemic (ɛkˈdɛmɪk) *adj* not indigenous or endemic; foreign: *an ecdemic disease*

ecdysiast (ɛkˈdɪzɪˌæst) *n* a facetious word for **stripper** (sense 1) [C20 (coined by H. L. Mencken) from ECDYSIS + *-ast*, variant of *-IST*]

ecdysis (ˈɛkdɪsɪs) *n, pl* **-ses** (-ˌsiːz) the periodic shedding of the cuticle in insects and other arthropods or the outer epidermal layer in reptiles. See also **ecdysone** [C19 New Latin, from Greek *ekdusis*, from *ekduein* to strip, from *ek-* EX-¹ + *duein* to put on] ▷ **ecˈdysial** *adj*

ecdysone (ɛkˈdaɪˌsəʊn) *n* a hormone secreted by the prothoracic gland of insects that controls

ecdysis and stimulates metamorphosis [C20 from German *ecdyson*, from Greek *ekdusis*; see ECDYSIS]

ecesis (ɪˈsiːsɪs) *n* the establishment of a plant in a new environment [C20 from Greek *oikēsis* a dwelling in, from *oikein* to inhabit; related to *oikos* a house]

ECG *abbreviation for* **1** electrocardiogram **2** electrocardiograph

echard (ˈɛkɑːd) *n* water that is present in the soil but cannot be absorbed or otherwise utilized by plants [C20 from Greek *ekhein* to hold back + *ardein* to water]

echelon (ˈɛʃəˌlɒn) *n* **1** a level of command, responsibility, etc (esp in the phrase **the upper echelons**) **2** *military* **a** a formation in which units follow one another but are offset sufficiently to allow each unit a line of fire ahead **b** a group formed in this way **3** *physics* a type of diffraction grating used in spectroscopy consisting of a series of plates of equal thickness arranged stepwise with a constant offset ▷ *vb* **4** to assemble in echelon [C18 from French *échelon*, literally: rung of a ladder, from Old French *eschiele* ladder, from Latin *scāla*; see SCALE³]

echeveria (ˌɛtʃɪˈvɪərɪə) *n* any of various tropical American crassulaceous plants of the genus *Echeveria*, cultivated for their colourful foliage [named after M. *Echeveri*, 19th-century Mexican botanical artist]

echidna (ɪˈkɪdnə) *n, pl* **-nas** *or* **-nae** (-niː) any of the spine-covered monotreme mammals of the genera *Tachyglossus* of Australia and *Zaglossus* of New Guinea: family *Tachyglossidae*. They have a long snout and claws for hunting ants and termites. Also called: **spiny anteater** [C19 from New Latin, from Latin: viper, from Greek *ekhidna*]

echinacea (ˌɛkɪˈneɪʃɪə) *n* **1** either of the two N American plants of the genus *Echinacea*, having flower heads with purple rays and black centres: family *Compositae* (composites). Also called: **purple coneflower** See **coneflower 2** the powdered root of either of these plants, used to stimulate the immune system [from New Latin, from Latin *echīnātus* prickly, from *echīnus* hedgehog]

echinate (ˈɛkɪˌneɪt) *or* **echinated** *adj* *biology* covered with spines, bristles, or bristle-like outgrowths

echino- *or before a vowel* **echin-** *combining form* indicating spiny or prickly: *echinoderm* [from New Latin, via Latin from Greek *ekhinos* sea urchin, hedgehog]

echinococcus (ɪˌkaɪnəˈkɒkəs) *n* any of the tapeworms constituting the genus *Echinococcus*, the larvae of which are parasitic in man and domestic animals

echinoderm (ɪˈkaɪnəʊˌdɜːm) *n* any of the marine invertebrate animals constituting the phylum *Echinodermata*, characterized by tube feet, a calcite body-covering (test), and a five-part symmetrical body. The group includes the starfish, sea urchins, and sea cucumbers ▷ eˌchinoˈdermal *or* eˌchinoˈdermatous *adj*

echinoid (ɪˈkaɪnɔɪd, ˈɛkə-) *n* **1** any of the echinoderms constituting the class *Echinoidea*, typically having a rigid ovoid body. The class includes the sea urchins and sand dollars ▷ *adj* **2** of or belonging to this class

echinus (ɪˈkaɪnəs) *n, pl* **-ni** (-naɪ) **1** *architect* an ovolo moulding between the shaft and the abacus of a Doric column **2** any of the sea urchins of the genus *Echinus*, such as *E. esculentus* (**edible sea urchin**) of the Mediterranean [C14 from Latin, from Greek *ekhinos*]

echium (ˈɛkɪəm) *n* any plant of the Eurasian and African genus *Echium* with bell-shaped flowers sometimes borne on single-sided spikes in a wide variety of colours; *E. vulgare* is viper's bugloss: family *Boraginaceae* [New Latin, from Greek *echion*, from *echis* viper, from its use as an antidote to a viper bite]

echo (ˈɛkəʊ) *n, pl* **-oes 1 a** the reflection of sound or other radiation by a reflecting medium, esp a

solid object **b** the sound so reflected **2** a repetition or imitation, esp an unoriginal reproduction of another's opinions **3** something that evokes memories, esp of a particular style or era **4** (*sometimes plural*) an effect that continues after the original cause has disappeared; repercussion: *the echoes of the French Revolution* **5** a person who copies another, esp one who obsequiously agrees with another's opinions **6 a** the signal reflected by a radar target **b** the trace produced by such a signal on a radar screen **7** the repetition of certain sounds or syllables in a verse line **8** the quiet repetition of a musical phrase **9** Also called: **echo organ** *or* **echo stop** a manual or stop on an organ that controls a set of quiet pipes that give the illusion of sounding at a distance **10** an electronic effect in recorded music that adds vibration or resonance ▷ *vb* **-oes**, **-oing**, **-oed 11** to resound or cause to resound with an echo: *the cave echoed their shouts* **12** (*intr*) (of sounds) to repeat or resound by echoes; reverberate **13** (*tr*) (of persons) to repeat (words, opinions, etc), in imitation, agreement, or flattery **14** (*tr*) (of things) to resemble or imitate (another style, earlier model, etc) **15** (*tr*) (of a computer) to display (a character) on the screen of a visual display unit as a response to receiving that character from a keyboard entry [C14 via Latin from Greek *ēkhō*; related to Greek *ēkhē* sound] ▷ ˈechoing *adj* ▷ ˈecholess *adj* ▷ ˈecho-ˌlike *adj*

Echo¹ (ˈɛkəʊ) *n* either of two US passive communications satellites, the first of which was launched in 1960

Echo² (ˈɛkəʊ) *n* *Greek myth* a nymph who, spurned by Narcissus, pined away until only her voice remained

Echo³ (ˈɛkəʊ) *n* *communications* code word for the letter *e*

echocardiogram (ˌɛkəʊˈkɑːdɪəʊˌgræm) *n* a visual display or record produced using echocardiography

echocardiography (ˌɛkəʊkɑːdɪˈɒgrəfɪ) *n* examination of the heart using ultrasound techniques

echo chamber *n* a room with walls that reflect sound. It is used to make acoustic measurements and as a source of reverberant sound to be mixed with direct sound for recording or broadcasting. Also called: **reverberation chamber**

echography (ɛˈkɒgrəfɪ) *n* medical examination of the internal structures of the body by means of ultrasound

echoic (ɛˈkəʊɪk) *adj* **1** characteristic of or resembling an echo **2** onomatopoeic; imitative

echoic memory *n* *psychol* the ability to recapture the exact impression of a sound shortly after the sound has finished. Compare **iconic memory**

echoism (ˈɛkəʊˌɪzəm) *n* **1** onomatopoeia as a source of word formation **2** phonetic assimilation of one vowel to the vowel in the preceding syllable

echolalia (ˌɛkəʊˈleɪlɪə) *n* *psychiatry* the tendency to repeat mechanically words just spoken by another person: can occur in cases of brain damage, mental retardation, and schizophrenia [C19 from New Latin, from ECHO + Greek *lalia* talk, chatter, from *lalein* to chatter] ▷ echolalic (ˌɛkəʊˈlælɪk) *adj*

echolocation (ˌɛkəʊləʊˈkeɪʃən) *n* determination of the position of an object by measuring the time taken for an echo to return from it and its direction

echo plate *n* (in sound recording or broadcasting) an electromechanical device for producing echo and reverberation effects

echopraxia (ˌɛkəʊˈpræksɪə) *or* **echopraxis** *n* the involuntary imitation of the actions of others

echo sounder *n* a navigation and position-finding device that determines depth by measuring the time taken for a pulse of high-frequency sound to reach the sea bed or a submerged object and for the echo to return ▷ echo sounding *n*

echovirus (ˈɛkəʊˌvaɪrəs) *or* **ECHO virus** *n* any of a

e

group of viruses that can cause symptoms of mild meningitis, the common cold, or infections of the intestinal and respiratory tracts [c20 from the initials of *Enteric Cytopathic Human Orphan* ("orphan" because originally believed to be unrelated to any disease) + VIRUS]

echt *German* (ɛçt; *English* ɛkt) *adj* real; genuine; authentic

éclair (eɪˈklɛə, ɪˈklɛə) *n* a finger-shaped cake of choux pastry, usually filled with cream and covered with chocolate [c19 from French, literally: lightning (probably so called because it does not last long), from Latin *éclairer*, from Latin *clārāre* to make bright, from *clārus* bright]

eclampsia (ɪˈklæmpsɪə) *n* **1** *pathol* a toxic condition of unknown cause that sometimes develops in the last three months of pregnancy, characterized by high blood pressure, abnormal weight gain and convulsions. Compare **pre-eclampsia 2** another name for **milk fever** (in cattle) [c19 from New Latin, from Greek *eklampsis* a shining forth, from *eklampein*, from *lampein* to shine] > **ecˈlamptic** *adj*

éclat (eɪˈklɑː; *French* ekla) *n* **1** brilliant or conspicuous success, effect, etc **2** showy display; ostentation **3** social distinction **4** approval; acclaim; applause [c17 from French, from *éclater* to burst; related to Old French *esclater* to splinter, perhaps of Germanic origin; compare SLIT]

eclectic (ɪˈklɛktɪk, ɛˈklɛk-) *adj* **1** (in art, philosophy, etc) selecting what seems best from various styles, doctrines, ideas, methods, etc **2** composed of elements drawn from a variety of sources, styles, etc ▷ *n* **3** a person who favours an eclectic approach, esp in art or philosophy [c17 from Greek *eklektikos*, from *eklegein* to select, from *legein* to gather] > **ecˈlectically** *adv*

eclecticism (ɪˈklɛktɪˌsɪzəm, ɛˈklɛk-) *n* **1** an eclectic system or method **2** the use or advocacy of such a system

eclipse (ɪˈklɪps) *n* **1** the total or partial obscuring of one celestial body by another. A **solar eclipse** occurs when the moon passes between the sun and the earth; a **lunar eclipse** when the earth passes between the sun and the moon. See also **total eclipse, partial eclipse, annular eclipse** Compare **occultation 2** the period of time during which such a phenomenon occurs **3** any dimming or obstruction of light **4** a loss of importance, power, fame, etc, esp through overshadowing by another ▷ *vb* **5** to cause an eclipse of **6** to cast a shadow upon; darken; obscure **7** to overshadow or surpass in importance, power, etc [c13 back formation from Old English *eclypsis,* from Latin *eclīpsis,* from Greek *ekleipsis* a forsaking, from *ekleipein* to abandon, from *leipein* to leave] > **eˈclipser** *n*

eclipse plumage *n* seasonal plumage that occurs in certain birds after the breeding plumage and before the winter plumage: characterized by dull coloration

eclipsing binary *or* **variable** *n* a binary star whose orbital plane lies in or near the line of sight so that one component is regularly eclipsed by its companion. See also **variable star**

eclipsis (ɪˈklɪpsɪs) *n* *linguistics* **1** a rare word for **ellipsis** (sense 1) **2** (in Gaelic) phonetic change of an initial consonant under the influence of a preceding word. Unvoiced plosives become voiced, while voiced plosives are changed to nasals

ecliptic (ɪˈklɪptɪk) *n* **1** *astronomy* **a** the great circle on the celestial sphere representing the apparent annual path of the sun relative to the stars. It is inclined at 23.45° to the celestial equator. The poles of the ecliptic lie on the celestial sphere due north and south of the plane of the ecliptic **b** (*as modifier*): *the ecliptic plane* **2** an equivalent great circle, opposite points of which pass through the Tropics of Cancer and Capricorn, on the terrestrial globe ▷ *adj* **3** of or relating to an eclipse > **eˈcliptically** *adv*

ecliptic latitude *n* *astronomy* another name for **celestial latitude**

ecliptic longitude *n* *astronomy* another name for **celestial longitude**

eclogite (ˈɛklədʒaɪt) *n* a rare coarse-grained basic rock consisting principally of garnet and pyroxene. Quartz, feldspar, etc, may also be present. It is thought to originate by metamorphism or igneous crystallization at extremely high pressure [c19 from Greek *eklogē* a selection]

eclogue (ˈɛklɒg) *n* a pastoral or idyllic poem, usually in the form of a conversation or soliloquy [c15 from Latin *ecloga* short poem, collection of extracts, from Greek *eklogē* selection, from *eklegein* to select; see ECLECTIC]

eclosion (ɪˈkləʊʒən) *n* the emergence of an insect larva from the egg or an adult from the pupal case [c19 from French *éclosion,* from *éclore* to hatch, ultimately from Latin *exclūdere* to shut out, EXCLUDE]

ECMO *abbreviation for* extracorporeal membrane oxygenation: a method of life support used to oxygenate the blood in newborn babies with lung failure, using a machine incorporating membranes that are impermeable to blood but permeable to oxygen and carbon dioxide

eco (ˈiːkəʊ) *n* **a** short for **ecology b** (*as modifier*): *an eco group*

eco- *combining form* denoting ecology or ecological: *ecocide; ecosphere*

ecocentric (ˌiːkəʊˈsɛntrɪk) *adj* having a serious concern for environmental issues: *ecocentric management*

ecocide (ˈiːkəˌsaɪd, ˈɛkə-) *n* total destruction of an area of the natural environment, esp by human agency

Ecofin (ˈɛkəʊˌfɪn) *n* the council of European finance ministers

ecofriendly (ˈiːkəʊˌfrɛndlɪ) *adj* having a beneficial effect on the environment or at least not causing environmental damage

ecol. *abbreviation for* **1** ecological **2** ecology

E. coli (ˌiːˈkəʊlaɪ) *n* short for *Escherichia coli*; see *Escherichia*

ecological (ˌiːkəˈlɒdʒɪkªl) *adj* **1** of or relating to ecology **2** (of a practice, policy, product, etc) tending to benefit or cause minimal damage to the environment > **ˌecoˈlogically** *adv*

ecological footprint *n* the amount of productive land appropriated on average by each person (in the world, a country, etc) for food, water, transport, housing, waste management, and other purposes

ecology (ɪˈkɒlədʒɪ) *n* **1** the study of the relationships between living organisms and their environment **2** the set of relationships of a particular organism with its environment **3** the study of the relationships between human groups and their physical environment ▷ Also called (for senses 1, 2): bionomics [c19 from German *Ökologie,* from Greek *oikos* house (hence, environment)] > **eˈcologist** *n*

e-commerce *or* **ecommerce** (ˈiːkɒmɜːs) *n* business transactions conducted on the internet [c20 from E-² + COMMERCE]

econ. *abbreviation for* **1** economical **2** economics **3** economy

econometrics (ɪˌkɒnəˈmɛtrɪks) *n* (*functioning as singular*) the application of mathematical and statistical techniques to economic problems and theories > **eˌconoˈmetric** *or* **eˌconoˈmetrical** *adj* > **econometrician** (ɪˌkɒnəməˈtrɪʃən) *or* **econometrist** (ɪˌkɒnəˈmɛtrɪst) *n*

economic (ˌiːkəˈnɒmɪk, ˌɛkə-) *adj* **1** of or relating to an economy, economics, or finance: *economic development; economic theories* **2** *Brit* capable of being produced, operated, etc, for profit; profitable: *the firm is barely economic* **3** concerning or affecting material resources or welfare: *economic pests* **4** concerned with or relating to the necessities of life; utilitarian **5** a variant of **economical 6** *informal* inexpensive; cheap

economical (ˌiːkəˈnɒmɪkªl, ˌɛkə-) *adj* **1** using the minimum required; not wasteful of time, effort, resources, etc: *an economical car; an economical style* **2** frugal; thrifty: *she was economical by nature* **3** a variant of **economic** (senses 1–4) **4** *euphemistic* deliberately withholding information (esp in the phrase **economical with the truth**)

economically (ˌiːkəˈnɒmɪkªlɪ, ˌɛkə-) *adv* **1** with economy or thrift; without waste **2** with regard to the economy of a person, country, etc

economic determinism *n* a doctrine that states that all cultural, social, political, and intellectual activities are a product of the economic organization of society

economic geography *n* the study of the geographical distribution of economic resources and their use

economic geology *n* the study of how geological deposits can be used as economic resources

economic indicator *n* a statistical measure representing an economic variable: *the retail price index is an economic indicator of the actual level of prices*

economic migrant *n* a person who moves from one region, place, or country to another in order to improve his or her standard of living

economic rent *n* **1** *economics* a payment to a factor of production (land, labour, or capital) in excess of that needed to keep it in its present use **2** (in Britain) the rent of a dwelling based on recouping the costs of providing it plus a profit sufficient to motivate the landlord to let it

economics (ˌiːkəˈnɒmɪks, ˌɛkə-) *n* **1** (*functioning as singular*) the social science concerned with the production and consumption of goods and services and the analysis of the commercial activities of a society. See also **macroeconomics, microeconomics 2** (*functioning as plural*) financial aspects: *the economics of the project are very doubtful*

economic sanctions *pl n* any actions taken by one nation or group of nations to harm the economy of another nation or group, often to force a political change

economic zone *n* another term for **exclusive economic zone**

economism (ɪˈkɒnəˌmɪzəm) *n* **1 a** a political theory that regards economics as the main factor in society, ignoring or reducing to simplistic economic terms other factors such as culture, nationality, etc **b** the belief that the main aim of a political group, trade union, etc, is to improve the material living standards of its members **2** (*often capital*) (in Tsarist Russia) a political belief that the sole concern of the working classes should be with improving their living conditions and not with political reforms

economist (ɪˈkɒnəmɪst) *n* **1** a specialist in economics **2** *archaic* a person who advocates or practises frugality

economistic (ɪˌkɒnəˈmɪstɪk) *adj* of or relating to economics or finances: *economistic issues*

economize *or* **economise** (ɪˈkɒnəˌmaɪz) *vb* (often foll by **on**) to limit or reduce (expense, waste, etc) > **eˌconomiˈzation** *or* **eˌconomiˈsation** *n*

economizer *or* **economiser** (ɪˈkɒnəˌmaɪzə) *n* **1** a device that uses the waste heat from a boiler flue to preheat the feed water **2** a person or thing that economizes

Economo's disease (ɪˈkɒnəməʊz) *n* *pathol* another name for **sleeping sickness** (sense 2) [c20 named after K. von *Economo* (1876–1931), Austrian neurologist]

economy (ɪˈkɒnəmɪ) *n, pl* **-mies 1** careful management of resources to avoid unnecessary expenditure or waste; thrift **2** a means or instance of this; saving **3** sparing, restrained, or efficient use, esp to achieve the maximum effect for the minimum effort: *economy of language* **4 a** the complex of human activities concerned with the production, distribution, and consumption of goods and services **b** a particular type or branch of such production, distribution, and consumption: *a socialist economy; an agricultural*

economy 5 the management of the resources, finances, income, and expenditure of a community, business enterprise, etc **6 a** a class of travel in aircraft, providing less luxurious accommodation than first class at a lower fare **b** (*as modifier*): *economy class* **7** (*modifier*) offering or purporting to offer a larger quantity for a lower price: *economy pack* **8** the orderly interplay between the parts of a system or structure: *the economy of nature* **9** *philosophy* the principle that, of two competing theories, the one with less ontological presupposition is to be preferred **10** *archaic* the management of household affairs; domestic economy [c16 via Latin from Greek *oikonomia* domestic management, from *oikos* house + *-nomia*, from *nemein* to manage]

economy-class syndrome *n* (not in technical usage) the development of a deep-vein thrombosis in the legs or pelvis of a person travelling for a long period of time in cramped conditions [c20 reference to the restricted legroom of cheaper seats on passenger aircraft]

economy of scale *n economics* a fall in average costs resulting from an increase in the scale of production

ecophysiology (ˌiːkəʊˌfɪzɪˈɒlədʒɪ) *n* the study of the physiology of organisms with respect to their adaptation to the environment

écorché (ˌeɪkɔːˈʃeɪ) *n* an anatomical figure without the skin, so that the muscular structure is visible [c19 French, literally: skinned]

ecoregion (ˈiːkəʊˌriːdʒən) *n* an area defined by its environmental conditions, esp climate, landforms, and soil characteristics

ecospecies (ˈiːkəʊˌspiːʃiːz, -ˌspiːsiːz, ˈɛkəʊ-) *n ecology* a species of plant or animal that can be divided into several ecotypes [c20 from ECO(LOGY) + SPECIES] > **ecospecific** (ˌiːkəʊspɪˈsɪfɪk, ˌɛkəʊ-) *adj*

ecosphere (ˈiːkəʊˌsfɪə, ˈɛkəʊ-) *n* the planetary ecosystem, consisting of all living organisms and their environment

écossaise (ˌeɪkɒˈseɪz; *French* ekosɛz) *n* **1** a lively dance in two-four time **2** the tune for such a dance [c19 French, literally: Scottish (dance)]

ecosystem (ˈiːkəʊˌsɪstəm, ˈɛkəʊ-) *n ecology* a system involving the interactions between a community of living organisms in a particular area and its nonliving environment [c20 from ECO(LOGY) + SYSTEM]

ecosystem services *pl n* the important benefits for human beings that arise from healthily functioning ecosystems, notably production of oxygen, soil genesis, and water detoxification

ecoterrorist (ˈiːkəʊˌtɛrərɪst) *n* a person who uses violence in order to achieve environmentalist aims [c20 from ECO- + TERRORIST]

ecotone (ˈiːkəˌtəʊn, ˈɛkə-) *n* the zone between two major ecological communities [c20 from ECO(LOGY) + *-tone*, from Greek *tonos* tension, TONE] > **ecoˌtonal** *adj*

ecotourism (ˈiːkəʊˌtʊərɪzəm) *n* tourism that is designed to contribute to the protection of the environment or at least minimize damage to it, often involving travel to areas of natural interest in developing countries or participation in environmental projects > **ˈecoˌtourist** *n*

ecotype (ˈiːkəˌtaɪp, ˈɛkə-) *n ecology* a group of organisms within a species that is adapted to particular environmental conditions and therefore exhibits behavioural, structural, or physiological differences from other members of the species > **ecotypic** (ˌiːkəˈtɪpɪk, ˌɛkə-) *adj* > **ˈecoˈtypically** *adv*

eco-warrior *n informal* a person who zealously pursues environmentalist aims [c20 from ECO- + WARRIOR]

ECOWAS (ɛˈkəʊəs) *n acronym for* Economic Community of West African States; an economic association established in 1975 among Benin, Burkina-Faso (then called Upper Volta), Côte d'Ivoire (then called Ivory Coast), The Gambia, Ghana, Guinea, Guinea-Bissau, Liberia, Mali, Mauritania, Niger, Nigeria, Senegal, Sierra Leone, and Togo. Cape Verdi and Mauritania have since joined

ECR *abbreviation for* efficient consumer response: the use of point-of-sale data to initiate the reordering of stock from a supplier

écraseur (ˌeɪkrɑːˈzɜː) *n* a surgical device consisting of a heavy wire loop placed around a part to be removed and tightened until it cuts through [c19 from French, from *écraser* to crush]

e-crime *n* criminal activity that involves the use of computers or networks such as the internet [c20 E-² + CRIME]

e-CRM *n* customer relationship management carried out on the internet

ecru (ˈɛkruː, ˈeɪkruː) *n* **1** a greyish-yellow to a light greyish colour; the colour of unbleached linen ▷ *adj* **2** of the colour ecru [c19 from French, from *é-* (intensive) + *cru* raw, from Latin *crūdus*; see CRUDE]

ECS *abbreviation for* European Communications Satellite

ECSC *abbreviation for* European Coal and Steel Community

ecstasy (ˈɛkstəsɪ) *n, pl* **-sies 1** (*often plural*) a state of exalted delight, joy, etc; rapture **2** intense emotion of any kind: *an ecstasy of rage* **3** *psychol* overpowering emotion characterized by loss of self-control and sometimes a temporary loss of consciousness: *often associated with orgasm, religious mysticism, and the use of certain drugs* **4** *archaic* a state of prophetic inspiration, esp of poetic rapture **5** *slang* 3,4-methylenedioxy-methamphetamine; MDMA: a powerful drug that acts as a stimulant and can produce hallucinations [c14 from Old French *extasie*, via Medieval Latin from Greek *ekstasis* displacement, trance, from *existanai* to displace, from *ex-* out + *histanai* to cause to stand]

ecstatic (ɛkˈstætɪk) *adj* **1** in a trancelike state of great rapture or delight **2** showing or feeling great enthusiasm: *ecstatic applause* ▷ *n* **3** a person who has periods of intense trancelike joy > **ecˈstatically** *adv*

ecstatics (ɛkˈstætɪks) *pl n* fits of delight or rapture

ECT *abbreviation for* **electroconvulsive therapy**

ectasia (ɛkˈteɪzɪə) *or* **ectasis** (ɛkˈteɪsɪs) *n pathol* the distension or dilation of a duct, vessel, or hollow viscus > **ecˈtatic** *adj*

ecthyma (ˈɛkθɪmə) *n pathol* a local inflammation of the skin characterized by flat ulcerating pustules [c19 from New Latin, from Greek *ekthuma* pustule, from *ekthuein* to break out, from *ek-* out + *thuein* to seethe]

ecto- *combining form* indicating outer, outside, external: *ectoplasm* [from Greek *ektos* outside, from *ek, ex* out]

ectoblast (ˈɛktəʊˌblæst) *n* another name for **ectoderm** *or* **epiblast** > **ˌectoˈblastic** *adj*

ectocrine (ˈɛktəʊˌkriːn, -krɪn) *n* a substance that is released by an organism into the external environment and influences the development, behaviour, etc, of members of the same or different species [c20 from ECTO- + *-crine*, as in *endocrine*]

ectoderm (ˈɛktəʊˌdɜːm) *or* **exoderm** *n* the outer germ layer of an animal embryo, which gives rise to epidermis and nervous tissue. See also **mesoderm, endoderm.** > **ˌectoˈdermal** *or* **ˌectoˈdermic** *adj*

ectoenzyme (ˌɛktəʊˈɛnzaɪm) *n* any of a group of enzymes secreted from the cells in which they are produced into the surrounding medium; extracellular enzyme. Also called: **exoenzyme**

ectogenesis (ˌɛktəʊˈdʒɛnəsɪs) *n* the growth of an organism outside the body in which it would normally be found, such as the growth of an embryo outside the mother's body or the growth of bacteria outside the body of a host > **ˌectoˈgenetic, ˌectoˈgenic** *or* **ectogenous** (ɛkˈtɒdʒɪnəs) *adj* > **ˌectoˈgenically** *adv*

ectomere (ˈɛktəʊˌmɪə) *n embryol* any of the blastomeres that later develop into ectoderm > **ectomeric** (ˌɛktəʊˈmɛrɪk) *adj*

ectomorph (ˈɛktəʊˌmɔːf) *n* a person with a thin body build: said to be correlated with cerebrotonia. Compare **endomorph, mesomorph** > **ˌectoˈmorphic** *adj* > **ˈectoˌmorphy** *n*

-ectomy *n combining form* indicating surgical excision of a part: *appendectomy* [from New Latin *-ectomia*, from Greek *ek-* out + -TOMY]

ectomycorrhiza (ˌɛktəʊˌmaɪkəˈraɪzə) *n* another name for **ectotrophic mycorrhiza**

ectoparasite (ˌɛktəʊˈpærəˌsaɪt) *n* a parasite, such as the flea, that lives on the outer surface of its host. Also called: **exoparasite** > **ectoparasitic** (ˌɛktəʊˌpærəˈsɪtɪk) *adj*

ectophyte (ˈɛktəʊˌfaɪt) *n* a parasitic plant that lives on the surface of its host > **ectophytic** (ˌɛktəʊˈfɪtɪk) *adj*

ectopia (ɛkˈtəʊpɪə) *n med* congenital displacement or abnormal positioning of an organ or part [c19 from New Latin, from Greek *ektopos* out of position, from *ek-* out of + *topos* place] > **ectopic** (ɛkˈtɒpɪk) *adj*

ectopic pregnancy *n pathol* the abnormal development of a fertilized egg outside the cavity of the uterus, usually within a Fallopian tube

ectoplasm (ˈɛktəʊˌplæzəm) *n* **1** *cytology* the outer layer of cytoplasm in some cells, esp protozoa, which differs from the inner cytoplasm (see **endoplasm**) in being a clear gel **2** *spiritualism* the substance supposedly emanating from the body of a medium during trances > **ˌectoˈplasmic** *adj*

ectoproct (ˈɛktəʊˌprɒkt) *n, adj* another word for **bryozoan** [from ECTO- + *-proct*, from Greek *prōktos* rectum]

ectosarc (ˈɛktəʊˌsɑːk) *n zoology* the ectoplasm of an amoeba or any other protozoan [c19 ECTO- + *-sarc*, from Greek *sarx* flesh] > **ˌectoˈsarcous** *adj*

ectotrophic mycorrhiza (ˌɛktəʊˈtrɒfɪk) *n botany* a type of mycorrhiza, typical of temperate and Boreal trees, in which the fungus forms a layer on the outside of the roots of the plant. Also called: **ectomycorrhiza** Compare **endotrophic mycorrhiza**

ectype (ˈɛkˌtaɪp) *n* **1** a copy as distinguished from a prototype **2** *architect* a cast embossed or in relief [c17 from Greek *ektupos* worked in relief, from *ek-* out of + *tupos* mould; see TYPE] > **ectypal** (ˈɛktɪpˀl) *adj*

écu (eɪˈkjuː; *French* eky) *n* **1** any of various former French gold or silver coins **2** a small shield [c18 from Old French *escu*, from Latin *scūtum* shield]

ECU (ˈeɪkjuː; *sometimes* ˈiːˈsiːˈjuː) *n acronym for* European Currency Unit: a former unit of currency based on the composite value of several different currencies in the European Union and functioning both as the reserve asset and accounting unit of the European Monetary System; replaced by the euro in 1999

Ecua. *abbreviation for* Ecuador

Ecuador (ˈɛkwəˌdɔː) *n* a republic in South America, on the Pacific: under the Incas when Spanish colonization began in 1532; gained independence in 1822; declared a republic in 1830. It consists chiefly of a coastal plain in the west, separated from the densely forested upper Amazon basin (Oriente) by ranges and plateaus of the Andes. Official language: Spanish; Quechua is also widely spoken. Religion: Roman Catholic majority. Currency: US dollar. Capital: Quito. Pop: 13 193 000 (2004 est.). Area: 283 560 sq km (109 483 sq miles)

Ecuadorean (ˌɛkwəˈdɔːrɪən) *adj* **1** of or relating to Ecuador or its inhabitants ▷ *n* **2** a native or inhabitant of Ecuador

ecumenical, oecumenical (ˌiːkjʊˈmɛnɪkˀl, ˌɛk-) *or* **ecumenic, oecumenic** *adj* **1** of or relating to the Christian Church throughout the world, esp with regard to its unity **2 a** tending to promote unity among Churches **b** of or relating to the international movement initiated among non-Catholic Churches in 1910 aimed at Christian

e

unity: embodied, since 1937, in the World Council of Churches **3** *rare* universal; general; worldwide [c16 via Late Latin from Greek *oikoumenikos*, from *oikein* to inhabit, from *oikos* house] > ˌ**ecu'menically** *or* ˌ**oecu'menically** *adv*
ecumenical council *n* an assembly of bishops and other ecclesiastics representative of the Christian Church throughout the world. Roman Catholic canon law states that an ecumenical council must be convened by the pope
ecumenism (ɪ'kjuːməˌnɪzəm, 'ɛkjʊm-), **ecumenicism** (ˌiːkjʊ'mɛnɪˌsɪzəm, ˌɛk-) *or* **ecumenicalism** *n* the aim of unity among all Christian churches throughout the world
écurie (*French* ekyri) *n* a team of motor-racing cars [c20 French, literally: a stable]
eczema ('ɛksɪmə, ɪg'ziːmə) *n pathol* a skin inflammation with lesions that scale, crust, or ooze a serous fluid, often accompanied by intense itching or burning [c18 from New Latin, from Greek *ekzema*, from *ek-* out + *zein* to boil; see YEAST] > **eczematous** (ɛk'sɛmətəs) *adj*
ed. *abbreviation for* **1** edited **2** (*pl* **eds**) edition **3** (*pl* **eds**) editor
-ed¹ *suffix* forming the past tense of most English verbs [Old English *-de, -ede, -ode, -ade*]
-ed² *suffix* forming the past participle of most English verbs [Old English *-ed, -od, -ad*]
-ed³ *suffix forming adjectives from nouns* possessing or having the characteristics of: *salaried; red-blooded* [Old English *-ede*]
edacious (ɪ'deɪʃəs) *adj chiefly humorous* devoted to eating; voracious; greedy [c19 from Latin *edāx* voracious, from *edere* to eat] > **e'daciously** *adv* > **edacity** (ɪ'dæsɪtɪ) *or* **e'daciousness** *n*
Edam ('iːdæm) *n* **1** a town in the NW Netherlands, in North Holland province, on the IJsselmeer: cheese, light manufacturing. Pop: 28 000 (2003 est; includes Volendam) **2** a hard round mild-tasting Dutch cheese, yellow in colour with a red outside covering
edaphic (ɪ'dæfɪk) *adj* of or relating to the physical and chemical conditions of the soil, esp in relation to the plant and animal life it supports. Compare **biotic** (sense 2) [c20 from Greek *edaphos* bottom, soil] > **e'daphically** *adv*
EDC *abbreviation for* European Defence Community
Edda ('ɛdə) *n* **1** Also called: **Elder Edda, Poetic Edda** a collection of mythological Old Norse poems made in the 12th century **2** Also called: **Younger Edda, Prose Edda** a treatise on versification together with a collection of Scandinavian myths, legends, and poems compiled by Snorri Sturluson (1179–1241), the Icelandic historian and poet [c18 Old Norse] > **Eddaic** (ɛ'deɪɪk) *adj*
Eddington limit ('ɛdɪŋtən) *n astronomy* the theoretical upper limit of luminosity that a star of a given mass can reach; occurs when the outward force of the radiation just balances the inward gravitational force [c20 named after A. S. *Eddington* (1882–1944), English astronomer and physicist]
eddo *or* **Chinese eddo** ('ɛdəʊ) *n, pl* **eddoes** other names for **taro**
eddy ('ɛdɪ) *n, pl* **-dies** **1** a movement in a stream of air, water, or other fluid in which the current doubles back on itself causing a miniature whirlwind or whirlpool **2** a deviation from or disturbance in the main trend of thought, life, etc, esp one that is relatively unimportant ▷ *vb* **-dies, -dying, -died** **3** to move or cause to move against the main current [c15 probably of Scandinavian origin; compare Old Norse *itha*; related to Old English *ed-* again, back, Old High German *it-*]
eddy current *n* an electric current induced in a massive conductor, such as the core of an electromagnet, transformer, etc, by an alternating magnetic field. Also called: **Foucault current**
Eddystone Rocks ('ɛdɪstən) *n* a dangerous group of rocks at the W end of the English Channel, southwest of Plymouth: lighthouse
Ede ('eɪdə) *n* a city in the central Netherlands, in Gelderland province. Pop: 105 000 (2003 est)
edelweiss ('eɪdᵊlˌvaɪs) *n* a small alpine flowering plant, *Leontopodium alpinum*, having white woolly oblong leaves and a tuft of attractive floral leaves surrounding the flowers: family *Asteraceae* (composites) [c19 German, literally: noble white]
edema (ɪ'diːmə) *n, pl* **-mata** (-mətə) the usual US spelling of **oedema**. > **edematous** (ɪ'dɛmətəs) *or* **e'demaˌtose** *adj*
Eden ('iːdᵊn) *n* **1** Also called: **Garden of Eden** *Old Testament* the garden in which Adam and Eve were placed at the Creation **2** a delightful place, region, dwelling, etc; paradise **3** a state of great delight, happiness, or contentment; bliss [c14 from Late Latin, from Hebrew *'ēdhen* place of pleasure] > **Edenic** (iː'dɛnɪk) *adj*
edentate (iː'dɛnteɪt) *n* **1** any of the placental mammals that constitute the order *Edentata*, which inhabit tropical regions of Central and South America. The order includes anteaters, sloths, and armadillos ▷ *adj* **2** of, relating to, or belonging to the order *Edentata* [c19 from Latin *ēdentātus* lacking teeth, from *ēdentāre* to render toothless, from *e-* out + *dēns* tooth]
edentulous (iː'dɛntʃʊləs) *or* **edentulate** (iː'dɛntʃʊlɪt) *adj* having no teeth
Edessa (ɪ'dɛsə) *n* **1** an ancient city on the N edge of the Syrian plateau, founded as a Macedonian colony by Seleucus I: a centre of early Christianity. Modern name: **Urfa** **2** a market town in Greece: ancient capital of Macedonia. Pop: 15 980 (latest est). Ancient name: **Aegae** ('iːgiː) Modern Greek name: **Édhessa**
edge (ɛdʒ) *n* **1** the border, brim, or margin of a surface, object, etc **2** a brink or verge: *the edge of a cliff; the edge of a breakthrough* **3** *maths* **a** a line along which two faces or surfaces of a solid meet **b** a line joining two vertices of a graph **4** the sharp cutting side of a blade **5** keenness, sharpness, or urgency: *the walk gave an edge to his appetite* **6** force, effectiveness, or incisiveness: *the performance lacked edge* **7** *dialect* **a** a cliff, ridge, or hillside **b** (*capital*) (in place names): *Hade Edge* **8** **have the edge on** *or* **over** to have a slight advantage or superiority (over) **9** **on edge** **a** nervously irritable; tense **b** nervously excited or eager **10** **set (someone's) teeth on edge** to make (someone) acutely irritated or uncomfortable ▷ *vb* **11** (*tr*) to provide an edge or border for **12** (*tr*) to shape or trim (the edge or border of something), as with a knife or scissors: *to edge a pie* **13** to push (one's way, someone, something, etc) gradually, esp edgeways **14** (*tr*) *cricket* to hit (a bowled ball) with the edge of the bat **15** (*tr*) to tilt (a ski) sideways so that one edge digs into the snow **16** (*tr*) to sharpen (a knife, etc) [Old English *ecg*; related to Old Norse *egg*, Old High German *ecka* edge, Latin *aciēs* sharpness, Greek *akis* point] > **'edgeless** *adj* > **'edger** *n*
Edgehill (ˌɛdʒ'hɪl) *n* a ridge in S Warwickshire: site of the indecisive first battle between Charles I and the Parliamentarians (1642) in the Civil War
edge tool *n* a tool with one or more cutting edges
edgeways ('ɛdʒˌweɪz) *or esp US and Canadian* **edgewise** ('ɛdʒˌwaɪz) *adv* **1** with the edge forwards or uppermost: *they carried the piano in edgeways* **2** on, by, with, or towards the edge: *he held it edgeways* **3** **get a word in edgeways** (*usually used with a negative*) to succeed in interrupting a conversation in which someone else is talking incessantly
edging ('ɛdʒɪŋ) *n* **1** anything placed along an edge to finish it, esp as an ornament, fringe, or border on clothing or along a path in a garden **2** the act of making an edge ▷ *adj* **3** relating to or used for making an edge: *edging shears*
edgy ('ɛdʒɪ) *adj* **-ier, -iest** **1** (*usually postpositive*) nervous, irritable, tense, or anxious **2** (of paintings, drawings, etc) excessively defined **3** innovative, or at the cutting edge, with the concomitant qualities of intensity and excitement > **'edgily** *adv* > **'edginess** *n*
edh (ɛð) *or* **eth** *n* a character of the runic alphabet (ð) used to represent the voiced dental fricative as in *then, mother, bathe*. It is used in modern phonetic transcription for the same purpose. Compare **theta** (sense 2), **thorn** (sense 5)
Édhessa (*Greek* 'ɛðɛsa) *n* transliteration of the Modern Greek name for **Edessa**
EDI *abbreviation for* electronic data interchange: an interactive electronic system that enables a supplier and customer to communicate easily
Ediacaran (ˌiːdiː'ækərən) *adj* **1** of, denoting, or formed in the last 50 million years of the Neoproterozoic era, during which a new texturally and chemically distinctive carbonate layer appeared, indicating climatic change ▷ *n* **2** **the** the Ediacaran period or rock system [c20 named after the Ediacara Hills in the Flinders mountain range in South Australia]
edible ('ɛdɪbᵊl) *adj* fit to be eaten; eatable [c17 from Late Latin *edibilis*, from Latin *edere* to eat] > ˌ**edi'bility** *or* **'edibleness** *n*
edibles ('ɛdɪbᵊlz) *pl n* articles fit to eat; food
edict ('iːdɪkt) *n* **1** a decree, order, or ordinance issued by a sovereign, state, or any other holder of authority **2** any formal or authoritative command, proclamation, etc [c15 from Latin *ēdictum*, from *ēdīcere* to declare] > **e'dictal** *adj* > **e'dictally** *adv*
Edict of Nantes *n* the law granting religious and civil liberties to the French Protestants, promulgated by Henry IV in 1598 and revoked by Louis XIV in 1685
edification (ˌɛdɪfɪ'keɪʃən) *n* **1** improvement, instruction, or enlightenment, esp when morally or spiritually uplifting **2** the act of edifying or state of being edified > ˌ**edifi'catory** *adj*
edifice ('ɛdɪfɪs) *n* **1** a building, esp a large or imposing one **2** a complex or elaborate institution or organization [c14 from Old French, from Latin *aedificium*, from *aedificāre* to build; see EDIFY] > **edificial** (ˌɛdɪ'fɪʃəl) *adj*
edify ('ɛdɪˌfaɪ) *vb* **-fies, -fying, -fied** (*tr*) to improve the morality, intellect, etc, of, esp by instruction [c14 from Old French *edifier*, from Latin *aedificāre* to construct, from *aedēs* a dwelling, temple + *facere* to make] > **'ediˌfier** *n* > **'ediˌfying** *adj* > **'ediˌfyingly** *adv*
edile ('iːdaɪl) *n* a variant spelling of **aedile**
Edinburgh ('ɛdɪnbərə, -brə) *n* **1** the capital of Scotland and seat of the Scottish Parliament (from 1999), in City of Edinburgh council area on the S side of the Firth of Forth: became the capital in the 15th century; castle; three universities (including University of Edinburgh, 1583); commercial and cultural centre, noted for its annual festival. Pop: 430 082 (2001) **2** **City of** a council area in central Scotland, created from part of Lothian region in 1996. Pop: 448 370 (2003 est). Area: 262 sq km (101 sq miles)
Edirne (ɛ'dirnɛ) *n* a city in NW Turkey: a Thracian town, rebuilt and renamed by the Roman emperor Hadrian. Pop: 126 000 (2005 est). Former name: **Adrianople**
edit ('ɛdɪt) *vb* (*tr*) **1** to prepare (text) for publication by checking and improving its accuracy, clarity, etc **2** to be in charge of (a publication, esp a periodical): *he edits the local newspaper* **3** to prepare (a film, tape, etc) by rearrangement, selection, or rejection of previously filmed or taped material **4** (*tr*) to modify (a computer file) by, for example, deleting, inserting, moving, or copying text **5** (often foll by *out*) to remove (incorrect or unwanted matter), as from a manuscript or film ▷ *n* **6** *informal* an act of editing: *give the book a final edit* [c18 back formation from EDITOR]
edition (ɪ'dɪʃən) *n* **1** *printing* **a** the entire number of copies of a book, newspaper, or other publication printed at one time from a single setting of type **b** a single copy from this number: *a first edition; the evening edition* **2** one of a number of printings of a book or other publication, issued at

separate times with alterations, amendments, etc. Compare **impression** (sense 6) **3 a** an issue of a work identified by its format: *a leather-bound edition of Shakespeare* **b** an issue of a work identified by its editor or publisher: *the Oxford edition of Shakespeare* **4** a particular instance of a television or radio programme broadcast ▷ *vb* **5** (*tr*) to produce multiple copies of (an original work of art) [c16 from Latin *ēditiō* a bringing forth, publishing, from *ēdere* to give out; see EDITOR]

editio princeps *Latin* (ɪˈdɪʃɪəʊ ˈprɪnsɛps) *n, pl* **editiones principes** (ɪˌdɪʃɪˈəʊniːz ˈprɪnsɪˌpiːz) the first printed edition of a work

editor (ˈɛdɪtə) *n* **1** a person who edits written material for publication **2** a person in overall charge of the editing and often the policy of a newspaper or periodical **3** a person in charge of one section of a newspaper or periodical: *the sports editor* **4** *films* **a** a person who makes a selection and arrangement of individual shots in order to construct the flowing sequence of images for a film **b** a device for editing film, including a viewer and a splicer **5** *television, radio* a person in overall control of a programme that consists of various items, such as a news or magazine style programme **6** a computer program that facilitates the deletion or insertion of data within information already stored in a computer [c17 from Late Latin: producer, exhibitor, from *ēdere* to give out, publish, from *ē-* out + *dāre* to give] > **'editor,ship** *n*

editorial (ˌɛdɪˈtɔːrɪəl) *adj* **1** of or relating to editing or editors **2** of, relating to, or expressed in an editorial **3** of or relating to the content of a publication rather than its commercial aspects ▷ *n* **4** an article in a newspaper, etc, expressing the opinion of the editor or the publishers > **,edi'torialist** *n* > **,edi'torially** *adv*

editorialize *or* **editorialise** (ˌɛdɪˈtɔːrɪəˌlaɪz) *vb* (*intr*) **1** to express an opinion in or as in an editorial **2** to insert one's personal opinions into an otherwise objective account > **,edi,toriali'zation** *or* **,edi,toriali'sation** *n* > **,edi'torial,izer** *or* **,edi'torial,iser** *n*

editor in chief *n* the controlling editor of a publication

EDM *surveying abbreviation for* electronic distance measurement

Edmonton (ˈɛdməntən) *n* a city in W Canada, capital of Alberta: oil industry. Pop: 782 101 (2001)

Edo (ˈɛdəʊ) *n* **1** (*pl* **Edo** *or* **Edos**) a member of a Negroid people of SW Nigeria around Benin, noted for their 16th-century bronze sculptures **2** Also called: **Bini** the language of this people, belonging to the Kwa branch of the Niger-Congo family

Edom (ˈiːdəm) *n* **1** a nomadic people descended from Esau **2** the son of Esau, who was the supposed ancestor of this nation **3** the ancient kingdom of this people, situated between the Dead Sea and the Gulf of Aqaba

Edomite (ˈiːdəˌmaɪt) *n* **1** an inhabitant of the ancient kingdom of Edom, whose people were hostile to the Israelites in Old Testament times **2** the ancient Semitic language of this people, closely related to Hebrew > **'Edom,itish** *or* **Edomitic** (ˌiːdəˈmɪtɪk) *adj*

EDT (in the US and Canada) *abbreviation for* Eastern Daylight Time

EDTA *n* ethylenediaminetetra-acetic acid; a colourless crystalline slightly soluble organic compound used in inorganic chemistry and biochemistry. It is a powerful chelating agent used to stabilize bleach in detergents. Formula: $[(HOOCCH_2)_2NCH_2]_2$

edu *an internet domain name for* an educational establishment

educable (ˈɛdjʊkəbᵊl) *or* **educatable** (ˈɛdjʊˌkeɪtəbᵊl) *adj* capable of being trained or educated; able to learn > **,educa'bility** *or* **,edu,cata'bility** *n*

educate (ˈɛdjʊˌkeɪt) *vb* (mainly *tr*) **1** (also *intr*) to

impart knowledge by formal instruction to (a pupil); teach **2** to provide schooling for (children): *I have educated my children at the best schools* **3** to improve or develop (a person, judgment, taste, skills, etc) **4** to train for some particular purpose or occupation [c15 from Latin *ēducāre* to rear, educate, from *dūcere* to lead]

educated (ˈɛdjʊˌkeɪtɪd) *adj* **1** having an education, esp a good one **2** displaying culture, taste, and knowledge; cultivated **3** (*prenominal*) based on experience or information (esp in the phrase **an educated guess**)

education (ˌɛdjʊˈkeɪʃən) *n* **1** the act or process of acquiring knowledge, esp systematically during childhood and adolescence **2** the knowledge or training acquired by this process: *his education has been invaluable to him* **3** the act or process of imparting knowledge, esp at a school, college, or university: *education is my profession* **4** the theory of teaching and learning: *a course in education* **5** a particular kind of instruction or training: *a university education; consumer education*

educational (ˌɛdjʊˈkeɪʃənᵊl) *adj* **1** providing knowledge; instructive or informative: *an educational toy* **2** of or relating to education > **,edu'cationally** *adv*

educationalist (ˌɛdjʊˈkeɪʃənəlɪst) *or* **educationist** *n* a specialist in educational theory or administration

educational psychology *n* the study of methods of training and teaching and their effectiveness, and of the problems experienced in learning formal material; in particular, the study of how to help people, esp school children, with learning problems to overcome their difficulties

Educational Welfare Officer *n* (in Britain) a local education authority worker whose job it is to find out whether difficulties outside school are contributing to a child's classroom problems or irregular attendance and who may intervene to help the child to benefit more from schooling. Former names: **school attendance officer, truancy officer**

educative (ˈɛdjʊkətɪv) *adj* producing or resulting in education: *an educative experience*

educator (ˈɛdjʊˌkeɪtə) *n* **1** a person who educates; teacher **2** a specialist in education; educationalist **3** (in South Africa) a school teacher

educatory (ˈɛdjʊkətərɪ, -trɪ, ˌɛdjʊˈkeɪtərɪ, -trɪ) *adj* educative or educational: *an educatory procedure*

educe (ɪˈdjuːs) *vb* (*tr*) *rare* **1** to evolve or develop, esp from a latent or potential state **2** to draw out or elicit (information, solutions, etc) [c15 from Latin *ēdūcere* to draw out, from *dūcere* to lead] > **e'ducible** *adj* > **eductive** (ɪˈdʌktɪv) *adj*

educt (ˈiːdʌkt) *n* a substance separated from another substance without chemical change. Compare **product** (sense 4) [c18 from Latin *ēductus*; see EDUCE]

eduction (ɪˈdʌkʃən) *n* **1** something educed **2** the act or process of educing **3** the exhaust stroke of a steam or internal-combustion engine. Compare **induction** [c17 from Latin *ēductiō*, from *ēdūcere* to EDUCE]

edulcorate (ɪˈdʌlkəˌreɪt) *vb* (*tr*) to free from soluble impurities by washing [c17 from Medieval Latin *ēdulcorāre*, from Late Latin *dulcor* sweetness] > **e,dulco'ration** *n*

edutainment (ˌɛdjʊˈteɪnmənt) *n* the presentation of informative or educational material in an entertaining style [c20 from EDU(CATION) + (ENTER)TAINMENT]

Edward (ˈɛdwəd) *n* **Lake** a lake in central Africa, between Uganda and the Democratic Republic of Congo (formerly Zaïre) in the Great Rift Valley: empties through the Semliki River into Lake Albert. Area: about 2150 sq km (830 sq miles). Former official name: Lake Amin

Edwardian (ɛdˈwɔːdɪən) *adj* **1** denoting, relating to, or having the style of life, architecture, dress, etc, current in Britain during the reign (1901–10) of Edward VII (1841–1910) ▷ *n* **2** a person who lived

during the reign of Edward VII > **Ed'wardianism** *n*

ee¹ (iː) *n, pl* **een** (iːn) a Scot word for **eye¹**

ee² *the internet domain name for* Estonia

EE *abbreviation for* **1** Early English **2** electrical engineer(ing) **3** (in New Zealand) **ewe** equivalent

e.e. *abbreviation for* errors excepted

-ee *suffix forming nouns* **1** indicating a person who is the recipient of an action (as opposed, esp in legal terminology, to the agent, indicated by *or* or *cr*): *assignee; grantee; lessee* **2** indicating a person in a specified state or condition: *absentee; employee* **3** indicating a diminutive form of something: *bootee* [via Old French *-e*, *-ee*, past participial endings, from Latin *-ātus*, *-āta* -ATE¹]

EEA *abbreviation for* **European Economic Area**

EE & MP *abbreviation for* Envoy Extraordinary and Minister Plenipotentiary

EEC *abbreviation for* European Economic Community (now subsumed within the European Union)

EEG *abbreviation for* **1** electroencephalogram **2** electroencephalograph

eejit (ˈiːdʒɪt) *n* a Scot and Irish word for **idiot** (sense 2)

EEK *abbreviation for* Estonian kroon: the standard monetary unit of Estonia

eel (iːl) *n* **1** any teleost fish of the order *Apodes* (or *Anguilliformes*), such as the European freshwater species *Anguilla anguilla*, having a long snakelike body, a smooth slimy skin, and reduced fins **2** any of various other animals with a long body and smooth skin, such as the mud eel and the electric eel **3** an evasive or untrustworthy person [Old English *ǣl*; related to Old Frisian *ēl*, Old Norse *āll*, Old High German *āl*] > **'eel-,like** *adj* > **'eely** *adj*

eelgrass (ˈiːlˌɡrɑːs) *n* **1** any of several perennial submerged marine plants of the genus *Zostera*, esp *Z. marina*, having grasslike leaves: family *Zosteraceae* **2** another name for **tape grass**

eelpout (ˈiːlˌpaʊt) *n* **1** any marine eel-like blennioid fish of the family *Zoarcidae*, such as *Zoarces viviparus* (**viviparous eelpout** or blenny) **2** another name for **burbot** [Old English *ǣlepūte*; related to Middle Dutch *aalpuit*]

eelworm (ˈiːlˌwɜːm) *n* any of various nematode worms, esp the wheatworm and the vinegar eel

e'en (iːn) *adv, n poetic or archaic* a contraction of **even²** and **evening**

e'er (ɛə) *adv poetic or archaic* a contraction of **ever**

-eer *or* **-ier** *suffix* **1** (forming nouns) indicating a person who is concerned with or who does something specified: *auctioneer; engineer; profiteer; mutineer* **2** (forming verbs) to be concerned with something specified: *electioneer* [from Old French *-ier*, from Latin *-arius* -ARY]

eerie (ˈɪərɪ) *adj* **eerier, eeriest** (esp of places, an atmosphere, etc) mysteriously or uncannily frightening or disturbing; weird; ghostly [c13 originally Scottish and Northern English, probably from Old English *earg* cowardly, miserable] > **'eerily** *adv* > **'eeriness** *n*

EFA *abbreviation for* **1** essential fatty acid ▷ *n* **2** European Fighter Aircraft

eff (ɛf) *vb* **1** euphemism for **fuck** (esp in the phrase **eff off**) **2** eff and blind *slang* to use obscene language > **'effing** *n, adj*

effable (ˈɛfəbᵊl) *adj archaic* capable of being expressed in words [c17 from Old French, from Late Latin *effābilis*, from Latin *effārī*, from *ex-* out + *fārī* to speak]

efface (ɪˈfeɪs) *vb* (*tr*) **1** to obliterate or make dim: *to efface a memory* **2** to make (oneself) inconspicuous or humble through modesty, cowardice, or obsequiousness **3** to rub out (a line, drawing, etc); erase [c15 from French *effacer*, literally: to obliterate the face; see FACE] > **ef'faceable** *adj* > **ef'facement** *n* > **ef'facer** *n*

effect (ɪˈfɛkt) *n* **1** something that is produced by a cause or agent; result **2** power or ability to influence or produce a result; efficacy: *with no effect* **3** the condition of being operative (esp in the phrases **in** or **into effect**): *the law comes into effect at*

e

midnight **4** **take effect** to become operative or begin to produce results **5** basic meaning or purpose (esp in the phrase **to that effect**) **6** an impression, usually one that is artificial or contrived (esp in the phrase **for effect**) **7** a scientific phenomenon: *the Doppler effect* **8** **in effect** **a** in fact; actually **b** for all practical purposes **9** the overall impression or result: *the effect of a painting* ▷ *vb* **10** (*tr*) to cause to occur; bring about; accomplish ▷ See also **effects** [C14 from Latin *effectus* a performing, tendency, from *efficere* to accomplish, from *facere* to do] > **ef'fecter** *n* > **ef'fectible** *adj*

effective (ɪ'fɛktɪv) *adj* **1** productive of or capable of producing a result **2** in effect; operative: *effective from midnight* **3** producing a striking impression; impressive: *an effective entrance* **4** (*prenominal*) actual rather than theoretical; real: *the effective income after deductions* **5** (of a military force, etc) equipped and prepared for action **6** *physics* (of an alternating quantity) having a value that is the square root of the mean of the squares of the magnitude measured at each instant over a defined period of time, usually one cycle. See also **root mean square** ▷ *n* **7** a serviceman who is equipped and prepared for action > **ef'fectively** *adv* > **ef'fectiveness** *n*

effector *or* **effecter** (ɪ'fɛktə) *n physiol* a nerve ending that terminates in a muscle or gland and provides neural stimulation causing contraction or secretion

effects (ɪ'fɛkts) *pl n* **1** Also called: **personal effects** personal property or belongings **2** lighting, sounds, etc, to accompany and enhance a stage, film, or broadcast production

effectual (ɪ'fɛktjʊəl) *adj* **1** capable of or successful in producing an intended result; effective **2** (of documents, agreements, etc) having legal force > **ef,fectu'ality** *or* **ef'fectualness** *n*

effectually (ɪ'fɛktjʊəlɪ) *adv* **1** with the intended effect; thoroughly **2** to all practical purposes; in effect

effectuate (ɪ'fɛktjʊ,eɪt) *vb* (*tr*) to cause to happen; effect; accomplish > **ef,fectu'ation** *n*

effeminate (ɪ'fɛmɪnɪt) *adj* **1** (of a man or boy) displaying characteristics regarded as typical of a woman; not manly **2** lacking firmness or vigour: *an effeminate piece of writing* [C14 from Latin *effēmināre* to make into a woman, from *fēmina* woman] > **ef'feminacy** *or* **ef'feminateness** *n* > **ef'feminately** *adv*

effendi (ɛ'fɛndɪ) *n, pl* **-dis** **1** (in the Ottoman Empire) a title of respect used to address men of learning or social standing **2** (in Turkey since 1934) the oral title of address equivalent to *Mr* [C17 from Turkish *efendi* master, from Modern Greek *aphentēs*, from Greek *authentēs* lord, doer; see AUTHENTIC]

efferent ('ɛfərənt) *adj* carrying or conducting outwards from a part or an organ of the body, esp from the brain or spinal cord. Compare **afferent** [C19 from Latin *efferre* to bear off, from *ferre* to bear] > **'efference** *n* > **'efferently** *adv*

effervesce (,ɛfə'vɛs) *vb* (*intr*) **1** (of a liquid) to give off bubbles of gas **2** (of a gas) to issue in bubbles from a liquid **3** to exhibit great excitement, vivacity, etc [C18 from Latin *effervescere* to foam up, from *fervescere* to begin to boil, from *fervēre* to boil, ferment] > **,effer'vescible** *adj* > **,effer'vescingly** *adv*

effervescent (,ɛfə'vɛsᵊnt) *adj* **1** (of a liquid) giving off bubbles of gas; bubbling **2** high-spirited; vivacious > **,effer'vescence** *n* > **,effer'vescently** *adv*

effete (ɪ'fi:t) *adj* **1** weak, ineffectual, or decadent as a result of overrefinement: *an effete academic* **2** exhausted of vitality or strength; worn out; spent **3** (of animals or plants) no longer capable of reproduction [C17 from Latin *effētus* having produced young, hence, exhausted by bearing, from *fētus* having brought forth; see FETUS] > **ef'fetely** *adv* > **ef'feteness** *n*

efficacious (,ɛfɪ'keɪʃəs) *adj* capable of or successful in producing an intended result; effective as a means, remedy, etc [C16 from Latin *efficāx* powerful, efficient, from *efficere* to achieve; see EFFECT] > **,effi'caciously** *adv* > **,effi'caciousness** *n*

efficacy ('ɛfɪkəsɪ) *n* the quality of being successful in producing an intended result; effectiveness

efficiency (ɪ'fɪʃənsɪ) *n, pl* **-cies** **1** the quality or state of being efficient; competence; effectiveness **2** the ratio of the useful work done by a machine, engine, device, etc, to the energy supplied to it, often expressed as a percentage. See also **thermal efficiency**

efficiency apartment *n US* a small flat or bedsit

efficient (ɪ'fɪʃənt) *adj* **1** functioning or producing effectively and with the least waste of effort; competent **2** *philosophy* producing a direct effect; causative [C14 from Latin *efficiēns* effecting] > **ef'ficiently** *adv*

efficient cause *n philosophy* that which produces an effect by a causal process. Compare **final cause** See also **cause** (sense 7)

effigy ('ɛfɪdʒɪ) *n, pl* **-gies** **1** a portrait of a person, esp as a monument or architectural decoration **2** a crude representation of someone, used as a focus for contempt or ridicule and often hung up or burnt in public (often in the phrases **burn** or **hang in effigy**) [C18 from Latin *effigiēs*, from *effingere* to form, portray, from *fingere* to shape] > **effigial** (ɪ'fɪdʒɪəl) *adj*

effleurage (,ɛflɜ:'rɑ:ʒ) *n* **1** a light stroking technique used in massage ▷ *vb* **2** (*intr*) to massage using this movement [C19 from French *effleurer* to stroke lightly]

effloresce (,ɛflɔ:'rɛs) *vb* (*intr*) **1** to burst forth into or as if into flower; bloom **2** to become powdery by loss of water or crystallization **3** to become encrusted with powder or crystals as a result of chemical change or the evaporation of a solution [C18 from Latin *efflōrēscere* to blossom, from *flōrēscere*, from *flōs* flower]

efflorescence (,ɛflɔ:'rɛsᵊns) *n* **1** a bursting forth or flowering **2** *chem, geology* **a** the process of efflorescing **b** the powdery substance formed as a result of this process, esp on the surface of rocks **3** any skin rash or eruption > **,efflo'rescent** *adj*

effluence ('ɛflʊəns) *or* **efflux** ('ɛflʌks) *n* **1** the act or process of flowing out **2** something that flows out

effluent ('ɛflʊənt) *n* **1** liquid discharged as waste, as from an industrial plant or sewage works **2** radioactive waste released from a nuclear power station **3** a stream that flows out of another body of water **4** something that flows out or forth ▷ *adj* **5** flowing out or forth [C18 from Latin *effluere* to run forth, from *fluere* to flow]

effluvium (ɛ'flu:vɪəm) *n, pl* **-via** (-vɪə) *or* **-viums** an unpleasant smell or exhalation, as of gaseous waste or decaying matter [C17 from Latin: a flowing out; see EFFLUENT] > **ef'fluvial** *adj*

effort ('ɛfət) *n* **1** physical or mental exertion, usually considerable when unqualified: *the rock was moved with effort* **2** a determined attempt: *our effort to save him failed* **3** achievement; creation: *a great literary effort* **4** *physics* an applied force acting against inertia [C15 from Old French *esfort*, from *esforcier* to force, ultimately from Latin *fortis* strong; see FORCE[1]] > **'effortful** *adj*

effort bargain *n* a bargain in which the reward to an employee is based on the effort that the employee puts in

effortless ('ɛfətlɪs) *adj* **1** requiring or involving little effort; easy **2** *archaic* making little effort; passive > **'effortlessly** *adv* > **'effortlessness** *n*

effrontery (ɪ'frʌntərɪ) *n, pl* **-ies** shameless or insolent boldness; impudent presumption; audacity; temerity [C18 from French *effronterie*, from Old French *esfront* barefaced, shameless, from Late Latin *effrons*, literally: putting forth one's forehead; see FRONT]

effulgent (ɪ'fʌldʒənt) *adj* radiant; brilliant [C18 from Latin *effulgēre* to shine forth, from *fulgēre* to shine] > **ef'fulgence** *n* > **ef'fulgently** *adv*

effuse *vb* (ɪ'fju:z) **1** to pour or flow out **2** to spread out; diffuse **3** (*intr*) to talk profusely, esp in an excited manner **4** to cause (a gas) to flow or (of a gas) to flow under pressure ▷ *adj* (ɪ'fju:s) **5** *botany* (esp of an inflorescence) spreading out loosely [C16 from Latin *effūsus* poured out, from *effundere* to shed, from *fundere* to pour]

effusiometer (ɪ,fju:zɪ'ɒmɪtə) *n physics* an apparatus for determining rates of effusion of gases, usually used for measuring molecular weights

effusion (ɪ'fju:ʒən) *n* **1** an unrestrained outpouring in speech or words **2** the act or process of being poured out **3** something that is poured out **4** the flow of a gas through a small aperture under pressure, esp when the density is such that the mean distance between molecules is large compared to the diameter of the aperture **5** *med* **a** the escape of blood or other fluid into a body cavity or tissue **b** the fluid that has escaped

effusive (ɪ'fju:sɪv) *adj* **1** extravagantly demonstrative of emotion; gushing **2** (of rock) formed by the solidification of magma > **ef'fusively** *adv* > **ef'fusiveness** *n*

Efik ('ɛfɪk) *n* **1** (*pl* **Efiks** *or* **Efik**) a member of a subgroup of the Ibibio people of SE Nigeria **2** the language spoken by this people, variously classified as belonging to the Benue-Congo or Kwa divisions of the Niger-Congo family

EFIS *aeronautics abbreviation for* **electronic flight information systems**

E-FIT ('i:fɪt) *n trademark* **1** a technique which uses psychological principles and computer technology to generate a likeness of a face: used by the police to trace suspects from witnesses' descriptions **2** an image generated by this technique [C20 from Electronic Facial Identification Technique]

EFL *abbreviation for* English as a Foreign Language

eft[1] (ɛft) *n* **1** a dialect or archaic name for a **newt** **2** any of certain terrestrial newts, such as *Diemictylus viridescens* (**red eft**) of eastern North America [Old English *efeta*]

eft[2] (ɛft) *adv archaic* **a** again **b** afterwards [Old English; see AFT, AFTER]

EFTA ('ɛftə) *n acronym for* European Free Trade Association; established in 1960 to eliminate trade tariffs on industrial products; now comprises Norway, Switzerland, Iceland, and Liechtenstein. Free trade was established between EFTA and the EC (now EU) in 1984. In 1994 EFTA (excluding Switzerland) and the EU together created the European Economic Area (EEA)

EFTPOS ('ɛftpɒs) *n acronym for* **electronic funds transfer at point of sale**

EFTS *computing abbreviation for* electronic funds transfer system

eftsoons (ɛft'su:nz) *adv archaic* **1** soon afterwards **2** repeatedly [Old English *eft sōna*, literally: afterwards soon]

eg *the internet domain name for* Egypt

Eg. *abbreviation for* **1** Egypt(ian) **2** Egyptology

e.g., eg. *or* **eg** *abbreviation for* exempli gratia [Latin: for example]

egad (ɪ'gæd, i:'gæd) *interj archaic* a mild oath or expression of surprise [C17 probably variant of *Ah God!*]

egalitarian (ɪ,gælɪ'tɛərɪən) *adj* **1** of, relating to, or upholding the doctrine of the equality of mankind and the desirability of political, social, and economic equality ▷ *n* **2** an adherent of egalitarian principles [C19 alteration of *equalitarian*, through influence of French *égal* EQUAL] > **e,gali'tarian,ism** *n*

Eger *n* **1** (*Hungarian* 'ɛgɛr) a city in N central Hungary. Pop: 56 696 (2003 est) **2** ('e:gər) the German name for **Cheb**

Egeria (ɪ'dʒɪərɪə) *n* a female adviser [C17 name of the mythical adviser of Numa Pompilius, king of Rome]

egest (i:'dʒɛst) *vb* (*tr*) to excrete (waste material) [C17 from Latin *ēgerere* to carry out, from *gerere* to carry] > **e'gestion** *n* > **e'gestive** *adj*

egesta (i:'dʒɛstə) *pl n* anything egested, as waste material from the body; excrement [C18 from Latin, literally: (things) carried out; see EGEST]

egg¹ (ɛg) *n* **1** the oval or round reproductive body laid by the females of birds, reptiles, fishes, insects, and some other animals, consisting of a developing embryo, its food store, and sometimes jelly or albumen, all surrounded by an outer shell or membrane **2** *Also called:* **egg cell** any female gamete; ovum **3** the egg of the domestic hen used as food **4** something resembling an egg, esp in shape or in being in an early stage of development **5** **good** (*or* **bad**) **egg** *old-fashioned informal* a good (or bad) person **a** an exclamation of delight (or dismay) **6** **lay an egg** *slang, chiefly US and Canadian* **a** to make a joke or give a performance, etc, that fails completely **b** (of a joke, performance, etc) to fail completely; flop **7** **put** *or* **have all one's eggs in one basket** to stake everything on a single venture **8** **teach one's grandmother to suck eggs** to presume to teach someone something that he knows already **9** **with egg on one's face** *informal* made to look ridiculous ▷ *vb* (*tr*) **10** to dip (food) in beaten egg before cooking **11** *US informal* to throw eggs at [C14 from Old Norse *egg*; related to Old English *æg*, Old High German *ei*]

egg² (ɛg) *vb* (*tr*; usually foll by *on*) to urge or incite, esp to daring or foolish acts [Old English *eggian*, from Old Norse *eggja* to urge; related to Old English *ecg* EDGE, Middle Low German *eggen* to harrow]

egg and dart, egg and tongue *or* **egg and anchor** *n* (in architecture and cabinetwork) **a** an ornamental moulding in which a half egg shape alternates with a dart, tongue, or anchor shape **b** (*as modifier*): *egg-and-dart moulding*

egg-and-spoon race *n* a race in which runners carry an egg balanced in a spoon

eggbeater ('ɛg,bi:tə) *n* **1** *Also called:* **eggwhisk** a kitchen utensil for beating eggs, whipping cream, etc; whisk **2** *chiefly US and Canadian* an informal name for **helicopter**

egg-binding *n* a condition with a variety of causes, such as lack of sunlight and a cold damp environment, that causes a female bird to be unable to lay an egg that she is carrying

egg-bound *adj* describing egg-bearing animals and birds that have difficulty passing their eggs

egg cup *n* a small cuplike container, used for holding a boiled egg while it is being eaten

egger *or* **eggar** ('ɛgə) *n* any of various widely distributed moths of the family *Lasiocampidae*, such as *Lasiocampa quercus* (**oak egger**) of Europe, having brown bodies and wings [C18 from EGG¹, from the egg-shaped cocoon]

egghead ('ɛg,hɛd) *n informal* an intellectual; highbrow

eggler ('ɛglə) *n archaic or dialect* an egg dealer: sometimes itinerant

eggnog (,ɛg'nɒg) *n* a drink that can be served hot or cold, made of eggs, milk, sugar, spice, and brandy, rum, or other spirit. *Also called:* **egg flip** [C19 from EGG¹ + NOG¹]

eggplant ('ɛg,plɑ:nt) *n* **1** a tropical Old World solanaceous plant, *Solanum melongena*, widely cultivated for its egg-shaped typically dark purple fruit **2** the fruit of this plant, which is cooked and eaten as a vegetable. *Also called:* **aubergine**

egg roll *n* a Chinese-American dish consisting of egg dough filled with a minced mixture of pork, bamboo shoots, onions, etc, and browned in deep fat

eggs Benedict *pl n* a dish consisting of toast, covered with a slice of ham, poached egg, and hollandaise sauce

eggshell ('ɛg,ʃɛl) *n* **1** the hard porous protective outer layer of a bird's egg, consisting of calcite and protein **2** a yellowish-white colour **3** a type of paper with a slightly rough finish **4** (*modifier*) (of paint) having a very slight sheen **5** **walk on eggshells** to be very cautious or diplomatic for fear of upsetting someone ▷ *adj* **6** of a yellowish-white colour: *eggshell paint*

eggshell porcelain *or* **china** *n* a type of very thin translucent porcelain originally made in China

egg slice *n* a spatula for removing omelettes, fried eggs, etc, from a pan

egg spoon *n* a small spoon for eating a boiled egg

egg timer *n* a device, typically a miniature hourglass, for timing the boiling of an egg

egg tooth *n* (in embryo birds and reptiles) a temporary tooth or (in birds) projection of the beak used for piercing the eggshell

egg white *n* the white of an egg; albumen

Egham ('ɛgəm) *n* a town in S England, in N Surrey on the River Thames. Pop: 27 666 (2001)

egis ('i:dʒɪs) *n* a rare spelling of **aegis**

eglandular (i:'glændjʊlə) *adj* having no glands [E-¹ + GLANDULAR]

eglantine ('ɛglən,taɪn) *n* another name for **sweetbrier** [C14 from Old French *aiglent*, ultimately from Latin *acus* needle, from *acer* sharp, keen]

EGM *abbreviation for* **extraordinary general meeting**

Egmont ('ɛgmɒnt) *n* an extinct volcano in New Zealand, in W central North Island in the **Egmont National Park**: an almost perfect cone. Height: 2518 m (8261 ft)

ego ('i:gəʊ, 'ɛgəʊ) *n, pl* **egos** **1** the self of an individual person; the conscious subject **2** *psychoanal* the conscious mind, based on perception of the environment from birth onwards: responsible for modifying the antisocial instincts of the id and itself modified by the conscience (superego) **3** one's image of oneself; morale: *to boost one's ego* **4** egotism; conceit [C19 from Latin: I]

ego boost *n* something such as praise, success, etc, that makes one feel better about oneself or raises one's morale

egocentric (,i:gəʊ'sɛntrɪk, ,ɛg-) *adj* **1** regarding everything only in relation to oneself; self-centred; selfish **2** *philosophy* pertaining to a theory in which everything is considered in relation to the self: *an egocentric universe* ▷ *n* **3** a self-centred person; egotist > ,egocen'tricity *n*

egocentrism (,i:gəʊ'sɛntrɪzəm, ,ɛgəʊ-) *n* **1** the condition or fact of being egocentric **2** *psychol* a stage in a child's development characterized by lack of awareness that other people's points of view differ from his own

ego ideal *n psychoanal* an internal ideal of personal perfection that represents what one wants to be rather than what one ought to be and is derived from one's early relationship with one's parents. See also **superego**

egoism ('i:gəʊ,ɪzəm, 'ɛg-) *n* **1** concern for one's own interests and welfare **2** *ethics* the theory that the pursuit of one's own welfare is the highest good. Compare **altruism 3** self-centredness; egotism

egoist ('i:gəʊɪst, 'ɛg-) *n* **1** a person who is preoccupied with his own interests; a selfish person **2** a conceited person; egotist **3** *ethics* a person who lives by the values of egoism > ,ego'istic *or* ,ego'istical *adj* > ,ego'istically *adv*

Egoli (ɛ'gəʊlɪ) *n* a local name for **Johannesburg** [from Zulu *eGoli* place of gold]

egomania (,i:gəʊ'meɪnɪə, ,ɛg-) *n psychiatry* **1** obsessive love for oneself and regard for one's own needs **2** any action dictated by this point of view > ,ego'mani,ac *n* > egomaniacal (,i:gəʊmə'naɪk³l, ,ɛg-) *adj*

egotism ('i:gə,tɪzəm, 'ɛgə-) *n* **1** an inflated sense of self-importance or superiority; self-centredness **2** excessive reference to oneself [C18 from Latin *ego* I + -ISM]

egotist ('i:gətɪst, 'ɛg-) *n* **1** a conceited boastful person **2** a self-interested person; egoist > ,ego'tistic *or* ,ego'tistical *adj* > ,ego'tistically *adv*

ego trip *informal* ▷ *n* **1** something undertaken to boost or draw attention to a person's own image or appraisal of himself ▷ *vb* ego-trip -trips, -tripping, -tripped (*intr*) **2** to act in this way

e-government *n* the provision of government information and services by means of the internet and other computer resources [C20 *electronic government*]

egregious (ɪ'gri:dʒəs, -dʒɪəs) *adj* **1** outstandingly bad; flagrant: *an egregious lie* **2** *archaic* distinguished; eminent [C16 from Latin *ēgregius* outstanding (literally: standing out from the herd), from *ē-* out + *grex* flock, herd] > e'gregiously *adv* > e'gregiousness *n*

egress *n* ('i:grɛs) **1** *Also called:* **egression** the act of going or coming out; emergence **2** a way out, such as a path; exit **3** the right or permission to go out or depart **4** *astronomy* another name for **emersion** (sense 2) ▷ *vb* (ɪ'grɛs) (*intr*) **5** to go forth; issue [C16 from Latin *ēgredī* to come forth, depart, from *gradī* to move, step]

egret ('i:grɪt) *n* any of various wading birds of the genera *Egretta, Hydranassa*, etc, that are similar to herons but usually have a white plumage and, in the breeding season, long feathery plumes (see **aigrette**): family *Ardeidae*, order *Ciconiiformes* [C15 from Old French *aigrette*, from Old Provençal *aigreta*, from *aigron* heron, of Germanic origin; compare Old High German *heigaro* HERON]

Egypt ('i:dʒɪpt) *n* a republic in NE Africa, on the Mediterranean and Red Sea: its history dates back about 5000 years. Occupied by the British from 1882, it became an independent kingdom in 1922 and a republic in 1953. Over 96 per cent of the total area is desert, with the chief areas of habitation and cultivation in the Nile delta and valley. Cotton is the main export. Official language: Arabic. Official religion: Muslim; Sunni majority. Currency: pound. Capital: Cairo. Pop: 73 389 000 (2004 est). Area: 997 739 sq km (385 229 sq miles). Official name: **Arab Republic of Egypt** Former official name (1958–71): **United Arab Republic**

Egyptian (ɪ'dʒɪpʃən) *adj* **1** of, relating to, or characteristic of Egypt, its inhabitants, or their dialect of Arabic **2** of, relating to, or characteristic of the ancient Egyptians, their language, or culture **3** (of type) having square slab serifs **4** *archaic* of or relating to the Gypsies ▷ *n* **5** a native or inhabitant of Egypt **6** a member of an indigenous non-Semitic people who established an advanced civilization in Egypt that flourished from the late fourth millennium BC **7** the extinct language of the ancient Egyptians, belonging to the Afro-Asiatic family of languages. It is recorded in hieroglyphic inscriptions, the earliest of which date from before 3000 BC. It was extinct by the fourth century AD. See also **Coptic 8** a large size of drawing paper **9** an archaic name for a **Gypsy**

Egyptian jasper *n* a type of jasper, generally with zones of colour, found in desert regions of Egypt

Egyptian Mau (maʊ) *n* a breed of medium-sized cat with a spotted coat of medium length [Arabic *mau* cat]

Egyptology (,i:dʒɪp'tɒlədʒɪ) *n* the study of the archaeology and language of ancient Egypt > Egyptological (ɪ,dʒɪptə'lɒdʒɪk³l) *adj* > ,Egyp'tologist *n*

eh¹ (eɪ) *interj* an exclamation used to express questioning surprise or to seek the repetition or confirmation of a statement or question: *Eh? What did you say?*

eh² *the internet domain name for* Western Sahara

EHF *abbreviation for* **extremely high frequency**

EHO (in Britain) *abbreviation for* **Environmental Health Officer**

E hoa (ɛ hɒ:ə) *n* **1** friend; pal ▷ *sentence substitute* **2** hello! [Māori]

EHV *abbreviation for* equine herpesvirus

EI *abbreviation for* **1** East Indian **2** East Indies **3** *social psychol* emotional intelligence **4** (in Canada) Employment Insurance

EIA *abbreviation for* equine infectious anaemia

EIB *abbreviation for* European Investment Bank

eider *or* **eider duck** ('aɪdə) *n* any of several sea ducks of the genus *Somateria*, esp *S. mollissima*, and related genera, which occur in the N hemisphere.

e

The male has black and white plumage, and the female is the source of eiderdown [c18 from Old Norse æthr; related to Swedish ejder, Dutch, German *Eider*]

eiderdown ('aɪdə,daʊn) *n* **1** the breast down of the female eider duck, with which it lines the nest, used for stuffing pillows, quilts, etc **2** a thick warm cover for a bed, made of two layers of material enclosing a soft filling **3** *US* a warm cotton fabric having a woollen nap

eidetic (aɪ'dɛtɪk) *adj psychol* **1** (of visual, or sometimes auditory, images) exceptionally vivid and allowing detailed recall of something previously perceived: thought to be common in children **2** relating to or subject to such imagery [c20 from Greek *eidētikos*, from *eidos* shape, form] > ei'detically *adv*

eidolon (aɪ'dəʊlɒn) *n, pl* -la (-lə) *or* -lons **1** an unsubstantial image; apparition; phantom **2** an ideal or idealized figure [c19 from Greek: phantom, IDOL]

Eid-ul-Adha ('iːdʊl,ɑːdə) *n* an annual Muslim festival marking the end of the pilgrimage to Mecca. Animals are sacrificed and their meat shared among the poor [from Arabic *id ul adha* festival of sacrifice]

Eid-ul-Fitr ('iːdʊl,fiːtə) *n* an annual Muslim festival marking the end of Ramadan, involving the exchange of gifts and a festive meal [from Arabic *id ul fitr* festival of fast-breaking]

Eifel ('aɪfəl; German 'aifəl) *n* a plateau region in W Germany, between the River Moselle and the Belgian frontier: quarrying

Eiffel Tower *n* a tower in Paris: designed by A G Eiffel; erected for the 1889 Paris Exposition. Height: 300 m (984 ft), raised in 1959 to 321 m (1052 ft)

eigen *combining form* characteristic; proper: *eigenvalue* [from German, literally: own]

eigenfrequency ('aɪgən,friː kwənsɪ) *n, pl* -cies *physics* a resonance frequency of a system

eigenfunction ('aɪgən,fʌŋkʃən) *n maths, physics* a function satisfying a differential equation, esp an allowed function for a system in wave mechanics

eigentone ('aɪgən,təʊn) *n* a characteristic acoustic resonance frequency of a system

eigenvalue ('aɪgən,væljuː) *n maths, physics* one of the particular values of a certain parameter for which a differential equation or matrix equation has an eigenfunction. In wave mechanics an eigenvalue is equivalent to the energy of a quantum state of a system

eigenvector ('aɪgən,vɛktə) *n maths, physics* a vector *x* satisfying an equation $Ax = \lambda x$, where *A* is a square matrix and λ is a constant

Eiger (German 'aigər) *n* a mountain in central Switzerland, in the Bernese Alps. Height: 3970 m (13 025 ft)

eight (eɪt) *n* **1** the cardinal number that is the sum of one and seven and the product of two and four. See also **number** (sense 1) **2** a numeral, 8, VIII, etc, representing this number **3** *music* the numeral 8 used as the lower figure in a time signature to indicate that the beat is measured in quavers **4** the amount or quantity that is one greater than seven **5** something representing, represented by, or consisting of eight units, such as a playing card with eight symbols on it **6** *rowing* **a** a racing shell propelled by eight oarsmen **b** the crew of such a shell **7** Also called: **eight o'clock** eight hours after noon or midnight **8** **have one over the eight** *slang* to be drunk **9** See **figure of eight** ▷ *determiner* **10** **a** amounting to eight **b** (*as pronoun*): *I could only find eight* ▷ Related prefixes: **octa-, octo-** [Old English *eahta*; related to Old High German *ahto*, Old Norse *ātta*, Old Irish *ocht*, Latin *octō*, Greek *okto*, Sanskrit *astau*]

eight ball *n US and Canadian* **1** (in pool) the black ball, marked with the number eight **2** **behind the eight ball** in a difficult situation; snookered

eighteen ('eɪ'tiːn) *n* **1** the cardinal number that is the sum of ten and eight and the product of two

and nine. See also **number** (sense 1) **2** a numeral, 18, XVIII, etc, representing this number **3** the amount or quantity that is eight more than ten **4** something represented by, representing, or consisting of 18 units **5** (*functioning as singular or plural*) a team of 18 players in Australian Rules football ▷ *determiner* **6** **a** amounting to eighteen: *eighteen weeks* **b** (*as pronoun*): *eighteen of them knew* [Old English *eahtatēne*; related to Old Norse *attjan*, Old High German *ahtozehan*]

eighteenmo ('eɪ'tiːnməʊ) *n, pl* -mos **1** Also called: **octodecimo** a book size resulting from folding a sheet of paper into 18 leaves or 36 pages. Often written: 18mo, 18° **2** a book of this size

eighteenth ('eɪ'tiːnθ) *adj* **1** (*usually prenominal*) **a** coming after the seventeenth in numbering or counting order, position, time, etc; being the ordinal number of *eighteen*: often written 18th **b** (*as noun*): *come on the eighteenth* ▷ *n* **2** **a** one of 18 approximately equal parts of something **b** (*as modifier*): *an eighteenth part* **3** the fraction that is equal to one divided by 18 (1/18)

eightfold ('eɪt,fəʊld) *adj* **1** equal to or having eight times as many or as much **2** composed of eight parts ▷ *adv* **3** by or up to eight times as much

eighth (eɪtθ) *adj* **1** (*usually prenominal*) **a** coming after the seventh and before the ninth in numbering or counting order, position, time, etc; being the ordinal number of *eight*: often written 8th **b** (*as noun*): *the eighth in line* ▷ *n* **2** **a** one of eight equal or nearly equal parts of an object, quantity, measurement, etc **b** (*as modifier*): *an eighth part* **3** the fraction equal to one divided by eight (1/8) **4** another word for **octave** ▷ *adv* **5** Also: **eighthly** after the seventh person, position, event, etc

eighth note *n music, US and Canadian* a note having the time value of an eighth of a semibreve. Also called (in Britain and certain other countries): **quaver**

eightieth ('eɪtɪɪθ) *adj* **1** (*usually prenominal*) **a** being the ordinal number of *eighty* in numbering or counting order, position, time, etc: often written 80th **b** (*as noun*): *the eightieth in succession* ▷ *n* **2** **a** one of 80 approximately equal parts of something **b** (*as modifier*): *an eightieth part* **3** the fraction equal to one divided by 80 (1/80)

eightsome reel ('eɪtsəm) *n* a Scottish dance for eight people

eightvo ('eɪtvəʊ) *n, pl* -vos *bookbinding* another word for **octavo**

eighty ('eɪtɪ) *n, pl* -ies **1** the cardinal number that is the product of ten and eight. See also **number** (sense 1) **2** a numeral, 80, LXXX, etc, representing this number **3** (*plural*) the numbers 80–89, esp a person's age or the year of a particular century **4** the amount or quantity that is eight times as big as ten **5** something represented by, representing, or consisting of 80 units ▷ *determiner* **6** **a** amounting to eighty: *eighty pages of nonsense* **b** (*as pronoun*): *eighty are expected* [Old English *eahtatig*; related to Old Frisian *achtig*, Old High German *ahtozug*]

eighty-seven *n cricket* a score traditionally regarded as being unlucky [possibly because 13 less than a century]

eikon ('aɪkɒn) *n* a variant spelling of **icon**

Eilat, Elat *or* **Elath** (eɪ'laːt) *n* a port in S Israel, on the Gulf of Aqaba: Israel's only outlet to the Red Sea. Pop: 43 500 (2003 est)

Eilean Donan Castle ('eɪlən 'dɒnən) *n* a castle near the Kyle of Lochalsh in Highland, Scotland: built in the 13th century; famous for its picturesque setting

Eilean Siar ('eɪlən 'sɪə) *n* the Scottish Gaelic name for **Western Isles**

eina ('eɪnaː) *interj South African* an exclamation of sudden pain [c19 Afrikaans, from Khoi]

Eindhoven (Dutch 'aɪnt,həʊvən, 'eɪnthoːvə) *n* a city in the SE Netherlands, in North Brabant province: radio and electrical industry. Pop: 206 000 (2003 est)

einkorn ('aɪn,kɔːn) *n* a variety of wheat, *Triticum monococcum*, of Greece and SW Asia, having pale red kernels, and cultivated in hilly regions as grain for horses [c20 from German, literally: one kernel]

Einsteinian (aɪn'staɪnɪən) *adj* of or relating to Albert Einstein, the US physicist and mathematician, born in Germany (1879–1955)

einsteinium (aɪn'staɪnɪəm) *n* a metallic transuranic element artificially produced from plutonium. Symbol: Es; atomic no.: 99; half-life of most stable isotope, ^{252}Es: 276 days [c20 New Latin, named after Albert Einstein (1879–1955), German-born US physicist and mathematician]

Einstein shift ('aɪnstaɪn) *n astronomy* a small displacement towards the red in the spectra, caused by the interaction between the radiation and the gravitational field of a massive body, such as the sun

Einstein's mass-energy law *n* the principle that mass (*m*) and energy (*E*) are equivalent according to the equation $E = mc^2$, where *c* is the velocity of light

Einstein's photoelectric law *n* the principle that the maximum energy of a photoelectron is *hv* – Φ, where *v* is the frequency of the incident radiation, *h* is the Planck constant, and Φ is the work function

Eire ('ɛərə) *n* **1** the Irish Gaelic name for **Ireland**[1]: often used to mean the **Republic of Ireland** **2** a former name for the **Republic of Ireland** (1937–49)

eirenic (aɪ'riːnɪk) *adj* a variant spelling of **irenic**

eirenicon *or* **irenicon** (aɪ'riːnɪ,kɒn) *n* a proposition that attempts to harmonize conflicting viewpoints [c19 from Greek, from *eirēnikos* of or concerning peace, from *eirēnē* peace]

eisegesis (,aɪsə'dʒiːsɪs) *n, pl* -ses (-siːz) the interpretation of a text, esp a biblical text, using one's own ideas. Compare **exegesis** [c19 from Greek *eis* into, in + *-egesis*, as in EXEGESIS]

Eisenach (German 'aizənax) *n* a city in central Germany, in Thuringia: birthplace of Johann Sebastian Bach. Pop: 44 081 (2003 est)

Eisenstadt (German 'aizənʃtat) *n* a town in E Austria, capital of Burgenland province: Hungarian until 1921. Pop: 11 334 (2001)

eish (eɪʃ) *interj South African* an exclamation expressive of surprise, agreement, disapproval, etc [from Zulu]

Eisk *or* **Eysk** (Russian jejsk) *n* variant transliterations of the Russian name for **Yeisk**

eisteddfod (aɪ'stɛdfəd; Welsh aɪ'stɛðvɒd) *n, pl* -fods *or* -fodau (Welsh aɪ,stɛð'vɒdaɪ) any of a number of annual festivals in Wales, esp the **Royal National Eisteddfod**, in which competitions are held in music, poetry, drama, and the fine arts [c19 from Welsh, literally: session, from *eistedd* to sit (from *sedd* seat) + *-fod*, from *bod* to be] > ,eistedd'fodic *adj*

either ('aɪðə, 'iːðə) *determiner* **1** one or the other (of two): *either coat will do* **b** (*as pronoun*): *either is acceptable* **2** both one and the other: *there were ladies at either end of the table* **3** (*coordinating*) used preceding two or more possibilities joined by "*or*": *you may have either cheese or a sweet* ▷ *adv* (*sentence modifier*) **4** (*used with a negative*) used to indicate that the clause immediately preceding is a partial reiteration of a previous clause: *John isn't a liar, but he isn't exactly honest either* [Old English *ægther*, short for *ǣghwæther* each of two; related to Old Frisian *ēider*, Old High German *ēogihweder*; see EACH, WHETHER]

USAGE *Either* is followed by a singular verb in good usage: *either is good; either of these books is useful*. Care should be taken to avoid ambiguity when using *either* to mean *both* or *each*, as in the following sentence: *a ship could be moored on either side of the channel*. Agreement between the verb and its subject in *either...or...* constructions follows the pattern given for *neither...nor...* See at **neither**

either-or *adj* presenting an unavoidable need to choose between two alternatives: *an either-or situation*

Eivissa (əɪˈβisə) *n* the Catalan name for **Ibiza**

ejaculate *vb* (ɪˈdʒækjʊˌleɪt) **1** to eject or discharge (semen) in orgasm **2** (*tr*) to utter abruptly; blurt out ▷ *n* (ɪˈdʒækjʊlɪt) **3** another word for **semen** [c16 from Latin *ējaculārī* to hurl out, from *jaculum* javelin, from *jacere* to throw] > e'jacu,lator *n*

ejaculation (ɪˌdʒækjʊˈleɪʃən) *n* **1** an abrupt emphatic utterance or exclamation **2** a discharge of semen > e'jaculatory *or* e'jaculative *adj*

ejaculatio praecox (ɪˌdʒækjʊˈleɪʃɪəʊ ˈpriːkɒks) *n* premature ejaculation during sexual intercourse [Latin]

eject (ɪˈdʒɛkt) *vb* **1** (*tr*) to drive or force out; expel or emit **2** (*tr*) to compel (a person) to leave; evict; dispossess **3** (*tr*) to dismiss, as from office **4** (*intr*) to leave an aircraft rapidly, using an ejection seat or capsule **5** (*tr*) *psychiatry* to attribute (one's own motivations and characteristics) to others [c15 from Latin *ejicere*, from *jacere* to throw] > e'jection *n*

ejecta (ɪˈdʒɛktə) *pl n* matter thrown out of a crater by an erupting volcano or during a meteorite impact [c19 Latin, literally: (things) ejected; see EJECT]

ejection seat *or* **ejector seat** *n* a seat, esp as fitted to military aircraft, that is fired by a cartridge or rocket to eject the occupant from the aircraft in an emergency

ejective (ɪˈdʒɛktɪv) *adj* **1** relating to or causing ejection **2** *phonetics* (of a plosive or fricative consonant, as in some African languages) pronounced with a glottal stop ▷ *n* **3** *phonetics* an ejective consonant > e'jectively *adv*

ejectment (ɪˈdʒɛktmənt) *n* **1** *property law* (formerly) an action brought by a wrongfully dispossessed owner seeking to recover possession of his land **2** the act of ejecting or state of being ejected; dispossession

ejector (ɪˈdʒɛktə) *n* **1** a person or thing that ejects **2** the mechanism in a firearm that ejects the empty cartridge or shell after firing

Ekaterinburg (Russian jɪkətɪrɪnˈburk) *n* a variant transliteration of the Russian name for Yekaterinburg

Ekaterinodar (Russian jɪkətɪrɪnaˈdar) *n* the former name (until 1920) of **Krasnodar**

Ekaterinoslav (Russian jɪkətɪrɪnaˈslaf) *n* the former name (1787–96, 1802–1926) of **Dnepropetrovsk**

eke[1] (iːk) *vb* (*tr*) *archaic* to increase, enlarge, or lengthen [Old English *eacan*; related to Old Norse *auka* to increase, Latin *augēre* to increase]

eke[2] (iːk) *sentence connector* *archaic* also; moreover [Old English *eac*; related to Old Norse, Gothic *auk* also, Old High German *ouh*, Latin *autem* but, *aut* or]

eke out *vb* (*tr, adverb*) **1** to make (a supply) last, esp by frugal use: *they eked out what little food was left* **2** to support (existence) with difficulty and effort **3** to add to (something insufficient), esp with effort: *to eke out an income with evening work*

EKG (in the US and Canada) *abbreviation for* **1** electrocardiogram **2** electrocardiograph

ekistics (ɪˈkɪstɪks) *n* (*functioning as singular*) the science or study of human settlements [c20 from Greek *oikistikos* of or concerning settlements, from *oikizein* to settle (a colony), from *oikos* a house] > e'kistic *or* e'kistical *adj* > ,ekis'tician *n*

Ekman layer (Swedish ˈɛkman) *n* the thin top layer of the sea that flows at 90° to the wind direction, discovered by Vagn Walfrid Ekman (1874–1954), Swedish oceanographer

Ekman Spiral *n* a complex interaction on the surface of the sea between wind, rotation of the earth, and friction forces, discovered by Vagn Walfrid Ekman (1874–1954)

ekpwele (ɛkˈpweɪleɪ) *or* **ekuele** (ɛɪˈkweɪleɪ) *n, pl* -le (-leɪ) a former monetary unit of Equatorial Guinea [from the native name in Equatorial Guinea]

ek se (ɛk seɪ) *sentence substitute* *South African* an expression used to seek agreement, for emphasis, etc [Afrikaans, literally: I say]

el (ɛl) *n* *US informal* a shortened form of **elevated railway** *or* **railroad**

El Aaiún (ɛl aɪˈjuːn) *n* a city in Western Sahara, controlled by Morocco: the capital of the former Spanish Sahara; port facilities for rich phosphate deposits nearby. Pop: 197 000 (2005 est). Moroccan (French) name: Laâyoune

elaborate *adj* (ɪˈlæbərɪt) **1** planned or executed with care and exactness; detailed **2** marked by complexity, ornateness, or detail ▷ *vb* (ɪˈlæbəˌreɪt) **3** (*intr*; usually foll by *on* or *upon*) to add information or detail (to an account); expand (upon) **4** (*tr*) to work out in detail; develop **5** (*tr*) to make more complicated or ornate **6** (*tr*) to produce by careful labour; create **7** (*tr*) *physiol* to change (food or simple substances) into more complex substances for use in the body [c16 from Latin *elabōrāre* to take pains, from *labōrāre* to toil] > e'laborately *adv* > e'laborateness *n* > e,labo'ration *n* > elaborative (ɪˈlæbərətɪv) *adj* > e'labo,rator *n*

elaeoptene (ˌɛlɪˈɒptiːn) *n* a variant spelling of **eleoptene**

elaiosome (ɪˈleɪəsəʊm) *n* an oil-rich body on seeds or fruits that attracts ants, which act as dispersal agents [from Greek *elaion* oil + -SOME[3]]

El Alamein *or* **Alamein** (ɛl ˈæləˌmeɪn) *n* a village on the N coast of Egypt, about 112 km (70 miles) west of Alexandria: scene of a decisive Allied victory over the Axis forces (1942)

Elam (ˈiːləm) *n* an ancient kingdom east of the River Tigris: established before 4000 BC; probably inhabited by a non-Semitic people

Elamite (ˈiːləˌmaɪt) *n* **1** an inhabitant of the ancient kingdom of Elam **2** Also called: Elamitic, Susian the extinct language of this people, of no known relationship, recorded in cuneiform inscriptions dating from the 25th to the 4th centuries BC ▷ *adj* **3** of or relating to Elam, its people, or their language

élan (eɪˈlɑːn, eɪˈlæn; French elɑ̃) *n* a combination of style and vigour: *he performed the concerto with élan* [c19 from French, from *élancer* to throw forth, ultimately from Latin *lancea* LANCE]

eland (ˈiːlənd) *n* **1** a large spiral-horned antelope, *Taurotragus oryx*, inhabiting bushland in eastern and southern Africa. It has a dewlap and a hump on the shoulders and is light brown with vertical white stripes **2** giant eland a similar but larger animal, *T. derbianus*, living in wooded areas of central and W Africa [c18 via Afrikaans from Dutch *eland* elk; related to Old Slavonic *jeleni* stag, Greek *ellos* fawn]

élan vital French (elɑ̃ vital) *n* a creative principle held by Henri Bergson to be present in all organisms and responsible for evolution. Compare **Bergsonism** [literally: vital impetus]

elapid (ˈɛləpɪd) *n* **1** any venomous snake of the mostly tropical family *Elapidae*, having fixed poison fangs at the front of the upper jaw and including the cobras, coral snakes, and mambas ▷ *adj* **2** of, relating to, or belonging to the *Elapidae* [c19 from New Latin *Elapidae*, from Medieval Greek *elaps, elops* a fish, sea serpent; perhaps related to Greek *lepis* scale]

elapse (ɪˈlæps) *vb* (*intr*) (of time) to pass by [c17 from Latin *ēlābī* to slip away, from *lābī* to slip, glide]

Elara (ɛˈlærə) *n* *astronomy* a small satellite of Jupiter in an intermediate orbit

elasmobranch (ɪˈlæsməˌbræŋk, ɪˈlæz-) *n* **1** any cartilaginous fish of the subclass *Elasmobranchii* (or *Selachii*), which includes the sharks, rays, dogfish, and skates ▷ *adj* **2** of, relating to, or belonging to the *Elasmobranchii* ▷ Also called: selachian [c19 from New Latin *elasmobranchii*, from Greek *elasmos* metal plate + *brankhia* gills]

elasmosaur (ɪˈlæzməˌsɔː) *n* a very long-necked extinct marine reptile: a type of plesiosaur [c19 from Greek *elasmos* metal plate + *sauros* lizard]

elastance (ɪˈlæstəns) *n* *physics* the reciprocal of capacitance. It is measured in reciprocal farads (darafs) [c19 from ELASTIC + -ANCE]

elastane (ɪˈlæsteɪn) *n* a synthetic fibre characterized by its ability to revert to its original shape after being stretched

elastase (ɪˈlæsteɪs) *n* an enzyme that digests elastin

elastic (ɪˈlæstɪk) *adj* **1** (of a body or material) capable of returning to its original shape after compression, expansion, stretching, or other deformation **2** capable of adapting to change: *an elastic schedule* **3** quick to recover from fatigue, dejection, etc; buoyant **4** springy or resilient: *an elastic walk* **5** (of gases) capable of expanding spontaneously **6** *physics* (of collisions) involving no overall change in translational kinetic energy **7** made of elastic ▷ *n* **8** tape, cord, or fabric containing interwoven strands of flexible rubber or similar substance allowing it to stretch and return to its original shape **9** *chiefly US and Canadian* something made of elastic, such as a rubber band or a garter [c17 from New Latin *elasticus* impulsive, from Greek *elastikos*, from *elaunein* to beat, drive] > e'lastically *adv*

elasticate (ɪˈlæstɪˌkeɪt) *vb* (*tr*) to insert elastic sections or thread into (a fabric or garment): *an elasticated waistband* > e,lasti'cation *n*

elastic band *n* another name for **rubber band**

elasticity (ɪlæˈstɪsɪtɪ, ˌiːlæ-) *n* **1** the property of a body or substance that enables it to resume its original shape or size when a distorting force is removed. See also **elastic limit** **2** the state or quality of being elastic; flexibility or buoyancy **3** a measure of the sensitivity of demand for goods or services to changes in price or other marketing variables, such as advertising

elasticize *or* **elasticise** (ɪˈlæstɪˌsaɪz) *vb* (*tr*) **1** to make elastic **2** another word for **elasticate**

elastic limit *n* the greatest stress that can be applied to a material without causing permanent deformation

elastic modulus *n* another name for **modulus of elasticity**

elastic rebound *n* *geology* a theory of earthquakes that envisages gradual deformation of the fault zone without fault slippage until friction is overcome, when the fault suddenly slips to produce the earthquake

elastin (ɪˈlæstɪn) *n* *biochem* a fibrous scleroprotein constituting the major part of elastic tissue, such as the walls of arteries [c19 from ELASTIC + -IN]

elastomer (ɪˈlæstəmə) *n* any material, such as natural or synthetic rubber, that is able to resume its original shape when a deforming force is removed [c20 from ELASTIC + -MER] > elastomeric (ɪˌlæstəˈmɛrɪk) *adj*

Elastoplast (ɪˈlæstəˌplɑːst) *n* trademark a gauze surgical dressing backed by adhesive tape

Elat *or* **Elath** (eɪˈlɑːt) *n* variant spellings of **Eilat**

elate (ɪˈleɪt) *vb* (*tr*) to fill with high spirits, exhilaration, pride or optimism [c16 from Latin *ēlāt-* stem of past participle of *efferre* to bear away, from *ferre* to carry]

elated (ɪˈleɪtɪd) *adj* full of high spirits, exhilaration, pride or optimism; very happy > e'latedly *adv* > e'latedness *n*

elater (ˈɛlətə) *n* **1** an elaterid beetle **2** *botany* a spirally thickened filament, occurring in liverwort capsules and horsetails, thought to aid dispersal of spores [c17 via New Latin from Greek: driver, from *elaunein* to beat, drive; compare ELASTIC]

elaterid (ɪˈlætərɪd) *n* **1** any of the beetles constituting the widely distributed family *Elateridae* (click beetles). The group includes the wireworms and certain fireflies ▷ *adj* **2** of, relating to, or belonging to the family *Elateridae* [c19 from New Latin *Elateridae*, from ELATER]

elaterin (ɪˈlætərɪn) *n* a white crystalline substance found in elaterium, used as a purgative [c19 from ELATERIUM + -IN]

elaterite (ɪ'lætəˌraɪt) *n* a dark brown naturally occurring bitumen resembling rubber [c19 from ELATER + -ITE[1]]

elaterium (ˌɛlə'tɪərɪəm) *n* a greenish sediment prepared from the juice of the squirting cucumber, used as a purgative [c16 from Latin, from Greek *elatērion* squirting cucumber, from *elatērios* purgative, from *elaunein* to drive]

elation (ɪ'leɪʃən) *n* joyfulness or exaltation of spirit, as from success, pleasure, or relief; high spirits

elative ('iːlətɪv) *adj* **1** (in the grammar of Finnish and other languages) denoting a case of nouns expressing a relation of motion or direction, usually translated by the English prepositions *out of* or *away from*. Compare **illative** (sense 3) ▷ *n* **2 a** the elative case **b** an elative word or speech element [c19 from Latin *ēlātus*, past participle of *efferre* to carry out; see ELATE]

E layer *n* another name for **E region**

Elba ('ɛlbə) *n* a mountainous island off the W coast of Italy, in the Mediterranean: Napoleon Bonaparte's first place of exile (1814–15). Pop: 27 722 (1991 est). Area: 223 sq km (86 sq miles)

Elbe (ɛlb; *German* 'ɛlbə) *n* a river in central Europe, rising in the N Czech Republic and flowing generally northwest through Germany to the North Sea at Hamburg. Length: 1165 km (724 miles). Czech name: **Labe**

Elbert ('ɛlbət) *n* **Mount** a mountain in central Colorado, in the Sawatch range. Height: 4399 m (14 431 ft)

Elbląg (*Polish* 'ɛlblɔŋk) *n* a port in N Poland: metallurgical industries. Pop: 129 000 (2005 est). German name: **Elbing** ('ɛlbɪŋ)

elbow ('ɛlbəʊ) *n* **1** the joint between the upper arm and the forearm, formed by the junction of the radius and ulna with the humerus **2** the corresponding joint or bone of birds or mammals **3** the part of a garment that covers the elbow **4** something resembling an elbow, such as a sharp bend in a road or river **5 at one's elbow** within easy reach **6 out at elbow(s)** ragged or impoverished **7 up to the elbows with** *or* **in** busily occupied with; deeply immersed in ▷ *vb* **8** (*tr*) to reject; dismiss. Also: **give the elbow 9** to make (one's way) by shoving, jostling, etc **10** (*tr*) to knock or shove with or as if with the elbow [Old English *elnboga*; see ELL[2], BOW[2]; related to Old Norse *olbogi*, Old High German *elinbogo*]

elbow grease *n facetious* vigorous physical labour, esp hard rubbing

elbowroom ('ɛlbəʊˌruːm, -ˌrʊm) *n* sufficient scope to move or function

Elbrus (ɪl'bruːs) *n* a mountain in SW Russia, on the border with Georgia, in the Caucasus Mountains, with two extinct volcanic peaks: the highest mountain in Europe. Height: 5642 m (18 510 ft)

Elburz Mountains (ɛl'bʊəz) *pl n* a mountain range in N Iran, parallel to the SW and S shores of the Caspian Sea. Highest peak: Mount Demavend, 5601 m (18 376 ft)

El Capitan (ɛl ˌkapɪ'tæn) *n* a mountain in E central California, in the Sierra Nevada: a monolith with a precipice rising over 1100 m (3600 ft) above the floor of the Yosemite Valley. Height: 2306 m (7564 ft)

Elche (*Spanish* 'eltʃe) *n* a town in S Spain, in Valencia: noted for Iberian and Roman archaeological finds and the medieval religious drama performed there annually: fruit growing, esp dates, pomegranates, figs. Pop: 207 163 (2003 est). Catalan name: **Elx**

eld (ɛld) *n archaic* **1** old age **2** olden days; antiquity [Old English *eldu*; related to Old Norse *elli*; see OLD]

elder[1] ('ɛldə) *adj* **1** born earlier; senior. Compare **older 2** (in piquet and similar card games) denoting or relating to the nondealer (the **elder hand**), who has certain advantages in the play **3** *archaic* **a** prior in rank, position, or office **b** of a previous time; former ▷ *n* **4** an older person; one's senior **5** *anthropol* a senior member of a tribe who has influence or authority **6** (in certain Protestant Churches) a lay office having teaching, pastoral, or administrative functions **7** another word for **presbyter** [Old English *eldra*, comparative of *eald* OLD; related to Old Norse *ellri*, Old High German *altiro*, Gothic *althiza*] > '**elder**ˌ**ship** *n*

elder[2] ('ɛldə) *n* **1** Also called: **elderberry** any of various caprifoliaceous shrubs or small trees of the genus *Sambucus*, having clusters of small white flowers and red, purple, or black berry-like fruits **2** any of various unrelated plants, such as box elder and marsh elder ▷ Compare **alder** [Old English *ellern*; related to Old Norse *elrir*, Old High German *erlīn*, Old Slavonic *jelĭcha*, Latin *alnus*]

elderberry ('ɛldəˌbɛrɪ) *n, pl* **-ries 1** the berry-like fruit of the elder, used for making wines, jellies, etc **2** another name for **elder[1]** (sense 1)

Elder Brethren *pl n* the senior members of the governing body of Trinity House

elderly ('ɛldəlɪ) *adj* (of people) **a** quite old; past middle age **b** (*as collective noun; preceded by* the): *the elderly*. Related adj: **geriatric**. > '**elderliness** *n*

elder statesman *n* an old, experienced, and eminent person, esp a politician, whose advice is often sought

eldest ('ɛldɪst) *adj* being the oldest, esp the oldest surviving child of the same parents [Old English *eldesta*, superlative of *eald* OLD]

ELDO ('ɛldəʊ) *n acronym for* European Launcher Development Organization

El Dorado (ɛl dɒ'rɑːdəʊ; *Spanish* el do'raðo) *n* **1** a fabled city in South America, rich in treasure and sought by Spanish explorers in the 16th century **2** Also: **eldorado** any place of great riches or fabulous opportunity [c16 from Spanish, literally: the gilded (place)]

ELDR *abbreviation for* European Democratic and Reform Party: a European political party since 1993

eldritch *or* **eldrich** ('ɛldrɪtʃ) *adj poetic, Scot* unearthly; weird [c16 perhaps from Old English *ælf* ELF + *rīce* realm; see RICH]

Elea ('iːlɪə) *n* (in ancient Italy) a Greek colony on the Tyrrhenian coast of Lucana

Eleanor Cross ('ɛlɪnə, -ˌnɔː) *n* any of the crosses erected at each place where the body of Eleanor of Castile (1246–90, Edward I's Spanish wife) rested between Nottingham (where she died) and London (where she is buried)

e-learning *n* an internet-based teaching system [c20 electronic *learning*]

Eleatic (ˌɛlɪ'ætɪk) *adj* **1** denoting or relating to a school of philosophy founded in Elea in Greece in the 6th century BC by Xenophanes, Parmenides, and Zeno. It held that one pure immutable Being is the only object of knowledge and that information obtained by the senses is illusory ▷ *n* **2** a follower of this school > **Eleaticism** (ˌɛlɪ'ætɪˌsɪzəm) *n*

elecampane (ˌɛlɪkæm'peɪn) *n* a perennial flowering plant, *Inula helenium*, of Europe, Asia, and North America having large hairy leaves and narrow yellow petals: family *Asteraceae* (composites) [c16 from Medieval Latin *enula campāna*, from *enula* (from Greek *helenion*) + *campānus* of the field]

elect (ɪ'lɛkt) *vb* **1** (*tr*) to choose (someone) to be (a representative or a public official) by voting: *they elected him Mayor* **2** to select; choose: *to elect to die rather than surrender* **3** (*tr*) (of God) to select or predestine for the grace of salvation ▷ *adj* **4** (*immediately postpositive*) voted into office but not yet installed: *the president elect* **5 a** chosen or choice; selected or elite **b** (*as collective noun*; preceded by *the*): *the elect* **6** *Christianity* **a** selected or predestined by God to receive salvation; chosen **b** (*as collective noun;* preceded by *the*): *the elect* [c15 from Latin *ēligere* to select, from *legere* to choose] > **e'lectable** *adj*

election (ɪ'lɛkʃən) *n* **1** the selection by vote of a person or persons from among candidates for a position, esp a political office **2** a public vote on an official proposition **3** the act or an instance of choosing **4** *Christianity* **a** the doctrine of Calvin that God chooses certain individuals for salvation without reference to their faith or works **b** the doctrine of Arminius and others that God chooses for salvation those who, by grace, persevere in faith and works

electioneer (ɪˌlɛkʃə'nɪə) *vb* (*intr*) **1** to be active in a political election or campaign ▷ *n* **2** a person who engages in this activity > **e**ˌ**lection'eering** *n, adj*

elective (ɪ'lɛktɪv) *adj* **1** of or based on selection by vote: *elective procedure* **2** selected by vote: *an elective official* **3** having the power to elect **4** open to choice; optional: *an elective course of study* ▷ *n* **5** an optional course or hospital placement undertaken by a medical student > **e'lectively** *adv* > **electivity** (ˌiːlɛk'tɪvɪtɪ) *or* **e'lectiveness** *n*

elector (ɪ'lɛktə) *n* **1** someone who is eligible to vote in the election of a government **2** (*often capital*) a member of the US electoral college **3** (*often capital*) (in the Holy Roman Empire) any of the German princes entitled to take part in the election of a new emperor > **e'lector**ˌ**ship** *n*

electoral (ɪ'lɛktərəl) *adj* relating to or consisting of electors > **e'lectorally** *adv*

electoral college *n* **1** (*often capitals*) *US* a body of electors chosen by the voters who formally elect the president and vice president **2** any body of electors with similar functions

electorate (ɪ'lɛktərɪt) *n* **1** the body of all qualified voters **2** the rank, position, or territory of an elector of the Holy Roman Empire **3** *Austral and NZ* the area represented by a Member of Parliament **4** *Austral and NZ* the voters in a constituency

Electra (ɪ'lɛktrə) *n Greek myth* the daughter of Agamemnon and Clytemnestra. She persuaded her brother Orestes to avenge their father by killing his murderess Clytemnestra and her lover Aegisthus

Electra complex *n psychoanal* the sexual attachment of a female child to her father. See also **penis envy**

Electra paradox *n logic* the supposed paradox that one may know something to be true of an object under one description but not another, as when Electra knew that Orestes was her brother but not that the man before her was her brother although he was Orestes. This shows the predicate "knows" to be intensional, that Electra's knowledge here is de dicto, and that the statement of it yields an opaque context. See also **de dicto**

electret (ɪ'lɛktrət) *n* a permanently polarized dielectric material; its electric field is similar to the magnetic field of a permanent magnet [c20 from *electr(icity* + *magn)et*]

electric (ɪ'lɛktrɪk) *adj* **1** of, derived from, produced by, producing, transmitting, or powered by electricity: *electric current; an electric cord; an electric blanket; an electric fence; an electric fire* **2** (of a musical instrument) amplified electronically: *an electric guitar; an electric mandolin* **3** very tense or exciting; emotionally charged: *an electric atmosphere* ▷ *n* **4** *informal* an electric train, car, etc **5** *Brit informal* electricity or electrical power **6** (*plural*) an electric circuit or electric appliances [c17 from New Latin *electricus* amber-like (because friction causes amber to become charged), from Latin *ēlectrum* amber, from Greek *ēlektron*, of obscure origin]

USAGE See at **electronic**

electrical (ɪ'lɛktrɪkᵊl) *adj* of, relating to, or concerned with electricity > **e'lectrically** *adv*

USAGE See at **electronic**

electrical engineering *n* the branch of engineering concerned with the practical applications of electricity > **electrical engineer** *n*

electric-arc furnace *n* another name for **arc furnace**

electric-arc welding *n* another name for **arc welding**

electric blanket *n* a blanket that contains an electric heating element, used to warm a bed

electric blue *n* **a** a strong metallic blue colour **b** (*as adjective*): *an electric-blue evening dress*

electric chair *n* (in the US) **a** an electrified chair for executing criminals **b** (usually preceded by *the*) execution by this method

electric charge *n* another name for **charge** (sense 25)

electric circuit *n* *physics* another name for **circuit** (sense 3a)

electric constant *n* the permittivity of free space, which has the value 8.854 187 × 10⁻¹² farad per metre. Symbol: ε_0 Also called: **absolute permittivity**

electric current *n* another name for **current** (sense 8)

electric discharge *n* *physics* another name for **discharge** (sense 20b)

electric-discharge lamp *n* another name for **fluorescent lamp**

electric displacement *n* *physics* the electric flux density when an electric field exists in free space into which a dielectric is introduced. Symbol: *D* Also called: **electric flux density**

electric eel *n* an eel-like freshwater cyprinoid fish, *Electrophorus electricus,* of N South America, having electric organs in the body: family *Electrophoridae*

electric eye *n* another name for **photocell**

electric field *n* a field of force surrounding a charged particle within which another charged particle experiences a force. Compare **magnetic field**

electric field strength *n* the strength or intensity of a force field at any point, usually measured in volts per metre. Symbol: *E*

electric fire *n* a device that provides heat for a room from an incandescent electric element

electric flux *n* the product of the electric displacement and the area across which it is displaced in an electric field. Symbol: Ψ

electric flux density *n* another name for **electric displacement**

electric furnace *n* any furnace in which the heat is provided by an electric current

electric guitar *n* an electrically amplified guitar, used mainly in pop music. Compare **acoustic guitar**

electric hare *n* (in greyhound racing) a model of a hare, mounted on an electrified rail, which the dogs chase

electrician (ɪlɛkˈtrɪʃən, ˌiːlɛk-) *n* a person whose occupation is the installation, maintenance, and repair of electrical devices

electricity (ɪlɛkˈtrɪsɪtɪ, ˌiːlɛk-) *n* **1** any phenomenon associated with stationary or moving electrons, ions, or other charged particles **2** the science concerned with electricity **3** an electric current or charge: *a motor powered by electricity* **4** emotional tension or excitement, esp between or among people

electric motor *n* a device that converts electrical energy to mechanical torque

electric needle *n* a surgical instrument for cutting tissue by the application of a high-frequency current

electric organ *n* **1** *music* **a** a pipe organ operated by electrical means **b** another name for **electronic organ 2** *zoology* a small group of modified muscle cells on the body of certain fishes, such as the electric eel, that gives an electric shock to any animal touching them

electric potential *n* **a** the work required to transfer a unit positive electric charge from an infinite distance to a given point against an electric field **b** the potential difference between the point and some other reference point. Symbol: *V* or φ Sometimes shortened to: **potential**

electric ray *n* any ray of the order *Torpediniformes,* of tropical and temperate seas, having a flat rounded body with an electric organ in each of the fins, close to the head

electric shock *n* the physiological reaction, characterized by pain and muscular spasm, to the passage of an electric current through the body. It can affect the respiratory system and heart rhythm. Sometimes shortened to: **shock**

electric storm *n* a violent atmospheric disturbance in which the air is highly charged with static electricity, causing a storm. Compare **thunderstorm**

electric strength *n* the maximum voltage sustainable by an insulating material, after which it loses its insulating properties

electric susceptibility *n* another name for **susceptibility** (sense 4a)

electrify (ɪˈlɛktrɪˌfaɪ) *vb* -fies, -fying, -fied (*tr*) **1** to adapt or equip (a system, device, etc) for operation by electrical power **2** to charge with or subject to electricity **3** to startle or excite intensely; shock or thrill > eˈlectriˌfiable *adj* > eˌlectrifiˈcation *n* > eˈlectriˌfier *n*

electro (ɪˈlɛktrəʊ) *n, pl* -tros short for **electroplate** or **electrotype**

electro- *or sometimes before a vowel* **electr-** *combining form* **1** electric or electrically: *electrocardiograph; electrocute* **2** electrolytic: *electroanalysis* [from New Latin, from Latin *ēlectrum* amber, from Greek *ēlektron*]

electroacoustic (ɪˌlɛktrəʊəˈkuːstɪk) *adj* another word for **acoustoelectronic**

electroactive (ɪˌlɛktrəʊˈæktɪv) *adj* (of living tissue) exhibiting electrical activity or responsive to electrical stimuli > eˌlectroacˈtivity *n*

electroanalysis (ɪˌlɛktrəʊəˈnælɪsɪs) *n* chemical analysis by electrolysis or electrodeposition > electroanalytic (ɪˌlɛktrəʊˌænəˈlɪtɪk) *or* eˌlectro‚anaˈlytical *adj*

electrocardiogram (ɪˌlɛktrəʊˈkɑːdɪəʊˌɡræm) *n* a tracing of the electric currents that initiate the heartbeat, used to diagnose possible heart disorders. Abbreviation: **ECG**

electrocardiograph (ɪˌlɛktrəʊˈkɑːdɪəʊˌɡrɑːf, -ˌɡræf) *n* an instrument for recording the electrical activity of the heart. Abbreviation: **ECG**
> eˌlectro‚cardioˈgraphic *adj*
> eˌlectro‚cardioˈgraphically *adv*
> electrocardiography (ɪˌlɛktrəʊˌkɑːdɪˈɒɡrəfɪ) *n*

electrocautery (ɪˌlɛktrəʊˈkɔːtərɪ) *n vet science* the use of an electrically heated metal instrument for cautery

electrochemical (ɪˌlɛktrəʊˈkɛmɪkᵊl) *adj* of or relating to electrochemistry
> eˌlectroˈchemically *adv*

electrochemical equivalent *n* the mass of an element liberated from its ions or converted into them by one coulomb of electric charge

electrochemical series *n* another name for **electromotive series**

electrochemistry (ɪˌlɛktrəʊˈkɛmɪstrɪ) *n* the branch of chemistry concerned with the study of electric cells and electrolysis > eˌlectroˈchemist *n*

electrochromatography (ɪˌlɛktrəʊkrəʊməˈtɒɡrəfɪ) *n* chromatography effected by the influence of an applied electric field > eˌlectrochroˈmatic *adj*

electroclash (ɪˈlɛktrəʊˌklæʃ) *n* **a** a type of electronic music, originating in the first decade of the 21st century, that combines modern techno with synthesizer music characteristic of the 1980s **b** (*as modifier*): *the electroclash scene*

electroconvulsive therapy (ɪˌlɛktrəʊkənˈvʌlsɪv) *n med* the treatment of certain psychotic conditions by passing an electric current through the brain to induce coma or convulsions. Abbreviation: **ECT** Also called: **electroshock therapy** See also **shock therapy**

electrocorticogram (ɪˌlɛktrəʊˈkɔːtɪkəʊˌɡræm) *n* a record of brain waves obtained by placing electrodes directly on the surface of the exposed cerebral cortex. Compare **electroencephalogram, electroencephalograph**

electrocute (ɪˈlɛktrəˌkjuːt) *vb* (*tr*) **1** to kill as a result of an electric shock **2** *US* to execute in the electric chair [C19 from ELECTRO- + (exe)cute] > eˌlectroˈcution *n*

electrocyte (ɪˈlɛktrəʊˌsaɪt) *n zoology* a specialized muscle or nerve cell that generates electricity, as found in an electric organ

electrode (ɪˈlɛktrəʊd) *n* **1** a conductor through which an electric current enters or leaves an electrolyte, an electric arc, or an electronic valve or tube **2** an element in a semiconducting device that emits, collects, or controls the movement of electrons or holes

electrode efficiency *n chem* the ratio of the amount of metal deposited in an electrolytic cell to that theoretically deposited according to Faraday's laws

electrodeposit (ɪˌlɛktrəʊdɪˈpɒzɪt) *vb* **1** (*tr*) to deposit (a metal) by electrolysis ▷ *n* **2** the deposit so formed > electrodeposition (ɪˌlɛktrəʊˌdɛpəˈzɪʃən) *n*

electrode potential *n chem* the potential difference developed when an electrode of an element is placed in a solution containing ions of that element

electrodialysis (ɪˌlɛktrəʊdaɪˈælɪsɪs) *n* dialysis in which electrolytes are removed from a colloidal solution by a potential difference between two electrodes separated by one or more membranes

electrodynamic (ɪˌlɛktrəʊdaɪˈnæmɪk) *adj* **1** operated by an electromotive force between current-carrying coils: *an electrodynamic wattmeter* **2** of or relating to electrodynamics

electrodynamics (ɪˌlɛktrəʊdaɪˈnæmɪks) *n* (*functioning as singular*) the branch of physics concerned with the interactions between electrical and mechanical forces

electrodynamometer (ɪˌlɛktrəʊˌdaɪnəˈmɒmɪtə) *n* an instrument that uses the interaction of the magnetic fields of two coils to measure electric current, voltage, or power

electroencephalogram (ɪˌlɛktrəʊɛnˈsɛfələˌɡræm) *n med* the tracing obtained from an electroencephalograph. Abbreviation: **EEG**

electroencephalograph (ɪˌlɛktrəʊɛnˈsɛfələˌɡrɑːf, -ˌɡræf) *n* an instrument for recording the electrical activity of the brain, usually by means of electrodes placed on the scalp: used to diagnose tumours of the brain, to study brain waves, etc. Abbreviation: **EEG** See also **brain wave**
> eˌlectroenˌcephaloˈgraphic *adj*
> eˌlectroenˌcephaloˈgraphically *adv*
> electroencephalography (ɪˌlɛktrəʊɛnˌsɛfəˈlɒɡrəfɪ) *n*

electroendosmosis (ɪˌlɛktrəʊˌɛndɒzˈməʊsɪs, -dɒs-) *n* another name for **electro-osmosis**

electrofluor (ɪˈlɛktrəʊˌfluːɔː) *n physics* a transparent material that stores electrical energy and subsequently releases it as light [C20 from ELECTRO- + FLUOR(ESCENCE)]

electroform (ɪˈlɛktrəˌfɔːm) *vb* to form (a metallic object) by electrolytic deposition on a mould or matrix

electrogen (ɪˈlɛktrəʊˌdʒɛn) *n* a molecule that emits electrons when it is illuminated
> eˌlectroˈgenic *adj*

electrograph (ɪˈlɛktrəʊˌɡrɑːf, -ˌɡræf) *n* **1** an apparatus for engraving metal printing cylinders, esp in gravure printing **2** the equipment used for the electrical transmission of pictures **3 a** a recording electrometer **b** a graph produced by this instrument **4** a visual record of the surface composition of a metal, obtained by placing an electrolyte-soaked paper over the metal and passing a current through the paper to an electrode on the other side > electrographic (ɪˌlɛktrəʊˈɡræfɪk) *adj* > eˌlectroˈgraphically *adv* > electrography (ɪlɛkˈtrɒɡrəfɪ, ˌiːlɛk-) *n*

electrojet (ɪˈlɛktrəʊˌdʒɛt) *n* a narrow belt of fast-moving ions in the ionosphere, under the influence of the earth's magnetic field, causing auroral displays

electrokinetic (ɪˌlɛktrəʊkɪˈnɛtɪk, -kaɪ-) *adj* of or

e

relating to the motion of charged particles and its effects

electrokinetics (ɪˌlɛktrəʊkɪˈnɛtɪks, -kaɪ-) *n* (functioning as singular) the branch of physics concerned with the motion of charged particles

electroluminescence (ɪˌlɛktrəʊˌluːmɪˈnɛsᵊns) *n* physics **a** the emission of light by a phosphor when activated by an alternating field or by a gas when activated by an electric discharge **b** the light emitted by this process
> eˌlectroˌlumiˈnescent *adj*

electrolyse *or US* **electrolyze** (ɪˈlɛktrəʊˌlaɪz) *vb* (tr) **1** to decompose (a chemical compound) by electrolysis **2** to destroy (living tissue, such as hair roots) by electrolysis [c19 back formation from ELECTROLYSIS on pattern of *analyse*]
> eˌlectroˈlysation *or US* eˌlectrolyˈzation *n*
> eˈlectroˌlyser *or US* eˈlectroˌlyzer *n*

electrolysis (ɪlɛkˈtrɒlɪsɪs) *n* **1** the conduction of electricity by a solution or melt, esp the use of this process to induce chemical changes **2** the destruction of living tissue, such as hair roots, by an electric current, usually for cosmetic reasons [c19 from ELECTRO- + -LYSIS]

electrolyte (ɪˈlɛktrəʊˌlaɪt) *n* **1** a solution or molten substance that conducts electricity **2 a** a chemical compound that dissociates in solution into ions **b** any of the ions themselves

electrolytic (ɪˌlɛktrəʊˈlɪtɪk) *adj* **1** physics **a** of, concerned with, or produced by electrolysis or electrodeposition **b** of, relating to, or containing an electrolyte ▷ *n* **2** electronics Also called: **electrolytic capacitor** a small capacitor consisting of two electrodes separated by an electrolyte
> eˌlectroˈlytically *adv*

electrolytic cell *n* any device in which electrolysis occurs. Sometimes shortened to: **cell**

electrolytic gas *n* a mixture of two parts of hydrogen and one part of oxygen by volume, formed by the electrolysis of water

electromagnet (ɪˌlɛktrəʊˈmægnɪt) *n* a magnet consisting of an iron or steel core wound with a coil of wire, through which a current is passed

electromagnetic (ɪˌlɛktrəʊmægˈnɛtɪk) *adj* **1** of, containing, or operated by an electromagnet: *an electromagnetic pump* **2** of, relating to, or consisting of electromagnetism: *electromagnetic moment* **3** of or relating to electromagnetic radiation: *the electromagnetic spectrum* > eˌlectromagˈnetically *adv*

electromagnetic field *n* a field of force associated with a moving electric charge equivalent to an electric field and a magnetic field at right angles to each other and to the direction of propagation

electromagnetic interaction *or* **force** *n* physics an interaction between charged particles arising from their electric and magnetic fields; its strength is about 100 times weaker than the strong interaction. See **interaction** (sense 2), **electroweak interaction**

electromagnetic moment *n* a measure of the magnetic strength of a magnet or current-carrying coil, expressed as the torque produced when the magnet or coil is set with its axis perpendicular to unit magnetic flux density. It is measured in ampere metres squared. Symbol: m Also called: **magnetic moment** Compare **magnetic dipole moment**

electromagnetic pump *n* a device for pumping liquid metals by placing a pipe between the poles of an electromagnet and passing a current through the liquid metal

electromagnetic radiation *n* radiation consisting of self-sustaining oscillating electric and magnetic fields at right angles to each other and to the direction of propagation. It does not require a supporting medium and travels through empty space at the speed of light. See also **photon**

electromagnetics (ɪˌlɛktrəʊmægˈnɛtɪks) *n* (functioning as singular) physics another name for **electromagnetism** (sense 2)

electromagnetic spectrum *n* the complete range of electromagnetic radiation from the longest radio waves (wavelength 10^5 metres) to the shortest gamma radiation (wavelength 10^{-13} metre)

electromagnetic unit *n* any unit that belongs to a system of electrical cgs units in which the magnetic constant is given the value of unity and is taken as a pure number. Abbreviations: EMU, e.m.u. Compare **electrostatic unit**

electromagnetic wave *n* a wave of energy propagated in an electromagnetic field. See also **electromagnetic radiation**

electromagnetism (ɪˌlɛktrəʊˈmægnɪˌtɪzəm) *n* **1** magnetism produced by an electric current **2** Also called: **electromagnetics** the branch of physics concerned with magnetism produced by electric currents and with the interaction of electric and magnetic fields

electromechanical (ɪˌlɛktrəʊmɪˈkænɪkᵊl) *adj* of, relating to, or concerning an electrically operated mechanical device > eˌlectromeˈchanically *adv*

electromerism (ɪˌlɛktrəʊˈmɛrɪzəm) *n* chem a type of tautomerism in which the isomers (**electromers**) differ in the distribution of charge in their molecules [c20 from ELECTRO- + (iso)merism]

electrometallurgy (ɪˌlɛktrəʊmɪˈtælədʒɪ, -ˈmɛtəˌlɜːdʒɪ) *n* metallurgy involving the use of electric-arc furnaces, electrolysis, and other electrical operations > eˌlectroˌmetalˈlurgical *adj* > eˌlectroˈmetalˌlurgist *n*

electrometer (ɪlɛkˈtrɒmɪtə, iːlɛk-) *n* an instrument for detecting or determining the magnitude of a potential difference or charge by the electrostatic forces between charged bodies > electrometric (ɪˌlɛktrəʊˈmɛtrɪk) *or* eˌlectroˈmetrical *adj* > eˌlectroˈmetrically *adv* > elecˈtrometry *n*

electromotive (ɪˌlɛktrəʊˈməʊtɪv) *adj* of, concerned with, producing, or tending to produce an electric current

electromotive force *n* physics **a** a source of energy that can cause a current to flow in an electrical circuit or device **b** the rate at which energy is drawn from this source when unit current flows through the circuit or device, measured in volts. Abbreviations: emf, EMF Symbol: E Compare **potential difference**

electromotive series *n* chem a series of the metals, together with hydrogen, ranged in the order of their electrode potentials

electromyography (ɪˌlɛktrəʊmaɪˈɒɡrəfɪ) *n* med a technique for recording the electrical activity of muscles: used in the diagnosis of nerve and muscle disorders

electron (ɪˈlɛktrɒn) *n* a stable elementary particle present in all atoms, orbiting the nucleus in numbers equal to the atomic number of the element in the neutral atom; a lepton with a negative charge of $1.602\,176\,462 \times 10^{-19}$ coulomb, a rest mass of $9.109\,381\,88 \times 10^{-31}$ kilogram, a radius of $2.817\,940\,285 \times 10^{-15}$ metre, and a spin of $\frac{1}{2}$ [c19 from ELECTRO- + -ON]

electron affinity *n* a measure of the ability of an atom or molecule to form a negative ion, expressed as the energy released when an electron is attached. Symbol: A

electron capture *n* physics **1** the transformation of an atomic nucleus in which an electron from the atom is spontaneously absorbed into the nucleus. A proton is changed into a neutron, thereby reducing the atomic number by 1. A neutrino is emitted. The process may be detected by the consequent emission of the characteristic X-rays of the resultant element. Former name: K-capture **2** the spontaneous or induced recombination of free electrons with ions or by transfer from other atoms or ions

electronegative (ɪˌlɛktrəʊˈnɛɡətɪv) *adj* **1** having a negative electric charge **2** (of an atom, group, molecule, etc) tending to gain or attract electrons and form negative ions or polarized bonds.

Compare **electropositive**

electronegativity (ɪˌlɛktrəʊˌnɛɡəˈtɪvɪtɪ) *n* **1** the state of being electronegative **2** a measure of the ability of a specified atom to attract electrons in a molecule

electron gun *n* a heated cathode with an associated system of electrodes and coils for producing and focusing a beam of electrons, used esp in cathode-ray tubes

electronic (ɪlɛkˈtrɒnɪk, iːlɛk-) *adj* **1** of, concerned with, using, or operated by devices in which electrons are conducted through a semiconductor, free space, or gas **2** of or concerned with electronics **3** of or concerned with electrons or an electron: *an electronic energy level in a molecule* **4** involving or concerned with the representation, storage, or transmission of information by electronic systems: *electronic mail; electronic shopping* > elecˈtronically *adv*

USAGE *Electronic* is used to refer to equipment, such as television sets, computers, etc, in which the current is controlled by transistors, valves, and similar components and also to the components themselves. *Electrical* is used in a more general sense, often to refer to the use of electricity as a whole as opposed to other forms of energy: *electrical engineering; an electrical appliance. Electric,* in many cases used interchangeably with *electrical,* is often restricted to the description of particular devices or to concepts relating to the flow of current: *electric fire; electric charge*

electronica (ɪlɛkˈtrɒnɪkə, iːlɛk-) *pl n* electronic equipment, systems, music, etc, collectively

electronic configuration *n* chem the arrangement of electrons in the orbitals of an atom or molecule

electronic countermeasures *pl n* military (in electronic warfare) actions intended to interfere with an enemy's use of electromagnetic radiation equipment

electronic editing *n* radio, television editing of a sound or vision tape recording by electronic rerecording rather than by physical cutting

electronic file cabinet *n* computing a device, controlled by software, for the storage and retrieval of information

electronic flash *n* photog an electronic device for producing a very bright flash of light by means of an electric discharge in a gas-filled tube

electronic flight information systems *pl n* (in an aircraft) the computer-operated visual displays on the flight deck, showing information about the aircraft's state and performance in flight

electronic footprint *n* computing data that identifies a computer that has connected to a particular website

electronic funds transfer at point of sale *n* a system for debiting a retail sale direct to the customer's bank, building-society, or credit-card account by means of a computer link using the telephone network. Acronym: EFTPOS

electronic game *n* any of various small hand-held computerized games, usually battery-operated, having a small screen on which graphics are displayed and buttons to operate the game

electronic graphics *n* (functioning as singular) (on television) the production of graphic designs and text by electronic means

electronic ignition *n* any system that uses an electronic circuit to supply the voltage to the sparking plugs of an internal-combustion engine

electronic keyboard *n* **1** a typewriter keyboard used to operate an electronic device such as a computer, word processor, etc **2** the full name for **keyboard** (sense 2)

electronic mail *n* the transmission and distribution of messages, information, facsimiles of documents, etc, from one computer terminal to another. Abbreviations: e-mail, email

electronic mailbox *n* a device used to store electronic mail

electronic music *n* a form of music consisting of sounds produced by oscillating electric currents either controlled from an instrument panel or keyboard or prerecorded on magnetic tape

electronic office *n* integrated computer systems designed to handle office work

electronic organ *n* *music* an electrophonic instrument played by means of a keyboard, in which sounds are produced and amplified by any of various electronic or electrical means. See also **synthesizer**

electronic organizer *n* See **personal organizer** (sense 2)

electronic point of sale *n* a computerized system for recording sales in retail shops, using a laser scanner at the cash till to read bar codes on the packages of the items sold. Acronym: EPOS

electronic programme guide *n* an on-screen guide that enables viewers of digital television to select programmes using a hand-held device. Abbreviation: EPG

electronic publishing *n* the publication of information on magnetic tape, disks, etc, so that it can be accessed by a computer

electronics (ɪlɛk'trɒnɪks, ˌiːlɛk-) *n* **1** (*functioning as singular*) the science and technology concerned with the development, behaviour, and applications of electronic devices and circuits **2** (*functioning as plural*) the circuits and devices of a piece of electronic equipment: *the electronics of a television set*

electronic signature *n* *computing* electronic proof of a person's identity

electronic surveillance *n* **1** the use of such electronic devices as television monitors, video cameras, etc, to prevent burglary, shop lifting, break-ins, etc **2** monitoring events, conversations, etc, at a distance by electronic means, esp by such covert means as wiretapping or bugging

electronic tag *n* another name for **tag¹** (sense 2)

electronic transfer of funds *n* the transfer of money from one bank or building-society account to another by means of a computer link using the telephone network. Abbreviation: ETF

electronic warfare *n* the military use of electronics to prevent or reduce an enemy's effective use and to protect friendly use of electromagnetic radiation equipment

electron lens *n* a system, such as an arrangement of electrodes or magnets, that produces a field for focusing a beam of electrons

electron micrograph *n* a photograph or image of a specimen taken using an electron microscope

electron microscope *n* a powerful type of microscope that uses electrons, rather than light, and electron lenses to produce a magnified image

electron multiplier *n* *physics* a device for amplifying and measuring a flux of electrons. Each electron hits an anode surface and releases secondary electrons that are accelerated to a second surface; after several such stages a measurable pulse of current is obtained

electron optics *n* (*functioning as singular*) the study and use of beams of electrons and of their deflection and focusing by electric and magnetic fields

electron paramagnetic resonance *n* *physics* another name for **electron spin resonance** Abbreviation: EPR

electron probe microanalysis *n* a technique for the analysis of a very small amount of material by bombarding it with a narrow beam of electrons and examining the resulting X-ray emission spectrum

electron spin resonance *n* a technique for investigating paramagnetic substances by subjecting them to high-frequency radiation in a strong magnetic field. Changes in the spin of unpaired electrons cause radiation to be absorbed at certain frequencies. Abbreviation: ESR See also **nuclear magnetic resonance**

electron telescope *n* an astronomical telescope with an attachment for converting the infrared radiation emitted from the surface of planets into a visible image

electron transport *n* *biochem* the metabolic process in mitochondria or chloroplasts, in which electrons are transferred in stages from energy-rich compounds to molecular oxygen with liberation of energy

electron tube *n* an electrical device, such as a valve, in which a flow of electrons between electrodes takes place. Also called: **vacuum tube** Sometimes shortened to: **tube**

electronvolt (ɪˌlɛktrɒn'vəʊlt) *n* a unit of energy equal to the work done on an electron accelerated through a potential difference of 1 volt. 1 electronvolt is equivalent to 1.602×10^{-19} joule. Symbol: eV

electro-osmosis *n* movement of liquid through a capillary tube or membrane under the influence of an electric field: used in controlling rising damp. Also called: **electroendosmosis**

electropalatography (ɪˌlɛktrəʊˌpælə'tɒgrəfɪ) *n* the study of the movements of the tongue during speech using touch-sensitive electrodes in the mouth linked to a computer

electrophilic (ɪˌlɛktrəʊ'fɪlɪk) *adj* *chem* having or involving an affinity for negative charge. Electrophilic reagents (**electrophiles**) are atoms, molecules, and ions that behave as electron acceptors. Compare **nucleophilic.** > **electrophile** (ɪ'lɛktrəˌfaɪl) *n*

electrophone (ɪ'lɛktrəˌfəʊn) *n* *music* any instrument whose sound is produced by the oscillation of an electric current, such as an electronic organ, synthesizer, etc > **electrophonic** (ɪˌlɛktrəʊ'fɒnɪk) *adj*

electrophoresis (ɪˌlɛktrəʊfə'riːsɪs) *n* the motion of charged particles in a colloid under the influence of an applied electric field. Also called: **cataphoresis** > **electrophoretic** (ɪˌlɛktrəʊfə'rɛtɪk) *adj*

electrophorus (ɪlɛk'trɒfərəs, ˌiːlɛk-) *n* an apparatus for generating static electricity. It consists of an insulating plate charged by friction and used to charge a metal plate by induction [C18 from ELECTRO- + -*phorus,* from Greek -*phoros* bearing, from *pherein* to bear]

electrophotography (ɪˌlɛktrəʊˌfə'tɒgrəfɪ) *n* photography in which an image is transferred onto paper by means of electrical rather than chemical processes > **electrophotographic** *adj*

electrophysiology (ɪˌlɛktrəʊˌfɪzɪ'ɒlədʒɪ) *n* the branch of medical science concerned with the electrical activity associated with bodily processes > **electrophysiological** *adj* > **electrophysiologist** *n*

electroplate (ɪ'lɛktrəʊˌpleɪt) *vb* **1** (*tr*) to plate (an object) by electrolysis ▷ *n* **2** electroplated articles collectively, esp when plated with silver ▷ *adj* **3** coated with metal by electrolysis; electroplated > **electroplater** *n*

electropositive (ɪˌlɛktrəʊ'pɒzɪtɪv) *adj* **1** having a positive electric charge **2** (of an atom, group, molecule, etc) tending to release electrons and form positive ions or polarized bonds. Compare **electronegative**

electroreceptor (ɪ'lɛktrəʊrɪˌsɛptə) *n* *zoology* an organ, present in some fishes, that detects electrical discharges

electrorheology (ɪˌlɛktrəʊrɪ'ɒlədʒɪ) *n* **1** the study of the flow of fluids under the influence of electric fields **2** the way in which fluid flow is influenced by an electric field > **electrorheological** *adj*

electroscope (ɪ'lɛktrəʊˌskəʊp) *n* an apparatus for detecting an electric charge, typically consisting of a rod holding two gold foils that separate when a charge is applied > **electroscopic** (ɪˌlɛktrəʊ'skɒpɪk) *adj*

electroshock therapy (ɪ'lɛktrəʊˌʃɒk) *n* another name for **electroconvulsive therapy**

electrostatic (ɪˌlɛktrəʊ'stætɪk) *adj* **1** of, concerned with, producing, or caused by static electricity **2** concerned with electrostatics > **electrostatically** *adv*

electrostatic field *n* an electric field associated with static electric charges

electrostatic generator *n* any device for producing a high voltage by building up a charge of static electricity

electrostatic lens *n* an electron lens consisting of a system of metal electrodes, the electrostatic field of which focuses the charged particles

electrostatic precipitation *n* *chem* the removal of suspended solid particles from a gas by giving them an electric charge and attracting them to charged plates

electrostatics (ɪˌlɛktrəʊ'stætɪks) *n* (*functioning as singular*) the branch of physics concerned with static charges and the electrostatic field

electrostatic unit *n* any unit that belongs to a system of electrical cgs units in which the electric constant is given the value of unity and is taken as a pure number. Abbreviations: ESU, e.s.u. Compare **electromagnetic unit**

electrostriction (ɪˌlɛktrəʊ'strɪkʃən) *n* the change in dimensions of a dielectric occurring as an elastic strain when an electric field is applied

electrosurgery (ɪˌlɛktrəʊ'sɜːdʒərɪ) *n* the surgical use of electricity, as in cauterization > **electrosurgical** *adj*

electrotechnics (ɪˌlɛktrəʊ'tɛknɪks) *n* (*functioning as singular*) another name for **electrotechnology** > **electrotechnical** *adj* > **electrotechnician** *n*

electrotechnology (ɪˌlɛktrəʊtɛk'nɒlədʒɪ) *n* the technological use of electric power

electrotherapeutics (ɪˌlɛktrəʊˌθɛrə'pjuːtɪks) *n* (*functioning as singular*) the branch of medical science concerned with the use of electrotherapy > **electrotherapeutic** *or* **electrotherapeutical** *adj*

electrotherapy (ɪˌlɛktrəʊ'θɛrəpɪ) *n* treatment in which electric currents are passed through the tissues to stimulate muscle function in paralysed patients > **electrotherapist** *n*

electrothermal (ɪˌlɛktrəʊ'θɜːməl) *or* **electrothermic** (ɪˌlɛktrəʊ'θɜːmɪk) *adj* concerned with both electricity and heat, esp the production of electricity by heat

electrothermal printer *n* *computing* a printer that produces characters by burning the image on specially coated paper. Also called: thermal printer

electrotint (ɪ'lɛktrəʊˌtɪnt) *n* a printing block made by drawing on a metal plate with varnish and electrolytically depositing a layer of metal on the nonvarnished areas of the plate

electrotonus (ɪlɛk'trɒtənəs, ˌiːlɛk-) *n* *physiol* the change in the state of irritability and conductivity of a nerve or muscle caused by the passage of an electric current [C19 from New Latin, from ELECTRO- + Latin *tonus* TONE] > **electrotonic** (ɪˌlɛktrəʊ'tɒnɪk) *adj*

electrotype (ɪ'lɛktrəʊˌtaɪp) *n* **1** a duplicate printing plate made by electrolytically depositing a layer of copper or nickel onto a mould of the original. Sometimes shortened to: **electro** ▷ *vb* **2** (*tr*) to make an electrotype of (printed matter, illustrations, etc) > **electrotyper** *n*

electrovalency (ɪˌlɛktrəʊ'veɪlənsɪ) *or* **electrovalence** *n* *chem* the valency of a substance in forming ions, equal to the number of electrons gained or lost > **electrovalent** *adj* > **electrovalently** *adv*

electrovalent bond *n* a type of chemical bond in which one atom loses an electron to form a positive ion and the other atom gains the electron to form a negative ion. The resulting ions are held together by electrostatic attraction. Also called: ionic bond Compare **covalent bond**

electroweak interaction (ɪˌlɛktrəʊ'wiːk) *n*

e

physics a type of fundamental interaction combining both the electromagnetic interaction and the weak interaction. See also **electromagnetic interaction, weak interaction**

electrum (ɪˈlɛktrəm) *n* an alloy of gold (55–88 per cent) and silver used for jewellery and ornaments [c14 from Latin, from Greek *ēlektron* amber]

electuary (ɪˈlɛktjʊərɪ) *n, pl* -aries *archaic* a paste taken orally, containing a drug mixed with syrup or honey [c14 from Late Latin *ēlēctuārium*, probably from Greek *ēkleikton* electuary, from *ekleikhein* to lick out, from *leikhein* to lick]

eleemosynary (ˌɛliːˈmɒsɪnərɪ) *adj* 1 of, concerned with, or dependent on charity 2 given as an act of charity [c17 from Church Latin *eleēmosyna* ALMS]

elegance (ˈɛlɪgəns) *or* **elegancy** *n, pl* -gances *or* -gancies 1 dignified grace in appearance, movement, or behaviour 2 good taste in design, style, arrangement, etc 3 something elegant; a refinement

elegant (ˈɛlɪgənt) *adj* 1 tasteful in dress, style, or design 2 dignified and graceful in appearance, behaviour, etc 3 cleverly simple; ingenious: *an elegant solution to a problem* [c16 from Latin *ēlegāns* tasteful, related to *ēligere* to select; see ELECT] > 'elegantly *adv*

elegiac (ˌɛlɪˈdʒaɪək) *adj* 1 resembling, characteristic of, relating to, or appropriate to an elegy 2 lamenting; mournful; plaintive 3 denoting or written in elegiac couplets or elegiac stanzas ▷ *n* 4 (*often plural*) an elegiac couplet or stanza > ele'giacally *adv*

elegiac couplet *n classical prosody* a couplet composed of a dactylic hexameter followed by a dactylic pentameter

elegiac stanza *n prosody* a quatrain in iambic pentameters with alternate lines rhyming

elegize *or* **elegise** (ˈɛlɪˌdʒaɪz) *vb* 1 to compose an elegy or elegies (in memory of) 2 (*intr*) to write elegiacally > 'elegist *n*

elegy (ˈɛlɪdʒɪ) *n, pl* -gies 1 a mournful or plaintive poem or song, esp a lament for the dead 2 poetry or a poem written in elegiac couplets or stanzas [c16 via French and Latin from Greek *elegeia*, from *elegos* lament sung to flute accompaniment]

■ USAGE Avoid confusion with **eulogy**

Eleia (ˈiːliːə) *n* a variant spelling of **Elia**

element (ˈɛlɪmənt) *n* 1 any of the 118 known substances (of which 93 occur naturally) that consist of atoms with the same number of protons in their nuclei. Compare **compound¹** (sense 1) 2 one of the fundamental or irreducible components making up a whole 3 a cause that contributes to a result; factor 4 any group that is part of a larger unit, such as a military formation 5 a small amount; hint: *an element of sarcasm in her voice* 6 a distinguishable section of a social group: *he belonged to the stable element in the expedition* 7 the most favourable environment for an animal or plant 8 the situation in which a person is happiest or most effective (esp in the phrases **in** or **out of one's element**) 9 the resistance wire and its former that constitute the electrical heater in a cooker, heater, etc 10 *electronics* another name for **component** (sense 2) 11 one of the four substances thought in ancient and medieval cosmology to constitute the universe (earth, air, water, or fire) 12 (*plural*) atmospheric conditions or forces, esp wind, rain, and cold: *exposed to the elements* 13 (*plural*) the first principles of a subject 14 *geometry* a point, line, plane, or part of a geometric figure 15 *maths* **a** any of the terms in a determinant or matrix **b** one of the infinitesimally small quantities summed by an integral, often represented by the expression following the integral sign: *in ∫ᵇₐf(x)dx, f(x)dx is an element of area* 16 *maths, logic* one of the objects or numbers that together constitute a set 17 *Christianity* the bread or wine consecrated in the Eucharist 18 *astronomy* any of the numerical quantities, such as the major axis or eccentricity, used in describing the

orbit of a planet, satellite, etc 19 one of the vertical or horizontal rods forming a television or VHF radio receiving aerial 20 *physics* a component of a compound lens [c13 from Latin *elementum* a first principle, alphabet, element, of uncertain origin]

elemental (ˌɛlɪˈmɛntᵊl) *adj* 1 fundamental; basic; primal: *the elemental needs of man* 2 motivated by or symbolic of primitive and powerful natural forces or passions: *elemental rites of worship* 3 of or relating to earth, air, water, and fire considered as elements 4 of or relating to atmospheric forces, esp wind, rain, and cold 5 of, relating to, or denoting a chemical element ▷ *n* 6 *rare* a spirit or force that is said to appear in physical form > ˌele'mentally *adv* > ˌele'mental,ism *n*

elementary (ˌɛlɪˈmɛntərɪ, -trɪ) *adj* 1 not difficult; simple; rudimentary 2 of or concerned with the first principles of a subject; introductory or fundamental 3 *maths* (of a function) having the form of an algebraic, exponential, trigonometric, or a logarithmic function, or any combination of these 4 *chem* another word for **elemental** (sense 5) > ˌele'mentarily *adv* > ˌele'mentariness *n*

elementary particle *n* any of several entities, such as electrons, neutrons, or protons, that are less complex than atoms and are regarded as the constituents of all matter. Also called: **fundamental particle**

elementary school *n* 1 *Brit* a former name for **primary school** 2 Also called (in the US): **grade school**, **grammar school** *US and Canadian* a state school in which instruction is given for the first six to eight years of a child's education

elemi (ˈɛlɪmɪ) *n, pl* -mis any of various fragrant resins obtained from tropical trees, esp trees of the family *Burseraceae*: used in making varnishes, ointments, inks, etc [c16 via Spanish from Arabic *al-lāmi* the elemi]

elenchus (ɪˈlɛŋkəs) *n, pl* -chi (-kaɪ) *logic* 1 refutation of an argument by proving the contrary of its conclusion, esp syllogistically 2 **Socratic elenchus** the drawing out of the consequences of a position in order to show them to be contrary to some accepted position [c17 from Latin, from Greek *elenkhos* refutation, from *elenkhein* to put to shame, refute]

elenctic (ɪˈlɛŋktɪk) *adj logic* refuting an argument by proving the falsehood of its conclusion. Compare **deictic** (sense 1)

eleoptene *or* **elaeoptene** (ˌɛlɪˈɒptiːn) *n* the liquid part of a volatile oil [c20 from Greek *elaion* oil + *ptēnos* having wings, volatile; related to Greek *petesthai* to fly]

elephant (ˈɛlɪfənt) *n, pl* -phants *or* -phant 1 either of the two proboscidean mammals of the family *Elephantidae*. The **African elephant** (*Loxodonta africana*) is the larger species, with large flapping ears and a less humped back than the **Indian elephant** (*Elephas maximus*), of S and SE Asia 2 *chiefly Brit* a size of writing paper, 23 by 28 inches [c13 from Latin *elephantus*, from Greek *elephas* elephant, ivory, of uncertain origin] > 'elephan,toid *adj*

elephant bird *n* another name for **aepyornis**

elephant fish *n* a large marine fish, *Callorhinchus milii*, of southwest Pacific waters, having a snout resembling an elephant's trunk. Also called: **reperepe**

elephant grass *n* any of various stout tropical grasses or grasslike plants, esp *Pennisetum purpureum*, and *Typha elephantina*, a type of reed mace

elephant gun *n* 1 a gun used in the hunting of elephants 2 *Austral slang* a surfboard for riding large waves

elephantiasis (ˌɛlɪfənˈtaɪəsɪs) *n pathol* a complication of chronic filariasis, in which nematode worms block the lymphatic vessels, usually in the legs or scrotum, causing extreme enlargement of the affected area. See also **filariasis** [c16 via Latin from Greek, from *elephas* ELEPHANT + -IASIS] > elephantiasic (ˌɛlɪˌfæntɪˈæsɪk,

ˌɛlɪfənˈtaɪəsɪk) *adj*

elephantine (ˌɛlɪˈfæntaɪn) *adj* 1 denoting, relating to, or characteristic of an elephant or elephants 2 huge, clumsy, or ponderous

elephants (ˈɛlɪfənts) *adj Austral slang* drunk; intoxicated [c20 shortened from *elephant's trunk*, rhyming slang for DRUNK]

elephant seal *n* either of two large earless seals, *Mirounga leonina* of southern oceans or *M. angustirostris* of the N Atlantic, the males of which have a long trunklike snout

elephant's-ear *n* 1 any aroid plant of the genus *Colocasia*, of tropical Asia and Polynesia, having very large heart-shaped leaves: grown for ornament and for their edible tubers. See also **taro** 2 any of various cultivated begonias with large showy leaves

elephant's-foot *or* **elephant foot** *n* a monocotyledonous plant, *Testudinaria elephantipes*, of southern Africa, with a very large starchy tuberous stem, covered in corky scales: family *Dioscoreaceae*

elephant shrew *n* any small active African mammal of the family *Macroscelididae* and order *Macroscelidea*, having an elongated nose, large ears, and long hind legs

Eleusinian mysteries *pl n* a mystical religious festival, held in September at Eleusis in classical times, in which initiates celebrated Persephone, Demeter, and Dionysus

Eleusis (ɪˈluːsɪs) *n* a town in Greece, in Attica about 23 km (14 miles) west of Athens, of which it is now an industrial suburb. Modern Greek name: Elevsís > Eleusinian (ˌɛljuˈsɪnɪən) *n, adj*

elevate (ˈɛlɪˌveɪt) *vb* (*tr*) 1 to move to a higher place 2 to raise in rank or status; promote 3 to put in a cheerful mood; elate 4 to put on a higher cultural plane; uplift: *to elevate the tone of a conversation* 5 to raise the axis of a gun 6 to raise the intensity or pitch of (the voice) 7 *RC Church* to lift up (the Host) at Mass for adoration [c15 from Latin *ēlevāre* from *levāre* to raise, from *levis* (adj) light] > ˌele'vatory *adj*

elevated (ˈɛlɪˌveɪtɪd) *adj* 1 raised to or being at a higher level 2 inflated or lofty; exalted: *an elevated opinion of oneself* 3 in a cheerful mood; elated 4 *informal* slightly drunk ▷ *n* 5 *US* short for **elevated railway** *or* **railroad**

elevated railway *or* **railroad** *n US* an urban railway track built on supports above a road

elevation (ˌɛlɪˈveɪʃən) *n* 1 the act of elevating or the state of being elevated 2 the height of something above a given or implied place, esp above sea level 3 a raised area; height 4 nobleness or grandeur; loftiness: *elevation of thought* 5 a drawing to scale of the external face of a building or structure. Compare **plan** (sense 3), **ground plan** (sense 1) 6 the external face of a building or structure 7 a ballet dancer's ability to leap high 8 *RC Church* the lifting up of the Host at Mass for adoration 9 *astronomy* another name for **altitude** (sense 3) 10 the angle formed between the muzzle of a gun and the horizontal 11 *surveying* the angular distance between the plane through a point of observation and an object above it. Compare **depression** (sense 7) 12 *linguistics* another term for **amelioration**. > ˌele'vational *adj*

elevator (ˈɛlɪˌveɪtə) *n* 1 a person or thing that elevates 2 *chiefly US* a mechanical hoist for raising something, esp grain or coal, often consisting of a chain of scoops linked together on a conveyor belt 3 *chiefly US and Canadian* a platform, compartment, or cage raised or lowered in a vertical shaft to transport persons or goods in a building. Also called (in Britain and certain other countries): **lift** 4 *chiefly US and Canadian* a large granary equipped with an elevator and, usually, facilities for cleaning and grading the grain 5 any muscle that raises a part of the body 6 a surgical instrument for lifting a part of the body 7 a control surface on the tailplane of an aircraft, for making it climb or descend

eleven (ɪˈlɛvᵊn) *n* **1** the cardinal number that is the sum of ten and one **2** a numeral 11, XI, etc, representing this number **3** something representing, represented by, or consisting of 11 units **4** (*functioning as singular or plural*) a team of 11 players in football, cricket, hockey, etc **5** Also called: **eleven o'clock** eleven hours after noon or midnight ▷ *determiner* **6 a** amounting to eleven: *eleven chances* **b** (*as pronoun*): *have another eleven today* [Old English *endleofan*; related to Old Norse *ellefo*, Gothic *ainlif*, Old Frisian *andlova*, Old High German *einlif*]

eleven-plus *n* (esp formerly) an examination, taken by children aged 11 or 12, that determines the type of secondary education a child will be given

elevenses (ɪˈlɛvᵊnzɪz) *pl n* (*sometimes functioning as singular*) *Brit informal* a light snack, usually with tea or coffee, taken mid-morning

eleventh (ɪˈlɛvᵊnθ) *adj* **1** (*usually prenominal*) **a** coming after the tenth in numbering or counting order, position, time, etc; being the ordinal number of *eleven*: often written 11th **b** (*as pronoun*): *the eleventh in succession* ▷ *n* **2 a** one of 11 equal or nearly equal parts of an object, quantity, measurement, etc **b** (*as modifier*): *an eleventh part* **3** the fraction equal to one divided by 11 (1/11) **4** *music* **a** an interval of one octave plus one fourth **b** See **eleventh chord**

eleventh chord *n* a chord much used in jazz, consisting of a major or minor triad upon which are superimposed the seventh, ninth, and eleventh above the root

eleventh hour *n* **a** the latest possible time; last minute **b** (*as modifier*): *an eleventh-hour decision*

elevon (ˈɛlɪˌvɒn) *n* an aircraft control surface that combines the functions of an elevator and aileron, usually fitted to tailless or delta-wing aircraft [C20 from ELEV(ATOR) + (AILER)ON]

Elevsís (ˌɛlɛfˈsɪs) *n* transliteration of the Modern Greek name for **Eleusis**

elf (ɛlf) *n*, *pl* **elves** (ɛlvz) **1** (in folklore) one of a kind of legendary beings, usually characterized as small, manlike, and mischievous **2** a mischievous or whimsical child [Old English *ælf*; related to Old Norse *elfr* elf, Middle Low German *alf* incubus, Latin *albus* white] > ˈelfˌlike *adj*

ELF *abbreviation for* **extremely low frequency**

El Faiyûm (ɛl faɪˈjuːm) *or* **Al Faiyûm** (æl faɪˈjuːm) *n* a city in N Egypt: a site of towns going back at least to the 12th dynasty. Pop: 311 000 (2005 est)

elf-cup *n* any of various cup-shaped ascomycetous fungi of the order *Pezizales*, often strikingly coloured, such as the **orange-peel elf-cup** (*Aleuria aurantia*), which is bright orange inside and dirty white outside, and the **scarlet elf-cup** (*Sarcoscypha coccinea*)

El Ferrol (*Spanish* ɛl fɛˈrrɔl) *n* a port in NW Spain, on the Atlantic: fortified naval base, with a deep natural harbour. Pop: 78 764 (2003 est). Former name: El Ferrol del Caudillo (dɛl kauˈðiλo)

elfin (ˈɛlfɪn) *adj* **1** of, relating to, or like an elf or elves **2** small, delicate, and charming

elfin forest *or* **woodland** *n* the zone of stunted wind-blown trees growing at high altitudes just above the timberline on tropical mountains. Also called: **krummholz**

elfish (ˈɛlfɪʃ) *or* **elvish** *adj* **1** of, relating to, or like an elf or elves; charmingly mischievous or sprightly; impish ▷ *n* **2** the supposed language of elves > ˈelfishly *or* ˈelvishly *adv* > ˈelfishness *or* ˈelvishness *n*

elfland (ˈɛlfˌlænd) *n* another name for **fairyland**

elflock (ˈɛlfˌlɒk) *n* a lock of hair, fancifully regarded as having been tangled by the elves

Elgin (ˈɛlgɪn) *n* a market town in NE Scotland, the administrative centre of Moray, on the River Lossie: ruined 13th-century cathedral; distilling, engineering. Pop: 20 829 (2001)

Elgin marbles *pl n* a group of 5th-century BC Greek sculptures originally decorating the Parthenon in Athens, brought to England by

Thomas Bruce, seventh Earl of Elgin (1766–1841), and now at the British Museum

El Gîza (ɛl ˈgiːzə) *or* **Gîza** *n* a city in NE Egypt, on the W bank of the Nile opposite Cairo: nearby are the Great Pyramid of Cheops (Khufu) and the Sphinx. Pop: 2 221 868 (1996)

Elgon (ˈɛlgɒn) *n* **Mount** an extinct volcano in E Africa, on the Kenya-Uganda border. Height: 4321m (14 178 ft)

Eli (ˈiːlaɪ) *n* *Old Testament* the highest priest at Shiloh and teacher of Samuel (I Samuel 1–3)

Elia *or* **Eleia** (ˈiːlɪə) *n* a department of SW Greece, in the W Peloponnese: in ancient times most of the region formed the state of Elis. Pop: 183 521 (2001). Area: 2681 sq km (1035 sq miles). Modern Greek name: Ilía

Elias (ɪˈlaɪəs) *n* *Bible* the Douay spelling of **Elijah**

eliche (*Italian* elike) *n* pasta in the form of spirals [Italian: literally, propellers]

elicit (ɪˈlɪsɪt) *vb* (*tr*) **1** to give rise to; evoke: *to elicit a sharp retort* **2** to bring to light: *to elicit the truth* [C17 from Latin *ēlicere* to lure forth, from *licere* to entice] > eˈlicitable *adj* > eˌliciˈtation *n* > eˈlicitor *n*

elide (ɪˈlaɪd) *vb* *phonetics* to undergo or cause to undergo elision [C16 from Latin *ēlīdere* to knock, from *laedere* to hit, wound] > eˈlidible *adj*

eligible (ˈɛlɪdʒəbᵊl) *adj* **1** fit, worthy, or qualified, as for an office or function **2** desirable and worthy of being chosen, esp as a spouse: *an eligible young man* [C15 from Late Latin *ēligibilis* able to be chosen, from *ēligere* to ELECT] > ˌeligiˈbility *n* > ˈeligibly *adv*

Elijah (ɪˈlaɪdʒə) *n* *Old Testament* a Hebrew prophet of the 9th century BC, who was persecuted for denouncing Ahab and Jezebel. (I Kings 17–21: 21; II Kings 1–2:18)

Elikón (ɛliˈkɔn) *n* transliteration of the Modern Greek name for **Helicon**

eliminate (ɪˈlɪmɪˌneɪt) *vb* (*tr*) **1** to remove or take out; get rid of **2** to reject as trivial or irrelevant; omit from consideration **3** to remove (a competitor, team, etc) from a contest, usually by defeat **4** *slang* to murder in a cold-blooded manner **5** *physiol* to expel (waste matter) from the body **6** *maths* to remove (an unknown variable) from two or more simultaneous equations [C16 from Latin *ēlīmināre* to turn out of the house, from *e-* out + *līmen* threshold] > eˈliminable *adj* > eˌliminaˈbility *n* > eˈliminant *n* > eˈliminative *or* eˈliminatory *adj* > eˈlimiˌnator *n*

USAGE *Eliminate* is sometimes wrongly used to talk about avoiding the repetition of something undesirable: *we must prevent* (not *eliminate*) *further mistakes of this kind*

elimination (ɪˌlɪmɪˈneɪʃən) *n* **1** the act of eliminating or the state of being eliminated **2** *logic* (qualified by the name of an operation) a syntactic rule specifying the conditions under which a formula or statement containing the specified operation may permit the derivation of others that do not contain it: *conjunction-elimination; universal elimination* **3** *chem* a type of chemical reaction involving the loss of a simple molecule, such as water or carbon dioxide

Elis (ˈiːlɪs) *n* an ancient city-state of SW Greece, in the NW Peloponnese: site of the ancient Olympic games

ELISA (ɪˈlaɪzə) *n acronym for* enzyme-linked immunosorbent assay: an immunological technique for accurately measuring the amount of a substance, for example in a blood sample

Élisabethville (ɪˈlɪzəbəθˌvɪl) *n* the former name (until 1966) of **Lubumbashi**

Elisavetgrad (*Russian* jɪlizaˈvjɛtgrət) *n* a former name (until 1924) of **Kirovograd**

Elisavetpol (*Russian* jɪlizaˈvjɛtpəlj) *n* a former name (until 1920) of **Kirovabad**

Elisha (ɪˈlaɪʃə) *n* *Old Testament* a Hebrew prophet of the 9th century BC: successor of Elijah (II Kings 3–9)

elision (ɪˈlɪʒən) *n* **1** the omission of a syllable or

vowel at the beginning or end of a word, esp when a word ending with a vowel is next to one beginning with a vowel **2** any omission of a part or parts [C16 from Latin *ēlīsiō*, from *ēlīdere* to ELIDE]

elite *or* **élite** (ɪˈliːt, eɪ-) *n* **1** (*sometimes functioning as plural*) the most powerful, rich, gifted, or educated members of a group, community, etc **2** Also called: **twelve pitch** a typewriter typesize having 12 characters to the inch ▷ *adj* **3** of, relating to, or suitable for an elite; exclusive [C18 from French, from Old French *eslit* chosen, from *eslire* to choose, from Latin *ēligere* to ELECT]

elitism (ɪˈliːtɪzəm, eɪ-) *n* **1 a** the belief that society should be governed by a select group of gifted and highly educated individuals **b** such government **2** pride in or awareness of being one of an elite group > eˈlitist *adj, n*

elixir (ɪˈlɪksə) *n* **1** an alchemical preparation supposed to be capable of prolonging life indefinitely (**elixir of life**) or of transmuting base metals into gold **2** anything that purports to be a sovereign remedy; panacea **3** an underlying principle; quintessence **4** a liquid containing a medicinal drug with syrup, glycerine, or alcohol added to mask its unpleasant taste [C14 from Medieval Latin, from Arabic *al iksīr* the elixir, probably from Greek *xērion* powder used for drying wounds, from *xēros* dry]

Elizabeth (ɪˈlɪzəbəθ) *n* **1** a city in NE New Jersey, on Newark Bay. Pop: 123 215 (2003 est) **2** a town in SE South Australia, near Adelaide. Pop: 34 000 (latest est)

Elizabethan (ɪˌlɪzəˈbiːθən) *adj* **1** of, characteristic of, or relating to England or its culture in the age of Elizabeth I (1533–1603; reigned 1558–1603) or to the United Kingdom or its culture in the age of Elizabeth II (born 1926; queen from 1952) **2** of, relating to, or designating a style of architecture used in England during the reign of Elizabeth I, characterized by moulded and sculptured ornament based on German and Flemish models ▷ *n* **3** a person who lived in England during the reign of Elizabeth I

Elizabethan sonnet *n* another term for **Shakespearean sonnet**

elk (ɛlk) *n*, *pl* **elks** *or* **elk 1** a large deer, *Alces alces*, of N Europe and Asia, having large flattened palmate antlers: also occurs in North America, where it is called a moose **2 American elk** another name for **wapiti 3** a stout pliable waterproof leather made from calfskin or horsehide [Old English *eolh*; related to Old Norse *elgr*, Old High German *elaho*, Latin *alcēs*, Greek *alkē*, *elaphos* deer]

El Khalil (ɛl xɒˈliːl) *n* transliteration of the Arabic name for **Hebron**

elkhound (ˈɛlkˌhaʊnd) *n* a powerful breed of dog of the spitz type with a thick grey coat and tightly curled tail. Also called: **Norwegian elkhound**

ell[1] (ɛl) *n* an obsolete unit of length equal to approximately 45 inches [Old English *eln* the forearm (the measure originally being from the elbow to the fingertips); related to Old High German *elina*, Latin *ulna*, Greek *ōlenē*]

ell[2] (ɛl) *n* **1** an extension to a building, usually at right angles and located at one end **2** a pipe fitting, pipe, or tube with a sharp right-angle bend [C20 a spelling of L, indicating a right angle]

Ellás (ɛˈlas) *n* transliteration of the Modern Greek name for **Greece**

Ellesmere Island (ˈɛlzmɪə) *n* a Canadian island in the Arctic Ocean: part of Nunavut; mountainous, with many glaciers. Area: 212 688 sq km (82 119 sq miles)

Ellesmere Port *n* a port in NW England, in NW Cheshire on the Mersey estuary and Manchester Ship Canal. Pop: 66 265 (2001)

Ellice Islands (ˈɛlɪs) *pl n* the former name (until 1975) of **Tuvalu**

ellipse (ɪˈlɪps) *n* a closed conic section shaped like a flattened circle and formed by an inclined plane that does not cut the base of the cone. Standard

e

equation $x^2/a^2 + y^2/b^2 = 1$, where $2a$ and $2b$ are the lengths of the major and minor axes. Area: πab [c18 back formation from ELLIPSIS]

ellipsis (ɪˈlɪpsɪs) *n, pl* **-ses** (-siːz) **1** Also called: **eclipsis** omission of parts of a word or sentence **2** *printing* a sequence of three dots (...) indicating an omission in text [c16 from Latin, from Greek *elleipsis* omission, from *elleipein* to leave out, from *leipein* to leave]

ellipsoid (ɪˈlɪpsɔɪd) *n* **a** a geometric surface, symmetrical about the three coordinate axes, whose plane sections are ellipses or circles. Standard equation: $x^2/a^2 + y^2/b^2 + z^2/c^2 = 1$, where $\pm a, \pm b, \pm c$ are the intercepts on the *x*-, *y*-, and *z*- axes **b** a solid having this shape: *the earth is an ellipsoid* ▷ **ellipsoidal** (ɪˌlɪpˈsɔɪdəl, ˌɛl-) *adj*

ellipsoid of revolution *n* a geometric surface produced by rotating an ellipse about one of its two axes and having circular plane surfaces perpendicular to the axis of revolution. Also called: **spheroid**

elliptical (ɪˈlɪptɪkəl) *adj* **1** relating to or having the shape of an ellipse **2** relating to or resulting from ellipsis **3** (of speech, literary style, etc) **a** very condensed or concise, often so as to be obscure or ambiguous **b** circumlocutory or long-winded ▷ Also (for senses 1, 2): **elliptic** > **elˈliptically** *adv* > **elˈlipticalness** *n*

◼ USAGE The use of *elliptical* to mean *circumlocutory* should be avoided as it may be interpreted wrongly as meaning *condensed* or *concise*

elliptic geometry *n* another name for **Riemannian geometry**

ellipticity (ɪlɪpˈtɪsɪtɪ, ˌɛl-) *n* the degree of deviation from a circle or sphere of an elliptical or ellipsoidal shape or path, measured as the ratio of the major to the minor axes

elm (ɛlm) *n* **1** any ulmaceous tree of the genus *Ulmus*, occurring in the N hemisphere, having serrated leaves and winged fruits (samaras): cultivated for shade, ornament, and timber **2** the hard heavy wood of this tree ▷ See also **slippery elm, wahoo¹, wych-elm** [Old English *elm*; related to Old Norse *almr*, Old High German *elm*, Latin *ulmus*]

El Mansûra (ɛl mænˈsuərə) or **Al Mansûrah** *n* a city in NE Egypt: scene of a battle (1250) in which the Crusaders were defeated by the Mamelukes and Louis IX of France was captured; cotton-manufacturing centre. Pop: 423 000 (2005 est)

El Minya (ɛl ˈmɪnjə) *n* a river port in central Egypt on the Nile. Pop: 225 000 (2005 est)

El Misti (ɛl ˈmiːstiː) *n* a volcano in S Peru, in the Andes. Height: 5852 m (19 199 ft)

El Niño (ɛl ˈniːnjəʊ) *n meteorol* a warming of the eastern tropical Pacific occurring every few years, which alters the weather pattern of the tropics [c20 from Spanish: The Child, ie Christ, referring to its original occurrence at Christmas time]

El Obeid (ɛl əʊˈbeɪd) *n* a city in the central Sudan, in Kordofan province: scene of the defeat of a British and Egyptian army by the Mahdi (1883). Pop: 423 000 (2005 est)

elocute (ˈɛləˌkjuːt) *vb (intr) facetious* to speak as if practising elocution; declaim [c19 back formation from ELOCUTION]

elocution (ˌɛləˈkjuːʃən) *n* the art of public speaking, esp of voice production, delivery, and gesture [c15 from Latin *ēlocūtiō* a speaking out, from *ēloquī*, from *loquī* to speak] > ˌelo'cutionary *adj* > ˌelo'cutionist *n*

Elohim (ɛˈləʊhɪm, ˌɛləʊˈhiːm) *n Old Testament* a Hebrew word for God or gods [c17 from Hebrew *'Elōhim*, plural (used to indicate uniqueness) of *'Elōah* God; probably related to *'El* God]

Elohist (ɛˈləʊhɪst) *n Old Testament* the supposed author or authors of one of the four main strands of text of the Pentateuch, identified chiefly by the use of the word *Elohim* for God instead of YHVH (Jehovah)

eloign or **eloin** (ɪˈlɔɪn) *vb (tr) archaic* to remove

(oneself, one's property, etc) to a distant place [c16 from Anglo-French *esloigner* to go far away; related to Latin *longē* (adv) far; compare ELONGATE] > e'loigner or e'loiner *n* > e'loignment or e'loinment *n*

elongate (ˈiːlɒŋɡeɪt) *vb* **1** to make or become longer; stretch ▷ *adj* **2** long and narrow; slender: *elongate leaves* **3** lengthened or tapered [c17 from Late Latin *ēlongāre* to keep at a distance, from *ē-* away + Latin *longē* (adv) far, but also later: to lengthen, as if from *ē-* + Latin *longus* (adj) long]

elongation (ˌiːlɒŋˈɡeɪʃən) *n* **1** the act of elongating or state of being elongated; lengthening **2** something that is elongated **3** *astronomy* the difference between the celestial longitude of the sun and that of a planet or the moon

elope (ɪˈləʊp) *vb (intr)* to run away secretly with a lover, esp in order to marry [c16 from Anglo-French *aloper*, perhaps from Middle Dutch *lōpen* to run; see LOPE] > e'lopement *n* > e'loper *n*

eloquence (ˈɛləkwəns) *n* **1** ease in using language to best effect **2** powerful and effective language **3** the quality of being persuasive or moving

eloquent (ˈɛləkwənt) *adj* **1** (of speech, writing, etc) characterized by fluency and persuasiveness **2** visibly or vividly expressive, as of an emotion: *an eloquent yawn* [c14 from Latin *ēloquēns*, from *ēloquī* to speak out, from *loquī* to speak] > 'eloquently *adv*

El Paso (ɛl ˈpæsəʊ) *n* a city in W Texas, on the Rio Grande opposite Ciudad Juárez, Mexico. Pop: 584 113 (2003 est)

El Salvador (ɛl ˈsælvəˌdɔː) *n* a republic in Central America, on the Pacific: colonized by the Spanish from 1524; declared independence in 1841, becoming a republic in 1856. It consists of coastal lowlands rising to a central plateau. Coffee constitutes over a third of the total exports. Official language: Spanish. Religion: Roman Catholic majority. Currency: US dollar. Capital: San Salvador. Pop: 6 614 000 (2004 est). Area: 21 393 sq km (8236 sq miles) > ˌSalva'doran, ˌSalva'dorean or ˌSalva'dorian *adj, n*

Elsan (ˈɛlsæn) *n trademark* a type of portable lavatory in which chemicals are used to kill bacteria and deodorize the sludge [c20 from the initials of E L Jackson, the manufacturer + SAN(ITATION)]

Elsass (ˈɛlzas) *n* the German name for **Alsace**

Elsass-Lothringen (ˈɛlzasˈloːtrɪŋən) *n* the German name for **Alsace-Lorraine**

else (ɛls) *determiner (postpositive; used after an indefinite pronoun or an interrogative)* **1** in addition; more: *there is nobody else here* **2** other; different: *where else could he be?* ▷ *adv* **3** or else **a** if not, then: *go away or else I won't finish my work today* **b** or something terrible will result: *used as a threat: sit down, or else!* [Old English *elles*, genitive of *el-* strange, foreign; related to Old High German *eli-* other, Gothic *alja*, Latin *alius*, Greek *allos*]

elsewhere (ˌɛlsˈwɛə) *adv* in or to another place; somewhere else [Old English *elles hwǣr*; see ELSE, WHERE]

Elsinore (ˈɛlsɪˌnɔː, ˌɛlsɪˈnɔː) *n* the English name for **Helsingør**

ELT *abbreviation for* English Language Teaching: the teaching of English specifically to students whose native language is not English

eluate (ˈɛljuˌeɪt) *n* a solution of adsorbed material in the eluent obtained during the process of elution

elucidate (ɪˈluːsɪˌdeɪt) *vb* to make clear (something obscure or difficult); clarify [c16 from Late Latin *ēlūcidāre* to enlighten; see LUCID] > eˌluci'dation *n* > e'luciˌdative or e'luciˌdatory *adj* > e'luciˌdator *n*

elude (ɪˈluːd) *vb (tr)* **1** to escape or avoid (capture, one's pursuers, etc), esp by cunning **2** to avoid fulfilment of (a responsibility, obligation, etc); evade **3** to escape discovery, or understanding by; baffle: *the solution eluded her* [c16 from Latin *ēlūdere*

to deceive, from *lūdere* to play] > e'luder *n* > elusion (ɪˈluːʒən) *n*

◼ USAGE *Elude* is sometimes wrongly used where *allude* is meant: *he was alluding* (not *eluding*) *to his previous visit to the city*

eluent or **eluant** (ˈɛljuːənt) *n* a solvent used for eluting

Elul (ɛˈluːl) *n* (in the Jewish calendar) the sixth month of the year according to biblical reckoning and the twelfth month of the civil year, usually falling within August and September [from Hebrew]

elusive (ɪˈluːsɪv) *adj* **1** difficult to catch: *an elusive thief* **2** preferring or living in solitude and anonymity **3** difficult to remember: *an elusive thought* > e'lusively *adv* > e'lusiveness *n*

◼ USAGE See at **illusory**

elusory (ɪˈluːsərɪ) *adj* **1** avoiding the issue; evasive: *elusory arguments* **2** difficult to grasp mentally; elusive: *elusory ideas*

elute (iːˈluːt, ɪˈluːt) *vb (tr)* to wash out (a substance) by the action of a solvent, as in chromatography [c18 from Latin *ēlūtus* rinsed out, from *ēluere* to wash clean, from *luere* to wash, LAVE] > e'lution *n*

elutriate (ɪˈluːtrɪˌeɪt) *vb (tr)* to purify or separate (a substance or mixture) by washing and straining or decanting [c18 from Latin *ēlūtriāre* to wash out, from *ēluere*, from *ē-* out + *lavere* to wash] > eˌlutri'ation *n* > e'lutriˌator *n*

eluviation (ɪˌluːvɪˈeɪʃən) *n* the process by which material suspended in water is removed from one layer of soil to another by the action of rainfall or chemical decomposition [c20 from ELUVIUM]

eluvium (ɪˈluːvɪəm) *n, pl* **-via** (-vɪə) a mass of sand, silt, etc: a product of the erosion of rocks that has remained in its place of origin [c19 New Latin, from Latin *ēluere* to wash out] > e'luvial *adj*

elver (ˈɛlvə) *n* a young eel, esp one migrating up a river from the sea. See also **leptocephalus** [c17 variant of *eelfare* migration of young eels, literally: eel-journey; see EEL, FARE]

elves (ɛlvz) *n* the plural of **elf**

elvish (ˈɛlvɪʃ) *adj* a variant of **elfish**

Elx (eltʃ) *n* the Catalan name for **Elche**

Ely (ˈiːlɪ) *n* **1** a cathedral city in E England, in E Cambridgeshire on the River Ouse. Pop: 13 954 (2001) **2** a former county of E England, part of Cambridgeshire since 1965

Elysée (eˈliːzeɪ) *n* a palace in Paris, in the Champs Elysées: official residence of the president of France

Elysian (ɪˈlɪzɪən) *adj* **1** of or relating to Elysium **2** *literary* delightful; glorious; blissful

Elysium (ɪˈlɪzɪəm) *n* **1** Also called: **Elysian fields** *Greek myth* the dwelling place of the blessed after death. See also **Islands of the Blessed 2** a state or place of perfect bliss [c16 from Latin, from Greek *Elūsion pedion* Elysian (that is, blessed) fields]

elytron (ˈɛlɪˌtrɒn) or **elytrum** (ˈɛlɪtrəm) *n, pl* **-tra** (-trə) either of the horny front wings of beetles and some other insects, which cover and protect the hind wings [c18 from Greek *elutron* sheath, covering] > 'elyˌtroid or 'elytrous *adj*

em (ɛm) *n printing* **1** Also called: **mutton, mut** the square of a body of any size of type, used as a unit of measurement **2** Also called: **pica em, pica** a unit of measurement used in printing, equal to one sixth of an inch [c19 from the name of the letter *M*]

em- *prefix* a variant of **en-¹** and **en-²** before *b, m,* and *p*

'em (əm) *pron* an informal variant of **them**

emaciate (ɪˈmeɪsɪˌeɪt) *vb (usually tr)* to become or cause to become abnormally thin [c17 from Latin *ēmaciāre* to make lean, from *macer* thin] > eˌmaci'ation *n*

emaciated (ɪˈmeɪsɪˌeɪtɪd) *adj* abnormally thin

emacs (ˈiːmæks) *n, pl* **emacsen** (ˈiːmæksən) *computing* a powerful computer program used for creating and editing text, functioning primarily through keyboard commands [c20 from *e(ditor mac(ro)s*]

e-mail *or* **email** ('i:meɪl) *n* **1** short for **electronic mail** ▷ *vb* (*tr*) **2** to contact (a person) by electronic mail **3** to send (a message, document, etc) by electronic mail > **e'mailer** *n*

emalangeni (ˌɛmɒːlɒːŋˈgeɪnɪ) *n* the plural of **lilangeni**

emanate ('ɛmɒˌneɪt) *vb* **1** (*intr; often foll by from*) to issue or proceed from or as from a source **2** (*tr*) to send forth; emit [c18 from Latin *ēmānāre* to flow out, from *mānāre* to flow] > **emanative** ('ɛmənətɪv) *adj* > **'emaˌnator** *n* > **emanatory** ('ɛməˌneɪtərɪ, -trɪ) *adj*

emanation (ˌɛməˈneɪʃən) *n* **1** an act or instance of emanating **2** something that emanates or is produced; effusion **3** a gaseous product of radioactive decay, such as radon > ˌema'national *adj*

emancipate (ɪˈmænsɪˌpeɪt) *vb* (*tr*) **1** to free from restriction or restraint, esp social or legal restraint **2** (*often passive*) to free from the inhibitions imposed by conventional morality **3** to liberate (a slave) from bondage [c17 from Latin *ēmancipāre* to give independence (to a son), from *mancipāre* to transfer property, from *manceps* a purchaser; see MANCIPLE] > e'manciˌpated *adj* > e'mancipative *adj* > e'mancipist *or* e'manciˌpator *n* > emancipatory (ɪˈmænsɪpətərɪ, -trɪ) *adj*

emancipation (ɪˌmænsɪˈpeɪʃən) *n* **1** the act of freeing or state of being freed; liberation **2** *informal* freedom from inhibition and convention > eˌmanci'pationist *n*

emarginate (ɪˈmɑːdʒɪˌneɪt) *or* **emarginated** *adj* having a notched tip or edge: *emarginate leaves* [c17 from Latin *ēmargināre* to deprive of its edge, from *margō* MARGIN] > eˌmargi'nately *adv* > eˌmargi'nation *n*

e-marketing *n* the practice of marketing by means of the internet [c20 electronic *marketing*]

emasculate *vb* (ɪˈmæskjʊˌleɪt) (*tr*) **1** to remove the testicles of; castrate; geld **2** to deprive of vigour, effectiveness, etc **3** *botany* to remove the stamens from (a flower) to prevent self-pollination for the purposes of plant breeding ▷ *adj* (ɪˈmæskjʊlɪt, -ˌleɪt) **4** castrated; gelded **5** deprived of strength, effectiveness, etc [c17 from Latin *ēmasculāre*, from *masculus* male; see MASCULINE] > eˌmascu'lation *n* > e'masculative *or* e'masculatory *adj* > e'mascuˌlator *n*

embalm (ɪmˈbɑːm) *vb* (*tr*) **1** to treat (a dead body) with preservatives, as by injecting formaldehyde into the blood vessels, to retard putrefaction **2** to preserve or cherish the memory of **3** *poetic* to give a sweet fragrance to [c13 from Old French *embaumer*; see BALM] > em'balmer *n* > em'balmment *n*

embank (ɪmˈbæŋk) *vb* (*tr*) to protect, enclose, or confine (a waterway, road, etc) with an embankment

embankment (ɪmˈbæŋkmənt) *n* a man-made ridge of earth or stone that carries a road or railway or confines a waterway. See also **levee**

embargo (ɛmˈbɑːgəʊ) *n*, *pl* -goes **1** a government order prohibiting the departure or arrival of merchant ships in its ports **2** any legal stoppage of commerce: *an embargo on arms shipments* **3** a restraint, hindrance, or prohibition ▷ *vb* -goes, -going, -goed (*tr*) **4** to lay an embargo upon **5** to seize for use by the state [c16 from Spanish, from *embargar*, from Latin IM- + *barra* BAR[1]]

embark (ɛmˈbɑːk) *vb* **1** to board (a ship or aircraft) **2** (*intr; usually foll by on or upon*) to commence or engage (in) a new project, venture, etc [c16 via French from Old Provençal *embarcar*, from EM- + *barca* boat, BARQUE] > ˌembar'kation *n* > em'barkment *n*

embarras de richesses *French* (ãbara də riʃɛs) *n* a superfluous abundance of options, from which one finds it difficult to select. Also called: *embarras de choix* (də ʃwa) [c18 literally: embarrassment of riches]

embarrass (ɪmˈbærəs) *vb* (*mainly tr*) **1** (*also intr*) to feel or cause to feel confusion or self-consciousness; disconcert; fluster **2** (*usually passive*) to involve in financial difficulties **3** *archaic* to make difficult; complicate **4** *archaic* to impede; obstruct; hamper [c17 (in the sense: to impede): via French and Spanish from Italian *imbarazzare*, from *imbarrare* to confine within bars; see EN-[1], BAR[1]] > em'barrassed *adj* > em'barrassedly *adv*

embarrassing (ɪmˈbærəsɪŋ) *adj* causing one to feel confusion or self-consciousness; disconcerting > em'barrassingly *adv*

embarrassment (ɪmˈbærəsmənt) *n* **1** the state of being embarrassed **2** something that embarrasses **3** a financial predicament **4** an excessive amount; superfluity

embassy ('ɛmbəsɪ) *n*, *pl* -sies **1** the residence or place of official business of an ambassador **2** an ambassador and his entourage collectively **3** the position, business, or mission of an ambassador **4** any important or official mission, duty, etc, esp one undertaken by an agent [c16 from Old French *ambassee*, from Old Italian *ambasciata*, from Old Provençal *ambaisada*, ultimately of Germanic origin; see AMBASSADOR]

embattle (ɪmˈbætᵊl) *vb* (*tr*) **1** to deploy (troops) for battle **2** to strengthen or fortify (a position, town, etc) **3** to provide (a building) with battlements [c14 from Old French *embataillier*; see EN-[1], BATTLE]

embattled (ɪmˈbætᵊld) *adj* **1** prepared for or engaged in conflict, controversy, or battle **2** *heraldry* having an indented edge resembling battlements

embay (ɪmˈbeɪ) *vb* (*tr; usually passive*) **1** to form into a bay **2** to enclose in or as if in a bay **3** (*esp of the wind*) to force (a ship, esp a sailing ship) into a bay

embayment (ɪmˈbeɪmənt) *n* a shape resembling a bay

Embden-Meyerhof pathway ('ɛmdənˈmaɪəˌhɒf) *n* the metabolic reaction sequence in glycolysis by which glucose is converted to pyruvic acid with production of ATP [c20 named after Gustav *Embden* (1874–1933) and Otto *Meyerhof* (1884–1951), German biochemists]

embed (ɪmˈbɛd) *vb* -beds, -bedding, -bedded **1** (*usually foll by in*) to fix or become fixed firmly and deeply in a surrounding solid mass: *to embed a nail in wood* **2** (*tr*) to surround closely: *hard rock embeds the roots* **3** (*tr*) to fix or retain (a thought, idea, etc) in the mind **4** (*often foll by with*) to assign a journalist or be assigned as one to accompany an active military unit **5** (*tr*) *grammar* to insert (a subordinate clause) into a sentence ▷ Also: **imbed** ▷ *n* **6** a journalist accompanying an active military unit > em'bedment *n*

embedding (ɪmˈbɛdɪŋ) *n* the practice of assigning or being assigned a journalist to accompany an active military unit

embellish (ɪmˈbɛlɪʃ) *vb* (*tr*) **1** to improve or beautify by adding detail or ornament; adorn **2** to make (a story) more interesting by adding detail **3** to provide (a melody, part, etc) with ornaments. See **ornament** (sense 5) [c14 from Old French *embelir*, from *bel* beautiful, from Latin *bellus*] > em'bellisher *n* > em'bellishment *n*

ember ('ɛmbə) *n* **1** a glowing or smouldering piece of coal or wood, as in a dying fire **2** the fading remains of a past emotion: *the embers of his love* [Old English *ǣmyrge*; related to Old Norse *eimyrja* ember, *eimr* smoke, Old High German *eimuria* ember]

Ember days *pl n* *RC and Anglican Church* any of four groups of three days (always Wednesday, Friday, and Saturday) of prayer and fasting, the groups occurring after Pentecost, after the first Sunday of Lent, after the feast of St Lucy (Dec 13), and after the feast of the Holy Cross (Sept 14) [Old English *ymbrendæg*, from *ymbren*, perhaps from *ymbryne* a (recurring) period, from *ymb* around + *ryne* a course + *dæg* day]

ember goose *n* (*not in ornithological use*) another name for the **great northern diver** [c18 from Norwegian *emmer-gaas*]

Ember week *n* a week in which Ember days fall

embezzle (ɪmˈbɛzᵊl) *vb* (*tr*) to convert (money or property entrusted to one) fraudulently to one's own use [c15 from Anglo-French *embeseiller* to destroy, from Old French *beseiller* to make away with, of uncertain origin] > em'bezzlement *n* > em'bezzler *n*

embitter (ɪmˈbɪtə) *vb* (*tr*) **1** to make (a person) resentful or bitter **2** to aggravate (an already hostile feeling, difficult situation, etc) > em'bittered *adj* > em'bitterer *n* > em'bitterment *n*

emblaze (ɪmˈbleɪz) *vb* (*tr*) *archaic* **1** to cause to light up; illuminate **2** to set fire to

emblazon (ɪmˈbleɪzᵊn) *vb* (*tr*) **1** to describe, portray, or colour (arms) according to the conventions of heraldry **2** to portray heraldic arms on (a shield, one's notepaper, etc) **3** to make bright or splendid, as with colours, flowers, etc **4** to glorify, praise, or extol, often so as to attract great publicity: *his feat was emblazoned on the front page* > em'blazonment *n*

emblazonry (ɪmˈbleɪzᵊnrɪ) *n* another name for **blazonry**

emblem ('ɛmbləm) *n* **1** a visible object or representation that symbolizes a quality, type, group, etc, esp the concrete symbol of an abstract idea: *the dove is an emblem of peace* **2** an allegorical picture containing a moral lesson, often with an explanatory motto or verses, esp one printed in an **emblem book** [c15 from Latin *emblēma* raised decoration, mosaic, from Greek, literally: something inserted, from *emballein* to insert, from *ballein* to throw] > ˌemblem'atic *or* ˌemblem'atical *adj* > ˌemblem'atically *adv*

emblematize (ɛmˈblɛməˌtaɪz), **emblemize** ('ɛmbləˌmaɪz), **emblematise** *or* **emblemise** *vb* (*tr*) **1** to function as an emblem of; symbolize **2** to represent by or as by an emblem

emblements ('ɛmbləmənts) *pl n* *law* **1** annual crops and vegetable products cultivated by man's labour **2** the profits from such crops [c15 from Old French *emblaement*, from *emblaer* to sow with grain, from Medieval Latin *imblādāre*, from *blāda* grain, of Germanic origin; compare Old English *blǣd* grain]

embody (ɪmˈbɒdɪ) *vb* -bodies, -bodying, -bodied (*tr*) **1** to give a tangible, bodily, or concrete form to (an abstract concept) **2** to be an example of or express (an idea, principle, etc), esp in action: *his gentleness embodies a Christian ideal* **3** (*often foll by in*) to collect or unite in a comprehensive whole, system, etc; comprise; include: *all the different essays were embodied in one long article* **4** to invest (a spiritual entity) with a body or with bodily form; render incarnate > em'bodiment *n*

embolden (ɪmˈbəʊldᵊn) *vb* (*tr*) to encourage; make bold

embolectomy (ˌɛmbəˈlɛktəmɪ) *n*, *pl* -mies the surgical removal of an embolus that is blocking a blood vessel

embolic (ɛmˈbɒlɪk) *adj* **1** of or relating to an embolus or embolism **2** *embryol* of, relating to, or resulting from invagination

embolism ('ɛmbəˌlɪzəm) *n* **1** the occlusion of a blood vessel by an embolus **2** *botany* the blocking of a xylem vessel by an air bubble **3** the insertion of one or more days into a calendar, esp the Jewish calendar; intercalation **4** *RC Church* a prayer inserted in the canon of the Mass between the Lord's Prayer and the breaking of the bread **5** another name (not in technical use) for **embolus** [c14 from Medieval Latin *embolismus*, from Late Greek *embolismos* intercalary; see EMBOLUS] > ˌembo'lismic *adj*

embolize *or* **embolise** ('ɛmbəˌlaɪz) *vb* (*tr*) to cause embolism in (a blood vessel) > ˌemboli'zation *or* ˌemboli'sation *n*

embolus ('ɛmbələs) *n*, *pl* -li (-ˌlaɪ) material, such as part of a blood clot or an air bubble, that is transported by the blood stream until it becomes lodged within a small vessel and impedes the circulation. Compare **thrombus** [c17 via Latin from Greek *embolos* stopper, from *emballein* to insert, from *ballein* to throw; see EMBLEM]

emboly ('ɛmbəlɪ) *n, pl* **-lies** another name for **invagination** (sense 3) [c19 from Greek *embolē* an insertion, from *emballein* to throw in; see EMBLEM]

embonpoint French (ābɔ̃pwɛ̃) *n* **1** plumpness or stoutness ▷ *adj* **2** plump; stout [c18 from phrase *en bon point* in good condition]

embosom (ɪm'bʊzəm) *vb* (*tr*) *archaic* **1** to enclose or envelop, esp protectively **2** to clasp to the bosom; hug **3** to cherish

emboss (ɪm'bɒs) *vb* **1** to mould or carve (a decoration or design) on (a surface) so that it is raised above the surface in low relief **2** to cause to bulge; make protrude [c14 from Old French *embocer*, from EM- + *boce* BOSS²] > em'bosser *n* > em'bossment *n*

embossed (ɪm'bɒsd) *adj* having a moulded or carved decoration or design on the surface so that it is raised above the surface in low relief

embothrium (ɪm'bʊθrɪəm) *n* any evergreen shrub of the genus *Embothrium*, esp *E. coccineum*, native to South America but widely cultivated as an ornamental for its scarlet flowers: family *Proteaceae*. Also called: Chilean firebush [c19 from EM- + Greek *bothrion* small pit (referring to its anthers)]

embouchure (ˌɒmbʊ'ʃʊə) *n* **1** the mouth of a river or valley **2** *music* **a** the correct application of the lips and tongue in playing a wind instrument **b** the mouthpiece of a wind instrument [c18 from French, from Old French *emboucher* to put to one's mouth, from *bouche* mouth, from Latin *bucca* cheek]

embourgeoisement (*French* āburʒwazmā) *n* the process of becoming middle-class; the assimilation into the middle class of traditionally working-class people [from French, from EN-¹ + BOURGEOIS¹]

embow (ɪm'bəʊ) *vb* (*tr*) to design or create (a structure) in the form of an arch or vault > em'bowed *adj* > em'bowment *n*

embowel (ɪm'baʊəl) *vb* *obsolete* **1** to bury or embed deeply **2** another word for **disembowel**

embower (ɪm'baʊə) *vb* (*tr*) *archaic* to enclose in or as in a bower

embrace¹ (ɪm'breɪs) *vb* (*mainly tr*) **1** (*also intr*) (of a person) to take or clasp (another person) in the arms, or (of two people) to clasp each other, as in affection, greeting, etc; hug **2** to accept (an opportunity, challenge, etc) willingly or eagerly **3** to take up (a new idea, faith, etc); adopt: *to embrace Judaism* **4** to comprise or include as an integral part: *geology embraces the science of mineralogy* **5** to encircle or enclose ▷ *n* **6** the act of embracing **7** (*often plural*) *euphemistic* sexual intercourse [c14 from Old French *embracier*, from EM- + *brace* a pair of arms, from Latin *bracchia* arms] > em'braceable *adj* > em'bracement *n* > em'bracer *n*

embrace² (ɪm'breɪs) *vb* (*tr*) *criminal law* to commit or attempt to commit embracery against (a jury, etc) [c15 back formation from EMBRACEOR]

embraceor or **embracer** (ɪm'breɪsə) *n* *criminal law* a person guilty of embracery [c15 from Old French *embraseor*, from *embraser* to instigate, literally: to set on fire, from *braser* to burn, from *brese* live coals]

embracery (ɪm'breɪsərɪ) *n* *criminal law* the offence of attempting by corrupt means to influence a jury or juror, as by bribery or threats

embranchment (ɪm'brɑ:ntʃmənt) *n* **1** the process of branching out, esp by a river **2** a branching out or ramification, as of a river or mountain range

embrangle (ɪm'bræŋgəl) *vb* (*tr*) *rare* to confuse or entangle [c17 from EM- + obsolete *brangle* to wrangle, perhaps a blend of BRAWL¹ + WRANGLE] > em'branglement *n*

embrasure (ɪm'breɪʒə) *n* **1** *fortifications* an opening or indentation, as in a battlement, for shooting through **2** an opening forming a door or

window, having splayed sides that increase the width of the opening in the interior [c18 from French, from obsolete *embraser* to widen, of uncertain origin] > em'brasured *adj*

embrocate ('ɛmbrəʊˌkeɪt) *vb* (*tr*) to apply a liniment or lotion to (a part of the body) [c17 from Medieval Latin *embrocāre*, from *embrocha* poultice, from Greek *embrokhē* lotion, infusion, from *brokhē* a moistening]

embrocation (ˌɛmbrəʊ'keɪʃən) *n* a drug or agent for rubbing into the skin; liniment

embroider (ɪm'brɔɪdə) *vb* **1** to do decorative needlework (upon) **2** to add fictitious or fanciful detail to (a story) **3** to add exaggerated or improbable details to (an account of an event, etc) [c15 from Old French *embroder*; see em- EN-¹, BROIDER] > em'broiderer *n*

embroidery (ɪm'brɔɪdərɪ) *n, pl* **-deries 1** decorative needlework done usually on loosely woven cloth or canvas, often being a picture or pattern **2** elaboration or exaggeration, esp in writing or reporting; embellishment

embroil (ɪm'brɔɪl) *vb* (*tr*) **1** to involve (a person, oneself, etc) in trouble, conflict, or argument **2** to throw (affairs) into a state of confusion or disorder; complicate; entangle [c17 from French *embrouiller*, from *brouiller* to mingle, confuse] > em'broiler *n* > em'broilment *n*

embrue (ɪm'bru:) *vb* **-brues, -bruing, -brued** a variant spelling of **imbrue**. > em'bruement *n*

embryectomy (ˌɛmbrɪ'ɛktəmɪ) *n, pl* **-mies** the surgical removal of an embryo

embryo ('ɛmbrɪˌəʊ) *n, pl* **-bryos 1** an animal in the early stages of development following cleavage of the zygote and ending at birth or hatching **2** the human product of conception up to approximately the end of the second month of pregnancy. Compare **fetus 3** a plant in the early stages of development: in higher plants, the plumule, cotyledons, and radicle within the seed **4** an undeveloped or rudimentary state (esp in the phrase **in embryo**) **5** something in an early stage of development: *an embryo of an idea* [c16 from Late Latin, from Greek *embruon*, from *bruein* to swell] > 'embry,oid *adj*

embryogeny (ˌɛmbrɪ'ɒdʒɪnɪ) *n* **1** Also called: **embryogenesis** (ˌɛmbrɪəʊ'dʒɛnəsɪs) the formation and development of an embryo **2** the study of these processes > embryogenic (ˌɛmbrɪəʊ'dʒɛnɪk) *adj*

embryol. abbreviation for embryology

embryology (ˌɛmbrɪ'ɒlədʒɪ) *n* **1** the branch of science concerned with the study of embryos **2** the structure and development of the embryo of a particular organism > embryological (ˌɛmbrɪə'lɒdʒɪk⁰l) or ,embryo'logic *adj* > ,embryo'logically *adv* > ,embry'ologist *n*

embryonic (ˌɛmbrɪ'ɒnɪk) or **embryonal** ('ɛmbrɪən⁰l) *adj* **1** of or relating to an embryo **2** in an early stage; rudimentary; undeveloped > ,embry'onically *adv*

embryo sac *n* the structure within a plant ovule that contains the egg cell: develops from the megaspore and contains the embryo plant and endosperm after fertilization

embus (ɪm'bʌs) *vb* **-buses, -busing, -bused** or **-busses, -bussing, -bussed** *military* to cause (troops) to board or (of troops) to board a transport vehicle

embusqué French (ābyske) *n, pl* **-qués** (-ke) a man who avoids military conscription by obtaining a government job [c20 from *embusquer* to lie in ambush, shirk]

emcee (ˌɛm'si:) *informal* ▷ *n* **1** a master of ceremonies ▷ *vb* **-cees, -ceeing, -ceed 2** to act as master of ceremonies (for or at) [c20 from the abbreviation MC]

em dash or **rule** *n* *printing* a dash (—) one em long

Emden (*German* 'ɛmdən) *n* a port in NW Germany, in Lower Saxony at the mouth of the River Ems. Pop: 51 445 (2003 est)

-eme *suffix forming nouns* *linguistics* indicating a

minimal distinctive unit of a specified type in a language: *morpheme; phoneme* [c20 via French, abstracted from PHONEME]

emend (ɪ'mɛnd) *vb* (*tr*) to make corrections or improvements in (a text) by critical editing [c15 from Latin *ēmendāre* to correct, from *ē-* out + *mendum* a mistake] > e'mendable *adj*

emendation (ˌi:mɛn'deɪʃən) *n* **1** a correction or improvement in a text **2** the act or process of emending > 'emen,dator *n* > emendatory (ɪ'mɛndətərɪ, -trɪ) *adj*

emerald ('ɛmərəld, 'ɛmrəld) *n* **1** a green transparent variety of beryl: highly valued as a gem **2 a** the clear green colour of an emerald **b** (*as adjective*): *an emerald carpet* **3** (formerly) a size of printer's type approximately equal to 6½ point **4** short for **emerald moth** [c13 from Old French *esmeraude*, from Latin *smaragdus*, from Greek *smaragdos*; related to Sanskrit *marakata* emerald]

Emerald Isle *n* a poetic name for **Ireland**

emerald moth *n* any of various green geometrid moths, esp the **large emerald** (*Geometra papilionaria*) a handsome pale green moth with white wavy markings

emerge (ɪ'mɜ:dʒ) *vb* (*intr*; often foll by *from*) **1** to come up to the surface of or rise from water or other liquid **2** to come into view, as from concealment or obscurity: *he emerged from the cave* **3** (foll by *from*) to come out (of) or live (through a difficult experience): *he emerged from his ordeal with dignity* **4** to become apparent: *several interesting things emerged from the report* [c17 from Latin *ēmergere* to rise up from, from *mergere* to dip] > e'merging *adj*

emergence (ɪ'mɜ:dʒəns) *n* **1** the act or process of emerging **2** an outgrowth, such as a prickle, that contains no vascular tissue and does not develop into stem, leaf, etc

emergency (ɪ'mɜ:dʒənsɪ) *n, pl* **-cies 1 a** an unforeseen or sudden occurrence, esp of a danger demanding immediate remedy or action **b** (*as modifier*): *an emergency exit* **2 a** a patient requiring urgent treatment **b** (*as modifier*): *an emergency ward* **3 state of emergency** a condition, declared by a government, in which martial law applies, usually because of civil unrest or natural disaster **4** NZ a player selected to stand by to replace an injured member of a team; reserve

emergency medical technician *n* US a member of the emergency services who is trained to provide basic emergency medical care before a patient is taken to a hospital. Abbreviation: EMT

emergent (ɪ'mɜ:dʒənt) *adj* **1** coming into being or notice: *an emergent political structure* **2** (of a nation) recently independent ▷ *n* **3** an aquatic plant with stem and leaves above the water > e'mergently *adv*

emergent evolution *n* philosophy the doctrine that, in the course of evolution, some entirely new properties, such as life and consciousness, appear at certain critical points, usually because of an unpredictable rearrangement of the already existing entities

emerging market *n* a financial or consumer market in a newly developing country or former communist country

emeritus (ɪ'mɛrɪtəs) *adj* (usually postpositive) retired or honourably discharged from full-time work, but retaining one's title on an honorary basis: *a professor emeritus* [c19 from Latin, from *merēre* to deserve; see MERIT]

emersed (ɪ'mɜ:st) *adj* (of the leaves or stems of aquatic plants) protruding above the surface of the water

emersion (ɪ'mɜ:ʃən) *n* **1** the act or an instance of emerging **2** Also called: **egress** astronomy the reappearance of a celestial body after an eclipse or occultation [c17 from Latin *ēmersus*, from *ēmergere*; see EMERGE]

emery ('ɛmərɪ) *n* **a** a hard greyish-black mineral consisting of corundum with either magnetite or haematite: used as an abrasive and polishing agent, esp as a coating on paper, cloth, etc Formula: Al_2O_3 **b** (*as modifier*): *emery paper* [c15 from

Old French *esmeril*, ultimately from Greek *smuris* powder for rubbing]

emery board *n* a strip of cardboard or wood with a rough surface of crushed emery, for filing one's nails

emery wheel *n* a grinding or polishing wheel consisting of, or the surface of which is coated with, abrasive emery particles

emesis ('ɛmɪsɪs) *n* the technical name for **vomiting** [C19 via New Latin from Greek, from *emein* to vomit]

emetic (ɪ'mɛtɪk) *adj* 1 causing vomiting ▷ *n* 2 an emetic agent or drug [C17 from Late Latin *ēmeticus*, from Greek *emetikos*, from *emein* to vomit] > e'metically *adv*

emetine ('ɛmə,ti:n, -tɪn) *or* **emetin** ('ɛmətɪn) *n* a white bitter poisonous alkaloid obtained from ipecacuanha: the hydrochloride is used to treat amoebic infections. Formula: $C_{29}H_{40}O_4N_2$ [C19 from French *émétine*; see EMETIC, -INE²]

emf *or* **EMF** *abbreviation for* electromotive force

-emia *n combining form* a US variant of **-aemia**

emigrant ('ɛmɪɡrənt) *n* **a** a person who leaves one place or country, esp a native country, to settle in another. Compare **immigrant** **b** (*as modifier*): *an emigrant worker*

emigrate ('ɛmɪˌɡreɪt) *vb* (*intr*) to leave one place or country, esp one's native country, in order to settle in another. Compare **immigrate** [C18 from Latin *ēmigrāre*, from *mīgrāre* to depart, MIGRATE] > 'emiˌgratory *adj*

emigration (ˌɛmɪ'ɡreɪʃən) *n* 1 the act or an instance of emigrating 2 emigrants considered collectively

émigré ('ɛmɪˌɡreɪ; *French* emigre) *n* an emigrant, esp one forced to leave his native country for political reasons [C18 from French, from *émigrer* to EMIGRATE]

Emilia-Romagna (ɪ'mi:lɪərəʊ'mɑ:njə; *Italian* e'mi:liaro'maɲɲa) *n* a region of N central Italy, on the Adriatic: rises from the plains of the Po valley in the north to the Apennines in the south. Capital: Bologna. Pop: 4 030 220 (2003 est). Area: 22 123 sq km (8628 sq miles)

eminence ('ɛmɪnəns) *n* 1 a position of superiority, distinction, high rank, or fame 2 a high or raised piece of ground 3 *anatomy* a projection of an organ or part ▷ Also: **eminency** [C17 from French, from Latin *ēminentia* a standing out; see EMINENT]

Eminence ('ɛmɪnəns) *or* **Eminency** *n, pl* **-nences** *or* **-nencies** (preceded by *Your* or *His*) a title used to address or refer to a cardinal

éminence grise *French* (eminɑ̃s ɡriz) *n, pl* **éminences grises** (eminɑ̃s ɡriz) a person who wields power and influence unofficially or behind the scenes [C19 literally: grey eminence, originally applied to Père Joseph (François Le Clerc du Tremblay; died 1638), French monk, secretary of Cardinal Richelieu]

eminent ('ɛmɪnənt) *adj* 1 above others in rank, merit, or reputation; distinguished: *an eminent scientist* 2 (*prenominal*) noteworthy, conspicuous, or outstanding: *eminent good sense* 3 projecting or protruding; prominent [C15 from Latin *ēminēre* to project, stand out, from *minēre* to stand] > 'eminently *adv*

eminent domain *n law* the right of a state to confiscate private property for public use, payment usually being made to the owners in compensation

eminently ('ɛmɪnəntlɪ) *adv* extremely: *eminently sensible*

emir (ɛ'mɪə) *n* (in the Islamic world) 1 an independent ruler or chieftain 2 a military commander or governor 3 a descendant of Mohammed ▷ Also spelt. amir [C17 via French from Spanish *emir*, from Arabic *'amīr* commander]

emirate (ɛ'mɪərɪt, 'ɛmɪrɪt) *n* 1 the rank or office of an emir 2 the government, jurisdiction, or territory of an emir

Emiscan (ˌɛmɪ'skæn) *n trademark* a computerized

radiological technique for examining the soft tissues of the body, esp the brain, to detect the presence of tumours, abscesses, etc

emissary ('ɛmɪsərɪ, -ɪsrɪ) *n, pl* **-saries** 1 **a** an agent or messenger sent on a mission, esp one who represents a government or head of state **b** (*as modifier*): *an emissary delegation* 2 an agent sent on a secret mission, as a spy ▷ *adj* 3 (of veins) draining blood from sinuses in the dura mater to veins outside the skull [C17 from Latin *ēmissārius* emissary, spy, from *ēmittere* to send out; see EMIT]

emission (ɪ'mɪʃən) *n* 1 the act of emitting or sending forth 2 energy, in the form of heat, light, radio waves, etc, emitted from a source 3 a substance, fluid, etc, that is emitted; discharge 4 a measure of the number of electrons emitted by a cathode or electron gun: *at 1000°C the emission is 3 mA*. See also **secondary emission, thermionic emission** 5 *physiol* any bodily discharge, esp an involuntary release of semen during sleep 6 an issue, as of currency [C17 from Latin *ēmissiō*, from *ēmittere* to send forth, EMIT] > e'missive *adj*

emission nebula *n* a type of nebula that emits visible radiation. See **nebula**

emission spectrum *n* the continuous spectrum or pattern of bright lines or bands seen when the electromagnetic radiation emitted by a substance is passed into a spectrometer. The spectrum is characteristic of the emitting substance and the type of excitation to which it is subjected. Compare **absorption spectrum**

emissivity (ˌɛmɪ'sɪvɪtɪ, ˌem-) *n* a measure of the ability of a surface to radiate energy; the ratio of the radiant flux emitted per unit area to that emitted by a black body at the same temperature. Symbol: ε

emit (ɪ'mɪt) *vb* **emits, emitting, emitted** (*tr*) 1 to give or send forth; discharge: *the pipe emitted a stream of water* 2 to give voice to; utter: *she emitted a shrill scream* 3 *physics* to give off (radiation or particles) 4 to put (currency) into circulation [C17 from Latin *ēmittere* to send out, from *mittere* to send]

emitter (ɪ'mɪtə) *n* 1 a person or thing that emits 2 a radioactive substance that emits radiation: *a beta emitter* 3 the region in a transistor in which the charge-carrying holes or electrons originate

Emmanuel (ɪ'mænjʊəl) *n* a variant spelling of **Immanuel**

Emmen ('ɛmən; *Dutch* 'ɛmə) *n* a city in the NE Netherlands, in Drenthe province: a new town developed since World War II. Pop: 108 000 (2003 est)

emmenagogue (ɪ'mɛnəˌɡɒɡ, -'mi:-) *n* 1 a drug or agent that increases menstrual flow ▷ *adj also* **emmenagogic** (ɪˌmɛnə'ɡɒdʒɪk) 2 inducing or increasing menstrual flow [C18 from Greek *emmēna* menses, (from *mēn* month) + -AGOGUE]

Emmenthal, Emmental ('ɛmənˌtɑ:l) *or* **Emmenthaler, Emmentaler** *n* a hard Swiss cheese with holes in it, similar to Gruyère [C20 named after *Emmenthal*, a valley in Switzerland]

emmer ('ɛmə) *n* a variety of wheat, *Triticum dicoccum*, grown in mountainous parts of Europe as a cereal crop and for livestock food: thought to be an ancestor of many other varieties of wheat [C20 from German; related to Old High German *amari* spelt]

emmet ('ɛmɪt) *n* 1 *Brit* an archaic or dialect word for **ant** 2 *Cornish dialect* a tourist or holiday-maker [Old English *æmette* ANT; related to Old Norse *meita*, Old High German *āmeiza*, Gothic *maitan*]

emmetropia (ˌɛmɪ'trəʊpɪə) *n* the normal condition of perfect vision, in which parallel light rays are focused on the retina without the need for accommodation [C19 from New Latin, from Greek *emmetros* in due measure + -ÓPIA] > emmetropic (ˌɛmɪ'trɒpɪk) *adj*

Emmy ('ɛmɪ) *n, pl* **-mys** *or* **-mies** (in the US) one of the gold-plated statuettes awarded annually for outstanding television performances and productions [C20 alteration of *Immy*, short for *image*

orthicon tube]

emo ('i:məʊ) *n* **a** a type of music combining traditional hard rock with personal and emotional lyrics **b** (*as modifier*): *emo bands* [C20 short for *emotional rock*]

emollient (ɪ'mɒljənt) *adj* 1 softening or soothing, esp to the skin 2 helping to avoid confrontation; calming ▷ *n* 3 any preparation or substance that has a softening or soothing effect, esp when applied to the skin [C17 from Latin *emollīre* to soften, from *mollis* soft] > e'mollience *n*

emolument (ɪ'mɒljʊmənt) *n* the profit arising from an office or employment, usually in the form of fees or wages [C15 from Latin *ēmolumentum* benefit; originally, fee paid to a miller, from *ēmolere*, from *molere* to grind]

emote (ɪ'məʊt) *vb* (*intr*) to display exaggerated emotion, as in acting; behave theatrically [C20 back formation from EMOTION] > e'moter *n*

emoticon (ɪ'məʊtɪˌkɒn) *n* any of several combinations of symbols used in electronic mail and text messaging to indicate the state of mind of the writer, such as :-) to express happiness [C20 from EMOT(ION) + ICON]

emotion (ɪ'məʊʃən) *n* any strong feeling, as of joy, sorrow, or fear [C16 from French, from Old French *esmovoir* to excite, from Latin *ēmovēre* to disturb, from *movēre* to MOVE] > e'motionless *adj*

emotional (ɪ'məʊʃənᵊl) *adj* 1 of, characteristic of, or expressive of emotion 2 readily or excessively affected by emotion 3 appealing to or arousing emotion: *an emotional piece of music* 4 caused, determined, or actuated by emotion rather than reason: *an emotional argument* > e,moti'on'ality *n* > e'motionally *adv*

emotional correctness *n* pressure on an individual to be seen to feel the same emotion as others

emotional intelligence *n* awareness of one's own emotions and moods and those of others, esp in managing people

emotionalism (ɪ'məʊʃənəˌlɪzəm) *n* 1 emotional nature, character, or quality 2 a tendency to yield readily to the emotions 3 an appeal to the emotions, esp an excessive appeal, as to an audience 4 a doctrine stressing the value of deeply felt responses in ethics and the arts > e'motionalist *n* > e,motional'istic *adj*

emotionalize *or* **emotionalise** (ɪ'məʊʃənəˌlaɪz) *vb* (*tr*) to make emotional; subject to emotional treatment > e,motionali'zation *or* e,motionali'sation *n*

emotional labour *n* work that requires good interpersonal skills

emotional literacy *n* the ability to deal with one's emotions and recognize their causes

emotive (ɪ'məʊtɪv) *adj* 1 tending to or designed to arouse emotion 2 of or characterized by emotion > e'motively *adv* > e'motiveness *or* ,emo'tivity *n*

USAGE *Emotional* is preferred to *emotive* when describing a display of emotion: *he was given an emotional (not emotive) welcome*

emotivism (ɪ'məʊtɪˌvɪzəm) *n ethics* the theory that moral utterances do not have a truth value but express the feelings of the speaker, so that *murder is wrong* is equivalent to *down with murder*. Also called: boo-hurrah theory Compare **prescriptivism, descriptivism**

empale (ɪm'peɪl) *vb* a less common spelling of **impale**. > em'palement *n* > em'paler *n*

empanel *or* **impanel** (ɪm'pænᵊl) *vb* **-els, -elling, -elled** *or US* **-els, -eling, -eled** (*tr*) *law* 1 to enter on a list (names of persons to be summoned for jury service) 2 to select (a jury) from the names on such a list > em'panelment *or* im'panelment *n*

empathic (ɛm'pæθɪk) *or* **empathetic** (ˌɛmpə'θɛtɪk) *adj* of or relating to empathy > em'pathically *or* ,empa'thetically *adv*

empathize *or* **empathise** ('ɛmpəˌθaɪz) *vb* (*intr*) to engage in or feel empathy

empathy ('ɛmpəθɪ) *n* 1 the power of

e

understanding and imaginatively entering into another person's feelings. See also **identification** (sense 3b) **2** the attribution to an object, such as a work of art, of one's own emotional or intellectual feelings about it [c20 from Greek *empatheia* affection, passion, intended as a rendering of German *Einfühlung*, literally: a feeling in; see EN-², -PATHY] > 'empathist *n*

empennage (ɛmˈpɛnɪdʒ; *French* ɑ̃pɛnaʒ) *n* the rear part of an aircraft, comprising the fin, rudder, and tailplane [c20 from French: feathering, from *empenner* to feather an arrow, from *penne* feather, from Latin *pinna*]

emperor (ˈɛmpərə) *n* **1** a monarch who rules or reigns over an empire **2** Also called: emperor moth any of several large saturniid moths with eyelike markings on each wing, esp *Saturnia pavonia* of Europe. See also **giant peacock moth 3** See **purple emperor** [c13 from Old French *empereor*, from Latin *imperātor* commander-in-chief, from *imperāre* to command, from IM- + *parāre* to make ready] > 'emperor,ship *n*

emperor penguin *n* an Antarctic penguin, *Aptenodytes forsteri*, with orange-yellow patches on the neck: the largest penguin, reaching a height of 1.3 m (4 ft)

empery (ˈɛmpərɪ) *n, pl* -peries *archaic* dominion or power; empire [c13 (in the sense: the status of an emperor): from Anglo-French *emperie*, from Latin *imperium* power; see EMPIRE]

emphasis (ˈɛmfəsɪs) *n, pl* -ses (-siːz) **1** special importance or significance **2** an object, idea, etc, that is given special importance or significance **3** stress made to fall on a particular syllable, word, or phrase in speaking **4** force or intensity of expression: *he spoke with special emphasis on the subject of civil rights* **5** sharpness or clarity of form or outline: *the sunlight gave emphasis to the shape of the mountain* [c16 via Latin from Greek: meaning, (in rhetoric) significant stress; see EMPHATIC]

emphasize *or* **emphasise** (ˈɛmfəˌsaɪz) *vb* (*tr*) to give emphasis or prominence to; stress

emphatic (ɪmˈfætɪk) *adj* **1** expressed, spoken, or done with emphasis **2** forceful and positive; definite; direct: *an emphatic personality* **3** sharp or clear in form, contour, or outline **4** important or significant; stressed: *the emphatic points in an argument* **5** *phonetics* denoting certain dental consonants of Arabic that are pronounced with accompanying pharyngeal constriction ▷ *n* **6** *phonetics* an emphatic consonant, as used in Arabic [c18 from Greek *emphatikos* expressive, forceful, from *emphainein* to exhibit, display, from *phainein* to show]

emphatically (ɪmˈfætɪkəlɪ, -klɪ) *adv* **1** with emphasis or force **2** definitely or unquestionably

emphysema (ˌɛmfɪˈsiːmə) *n pathol* **1** Also called: pulmonary emphysema a condition in which the air sacs of the lungs are grossly enlarged, causing breathlessness and wheezing **2** the abnormal presence of air in a tissue or part [c17 from New Latin, from Greek *emphusēma* a swelling up, from *emphusan* to inflate, from *phusan* to blow] > emphysematous (ˌɛmfɪˈsɛmətəs, -ˈsiː-) *adj*

empire (ˈɛmpaɪə) *n* **1** an aggregate of peoples and territories, often of great extent, under the rule of a single person, oligarchy, or sovereign state **2** any monarchy that for reasons of history, prestige, etc, has an emperor rather than a king as head of state **3** the period during which a particular empire exists **4** supreme power; sovereignty. **5** a large industrial organization with many ramifications, esp a multinational corporation ▷ Related adj: **imperial** [c13 from Old French, from Latin *imperium* rule, from *imperāre* to command, from *parāre* to prepare]

Empire (ˈɛmpaɪə) *n* the **1** See **British Empire 2** *French history* **a** the period of imperial rule in France from 1804 to 1815 under Napoleon Bonaparte (1769–1821) **b** Also called: Second Empire the period from 1852 to 1870 when Napoleon III (1808–73) ruled as emperor ▷ *adj* **3**

denoting, characteristic of, or relating to the British Empire **4** denoting, characteristic of, or relating to either French Empire, esp the first: in particular, denoting the neoclassical style of architecture and furniture and the high-waisted style of women's dresses characteristic of the period

empire-builder *n informal* a person who seeks extra power for its own sake, esp by increasing the number of his subordinates or staff > 'empire-,building *n, adj*

Empire Day *n* the former name of **Commonwealth Day**

Empire State *n* nickname of **New York** (state)

empiric (ɛmˈpɪrɪk) *n* **1** a person who relies on empirical methods **2** a medical quack; charlatan ▷ *adj* **3** a variant of **empirical** [c16 from Latin *empīricus*, from Greek *empeirikos* practised, from *peiran* to attempt]

empirical (ɛmˈpɪrɪkˀl) *adj* **1** derived from or relating to experiment and observation rather than theory **2** (of medical treatment) based on practical experience rather than scientific proof **3** *philosophy* **a** (of knowledge) derived from experience rather than by logic from first principles. Compare **a priori, a posteriori b** (of a proposition) subject, at least theoretically, to verification. Compare **analytic** (sense 4), **synthetic** (sense 4) **4** of or relating to medical quackery ▷ *n* **5** *statistics* the posterior probability of an event derived on the basis of its observed frequency in a sample. Compare **mathematical probability** See also **posterior probability**. > em'pirically *adv* > em'piricalness *n*

empirical formula *n* **1** a chemical formula indicating the proportion of each element present in a molecule: $C_6H_{12}O_6$ *is the molecular formula of sucrose whereas* CH_2O *is its empirical formula.* Compare **molecular formula, structural formula 2** a formula or expression obtained from experimental data rather than theory

empiricism (ɛmˈpɪrɪˌsɪzəm) *n* **1** *philosophy* the doctrine that all knowledge of matters of fact derives from experience and that the mind is not furnished with a set of concepts in advance of experience. Compare **intuitionism, rationalism 2** the use of empirical methods **3** medical quackery; charlatanism > em'piricist *n, adj*

emplace (ɪmˈpleɪs) *vb* (*tr*) to put in place or position

emplacement (ɪmˈpleɪsmənt) *n* **1** a prepared position for the siting of a gun or other weapon **2** the act of putting or state of being put in place [c19 from French, from obsolete *emplacer* to put in position, from PLACE]

emplane (ɪmˈpleɪn) *vb* to board or put on board an aeroplane

employ (ɪmˈplɔɪ) *vb* (*tr*) **1** to engage or make use of the services of (a person) in return for money; hire **2** to provide work or occupation for; keep busy; occupy: *collecting stamps employs a lot of his time* **3** to use as a means: *to employ secret measures to get one's ends* ▷ *n* **4** the state of being employed (esp in the phrase **in someone's employ**) [c15 from Old French *emploier*, from Latin *implicāre* to entangle, engage, from *plicāre* to fold]

employee (ɛmˈplɔɪiː, ˌɛmplɔɪˈiː:) *or sometimes US* **employe** *n* a person who is hired to work for another or for a business, firm, etc, in return for payment. Also called (esp formerly): employé

employee association *n* an organization, other than a trade union, whose members comprise employees of a single employing organization. The aims of the association may be social, recreational, or professional

employer (ɪmˈplɔɪə) *n* **1** a person, business, firm, etc, that employs workers **2** a person who employs; user

employers' association *n* a body of employers, usually from the same sector of the economy, associated to further the interests of member companies by conducting negotiations with trade

unions, providing advice, making representations to other bodies, etc

employment (ɪmˈplɔɪmənt) *n* **1** the act of employing or state of being employed **2** the work or occupation in which a person is employed **3** the purpose for which something is used

employment agency *n* a private firm whose business is placing people in jobs

employment equity *n* **1** *South African* a policy or programme designed to reserve jobs for people formerly disadvantaged under apartheid **2** *Canadian* a policy or programme designed to ensure equal opportunity in employment

employment exchange *n Brit* a former name for **employment office**

employment office *n Brit* any of a number of government offices established to collect and supply to the unemployed information about job vacancies and to employers information about availability of prospective workers. Former names: employment exchange, labour exchange See also **Jobcentre**

employment tribunal *n* (in England, Scotland, and Wales) a tribunal that rules on disputes between employers and employees regarding unfair dismissal, redundancy, etc. See also **industrial tribunal**

empoison (ɪmˈpɔɪzˀn) *vb* (*tr*) **1** *rare* to embitter or corrupt **2** an archaic word for **poison** (senses 6–9) > em'poisonment *n*

empolder (ɪmˈpəʊldə) *vb* a variant spelling of **impolder**

emporium (ɛmˈpɔːrɪəm) *n, pl* -riums, -ria (-rɪə) a large and often ostentatious retail shop offering for sale a wide variety of merchandise [c16 from Latin, from Greek *emporion*, from *emporos* merchant, from *poros* a journey]

empoverish (ɪmˈpɒvərɪʃ) *vb* an obsolete spelling of **impoverish**. > em'poverisher *n* > em'poverishment *n*

empower (ɪmˈpaʊə) *vb* (*tr*) **1** to give or delegate power or authority to; authorize **2** to give ability to; enable or permit

empowerment (ɪmˈpaʊəmənt) *n* **1** the giving or delegation of power or authority; authorization **2** the giving of an ability; enablement or permission **3** (in South Africa) a policy of providing special opportunities in employment, training, etc for Blacks and others disadvantaged under apartheid

empress (ˈɛmprɪs) *n* **1** the wife or widow of an emperor **2** a woman who holds the rank of emperor in her own right **3** a woman of great power and influence [c12 from Old French *empereriz*, from Latin *imperātrix* feminine of *imperātor* EMPEROR]

emprise (ɛmˈpraɪz) *n archaic* **1** a chivalrous or daring enterprise; adventure **2** chivalrous daring or prowess [c13 from Old French, from *emprendre* to undertake; see ENTERPRISE]

empt (ɛmpt, ɛmt) *vb* (*tr*) *dialect* to empty [from Old English *æmtian* to be without duties; compare EMPTY]

empty (ˈɛmptɪ) *adj* -tier, -tiest **1** containing nothing **2** without inhabitants; vacant or unoccupied **3** carrying no load, passengers, etc **4** without purpose, substance, or value: *an empty life* **5** insincere or trivial: *empty words* **6** not expressive or vital; vacant: *she has an empty look* **7** *informal* hungry **8** (*postpositive, foll by of*) devoid; destitute: *a life empty of happiness* **9** *informal* drained of energy or emotion: *after the violent argument he felt very empty* **10** *maths, logic* (of a set or class) containing no members **11** *philosophy, logic* (of a name or description) having no reference ▷ *vb* -ties, -tying, -tied **12** to make or become empty **13** (when *intr*, foll by *into*) to discharge (contents) **14** (*tr*; often foll by *of*) to unburden or rid (oneself): *to empty oneself of emotion* ▷ *n, pl* -ties **15** an empty container, esp a bottle [Old English *æmtig*, from *æmetta* free time, from *æ-* without + *-metta*, from *mōtan* to be obliged to; see MUST¹] > 'emptiable *adj*

> 'emptier *n* > 'emptily *adv* > 'emptiness *n*

empty cow *n* a cow that does not produce calves during the breeding season

empty-handed *adj* **1** carrying nothing in the hands **2** having gained nothing: *they returned from the negotiations empty-handed*

empty-headed *adj* lacking intelligence or sense; frivolous

empty-nester *n informal* a married person whose children have grown up and left home

empty-nest syndrome *n informal* a condition, often involving depression, loneliness, etc, experienced by parents living in a home from which the children have grown up and left

Empty Quarter *n* another name for **Rub' al Khali**

empyema (ˌɛmpaɪˈiːmə) *n, pl* -emata (-ˈiːmətə) *or* -emas a collection of pus in a body cavity, esp in the chest [C17 from Medieval Latin, from Greek *empuēma* abscess, from *empuein* to suppurate, from *puon* pus] > ˌempyˈemic *adj*

empyrean (ˌɛmpaɪˈriːən) *n* **1** *archaic* the highest part of the (supposedly spherical) heavens, thought in ancient times to contain the pure element of fire and by early Christians to be the abode of God and the angels **2** *poetic* the heavens or sky ▷ *adj also* **empyreal 3** of or relating to the sky, the heavens, or the empyrean **4** heavenly or sublime **5** *archaic* composed of fire [C17 from Medieval Latin *empyreus*, from Greek *empuros* fiery, from *pur* fire]

empyreuma (ˌɛmpɪˈruːmə) *n, pl* -mata (-mətə) the smell and taste associated with burning vegetable and animal matter [C17 from Greek, from *empureuein* to set on fire]

Ems (ɛmz) *or* **Bad Ems** *n* **1** a town in W Germany, in the Rhineland-Palatinate: famous for the **Ems Telegram** (1870), Bismarck's dispatch that led to the outbreak of the Franco-Prussian War. Pop: 9666 (2003 est) **2** a river in W Germany, rising in the Teutoburger Wald and flowing generally north to the North Sea. Length: about 370 km (230 miles)

EMS *abbreviation for* **1** European Monetary System **2** enhanced messaging service: a system used for sending text messages containing special text formatting, animations, etc, to and from mobile phones

EMT *US abbreviation for* emergency medical technician

emu (ˈiːmjuː) *n* a large Australian flightless bird, *Dromaius novaehollandiae*, similar to the ostrich but with three-toed feet and grey or brown plumage: order *Casuariiformes*. See also **ratite** [C17 changed from Portuguese *ema* ostrich, from Arabic *Na-ʼamah* ostrich]

EMU 1 *abbreviation for* European Monetary Union **2** *abbreviation for* Economic and Monetary Union **3** See **e.m.u.**

e.m.u. *or* **EMU** *abbreviation for* electromagnetic unit

emu-bob *Austral informal* ▷ *vb* -bobs, -bobbing, -bobbed **1** (*intr*) to bend over to collect litter or small pieces of wood ▷ *n* **2** Also called: emu parade a parade of soldiers or schoolchildren for litter collection > ˈemu-bobbing *n*

emu bush *n* any of various Australian shrubs, esp those of the genus *Eremophila* (family *Myoporaceae*), whose fruits are eaten by emus

emulate (ˈɛmjʊˌleɪt) *vb* (*tr*) **1** to attempt to equal or surpass, esp by imitation **2** to rival or compete with **3** to make one computer behave like (another different type of computer) so that the imitating system can operate on the same data and execute the same programs as the imitated system [C16 from Latin *aemulārī*, from *aemulus* competing with; probably related to *imitārī* to IMITATE] > ˈemulative *adj* > ˈemulatively *adv* > ˈemuˌlator *n*

emulation (ˌɛmjʊˈleɪʃən) *n* **1** the act of emulating or imitating **2** the effort or desire to equal or surpass another or others **3** *archaic* jealous rivalry

emulous (ˈɛmjʊləs) *adj* **1** desiring or aiming to equal or surpass another; competitive **2** characterized by or arising from emulation or imitation **3** *archaic* envious or jealous [C14 from Latin *aemulus* rivalling; see EMULATE] > ˈemulously *adv* > ˈemulousness *n*

emulsifier (ɪˈmʌlsɪˌfaɪə) *n* an agent that forms or preserves an emulsion, esp any food additive, such as lecithin, that prevents separation of sauces or other processed foods

emulsify (ɪˈmʌlsɪˌfaɪ) *vb* -fies, -fying, -fied to make or form into an emulsion > eˌmulsiˈfiable *or* eˈmulsible *adj* > eˌmulsifiˈcation *n*

emulsion (ɪˈmʌlʃən) *n* **1** *photog* a light-sensitive coating on a base, such as paper or film, consisting of fine grains of silver bromide suspended in gelatine **2** *chem* a colloid in which both phases are liquids: *an oil-in-water emulsion* **3** Also called: emulsion paint a type of paint in which the pigment is suspended in a vehicle, usually a synthetic resin, that is dispersed in water as an emulsion. It usually gives a mat finish **4** *pharmacol* a mixture in which an oily medicine is dispersed in another liquid **5** any liquid resembling milk [C17 from New Latin *ēmulsiō*, from Latin *ēmulsus* milked out, from *ēmulgēre* to milk out, drain out, from *mulgēre* to milk] > eˈmulsive *adj*

emulsoid (ɪˈmʌlsɔɪd) *n chem* a sol with a liquid disperse phase

emunctory (ɪˈmʌŋktərɪ) *adj* **1** of or relating to a bodily organ or duct having an excretory function ▷ *n, pl* -ries **2** an excretory organ or duct, such as a skin pore [C16 from New Latin *ēmunctōrium*, from Latin *ēmungere* to wipe clean, from *mungere* to wipe]

emu oil *n* an oil obtained from the fat of the emu, traditionally used as an emollient by native Australians to relieve pain and speed the healing process

emu parade *n* **1** *Austral* an army exercise devoted to emu-bobbing **2** Also called: emu walk an organized session of combing an area for clues, esp by the police

emu-wren *n* any Australian wren of the genus *Stipiturus*, having long plumy tail feathers

EMV *abbreviation for* expected monetary value: the product of the monetary outcome of a particular decision in a decision tree and the probability of this outcome happening

en (ɛn) *n printing* a unit of measurement, half the width of an em. Also called: nut See also **ennage**

EN (in Britain) *abbreviation for* **1** enrolled nurse **2** English Nature

en-¹ *or* **em-** *prefix forming verbs* **1** (*from nouns*) **a** put in or on: *entomb; enthrone* **b** go on or into: *enplane* **c** surround or cover with: *enmesh* **d** furnish with: *empower* **2** (*from adjectives and nouns*) cause to be in a certain condition: *enable; encourage; enrich; enslave* [via Old French from Latin *in-* IN-²]

en-² *or* **em-** *prefix forming nouns and adjectives* in; into; inside: *endemic* [from Greek (often via Latin); compare IN-¹, IN-²]

-en¹ *suffix forming verbs from adjectives and nouns* cause to be; become; cause to have: *blacken; heighten* [Old English *-n-*, as in *fæst-n-ian* to fasten, of common Germanic origin; compare Icelandic *fastna*]

-en² *suffix forming adjectives from nouns* of; made of; resembling: *ashen; earthen; wooden* [Old English *-en*; related to Gothic *-eins*, Latin *-īnus* -INE¹]

enable (ɪnˈeɪbəl) *vb* (*tr*) **1** to provide (someone) with adequate power, means, opportunity, or authority (to do something) **2** to make possible **3** to put (a digital electronic circuit element) into an operative condition by supplying a suitable input pulse > enˈablement *n* > enˈabler *n*

enabling act *n* a legislative act conferring certain specified powers on a person or organization

enact (ɪnˈækt) *vb* (*tr*) **1** to make into an act or statute **2** to establish by law; ordain or decree **3** to represent or perform in or as if in a play; to act out > enˈactable *adj* > enˈactive *or* enˈactory *adj* > enˈactment *or* enˈaction *n* > enˈactor *n*

enalapril (ɪˈnæləprɪl) *n* an ACE inhibitor used to treat high blood pressure and congestive heart failure

enamel (ɪˈnæməl) *n* **1** a coloured glassy substance, translucent or opaque, fused to the surface of articles made of metal, glass, etc, for ornament or protection **2** an article or articles ornamented with enamel **3** an enamel-like paint or varnish **4** any smooth glossy coating resembling enamel **5** another word for **nail polish 6** the hard white calcified substance that covers the crown of each tooth **7** (*modifier*) **a** decorated or covered with enamel: *an enamel ring* **b** made with enamel: *enamel paste* ▷ *vb* -els, -elling, -elled *or US* -els, -eling, -eled (*tr*) **8** to inlay, coat, or otherwise decorate with enamel **9** to ornament with glossy variegated colours, as if with enamel **10** to portray in enamel [C15 from Old French *esmail*, of Germanic origin; compare Old High German *smalz* lard; see SMELT¹] > eˈnameller, eˈnamellist *or US* eˈnameler, eˈnamelist *n* > eˈnamelˌwork *n*

enamour *or US* **enamor** (ɪnˈæmə) *vb* (*tr; usually passive* and foll by *of*) to inspire with love; captivate; charm [C14 from Old French *enamourer*, from *amour* love, from Latin *amor*]

enamoured *or US* **enamored** (ɪnˈæməd) *adj* in love; captivated; charmed

enantiomer (ɛnˈæntɪəmə) *n chem* a molecule that exhibits stereoisomerism because of the presence of one or more chiral centres

enantiomorph (ɛnˈæntɪəˌmɔːf) *n* either of the two crystal forms of a substance that are mirror images of each other [C19 from Greek *enantios* opposite + -MORPH] > enˌantioˈmorphic *adj* > enˌantioˈmorphism *n*

enarthrosis (ˌɛnɑːˈθrəʊsɪs) *n, pl* -ses (-siːz) *anatomy* a ball-and-socket joint, such as that of the hip [C17 via New Latin from Greek, from *arthrōsis*, from *arthron* a joint + -OSIS] > enarˈthrodial *adj*

enate (ˈiːneɪt) *adj also* **enatic** (iːˈnætɪk) **1** *biology* growing out or outwards **2** related on the side of the mother ▷ *n* **3** a relative on the mother's side [C17 from Latin *ēnātus*, from *ēnāscī* to be born from, from *nāscī* to be born]

en attendant *French* (ān atādā) *adv* in the meantime; while waiting

en bloc *French* (ā blɔk) *adv* in a lump or block; as a body or whole; all together

en brochette *French* (ā brɔʃɛt) *adj, adv* (esp of meat) roasted or grilled on a skewer [literally: on a skewer]

en brosse *French* (ā brɔs) *adj, adv* (of the hair) cut very short so that the hair stands up stiffly [literally: in the style of a brush]

enc. *abbreviation for* **1** enclosed **2** enclosure

encaenia (ɛnˈsiːnɪə) *n rare* a festival of dedication or commemoration [C14 via Late Latin from Greek *enkainia*, from *kainos* new]

encage (ɪnˈkeɪdʒ) *vb* (*tr*) to confine in or as in a cage

encamp (ɪnˈkæmp) *vb* (*tr*) to lodge or cause to lodge in a camp

encampment (ɪnˈkæmpmənt) *n* **1** the act of setting up a camp **2** the place where a camp, esp a military camp, is set up

encapsulate *or* **incapsulate** (ɪnˈkæpsjʊˌleɪt) *vb* **1** to enclose or be enclosed in or as if in a capsule **2** (*tr*) to sum up in a short or concise form > enˌcapsuˈlation *or* inˌcapsuˈlation *n*

encarnalize *or* **encarnalise** (ɪnˈkɑːnəˌlaɪz) *vb* (*tr*) *rare* **1** to provide with a bodily form; incarnate **2** to make carnal, gross, or sensual

encase *or* **incase** (ɪnˈkeɪs) *vb* (*tr*) to place or enclose in or as if in a case > enˈcasement *or* inˈcasement *n*

encash (ɪnˈkæʃ) *vb* (*tr*) *Brit formal* to exchange (a cheque) for cash > enˈcashable *adj* > enˈcashment *n*

encastré (ɛnˈkɑːstreɪ) *adj civil engineering* (of a beam) fixed at the ends; built into its supports [from French, past participle of *encastrer*, from Latin *incastrare* to cut in; see CASTRATE]

encaustic (ɪnˈkɒstɪk) *ceramics* ▷ *adj* **1** decorated by any process involving burning in colours, esp by inlaying coloured clays and baking or by fusing wax colours to the surface ▷ *n* **2** the process of burning in colours **3** a product of such a process [c17 from Latin *encausticus*, from Greek *enkaustikos*, from *enkaiein* to burn in, from *kaiein* to burn] > en'caustically *adv*

-ence or **-ency** *suffix forming nouns* indicating an action, state, condition, or quality: *benevolence*; *residence*; *patience* [via Old French from Latin *-entia*, from *-ēns*, present participial ending]

enceinte[1] (ɒnˈsænt; *French* ãsɛ̃t) *adj* another word for **pregnant** [c17 from French, from Latin *inciēns* pregnant; related to Greek *enkuos*, from *kuein* to be pregnant]

enceinte[2] (ɒnˈsænt; *French* ãsɛ̃t) *n* **1** a boundary wall enclosing a defended area **2** the area enclosed [c18 from French: enclosure, from *enceindre* to encompass, from Latin *incingere*, from *cingere* to gird]

Enceladus[1] (ɛnˈsɛlədəs) *n Greek myth* a giant who was punished for his rebellion against the gods by a fatal blow from a stone cast by Athena. He was believed to be buried under Mount Etna in Sicily

Enceladus[2] *n* a very bright satellite of Saturn

encephalalgia (ɛnˌsɛfəˈlældʒɪə) *n med* pain in the head; headache

encephalic (ˌɛnsɪˈfælɪk, ˌɛnkɪ-) *adj* of or relating to the brain

encephalin (ɛnˈsɛfəlɪn) *n* a variant of **enkephalin**

encephalitis (ˌɛnsɛfəˈlaɪtɪs, ˌɛnkef-) *n* inflammation of the brain > encephalitic (ˌɛnsɛfəˈlɪtɪk) *adj*

encephalitis lethargica (lɪˈθɑːdʒɪkə) *n pathol* a technical name for sleeping sickness (sense 2)

encephalo- or before a vowel **encephal-** *combining form* indicating the brain: *encephalogram*; *encephalitis* [from New Latin, from Greek *enkephalos*, from *en-* in + *kephalē* head]

encephalogram (ɛnˈsɛfələˌgræm) *n* **1** an X-ray photograph of the brain, esp one (a **pneumoencephalogram**) taken after replacing some of the cerebrospinal fluid with air or oxygen so that the brain cavities show clearly **2** short for **electroencephalogram**

encephalograph (ɛnˈsɛfələˌgrɑːf, -ˌgræf) *n* **1** short for **electroencephalograph 2** any other apparatus used to produce an encephalogram

encephalography (ˌɛnsɛfəˈlɒgrəfɪ) *n* **1** the branch of medical science concerned with taking and analysing X-ray photographs of the brain **2** another name for **electroencephalography** > encephalographic (ɛnˌsɛfələˈgræfɪk) *adj* > en,cepha'lo'graphically *adv*

encephaloma (ˌɛnsɛfəˈləʊmə) *n, pl* -mas or -mata (-mətə) a brain tumour

encephalomyelitis (ɛnˌsɛfələʊˌmaɪəˈlaɪtɪs) *n* acute inflammation of the brain and spinal cord > encephalomyelitic (ɛnˌsɛfələʊˌmaɪəˈlɪtɪk) *adj*

encephalon (ɛnˈsɛfəˌlɒn) *n, pl* -la (-lə) a technical name for **brain** [c18 from New Latin, from Greek *enkephalos* brain (literally: that which is in the head), from *en-* + *kephalē* head] > en'cephalous *adj*

encephalopathy (ɛnˌsɛfəˈlɒpəθɪ) *n* any degenerative disease of the brain, often associated with toxic conditions. See also **BSE**

enchain (ɪnˈtʃeɪn) *vb* (*tr*) **1** to bind with chains **2** to hold fast or captivate (the attention, etc) > en'chainment *n*

enchant (ɪnˈtʃɑːnt) *vb* (*tr*) **1** to cast a spell on; bewitch **2** to delight or captivate utterly; fascinate; charm [c14 from Old French *enchanter*, from Latin *incantāre* to chant a spell, from *cantāre* to chant, from *canere* to sing] > en'chanter *n* > en'chantress *fem n*

enchanted (ɪnˈtʃɑːntɪd) *adj* **1** under a spell; bewitched; magical **2** utterly delighted or captivated; fascinated; charmed

enchanter's nightshade *n* any of several onagraceous plants of the genus *Circaea*, esp *C. lutetiana*, having small white flowers and bristly fruits

enchanting (ɪnˈtʃɑːntɪŋ) *adj* pleasant; delightful > en'chantingly *adv*

enchantment (ɪnˈtʃɑːntmənt) *n* **1** the act of enchanting or state of being enchanted **2** a magic spell or act of witchcraft **3** great charm or fascination

enchase (ɪnˈtʃeɪs) *vb* (*tr*) a less common word for **chase** (sense 3) [c15 from Old French *enchasser* to enclose, set, from EN-[1] + *casse* CASE[2]] > en'chaser *n*

enchilada (ˌɛntʃɪˈlɑːdə) *n* a Mexican dish consisting of a tortilla fried in hot fat, filled with meat, and served with a chilli sauce [c19 American Spanish, feminine of *enchilado* seasoned with chilli, from *enchilar* to spice with chilli, from *chile* CHILLI]

enchiridion (ˌɛnkaɪˈrɪdɪən) *n, pl* -ions or -ia (-ɪə) *rare* a handbook or manual [c16 from Late Latin, from Greek *enkheiridion*, from EN-[2] + *kheir* hand]

enchondroma (ˌɛnkɒnˈdrəʊmə) *n, pl* -mas or -mata (-mətə) *pathol* a benign cartilaginous tumour, most commonly in the bones of the hands or feet [c19 New Latin from Greek, from EN-[2] + *khondros* cartilage] > ,enchon'dromatous *adj*

enchorial (ɛnˈkɔːrɪəl) or **enchoric** (ɛnˈkɒrɪk) *adj* of or used in a particular country: used esp of the popular (demotic) writing of the ancient Egyptians [c19 via Late Latin from Greek *enkhōrios*, from EN-[2] + *khōra* country]

-enchyma *n combining form* denoting cellular tissue: *aerenchyma* [c20 abstracted from PARENCHYMA]

encipher (ɪnˈsaɪfə) *vb* (*tr*) to convert (a message, document, etc) from plain text into code or cipher; encode > en'cipherer *n* > en'cipherment *n*

encircle (ɪnˈsɜːkᵊl) *vb* (*tr*) to form a circle around; enclose within a circle; surround > en'circlement *n* > en'circling *adj*

encl. *abbreviation for* **1** enclosed **2** enclosure

en clair *French* (ã klɛr) *adv, adj* in ordinary language; not in cipher [literally: in clear]

enclasp (ɪnˈklɑːsp) *vb* (*tr*) to clasp; embrace

enclave (ˈɛnkleɪv) *n* a part of a country entirely surrounded by foreign territory: viewed from the position of the surrounding territories. Compare **exclave** [c19 from French, from Old French *enclaver* to enclose, from Vulgar Latin *inclāvāre* (unattested) to lock up, from Latin IN-[2] + *clavis* key]

enclitic (ɪnˈklɪtɪk) *adj* **1 a** denoting or relating to a monosyllabic word or form that is treated as a suffix of the preceding word, as Latin *-que* in *populusque* **b** (in classical Greek) denoting or relating to a word that throws an accent back onto the preceding word ▷ *n* **2** an enclitic word or linguistic form ▷ Compare **proclitic** [c17 from Late Latin *encliticus*, from Greek *enklitikos*, from *enklinein* to cause to lean, from EN-[2] + *klinein* to lean] > en'clitically *adv*

enclose or **inclose** (ɪnˈkləʊz) *vb* (*tr*) **1** to close; hem in; surround **2** to surround (land) with or as if with a fence **3** to put in an envelope or wrapper, esp together with a letter **4** to contain or hold > en'closable or in'closable *adj* > en'closer or in'closer *n*

enclosed order *n* a Christian religious order that does not permit its members to go into the outside world

enclosure or **inclosure** (ɪnˈkləʊʒə) *n* **1** the act of enclosing or state of being enclosed **2** a region or area enclosed by or as if by a fence **3 a** the act of appropriating land, esp common land, by putting a hedge or other barrier around it **b** *history* such acts as were carried out at various periods in England, esp between the 12th and 14th centuries and finally in the 18th and 19th centuries **4** a fence, wall, etc, that serves to enclose **5** something, esp a supporting document, enclosed within an envelope or wrapper, esp together with a letter **6** *Brit* a section of a sports ground, racecourse, etc, allotted to certain spectators

encode (ɪnˈkəʊd) *vb* (*tr*) **1** to convert (a message) from plain text into code **2** *computing* to convert (characters and symbols) into a digital form as a

series of impulses. Compare **decode** (sense 2) **3** to convert (an electrical signal) into a form suitable for transmission **4** to convert (a nerve signal) into a form that can be received by the brain **5** to use (a word, phrase, etc, esp of a foreign language) in the construction appropriate to it in that language > en'codement *n* > en'coder *n*

encomiast (ɛnˈkəʊmɪˌæst) *n* a person who speaks or writes an encomium [c17 from Greek *enkōmiastēs*, from *enkōmiazein* to utter an ENCOMIUM] > en,comi'astic or en,comi'astical *adj* > en,comi'astically *adv*

encomium (ɛnˈkəʊmɪəm) *n, pl* -miums or -mia (-mɪə) a formal expression of praise; eulogy; panegyric [c16 from Latin, from Greek *enkōmion*, from EN-[2] + *kōmos* festivity]

encompass (ɪnˈkʌmpəs) *vb* (*tr*) **1** to enclose within a circle; surround **2** to bring about; cause to happen; contrive: *he encompassed the enemy's ruin* **3** to include entirely or comprehensively: *this book encompasses the whole range of knowledge* > en'compassment *n*

encopresis (ˌɛnkəʊˈpriːsɪs) *n* involuntary discharge of faeces, esp when associated with psychiatric disturbance [c20 from New Latin, from Greek EN-[2] + COPR(O)-, + *-esis* as in ENURESIS] > encopretic (ˌɛnkəʊˈprɛtɪk) *adj*

encore (ˈɒŋkɔː) *interj* **1** again; once more: used by an audience to demand an extra or repeated performance ▷ *n* **2** an extra or repeated performance given in response to enthusiastic demand ▷ *vb* **3** (*tr*) to demand an extra or repeated performance of (a work, piece of music, etc) by (a performer) [c18 from French: still, again, perhaps from Latin *in hanc hōram* until this hour]

encounter (ɪnˈkaʊntə) *vb* **1** to come upon or meet casually or unexpectedly **2** to come into conflict with (an enemy, army, etc) in battle or contest **3** (*tr*) to be faced with; contend with: *he encounters many obstacles in his work* ▷ *n* **4** a meeting with a person or thing, esp when casual or unexpected **5** a hostile meeting; contest or conflict [c13 from Old French *encontrer*, from Vulgar Latin *incontrāre* (unattested), from Latin IN-[2] + *contrā* against, opposite] > en'counterer *n*

encounter group *n* a group of people who meet in order to develop self-awareness and mutual understanding by openly expressing their feelings, by confrontation, physical contact, etc

encourage (ɪnˈkʌrɪdʒ) *vb* (*tr*) **1** to inspire (someone) with the courage or confidence (to do something) **2** to stimulate (something or someone to do something) by approval or help; support > en'couragement *n* > en'courager *n* > en'couraging *adj* > en'couragingly *adv*

encrinite (ˈɛnkrɪˌnaɪt) *n* (in the US) a sedimentary rock formed almost exclusively from the skeletal plates of crinoids. Sometimes shortened to: **crinite** [c19 from New Latin *encrinus* (from Greek EN-[2] + *krinon* lily) + -ITE[1]]

encroach (ɪnˈkrəʊtʃ) *vb* (*intr*) **1** (often foll by *on* or *upon*) to intrude gradually, stealthily, or insidiously upon the rights, property, etc, of another **2** to advance beyond the usual or proper limits [c14 from Old French *encrochier* to seize, literally: fasten upon with hooks, from EN-[1] + *croc* hook, of Germanic origin; see CROOK] > en'croacher *n* > en'croachingly *adv* > en'croachment *n*

encrust or **incrust** (ɪnˈkrʌst) *vb* **1** (*tr*) to cover or overlay with or as with a crust or hard coating **2** to form or cause to form a crust or hard coating **3** (*tr*) to decorate lavishly, as with jewels > ,encrus'tation or ,incrus'tation *n*

encrypt (ɪnˈkrɪpt) *vb* (*tr*) **1** to put (a message) into code **2** to put (computer data) into a coded form **3** to distort (a television or other signal) so that it cannot be understood without the appropriate decryption equipment [c20 from EN-[1] + *crypt*, as in CRYPTO-] > en'crypted *adj* > en'cryption *n*

enculturation (ɛnˌkʌltʃʊˈreɪʃən) *n* another word for **socialization** > enculturative (ɛnˈkʌltʃʊrətɪv) *adj*

encumber or **incumber** (ɪnˈkʌmbə) vb (tr) **1** to hinder or impede; make difficult; hamper: *encumbered with parcels after going shopping at Christmas; his stupidity encumbers his efforts to learn* **2** to fill with superfluous or useless matter **3** to burden with debts, obligations, etc [C14 from Old French *encombrer*, from EN-¹ + *combre* a barrier, from Late Latin *combrus*, of uncertain origin] > en'cumberingly or in'cumberingly adv

encumbrance or **incumbrance** (ɪnˈkʌmbrəns) n **1** a thing that impedes or is burdensome; hindrance **2** law a burden or charge upon property, such as a mortgage or lien **3** rare a dependent person, esp a child

encumbrancer (ɪnˈkʌmbrənsə) n law a person who holds an encumbrance on property belonging to another

-ency suffix forming nouns a variant of **-ence**: *fluency; permanency*

encyclical (ɛnˈsɪklɪkəl) n **1** a letter sent by the pope to all Roman Catholic bishops throughout the world ▷ adj also **encyclic 2** (of letters) intended for general or wide circulation [C17 from Late Latin *encyclicus*, from Greek *enkuklios* general, from *kuklos* circle]

encyclopedia or **encyclopaedia** (ɛnˌsaɪkləˈpiːdɪə) n a book, often in many volumes, containing articles on various topics, often arranged in alphabetical order, dealing either with the whole range of human knowledge or with one particular subject: *a medical encyclopedia* [C16 from New Latin *encyclopaedia*, erroneously for Greek *enkuklios paideia* general education, from *enkuklios* general (see ENCYCLICAL), + *paideia* education, from *pais* child]

encyclopedic or **encyclopaedic** (ɛnˌsaɪkləˈpiːdɪk) adj **1** of, characteristic of, or relating to an encyclopedia **2** covering a wide range of knowledge; comprehensive > en,cyclo'pedically or en,cyclo'paedically adv

encyclopedist or **encyclopaedist** (ɛnˌsaɪkləˈpiːdɪst) n a person who compiles or contributes to an encyclopedia > en,cyclo'pedism or en,cyclo'paedism n

encyst (ɛnˈsɪst) vb biology to enclose or become enclosed by a cyst, thick membrane, or shell > en'cysted adj > en'cystment or ,encys'tation n

end¹ (ɛnd) n **1** the extremity of the length of something, such as a road, line, etc **2** the surface at either extremity of a three-dimensional object **3** the extreme extent, limit, or degree of something **4** the most distant place or time that can be imagined: *the ends of the earth* **5** the time at which something is concluded **6 a** the last section or part **b** (as modifier): *the end office*. Related adjs: **final, terminal, ultimate 7** a share or part: *his end of the bargain* **8** (often plural) a remnant or fragment (esp in the phrase **odds and ends**) **9** a final state, esp death; destruction **10** the purpose of an action or existence **11** sport either of the two defended areas of a playing field, rink, etc **12** bowls, curling a section of play from one side of the rink to the other **13** American football a player at the extremity of the playing line; wing **14** all ends up totally or completely **15** a sticky end informal an unpleasant death **16** at a loose end or (US and Canadian) at loose ends without purpose or occupation **17** at an end exhausted or completed **18** at the end of the day See day (sense 10) **19** come to an end to become completed or exhausted **20** end on **a** with the end pointing towards one **b** with the end adjacent to the end of another object **21** go off the deep end informal to lose one's temper; react angrily **22** in the end finally **23** make (both) ends meet to spend no more than the money one has **24** no end (of) informal (intensifier): *I had no end of work* **25** on end **a** upright **b** without pause or interruption **26** the end informal **a** the worst, esp something that goes beyond the limits of endurance **b** chiefly US the best in quality **27** the end of the road the point beyond which survival or continuation is impossible **28** throw (someone) in at the deep end to put (someone) into a new situation, job, etc, without preparation or introduction ▷ vb **29** to bring or come to a finish; conclude **30** to die or cause to die **31** (tr) to surpass; outdo: *a novel to end all novels* **32** end it all informal to commit suicide ▷ See also **end up** [Old English *ende*; related to Old Norse *endir*, Gothic *andeis*, Old High German *endi*, Latin *antiae* forelocks, Sanskrit *antya* last] > 'ender n

end² (ɛnd) vb (tr) Brit to put (hay or grain) into a barn or stack [Old English *innian*; related to Old High German *innōn*; see INN]

end- combining form a variant of **endo-** before a vowel

-end suffix forming nouns See **-and**

end-all n short for **be-all and end-all**

endamage (ɛnˈdæmɪdʒ) vb (tr) to cause injury to; damage > en'damagement n

endamoeba or US **endameba** (ˌɛndəˈmiːbə) n, pl -bae (-biː) or -bas variants of **entamoeba**

endanger (ɪnˈdeɪndʒə) vb (tr) to put in danger or peril; imperil > en'dangerment n

endangered (ɪnˈdeɪndʒəd) adj in danger: used esp of animals in danger of extinction: *the giant panda is an endangered species*

endarch (ˈɛndˌɑːk) adj botany (of a xylem strand) having the first-formed xylem internal to that formed later. Compare **exarch** [C20 from ENDO- + Greek *arkhē* beginning]

en dash or **rule** n printing a dash (–) one en long

end-blown adj music (of a recorder) held downwards and blown through one end

endbrain (ˈɛndˌbreɪn) n anatomy another name for **telencephalon**

endear (ɪnˈdɪə) vb (tr) to cause to be beloved or esteemed

endearing (ɪnˈdɪərɪŋ) adj giving rise to love or esteem; charming > en'dearingly adv

endearment (ɪnˈdɪəmənt) n **1** something that endears, such as an affectionate utterance **2** the act or process of endearing or the condition of being endeared

endeavour or US **endeavor** (ɪnˈdɛvə) vb **1** to try (to do something) ▷ n **2** an effort to do or attain something [C14 *endeveren*, from EN-¹ + *-deveren* from *dever* duty, from Old French *deveir*; see DEVOIRS] > en'deavourer or US en'deavorer n

endemic (ɛnˈdɛmɪk) adj also **endemial** (ɛnˈdɛmɪəl) or **endemical 1** present within a localized area or peculiar to persons in such an area ▷ n **2** an endemic disease or plant [C18 from New Latin *endēmicus*, from Greek *endēmos* native, from EN-² + *dēmos* the people] > en'demically adv > 'endemism or ,ende'micity n

Enderby Land (ˈɛndəbɪ) n part of the coastal region of Antarctica, between Kemp Land and Queen Maud Land: the westernmost part of the Australian Antarctic Territory (claims are suspended under the Antarctic Treaty); discovered in 1831

endergonic (ˌɛndəˈɡɒnɪk) adj (of a biochemical reaction) requiring energy to proceed. Compare **exergonic** [C20 from END(O-) + Greek *ergon* work + -IC]

endermic (ɛnˈdɜːmɪk) adj (of a medicine) acting by absorption through the skin [C19 from EN-² + Greek *derma* skin]

endgame (ˈɛndˌɡeɪm) n **1** Also called: **ending** the closing stage of a game of chess, in which only a few pieces are left on the board **2** the closing stage of any of certain other games

ending (ˈɛndɪŋ) n **1** the act of bringing to or reaching an end **2** the last part of something, as a book, film, etc **3** the final part of a word, esp a suffix **4** chess another word for **endgame**

endive (ˈɛndaɪv) n a plant, *Cichorium endivia*, cultivated for its crisp curly leaves, which are used in salads: family *Asteraceae* (composites). Compare **chicory** [C15 from Old French, from Medieval Latin *endīvia*, variant of Latin *intubus, entubus*, of uncertain origin]

endless (ˈɛndlɪs) adj **1** having or seeming to have no end; eternal or infinite **2** continuing too long or continually recurring **3** formed with the ends joined: *an endless belt* > 'endlessly adv > 'endlessness n

endlong (ˈɛndˌlɒŋ) adv archaic lengthways or on end

end matter n another name for **back matter**

endmost (ˈɛndˌməʊst) adj nearest the end; most distant

endo- or before a vowel **end-** combining form inside; within: *endocrine* [from Greek, from *endon* within]

endobiotic (ˌɛndəʊbaɪˈɒtɪk) adj formed within a host cell

endoblast (ˈɛndəʊˌblæst) n **1** embryol a less common name for **endoderm 2** another name for **hypoblast** (sense 1) > ,endo'blastic adj

endocardial (ˌɛndəʊˈkɑːdɪəl) or **endocardiac** adj **1** of or relating to the endocardium **2** within the heart

endocarditis (ˌɛndəʊkɑːˈdaɪtɪs) n inflammation of the endocardium > endocarditic (ˌɛndəʊkɑːˈdɪtɪk) adj

endocardium (ˌɛndəʊˈkɑːdɪəm) n, pl -dia (-dɪə) the membrane that lines the cavities of the heart and forms part of the valves [C19 from New Latin, from ENDO- + Greek *kardia* heart]

endocarp (ˈɛndəˌkɑːp) n the inner, usually woody, layer of the pericarp of a fruit, such as the stone of a peach or cherry > ,endo'carpal or ,endo'carpic adj

endocentric (ˌɛndəʊˈsɛntrɪk) adj grammar (of a construction) fulfilling the grammatical role of one of its constituents; as in *three blind mice*, where the whole noun phrase fulfils the same role as its head noun *mice*. Compare **exocentric**

endocranial cast (ˌɛndəʊˈkreɪnɪəl) n a cast made of the inside of a cranial cavity to show the size and shape of the brain: used esp in anthropology. Sometimes shortened to: **endocast**

endocranium (ˌɛndəʊˈkreɪnɪəm) n, pl -nia (-nɪə) anatomy the thick fibrous membrane that lines the cranial cavity and forms the outermost layer of the dura mater

endocrine (ˈɛndəʊˌkraɪn, -krɪn) adj also **endocrinal** (ˌɛndəʊˈkraɪnəl) or **endocrinic** (ˌɛndəʊˈkrɪnɪk) or **endocrinous** (ɛnˈdɒkrɪnəs) **1** of or denoting endocrine glands or their secretions: *endocrine disorders* ▷ n **2** an endocrine gland ▷ Compare **exocrine** [C20 from ENDO- + -crine, from Greek *krinein* to separate]

endocrine gland n any of the glands that secrete hormones directly into the bloodstream, including the pituitary, pineal, thyroid, parathyroid, adrenal, testes, ovaries, and the pancreatic islets of Langerhans. Also called: **ductless gland**

endocrinology (ˌɛndəʊkraɪˈnɒlədʒɪ, -krɪ-) n the branch of medical science concerned with the endocrine glands and their secretions > endocrinologic (ˌɛndəʊˌkrɪnəˈlɒdʒɪk) or ,endo,crino'logical adj > ,endocri'nologist n

endocrinopathy (ˌɛndəʊkrɪˈnɒpəθɪ) n any disease due to disorder of the endocrine system > endocrinopathic (ˌɛndəʊˌkrɪnəʊˈpæθɪk) adj

endocuticle (ˈɛndəʊˌkjuːtɪkəl) n the inner layer of the cuticle of an insect

endocytosis (ˌɛndəʊsaɪˈtəʊsɪs) n the process by which a living cell takes up molecules bound to its surface

endoderm (ˈɛndəʊˌdɜːm) or **entoderm** n the inner germ layer of an animal embryo, which gives rise to the lining of the digestive and respiratory tracts. See also **ectoderm, mesoderm** > ,endo'dermal, ,endo'dermic, ,ento'dermal or ,ento'dermic adj

endodermis (ˌɛndəʊˈdɜːmɪs) n botany the specialized innermost layer of cortex in roots and some stems, which controls the passage of water and dissolved substances between the cortex and stele [C19 from New Latin, from ENDO- + Greek *derma* skin]

endodontics (ˌɛndəʊˈdɒntɪks) n (functioning as singular) the branch of dentistry concerned with diseases of the dental pulp [C19 from New Latin *endodontia*, from ENDO- + Greek *odōn* tooth] > ˌendoˈdontal *or* ˌendoˈdontic *adj* > ˌendoˈdontist *n*

endoenzyme (ˌendəʊˈenzaɪm) *n* any of a group of enzymes, esp endopeptidases, that act upon inner chemical bonds in a chain of molecules. Compare **exoenzyme** (sense 1)

endoergic (ˌendəʊˈɜːdʒɪk) *adj* (of a nuclear reaction) occurring with absorption of energy, as opposed to *exoergic*. Compare **endothermic** [from ENDO- + -*ergic* from Greek *ergon* work]

end of steel *n Canadian* **1** a point up to which railway tracks have been laid **2** a town located at such a point

endogamy (enˈdɒɡəmɪ) *n* **1** *anthropol* marriage within one's own tribe or similar unit. Compare **exogamy** (sense 1) **2** pollination between two flowers on the same plant > enˈdogamous *or* endogamic (ˌendəʊˈɡæmɪk) *adj*

endogen (ˈendəʊˌdʒen) *n* a former name for **monocotyledon**

endogenous (enˈdɒdʒɪnəs) *adj* **1** *biology* developing or originating within an organism or part of an organism: *endogenous rhythms* **2** having no apparent external cause: *endogenous depression* > enˈdogenously *adv* > enˈdogeny *n*

endolithic (ˌendəʊˈlɪθɪk) *adj* (of organisms, such as algae) growing inside rock

endolymph (ˈendəʊˌlɪmf) *n* the fluid that fills the membranous labyrinth of the internal ear > endolymphatic (ˌendəʊlɪmˈfætɪk) *adj*

endometriosis (ˌendəʊˌmiːtrɪˈəʊsɪs) *n pathol* the presence of endometrium in areas other than the lining of the uterus, as on the ovaries, resulting in premenstrual pain

endometritis (ˌendəʊmɪˈtraɪtɪs) *n* inflammation of the endometrium, which is caused by infection, as by bacteria, foreign bodies, etc

endometrium (ˌendəʊˈmiːtrɪəm) *n, pl* -tria (-trɪə) the mucous membrane that lines the uterus [C19 New Latin, from ENDO- + Greek *mētra* uterus] > endoˈmetrial *adj*

endomitosis (ˌendəʊmaɪˈtəʊsɪs) *n biology* the division of chromosomes but not of the cell nucleus, resulting in a polyploid cell

endomorph (ˈendəʊˌmɔːf) *n* **1** a person with a fat and heavy body build: said to be correlated with viscerotonia. Compare **ectomorph, mesomorph 2** a mineral that naturally occurs enclosed within another mineral, as within quartz > endoˈmorphic *adj* > ˈendoˌmorphy *n*

endomorphism (ˌendəʊˈmɔːˌfɪzəm) *n geology* changes in a cooling body of igneous rock brought about by assimilation of fragments of, or chemical reaction with, the surrounding country rock

endoneurium (ˌendəʊˈnjʊərɪəm) *n* the delicate connective tissue surrounding nerve fibres within a bundle [New Latin, from ENDO- + NEURO- + -IUM]

endonuclease (ˌendəʊˈnjuːklɪˌeɪz) *n* an enzyme that is responsible for scission of a nucleic acid chain, the action of which is not confined to the terminal nucleotide. Compare **exonuclease**

endoparasite (ˌendəʊˈpærəˌsaɪt) *n* a parasite, such as the tapeworm, that lives within the body of its host > endoparasitic (ˌendəʊˌpærəˈsɪtɪk) *adj*

endopeptidase (ˌendəʊˈpeptɪˌdeɪz) *n* any proteolytic enzyme, such as pepsin, that splits a protein into smaller peptide fragments. Also called: proteinase Compare **exopeptidase**

endophyte (ˈendəʊˌfaɪt) *n* a fungus, or occasionally an alga or other organism, that lives within a plant > endophytic (ˌendəʊˈfɪtɪk) *adj* > ˌendoˈphytically *adv*

endoplasm (ˈendənˌplæzəm) *n cytology* the inner cytoplasm in some cells, esp protozoa, which is more granular and fluid than the outer cytoplasm (see **ectoplasm** (sense 1)) > ˌendoˈplasmic *adj*

endoplasmic reticulum *n* an extensive intracellular membrane system whose functions include synthesis and transport of lipids and, in regions where ribosomes are attached, of proteins

end organ *n anatomy* the expanded end of a peripheral motor or sensory nerve

endorphin (enˈdɔːfɪn) *n* any of a class of polypeptides, including enkephalin, occurring naturally in the brain, that bind to pain receptors and so block pain sensation [C20 from ENDO- + MORPHINE]

endorse *or* **indorse** (ɪnˈdɔːs) *vb* (tr) **1** to give approval or sanction to **2** to sign (one's name) on the back of (a cheque, etc) to specify oneself as payee **3** *commerce* **a** to sign the back of (a negotiable document) to transfer ownership of the rights to a specified payee **b** to specify (a designated sum) as transferable to another as payee **4** to write (a qualifying comment, recommendation, etc) on the back of a document **5** to sign (a document), as when confirming receipt of payment **6** *chiefly Brit* to record (a conviction) on (a driving licence) [C16 from Old French *endosser* to put on the back, from EN-¹ + *dos* back, from Latin *dorsum*] > enˈdorsable *or* inˈdorsable *adj* > enˈdorser, enˈdorsor, inˈdorser *or* inˈdorsor *n*

endorsee (ˌɪnˌdɔːˈsiː, ˌendɔː-) *or* **indorsee** *n* the person in whose favour a negotiable instrument is endorsed

endorsement *or* **indorsement** (ɪnˈdɔːsmənt) *n* **1** the act or an instance of endorsing **2** something that endorses, such as a signature or qualifying comment **3** approval or support **4** a record of a motoring offence on a driving licence **5** *insurance* a clause in or amendment to an insurance policy allowing for alteration of coverage

endoscope (ˈendəʊˌskəʊp) *n* a long slender medical instrument used for examining the interior of hollow organs including the lung, stomach, bladder, and bowel > endoscopic (ˌendəʊˈskɒpɪk) *adj* > endoscopist (enˈdɒskəpɪst) *n* > enˈdoscopy *n*

endoskeleton (ˌendəʊˈskelɪtən) *n* the internal skeleton of an animal, esp the bony or cartilaginous skeleton of vertebrates. Compare **exoskeleton**. > endoˈskeletal *adj*

endosmosis (ˌendɒsˈməʊsɪs, -dɒz-) *n biology* osmosis in which water enters a cell or organism from the surrounding solution. Compare **exosmosis**. > endosmotic (ˌendɒsˈmɒtɪk, -dɒz-) *adj* > ˌendosˈmotically *adv*

endosperm (ˈendəʊˌspɜːm) *n* the tissue within the seed of a flowering plant that surrounds and nourishes the developing embryo > endoˈspermic *adj*

endospore (ˈendəʊˌspɔː) *n* **1** a small asexual spore produced by some bacteria and algae **2** the innermost wall of a spore or pollen grain > endosporous (enˈdɒspərəs, ˌendəʊˈspɔːrəs) *adj*

endosteum (enˈdɒstɪəm) *n, pl* -tea (-tɪə) a highly vascular membrane lining the marrow cavity of long bones, such as the femur and humerus [C19 New Latin, from ENDO- + Greek *osteon* bone] > enˈdosteal *adj*

endostosis (ˌendɒsˈtəʊsɪs) *n, pl* -ses (-siːz) the conversion of cartilage into bone

endosymbiosis (ˌendəʊˌsɪmbɪˈəʊsɪs) *n* a type of symbiosis in which one organism lives inside the other, the two typically behaving as a single organism. It is believed to be the means by which such organelles as mitochondria and chloroplasts arose within eukaryotic cells > ˌendoˌsymbiˈotic *adj*

endothecium (ˌendəʊˈθiːʃɪəm, -sɪəm) *n, pl* -cia (-ʃɪə, -sɪə) *botany* **1** the inner mass of cells of the developing capsule in mosses **2** the fibrous tissue of the inner wall of an anther [C19 New Latin, from ENDO- + Greek *thēkion* case; see THECA] > ˌendoˈthecial *adj*

endothelioma (ˌendəʊˌθiːlɪˈəʊmə) *n, pl* -mata (-mətə) *pathol* a tumour originating in endothelial tissue, such as the lining of blood vessels

endothelium (ˌendəʊˈθiːlɪəm) *n, pl* -lia (-lɪə) a tissue consisting of a single layer of cells that lines the blood and lymph vessels, heart, and some other cavities [C19 New Latin, from ENDO- + -*thelium*, from Greek *thēlē* nipple] > ˌendoˈthelial *adj* > ˌendoˈtheliˌoid *adj*

endothermic (ˌendəʊˈθɜːmɪk) *or* **endothermal** *adj* (of a chemical reaction or compound) occurring or formed with the absorption of heat. Compare **exothermic, endoergic** > ˌendoˈthermically *adv* > ˌendoˈthermism *n*

endotoxin (ˌendəʊˈtɒksɪn) *n* a toxin contained within the protoplasm of an organism, esp a bacterium, and liberated only at death > ˌendoˈtoxic *adj*

endotracheal anaesthesia (ˌendəʊˈtrækɪəl) *n* a method of administering gaseous anaesthetics to animals through a tube inserted into the trachea

endotrophic mycorrhiza (ˌendəʊˈtrɒfɪk) *n botany* the most widespread and common type of mycorrhiza, in which the fungus lives within the cells of the roots of the plant. Also called: endomycorrhiza, arbuscular mycorrhiza Compare **ectotrophic mycorrhiza**

endow (ɪnˈdaʊ) *vb* (tr) **1** to provide with or bequeath a source of permanent income **2** (usually foll by *with*) to provide with (qualities, characteristics, etc) **3** *obsolete* to provide with a dower [C14 from Old French *endouer*, from EN-¹ + *douer*, from Latin *dōtāre*, from *dōs* dowry] > enˈdower *n*

endowment (ɪnˈdaʊmənt) *n* **1 a** the source of income with which an institution, etc, is endowed **b** the income itself **2** the act or process of endowing **3** (*usually plural*) natural talents or qualities

endowment assurance *or* **insurance** *n* a form of life insurance that provides for the payment of a specified sum directly to the policyholder at a designated date or to his beneficiary should he die before this date

endowment mortgage *n* an arrangement whereby a person takes out a mortgage and pays the capital repayment instalments into a life assurance policy and only the interest to the mortgagee during the term of the policy. The loan is repaid by the policy either when it matures or on the prior death of the policyholder

endozoic (ˌendəʊˈzəʊɪk) *adj botany* **1** (of a plant) living within an animal **2** denoting seed dispersal in which the seeds are swallowed by an animal and subsequently pass out in the faeces

endpaper (ˈendˌpeɪpə) *n* either of two leaves at the front and back of a book pasted to the inside of the board covers and the first leaf of the book to secure the binding

end pin *n music* the adjustable metal spike attached to the bottom of a cello, double bass, etc, that supports it while it is being played

endplate (ˈendˌpleɪt) *n* **1** any usually flat platelike structure at the end of something **2** *physiol* the flattened end of a motor nerve fibre, which transmits impulses to muscle

endplay (ˈendˌpleɪ) *bridge* ▷ *n* **1** a way of playing the last few tricks in a hand so that an opponent is forced to make a particular lead ▷ *vb* (tr) **2** to force (an opponent) to make a particular lead near the end of a hand: *declarer endplayed West for the jack of spades*

end point *n* **1** *chem* the point at which a titration is complete, usually marked by a change in colour of an indicator **2** the point at which anything is complete

end product *n* the final result or outcome of a process, series, endeavour, etc, esp in manufacturing

end-stopped *adj* (of verse) having a pause at the end of each line

endue *or* **indue** (ɪnˈdjuː) *vb* -dues, -duing, -dued (tr) **1** (usually foll by *with*) to invest or provide, as with some quality or trait **2** *rare* (foll by *with*) to clothe or dress (in) [C15 from Old French *enduire*, from Latin *indūcere*, from *dūcere* to lead]

end up *vb* (adverb) **1** (copula) to become eventually; turn out to be: *he ended up a thief* **2** (intr) to arrive, esp by a circuitous or lengthy route or process:

he ended up living in New Zealand

endurance (ɪnˈdjʊərəns) *n* **1** the capacity, state, or an instance of enduring **2** something endured; a hardship, strain, or privation

endure (ɪnˈdjʊə) *vb* **1** to undergo (hardship, strain, privation, etc) without yielding; bear **2** (*tr*) to permit or tolerate **3** (*intr*) to last or continue to exist [c14 from Old French *endurer*, from Latin *indūrāre* to harden, from *dūrus* hard] ▷ en'durable *adj* ▷ en,dura'bility *or* en'durableness *n* ▷ en'durably *adv*

enduring (ɪnˈdjʊərɪŋ) *adj* **1** permanent; lasting **2** having forbearance; long-suffering ▷ en'duringly *adv* ▷ en'duringness *n*

end user *n* **1 a** (in international trading) the person, organization, or nation that will be the ultimate recipient of goods, esp such as arms or advanced technology **b** (*as modifier*): *an end-user certificate* **2** *computing* the ultimate destination, such as a program or operator, of information that is being transferred within a system

endways (ˈɛndˌweɪz) *or esp US and Canadian* **endwise** (ˈɛndˌwaɪz) *adv* **1** having the end forwards or upwards ▷ *adj* **2** vertical or upright **3** lengthways **4** standing or lying end to end

Endymion (ɛnˈdɪmɪən) *n Greek myth* a handsome youth who was visited every night by the moon goddess Selene, who loved him

endysis (ɛnˈdaɪsɪs) *n zoology* the formation of new layers of integument after ecdysis

end zone *n American football* the area behind the goals at each end of the field that the ball must cross for a touchdown to be awarded

ENE *symbol for* east-northeast

-ene *n combining form* (in chemistry) indicating an unsaturated compound containing double bonds: *benzene; ethylene* [from Greek *-ēnē*, feminine patronymic suffix]

ENEA *abbreviation for* European Nuclear Energy Agency: the European body responsible for the development of nuclear-generated electric power

enema (ˈɛnɪmə) *n, pl* **-mas** *or* **-mata** (-mətə) *med* **1** the introduction of liquid into the rectum to evacuate the bowels, medicate, or nourish **2** the liquid so introduced [c15 from New Latin, from Greek: injection, from *enienai* to send in, from *hienai* to send]

enemy (ˈɛnəmɪ) *n, pl* **-mies 1** a person hostile or opposed to a policy, cause, person, or group, esp one who actively tries to do damage; opponent **2 a** an armed adversary; opposing military force **b** (*as modifier*): *enemy aircraft* **3 a** a hostile nation or people **b** (*as modifier*): *an enemy alien* **4** something that harms or opposes; adversary: *courage is the enemy of failure* ▷ *Related adjective:* **inimical** [c13 from Old French *enemi*, from Latin *inimīcus* hostile, from IN-¹ + *amīcus* friend]

energetic (ˌɛnəˈdʒɛtɪk) *adj* having or showing much energy or force; vigorous ▷ ˌener'getically *adv*

energetics (ˌɛnəˈdʒɛtɪks) *n* (*functioning as singular*) the branch of science concerned with energy and its transformations

energid (ˈɛnədʒɪd) *n biology* a nucleus and the cytoplasm associated with it in a syncytium [c19 adapted from German, from ENERGY + -ID¹]

energize *or* **energise** (ˈɛnəˌdʒaɪz) *vb* **1** to have or cause to have energy; invigorate **2** (*tr*) to apply a source of electric current or electromotive force to (a circuit, field winding, etc) ▷ 'ener,gizer *or* 'ener,giser *n*

energumen (ˌɛnəˈgjuːmɛn) *n* **1** a person thought to be possessed by an evil spirit **2** a fanatic or zealot [c18 via Late Latin from Greek *energoumenos* having been worked on, from *energein* to be in action, from *energos* effective; see ENERGY]

energy (ˈɛnədʒɪ) *n, pl* **-gies 1** intensity or vitality of action or expression; forcefulness **2** capacity or tendency for intense activity; vigour **3** vigorous or intense action; exertion **4** *physics* **a** the capacity of a body or system to do work **b** a measure of this capacity, expressed as the work that it does in changing to some specified

reference state. It is measured in joules (SI units). Symbol: *E* **5** a source of power. See also **kinetic energy, potential energy** [c16 from Late Latin *energīa*, from Greek *energeia* activity, from *energos* effective, from EN-² + *ergon* work]

energy band *n physics* a range of energies associated with the quantum states of electrons in a crystalline solid. In a semiconductor or an insulator there is a **valence band** containing many states, most of which are occupied. Above this is a **forbidden band** with only a few isolated states caused by impurities. Above this is a **conduction band** containing many states most of which are empty. In a metal there is a continuous **valence-conduction band**. See also **energy gap**

energy conversion *n* the process of changing one form of energy into another, such as nuclear energy into heat or solar energy into electrical energy

energy crop *n* a crop that is grown because it can be used as fuel

energy drink *n* a soft drink containing ingredients designed to boost the drinker's energy, esp after exercise

energy gap *n physics* the difference of energy between the bottom of the conduction band and the top of the valence band of the electrons in a crystalline solid. For values below about 2eV the substance is considered to be a semiconductor whilst for higher values it is considered to be an insulator

energy level *n physics* **1** a constant value of energy in the distribution of energies among a number of atomic particles **2** the energy of a quantum state of a system. The terms **energy level** and **energy state** are often used loosely to mean **quantum state**. This is avoided in precise communication

energy-smart *adj* using electrical power in an efficient or economical way

enervate *vb* (ˈɛnəˌveɪt) **1** (*tr*) to deprive of strength or vitality; weaken physically or mentally; debilitate ▷ *adj* (ɪˈnɜːvɪt) **2** deprived of strength or vitality; weakened [c17 from Latin *ēnervāre* to remove the nerves from, from *nervus* nerve, sinew] ▷ ˌener'vation *n* ▷ 'ener,vative *adj* ▷ 'ener,vator *n*

enervating (ˈɛnəˌveɪtɪŋ) *adj* tending to deprive of strength or vitality; physically or mentally weakening; debilitating

Enewetak (ˌɛnɪˈweɪtɒk, əˈniːwɛˌtɔːk) *n* the official name for **Eniwetok**

enface (ɪnˈfeɪs) *vb* (*tr*) to write, print, or stamp (something) on the face of (a document) ▷ en'facement *n*

en face *French* (ɑ̃ fas) *adj* **1** facing forwards **2** opposite; facing

en famille *French* (ɑ̃ famij) *adv* **1** with one's family; at home **2** in a casual way; informally

enfant sauvage *French* (ɑ̃fɑ̃ sovaʒ) *n, pl enfants sauvages* (ɑ̃fɑ̃ sovaʒ) a person given to naive, undisciplined, or unpredictable behaviour, largely because of youth and inexperience [c20 literally: wild child]

enfant terrible *French* (ɑ̃fɑ̃ tɛriblə) *n, pl enfants terribles* (ɑ̃fɑ̃ tɛriblə) a person given to unconventional conduct or indiscreet remarks [c19 literally: terrible child]

enfeeble (ɪnˈfiːbəl) *vb* (*tr*) to make weak; deprive of strength ▷ en'feeblement *n* ▷ en'feebler *n*

enfeoff (ɪnˈfiːf) *vb* (*tr*) **1** *property law* to invest (a person) with possession of a freehold estate in land **2** (in feudal society) to take (someone) into vassalage by giving a fee or fief in return for certain services [c14 from Anglo-French *enfeoffer*; see FIEF] ▷ en'feoffment *n*

en fête *French* (ɑ̃ fɛt) *adv* **1** dressed for a festivity **2** engaged in a festivity [c19 literally: in festival]

Enfield (ˈɛnfiːld) *n* a borough of Greater London: a N residential suburb. Pop: 280 300 (2003 est). Area: 55 sq km (31 sq miles)

Enfield rifle *n* **1** a breech-loading bolt-action magazine rifle, usually .303 calibre, used by the

British army until World War II and by other countries **2** a 19th-century muzzle-loading musket used by the British army [c19 from ENFIELD, where it was first made]

enfilade (ˌɛnfɪˈleɪd) *military* ▷ *n* **1** a position or formation subject to fire from a flank along the length of its front ▷ *vb* (*tr*) **2** to subject (a position or formation) to fire from a flank **3** to position (troops or guns) so as to be able to fire at a flank [c18 from French: suite, from *enfiler* to thread on string, from *fil* thread]

enfleurage *French* (ɑ̃flœraʒ) *n* the process of exposing odourless oils to the scent of fresh flowers, used in perfume-making [c19 literally: inflowering]

enfold *or* **infold** (ɪnˈfəʊld) *vb* (*tr*) **1** to cover by enclosing **2** to embrace **3** to form with or as with folds ▷ en'folder *or* in'folder *n* ▷ en'foldment *or* in'foldment *n*

enforce (ɪnˈfɔːs) *vb* (*tr*) **1** to ensure observance of or obedience to (a law, decision, etc) **2** to impose (obedience, loyalty, etc) by or as by force **3** to emphasize or reinforce (an argument, demand, etc) ▷ en'forceable *adj* ▷ en,force'ability *n* ▷ enforcedly (ɪnˈfɔːsɪdlɪ) *adv* ▷ en'forcement *n* ▷ en'forcer *n*

enfranchise (ɪnˈfræntʃaɪz) *vb* (*tr*) **1** to grant the power of voting to, esp as a right of citizenship **2** to liberate, as from servitude **3** (in England) to invest (a town, city, etc) with the right to be represented in Parliament **4** *English law* to convert (leasehold) to freehold ▷ en'franchisement *n* ▷ en'franchiser *n*

eng (ɛŋ) *n phonetics* another name for **agma**

ENG *abbreviation for* electronic news gathering: TV news obtained at the point of action by means of modern video equipment

eng. *abbreviation for* **1** engineer **2** engineering

Eng. *abbreviation for* **1** England **2** English

Engadine (ˈɛŋgəˌdiːn) *n* the upper part of the valley of the River Inn in Switzerland, in Graubünden canton: tourist and winter sports centre

engage (ɪnˈgeɪdʒ) *vb* (*mainly tr*) **1** to secure the services of; employ **2** to secure for use; reserve: *engage a room* **3** to involve (a person or his attention) intensely; engross; occupy **4** to attract (the affection) of (a person): *her innocence engaged him* **5** to draw (somebody) into conversation **6** (*intr*) to take part; participate: *he engages in many sports* **7** to promise (to do something) **8** (*also intr*) *military* to begin an action with (an enemy) **9** to bring (a mechanism) into operation: *he engaged the clutch* **10** (*also intr*) to undergo or cause to undergo interlocking, as of the components of a driving mechanism, such as a gear train **11** *machinery* to locate (a locking device) in its operative position or to advance (a tool) into a workpiece to commence cutting [c15 from Old French *engagier*, from EN-¹ + *gage* a pledge, see GAGE¹] ▷ en'gager *n*

engagé *French* (ɑ̃gaʒe) *adj* (of a writer or artist, esp a man) morally or politically committed to some ideology

engaged (ɪnˈgeɪdʒd) *adj* **1** pledged to be married; betrothed **2** employed, occupied, or busy **3** *architect* built against or attached to a wall or similar structure: *an engaged column* **4** (of a telephone line) already in use ▷ engagedly (ɪnˈgeɪdʒɪdlɪ) *adv*

engaged tone *n Brit* a repeated single note heard on a telephone when the number called is already in use. US and Canadian equivalent: **busy signal** Compare **ringing tone, dialling tone**

engagée *French* (ɑ̃gaʒe) *adj* (of a female writer or artist) morally or politically committed to some ideology

engagement (ɪnˈgeɪdʒmənt) *n* **1** a pledge of marriage; betrothal **2** an appointment or arrangement, esp for business or social purposes **3** the act of engaging or condition of being engaged **4** a promise, obligation, or other condition that binds **5** a period of employment,

e

esp a limited period **6** an action; battle **7** (*plural*) financial obligations

engagement ring *n* a ring given by a man to a woman as a token of their betrothal

engaging (ɪnˈɡeɪdʒɪŋ) *adj* pleasing, charming, or winning > en'gagingly *adv* > en'gagingness *n*

en garde *French* (ɑ̃ ɡard) *interj* **1** on guard; a call to a fencer to adopt a defensive stance in readiness for an attack or bout ▷ *adj* **2** (of a fencer) in such a stance

engender (ɪnˈdʒɛndə) *vb* **1** (*tr*) to bring about or give rise to; produce or cause **2** to be born or cause to be born; bring or come into being [C14 from Old French *engendrer*, from Latin *ingenerāre*, from *generāre* to beget] > en'genderer *n* > en'genderment *n*

engine (ˈɛndʒɪn) *n* **1** any machine designed to convert energy, esp heat energy, into mechanical work: *a steam engine; a petrol engine* **2 a** a railway locomotive **b** (*as modifier*): *the engine cab* **3** *military* any of various pieces of equipment formerly used in warfare, such as a battering ram or gun **4** *obsolete* any instrument or device: *engines of torture* [C13 from Old French *engin*, from Latin *ingenium* nature, talent, ingenious contrivance, from IN-[2] + *-genium*, related to *gignere* to beget, produce]

engine driver *n chiefly Brit* a person who drives a railway locomotive; train driver

engineer (ˌɛndʒɪˈnɪə) *n* **1** a person trained in any branch of the profession of engineering **2** the originator or manager of a situation, system, etc **3** a mechanic; person who repairs or services machines **4** *US and Canadian* the driver of a railway locomotive **5** an officer responsible for a ship's engines **6** Informal name: **sapper** a member of the armed forces, esp the army, trained in engineering and construction work ▷ *vb* (*tr*) **7** to originate, cause, or plan in a clever or devious manner: *he engineered the minister's downfall* **8** to design, plan, or construct as a professional engineer [C14 *enginer*, from Old French *engigneor*, from *engignier* to contrive, ultimately from Latin *ingenium* skill, talent; see ENGINE]

engineering (ˌɛndʒɪˈnɪərɪŋ) *n* the profession of applying scientific principles to the design, construction, and maintenance of engines, cars, machines, etc (**mechanical engineering**), buildings, bridges, roads, etc (**civil engineering**), electrical machines and communication systems (**electrical engineering**), chemical plant and machinery (**chemical engineering**), or aircraft (**aeronautical engineering**). See also **military engineering**

engineer officer *n* a ship's officer who is qualified to be in charge of the vessel's propulsion and other machinery

engine pod *n aeronautics* an aircraft turbojet unit comprising the engine and its cowling suspended by a pylon, often below the wing

engine room *n* a place where engines are housed, esp on a ship

enginery (ˈɛndʒɪnrɪ) *n, pl* -ries **1** a collection or assembly of engines; machinery **2** engines employed in warfare **3** *rare* skilful manoeuvring or contrivance

englacial (ɪnˈɡleɪsɪəl) *adj* embedded in, carried by, or running through a glacier: *englacial drift; an englacial river* > en'glacially *adv*

England (ˈɪŋɡlənd) *n* the largest division of Great Britain, bordering on Scotland and Wales: unified in the mid-tenth century and conquered by the Normans in 1066; united with Wales in 1536 and Scotland in 1707; monarchy overthrown in 1649 but restored in 1660. Capital: London. Pop: 49 855 700 (2003 est). Area: 130 439 sq km (50 352 sq miles). See **United Kingdom, Great Britain**

Engler degrees (ˈɛŋlə) *n* (*functioning as singular*) a scale of measurement of viscosity based on the ratio of the time taken by a particular liquid to flow through a standard orifice to the time taken by water to flow through the same orifice [named after C. *Engler* (1842–1925), German chemist, who proposed it]

English (ˈɪŋɡlɪʃ) *n* **1** the official language of Britain, the US, most parts of the Commonwealth, and certain other countries. It is the native language of over 280 million people and is acquired as a second language by many more. It is an Indo-European language belonging to the West Germanic branch. See also **Middle English, Old English, Modern English 2** the **English** (*functioning as plural*) the natives or inhabitants of England collectively **3** (formerly) a size of printer's type approximately equal to 14 point **4** an old style of black-letter typeface **5** (*often not capital*) the usual US and Canadian term for **side** (in billiards) ▷ *adj* **6** denoting, using, or relating to the English language **7** relating to or characteristic of England or the English ▷ *vb* (*tr*) **8** *archaic* to translate or adapt into English ▷ *Related prefix*: **Anglo-**. > 'Englishness *n*

English bond *n* a bond used in brickwork that has a course of headers alternating with a course of stretchers

English Canadian *n* a Canadian citizen whose first language is English, esp one of English descent

English Channel *n* an arm of the Atlantic Ocean between S England and N France, linked with the North Sea by the Strait of Dover. Length: about 560 km (350 miles). Width: between 32 km (20 miles) and 161 km (100 miles)

English flute *n music* another name for **recorder** (sense 4)

English Heritage *n* an organization, partly funded by government aid, that looks after ancient monuments and historic buildings in England. Official name: **The Historic Buildings and Monuments Commission for England**

English horn *n music* another name for **cor anglais**

Englishism (ˈɪŋɡlɪˌʃɪzəm) *n chiefly US* **1** an English custom, practice, etc **2** a word or expression not found in forms of English other than British English; Anglicism **3** high regard for English customs, institutions, etc

Englishman (ˈɪŋɡlɪʃmən) *n, pl* -men a male native or inhabitant of England

Englishman's tie *or* **knot** *n* a type of knot for tying together heavy ropes

Englishry (ˈɪŋɡlɪʃrɪ) *n now rare* **1** people of English descent, esp in Ireland **2** the fact or condition of being an Englishman or Englishwoman, esp by birth

English self *n* a breed of short-haired guinea pig that is a single colour throughout

English setter *n* a breed of setter having a white coat speckled with liver, brown, or yellowish markings

English springer spaniel *n* See **springer spaniel**

Englishwoman (ˈɪŋɡlɪʃˌwʊmən) *n, pl* -women a female native or inhabitant of England

englut (ɪnˈɡlʌt) *vb* -gluts, -glutting, -glutted (*tr*) *literary* **1** to devour ravenously; swallow eagerly **2** to glut or sate (oneself); surfeit; satiate

engorge (ɪnˈɡɔːdʒ) *vb* (*tr*) **1** *pathol* to congest with blood **2** to eat (food) ravenously or greedily **3** to gorge (oneself); glut; satiate > en'gorgement *n*

engr *abbreviation for* **1** engineer **2** engraver

engraft *or* **ingraft** (ɪnˈɡrɑːft) *vb* (*tr*) **1** to graft (a shoot, bud, etc) onto a stock **2** to incorporate in a firm or permanent way; implant: *they engrafted their principles into the document* > ˌengraf'tation, ˌingraf'tation, en'graftment *or* in'graftment *n*

engrail (ɪnˈɡreɪl) *vb* (*tr*) to decorate or mark (the edge of) (a coin) with small carved notches [C14 from Old French *engresler*, from EN-[1] + *gresle* slim, from Latin *gracilis* slender, graceful] > en'grailment *n*

engrain (ɪnˈɡreɪn) *vb* a variant spelling of **ingrain**

engram (ˈɛnɡræm) *n psychol* the physical basis of an individual memory in the brain. See also **memory trace** [C20 from German *Engramm*, from Greek *en-* IN + *gramma* letter] > en'grammic *or* ˌengram'matic *adj*

engrave (ɪnˈɡreɪv) *vb* (*tr*) **1** to inscribe (a design, writing, etc) onto (a block, plate, or other surface used for printing) by carving, etching with acid, or other process **2** to print (designs or characters) from a printing plate so made **3** to fix deeply or permanently in the mind [C16 from EN-[1] + GRAVE[3], on the model of French *engraver*] > en'graver *n*

engraving (ɪnˈɡreɪvɪŋ) *n* **1** the art of a person who engraves **2** a block, plate, or other surface that has been engraved **3** a print made from such a surface. Related adj: **glyptic**

engross (ɪnˈɡrəʊs) *vb* (*tr*) **1** to occupy one's attention completely; absorb **2** to write or copy (manuscript) in large legible handwriting **3** *law* to write or type out formally (a deed, agreement, or other document) preparatory to execution **4** another word for **corner** (sense 21b) [C14 (in the sense: to buy up wholesale): from Old French *en gros* in quantity; C15 (in the sense: to write in large letters): probably from Medieval Latin *ingrossāre*; both from Latin *grossus* thick, GROSS] > en'grossed *adj* > engrossedly (ɪnˈɡrəʊsɪdlɪ) *adv* > en'grosser *n*

engrossing (ɪnˈɡrəʊsɪŋ) *adj* so interesting as to occupy one's attention completely; absorbing

engrossment (ɪnˈɡrəʊsmənt) *n* **1** a deed or other document that has been engrossed **2** the state of being engrossed

engulf *or* **ingulf** (ɪnˈɡʌlf) *vb* (*tr*) **1** to immerse, plunge, bury, or swallow up **2** (*often passive*) to overwhelm: *engulfed by debts* > en'gulfment *n*

enhance (ɪnˈhɑːns) *vb* (*tr*) to intensify or increase in quality, value, power, etc; improve; augment [C14 from Old French *enhaucier*, from EN-[1] + *haucier* to raise, from Vulgar Latin *altiāre* (unattested), from Latin *altus* high] > en'hancement *n* > en'hancer *n* > en'hancive *adj*

enhanced oil recovery *n* any of several techniques that make it possible to recover more oil than can be obtained by natural pressure, such as the injection of fluid or gases into an oilfield to force more oil to the surface

enhanced radiation weapon *n* a technical name for **neutron bomb**

enharmonic (ˌɛnhɑːˈmɒnɪk) *adj music* **1** denoting or relating to a small difference in pitch between two notes such as A flat and G sharp: not present in instruments of equal temperament such as the piano, but significant in the intonation of stringed and wind instruments **2** denoting or relating to enharmonic modulation [C17 from Latin *enharmonicus*, from Greek *enarmonios*, from EN-[2] + *harmonia*; see HARMONY] > ˌenhar'monically *adv*

enharmonic modulation *n music* a change of key achieved by regarding a note in one key as an equivalent note in another. Thus E flat in the key of A flat could be regarded as D sharp in the key of B major

Enid (ˈiːnɪd) *n* (in Arthurian legend) the faithful wife of Geraint

enigma (ɪˈnɪɡmə) *n* a person, thing, or situation that is mysterious, puzzling, or ambiguous [C16 from Latin *aenigma*, from Greek *ainigma*, from *ainissesthai* to speak in riddles, from *ainos* fable, story] > enigmatic (ˌɛnɪɡˈmætɪk) *or* ˌenig'matical *adj* > ˌenig'matically *adv*

enigmatize *or* **enigmatise** (ɪˈnɪɡməˌtaɪz) *vb* (*tr*) to make enigmatic

enisle (ɪnˈaɪl) *vb* (*tr*) *poetic* to put on or make into an island

Eniwetok (ˌɛnəˈwiːtɒk, əˈniːwɪˌtɔːk) *n* an atoll in the W Pacific Ocean, in the NW Marshall Islands: taken by the US from Japan in 1944; became a naval base and later a testing ground for atomic weapons. Pop: 715 (latest est). Official name: **Enewetak**

enjambment *or* **enjambement** (ɪnˈdʒæmmənt; *French* ɑ̃ʒɑ̃bmɑ̃) *n prosody* the running over of a sentence from one line of verse into the next [C19 from French, literally: a straddling, from *enjamber* to straddle, from EN-[1] + *jambe* leg; see JAMB] > en'jambed *adj*

enjoin (ɪnˈdʒɔɪn) *vb (tr)* **1** to order (someone) to do (something); urge strongly; command **2** to impose or prescribe (a condition, mode of behaviour, etc) **3** *law* to require (a person) to do or refrain from doing (some act), esp by issuing an injunction [c13 from Old French *enjoindre,* from Latin *injungere* to fasten to, from IN-² + *jungere* to JOIN] > enˈjoiner *n* > enˈjoinment *n*

enjoy (ɪnˈdʒɔɪ) *vb (tr)* **1** to receive pleasure from; take joy in **2** to have the benefit of; use with satisfaction **3** to have as a condition; experience: *the land enjoyed a summer of rain* **4** *archaic* to have sexual intercourse with **5** *enjoy oneself* to have a good time [c14 from Old French *enjoir,* from EN-¹ + *joir* to find pleasure in, from Latin *gaudēre* to rejoice] > enˈjoyable *adj* > enˈjoyableness *n* > enˈjoyably *adv* > enˈjoyer *n*

enjoyment (ɪnˈdʒɔɪmənt) *n* **1** the act or condition of receiving pleasure from something **2** the use or possession of something that is satisfying or beneficial **3** something that provides joy or satisfaction **4** the possession or exercise of a legal right

enkephalin (ɛnˈkɛfəlɪn) *or* **encephalin** (ɛnˈsɛfəlɪn) *n* a chemical occurring in the brain, having effects similar to those of morphine. See also **endorphin**

enkindle (ɪnˈkɪndəl) *vb (tr)* **1** to set on fire; kindle **2** to excite to activity or ardour; arouse > enˈkindler *n*

enlace (ɪnˈleɪs) *vb (tr)* **1** to bind or encircle with or as with laces **2** to entangle; intertwine > enˈlacement *n*

enlarge (ɪnˈlɑːdʒ) *vb* **1** to make or grow larger in size, scope, etc; increase or expand **2** *(tr)* to make (a photographic print) of a larger size than the negative **3** *(intr; foll by on or upon)* to speak or write (about) in greater detail; expatiate (on) > enˈlargeable *adj*

enlargement (ɪnˈlɑːdʒmənt) *n* **1** the act of enlarging or the condition of being enlarged **2** something that enlarges or is intended to enlarge **3** a photographic print that is larger than the negative from which it is made

enlarger (ɪnˈlɑːdʒə) *n* an optical instrument for making enlarged photographic prints in which a negative is brightly illuminated and its enlarged image is focused onto a sheet of sensitized paper

enlighten (ɪnˈlaɪtən) *vb (tr)* **1** to give information or understanding to; instruct; edify **2** to free from ignorance, prejudice, or superstition **3** to give spiritual or religious revelation to **4** *poetic* to shed light on > enˈlightener *n* > enˈlightening *adj*

enlightened (ɪnˈlaɪtənd) *adj* **1** factually well-informed, tolerant of alternative opinions, and guided by rational thought: *an enlightened administration; enlightened self-interest* **2** privy to or claiming a sense of spiritual or religious revelation of truth: *the search for an enlightened spiritual master*

enlightenment (ɪnˈlaɪtənmənt) *n* **1** the act or means of enlightening or the state of being enlightened **2** *Buddhism* the awakening to ultimate truth by which man is freed from the endless cycle of personal reincarnations to which all men are otherwise subject **3** *Hinduism* a state of transcendent divine experience represented by Vishnu: regarded as a goal of all religion

Enlightenment (ɪnˈlaɪtənmənt) *n* **the** an 18th-century philosophical movement stressing the importance of reason and the critical reappraisal of existing ideas and social institutions

enlist (ɪnˈlɪst) *vb* **1** to enter or persuade to enter into an engagement to serve in the armed forces **2** *(tr)* to engage or secure (a person, his services, or his support) for a venture, cause, etc **3** *(intr; foll by in)* to enter into or join an enterprise, cause, etc > enˈlister *n* > enˈlistment *n*

enlisted man *n US* a serviceman who holds neither a commission nor a warrant and is not under training for officer rank as a cadet or midshipman

enliven (ɪnˈlaɪvən) *vb (tr)* **1** to make active, vivacious, or spirited; invigorate **2** to make cheerful or bright; gladden or brighten > enˈlivener *n* > enˈlivening *adj* > enˈlivenment *n*

en masse (French ã mas) *adv* in a group, body, or mass; as a whole; all together [c19 from French]

enmesh, inmesh (ɪnˈmɛʃ) *or* **immesh** *vb (tr)* to catch or involve in or as if in a net or snare; entangle > enˈmeshment *n*

enmity (ˈɛnmɪtɪ) *n, pl* -ties a feeling of hostility or ill will, as between enemies; antagonism [c13 from Old French *enemistié,* from *enemi* ENEMY]

ennage (ˈɛnɪdʒ) *n printing* the total number of ens in a piece of matter to be set in type

ennead (ˈɛnɪˌæd) *n* **1** a group or series of nine **2** the sum of or number nine [c17 from Greek *enneas,* from *ennea* nine] > enneˈadic *adj*

enneagon (ˈɛnɪəgən) *n* another name for **nonagon**

enneahedron (ˌɛnɪəˈhiːdrən) *n, pl* -drons *or* -dra (-drə) a solid figure having nine plane faces. See also **polyhedron.** > ˌenneaˈhedral *adj*

Ennerdale Water (ˈɛnəˌdeɪl) *n* a lake in NW England, in Cumbria in the Lake District. Length: 4 km (2.5 miles)

Ennis (ˈɛnɪs) *n* a town in the W Republic of Ireland, county town of Co Clare. Pop: 22 051 (2002)

Enniskillen (ˌɛnɪsˈkɪlɪn) *or formerly* **Inniskilling** *n* a town in SW Northern Ireland, in Fermanagh, on an island in the River Erne: scene of the defeat of James II's forces in 1689. Pop: 13 599 (2001)

ennoble (ɪˈnəʊbəl) *vb (tr)* **1** to make noble, honourable, or excellent; dignify; exalt **2** to raise to a noble rank; confer a title of nobility upon > enˈnoblement *n* > enˈnobler *n* > enˈnobling *adj*

ennog (ˈɛnɒg) *n Northern English dialect* a back alley

ennui (ˈɒnwiː; French ãɥi) *n* a feeling of listlessness and general dissatisfaction resulting from lack of activity or excitement [c18 from French: apathy, from Old French *enui* annoyance, vexation; see ANNOY]

ennuied, ennuyed (ˈɒnwiːd) *or* **ennuyé** (French ãɥije) *adj* affected with ennui; bored

ENO abbreviation for English National Opera

Enoch (ˈiːnɒk) *n Old Testament* **1** the eldest son of Cain after whom the first city was named (Genesis 4:17) **2** the father of Methuselah: said to have walked with God and to have been taken by God at the end of his earthly life (Genesis 5:24)

enol (ˈiːnɒl) *n* any organic compound containing the group -CH:CO-, often existing in chemical equilibrium with the corresponding keto form. See **keto-enol tautomerism** [c19 from -ENE + -OL¹] > eˈnolic *adj*

enology (iːˈnɒlədʒɪ) *n* the usual US spelling of **oenology**

enormity (ɪˈnɔːmɪtɪ) *n, pl* -ties **1** the quality or character of being outrageous; extreme wickedness **2** an act of great wickedness; atrocity **3** *informal* vastness of size or extent [c15 from Old French *enormite,* from Late Latin *ēnormitās* hugeness; see ENORMOUS]

> USAGE In modern English, it is common to talk about the *enormity* of something such as a task or a problem, but one should not talk about the *enormity* of an object or area: *distribution is a problem because of India's enormous size* (not *India's enormity*).

enormous (ɪˈnɔːməs) *adj* **1** unusually large in size, extent, or degree; immense; vast **2** *archaic* extremely wicked; heinous [c16 from Latin *ēnormis,* from *ē-* out of, away from + *norma* rule, pattern] > eˈnormously *adv* > eˈnormousness *n*

Enos (ˈiːnɒs) *n Old Testament* a son of Seth (Genesis 4:26; 5:6)

e-nose (ˈiːnəʊz) *n* an electronic device which can detect bacteria, disease, etc by means of a computerized chemical sensing system [c20 E(LECTRONIC) + NOSE (sense 1)]

enosis (ˈɛnəʊsɪs) *n* the union of Greece and Cyprus: the aim of a group of Greek Cypriots [c20

Modern Greek: from Greek *henoun* to unite, from *heis* one]

enough (ɪˈnʌf) *determiner* **1 a** sufficient to answer a need, demand, supposition, or requirement; adequate: *enough cake* **b** *(as pronoun)*: *enough is now known* **2** that's enough! that will do: used to put an end to an action, speech, performance, etc ▷ *adv* **3** so as to be adequate or sufficient; as much as necessary: *you have worked hard enough* **4** *(not used with a negative)* very or quite; rather: *she was pleased enough to see me* **5** (intensifier): *oddly enough; surprisingly enough* **6** just adequately; tolerably: *he did it well enough* [Old English *genōh*; related to Old Norse *gnōgr,* Gothic *ganōhs,* Old High German *ginuog*]

enounce (ɪˈnaʊns) *vb (tr) formal* **1** to enunciate **2** to pronounce [c19 from French *énoncer,* from Latin *ēnuntiāre* ENUNCIATE] > eˈnouncement *n*

enow (ɪˈnaʊ) *adj, adv* an archaic word for **enough**

en passant (ɒn pæˈsɑːnt; French ã pasã) *adv* in passing: in chess, said of capturing a pawn that has made an initial move of two squares to its fourth rank, bypassing the square where an enemy pawn on its own fifth rank could capture it. The capture is made as if the captured pawn had moved one square instead of two [c17 from French]

en pension (French ã pãsjõ) *adv* in lodgings with all meals provided

enphytotic (ˌɛnfaɪˈtɒtɪk) *adj* (of plant diseases) causing a constant amount of damage each year [c20 from EN-² + -PHYTE + -OTIC]

enplane (ɛnˈpleɪn) *vb (intr)* to board an aircraft

en plein (French ã plɛ̃) *adj (postpositive), adv* (of a gambling bet) placed entirely on a single number, etc [from French: in full]

enprint (ˈɛnprɪnt) *n* a standard photographic print (5 × 3.5 in) produced from a negative

en prise (French ã priz) *adj (postpositive), adv* (of a chess piece) exposed to capture [c19 from French; see PRIZE¹]

enquire (ɪnˈkwaɪə) *vb* a variant of **inquire** > enˈquirer *n* > enˈquiry *n*

enrage (ɪnˈreɪdʒ) *vb (tr)* to provoke to fury; put into a rage; anger > enˈraged *adj* > enragedly (ɪnˈreɪdʒɪdlɪ) *adv* > enˈragement *n*

en rapport (French ã rapɔr) *adj (postpositive), adv* in sympathy, harmony, or accord

enrapture (ɪnˈræptʃə) *vb (tr)* to fill with delight; enchant

enrich (ɪnˈrɪtʃ) *vb (tr)* **1** to increase the wealth of **2** to endow with fine or desirable qualities: *to enrich one's experience by travelling* **3** to make more beautiful; adorn; decorate: *a robe enriched with jewels* **4** to improve in quality, colour, flavour, etc **5** to increase the food value of by adding nutrients: *to enrich dog biscuits with calcium* **6** to make (soil) more productive, esp by adding fertilizer **7** *physics* to increase the concentration or abundance of one component or isotope in (a solution or mixture); concentrate: *to enrich a solution by evaporation; enrich a nuclear fuel* > enˈriched *adj* > enˈricher *n* > enˈrichment *n*

enrobe (ɪnˈrəʊb) *vb (tr)* to dress in or as if in a robe; attire > enˈrober *n*

enrol *or US* **enroll** (ɪnˈrəʊl) *vb* -rols *or US* -rolls, -rolling, -rolled *(mainly tr)* **1** to record or note in a roll or list **2** *(also intr)* to become or cause to become a member; enlist; register **3** to put on record; record **4** *rare* to roll or wrap up > enrolˈlee *n* > enˈroller *n*

enrolment *or US* **enrollment** (ɪnˈrəʊlmənt) *n* **1** the act of enrolling or state of being enrolled **2** a list of people enrolled **3** the total number of people enrolled

enroot (ɪnˈruːt) *vb (tr; usually passive)* **1** to establish (plants) by fixing their roots in the earth **2** to fix firmly, implant, or embed

en route (ɒn ˈruːt; French ã rut) *adv* on or along the way; on the road [c18 from French]

ens (ɛnz) *n, pl* entia (ˈɛnʃɪə) *metaphysics* **1** being or existence in the most general abstract sense **2** a real thing, esp as opposed to an attribute; entity [c16 from Late Latin, literally: being, from Latin *esse* to be]

Ens. *abbreviation for* Ensign

ENSA (ˈɛnsə) *n acronym for* Entertainments National Service Association: a British organization providing entertainment for the armed forces during World War II

ensample (ɛnˈsɑːmpᵊl) *n* an archaic word for **example**

ensanguine (ɪnˈsæŋɡwɪn) *vb* (*tr*) *literary* to cover or stain with or as with blood

Enschede (*Dutch* ˈɛnsxədeː) *n* a city in the E Netherlands, in Overijssel province: a major centre of the Dutch cotton industry. Pop: 152 000 (2003 est)

ensconce (ɪnˈskɒns) *vb* (*tr; often passive*) **1** to establish or settle firmly or comfortably: *ensconced in a chair* **2** to place in safety; hide [c16 see EN-¹, SCONCE²]

ensemble (ɒnˈsɒmbᵊl; *French* ɑ̃sɑ̃blə) *n* **1** all the parts of something considered together and in relation to the whole **2** a person's complete costume; outfit **3 a** the cast of a play other than the principals; supporting players **b** (*as modifier*): *an ensemble role* **4** *music* **a** a group of soloists singing or playing together **b** (*as modifier*): *an ensemble passage* **5** *music* the degree of precision and unity exhibited by a group of instrumentalists or singers performing together: *the ensemble of the strings is good* **6** the general or total effect of something made up of individual parts **7** *physics* **a** a set of systems (such as a set of collections of atoms) that are identical in all respects apart from the motions of their constituents **b** a single system (such as a collection of atoms) in which the properties are determined by the statistical behaviour of its constituents ▷ *adv* **8** all together or at once ▷ *adj* **9** (of a film or play) involving several separate but often interrelated story lines: *ensemble comedy drama* **10** involving no individual star but several actors whose roles are of equal importance: *fine ensemble playing* [c15 from French: together, from Latin *insimul*, from IN-² + *simul* at the same time]

enshrine *or* **inshrine** (ɪnˈʃraɪn) *vb* (*tr*) **1** to place or enclose in or as if in a shrine **2** to hold as sacred; cherish; treasure ▷ enˈshrinement *n*

enshroud (ɪnˈʃraʊd) *vb* (*tr*) to cover or hide with or as if with a shroud: *the sky was enshrouded in mist*

ensiform (ˈɛnsɪˌfɔːm) *adj biology* shaped like a sword blade: *ensiform leaves* [c16 from Latin *ensis* sword]

ensign (ˈɛnsaɪn) *n* **1** (*also* ˈɛnsən) a flag flown by a ship, branch of the armed forces, etc, to indicate nationality, allegiance, etc. See also **Red Ensign**, **White Ensign 2** any flag, standard, or banner **3** a standard-bearer **4** a symbol, token, or emblem; sign **5** (in the US Navy) a commissioned officer of the lowest rank **6** (in the British infantry) a colours bearer **7** (formerly in the British infantry) a commissioned officer of the lowest rank [c14 from Old French *enseigne*, from Latin INSIGNIA] ▷ ˈensignˌship *or* ˈensigncy *n*

ensilage (ˈɛnsɪlɪdʒ) *n* **1** the process of ensiling green fodder **2** a less common name for **silage**

ensile (ɛnˈsaɪl, ˈɛnsaɪl) *vb* (*tr*) **1** to store and preserve (green fodder) in an enclosed pit or silo **2** to turn (green fodder) into silage by causing it to ferment in a closed pit or silo [c19 from French *ensiler*, from Spanish *ensilar*, from EN-¹ + *silo* SILO] ▷ enˌsilaˈbility *n*

enslave (ɪnˈsleɪv) *vb* (*tr*) to make a slave of; reduce to slavery; subjugate ▷ enˈslavement *n* ▷ enˈslaver *n*

ensnare *or* **insnare** (ɪnˈsnɛə) *vb* (*tr*) **1** to catch or trap in a snare **2** to trap or gain power over someone by dishonest or underhand means ▷ enˈsnarement *n* ▷ enˈsnarer *n*

ensoul *or* **insoul** (ɪnˈsəʊl) *vb* (*tr*) **1** to endow with a soul **2** to cherish within the soul ▷ enˈsoulment *or* inˈsoulment *n*

ensphere *or* **insphere** (ɪnˈsfɪə) *vb* (*tr*) **1** to enclose in or as if in a sphere **2** to make spherical in form

enstatite (ˈɛnstəˌtaɪt) *n* a grey, green, yellow, or brown pyroxene mineral consisting of magnesium silicate in orthorhombic crystalline form. Formula: $Mg_2Si_2O_6$ [c19 from Greek *enstatēs* adversary (referring to its refractory quality) + -ITE¹]

ensue (ɪnˈsjuː) *vb* -sues, -suing, -sued **1** (*intr*) to follow; come next or afterwards **2** (*intr*) to follow or occur as a consequence; result **3** (*tr*) *obsolete* to pursue [c14 from Anglo-French *ensuer*, from Old French *ensuivre*, from EN-¹ + *suivre* to follow, from Latin *sequī*]

ensuing (ɪnˈsjuːɪŋ) *adj* **1** following subsequently or in order **2** following or occurring as a consequence; resulting

en suite *French* (ɑ̃ sɥit) *adv* as part of a set; forming a unit: *a hotel room with bathroom en suite* [c19 literally: in sequence]

ensure (ɛnˈʃʊə, -ˈʃɔː) *or esp US* **insure** *vb* (*tr*) **1** (*may take a clause as object*) to make certain or sure; guarantee: *this victory will ensure his happiness* **2** to make safe or secure; protect ▷ enˈsurer *n*

enswathe (ɪnˈsweɪð) *vb* (*tr*) to bind or wrap; swathe ▷ enˈswathement *n*

ENT *med abbreviation for* ear, nose, and throat

-ent *suffix forming adjectives and nouns* causing or performing an action or existing in a certain condition; the agent that performs an action: *astringent; dependent* [from Latin *-ent-, -ens*, present participial ending]

entablature (ɛnˈtæblətʃə) *n architect* **1** the part of a classical temple above the columns, having an architrave, a frieze, and a cornice **2** any construction of similar form [c17 from French, from Italian *intavolatura* something put on a table, hence, something laid flat, from *tavola* table, from Latin *tabula* TABLE]

entablement (ɪnˈteɪbᵊlmənt) *n* the platform of a pedestal, above the dado, that supports a statue [c17 from Old French]

entail (ɪnˈteɪl) *vb* (*tr*) **1** to bring about or impose by necessity; have as a necessary consequence: *this task entails careful thought* **2** *property law* to restrict (the descent of an estate) to a designated line of heirs **3** *logic* to have as a necessary consequence ▷ *n* **4** *property law* **a** the restriction imposed by entailing an estate **b** an estate that has been entailed [c14 *entaillen*, from EN-¹ + *taille* limitation, TAIL²] ▷ enˈtailer *n*

entailment (ɪnˈteɪlmənt) *n* **1** the act of entailing or the condition of being entailed **2** *philosophy, logic* **a** a relationship between propositions such that one must be true if the others are **b** a proposition whose truth depends on such a relationship. Usual symbol: → See **fish-hook** (sense 2)

entamoeba (ˌɛntəˈmiːbə), **endamoeba**, *US* **entameba**, **endameba** *n*, *pl* -bae (-biː) *or* -bas any parasitic amoeba of the genus *Entamoeba* (or *Endamoeba*), esp *E. histolytica*, which lives in the intestines of man and causes amoebic dysentery

entangle (ɪnˈtæŋɡᵊl) *vb* (*tr*) **1** to catch or involve in or as if in a tangle; ensnare or enmesh **2** to make tangled or twisted; snarl **3** to make complicated; confuse **4** to involve in difficulties; entrap ▷ enˈtangler *n*

entanglement (ɪnˈtæŋɡᵊlmənt) *n* **1** something that entangles or is itself entangled **2** a sexual relationship regarded as unfortunate, damaging, or compromising

entasis (ˈɛntəsɪs) *n, pl* -ses (-siːz) **1** a slightly convex curve given to the shaft of a column, pier, or similar structure, to correct the illusion of concavity produced by a straight shaft **2** Also called: **entasia** (ɛnˈteɪzɪə) *physiol* an involuntary or spasmodic muscular contraction [c18 from Greek, from *enteinein* to stretch tight, from *teinein* to stretch]

Entebbe (ɛnˈtɛbɪ) *n* a town in S Uganda, on Lake Victoria: British administrative centre of Uganda

(1893–1958); international airport. Pop: 57 518 (2002 est)

entelechy (ɛnˈtɛlɪkɪ) *n, pl* -chies *metaphysics* **1** (in the philosophy of Aristotle) actuality as opposed to potentiality **2** (in the system of Leibnitz) the soul or principle of perfection of an object or person; a monad or basic constituent **3** something that contains or realizes a final cause, esp the vital force thought to direct the life of an organism [c17 from Late Latin *entelechia*, from Greek *entelekheia*, from EN-² + *telos* goal, completion + *ekhein* to have]

entellus (ɛnˈtɛləs) *n* an Old World monkey, *Presbytes entellus*, of S Asia. This langur is regarded as sacred in India. Also called: **hanuman** [c19 New Latin, apparently from the name of the aged Sicilian character in Book V of Virgil's *Aeneid*]

entente (*French* ɑ̃tɑ̃t) *n* **1** short for **entente cordiale 2** the parties to an entente cordiale collectively [c19 French: understanding]

entente cordiale (*French* ɑ̃tɑ̃t kɔrdjal) *n* **1** a friendly understanding between political powers: less formal than an alliance **2** (*often capitals*) the understanding reached by France and Britain in April 1904, which settled outstanding colonial disputes [c19 French: cordial understanding]

enter (ˈɛntə) *vb* **1** to come or go into (a place, house, etc) **2** to penetrate or pierce **3** (*tr*) to introduce or insert **4** to join (a party, organization, etc) **5** (when *intr*, foll by *into*) to become involved or take part (in): *to enter a game; to enter into an agreement* **6** (*tr*) to record (an item such as a commercial transaction) in a journal, account, register, etc **7** (*tr*) to record (a name, etc) on a list **8** (*tr*) to present or submit: *to enter a proposal* **9** (*intr*) *theatre* to come on stage: used as a stage direction: *enter Juliet* **10** (when *intr*, often foll by *into, on*, or *upon*) to begin; start: *to enter upon a new career* **11** (*intr*; often foll by *upon*) to come into possession (of) **12** (*tr*) to place (evidence, a plea, etc) before a court of law or upon the court records **13** (*tr*) *law* **a** to go onto and occupy (land) **b** *chiefly US* to file a claim to (public lands) [c13 from Old French *entrer*, from Latin *intrāre* to go in, from *intrā* within] ▷ ˈenterable *adj* ▷ ˈenterer *n*

enterectomy (ˌɛntəˈrɛktəmɪ) *n, pl* -mies surgical excision of part of the intestine

enteric (ɛnˈtɛrɪk) *or* **enteral** (ˈɛntərəl) *adj* intestinal [c19 from Greek *enterikos*, from *enteron* intestine] ▷ ˈenterally *adv*

enteric fever *n* another name for **typhoid fever**

enter into *vb* (*intr, preposition*) **1** to be considered as a necessary part of (one's plans, calculations, etc) **2** to be in sympathy with: *he enters into his patient's problems*

enteritis (ˌɛntəˈraɪtɪs) *n* inflammation of the small intestine

entero- *or before a vowel* **enter-** *combining form* indicating an intestine: *enterovirus; enteritis* [from New Latin, from Greek *enteron* intestine]

enterobacterium (ˌɛntərəʊbækˈtɪərɪəm) *n, pl* -ria (-rɪə) any of a class of Gram-negative rodlike bacteria that occur in the gastrointestinal tract

enterobiasis (ˌɛntərəʊˈbaɪəsɪs) *n* a disease, common in children, caused by infestation of the large intestine with nematodes of the genus *Enterobius*, esp the pinworm (*E. vermicularis*)

enterocolitis (ˌɛntərəʊkɒˈlaɪtɪs) *n* inflammation of the small intestine and colon

enterogastrone (ˌɛntərəʊˈɡæstrəʊn) *n* a hormone liberated by the upper intestinal mucosa when stimulated by fat: reduces peristalsis and secretion in the stomach [c20 from ENTERO- + GASTRO- + (HORM)ONE]

enterokinase (ˌɛntərəʊˈkaɪneɪz) *n* an enzyme in intestinal juice that converts trypsinogen to trypsin

enteron (ˈɛntəˌrɒn) *n, pl* -tera (-tərə) the alimentary canal, esp of an embryo or a coelenterate [c19 via New Latin from Greek: intestine; related to Latin *inter* between]

enterostomy (ˌɛntəˈrɒstəmɪ) *n, pl* -mies surgical

formation of a permanent opening into the intestine through the abdominal wall, used as an artificial anus, for feeding, etc

enterotomy (ˌɛntəˈrɒtəmɪ) *n, pl* -mies surgical incision into the intestine

enterovirus (ˌɛntərəʊˈvaɪrəs) *n, pl* -viruses any of a group of viruses that occur in and cause diseases of the gastrointestinal tract

enterprise (ˈɛntəˌpraɪz) *n* 1 a project or undertaking, esp one that requires boldness or effort 2 participation in such projects 3 readiness to embark on new ventures; boldness and energy 4 a initiative in business b (*as modifier*): *the enterprise culture* 5 a business unit; a company or firm [C15 from Old French *entreprise* (n), from *entreprendre* from *entre-* between (from Latin: INTER-) + *prendre* to take, from Latin *prehendere* to grasp] > ˈenterˌpriser *n*

Enterprise Allowance Scheme *n* (in Britain) a scheme to provide a weekly allowance to an unemployed person who wishes to set up a business and is willing to invest a specified amount in it during its first year

Enterprise Investment Scheme *n* (in Britain) a scheme to provide tax relief on investments in certain small companies: came into operation in 1994, when it replaced the Business Expansion Scheme

enterprise zone *n* a designated zone in a depressed area, esp an inner urban area, where firms are given tax concessions and various planning restrictions are lifted, in order to attract new industry and business to the area: first introduced in Britain in 1981

enterprising (ˈɛntəˌpraɪzɪŋ) *adj* ready to embark on new ventures; full of boldness and initiative > ˈenterˌprisingly *adv*

entertain (ˌɛntəˈteɪn) *vb* 1 to provide amusement for (a person or audience) 2 to show hospitality to (guests) 3 (*tr*) to hold in the mind: *to entertain an idea* [C15 from Old French *entretenir*, from *entre-* mutually + *tenir* to hold, from Latin *tenēre*]

entertainer (ˌɛntəˈteɪnə) *n* 1 a professional singer, comedian, or other performer who takes part in public entertainments 2 any person who entertains

entertaining (ˌɛntəˈteɪnɪŋ) *adj* serving to entertain or give pleasure; diverting; amusing > ˌenterˈtainingly *adv*

entertainment (ˌɛntəˈteɪnmənt) *n* 1 the act or art of entertaining or state of being entertained 2 an act, production, etc, that entertains; diversion; amusement

enthalpy (ˈɛnθəlpɪ, ɛnˈθæl-) *n* a thermodynamic property of a system equal to the sum of its internal energy and the product of its pressure and volume. Symbol: *H* Also called: heat content, total heat [C20 from Greek *enthalpein* to warm in, from EN-² + *thalpein* to warm]

enthetic (ɛnˈθɛtɪk) *adj* (esp of infectious diseases) introduced into the body from without [C19 from Greek *enthetikos*, from *entithenai* to put in]

enthral or *US* **enthrall** (ɪnˈθrɔːl) *vb* -thrals or *US* -thralls, -thralling, -thralled (*tr*) 1 to hold spellbound; enchant; captivate 2 *obsolete* to hold as thrall; enslave [C16 from EN-¹ + THRALL] > enˈthraller *n* > enˈthralment or *US* enˈthrallment *n*

enthralling (ɪnˈθrɔːlɪŋ) *adj* holding the attention completely; fascinating; spellbinding

enthrone (ɛnˈθrəʊn) *vb* -tr 1 to place on a throne 2 to honour or exalt 3 to assign authority to > enˈthronement *n*

enthuse (ɪnˈθjuːz) *vb* to feel or show or cause to feel or show enthusiasm

enthusiasm (ɪnˈθjuːzɪˌæzəm) *n* 1 ardent and lively interest or eagerness 2 an object of keen interest; passion 3 *archaic* extravagant or unbalanced religious fervour 4 *obsolete* possession or inspiration by a god [C17 from Late Latin *enthūsiasmus*, from Greek *enthousiasmos*, from *enthousiazein* to be possessed by a god, from *entheos* inspired, from EN-² + *theos* god]

enthusiast (ɪnˈθjuːzɪˌæst) *n* 1 a person filled with or motivated by enthusiasm; fanatic 2 *archaic* a religious visionary, esp one whose zeal for religion is extravagant or unbalanced

enthusiastic (ɪnˌθjuːzɪˈæstɪk) *adj* filled with or motivated by enthusiasm; fanatical; keen > enˌthusiˈastically *adv*

enthymeme (ˈɛnθɪˌmiːm) *n logic* 1 an incomplete syllogism, in which one or more premises are unexpressed as their truth is considered to be self-evident 2 any argument some of whose premises are omitted as obvious [C16 via Latin from Greek *enthumēma*, from *enthumeisthai* to have in the mind (literally: to have in the mind), from EN-² + *thumos* mind] > ˌenthyˈmematic or ˌenthyˈmematical *adj*

entice (ɪnˈtaɪs) *vb* (*tr*) to attract or draw towards oneself by exciting hope or desire; tempt; allure [C13 from Old French *enticier*, from Vulgar Latin *intitiāre* (unattested) to incite, from Latin *titiō* firebrand] > enˈticement *n* > enˈticer *n* > enˈticing *adj* > enˈticingly *adv* > enˈticingness *n*

entire (ɪnˈtaɪə) *adj* 1 (*prenominal*) whole; complete: *the entire project is going well* 2 (*prenominal*) without reservation or exception; total: *you have my entire support* 3 not broken or damaged; intact 4 consisting of a single piece or section; undivided; continuous 5 (of leaves, petals, etc) having a smooth margin not broken up into teeth or lobes 6 not castrated: *an entire horse* 7 *obsolete* of one substance or kind; unmixed; pure ▷ *n* 8 a less common word for **entirety** 9 an uncastrated horse 10 *philately* a a complete item consisting of an envelope, postcard, or wrapper with stamps affixed b on entire (of a stamp) placed on an envelope, postcard, etc, and bearing postal directions [C14 from Old French *entier*, from Latin *integer* whole, from IN-¹ + *tangere* to touch] > enˈtireness *n*

entirely (ɪnˈtaɪəlɪ) *adv* 1 without reservation or exception; wholly; completely 2 solely or exclusively; only

entirety (ɪnˈtaɪərɪtɪ) *n, pl* -ties 1 the state of being entire or whole; completeness 2 a thing, sum, amount, etc, that is entire; whole; total

entitle (ɪnˈtaɪtˀl) *vb* (*tr*) 1 to give (a person) the right to do or have something; qualify; allow 2 to give a name or title to 3 to confer a title of rank or honour upon [C14 from Old French *entituler*, from Late Latin *intitulāre*, from Latin *titulus* TITLE] > enˈtitlement *n*

entity (ˈɛntɪtɪ) *n, pl* -ties 1 something having real or distinct existence; a thing, esp when considered as independent of other things 2 existence or being 3 the essence or real nature [C16 from Medieval Latin *entitās*, from *ēns* being; see ENS] > entitative (ˈɛntɪtətɪv) *adj*

ento- *combining form* inside; within: *entoderm* [New Latin, from Greek *entos* within]

entoblast (ˈɛntəʊˌblæst) *n* 1 *embryol* a less common name for **endoderm** 2 a less common name for **hypoblast**. > entoblastic (ˌɛntəʊˈblæstɪk) *adj*

entoderm (ˈɛntəʊˌdɜːm) *n embryol* another name for **endoderm**. > ˌentoˈdermal or ˌentoˈdermic *adj*

entoil (ɪnˈtɔɪl) *vb* (*tr*) an archaic word for **ensnare** > enˈtoilment *n*

entomb (ɪnˈtuːm) *vb* (*tr*) 1 to place in or as if in a tomb; bury; inter 2 to serve as a tomb for > enˈtombment *n*

entomic (ɛnˈtɒmɪk) *adj* denoting or relating to insects [C19 from Greek *entomon* (see ENTOMO-) + -IC]

entomo- *combining form* indicating an insect: *entomology* [from Greek *entomon* insect (literally: creature cut into sections), from *en-* in + *-tomon*, from *temnein* to cut]

entomol. or **entom.** *abbreviation for* entomology

entomologize or **entomologise** (ˌɛntəˈmɒləˌdʒaɪz) *vb* (*intr*) to collect or study insects

entomology (ˌɛntəˈmɒlədʒɪ) *n* the branch of science concerned with the study of insects

> entomological (ˌɛntəməˈlɒdʒɪkˀl) or ˌentomoˈlogic *adj* > ˌentomoˈlogically *adv* > ˌentoˈmologist *n*

entomophagous (ˌɛntəˈmɒfəgəs) *adj* feeding mainly on insects; insectivorous

entomophilous (ˌɛntəˈmɒfɪləs) *adj* (of flowering plants) pollinated by insects. Compare **anemophilous**. > ˌentoˈmophily *n*

entomostracan (ˌɛntəˈmɒstrəkən) *n* 1 any small crustacean of the group (formerly subclass) *Entomostraca*, including the branchiopods, ostracods, and copepods ▷ *adj* 2 of, relating to, or belonging to the *Entomostraca* [C19 from New Latin ENTOMO- + Greek *ostrakon* shell; see OSTRACIZE] > ˌentoˈmostracous *adj*

entophyte (ˈɛntəʊˌfaɪt) *n botany* a variant of **endophyte**. > entophytic (ˌɛntəʊˈfɪtɪk) *adj*

entopic (ɛnˈtɒpɪk) *adj anatomy* situated in its normal place or position. See also **ectopia** [from Greek *entopos* in a place, from *topos* place]

entoptic (ɛnˈtɒptɪk) *adj* (of visual sensation) resulting from structures within the eye itself [ENTO- + OPTIC]

entourage (ˈɒntʊˌrɑːʒ; *French* āturaʒ) *n* 1 a group of attendants or retainers, esp such as surround an important person; retinue 2 surroundings or environment [C19 from French, from *entourer* to surround, from *entour* around, from *tour* circuit; see TOUR, TURN]

entozoic (ˌɛntəʊˈzəʊɪk) *adj* 1 of or relating to an entozoon 2 living inside an animal: *entozoic fungi*

entozoon (ˌɛntəʊˈzəʊɒn) or **entozoan** *n, pl* -zoa (-ˈzəʊə) any animal, such as a tapeworm, that lives within another animal, usually as a parasite

entr'acte (ɒnˈtrækt; *French* ātrakt) *n* 1 an interval between two acts of a play or opera 2 (esp formerly) an entertainment during an interval, such as dancing between acts of an opera [C19 French, literally: between-act]

entrails (ˈɛntreɪlz) *pl n* 1 the internal organs of a person or animal; intestines; guts 2 the innermost parts of anything [C13 from Old French *entrailles*, from Medieval Latin *intrālia*, changed from Latin *interānea* intestines, ultimately from *inter* between]

entrain¹ (ɪnˈtreɪn) *vb* to board or put aboard a train > enˈtrainment *n*

entrain² (ɪnˈtreɪn) *vb* (*tr*) 1 (of a liquid or gas) to carry along (drops of liquid, bubbles, etc), as in certain distillations 2 to disperse (air bubbles) through concrete in order to increase its resistance to frost 3 *zoology* to adjust (an internal rhythm of an organism) so that it synchronizes with an external cycle, such as that of light and dark > enˈtrainment *n*

entrammel (ɪnˈtræməl) *vb* -mels, -melling, -melled or *US* -els, -eling, -eled (*tr*) to hamper or obstruct by entangling

entrance¹ (ˈɛntrəns) *n* 1 the act or an instance of entering; entry 2 a place for entering, such as a door or gate 3 a the power, liberty, or right of entering; admission b (*as modifier*): *an entrance fee* 4 the coming of an actor or other performer onto a stage [C16 from French, from *entrer* to ENTER]

entrance² (ɪnˈtrɑːns) *vb* (*tr*) 1 to fill with wonder and delight; enchant 2 to put into a trance; hypnotize > enˈtrancement *n* > enˈtrancing *adj*

entrant (ˈɛntrənt) *n* 1 a person who enters 2 a new member of a group, society, or association 3 a person who enters a competition or contest; competitor [C17 from French, literally: entering, from *entrer* to ENTER]

entrap (ɪnˈtræp) *vb* -traps, -trapping, -trapped (*tr*) 1 to catch or snare in or as if in a trap 2 to lure or trick into danger, difficulty, or embarrassment > enˈtrapper *n*

entrapment (ɪnˈtræpmənt) *n* the luring, by a police officer, of a person into committing a crime so that he may be prosecuted for it

entreat or **intreat** (ɪnˈtriːt) *vb* 1 to ask (a person) earnestly; beg or plead with; implore 2 to make an earnest request or petition for (something) 3 an archaic word for **treat** (sense 4) [C15 from Old

French *entraiter,* from EN-[1] + *traiter* to TREAT]
> en'treatingly *or* in'treatingly *adv* > en'treatment *or* in'treatment *n*

entreaty (ɪnˈtriːtɪ) *n, pl* -treaties an earnest request or petition; supplication; plea

entrechat (*French* ɑ̃trəʃa) *n* a leap in ballet during which the dancer repeatedly crosses his feet or beats them together [C18 from French, from earlier *entrechase,* changed by folk etymology from Italian (*capriola*) *intrecciata,* literally: entwined (caper), from *intrecciare* to interlace, from IN-[2] + *treccia* TRESS]

entrecôte (*French* ɑ̃trəkot) *n* a beefsteak cut from between the ribs [C19 French *entrecôte,* from *entre-* INTER- + *côte* rib, from Latin *costa*]

Entre-Deux-Mers (*French* ɑ̃trədømɛr) *n* any wine produced in the area of the Gironde between the rivers Dordogne and Garonne in S France

entrée (ˈɒntreɪ) *n* 1 a dish served before a main course 2 *chiefly US* the main course of a meal 3 the power or right of entry [C18 from French, from *entrer* to ENTER; in cookery, so called because formerly the course was served after an intermediate course called the *relevé* (remove)]

entremets (*French* ɑ̃trəmɛ) *n, pl* -mets (*French* -mɛ) 1 a dessert 2 a light dish, formerly served at formal dinners between the main course and the dessert [C18 from French, from Old French *entremes,* from *entre-* between, INTER- + *mes* dish, MESS]

entrench *or* **intrench** (ɪnˈtrɛntʃ) *vb* 1 (*tr*) to construct (a defensive position) by digging trenches around it 2 (*tr*) to fix or establish firmly, esp so as to prevent removal or change 3 (*intr; foll by on or upon*) to trespass or encroach; infringe > en'trenched *or* in'trenched *adj* > en'trencher *or* in'trencher *n*

entrenchment *or* **intrenchment** (ɪnˈtrɛntʃmənt) *n* 1 the act of entrenching or state of being entrenched 2 a position protected by trenches 3 one of a series of deep trenches constructed as a shelter from gunfire

entre nous (*French* ɑ̃trə nu) *adv* between ourselves; in confidence [C17 from French]

entrepôt (*French* ɑ̃trəpo) *n* 1 a warehouse for commercial goods 2 a a trading centre or port at a geographically convenient location, at which goods are imported and re-exported without incurring liability for duty b (*as modifier*): *an entrepôt trade* [C18 French, from *entreposer* to put in, from *entre-* between, INTER- + *poser* to place (see POSE[1]); formed on the model of DEPOT]

entrepreneur (ˌɒntrəprəˈnɜː; *French* ɑ̃trəprənœr) *n* 1 the owner or manager of a business enterprise who, by risk and initiative, attempts to make profits 2 a middleman or commercial intermediary [C19 from French, from *entreprendre* to undertake; see ENTERPRISE] > ˌentrepreˈneurial *adj* > ˌentrepreˈneurship *n*

entresol (ˈɒntrəˌsɒl; *French* ɑ̃trəsɔl) *n* another name for **mezzanine** (sense 1) [C18 from French, literally: between floors, from *entre-* INTER- + *sol* floor, ground, from Latin *solum*]

entropy (ˈɛntrəpɪ) *n, pl* -pies 1 a thermodynamic quantity that changes in a reversible process by an amount equal to the heat absorbed or emitted divided by the thermodynamic temperature. It is measured in joules per kelvin. Symbol: *S* See also **law of thermodynamics** (sense 1) 2 a statistical measure of the disorder of a closed system expressed by $S = k \log P + c$ where P is the probability that a particular state of the system exists, k is the Boltzmann constant, and c is another constant 3 lack of pattern or organization; disorder 4 a measure of the efficiency of a system, such as a code or language, in transmitting information [C19 from EN-[2] + -TROPE]

entrust *or* **intrust** (ɪnˈtrʌst) *vb* (*tr*) 1 (usually foll by *with*) to invest or charge (with a duty, responsibility, etc) 2 (often foll by *to*) to put into the care or protection of someone > enˈtrustment *n*

or inˈtrustment *n*

▌ **USAGE** It is usually considered incorrect to talk about *entrusting* someone *to* do something: *the army cannot be trusted* (not *entrusted*) *to carry out orders*

entry (ˈɛntrɪ) *n, pl* -tries 1 the act or an instance of entering; entrance 2 a point or place for entering, such as a door, gate, etc 3 a the right or liberty of entering; admission; access b (*as modifier*): *an entry permit* 4 the act of recording an item, such as a commercial transaction, in a journal, account, register, etc 5 an item recorded, as in a diary, dictionary, or account 6 a a person, horse, car, etc, entering a competition or contest; competitor b (*as modifier*): *an entry fee* 7 the competitors entering a contest considered collectively: *a good entry this year for the speed trials* 8 the people admitted at one time to a school, college, or course of study, etc, considered collectively; intake 9 the action of an actor in going on stage or his manner of doing this 10 *criminal law* the act of unlawfully going onto the premises of another with the intention of committing a crime 11 *property law* the act of going upon another person's land with the intention of asserting the right to possession 12 any point in a piece of music, esp a fugue, at which a performer commences or resumes playing or singing 13 *cards* a card that enables one to transfer the lead from one's own hand to that of one's partner or to the dummy hand 14 *English dialect* a passage between the backs of two rows of terraced houses [C13 from Old French *entree,* past participle of *entrer* to ENTER]

entryism (ˈɛntriːɪzəm) *n* the policy or practice of members of a particular political group joining an existing political party with the intention of changing its principles and policies, instead of forming a new party > ˈentryist *n, adj*

entry-level *adj* 1 (of a job or worker) at the most elementary level in a career structure 2 (of a product) characterized by being at the most appropriate level for use by a beginner: *an entry-level camera*

entwine *or* **intwine** (ɪnˈtwaɪn) *vb* (of two or more things) to twine together or (of one or more things) to twine around (something else) > enˈtwinement *or* inˈtwinement *n*

enucleate *vb* (ɪˈnjuːklɪˌeɪt) (*tr*) 1 *biology* to remove the nucleus from (a cell) 2 *surgery* to remove (a tumour or other structure) from its capsule without rupturing it 3 *archaic* to explain or disclose ▷ *adj* (ɪˈnjuːklɪɪt, -ˌeɪt) 4 (of cells) deprived of their nuclei [C16 from Latin *ēnucleāre* to remove the kernel, from *nucleus* kernel] > eˌnucleˈation *n*

Enugu (ɛˈnuːguː) *n* a city in S Nigeria, capital of Enugu state: capital of the former Eastern region and of the breakaway state of Biafra during the Civil War (1967–70): coal-mining. Pop: 549 000 (2005 est)

E number *n* any of a series of numbers with the prefix E indicating a specific food additive recognized by the European Union and used on labels of processed food

enumerate (ɪˈnjuːməˌreɪt) *vb* 1 (*tr*) to mention separately or in order; name one by one; list 2 (*tr*) to determine the number of; count 3 *Canadian* to compile or enter (a name or names) in a voting list for an area [C17 from Latin *ēnumerāre,* from *numerāre* to count, reckon; see NUMBER] > eˈnumerable *adj* > eˌnumerˈation *n* > eˈnumerative *adj*

enumerator (ɪˈnjuːməˌreɪtə) *n* 1 a person or thing that enumerates 2 *Canadian* a person who compiles the voting list for an area 3 *Brit* a person who issues and retrieves forms during a census of population

enunciable (ɪˈnʌnsɪəbᵊl) *adj* capable of being enunciated

enunciate (ɪˈnʌnsɪˌeɪt) *vb* 1 to articulate or

pronounce (words), esp clearly and distinctly 2 (*tr*) to state precisely or formally [C17 from Latin *ēnuntiāre* to declare, from *nuntiāre* to announce, from *nuntius* messenger] > eˌnunciˈation *n* > eˈnunciative *or* eˈnunciatory *adj* > eˈnunciatively *adv* > eˈnunciˌator *n*

enure (ɪˈnjʊə) *vb* a variant spelling of **inure** > enˈurement *n*

enuresis (ˌɛnjʊˈriːsɪs) *n* involuntary discharge of urine, esp during sleep [C19 from New Latin, from Greek EN-[2] + *ourein* to urinate, from *ouron* urine] > enuretic (ˌɛnjʊˈrɛtɪk) *adj, n*

envelop (ɪnˈvɛləp) *vb* -lops, -loping, -loped (*tr*) 1 to wrap or enclose in or as if in a covering 2 to conceal or obscure, as from sight or understanding: *a plan enveloped in mystery* 3 to surround or partially surround (an enemy force) [C14 from Old French *envoluper,* from EN-[1] + *voluper, voloper,* of obscure origin] > enˈvelopment *n*

envelope (ˈɛnvəˌləʊp, ˈɒn-) *n* 1 a flat covering of paper, usually rectangular in shape and with a flap that can be folded over and sealed, used to enclose a letter, etc 2 any covering or wrapper 3 *biology* any enclosing structure, such as a membrane, shell, or skin 4 the bag enclosing the gas in a balloon 5 *maths* a curve or surface that is tangent to each one of a group of curves or surfaces 6 *electronics* the sealed glass or metal housing of a valve, electric light, etc 7 *telecomm* the outer shape of a modulated wave, formed by the peaks of successive cycles of the carrier wave 8 push the envelope *informal* to push the boundaries of what is possible [C18 from French *enveloppe,* from *envelopper* to wrap around; see ENVELOP; sense 8 from aeronautics jargon, referring to graphs of aircraft performance]

envenom (ɪnˈvɛnəm) *vb* (*tr*) 1 to fill or impregnate with venom; make poisonous 2 to fill with bitterness or malice

enviable (ˈɛnviəbᵊl) *adj* exciting envy; fortunate or privileged > ˈenviableness *n* > ˈenviably *adv*

envious (ˈɛnviəs) *adj* feeling, showing, or resulting from envy [C13 from Anglo-Norman, ultimately from Latin *invidiōsus* full of envy, INVIDIOUS; see ENVY] > ˈenviously *adv* > ˈenviousness *n*

enviro (ɪnˈvaɪrəʊ) *n, pl* enviros *informal* an environmentalist

environ (ɪnˈvaɪrən) *vb* (*tr*) to encircle or surround [C14 from Old French *environner* to surround, from *environ* around, from EN-[1] + *viron* a circle, from *virer* to turn, VEER[1]]

environment (ɪnˈvaɪrənmənt) *n* 1 external conditions or surroundings, esp those in which people live or work 2 *ecology* the external surroundings in which a plant or animal lives, which tend to influence its development and behaviour 3 the state of being environed; encirclement 4 *computing* an operating system, program, or integrated suite of programs that provides all the facilities necessary for a particular application: *a word-processing environment* > enˌvironˈmental *adj* > enˌvironˈmentally *adv*

environmental audit *n* the systematic examination of an organization's interaction with the environment, to assess the success of its conservation or antipollution programme

Environmental Health Officer *n* (in Britain) an employee of the Environmental Health Service. Former names: public health inspector, sanitary inspector

Environmental Health Service *n* (in Britain) a service provided by a local authority, which deals with prevention of the spread of communicable diseases, food safety and hygiene, control of infestation by insects or rodents, etc

environmentalism (ɪnˌvaɪrənˈmɛntəˌlɪzəm) *n* *psychol* the belief that a person's behaviour is affected chiefly by his environment. Compare **hereditarianism**

environmentalist (ɪnˌvaɪrənˈmɛntəlɪst) *n* 1 an adherent of environmentalism 2 a person who is concerned with the maintenance of ecological balance and the conservation of the environment **3** a person concerned with issues that affect the environment, such as pollution

environs (ɪnˈvaɪrənz) *pl n* a surrounding area or region, esp the suburbs or outskirts of a town or city; vicinity

envisage (ɪnˈvɪzɪdʒ) *vb* (*tr*) **1** to form a mental image of; visualize; contemplate **2** to conceive of as a possibility in the future; foresee **3** *archaic* to look in the face of; confront [C19 from French *envisager*, from EN-¹ + *visage* face, VISAGE] > en'visagement *n*

> **USAGE** It was formerly considered incorrect to use a clause after *envisage* as in *it is envisaged that the new centre will cost £40 million*, but this use is now acceptable

envision (ɪnˈvɪʒən) *vb* (*tr*) to conceive of as a possibility in the future; foresee

envoy¹ (ˈɛnvɔɪ) *n* **1** Formal name: envoy extraordinary and minister plenipotentiary a diplomat of the second class, ranking between an ambassador and a minister resident **2** an accredited messenger, agent, or representative [C17 from French *envoyé*, literally: sent, from *envoyer* to send, from Vulgar Latin *inviāre* (unattested) to send on a journey, from IN-² + *via* road] > 'envoyship *n*

envoy² *or* **envoi** (ˈɛnvɔɪ) *n* **1** a brief dedicatory or explanatory stanza concluding certain forms of poetry, notably ballades **2** a postscript in other forms of verse or prose [C14 from Old French *envoye*, from *envoyer* to send; see ENVOY¹]

envy (ˈɛnvɪ) *n, pl* -vies **1** a feeling of grudging or somewhat admiring discontent aroused by the possessions, achievements, or qualities of another **2** the desire to have for oneself something possessed by another; covetousness **3** an object of envy ▷ *vb* -vies, -vying, -vied **4** to be envious of (a person or thing) [C13 via Old French from Latin *invidia*, from *invidēre* to eye maliciously, from IN-² + *vidēre* to see] > 'envier *n* > 'envyingly *adv*

enwind (ɪnˈwaɪnd) *vb* -winds, -winding, -wound (*tr*) to wind or coil around; encircle

enwomb (ɪnˈwuːm) *vb* (*tr; often passive*) to enclose in or as if in a womb

enwrap *or* **inwrap** (ɪnˈræp) *vb* -wraps, -wrapping, -wrapped (*tr*) **1** to wrap or cover up; envelop **2** (*usually passive*) to engross or absorb: *enwrapped in thought*

enwreath (ɪnˈriːð) *vb* (*tr*) to surround or encircle with or as with a wreath or wreaths

Enzed (ˈɛnˈzɛd) *n Austral and NZ informal* **1** New Zealand **2** Also called: Enzedder a New Zealander

enzootic (ˌɛnzəʊˈɒtɪk) *adj* **1** (of diseases) affecting animals within a limited region ▷ *n* **2** an enzootic disease ▷ Compare **epizootic** [C19 from EN-² + Greek *zōion* animal + -OTIC] > enzo'otically *adv*

enzyme (ˈɛnzaɪm) *n* any of a group of complex proteins or conjugated proteins that are produced by living cells and act as catalysts in specific biochemical reactions [C19 from Medieval Greek *enzumos* leavened, from Greek EN-² + *zumē* leaven] > enzymatic (ˌɛnzaɪˈmætɪk, -zɪ-) *or* enzymic (ɛnˈzaɪmɪk, -ˈzɪm-) *adj*

enzyme-linked immunosorbent assay (ˌɪmjʊnəʊˈsɔːbənt) *n* the full name for **ELISA**

enzymology (ˌɛnzaɪˈmɒlədʒɪ) *n* the branch of science concerned with the study of enzymes > enzymological (ˌɛnzaɪməˈlɒdʒɪkᵊl) *adj* > ˌenzy'mologist *n*

enzymolysis (ˌɛnzaɪˈmɒlɪsɪs) *n* a biochemical decomposition, such as a fermentation, that is catalysed by an enzyme > enzymolytic (ˌɛnzaɪməˈlɪtɪk) *adj*

e.o. *abbreviation for* ex officio

eo- *combining form* early or primeval: *Eocene; eohippus* [from Greek, from *ēōs* dawn]

eobiont (ˌiːəʊˈbaɪənt) *n* a hypothetical chemical precursor of a living cell [C20 from EO- + Greek

biōnt stem of present participle of *biōn* to live, from *bios* life]

EOC *abbreviation for* **Equal Opportunities Commission**

Eocene (ˈiːəʊˌsiːn) *adj* **1** of, denoting, or formed in the second epoch of the Tertiary period, which lasted for 20 000 000 years, during which hooved mammals appeared ▷ *n* **2** the the Eocene epoch or rock series [C19 from EO- + -CENE]

Eogene (ˈiːəʊˌdʒiːn) *adj, n* another word for **Palaeogene**

eohippus (ˌiːəʊˈhɪpəs) *n, pl* -puses the earliest horse: an extinct Eocene dog-sized animal of the genus with four-toed forelegs, three-toed hindlegs, and teeth specialized for browsing [C19 New Latin, from EO- + Greek *hippos* horse]

Eolian (iːˈəʊlɪən) *adj, n* a variant spelling of **Aeolian**

Eolic (iːˈɒlɪk, ɪˈəʊlɪk) *adj, n* a variant spelling of **Aeolic**

eolipile (iːˈɒlɪˌpaɪl) *n* a variant spelling of **aeolipile**

eolith (ˈiːəʊlɪθ) *n* a stone, usually crudely broken, used as a primitive tool in Eolithic times

Eolithic (ˌiːəʊˈlɪθɪk) *adj* denoting, relating to, or characteristic of the early part of the Stone Age, characterized by the use of crude stone tools

e.o.m. *commerce abbreviation for* end of the month

eon (ˈiːən, ˈiːɒn) *n* **1** the usual US spelling of **aeon 2** *geology* the longest division of geological time, comprising two or more eras

eonian (iːˈəʊnɪən) *adj* **1** the usual US spelling of **aeonian 2** *geology* of or relating to an eon

eonism (ˈiːəˌnɪzəm) *n psychiatry* the adoption of female dress and behaviour by a male. See also **transvestite** [C19 named after Charles Éon de Beaumont (died 1810), French transvestite]

Eos (ˈiːɒs) *n Greek myth* the winged goddess of the dawn, the daughter of Hyperion. Roman counterpart: Aurora

eosin (ˈiːəʊsɪn) *or* **eosine** (ˈiːəʊsɪn, -ˌsiːn) *n* **1** Also called: bromeosin a red crystalline water-insoluble derivative of fluorescein. Its soluble salts are used as dyes. Formula: $C_{20}H_8Br_4O_5$ **2** any of several similar dyes [C19 from Greek *ēōs* dawn + -IN; referring to the colour it gives to silk] > ˌeo'sinic *adj* > 'eosin-ˌlike *adj*

eosinophil (ˌiːəʊˈsɪnəfɪl) *or* **eosinophile** (ˌiːəʊˈsɪnəˌfaɪl) *n* a leucocyte with a multilobed nucleus and coarse granular cytoplasm that stains readily with acidic dyes such as eosin > ˌeoˌsino'philic *or* eosinophilous (ˌiːəʊsɪˈnɒfɪləs) *adj*

eosinophilia (ˌiːəʊˌsɪnəˈfɪlɪə) *n* the presence of abnormally large numbers of eosinophils in the blood, occurring in various diseases and in response to certain drugs

-eous *suffix of adjectives* relating to or having the nature of: *gaseous*. Compare **-ious** [from Latin *-eus*]

Eozoic (ˌiːəʊˈzəʊɪk) *adj archaic* of or formed in the part of the Precambrian era during which life first appeared

ep (ɛp) *abbreviation for* episode

EP *n* **1** an extended-play single, one of the formats in which music is sold, usually comprising four or five tracks ▷ *abbreviation for* **2** Eastern (Cape) Province

Ep. *abbreviation for* Epistle

ep- *prefix* variant of **epi-** before a vowel: *epexegesis*

EPA *abbreviation for* eicosapentaenoic acid: a fatty acid, found in certain fish oils, that can reduce blood cholesterol

epact (ˈiːpækt) *n* **1** the difference in time, about 11 days, between the solar year and the lunar year **2** the number of days between the beginning of the calendar year and the new moon immediately preceding this **3** the difference in time between the calendar month and the synodic month [C16 via Late Latin from Greek *epaktē*, from *epagein* to bring in, intercalate, from *agein* to lead]

epanalepsis (ˌɛpænəˈlɛpsɪs) *n rhetoric* the repetition, after a more or less lengthy passage of subordinate or parenthetic text, of a word or clause that was used before [C16 from Greek, from

EPI- + ANA- + *lēpis* taking, from *lambanein* to take up] > ˌepana'leptic *adj*

epanaphora (ˌɛpəˈnæfərə) *n rhetoric* another word for **anaphora**. > ˌepan'aphoral *adj*

epanorthosis (ˌɛpænɔːˈθəʊsɪs) *n rhetoric* the almost immediate replacement of a preceding word or phrase by a more correct or more emphatic one, as for example in *thousands, nay, millions* [C16 from Greek: correction, from EPI- + ANA- + *orthos* straight] > ˌepanor'thotic *adj*

eparch (ˈɛpɑːk) *n* **1** a bishop or metropolitan in charge of an eparchy (sense 1) **2** a government official in charge of an eparchy (senses 2 or 3) [C17 from Greek *eparkhos*, from *epi-* over, on + -ARCH]

eparchy (ˈɛpɑːkɪ) *or* **eparchate** (ˈɛpɑːkɪt) *n, pl* -chies *or* -chates **1** a diocese of the Eastern Christian Church **2** (in ancient Greece) a province **3** (in modern Greece) a subdivision of a province > ep'archial *adj*

e-passport *n* a passport with an embedded microchip carrying information about the holder [C20 from E-² + PASSPORT]

épatant *French* (epatɑ̃) *adj* startling or shocking, esp through being unconventional [C20 from present participle of *épater* to flabbergast]

epaulette *or US* **epaulet** (ˈɛpəˌlɛt, -lɪt) *n* a piece of ornamental material on the shoulder of a garment, esp a military uniform [C18 from French *épaulette*, from *épaule* shoulder, from Latin *spatula* shoulder blade; see SPATULA]

e-payment *n* a digital payment for a transaction made on the internet

épée (ˈɛpeɪ; *French* epe) *n* a sword similar to the foil but with a larger guard and a heavier blade of triangular cross section [C19 from French: sword, from Latin *spatha*, from Greek *spathē* blade; see SPADE¹]

épéeist (ˈɛpeɪɪst) *n fencing* a person who uses or specializes in using an épée

epeiric (ɪˈpaɪrɪk) *adj geology* in, of, or relating to a continent: *an epeiric sea* [C20 from Greek *ēpeiros* continent + -IC]

epeirogeny (ˌɛpaɪˈrɒdʒɪnɪ) *or* **epeirogenesis** (ˌɪˌpaɪrəʊˈdʒɛnɪsɪs) *n* the formation and submergence of continents by broad relatively slow displacements of the earth's crust. Also called: epirogeny [C19 from Greek *ēpeiros* continent + -GENY] > epeirogenic (ˌɪˌpaɪrəʊˈdʒɛnɪk) *or* epeirogenetic (ˌɪˌpaɪrəʊdʒɪˈnɛtɪk) *adj*

epencephalon (ˌɛpɛnˈsɛfəˌlɒn) *n, pl* -la (-lə) *anatomy* **1** the cerebellum and pons Varolii **2** the part of the embryonic brain that develops into this; metencephalon [C19 New Latin; see EPI-, ENCEPHALON] > ˌepence'phalic (ˌɛpɛnsɛˈfælɪk) *adj*

ependyma (ɪˈpɛndɪmə) *n* the membrane lining the ventricles of the brain and the central canal of the spinal cord > e'pendymal *adj*

epenthesis (ɛˈpɛnθɪsɪs) *n, pl* -ses (-ˌsiːz) the insertion of a sound or letter into a word [C17 via Late Latin from Greek, from *epentithenai* to insert, from EPI- + EN-² + *tithenai* to place] > epenthetic (ˌɛpɛnˈθɛtɪk) *adj*

epergne (ɪˈpɜːn) *n* an ornamental centrepiece for a table: a stand with holders for sweetmeats, fruit, flowers, etc [C18 probably from French *épargne* a saving, from *épargner* to economize, of Germanic origin; compare SPARE]

epexegesis (ɛˌpɛksɪˈdʒiːsɪs) *n, pl* -ses (-ˌsiːz) *rhetoric* **1** the addition of a phrase, clause, or sentence to a text to provide further explanation **2** the phrase, clause, or sentence added for this purpose [C17 from Greek; see EPI-, EXEGESIS] > epexegetic (ɛˌpɛksɪˈdʒɛtɪk) *or* epˌexe'getical *adj* > epˌexe'getically *adv*

EPG *abbreviation for* electronic programme guide

Eph. *or* **Ephes.** *Bible abbreviation for* Ephesians

eph- *prefix* a variant of **epi-** before an aspirate: *ephedra; ephedrine*

ephah *or* **epha** (ˈiːfə) *n* a Hebrew unit of dry measure equal to approximately one bushel or about 33 litres [C16 from Hebrew *'ephāh*, of Egyptian origin]

ephebe (ɪˈfiːb, ˈɛfiːb) *n* (in ancient Greece) a youth about to enter full citizenship, esp one undergoing military training [C19 from Latin *ephēbus*, from Greek *ephēbos*, from *hēbē* young manhood] > eˈphebic *adj*

ephedra (ɪˈfɛdrə) *n* any gymnosperm shrub of the genus *Ephedra*, of warm regions of America and Eurasia: the source of ephedrine: family *Ephedraceae*, phylum *Gnetophyta* [C18 New Latin, from Latin, from Greek *ephedros* a sitting upon, from EPI- + *hedra* seat]

ephedrine or **ephedrin** (ɪˈfɛdrɪn, ˈɛfɪˌdriːn, -drɪn) *n* a white crystalline alkaloid obtained from plants of the genus *Ephedra*: used for the treatment of asthma and hay fever; l-phenyl-2-methylaminopropanol. Formula: $C_6H_5CH(OH)CH(NHCH_3)CH_3$ [C19 from New Latin EPHEDRA + -INE²]

ephemera (ɪˈfɛmərə) *n, pl* -eras *or* -erae (-əˌriː) 1 a mayfly, esp one of the genus *Ephemera* 2 something transitory or short-lived 3 (*functioning as plural*) a class of collectable items not originally intended to last for more than a short time, such as tickets, posters, postcards, or labels 4 a plural of **ephemeron** [C16; see EPHEMERAL]

ephemeral (ɪˈfɛmərəl) *adj* 1 lasting for only a short time; transitory; short-lived: *ephemeral pleasure* ▷ *n* 2 a short-lived organism, such as the mayfly 3 a plant that completes its life cycle in less than one year, usually less than six months [C16 from Greek *ephēmeros* lasting only a day, from *hēmera* day] > eˈphemerally *adv* > eˌphemerˈality *or* eˈphemeralness *n*

ephemerid (ɪˈfɛmərɪd) *n* any insect of the order *Ephemeroptera* (or *Ephemerida*), which comprises the mayflies. Also called: **ephemeropteran** [C19 from New Latin *Ephēmerida*, from Greek *ephēmeros* short-lived + -ID²]

ephemeris (ɪˈfɛmərɪs) *n, pl* ephemerides (ˌɛfɪˈmɛrɪˌdiːz) 1 a table giving the future positions of a planet, comet, or satellite 2 an annual publication giving the positions of the sun, moon, and planets during the course of a year, information concerning eclipses, astronomical constants, etc 3 *obsolete* a diary or almanac [C16 from Latin, from Greek: diary, journal; see EPHEMERAL]

ephemeris time *n* time that is based on the orbit of the earth around the sun rather than the axial rotation of the earth, one **ephemeris second** being 1/31 556 925.9747 of the tropical year 1900. It was used from 1960 to 1983 as an astronomical timescale but has been replaced by terrestrial dynamical time and barycentric dynamic time

ephemeron (ɪˈfɛməˌrɒn) *n, pl* -era (-ərə) *or* -erons (*usually plural*) something transitory or short-lived [C16 see EPHEMERAL]

ephemeropteran (iːˌfɛməˈrɒptərən) *n* 1 another word for **ephemerid** ▷ *adj* 2 of or relating to the *Ephemeroptera*

Ephesian (ɪˈfiːʒən) *adj* 1 of or relating to Ephesus ▷ *n* 2 an inhabitant or native of Ephesus

Ephesians (ɪˈfiːʒnz) *n* (*functioning as singular*) a book of the New Testament (in full **The Epistle of Paul the Apostle to the Ephesians**), containing an exposition of the divine plan for the world and the consummation of this in Christ

Ephesus (ˈɛfɪsəs) *n* (in ancient Greece) a major trading city on the W coast of Asia Minor: famous for its temple of Artemis (Diana); sacked by the Goths (262 AD)

ephod (ˈiːfɒd) *n Old Testament* an embroidered vestment believed to resemble an apron with shoulder straps, worn by priests in ancient Israel [C14 from Hebrew *ōphōdh*]

ephor (ˈɛfɔː) *n, pl* -ors *or* -ori (-əˌraɪ) (in ancient Greece) one of a board of senior magistrates in any of several Dorian states, esp the five Spartan ephors, who were elected by vote of all full citizens and who wielded effective power [C16 from Greek *ephoros*, from *ephoran* to supervise, from EPI- + *horan* to look] > ˈephoral *adj* > ˈephorate *n*

Ephraim (ˈiːfreɪɪm) *n Old Testament* 1 a the younger son of Joseph, who received the principal blessing of his grandfather Jacob (Genesis 48:8–22) b the tribe descended from him c the territory of this tribe, west of the River Jordan 2 the northern kingdom of Israel after the kingdom of Solomon had been divided into two

Ephraimite (ˈiːfreɪɪˌmaɪt) *n* a member of the tribe of Ephraim

epi-, eph- *or before a vowel* **ep-** *prefix* 1 on; upon; above; over: *epidermis; epicentre* 2 in addition to: *epiphenomenon* 3 after: *epigenesis; epilogue* 4 near; close to: *epicalyx* [from Greek, from *epi* (prep)]

epibiosis (ˌɛpɪbaɪˈəʊsɪs) *n* any relationship between two organisms in which one grows on the other but is not parasitic on it. See also **epiphyte, epizoite.** > epibiotic (ˌɛpɪbaɪˈɒtɪk) *adj*

epiblast (ˈɛpɪˌblæst) *n embryol* the outermost layer of an embryo, which becomes the ectoderm at gastrulation. Also called: **ectoblast** > ˌepiˈblastic *adj*

epiblem (ˈɛpɪblɛm) *n botany* the outermost cell layer of a root; epidermis

epiboly (ɪˈpɪbəlɪ) *n, pl* -lies *embryol* a process that occurs during gastrulation in vertebrates, in which cells on one side of the blastula grow over and surround the remaining cells and yolk and eventually form the ectoderm [C19 from Greek *epibolē* a laying on, from *epiballein* to throw on, from EPI- + *ballein* to throw] > epibolic (ˌɛpɪˈbɒlɪk) *adj*

epic (ˈɛpɪk) *n* 1 a long narrative poem recounting in elevated style the deeds of a legendary hero, esp one originating in oral folk tradition 2 the genre of epic poetry 3 any work of literature, film, etc, having heroic deeds for its subject matter or having other qualities associated with the epic: *a Hollywood epic* 4 an episode in the lives of men in which heroic deeds are performed or attempted: *the epic of Scott's expedition to the South Pole* ▷ *adj* 5 denoting, relating to, or characteristic of an epic or epics 6 of heroic or impressive proportions: *an epic voyage* [C16 from Latin *epicus*, from Greek *epikos*, from *epos* speech, word, song]

epicalyx (ˌɛpɪˈkeɪlɪks, -ˈkæl-) *n, pl* -lyxes *or* -lyces (-lɪˌsiːz) *botany* a series of small sepal-like bracts forming an outer calyx beneath the true calyx in some flowers

epicanthus (ˌɛpɪˈkænθəs) *n, pl* -thi (-θaɪ) a fold of skin extending vertically over the inner angle of the eye: characteristic of Mongolian peoples and a congenital anomaly among other races. Also called: **epicanthic fold** [C19 New Latin, from EPI- + Latin *canthus* corner of the eye, from Greek *kanthos*] > ˌepiˈcanthic *adj*

epicardium (ˌɛpɪˈkɑːdɪəm) *n, pl* -dia (-dɪə) *anatomy* the innermost layer of the pericardium, in direct contact with the heart [C19 New Latin, from EPI- + Greek *kardia* heart] > ˌepiˈcardiac *or* ˌepiˈcardial *adj*

epicarp (ˈɛpɪˌkɑːp) *or* **exocarp** *n* the outermost layer of the pericarp of fruits: forms the skin of a peach or grape [C19 from French *épicarpe*, from EPI- + Greek *karpos* fruit]

epicedium (ˌɛpɪˈsiːdɪəm) *n, pl* -dia (-dɪə) *rare* a funeral ode [C16 Latin, from Greek *epikēdeion*, from EPI- + *kēdos* care]

epicene (ˈɛpɪˌsiːn) *adj* 1 having the characteristics of both sexes; hermaphroditic 2 of neither sex; sexless 3 effeminate 4 *grammar* a denoting a noun that may refer to a male or a female, such as *teacher* as opposed to *businessman* or *shepherd* b (in Latin, Greek, etc) denoting a noun that retains the same grammatical gender regardless of the sex of the referent ▷ *n* 5 an epicene person or creature 6 an epicene noun [C15 from Latin *epicoenus*, from Greek *epikoinos* common to many, from *koinos* common] > ˌepiˈcenism *n*

epicentre *or US* **epicenter** (ˈɛpɪˌsɛntə) *n* 1 the point on the earth's surface directly above the focus of an earthquake or underground nuclear explosion. Compare **focus** (sense 6) 2 *informal* the absolute centre of something: *the epicentre of world sprinting* [C19 from New Latin *epicentrum*, from Greek *epikentros* over the centre, from EPI- + *kentron* needle; see CENTRE] > ˌepiˈcentral *adj*

epiclesis (ˌɛpɪˈkliːsɪs) *n, pl* -ses (-siːz) *Christianity* the invocation of the Holy Spirit to consecrate the bread and wine of the Eucharist [C19 from Greek, from EPI- + *klēsis* a prayer, from *kalein* to call]

epicontinental (ˌɛpɪˌkɒntɪˈnɛntᵊl) *adj* (esp of a sea) situated on a continental shelf or continent

epicotyl (ˌɛpɪˈkɒtɪl) *n* the part of an embryo plant stem above the cotyledons but beneath the terminal bud [C19 from EPI- + Greek *kotulē*; see COTYLEDON]

epicrisis (ˈɛpɪˌkraɪsɪs) *n pathol* a secondary crisis occurring in the course of a disease [C20 from EPI- + CRISIS]

epicritic (ˌɛpɪˈkrɪtɪk) *adj* (of certain nerve fibres of the skin) serving to perceive and distinguish fine variations of temperature or touch [C20 from Greek *epikritikos* decisive, from *epikrinein* to decide, from EPI- + *krinein* to judge]

epic simile *n* an extended simile, as used in the epic poetry of Homer and other writers

epicure (ˈɛpɪˌkjʊə) *n* 1 a person who cultivates a discriminating palate for the enjoyment of good food and drink; gourmet 2 a person devoted to sensual pleasures [C16 from Medieval Latin *epicūrus*, after Epicurus; see EPICUREAN] > ˈepicurˌism *n*

epicurean (ˌɛpɪkjʊˈriːən) *adj* 1 devoted to sensual pleasures, esp food and drink; hedonistic 2 suitable for an epicure: *an epicurean feast* ▷ *n* 3 an epicure; gourmet > ˌepicuˈreanism *n*

Epicurean (ˌɛpɪkjʊˈriːən) *adj* 1 of or relating to the philosophy of Epicurus, the Greek philosopher (341–270 BC), who held that the highest good is pleasure ▷ *n* 2 a follower of the philosophy of Epicurus > ˌEpicuˈreanism *n*

epicuticle (ˈɛpɪˌkjuːtɪkᵊl) *n* 1 *botany* a waxy layer on the surface of the cuticle 2 *zoology* the outermost lipoprotein layer of the insect cuticle

epicycle (ˈɛpɪˌsaɪkᵊl) *n* 1 *astronomy* (in the Ptolemaic system) a small circle, around which a planet was thought to revolve, whose centre describes a larger circle (the **deferent**) centred on the earth 2 a circle that rolls around the inside or outside of another circle, so generating an epicycloid or hypocycloid [C14 from Late Latin *epicyclus*, from Greek *epikuklos*; see EPI-, CYCLE] > epicyclic (ˌɛpɪˈsaɪklɪk, -ˈsɪklɪk) *or* ˌepiˈcyclical *adj*

epicyclic train *n* a cluster of gears consisting of a central gearwheel with external teeth (the sun), a coaxial gearwheel of greater diameter with internal teeth (the annulus), and one or more planetary gears engaging with both of them to provide a large gear ratio in a compact space

epicycloid (ˌɛpɪˈsaɪklɔɪd) *n* the curve described by a point on the circumference of a circle as this circle rolls around the outside of another fixed circle, the two circles being coplanar. Compare **hypocycloid, cycloid** (sense 4) > ˌepiˈcloidal *adj*

epicycloidal wheel *n* one of the planetary gears of an epicyclic train

Epidaurus (ˌɛpɪˈdɔːrəs; *Greek* ɛpiˈðaurɔs) *n* an ancient port in Greece, in the NE Peloponnese, in Argolis on the Saronic Gulf

epideictic (ˌɛpɪˈdaɪktɪk) *adj* designed to display something, esp the skill of the speaker in rhetoric. Also: **epidictic** (ˌɛpɪˈdɪktɪk) [C18 from Greek *epideiktikos*, from *epideiknunai* to display, show off, from *deiknunai* to show]

epidemic (ˌɛpɪˈdɛmɪk) *adj* 1 (esp of a disease) attacking or affecting many persons simultaneously in a community or area ▷ *n* 2 a widespread occurrence of a disease: *an influenza epidemic* 3 a rapid development, spread, or growth of something, esp something unpleasant: *an epidemic of strikes* [C17 from French *épidémique*, via Late Latin from Greek *epidēmia* literally: among the people, from EPI- + *dēmos* people] > ˌepiˈdemically *adv*

epidemic encephalitis *n pathol* a technical name for **sleeping sickness** (sense 2)

epidemic meningitis n another name for **cerebrospinal meningitis**

epidemic parotitis n another name for **mumps**

epidemiology (ˌɛpɪˌdiːmɪˈɒlədʒɪ) n the branch of medical science concerned with the occurrence, transmission, and control of epidemic diseases > epidemiological (ˌɛpɪˌdiːmɪəˈlɒdʒɪkəl) adj > ˌepiˌdemioˈlogically adv > ˌepiˌdemiˈologist n

epidermis (ˌɛpɪˈdɜːmɪs) n 1 Also called: **cuticle** the thin protective outer layer of the skin, composed of stratified epithelial tissue 2 the outer layer of cells of an invertebrate 3 the outer protective layer of cells of a plant, which may be thickened by a cuticle [C17 via Late Latin from Greek, from EPI- + derma skin] > ˌepiˈdermal, ˌepiˈdermic or ˌepiˈdermoid adj

epidermolysis bullosa (ˌɛpɪdɜːˈmɒlɪsɪs bʊˈləʊzə) n a group of genetic disorders causing blistering of the skin and mucous membranes. In simple cases the blistering is induced by injury, but in serious cases it occurs spontaneously

epidiascope (ˌɛpɪˈdaɪəˌskəʊp) n an optical device for projecting a magnified image onto a screen. See also **episcope**

epididymis (ˌɛpɪˈdɪdɪmɪs) n, pl -didymides (-dɪˈdɪmɪˌdiːz) anatomy a convoluted tube situated along the posterior margin of each testis, in which spermatozoa are stored and conveyed to the vas deferens [C17 from Greek epididumis, from EPI- + didumos twin, testicle; see DIDYMOUS] > ˌepiˈdidymal adj

epidote (ˈɛpɪˌdəʊt) n a green mineral consisting of hydrated calcium iron aluminium silicate in monoclinic crystalline form: common in metamorphic rocks. Formula: $Ca_2(Al,Fe)_3(SiO_4)_3(OH)$ [C19 from French épidote, ultimately from Greek epididonai to increase, from didonai to give; so called because two sides of its crystal are longer than the other two sides] > epidotic (ˌɛpɪˈdɒtɪk) adj

epidural (ˌɛpɪˈdjʊərəl) adj 1 Also: **extradural** upon or outside the dura mater ▷ n 2 Also called: **epidural anaesthesia** a injection of anaesthetic into the space outside the dura mater enveloping the spinal cord b anaesthesia induced by this method [C19 from EPI- + DUR(A MATER) + -AL[1]]

epifocal (ˌɛpɪˈfəʊkəl) adj geology situated or occurring at an epicentre

epigamic (ˌɛpɪˈɡæmɪk) adj zoology attractive to the opposite sex: epigamic coloration

epigastrium (ˌɛpɪˈɡæstrɪəm) n, pl -tria (-trɪə) the upper middle part of the abdomen, above the navel and below the breast [C17 from New Latin, from Greek EPI- + gastrion, from gastēr stomach] > ˌepiˈgastric or ˌepiˈgastrial adj

epigeal (ˌɛpɪˈdʒiːəl), **epigean** or **epigeous** adj 1 of or relating to seed germination in which the cotyledons appear above the ground because of the growth of the hypocotyl 2 living or growing on or close to the surface of the ground [C19 from Greek epigeios of the earth, from EPI- + gē earth]

epigene (ˈɛpɪˌdʒiːn) adj formed or taking place at or near the surface of the earth. Compare **hypogene** [C19 from French épigène, ultimately from Greek epigignesthai to be born after, from gignesthai to be born]

epigenesis (ˌɛpɪˈdʒɛnɪsɪs) n 1 the widely accepted theory that an individual animal or plant develops by the gradual differentiation and elaboration of a fertilized egg cell. Compare **preformation** (sense 2) 2 the formation or alteration of rocks after the surrounding rock has been formed 3 alteration of the mineral composition of a rock by external agents: a type of metamorphism > ˌepiˈgenesist or epigenist (ɪˈpɪdʒɪnɪst) n

epigenetic (ˌɛpɪdʒɪˈnɛtɪk) adj 1 of or relating to epigenesis 2 denoting processes by which heritable modifications in gene function occur without a change in the sequence of the DNA > ˌepigeˈnetically adv

epigenetics (ˌɛpɪdʒɪˈnɛtɪks) n (functioning as sing)

the study of heritable changes that occur without a change in the DNA sequence

epigenous (ɪˈpɪdʒɪnəs) adj biology growing on the surface, esp the upper surface, of an organism or part: an epigenous fungus

epigeous (ˌɛpɪˈdʒiːəs) adj a variant of **epigeal**

epiglottis (ˌɛpɪˈɡlɒtɪs) n, pl -tises or -tides (-tɪˌdiːz) a thin cartilaginous flap that covers the entrance to the larynx during swallowing, preventing food from entering the trachea > ˌepiˈglottal or ˌepiˈglottic adj

epignathous (ˌɛpɪɡˈneɪθəs) adj zoology having a protruding upper jaw

epigone (ˈɛpɪˌɡəʊn) or **epigon** (ˈɛpɪˌɡɒn) n rare an inferior follower or imitator [C19 from Greek epigonos one born after, from epigignesthai; see EPIGENE]

Epigoni (ɪˈpɪɡəˌnaɪ) pl n, sing -onus (-ənəs) Greek myth the descendants of the Seven against Thebes, who undertook a second expedition against the city and eventually captured and destroyed it [C20 from Greek epigonoi those born after]

epigram (ˈɛpɪˌɡræm) n 1 a witty, often paradoxical remark, concisely expressed 2 a short, pungent, and often satirical poem, esp one having a witty and ingenious ending [C15 from Latin epigramma, from Greek: inscription, from epigraphein to write upon, from graphein to write] > ˌepigramˈmatic adj > ˌepigramˈmatically adv

epigrammatize or **epigrammatise** (ˌɛpɪˈɡræməˌtaɪz) vb to make an epigram or epigrams (about) > ˌepiˈgrammatism n > ˌepiˈgrammatist n

epigraph (ˈɛpɪˌɡrɑːf, -ˌɡræf) n 1 a quotation at the beginning of a book, chapter, etc, suggesting its theme 2 an inscription on a monument or building [C17 from Greek epigraphē; see EPIGRAM] > epigraphic (ˌɛpɪˈɡræfɪk) or ˌepiˈgraphical adj > ˌepiˈgraphically adv

epigraphy (ɪˈpɪɡrəfɪ) n 1 the study of ancient inscriptions 2 epigraphs collectively > eˈpigraphist or eˈpigrapher n

epigynous (ɪˈpɪdʒɪnəs) adj (of flowers) having the receptacle enclosing and fused with the gynoecium so that the other floral parts arise above it [C19 from EPI- + Greek gunē (female organ, pistil) + -OUS] > eˈpigyny n

epilate (ˈɛpɪˌleɪt) vb (tr) rare to remove hair from [C19 from French épiler (modelled on dépiler DEPILATE) + -ATE[1]] > ˌepiˈlation n

epilator (ˈɛpɪˌleɪtə) n an electrical appliance consisting of a metal spiral head that rotates at high speed, plucking unwanted hair

epilepsy (ˈɛpɪˌlɛpsɪ) n a disorder of the central nervous system characterized by periodic loss of consciousness with or without convulsions. In some cases it is due to brain damage but in others the cause is unknown. See also **grand mal, petit mal** [C16 from Late Latin epilēpsia, from Greek, from epilambanein to attack, seize, from lambanein to take]

epileptic (ˌɛpɪˈlɛptɪk) adj 1 of, relating to, or having epilepsy ▷ n 2 a person who has epilepsy > ˌepiˈleptically adv

epileptogenic (ˌɛpɪˌlɛptəʊˈdʒɛnɪk) adj causing an epileptic attack

epileptoid (ˌɛpɪˈlɛptɔɪd) or **epileptiform** (ˌɛpɪˈlɛptɪˌfɔːm) adj resembling epilepsy

epilimnion (ˌɛpɪˈlɪmnɪən) n the upper layer of water in a lake [C20 from EPI- + Greek limnion, diminutive of limnē lake]

epilithic (ˌɛpɪˈlɪθɪk) adj (of plants) growing on the surface of rock

epilogue (ˈɛpɪˌlɒɡ) n 1 a a speech, usually in verse, addressed to the audience by an actor at the end of a play b the actor speaking this 2 a short postscript to any literary work, such as a brief description of the fates of the characters in a novel 3 Brit (esp formerly) the concluding programme of the day on a radio or television station, often having a religious content [C15 from Latin epilogus, from Greek epilogos, from logos word,

speech] > epilogist (ɪˈpɪlədʒɪst) n

epimere (ˈɛpɪˌmɪə) n embryol the dorsal part of the mesoderm of a vertebrate embryo, consisting of a series of segments (somites)

epimerism (ɪˈpɪməˌrɪzəm) n optical isomerism in which isomers (**epimers**) can form about asymmetric atoms within the molecule, esp in carbohydrates [C20 German Epimer (see EPI-, -MER) + -ISM] > epimeric (ˌɛpɪˈmɛrɪk) adj

epimorphosis (ˌɛpɪmɔːˈfəʊsɪs) n a type of development in animals, such as certain insect larvae, in which segmentation of the body is complete before hatching > ˌepiˈmorphic adj

epimysium (ˌɛpɪˈmɪzɪəm) n, pl -sia (-zɪə) anatomy the sheath of connective tissue that encloses a skeletal muscle [from New Latin, from EPI- + Greek mus mouse, MUSCLE]

epinasty (ˈɛpɪˌnæstɪ) n, pl -ties increased growth of the upper surface of a plant part, such as a leaf, resulting in a downward bending of the part. Compare **hyponasty** [C19 from EPI- + -nasty, from Greek nastos pressed down, from nassein to press] > ˌepiˈnastic adj

epinephrine (ˌɛpɪˈnɛfrɪn, -riːn) or **epinephrin** n a US name for **adrenaline** [C19 from EPI- + nephro- + -INE[2]]

epineurium (ˌɛpɪˈnjʊərɪəm) n a sheath of connective tissue around two or more bundles of nerve fibres [C19 from New Latin, from EPI- + Greek neuron nerve + -IUM] > ˌepiˈneurial adj

epipelagic (ˌɛpɪpəˈlædʒɪk) adj of, relating to, or inhabiting the upper zone of the ocean from just below the surface to approximately 100 metres deep

epipetalous (ˌɛpɪˈpɛtələs) adj botany (of stamens) attached to the petals

Epiph. abbreviation for Epiphany

epiphany (ɪˈpɪfənɪ) n, pl -nies 1 the manifestation of a supernatural or divine reality 2 any moment of great or sudden revelation [C17 via Church Latin from Greek epiphaneia an appearing, from EPI- + phainein to show] > epiphanic (ˌɛpɪˈfænɪk) adj

Epiphany (ɪˈpɪfənɪ) n, pl -nies a Christian festival held on Jan 6, commemorating, in the Western Church, the manifestation of Christ to the Magi and, in the Eastern Church, the baptism of Christ

epiphenomenalism (ˌɛpɪfɪˈnɒmɪnəˌlɪzəm) n the dualistic doctrine that consciousness is merely a by-product of physiological processes and has no power to affect them. Compare **interactionism, parallelism**. > ˌepipheˈnomenalist n, adj

epiphenomenon (ˌɛpɪfɪˈnɒmɪnən) n, pl -na (-nə) 1 a secondary or additional phenomenon; by-product 2 pathol an unexpected or atypical symptom or occurrence during the course of a disease > ˌepipheˈnomenal adj > ˌepipheˈnomenally adv

epiphragm (ˈɛpɪˌfræm) n a disc of calcium phosphate and mucilage secreted by snails over the aperture of their shells before hibernation [C19 via New Latin from Greek epiphragma a lid, from epiphrassein, from EPI- + phrassein to place in an enclosure]

epiphyllous (ˌɛpɪˈfɪləs) adj botany (of plants) growing on, or attached to, the leaf of another plant

epiphysis (ɪˈpɪfɪsɪs) n, pl -ses (-ˌsiːz) 1 the end of a long bone, initially separated from the shaft (diaphysis) by a section of cartilage that eventually ossifies so that the two portions fuse together 2 Also called: epiphysis cerebri (ˈsɛrɪbraɪ) the technical name for **pineal gland** [C17 via New Latin from Greek: a growth upon, from EPI- + phusis growth, from phuein to bring forth, produce] > epiphyseal or epiphysial (ˌɛpɪˈfɪzɪəl) adj

epiphyte (ˈɛpɪˌfaɪt) n a plant that grows on another plant but is not parasitic on it > epiphytic (ˌɛpɪˈfɪtɪk), ˌepiˈphytal or ˌepiˈphytical adj > ˌepiˈphytically adv

epiphytotic (ˌɛpɪfaɪˈtɒtɪk) adj (of plant diseases and parasites) affecting plants over a wide

e

geographical region [from EPI- + -PHYTE + -OTIC]

epirogeny (ˌɛpaɪˈrɒdʒɪnɪ) *n* a variant spelling of **epeirogeny**. ▷ epirogenic (ˌɪˌpaɪrəʊˈdʒɛnɪk) *or* epirogenetic (ˌɪˌpaɪrəʊdʒɪˈnɛtɪk) *adj*

Epirus (ɪˈpaɪərəs) *n* **1** a region of NW Greece, part of ancient Epirus ceded to Greece after independence in 1830 **2** (in ancient Greece) a region between the Pindus mountains and the Ionian Sea, straddling the modern border with Albania

Epis. *Bible abbreviation for* Also: Epist. Epistle

episcopacy (ɪˈpɪskəpəsɪ) *n, pl* -cies **1** government of a Church by bishops **2** another word for **episcopate**

episcopal (ɪˈpɪskəpəl) *adj* of, denoting, governed by, or relating to a bishop or bishops [c15 from Church Latin *episcopālis,* from *episcopus* BISHOP] ▷ eˈpiscopally *adv*

Episcopal (ɪˈpɪskəpəl) *adj* belonging to or denoting the Episcopal Church ▷ Eˈpiscopally *adv*

Episcopal Church *n* an autonomous branch of the Anglican Communion in Scotland and the US

episcopalian (ɪˌpɪskəˈpeɪlɪən) *adj also* episcopal **1** practising or advocating the principle of Church government by bishops ▷ *n* **2** an advocate of such Church government ▷ eˌpiscoˈpalianism *n*

Episcopalian (ɪˌpɪskəˈpeɪlɪən) *adj* **1** belonging to or denoting the Episcopal Church ▷ *n* **2** a member or adherent of this Church

episcopalism (ɪˈpɪskəpəˌlɪzəm) *n* the belief that a Church should be governed by bishops

episcopate (ɪˈpɪskəpɪt, -ˌpeɪt) *n* **1** the office, status, or term of office of a bishop **2** bishops collectively

episcope (ˈɛpɪˌskəʊp) *n Brit* an optical device that projects an enlarged image of an opaque object, such as a printed page or photographic print, onto a screen by means of reflected light. US and Canadian name: opaque projector See also **epidiascope**

episematic (ˌɛpɪsɪˈmætɪk) *adj zoology* (esp of coloration) aiding recognition between animals of the same species

episiotomy (əˌpiːzɪˈɒtəmɪ) *n, pl* -mies surgical incision into the perineum during the late stages of labour to prevent its laceration during childbirth and to make delivery easier [c20 from *episio-,* from Greek *epision* pubic region + -TOMY]

episode (ˈɛpɪˌsəʊd) *n* **1** an incident, event, or series of events **2** any one of the sections into which a serialized novel or radio or television programme is divided **3** an incident, sequence, or scene that forms part of a narrative but may be a digression from the main story **4** (in ancient Greek tragedy) a section between two choric songs **5** *music* a contrasting section between statements of the subject, as in a fugue or rondo [c17 from Greek *epeisodion* something added, from *epi-* (in addition) + *eisodios* coming in, from *eis-* in + *hodos* road]

episodic (ˌɛpɪˈsɒdɪk) *or* episodical *adj* **1** resembling or relating to an episode **2** divided into or composed of episodes **3** irregular, occasional, or sporadic ▷ ˌepiˈsodically *adv*

episome (ˈɛpɪˌsəʊm) *n* a unit of genetic material (DNA) in bacteria, such as a plasmid, that can either replicate independently or can be integrated into the host chromosome

epispastic (ˌɛpɪˈspæstɪk) *med* ▷ *adj* **1** producing a serous discharge or a blister ▷ *n* **2** an epispastic agent [c17 from Greek *epispastikos,* from *epispan* to attract, from *span* to draw; alluding to the ancient belief that blisters consisted of humours drawn to the surface of the skin]

Epist. *or* **Epis.** *Bible abbreviation for* Epistle

epistasis (ɪˈpɪstəsɪs) *n* **1** *obsolete* scum on the surface of a liquid, esp on an old specimen of urine **2** *med* the arrest or checking of a bodily discharge, esp bleeding **3** Also called: hypostasis *genetics* the suppression by a gene of the effect of another gene that is not its allele [c19 from Greek: a stopping, from *ephistanai* to stop, from EPI- +

histanai to put] ▷ **epistatic** (ˌɛpɪˈstætɪk) *adj*

epistaxis (ˌɛpɪˈstæksɪs) *n* the technical name for **nosebleed** [c18 from Greek: a dropping, from *epistazein* to drop on, from *stazein* to drip]

epistemic (ˌɛpɪˈstiːmɪk) *adj* **1** of or relating to knowledge or epistemology **2** denoting the branch of modal logic that deals with the formalization of certain epistemological concepts, such as knowledge, certainty, and ignorance. See also **doxastic** [c20 from Greek *epistēmē* knowledge] ▷ ˌepisˈtemically *adv*

epistemics (ˌɛpɪˈstiːmɪks, -ˈstɛm-) *n* (*functioning as singular*) *chiefly Brit* the interdisciplinary study of knowledge and human information-processing, using the formal techniques of logic, linguistics, philosophy, and psychology. Compare **artificial intelligence**

epistemological (ɪˌpɪstɪməˈlɒdʒɪkəl) *adj* **1** concerned with or arising from epistemology **2** (of a philosophical problem) requiring an account of how knowledge of the given subject could be obtained ▷ eˌpistemoˈlogically *adv*

epistemology (ɪˌpɪstɪˈmɒlədʒɪ) *n* the theory of knowledge, esp the critical study of its validity, methods, and scope [c19 from Greek *epistēmē* knowledge] ▷ eˌpisteˈmologist *n*

episternum (ˌɛpɪˈstɜːnəm) *n, pl* -na (-nə) **1** the manubrium of the sternum in mammals **2** another name for **interclavicle**. ▷ ˌepiˈsternal *adj*

epistle (ɪˈpɪsəl) *n* **1** a letter, esp one that is long, formal, or didactic **2** a literary work in letter form, esp a dedicatory verse letter of a type originated by Horace [Old English *epistol,* via Latin from Greek *epistolē,* from *epistellein* to send to, from *stellein* to prepare, send]

Epistle (ɪˈpɪsəl) *n* **1** *New Testament* any of the apostolic letters of Saints Paul, Peter, James, Jude, or John **2** a reading from one of the Epistles, forming part of the Eucharistic service in many Christian Churches

epistler (ɪˈpɪslə, ɪˈpɪstlə) *or* **epistoler** (ɪˈpɪstələ) *n* (*often capital*) **1** a writer of an epistle or epistles **2** the person who reads the Epistle in a Christian religious service

epistolary (ɪˈpɪstələrɪ) *or archaic* **epistolatory** *adj* **1** relating to, denoting, conducted by, or contained in letters **2** (of a novel or other work) constructed in the form of a series of letters

epistrophe (ɪˈpɪstrəfɪ) *n rhetoric* repetition of a word at the end of successive clauses or sentences [c17 New Latin, from Greek, from EPI- + *strophē* a turning]

epistyle (ˈɛpɪˌstaɪl) *n* another name for **architrave** (sense 1) [c17 via Latin *epistȳlium* from Greek *epistulion,* from EPI- + *stulos* column, STYLE]

epitaph (ˈɛpɪˌtɑːf, -ˌtæf) *n* **1** a commemorative inscription on a tombstone or monument **2** a speech or written passage composed in commemoration of a dead person **3** a final judgment on a person or thing [c14 via Latin from Greek *epitaphion,* from *epitaphios* over a tomb, from EPI- + *taphos* tomb] ▷ epitaphic (ˌɛpɪˈtæfɪk) *adj* ▷ ˈepiˌtaphist *n*

epitasis (ɪˈpɪtəsɪs) *n* (in classical drama) the part of a play in which the main action develops. Compare **protasis** (sense 2), **catastrophe** (sense 2) [c16 from Greek: a stretching, intensification, from *teinein* to stretch]

epitaxial transistor (ˌɛpɪˈtæksɪəl) *n* a transistor made by depositing a thin pure layer of semiconductor material (**epitaxial layer**) onto a crystalline support by epitaxy. The layer acts as one of the electrode regions, usually the collector

epitaxy (ˈɛpɪˌtæksɪ) *or* **epitaxis** *n* the growth of a thin layer on the surface of a crystal so that the layer has the same structure as the underlying crystal ▷ **epitaxial** (ˌɛpɪˈtæksɪəl) *adj*

epithalamium (ˌɛpɪθəˈleɪmɪəm) *or* **epithalamion** *n, pl* -mia (-mɪə) a poem or song written to celebrate a marriage; nuptial ode [c17 from Latin, from Greek *epithalamion* marriage song, from *thalamos* bridal chamber] ▷ **epithalamic** (ˌɛpɪθəˈlæmɪk) *adj*

epitheca (ˌɛpɪˈθiːkə) *n, pl* -cae (-siː) the outer and older layer of the cell wall of a diatom. Compare **hypotheca** [c19 from EPI- + THECA]

epithelioma (ˌɛpɪˌθiːlɪˈəʊmə) *n, pl* -mas *or* -mata (-mətə) *pathol* a malignant tumour of epithelial tissue ▷ epitheliomatous (ˌɛpɪˌθiːlɪˈɒmətəs) *adj*

epithelium (ˌɛpɪˈθiːlɪəm) *n, pl* -liums *or* -lia (-lɪə) an animal tissue consisting of one or more layers of closely packed cells covering the external and internal surfaces of the body. The cells vary in structure according to their function, which may be protective, secretory, or absorptive [c18 New Latin, from EPI- + Greek *thēlē* nipple] ▷ ˌepiˈthelial *adj*

epithet (ˈɛpɪˌθɛt) *n* a descriptive word or phrase added to or substituted for a person's name: "Lackland" is an epithet for King John [c16 from Latin *epitheton,* from Greek, from *epitithenai* to add, from *tithenai* to put] ▷ ˌepiˈthetic *or* ˌepiˈthetical *adj*

epitome (ɪˈpɪtəmɪ) *n* **1** a typical example of a characteristic or class; embodiment; personification: *he is the epitome of sloth* **2** a summary of a written work; abstract [c16 via Latin from Greek *epitomē,* from *epitemnein* to abridge, from EPI- + *temnein* to cut] ▷ epitomical (ˌɛpɪˈtɒmɪkəl) *or* ˌepiˈtomic *adj*

epitomize *or* **epitomise** (ɪˈpɪtəˌmaɪz) *vb* (*tr*) **1** to be a personification of; typify **2** to make an epitome of ▷ eˈpitomist *n* ▷ eˌpitomiˈzation *or* eˌpitomiˈsation ▷ eˈpitoˌmizer *or* eˈpitoˌmiser *n*

epitope (ˈɛpɪˌtəʊp) *n* the site on an antigen at which a specific antibody becomes attached

epizoic (ˌɛpɪˈzəʊɪk) *adj* **1** (of an animal or plant) growing or living on the exterior of a living animal **2** (of plants) having seeds or fruit dispersed by animals ▷ ˌepiˈzoism *n*

epizoite (ˌɛpɪˈzəʊɪt) *n* an organism that lives on an animal but is not parasitic on it

epizoon (ˌɛpɪˈzəʊɒn) *n, pl* -zoa (-ˈzəʊə) an animal, such as a parasite, that lives on the body of another animal [c19 New Latin, from EPI- + Greek *zōion* animal] ▷ ˌepiˈzoan *adj*

epizootic (ˌɛpɪzəʊˈɒtɪk) *adj* **1** (of a disease) suddenly and temporarily affecting a large number of animals over a large area ▷ *n* **2** an epizootic disease. Compare **enzootic** ▷ ˌepizoˈotically *adv*

e pluribus unum *Latin* (eɪ ˈplʊərɪbʊs ˈuːnʊm) one out of many: the motto of the USA

EPNS *abbreviation for* electroplated nickel silver

EPO *abbreviation for* erythropoietin

epoch (ˈiːpɒk) *n* **1** a point in time beginning a new or distinctive period: *the invention of nuclear weapons marked an epoch in the history of warfare* **2** a long period of time marked by some predominant or typical characteristic; era **3** *astronomy* a precise date to which information, such as coordinates, relating to a celestial body is referred **4** *geology* a unit of geological time within a period during which a series of rocks is formed: *the Pleistocene epoch* **5** *physics* the displacement of an oscillating or vibrating body at zero time [c17 from New Latin *epocha,* from Greek *epokhē* cessation, related to *ekhein* to hold, have] ▷ **epochal** (ˈɛpˌɒkəl) *adj* ▷ ˈepˌochally *adv*

epoch-making *adj* of great importance; momentous

epode (ˈɛpəʊd) *n Greek prosody* **1** the part of a lyric ode that follows the strophe and the antistrophe **2** a type of lyric poem composed of couplets in which a long line is followed by a shorter one, invented by Archilochus [c16 via Latin from Greek *epōidos* a singing after, from *epaidein* to sing after, from *aidein* to sing]

eponym (ˈɛpənɪm) *n* **1** a name, esp a place name, derived from the name of a real or mythical person, as for example *Constantinople* from *Constantine I* **2** the name of the person from which such a name is derived: *in the Middle Ages, "Brutus" was thought to be the eponym of "Britain."* [c19 from Greek *epōnumos* giving a significant name]

> ˌepoˈnymic *adj*

eponymous (ɪˈpɒnɪməs) *adj* **1** (of a person) being the person after whom a literary work, film, etc, is named: *the eponymous heroine in the film of Jane Eyre* **2** (of a literary work, film, etc) named after its central character or creator: *the Stooges' eponymous debut album* > eˈponymously *adv*

eponymy (ɪˈpɒnɪmɪ) *n* the derivation of names of places, etc, from those of persons

epopee (ˈɛpəʊˌpiː; *French* epɔpe) *or* **epopoeia** (ˌɛpəˈpiːə) *n* **1** an epic poem **2** epic poetry in general [c17 from French *épopée*, from Greek *epopoiia*, from EPOS + *poiein* to make]

epos (ˈɛpɒs) *n* **1** a body of poetry in which the tradition of a people is conveyed, esp a group of poems concerned with a common epic theme **2** another word for **epic** (sense 1) [c19 via Latin from Greek: speech, word, epic poem, song; related to Latin *vōx* VOICE]

EPOS (ˈiːpɒs) *n acronym for* **electronic point of sale**

epoxide (ɪˈpɒksaɪd) *n* **a** a compound containing an oxygen atom joined to two different groups that are themselves joined to other groups **b** (*as modifier*): *epoxide resin* [c20 from EPI- + OXIDE]

epoxy (ɪˈpɒksɪ) *adj chem* **1** of, consisting of, or containing an oxygen atom joined to two different groups that are themselves joined to other groups: *epoxy group* **2** of, relating to, or consisting of an epoxy resin ▷ *n, pl* epoxies **3** short for **epoxy resin** [c20 from EPI- + OXY-²]

epoxy *or* **epoxide resin** *n* any of various tough resistant thermosetting synthetic resins containing epoxy groups: used in surface coatings, laminates, and adhesives

EPP *abbreviation for* executive pension plan

EPP-ED *abbreviation for* European People's Party and European Democrats: a mainstream centre and centre-right political group in the European Parliament

Epping (ˈɛpɪŋ) *n* a town in E England, in Essex, on the edge of Epping Forest: a residential centre for London. Pop: 9889 (2001)

Epping Forest (ˈɛpɪŋ) *n* a forest in E England, northeast of London: formerly a royal hunting ground

EPR *abbreviation for* **electron paramagnetic resonance**

EPROM (ˈiːprɒm) *n computing acronym for* erasable programmable read-only memory

eps *abbreviation for* earnings per share

epsilon (ˈɛpsɪˌlɒn, ɛpˈsaɪlən) *n* the fifth letter of the Greek alphabet (E, ε), a short vowel, transliterated as *e* [Greek *e psilon*, literally: simple *e*]

Epsilon (ˈɛpsɪˌlɒn, ɛpˈsaɪlən) *n* (*foll by the genitive case of a specified constellation*) the fifth brightest star in a constellation: *Epsilon Aurigae*

Epsom (ˈɛpsəm) *n* a town in SE England, in Surrey: famous for its mineral springs and for horse racing. Pop (with Ewell): 64 492 (2001)

Epsom salts *n* (*functioning as singular or plural*) a medicinal preparation of hydrated magnesium sulphate, used as a purgative [c18 named after EPSOM, where they occur naturally in the water]

Epstein-Barr virus (ˈɛpstaɪn ˈbɑː) *n* a virus belonging to the herpes family that causes infectious mononucleosis; it is also implicated in the development of Burkitt's lymphoma and Hodgkin's disease. Abbreviation: EBV [c20 named after Sir M A *Epstein* (born 1921), and Yvonne M *Barr* (born 1932), British pathologists who discovered the virus]

epulis (ɛˈpuːlɪs) *n* **1** *pathol* a swelling of the gum, usually as a result of fibrous hyperplasia **2** *vet science* a benign tumour attached to the jaw of an animal, esp a dog

epyllion (ɪˈpɪlɪən) *n, pl* -lia (-lɪə) a miniature epic [c19 from Greek, diminutive of EPOS]

EPZ *abbreviation for* export processing zone: an industrial area containing many foreign-owned factories

EQ *abbreviation for* **1** emotional quotient, a

(notional) measure of a person's adequacy in such areas as self-awareness, empathy, and dealing sensitively with other people [late c20 by analogy with IQ] **2** equalization, the electronic balancing of sound frequencies on audio recording equipment or hi-fi to reduce distortion or achieve a specific effect

eq. *abbreviation for* **1** equal **2** equation **3** equivalent

EQC (in New Zealand) *abbreviation for* Earthquake Commission

equable (ˈɛkwəbəl) *adj* **1** even-tempered; placid **2** unvarying; uniform: *an equable climate* [c17 from Latin *aequābilis*, from *aequāre* to make equal] > ˌequaˈbility *or* ˈequableness *n* > ˈequably *adv*

equal (ˈiːkwəl) *adj* **1** (often foll by to or with) identical in size, quantity, degree, intensity, etc; the same (as) **2** having identical privileges, rights, status, etc: *all men are equal before the law* **3** having uniform effect or application: *equal opportunities* **4** evenly balanced or proportioned: *the game was equal between the teams* **5** (usually foll by to) having the necessary or adequate strength, ability, means, etc (for): *to be equal to one's work* **6** another word for **equivalent** (sense 3a) ▷ *n* **7** a person or thing equal to another, esp in merit, ability, etc: *he has no equal when it comes to boxing* ▷ *vb* equals, equalling, equalled *or US* equals, equaling, equaled **8** (*tr*) to be equal to; correspond to; match: *my offer equals his* **9** (*intr; usually foll by out*) to become equal or level **10** (*tr*) to make, perform, or do something equal to: *to equal the world record* **11** (*tr*) *archaic* to make equal [c14 from Latin *aequālis*, from *aequus* level, of obscure origin] > ˈequally *adv*

⏐ **USAGE** The use of *more equal* as in *from now on their relationship will be a more equal one* is acceptable in modern English usage. *Equally* is preferred to *equally as* in sentences such as *reassuring the victims is equally important*. *Just as* is preferred to *equally as* in sentences such as *their surprise was just as great as his*

equal-area *n* (*modifier*) (of a map projection) showing area accurately and therefore distorting shape and direction. Also: homologographic

equali (ɪˈkwɑːliː) *pl n music* pieces for a group of instruments of the same kind: *Beethoven's Equali for four trombones* [Italian: old pl form of *uguale* equal]

equalitarian (ɪˌkwɒlɪˈtɛərɪən) *adj, n* a less common word for **egalitarian** > eˌqualiˈtarianism *n*

equality (ɪˈkwɒlɪtɪ) *n, pl* -ties **1** the state of being equal **2** *maths* a statement, usually an equation, indicating that quantities or expressions on either side of an equal sign are equal

equalization payment *or* **grant** *n Canadian* a financial grant made by the federal government to a poorer province in order to facilitate a level of services equal to that of a richer province

equalize *or* **equalise** (ˈiːkwəˌlaɪz) *vb* **1** (*tr*) to make equal or uniform; regularize **2** (*intr*) (in sports) to reach the same score as one's opponent or opponents > ˌequaliˈzation *or* ˌequaliˈsation *n*

equalizer *or* **equaliser** (ˈiːkwəˌlaɪzə) *n* **1** a person or thing that equalizes, esp a device to counterbalance opposing forces **2** an electronic network introduced into a transmission circuit to alter its response, esp to reduce distortion by equalizing its response over a specified frequency range **3** *sport* a goal, point, etc, that levels the score **4** *US slang* a weapon, esp a gun

Equal Opportunities Commission *n* (in Britain) a body appointed by the Government to enforce the provisions of the Equal Pay Act 1970 and the Sex Discrimination Act 1975. Abbreviation: EOC

equal opportunity *n* **a** the offering of employment, pay, or promotion equally to all, without discrimination as to sex, race, colour, disability, etc **b** (*as modifier*): *our equal-opportunity policy; an equal-opportunities employer*

equal pay *n* the right of a man or woman to receive the same pay as a person of the opposite

sex doing the same or similar work for the same or a similar employer

equal sign *or* **equals sign** *n* the symbol =, used to indicate a mathematical equality

equanimity (ˌiːkwəˈnɪmɪtɪ, ˌɛkwə-) *n* calmness of mind or temper; composure [c17 from Latin *aequanimitās*, from *aequus* even, EQUAL + *animus* mind, spirit] > equanimous (ɪˈkwænɪməs) *adj* > eˈquanimously *adv*

equate (ɪˈkweɪt) *vb* (*mainly tr*) **1** to make or regard as equivalent or similar, esp in order to compare or balance **2** *maths* to indicate the equality of; form an equation from **3** (*intr*) to be equal; correspond [c15 from Latin *aequāre* to make EQUAL] > eˈquatable *adj* > eˌquataˈbility *n*

equation (ɪˈkweɪʒən, -ʃən) *n* **1** a mathematical statement that two expressions are equal: it is either an **identity** in which the variables can assume any value, or a **conditional equation** in which the variables have only certain values (roots) **2** the act of regarding as equal; equating **3** the act of making equal or balanced; equalization **4** a situation, esp one regarded as having a number of conflicting elements: *what you want doesn't come into the equation* **5** the state of being equal, equivalent, or equally balanced **6** a situation or problem in which a number of factors need to be considered **7** See **chemical equation 8** *astronomy* See **personal equation**. > eˈquational *adj* > eˈquationally *adv*

equation of state *n* any equation that expresses the relationship between the temperature, pressure, and volume of a substance

equation of time *n* the difference between apparent solar time and mean solar time, being at a maximum in February (over 14 minutes) and November (over 16 minutes)

equator (ɪˈkweɪtə) *n* **1** the great circle of the earth with a latitude of 0°, lying equidistant from the poles; dividing the N and S hemispheres **2** a circle dividing a sphere or other surface into two equal symmetrical parts **3** See **magnetic equator 4** *astronomy* See **celestial equator** [c14 from Medieval Latin (*circulus*) *aequātor* (*diei et noctis*) (circle) that equalizes (the day and night), from Latin *aequāre* to make EQUAL]

equatorial (ˌɛkwəˈtɔːrɪəl) *adj* **1** of, like, or existing at or near the equator **2** *astronautics* lying in the plane of the equator: *an equatorial orbit* **3** *astronomy* of or referring to the celestial equator: *equatorial coordinates* ▷ *n* **4** an equatorial mounting > ˌequaˈtorially *adv*

Equatorial Guinea *n* a republic of W Africa, consisting of Río Muni on the mainland and the island of Bioko in the Gulf of Guinea, with four smaller islands: ceded by Portugal to Spain in 1778; gained independence in 1968. Official languages: Spanish and French. Religion: Roman Catholic majority. Currency: franc. Capital: Malabo. Pop: 507 000 (2004 est). Area: 28 049 sq km (10 830 sq miles). Former name (until 1964): Spanish Guinea

equatorial mounting *n* an astronomical telescope mounting that allows motion of the telescope about two mutually perpendicular axes, one of which is parallel to the earth's axis

equerry (ˈɛkwərɪ; *at the British court* ɪˈkwɛrɪ) *n, pl* -ries **1** an officer attendant upon the British sovereign **2** (formerly) an officer in a royal household responsible for the horses [c16 alteration (through influence of Latin *equus* horse) of earlier *escuirie*, from Old French: stable, group of squires, from *escuyer* SQUIRE]

equestrian (ɪˈkwɛstrɪən) *adj* **1** of or relating to horses and riding **2** on horseback; mounted **3** depicting or representing a person on horseback: *an equestrian statue* **4** of, relating to, or composed of Roman equites **5** of, relating to, or composed of knights, esp the imperial free knights of the Holy Roman Empire ▷ *n* **6** a person skilled in riding and horsemanship [c17 from Latin *equestris*, from *eques* horseman, knight, from *equus* horse]

e

> e'questrian,ism *n*

equestrienne (ˌɪkwɛstrɪˈɛn) *n* a female rider on horseback, esp one in a circus who performs acrobatics

equi- *combining form* equal or equally: *equidistant; equilateral*

equiangular (ˌiːkwɪˈæŋɡjʊlə) *adj* having all angles equal

equidistant (ˌiːkwɪˈdɪstənt) *adj* distant by equal amounts from two or more places > ˌequiˈdistance *n* > ˌequiˈdistantly *adv*

equilateral (ˌiːkwɪˈlætərəl) *adj* 1 having all sides of equal length: *an equilateral triangle* ▷ *n* 2 a geometric figure having all its sides of equal length 3 a side that is equal in length to other sides > ˌequiˈlaterally *adv*

equilibrant (ɪˈkwɪlɪbrənt) *n* a force capable of balancing another force and producing equilibrium

equilibrate (ˌiːkwɪˈlaɪbreɪt, ɪˈkwɪlɪˌbreɪt) *vb* to bring to or to be in equilibrium; balance [c17 from Late Latin *aequilibrāre,* from *aequilibris* in balance; see EQUILIBRIUM] > equilibration (ˌiːkwɪlaɪˈbreɪʃən, ɪˌkwɪlɪ-) *n* > equilibrator (ɪˈkwɪlɪˌbreɪtə) *n*

equilibrist (ɪˈkwɪlɪbrɪst) *n* a person who performs balancing feats, esp on a high wire > eˌquiliˈbristic *adj*

equilibrium (ˌiːkwɪˈlɪbrɪəm) *n, pl* -riums *or* -ria (-rɪə) 1 a stable condition in which forces cancel one another 2 a state or feeling of mental balance; composure 3 any unchanging condition or state of a body, system, etc, resulting from the balance or cancelling out of the influences or processes to which it is subjected. See **thermodynamic equilibrium** 4 *physics* a state of rest or uniform motion in which there is no resultant force on a body 5 *chem* the condition existing when a chemical reaction and its reverse reaction take place at equal rates 6 *physics* the condition of a system that has its total energy distributed among its component parts in the statistically most probable manner 7 *physiol* a state of bodily balance, maintained primarily by special receptors in the inner ear 8 the economic condition in which there is neither excess demand nor excess supply in a market [c17 from Latin *aequilībrium,* from *aequi-* EQUI- + *lībra* pound, balance]

equimolecular (ˌiːkwɪməˈlɛkjʊlə) *adj* (of substances, solutions, etc) containing equal numbers of molecules

equine (ˈɛkwaɪn) *adj* 1 of, relating to, or resembling a horse 2 of, relating to, or belonging to the family *Equidae,* which comprises horses, zebras, and asses [c18 from Latin *equīnus,* from *equus* horse] > ˈequinely *adv*

equine distemper *n* another name for **strangles**

equine herpesvirus *n vet science* a viral disease of horses that may cause respiratory signs, abortion, neonatal death, and paresis. A vaccine is available against this disease. Abbreviation: EHV

equine infectious anaemia *n vet science* a viral disease of horses, donkeys, and mules characterized by fever, anaemia, jaundice, depression, and weight loss. Abbreviation: EIA

equine influenza *n vet science* a respiratory disease of horses, caused by the *Orthomyxoviridae type A* virus, characterized by a fever and persistent cough

equinoctial (ˌiːkwɪˈnɒkʃəl) *adj* 1 relating to or occurring at either or both equinoxes 2 (of a plant) having flowers that open and close at specific regular times 3 *astronomy* of or relating to the celestial equator ▷ *n* 4 a storm or gale at or near an equinox 5 another name for **celestial equator** [c14 from Latin *aequinoctiālis* concerning the EQUINOX]

equinoctial circle *or* **line** *n* another name for **celestial equator**

equinoctial point *n* either of the two points at which the celestial equator intersects the ecliptic

equinox (ˈiːkwɪˌnɒks, ˈɛkwɪˌnɒks) *n* 1 either of the two occasions, six months apart, when day and night are of equal length. See **vernal equinox, autumnal equinox** 2 another name for **equinoctial point** [c14 from Medieval Latin *equinoxium,* changed from Latin *aequinoctium,* from *aequi-* EQUI- + *nox* night]

equinumerous (ˌiːkwɪˈnjuːmərəs) *adj logic* having the same number of members

equip (ɪˈkwɪp) *vb* equips, equipping, equipped (tr) 1 to furnish with (necessary supplies, etc) 2 (*usually passive*) to provide with abilities, understanding, etc: *her son was never equipped to be a scholar* 3 to dress out; attire [c16 from Old French *eschiper* to embark, fit out (a ship), of Germanic origin; compare Old Norse *skipa* to put in order, *skip* SHIP] > eˈquipper *n*

equipage (ˈɛkwɪpɪdʒ) *n* 1 a horse-drawn carriage, esp one elegantly equipped and attended by liveried footmen 2 (formerly) the stores and equipment of a military unit 3 *archaic* a a set of useful articles b a group of attendants; retinue

equipartition (ˌɛkwɪpɑːˈtɪʃən) *n* the equal division of the energy of a system in thermal equilibrium between different degrees of freedom. This principle was assumed to be exact in classical physics, but quantum theory shows that it is true only in certain special cases

équipe (eɪˈkiːp) *n* (esp in motor racing) a team [French]

equipment (ɪˈkwɪpmənt) *n* 1 an act or instance of equipping 2 the items so provided 3 a set of tools, devices, kit, etc, assembled for a specific purpose, such as a soldier's kit and weapons

equipoise (ˈɛkwɪˌpɔɪz) *n* 1 even balance of weight or other forces; equilibrium 2 a counterbalance; counterpoise ▷ *vb* 3 (tr) to offset or balance in weight or force; balance

equipollent (ˌiːkwɪˈpɒlənt) *adj* 1 equal or equivalent in significance, power, or effect 2 *logic* (of two propositions) logically deducible from each other; equivalent 3 *maths, logic* (of two classes) having the same cardinality ▷ *n* 4 something that is equipollent [c15 from Latin *aequipollēns* of equal importance, from EQUI- + *pollēre* to be able, be strong] > ˌequiˈpollence *or* ˌequiˈpollency *n* > ˌequiˈpollently *adv*

equiponderate (ˌiːkwɪˈpɒndəˌreɪt) *vb* (tr) to equal or balance in weight, power, force, etc; offset; counterbalance [c17 from Medieval Latin *aequiponderāre,* from Latin EQUI- + *ponderāre* to weigh] > ˌequiˈponderance *or* ˌequiˈponderancy *n* > ˌequiˈponderant *adj*

equipotential (ˌiːkwɪpəˈtɛnʃəl) *adj* 1 having the same electric potential or uniform electric potential 2 Also: **equipotent** (ˌiːkwɪˈpəʊtᵊnt) equivalent in power or effect ▷ *n* 3 an equipotential line or surface > ˌequipoˌtentiˈality *n*

equiprobable (ˌiːkwɪˈprɒbəbᵊl) *adj* equally probable > ˌequiˌprobaˈbility *n*

equisetum (ˌɛkwɪˈsiːtəm) *n, pl* -tums *or* -ta (-tə) any tracheophyte plant of the genus *Equisetum,* which comprises the horsetails [c19 New Latin, changed from Latin *equisaetum,* from *equus* horse + *saeta* bristle]

equitable (ˈɛkwɪtəbᵊl) *adj* 1 impartial or reasonable; fair; just: *an equitable decision* 2 *law* relating to or valid in equity, as distinct from common law or statute law 3 *law* (formerly) recognized in a court of equity only, as claims, rights, etc [c17 from French *équitable,* from *équité* EQUITY] > ˈequitableness *n* > ˈequitably *adv*

equitant (ˈɛkwɪtᵊnt) *adj* (of a leaf) having the base folded around the stem so that it overlaps the leaf above and opposite [c19 from Latin *equitāns* riding, from *equitāre* to ride, from *equus* horse]

equitation (ˌɛkwɪˈteɪʃən) *n* the study and practice of riding and horsemanship [c16 from Latin *equitātiō,* from *equitāre* to ride, from *equus* horse]

equites (ˈɛkwɪˌtiːz) *pl n* (in ancient Rome) 1 the cavalry 2 members of a social order distinguished by wealth and ranking just below the senators

Also called: knights [from Latin, plural of *eques* horseman, from *equus* horse]

equities (ˈɛkwɪtɪz) *pl n* another name for **ordinary shares**

equity (ˈɛkwɪtɪ) *n, pl* -ties 1 the quality of being impartial or reasonable; fairness 2 an impartial or fair act, decision, etc 3 *law* a system of jurisprudence founded on principles of natural justice and fair conduct. It supplements the common law and mitigates its inflexibility, as by providing a remedy where none exists at law 4 *law* an equitable right or claim: *equity of redemption* 5 the interest of ordinary shareholders in a company 6 the market value of a debtor's property in excess of all debts to which it is liable [c14 from Old French *equite,* from Latin *aequitās,* from *aequus* level, EQUAL]

Equity (ˈɛkwɪtɪ) *n* the actors' trade union. Full name: Actors' Equity Association

equity capital *n* the part of the share capital of a company owned by ordinary shareholders or in certain circumstances by other classes of shareholder

equity-linked policy *n* an insurance or assurance policy in which premiums are invested partially or wholly in ordinary shares for the eventual benefit of the beneficiaries of the policy

equity of redemption *n property law* the right that a mortgager has in equity to redeem his property on payment of the sum owing, even though the sum is overdue. See also **foreclose**

equiv. *abbreviation for* equivalent

equivalence (ɪˈkwɪvələns) *or* **equivalency** *n* 1 the state of being equivalent or interchangeable 2 *maths, logic* a the relationship between two statements, each of which implies the other b the binary truth-function that takes the value *true* when both component sentences are true or when both are false, corresponding to English *if and only if.* Symbol: ≡ or ↔, as in $-(p \wedge q) \equiv -p \vee -q$. Also called: biconditional

equivalence relation *n logic, maths* a relation that is reflexive, symmetric, and transitive: it imposes a partition on its domain of definition so that two elements belong to the same subset if and only if the relation holds between them

equivalency (ˌɛkwɪˈveɪlənsɪ) *or* **equivalence** *n chem* the state of having equal valencies > ˌequiˈvalent *adj*

equivalent (ɪˈkwɪvələnt) *adj* 1 equal or interchangeable in value, quantity, significance, etc 2 having the same or a similar effect or meaning 3 *maths* a having a particular property in common; equal b (of two equations or inequalities) having the same set of solutions c (of two sets) having the same cardinal number 4 *maths, logic* (of two propositions) having an equivalence between them ▷ *n* 5 something that is equivalent 6 short for **equivalent weight** [c15 from Late Latin *aequivalēns,* from *aequivalēre* to be equally significant, from Latin *aequi-* EQUI- + *valēre* to be worth] > eˈquivalently *adv*

equivalent air speed *n* the speed at sea level that would produce the same Pitot-static tube reading as that measured at altitude

equivalent circuit *n* an arrangement of simple electrical components that is electrically equivalent to a complex circuit and is used to simplify circuit analysis

equivalent focal length *n optics* the ratio of the size of an image of a small distant object near the optical axis to the angular distance of the object in radians

equivalent weight *n* the weight of an element or compound that will combine with or displace 8 grams of oxygen or 1.007 97 grams of hydrogen. Also called: gram equivalent

equivocal (ɪˈkwɪvəkᵊl) *adj* 1 capable of varying interpretations; ambiguous 2 deliberately misleading or vague; evasive 3 of doubtful character or sincerity; dubious [c17 from Late Latin *aequivocus,* from Latin EQUI- + *vōx* voice]

> e'quivocally *adv* > e,quivo'cality *or* e'quivocalness *n*

equivocate (ɪ'kwɪvəˌkeɪt) *vb* (*intr*) to use vague or ambiguous language, esp in order to avoid speaking directly or honestly; hedge [C15 from Medieval Latin *aequivocāre*, from Late Latin *aequivocus* ambiguous, EQUIVOCAL]
> e'quivoˌcatingly *adv* > e'quivoˌcator *n*
> e'quivocatory *adj*

equivocation (ɪˌkwɪvə'keɪʃən) *n* **1** the act or an instance of equivocating **2** *logic* a fallacy based on the use of the same term in different senses, esp as the middle term of a syllogism, as *the badger lives in the bank, and the bank is in the High Street, so the badger lives in the High Street*

equivoque *or* **equivoke** ('ɛkwɪˌvəʊk) *n* **1** a play on words; pun **2** an ambiguous phrase or expression **3** double meaning; ambiguity [C14 *equivoc* EQUIVOCAL]

Equuleus (ɛ'kwʊlɪəs) *n, Latin genitive* Equulei (ɛ'kwʊlɪˌaɪ) a small faint constellation in the N hemisphere between Pegasus and Aquarius [from Latin: a young horse, from *equus* horse]

er¹ (ə, ɜː) *interj* a sound made when hesitating in speech

er² *the internet domain name for* Eritrea

Er *the chemical symbol for* erbium

ER *abbreviation for* **1** (in the US) Emergency Room (in hospitals) **2** Elizabeth Regina [Latin: Queen Elizabeth] **3** Eduardus Rex [Latin: King Edward]

-er¹ *suffix forming nouns* **1** a person or thing that performs a specified action: *reader; decanter; lighter* **2** a person engaged in a profession, occupation, etc: *writer; baker; bootlegger* **3** a native or inhabitant of: *islander; Londoner; villager* **4** a person or thing having a certain characteristic: *newcomer; double-decker; fiver* [Old English *-ere*; related to German *-er*, Latin *-ārius*]

-er² *suffix* forming the comparative degree of adjectives (*deeper, freer, sunnier*, etc) and adverbs (*faster, slower*, etc) [Old English *-rd, -re* (adj), *-or* (adv)]

era ('ɪərə) *n* **1** a period of time considered as being of a distinctive character; epoch **2** an extended period of time the years of which are numbered from a fixed point or event: *the Christian era* **3** a point in time, esp one beginning a new or distinctive period: *the discovery of antibiotics marked an era in modern medicine* **4** *geology* a major division of geological time, divided into several periods: *the Mesozoic era* [C17 from Latin *aera* counters, plural of *aes* brass, pieces of brass money]

ERA ('iːrə) *n, abbreviation or acronym for* **1** (in Britain) Education Reform Act: the 1988 act which established the key elements of the National Curriculum **2** (in the US) Equal Rights Amendment: a proposed amendment to the US Constitution enshrining equality between the sexes

eradiate (ɪ'reɪdɪˌeɪt) *vb* a less common word for **radiate** Compare **irradiate**. > e,radi'ation *n*

eradicate (ɪ'rædɪˌkeɪt) *vb* (*tr*) **1** to obliterate; stamp out **2** to pull or tear up by the roots [C16 from Latin *ērādīcāre* to uproot, from EX-¹ + *rādīx* root] > e'radicably *adj* > e'radicably *adv*
> e,radi'cation *n* > e'radicative *adj* > e'radiˌcator *n*

erase (ɪ'reɪz) *vb* **1** to obliterate or rub out (something written, typed, etc) **2** (*tr*) to destroy all traces of; remove completely: *time erases grief* **3** to remove (a recording) from (magnetic tape) **4** (*tr*) *computing* to replace (data) on a storage device with characters representing an absence of data [C17 from Latin *ērādere* to scrape off, from EX-¹ + *rādere* to scratch, scrape] > e'rasable *adj*

eraser (ɪ'reɪzə) *n* an object, such as a piece of rubber or felt, used for erasing something written, typed, etc: *a pencil eraser*

erasion (ɪ'reɪʒən) *n* **1** the act of erasing; erasure **2** the surgical scraping away of tissue, esp of bone

Erastianism (ɪ'ræstɪəˌnɪzəm) *n* the theory that the state should have authority over the church in ecclesiastical matters [C17 named after Thomas *Erastus* (1524–83), Swiss theologian to whom such

views were attributed] > E'rastian *n, adj*

erasure (ɪ'reɪʒə) *n* **1** the act or an instance of erasing **2** the place or mark, as on a piece of paper, where something has been erased

Erato ('ɛrəˌtəʊ) *n Greek myth* the Muse of love poetry

Erbil, Irbil ('ɜːbɪl) *or* **Arbil** *n* a city in N Iraq: important in Assyrian times. Pop: 870 000 (2005 est). Ancient name: Arbela

erbium ('ɜːbɪəm) *n* a soft malleable silvery-white element of the lanthanide series of metals: used in special alloys, room-temperature lasers, and as a pigment. Symbol: Er; atomic no.: 68; atomic wt.: 167.26; valency: 3; relative density: 9.006; melting pt.: 1529°C; boiling pt.: 2868°C [C19 from New Latin, from (*Ytt*)*erb*(*y*), Sweden, where it was first found + -IUM]

Erciyas Daği (*Turkish* 'ɛrdʒijas da·'i) *n* an extinct volcano in central Turkey. Height 3916 m (12 848 ft)

ERCP *abbreviation for* endoscopic retrograde cholangiopancreatography

ERDF *abbreviation for* European Regional Development Fund: a fund to provide money for specific projects for work on the infrastructure in countries of the European Union

ere (ɛə) *conj, prep* a poetic word for **before** [Old English *ǣr*; related to Old Norse *ār* early, Gothic *airis* earlier, Old High German *ēr* earlier, Greek *eri* early]

Erebus¹ ('ɛrɪbəs) *n Greek myth* **1** the god of darkness, son of Chaos and brother of Night **2** the darkness below the earth, thought to be the abode of the dead or the region they pass through on their way to Hades

Erebus² ('ɛrɪbəs) *n* **Mount** a volcano in Antarctica, on Ross Island: discovered by Sir James Ross in 1841 and named after his ship. Height: 3794 m (12 448 ft)

Erechtheum (ɪ'rɛkθɪəm, ˌɛrək'θiːəm) *or* **Erechtheion** (ɪ'rɛkθɪən, ˌɛrək'θiːən) *n* a temple on the Acropolis at Athens, which has a porch of caryatids

Erechtheus (ɛ'rɛkθjuːs, -θɪəs) *n Greek myth* a king of Athens who sacrificed one of his daughters because the oracle at Delphi said this was the only way to win the war against the Eleusinians

erect (ɪ'rɛkt) *adj* **1** upright in posture or position; not bent or leaning: *an erect stance* **2** (of an optical image) having the same orientation as the object; not inverted **3** *physiol* (of the penis, clitoris, or nipples) firm or rigid after swelling with blood, esp as a result of sexual excitement **4** (of plant parts) growing vertically or at right angles to the parts from which they arise ▷ *vb* (*mainly tr*) **5** to put up; construct; build **6** to raise to an upright position; lift up: *to erect a flagpole* **7** to found or form; set up **8** (*also intr*) *physiol* to become or cause to become firm or rigid by filling with blood **9** to hold up as an ideal; exalt **10** *optics* to change (an inverted image) to an upright position **11** to draw or construct (a line, figure, etc) on a given line or figure, esp at right angles to it [C14 from Latin *ērigere* to set up, from *regere* to control, govern]
> e'rectable *adj* > e'rectly *adv* > e'rectness *n*

erectile (ɪ'rɛktaɪl) *adj* **1** *physiol* (of tissues or organs, such as the penis or clitoris) capable of becoming rigid or erect as the result of being filled with blood **2** capable of being erected
> erectility (ɪrɛk'tɪlɪtɪ, ˌiːrɛk-) *n*

erectile impotence *n* impotence caused by the inability of the penis to become sufficiently firm to penetrate the vagina

erection (ɪ'rɛkʃən) *n* **1** the act of erecting or the state of being erected **2** something that has been erected; a building or construction **3** *physiol* the enlarged state or condition of erectile tissues or organs, esp the penis, when filled with blood **4** an erect penis

erector *or* **erecter** (ɪ'rɛktə) *n* **1** *anatomy* any muscle that raises a part or makes it erect **2** a person or thing that erects

E region *or* **layer** *n* a region of the ionosphere,

extending from a height of 90 to about 150 kilometres. It reflects radio waves of medium wavelength. Also called: Heaviside layer, Kennelly-Heaviside layer See also **ionosphere**

erelong (ɛə'lɒŋ) *adv archaic or poetic* before long; soon

eremite ('ɛrɪˌmaɪt) *n* a Christian hermit or recluse. Compare **coenobite** [C13 see HERMIT]
> eremitic (ˌɛrɪ'mɪtɪk) *or* ˌere'mitical *adj*
> eremitism ('ɛrɪmaɪˌtɪzəm) *n*

erepsin (ɪ'rɛpsɪn) *n* a mixture of proteolytic enzymes secreted by the small intestine [C20 *er-*, from Latin *ēripere* to snatch (from *rapere* to seize) + (P)EPSIN]

erethism ('ɛrɪˌθɪzəm) *n* **1** *physiol* an abnormally high degree of irritability or sensitivity in any part of the body **2** *psychiatry* **a** a personality disorder resulting from mercury poisoning **b** an abnormal tendency to become aroused quickly, esp sexually, as the result of a verbal or psychic stimulus [C18 from French *érethisme*, from Greek *erethismos* irritation, from *erethizein* to excite, irritate] > ˌere'thismic, ˌere'thistic *or* ˌere'thitic *adj*

Eretria (ɪ'rɛtrɪə) *n* an ancient city in Greece, on the S coast of Euboea: founded as an Ionian colony; destroyed by the Persians in 490 BC following which it never regained its former significance

Eretz Yisrael *or* **Eretz Israel** *Hebrew* ('ɛrets jis'raeɪl; *Yiddish* 'ɛrets jisra'eɪl) *n Judaism* **1** the Holy Land; Israel **2** the concept, favoured by some extreme Zionists, of a Jewish state the territory of which matched the largest expanse of biblical Israel [literally: Land of Israel]

erev ('ɛrev) *n* (*in combination*) *Judaism* the day before; the eve of: *erev Shabbat* (the Sabbath eve, ie, Friday); *erev Pesach* (the day before Passover) [from Hebrew]

Erevan (*Russian* jɪrɪ'van) *n* a variant spelling of **Yerevan**

erewhile (ɛə'waɪl) *or* **erewhiles** *adv archaic* a short time ago; a little while before

erf (ɜːf) *n, pl* **erven** ('ɜːvən) *South African* a plot of land, usually urban, marked off for building purposes [Afrikaans]

Erf (ɜːf) *abbreviation for* electrorheological fluid: a man-made liquid that thickens or solidifies when an electric current passes through it and returns to a liquid when the current ceases

Erfurt (*German* 'ɛrfʊrt) *n* an industrial city in central Germany, the capital of Thuringia: university (1392). Pop: 201 645 (2003 est)

erg¹ (ɜːg) *n* the cgs unit of work or energy. 1 erg is equivalent to 10^{-7} joule [C19 from Greek *ergon* work]

erg² (ɜːg) *n, pl* **ergs** *or* **areg** an area of shifting sand dunes in a desert, esp the Sahara [C19 from Arabic *'irj*]

erg³ (ɜːg) *n informal* short for **ergometer** (sense 2)

ergative ('ɜːgətɪv) *linguistics* ▷ *adj* **1** denoting a type of verb that takes the same noun as either direct object or as subject, with equivalent meaning. Thus, "fuse" is an ergative verb: "He fused the lights" and "The lights fused" have equivalent meaning **2** denoting a case of nouns in certain languages, for example, Inuktitut or Basque, marking a noun used interchangeably as either the direct object of a transitive verb or the subject of an intransitive verb **3** denoting a language that has ergative verbs or ergative nouns ▷ *n* **4** an ergative verb **5** an ergative noun or case of nouns [C20 from Greek *ergatēs* a workman + -IVE]

ergatocracy (ˌɜːgə'tɒkrəsɪ) *n, pl* **-cies** *rare* government by the workers [C20 from Greek *ergatēs* a workman, from *ergon* work, deed + -CRACY]

ergo¹ ('ɜːgəʊ) *sentence connector* therefore; hence [C14 from Latin: therefore]

ergo² ('ɜːgəʊ) *n informal* short for **ergometer** (sense 2)

ergograph ('ɜːgəˌgrɑːf, -ˌgræf) *n* an instrument that measures and records the amount of work a muscle does during contraction, its rate of fatigue, etc

e

ergometer (ɜːˈɡɒmɪtə) *n* **1** a dynamometer **2** Also called (informal): **erg**, **ergo** a type of exercise machine in which the action of rowing is simulated by the pulling of a strong flexible cord wound round a flywheel [C20 from Greek *ergon* work + -METER]

ergonomic (ˌɜːɡəˈnɒmɪk) *adj* **1** of or relating to ergonomics **2** designed to minimize physical effort and discomfort, and hence maximize efficiency

ergonomics (ˌɜːɡəˈnɒmɪks) *n* (*functioning as singular*) the study of the relationship between workers and their environment, esp the equipment they use. Also called: biotechnology [C20 from Greek *ergon* work + (ECO)NOMICS] > **ergonomist** (ɜːˈɡɒnəmɪst) *n*

ergosterol (ɜːˈɡɒstəˌrɒl) *n* a plant sterol that is converted into vitamin D by the action of ultraviolet radiation. Formula: $C_{28}H_{43}OH$

ergot (ˈɜːɡət, -ɡɒt) *n* **1** a disease of cereals and other grasses caused by ascomycete fungi of the genus *Claviceps*, in which the seeds or grain of the plants are replaced by the spore-containing bodies (sclerotia) of the fungus **2** any fungus causing this disease **3** the dried sclerotia of *C. purpurea*, used as the source of certain alkaloids used to treat haemorrhage, facilitate uterine contraction in childbirth, etc [C17 from French: spur (of a cock), of unknown origin]

ergotism (ˈɜːɡəˌtɪzəm) *n* ergot poisoning, producing either burning pains and eventually gangrene in the limbs or itching skin and convulsions. Also called: Saint Anthony's fire

eric *or* **eriach** (ˈɛrɪk) *n* (in old Irish law) a fine paid by a murderer to the family of his victim. Compare **wergild** [C16 from Irish *eiric*]

erica (ˈɛrɪkə) *n* any shrub of the ericaceous genus *Erica*, including the heaths and some heathers [C19 via Latin from Greek *ereikē* heath]

ericaceous (ˌɛrɪˈkeɪʃəs) *adj* of, relating to, or belonging to the *Ericaceae*, a family of trees and shrubs with typically bell-shaped flowers: includes heather, rhododendron, azalea, and arbutus [C19 from New Latin *Erīcāceae*, from Latin *erīca* heath, from Greek *ereikē*]

ericoid (ˈɛrɪˌkɔɪd) *adj botany* (of leaves) small and tough, resembling those of heather

Eridanus (ɛˈrɪdənəs) *n*, *Latin genitive* Eridani (ɛˈrɪdəˌnaɪ) a long twisting constellation in the S hemisphere extending from Orion to Hydrus and containing the first magnitude star Achernar [from Greek *Eridanos* river in Italy (sometimes identified with the Po) into which, according to legend, Phaëthon fell]

Erie[1] (ˈɪərɪ) *n* **1** (*pl* Eries *or* Erie) a member of a North American Indian people formerly living south of Lake Erie **2** the language of this people, possibly belonging to the Iroquoian family

Erie[2] (ˈɪərɪ) *n* **1** Lake a lake between the US and Canada: the southernmost and the shallowest of the Great Lakes; empties by the Niagara River into Lake Ontario. Area: 25 718 sq km (9930 sq miles) **2** a port in NW Pennsylvania, on Lake Erie. Pop: 101 373 (2003 est)

Erie Canal *n* a canal in New York State between Albany and Buffalo, linking the Hudson River with Lake Erie. Length: 579 km (360 miles)

erigeron (ɪˈrɪdʒərən, -ˈrɪɡ-) *n* any plant of the genus *Erigeron*, whose flowers resemble asters but have narrower rays: family *Asteraceae* (composites). See also **fleabane** (sense 1) [C17 via Latin from Greek, from *ēri* early + *gerōn* old man; from the white down characteristic of some species]

Erin (ˈɪərɪn, ˈɛərɪn) *n* an archaic or poetic name for **Ireland**[1] [from Irish Gaelic *Éirinn*, dative of *Ériu* Ireland]

erinaceous (ˌɛrɪˈneɪʃəs) *adj* of, relating to, or resembling hedgehogs [C18 from Latin *ērināceus* hedgehog]

eringo (ɪˈrɪŋɡəʊ) *n*, *pl* -goes *or* -gos a variant spelling of **eryngo**

erinus (ɪˈraɪnəs) *n* any plant of the scrophulariaceous genus *Erinus*, native to S Africa and S Europe, esp *E. alpinus*, grown as a rock plant for its white, purple, or carmine flowers [New Latin, from Greek *erinos*, an unidentified plant]

Erinyes (ɪˈrɪnɪˌiːz) *pl n*, *sing* Erinys (ɪˈrɪnɪs, ɪˈraɪ-) *myth* another name for the **Furies**

eriostemon (ɛrɪˈɒstəmən) *n* Austral any rutaceous shrub of the mainly Australian genus *Eriostemon*, having waxy white or pink flowers. Also called: **wax flower** [New Latin, from Greek *erion* wool + *stemon* stamen]

Eris (ˈɛrɪs) *n* Greek myth the goddess of discord, sister of Ares

Eriskay pony (ˌɛrɪsˈkeɪ) *n* a breed of medium-sized pony, typically grey, with a dense waterproof coat. The Eriskay is the only surviving variety of the native ponies of the Western Isles of Scotland

eristic (ɛˈrɪstɪk) *adj also* **eristical** **1** of, relating, or given to controversy or logical disputation, esp for its own sake ▷ *n* **2** a person who engages in logical disputes; a controversialist **3** the art or practice of logical disputation, esp if specious [C17 from Greek *eristikos*, from *erizein* to wrangle, from *eris* discord]

Eritrea (ˌɛrɪˈtreɪə) *n* a small country in NE Africa, on the Red Sea: became an Italian colony in 1890; federated with Ethiopia (1952–9); an independence movement was engaged in war with the Ethiopian government from 1961 until independence was gained in 1993; consists of hot and arid coastal lowlands, rising to the foothills of the Ethiopian highlands. Languages: Tigrinya, Arabic, English, Afar, and others. Religions: Muslim and Christian. Currency: nakfa. Capital: Asmara. Pop: 4 296 000 (2004 est). Area: 117 400 sq km (45 300 sq miles)

Eritrean (ˌɛrɪˈtreɪən) *adj* **1** of or relating to Eritrea or its inhabitants ▷ *n* **2** a native or inhabitant of Eritrea

Erivan (*Russian* jɪrɪˈvan) *n* a variant spelling of **Yerevan**

erk (ɜːk) *n* Brit slang an aircraftman or naval rating [C20 perhaps a corruption of *AC* (aircraftman)]

erlang (ˈɜːlæŋ) *n* a unit of traffic intensity in a telephone system equal to the intensity for a specific period when the average number of simultaneous calls is unity. Abbreviation: e [C20 named after A K *Erlang* (1878–1929), Danish mathematician]

Erlangen (*German* ˈɛrlaŋən) *n* a town in central Germany, in Bavaria: university (1743). Pop: 102 449 (2003 est)

Erlenmeyer flask (ˈɜːlənˌmaɪə) *n* a flask, for use in a laboratory, with a narrow neck, wide base, and conical shape; conical flask [C19 named after Emil *Erlenmeyer* (1825–1909), German chemist]

erlking (ˈɜːlˌkɪŋ) *n* German myth a malevolent spirit who carries children off to death [C18 from German *Erlkönig*, literally: alder king, coined in 1778 by Herder, a mistranslation of Danish *ellerkonge* king of the elves]

ERM *abbreviation for* **Exchange Rate Mechanism**

ermine (ˈɜːmɪn) *n*, *pl* -mines *or* -mine **1** the stoat in northern regions, where it has a white winter coat with a black-tipped tail **2** the fur of this animal **3** one of the two principal furs used on heraldic shields, conventionally represented by a white field flecked with black ermine tails. Compare **vair** **4** the dignity or office of a judge, noble, or king **5** short for **ermine moth** [C12 from Old French *hermine*, from Medieval Latin *Armenius* (*mūs*) Armenian (mouse)]

ermine moth *n* **1** Also called: **ermine** an arctiid moth of the genus *Spilosoma*, characterized by dark spots on the light coloured wings, and producing woolly bear caterpillars **2** small ermine an unrelated micro, *Yponomeuta padella*

Ermite (ˈɜːmaɪt) *n* a salty blue cheese made in Quebec, Canada [via Canadian French from French *ermite* hermit, the cheese being made originally by monks]

erne *or* **ern** (ɜːn) *n* another name for the (European) **sea eagle** [Old English *earn*; related to Old Norse *örn* eagle, Old High German *aro* eagle, Greek *ornis* bird]

Erne (ɜːn) *n* a river in N central Republic of Ireland, rising in County Cavan and flowing north across the border, through **Upper Lough Erne** and **Lower Lough Erne** and then west to Donegal Bay. Length: about 96 km (60 miles)

Ernie (ˈɜːnɪ) *n* (in Britain) a machine that randomly selects winning numbers of Premium Bonds [C20 acronym of Electronic Random Number Indicator Equipment]

ERO (in New Zealand) *abbreviation for* Education Review Office

erode (ɪˈrəʊd) *vb* **1** to grind or wear down or away or become ground or worn down or away **2** to deteriorate or cause to deteriorate: *jealousy eroded the relationship* **3** (*tr; usually passive*) pathol to remove (tissue) by ulceration [C17 from Latin *ērōdere*, from EX-[1] + *rōdere* to gnaw] > e'**rodent** *adj*, *n* > e'**rodible** *adj*

erogenous (ɪˈrɒdʒɪnəs) *or* **erogenic** (ˌɛrəˈdʒɛnɪk) *adj* **1** sensitive to sexual stimulation: *erogenous zones of the body* **2** arousing sexual desire or giving sexual pleasure [C19 from Greek *erōs* love, desire + -GENOUS] > **erogeneity** (ˌɛrədʒɪˈniːɪtɪ) *n*

Eros (ˈɪərɒs, ˈɛrɒs) *n* **1** Greek myth the god of love, son of Aphrodite. Roman counterpart: **Cupid** **2** Also called: **life instinct** (in Freudian theory) the group of instincts, esp sexual, that govern acts of self-preservation and that tend towards uninhibited enjoyment of life. Compare **Thanatos** [Greek: desire, sexual love]

Eros–433 *n* an asteroid with an orbital period around the sun of 1.76 years. The NEAR Shoemaker spacecraft made the first asteroid landing on Eros on 12 Feb 2001

erose (ɪˈrəʊs, -ˈrəʊz) *adj* jagged or uneven, as though gnawed or bitten: *erose leaves* [C18 from Latin *ērōsus* eaten away, from *ērōdere* to ERODE] > e'**rosely** *adv*

erosion (ɪˈrəʊʒən) *n* **1** the wearing away of rocks and other deposits on the earth's surface by the action of water, ice, wind, etc **2** the act or process of eroding or the state of being eroded > e'**rosive** *or* e'**rosional** *adj*

erotema (ˌɛrəʊˈtiːmə), **eroteme** (ˈɛrəʊˌtiːm) *or* **erotesis** (ˌɛrəʊˈtiːsɪs) *n* rhetoric a rhetorical question [C16 New Latin, from Greek, from *erōtaein* to ask]

erotetic (ˌɛrəʊˈtɛtɪk) *adj* **1** rhetoric pertaining to a rhetorical question **2** grammar, philosophy pertaining to questions; interrogative

erotic (ɪˈrɒtɪk) *adj also* **erotical** **1** of, concerning, or arousing sexual desire or giving sexual pleasure **2** marked by strong sexual desire or being especially sensitive to sexual stimulation ▷ *n* **3** a person who has strong sexual desires or is especially responsive to sexual stimulation [C17 from Greek *erōtikos* of love, from *erōs* love] > e'**rotically** *adv*

erotica (ɪˈrɒtɪkə) *pl n* explicitly sexual literature or art [C19 from Greek *erōtika*, neuter plural of *erōtikos* EROTIC]

eroticism (ɪˈrɒtɪˌsɪzəm) *or* **erotism** (ˈɛrəˌtɪzəm) *n* **1** erotic quality or nature **2** the use of sexually arousing or pleasing symbolism in literature or art **3** sexual excitement or desire **4** a tendency to exalt sex **5** psychol an overt display of sexual behaviour

eroticize *or* **eroticise** (ɪˈrɒtɪˌsaɪz) *vb* (*tr*) to regard or present in a sexual way > e,**rotici'zation** *or* e,**rotici'sation** *n*

eroto- *combining form* denoting erotic desire, excitement, etc: *erotogenic*; *erotology* [from Greek *erōt-*, *erōs* love]

erotogenic (ɪˌrɒtəˈdʒɛnɪk) *adj* originating from or causing sexual stimulation; erogenous

erotology (ˌɛrəˈtɒlədʒɪ) *n* **1** the study of erotic stimuli and sexual behaviour **2** a description of such stimuli and behaviour > **erotological** (ˌɛrətəˈlɒdʒɪkᵊl) *adj* > ˌerot'**ologist** *n*

erotomania (ɪˌrɒtəʊˈmeɪnɪə) *n* **1** abnormally strong sexual desire **2** a condition in which a person is obsessed with another person and groundlessly believes that person to be in love with him or her > eˌrotoˈmaniac *n*

err (ɜː) *vb* (*intr*) **1** to make a mistake; be incorrect **2** to stray from the right course or accepted standards; sin **3** to act with bias, esp favourable bias: *to err on the side of justice* [c14 *erren* to wander, stray, from Old French *errer*, from Latin *errāre*]

errancy (ˈɛrənsɪ) *n, pl* **-cies 1** the state or an instance of erring or a tendency to err **2** *Christianity* the holding of views at variance with accepted doctrine

errand (ˈɛrənd) *n* **1** a short trip undertaken to perform a necessary task or commission (esp in the phrase **run errands**) **2** the purpose or object of such a trip [Old English *ǣrende*; related to *ār* messenger, Old Norse *erendi* message, Old High German *ārunti*, Swedish *ärende*]

errand boy *n* (in Britain, esp formerly) a boy employed by a shopkeeper to deliver goods and run other errands

errant (ˈɛrənt) *adj* (*often postpositive*) **1** *archaic or literary* wandering in search of adventure **2** erring or straying from the right course or accepted standards [c14 from Old French: journeying, from Vulgar Latin *iterāre* (unattested), from Latin *iter* journey; influenced by Latin *errāre* to ERR] > ˈerrantly *adv*

errantry (ˈɛrəntrɪ) *n, pl* **-ries** the way of life of a knight errant

errata (ɪˈrɑːtə) *n* the plural of **erratum**

erratic (ɪˈrætɪk) *adj* **1** irregular in performance, behaviour, or attitude; inconsistent and unpredictable **2** having no fixed or regular course; wandering ▷ *n* **3** a piece of rock that differs in composition, shape, etc, from the rock surrounding it, having been transported from its place of origin, esp by glacial action **4** an erratic person or thing [c14 from Latin *errāticus*, from *errāre* to wander, ERR] > erˈratically *adv*

erratum (ɪˈrɑːtəm) *n, pl* **-ta** (-tə) **1** an error in writing or printing **2** another name for **corrigendum** [c16 from Latin: mistake, from *errāre* to ERR]

errhine (ˈɛraɪn, ˈɛrɪn) *medical obsolete* ▷ *adj* **1** causing nasal secretion ▷ *n* **2** an errhine drug or agent [c17 from Greek *errhinos*, from EN-² + *rhis* nose]

Er Rif (ɛə rɪf) *n* a mountainous region of N Morocco, near the Mediterranean coast

erroneous (ɪˈrəʊnɪəs) *adj* based on or containing error; mistaken; incorrect [c14 (in the sense: deviating from what is right), from Latin *errōneus*, from *errāre* to wander] > erˈroneously *adv* > erˈroneousness *n*

error (ˈɛrə) *n* **1** a mistake or inaccuracy, as in action or speech **2** an incorrect belief or wrong judgment **3** the condition of deviating from accuracy or correctness, as in belief, action, or speech **4** deviation from a moral standard; wrongdoing: *he saw the error of his ways* **5** *maths, statistics* a measure of the difference between some quantity and an approximation to or estimate of it, often expressed as a percentage: *an error of 5%* **6** *statistics* See **type I error, type II error** [c13 from Latin, from *errāre* to ERR] > ˈerror-ˌfree *adj*

error correction *n computing* the automatic correction of errors in data that arise from missing or distorted digital pulses

error message *n* a message displayed on a visual display unit, printout, etc, indicating that an incorrect instruction has been given to the computer

error of closure *n surveying* the amount by which a computed, plotted, or observed quantity or position differs from the true or established one, esp when plotting a closed traverse. Also called: **closing error**

ERS *abbreviation for* earnings related supplement

ersatz (ˈɛəzæts, ˈɜː-) *adj* **1** made in imitation of some natural or genuine product; artificial ▷ *n* **2** an ersatz substance or article [c20 German, from *ersetzen* to substitute]

Erse (ɜːs) *n* **1** another name for Irish **Gaelic** ▷ *adj* **2** of or relating to the Irish Gaelic language [c14 from Lowland Scots *Erisch* Irish; Irish being regarded as the literary form of Gaelic]

erst (ɜːst) *adv archaic* **1** long ago; formerly **2** at first [Old English *ǣrest* earliest, superlative of *ǣr* early; see ERE; related to Old High German *ērist*, Dutch *eerst*]

erstwhile (ˈɜːstˌwaɪl) *adj* **1** former; one-time: *my erstwhile companions* ▷ *adv* **2** *archaic* long ago; formerly

erubescence (ˌɛrʊˈbɛsᵊns) *n* the process of growing red or a condition of redness [c18 from Latin *ērubescentia* blushing, from *rubēscere* to grow red, from *ruber* red] > ˌeruˈbescent *adj*

erucic acid (ɪˈruːsɪk) *n* a crystalline fatty acid derived from the oils of rapeseed, mustard seed, and wallflower seed

eruct (ɪˈrʌkt) *or* **eructate** *vb* **1** to raise (gas and often a small quantity of acid) from the stomach; belch **2** (of a volcano) to pour out (fumes or volcanic matter) [c17 from Latin *ēructāre*, from *ructāre* to belch] > eructation (ˌiːrʌkˈteɪʃən, ˌiːrʌk-) *n* > eˈructative (ɪˈrʌktətɪv) *adj*

erudite (ˈɛrʊˌdaɪt) *adj* having or showing extensive scholarship; learned [c15 from Latin *ērudītus*, from *ērudīre* to polish, from EX-¹ + *rudis* unpolished, rough] > ˈeruˌditely *adv* > erudition (ˌɛrʊˈdɪʃən) *or* ˈeruˌditeness *n*

erumpent (ɪˈrʌmpənt) *adj* bursting out or (esp of plant parts) developing as though bursting through an overlying structure [c17 from Latin *ērumpere* to burst forth, from *rumpere* to burst]

erupt (ɪˈrʌpt) *vb* **1** to eject (steam, water, and volcanic material such as lava and ash) violently or (of volcanic material, etc) to be so ejected **2** (*intr*) (of a skin blemish) to appear on the skin; break out **3** (*intr*) (of a tooth) to emerge through the gum and become visible during the normal process of tooth development **4** (*intr*) to burst forth suddenly and violently, as from restraint: *to erupt in anger* [c17 from Latin *ēruptus* having burst forth, from *ērumpere*, from *rumpere* to burst] > eˈruptible *adj* > eˈruption *n*

eruptive (ɪˈrʌptɪv) *adj* **1** erupting or tending to erupt **2** resembling or of the nature of an eruption **3** (of rocks) formed from such products as ash and lava resulting from volcanic eruptions **4** (of a disease) characterized by skin eruptions > eˈruptively *adv* > eˌrupˈtivity *or* eˈruptiveness *n*

eruv (ˈɛərʊːv, ˈɛrʊːv) *n Judaism* an area, circumscribed by a symbolic line, within which certain activities forbidden to Orthodox Jews on the Sabbath are permitted [c20 from Hebrew, literally: mixture, mixing]

-ery *or* **-ry** *suffix forming nouns* **1** indicating a place of business or some other activity: *bakery; brewery; refinery* **2** indicating a class or collection of things: *cutlery; greenery* **3** indicating qualities or actions collectively: *snobbery; trickery* **4** indicating a practice or occupation: *husbandry* **5** indicating a state or condition: *slavery* [from Old French *-erie*; see -ER¹, -Y³]

Erymanthian boar (ˌɛrɪˈmænθɪən) *n Greek myth* a wild boar that ravaged the district around Mount Erymanthus: captured by Hercules as his fourth labour

Erymanthus (ˌɛrɪˈmænθəs) *n* **Mount** a mountain in SW Greece, in the NW Peloponnese. Height: 2224 m (7297 ft). Modern Greek name: Erímanthos (eˈrimanθɒs)

eryngium (ɪˈrɪndʒɪəm) *n* any plant of the temperate and subtropical perennial umbelliferous genus *Eryngium*, with distinctive spiny foliage, metallic blue flower heads, and bluish stems, several species of which are grown as garden plants. See also **sea holly** [New Latin, from Greek *ērynggion* a species of thistle]

eryngo (ɪˈrɪŋgəʊ) *n, pl* **-goes** or **-gos** any umbelliferous plant of the genus *Eryngium*, such as the sea holly, having toothed or lobed leaves. Also called: eringo [c16 from Latin *ēryngion* variety of thistle, from Greek *ērungion*, diminutive of *ērungos* thistle]

erysipelas (ˌɛrɪˈsɪpɪləs) *n* an acute streptococcal infectious disease of the skin, characterized by fever, headache, vomiting, and purplish raised lesions, esp on the face. Also called: Saint Anthony's fire [c16 from Latin, from Greek *erusipelas*, from Greek *erusi-* red + *-pelas* skin] > erysipelatous (ˌɛrɪsɪˈpɛlətəs) *adj*

erysipeloid (ˌɛrɪˈsɪpɪˌlɔɪd) *n* an infective dermatitis mainly affecting the hands, characterized by inflammation and caused by the microorganism *Erysipelothrix rhusiopathiae* on contaminated meat, poultry, or fish: most prevalent among fishermen and butchers

erythema (ˌɛrɪˈθiːmə) *n pathol* redness of the skin, usually occurring in patches, caused by irritation or injury to the tissue [c18 from New Latin, from Greek *eruthēma*, from *eruthros* red] > erythematic (ˌɛrɪθɪˈmætɪk), erythematous (ˌɛrɪˈθiːmətəs) *or* ˌeryˈthemal *adj*

erythraemia *or esp US* **erythremia** (ˌɛrɪˈθriːmɪə) *n med* another name for **polycythaemia vera** (see **polycythaemia**)

erythrism (ˈɛrɪθrɪzəm) *n* abnormal red coloration, as in plumage or hair > erythrismal (ˌɛrɪˈθrɪzməl) *adj*

erythrite (ɪˈrɪθraɪt) *n* **1** Also called: cobalt bloom a pink to purple secondary mineral consisting of hydrated cobalt arsenate in monoclinic crystalline form. Formula: $Co_3(AsO_4)_2.8H_2O$ **2** another name for **erythritol**

erythritol (ɪˈrɪθrɪˌtɒl) *or* **erythrite** *n* a sweet crystalline compound extracted from certain algae and lichens and used in medicine to dilate the blood vessels of the heart; 1,2,3,4-butanetetrol. Formula: $C_4H_{10}O_4$

erythro- *or* **erythr-** *combining form* red: *erythrocyte* [from Greek *eruthros* red]

erythroblast (ɪˈrɪθrəʊˌblæst) *n* a nucleated cell in bone marrow that develops into an erythrocyte > eˌrythroˈblastic *adj*

erythroblastosis (ɪˌrɪθrəʊblæˈstəʊsɪs) *n* **1** the abnormal presence of erythroblasts in the circulating blood **2** Also called: erythroblastosis fetalis an anaemic blood disease of a fetus or newborn child, characterized by erythroblasts in the circulating blood: caused by a blood incompatibility between mother and fetus

erythrocyte (ɪˈrɪθrəʊˌsaɪt) *n* a blood cell of vertebrates that transports oxygen and carbon dioxide, combined with the red pigment haemoglobin, to and from the tissues. Also called: red blood cell > erythrocytic (ɪˌrɪθrəʊˈsɪtɪk) *adj*

erythrocytometer (ɪˌrɪθrəʊsaɪˈtɒmɪtə) *n* an instrument for counting the number or measuring the size of red blood cells in a sample of blood > eˌrythrocyˈtometry *n*

erythromelalgia (ɪˌrɪθrəʊmɛlˈældʒə) *n* a condition resulting from excessive dilation of the blood vessels, usually affecting the extremities, which feel hot and painful

erythromycin (ɪˌrɪθrəʊˈmaɪsɪn) *n* an antibiotic used in treating certain infections, sometimes as an alternative to penicillin. It is obtained from the bacterium *Streptomyces erythreus*. Formula: $C_{37}M_{67}NO_{13}$ [c20 from ERYTHRO- + Greek *mukēs* fungus + -IN]

erythronium (ˌɛrɪˈθrəʊnɪəm) *n* any plant of the bulbous genus *Erythronium*, with decoratively mottled leaves and cyclamen-like yellow, rose, purple, or white flowers: family *Liliaceae*. See also **dogtooth violet** [New Latin, from Greek *erythros* red]

erythropenia (ɪˌrɪθrəʊˈpiːnɪə) *n* the presence of decreased numbers of erythrocytes in the blood, as occurs in some forms of anaemia. Also called: erythrocytopenia [from ERYTHRO- + Greek *penia* poverty]

e

erythropoiesis (ɪˌrɪθrəʊpɔɪˈiːsɪs) *n physiol* the formation of red blood cells [C19 from ERYTHRO- + Greek *poiēsis* a making, from *poiein* to make] > eˌrythropoiˈetic *adj*

erythropoietin (ɪˌrɪθrəʊpɔɪˈiːtɪn) *n* a hormone, secreted by the kidney in response to low levels of oxygen in the tissues, that increases the rate of erythropoiesis. It has been used as a performance-enhancing drug for athletes and racehorses. Abbreviation: EPO

erythropsia (ˌɛrɪˈθrɒpsɪə) *n med* a defect of vision in which objects appear red

Erzgebirge (German ˈeːrtsɡəbɪrɡə) *pl n* a mountain range on the border between Germany and the Czech Republic: formerly rich in mineral resources. Highest peak: Mount Klínovec (Keilberg), 1244 m (4081 ft). Czech name: Krušné Hory. Also called: Ore Mountains

Erzurum (ˈɛəzʊrʊm) *n* a city in E Turkey: a strategic centre; scene of two major battles against Russian forces (1877 and 1916); important military base and a closed city to unofficial visitors. Pop: 436 000 (2005 est)

es *the internet domain name for* Spain

Es *the chemical symbol for* einsteinium

ES *international car registration for* El Salvador

-es *suffix* **1** a variant of **-s**[1] for nouns ending in *ch, s, sh, z,* postconsonantal *y*, for some nouns ending in a vowel, and nouns in *f* with *v* in the plural: *ashes; heroes; calves* **2** a variant of **-s**[1] for verbs ending in *ch, s, sh, z,* postconsonantal *y*, or a vowel: *preaches; steadies; echoes*

ESA *abbreviation for* **1** Environmentally Sensitive Area: an area which contains a natural feature, such as the habitat of a rare species, and which is protected by government regulations **2** European Space Agency

Esaki diode (ɪˈsɑːkɪ) *n* another name for **tunnel diode** [named after L *Esaki* (born 1925), its Japanese designer]

Esau (ˈiːsɔː) *n Bible* son of Isaac and Rebecca and twin brother of Jacob, to whom he sold his birthright (Genesis 25)

ESB *abbreviation for* electrical stimulation of the brain

Esbjerg (Danish ˈɛsbjɛr) *n* a port in SW Denmark, in Jutland on the North Sea: Denmark's chief fishing port. Pop: 72 550 (2004 est)

escadrille (ˌɛskəˈdrɪl; French ɛskadrij) *n* **1** a French squadron of aircraft, esp in World War I **2** a small squadron of ships [from French: flotilla, from Spanish *escuadrilla*, from *escuadra* SQUADRON]

escalade (ˌɛskəˈleɪd) *n* **1** an assault by the use of ladders, esp on a fortification ▷ *vb* **2** to gain access to (a place) by the use of ladders [C16 from French, from Italian *scalata*, from *scalare* to mount, SCALE[3]] > ˌescaˈlader *n*

escalate (ˈɛskəˌleɪt) *vb* to increase or be increased in extent, intensity, or magnitude: *to escalate a war; prices escalated because of inflation* [C20 back formation from ESCALATOR] > ˌescaˈlation *n*

escalator (ˈɛskəˌleɪtə) *n* **1** a moving staircase consisting of stair treads fixed to a conveyor belt, for transporting passengers between levels, esp between the floors of a building **2** short for **escalator clause** [C20 originally a trademark]

escalator clause *n* a clause in a contract stipulating an adjustment in wages, prices, etc, in the event of specified changes in conditions, such as a large rise in the cost of living or price of raw materials

escallonia (ˌɛskəˈləʊnɪə) *n* any evergreen shrub of the South American saxifragaceous genus *Escallonia*, with white or red flowers: cultivated for ornament [C19 from *Escallon*, 18th-century Spanish traveller who discovered it]

escallop (ɛˈskɒləp, ɛˈskæl-) *n, vb* another word for **scallop**

escalope (ˈɛskəˌlɒp) *n* a thin slice of meat, usually veal, coated with egg and breadcrumbs, fried, and served with a rich sauce [C19 from Old French: shell]

escapade (ˈɛskəˌpeɪd, ˌɛskəˈpeɪd) *n* **1** a wild or exciting adventure, esp one that is mischievous or unlawful; scrape **2** any lighthearted or carefree episode; prank; romp [C17 from French, from Old Italian *scappata*, from Vulgar Latin *ex-cappāre* (unattested) to ESCAPE]

escape (ɪˈskeɪp) *vb* **1** to get away or break free from (confinements, captors, etc): *the lion escaped from the zoo* **2** to manage to avoid (imminent danger, punishment, evil, etc): *to escape death* **3** (*intr;* usually foll by *from*) (of gases, liquids, etc) to issue gradually, as from a crack or fissure; seep; leak: *water was escaping from the dam* **4** (*tr*) to elude; be forgotten by: *the actual figure escapes me* **5** (*tr*) to be articulated inadvertently or involuntarily: *a roar escaped his lips* **6** (*intr*) (of cultivated plants) to grow wild ▷ *n* **7** the act of escaping or state of having escaped **8** avoidance of injury, harm, etc: *a narrow escape* **9 a** a means or way of escape **b** (*as modifier*): *an escape route* **10** a means of distraction or relief, esp from reality or boredom: *angling provides an escape for many city dwellers* **11** a gradual outflow; leakage; seepage **12** Also called: **escape valve, escape cock** a valve that releases air, steam, etc, above a certain pressure; relief valve or safety valve **13** a plant that was originally cultivated but is now growing wild [C14 from Old Northern French *escaper*, from Vulgar Latin *excappāre* (unattested) to escape (literally: to remove one's cloak, hence free oneself), from EX-[1] + Late Latin *cappa* cloak] > esˈcapable *adj* > esˈcaper *n*

escape clause *n* a clause in a contract freeing one of the parties from his obligations in certain circumstances

escapee (ɪˌskeɪˈpiː) *n* a person who has escaped, esp an escaped prisoner

escape hatch *n* a means of escape in an emergency, esp from a submarine

escape mechanism *n psychol* any emotional or mental mechanism that enables a person to avoid acknowledging unpleasant or threatening realities. See also **escapism**

escapement (ɪˈskeɪpmənt) *n* **1** *horology* a mechanism consisting of an escape wheel and anchor, used in timepieces to provide periodic impulses to the pendulum or balance **2** any similar mechanism that regulates movement, usually consisting of toothed wheels engaged by rocking levers **3** (in a piano) the mechanism that allows the hammer to clear the string after striking, so that the string can vibrate **4** an overflow channel **5** *rare* an act or means of escaping

escape pipe *n* a pipe for overflowing water, escaping steam, etc

escape road *n* a road, usually ending in a pile of sand, provided on a hill for a driver to drive into if his brakes fail or on a bend if he loses control of the turn

escape routine *n computing* a means of leaving a computer-program sequence before its end, in order to commence another sequence

escape shaft *n* a shaft in a mine through which miners can escape if the regular shaft is blocked

escape velocity *n* the minimum velocity that a body must have in order to escape from the gravitational field of the earth or other celestial body

escape wheel *n horology* a toothed wheel that engages intermittently with a balance wheel or pendulum, causing the mechanism to oscillate and thereby moving the hands of a clock or watch. Also called: **scapewheel**

escapism (ɪˈskeɪpɪzəm) *n* an inclination to or habit of retreating from unpleasant or unacceptable reality, as through diversion or fantasy > esˈcapist *n, adj*

escapologist (ˌɛskəˈpɒlədʒɪst) *n* an entertainer who specializes in freeing himself or herself from confinement. Also called: escape artist > ˌescaˈpology *n*

escargot *French* (ɛskarɡo) *n* a variety of edible snail, usually eaten with a sauce made of melted butter and garlic

escarole (ˈɛskərəʊl) *n US and Canadian* a variety of endive with broad leaves, used in salads [C20 French from Italian *scar(i)ola*, from Latin *esca* food]

escarp (ɪˈskɑːp) *n* **1** *fortifications* the inner side of the ditch separating besiegers and besieged. Compare **counterscarp** ▷ *vb* **2** a rare word for **scarp** (sense 3) [C17 from French *escarpe*; see SCARP]

escarpment (ɪˈskɑːpmənt) *n* **1 a** the long continuous steep face of a ridge or plateau formed by erosion; scarp **b** any steep slope, such as one resulting from faulting **2** a steep artificial slope immediately in front of the rampart of a fortified place

Escaut (ɛsko) *n* the French name for the **Scheldt**

-escent *suffix forming adjectives* beginning to be, do, show, etc: *convalescent; luminescent* [via Old French from Latin *-ēscent-*, stem of present participial suffix of *-ēscere*, ending of inceptive verbs] > **-escence** *suffix forming nouns*

eschalot (ˌɛʃəˌlɒt, ˌɛʃəˈlɒt) *n* another name for **shallot** [C18 from Old French *eschalotte* a little SCALLION]

eschar (ˈɛskɑː) *n* a dry scab or slough, esp one following a burn or cauterization of the skin [C16 from Late Latin *eschara* scab, from Greek *eskhara* hearth, pan of hot coals (which could inflict burns); see SCAR[1]]

escharotic (ˌɛskəˈrɒtɪk) *med* ▷ *adj* **1** capable of producing an eschar ▷ *n* **2** a caustic or corrosive agent

eschatology (ˌɛskəˈtɒlədʒɪ) *n* the branch of theology or biblical exegesis concerned with the end of the world [C19 from Greek *eskhatos* last] > eschatological (ˌɛskətəˈlɒdʒɪk[ə]l) *adj* > ˌeschatoˈlogically *adv* > ˌeschaˈtologist *n*

escheat (ɪsˈtʃiːt) *law* ▷ *n* **1** (in England before 1926) the reversion of property to the Crown in the absence of legal heirs **2** (in feudal times) the reversion of property to the feudal lord in the absence of legal heirs or upon outlawry of the tenant **3** the property so reverting ▷ *vb* **4** to take (land) by escheat or (of land) to revert by escheat [C14 from Old French *eschete*, from *escheoir* to fall to the lot of, from Late Latin *excadere* (unattested), from Latin *cadere* to fall] > esˈcheatable *adj* > esˈcheatage *n*

Escher figure (ˈɛʃə) *n* another name for **impossible figure** [named after M C *Escher* (1898–1970), Dutch graphic artist who produced many such drawings]

Escherichia (ˌɛʃəˈrɪkɪə) *n* a genus of Gram-negative rodlike bacteria that are found in the intestines of humans and many animals, esp E. coli, which is sometimes pathogenic and is widely used in genetic research [C19 named after Theodor *Escherich* (1857–1911), German paediatrician who first described *E. coli*]

eschew (ɪsˈtʃuː) *vb* (*tr*) to keep clear of or abstain from (something disliked, injurious, etc); shun; avoid [C14 from Old French *eschiver*, of Germanic origin; compare Old High German *skiuhan* to frighten away; see SHY[1], SKEW] > esˈchewal *n* > esˈchewer *n*

eschscholtzia or **eschscholzia** (ɛˈʃɒltsɪə) *n* See **California poppy** [named after J F von *Eschscholtz* (1743–1831), German naturalist]

escolar (ˌɛskəˈlɑː) *n, pl* -lars or -lar any slender spiny-finned fish of the family *Gempylidae*, of warm and tropical seas: similar and closely related to the scombroid fishes. Also called: snake mackerel [from Spanish: SCHOLAR; so called from the rings round its eyes, suggestive of spectacles]

Escorial (ˌɛskɒrɪˈɑːl, ɛˈskɔːrɪəl) or **Escurial** *n* a village in central Spain, northwest of Madrid: site of an architectural complex containing a monastery, palace, and college, built by Philip II between 1563 and 1584

escort *n* (ˈɛskɔːt) **1** one or more persons, soldiers, vehicles, etc, accompanying another or others for protection, guidance, restraint, or as a mark of honour **2** a man or youth who accompanies a woman or girl: *he was her escort for the evening* **3 a** a person, esp a young woman, who may be hired to accompany another for entertainment, etc **b** (*as modifier*): *an escort agency* ▷ *vb* (ɪsˈkɔːt) **4** (*tr*) to accompany or attend as an escort [C16 from French *escorte*, from Italian *scorta*, from *scorgere* to guide, from Latin *corrigere* to straighten; see CORRECT]

escribe (ɪˈskraɪb) *vb* (*tr*) to draw (a circle) so that it is tangential to one side of a triangle and to the other two sides produced [C16 (meaning: to write out): from EX-¹ + Latin *scrībere* to write]

escritoire (ˌɛskrɪˈtwɑː) *n* a writing desk with compartments and drawers, concealed by a hinged flap, on a chest of drawers or plain stand [C18 from French, from Medieval Latin *scriptōrium* writing room in a monastery, from Latin *scrībere* to write]

escrow (ˈɛskrəʊ, ɛˈskrəʊ) *law* ▷ *n* **1** money, goods, or a written document, such as a contract bond, delivered to a third party and held by him pending fulfilment of some condition **2** the state or condition of being an escrow (esp in the phrase **in escrow**) ▷ *vb* (*tr*) **3** to place (money, a document, etc) in escrow [C16 from Old French *escroe*, of Germanic origin; see SCREED, SHRED, SCROLL]

escuage (ˈɛskjʊɪdʒ) *n* (in medieval Europe) another word for **scutage** [C16 from Old French, from *escu* shield, from Latin *scūtum*]

escudo (ɛˈskuːdəʊ; *Portuguese* ɪʃˈkuðu) *n*, *pl* -dos (-dəʊz; *Portuguese* -ðuʃ) **1** the standard monetary unit of Cape Verde, divided into 100 centavos **2** the former standard monetary unit of Portugal, divided into 100 centavos; replaced by the euro in 2002 **3** a former monetary unit of Chile, divided into 100 centesimos **4** an old Spanish silver coin worth 10 reals [C19 Spanish, literally: shield, from Latin *scūtum*]

esculent (ˈɛskjʊlənt) *n* **1** any edible substance ▷ *adj* **2** edible [C17 from Latin *ēsculentus* good to eat, from *ēsca* food, from *edere* to eat]

Escurial (ɛˌskjʊərɪˈɑːl, ɛˈskjʊərɪəl) *n* a variant of **Escorial**

escutcheon (ɪˈskʌtʃən) *n* **1** a shield, esp a heraldic one that displays a coat of arms **2** Also called: **escutcheon plate** a plate or shield that surrounds a keyhole, door handle, light switch, etc, esp an ornamental one protecting a door or wall surface **3** the place on the stern or transom of a vessel where the name is shown **4 blot on one's escutcheon** a stain on one's honour [C15 from Old Northern French *escuchon*, ultimately from Latin *scūtum* shield] > esˈcutcheoned *adj*

Esd. *Bible abbreviation for* Esdras

ESDA or **Esda** (ˈɛzdə) *n acronym for* Electrostatic Deposition Analysis: a technique used to check the sequence in which a statement written in police custody was made. The chronology of the statement is arrived at by the examination of indentations on subsequent pages

Esdraelon (ˌɛsdreɪˈiːlɒn) *n* a plain in N Israel, east of Mount Carmel. Also called: (Plain of) Jezreel

Esdras (ˈɛzdræs) *n* **1** either of two books of the Apocrypha, I and II Esdras called III and IV Esdras in the Douay Bible **2** either of two books of the Douay Bible Old Testament, I and II Esdras corresponding to the books of Ezra and Nehemiah in the Authorized Version

ESE *symbol for* east-southeast

-ese *suffix forming adjectives and nouns* indicating place of origin, language, or style: *Cantonese; Japanese; journalese*

esemplastic (ˌɛsɛmˈplæstɪk) *adj literature* making into one; unifying [C19 (first used by Samuel Taylor Coleridge): from Greek *es, eis* into + *em*, from *hen*, neuter of *heis* one + -PLASTIC]

eserine (ˈɛsəriːn, -rɪn) *n* another name for **physostigmine** [C19 *eser-*, of African origin + -INE²]

Eṣfahãn (ˌɛsfəˈhɑːn) *n* a variant of **Isfahan**

Esher (ˈiːʃə) *n* a town in SE England, in NE Surrey near London: racecourse. Pop: 25 172 (2001)

esker (ˈɛskə) or **eskar** (ˈɛskɑː, -kə) *n* a long winding ridge of gravel, sand, etc, originally deposited by a meltwater stream running under a glacier. Also called: **os** [C19 from Old Irish *escir* ridge]

Eskilstuna (*Swedish* ˈɛskilstuːna) *n* an industrial city in SE Sweden. Pop: 91 137 (2004 est)

Eskimo (ˈɛskɪˌməʊ) *n* **1** (*pl* -mos or -mo) a member of a group of peoples inhabiting N Canada, Greenland, Alaska, and E Siberia, having a material culture adapted to an extremely cold climate **2** the language of these peoples **3** a family of languages that includes Eskimo and Aleut ▷ *adj* **4** relating to, denoting, or characteristic of the Eskimos ▷ Former spelling: Esquimau See also **Inuit, Inuktitut** [C18 from Algonquian *Esquimawes*]

USAGE Eskimo is considered by many to be offensive, and in North America the term *Inuit* is usually preferred. *Inuit*, however, can be accurately applied only to those Aboriginal peoples inhabiting parts of Northern Canada, Alaska, and Greenland (as distinguished from those in Asia or the Aleutian Islands)

Eskimo dog *n* a large powerful breed of sled dog with a long thick coat and curled tail

Eskişehir (*Turkish* ɛsˈkiʃɛˌhir) *n* an industrial city in NW Turkey: founded around hot springs in Byzantine times. Pop: 519 000 (2005 est)

Esky (ˈɛskɪ) *n*, *pl* -kies (*sometimes not capital*) *Austral trademark* a portable insulated container for keeping food and drink cool [C20 from ESKIMO]

ESL *abbreviation for* English as a second language

ESN *abbreviation for* educationally subnormal; formerly used to designate a person of limited intelligence who needs special schooling

ESO *abbreviation for* European Southern Observatory

esophagus (iːˈsɒfəgəs) *n*, *pl* -gi (-ˌdʒaɪ) or -guses the US spelling of **oesophagus**. > esophageal (iːˌsɒfəˈdʒiːəl) *adj*

esoteric (ˌɛsəʊˈtɛrɪk) *adj* **1** restricted to or intended for an enlightened or initiated minority, esp because of abstruseness or obscurity: *an esoteric cult.* Compare **exoteric 2** difficult to understand; abstruse: *an esoteric statement* **3** not openly admitted; private: *esoteric aims* [C17 from Greek *esōterikos*, from *esōterō* inner] > ˌeso'terically *adv* > ˌeso'teri,cism *n*

esp *abbreviation for* especially

ESP *abbreviation for* **1 extrasensory perception 2** English for Specific (or Special) Purposes: the technique of teaching English to students who need it for a particular purpose, such as business dealings **3** electronic stability programme: an electronic system that automatically stabilizes a road vehicle that is being oversteered or is in danger of rolling over by selectively applying individual brakes

espadrille (ˌɛspəˈdrɪl) *n* a light shoe with a canvas upper, esp with a braided cord sole [C19 from French, from Provençal *espardilho*, diminutive of *espart* ESPARTO; so called from the use of esparto for the soles of such shoes]

espalier (ɪˈspæljə) *n* **1** an ornamental shrub or fruit tree that has been trained to grow flat, as against a wall **2** the trellis, framework, or arrangement of stakes on which such plants are trained **3** the method used to produce such plants ▷ *vb* **4** (*tr*) to train (a plant) on an espalier [C17 from French: trellis, from Old Italian: shoulder supports, from *spalla* shoulder, from Late Latin SPATULA]

España (esˈpaɲa) *n* the Spanish name for **Spain**

esparto or **esparto grass** (ɛˈspɑːtəʊ) *n*, *pl* -tos any of various grasses, esp *Stipa tenacissima* of S Europe and N Africa, that yield a fibre used to make ropes, mats, etc [C18 from Spanish, via Latin

from Greek *sparton* rope made of rushes, from *spartos* a kind of rush]

especial (ɪˈspɛʃəl) *adj* (*prenominal*) **1** unusual; notable; exceptional: *he paid especial attention to her that evening* **2** applying to one person or thing in particular; not general; specific; peculiar: *he had an especial dislike of relatives* [C14 from Old French, from Latin *speciālis* individual; see SPECIAL]

USAGE Especial and especially have a more limited use than special and specially. Special is always used in preference to especial when the sense is one of being out of the ordinary: *a special lesson; he has been specially trained.* Special is also used when something is referred to as being for a particular purpose: *the word was specially underlined for you.* Where an idea of pre-eminence or individuality is involved, either especial or special may be used: *he is my especial (or special) friend; he is especially (or specially) good at his job.* In informal English, however, special is usually preferred in all contexts

especially (ɪˈspɛʃəlɪ) *adv* **1** in particular; specifically: *for everyone's sake, especially your children's* **2** very much: *especially useful for vegans*

esperance (ˈɛspərəns) *n archaic* hope or expectation [C15 from Old French, from Vulgar Latin *sperantia* (unattested), from Latin *spērāre* to hope, from *spēs* hope]

Esperanto (ˌɛspəˈræntəʊ) *n* an international artificial language based on words common to the chief European languages, invented in 1887 [C19 literally: the one who hopes, pseudonym of Dr L L Zamenhof (1859–1917), Polish philologist who invented it] > ˌEspe'rantist *n, adj*

espial (ɪˈspaɪəl) *n archaic* **1** the act or fact of being seen or discovered **2** the act of noticing **3** the act of spying upon; secret observation

espionage (ˈɛspɪəˌnɑːʒ, ˌɛspɪəˈnɑːʒ, ˈɛspɪənɪdʒ) *n* **1** the systematic use of spies to obtain secret information, esp by governments to discover military or political secrets **2** the act or practice of spying [C18 from French *espionnage*, from *espionner* to spy, from *espion* spy, from Old Italian *spione*, of Germanic origin; compare German *spähen* to SPY]

Espírito Santo (*Portuguese* ɪʃˈpiritu ˈsɐ̃ntu) *n* a state of E Brazil, on the Atlantic: swampy coastal plain with mountains in the west; heavily forested. Capital: Vitória. Pop: 3 201 722 (2002). Area: 45 597 sq km (17 601 sq miles)

Espíritu Santo (esˈpiritu ˈsæntəʊ) *n* an island in the SW Pacific: the largest and westernmost of the Vanuatu islands. Pop: 25 581 (latest est). Area: 4856 sq km (1875 sq miles)

esplanade (ˌɛspləˈneɪd, -ˈnɑːd) *n* **1** a long open level stretch of ground for walking along, esp beside the seashore. Compare **promenade** (sense 1) **2** an open area in front of a fortified place, in which attackers are exposed to the defenders' fire [C17 from French, from Old Italian *spianata*, from *spianare* to make level, from Latin *explānāre*; see EXPLAIN]

Espoo (*Finnish* ˈespoː) *n* a city in S Finland. Pop: 224 231 (2003 est)

espousal (ɪˈspaʊzᵊl) *n* **1** adoption or support: *an espousal of new beliefs* **2** (*sometimes plural*) *archaic* a marriage or betrothal ceremony

espouse (ɪˈspaʊz) *vb* (*tr*) **1** to adopt or give support to (a cause, ideal, etc): *to espouse socialism* **2** *archaic* (esp of a man) to take as spouse; marry [C15 from Old French *espouser*, from Latin *spōnsāre* to affiance, *espouse*] > es'pouser *n*

espressivo (ˌɛsprɛˈsiːvəʊ) *adj, adv music* (to be performed) in an expressive manner [Italian]

espresso (ɛˈspresəʊ) *n, pl* -sos **1** strong coffee made by forcing steam or boiling water through ground coffee beans **2** an apparatus for making coffee in this way [C20 Italian, short for *caffè espresso*, literally: pressed coffee]

e

esprit (ɛ'spriː) *n* spirit and liveliness, esp in wit [c16 from French, from Latin *spīritus* a breathing, SPIRIT¹]

esprit de corps (ɛ'spriː də 'kɔː; *French* ɛspri də kɔr) *n* consciousness of and pride in belonging to a particular group; the sense of shared purpose and fellowship

espy (ɪ'spaɪ) *vb* **-pies, -pying, -pied** (*tr*) to catch sight of or perceive (something distant or previously unnoticed); detect: *to espy a ship on the horizon* [c14 from Old French *espier* to SPY, of Germanic origin] > **es'pier** *n*

Esq. *abbreviation for* esquire: used esp in correspondence

-esque *suffix forming adjectives* indicating a specified character, manner, style, or resemblance: *picturesque; Romanesque; statuesque; Chaplinesque* [via French from Italian *-esco*, of Germanic origin; compare -ISH]

Esquiline ('ɛskwə,laɪn) *n* one of the seven hills on which ancient Rome was built

Esquimau ('ɛskɪ,məʊ) *n, pl* **-maus** or **-mau**, *adj* a former spelling of **Eskimo**

esquire (ɪ'skwaɪə) *n* **1** *chiefly Brit* a title of respect, usually abbreviated *Esq.*, placed after a man's name **2** (in medieval times) the attendant and shield bearer of a knight, subsequently often knighted himself **3** *rare* a male escort [c15 from Old French *escuier*, from Late Latin *scūtārius* shield bearer, from Latin *scūtum* shield]

ESR *abbreviation for* **1 electron spin resonance 2** erythrocyte sedimentation rate: the rate at which red blood cells settle in a vertical tube, used to detect the presence of disease

ESRC *abbreviation for* Economic and Social Research Council

ESRO ('ɛzrəʊ) *n acronym for* European Space Research Organization

-ess *suffix forming nouns* indicating a female: *waitress; lioness* [via Old French from Late Latin *-issa*, from Greek]

USAGE The suffix *-ess* in such words as *poetess, authoress* is now often regarded as disparaging; a sexually neutral term *poet, author* is preferred

Essaouira (,ɛsɑ'wɪərə) *n* a port in SW Morocco on the Atlantic. Pop: 84 000 (2003). Former name (until 1956): **Mogador**

essay *n* ('ɛseɪ; *for senses* 2,3 *also* ɛ'seɪ) **1** a short literary composition dealing with a subject analytically or speculatively **2** an attempt or endeavour; effort **3** a test or trial ▷ *vb* (ɛ'seɪ) (*tr*) **4** to attempt or endeavour; try **5** to test or try out [c15 from Old French *essaier* to attempt, from *essai* an attempt, from Late Latin *exagium* a weighing, from Latin *agere* to do, compel, influenced by *exigere* to investigate]

essayist ('ɛseɪɪst) *n* a person who writes essays

esse ('ɛsɪ) *n philosophy* **1** existence **2** essential nature; essence [c17 from Latin: to be]

Essen (*German* 'ɛsən) *n* a city in W Germany, in North Rhine-Westphalia: the leading administrative centre of the Ruhr; university. Pop: 589 499 (2003 est)

essence ('ɛsəns) *n* **1** the characteristic or intrinsic feature of a thing, which determines its identity; fundamental nature **2** the most distinctive element of a thing: *the essence of a problem* **3** a perfect or complete form of something, esp a person who typifies an abstract quality: *he was the essence of gentility* **4** *philosophy* **a** the unchanging and unchangeable nature of something which is necessary to its being the thing it is; its necessary properties. Compare **accident** (sense 4) **b** the properties in virtue of which something is called by its name **c** the nature of something as distinct from, and logically prior to, its existence **5** *theol* an immaterial or spiritual entity **6 a** the constituent of a plant, usually an oil, alkaloid, or glycoside, that determines its chemical or pharmacological properties **b** an alcoholic solution of such a substance **7** a substance,

usually a liquid, containing the properties of a plant or foodstuff in concentrated form: *vanilla essence* **8** a rare word for **perfume 9** in essence essentially; fundamentally **10** of the essence indispensable; vitally important [c14 from Medieval Latin *essentia*, from Latin: the being (of something), from *esse* to be]

Essene ('ɛsiːn, ɛ'siːn) *n Judaism* a member of an ascetic sect that flourished in Palestine from the second century BC to the second century AD, living in strictly organized communities > **Essenian** (ɛ'siːnɪən) *or* **Essenic** (ɛ'sɛnɪk) *adj*

essential (ɪ'sɛnʃəl) *adj* **1** vitally important; absolutely necessary **2** basic; fundamental: *the essential feature* **3** completely realized; absolute; perfect: *essential beauty* **4** *biochem* (of an amino acid or a fatty acid) necessary for the normal growth of an organism but not synthesized by the organism and therefore required in the diet **5** derived from or relating to an extract of a plant, drug, etc: *an essential oil* **6** *logic* (of a property) guaranteed by the identity of the subject; necessary. Thus, if having the atomic number 79 is an essential property of gold, nothing can be gold unless it has that atomic number **7** *music* denoting or relating to a note that belongs to the fundamental harmony of a chord or piece **8** *pathol* (of a disease) having no obvious external cause: *essential hypertension* **9** *geology* (of a mineral constituent of a rock) necessary for defining the classification of a rock. Its absence alters the rock's name and classification ▷ *n* **10** something fundamental or indispensable: *a sharp eye is an essential for a printer* **11** *music* an essential note > **essentiality** (ɪ,sɛnʃɪ'ælɪtɪ) *or* **es'sentialness** *n*

essential element *n biochem* any chemical element required by an organism for healthy growth. It may be required in large amounts (see **macronutrient**) or in very small amounts (see **trace element**)

essential fatty acid *n biochem* any fatty acid required by the body in manufacturing prostaglandins, found in such foods as oily fish and nuts. Abbreviation: **EFA**

essentialism (ɪ'sɛnʃə,lɪzəm) *n* **1** *philosophy* one of a number of related doctrines which hold that there are necessary properties of things, that these are logically prior to the existence of the individuals which instantiate them, and that their classification depends upon their satisfaction of sets of necessary conditions **2** the doctrine that education should concentrate on teaching basic skills and encouraging intellectual self-discipline > **es'sentialist** *n*

essentially (ɪ'sɛnʃəlɪ) *adv* in a fundamental or basic way; in essence

essential oil *n* any of various volatile organic oils present in plants, usually containing terpenes and esters and having the odour or flavour of the plant from which they are extracted: used in flavouring and perfumery. Compare **fixed oil** See also **oleoresin**

Essequibo (,ɛsɪ'kwiːbəʊ) *n* a river in Guyana, rising near the Brazilian border and flowing north to the Atlantic: drains over half of Guyana. Length: 1014 km (630 miles)

Essex ('ɛsɪks) *n* **1** a county of SE England, on the North Sea and the Thames estuary; the geographical and ceremonial county includes Thurrock and Southend-on-Sea, which became independent unitary authorities in 1998. Administrative centre: Chelmsford. Pop (excluding unitary authorities): 1 324 100 (2003 est). Area (excluding unitary authorities): 3446 sq km (1310 sq miles) **2** an Anglo-Saxon kingdom that in the early 7th century AD comprised the modern county of Essex and much of Hertfordshire and Surrey. By the late 8th century, Essex had become a dependency of the kingdom of Mercia

Essex girl *n informal derogatory* a young working-class woman from the Essex area, typically

considered as being unintelligent, materialistic, devoid of taste, and sexually promiscuous

Essex Man *n informal derogatory* a working man, typically a Londoner who has moved out to Essex, who flaunts his new-found success and status

Esslingen ('ɛs,lɪŋən) *n* a town in SW Germany, on the River Neckar: Gothic church, medieval buildings. Pop: 91 980 (2003 est)

essonite ('ɛsə,naɪt) *n* a variant spelling of **hessonite**

Essonne (*French* ɛsɔn) *n* a department of N France, south of Paris in Île-de-France region: formed in 1964. Capital: Évry. Pop: 1 153 434 (2003 est). Area: 1811 sq km (706 sq miles)

est¹ (ɛst) *n* a treatment intended to help people towards psychological growth, in which they spend many hours in large groups, deprived of food and water and hectored by stewards [Erhard Seminars Training; after Werner Erhard, American businessman, who devised the system]

est² *abbreviation for* **1** Also: **estab** established **2** estimate(d)

EST *abbreviation for* **1 Eastern Standard Time 2** electric-shock treatment **3** *international car registration for* Estonia

-est¹ *suffix* forming the superlative degree of adjectives and adverbs: *shortest; fastest* [Old English *-est, -ost*]

-est² *or* **-st** *suffix* forming the archaic second person singular present and past indicative tense of verbs: *thou goest; thou hadst* [Old English *-est, -ast*]

establish (ɪ'stæblɪʃ) *vb* (*usually tr*) **1** to make secure or permanent in a certain place, condition, job, etc: *to establish one's usefulness; to establish a house* **2** to create or set up (an organization, etc) on or as if on a permanent basis: *to establish a company* **3** to prove correct or free from doubt; validate: *to establish a fact* **4** to cause (a principle, theory, etc) to be widely or permanently accepted: *to establish a precedent* **5** to give (a Church) the status of a national institution **6** (of a person) to become recognized and accepted: *he established himself as a reliable GP* **7** (in works of imagination) to cause (a character, place, etc) to be credible and recognized: *the first scene established the period* **8** *cards* to make winners of (the remaining cards of a suit) by forcing out opponents' top cards **9** *botany* (*also intr*) **a** to cause (a plant) to grow or (of a plant) to grow in a new place: *the birch scrub has established over the past 25 years* **b** to become or cause to become a sapling or adult plant from a seedling [c14 from Old French *establir*, from Latin *stabilīre* to make firm, from *stabilis* STABLE²] > **es'tablisher** *n*

Established Church *n* a Church that is officially recognized as a national institution, esp the Church of England

establishment (ɪ'stæblɪʃmənt) *n* **1** the act of establishing or state of being established **2 a** a business organization or other large institution **b** the place where a business is carried on **3** the staff and equipment of a commercial or other organization **4** the approved size, composition, and equipment of a military unit, government department, business division, etc, as formally promulgated **5** any large organization, institution, or system **6** a household or place of residence **7** a body of employees or servants **8** (*modifier*) belonging to or characteristic of the Establishment; orthodox or conservative: *the establishment view of history*

Establishment (ɪ'stæblɪʃmənt) *n* **the** a group or class of people having institutional authority within a society, esp those who control the civil service, the government, the armed forces, and the Church: usually identified with a conservative outlook

establishmentarian (ɪ,stæblɪʃmən'tɛərɪən) *adj* **1** denoting or relating to an Established Church, esp the Church of England **2** denoting or relating to the principle of a Church being officially recognized as a national institution ▷ *n* **3** an upholder of this principle, esp as applied to the

Church of England > es̩tablishmen'tarianism *n*

estaminet French (ɛstamine) *n* a small café, bar, or bistro, esp a shabby one [c19 from French, perhaps from Walloon dialect *staminet* manger]

estancia (ɪ'stænsɪə; *Spanish* es'tansia) *n* (in Spanish America) a large estate or cattle ranch [c18 from American Spanish, from Spanish: dwelling, from Vulgar Latin *stantia* (unattested) a remaining, from Latin *stāre* to stand]

estate (ɪ'steɪt) *n* **1** a large piece of landed property, esp in the country **2** *chiefly Brit* a large area of property development, esp of new houses or (**trading estate**) of factories **3** *property law* **a** property or possessions **b** the nature of interest that a person has in land or other property, esp in relation to the right of others **c** the total extent of the real and personal property of a deceased person or bankrupt **4** Also called: **estate of the realm** an order or class of persons in a political community, regarded collectively as a part of the body politic: usually regarded as being the lords temporal (peers), lords spiritual, and commons. See also **States General, fourth estate** **5** state, period, or position in life, esp with regard to wealth or social standing: *youth's estate; a poor man's estate* [c13 from Old French *estat*, from Latin *status* condition, STATE]

estate agent *n* **1** *Brit* an agent concerned with the valuation, management, lease, and sale of property. Usual US and Canadian name: **real-estate agent** **2** the administrator of a large landed property, acting on behalf of its owner; estate manager

estate car *n* *Brit* a car with a comparatively long body containing a large carrying space, reached through a rear door: usually the back seats can be folded forward to increase the carrying space. Also called (esp US, Canadian, Austral, and NZ): **station wagon**

estate duty *n* another name for **death duty**

Estates General *n* See **States General**

esteem (ɪ'sti:m) *vb* (tr) **1** to have great respect or high regard for: *to esteem a colleague* **2** *formal* to judge or consider; deem: *to esteem an idea improper* ▷ *n* **3** high regard or respect; good opinion **4** *archaic* judgment; opinion [c15 from Old French *estimer*, from Latin *aestimāre* ESTIMATE] > **es'teemed** *adj*

ester ('ɛstə) *n* *chem* any of a class of compounds produced by reaction between acids and alcohols with the elimination of water. Esters with low molecular weights, such as ethyl acetate, are usually volatile fragrant liquids; fats are solid esters [c19 from German, probably a contraction of *Essigäther* acetic ether, from *Essig* vinegar (ultimately from Latin *acētum*) + *Äther* ETHER]

esterase ('ɛstə̩reɪs, -̩reɪz) *n* any of a group of enzymes that hydrolyse esters into alcohols and acids

esterify (ɛ'stɛrə̩faɪ) *vb* -**fies**, -**fying**, -**fied** *chem* to change or cause to change into an ester > es̩terifi'cation *n*

Esth. *Bible abbreviation for* Esther

Esther ('ɛstə) *n Old Testament* **1** a beautiful Jewish woman who became queen of Persia and saved her people from massacre **2** the book in which this episode is recounted

esthesia (i:s'θi:zɪə) *n* a US spelling of **aesthesia**

esthete ('i:sθi:t) *n* a US spelling of **aesthete** > **esthetic** (ɛs'θɛtɪk) or **es'thetical** *adj* > **es'thetically** *adv* > **esthetician** (̩i:sθɪ'tɪʃən) *n* > **es'theti̩cism** *n* > **es'thetics** *n*

Esthonia (ɛs'stəʊnɪə, ɛ'stəʊ-) *n* See **Estonia**

estimable ('ɛstɪməbᵊl) *adj* worthy of respect; deserving of admiration: *my estimable companion* > 'estimableness *n* > 'estimably *adv*

estimate *vb* ('ɛstɪ̩meɪt) **1** to form an approximate idea of (distance, size, cost, etc); calculate roughly; gauge **2** (tr; may take a clause as object) to form an opinion about; judge: *to estimate one's chances* **3** to submit (an approximate price) for (a job) to a prospective client **4** (tr) *statistics* to assign

---

a value (a **point estimate**) or range of values (an **interval estimate**) to a parameter of a population on the basis of sampling statistics. See **estimator** ▷ *n* ('ɛstɪmɪt) **5** an approximate calculation **6** a statement indicating the likely charge for or cost of certain work **7** a judgment; appraisal; opinion [c16 from Latin *aestimāre* to assess the worth of, of obscure origin] > 'estimative *adj*

estimation (̩ɛstɪ'meɪʃən) *n* **1** a considered opinion; judgment: *what is your estimation of the situation?* **2** esteem; respect **3** the act of estimating

estimator ('ɛstɪ̩meɪtə) *n* **1** a person or thing that estimates **2** *statistics* a derived random variable that generates estimates of a parameter of a given distribution, such as $\bar{X}$, the mean of a number of identically distributed random variables X_i. If $\bar{X}$ is unbiased, $\bar{x}$, the observed value should be close to $E(X_i)$. See also **sampling statistic**

estipulate (ɪ'stɪpjʊlɪt, -̩leɪt) *adj* a variant of **exstipulate**

estival (i:'staɪvᵊl, 'ɛstɪ-) *adj* the usual US spelling of **aestival**

estivate ('i:stɪ̩veɪt, 'ɛs-) *vb* (intr) the usual US spelling of **aestivate**. > 'esti̩vator *n*

estivation (̩i:stɪ'veɪʃən, ̩ɛs-) *n* the usual US spelling of **aestivation**

Estonia (ɛ'stəʊnɪə) or **Esthonia** (ɛ'stəʊnɪə, ɛ'stəʊ-) *n* a republic in NE Europe, on the Gulf of Finland and the Baltic: low-lying with many lakes and forests, it includes numerous islands in the Baltic Sea. It was under Scandinavian and Teutonic rule from the 13th century to 1721, when it passed to Russia: it was an independent republic from 1920 to 1940, when it was annexed by the Soviet Union; became independent in 1991 and joined the EU in 2004. Official language: Estonian. Religion: believers are mostly Christian. Currency: kroon. Capital: Tallinn. Pop: 1 308 000 (2004 est). Area: 45 227 sq km (17 462 sq miles)

Estonian (ɛ'stəʊnɪən) or **Esthonian** (ɛ'stəʊnɪən, ɛ'stəʊ-) *adj* **1** of, relating to, or characteristic of Estonia, its people, or their language ▷ *n* **2** the official language of Estonia: belongs to the Finno-Ugric family **3** a native or inhabitant of Estonia

estop (ɪ'stɒp) *vb* -**tops**, -**topping**, -**topped** (tr) *law* to preclude by estoppel **2** *archaic* to stop [c15 from Old French *estoper* to plug, ultimately from Latin *stuppa* tow; see STOP] > es'toppage *n*

estoppel (ɪ'stɒpᵊl) *n law* a rule of evidence whereby a person is precluded from denying the truth of a statement of facts he has previously asserted. See also **conclusion** [c16 from Old French *estoupail* plug, from *estoper* to stop up; see ESTOP]

Estoril ('ɛʃtɔ:̩ri:l) *n* a resort in W Portugal, near Lisbon, on the Atlantic Ocean: noted esp for a famous avenue of palm trees leading to the seafront. Pop: 24 850 (1991)

estovers (ɛ'stəʊvəz) *pl n law* a right allowed by law to tenants of land to cut timber, esp for fuel and repairs [c15 from Anglo-French, plural of *estover*, *n* use of Old French *estovoir* to be necessary, from Latin *est opus* there is need]

estrade (ɪs'trɑ:d) *n* a dais or raised platform [c17 from French, from Spanish *estrado* carpeted floor, from Latin: STRATUM]

estradiol (̩ɛstrə'daɪɒl, ̩i:strə-) *n* the US spelling of **oestradiol**

estragon ('ɛstrə̩gɒn) *n* another name for **tarragon**

estrange (ɪ'streɪndʒ) *vb* (tr) **1** (usually passive; often foll by *from*) to separate and live apart from (one's spouse): *he is estranged from his wife* **2** (usually passive; often foll by *from*) to antagonize or lose the affection of (someone previously friendly); alienate [c15 from Old French *estranger*, from Late Latin *extrāneāre* to treat as a stranger, from Latin *extrāneus* foreign; see STRANGE] > es'trangement *n*

estranged (ɪ'streɪndʒd) *adj* **1** separated and living apart from one's spouse **2** no longer friendly; alienated

estray (ɪ'streɪ) *n law* a stray domestic animal of

---

unknown ownership [c16 from Anglo-French, from Old French *estraier* to STRAY]

estreat (ɪ'stri:t) *law* ▷ *n* **1** a true copy of or extract from a court record **2** to enforce (a recognizance that has been forfeited) by sending an extract of the court record to the proper authority [c14 from Old French *estraite*, feminine of *estrait* extracted, from *estraire* to EXTRACT]

Estrela mountain dog (ɪs'trɛlə) *n* a sturdy well-built dog of a Portuguese breed with a long thick coat and a thick tuft of hair round the neck, often used as a guard dog [c20 after the Estrela mountain range in Portugal]

Estremadura (*Portuguese* ɪʃtrəmə'ðurə) *n* a region of W Spain: arid and sparsely populated except in the valleys of the Tagus and Guardiana rivers. Area: 41 593 sq km (16 059 sq miles). Spanish name: Extremadura

estrin ('ɛstrɪn, 'i:strɪn) *n* the US spelling of **oestrin**

estriol ('ɛstrɪ̩ɒl, 'i:strɪ-) *n* the usual US spelling of **oestriol**

estrogen ('ɛstrədʒən, 'i:strə-) *n* the usual US spelling of **oestrogen**. > estrogenic (̩ɛstrə'dʒɛnɪk, ̩i:strə-) *adj* > ̩estro'genically *adv*

estrone ('ɛstrəʊn, 'i:strəʊn) *n* the usual US spelling of **oestrone**

estrus ('ɛstrəs, 'i:strəs) *n* the usual US spelling of **oestrus**. > 'estrous *adj*

estuarine ('ɛstjʊə̩raɪn, -rɪn) *adj* **1** formed or deposited in an estuary: *estuarine muds* **2** growing in, inhabiting, or found in an estuary: *an estuarine fauna*

estuary ('ɛstjʊərɪ) *n*, *pl* -**aries** **1** the widening channel of a river where it nears the sea, with a mixing of fresh water and salt (tidal) water **2** an inlet of the sea [c16 from Latin *aestuārium* marsh, channel, from *aestus* tide, billowing movement, related to *aestās* summer] > estuarial (̩ɛstjʊ'ɛərɪəl) *adj*

estuary English *n* a variety of standard British English in which the pronunciation reflects various features characteristic of London and the Southeast of England [c20 from the area around the Thames ESTUARY where it originated]

e.s.u. or **ESU** abbreviation for electrostatic unit

esurient (ɪ'sjʊərɪənt) *adj* greedy; voracious [c17 from Latin *ēsurīre* to be hungry, from *edere* to eat] > e'surience or e'suriency *n* > e'suriently *adv*

E. Sussex abbreviation for East Sussex

et the internet domain name for Ethiopia

Et the chemical symbol for ethyl

ET **1** abbreviation for Employment Training: a government scheme offering training in technological and business skills to unemployed people **2** international car registration for Egypt

-et suffix of nouns small or lesser: *islet; baronet* [from Old French *-et, -ete*]

eta[1] ('i:tə) *n* the seventh letter in the Greek alphabet (H, η), a long vowel sound, transliterated as *e* or *ē* [Greek, of Phoenician origin; compare Hebrew HETH]

eta[2] ('eɪtə) *n*, *pl* **eta** or **etas** (in Japan, formerly) a member of a class of outcasts who did menial and dirty tasks [c19 Japanese]

ETA[1] abbreviation for estimated time of arrival

ETA[2] ('ɛtə) *n* acronym for Euzkadi ta Askatsuna: an organization of militant Basque nationalists attempting to gain independence for the Basques, esp those ruled by Spain, until a cease-fire in 1998, by means of guerrilla warfare [Basque, literally: Basque Nation and Liberty]

etaerio (ɛ'tɪərɪəʊ) *n* an aggregate fruit, as one consisting of drupes (raspberry) or achenes (traveller's joy) [c19 from French *etairion*, from Greek *hetaireia* association]

étagère French (etaʒɛr) *n* a stand with open shelves for displaying ornaments, etc [c19 from French, from *étage* shelf; see STAGE]

e-tail ('i:teɪl) or **e-tailing** ('i:teɪlɪŋ) *n* retail conducted via the internet [c20 E-² + (RE)TAIL] > e-tailer *n*

et al. abbreviation for **1** et alibi [Latin: and

elsewhere] **2** et alii [Latin: and others]

etalon (ˈɛtəˌlɒn) *n physics* a device used in spectroscopy to measure wavelengths by interference effects produced by multiple reflections between parallel half-silvered glass or quartz plates [c20 French *étalon* a fixed standard of weights and measures, from Old French *estalon*; see STALLION]

etamine (ˈɛtəˌmiːn) or **etamin** (ˈɛtəmɪn) *n* a cotton or worsted fabric of loose weave, used for clothing, curtains, etc [c18 from French, from Latin *stāminea*, from *stāmineus* made of threads, from *stamen* thread, warp]

etc *abbreviation for* et cetera

et cetera or **etcetera** (ɪtˈsɛtrə) **1** and the rest; and others; and so forth: used at the end of a list to indicate that other items of the same class or type should be considered or included **2** the like; or something else similar. Abbreviations: etc, &c See also **etceteras** [from Latin, from *et* and + *cetera* the other (things)]

> USAGE It is unnecessary to use *and* before *etc* as *etc* (*et cetera*) already means *and other things*. The repetition of *etc*, as in *he brought paper, ink, notebooks, etc, etc*, is avoided except in informal contexts

etceteras (ɪtˈsɛtrəz) *pl n* miscellaneous extra things or persons

etch (ɛtʃ) *vb* **1** (*tr*) to wear away the surface of (a metal, glass, etc) by chemical action, esp the action of an acid **2** to cut or corrode (a design, decoration, etc) on (a metal or other plate to be used for printing) by using the action of acid on parts not covered by wax or other acid-resistant coating **3** (*tr*) to cut with or as if with a sharp implement: *he etched his name on the table* **4** (*tr; usually passive*) to imprint vividly: *the event was etched on her memory* [c17 from Dutch *etsen*, from Old High German *azzen* to feed, bite] > **etcher** *n*

etchant (ˈɛtʃənt) *n* any acid or corrosive used for etching

etching (ˈɛtʃɪŋ) *n* **1** the art, act, or process of preparing etched surfaces or of printing designs from them **2** an etched plate **3** an impression made from an etched plate

ETD *abbreviation for* estimated time of departure

Eteocles (ɪˈtiːəˌkliːz, ˈɛtɪə-) *n Greek myth* a son of Oedipus and Jocasta. He expelled his brother Polynices from Thebes; they killed each other in single combat when Polynices returned as leader of the Seven against Thebes

eternal (ɪˈtɜːnəl) *adj* **1 a** without beginning or end; lasting for ever: *eternal life* **b** (*as noun*): *the eternal* **2** (*often capital*) denoting or relating to that which is without beginning and end, regarded as an attribute of God **3** unchanged by time, esp being true or valid for all time; immutable: *eternal truths* **4** seemingly unceasing; occurring again and again: *eternal bickering* [c14 from Late Latin *aeternālis*, from Latin *aeternus*; related to Latin *aevum* age] > ˌeterˈnality or eˈternalness *n* > eˈternally *adv*

Eternal City *n* the Rome

eternalize (ɪˈtɜːnəˌlaɪz), **eternize** (ɪˈtɜːnaɪz) or **eternalise, eternise** *vb* (*tr*) **1** to make eternal **2** to make famous for ever; immortalize > eˌternaliˈzation, eˌterniˈzation, eˌternaliˈsation or eˌterniˈsation *n*

eternal triangle *n* an emotional relationship in which there are conflicts involving a man and two women or a woman and two men

eterne (ɪˈtɜːn) *adj* an archaic or poetic word for **eternal** [c14 from Old French, from Latin *aeternus*]

eternity (ɪˈtɜːnɪtɪ) *n, pl* **-ties 1** endless or infinite time **2** the quality, state, or condition of being eternal **3** (*usually plural*) any of the aspects of life and thought that are considered to be timeless, esp timeless and true **4** *theol* the condition of timeless existence, believed by some to characterize the afterlife **5** a seemingly endless period of time: *an eternity of waiting*

eternity ring *n* a ring given as a token of lasting

affection, esp one set all around with stones to symbolize continuity

etesian (ɪˈtiːʒɪən) *adj* (of NW winds) recurring annually in the summer in the E Mediterranean [c17 from Latin *etēsius* yearly, from Greek *etēsios*, from *etos* year]

ETF *abbreviation for* **electronic transfer of funds**

eth (ɛð, ɛθ) *n* a variant of **edh**

ETH *international car registration for* Ethiopia

Eth. *abbreviation for* Ethiopia(n)

-eth[1] *suffix* forming the archaic third person singular present indicative tense of verbs: *goeth; taketh* [Old English *-eth, -th*]

-eth[2] or **-th** *suffix forming ordinal numbers* a variant of **-th**[2]: *twentieth*

ethambutol (ɛˈθæmbjʊˌtɒl) *n* a compound used in the treatment of tuberculosis [from ETH(YLENE) + AM(INE) + BUT(AN)OL]

ethanal (ˈɛθəˌnæl, ˈiːθə-) *n* the modern name for **acetaldehyde**

ethane (ˈiːθeɪn, ˈɛθ-) *n* a colourless odourless flammable gaseous alkane obtained from natural gas and petroleum: used as a fuel and in the manufacture of organic chemicals. Formula: C_2H_6 [c19 from ETH(YL) + -ANE]

ethanedioic acid (ˌiːθeɪndaɪˈɒɪk, ˌɛθ-) *n* the technical name for **oxalic acid** [c20 from ETHANE + DI-[1] + -O- + -IC]

ethanediol (ˈiːθeɪnˌdaɪɒl, ˈɛθ-) *n* a clear colourless syrupy soluble liquid substance, used as an antifreeze and solvent. Formula: CH_2OHCH_2OH. Also called: **glycol, ethylene glycol** [c20 from ETHANE + DI-[1] + -OL[1]]

ethanoic acid (ˌɛθəˈnəʊɪk, ˌiːθə-) *n* the modern name for **acetic acid**

ethanol (ˈɛθəˌnɒl, ˈiːθə-) *n* the technical name for **alcohol** (sense 1)

ethanoyl (ˈɛθəˌnɔɪl) *n* (*modifier*) of, consisting of, or containing the monovalent group CH_3CO-: *ethanoyl group or radical* [c20 from ETH(YL) + -OYL]

ethanoyl chloride *n* another name for **acetyl chloride**

ethene (ˈɛθiːn) *n* the technical name for **ethylene**

ether (ˈiːθə) *n* **1** Also called: **diethyl ether, ethyl ether, ethoxyethane** a colourless volatile highly flammable liquid with a characteristic sweetish odour, made by the reaction of sulphuric acid with ethanol: used as a solvent and anaesthetic. Formula: $C_2H_5OC_2H_5$ **2** any of a class of organic compounds with the general formula ROR′ where R and R′ are alkyl groups, as in diethyl ether $C_2H_5OC_2H_5$ **3** the ether the hypothetical medium formerly believed to fill all space and to support the propagation of electromagnetic waves **4** *Greek myth* the upper regions of the atmosphere; clear sky or heaven **5** a rare word for **air** ⊳ Also (for senses 3-5): **aether** [c17 from Latin *aether*, from Greek *aithēr*, from *aithein* to burn] > **etheric** (iˈθɛrɪk) *adj*

ethereal (ɪˈθɪərɪəl) *adj* **1** extremely delicate or refined; exquisite **2** almost as light as air; impalpable; airy **3** celestial or spiritual **4** of, containing, or dissolved in an ether, esp diethyl ether: *an ethereal solution* **5** of or relating to the ether [c16 from Latin *aethereus*, from Greek *aitherios*, from *aithēr* ETHER] > eˌthereˈality or eˈtherealness *n* > eˈthereally *adv*

etherealize or **etherealise** (ɪˈθɪərɪəˌlaɪz) *vb* (*tr*) **1** to make or regard as being ethereal **2** to add ether to or make into ether or something resembling ether > eˌtherealiˈzation or eˌtherealiˈsation *n*

etherify (ˈiːθərɪˌfaɪ, iːˈθɛrɪ-) *vb* **-fies, -fying, -fied** (*tr*) to change (a compound, such as an alcohol) into an ether > eˌtherifiˈcation *n*

etherize or **etherise** (ˈiːθəˌraɪz) *vb* (*tr*) *obsolete* to subject (a person) to the anaesthetic influence of ether fumes; anaesthetize > ˌetheriˈzation or ˌetheriˈsation *n* > ˈetherˌizer or ˈetherˌiser *n*

Ethernet (ˈiːθəˌnɛt) *n trademark computing* a widely used type of local area network

ethic (ˈɛθɪk) *n* **1** a moral principle or set of moral values held by an individual or group: *the Puritan*

ethic ⊳ *adj* **2** another word for **ethical** ⊳ See also **ethics** [c15 from Latin *ēthicus*, from Greek *éthikos*, from *ēthos* custom; see ETHOS]

ethical (ˈɛθɪkəl) *adj* **1** in accordance with principles of conduct that are considered correct, esp those of a given profession or group **2** of or relating to ethics **3** (of a medicinal agent) available legally only with a doctor's prescription or consent > ˈethically *adv* > ˈethicalness or ˌethiˈcality *n*

ethical investment *n* an investment in a company whose activities or products are not considered by the investor to be unethical

ethicize or **ethicise** (ˈɛθɪˌsaɪz) *vb* (*tr*) to make or consider as ethical

ethics (ˈɛθɪks) *n* **1** (*functioning as singular*) the philosophical study of the moral value of human conduct and of the rules and principles that ought to govern it; moral philosophy. See also **meta-ethics 2** (*functioning as plural*) a social, religious, or civil code of behaviour considered correct, esp that of a particular group, profession, or individual **3** (*functioning as plural*) the moral fitness of a decision, course of action, etc: *he doubted the ethics of their verdict* > **ethicist** *n*

Ethiop (ˈiːθɪˌɒp) or **Ethiope** (ˈiːθɪˌəʊp) *adj* archaic words for **Black**[1]

Ethiopia (ˌiːθɪˈəʊpɪə) *n* a state in NE Africa, on the Red Sea: consolidated as an empire under Menelik II (1889-1913); federated with Eritrea from 1952 until 1993; Emperor Haile Selassie was deposed by the military in 1974 and the monarchy was abolished in 1975; an independence movement in Eritrea was engaged in war with the government from 1961 until 1993. It lies along the Great Rift Valley and consists of deserts in the southeast and northeast and a high central plateau with many rivers (including the Blue Nile) and mountains rising over 4500 m (15 000 ft); the main export is coffee. Language: Amharic. Religion: Christian majority. Currency: birr. Capital: Addis Ababa. Pop: 72 420 000 (2004 est). Area: 1 128 215 sq km (435 614 sq miles). Former name: **Abyssinia**

Ethiopian (ˌiːθɪˈəʊpɪən) *adj* **1** of, relating to, or characteristic of Ethiopia, its people, or any of their languages **2** of or denoting a zoogeographical region consisting of Africa south of the Sahara **3** *anthropol obsolete* of or belonging to a postulated racial group characterized by dark skin, an oval elongated face, and thin lips, living chiefly in Africa south of the Sahara ⊳ *n* **4** a native or inhabitant of Ethiopia **5** any of the languages of Ethiopia, esp Amharic ⊳ *n, adj* **6** an archaic word for **Black**[1]

Ethiopic (ˌiːθɪˈɒpɪk, -ˈəʊpɪk) *n* **1** the ancient language of Ethiopia, belonging to the Semitic subfamily of the Afro-Asiatic family: a Christian liturgical language. See also **Ge'ez 2** the group of languages developed from this language, including Amharic, Tigre, and Tigrinya ⊳ *adj* **3** denoting or relating to this language or group of languages **4** a less common word for **Ethiopian**

ethmoid (ˈɛθmɔɪd) *anatomy* ⊳ *adj* also **ethmoidal 1** denoting or relating to a bone of the skull that forms part of the eye socket and the nasal cavity ⊳ *n* **2** the ethmoid bone [c18 from Greek *ēthmoeidēs* like a sieve, from *ēthmos* sieve, from *ēthein* to sift]

ethnarch (ˈɛθnɑːk) *n* the ruler of a people or province, as in parts of the Roman and Byzantine Empires [c17 from Greek *ethnarkhēs*, from *ethnos* nation + *arkhein* to rule] > ˈethnarchy *n*

ethnic (ˈɛθnɪk) or **ethnical** *adj* **1** relating to or characteristic of a human group having racial, religious, linguistic, and certain other traits in common **2** relating to the classification of mankind into groups, esp on the basis of racial characteristics **3** denoting or deriving from the cultural traditions of a group of people: *the ethnic dances of Slovakia* **4** characteristic of another culture, esp a peasant culture: *the ethnic look; ethnic food* ⊳ *n* **5** *chiefly US and Austral* a member of an ethnic group, esp a minority group [c14 (in the senses: heathen, Gentile): from Late Latin *ethnicus*, from Greek *ethnikos,* from *ethnos* race] > **'ethnically** *adv* > **ethnicity** (εθ'nɪsɪtɪ) *n*

ethnic cleansing *n euphemistic* the violent removal by one ethnic group of other ethnic groups from the population of a particular area: used esp of the activities of Serbs against Croats and Muslims in the former Yugoslavia

ethnic minority *n* an immigrant or racial group regarded by those claiming to speak for the cultural majority as distinct and unassimilated

ethno- *combining form* indicating race, people, or culture: *ethnology* [via French from Greek *ethnos* race]

ethnobiology (ˌɛθnəʊbaɪ'ɒlədʒɪ) *n* the branch of biology involving the study of the uses of plants and animals in various human societies

ethnobotany (ˌɛθnəʊ'bɒtənɪ) *n* the branch of botany concerned with the use of plants in folklore, religion, etc > ˌethno'botanist *n*

ethnocentrism (ˌɛθnəʊ'sɛnˌtrɪzəm) *n* belief in the intrinsic superiority of the nation, culture, or group to which one belongs, often accompanied by feelings of dislike for other groups > ˌethno'centric *adj* > ˌethno'centrically *adv* > ˌethnocen'tricity *n*

ethnogeny (εθ'nɒdʒɪnɪ) *n* the branch of ethnology that deals with the origin of races or peoples > **ethnogenic** (ˌɛθnəʊ'dʒɛnɪk) *adj* > eth'nogenist *n*

ethnography (εθ'nɒɡrəfɪ) *n* the branch of anthropology that deals with the scientific description of individual human societies > eth'nographer *n* > **ethnographic** (ˌɛθnəʊ'ɡræfɪk) *or* ˌethno'graphical *adj* > ˌethno'graphically *adv*

ethnology (εθ'nɒlədʒɪ) *n* the branch of anthropology that deals with races and peoples, their relations to one another, their origins, and their distinctive characteristics > **ethnologic** (ˌɛθnə'lɒdʒɪk) *or* ˌethno'logical *adj* > ˌethno'logically *adv* > eth'nologist *n*

ethnomethodology (ˌɛθnəʊmɛθə'dɒlədʒɪ) *n* a method of studying linguistic communication that emphasizes common-sense views of conversation and the world. Compare **phenomenology**

ethnomusicology (ˌɛθnəʊmjuːzɪ'kɒlədʒɪ) *n* the study of the music of different cultures > ˌethnomusi'cologist *n*

ethology (ɪ'θɒlədʒɪ) *n* the study of the behaviour of animals in their normal environment [C17 (in the obsolete sense: mimicry): via Latin from Greek *ēthologia,* from *ēthos* character; current sense, C19] > **ethological** (ˌɛθə'lɒdʒɪkᵊl) *adj* > etho'logically *adv* > e'thologist *n*

ethonone ('ɛθəˌnəʊn) *n* another name for **ketene**

ethos ('iːθɒs) *n* the distinctive character, spirit, and attitudes of a people, culture, era, etc: *the revolutionary ethos* [C19 from Late Latin: habit, from Greek]

ethoxide (iːθ'ɒksaɪd) *n* any of a class of saltlike compounds with the formula MOC₂H₅, where M is a metal atom. Also called: ethylate [C20 from *ethox(yl)* (from ETH(YL) + OX(YGEN) + -YL) + -IDE]

ethoxyethane (ɛˌθɒksɪ'iːθeɪn) *n* the technical name for **ether** (sense 1) [C20 from ETH(YL) + OXY-² + ETHANE]

ethyl ('iːθaɪl, 'ɛθɪl) *n* (*modifier*) of, consisting of, or containing the monovalent group C₂H₅: *ethyl group or radical* [C19 from ETH(ER) + -YL] > **ethylic** (ɪ'θɪlɪk) *adj*

ethyl acetate *n* a colourless volatile flammable fragrant liquid ester, made from acetic acid and ethanol: used in perfumes and flavourings and as a solvent for plastics, etc Formula: CH₃COOC₂H₅

ethyl alcohol *n* another name for **alcohol** (sense 1)

ethylate ('ɛθɪˌleɪt) *vb* **1** to undergo or cause to undergo a chemical reaction in which an ethyl group is introduced into a molecule ▷ *n* **2** another name for an **ethoxide**. > ˌethyl'ation *n*

ethyl carbamate *n* a colourless odourless crystalline ester that is used in the manufacture of pesticides, fungicides, and pharmaceuticals. Formula: CO(NH₂)OC₂H₅. Also called: **urethane**

ethylene ('ɛθɪˌliːn) *n* a colourless flammable gaseous alkene with a sweet odour, obtained from petroleum and natural gas and used in the manufacture of polythene and many other chemicals. Formula: CH₂:CH₂. Also called: **ethene** > **ethylenic** (ˌɛθɪ'liːnɪk) *adj*

ethylene glycol *n* another name for **ethanediol**

ethylene group *or* **radical** *n chem* the divalent group, -CH₂CH₂-, derived from ethylene

ethylene series *n chem* the homologous series of unsaturated hydrocarbons that contain one double bond and have the general formula, CₙH₂ₙ; alkene series

ethyl ether *n* a more formal name for **ether** (sense 1)

ethyne ('iːθaɪn, 'ɛθaɪn) *n* another name for **acetylene** [C20 from ETHYL + -INE²]

etiolate ('iːtɪəʊˌleɪt) *vb* **1** *botany* to whiten (a green plant) through lack of sunlight **2** to become or cause to become pale and weak, as from malnutrition [C18 from French *étioler* to make pale, probably from Old French *estuble* straw, from Latin *stipula*] > ˌetio'lation *n*

etiology (ˌiːtɪ'ɒlədʒɪ) *n, pl* -gies a variant spelling of **aetiology**. > **etiological** (ˌiːtɪə'lɒdʒɪkᵊl) *adj* > ˌetio'logically *adv* > eti'ologist *n*

etiquette ('ɛtɪˌkɛt, ˌɛtɪ'kɛt) *n* **1** the customs or rules governing behaviour regarded as correct or acceptable in social or official life **2** a conventional but unwritten code of practice followed by members of any of certain professions or groups: *medical etiquette* [C18 from French, from Old French *estiquette* label, from *estiquier* to attach; see STICK²]

Etna ('ɛtnə) *n* **Mount** an active volcano in E Sicily: the highest volcano in Europe and the highest peak in Italy south of the Alps. Height: 3323 m (10 902 ft)

Eton ('iːtᵊn) *n* **1** a town in S England, in Windsor and Maidenhead unitary authority, Berkshire, near the River Thames: site of **Eton College,** a public school for boys founded in 1440. Pop: 3821 (2001 est) **2** this college

Eton collar *n* a broad stiff white collar worn outside an Eton jacket

Eton crop *n* a short mannish hairstyle worn by women in the 1920s

Etonian (iː'təʊnɪən) *adj* **1** a pupil of Eton College ▷ *adj* **2** of or relating to Eton College

Eton jacket *n* a waist-length jacket with a V-shaped back, open in front, formerly worn by pupils of Eton College

etonogestrel (ˌɪtɒnəʊ'dʒɛstrəl) *n* a progestogen used as a male contraceptive, released from two tiny rods placed under the skin

étrier (French etrije) *n mountaineering* a short portable ladder or set of webbing loops that can be attached to a karabiner or fifi hook. US name: stirrup [C20 from French: stirrup]

Etruria (ɪ'trʊərɪə) *n* **1** an ancient country of central Italy, between the Rivers Arno and Tiber, roughly corresponding to present-day Tuscany and part of Umbria **2** a factory established in Staffordshire by Josiah Wedgwood in 1769

Etruscan (ɪ'trʌskən) *or* **Etrurian** (ɪ'trʊərɪən) *n* **1** a member of an ancient people of central Italy whose civilization influenced the Romans, who had suppressed them by about 200 BC **2** the non-Indo-European language of the ancient Etruscans, whose few surviving records have not been fully interpreted ▷ *adj* **3** of, relating to, or characteristic of Etruria, the Etruscans, their culture, or their language

et seq. *abbreviation for* **1** et sequens [Latin: and the following] **2** *Also:* et seqq et sequentia [Latin: and those that follow]

-ette *suffix of nouns* **1** small: *cigarette; kitchenette* **2** female: *majorette* **3** (esp in trade names) imitation: *Leatherette* [from French, feminine of -ET]

étude ('eɪtjuːd; *French* etyd) *n* a short musical composition for a solo instrument, esp one designed as an exercise or exploiting technical virtuosity [C19 from French: STUDY]

étui (ɛ'twiː) *n, pl* **étuis** a small usually ornamented case for holding needles, cosmetics, or other small articles [C17 from French, from Old French *estuier* to enclose; see TWEEZERS]

ety., etym. *or* **etymol.** *abbreviation for* **1** etymological **2** etymology

etymologize *or* **etymologise** (ˌɛtɪ'mɒləˌdʒaɪz) *vb* to trace, state, or suggest the etymology of (a word)

etymology (ˌɛtɪ'mɒlədʒɪ) *n, pl* -gies **1** the study of the sources and development of words and morphemes **2** an account of the source and development of a word or morpheme [C14 via Latin from Greek *etumologia;* see ETYMON, -LOGY] > **etymological** (ˌɛtɪmə'lɒdʒɪkᵊl) *adj* > ˌety'mologically *adv* > ety'mologist *n*

etymon ('ɛtɪˌmɒn) *n, pl* -mons *or* -ma (-mə) a form of a word or morpheme, usually the earliest recorded form or a reconstructed form, from which another word or morpheme is derived: *the etymon of English "ewe" is Indo-European "*owi"* [C16 via Latin, from Greek *etumon* basic meaning, from *etumos* true, actual]

e-type *n informal* a person who works in or is interested in electronics [C20 electronics]

Etzel ('ɛtsᵊl) *n German legend* a great king who, according to the *Nibelungenlied,* was the second husband of Kriemhild after the death of Siegfried: identified with Attila the Hun. Compare **Atli**

eu *the internet domain name for* the European Union

Eu *the chemical symbol for* europium

EU *abbreviation for* **European Union**

eu- *combining form* well, pleasant, or good: *eupeptic; euphony* [via Latin from Greek, from *eus* good]

eubacteria (ˌjuːbæk'tɪərɪə) *pl n, sing* -rium (-rɪəm) a large group of bacteria characterized by a rigid cell wall and, in motile types, flagella; the true bacteria [C20 via New Latin from Greek, from EU- (in the sense: true) + BACTERIUM]

Euboea (juː'bɪə) *n* an island in the W Aegean Sea: the largest island after Crete of the Greek archipelago; linked with the mainland by a bridge across the Euripus channel. Capital: Chalcis. Pop: 198 130 (2001). Area: 3908 sq km (1509 sq miles). Modern Greek name: Évvoia Former English name: Negropont

Euboean (juː'bɪən) *adj* **1** of or relating to the Greek island of Euboea ▷ *n* **2** a native or inhabitant of Euboea

eucaine (juː'keɪn) *n* a crystalline optically active substance formerly used as a local anaesthetic. Formula: C₁₅H₂₁NO₂

eucalyptol (ˌjuːkə'lɪptɒl) *or* **eucalyptole** (ˌjuːkə'lɪptəʊl) *n* a colourless oily liquid with a camphor-like odour and a spicy taste; it is obtained from eucalyptus oil and used in perfumery and as a flavouring. Formula: C₁₀H₁₈O. Also called: cineol

eucalyptus (ˌjuːkə'lɪptəs) *or* **eucalypt** ('juːkəˌlɪpt) *n, pl* -lyptuses *or* -lypti (-'lɪptaɪ) *or* -lypts any myrtaceous tree of the mostly Australian genus *Eucalyptus,* such as the blue gum and ironbark, widely cultivated for the medicinal oil in their leaves (**eucalyptus oil**), timber, and ornament [C19 New Latin, from EU- + Greek *kaluptos* covered, from *kaluptein* to cover, hide]

eucaryote (juː'kærɪɒt) *n* a variant spelling of **eukaryote**

eucharis ('juːkərɪs) *n* any amaryllidaceous plant of the South American genus *Eucharis,* cultivated for their large white fragrant flowers [C19 New Latin, from Late Latin: charming, from Greek *eukharis,* from EU- + *kharis* grace]

Eucharist ('juːkərɪst) *n* **1** the Christian sacrament in which Christ's Last Supper is commemorated by the consecration of bread and wine **2** the consecrated elements of bread and wine offered in the sacrament **3** Mass, esp when regarded as the

e

service where the sacrament of the Eucharist is administered [c14 via Church Latin from Greek *eukharistia*, from *eukharistos* thankful, from EU- + *kharizesthai* to show favour, from *kharis* favour]
> ˌEuchaˈristic *or* Euchaˈristical *adj*
> ˌEuchaˈristically *adv*

euchlorine (juːˈklɔːriːn) *or* **euchlorin** (juːˈklɔːrɪn) *n* an explosive gaseous mixture of chlorine and chlorine dioxide

euchre (ˈjuːkə) *n* **1** a US and Canadian card game similar to écarté for two to four players, using a poker pack with joker **2** an instance of euchring another player, preventing him from making his contracted tricks ▷ *vb* (tr) **3** to prevent (a player) from making his contracted tricks **4** (usually foll by *out*) *US, Canadian, Austral, and NZ informal* to outwit or cheat **5** *Austral and NZ informal* to ruin or exhaust [c19 of unknown origin]

euchromatin (juːˈkrəʊmətɪn) *n* the part of a chromosome that constitutes the major genes and does not stain strongly with basic dyes when the cell is not dividing. Compare **heterochromatin**
> euchromatic (ˌjuːkrəʊˈmætɪk) *adj*

Euclid (ˈjuːklɪd) *n* the works of Euclid (Greek mathematician of Alexandria, 3rd century BC), esp his system of geometry

Euclidean *or* **Euclidian** (juːˈklɪdɪən) *adj* of or relating to Euclid, the 3rd century BC Greek mathematician, or his system of geometry

eucryphia (juːˈkrɪfɪə) *n* any tree or shrub of the mostly evergreen genus *Eucryphia*, native to Australia and S America, having leaves of a dark lustrous green and white flowers: family *Eucryphiaceae* [from Greek *eu* well + *kryphios* hidden, from *kryptein* to hide, referring to the sepals being joined at the top]

eudemon *or* **eudaemon** (juːˈdiːmən) *n* a benevolent spirit or demon [c17 from Greek *eudaimōn*, from EU- + *daimōn* in-dwelling spirit; see DEMON]

eudemonia *or* **eudaemonia** (ˌjuːdɪˈməʊnɪə) *n* happiness, esp (in the philosophy of Aristotle) that resulting from a rational active life

eudemonics *or* **eudaemonics** (ˌjuːdɪˈmɒnɪks) *n* (functioning as singular) **1** the art or theory of happiness **2** another word for **eudemonism**
> ˌeudeˈmonic *or* ˌeudaeˈmonic *adj*

eudemonism *or* **eudaemonism** (juːˈdiːməˌnɪzəm) *n philosophy* an ethical doctrine holding that the value of moral action lies in its capacity to produce happiness > euˈdemonist *or* euˈdaemonist *n* > euˌdemonˈistic, euˌdaemonˈistic, euˌdemonˈistical *or* euˌdaemonˈistical *adj*
> euˌdemonˈistically *or* euˌdaemonˈistically *adv*

eudicotyledon (ˌjuːdaɪˌkɒtɪˈliːdˀn) *n* any plant belonging to one of the two major groups of flowering plants, comprising over 60 per cent of all plants, normally having net-veined leaves and two cotyledons in the seed

eudiometer (ˌjuːdɪˈɒmɪtə) *n* a graduated glass tube used in the study and volumetric analysis of gas reactions [c18 from Greek *eudios*, literally: clear skied (from EU- + *Dios*, genitive of *Zeus* god of the heavens) + -METER] > eudiometric (ˌjuːdɪəˈmɛtrɪk) *or* ˌeudioˈmetrical *adj* > ˌeudiˈometry *n*

eugarie (ˈjuːɡərɪ) *n Queensland dialect* another name for **pipi**

eugenics (juːˈdʒɛnɪks) *n* (functioning as singular) the study of methods of improving the quality of the human race, esp by selective breeding [c19 from Greek *eugenēs* well-born, from EU- + -*genēs* born; see -GEN] > euˈgenic *adj* > euˈgenically *adv* > euˈgenicist *n* > euˈgenist *n, adj*

eugenol (ˈjuːdʒɪˌnɒl) *n* a colourless or pale yellow oily liquid substance with a spicy taste and an odour of cloves, used in perfumery; 4-allyl-2-methoxyphenol. Formula: $C_{10}H_{12}O_2$ [c19 *eugen-*, from *Eugenia caryophyllata* kind of clove from which oil may be obtained + -OL[1]]

euglena (juːˈgliːnə) *n* any freshwater unicellular organism of the genus *Euglena*, moving by means

of flagella and typically having holophytic nutrition. It has been variously regarded as an alga or a protozoan but is now usually classified as a protoctist (phylum *Euglenophyta*) [c19 from New Latin, from EU- + Greek *glēnē* eyeball, socket of a joint] > euˈglenoid *adj, n*

euhemerism (juːˈhiːməˌrɪzəm) *n* **1** the theory that gods arose out of the deification of historical heroes **2** any interpretation of myths that derives the gods from outstanding men and seeks the source of mythology in history [c19 named after *Euhemerus* (?300 BC), Greek philosopher who propounded this theory] > euˈhemerist *n* > euˌhemerˈistic *adj* > euˌhemerˈistically *adv*

euhemerize *or* **euhemerise** (juːˈhiːməˌraɪz) *vb* to deal with or explain (myths) by euhemerism

eukaryote *or* **eucaryote** (juːˈkærɪɒt) *n* any member of the Eukarya, a domain of organisms having cells each with a distinct nucleus within which the genetic material is contained. Eukaryotes include protoctists, fungi, plants, and animals. Compare **prokaryote** [from EU- + KARYO- + -*ote* as in *zygote*] > eukaryotic *or* eucaryotic (ˌjuːkærɪˈɒtɪk) *adj*

eulachon (ˈjuːləˌkɒn) *or* **eulachan** *n, pl* -chons, -chon *or* -chans, -chan another name for **candlefish** [from Chinook Jargon *ulâkân*]

Eulenspiegel (ˈɔɪlənˌʃpiːɡˀl) *n* See **Till Eulenspiegel**

Euler's circles (ˈɔɪləz) *pl n logic* a diagram in which the terms of categorial statements are represented by circles whose inclusion in one another represents the inclusion of the extensions of the terms in one another. Compare **Venn diagram** [named after *Leonhard Euler* (1707–83), Swiss mathematician]

eulogia (juːˈləʊdʒɪə) *n* **1** *Eastern Christian Church* blessed bread distributed to members of the congregation after the liturgy, esp to those who have not communed **2** *archaic* a blessing or something blessed [c18 from Greek: blessing; see EULOGY]

eulogize *or* **eulogise** (ˈjuːləˌdʒaɪz) *vb* to praise (a person or thing) highly in speech or writing > ˈeulogist, ˈeuloˌgizer *or* ˈeuloˌgiser *n* > ˌeuloˈgistic *or* ˌeuloˈgistical *adj* > ˌeuloˈgistically *adv*

eulogy (ˈjuːlədʒɪ) *n, pl* -gies **1** a formal speech or piece of writing praising a person or thing, esp a person who has recently died **2** high praise or commendation. Also called (archaic): eulogium (juːˈləʊdʒɪəm) [c16 from Late Latin *eulogia*, from Greek: praise, from EU- + -LOGY; influenced by Latin *ēlogium* short saying, inscription]

◼◼◼ USAGE Avoid confusion with **elegy**

Eumenides (juːˈmɛnɪˌdiːz) *pl n* another name for the **Furies**, used by the Greeks as a euphemism [from Greek, literally: the benevolent ones, from *eumenēs* benevolent, from EU- + *menos* spirit]

eumung (ˈjuːmʌŋ) *or* **eumong** (ˈjuːmɒŋ) *n* any of various Australian acacias [from a native Australian language]

eunuch (ˈjuːnək) *n* **1** a man who has been castrated, esp (formerly) for some office such as a guard in a harem **2** *informal* an ineffective man: *a political eunuch* [c15 via Latin from Greek *eunoukhos* attendant of the bedchamber, from *eunē* bed + *ekhein* to have, keep]

euonymus (juːˈɒnɪməs) *or* **evonymus** *n* any tree or shrub of the N temperate genus *Euonymus,* such as the spindle tree, whose seeds are each enclosed in a fleshy, typically red, aril: family *Celastraceae* [c18 from Latin: spindle tree, from Greek *euōnumos* fortunately named, from EU- + *onoma* NAME]

eupatorium (ˌjuːpəˈtɔːrɪəm) *n* any plant of the genus *Eupatorium,* of N temperate regions and tropical America: cultivated for their ornamental clusters of purple, pink, or white flowers: family *Asteraceae* (composites) [c16 from New Latin, from Greek *eupatorion* hemp agrimony, from *Eupator* surname of Mithridates VI, king of Pontus and traditionally the first to have used it medicinally]

eupatrid (juːˈpætrɪd) *n, pl* -patridae (-ˈpætrɪˌdiː) *or* -patrids (in ancient Greece) a hereditary noble or

landowner [c19 via Latin from Greek *eupatridēs,* literally: having a good father, from EU- + *patēr* father]

Eupen and Malmédy (French øpɛn malmedi) *n* a region of Belgium in Liège province: ceded by Germany in 1919. Pop: 29 372 (2004 est)

eupepsia (juːˈpɛpsɪə) *or* **eupepsy** (juːˈpɛpsɪ) *n physiol* good digestion [c18 from New Latin, from Greek, from EU- + *pepsis* digestion, from *peptein* to digest] > euˈpeptic *adj*

euphausiid (juːˈfɔːzɪɪd) *n* any small pelagic shrimplike crustacean of the order *Euphausiacea*: an important constituent of krill [c19 from New Latin *Euphausiacea,* perhaps from Greek EU- + *pha-* from *phainein* to reveal, show + *ousia* substance, stuff]

euphemism (ˈjuːfɪˌmɪzəm) *n* **1** an inoffensive word or phrase substituted for one considered offensive or hurtful, esp one concerned with religion, sex, death, or excreta. Examples of euphemisms are *sleep with* for *have sexual intercourse with; departed* for *dead; relieve oneself* for *urinate* **2** the use of such inoffensive words or phrases [c17 from Greek *euphēmismos,* from EU- + *phēmē* speech] > ˌeupheˈmistic *adj* > ˌeupheˈmistically *adv*

euphemize *or* **euphemise** (ˈjuːfɪˌmaɪz) *vb* to speak in euphemisms or refer to by means of a euphemism > ˈeupheˌmizer *or* ˈeupheˌmiser *n*

euphonic (juːˈfɒnɪk) *or* **euphonious** (juːˈfəʊnɪəs) *adj* **1** denoting or relating to euphony; pleasing to the ear **2** (of speech sounds) altered for ease of pronunciation > euˈphonically *or* euˈphoniously *adv* > euˈphoniousness *n*

euphonium (juːˈfəʊnɪəm) *n* a brass musical instrument with four valves; the tenor of the tuba family. It is used mainly in brass bands [c19 New Latin, from EUPH(ONY + HARM)ONIUM]

euphonize *or* **euphonise** (ˈjuːfəˌnaɪz) *vb* **1** to make pleasant to hear; render euphonious **2** to change (speech sounds) so as to facilitate pronunciation

euphony (ˈjuːfənɪ) *n, pl* -nies **1** the alteration of speech sounds, esp by assimilation, so as to make them easier to pronounce **2** a pleasing sound, esp in speech [c17 from Late Latin *euphōnia,* from Greek, from EU- + *phōnē* voice]

euphorbia (juːˈfɔːbɪə) *n* any plant of the genus *Euphorbia,* such as the spurges and poinsettia: family *Euphorbiaceae* [c14 *euforbia*: from Latin *euphorbea* African plant named after *Euphorbus,* first-century AD Greek physician]

euphorbiaceous (juːˌfɔːbɪˈeɪʃəs) *adj* of, relating to, or belonging to the *Euphorbiaceae,* a family of plants typically having capsular fruits: includes the spurges, the castor oil and cassava plants, cascarilla, and poinsettia

euphoria (juːˈfɔːrɪə) *n* a feeling of great elation, esp when exaggerated [c19 from Greek: good ability to endure, from EU- + *pherein* to bear] > euphoric (juːˈfɒrɪk) *adj*

euphoriant (juːˈfɔːrɪənt) *adj* **1** relating to or able to produce euphoria ▷ *n* **2** a euphoriant drug or agent

euphotic (juːˈfəʊtɪk, -ˈfɒt-) *adj ecology* denoting or relating to the uppermost part of a sea or lake down to about 100 metres depth, which receives enough light to enable photosynthesis to take place [c20 from EU- + PHOTIC]

euphrasy (ˈjuːfrəsɪ) *n, pl* -sies another name for **eyebright** [c15 *eufrasie*: from Medieval Latin *eufrasia,* from Greek *euphrasia* gladness, from *euphrainein* to make glad, from EU- + *phrēn* mind]

Euphrates (juːˈfreɪtiːz) *n* a river in SW Asia, rising in E Turkey and flowing south across Syria and Iraq to join the Tigris, forming the Shatt-al-Arab, which flows to the head of the Persian Gulf: important in ancient times for the extensive irrigation of its valley (in Mesopotamia). Length: 3598 km (2235 miles)

euphroe *or* **uphroe** (ˈjuːfrəʊ, -vrəʊ) *n nautical* a wooden block with holes through which the lines of a crowfoot are rove [c19 from Dutch *juffrouw* maiden, earlier *joncfrouwe* (from *jonc* YOUNG + *frouwe* woman)]

Euphrosyne (juːˈfrɒzɪˌniː) *n Greek myth* one of the three Graces [from Greek: mirth, merriment]

euphuism (ˈjuːfjuːˌɪzəm) *n* **1** an artificial prose style of the Elizabethan period, marked by extreme use of antithesis, alliteration, and extended similes and allusions **2** any stylish affectation in speech or writing, esp a rhetorical device or expression [c16 after *Euphues*, prose romance by John Lyly] > **euphuist** *n* > ˌeuphuˈistic or ˌeuphuˈistical *adj* > ˌeuphuˈistically *adv*

euplastic (juːˈplæstɪk) *adj* healing quickly and well [c19 from Greek *euplastos* readily moulded; see EU-, PLASTIC]

euploid (ˈjuːplɔɪd) *adj* **1** having chromosomes present in an exact multiple of the haploid number ▷ *n* **2** a euploid cell or individual ▷ Compare **aneuploid** [c20 from EU- + -*ploid*, as in HAPLOID] > **euploidy** *n*

eupnoea *or US* **eupnea** (juːpˈnɪə) *n physiol* normal relaxed breathing. Compare **dyspnoea** [c18 from New Latin, from Greek *eupnoia*, from *eupnous* breathing easily, from EU- + *pnoē*, from *pnein* to breathe] > **eupˈnoeic** *or US* **eupˈneic** *adj*

eur- *combining form* a variant of **euro-** before a vowel

Eurasia (jʊəˈreɪʃə, -ʒə) *n* the continents of Europe and Asia considered as a whole

Eurasian (jʊəˈreɪʃən, -ʒən) *adj* **1** of or relating to Eurasia **2** of mixed European and Asian descent ▷ *n* **3** a person of mixed European and Asian descent

Euratom (jʊəˈrætəm) *n* short for **European Atomic Energy Community**; an authority established by the European Economic Community (now the European Union) to develop peaceful uses of nuclear energy

Eure (*French* œr) *n* a department of N France, in Haute-Normandie region. Capital: Évreux. Pop: 550 056 (2003 est). Area: 6037 sq km (2354 sq miles)

Eure-et-Loir (*French* œrelwar) *n* a department of N central France, in Centre region. Capital: Chartres. Pop: 412 094 (2003 est). Area: 5940 sq km (2317 sq miles)

eureka (jʊˈriːkə) *interj* an exclamation of triumph on discovering or solving something [c17 from Greek *heurēka* I have found (it), from *heuriskein* to find; traditionally the exclamation of Archimedes when he realized, during bathing, that the volume of an irregular solid could be calculated by measuring the water displaced when it was immersed]

eureka moment *n informal* a moment at which a person realizes or solves something

Eureka Stockade *n* a violent incident in Ballarat, Australia, in 1854 between gold miners and the military, as a result of which the miners won their democratic rights in the state parliament

eurhythmic (juːˈrɪðmɪk), **eurhythmical,** *esp US* **eurythmic, eurythmical** *adj* **1** having a pleasing and harmonious rhythm, order, or structure **2** of or relating to eurhythmics

eurhythmics *or esp US* **eurythmics** (juːˈrɪðmɪks) *n (functioning as singular)* **1** a system of training through physical movement to music, originally taught by Émile Jaques-Dalcroze, to develop grace and musical understanding **2** dancing of this style, expressing the rhythm and spirit of the music through body movement

eurhythmy *or esp US* **eurythmy** (juːˈrɪðmɪ) *n* **1** rhythmic movement **2** harmonious structure [c17 from Latin *eurythmia*, from Greek *eurhuthmia*, from EU- + *rhuthmos* proportion, RHYTHM]

euripus (jʊˈraɪpəs) *n, pl* -**pi** (-paɪ) a strait or channel with a strong current or tide [c17 from Latin, from Greek *Ēuripos* the strait between Boeotia and Euboea, from *ripē* force, rush]

euro (ˈjʊərəʊ) *n, pl* -**os** the official currency unit, divided into 100 cents, of the member countries of the European Union who have adopted European Monetary Union; these are Austria, Belgium,

Finland, France, Germany, Greece, Ireland, Italy, Luxembourg, the Netherlands, Portgual, and Spain; also used by Andorra, Bosnia-Herzegovina, French Guiana, Guadeloupe, Kosovo, Martinique, Mayotte, Monaco, Montenegro, Réunion, San Marino, and the Vatican City

euro- (ˈjʊərəʊ-) *or before a vowel* **eur-** *combining form* (*sometimes capital*) Europe or European: *eurodollar*

euro-ad *n* an advertisement designed to be suitable for all countries in the European Union

Eurobeach (ˈjʊərəʊˌbiːtʃ) *n* a beach that has been designated as suitable for bathing from because it meets the limits set by European Union regulations for bacteria in bathing areas

eurobond (ˈjʊərəʊˌbɒnd) *n* (*sometimes capital*) a bond issued in a eurocurrency

Eurocentric (ˌjʊərəʊˈsɛntrɪk) *adj* chiefly concerned with or concentrating on Europe and European culture: *the Eurocentric curriculum*

eurocheque (ˈjʊərəʊˌtʃɛk) *n* (*sometimes capital*) a cheque drawn on a European bank that can be cashed at any bank or bureau de change displaying the EC sign or that can be used to pay for goods or services at any outlet displaying this sign

Euroclydon (jʊˈrɒklɪˌdɒn) *n* **1** a stormy wind from the north or northeast that occurs in the Levant, which caused the ship in which St Paul was travelling to be wrecked (Acts 27:14) **2** any stormy wind [c17 from Greek *eurokludōn*, from *Euros* EURUS + Greek *akulōn* (unattested) north wind, from Latin *aquilō*]

euro-commercial paper (ˌjuːrəʊkəˈmɜːʃəl) *n* commercial paper issued in a eurocurrency

Eurocommunism (ˌjʊərəʊˈkɒmjʊˌnɪzəm) *n* the policies, doctrines, and practices of Communist Parties in Western Europe in the 1970s and 1980s, esp those rejecting democratic centralism and favouring nonalignment with the Soviet Union and China > ˌEuroˈcommunist *n, adj*

eurocrat (ˈjʊərəˌkræt) *n* (*sometimes capital*) a member, esp a senior member, of the administration of the European Union

eurocreep (ˈjʊərəˌkriːp) *n* the gradual introduction of the euro into use in Britain

eurocurrency (ˈjʊərəʊˌkʌrənsɪ) *n* (*sometimes capital*) **a** the currency of any country held on deposit in Europe outside its home market: used as a source of short- or medium-term finance, esp in international trade, because of easy convertibility **b** (*as modifier*): *the eurocurrency market*

eurodeposit (ˌjʊərəʊdɪˈpɒzɪt) *n* (*sometimes capital*) a deposit of the currency of any country in the eurocurrency market

eurodollar (ˈjʊərəʊˌdɒlə) *n* (*sometimes capital*) a US dollar held as part of a European holding. See **eurocurrency**

Euroland (ˈjʊərəʊˌlænd) *n* the geographical area containing the countries that have joined the European single currency

euromarket (ˈjʊərəʊˌmɑːkɪt) *n* **1** a market for financing international trade backed by the central banks and commercial banks of the European Union **2** the European Union treated as one large market for the sale of goods and services

Euro MP *n informal* a member of the European Parliament

Euronext (ˈjʊərəʊˌnɛkst) *n* a European stock exchange formed by the amalgamation of the Paris, Brussels, and Amsterdam bourses

euronote (ˈjuːˌrəʊˌnəʊt) *n* a form of euro-commercial paper consisting of short-term negotiable bearer notes

Europa[1] (jʊˈrəʊpə) *n Greek myth* a Phoenician princess who had three children by Zeus in Crete, where he had taken her after assuming the guise of a white bull. Their offspring were Rhadamanthus, Minos, and Sarpedon

Europa[2] (jʊˈrəʊpə) *n* the smallest of the four Galilean satellites of Jupiter. Diameter: 3138 km; orbital radius: 671 000 km

Europe (ˈjʊərəp) *n* **1** the second smallest

continent, forming the W extension of Eurasia: the border with Asia runs from the Urals to the Caspian and the Black Sea. The coastline is generally extremely indented and there are several peninsulas (notably Scandinavia, Italy, and Iberia) and offshore islands (including the British Isles and Iceland). It contains a series of great mountain systems in the south (Pyrenees, Alps, Apennines, Carpathians, Caucasus), a large central plain, and a N region of lakes and mountains in Scandinavia. Pop: 724 722 000 (2005 est). Area: about 10 400 000 sq km (4 000 000 sq miles) **2** *Brit* the continent of Europe except for the British Isles **3** *Brit* the European Union: *when did Britain go into Europe?*

European (ˌjʊərəˈpɪən) *adj* **1** of or relating to Europe or its inhabitants **2** native to or derived from Europe ▷ *n* **3** a native or inhabitant of Europe **4** a person of European descent **5** a supporter of the European Union or of political union of the countries of Europe or a part of it > ˌEuroˈpeanˌism *n*

European Central Bank *n* the central bank of the European Union, established in 1998 to oversee the process of European Monetary Union and subsequently to direct monetary policy within the countries using the euro. Abbreviation: **ECB**

European Commission *n* the executive body of the European Union formed in 1967, which initiates action in the EU and mediates between member governments. Former name (until 1993): Commission of the European Communities

European Community *or* **Communities** *n* an economic and political association of European States that came into being in 1967, when the legislative and executive bodies of the European Economic Community merged with those of the European Coal and Steel Community and the European Atomic Energy Community: subsumed into the **European Union** in 1993. Abbreviation: **EC**

European Council *n* an executive body of the European Union, made up of the President of the European Commission and representatives of the member states, including the foreign and other ministers. The Council acts at the request of the Commission

European Currency Unit *n* See **ECU**

European Economic Area *n* a free-trade area created in 1994 by an agreement between the European Free Trade Association (EFTA), excluding Switzerland, and the European Union (EU). Abbreviation: **EEA**

European Economic Community *n* the former W European economic association created by the Treaty of Rome in 1957; in 1967 its executive and legislative bodies merged with those of the European Coal and Steel Community and the European Atomic Energy Community to form the European Community (now part of the European Union). Informal name: **Common Market** Abbreviation: **EEC**

European Free Trade Association *n* See **EFTA**

Europeanize *or* **Europeanise** (ˌjʊərəˈpɪəˌnaɪz) *vb* (*tr*) **1** to make European in culture, dress, etc **2** to integrate (a country, economy, etc) into the European Union > ˌEuroˌpeaniˈzation *or* ˌEuroˌpeaniˈsation *n*

European Monetary Institute *n* an organization set up in 1991 to coordinate economic and monetary policy within the European Union: superseded by the European Central Bank in 1998

European Monetary System *n* the system used in the European Union for stabilizing exchange rates between the currencies of member states and financing the balance-of-payments support mechanism. The original Exchange Rate Mechanism was formed in 1979 but superseded in 1999 when the euro was adopted as official currency of 11 EU member states. A new exchange rate mechanism (ERM II) based on the euro is

e

used to regulate the currencies of participating states that have not adopted the euro. Abbreviation: EMS

European Monetary Union *n* the agreement between members of the European Union to establish a common currency. The current participating members are Austria, Belgium, Finland, France, Germany, Greece, Ireland, Italy, Luxembourg, the Netherlands, Portugal, and Spain. Abbreviation: EMU

European Parliament *n* the assembly of the European Union in Strasbourg. It consists of 626 directly elected members and its role is largely advisory

European plan *n US* a hotel rate of charging covering room and service but not meals. Compare **American plan**

European Recovery Programme *n* the official name for the **Marshall Plan**

European Union *n* an organization created in 1993 with the aim of achieving closer economic and political union between member states of the European Community. The current members are Austria, Belgium, Cyprus, the Czech Republic, Denmark, Estonia, Finland, France, Germany, Greece, Hungary, Ireland, Italy, Latvia, Lithuania, Luxembourg, Malta, the Netherlands, Poland, Portugal, Slovakia, Slovenia, Spain, Sweden, and the UK. Abbreviation: EU

European wasp *n Austral* a large black-and-yellow banded wasp, *Vespula germanica*, native to Europe, North Africa, and Asia, now established in Australasia and the US

Europhile ('jʊərəʊˌfaɪl) (*sometimes not capital*) ▷ *n* **1** a person who admires Europe, Europeans, or the European Union ▷ *adj* **2** marked by or possessing admiration for Europe, Europeans, or the European Union

Europhilia (ˌjʊərəʊˈfɪlɪə) *n* (*sometimes not capital*) admiration for Europe, Europeans, or the European Union

Europhobia (ˌjʊərəʊˈfəʊbɪə) *n* (*sometimes not capital*) dislike for or hostility to Europe, Europeans, or the European Union

Europhobic (ˌjʊərəʊˈfəʊbɪk) *adj* (*sometimes not capital*) hostile to Europe, Europeans, or the European Union

europium (jʊˈrəʊpɪəm) *n* a soft ductile reactive silvery-white element of the lanthanide series of metals: used as the red phosphor in colour television and in lasers. Symbol: Eu; atomic no.: 63; atomic wt.: 151.965; valency: 2 or 3; relative density: 5.244; melting pt.: 822°C; boiling pt.: 1527°C [C20 named after EUROPE + -IUM]

Europol ('jʊərəʊˌpɒl) *n acronym for* European Police Office, an international association devoted to fighting cross-border organized crime within the European Union

Europoort (*Dutch* 'øːroːpoːrt) *n* a port in the Netherlands near Rotterdam: developed in the 1960s; handles chiefly oil

Euro-sceptic (ˌjʊərəʊˈskɛptɪk) (in Britain) ▷ *n* **1** a person who is opposed to closer links with the European Union ▷ *adj* **2** opposing closer links with the European Union: *Euro-sceptic MPs*

Eurostat ('jʊərəʊˌstæt) *n* an organization within the European Union that collects and collates statistical information relating to member states. Full name: **Statistical Office of the European Communities**

Eurosterling ('jʊərəʊˌstɜːlɪŋ) *n* sterling as part of a European holding. See **eurocurrency**

Eurotax ('jʊərəʊˌtæks) *n* a tax imposed by the European Union

Eurotrack ('jʊərəʊˌtræk) *n* short for **Financial Times Stock Exchange Eurotrack 100 Index**

Eurotunnel ('jʊərəʊˌtʌnəl) *n* another name for **Channel Tunnel**

Eurovision ('jʊərəʊˌvɪʒən) *n* **a** the network of the European Broadcasting Union for the exchange of news and television programmes amongst its member organizations and for the relay of news

and programmes from outside the network **b** (*as modifier*): *the Eurovision song contest*

Eurozone ('jʊərəʊˌzəʊn) *n* another name for **Euroland**

Eurus ('jʊərəs) *n Greek myth* the east or southeast wind personified [Latin, from Greek *euros*]

eury- *combining form* broad or wide: *eurythermal* [New Latin, from Greek, from *eurus* wide]

Euryale (jʊˈraɪəlɪ) *n Greek myth* one of the three Gorgons

Eurydice (jʊˈrɪdɪsɪ) *n Greek myth* a dryad married to Orpheus, who sought her in Hades after she died. She could have left Hades with him had he not broken his pact and looked back at her

euryhaline (ˌjʊərɪˈheɪliːn, -laɪn) *adj* (of certain aquatic animals) able to tolerate a wide range of salinity. Compare **stenohaline**

eurypterid (jʊˈrɪptərɪd) *n* any large extinct scorpion-like aquatic arthropod of the group *Eurypterida*, of Palaeozoic times, thought to be related to the horseshoe crabs [C19 from New Latin *Eurypterida*, from EURY- + Greek *pteron* wing, feather]

Eurystheus (jʊˈrɪsθjuːs, -θɪəs) *n Greek myth* a grandson of Perseus, who, through the favour of Hera, inherited the kingship of Mycenae, which Zeus had intended for Hercules

eurythermal (ˌjʊərɪˈθɜːməl), **eurythermic** *or* **eurythermous** *adj* (of organisms) able to tolerate a wide range of temperatures in the environment. Compare **stenothermal**

eurythmics (juːˈrɪðmɪks) *n* a variant spelling (esp US) of **eurhythmics**. > eu'rythmic *or* eu'rythmical *adj* > eu'rythmy *n*

eurytopic (ˌjʊərɪˈtɒpɪk) *adj* **1** *ecology* (of a species) able to tolerate a wide range of environments **2** *ecology* having a wide geographical distribution. Compare **stenotopic** [C20 from EURY- + *top* from Greek *topos* place + -IC]

eusporangiate (ˌjuːspɔːˈrændʒɪɪt) *adj* (of ferns) having each sporangium developing from a group of cells, rather than a single cell, and with no specialized disperal of spores. Compare **leptosporangiate** [from New Latin *eusporangiātus* (unattested), from EU- + SPORANGIUM]

Eustachian tube (juːˈsteɪʃən) *n* a tube that connects the middle ear with the nasopharynx and equalizes the pressure between the two sides of the eardrum [C18 named after Bartolomeo *Eustachio*, 16th-century Italian anatomist]

eustatic (juːˈstætɪk) *adj* denoting or relating to worldwide changes in sea level, caused by the melting of ice sheets, movements of the ocean floor, sedimentation, etc [C20 from Greek, from EU- + STATIC] > **eustasy** ('juːstəsɪ) *n* > eu'statically *adv*

eutaxia (juːˈtæksɪə) *n engineering* the condition of being easily melted

eutectic (juːˈtɛktɪk) *adj* **1** (of a mixture of substances, esp an alloy) having the lowest freezing point of all possible mixtures of the substances **2** concerned with or suitable for the formation of eutectic mixtures ▷ *n* **3** a eutectic mixture **4** the temperature on a phase diagram at which a eutectic mixture forms [C19 from Greek *eutēktos* melting readily, from EU- + *tēkein* to melt]

eutectoid (juːˈtɛktɔɪd) *n* **1** a mixture of substances similar to a eutectic, but forming two or three constituents from a solid instead of from a melt ▷ *adj* **2** concerned with or suitable for eutectoid mixtures [C20 from EUTECT(IC) + -OID]

Euterpe (juːˈtɜːpɪ) *n Greek myth* the Muse of lyric poetry and music > Eu'terpean *adj*

euthanasia (ˌjuːθəˈneɪzɪə) *n* the act of killing someone painlessly, esp to relieve suffering from an incurable illness. Also called: mercy killing [C17 via New Latin from Greek: easy death, from EU- + *thanatos* death]

euthenics (juːˈθɛnɪks) *n* (*functioning as singular*) the study of the control of the environment, esp with a view to improving the health and living standards of the human race [C20 from Greek

euthēnein to thrive] > eu'thenist *n*

eutherian (juːˈθɪərɪən) *adj* **1** of, relating to, or belonging to the *Eutheria*, a subclass of mammals all of which have a placenta and reach an advanced state of development before birth. The group includes all mammals except monotremes and marsupials ▷ *n* **2** any eutherian mammal ▷ Compare **metatherian**, **prototherian** [C19 from New Latin *Euthēria*, from Greek EU- + *thēria*, plural of *thērion* beast]

euthymia (juːˈθɪmɪə) *n psychol* a pleasant state of mind [EU- + -THYMIA]

eutrophic (juːˈtrɒfɪk, -ˈtrəʊ-) *adj* (of lakes and similar habitats) rich in organic and mineral nutrients and supporting an abundant plant life, which in the process of decaying depletes the oxygen supply for animal life. Compare **oligotrophic** [C18 probably from *eutrophy*, from Greek *eutrophia* sound nutrition, from *eutrophos* well-fed, from EU- + *trephein* to nourish] > 'eutrophy *n*

eutrophication (juːˌtrɒfɪˈkeɪʃən) *n* a process by which pollution from such sources as sewage effluent or leachate from fertilized fields causes a lake, pond, or fen to become overrich in organic and mineral nutrients, so that algae and cyanobacteria grow rapidly and deplete the oxygen supply

euxenite ('juːksɪˌnaɪt) *n* a rare brownish-black mineral containing erbium, cerium, uranium, columbium, and yttrium [C19 from Greek *euxenos* hospitable (literally: well-disposed to strangers), from EU- + *xenos* stranger; from its containing a number of rare elements]

Euxine Sea ('juːksaɪn) *n* another name for the **Black Sea**

eV *abbreviation for* electronvolt

EV *abbreviation for* English Version (of the Bible)

EVA *astronautics abbreviation for* extravehicular activity

evacuant (ɪˈvækjʊənt) *adj* **1** serving to promote excretion, esp of the bowels ▷ *n* **2** an evacuant agent

evacuate (ɪˈvækjʊˌeɪt) *vb* (*mainly tr*) **1** (*also intr*) to withdraw or cause to withdraw from (a place of danger) to a place of greater safety **2** to make empty by removing the contents of **3** (*also intr*) *physiol* **a** to eliminate or excrete (faeces); defecate **b** to discharge (any waste product) from (a part of the body) **4** (*tr*) to create a vacuum in (a bulb, flask, reaction vessel, etc) [C16 from Latin *ēvacuāre* to void, from *vacuus* empty] > e,vacu'ation *n* > e'vacuative *adj* > e'vacu,ator *n*

evacuee (ɪ,vækjʊˈiː) *n* a person evacuated from a place of danger, esp in wartime

evade (ɪˈveɪd) *vb* (*mainly tr*) **1** to get away from or avoid (imprisonment, captors, etc); escape **2** to get around, shirk, or dodge (the law, a duty, etc) **3** (*also intr*) to avoid answering (a question) [C16 from French *évader*, from Latin *ēvādere* to go forth, from *vādere* to go] > e'vadable *adj* > e'vader *n* > e'vadingly *adv*

evaginate (ɪˈvædʒɪˌneɪt) *vb* (*tr*) *med* to turn (an organ or part) inside out; turn the outer surface of (an organ or part) back on itself [C17 from Late Latin *ēvāgināre* to unsheathe, from *vāgīna* sheath] > e,vagi'nation *n*

evaluate (ɪˈvæljʊˌeɪt) *vb* (*tr*) **1** to ascertain or set the amount or value of **2** to judge or assess the worth of; appraise **3** *maths, logic* to determine the unique member of the range of a function corresponding to a given member of its domain [C19 back formation from *evaluation*, from French, from *evaluer* to evaluate; see VALUE] > e,valu'ation *n* > e'valu,ator *n*

evaluative (ɪˈvæljʊətɪv) *adj* **1** of, denoting, or based on an act of evaluating **2** *philosophy* expressing an attitude or value judgment; emotive

evanesce (ˌɛvəˈnɛs) *vb* (*intr*) (of smoke, mist, etc) to fade gradually from sight; vanish [C19 from Latin *ēvānēscere* to disappear; see VANISH]

evanescent (ˌɛvəˈnɛsᵊnt) *adj* **1** passing out of sight; fading away; vanishing **2** ephemeral or transitory > ˌevaˈ**nescence** *n* > ˌevaˈ**nescently** *adv*

evangel (ɪˈvændʒəl) *n* **1** *archaic* the gospel of Christianity **2** (*often capital*) any of the four Gospels of the New Testament **3** any body of teachings regarded as central or basic **4** *US* an evangelist [C14 from Church Latin *ēvangelium*, from Greek *evangelion* good news, from EU- + *angelos* messenger; see ANGEL]

evangelical (ˌiːvænˈdʒɛlɪkᵊl) *Christianity* ▷ *adj* **1** of, based upon, or following from the Gospels **2** denoting or relating to any of certain Protestant sects or parties, which emphasize the importance of personal conversion and faith in atonement through the death of Christ as a means of salvation **3** another word for **evangelistic** ▷ *n* **4** an upholder of evangelical doctrines or a member of an evangelical sect or party, esp the Low-Church party of the Church of England > ˌevanˈ**gelicalism** *n* > ˌevanˈ**gelically** *adv*

evangelism (ɪˈvændʒɪˌlɪzəm) *n* **1** (in Protestant churches) the practice of spreading the Christian gospel. RC Church term: **evangelization** *or* **evangelisation** **2** ardent or missionary zeal for a cause **3** the work, methods, or characteristic outlook of a revivalist or evangelist preacher **4** a less common word for **evangelicalism**

evangelist (ɪˈvændʒɪlɪst) *n* **1** an occasional preacher, sometimes itinerant and often preaching at meetings in the open air **2** a preacher of the Christian gospel **3** any zealous advocate of a cause **4** another word for **revivalist** (sense 1)

Evangelist (ɪˈvændʒɪlɪst) *n* **1** any of the writers of the New Testament Gospels: Matthew, Mark, Luke, or John **2** a senior official or dignitary of the Mormon Church

evangelistic (ɪˌvændʒɪˈlɪstɪk) *adj* **1** denoting, resembling, or relating to evangelists or their methods and attitudes: *evangelistic zeal* **2** zealously advocating a cause **3** (*often capital*) of or relating to all or any of the four Evangelists > eˌvangeˈ**listically** *adv*

evangelize *or* **evangelise** (ɪˈvændʒɪˌlaɪz) *vb* **1** to preach the Christian gospel or a particular interpretation of it (to) **2** (*intr*) to advocate a cause with the object of making converts > eˌvangeliˈ**zation** *or* eˌvangeliˈ**sation** *n* > eˈvangeˌ**lizer** *or* eˈvangeˌ**liser** *n*

evanish (ɪˈvænɪʃ) *vb* a poetic word for **vanish** [C15 from Old French *esvanir*, from Latin *ēvānēscere* to VANISH] > eˈ**vanishment** *n*

Evanston (ˈɛvənstən) *n* a city in NE Illinois, on Lake Michigan north of Chicago: Northwestern University (1851). Pop: 74 360 (2003 est)

Evansville (ˈɛvənzˌvɪl) *n* a city in SW Indiana, on the Ohio River. Pop: 117 881 (2003 est)

evaporate (ɪˈvæpəˌreɪt) *vb* **1** to change or cause to change from a liquid or solid state to a vapour. Compare **boil**[1] (sense 1) **2** to lose or cause to lose liquid by vaporization leaving a more concentrated residue **3** to disappear or cause to disappear: *all her doubts evaporated* **4** (*tr*) to deposit (a film, metal, etc) by vaporization of a liquid or solid and the subsequent condensation of its vapour [C16 from Late Latin *ēvapōrāre*, from Latin *vapor* steam; see VAPOUR] > eˈ**vaporable** *adj* > eˌvaporaˈ**bility** *n* > eˌvapoˈ**ration** *n* > eˈ**vaporative** *adj* > eˈvapoˌ**rator** *n*

evaporated milk *n* thick unsweetened tinned milk from which some of the water has been evaporated

evaporimeter (ɪˌvæpəˈrɪmɪtə) *or* **evaporometer** (ɪˌvæpəˈrɒmɪtə) *n* another name for **atmometer**

evaporite (ɪˈvæpəˌraɪt) *n* any sedimentary rock, such as rock salt, gypsum, or anhydrite, formed by evaporation of former seas or salt-water lakes [C20 EVAPORATION + -ITE[1]]

evapotranspiration (ɪˌvæpəʊˌtrænspəˈreɪʃən) *n* the return of water vapour to the atmosphere by evaporation from land and water surfaces and by the transpiration of vegetation

evasion (ɪˈveɪʒən) *n* **1** the act of evading or escaping, esp from a distasteful duty, responsibility, etc, by trickery, cunning, or illegal means: *tax evasion* **2** trickery, cunning, or deception used to dodge a question, duty, etc; means of evading [C15 from Late Latin *ēvāsiō*, from Latin *ēvādere* to go forth; see EVADE]

evasive (ɪˈveɪsɪv) *adj* **1** tending or seeking to evade; avoiding the issue; not straightforward **2** avoiding or seeking to avoid trouble or difficulties: *to take evasive action* **3** hard to catch or obtain; elusive > eˈ**vasively** *adv* > eˈ**vasiveness** *n*

eve (iːv) *n* **1 a** the evening or day before some special event or festival **b** (*capital when part of a name*): *New Year's Eve* **2** the period immediately before an event: *on the eve of civil war* **3** an archaic word for **evening** [C13 variant of EVEN[2]]

Eve (iːv) *n* *Old Testament* the first woman; mother of the human race, fashioned by God from the rib of Adam (Genesis 2:18-25)

evection (ɪˈvɛkʃən) *n* irregularity in the moon's motion caused by perturbations of the sun and planets [C17 from Latin *ēvectiō* a going up, from *ēvehere* to lead forth, from *vehere* to carry] > eˈ**vectional** *adj*

even[1] (ˈiːvᵊn) *adj* **1** level and regular; flat: *an even surface* **2** (*postpositive; foll by with*) on the same level or in the same plane (as): *one surface even with another* **3** without variation or fluctuation; regular; constant: *an even rate of progress* **4** not readily moved or excited; placid; calm: *an even temper* **5** equally balanced between two sides: *an even game* **6** equal or identical in number, quantity, etc: *two even spoonfuls of sugar* **7 a** (of a number) divisible by two **b** characterized or indicated by such a number: *maps are on the even pages*. Compare **odd** (sense 4) **8** relating to or denoting two or either of two alternatives, events, etc, that have an equal probability: *an even chance of missing or catching a train* **9** having no balance of debt; neither owing nor being owed **10** just and impartial; fair: *an even division* **11** exact in number, amount, or extent: *an even pound* **12** equal, as in score; level: *now the teams are even* **13** *maths* (of a function) unchanged in value when the sign of the independent variable is changed, as in $y = z^2$. Compare **odd** (sense 8) **14** **even money a** a bet in which the winnings are the same as the amount staked **b** (*as modifier*): *the even-money favourite* **15** **get even (with)** *informal* to exact revenge (on); settle accounts (with) **16** **of even date** *legal, formal, or obsolete* of the same or today's date ▷ *adv* **17** (intensifier; used to suggest that the content of a statement is unexpected or paradoxical): *even an idiot can do that* **18** (intensifier; used with comparative forms): *this is even better* **19** notwithstanding; in spite of: *even having started late she soon caught him up* **20** used to introduce a more precise version of a word, phrase, or statement: *he is base, even depraved* **21** used preceding a clause of supposition or hypothesis to emphasize the implication that whether or not the condition in it is fulfilled, the statement in the main clause remains valid: *even if she died he wouldn't care* **22** *archaic* that is to say; namely (used for emphasis): *he, even he, hath spoken these things* **23** *archaic* all the way; fully: *I love thee even unto death* **24** **even as** (*conjunction*) at the very same moment or in the very same way that: *even as I spoke, it thundered* **25** **even so** in spite of any assertion to the contrary: nevertheless ▷ *vb* **26** to make or become even ▷ See also **break even, even out, evens, even up** [Old English *efen*; related to Old Norse *jafn* even, equal, Gothic *ibns*, Old High German *eban*] > ˈ**evener** *n* > ˈ**evenly** *adv* > ˈ**evenness** *n*

even[2] (ˈiːvᵊn) *n* an archaic word for **eve** *or* **evening** [Old English *ǣfen*; related to Old Frisian *ēvend*, Old High German *āband*]

evenfall (ˈiːvᵊnˌfɔːl) *n* *archaic* early evening; dusk

even-handed *adj* dealing fairly with all; impartial > ˌeven-ˈ**handedly** *adv* > ˌeven-ˈ**handedness** *n*

evening (ˈiːvnɪŋ) *n* **1** the latter part of the day, esp from late afternoon until nightfall **2** the latter or concluding period: *the evening of one's life* **3** the early part of the night spent in a specified way: *an evening at the theatre* **4** an entertainment, meeting, or reception held in the early part of the night **5** *Southern US and Brit dialect* the period between noon and sunset **6** (*modifier*) of, used, or occurring in the evening: *the evening papers* ▷ See also **evenings** [Old English *ǣfnung*; related to Old Frisian *ēvend*, Old High German *āband*]

evening class *n* a class held in the evenings at certain colleges, normally for adults

evening dress *n* attire for wearing at a formal occasion during the evening, esp (for men) a dinner jacket and black tie, or (less commonly, for women) a floor-length gown

evening primrose *n* any onagraceous plant of the genus *Oenothera*, native to North America but widely cultivated and naturalized, typically having yellow flowers that open in the evening

evening primrose oil *n* an oil, obtained from the seeds of the evening primrose, that is claimed to stimulate the production of prostaglandins

evenings (ˈiːvnɪŋz) *adv* *informal* in the evening, esp regularly

evening star *n* a planet, usually Venus, seen just after sunset during the time that the planet is east of the sun. Compare **morning star**

Evenki (əˈvɛŋkɪ) *n* **1** (*pl* **Evenki**) a Tungus people of E Siberia **2** the language of this people

even out *vb* (*adverb*) to make or become even, as by the removal of bumps, inequalities, etc

evens (ˈiːvənz) *adj, adv* **1** (of a bet) winning the same as the amount staked if successful **2** (of a runner) offered at such odds

evensong (ˈiːvᵊnˌsɒŋ) *n* **1** Also called: **Evening Prayer, vespers** *Church of England* the daily evening service of Bible readings and prayers prescribed in the Book of Common Prayer **2** *archaic* another name for **vespers** **3** an archaic or poetic word for **evening**

event (ɪˈvɛnt) *n* **1** anything that takes place or happens, esp something important; happening; incident **2** the actual or final outcome; result (esp in the phrases **in the event, after the event**) **3** any one contest in a programme of sporting or other contests: *the high jump is his event* **4** *philosophy* **a** an occurrence regarded as a bare instant of space-time as contrasted with an object which fills space and has endurance **b** an occurrence regarded in isolation from, or contrasted with, human agency. Compare **act** (sense 8) **5** **in any event** *or* **at all events** regardless of circumstances; in any case **6** **in the event of** in case of; if (such a thing) happens: *in the event of rain the race will be cancelled* **7** **in the event that** if it should happen that ▷ *vb* **8** to take part or ride (a horse) in eventing [C16 from Latin *ēventus* a happening, from *ēvenīre* to come forth, happen, from *venīre* to come]

even-tempered *adj* not easily angered or excited; calm

eventful (ɪˈvɛntfʊl) *adj* full of events or incidents: *an eventful day* > eˈ**ventfully** *adv* > eˈ**ventfulness** *n*

event horizon *n* *astronomy* the surface around a black hole enclosing the space from which electromagnetic radiation cannot escape due to gravitational attraction. For a non-rotating black hole, the radius is proportional to the mass of the black hole

eventide (ˈiːvᵊnˌtaɪd) *n* *archaic or poetic* another word for **evening**

eventide home (ˈiːvᵊnˌtaɪd) *n* *euphemistic* an old people's home

eventing (ɪˈvɛntɪŋ) *n* the sport of taking part in equestrian competitions (esp **three-day events**), usually consisting of three sections: dressage, cross-country riding, and showjumping > eˈ**venter** *n*

eventration (ˌiːvɛnˈtreɪʃən) *n* *pathol* protrusion of

the bowel through the abdomen

event television *n* television programmes focusing on events that attract media attention and high ratings

event theatre *n* spectacular and extravagantly-mounted theatrical productions collectively

eventual (ɪ'vɛntʃʊəl) *adj* (*prenominal*) happening in due course of time; ultimate: *the eventual outcome*

eventuality (ɪˌvɛntʃʊ'ælɪtɪ) *n, pl* **-ties** a possible event, occurrence, or result; contingency

eventually (ɪ'vɛntʃʊəlɪ) *adv* 1 at the very end; finally 2 (*as sentence modifier*) after a long time or long delay: *eventually, he arrived*

eventuate (ɪ'vɛntʃʊˌeɪt) *vb* (*intr*) 1 (often foll by *in*) to result ultimately (in) 2 to come about as a result: *famine eventuated from the crop failure* > e,ventu'ation *n*

even up *vb* (*adverb*) to make or become equal, esp in respect of claims or debts; settle or balance

ever ('ɛvə) *adv* 1 at any time: *have you ever seen it?* 2 by any chance; in any case: *how did you ever find out?* 3 at all times; always: *ever busy* 4 in any possible way or manner: *come as fast as ever you can* 5 *informal, chiefly Brit* (intensifier, in the phrases **ever so, ever such,** and **ever such a**): *ever so good; ever such bad luck; ever such a waste* 6 **ever and again** (*or* **anon**) *archaic* now and then; from time to time 7 **is he** *or* **she ever!** *US and Canadian slang* he or she displays the quality concerned in abundance ▷ See also **forever** [Old English *ǣfre*, of uncertain origin]

Everest ('ɛvərɪst) *n* 1 **Mount** a mountain in S Asia on the border between Nepal and Tibet, in the Himalayas: the highest mountain in the world; first climbed by members of a British-led expedition (1953). Height: established as 8848 m (29 028 ft) for many years, but the latest of a series of more recent reassessments (in 1999), not currently accepted by all authorities or by either of the controlling governments, puts it at 8850 m (29 035 ft). Nepalese name: **Sagarmatha** Chinese name: **Qomolangma** 2 any high point of ambition or achievement [C19 named after Sir G. *Everest* (1790–1866), Surveyor-General of India]

Everglades ('ɛvəˌɡleɪdz) *pl n* **the** a subtropical marshy region of Florida, south of Lake Okeechobee: contains the **Everglades National Park** established to preserve the flora and fauna of the swamps. Area: over 13 000 sq km (5000 sq miles)

evergreen ('ɛvəˌɡriːn) *adj* 1 (of certain trees and shrubs) bearing foliage throughout the year; continually shedding and replacing leaves. Compare **deciduous** 2 remaining fresh and vital ▷ *n* 3 an evergreen tree or shrub

evergreen fund *n* a fund that provides capital for new companies and makes regular injections of capital to support their development

everlasting (ˌɛvə'lɑːstɪŋ) *adj* 1 never coming to an end; eternal 2 lasting for an indefinitely long period 3 lasting so long or occurring so often as to become tedious ▷ *n* 4 endless duration; eternity 5 Also called: **everlasting flower** another name for **immortelle**. See also **cat's-foot** > ,ever'lastingly *adv* > ,ever'lastingness *n*

evermore (ˌɛvə'mɔː) *adv* (often preceded by *for*) all time to come

evernet ('ɛvəˌnɛt) *n* a hypothetical form of internet that is continuously accessible using a wide variety of devices [C20 from EVER + (INTER)NET]

evert (ɪ'vɜːt) *vb* (*tr*) to turn (an eyelid, the intestines, or some other bodily part) outwards or inside out [C16 from Latin *ēvertere* to overthrow, from *vertere* to turn] > e'versible *adj* > e'version *n*

evertor (ɪ'vɜːtə) *n* any muscle that turns a part outwards

every ('ɛvrɪ) *determiner* 1 each one (of the class specified), without exception: *every child knows it* 2 (*not used with a negative*) the greatest or best possible: *every hope of success* 3 each: used before a noun phrase to indicate the recurrent, intermittent, or serial nature of a thing: *every third*

day; *every now and then*; *every so often* 4 every bit (used in comparisons with *as*) quite; just; equally: *every bit as funny as the other show* 5 **every other** each alternate; every second: *every other day* 6 **every which way a** in all directions; everywhere **b** *US and Canadian* from all sides: *stones coming at me every which way* [C15 *everich*, from Old English *ǣfre ǣlc*, from *ǣfre* EVER + *ǣlc* EACH]

everybody ('ɛvrɪˌbɒdɪ) *pron* every person; everyone

▐▐ USAGE See at **everyone**

everyday ('ɛvrɪˌdeɪ) *adj* 1 happening each day; daily 2 commonplace or usual; ordinary 3 suitable for or used on ordinary days as distinct from Sundays or special days

Everyman ('ɛvrɪˌmæn) *n* 1 a medieval English morality play in which the central figure represents mankind, whose earthly destiny is dramatized from the Christian viewpoint 2 (*often not capital*) the ordinary person; common man

everyone ('ɛvrɪˌwʌn, -wən) *pron* every person; everybody

▐▐ USAGE *Everyone* and *everybody* are interchangeable, as are *no one* and *nobody*, and *someone* and *somebody*. Care should be taken to distinguish between *everyone* and *someone* as single words and *every one* and *some one* as two words, the latter form correctly being used to refer to each individual person or thing in a particular group: *every one of them is wrong*

every one *pron* each person or thing in a group, without exception: *every one of the large cats is a fast runner*

everyplace ('ɛvrɪˌpleɪs) *adv US* an informal word for **everywhere**

everything ('ɛvrɪˌθɪŋ) *pron* 1 the entirety of a specified or implied class: *she lost everything in the War* 2 a great deal, esp of something very important: *she means everything to me*

everywhere ('ɛvrɪˌwɛə) *adv* to or in all parts or places

Evesham ('iːvʃəm) *n* a town in W central England, in W Worcestershire, on the River Avon: scene of the Battle of Evesham in 1265 (Lord Edward's defeat of Simon de Montfort and the barons); centre of the **Vale of Evesham**, famous for market gardens and orchards. Pop: 22 179 (2001)

Eve's pudding *n Brit* a baked sponge pudding with a layer of apple at the bottom

Évian-les-Bains *or* **Évian** (French evjãlebɛ̃) *n* a resort and spa town in E France, on Lake Geneva opposite Lausanne; noted for its bottled mineral waters. Pop: 7273 (1999)

evict (ɪ'vɪkt) *vb* (*tr*) 1 to expel (a tenant) from property by process of law; turn out 2 to recover (property or the title to property) by judicial process or by virtue of a superior title [C15 from Late Latin *ēvincere*, from Latin: to vanquish utterly, from *vincere* to conquer] > e'viction *n* > e'victor *n* > e'vic'tee *n*

evidence ('ɛvɪdəns) *n* 1 ground for belief or disbelief; data on which to base proof or to establish truth or falsehood 2 a mark or sign that makes evident: *his pallor was evidence of ill health* 3 *law* matter produced before a court of law in an attempt to prove or disprove a point in issue, such as the statements of witnesses, documents, material objects, etc. See also **circumstantial evidence, direct evidence** 4 **turn queen's (king's, state's) evidence** (of an accomplice) to act as witness for the prosecution and testify against those associated with him in crime 5 **in evidence** on display; conspicuous: *her new ring was in evidence* ▷ *vb* (*tr*) 6 to make evident; show clearly 7 to give proof of or evidence for

evident ('ɛvɪdənt) *adj* easy to see or understand; readily apparent [C14 from Latin *ēvidēns*, from *vidēre* to see]

evidential (ˌɛvɪ'dɛnʃəl) *adj* relating to, serving as, or based on evidence > ,evi'dentially *adv*

evidently ('ɛvɪdəntlɪ) *adv* 1 without question; clearly; undoubtedly 2 to all appearances; apparently: *they are evidently related*

evil ('iːvəl) *adj* 1 morally wrong or bad; wicked: *an evil ruler* 2 causing harm or injury; harmful: *an evil plan* 3 marked or accompanied by misfortune; unlucky: *an evil fate* 4 (of temper, disposition, etc) characterized by anger or spite 5 not in high esteem; infamous: *an evil reputation* 6 offensive or unpleasant: *an evil smell* 7 *slang* good; excellent ▷ *n* 8 the quality or an instance of being morally wrong; wickedness: *the evils of war* 9 (*sometimes capital*) a force or power that brings about wickedness or harm: *evil is strong in the world* 10 *archaic* an illness or disease, esp scrofula (the **king's evil**) ▷ *adv* 11 (*now usually in combination*) in an evil manner; badly: *evil-smelling* [Old English *yfel*, of Germanic origin; compare Old Frisian *evel*, Old High German *ubil* evil, Old Irish *adbal* excessive] > 'evilly *adv* > 'evilness *n*

evildoer ('iːvəlˌduːə) *n* a person who does evil > 'evil,doing *n*

evil eye *n* **the** 1 a look or glance superstitiously supposed to have the power of inflicting harm or injury 2 the power to inflict harm, etc, by such a look > ,evil-'eyed *adj*

evil-minded *adj* inclined to evil thoughts; wicked; malicious or spiteful > ,evil-'mindedly *adv* > ,evil-'mindedness *n*

Evil One *n* **the** the devil; Satan

evince (ɪ'vɪns) *vb* (*tr*) to make evident; show (something, such as an emotion) clearly [C17 from Latin *ēvincere* to overcome; see EVICT] > e'vincible *adj* > e'vincive *adj*

▐▐ USAGE *Evince* is sometimes wrongly used where *evoke* is meant: *the proposal evoked* (not *evinced*) *a storm of protest*

eviscerate (ɪ'vɪsəˌreɪt) *vb* 1 (*tr*) to remove the internal organs of; disembowel 2 (*tr*) to deprive of meaning or significance 3 (*tr*) *surgery* to remove the contents of (the eyeball or other organ) 4 (*intr*) *surgery* (of the viscera) to protrude through a weakened abdominal incision after an operation ▷ *adj* 5 having been disembowelled [C17 from Latin *ēviscerāre* to disembowel, from *viscera* entrails] > e,viscer'ation *n* > e'viscer,ator *n*

evitable ('ɛvɪtəbəl) *adj rare* able to be avoided [C16 from Latin *ēvītābilis*, from *ēvītāre*, from *vītāre* to avoid]

evite (ɪ'vaɪt) *vb* an archaic word for **avoid**

evo ('iːvəʊ) *n Austral* an informal word for **evening**

evocation (ˌɛvə'keɪʃən) *n* 1 the act or an instance of evoking 2 *French law* the transference of a case from an inferior court for adjudication by a higher tribunal 3 another word for **induction** (sense 6) [C17 from Latin *ēvocātiō* a calling forth, from *ēvocāre* to EVOKE]

evocative (ɪ'vɒkətɪv) *adj* tending or serving to evoke > e'vocatively *adv* > e'vocativeness *n*

evocator ('ɛvəˌkeɪtə) *n* 1 a person or thing that evokes 2 *embryol* a substance or tissue that induces morphogenesis

evoke (ɪ'vəʊk) *vb* (*tr*) 1 to call or summon up (a memory, feeling, etc), esp from the past 2 to call forth or provoke; elicit: *his words evoked an angry reply* 3 to cause (spirits) to appear; conjure up [C17 from Latin *ēvocāre* to call forth, from *vocāre* to call] > evocable ('ɛvəkəbəl) *adj* > e'voker *n*

▐▐ USAGE See at **evince** and **invoke**

evolute ('ɛvəˌluːt) *n* 1 a geometric curve that describes the locus of the centres of curvature of another curve (the **involute**). The tangents to the evolute are at right angles to the involute ▷ *adj* 2 *biology* having the margins rolled outwards [C19 from Latin *ēvolūtus* unrolled, from *ēvolvere* to roll out, EVOLVE]

evolution (ˌiːvə'luːʃən) *n* 1 *biology* a gradual change in the characteristics of a population of animals or plants over successive generations: accounts for the origin of existing species from ancestors unlike them. See also **natural selection** 2 a gradual development, esp to a more complex form 3 the act of throwing off, as heat, gas, vapour, etc 4 a pattern formed by a series of movements or something similar 5 an algebraic operation in which the root of a number, expression, etc, is extracted. Compare **involution** (sense 6) 6 *military* an exercise carried out in accordance with a set procedure or plan [C17 from Latin *ēvolūtiō* an unrolling, from *ēvolvere* to EVOLVE] > ˌ**evoˈlutionary** *or* ˌ**evoˈlutional** *adj*

evolutionary algorithm *n computing* a computer program that is designed to evolve and improve in response to input

evolutionist (ˌiːvəˈluːʃənɪst) *n* 1 a person who believes in a theory of evolution, esp Darwin's theory of the evolution of plant and animal species ▷ *adj* 2 of or relating to a theory of evolution > ˌ**evoˈlutionism** *n* > ˌ**evolutionˈistic** *adj*

evolutive (ɪˈvɒljʊtɪv) *adj* relating to, tending to, or promoting evolution

evolve (ɪˈvɒlv) *vb* 1 to develop or cause to develop gradually 2 (*intr*) (of animal or plant species) to undergo evolution 3 (*tr*) to yield, emit, or give off (heat, gas, vapour, etc) [C17 from Latin *ēvolvere* to unfold, from *volvere* to roll] > **eˈvolvable** *adj* > **eˈvolvement** *n* > **eˈvolver** *n*

evonymus (ɛˈvɒnɪməs) *n* a variant of **euonymus**

Évora (*Portuguese* ˈɛvura) *n* a city in S central Portugal: ancient Roman settlement; occupied by the Moors from 712 to 1166; residence of the Portuguese court in 15th and 16th centuries. Pop: 56 525 (2001). Ancient name: **Ebora** (ˈiːbərə)

e-voting *n* the application of electronic technology to cast and count votes in an election

Évreux (*French* evrø) *n* an industrial town in NW France: severely damaged in World War II; cathedral (12th–16th centuries). Pop: 51 198 (1999)

Évros (ˈɛvrɒs) *n* transliteration of the Modern Greek name for the **Maritsa**

evulsion (ɪˈvʌlʃən) *n rare* the act of extracting by force [C17 from Latin *ēvulsiō*, from *ēvellere*, from *vellere* to pluck]

Évvoia (ˈɛvia) *n* transliteration of the Modern Greek name for **Euboea**

evzone (ˈɛvzəʊn) *n* a soldier in an elite Greek infantry regiment [C19 from Modern Greek, from Greek *euzōnos* literally: well-girt, from EU- + *zōnē* girdle]

EW *international car registration for* Estonia

e-wallet *n* computer software in which digital cash may be stored for use in paying for transactions on the internet

ewe (juː) *n* **a** a female sheep **b** (*as modifier*): *a ewe lamb* [Old English *ēowu*; related to Old Norse *ǣr* ewe, Old High German *ou*, Latin *ovis* sheep, Sanskrit *avi*]

Ewe (ˈɛwɛ) *n* 1 (*pl* **Ewe** *or* **Ewes**) a member of a Negroid people of W Africa living chiefly in the forests of E Ghana, Togo, and Benin 2 the language of this people, belonging to the Kwa branch of the Niger-Congo family

ewe equivalent *n NZ* the basic measure for calculating stock unit: *one Jersey cow is equal to 6.5 ewe equivalents*

ewe-neck *n* 1 a condition in horses in which the neck is straight and sagging rather than arched 2 a horse or other animal with this condition > ˈ**ewe-ˌnecked** *adj*

ewer (ˈjuːə) *n* a large jug or pitcher with a wide mouth [C14 from Old French *evier*, from Latin *aquārius* water carrier, from *aqua* water]

EWO *abbreviation for* **Educational Welfare Officer**

ex[1] (ɛks) *prep* 1 *finance* not participating in; excluding; without: *ex bonus; ex dividend; ex rights* 2 *commerce* without charge to the buyer until removed from: *ex quay; ex ship; ex works* [C19 from Latin: out of, from]

ex[2] (ɛks) *n informal* (a person's) former wife, husband, etc

Ex. *Bible abbreviation for* Exodus

ex-[1] *prefix* 1 out of; outside of; from: *exclosure; exurbia* 2 former: *ex-wife* [from Latin, from *ex* (prep), identical in meaning and origin with Greek *ex, ek*; see EC-]

ex-[2] *combining form* a variant of **exo-** before a vowel: *exergonic*

exa- *prefix* denoting 10^{18}: *exametres*. Symbol: E

exabyte (ˈɛksəˌbaɪt) *n computing* 10^{18} or 2^{60} bytes

exacerbate (ɪɡˈzæsəˌbeɪt, ɪkˈsæs-) *vb* (*tr*) 1 to make (pain, disease, emotion, etc) more intense; aggravate 2 to exasperate or irritate (a person) [C17 from Latin *exacerbāre* to irritate, from *acerbus* bitter] > **exˌacerˈbation** *n*

exact (ɪɡˈzækt) *adj* 1 correct in every detail; strictly accurate: *an exact copy* 2 precise, as opposed to approximate; neither more nor less: *the exact sum* 3 (*prenominal*) specific; particular: *this exact spot* 4 operating with very great precision: *exact instruments* 5 allowing no deviation from a standard; rigorous; strict: *an exact mind* 6 based mainly on measurement and the formulation of laws, as opposed to description and classification: *physics is an exact science* ▷ *vb* (*tr*) 7 to force or compel (payment or performance); extort: *to exact tribute* 8 to demand as a right; insist upon: *to exact respect* 9 to call for or require: *this work exacts careful effort* [C16 from Latin *exactus* driven out, from *exigere* to drive forth, from *agere* to drive] > **exˈactable** *adj* > **exˈactness** *n* > **exˈactor** *or* **exˈacter** *n*

exacting (ɪɡˈzæktɪŋ) *adj* making rigorous or excessive demands: *an exacting job* > **exˈactingly** *adv* > **exˈactingness** *n*

exaction (ɪɡˈzækʃən) *n* 1 the act or an instance of exacting, esp money 2 an excessive or harsh demand, esp for money; extortion 3 a sum or payment exacted

exactitude (ɪɡˈzæktɪˌtjuːd) *n* the quality of being exact; precision; accuracy

exactly (ɪɡˈzæktlɪ) *adv* 1 in an exact manner; accurately or precisely 2 in every respect; just: *it is exactly what I want* 3 **not exactly** *ironic* not at all; by no means ▷ *sentence substitute* 4 just so! precisely!

exacum (ˈɛksəkəm) *n* any plant of the annual or perennial tropical genus *Exacum*; some are grown as greenhouse biennials for their bluish-purple platter-shaped flowers: family *Gentianaceae* [Latin, a name for centaury, from *ex* out + *agere* to drive]

exaggerate (ɪɡˈzædʒəˌreɪt) *vb* 1 to regard or represent as larger or greater, more important or more successful, etc, than is true 2 (*tr*) to make greater, more noticeable, etc, than usual [C16 from Latin *exaggerāre* to magnify, from *aggerāre* to heap, from *agger* heap] > **exˈaggerˌatingly** *adv* > **exˌaggerˈation** *n* > **exˈaggerative** *or* **exˈaggeratory** *adj* > **exˈaggerˌator** *n*

exaggerated (ɪɡˈzædʒəˌreɪtɪd) *adj* 1 unduly or excessively magnified; enlarged beyond truth or reasonableness 2 *pathol* abnormally enlarged: *an exaggerated spleen* > **exˈaggerˌatedly** *adv*

ex all *adv finance* without the right to any benefits: *shares quoted ex all*

exalt (ɪɡˈzɔːlt) *vb* (*tr*) 1 to raise or elevate in rank, position, dignity, etc 2 to praise highly; glorify; extol 3 to stimulate the mind or imagination of; excite 4 to increase the intensity of (a colour, etc) 5 to fill with joy or delight; elate 6 *obsolete* to lift up physically [C15 from Latin *exaltāre* to raise, from *altus* high] > **exˈalter** *n*

> USAGE *Exalt* is sometimes wrongly used where *exult* is meant: *he was exulting* (not *exalting*) *in his win earlier that day*

exaltation (ˌɛɡzɔːlˈteɪʃən) *n* 1 the act of exalting or state of being exalted 2 a feeling of intense well-being or exhilaration; elation; rapture 3 a flock of larks

exalted (ɪɡˈzɔːltɪd) *adj* 1 high or elevated in rank, position, dignity, etc 2 elevated in character; noble; lofty: *an exalted ideal* 3 *informal* excessively high; inflated: *he has an exalted opinion of himself* 4 intensely excited > **exˈaltedly** *adv* > **exˈaltedness** *n*

exam (ɪɡˈzæm) *n* short for **examination**

examen (ɪɡˈzeɪmɛn) *n RC Church* an examination of conscience, usually made daily by Jesuits and others [C17 from Latin: tongue of a balance, from *exigere* to thrust out, from *agere* to thrust]

examination (ɪɡˌzæmɪˈneɪʃən) *n* 1 the act of examining or state of being examined 2 *education* **a** written exercises, oral questions, or practical tasks, set to test a candidate's knowledge and skill **b** (*as modifier*): *an examination paper* 3 *med* **a** physical inspection of a patient or parts of his body, in order to verify health or diagnose disease **b** laboratory study of secretory or excretory products, tissue samples, etc, esp in order to diagnose disease 4 *law* the formal interrogation of a person on oath, esp of an accused or a witness > **exˌamiˈnational** *adj*

examine (ɪɡˈzæmɪn) *vb* (*tr*) 1 to look at, inspect, or scrutinize carefully or in detail; investigate 2 *education* to test the knowledge or skill of (a candidate) in (a subject or activity) by written or oral questions or by practical tests 3 *law* to interrogate (a witness or accused person) formally on oath 4 *med* to investigate the state of health of (a patient) [C14 from Old French *examiner*, from Latin *exāmināre* to weigh, from *exāmen* means of weighing; see EXAMEN] > **exˈaminable** *adj* > **exˈaminer** *n* > **exˈamining** *adj*

examinee (ɪɡˌzæmɪˈniː) *n* a person who takes an examination

examine-in-chief *vb* (*tr*) *law* to examine (one's own witness) in attempting to adduce a case. Compare **cross-examine**. > **exˌamiˈnation-in-chief** *n*

example (ɪɡˈzɑːmpᵊl) *n* 1 a specimen or instance that is typical of the group or set of which it forms part; sample 2 a person, action, thing, etc, that is worthy of imitation; pattern: *you must set an example to the younger children* 3 a precedent, illustration of a principle, or model: *an example in a maths book* 4 a punishment or the recipient of a punishment serving or intended to serve as a warning: *the headmaster made an example of him* 5 **for example** as an illustration; for instance ▷ *vb* 6 (*tr; now usually passive*) to present an example of; exemplify [C14 from Old French, from Latin *exemplum* pattern, from *eximere* to take out, from EX-[1] + *emere* to purchase]

exanimate (ɪɡˈzænɪmɪt, -ˌmeɪt) *adj rare* lacking life; inanimate [C16 from Latin *exanimāre* to deprive of air, from *anima* breath, spirit] > **exˌaniˈmation** *n*

exanthema (ˌɛksænˈθiːmə) *or* **exanthem** (ɛkˈsænθəm) *n, pl* **-themata** (-ˈθiːmətə) *or* **-themas** *or* **-thems** a skin eruption or rash occurring as a symptom in a disease such as measles or scarlet fever [C17 via Late Latin from Greek, from *exanthein* to burst forth, from *anthein* to blossom, from *anthos* flower] > **exanthematous** (ˌɛksænˈθɛmətəs) *or* **exanthematic** (ɛkˌsænθɪˈmætɪk) *adj*

exarate (ˈɛksəˌreɪt) *adj* (of the pupa of such insects as ants and bees) having the legs, wings, antennae, etc, free and movable [C19 from Latin *exarātus*, literally: ploughed up (apparently referring to the way this type of pupa throws off the larval skin), from *exarāre*, from *arā* plough]

exarch[1] (ˈɛksɑːk) *n* 1 the head of certain autonomous Orthodox Christian Churches, such as that of Bulgaria and Cyprus 2 any of certain Eastern Orthodox bishops, lower in rank than a patriarch but higher than a metropolitan 3 the governor of a province in the Byzantine Empire [C16 from Late Latin *exarchus* overseer, from Greek *exarkhos*, from *exarkhein* to take the lead, from *arkhein* to rule] > **exˈarchal** *adj*

exarch[2] (ˈɛksɑːk) *adj botany* (of a xylem strand) having the first-formed xylem external to that formed later. Compare **endarch, mesarch** [C19 from EX-[1] (outside) + Greek *arkhē* beginning, origin]

exarchate (ˈɛksɑːˌkeɪt, ɛkˈsɑːkeɪt) *or* **exarchy** (ˈɛksɑːkɪ) *n, pl* **-chates** *or* **-chies** the office, rank, or jurisdiction of an exarch

exasperate (ɪɡˈzɑːspəˌreɪt) *vb* (*tr*) 1 to cause great irritation or anger to; infuriate 2 to cause (an unpleasant feeling, condition, etc) to worsen; aggravate ▷ *adj* 3 *botany* having a rough prickly surface because of the presence of hard projecting

e

points [c16 from Latin *exasperāre* to make rough, from *asper* rough] > ex'asper,atedly *adv* > ex'asper,ater *n* > ex'asper,ating *adj* > ex'asper,atingly *adv* > ex,asper'ation *n*

exbi- *combining form computing* denoting 2 to the power 60 [c20 from EX(A-) + BI(NARY)]

Exc. *abbreviation for* Excellency

Excalibur (ɛkˈskælɪbə) *n* (in Arthurian legend) the magic sword of King Arthur [c14 from Old French *Escalibor*, from Medieval Latin *Caliburnus*, from Welsh *Caledvwlch*, perhaps related to Irish *Caladbolg* a legendary sword (literally: hard belly, hence, voracious)]

ex cathedra (ɛks kəˈθiːdrə) *adj, adv* 1 with authority 2 *RC Church* (of doctrines of faith or morals) defined by the pope as infallibly true, to be accepted by all Catholics [Latin, literally: from the chair]

excaudate (ɛksˈkɔːdeɪt) *adj zoology* having no tail or tail-like process; tailless

excavate (ˈɛkskəˌveɪt) *vb* 1 to remove (soil, earth, etc) by digging; dig out 2 to make (a hole, cavity, or tunnel) in (solid matter) by hollowing or removing the centre or inner part: *to excavate a tooth* 3 to unearth (buried objects) methodically in an attempt to discover information about the past [c16 from Latin *excavāre*, from *cavāre* to make hollow, from *cavus* hollow] > ,exca'vation *n*

excavator (ˈɛkskəˌveɪtə) *n* 1 a powered machine for digging earth, gravel, sand, etc, esp a caterpillar tractor so equipped 2 any person, animal, or thing that excavates

exceed (ɪkˈsiːd) *vb* 1 to be superior to (a person or thing), esp in size or quality; excel 2 (*tr*) to go beyond the limit or bounds of 3 to be greater in degree or quantity than (a person or thing) [c14 from Latin *excēdere* to go beyond, from *cēdere* to go] > ex'ceedable *adj* > ex'ceeder *n*

exceeding (ɪkˈsiːdɪŋ) *adj* 1 very great; exceptional or excessive ▷ *adv* 2 an archaic word for **exceedingly**

exceedingly (ɪkˈsiːdɪŋlɪ) *adv* to a very great or unusual degree; extremely; exceptionally

excel (ɪkˈsɛl) *vb* -cels, -celling, -celled 1 to be superior to (another or others); surpass 2 (*intr*; foll by *in* or *at*) to be outstandingly good or proficient: *he excels at tennis* [c15 from Latin *excellere* to rise up]

excellence (ˈɛksələns) *n* 1 the state or quality of excelling or being exceptionally good; extreme merit; superiority 2 an action, characteristic, feature, etc, in which a person excels

Excellency (ˈɛksələnsɪ) or **Excellence** *n, pl* -lencies *or* -lences 1 (usually preceded by *Your, His,* or *Her*) a title used to address or refer to a high-ranking official, such as an ambassador or governor 2 *RC Church* a title of bishops and archbishops in many non-English-speaking countries

excellent (ˈɛksələnt) *adj* exceptionally good; extremely meritorious; superior > 'excellently *adv*

excelsior (ɪkˈsɛlsɪˌɔː) *interj, adv, n* 1 excellent: used as a motto and as a trademark for various products, esp in the US for fine wood shavings used for packing breakable objects 2 upwards [c19 from Latin: higher]

except (ɪkˈsɛpt) *prep* 1 Also: **except for** other than; apart from; with the exception of: *he likes everyone except you; except for this mistake, you did very well* 2 **except that** (conjunction) but for the fact that; were it not true that ▷ *conj* 3 an archaic word for **unless** 4 *informal; not standard in the US* except that; but for the fact that: *I would have arrived earlier, except I lost my way* ▷ *vb* 5 (*tr*) to leave out; omit; exclude 6 (*intr*; often foll by *to*) *rare* to take exception, object [c14 from Old French *excepter* to leave out, from Latin *exceptāre*, from *excipere* to take out, from *capere* to take]

excepting (ɪkˈsɛptɪŋ) *prep* 1 excluding; except; except for (esp in the phrase **not excepting**) ▷ *conj* 2 an archaic word for **unless**

> USAGE The use of *excepting* is considered by many people to be

acceptable only after *not, only,* or *without*. Elsewhere *except* is preferred: *every country agreed to the proposal except* (not *excepting*) *Spain; he was well again except for* (not *excepting*) *a slight pain in his chest*

exception (ɪkˈsɛpʃən) *n* 1 the act of excepting or fact of being excepted; omission 2 anything excluded from or not in conformance with a general rule, principle, class, etc 3 criticism, esp when it is adverse; objection 4 *law* (formerly) a formal objection in the course of legal proceedings 5 *law* a clause or term in a document that restricts the usual legal effect of the document 6 **take exception a** (usually foll by *to*) to make objections (to); demur (at) **b** (often foll by *at*) to be offended (by); be resentful (at)

exceptionable (ɪkˈsɛpʃənəbəl) *adj* open to or subject to objection; objectionable > ex'ceptionableness *n* > ex'ceptionably *adv*

exceptional (ɪkˈsɛpʃənəl) *adj* 1 forming an exception; not ordinary 2 having much more than average intelligence, ability, or skill > ex'ceptionally *adv*

exceptionalism (ɪkˈsɛpʃənəˌlɪzm) *n* an attitude to other countries, cultures, etc based on the idea of being quite distinct from, and often superior to, them in vital ways

exceptive (ɪkˈsɛptɪv) *adj* relating to or forming an exception

excerpt *n* (ˈɛksɜːpt) 1 a part or passage taken from a book, speech, play, etc, and considered on its own; extract ▷ *vb* (ɛkˈsɜːpt) 2 (*tr*) to take (a part or passage) from a book, speech, play, etc [c17 from Latin *excerptum*, literally: (something) picked out, from *excerpere* to select, from *carpere* to pluck] > ex'cerptor *n* > ex'cerptible *adj* > ex'cerption *n*

excess *n* (ɪkˈsɛs, ˈɛksɛs) 1 the state or act of going beyond normal, sufficient, or permitted limits 2 an immoderate or abnormal amount, number, extent, or degree too much or too many: *an excess of tolerance* 3 the amount, number, extent, or degree by which one thing exceeds another 4 *chem* a quantity of a reagent that is greater than the quantity required to complete a reaction: *add an excess of acid* 5 overindulgence or intemperance 6 *insurance, chiefly Brit* a specified contribution towards the cost of a claim, stipulated on certain insurance policies as being payable by the policyholder 7 **in excess of** more than; over 8 **to excess** to an inordinate extent: *he drinks to excess* ▷ *adj* (usually prenominal) (ˈɛksɛs, ɪkˈsɛs) 9 more than normal, necessary, or permitted; surplus: *excess weight* 10 payable as a result of previous underpayment: *excess postage* [c14 from Latin *excessus*, from *excēdere* to go beyond; see EXCEED]

excess demand *n economics* a situation in which the market demand for a commodity is greater than its market supply, thus causing its market price to rise

excessive (ɪkˈsɛsɪv) *adj* exceeding the normal or permitted extents or limits; immoderate; inordinate > ex'cessively *adv* > ex'cessiveness *n*

excess luggage or **baggage** *n* luggage that is greater in weight or in number of pieces than an airline, etc, will carry free

excess supply *n economics* a situation in which the market supply of a commodity is greater than the market demand for it, thus causing its market price to fall

exchange (ɪksˈtʃeɪndʒ) *vb* 1 (*tr*) to give up, part with, or transfer (one thing) for an equivalent: *to exchange gifts; to exchange francs for dollars* 2 (*tr*) to give and receive (information, ideas, etc); interchange 3 (*tr*) to replace (one thing) with another, esp to replace unsatisfactory goods 4 to transfer or hand over (goods) in return for the equivalent value in kind rather than in money; barter; trade 5 (*tr*) *chess* to capture and surrender (pieces, usually of the same value) in a single sequence of moves ▷ *n* 6 the act or process of exchanging 7 **a** anything given or received as an

equivalent, replacement, or substitute for something else **b** (*as modifier*): *an exchange student* 8 an argument or quarrel; altercation: *the two men had a bitter exchange* 9 Also called: **telephone exchange** a switching centre in which telephone lines are interconnected 10 **a** a place where securities or commodities are sold, bought, or traded, esp by brokers or merchants: *a stock exchange; a corn exchange* **b** (*as modifier*): *an exchange broker* 11 **a** the system by which commercial debts between parties in different places are settled by commercial documents, esp bills of exchange, instead of by direct payment of money **b** the percentage or fee charged for accepting payment in this manner 12 a transfer or interchange of sums of money of equivalent value, as between different national currencies or different issues of the same currency 13 (*often plural*) the cheques, drafts, bills, etc, exchanged or settled between banks in a clearing house 14 *chess* the capture by both players of pieces of equal value, usually on consecutive moves 15 **win** (*or* **lose**) **the exchange** *chess* to win (or lose) a rook in return for a bishop or knight 16 *med* another word for **transfusion** (sense 2) 17 *physics* a process in which a particle is transferred between two nucleons, such as the transfer of a meson between two nucleons ▷ See also **bill of exchange, exchange rate, foreign exchange, labour exchange** [c14 from Anglo-French *eschaungier*, from Vulgar Latin *excambiāre* (unattested), from Latin *cambīre* to barter] > ex'changeable *adj* > ex,changea'bility *n* > ex'changeably *adv*

exchange force *n physics* 1 a force between two elementary particles resulting from the exchange of a virtual particle 2 the force causing the alignment of the magnetic dipole moments of atoms in ferromagnetic materials

exchanger (ɪksˈtʃeɪndʒə) *n* a person or thing that exchanges

exchange rate *n* the rate at which the currency unit of one country may be exchanged for that of another

Exchange Rate Mechanism *n* 1 the mechanism formerly used in the European Monetary System in which participating governments committed themselves to maintain the values of their currencies in relation to the ECU. Abbreviation: ERM 2 Also: **Exchange Rate Mechanism II** the mechanism used to stabilize the currencies of European Union states that have not adopted the euro but wish to maintain the value of their currency in relation to it. Abbreviation: ERM II

exchequer (ɪksˈtʃɛkə) *n* 1 (*often capital*) *government* (in Britain and certain other countries) the accounting department of the Treasury, responsible for receiving and issuing funds 2 *informal* personal funds; finances [c13 (in the sense: chessboard, counting table): from Old French *eschequier*, from *eschec* CHECK]

Exchequer (ɪksˈtʃɛkə) *n* See **Court of Exchequer**

excide (ɪkˈsaɪd) *vb* (*tr*) *rare* to cut out; excise [c18 from Latin *excīdere* to cut off, from *caedere* to cut]

excimer (ˈɛkˌsaɪmə) *n physics* an excited dimer formed by the association of excited and unexcited molecules, which would remain dissociated in the ground state

excipient (ɪkˈsɪpɪənt) *n* a substance, such as sugar or gum, used to prepare a drug or drugs in a form suitable for administration [c18 from Latin *excipiēns* excepting, from *excipere* to EXCEPT]

excisable (ɪkˈsaɪzəbəl) *adj* liable to an excise tax

excise[1] *n* (ˈɛksaɪz, ɛkˈsaɪz) 1 Also called: **excise tax** a tax on goods, such as spirits, produced for the home market 2 a tax paid for a licence to carry out various trades, sports, etc 3 *Brit* that section of the government service responsible for the collection of excise, now the Board of Customs and Excise [c15 probably from Middle Dutch *excijs*, probably from Old French *assise* a sitting, assessment, from Latin *assīdēre* to sit beside, assist in judging, from *sedēre* to sit] > ex'cisable *adj*

excise² (ɪk'saɪz) *vb (tr)* **1** to delete (a passage, sentence, etc); expunge **2** to remove (an organ, structure, or part) surgically [C16 from Latin *excīdere* to cut down; see EXCIDE] > **excision** (ɪk'sɪʒən) *n*

exciseman ('ɛksaɪz,mæn) *n, pl* **-men** *Brit* (formerly) a government agent whose function was to collect excise and prevent smuggling

excitable (ɪk'saɪtəbᵊl) *adj* **1** easily excited; volatile **2** (esp of a nerve) ready to respond to a stimulus > **ex,cita'bility** *or* **ex'citableness** *n* > **ex'citably** *adv*

excitant (ɪk'saɪtᵊnt, 'ɛksɪtənt) *adj also* **excitative** (ɪk'saɪtətɪv) *or* **excitatory** (ɪk'saɪtətərɪ) **1** able to excite or stimulate ▷ *n* **2** something, such as a drug or other agent, able to excite; stimulant

excitation (,ɛksɪ'teɪʃən) *n* **1** the act or process of exciting or state of being excited **2** a means of exciting or cause of excitement **3 a** the current in a field coil of a generator, motor, etc, or the magnetizing current in a transformer **b** (*as modifier*): *an excitation current* **4** the action of a stimulus on an animal or plant organ, inducing it to respond

excite (ɪk'saɪt) *vb (tr)* **1** to arouse (a person) to strong feeling, esp to pleasurable anticipation or nervous agitation **2** to arouse or elicit (an emotion, response, etc); evoke: *her answers excited curiosity* **3** to cause or bring about; stir up: *to excite a rebellion* **4** to arouse sexually **5** *physiol* to cause a response in or increase the activity of (an organ, tissue, or part); stimulate **6** to raise (an atom, molecule, electron, nucleus, etc) from the ground state to a higher energy level **7** to supply electricity to (the coils of a generator or motor) in order to create a magnetic field **8** to supply a signal to a stage of an active electronic circuit [C14 from Latin *excitāre*, from *excīēre* to stimulate, from *ciēre* to set in motion, rouse]

excited (ɪk'saɪtɪd) *adj* **1** emotionally aroused, esp to pleasure or agitation **2** characterized by excitement **3** sexually aroused **4** (of an atom, molecule, etc) occupying an energy level above the ground state > **ex'citedly** *adv* > **ex'citedness** *n*

excitement (ɪk'saɪtmənt) *n* **1** the state of being excited **2** a person or thing that excites; stimulation or thrill

exciter (ɪk'saɪtə) *n* **1** a person or thing that excites **2** a small generator that excites a larger machine **3** an oscillator producing a transmitter's carrier wave

exciting (ɪk'saɪtɪŋ) *adj* causing excitement; stirring; stimulating > **ex'citingly** *adv*

exciton ('ɛksaɪ,tɒn) *n* a mobile neutral entity in a crystalline solid consisting of an excited electron bound to the hole produced by its excitation [C20 from EXCIT(ATION) + -ON]

excitor (ɪk'saɪtə) *n* **1** a nerve that, when stimulated, causes increased activity in the organ or part it supplies **2** a variant spelling of **exciter**

exclaim (ɪk'skleɪm) *vb* to cry out or speak suddenly or excitedly, as from surprise, delight, horror, etc [C16 from Latin *exclāmāre*, from *clāmāre* to shout] > **ex'claimer** *n*

exclamation (,ɛksklə'meɪʃən) *n* **1** an abrupt, emphatic, or excited cry or utterance; interjection; ejaculation **2** the act of exclaiming > **,excla'mational** *adj*

exclamation mark *or US* **point** *n* **1** the punctuation mark ! used after exclamations and vehement commands **2** this mark used for any other purpose, as to draw attention to an obvious mistake, in road warning signs, (in chess commentaries) beside the notation of a move considered a good one, (in mathematics) as a symbol of the factorial function, or (in logic) occurring with an existential quantifier

exclamatory (ɪk'sklæmətərɪ, -trɪ) *adj* using, containing, or relating to exclamations > **ex'clamatorily** *adv*

exclaustration (,ɛksklɔː'streɪʃən) *n* the return of a monk or nun to the outside world after being released from his or her religious vows [from EX-¹ + Latin *claustrum* cloister]

exclave ('ɛkskleɪv) *n* a part of a country entirely surrounded by foreign territory: viewed from the position of the home country. Compare **enclave** [C20 from EX-¹ + *-clave*, on the model of ENCLAVE]

exclosure (ɪk'skləʊʒə) *n* an area of land, esp in a forest, fenced round to keep out unwanted animals

exclude (ɪk'skluːd) *vb (tr)* **1** to keep out; prevent from entering **2** to reject or not consider; leave out **3** to expel forcibly; eject **4** to debar from school, either temporarily or permanently, as a form of punishment [C14 from Latin *exclūdere*, from *claudere* to shut] > **ex'cludable** *or* **ex'cludible** *adj* > **ex'cluder** *n*

excluded middle *n logic* the principle that every proposition is either true or false, so that there is no third truth-value and no statements lack truth-value

excluding (ɪk'skluːdɪŋ) *prep* excepting

exclusion (ɪk'skluːʒən) *n* the act or an instance of excluding or the state of being excluded > **ex'clusionary** *adj*

exclusionist (ɪk'skluːʒənɪst) *adj* **1** *chiefly US* denoting or relating to a policy of excluding various types of immigrants, imports, etc ▷ *n* **2** a supporter of a policy of exclusion > **ex'clusion,ism** *n*

exclusion principle *n* See **Pauli exclusion principle**

exclusive (ɪk'skluːsɪv) *adj* **1** excluding all else; rejecting other considerations, possibilities, events, etc: *an exclusive preoccupation with money* **2** belonging to a particular individual or group and to no other; not shared: *exclusive rights; an exclusive story* **3** belonging to or catering for a privileged minority, esp a fashionable clique: *an exclusive restaurant* **4** (*postpositive*; foll by *to*) limited (to); found only (in): *this model is exclusive to Harrods* **5** single; unique; only: *the exclusive means of transport on the island was the bicycle* **6** separate and incompatible: *mutually exclusive principles* **7** (*immediately postpositive*) not including the numbers, dates, letters, etc, mentioned: *1980–84 exclusive* **8** (*postpositive*; foll by *of*) except (for); not taking account (of): *exclusive of bonus payments, you will earn this amount* **9** *commerce* (of a contract, agreement, etc) binding the parties to do business only with each other with respect to a class of goods or services **10** *logic* (of a disjunction) true if only one rather than both of its component propositions is true. Compare **inclusive** (sense 5) ▷ *n* **11** an exclusive story; a story reported in only one newspaper > **ex'clusively** *adv* > **exclusivity** (,ɛkskluː'sɪvɪtɪ) *or* **ex'clusiveness** *n*

Exclusive Brethren *pl n* one of the two main divisions of the Plymouth Brethren, which, in contrast to the Open Brethren, restricts its members' contacts with those outside the sect

exclusive economic zone *n* the coastal water and sea bed around a country's shores, to which it claims exclusive rights for oil exploration, fishing, etc. Sometimes shortened to: **economic zone**

exclusive or *n logic* the connective that gives the value *true* to a disjunction if one or other, but not both, of the disjuncts are true. Also called: **exclusive disjunction**. Compare **inclusive or**

exclusive OR circuit *or* **gate** *n electronics* a computer logic circuit having two or more input wires and one output wire and giving a high-voltage output signal if a low-voltage signal is fed to one or more, but not all, of the input wires. Compare **OR circuit**

excogitate (ɛks'kɒdʒɪ,teɪt) *vb (tr)* **1** to devise, invent, or contrive **2** to think out in detail [C16 from Latin *excōgitāre*, from *cōgitāre* to ponder, COGITATE] > **ex'cogitable** *adj* > **ex,cogi'tation** *n* > **ex'cogitative** *adj* > **ex'cogi,tator** *n*

excommunicate *RC Church* ▷ *vb* (,ɛkskə'mjuːnɪ,keɪt) **1** (*tr*) to sentence (a member of the Church) to exclusion from the communion of believers and from the privileges and public prayers of the Church ▷ *adj* (,ɛkskə'mjuːnɪkɪt, -,keɪt) **2** having incurred such a sentence ▷ *n* (,ɛkskə'mjuːnɪkɪt, -,keɪt) **3** an excommunicated person [C15 from Late Latin *excommūnicāre*, literally: to exclude from the community, from Latin *commūnis* COMMON] > **,excom'municable** *adj* > **,excom,muni'cation** *n* > **,excom'municative** *or* **,excom'municatory** *adj* > **,excom'municator** *n*

excoriate (ɪk'skɔːrɪ,eɪt) *vb (tr)* **1** to strip (the skin) from (a person or animal); flay **2** *med* to lose (a superficial area of skin), as by scratching, the application of chemicals, etc **3** to censure severely [C15 from Late Latin *excoriāre* to strip, flay, from Latin *corium* skin, hide] > **ex,cori'ation** *n*

excrement ('ɛkskrɪmənt) *n* waste matter discharged from the body, esp faeces; excreta [C16 from Latin *excrēmentum*, from *excernere* to sift, EXCRETE] > **excremental** (,ɛkskrɪ'mɛntᵊl) *or* **excrementitious** (,ɛkskrɪmɛn'tɪʃəs) *adj*

excrescence (ɪk'skrɛsᵊns) *n* a projection or protuberance, esp an outgrowth from an organ or part of the body > **excrescential** (,ɛkskrɪ'sɛnʃəl) *adj*

excrescency (ɪk'skrɛsənsɪ) *n, pl* **-cies** **1** the state or condition of being excrescent **2** another word for **excrescence**

excrescent (ɪk'skrɛsᵊnt) *adj* **1** denoting, relating to, or resembling an abnormal outgrowth **2** uselessly added; not essential; superfluous **3** denoting or relating to a speech sound or letter inserted into a word without etymological justification, such as the *b* in *nimble* [C17 from Latin *excrēscēns*, from *excrēscere*, from *crēscere* to grow] > **ex'crescently** *adv*

excreta (ɪk'skriːtə) *pl n* waste matter, such as urine, faeces, or sweat, discharged from the body; excrement [C19 New Latin, from Latin *excernere* to EXCRETE] > **ex'cretal** *adj*

excrete (ɪk'skriːt) *vb* **1** to discharge (waste matter, such as urine, sweat, carbon dioxide, or faeces) from the body through the kidneys, skin, lungs, bowels, etc **2** (of plants) to eliminate (waste matter, such as carbon dioxide and salts) through the leaves, roots, etc [C17 from Latin *excernere* to separate, discharge, from *cernere* to sift] > **ex'creter** *n* > **ex'cretion** *n* > **ex'cretive** *or* **ex'cretory** *adj*

e

excruciate (ɪk'skruːʃɪ,eɪt) *vb (tr)* **1** to inflict mental suffering on; torment **2** *obsolete* to inflict physical pain on [C16 from Latin *excruciāre*, from *cruciāre* to crucify, from *crux* cross] > **ex,cruci'ation** *n*

excruciating (ɪk'skruːʃɪ,eɪtɪŋ) *adj* **1** unbearably painful; agonizing **2** intense; extreme: *he took excruciating pains to do it well* **3** *informal* irritating; trying **4** *humorous* very bad: *an excruciating pun* > **ex'cruci,atingly** *adv*

exculpate ('ɛkskʌl,peɪt, ɪk'skʌlpeɪt) *vb (tr)* to free from blame or guilt; vindicate or exonerate [C17 from Medieval Latin *exculpāre*, from Latin EX-¹ + *culpāre* to blame, from *culpa* fault, blame] > **exculpable** (ɪk'skʌlpəbᵊl) *adj* > **,excul'pation** *n* > **ex'culpatory** *adj*

excurrent (ɛk'skʌrənt) *adj* **1** *zoology* having an outward flow, as certain pores in sponges, ducts, etc **2** *botany* **a** (of veins) extending beyond the margin of the leaf **b** having an undivided main stem or trunk, as the spruce and other conifers **3** flowing or running in an outward direction [C19 from Latin *excurrere* to run forth; see EXCURSION]

excursion (ɪk'skɜːʃən, -ʒən) *n* **1** a short outward and return journey, esp for relaxation, sightseeing, etc; outing **2** a group of people going on such a journey **3** (*modifier*) of or relating to special reduced rates offered on certain journeys by rail: *an excursion ticket* **4** a digression or deviation: *an excursion into politics* **5** (formerly) a raid or attack **6** *physics* **a** a movement from an equilibrium position, as in an oscillation **b** the magnitude of this displacement **7** the normal movement of a movable bodily organ or part from its resting position, such as the lateral movement of the lower jaw **8** *machinery* the locus of a point on a moving part, esp the deflection of a whirling shaft [C16 from Latin *excursiō* an attack, from *excurrere* to run out, from *currere* to run]

excursionist (ɪk'skɜːʃənɪst, -ʒənɪst) *n* a person who goes on an excursion

excursive (ɪk'skɜːsɪv) *adj* **1** tending to digress **2** involving detours; rambling [C17 from Latin *excursus*, from *excurrere* to run forth] > ex'cursively *adv* > ex'cursiveness *n*

excursus (ɛk'skɜːsəs) *n, pl* -suses *or* -sus an incidental digression from the main topic under discussion or from the main story in a narrative [C19 from Latin: a running forth, from *excurrere* to run out]

excusatory (ɪk'skjuːzətərɪ, -trɪ) *adj* tending to or intended to excuse; apologetic

excuse *vb* (ɪk'skjuːz) (*tr*) **1** to pardon or forgive: *he always excuses her unpunctuality* **2** to seek pardon or exemption for (a person, esp oneself): *to excuse oneself for one's mistakes* **3** to make allowances for; judge leniently: *to excuse someone's ignorance* **4** to serve as an apology or explanation for; vindicate or justify: *her age excuses her behaviour* **5** to exempt from a task, obligation, etc: *you are excused making breakfast* **6** to dismiss or allow to leave: *he asked them to excuse him* **7** to seek permission for (someone, esp oneself) to leave: *he excused himself and left* **8** be excused *euphemistic* to go to the lavatory **9** excuse me! an expression used to catch someone's attention or to apologize for an interruption, disagreement, or social indiscretion ▷ *n* (ɪk'skjuːs) **10** an explanation offered in defence of some fault or offensive behaviour or as a reason for not fulfilling an obligation, etc **11** *informal* an inferior example of something specified; makeshift: *she is a poor excuse for a hostess* **12** the act of excusing [C13 from Latin *excusāre*, from EX-[1] + -*cūsare*, from *causa* cause, accusation] > ex'cusable *adj* > ex'cusableness *n* > ex'cusably *adv*

excuse-me *n* a dance in which a person may take another's partner

ex-directory *adj chiefly Brit* not listed in a telephone directory, by request, and not disclosed to inquirers. US and Canadian term: unlisted

ex div. *abbreviation for* ex dividend

ex dividend *adv* without the right to the current dividend: *to quote shares ex dividend*. Compare **cum dividend**

exeat ('ɛksɪət) *n Brit* **1** leave of absence from school or some other institution **2** a bishop's permission for a priest to leave his diocese in order to take up an appointment elsewhere [C18 Latin, literally: he may go out, from *exīre*]

exec. *abbreviation for* **1** executive **2** executor

execrable ('ɛksɪkrəbᵊl) *adj* **1** deserving to be execrated; abhorrent **2** of very poor quality: *an execrable meal* [C14 from Latin *exsecrābilis*, from *exsecrārī* to EXECRATE] > 'execrableness *n* > 'execrably *adv*

execrate ('ɛksɪˌkreɪt) *vb* **1** (*tr*) to loathe; detest; abhor **2** (*tr*) to profess great abhorrence for; denounce; deplore **3** to curse (a person or thing); damn [C16 from Latin *exsecrārī* to curse, from EX-[1] + -*secrārī* from *sacer* SACRED] > ˌexe'cration *n* > 'exeˌcrative *or* 'exeˌcratory *adj* > 'exeˌcratively *adv*

executable (ɪg'zɛkjʊtəbᵊl) *adj* **1** (of a computer program) able to be run ▷ *n* **2** a file containing a program that will run as soon as it is opened

executant (ɪg'zɛkjʊtənt) *n* a performer, esp of musical works

executary (ɪg'zɛkjʊtrɪ) *n, pl* -aries a person whose job comprises tasks appropriate to a middle-management executive as well as those traditionally carried out by a secretary [C20 from EXECU(TIVE) + (SECRE)TARY]

execute ('ɛksɪˌkjuːt) *vb* (*tr*) **1** to put (a condemned person) to death; inflict capital punishment upon **2** to carry out; complete; perform; do: *to execute an order* **3** to perform; accomplish; effect: *to execute a pirouette* **4** to make or produce: *to execute a drawing* **5** to carry into effect (a judicial sentence, the law, etc); enforce **6** *law* to comply with legal formalities in order to render (a deed, etc) effective, as by signing, sealing, and delivering **7** to sign (a will) in the presence of witnesses and in accordance with other legal formalities **8** to carry out the terms of (a contract, will, etc) [C14 from Old French *executer*, back formation from *executeur* EXECUTOR] > 'exeˌcuter *n*

execution (ˌɛksɪ'kjuːʃən) *n* **1** the act or process of executing **2** the carrying out or undergoing of a sentence of death **3** the style or manner in which something is accomplished or performed; technique: *as a pianist his execution is poor* **4 a** the enforcement of the judgment of a court of law **b** the writ ordering such enforcement

executioner (ˌɛksɪ'kjuːʃənə) *n* **1** an official charged with carrying out the death sentence passed upon a condemned person **2** an assassin, esp one appointed by a political or criminal organization

executive (ɪg'zɛkjʊtɪv) *n* **1 a** a person or group responsible for the administration of a project, activity, or business **b** (*as modifier*): *executive duties* **2 a** the branch of government responsible for carrying out laws, decrees, etc; administration **b** any administration. Compare **judiciary, legislature** ▷ *adj* **3** having the function or purpose of carrying plans, orders, laws, etc, into practical effect **4** of, relating to, or designed for an executive: *the executive suite* **5** *informal* of the most expensive or exclusive type: *executive housing* > ex'ecutively *adv*

Executive Council *n* (in Australia and New Zealand) a body consisting of ministers of the Crown presided over by the Governor or Governor-General that formally approves Cabinet decisions, etc

executive director *n* a member of the board of directors of a company who is also an employee (usually full-time) of that company and who often has a specified area of responsibility, such as finance or production. Compare **nonexecutive director**

executive officer *n* **1** the second-in-command of any of certain military units. Abbreviation (US): XO **2** a specialist seaman officer, responsible under the captain for the routine efficient running of the ship in the US, British (formerly), and certain other navies

executive session *n US government* a session of the Senate for the discussion of executive business, such as the ratification of treaties: formerly held in secret

executor (ɪg'zɛkjʊtə) *n* **1** *law* a person appointed by a testator to carry out the wishes expressed in his will **2** a person who executes [C13 from Anglo-French *executour*, from Latin *execūtor*, from EX-[1] + *sequi* follow] > exˌecu'torial *adj* > ex'ecutorˌship *n*

executory (ɪg'zɛkjʊtərɪ, -trɪ) *adj* **1** (of a law, agreement, etc) coming into operation at a future date; not yet effective: *an executory contract* **2** executive; administrative

executrix (ɪg'zɛkjʊtrɪks) *n, pl* **executrices** (ɪgˌzɛkjʊ'traɪsiːz) *or* **executrixes** *law* a female executor

exedra ('ɛksɪdrə, ɛk'siː-) *n* **1** a building, room, portico, or apse containing a continuous bench, used in ancient Greece and Rome for holding discussions **2** an outdoor bench in a recess [C18 via Latin from Greek, from *hedra* seat]

exegesis (ˌɛksɪ'dʒiːsɪs) *n, pl* -ses (-siːz) explanation or critical interpretation of a text, esp of the Bible. Compare **eisegesis** [C17 from Greek, from *exēgeisthai* to interpret, from EX-[1] + *hēgeisthai* to guide]

exegete ('ɛksɪˌdʒiːt) *or* **exegetist** (ˌɛksɪ'dʒiːtɪst, -'dʒɛt-) *n* a person who practises exegesis [C18 from Greek *exēgētēs*, from *exēgeisthai* to interpret; see EXEGESIS]

exegetic (ˌɛksɪ'dʒɛtɪk) *or* **exegetical** *adj* of or relating to exegesis; expository > ˌexe'getically *adv*

exegetics (ˌɛksɪ'dʒɛtɪks) *n* (*functioning as singular*) the scientific study of exegesis and exegetical methods

exemplar (ɪg'zɛmplə, -plɑː) *n* **1** a person or thing to be copied or imitated **2** a typical specimen or instance **3** a copy of a book or text on which further printings have been based [C14 from Latin *exemplarium* model, from *exemplum* EXAMPLE]

exemplary (ɪg'zɛmplərɪ) *adj* **1** fit for imitation; model: *an exemplary performance* **2** serving as a warning; admonitory: *an exemplary jail sentence* **3** representative; typical: *an action exemplary of his conduct* > ex'emplarily *adv* > ex'emplariness *n*

exemplary damages *pl n law* damages awarded to a plaintiff above the value of actual loss sustained so that they serve also as a punishment to the defendant and a deterrent to others

exemplify (ɪg'zɛmplɪˌfaɪ) *vb* -fies, -fying, -fied (*tr*) **1** to show by example **2** to serve as an example of **3** *law* **a** to make an official copy of (a document from public records) under seal **b** to transcribe (a legal document) [C15 via Old French from Medieval Latin *exemplificāre*, from Latin *exemplum* EXAMPLE + *facere* to make] > ex'empliˌfiable *adj* > exˌemplifi'cation *n* > ex'emplifiˌcative *adj* > ex'empliˌfier *n*

exempli gratia *Latin* (ɪg'zɛmplaɪ 'grɑːtɪˌɑː) for the sake of example. Abbreviations: e.g., eg., eg

exemplum (ɪg'zɛmpləm) *n, pl* -pla (-plə) **1** an anecdote that supports a moral point or sustains an argument, used esp in medieval sermons **2** an example or illustration [from Latin: EXAMPLE]

exempt (ɪg'zɛmpt) *vb* **1** (*tr*) to release from an obligation, liability, tax, etc; excuse: *to exempt a soldier from drill* ▷ *adj* (*sometimes postpositive*) **2** freed from or not subject to an obligation, liability, tax, etc; excused: *exempt gilts; tax-exempt bonus* **3** *obsolete* set apart; remote ▷ *n* **4** a person who is exempt from an obligation, tax, etc [C14 from Latin *exemptus* removed, from *eximere* to take out, from *emere* to buy, obtain] > ex'emption *n*

exenterate *vb* (ɪg'zɛntəˌreɪt) (*tr*) **1** *surgery* to remove (internal organs, an eyeball, etc); eviscerate **2** a rare word for **disembowel** ▷ *adj* (ɪg'zɛntəˌreɪt, -rɪt) **3** *rare* having been disembowelled [C17 from Latin *exenterāre*, from EX-[1] + Greek *enteron* intestine] > exˌenter'ation *n*

exequatur (ˌɛksɪ'kweɪtə) *n* **1** an official authorization issued by a host country to a consular agent, permitting him to perform his official duties **2** an act by which the civil governments of certain nations permit the laws of the Roman Catholic Church to take effect in their territories [C18 from Latin, literally: let him perform, from *exequī* to perform, from EX-[1] + *sequī* to follow]

exequies ('ɛksɪkwɪz) *pl n, sing* -quy the rites and ceremonies used at funerals [C14 from Latin *exequiae* (plural) funeral procession, rites, from *exequī* to follow to the end, from *sequī* to follow]

exercise ('ɛksəˌsaɪz) *vb* (*mainly tr*) **1** to put into use; employ: *to exercise tact* **2** (*intr*) to take exercise or perform exercises; exert one's muscles, etc, esp in order to keep fit **3** to practise using in order to develop or train: *to exercise one's voice* **4** to perform or make proper use of: *to exercise one's rights* **5** to bring to bear; exert: *to exercise one's influence* **6** (*often passive*) to occupy the attentions of, esp so as to worry or vex: *to be exercised about a decision* **7** *military* to carry out or cause to carry out, manoeuvres, simulated combat operations, etc ▷ *n* **8** physical exertion, esp for the purpose of development, training, or keeping fit **9** mental or other activity or practice, esp in order to develop a skill **10** a set of movements, questions, tasks, etc, designed to train, improve, or test one's ability in a particular field: *piano exercises* **11** a performance or work of art done as practice or to demonstrate a technique **12** the performance of a function; discharge: *the exercise of one's rights* **13** (*sometimes plural*) *military* a manoeuvre or simulated combat operation carried out for training and evaluation **14** (*usually plural*) *US and Canadian* a ceremony or formal routine, esp at a school or college: *opening exercises; graduation exercises* **15** *gymnastics* a particular type of event, such as performing on the horizontal bar [C14 from Old French *exercice*, from Latin *exercitium*, from *exercēre* to drill, from EX-[1] + *arcēre* to ward off]

> ˈexerˌcisable *adj*
exercise bike *or* **cycle** *n* a stationary exercise machine that is pedalled like a bicycle as a method of increasing cardiovascular fitness
exercise book *n* a notebook used by students
exercise price *n stock exchange* the price at which the holder of a traded option may exercise his right to buy (or sell) a security
exerciser (ˈɛksəˌsaɪzə) *n* **1** a device with springs or elasticated cords for muscular exercise **2** a person or thing that exercises
exercitation (ɪɡˌzɜːsɪˈteɪʃən) *n* a rare word for **exercise** [C14 from Latin *exercitātiō*, from *exercitāre* frequentative of *exercēre* to EXERCISE]
exergonic (ˌɛksəˈɡɒnɪk) *adj* (of a biochemical reaction) producing energy and therefore occurring spontaneously. Compare **endergonic** [C20 from EX(O)- + Greek *ergon* work + -IC]
exergue (ɛkˈsɜːɡ) *n* a space on the reverse of a coin or medal below the central design, often containing the date, place of minting, etc [C17 from French, from Medieval Latin *exergum*, from Greek *ex* outside + *ergon* work] > exˈergual *adj*
exert (ɪɡˈzɜːt) *vb (tr)* **1** to use (influence, authority, etc) forcefully or effectively **2** to apply (oneself) diligently; make a strenuous effort [C17 (in the sense: push forth, emit): from Latin *exserere* to thrust out, from EX-[1] + *serere* to bind together, entwine] > exˈertion *n* > exˈertive *adj*
Exeter (ˈɛksɪtə) *n* a city in SW England, administrative centre of Devon; university (1955). Pop: 106 772 (2001)
exeunt *Latin* (ˈɛksɪˌʌnt) they go out: used as a stage direction
exeunt omnes *Latin* (ˈɛksɪˌʌnt ˈɒmneɪz) they all go out: used as a stage direction
exfoliant (ɛksˈfəʊlɪənt) *n* a gently abrasive cosmetic product designed to remove dead cells from the skin's surface [C20 from EXFOLIATE + -ANT]
exfoliate (ɛksˈfəʊlɪˌeɪt) *vb* **1** *(tr)* to wash (a part of the body) with a granular cosmetic preparation in order to remove dead cells from the skin's surface **2** (of bark, skin, etc) to peel off in (layers, flakes, or scales) **3** *(intr)* (of rocks or minerals) to shed the thin outermost layer because of weathering or heating **4** (of some minerals, esp mica) to split or cause to split into thin flakes [C17 from Late Latin *exfoliāre* to strip off leaves, from Latin *folium* leaf] > exˌfoliˈation *n* > exˈfoliative *adj*
ex gratia (ˈɡreɪʃə) *adj* given as a favour or gratuitously where no legal obligation exists: *an ex gratia payment* [New Latin, literally: out of kindness]
exhalant (ɛksˈheɪlənt, ɪɡˈzeɪ-) *adj* **1** emitting a vapour or liquid; exhaling: *exhalant duct* ▷ *n* **2** an organ or vessel that emits a vapour or liquid
exhale (ɛksˈheɪl, ɪɡˈzeɪl) *vb* **1** to expel (breath, tobacco smoke, etc) from the lungs; breathe out **2** to give off (air, vapour, fumes, etc) or (of air, vapour, etc) to be given off; emanate [C14 from Latin *exhālāre* to breathe out, from *hālāre* to breathe] > exˈhalable *adj* > ˌexhaˈlation *n*
exhaust (ɪɡˈzɔːst) *vb (mainly tr)* **1** to drain the energy of; tire out **2** to deprive of resources, etc: *a nation exhausted by war* **3** to deplete totally; expend; consume: *to exhaust food supplies* **4** to empty (a container) by drawing off or pumping out (the contents) **5** to develop or discuss thoroughly so that no further interest remains: *to exhaust a topic of conversation* **6** to remove gas from (a vessel, etc) in order to reduce the pressure or create a vacuum; evacuate **7** to remove or use up the active ingredients from (a drug, solution, etc) **8** to destroy the fertility of (soil) by excessive cultivation **9** *(intr)* (of steam or other gases) to be emitted or to escape from an engine after being expanded ▷ *n* **10** gases ejected from an engine as waste products **11** **a** the expulsion of expanded gas or steam from an engine **b** (*as modifier*): *exhaust stroke* **12** **a** the parts of an engine through which the exhausted gases or steam pass **b** (*as modifier*): *exhaust valve; exhaust pipe* [C16 from Latin *exhaustus* made empty, from *exhaurīre* to draw out, from *haurīre* to draw, drain] > exˈhausted *adj* > exˈhauster *n* > exˈhaustible *adj* > exˌhaustiˈbility *n* > exˈhausting *adj*
exhaustion (ɪɡˈzɔːstʃən) *n* **1** extreme tiredness; fatigue **2** the condition of being used up; consumption: *exhaustion of the earth's resources* **3** the act of exhausting or the state of being exhausted
exhaustive (ɪɡˈzɔːstɪv) *adj* **1** comprehensive in scope; thorough: *an exhaustive survey* **2** tending to exhaust > exˈhaustively *adv* > exˈhaustiveness *n*
exhaust stroke *n* another name for **scavenge stroke**
exhibit (ɪɡˈzɪbɪt) *vb (mainly tr)* **1** (*also intr*) to display (something) to the public for interest or instruction: *this artist exhibits all over the world* **2** to manifest; display; show: *the child exhibited signs of distress* **3** *law* to produce (a document or object) in court to serve as evidence ▷ *n* **4** an object or collection exhibited to the public **5** *law* a document or object produced in court and referred to or identified by a witness in giving evidence [C15 from Latin *exhibēre* to hold forth, from *habēre* to have] > exˈhibitory *adj*
exhibition (ˌɛksɪˈbɪʃən) *n* **1** a public display of art, products, skills, activities, etc: *a judo exhibition* **2** the act of exhibiting or the state of being exhibited **3** **make an exhibition of oneself** to behave so foolishly in public that one excites notice or ridicule **4** *Brit* a scholarship awarded to a student at a university or school
exhibitioner (ˌɛksɪˈbɪʃənə) *n Brit* a student who has been awarded an exhibition
exhibitionism (ˌɛksɪˈbɪʃəˌnɪzəm) *n* **1** a compulsive desire to attract attention to oneself, esp by absurd or exaggerated behaviour or boasting **2** *psychiatry* a compulsive desire to expose one's genital organs publicly > ˌexhiˈbitionist *n, adj* > ˌexhiˌbitionˈistic *adj*
exhibition killing *n* the murder of a hostage by terrorists, filmed for broadcasting on television or the internet
exhibitive (ɪɡˈzɪbɪtɪv) *adj* (*usually postpositive* and foll by *of*) illustrative or demonstrative: *a masterpiece exhibitive of his talent* > exˈhibitively *adv*
exhibitor (ɪɡˈzɪbɪtə) *n* **1** a person or thing that exhibits **2** an individual or company that shows films, esp the manager or owner of a cinema
exhilarant (ɪɡˈzɪlərənt) *adj* **1** exhilarating; invigorating ▷ *n* **2** something that exhilarates
exhilarate (ɪɡˈzɪləˌreɪt) *vb (tr)* to make lively and cheerful; gladden; elate [C16 from Latin *exhilarāre*, from *hilarāre* to cheer; see HILARIOUS] > exˌhilaˈration *n* > exˈhilarative *or* exˈhilaratory *adj*
exhilarating (ɪɡˈzɪləˌreɪtɪŋ) *adj* causing strong feelings of excitement and happiness: *an exhilarating helicopter trip* > exˈhilaˌratingly *adv*
exhort (ɪɡˈzɔːt) *vb* to urge or persuade (someone) earnestly; advise strongly [C14 from Latin *exhortārī*, from *hortārī* to urge] > **exhortative** (ɪɡˈzɔːtətɪv) *or* exˈhortatory *adj* > exˈhorter *n*
exhortation (ˌɛɡzɔːˈteɪʃən) *n* **1** the act or process of exhorting **2** a speech or written passage intended to persuade, inspire, or encourage
exhume (ɛksˈhjuːm) *vb (tr)* **1** to dig up (something buried, esp a corpse); disinter **2** to reveal; disclose; unearth: *don't exhume that old argument* [C18 from Medieval Latin *exhumāre*, from Latin EX-[1] + *humāre* to bury, from *humus* the ground] > **exhumation** (ˌɛkshjʊˈmeɪʃən) *n* > exˈhumer *n*
ex hypothesi (ɛks haɪˈpɒθəsɪ) *adv* in accordance with or following from the hypothesis stated [C17 New Latin]
exigency (ˈɛksɪdʒənsɪ, ɪɡˈzɪdʒənsɪ) *or* **exigence** (ˈɛksɪdʒəns) *n, pl* **-gencies** *or* **-gences** **1** the state of being exigent; urgency **2** (*often plural*) an urgent demand; pressing requirement **3** an emergency
exigent (ˈɛksɪdʒənt) *adj* **1** urgent; pressing **2** exacting; demanding [C15 from Latin *exigere* to drive out, weigh out, from *agere* to drive, compel] > ˈexigently *adv*
exigible (ˈɛksɪdʒəbᵊl) *adj* liable to be exacted or required: *part of the debt is exigible this month* [C17 from French, from *exiger* to demand, from Latin *exigere*; see EXIGENT]
exiguous (ɪɡˈzɪɡjʊəs, ɪkˈsɪɡ-) *adj* scanty or slender; meagre: *an exiguous income* [C17 from Latin *exiguus*, from *exigere* to weigh out; see EXIGENT] > **exiguity** (ˌɛksɪˈɡjuːɪtɪ) *or* exˈiguousness *n* > exˈiguously *adv*
exile (ˈɛɡzaɪl, ˈɛksaɪl) *n* **1** a prolonged, usually enforced absence from one's home or country; banishment **2** the expulsion of a person from his native land by official decree **3** a person banished or living away from his home or country; expatriate ▷ *vb* **4** to expel from home or country, esp by official decree as a punishment; banish [C13 from Latin *exsilium* banishment, from *exsul* banished person; perhaps related to Greek *alasthai* to wander] > **exilic** (ɛɡˈzɪlɪk, ɛkˈsɪlɪk) *or* exˈilian *adj*
Exile (ˈɛɡzaɪl, ˈɛksaɪl) *n* **the** another name for the **Babylonian captivity** (of the Jews)
eximious (ɛɡˈzɪmɪəs) *adj rare* distinguished; eminent [C16 from Latin *eximius*, from *eximere* to take out, from *emere* to purchase] > exˈimiously *adv*
exine (ˈɛksɪn, -aɪn) *or* **extine** (ˈɛkstɪn, -tiːn, -taɪn) *n botany* the outermost coat of a pollen grain or a spore. Compare **intine**
exist (ɪɡˈzɪst) *vb (intr)* **1** to have being or reality; to be **2** to eke out a living; stay alive; survive: *I can barely exist on this wage* **3** to be living; live **4** to be present under specified conditions or in a specified place: *sharks exist in the Pacific* **5** *philosophy* **a** to be actual rather than merely possible **b** to be a member of the domain of some theory, an element of some possible world, etc **c** to have contingent being while free, responsible, and aware of one's situation [C17 from Latin *exsistere* to step forth, from EX-[1] + *sistere* to stand] > exˈisting *adj*
existence (ɪɡˈzɪstəns) *n* **1** the fact or state of existing; being **2** the continuance or maintenance of life; living, esp in adverse circumstances: *a struggle for existence; she has a wretched existence* **3** something that exists; a being or entity **4** everything that exists, esp that is living
existent (ɪɡˈzɪstənt) *adj* **1** in existence; extant; current **2** having existence; living ▷ *n* **3** a person or a thing that exists
existential (ˌɛɡzɪˈstɛnʃəl) *adj* **1** of or relating to existence, esp human existence **2** *philosophy* pertaining to what exists, and is thus known by experience rather than reason; empirical as opposed to theoretical **3** *logic* denoting or relating to a formula or proposition asserting the existence of at least one object fulfilling a given condition; containing an existential quantifier **4** of or relating to existentialism ▷ *n logic* **5** **a** an existential statement or formula **b** short for **existential quantifier.** > ˌexisˈtentially *adv*
existentialism (ˌɛɡzɪˈstɛnʃəˌlɪzəm) *n* a modern philosophical movement stressing the importance of personal experience and responsibility and the demands that they make on the individual, who is seen as a free agent in a deterministic and seemingly meaningless universe > ˌexisˈtentialist *adj, n*
existential quantifier *n logic* a formal device, for which the conventional symbol is ∃, which indicates that the open sentence that follows is true of at least one member of the relevant universe of interpretation, as (∃*x*) *Fx* meaning "something is (an) F," "something Fs," or "there are (some) Fs."
exit (ˈɛɡzɪt, ˈɛksɪt) *n* **1** a way out; door or gate by which people may leave **2** the act or an instance of going out; departure **3** **a** the act of leaving or right to leave a particular place **b** (*as modifier*): *an exit visa* **4** departure from life; death **5** *theatre* the act of going offstage **6** (in Britain) a point at which vehicles may leave or join a motorway **7** *bridge* **a** the act of losing the lead deliberately **b** a card enabling one to do this ▷ *vb (intr)* **8** to go away or out; depart; leave **9** *theatre* to go offstage:

e

used as a stage direction: *exit Hamlet* **10** *bridge* to lose the lead deliberately **11** (*sometimes tr*) *computing* to leave (a computer program or system) [c17 from Latin *exitus* a departure, from *exīre* to go out, from EX-¹ + *īre* to go]

Exit ('ɛgzɪt, 'ɛksɪt) *n* (in Britain) a society that seeks to promote the legitimization of voluntary euthanasia

exitance ('ɛksɪtəns) *n* a measure of the ability of a surface to emit radiation. See **luminous exitance, radiant exitance**

exit poll *n* a poll taken by an organization by asking people how they voted in an election as they leave a polling station

exit pupil *n* the smallest cross section of the beam of light from the eyepiece of a telescope through which all the light from the eyepiece passes. Its diameter is equal to the ratio of the focal length of the eyepiece to the focal ratio of the telescope

exit strategy *n* **1** a method or plan for extricating oneself from an undesirable situation **2** a plan and timetable for withdrawal from a military engagement **3** the method by which an investor intends to cash out of an investment

ex lib. *abbreviation for* ex libris

ex libris (ɛks 'liːbrɪs) *adj* **1** from the collection or library of: frequently printed on bookplates ▷ *n* *ex-libris* **2** a bookplate bearing the owner's name, etc [c19 from Latin, literally: from the books (of)]

Exmoor ('ɛksˌmʊə, -ˌmɔː) *n* **1** a high moorland in SW England, in W Somerset and N Devon: chiefly grazing ground for Exmoor ponies, sheep, and red deer **2** a small stocky breed of pony with a fawn-coloured nose, originally from Exmoor

Exmouth ('ɛksməθ) *n* a town in SW England, in Devon, at the mouth of the River Exe: tourism, fishing. Pop: 32 972 (2001)

ex new *adv, adj* (of shares, etc) without the right to take up any scrip issue or rights issue. Compare **cum new**

exo ('ɛksəʊ) *adj Austral* an informal word for **excellent**

exo- *combining form* external, outside, or beyond: *exobiology; exothermal* [from Greek *exō* outside]

exobiology (ˌɛksəʊbaɪ'ɒlədʒɪ) *n* another name for **astrobiology**. > ˌexobi'ologist *n*

exocarp ('ɛksəʊˌkɑːp) *n* another name for **epicarp**

exocentric (ˌɛksəʊ'sɛntrɪk) *adj grammar* (of a construction) not fulfilling the grammatical role of any of its constituents; as in *until last Easter*, where the constituents are prepositional, adjectival, and nominal, while the whole construction is adverbial. Compare **endocentric**

Exocet ('ɛksəʊsɛt) *n trademark* a tactical missile with a high-explosive warhead, which is guided by computer and radar, travels at a very low altitude at high subsonic speed, and has a range of up to 70 km. It may be launched from a ship, aircraft, or submarine [c20 from French, from New Latin *Exocoetus volitans* flying fish]

exocrine ('ɛksəʊˌkraɪn, -krɪn) *adj* **1** of or relating to exocrine glands or their secretions ▷ *n* **2** an exocrine gland ▷ Compare **endocrine** [c20 EXO- + *-crine* from Greek *krinein* to separate]

exocrine gland *n* any gland, such as a salivary or sweat gland, that secretes its products through a duct onto an epithelial surface

exocuticle ('ɛksəʊˌkjuːtɪkªl) *n* the layer of an insect's cuticle between the epicuticle and the endocuticle, which is often hard and dark

exocytosis (ˌɛksəʊsaɪ'təʊsɪs) *n* a process by which material is exported from a biological cell

Exod. *Bible abbreviation for* Exodus

exoderm ('ɛksəʊˌdɜːm) *n embryol* another name for **ectoderm**

exodontics (ˌɛksəʊ'dɒntɪks) *n* (*functioning as singular*) the branch of dental surgery concerned with the extraction of teeth. Also called: **exodontia** (ˌɛksəʊ'dɒnʃə) [c20 New Latin, from EX-¹ + *-odontia*, from Greek *odōn* tooth] > ˌexo'dontist *n*

exodus ('ɛksədəs) *n* the act or an instance of

going out [c17 via Latin from Greek *exodos* from EX-¹ + *hodos* way]

Exodus ('ɛksədəs) *n* **1 the** the departure of the Israelites from Egypt led by Moses **2** the second book of the Old Testament, recounting the events connected with this and the divine visitation of Moses at Mount Sinai

exoenzyme (ˌɛksəʊ'ɛnzaɪm) *n* **1** any enzyme, esp an exopeptidase, that acts upon terminal chemical bonds in a chain of molecules. Compare **endoenzyme 2** another name for **ectoenzyme**

exoergic (ˌɛksəʊ'ɜːdʒɪk) *adj* (of a nuclear reaction) occurring with evolution of energy. Compare **endoergic, exothermic** [EXO- + *-ergic*, from Greek *ergon* work]

ex off. *abbreviation for* ex officio

ex officio ('ɛks ə'fɪʃɪəʊ, ə'fɪsɪəʊ) *adv, adj* by right of position or office. Abbreviation: **ex off.** [Latin]

exogamy (ɛk'sɒgəmɪ) *n* **1** *sociol, anthropol* the custom or an act of marrying a person belonging to another tribe, clan, or similar social unit. Compare **endogamy 2** *biology* fusion of gametes from parents that are not closely related > exogamous (ɛk'sɒgəməs) *or* exogamic (ˌɛksəʊ'gæmɪk) *adj*

exogenous (ɛk'sɒdʒɪnəs) *adj* **1** having an external origin **2** *biology* **a** developing or originating outside an organism or part of an organism **b** of or relating to external factors, such as light, that influence an organism **3** *psychiatry* (of a mental illness) caused by external factors > ex'ogenously *adv*

exon¹ ('ɛksɒn) *n Brit* one of the four officers who command the Yeomen of the Guard [c17 a pronunciation spelling of French *exempt* EXEMPT]

exon² ('ɛksɒn) *n* any segment of a discontinuous gene the segments of which are separated by introns. Compare **intron** [c20 from EX-¹ + -ON] > ex'onic *adj*

exonerate (ɪg'zɒnəˌreɪt) *vb* (*tr*) **1** to clear or absolve from blame or a criminal charge **2** to relieve from an obligation or task; exempt [c16 from Latin *exonerāre* to free from a burden, from *onus* a burden] > exˌoner'ation *n* > ex'onerative *adj* > ex'onerˌator *n*

exonuclease (ˌɛksəʊ'njuːkliˌeɪz) *n* an enzyme that is capable of detaching the terminal nucleotide from a nucleic acid chain. Compare **endonuclease**

exonym ('ɛksəˌnɪm) *n* a name given to a place by foreigners: *Londres is an exonym of London* [c20 from Greek EX-¹ + -ONYM]

exoparasite (ˌɛksəʊ'pærəˌsaɪt) *n* another word for **ectoparasite**. > exoparasitic (ˌɛksəʊˌpærə'sɪtɪk) *adj*

exopeptidase (ˌɛksəʊ'pɛptɪˌdeɪz) *n* any proteolytic enzyme, such as erepsin, that acts on the terminal bonds in a peptide chain. Compare **endopeptidase**

exophoric (ˌɛksəʊ'fɒrɪk) *adj grammar* denoting or relating to a pronoun such as "I" or "you", the meaning of which is determined by reference outside the discourse rather than by a preceding or following expression. Compare **anaphora** [from EXO- + Greek *pherein* to carry]

exophthalmic goitre *n* a form of hyperthyroidism characterized by enlargement of the thyroid gland, protrusion of the eyeballs, increased basal metabolic rate, and weight loss. Also called: **Graves' disease**

exophthalmos (ˌɛksɒf'θælmɒs), **exophthalmus** (ˌɛksɒf'θælməs) *or* **exophthalmia** (ˌɛksɒf'θælmɪə) *n* abnormal protrusion of the eyeball, as caused by hyperthyroidism. Also called: **proptosis, ocular proptosis** [c19 via New Latin from Greek, from EX-¹ + *ophthalmos* eye] > exoph'thalmic *adj*

exoplanet ('ɛksəʊˌplænɪt) *n* a planet that orbits a star in a solar system other than that of Earth

exoplasm ('ɛksəʊˌplæzəm) *n* another name for **ectoplasm**

exor. *Brit abbreviation for* executor

exorable ('ɛksərəbªl) *adj* able to be persuaded or moved by pleading [c16 from Latin *exōrābilis*, from

exōrāre to persuade, from *ōrāre* to beseech] > ˌexora'bility *n*

exorbitant (ɪg'zɔːbɪtªnt) *adj* (of prices, demands, etc) in excess of what is reasonable; excessive; extravagant; immoderate [c15 from Late Latin *exorbitāre* to deviate, from Latin *orbita* track] > ex'orbitance *n* > ex'orbitantly *adv*

exorcize *or* **exorcise** ('ɛksɔːˌsaɪz) *vb* (*tr*) to expel or attempt to expel (one or more evil spirits) from (a person or place believed to be possessed or haunted), by prayers and religious rites [c15 from Late Latin *exorcizāre*, from Greek *exorkizein*, from EX-¹ + *horkizein* to adjure] > 'exorˌcizer *or* 'exorˌciser *n* > 'exorcism *n* > 'exorcist *n*

exordium (ɛk'sɔːdɪəm) *n, pl* **-diums, -dia** (-dɪə) an introductory part or beginning, esp of an oration or discourse [c16 from Latin, from *exōrdīrī* to begin, from *ōrdīrī* to begin] > ex'ordial *adj*

exoskeleton (ˌɛksəʊ'skɛlɪtªn) *n* the protective or supporting structure covering the outside of the body of many animals, such as the thick cuticle of arthropods. Compare **endoskeleton** > ˌexo'skeletal *adj*

exosmosis (ˌɛksɒz'məʊsɪs, -sɒs-) *n biology* osmosis in which water flows from a cell or organism into the surrounding solution. Compare **endosmosis** > exosmotic (ˌɛksɒz'mɒtɪk, -sɒs-) *or* exosmic (ɛk'sɒzmɪk, -'sɒs-) *adj*

exosphere ('ɛksəʊˌsfɪə) *n* the outermost layer of the earth's atmosphere. It extends from about 400 km above the earth's surface

exospore ('ɛksəʊˌspɔː) *n* the outer layer of the spores of some algae and fungi > ˌexo'sporous *adj*

exostosis (ˌɛksɒ'stəʊsɪs) *n, pl* **-ses** (-siːz) an abnormal bony outgrowth from the surface of a bone [c18 via New Latin from Greek, from EX-¹ + *osteon* bone]

exoteric (ˌɛksəʊ'tɛrɪk) *adj* **1** intelligible to or intended for more than a select or initiated minority **2** external; exterior [c17 from Latin *exōtericus* external, from Greek *exōterikos*, from *exōterō* further outside; see EXO-] > ˌexo'terically *adv* > ˌexo'teriˌcism *n*

exothermic (ˌɛksəʊ'θɜːmɪk) *or* **exothermal** *adj* (of a chemical reaction or compound) occurring or formed with the evolution of heat. Compare **endothermic, exoergic**. > ˌexo'thermically *or* ˌexo'thermally *adv*

exotic (ɪg'zɒtɪk) *adj* **1** originating in a foreign country, esp one in the tropics; not native: *an exotic plant* **2** having a strange or bizarre allure, beauty, or quality **3** *NZ* (of trees, esp pine trees) native to the northern hemisphere but cultivated in New Zealand **4** of or relating to striptease ▷ *n* **5** an exotic person or thing [c16 from Latin *exōticus*, from Greek *exōtikos* foreign, from *exō* outside] > ex'otically *adv* > ex'otiˌcism *n* > ex'oticness *n*

exotica (ɪg'zɒtɪkə) *pl n* exotic objects, esp when forming a collection [c19 Latin, neuter plural of *exōticus*; see EXOTIC]

exotic dancer *n* a striptease or belly dancer

exotoxin (ˌɛksəʊ'tɒksɪn) *n* a toxin produced by a microorganism and secreted into the surrounding medium > ˌexo'toxic *adj*

exp *maths symbol for* exponential (sense 2)

expand (ɪk'spænd) *vb* **1** to make or become greater in extent, volume, size, or scope; increase **2** to spread out or be spread out; unfold; stretch out **3** (*intr; often foll by on*) to enlarge or expatiate on (a story, topic, etc) in detail **4** (*intr*) to become increasingly relaxed, friendly, or talkative **5** *maths* to express (a function or expression) as the sum or product of terms [c15 from Latin *expandere* to spread out, from *pandere* to spread, extend] > ex'pandable *adj*

expanded (ɪk'spændɪd) *adj* **1** Also: **extended** (of printer's type) wider than usual for a particular height. Compare **condensed 2** (of a plastic) having been foamed during manufacture by the introduction of a gas in order to make a light packaging material or heat insulator: *expanded polystyrene*. See also **expanded metal**

expanded metal *n* an open mesh of metal produced by stamping out alternating slots in a metal sheet and stretching it into an open pattern. It is used for reinforcing brittle or friable materials and in fencing

expander (ɪk'spændə) *n* **1** a device for exercising and developing the muscles of the body: *a chest expander* **2** an electronic device for increasing the variations in signal amplitude in a transmission system according to a specified law. Compare **compressor** (sense 5), **compander**

expanding universe theory *n* the theory, developed from the observed red shifts of celestial bodies, that the space between galaxies is expanding, so that they appear to recede from us at velocities that increase with their distance. See also **oscillating universe theory**

expanse (ɪk'spæns) *n* **1** an uninterrupted surface of something that spreads or extends, esp over a wide area; stretch: *an expanse of water* **2** expansion or extension [C17 from New Latin *expansum* the heavens, from Latin *expansus* spread out, from *expandere* to EXPAND]

expansible (ɪk'spænsəbᵊl) *adj* able to expand or be expanded > **ex͵pansi'bility** *n*

expansile (ɪk'spænsaɪl) *adj* **1** able to expand or cause expansion **2** of or relating to expansion

expansion (ɪk'spænʃən) *n* **1** the act of expanding or the state of being expanded **2** something expanded; an expanded surface or part **3** the degree, extent, or amount by which something expands **4** an increase, enlargement, or development, esp in the activities of a company **5** *maths* **a** the form of an expression or function when it is written as the sum or product of its terms **b** the act or process of determining this expanded form **6** the part of an engine cycle in which the working fluid does useful work by increasing in volume **7** the increase in the dimensions of a body or substance when subjected to an increase in temperature, internal pressure, etc > **ex'pansionary** *adj*

expansion bend *n* *engineering* a loop in a pipe conveying hot fluid that provides flexibility which takes up thermal expansion and thus reduces temperature-induced stress in the pipe to an acceptable level

expansion bolt *n* a bolt that expands on tightening, enabling it to be secured into an unthreaded hole

expansionism (ɪk'spænʃə͵nɪzəm) *n* the doctrine or practice of expanding the economy or territory of a country > **ex'pansionist** *n, adj* > **ex͵pansion'istic** *adj*

expansion joint *n* *engineering* a gap in steel or concrete to allow for thermal expansion

expansion slot *n* a physical electronic interface provided in a computer system to enable extra facilities to be added easily at a later date

expansive (ɪk'spænsɪv) *adj* **1** able or tending to expand or characterized by expansion **2** wide; extensive **3** friendly, open, or talkative: *an expansive person* **4** grand or extravagant: *an expansive way of life* **5** *psychiatry* lacking restraint in the expression of feelings, esp in having delusions of grandeur or being inclined to overvalue oneself or one's work > **ex'pansively** *adv* > **ex'pansiveness** *n*

expansivity (͵ɛkspæn'sɪvɪtɪ) *n* **1** the quality of being expansive **2** another name for **coefficient of expansion**

ex parte (ɛks 'pɑːtɪ) *adj* *law* (of an application in a judicial proceeding) on behalf of one side or party only: *an ex parte injunction* [Latin]

expat (͵ɛks'pæt) *n, adj* *informal* short for **expatriate**

expatiate (ɪk'speɪʃɪ͵eɪt) *vb* (*intr*) **1** (foll by *on* or *upon*) to enlarge (on a theme, topic, etc) at length or in detail; elaborate (on) **2** *rare* to wander about [C16 from Latin *exspatiārī* to digress, from *spatiārī* to walk about] > **ex͵pati'ation** *n* > **ex'pati͵ator** *n*

expatriate *adj* (ɛks'pætrɪɪt, -͵eɪt) **1** resident in a foreign country **2** exiled or banished from one's native country ▷ *n* (ɛks'pætrɪɪt, -͵eɪt) **3** a person who lives in a foreign country **4** an exile ▷ *vb* (ɛks'pætrɪ͵eɪt) (*tr*) **5** to exile (oneself) from one's native country or cause (another) to go into exile **6** to deprive (oneself or another) of citizenship [C18 from Medieval Latin *expatriāre*, from Latin EX-[1] + *patria* native land] > **ex͵patri'ation** *n*

expect (ɪk'spɛkt) *vb* (*tr; may take a clause as object or an infinitive*) **1** to regard as probable or likely; anticipate: *he expects to win* **2** to look forward to or be waiting for: *we expect good news today* **3** to decide that (something) is requisite or necessary: *the boss expects us to work late* ▷ See also **expecting** [C16 from Latin *exspectāre* to watch for, from *spectāre* to look at] > **ex'pectable** *adj* > **ex'pectably** *adv*

expectancy (ɪk'spɛktənsɪ) *or* **expectance** *n* **1** something expected, esp on the basis of a norm or average: *life expectancy* **2** anticipation; expectation **3** the prospect of a future interest or possession, esp in property: *an estate in expectancy*

expectant (ɪk'spɛktənt) *adj* **1** expecting, anticipating, or hopeful: *an expectant glance* **2** having expectations, esp of possession of something or prosperity **3** pregnant: *an expectant mother* ▷ *n* **4** a person who expects something **5** *obsolete* a candidate for office, esp for ecclesiastical preferment > **ex'pectantly** *adv*

expectation (͵ɛkspɛk'teɪʃən) *n* **1** the act or state of expecting or the state of being expected **2** (*usually plural*) something looked forward to, whether feared or hoped for: *their worst expectations* **3** an attitude of expectancy or hope; anticipation **4** *statistics* another term for **expected value.** > **expectative** (ɪk'spɛktətɪv) *adj*

expected frequency *n* *statistics* the number of occasions on which an event may be presumed to occur on average in a given number of trials

expected utility *n* *statistics* the weighted average utility of the possible outcomes of a probabilistic situation; the sum or integral of the product of the probability distribution and the utility function

expected value *n* *statistics* the sum or integral of all possible values of a random variable, or any given function of it, multiplied by the respective probabilities of the values of the variable. Symbol: $E(X)$. $E(X)$ is the mean of the distribution; $E(X–c) = E(X)–c$ where c is a constant. Also called: **mathematical expectation**

expecting (ɪk'spɛktɪŋ) *adj* *informal* pregnant

expectorant (ɪk'spɛktərənt) *med* ▷ *adj* **1** promoting the secretion, liquefaction, or expulsion of sputum from the respiratory passages ▷ *n* **2** an expectorant drug or agent

expectorate (ɪk'spɛktə͵reɪt) *vb* to cough up and spit out (sputum from the respiratory passages) [C17 from Latin *expectorāre*, literally: to drive from the breast, expel, from *pectus* breast] > **ex͵pecto'ration** *n* > **ex'pecto͵rator** *n*

expediency (ɪk'spiːdɪənsɪ) *or* **expedience** *n, pl* **-encies** *or* **-ences** **1** appropriateness; suitability **2** the use of or inclination towards methods that are advantageous rather than fair or just **3** another word for **expedient** (sense 3)

expedient (ɪk'spiːdɪənt) *adj* **1** suitable to the circumstances; appropriate **2** inclined towards methods or means that are advantageous rather than fair or just ▷ *n also* **expediency** **3** something suitable or appropriate, esp something used during an urgent situation [C14 from Latin *expediēns* setting free; see EXPEDITE] > **ex'pediently** *adv*

expediential (ɪk͵spiːdɪ'ɛnʃəl) *adj* denoting, based on, or involving expediency > **ex͵pedi'entially** *adv*

expedite ('ɛkspɪ͵daɪt) *vb* (*tr*) **1** to hasten the progress of; hasten or assist **2** to do or process (something, such as business matters) with speed and efficiency **3** *rare* to dispatch (documents, messages, etc) ▷ *adj* *obsolete* **4** unimpeded or prompt; expeditious **5** alert or prepared [C17 from Latin *expedīre*, literally: to free the feet (as from a snare), hence, liberate, from EX-[1] + *pēs* foot]

expediter *or* **expeditor** ('ɛkspɪ͵daɪtə) *n* a person who expedites something, esp a person employed in an industry to ensure that work on each job progresses efficiently

expedition (͵ɛkspɪ'dɪʃən) *n* **1** an organized journey or voyage for a specific purpose, esp for exploration or for a scientific or military purpose **2** the people and equipment comprising an expedition **3** a pleasure trip; excursion **4** promptness in acting; dispatch [C15 from Latin *expedītiō*, from *expedīre* to prepare, EXPEDITE]

expeditionary (͵ɛkspɪ'dɪʃənərɪ) *adj* relating to or constituting an expedition, esp a military one

expeditious (͵ɛkspɪ'dɪʃəs) *adj* characterized by or done with speed and efficiency; prompt; quick > **͵expe'ditiously** *adv* > **͵expe'ditiousness** *n*

expel (ɪk'spɛl) *vb* **-pels, -pelling, -pelled** (*tr*) **1** to eject or drive out with force **2** to deprive of participation in or membership of a school, club, etc [C14 from Latin *expellere* to drive out, from *pellere* to thrust, drive] > **ex'pellable** *adj* > **expellee** (͵ɛkspɛ'liː) *n* > **ex'peller** *n*

expellant *or* **expellent** (ɪk'spɛlənt) *adj* **1** forcing out or having the capacity to force out ▷ *n* **2** a medicine used to expel undesirable substances or organisms from the body, esp worms from the digestive tract

expellers (ɪk'spɛləz) *pl n* the residue remaining after an oilseed has been crushed to expel the oil, used for animal fodder Compare **extractions**

expend (ɪk'spɛnd) *vb* (*tr*) **1** to spend; disburse **2** to consume or use up [C15 from Latin *expendere*, from *pendere* to weigh] > **ex'pender** *n*

expendable (ɪk'spɛndəbᵊl) *adj* **1** that may be expended or used up **2** not essential; not worth preserving **3** able to be sacrificed to achieve an objective, esp a military one ▷ *n* **4** something that is expendable > **ex͵penda'bility** *n*

expenditure (ɪk'spɛndɪtʃə) *n* **1** something expended, such as time or money **2** the act of expending

e

expense (ɪk'spɛns) *n* **1** a particular payment of money; expenditure **2** money needed for individual purchases; cost; charge **3** (*plural*) incidental money spent in the performance of a job, commission, etc, usually reimbursed by an employer or allowable against tax **4** something requiring money for its purchase or upkeep **5** **at the expense of** to the detriment of: *he succeeded at the expense of his health* ▷ *vb* **6** (*tr*) *US and Canadian* to treat as an expense for book-keeping or tax purposes [C14 from Late Latin *expēnsa*, from Latin *expēnsus* weighed out; see EXPEND]

expense account *n* **1** an arrangement by which expenses incurred in the course of a person's work are refunded by his employer or deducted from his income for tax purposes **2** a record of such expenses **3** (*modifier*) *informal* paid for by an employer or by money allowable against tax

expensive (ɪk'spɛnsɪv) *adj* high-priced; costly; dear > **ex'pensively** *adv* > **ex'pensiveness** *n*

experience (ɪk'spɪərɪəns) *n* **1** direct personal participation or observation; actual knowledge or contact: *experience of prison life* **2** a particular incident, feeling, etc, that a person has undergone: *an experience to remember* **3** accumulated knowledge, esp of practical matters: *a man of experience* **4** **a** the totality of characteristics, both past and present, that make up the particular quality of a person, place, or people **b** the impact made on an individual by the culture of a people, nation, etc: *the American experience* **5** *philosophy* **a** the content of a perception regarded as independent of whether the apparent object actually exists. Compare **sense datum** **b** the faculty by which a person acquires knowledge of contingent facts about the world, as contrasted with reason **c** the totality of a person's perceptions, feelings, and memories ▷ *vb* (*tr*) **6** to participate in or undergo **7** to be emotionally or aesthetically moved by; feel: *to experience beauty* [C14 from Latin *experientia*, from *experīrī* to prove; related to Latin *perīculum* PERIL] > **ex'perienceable** *adj*

experienced (ɪk'spɪərɪənst) *adj* having become skilful or knowledgeable from extensive contact or participation or observation
experience table *n insurance* an actuarial table, esp a mortality table based on past statistics
experiential (ɪkˌspɪərɪ'ɛnʃəl) *adj philosophy* relating to or derived from experience; empirical > **exˌperi'entially** *adv*
experiment *n* (ɪk'spɛrɪmənt) **1** a test or investigation, esp one planned to provide evidence for or against a hypothesis: *a scientific experiment* **2** the act of conducting such an investigation or test; experimentation; research **3** an attempt at something new or different; an effort to be original: *a poetic experiment* **4** an obsolete word for **experience** ▷ *vb* (ɪk'spɛrɪˌmɛnt) **5** (*intr*) to make an experiment or experiments [C14 from Latin *experīmentum* proof, trial, from *experīrī* to test; see EXPERIENCE] > **ex'periˌmenter** *n*
experimental (ɪkˌspɛrɪ'mɛntᵊl) *adj* **1** relating to, based on, or having the nature of experiment: *an experimental study* **2** based on or derived from experience; empirical: *experimental evidence* **3** tending to experiment: *an experimental artist* **4** tentative or provisional > **exˌperi'mentally** *adv*
experimental condition *n statistics* one of the distinct states of affairs or values of the independent variable for which the dependent variable is measured in order to carry out statistical tests or calculations. Also called: **condition**
experimentalism (ɪkˌspɛrɪ'mɛntəˌlɪzəm) *n* employment of or reliance upon experiments; empiricism > **exˌperi'mentalist** *n*
experimentalize *or* **experimentalise** (ɪkˌspɛrɪ'mɛntəˌlaɪz) *vb* (*intr*) to engage in experiments
experimental psychology *n* the scientific study of the individual behaviour of man and other animals, esp of perception, learning, memory, motor skills, and thinking
experimentation (ɪkˌspɛrɪmɛn'teɪʃən) *n* the act, process, or practice of experimenting
experimenter effect *n psychol* the influence of an experimenter's expectations on his results
expert ('ɛkspɜːt) *n* **1** a person who has extensive skill or knowledge in a particular field ▷ *adj* **2** skilful or knowledgeable **3** of, involving, or done by an expert: *an expert job* [C14 from Latin *expertus* known by experience, from *experīrī* to test; see EXPERIENCE] > **'expertly** *adv* > **'expertness** *n*
expertise (ˌɛkspɜː'tiːz) *n* special skill, knowledge, or judgment; expertness [C19 from French: expert skill, from EXPERT]
expertize *or* **expertise** ('ɛkspɜːˌtaɪz) *vb US* to act as an expert or give an expert opinion (on)
expert system *n* a computer program that can offer intelligent advice or make intelligent decisions using rule-based programs
expiable ('ɛkspɪəbᵊl) *adj* capable of being expiated or atoned for
expiate ('ɛkspɪˌeɪt) *vb* (*tr*) to atone for or redress (sin or wrongdoing) [C16 from Latin *expiāre*, from *pius* dutiful; see PIOUS] > **'expiˌator** *n*
expiation (ˌɛkspɪ'eɪʃən) *n* the act, process, or a means of expiating; atonement
expiatory ('ɛkspɪətərɪ, -trɪ) *adj* **1** capable of making expiation **2** given or offered in expiation
expiration (ˌɛkspɪ'reɪʃən) *n* **1** the finish of something; ending; expiry **2** the act, process, or sound of breathing out **3** *rare* a last breath; death
expiratory (ɪk'spaɪərətərɪ, -trɪ) *adj* relating to the expulsion of air from the lungs during respiration
expire (ɪk'spaɪə) *vb* **1** (*intr*) to finish or run out; cease; come to an end **2** to breathe out (air); exhale **3** (*intr*) to die [C15 from Old French *expirer*, from Latin *exspīrāre* to breathe out, from *spīrāre* to breathe] > **ex'pirer** *n*
expiry (ɪk'spaɪərɪ) *n, pl* **-ries 1 a** a coming to an end, esp of a contract period; termination: *expiry of a lease* **b** (*as modifier*): *the expiry date* **2** death
explain (ɪk'spleɪn) *vb* **1** (when *tr, may take a clause as object*) to make (something) comprehensible, esp by giving a clear and detailed account of the relevant structure, operation, surrounding circumstances, etc **2** (*tr*) to justify or attempt to justify (oneself) by giving reasons for one's actions or words [C15 from Latin *explānāre* to flatten, from *plānus* level] > **ex'plainable** *adj* > **ex'plainer** *n*
explain away *vb* (*tr, adverb*) to offer excuses or reasons for (bad conduct, mistakes, etc)
explanation (ˌɛkspləˈneɪʃən) *n* **1** the act or process of explaining **2** a statement or occurrence that explains **3** a clarification of disputed terms or points; reconciliation
explanatory (ɪk'splænətərɪ, -trɪ) *or* **explanative** *adj* serving or intended to serve as an explanation > **ex'planatorily** *adv*
explant (ɛks'plɑːnt) *vb* **1** to transfer (living tissue) from its natural site to a new site or to a culture medium ▷ *n* **2** a piece of tissue treated in this way > **ˌexplan'tation** *n*
expletive (ɪk'spliːtɪv) *n* **1** an exclamation or swearword; an oath or a sound expressing an emotional reaction rather than any particular meaning **2** any syllable, word, or phrase conveying no independent meaning, esp one inserted in a line of verse for the sake of the metre ▷ *adj also* **expletory** (ɪk'spliːtərɪ) **3** expressing no particular meaning, esp when filling out a line of verse [C17 from Late Latin *explētīvus* for filling out, from *explēre*, from *plēre* to fill] > **ex'pletively** *adv*
explicable ('ɛksplɪkəbᵊl, ɪk'splɪk-) *adj* capable of being explained
explicate ('ɛksplɪˌkeɪt) *vb* (*tr*) *formal* **1** to make clear or explicit; explain **2** to formulate or develop (a theory, hypothesis, etc) [C16 from Latin *explicāre* to unfold, from *plicāre* to fold] > **explicative** (ɪk'splɪkətɪv) *or* **explicatory** (ɪk'splɪkətərɪ, -trɪ) *adj* > **'expliˌcator** *n*
explication (ˌɛksplɪ'keɪʃən) *n* **1** the act or process of explicating **2** analysis or interpretation, esp of a literary passage or work or philosophical doctrine **3** a comprehensive description
explication de texte *French* (ɛksplikasjɔ̃ də tɛkst) *n, pl* ***explications de texte*** (ɛksplikasjɔ̃ də tɛkst) a close textual analysis of a literary work [literally: explanation of (the) text]
explicit[1] (ɪk'splɪsɪt) *adj* **1** precisely and clearly expressed, leaving nothing to implication; fully stated: *explicit instructions* **2** graphically detailed, leaving little to the imagination: *sexually explicit scenes* **3** openly expressed without reservations; unreserved **4** *maths* (of a function) having an equation of the form $y=f(x)$, in which y is expressed directly in terms of x, as in $y=x^4+x+z$ Compare **implicit** (sense 4) [C17 from Latin *explicitus* unfolded, from *explicāre*; see EXPLICATE] > **ex'plicitly** *adv* > **ex'plicitness** *n*
explicit[2] (ɪk'splɪsɪt) the end; an indication, used esp by medieval scribes, of the end of a book, part of a manuscript, etc [Late Latin, probably short for *explicitus est liber* the book is unfolded (or complete); shortened by analogy with INCIPIT]
explode (ɪk'spləʊd) *vb* **1** to burst or cause to burst with great violence as a result of internal pressure, esp through the detonation of an explosive; blow up **2** to destroy or be destroyed in this manner **3** (of a gas) to undergo or cause (a gas) to undergo a sudden violent expansion, accompanied by heat, light, a shock wave, and a loud noise, as a result of a fast uncontrolled exothermic chemical or nuclear reaction **4** (*intr*) to react suddenly or violently with emotion, etc **5** (*intr*) (esp of a population) to increase rapidly **6** (*tr*) to show (a theory, etc) to be baseless; refute and make obsolete **7** (*tr*) *phonetics* to pronounce (a stop) with audible plosion ▷ Compare **implode** [C16 from Latin *explōdere* to drive off by clapping, hiss (an actor) off, from EX-[1] + *plaudere* to clap] > **ex'ploder** *n*
exploded view *n* a drawing or photograph of a complicated mechanism that shows the individual parts separately, usually indicating their relative positions
exploding star *n* an irregular variable star, such as a nova, supernova, or flare star, in which rapid increases in luminosity occur, caused by some form of explosion
exploit *n* ('ɛksplɔɪt) **1** a notable deed or feat, esp one that is noble or heroic ▷ *vb* (ɪk'splɔɪt) (*tr*) **2** to take advantage of (a person, situation, etc), esp unethically or unjustly for one's own ends **3** to make the best use of: *to exploit natural resources* [C14 from Old French: accomplishment, from Latin *explicitum* (something) unfolded, from *explicāre* to EXPLICATE] > **ex'ploitable** *adj* > **ˌexploi'tation** *n* > **ex'ploitive** *or* **ex'ploitative** *adj*
exploration (ˌɛksplə'reɪʃən) *n* **1** the act or process of exploring **2** *med* examination of an organ or part for diagnostic purposes **3** an organized trip into unfamiliar regions, esp for scientific purposes; expedition > **exploratory** (ɪk'splɒrətərɪ, -trɪ) *or* **ex'plorative** *adj*
explore (ɪk'splɔː) *vb* **1** (*tr*) to examine or investigate, esp systematically **2** to travel to or into (unfamiliar or unknown regions), esp for organized scientific purposes **3** (*tr*) *med* to examine (an organ or part) for diagnostic purposes **4** (*tr*) *obsolete* to search for or out [C16 from Latin *explōrāre*, from EX-[1] + *plōrāre* to cry aloud; probably from the shouts of hunters sighting prey] > **ex'plorer** *n*
Explorer[1] (ɪk'splɔːrə) *n US* a member of the senior branch of the Scouts. Brit equivalent: **Venture Scout**
Explorer[2] (ɪk'splɔːrə) *n* any of the first series of US satellites. **Explorer 1**, launched in 1958, confirmed the existence of intense radiation belts around the earth
explosion (ɪk'spləʊʒən) *n* **1** the act or an instance of exploding **2** a violent release of energy resulting from a rapid chemical or nuclear reaction, esp one that produces a shock wave, loud noise, heat, and light. Compare **implosion** (sense 1) **3** a sudden or violent outburst of activity, noise, emotion, etc **4** a rapid increase, esp in a population **5** *phonetics* another word for **plosion** [C17 from Latin *explōsiō*, from *explōdere* to EXPLODE]
explosion welding *n engineering* the welding of two parts forced together by a controlled explosion
explosive (ɪk'spləʊsɪv) *adj* **1** of, involving, or characterized by an explosion or explosions **2** capable of exploding or tending to explode **3** potentially violent or hazardous; dangerous **4** *phonetics* another word for **plosive** ▷ *n* **5** a substance that decomposes rapidly under certain conditions with the production of gases, which expand by the heat of the reaction. The energy released is used in firearms, blasting, and rocket propulsion **6** a plosive consonant; stop > **ex'plosively** *adv* > **ex'plosiveness** *n*
explosive forming *n engineering* a rapid method of forming a metal object in which components are made by subjecting the metal to very high pressures generated by a controlled explosion
expo ('ɛkspəʊ) *n, pl* **-pos** short for **exposition** (sense 3)
exponent (ɪk'spəʊnənt) *n* **1** (usually foll by *of*) a person or thing that acts as an advocate (of an idea, cause, etc) **2** a person or thing that explains or interprets **3** a performer or interpretive artist, esp a musician **4** Also called: **power, index** *maths* a number or variable placed as a superscript to the right of another number or quantity indicating the number of times the number or quantity is to be multiplied by itself ▷ *adj* **5** offering a declaration, or interpretation [C16 from Latin *expōnere* to set out, expound, from *pōnere* to set, place]
exponential (ˌɛkspəʊ'nɛnʃəl) *adj* **1** *maths* (of a function, curve, series, or equation) of, containing, or involving one or more numbers or quantities raised to an exponent, esp e^x **2** *maths* raised to the power of e, the base of natural

logarithms. Symbol: **exp** **3** of or involving an exponent or exponents **4** *informal* very rapid ▷ *n* **5** *maths* an exponential function, etc > ˌ**expoˈnentially** *adv*
exponential distribution *n statistics* a continuous single-parameter distribution used esp when making statements about the length of life of certain materials or waiting times between randomly occurring events. Its density function is $p(x) = \lambda e^{-\lambda x}$ for positive λ and nonnegative *x*, and it is a special case of the gamma distribution
exponential horn *n* a horn for the radiation of acoustic or high-frequency electromagnetic waves, of which the cross-sectional area increases exponentially with the length
export *n* (ˈɛkspɔːt) **1** (*often plural*) **a** goods (**visible exports**) or services (**invisible exports**) sold to a foreign country or countries **b** (*as modifier*): *an export licence; export finance* ▷ *vb* (ɪkˈspɔːt, ˈɛkspɔːt) **2** to sell (goods or services) or ship (goods) to a foreign country or countries **3** (*tr*) to transmit or spread (an idea, social institution, etc) abroad ▷ Compare **import** [C15 from Latin *exportāre* to carry away, from *portāre* to carry] > **exˈportable** *adj* > **exˌportaˈbility** *n* > **exˈporter** *n*
exportation (ˌɛkspɔːˈteɪʃən) *n* **1** the act, business, or process of exporting goods or services **2** *chiefly US* an exported product or service
export reject *n* an article that fails to meet a standard of quality required for export and that is sold on the home market
expose (ɪkˈspəʊz) *vb* (*tr*) **1** to display for viewing; exhibit **2** to bring to public notice; disclose; reveal: *to expose the facts* **3** to divulge the identity of; unmask **4** (foll by *to*) to make subject or susceptible (to attack, criticism, etc) **5** to abandon (a child, animal, etc) in the open to die **6** (foll by *to*) to introduce (to) or acquaint (with) **7** *photog* to subject (a photographic film or plate) to light, X-rays, or some other type of actinic radiation **8** *RC Church* to exhibit (the consecrated Eucharistic Host or a relic) for public veneration **9** **expose oneself** to display one's sexual organs in public [C15 from Old French *exposer*, from Latin *expōnere* to set out; see EXPONENT] > **exˈposable** *adj* > **exˈposal** *n* > **exˈposer** *n*
exposé (ɛksˈpəʊzeɪ) *n* **1** the act or an instance of bringing a scandal, crime, etc, to public notice **2** an article, book, or statement that discloses a scandal, crime, etc
exposed (ɪkˈspəʊzd) *adj* **1** not concealed; displayed for viewing **2** without shelter from the elements **3** susceptible to attack or criticism; vulnerable **4** *mountaineering* (of a climb, pitch, or move) performed on a high, sheer, and unsheltered rock face > **exˈposedness** *n*
exposition (ˌɛkspəˈzɪʃən) *n* **1** a systematic, usually written statement about, commentary on, or explanation of a specific subject **2** the act of expounding or setting forth information or a viewpoint **3** a large public exhibition, esp of industrial products or arts and crafts **4** the act of exposing or the state of being exposed **5** the part of a play, novel, etc, in which the theme and main characters are introduced **6** *music* the first statement of the subjects or themes of a movement in sonata form or a fugue **7** *RC Church* the exhibiting of the consecrated Eucharistic Host or a relic for public veneration [C14 from Latin *expositiō* a setting forth, from *expōnere* to display; see EXPONENT] > ˌ**expoˈsitional** *adj*
expositor (ɪkˈspɒzɪtə) *n* a person who expounds
expository (ɪkˈspɒzɪtərɪ, -trɪ) *or* **expositive** *adj* of, involving, or assisting in exposition; explanatory > **exˈpositorily** *or* **exˈpositively** *adv*
ex post facto (ɛks pəʊst ˈfæktəʊ) *adj* having retrospective effect: *an ex post facto law* [C17 from Latin *ex* from + *post* afterwards + *factus* done, from *facere* to do]
expostulate (ɪkˈspɒstjʊˌleɪt) *vb* (*intr;* usually foll by *with*) to argue or reason (with), esp in order to dissuade from an action or intention [C16 from Latin *expostulāre* to require, from *postulāre* to demand; see POSTULATE] > **exˈpostuˌlatingly** *adv* > **exˌpostuˈlation** *n* > **exˈpostuˌlator** *n* > **exˈpostulatory** *or* **exˈpostulative** *adj*
exposure (ɪkˈspəʊʒə) *n* **1** the act of exposing or the condition of being exposed **2** the position or outlook of a house, building, etc; aspect: *the bedroom has a southern exposure* **3** lack of shelter from the weather, esp the cold: *to die of exposure* **4** a surface that is exposed: *an exposure of granite* **5** *mountaineering* the degree to which a climb, etc is exposed (see **exposed** (sense 4)) **6** *photog* **a** the act of exposing a photographic film or plate to light, X-rays, etc **b** an area on a film or plate that has been exposed to light, etc **c** (*as modifier*): *exposure control* **7** *photog* **a** the intensity of light falling on a photographic film or plate multiplied by the time for which it is exposed **b** a combination of lens aperture and shutter speed used in taking a photograph **8** appearance or presentation before the public, as in a theatre, on television, or in films **9** See **indecent exposure**
exposure meter *n photog* an instrument for measuring the intensity of light, usually by means of a photocell, so that the suitable camera settings of shutter speed and f-number (or lens aperture) can be determined. Also called: **light meter**
expound (ɪkˈspaʊnd) *vb* (when *intr*, foll by *on* or *about*) to explain or set forth (an argument, theory, etc) in detail: *to expound on one's theories* [C13 from Old French *espondre*, from Latin *expōnere* to set forth, from *pōnere* to put] > **exˈpounder** *n*
express (ɪkˈsprɛs) *vb* (*tr*) **1** to transform (ideas) into words; utter; verbalize **2** to show or reveal; indicate: *tears express grief* **3** to communicate (emotion, etc) without words, as through music, painting, etc **4** to indicate through a symbol, formula, etc **5** to force or squeeze out: *to express the juice from an orange* **6** to send by rapid transport or special messenger **7** **express oneself** to communicate one's thoughts or ideas ▷ *adj* (*prenominal*) **8** clearly indicated or shown; explicitly stated: *an express wish* **9** done or planned for a definite reason or goal; particular: *an express purpose* **10** of, concerned with, or designed for rapid transportation of people, merchandise, mail, money, etc: *express delivery; an express depot* ▷ *n* **11** **a** a system for sending merchandise, mail, money, etc, rapidly **b** merchandise, mail, etc, conveyed by such a system **c** *chiefly US and Canadian* an enterprise operating such a system **12** Also called: **express train** a fast train stopping at none or only a few of the intermediate stations between its two termini **13** See **express rifle** ▷ *adv* **14** by means of a special delivery or express delivery: *it went express* [C14 from Latin *expressus*, literally: squeezed out, hence, prominent, from *exprimere* to force out, from EX-[1] + *premere* to press] > **exˈpresser** *n* > **exˈpressible** *adj*
expressage (ɪkˈsprɛsɪdʒ) *n* **1** the conveyance of merchandise by express **2** the fee charged for such conveyance
expression (ɪkˈsprɛʃən) *n* **1** the act or an instance of transforming ideas into words **2** a manifestation of an emotion, feeling, etc, without words: *tears are an expression of grief* **3** communication of emotion through music, painting, etc **4** a look on the face that indicates mood or emotion: *a joyful expression* **5** the choice of words, phrases, syntax, intonation, etc, in communicating **6** a particular phrase used conventionally to express something: *a dialect expression* **7** the act or process of forcing or squeezing out a liquid **8** *maths* a variable, function, or some combination of constants, variables, or functions **9** *genetics* the effect of a particular gene on the phenotype > **exˈpressional** *adj* > **exˈpressionless** *adj* > **exˈpressionlessly** *adv*
expressionism (ɪkˈsprɛʃəˌnɪzəm) *n* (*sometimes capital*) an artistic and literary movement originating in Germany at the beginning of the 20th century, which sought to express emotions rather than to represent external reality: characterized by the use of symbolism and of exaggeration and distortion > **exˈpressionist** *n, adj* > **exˌpressionˈistic** *adj*
expression mark *n* one of a set of musical directions, usually in Italian, indicating how a piece or passage is to be performed
expressive (ɪkˈsprɛsɪv) *adj* **1** of, involving, or full of expression **2** (*postpositive;* foll by *of*) indicative or suggestive (of): *a look expressive of love* **3** having a particular meaning, feeling, or force; significant > **exˈpressively** *adv* > **exˈpressiveness** *n*
expressivity (ˌɛksprɛˈsɪvɪtɪ) *n* **1** (esp of a work of art) the quality of being expressive **2** *genetics* the strength of the effect of a gene on the phenotype
expressly (ɪkˈsprɛslɪ) *adv* **1** for an express purpose; with specific intentions **2** plainly, exactly, or unmistakably
expresso (ɪkˈsprɛsəʊ) *n* a variant of **espresso**
express rifle *n* a high-velocity hunting rifle for big game shooting
expressway (ɪkˈsprɛsˌweɪ) *n* a motorway
expropriate (ɛksˈprəʊprɪˌeɪt) *vb* (*tr*) to deprive (an owner) of (property), esp by taking it for public use. See also **eminent domain** [C17 from Medieval Latin *expropriāre* to deprive of possessions, from *proprius* own] > **exˈpropriable** *adj* > **exˌpropriˈation** *n* > **exˈpropriˌator** *n*
exptl *abbreviation for* experimental
expulsion (ɪkˈspʌlʃən) *n* the act of expelling or the fact or condition of being expelled [C14 from Latin *expulsiō* a driving out, from *expellere* to EXPEL]
expulsive (ɪkˈspʌlsɪv) *adj* tending expel
expunge (ɪkˈspʌndʒ) *vb* (*tr*) **1** to delete or erase; blot out; obliterate **2** to wipe out or destroy [C17 from Latin *expungere* to blot out, from *pungere* to prick] > **expunction** (ɪkˈspʌŋkʃən) *n* > **exˈpunger** *n*
expurgate (ˈɛkspəˌɡeɪt) *vb* (*tr*) to amend (a book, text, etc) by removing (obscene or offensive sections) [C17 from Latin *expurgāre* to clean out, from *purgāre* to purify; see PURGE] > ˌ**expurˈgation** *n* > ˈ**expurˌgator** *n* > **expurgatory** (ɛksˈpɜːɡətərɪ, -trɪ) *or* **expurgatorial** (ɛkˌspɜːɡəˈtɔːrɪəl) *adj*
exquisite (ɪkˈskwɪzɪt, ˈɛkskwɪzɪt) *adj* **1** possessing qualities of unusual delicacy and fine craftsmanship **2** extremely beautiful and pleasing: *an exquisite face* **3** outstanding or excellent: *an exquisite victory* **4** sensitive; discriminating: *exquisite taste* **5** fastidious and refined **6** intense or sharp in feeling: *exquisite pleasure; exquisite pain* ▷ *n* **7** *obsolete* a dandy [C15 from Latin *exquīsītus* excellent, from *exquīrere* to search out, from *quaerere* to seek] > **exˈquisitely** *adv* > **exˈquisiteness** *n*
exr *abbreviation for* executor
exsanguinate (ɪkˈsæŋɡwɪneɪt) *vb* (*tr*) *rare* to drain the blood from [C19 from Latin *exsanguināre*] > **exˌsanguinˈation** *n*
exsanguine (ɪkˈsæŋɡwɪn) *or* **exsanguinous** *adj* without blood; anaemic [C17 from Latin *exsanguis*, from *sanguis* blood] > ˌ**exsanˈguinity** *n*
exscind (ɛkˈsɪnd) *vb* (*tr*) to cut off or out; excise [C17 *exscind*, from Latin *exscindere* to extirpate, destroy, from *scindere* to cut, tear, split]
exsect (ɛkˈsɛkt) *vb* (*tr*) to cut out [C17 *exsect*, from Latin *exsecāre* to cut away, from *secāre* to cut] > **exsection** (ɛkˈsɛkʃən) *n*
exsert (ɛkˈsɜːt) *vb* **1** (*tr*) to thrust out; protrude ▷ *adj also* **exserted** **2** protruded, stretched out, or (esp of stamens) projecting beyond the corolla of a flower [C19 from Latin *exserere* to thrust out; see EXERT] > **exˈsertion** *n* > **exsertile** (ɛkˈsɜːtaɪl) *adj*
ex-service *adj* having formerly served in the armed forces
ex-serviceman *n, pl* **-men** a man who has served in the army, navy, or air force
ex-servicewoman *n, pl* **-women** a woman who has served in the army, navy, or air force
exsiccate (ˈɛksɪˌkeɪt) *vb* to dry up; desiccate [C15 from Latin *exsiccāre*, from *siccus* dry] > ˌ**exsicˈcation** *n* > ˈ**exsiccative** *adj* > ˈ**exsicˌcator** *n*

e

ex silentio *Latin* (ɛks sɪ'lɛnʃɪˌəʊ) *adv, adj* (of a theory, assumption, etc) based on a lack of evidence to the contrary [literally: from silence]
exstipulate (ɛk'stɪpjʊlɪt, -ˌleɪt) *or* **estipulate** *adj* (of a flowering plant) having no stipules
exstrophy ('ɛkstrəfɪ) *n med* congenital eversion of a hollow organ, esp the urinary bladder [C19 from Greek EX-[1] + *strophein* to turn]
ext *abbreviation for* **1** extinct **2** extract
extant (ɛk'stænt, 'ɛkstənt) *adj* **1** still in existence; surviving **2** *archaic* standing out; protruding [C16 from Latin *exstāns* standing out, from *exstāre*, from *stāre* to stand]

USAGE *Extant* is sometimes wrongly used simply to say that something exists, without any connotation of survival: *plutonium is perhaps the deadliest element in existence* (not *the deadliest element extant*)

extemporaneous (ɪkˌstɛmpə'reɪnɪəs) *or* **extemporary** (ɪk'stɛmpərərɪ, -prərɪ) *adj* **1** spoken, performed, etc, without planning or preparation; impromptu; extempore **2** done in a temporary manner; improvised > **exˌtempo'raneously** *or* **ex'temporarily** *adv* > **exˌtempo'raneousness** *or* **ex'temporariness** *n*
extempore (ɪk'stɛmpərɪ) *adv, adj* without planning or preparation; impromptu [C16 from Latin *ex tempore* instantaneously, from EX-[1] out of + *tempus* time]
extemporize *or* **extemporise** (ɪk'stɛmpəˌraɪz) *vb* **1** to perform, speak, or compose (an act, speech, piece of music, etc) without planning or preparation **2** to use (a temporary solution) for an immediate need; improvise > **exˌtempori'zation** *or* **exˌtempori'sation** *n* > **ex'tempoˌrizer** *or* **ex'tempoˌriser** *n*
extend (ɪk'stɛnd) *vb* **1** to draw out or be drawn out; stretch **2** to last for a certain time: *his schooling extended for three years* **3** (*intr*) to reach a certain point in time or distance: *the land extends five miles* **4** (*intr*) to exist or occur: *the trees extended throughout the area* **5** (*tr*) to increase (a building, etc) in size or area; add to or enlarge **6** (*tr*) to broaden the meaning or scope of: *the law was extended* **7** (*tr*) to put forth, present, or offer: *to extend greetings* **8** to stretch forth (an arm, etc) **9** (*tr*) to lay out (a body) at full length **10** (*tr*) to strain or exert (a person or animal) to the maximum **11** (*tr*) to prolong (the time originally set) for payment of (a debt or loan), completion of (a task), etc **12** (*tr*) *book-keeping* **a** to carry forward **b** to calculate the amount of (a total, balance, etc) **13** (*tr*) *law* (formerly in England) to value or assess (land) [C14 from Latin *extendere* to stretch out, from *tendere* to stretch] > **ex'tendible** *or* **ex'tendable** *adj* > **exˌtendi'bility** *or* **exˌtenda'bility** *n*
extended (ɪk'stɛndɪd) *adj* **1** stretched out in time, space, influence, application, etc **2** (of a horse's pace) free-moving and with long steps: *an extended trot* **3** *printing* another word for **expanded** (sense 1) > **ex'tendedly** *adv* > **ex'tendedness** *n*
extended family *n sociol, anthropol* a social unit that contains the nuclear family together with blood relatives, often spanning three or more generations
extended-play *adj* denoting an EP record
extender (ɪk'stɛndə) *n* **1** a person or thing that extends **2** a substance, such as French chalk or china clay, added to paints to give them body and decrease their rate of settlement **3** a substance added to glues and resins to dilute them or to modify their viscosity **4** a substance added to elastomers to assist the plasticizer **5** *printing* the part of certain lower case letters that extends either above (the ascender) or below (the descender) the body of the letter
extensible (ɪk'stɛnsəbᵊl) *or* **extensile** (ɪk'stɛnsaɪl) *adj* capable of being extended > **exˌtensi'bility** *or* **ex'tensibleness** *n*
extension (ɪk'stɛnʃən) *n* **1** the act of extending or the condition of being extended **2** something that can be extended or that extends another object **3** the length, range, etc, over which something is extended; extent **4** an additional telephone set connected to the same telephone line as another set or other sets **5** a room or rooms added to an existing building **6** a delay, esp one agreed by all parties, in the date originally set for payment of a debt or completion of a contract **7** the property of matter by which it occupies space; size **8 a** the act of straightening or extending an arm or leg **b** its position after being straightened or extended **9** *med* a steady pull applied to a fractured or dislocated arm or leg to restore it to its normal position. See also **traction** (sense 3) **10 a** a service by which some of the facilities of an educational establishment, library, etc, are offered to outsiders **b** (*as modifier*): *a university extension course* **11** *logic* **a** the class of entities to which a given word correctly applies: thus, the extension of *satellite of Mars* is the set containing only Deimos and Phobos. Compare **intension** (sense 1a) **b conservative extension** a formal theory that includes among its theorems all the theorems of a given theory [C14 from Late Latin *extensiō* a stretching out; see EXTEND]
extensional (ɪk'stɛnʃənᵊl) *adj* **1** relating to or characterized by extension **2** *logic* explicable solely in terms of extensions; ignoring differences of meaning that do not affect the extension. See also **extensionality, substitutivity, transparent context.** > **ex'tensionally** *adv* > **ex'tensionalism** *n*
extensionality (ɪkˌstɛnʃə'nælɪtɪ) *n logic* the principle that sets are definable in terms of their elements alone, whatever way they may have been selected. Thus {a, b}={b, a}={first two letters of the alphabet}
extension ring *or* **tube** *n photog* a spacer element that can be fixed between the camera body and the lens to increase the distance between film and lens and allow closer focus than would be possible without it
extensity (ɪk'stɛnsɪtɪ) *n* **1** *psychol* that part of sensory perception relating to the spatial aspect of objects **2** *rare* the condition of being extensive
extensive (ɪk'stɛnsɪv) *adj* **1** having a large extent, area, scope, degree, etc; vast: *extensive deserts; an extensive inheritance* **2** widespread: *extensive coverage in the press* **3** *agriculture* involving or farmed with minimum expenditure of capital or labour, esp depending on a large area of land. Compare **intensive** (sense 3) **4** *physics* of or relating to a property, measurement, etc, of a macroscopic system that is proportional to the size of the system: *heat is an extensive property*. Compare **intensive** (sense 7) **5** *logic* **a** of or relating to logical extension **b** (of a definition) in terms of the objects to which the term applies rather than its meaning > **ex'tensively** *adv* > **ex'tensiveness** *n*
extensometer (ˌɛkstɛn'sɒmɪtə) *or* **extensimeter** (ˌɛkstɛn'sɪmɪtə) *n* an apparatus for studying small changes of length, as in the thermal expansion or mechanical compression of a solid
extensor (ɪk'stɛnsə, -sɔː) *n* any muscle that stretches or extends an arm, leg, or other bodily part. Compare **flexor** [C18 from New Latin, from Latin *extensus* stretched out]
extent (ɪk'stɛnt) *n* **1** the range over which something extends; scope: *the extent of the damage* **2** an area or volume: *a vast extent of concrete* **3** *US law* a writ authorizing a person to whom a debt is due to assume temporary possession of his debtor's lands **4** *logic* another word for **extension** (sense 11) [C14 from Old French *extente*, from Latin *extentus* extensive, from *extendere* to EXTEND]
extenuate (ɪk'stɛnjʊˌeɪt) *vb* (*tr*) **1** to represent (an offence, a fault, etc) as being less serious than it appears, as by showing mitigating circumstances **2** to cause to be or appear less serious; mitigate **3** to underestimate or make light of **4** *archaic* **a** to emaciate or weaken **b** to dilute or thin out [C16 from Latin *extenuāre* to make thin, from *tenuis* thin, frail] > **ex'tenuˌating** *adj* > **exˌtenu'ation** *n* > **ex'tenuˌator** *n* > **ex'tenuatory** *adj*
exterior (ɪk'stɪərɪə) *n* **1** a part, surface, or region that is on the outside **2** the observable outward behaviour or appearance of a person **3** a film or scene shot outside a studio ▷ *adj* **4** of, situated on, or suitable for the outside: *exterior cleaning* **5** coming or acting from without; external: *exterior complications* **6** of or involving foreign nations [C16 from Latin, comparative of *exterus* on the outside, from *ex* out of] > **ex'teriorly** *adv*
exterior angle *n* **1** an angle of a polygon contained between one side extended and the adjacent side **2** any of the four angles made by a transversal that are outside the region between the two intersected lines
exteriorize *or* **exteriorise** (ɪk'stɪərɪəˌraɪz) *vb* (*tr*) **1** *surgery* to expose (an attached organ or part) outside a body cavity, esp in order to remove it from an operating area **2** another word for **externalize.** > **exˌteriori'zation** *or* **exˌteriori'sation** *n*
exterminate (ɪk'stɜːmɪˌneɪt) *vb* (*tr*) to destroy (living things, esp pests or vermin) completely; annihilate; eliminate [C16 from Latin *extermināre* to drive away, from *terminus* boundary] > **ex'terminable** *adj* > **exˌtermi'nation** *n* > **ex'terminative** *or* **ex'terminatory** *adj* > **ex'termiˌnator** *n*
extern *or* **externe** ('ɛkstɜːn, ɪk'stɜːn) *n US* a person, such as a physician at a hospital, who has an official connection with an institution but does not reside in it [C16 from Latin *externus* EXTERNAL]
external (ɪk'stɜːnᵊl) *adj* **1** of, situated on, or suitable for the outside; outer **2** coming or acting from without: *external evidence from an independent source* **3** of or involving foreign nations; foreign **4** of, relating to, or designating a medicine that is applied to the outside of the body **5** *anatomy* situated on or near the outside of the body: *the external ear* **6** *education* denoting assessment by examiners who are not employed at the candidate's place of study **7** *Austral and NZ* (of a student) studying a university subject extramurally **8** *philosophy* (of objects, etc) taken to exist independently of a perceiving mind ▷ *n* **9** (*often plural*) an external circumstance or aspect, esp one that is superficial or inessential **10** *Austral and NZ* a student taking an extramural subject [C15 from Latin *externus* outward, from *exterus* on the outside, from *ex* out of] > **ex'ternally** *adv*
External Affairs *pl n Canadian* (formerly) the Canadian federal Foreign Affairs department
external-combustion engine *n* a heat engine in which the working fluid is heated in an external boiler or heat exchanger and is thus isolated from the process of fuel combustion
external ear *n* the part of the ear consisting of the auricle and the auditory canal
externalism (ɪk'stɜːnəˌlɪzəm) *n* **1** exaggerated emphasis on outward form, esp in religious worship **2** a philosophical doctrine holding that only objects that can be perceived by the senses are real; phenomenalism > **ex'ternalist** *n*
externality (ˌɛkstɜː'nælɪtɪ) *n, pl* **-ties 1** the state or condition of being external **2** something external **3** *philosophy* the quality of existing independently of a perceiving mind **4** an economic effect that results from an economic choice but is not reflected in market prices
externalize (ɪk'stɜːnəˌlaɪz), **exteriorize** (ɪk'stɪərɪəˌraɪz), **externalise** *or* **exteriorise** *vb* (*tr*) **1** to make external; give outward shape to **2** *psychol* to attribute (one's own feelings) to one's surroundings > **exˌternali'zation, exˌteriori'zation, exˌternali'sation** *or* **exˌteriori'sation** *n*
exteroceptor ('ɛkstərəʊˌsɛptə) *n* any sensory organ or part of the body, such as the eye, able to receive stimuli from outside the body. Compare **interoceptor, proprioceptor** [C20 *extero-*, from Latin *exterus* EXTERIOR + (RE)CEPTOR] > **ˌextero'ceptive** *adj*
exterritorial (ˌɛkstɛrɪ'tɔːrɪəl) *adj* a variant of

extraterritorial. ⊳ ˌexˌterriˌtori'ality *n*
⊳ ˌexterri'torially *adv*

extinct (ɪk'stɪŋkt) *adj* **1** (of an animal or plant species) having no living representative; having died out **2** quenched or extinguished **3** (of a volcano) no longer liable to erupt; inactive **4** void or obsolete: *an extinct political office* [c15 from Latin *exstinctus* quenched, from *exstinguere* to EXTINGUISH]

extinction (ɪk'stɪŋkʃən) *n* **1** the act of making extinct or the state of being extinct **2** the act of extinguishing or the state of being extinguished **3** complete destruction; annihilation **4** *physics* reduction of the intensity of radiation as a result of absorption or scattering by matter **5** *astronomy* the dimming of light from a celestial body as it passes through an absorbing or scattering medium, such as the earth's atmosphere or interstellar dust **6** *psychol* a process in which the frequency or intensity of a learned response is decreased as a result of reinforcement being withdrawn. Compare **habituation**

extinctive (ɪk'stɪŋktɪv) *adj* tending or serving to extinguish or make extinct

extine ('ɛkstɪn, -tiːn, -taɪn) *n* another name for **exine** [c19 from Latin *extimus* outermost + -INE[1]]

extinguish (ɪk'stɪŋgwɪʃ) *vb* (*tr*) **1** to put out or quench (a light, flames, etc) **2** to remove or destroy entirely; annihilate **3** *archaic* to eclipse or obscure by or as if by superior brilliance **4** *law* to discharge (a debt) [c16 from Latin *exstinguere*, from *stinguere* to quench] ⊳ ex'tinguishable *adj* ⊳ ex'tinguisher *n* ⊳ ex'tinguishment *n*

extinguishant (ɪk'stɪŋgwɪʃənt) *n* a substance, such as a liquid, foam, powder, etc, used in extinguishing fires

extirpate ('ɛkstəˌpeɪt) *vb* (*tr*) **1** to remove or destroy completely **2** to pull up or out; uproot **3** to remove (an organ or part) surgically [c16 from Latin *exstirpāre* to root out, from *stirps* root, stock] ⊳ ˌextir'pation *n* ⊳ 'extirˌpative *adj* ⊳ 'extirˌpator *n*

extol or *US* **extoll** (ɪk'stəʊl) *vb* -tols, -tolling, -tolled or *US* -tolls, -tolling, -tolled (*tr*) to praise lavishly; exalt [c15 from Latin *extollere* to elevate, from *tollere* to raise] ⊳ ex'toller *n* ⊳ ex'tollingly *adv* ⊳ ex'tolment *n*

extort (ɪk'stɔːt) *vb* (*tr*) **1** to secure (money, favours, etc) by intimidation, violence, or the misuse of influence or authority **2** to obtain by importunate demands **3** to overcharge for (something, esp interest on a loan) [c16 from Latin *extortus* wrenched out, from *extorquēre* to wrest away, from *torquēre* to twist, wrench] ⊳ ex'torter *n* ⊳ ex'tortive *adj*

extortion (ɪk'stɔːʃən) *n* the act of securing money, favours, etc by intimidation or violence; blackmail ⊳ ex'tortioner *n* or ex'tortionist *n*

extortionate (ɪk'stɔːʃənɪt) *adj* **1** (of prices, etc) excessive; exorbitant **2** (of persons) using extortion ⊳ ex'tortionately *adv*

extra ('ɛkstrə) *adj* **1** being more than what is usual or expected; additional ⊳ *n* **2** a person or thing that is additional **3** something for which an additional charge is made: *the new car had many extras* **4** an additional edition of a newspaper, esp to report a new development or crisis **5** *films* an actor or person temporarily engaged, usually for crowd scenes **6** *cricket* a run not scored from the bat, such as a wide, no-ball, bye, or leg bye **7** *US* something that is better than usual in quality ⊳ *adv* **8** unusually; exceptionally: *an extra fast car* [c18 perhaps shortened from EXTRAORDINARY]

extra- *prefix* outside or beyond an area or scope: *extrasensory; extraterritorial* [from Latin *extrā* outside, beyond, changed from *extera*, from *exterus* outward]

extracanonical (ˌɛkstrəkə'nɒnɪkəl) *adj* Christianity not included in the canon of Scripture

extracellular (ˌɛkstrə'sɛljʊlə) *adj biology* situated or occurring outside a cell or cells ⊳ ˌextra'cellularly *adv*

extracorporeal (ˌɛkstrəkɔː'pɔːrɪəl) *adj* outside the body

extra cover *n cricket* a fielding position between cover and mid-off

extract *vb* (ɪk'strækt) (*tr*) **1** to withdraw, pull out, or uproot by force **2** to remove or separate **3** to derive (pleasure, information, etc) from some source or situation **4** to deduce or develop (a doctrine, policy, etc) **5** *informal* to extort (money, etc) **6** to obtain (a substance) from a mixture or material by a chemical or physical process, such as digestion, distillation, the action of a solvent, or mechanical separation **7** to cut out or copy out (an article, passage, quotation, etc) from a publication **8** to determine the value of (the root of a number) ⊳ *n* ('ɛkstrækt) **9** something extracted, such as a part or passage from a book, speech, etc **10** a preparation containing the active principle or concentrated essence of a material: *beef extract; yeast extract* **11** *pharmacol* a solution of plant or animal tissue containing the active principle [c15 from Latin *extractus* drawn forth, from *extrahere*, from *trahere* to drag] ⊳ ex'tractable *adj* ⊳ exˌtracta'bility *n*

> USAGE *Extract* is sometimes wrongly used where *extricate* would be better: *he will find it difficult extricating* (not *extracting*) *himself from this situation*

extraction (ɪk'strækʃən) *n* **1** the act of extracting or the condition of being extracted **2** something extracted; an extract **3 a** the act or an instance of extracting a tooth or teeth **b** a tooth or teeth extracted **4** origin, descent, lineage, or ancestry

extractions (ɪk'strækʃənz) *pl n* the residue remaining after an oilseed has had the oil extracted by a solvent. Used as a feed for animals: *groundnut extractions*. Compare **expellers**

extractive (ɪk'stræktɪv) *adj* **1** tending or serving to extract **2** of, involving, or capable of extraction ⊳ *n* **3** something extracted or capable of being extracted **4** the part of an extract that is insoluble

extractor (ɪk'stræktə) *n* **1** a person or thing that extracts **2** an instrument for pulling something out or removing tight-fitting components **3** a device for extracting liquid from a solid, esp a centrifugal dryer **4** short for **extractor fan** **5** a fitting in many firearms for removing spent cartridges from the chamber

extractor fan or **extraction fan** *n* a fan used in kitchens, bathrooms, workshops, etc, to remove stale air or fumes

extracurricular (ˌɛkstrəkə'rɪkjʊlə) *adj* **1** taking place outside the normal school timetable **2** beyond the regular duties, schedule, etc

extraditable ('ɛkstrəˌdaɪtəbəl) *adj* **1** (of a crime) rendering the offender liable to extradition: *an extraditable offence* **2** (of a person) subject to extradition

extradite ('ɛkstrəˌdaɪt) *vb* (*tr*) **1** to surrender (an alleged offender) for trial to a foreign state **2** to procure the extradition of [c19 back formation from EXTRADITION]

extradition (ˌɛkstrə'dɪʃən) *n* the surrender of an alleged offender or fugitive to the state in whose territory the alleged offence was committed [c19 from French, from Latin *trāditiō* a handing over; see TRADITION]

extrados (ɛk'streɪdɒs) *n*, *pl* -dos (-dɒz) or -doses *architect* the outer curve or surface of an arch or vault. Compare **intrados** [c18 from French, from EXTRA- + *dos* back, from Latin *dorsum*]

extradural (ˌɛkstrə'djʊərəl) *adj* another word for **epidural** (sense 1)

extrafloral (ˌɛkstrə'flɔːrəl) *adj* produced or occurring outside a flower: *extrafloral nectar*

extragalactic (ˌɛkstrəgə'læktɪk) *adj* occurring or existing beyond the Galaxy

extragalactic nebula *n* the former name for **galaxy**

extrajudicial (ˌɛkstrədʒuː'dɪʃəl) *adj* **1** outside the ordinary course of legal proceedings: *extrajudicial evidence* **2** beyond the jurisdiction or authority of the court

extramarital (ˌɛkstrə'mærɪtəl) *adj* (esp of sexual relations) occurring outside marriage

extramundane (ˌɛkstrə'mʌndeɪn) *adj* not of the physical world or universe

extramural (ˌɛkstrə'mjʊərəl) *adj* **1** connected with but outside the normal courses or programme of a university, college, etc: *extramural studies* **2** located beyond the boundaries or walls of a city, castle, etc ⊳ ˌextra'murally *adv*

extraneous (ɪk'streɪnɪəs) *adj* **1** not essential **2** not pertinent or applicable; irrelevant **3** coming from without; of external origin **4** not belonging; unrelated to that to which it is added or in which it is contained [c17 from Latin *extrāneus* external, from *extrā* outside] ⊳ ex'traneously *adv* ⊳ ex'traneousness *n*

extranet ('ɛkstrəˌnɛt) *n computing* an intranet that is modified to allow outsiders access to it, esp one belonging to a business that allows access to customers [c20 from EXTRA- + NET[1] (sense 8), modelled on INTRANET]

extranuclear (ˌɛkstrə'njuːklɪə) *adj biology* situated or occurring in part of a cell outside the nucleus

extraordinary (ɪk'strɔːdənrɪ, -dənərɪ) *adj* **1** very unusual, remarkable, or surprising **2** not in an established manner, course, or order **3** employed for particular events or purposes **4** (*usually postpositive*) (of an official, etc) additional or subordinate to the usual one: *a minister extraordinary* [c15 from Latin *extraordinārius* beyond what is usual; see ORDINARY] ⊳ ex'traordinarily *adv* ⊳ ex'traordinariness *n*

extraordinary general meeting *n* a meeting specially called to discuss a particular item of a company's business, usually one of some importance. The meeting may be called by a group of shareholders or by the directors. Abbreviation: **EGM**

extraordinary ray *n optics* the plane-polarized ray of light that does not obey the laws of refraction in a doubly refracting crystal. See **double refraction** Compare **ordinary ray**

extrapolate (ɪk'stræpəˌleɪt) *vb* **1** *maths* to estimate (a value of a function or measurement) beyond the values already known, by the extension of a curve. Compare **interpolate** (sense 4) **2** to infer (something not known) by using but not strictly deducing from the known facts [c19 EXTRA- + *-polate*, as in INTERPOLATE] ⊳ exˌtrapo'lation *n* ⊳ ex'trapolative or ex'trapolatory *adj* ⊳ ex'trapoˌlator *n*

extraposition (ˌɛkstrəpə'zɪʃən) *n* **1** placement of something outside something else **2** *transformational grammar* a rule that moves embedded clauses out to the end of the main clause, converting, for example, *A man who will help has just arrived* into *A man has just arrived who will help*

extrasensory (ˌɛkstrə'sɛnsərɪ) *adj* of or relating to extrasensory perception

extrasensory perception *n* the supposed ability of certain individuals to obtain information about the environment without the use of normal sensory channels. Also called: **cryptaesthesia** See also **clairvoyance** (sense 1), **telepathy** Abbreviation: **ESP**

extrasolar (ˌɛkstrə'səʊlə) *adj* occurring or existing beyond the earth's solar system

extraterrestrial (ˌɛkstrətɪ'rɛstrɪəl) *adj* **1** occurring or existing beyond the earth's atmosphere ⊳ *n* **2** (in science fiction) a being from beyond the earth's atmosphere

extraterritorial (ˌɛkstrəˌtɛrɪ'tɔːrɪəl) or **exterritorial** *adj* **1** beyond the limits of a country's territory **2** of, relating to, or possessing extraterritoriality ⊳ ˌextraˌterri'torially or ˌexterri'torially *adv*

extraterritoriality (ˌɛkstrəˌtɛrɪˌtɔːrɪ'ælɪtɪ) *n international law* **1** the privilege granted to some aliens, esp diplomats, of being exempt from the jurisdiction of the state in which they reside **2** the right or privilege of a state to exercise authority in certain circumstances beyond the limits of its territory

e

extra time *n sport* an additional period played at the end of a match, to compensate for time lost through injury or (in certain circumstances) to allow the teams to achieve a conclusive result

extrauterine (ˌɛkstrəˈjuːtəˌraɪn) *adj* situated or developing outside the cavity of the uterus

extravagance (ɪkˈstrævɪɡəns) *n* **1** excessive outlay of money; wasteful spending **2** immoderate or absurd speech or behaviour

extravagant (ɪkˈstrævɪɡənt) *adj* **1** spending money excessively or immoderately **2** going beyond usual bounds; unrestrained: *extravagant praise* **3** ostentatious; showy **4** exorbitant in price; overpriced [c14 from Medieval Latin *extravagāns,* from Latin EXTRA- + *vagārī* to wander] > ex'travagantly *adv*

Extravagantes (ɪkˌstrævəˈɡæntiːz) *pl n RC Church* decretals circulating outside some recognized collection of canon law. Those of John XXII and the so-called Extravagantes communes form part of the Corpus Juris Canonici [Latin: wandering, circulating]

extravaganza (ɪkˌstrævəˈɡænzə) *n* **1** an elaborately staged and costumed light entertainment **2** any lavish or fanciful display, literary or other composition, etc [c18 from Italian: EXTRAVAGANCE]

extravagate (ɪkˈstrævəˌɡeɪt) *vb* (*intr*) *archaic* **1** to exceed normal limits or propriety **2** to roam at will [c17 from Latin *extravagārī*; see EXTRAVAGANT] > ex,trava'gation *n*

extravasate (ɪkˈstrævəˌseɪt) *vb* **1** *pathol* to cause (blood or lymph) to escape or (of blood or lymph) to escape into the surrounding tissues from their proper vessels **2** to exude (molten material, such as lava) or (of molten material) to be exuded ▷ *n* **3** *pathol* the material extravasated [c17 from Latin EXTRA- + *vās* vessel] > ex,trava'sation *n*

extravascular (ˌɛkstrəˈvæskjʊlə) *adj anatomy* situated or occurring outside a lymph or blood vessel

extravehicular (ˌɛkstrəvɪˈhɪkjʊlə) *adj* occurring or used outside a spacecraft, either in space or on the surface of the moon or another planet

extraversion (ˌɛkstrəˈvɜːʃən) *n* a variant spelling of **extroversion**. > ,extra'versive *adj*

extravert (ˈɛkstrəˌvɜːt) *n, adj* a variant spelling of **extrovert**

extra virgin *adj* (of olive oil) of the highest quality, extracted by cold pressing rather than chemical treatment

Extremadura (estremaˈðura) *n* the Spanish name for **Estremadura**

extremal (ɪkˈstriːml̩) *n maths, logic* the clause in a recursive definition that specifies that no items other than those generated by the stated rules fall within the definition, as in *1 is an integer, if n is an integer so is n+1, and nothing else is*

extreme (ɪkˈstriːm) *adj* **1** being of a high or of the highest degree or intensity: *extreme cold; extreme difficulty* **2** exceeding what is usual or reasonable; immoderate: *extreme behaviour* **3** very strict, rigid, or severe **4** (*prenominal*) farthest or outermost in direction: *the extreme boundary* **5** *meteorol* of, relating to, or characteristic of a continental climate ▷ *n* **6** the highest or furthest degree (often in the phrases **in the extreme, go to extremes**) **7** (*often plural*) either of the two limits or ends of a scale or range of possibilities **8** *maths* **a** the first or last term of a series or a proportion **b** a maximum or minimum value of a function **9** *logic* the subject or predicate of the conclusion of a syllogism [c15 from Latin *extrēmus* outermost, from *exterus* on the outside; see EXTERIOR] > ex'tremeness *n*

extreme fighting *n* a combat sport incorporating techniques from a range of martial arts, with little if any regulation of the types of blows permissible

extremely (ɪkˈstriːmlɪ) *adv* **1** to the extreme; exceedingly **2** (*intensifier*): *I behaved extremely badly*

USAGE See at **very**

extremely high frequency *n* a radio frequency between 30 000 and 300 000 megahertz. Abbreviation: EHF

extremely low frequency *n* a radio frequency or radio-frequency band below 3 kilohertz. Abbreviation: ELF

extreme programming *n* a discipline of software engineering following a specific structure, designed to simplify and speed up the development process. Abbreviation: XP

extreme sport *n* a sport that is physically hazardous, such as bungee jumping or snowboarding

extreme unction *n RC Church* a former name for **anointing of the sick**

extremist (ɪkˈstriːmɪst) *n* **1** a person who favours or resorts to immoderate, uncompromising, or fanatical methods or behaviour, esp in being politically radical ▷ *adj* **2** of, relating to, or characterized by immoderate or excessive actions, opinions, etc > ex'tremism *n*

extremity (ɪkˈstrɛmɪtɪ) *n, pl* -ties **1** the farthest or outermost point or section; termination **2** the greatest or most intense degree **3** an extreme condition or state, as of adversity or disease **4** a limb, such as a leg, arm, or wing, or the part of such a limb farthest from the trunk **5** (*usually plural*) archaic a drastic or severe measure

extremophile (ɪkˈstrɛməˌfaɪl) *n* a microbe that lives in an environment once thought to be uninhabitable, for example in boiling or frozen water

extricate (ˈɛkstrɪˌkeɪt) *vb* (*tr*) to remove or free from complication, hindrance, or difficulty; disentangle [c17 from Latin *extrīcāre* to disentangle, from EX-¹ + *trīcae* trifles, vexations] > 'extricable *adj* > ,extri'cation *n*

USAGE See at **extract**

extrinsic (ɛkˈstrɪnsɪk) *adj* **1** not contained or included within; extraneous **2** originating or acting from outside; external [c16 from Late Latin *extrinsecus* (adj) outward, from Latin (adv) from without, on the outward side, from *exter* outward + *secus* alongside, related to *sequī* to follow] > ex'trinsically *adv*

extrorse (ɛkˈstrɔːs) or **extrorsal** *adj botany* turned or opening outwards or away from the axis: *extrorse anthers* [c19 from Late Latin *extrorsus* in an outward direction, from Latin EXTRA- + *versus* turned towards]

extroversion or **extraversion** (ˌɛkstrəˈvɜːʃən) *n* **1** *psychol* the directing of one's interest outwards, esp towards social contacts **2** *pathol* a turning inside out of an organ or part ▷ Compare **introversion** [c17 from *extro-* (variant of EXTRA-, contrasting with INTRO-) + *-version,* from Latin *vertere* to turn] > ,extro'versive or ,extra'versive *adj* > ,extro'versively or ,extra'versively *adv*

extrovert or **extravert** (ˈɛkstrəˌvɜːt) *psychol* ▷ *n* **1** a person concerned more with external reality than inner feelings ▷ *adj* **2** of or characterized by extroversion: *extrovert tendencies* ▷ Compare **introvert** [c20 from *extro-* (variant of EXTRA-, contrasting with INTRO-) + *-vert,* from Latin *vertere* to turn] > 'extro,verted or 'extra,verted *adj*

extrude (ɪkˈstruːd) *vb* **1** (*tr*) to squeeze or force out **2** (*tr*) to produce (moulded sections of plastic, metal, etc) by ejection under pressure through a suitably shaped nozzle or die **3** (*tr*) to chop up or pulverize (an item of food) and re-form it to look like a whole **4** a less common word for **protrude** [c16 from Latin *extrūdere* to thrust out, from *trūdere* to push, thrust] > ex'truded *adj*

extrusion (ɪkˈstruːʒən) *n* **1** the act or process of extruding **2** the movement of magma onto the surface of the earth through volcano craters and cracks in the earth's crust, forming igneous rock **b** any igneous rock formed in this way **3** a component or length of material formed by the process of extruding [c16 from Medieval Latin *extrūsiō,* from *extrūdere* to EXTRUDE] > ex'trusible *adj*

extrusive (ɪkˈstruːsɪv) *adj* **1** tending to extrude **2** (of igneous rocks) formed from magma issuing from volcanoes or cracks in the earth's crust; volcanic. Compare **intrusive** (sense 2)

exuberant (ɪɡˈzjuːbərənt) *adj* **1** abounding in vigour and high spirits; full of vitality **2** lavish or effusive; excessively elaborate **3** growing luxuriantly or in profusion [c15 from Latin *exūberāns,* from *ūberāre* to be fruitful, from *ūber* fertile] > ex'uberance *n* > ex'uberantly *adv*

exuberate (ɪɡˈzjuːbəˌreɪt) *vb* (*intr*) *rare* **1** to be exuberant **2** to abound or grow in profusion [c15 from Latin *exūberāre* to be abundant; see EXUBERANT]

exudation (ˌɛksjʊˈdeɪʃən) *n* **1** the act of exuding or oozing out **2** Also called: exudate (ˈɛksjʊˌdeɪt) a fluid with a high content of protein in a body cavity. Compare **transudate**. > exudative (ɪɡˈzjuːdətɪv) *adj*

exude (ɪɡˈzjuːd) *vb* **1** to release or be released through pores, incisions, etc, as sweat from the body or sap from trees **2** (*tr*) to make apparent by mood or behaviour: *he exuded confidence* [c16 from Latin *exsūdāre,* from *sūdāre* to sweat]

exult (ɪɡˈzʌlt) *vb* (*intr*) **1** to be joyful or jubilant, esp because of triumph or success; rejoice **2** (often foll by *over*) to triumph (over); take delight in the defeat (of) [c16 from Latin *exsultāre* to jump or leap for joy, from *saltāre* to leap] > exultation (ˌɛɡzʌlˈteɪʃən) *n* > ex'ultingly *adv*

USAGE See at **exalt**

exultant (ɪɡˈzʌltənt) *adj* elated or jubilant, esp because of triumph or success > ex'ultance or ex'ultancy *n* > ex'ultantly *adv*

exurbia (ɛksˈɜːbɪə) *n chiefly US* the region outside the suburbs of a city, consisting of residential areas (**exurbs**) that are occupied predominantly by rich commuters (**exurbanites**). Compare **stockbroker belt** [c20 from EX-¹ + Latin *urbs* city, on pattern of *suburbia*] > ex'urban *adj*

exuviae (ɪɡˈzjuːvɪˌiː) *pl n* layers of skin or cuticle shed by animals during ecdysis [c17 from Latin: something stripped off (the body), from *exuere* to strip off] > ex'uvial *adj*

exuviate (ɪɡˈzjuːvɪˌeɪt) *vb* to shed (a skin or similar outer covering) > ex,uvi'ation *n*

ex voto *Latin* (ɛks ˈvəʊtəʊ) *adv, adj* **1** in accordance with a vow ▷ *n* **2** an offering made in fulfilment of a vow

ex works *adv, adj* (**ex-works** when prenominal) *Brit* (of a price, value, etc) excluding the cost of delivery from the factory and sometimes excluding the commission or profit of the distributor or retailer

-ey *suffix* a variant of -Y¹, -Y²

Eyam (iːm) *n* a village in N central England, in Derbyshire. When plague reached the village in 1665 the inhabitants, led by the Rev Mompesson, isolated themselves to prevent it spreading further: as a result most of them died, including Mompesson's family

eyas (ˈaɪəs) *n* a nestling hawk or falcon, esp one reared for training in falconry [c15 mistaken division of earlier *a nyas,* from Old French *niais* nestling, from Latin *nīdus* nest]

eye¹ (aɪ) *n* **1** the organ of sight of animals, containing light-sensitive cells associated with nerve fibres, so that light entering the eye is converted to nervous impulses that reach the brain. In man and other vertebrates the iris controls the amount of light entering the eye and the lens focuses the light onto the retina. Related adjs: **ocular, oculate, ophthalmic, optic 2** (*often plural*) the ability to see; sense of vision: *weak eyes* **3** the visible external part of an eye, often including the area around it: *heavy-lidded eyes; piercing eyes* **4** a look, glance, expression, or gaze: *a stern eye* **5** a sexually inviting or provocative look (esp in the phrases **give (someone) the (glad) eye, make eyes at**) **6** attention or observation (often in the phrases **catch someone's eye, keep an eye on, cast an eye over**) **7** ability to recognize, judge, or appreciate: *an eye for antiques* **8** (*often plural*) opinion, judgment, point of view, or authority: *in* *the eyes of the law* **9** a structure or marking having the appearance of an eye, such as the bud on a twig or potato tuber or a spot on a butterfly wing **10** a small loop or hole, as at one end of a needle **11** a small area of low pressure and calm in the centre of a tornado or cyclone **12** See **photocell 13** *informal* See **private eye 14 all eyes** *informal* acutely vigilant or observant: *the children were all eyes* **15 (all) my eye** *informal* rubbish; nonsense **16 an eye for an eye** retributive or vengeful justice; retaliation **17 cut one's eye after, at,** *or* **on (someone)** *Caribbean* to look rudely at (a person) and then turn one's face away sharply while closing one's eyes: *a gesture of contempt* **18** *NZ* **eyes out** with every possible effort: *he went at the job eyes out* **19 get one's eye in** *chiefly sport* to become accustomed to the conditions, light, etc, with a consequent improvement in one's performance **20 half an eye a** a modicum of perceptiveness **b** continuing unobtrusive observation or awareness: *the dog had half an eye on the sheep* **21 have eyes for** to be interested in: *she has eyes only for him* **22 in one's mind's eye** pictured within the mind; imagined or remembered vividly **23 in the public eye** exposed to public curiosity or publicity **24 keep an eye open** *or* **out (for)** to watch with special attention (for) **25 keep one's eyes peeled** (*or* **skinned**) to watch vigilantly (for) **26 look (someone) in the eye** to look openly and without shame or embarrassment at **27 make (sheep's) eyes (at)** *old-fashioned* to ogle amorously **28 more than meets the eye** hidden motives, meaning, or facts **29 pick the eyes out (of)** *Austral and NZ* to select the best parts or pieces (of) **30 see eye to eye (with)** to agree (with) **31 set, lay,** *or* **clap eyes on** (*usually used with a negative*) to see: *she had never laid eyes on him before* **32 the eye of the wind** *nautical* the direction from which the wind is blowing **33 turn a blind eye to** *or* **close one's eyes to** to pretend not to notice or ignore deliberately **34 up to one's eyes (in)** extremely busy (with) **35 with a … eye** in a … manner: *he regards our success with a jealous eye* **36 with** *or* **having an eye to** (*preposition*) **a** regarding; with reference to: *with an eye to one's own interests* **b** with the intention or purpose of **37 with one's eyes open** in the full knowledge of all relevant facts **38 with one's eyes shut a** with great ease, esp as a result of thorough familiarity **b** without being aware of all the facts ▷ *vb* **eyes, eyeing** *or* **eying, eyed** (*tr*) **39** to look at carefully or warily **40** Also: **eye up** to look at in a manner indicating sexual interest; ogle ▷ See also **eyes** [Old English *ēage*; related to Old Norse *auga*, Old High German *ouga*, Sanskrit *akṣi*] > **'eyeless** *adj* > **'eye,like** *adj*

eye² (aɪ) *n* another word for **nye**

eyeball ('aɪ,bɔːl) *n* **1** the entire ball-shaped part of the eye **2 eyeball to eyeball** in close confrontation ▷ *vb* **3** (*tr*) *slang* to stare at

eyebank ('aɪ,bæŋk) *n* a place in which corneas are stored for use in corneal grafts

eyebath ('aɪ,bɑːθ) *n* a small vessel with a rim shaped to fit round the eye, used for applying medicated or cleansing solutions to the eyeball. Also called (US and Canadian): **eyecup**

eyeblack ('aɪ,blæk) *n* another name for **mascara**

eyebolt ('aɪ,bəʊlt) *n* a threaded bolt, the head of which is formed into a ring or eye for lifting, pulling, or securing

eyebright ('aɪ,braɪt) *n* any scrophulariaceous annual plant of the genus *Euphrasia*, esp *E. nemorosa*, having small white-and-purple two-lipped flowers: formerly used in the treatment of eye disorders. Also called: **euphrasy**

eyebrow ('aɪ,braʊ) *n* **1** the transverse bony ridge over each eye **2** the arch of hair that covers this ridge. Related adj: **superciliary 3 raise an eyebrow** See **raise** (sense 31)

eyebrow pencil *n* a cosmetic in pencil form for applying colour and shape to the eyebrows

eye candy *n informal* **1** a person who is attractive to look at, but lacking in intelligence or depth **2** something intended to be attractive to the eye without being demanding or contributing anything essential

eye-catching *adj* tending to attract attention; striking > **'eye-,catcher** *n*

eye contact *n* a direct look between two people; meeting of eyes

eyecup ('aɪ,kʌp) *n US and Canadian* a small vessel with a rim shaped to fit round the eye, used for applying medicated or cleansing solutions to the eyeball. Also called (in Britain and certain other countries): **eyebath**

eyed (aɪd) *adj* **a** having an eye or eyes (as specified) **b** (*in combination*): *one-eyed; brown-eyed*

eye dog *n NZ* a dog trained to control sheep by staring fixedly at them. Also called: **strong-eye dog** See also **seeing-eye dog**

eyeful ('aɪfʊl) *n informal* **1** a view, glance, or gaze **2** a very attractive sight, esp a woman

eyeglass ('aɪ,glɑːs) *n* **1** a lens for aiding or correcting defective vision, esp a monocle **2** another word for **eyepiece**

eyeglasses ('aɪ,glɑːsɪz) *pl n Now chiefly US* another word for **spectacles**

eyehole ('aɪ,həʊl) *n* **1** a hole through which something, such as a rope, hook, or bar, is passed **2** the cavity that contains the eyeball; eye socket **3** another word for **peephole**

eyehook ('aɪ,hʊk) *n* a hook attached to a ring at the extremity of a rope or chain

eyelash ('aɪ,læʃ) *n* **1** any one of the short curved hairs that grow from the edge of the eyelids **2** a row or fringe of these hairs. Related adj: **ciliary**

eyelet ('aɪlɪt) *n* **1** a small hole for a lace or cord to be passed through or for a hook to be inserted into **2** a small metal ring or tube with flared ends bent back, reinforcing an eyehole in fabric **3** a chink or small opening, such as a peephole in a wall **4** *embroidery* **a** a small hole with finely stitched edges, forming part of an ornamental pattern **b** Also called: **eyelet embroidery** a piece of embroidery decorated with such work **5** fabric decorated with such work produced by machine **6** a small eye or eyelike marking ▷ *vb* **7** (*tr*) to supply with an eyelet or eyelets [c14 from Old French *oillet*, literally: a little eye, from *oill* eye, from Latin *oculus* eye; see EYE¹]

eyeleteer (,aɪlɪ'tɪə) *n* a small bodkin or other pointed tool for making eyelet holes

eyelevel ('aɪ,lɛvᵊl) *adj* level with a person's eyes when looking straight ahead: *an eyelevel grill*

eyelid ('aɪ,lɪd) *n* **1** either of the two muscular folds of skin that can be moved to cover the exposed portion of the eyeball. Related adj: **palpebral 2** Also called: **clamshell** *aeronautics* a set of movable parts at the rear of a jet engine that redirect the exhaust flow to assist braking during landing

eyeliner ('aɪ,laɪnə) *n* a cosmetic used to outline the eyes

eye of day *n poetic* the sun

eye-opener *n informal* **1** something startling or revealing **2** *US and Canadian* an alcoholic drink taken early in the morning

eyepiece ('aɪ,piːs) *n* the lens or combination of lenses in an optical instrument nearest the eye of the observer

eye-popping *adj informal* so amazing or astonishing as to make one's eyes protrude

eye rhyme *n* a rhyme involving words that are similar in spelling but not in sound, such as *stone* and *none*

eyes (aɪz) *pl n nautical* the part of the bows of a ship that are furthest forward at the level of the main deck

eyes front *interj* **1** *military* a command to troops to look ahead **2** a demand for attention

eyeshade ('aɪ,ʃeɪd) *n* an opaque or tinted translucent visor, worn on the head like a cap to protect the eyes from glare

eye shadow *n* a coloured cosmetic put around the eyes so as to enhance their colour or shape

eyeshot ('aɪ,ʃɒt) *n* range of vision; view

eyesight ('aɪ,saɪt) *n* the ability to see; faculty of sight

eyes left *interj military* a command to troops to look left, esp as a salute when marching

eye socket *n* the nontechnical name for **orbit** (sense 3)

eyesore ('aɪ,sɔː) *n* something very ugly

eye splice *n* an eye formed in a rope by splicing the end into its standing part

eyespot ('aɪ,spɒt) *n* **1** a small area of light-sensitive pigment in some protozoans, algae, and other simple organisms **2** an eyelike marking, as on the wings of certain butterflies

eyes right *interj military* a command to troops to look right, esp as a salute when marching

eyestalk ('aɪ,stɔːk) *n* a movable stalk bearing a compound eye at its tip: occurs in crustaceans and some molluscs

eyestrain ('aɪ,streɪn) *n* fatigue or irritation of the eyes, resulting from excessive use, as from prolonged reading of small print, or uncorrected defects of vision

Eyetie ('aɪtaɪ) *n, adj Brit slang offensive* Italian [c20 based on a jocular mispronunciation of *Italian*]

eyetooth (,aɪ'tuːθ) *n, pl* **-teeth 1** either of the two canine teeth in the upper jaw **2 give one's eyeteeth for** to go to any lengths to achieve or obtain (something)

eyewash ('aɪ,wɒʃ) *n* **1** a mild solution for applying to the eyes for relief of irritation, etc **2** *informal* nonsense; rubbish

eyewitness ('aɪ,wɪtnɪs) *n* **a** a person present at an event who can describe what happened **b** (*as modifier*): *an eyewitness account*

eyot (aɪt) *n Brit rare* island [variant of AIT]

eyra ('eərə, 'aɪərə) *n* a reddish-brown variety of the jaguarondi [c19 from American Spanish, from Tupi *eirara*]

eyre (εə) *n English legal history* **1** any of the circuit courts held in each shire from 1176 until the late 13th century **2 justices in eyre** the justices travelling on circuit and presiding over such courts [c13 from Old French *erre* journey, from *errer* to travel, from Latin *errāre* to wander]

Eyre (εə) *n* **Lake** a shallow salt lake or salt flat in NE central South Australia, about 11 m (35 ft) below sea level, divided into two areas (North and South); it usually contains little or no water. Maximum area: 9600 sq km (3700 sq miles) [c19 named after Edward John *Eyre* (1815–1901), British explorer and colonial administrator]

Eyre Peninsula *n* a peninsula of South Australia, between the Great Australian Bight and Spencer Gulf

eyrie ('ɪərɪ, 'εərɪ, 'aɪərɪ) *or* **aerie** *n* **1** the nest of an eagle or other bird of prey, built in a high inaccessible place **2** the brood of a bird of prey, esp an eagle **3** any high isolated position or place [c16 from Medieval Latin *airea*, from Latin *ārea* open field, hence nest]

eyrir ('eɪrɪə) *n, pl* **aurar** ('ɔːrɑː) an Icelandic monetary unit worth one hundredth of a krona [Old Norse: ounce (of silver), money; related to Latin *aureus* golden]

Ez. *or* **Ezr.** *Bible abbreviation for* Ezra

Ezek. *Bible abbreviation for* Ezekiel

Ezekiel (ɪ'ziːkɪəl) *n Old Testament* **1** a Hebrew prophet of the 6th century BC, exiled to Babylon in 597 BC **2** the book containing his oracles, which describe the downfall of Judah and Jerusalem and their subsequent restoration. Douay spelling: **Ezechiel**

e-zine ('iːziːn) *n* a magazine available only in electronic form, for example on the World Wide Web

Ezra ('εzrə) *n Old Testament* **1** a Jewish priest of the 5th century BC, who was sent from Babylon by the Persian king Artaxerxes I to reconstitute observance of the Jewish law and worship in Jerusalem after the captivity **2** the book recounting his efforts to perform this task

e

Ff

f or **F** (εf) *n, pl* **f's, F's** or **Fs 1** the sixth letter and fourth consonant of the modern English alphabet **2** a speech sound represented by this letter, usually a voiceless labio-dental fricative, as in *fat*

f *symbol for* **1** *music* forte: an instruction to play loudly **2** *physics* frequency **3** (formerly in the Netherlands) guilder [from Dutch: florin] **4** *maths* function (of) **5** *physics* femto- **6** *chess* See **algebraic notation**

f, f/ or **f:** *symbol for* f-number

F *symbol for* **1** *music* **a** a note having a frequency of 349.23 hertz (**F above middle C**) or this value multiplied or divided by any power of 2; the fourth note of the scale of C major **b** a key, string, or pipe producing this note **c** the major or minor key having this note as its tonic **2** Fahrenheit **3** Fellow **4** *chem* fluorine **5** Helmholtz function **6** *physics* force **7** franc(s) **8** farad(s) **9** *genetics* a generation of filial offspring, F_1 being the first generation of offspring, F_2 being the second generation, etc **10** *international car registration for* France

f. or **F.** *abbreviation for* **1** fathom(s) **2** female **3** *grammar* feminine **4** (*pl* ff. or FF.) folio **5** (*pl* ff.) following (page)

F- *abbreviation for* fighter: F-106

fa (fɑː) *n music* a variant spelling of **fah**

FA *abbreviation for* **1** *military* field artillery **2** (in Britain) Football Association. See also **FA Cup**

f.a. or **FA** *abbreviation for* fanny adams

faa or **fa'** (fɔː) *vb* a Scot word for **fall**

FAA *abbreviation for* **1** Fleet Air Arm **2** (in the US) Federal Aviation Administration **3** Fellow of the Australian Academy (of Science)

fab (fæb) *adj, interj informal, chiefly Brit* short for **fabulous**: an expression of approval or enthusiasm

FAB *abbreviation for* flavoured alcoholic beverage

F.A.B. *interj Brit* an expression of agreement to, or acknowledgment of, a command [c20 from British television series *Thunderbirds*]

fabaceous (fəˈbeɪʃəs) *adj* a less common term for **leguminous** [c18 from Late Latin *fabāceus* of beans, from Latin *faba* bean]

Fabian (ˈfeɪbɪən) *adj* **1** of, relating to, or resembling the delaying tactics of the Roman general Q. Fabius Maximus (died 203 bc) who withstood Hannibal while avoiding a pitched battle; cautious; circumspect ▷ *n* **2** a member of or sympathizer with the Fabian Society [c19 from Latin *Fabiānus* of Fabius]

Fabianism (ˈfeɪbɪəˌnɪzəm) *n* the beliefs, principles, or practices of the Fabian Society ▷ **ˈFabianist** *n, adj*

Fabian Society *n* an association of British socialists advocating the establishment of democratic socialism by gradual reforms within the law: founded in 1884

fable (ˈfeɪbˀl) *n* **1** a short moral story, esp one with animals as characters **2** a false, fictitious, or improbable account; fiction or lie **3** a story or legend about supernatural or mythical characters or events **4** legends or myths collectively. Related *adj:* **fabulous 5** *archaic* the plot of a play or of an epic or dramatic poem ▷ *vb* **6** to relate or tell (fables) **7** (*intr*) to speak untruthfully; tell lies **8** (*tr*) to talk about or describe in the manner of a fable: *ghosts are fabled to appear at midnight* [c13 from Latin *fābula* story, narrative, from *fārī* to speak, say] ▷ **ˈfabler** *n*

fabled (ˈfeɪbˀld) *adj* **1** made famous in fable **2** fictitious

fabliau (ˈfæblɪˌəʊ; French fablijo) *n, pl* **fabliaux** (ˈfæblɪˌəʊz; French fablijo) a comic usually ribald verse tale, of a kind popular in France in the 12th and 13th centuries [c19 from French: a little tale, from *fable* tale]

Fablon (ˈfæblən, -lɒn) *n trademark* a brand of adhesive-backed plastic material used to cover and decorate shelves, worktops, etc, and for handicraft purposes

fabric (ˈfæbrɪk) *n* **1** any cloth made from yarn or fibres by weaving, knitting, felting, etc **2** the texture of a cloth **3** a structure or framework: *the fabric of society* **4** a style or method of construction **5** *rare* a building **6** the texture, arrangement, and orientation of the constituents of a rock [c15 from Latin *fabrica* workshop, from *faber* craftsman]

fabricant (ˈfæbrɪkənt) *n archaic* a manufacturer

fabricate (ˈfæbrɪˌkeɪt) *vb* (*tr*) **1** to make, build, or construct **2** to devise, invent, or concoct (a story, lie, etc) **3** to fake or forge [c15 from Latin *fabricāre* to build, make, from *fabrica* workshop; see FABRIC] ▷ **ˌfabriˈcation** *n* ▷ **ˈfabricative** *adj* ▷ **ˈfabriˌcator** *n*

Fabrikoid (ˈfæbrɪˌkɔɪd) *n trademark* a waterproof fabric made of cloth coated with pyroxylin

fabulist (ˈfæbjʊlɪst) *n* **1** a person who invents or recounts fables **2** a person who lies or falsifies

fabulous (ˈfæbjʊləs) *adj* **1** almost unbelievable; astounding; legendary: *fabulous wealth* **2** *informal* extremely good: *a fabulous time at the party* **3** of, relating to, or based upon fable: *a fabulous beast* [c15 from Latin *fābulōsus* celebrated in fable, from *fābula* FABLE] ▷ **ˈfabulously** *adv* ▷ **ˈfabulousness** *n*

façade or **facade** (fəˈsɑːd, fæ-) *n* **1** the face of a building, esp the main front **2** a front or outer appearance, esp a deceptive one [c17 from French, from Italian *facciata*, from *faccia* FACE]

face (feɪs) *n* **1 a** the front of the head from the forehead to the lower jaw; visage **b** (*as modifier*): *face flannel; face cream* **2 a** the expression of the countenance; look: *a sad face* **b** a distorted expression, esp to indicate disgust; grimace: *she made a face* **3** *informal* make-up (esp in the phrase **put one's face on**) **4** outward appearance: *the face of the countryside is changing* **5** appearance or pretence (esp in the phrases **put a bold, good, bad,** etc, **face on**) **6** worth in the eyes of others; dignity (esp in the phrases **lose** or **save face**) **7** *informal* impudence or effrontery **8** the main side of an object, building, etc, or the front: *the face of a palace; a cliff face* **9** the marked surface of an instrument, esp the dial of a timepiece **10** the functional or working side of an object, as of a tool or playing card **11 a** the exposed area of a mine from which coal, ore, etc, may be mined **b** (*as modifier*): *face worker* **12** the uppermost part or surface: *the face of the earth* **13** Also called: **side** any one of the plane surfaces of a crystal or other solid figure **14** *mountaineering* a steep side of a mountain, bounded by ridges **15** either of the surfaces of a coin, esp the one that bears the head of a ruler **16** *Brit slang* a well-known or important person **17** Also called: **typeface** *printing* **a** the printing surface of any type character **b** the style, the design, or sometimes the size of any type fount **c** the print made from type **18** *nautical, aeronautics* the aft or near side of a propeller blade **19 fly in the face of** to act in defiance of **20 in one's face** directly opposite or against one **21 in (the) face of** despite **22 look (someone) in the face** to look directly at a person without fear or shame **23 on the face of it** to all appearances **24 set one's face against** to oppose with determination **25 show one's face** to make an appearance **26 shut one's face** *slang* (*often imperative*) to be silent **27 to someone's face** in someone's presence; directly and openly: *I told him the truth to his face* **28 until one is blue in the face** *informal* to the utmost degree; indefinitely ▷ *vb* **29** (when *intr*, often foll by *to, towards,* or *on*) to look or be situated or placed (in a specified direction): *the house faces on the square* **30** to be opposite: *facing page 9* **31** (*tr*) to meet or be confronted by: *in his work he faces many problems* **32** (*tr*) to accept or deal with something: *let's face it, you're finished* **33** (*tr*) to provide with a surface of a different material: *the cuffs were faced with velvet* **34** to dress the surface of (stone or other material) **35** (*tr*) to expose (a card) with the face uppermost **36** *military, chiefly US* to order (a formation) to turn in a certain direction or (of a formation) to turn as required: *right face!* **37** *ice hockey* **a** (of the referee) to drop (the puck) between two opposing players, as when starting or restarting play. See also **face-off b** to start or restart play in this manner **38** face the music *informal* to confront the consequences of one's actions ▷ See also **face down, face out, face up to** [c13 from Old French, from Vulgar Latin *facia* (unattested), from Latin *faciēs* form, related to *facere* to make] ▷ **ˈfaceable** *adj*

FACE *abbreviation for* Fellow of the Australian College of Education

face-ache *n* **1** neuralgia **2** *slang* an ugly or miserable-looking person

facebar (ˈfeɪsˌbɑː) *n* a wrestling hold in which a wrestler stretches the skin on his opponent's face backwards

face card *n* (in a pack of playing cards) a king, queen, or jack of any suit. Also called (in Britain and certain other countries): **court card**

face-centred *adj* (of a crystal) having a lattice point at the centre of each face of each unit cell as well as at the corners. Compare **body-centred**

face cloth or **face flannel** n Brit a small piece of cloth used to wash the face and hands. US equivalent: **washcloth**

face down vb (tr, adverb) to confront and force (someone or something) to back down

face flies n flies (musca autumnalis) that attack cattle, feeding off their eye secretions

face-harden vb (tr) to harden the surface of (steel or iron) by the addition of carbon at high temperature

faceless ('feɪslɪs) adj 1 without a face 2 without identity; anonymous > **facelessness** n

face-lift n 1 a cosmetic surgical operation for tightening sagging skin and smoothing unwanted wrinkles on the face 2 any improvement or renovation, as of a building, etc

facemail ('feɪs,meɪl) n a computer program which uses an electronically generated face to deliver messages on screen

face-off n 1 ice hockey the method of starting a game, in which the referee drops the puck, etc between two opposing players 2 a confrontation ▷ vb **face off** (adverb) 3 to start play by (a face-off)

face out vb (tr, adverb) 1 to endure (trouble) 2 to defy or act boldly in spite of (criticism, blame, etc) 3 Also (esp US and Canadian): **face down** to cause to concede by a bold stare

face pack n a cream treatment that cleanses and tones the skin

faceplate ('feɪs,pleɪt) n 1 a perforated circular metal plate that can be attached to the headstock of a lathe in order to hold flat or irregularly shaped workpieces 2 Also called: **surface plate** a flat rigid plate used to check the flatness and squareness of the faces of a component 3 the part of a cathode-ray tube carrying the phosphor screen

face powder n a flesh-tinted cosmetic powder worn to make the face look less shiny, softer, etc

faceprint ('feɪs,prɪnt) n a digitally recorded representation of a person's face that can be used for security purposes because it is as individual as a fingerprint

facer ('feɪsə) n 1 a person or thing that faces 2 a lathe tool used to turn a face perpendicular to the axis of rotation 3 Brit informal a difficulty or problem

face recognition n the ability of a computer to scan, store, and recognize human faces for use in identifying people

face-saver n something that serves to maintain the dignity or prestige of someone or something

face-saving adj maintaining dignity or prestige

facet ('fæsɪt) n 1 any of the surfaces of a cut gemstone 2 an aspect or phase, as of a subject or personality 3 architect the raised surface between the flutes of a column 4 any of the lenses that make up the compound eye of an insect or other arthropod 5 anatomy any small smooth area on a hard surface, as on a bone ▷ vb **-ets, -eting, -eted** or **-ets, -etting, -etted** 6 (tr) to cut facets in (a gemstone) [c17 from French facette a little FACE]

facetiae (fə'si:ʃɪ,i:) pl n 1 humorous or witty sayings 2 obscene or coarsely witty books [c17 from Latin: jests, plural of facētia witticism, from facētus elegant]

face time n the time spent dealing with someone else face to face, esp in a place of work

facetious (fə'si:ʃəs) adj 1 characterized by levity of attitude and love of joking: a facetious person 2 jocular or amusing, esp at inappropriate times: facetious remarks [c16 from Old French facetieux, from facetie witty saying; see FACETIAE] > fa'cetiously adv > fa'cetiousness n

face to face adv, adj (**face-to-face** as adjective) 1 opposite one another 2 in confrontation

face up to vb (intr, adverb + preposition) to accept (an unpleasant fact, reality, etc)

face validity n psychol the extent to which a psychological test appears to measure what it is intended to measure

face value n 1 the value written or stamped on the face of a commercial paper or coin 2 apparent worth or value, as opposed to real worth

facia ('feɪʃɪə) n a variant spelling of **fascia** > 'facial adj

facial ('feɪʃəl) adj 1 of or relating to the face ▷ n 2 a beauty treatment for the face, involving cleansing, massage, and cosmetic packs > 'facially adv

facial angle n the angle formed between a line from the base of the nose to the opening of the ear and a line from the base of the nose to the most prominent part of the forehead: often used in comparative anthropology

facial eczema n a disease of sheep and cattle, occurring in warm areas of North Island, New Zealand. It is caused by a fungus, Pithomyces chartarum, and causes impairment of liver function and reddening, itching, scab formation, and swelling of the skin, esp on the face

facial index n the ratio of the length of the face to the width of the face multiplied by 100: often used in comparative anthropology. Compare **cranial index**

facial nerve n the seventh cranial nerve, supplying the muscles controlling facial expression, glands of the palate and nose, and the taste buds in the anterior two-thirds of the tongue

-facient suffix forming adjectives and nouns indicating a state or quality: absorbefacient; rubefacient [from Latin facient-, faciēns, present participle of facere to do]

facies ('feɪʃɪ,i:z) n, pl **-cies** 1 the general form and appearance of an individual or a group of plants or animals 2 the characteristics of a rock or series of rocks reflecting their appearance, composition, and conditions of formation 3 med the general facial expression of a patient, esp when typical of a specific disease or disorder. See **Hippocratic facies** [c17 from Latin: appearance, FACE]

facile ('fæsaɪl) adj 1 easy to perform or achieve 2 working or moving easily or smoothly 3 without depth; superficial: a facile solution 4 archaic relaxed in manner; easygoing [c15 from Latin facilis easy, from facere to do] > 'facilely adv > 'facileness n

facile princeps (Latin 'fæsɪlɪ 'prɪnseps) n an obvious leader [literally: easily first]

facilitate (fə'sɪlɪ,teɪt) vb (tr) to make easier; assist the progress of > fa'cilitative adj > fa'cili,tator n

facilitation (fə,sɪlɪ'teɪʃən) n 1 the act or process of facilitating 2 physiol the increased ease of transmission of impulses in a nerve fibre, caused by prior excitation

facility (fə'sɪlɪtɪ) n, pl **-ties** 1 ease of action or performance; freedom from difficulty 2 ready skill or ease deriving from practice or familiarity 3 (often plural) the means or equipment facilitating the performance of an action 4 rare easy-going disposition 5 military an organization or building offering supporting capability 6 (usually plural) a euphemistic word for **lavatory** [c15 from Latin facilitās, from facilis easy; see FACILE]

facing ('feɪsɪŋ) n 1 a piece of material used esp to conceal the seam of a garment and prevent fraying 2 (usually plural) a piece of additional cloth, esp in a different colour, on the collar, cuffs, etc, of the jacket of a military uniform, formerly used to denote the regiment 3 an outer layer or coat of material applied to the surface of a wall 4 marketing an area of retail shelf space

façonné or **faconne** ('fæsə,neɪ) adj 1 denoting a fabric with the design woven in ▷ n 2 such a fabric [c19 French, from façonner to fashion]

facsimile (fæk'sɪmɪlɪ) n 1 a an exact copy or reproduction b (as modifier): a facsimile publication 2 an image produced by facsimile transmission ▷ vb **-les, -leing, -led** 3 (tr) to make an exact copy of [c17 from Latin fac simile! make something like it!, from facere to make + similis similar, like]

facsimile machine n a machine which transmits and receives documents in facsimile

transmission. Often shortened to: **fax, fax machine**

facsimile transmission n an international system of transmitting a written, printed, or pictorial document over the telephone system by scanning it photoelectrically and reproducing the image after transmission. Often shortened to: **fax**

fact (fækt) n 1 an event or thing known to have happened or existed 2 a truth verifiable from experience or observation 3 a piece of information: get me all the facts of this case 4 law (often plural) an actual event, happening, etc, as distinguished from its legal consequences. Questions of fact are decided by the jury, questions of law by the court or judge 5 philosophy a proposition that may be either true or false, as contrasted with an evaluative statement 6 **after** (or **before**) **the fact** criminal law after (or before) the commission of the offence: an accessory after the fact 7 **as a matter of fact, in fact, in point of fact** in reality or actuality 8 **fact of life** an inescapable truth, esp an unpleasant one 9 **the fact of the matter** the truth [c16 from Latin factum something done, from factus made, from facere to make] > 'factful adj

fact-finding adj having the purpose of ascertaining facts: a fact-finding tour of the Northeast

factice ('fæktɪs) n a soft rubbery material made by reacting sulphur or sulphur chloride with vegetable oil [c19 from Greek faktis from Latin factīcius FACTITIOUS]

faction¹ ('fækʃən) n 1 a group of people forming a minority within a larger body, esp a dissentious group 2 strife or dissension within a group [c16 from Latin factiō a making, from facere to make, do] > 'factional adj > 'factional,ism n > 'factionalist n

faction² ('fækʃən) n a television programme, film, or literary work comprising a dramatized presentation of actual events [c20 a blend of FACT and FICTION]

faction fight n South African a fight between rival Black groups, usually originating in tribal or clan feuds

factious ('fækʃəs) adj given to, producing, or characterized by faction > 'factiously adv > 'factiousness n

⬛ USAGE See at **fractious**

factitious (fæk'tɪʃəs) adj 1 artificial rather than natural: factitious demands created by the mass media 2 not genuine; sham: factitious enthusiasm [c17 from Latin factīcius, from facere to make, do] > fac'titiously adv > fac'titiousness n

factitive ('fæktɪtɪv) adj grammar denoting a verb taking a direct object as well as a noun in apposition, as for example elect in they elected John president, where John is the direct object and president is the complement [c19 from New Latin factītīvus, from Latin factītāre to do frequently, from facere to do] > 'factitively adv

factive ('fæktɪv) adj logic, linguistics, philosophy (of a linguistic context) giving rise to the presupposition that a sentence occurring in that context is true, as John regrets that Mary did not attend

factoid ('fæktɔɪd) n a piece of unreliable information believed to be true because of the way it is presented or repeated in print [c20 coined by Norman Mailer (born 1923), US author, from FACT + -OID]

factor ('fæktə) n 1 an element or cause that contributes to a result 2 maths a one of two or more integers or polynomials whose product is a given integer or polynomial: 2 and 3 are factors of 6 b an integer or polynomial that can be exactly divided into another integer or polynomial: 1, 2, 3, and 6 are all factors of 6 3 (foll by identifying numeral) med any of several substances that participate in the clotting of blood: factor VIII 4 a person who acts on another's behalf, esp one who transacts business for another 5 commerce a business that makes loans in return for or on security of trade debts 6 former name for a **gene** 7 commercial law a person to whom goods are

f

consigned for sale and who is paid a factorage **8** (in Scotland) the manager of an estate ▷ *vb* **9** (*intr*) to engage in the business of a factor ▷ See also **factor in** [c15 from Latin: one who acts, from *facere* to do] > ˈfactorable *adj* > ˌfactoraˈbility *n* > ˈfactorˌship *n*

USAGE *Factor* (sense 1) should only be used to refer to something which contributes to a result. It should not be used to refer to a part of something such as a plan or arrangement; instead a word such as *component* or *element* should be used

factor VIII *n* a protein that participates in the clotting of blood. It is extracted from donated serum and used in the treatment of the commonest type of haemophilia, in which it is absent

factorage (ˈfæktərɪdʒ) *n* the commission payable to a factor

factor analysis *n statistics* any of several techniques for deriving from a number of given variables a smaller number of different, more useful, variables

factor cost *n* (in social accounting) valuation of goods and services at their overall commercial cost, including markups but excluding indirect taxes and subsidies

factorial (fækˈtɔːrɪəl) *maths* ▷ *n* **1** the product of all the positive integers from one up to and including a given integer. Factorial zero is assigned the value of one: *factorial four is* $1 \times 2 \times 3 \times 4$. Symbol: *n*!, where *n* is the given integer ▷ *adj* **2** of or involving factorials or factors > facˈtorially *adv*

factor in *vb* (*tr, adverb*) *chiefly US* to take account of (something) when making a calculation

factoring (ˈfæktərɪŋ) *n* **1** the business of a factor **2** the business of purchasing debts from clients at a discount and making a profit from their collection

factorize *or* **factorise** (ˈfæktəˌraɪz) *vb* (*tr*) *maths* to resolve (an integer or polynomial) into factors > ˌfactoriˈzation *or* ˌfactoriˈsation *n*

factor of production *n* a resource or input entering the production of wealth, such as land, labour, capital, etc. Also called: **agent of production**

factor of safety *n* the ratio of the breaking stress of a material or structure to the calculated maximum stress when in use. Also called: **safety factor**

factory (ˈfæktərɪ) *n, pl* -**ries 1 a** a building or group of buildings containing a plant assembly for the manufacture of goods **b** (*as modifier*): *a factory worker* **2** *rare* a trading station maintained by factors in a foreign country **3** *Canadian* (formerly) a main trading station for the exchange and transshipment of furs [c16 from Late Latin *factorium*; see FACTOR] > ˈfactory-ˌlike *adj*

factory farm *n* a farm in which animals are bred and fattened using modern industrial methods > **factory farming** *n*

factory outlet *or* **factory shop** *n* a usually low-rent site leased by a factory to sell its end-of-line or damaged stock direct to the customer at reduced prices

factory ship *n* a fishing boat that processes the fish that are caught

factotum (fækˈtəʊtəm) *n* a person employed to do all kinds of work [c16 from Medieval Latin, from Latin *fac*! do! + *tōtum*, from *tōtus* (adj) all]

facts and figures *pl n* details; precise information

factsheet (ˈfæktˌʃiːt) *n* a printed sheet containing information relating to items covered in a television or radio programme

facts of life *pl n* **the** the details of sexual behaviour and reproduction, esp as told to children

factual (ˈfæktʃʊəl) *adj* **1** of, relating to, or characterized by facts **2** of the nature of fact; real;

actual > ˈfactualism *n* > ˈfactualist *n* > ˌfactualˈistic *adj* > ˈfactually *adv* > ˈfactualness *or* ˌfactuˈality *n*

facture (ˈfæktʃə) *n rare* **1** construction **2** workmanship; quality [c15 from Old French, from Latin *factūra*]

facula (ˈfækjʊlə) *n, pl* -**lae** (-ˌliː) any of the bright areas on the sun's surface, usually appearing just before a sunspot and subject to the same 11-year cycle [c18 from Latin: little torch, from *fax* torch] > ˈfacular *adj*

facultative (ˈfækəltətɪv) *adj* **1** empowering but not compelling the doing of an act **2** *philosophy* that may or may not occur **3** *insurance* denoting a form of reinsurance in which the reinsurer has no obligation to accept a particular risk nor the insurer to reinsure, terms and conditions being negotiated for each reinsurance **4** *biology* able to exist under more than one set of environmental conditions: *a facultative parasite can exist as a parasite or a saprotroph.* Compare **obligate** (sense 4) **5** of or relating to a faculty > ˈfacultatively *adv*

faculty (ˈfækəltɪ) *n, pl* -**ties 1** one of the inherent powers of the mind or body, such as reason, memory, sight, or hearing **2** any ability or power, whether acquired or inherent **3** a conferred power or right **4 a** a department within a university or college devoted to a particular branch of knowledge **b** the staff of such a department **c** *chiefly US and Canadian* all the teaching staff at a university, college, school, etc **5** all members of a learned profession **6** *archaic* occupation [c14 (in the sense: department of learning): from Latin *facultās* capability; related to Latin *facilis* easy]

Faculty of Advocates *n law* the college or society of advocates in Scotland

FA Cup *n soccer* (in England) **1** an annual knockout competition for a silver trophy, open to all member teams of the Football Association **2** the trophy itself

fad (fæd) *n informal* **1** an intense but short-lived fashion; craze **2** a personal idiosyncrasy or whim [c19 of uncertain origin] > ˈfaddish *adj* > ˈfaddishness *n* > ˈfaddism *n* > ˈfaddist *n*

FAD *n biochem* flavin adenine dinucleotide: an ester of riboflavin with ADP that acts as the prosthetic group for many flavoproteins. See also **FMN**

faddy (ˈfædɪ) *adj* -**dier**, -**diest** of, having, or involving personal and often transitory whims, esp about food

fade (feɪd) *vb* **1** to lose or cause to lose brightness, colour, or clarity **2** (*intr*) to lose freshness, vigour, or youth; wither **3** (*intr*; usually foll by *away* or *out*) to vanish slowly; die out **4 a** to decrease the brightness or volume of (a television or radio programme or film sequence) or (of a television programme, etc) to decrease in this way **b** to decrease the volume of (a sound) in a recording system or (of a sound) to be so reduced in volume **5** (*intr*) (of the brakes of a vehicle) to lose power **6** to cause (a golf ball) to move with a controlled left-to-right trajectory or (of a golf ball) to veer gradually from left to right ▷ *n* **7** the act or an instance of fading [c14 from *fade* (adj) dull, from Old French, from Vulgar Latin *fatidus* (unattested), probably blend of Latin *vapidus* VAPID + Latin *fatuus* FATUOUS] > ˈfadable *adj* > ˈfadedness *n* > ˈfader *n*

fade-in *n* **1** *films* an optical effect in which a shot appears gradually out of darkness **2** a gradual increase in the volume in a radio or television broadcast ▷ *vb* **fade in** (*adverb*) **3** Also: **fade up** to increase or cause to increase gradually, as vision or sound in a film or broadcast

fadeless (ˈfeɪdlɪs) *adj* not subject to fading

fade-out *n* **1** *films* an optical effect in which a shot slowly disappears into darkness **2** a gradual reduction in signal strength in a radio or television broadcast **3** a gradual and temporary loss of a received radio or television signal due to atmospheric disturbances, magnetic storms, etc **4** a slow or gradual disappearance ▷ *vb* **fade out**

(*adverb*) **5** to decrease or cause to decrease gradually, as vision or sound in a film or broadcast

fadge (fædʒ) *vb* (*intr*) *archaic or dialect* **1** to agree **2** to succeed ▷ *n* **3** *NZ* a package of wool in a wool-bale that weighs less than 100 kilograms [c16 of uncertain origin]

fading (ˈfeɪdɪŋ) *n* a variation in the strength of received radio signals due to variations in the conditions of the transmission medium

fado *Portuguese* (ˈfɑːdu) *n* a type of melancholy Portuguese folk song [literally: FATE]

fadometer (fəˈdɒmɪtə) *n chem* an instrument used to determine the resistance to fading of a pigment or dye

fae (feɪ) *prep* a Scot word for **from**

faecal *or esp US* **fecal** (ˈfiːkəl) *adj* of, relating to, or consisting of faeces

faeces *or esp US* **feces** (ˈfiːsiːz) *pl n* bodily waste matter derived from ingested food and the secretions of the intestines and discharged through the anus [c15 from Latin *faecēs*, plural of *faex* sediment, dregs]

faena *Spanish* (faˈena) *n* bullfighting the matador's final series of passes with sword and cape before the kill [literally: task, from obsolete Catalan (modern *feina*), from Latin *facienda* things to be done, from *facere* to do]

Faenza (*Italian* faˈɛntsa) *n* a city in N Italy, in Emilia-Romagna: famous in the 15th and 16th centuries for its majolica earthenware, esp faïence. Pop: 53 641 (2001)

faerie *or* **faery** (ˈfeɪərɪ, ˈfɛərɪ) *n, pl* -**ries** *archaic or poetic* **1** the land of fairies **2** enchantment ▷ *adj, n* **3** a variant of **fairy**

Faeroes *or* **Faroes** (ˈfɛərəʊz) *pl n* a group of 21 basalt islands in the North Atlantic between Iceland and the Shetland Islands: a self-governing community within the kingdom of Denmark; fishing. Capital: Thorshavn. Pop: 47 000 (2003 est). Area: 1400 sq km (540 sq miles). Also called: **Faeroe Islands** *or* **Faroe Islands**

Faeroese *or* **Faroese** (ˌfɛərəʊˈiːz) *adj* **1** of, relating to, or characteristic of the Faeroes, their inhabitants, or their language ▷ *n* **2** the chief language of the Faeroes, closely related to Icelandic, although they are not mutually intelligible **3** (*pl* -**ese**) a native or inhabitant of the Faeroes

faff (fæf) *vb* (*intr*; often foll by *about*) *Brit informal* to dither or fuss [c19 of obscure origin]

Fafnir (ˈfæfnɪə, ˈfæv-) *n Norse myth* the son of Hreidmar, whom he killed to gain the cursed treasure of Andvari. He became a dragon and was slain by Sigurd while guarding the treasure

fag¹ (fæg) *n* **1** *informal* a boring or wearisome task: *it's a fag having to walk all that way* **2** *Brit* (esp formerly) a young public school boy who performs menial chores for an older boy or prefect ▷ *vb* **fags, fagging, fagged 3** (when *tr*, often foll by *out*) *informal* to become or cause to become exhausted by hard toil or work **4** (*usually intr*) *Brit* to do or cause to do menial chores in a public school: *Brown fags for Lee* [c18 of obscure origin]

fag² (fæg) *n* **1** *Brit* a slang word for **cigarette 2** a fag end, as of cloth [c16 (in the sense: something hanging loose, flap): of obscure origin]

fag³ (fæg) *n slang, chiefly US and Canadian* short for **faggot²**

fagaceous (fəˈɡeɪʃəs) *adj* of, relating to, or belonging to the *Fagaceae*, a family of trees, including beech, oak, and chestnut, whose fruit is partly or wholly enclosed in a husk (cupule) [c19 from New Latin *Fāgāceae*, from Latin *fāgus* beech]

fag end *n* **1** the last and worst part, esp when it is of little use **2** *Brit informal* the stub of a cigarette [c17 see FAG²]

faggot¹ *or esp US* **fagot** (ˈfæɡət) *n* **1** a bundle of sticks or twigs, esp when bound together and used as fuel **2** a bundle of iron bars, esp a box formed by four pieces of wrought iron and filled with scrap to be forged into wrought iron **3** a ball of chopped meat, usually pork liver, bound with herbs and bread and eaten fried **4** a bundle of anything ▷ *vb* (*tr*) **5** to collect into a bundle or bundles **6** *needlework* to do faggoting on (a garment, piece of cloth, etc) [C14 from Old French, perhaps from Greek *phakelos* bundle]

faggot² ('fægət) *n slang, chiefly US and Canadian* a male homosexual. Often shortened to: **fag** [C20 special use of FAGGOT¹] > 'faggoty *adj*

faggoting *or esp US* **fagoting** ('fægətɪŋ) *n* **1** decorative needlework done by tying vertical threads together in bundles **2** a decorative way of joining two hems by crisscross stitches

faggot vote *n* (*formerly*) a vote created by the allotting of property to a person to give him the status of an elector [C19 perhaps from the former use of FAGGOT¹ meaning a person spuriously entered on a military roll]

fag hag *n slang, usually derogatory* a heterosexual woman who prefers the company of homosexual men

fah *or* **fa** (fɑː) *n music* **1** (in the fixed system of solmization) the note F **2** (in tonic sol-fa) the fourth degree of any major scale; subdominant [C14 see GAMUT]

FAHA *abbreviation for* Fellow of the Australian Academy of the Humanities

fahlband ('fɑːl,bænd) *n* a thin bed of schistose rock impregnated with metallic sulphides [C19 from German: pale band]

Fahrenheit ('færən,haɪt) *adj* of or measured according to the Fahrenheit scale of temperature. Symbol: F [named after G. D. *Fahrenheit* (1686–1736), German physicist and inventor of the scale]

Fahrenheit scale *n* a scale of temperatures in which 32° represents the melting point of ice and 212° represents the boiling point of pure water under standard atmospheric pressure. Compare **Celsius scale**

FAI *abbreviation for* **1** Fédération aéronautique internationale [French: International Aeronautical Federation] **2** Football Association of Ireland

Faial *or* **Fayal** (*Portuguese* fə'ial) *n* an island in the central Azores archipelago. Chief town: Horta. Area: 171 sq km (66 sq miles)

faïence (faɪ'ɑːns, feɪ-) *n* **a** a tin-glazed earthenware, usually that of French, German, Italian, or Scandinavian origin **b** (*as modifier*): *a faïence cup* [C18 from French, strictly: pottery from FAENZA]

fail¹ (feɪl) *vb* **1** to be unsuccessful in an attempt (at something or to do something) **2** (*intr*) to stop operating or working properly: *the steering failed suddenly* **3** to judge or be judged as being below the officially accepted standard required for success in (a course, examination, etc) **4** (*tr*) to prove disappointing, undependable, or useless to (someone) **5** (*tr*) to neglect or be unable (to do something) **6** (*intr*) to prove partly or completely insufficient in quantity, duration, or extent **7** (*intr*) to weaken; fade away **8** (*intr*) to go bankrupt or become insolvent ▷ *n* **9** a failure to attain the required standard, as in an examination **10** *without fail* definitely; with certainty [C13 from Old French *faillir*, ultimately from Latin *fallere* to disappoint; probably related to Greek *phēlos* deceitful]

fail² (fel) *n Scot* a turf; sod [perhaps from Scottish Gaelic *fàl*]

failed state *n* a weak state where social and political structures have collapsed to the point where the government has little or no control

failing ('feɪlɪŋ) *n* **1** a weak point; flaw ▷ *prep* **2** (*used to express a condition*) in default of: *failing a solution this afternoon, the problem will have to wait until Monday* > 'failingly *adv*

faille (feɪl; *French* faj) *n* a soft light ribbed fabric of silk, rayon, or taffeta [C16 from French: head covering, hence, fabric used for this, of obscure origin]

fail-safe *adj* **1** designed to return to a safe condition in the event of a failure or malfunction **2** (of a nuclear weapon) capable of being deactivated in the event of a failure or accident **3** unlikely to fail; foolproof ▷ *vb* **4** (*intr*) to return to a safe condition in the event of a failure or malfunction

failure ('feɪljə) *n* **1** the act or an instance of failing **2** a person or thing that is unsuccessful or disappointing: *the evening was a failure* **3** nonperformance of something required or expected: *failure to attend will be punished* **4** cessation of normal operation; breakdown: *a power failure* **5** an insufficiency or shortage: *a crop failure* **6** a decline or loss, as in health or strength **7** the fact of not reaching the required standard in an examination, test, course, etc **8** the act or process of becoming bankrupt or the state of being bankrupt

fain (feɪn) *adv* **1** (*usually with* would) *archaic* willingly; gladly: *she would fain be dead* ▷ *adj* **2** *obsolete* **a** willing or eager **b** compelled [Old English *fægen*; related to Old Norse *fegiun* happy, Old High German *gifehan* to be glad, Gothic *fahehs* joy; see FAWN²]

fainéant ('feɪnɪənt; *French* fenɛɑ̃) *n* **1** a lazy person; idler ▷ *adj* **2** indolent [C17 from French, modification of earlier *fait-nient* (he) does nothing, by folk etymology from Old French *faignant* shirker, from *faindre* to be lazy] > 'faineance *or* 'faineancy *n*

fainites ('feɪnaɪts) *or* **fains** (feɪnz) *interj dialect* a cry for truce or respite from the rules of a game [C19 from *fains* I I decline, from *feine* feign, from Old French *se feindre* in the sense: back out, esp in battle]

fáinne ('faːɲə) *n Irish* a small ring-shaped metal badge worn by advocates of the Irish language [Irish Gaelic, literally: ring]

faint (feɪnt) *adj* **1** lacking clarity, brightness, volume, etc: *a faint noise* **2** lacking conviction or force; weak: *faint praise* **3** feeling dizzy or weak as if about to lose consciousness **4** without boldness or courage; timid (esp in the combination **faint-hearted**) **5** *not the faintest* (*idea or notion*) no idea whatsoever: *I haven't the faintest* ▷ *vb* (*intr*) **6** to lose consciousness, esp momentarily, as through weakness **7** *archaic or poetic* to fail or become weak, esp in hope or courage ▷ *n* **8** a sudden spontaneous loss of consciousness, usually momentary, caused by an insufficient supply of blood to the brain. Technical name: syncope [C13 from Old French, from *faindre* to be idle] > 'fainter *n* > 'faintingly *adv* > 'faintish *adj* > 'faintishness *n* > 'faintly *adv* > 'faintness *n*

faints (feɪnts) *pl n* a variant spelling of **feints**

fair¹ (fɛə) *adj* **1** free from discrimination, dishonesty, etc; just; impartial **2** in conformity with rules or standards; legitimate: *a fair fight* **3** (of the hair or complexion) light in colour **4** beautiful or lovely to look at **5** moderately or quite good: *a fair piece of work* **6** unblemished; untainted **7** (of the tide or wind) favourable to the passage of a vessel **8** sunny, fine, or cloudless **9** (*prenominal*) *informal* thorough; real: *a fair battle to get to the counter* **10** pleasant or courteous **11** apparently good or valuable, but really false: *fair words* **12** open or unobstructed: *a fair passage* **13** (of handwriting) clear and legible **14** *a fair crack of the whip or* (*Austral*) *a fair shake of the dice*, a fair go *informal* a fair opportunity; fair chance **15** *fair and square* in a correct or just way **16** *fair do's* **a** equal shares or treatment **b** an expression of appeal for equal shares or treatment **17** *fair enough!* an expression of agreement **18** *fair go! Austral and NZ informal* come off it!; I don't believe it! **19** *fair to middling* about average ▷ *adv* **20** in a fair way; correctly: *act fair, now!* **21** absolutely or squarely; quite: *the question caught him fair off his guard* **22** *dialect* really or very: *fair tired* ▷ *vb* **23** (*intr*) *dialect* (of the weather) to become fine and mild ▷ *n* **24** *archaic* a person or thing that is beautiful or valuable, esp a woman [Old English *fæger*; related to Old Norse *fagr*, Old Saxon, Old High German *fagar*, Gothic *fagrs* suitable] > 'fairness *n*

fair² (fɛə) *n* **1** a travelling entertainment with sideshows, rides, etc, esp one that visits places at the same time each year **2** a gathering of producers and dealers in a given class of products to facilitate business: *a book fair* **3** an event including amusements and the sale of goods, esp for a charity; bazaar **4** a regular assembly at a specific place for the sale of goods, esp livestock [C13 from Old French *feire*, from Late Latin *fēria* holiday, from Latin *fēriae* days of rest: related to *festus* FESTAL]

Fairbanks ('fɛə,bæŋks) *n* a city in central Alaska, at the terminus of the Alaska Highway. Pop: 30 970 (2003 est)

fair copy *n* a clean copy of a document on which all corrections have been made

fairfaced ('fɛə,feɪst) *adj* (of brickwork) having a neat smooth unplastered surface

fair game *n* **1** a legitimate object for ridicule or attack **2** *hunting archaic* quarry that may legitimately be pursued according to the rules of a particular sport

fairground ('fɛə,graʊnd) *n* an open space used for a fair or exhibition

fair-haired boy *n* the usual US name for **blue-eyed boy**

fairing¹ ('fɛərɪŋ) *n* an external metal structure fitted around parts of an aircraft, car, vessel, etc, to reduce drag. Also called: **fillet** Compare **cowling** [C20 FAIR¹ + -ING]

fairing² ('fɛərɪŋ) *n* **1** *archaic* a present, esp from a fair **2** a sweet circular biscuit made with butter

fairish ('fɛərɪʃ) *adj* **1** moderately good, well, etc **2** (of the hair, complexion, etc) moderately light in colour

Fair Isle *n* an intricate multicoloured pattern knitted with Shetland wool into various garments, such as sweaters [C19 named after one of the Shetland Islands where the pattern originated]

fairlead ('fɛə,liːd) *or* **fairleader** *n nautical* a block or ring through which a line is rove to keep it clear of obstructions, prevent chafing, or maintain it at an angle Also called: **leader**

fairly ('fɛəlɪ) *adv* **1** (*not used with a negative*) moderately **2** as deserved; justly **3** (*not used with a negative*) positively; absolutely: *the hall fairly rang with applause* **4** *archaic* clearly **5** *obsolete* courteously

fair-minded *adj* just or impartial > ,fair-'mindedness *n*

fair play *n* **1** an established standard of decency, honesty, etc **2** abidance by this standard

fair rent *n* (in Britain) the rent for a private tenancy, fixed and registered by a rent officer, and based on the size, condition, and usefulness of the property, but not its scarcity value

fair sex *n the* women collectively

fair-spoken *adj* civil, courteous, or elegant in speech > ,fair-'spokenness *n*

fair trade *n* **a** the practice of directly benefiting producers in the developing world by buying straight from them at a guaranteed price **b** (*as modifier*): *fair-trade coffee*

fairway ('fɛə,weɪ) *n* **1** (on a golf course) the areas of shorter grass between the tees and greens, esp the avenue approaching a green bordered by rough **2** *nautical* **a** the navigable part of a river, harbour, etc **b** the customary course followed by vessels

fair-weather *adj* **1** suitable for use in fair weather only **2** not reliable or present in situations of hardship or difficulty (esp in the phrase **fair-weather friend**)

Fairweather ('fɛə,wɛðə) *n* **Mount** a mountain in W North America, on the border between Alaska and British Columbia. Height: 4663 m (15 300 ft)

fairy ('fɛərɪ) *n, pl* fairies **1** an imaginary supernatural being, usually represented in diminutive human form and characterized as

f

clever, playful, and having magical powers **2** *slang* a male homosexual **3 away with the fairies** *informal* out of touch with reality ▷ *adj* (*prenominal*) **4** of or relating to a fairy or fairies **5** resembling a fairy or fairies, esp in being enchanted or delicate [c14 from Old French *faerie* fairyland, from *feie* fairy, from Latin *Fāta* the Fates; see FATE, FAY¹] > ˈfairy-ˌlike *adj*

fairy cycle *n* a child's bicycle

fairyfloss (ˈfɛərɪˌflɒs) *n* *Austral* a very light fluffy confection made from coloured spun sugar, usually held on a stick. Also called (chiefly Brit): **candyfloss**, (US and Canadian) **cotton candy**

fairy godmother *n* **1** a character in certain fairy stories who brings unexpected benefits to the hero or heroine **2** any benefactress, esp an unknown one

fairyland (ˈfɛərɪˌlænd) *n* **1** the imaginary domain of the fairies; an enchanted or wonderful place **2** a fantasy world, esp one resulting from a person's wild imaginings

fairy lights *pl n* small coloured electric bulbs strung together and used for decoration, esp on a Christmas tree

fairy penguin *n* a small penguin, *Eudyptula minor*, with a bluish head and back, found on the Australian coast. Also called: **little penguin**, **blue penguin**, **korora**

fairy ring *n* **1** a ring of dark luxuriant vegetation in grassy ground corresponding to the edge of an underground fungal mycelium: popularly associated with the dancing of fairies: seasonally marked by a ring of mushrooms **2** short for **fairy ring mushroom**, *Marasmius oreades*, a dainty buff-coloured edible basidiomycetous fungus, characteristically forming rings in grassland

fairy shrimp *n* any small freshwater branchiopod crustacean of the genera *Chirocephalus*, *Artemia*, etc, having a transparent body with many appendages and habitually swimming on its back: order *Anostraca*

fairy swallow *n* (*sometimes capitals*) a variety of domestic fancy pigeon having blue-and-white plumage and heavily muffed feet

fairy tale *or* **story** *n* **1** a story about fairies or other mythical or magical beings, esp one of traditional origin told to children **2** a highly improbable account

fairy-tale *adj* **1** of or relating to a fairy tale **2** resembling a fairy tale, esp in being extremely happy or fortunate: *a true story with a fairy-tale ending* **3** highly improbable: *he came out with a fairy-tale account of his achievements*

Faisalabad (faɪˈʒɑːləˌbɑːd) *n* a city in NE Pakistan: commercial and manufacturing centre of a cotton- and wheat-growing region; university (1961). Pop: 2 533 000 (2005 est). Former name (until 1979): **Lyallpur**

fait accompli *French* (fɛt akɔ̃pli) *n, pl* **faits accomplis** (fez akɔ̃pli) something already done and beyond alteration [literally: accomplished fact]

faites vos jeux *French* (fɛt vo ʒø) place your bets! (a phrase used by croupiers in roulette and other casino gambling games)

faith (feɪθ) *n* **1** strong or unshakeable belief in something, esp without proof or evidence **2** a specific system of religious beliefs: *the Jewish faith* **3** *Christianity* trust in God and in his actions and promises **4** a conviction of the truth of certain doctrines of religion, esp when this is not based on reason **5** complete confidence or trust in a person, remedy, etc **6** any set of firmly held principles or beliefs **7** allegiance or loyalty, as to a person or cause (esp in the phrases **keep faith**, **break faith**) **8 bad faith** insincerity or dishonesty **9 good faith** honesty or sincerity, as of intention in business (esp in the phrase **in good faith**) ▷ *interj* **10** *archaic* indeed; really (also in the phrases **by my faith**, **in faith**) [c12 from Anglo-French *feid*, from Latin *fidēs* trust, confidence]

faith community *n* a community of people sharing the same religious faith

faither (ˈfeðər) *n* a Scot word for **father**

faithful (ˈfeɪθfʊl) *adj* **1** having faith; remaining true, constant, or loyal **2** maintaining sexual loyalty to one's lover or spouse **3** consistently reliable: *a faithful worker* **4** reliable or truthful: *a faithful source* **5** accurate in detail: *a faithful translation* ▷ *n* **6 the faithful a** the believers in and loyal adherents of a religious faith, esp Christianity **b** any group of loyal and steadfast followers > ˈfaithfully *adv* > ˈfaithfulness *n*

faith healing *n* treatment of a sick person through the supposed power of religious faith > **faith healer** *n*

faithless (ˈfeɪθlɪs) *adj* **1** unreliable or treacherous **2** dishonest or disloyal **3** having no faith or trust **4** lacking faith, esp religious faith > ˈfaithlessly *adv* > ˈfaithlessness *n*

faith school *n* *Brit* a school that provides a general education within a framework of a specific religious belief

faitour (ˈfeɪtə) *n* *obsolete* an impostor [c14 from Anglo-French: cheat, from Old French *faitor*, from Latin: FACTOR]

Faiyûm *or* **Fayum** (faɪˈjuːm) *n* See **El Faiyûm**

fajitas (fəˈhiːtəz) *pl n* a Mexican dish of soft tortillas wrapped around fried strips of meat, vegetables, etc [Mexican Spanish]

fake¹ (feɪk) *vb* **1** (*tr*) to cause (something inferior or not genuine) to appear more valuable, desirable, or real by fraud or pretence **2** to pretend to have (an illness, emotion, etc): *to fake a headache* **3** to improvise (music, stage dialogue, etc) ▷ *n* **4** an object, person, or act that is not genuine; sham, counterfeit, or forgery ▷ *adj* **5** not genuine; spurious [originally (C18) thieves' slang to mug or do someone; probably via Polari from Italian *facciare* to make or do] > ˈfaker *n* > ˈfakery *n*

fake² (feɪk) *nautical* ▷ *vb* **1** (*tr*; usually foll by *down*) to coil (a rope) on deck ▷ *n* **2** one round of a coil of rope [Middle English *faken*, perhaps via Lingua Franca from Italian *facciare* to make or do; see FAKE¹]

fakir, faqir (fəˈkɪə, ˈfeɪkə) *or* **fakeer** (fəˈkɪə) *n* **1** a Muslim ascetic who rejects wordly possessions **2** a Hindu religious mendicant or holy man [c17 from Arabic *faqīr* poor]

fa-la *or* **fal la** (fɑːˈlɑː) *n* (esp in 16th-century songs) a refrain sung to the syllables *fa-la-la*

falafel *or* **felafel** (fəˈlɑːfəl) *n* a ball or cake of ground spiced chickpeas, deep-fried and often served with pitta bread [c20 from Arabic *felāfil*]

Falange (ˈfælændʒ; *Spanish* faˈlanxe) *n* the Fascist movement founded in Spain in 1933; the one legal party in Spain under the regime (1939–75) of Francisco Franco (1892–1975), the Spanish general and statesman [Spanish: PHALANX] > **Faˈlangist** *n, adj*

Falasha (fəˈlæʃə) *n, pl* **-sha** *or* **-shas** a member of a tribe of Black Ethiopian Jews [from Amharic, from *fälasi* stranger]

falbala (ˈfælbələ) *n* a gathered flounce, frill, or ruffle [c18 from French, from (dialect) *ferbelà*; see FURBELOW]

falcate (ˈfælkeɪt) *or* **falciform** (ˈfælsɪˌfɔːm) *adj* *biology* shaped like a sickle [c19 from Latin *falcātus*, from *falx* sickle]

falchion (ˈfɔːltʃən, ˈfɔːlʃən) *n* **1** a short and slightly curved medieval sword broader towards the point **2** an archaic word for **sword** [c14 from Italian *falcione*, from *falce*, from Latin *falx* sickle]

falcon (ˈfɔːlkən, ˈfɔːlkən) *n* **1** any diurnal bird of prey of the family *Falconidae*, esp any of the genus *Falco* (gyrfalcon, peregrine falcon, etc), typically having pointed wings and a long tail **2 a** any of these or related birds, trained to hunt small game **b** the female of such a bird (compare **tercel**). Related adj: **falconine 3** a light-medium cannon used from the 15th to 17th centuries [c13 from Old French *faucon*, from Late Latin *falcō* hawk, probably of Germanic origin; perhaps related to Latin *falx* sickle]

falconer (ˈfɔːlkənə, ˈfɔːlkə-) *n* a person who breeds or trains hawks or who follows the sport of falconry

falconet (ˈfɔːlkəˌnɛt, ˈfɔːlkə-) *n* **1** any of various small falcons, esp any of the Asiatic genus *Microhierax* **2** a small light cannon used from the 15th to 17th centuries

falcon-gentle *or* **falcon-gentil** *n* *falconry* a female falcon, esp a female peregrine falcon [c14 from Old French *faucon-gentil* literally: noble falcon]

falconiform (fælˈkəʊnɪˌfɔːm) *adj* of, relating to, or belonging to the order *Falconiformes*, which includes the vultures, hawks, eagles, buzzards, and falcons

falconine (ˈfɔːlkəˌnaɪn, ˈfɔːlkə-) *adj* **1** of, relating to, or resembling a falcon **2** of, relating to, or belonging to the family *Falconidae*, which includes the falcons

falconry (ˈfɔːlkənrɪ, ˈfɔːlkən-) *n* **1** the art of keeping falcons and training them to return from flight to a lure or to hunt quarry **2** the sport of causing falcons to return from flight to their trainer and to hunt quarry under his direction

falcula (ˈfælkjʊlə) *n, pl* **-lae** (-liː) *zoology* a sharp curved claw, esp of a bird > **falculate** *adj*

falderal (ˈfældɪˌræl), **falderol** (ˈfældɪˌrɒl) *or* **folderol** (ˈfɒldɪˌrɒl) *n* **1** a showy but worthless trifle **2** foolish nonsense **3** a nonsensical refrain in old songs

faldstool (ˈfɔːldˌstuːl) *n* a backless seat, sometimes capable of being folded, used by bishops and certain other prelates [c11 *fyldestol*, probably a translation of Medieval Latin *faldistolium* folding stool, of Germanic origin; compare Old High German *faldstuol*]

Falerii (fəˈlɪərɪˌaɪ) *n* an ancient city of S Italy, in Latium: important in pre-Roman times

Faliraki (ˌfælɪˈrɑːkɪ) *n* a coastal resort in SE Greece, on Rhodes. Pop: 400 (2000 est)

Faliscan (fəˈlɪskən) *n* an ancient language of Italy, spoken in the area north of the Tiber. It was closely related to Latin, which displaced it before 200 BC

Falkirk (ˈfɔːlkɜːk) *n* **1** a town in Scotland, the administrative centre of Falkirk council area: scene of Edward I's defeat of Wallace (1298) and Prince Charles Edward's defeat of General Hawley (1746); iron works. Pop: 32 379 (2001) **2** a council area in central Scotland, on the Firth of Forth: created in 1996 from part of Central Region: largely agricultural, with heavy industry in Falkirk and Grangemouth. Administrative centre: Falkirk. Pop: 145 920 (2003 est). Area: 299 sq km (115 sq miles)

Falkland Islands (ˈfɔːlklənd) *pl n* a group of over 100 islands in the S Atlantic: a UK Overseas Territory; invaded by Argentina, who had long laid claim to the islands, on 2 April 1982; recaptured by a British expeditionary force on 14 June 1982. Chief town: Stanley. Pop: 3000 (2003 est). Area: about 12 200 sq km (4700 sq miles). Spanish name: **Islas Malvinas**

Falkland Islands Dependencies *pl n* the former name (until 1985) for South Georgia and the South Sandwich Islands

fall (fɔːl) *vb* **falls**, **falling**, **fell** (fɛl) **fallen** (ˈfɔːlən) (*mainly intr*) **1** to descend by the force of gravity from a higher to a lower place **2** to drop suddenly from an erect position **3** to collapse to the ground, esp in pieces **4** to become less or lower in number, quality, etc: *prices fell in the summer* **5** to become lower in pitch **6** to extend downwards: *her hair fell to her waist* **7** to be badly wounded or killed **8** to slope in a downward direction **9** *Christianity* to yield to temptation or sin **10** to diminish in status, estimation, etc **11** to yield to attack: *the city fell under the assault* **12** to lose power: *the government fell after the riots* **13** to pass into or take on a specified condition: *to fall asleep; fall in love* **14** to adopt a despondent expression: *her face fell* **15** to be averted: *her gaze fell* **16** to come by chance or presumption: *suspicion fell on the butler* **17** to occur; take place: *night fell; Easter falls early this year* **18** (of payments) to be due **19** to be directed to a specific point **20** (foll by *back, behind*, etc) to move in a specified direction **21** to occur at a specified place: *the accent falls on the last syllable* **22** (foll by *to*) to return (to); be inherited (by): *the estate falls to the eldest son* **23** (often foll by *into, under*, etc) to be classified or included: *the subject falls into two main areas* **24** to issue forth: *a curse fell from her lips* **25** (of animals, esp lambs) to be born **26** *Brit dialect* to become pregnant **27** *(tr) Austral and NZ dialect* to fell (trees) **28** *cricket* (of a batsman's wicket) to be taken by the bowling side: *the sixth wicket fell for 96* **29** *archaic* to begin to do: *fall a-doing; fall to doing* **30** **fall flat** to fail to achieve a desired effect **31** **fall foul of** **a** to come into conflict with **b** *nautical* to come into collision with **32** **fall short** **a** to prove inadequate **b** (often foll by *of*) to fail to reach or measure up to (a standard) ▷ *n* **33** an act or instance of falling **34** something that falls: *a fall of snow* **35** *chiefly US* autumn **36** the distance that something falls: *a hundred-foot fall* **37** a sudden drop from an upright position **38** *(often plural)* **a** a waterfall or cataract **b** *(capital when part of a name)*: *Niagara Falls* **39** a downward slope or decline **40** a decrease in value, number, etc **41** a decline in status or importance **42** a moral lapse or failing **43** a capture or overthrow: *the fall of the city* **44** a long false hairpiece; switch **45** a piece of loosely hanging material, such as a veil on a hat **46** *machinery, nautical* the end of a tackle to which power is applied to hoist it **47** *nautical* one of the lines of a davit for holding, lowering, or raising a boat **48** Also called: **pinfall** *wrestling* a scoring move, pinning both shoulders of one's opponent to the floor for a specified period **49** *hunting* **a** another word for **deadfall** **b** *(as modifier)*: *a fall trap* **50** **a** the birth of an animal **b** the animals produced at a single birth **51** **take the fall** *slang, chiefly US* to be blamed, punished, or imprisoned ▷ See also **fall about, fall among, fall apart, fall away, fall back, fall behind, fall down, fall for, fall in, fall off, fall on, fallout, fall over, fall through, fall to** [Old English *feallan*; related to Old Norse *falla*, Old Saxon, Old High German *fallan* to fall; see FELL[2]]

Fall (fɔːl) *n the theol* Adam's sin of disobedience and the state of innate sinfulness ensuing from this for himself and all mankind. See also **original sin**

fall about *vb (intr, adverb)* to laugh in an uncontrolled manner: *we fell about when we saw him*

fallacious (fəˈleɪʃəs) *adj* **1** containing or involving a fallacy; illogical; erroneous **2** tending to mislead **3** delusive or disappointing: *a fallacious hope* > falˈlaciously *adv* > falˈlaciousness *n*

fallacy (ˈfæləsɪ) *n, pl* **-cies** **1** an incorrect or misleading notion or opinion based on inaccurate facts or invalid reasoning **2** unsound or invalid reasoning **3** the tendency to mislead **4** *logic* an error in reasoning that renders an argument logically invalid [c15 from Latin *fallācia*, from *fallax* deceitful, from *fallere* to deceive]

fallacy of many questions *n logic* the rhetorical trick of asking a question that cannot be answered without admitting a presupposition that may be false, as *have you stopped beating your wife?*

fallal (fælˈlæl) *n* a showy ornament, trinket, or article of dress [c18 perhaps based on FALBALA] > falˈlalery *n*

fall among *vb (intr, preposition)* to enter the company of (a group of people), esp by chance: *he fell among thieves*

fall apart *vb (intr, adverb)* **1** to break owing to long use or poor construction: *the chassis is falling apart* **2** to become disorganized and ineffective: *since you resigned, the office has fallen apart*

fall away *vb (intr, adverb)* **1** (of friendship) to be withdrawn **2** to slope down

fall back *vb (intr, adverb)* **1** to recede or retreat **2** (foll by *on* or *upon*) to have recourse (to) ▷ *n* **fall-back** **3** a retreat **4** a reserve, esp money, that can be called upon in need **5** **a** anything to which one can have recourse as a second choice **b** *(as modifier)*: *a fall-back position*

fall behind *vb (intr, adverb)* **1** to drop back; fail to keep up **2** to be in arrears, as with a payment

fall down *vb (intr, adverb)* **1** to drop suddenly or collapse **2** (often foll by *on*) *informal* to prove unsuccessful; fail

fallen (ˈfɔːlən) *vb* **1** the past participle of **fall** ▷ *adj* **2** having sunk in reputation or honour: *a fallen woman* **3** killed in battle with glory: *our fallen heroes* **4** defeated

fallen arch *n* collapse of the arch formed by the instep of the foot, resulting in flat feet

faller (ˈfɔːlə) *n* **1** any device that falls or operates machinery by falling, as in a spinning machine **2** one that falls, esp a horse that falls at a fence in a steeplechase **3** *US and Canadian* a person who fells trees

fallfish (ˈfɔːlˌfɪʃ) *n, pl* **-fish** *or* **-fishes** a large North American freshwater cyprinid fish, *Semotilus corporalis*, resembling the chub

fall for *vb (intr, preposition)* **1** to become infatuated with (a person) **2** to allow oneself to be deceived by (a lie, trick, etc)

fall guy *n informal* **1** a person who is the victim of a confidence trick **2** a scapegoat

fallible (ˈfælɪbᵊl) *adj* **1** capable of being mistaken; erring **2** liable to mislead [c15 from Medieval Latin *fallibilis*, from Latin *fallere* to deceive] > ˌfalliˈbility *or* ˈfallibleness *n* > ˈfallibly *adv*

fall in *vb (intr, adverb)* **1** to collapse; no longer act as a support **2** to adopt a military formation, esp as a soldier taking his place in a line **3** (of a lease) to expire **4** (of land) to come into the owner's possession on the expiry of the lease **5** (often foll by *with*) **a** to meet and join **b** to agree with or support a person, suggestion, etc **6** *Austral and NZ* to make a mistake or come to grief **7** *NZ* to become pregnant ▷ *sentence substitute* **8** the order to adopt a military formation

falling band *n* a man's large flat collar, often lace-trimmed, worn during the 17th century

falling sickness *or* **evil** *n* a former name (nontechnical) for **epilepsy**

falling star *n* an informal name for **meteor**

fall line *n* **1** *skiing* the natural downward course between two points on a slope **2** the edge of a plateau

Fall Line *n* a natural junction, running parallel to the E coast of the US, between the hard rocks of the Appalachians and the softer coastal plain, along which rivers form falls and rapids

fall off *vb (intr)* **1** to drop unintentionally to the ground from (a high object, bicycle, etc), esp after losing one's balance **2** *(adverb)* to diminish in size, intensity, etc; decline or weaken: *business fell off after Christmas* **3** *(adverb) nautical* to allow or cause a vessel to sail downwind of her former heading ▷ *n* **fall-off** **4** a decline or drop

fall on *vb (intr, preposition)* **1** Also: **fall upon** to attack or snatch (an army, booty, etc) **2** **fall flat on one's face** to fail, esp in a ridiculous or humiliating manner **3** **fall on one's feet** to emerge unexpectedly well from a difficult situation

Fallopian tube (fəˈləʊpɪən) *n* either of a pair of slender tubes through which ova pass from the ovaries to the uterus in female mammals. See **oviduct** Related adjs: **oviducal, oviductal** [c18 named after Gabriello *Fallopio* (1523–62), Italian anatomist who first described the tubes]

Fallot's tetralogy (ˈfæləʊz) *n* a congenital heart disease in which there are four defects: pulmonary stenosis, enlarged right ventricle, a ventricular septal defect, and an aorta whose origin lies over the septal defect. In babies suffering this disease the defects can be corrected by surgery [c20 named after E. L. A. *Fallot* (1850–1911), French physician]

fallout (ˈfɔːlˌaʊt) *n* **1** the descent of solid material in the atmosphere onto the earth, esp of radioactive material following a nuclear explosion **2** any solid particles that so descend **3** *informal* side-effects; secondary consequences ▷ *vb* **fall out** *(intr, adverb)* **4** *informal* to quarrel or disagree **5** *(intr)* to happen or occur **6** *military* to leave a parade or disciplinary formation ▷ *sentence substitute* **7** *military* the order to leave a parade or disciplinary formation

fall over *vb (intr, adverb)* **1** to lose one's balance and collapse to the ground **2** to fall from an upright position: *the vase fell over* **3** **fall over oneself** to do everything within one's power: *he fell over himself to be as helpful as possible*

fallow[1] (ˈfæləʊ) *adj* **1** (of land) left unseeded after being ploughed and harrowed to regain fertility for a crop **2** (of an idea, state of mind, etc) undeveloped or inactive, but potentially useful ▷ *n* **3** land treated in this way ▷ *vb* **4** *(tr)* to leave (land) unseeded after ploughing and harrowing it [Old English *fealga*; related to Greek *polos* ploughed field] > ˈfallowness *n*

fallow[2] (ˈfæləʊ) *adj* of a light yellowish-brown colour [Old English *fealu*; related to Old Norse *fölr*, Old Saxon, Old High German *falo*, Latin *pallidus* Greek *polios* grey]

fallow deer *n* either of two deer, *Dama dama* or *D. mesopotamica*, native to the Mediterranean region and Persia respectively. The antlers are flattened and the summer coat is reddish with white spots

fall through *vb (intr, adverb)* to miscarry or fail

fall to *vb (intr)* **1** *(adverb)* to begin some activity, as eating, working, or fighting **2** *(preposition)* to devolve on (a person): *the task fell to me* **3** **fall to the ground** (of a plan, theory, etc) to be rendered invalid, esp because of lack of necessary information

Fallujah (fəˈlʊdʒə) a town in central Iraq, about 60 km W of Baghdad; a centre of resistance against the US-led invasion of Iraq, from 2003. Pop: 223 000 (2005 est)

Falmouth (ˈfælməθ) *n* a port and resort in SW England, in S Cornwall. Pop: 21 635 (2001)

false (fɔːls) *adj* **1** not in accordance with the truth or facts **2** irregular or invalid: *a false start* **3** untruthful or lying: *a false account* **4** not genuine, real, or natural; artificial; fake: *false eyelashes* **5** being or intended to be misleading or deceptive: *a false rumour* **6** disloyal or treacherous: *a false friend* **7** based on mistaken or irrelevant ideas or facts: *false pride; a false argument* **8** *(prenominal)* (esp of plants) superficially resembling the species specified: *false hellebore* **9** serving to supplement or replace, often temporarily: *a false keel* **10** *music* **a** (of a note, interval, etc) out of tune **b** (of the interval of a perfect fourth or fifth) decreased by a semitone **c** (of a cadence) interrupted or imperfect ▷ *adv* **11** in a false or dishonest manner (esp in the phrase **play (someone) false**) [Old English *fals*, from Latin *falsus*, from *fallere* to deceive] > ˈfalsely *adv* > ˈfalseness *n*

false acacia *n* another name for the **locust tree** (see **locust** (sense 2))

false alarm *n* **1** a needless alarm given in error or with intent to deceive **2** an occasion on which danger is perceived but fails to materialize

false ankylosis *n* a nontechnical name for **pseudoarthrosis**

False Bay *n* a bay in SW South Africa, near the Cape of Good Hope

false bedding *n* another name for **cross bedding**

false-card *vb (intr) bridge* to play a misleading card, esp a high loser, in order to deceive an opponent

false cirrus *n* a type of thick cirrus cloud spreading from the top of a cumulonimbus cloud

false colour *n* colour used in a computer or photographic display to help in interpreting the image, as in the use of red to show high temperatures and blue to show low temperatures in an infrared image converter

f

false colours *pl n* **1** a flag to which one is not entitled, flown esp in order to deceive: *the ship was sailing under false colours* **2** an assumed or misleading name or guise: *to trade under false colours*

false dawn *n* zodiacal light appearing just before sunrise

false diamond *n* any of a number of semiprecious stones that resemble diamond, such as zircon and white topaz

false friend *n* a word or expression in one language that, because it resembles one in another language, is often wrongly taken to have the same meaning, for example, the French *agenda* which means *diary*, not *agenda*

false fruit *n* another name for **pseudocarp**

falsehood ('fɔːls,hʊd) *n* **1** the quality of being untrue **2** an untrue statement; lie **3** the act of deceiving or lying

false imprisonment *n law* the restraint of a person's liberty without lawful authority

false joint *n* a nontechnical name for **pseudoarthrosis**

false keel *n* an extension to the keel of a vessel either for protecting the keel from damage or for reducing leeway

false memory syndrome *n* an alleged condition in which a person undergoing psychotherapy erroneously believes in traumatic events in his or her childhood. See also **recovered memory**

false negative *n* **1** a result in a medical test that wrongly indicates the absence of the condition being tested for **2** a person from whom such a result is obtained

false position *n* a situation in which a person is forced to act or seems to be acting against his principles or interests

false positive *n* **1** a result in a medical test that wrongly indicates the presence of the condition being tested for **2** a person from whom such a result is obtained

false pregnancy *n* another name for **phantom pregnancy**

false pretences *pl n* **1** *criminal law* a former name for **deception** (see **obtaining by deception**) **2** a similar misrepresentation used to obtain anything, such as trust or affection (esp in the phrase **under false pretences**)

false relation *n music* a harmonic clash that occurs when a note in one part sounds simultaneously with or immediately before or after its chromatically altered (sharpened or flattened) equivalent appearing in another part. Also called (esp US): **cross relation**

false ribs *pl n* any of the lower five pairs of ribs in man, attached behind to the thoracic vertebrae but in front not attached directly to the breastbone. See **floating rib**

false scorpion *n* any small predatory arachnid of the order *Pseudoscorpionida*, which includes the **book scorpion** and is named from the claw-shaped palps, which are poison organs

false step *n* **1** an unwise action **2** a stumble; slip

false teeth *pl n* a denture, esp a removable complete set of artificial teeth for one or both jaws

falsetto (fɔːlˈsɛtəʊ) *n, pl* -tos a form of vocal production used by male singers to extend their range upwards beyond its natural compass by limiting the vibration of the vocal cords [c18 from Italian, from *falso* FALSE]

false vampire *n* any large insectivorous bat of the family *Megadermatidae*, of Africa, S and SE Asia, and Australia. They eat insects and small vertebrates but do not feed on blood

falsework ('fɔːls,wɜːk) *n* a framework supporting something under construction

falsies ('fɔːlsɪz) *pl n informal* pads of soft material, such as foam rubber, worn to exaggerate the size of or simulate the appearance of a woman's breasts

falsify ('fɔːlsɪ,faɪ) *vb (tr)* -fies, -fying, -fied **1** to make (a report, evidence, accounts, etc) false or inaccurate by alteration, esp in order to deceive **2** to prove false; disprove [c15 from Old French *falsifier*, from Late Latin *falsificāre*, from Latin *falsus* FALSE + *facere* to make] > 'falsi,fiable *adj* > falsification (,fɔːlsɪfɪˈkeɪʃən) *n* > 'falsi,fier *n*

falsity ('fɔːlsɪtɪ) *n, pl* -ties **1** the state of being false or untrue **2** something false; a lie or deception

Falstaffian (fɔːlˈstɑːfɪən) *adj* jovial, plump, and dissolute [c19 after Sir John *Falstaff*, a character in Shakespeare's *Henry IV, Parts I–II* (1597)]

Falster ('fɑːlstə) *n* an island in the Baltic Sea, part of SE Denmark. Chief town: Nykøbing. Pop: 43 537 (2003 est). Area: 513 sq km (198 sq miles)

faltboat ('fælt,bəʊt) *n* a collapsible boat made of waterproof material stretched over a light framework [German *Faltboot*, from *falten* to FOLD[1] + *Boot* BOAT]

falter ('fɔːltə) *vb* **1** *(intr)* to be hesitant, weak, or unsure; waver **2** *(intr)* to move unsteadily or hesitantly; stumble **3** to utter haltingly or hesitantly; stammer ▷ *n* **4** uncertainty or hesitancy in speech or action **5** a quavering or irregular sound [c14 probably of Scandinavian origin; compare Icelandic *faltrast*] > 'falterer *n* > 'falteringly *adv*

Falun (,fɑːˈluːn) *n* a city in central Sweden: iron and pyrites mines. Pop: 55 009 (2004 est)

Falun Gong (,fæluːn ˈguːn) *n* a modern religious movement combining aspects of Buddhism and Taoism, especially the practice of qi gong, founded by Li Hongzhi in 1992 [c20 from Chinese, *falun* dharma wheel (from *fa* law, *lun* wheel) + *gong* practice]

Famagusta (,fæməˈɡʊstə) *n* a port in E Cyprus, on **Famagusta Bay**: became one of the richest cities in Christendom in the 14th century. Pop: 67 167 (1994)

fame (feɪm) *n* **1** the state of being widely known or recognized; renown; celebrity **2** *archaic* rumour or public report ▷ *vb* **3** *(tr; now usually passive)* to make known or famous; celebrate: *he was famed for his ruthlessness* [c13 from Latin *fāma* report; related to *fārī* to say] > **famed** *adj*

familial (fəˈmɪlɪəl) *adj* **1** of or relating to the family **2** occurring in the members of a family: *a familial disease*

familiar (fəˈmɪlɪə) *adj* **1** well-known; easily recognized: *a familiar figure* **2** frequent or customary: *a familiar excuse* **3** *(postpositive; foll by with)* acquainted **4** friendly; informal **5** close; intimate **6** more intimate than is acceptable; presumptuous **7** an archaic word for **familial** ▷ *n* **8** Also called: familiar spirit a supernatural spirit often assuming animal form, supposed to attend and aid a witch, wizard, etc **9** a person, attached to the household of the pope or a bishop, who renders service in return for support **10** an officer of the Inquisition who arrested accused persons **11** a friend or frequent companion [c14 from Latin *familiāris* domestic, from *familia* FAMILY] > faˈmiliarly *adv* > faˈmiliarness *n*

familiarity (fə,mɪlɪˈærɪtɪ) *n, pl* -ties **1** reasonable knowledge or acquaintance, as with a subject or place **2** close acquaintance or intimacy **3** undue intimacy **4** *(sometimes plural)* an instance of unwarranted intimacy

familiarize *or* **familiarise** (fəˈmɪljə,raɪz) *vb (tr)* **1** to make (oneself or someone else) familiar, as with a particular subject **2** to make (something) generally known or accepted > fa,miliari'zation *or* fa,miliari'sation *n* > faˈmiliar,izer *or* faˈmiliar,iser *n*

Familist ('fæmɪlɪst) *n* a member of the Family of Love, a mystical Christian religious sect of the 16th and 17th centuries based upon love > 'Fami,lism *n*

famille French (famij) *n* a type of Chinese porcelain characterized either by a design on a background of yellow (*famille jaune*) or black (*famille noire*) or by a design in which the predominant colour is pink (*famille rose*) or green (*famille verte*) [c19 literally: family]

family ('fæmɪlɪ, 'fæmlɪ) *n, pl* -lies **1 a** a primary social group consisting of parents and their offspring, the principal function of which is provision for its members **b** *(as modifier)*: *family quarrels; a family unit* **2** one's wife or husband and one's children **3** one's children, as distinguished from one's husband or wife **4** a group of persons related by blood; a group descended from a common ancestor. Compare **extended family 5** all the persons living together in one household **6** any group of related things or beings, esp when scientifically categorized **7** *biology* any of the taxonomic groups into which an order is divided and which contains one or more genera. *Felidae* (cat family) and *Canidae* (dog family) are two families of the order *Carnivora* **8** *ecology* a group of organisms of the same species living together in a community **9** a group of historically related languages assumed to derive from one original language **10** *chiefly US* an independent local group of the Mafia **11** *maths* a group of curves or surfaces whose equations differ from a given equation only in the values assigned to one or more constants in each curve: *a family of concentric circles* **12** *physics* the isotopes, collectively, that comprise a radioactive series **13 in the family way** *informal* pregnant [c15 from Latin *familia* a household, servants of the house, from *famulus* servant]

family allowance *n* **1** (in Britain) a former name for **child benefit 2** *(capitals) Canadian* a regular government payment to the parents of children up to a certain age. Also called (in Britain and certain other countries): **child benefit**

family balancing *n US* the choosing of the sex of a future child on the basis of how many children of each sex a family already has

family Bible *n* a large Bible used for family worship in which births, marriages, and deaths are recorded

family circle *n* **1** members of a family regarded as a closed group **2** *chiefly US* the cheap seating area in a theatre behind or above the dress circle

Family Compact *n Canadian* **1 the** the ruling oligarchy in Upper Canada in the early 19th century **2** *(often not capital)* any influential clique

family credit *n* (formerly, in Britain) a means-tested allowance paid to low-earning families with one or more dependent children and one or both parents in work: replaced by Working Families' Tax Credit in 1999

Family Division *n Brit law* a division of the High Court of Justice dealing with divorce, the rights of access to children, etc

family doctor *n* See **general practitioner**

family grouping *n* a system, used usually in the infant school, of grouping children of various ages together, esp for project work. Also called: **vertical grouping**

family man *n* a man who is married and has children, esp one who is devoted to his family

family name *n* **1** a surname, esp when regarded as representing the family honour **2** a first or middle name frequently used in a family, often originally a surname

family planning *n* the control of the number of children in a family and of the intervals between them, esp by the use of contraceptives. See also **birth control**

family skeleton *n* a closely guarded family secret

family support *n NZ* a means-tested allowance for families in need

family therapy *n* a form of psychotherapy in which the members of a family participate, with the aim of improving communications between them and the ways in which they relate to each other

family tree *n* a chart showing the genealogical relationships and lines of descent of a family. Also called: **genealogical tree**

famine ('fæmɪn) *n* **1** a severe shortage of food, as through crop failure or overpopulation **2** acute shortage of anything **3** violent hunger [C14 from Old French, via Vulgar Latin, from Latin *famēs* hunger]

famish ('fæmɪʃ) *vb* **1** (*now usually passive*) to be or make very hungry or weak **2** *archaic* to die or cause to die from starvation **3** *Irish* to make very cold: *I was famished with the cold* [C14 from Old French *afamer*, via Vulgar Latin, from Latin *famēs* FAMINE] > '**famishment** *n*

famous ('feɪməs) *adj* **1** known to or recognized by many people; renowned **2** *informal* excellent; splendid **3** *archaic* of ill repute [C14 from Latin *fāmōsus*; see FAME] > '**famousness** *n*

famously ('feɪməslɪ) *adv* **1** well-known: *her famously relaxed manner* **2** very well: *the two got on famously*

famulus ('fæmjʊləs) *n*, *pl* **-li** (-ˌlaɪ) (formerly) the attendant of a sorcerer or scholar [C19 from Latin: servant]

fan¹ (fæn) *n* **1 a** any device for creating a current of air by movement of a surface or number of surfaces, esp a rotating device consisting of a number of blades attached to a central hub **b** a machine that rotates such a device **2** any of various hand-agitated devices for cooling onself, esp a collapsible semicircular series of flat segments of paper, ivory, etc **3** something shaped like such a fan, such as the tail of certain birds **4** *agriculture* **a** a kind of basket formerly used for winnowing grain **b** a machine equipped with a fan for winnowing or cleaning grain ▷ *vb* **fans**, **fanning**, **fanned** (*mainly tr*) **5** to cause a current of air, esp cool air, to blow upon, as by means of a fan: *to fan one's face* **6** to agitate or move (air, smoke, etc) with or as if with a fan **7** to make fiercer, more ardent, etc: *fan one's passion* **8** (*also intr*; often foll by *out*) to spread out or cause to spread out in the shape of a fan **9 a** to fire (an automatic gun) continuously by keeping the trigger depressed **b** to fire (a nonautomatic gun) several times by repeatedly chopping back the hammer with the palm **10** to winnow (grain) by blowing the chaff away from it [Old English *fann*, from Latin *vannus*] > '**fanlike** *adj* > '**fanner** *n*

fan² (fæn) *n* **1** an ardent admirer of a pop star, film actor, football team, etc **2** a devotee of a sport, hobby, etc [C17, re-formed C19 from FAN(ATIC)]

Fanagalo ('fænəgələʊ) *or* **Fanakalo** *n* (in South Africa) a Zulu-based pidgin with English and Afrikaans components, esp associated with the mines [C20 from Fanagalo *fana go lo*, literally: to be like this; compare Zulu *fand* to be like, *ka-lo* of this]

fanatic (fəˈnætɪk) *n* **1** a person whose enthusiasm or zeal for something is extreme or beyond normal limits **2** *informal* a person devoted to a particular hobby or pastime; fan: *a jazz fanatic* ▷ *adj* **3** a variant of **fanatical** [C16 from Latin *fānāticus* belonging to a temple, hence, inspired by a god, frenzied, from *fānum* temple]

fanatical (fəˈnætɪkᵊl) *adj* surpassing what is normal or accepted in enthusiasm for or belief in something; excessively or unusually dedicated or devoted > fa'**natically** *adv*

fanaticism (fəˈnætɪˌsɪzəm) *n* wildly excessive or irrational devotion, dedication, or enthusiasm

fanaticize *or* **fanaticise** (fəˈnætɪˌsaɪz) *vb* to make or become fanatical

fanbase ('fænˌbeɪs) *n* the body of admirers of a particular pop singer, football team, etc

fan belt *n* any belt that drives a fan, esp the belt that drives a cooling fan together with a dynamo or alternator in a car engine

fancied ('fænsɪd) *adj* **1** imaginary; unreal **2** thought likely to win or succeed: *a fancied runner*

fancier ('fænsɪə) *n* **1** a person with a special interest in something **2** a person who breeds plants or animals, often as a pastime: *a bird fancier*

fanciful ('fænsɪfʊl) *adj* **1** not based on fact; dubious or imaginary: *fanciful notions* **2** made or designed in a curious, intricate, or imaginative way **3** indulging in or influenced by fancy;

whimsical > '**fancifully** *adv* > '**fancifulness** *n*

fan club *n* **1** an organized group of admirers of a particular pop singer, film star, etc **2** be a member of someone's fan club *informal* to approve of someone strongly

fancy ('fænsɪ) *adj* **-cier**, **-ciest 1** not plain; ornamented or decorative: *a fancy cake; fancy clothes* **2** requiring skill to perform; intricate: *a fancy dance routine* **3** arising in the imagination; capricious or illusory **4** (*often used ironically*) superior in quality or impressive: *a fancy course in business administration* **5** higher than expected: *fancy prices* **6** (of a domestic animal) bred for particular qualities ▷ *n*, *pl* **-cies 7** a sudden capricious idea; whim **8** a sudden or irrational liking for a person or thing **9** the power to conceive and represent decorative and novel imagery, esp in poetry. Fancy was held by Coleridge to be more casual and superficial than imagination. See **imagination** (sense 4) **10** an idea or thing produced by this **11** a mental image **12** taste or judgment, as in art of dress **13** Also called: **fantasy, fantasia** *music* a composition for solo lute, keyboard, etc, current during the 16th and 17th centuries **14 the fancy** *archaic* those who follow a particular sport, esp prize fighting ▷ *vb* **-cies**, **-cying**, **-cied** (*tr*) **15** to picture in the imagination **16** to suppose; imagine: *I fancy it will rain* **17** (*often used with a negative*) to like: *I don't fancy your chances!* **18** (*reflexive*) to have a high or ill-founded opinion of oneself: *he fancied himself as a doctor* **19** *informal* to have a wish for; desire: *she fancied some chocolate* **20** *Brit informal* to be physically attracted to (another person) **21** to breed (animals) for particular characteristics ▷ *interj* **22** Also: **fancy that!** an exclamation of surprise or disbelief [C15 *fantsy*, shortened from *fantasie*; see FANTASY] > '**fancily** *adv* > '**fanciness** *n*

fancy dress *n* **a** costume worn at masquerades, etc, usually representing a particular role, historical figure, etc **b** (*as modifier*): *a fancy-dress ball*

fancy-free *adj* having no commitments; carefree

fancy goods *pl n* small decorative gifts; knick-knacks

fancy man *n* *slang* **1** a woman's lover **2** a pimp

fancy woman *n* *slang* a mistress or prostitute

fancywork ('fænsɪˌwɜːk) *n* any ornamental needlework, such as embroidery or crochet

fan dance *n* a dance in which large fans are manipulated in front of the body, partially revealing or suggesting nakedness

fandangle (fænˈdæŋɡᵊl) *n* *informal* **1** elaborate ornament **2** nonsense [C19 perhaps from FANDANGO]

fandango (fænˈdæŋɡəʊ) *n*, *pl* **-gos 1** an old Spanish courtship dance in triple time between a couple who dance closely and provocatively **2** a piece of music composed for or in the rhythm of this dance [C18 from Spanish, of uncertain origin]

fane (feɪn) *n* *archaic or poetic* a temple or shrine [C14 from Latin *fānum*]

fanfare ('fænfeə) *n* **1** a flourish or short tune played on brass instruments, used as a military signal, at a ceremonial event, etc **2** an ostentatious flourish or display [C17 from French, back formation from *fanfarer* to play a flourish on trumpets; see FANFARONADE]

fanfaronade (ˌfænfərəˈnɑːd) *n* *rare* boasting or flaunting behaviour; bluster [C17 via French from Spanish *fanfaronada*, from *fanfarron* boaster, from Arabic *farfār* garrulous]

fang¹ (fæŋ) *n* **1** the long pointed hollow or grooved tooth of a venomous snake through which venom is injected **2** any large pointed tooth, esp the canine or carnassial tooth of a carnivorous mammal **3** the root of a tooth **4** (*usually plural*) *Brit informal* tooth: *clean your fangs* [Old English *fang* what is caught, prey; related to Old Norse *fang* a grip, German *Fang* booty] > **fanged** *adj* > **fangless** *adj* > '**fang,like** *adj*

fang² (fæŋ) *Austral informal* ▷ *vb* (*intr*) **1** to drive at great speed ▷ *n* **2** an act or instance of driving in such a way: *we took the car for a fang* [C20 from Juan

Manuel *Fangio* (1911–95), Argentinian racing driver who was world champion five times]

fanfic ('fænˌfɪk) *n* fiction written around previously established characters invented by other authors

Fang (fæŋ, fɑːŋ) *n* **1** (*pl* **Fangs** *or* **Fang**) a member of a Negroid people of W Africa, living chiefly in the rain forests of Gabon and Rio Muni: noted for their use of iron and copper money and for their sculpture **2** the language of this people, belonging to the Bantu group of the Niger-Congo family

fango ('fæŋɡəʊ) *n* mud from thermal springs in Italy, used in the treatment of rheumatic disease [from Italian]

fan heater *n* a space heater consisting of an electrically heated element with an electrically driven fan to disperse the heat by forced convection

fanion ('fænjən) *n* a small flag used by surveyors to mark stations [C18 from French, from *fanon* maniple, of Germanic origin]

fanjet ('fænˌdʒɛt) *n* another name for **turbofan** (senses 1, 2)

fankle ('fæŋkᵊl) *Scot dialect* ▷ *vb* (*tr*) **1** to entangle ▷ *n* **2** a tangle; confusion [from *fank* a coil of rope, from *fang*, obsolete variant of VANG]

fanlight ('fænˌlaɪt) *n* **1** a semicircular window over a door or window, often having sash bars like the ribs of a fan **2** a small rectangular window over a door. US name: **transom 3** another name for **skylight**

fan mail *n* mail sent to a famous person, such as a pop musician or film star, by admirers

fanny ('fænɪ) *n*, *pl* **-nies** *slang* **1** *taboo, Brit* the female genitals **2** *chiefly US and Canadian* the buttocks [C20 perhaps from *Fanny*, pet name from *Frances*]

USAGE Despite the theory that this word derives from the name 'Fanny', its use in British English is still considered taboo by many people, and is likely to cause offence. In the US the word refers to the buttocks. Serious misunderstanding may therefore arise when what people in Britain know as a 'bumbag' is referred to in the US as a 'fanny pack'

fanny adams *n* *Brit slang* **1** (usually preceded by *sweet*) absolutely nothing at all. Often shortened to: **f.a.**, **FA** *or* **SFA 2** *chiefly nautical* (formerly) tinned meat, esp mutton [C19 from the name of a young murder victim whose body was cut up into small pieces. For sense 1: a euphemism for *fuck all*]

fanon ('fænən) *n* *RC Church* **1** a collar-shaped vestment worn by the pope when celebrating mass **2** (formerly) various pieces of embroidered fabric used in the liturgy [Middle English, of Germanic origin; related to Old High German *fano* cloth]

fan palm *n* any of various palm trees, such as the talipot and palmetto, that have fan-shaped leaves. Compare **feather palm**

fantail ('fænˌteɪl) *n* **1** a breed of domestic pigeon having a large tail that can be opened like a fan **2** any Old World flycatcher of the genus *Rhipidura*, of Australia, New Zealand, and SE Asia, having a broad fan-shaped tail **3** a tail shaped like an outspread fan **4** *architect* a part or structure having a number of components radiating from a common centre **5** a burner that ejects fuel to produce a wide flat flame in a lamp or furnace **6** a flat jet of air and coal dust projected into the air stream of a pulverized-coal furnace **7** an auxiliary sail on the upper portion of a windmill that turns the mill to face the wind **8** *US* a curved part of the deck projecting aft of the sternpost of a ship > '**fan,tailed** *adj*

fan-tan *n* **1** a Chinese gambling game in which a random number of counters are placed under a bowl and wagers laid on how many will remain after they have been divided by four **2** a card

f

game played in sequence, the winner being the first to use up all his cards [C19 from Chinese (Cantonese) *fan t'an* repeated divisions, from *fan* times + *t'an* division]
fantasia (fæn'teɪzɪə, ˌfæntə'zɪə) *n* **1** any musical composition of a free or improvisatory nature **2** a potpourri of popular tunes woven freely into a loosely bound composition **3** another word for **fancy** (sense 13) [C18 from Italian: fancy; see FANTASY]
fantasist ('fæntəsɪst) *n* **1** a person who indulges in fantasies **2** a person who writes musical or literary fantasies
fantasize *or* **fantasise** ('fæntəˌsaɪz) *vb* **1** (when *tr*, takes a clause as object) to conceive extravagant or whimsical ideas, images, etc **2** (*intr*) to conceive pleasant or satisfying mental images
fantasm ('fæntæzəm) *n* an archaic spelling of **phantasm**. > **fan'tasmal** *or* **fan'tasmic** *adj* > **fan'tasmally** *or* **fan'tasmically** *adv*
fantast ('fæntæst) *n* a dreamer or visionary [C16 from German *Phantast*, from Greek *phantastēs* boaster; English word influenced in meaning by FANTASTIC]
fantastic (fæn'tæstɪk) *adj* also **fantastical** **1** strange, weird, or fanciful in appearance, conception, etc **2** created in the mind; illusory **3** extravagantly fanciful; unrealistic: *fantastic plans* **4** incredible or preposterous; absurd: *a fantastic verdict* **5** *informal* very large or extreme; great: *a fantastic fortune; he suffered fantastic pain* **6** *informal* very good; excellent **7** of, given to, or characterized by fantasy **8** not constant; capricious; fitful: *given to fantastic moods* ▷ *n* **9** *archaic* a person who dresses or behaves eccentrically [C14 *fantastik* imaginary, via Late Latin from Greek *phantastikos* capable of imagining, from *phantazein* to make visible] > ˌ**fantasti'cality** *or* **fan'tasticalness** *n*
fantastically (fæn'tæstɪkəlɪ) *adv* **1** in a fantastic manner **2** *informal* (intensifier): *it's fantastically cheap*
fantasy *or* **phantasy** ('fæntəsɪ) *n, pl* **-sies** **1** **a** imagination unrestricted by reality **b** (*as modifier*): *a fantasy world* **2** a creation of the imagination, esp a weird or bizarre one **3** *psychol* **a** a series of pleasing mental images, usually serving to fulfil a need not gratified in reality **b** the activity of forming such images **4** a whimsical or far-fetched notion **5** an illusion, hallucination, or phantom **6** a highly elaborate imaginative design or creation **7** *music* another word for **fantasia**[1] (sense 2), **fancy** (sense 13), (rarely) **development** (sense 5) **8** **a** literature having a large fantasy content **b** a prose or dramatic composition of this type **9** (*modifier*) of or relating to a competition, often in a newspaper, in which a participant selects players for an imaginary ideal team, and points are awarded according to the actual performances of the chosen players: *fantasy football* ▷ *vb* **-sies, -sying, -sied** **10** a less common word for **fantasize** [C14 *fantasie*, from Latin *phantasia*, from Greek *phantazein* to make visible]
Fanti ('fæntɪ) *n* **1** a language of Ghana: one of the two chief dialects of Akan. Compare **Twi** **2** (*pl* **-tis** *or* **-ti**) a member of a Negroid people who speak this language, inhabiting the rain forests of Ghana and the Ivory Coast
fantoccini (ˌfæntə'tʃiːnɪ) *pl n* **1** marionettes **2** puppet shows in which they are used [C18 from Italian: little puppets, plural of *fantoccino*, from *fantoccio* puppet, from *fante* boy, from Latin *infāns* INFANT]
fantod ('fæntəd) *n* **1** crotchety or faddish behaviour **2** (*pl*) a state of restlessness or unease [C19 of uncertain origin]
fantom ('fæntəm) *n* an archaic spelling of **phantom**
fantoosh (fæn'tuːʃ) *adj Scot* pretentious; ostentatious [of uncertain origin]
fan tracery *n architect* the carved ornamentation on fan vaulting
fan vaulting *n architect* vaulting having ribs that radiate like those of a fan and spring from the top of a capital or corbel. Also called: **palm vaulting**
fan worm *n* any tube-dwelling polychaete worm of the family *Sabellidae*, having long tentacles that spread into a fan when the worm emerges from its tube
FANY ('fænɪ) *n* **1** *acronym for* First Aid Nursing Yeomanry **2** Also called: **Fany, Fanny** *pl* **FANYs, Fanys, Fannies** a member of this organization
fanzine ('fænˌziːn) *n* a small-circulation magazine produced by amateurs for fans of a specific interest, pop group, etc [C20 from FAN[2] + (MAGA)ZINE]
FAO *abbreviation for* **1** Food and Agriculture Organization (of the United Nations) **2** for the attention of
FAQ *computing abbreviation for* frequently asked question *or* questions: a text file containing basic information on a particular subject
f.a.q. *commerce abbreviation for* fair average quality
faqir (fə'kɪə, 'feɪkə) *n* a variant spelling of **fakir**
far (fɑː) *adv* **farther** *or* **further**, **farthest** *or* **furthest** **1** at, to, or from a great distance **2** at or to a remote time: *far in the future* **3** to a considerable degree; very much: *a far better plan* **4** **as far as** **a** to the degree or extent that **b** to the distance or place of **5** **by far** by a considerable margin **6** **far and away** by a very great margin **7** **far and wide** over great distances; everywhere **8** **far be it from me** I would not presume; on no account: *far be it from me to tell you what to do* **9** **far gone** **a** in an advanced state of deterioration **b** *informal* extremely drunk **10** **go far** **a** to be successful; achieve much: *your son will go far* **b** to be sufficient or last long: *the wine didn't go far* **11** **go too far** to exceed reasonable limits **12** **how far?** to what extent, distance, or degree? **13** **in so far as** to the degree or extent that **14** **so far** **a** up to the present moment **b** up to a certain point, extent, degree, etc **15** **so far, so good** an expression of satisfaction with progress made ▷ *adj* (*prenominal*) **16** remote in space or time: *a far country; in the far past* **17** extending a great distance; long **18** more distant: *the far end of the room* **19** **a far cry** **a** a long way **b** something very different **20** **far from** in a degree, state, etc, remote from: *he is far from happy* [Old English *feorr*; related to Old Frisian *fir*, Old High German *ferro*, Latin *porro* forwards, Greek *pera* further] > **'farness** *n*
farad ('færəd, -æd) *n physics* the derived SI unit of electric capacitance; the capacitance of a capacitor between the plates of which a potential of 1 volt is created by a charge of 1 coulomb. Symbol: F [C19 named after Michael *Faraday* (1791–1867), English physicist and chemist]
faraday ('færəˌdeɪ) *n* a quantity of electricity, used in electrochemical calculations, equivalent to unit amount of substance of electrons. It is equal to the product of the Avogadro number and the charge on the electron and has the value 96 487 coulombs per mole. Symbol: F [C20 named after Michael *Faraday* (1791–1867), English physicist and chemist]
Faraday cage *n* an earthed conducting cage or container used to protect electrical equipment against electric fields [C20 named after Michael *Faraday* (1791–1867), English physicist and chemist]
faradic (fə'rædɪk) *or* **faradaic** (ˌfærə'deɪɪk) *adj* of or concerned with an intermittent asymmetric alternating current such as that induced in the secondary winding of an induction coil [C19 from French *faradique*, from Michael *Faraday* (1791–1867), English physicist and chemist]
faradism ('færəˌdɪzəm) *n* the therapeutic use of faradic currents
faradize *or* **faradise** ('færəˌdaɪz) *vb* (*tr*) *obsolete* to treat (an organ or part) with faradic currents > ˌ**faradi'zation** *or* ˌ**faradi'sation** *n* > **'faraˌdizer** *or* **'faraˌdiser** *n*
farandole ('færənˌdəʊl; *French* farɑ̃dɔl) *n* **1** a lively dance in six-eight or four-four time from Provence **2** a piece of music composed for or in the rhythm of this dance [C19 from French, from Provençal *farandoulo*, of uncertain origin; compare Spanish *farándula* itinerant group of actors]
faraway ('fɑːrəˌweɪ) *adj* (**far away** *when postpositive*) **1** very distant; remote **2** dreamy or absent-minded
FARC (fɑːk) *n acronym for Fuerzas Armadas Revolucionarias de Colombia*, Revolutionary Armed Forces of Colombia, a Marxist revolutionary guerrilla force engaging in armed struggle against the government of Colombia
farce (fɑːs) *n* **1** a broadly humorous play based on the exploitation of improbable situations **2** the genre of comedy represented by works of this kind **3** a ludicrous situation or action **4** Also: **farcemeat** another name for **forcemeat** ▷ *vb* (*tr*) *obsolete* **5** to enliven (a speech, etc) with jokes **6** to stuff (meat, fowl, etc) with forcemeat [C14 (in the sense: stuffing): from Old French, from Latin *farcīre* to stuff, interpolate passages (in the mass, in religious plays, etc)]
farceur *French* (farsœr) *n* **1** a writer of or performer in farces **2** a joker > **far'ceuse** *fem n*
farci (fɑː'siː) *adj* (of food) stuffed [French: stuffed; see FARCE]
farcical ('fɑːsɪkəl) *adj* **1** ludicrous; absurd **2** of or relating to farce > ˌ**farci'cality** *or* **'farcicalness** *n* > **'farcically** *adv*
farcy ('fɑːsɪ) *n, pl* **-cies** *vet science* a form of glanders in which lymph vessels near the skin become thickened, with skin lesions and abscess-forming nodules, caused by a bacterium, *Burkholderia mallei* [C15 from Old French *farcin*, from Late Latin *farcīminum* glanders, from Latin *farcīmen* a sausage, from *farcīre* to stuff]
fard (fɑːd) *n archaic* paint for the face, esp white paint [C15 from Old French *farder* to use facial cosmetics, of Germanic origin]
fardel ('fɑːdəl) *n archaic* a bundle or burden [C13 from Old French *farde*, ultimately from Arabic *fardah*]
fare (fɛə) *n* **1** the sum charged or paid for conveyance in a bus, train, aeroplane, etc **2** a paying passenger, esp when carried by taxi **3** a range of food and drink; diet ▷ *vb* (*intr*) **4** to get on (as specified); manage: *he fared well* **5** (with *it* as a subject) to turn out or happen as specified: *it fared badly with him* **6** *archaic* to eat: *we fared sumptuously* **7** (often foll by *forth*) *archaic* to go or travel [Old English *faran*; related to Old Norse *fara* to travel, Old High German *faran* to go, Greek *poros* ford] > **'farer** *n*
Far East *n* **the** the countries of E Asia, usually including China, Japan, North and South Korea, Indonesia, Malaysia, and the Philippines: sometimes extended to include all territories east of Afghanistan
Far Eastern *adj* of or relating to the Far East (E Asia) or its inhabitants
Fareham ('fɛərəm) *n* a market town in S England, in S Hampshire. Pop: 37 440 (2001 est)
fare stage *n* **1** a section of a bus journey for which a set charge is made **2** a bus stop marking the end of such a section
fare-thee-well *or* **fare-you-well** *n informal, chiefly US* a state of perfection: *the steak was cooked to a fare-thee-well*
farewell (ˌfɛə'wɛl) *sentence substitute* **1** goodbye; adieu ▷ *n* **2** a parting salutation **3** an act of departure; leave-taking **4** (*modifier*) expressing leave-taking: *a farewell speech* ▷ *vb* (*tr*) **5** *Austral and NZ* to honour (a person) at his departure, retirement, etc
far-fetched *adj* improbable in nature; unlikely
far-flung *adj* **1** widely distributed **2** far distant; remote
Faridabad (fæ'rɪdəbæd) *n* a city in NE India, in Haryana: industrial centre. Pop: 1 054 981 (2001)
farina (fə'riːnə) *n* **1** flour or meal made from any kind of cereal grain **2** *chiefly Brit* starch, esp prepared from potato flour [C18 from Latin *fār*

spelt, coarse meal]

farinaceous (ˌfærɪˈneɪʃəs) *adj* **1** consisting or made of starch, such as bread, macaroni, and potatoes **2** having a mealy texture or appearance **3** containing starch: *farinaceous seeds*

farinose (ˈfærɪˌnəʊs, -ˌnəʊz) *adj* **1** similar to or yielding farina **2** *botany* covered with very short hairs resembling a whitish mealy dust
> ˈfariˌnosely *adv*

farl *or* **farle** (fɑːl) *n* a thin cake of oatmeal, often triangular in shape [c18 from earlier *fardel* fourth part, from Old English *fēortha* fourth + Middle English *del* part]

farm (fɑːm) *n* **1 a** a tract of land, usually with house and buildings, cultivated as a unit or used to rear livestock **b** (*as modifier*): *farm produce* **c** (*in combination*): *farmland* **2** a unit of land or water devoted to the growing or rearing of some particular type of vegetable, fruit, animal, or fish: *a fish farm* **3** an installation for storage **4** a district of which one or more taxes are leased **5** *history* **a** a fixed sum paid by an individual or group for the right of collecting and retaining taxes, rents, etc **b** a fixed sum paid regularly by a town, county, etc, in lieu of taxes **c** the leasing of a source of revenue to an individual or group **d** a fixed tax, rent, etc, paid regularly ▷ *vb* **6** (*tr*) **a** to cultivate (land) **b** to rear (stock, etc) on a farm **7** (*intr*) to engage in agricultural work, esp as a way of life **8** (*tr*) to look after a child for a fixed sum **9 a** to collect the moneys due and retain the profits from (a tax district, business, etc) for a specified period on payment of a sum or sums **b** to operate (a franchise) under similar conditions ▷ See also **farm out** [c13 from Old French *ferme* rented land, ultimately from Latin *firmāre* to settle]
> ˈfarmable *adj*

farm-bike *n* NZ a motorcycle built for off-road travel

farmed (fɑːmd) *adj* (of fish and game) reared on a farm rather than caught in the wild

farmer (ˈfɑːmə) *n* **1** a person who operates or manages a farm **2** a person who obtains the right to collect and retain a tax, rent, etc, or operate a franchise for a specified period on payment of a fee **3** a person who looks after a child for a fixed sum

farmer-general *n, pl* farmers-general (in France before 1789) a member of a group allowed to farm certain taxes > ˈfarmer-ˈgeneralˌship *n*

farmer's lung *n* inflammation of the alveoli of the lungs caused by an allergic response to fungal spores in hay

farmers' market *n* a market at which farm produce is sold directly to the public by the producer

farm-gate sale *n* NZ the sale of produce direct from the producer

farm hand *n* a person who is hired to work on a farm

farmhouse (ˈfɑːmˌhaʊs) *n* **1** a house attached to a farm, esp the dwelling from which the farm is managed **2** Also called: farmhouse loaf *Brit* a large white loaf, baked in a tin, with slightly curved sides and top

farming (ˈfɑːmɪŋ) *n* **a** the business, art, or skill of agriculture **b** (*as modifier*): *farming methods*

farmland (ˈfɑːmˌlænd) *n* land used or suitable for farming

farm out *vb* (*tr, adverb*) **1** to send (work) to be done by another person, firm, etc; subcontract **2** to put (a child, etc) into the care of a private individual; foster **3** to lease to another for a rent or fee the right to operate (a business for profit, land, etc) or the right to collect (taxes)

farmstead (ˈfɑːmˌstɛd) *n* a farm or the part of a farm comprising its main buildings together with adjacent grounds

farm team *n US and Canadian* a sports team in a smaller or lower league that is affiliated to one in a larger or higher league

farm-toun (ˈfærmˌtʊn, ˈfɑːmˌtʊn) *n Scot* a

farmhouse together with its outbuildings

farmyard (ˈfɑːmˌjɑːd) *n* **a** an area surrounded by or adjacent to farm buildings **b** (*as modifier*): *farmyard animals*

farnarkel (ˈfɑːnɑːkəl) *vb* (*intr; often foll by around*) *Austral slang* to spend time or act in a careless or inconsequential manner; waste time [c20 coined by the New Zealand-born comedian John Clarke as the name of a fictitious sport of doing nothing for which he commentated in an Australian TV series] > ˈfarnarkeling *n*

Farnborough (ˈfɑːnbərə, -brə) *n* a town in S England, in NE Hampshire: military base, with an aeronautical research centre. Pop: 57 147 (2001)

farnesol (ˈfɑːnɪˌsɒl) *n* a colourless aromatic sesquiterpene alcohol found in many essential oils and used in the form of its derivatives in perfumery; 3,7,11-trimethyl-2,6,10-dodecatrienol. Formula: $C_{15}H_{26}O$ [c20 from New Latin (*Acacia*) *farnesiāna*; named after Odoardo *Farnese*, c17 Italian cardinal]

Farnham (ˈfɑːnəm) *n* a town in S England, in NW Surrey. Pop: 36 296 (2001)

Far North *n* **the** the Arctic and sub-Arctic regions of the world

faro (ˈfɛərəʊ) *n* a gambling game in which players bet against the dealer on what cards he will turn up [c18 probably spelling variant of *Pharaoh*]

Faro (ˈfɑːrəʊ) *n* a port and resort in S Portugal: destroyed by earthquakes in 1722 and 1755. Pop: 58 051 (2001)

Faroes (ˈfɛərəʊz) *n* a variant spelling of **Faeroes**

Faroese (ˌfɛərəʊˈiːz) *adj, n* a variant spelling of **Faeroese**

far-off *adj* (**far off** when postpositive) remote in space or time; distant

farouche *French* (faruʃ) *adj* **1** sullen or shy **2** socially inept [c18 from French, from Old French *faroche*, from Late Latin *forasticus* from without, from Latin *foras* out of doors]

far-out *slang* ▷ *adj* (**far out** when postpositive) **1** bizarre or avant-garde **2** excellent; wonderful ▷ *interj* **far out 3** an expression of amazement or delight

Farquhar Islands (ˈfɑːkwə, -kə) *pl n* an island group in the Indian Ocean: administratively part of the Seychelles

farrago (fəˈrɑːgəʊ) *n, pl* -gos *or* -goes a hotchpotch [c17 from Latin: mash for cattle (hence, a mixture), from *fār* spelt] > farraginous (fəˈrædʒɪnəs) *adj*

far-reaching *adj* extensive in influence, effect, or range

farrier (ˈfærɪə) *n chiefly Brit* **1** a person who shoes horses **2** *archaic* another name for **veterinary surgeon 3** *military* a noncommissioned officer who looks after horses [c16 from Old French *ferrier*, from Latin *ferrārius* smith, from *ferrum* iron]

farriery (ˈfærɪərɪ) *n, pl* -eries *chiefly Brit* the art, work, or establishment of a farrier

farrow[1] (ˈfærəʊ) *n* **1** a litter of piglets ▷ *vb* **2** (of a sow) to give birth to (a litter) [Old English *fearh*; related to Old High German *farah* young pig, Latin *porcus* pig, Greek *porkos*]

farrow[2] (ˈfærəʊ) *adj* (of a cow) not calving in a given year [c15 from Middle Dutch *verwe-* (unattested) cow that has ceased to bear; compare Old English *fearr* ox]

far-seeing *adj* having shrewd judgment; far-sighted

Farsi (ˈfɑːsiː) *n* the Indo-European language of modern Iran. See also **Persian** (sense 4)

far-sighted *adj* **1** possessing prudence and foresight **2** *med* of, relating to, or suffering from hyperopia **3** another word for **long-sighted.** > ˌfar-ˈsightedly *adv* > ˌfar-ˈsightedness *n*

fart (fɑːt) *slang* ▷ *n* **1** an emission of intestinal gas from the anus, esp an audible one **2** a contemptible person ▷ *vb* (*intr*) **3** to expel intestinal gas from the anus; to break wind **4 fart about** *or* **around a** to behave foolishly or aimlessly **b** to waste time [Middle English *farten*;

related to Old Norse *freta*, Old High German *ferzan* to break wind, Sanskrit *pardatē* he breaks wind]

farther (ˈfɑːðə) *adv* **1** to or at a greater distance in space or time **2** in addition ▷ *adj* **3** more distant or remote in space or time **4** additional [c13 see FAR, FURTHER]

> **USAGE** *Farther, farthest, further,* and *furthest* can all be used to refer to literal distance, but *further* and *furthest* are regarded as more correct for figurative senses denoting greater or additional amount, time, etc: *further to my letter. Further* and *furthest* are also preferred for figurative distance

farthermost (ˈfɑːðəˌməʊst) *adj* most distant or remote

farthest (ˈfɑːðɪst) *adv* **1** to or at the greatest distance in space or time ▷ *adj* **2** most distant in space or time **3** most extended [c14 *ferthest*, from *ferther* FURTHER]

farthing (ˈfɑːðɪŋ) *n* **1** a former British bronze coin, worth a quarter of an old penny, that ceased to be legal tender in 1961 **2** something of negligible value; jot [Old English *fēorthing* from *fēortha* FOURTH + -ING[1]]

farthingale (ˈfɑːðɪŋˌgeɪl) *n* a hoop or framework worn under skirts, esp in the Elizabethan period, to shape and spread them [c16 from French *verdugale*, from Old Spanish *verdugado*, from *verdugo* rod]

fartlek (ˈfɑːtlɛk) *n sport* another name for **interval training** [Swedish, literally: speed play]

FAS *or* **f.a.s.** *abbreviation for* free alongside ship

fasces (ˈfæsiːz) *pl n, sing* -cis (-sɪs) **1** (in ancient Rome) one or more bundles of rods containing an axe with its blade protruding; a symbol of a magistrate's power **2** (in modern Italy) such an object used as the symbol of Fascism [c16 from Latin, plural of *fascis* bundle]

fascia *or* **facia** (ˈfeɪʃɪə) *n, pl* -ciae (-ʃɪˌiː) **1** the flat surface above a shop window **2** *architect* a flat band or surface, esp a part of an architrave or cornice **3** (ˈfæʃɪə) fibrous connective tissue occurring in sheets beneath the surface of the skin and between muscles and groups of muscles **4** *biology* a distinctive band of colour, as on an insect or plant **5** *Brit* a less common name for **dashboard** (sense 1) [c16 from Latin: band: related to *fascis* bundle; see FASCES] > ˈfascial *or* ˈfacial *adj*

fasciate (ˈfæʃɪˌeɪt) *or* **fasciated** *adj* **1** *botany* **a** (of stems and branches) abnormally flattened due to coalescence **b** growing in a bundle **2** (of birds, insects, etc) marked by distinct bands of colour [c17 probably from New Latin *fasciātus* (unattested) having bands; see FASCIA] > ˈfasciately *adv*

fasciation (ˌfæʃɪˈeɪʃən) *n botany* an abnormal flattening of stems due to failure of the lateral branches to separate from the main stem

fascicle (ˈfæsɪkəl) *n* **1** a bundle or cluster of branches, leaves, etc **2** Also called: fasciculus *anatomy* a small bundle of fibres, esp nerve fibres **3** *printing* another name for **fascicule 4** any small bundle or cluster [c15 from Latin *fasciculus* a small bundle, from *fascis* a bundle] > fascicular (fəˈsɪkjʊlə) *or* fasciculate (fəˈsɪkjʊˌleɪt, -lɪt) *adj* > fasˈciculately *adv* > fasˌcicuˈlation *n*

fascicule (ˈfæsɪˌkjuːl) *n* one part of a printed work that is published in instalments. Also called: fascicle, fasciculus

fasciculus (fəˈsɪkjʊləs) *n, pl* -li (-ˌlaɪ) another name for **fascicle** (sense 2) *or* **fascicule**

fasciitis (ˌfæʃɪˈaɪtɪs) *n* inflammation of the fascia of a muscle

fascinate (ˈfæsɪˌneɪt) *vb* (*mainly tr*) **1** to attract and delight by arousing interest or curiosity: *his stories fascinated me for hours.* **2** to render motionless, as with a fixed stare or by arousing terror or awe **3** *archaic* to put under a spell [c16 from Latin *fascināre*, from *fascinum* a bewitching] > ˈfasciˌnatedly *adv* > ˌfasciˈnation *n* > ˈfascinative *adj*

> **USAGE** A person can be fascinated by

or *with* another person or thing. It is correct to speak of someone's fascination *with* a person or thing; one can also say a person or thing has a fascination *for* someone

fascinating ('fæsɪˌneɪtɪŋ) *adj* 1 arousing great interest 2 enchanting or alluring: *a fascinating woman* > **'fasciˌnatingly** *adv*

fascinator ('fæsɪˌneɪtə) *n rare* a lace or crocheted head covering for women

fascine (fæ'siːn, fə-) *n* a bundle of long sticks used for filling in ditches and in the construction of embankments, roads, fortifications, etc [C17 from French, from Latin *fascīna*; see FASCES]

fascism ('fæʃɪzəm) *n* (*sometimes capital*) 1 any ideology or movement inspired by Italian Fascism, such as German National Socialism; any right-wing nationalist ideology or movement with an authoritarian and hierarchical structure that is fundamentally opposed to democracy and liberalism 2 any ideology, movement, programme, tendency, etc, that may be characterized as right-wing, chauvinist, authoritarian, etc 3 prejudice in relation to the subject specified: *body fascism* [C20 from Italian *fascismo*, from *fascio* political group, from Latin *fascis* bundle; see FASCES]

Fascism ('fæʃɪzəm) *n* the political movement, doctrine, system, or regime (1922–43) in Italy of the dictator Benito Mussolini (1883–1945). Fascism encouraged militarism and nationalism, organizing the country along hierarchical authoritarian lines

fascist ('fæʃɪst) (*sometimes capital*) *n* 1 an adherent or practitioner of fascism 2 any person regarded as having right-wing authoritarian views ▷ *adj also* **fascistic** (fə'ʃɪstɪk) 3 characteristic of or relating to fascism > **fa'scistically** *adv*

Fascist ('fæʃɪst) *n* 1 a supporter or member of the Italian Fascist movement ▷ *adj* 2 of or relating to Italian Fascism

fash (fæʃ) *Scot* ▷ *n* 1 worry; trouble; bother ▷ *vb* 2 to trouble; bother; annoy [C16 from obsolete French *fascher* to annoy, ultimately from Latin *fastīdium* disgust, aversion]

fashion ('fæʃən) *n* 1 a style in clothes, cosmetics, behaviour, etc, esp the latest or most admired style b (*as modifier*): *a fashion magazine* 2 (*modifier*) (esp of accessories) designed to be in the current fashion, but not necessarily to last 3 a manner of performance; mode; way: *in a striking fashion* b (*in combination*): *crab-fashion* 4 a way of life that revolves around the activities, dress, interests, etc, that are most fashionable 5 shape, appearance, or form 6 sort; kind; type 7 **after** *or* **in a fashion** a in some manner, but not very well: *I mended it, after a fashion* b of a low order; of a sort: *he is a poet, after a fashion* 8 **after the fashion of** like; similar to 9 **of fashion** of high social standing ▷ *vb* (*tr*) 10 to give a particular form to 11 to make suitable or fitting 12 *obsolete* to contrive; manage [C13 *facioun* form, manner, from Old French *faceon*, from Latin *factiō* a making, from *facere* to make] > **'fashioner** *n*

fashionable ('fæʃənəbᵊl) *adj* 1 conforming to fashion; in vogue 2 of, characteristic of, or patronized by people of fashion: *a fashionable café* 3 (usually foll by *with*) patronized (by); popular (with) > **ˌfashiona'bility** *or* **'fashionableness** *n* > **'fashionably** *adv*

fashion-forward *adj* relating to, anticipating, or reflecting the most up-to-date fashion trends

fashion house *n* an establishment in which fashionable clothes are designed, made, and sold

fashion icon *n* a person or thing that is very well known as being highly fashionable

fashionista (ˌfæʃə'niːstə) *n informal* a person who follows trends in the fashion industry obsessively and strives continually to adopt the latest fashions [C20 from FASHION + *-ista* as in SANDINISTA]

fashion plate *n* 1 an illustration of the latest fashion in dress 2 a fashionably dressed person

fashion victim *n informal* a person who slavishly follows fashion

fashiony ('fæʃənɪ) *adj informal* of or relating to fashion; fashionable; trendy: *a more upbeat fashiony look*

Fashoda (fə'ʃəʊdə) *n* a small town in SE Sudan: scene of a diplomatic incident (1898) in which French occupation of the fort at Fashoda caused a crisis between France and Great Britain. Modern name: **Kodok**

FASSA *abbreviation for* Fellow of the Academy of Social Sciences in Australia

fast[1] (fɑːst) *adj* 1 acting or moving or capable of acting or moving quickly; swift 2 accomplished in or lasting a short time: *fast work; a fast visit* 3 (*prenominal*) adapted to or facilitating rapid movement: *the fast lane of a motorway* 4 requiring rapidity of action or movement: *a fast sport* 5 (of a clock, etc) indicating a time in advance of the correct time 6 given to an active dissipated life 7 of or characteristic of such activity: *a fast life* 8 not easily moved; firmly fixed; secure 9 firmly fastened, secured, or shut 10 steadfast; constant (esp in the phrase **fast friends**) 11 *sport* (of a playing surface, running track, etc) conducive to rapid speed, as of a ball used on it or of competitors playing or racing on it 12 that will not fade or change colour readily: *a fast dye* 13 a proof against fading: *the colour is fast to sunlight* b (*in combination*): *washfast* 14 *photog* a requiring a relatively short time of exposure to produce a given density: *a fast film* b permitting a short exposure time: *a fast shutter* 15 *cricket* (of a bowler) characteristically delivering the ball rapidly 16 *informal* glib or unreliable; deceptive: *a fast talker* 17 *archaic* sound; deep: *a fast sleep* 18 *informal* a deceptive or unscrupulous trick (esp in the phrase **pull a fast one**) 19 **fast worker** a person who achieves results quickly, esp in seductions ▷ *adv* 20 quickly; rapidly 21 soundly; deeply: *fast asleep* 22 firmly; tightly 23 in quick succession 24 in advance of the correct time: *my watch is running fast* 25 in a reckless or dissipated way 26 **fast by** *or* **beside** *archaic* close or hard by; very near 27 **play fast and loose** *informal* to behave in an insincere or unreliable manner ▷ *interj* 28 *archery* (said by the field captain to archers) stop shooting! [Old English *fæst* strong, tight; related to Old High German *festi* firm, Old Norse *fastr*]

fast[2] (fɑːst) *vb* 1 (*intr*) to abstain from eating all or certain foods or meals, esp as a religious observance ▷ *n* 2 an act or period of fasting [Old English *fæstan*; related to Old High German *fastēn* to fast, Gothic *fastan*] > **'faster** *n*

fastback ('fɑːstˌbæk) *n* 1 a car having a back that forms one continuous slope from roof to rear 2 *Brit* a type of pig developed from the landrace or large white and bred for lean meat

fastball ('fɑːstˌbɔːl) *n baseball* a ball pitched at the pitcher's top speed

fast-breeder reactor *n* a nuclear reactor that uses little or no moderator and produces more fissionable material than it consumes. See also **breeder reactor, fast reactor**

fast casual *n* a style of fast food involving healthier, fresher, and more varied dishes than traditional fast food, served in more attractive surroundings

fasten ('fɑːsᵊn) *vb* 1 to make or become fast or secure 2 to make or become attached or joined 3 to close or become closed by fixing firmly in place, locking, etc 4 (*tr*; foll by *in* or *up*) to enclose or imprison 5 (*tr*; usually foll by *on*) to cause (blame, a nickname, etc) to be attached (to); place (on) or impute (to) 6 (usually foll by *on* or *upon*) to direct or be directed in a concentrated way; fix: *he fastened his gaze on the girl* 7 (*intr*; usually foll by *on*) take firm hold (of) [Old English *fæstnian*; related to Old Norse *fastna* to pledge, Old High German *fastinōn* to make fast; see FAST[1]] > **'fastener** *n*

fastening ('fɑːsᵊnɪŋ) *n* something that fastens, such as a clasp or lock

fast follower *n* a company that is quick to pick up good new ideas from other companies

fast food *n* 1 food that requires little preparation before being served ▷ *adj* **fast-food** 2 (of a restaurant, café, etc) serving such food

fast-forward *n* 1 (*sometimes not hyphenated*) the control on a tape deck or video recorder used to wind the tape or video forward at speed 2 *informal* a state of urgency or rapid progress: *my mind went into fast forward* ▷ *vb* 3 (*tr*) to wind (a video or tape) forward using the fast-forward control 4 to deal with speedily: *fast-forward the trials of the new drug* 5 (*intr*) to move forward through a tape or video using the fast-forward control 6 (usually foll by *to*) to direct one's attention towards a particular time or event, ignoring intervening material: *fast-forward to the summer of 2001* [C20 from the fast-forward wind control in a tape deck]

fastidious (fæ'stɪdɪəs) *adj* 1 very critical; hard to please 2 excessively particular about details 3 exceedingly delicate; easily disgusted [C15 from Latin *fastīdiōsus* scornful, from *fastīdium* loathing, from *fastus* pride + *taedium* weariness] > **fas'tidiously** *adv* > **fas'tidiousness** *n*

fastie ('fɑːstɪ) *n Austral slang* 1 a deceitful act 2 **pull a fastie** to play a sly trick

fastigiate (fæ'stɪdʒɪɪt, -ˌeɪt) *or* **fastigiated** *adj biology* 1 (of plants) having erect branches, often appearing to form a single column with the stem 2 (of parts or organs) united in a tapering group [C17 from Medieval Latin *fastīgiātus* lofty, from Latin *fastīgium* height]

fast lane *n* 1 the outside lane on a motorway or dual carriageway for vehicles overtaking or travelling at high speed 2 *informal* the quickest but most competitive route to success

fast motion *n films* action that appears to have occurred at a faster speed than that at which it was filmed. Compare **slow motion** (sense 1)

fastness ('fɑːstnɪs) *n* 1 a stronghold; fortress 2 the state or quality of being firm or secure 3 the ability of a dye to remain permanent and not run or fade 4 *archaic* swiftness [Old English *fæstnes*; see FAST[1]]

fast neutron *n physics* a a neutron produced by nuclear fission that has lost little energy by collision; a neutron with a kinetic energy in excess of 0.1 MeV b a neutron with a kinetic energy in excess of 1.5 MeV, the fission threshold of uranium-238

fast reactor *n* a nuclear reactor using little or no moderator, fission being caused by fast neutrons

fast talk *slang* ▷ *n* 1 fervent, deceptive patter ▷ *vb* **fast-talk** 2 to influence (a person) by means of such patter

fast-track *adj* 1 denoting the quickest or most direct route or system: *fast-track executives; a fast-track procedure for libel claims* ▷ *vb* 2 (*tr*) to speed up the progress of (a project or person)

fat (fæt) *n* 1 any of a class of naturally occurring soft greasy solids that are esters of glycerol and certain fatty acids. They are present in some plants and in the adipose tissue of animals, forming a reserve energy source, and are used in making soap and paint and in the food industry. See also **oil** (sense 1) 2 vegetable or animal tissue containing fat. Related adjs: **adipose, lipoid, stearic** 3 corpulence, obesity, or plumpness 4 the best or richest part of something 5 a part in a play that gives an actor a good opportunity to show his talents 6 **chew the fat** *slang* a to argue over a point b to talk idly; gossip 7 **the fat is in the fire** an irrevocable action has been taken, esp one from which dire consequences are expected 8 **the fat of the land** the best that is obtainable ▷ *adj* **fatter, fattest** 9 having much or too much flesh or fat 10 consisting of or containing fat; greasy: *fat pork* 11 profitable; lucrative: *a fat year* 12 affording great opportunities: *a fat part in the play* 13 fertile or productive: *a fat land* 14 thick, broad, or extended: *a fat log of wood* 15 having a high content of a particular material or ingredient, such as resin in wood or oil in paint **16** plentifully supplied: *a fat larder* **17** *slang* empty; stupid: *get this into your fat head* **18** *slang* very little or none; minimal (in phrases such as **a fat chance**, **a fat lot of good**, etc) ▷ *vb* **fats**, **fatting**, **fatted 19** to make or become fat; fatten [Old English *fǣtt*, past participle of *fǣtan* to cram; related to Old Norse *feita*, Old High German *feizen* to fatten; compare Gothic *fētjan* to adorn] > ˈfatless *adj* > ˈfatˌlike *adj* > ˈfatly *adv* > ˈfatness *n* > ˈfattish *adj*

Fatah (ˈfætə) *n* **Al** a Palestinian terrorist organization, founded in 1956, with the aim of destroying the state of Israel: it has splintered into rival factions since 1988

fatal (ˈfeɪtəl) *adj* **1** resulting in or capable of causing death: *a fatal accident* **2** bringing ruin; disastrous **3** decisively important; fateful **4** decreed by fate; destined; inevitable [c14 from Old French *fatal* or Latin *fātālis*, from *fātum*, see FATE]

fatalism (ˈfeɪtəˌlɪzəm) *n* **1** the philosophical doctrine that all events are predetermined so that man is powerless to alter his destiny **2** the acceptance of and submission to this doctrine **3** a lack of effort or action in the face of difficulty > ˈfatalist *n* > ˌfatalˈistic *adj* > ˌfatalˈistically *adv*

fatality (fəˈtælɪtɪ) *n*, *pl* -ties **1** an accident or disaster resulting in death **2** a person killed in an accident or disaster **3** the power of causing death or disaster; deadliness **4** the quality or condition of being fated **5** something caused or dictated by fate

fatally (ˈfeɪtəlɪ) *adv* **1** resulting in death or disaster: *fatally wounded in battle* **2** as decreed by fate; inevitably

Fata Morgana (ˈfɑːtə mɔːˈgɑːnə; *Italian* ˈfaːta mɔrˈgaːna) *n* a mirage, esp one in the Strait of Messina attributed to the sorcery of Morgan le Fay [c19 from Italian: MORGAN LE FAY]

fatback (ˈfætˌbæk) *n* the fat, usually salted, from the upper part of a side of pork

fat body *n* *zoology* **1** a mass of fatty tissue in insects, used as an energy source during hibernation and metamorphosis **2** a similar tissue mass in amphibians and reptiles

fat camp *n* a residential camp at which children undergo a programme of exercise, diet change, etc, intended to help them lose weight

fat cat *n* *slang* **a** a very wealthy or influential person **b** (*as modifier*): *a fat-cat industrialist*

fate (feɪt) *n* **1** the ultimate agency that predetermines the course of events **2** the inevitable fortune that befalls a person or thing; destiny **3** the end or final result **4** a calamitous or unfavourable outcome or result; death, destruction, or downfall ▷ *vb* **5** (*tr; usually passive*) to predetermine; doom: *he was fated to lose the game* [c14 from Latin *fātum* oracular utterance, from *fārī* to speak]

fated (ˈfeɪtɪd) *adj* **1** destined **2** doomed to death or destruction

fateful (ˈfeɪtfʊl) *adj* **1** having important consequences; decisively important **2** bringing death or disaster **3** controlled by or as if by fate **4** prophetic > ˈfatefully *adv* > ˈfatefulness *n*

Fates (feɪts) *pl n* **1** *Greek myth* the three goddesses who determine the destinies of the lives of man, which are likened to skeins of thread that they spin, measure out, and at last cut. See **Atropos**, **Clotho**, **Lachesis 2** *Norse myth* another name for the **Norns** (see **Norn¹**)

fat-finger *vb* (*intr*) *informal* **1** to make a mistake by pressing the wrong key on a keyboard or number pad **2** to make an error that causes further problems

fath. *abbreviation for* fathom

fathead (ˈfætˌhɛd) *n* *informal* a stupid person; fool > ˈfatˌheaded *adj*

fat hen *n* a common plant, *Chenopodium album*, with small green flowers and whitish scales on the stem and leaves: family Chenopodiaceae (chenopods). Also called (US): pigweed, lamb's-quarters

father (ˈfɑːðə) *n* **1** a male parent **2** a person who founds a line or family; forefather **3** any male acting in a paternal capacity. Related adj: **paternal 4** (*often capital*) a respectful term of address for an old man **5** a male who originates something: *the father of modern psychology* **6** a leader of an association, council, etc; elder: *a city father* **7** *Brit* the eldest or most senior member in a society, profession, etc: *father of the bar* **8** (*often plural*) a senator or patrician in ancient Rome **9** the father of *informal* a very large, severe, etc, example of a specified kind: *the father of a whipping* ▷ *vb* (*tr*) **10** to procreate or generate (offspring); beget **11** to create, found, originate, etc **12** to act as a father to **13** to acknowledge oneself as father or originator of **14** (foll by *on* or *upon*) to impose or place without a just reason [Old English *fæder*; related to Old Norse *fathir*, Old Frisian *feder*, Old High German *fater*, Latin *pater*, Greek *patēr*, Sanskrit *pitr*] > ˈfathering *n*

Father (ˈfɑːðə) *n* **1** God, esp when considered as the first person of the Christian Trinity **2** Also called: Church Father any of the writers on Christian doctrine of the pre-Scholastic period **3** a title used for Christian priests

Father Christmas *n* another name for **Santa Claus**

father confessor *n* **1** *Christianity* a priest who hears confessions and advises on religious or moral matters **2** any person to whom one tells private matters

fatherhood (ˈfɑːðəˌhʊd) *n* the state or responsibility of being a father

father-in-law *n*, *pl* fathers-in-law the father of one's wife or husband

fatherland (ˈfɑːðəˌlænd) *n* **1** a person's native country **2** the country of a person's ancestors

father lasher *n* a large sea scorpion, *Myoxocephalus scorpius*, occurring in British and European coastal waters. Also called: short-spined sea scorpion

fatherless (ˈfɑːðəlɪs) *adj* having no father

fatherly (ˈfɑːðəlɪ) *adj* of, resembling, or suitable to a father > ˈfatherliness *n*

father of the chapel *n* (in British trade unions in the publishing and printing industries) a shop steward. Abbreviation: FoC

Father of the House *n* (in Britain) the longest-serving member of the House of Commons

Father's Day *n* a day observed as a day in honour of fathers; in Britain the third Sunday in June

Father Time *n* time personified as an old bearded man, usually carrying a scythe and an hourglass

fathom (ˈfæðəm) *n* **1** a unit of length equal to six feet (1.829 metres), used to measure depths of water **2** *mining* a unit of volume usually equal to six cubic feet, used in measuring ore bodies **3** *forestry* a unit of volume equal to six cubic feet, used for measuring timber ▷ *vb* (*tr*) **4** to measure the depth of, esp with a sounding line; sound **5** to penetrate (a mystery, problem, etc); discover the meaning of [Old English *fæthm*; related to Old Frisian *fethem* outstretched arms, Old Norse *fathmr* embrace, Old High German *fadum* cubit, Latin *patēre* to gape] > ˈfathomable *adj* > ˈfathomer *n*

Fathometer (fəˈðɒmɪtə) *n* *trademark* a type of echo sounder used for measuring the depth of water

fathomless (ˈfæðəmlɪs) *adj* another word for **unfathomable**. > ˈfathomlessly *adv* > ˈfathomlessness *n*

fatidic (feɪˈtɪdɪk) or **fatidical** *adj* *rare* prophetic [c17 from Latin *fātidicus*, from *fātum* FATE + *dīcere* to say] > faˈtidically *adv*

fatigue (fəˈtiːg) *n* **1** physical or mental exhaustion due to exertion **2** a tiring activity or effort **3** *physiol* the temporary inability of an organ or part to respond to a stimulus because of overactivity **4** the progressive cracking of a material subjected to alternating stresses, esp vibrations **5** the temporary inability to respond to a situation or perform a function, because of overexposure or overactivity: *compassion fatigue* **6 a** any of the mainly domestic duties performed by military personnel, esp as a punishment **b** (*as modifier*): *fatigue duties* **7** (*pl*) special clothing worn by military personnel to carry out such duties ▷ *vb* **-tigues**, **-tiguing**, **-tigued 8** to make or become weary or exhausted **9** to crack or break (a material or part) by inducing fluctuating stresses in it, or (of a metal or part) to become weakened or fail as a result of fluctuating stresses [c17 from French, from *fatiguer* to tire, from Latin *fatīgāre*] > ˈfatigable (ˈfætɪgəbəl) *adj* > faˈtigueless *adj*

Fátima (*Portuguese* ˈfatimə) *n* a village in central Portugal: Roman Catholic shrine and pilgrimage centre

Fatimid (ˈfætɪmɪd) *n* **1** a member of the Moslem dynasty, descended from Fatima, daughter of Mohammed, and Ali, her husband, that ruled over North Africa and parts of Egypt and Syria (909–1171) **2** Also called: Fatimite (ˈfætɪˌmaɪt) a descendant of Fatima and Ali

fat lamb *n* *Austral and NZ* a lamb bred for its tender meat, esp for export trade

fatling (ˈfætlɪŋ) *n* a young farm animal fattened for killing

fat mouse *n* any nocturnal African mouse of the genus *Steatomys*, of dry regions: eaten as a delicacy by Africans because of their high fat content: family *Muridae*

Fatshan (ˈfɑːtˈʃɑːn) *n* a variant transliteration of the Chinese name for **Foshan**

fatshedera (fætsˈhɛdərə) *n* an evergreen garden shrub with shiny green leaves and umbels of pale green flowers; a bigeneric hybrid between *Fatsia japonica moseri* and *Hedera hibernica*: family *Araliaceae*

fatsia (ˈfætsɪə) *n* any shrub of the araliaceous genus *Fatsia*, esp *F. japonica*, with large deeply palmate leaves and umbels of white flowers [New Latin, from the Japanese name]

fatso (ˈfætsəʊ) *n*, *pl* -sos *or* -soes *slang* a fat person: used as an insulting or disparaging term of address

fat-soluble *adj* soluble in nonpolar substances, such as ether, chloroform, and oils. Fat-soluble compounds are often insoluble in water

fat stock *n* livestock fattened and ready for market

fat tax *n* *informal* a tax levied in the form of higher duties or VAT on foods with a high fat content

fatten (ˈfætən) *vb* **1** to grow or cause to grow fat or fatter **2** (*tr*) to cause (an animal or fowl) to become fat by feeding it **3** (*tr*) to make fuller or richer **4** (*tr*) to enrich (soil) by adding fertilizing agents > ˈfattenable *adj* > ˈfattener *n* > ˈfattening *adj*

fattism (ˈfætɪzəm) *n* discrimination on the basis of weight, esp prejudice against those considered to be overweight [c20 from FAT + -ISM, on the model of RACISM] > ˈfattist *n*, *adj*

fatty (ˈfætɪ) *adj* -tier, -tiest **1** containing, consisting of, or derived from fat **2** having the properties of fat; greasy; oily **3** (*esp of tissues, organs, etc*) characterized by the excessive accumulation of fat ▷ *n*, *pl* -ties **4** *informal* a fat person > ˈfattily *adv* > ˈfattiness *n*

fatty acid *n* **1** any of a class of aliphatic carboxylic acids, such as palmitic acid, stearic acid, and oleic acid, that form part of a lipid molecule **2** another name for **carboxylic acid**, esp a naturally occurring one

fatty degeneration *n* *pathol* the abnormal formation of tiny globules of fat within the cytoplasm of a cell

fatty oil *n* another name for **fixed oil**

fatuity (fəˈtjuːɪtɪ) *n*, *pl* -ties **1** complacent foolishness; inanity **2** a fatuous remark, act, sentiment, etc **3** *archaic* idiocy > faˈtuitous *adj*

fatuous (ˈfætjʊəs) *adj* complacently or inanely foolish [c17 from Latin *fatuus*; related to *fatiscere* to gape] > ˈfatuously *adv* > ˈfatuousness *n*

fatwa *or* **fatwah** ('fætwɑ:) *n* a religious decree issued by a Muslim leader [Arabic]

faubourg ('fəʊbʊəg; *French* fubur) *n* a suburb or quarter, esp of a French city [c15 from French *fauxbourg*, perhaps a modification through folk etymology of Old French *forsborc*, from Latin *foris* outside + Old French *borc* BURG]

faucal ('fɔ:k²l) *or* **faucial** ('fɔ:ʃəl) *adj* 1 anatomy of or relating to the fauces 2 *phonetics* articulated in that part of the vocal tract between the back of the mouth and the larynx; pharyngeal

fauces ('fɔ:si:z) *n, pl* -ces *anatomy* the area between the cavity of the mouth and the pharynx, including the surrounding tissues [c16 from Latin: throat]

faucet ('fɔ:sɪt) *n* 1 a tap fitted to a barrel 2 *US and Canadian* a valve by which a fluid flow from a pipe can be controlled by opening and closing an orifice. Also called (in Britain and certain other countries): **tap** [c14 from Old French *fausset*, from Provençal *falset*, from *falsar* to bore]

faugh (fɔ:) *interj* an exclamation of disgust, scorn, etc

Faulknerian (fɔ:k'nɪərɪən) *adj* of, relating to, or like William Faulkner (1897–1962), the US novelist and short-story writer, his works, ideas, etc

fault (fɔ:lt) *n* 1 an imperfection; failing or defect; flaw 2 a mistake or error 3 an offence; misdeed 4 responsibility for a mistake or misdeed; culpability 5 *electronics* a defect in a circuit, component, or line, such as a short circuit 6 *geology* a fracture in the earth's crust resulting in the relative displacement and loss of continuity of the rocks on either side of it 7 *tennis, squash, badminton* an invalid serve, such as one that lands outside a prescribed area 8 (in showjumping) a penalty mark given for failing to clear or refusing a fence, exceeding a time limit, etc 9 *hunting* an instance of the hounds losing the scent 10 deficiency; lack; want 11 **at fault** a guilty of error; culpable b perplexed c (of hounds) having temporarily lost the scent 12 **find fault (with)** to seek out minor imperfections or errors (in); carp (at) 13 **to a fault** excessively ▷ *vb* 14 *geology* to undergo or cause to undergo a fault 15 (*tr*) to find a fault in, criticize, or blame 16 (*intr*) to commit a fault [c13 from Old French *faute*, from Vulgar Latin *fallita* (unattested), ultimately from Latin *fallere* to fail]

fault-finding *n* 1 continual and usually trivial criticism 2 the systematic investigation of malfunctions in electronic apparatus ▷ *adj* 3 given to finding fault > **'fault-,finder** *n*

faultless ('fɔ:ltlɪs) *adj* without fault; perfect or blameless > **'faultlessly** *adv* > **'faultlessness** *n*

fault line *n* 1 Also called: **fault plane** *geology* the surface of a fault fracture along which the rocks have been displaced 2 a potentially disruptive division or area of contention: *Europe remains the main fault line in the Tory Party*

fault tree *n* a diagram providing a model of the interactions between the components of a system when a failure occurs

faulty ('fɔ:ltɪ) *adj* faultier, faultiest 1 defective or imperfect 2 *archaic* culpable > **'faultily** *adv* > **'faultiness** *n*

faun (fɔ:n) *n* (in Roman legend) a rural deity represented as a man with a goat's ears, horns, tail, and hind legs [c14 back formation from *Faunes* (plural), from Latin FAUNUS] > **'faun,like** *adj*

fauna ('fɔ:nə) *n, pl* -nas *or* -nae (-ni:) 1 all the animal life of a given place or time, esp when distinguished from the plant life (flora) 2 a descriptive list of such animals [c18 from New Latin, from Late Latin *Fauna* a goddess, sister of FAUNUS] > **'faunal** *adj* > **'faunally** *adv*

faunula ('fɔ:njʊlə) *or* **faunule** ('fɔ:nju:l) *n, pl* -ulae (-ju:li:) *or* -ules 1 the fauna of a small single environment 2 fossil fauna, dominated by representatives of a single community, found in a single stratum or in several thin adjacent strata [c20 from FAUNA + -ULE]

Faunus ('fɔ:nəs) *n* an ancient Italian deity of pastures and forests, later identified with the Greek Pan

faur (fɔ:r) *adj* a Scot word for **far**

Faust (faʊst) *or* **Faustus** ('faʊstəs) *n German legend* a magician and alchemist who sells his soul to the devil in exchange for knowledge and power

Faustian ('faʊstɪən) *adj* of or relating to Faust, esp reminiscent of his bargain with the devil

faut (fɔ:t) *n, vb* a Scot word for **fault**

faute de mieux *French* (fot də mjø; *English* ,fəʊt də 'mjɜ:) for lack of anything better

fauteuil ('fəʊtɜ:ɪ; *French* fotœj) *n* an armchair, the sides of which are not upholstered [c18 from French, from Old French *faudestuel*, folding chair, of Germanic origin; see FALDSTOOL]

Fauve (*French* fov) *n* 1 one of a group of French painters prominent from 1905, including Henri Matisse (1869–1954), Maurice de Vlaminck (1876–1958), and André Derain (1880–1954), characterized by the use of bright colours and simplified forms ▷ *adj* 2 (*often not capital*) of this group or its style [c20 from French, literally: wild beast, alluding to the violence of colours, etc] > **'Fauvism** *n* > **'Fauvist** *n, adj*

faux-naïf *French* (fonaif) *adj* 1 appearing or seeking to appear simple and unsophisticated: *a faux-naïf narration* ▷ *n* 2 a person who pretends to be naïve [French: false naïve]

faux pas (,fəʊ 'pɑ:; *French* fo pɑ) *n, pl* **faux pas** (,fəʊ 'pɑ:z; *French* fo pɑ) a social blunder or indiscretion [c17 from French: false step]

fava bean ('fɑ:və) *n US and Canadian* 1 an erect annual Eurasian bean plant, *Vicia faba*, cultivated for its large edible flattened seeds, used as a vegetable 2 the seed of this plant. Also called: **broad bean** [c20 Italian *fava* from Latin *faba* bean]

fave (feɪv) *adj, n informal* short for **favourite** (senses 1, 2)

favela (fɑ:'veɪlə) *n* (in Brazil) a shanty or shantytown [c20 from Portuguese]

faveolate (fə'vi:ə,leɪt) *or* **favose** ('fævəʊs) *adj* pitted with cell-like cavities [c19 from New Latin *faveolus* a little honeycomb, blend of Latin *favus* honeycomb + *alveolus* a small hollow]

favonian (fə'vəʊnɪən) *adj* 1 of or relating to the west wind 2 *poetic* favourable [c17 from Latin *Favōniānus*]

favorite son *n* (in the US) a politician popular in his home state but little admired beyond it

favour *or US* **favor** ('feɪvə) *n* 1 an approving attitude; good will 2 an act performed out of good will, generosity, or mercy 3 prejudice and partiality; favouritism 4 a condition of being regarded with approval or good will (esp in the phrases **in favour, out of favour**) 5 *archaic* leave; permission 6 a token of love, goodwill, etc 7 a small gift or toy given to a guest at a party 8 *history* a badge or ribbon worn or given to indicate loyalty, often bestowed on a knight by a lady 9 *obsolete, chiefly Brit* a communication, esp a business letter 10 *archaic* appearance 11 **find favour with** to be approved of by someone 12 **in favour of** a approving b to the benefit of c (of a cheque, etc) made out to d in order to show preference for: *I rejected him in favour of George* ▷ *vb* (*tr*) 13 to regard with especial kindness or approval 14 to treat with partiality or favouritism 15 to support; advocate 16 to perform a favour for; oblige 17 to help; facilitate 18 *informal* to resemble: *he favours his father* 19 to wear habitually: *she favours red* 20 to treat gingerly or with tenderness; spare: *a footballer favouring an injured leg* ▷ See also **favours** [c14 from Latin, from *favēre* to protect] > **'favourer** *or US* **'favorer** *n* > **'favouringly** *or US* **favoringly** *adv*

favourable *or US* **favorable** ('feɪvərəb²l, 'feɪvrə-) *adj* 1 advantageous, encouraging, or promising 2 giving consent > **'favourableness** *or US* **'favorableness** *n* > **'favourably** *or US* **favorably** *adv*

favourable pressure gradient *n engineering* a decrease of pressure in the direction of flow

-favoured *adj* (*in combination*) having an appearance (as specified): *ill-favoured*

favourite *or US* **favorite** ('feɪvərɪt, 'feɪvrɪt) *adj* 1 (*prenominal*) most liked; preferred above all others ▷ *n* 2 a a person or thing regarded with especial preference or liking b (*as modifier*): *a favourite book* 3 *sport* a competitor thought likely to win 4 (*pl*) *computing* a place on certain browsers that allows internet users to list the addresses of websites they find and like with a click of the mouse so that they can revisit them merely by opening the list and clicking on the address 5 **play favourites** to display favouritism [c16 from Italian *favorito*, from *favorire* to favour, from Latin *favēre*]

favouritism *or US* **favoritism** ('feɪvərɪ,tɪzəm, 'feɪvrɪ-) *n* 1 the practice of giving special treatment to a person or group 2 the state of being treated as a favourite

favours *or US* **favors** ('feɪvəz) *pl n* sexual intimacy, as when consented to by a woman

Favrile glass (fə'vri:l) *n* a type of iridescent glass developed by L.C. Tiffany

favus ('feɪvəs) *n* an infectious fungal skin disease of man and some domestic animals, characterized by formation of a honeycomb-like mass of roundish dry cup-shaped crusts [c19 from New Latin, from Latin: honeycomb]

fawn¹ (fɔ:n) *n* 1 a young deer of either sex aged under one year 2 a a light greyish-brown colour b (*as adjective*): *a fawn raincoat* 3 **in fawn** (of deer) pregnant ▷ *vb* 4 (of deer) to bear (young) [c14 from Old French *faon*, from Latin *fētus* offspring; see FETUS] > **'fawn,like** *adj*

fawn² (fɔ:n) *vb* (*intr; often foll by on or upon*) 1 to seek attention and admiration (from) by cringing and flattering 2 (of animals, esp dogs) to try to please by a show of extreme friendliness and fondness (towards) [Old English *fægnian* to be glad, from *fægen* glad; see FAIN] > **'fawner** *n* > **'fawningly** *adv* > **'fawningness** *n*

fawn lily *n* another name for **dogtooth violet**

fax (fæks) *n* 1 Also: **fax machine** short for **facsimile machine** 2 short for **facsimile transmission** 3 a message or document sent by fax ▷ *vb* 4 (*tr*) to send (a message, document, etc) by fax

fay¹ (feɪ) *n* 1 a fairy or sprite ▷ *adj* 2 of or resembling a fay 3 *informal* pretentious or precious [c14 from Old French *feie*, ultimately from Latin *fātum* FATE]

fay² (feɪ) *vb* to fit or be fitted closely or tightly [Old English *fēgan* to join; related to Old High German *fuogen*, Latin *pangere* to fasten]

fay³ (feɪ) *n* an obsolete word for **faith** [c13 from Anglo-French *feid*; see FAITH]

Fayal (*Portuguese* fə'ial) *n* a variant spelling of **Faial**

fayalite ('feɪə,laɪt, faɪ'ɑ:laɪt) *n* a rare brown or black mineral of the olivine group, consisting of iron silicate. Formula: Fe_2SiO_4 [c19 named after FAYAL]

fayre (fɛə) *n* a pseudo-archaic spelling of **fair²** or **fare**

Fayum (faɪ'ju:m) *n* See **El Faiyûm**

faze (feɪz) *vb* (*tr*) to disconcert; worry; disturb [c19 variant of FEEZE]

fazed (feɪzd) *adj* disconcerted; worried; disturbed

FBA *abbreviation for* Fellow of the British Academy

FBI (in the US) *abbreviation for* Federal Bureau of Investigation; an agency of the Justice Department responsible for investigating violations of Federal laws

FBL *abbreviation for* fly-by-light

FBW *aeronautics abbreviation for* fly-by-wire

fc *printing abbreviation for* follow copy

FC *text messaging abbreviation for* 1 (in Britain) Football Club 2 (in Canada) Federal Court 3 fingers crossed

FCA (in Britain) *abbreviation for* Fellow of the Institute of Chartered Accountants

fcap *abbreviation for* foolscap

FCC (in the US) *abbreviation for* Federal Communications Commission

FCCA (in Britain) *abbreviation for* Fellow of the Chartered Association of Certified Accountants

FCII (in Britain) *abbreviation for* Fellow of the Chartered Insurance Institute

F clef *n* another name for **bass clef**

FCO *abbreviation for* Foreign and Commonwealth Office

FD *abbreviation for* Fidei Defensor [Latin: Defender of the Faith]

FDA (in the US) *abbreviation for* Food and Drug Administration: a federal agency responsible for monitoring trading and safety standards in the food and drug industries

F distribution *n statistics* a continuous distribution obtained from the ratio of two chi-square distributions and used esp to test the equality of the variances of two normally distributed variances

fdm *abbreviation for* frequency-division multiplex. See **multiplex**

FDP *abbreviation for* Freie Demokratische Partei [German: Free Democratic Party]

Fe *the chemical symbol for* iron [from New Latin *ferrum*]

feal (fiːl) *adj* an archaic word for **faithful** [C16 from Old French *feeil*, from Latin *fidēlis*]

fealty (ˈfiːəltɪ) *n, pl* **-ties** (in feudal society) the loyalty sworn to one's lord on becoming his vassal. See **homage** (sense 2) [C14 from Old French *fealte*, from Latin *fidēlitās* FIDELITY]

fear (fɪə) *n* **1** a feeling of distress, apprehension, or alarm caused by impending danger, pain, etc **2** a cause of this feeling **3** awe; reverence: *fear of God* **4** concern; anxiety **5** possibility; chance: *there is no fear of that happening* **6 for fear of, that** *or* **lest** to forestall or avoid **7 no fear** certainly not **8 put the fear of God into** to frighten ▷ *vb* **9** to be afraid (to do something) or of (a person or thing); dread **10** (*tr*) to revere; respect **11** (*tr; takes a clause as object*) to be sorry: used to lessen the effect of an unpleasant statement: *I fear that you have not won* **12** (*intr; foll by for*) to feel anxiety about something **13** an archaic word for **frighten** [Old English *fǣr*; related to Old High German *fāra*, Old Norse *fār* hostility, Latin *perīculum* danger] > ˈ**fearer** *n* > ˈ**fearless** *adj* > ˈ**fearlessly** *adv* > ˈ**fearlessness** *n*

fearful (ˈfɪəfʊl) *adj* **1** having fear; afraid **2** causing fear; frightening **3** *informal* very unpleasant or annoying: *a fearful cold* > ˈ**fearfulness** *n*

fearfully (ˈfɪəfʊlɪ) *adv* **1** in a fearful manner **2** (intensifier): *you're fearfully kind*

fearnought *or* **fearnaught** (ˈfɪəˌnɔːt) *n* **1** a heavy woollen fabric **2** a coat made of such fabric

fearsome (ˈfɪəsəm) *adj* **1** frightening **2** timorous; afraid > ˈ**fearsomely** *adv* > ˈ**fearsomeness** *n*

feasibility study *n* a study designed to determine the practicability of a system or plan

feasible (ˈfiːzəbəl) *adj* **1** able to be done or put into effect; possible **2** likely; probable: *a feasible excuse* [C15 from Anglo-French *faisable*, from *faire* to do, from Latin *facere*] > ˌ**feasiˈbility** *or* ˈ**feasibleness** *n* > ˈ**feasibly** *adv*

feast (fiːst) *n* **1** a large and sumptuous meal, usually given as an entertainment for several people **2** a periodic religious celebration **3** something extremely pleasing or sumptuous: *a feast for the eyes* **4 movable feast** a festival or other event of variable date ▷ *vb* **5** (*intr*) **a** to eat a feast **b** (usually foll by *on*) to enjoy the eating (of), as if feasting: *to feast on cakes* **6** (*tr*) to give a feast to **7** (*intr; foll by on*) to take great delight (in): *to feast on beautiful paintings* **8** (*tr*) to regale or delight: *to feast one's mind or one's eyes* [C13 from Old French *feste*, from Latin *festa*, neuter plural (later assumed to be feminine singular) of *festus* joyful; related to Latin *fānum* temple, *fēriae* festivals] > ˈ**feaster** *n*

Feast of Dedication *n Judaism* a literal translation of **Chanukah**

Feast of Lanterns *n* **1** *Hinduism* another name for **Diwali** **2** Also called: **Festival of Lanterns** *Japanese Buddhism* another name for **Bon**[1]

Feast of Lights *n Judaism* an English name for **Hanukkah**

Feast of Tabernacles *n Judaism* a literal translation of **Sukkoth**

Feast of Weeks *n Judaism* a literal translation of **Shavuot**

feat[1] (fiːt) *n* a remarkable, skilful, or daring action; exploit; achievement: *feats of strength* [C14 from Anglo-French *fait*, from Latin *factum* deed; see FACT]

feat[2] (fiːt) *adj archaic* **1** another word for **skilful** **2** another word for **neat**[1] *or* **suitable** [C14 from Old French *fet*, from Latin *factus* made, from *facere* to make] > ˈ**featly** *adv*

feather (ˈfɛðə) *n* **1** any of the flat light waterproof epidermal structures forming the plumage of birds, each consisting of a hollow shaft having a vane of barbs on either side. They are essential for flight and help maintain body temperature **2** something resembling a feather, such as a tuft of hair or grass **3** *archery* **a** a bird's feather or artificial substitute fitted to an arrow to direct its flight **b** the feathered end of an arrow, opposite the head **4** a strip, spline, or tongue of wood fitted into a groove **5** the wake created on the surface of the water by the raised periscope of a submarine **6** *rowing* the position of an oar turned parallel to the water between strokes. Compare **square** (sense 8) **7** a step in ballroom dancing in which a couple maintain the conventional hold but dance side by side **8** condition of spirits; fettle: *in fine feather* **9** something of negligible value; jot: *I don't care a feather* **10 birds of a feather** people of the same type, character, or interests **11 feather in one's cap** a cause for pleasure at one's achievements: *your promotion is a feather in your cap* **12 not take** *or* **knock a feather out of (someone)** *Irish* to fail to upset or injure (someone): *it didn't take a feather out of him* ▷ *vb* **13** (*tr*) to fit, cover, or supply with feathers **14** *rowing* to turn (an oar) parallel to the water during recovery between strokes, principally in order to lessen wind resistance. Compare **square** (sense 41) **15** (in canoeing) to turn (a paddle) parallel to the direction of the canoe between strokes, while keeping it in the water, principally in order to move silently **16** to change the pitch of (an aircraft propeller) so that the chord lines of the blades are in line with the airflow **17** (*tr*) to join (two boards) by means of a tongue-and-groove joint **18** (*intr*) (of a bird) to grow feathers **19** (*intr*) to move or grow like feathers **20 feather one's nest** to provide oneself with comforts, esp financial ▷ See also **feathers** [Old English *fether*; related to Old Frisian *fethere*, Old Norse *fjöthr* feather, Old High German *fedara* wing, Greek *petesthai* to fly, Sanskrit *patati* he flies] > ˈ**featherless** *adj* > ˈ**feather-ˌlike** *adj* > ˈ**feathery** *adj*

feather bed *n* **1** a mattress filled with feathers or down ▷ *vb* **featherbed -beds, -bedding, -bedded** **2** (*tr*) to pamper; spoil **3** (*intr*) *US* to be subject to or engage in featherbedding

featherbedding (ˈfɛðəˌbɛdɪŋ) *n* the practice of limiting production, duplicating work, or overmanning, esp in accordance with a union contract, in order to prevent redundancies or create jobs

featherbrain (ˈfɛðəˌbreɪn) *or* **featherhead** *n* a frivolous or forgetful person > ˈ**featherˌbrained** *or* ˈ**featherˌheaded** *adj*

featheredge (ˈfɛðərˌɛdʒ) *n* a board or plank that tapers to a thin edge at one side > ˈ**featherˌedged** *adj*

feather grass *n* a perennial grass, *Stipa pennata*, native to the steppes of Europe and N Asia, cultivated as an ornament for its feathery inflorescence

feathering (ˈfɛðərɪŋ) *n* **1** the plumage of a bird; feathers **2** another word for **feathers** (sense 2) **3** *printing* **a** an imperfection in print caused by the spreading of ink **b** the use of additional space between lines in typesetting in order to fill the page

feather palm *n* any of various palm trees, such as the wax palm and date palm, that have pinnate or feather-like leaves. Compare **fan palm**

feathers (ˈfɛðəz) *pl n* **1** the plumage of a bird **2** Also called: **feathering** the long hair on the legs or tail of certain breeds of horses and dogs **3** *informal* dress; attire: *her best feathers* **4 ruffle feathers** to cause upset or offence

feather star *n* any free-swimming crinoid echinoderm of the genus *Antedon* and related genera, living on muddy sea bottoms and having ten feathery arms radiating from a small central disc

featherstitch (ˈfɛðəˌstɪtʃ) *n* **1** a zigzag embroidery stitch ▷ *vb* **2** to decorate (cloth) with featherstitch

feather-veined *adj* (of a leaf) having a network of veins branching from the midrib to the margin

featherweight (ˈfɛðəˌweɪt) *n* **1 a** something very light or of little importance **b** (*as modifier*): *featherweight considerations* **2 a** a professional boxer weighing 118–126 pounds (53.5–57 kg) **b** an amateur boxer weighing 54–57 kg (119–126 pounds) **c** (*as modifier*): *the featherweight challenger* **3** a wrestler in a similar weight category (usually 126–139 pounds (57–63 kg))

featly (ˈfiːtlɪ) *adv archaic* **1** neatly **2** fitly > ˈ**featliness** *n*

feature (ˈfiːtʃə) *n* **1** any one of the parts of the face, such as the nose, chin, or mouth **2** a prominent or distinctive part or aspect, as of a landscape, building, book, etc **3** the principal film in a programme at a cinema **4** an item or article appearing regularly in a newspaper, magazine, etc: *a gardening feature* **5** Also called: **feature story** a prominent story in a newspaper, etc: *a feature on prison reform* **6** a programme given special prominence on radio or television as indicated by attendant publicity **7** an article offered for sale as a special attraction, as in a large retail establishment **8** *archaic* general form or make-up **9** *linguistics* a quality of a linguistic unit at some level of description: *grammatical feature; semantic feature* ▷ *vb* **10** (*tr*) to have as a feature or make a feature of **11** to give prominence to (an actor, famous event, etc) in a film or (of an actor, etc) to have prominence in a film **12** (*tr*) *US informal* to imagine; consider: *I can't feature that happening* [C14 from Anglo-French *feture*, from Latin *factūra* a making, from *facere* to make]

f

featured *adj* (*in combination*) having features as specified: *heavy-featured*

feature-length *adj* (of a film or programme) similar in extent to a feature although not classed as such

featureless (ˈfiːtʃəlɪs) *adj* without distinctive points or qualities; undistinguished > ˈ**featurelessness** *n*

feaze[1] (fiːz) *vb nautical* to make or become unravelled or frayed [C16 perhaps from obsolete Dutch *vese* fringe, from Middle Dutch *vese, veze* fringe; related to Old English *fæs*]

feaze[2] (fiːz) *vb, n* a variant of **feeze** *or* **faze**

Feb *abbreviation for* February

febri *combining form* indicating fever: *febrifuge* [from Latin *febris* fever]

febricity (fɪˈbrɪsɪtɪ) *n rare* the condition of having a fever [C19 from Medieval Latin *febricitās*, from Latin *febris* fever]

febrifacient (ˌfɛbrɪˈfeɪʃənt) *adj* **1** producing fever ▷ *n* **2** something that produces fever

febrific (fɪˈbrɪfɪk) *or* **febriferous** *adj* causing or having a fever

febrifuge (ˈfɛbrɪˌfjuːdʒ) *n* **1** any drug or agent for reducing fever ▷ *adj* **2** serving to reduce fever [C17 from Medieval Latin *febrifugia* feverfew; see FEBRI-, -FUGE] > **febrifugal** (fɪˈbrɪfjʊgəl, ˌfɛbrɪˈfjuːgəl) *adj*

febrile (ˈfiːbraɪl) *adj* of or relating to fever; feverish [C17 from medical Latin *febrīlis*, from Latin *febris* fever] > **febrility** (fɪˈbrɪlɪtɪ) *n*

February (ˈfɛbrʊərɪ) *n, pl* **-aries** the second month of the year, consisting of 28 or (in a leap year) 29 days [C13 from Latin *Februārius mēnsis* month of expiation, from *februa* Roman festival of purification held on February 15, from plural of *februum* a purgation]

February Revolution *n* another name for the **Russian Revolution** (sense 1)

fec. *abbreviation for* fecit

fecal ('fiːkᵊl) *adj* the usual US spelling of **faecal**

feces ('fiːsiːz) *pl n* the usual US spelling of **faeces**

fecht (fɛxt) *vb, n* a Scot word for **fight**. > '**fechter** *n*

fecit *Latin* ('feɪkɪt) (he or she) made it: used formerly on works of art next to the artist's name. Abbreviation: **fec**

feck[1] (fɛk) *n Scot obsolete* **a** worth; value **b** amount; quantity **c** the greater part; the majority [C15 (Scottish dialect) *fek*, short for EFFECT]

feck[2] (fɛk) *vb, n, interj slang* a variant of **fuck**

fecking ('fɛkɪŋ) *or* **feckin** ('fɛkɪn) *adj, adv chiefly Irish slang* (intensifier): *a fecking eejit; it's fecking hot* [C20 a euphemism for FUCKING]

feckless ('fɛklɪs) *adj* feeble; weak; ineffectual; irresponsible [C16 from obsolete *feck* value, effect + -LESS] > '**fecklessly** *adv* > '**fecklessness** *n*

fecula ('fɛkjʊlə) *n, pl* **-lae** (-ˌliː) **1** starch obtained by washing the crushed parts of plants, such as the potato **2** faecal material, esp of insects [C17 from Latin: burnt tartar, appearing as a crust in wine, from *faex* sediment]

feculent ('fɛkjʊlənt) *adj* **1** filthy, scummy, muddy, or foul **2** of the nature of or containing waste matter [C15 from Latin *faeculentus*; see FAECES] > '**feculence** *n*

fecund ('fiːkənd, 'fɛk-) *adj* **1** greatly productive; fertile **2** intellectually productive; prolific [C14 from Latin *fēcundus*; related to Latin *fētus* offspring]

fecundate ('fiːkənˌdeɪt, 'fɛk-) *vb (tr)* **1** to make fruitful **2** to fertilize; impregnate [C17 from Latin *fēcundāre* to fertilize] > ˌ**fecun'dation** *n* > '**fecunˌdator** *n* > **fecundatory** (fɪ'kʌndətərɪ, -trɪ) *adj*

fecundity (fɪ'kʌndɪtɪ) *n* **1** fertility; fruitfulness **2** intellectual fruitfulness; creativity

fed[1] (fɛd) *vb* **1** the past tense and past participle of **feed** **2** **fed to death** *or* **fed (up) to the (back) teeth** *informal* bored or annoyed

fed[2] (fɛd) *n US slang* an agent of the FBI

Fed (fɛd) *n* **the** *US informal* the Federal Reserve Bank or Federal Reserve Board

Fed. *or* **fed.** *abbreviation for* **1** Federal **2** Federation **3** Federated

fedayee (fə'dɑːjiː) *n, pl* **-yeen** (-jiːn) (*sometimes capital*) (in Arab states) a commando, esp one fighting against Israel [from Arabic *fidā'i* one who risks his life in a cause, from *fidā'* redemption]

federal ('fɛdərəl) *adj* **1** of or relating to a form of government or a country in which power is divided between one central and several regional governments **2** of or relating to a treaty between provinces, states, etc, that establishes a political unit in which power is so divided **3** of or relating to the central government of a federation **4** of or relating to any union or association of parties or groups that retain some autonomy **5** (of a university) comprised of relatively independent colleges ▷ *n* **6** a supporter of federal union or federation [C17 from Latin *foedus* league] > '**federally** *adv*

Federal ('fɛdərəl) *adj* **1** **a** of or relating to the Federalist party or Federalism **b** characteristic of or supporting the Union government during the American Civil War ▷ *n* **2** **a** a supporter of the Union government during the American Civil War **b** a Federalist

Federal Bureau of Investigation *n* See **FBI**

federal district *or* **territory** *n* an area used as the seat of central government in a federal system

Federal Government *n* the national government of a federated state, such as that of Australia located in Canberra

federalism ('fɛdərəˌlɪzəm) *n* **1** the principle or a system of federal union **2** advocacy of federal union > '**federalist** *n, adj* > ˌ**federal'istic** *adj*

Federalism ('fɛdərəˌlɪzəm) *n US history* the principles and policies of the Federalist party

Federalist ('fɛdərəlɪst) *US history* ▷ *n* **1** a supporter or member of the Federalist party ▷ *adj also* **Federal'istic** **2** characteristic of the Federalists

Federalist Party *or* **Federal Party** *n* the American political party founded in 1787 and led initially by Alexander Hamilton. It took an active part in the shaping of the US Constitution and thereafter favoured strong centralized government and business interests

federalize *or* **federalise** ('fɛdərəˌlaɪz) *vb (tr)* **1** to unite in a federation or federal union; federate **2** to subject to federal control > ˌ**federali'zation** *or* ˌ**federali'sation** *n*

Federal Republic of Germany *n* the official name of **Germany,** formerly of West Germany

Federal Reserve note *n* a bank note issued by the Federal Reserve Banks and now serving as the prevailing paper currency in circulation in the US

Federal Reserve System *n* (in the US) a banking system consisting of twelve **Federal Reserve Districts**, each containing member banks regulated and served by a **Federal Reserve Bank**. It operates under the supervision of the **Federal Reserve Board** and performs functions similar to those of the Bank of England

federate *vb* ('fɛdəˌreɪt) **1** to unite or cause to unite in a federal union ▷ *adj* ('fɛdərɪt) **2** federal; federated > '**federative** *adj*

Federated Malay States *pl n* See **Malay States**

federation (ˌfɛdə'reɪʃən) *n* **1** the act of federating **2** the union of several provinces, states, etc, to form a federal union **3** a political unit formed in such a way **4** any league, alliance, or confederacy **5** a union of several parties, groups, etc **6** any association or union for common action

Federation (ˌfɛdə'reɪʃən) *n Austral* **1** **the** the federation of the Australian colonies in 1901 **2** a style of domestic architecture of that period, characterized by red brick, terracotta roof tiles, sinuous curves, and heavy window frames

Federation of Rhodesia and Nyasaland *n* a federation (1953–63) of Northern Rhodesia, Southern Rhodesia, and Nyasaland

Federation wheat *n Austral* an early-maturing drought-resistant variety of wheat developed by William Farrar in 1902

fedora (fɪ'dɔːrə) *n* a soft felt or velvet medium-brimmed hat, usually with a band [C19 allegedly named after *Fédora* (1882), play by Victorien Sardou (1831–1908)]

fed up *adj* (*usually postpositive*) *informal* annoyed, discontented, or bored: *I'm fed up with your conduct*

fee (fiː) *n* **1** a payment asked by professional people or public servants for their services: *a doctor's fee; school fees* **2** a charge made for a privilege: *an entrance fee* **3** *property law* **a** an interest in land capable of being inherited. See **fee simple, fee tail** **b** the land held in fee **4** (in feudal Europe) the land granted by a lord to his vassal **5** an obsolete word for a **gratuity** **6** **in fee** **a** *law* (of land) in absolute ownership **b** *archaic* in complete subjection ▷ *vb* **fees, feeing, feed** **7** *rare* to give a fee to **8** *chiefly Scot* to hire for a fee [C14 from Old French *fie*, of Germanic origin; see FIEF] > '**feeless** *adj*

feeble ('fiːbᵊl) *adj* **1** lacking in physical or mental strength; frail; weak **2** inadequate; unconvincing: *feeble excuses* **3** easily influenced or indecisive [C12 from Old French *feble, fleible*, from Latin *flēbilis* to be lamented, from *flēre* to weep] > '**feebleness** *n* > '**feebly** *adv*

feeble-minded *adj* **1** lacking in intelligence; stupid **2** mentally defective **3** lacking decision; irresolute > ˌ**feeble-'mindedly** *adv* > ˌ**feeble-'mindedness** *n*

feed (fiːd) *vb* **feeds, feeding, fed** (fɛd) (*mainly tr*) **1** to give food to: *to feed the cat* **2** to give as food: *to feed meat to the cat* **3** (*intr*) to eat food: *the horses feed at noon* **4** to provide food for: *these supplies can feed 10 million people* **5** to provide what is necessary for the existence or development of: *to feed one's imagination* **6** to gratify; satisfy: *to feed one's eyes on a beautiful sight* **7** (*also intr*) to supply (a machine, furnace, etc) with (the necessary materials or fuel) for its operation, or (of such materials) to flow or move forwards into a machine, etc **8** to use (land) as grazing **9** *theatre informal* to cue (an actor, esp a comedian) with lines or actions **10** *sport* to pass a ball to (a team-mate) **11** *electronics* to introduce (electrical energy) into a circuit, esp by means of a feeder **12** (*also intr*; foll by *on* or *upon*) to eat or cause to eat ▷ *n* **13** the act or an instance of feeding **14** food, esp that of animals or babies **15** the process of supplying a machine or furnace with a material or fuel **16** the quantity of material or fuel so supplied **17** the rate of advance of a cutting tool in a lathe, drill, etc **18** a mechanism that supplies material or fuel or controls the rate of advance of a cutting tool **19** *theatre informal* a performer, esp a straight man, who provides cues **20** an informal word for **meal** [Old English *fēdan*; related to Old Norse *fætha* to feed, Old High German *fuotan*, Gothic *fōthjan*; see FOOD, FODDER] > '**feedable** *adj*

feedback ('fiːdˌbæk) *n* **1** **a** the return of part of the output of an electronic circuit, device, or mechanical system to its input, so modifying its characteristics. In **negative feedback** a rise in output energy reduces the input energy; in **positive feedback** an increase in output energy reinforces the input energy **b** that part of the output signal fed back into the input **2** the return of part of the sound output by a loudspeaker to the microphone or pick-up so that a high-pitched whistle is produced **3** the whistling noise so produced **4** **a** the effect of the product of a biological pathway on the rate of an earlier step in that pathway **b** the substance or reaction causing such an effect, such as the release of a hormone in a biochemical pathway **5** information in response to an inquiry, experiment, etc: *there was little feedback from our questionnaire* ▷ *vb* **feed back** ▷ *adv* **6** (*tr*) to return (part of the output of a system) to its input **7** to offer or suggest (information, ideas, etc) in reaction to an inquiry, experiment, etc

feedbag ('fiːdˌbæg) *n* **1** any bag in which feed for livestock is sacked **2** *US and Canadian* a bag, fastened around the head of a horse and covering the nose, in which feed is placed. Also called (in Britain and certain other countries): **nosebag**

feeder ('fiːdə) *n* **1** a person or thing that feeds or is fed **2** a child's feeding bottle or bib **3** *agriculture, chiefly US and Canadian* a head of livestock being fattened for slaughter **4** a person or device that feeds the working material into a system or machine **5** a tributary channel, esp one that supplies a reservoir or canal with water **6** **a** a road, service, etc, that links secondary areas to the main traffic network **b** (*as modifier*): *a feeder bus* **7** **a** a transmission line connecting an aerial to a transmitter or receiver **b** a power line for transmitting electrical power from a generating station to a distribution network

feeding bottle *n* a bottle fitted with a rubber teat from which infants or young animals suck liquids. Also called: **nursing bottle**

feeding frenzy *n* **1** a phenomenon in which aquatic predators, esp sharks, become so excited when eating that they attack each other **2** a period of intense excitement over or interest in a person or thing: *the media erupt into a feeding frenzy*

feedlot ('fiːdˌlɒt) *n* an area or building where livestock are fattened rapidly for market

feedstock ('fiːdˌstɒk) *n* the main raw material used in the manufacture of a product

feedstuff ('fiːdˌstʌf) *or* **feedingstuff** ('fiːdɪŋˌstʌf) *n* any material used as a food, esp for animals

feedthrough ('fiːdˌθruː) *n electronics* a conductor used to connect two sides of a part, such as a printed circuit board

feedwater ('fiːdˌwɔːtə) *n* water, previously

purified to prevent scale deposit or corrosion, that is fed to boilers for steam generation

feel (fiːl) *vb* **feels, feeling, felt** (fɛlt) **1** to perceive (something) by touching **2** to have a physical or emotional sensation of (something): *to feel heat; to feel anger* **3** (*tr*) to examine (something) by touch **4** (*tr*) to find (one's way) by testing or cautious exploration **5** (*copula*) to seem or appear in respect of the sensation given: *I feel tired; it feels warm* **6** to have an indistinct, esp emotional conviction; sense (esp in the phrase **feel in one's bones**) **7** (*intr*; foll by *for*) to show sympathy or compassion (towards): *I feel for you in your sorrow* **8** to believe, think, or be of the opinion (that): *he feels he must resign* **9** (*tr*; often foll by *up*) *slang* to pass one's hands over the sexual organs of **10** **feel like** to have an inclination (for something or doing something): *I don't feel like going to the pictures* **11** **feel (quite) oneself** to be fit and sure of oneself **12** **feel up to** (*usually used with a negative or in a question*) to be fit enough for (something or doing something): *I don't feel up to going out tonight* ▷ *n* **13** the act or an instance of feeling, esp by touching **14** the quality of or an impression from something perceived through feeling: *the house has a homely feel about it* **15** the sense of touch: *the fabric is rough to the feel* **16** an instinctive aptitude; knack: *she's got a feel for this sort of work* [Old English *fēlan*; related to Old High German *fuolen*, Old Norse *fālma* to grope, Latin *palma* PALM[1]]

feeler ('fiːlə) *n* **1** a person or thing that feels **2** an organ in certain animals, such as an antenna or tentacle, that is sensitive to touch **3** a remark designed to probe the reactions or intentions of other people

feeler gauge *n* a thin metal strip of known thickness used to measure a narrow gap or to set a gap between two parts

feel-good *adj* causing or characterized by a feeling of self-satisfaction: *feel-good factor*

feeling ('fiːlɪŋ) *n* **1** the sense of touch **2 a** the ability to experience physical sensations, such as heat, pain, etc **b** the sensation so experienced **3** a state of mind **4** a physical or mental impression: *a feeling of warmth* **5** fondness; sympathy: *to have a great deal of feeling for someone* **6** an ability to feel deeply: *a person of feeling* **7** a sentiment: *a feeling that the project is feasible* **8** an impression or mood; atmosphere: *the feeling of a foreign city* **9** an emotional disturbance, esp anger or dislike: *a lot of bad feeling about the increase in taxes* **10** intuitive appreciation and understanding: *a feeling for words* **11** sensibility in the performance of something **12** (*plural*) emotional or moral sensitivity, as in relation to principles or personal dignity (esp in the phrase **hurt** or **injure the feelings of**) **13** **have feelings for** to be emotionally or sexually attracted to ▷ *adj* **14** sentient; sensitive **15** expressing or containing emotion **16** warm-hearted; sympathetic > '**feelingly** *adv*

feen (fiːn) *n Irish dialect* an informal word for **man**

fee simple *n property law* an absolute interest in land over which the holder has complete freedom of disposition during his life. Compare **fee tail** [c15 from Anglo-French: fee (or fief) simple]

feet (fiːt) *n* **1** the plural of **foot** **2** **at (someone's) feet** as someone's disciple **3** **be run** *or* **rushed off one's feet** to be very busy **4** **carry** *or* **sweep off one's feet** to fill with enthusiasm **5** **feet of clay** a weakness that is not widely known **6** **get one's feet wet** to begin to participate in something **7** **have** (*or* **keep**) **one's feet on the ground** to be practical and reliable **8** **on one's** *or* **its feet** **a** standing up **b** in good health **c** (of a business, company, etc) thriving **9** **put one's feet up** to rest **10** **stand on one's own feet** to be independent > '**feetless** *adj*

fee tail *n property law* **a** a freehold interest in land restricted to a particular line of heirs **b** an estate in land subject to such restriction. Compare **fee simple** [c15 from Anglo-French *fee tailé* fee (or fief) determined, from *taillier* to cut]

feeze *or* **feaze** (fiːz) *dialect* ▷ *vb* **1** (*tr*) to beat **2** to drive off **3** *chiefly US* to disconcert; worry ▷ *n* **4** a rush **5** *chiefly US* a state of agitation [Old English *fēsian*]

FEI *abbreviation for* Fédération Équestre Internationale: the international governing body of equestrian sports [from French]

feign (feɪn) *vb* **1** to put on a show of (a quality or emotion); pretend: *to feign innocence* **2** (*tr*) to make up; invent: *to feign an excuse* **3** (*tr*) to copy; imitate: *to feign someone's laugh* [c13 from Old French *feindre* to pretend, from Latin *fingere* to form, shape, invent] > '**feigner** *n* > '**feigningly** *adv*

feijoa (fiː'dʒəʊə) *n* **1** an evergreen myrtaceous shrub, *Feijoa sellowiana*, of South America **2** the fruit of this shrub [c19 from New Latin, named after J. da Silva Feijo, 19th-century Spanish botanist]

feint[1] (feɪnt) *n* **1** a mock attack or movement designed to distract an adversary, as in a military manoeuvre or in boxing, fencing, etc **2** a misleading action or appearance ▷ *vb* **3** (*intr*) to make a feint [c17 from French *feinte*, from *feint* pretended, from Old French *feindre* to FEIGN]

feint[2] (feɪnt) *n printing* the narrowest rule used in the production of ruled paper [c19 variant of FAINT]

feints *or* **faints** (feɪnts) *pl n* the leavings of the second distillation of Scotch malt whisky

feisty ('faɪstɪ) *adj* **feistier, feistiest** *informal* **1** lively, resilient, and self-reliant **2** *US and Canadian* frisky **3** *US and Canadian* irritable [c19 from dialect *feist*, *fist* small dog; related to Old English *fisting* breaking wind]

felafel (fəl'ɑːfəl) *n* a variant spelling of **falafel**

Feldenkrais method ('fɛldᵊn,kraɪs) *n* a system of gentle movements that promote flexibility, coordination, and self-awareness [c20 after Moshe *Feldenkrais* (1904–84), Russian-born engineer who developed it]

feldsher, feldscher *or* **feldschar** ('fɛldʃə) *n* (in Russia) a medical doctor's assistant [c19 Russian, from German *Feldscher* a field surgeon, from *Feld* field + *Scherer* surgeon, from *scheren* to shear]

feldspar ('fɛld,spɑː, 'fɛl,spɑː) *or* **felspar** *n* any of a group of hard rock-forming minerals consisting of aluminium silicates of potassium, sodium, calcium, or barium: the principal constituents of igneous rocks. The group includes orthoclase, microcline, and the plagioclase minerals [c18 from German *feldspat(h)*, from *feld* field + *spat(h)* SPAR[3]] > **feldspathic** (fɛld'spæθɪk, fɛl'spæθ-), **fel'spathic**, '**feldspath,ose**, '**felspath,ose** *adj*

feldspathoid ('fɛldspə,θɔɪd) *n* any of a group of rock-forming minerals, such as leucite and sodalite, that are similar to feldspars but contain less silica

felicific (,fiːlɪ'sɪfɪk) *adj* making or tending to make happy [c19 from Latin *fēlix* happy + *facere* to make]

felicitate (fɪ'lɪsɪ,teɪt) *vb* to wish joy to; congratulate > **fe'lici,tator** *n*

felicitation (fɪ,lɪsɪ'teɪʃən) *n* a less common word for **congratulation**

felicitous (fɪ'lɪsɪtəs) *adj* **1** well-chosen; apt **2** possessing an agreeable style **3** producing or marked by happiness > **fe'licitously** *adv* > **fe'licitousness** *n*

felicity (fɪ'lɪsɪtɪ) *n*, *pl* **-ties** **1** happiness; joy **2** a cause of happiness **3** an appropriate expression or style **4** the quality or display of such expressions or style **5** *philosophy* appropriateness (of a speech act). The performative *I appoint you ambassador* can only possess felicity if uttered by one in whom the authority for such appointments is vested [c14 from Latin *fēlīcitās* happiness, from *fēlix* happy]

feline ('fiːlaɪn) *adj* **1** of, relating to, or belonging to the *Felidae*, a family of predatory mammals, including cats, lions, leopards, and cheetahs, typically having a round head and retractile claws: order *Carnivora* (carnivores) **2** resembling or suggestive of a cat, esp in stealth or grace ▷ *n also* **felid** ('fiːlɪd) **3** any animal belonging to the family *Felidae*; a cat [c17 from Latin *fēlīnus*, from *fēlēs* cat] > '**felinely** *adv* > '**felineness** *or* **felinity** (fɪ'lɪnɪtɪ) *n*

Felixstowe ('fiːlɪk,stəʊ) *n* a port and resort in E England, in Suffolk: ferry connections to Rotterdam and Zeebrugge. Pop: 29 349 (2001)

fell[1] (fɛl) *vb* the past tense of **fall**

fell[2] (fɛl) *vb* (*tr*) **1** to cut or knock down: *to fell a tree; to fell an opponent* **2** *needlework* to fold under and sew flat (the edges of a seam) ▷ *n* **3** *US and Canadian* the timber felled in one season **4** a seam finished by felling [Old English *fellan*; related to Old Norse *fella*, Old High German *fellen*; see FALL] > '**fellable** *adj*

fell[3] (fɛl) *adj* **1** *archaic* cruel or fierce; terrible **2** *archaic* destructive or deadly: *a fell disease* **3** **one fell swoop** a single hasty action or occurrence [C13 *fel*, from Old French: cruel, from Medieval Latin *fellō* villain; see FELON[1]] > '**fellness** *n*

fell[4] (fɛl) *n* an animal skin or hide [Old English; related to Old High German *fel* skin, Old Norse *berfjall* bearskin, Latin *pellis* skin; see PEEL[1]]

fell[5] (fɛl) *n* (*often plural*) *Northern English and Scot* **a** a mountain, hill, or tract of upland moor **b** (*in combination*): *fell-walking* [c13 from Old Norse *fjall*; related to Old High German *felis* rock]

fella ('fɛlə) *n* a nonstandard variant of **fellow**

fellah ('fɛlə) *n*, *pl* **fellahs, fellahin** *or* **fellaheen** (,fɛlə'hiːn) a peasant in Arab countries [c18 from Arabic, dialect variant of *fallāh*, from *falaha* to cultivate]

fellate (fɛ'leɪt, fɪ-) *vb* (*tr*) to perform fellatio on (a person) [c20 back formation from FELLATIO]

fellatio (fɪ'leɪʃɪəʊ, fɛ-) *or* **fellation** *n* a sexual activity in which the penis is stimulated by the partner's mouth. Compare **cunnilingus** [c19 New Latin, from Latin *fellāre* to suck] > **fel'lator** *n* > **fel'latrix** *fem n*

feller[1] ('fɛlə) *n* **1** a person or thing that fells **2** an attachment on a sewing machine for felling seams

feller[2] ('fɛlə) *n* a nonstandard variant of **fellow**

Felling ('fɛlɪŋ) *n* a town in NE England, in Gateshead unitary authority, Tyne and Wear; formerly noted for coal mining. Pop: 34 196 (2001)

Felliniesque (fə'liːnɪ,ɛsk) *adj* referring to or reminiscent of the work of the Italian film-maker Federic Fellini (1920–93)

fellmonger ('fɛl,mʌŋgə) *n* a person who deals in animal skins or hides > '**fell,mongering** *or* '**fell,mongery** *n*

felloe ('fɛləʊ) *or* **felly** ('fɛlɪ) *n*, *pl* **-loes** *or* **-lies** a segment or the whole rim of a wooden wheel to which the spokes are attached and onto which a metal tyre is usually shrunk [Old English *felge*; related to Old High German *felga*, Middle Dutch *velge*, of unknown origin]

fellow ('fɛləʊ) *n* **1** a man or boy **2** an informal word for **boyfriend** **3** *informal* one or oneself: *a fellow has to eat* **4** a person considered to be of little importance or worth **5 a** (*often plural*) a companion; comrade; associate **b** (*as modifier*): *fellow travellers* **6** (at Oxford and Cambridge universities) a member of the governing body of a college, who is usually a member of the teaching staff **7** a member of the governing body or established teaching staff at any of various universities or colleges **8** a postgraduate student employed, esp for a fixed period, to undertake research and, often, to do some teaching **9 a** a person in the same group, class, or condition: *the surgeon asked his fellows* **b** (*as modifier*): *fellow students; a fellow sufferer* **10** one of a pair; counterpart; mate: *looking for the glove's fellow* [Old English *fēolaga*, from Old Norse *félagi*, one who lays down money, from *fē* money + *lag* a laying down]

Fellow ('fɛləʊ) *n* a member of any of various learned societies: *Fellow of the British Academy*

fellow feeling *n* **1** mutual sympathy or friendship **2** an opinion held in common

fellowship ('fɛləʊʃɪp) *n* **1** the state of sharing

f

mutual interests, experiences, activities, etc **2** a society of people sharing mutual interests, experiences, activities, etc; club **3** companionship; friendship **4** the state or relationship of being a fellow **5 a** mutual trust and charitableness between Christians **b** a Church or religious association **6** *education* **a** a financed research post providing study facilities, privileges, etc, often in return for teaching services **b** a foundation endowed to support a postgraduate research student **c** an honorary title carrying certain privileges awarded to a postgraduate student **7** (*often capital*) the body of fellows in a college, university, etc

fellow traveller *n* **1** a companion on a journey **2** a non-Communist who sympathizes with Communism

fell pony *n* a British breed of large and heavy ponies, found in the hills of N England

felo de se (ˈfiːləʊ dɪ ˈsiː, ˈfɛləʊ) *n, pl* **felones de se** (ˈfiːləʊˌniːz dɪ ˈsiː, ˈfɛl-) *or* **felos de se** *law* **a** suicide **b** a person who commits suicide [c17 from Anglo-Latin, from *felō* felon + Latin *dē* of + *sē* oneself]

felon[1] (ˈfɛlən) *n* **1** *criminal law* (formerly) a person who has committed a felony **2** *obsolete* a wicked person ▷ *adj* **3** *archaic or poetic* evil; cruel [c13 from Old French: villain, from Medieval Latin *fellō*, of uncertain origin]

felon[2] (ˈfɛlən) *n* a purulent inflammation of the end joint of a finger, sometimes affecting the bone [c12 from Medieval Latin *fellō* sore, perhaps from Latin *fel* poison]

felonious (fɪˈləʊnɪəs) *adj* **1** *criminal law* of, involving, or constituting a felony **2** *obsolete* wicked; base > **feˈloniously** *adv* > **feˈloniousness** *n*

felonry (ˈfɛlənrɪ) *n, pl* **-ries** **1** felons collectively **2** (formerly) the convict population of a penal colony, esp in Australia

felony (ˈfɛlənɪ) *n, pl* **-nies** (formerly) a serious crime, such as murder or arson. All distinctions between felony and misdemeanour were abolished in England and Wales in 1967

felsite (ˈfɛlsaɪt) *or* **felstone** (ˈfɛlˌstəʊn) *n* any fine-grained igneous rock consisting essentially of quartz and feldspar [c18 FELS(PAR) + -ITE[1]] > **felsitic** (fɛlˈsɪtɪk) *adj*

felspar (ˈfɛlˌspɑː) *n* a variant (esp Brit) of **feldspar** > **felspathic** (fɛlˈspæθɪk) *or* **felspathose** *adj*

felt[1] (fɛlt) *vb* the past tense and past participle of **feel**

felt[2] (fɛlt) *n* **1 a** a matted fabric of wool, hair, etc, made by working the fibres together under pressure or by heat or chemical action **b** (*as modifier*): *a felt hat* **2** any material, such as asbestos, made by a similar process of matting ▷ *vb* **3** (*tr*) to make into or cover with felt **4** (*intr*) to become matted [Old English; related to Old Saxon *filt*, Old High German *filz* felt, Latin *pellere* to beat, Greek *pelas* close; see ANVIL, FILTER]

felting (ˈfɛltɪŋ) *n* **1** felted material; felt **2** the process of making felt **3** materials for making felt

felt-tip pen *n* a pen having a writing point made from pressed fibres. Also called: **fibre-tip pen**

felucca (fɛˈlʌkə) *n* a narrow lateen-rigged vessel of the Mediterranean [c17 from Italian *felucca*, probably from obsolete Spanish *faluca*, probably from Arabic *fulūk* ships, from Greek *epholkion* small boat, from *ephelkein* to tow]

felwort (ˈfɛlˌwɜːt) *n* a biennial gentianaceous plant, *Gentianella amarella*, of Europe and SW China, having purple flowers and rosettes of leaves [Old English *feldwyrt*; see FIELD, WORT]

fem *abbreviation for* **1** female **2** feminine

female (ˈfiːmeɪl) *adj* **1** of, relating to, or designating the sex producing gametes (ova) that can be fertilized by male gametes (spermatozoa) **2** of, relating to, or characteristic of a woman: *female charm* **3** for or composed of women or girls: *female suffrage; a female choir* **4** (of reproductive organs such as the ovary and carpel) capable of producing female gametes **5** (of gametes such as the ovum)

capable of being fertilized by a male gamete in sexual reproduction **6** (of flowers) lacking, or having nonfunctional, stamens **7** having an internal cavity into which a projecting male counterpart can be fitted: *a female thread* ▷ *n* **8 a** a female animal or plant **b** *mildly offensive* a woman or girl [c14 from earlier *femelle* (influenced by *male*), from Latin *fēmella* a young woman, from *fēmina* a woman] > **ˈfemaleness** *n*

female impersonator *n* a male theatrical performer who acts as a woman

female suffrage *n* *chiefly US* another name for **women's suffrage**

feme (fɛm) *n* *law* a woman or wife [c16 from Anglo-French, ultimately from Latin *fēmina* woman]

feme covert *n* *law* a married woman [c16 from Anglo-French: a covered woman, one protected by marriage]

feme sole *n* *law* **1** a single woman, whether spinster, widow, or divorcee **2** a woman whose marriage has been annulled or is otherwise independent of her husband, as by owning her own property [c16 from Anglo-French: a woman alone]

femineity (ˌfɛmɪˈneɪɪtɪ) *n* the quality of being feminine; womanliness

feminine (ˈfɛmɪnɪn) *adj* **1** suitable to or characteristic of a woman: *a feminine fashion* **2** possessing qualities or characteristics considered typical of or appropriate to a woman **3** effeminate; womanish **4** *grammar* **a** denoting or belonging to a gender of nouns, occurring in many inflected languages, that includes all kinds of referents as well as some female animate referents **b** (*as noun*): German *Zeit* "time" and *Ehe* "marriage" are feminines [c14 from Latin *fēminīnus*, from *fēmina* woman] > **ˈfemininely** *adv* > **ˈfeminineness** *n*

feminine ending *n* *prosody* an unstressed syllable at the end of a line of verse

feminine rhyme *n* *prosody* a rhyme between words in which one, two, or more unstressed syllables follow a stressed one, as in *elation, nation* or *merrily, verily*. Compare **masculine rhyme**

femininity (ˌfɛmɪˈnɪnɪtɪ) *n* **1** the quality of being feminine **2** womanhood

feminism (ˈfɛmɪˌnɪzəm) *n* a doctrine or movement that advocates equal rights for women

feminist (ˈfɛmɪnɪst) *n* **1** a person who advocates equal rights for women ▷ *adj* **2** of, relating to, or advocating feminism

feminize *or* **feminise** (ˈfɛmɪˌnaɪz) *vb* **1** to make or become feminine **2** to cause (a male animal) to develop female characteristics > ˌfemi niˈzation *or* ˌfeminiˈsation *n*

femme French (fam; English fɛm) *n* a woman or wife

femme de chambre French (fam də ʃɑ̃brə) *n, pl* **femmes de chambre** (fam də ʃɑ̃brə) **1** a chambermaid **2** *rare* a personal maid [c18 woman of the bedroom]

femme fatale French (fam fatal; English ˈfɛm fəˈtæl, -ˈtɑːl) *n, pl* **femmes fatales** (fam fatal; English ˈfɛm fəˈtæl, -ˈtɑːlz) an alluring or seductive woman, esp one who causes men to love her to their own distress [fatal woman]

femmy (ˈfɛmɪ) *adj* **-mier, -miest** *informal* markedly or exaggeratedly feminine in appearance, manner, etc

femoral (ˈfɛmərəl) *adj* of or relating to the thigh or femur

femto- *prefix* denoting 10⁻¹⁵: *femtometer*. Symbol: f [from Danish or Norwegian *femten* fifteen]

femur (ˈfiːmə) *n, pl* **femurs** *or* **femora** (ˈfɛmərə) **1** the longest thickest bone of the human skeleton, articulating with the pelvis above and the knee below. Nontechnical name: **thighbone 2** the corresponding bone in other vertebrates **3** the segment of an insect's leg nearest to the body [c18 from Latin: thigh]

fen[1] (fɛn) *n* low-lying flat land that is marshy or artificially drained [Old English *fenn*; related to

Old High German *fenna*, Old Norse *fen*, Gothic *fani* clay, Sanskrit *panka* mud]

fen[2] (fɛn) *n, pl* **fen** a monetary unit of the People's Republic of China, worth one hundredth of a yuan [from Mandarin Chinese]

fence (fɛns) *n* **1** a structure that serves to enclose an area such as a garden or field, usually made of posts of timber, concrete, or metal connected by wire, netting, rails, or boards **2** *slang* a dealer in stolen property **3** an obstacle for a horse to jump in steeplechasing or showjumping **4** *machinery* a guard or guide, esp in a circular saw or plane **5** a projection usually fitted to the top surface of a sweptback aircraft wing to prevent movement of the airflow towards the wing tips **6 mend one's fences a** *chiefly US and Canadian* to restore a position or reputation that has been damaged, esp in politics **b** to re-establish friendly relations (with someone) **7** (**sit**) **on the fence** (to be) unable or unwilling to commit oneself **8 over the fence** *Austral and NZ* *informal* unreasonable, unfair, or unjust ▷ *vb* **9** (*tr*) to construct a fence on or around (a piece of land, etc) **10** (*tr; foll by in or off*) to close (in) or separate (off) with or as if with a fence: *he fenced in the livestock* **11** (*intr*) to fight using swords or foils **12** (*intr*) to evade a question or argument, esp by quibbling over minor points **13** (*intr*) to engage in skilful or witty debate, repartee, etc **14** (*intr*) *slang* to receive stolen property **15** (*tr*) *archaic* to ward off or keep out [c14 *fens*, shortened from *defens* DEFENCE] > **ˈfenceless** *adj* > **ˈfenceˌlike** *adj*

fencer (ˈfɛnsə) *n* **1** a person who fights with a sword, esp one who practises the art of fencing **2** *chiefly Austral and NZ* a person who erects and repairs fences

fencible (ˈfɛnsəbᵊl) *adj* **1** a Scot word for **defensible** ▷ *n* **2** (formerly) a person who undertook military service in immediate defence of his homeland only

fencing (ˈfɛnsɪŋ) *n* **1** the practice, art, or sport of fighting with swords, esp the sport of using foils, épées, or sabres under a set of rules to score points **2 a** wire, stakes, etc, used as fences **b** fences collectively **3** skilful or witty debate **4** the avoidance of direct answers; evasiveness **5** *slang* the business of buying and selling stolen property

fencing wire *n* a heavy-gauge galvanized wire used for farm fences

fend (fɛnd) *vb* **1** (*intr; foll by for*) to give support (to someone, esp oneself); provide (for) **2** (*tr; usually foll by off*) to ward off or turn aside (blows, questions, attackers, etc) **3** (*tr*) *archaic* to defend or resist **4** (*intr*) *Scot and Northern English dialect* to struggle; strive ▷ *n* **5** *Scot and Northern English dialect* a shift or effort [c13 *fenden*, shortened from *defenden* to DEFEND]

Fendalton tractor (ˌfɛnˈdɔːltən) *n* *NZ informal* a four-wheel drive recreational vehicle. Also called: **Fendalton shopping cart** [from the name of a wealthy suburb of Christchurch]

fender (ˈfɛndə) *n* **1** a low metal frame which confines falling coals to the hearth **2** *chiefly US* a metal frame fitted to the front of locomotives to absorb shock, clear the track, etc **3** a cushion-like device, such as a car tyre hung over the side of a vessel to reduce damage resulting from accidental contact or collision **4** *US and Canadian* the part of a car body that surrounds the wheels. Also called (in Britain and certain other countries): **wing** > **ˈfendered** *adj*

Fender (ˈfɛndə) *n* *trademark* a type of solid-body electric guitar [c20 named after Leo *Fender*, its US inventor (1951)]

fender pile *n* an upright, usually freestanding, pile driven into the sea bed or a riverbed beside a berth to protect the dock wall or wharf from the impact of vessels

fenestella (ˌfɛnɪˈstɛlə) *n, pl* **-lae** (-liː) **1** *RC Church* a small aperture in the front of an altar, containing relics **2** *ecclesiast* a niche in the side wall of a chancel, in which the credence or piscina are set

3 *architect* a small window or an opening in a wall [C18 from Latin: a little window, from *fenestra* window]

fenestra (fɪˈnɛstrə) *n, pl* -trae (-triː) **1** *biology* a small opening in or between bones, esp one of the openings between the middle and inner ears **2** *zoology* a transparent marking or spot, as on the wings of moths **3** *architect* a window or window-like opening in the outside wall of a building [C19 via New Latin from Latin: wall opening, window] > feˈnestral *adj*

fenestrated (fɪˈnɛsˌtreɪtɪd, ˈfɛnɪˌstreɪtɪd) *or* **fenestrate** *adj* **1** *architect* having windows or window-like openings **2** *biology* perforated or having fenestrae

fenestration (ˌfɛnɪˈstreɪʃən) *n* **1** the arrangement and design of windows in a building **2** a surgical operation to restore hearing by making an artificial opening into the labyrinth of the ear

F Eng *abbreviation for* Fellow of the Fellowship of Engineering

feng shui (ˈfʌŋ ˈʃweɪ) *n* the Chinese art of determining the most propitious design and placement of a grave, building, room, etc, so that the maximum harmony is achieved between the flow of chi of the environment and that of the user, believed to bring good fortune [C20 from Chinese *feng* wind + *shui* water]

Fenian (ˈfiːnɪən) *n* **1** (formerly) a member of an Irish revolutionary organization founded in the US in the 19th century to fight for an independent Ireland **2** *Irish myth* one of the Fianna **3** *derogatory, offensive* an Irish Catholic or a person of Irish Catholic descent ▷ *adj* **4** of or relating to the Fenians [C19 from Irish Gaelic *fêinne*, plural of *fian* band of warriors] > ˈFenianism *n*

fennec (ˈfɛnɛk) *n* a very small nocturnal fox, *Fennecus zerda*, inhabiting deserts of N Africa and Arabia, having pale fur and enormous ears [C18 from Arabic *fenek* fox]

fennel (ˈfɛnᵊl) *n* **1** a strong-smelling yellow-flowered umbelliferous plant, *Foeniculum vulgare*, whose seeds and feathery leaves are used to season and flavour food. See also **finocchio 2** another name for **mayweed** [Old English *fenol*, from Latin *faeniculum* fennel, diminutive of *faenum* hay]

fennelflower (ˈfɛnᵊlˌflaʊə) *n* any of various Mediterranean ranunculaceous plants of the genus *Nigella*, having finely divided leaves and white, blue, or yellow flowers. See also **love-in-a-mist**

fenny (ˈfɛnɪ) *adj* **1** boggy or marshy: *fenny country* **2** found in, characteristic of, or growing in fens

Fenrir (ˈfɛnrɪə), **Fenris** (ˈfɛnrɪs) *or* **Fenriswolf** (ˈfɛnrɪsˌwʊlf) *n Norse myth* an enormous wolf, fathered by Loki, which killed Odin

Fens (fɛnz) *pl n* **the** a flat low-lying area of E England, west and south of the Wash: consisted of marshes until reclaimed in the 17th to 19th centuries

fentanyl (ˈfɛntəˌnaɪl) *n* a narcotic drug used in medicine to relieve pain

fenugreek (ˈfɛnjʊˌgriːk) *n* an annual heavily scented Mediterranean leguminous plant, *Trigonella foenum-graecum*, with hairy stems and white flowers: cultivated for forage and for its medicinal seeds [Old English *fēnogrēcum*, from Latin *fenum Graecum* literally: Greek hay]

feoff (fiːf) *medieval history* ▷ *n* **1** a variant spelling of **fief** ▷ *vb* **2** (*tr*) to invest with a benefice or fief [C13 from Anglo-French *feoffer*, from *feoff* a FIEF] > ˈfeoffor *or* ˈfeoffer *n*

feoffee (fɛˈfiː, ˌfiːˈfiː) *n* (in feudal society) a vassal granted a fief by his lord

feoffment (ˈfiːfmənt) *n* (in medieval Europe) a lord's act of granting a fief to his man

-fer *n combining form* indicating a person or thing that bears something specified: *crucifer; conifer* [from Latin, from *ferre* to bear]

feral¹ (ˈfɪərəl, ˈfɛr-) *adj* **1** Also: **ferine** (of animals and plants) existing in a wild or uncultivated state, esp after being domestic or cultivated **2** Also: **ferine** savage; brutal **3** *Austral derogatory slang* (of a person) tending to be interested in environmental issues and having a rugged, unkempt appearance ▷ *n* **4** *Austral derogatory slang* a person who displays such tendencies and appearance **5** *Austral slang* disgusting **6** *Austral slang* excellent [C17 from Medieval Latin *ferālis*, from Latin *fera* a wild beast, from *ferus* savage] > ferity (ˈfɛrɪtɪ) *n*

feral² (ˈfɪərəl, ˈfɛr-) *adj archaic* **1** *astrology* associated with death **2** gloomy; funereal [C17 from Latin *fērālis* relating to corpses; perhaps related to *ferre* to carry]

feral child *n* a neglected child who engages in lawless or anti-social behaviour

ferbam (ˈfɜːbæm) *n* a black slightly water-soluble fluffy powder used as a fungicide. Formula: [(CH₃)₂NCSS]₃Fe [C20 from *fer*(*ric* dimethyldithiocar)*bam*(*ate*)]

fer-de-lance (ˌfɛədəˈlɑːns) *n* a large highly venomous tropical American snake, *Trimeresurus* (*or Bothops*) *atrox*, with a greyish-brown mottled coloration: family *Crotalidae* (pit vipers) [C19 from French, literally: iron (head) of a lance]

fere (fɪə; *Scot* fiːr) *n Scot* **1** a companion **2** Also: **fier** a husband or wife [Old English *gefêra*, from *fêran* to travel; see FARE]

feretory (ˈfɛrɪtərɪ, -trɪ) *n, pl* -ries *chiefly RC Church* **1** a shrine, usually portable, for a saint's relics **2** the chapel in which a shrine is kept [C14 from Middle French *fiertre*, from Latin *feretrum* a bier, from Greek *pheretron*, from *pherein* to bear]

Fergana *or* **Ferghana** (fəˈgɑːnə) *n* **1** a region of W central Asia, surrounded by high mountains and accessible only from the west; mainly in Uzbekistan and partly in Tajikistan and Kyrgyzstan **2** the chief city of this region, in E Uzbekistan. Pop: 230 000 (2005 est)

Fergus (ˈfɜːgəs) *n* (in Irish legend) a warrior king of Ulster, who was supplanted by Conchobar

feria (ˈfɪərɪə) *n, pl* -rias *or* -riae (-rɪˌiː) *RC Church* a weekday, other than Saturday, on which no feast occurs [C19 from Late Latin: day of the week (as in *prīma fēria* Sunday), singular of Latin *fēriae* festivals]

ferial (ˈfɪərɪəl) *adj* **1** of or relating to a feria **2** *rare* of or relating to a holiday

ferine (ˈfɪəraɪn) *adj* another word for **feral** [C17 from Latin *ferīnus*, of wild animals, from *fera* wild beast]

ferity (ˈfɛrɪtɪ) *n, pl* -ties *rare* **1** the state of being wild or uncultivated **2** savagery; ferocity [C16 from Latin *feritās*, from *ferus* savage, untamed]

ferly (ˈfɛrlɪ) *Scot* ▷ *adj* **1** wonderful; strange ▷ *n, pl* -lies **2** a wonder; something strange or marvellous ▷ *vb* -lies, -lying, -lied (*intr*) **3** to wonder; be surprised [Old English *fǣrlic* sudden]

Fermanagh (fəˈmænə) *n* a district and historical county of SW Northern Ireland: contains the Upper and Lower Lough Erne. Pop: 58 705 (2003 est). Area (excluding water): 1700 sq km (656 sq miles)

fermata (fəˈmɑːtə) *n, pl* -tas *or* -te (-tɪ) *music* another word for **pause** (sense 5) [from Italian, from *fermare* to stop, from Latin *firmāre* to establish; see FIRM¹]

Fermat's last theorem (fɜːˈmæts) *n* (in number theory) the hypothesis that the equation $x^n + y^n = z^n$ has no integral solutions for n greater than two [named after Pierre de *Fermat* (1601–65), French mathematician]

Fermat's principle *n physics* the principle that a ray of light passes from one point to another in such a way that the time taken is a minimum

ferment *n* (ˈfɜːmɛnt) **1** any agent or substance, such as a bacterium, mould, yeast, or enzyme, that causes fermentation **2** another word for **fermentation 3** commotion; unrest ▷ *vb* (fəˈmɛnt) **4** to undergo or cause to undergo fermentation **5** to stir up or seethe with excitement [C15 from Latin *fermentum* yeast, from *fervēre* to seethe] > ferˈmentable *adj* > ferˌmentaˈbility *n* > ferˈmenter *n*

▪ **USAGE** See at **foment**

fermentation (ˌfɜːmɛnˈteɪʃən) *n* a chemical reaction in which a ferment causes an organic molecule to split into simpler substances, esp the anaerobic conversion of sugar to ethyl alcohol by yeast. Also called: **ferment** Related adj: **zymotic** > ferˈmentative *adj* > ferˈmentatively *adv* > ferˈmentativeness *n*

fermentation lock *n* a valve placed on the top of bottles of fermenting wine to allow bubbles to escape

fermi (ˈfɜːmɪ) *n* a unit of length used in nuclear physics equal to 10^{-15} metre

Fermi-Dirac statistics *n physics* the branch of quantum statistics used to calculate the permitted energy arrangements of the particles in a system in terms of the exclusion principle. Compare **Bose-Einstein statistics** [C20 named after Enrico *Fermi* (1901–54), Italian nuclear physicist and Paul *Dirac* (1902–84), English physicist]

Fermi energy *or* **level** *n* the level in the distribution of electron energies in a solid at which a quantum state is equally likely to be occupied or empty [C20 named after Enrico *Fermi* (1901–54), Italian nuclear physicist]

fermion (ˈfɜːmɪˌɒn) *n* any of a group of elementary particles, such as a nucleon, that has half-integral spin and obeys Fermi-Dirac statistics. Compare **boson** [C20 named after Enrico *Fermi* (1901–54), Italian nuclear physicist; see -ON]

fermium (ˈfɜːmɪəm) *n* a transuranic element artificially produced by neutron bombardment of plutonium. Symbol: Fm; atomic no: 100; half-life of most stable isotope, ^{257}Fm: 80 days (approx) [C20 named after Enrico *Fermi* (1901–54), Italian nuclear physicist]

fern (fɜːn) *n* **1** any tracheophyte plant of the phylum *Filicinophyta*, having roots, stems, and fronds and reproducing by spores formed in structures (sori) on the fronds. See also **tree fern 2** any of certain similar but unrelated plants, such as the sweet fern [Old English *fearn*; related to Old High German *farn*, Sanskrit *parná* leaf] > ˈfernˌlike *adj* > ˈferny *adj*

Fernando de Noronha (Portuguese ferˈnəndu di noˈrɔɲa) *n* a volcanic island in the S Atlantic northeast of Cape São Roque: constitutes a federal territory of Brazil; a penal colony since the 18th century; inhabited by military personnel. Area: 26 sq km (10 sq miles)

Fernando Po (fəˈnændəʊ pəʊ) *n* a former name (until 1973) of **Bioko**

fernbird (ˈfɜːnˌbɜːd) *n* a small brown and white New Zealand swamp bird, *Bowdleria punctata*, with a fernlike tail. Also called (NZ): **matata**

fernery (ˈfɜːnərɪ) *n, pl* -eries **1** a place where ferns are grown **2** a collection of ferns grown in such a place

fern root *n* another name for **aruhe**

fern seed *n* the minute particles by which ferns reproduce themselves, formerly thought to be invisible. Possession of them was thought to make a person invisible

ferocious (fəˈrəʊʃəs) *adj* savagely fierce or cruel: *a ferocious tiger; a ferocious argument* [C17 from Latin *ferox* fierce, untamable, warlike] > feˈrociously *adv* > ferocity (fəˈrɒsɪtɪ) *or* feˈrociousness *n*

-ferous *adj combining form* bearing or producing: *coniferous; crystalliferous*. Compare **-gerous** [from -FER + -OUS]

Ferrara (fəˈrɑːrə; Italian ferˈrara) *n* a city in N Italy, in Emilia-Romagna: a centre of the Renaissance under the House of Este; university (1391). Pop: 130 992 (2001)

ferrate (ˈfɛreɪt) *n* a salt containing the divalent ion, FeO_4^{2-}. Ferrates are derivatives of the hypothetical acid H_2FeO_4 [C19 from Latin *ferrum* iron]

ferredoxin (ˌfɛrɪˈdɒksɪn) *n* an iron- and sulphur-containing protein found in plants and

f

microorganisms and involved in photosynthesis and nitrogen fixation

ferreous ('fɛrɪəs) *adj* containing or resembling iron: *a ferreous alloy; a ferreous substance* [c17 from Latin *ferreus* made of iron, from *ferrum* iron]

ferret[1] ('fɛrɪt) *n* **1** a domesticated albino variety of the polecat *Mustela putorius*, bred for hunting rats, rabbits, etc **2 black-footed ferret** a musteline mammal, *Mustela nigripes*, of W North America, closely related to the weasels ▷ *vb* **-rets, -reting, -reted** **3** to hunt (rabbits, rats, etc) with ferrets **4** (*tr; usually foll by out*) to drive from hiding: *to ferret out snipers* **5** (*tr; usually foll by out*) to find by persistent investigation **6** (*intr*) to search around [c14 from Old French *furet*, from Latin *fur* thief] > **'ferreter** *n* > **'ferrety** *adj*

ferret[2] ('fɛrɪt) *or* **ferreting** *n* silk binding tape [c16 from Italian *fioretti* floss silk, plural of *fioretto*: a little flower, from *fiore* flower, from Latin *flōs*]

ferret badger *n* any small badger of the genus *Melogale*, of SE Asia, resembling a ferret in appearance and smell

ferri- *combining form* indicating the presence of iron, esp in the trivalent state: *ferricyanide; ferriferous.* Compare **ferro-** [from Latin *ferrum* iron]

ferriage ('fɛrɪɪdʒ) *n* **1** transportation by ferry **2** the fee charged for passage on a ferry

ferric ('fɛrɪk) *adj* of or containing iron in the trivalent state: *ferric oxide*; designating an iron (III) compound [c18 from Latin *ferrum* iron]

ferric oxide *n* a red crystalline insoluble oxide of iron that occurs as haematite and rust and is made by heating ferrous sulphate: used as a pigment and metal polish (**jeweller's rouge**), and as a sensitive coating on magnetic tape. Formula: Fe_2O_3. Systematic name: **iron (III) oxide**

ferricyanic acid (ˌfɛrɪsaɪ'ænɪk) *n* a brown soluble unstable solid tribasic acid, usually known in the form of ferricyanide salts. Formula: $H_3Fe(CN)_6$

ferricyanide (ˌfɛrɪ'saɪəˌnaɪd) *n* any salt of ferricyanic acid

ferriferous (fɛ'rɪfərəs) *adj* producing or yielding iron; iron-bearing: *a ferriferous rock*

ferrimagnetism (ˌfɛrɪ'mægnɪˌtɪzəm) *n* a phenomenon exhibited by certain substances, such as ferrites, in which the magnetic moments of neighbouring ions are antiparallel and unequal in magnitude. The substances behave like ferromagnetic materials. See also **antiferromagnetism.** > **ferrimagnetic** (ˌfɛrɪmæg'nɛtɪk) *adj*

Ferris wheel ('fɛrɪs) *n* a fairground wheel having seats freely suspended from its rim; the seats remain horizontal throughout its rotation [c19 named after G.W.G. *Ferris* (1859–96), American engineer]

ferrite ('fɛraɪt) *n* **1** any of a group of ferromagnetic highly resistive ceramic compounds with the formula MFe_2O_4, where M is usually a metal such as cobalt or zinc **2** any of the body-centred cubic allotropes of iron, such as alpha iron, occurring in steel, cast iron, etc **3** any of various microscopic grains, probably composed of iron compounds, in certain igneous rocks [c19 from FERRI- + -ITE[1]]

ferrite-rod aerial *n* a type of aerial, normally used in radio reception, consisting of a small coil of wire mounted on a ferrite core, the coil serving as a tuning inductance

ferritin ('fɛrɪtɪn) *n biochem* a protein that contains iron and plays a part in the storage of iron in the body. It occurs in the liver and spleen [c20 from FERRITE + -IN]

ferro- *combining form* **1** indicating a property of iron or the presence of iron: *ferromagnetism; ferromanganese* **2** indicating the presence of iron in the divalent state: *ferrocyanide.* Compare **ferri-** [from Latin *ferrum* iron]

ferrocene ('fɛrəʊˌsiːn) *n* a reddish-orange insoluble crystalline compound. Its molecules have an iron atom sandwiched between two cyclopentadiene rings. Formula: $Fe(C_5H_5)_2$ [c20

from FERRO- + C(YCLOPENTADI)ENE]

ferrochromium (ˌfɛrəʊ'krəʊmɪəm) *or* **ferrochrome** *n* an alloy of iron and chromium (60–72 per cent), used in the production of very hard steel

ferroconcrete (ˌfɛrəʊ'kɒnkriːt) *n* another name for **reinforced concrete**

ferrocyanic acid (ˌfɛrəʊsaɪ'ænɪk) *n* a white volatile unstable solid tetrabasic acid, usually known in the form of ferrocyanide salts. Formula: $H_4Fe(CN)_6$

ferrocyanide (ˌfɛrəʊ'saɪəˌnaɪd) *n* any salt of ferrocyanic acid, such as potassium ferrocyanide, $K_4Fe(CN)_6$

ferroelectric (ˌfɛrəʊɪ'lɛktrɪk) *adj* **1** (of a substance) exhibiting spontaneous polarization that can be reversed by the application of a suitable electric field **2** of or relating to ferroelectric substances ▷ *n* **3** a ferroelectric substance > **ˌferro'lectrically** *adv* > **ferroelectricity** (ˌfɛrəʊɪlɛk'trɪsɪtɪ, -,iːlɛk-) *n*

Ferrol (Spanish fɛ'rrɔl) *n* See **El Ferrol**

ferromagnesian (ˌfɛrəʊmæg'niːʒən) *adj* (of minerals such as biotite) containing a high proportion of iron and magnesium

ferromagnetism (ˌfɛrəʊ'mægnɪˌtɪzəm) *n* the phenomenon exhibited by substances, such as iron, that have relative permeabilities much greater than unity and increasing magnetization with applied magnetizing field. Certain of these substances retain their magnetization in the absence of the applied field. The effect is caused by the alignment of electron spin in regions called domains. Compare **diamagnetism, paramagnetism** See also **magnet, Curie-Weiss law** > **ferromagnetic** (ˌfɛrəʊmæg'nɛtɪk) *adj*

ferromanganese (ˌfɛrəʊ'mæŋgəˌniːz) *n* an alloy of iron and manganese, used in making additions of manganese to cast iron and steel

ferromolybdenum (ˌfɛrəʊmɒ'lɪbdɪnəm) *n* an alloy of iron and molybdenum used in making alloy steels

ferronickel (ˌfɛrəʊ'nɪkəl) *n* an alloy of iron and nickel used in making nickel steels

ferrosilicon (ˌfɛrəʊ'sɪlɪkən) *n* an alloy of iron and silicon, used in making cast iron and steel

ferrotype ('fɛrəʊˌtaɪp) *n* **1** a photographic print produced directly in a camera by exposing a sheet of iron or tin coated with a sensitized enamel **2** the process by which such a print is produced ▷ Also called: **tintype**

ferrous ('fɛrəs) *adj* of or containing iron in the divalent state; designating an iron (II) compound [c19 from FERRI- + -OUS]

ferrous sulphate *n* an iron salt with a saline taste, usually obtained as greenish crystals of the heptahydrate, which are converted to the white monohydrate above 100°C: used in inks, tanning, water purification, and in the treatment of anaemia. Formula: $FeSO_4$. Systematic name: **iron (II) sulphate** Also called: **copperas, green vitriol**

ferruginous (fɛ'ruːdʒɪnəs) *adj* **1** (of minerals, rocks, etc) containing iron: *a ferruginous clay* **2** rust-coloured [c17 from Latin *ferrūgineus* of a rusty colour, from *ferrūgō* iron rust, from *ferrum* iron]

ferruginous duck *n* a common European duck, *Aythya nyroca*, having reddish-brown plumage with white wing bars

ferrule *or* **ferule** ('fɛruːl, -rəl) *n* **1** a metal ring, tube, or cap placed over the end of a stick, handle, or post for added strength or stability or to increase wear **2** a side opening in a pipe that gives access for inspection or cleaning **3** a bush, gland, small length of tube, etc, esp one used for making a joint ▷ *vb* **4** (*tr*) to equip (a stick, etc) with a ferrule [c17 from Middle English *virole*, from Old French *virol*, from Latin *viriola* a little bracelet, from *viria* bracelet; influenced by Latin *ferrum* iron]

ferry ('fɛrɪ) *n, pl* **-ries 1** Also called: **ferryboat** a vessel for transporting passengers and usually vehicles across a body of water, esp as a regular service **2 a** such a service **b** (*in combination*): *a*

ferryman 3 a legal right to charge for transporting passengers by boat **4** the act or method of delivering aircraft by flying them to their destination ▷ *vb* **-ries, -rying, -ried 5** to transport or go by ferry **6** to deliver (an aircraft) by flying it to its destination **7** (*tr*) to convey (passengers, goods, etc): *the guests were ferried to the church in taxis* [Old English *ferian* to carry, bring; related to Old Norse *ferja* to transport, Gothic *farjan*; see FARE]

fertigate ('fɜːtɪˌgeɪt) *vb* **-ates, -ating, -ated** to fertilize and irrigate at the same time, by adding fertilizers to the water supply [c20 from FERTILIZE + IRRIGATE] > **ˌferti'gation** *n*

fertile ('fɜːtaɪl) *adj* **1** capable of producing offspring **2 a** (of land) having nutrients capable of sustaining an abundant growth of plants **b** (of farm animals) capable of breeding stock **3** *biology* **a** capable of undergoing growth and development: *fertile seeds; fertile eggs* **b** (of plants) capable of producing gametes, spores, seeds, or fruits **4** producing many offspring; prolific **5** highly productive; rich; abundant: *a fertile brain* **6** *physics* (of a substance) able to be transformed into fissile or fissionable material, esp in a nuclear reactor **7** conducive to productiveness: *fertile rain* [c15 from Latin *fertilis*, from *ferre* to bear] > **'fertilely** *adv* > **'fertileness** *n*

Fertile Crescent *n* an area of fertile land in the Middle East, extending around the Rivers Tigris and Euphrates in a semicircle from Israel to the Persian Gulf, where the Sumerian, Babylonian, Assyrian, Phoenician, and Hebrew civilizations flourished

fertility (fɜː'tɪlɪtɪ) *n* **1** the ability to produce offspring, esp abundantly **2** the state or quality of being fertile

fertility cult *n* the practice in some settled agricultural communities of performing religious or magical rites to ensure good weather and crops and the perpetuity of the tribe

fertility symbol *n* an object, esp a phallic symbol, used in fertility-cult ceremonies to symbolize regeneration

fertilization *or* **fertilisation** (ˌfɜːtɪlaɪ'zeɪʃən) *n* **1** the union of male and female gametes, during sexual reproduction, to form a zygote **2** the act or process of fertilizing **3** the state of being fertilized

fertilize *or* **fertilise** ('fɜːtɪˌlaɪz) *vb* (*tr*) **1** to provide (an animal, plant, or egg cell) with sperm or pollen to bring about fertilization **2** to supply (soil or water) with mineral and organic nutrients to aid the growth of plants **3** to make fertile or productive > **'ferti,lizable** *or* **'ferti,lisable** *adj*

fertilizer *or* **fertiliser** ('fɜːtɪˌlaɪzə) *n* **1** any substance, such as manure or a mixture of nitrates, added to soil or water to increase its productivity **2** an object or organism such as an insect that fertilizes an animal or plant

ferula ('fɛrʊlə, 'fɛrjʊ-) *n, pl* **-las** *or* **-lae** (-ˌliː) **1** any large umbelliferous plant of the Mediterranean genus *Ferula*, having thick stems and dissected leaves: cultivated as the source of several strongly scented gum resins, such as galbanum **2** a rare word for **ferule**[1] [c14 from Latin: giant fennel] > **ferulaceous** (ˌfɛrʊ'leɪʃəs, ˌfɛrjʊ-) *adj*

ferule[1] ('fɛruːl, -rəl) *n* **1** a flat piece of wood, such as a ruler, used in some schools to cane children on the hand ▷ *vb* **2** (*tr*) *rare* to punish with a ferule [c16 from Latin *ferula* giant fennel, whip, rod; the stalk of the plant was used for punishment]

ferule[2] ('fɛruːl, -rəl) *n* a variant spelling of **ferrule**

fervency ('fɜːvənsɪ) *n, pl* **-cies** another word for **fervour**

fervent ('fɜːvənt) *or* **fervid** ('fɜːvɪd) *adj* **1** intensely passionate; ardent: *a fervent desire to change society* **2** *archaic or poetic* boiling, burning, or glowing: *fervent heat* [c14 from Latin *fervēre* to boil, glow] > **'fervently** *or* **'fervidly** *adv* > **'ferventness** *or* **'fervidness** *n*

Fervidor French (fɛrvidɔr) *n* another name for

Thermidor [probably from *ferveur* heat + THERMIDOR]
fervour *or US* **fervor** ('fɜːvə) *n* **1** great intensity of feeling or belief; ardour; zeal **2** *rare* intense heat [c14 from Latin *fervor* heat, from *fervēre* to glow, boil]
Fès (fɛs) *or* **Fez** *n* a city in N central Morocco, traditional capital of the north: became an independent kingdom in the 11th century, at its height in the 14th century; religious centre; university (850). Pop: 664 000 (2003)
Fescennine ('fɛsɪˌnaɪn) *adj rare* scurrilous or obscene [c17 from Latin *Fescennīnus* of *Fescennia*, a city in Etruria noted for the production of mocking or obscene verse]
fescue ('fɛskjuː) *or* **fescue grass** *n* any grass of the genus *Festuca*: widely cultivated as pasture and lawn grasses, having stiff narrow leaves. See also **meadow fescue, sheep's fescue** [c14 from Old French *festu*, ultimately from Latin *festūca* stem, straw]
fess (fɛs) *vb* (*intr*; foll by *up*) *informal, chiefly US* to make a confession [c19 shortened from CONFESS]
fesse *or* **fess** (fɛs) *n heraldry* an ordinary consisting of a horizontal band across a shield, conventionally occupying a third of its length and being wider than a bar [c15 from Anglo-French *fesse*, from Latin *fascia* band, fillet]
fesse point *n heraldry* the midpoint of a shield
fest (fɛst) *n* **a** a meeting or event at which the emphasis is on a particular activity: *a fashion fest* **b** (*in combination*): *schmaltz-fest; lovefest* [c19 from German *Fest* festival]
festal ('fɛstᵊl) *adj* another word for **festive** [c15 from Latin *festum* holiday, banquet; see FEAST] > 'festally *adv*
fester ('fɛstə) *vb* **1** to form or cause to form pus **2** (*intr*) to become rotten; decay **3** to become or cause to become bitter, irritated, etc, esp over a long period of time; rankle: *resentment festered his imagination* **4** (*intr*) *informal* to be idle or inactive ▷ *n* **5** a small ulcer or sore containing pus [c13 from Old French *festre* suppurating sore, from Latin: FISTULA]
festina lente *Latin* (fɛs'tiːnə 'lɛntɪ) hasten slowly
festination (ˌfɛstɪ'neɪʃən) *n* an involuntary quickening of gait, as in some persons with Parkinson's disease [c16 from Latin *festīnātiō*, from *festīnāre* to hasten]
festival ('fɛstɪvᵊl) *n* **1** a day or period set aside for celebration or feasting, esp one of religious significance **2** any occasion for celebration, esp one which commemorates an anniversary or other significant event **3** an organized series of special events and performances, usually in one place: *a festival of drama* **4** *archaic* a time of revelry; merrymaking **5** (*modifier*) relating to or characteristic of a festival [c14 from Church Latin *fēstīvālis* of a feast, from Latin *festīvus* FESTIVE]
Festival Hall *n* a concert hall in London, on the South Bank of the Thames: constructed for the 1951 Festival of Britain; completed 1964–65. Official name: **Royal Festival Hall**
festive ('fɛstɪv) *adj* appropriate to or characteristic of a holiday, etc; merry [c17 from Latin *festīvus* joyful, from *festus* of a FEAST] > 'festively *adv* > 'festiveness *n*
festive season *n* the period immediately leading up to Christmas and ending just after New Year
festivity (fɛs'tɪvɪtɪ) *n, pl* **-ties** **1** merriment characteristic of a festival, party, etc **2** any festival or other celebration **3** (*plural*) festive proceedings; celebrations
festoon (fɛ'stuːn) *n* **1** a decorative chain of flowers, ribbons, etc, suspended in loops; garland **2** a carved or painted representation of this, as in architecture, furniture, or pottery **3** **a** the scalloped appearance of the gums where they meet the teeth **b** a design carved on the base material of a denture to simulate this **4** **a** either of two *Zerynthia* species of white pierid butterfly of southern Europe, typically mottled red, yellow, and brown **b** an ochreous brown moth, *Apoda avellana* the unusual sluglike larvae of which feed on oak leaves ▷ *vb* (*tr*) **5** to decorate or join together with festoons **6** to form into festoons [c17 from French *feston*, from Italian *festone* ornament for a feast, from *festa* FEAST]
festoon blind *n* a window blind consisting of vertical rows of horizontally gathered fabric that may be drawn up to form a series of ruches
festoonery (fɛ'stuːnərɪ) *n* an arrangement of festoons
festschrift ('fɛstˌʃrɪft) *n, pl* **-schriften** (-ʃrɪftən) *or* **-schrifts** a collection of essays or learned papers contributed by a number of people to honour an eminent scholar, esp a colleague [German, from *Fest* celebration, FEAST + *Schrift* writing]
festy ('fɛstɪ) *adj Austral slang* **1** dirty; malodorous **2** very bad [c20 shortened form of *festering*]
FET *abbreviation for* **field-effect transistor**
feta ('fɛtə) *n* a white sheep or goat cheese popular in Greece [Modern Greek, from the phrase *turi pheta*, from *turi* cheese + *pheta*, from Italian *fetta* a slice]
fetal *or* **foetal** ('fiːtᵊl) *adj* of, relating to, or resembling a fetus
fetal alcohol syndrome *n* a condition in newborn babies caused by excessive intake of alcohol by the mother during pregnancy: characterized by various defects including mental retardation
fetal diagnosis *n* prenatal determination of genetic or chemical abnormalities in a fetus, esp by amniocentesis
fetal position *n* a bodily position similar to that of a fetus in the womb, with the knees up towards the chest and the head bent forward
fetation *or* **foetation** (fiː'teɪʃən) *n* **1** the state of pregnancy **2** the process of development of a fetus
fetch[1] (fɛtʃ) *vb* (*mainly tr*) **1** to go after and bring back; get: *to fetch help* **2** to cause to come; bring or draw forth: *the noise fetched him from the cellar* **3** (*also intr*) to cost or sell for (a certain price): *the table fetched six hundred pounds* **4** to utter (a sigh, groan, etc) **5** *informal* to deal (a blow, slap, etc) **6** (*also intr*) *nautical* to arrive at or proceed by sailing **7** *informal* to attract: *to be fetched by an idea* **8** (used esp as a command to dogs) to retrieve (shot game, an object thrown, etc) **9** *rare* to draw in (a breath, gasp, etc), esp with difficulty **10** **fetch and carry** to perform menial tasks or run errands ▷ *n* **11** the reach, stretch, etc, of a mechanism **12** a trick or stratagem **13** the distance in the direction of the prevailing wind that air or water can travel continuously without obstruction [Old English *feccan*; related to Old Norse *feta* to step, Old High German *sih fazzōn* to climb]
fetch[2] (fɛtʃ) *n* the ghost or apparition of a living person [c18 of unknown origin]
fetcher ('fɛtʃə) *n* **1** a person or animal that fetches **2** *rugby informal* a flanker who specializes in winning the ball rather than running with it
fetching ('fɛtʃɪŋ) *adj informal* **1** attractively befitting: *a fetching hat* **2** charming: *a fetching personality* > 'fetchingly *adv*
fetch up *vb* (*adverb*) **1** (*intr*; usually foll by *at* or *in*) *informal* to arrive (at) or end up (in): *to fetch up in New York* **2** (*intr*) *nautical* to stop suddenly, as from running aground: *to fetch up on a rock* **3** *slang* to vomit (food, etc) **4** (*tr*) *Brit dialect* to rear (children, animals, etc)
fête *or* **fete** (feɪt) *n* **1** a gala, bazaar, or similar entertainment, esp one held outdoors in aid of charity **2** a feast day or holiday, esp one of religious significance **3** *Caribbean informal* an organized group entertainment, esp a party or a dance ▷ *vb* **4** (*tr*) to honour or entertain with or as if with a fête: *the author was fêted by his publishers* **5** (*intr*) *Caribbean informal* to join in a fête [c18 from French: FEAST]
fête champêtre *French* (fɛt ʃɑ̃pɛtrə) *n, pl* ***fêtes champêtres*** (fɛt ʃɑ̃pɛtrə) **1** a garden party, picnic, or similar outdoor entertainment **2** Also called: **fête galante** (fɛt galɑ̃t) *arts* **a** a genre of painting popular in France from the early 18th century, characterized by the depiction of figures in pastoral settings. Watteau was its most famous exponent **b** a painting in this genre [c18 from French, literally: country festival]
fetial ('fiːʃəl) *n, pl* **fetiales** (ˌfiːʃɪ'eɪliːz) **1** (in ancient Rome) any of the 20 priestly heralds involved in declarations of war and in peace negotiations ▷ *adj* **2** of or relating to the fetiales **3** a less common word for **heraldic** [c16 from Latin *fētiālis*, probably from Old Latin *fētis* treaty]
feticide *or* **foeticide** ('fiːtɪˌsaɪd) *n* the destruction of a fetus in the uterus; aborticide > ˌfeti'cidal *or* ˌfoeti'cidal *adj*
fetid *or* **foetid** ('fɛtɪd, 'fiː-) *adj* having a stale nauseating smell, as of decay [c16 from Latin *fētidus*, from *fētēre* to stink; related to *fūmus* smoke] > 'fetidly *or* 'foetidly *adv* > 'fetidness *or* 'foetidness *n*
fetiparous *or* **foetiparous** (fɪ'tɪpərəs) *adj* (of marsupials, such as the kangaroo) giving birth to incompletely developed offspring [c19 from FETUS + -PAROUS]
fetish *or* **fetich** ('fɛtɪʃ, 'fiːtɪʃ) *n* **1** something, esp an inanimate object, that is believed in certain cultures to be the embodiment or habitation of a spirit or magical powers **2** **a** a form of behaviour involving fetishism **b** any object that is involved in fetishism **3** any object, activity, etc, to which one is excessively or irrationally devoted: *to make a fetish of cleanliness* [c17 from French *fétiche*, from Portuguese *feitiço* (n) sorcery, from adj: artificial, from Latin *factīcius* made by art, FACTITIOUS] > 'fetish-ˌlike *or* 'fetich-ˌlike *adj*
fetishism *or* **fetichism** ('fɛtɪˌʃɪzəm, 'fiː-) *n* **1** a condition in which the handling of an inanimate object or a specific part of the body other than the sexual organs is a source of sexual satisfaction **2** belief in or recourse to a fetish for magical purposes **3** excessive attention or attachment to something > 'fetishist *or* 'fetichist *n* > ˌfetish'istic *or* ˌfetich'istic *adj*
fetishize *or* **fetishise** ('fɛtɪʃˌaɪz) *vb* (*tr*) to be excessively or irrationally devoted to (an object, activity, etc) > ˌfetishi'zation *or* ˌfetishi'sation *n*
fetlock ('fɛtˌlɒk) *or* **fetterlock** *n* **1** a projection behind and above a horse's hoof: the part of the leg between the cannon bone and the pastern **2** Also called: **fetlock joint** the joint at this part of the leg **3** the tuft of hair growing from this part [C14 *fetlak*; related to Middle High German *vizzeloch* fetlock, from *vizzel* pastern + *-och*; see FOOT]
fetor *or* **foetor** ('fiːtə, -tɔː) *n* an offensive stale or putrid odour; stench [c15 from Latin, from *fētēre* to stink]
fetoscope ('fiːtəʊˌskəʊp) *n* a fibreoptic instrument that can be passed through the abdomen of a pregnant woman to enable examination of the fetus and withdrawal of blood for sampling in prenatal diagnosis > **fetoscopy** (fiː'tɒskəpɪ) *n*
fetter ('fɛtə) *n* **1** (*often plural*) a chain or bond fastened round the ankle; shackle **2** (*usually plural*) a check or restraint: *in fetters* ▷ *vb* (*tr*) **3** to restrict or confine **4** to bind in fetters [Old English *fetor*; related to Old Norse *fjöturr* fetter, Old High German *fezzera*, Latin *pedica* fetter, *impedīre* to hinder] > 'fetterer *n* > 'fetterless *adj*
fetter bone *n* another name for **pastern** (sense 2)
fetterlock ('fɛtəˌlɒk) *n* another name for **fetlock**
fettle ('fɛtᵊl) *vb* (*tr*) **1** to remove (excess moulding material and casting irregularities) from a cast component **2** to line or repair (the walls of a furnace) **3** *Brit dialect* **a** to prepare or arrange (a thing, oneself, etc), esp to put a finishing touch to **b** to repair or mend (something) ▷ *n* **4** state of health, spirits, etc (esp in the phrase **in fine fettle**) **5** another name for **fettling** [C14 (in the sense: to put in order): back formation from *fetled* girded up, from Old English *fetel* belt]
fettler ('fɛtlə) *n Brit, Austral* a person employed to

f

maintain railway tracks

fettling ('fɛtlɪŋ) *n* a refractory material used to line the hearth of puddling furnaces. Also called: **fettle**

fettucine, fettuccine *or* **fettuccini** (ˌfɛtuˈtʃiːnɪ) *n* a type of pasta in the form of narrow ribbons [Italian *fettuccine*, plural of *fettuccina*, diminutive of *fetta* slice]

fetus *or* **foetus** ('fiːtəs) *n, pl* **-tuses** the embryo of a mammal in the later stages of development, when it shows all the main recognizable features of the mature animal, esp a human embryo from the end of the second month of pregnancy until birth. Compare **embryo** (sense 2) [c14 from Latin: offspring, brood]

feu (fjuː) *n* **1** *Scot legal history* **a** a feudal tenure of land for which rent was paid in money or grain instead of by the performance of military service **b** the land so held **2** *Scots law* a right to the use of land in return for a fixed annual payment (**feu duty**) [c15 from Old French; see FEE]

feuar ('fjuə) *n Scot* the tenant of a feu

feud¹ (fjuːd) *n* **1** long and bitter hostility between two families, clans, or individuals; vendetta **2** a quarrel or dispute ▷ *vb* **3** (*intr*) to take part in or carry on a feud [c13 *fede*, from Old French *feide*, from Old High German *fēhida*; related to Old English *fæhth* hostility; see FOE]

feud² *or* **feod** (fjuːd) *n feudal law* land held in return for service [c17 from Medieval Latin *feodum*, of Germanic origin; see FEE]

feudal¹ ('fjuːdªl) *adj* **1** of, resembling, relating to, or characteristic of feudalism or its institutions **2** of, characteristic of, or relating to a fief. Compare **allodial 3** *disparaging* old-fashioned, reactionary, etc [c17 from Medieval Latin *feudālis*, from *feudum* FEUD²]

feudal² ('fjuːdªl) *adj* of or relating to a feud or quarrel

feudalism ('fjuːdəˌlɪzəm) *n* **1** Also called: **feudal system** the legal and social system that evolved in W Europe in the 8th and 9th centuries, in which vassals were protected and maintained by their lords, usually through the granting of fiefs, and were required to serve under them in war. See also **vassalage, fief 2** any social system or society, such as medieval Japan or Ptolemaic Egypt, that resembles medieval European feudalism
> **'feudalist** *n* > **ˌfeudal'istic** *adj*

feudality (fjuːˈdælɪtɪ) *n, pl* **-ties 1** the state or quality of being feudal **2** a fief or fee

feudalize *or* **feudalise** ('fjuːdəˌlaɪz) *vb* (*tr*) to make feudal; create feudal institutions in (a society) > **ˌfeudali'zation** *or* **ˌfeudali'sation** *n*

feudatory ('fjuːdətərɪ, -trɪ) (in feudal Europe) *n* **1** a person holding a fief; vassal ▷ *adj* **2** relating to or characteristic of the relationship between lord and vassal **3** (esp of a kingdom) under the overlordship of another sovereign [c16 from Medieval Latin *feudātor*]

feu de joie *French* (fø də ʒwa) *n, pl* **feux de joie** (fø) a salute of musketry fired successively by each man in turn along a line and back [c18 literally: fire of joy]

feudist ('fjuːdɪst) *n US* a person who takes part in a feud or quarrel

Feuillant *French* (fœjɑ̃) *n French history* a member of a club formed in 1791 by Lafayette advocating a limited constitutional monarchy: forced to disband in 1792 as the revolution became more violent and antimonarchical [from the convent of Notre Dame des *Feuillants*, where meetings were held]

feuilleton ('fɔɪˌtɒn; *French* fœjtɔ̃) *n* **1** the part of a European newspaper carrying reviews, serialized fiction, etc **2** such a review or article [c19 from French, from *feuillet* sheet of paper, diminutive of *feuille* leaf, from Latin *folium*] > **'feuilletonism** *n* > **'feuilletonist** *n* > **ˌfeuilleton'istic** *adj*

fever ('fiːvə) *n* **1** an abnormally high body temperature, accompanied by a fast pulse rate, dry skin, etc. Related adjs: **febrile, pyretic 2** any

of various diseases, such as yellow fever or scarlet fever, characterized by a high temperature **3** intense nervous excitement or agitation: *she was in a fever about her party* ▷ *vb* **4** (*tr*) to affect with or as if with fever [Old English *fēfor*, from Latin *febris*] > **'fevered** *adj* > **'feverless** *adj*

fever blister *or* **sore** *n* another name for **cold sore**

feverfew ('fiːvəˌfjuː) *n* a bushy European strong-scented perennial plant, *Tanacetum parthenium*, with white flower heads, formerly used medicinally: family *Asteraceae* (composites) [Old English *feferfuge*, from Late Latin *febrifugia*, from Latin *febris* fever + *fugāre* to put to flight]

feverish ('fiːvərɪʃ) *or* **feverous** *adj* **1** suffering from fever, esp a slight fever **2** in a state of restless excitement **3** of, relating to, caused by, or causing fever > **'feverishly** *or* **'feverously** *adv* > **'feverishness** *n*

fever pitch *n* a state of intense excitement: *things were at fever pitch with the election coming up*

fever therapy *n* a former method of treating disease by raising the body temperature. Compare **cryotherapy**

fever tree *n US* **1** any of several trees that produce a febrifuge or tonic, esp *Pinckneya pubens*, a rubiaceous tree of SE North America **2** a tall leguminous swamp tree, *Acacia xanthophloea*, of southern Africa, with fragrant yellow flowers

feverwort ('fiːvəˌwɜːt) *n US* any of several plants considered to have medicinal properties, such as horse gentian and boneset

few (fjuː) *determiner* **1 a** a small number of; hardly any: *few men are so cruel* **b** (*as pronoun; functioning as plural*): *many are called but few are chosen* **2** (preceded by *a*) **a** a small number of: *a few drinks* **b** (*as pronoun; functioning as plural*): *a few of you* **3 a** good few *informal* several **4 a** at great intervals; widely spaced **b** not abundant; scarce **5** have a few (too many) to consume several (or too many) alcoholic drinks **6** not or quite a few *informal* several ▷ *n* **7** the few a small number of people considered as a class: *the few who fell at Thermopylae*. Compare **many** (sense 4) [Old English *fēawa*; related to Old High German *fao* little, Old Norse *fār* little, silent] > **'fewness** *n*

▣ USAGE See at **less**

fey (feɪ) *adj* **1** interested in or believing in the supernatural **2** attuned to the supernatural; clairvoyant; visionary **3** *chiefly Scot* fated to die; doomed **4** *chiefly Scot* in a state of high spirits or unusual excitement, formerly believed to presage death [Old English *fæge* marked out for death; related to Old Norse *feigr* doomed, Old High German *feigi*] > **'feyness** *n*

Feynman diagram ('faɪnmən) *n physics* a graphical representation of the interactions between elementary particles [c20 named after Richard *Feynman* (1918–88), US physicist]

fez (fɛz) *n, pl* **fezzes** an originally Turkish brimless felt or wool cap, shaped like a truncated cone, usually red and with a tassel [c19 via French from Turkish, from FEZ] > **fezzed** *adj*

Fez (fɛz) *n* a variant of **Fès**

Fezzan (fɛˈzɑːn) *n* a region of SW Libya, in the Sahara: a former province (until 1963)

ff *symbol for* **1** folios **2** following (pages, lines, etc) **3** *music* fortissimo: an instruction to play very loudly

ffa *commerce abbreviation for* free from alongside (ship)

F-factor *n informal* the quality of being attractive to members of the opposite sex [c20 from *fanciability factor*]

Ffestiniog (fɛsˈtɪnjɒg) *n* a town in N Wales, in Gwynedd: tourist attractions include former slate quarries and a narrow-gauge railway at nearby Blaenau Ffestiniog. Pop: 800 (latest est)

fi *the internet domain name for* Finland

FI *abbreviation for* Falkland Islands

FIA *abbreviation for* **1** (in Britain) Fellow of the Institute of Actuaries **2** *motor racing* Fédération

Internationale l'Automobile, Formula One's governing body [(for sense 2) from French]

fiacre (fɪˈɑːkrə) *n* a small four-wheeled horse-drawn carriage, usually with a folding roof [c17 named after the Hotel de St Fiacre, Paris, where these vehicles were first hired out]

fiancé (fɪˈɒnseɪ) *n* a man who is engaged to be married [c19 from French, from Old French *fiancier* to promise, betroth, from *fiance* a vow, from *fier* to trust, from Latin *fidere*]

fiancée (fɪˈɒnseɪ) *n* a woman who is engaged to be married

fianchetto (ˌfɪənˈtʃɛtəʊ, -ˈkɛtəʊ) *chess* ▷ *n, pl* **-tos, -ti** (-tiː) **1** the development of a bishop on the second rank of the neighbouring knight's file or the third rank of the nearer rook's file ▷ *vb* **-toes, -toing, -toed 2** to develop (a bishop) thus [c19 from Italian diminutive of *fianco* FLANK]

Fianna ('fiːənə) *pl n* a legendary band of Irish warriors noted for their heroic exploits, attributed to the 2nd and 3rd centuries AD. Also called: **Fenians**

Fianna Fáil ('fiːənə 'fɑːl) *n* one of the major Irish political parties, founded by de Valera in 1926 as a republican party [from Irish Gaelic *Fianna* warriors + *Fáil* of Ireland, from *Fál* an ancient and poetic name for Ireland]

fiasco (fɪˈæskəʊ) *n, pl* **-cos** *or* **-coes** a complete failure, esp one that is ignominious or humiliating [c19 from Italian, literally: FLASK; sense development obscure]

fiat ('faɪət, -æt) *n* **1** official sanction; authoritative permission **2** an arbitrary order or decree **3** *chiefly literary* any command, decision, or act of will that brings something about [c17 from Latin, literally: let it be done, from *fierī* to become]

fiat money *n chiefly US* money declared by a government to be legal tender though it is not convertible into standard specie

fib (fɪb) *n* **1** a trivial and harmless lie ▷ *vb* **fibs, fibbing, fibbed 2** (*intr*) to tell such a lie [c17 perhaps from *fibble-fable* an unlikely story; see FABLE] > **'fibber** *n*

fiber ('faɪbə) *n* the usual US spelling of **fibre**

Fibonacci sequence *or* **series** (ˌfiːbəˈnɑːtʃɪ) *n* the infinite sequence of numbers, 0, 1, 1, 2, 3, 5, 8, etc, in which each member (**Fibonacci number**) is the sum of the previous two [named after Leonardo *Fibonacci* (?1170–?1250), Italian mathematician]

fibre *or US* **fiber** ('faɪbə) *n* **1** a natural or synthetic filament that may be spun into yarn, such as cotton or nylon **2** cloth or other material made from such yarn **3** a long fine continuous thread or filament **4** the structure of any material or substance made of or as if of fibres; texture **5** essential substance or nature: *all the fibres of his being were stirred* **6** strength of character (esp in the phrase **moral fibre**) **7** See **dietary fibre 8** *botany* **a** a narrow elongated thick-walled cell: a constituent of sclerenchyma tissue **b** such tissue extracted from flax, hemp, etc, used to make linen, rope, etc **c** a very small root or twig **9** *anatomy* any thread-shaped structure, such as a nerve fibre [c14 from Latin *fibra* filament, entrails] > **'fibred** *or US* **'fibered** *adj* > **'fibreless** *or US* **'fiberless** *adj*

fibreboard *or US* **fiberboard** ('faɪbəˌbɔːd) *n* a building material made of compressed wood or other plant fibres, esp one in the form of a thin semirigid sheet

fibrefill *or US* **fiberfill** ('faɪbəˌfɪl) *n* a synthetic fibre used as a filling for pillows, quilted materials, etc

fibreglass *or US* **fiberglass** ('faɪbəˌglɑːs) *n* **1** material consisting of matted fine glass fibres, used as insulation in buildings, in fireproof fabrics, etc **2** a fabric woven from this material or a light strong material made by bonding fibreglass with a synthetic resin; used for car bodies, boat hulls, etc. Also called: **glass fibre**

fibre optics *n* (*functioning as singular*) the transmission of information modulated on light carried down very thin flexible fibres of glass. See also **optical fibre.** > ˌ**fibre'optic** *adj*

fibrescope *or US* **fiberscope** ('faɪbəˌskəʊp) *n* an endoscope that transmits images of the interior of a hollow organ by fibre optics

fibriform ('faɪbrɪˌfɔːm, 'fɪb-) *adj* having the form of a fibre or fibres

fibril ('faɪbrɪl) *or* **fibrilla** (faɪ'brɪlə, fɪ-) *n, pl* **-brils** *or* **-brillae** (-'brɪliː) **1** a small fibre or part of a fibre **2** *biology* a threadlike structure, such as a root hair or a thread of muscle tissue [C17 from New Latin *fibrilla* a little FIBRE] > '**fibrilar, fi'brillar** *or* **fi'brillose** *adj* > **fi'brilliˌform** *adj*

fibrillation (ˌfaɪbrɪ'leɪʃən, ˌfɪb-) *n* **1** a local and uncontrollable twitching of muscle fibres, esp of the heart, not affecting the entire muscle. **Atrial fibrillation** results in rapid and irregular heart and pulse rate. In **ventricular fibrillation**, the heart stops beating **2** irregular twitchings of the muscular wall of the heart, often interfering with the normal rhythmic contractions

fibrin ('fɪbrɪn) *n* a white insoluble elastic protein formed from fibrinogen when blood clots: forms a network that traps red cells and platelets

fibrinogen (fɪ'brɪnədʒən) *n* a soluble protein, a globulin, in blood plasma, converted to fibrin by the action of the enzyme thrombin when blood clots > **fibrinogenic** (ˌfaɪbrɪnəʊ'dʒɛnɪk) *or* **fibrinogenous** (ˌfaɪbrɪ'nɒdʒənəs) *adj*

fibrinolysis (ˌfɪbrɪ'nɒlɪsɪs) *n* the breakdown of fibrin in blood clots, esp by enzymes > **fibrinolytic** (ˌfaɪbrɪnəʊ'lɪtɪk) *adj*

fibrinous ('fɪbrɪnəs) *adj* of, containing, or resembling fibrin

fibro ('faɪbrəʊ) *n Austral informal* **1 a** short for **fibrocement b** (*as modifier*): *a fibro shack* **2** a house built of fibrocement

fibro- *combining form* **1** indicating fibrous tissue: *fibroin; fibrosis* **2** indicating fibre: *fibrocement* [from Latin *fibra* FIBRE]

fibroblast ('faɪbrəʊˌblæst) *n* a cell in connective tissue that synthesizes collagen > ˌ**fibro'blastic** *adj*

fibrocement (ˌfaɪbrəʊsɪ'mɛnt) *n* (formerly) cement combined with asbestos fibre, used esp in sheets for building

fibroid ('faɪbrɔɪd) *adj* **1** *anatomy* (of structures or tissues) containing or resembling fibres ▷ *n* **2** a benign tumour, composed of fibrous and muscular tissue, occurring in the wall of the uterus and often causing heavy menstruation

fibroin ('faɪbrəʊɪn) *n* a tough elastic protein that is the principal component of spiders' webs and raw silk

Fibrolite ('faɪbrəlaɪt) *n NZ trademark* a type of building board containing asbestos and cement

fibroma (faɪ'brəʊmə) *n, pl* **-mata** (-mətə) *or* **-mas** a benign tumour derived from fibrous connective tissue > **fibromatous** (faɪ'brɒmətəs) *adj*

fibromyalgia (ˌfaɪbrəʊmaɪ'ældʒɪə) *n* a rheumatoid disorder characterized by muscle pain and headaches

fibrosis (faɪ'brəʊsɪs) *n* the formation of an abnormal amount of fibrous tissue in an organ or part as the result of inflammation, irritation, or healing > **fibrotic** (faɪ'brɒtɪk) *adj*

fibrositis (ˌfaɪbrə'saɪtɪs) *n* inflammation of white fibrous tissue, esp that of muscle sheaths

fibrous ('faɪbrəs) *adj* consisting of, containing, or resembling fibres: *fibrous tissue* > '**fibrously** *adv* > '**fibrousness** *n*

fibrovascular (ˌfaɪbrəʊ'væskjʊlə) *adj botany* (of a vascular bundle) surrounded by sclerenchyma or within sclerenchymatous tissue

fibula ('fɪbjʊlə) *n, pl* **-lae** (-ˌliː) *or* **-las** **1** the outer and thinner of the two bones between the knee and ankle of the human leg. Compare **tibia** **2** the corresponding bone in other vertebrates **3** a metal brooch resembling a safety pin, often highly decorated, common in Europe after 1300 BC [C17 from Latin: clasp, probably from *figere* to fasten] > '**fibular** *adj*

-fic *suffix forming adjectives* causing, making, or producing: *honorific* [from Latin *-ficus*, from *facere* to do, make]

fiche (fiːʃ) *n* See **microfiche, ultrafiche**

fichu ('fiːʃuː) *n* a woman's shawl or scarf of some light material, worn esp in the 18th century [C19 from French: small shawl, from *ficher* to fix with a pin, from Latin *figere* to fasten, FIX]

fickle ('fɪkᵊl) *adj* changeable in purpose, affections, etc; capricious [Old English *ficol* deceitful; related to *fician* to wheedle, *befician* to deceive] > '**fickleness** *n*

fico ('fiːkəʊ) *n, pl* **-coes** *archaic* **1** a worthless trifle **2** another word for **fig**[1] (sense 7) [C16 from Italian: FIG[1]]

fictile ('fɪktaɪl) *adj* **1** moulded or capable of being moulded from clay; plastic **2** made of clay by a potter **3** relating to the craft of pottery [C17 from Latin *fictilis* that can be moulded, hence, made of clay, from *fingere* to shape]

fiction ('fɪkʃən) *n* **1** literary works invented by the imagination, such as novels or short stories **2** an invented story or explanation; lie **3** the act of inventing a story or explanation **4** *law* something assumed to be true for the sake of convenience, though probably false [C14 from Latin *fictiō* a fashioning, hence something imaginary, from *fingere* to shape] > '**fictional** *adj* > '**fictionally** *adv* > ˌ**fiction'eer** *or* '**fictionist** *n*

fictionalize *or* **fictionalise** ('fɪkʃənəˌlaɪz) *vb* (*tr*) to make into fiction or give a fictional aspect to > ˌ**fictionali'zation** *or* ˌ**fictionali'sation** *n*

fictitious (fɪk'tɪʃəs) *adj* **1** not genuine or authentic; assumed; false: *to give a fictitious address* **2** of, related to, or characteristic of fiction; created by the imagination > **fic'titiously** *adv* > **fic'titiousness** *n*

fictive ('fɪktɪv) *adj* **1** of, relating to, or able to create fiction **2** a rare word for **fictitious** > '**fictively** *adv*

ficus ('fiːkəs) *n* any plant of the genus *Ficus*, which includes the edible fig and several greenhouse and house plants. See **rubber plant, weeping ivy**

fid (fɪd) *n nautical* **1** a spike for separating strands of rope in splicing **2** a wooden or metal bar for supporting the heel of a topmast [C17 of unknown origin]

-fid *adj combining form* divided into parts or lobes: *bifid; pinnatifid* [from Latin *-fidus*, from *findere* to split]

Fid. Def. *or* **FID DEF** *abbreviation for* Fidei Defensor

fiddle ('fɪdᵊl) *n* **1** *informal or sometimes when used of a classical violin disparaging* any instrument of the viol or violin family, esp the violin **2** a violin played as a folk instrument **3** time-wasting or trifling behaviour; nonsense; triviality **4** *nautical* a small railing around the top of a table to prevent objects from falling off it in bad weather **5** *Brit informal* an illegal or fraudulent transaction or arrangement **6** *Brit informal* a manually delicate or tricky operation **7** **at** *or* **on the fiddle** *informal* engaged in an illegal or fraudulent undertaking **8** **face as long as a fiddle** *informal* a dismal or gloomy facial expression **9** **fit as a fiddle** *informal* in very good health **10** **play second fiddle** *informal* to be subordinate; play a minor part ▷ *vb* **11** to play (a tune) on the fiddle **12** (*intr; often foll by with*) to make restless or aimless movements with the hands **13** (when *intr*, often foll by *about* or *around*) *informal* to spend (time) or act in a careless or inconsequential manner; waste (time) **14** (often foll by *with*) *informal* to tamper or interfere (with) **15** *informal* to contrive to do (something) by illicit means or deception: *he fiddled his way into a position of trust* **16** (*tr*) *informal* to falsify (accounts, etc); swindle [Old English *fithele*, probably from Medieval Latin *vitula*, from Latin *vītulārī* to celebrate; compare Old High German *fidula* fiddle; see VIOLA[1]]

fiddle-back *n* **1** a chair with a fiddle-shaped back **2** a chasuble with a fiddle-shaped front

fiddle-de-dee, fiddlededee *or* **fiddlededeedee** (ˌfɪdᵊldɪ'diː) *interj rare* an exclamation of impatience, disbelief, or disagreement

fiddle-faddle ('fɪdᵊlˌfædᵊl) *n, interj* **1** trivial matter; nonsense ▷ *vb* **2** (*intr*) to fuss or waste time, esp over trivial matters [C16 reduplication of FIDDLE] > '**fiddle-ˌfaddler** *n*

fiddlehead ('fɪdᵊlˌhɛd) *or* **fiddleneck** *n* **1** *nautical* an ornamental carving, in the shape of the scroll at the head end of a fiddle, fitted to the top of the stem or cutwater **2** *US and Canadian* the edible coiled tip of a young fern frond

fiddle pattern *n* the style of a spoon or fork with a violin-shaped handle

fiddler ('fɪdlə) *n* **1** a person who plays the fiddle, esp in folk music **2** See **fiddler crab** **3** a person who wastes time or acts aimlessly **4** *informal* a cheat or petty rogue

fiddler crab *n* any of various burrowing crabs of the genus *Uca* of American coastal regions, the males of which have one of their anterior pincer-like claws very much enlarged [C19 referring to the rapid fiddling movement of the enlarged anterior claw of the males, used to attract females]

fiddlestick ('fɪdᵊlˌstɪk) *n* **1** *informal* a violin bow **2** any meaningless or inconsequential thing; trifle **3** **fiddlesticks!** an expression of annoyance or disagreement

fiddlewood ('fɪdᵊlˌwʊd) *n* **1** any of various tropical American verbenaceous trees of the genus *Citharexylum* and related genera **2** the hard durable wood of any of these trees

fiddling ('fɪdlɪŋ) *adj* trifling or insignificant; petty

fiddly ('fɪdlɪ) *adj* **-dlier, -dliest** small and awkward to do or handle

FIDE *abbreviation for* Fédération Internationale des Echecs: International Chess Federation

fideicommissary (ˌfɪdɪaɪ'kɒmɪsərɪ) *civil law* ▷ *n, pl* **-saries** **1** a person who receives a fideicommissum ▷ *adj* **2** of, relating to, or resembling a fideicommissum

fideicommissum (ˌfɪdɪaɪkə'mɪsəm) *n, pl* **-sa** (-sə) *civil law* a gift of property, usually by will, to be held on behalf of another who cannot receive the gift directly [C18 from Late Latin: (something) bequeathed in trust, from Latin *fidēs* trust, faith + *committere* to entrust]

Fidei Defensor *Latin* ('faɪdɪˌaɪ dɪ'fɛnsɔː) *n* defender of the faith; a title given to Henry VIII by Pope Leo X, and appearing on Brit coins as FID DEF or FD

fideism ('fiːdeɪˌɪzəm) *n* the theological doctrine that religious truth is a matter of faith and cannot be established by reason. Compare **natural theology** [C19 from Latin *fidēs* faith] > '**fideist** *n* > ˌ**fide'istic** *adj*

Fidelism (fiː'dɛlɪzəm) *n* belief in, adherence to, or advocacy of the principles of Fidel Castro, the Cuban Communist statesman (born 1927). Also called: **Castroism** > **Fi'delist** *n*

fidelity (fɪ'dɛlɪtɪ) *n, pl* **-ties** **1** devotion to duties, obligations, etc; faithfulness **2** loyalty or devotion, as to a person or cause **3** faithfulness to one's spouse, lover, etc **4** adherence to truth; accuracy in reporting detail **5** *electronics* the degree to which the output of a system, such as an amplifier or radio, accurately reproduces the characteristics of the input signal. See also **high fidelity** [C15 from Latin *fidēlitās*, from *fidēlis* faithful, from *fidēs* faith, loyalty]

fidge (fɪdʒ) *vb* (*intr*) an obsolete word for **fidget** [C18 probably variant of dialect *fitch* to FIDGET]

fidget ('fɪdʒɪt) *vb* **1** (*intr*) to move about restlessly **2** (*intr; often foll by with*) to make restless or uneasy movements (with something); fiddle: *he fidgeted with his pen* **3** (*tr*) to cause to fidget **4** (*tr*) to cause to worry; make uneasy ▷ *n* **5** (*often plural*) a state of restlessness or unease, esp as expressed in continual motion: *he's got the fidgets* **6** a person who fidgets [C17 from earlier *fidge*, probably from Old Norse *fikjast* to desire eagerly] > '**fidgetingly** *adv* > '**fidgety** *adj*

fiducial (fɪ'djuːʃɪəl) *adj* **1** *physics* used as a standard of reference or measurement: *a fiducial point* **2** of or

f

based on trust or faith **3** *law* a less common word for **fiduciary** [c17 from Late Latin *fidūciālis* , from Latin *fidūcia* confidence, reliance, from *fidere* to trust] ▷ fi'ducially *adv*

fiduciary (fɪ'djuːʃərɪ) *law* ▷ *n*, *pl* -aries **1** a person bound to act for another's benefit, as a trustee in relation to his beneficiary ▷ *adj* **2 a** having the nature of a trust **b** of or relating to a trust or trustee [c17 from Latin *fidūciārius* relating to something held in trust, from *fidūcia* trust; see FIDUCIAL] ▷ fi'duciarily *adv*

fiduciary issue *n* an issue of banknotes not backed by gold

fidus Achates ('faɪdəs ə'keɪtiːz) *n* a faithful friend or companion [Latin, literally: faithful Achates, the name of the faithful companion of Aeneas in Virgil's *Aeneid*]

fie (faɪ) *interj obsolete or facetious* an exclamation of distaste or mock dismay [c13 from Old French *fi*, from Latin *fi*, exclamation of disgust]

fief *or* **feoff** (fiːf) *n* (in feudal Europe) the property or fee granted to a vassal for his maintenance by his lord in return for service [c17 from Old French *fie*, of Germanic origin; compare Old English *fēo* cattle, money, Latin *pecus* cattle, *pecūnia* money, Greek *pokos* fleece]

fiefdom ('fiːfdəm) *n* **1** (in feudal Europe) the property owned by a lord **2** an area over which a person or organization exerts authority or influence

field (fiːld) *n* **1** an open tract of uncultivated grassland; meadow. Related adj: **campestral 2** a piece of land cleared of trees and undergrowth, usually enclosed with a fence or hedge and used for pasture or growing crops: *a field of barley* **3** a limited or marked off area, usually of mown grass, on which any of various sports, athletic competitions, etc, are held: *a soccer field* **4** an area that is rich in minerals or other natural resources: *a coalfield* **5** short for **battlefield, airfield 6** the mounted followers that hunt with a pack of hounds **7 a** all the runners in a particular race or competitors in a competition **b** the runners in a race or competitors in a competition excluding the favourite **8** *cricket* the fielders collectively, esp with regard to their positions **9** a wide or open expanse: *a field of snow* **10 a** an area of human activity: *the field of human knowledge* **b** a sphere or division of knowledge, interest, etc: *his field is physics* **11 a** a place away from the laboratory, office, library, etc, usually out of doors, where practical work is done or original material or data collected **b** (*as modifier*): *a field course* **12** the surface or background, as of a flag, coin, or heraldic shield, on which a design is displayed **13** Also called: **field of view** the area within which an object may be observed with a telescope, microscope, etc **14** *physics* **a** See **field of force b** a region of space that is a vector field **c** a region of space under the influence of some scalar quantity, such as temperature **15** *maths* a set of entities subject to two binary operations, addition and multiplication, such that the set is a commutative group under addition and the set, minus the zero, is a commutative group under multiplication and multiplication is distributive over addition **16** *maths, logic* the set of elements that are either arguments or values of a function; the union of its domain and range **17** *computing* a set of one or more characters comprising a unit of information **b** a predetermined section of a record **18** *television* one of two or more sets of scanning lines which when interlaced form the complete picture **19** *obsolete* the open country: *beasts of the field* **20 hold** *or* **keep the field** to maintain one's position in the face of opposition **21 in the field a** *military* in an area in which operations are in progress **b** actively or closely involved with or working on something (rather than being in a more remote or administrative position) **22 lead the field** to be in the leading or most pre-eminent position **23 leave the field**

informal to back out of a competition, contest, etc **24 take the field** to begin or carry on activity, esp in sport or military operations **25 play the field** *informal* to disperse one's interests or attentions among a number of activities, people, or objects **26** (*modifier*) *military* of or relating to equipment, personnel, etc, specifically designed or trained for operations in the field: *a field gun; a field army* ▷ *vb* **27** (*tr*) *sport* to stop, catch, or return (the ball) as a fielder **28** (*tr*) *sport* to send (a player or team) onto the field to play **29** (*intr*) *sport* (of a player or team) to act or take turn as a fielder or fielders **30** (*tr*) *military* to put (an army, a unit, etc) in the field **31** (*tr*) to enter (a person) in a competition: *each party fielded a candidate* **32** (*tr*) *informal* to deal with or handle, esp adequately and by making a reciprocal gesture: *to field a question* [Old English *feld*; related to Old Saxon, Old High German *feld*, Old English *fold* earth, Greek *platus* broad]

field ambulance *n military* a mobile medical unit that accepts casualties from forward units, treating the lightly wounded and stabilizing the condition of the seriously wounded before evacuating them to a hospital

field army *n military* the largest formation of a land force, usually consisting of two or more corps with supporting arms and services

field artillery *n* artillery capable of deployment in support of front-line troops, due mainly to its mobility

field battery *n* a small unit of usually four field guns

field boot *n* a close-fitting knee-length boot

field captain *n* the senior official at an archery meeting, responsible for safety

field centre *n* a research centre equipped for field studies, usually located in or near an area of scientific interest

field corn *n US* any variety of corn that is grown as a feed for livestock

field cornet *n South African* a commander of burgher troops called up in time of war or in an emergency, esp during the 19th century. Often shortened to: **cornet**

fieldcraft ('fiːld,krɑːft) *n* ability and experience in matters concerned with living out-of-doors, esp in a wild area

field day *n* **1** a day spent in some special outdoor activity, such as nature study or sport **2** a day-long competition between amateur radio operators using battery or generator power, the aim being to make the most contacts with other operators around the world **3** *military* a day devoted to manoeuvres or exercises, esp before an audience **4** *informal* a day or time of exciting or successful activity: *the children had a field day with their new toys* **5** *Austral* **a** a day or series of days devoted to the demonstration of farm machinery in country centres **b** a combined open day and sale on a stud property

field drain *or* **tile** *n* an underground earthenware pipe used for draining fields

field-effect transistor *n* a unipolar transistor consisting of three or more electrode regions, the source, one or more gates, and the drain. A current flowing in a channel between the highly doped source and drain is controlled by the electric field arising from a voltage applied between source and gate. Abbreviation: **FET** See also **JFET, IGFET**

field emission *n* the emission of electrons from a solid or liquid subjected to a high electric field

fielder ('fiːldə) *n cricket, baseball* **a** a player in the field **b** a member of the fielding rather than the batting side

field event *n* a competition, such as the discus, high jump, etc, that takes place on a field or similar area as opposed to those on the running track

fieldfare ('fiːld,feə) *n* a large Old World thrush, *Turdus pilaris*, having a pale grey head and rump, brown wings and back, and a blackish tail [Old

English *feldefare*; see FIELD, FARE]

field glass *n* **1** a small telescope often incorporating a prism and held in one hand **2** a former name for **field glasses**

field glasses *pl n* another name for **binoculars** Former name: **field glass**

field goal *n* **1** *basketball* a goal scored while the ball is in normal play rather than from a free throw **2** *American football* a score of three points made by kicking the ball through the opponent's goalposts above the crossbar

field guidance *n* a method of guiding a missile to a point within a gravitational or radio field by means of the properties of the field

field gun *n* a gun specially designed for service in direct support of front-line troops

field hockey *n US and Canadian* hockey played on a field, as distinguished from ice hockey

field-holler *n* a cry employing falsetto, portamento, and sudden changes of pitch, used in African-American work songs, later integrated into the techniques of the blues

field hospital *n* a temporary hospital set up near a battlefield equipped to provide remedial surgery and post-operative care

field layer *n* See **layer** (sense 2)

field magnet *n* a permanent magnet or an electromagnet that produces the magnetic field in a generator, electric motor, or similar device

field marshal *n* an officer holding the highest rank in the British and certain other armies

fieldmouse ('fiːld,maʊs) *n*, *pl* -mice **1** any nocturnal mouse of the genus *Apodemus*, inhabiting woods, fields, and gardens of the Old World: family *Muridae*. They have yellowish-brown fur and feed on fruit, vegetables, seeds, etc **2** a former name for **vole**[1]

field officer *n* an officer holding **field rank**, namely that of major, lieutenant colonel, or colonel

field of fire *n* the area that a weapon or group of weapons can cover with fire from a given position

field of force *n* the region of space surrounding a body, such as a charged particle or a magnet, within which it can exert a force on another similar body not in contact with it. See also **electric field, magnetic field, gravitational field**

field of honour *n* the place or scene of a battle or duel, esp of jousting tournaments in medieval times

fieldpiece ('fiːld,piːs) *n* a former name for **field gun**

field poppy *n* another name for **corn poppy**

field post office *n* a place to which mail intended for military units in the field is sent to be sorted and forwarded. Abbreviation: **FPO**

fieldsman ('fiːldzmən) *n*, *pl* -men *cricket* another name for **fielder**

field spaniel *n* a robust, low-slung breed of spaniel developed by crossing the cocker spaniel with the Sussex spaniel

field sports *pl n* sports carried on in the open countryside, such as hunting, shooting, or fishing

fieldstone ('fiːld,stəʊn) *n* building stone found in fields

field strength *n* **1** *radio, television* the intensity of an electromagnetic wave at any point in the area covered by a radio or television transmitter **2** *physics* the intensity of an electric or magnetic field. See **intensity**

field study *n* (*often plural*) a research project carried out in the field. See **field** (sense 11)

field tile *n Brit and NZ* an earthenware drain used in farm drainage

field trial *n* **1** *hunting* a test of or contest between gun dogs to determine their proficiency and standard of training in retrieving or pointing **2** (*often plural*) a test to display performance, efficiency, or durability, as of a vehicle or invention

field trip *n* an expedition, as by a group of

students or research workers, to study something at first hand
field winding ('waɪndɪŋ) *n* the insulated current-carrying coils on a field magnet that produce the magnetic field intensity required to set up the electrical excitation in a generator or motor
fieldwork ('fiːldˌwɜːk) *n military* a temporary structure used in defending or fortifying a place or position
field work *n* an investigation or search for material, data, etc, made in the field as opposed to the classroom, laboratory, or official headquarters > **field worker** *n*
fiend (fiːnd) *n* **1** an evil spirit; demon; devil **2** a person who is extremely wicked, esp in being very cruel or brutal **3** *informal* **a** a person who is intensely interested in or fond of something: *a fresh-air fiend; he is a fiend for cards* **b** an addict: *a drug fiend* **4** (*Informal*) a mischievous or spiteful person, esp a child [Old English *fēond*; related to Old Norse *fjāndi* enemy, Gothic *fijands*, Old High German *fiant*] > **'fiendˌlike** *adj*
Fiend (fiːnd) *n* **the** the devil; Satan
fiendish ('fiːndɪʃ) *adj* **1** of or like a fiend **2** diabolically wicked or cruel **3** *informal* extremely difficult or unpleasant: *a fiendish problem* > **'fiendishly** *adv* > **'fiendishness** *n*
fier *or* **fiere** (fiːr) *n Scot* variant spellings of **fere**
fierce (fɪəs) *adj* **1** having a violent and unrestrained nature; savage: *a fierce dog* **2** wild or turbulent in force, action, or intensity: *a fierce storm* **3** vehement, intense, or strong: *fierce competition* **4** *informal* very disagreeable or unpleasant [C13 from Old French *fiers*, from Latin *ferus*] > **'fiercely** *adv* > **'fierceness** *n*
fieri facias ('faɪəˌraɪ 'feɪʃɪəs) *n law* a writ ordering a levy on the belongings of an adjudged debtor to satisfy the debt [C15 from Latin, literally: cause (it) to be done]
fiery ('faɪərɪ) *adj* **fierier, fieriest 1** of, containing, or composed of fire **2** resembling fire in heat, colour, ardour, etc: *a fiery desert wind; a fiery speaker* **3** easily angered or aroused: *a fiery temper* **4** (of food) producing a burning sensation: *a fiery curry* **5** (of the skin or a sore) inflamed **6** flammable or containing flammable gas **7** (of a cricket pitch) making the ball bounce dangerously high > **'fierily** *adv* > **'fieriness** *n*
fiery cross *n* **1** a burning cross, used as a symbol by the Ku Klux Klan **2** a wooden cross with ends charred or dipped in blood formerly used by Scottish Highlanders to summon the clans to battle
Fiesole (*Italian* 'fiɛːzole) *n* a town in central Italy, in Tuscany near Florence: Etruscan and Roman remains. Pop: 14 085 (2001). Ancient name: **Faesulae** ('fiːsʊliː)
fiesta (fɪ'ɛstə; *Spanish* 'fjesta) *n* (esp in Spain and Latin America) **1** a religious festival or celebration, esp on a saint's day **2** a holiday or carnival [Spanish, from Latin *festa*, plural of *festum* festival; see FEAST]
FIFA ('fiːfə) *n acronym for* Fédération Internationale de Football Association [from French]
fife (faɪf) *n* **1** a small high-pitched flute similar to the piccolo and usually having no keys, used esp in military bands ▷ *vb* **2** to play (music) on a fife [C16 from Old High German *pfīfa*; see PIPE¹] > **'fifer** *n*
Fife (faɪf) *n* a council area and historical county of E central Scotland, bordering on the North Sea between the Firths of Tay and Forth: coastal lowlands in the north and east, with several ranges of hills; mainly agricultural. Administrative centre: Glenrothes. Pop: 352 040 (2003 est). Area: 1323 sq km (511 sq miles)
fife rail *n nautical* a rail at the base of a mast of a sailing vessel, fitted with pins for belaying running rigging. Compare **pin rail** [C18 of unknown origin]
fifi hook ('fiːfiː) *n mountaineering* a metal hook at the top of an étrier for attaching it to a peg and also connected by a cord to the climber's harness to pull the étrier up and prevent it being dropped [C20 of unknown origin]
FIFO ('faɪfəʊ) *n acronym for* first in, first out (as an accounting principle in costing stock). Compare **LIFO**
fifteen ('fɪf'tiːn) *n* **1** the cardinal number that is the sum of ten and five **2** a numeral, 15, XV, etc, representing this number **3** something represented by, representing, or consisting of 15 units **4** a rugby football team ▷ *determiner* **5 a** amounting to fifteen: *fifteen jokes* **b** (*as pronoun*): *fifteen of us danced* [Old English *fīftēne*]
Fifteen ('fɪf'tiːn) *n* **the** *Brit history* the Jacobite rising of 1715
fifteenth ('fɪf'tiːnθ) *adj* **1 a** coming after the fourteenth in order, position, time, etc. Often written: 15th **b** (*as noun*): *the fifteenth of the month* ▷ *n* **2 a** one of 15 equal or nearly equal parts of something **b** (*as modifier*): *a fifteenth part* **3** the fraction equal to one divided by 15 (1/15) **4 a** an interval of two octaves **b** one of two notes constituting such an interval in relation to the other, esp the one higher in pitch **c** an organ stop of diapason quality sounding a note two octaves higher than that normally produced by the key depressed; a two-foot stop
fifth (fɪfθ) *adj* (*usually prenominal*) **1 a** coming after the fourth in order, position, time, etc. Often written: 5th **b** (*as noun*): *he came on the fifth* ▷ *n* **2 a** one of five equal or nearly equal parts of an object, quantity, measurement, etc **b** (*as modifier*): *a fifth part* **3** the fraction equal to one divided by five (1/5) **4** *music* **a** the interval between one note and another five notes away from it counting inclusively along the diatonic scale **b** one of two notes constituting such an interval in relation to the other. See also **perfect** (sense 9), **diminished** (sense 2), **interval** (sense 5) **5** an additional high gear fitted to some motor vehicles ▷ *adv* **6** Also: **fifthly** after the fourth person, position, event, etc ▷ *sentence connector* **7** Also: **fifthly** as the fifth point: linking what follows with the previous statements, as in a speech or argument [Old English *fifta*]
Fifth Amendment *n* **1** an amendment to the US Constitution stating that no person may be compelled to testify against himself and that no person may be tried for a second time on a charge for which he has already been acquitted **2 take the fifth (amendment)** *US* to refuse to answer a question on the grounds that it might incriminate oneself
fifth column *n* **1** (originally) a group of Falangist sympathizers in Madrid during the Spanish Civil War who were prepared to join the four columns of insurgents marching on the city **2** any group of hostile or subversive infiltrators; an enemy in one's midst > **fifth columnist** *n*
fifth disease *n* a mild infectious disease of childhood, caused by a virus, characterized by fever and a red rash spreading from the cheeks to the limbs and trunk. Also called: **slapped-cheek disease** Technical name: **erythema infectiosum** [C20 from its being among the five most common childhood infections]
fifth force *n* a hypothetical non-Newtonian repulsive component of the force of gravity, postulated as an addition to the four known fundamental forces (gravitational, electromagnetic, strong, and weak)
fifth-generation *adj* denoting developments in computer design to produce machines with artifical intelligence
Fifth Republic *n* the French republic established in 1958 as the successor to the Fourth Republic. Its constitution is characterized by the strong position of the president
fifth wheel *n* **1** a spare wheel for a four-wheeled vehicle **2 a** the coupling table of an articulated vehicle **b** a steering bearing that enables the front axle of a horse-drawn vehicle to rotate relative to the body **3** a superfluous or unnecessary person or thing
fiftieth ('fɪftɪɪθ) *adj* **1 a** being the ordinal number of *fifty* in order, position, time, etc. Often written: 50th **b** (*as noun*): *the fiftieth in the series* ▷ *n* **2 a** one of 50 equal or approximately equal parts of something **b** (*as modifier*): *a fiftieth part* **3** the fraction equal to one divided by 50 (1/50)
fifty ('fɪftɪ) *n, pl* **-ties 1** the cardinal number that is the product of ten and five **2** a numeral, 50, L, etc, representing this number **3** something represented by, representing, or consisting of 50 units ▷ *determiner* **4 a** amounting to fifty: *fifty people* **b** (*as pronoun*): *fifty should be sufficient* [Old English *fīftig*]
fifty-fifty *adj, adv informal* shared or sharing equally; in equal parts
fig¹ (fɪg) *n* **1** any moraceous tree or shrub of the tropical and subtropical genus *Ficus*, in which the flowers are borne inside a pear-shaped receptacle **2** the fruit of any of these trees, esp of *F. carica*, which develops from the receptacle and has sweet flesh containing numerous seedlike structures **3** any of various plants or trees having a fruit similar to this **4 Hottentot** *or* **sour fig** a succulent plant, *Mesembryanthemum edule*, of southern Africa, having a capsular fruit containing edible pulp: family *Aizoaceae* **5** (*used with a negative*) something of negligible value; jot: *I don't care a fig for your opinion* **6** Also: **feg** *dialect* a piece or segment from an orange **7** Also called: **fico** an insulting gesture made with the thumb between the first two fingers or under the upper teeth [C13 from Old French *figue*, from Old Provençal *figa*, from Latin *ficus* fig tree]
fig² (fɪg) *slang* ▷ *vb* **figs, figging, figged** (*tr*) **1** (foll by *out* or *up*) to dress (up) or rig (out) **2** to administer stimulating drugs to (a horse) ▷ *n* **3** dress, appearance, or array (esp in the phrase **in full fig**) **4** physical condition or form: *in bad fig* [C17 *feague*, of uncertain origin] **f**
fig.³ *abbreviation for* **1** figurative(ly) **2** figure
fig-bird *n* any Australian oriole of the genus *Sphecotheres*, feeding on figs and other fruit
fight (faɪt) *vb* **fights, fighting, fought 1** to oppose or struggle against (an enemy) in battle **2** to oppose or struggle against (a person, thing, cause, etc) in any manner **3** (*tr*) to engage in or carry on (a battle, contest, etc) **4** (when *intr* often foll by *for*) to uphold or maintain (a cause, ideal, etc) by fighting or struggling: *to fight for freedom* **5** (*tr*) to make or achieve (a way) by fighting **6** (*intr*) *boxing* **a** to box, as for a living **b** to use aggressive rough tactics **7** to engage (another or others) in combat **8 fight it out** to contend or struggle until a decisive result is obtained **9 fight shy of** to keep aloof from ▷ *n* **10** a battle, struggle, or physical combat **11** a quarrel, dispute, or contest **12** resistance (esp in the phrase **to put up a fight**) **13** the desire to take part in physical combat (esp in the phrase **to show fight**) **14** a boxing match ▷ See also **fight back, fight off** [Old English *feohtan*; related to Old Frisian *fiuchta*, Old Saxon, Old High German *fehtan* to fight] > **'fighting** *n, adj*
fight back *vb* (*adverb*) **1** (*intr*) to resist an attack **2** (*intr*) to counterattack **3** (*tr*) to struggle to repress: *she tried to fight back her tears* ▷ *n* **fightback 4** an act or campaign of resistance **5** a counterattack
fighter ('faɪtə) *n* **1** a person who fights, esp a professional boxer **2** a person who has determination **3** *military* an armed aircraft designed for destroying other aircraft
fighter-bomber *n* a high-performance aircraft that combines the roles of fighter and bomber
fighting chance *n* a slight chance of success dependent on a struggle
fighting cock *n* **1** another name for **gamecock 2** a pugnacious person
fighting fish *n* any of various labyrinth fishes of the genus *Betta*, esp the Siamese fighting fish
fighting top *n* one of the gun platforms on the lower masts of sailing men-of-war, used in

attacking the crew of an enemy ship with swivel guns and muskets

fight off *vb (tr, adverb)* **1** to repulse; repel **2** to struggle to avoid or repress: *to fight off a cold*

fight-or-flight *n (modifier)* involving or relating to an involuntary response to stress in which the hormone adrenaline is secreted into the blood in readiness for physical action, such as fighting or running away

figjam (ˈfɪɡˌdʒæm) *n Austral slang* a very conceited person [C20 from *f(uck) I('m) g(ood) j(ust) a(sk) m(e)*]

fig leaf *n* **1** a leaf from a fig tree **2** a representation of a leaf, usually a vine leaf rather than an actual fig leaf, used in painting or sculpture to cover the genitals of nude figures **3** a device intended to conceal something regarded as shameful or indecent

fig marigold *n* an erect species of mesembryanthemum, *M. tricolor*, grown as a garden annual for its red-orange flowers with yellow centres

figment (ˈfɪɡmənt) *n* a fantastic notion, invention, or fabrication: *a figment of the imagination* [C15 from Late Latin *figmentum* a fiction, from Latin *fingere* to shape]

figuline (ˈfɪɡjʊˌlaɪn) *rare* ▷ *adj* **1** of or resembling clay ▷ *n* **2** an article made of clay [C17 from Latin *figulīnus* of a potter, from *figulus* a potter, from *fingere* to mould]

figural (ˈfɪɡərəl) *adj* composed of or relating to human or animal figures

figurant (ˈfɪɡjʊrənt) *n* **1** a ballet dancer who does group work but no solo roles **2** *theatre* a minor character, esp one who does not speak [C18 from French, from *figurer* to represent, appear, FIGURE] > **figurante** (ˌfɪɡjʊˈrɒnt) *fem n*

figurate (ˈfɪɡjʊrɪt) *adj* **1** *music* exhibiting or produced by figuration; florid or decorative **2** having a definite or particular shape or figure [C15 from Latin *figūrāre* to shape] > **ˈfigurately** *adv*

figuration (ˌfɪɡəˈreɪʃən) *n* **1** *music* **a** the employment of characteristic patterns of notes, esp in variations on a theme **b** decoration or florid ornamentation in general **2** the act or an instance of representing figuratively, as by means of allegory or emblem **3** a figurative or emblematic representation **4** the act of decorating with a design

figurative (ˈfɪɡərətɪv) *adj* **1** of the nature of, resembling, or involving a figure of speech; not literal; metaphorical **2** using or filled with figures of speech **3** representing by means of an emblem, likeness, figure, etc **4** (in painting, sculpture, etc) of, relating to, or characterized by the naturalistic representation of the external world > **ˈfiguratively** *adv* > **ˈfigurativeness** *n*

figure (ˈfɪɡə; *US* ˈfɪɡjər) *n* **1** any written symbol other than a letter, esp a whole number **2** another name for **digit** (sense 2) **3** an amount expressed numerically: *a figure of 1800 was suggested* **4** (*plural*) calculations with numbers: *he's good at figures* **5** visible shape or form; outline **6** the human form, esp as regards size or shape: *a girl with a slender figure* **7** a slim bodily shape (esp in the phrases **keep** *or* **lose one's figure**) **8** a character or personage, esp a prominent or notable one; personality: *a figure in politics* **9** the impression created by a person through behaviour (esp in the phrase **to cut a fine, bold, etc, figure**) **10** **a** a person as impressed on the mind: *the figure of Napoleon* **b** (*in combination*): *father-figure* **11** a representation in painting or sculpture, esp of the human form **12** an illustration or explanatory diagram in a text **13** a representative object or symbol; emblem **14** a pattern or design, as on fabric or in wood **15** a predetermined set of movements in dancing or skating **16** *geometry* any combination of points, lines, curves, or planes. A **plane figure**, such as a circle, encloses an area; a **solid figure** such as a sphere, encloses a volume **17** *rhetoric* See **figure of speech** **18** *logic* one of the four possible arrangements of the three terms in the premises of a syllogism. Compare **mood[2]** (sense 2) **19** *music* **a** a numeral written above or below a note in a part. See **figured bass, thorough bass** **b** a characteristic short pattern of notes ▷ *vb* **20** (when *tr*, often foll by *up*) to calculate or compute (sums, amounts, etc) **21** (*tr; usually takes a clause as object*) *informal, chiefly US, Canadian, and NZ* to think or conclude; consider **22** (*tr*) to represent by a diagram or illustration **23** (*tr*) to pattern or mark with a design **24** (*tr*) to depict or portray in a painting, etc **25** (*tr*) *rhetoric* to express by means of a figure of speech **26** (*tr*) to imagine **27** (*tr*) *music* **a** to decorate (a melody line or part) with ornamentation **b** to provide figures above or below (a bass part) as an indication of the accompanying harmonies required. See **figured bass, thorough bass** **28** (*intr;* usually foll by *in*) to be included: *his name figures in the article* **29** (*intr*) *informal* to accord with expectation; be logical: *it figures that he wouldn't come* **30** **go figure** *informal* an expression of surprise, astonishment, wonder, etc ▷ See also **figure on, figure out** [C13 from Latin *figūra* a shape, from *fingere* to mould] > **ˈfigureless** *adj* > **ˈfigurer** *n*

figured (ˈfɪɡəd) *adj* **1** depicted as a figure in graphic art, painting, or sculpture **2** decorated or patterned with a design **3** having a form **4** *music* **a** ornamental **b** (of a bass part) provided with numerals indicating accompanying harmonies

figured bass (beɪs) *n* a shorthand method of indicating a thorough-bass part in which each bass note is accompanied by figures indicating the intervals to be played in the chord above it in the realization

figure-ground phenomenon *n* the division of the perceptual field into background and objects that appear to stand out against it. The concept was evolved by the Gestalt psychologists, who invented *ambiguous* figures in which the same part could be seen either as figure or ground

figurehead (ˈfɪɡəˌhɛd) *n* **1** a person nominally having a prominent position, but no real authority **2** a carved bust or full-length figure at the upper end of the stems of some sailing vessels

figure of eight *or* **figure eight** *n* **1** an outline of the number 8 traced on ice by a skater **2** a flight manoeuvre by an aircraft outlining a figure 8 **3** **a** a knot in the shape of a figure 8 made to prevent the unreeving of a rope **b** a climber's knot in the shape of a figure 8 made with a doubled rope to provide a secure loop **c** an angler's knot sometimes used to attach a fly to a leader or dropper

figure of merit *n* **1** *aeronautics* a measure of the efficiency of a helicopter in hover **2** *electrical engineering* a measure of the efficiency of a component, such as a circuit

figure of speech *n* an expression of language, such as simile, metaphor, or personification, by which the usual or literal meaning of a word is not employed

figure on *or* **upon** *vb (intr, preposition) informal, chiefly US and Canadian* **1** to depend on (support or help) **2** to take into consideration

figure out *vb (tr, adverb; may take a clause as object) informal* **1** to calculate or reckon **2** to understand

figure skating *n* ice skating in which the skater traces outlines of selected patterns > **figure skater** *n*

figurine (ˌfɪɡəˈriːn) *n* a small carved or moulded figure; statuette [C19 from French, from Italian *figurina* a little FIGURE]

figwort (ˈfɪɡˌwɜːt) *n* any scrophulariaceous plant of the N temperate genus *Scrophularia*, having square stems and small brown or greenish flowers

Fiji (ˈfiːdʒiː, fiːˈdʒiː) *n* **1** an independent republic, consisting of 844 islands (chiefly Viti Levu and Vanua Levu) in the SW Pacific: a British colony (1874–1970); a member of the Commonwealth (1970–87 and from 1997); the large islands are of volcanic origin, surrounded by coral reefs; smaller ones are of coral. Official language: English. Religion: Christian and Hindu. Currency: dollar. Capital: Suva. Pop: 847 000 (2004 est). Area: 18 272 sq km (7055 sq miles) ▷ *n, adj* **2** another word for **Fijian**

Fijian (fiːˈdʒiːən) *n* **1** a member of the indigenous people of mixed Melanesian and Polynesian descent inhabiting Fiji **2** the language of this people, belonging to the Malayo-Polynesian family ▷ *adj* **3** of, relating to, or characteristic of Fiji or its inhabitants ▷ Also: **Fiji**

filagree (ˈfɪləˌɡriː) *n, adj, vb* a less common variant of **filigree**

filament (ˈfɪləmənt) *n* **1** the thin wire, usually tungsten, inside a light bulb that emits light when heated to incandescence by an electric current **2** *electronics* a high-resistance wire or ribbon, forming the cathode in some valves **3** a single strand of a natural or synthetic fibre; fibril **4** *botany* **a** the stalk of a stamen **b** any of the long slender chains of cells into which some algae and fungi are divided **5** *ornithol* the barb of a down feather **6** *anatomy* any slender structure or part, such as the tail of a spermatozoon; filum **7** *astronomy* **a** a long structure of relatively cool material in the solar corona **b** a long large-scale cluster of galaxies [C16 from New Latin *fīlāmentum*, from Medieval Latin *fīlāre* to spin, from Latin *fīlum* thread] > **filamentary** (ˌfɪləˈmɛntərɪ, -trɪ) *or* **ˌfilaˈmentous** *adj*

filar (ˈfaɪlə) *adj* **1** of thread **2** (of an optical instrument) having fine threads across the eyepiece forming a reticle or set of cross wires [C19 from Latin *fīlum* thread]

filaria (fɪˈlɛərɪə) *n, pl* **-iae** (-ɪˌiː) any parasitic nematode worm of the family *Filariidae*, living in the blood and tissues of vertebrates and transmitted by insects: the cause of filariasis [C19 New Latin (former name of genus), from Latin *fīlum* thread] > **fiˈlarial** *or* **fiˈlarian** *adj*

filariasis (ˌfɪləˈraɪəsɪs, fɪˌlɛərɪˈeɪsɪs) *n* a disease common in tropical and subtropical countries resulting from infestation of the lymphatic system with the nematode worms *Wuchereria bancrofti* or *Brugia malayi*, transmitted by mosquitoes: characterized by inflammation and obstruction of the lymphatic vessels. See also **elephantiasis** [C19 from New Latin; see FILARIA]

filature (ˈfɪlətʃə) *n* **1** the act or process of spinning silk, etc, into threads **2** the reel used for this **3** a place where such spinning or reeling is done [C18 from Medieval Latin *fīlātūra* the art of spinning, from *fīlāre* to spin thread; see FILAMENT]

filbert (ˈfɪlbət) *n* **1** any of several N temperate shrubs of the genus *Corylus*, esp *C. maxima*, that have edible rounded brown nuts: family *Corylaceae* **2** Also called: **hazelnut, cobnut** the nut of any of these shrubs ▷ See also **hazel** (senses 1, 3) [C14 named after St Philbert, 7th-century Frankish abbot, because the nuts are ripe around his feast day, Aug 22]

filch (fɪltʃ) *vb* (*tr*) to steal or take surreptitiously in small amounts; pilfer [C16 *filchen* to steal, attack, perhaps from Old English *gefylce* band of men] > **ˈfilcher** *n*

file[1] (faɪl) *n* **1** a folder, box, etc, used to keep documents or other items in order **2** the documents, etc, kept in this way **3** documents or information about a specific subject, person, etc: *we have a file on every known thief* **4** an orderly line or row **5** a line of people in marching formation, one behind another. Compare **rank[1]** (sense 6) **6** any of the eight vertical rows of squares on a chessboard **7** *computing* a named collection of information, in the form of text, programs, graphics, etc, held on a permanent storage device such as a magnetic disk **8** *obsolete* a list or catalogue **9** **on file** recorded or catalogued for reference, as in a file ▷ *vb* **10** to place (a document, letter, etc) in a file **11** (*tr*) to put on record, esp to place (a legal document) on public or official record; register **12** (*tr*) to bring (a suit, esp a divorce suit) in a court of law **13** (*tr*) to submit (copy) to a newspaper or news agency **14** (*intr*) to march or walk in a file or files: *the ants filed down the hill* [C16 (in the sense: string on which documents are hung): from Old French *filer*, from Medieval Latin *filāre*; see FILAMENT] > ˈ**filer** *n*

file² (faɪl) *n* **1** a hand tool consisting essentially of a steel blade with small cutting teeth on some or all of its faces. It is used for shaping or smoothing metal, wood, etc **2** *rare, Brit slang* a cunning or deceitful person ▷ *vb* **3** (*tr*) to shape or smooth (a surface) with a file [Old English *fīl*; related to Old Saxon *fīla*, Old High German *fīhala* file, Greek *pikros* bitter, sharp] > ˈ**filer** *n*

file³ (faɪl) *vb* (*tr*) *obsolete* to pollute or defile [Old English *fȳlan*; related to Middle Low German *vülen*; see DEFILE¹, FILTH, FOUL]

filecard (ˈfaɪlˌkɑːd) *n* a type of brush with sharp steel bristles, used for cleaning the teeth of a file

filefish (ˈfaɪlˌfɪʃ) *n, pl* **-fish** *or* **-fishes** any tropical triggerfish, such as *Alutera scripta*, having a narrow compressed body and a very long dorsal spine [C18 referring to its file-like scales]

filename (ˈfaɪlˌneɪm) *n* an arrangement of characters that enables a computer system to permit the user to have access to a particular file

file server *n computing* the central unit of a local area network that controls its operation and provides access to separately stored data files

file sharing *n* the practice of sharing computer data or space on a network

filet (ˈfɪlɪt, ˈfɪleɪ; *French* filɛ) *n* a variant spelling of **fillet** (senses 1–3) [C20 from French: net, from Old Provençal *filat*, from *fil* thread, from Latin *fīlum*]

filet mignon (ˈfɪleɪ ˈmiːnjɒn) *n* a small tender boneless cut of beef from the inside of the loin [from French, literally: dainty fillet]

file transfer protocol *n* See **FTP**

filial (ˈfɪljəl) *adj* **1** of, resembling, or suitable to a son or daughter: *filial affection* **2** *genetics* designating any of the generations following the parental generation. Abbrev: **F**; F_1 indicates the first filial generation, F_2 the second, etc [C15 from Late Latin *filiālis*, from Latin *filius* son] > ˈ**filially** *adv* > ˈ**filialness** *n*

filiate (ˈfɪlɪˌeɪt) *vb* (*tr*) **1** *law* to fix judicially the paternity of (a child, esp one born out of wedlock) **2** *law* a less common word for **affiliate** **3** *archaic* to affiliate or associate [C18 from Medieval Latin *filiātus* acknowledged as a son, from Latin *filius* son]

filiation (ˌfɪlɪˈeɪʃən) *n* **1** line of descent; lineage; derivation **2** the fact of being the child of certain parents **3** *law* the act or process of filiating **4** *law* a less common word for **affiliation order** **5** the set of rules governing the attachment of children to their parents and its social consequences

filibeg, fillibeg *or* **philibeg** (ˈfɪlɪˌbɛg) *n* the kilt worn by Scottish Highlanders [C18 from Scottish Gaelic *fēileadhbeag*, from *fēileadh* kilt + *beag* small]

filibuster (ˈfɪlɪˌbʌstə) *n* **1** the process or an instance of obstructing legislation by means of long speeches and other delaying tactics **2** Also called: **filibusterer** a legislator who engages in such obstruction **3** a buccaneer, freebooter, or irregular military adventurer, esp a revolutionary in a foreign country ▷ *vb* **4** to obstruct (legislation) with delaying tactics **5** (*intr*) to engage in unlawful and private military action [C16 from Spanish *filibustero*, from French *flibustier* probably from Dutch *vrijbuiter* pirate, literally: one plundering freely; see FREEBOOTER] > ˈ**fili,busterer** *n* > ˈ**fili,busterism** *n*

filicide (ˈfɪlɪˌsaɪd) *n* **1** the act of killing one's own son or daughter **2** a person who does this [C17 from Latin *filius* son or *filia* daughter + -CIDE] > ˌ**filiˈcidal** *adj*

filiform (ˈfɪlɪˌfɔːm, ˈfaɪ-) *adj biology* having the form of a thread [C18 from Latin *fīlum* thread]

filigree (ˈfɪlɪˌgriː), **filagree** *or* **fillagree** *n* **1** delicate ornamental work of twisted gold, silver, or other wire **2** any fanciful delicate ornamentation ▷ *adj* **3** made of or as if with filigree ▷ *vb* **-grees, -greeing, -greed** **4** (*tr*) to decorate with or as if with filigree [C17 from earlier *filigreen*, from French *filigrane*, from Latin *fīlum* thread + *grānum* GRAIN]

filing clerk *n* an employee who maintains office files

filings (ˈfaɪlɪŋz) *pl n* shavings or particles removed by a file: *iron filings*

Filipino (ˌfɪlɪˈpiːnəʊ) *n* **1** *pl* **-nos** Also (feminine): **Filipina** a native or inhabitant of the Philippines **2** another name for **Tagalog** ▷ *adj* **3** of or relating to the Philippines or their inhabitants

fill (fɪl) *vb* (*mainly tr; often foll by up*) **1** (*also intr*) to make or become full: *to fill up a bottle; the bath fills in two minutes* **2** to occupy the whole of: *the party filled two floors of the house* **3** to plug (a gap, crevice, cavity, etc) **4** to meet (a requirement or need) satisfactorily **5** to cover (a page or blank space) with writing, drawing, etc **6** to hold and perform the duties of (an office or position) **7** to appoint or elect an occupant to (an office or position) **8** *building trades* to build up (ground) with fill **9** (*also intr*) to swell or cause to swell with wind, as in manoeuvring the sails of a sailing vessel **10** to increase the bulk of by adding an inferior substance **11** *poker* to complete (a full house, etc) by drawing the cards needed **12** *chiefly US and Canadian* to put together the necessary materials for (a prescription or order) **13** **fill the bill** *informal* to serve or perform adequately ▷ *n* **14** material such as gravel, stones, etc, used to bring an area of ground up to a required level **15** **one's fill** the quantity needed to satisfy one: *to eat your fill* ▷ See also **fill away, fill in, fill out, fill up** [Old English *fyllan*; related to Old Frisian *fella*, Old Norse *fylla*, Gothic *fulljan*, Old High German *fullen*; see FULL¹, FULFIL]

fillagree (ˈfɪləˌgriː) *n, adj, vb* a less common variant of **filigree**

fill away *vb* (*intr, adverb*) *nautical* to cause a vessel's sails to fill, either by steering it off the wind or by bracing the yards

fille de joie *French* (fij də ʒwa) *n, pl* ***filles de joie*** (fij də ʒwa) a prostitute [girl of pleasure]

filled gold *n* another name (esp US) for **rolled gold**

filler (ˈfɪlə) *n* **1** a person or thing that fills **2** an object or substance used to add weight or size to something or to fill in a gap **3** a paste, used for filling in cracks, holes, etc, in a surface before painting **4** *architect* a small joist inserted between and supported by two beams **5 a** the inner portion of a cigar **b** the cut tobacco for making cigarettes **6** *journalism* articles, photographs, etc, to fill space between more important articles in the layout of a newspaper or magazine **7** *informal* something, such as a musical selection, to fill time in a broadcast or stage presentation **8** a small radio or television transmitter used to fill a gap in coverage

filler cap *n* a device sealing the filling pipe to the petrol tank in a motor vehicle

filler metal *n* metal supplied in the form of a welding rod, sometimes flux coated, melted by an arc or a flame into a joint between components to be joined

fillet (ˈfɪlɪt) *n* **1 a** Also called: **fillet steak** a strip of boneless meat, esp the undercut of a sirloin of beef **b** the boned side of a fish **c** the white meat of breast and wing of a chicken **2** a narrow strip of any material **3** a thin strip of ribbon, lace, etc, worn in the hair or around the neck **4** a narrow flat moulding, esp one between other mouldings **5** a narrow band between two adjacent flutings on the shaft of a column **6** Also called: **fillet weld** a narrow strip of welded metal of approximately triangular cross-section used to join steel members at right angles **7** *heraldry* a horizontal division of a shield, one quarter of the depth of the chief **8** Also called: **listel, list** the top member of a cornice **9** *anatomy* a band of sensory nerve fibres in the brain connected to the thalamus. Technical name: **lemniscus** **10 a** a narrow decorative line, impressed on the cover of a book **b** a wheel tool used to impress such lines **11** another name for **fairing¹** ▷ *vb* **-lets, -leting, -leted** (*tr*) **12** to cut or prepare (meat or fish) as a fillet **13** to cut fillets from (meat or fish) **14** *anatomy* to surgically remove a bone from (part of the body) so that only soft tissue remains **15** to bind or decorate with or as if with a fillet ▷ Also (for senses 1–3): **filet** [C14 from Old French *filet*, from *fil* thread, from Latin *fīlum*]

fill in *vb* (*adverb*) **1** (*tr*) to complete (a form, drawing, etc) **2** (*intr*) to act as a substitute: *a girl is filling in while the typist is away* **3** (*tr*) to put material into (a hole or cavity), esp so as to make it level with a surface **4** (*tr*) *informal* to inform with facts or news **5** (*tr*) *Brit slang* to attack and injure severely ▷ *n* **fill-in** **6** a substitute **7** *US informal* a briefing to complete one's understanding

filling (ˈfɪlɪŋ) *n* **1** the substance or thing used to fill a space or container: *pie filling* **2** *dentistry* **a** any of various substances (metal, plastic, etc) for inserting into the prepared cavity of a tooth **b** the cavity of a tooth so filled **3** *textiles* another term for **weft** ▷ *adj* **4** (of food or a meal) substantial and satisfying

filling station *n* a place where petrol and other supplies for motorists are sold

fillip (ˈfɪlɪp) *n* **1** something that adds stimulation or enjoyment **2** the action of holding a finger towards the palm with the thumb and suddenly releasing it outwards to produce a snapping sound **3** a quick blow or tap made by a finger snapped in this way ▷ *vb* **4** (*tr*) to stimulate or excite **5** (*tr*) to strike or project sharply with a fillip **6** (*intr*) to make a fillip [C15 *philippe*, of imitative origin]

fillister, filister *or* **fillester** (ˈfɪlɪstə) *n* **1** Also called: **fillister plane** an adjustable plane for cutting rabbets, grooves, etc **2** Also called: **sash fillister** a rabbet or groove, esp one in a window sash bar for a pane of glass [C19 of unknown origin]

fill light *n photog* a light that supplements the key light without changing its character, used esp to lighten shadows

fill out *vb* (*adverb*) **1** to make or become fuller, thicker, or rounder: *her figure has filled out since her marriage* **2** to make more substantial: *the writers were asked to fill their stories out* **3** (*tr*) to complete (a form, application, etc)

fill up *vb* (*adverb*) **1** (*tr*) to complete (a form, application, etc) **2** to make or become completely full ▷ *n* **fill-up** **3** the act of filling something completely, esp the petrol tank of a car

filly (ˈfɪlɪ) *n, pl* **-lies** **1** a female horse or pony under the age of four **2** *informal rare* a spirited girl or young woman [C15 from Old Norse *fylja*; related to Old High German *fulihha*; see FOAL]

film (fɪlm) *n* **1 a** a sequence of images of moving objects photographed by a camera and providing the optical illusion of continuous movement when projected onto a screen **b** a form of entertainment, information, etc, composed of such a sequence of images and shown in a cinema, etc **c** (*as modifier*): *film techniques* **2** a thin flexible strip of cellulose coated with a photographic emulsion, used to make negatives and transparencies **3** a thin coating or layer **4** a thin sheet of any material, as of plastic for packaging **5** a fine haze, mist, or blur **6** a gauzy web of filaments or fine threads **7** *pathol* an abnormally opaque tissue, such as the cornea in some eye diseases ▷ *vb* **8 a** to photograph with a cine camera **b** to make a film of (a screenplay, event, etc) **9** (often foll by *over*) to cover or become covered or coated with a film [Old English *filmen* membrane; related to Old Frisian *filmene*, Greek *pelma* sole of the foot; see FELL⁴]

film colour *n physiol* a misty appearance produced when no lines or edges are present in the visual field

filmi (ˈfɪlmɪ) *adj Hinglish* **1** of or relating to the Indian film industry or Indian films **2**

f

filmic | finalize

containing the high drama typical of Indian films [Hindi]

filmic ('fɪlmɪk) *adj* **1** of or relating to films or the cinema **2** having characteristics that are suggestive of films or the cinema > '**filmically** *adv*

film library *n* a collection of films as archives or for loan or hire

film-maker *n* a person who directs or produces films for the cinema or television

film noir (nwɑː) *n* a gangster thriller, made esp in the 1940s in Hollywood characterized by contrasty lighting and often somewhat impenetrable plots [C20 French, literally: black film]

filmography (fɪlˈmɒɡrəfɪ) *n* **1** a list of the films made by a particular director, actor, etc **2** any writing that deals with films or the cinema

film pack *n* a box containing several sheets of film for use in a plate camera

film set *n* the scenery and props as arranged for shooting a film

filmset ('fɪlmˌsɛt) *vb* **-sets, -setting, -set** (*tr*) to set (type matter) by filmsetting > '**filmˌsetter** *n*

filmsetting ('fɪlmˌsɛtɪŋ) *n printing* typesetting by exposing type characters onto photographic film from which printing plates are made

film speed *n* **1** the sensitivity to light of a photographic film, specified in terms of the film's ISO rating **2** the rate at which the film passes through a motion picture camera or projector

film star *n* a popular film actor or actress

film strip *n* a strip of film composed of different images projected separately as slides

filmy ('fɪlmɪ) *adj* **filmier, filmiest 1** composed of or resembling film; transparent or gauzy **2** covered with or as if with a film; hazy; blurred > '**filmily** *adv* > '**filminess** *n*

filmy fern *n* any fern of the family *Hymenophyllaceae*, growing in humid regions and having thin translucent leaves

filo ('fiːləʊ) *n* a type of Greek flaky pastry in very thin sheets [C20 Modern Greek *phullon* leaf]

Filofax ('faɪləʊˌfæks) *n trademark* a type of loose-leaf ring binder with sets of different-coloured paper, used as a portable personal filing system, including appointments, addresses, etc

filoplume ('fɪləˌpluːm, 'faɪ-) *n ornithol* any of the hairlike feathers that lack vanes and occur between the contour feathers [C19 from New Latin *filoplūma*, from Latin *filum* thread + *plūma* feather]

filose ('faɪləʊs, -ləʊz) *adj biology* resembling or possessing a thread or threadlike process: *filose pseudopodia* [C19 from Latin *filum* thread]

filoselle (ˌfɪləʊ'sɛl) *n* soft silk thread, used esp for embroidery [C17 from French: silk, silkworm, from Italian *filosello*, perhaps from Latin *folliculus* little bag]

filovirus ('faɪləʊˌvaɪrəs) *n* any member of a family of viruses that includes the agents responsible for Ebola virus disease and Marburg disease [C20 from Latin *filum* thread + VIRUS]

fils¹ *French* (fis) an addition to a French surname to specify the son rather than the father of the same name: *a book by Dumas fils.* Compare *père* [French: son]

fils² (fɪls), **fil** (fɪl) *n, pl* **fils a** a fractional monetary unit of Bahrain, Iraq, Jordan, and Kuwait, worth one thousandth of a dinar **b** a fractional monetary unit of the United Arab Emirates, worth one hundredth of a dirham **c** a fractional monetary unit of Yemen, worth one hundredth of a riyal [from Arabic]

filter ('fɪltə) *n* **1** a porous substance, such as paper or sand, that allows fluid to pass but retains suspended solid particles: used to clean fluids or collect solid particles **2** any device containing such a porous substance for separating suspensions from fluids **3** any of various porous substances built into the mouth end of a cigarette or cigar for absorbing impurities such as tar **4** any electronic, optical, or acoustic device that blocks signals or radiations of certain frequencies while allowing others to pass. See also **band-pass**

filter 5 any transparent disc of gelatine or glass used to eliminate or reduce the intensity of given frequencies from the light leaving a lamp, entering a camera, etc **6** *Brit* a traffic signal at a road junction consisting of a green arrow which when illuminated permits vehicles to turn either left or right when the main signals are red ▷ *vb* **7** (often foll by *out*) to remove or separate (suspended particles, wavelengths of radiation, etc) from (a liquid, gas, radiation, etc) by the action of a filter **8** (*tr*) to obtain by filtering **9** (*intr foll by through*) to pass (through a filter or something like a filter): *dust filtered through the screen* **10** (*intr*) to flow slowly; trickle [C16 *filtre* from Medieval Latin *filtrum* piece of felt used as a filter, of Germanic origin; see FELT²]

filterable ('fɪltərəbəl) *or* **filtrable** ('fɪltrəbəl) *adj* **1** capable of being filtered **2** (of most viruses and certain bacteria) capable of passing through the pores of a fine filter > ˌfiltera'bility *or* 'filterableness *n*

filter bed *n* **1** a layer of sand or gravel in a tank or reservoir through which a liquid is passed so as to purify it. Compare **bacteria bed 2** any layer of material through which a liquid is passed so as to filter it

filter cake *n chem* the solid material accumulated by a filter press

filter feeding *n zoology* a method of feeding occurring in some aquatic animals, such as planktonic invertebrates and whalebone whales, in which minute food particles are filtered from the surrounding water > **filter feeder** *n*

filter out *or* **through** *vb* (*intr, adverb*) to become known gradually; leak: *rumours filtered out about the divorce*

filter paper *n* a porous paper used for filtering liquids

filter press *n* an apparatus used for filtration consisting of a set of frames covered with filter cloth on both sides, between which the liquid to be filtered is pumped

filter pump *n* a vacuum pump used to assist laboratory filtrations in which a jet of water inside a glass tube entrains air molecules from the system to be evacuated

filter tip *n* **1** an attachment to the mouth end of a cigarette for trapping impurities such as tar during smoking. It consists of any of various dense porous substances, such as cotton **2** a cigarette having such an attachment > 'filter-ˌtipped *adj*

filth (fɪlθ) *n* **1** foul or disgusting dirt; refuse **2** extreme physical or moral uncleanliness; pollution **3** vulgarity or obscenity, as in language **4** *the derogatory slang* the police [Old English *fȳlth*; related to Old Saxon, Old High German *fūlitha*; see FOUL, DEFILE]

filthy ('fɪlθɪ) *adj* **filthier, filthiest 1** characterized by or full of filth; very dirty or obscene **2** offensive or vicious: *that was a filthy trick to play* **3** *informal, chiefly Brit* extremely unpleasant: *filthy weather* ▷ *adv* **4** extremely; disgustingly: *filthy rich* > 'filthily *adv* > 'filthiness *n*

filtrate ('fɪltreɪt) *n* **1** a liquid or gas that has been filtered ▷ *vb* **2** another name for **filter** (sense 7) [C17 from Medieval Latin *filtrāre* to FILTER] > 'filtratable *adj*

filtration (fɪl'treɪʃən) *n* the act or process of filtering

filum ('faɪləm) *n, pl* **-la** (-lə) *anatomy* any threadlike structure or part [Latin: thread, cord, fibre]

fimble ('fɪmbəl) *n* the male plant of the hemp, which matures before the female plant [C15 from Middle Dutch *femeel*, from Old French *chanvre femelle* female hemp, from *chanvre* hemp + *femelle* FEMALE]

fimbria ('fɪmbrɪə) *n, pl* **-briae** (-brɪˌiː) *anatomy* a fringe or fringelike margin or border, esp at the opening of the Fallopian tubes [C18 from Late Latin, from Latin *fimbriae* threads, shreds] > 'fimbrial *adj*

fimbriate ('fɪmbrɪɪt, -ˌeɪt), **fimbriated** *or* **fimbrillate** ('fɪmbrɪlɪt, -ˌleɪt) *adj* having a fringed margin, as some petals, antennae, etc > ˌfimbri'ation *n*

fimicolous (fɪ'mɪkələs) *adj biology* (esp of fungi) growing in or on dung [C19 from Latin *fimus* dung + *colere* to inhabit]

fin¹ (fɪn) *n* **1** any of the firm appendages that are the organs of locomotion and balance in fishes and some other aquatic animals. Most fishes have paired and unpaired fins, the former corresponding to the limbs of higher vertebrates **2** a part or appendage that resembles a fin **3** a *Brit* a vertical surface to which the rudder is attached, usually placed at the rear of an aeroplane to give stability about the vertical axis. US name: **vertical stabilizer b** a tail surface fixed to a rocket or missile to give stability **4** *nautical* a fixed or adjustable blade projecting under water from the hull of a vessel to give it stability or control **5** a projecting rib to dissipate heat from the surface of an engine cylinder, motor casing, or radiator **6** (often plural) another name for **flipper** (sense 2) ▷ *vb* **fins, finning, finned 7** (*tr*) to provide with fins **8** (*tr*) to remove the fins from (a dead fish) **9** (*intr*) (esp of a whale) to agitate the fins violently in the water [Old English *finn*; related to Middle Dutch *vinne*, Old Swedish *fina*, Latin *pinna* wing] > 'finless *adj*

fin² (fɪn) *n US slang* a five-dollar bill [from Yiddish *finf* five, ultimately from Old High German *funf, finf*]

FIN *international car registration for* Finland

fin. *abbreviation for* **1** finance **2** financial

Fin *abbreviation for* **1** Finland **2** Finnish

finable *or* **fineable** ('faɪnəbəl) *adj* liable to a fine > 'finableness *or* 'fineableness *n*

finagle (fɪ'neɪɡəl) *vb informal* **1** (*tr*) to get or achieve by trickery, craftiness, or persuasion; wangle **2** to use trickery or craftiness on (a person) [C20 probably changed from dialect *fainaigue*] > fi'nagler *n*

final ('faɪnəl) *adj* **1** of or occurring at the end; concluding; ultimate; last **2** having no possibility for further discussion, action, or change; conclusive; decisive: *a final decree of judgment* **3** relating to or constituting an end or purpose: *a final clause may be introduced by "in order to"* **4** *phonetics* at the end of a word: *"cat" has a final "t"*. Compare **medial** (sense 1), **initial** (sense 1) **5** *music* another word for **perfect** (sense 9b) ▷ *n* **6** a terminal or last thing; end **7** a deciding contest between the winners of previous rounds in a competition **8** *music* the tonic note of a church mode ▷ See also **finals** [C14 from Latin *finālis*, from *finis* limit, boundary]

final cause *n philosophy* the end or purpose of a thing or process, as opposed to its efficient cause. See **cause** (sense 7)

finale (fɪ'nɑːlɪ) *n* **1** the concluding part of any performance or presentation **2** the closing section or movement of a musical composition [C18 from Italian, n use of adj *finale*, from Latin *finālis* FINAL]

finalism ('faɪnəˌlɪzəm) *n philosophy* the doctrine that final causes determine the course of all events > ˌfina'listic *adj*

finalist ('faɪnəlɪst) *n* a contestant who has reached the last and decisive stage of a sports or other competition

finality (faɪ'nælɪtɪ) *n, pl* **-ties 1** the condition or quality of being final or settled; conclusiveness: *the finality of death* **2** a final or conclusive act **3** *metaphysics* the doctrine of the efficacy of final causes. Compare **teleology**

finalize *or* **finalise** ('faɪnəˌlaɪz) *vb* **1** (*tr*) to put into final form; settle: *to finalize plans for the merger* **2** (*intr*) to complete arrangements or negotiations; reach agreement on a transaction > ˌfinali'zation *or* ˌfinali'sation *n*

■ USAGE Although *finalize* has been in widespread use for some time, many speakers and writers still prefer to use *complete, conclude,* or *make final,* esp in formal contexts

finally ('faɪnəlɪ) *adv* **1** after a long delay; at last; eventually **2** at the end or final point; lastly **3** completely; conclusively; irrevocably ▷ *sentence connector* **4** in the end; lastly: *finally, he put his tie on* **5** as the last or final point: linking what follows with the previous statements, as in a speech or argument

finals ('faɪnəlz) *pl n* **1** the deciding part or parts of a sports or other competition **2** *education* the last examination series in an academic or professional course

final-salary *adj* another name for **defined-benefit**

finance (fɪ'næns, 'faɪnæns) *n* **1** the system of money, credit, etc, esp with respect to government revenues and expenditures **2** funds or the provision of funds **3** (*plural*) funds; financial condition ▷ *vb* **4** (*tr*) to provide or obtain funds, capital, or credit for **5** (*intr*) to manage or secure financial resources [C14 from Old French, from *finer* to end, settle by payment]

finance bill *n* a legislative bill providing money for the public treasury

finance company *or* **house** *n* an enterprise engaged in the loan of money against collateral or speculatively to manufacturers and retailers, esp one specializing in the financing of hire-purchase contracts

financial (fɪ'nænʃəl, faɪ-) *adj* **1** of or relating to finance or finances **2** of or relating to persons who manage money, capital, or credit **3** *Austral and NZ informal* having money; in funds **4** *Austral and NZ* (of a club member) fully paid-up ▷ fi'nancially *adv*

financial futures *pl n* futures in a stock-exchange index, currency exchange rate, or interest rate enabling banks, building societies, brokers, and speculators to hedge their involvement in these markets

Financial Ombudsman *n* any of five British ombudsmen: the **Banking Ombudsman**, set up in 1986 to investigate complaints from bank customers; the **Building Society Ombudsman**, set up in 1987 to investigate complaints from building society customers; the **Insurance Ombudsman**, set up in 1981 to investigate complaints by policyholders (since 1988 this ombudsman has also operated a **Unit Trust Ombudsman** scheme); the **Investment Ombudsman** set up in 1989 to investigate complaints by investors (the **Personal Investment Authority Ombudsman** is responsible for investigating complaints by personal investors); and the **Pensions Ombudsman**, set up in 1993 to investigate complaints regarding pension schemes

Financial Services Authority *n* (in the United Kingdom) a regulatory body that oversees London's financial markets, each of which has its own self-regulatory organization: it succeeded the Securities and Investments Board. Abbreviation: **FSA**

Financial Times Industrial Ordinary Share Index *n* an index of share prices produced by the *Financial Times*, designed to reflect general price trends: based on the average price of thirty British shares

Financial Times Stock Exchange 100 Index *n* an index of share prices produced by the *Financial Times* based on an average of 100 securities and giving the best indication of daily movements. Abbreviation: **FTSE 100 Index** Informal name: Footsie

Financial Times Stock Exchange Eurotrack 100 Index *n* an index of share prices produced by the *Financial Times* of 100 companies from Continental Europe, designed to reflect the wider European market. Usually shortened to: **Eurotrack**

financial year *n Brit* **1** any annual period at the end of which a firm's accounts are made up **2** the annual period ending April 5, over which Budget estimates are made by the British Government and which functions as the income-tax year. US and Canadian equivalent: **fiscal year**

financier (fɪ'nænsɪə, faɪ-) *n* a person who is engaged or skilled in large-scale financial operations

financing gap *n* the difference between a country's requirements for foreign exchange to finance its debts and imports and its income from overseas

finback ('fɪn,bæk) *n* another name for **rorqual**

finch (fɪntʃ) *n* **1** any songbird of the family *Fringillidae*, having a short stout bill for feeding on seeds and, in most species, a bright plumage in the male. Common examples are the goldfinch, bullfinch, chaffinch, siskin, and canary **2** any of various similar or related birds. Related adj: **fringilline** [Old English *finc*; related to Old High German *finko*, Middle Dutch *vinker*, Greek *spingos*]

Finchley ('fɪntʃlɪ) *n* a residential district of N London, part of the Greater London borough of Barnet from 1965

find (faɪnd) *vb* finds, finding, found (faʊnd) (*mainly tr*) **1** to meet with or discover by chance **2** to discover or obtain, esp by search or effort: *to find happiness* **3** (*may take a clause as object*) to become aware of; realize: *he found much knew* **4** (*may take a clause as object*) to regard as being; consider: *I find this wine a little sour* **5** to look for and point out (something to be criticized): *to find fault* **6** (*also intr*) *law* to determine an issue after judicial inquiry and pronounce a verdict (upon): *the court found the accused guilty* **7** to regain (something lost or not functioning): *to find one's tongue* **8** to reach (a target): *the bullet found its mark* **9** to provide, esp with difficulty: *we'll find room for you too* **10** to be able to pay: *I can't find that amount of money* **11** find oneself to realize and accept one's real character; discover one's true vocation **12** find one's feet to become capable or confident, as in a new job ▷ *n* **13** a person, thing, etc, that is found, esp a valuable or fortunate discovery [Old English *findan*; related to Old Norse *finna*, Gothic *finthan*, Old High German *fintan* to find] ▷ **findable** *adj*

finder ('faɪndə) *n* **1** a person or thing that finds **2** *physics* a small low-power wide-angle telescope fitted to a more powerful larger telescope, used to locate celestial objects to be studied by the larger instrument **3** *photog* short for **viewfinder 4** finders keepers *informal* whoever finds something has the right to keep it

fin de siècle *French* (fɛ̃ də sjɛklə) *n* **1** the end of the 19th century, when traditional social, moral, and artistic values were in transition ▷ *adj* fin-de-siècle **2** of or relating to the close of the 19th century **3** decadent, esp in artistic tastes

finding ('faɪndɪŋ) *n* **1** a thing that is found or discovered **2** *law* the conclusion reached after a judicial inquiry; verdict **3** (*plural*) *US* the tools and equipment of an artisan

find out *vb* (*adverb*) **1** to gain knowledge of (something); learn: *he found out what he wanted* **2** to detect the crime, deception, etc, of (someone)

find the lady *n* another name for **three-card trick**

fine¹ (faɪn) *adj* **1** excellent or choice in quality; very good of its kind: *a fine speech* **2** superior in skill, ability, or accomplishment: *a fine violinist* **3** (of weather) clear and dry **4** enjoyable or satisfying: *a fine time* **5** (*postpositive*) *informal* quite well; in satisfactory health: *I feel fine* **6** satisfactory; acceptable: *that's fine by me* **7** of delicate composition or careful workmanship: *fine crystal* **8** (of precious metals) pure or having a high or specified degree of purity: *fine silver; gold 98 per cent fine* **9** subtle in perception, discriminating: *a fine eye for antique brasses* **10** abstruse or subtle: *a fine point in argument* **11** very thin or slender: *fine hair* **12** very small: *fine dust; fine print* **13** (of edges, blades, etc) sharp; keen **14** ornate, showy, or smart **15** good-looking; handsome: *a fine young woman* **16** polished, elegant, or refined: *a fine gentleman* **17** morally upright and commendable: *a fine man* **18** *cricket* (of a fielding position) oblique to and behind the wicket: *fine leg* **19** (*prenominal*) *informal* disappointing or terrible: *a fine mess* ▷ *adv* **20** *informal* quite well; all right: *that suits me fine* **21** a nonstandard word for **finely 22** *billiards, snooker* (of a stroke on the cue ball) so as to merely brush the object ball **23** cut it fine to allow little margin of time, space, etc ▷ *vb* **24** to make or become finer; refine **25** (often foll by *down* or *away*) to make or become smaller **26** (*tr*) to clarify (wine, etc) by adding finings **27** (*tr*) *billiards, snooker* to hit (a cue ball) fine **28** (*intr*; foll by *up*) *Austral and NZ informal* (of the weather) to become fine [C13 from Old French *fin*, from Latin *finis* end, boundary, as in *finis honōrum* the highest degree of honour]

fine² (faɪn) *n* **1** a certain amount of money exacted as a penalty: *a parking fine* **2** a payment made by a tenant at the start of his tenancy to reduce his subsequent rent; premium **3** *feudal law* a sum of money paid by a man to his lord, esp for the privilege of transferring his land to another **4** a method of transferring land in England by bringing a fictitious law suit: abolished 1833 **5** in fine **a** in short; briefly **b** in conclusion; finally ▷ *vb* **6** (*tr*) to impose a fine on [C12 (in the sense: conclusion, settlement): from Old French *fin*; see FINE¹]

fine³ ('fiːneɪ) *n music* **1** the point at which a piece is to end, usually after a *da capo* or *dal segno* **2** an ending or finale [Italian, from Latin *finis* end]

fine⁴ *French* (fin) *n* brandy of ordinary quality [literally: fine]

fineable ('faɪnəbəl) *adj* a variant spelling of **finable**. ▷ **'fineableness** *n*

fine art *n* **1** art produced chiefly for its aesthetic value, as opposed to applied art **2** (*often plural*) Also called: **beaux arts** any of the fields in which such art is produced, such as painting, sculpture, and engraving

fine-cut *adj* (of tobacco) finely cut or shredded

fine-draw *vb* -draws, -drawing, -drew, -drawn (*tr*) **1** to sew together so finely that the join is scarcely noticeable **2** to carry out the last drawing-out operation on (wire, tube, etc) to reduce its diameter

fine-drawn *adj* **1** (of arguments, distinctions, etc) precise or subtle **2** (of wire) drawn out until very fine; attenuated **3** (of features) delicate or refined

Fine Gael ('fɪnə 'gɛːl) *n* one of the major political parties in the Republic of Ireland, formed in 1933 [from Irish Gaelic *fine* tribe, race + *Gael* of the Gaels]

fine-grain *adj photog* having or producing an image with grain of inconspicuous size: *a fine-grain image; a fine-grain developer*

fine-grained *adj* **1** (of wood, leather, etc) having a fine smooth even grain **2** detailed, in-depth, or involving fine detail

fine leg *n cricket* **a** a fielding position between long leg and square leg **b** a fielder in this position

finely ('faɪnlɪ) *adv* **1** into small pieces; minutely **2** precisely or subtly **3** splendidly or delicately

fineness ('faɪnnɪs) *n* **1** the state or quality of being fine **2** a measurement of the purity of precious metal, expressed as the number of parts per thousand that is precious metal

fine print *n* matter set in small type, as in a contract, esp considered as containing unfavourable conditions that the signer might overlook. Also called: **small print**

finery¹ ('faɪnərɪ) *n* elaborate or showy decoration, esp clothing and jewellery

finery² ('faɪnərɪ) *n, pl* -eries a hearth for converting cast iron into wrought iron [C17 from Old French *finerie*, from *finer* to refine; see FINE¹]

fines herbes (*French* finz ɛrb) *pl n* a mixture of finely chopped herbs, used to flavour omelettes, salads, etc

f

finespun ('faɪnˌspʌn) *adj* **1** spun or drawn out to a fine thread **2** excessively subtle or refined; not practical

finesse (fɪ'nɛs) *n* **1** elegant skill in style or performance **2** subtlety and tact in handling difficult situations **3** *bridge, whist* an attempt to win a trick when opponents hold a high card in the suit led by playing a lower card, hoping the opponent who has already played holds the missing card **4** a trick, artifice, or strategy ▷ *vb* **5** to manage or bring about with finesse **6** to play (a card) as a finesse [c15 from Old French, from *fin* fine, delicate; see FINE¹]

fine structure *n* the splitting of a spectral line into two or more closely spaced components as a result of interaction between the spin and orbital angular momenta of the atomic electrons. Compare **hyperfine structure**

fine-tooth comb *or* **fine-toothed comb** *n* **1** a comb with fine teeth set closely together **2** **go over** (*or* **through**) **with a fine-tooth(ed) comb** to examine very thoroughly

fine-tune *vb* (*tr*) to make fine adjustments to (something) in order to obtain optimum performance

finfoot ('fɪnˌfʊt) *n, pl* **-foots** any aquatic bird of the tropical and subtropical family *Heliornithidae*, having broadly lobed toes, a long slender head and neck, and pale brown plumage: order *Gruiformes* (cranes, rails etc). Also called: **sungrebe**

Fingal's Cave ('fɪŋgəlz) *n* a cave in W Scotland, on Staffa Island in the Inner Hebrides: basaltic pillars. Length: 69 m (227 ft). Height: 36 m (117 ft)

finger ('fɪŋgə) *n* **1 a** any of the digits of the hand, often excluding the thumb. Technical name: **digitus manus b** (*as modifier*): *a finger bowl* **c** (*in combination*): *a fingernail*. Related adj: **digital 2** the part of a glove made to cover a finger **3** something that resembles a finger in shape or function: *a finger of land* **4** Also called: **digit** the length or width of a finger used as a unit of measurement **5** a quantity of liquid in a glass, etc, as deep as a finger is wide; tot **6** a projecting machine part, esp one serving as an indicator, guide, or guard **7 burn one's fingers** to suffer from having meddled or been rash **8 get** *or* **pull one's finger out** *Brit informal* to begin or speed up activity, esp after initial delay or slackness **9 have a** (*or* **one's**) **finger in the pie a** to have an interest in or take part in some activity **b** to meddle or interfere **10 lay a finger on** (*usually negative*) to harm **11 lay** *or* **put one's finger on** to indicate, identify, or locate accurately **12 not lift** (*or* **raise**) **a finger** (*foll by an infinitive*) not to make any effort (to do something) **13 let slip through one's fingers** to allow to escape; miss narrowly **14 point the finger at** to accuse or blame **15 put the finger on** *informal* **a** to inform on or identify, esp for the police **b** to choose (the victim or location of an intended crime) **16 twist** *or* **wrap around one's little finger** to have easy and complete control or influence over ▷ *vb* **17** (*tr*) to touch or manipulate with the fingers; handle **18** (*tr*) *informal, chiefly US* to identify as a criminal or suspect **19** (*intr*) to extend like a finger **20** to use one's fingers in playing (an instrument, such as a piano or clarinet) **21** to indicate on (a composition or part) the fingering required by a pianist, harpsichordist, etc **22** (*tr; usually passive*) to arrange the keys of (a clarinet, flute, etc) for playing in a certain way [Old English; related to Old Norse *fingr*, Gothic *figgrs*, Old High German *fingar*; see FIVE, FIST] > 'fingerer *n* > 'fingerless *adj*

fingerboard ('fɪŋgəˌbɔːd) *n* the long strip of hard wood on a violin, guitar, or related stringed instrument upon which the strings are stopped by the fingers

finger bowl *n* a small bowl filled with water for rinsing the fingers at the table after a meal

fingerbreadth ('fɪŋgəˌbrɛdθ, -ˌbrɛtθ) *or* **finger's breadth** *n* the width of a finger, used as an indication of length

finger buffet ('bʊfeɪ) *n* a buffet meal at which food that may be picked up with the fingers (**finger food**), such as canapés or vol-au-vents, is served

fingered ('fɪŋgəd) *adj* **1** marked or dirtied by handling **2 a** having a finger or fingers **b** (*in combination*): *nine-fingered; red-fingered* **3** (of a musical part) having numerals indicating the necessary fingering

fingering¹ ('fɪŋgərɪŋ) *n* **1** the technique or art of using one's fingers in playing a musical instrument, esp the piano **2** the numerals in a musical part indicating this

fingering² ('fɪŋgərɪŋ) *n* fine wool for knitting [c17 from earlier *fingram*, perhaps from Old French *fin grain* fine grain]

fingerling ('fɪŋgəlɪŋ) *n* **1** a very young fish, esp the parr of salmon or trout **2** a diminutive creature or object

fingermark ('fɪŋgəˌmɑːk) *n* a mark left by dirty or greasy fingers on paintwork, walls, etc

fingernail ('fɪŋgəˌneɪl) *n* a thin horny translucent plate covering part of the dorsal surface of the end joint of each finger. Related adjs: **ungual, ungular**

finger painting *n* **1** the process or art of painting with **finger paints** of starch, glycerine, and pigments, using the fingers, hand, or arm **2** a painting made in this way

finger post *n* a signpost showing a pointing finger or hand

fingerprint ('fɪŋgəˌprɪnt) *n* **1** an impression of the pattern of ridges on the palmar surface of the end joint of each finger and thumb **2** any identifying characteristic **3** *biochem* the pattern of fragments obtained when a protein is digested by a proteolytic enzyme, usually observed following two-dimensional separation by chromatography and electrophoresis ▷ *vb* **4** (*tr*) to take an inked impression of the fingerprints of (a person) **5** to take a sample of (a person's) DNA

fingerstall ('fɪŋgəˌstɔːl) *n* a protective covering for a finger. Also called: **cot, fingertip**

finger tight *adj* made as tight as possible by hand

fingertip ('fɪŋgəˌtɪp) *n* **1** the end joint or tip of a finger **2** another term for **fingerstall 3 at one's fingertips** readily available and within one's mental grasp

fingertip search *n* a detailed search made by passing the fingers over the scene of a crime or incident

finger trouble *n* *computing* trouble caused by operator error, such as striking the wrong key

finger wave *n* *hairdressing* a wave set in wet hair by using fingers and comb only

Fingo ('fɪŋgəʊ) *n, pl* **-go** *or* **-gos** a member of a Xhosa-speaking people settled in southern Africa in the Ciskei and Transkei: originally refugees from the Zulu wars of conquest

finial ('faɪnɪəl) *n* **1** an ornament on top of a spire, gable, etc, esp in the form of a foliated fleur-de-lys **2** an ornament at the top of a piece of furniture, etc [c14 from *finial* (adj), variant of FINAL] > 'finialed *adj*

finical ('fɪnɪk³l) *adj* another word for **finicky** > ˌfini'cality *n* > 'finically *adv* > 'finicalness *n*

finicky ('fɪnɪkɪ) *or* **finicking** *adj* **1** excessively particular, as in tastes or standards; fussy **2** full of trivial detail; overelaborate [c19 from FINICAL]

fining ('faɪnɪŋ) *n* **1** the process of removing undissolved gas bubbles from molten glass **2** the process of clarifying liquors by the addition of a coagulant **3** (*plural*) a substance, such as isinglass, added to wine, beer, etc, to clarify it [c17 from FINE¹ (in the sense: to clarify, refine)]

finis ('fɪnɪs) *n* the end; finish: used at the end of books, films, etc [c15 from Latin]

finish ('fɪnɪʃ) *vb* (*mainly tr*) **1** to bring to an end; complete, conclude, or stop **2** (*intr*; sometimes foll by *up*) to be at or come to the end; use up **3** to bring to a desired or complete condition **4** to put a particular surface texture on (wood, cloth, etc) **5** (*often foll by off*) to destroy or defeat completely **6** to train (a person) in social graces and talents **7** (*intr*; foll by *with*) **a** to end a relationship or association **b** to stop punishing a person: *I haven't finished with you yet!* ▷ *n* **8** the final or last stage or part; end **9 a** the death, destruction, or absolute defeat of a person or one side in a conflict: *a fight to the finish* **b** the person, event, or thing that brings this about **10 a** the surface texture or appearance of wood, cloth, etc: *a rough finish* **b** a preparation, such as varnish, used to produce such a texture **11** a thing, event, etc, that completes **12** completeness and high quality of workmanship **13** refinement in social graces **14** *sport* ability to sprint at the end of a race: *he has a good finish* [c14 from Old French *finir*, from Latin *finīre* see FINE¹]

finished ('fɪnɪʃt) *adj* **1** perfected **2** (*predicative*) at the end of a task, activity, etc: *they were finished by four* **3** (*predicative*) without further hope of success or continuation: *she was finished as a prima ballerina*

finisher ('fɪnɪʃə) *n* **1** a craftsman who carries out the final tasks in a manufacturing process **2** *boxing* a knockout blow

finishing ('fɪnɪʃɪŋ) *n football* the act or skill of goal scoring: *Brattbakk's finishing is deadly*

finishing school *n* a private school for girls that prepares them for society by teaching social graces and accomplishments

Finistère (ˌfɪnɪ'stɛə; *French* finistɛr) *n* a department of NW France, at the tip of the Breton peninsula. Capital: Quimper. Pop: 863 798 (2003 est). Area: 7029 sq km (2741 sq miles)

Finisterre (ˌfɪnɪ'stɛə) *n* **1 Cape.** a headland in NW Spain: the westernmost point of the Spanish mainland **2** an English name for **Finistère**

finite ('faɪnaɪt) *adj* **1** bounded in magnitude or spatial or temporal extent: *a finite difference* **2** *maths, logic* having a number of elements that is a natural number; able to be counted using the natural numbers less than some natural number. Compare **denumerable, infinite** (sense 4) **3 a** limited or restricted in nature: *human existence is finite* **b** (*as noun*): *the finite* **4** denoting any form or occurrence of a verb inflected for grammatical features such as person, number, and tense [c15 from Latin *finītus* limited, from *finīre* to limit, end] > 'finitely *adv* > 'finiteness *n*

finitism ('faɪnaɪˌtɪzəm) *n philosophy, logic* the view that only those entities may be admitted to mathematics that can be constructed in a finite number of steps, and only those propositions entertained whose truth can be proved in a finite number of steps. Compare **intuitionism**

fink (fɪŋk) *slang, chiefly US and Canadian* ▷ *n* **1** a strikebreaker; blackleg **2** an informer, such as one working for the police; spy **3** an unpleasant, disappointing, or contemptible person ▷ *vb* **4** (*intr*; often foll by *on*) to inform (on someone), as to the police [c20 of uncertain origin]

fin keel *n* a projection from the keel of a vessel to give it additional stability

fink out *vb* (*intr, adverb*) *slang, chiefly US* to fail to carry something out or through; give up

Finland ('fɪnlənd) *n* **1** a republic in N Europe, on the Baltic Sea: ceded to Russia by Sweden in 1809; gained independence in 1917; Soviet invasion successfully withstood in 1939–40, with the loss of Karelia; a member of the European Union. It is generally low-lying, with about 50 000 lakes, extensive forests, and peat bogs. Official languages: Finnish and Swedish. Religion: Christian, Lutheran majority. Currency: euro. Capital: Helsinki. Pop: 5 216 000 (2004 est). Area: 337 000 sq km (130 120 sq miles). Finnish name: **Suomi 2 Gulf of** an arm of the Baltic Sea between Finland, Estonia, and Russia

Finlandization *or* **Finlandisation** (ˌfɪnləndaɪ'zeɪʃən) *n* neutralization of a small country by a superpower, using conciliation, as the former Soviet Union did in relation to Finland

Finn¹ (fɪn) *n* **1** a native, inhabitant, or citizen of Finland **2** a speaker of a Finnic language, esp one of the original inhabitants of Russia, who were pushed northwards during the Slav migrations [Old English *Finnas* (plural); related to Old Norse *Finnr* Finn, Latin *Fennī* the Finns, Greek *Phinnoi*]

Finn² (fɪn) *n* known as **Finn MacCool** (in Irish legend) chief of the Fianna, father of the heroic poet Ossian

finnan haddock ('fɪnən) or **haddie** ('hædɪ) *n* smoked haddock [c18 *finnan* after *Findon*, a village in Scotland south of Aberdeen + HADDOCK]

finned (fɪnd) *adj* having one or more fins or finlike parts

finner ('fɪnə) *n* another name for **rorqual** [c18 from FIN¹ + -ER¹]

Finnic ('fɪnɪk) *n* **1** one of the two branches of the Finno-Ugric family of languages, including Finnish and several languages of NE Europe. Compare **Ugric** ▷ *adj* **2** of or relating to this group of languages or to the Finns

Finnish ('fɪnɪʃ) *adj* **1** of, relating to, or characteristic of Finland, the Finns, or their language ▷ *n* **2** the official language of Finland, also spoken in Estonia and NW Russia, belonging to the Finno-Ugric family

Finnmark ('fɪn,mɑːk) *n* a county of N Norway: the largest, northernmost, and least populated county; mostly a barren plateau. Capital: Vadsø. Pop: 73 210 (2004 est). Area: 48 649 sq km (18 779 sq miles)

finnock ('fɪnək) *n* a young sea trout on its first return to fresh water [originally Scot: from Gaelic *fionnag*, from *fionn* white]

Finno-Ugric ('fɪnəʊ'uːɡrɪk, -'juː-) or **Finno-Ugrian** *n* **1** a family of languages spoken in Scandinavia, Hungary, and NE Europe, including Finnish, Estonian, Hungarian, Ostyak, and Vogul: generally regarded as a subfamily of Uralic. See also **Ural-Altaic** ▷ *adj* **2** of, relating to, speaking, or belonging to this family of languages

finny ('fɪnɪ) *adj* **-nier, -niest 1** *poetic* relating to or containing many fishes **2** having or resembling a fin or fins

fino ('fiːnəʊ) *n* a very dry sherry [from Spanish: FINE¹]

finocchio or **finochio** (fɪ'nɒkɪˌəʊ) *n* a variety of fennel, *Foeniculum vulgare dulce*, with thickened stalks that resemble celery and are eaten as a vegetable, esp in S Europe. Also called: Florence fennel [c18 from Italian: FENNEL]

Finsteraarhorn (German ˌfɪnstər'aːrhɔrn) *n* a mountain in S central Switzerland: highest peak in the Bernese Alps. Height: 4274 m (14 022 ft)

fiord (fjɔːd) *n* a variant spelling of **fjord**

fiorin ('faɪərɪn) *n* a temperate perennial grass, *Agrostis stolonifera*. Also called: **creeping bent grass** See **bent grass** [c19 from Irish Gaelic *fiorthann* wheat grass]

fioritura (ˌfjɔːrɪ'tʊərə, fiː'ərɪ-) *n*, *pl* **-ture** (-'tʊəreɪ) *music* embellishment, esp ornamentation added by the performer [Italian: a blossoming]

fipple ('fɪp'l) *n* **1** a wooden plug forming a flue in the end of a pipe, as the mouthpiece of a recorder **2** a similar device in an organ pipe with a flutelike tone [c17 of unknown origin]

fipple flute *n* an end-blown flute provided with a fipple, such as the recorder or flageolet

fir (fɜː) *n* **1** any pyramidal coniferous tree of the N temperate genus *Abies*, having single needle-like leaves and erect cones: family Pinaceae. See also **red fir, silver fir, balsam fir 2** any of various other trees of the family Pinaceae, such as the Douglas fir **3** the wood of any of these trees [Old English *furh*; related to Old Norse *fura*, Old High German *foraha* fir, Latin *quercus* oak]

fire (faɪə) *n* **1** the state of combustion in which inflammable material burns, producing heat, flames, and often smoke **2 a** a mass of burning coal, wood, etc, used esp in a hearth to heat a room **b** (*in combination*): *firewood; firelighter* **3** a destructive conflagration, as of a forest, building, etc **4** a device for heating a room, etc **5** something resembling a fire in light or brilliance: *a diamond's fire* **6** a flash or spark of or as if of fire **7**

a the act of discharging weapons, artillery, etc **b** the shells, etc, fired **8** a burst or rapid volley: *a fire of questions* **9** intense passion; ardour **10** liveliness, as of imagination, thought, etc **11** a burning sensation sometimes produced by drinking strong alcoholic liquor **12** fever and inflammation **13** a severe trial or torment (esp in the phrase **go through fire and water**) **14** **catch fire** to ignite **15** **draw someone's fire** to attract the criticism or censure of someone **16** **hang fire a** to delay firing **b** to delay or be delayed **17** **no smoke without fire** the evidence strongly suggests something has indeed happened **18** **on fire a** in a state of ignition **b** ardent or eager **c** *informal* playing or performing at the height of one's abilities **19** **open fire** to start firing a gun, artillery, etc **20** **play with fire** to be involved in something risky **21** **set fire to** or **set on fire a** to ignite **b** to arouse or excite **22** **set the world** or (*Brit*) **the Thames** or (*Scot*) **the heather on fire** *informal* to cause a great sensation **23** **under fire** being attacked, as by weapons or by harsh criticism **24** (*modifier*) *astrology* of or relating to a group of three signs of the zodiac, Aries, Leo, and Sagittarius. Compare **earth** (sense 10), **air** (sense 20), **water** (sense 12) ▷ *vb* **25** to discharge (a firearm or projectile) or (of a firearm, etc) to be discharged **26** to detonate (an explosive charge or device) or (of such a charge or device) to be detonated **27** (*tr*) *informal* to dismiss from employment **28** (*tr*) *ceramics* to bake in a kiln to harden the clay, fix the glaze, etc **29** to kindle or be kindled; ignite **30** (*tr*) to provide with fuel: *oil fires the heating system* **31** (*intr*) to tend a fire **32** (*tr*) to subject to heat **33** (*tr*) to heat slowly so as to dry **34** (*tr*) to arouse to strong emotion **35** to glow or cause to glow **36** (*intr*) (of an internal-combustion engine) to ignite **37** (*intr*) (of grain) to become blotchy or yellow before maturity **38** *vet science* another word for **cauterize 39** (*intr*) *Austral informal* (of a sportsman, etc) to play well or with enthusiasm ▷ *sentence substitute* **40** a cry to warn others of a fire **41** the order to begin firing a gun, artillery, etc [Old English *fȳr*; related to Old Saxon *fiur*, Old Norse *fūrr*, Old High German *fūir*, Greek *pur*] ▷ **'fireable** *adj* ▷ **'fireless** *adj* ▷ **'firer** *n*

fire alarm *n* **1** a device to give warning of fire, esp a bell, siren, or hooter **2** a shout to warn that a fire has broken out

fire-and-brimstone *adj* (of a sermon, preacher, etc) zealous, esp in threatening eternal damnation

fire ant *n* any mound-building predatory ant of the genus *Solenopsis*, of tropical and subtropical America, that can inflict a painful sting

firearm ('faɪərˌɑːm) *n* a weapon, esp a portable gun or pistol, from which a projectile can be discharged by an explosion caused by igniting gunpowder, etc

fire away *vb* (*intr, adverb; often imperative*) *informal* to begin to speak or to ask questions

fireback ('faɪəˌbæk) *n* **1** Also called: **reredos** an ornamental iron slab against the back wall of a hearth **2** any pheasant of the genus *Lophura*, of SE Asia

fireball ('faɪəˌbɔːl) *n* **1** a ball-shaped discharge of lightning **2** the bright spherical region of hot ionized gas at the centre of a nuclear explosion **3** *astronomy* another name for **bolide 4** *slang* an energetic person

firebase ('faɪəˌbeɪs) *n* an artillery base supporting advancing troops

firebird ('faɪəˌbɜːd) *n* *chiefly US* any of various songbirds having a bright red plumage, esp the Baltimore oriole

fire blanket *n* a large blanket-like piece of fire resistant material such as fibreglass used in smothering a fire

fire blight *n* a disease of apples, pears, and similar fruit trees, caused by the bacterium *Erwinia amylovora* and characterized by blackening of the blossoms and leaves, and cankers on the

branches

fireboat ('faɪəˌbəʊt) *n* a motor vessel with fire-fighting apparatus

firebomb ('faɪəˌbɒm) *n* another name for **incendiary** (sense 6)

firebox ('faɪəˌbɒks) *n* **1** the furnace chamber of a boiler in a steam locomotive **2** an obsolete word for **tinderbox**

firebrand ('faɪəˌbrænd) *n* **1** a piece of burning or glowing wood or other material **2** a person who causes unrest or is very energetic

firebrat ('faɪəˌbræt) *n* a small primitive wingless insect, *Thermobia domestica*, that occurs in warm buildings, feeding on starchy food scraps, fabric, etc: order Thysanura (bristletails)

firebreak ('faɪəˌbreɪk) *n* **1** Also: **fireguard, fire line** a strip of open land in forest or prairie, to arrest the advance of a fire **2** a measure taken to arrest the advance of anything dangerous or harmful

firebrick ('faɪəˌbrɪk) *n* a refractory brick made of fire clay, used for lining furnaces, flues, etc

fire brigade *n* *chiefly Brit* an organized body of firefighters

firebug ('faɪəˌbʌɡ) *n* *informal* a person who deliberately sets fire to property

fire clay *n* a heat-resistant clay used in the making of firebricks, furnace linings, etc

fire company *n* **1** an insurance company selling policies relating to fire risk **2** US an organized body of firemen

fire control *n* *military* the procedures by which weapons are brought to engage a target

firecracker ('faɪəˌkrækə) *n* **1** a small cardboard container filled with explosive powder and lit by a fuse ▷ *adj* **2** impressively energetic: *a firecracker start to the race*

firecrest ('faɪəˌkrest) *n* a small European warbler, *Regulus ignicapillus*, having a crown striped with yellow, black, and white

fire-cure *vb* (*tr*) to cure (tobacco) by exposure to the smoke and heat of an open fire

firedamp ('faɪəˌdæmp) *n* a mixture of hydrocarbons, chiefly methane, formed in coal mines. It forms explosive mixtures with air. See also **afterdamp**

fire department *n* US and Canadian the department of a local authority responsible for the prevention and extinguishing of fires

firedog ('faɪəˌdɒɡ) *n* either of a pair of decorative metal stands used to support logs in an open fire

fire door *n* **1** a door made of noncombustible material, the purpose of which is to prevent a fire from spreading within a building **2** a similar door, leading to the outside of a building, that can be easily opened from inside; emergency exit

firedrake ('faɪəˌdreɪk) or **firedragon** ('faɪəˌdræɡən) *n* *myth* a fire-breathing dragon

fire drill *n* a rehearsal of duties or escape procedures to be followed in case of fire

fire-eater *n* **1** a performer who simulates the swallowing of fire **2** a belligerent person ▷ **'fire-ˌeating** *n, adj*

fire engine *n* a heavy road vehicle that carries firemen and fire-fighting equipment to a fire

fire escape *n* a means of evacuating persons from a building in the event of fire, esp a metal staircase outside the building

fire-extinguisher *n* a portable device for extinguishing fires, usually consisting of a canister with a directional nozzle used to direct a spray of water, chemically generated foam, inert gas, or fine powder onto the fire

firefight ('faɪəˌfaɪt) *n* a brief small-scale engagement between opposing military ground forces using short-range light weapons

firefighter ('faɪəˌfaɪtə) *n* a person who fights fires, usually a public employee or trained volunteer

firefighting ('faɪəˌfaɪtɪŋ) *n* **1 a** the occupation of attempting to control and extinguish fires **b** (*as modifier*): *firefighting equipment* **2** the practice of reacting to urgent problems as they arise, as

f

opposed to planning for the future

firefly ('faɪəˌflaɪ) *n, pl* **-flies** 1 any nocturnal beetle of the family *Lampyridae*, common in warm and tropical regions, having luminescent abdominal organs. See also **glow-worm** 2 any tropical American click beetle of the genus *Pyrophorus*, esp *P. noctiluca*, that have luminescent thoracic organs

fireguard ('faɪəˌgɑːd) *n* 1 Also called: **fire screen** a metal panel or meshed frame put before an open fire to protect against falling logs, sparks, etc 2 a less common word for **firebreak**

fire hall *n US and Canadian* a fire station

fire hydrant *n* a hydrant for use as an emergency supply for fighting fires, esp one in a street. Also called (esp US and NZ): **fireplug**

fire insurance *n* insurance covering damage or loss caused by fire or lightning

fire irons *pl n* metal fireside implements, such as poker, shovel, and tongs

fireless cooker *n* an insulated container that retains enough heat to cook food or keep it warm

firelock ('faɪəˌlɒk) *n* 1 an obsolete type of gunlock with a priming mechanism ignited by sparks 2 a gun or musket having such a lock

fireman ('faɪəmən) *n, pl* **-men** 1 a man who fights fires, usually a public employee or trained volunteer 2 **a** (on steam locomotives) the man who stokes the fire and controls the injectors feeding water to the boiler **b** (on diesel and electric locomotives) the driver's assistant 3 a man who tends furnaces; stoker 4 Also called: **deputy** a mine official responsible for safety precautions. US equivalent: **fire boss** 5 *US navy* a junior rating who works on marine engineering equipment

fire marshal *n US* 1 a public official responsible for investigating the causes of fires, enforcing fire prevention laws, etc 2 the head of a fire prevention organization

Firenze (fi'rɛntse) *n* the Italian name for **Florence**

fire opal *n* an orange-red translucent variety of opal, valued as a gemstone

firepan ('faɪəˌpæn) *n* a metal container for a fire in a room

fireplace ('faɪəˌpleɪs) *n* 1 an open recess in a wall of a room, at the base of a chimney, etc, for a fire; hearth 2 *Austral* an authorized place or installation for outside cooking, esp by a roadside

fireplug ('faɪəˌplʌg) *n* another name (esp US and NZ) for **fire hydrant**

fire power *n military* 1 the amount of fire that may be delivered by a unit or weapon 2 the capability of delivering fire

fireproof ('faɪəˌpruːf) *adj* 1 capable of resisting damage by fire ▷ *vb* 2 *(tr)* to make resistant to fire

fire raiser *n* a person who deliberately sets fire to property > **fire raising** *n*

fire sale *n* 1 a sale of goods at reduced prices after a fire at a shop or factory 2 any instance of offering goods or assets at greatly reduced prices to ensure a quick sale

fire screen *n* 1 a decorative screen placed in the hearth when there is no fire 2 a screen placed before a fire to protect the face from intense heat

fire ship *n* a vessel loaded with explosives and used, esp formerly, as a bomb by igniting it and directing it to drift among an enemy's warships

fireside ('faɪəˌsaɪd) *n* 1 the hearth 2 family life; the home

fire station *n* a building where fire-fighting vehicles and equipment are stationed and where firefighters on duty wait. Also called (US): **firehouse, station house**

firestone ('faɪəˌstəʊn) *n* a sandstone that withstands intense heat, esp one used for lining kilns, furnaces, etc

firestorm ('faɪəˌstɔːm) *n* an uncontrollable blaze sustained by violent winds that are drawn into the column of rising hot air over the burning area: often the result of heavy bombing

firethorn ('faɪəˌθɔːn) *n* any rosaceous evergreen spiny shrub of the genus *Pyracantha*, of SE Europe and Asia, having bright red or orange fruits: cultivated for ornament

fire trail *n Austral* a permanent track cleared through the bush to provide access for fire-fighting

firetrap ('faɪəˌtræp) *n* a building that would burn easily or one without fire escapes

fire walking *n* a religious rite in which people walk barefoot over white-hot ashes, stones, etc

firewall *n* 1 a fireproof wall or partition used to impede the progress of a fire, as from one room or compartment to another 2 *computing* a computer system that isolates another computer from the internet in order to prevent unauthorized access

firewarden ('faɪəˌwɔːdᵊn) *n US and Canadian* an officer responsible for fire prevention and control in an area, esp in a forest

fire watcher *n* a person who watches for fires, esp those caused by aerial bombardment

firewater ('faɪəˌwɔːtə) *n* any strong spirit, esp whisky

fireweed ('faɪəˌwiːd) *n* 1 any of various plants that appear as first vegetation in burnt-over areas, esp rosebay willowherb 2 Also called: **pilewort** a weedy North American plant, *Erechtites hieracifolia*, having small white or greenish flowers: family *Asteraceae* (composites) ▷ *n* an Australian rainforest tree, *Stenocarpus sinuatus*, having whorls of bright red flowers

firework ('faɪəˌwɜːk) *n* a device, such as a Catherine wheel, Roman candle, or rocket, in which combustible materials are ignited and produce coloured flames, sparks, and smoke, sometimes accompanied by bangs

fireworks ('faɪəˌwɜːks) *pl n* 1 a show in which large numbers of fireworks are let off simultaneously 2 *informal* an exciting or spectacular exhibition, as of musical virtuosity or wit 3 *informal* a burst of temper

firie ('faɪərɪ) *n Austral informal* a firefighter

firing ('faɪərɪŋ) *n* 1 the process of baking ceramics, etc, in a kiln or furnace: *a second firing* 2 the act of stoking a fire or furnace 3 a discharge of a firearm 4 something used as fuel, such as coal or wood 5 *US* a scorching of plants, as a result of disease, drought, or heat

firing line *n* 1 *military* **a** the positions from which fire is delivered **b** the soldiers occupying these positions 2 the leading or most advanced position in an activity

firing order *n* the sequence of ignition in the cylinders of an internal-combustion engine

firing party *n* 1 a military detachment detailed to fire a salute at a funeral 2 another name for **firing squad**

firing pin *n* the part of the firing mechanism of a firearm that ignites the charge by striking the primer

firing squad *n* a small military detachment formed to implement a death sentence by shooting

firkin ('fɜːkɪn) *n* 1 a small wooden barrel or similar container 2 *Brit* a unit of capacity equal to nine gallons [C14 *fir*, from Middle Dutch *vierde* FOURTH + -KIN]

firm[1] (fɜːm) *adj* 1 not soft or yielding to a touch or pressure; rigid; solid 2 securely in position; stable or stationary 3 definitely established; decided; settled 4 enduring or steady; constant 5 having determination or strength; resolute 6 (of prices, markets, etc) tending to rise ▷ *adv* 7 in a secure, stable, or unyielding manner: *he stood firm over his obligation to pay* ▷ *vb* 8 (sometimes foll by *up*) to make or become firm 9 *(intr) Austral horse racing* (of a horse) to shorten in odds [C14 from Latin *firmus*] > '**firmly** *adv* > '**firmness** *n*

firm[2] (fɜːm) *n* 1 a business partnership 2 any commercial enterprise 3 a team of doctors and their assistants 4 *Brit slang* **a** a gang of criminals **b** a gang of football hooligans [C16 (in the sense: signature): from Spanish *firma* signature, title of a partnership or business concern, from *firmar* to sign, from Latin *firmāre* to confirm, from *firmus* firm]

firmament ('fɜːməmənt) *n* the expanse of the sky; heavens [C13 from Late Latin *firmāmentum* sky (considered as fixed above the earth), from Latin: prop, support, from *firmāre* to make FIRM[1]] > **firmamental** (ˌfɜːmə'mɛntᵊl) *adj*

firman (fɜː'mɑːn, 'fɜː-) *n* 1 an edict of an Oriental sovereign 2 any authoritative grant of permission [C17 from Persian *fermān*]

firmer chisel ('fɜːmə) *n* a chisel or gouge with a thin blade, used on wood. Sometimes shortened to: **firmer**

firmware ('fɜːmˌwɛə) *n computing* a fixed form of software programmed into a read-only memory

firn (fɪən) *n* another name for **névé** (sense 1) [C19 from German (Swiss dialect) *firn* of the previous year, from Old High German *firni* old]

firn line *n* 1 Also called: **firn limit** the zone of a glacier between the lower region of solid ice and the upper region of névé, above which ablation occurs 2 the snow line on a glacier

firry ('fɜːrɪ) *adj* 1 of, relating to, or made from fir trees 2 abounding in or dominated by firs

first (fɜːst) *adj (usually prenominal)* 1 **a** coming before all others; earliest, best, or foremost **b** *(as noun)*: *I was the first to arrive* 2 preceding all others in numbering or counting order; the ordinal number of *one*. Often written: 1st 3 rated, graded, or ranked above all other levels 4 denoting the lowest forward ratio of a gearbox in a motor vehicle 5 *music* **a** denoting the highest part assigned to one of the voice parts in a chorus or one of the sections of an orchestra: *first soprano; the first violins* **b** denoting the principal player in a specific orchestral section: *he plays first horn* 6 **first thing** as the first action of the day: *I'll see you first thing tomorrow* 7 **first things first** things must be done in order of priority 8 **the first thing, idea,** etc *(in negative constructions)* even one thing, etc: *he doesn't know the first thing about me* ▷ *n* 9 the beginning; outset: *I knew you were a rogue from the first; I couldn't see at first because of the mist* 10 *education, chiefly Brit* an honours degree of the highest class. Full term: **first-class honours degree** 11 something which has not occurred before: *a first for the company* 12 the lowest forward ratio of a gearbox in a motor vehicle; low gear 13 *music* **a** the highest part in a particular section of a chorus or orchestra **b** the instrument or voice taking such a part **c** the chief or leading player in a section of an orchestra; principal 14 *music* a rare word for **prime** (sense 11) ▷ *adv* 15 before anything else in order, time, preference, importance, etc: *do this first; first, remove the head and tail of the fish* 16 **first and last** on the whole; overall 17 **from first to last** throughout 18 for the first time: *I've loved you since I first saw you* 19 *(sentence modifier)* in the first place or beginning of a series of actions: *first I want to talk about criminality* ▷ See also **firsts** [Old English *fyrest*; related to Old Saxon *furist*, Old Norse *fyrstr*, German *Fürst* prince, one who is first in rank]

first aid *n* 1 **a** immediate medical assistance given in an emergency **b** *(as modifier)*: *first-aid box* 2 (in Barbados) a small shop that sells domestic items after hours

first base *n* 1 *baseball* **a** the base that a runner must reach safely to score a hit, and the first of the three bases he must reach safely on the way to home plate in order to score a run **b** the fielding position nearest this base 2 **get to first base** *informal, chiefly US and Canadian* to accomplish the first step of an undertaking

first blood *n* 1 the first killing or wounding in a fight or war 2 the first damage or reverse inflicted on an opponent in a conflict

first-born *adj* 1 eldest of the children in a family ▷ *n* 2 the eldest child in a family

first cause *n* 1 a source or cause of something 2 *(often capitals)* (esp in philosophy) God considered as the uncaused creator of all beings apart from himself

first class n **1** the class or grade of the best or highest value, quality, etc ▷ adj (**first-class** when prenominal) **2** of the best or highest class or grade: a first-class citizen **3** excellent; first-rate **4** of or denoting the most comfortable and expensive class of accommodation in a hotel, aircraft, train, etc **5 a** (in Britain) of or relating to mail that is processed most quickly **b** (in the US and Canada) of or relating to mail that consists mainly of written letters, cards, etc **6** education See **first** (sense 10) ▷ adv **first-class 7** by first-class mail, means of transportation, etc

first-day cover n philately a cover, usually an envelope, postmarked on the first day of the issue of its stamps

first-degree burn n pathol See **burn** (sense 22)

First Empire n the period of imperial rule in France (1804–14) under Napoleon Bonaparte

first estate n the first of the three estates of the realm, such as the Lords Spiritual in England or the clergy in France until the revolution

First Fleet n Austral the fleet of convict ships that arrived at Port Jackson in 1788 > First Fleeter n

first floor n **1** Brit the floor or storey of a building immediately above the ground floor. US and Canadian term: **second floor 2** US and Canadian another term for **ground floor**

first-foot chiefly Scot ▷ n also **first-footer 1** the first person to enter a household in the New Year. By Hogmanay tradition a dark-haired man who crosses the threshold at midnight brings good luck ▷ vb **2** to enter (a house) as first-foot > 'first-'footing n

first four ships pl n NZ **1** the earliest settlers' ships to arrive in the Canterbury Province **2 come with the first four ships** to be a founder member of Canterbury

first fruits pl n **1** the first results, products, or profits of an undertaking **2** fruit that ripens first

first-hand adj, adv **1** from the original source; direct or directly: first-hand news; he got the news first-hand **2** at first hand from the original source; directly

First International n an association of socialists and labour leaders founded in London in 1864 and dissolved in Philadelphia in 1876. Official name: International Workingmen's Association

first lady n (often capitals) **1** (in the US) the wife or official hostess of a chief executive, esp of a state governor or a president **2** a woman considered to be at the top of her profession or art: the first lady of jazz

first language n a person's native language

first lieutenant n **1** the officer responsible for the upkeep and maintenance of a warship, esp the executive officer of a smaller ship in the Royal Navy **2** an officer holding commissioned rank in the US Army, Air Force, Marine Corps, or in certain other forces, senior to a second lieutenant and junior to a captain

first light n the time when light first appears in the morning; dawn

first-line adj acting or used as a first resort: first-line treatment; first-line batsmen

firstling ('f3:stlɪŋ) n the first, esp the first offspring

first-loss policy n an insurance policy for goods in which a total loss is extremely unlikely and the insurer agrees to provide cover for a sum less than the total value of the property

firstly ('f3:stlɪ) adv coming before other points, questions, etc

first mate n an officer second in command to the captain of a merchant ship. Also called: **first officer**

First Minister n **1** the chief minister of the Northern Ireland Assembly **2** the chief minister of the Scottish Parliament

first mortgage n a mortgage that has priority over other mortgages on the same property, except for taxation and other statutory liabilities

First Mover n the Aristotelian conception of God as the unmoved mover of everything else

first name n a name given to a person at birth, as opposed to a surname. Also called: **Christian name, forename, given name**

First Nation n (also without capitals) Canadian another name for **band¹** (sense 5)

first night n **a** the first public performance of a play or other production **b** (as modifier): first-night nerves

first-nighter n a member of an opening night audience, esp one who habitually attends first nights

first offender n a person convicted of any criminal offence for the first time

first officer n **1** another name for **first mate 2** the member of an aircraft crew who is second in command to the captain

first-order adj logic quantifying only over individuals and not over predicates or clauses: **first-order predicate calculus** studies the logical properties of such quantification

first-past-the-post n (modifier) of or relating to a voting system in which a candidate may be elected by a simple majority rather than an absolute majority. Compare **proportional representation**

First Peoples pl n Canadian a collective term for the Native Canadian peoples, the Inuit, and the Métis

first person n a grammatical category of pronouns and verbs used by the speaker to refer to or talk about himself, either alone (**first person singular**) or together with others (**first person plural**)

first post n Brit the first of two military bugle calls ordering or giving notice of the time to retire for the night. The second is called **last post**

first principle n (usually plural) **1** one of the fundamental assumptions on which a particular theory or procedure is thought to be based **2** an axiom of a mathematical or scientific theory

first quarter n one of the four principal phases of the moon, occurring between new moon and full moon, when half of the lighted surface is visible from earth. Compare **last quarter**

first-rate adj **1** of the best or highest rated class or quality **2** informal very good; excellent ▷ adv **3** not standard very well; excellently

first reading n the introduction of a bill in a legislative assembly

first refusal n the chance of buying a house, merchandise, etc, before the offer is made to other potential buyers

First Republic n the republic in France, which lasted from the abolition of the monarchy in 1792 until Napoleon Bonaparte proclaimed himself emperor in 1804

firsts (f3:sts) pl n saleable goods of the highest quality

first school n Brit a school for children aged between 5 and 8 or 9. Compare **middle school**

First Secretary n the chief minister of the National Assembly for Wales

first-strike adj (of a nuclear missile) intended for use in an opening attack calculated to destroy the enemy's nuclear weapons

first string n **1** the top player of a team in an individual sport, such as squash ▷ adj **first-string 2** being a regular member of a team rather than a substitute or reserve **3** being the top player of a team in an individual sport **4** of high rating; first-class

first water n **1** the finest quality of diamond or other precious stone **2** the highest grade or best quality **3** the most extreme kind: a fool of the first water

First World War n another name for **World War I**

firth (f3:θ) or **frith** n a relatively narrow inlet of the sea, esp in Scotland [c15 from Old Norse fjörthr FIORD]

fisc (fisk) n rare a state or royal treasury [c16 from Latin fiscus treasury, originally money-bag]

fiscal ('fɪskəl) adj **1** of or relating to government finances, esp tax revenues **2** of or involving financial matters ▷ n **3 a** (in some countries) a public prosecutor **b** Scot short for **procurator fiscal 4** a postage or other stamp signifying payment of a tax [c16 from Latin fiscālis concerning the state treasury, from fiscus public money; see FISC] > 'fiscally adv

fiscal drag n economics the process by which, during inflation, rising incomes draw people into higher tax brackets, so that their real incomes may fall; this acts as a restraint on the expansion of the economy

fiscal year n US and Canadian **1** any annual period at the end of which a firm's accounts are made up **2** the annual period ending April 5, over which Budget estimates are made by the British Government and which functions as the income-tax year. Also called (in Britain and certain other countries): **financial year**

fish (fɪʃ) n, pl fish or fishes **1 a** any of a large group of cold-blooded aquatic vertebrates having jaws, gills, and usually fins and a skin covered in scales: includes the sharks and rays (class Chondrichthyes: **cartilaginous fishes**) and the teleosts, lungfish, etc (class Osteichthyes: **bony fishes**) **b** (in combination): fishpond. Related adjs: **ichthyic, ichthyoid, piscine 2** any of various similar but jawless vertebrates, such as the hagfish and lamprey **3** (not in technical use) any of various aquatic invertebrates, such as the cuttlefish, jellyfish, and crayfish **4** the flesh of fish used as food **5** informal a person of little emotion or intelligence: a poor fish **6** short for **fishplate 7** Also called: tin fish an informal word for **torpedo** (sense 1) **8 a fine kettle of fish** an awkward situation; mess **9 drink like a fish** to drink (esp alcohol) to excess **10 have other fish to fry** to have other activities to do, esp more important ones **11 like a fish out of water** out of one's usual place **12 neither fish, flesh, nor fowl** neither this nor that **13 make fish of one and flesh of another** Irish to discriminate unfairly between people ▷ vb **14** (intr) to attempt to catch fish, as with a line and hook or with nets, traps, etc **15** (tr) to fish in (a particular area of water) **16** to search (a body of water) for something or to search for something, esp in a body of water **17** (intr; foll by for) to seek something indirectly: to fish for compliments ▷ See also **fish out** [Old English fisc; related to Old Norse fiskr, Gothic fiscs, Russian piskar, Latin piscis] > 'fishable adj > 'fish,like adj

FISH (fɪʃ) n acronym for fluorescence in situ hybridization, a technique for detecting and locating gene mutations and chromosome abnormalities

fish and brewis n Canadian a Newfoundland dish of cooked salt cod and soaked hard bread

fish and chips n fish fillets coated with batter and deep-fried, eaten with potato chips

fish-and-chip shop n (esp in Britain) a place where fish and chips are cooked and sold

fishbolt ('fɪʃ,bəʊlt) n a bolt used for fastening a fishplate to a rail

fishbone fern ('fɪʃ,bəʊn) n a common Australian fern, Nephrolepis cordifolia, having fronds with many pinnae

fishbowl ('fɪʃ,bəʊl) n another name for **goldfish bowl**

fishcake n a fried ball of flaked fish mixed with mashed potatoes

fish eagle n another name for the **osprey**

fisher ('fɪʃə) n **1** a person who fishes; fisherman **2** Also called: pekan **a** a large North American marten, Martes pennanti, having thick dark brown fur **b** the fur of this animal **3 fisher of men** an evangelist

fisherman ('fɪʃəmən) n, pl -men **1** a person who fishes as a profession or for sport **2** a vessel used for fishing

fisherman's bend n a knot used to fasten a rope to an anchor, ring, or spar

f

fisherman's knot *n* a knot for joining two ropes of equal thickness consisting of an overhand knot or double overhand knot by each rope round the other, so that the two knots jam when pulled tight

fishery ('fɪʃərɪ) *n, pl* **-eries 1 a** the industry of catching, processing, and selling fish **b** a place where this is carried on **2** a place where fish are reared **3** a fishing ground **4** another word for **piscary** (sense 2)

Fishes ('fɪʃɪz) *n* **the** the constellation Pisces, the twelfth sign of the zodiac

fisheye lens ('fɪʃ,aɪ) *n photog* a lens of small focal length, having a highly curved protruding front element, that covers an angle of view of almost 180°. It yields a circular image having considerable linear distortion

fishfinger ('fɪʃ,fɪŋgə) or *US and Canadian* **fish stick** *n* an oblong piece of filleted or minced fish coated in breadcrumbs

fish flake *n Canadian* a platform on which fish are dried

fishgig ('fɪʃ,gɪg) *n* a pole with barbed prongs for impaling fish. Also: **fizgig** [C17 of uncertain origin; perhaps altered from Spanish *fisga* harpoon]

Fishguard ('fɪʃ,gɑːd) *n* a port and resort in SW Wales, in Pembrokeshire: ferry connections to Cork and Rosslare. Pop: 3193 (2001)

fish hawk *n* another name for the **osprey**

fish-hook *n* **1** a sharp hook used in angling, esp one with a barb **2** *logic* a symbol (−ɔ) for entailment

fishing ('fɪʃɪŋ) *n* **1 a** the occupation of catching fish **b** (*as modifier*): *a fishing match* **2** another word for **piscary** (sense 2) Related adj: **piscatorial**

fishing ground *n* an area of water that is good for fishing

fishing rod *n* a long tapered flexible pole, often in jointed sections, for use with a fishing line and, usually, a reel

fishing tackle *n* all the equipment, such as rods, lines, bait, etc, used in angling

fish joint *n* a connection formed by fishplates at the meeting point of two rails, beams, etc, as on a railway

fish ladder *n* a row of ascending pools or weirs connected by short falls to allow fish to pass barrages or dams

fish louse *n* any small flat rounded crustacean of the subclass *Branchiura*, having sucking mouth parts: parasites of fish

fishmeal ('fɪʃ,miːl) *n* ground dried fish used as feed for farm animals, as a fertilizer, etc

fishmonger ('fɪʃ,mʌŋgə) *n chiefly Brit* a retailer of fish

fishnet ('fɪʃ,nɛt) *n* **1** *chiefly US and Canadian* a net for catching fish **2 a** an open mesh fabric resembling netting **b** (*as modifier*): *fishnet tights*

fish out *vb* (*tr, adverb*) to find or extract (something)

fishplate ('fɪʃ,pleɪt) *n* a flat piece of metal joining one rail, stanchion, or beam to another

fishskin disease ('fɪʃ,skɪn) *n pathol* a nontechnical name for **ichthyosis**

fishtail ('fɪʃ,teɪl) *n* **1** an aeroplane manoeuvre in which the tail is moved from side to side to reduce speed **2** a nozzle having a long narrow slot at the top, placed over a Bunsen burner to produce a thin fanlike flame **3** (*intr*) (of an aeroplane) to slow an aeroplane by moving the tail from side to side **4** to drive with the rear of the vehicle moving from side to side in an uncontrolled fashion

fish tail *n* a step in ballroom dancing in which the feet are quickly crossed

fishway ('fɪʃ,weɪ) *n US and Canadian* another name for **fish ladder**

fishwife ('fɪʃ,waɪf) *n, pl* **-wives 1** a woman who sells fish **2** a coarse scolding woman > 'fish,wifely *adj*

fishy ('fɪʃɪ) *adj* **fishier, fishiest 1** of, involving, or suggestive of fish **2** abounding in fish **3** *informal* suspicious, doubtful, or questionable: *their leaving at the same time looked fishy* **4** dull and lifeless: *a fishy*

look > 'fishily *adv* > 'fishiness *n*

fissi- *combining form* indicating a splitting or cleft: *fissirostral* [from Latin *fissus*, past participle of *findere* to split]

fissile ('fɪsaɪl) *adj* **1** *Brit* capable of undergoing nuclear fission as a result of the impact of slow neutrons **2** *US and Canadian* capable of undergoing nuclear fission as a result of any process. Another word for: **fissionable 3** tending to split or capable of being split [C17 from Latin *fissilis*, from *fissus* split; see FISSI-] > **fissility** (fɪ'sɪlɪtɪ) *n*

fission ('fɪʃən) *n* **1** the act or process of splitting or breaking into parts **2** *biology* a form of asexual reproduction in single-celled animals and plants involving a division into two or more equal parts that develop into new cells **3** short for **nuclear fission** [C19 from Latin *fissiō* a cleaving]

fissionable ('fɪʃənəbᵊl) *adj* capable of undergoing nuclear fission as a result of any process. Compare **fissile** (sense 1) > ,fissiona'bility *n*

fission bomb *n* a bomb in which the energy is supplied by nuclear fission. See **atomic bomb**

fission-fusion bomb *n* another name for **fusion bomb**

fission product *n* a nuclide produced either directly by nuclear fission or by the radioactive decay of such a nuclide

fission reactor *n* a nuclear reactor in which a fission reaction takes place

fission-track dating *n* the dating of samples of minerals by comparing the tracks in them by fission fragments of the uranium nuclei they contain, before and after irradiation by neutrons

fissipalmate (,fɪsɪ'pælmeɪt) *adj* (of some birds' feet) partially webbed, having lobes and fringes on separate toes

fissiparous (fɪ'sɪpərəs) *adj* **1** *biology* reproducing by fission **2** having a tendency to divide into groups or factions > fis'siparously *adv* > fis'siparousness *n*

fissiped ('fɪsɪ,pɛd) or **fissipedal** (fɪ'sɪpɪdᵊl, ,fɪsɪ'piːdᵊl) *adj* **1** having toes that are separated from one another, as dogs, cats, bears, and similar carnivores ▷ *n* **2** a fissiped animal ▷ Compare **pinniped**

fissirostral (,fɪsɪ'rɒstrəl) *adj* **1** (of the beaks of some birds) broad and deeply cleft **2** having such a beak, as swifts and swallows

fissure ('fɪʃə) *n* **1** any long narrow cleft or crack, esp in a rock **2** a weakness or flaw indicating impending disruption or discord: *fissures in a decaying empire* **3** *anatomy* a narrow split or groove that divides an organ such as the brain, lung, or liver into lobes. See also **sulcus 4** a small unnatural crack in the skin or mucous membrane, as between the toes or at the anus **5** a minute crack in the surface of a tooth, caused by imperfect joining of enamel during development ▷ *vb* **6** to crack or split apart [C14 from medical Latin *fissūra*, from Latin *fissus* split]

fissure eruption *n* the emergence of lava from a fissure in the ground rather than from a volcanic cone or vent

fissure of Rolando (rəʊ'lændəʊ) *n* another name for **central sulcus** [C19 named after L. *Rolando* (died 1831), Italian anatomist]

fissure of Sylvius ('sɪlvɪəs) *n* a deep horizontal cleft in each cerebral hemisphere: marks the separation of the temporal lobe from the frontal and parietal lobes [named after Franciscus *Sylvius* (died 1652), German anatomist]

fist (fɪst) *n* **1** a hand with the fingers clenched into the palm, as for hitting **2** Also called: **fistful** the quantity that can be held in a fist or hand **3** an informal word for **hand** or **index** (sense 9) ▷ *vb* **4** (*tr*) to hit with the fist [Old English *fȳst*; related to Old Frisian *fest*, Old Saxon, Old High German *fūst*; see FIVE]

fistic ('fɪstɪk) *adj* of or relating to fisticuffs or boxing

fisticuffs ('fɪstɪ,kʌfs) *pl n* combat with the fists

[C17 probably from *fisty* with the fist + CUFF²]

fistmele ('fɪst,miːl) *n archery* a measure of the width of a hand and the extended thumb, used to calculate the approximate height of the string of a braced bow [C17 from FIST + *mele*, variant of obsolete *meal* measure]

fistula ('fɪstjʊlə) *n, pl* **-las** or **-lae** (-,liː) **1** *pathol* an abnormal opening between one hollow organ and another or between a hollow organ and the surface of the skin, caused by ulceration, congenital malformation, etc **2** *obsolete* any musical wind instrument; a pipe [C14 from Latin: pipe, tube, hollow reed, ulcer]

fistulous ('fɪstjʊləs), **fistular** ('fɪstjʊlə) or **fistulate** ('fɪstjʊlɪt) *adj* **1** *pathol* containing, relating to, or resembling a fistula **2** hollow, esp slender and hollow; reedlike or tubular **3** containing tubes or tubelike parts

fit¹ (fɪt) *vb* **fits, fitting, fitted** or *US* **fit 1** to be appropriate or suitable for (a situation, etc) **2** to be of the correct size or shape for (a connection, container, etc) **3** (*tr*) to adjust in order to render appropriate **4** (*tr*) to supply with that which is needed **5** (*tr*) to try clothes on (someone) in order to make adjustments if necessary **6** (*tr*) to make competent or ready: *the experience helped to fit him for the task* **7** (*tr*) to locate with care **8** (*intr*) to correspond with the facts or circumstances ▷ *adj* **fitter, fittest 9** suitable to a purpose or design; appropriate **10** having the right qualifications; qualifying **11** in good health **12** worthy or deserving: *a book fit to be read* **13** (foll by an infinitive) in such an extreme condition that a specified consequence is likely: *she was fit to scream* **14** *informal* (of a person) sexually attractive ▷ *n* **15** the manner in which something fits **16** the act or process of fitting **17** *statistics* the correspondence between observed and predicted characteristics of a distribution or model. See **goodness of fit** ▷ See also **fit in, fit out, fit up** [C14 probably from Middle Dutch *vitten*; related to Old Norse *fitja* to knit] > 'fittable *adj*

fit² (fɪt) *n* **1** *pathol* a sudden attack or convulsion, such as an epileptic seizure **2** a sudden spell of emotion: *a fit of anger* **3** an impulsive period of activity or lack of activity; mood: *a fit of laziness* **4** **give (a person) a fit** to surprise (a person) in an outrageous manner **5** **have** or **throw a fit** *informal* to become very angry or excited **6** **in** or **by fits and starts** in spasmodic spells; irregularly ▷ *vb* **fits, fitting, fitted 7** (*intr*) *informal* to have a sudden attack or convulsion, such as an epileptic seizure [Old English *fitt* conflict; see FIT³]

fit³ (fɪt) *n archaic* a story or song or a section of a story or song [Old English *fitt*; related to Old Norse *fit* hem, Old High German *fizza* yarn]

fitch (fɪtʃ) or **fitchet** ('fɪtʃɪt) *n* **1** another name for **polecat** (sense 1) **2** the fur of the polecat or ferret [C16 probably from *ficheux* FITCHEW]

fitchew ('fɪtʃuː) *n* an archaic name for **polecat** [C14 *ficheux*, from Old French *ficheau*, from Middle Dutch *vitsau*, of obscure origin]

fitful ('fɪtfʊl) *adj* characterized by or occurring in irregular spells: *fitful sleep* > 'fitfully *adv* > 'fitfulness *n*

fit in *vb* **1** (*tr*) to give a place or time to: *if my schedule allows it, I'll fit you in* **2** (*intr, adverb*) to belong or conform, esp after adjustment

fitly ('fɪtlɪ) *adv* in a proper manner or place or at a proper time

fitment ('fɪtmənt) *n* **1** *machinery* an accessory attached to an assembly of parts **2** *chiefly Brit* a detachable part of the furnishings of a room

fitna ('fɪtnɑː) *n* a state of trouble or chaos [Arabic]

fitness ('fɪtnɪs) *n* **1** the state of being fit **2** *biology* **a** the degree of adaptation of an organism to its environment, determined by its genetic constitution **b** the ability of an organism to produce viable offspring capable of surviving to the next generation

fit out *vb* **1** (*tr, adverb*) to equip; supply with necessary or new equipment, clothes, etc ▷ *n* **fit-**

out 2 the act of equipping or supplying with necessary or new equipment; refurbishment

fitted ('fɪtɪd) adj **1** designed for excellent fit: a fitted suit **2** (of a carpet) cut, sewn, or otherwise adapted to cover a floor completely **3 a** (of furniture) built to fit a particular space: a fitted cupboard **b** (of a room) equipped with fitted furniture: a fitted kitchen **4** (of sheets) having ends that are elasticated and shaped to fit tightly over a mattress **5** having accessory parts

fitter ('fɪtə) n **1** a person who fits a garment, esp when it is made for a particular person **2** a person who is skilled in the assembly and adjustment of machinery, esp of a specified sort: an electrical fitter **3** a person who supplies something for an expedition, activity, etc

fitting ('fɪtɪŋ) adj **1** appropriate or proper; suitable ▷ n **2** an accessory or part: an electrical fitting **3** (plural) furnishings or accessories in a building **4** work carried out by a fitter **5** the act of trying on clothes so that they can be adjusted to fit **6** Brit size in clothes or shoes: a narrow fitting > 'fittingly adv > 'fittingness n

fit up vb (tr, adverb) **1** (often foll by with) to equip or provide: the optician will soon fit you up with a new pair of glasses **2** Brit slang to incriminate (someone) on a false charge; frame ▷ n **fit-up 3** theatre slang a stage and accessories that can be erected quickly for plays **4** Brit slang a frame-up

Fitzgerald-Lorentz contraction (fɪts'dʒɛrəldlɔː'rɛnts) n physics the contraction that a moving body exhibits when its velocity approaches that of light [C19 named after G. F. Fitzgerald (1851–1901), Irish physicist and H. A. Lorentz (1853–1928), Dutch physicist]

Fitzrovia (fɪts'rəʊvɪə) n informal the district north of Oxford Street, London, around Fitzroy Square and its pubs, noted in the 1930s and 40s as a haunt of poets

Fitzwilliam Museum (ˌfɪts'wɪljəm) n a museum, attached to Cambridge University and founded in 1816, noted esp for its paintings and collections devoted to the applied arts [C19 named after the 7th Viscount Fitzwilliam of Merrion, who donated the first collection]

Fiume ('fiuːme) n the Italian name for **Rijeka**

five (faɪv) n **1** the cardinal number that is the sum of four and one **2** a numeral, 5, V, etc, representing this number **3** the amount or quantity that is one greater than four **4** something representing, represented by, or consisting of five units, such as a playing card with five symbols on it ▷ determiner **5 a** amounting to five: five minutes **b** (as pronoun): choose any five you like Related prefixes: **penta-, quinque-** ▷ See also **fives** [Old English fīf; related to Old Norse fimm, Gothic fimf, Old High German finf, Latin quinque, Greek pente, Sanskrit pañca]

five-a-side n **a** a version of soccer with five players on each side **b** (as modifier): a five-a-side tournament

5BX n a fitness exercise programme originally devised in the Canadian Air Force [from 5 b(asic) (e)x(ercises)]

five by five interj an expression used in telecommunications to state that a signal is being received clearly

five-eighth n **1** Austral (in rugby) a player positioned between the scrum-half and the inside -centre **2** NZ (in rugby) either of two players positioned between the halfback and the centre

five-faced bishop n Brit another name for **moschatel**

five-finger n any of various plants having five-petalled flowers or five lobed leaves, such as cinquefoil and Virginia creeper

fivefold ('faɪvˌfəʊld) adj **1** equal to or having five times as many or as much **2** composed of five parts ▷ adv **3** by or up to five times as many or as much

five hundred n a card game for three players, with 500 points for game

five Ks pl n the items traditionally worn or carried by Sikhs, each possessing a symbolic importance. See **Kachera, Kangha, Kara, Kesh, Kirpan** [translation of Punjabi panch kakke]

Five Nations pl n (formerly) a confederacy of North American Indian peoples living mainly in and around present-day New York state, consisting of the Cayugas, Mohawks, Oneidas, Onondagas, and Senecas. Also called: **Iroquois** See also **Six Nations**

Five Nations Championship n rugby Union a former annual competition involving the national sides of England, France, Ireland, Scotland, and Wales; replaced by the **Six Nations Championship** in 2000

five-o'clock shadow n beard growth visible late in the day on a man's shaven face

fivepenny ('faɪvpənɪ) adj (prenominal) US (of a nail) one and three-quarters of an inch in length

fivepins ('faɪvˌpɪnz) n (functioning as singular) a bowling game using five pins, played esp in Canada. Also called: **five-pin bowling** > 'five,pin adj

fiver ('faɪvə) n informal **1** (in Britain) a five-pound note **2** (in the US) a five-dollar bill

fives (faɪvz) n (functioning as singular) a ball game similar to squash but played with bats or the hands

five-spot n (in the US) a five-dollar bill

five-star adj (of a hotel) first-class, top-quality, or offering exceptional luxury

five stones n the game of jacks played with five stones

Five Towns n the the name given in his fiction by Arnold Bennett to the Potteries towns (actually six in number) of Burslem, Fenton, Hanley, Longton, Stoke-upon-Trent, and Tunstall, now part of the city of Stoke-on-Trent

Five-Year Plan n (formerly in socialist economies) a government plan for economic development over a period of five years

fix (fɪks) vb (mainly tr) **1** (also intr) to make or become firm, stable, or secure **2** to attach or place permanently **3** (often foll by up) to settle definitely; decide **4** to hold or direct (eyes, attention, etc) steadily: he fixed his gaze on the woman **5** to call to attention or rivet **6** to make rigid: to fix one's jaw **7** to place or ascribe: to fix the blame on someone **8** to mend or repair **9** informal to provide with: how are you fixed for supplies? **10** informal to influence (a person, outcome of a contest, etc) unfairly, as by bribery **11** slang to take revenge on; get even with, esp by killing **12** informal to give (someone) his just deserts: that'll fix him **13** informal to arrange or put in order **14** informal to prepare: to fix a meal **15** dialect or informal to spay or castrate (an animal) **16** US dialect or informal to prepare oneself: I'm fixing to go out **17** photog to treat (a film, plate, or paper) with fixer to make permanent the image rendered visible by developer **18** cytology to kill, preserve, and harden (tissue, cells, etc) for subsequent microscopic study **19 a** to convert (atmospheric nitrogen) into nitrogen compounds, as in the manufacture of fertilizers or the action of bacteria in the soil **b** to convert (carbon dioxide) into organic compounds, esp carbohydrates, as occurs in photosynthesis in plants and some microorganisms **20** to reduce (a substance) to a solid or condensed state or a less volatile state **21** (intr) slang to inject a drug ▷ n **22** informal a predicament; dilemma **23** the ascertaining of the navigational position, as of a ship, by radar, observation, etc **24** slang an intravenous injection of a drug, esp heroin **25** informal an act or instance of bribery ▷ See also **fix up** [C15 from Medieval Latin fixāre, from Latin fixus fixed, from fīgere] > 'fixable adj

fixate ('fɪkseɪt) vb **1** to become or cause to become fixed **2** to direct the eye or eyes at a point in space so that the image of the point falls on the centre (fovea) of the eye or eyes **3** psychol to engage in fixation **4** (tr; usually passive) informal to obsess or preoccupy [C19 from Latin fixus fixed + -ATE[1]]

fixation (fɪk'seɪʃən) n **1** the act of fixing or the state of being fixed **2** a preoccupation or obsession **3** psychol **a** the act of fixating **b** (in psychoanalytical schools) a strong attachment of a person to another person or an object in early life **4** chem **a** the conversion of nitrogen in the air into a compound, esp a fertilizer **b** the conversion of a free element into one of its compounds **5** the reduction of a substance from a volatile or fluid form to a nonvolatile or solid form

fixative ('fɪksətɪv) adj **1** serving or tending to fix ▷ n **2** a fluid usually consisting of a transparent resin, such as shellac, dissolved in alcohol and sprayed over drawings to prevent smudging **3** cytology a fluid, such as formaldehyde or ethanol, that fixes tissues and cells for microscopic study **4** a substance added to a liquid, such as a perfume, to make it less volatile

fixed (fɪkst) adj **1** attached or placed so as to be immovable **2** not subject to change; stable: fixed prices **3** steadily directed: a fixed expression **4** established as to relative position: a fixed point **5** not fluctuating; always at the same time: a fixed holiday **6** (of ideas, notions, etc) firmly maintained **7** (of an element) held in chemical combination: fixed nitrogen **8** (of a substance) nonvolatile **9** arranged **10** astrology of, relating to, or belonging to the group consisting of the four signs of the zodiac Taurus, Leo, Scorpio, and Aquarius, which are associated with stability. Compare **cardinal** (sense 9), **mutable** (sense 2) **11** informal equipped or provided for, as with money, possessions, etc **12** informal illegally arranged: a fixed trial > fixedly ('fɪksɪdlɪ) adv > 'fixedness n

fixed assets pl n nontrading business assets of a relatively permanent nature, such as plant, fixtures, or goodwill. Also called: **capital assets** Compare **current assets**

fixed charge n **1** an invariable expense usually at regular intervals, such as rent **2** a legal charge on specific assets or property, as of a company

fixed costs pl n **1** another name for **overheads 2** costs that do not vary with output

fixed-head coupé n another name (esp Brit) for **coupé** (sense 1)

fixed idea n an idea, esp one of an obsessional nature, that is persistently maintained and not subject to change. Also called: idée fixe

fixed oil n a natural animal or vegetable oil that is not volatile: a mixture of esters of fatty acids, usually triglycerides. Also called: **fatty oil** Compare **essential oil**

fixed point n **1** physics a reproducible invariant temperature; the boiling point, freezing point, or triple point of a substance, such as water, that is used to calibrate a thermometer or define a temperature scale **2** maths a point that is not moved by a given transformation

fixed-point representation n computing the representation of numbers by a single set of digits such that the radix point has a predetermined location, the value of the number depending on the position of each digit relative to the radix point. Compare **floating-point representation**

fixed satellite n a satellite in a geostationary orbit

fixed star n **1** any of the stars in the Ptolemaic system, all of which were thought to be attached to an outer crystal sphere thus explaining their apparent lack of movement **2** an extremely distant star whose position appears to be almost stationary over a long period of time

fixer ('fɪksə) n **1** a person or thing that fixes **2** photog a solution containing one or more chemical compounds that is used, in fixing, to dissolve unexposed silver halides. It sometimes has an additive to stop the action of developer **3** slang a person who makes arrangements, esp by underhand or illegal means

fixing ('fɪksɪŋ) n a means of attaching one thing to another, as a pipe to a wall, slate to a roof, etc

fixings ('fɪksɪŋz) pl n chiefly US and Canadian **1**

f

apparatus or equipment **2** accompaniments for a dish; trimmings

fixity ('fɪksɪtɪ) *n, pl* **-ties** **1** the state or quality of being fixed; stability **2** something that is fixed; a fixture

fixture ('fɪkstʃə) *n* **1** an object firmly fixed in place, esp a household appliance **2** a person or thing regarded as fixed in a particular place or position **3** *property law* an article attached to land and regarded as part of it **4** a device to secure a workpiece in a machine tool **5** *chiefly Brit* **a** a sports match or social occasion **b** the date of such an event **6** *rare* the act of fixing [C17 from Late Latin *fixūra* a fastening (with *-t-* by analogy with *mixture*)] > '**fixtureless** *adj*

fix up *vb (tr, adverb)* **1** to arrange: *let's fix up a date* **2** (often foll by *with*) to provide: *I'm sure we can fix you up with a room* **3** *informal* to repair or rearrange

fizgig ('fɪz,gɪg) *n* **1** a frivolous or flirtatious girl **2** a firework or whirling top that fizzes as it moves **3** a variant of **fishgig** **4** *Austral slang* a police informer ▷ *vb* **5** *(intr) Austral slang* to inform on criminals to the police [C16 probably from obsolete *fise* a breaking of wind + *gig* girl]

fizz (fɪz) *vb (intr)* **1** to make a hissing or bubbling sound **2** (of a drink) to produce bubbles of carbon dioxide, either through fermentation or aeration ▷ *n* **3** a hissing or bubbling sound **4** the bubbly quality of a drink; effervescence **5** any effervescent drink [C17 of imitative origin] > '**fizzy** *adj* > '**fizziness** *n*

fizzer ('fɪzə) *n* **1** anything that fizzes **2** *Austral slang* a person or thing that disappoints, fails to succeed, etc: *the horse proved to be a fizzer*

fizzle ('fɪzᵊl) *vb (intr)* **1** to make a hissing or bubbling sound **2** (often foll by *out*) *informal* to fail or die out, esp after a promising start ▷ *n* **3** a hissing or bubbling sound; fizz **4** *informal* an outright failure; fiasco [C16 probably from obsolete *fist* to break wind]

fj *the internet domain name for* Fiji

fjeld *or* **field** (fjɛld) *n* a high rocky plateau with little vegetation in Scandinavian countries [C19 Norwegian; related to Old Norse *fjall* mountain; see FELL[5]]

FJI *international car registration for* Fiji

fjord *or* **fiord** (fjɔːd) *n* (esp on the coast of Norway) a long narrow inlet of the sea between high steep cliffs formed by glacial action [C17 from Norwegian, from Old Norse *fjörthr*; see FIRTH, FORD]

fk *the internet domain name for* Falkland Islands

FL *abbreviation for* **1** Flight Lieutenant **2** Florida **3** *international car registration for* Liechtenstein [(for sense 3) from German *Fürstentum Liechtenstein* Principality of Liechtenstein]

fl. *abbreviation for* **1** *floruit* **2** (formerly in the Netherlands) *symbol for* guilder

Fla. *abbreviation for* Florida

flab (flæb) *n* unsightly or unwanted fat on the body; flabbiness [C20 back formation from FLABBY]

flabbergast ('flæbə,gɑːst) *vb (tr) informal* to overcome with astonishment; amaze utterly; astound [C18 of uncertain origin]

flabbergasted ('flæbə,gɑːstɪd) *adj informal* overcome with astonishment; amazed; astounded

flabby ('flæbɪ) *adj* **-bier, -biest** **1** lacking firmness; loose or yielding: *flabby muscles* **2** having flabby flesh, esp through being overweight **3** lacking vitality; weak; ineffectual [C17 alteration of *flappy*, from FLAP + -Y[1]; compare Dutch *flabbe* drooping lip] > '**flabbily** *adv* > '**flabbiness** *n*

flabellate (flə'bɛlɪt, -eɪt) *or* **flabelliform** (flə'bɛlɪ,fɔːm) *adj biology* shaped like a fan

flabellum (flə'bɛləm) *n, pl* **-la** (-lə) **1** a fan-shaped organ or part, such as the tip of the proboscis of a honeybee **2** *RC Church* a large ceremonial fan [C19 from Latin: small fan, from *flābra* breezes, from *flāre* to blow]

flaccid ('flæksɪd, 'flæs-) *adj* lacking firmness; soft and limp; flabby [C17 from Latin *flaccidus*, from *flaccus*] > **flac'cidity** *or* '**flaccidness** *n* > '**flaccidly** *adv*

flack[1] (flæk) *n chiefly US and Canadian* a press or publicity agent [C20 of unknown origin]

flack[2] (flæk) *n* a variant spelling of **flak**

flacon (*French* flakɔ̃) *n* a small stoppered bottle or flask, such as one used for perfume [C19 from French; see FLAGON]

flag[1] (flæg) *n* **1** a piece of cloth, esp bunting, often attached to a pole or staff, decorated with a design and used as an emblem, symbol, or standard or as a means of signalling **2** a small paper flag, emblem, or sticker sold on flag days **3** an indicator, that may be set or unset, used to indicate a condition or to stimulate a particular reaction in the execution of a computer program **4** *informal* short for **flag officer, flagship** **5** *journalism* another name for **masthead** (sense 2) **6** the fringe of long hair, tapering towards the tip, on the underside of the tail of certain breeds of dog, such as setters **7** the conspicuously marked tail of a deer **8** a less common name for **bookmark** **9** *Austral and NZ* the part of a taximeter that is raised when a taxi is for hire **10** the pennant-shaped pattern that is formed when a price fluctuation is plotted on a chart, interrupting the steady rise or fall that precedes and then follows it **11** **the** (in Victoria, Australia) the Australian Rules premiership **12** **fly the flag** to represent or show support for one's country, an organization, etc **13** **show the flag** **a** to assert a claim, as to a territory or stretch of water, by military presence **b** *informal* to be present; make an appearance **14** **strike** (*or* **lower**) **the flag** **a** to relinquish command, esp of a ship **b** to submit or surrender ▷ *vb* **flags, flagging, flagged** *(tr)* **15** to decorate or mark with a flag or flags **16** (often foll by *down*) to warn or signal (a vehicle) to stop **17** to send or communicate (messages, information, etc) by flag **18** to decoy (game or wild animals) by waving a flag or similar object so as to attract their attention **19** to mark (a page in a book, card, etc) for attention by attaching a small tab or flag **20** (foll by *away* or *by*) *NZ* to consider unimportant; brush aside ▷ See also **flag out, flags, flag up** [C16 of uncertain origin] > '**flagger** *n* > '**flagless** *adj*

flag[2] (flæg) *n* **1** any of various plants that have long swordlike leaves, esp the iris *Iris pseudacorus* (**yellow flag**) **2** the leaf of any such plant ▷ See also **sweet flag** [C14 probably of Scandinavian origin; compare Dutch *flag*, Danish *flæg* yellow iris]

flag[3] (flæg) *vb* **flags, flagging, flagged** *(intr)* **1** to hang down; become limp; droop **2** to decline in strength or vigour; become weak or tired [C16 of unknown origin]

flag[4] (flæg) *n* **1** short for **flagstone** ▷ *vb* **flags, flagging, flagged** **2** *(tr)* to furnish (a floor) with flagstones

flag captain *n* the captain of a flagship

flag day *n Brit* a day on which money is collected by a charity and small flags, emblems, or stickers are given to contributors

Flag Day *n* June 14, the annual holiday in the US to celebrate the adoption in 1777 of the Stars and Stripes

flagellant ('flædʒɪlənt, flə'dʒɛlənt) *or* **flagellator** ('flædʒɪ,leɪtə) *n* **1** a person who whips himself or others either as part of a religious penance or for sexual gratification **2** *(often capital)* (in medieval Europe) a member of a religious sect who whipped themselves in public [C16 from Latin *flagellāre* to whip, from FLAGELLUM] > '**flagellant,ism** *n*

flagellate *vb* ('flædʒɪ,leɪt) **1** *(tr)* to whip; scourge; flog ▷ *adj* ('flædʒɪlɪt, -,leɪt) *also* **flagellated** **2** possessing one or more flagella **3** resembling a flagellum; whiplike ▷ *n* ('flædʒɪlɪt, -,leɪt) **4** a flagellate organism, esp any protozoan of the phylum *Zoomastigina* > ,**flagel'lation** *n*

flagelliform (flə'dʒɛlɪ,fɔːm) *adj* slender, tapering, and whiplike, as the antennae of certain insects

flagellin (flə'dʒɛlɪn) *n* the structural protein of bacterial flagella

flagellum (flə'dʒɛləm) *n, pl* **-la** (-lə) *or* **-lums** **1** *biology* a long whiplike outgrowth from a cell that acts as an organ of locomotion: occurs in some protozoans, gametes, spores, etc **2** *botany* a long thin supple shoot or runner **3** *zoology* the terminal whiplike part of an arthropod's appendage, esp of the antenna of many insects [C19 from Latin: a little whip, from *flagrum* a whip, lash] > **fla'gellar** *adj*

flageolet[1] (,flædʒə'lɛt) *n* a high-pitched musical instrument of the recorder family having six or eight finger holes [C17 from French, modification of Old French *flajolet* a little flute, from *flajol* flute, from Vulgar Latin *flabeolum* (unattested), from Latin *flāre* to blow]

flageolet[2] *or* **flageolet bean** ('flædʒə,leɪ) *n* the pale green immature seed of a haricot bean, cooked and eaten as a vegetable [C19 from French *fageolet*, from Latin *phaseolus* bean; perhaps influenced by FLAGEOLET[1]]

flag fall *n Austral* the minimum charge for hiring a taxi, to which the rate per kilometre is added

flagging ('flægɪŋ) *n* flagstones or a flagged area

flaggy[1] ('flægɪ) *adj* **-gier, -giest** drooping; limp

flaggy[2] ('flægɪ) *adj* made of or similar to flagstone

flagitious (flə'dʒɪʃəs) *adj* atrociously wicked; vicious; outrageous [C14 from Latin *flāgitiōsus* infamous, from *flāgitium* a shameful act; related to Latin *flagrum* whip] > **fla'gitiously** *adv* > **fla'gitiousness** *n*

flag lieutenant *n* an admiral's ADC

flagman ('flægmən) *n, pl* **-men** a person who has charge of, carries, or signals with a flag, esp a railway employee

flag of convenience *n* a national flag flown by a ship registered in that country to gain financial or legal advantage

flag officer *n* **1** an officer in certain navies of the rank of rear admiral or above and entitled to fly its flag **2** the head of a boat or yacht club

flag of truce *n* a white flag indicating the peaceful intent of its bearer or an invitation to an enemy to negotiate

flagon ('flægən) *n* **1** a large bottle of wine, cider, etc **2** a vessel having a handle, spout, and narrow neck [C15 from Old French *flascon*, from Late Latin *flascō*, probably of Germanic origin; see FLASK]

flag out *vb (adverb)* to register (a commercial vehicle) in a country other than the one in which it operates, usually in order to take advantage of favourable rates of taxation

flagpole ('flæg,pəʊl) *or* **flagstaff** ('flæg,stɑːf) *n, pl* **-poles, -staffs** *or* **-staves** (-,steɪvz) a pole or staff on which a flag is hoisted and displayed

flag rank *n* the rank of a flag officer

flagrant ('fleɪgrənt) *adj* **1** openly outrageous **2** *obsolete* burning or blazing [C15 from Latin *flagrāre* to blaze, burn] > '**flagrancy,** '**flagrance** *or* '**flagrantness** *n* > '**flagrantly** *adv*

flagrante delicto (flə'græntɪ dɪ'lɪktəʊ) *adv* See **in flagrante delicto**

flags (flægz) *pl n rare* the long feathers on the leg of a hawk or falcon

flagship ('flæg,ʃɪp) *n* **1** a ship, esp in a fleet, aboard which the commander of the fleet is quartered **2** the most important ship belonging to a shipping company **3** a single item from a related group considered as the most important, often in establishing a public image

flagstone ('flæg,stəʊn) *or* **flag** *n* **1** a hard fine-textured rock, such as a sandstone or shale, that can be split up into slabs for paving **2** a slab of such a rock [C15 *flag* (in the sense: sod, turf), from Old Norse *flaga* slab; compare Old English *flæcg* plaster, poultice]

flag up *vb (tr; adverb)* to bring (something) to someone's attention; point out

flag-waving *n informal* **a** an emotional appeal or display intended to arouse patriotic or nationalistic feeling **b** *(as modifier)*: *a flag-waving speech* > '**flag-,waver** *n*

flail (fleɪl) *n* **1** an implement used for threshing grain, consisting of a wooden handle with a free-swinging metal or wooden bar attached to it **2** a weapon so shaped used in the Middle Ages ▷ *vb* **3** (*tr*) to beat or thrash with or as if with a flail **4** to move or be moved like a flail; thresh about: *with arms flailing* [C12 *fleil*, ultimately from Late Latin *flagellum* flail, from Latin: whip]

flair¹ (fleə) *n* **1** natural ability; talent; aptitude **2** instinctive discernment; perceptiveness **3** stylishness or elegance; dash: *to dress with flair* **4** *hunting rare* **a** the scent left by quarry **b** the sense of smell of a hound [C19 from French, literally: sense of smell, from Old French: scent, from *flairier* to give off a smell, ultimately from Latin *frāgrāre* to smell sweet; see FRAGRANT]

flair² (fler) *n* a Scot word for **floor**

flak *or* **flack** (flæk) *n* **1** anti-aircraft fire or artillery **2** *informal* a great deal of adverse criticism [C20 from German Fl(ieger)a(bwehr)k(anone), literally: aircraft defence gun]

flake¹ (fleɪk) *n* **1** a small thin piece or layer chipped off or detached from an object or substance; scale **2** a small piece or particle: *a flake of snow* **3** a thin layer or stratum **4** *archaeol* **a** a fragment removed by chipping or hammering from a larger stone used as a tool or weapon. See also **blade** **b** (*as modifier*): *flake tool* **5** *slang, chiefly US* an eccentric, crazy, or unreliable person ▷ *vb* **6** to peel or cause to peel off in flakes; chip **7** to cover or become covered with or as with flakes **8** (*tr*) to form into flakes [C14 of Scandinavian origin; compare Norwegian *flak* disc, Middle Dutch *vlacken* to flutter] ▷ **ˈflaker** *n*

flake² (fleɪk) *n* a rack or platform for drying fish or other produce [C14 from Old Norse *flaki*; related to Dutch *vlaak* hurdle]

flake³ (fleɪk) *vb nautical* another word for **fake**

flake⁴ (fleɪk) *n* (in Australia) the commercial name for the meat of the gummy shark

flake out *vb* (*intr, adverb*) *informal* to collapse or fall asleep as through extreme exhaustion

flake white *n* a pigment made from flakes of white lead

flak jacket *n* a reinforced sleeveless jacket for protection against gunfire or shrapnel worn by soldiers, policemen, etc

flaky (ˈfleɪkɪ) *adj* **flakier, flakiest** **1** like or made of flakes **2** tending to peel off or break easily into flakes **3** Also: **flakey** *US slang* eccentric; crazy ▷ **ˈflakily** *adv* ▷ **ˈflakiness** *n*

flaky pastry *n* a rich pastry in the form of very thin layers, used for making pies, small cakes, etc

flam¹ (flæm) *now chiefly dialect* ▷ *n* **1** a falsehood, deception, or sham **2** nonsense; drivel ▷ *vb* **flams, flamming, flammed** **3** (*tr*) to cheat or deceive [C16 probably short for FLIMFLAM]

flam² (flæm) *n* a drumbeat in which both sticks strike the head almost simultaneously but are heard to do so separately [C18 probably imitative of the sound]

flambé *or* **flambée** (ˈflɑːmbeɪ, ˈflæm-; *French* flɑ̃be) *adj* **1** (of food, such as steak or pancakes) served in flaming brandy ▷ *vb* **-béing, -béeing, -béd, -béed** **2** (*tr*) to pour brandy over (food) and ignite it [French, past participle of *flamber* to FLAME]

flambeau (ˈflæmbəʊ) *n, pl* **-beaux** (-bəʊ, -bəʊz) *or* **-beaus** **1** a burning torch, as used in night processions **2** a large ornamental candlestick [C17 from Old French: torch, literally: a little flame, from *flambe* FLAME]

Flamborough Head (ˈflæmbərə, -brə) *n* a chalk promontory in NE England, on the coast of the East Riding of Yorkshire

flamboyant (flæmˈbɔɪənt) *adj* **1** elaborate or extravagant; florid; showy **2** rich or brilliant in colour; resplendent **3** of, denoting, or relating to the French Gothic style of architecture characterized by flamelike tracery and elaborate carving ▷ *n* **4** another name for **royal poinciana** [C19 from French: flaming, from *flamboyer* to

FLAME] ▷ flam'boyance *or* flam'boyancy *n* ▷ flam'boyantly *adv*

flame (fleɪm) *n* **1** a hot usually luminous body of burning gas often containing small incandescent particles, typically emanating in flickering streams from burning material or produced by a jet of ignited gas **2** (*often plural*) the state or condition of burning with flames: *to burst into flames* **3** a brilliant light; fiery glow **4** a strong reddish-orange colour **b** (*as adjective*): *a flame carpet* **5** intense passion or ardour; burning emotion **6** *informal* a lover or sweetheart (esp in the phrase **an old flame**) **7** *informal* an abusive message sent by electronic mail, esp to express anger or criticism of an internet user by sending him or her large numbers of messages ▷ *vb* **8** to burn or cause to burn brightly; give off or cause to give off flame **9** (*intr*) to burn or glow as if with fire; become red or fiery: *his face flamed with anger* **10** (*intr*) to show great emotion; become angry or excited **11** (*tr*) to apply a flame to (something) **12** (*tr*) *archaic* to set on fire, either physically or with emotion **13** *informal* to send an abusive message by electronic mail ▷ See also **flameout** [C14 from Anglo-French *flaume*, from Old French *flambe*, modification of *flamble*, from Latin *flammula* a little flame, from *flamma* flame] ▷ **ˈflamer** *n* ▷ **ˈflameless** *adj* ▷ **ˈflamelet** *n* ▷ **ˈflameˌlike** *adj* ▷ **ˈflamy** *adj*

flame-arc light *n electrical engineering* an arc light that uses flame carbons to colour the arc

flame carbon *n electrical engineering* a carbon electrode containing metallic salts that colour the arc in a flame-arc light

flame cell *n* an organ of excretion in flatworms: a hollow cup-shaped cell containing a bunch of cilia, whose movement draws in waste products and wafts them to the outside through a connecting tubule

flame cutting *n engineering* a method of cutting ferrous metals in which the metal is heated by a torch to about 800°C and is oxidized by a stream of oxygen from the torch

flame gun *n* a type of flame-thrower for destroying garden weeds

flame hardening *n engineering* the surface hardening of ferrous metals by heating the metal with an oxyacetylene flame followed by rapid cooling

flame lamp *n electrical engineering* a filament lamp in which the bulb resembles the shape of a flame

flamen (ˈfleɪmɛn) *n, pl* **flamens** *or* **flamines** (ˈflæmɪˌniːz) (in ancient Rome) any of 15 priests who each served a particular deity [C14 from Latin; probably related to Old English *blōtan* to sacrifice, Gothic *blotan* to worship]

flamenco (fləˈmɛŋkəʊ) *n, pl* **-cos** **1** a type of dance music for vocal soloist and guitar, characterized by elaborate melody and sad mood **2** the dance performed to such music [from Spanish: like a gipsy, literally: Fleming, from Middle Dutch *Vlaminc* Fleming]

flame-of-the-forest *n* **1** (esp in Malaysia) another name for **royal poinciana** **2** a leguminous tree, *Butea frondosa*, native to E India and Myanmar, having hanging clusters of scarlet flowers

flameout (ˈfleɪmˌaʊt) *n* **1** the failure of an aircraft jet engine in flight due to extinction of the flame ▷ *vb* **flame out** (*adverb*) **2** (of a jet engine) to fail in flight or to cause (a jet engine) to fail in flight

flameproof (ˈfleɪmˌpruːf) *adj* **1** not liable to catch fire or be damaged by fire **2** (of electrical apparatus) designed so that an internal explosion will not ignite external flammable gas

flame retarder *n* a material that, while not incombustible, does not itself maintain combustion without an external heat source and therefore retards the spread of fire

flame test *n* a test for detecting the presence of certain metals in compounds by the coloration they give to a flame. Sodium, for example, turns a flame yellow

flame-thrower *n* a weapon that ejects a stream or spray of burning fluid

flame tree *n* any of various tropical trees with red or orange flowers, such as flame-of-the-forest

flaming (ˈfleɪmɪŋ) *adj* **1** burning with or emitting flames **2** glowing brightly; brilliant **3** intense or ardent; vehement; passionate: *a flaming temper* **4** (*intensifier*): *you flaming idiot* **5** an obsolete word for **flagrant**. ▷ **ˈflamingly** *adv*

flamingo (fləˈmɪŋgəʊ) *n, pl* **-gos** *or* **-goes** **1** any large wading bird of the family *Phoenicopteridae*, having a pink-and-red plumage and downward-bent bill and inhabiting brackish lakes: order *Ciconiiformes* **2 a** a reddish-orange colour **b** (*as adjective*): *flamingo gloves* [C16 from Portuguese *flamengo*, from Provençal *flamenc*, from Latin *flamma* flame + Germanic suffix *-ing* denoting descent from or membership of; compare *-ING³*]

Flaminian Way (fləˈmɪnɪən) *n* an ancient road in Italy, extending north from Rome to Rimini: constructed in 220 BC by Gaius Flaminius. Length: over 322 km (200 miles). Latin name: Via Flaminia

flammable (ˈflæməbəl) *adj* liable to catch fire; readily combustible; inflammable ▷ ˌflammaˈbility *n*

USAGE *Flammable* and *inflammable* are interchangeable when used of the properties of materials. *Flammable* is, however, often preferred for warning labels as there is less likelihood of misunderstanding (*inflammable* being sometimes taken to mean *not flammable*). *Inflammable* is preferred in figurative contexts: *this could prove to be an inflammable situation*

flan (flæn) *n* **1** an open pastry or sponge tart filled with fruit or a savoury mixture **2** a piece of metal ready to receive the die or stamp in the production of coins; shaped blank; planchet [C19 from French, from Old French *flaon*, from Late Latin *fladō* flat cake, of Germanic origin]

flanch (flæntʃ) *n* a variant of **flaunch**

Flanders (ˈflɑːndəz) *n* a powerful medieval principality in the SW part of the Low Countries, now in the Belgian provinces of East and West Flanders, the Netherlands province of Zeeland, and the French department of the Nord; scene of battles in many wars

Flanders poppy *n* another name for **corn poppy**

flânerie *French* (flɑnri) *n* aimless strolling or lounging; idleness [C19 from *flâner* to stroll, dawdle, ultimately from Old Norse *flana* to wander about]

flâneur *French* (flɑnœr) *n* an idler or loafer [C19 see FLÂNERIE]

flange (flændʒ) *n* **1** a projecting disc-shaped collar or rim on an object for locating or strengthening it or for attaching it to another object **2** a flat outer face of a rolled-steel joist, esp of an I- or H-beam **3** a tool for forming a flange ▷ *vb* **4** (*tr*) to attach or provide (a component) with a flange **5** (*intr*) to take the form of a flange [C17 probably changed from earlier *flaunche* curved segment at side of a heraldic field, from French *flanc* FLANK] ▷ **flanged** *adj* ▷ **ˈflangeless** *adj* ▷ **ˈflanger** *n*

flange coupling *n engineering* a driving coupling between rotating shafts that consists of flanges (or **half couplings**) one of which is fixed at the end of each shaft, the two flanges being bolted together with a ring of bolts to complete the drive

flanged rail *n* another name for **flat-bottomed rail**

flank (flæŋk) *n* **1** the side of a man or animal between the ribs and the hip **2** (loosely) the outer part of the human thigh **3** a cut of beef from the flank **4** the side of anything, such as a mountain or building **5** the side of a naval or military formation ▷ *vb* **6** (when *intr*, often foll by *on* or *upon*) to be located at the side of (an object, building, etc) **7** *military* to position or guard on or beside the flank of (a formation, etc) **8** *military* to

f

move past or go round (a flank) [C12 from Old French *flanc*, of Germanic origin]

flanker (ˈflæŋkə) *n* **1** one of a detachment of soldiers detailed to guard the flanks, esp of a formation **2** a projecting fortification, used esp to protect or threaten a flank **3** *rugby* a wing forward

flannel (ˈflænᵊl) *n* **1** a soft light woollen fabric with a slight nap, used for clothing **2** (*plural*) trousers or other garments made of flannel **3** See **cotton flannel** **4** *Brit* a small piece of cloth used to wash the face and hands; face cloth. US and Canadian equivalent: **washcloth** **5** *Brit informal* indirect or evasive talk; deceiving flattery ▷ *vb* **-nels, -nelling, -nelled** *or US* **-nels, -neling, -neled** (*tr*) **6** to cover or wrap with flannel **7** to rub, clean, or polish with flannel **8** *Brit informal* to talk evasively to; flatter in order to mislead [C14 probably variant of *flanen* sackcloth, from Welsh *gwlanen* woollen fabric, from *gwlân* wool] > ˈ**flannelly** *adj*

flannelboard (ˈflænᵊlˌbɔːd) *or* **flannelgraph** (ˈflænᵊlˌɡrɑːf, -ˌɡræf) *n* a visual aid used in teaching consisting of a board covered with flannel to which pictures, diagrams, etc will stick when pressed on

flannelette (ˌflænᵊˈlɛt) *n* a cotton imitation of flannel

flannel flower *n* any Australian plant of the umbelliferous genus *Actinotus* having white flannel-like bracts beneath the flowers

flap (flæp) *vb* **flaps, flapping, flapped** **1** to move (wings or arms) up and down, esp in or as if in flying, or (of wings or arms) to move in this way **2** to move or cause to move noisily back and forth or up and down **3** (*intr*) *informal* to become agitated or flustered; panic **4** to deal (a person or thing) a blow with a broad flexible object **5** (*tr*; sometimes foll by *down*) to toss, fling, slam, etc, abruptly or noisily **6** (*tr*) *phonetics* to pronounce (an (r) sound) by allowing the tongue to give a single light tap against the alveolar ridge or uvula ▷ *n* **7** the action, motion, or noise made by flapping **8** a piece of material, etc, attached at one edge and usually used to cover an opening, as on a tent, envelope, or pocket **9** a blow dealt with a flat object; slap **10** a movable surface fixed to the trailing edge of an aircraft wing that increases lift during takeoff and drag during landing **11** *surgery* a piece of tissue partially connected to the body, either following an amputation or to be used as a graft **12** *informal* a state of panic, distress, or agitation **13** *phonetics* an (r) produced by allowing the tongue to give a single light tap against the alveolar ridge or uvula [C14 probably of imitative origin]

flapdoodle (ˈflæpˌduːdᵊl) *n slang* foolish talk; nonsense [C19 of unknown origin]

flapjack (ˈflæpˌdʒæk) *n* **1** a chewy biscuit made with rolled oats **2** *US, Canadian & NZ* another word for **pancake** [C17 from FLAP (in the sense: toss) + JACK[1]]

flapper (ˈflæpə) *n* **1** a person or thing that flaps **2** (in the 1920s) a young woman, esp one flaunting her unconventional dress and behaviour

flare (flɛə) *vb* **1** to burn or cause to burn with an unsteady or sudden bright flame **2** to spread or cause to spread outwards from a narrow to a wider shape **3** (*tr*) to make a conspicuous display of **4** to increase the temperature of (a molten metal or alloy) until a gaseous constituent of the melt burns with a characteristic flame or (of a molten metal or alloy) to show such a flame **5** (*tr*; sometimes foll by *off*) (in the oil industry) to burn off (unwanted gas) at an oil well ▷ *n* **6** an unsteady flame **7** a sudden burst of flame **8** **a** a blaze of light or fire used to illuminate, identify, alert, signal distress, etc **b** the device producing such a blaze **9** a spreading shape or anything with a spreading shape **10** a sudden outburst, as of emotion **11** *optics* **a** the unwanted light reaching the image region of an optical device by reflections inside the instrument, etc **b** the fogged area formed on a negative by such reflections. See also **solar flare** **12** *astronomy* short for **solar flare** **13** *aeronautics* the final transition phase of an aircraft landing, from the steady descent path to touchdown **14** an open flame used to burn off unwanted gas at an oil well [C16 (to spread out): of unknown origin] > **flared** *adj*

flare path *n* an airstrip illuminated for use at night or in bad weather

flares (flɛəz) *pl n informal* trousers with legs that widen below the knee

flare star *n* a red dwarf star in which outbursts, thought to be analogous to solar flares, occur, increasing the luminosity by several magnitudes in a few minutes

flare-up *n* **1** a sudden burst of fire or light **2** *informal* a sudden burst of emotion or violence ▷ *vb* **flare up** (*intr, adverb*) **3** to burst suddenly into fire or light **4** *informal* to burst into anger

flash (flæʃ) *n* **1** a sudden short blaze of intense light or flame **2** a sudden occurrence or display, esp one suggestive of brilliance **3** a very brief space of time: *over in a flash* **4** an ostentatious display **5** Also called: **newsflash** a short news announcement concerning a new event **6** Also called: **patch** *chiefly Brit* an insignia or emblem worn on a uniform, vehicle, etc, to identify its military formation **7** a patch of bright colour on a dark background, such as light marking on an animal **8** a volatile mixture of inorganic salts used to produce a glaze on bricks or tiles **9** **a** a sudden rush of water down a river or watercourse **b** a device, such as a sluice, for producing such a rush **10** *photog informal* short for **flashlight** (sense 2) *or* **flash photography** **11** a ridge of thin metal or plastic formed on a moulded object by the extrusion of excess material between dies **12** *Yorkshire and Lancashire dialect* a pond, esp one produced as a consequence of subsidence **13** (*modifier*) involving, using, or produced by a flash of heat, light, etc: *flash blindness* **14** **flash in the pan** a project, person, etc, that enjoys only short-lived success, notoriety, etc ▷ *adj* **15** *informal* ostentatious or vulgar **16** *informal* of or relating to gamblers and followers of boxing and racing **17** sham or counterfeit **18** *informal* relating to or characteristic of the criminal underworld **19** brief and rapid: *flash freezing* ▷ *vb* **20** to burst or cause to burst suddenly or intermittently into flame **21** to emit or reflect or cause to emit or reflect light suddenly or intermittently **22** (*intr*) to move very fast: *he flashed by on his bicycle* **23** (*intr*) to come rapidly (into the mind or vision) **24** (*intr*; foll by *out* or *up*) to appear like a sudden light **25** **a** to signal or communicate very fast: *to flash a message* **b** to signal by use of a light, such as car headlights **26** (*tr*) *informal* to display ostentatiously **27** (*tr*) *informal* to show suddenly and briefly **28** (*intr*) *Brit slang* to expose oneself indecently **29** (*tr*) to cover (a roof) with flashing **30** to send a sudden rush of water down (a river, etc), or to carry (a vessel) down by this method **31** (in the making of glass) to coat (glass) with a thin layer of glass of a different colour **32** (*tr*) to subject to a brief pulse of heat or radiation **33** (*tr*) to change (a liquid) to a gas by causing it to hit a hot surface **34** *obsolete* to splash or dash (water) [C14 (in the sense: to rush, as of water): of unknown origin]

flashback (ˈflæʃˌbæk) *n* **1** a transition in a novel, film, etc, to an earlier scene or event ▷ *vb* **flash back** **2** (*intr, adverb*) to return in a novel, film, etc, to a past event

flashboard (ˈflæʃˌbɔːd) *n* a board or boarding that is placed along the top of a dam to increase its height and capacity. Also called: **stop log, stop plank**

flashbulb (ˈflæʃˌbʌlb) *n photog* a small expendable glass light bulb formerly used to produce a bright flash of light. Also called: **photoflash** Compare **electronic flash**

flashbulb memory *n psychol* the clear recollections that a person may have of the circumstances associated with a dramatic event

flash burn *n pathol* a burn caused by momentary exposure to intense radiant heat

flash card *n* a card on which are written or printed words for children to look at briefly, used as an aid to learning

flash drive *n* a pocket-sized portable computer hard drive and data storage device. See also **key drive, pen drive, thumb drive, USB drive**

flash eliminator *or* **suppressor** *n* a device fitted to the muzzle of a firearm to reduce the flash made by the ignited propellant gases

flasher (ˈflæʃə) *n* **1** something that flashes, such as a direction indicator on a vehicle **2** *Brit slang* a person who indecently exposes himself

flash flood *n* a sudden short-lived torrent, usually caused by a heavy storm, esp in desert regions

flash gun *n* a type of electronic flash, attachable to or sometimes incorporated in a camera, that emits a very brief flash of light when the shutter is open

flashing (ˈflæʃɪŋ) *n* a weatherproof material, esp thin sheet metal, used to cover the valleys between the slopes of a roof, the junction between a chimney and a roof, etc

flashlight (ˈflæʃˌlaɪt) *n* **1** *chiefly US and Canadian* a small portable electric lamp powered by one or more dry batteries. Also called (in Britain and certain other couontries): **torch** **2** *photog* the brief bright light emitted by an electronic flash unit. Sometimes shortened to: **flash** **3** *chiefly US and Canadian* a light that flashes, used for signalling, in a lighthouse, etc

flash mob *n* a group of people coordinated by email to meet to perform some predetermined action at a particular place and time and then disperse quickly > ˈ**flash**ˌ**mobbing** *n*

flashover (ˈflæʃˌəʊvə) *n* **1** an electric discharge over or around the surface of an insulator **2** the sudden and rapid spread of fire through the air, caused by the ignition of smoke or fumes from surrounding objects

flash photography *n* photography in which a flashbulb or electronic flash is used to provide momentary illumination of a dark or insufficiently lit subject

flash photolysis *n physics* a technique for producing and investigating free radicals. A low-pressure gas is subjected to a flash of radiation to produce the radicals, subsequent flashes being used to identify them and assess their lifetimes by absorption spectroscopy

flash point *or* **flashing point** *n* **1** the lowest temperature at which the vapour above a liquid can be ignited in air **2** a critical moment beyond which a situation will inevitably erupt into violence: *the political mood has reached flash point*

flash set *n civil engineering* undesirably rapid setting of cement in concrete

flash smelting *n* a smelting process for sulphur-containing ores in which the dried and powdered ore, mixed with oxygen, is ignited on discharge from a nozzle, melts, and drops to the bottom of a settling chamber. Sulphur is released mainly in its solid form, thus reducing atmospheric pollution

flashy (ˈflæʃɪ) *adj* **flashier, flashiest** **1** brilliant and dazzling, esp for a short time or in a superficial way **2** cheap and ostentatious > ˈ**flashily** *adv* > ˈ**flashiness** *n*

flask (flɑːsk) *n* **1** a bottle with a narrow neck, esp used in a laboratory or for wine, oil, etc **2** Also called: **hip flask** a small flattened container of glass or metal designed to be carried in a pocket, esp for liquor **3** See **powder flask** **4** a container packed with sand to form a mould in a foundry **5** See **vacuum flask** **6** Also called: **cask, coffin** *engineering* a container used for transporting irradiated nuclear fuel [C14 from Old French *flasque, flaske*, from Medieval Latin *flasca, flasco*, perhaps of Germanic origin; compare Old English *flasce, flaxe*]

flasket ('flɑːskɪt) *n* **1** a long shallow basket **2** a small flask [C15 from Old French *flasquet* a little FLASK]

flat[1] (flæt) *adj* **flatter, flattest 1** horizontal; level: *flat ground* **2** even or smooth, without projections or depressions: *a flat surface* **3** lying stretched out at full length; prostrate **4** having little depth or thickness; shallow **5** (*postpositive*; often foll by *against*) having a surface or side in complete contact with another surface: *flat against the wall* **6** spread out, unrolled, or levelled **7** (of a tyre) deflated, either partially or completely **8** (of shoes) having an unraised or only slightly raised heel **9** *chiefly Brit* **a** (of races, racetracks, or racecourses) not having obstacles to be jumped **b** of, relating to, or connected with flat racing as opposed to steeplechasing and hurdling: *flat jockeys earn more* **10** without qualification; total **11** without possibility of change; fixed: *a flat rate* **12** (*prenominal or immediately postpositive*) neither more nor less; exact: *he did the journey in thirty minutes flat* **13** unexciting or lacking point or interest: *a flat joke* **14** without variation or resonance; monotonous: *a flat voice* **15** (of food) stale or tasteless **16** (of beer, sparkling wines, etc) having lost effervescence, as by exposure to air **17** (of trade, business, a market, etc) commercially inactive; sluggish **18** (of a battery) fully discharged; dead **19** (of a print, photograph, or painting) lacking contrast or shading between tones **20** (of paint) without gloss or lustre; matt **21** (of a painting) lacking perspective **22** (of lighting) diffuse **23** *music* **a** (*immediately postpositive*) denoting a note of a given letter name (or the sound it represents) that has been lowered in pitch by one chromatic semitone: *B flat* **b** (of an instrument, voice, etc) out of tune by being too low in pitch. Compare **sharp** (sense 12) **24** *phonetics* another word for **lenis 25 flat a** *phonetics* the vowel sound of *a* as in the usual US or S Brit pronunciation of *hand, cat*, usually represented by the symbol (æ) ▷ *adv* **26** in or into a prostrate, level, or flat state or position: *he held his hand out flat* **27** completely or utterly; absolutely **28** exactly; precisely: *in three minutes flat* **29** *music* **a** lower than a standard pitch **b** too low in pitch. Compare **sharp** (sense 18) **30 fall flat** to fail to achieve a desired effect, etc **31 flat out** *informal* **a** with the maximum speed or effort **b** totally exhausted ▷ *n* **32** a flat object, surface, or part **33** (*often plural*) a low-lying tract of land, esp a marsh or swamp **34** (*often plural*) a mud bank exposed at low tide **35** *music* **a** an accidental that lowers the pitch of the following note by one chromatic semitone. Usual symbol: ♭ **b** a note affected by this accidental. Compare **sharp** (sense 19) **36** *theatre* a rectangular wooden frame covered with painted canvas, etc, used to form part of a stage setting **37** a punctured car tyre **38** (*often cap*; preceded by *the*) *chiefly Brit* **a** flat racing, esp as opposed to steeplechasing and hurdling **b** the season of flat racing **39** *nautical* a flatboat or lighter **40** *US and Canadian* a shallow box or container, used for holding plants, growing seedlings, etc ▷ *vb* **flats, flatting, flatted 41** to make or become flat **42** *music* the usual US word for **flatten** (sense 3) ▷ See also **flats** [C14 from Old Norse *flatr*; related to Old High German *flaz* flat, Greek *platus* flat, broad] > '**flatly** *adv* > '**flatness** *n*

flat[2] (flæt) *n* **1** a set of rooms comprising a residence entirely on one floor of a building. Usual US and Canadian name: **apartment 2** *Brit and NZ* a portion of a house used as separate living quarters **3** *NZ* a house shared with people who are not members of one's own family ▷ *vb* **flats, flatting, flatted** (*intr*) **4** *Austral and NZ* to live in a flat (with someone) [Old English *flett* floor, hall, house; related to FLAT[1]]

flat-bed lorry ('flæt,bɛd) *n* a lorry with a flat platform for its body

flat-bed press *n* a printing machine on which the type forme is carried on a flat bed under a revolving paper-bearing cylinder. Also called: **cylinder press**

flat-bed scanner *n* a computer-controlled device which electronically scans images placed on its flat plate, allowing them to be stored in digital form

flatboat ('flæt,bəʊt) *n* any boat with a flat bottom, usually for transporting goods on a canal or river

flat-bottomed rail *n* *railways* a rail having a cross section like an inverted T, with the top extremity enlarged slightly to form the head. Also called: **flanged rail**

flatbread ('flæt,brɛd) *n* a type of thin unleavened bread

flat cap *n* **1** another name for **cloth cap** (sense 1) **2** an Elizabethan man's hat with a narrow down-turned brim

flat-coated retriever *n* a medium-sized variety of retriever having a dense flat black or liver-coloured coat with feathered legs and tail

flat dog *n* *Austral* another name for **crocodile**

flat-earther *n* *informal* a person who does not accept or is out of touch with the realities of modern life

flatette (,flæt'ɛt) *n* *Austral* a very small flat

flatfish ('flæt,fɪʃ) *n, pl* **-fish** *or* **-fishes** any marine spiny-finned fish of the order *Heterosomata*, including the halibut, plaice, turbot, and sole, all of which (when adult) swim along the sea floor on one side of the body, which is highly compressed and has both eyes on the uppermost side

flatfoot ('flæt,fʊt) *n* **1** Also called: **splayfoot** a condition in which the entire sole of the foot is able to touch the ground because of flattening of the instep arch **2** *pl* **-foots** *or* **-feet** a slang word (usually derogatory) for a **policeman**

flat-footed (,flæt'fʊtɪd) *adj* **1** having flatfoot **2** *Brit informal* **a** clumsy or awkward **b** downright and uncompromising **3** *informal* off guard or unawares (often in the phrase **catch flat-footed**) > ,**flat-'footedly** *adv* > ,**flat-'footedness** *n*

flathead ('flæt,hɛd) *n, pl* **-head** *or* **-heads** any Pacific scorpaenoid food fish of the family *Platycephalidae*, which resemble gurnards

flatiron ('flæt,aɪən) *n* (formerly) an iron for pressing clothes that was heated by being placed on a stove, etc

flat knot *n* another name for **reef knot**

flatlet ('flætlɪt) *n* a flat having only a few rooms

flatline ('flæt,laɪn) *vb* (*intr*) *informal* **1** to die or be so near death that the display of one's vital signs on medical monitoring equipment shows a flat line rather than peaks and troughs **2** to remain at a continuous low level

flatling ('flætlɪŋ) *archaic or dialect* ▷ *adv* **1** in a flat or prostrate position ▷ *adj* ▷ *adv* **2** with the flat side, as of a sword Also (for adv): **flatlings**

flatmate ('flæt,meɪt) *n* *Brit* a person with whom one shares a flat

flat-pack *adj* (of a piece of furniture, equipment, or other construction) supplied in pieces packed into a flat box for assembly by the buyer

flat racing *n* **a** the racing of horses on racecourses without jumps **b** (*as modifier*): *the flat-racing season*

flats (flæts) *or* **flatties** ('flætɪz) *pl n* shoes with flat heels or no heels

flatscreen ('flæt,skriːn) *n* **a** a slimline television set or computer monitor with a flat screen **b** (*as modifier*): *a flatscreen television*

flat-share *n* **1** the state of living in a flat where each occupant shares the facilities and expenses ▷ *vb* (*intr*) **2** to live in a flat with other people who are not relatives

flat spin *n* **1** an aircraft spin in which the longitudinal axis is more nearly horizontal than vertical **2** *informal* a state of confusion; dither

flat spot *n* **1** *engineering* a region of poor acceleration over a narrow range of throttle openings, caused by a weak mixture in the carburettor **2** any narrow region of poor performance in a mechanical device

flatten ('flætᵊn) *vb* **1** (sometimes foll by *out*) to make or become flat or flatter **2** (*tr*) *informal* **a** to knock down or injure; prostrate **b** to crush or subdue: *failure will flatten his self-esteem* **3** (*tr*) *music* to lower the pitch of (a note) by one chromatic semitone. Usual US word: **flat 4** (*intr*; foll by *out*) to manoeuvre an aircraft into horizontal flight, esp after a dive > '**flattener** *n*

flatter[1] ('flætə) *vb* **1** to praise insincerely, esp in order to win favour or reward **2** to show to advantage: *that dress flatters her* **3** (*tr*) to make to appear more attractive, etc, than in reality **4** to play upon or gratify the vanity of (a person): *it flatters her to be remembered* **5** (*tr*) to beguile with hope; encourage, esp falsely **6** (*tr*) to congratulate or deceive (oneself) [C13 probably from Old French *flater* to lick, fawn upon, of Frankish origin] > '**flatterable** *adj* > '**flatterer** *n* > '**flatteringly** *adv*

flatter[2] ('flætə) *n* **1** a blacksmith's tool, resembling a flat-faced hammer, that is placed on forged work and struck to smooth the surface of the forging **2** a die with a narrow rectangular orifice for drawing flat sections

flattery ('flætərɪ) *n, pl* **-teries 1** the act of flattering **2** excessive or insincere praise

flattie ('flætɪ) *n* *NZ informal* a flounder or other flatfish

flatties ('flætɪz) *pl n* another word for **flats**

flatting ('flætɪŋ) *n* **1** *metallurgy* the process of flattening metal into a sheet by rolling **2** *NZ* the practice of sharing a house with people who are not members of one's own family **3** *NZ* to leave the parental home and live independently in a flat, usually with people of the same age group

flattish ('flætɪʃ) *adj* somewhat flat

flattop ('flæt,tɒp) *n* *US* an informal name for **aircraft carrier**

flat top *n* a style of haircut in which the hair is cut shortest on the top of the head so that it stands up from the scalp and appears flat from the crown to the forehead

flat tuning *n* the condition of a radio receiver that does not discriminate sharply between signals on different frequencies

flatulent ('flætjʊlənt) *adj* **1** suffering from or caused by an excessive amount of gas in the alimentary canal, producing uncomfortable distension **2** generating excessive gas in the alimentary canal **3** pretentious or windy in style [C16 from New Latin *flātulentus*, from Latin: FLATUS] > '**flatulence** *or* '**flatulency** *n* > '**flatulently** *adv*

flatus ('fleɪtəs) *n, pl* **-tuses** gas generated in the alimentary canal [C17 from Latin: a blowing, snorting, from *flāre* to breathe, blow]

flatware ('flæt,wɛə) *n* *US and Canadian* **1** cutlery **2** any relatively flat tableware such as plates, saucers, etc. Compare **hollowware**

flatways ('flæt,weɪz) *or US* **flatwise** *adv* with the flat or broad side down or in contact with another surface

flatworm ('flæt,wɜːm) *n* any parasitic or free-living invertebrate of the phylum *Platyhelminthes*, including planarians, flukes, and tapeworms, having a flattened body with no circulatory system and only one opening to the intestine

flat-woven *adj* (of a carpet) woven without pile

flaunch (flɔːntʃ) *n* a cement or mortar slope around a chimney top, manhole, etc, to throw off water. Also called: **flaunching** [C18 variant of FLANGE]

flaunt (flɔːnt) *vb* **1** to display (possessions, oneself, etc) ostentatiously; show off **2** to wave or cause to wave freely; flutter ▷ *n* **3** the act of flaunting [C16 perhaps of Scandinavian origin; compare Norwegian dialect *flanta* to wander about] > '**flaunter** *n* > '**flauntingly** *adv*

USAGE *Flaunt* is sometimes wrongly used where *flout* is meant: *they must be* prevented from flouting (not *flaunting*) the law

flaunty ('flɔːntɪ) *adj* **flauntier, flauntiest** *chiefly US* characterized by or inclined to ostentatious display or flaunting > '**flauntily** *adv* > '**flauntiness** *n*

flautist ('flɔːtɪst) *or US and Canadian* **flutist** ('fluːtɪst) *n* a player of the flute [c19 from Italian *flautista*, from *flauto* FLUTE]

flavescent (flə'vɛsᵊnt) *adj* turning yellow; yellowish [c19 from Latin *flāvēscere* to become yellow, from *flāvēre* to be yellow, from *flāvus* yellow]

flavin *or* **flavine** ('fleɪvɪn) *n* **1** a heterocyclic ketone that forms the nucleus of certain natural yellow pigments, such as riboflavin. Formula: $C_{10}H_6N_4O_2$. See **flavoprotein** **2** any yellow pigment based on flavin **3** another name for **quercetin** [c19 from Latin *flāvus* yellow]

flavine ('fleɪvɪn) *n* **1** another name for **acriflavine hydrochloride** **2** a variant spelling of **flavin**

flavivirus ('fleɪvɪˌvaɪrəs) *n* a type of arbovirus that causes a wide range of diseases in humans, including yellow fever, dengue, and West Nile fever. It is spread by ticks or mosquitoes

flavone ('fleɪvəʊn) *n* **1** a crystalline compound occurring in plants. Formula: $C_{15}H_{10}O_2$ **2** any of a class of yellow plant pigments derived from flavone [c19 from German *Flavon*, from Latin *flāvus* yellow + -ONE]

flavonoid ('fleɪvəˌnɔɪd) *n* any of a group of organic compounds that occur as pigments in fruit and flowers [c20 from FLAVONE + -OID]

flavonol ('fleɪvəˌnɒl) *n* a flavonoid that occurs in red wine and is said to offer protection against heart disease

flavoprotein (ˌfleɪvəʊ'prəʊtiːn) *n* any of a group of enzymes that contain a derivative of riboflavin linked to a protein and catalyse oxidation in cells. Also called: **cytochrome reductase** See also **FMN, FAD** [c20 from FLAVIN + PROTEIN]

flavopurpurin (ˌfleɪvəʊ'pɜːpjʊrɪn) *n* a yellow crystalline dye derived from anthraquinone. Formula: $C_{14}H_5O_2(OH)_3$ [c20 from Latin *flāvus* yellow + PURPURIN]

flavorous ('fleɪvərəs) *adj* having flavour; tasty

flavour *or US* **flavor** ('fleɪvə) *n* **1** taste perceived in food or liquid in the mouth **2** a substance added to food, etc, to impart a specific taste **3** a distinctive quality or atmosphere; suggestion **4** a type or variety **5** *physics* a property of quarks that enables them to be differentiated into six types: up, down, strange, charm, bottom (or beauty), and top (or truth) **6** **flavour of the month** a person or thing that is the most popular at a certain time ▷ *vb* **7** (*tr*) to impart a flavour, taste, or quality to [c14 from Old French *flaour*, from Late Latin *flātor* (unattested) bad smell, breath, from Latin *flāre* to blow] > '**flavourer** *or US* '**flavorer** *n* > '**flavourless** *or US* '**flavorless** *adj* > '**flavoursome** *or US* '**flavorsome** *adj*

flavour enhancer *n* another term for **monosodium glutamate**

flavourful *or US* **flavorful** ('fleɪvəfʊl) *adj* having a full pleasant taste or flavour > '**flavourfully** *or US* '**flavorfully** *adv*

flavouring *or* **flavoring** ('fleɪvərɪŋ) *n* a substance used to impart a particular flavour to food

flaw[1] (flɔː) *n* **1** an imperfection, defect, or blemish **2** a crack, breach, or rift **3** *law* an invalidating fault or defect in a document or proceeding ▷ *vb* **4** to make or become blemished, defective, or imperfect [c14 probably from Old Norse *flaga* stone slab; related to Swedish *flaga* chip, flake, flaw] > '**flawless** *adj* > '**flawlessly** *adv* > '**flawlessness** *n*

flaw[2] (flɔː) *n* **1 a** a sudden short gust of wind; squall **b** a spell of bad, esp windy, weather **2** *obsolete* an outburst of strong feeling [c16 of Scandinavian origin; related to Norwegian *flaga* squall, gust, Middle Dutch *vlāghe*] > '**flawy** *adj*

flax (flæks) *n* **1** any herbaceous plant or shrub of the genus *Linum*, esp *L. usitatissimum*, which has blue flowers and is cultivated for its seeds (flaxseed) and for the fibres of its stems: family *Linaceae* **2** the fibre of this plant, made into thread and woven into linen fabrics **3** any of various similar plants **4** NZ a swamp plant producing a fibre that is used by Māoris for decorative work, baskets, etc. Also called: **harakeke** [Old English *fleax*; related to Old Frisian *flax*, Old High German *flahs* flax, Greek *plekein* to plait]

flaxen ('flæksən) *or* **flaxy** *adj* **1** of, relating to, or resembling flax **2** of a soft yellow colour: *flaxen hair*

flax kit *n* NZ a basket woven from flax fibres

flaxseed ('flæksˌsiːd) *n* the seed of the flax plant, which yields linseed oil. Also called: **linseed**

flay (fleɪ) *vb* (*tr*) **1** to strip off the skin or outer covering of, esp by whipping; skin **2** to attack with savage criticism **3** to strip of money or goods, esp by cheating or extortion [Old English *flēan*; related to Old Norse *flā* to peel, Lithuanian *plēšti* to tear] > '**flayer** *n*

flaysome ('fleɪsəm) *adj* *Northern English dialect* frightening

fld *abbreviation for* field

fl. dr. *abbreviation for* fluid dram

flea (fliː) *n* **1** any small wingless parasitic blood-sucking insect of the order *Siphonaptera*, living on the skin of mammals and birds and noted for its power of leaping **2** any of various invertebrates that resemble fleas, such as the water flea and flea beetle **3** **flea in one's ear** *informal* a sharp rebuke [Old English *flēah*; related to Old Norse *flō*, Old High German *flōh*]

fleabag ('fliːˌbæg) *n* *slang* **1** *Brit* a dirty or unkempt person, esp a woman **2** *US* a cheap or dirty hotel

fleabane ('fliːˌbeɪn) *n* **1** any of several plants of the genus *Erigeron*, such as *E. acer*, having purplish tubular flower heads with orange centres: family *Asteraceae* (composites) **2** any of several plants of the related genus *Pulicaria*, esp the Eurasian *P. dysenterica*, which has yellow daisy-like flower heads **3** **Canadian fleabane** a related plant, *Conyza* (or *Erigeron*) *canadensis*, with small white tubular flower heads. US name: **horseweed** **4** any of various other plants reputed to ward off fleas

flea beetle *n* any small common beetle of the genera *Phyllotreta*, *Chalcoides*, etc, having enlarged hind legs and capable of jumping: family *Chrysomelidae*. The larvae of many species are very destructive to turnips and other cruciferous vegetables

fleabite ('fliːˌbaɪt) *n* **1** the bite of a flea **2** a slight or trifling annoyance or discomfort

flea-bitten *adj* **1** bitten by or infested with fleas **2** *informal* shabby or decrepit; mean **3** (of the coat of a horse) having reddish-brown spots on a lighter background

fleam (fliːm) *n* *archaic* a lancet used for letting blood [c16 from Old French *flieme*, alteration of Late Latin *phlebotomus* lancet (literally: vein cutter); see PHLEBOTOMY]

flea market *n* an open-air market selling cheap and often second-hand goods

fleapit ('fliːˌpɪt) *n* *informal* a shabby cinema or theatre

fleawort ('fliːˌwɜːt) *n* **1** any of various plants of the genus *Senecio*, esp *S. integrifolius*, a European species with yellow daisy-like flowers and rosettes of downy leaves: family *Asteraceae* (composites) **2** a Eurasian plantain, *Plantago psyllium* (or *P. indica*), whose seeds resemble fleas and were formerly used as a flea repellent **3** another name for **ploughman's spikenard**

flèche (fleɪʃ, flɛʃ) *n* **1** Also called: **spirelet** a slender spire, esp over the intersection of the nave and transept ridges of a church roof **2** a pointed part of a fortification directed towards the attackers **3** *fencing* a short running attack [c18 from French: spire (literally: arrow), probably of Germanic origin; related to Middle Low German *flieke* long arrow]

fléchette (fleɪ'ʃɛt) *n* a steel dart or missile dropped from an aircraft, as in World War I [from French; see FLÈCHE]

fleck (flɛk) *n* **1** a small marking or streak; speckle **2** a small particle; speck: *a fleck of dust* ▷ *vb* **3** (*tr*) Also: **flecker** to mark or cover with flecks; speckle [c16 probably from Old Norse *flekkr* stain, spot; related to Old High German *flec* spot, plot of land]

flection ('flɛkʃən) *n* **1** the act of bending or the state of being bent **2** something bent; bend **3** *grammar* a less common word for **inflection** ▷ See also **flexion** [c17 from Latin *flexiō* a bending, from *flectere* to curve, bow] > '**flectional** *adj* > '**flectionless** *adj*

fled (flɛd) *vb* the past tense and past participle of **flee**

fledge (flɛdʒ) *vb* **1** (*tr*) to feed and care for (a young bird) until it is able to fly **2** (*tr*) Also called: **fletch** to fit (something, esp an arrow) with a feather or feathers **3** (*intr*) (of a young bird) to grow feathers **4** (*tr*) to cover or adorn with or as if with feathers [Old English *-flycge*, as in *unflycge* unfledged; related to Old High German *flucki* able to fly; see FLY[1]]

fledgling *or* **fledgeling** ('flɛdʒlɪŋ) *n* **1** a young bird that has just fledged **2** a young and inexperienced person

fledgy ('flɛdʒɪ) *adj* **fledgier, fledgiest** *rare* feathery or feathered

flee[1] (fliː) *vb* **flees, fleeing, fled** **1** to run away from (a place, danger, etc); fly: *to flee the country* **2** (*intr*) to run or move quickly; rush; speed: *she fled to the door* [Old English *flēon*; related to Old Frisian *fliā*, Old High German *fliohan*, Gothic *thliuhan*] > '**fleer** *n*

flee[2] (fliː) *vb* **1** a Scot word for **fly**[1] ▷ *n* **2** a Scot word for **fly**[2]

fleece (fliːs) *n* **1** the coat of wool that covers the body of a sheep or similar animal and consists of a mass of crinkly hairs **2** the wool removed from a single sheep **3** something resembling a fleece in texture or warmth **4** sheepskin or a fabric with soft pile, used as a lining for coats, etc **5** a warm polyester fabric with a brushed nap, used for outdoor garments **6** a jacket or top made from such a fabric ▷ *vb* (*tr*) **7** to defraud or charge exorbitantly; swindle **8** another term for **shear** (sense 1) [Old English *flēos*; related to Middle High German *vlius*, Dutch *vlies* fleece, Latin *plūma* feather, down]

fleecie ('fliːsɪ) *n* NZ a person who collects fleeces after shearing and prepares them for baling. Also called: **fleece-oh**

fleecy ('fliːsɪ) *adj* **fleecier, fleeciest** of or resembling fleece; woolly > '**fleecily** *adv* > '**fleeciness** *n*

fleein' ('fliːɪn) *adj* *Scot dialect* drunk [literally: flying, from FLEE[2]]

fleer (flɪə) *archaic* ▷ *vb* **1** to grin or laugh at; scoff; sneer ▷ *n* **2** a derisory glance or grin [c14 of Scandinavian origin; compare Norwegian *flire* to snigger] > '**fleeringly** *adv*

fleet[1] (fliːt) *n* **1** a number of warships organized as a tactical unit **2** all the warships of a nation **3** a number of aircraft, ships, buses, etc, operating together or under the same ownership [Old English *flēot* ship, flowing water, from *flēotan* to FLOAT]

fleet[2] (fliːt) *adj* **1** rapid in movement; swift **2** *poetic* fleeting; transient ▷ *vb* **3** (*intr*) to move rapidly **4** (*intr*) *archaic* to fade away smoothly; glide **5** (*tr*) *nautical* **a** to change the position of (a hawser) **b** to pass (a messenger or lead) to a hawser from a winch for hauling in **c** to spread apart (the blocks of a tackle) **6** (*intr*) *obsolete* to float or swim **7** (*tr*) *obsolete* to cause (time) to pass rapidly [probably Old English *flēotan* to float, glide rapidly; related to Old High German *fliozzan* to flow, Latin *pluere* to rain] > '**fleetly** *adv* > '**fleetness** *n*

fleet[3] (fliːt) *n* *chiefly Southeastern Brit* a small coastal inlet; creek [Old English *flēot* flowing water; see FLEET[1]]

Fleet (fliːt) *n* **the** **1** a stream that formerly ran into the Thames between Ludgate Hill and Fleet Street and is now a covered sewer **2** Also called: **Fleet Prison** (formerly) a London prison, esp used for holding debtors

fleet admiral *n* an officer holding the most senior commissioned rank in the US and certain other navies

Fleet Air Arm *n* the aviation branch of the Royal Navy. Abbreviation: **FAA**

fleet chief petty officer *n* a noncommissioned officer in the Royal Navy comparable in rank to a warrant officer in the British Army or Royal Air Force

fleeting ('fli:tɪŋ) *adj* rapid and transient: *a fleeting glimpse of the sea* > **'fleetingly** *adv* > **'fleetingness** *n*

fleet rate *or* **fleet rating** *n* a reduced rate quoted by an insurance company to underwrite the risks to a fleet of vehicles, aircraft, etc

Fleet Street *n* **1** a street in central London in which many newspaper offices were formerly situated **2** British journalism or journalists collectively

Fleetwood ('fli:twʊd) *n* a fishing port in NW England, in Lancashire. Pop: 26 841 (2001)

fleishik *or* **fleishig** ('fleɪʃɪk, 'flaɪ-) *adj* Judaism (of food) containing or derived from meat or meat products and therefore to be prepared and eaten separately from dairy foods. Also: **meaty** Compare **milchik** See also **kashruth**

Flem. *abbreviation for* Flemish

Fleming ('flɛmɪŋ) *n* a native or inhabitant of Flanders or a Flemish-speaking Belgian. Compare **Walloon** [c14 from Middle Dutch *Vlaminc*]

Fleming's rules *pl n* physics two rules used as mnemonics for the relationship between the directions of current flow, motion, and magnetic field in electromagnetic induction. The hand is held with the thumb, first, and second fingers at right angles, respectively indicating the directions of motion, field, and electric current. The left hand is used for electric motors and the right hand for dynamos [c19 named after Sir John Ambrose *Fleming* (1849–1945), English electrical engineer, who devised them]

Flemish ('flɛmɪʃ) *n* **1** one of the two official languages of Belgium, almost identical in form with Dutch **2 the** (*functioning as plural*) the Flemings collectively ▷ *adj* **3** of, relating to, or characteristic of Flanders, the Flemings, or their language

Flemish bond *n* a bond used in brickwork that has alternating stretchers and headers in each course, each header being placed centrally over a stretcher

Flemish Brabant *n* a province of central Belgium, formed in 1995 from the N part of Brabant province: densely populated and intensively farmed, with large industrial centres. Pop: 1 031 904 (2004 est). Area: 2106 sq km (813 sq miles)

Flensburg (*German* 'flɛnsbʊrk) *n* a port in N Germany, in Schleswig-Holstein: taken from Denmark by Prussia in 1864; voted to remain German in 1920. Pop: 85 300 (2003 est)

flense (flɛns), **flench** (flɛntʃ) *or* **flinch** (flɪntʃ) *vb* (*tr*) to strip (a whale, seal, etc) of (its blubber or skin) [c19 from Danish *flense*; related to Dutch *flensen*] > **'flenser**, **'flencher** *or* **'flincher** *n*

flesh (flɛʃ) *n* **1** the soft part of the body of an animal or human, esp muscular tissue, as distinct from bone and viscera. Related adj: **sarcoid 2** *informal* excess weight; fat **3** *archaic* the edible tissue of animals as opposed to that of fish or, sometimes, fowl; meat **4** the thick usually soft part of a fruit or vegetable, as distinct from the skin, core, stone, etc **5** the human body and its physical or sensual nature as opposed to the soul or spirit. Related adj: **carnal 6** mankind in general **7** animate creatures in general **8** one's own family; kin (esp in the phrase **one's own flesh and blood**) **9** a yellowish-pink to greyish-yellow colour **10** *Christian Science* belief on the physical plane which is considered erroneous, esp the belief that matter has sensation **11** (*modifier*) *tanning* of or relating to the inner or under layer of a skin or hide: *a flesh split* **12 in the flesh** in person; actually present **13 make one's flesh creep** (esp of something ghostly) to frighten and horrify one **14 press the flesh** *informal* to shake hands, usually with large numbers of people, esp in political campaigning ▷ *vb* **15** (*tr*) *hunting* to stimulate the hunting instinct of (hounds or falcons) by giving them small quantities of raw flesh **16** to wound the flesh of with a weapon **17** *archaic or poetic* to accustom or incite to bloodshed or battle by initial experience **18** *tanning* to remove the flesh layer of (a hide or skin) **19** to fatten; fill out [Old English *flǣsc*; related to Old Norse *flesk* ham, Old High German *fleisk* meat, flesh]

flesher ('flɛʃə) *n* **1** a person or machine that fleshes hides or skins **2** *Scot* a person who sells meat; butcher

flesh fly *n* any dipterous fly of the genus *Sarcophaga*, esp *S. carnaria*, whose larvae feed on carrion or the tissues of living animals: family *Calliphoridae*

fleshings ('flɛʃɪŋz) *pl n* **1** flesh-coloured tights **2** bits of flesh scraped from the hides or skins of animals

fleshly ('flɛʃlɪ) *adj* **-lier, -liest 1** relating to the body, esp its sensual nature; carnal: *fleshly desire* **2** worldly as opposed to spiritual **3** fleshy; fat > **'fleshliness** *n*

flesh out *vb* (*adverb*) **1** (*tr*) to give substance to (an argument, description, etc) **2** (*intr*) to expand or become more substantial

fleshpots ('flɛʃˌpɒts) *pl n often facetious* **1** luxurious or self-indulgent living **2** places, such as striptease clubs, where bodily desires are gratified or titillated [c16 from the Biblical use as applied to Egypt (Exodus 16:3)]

flesh wound (wu:nd) *n* a wound affecting superficial tissues

fleshy ('flɛʃɪ) *adj* **fleshier, fleshiest 1** fat; plump **2** related to or resembling flesh **3** *botany* (of some fruits, leaves, etc) thick and pulpy > **'fleshiness** *n*

fletch (flɛtʃ) *vb* another word for **fledge** (sense 2) [c17 probably back formation from FLETCHER]

fletcher ('flɛtʃə) *n* a person who makes arrows [c14 from Old French *flechier*, from *fleche* arrow; see FLÈCHE]

Fletcherism ('flɛtʃəˌrɪzəm) *n* the practice of chewing food thoroughly and drinking liquids in small sips to aid digestion [c20 named after Horace *Fletcher* (1849–1919), American nutritionist]

fletchings ('flɛtʃɪŋz) *pl n* arrow feathers [plural of *fletching*, from FLETCH]

fleur-de-lys *or* **fleur-de-lis** (ˌflɜː'də'li:) *n, pl* **fleurs-de-lys** *or* **fleurs-de-lis** (ˌflɜː'də'li:z) **1** *heraldry* a charge representing a lily with three distinct petals **2** another name for **iris** (sense 2) [c19 from Old French *flor de lis*, literally: lily flower]

fleurette *or* **fleuret** (flʊə'rɛt, flɜː-) *n* an ornament resembling a flower [c19 French, literally: a small flower, from *fleur* flower]

fleuron ('flʊərɒn, -rən, 'flɜː-) *n* **1** another name for **flower** (sense 8) **2** *cookery* a decorative piece of pastry [c14 from French, from Old French *floron*, from *flor* FLOWER]

Flevoland (*Dutch* 'fle:volant) *n* a province of the central Netherlands, created in 1986 on land reclaimed from the IJsselmeer (formerly the Zuiderzee); entirely below sea level. Capital: Lelystad. Pop: 352 000 (2003 est). Area: 1420 sq km (548 sq miles)

flew¹ (flu:) *vb* the past tense of **fly** (sense 1)

flew² (flu:) *n* a variant spelling of **flue³**

flews (flu:z) *pl n* the fleshy hanging upper lip of a bloodhound or similar dog [c16 of unknown origin]

flex (flɛks) *n* **1** *Brit* a flexible insulated electric cable, used esp to connect appliances to mains. US and Canadian name: **cord 2** *informal* flexibility or pliability ▷ *vb* **3** to bend or be bent: *he flexed his arm; his arm flexed* **4** to contract (a muscle) or (of a muscle) to contract **5** (*intr*) to work according to flexitime **6** to test or display (one's authority or strength) [c16 from Latin *flexus* bent, winding, from *flectere* to bend, bow]

flexecutive (flɛg'zɛkjʊtɪv) *n* an executive to whom the employer allows flexibility about times and locations of working [c20 from FLEX(IBLE) + (EX)ECUTIVE]

flexible ('flɛksɪbəl) *adj* Also: **flexile** ('flɛksaɪl) **1** able to be bent easily without breaking; pliable **2** adaptable or variable: *flexible working hours* **3** able to be persuaded easily; tractable > ˌflexi'bility *or* 'flexibleness *n* > 'flexibly *adv*

flexion ('flɛkʃən) *n* **1** the act of bending a joint or limb **2** the condition of the joint or limb so bent **3** a variant spelling of **flection**. > 'flexional *adj* > 'flexionless *adj*

flexitarian (ˌflɛksɪ'tɛərɪən) *n* **1** a person who eats a predominantly vegetarian diet, but who eats meat or fish occasionally ▷ *adj* **2** of or relating to a flexitarian: *flexitarian fare* > ˌflexi'tarianˌism *n* [c21 from FLEXI(BLE) + (VEGE)TARIAN]

flexitime ('flɛksɪˌtaɪm) *or* **flextime** ('flɛksˌtaɪm) *n* a system permitting flexibility of working hours at the beginning or end of the day, provided an agreed period of each day (**core time**) is spent at work

flexo ('flɛksəʊ) *n, adj, adv* short for **flexography, flexographic** *or* **flexographically**

flexography (flɛk'sɒɡrəfɪ) *n* **1** a method of rotary letterpress printing using a resilient printing plate and solvent-based ink: used characteristically for printing on metal foil or plastic **2** matter printed by this method ▷ Abbreviation: **flexo** > **flexographic** (ˌflɛksə'ɡræfɪk) *adj* > ˌflexo'graphically *adv*

flexor ('flɛksə) *n* any muscle whose contraction serves to bend a joint or limb. Compare **extensor** [c17 New Latin; see FLEX]

flexuous ('flɛksjʊəs) *or* **flexuose** ('flɛksjʊˌəʊs) *adj* **1** full of bends or curves; winding **2** variable; unsteady [c17 from Latin *flexuōsus* full of bends, tortuous, from *flexus* a bending; see FLEX] > 'flexuously *adv*

flexure ('flɛkʃə) *n* **1** the act of flexing or the state of being flexed **2** a bend, turn, or fold > 'flexural *adj*

flex-wing *n aeronautics* a collapsible fabric delta wing, as used with hang-gliders

fley *or* **flay** (fleɪ) *vb Scot and Northern English dialect* **1** to be afraid or cause to be afraid **2** (*tr*) to frighten away; scare [Old English *āflēgan* to put to flight; related to Old Norse *fleygja*]

flibbert ('flɪbət) *n Southwest English dialect* a small piece or bit

flibbertigibbet ('flɪbətɪˌdʒɪbɪt) *n* an irresponsible, silly, or gossipy person [c15 of uncertain origin]

flick¹ (flɪk) *vb* **1** (*tr*) to touch with or as if with the finger or hand in a quick jerky movement **2** (*tr*) to propel or remove by a quick jerky movement, usually of the fingers or hand: *to flick a piece of paper at someone* **3** to move or cause to move quickly or jerkily **4** (*intr; foll by through*) to read or look at (a book, newspaper, etc) quickly or idly **5** to snap or click (the fingers) to produce a sharp sound ▷ *n* **6** a tap or quick stroke with the fingers, a whip, etc **7** the sound made by such a stroke **8** a fleck, streak, or particle [c15 of imitative origin; compare French *flicflac*]

flick² (flɪk) *n slang* **1** a cinema film **2** (*plural*) **the the cinema**: *what's on at the flicks tonight?*

flicker¹ ('flɪkə) *vb* **1** (*intr*) to shine with an unsteady or intermittent light **2** (*intr*) to move quickly to and fro; quiver, flutter, or vibrate **3** (*tr*) to cause to flicker ▷ *n* **4** an unsteady or brief light or flame **5** a swift quivering or fluttering movement **6** a visual sensation, often seen in a television image, produced by periodic fluctuations in the brightness of light at a frequency below that covered by the persistence of

f

vision **7** (*plural*) **the** a US word for **flick²** (sense 2) [Old English *flicorian*; related to Dutch *flikkeren*, Old Norse *flökra* to flutter] > **'flickery** *adj*

flicker² ('flɪkə) *n* any North American woodpecker of the genus *Colaptes*, esp *C. auratus* (**yellow-shafted flicker**), which has a yellow undersurface to the wings and tail [C19 perhaps imitative of the bird's call]

flick knife *n* a knife with a retractable blade that springs out when a button is pressed. US and Canadian word: **switchblade**

flick-pass *n* **1** *rugby* a movement in which the ball is passed quickly to another player by flicking it out of the hand; often performed with only one hand **2** *hockey, ice hockey* an instance of passing the puck using a short backhand movement, esp over the stick of a defender **3** *Austral* an instance of passing of undesirable or unwanted duties, responsibility, etc, to someone else ▷ *vb* **flick-pass** (*tr*) **4** *rugby, hockey, ice hockey* to pass (a ball or puck) quickly with a flick-pass **5** to pass (undesirable or unwanted duties, responsibility, etc) to someone else

flier ('flaɪə) *n* a variant spelling of **flyer**

flight¹ (flaɪt) *n* **1** the act, skill, or manner of flying **2** a journey made by a flying animal or object **3 a** a scheduled airline journey **b** an aircraft flying on such a journey **4** a group of flying birds or aircraft **5** the basic tactical unit of a military air force **6** a journey through space, esp of a spacecraft **7** rapid movement or progress **8** a soaring mental journey above or beyond the normal everyday world **9 a** a single line of hurdles across a track in a race **b** a series of such hurdles **10** a bird's wing or tail feather; flight feather **11** a feather or plastic attachment fitted to an arrow or dart to give it stability in flight **12** See **flight arrow 13** the distance covered by a flight arrow **14** *sport, esp cricket* a flighted movement imparted to a ball, dart, etc **b** the ability to flight a ball **15** *angling* a device on a spinning lure that revolves rapidly **16** a set of steps or stairs between one landing or floor and the next **17** a large enclosed area attached to an aviary or pigeon loft where the birds may fly but not escape ▷ *vb* **18** (*tr*) *sport* to cause (a ball, dart, etc) to float slowly or deceptively towards its target **19** (*intr*) (of wild fowl) to fly in groups **20** (*tr*) to shoot (a bird) in flight **21** (*tr*) to fledge (an arrow or a dart) [Old English *flyht*; related to Middle Dutch *vlucht*, Old Saxon *fluht*]

flight² (flaɪt) *n* **1** the act of fleeing or running away, as from danger **2** *take to flight* to cause to run away; rout **3** *take (to) flight* to run away or withdraw hastily; flee [Old English *flyht* (unattested); related to Old Frisian *flecht*, Old High German *fluht*, Old Norse *flötti*]

flight arrow *n* a long thin arrow used for shooting long distances. Often shortened to: **flight**

flight attendant *n* a person who attends to the needs of passengers on a commercial flight

flight capital *n* funds transferred abroad in order to avoid high taxes or to provide for a person's needs if flight from the country becomes necessary

flight deck *n* **1** the crew compartment in an airliner. Compare **cockpit** (sense 1) **2** the upper deck of an aircraft carrier from which aircraft take off and on which they land

flight engineer *n* the member of an aircraft crew who is responsible for the operation of the aircraft's systems, including the engines, during flight

flight feather *n* any of the large stiff feathers that cover the wings and tail of a bird and are adapted for flying

flight formation *n* two or more aircraft flying together in a set pattern

flightless ('flaɪtlɪs) *adj* (of certain birds and insects) unable to fly. See also **ratite**

flight level *n* *aeronautics* a specified height at which an aircraft is allowed to fly

flight lieutenant *n* an officer holding a commissioned rank senior to a flying officer and junior to a squadron leader in the RAF and certain other air forces

flight line *n* an area of an airfield or airport on which aircraft, esp military aircraft, are parked and serviced

flight management systems *pl n* a suite of computer programs in a computer on board an aircraft used to calculate the most economical flying speeds and altitudes during a flight and to identify possible choices in emergencies

flight path *n* the course through the air of an aircraft, rocket, or projectile. Compare **approach** (sense 10), **glide path**

flight plan *n* a written statement of the details of a proposed aircraft flight

flight recorder *n* an electronic device fitted to an aircraft for storing information concerning its performance in flight. It is often used to determine the cause of a crash. Also called: **black box**

flight sergeant *n* a noncommissioned officer in the Royal Air Force junior in rank to a master aircrew

flight simulator *n* a ground-training device that reproduces exactly the conditions experienced on the flight deck of an aircraft. Compare **Link trainer**

flight strip *n* **1** a strip of cleared land used as an emergency runway for aircraft **2** another name for **runway** (sense 1) **3** a strip of continuous aerial photographs

flight surgeon *n* a medical officer specializing in aviation medicine in the US and certain other air forces

flighty ('flaɪtɪ) *adj* **flightier, flightiest 1** frivolous and irresponsible; capricious; volatile **2** mentally erratic, unstable, or wandering **3** flirtatious; coquettish > **'flightily** *adv* > **'flightiness** *n*

flim (flɪm) *n Northern English dialect* a five-pound note

flimflam ('flɪm,flæm) *informal* ▷ *n* **1 a** nonsense; foolishness **b** (*as modifier*): *flimflam arguments* **2** a deception; swindle ▷ *vb* **-flams, -flamming, -flammed 3** (*tr*) to deceive; trick; swindle; cheat [C16 probably of Scandinavian origin; compare Old Norse *flīm* mockery, Norwegian *flire* to giggle] > **'flim,flammer** *n*

flimsy ('flɪmzɪ) *adj* **-sier, -siest 1** not strong or substantial; fragile **2** light and thin **3** unconvincing or inadequate; weak: *a flimsy excuse* ▷ *n* **4** thin paper used for making carbon copies of a letter, etc **5** a copy made on such paper **6** a slang word for **banknote** [C17 of uncertain origin] > **'flimsily** *adv* > **'flimsiness** *n*

flinch¹ (flɪntʃ) *vb* (*intr*) **1** to draw back suddenly, as from pain, shock, etc; wince: *he flinched as the cold water struck him* **2** (*often foll by from*) to avoid contact (with); shy away: *he never flinched from his duty* ▷ *n* **3** the act or an instance of drawing back **4** a card game in which players build sequences [C16 from Old French *flenchir*; related to Middle High German *lenken* to bend, direct] > **'flincher** *n* > **'flinchingly** *adv*

flinch² (flɪntʃ) *vb* a variant of **flense**

flinders ('flɪndəz) *pl n rare* small fragments or splinters (esp in the phrase **fly into flinders**) [C15 probably of Scandinavian origin; compare Norwegian *flindra* thin piece of stone]

Flinders bar ('flɪndəz) *n navigation* a bar of soft iron mounted on a binnacle to compensate for local magnetism causing error to the compass [C19 named after Matthew *Flinders* (died 1814), English navigator]

Flinders Island *n* an island off the coast of NE Tasmania: the largest of the Furneaux Islands. Pop: 850 (2004 est). Area: 2077 sq km (802 sq miles)

Flinders Range *n* a mountain range in E South Australia, between Lake Torrens and Lake Frome.

Highest peak: 1188 m (3898 ft)

fling (flɪŋ) *vb* **flings, flinging, flung** (flʌŋ) (*mainly tr*) **1** to throw, esp with force or abandon; hurl or toss **2** to put or send without warning or preparation: *to fling someone into jail* **3** (*also intr*) to move (oneself or a part of the body) with abandon or speed: *he flung himself into a chair* **4** (usually foll by *into*) to apply (oneself) diligently and with vigour (to) **5** to cast aside; disregard **6** to utter violently or offensively **7** *poetic* to give out; emit ▷ *n* **8** the act or an instance of flinging; toss; throw **9** a period or occasion of unrestrained, impulsive, or extravagant behaviour: *to have a fling* **10** any of various vigorous Scottish reels full of leaps and turns, such as the Highland fling **11** a trial; try [C13 of Scandinavian origin; related to Old Norse *flengja* to flog, Swedish *flänga*, Danish *flænge*] > **'flinger** *n*

flint (flɪnt) *n* **1** an impure opaque microcrystalline greyish-black form of quartz that occurs in chalk. It produces sparks when struck with steel and is used in the manufacture of pottery, flint glass, and road-construction materials. Formula: SiO_2 **2** any piece of flint, esp one used as a primitive tool or for striking fire **3** a small cylindrical piece of an iron alloy, used in cigarette lighters **4** Also called: **flint glass, white flint** colourless glass other than plate glass **5** See **optical flint** ▷ *vb* **6** (*tr*) to fit or provide with a flint [Old English; related to Old High German *flins*, Old Swedish *flinta* splinter of stone, Latin *splendēre* to shine]

Flint (flɪnt) *n* **1** a town in NE Wales, in Flintshire, on the Dee estuary. Pop: 11 936 (2001) **2** a city in SE Michigan: closure of the car production plants led to a high level of unemployment. Pop: 120 292 (2003 est)

flint glass *n* another name for **optical flint, flint** (sense 4)

flintlock ('flɪnt,lɒk) *n* **1** an obsolete gunlock in which the charge is ignited by a spark produced by a flint in the hammer **2** a firearm having such a lock

Flintshire ('flɪntʃɪə, -ʃə) *n* a county of NE Wales, on the Irish Sea and the Dee estuary: became part of Clwyd in 1974, reinstated with reduced borders in 1996: includes the industrialized Deeside region in the E and the Clwydian Hills in the SW. Administrative centre: Mold. Pop: 149 400 (2003 est). Area: 437 sq km (169 sq miles)

flinty ('flɪntɪ) *adj* **flintier, flintiest 1** of, relating to, or resembling flint **2** hard or cruel; obdurate; unyielding > **'flintily** *adv* > **'flintiness** *n*

flip (flɪp) *vb* **flips, flipping, flipped 1** to throw (something light or small) carelessly or briskly; toss **2** to throw or flick (an object such as a coin) so that it turns or spins in the air **3** to propel by a sudden movement of the finger; flick **4** (foll by *through*) to read or look at (a book, newspaper, etc) quickly, idly, or incompletely **5** (*intr*) (of small objects) to move or bounce jerkily **6** (*intr*) to make a snapping movement or noise with the finger and thumb **7** (*intr*) *slang* to fly into a rage or an emotional outburst (also in the phrases **flip one's lid, flip one's top**) **8** (*intr*) *slang* to become ecstatic or very excited ▷ *n* **9** a snap or tap, usually with the fingers **10** a rapid jerk **11** a somersault, esp one performed in the air, as in a dive, rather than from a standing position **12** same as **nog¹** (sense 1) ▷ *adj* **13** *informal* impertinent, flippant, or pert [C16 probably of imitative origin; see FILLIP]

flip chart *n* a pad, containing large sheets of paper that can be easily turned over, mounted on a stand and used to present reports, data, etc

flip-flop *n* **1** a backward handspring **2** Also called: **bistable** an electronic device or circuit that can assume either of two stable states by the application of a suitable pulse **3** *informal, chiefly US* a complete change of opinion, policy, etc **4** a repeated flapping or banging noise **5** Also called (US, Canadian, Austral, and NZ): **thong** a rubber-soled sandal attached to the foot by a thong between the big toe and the next toe ▷ *vb* **-flops, -flopping, -flopped** (*intr*) **6** *informal, chiefly US* to make a complete change of opinion, policy, etc **7** to move with repeated flaps ▷ *adv* **8** with repeated flappings: *to go flip-flop* [C16 reduplication of FLIP]

flip-flopper *n US informal* a person who makes a complete change of policy, opinion, etc

flippant (ˈflɪpənt) *adj* **1** marked by inappropriate levity; frivolous or offhand **2** impertinent; saucy **3** *obsolete* talkative or nimble [C17 perhaps from FLIP] > ˈ**flippancy** *n* > ˈ**flippantly** *adv*

flipper (ˈflɪpə) *n* **1** the flat broad limb of seals, whales, penguins, and other aquatic animals, specialized for swimming **2** (*often plural*) Also called: **fin** either of a pair of rubber paddle-like devices worn on the feet as an aid in swimming, esp underwater **3** *cricket* a ball bowled with topspin imparted by the action of the bowler's wrist

flipping (ˈflɪpɪŋ) *adj, adv Brit slang* (intensifier): *a flipping idiot; it's flipping cold* [C19 perhaps a euphemism for FUCKING]

flippy (ˈflɪpɪ) *adj* **-pier, -piest** *informal* (of clothes) tending to move to and fro as the wearer walks: *little flippy skirts*

flip side *n* **1** another term for **B-side** **2** another, less familiar aspect of a person or thing: *the flip side of John Lennon*

flip-up *adj* (*prenominal*) able to be opened by being flipped upwards

flirt (flɜːt) *vb* **1** (*intr*) to behave or act amorously without emotional commitment; toy or play with another's affections; dally **2** (*intr*; usually foll by *with*) to deal playfully or carelessly (with something dangerous or serious); trifle **3** (*intr*; usually foll by *with*) to think casually (about); toy (with): *to flirt with the idea of leaving* **4** (*intr*) to move jerkily; dart; flit **5** (*tr*) to subject to a sudden swift motion; flick or toss ▷ *n* **6** a person who acts flirtatiously [C16 of uncertain origin] > ˈ**flirter** *n* > ˈ**flirty** *adj* > ˈ**flirtingly** *adv*

flirtation (flɜːˈteɪʃən) *n* **1** behaviour intended to arouse sexual feelings or advances without emotional commitment; coquetry **2** any casual involvement without commitment

flirtatious (flɜːˈteɪʃəs) *adj* **1** given to flirtation **2** expressive of playful sexual invitation: *a flirtatious glance* > flirˈ**tatiously** *adv* > flirˈ**tatiousness** *n*

flit (flɪt) *vb* **flits, flitting, flitted** (*intr*) **1** to move along rapidly and lightly; skim or dart **2** to fly rapidly and lightly; flutter **3** to pass quickly; fleet: *a memory flitted into his mind* **4** *Scot and Northern English dialect* to move house **5** *Brit informal* to depart hurriedly and stealthily in order to avoid obligations **6** an informal word for **elope** ▷ *n* **7** the act or an instance of flitting **8** *slang, chiefly US* a male homosexual **9** *Brit informal* a hurried and stealthy departure in order to avoid obligations (esp in the phrase **do a flit**) **10** See **moonlight flit** [C12 from Old Norse *flytja* to carry] > ˈ**flitter** *n*

flitch (flɪtʃ) *n* **1** a side of pork salted and cured **2** a steak cut from the side of certain fishes, esp halibut **3** a piece of timber cut lengthways from a tree trunk, esp one that is larger than 4 by 12 inches ▷ *vb* **4** (*tr*) to cut (a tree trunk) into flitches [Old English *flicce*; related to Old Norse *flikki*, Middle Low German *vlicke*, Norwegian *flika*; see FLESH]

flite *or* **flyte** (flaɪt; *Scot* fləɪt) *Scot and Northern English dialect* ▷ *vb* **1** (*tr*) to scold or rail at ▷ *n* **2** a dispute or scolding [Old English *flītan* to wrangle, of Germanic origin; related to Old Frisian *flīt* strife, Old High German *flīz* strife]

flitter (ˈflɪtə) *vb* a less common word for **flutter**

flittermouse (ˈflɪtəˌmaʊs) *n, pl* **-mice** a dialect name for **bat**[2] (the animal) [C16 translation of German *Fledermaus*; see FLITTER, MOUSE]

flivver (ˈflɪvə) *n* an old, cheap, or battered car [C20 of unknown origin]

float (fləʊt) *vb* **1** to rest or cause to rest on the surface of a fluid or in a fluid or space without sinking; be buoyant or cause to exhibit buoyancy: *to float a ship* **2** to move or cause to move buoyantly, lightly, or freely across a surface or through air, water, etc; drift: *fog floated across the road* **3** to move about aimlessly, esp in the mind: *thoughts floated before him* **4** to suspend or be suspended without falling; hang **5** (*tr*) **a** to launch or establish (a commercial enterprise, etc) **b** to offer for sale (stock or bond issues, etc) on the stock market **6** (*tr*) *finance* to allow (a currency) to fluctuate against other currencies in accordance with market forces **7** (*tr*) to flood, inundate, or irrigate (land), either artificially or naturally **8** (*tr*) to spread, smooth, or level (a surface of plaster, rendering, etc) ▷ *n* **9** something that floats **10** *angling* an indicator attached to a baited line that sits on the water and moves when a fish bites **11** a small hand tool with a rectangular blade used for floating plaster, etc **12** *chiefly US* any buoyant object, such as a platform or inflated tube, used offshore by swimmers or, when moored alongside a pier, as a dock by vessels **13** Also called: **paddle** a blade of a paddle wheel **14** *Brit* a buoyant garment or device to aid a person in staying afloat **15** a hollow watertight structure fitted to the underside of an aircraft to allow it to land on water **16** another name for **air bladder** (sense 2) **17** an exhibit carried in a parade, esp a religious parade **18** a motor vehicle used to carry a tableau or exhibit in a parade, esp a civic parade **19** a small delivery vehicle, esp one powered by batteries: *a milk float* **20** *Austral and NZ* a vehicle for transporting horses **21** *banking, chiefly US* the total value of uncollected cheques and other commercial papers **22** *chiefly US and Canadian* a sum to be applied to minor expenses; petty cash **23** a sum of money used by shopkeepers to provide change at the start of the day's business, this sum being subtracted from the total at the end of the day when calculating the day's takings **24** the hollow floating ball of a ballcock **25** *engineering* a hollow cylindrical structure in a carburettor that actuates the fuel valve **26** *chiefly US and Canadian* a carbonated soft drink with a scoop of ice cream in it **27** (in textiles) a single thread brought to or above the surface of a woven fabric, esp to form a pattern **28** *forestry* a measure of timber equal to eighteen loads ▷ See also **float off, floats** [Old English *flotian*; related to Old Norse *flota*, Old Saxon *flotōn*; see FLEET[2]] > ˈ**floatable** *adj* > ˌ**floataˈbility** *n*

floatage (ˈfləʊtɪdʒ) *n* a variant spelling of **flotage**

floatation (fləʊˈteɪʃən) *n* a variant spelling of **flotation**

float chamber *n* a chamber in a carburettor in which a floating valve controls the entry and level of petrol

floatcut file (ˈfləʊtˌkʌt) *n engineering* a file having rows of parallel teeth

floatel (fləʊˈtɛl) *n* a variant spelling of **flotel**

floater (ˈfləʊtə) *n* **1** a person or thing that floats **2** any of a number of dark spots that appear in one's vision as a result of dead cells or fragments in the lens or vitreous humour of the eye **3** *US and Canadian* **a** a person of no fixed political opinion **b** a person who votes illegally in more than one district at one election **c** a voter who can be bribed **4** Also called: **floating policy** *US and Canadian insurance* a policy covering loss or theft of or damage to movable property, such as jewels or furs, regardless of its location **5** *US informal* a person who often changes employment, residence, etc; drifter **6** *Austral* a loose gold- or opal-bearing rock **7** *Austral* (esp in Adelaide) a meat pie in a plate of pea soup

float-feed *adj* (of a fuel system) controlled by a float operating a needle valve

float glass *n* a type of flat polished transparent glass made by allowing the molten glass to harden as it floats on liquid of higher density

floating (ˈfləʊtɪŋ) *adj* **1** having little or no attachment **2** (of an organ or part) displaced from the normal position or abnormally movable: *a floating kidney* **3** not definitely attached to one place or policy; uncommitted or unfixed: *the floating vote* **4** *finance* **a** (of capital) not allocated or invested; available for current use **b** (of debt) short-term and unfunded, usually raised by a government or company to meet current expenses **c** (of a currency) free to fluctuate against other currencies in accordance with market forces **5** *machinery* operating smoothly through being free from external constraints **6** (of an electronic circuit or device) not connected to a source of voltage > ˈ**floatingly** *adv*

floating assets *pl n* another term for **current assets**

floating charge *n chiefly Brit* an unsecured charge on the assets of an enterprise that allows such assets to be used commercially until the enterprise ceases to operate or the creditor intervenes to demand collateral

floating debt *n* short-term government borrowing, esp by the issue of three-month Treasury bills

floating dock *n* a large boxlike structure that can be submerged to allow a vessel to enter it and then floated to raise the vessel out of the water for maintenance or repair. Also called: **floating dry dock**

floating heart *n* any perennial aquatic freshwater plant of the genus *Nymphoides*, esp *N. lacunosum*, having floating heart-shaped leaves: family *Menyanthaceae*

floating island *n* a floating mass of soil held together by vegetation

floating-point representation *n computing* the representation of numbers by two sets of digits (*a*, *b*), the set *a* indicating the significant digits, the set *b* giving the position of the radix point. The number is the product ar^b, where *r* is the base of the number system used. Compare **fixed-point representation**

f

floating policy *n* **1** (in marine insurance) a policy covering loss of or damage to specified goods irrespective of the ship in which they are consigned **2** another term for **floater** (sense 4)

floating-rate note *n* a eurobond, often issued as a negotiable bearer bond, that has a floating rate of interest

floating rib *n* any rib of the lower two pairs of ribs in man, which are not attached to the breastbone

floating voter *n* a person who does not vote consistently for any single political party

float off *vb* (*tr, adverb*) to offer (shares in a subsidiary company) for sale on the stock market separately from the main company

floats (fləʊts) *pl n theatre* another word for **footlights**

floaty (ˈfləʊtɪ) *adj* **floatier, floatiest** **1** filmy and light: *floaty material* **2** capable of floating; buoyant **3** (of a vessel) riding high in the water; of shallow draught

floc (flɒk) *n* another word for **floccule** [C20 from Latin *floccus* a tuft of wool, FLOCK[2]]

floccose (ˈflɒkəʊs) *adj* consisting of or covered with woolly tufts or hairs: *floccose growths of bacteria* [C18 from Latin *floccōsus* full of flocks of wool]

flocculant (ˈflɒkjʊlənt) *n* a substance added to a suspension to enhance aggregation of the suspended particles

flocculate (ˈflɒkjʊˌleɪt) *vb* to form or be formed into an aggregated flocculent mass > ˌ**flocculˈlation** *n*

floccule (ˈflɒkjuːl), **flocculus, flock** *or* **floc** *n* **1** a small aggregate of flocculent material **2** something resembling a tuft of wool [C19 from Late Latin *flocculus* a little tuft; see FLOCK[2]]

flocculent (ˈflɒkjʊlənt) *adj* **1** like wool; fleecy **2** *chem* aggregated in woolly cloudlike masses: *a flocculent precipitate* **3** *biology* covered with tufts or flakes of a waxy or wool-like substance > ˈ**flocculence** *or* ˈ**flocculency** *n* > ˈ**flocculently** *adv*

flocculus ('flɒkjʊləs) *n, pl* -li (-,laɪ) **1** a marking on the sun's surface or in its atmosphere, as seen on a spectroheliogram. It consists of calcium when lighter than the surroundings and of hydrogen when darker **2** *anatomy* a tiny ovoid prominence on each side of the cerebellum **3** another word for **floccule**

floccus ('flɒkəs) *n, pl* flocci ('flɒksaɪ) **1** a downy or woolly covering, as on the young of certain birds **2** a small woolly tuft of hair ▷ *adj* **3** (of a cloud) having the appearance of woolly tufts at odd intervals in its structure [c19 from Latin: tuft of hair or wool, FLOCK²]

flock¹ (flɒk) *n* (*sometimes functioning as plural*) **1** a group of animals of one kind, esp sheep or birds **2** a large number of people; crowd **3** a body of Christians regarded as the pastoral charge of a priest, a bishop, the pope, etc **4** *rare* a band of people; group ▷ *vb* (*intr*) **5** to gather together or move in a flock **6** to go in large numbers: *people flocked to the church* [Old English *flocc*; related to Old Norse *flokkr* crowd, Middle Low German *vlocke*]

flock² (flɒk) *n* **1** a tuft, as of wool, hair, cotton, etc **2 a** waste from fabrics such as cotton, wool, or other cloth used for stuffing mattresses, upholstered chairs, etc **b** (*as modifier*): *flock mattress* **3** very small tufts of wool applied to fabrics, wallpaper, etc, to give a raised pattern **4** another word for **floccule** ▷ *vb* **5** to fill, cover, or ornament with flock [c13 from Old French *floc*, from Latin *floccus*; probably related to Old High German *floccho* down, Norwegian *flugsa* snowflake] > 'flocky *adj*

flock paper *n* a type of wallpaper with a raised pattern. See also **flock²** (sense 3)

Flodden ('flɒdⁿn) *n* a hill in Northumberland where invading Scots were defeated by the English in 1513 and James IV of Scotland was killed. Also called: **Flodden Field**

floe (fləʊ) *n* See **ice floe** [c19 probably from Norwegian *flo* slab, layer, from Old Norse; see FLAW¹]

flog (flɒg) *vb* flogs, flogging, flogged **1** (*tr*) to beat harshly, esp with a whip, strap, etc **2** (*tr*) *Brit slang* to sell **3** (*intr*) (of a sail) to flap noisily in the wind **4** (*intr*) to make progress by painful work **5** *NZ* to steal **6 flog a dead horse** *chiefly Brit* **a** to harp on some long discarded subject **b** to pursue the solution of a problem long realized to be insoluble **7 flog to death** to persuade a person so persistently of the value of (an idea or venture) that he loses interest in it [c17 probably from Latin *flagellāre*; see FLAGELLANT] > 'flogger *n* > 'flogging *n*

flokati (flə'kɑːtɪ) *n* a Greek hand-woven shaggy woollen rug [c20 from Modern Greek *phlokatē* a peasant's blanket]

flong (flɒŋ) *n* **1** *printing* a material, usually pulped paper or cardboard, used for making moulds in stereotyping **2** *journalism slang* material that is not urgently topical [c20 variant of FLAN]

flood (flʌd) *n* **1 a** the inundation of land that is normally dry through the overflowing of a body of water, esp a river **b** the state of a river that is at an abnormally high level (esp in the phrase **in flood**). Related adj: **diluvial 2** a great outpouring or flow **3 a** the rising of the tide from low to high water **b** (*as modifier*): *the flood tide*. Compare **ebb** (sense 3) **4** *theatre* short for **floodlight 5** *archaic* a large body of water, as the sea or a river ▷ *vb* **6** (of water) to inundate or submerge (land) or (of land) to be inundated or submerged **7** to fill up or be filled to overflowing, as with a flood **8** (*intr*) to flow; surge **9** to supply an excessive quantity of petrol to (a carburettor or petrol engine) or (of a carburettor, etc) to be supplied with such an excess **10** (*intr*) to rise to a flood; overflow **11** (*intr*) **a** to bleed profusely from the uterus, as following childbirth **b** to have an abnormally heavy flow of blood during a menstrual period [Old English *flōd*; related to Old Norse *flōth*, Gothic *flōdus*, Old High German *fluot* flood, Greek *plōtos* navigable; see

FLOW, FLOAT] > 'floodable *adj* > 'flooder *n* > 'floodless *adj*

Flood (flʌd) *n Old Testament* **the** the flood extending over all the earth from which Noah and his family and livestock were saved in the ark. (Genesis 7–8); the Deluge

flood basalt *n* a very extensive lava flow of basaltic composition that has issued from a fissure, often to be found as part of a series of such flows one on top of another, forming a plateau. See **fissure eruption**

flood control *n* the technique or practice of preventing or controlling floods with dams, artificial channels, etc

flooded gum *n* any of various eucalyptus trees of Australia, esp *Eucalyptus saligna* (the Sydney blue gum), that grow in damp soil

floodgate ('flʌd,geɪt) *n* **1** Also called: **head gate, water gate** a gate in a sluice that is used to control the flow of water. See also **sluicegate 2** (*often plural*) a control or barrier against an outpouring or flow

flooding ('flʌdɪŋ) *n* **1** the submerging of land under water, esp due to heavy rain, a lake or river overflowing, etc **2** *psychol* a method of eliminating anxiety in a given situation, by exposing a person to the situation until the anxiety subsides

floodlight ('flʌd,laɪt) *n* **1** a broad intense beam of artificial light, esp as used in the theatre or to illuminate the exterior of buildings **2** the lamp or source producing such light ▷ *vb* **-lights, -lighting, -lit 3** (*tr*) to illuminate by or as if by a floodlight

flood plain *n* the flat area bordering a river, composed of sediment deposited during flooding

floor (flɔː) *n* **1** Also called: **flooring** the inner lower surface of a room **2** a storey of a building: *the second floor* **3** a flat bottom surface in or on any structure: *the floor of a lift; a dance floor* **4** the bottom surface of a tunnel, cave, river, sea, etc **5** *mining* an underlying stratum **6** *nautical* the bottom, or the lowermost framing members at the bottom, of a vessel **7** that part of a legislative hall in which debate and other business is conducted **8** the right to speak in a legislative or deliberative body (esp in the phrases **get, have,** or **be given the floor**) **9** the room in a stock exchange where trading takes place **10** the earth; ground **11** a minimum price charged or paid: *a wage floor* **12 take the floor** to begin dancing on a dance floor ▷ *vb* **13** to cover with or construct a floor **14** (*tr*) to knock to the floor or ground **15** (*tr*) *informal* to disconcert, confound, or defeat: *to be floored by a problem* [Old English *flōr*; related to Old Norse *flōrr*, Middle Low German *vlōr* floor, Latin *plānus* level, Greek *planan* to cause to wander]

floorage ('flɔːrɪdʒ) *n* an area of floor; floor space

floorboard ('flɔː,bɔːd) *n* one of the boards forming a floor

floor-filler *n* *informal* a dance recording that is so catchy and popular that everyone in the place where it is played wants to dance

flooring ('flɔːrɪŋ) *n* **1** the material used in making a floor, esp the surface material **2** another word for **floor** (sense 1)

flooring saw *n* a type of saw curved at the end for cutting through floorboards

floor leader *n* *US government* a member of a legislative body who organizes his party's activities

floor manager *n* **1** the stage manager employed in the production of a television programme **2** a person in overall charge of one floor of a large shop or department store

floor plan *n* a drawing to scale of the arrangement of rooms on one floor of a building. Compare **elevation** (sense 5)

floor show *n* a series of entertainments, such as singing, dancing, and comedy acts, performed in a nightclub

floor trading *n* trading by personal contact on

the floor of a market or exchange. Compare **screen trading**

floorwalker ('flɔː,wɔːkə) *n* the US name for **shopwalker**

floozy, floozie *or* **floosie** ('fluːzɪ) *n, pl* -zies *or* -sies *slang* a disreputable woman [c20 of unknown origin]

flop (flɒp) *vb* flops, flopping, flopped **1** (*intr*) to bend, fall, or collapse loosely or carelessly **2** (when *intr*, often foll by *into, onto,* etc) to fall, cause to fall, or move with a sudden noise **3** (*intr*) *informal* to fail; be unsuccessful: *the scheme flopped* **4** (*intr*) to fall flat onto the surface of water, hitting it with the front of the body **5** (*intr;* often foll by *out*) *slang* to go to sleep ▷ *n* **6** the act of flopping **7** *informal* a complete failure **8** *US and Canadian slang* a place to sleep **9** *athletics* See **Fosbury flop** [c17 variant of FLAP]

flophouse ('flɒp,haʊs) *n* *US and Canadian slang* a cheap lodging house, esp one used by tramps. Also called (in Britain and certain other countries): **dosshouse**

floppy ('flɒpɪ) *adj* -pier, -piest **1** limp or hanging loosely: *a dog with floppy ears* ▷ *n, pl* -pies **2** short for **floppy disk**. > 'floppily *adv* > 'floppiness *n*

floppy disk *n* a flexible removable magnetic disk that stores information and can be used to store data for use in a microprocessor. Also called: **diskette, flexible disk**

flops *or* **FLOPS** *n* acronym for floating-point operations per second: used as a measure of computer processing power (in combination with a prefix): *megaflops; gigaflops*

flop sweat *n* *informal* a sudden heavy perspiration caused by embarrassment

flor. *abbreviation for* **floruit**

flora ('flɔːrə) *n, pl* -ras *or* -rae (-riː) **1** all the plant life of a given place or time **2** a descriptive list of such plants, often including a key for identification **3** short for **intestinal flora** [c18 from New Latin, from Latin *Flōra* goddess of flowers, from *flōs* FLOWER]

Flora ('flɔːrə) *n* the Roman goddess of flowers [c16 from Latin, from *flōs* flower]

floral ('flɔːrəl) *adj* **1** decorated with or consisting of flowers or patterns of flowers **2** of, relating to, or associated with flowers: *floral leaves* > 'florally *adv*

floral envelope *n* the part of a flower that surrounds the stamens and pistil: the calyx and corolla (considered together) or the perianth

Floréal *French* (flɔreal) *n* the month of flowers: the eighth month of the French revolutionary calendar, extending from April 21 to May 20 [c19 ultimately from Latin *flōreus* of flowers, from *flōs* a flower]

floreat *Latin* ('flɒrɪæt) *vb* (*intr*) *pl* floreant may (a person, institution, etc) flourish: *floreat Oxonia!*

floreated ('flɔːrɪ,eɪtɪd) *adj* a variant spelling of **floriated**

Florence ('flɒrəns) *n* a city in central Italy, on the River Arno in Tuscany: became an independent republic in the 14th century; under Austrian and other rule intermittently from 1737 to 1859; capital of Italy 1865–70. It was the major cultural and artistic centre of the Renaissance and is still one of the world's chief art centres. Pop: 356 118 (2001). Ancient name: **Florentia** (flɒ'rɛntsɪə, -'rɛntɪə) Italian name: **Firenze**

Florence fennel *n* another name for **finocchio**

Florence flask *n* a round flat-bottomed glass flask with a long neck, used in chemical experiments

Florentine ('flɒrən,taɪn) *adj* **1** of or relating to Florence **2** (*usually postpositive*) (of food) served or prepared with spinach ▷ *n* **3** a native or inhabitant of Florence **4** a biscuit containing nuts and dried fruit and coated with chocolate **5** a type of domestic fancy pigeon somewhat resembling the Modena

Flores ('flɔːrɛs) *n* **1** an island in Indonesia, one of the Lesser Sunda Islands, between the Flores Sea and the Savu Sea: mountainous, with active volcanoes and unexplored forests. Chief town: Ende. Area: 17 150 sq km (6622 sq miles) **2** (*also Portuguese* 'flor**ı**ʃ) an island in the Atlantic, the westernmost of the Azores. Chief town: Santa Cruz. Area: 142 sq km (55 sq miles)

florescence (flɔːˈrɛsəns) *n* the process, state, or period of flowering [C18 from New Latin *flōrēscentia*, from Latin *flōrēscere* to come into flower]

Flores Sea *n* a part of the Pacific Ocean in Indonesia between Celebes and the Lesser Sunda Islands

floret ('flɔːrɪt) *n* a small flower, esp one of many making up the head of a composite flower [C17 from Old French *florete* a little flower, from *flor* FLOWER]

Florianópolis (Portuguese floriəˈnɔpulis) *n* a port in S Brazil, capital of Santa Catarina state, on the W coast of Santa Catarina Island. Pop: 884 000 (2005 est)

floriated *or* **floreated** ('flɔːrɪˌeɪtɪd) *adj architect* having ornamentation based on flowers and leaves [C19 from Latin *flōs* FLOWER]

floribunda (ˌflɔːrɪˈbʌndə) *n* any of several varieties of cultivated hybrid roses whose flowers grow in large sprays [C19 from New Latin, feminine of *flōribundus* flowering freely]

floriculture ('flɔːrɪˌkʌltʃə) *n* the cultivation of flowering plants > ˌflori'cultural *adj* > ˌflori'culturist *n*

florid ('flɒrɪd) *adj* **1** having a red or flushed complexion **2** excessively ornate; flowery: *florid architecture* **3** an archaic word for **flowery** [C17 from Latin *flōridus* blooming] > flo'ridity *or* 'floridness *n* > 'floridly *adv*

Florida ('flɒrɪdə) *n* **1** a state of the southeastern US, between the Atlantic and the Gulf of Mexico: consists mostly of a low-lying peninsula ending in the **Florida Keys** a chain of small islands off the coast of S Florida, extending southwest for over 160 km (100 miles). Capital: Tallahassee. Pop: 17 019 068 (2003 est). Area: 143 900 sq km (55 560 sq miles). Abbreviations: **Fla,** (with zip code) **FL 2 Straits of** a sea passage between the Florida Keys and Cuba, linking the Atlantic with the Gulf of Mexico

Floridian (flɒˈrɪdɪən) *n* **1** a native or inhabitant of Florida ▷ *adj* **2** of or relating to Florida or its inhabitants

floriferous (flɔːˈrɪfərəs) *adj* bearing or capable of bearing many flowers

florigen ('flɒrɪdʒən) *n* the hypothetical plant hormone that induces flowering, thought to be synthesized in the leaves as a photoperiodic response and transmitted to the flower buds [C20 from Latin *flōr-, flōs* FLOWER + -GEN]

florilegium (ˌflɒrɪˈliːdʒɪəm) *n, pl* -gia (-dʒɪə) **1** (formerly) a lavishly illustrated book on flowers **2** *rare* an anthology [C17 Modern Latin, from Latin *florilegus* flower-collecting, from *flōs* flower + *legere* to collect]

florin ('flɒrɪn) *n* **1** a former British coin, originally silver and later cupronickel, equivalent to ten (new) pence **2** the standard monetary unit of Aruba, divided into 100 cents **3** (formerly) another name for **guilder** (sense 1) **4** any of various gold coins of Florence, Britain, or Austria [C14 from French, from Old Italian *fiorino* Florentine coin, from *fiore* flower, from Latin *flōs*]

florist ('flɒrɪst) *n* a person who grows or deals in flowers

floristic (flɒˈrɪstɪk) *adj* of or relating to flowers or a flora > flo'ristically *adv*

floristics (flɒˈrɪstɪks) *n* (*functioning as singular*) the branch of botany concerned with the types, numbers, and distribution of plant species in a particular area

-florous *adj combining form* indicating number or type of flowers: *tubuliflorous*

floruit *Latin* ('flɒruːɪt) *vb* (he or she) flourished: used to indicate the period when a historical figure, whose birth and death dates are unknown,

was most active. Abbreviations: *fl., flor*

florula ('flɒrjʊlə) *or* **florule** ('flɒrjuːl) *n, pl* -ulae (-juːliː) *or* -ules **1** the flora of a small single environment **2** a fossil flower found in a single stratum or in several thin adjacent strata [C19 FLORA + -ULE]

flory ('flɔːrɪ) *or* **fleury** ('flʊərɪ, 'flɜːrɪ) *adj* (*usually postpositive*) *heraldry* containing a fleur-de-lys [C15 from Old French *floré*, from *flor* FLOWER]

flos ferri ('flɒs 'fɛrɪ) *n* a variety of aragonite that is deposited from hot springs in the form of a white branching mass [C18 from New Latin, literally: flower of iron]

floss (flɒs) *n* **1** the mass of fine silky fibres obtained from cotton and similar plants **2** any similar fine silky material, such as the hairlike styles and stigmas of maize or the fibres prepared from silkworm cocoons **3** untwisted silk thread used in embroidery, etc **4** See **dental floss** ▷ *vb* **5** (*tr*) to clean (between one's teeth) with dental floss [C18 perhaps from Old French *flosche* down]

flossy ('flɒsɪ) *adj* flossier, flossiest **1** consisting of or resembling floss **2** *US and Canadian slang* (esp of dress) showy

flotage *or* **floatage** ('fləʊtɪdʒ) *n* **1** the act or state of floating; flotation **2** buoyancy; power or ability to float **3** objects or material that float on the surface of the water; flotsam

flotation *or* **floatation** (fləʊˈteɪʃən) *n* **1 a** the launching or financing of a commercial enterprise by bond or share issues **b** the raising of a loan or new capital by bond or share issues **2** power or ability to float; buoyancy **3** Also called: **froth flotation** a process to concentrate the valuable ore in low-grade ores. The ore is ground to a powder, mixed with water containing surface-active chemicals, and vigorously aerated. The bubbles formed trap the required ore fragments and carry them to the surface froth, which is then skimmed off

flotation bags *pl n* bags inflated to keep a spacecraft or helicopter afloat and upright when it lands in the sea

flotation tank *or* **chamber** *n* an enclosed ventilated tank filled with a saline solution at body temperature, in which a person floats in darkness in order to relax or meditate

flote grass (fləʊt) *n* an aquatic perennial grass, *Glyceria fluitans*, whose metre-long stems and pale green leaves are often seen floating in still or sluggish water. The related **sweet grass** (*G. plicata*) has broader, darker leaves and owes its name to the fact that cattle like to eat it [C16 *flote* obsolete spelling of FLOAT]

flotel *or* **floatel** (fləʊˈtɛl) *n* (in the oil industry) an oil rig or boat used as accommodation for workers in off-shore oil fields [C20 from *float* + *hotel*]

flotilla (flə'tɪlə) *n* a small fleet or a fleet of small vessels [C18 from Spanish *flota* fleet, from French *flotte*, ultimately from Old Norse *floti*]

flotsam ('flɒtsəm) *n* **1** wreckage from a ship found floating. Compare **jetsam** (sense 1), **lagan 2** useless or discarded objects; odds and ends (esp in the phrase **flotsam and jetsam**) **3** vagrants [C16 from Anglo-French *floteson*, from *floter* to FLOAT]

flounce¹ (flaʊns) *vb* **1** (*intr; often foll by about, away, out,* etc) to move or go with emphatic or impatient movements ▷ *n* **2** the act of flouncing [C16 of Scandinavian origin; compare Norwegian *flunsa* to hurry, Swedish *flunsa* to splash]

flounce² (flaʊns) *n* an ornamental gathered ruffle sewn to a garment by its top edge [C18 from Old French *fronce* wrinkle, from *froncir* to wrinkle, of Germanic origin]

flouncing ('flaʊnsɪŋ) *n* material, such as lace or embroidered fabric, used for making flounces

flounder¹ ('flaʊndə) *vb* (*intr*) **1** to struggle; to move with difficulty, as in mud **2** to behave awkwardly; make mistakes ▷ *n* **3** the act of floundering [C16 probably a blend of FOUNDER² + BLUNDER; perhaps influenced by FLOUNDER²]

▮ **USAGE** *Flounder* is sometimes wrongly used where *founder* is meant: *the project foundered* (not *floundered*) *because of a lack of funds*

flounder² ('flaʊndə) *n, pl* -der *or* -ders **1** Also called: **fluke** a European flatfish, *Platichthys flesus* having a greyish-brown body covered with prickly scales: family *Pleuronectidae*: an important food fish **2** *US and Canadian* any flatfish of the families *Bothidae* (turbot, etc) and *Pleuronectidae* (plaice, halibut, sand dab, etc) [C14 probably of Scandinavian origin; compare Old Norse *flythra*, Norwegian *flundra*]

flour ('flaʊə) *n* **1** a powder, which may be either fine or coarse, prepared by sifting and grinding the meal of a grass, esp wheat **2** any finely powdered substance ▷ *vb* **3** (*tr*) to make (grain) into flour **4** (*tr*) to dredge or sprinkle (food or cooking utensils) with flour **5** (of mercury) to break into fine particles on the surface of a metal rather than amalgamating, or to produce such an effect on (a metal). The effect is caused by impurities, esp sulphur [C13 *flur* finer portion of meal, FLOWER] > 'floury *adj*

flourish ('flʌrɪʃ) *vb* **1** (*intr*) to thrive; prosper **2** (*intr*) to be at the peak of condition **3** (*intr*) to be healthy **4** to wave or cause to wave in the air with sweeping strokes **5** to display or make a display **6** to play (a fanfare, etc) on a musical instrument **7** (*intr*) to embellish writing, characters, etc, with ornamental strokes **8** to add decorations or embellishments to (speech or writing) **9** (*intr*) an obsolete word for **blossom** ▷ *n* **10** the act of waving or brandishing **11** a showy gesture **12** an ornamental embellishment in writing **13** a display of ornamental language or speech **14** a grandiose passage of music **15** an ostentatious display or parade **16** *obsolete* **a** the state of flourishing **b** the state of flowering [C13 from Old French *florir*, ultimately from Latin *flōrēre* to flower, from *flōs* a flower] > 'flourisher *n*

flour mite *n* any of several mites that infest flour and other stored organic materials and may be a serious pest; some may cause itching in persons handling infected material

flour moth *n* a pyralid moth, *Ephestia Kuehniella*, the larvae of which are an important pest of flour mills and granaries

flout (flaʊt) *vb* (when *intr,* usually foll by *at*) to show contempt (for); scoff or jeer (at) [C16 perhaps from Middle English *flouten* to play the flute, from Old French *flauter* compare Dutch *fluiten*; see FLUTE] > 'flouter *n* > 'floutingly *adv*

▮ **USAGE** See at **flaunt**

flow (fləʊ) *vb* (*mainly intr*) **1** (of liquids) to move or be conveyed as in a stream **2** (of blood) to circulate around the body **3** to move or progress freely as if in a stream **4** to proceed or be produced continuously and effortlessly: *ideas flowed from her pen* **5** to show or be marked by smooth or easy movement **6** to hang freely or loosely: *her hair flowed down her back* **7** to be present in abundance: *wine flows at their parties* **8** an informal word for **menstruate 9** (of tide water) to advance or rise. Compare **ebb** (sense 1) **10** (*tr*) to cover or swamp with liquid; flood **11** (of rocks such as slate) to yield to pressure without breaking so that the structure and arrangement of the constituent minerals are altered ▷ *n* **12** the act, rate, or manner of flowing: *a fast flow* **13** a continuous stream or discharge **14** continuous progression **15** the advancing of the tide **16** a stream of molten or solidified lava **17** the amount of liquid that flows in a given time **18** an informal word for **menstruation 19** *Scot* **a** a marsh or swamp **b** an inlet or basin of the sea **c** (*capital when part of a name*): *Scapa Flow* **20** flow of spirits natural happiness [Old English *flōwan*; related to Old Norse *flōa*, Middle Low German *vlōien*, Greek *plein* to float, Sanskrit *plavate* he swims]

flowage ('fləʊɪdʒ) *n* **1** the act of flowing or

f

overflowing or the state of having overflowed **2** the liquid that flows or overflows **3** a gradual deformation or motion of certain solids, such as asphalt, which flow without fracture

flow chart *or* **sheet** *n* a diagrammatic representation of the sequence of operations or equipment in an industrial process, computer program, etc

Flow Country *n* an area of moorland and peat bogs in northern Scotland known for its wildlife, now partly afforested

flower ('flaʊə) *n* **1 a** a bloom or blossom on a plant **b** a plant that bears blooms or blossoms **2** the reproductive structure of angiosperm plants, consisting normally of stamens and carpels surrounded by petals and sepals all borne on the receptacle (one or more of these structures may be absent). In some plants it is conspicuous and brightly coloured and attracts insects or other animals for pollination. Related adj: **floral** Related prefix: **antho- 3** any similar reproductive structure in other plants **4** the prime; peak **5** the choice or finest product, part, or representative **6** a decoration or embellishment **7** *printing* a type ornament, used with others in borders, chapter headings, etc **8** *Also called:* **fleuron** an embellishment or ornamental symbol depicting a flower **9** (*plural*) fine powder, usually produced by sublimation: *flowers of sulphur* ▷ *vb* **10** (*intr*) to produce flowers; bloom **11** (*intr*) to reach full growth or maturity **12** (*tr*) to deck or decorate with flowers or floral designs [c13 from Old French *flor*, from Latin *flōs*; see BLOW³] > '**flower-** ˌlike *adj*

flowerage ('flaʊərɪdʒ) *n* now rare **1** a mass of flowers **2** the process or act of flowering

flowerbed ('flaʊəˌbɛd) *n* a plot of ground in which flowers are grown in a garden, park, etc

flower bug *n* any of a number of bugs of the family *Cimicidae*, related to the debris bugs but frequenting flowers and feeding on the small insects found there

flower-de-luce ('flaʊədə'luːs) *n*, *pl* flowers-de-luce an archaic name for the **iris** (sense 2) and **lily** (sense 1) [c16 anglicized variant of French *fleur de lis*]

flowered ('flaʊəd) *adj* **1** having or abounding in flowers **2** decorated with flowers or a floral design

flowerer ('flaʊərə) *n* a plant that flowers at a specified time or in a specified way: *a late flowerer*

floweret ('flaʊərɪt) *n* another name for **floret**

flower girl *n* **1** a girl or woman who sells flowers in the street **2** *US and Scot* a young girl who carries flowers in a procession, esp at weddings

flower head *n* an inflorescence in which stalkless florets are crowded together at the tip of the stem

flowering ('flaʊərɪŋ) *adj* (of certain species of plants) capable of producing conspicuous flowers: *a flowering ash*

flowering currant *n* an ornamental shrub, *Ribes sanguineum*, growing to 2 to 3 metres (6 to 9ft) in height, with red, crimson, yellow, or white flowers: family *Saxifragaceae*

flowering maple *n* any tropical shrub of the malvaceous genus *Abutilon*, esp *A. hybridum*, having lobed leaves like those of the maple and brightly coloured flowers

flowerless ('flaʊəlɪs) *adj* designating any plant that does not produce seeds. See **cryptogam**

flower-of-an-hour *n* a malvaceous Old World herbaceous plant, *Hibiscus trionum*, having pale yellow flowers with a bladder-like calyx. Also called: **bladder ketmia**

flower-pecker *n* any small songbird of the family *Dicaeidae*, of SE Asia and Australasia, typically feeding on nectar, berries, and insects

flowerpot ('flaʊəˌpɒt) *n* a pot in which plants are grown

flower power *n* informal a youth cult of the late 1960s advocating peace and love, using the flower

as a symbol; associated with drug-taking. Its adherents were known as **flower children** or **flower people**

flowers of sulphur *pl n* minute crystals of sulphur obtained by condensing sulphur vapour on a cold surface

flowery ('flaʊərɪ) *adj* **1** abounding in flowers **2** decorated with flowers or floral patterns **3** like or suggestive of flowers: *a flowery scent* **4** (of language or style) elaborate; ornate > '**floweriness** *n*

flowmeter ('flaʊˌmiːtə) *n* an instrument that measures the rate of flow of a liquid or gas within a pipe or tube

flown¹ (fləʊn) *vb* the past participle of **fly**

flown² (fləʊn) *adj* relating to coloured (usually blue) decoration on porcelain that, during firing, has melted into the surrounding glaze giving a halo-like effect [probably from the obsolete past participle of FLOW]

flow-on *n* Austral and NZ a wage or salary increase granted to one group of workers as a consequence of a similar increase granted to another group

flow sheet *n* another name for **flow chart**

fl. oz. *abbreviation for* fluid ounce

FLQ (in Canada) *abbreviation for* Front de Libération du Québec: a Quebec separatist organization using terrorist tactics, esp in the 1960s and 1970s

flu (fluː) *n* informal **1** (often preceded by *the*) short for **influenza 2** any of various viral infections, esp a respiratory or intestinal infection

flub (flʌb) *informal* ▷ *n* **1** an embarrassing mistake or blunder ▷ *vb* **flubs, flubbing, flubbed 2** (*intr*) to blunder or make an embarrassing mistake [c20 of origin unknown]

fluctuant ('flʌktjʊənt) *adj* inclined to vary or fluctuate; unstable

fluctuate ('flʌktjʊˌeɪt) *vb* **1** to change or cause to change position constantly; be or make unstable; waver or vary **2** (*intr*) to rise and fall like a wave; undulate [c17 from Latin *fluctuāre*, from *fluctus* a wave, from *fluere* to flow]

fluctuation (ˌflʌktjʊ'eɪʃən) *n* **1** constant change; vacillation; instability **2** undulation **3** a variation in an animal or plant that is determined by environment rather than heredity

flue¹ (fluː) *n* **1** a shaft, tube, or pipe, esp as used in a chimney, to carry off smoke, gas, etc **2** *music* the passage in an organ pipe or flute within which a vibrating air column is set up. See also **flue pipe** [c16 of unknown origin]

flue² (fluː) *n* loose fluffy matter; down [c16 from Flemish *vluwe*, from Old French *velu* shaggy]

flue³ *or* **flew** (fluː) *n* a type of fishing net [Middle English, from Middle Dutch *vlūwe*]

flue⁴ (fluː) *n* another word for **fluke¹** (senses 1, 3) > flued *adj*

flue-cure *vb* (*tr*) to cure (tobacco) by means of radiant heat from pipes or flues connected to a furnace

flue gas *n* the smoke in the uptake of a boiler fire: it consists mainly of carbon dioxide, carbon monoxide, and nitrogen

fluellen *or* **fluellin** (flʊ'ɛlən) *n* **1** either of two weedy scrophulariaceous annuals related to the toadflaxes, **round-leaved fluellen** (*Kickxia spuria*) and **sharp-leaved fluellen** (*K. elatine*) **2** obsolete any of several speedwells, especially *Veronica officinalis* [c16 shortened from Welsh *Ilysiau Llewelyn* Llewelyn's flower]

fluency ('fluːənsɪ) *n* the quality of being fluent, esp facility in speech or writing

fluent ('fluːənt) *adj* **1** able to speak or write a specified foreign language with facility **2** spoken or written with facility: *his French is fluent* **3** easy and graceful in motion or shape **4** flowing or able to flow freely [c16 from Latin: flowing, from *fluere* to flow] > '**fluently** *adv*

flue pipe *or* **flue** *n* an organ pipe or tubular instrument of the flute family whose sound is produced by the passage of air across a sharp-edged fissure in the side. This sets in motion a

vibrating air column within the pipe or instrument

flue stop *n* an organ stop controlling a set of flue pipes

fluey ('fluːɪ) *adj* informal involved in, caused by, or like influenza

fluff (flʌf) *n* **1** soft light particles, such as the down or nap of cotton or wool **2** any light downy substance **3** an object, matter, etc, of little importance; trifle **4** informal a mistake, esp in speaking or reading lines or performing music **5** informal a young woman (esp in the phrase **a bit of fluff**) ▷ *vb* **6** to make or become soft and puffy by shaking or patting; puff up **7** informal to make a mistake in performing (an action, dramatic speech, music, etc) [c18 perhaps from FLUE²]

fluffer ('flʌfə) *n* a person employed on a pornographic film set to ensure that male actors are kept aroused

fluffy ('flʌfɪ) *adj* fluffier, fluffiest **1** of, resembling, or covered with fluff **2** soft and light: *fluffy hair* **3 a** sentimental or overromantic; not very intelligent **b** characterized by nonviolent methods > '**fluffily** *adv* > '**fluffiness** *n*

flugelhorn ('fluːɡ°lˌhɔːn) *n* a type of valved brass instrument consisting of a tube of conical bore with a cup-shaped mouthpiece, used esp in brass bands. It is a transposing instrument in B flat or C, and has the same range as the cornet in B flat [German *Flügelhorn*, from *Flügel* wing + *Horn* HORN]

fluid ('fluːɪd) *n* **1** a substance, such as a liquid or gas, that can flow, has no fixed shape, and offers little resistance to an external stress ▷ *adj* **2** capable of flowing and easily changing shape **3** of, concerned with, or using a fluid or fluids **4** constantly changing or apt to change **5** smooth in shape or movement; flowing [c15 from Latin *fluidus*, from *fluere* to flow] > '**fluidal** *adj* > '**fluidness** *n* > '**fluidly** *or* '**fluidally** *adv*

fluid dram *n* another name for **drachm**

fluid drive *n* a type of coupling for transmitting power from the engine of a motor vehicle to the transmission, using a torque converter. Also called: **fluid coupling, fluid clutch, fluid flywheel**

fluidextract ('fluːɪd'ɛkstrækt) *n* an alcoholic solution of a vegetable drug, one millilitre of which has an activity equivalent to one gram of the powdered drug

fluidics (fluː'ɪdɪks) *n* (functioning as singular) the study and use of systems in which the flow of fluids in tubes simulates the flow of electricity in conductors. Such systems are used in place of electronics in certain applications, such as the control of apparatus > flu'idic *adj*

fluidity (fluː'ɪdɪtɪ) *n* **1** the state of being fluid **2** physics the reciprocal of viscosity

fluidize *or* **fluidise** ('fluːɪˌdaɪz) *vb* (*tr*) to make fluid, esp to make (solids) fluid by pulverizing them so that they can be transported in a stream of gas as if they were liquids: *fluidized coal* > ˌfluidi'zation *or* ˌfluidi'sation *n* > '**fluidˌizer** *or* '**fluidˌiser** *n*

fluidized bed *n* chemical engineering a bed of fluidized solids used as a heat exchanger or mass transfer medium

fluid lubrication *n* engineering lubrication in which bearing surfaces are separated by an oil film sustained by the motion of the parts

fluid mechanics *n* (functioning as singular) the study of the mechanical and flow properties of fluids, esp as they apply to practical engineering. Also called: **hydraulics** See also **hydrodynamics**, **hydrostatics, hydrokinetics**

fluid ounce *n* a unit of capacity equal to the volume of one avoirdupois ounce of distilled water at 62°F: there are twenty fluid ounces in an Imperial pint and sixteen in a US pint

fluid pressure *n* the pressure exerted by a fluid at any point inside it. The difference of pressure between two levels is determined by the product of the difference of height, the density, and the acceleration of free fall

fluke[1] (fluːk) n 1 Also called: flue a flat bladelike projection at the end of the arm of an anchor 2 either of the two lobes of the tail of a whale or related animal 3 Also called: flue the barb or barbed head of a harpoon, arrow, etc [c16 perhaps a special use of FLUKE[3] (in the sense: a flounder)]

fluke[2] (fluːk) n 1 an accidental stroke of luck 2 any chance happening ▷ vb 3 (tr) to gain, make, or hit by a fluke [c19 of unknown origin]

fluke[3] (fluːk) n 1 any parasitic flatworm, such as the blood fluke and liver fluke, of the classes *Monogenea* and *Digenea* (formerly united in a single class *Trematoda*) 2 another name for **flounder**[1] (sense 1) [Old English *flōc*; related to Old Norse *flōki* flounder, Old Saxon *flaka* sole, Old High German *flah* smooth]

fluky or **flukey** ('fluːkɪ) adj flukier, flukiest informal 1 done or gained by an accident, esp a lucky one 2 variable; uncertain: *fluky weather* > '**flukiness** n

flume (fluːm) n 1 a ravine through which a stream flows 2 a narrow artificial channel made for providing water for power, floating logs, etc 3 a slide in the form of a long and winding tube with a stream of water running through it that descends into a purpose-built pool ▷ vb 4 (tr) to transport (logs) in a flume [c12 from Old French *flum*, ultimately from Latin *flūmen* stream, from *fluere* to flow]

flummery ('flʌmərɪ) n, pl -meries 1 informal meaningless flattery; nonsense 2 chiefly Brit a cold pudding of oatmeal, etc [c17 from Welsh *llymru*]

flummox ('flʌməks) vb (tr) to perplex or bewilder [c19 of unknown origin]

flung (flʌŋ) vb the past tense and past participle of **fling**

flunitrazepam (ˌfluːnaɪˈtræzəˌpæm) n a drug similar to diazepam, used in treating long-term insomnia

flunk (flʌŋk) informal, chiefly US, Canadian, and NZ ▷ vb 1 to fail or cause to fail to reach the required standard in (an examination, course, etc) 2 (intr; foll by out) to be dismissed from a school or college through failure in examinations ▷ n 3 a low grade below the pass standard [c19 perhaps from FLINCH[1] + FUNK[1]]

flunky or **flunkey** ('flʌŋkɪ) n, pl flunkies or flunkeys 1 a servile or fawning person 2 a person who performs menial tasks 3 usually derogatory a manservant in livery [c18 of unknown origin]

Fluon ('fluːɒn) n a trademark for polytetrafluoroethylene

fluor ('fluːɔː) n another name for **fluorspar** [c17 from Latin: a flowing; so called from its use as a metallurgical flux]

fluor- combining form a variant of **fluoro-** before a vowel: *fluorene; fluorine*

fluorapatite (ˌfluːəˈræpətaɪt) n a mineral consisting of calcium fluorophosphate; the most common form of apatite

fluorene ('fluːəriːn) n a white insoluble crystalline solid used in making dyes. Formula: $(C_6H_4)_2CH_2$

fluoresce (ˌfluːəˈrɛs) vb (intr) to exhibit fluorescence [c19 back formation from FLUORESCENCE]

fluorescein or **fluoresceine** (ˌfluːəˈrɛsɪɪn) n an orange-red crystalline compound that in aqueous solution exhibits a greenish-yellow fluorescence in reflected light and is reddish-orange in transmitted light: used as a marker in sea water and as an indicator. Formula: $C_{20}H_{12}O_5$

fluorescence (ˌfluːəˈrɛsəns) n 1 physics a the emission of light or other radiation from atoms or molecules that are bombarded by particles, such as electrons, or by radiation from a separate source. The bombarding radiation produces excited atoms, molecules, or ions and these emit photons as they fall back to the ground state b such an emission of photons that ceases as soon as the bombarding radiation is discontinued c such an emission of photons for which the average lifetime of the excited atoms and

molecules is less than about 10^{-8} seconds 2 the radiation emitted as a result of fluorescence. Compare **phosphorescence** [c19 FLUOR + -escence (as in *opalescence*)]

fluorescent (ˌfluːəˈrɛsᵊnt) adj exhibiting or having the property of fluorescence

fluorescent lamp n 1 a type of lamp in which an electrical gas discharge is maintained in a tube with a thin layer of phosphor on its inside surface. The gas, which is often mercury vapour, emits ultraviolet radiation causing the phosphor to fluoresce 2 a type of lamp in which an electrical discharge is maintained in a tube containing a gas such as neon, mercury vapour, or sodium vapour at low pressure. Gas atoms in the discharge are struck by electrons and fluoresce

fluorescent screen n a transparent screen coated on one side with a phosphor that fluoresces when exposed to X-rays or cathode rays

fluoric (fluːˈɔːrɪk) adj of, concerned with, or produced from fluorine or fluorspar

fluoridate ('fluːərɪˌdeɪt) vb to subject (water) to fluoridation

fluoridation (ˌfluːərɪˈdeɪʃən) n the addition of about one part per million of fluorides to the public water supply as a protection against tooth decay

fluoride ('fluːəˌraɪd) n 1 any salt of hydrofluoric acid, containing the fluoride ion, F^- 2 any compound containing fluorine, such as methyl fluoride

fluorinate ('fluːərɪˌneɪt) vb to treat or combine with fluorine > ˌfluori'nation n

fluorine ('fluːəriːn) or **fluorin** ('fluːərɪn) n a toxic pungent pale yellow gas of the halogen group that is the most electronegative and reactive of all the elements, occurring principally in fluorspar and cryolite: used in the production of uranium, fluorocarbons, and other chemicals. Symbol: F; atomic no: 9; atomic wt: 18.9984032; valency: 1; density: 1.696 kg/m³; relative density: 1.108; freezing pt: –219.62°C; boiling pt: –188.13°C

fluorite ('fluːəraɪt) n US and Canadian a white or colourless mineral sometimes fluorescent and often tinted by impurities, found in veins and as deposits from hot gases. It is used in the manufacture of glass, enamel, and jewellery, and is the chief ore of fluorine. Composition: calcium fluoride. Formula: CaF_2. Crystal structure: cubic. Also called (in Britain and certain other countries): **fluorspar, fluor**

fluoro- or before a vowel **fluor-** combining form 1 indicating the presence of fluorine: *fluorocarbon* 2 indicating fluorescence: *fluorography*

fluorocarbon (ˌfluːərəʊˈkɑːbᵊn) n any compound derived by replacing all or some of the hydrogen atoms in hydrocarbons by fluorine atoms. Many of them are used as lubricants, solvents, and coatings. See also **Freon, polytetrafluoroethylene, CFC**

fluorochrome ('fluːərəʊˌkrəʊm) n a chemical entity, such as a molecule or group, that exhibits fluorescence

fluorography (fluːəˈrɒɡrəfɪ) n the photographic recording of fluoroscopic images

fluorometer (ˌfluːəˈrɒmɪtə) or **fluorimeter** (ˌfluːəˈrɪmɪtə) n 1 an instrument for inducing fluorescence by irradiation and for examination of the emission spectrum of the resulting fluorescent light 2 a device for detecting and measuring ultraviolet radiation by determining the amount of fluorescence that it produces from a phosphor > **fluorometric** (ˌfluːərəʊˈmɛtrɪk) or **fluorimetric** (ˌfluːərɪˈmɛtrɪk) adj > ˌfluo'rometry or ˌfluo'rimetry n

fluorophore ('fluːərəʊˌfɔː) n a chemical group responsible for fluorescence

fluoroscope ('fluːərəˌskəʊp) n a device consisting of a fluorescent screen and an X-ray source that enables an X-ray image of an object, person, or part to be observed directly > **fluoroscopic** (ˌfluːərəˈskɒpɪk) adj > ˌfluoro'scopically adv

fluoroscopy (fluːəˈrɒskəpɪ) n examination of a person or object by means of a fluoroscope

fluorosis (fluːəˈrəʊsɪs) n fluoride poisoning, due to ingestion of too much fluoride in drinking water over a long period or to ingestion of pesticides containing fluoride salts. Chronic fluorosis results in mottling of the teeth of children

fluorspar ('fluːəˌspɑː), **fluor** or US and Canadian **fluorite** n a white or colourless mineral sometimes fluorescent and often tinted by impurities, found in veins and as deposits from hot gases. It is used in the manufacture of glass, enamel, and jewellery, and is the chief ore of fluorine. Composition: calcium fluoride. Formula: CaF_2. Crystal structure: cubic

fluoxetine (fluːˈɒksɪˌtiːn) n a drug that prolongs the action of serotonin in the brain. It is used as an antidepressant

flurry ('flʌrɪ) n, pl -ries 1 a sudden commotion or burst of activity 2 a light gust of wind or rain or fall of snow 3 stock exchange a sudden brief increase in trading or fluctuation in stock prices 4 the death spasms of a harpooned whale ▷ vb -ries, -rying, -ried 5 to confuse or bewilder or be confused or bewildered [c17 from obsolete *flurr* to scatter, perhaps formed on analogy with HURRY]

flush[1] (flʌʃ) vb 1 to blush or cause to blush 2 to flow or flood or cause to flow or flood with or as if with water 3 to glow or shine or cause to glow or shine with a rosy colour 4 to send a volume of water quickly through (a pipe, channel, etc) or into (a toilet) for the purpose of cleansing, emptying, etc 5 to cause (soluble substances in the soil) to be washed towards the surface, as by the action of underground springs, or (of such substances) to be washed towards the soil surface 6 (tr; usually passive) to excite or elate ▷ n 7 a rosy colour, esp in the cheeks; blush 8 a sudden flow or gush, as of water 9 a feeling of excitement or elation: *the flush of success* 10 early bloom; freshness: *the flush of youth* 11 redness of the skin, esp of the face, as from the effects of a fever, alcohol, etc 12 ecology an area of boggy land fed by ground water ▷ adj 13 having a ruddy or heightened colour [c16 (in the sense: to gush forth): perhaps from FLUSH[3]] > 'flusher n

flush[2] (flʌʃ) adj (usually postpositive) 1 level or even with another surface 2 directly adjacent; continuous 3 informal having plenty of money 4 informal abundant or plentiful, as money 5 full of vigour 6 full to the brim or to the point of overflowing 7 printing having an even margin, right or left, with no indentations 8 (of a blow) accurately delivered 9 (of a vessel) having no superstructure built above the flat level of the deck ▷ adv 10 so as to be level or even 11 directly or squarely ▷ vb (tr) 12 to cause (surfaces) to be on the same level or in the same plane 13 to enrich the diet of (an ewe) during the breeding season ▷ n 14 a period of fresh growth of leaves, shoots, etc [c18 probably from FLUSH[1] (in the sense: spring out)] > 'flushness n

flush[3] (flʌʃ) vb (tr) to rouse (game, wild creatures, etc) and put to flight [c13 *flusshen*, perhaps of imitative origin]

flush[4] (flʌʃ) n (in poker and similar games) a hand containing only one suit [c16 from Old French *flus*, from Latin *fluxus* FLUX]

flushing ('flʌʃɪŋ) n an extra feeding given to ewes before mating to increase the lambing percentage

Flushing ('flʌʃɪŋ) n a port in the SW Netherlands, in Zeeland province, on Walcheren Island, at the mouth of the West Scheldt river: the first Dutch city to throw off Spanish rule (1572). Pop: 45 000 (2003 est). Dutch name: **Vlissingen**

flushwork ('flʌʃˌwɜːk) n architect decorative treatment of the surface of an outside wall with flints split to show their smooth black surface, combined with dressed stone to form patterns such as tracery or initials

fluster ('flʌstə) vb 1 to make or become confused, nervous, or upset ▷ n 2 a state of confusion or

f

agitation [C15 probably of Scandinavian origin; compare Icelandic *flaustr* to hurry, *flaustra* to bustle]

flute (fluːt) *n* **1** a wind instrument consisting of an open cylindrical tube of wood or metal having holes in the side stopped either by the fingers or by pads controlled by keys. The breath is directed across a mouth hole cut in the side, causing the air in the tube to vibrate. Range: about three octaves upwards from middle C **2** any pipe blown directly on the principle of a flue pipe, either by means of a mouth hole or through a fipple **3** *architect* a rounded shallow concave groove on the shaft of a column, pilaster, etc **4** a groove or furrow in cloth, etc **5** a tall narrow wineglass **6** anything shaped like a flute ▷ *vb* **7** to produce or utter (sounds) in the manner or tone of a flute **8** (*tr*) to make grooves or furrows in [C14 from Old French *flahute*, via Old Provençal, from Vulgar Latin *flabeolum* (unattested); perhaps also influenced by Old Provençal *laut* lute; see FLAGEOLET] > **'flute,like** *adj* > **'fluty** *adj*

fluted ('fluːtɪd) *adj* **1** (esp of the shaft of a column) having flutes **2** sounding like a flute

fluter ('fluːtə) *n* **1** a craftsman who makes flutes or fluting **2** a tool used to make flutes or fluting **3** a less common word, used esp in folk music, for **flautist**

fluting ('fluːtɪŋ) *n* **1** a design or decoration of flutes on a column, pilaster, etc **2** grooves or furrows, as in cloth

flutist ('fluːtɪst) *n Now chiefly US and Canadian* a variant of **flautist**

flutter ('flʌtə) *vb* **1** to wave or cause to wave rapidly; flap **2** (*intr*) (of birds, butterflies, etc) to flap the wings **3** (*intr*) to move, esp downwards, with an irregular motion **4** (*intr*) *pathol* (of the auricles of the heart) to beat abnormally rapidly, esp in a regular rhythm **5** to be or make nervous or restless **6** (*intr*) to move about restlessly **7** *swimming* to cause (the legs) to move up and down in a flutter kick or (of the legs) to move in this way **8** (*tr*) *Brit informal* to wager or gamble (a small amount of money) ▷ *n* **9** a quick flapping or vibrating motion **10** a state of nervous excitement or confusion **11** excited interest; sensation; stir **12** *Brit informal* a modest bet or wager **13** *pathol* an abnormally rapid beating of the auricles of the heart (200 to 400 beats per minute), esp in a regular rhythm, sometimes resulting in heart block **14** *electronics* a slow variation in pitch in a sound-reproducing system, similar to wow but occurring at higher frequencies **15** a potentially dangerous oscillation of an aircraft, or part of an aircraft, caused by the interaction of aerodynamic forces, structural elastic reactions, and inertia **16** *swimming* See **flutter kick** **17** Also called: **flutter tonguing** *music* a method of sounding a wind instrument, esp the flute, with a rolling movement of the tongue [Old English *floterian* to float to and fro; related to German *flattern*; see FLOAT] > **'flutterer** *n* > **'flutteringly** *adv*

flutterboard ('flʌtə,bɔːd) *n US and Canadian* an oblong board or piece of polystyrene plastic used by swimmers in training or practice. Brit word: **float**

flutter kick *n* a type of kick used in certain swimming strokes, such as the crawl, in which the legs are held straight and alternately moved up and down rapidly in the water

fluttery ('flʌtərɪ) *adj* **1** flapping rapidly; fluttering **2** showing nervousness or excitement **3** light or insubstantial

fluvial ('fluːvɪəl) *or* **fluviatile** ('fluːvɪə,taɪl, -tɪl) *adj* of, relating to, or occurring in a river: *fluvial deposits* [C14 from Latin *fluviālis*, from *fluvius* river, from *fluere* to flow]

fluviomarine (,fluːvɪ,əʊmə'riːn) *adj* **1** (of deposits) formed by joint action of the sea and a river or stream **2** (esp of fish) able to live in both rivers and the sea [C19 *fluvio-*, from Latin *fluvius* river + MARINE]

fluvioterrestrial (,fluːvɪəʊtə'rɛstrɪəl) *adj* (of animals) able to live in rivers and on land

fluvoxamine (fluː'vɒksəmiːn) *n* an antidepressant drug that acts by preventing the re-uptake after release of serotonin in the brain, thereby prolonging its action. See **SSRI**

flux (flʌks) *n* **1** a flow or discharge **2** continuous change; instability **3** a substance, such as borax or salt, that gives a low melting-point mixture with a metal oxide. It is used for cleaning metal surfaces during soldering, etc, and for protecting the surfaces of liquid metals **4** *metallurgy* a chemical used to increase the fluidity of refining slags in order to promote the rate of chemical reaction **5** a similar substance used in the making of glass **6** *physics* **a** the rate of flow of particles, energy, or a fluid, through a specified area, such as that of neutrons (**neutron flux**) or of light energy (**luminous flux**) **b** the strength of a field in a given area expressed as the product of the area and the component of the field strength at right angles to the area: *magnetic flux; electric flux* **7** *pathol* an excessive discharge of fluid from the body, such as watery faeces in diarrhoea **8** the act or process of melting; fusion **9** (in the philosophy of Heraclitus) the state of constant change in which all things exist ▷ *vb* **10** to make or become fluid **11** (*tr*) to apply flux to (a metal, soldered joint, etc) **12** (*tr*) an obsolete word for **purge** [C14 from Latin *fluxus* a flow, from *fluere* to flow]

flux density *n physics* the amount of flux per unit of cross-sectional area

fluxion ('flʌkʃən) *n* **1** *maths obsolete* the rate of change of a function, especially the instantaneous velocity of a moving body; derivative **2** a less common word for **flux** (senses 1, 2) [C16 from Late Latin *fluxiō* a flowing] > **'fluxional** *or* **'fluxionary** *adj* > **'fluxionally** *adv*

fluxmeter ('flʌks,miːtə) *n* any instrument for measuring magnetic flux, usually by measuring the charge that flows through a coil when the flux changes

fly[1] (flaɪ) *vb* **flies, flying, flew, flown** **1** (*intr*) (of birds, aircraft, etc) to move through the air in a controlled manner using aerodynamic forces **2** to travel over (an area of land or sea) in an aircraft **3** to operate (an aircraft or spacecraft) **4** to float, flutter, or be displayed in the air or cause to float, etc, in this way: *to fly a kite* **5** to transport or be transported by or through the air by aircraft, wind, etc **6** (*intr*) to move or be moved very quickly, forcibly, or suddenly: *she came flying towards me* **7** (*intr*) to pass swiftly: *time flies* **8** to escape from (an enemy, place, etc); flee **9** (*intr*; may be foll by *at* or *upon*) to attack a person **10** (*intr*) to have a sudden outburst: *he flew into a rage again* **11** (*intr*) (of money, etc) to vanish rapidly **12** (*tr*) *falconry* (of hawks) to fly at (quarry) in attack: *peregrines fly rooks* **13** (*tr*) *theatre* to suspend (scenery) above the stage so that it may be lowered into view **14** **fly a kite** **a** to procure money by an accommodation bill **b** to release information or take a step in order to test public opinion **15** **fly high** *informal* **a** to have a high aim **b** to prosper or flourish **16** **fly in the face of** See **face** (sense 19) **17** **fly off the handle** *informal* to lose one's temper **18** **fly the coop** *US and Canadian informal* to leave suddenly **19** **go fly a kite** *US and Canadian informal* go away **20** **let fly** *informal* **a** to lose one's temper (with a person) **b** to shoot or throw (an object) ▷ *n, pl* **flies** **21** (*often plural*) Also called: **fly front** a closure that conceals a zip, buttons, or other fastening, by having one side overlapping, as on trousers **22** Also called: **fly sheet** **a** a flap forming the entrance to a tent **b** a piece of canvas drawn over the ridgepole of a tent to form an outer roof **23** a small air brake used to control the chiming of large clocks **24** the horizontal weighted arm of a fly press **25** **a** the outer edge of a flag **b** the distance from the outer edge of a flag to the staff. Compare **hoist** (sense 9) **26** *Brit* a light one-horse covered carriage formerly let out on hire **27** *Austral and NZ* an attempt: *I'll give it a fly* **28** *printing* **a** a device for transferring printed sheets from the press to a flat pile **b** Also called: **flyhand** a person who collects and stacks printed matter from a printing press **c** a piece of paper folded once to make four pages, with printing only on the first page **29** (*plural*) *theatre* the space above the stage out of view of the audience, used for storing scenery, etc **30** *rare* the act of flying [Old English *flēogan*; related to Old Frisian *fliāga*, Old High German *fliogan*, Old Norse *fljūga*] > **'flyable** *adj*

fly[2] (flaɪ) *n, pl* **flies** **1** any dipterous insect, esp the housefly, characterized by active flight. See also **horsefly, blowfly, tsetse fly, crane fly** **2** any of various similar but unrelated insects, such as the caddis fly, firefly, dragonfly, and chalcid fly **3** *angling* a lure made from a fish-hook dressed with feathers, tinsel, etc, to resemble any of various flies or nymphs: used in fly-fishing. See also **dry fly, wet fly** **4** (in southern Africa) an area that is infested with the tsetse fly **5** **drink with the flies** *Austral slang* to drink alone **6** **fly in amber** See **amber** (sense 2) **7** **fly in the ointment** *informal* a slight flaw that detracts from value, completeness, or enjoyment **8** **fly on the wall** a person who watches others, while not being noticed himself **9** **there are no flies on him, her, etc** *informal* he, she, etc, is no fool [Old English *flēoge*; related to Old Norse *fluga* Old High German *flioga*; see FLY[1]] > **'flyless** *adj*

fly[3] (flaɪ) *adj* **flyer, flyest** *slang* **1** *chiefly Brit* knowing and sharp; smart **2** *chiefly Scot* furtive or sneaky **3** *chiefly Scot* in secret; sneakily [C19 of uncertain origin]

fly agaric *n* a saprotrophic agaricaceous woodland fungus, *Amanita muscaria*, having a scarlet cap with white warts and white gills: poisonous but rarely fatal. See also **amanita** [so named from its use as a poison on flypaper]

fly ash *n* fine solid particles of ash carried into the air during combustion, esp the combustion of pulverized fuel in power stations

flyaway ('flaɪə,weɪ) *adj* **1** (of hair or clothing) loose and fluttering **2** frivolous or flighty; giddy ▷ *n* **3** a person who is frivolous or flighty

flyback ('flaɪ,bæk) *n* the fast return of the spot on a cathode-ray tube after completion of each trace

flyblow ('flaɪ,bləʊ) *vb* **-blows, -blowing, -blew, -blown** **1** (*tr*) to contaminate, esp with the eggs or larvae of the blowfly; taint ▷ *n* **2** (*usually plural*) the egg or young larva of a blowfly, deposited on meat, paper, etc

flyblown ('flaɪ,bləʊn) *adj* **1** covered with flyblows **2** contaminated; tainted

flyboat ('flaɪ,bəʊt) *n* any small swift boat

flybook ('flaɪ,bʊk) *n* a small case or wallet used by anglers for storing artificial flies

flyby ('flaɪ,baɪ) *n, pl* **-bys** a flight past a particular position or target, esp the close approach of a spacecraft to a planet or satellite for investigation of conditions

fly-by-light *n* aircraft control through systems operated by optical fibres rather than mechanical rods. Abbreviation: **FBL**

fly-by-night *informal* ▷ *adj* **1** unreliable or untrustworthy, esp in finance **2** brief; impermanent ▷ *n also* **fly-by-nighter** **3** an untrustworthy person, esp one who departs secretly or by night to avoid paying debts **4** a person who goes out at night to places of entertainment

fly-by-wire *n* aircraft control through systems operated by electronic circuits rather than mechanical rods. Abbreviation: **FBW**

flycatcher ('flaɪ,kætʃə) *n* **1** any small insectivorous songbird of the Old World subfamily *Muscicapinae*, having small slender bills fringed with bristles: family *Muscicapidae*. See also **spotted flycatcher** **2** any American passerine bird of the family *Tyrannidae*

fly-drive *adj, adv* describing a type of package-deal

holiday in which the price includes outward and return flights and car hire while away

flyer *or* **flier** ('flaɪə) *n* **1** a person or thing that flies or moves very fast **2** an aviator or pilot **3** *informal* a long flying leap; bound **4** a fast-moving machine part, esp one having periodic motion **5** a rectangular step in a straight flight of stairs. Compare **winder** (sense 5) **6** *athletics* an informal word for **flying start 7** *chiefly US* a speculative business transaction **8** a small handbill

fly-fish *vb* (*intr*) *angling* to fish using artificial flies as lures. See **dry fly, wet fly.** ▷ **'fly-,fisher** *n* ▷ **'fly-,fishing** *n*

fly half *n rugby* another name for **stand-off half**

flying ('flaɪɪŋ) *adj* **1** (*prenominal*) hurried; fleeting: *a flying visit* **2** (*prenominal*) designed for fast action **3** (*prenominal*) moving or passing quickly on or as if on wings: *a flying leap; the flying hours* **4** hanging, waving, or floating freely: *flying hair* **5** *nautical* (of a sail) not hauled in tight against the wind ▷ *n* **6** the act of piloting, navigating, or travelling in an aircraft **7** (*modifier*) relating to, capable of, accustomed to, or adapted for flight: *a flying machine*. Related adj: **volar**

flying boat *n* a seaplane in which the fuselage consists of a hull that provides buoyancy in the water

flying bomb *n* another name for the **V-1**

flying bridge *n* an auxiliary bridge of a vessel, usually built above or far outboard of the main bridge

flying buttress *n* a buttress supporting a wall or other structure by an arch or part of an arch that transmits the thrust outwards and downwards. Also called: **arc-boutant**

flying circus *n* **1** an exhibition of aircraft aerobatics **2** the aircraft and men who take part in such exhibitions

flying colours *pl n* conspicuous success; triumph: *he passed his test with flying colours*

flying doctor *n* (in areas of sparse or scattered population) a doctor who visits patients by aircraft

Flying Dutchman *n legend* **1** a phantom ship sighted in bad weather, esp off the Cape of Good Hope **2** the captain of this ship

flying field *n* a small airport; an airfield

flying fish *n* any marine teleost fish of the family *Exocoetidae*, common in warm and tropical seas, having enlarged winglike pectoral fins used for gliding above the surface of the water

flying fox *n* **1** any large fruit bat, esp any of the genus *Pteropus* of tropical Africa and Asia: family *Pteropodidae* **2** *Austral and NZ* a cable mechanism used for transportation across a river, gorge, etc **3** a cable mechanism ridden for fun at an adventure playground, etc

flying frog *n* any of several tropical frogs of the family *Rhacophoridae*, esp *Rhacophorus reinwardtii* of Malaya, that glide between trees by means of long webbed digits

flying gurnard *n* any marine spiny-finned gurnard-like fish of the mostly tropical family *Dactylopteridae*, having enlarged fan-shaped pectoral fins used to glide above the surface of the sea

flying jib *n* the jib set furthest forward or outboard on a vessel with two or more jibs

flying lemur *n* either of the two arboreal mammals of the genus *Cynocephalus*, family *Cynocephalidae*, and order *Dermoptera*, of S and SE Asia. They resemble lemurs but have a fold of skin between the limbs enabling movement by gliding leaps. Also called: **colugo**

flying lizard *or* **dragon** *n* any lizard of the genus *Draco*, of S and SE Asia, having an extensible fold of skin on each side of the body, used to make gliding leaps: family *Agamidae* (agamas)

flying mare *n* a wrestling throw in which a wrestler seizes his opponent's arm or head (**flying head mare**) and turns to throw him over his shoulder

flying officer *n* an officer holding commissioned rank senior to a pilot officer but junior to a flight lieutenant in the British and certain other air forces

flying phalanger *n* any nocturnal arboreal phalanger of the genus *Petaurus*, of E Australia and New Guinea, having black-striped greyish fur and moving with gliding leaps using folds of skin between the hind limbs and forelimbs. Also called: **glider**

flying picket *n* (in industrial disputes) a member of a group of pickets organized to be able to move quickly from place to place

flying saucer *n* any disc-shaped flying object alleged to come from outer space

flying-spot *adj* denoting an electronic system in which a rapidly moving spot of light is used to encode or decode data, for example to obtain a television signal by scanning a photographic film or slide

flying squad *n* a small group of police, soldiers, etc, ready to move into action quickly

flying squirrel *n* any nocturnal sciurine rodent of the subfamily *Petauristinae*, of Asia and North America. Furry folds of skin between the forelegs and hind legs enable these animals to move by gliding leaps

flying start *n* **1** Also called (informal): **flyer** (in sprinting) a start by a competitor anticipating the starting signal **2** a start to a race or time trial in which the competitor is already travelling at speed as he passes the starting line **3** any promising beginning **4** an initial advantage over others

flying wing *n* **1** an aircraft consisting mainly of one large wing and no fuselage or tailplane **2** (in Canadian football) the twelfth player, who has a variable position behind the scrimmage line

flyleaf ('flaɪ,liːf) *n, pl* **-leaves** the inner leaf of the endpaper of a book, pasted to the first leaf

flyman ('flaɪmən) *n, pl* **-men** *theatre* a stagehand who operates the scenery, curtains, etc, in the flies

fly orchid *n* a European orchid, *Ophrys insectifera*, whose flowers resemble and attract certain wasps: found in wood margins and scrub on lime-rich soils

flyover ('flaɪ,əʊvə) *n* **1** Also called: **overpass** *Brit* **a** an intersection of two roads at which one is carried over the other by a bridge **b** such a bridge **2** the US name for a **fly-past**

flypaper ('flaɪ,peɪpə) *n* paper with a sticky and poisonous coating, usually hung from the ceiling to trap flies

fly-past *n* a ceremonial flight of aircraft over a given area. Also called (esp US): **flyover**

flyposting ('flaɪ,pəʊstɪŋ) *n* the posting of advertising or political bills, posters, etc in unauthorized places

fly press *n* a hand-operated press in which a horizontal beam with heavy steel balls attached to the ends gives additional momentum to the descending member used to punch or compress material

Fly River *n* a river in W Papua New Guinea, flowing southeast to the Gulf of Papua. Length: about 1300 km (800 miles)

fly rod *n* a light flexible rod, now usually made of fibreglass or split cane, used in fly-fishing

Flysch (fliʃ) *n* (*sometimes not capital*) a marine sedimentary facies consisting of a sequence of sandstones, conglomerates, marls, shales, and clays that were formed by erosion during a period of mountain building and subsequently deformed as the mountain building continued. The phenomenon was first observed in the Alps [Swiss German]

flyscreen ('flaɪ,skriːn) *n* a wire-mesh screen over a window to prevent flies from entering a room

fly sheet *n* **1** another name for **fly** (sense 22) **2** a short handbill or circular

flyspeck ('flaɪ,spɛk) *n* **1** the small speck of the excrement of a fly **2** a small spot or speck ▷ *vb* **3** (*tr*) to mark with flyspecks

fly spray *n* a liquid used to destroy flies and other insects, sprayed from an aerosol

flystrike ('flaɪstraɪk) *n* the infestation of wounded sheep by blowflies or maggots

flyte (flaɪt; *Scot* fleɪt) *vb* a variant spelling of **flite**

fly-tipping *n* the deliberate dumping of rubbish in an unauthorized place

flytrap ('flaɪ,træp) *n* **1** any of various insectivorous plants, esp Venus's flytrap **2** a device for catching flies

fly way *n* the usual route used by birds when migrating

flyweight ('flaɪ,weɪt) *n* **1 a** a professional boxer weighing not more than 112 pounds (51 kg) **b** an amateur boxer weighing 48–51 kg (106–112 pounds) **c** (*as modifier*): *a flyweight contest* **2** (in Olympic wrestling) a wrestler weighing not more than 115 pounds (52 kg)

flywheel ('flaɪ,wiːl) *n* a heavy wheel that stores kinetic energy and smooths the operation of a reciprocating engine by maintaining a constant speed of rotation over the whole cycle

fm *abbreviation for* **1** fathom **2** from **3** *the internet domain name for* Micronesia

Fm *the chemical symbol for* fermium

FM *abbreviation for* **1** frequency modulation **2** Field Marshal **3** *aeronautics* figure of merit

FMCG *abbreviation for* fast-moving consumer goods

FMD *abbreviation for* **foot-and-mouth disease**

FMN *n biochem* flavin mononucleotide; a phosphoric ester of riboflavin that acts as the prosthetic group for many flavoproteins. See also **FAD**

FMRI *abbreviation for* functional magnetic resonance imaging: a technique that directly measures the blood flow in the brain, thereby providing information on brain activity

FMS *aeronautics abbreviation for* flight management systems

f-number *or* **f number** *n photog* the numerical value of the relative aperture. If the relative aperture is f8, 8 is the f-number and indicates that the focal length of the lens is 8 times the size of the lens aperture. See also **T-number**

fo *the internet domain name for* Faeroe Islands

FO *abbreviation for* **1** *army* Field Officer **2** *air force* Flying Officer **3** Foreign Office **4** *international car registration for* Faeroe Islands [(for sense 4) from Faeroese *Føroyar*]

fo. *abbreviation for* folio

foal (fəʊl) *n* **1** the young of a horse or related animal ▷ *vb* **2** to give birth to (a foal) [Old English *fola*; related to Old Frisian *fola*, Old High German *folo* foal, Latin *pullus* young creature, Greek *pōlos* foal]

foam (fəʊm) *n* **1** a mass of small bubbles of gas formed on the surface of a liquid, such as the froth produced by agitating a solution of soap or detergent in water **2** frothy saliva sometimes formed in and expelled from the mouth, as in rabies **3** the frothy sweat of a horse or similar animal **4 a** any of a number of light cellular solids made by creating bubbles of gas in the liquid material and solidifying it: used as insulators and in packaging **b** (*as modifier*): *foam rubber; foam plastic* **5** a colloid consisting of a gas suspended in a liquid **6** a mixture of chemicals sprayed from a fire extinguisher onto a burning substance to create a stable layer of bubbles which smothers the flames **7** a poetic word for the **sea** ▷ *vb* **8** to produce or cause to produce foam; froth **9** (*intr*) to be very angry (esp in the phrase **foam at the mouth**) [Old English *fām*; related to Old High German *feim*, Latin *spūma*, Sanskrit *phena*] ▷ **'foamless** *adj* ▷ **'foam,like** *adj*

foamflower ('fəʊm,flaʊə) *n* a perennial saxifragaceous plant, *Tiarella cordifolia*, of North America and Asia, having spring-blooming white flowers

foamy ('fəʊmɪ) *adj* **foamier, foamiest** of,

f

resembling, consisting of, or covered with foam > **'foamily** *adv* > **'foaminess** *n*

fob¹ (fɒb) *n* **1** a chain or ribbon by which a pocket watch is attached to a waistcoat **2** any ornament hung on such a chain **3** a small pocket in a man's waistcoat, for holding a watch **4** a metal or plastic tab on a key ring [c17 probably of Germanic origin; compare German dialect *Fuppe* pocket]

fob² (fɒb) *vb* **fobs, fobbing, fobbed** an archaic word for **cheat** [c15 probably from German *foppen* to trick]

f.o.b.³ or **FOB** *commerce* abbreviation for free on board

fob off *vb* (*tr, adverb*) **1** to appease or trick (a person) with lies or excuses **2** to dispose of (goods) by trickery

FoC abbreviation for father of the chapel

focaccia (fəˈkætʃə) *n* a flat Italian bread made with olive oil and yeast [from Italian]

focal ('fəʊkəl) *adj* **1** of or relating to a focus **2** situated at, passing through, or measured from the focus > **'focally** *adv*

focal infection *n* a bacterial infection limited to a specific part of the body, such as the tonsils or a gland

focalize or **focalise** ('fəʊkəˌlaɪz) *vb* a less common word for **focus**. > ˌfocali'zation or ˌfocali'sation *n*

focal length or **distance** *n* the distance from the focal point of a lens or mirror to the reflecting surface of the mirror or the centre point of the lens

focal plane *n* **1** the plane that is perpendicular to the axis of a lens or mirror and passes through the focal point **2** the plane in a telescope, camera, or other optical instrument in which a real image is in focus

focal point *n* **1** Also called: **principal focus, focus** the point on the axis of a lens or mirror to which parallel rays of light converge or from which they appear to diverge after refraction or reflection **2** a central point of attention or interest

focal ratio *n* *photog* another name for **f-number**

focometer (fəʊˈkɒmɪtə) *n* an instrument for measuring the focal length of a lens

fo'c's'le or **fo'c's'le** ('fəʊksəl) *n* a variant spelling of **forecastle**

focus ('fəʊkəs) *n, pl* **-cuses** or **-ci** (-saɪ, -kaɪ, -kiː) **1** a point of convergence of light or other electromagnetic radiation, particles, sound waves, etc, or a point from which they appear to diverge **2** another name for **focal point** (sense 1), **focal length 3** *optics* the state of an optical image when it is distinct and clearly defined or the state of an instrument producing this image **4** a point upon which attention, activity, etc, is directed or concentrated **5** *geometry* a fixed reference point on the concave side of a conic section, used when defining its eccentricity **6** the point beneath the earth's surface at which an earthquake or underground nuclear explosion originates. Compare **epicentre 7** *pathol* the main site of an infection or a localized region of diseased tissue ▷ *vb* **-cuses, -cusing, -cused** or **-cusses, -cussing, -cussed 8** to bring or come to a focus or into focus **9** (*tr*; often foll by *on*) to fix attention (on); concentrate [c17 via New Latin from Latin: hearth, fireplace] > **'focusable** *adj* > **'focuser** *n*

focused strategy *n* a business strategy in which an organization divests itself of all but its core activities, using the funds raised to enhance the distinctive abilities that give it an advantage over its rivals

focus group *n* a group of people brought together to give their opinions on a particular issue or product, often for the purpose of market research

focus puller *n* *films* the member of a camera crew who adjusts the focus of the lens as the camera is tracked in or out

fodder ('fɒdə) *n* **1** bulk feed for livestock, esp hay, straw, etc **2** raw experience or material: *fodder for the imagination* ▷ *vb* **3** (*tr*) to supply (livestock) with

fodder [Old English *fōdor*; related to Old Norse *fōthr*, Old High German *fuotar*; see FOOD, FORAGE]

foe (fəʊ) *n* *formal or literary* another word for **enemy** [Old English *fāh* hostile; related to Old High German *fēhan* to hate, Old Norse *feikn* dreadful; see FEUD¹]

FoE or **FOE** abbreviation for Friends of the Earth

foehn (fɜːn; *German* føːn) *n* *meteorol* a variant spelling of **föhn**

foeman ('fəʊmən) *n, pl* **-men** *archaic or poetic* an enemy in war; foe

foetal ('fiːtəl) *adj* a variant spelling of **fetal**

foetation (fiːˈteɪʃən) *n* a variant spelling of **fetation**

foeticide ('fiːtɪˌsaɪd) *n* a variant spelling of **feticide**. > ˌfoeti'cidal *adj*

foetid ('fɛtɪd, 'fiː-) *adj* a variant spelling of **fetid** > **'foetidly** *adv* > **'foetidness** *n*

foetor ('fiːtə) *n* a variant spelling of **fetor**

foetus ('fiːtəs) *n, pl* **-tuses** a variant spelling of **fetus**

fog¹ (fɒg) *n* **1** a mass of droplets of condensed water vapour suspended in the air, often greatly reducing visibility, corresponding to a cloud but at a lower level **2** a cloud of any substance in the atmosphere reducing visibility **3** a state of mental uncertainty or obscurity **4** *photog* a blurred or discoloured area on a developed negative, print, or transparency caused by the action of extraneous light, incorrect development, etc **5** a colloid or suspension consisting of liquid particles dispersed in a gas ▷ *vb* **fogs, fogging, fogged 6** to envelop or become enveloped with or as if with fog **7** to confuse or become confused **8** *photog* to produce fog on (a negative, print, or transparency) or (of a negative, print, or transparency) to be affected by fog [c16 perhaps back formation from *foggy* damp, boggy, from FOG²]

fog² (fɒg) *n* **a** a second growth of grass after the first mowing **b** grass left to grow long in winter [c14 probably of Scandinavian origin; compare Norwegian *fogg* rank grass]

fog bank *n* a distinct mass of fog, esp at sea

fogbound ('fɒgˌbaʊnd) *adj* **1** prevented from operation by fog: *the airport was fogbound* **2** obscured by or enveloped in fog: *the skyscraper was fogbound*

fogbow ('fɒgˌbəʊ) *n* a faint arc of light sometimes seen in a fog bank. Also called: **seadog, white rainbow**

fogdog ('fɒgˌdɒg) *n* a whitish spot sometimes seen in fog near the horizon. Also called: **seadog**

fogey or **fogy** ('fəʊgɪ) *n, pl* **-geys** or **-gies** an extremely fussy, old-fashioned, or conservative person (esp in the phrase **old fogey**) [c18 of unknown origin] > **'fogeyish** or **'fogyish** *adj* > **'fogeyism** or **'fogyism** *n*

fog fever *n* *vet science* an acute respiratory disease of cattle, with a high mortality, that can occur after grazing fog

foggage ('fɒgɪdʒ) *n* grass grown for winter grazing

fogged (fɒgd) or **foggy** *adj* *photog* affected or obscured by fog

Foggia (*Italian* 'fɔddʒa) *n* a city in SE Italy, in Apulia: seat of Emperor Frederick II; centre for Carbonari revolutionary societies in the revolts of 1820, 1848, and 1860. Pop: 155 203 (2001)

foggy ('fɒgɪ) *adj* **-gier, -giest 1** thick with fog **2** obscure or confused **3** another word for **fogged 4** not the foggiest (idea or notion) no idea whatsoever > **'foggily** *adv* > **'fogginess** *n*

foghorn ('fɒgˌhɔːn) *n* **1** a mechanical instrument sounded at intervals to serve as a warning to vessels in fog **2** *informal* a loud deep resounding voice

fog lamp *n* a powerful light for use in foggy conditions, usually positioned low down on the front or rear of a road vehicle

fog level *n* the density produced by the development of photographic materials that have not been exposed to light or other actinic

radiation. It forms part of the characteristic curve of a particular material

fog light *n* another word for **fog lamp**

fog signal *n* a signal used to warn railway engine drivers in fog, consisting of a detonator placed on the line

föhn or **foehn** (fɜːn; *German* føːn) *n* a warm dry wind blowing down the northern slopes of the Alps. It originates as moist air blowing from the Mediterranean, rising on reaching the Alps and cooling at the saturated adiabatic lapse rate, and descending on the leeward side, warming at the dry adiabatic lapse rate, thus gaining heat. See also **lapse rate** [German, from Old High German *phōnno*, from Latin *favōnius*; related to *fovēre* to warm]

FOI abbreviation for freedom of information

foible ('fɔɪbəl) *n* **1** a slight peculiarity or minor weakness; idiosyncrasy **2** the most vulnerable part of a sword's blade, from the middle to the tip. Compare **forte¹** (sense 2) [c17 from obsolete French, from obsolete adj: FEEBLE]

foie gras (*French* fwa gra) *n* See **pâté de foie gras**

foil¹ (fɔɪl) *vb* (*tr*) **1** to baffle or frustrate (a person, attempt, etc) **2** *hunting* (of hounds, hunters, etc) to obliterate the scent left by a hunted animal or (of a hunted animal) to run back over its own trail **3** *archaic* to repulse or defeat (an attack or assailant) ▷ *n* **4** *hunting* any scent that obscures the trail left by a hunted animal **5** *archaic* a setback or defeat [c13 *foilen* to trample, from Old French *fouler*, from Old French *fuler* tread down, FULL²] > **'foilable** *adj*

foil² (fɔɪl) *n* **1** metal in the form of very thin sheets: *gold foil; tin foil* **2** the thin metallic sheet forming the backing of a mirror **3** a thin leaf of shiny metal set under a gemstone to add brightness or colour **4** a person or thing that gives contrast to another **5** *architect* a small arc between cusps, esp as used in Gothic window tracery **6** short for **aerofoil** or **hydrofoil** ▷ *vb* (*tr*) **7** to back or cover with foil **8** Also: **foliate** *architect* to ornament (windows) with foils [c14 from Old French *foille*, from Latin *folia* leaves, plural of *folium*]

foil³ (fɔɪl) *n* a light slender flexible sword tipped by a button and usually having a bell-shaped guard [c16 of unknown origin]

foilsman ('fɔɪlzmən) *n, pl* **-men** *fencing* a person who uses or specializes in using a foil

foin (fɔɪn) *archaic* ▷ *n* **1** a thrust or lunge with a weapon ▷ *vb* **2** to thrust with a weapon [c14 probably from Old French *foine*, from Latin *fuscina* trident]

Foism ('fəʊˌɪzəm) *n* Chinese Buddhism, the version introduced from India from the 4th century AD onwards and essentially belonging to the Mahayana school [from Mandarin Chinese *fo* BUDDHA] > **'Foist** *n, adj*

foison ('fɔɪzən) *n* *archaic or poetic* a plentiful supply or yield [c13 from Old French, from Latin *fūsiō* a pouring out, from *fundere* to pour; see FUSION]

foist (fɔɪst) *vb* (*tr*) **1** (often foll by *off* or *on*) to sell or pass off (something, esp an inferior article) as genuine, valuable, etc **2** (usually foll by *in* or *into*) to insert surreptitiously or wrongfully [c16 probably from obsolete Dutch *vuisten* to enclose in one's hand, from Middle Dutch *vuist* fist]

fol. abbreviation for **1** folio **2** following

folacin ('fɒləsɪn) *n* another name for **folic acid** [c20 from FOL(IC) AC(ID) + -IN]

fold¹ (fəʊld) *vb* **1** to bend or be bent double so that one part covers another: *to fold a sheet of paper* **2** (*tr*) to bring together and intertwine (the arms, legs, etc): *she folded her hands* **3** (*tr*) (of birds, insects, etc) to close (the wings) together from an extended position **4** (*tr*; often foll by *up* or *in*) to enclose in or as if in a surrounding material **5** (*tr*; foll by *in*) to clasp (a person) in the arms **6** (*tr*; usually foll by *round, about, etc*) to wind (around); entwine **7** (*tr*) *poetic* to cover completely: *night folded the earth* **8** Also: **fold in** (*tr*) to mix (a whisked mixture) with other ingredients by gently turning one part over the other with a spoon **9** to produce a bend (in stratified rock) or (of stratified rock) to display a bend **10** (*intr*; often foll by *up*) *informal* to collapse; fail ▷ *n* **11** a piece or section that has been folded **12** a mark, crease, or hollow made by folding **13** a hollow in undulating terrain **14** a bend in stratified rocks that results from movements within the earth's crust and produces such structures as anticlines and synclines **15** *anatomy* another word for **plica** (sense 1) **16** a coil, as in a rope, etc **17** an act of folding ▷ See also **fold up** [Old English *fealdan*; related to Old Norse *falda* , Old High German *faldan*, Latin *duplus* double, Greek *haploos* simple] > **'foldable** *adj*

fold² (fəʊld) *n* **1 a** a small enclosure or pen for sheep or other livestock, where they can be gathered **b** the sheep or other livestock gathered in such an enclosure **c** a flock of sheep **d** a herd of Highland cattle **2** a church or the members of it **3** any group or community sharing a way of life or holding the same values ▷ *vb* **4** (*tr*) to gather or confine (sheep or other livestock) in a fold [Old English *falod*; related to Old Saxon *faled*, Middle Dutch *vaelt*]

-fold *suffix forming adjectives and adverbs* having so many parts, being so many times as much or as many, or multiplied by so much or so many: *threefold; three-hundredfold* [Old English *-fald, -feald*]

fold-and-thrust belt *n geology* a linear or arcuate region of the earth's surface that has been subjected to severe folding and thrust faulting

foldaway ('fəʊldə,weɪ) *adj* (*prenominal*) (of a bed) able to be folded and put away when not in use

foldback ('fəʊld,bæk) *n* (in multitrack recording) a process for returning a signal to a performer instantly. Also called: **cueing**

foldboat ('fəʊld,bəʊt) *n* another name for **faltboat**

folded dipole *n* a type of aerial, widely used with television and VHF radio receivers, consisting of two parallel dipoles connected together at their outer ends and fed at the centre of one of them. The length is usually half the operating wavelength

folder ('fəʊldə) *n* **1** a binder or file for holding loose papers, etc **2** a folded circular **3** a machine for folding printed sheets **4** a person or thing that folds **5** *computing* another name for **directory** (sense 5)

folderol ('fɒldə,rɒl) *n* a variant of **falderal**

folding door *n* a door in the form of two or more vertical hinged leaves that can be folded one against another

folding money *n informal* paper money

folding press *n* a fall in wrestling won by folding one's opponent's legs up to his head and pressing his shoulders to the floor

foldout ('fəʊld,aʊt) *n printing* another name for **gatefold**

fold up *vb* (*adverb*) **1** (*tr*) to make smaller or more compact **2** (*intr*) to collapse, as with laughter or pain

foley *or* **foley artist** ('fəʊlɪ) *n films* the US name for **footsteps editor** [C20 named after the inventor of the technique]

folia ('fəʊlɪə) *n* the plural of **folium**

foliaceous (,fəʊlɪ'eɪʃəs) *adj* **1** having the appearance of the leaf of a plant **2** bearing leaves or leaflike structures **3** *geology* (of certain rocks, esp schists) consisting of thin layers; foliated [C17 from Latin *foliāceus*]

foliage ('fəʊlɪɪdʒ) *n* **1** the green leaves of a plant **2** sprays of leaves used for decoration **3** an ornamental leaflike design [C15 from Old French *fuellage*, from *fuelle* leaf; influenced in form by Latin *folium*] > **'foliaged** *adj*

foliar ('fəʊlɪə) *adj* of or relating to a leaf or leaves [C19 from French *foliaire*, from Latin *folium* leaf]

foliate *adj* ('fəʊlɪɪt, -,eɪt) **1 a** relating to, possessing, or resembling leaves **b** in combination: *trifoliate* **2** (of certain metamorphic

rocks, esp schists) having the constituent minerals arranged in thin leaflike layers ▷ *vb* ('fəʊlɪ,eɪt) **3** (*tr*) to ornament with foliage or with leaf forms such as foils **4** to hammer or cut (metal) into thin plates or foil **5** (*tr*) to coat or back (glass, etc) with metal foil **6** (*tr*) to number the leaves of (a book, manuscript, etc). Compare **paginate 7** (*intr*) (of plants) to grow leaves [C17 from Latin *foliātus* leaved, leafy]

foliated ('fəʊlɪ,eɪtɪd) *adj* **1** *architect* ornamented with or made up of foliage or foils **2** (of rocks and minerals, esp schists) composed of thin easily separable layers **3** (esp of parts of animals or plants) resembling a leaf

foliation (,fəʊlɪ'eɪʃən) *n* **1** *botany* **a** the process of producing leaves **b** the state of being in leaf **c** the arrangement of leaves in a leaf bud; vernation **2** *architect* **a** ornamentation consisting of foliage **b** ornamentation consisting of cusps and foils **3** any decoration with foliage **4** the consecutive numbering of the leaves of a book **5** *geology* the arrangement of the constituents of a rock in leaflike layers, as in schists

folic acid ('fəʊlɪk, 'fɒl-) *n* any of a group of vitamins of the B complex, including pteroylglutamic acid and its derivatives: used in the treatment of megaloblastic anaemia. Also called: **folacin** [C20 from Latin *folium* leaf; so called because it may be obtained from green leaves] > **'folate** *n, adj*

folie à deux ('fɒlɪ æ 'dɜː) *n psychiatry* mental illness occurring simultaneously in two intimately related persons who share some of the elements of the illness, such as delusions [French: madness involving two (people)]

folie de grandeur *French* (fɔlɪ də grãdœr) *n* delusions of grandeur [literally: madness of grandeur]

folio ('fəʊlɪəʊ) *n, pl* **-lios 1** a sheet of paper folded in half to make two leaves for a book or manuscript **2** a book or manuscript of the largest common size made up of such sheets **3** a leaf of paper or parchment numbered on the front side only **4** a page number in a book **5** *law* a unit of measurement of the length of legal documents, determined by the number of words, generally 72 or 90 in Britain and 100 in the US **6** *NZ* a collection of related material ▷ *adj* **7** relating to or having the format of a folio: *a folio edition* ▷ *vb* **-lios, -lioing, -lioed 8** (*tr*) to number the leaves of (a book) consecutively [C16 from Latin phrase *in foliō* in a leaf, from *folium* leaf]

foliolate ('fəʊlɪə,leɪt, fəʊ'lɪəlɪt, -,leɪt) *adj botany* possessing or relating to leaflets [C19 from Late Latin *foliolum* little leaf, from Latin *folium* leaf]

foliose ('fəʊlɪ,əʊs, -,əʊz) *adj* another word for **foliaceous** (senses 1, 2) [C18 from Latin *foliōsus* full of leaves]

folium ('fəʊlɪəm) *n, pl* **-lia** (-lɪə) **1** a plane geometrical curve consisting of a loop whose two ends, intersecting at a node, are asymptotic to the same line. Standard equation: $x^3 + y^3 = 3axy$ where $x = y + a$ is the equation of the asymptote **2** any thin leaflike layer, esp of some metamorphic rocks [C19 from Latin, literally: leaf]

folk (fəʊk) *n, pl* **folk** *or* **folks 1** (*functioning as plural; often plural in form*) people in general, esp those of a particular group or class: *country folk* **2** (*functioning as plural; usually plural in form*) *informal* members of a family **3** (*functioning as singular*) *informal* short for **folk music 4** a people or tribe **5** (*modifier*) relating to, originating from, or traditional to the common people of a country: *a folk song* [Old English *folc*; related to Old Saxon, Old Norse, Old High German *folk*] > **'folkish** *adj* > **'folkishness** *n*

folk art *n* the visual arts, music, drama, dance, or literature originating from, or traditional to, the common people of a country

folk dance *n* **1** any of various traditional rustic dances often originating from festivals or rituals **2** a piece of music composed for such a dance ▷ *vb* **folk-dance** (*intr*) **3** to perform a folk dance > **folk**

dancing *n*

Folkestone ('fəʊkstən) *n* a port and resort in SE England, in E Kent. Pop: 45 273 (2001)

Folketing ('fɒlkətɪŋ; *Danish* 'fɔlgəteŋ) *n* the unicameral Danish parliament [Danish, from *folk* the people, FOLK + Old Norse *thing* assembly]

folk etymology *n* **1** the gradual change in the form of a word through the influence of a more familiar word or phrase with which it becomes associated, as for example *sparrow-grass* for *asparagus* **2** a popular but erroneous conception of the origin of a word

folkie *or* **folky** ('fəʊkɪ) *n, pl* **-ies** a devotee of folk music

folklore ('fəʊk,lɔː) *n* **1** the unwritten literature of a people as expressed in folk tales, proverbs, riddles, songs, etc **2** the body of stories and legends attached to a particular place, group, activity, etc: *Hollywood folklore; rugby folklore* **3** the anthropological discipline concerned with the study of folkloric materials > **'folk,loric** *adj* > **'folk,lorist** *n, adj* > **,folklor'istic** *adj*

folk medicine *n* the traditional art of medicine as practised among rustic communities and primitive peoples, consisting typically of the use of herbal remedies, fruits and vegetables thought to have healing power, etc

folk memory *n* the memory of past events as preserved in a community

folkmoot ('fəʊk,muːt) *or* **folkmote, folkmot** ('fəʊk,məʊt) *n* (in early medieval England) an assembly of the people of a district, town, or shire [Old English *folcmōt*, from *folc* FOLK + *mōt* from *mētan* to MEET¹]

folk music *n* **1** music that is passed on from generation to generation by oral tradition. Compare **art music 2** any music composed in the idiom of this oral tradition

folk-rock *n* a style of rock music influenced by folk, including traditional material arranged for electric instruments

folk singer *n* a person who sings folk songs or other songs in the folk idiom > **folk singing** *n*

folk song *n* **1** a song of which the music and text have been handed down by oral tradition among the common people **2** a modern song which employs or reflects the folk idiom

folksy ('fəʊksɪ) *adj* **-sier, -siest 1** of or like ordinary people; sometimes used derogatorily to describe affected simplicity **2** *informal, chiefly US and Canadian* friendly; affable **3** of or relating to folk art > **'folksiness** *n*

folk tale *or* **story** *n* a tale or legend originating among a people and typically becoming part of an oral tradition

folkways ('fəʊk,weɪz) *pl n sociol* traditional and customary ways of living

folk weave *n* a type of fabric with a loose weave

foll *abbreviation for* followed

follicle 1 any small sac or cavity in the body having an excretory, secretory, or protective function: *a hair follicle* **2** *botany* a dry fruit, formed from a single carpel, that splits along one side only to release its seeds: occurs in larkspur and columbine [C17 from Latin *folliculus* small bag, from *follis* pair of bellows, leather money-bag] > **follicular** (fɒ'lɪkjʊlə), **folliculate** (fɒ'lɪkjʊ,leɪt) *or* **fol'licu,lated** *adj*

follicle-stimulating hormone *n* a gonadotrophic hormone secreted by the pituitary gland that stimulates maturation of ovarian follicles in female mammals and growth of seminiferous tubules in males. Abbreviation: FSH See also **luteinizing hormone, prolactin**

folliculin (fɒ'lɪkjʊlɪn) *n* another name for oestrone

follow ('fɒləʊ) *vb* **1** to go or come after in the same direction **2** (*tr*) to accompany; attend **3** to come after as a logical or natural consequence **4** (*tr*) to keep to the course or track of **5** (*tr*) to act in accordance with; obey **6** (*tr*) to accept the ideas or beliefs of (a previous authority, etc) **7** to

f

understand (an explanation, argument, etc): *the lesson was difficult to follow* **8** to watch closely or continuously **9** (*tr*) to have a keen interest in: *to follow athletics* **10** (*tr*) to help in the cause of or accept the leadership of: *the men who followed Napoleon* **11** (*tr*) *rare* to earn a living at or in: *to follow the Navy* **12 follow suit** *cards* **a** to play a card of the same suit as the card played immediately before it **b** to do the same as someone else ▷ *n* **13** *billiards, snooker* **a** a forward spin imparted to a cue ball causing it to roll after the object ball **b** a shot made in this way ▷ See also **follow-on, follow out, follow through, follow up** [Old English *folgian*; related to Old Frisian *folgia*, Old Saxon *folgōn*, Old High German *folgēn*] > **'followable** *adj*

follower ('fɒləʊə) *n* **1** a person who accepts the teachings of another; disciple; adherent: *a follower of Marx* **2** an attendant or henchman **3** an enthusiast or supporter, as of a sport or team **4** (*esp formerly*) a male admirer **5** *rare* a pursuer **6** a machine part that derives its motion by following the motion of another part

following ('fɒləʊɪŋ) *adj* **1 a** (*prenominal*) about to be mentioned, specified, etc **b** (*as noun*): *will the following please raise their hands?* **2** (of winds, currents, etc) moving in the same direction as the course of a vessel ▷ *n* **3** a group of supporters or enthusiasts ▷ *prep* **4** as a result of

USAGE The use of *following* to mean *as a result of* is very common in journalism, but should be avoided in other kinds of writing

follow-my-leader *n* a game in which the players must repeat the actions of the leader. US, Canadian, and Irish name: **follow-the-leader**

follow-on *cricket* ▷ *n* **1** an immediate second innings forced on a team scoring a prescribed number of runs fewer than its opponents in the first innings ▷ *vb* **follow on 2** (*intr, adverb*) (of a team) to play a follow-on

follow out *vb* (*tr, adverb*) to implement (an idea or action) to a conclusion

followship ('fɒləʊʃɪp) *n* the practice of doing what other people suggest, rather than taking the lead

follow through *vb* (*adverb*) **1** *sport* to complete (a stroke or shot) by continuing the movement to the end of its arc **2** (*tr*) to pursue (an aim) to a conclusion ▷ *n* **follow-through 3** *sport* **a** the act of following through **b** the part of the stroke after the ball has been hit **4** the completion of a procedure, esp after a first action

follow up *vb* (*tr, adverb*) **1** to pursue or investigate (a person, evidence, etc) closely **2** to continue (action) after a beginning, esp to increase its effect ▷ *n* **follow-up 3 a** something done to reinforce an initial action **b** (*as modifier*): *a follow-up letter* **4** *med* a routine examination of a patient at various intervals after medical or surgical treatment

folly ('fɒlɪ) *n, pl* **-lies 1** the state or quality of being foolish; stupidity; rashness **2** a foolish action, mistake, idea, etc **3** a building in the form of a castle, temple, etc, built to satisfy a fancy or conceit, often of an eccentric kind **4** (*plural*) *theatre* an elaborately costumed revue **5** *archaic* **a** evil; wickedness **b** lewdness; wantonness [c13 from Old French *folie* madness, from *fou* mad; see FOOL¹]

Folsom man ('fɒlsəm) *n* a type of early man from a North American culture of the Pleistocene period, thought to have used flint tools and to have subsisted mainly by hunting bison [c20 named after *Folsom*, a settlement in New Mexico, where archaeological evidence was found]

Fomalhaut ('fəʊmə,lɔːt) *n* the brightest star in the constellation Piscis Austrinus, possessing a protoplanetary disc. Distance: 25 light years. Spectral type A3V [c16 from Arabic *fum'l-hūt* mouth of the fish, referring to its position in the constellation]

foment (fə'mɛnt) *vb* (*tr*) **1** to encourage or instigate (trouble, discord, etc); stir up **2** *med* to

apply heat and moisture to (a part of the body) to relieve pain and inflammation [c15 from Late Latin *fōmentāre*, from Latin *fōmentum* a poultice, ultimately from *fovēre* to foster] > **fomentation** (,fəʊmɛn'teɪʃən) *n* > **fo'menter** *n*

USAGE Both *foment* and *ferment* can be used to talk about stirring up trouble: *he was accused of fomenting/fermenting unrest.* Only *ferment* can be used intransitively or as a noun: *his anger continued to ferment* (not *foment*); *rural areas were unaffected by the ferment in the cities*

fomes ('fəʊmiːz) *n, pl* **-mites** (-mɪtiːz) *med* any material, such as bedding or clothing, that may harbour pathogens and therefore convey disease [c18 from Latin *fōmes* tinder]

fond¹ (fɒnd) *adj* **1** (*postpositive*; foll by *of*) predisposed (to); having a liking (for) **2** loving; tender **3** indulgent; doting **4** (of hopes, wishes, etc) cherished but unlikely to be realized **5** *archaic or dialect* **a** foolish **b** credulous [c14 *fonned*, from *fonnen* to be foolish, from *fonne* a fool] > **'fondly** *adv* > **'fondness** *n*

fond² (fɒnd; French fɔ̃) *n* **1** the background of a design, as in lace **2** *obsolete* fund; stock [c17 from French, from Latin *fundus* bottom; see FUND]

fondant ('fɒndənt) *n* **1** a thick flavoured paste of sugar and water, used in sweets and icings **2** a sweet made of this mixture ▷ *adj* **3** (of a colour) soft; pastel [c19 from French, literally: melting, from *fondre* to melt, from Latin *fundere*; see FOUND³]

fondle ('fɒndəl) *vb* **1** (*tr*) to touch or stroke tenderly; caress **2** (*intr*) *archaic* to act in a loving manner [c17 from (obsolete) vb *fond* to fondle; see FOUND¹] > **'fondler** *n* > **'fondlingly** *adv*

fondue ('fɒndjuː; French fɔ̃dy) *n* a Swiss dish, consisting of cheese melted in white wine or cider, into which small pieces of bread are dipped and then eaten [c19 from French, feminine of *fondu* melted, from *fondre* to melt; see FONDANT]

fondue Bourguignonne ('bʊəgɪ,njɒn; French burgiɲɔn) *n* a dish consisting of pieces of steak impaled on forks, cooked in oil at the table and dipped in sauces [French: Burgundy fondue]

FONE *text messaging abbreviation for* phone

Fonseca (Spanish fɒn'seka) *n* **Gulf of** an inlet of the Pacific Ocean in W Central America

fons et origo *Latin* (fɒnz ɛt 'ɒrɪgəʊ) *n* the source and origin

font¹ (fɒnt) *n* **1 a** a large bowl for baptismal water, usually mounted on a pedestal **b** a receptacle for holy water **2** the reservoir for oil in an oil lamp **3** *archaic or poetic* a fountain or well [Old English, from Church Latin *fons*, from Latin: fountain] > **'fontal** *adj*

font² (fɒnt) *n* *printing* a complete set of type of one style and size. Also called: **fount**

font² (fɒnt) *n* *printing* a complete set of type of one style and size [c16 from Old French *fonte* a founding, casting, from Vulgar Latin *funditus* (unattested) a casting, from Latin *fundere* to melt; see FOUND³]

Fontainebleau ('fɒntɪn,bləʊ; French fɔ̃tɛnblo) *n* a town in N France, in the **Forest of Fontainebleau**: famous for its palace (now a museum), one of the largest royal residences in France, built largely by Francis I (16th century). Pop: 15 942 (1999)

fontanelle *or chiefly US* **fontanel** (,fɒntə'nɛl) *n* *anatomy* any of several soft membranous gaps between the bones of the skull in a fetus or infant [c16 (in the sense: hollow between muscles): from Old French *fontanele*, literally: a little spring, from *fontaine* FOUNTAIN]

Fonthill Abbey ('fɒnthɪl) *n* a ruined Gothic Revival mansion in Wiltshire: rebuilt (1790–1810) for William Beckford by James Wyatt; the main tower collapsed in 1800 and, after rebuilding, again in 1827

fontina (fɒn'tiːnə) *n* a semihard, pale yellow, mild Italian cheese made from cow's milk [c20 from Italian dialect, of unknown origin]

Foochow ('fuː'tʃaʊ) *n* a variant transliteration of the Chinese name for **Fuzhou**

food (fuːd) *n* **1** any substance containing nutrients, such as carbohydrates, proteins, and fats, that can be ingested by a living organism and metabolized into energy and body tissue. Related adj: **alimentary 2** nourishment in more or less solid form as opposed to liquid form: *food and drink* **3** anything that provides mental nourishment or stimulus: *food for thought* [Old English *fōda*; related to Old Frisian *fōdia* to nourish, feed, Old Norse *fœthi*, Gothic *fōdeins* food; see FEED, FODDER] > **'foodless** *adj*

food additive *n* any of various natural or synthetic substances, such as salt, monosodium glutamate, or citric acid, used in the commercial processing of food as preservatives, antioxidants, emulsifiers, etc, in order to preserve or add flavour, colour, or texture to processed food

food body *n* *botany* a mass of nutrients attached to a seed coat, which attracts ants and thus aids dispersal of the seed

food chain *n* **1** *ecology* a sequence of organisms in an ecosystem in which each species is the food of the next member of the chain **2** *informal* the hierarchy in an organization or society

food combining *n* the practice of keeping carbohydrates separate from proteins in one's daily diet, as a way of losing weight and also for some medical conditions

food conversion ratio *n* a ratio expressing the weight of food required to produce a unit gain in the live weight of an animal

food group *n* any of the categories into which different foods may be placed according to the type of nourishment they supply, such as carbohydrates or proteins

foodie *or* **foody** ('fuːdɪ) *n, pl* **-ies** a person having an enthusiastic interest in the preparation and consumption of good food

food mile *n* a unit used to measure the distance that a food product travels from where it is produced to where it is sold or consumed

food poisoning *n* an acute illness typically characterized by gastrointestinal inflammation, vomiting, and diarrhoea, caused by food that is either naturally poisonous or contaminated by pathogenic bacteria (esp *Salmonella*)

food pollen *n* infertile pollen produced by some plants that attracts insects and thus aids pollination

food processor *n* *cookery* an electric domestic appliance designed to speed the preparation and mixing of ingredients by automatic chopping, grating, blending, etc

foodstuff ('fuːd,stʌf) *n* any material, substance, etc, that can be used as food

food stylist *n* a person who prepares food for photographs used in magazines, cookery books, etc

food vacuole *n* *biology* a cavity surrounding ingested food particles in some protozoans

food web *n* a combination of food chains that integrate to form a network

fool¹ (fuːl) *n* **1** a person who lacks sense or judgement **2** a person who is made to appear ridiculous **3** (*formerly*) a professional jester living in a royal or noble household **4** *obsolete* an idiot or imbecile **5 form the fool** *Caribbean* to play the fool or behave irritatingly **6 no fool** a wise or sensible person **7 play** *or* **act the fool** to deliberately act foolishly; indulge in buffoonery ▷ *vb* **8** (*tr*) to deceive (someone), esp in order to make him look ridiculous **9** (*intr*; foll by *with, around with*, or *about with*) *informal* to act or play (with) irresponsibly or aimlessly: *to fool around with a woman* **10** (*intr*) to speak or act in a playful, teasing, or jesting manner **11** (*tr*; foll by *away*) to squander; fritter **12 fool along** US to move or proceed in a leisurely way ▷ *adj* **13** *informal* short for **foolish** [c13 from Old French *fol* mad person, from Late Latin *follis* empty-headed fellow, from

Latin: bellows; related to Latin *flāre* to blow]

fool² (fuːl) *n chiefly Brit* a dessert made from a purée of fruit with cream or custard: *gooseberry fool* [c16 perhaps from FOOL¹]

foolery ('fuːlərɪ) *n, pl* **-eries** 1 foolish behaviour 2 an instance of this, esp a prank or trick

foolhardy ('fuːl,hɑːdɪ) *adj* **-hardier, -hardiest** heedlessly rash or adventurous [c13 from Old French *fol hardi*, from *fol* foolish + *hardi* bold] ▷ 'fool,hardily *adv* ▷ 'fool,hardiness *n*

foolish ('fuːlɪʃ) *adj* 1 unwise; silly 2 resulting from folly or stupidity 3 ridiculous or absurd; not worthy of consideration 4 weak-minded; simple 5 an archaic word for **insignificant**. ▷ 'foolishly *adv* ▷ 'foolishness *n*

foolproof ('fuːl,pruːf) *adj* 1 proof against failure; infallible: *a foolproof idea* 2 (esp of machines) proof against human misuse, error, etc

foolscap ('fuːlz,kæp) *n* 1 *chiefly Brit* a size of writing or printing paper, 13½ by 17 inches or 13¼ by 16½ inches 2 a book size, 4¼ by 6¾ inches (**foolscap octavo**) or (*chiefly Brit*) 6¾ by 8½ inches (**foolscap quarto**) 3 a variant spelling of **fool's cap** [c17 see FOOL¹, CAP; so called from the watermark formerly used on this kind of paper]

fool's cap *n* 1 a hood or cap with bells or tassels, worn by court jesters 2 a dunce's cap

fool's errand *n* a fruitless undertaking

fool's gold *n* any of various yellow minerals, esp pyrite or chalcopyrite, that can be mistaken for gold

fool's mate *n chess* a checkmate achieved by Black's second move: the quickest possible mate

fool's paradise *n* illusory happiness

fool's-parsley *n* an evil-smelling Eurasian umbelliferous plant, *Aethusa cynapium*, with small white flowers: contains the poison coniine

foo-pah ('fuː,pɑː) *n* an Irish word for **faux pas**

foosball ('fuːs,bɔːl) *n US and Canadian* a game, often played in bars, in which opponents on either side of a purpose-built table attempt to strike a ball into the other side's goal by moving horizontal bars to which miniatures of footballers are attached. Also called (esp in Britain): **table football**

foot (fʊt) *n, pl* **feet** (fiːt) 1 the part of the vertebrate leg below the ankle joint that is in contact with the ground during standing and walking. Related adj: **pedal** 2 any of various organs of locomotion or attachment in invertebrates, including molluscs 3 *botany* the lower part of some plant structures, as of a developing moss sporophyte embedded in the parental tissue 4 a a unit of length equal to one third of a yard or 12 inches. 1 Imperial foot is equivalent to 0.3048 metre. Abbreviation: **ft** b any of various units of length used at different times and places, typically about 10 per cent greater than the Imperial foot 5 any part resembling a foot in form or function: *the foot of a chair* 6 the lower part of something; base; bottom: *the foot of the page; the foot of a hill* 7 the end of a series or group: *the foot of the list* 8 manner of walking or moving; tread; step: *a heavy foot* 9 a infantry, esp in the British army b (*as modifier*): *a foot soldier* 10 any of various attachments on a sewing machine that hold the fabric in position, such as a presser foot for ordinary sewing and a zipper foot 11 *music* a a unit used in classifying organ pipes according to their pitch, in terms of the length of an equivalent column of air b this unit applied to stops and registers on other instruments 12 *printing* a the margin at the bottom of a page b the undersurface of a piece of type 13 *prosody* a group of two or more syllables in which one syllable has the major stress, forming the basic unit of poetic rhythm 14 a foot in the door an action, appointment, etc, that provides an initial step towards a desired goal, esp one that is not easily attainable 15 kick with the wrong foot *Scot and Irish* to be of the opposite religion to that which is regarded as acceptable or to that of the person who is speaking 16 my foot! an expression of disbelief, often of the speaker's own preceding statement: *he didn't know, my foot! Of course he did!* 17 of foot *archaic* in manner of movement: *fleet of foot* 18 on foot a walking or running b in progress; astir; afoot 19 one foot in the grave *informal* near to death 20 on the wrong (or right) foot *informal* in an inauspicious (or auspicious) manner 21 put a foot wrong to make a mistake 22 put one's best foot forward a to try to do one's best b to hurry 23 put one's foot down *informal* a to act firmly b to increase speed (in a motor vehicle) by pressing down on the accelerator 24 put one's foot in it *informal* to blunder 25 set on foot to initiate or start (something) 26 tread under foot to oppress 27 under foot on the ground; beneath one's feet ▷ vb 28 to dance to music (esp in the phrase **foot it**) 29 (*tr*) to walk over or set foot on; traverse (esp in the phrase **foot it**) 30 (*tr*) to pay the entire cost of (esp in the phrase **foot the bill**) 31 (usually foll by *up*) *archaic or dialect* to add up ▷ See also **feet, foots** [Old English *fōt*; related to Old Norse *fōtr*, Gothic *fōtus*, Old High German *fuoz*, Latin *pēs*, Greek *pous*, Sanskrit *pad*] ▷ 'footless *adj*

USAGE In front of another noun, the plural for the unit of length is *foot*: *a 20-foot putt; his 70-foot ketch*. Foot can also be used instead of *feet* when mentioning a quantity and in front of words like *tall*: *four foot of snow; he is at least six foot tall*

footage ('fʊtɪdʒ) *n* 1 a length or distance measured in feet 2 a the extent of film material shot and exposed b the sequences of filmed material 3 a payment, by the linear foot of work done b the amount paid

foot-and-mouth disease *n* an acute highly infectious viral disease of cattle, pigs, sheep, and goats, characterized by the formation of vesicular eruptions in the mouth and on the feet, esp around the hoofs. Also called: **hoof-and-mouth disease, aphtha, aphthous fever** Technical name **contagious stomatitis**

football ('fʊt,bɔːl) *n* 1 a any of various games played with a round or oval ball and usually based on two teams competing to kick, head, carry, or otherwise propel the ball into each other's goal, territory, etc. See **association football, rugby, Australian Rules, American football, Gaelic football** b (*as modifier*): *a football ground; a football supporter* 2 the ball used in any of these games or their variants 3 a problem, issue, etc, that is continually passed from one group or person to another and treated as a pretext for argument instead of being resolved ▷ 'foot,baller *n*

footboard ('fʊt,bɔːd) *n* 1 a treadle or foot-operated lever on a machine 2 a vertical board at the foot of a bed

footboy ('fʊt,bɔɪ) *n* a boy servant; page

foot brake *n* a brake operated by applying pressure to a foot pedal. Also called: **pedal brake**

footbridge ('fʊt,brɪdʒ) *n* a narrow bridge for the use of pedestrians

foot-candle *n* a former unit of illumination, equal to one lumen per square foot or 10.764 lux

footcloth ('fʊt,klɒθ) *n* an obsolete word for **caparison** (sense 1)

-footed *adj* 1 having a foot or feet as specified: *four-footed* 2 having a tread as specified: *heavy-footed*

footer¹ ('fʊtə) *n* 1 *archaic* a person who goes on foot; walker 2 (*in combination*) a person or thing of a specified length or height in feet: *a six-footer*

footer² ('fʊtə) *n Brit informal* short for **football** (the game)

footer³ or **fouter** ('fuːtər, 'fuːtə) *Scot* ▷ *vb* (*intr*) 1 to potter; occupy oneself trivially or to little effect ▷ *n* 2 a person who footers [perhaps from French *foutre*; see FOOTLE]

footfall ('fʊt,fɔːl) *n* the sound of a footstep

foot fault *n tennis* a fault that occurs when the server fails to keep both feet behind the baseline until he has served

footgear ('fʊt,ɡɪə) *n* another name for **footwear**

foothill ('fʊt,hɪl) *n* (*often plural*) a lower slope of a mountain or a relatively low hill at the foot of a mountain

foothold ('fʊt,həʊld) *n* 1 a ledge, hollow, or other place affording a secure grip for the foot, as during climbing 2 a secure position from which further progress may be made

footie ('fʊtɪ) *n* a variant spelling of **footy**

footing ('fʊtɪŋ) *n* 1 the basis or foundation on which something is established 2 the relationship or status existing between two persons, groups, etc 3 a secure grip by or for the feet 4 the lower part of a foundation of a column, wall, building, etc 5 *chiefly US* a the act of adding a column of figures b the total obtained 6 *rare* a fee paid upon entrance into a craft, society, etc, or such an entrance itself

foot-lambert *n* a former unit of luminance equal to the luminance of a surface emitting or reflecting 1 lumen per square foot. A completely reflecting surface illuminated by 1 foot-candle has a luminance of 1 foot-lambert. Abbreviation: **ft-L**

footle ('fuːtᵊl) *informal* ▷ *vb* (*intr*) 1 (often foll by *around* or *about*) to loiter aimlessly; potter 2 to talk nonsense ▷ *n* 3 *rare* foolishness [c19 probably from French *foutre* to copulate with, from Latin *futuere*]

footlights ('fʊt,laɪts) *pl n theatre* 1 lights set in a row along the front of the stage floor and shielded on the audience side 2 *informal* the acting profession; the stage

footling ('fuːtlɪŋ) *adj informal* silly, trivial, or petty

footloose ('fʊt,luːs) *adj* 1 free to go or do as one wishes 2 eager to travel; restless: *to feel footloose*

footman ('fʊtmən) *n, pl* **-men** 1 a male servant, esp one in livery 2 a low four-legged metal stand used in a fireplace for utensils, etc 3 (*formerly*) a foot soldier 4 any of several arctiid moths related to the tiger moths, esp the **common footman** (*Eilema lurideola*), with yellowish hind wings and brown forewings with a yellow front stripe; they produce woolly bear larvae

footmark ('fʊt,mɑːk) *n* a mark or trace of mud, wetness, etc, left by a person's foot on a surface

footnote ('fʊt,nəʊt) *n* 1 a note printed at the bottom of a page, to which attention is drawn by means of a reference mark in the body of the text 2 an additional comment, as to a main statement ▷ *vb* 3 (*tr*) to supply (a page, book, etc) with footnotes

footpace ('fʊt,peɪs) *n* 1 a normal or walking pace 2 Also called (in the Roman Catholic Church): **predella** the platform immediately before an altar at the top of the altar steps

footpad ('fʊt,pæd) *n archaic* a robber or highwayman, on foot rather than horseback

footpath ('fʊt,pɑːθ) *n* 1 a narrow path for walkers only 2 *chiefly Austral and NZ* another word for **pavement**

footplate ('fʊt,pleɪt) *n chiefly Brit* a a platform in the cab of a locomotive on which the crew stand to operate the controls b (*as modifier*): *a footplate man*

foot-pound *n* an fps unit of work or energy equal to the work done when a force of 1 pound moves through a distance of 1 foot. Abbreviation: **ft-lb**

foot-poundal *n* a unit of work or energy equal to the work done when a force of one poundal moves through a distance of one foot: it is equal to 0.042 14 joule

foot-pound-second *n* See **fps units**

footprint ('fʊt,prɪnt) *n* 1 an indentation or outline of the foot of a person or animal on a surface 2 the shape and size of the area something occupies: *enlarging the footprint of the building; a computer with a small footprint* 3 *computing* the amount of resources such as disk space and memory, that an application requires ▷ See also **electronic footprint** 4 an identifying characteristic on land or water, such as the area in which an aircraft's sonic boom can be heard or the area covered by the down-blast of a hovercraft **5** the area in which the signal from a direct broadcasting satellite is receivable

footrest (ˈfʊtˌrɛst) *n* something that provides a support for the feet, such as a low stool, rail, etc

footrope (ˈfʊtˌrəʊp) *n nautical* **1** the part of a boltrope to which the foot of a sail is stitched **2** a rope fixed so as to hang below a yard to serve as a foothold

foot rot *n vet science* See **rot**[1] (sense 11)

foot rule *n* a rigid measure, one foot in length

foots (fʊts) *pl n* (*sometimes singular*) the sediment that accumulates at the bottom of a vessel containing any of certain liquids, such as vegetable oil or varnish; dregs

footsie (ˈfʊtsɪ) *n informal* flirtation involving the touching together of feet, knees, etc (esp in the phrase **play footsie**)

Footsie (ˈfʊtsɪ) *n* an informal name for **Financial Times Stock Exchange 100 Index**

footslog (ˈfʊtˌslɒg) *vb* **-slogs, -slogging, -slogged** (*intr*) to march; tramp > ˈ**foot**ˌ**slogger** *n*

foot soldier *n* an infantryman

footsore (ˈfʊtˌsɔː) *adj* having sore or tired feet, esp from much walking > ˈ**foot**ˌ**soreness** *n*

footstalk (ˈfʊtˌstɔːk) *n* a small supporting stalk in animals and plants; a pedicel, peduncle, or pedicle

footstall (ˈfʊtˌstɔːl) *n* **1** the pedestal, plinth, or base of a column, pier, or statue **2** the stirrup on a sidesaddle

footstep (ˈfʊtˌstɛp) *n* **1** the action of taking a step in walking **2** the sound made by stepping or walking **3** the distance covered with a step; pace **4** a footmark **5** a single stair; step **6** to continue the tradition or example of another

footsteps editor *n Brit films* the technician who adds sound effects, such as doors closing, rain falling, etc, during the postproduction sound-dubbing process. US name: **foley** *or* **foley artist**

footstock (ˈfʊtˌstɒk) *n* another name for **tailstock**

footstool (ˈfʊtˌstuːl) *n* a low stool used for supporting or resting the feet of a seated person

foot-ton *n* a unit of work or energy equal to 2240 foot-pounds

foot traffic *n* **1** the wear and tear caused to a surface by people walking on it **2** *US and Canadian* the activity of pedestrians in a particular area

foot valve *n* **1** another name for **suction valve** **2** a nonreturn valve at the inlet end of a pipe

footwall (ˈfʊtˌwɔːl) *n* the rocks on the lower side of an inclined fault plane or mineral vein. Compare **hanging wall**

footway (ˈfʊtˌweɪ) *n* a way or path for pedestrians, such as a raised walk along the edge of a bridge

footwear (ˈfʊtˌwɛə) *n* anything worn to cover the feet

footwork (ˈfʊtˌwɜːk) *n* **1** skilful use of the feet, as in sports, dancing, etc **2** *informal* clever manoeuvring **3** *informal* preliminary groundwork

footworn (ˈfʊtˌwɔːn) *adj* **1** Also: **footweary** footsore **2** worn away by the feet: *a footworn staircase*

footy *or* **footie** (ˈfʊtɪ) *n informal* **a** football **b** (*as modifier*): *footy boots*

foo yong (ˈfuː ˈjɒŋ), **foo yoong** (ˈfuː ˈjʊŋ) *or* **foo yung, fu yung** (ˈfuː ˈjʌŋ) *n* a Chinese dish made of eggs mixed with chicken, crab meat, etc, and cooked like an omelette [from Chinese *fu yung* hibiscus]

foozle (ˈfuːzᵊl) *Chiefly golf* ▷ *vb* **1** to bungle (a shot) ▷ *n* **2** a bungled shot [c19 perhaps from German dialect *fuseln* to do slipshod work] > ˈ**foozler** *n*

fop (fɒp) *n* a man who is excessively concerned with fashion and elegance [c15 related to German *foppen* to trick; see FOB[2]] > ˈ**foppish** *adj* > ˈ**foppishly** *adv* > ˈ**foppishness** *n*

foppery (ˈfɒpərɪ) *n, pl* **-peries** the clothes, affectations, obsessions, etc, of or befitting a fop

for (fɔː; *unstressed* fə) *prep* **1** intended to reach; directed or belonging to: *there's a phone call for you* **2** to the advantage of: *I only did it for you* **3** in the direction of: *heading for the border* **4** over a span of (time or distance): *working for six days* **5** in favour of; in support of: *those for the proposal* **6** in order to get or achieve: *I do it for money; he does it for pleasure* **7** appropriate to; designed to meet the needs of; meant to be used in: *these kennels are for puppies* **8** in exchange for; at a cost of; to the amount of: *I got it for hardly any money* **9** such as explains or results in: *his reason for changing his job was not given* **10** in place of: *a substitute for the injured player* **11** because of; through: *she wept for pure relief* **12** with regard or consideration to the usual characteristics of: *he's short for a man; it's cool for this time of year* **13** concerning; as regards: *desire for money* **14** as being: *we took him for the owner* **15** at a specified time: *a date for the next evening* **16** to do or partake of: *an appointment for supper* **17** in the duty or task of: *that's for him to say* **18** to allow of: *too big a job for us to handle* **19** despite; notwithstanding: *she's a good wife, for all her nagging* **20** in order to preserve, retain, etc: *to fight for survival* **21** as a direct equivalent to: *word for word* **22** in order to become or enter: *to go for a soldier* **23** in recompense for: *I paid for it last week* **24** **for it** *Brit informal* liable for punishment or blame: *you'll be for it if she catches you* **25** **nothing for it** no choice; no other course ▷ *conj* **26** (*coordinating*) for the following reason; because; seeing that: *I couldn't stay, for the area was violent* [Old English; related to Old Norse *fyr* for, Old High German *fora* before, Latin *per* through, *prō* before, Greek *pro* before, in front]

f.o.r. *or* **FOR** *commerce abbreviation for* free on rail

for- *prefix* **1** indicating rejection or prohibition: *forbear; forbid* **2** indicating falsity or wrongness: *forswear* **3** used to give intensive force: *forgive; forlorn* [Old English *for-*; related to German *ver-*, Latin *per-*, Greek *peri-*]

forage (ˈfɒrɪdʒ) *n* **1** food for horses or cattle, esp hay or straw **2** the act of searching for food or provisions **3** *military* a raid or incursion ▷ *vb* **4** to search (the countryside or a town) for food, provisions, etc **5** (*intr*) *military* to carry out a raid **6** (*tr*) to obtain by searching about **7** (*tr*) to give food or other provisions to **8** (*tr*) to feed (cattle or horses) with such food [c14 from Old French *fourrage*, probably of Germanic origin; see FOOD, FODDER] > ˈ**forager** *n*

forage cap *n* a soldier's undress cap

forage mite *n* a mite normally occurring in forage but sometimes infesting the skin of mammals, esp horses, and birds

foramen (fɒˈreɪmɛn) *n, pl* **-ramina** (-ˈræmɪnə) *or* **-ramens** a natural hole, esp one in a bone through which nerves and blood vessels pass [c17 from Latin, from *forāre* to bore, pierce] > **foraminal** (fɒˈræmɪnᵊl) *adj*

foramen magnum *n* the large opening at the base of the skull through which the spinal cord passes [New Latin: large hole]

foraminifer (ˌfɒrəˈmɪnɪfə) *n* any marine protozoan of the phylum *Foraminifera*, having a shell with numerous openings through which cytoplasmic processes protrude. Often shortened to: **foram** See also **globigerina, nummulite** [c19 from New Latin, from FORAMEN + -FER] > **foraminiferal** (fɒˌræmɪˈnɪfərəl) *or* **fo**ˌ**rami**ˈ**niferous** *adj*

forasmuch as (fərəzˈmʌtʃ) *conj* (*subordinating*) *archaic or legal* seeing that; since

foray (ˈfɒreɪ) *n* **1** a short raid or incursion **2** a first attempt or new undertaking ▷ *vb* **3** to raid or ravage (a town, district, etc) [c14 from *forrayen* to pillage, from Old French *forreier*, from *forrier* forager, from *fuerre* fodder; see FORAGE] > ˈ**forayer** *n*

forb (fɔːb) *n* any herbaceous plant that is not a grass [c20 from Greek *phorbē* food, from *pherbein* to graze]

forbade (fəˈbæd, -ˈbeɪd) *or* **forbad** (fəˈbæd) *vb* the past tense of **forbid**

forbear[1] (fɔːˈbɛə) *vb* **-bears, -bearing, -bore, -borne** **1** (when *intr*, often foll by *from* or an infinitive) to cease or refrain (from doing something) **2** *archaic* to tolerate or endure (misbehaviour, mistakes, etc) [Old English *forberan*; related to Gothic *frabairan* to endure] > **for**ˈ**bearer** *n* > **for**ˈ**bearingly** *adv*

forbear[2] (ˈfɔːˌbɛə) *n* a variant spelling of **forebear**

forbearance (fɔːˈbɛərəns) *n* **1** the act of forbearing **2** self-control; patience **3** *law* abstention from or postponement of the enforcement of a legal right, esp by a creditor allowing his debtor time to pay

forbid (fəˈbɪd) *vb* **-bids, -bidding, -bade** *or* **-bad, -bidden** *or* **-bid** (*tr*) **1** to prohibit (a person) in a forceful or authoritative manner (from doing something or having something) **2** to make impossible; hinder **3** to shut out or exclude **4** **God forbid!** may it not happen [Old English *forbēodan*; related to Old High German *farbiotan*, Gothic *faurbiudan*; see FOR-, BID] > **for**ˈ**biddance** *n* > **for**ˈ**bidder** *n*

forbidden (fəˈbɪdᵊn) *adj* **1** not permitted by order or law **2** *physics* involving a change in quantum numbers that is not permitted by certain rules derived from quantum mechanics, esp rules for changes in the electrical dipole moment of the system

> USAGE It was formerly considered incorrect to talk of *forbidding* someone *from* doing something, but in modern usage either *from* or *to* can be used: *he was forbidden from entering/to enter the building*

forbidden band *n* See **energy band**

Forbidden City *n* **the** **1** Lhasa, Tibet: once famed for its inaccessibility and hostility to strangers **2** a walled section of Beijing, China, enclosing the Imperial Palace and associated buildings of the former Chinese Empire

forbidden fruit *n* any pleasure or enjoyment regarded as illicit, esp sexual indulgence

forbidden transition *n physics* an electronic transition in an atom, molecule, etc, that is not permitted by electric dipole selection rules

forbidding (fəˈbɪdɪŋ) *adj* **1** hostile or unfriendly **2** dangerous or ominous > **for**ˈ**biddingly** *adv* > **for**ˈ**biddingness** *n*

forbore (fɔːˈbɔː) *vb* the past tense of **forbear**

forborne (fɔːˈbɔːn) *vb* the past participle of **forbear**

forby *or* **forbye** (fɔːˈbaɪ; *Scot* fərˈbaɪ) *prep, adv Scot* **1** besides; in addition (to) **2** *obsolete* near; nearby

force[1] (fɔːs) *n* **1** strength or energy; might; power: *the force of the blow* **2** exertion or the use of exertion against a person or thing that resists; coercion **3** *physics* **a** a dynamic influence that changes a body from a state of rest to one of motion or changes its rate of motion. The magnitude of the force is equal to the product of the mass of the body and its acceleration **b** a static influence that produces an elastic strain in a body or system or bears weight. Symbol: F **4** *physics* any operating influence that produces or tends to produce a change in a physical quantity: *electromotive force* **5** **a** intellectual, social, political, or moral influence or strength **b** a person or thing with such influence **6** vehemence or intensity **7** a group of persons organized for military or police functions **8** (*sometimes capital*; preceded by *the*) *informal* the police force **9** a group of persons organized for particular duties or tasks: *a workforce* **10** *criminal law* violence unlawfully committed or threatened **11** *philosophy, logic* that which an expression is normally used to achieve. See **speech act, illocution, perlocution** **12** **in force** **a** (of a law) having legal validity or binding effect **b** in great strength or numbers **13** **join forces** to combine strengths, efforts, etc ▷ *vb* (*tr*) **14** to compel or cause (a person, group, etc) to do something through effort, superior strength, etc; coerce **15** to acquire, secure, or produce through effort, superior strength, etc **16** to propel or drive despite resistance **17** to break down or open (a lock, safe, door, etc) **18** to impose or inflict **19** to cause (plants or farm animals) to grow or fatten artificially at an increased rate **20** to strain or exert to the utmost **21** to rape; ravish **22** *cards* **a** to compel (a player) to trump in order to take a trick **b** to compel a player by the lead of a particular suit to play (a certain card) **c** (in bridge) to induce (a bid) from one's partner by bidding in a certain way **23 force down** to compel an aircraft to land **24 force a smile** to make oneself smile **25 force the pace** to adopt a high speed or rate of procedure [c13 from Old French, from Vulgar Latin *fortia* (unattested), from Latin *fortis* strong] > **'forceable** *adj* > **'forceless** *adj* > **'forcer** *n* > **'forcingly** *adv*

force² (fɔːs) *n* (in northern England) a waterfall [c17 from Old Norse *fors*]

forced (fɔːst) *adj* **1** done because of force; compulsory: *forced labour* **2** false or unnatural **3** due to an emergency or necessity **4** *physics* caused by an external agency > **'forcedly** ('fɔːsɪdlɪ) *adv* > **'forcedness** *n*

forced development *n* the processing of underexposed photographic film to increase the image density

force de frappe (*French* fɔrs də frap) *n* a military strike force, esp the independent nuclear strike force of France [c20 literally: striking force]

forced march *n military* a march in which normal needs are subordinated to the need for speed

forced perspective *n* the use of objects or images that are larger or smaller than they should be, to suggest that they are nearer or further away than they really are

force-feed *vb* -feeds, -feeding, -fed (tr) **1** to force (a person or animal) to eat or swallow food **2** to force (someone) to receive opinions, propaganda, etc ▷ *n* **force feed 3** a method of lubrication in which a pump forces oil into the bearings of an engine, etc

force-field analysis *n* a decision-making technique, often presented graphically, that identifies all the positive and negative forces impinging on a problem

forceful ('fɔːsful) *adj* **1** powerful **2** persuasive or effective > **'forcefully** *adv* > **'forcefulness** *n*

force majeure ('fɔːs mæ'ʒɜː, -'dʒʊə) *n law* irresistible force or compulsion such as will excuse a party from performing his part of a contract [from French: superior force]

forcemeat ('fɔːs,miːt) *n* a mixture of chopped or minced ingredients used for stuffing. Also called: farce, farcemeat [c17 from *force* (see FARCE) + MEAT]

forceps ('fɔːsɪps) *n, pl* -ceps *or* -cipes (-sɪ,piːz) **1 a** a surgical instrument in the form of a pair of pincers, used esp in the delivery of babies **b** (*as modifier*): *a forceps baby* **2** any pincer-like instrument **3** any part or structure of an organism shaped like a forceps [c17 from Latin, from *formus* hot + *capere* to seize] > **'forceps-like** *adj*

force pump *n* a pump that ejects fluid under pressure. Compare **lift pump**

force-ripe *Caribbean* ▷ *adj* **1** (of fruit) prematurely picked and ripened by squeezing or warm storage **2** precocious, esp sexually ▷ *vb* **3** (tr) to ripen (prematurely picked fruit) by squeezing or warm storage

Forces ('fɔːsɪz) *pl n* (usually preceded by *the*) the armed services of a nation

forcible ('fɔːsəbᵊl) *adj* **1** done by, involving, or having force **2** convincing or effective: *a forcible argument* > **'forcibleness** *or* ,forci'bility *n* > **'forcibly** *adv*

forcing bid *n contract bridge* a bid, often at a higher level than is required, that is understood to oblige the bidder's partner to reply

forcing frequency *n physics* the frequency of an oscillating force applied to a system. Compare **natural frequency**

forcing house *n* a place where growth or maturity (as of fruit, animals, etc) is artificially hastened

ford (fɔːd) *n* **1** a shallow area in a river that can be crossed by car, horseback, etc ▷ *vb* **2** (tr) to cross (a river, brook, etc) over a shallow area [Old English; related to Old Frisian *forda*, Old High German *furt* ford, Latin *porta* door, *portus* PORT¹] > **'fordable** *adj*

fordo *or* **foredo** (fɔː'duː) *vb* -does, -doing, -did, -done (tr) *archaic* **1** to destroy **2** to exhaust [Old English *fordōn*; related to Old Saxon *fardōn*, Old High German *fartuon*, Dutch *verdoen*; see FOR-, DO¹]

fore¹ (fɔː) *adj* **1** (*usually in combination*) located at, in, or towards the front: *the forelegs of a horse* ▷ *n* **2** the front part **3** something located at, in, or towards the front **4** short for **foremast 5 fore and aft** located at or directed towards both ends of a vessel: *a fore-and-aft rig* **6 to the fore a** to or into the front or conspicuous position **b** *Scot and Irish* alive or active: *is your grandfather still to the fore?* ▷ *adv* **7** at or towards a ship's bow **8** *obsolete* before ▷ *prep* ▷ *conj* **9** a less common word for **before** [Old English; related to Old Saxon, Old High German *fora*, Gothic *faura*, Greek *para*, Sanskrit *pura*]

fore² (fɔː) *interj* (in golf) a warning shout made by a player about to make a shot [c19 probably short for BEFORE]

fore- *prefix* **1** before in time or rank: *foresight; forefather* **2** at or near the front; before in place: *forehead* [Old English, from *fore* (adv)]

fore-and-after *n nautical* **1** any vessel with a fore-and-aft rig **2** a double-ended vessel

forearm¹ ('fɔːr,ɑːm) *n* the part of the arm from the elbow to the wrist. Related adjs: **cubital, radial** [c18 from FORE- + ARM¹]

forearm² (fɔːr'ɑːm) *vb* (tr) to prepare or arm (someone, esp oneself) in advance [c16 from FORE- + ARM²]

forearm smash ('fɔːr,ɑːm) *n* a blow like a punch delivered with the forearm in certain types of wrestling

forebear *or* **forbear** ('fɔː,bɛə) *n* an ancestor; forefather

forebode (fɔː'bəʊd) *vb* **1** to warn of or indicate (an event, result, etc) in advance **2** to have an intuition or premonition of (an event) > **fore'boder** *n*

foreboding (fɔː'bəʊdɪŋ) *n* **1** a feeling of impending evil, disaster, etc **2** an omen or portent ▷ *adj* **3** presaging something > **fore'bodingly** *adv* > **fore'bodingness** *n*

forebrain ('fɔː,breɪn) *n* the nontechnical name for **prosencephalon**

forecast ('fɔː,kɑːst) *vb* -casts, -casting, -cast *or* -casted **1** to predict or calculate (weather, events, etc), in advance **2** (tr) to serve as an early indication of **3** (tr) to plan in advance ▷ *n* **4** a statement of probable future weather conditions calculated from meteorological data **5** a prophecy or prediction **6** the practice or power of forecasting > **'fore,caster** *n*

forecastle, fo'c's'le *or* **fo'c'sle** ('fəʊksᵊl) *n* the part of a vessel at the bow where the crew is quartered and stores, machines, etc, may be stowed

foreclose (fɔː'kləʊz) *vb* **1** *law* to deprive (a mortgagor, etc) of the right to redeem (a mortgage or pledge) **2** (tr) to shut out; bar **3** (tr) to prevent or hinder **4** (tr) to answer or settle (an obligation, promise, etc) in advance **5** (tr) to make an exclusive claim to [c15 from Old French *forclore*, from *for-* out + *clore* to close, from Latin *claudere*] > **fore'closable** *adj* > **foreclosure** (fɔː'kləʊʒə) *n*

forecourse ('fɔː,kɔːs) *n nautical* the lowest foresail on a square-rigged vessel

forecourt ('fɔː,kɔːt) *n* **1** a courtyard in front of a building, as one in a filling station **2** Also called: **front court** the front section of the court in tennis, badminton, etc, esp the area between the service line and the net

foredeck ('fɔː,dɛk) *n nautical* the deck between the bridge and the forecastle

foredo (fɔː'duː) *vb* -does, -doing, -did, -done (tr) a variant spelling of **fordo**

foredoom (fɔː'duːm) *vb* (tr) to doom or condemn beforehand

fore-edge *n* the outer edge of the pages of a book

forefather ('fɔː,fɑːðə) *n* an ancestor, esp a male > **'fore,fatherly** *adj*

forefend (fɔː'fɛnd) *vb* (tr) a variant spelling of **forfend**

forefinger ('fɔː,fɪŋgə) *n* the finger next to the thumb. Also called: index finger

forefoot ('fɔː,fʊt) *n, pl* -feet **1** either of the front feet of a quadruped **2** *nautical* the forward end of the keel

forefront ('fɔː,frʌnt) *n* **1** the extreme front **2** the position of most prominence, responsibility, or action

foregather *or* **forgather** (fɔː'gæðə) *vb* (intr) **1** to gather together; assemble **2** *rare* to meet, esp unexpectedly **3** (foll by *with*) to socialize

forego¹ (fɔː'gəʊ) *vb* -goes, -going, -went, -gone to precede in time, place, etc [Old English *foregān*] > **fore'goer** *n*

forego² (fɔː'gəʊ) *vb* -goes, -going, -went, -gone (tr) a variant spelling of **forgo**. > **fore'goer** *n*

foregoing (fɔː'gəʊɪŋ) *adj* (*prenominal*) (esp of writing or speech) going before; preceding

foregone (fɔː'gɒn, 'fɔː,gɒn) *adj* gone or completed; past > **fore'goneness** *n*

foregone conclusion *n* an inevitable result or conclusion

foreground ('fɔː,graʊnd) *n* **1** the part of a scene situated towards the front or nearest to the viewer **2** the area of space in a perspective picture, depicted as nearest the viewer **3** a conspicuous or active position ▷ *vb* **4** (tr) to emphasize (an issue, idea, or word)

foregut ('fɔː,gʌt) *n* **1** the anterior part of the digestive tract of vertebrates, between the buccal cavity and the bile duct **2** the anterior part of the digestive tract of arthropods ▷ See also **midgut, hindgut**

forehand ('fɔː,hænd) *adj* (*prenominal*) **1** *sport* **a** (of a stroke) made with the racket held so that the wrist is facing the direction of the stroke **b** of or relating to the right side of a right-handed player or the left side of a left-handed player **2** foremost or paramount **3** done or given beforehand ▷ *n* **4** *sport* **a** a forehand stroke **b** the side on which such strokes are made **5** the part of a horse in front of the saddle **6** a frontal position ▷ *adv* **7** *sport* with a forehand stroke ▷ *vb* **8** *sport* to play (a shot) forehand

forehanded (,fɔː'hændɪd) *adj* **1** *US* **a** thrifty **b** well-off ▷ *adv* ▷ *adj* **2** *sport* a less common word for **forehand.** > **fore'handedly** *adv* > **fore'handedness** *n*

forehead ('fɒrɪd, 'fɔː,hɛd) *n* the part of the face between the natural hairline and the eyes, formed skeletally by the frontal bone of the skull; brow. Related adj: **frontal** [Old English *forhēafod*; related to Old Frisian *forhāfd*, Middle Low German *vorhōved*]

forehock ('fɔː,hɒk) *n* a foreleg cut of bacon or pork

foreign ('fɒrɪn) *adj* **1** of, involving, located in, or coming from another country, area, people, etc: *a foreign resident* **2** dealing or concerned with another country, area, people, etc **3** not pertinent or related **4** not familiar; strange **5** in an abnormal place or position: *foreign bodies* **6** *law* outside the jurisdiction of a particular state; alien [c13 from Old French *forain*, from Vulgar Latin *forānus* (unattested) situated on the outside, from Latin *foris* outside] > **'foreignly** *adv* > **'foreignness** *n*

foreign affairs *pl n* **1** matters abroad that involve the homeland, such as relations with another country **2** matters that do not involve the homeland

foreign aid *n* economic and other assistance given by one country to another

foreign bill *or* **draft** *n* a bill of exchange that is drawn in one country and made payable in another: used extensively in foreign trade. Compare **inland bill**

f

foreign correspondent n *journalism* a reporter who visits or resides in a foreign country in order to report on its affairs

foreigner ('fɒrɪnə) n **1** a person from a foreign country; alien **2** an outsider or interloper **3** something from a foreign country, such as a ship or product

foreign exchange n **1** the system by which one currency is converted into another, enabling international transactions to take place without the physical transportation of gold **2** foreign bills and currencies

foreignism ('fɒrɪˌnɪzəm) n **1** a custom, mannerism, idiom, etc, that is foreign **2** imitation of something foreign

foreign legion n a body of foreign volunteers serving in an army, esp that of France

foreign minister or **secretary** n (often capitals) a cabinet minister who is responsible for a country's dealings with other countries. US equivalent: **secretary of state** > **foreign ministry** n

foreign mission n **1** a body of persons sent to a non-Christian country in order to propagate Christianity **2** a diplomatic or other mission sent by one country to another

foreign office n the ministry of a country or state that is concerned with dealings with other states. US equivalent: **State Department** Canadian equivalent: **(department of) external affairs**

foreign service n *chiefly US* the diplomatic and usually consular personnel of a foreign affairs ministry or foreign office collectively who represent their country abroad, deal with foreign diplomats at home, etc

forejudge[1] (fɔːˈdʒʌdʒ) vb to judge (someone or an event, circumstance, etc) before the facts are known; prejudge

forejudge[2] (fɔːˈdʒʌdʒ) vb *law* a variant spelling of **forjudge**. > **fore'judgment** n

foreknow (fɔːˈnəʊ) vb **-knows, -knowing, -knew, -known** (tr) to know in advance > **fore'knowable** adj > **fore'knowledge** n > **fore'knowingly** adv

foreland ('fɔːlənd) n **1** a headland, cape, or coastal promontory **2** land lying in front of something, such as water

Foreland ('fɔːlənd) n either of two headlands (**North Foreland** and **South Foreland**) in SE England, on the coast of Kent

foreleg ('fɔːˌlɛg) n either of the front legs of a horse, sheep, or other quadruped

forelimb ('fɔːˌlɪm) n either of the front or anterior limbs of a four-limbed vertebrate: a foreleg, flipper, or wing

forelock[1] ('fɔːˌlɒk) n **1** a lock of hair growing or falling over the forehead **2** a lock of a horse's mane that grows forwards between the ears

forelock[2] ('fɔːˌlɒk) n **1** a wedge or peg passed through the tip of a bolt to prevent withdrawal ▷ vb **2** (tr) to secure (a bolt) by means of a forelock

foreman ('fɔːmən) n, pl **-men 1** a person, often experienced, who supervises other workmen. Female equivalent: **forewoman 2** *law* the principal juror, who presides at the deliberations of a jury > **'foreman,ship** n

foremast ('fɔːˌmɑːst; *nautical* 'fɔːməst) n the mast nearest the bow on vessels with two or more masts

foremilk ('fɔːˌmɪlk) n **1** another word for **colostrum 2** the first milk drawn from a cow's udder prior to milking

foremost ('fɔːˌməʊst) adj, adv first in time, place, rank, etc [Old English *formest*, from *forma* first; related to Old Saxon *formo* first, Old High German *fruma* advantage]

foremother ('fɔːˌmʌðə) n a female ancestor

forename ('fɔːˌneɪm) n a first or Christian name

forenamed ('fɔːˌneɪmd) adj (prenominal) named or mentioned previously; aforesaid

forenoon ('fɔːˌnuːn) n **a** the daylight hours before or just before noon **b** (as modifier): a forenoon conference

forensic (fəˈrɛnsɪk) adj relating to, used in, or connected with a court of law: forensic science [c17 from Latin *forēnsis* public, from FORUM] > **forensicality** (fəˌrɛnsɪˈkælɪtɪ) n > **fo'rensically** adv

forensic accountant n an accountant who specializes in applying accountancy skills to the purposes of the law

forensic medicine n the applied use of medical knowledge or practice, esp pathology, to the purposes of the law, as in determining the cause of death. Also called: **medical jurisprudence, legal medicine**

forensics (fəˈrɛnsɪks) n (functioning as singular or plural) the art or study of formal debating

foreordain (ˌfɔːrɔːˈdeɪn) vb (tr; may take a clause as object) to determine (events, results, etc) in the future > **foreor'dainment** or **foreordination** (ˌfɔːrɔːdɪˈneɪʃən) n

forepart ('fɔːˌpɑːt) n the first or front part in place, order, or time

forepaw ('fɔːˌpɔː) n either of the front feet of most land mammals that do not have hoofs

forepeak ('fɔːˌpiːk) n *nautical* the interior part of a vessel that is furthest forward

foreplay ('fɔːˌpleɪ) n mutual sexual stimulation preceding sexual intercourse

forequarter ('fɔːˌkwɔːtə) n the front portion, including the leg, of half of a carcass, as of beef or lamb

forequarters ('fɔːˌkwɔːtəz) pl n the part of the body of a horse or similar quadruped that consists of the forelegs, shoulders, and adjoining parts

forereach (fɔːˈriːtʃ) vb **1** (intr) *nautical* to keep moving under momentum without engine or sails **2** (tr) to surpass or outdo

forerun (fɔːˈrʌn) vb **-runs, -running, -ran, -run** (tr) **1** to serve as a herald for **2** to go before; precede **3** to prevent or forestall

forerunner ('fɔːˌrʌnə) n **1** a person or thing that precedes another; precursor **2** a person or thing coming in advance to herald the arrival of someone or something; harbinger **3** an indication beforehand of something to follow; omen; portent

foresaid ('fɔːˌsɛd) adj a less common word for **aforesaid**

foresail ('fɔːˌseɪl; *nautical* 'fɔːsəl) n *nautical* **1** the aftermost headsail of a fore-and-aft rigged vessel **2** the lowest sail set on the foremast of a square-rigged vessel

foresee (fɔːˈsiː) vb **-sees, -seeing, -saw, -seen** (tr; may take a clause as object) to see or know beforehand > **fore'seeable** adj > **fore'seer** n

foreshadow (fɔːˈʃædəʊ) vb (tr) to show, indicate, or suggest in advance; presage > **fore'shadower** n

foreshank ('fɔːˌʃæŋk) n **1** the top of the front leg of an animal **2** a cut of meat from this part

foresheet ('fɔːˌʃiːt) n **1** the sheet of a foresail **2** (plural) the part forward of the foremost thwart of a boat

foreshock ('fɔːˌʃɒk) n a relatively small earthquake heralding the arrival of a much larger one. Some large earthquakes are preceded by a series of foreshocks. Compare **aftershock**

foreshore ('fɔːˌʃɔː) n **1** the part of the shore that lies between the limits for high and low tides **2** the part of the shore that lies just above the high-water mark

foreshorten (fɔːˈʃɔːtən) vb (tr) **1** to represent (a line, form, object, etc) as shorter than actual length in order to give an illusion of recession or projection, in accordance with the laws of linear perspective **2** to make shorter or more condensed; reduce or abridge

foreshow (fɔːˈʃəʊ) vb **-shows, -showing, -showed, -shown** (tr) *archaic* to indicate in advance; foreshadow

foreside (fɔːˈsaɪd) n **1** the front or upper side or part **2** *US* land extending along the sea

foresight ('fɔːˌsaɪt) n **1** provision for or insight into future problems, needs, etc **2** the act or ability of foreseeing **3** the act of looking forward **4** *surveying* a reading taken looking forwards to a new station, esp in levelling from a point of known elevation to a point the elevation of which is to be determined. Compare **backsight 5** the front sight on a firearm > **ˌfore'sighted** adj > **ˌfore'sightedly** adv > **ˌfore'sightedness** n

foreskin ('fɔːˌskɪn) n *anatomy* the nontechnical name for **prepuce** (sense 1) Related adj: **preputial**

forespeak (fɔːˈspiːk) vb **-speaks, -speaking, -spoke, -spoken** (tr) *rare* **1** to predict; foresee **2** to arrange or speak of in advance

forespent (fɔːˈspɛnt) adj a variant spelling of **forspent**

forest ('fɒrɪst) n **1** a large wooded area having a thick growth of trees and plants **2** the trees of such an area **3** NZ an area planted with exotic pines or similar trees. Compare **bush**[1] (sense 4) **4** something resembling a large wooded area, esp in density: a forest of telegraph poles **5** *law* (formerly) an area of woodland, esp one owned by the sovereign and set apart as a hunting ground with its own laws and officers. Compare **park** (sense 5) **6** (modifier) of, involving, or living in a forest or forests: a forest glade ▷ vb **7** (tr) to create a forest (in); plant with trees [c13 from Old French, from Medieval Latin *forestis* unfenced woodland, from Latin *foris* outside] > **'forestal** or **foresteal** (fəˈrɛstəl) adj > **'forested** adj > **'forestless** adj > **'forest-ˌlike** adj

forestall (fɔːˈstɔːl) vb (tr) **1** to delay, stop, or guard against beforehand **2** to anticipate **3 a** to prevent or hinder sales at (a market, etc) by buying up merchandise in advance, etc **b** to buy up (merchandise) for profitable resale. Compare **corner** (sense 21) [c14 forestallen to waylay, from Old English foresteall an ambush, from fore- in front of + steall place] > **fore'staller** n > **fore'stalment** or esp US **fore'stallment** n

forestation (ˌfɒrɪˈsteɪʃən) n the planting of trees over a wide area

forestay ('fɔːˌsteɪ) n *nautical* an adjustable stay leading from the truck of the foremast to the deck, stem, or bowsprit, for controlling the motion or bending of the mast

forestaysail (fɔːˈsteɪˌseɪl; *nautical* fɔːˈsteɪsʲl) n *nautical* the triangular headsail set aftermost on a vessel

forester ('fɒrɪstə) n **1** a person skilled in forestry or in charge of a forest **2** any of various Old World moths of the genus Ino, characterized by brilliant metallic green wings: family Zygaenidae **3** a person or animal that lives in a forest **4** (capital) a member of the Ancient Order of Foresters, a friendly society

forest park n NZ a recreational reserve which may include bush and exotic trees

forest ranger n *chiefly US and Canadian* a government official who patrols and protects forests, wildlife, etc

forestry ('fɒrɪstrɪ) n **1** the science of planting and caring for trees **2** the planting and management of forests **3** *rare* forest land

foretaste n ('fɔːˌteɪst) **1** an early but limited experience or awareness of something to come ▷ vb (fɔːˈteɪst) **2** (tr) to have a foretaste of

foretell (fɔːˈtɛl) vb **-tells, -telling, -told** (tr; may take a clause as object) to tell or indicate (an event, a result, etc) beforehand; predict > **fore'teller** n

forethought ('fɔːˌθɔːt) n **1** advance consideration or deliberation **2** thoughtful anticipation of future events > **fore'thoughtful** adj > **fore'thoughtfully** adv > **fore'thoughtfulness** n

foretime ('fɔːˌtaɪm) n time already gone; the past

foretoken n ('fɔːˌtəʊkən) **1** a sign of a future event ▷ vb (fɔːˈtəʊkən) **2** (tr) to foreshadow

foretooth ('fɔːˌtuːθ) n, pl **-teeth** (-ˌtiːθ) *dentistry* another word for an **incisor**

foretop ('fɔːˌtɒp; *nautical* 'fɔːtəp) n *nautical* a platform at the top of the foremast

fore-topgallant (ˌfɔːtɒpˈgælənt; *nautical* ˌfɔːtəˈgælənt) adj *nautical* of, relating to, or being the topmost portion of a foremast, above the topmast: the fore-topgallant mast

fore-topmast (fɔːˈtɒpˌmɑːst; *nautical* fɔːˈtɒpməst)

n nautical a mast stepped above a foremast
fore-topsail (fɔːˈtɒpˌseɪl; *nautical* fɔːˈtɒpsᵊl) *n nautical* a sail set on a fore-topmast
foretriangle (ˈfɔːtraɪˌæŋgᵊl) *n* the triangular area formed by the deck, foremast, and headstay of a sailing vessel
4EVA *abbreviation for text messaging* for ever
forever (fɔːˈrɛvə, fə-) *adv* **1** Also: **for ever** without end; everlastingly; eternally **2** at all times; incessantly **3** *informal* for a very long time ▷ *n* **4** (*as object*) *informal* a very long time **5** ...**forever!** an exclamation expressing support or loyalty

USAGE *Forever* and *for ever* can both be used to say that something is without end. For all other meanings, *forever* is the preferred form

for evermore *or* **forevermore** (fɔːˌrɛvəˈmɔː, fə-) *adv* a more emphatic or emotive term for **forever**
forewarn (fɔːˈwɔːn) *vb* (*tr*) to warn beforehand > foreˈ**warner** *n* > foreˈ**warningly** *adv*
forewent (fɔːˈwɛnt) *vb* the past tense of **forego**
forewind (ˈfɔːˌwɪnd) *n nautical* a favourable wind
forewing (ˈfɔːˌwɪŋ) *n* either wing of the anterior pair of an insect's two pairs of wings
foreword (ˈfɔːˌwɜːd) *n* an introductory statement to a book [C19 literal translation of German *Vorwort*]
foreworn (fɔːˈwɔːn) *adj* a variant spelling of **forworn**
forex (ˈfɒrɛks) *n* short for **foreign exchange**
foreyard (ˈfɔːˌjɑːd) *n nautical* a yard for supporting the foresail of a square-rigger
forfaiting (ˈfɔːˌfeɪtɪŋ) *n* the financial service of discounting, without recourse, a promissory note, bill of exchange, letter of credit, etc, received from an overseas buyer by an exporter; a form of debt discounting [C20 from French *forfaire* to forfeit or surrender]
Forfar (ˈfɔːfər, -fɑː) *n* a market town in E Scotland, the administrative centre of Angus: site of a castle, residence of Scottish kings between the 11th and 14th centuries. Pop: 13 206 (2001)
forfeit (ˈfɔːfɪt) *n* **1** something lost or given up as a penalty for a fault, mistake, etc **2** the act of losing or surrendering something in this manner **3** *law* something confiscated as a penalty for an offence, breach of contract, etc **4** (*sometimes plural*) **a** a game in which a player has to give up an object, perform a specified action, etc, if he commits a fault **b** an object so given up ▷ *vb* **5** (*tr*) to lose or be liable to lose in consequence of a mistake, fault, etc **6** (*tr*) *law* **a** to confiscate as punishment **b** to surrender (something exacted as a penalty) ▷ *adj* **7** surrendered or liable to be surrendered as a penalty [C13 from Old French *forfet* offence, from *forfaire* to commit a crime, from Medieval Latin *foris facere* to act outside (what is lawful), from Latin *foris* outside + *facere* to do] > ˈ**forfeitable** *adj* > ˈ**forfeiter** *n*
forfeiture (ˈfɔːfɪtʃə) *n* **1** something forfeited **2** the act of forfeiting or paying a penalty
forfend *or* **forefend** (fɔːˈfɛnd) *vb* (*tr*) **1** *US* to protect or secure **2** *obsolete* to prohibit or prevent
forfex (ˈfɔːfɛks) *n entomol* a pair of pincers, esp the paired terminal appendages of an earwig [C18 Latin: a pair of scissors]
forficate (ˈfɔːfɪkɪt, -ˌkeɪt) *adj* (esp of the tails of certain birds) deeply forked [C19 from Latin *forfex* scissors]
forfochen (fərˈfoxᵊn) *adj Scot* exhausted [a variant of earlier *forfoughten* worn out by fighting]
forgat (fəˈgæt) *vb archaic* a past tense of **forget**
forgather (fɔːˈgæðə) *vb* a variant spelling of **foregather**
forgave (fəˈgeɪv) *vb* the past tense of **forgive**
forge[1] (fɔːdʒ) *n* **1** a place in which metal is worked by heating and hammering; smithy **2** a hearth or furnace used for heating metal **3** a machine used to shape metals by hammering ▷ *vb* **4** (*tr*) to shape (metal) by heating and hammering **5** (*tr*) to form, shape, make, or fashion (objects, articles, etc) **6** (*tr*) to invent or devise (an agreement, understanding, etc) **7** to make or produce a fraudulent imitation of (a signature, banknote, etc) or to commit forgery [C14 from Old French *forgier* to construct, from Latin *fabricāre*, from *faber* craftsman] > ˈ**forgeable** *adj* > ˈ**forger** *n*
forge[2] (fɔːdʒ) *vb* (*intr*) **1** to move at a steady and persevering pace **2** to increase speed; spurt [C17 of unknown origin]
forgery (ˈfɔːdʒərɪ) *n, pl* **-geries 1** the act of reproducing something for a deceitful or fraudulent purpose **2** something forged, such as a work of art or an antique **3** *criminal law* **a** the false making or altering of any document, such as a cheque or character reference (and including a postage stamp), or any tape or disc on which information is stored, intending that anyone shall accept it as genuine and so act to his or another's prejudice **b** something forged **4** *criminal law* the counterfeiting of a seal or die with intention to defraud
forget (fəˈgɛt) *vb* **-gets, -getting, -got, -gotten** *or archaic or dialect* **-got 1** (*when tr, may take a clause as object or an infinitive*) to fail to recall (someone or something once known); be unable to remember **2** (*tr; may take a clause as object or an infinitive*) to neglect, usually as the result of an unintentional error **3** (*tr*) to leave behind by mistake **4** (*tr*) to disregard intentionally **5** (*when tr, may take a clause as object*) to fail to mention **6 forget oneself a** to act in an improper manner **b** to be unselfish **c** to be deep in thought **7 forget it!** an exclamation of annoyed or forgiving dismissal of a matter or topic [Old English *forgietan*; related to Old Frisian *forgeta*, Old Saxon *fargetan*, Old High German *firgezzan*] > forˈ**gettable** *adj* > forˈ**getter** *n*
forgetful (fəˈgɛtfʊl) *adj* **1** tending to forget **2** (*often postpositive; foll by of*) inattentive (to) or neglectful (of) **3** *poetic* causing loss of memory > forˈ**getfully** *adv* > forˈ**getfulness** *n*
forget-me-not *n* any temperate low-growing plant of the mainly European boraginaceous genus *Myosotis*, having clusters of small typically blue flowers. Also called: **scorpion grass**
forging (ˈfɔːdʒɪŋ) *n* **1** the process of producing a metal component by hammering **2** the act of a forger **3** a metal component produced by this process **4** the collision of a horse's hind shoe and fore shoe
forgive (fəˈgɪv) *vb* **-gives, -giving, -gave, -given 1** to cease to blame or hold resentment against (someone or something) **2** to grant pardon for (a mistake, wrongdoing, etc) **3** (*tr*) to free or pardon (someone) from penalty **4** (*tr*) to free from the obligation of (a debt, payment, etc) [Old English *forgiefan*; see FOR-, GIVE] > forˈ**givable** *adj* > forˈ**givably** *adv* > forˈ**giver** *n*
forgiveness (fəˈgɪvnɪs) *n* **1** the act of forgiving or the state of being forgiven **2** willingness to forgive
forgiving (fəˈgɪvɪŋ) *adj* willing to forgive; merciful > forˈ**givingly** *adv* > forˈ**givingness** *n*
forgo *or* **forego** (fɔːˈgəʊ) *vb* **-goes, -going, -went, -gone** (*tr*) **1** to give up or do without **2** *archaic* to leave [Old English *forgān*; see FOR-, GO[1]] > forˈ**goer** *or* foreˈ**goer** *n*
forgot (fəˈgɒt) *vb* **1** the past tense of **forget 2** *archaic or dialect* a past participle of **forget**
forgotten (fəˈgɒtᵊn) *vb* a past participle of **forget**
forint (*Hungarian* ˈforint) *n* the standard monetary unit of Hungary, divided into 100 fillér [from Hungarian, from Italian *fiorino* FLORIN]
forjudge *or* **forejudge** (fɔːˈdʒʌdʒ) *vb* (*tr*) *law* **1** to deprive of a right by the judgment of a court **2** *chiefly US* to expel (an officer or attorney) from court for misconduct > forˈ**judgment** *or* foreˈ**judgment** *n*
fork (fɔːk) *n* **1** a small usually metal implement consisting of two, three, or four long thin prongs on the end of a handle, used for lifting food to the mouth or turning it in cooking, etc **2** an agricultural tool consisting of a handle and three or four metal prongs, used for lifting, digging, etc **3** a pronged part of any machine, device, etc **4** (of a road, river, etc) **a** a division into two or more branches **b** the point where the division begins **c** such a branch **5** *chiefly US* the main tributary of a river **6** *chess* a position in which two pieces are forked ▷ *vb* **7** (*tr*) to pick up, dig, etc, with a fork **8** (*tr*) *chess* to place (two enemy pieces) under attack with one of one's own pieces, esp a knight **9** (*tr*) to make into the shape of a fork **10** (*intr*) to be divided into two or more branches **11** to take one or other branch at a fork in a road, river, etc [Old English *forca*, from Latin *furca*] > ˈ**forkful** *n*
forked (fɔːkt, ˈfɔːkɪd) *adj* **1 a** having a fork or forklike parts **b** (*in combination*): *two-forked* **2** having sharp angles; zigzag **3** insincere or equivocal (esp in the phrase **forked tongue**) > **forkedly** (ˈfɔːkɪdlɪ) *adv* > ˈ**forkedness** *n*
forked lightning *n* a zigzag form of lightning. Also called: **chain lightning**
fork-lift truck *n* a vehicle having two power-operated horizontal prongs that can be raised and lowered for loading, transporting, and unloading goods, esp goods that are stacked on wooden pallets. Sometimes shortened to: **forklift**
fork out, over *or* **up** *vb* (*adverb*) *slang* to pay (money, goods, etc), esp with reluctance
Forlì (*Italian* forˈli) *n* a city in N Italy, in Emilia-Romagna. Pop: 108 335 (2001). Ancient name: **Forum Livii** (ˈlɪvɪaɪ)
forlorn (fəˈlɔːn) *adj* **1** miserable, wretched, or cheerless; desolate **2** deserted; forsaken **3** (*postpositive; foll by of*) destitute; bereft: *forlorn of hope* **4** desperate: *the last forlorn attempt* [Old English *forloren* lost, from *forlēosan* to lose; related to Old Saxon *farliosan*, Gothic *fraliusan*, Greek *luein* to release] > forˈ**lornly** *adv* > forˈ**lornness** *n*
forlorn hope *n* **1** a hopeless or desperate enterprise **2** a faint hope **3** *obsolete* a group of soldiers assigned to an extremely dangerous duty [C16 (in the obsolete sense): changed (by folk etymology) from Dutch *verloren hoop* lost troop, from *verloren*, past participle of *verliezen* to lose + *hoop* troop (literally: heap)]
form (fɔːm) *n* **1** the shape or configuration of something as distinct from its colour, texture, etc **2** the particular mode, appearance, etc, in which a thing or person manifests itself **3** a type or kind **4 a** a printed document, esp one with spaces in which to insert facts or answers **b** (*as modifier*): *a form letter* **5** physical or mental condition, esp good condition, with reference to ability to perform: *off form* **6** the previous record of a horse, athlete, etc, esp with regard to fitness **7** *Brit slang* a criminal record **8** style, arrangement, or design in the arts, as opposed to content **9** a fixed mode of artistic expression or representation in literary, musical, or other artistic works **10** a mould, frame, etc, that gives shape to something **11** organized structure or order, as in an artistic work **12** *education, chiefly Brit* a group of children who are taught together; class **13** manner, method, or style of doing something, esp with regard to recognized standards **14** behaviour or procedure, esp as governed by custom or etiquette: *good form* **15** formality or ceremony **16** a prescribed set or order of words, terms, etc, as in a religious ceremony or legal document **17** *philosophy* **a** the structure of anything as opposed to its constitution or content **b** essence as opposed to matter **c** (*often capital*) (in the philosophy of Plato) the ideal universal that exists independently of the particulars which fall under it. See also **Form d** (in the philosophy of Aristotle) the constitution of matter to form a substance; by virtue of this its nature can be understood **18** See **logical form 19** *Brit* a bench, esp one that is long, low, and backless **20** the nest or hollow in which a hare lives **21** a group of organisms within a species that differ from similar groups by trivial differences, as of colour **22** *linguistics* **a** the phonological or orthographic shape or appearance of a linguistic element, such as a word **b** a

f

linguistic element considered from the point of view of its shape or sound rather than, for example, its meaning **23** *crystallog* See **crystal form 24** *taxonomy* a group distinguished from other groups by a single characteristic: ranked below a variety ▷ *vb* **25** to give shape or form to or to take shape or form, esp a specified or particular shape **26** to come or bring into existence **27** to make, produce, or construct or be made, produced, or constructed **28** to construct or develop in the mind **29** (*tr*) to train, develop, or mould by instruction, discipline, or example **30** (*tr*) to acquire, contract, or develop: *to form a habit* **31** (*tr*) to be an element of, serve as, or constitute **32** (*tr*) to draw up; organize: *to form a club* [c13 from Old French *forme*, from Latin *forma* shape, model] ▷ ˈformable *adj*

Form (fɔːm) *n* (in the philosophy of Plato) an ideal archetype existing independently of those individuals which fall under it, supposedly explaining their common properties and serving as the only objects of true knowledge as opposed to the mere opinion obtainable of matters of fact. Also called: **Idea**

-form *adj combining form* having the shape or form of or resembling: *cruciform; vermiform* [from New Latin *-formis*, from Latin, from *fōrma* FORM]

formal¹ (ˈfɔːməl) *adj* **1** of, according to, or following established or prescribed forms, conventions, etc **2** characterized by observation of conventional forms of ceremony, behaviour, dress, etc: *a formal dinner* **3** methodical, precise, or stiff **4** suitable for occasions organized according to conventional ceremony **5** denoting or characterized by idiom, vocabulary, etc, used by educated speakers and writers of a language **6** acquired by study in academic institutions **7** regular or symmetrical in form **8** of or relating to the appearance, form, etc, of something as distinguished from its substance **9** logically deductive **10** *philosophy* **a** of or relating to form as opposed to matter or content **b** pertaining to the essence or nature of something **c** (in the writings of Descartes) pertaining to the correspondence between an image or idea and its object **d** being in the formal mode **11** denoting a second-person pronoun in some languages used when the addressee is a stranger, social superior, etc: *in French the pronoun "vous" is formal, while "tu" is informal* [c14 from Latin *formālis*] ▷ ˈformally *adv* ▷ ˈformalness *n*

formal² (ˈfɔːmæl) *n* another name for **methylal** [c19 from FORM(IC) + -AL³]

formaldehyde (fɔːˈmældɪˌhaɪd) *n* a colourless poisonous irritating gas with a pungent characteristic odour, made by the oxidation of methanol and used as formalin and in the manufacture of synthetic resins. Formula: HCHO. Systematic name: **methanal** [c19 FORM(IC) + ALDEHYDE; on the model of German *Formaldehyd*]

formal equivalence *n logic* the relation that holds between two open sentences when their universal closures are materially equivalent

formalin (ˈfɔːməlɪn) *or* **formol** (ˈfɔːmɒl) *n* a 40 per cent solution of formaldehyde in water, used as a disinfectant, preservative for biological specimens, etc

formalism (ˈfɔːməˌlɪzəm) *n* **1** scrupulous or excessive adherence to outward form at the expense of inner reality or content **2 a** the mathematical or logical structure of a scientific argument as distinguished from its subject matter **b** the notation, and its structure, in which information is expressed **3** *theatre* a stylized mode of production **4** (in Marxist criticism) excessive concern with artistic technique at the expense of social values, etc **5** the philosophical theory that a mathematical statement has no meaning but that its symbols, regarded as physical objects, exhibit a structure that has useful applications. Compare **logicism, intuitionism.** ▷ ˈformalist *n* ▷ ˌformalˈistic *adj*

▷ ˌformalˈistically *adv*

formality (fɔːˈmælɪtɪ) *n, pl* **-ties 1** a requirement of rule, custom, etiquette, etc **2** the condition or quality of being formal or conventional **3** strict or excessive observance of form, ceremony, etc **4** an established, proper, or conventional method, act, or procedure

formalize *or* **formalise** (ˈfɔːməˌlaɪz) *vb* **1** to be or make formal **2** (*tr*) to make official or valid **3** (*tr*) to give a definite shape or form to **4** *logic* to extract the logical form of (an expression), to express in the symbols of some formal system ▷ ˌformaliˈzation *or* ˌformaliˈsation *n* ▷ ˈformalˌizer *or* ˈformalˌiser *n*

formal language *n* **1** a language designed for use in situations in which natural language is unsuitable, as for example in mathematics, logic, or computer programming. The symbols and formulas of such languages stand in precisely specified syntactic and semantic relations to one another **2** *logic* a logistic system for which an interpretation is provided: distinguished from formal calculus in that the semantics enable it to be regarded as *about* some subject matter

formal logic *n* **1** the study of systems of deductive argument in which symbols are used to represent precisely defined categories of expressions. Also called: **symbolic logic** Compare **philosophical logic 2** a specific formal system that can be interpreted as representing a fragment of natural argument

formal mode *n philosophy* the style in which words are explicitly mentioned rather than used of their subject matter. *"Fido" is a dog's name* is in the formal mode, while *"Fido is a dog"* is in the material mode. See also **mention** (sense 7)

formal system *n logic* an uninterpreted symbolic system whose syntax is precisely defined, and on which a relation of deducibility is defined in purely syntactic terms; a logistic system. Also called: **formal theory, formal calculus** Compare **formal language**

formant (ˈfɔːmənt) *n acoustics, phonetics* any of several frequency ranges within which the partials of a sound, esp a vowel sound, are at their strongest, thus imparting to the sound its own special quality, tone colour, or timbre

format (ˈfɔːmæt) *n* **1** the general appearance of a publication, including type style, paper, binding, etc **2** an approximate indication of the size of a publication as determined by the number of times the original sheet of paper is folded to make a leaf. See also **duodecimo, quarto 3** style, plan, or arrangement, as of a television programme **4** *computing* **a** the defined arrangement of data encoded in a file or for example on magnetic disk or CD-ROM, essential for the correct recording and recovery of data on different devices **b** the arrangement of text on printed output or a display screen, or a coded description of such an arrangement ▷ *vb* **-mats, -matting, -matted** (*tr*) **5** to arrange (a book, page, etc) into a specified format [c19 via French from German, from Latin *liber formātus* volume formed]

formate (ˈfɔːmeɪt) *n* any salt or ester of formic acid containing the ion HCOO⁻ or the group HCOO– [c19 from FORM(IC) + -ATE¹]

formation (fɔːˈmeɪʃən) *n* **1** the act of giving or taking form, shape, or existence **2** something that is formed **3** the manner in which something is formed or arranged **4** a formal arrangement of a number of persons or things acting as a unit, such as a troop of soldiers, aircraft in flight, or a football team **5** *geology* **a** the fundamental lithostratigraphic unit **b** a series of rocks with certain characteristics in common **6** *ecology* a community of plants, such as a tropical rainforest, extending over a very large area ▷ forˈmational *adj*

formation dance *n* any dance in which a number of couples form a certain arrangement, such as two facing lines or a circle, and perform a

series of figures within or based on that arrangement ▷ **formation dancing** *n*

formation rules *pl n logic* the set of rules that specify the syntax of a formal system; the algorithm that generates the well-formed formulae

formative (ˈfɔːmətɪv) *adj* **1** of or relating to formation, development, or growth: *formative years* **2** shaping; moulding: *a formative experience* **3** (of tissues and cells in certain parts of an organism) capable of growth and differentiation **4** functioning in the formation of derived, inflected, or compound words **5** an inflectional or derivational affix **6** (in generative grammar) any of the minimum units of a sentence that have syntactic function ▷ ˈformatively *adv* ▷ ˈformativeness *n*

formative assessment *n* ongoing assessment of a pupil's educational development within a particular subject area. Compare **summative assessment**

form class *n* **1** another term for **part of speech 2** a group of words distinguished by common inflections, such as the weak verbs of English

form criticism *n* literary criticism concerned esp with analysing the Bible in terms of the literary forms used, such as proverbs, songs, or stories, and relating them to their historical forms and background ▷ **form critic** *n* ▷ **form critical** *adj*

form drag *n* the drag on a body moving through a fluid as a result of the shape of the body. It can be reduced by streamlining

forme *or US* **form** (fɔːm) *n printing* type matter, blocks, etc, assembled in a chase and ready for printing [c15 from French: FORM]

former¹ (ˈfɔːmə) *adj* (prenominal) **1** belonging to or occurring in an earlier time **2** having been at a previous time **3** denoting the first or first mentioned of two **4** near the beginning ▷ *n* **5 the former** the first or first mentioned of two: distinguished from *latter*

former² (ˈfɔːmə) *n* **1** a person or thing that forms or shapes **2** *electrical engineering* a tool for giving a coil or winding the required shape, sometimes consisting of a frame on which the wire can be wound, the frame then being removed

formerly (ˈfɔːməlɪ) *adv* **1** at or in a former time; in the past **2** *obsolete* in the immediate past; just now

form genus *n* a group of species (**form species**) that have similar structural characteristics but are not closely related

formic (ˈfɔːmɪk) *adj* **1** of, relating to, or derived from ants **2** of, containing, or derived from formic acid [c18 from Latin *formīca* ant; the acid occurs naturally in ants]

Formica (fɔːˈmaɪkə) *n trademark* any of various laminated plastic sheets, containing melamine, used esp for heat-resistant surfaces that can be easily cleaned

formic acid *n* a colourless corrosive liquid carboxylic acid found in some insects, esp ants, and many plants: used in dyeing textiles and the manufacture of insecticides and refrigerants. Formula: HCOOH. Systematic name: **methanoic acid**

formicary (ˈfɔːmɪkərɪ) *or* **formicarium** (ˌfɔːmɪˈkɛərɪəm) *n, pl* **-caries, -caria** (-ˈkɛərɪə) less common names for **ant hill** [c19 from Medieval Latin *formīcārium* see FORMIC]

formicate (ˈfɔːmɪˌkeɪt) *vb* (*intr*) now rare **1** to crawl around like ants **2** to swarm with ants or other crawling things [c17 from Latin *formīcāre*, from *formīca* ant]

formication (ˌfɔːmɪˈkeɪʃən) *n* a sensation of insects crawling on the skin; symptom of a nerve disorder

formidable (ˈfɔːmɪdəbˀl) *adj* **1** arousing or likely to inspire fear or dread **2** extremely difficult to defeat, overcome, manage, etc **3** tending to inspire awe or admiration because of great size, strength, excellence, etc [c15 from Latin *formīdābilis*, from *formīdāre* to dread, from *formīdō* fear] > ˌformidaˈbility *or* ˈformidableness *n* > ˈformidably *adv*

formless (ˈfɔːmlɪs) *adj* without a definite shape or form; amorphous > ˈformlessly *adv* > ˈformlessness *n*

form letter *n* a single copy of a letter that has been mechanically reproduced in large numbers for circulation

Formosa (fɔːˈməʊsə) *n* the former name of Taiwan

Formosa Strait *n* an arm of the Pacific between Taiwan and mainland China, linking the East and South China Seas. Also called: Taiwan Strait

formula (ˈfɔːmjʊlə) *n, pl* -las, -lae (-ˌliː) **1** an established form or set of words, as used in religious ceremonies, legal proceedings, etc **2** *maths, physics* a general relationship, principle, or rule stated, often as an equation, in the form of symbols **3** *chem* a representation of molecules, radicals, ions, etc, expressed in the symbols of the atoms of their constituent elements. See molecular formula, empirical formula, structural formula **4 a** a method, pattern, or rule for doing or producing something, often one proved to be successful **b** (*as modifier*): *formula fiction* **5 a** a prescription for making up a medicine, baby's food, etc **b** a substance prepared according to such a prescription **6** *motor racing* the specific category in which a particular type of car competes, judged according to engine size, weight, and fuel capacity [C17 from Latin: diminutive of *forma* FORM] > **formulaic** (ˌfɔːmjʊˈleɪɪk) *adj*

Formula One *n* **1** the top class of professional motor racing **2** the most important world championship in motor racing

formularize *or* **formularise** (ˈfɔːmjʊləˌraɪz) *vb* a less common word for **formulate** (sense 1) > ˌformulariˈzation *or* ˌformulariˈsation *n* > ˈformulaˌizer *or* ˈformulaˌiser *n*

formulary (ˈfɔːmjʊlərɪ) *n, pl* -laries **1** a book or system of prescribed formulas, esp relating to religious procedure or doctrine **2** a formula **3** *pharmacol* a book containing a list of pharmaceutical products, with their formulas and means of preparation > *adj* **4** of, relating to, or of the nature of a formula

formulate (ˈfɔːmjʊˌleɪt) *vb* (*tr*) **1** to put into or express in systematic terms; express in or as if in a formula **2** to devise > ˈformuˌlator *n*

formulation (ˌfɔːmjʊˈleɪʃən) *n* (*tr*) **1** the act or process of formulating **2** any mixture or substance prepared according to a particular formula **3** a medicinal preparation administered in a specific form, such as a tablet, linctus, ointment, or injection

formulism (ˈfɔːmjʊˌlɪzəm) *n* adherence to or belief in formulas > ˈformulist *n, adj* > ˌformuˈlistic *adj*

formwork (ˈfɔːmˌwɜːk) *n* an arrangement of wooden boards, bolts, etc, used to shape reinforced concrete while it is setting. Also called (esp Brit): shuttering

formyl (ˈfɔːmaɪl) *n* (*modifier*) of, consisting of, or containing the monovalent group HCO-: *a formyl group or radical* [C19 from FORM(IC) + -YL]

Fornax (ˈfɔːnæks) *n, Latin genitive* Fornacis (fɔːˈneɪsɪs, -ˈnæs-) a faint constellation in the S hemisphere lying between Cetus and Phoenix [Latin: oven, kiln]

fornenst (fɔːˈnɛnst) *prep Scot and Northeast English dialect* situated against or facing towards [from Scottish, from FORE[1] + *anenst* a variant of archaic ANENT]

fornicate[1] (ˈfɔːnɪˌkeɪt) *vb* (*intr*) to indulge in or commit fornication [C16 from Late Latin *fornicārī*, from Latin *fornix* vault, brothel situated therein] > ˈforniˌcator *n*

fornicate[2] (ˈfɔːnɪkɪt, -ˌkeɪt) *or* **fornicated** *adj* *biology* arched or hoodlike in form [C19 from Latin *fornicātus* arched, from *fornix* vault]

fornication (ˌfɔːnɪˈkeɪʃən) *n* **1** voluntary sexual intercourse outside marriage **2** *law* voluntary sexual intercourse between two persons of the opposite sex, where one is or both are unmarried **3** *Bible* sexual immorality in general, esp adultery

fornix (ˈfɔːnɪks) *n, pl* -nices (-nɪˌsiːz) *anatomy* any archlike structure, esp the arched band of white fibres at the base of the brain [C17 from Latin; see FORNICATE[a]] > ˈfornical *adj*

forsake (fəˈseɪk) *vb* -sakes, -saking, -sook (-ˈsʊk) -saken (-ˈseɪkən) (*tr*) **1** to abandon **2** to give up (something valued or enjoyed) [Old English *forsacan*] > forˈsaker *n*

forsaken (fəˈseɪkən) *vb* **1** the past participle of **forsake** > *adj* **2** completely deserted or helpless; abandoned > forˈsakenly *adv* > forˈsakenness *n*

forsook (fəˈsʊk) *vb* the past tense of **forsake**

forsooth (fəˈsuːθ) *adv archaic* in truth; indeed [Old English *forsōth*]

forspeak (fɔːˈspiːk) *vb* -speaks, -speaking, -spoke -spoken (*tr*) *Scot archaic* to bewitch

forspent *or* **forespent** (fɔːˈspɛnt) *adj archaic* tired out; exhausted

forsterite (ˈfɔːstəˌraɪt) *n* a white, yellow, or green mineral of the olivine group consisting of magnesium silicate. Formula: Mg_2SiO_4 [C19 named after J. R. Forster (1729–98), German naturalist]

forswear (fɔːˈsweə) *vb* -swears, -swearing, -swore, -sworn **1** (*tr*) to reject or renounce with determination or as upon oath **2** (*tr*) to deny or disavow absolutely or upon oath: *he forswore any knowledge of the crime* **3** to perjure (oneself) [Old English *forswearian*] > forˈswearer *n*

forsworn (fɔːˈswɔːn) *vb* the past participle of **forswear**. > forˈswornness *n*

forsythia (fɔːˈsaɪθɪə) *n* any oleaceous shrub of the genus *Forsythia*, native to China, Japan, and SE Europe but widely cultivated for its showy yellow bell-shaped flowers, which appear in spring before the foliage [C19 New Latin, named after William Forsyth (1737–1804), English botanist]

fort (fɔːt) *n* **1** a fortified enclosure, building, or position able to be defended against an enemy **2** hold the fort *informal* to maintain or guard something temporarily [C15 from Old French, from *fort* (adj) strong, from Latin *fortis*]

Fortaleza (Portuguese fortaˈleza) *n* a port in NE Brazil, capital of Ceará state. Pop: 3 261 000 (2005 est). Also called: Ceará

fortalice (ˈfɔːtəlɪs) *n* a small fort or outwork of a fortification [C15 from Medieval Latin *fortalitia*, from Latin *fortis* strong; see FORTRESS]

Fort-de-France (French fɔrdəfrɑ̃s) *n* the capital of Martinique, a port on the W coast: commercial centre of the French Antilles. Pop: 94 049 (1999 est)

forte[1] (fɔːt, ˈfɔːteɪ) *n* **1** something at which a person excels **2** *fencing* the stronger section of a sword blade, between the hilt and the middle. Compare **foible** [C17 from French *fort*, from *fort* (adj) strong, from Latin *fortis*]

forte[2] (ˈfɔːtɪ) *music* > *adj, adv* **1** loud or loudly. Symbol: f > *n* **2** a loud passage in music [C18 from Italian, from Latin *fortis* strong]

fortepiano (ˌfɔːtɪˈpjænəʊ) *n* an early type of piano popular in the late 18th century [from Italian, loud-soft]

forte-piano (ˌfɔːtɪˈpjɑːnəʊ) *music* > *adj, adv* **1** loud and then immediately soft. Symbol: fp > *n* **2** a note played in this way

forth (fɔːθ) *adv* **1** forward in place, time, order, or degree **2** out, as from concealment, seclusion, or inaction **3** away, as from a place or country **4** and so on; et cetera > *prep* **5** *archaic* out of; away from [Old English; related to Middle High German *vort*; see FOR, FURTHER]

Forth (fɔːθ) *n* **1** Firth of an inlet of the North Sea in SE Scotland: spanned by a cantilever railway bridge 1600 m (almost exactly 1 mile) long (1889), and by a road bridge (1964) **2** a river in S Scotland, flowing generally east to the Firth of Forth. Length: about 104 km (65 miles)

forthcoming (ˌfɔːθˈkʌmɪŋ) *adj* **1** approaching in time: *the forthcoming debate* **2** about to appear: *his forthcoming book* **3** available or ready **4** open or sociable > ˌforthˈcomingness *n*

forthright (ˈfɔːθˌraɪt) *adj* **1** direct and outspoken > *adv* (ˌfɔːθˈraɪt, ˈfɔːθˌraɪt) *also* forthrightly **2** in a direct manner; frankly **3** at once > ˈforthˌrightness *n*

forthwith (ˌfɔːθˈwɪθ, -ˈwɪð) *adv* at once; immediately

fortieth (ˈfɔːtɪɪθ) *adj* **1 a** being the ordinal number of *forty* in numbering or counting order, position, time, etc. Often written: 40th **b** (*as noun*): *he was the fortieth* > *n* **2 a** one of 40 approximately equal parts of something **b** (*as modifier*): *a fortieth part* **3** the fraction equal to one divided by 40 (1/40) [Old English *fēowertigotha*]

fortification (ˌfɔːtɪfɪˈkeɪʃən) *n* **1** the act, art, or science of fortifying or strengthening **2 a** a wall, mound, etc, used to fortify a place **b** such works collectively **3** any place that can be militarily defended

fortified pa *n* NZ *history* a Māori hilltop dwelling with trenches and palisades for defensive occupation

fortified wine *n* wine treated by the addition of brandy or alcohol, such as port, marsala, and sherry

fortify (ˈfɔːtɪˌfaɪ) *vb* -fies, -fying, -fied (*mainly tr*) **1** (*also intr*) to make (a place) defensible, as by building walls, digging trenches, etc **2** to strengthen physically, mentally, or morally **3** to strengthen, support, or reinforce (a garment, structure, etc) **4** to add spirits or alcohol to (wine), in order to produce sherry, port, etc **5** to increase the nutritious value of (a food), as by adding vitamins and minerals **6** to support or confirm: *to fortify an argument with facts* [C15 from Old French *fortifier*, from Late Latin *fortificāre*, from Latin *fortis* strong + *facere* to make] > ˈfortiˌfiable *adj* > ˈfortiˌfier *n* > ˈfortiˌfyingly *adv*

fortis (ˈfɔːtɪs) *phonetics* > *adj* **1** (of a consonant) articulated with considerable muscular tension of the speech organs or with a great deal of breath pressure or plosion > *n, pl* -tes (-tiːz) **2** a consonant, such as English p or f, pronounced with considerable muscular force or breath pressure > Compare **lenis** [Latin: strong]

fortissimo (fɔːˈtɪsɪˌməʊ) *music* > *adj, adv* **1** very loud. Symbol: ff > *n* **2** a very loud passage in music [C18 from Italian, from Latin *fortissimus*, from *fortis* strong]

fortitude (ˈfɔːtɪˌtjuːd) *n* strength and firmness of mind; resolute endurance [C15 from Latin *fortitūdō* courage] > ˌfortiˈtudinous *adj*

Fort Knox (nɒks) *n* a military reservation in N Kentucky: site of the US Gold Bullion Depository. Pop: 38 280 (latest est)

Fort Lamy (ˈfɔːt ˈlɑːmɪ; French fɔr lami) *n* the former name (until 1973) of **Ndjamena**

Fort Lauderdale (ˈlɔːdəˌdeɪl) *n* a city in SE Florida, on the Atlantic. Pop: 162 917 (2003 est)

fortnight (ˈfɔːtˌnaɪt) *n* a period of 14 consecutive days; two weeks [Old English *fēowertīene niht* fourteen nights]

fortnightly (ˈfɔːtˌnaɪtlɪ) *chiefly Brit* > *adj* **1** occurring or appearing once each fortnight > *adv* **2** once a fortnight > *n, pl* -lies **3** a publication issued at intervals of two weeks

FORTRAN *or* **Fortran** (ˈfɔːtræn) *n* a high-level computer programming language for mathematical and scientific purposes, designed to facilitate and speed up the solving of complex problems [C20 from *for(mula) tran(slation)*]

fortress (ˈfɔːtrɪs) *n* **1** a large fort or fortified town **2** a place or source of refuge or support > *vb* **1** (*tr*) to protect with or as if with a fortress [C13 from Old French *forteresse*, from Medieval Latin *fortalitia*, from Latin *fortis* strong]

Fort Sumter (ˈsʌmtə) *n* a fort in SE South Carolina, guarding Charleston Harbour. Its capture by Confederate forces (1861) was the first action of the Civil War

fortuitism (fɔːˈtjuːɪˌtɪzəm) *n philosophy* the doctrine that evolutionary adaptations are the result of chance. Compare **tychism**. ▷ for'tuitist *n, adj*

fortuitous (fɔːˈtjuːɪtəs) *adj* happening by chance, esp by a lucky chance; unplanned; accidental [c17 from Latin *fortuitus* happening by chance, from *forte* by chance, from *fors* chance, luck] ▷ for'tuitously *adv* ▷ for'tuitousness *n*

fortuity (fɔːˈtjuːɪtɪ) *n, pl* -ties 1 a chance or accidental occurrence 2 fortuitousness 3 chance or accident

Fortuna (fɔːˈtjuːnə) *n* the Roman goddess of fortune and good luck. Greek counterpart: Tyche

fortunate (ˈfɔːtʃənɪt) *adj* 1 having good luck; lucky 2 occurring by or bringing good fortune or luck; auspicious ▷ 'fortunateness *n*

fortunately (ˈfɔːtʃənɪtlɪ) *adv* 1 (*sentence modifier*) it is fortunate that; luckily 2 in a fortunate manner

fortune (ˈfɔːtʃən) *n* 1 an amount of wealth or material prosperity, esp, when unqualified, a great amount 2 small fortune a large sum of money 3 a power or force, often personalized, regarded as being responsible for human affairs; chance 4 luck, esp when favourable 5 (*often plural*) a person's lot or destiny ▷ *vb* 6 *archaic* a (*tr*) to endow with great wealth b (*intr*) to happen by chance [c13 from Old French, from Latin *fortūna*, from *fors* chance] ▷ 'fortuneless *adj*

fortune-hunter *n* a person who seeks to secure a fortune, esp through marriage ▷ 'fortune-,hunting *adj, n*

fortune-teller *n* a person who makes predictions about the future as by looking into a crystal ball, reading palms, etc ▷ 'fortune-,telling *adj, n*

Fort Wayne (weɪn) *n* a city in NE Indiana. Pop: 219 495 (2003 est)

Fort William (ˈwɪljəm) *n* a town in W Scotland, in Highland at the head of Loch Linnhe: tourist centre; the fort itself, built in 1655 and renamed after William III in 1690, was demolished in 1866. Pop: 9908 (2001)

Fort Worth (wɜːθ) *n* a city in N Texas, at the junction of the Clear and West forks of the Trinity River: aircraft works, electronics. Pop: 585 122 (2003 est)

forty (ˈfɔːtɪ) *n, pl* -ties 1 the cardinal number that is the product of ten and four. See also **number** (sense 1) 2 a numeral, 40, XL, etc, representing this number 3 something representing, represented by, or consisting of 40 units ▷ *determiner* 4 a amounting to forty b (*as pronoun*): *there were forty in the herd* [Old English *fēowertig*]

forty-five *n* 1 a gramophone record played at 45 revolutions per minute 2 *US and Canadian* a pistol having .45 calibre

Forty-Five *n* the *Brit history* another name for the **Jacobite Rebellion** (sense 2)

forty-niner *n* (*sometimes capital*) *US history* a prospector who took part in the California gold rush of 1849

forty-ninth parallel *n Canadian* an informal name for the border with the USA., which is in part delineated by the parallel line of latitude at 49°N

forty winks *n* (*functioning as singular or plural*) *informal* a short light sleep; nap

forum (ˈfɔːrəm) *n, pl* -rums, -ra (-rə) 1 a meeting or assembly for the open discussion of subjects of public interest 2 a medium for open discussion, such as a magazine 3 a public meeting place for open discussion 4 a court; tribunal 5 (in South Africa) a pressure group of community leaders or representatives, esp Black leaders or representatives 6 (in ancient Italy) an open space, usually rectangular in shape, serving as a city's marketplace and centre of public business [c15 from Latin: public place; related to Latin *foris* outside]

Forum *or* **Forum Romanum** (rəʊˈmɑːnəm) *n* **the** the main forum of ancient Rome, situated between the Capitoline and the Palatine Hills

forward (ˈfɔːwəd) *adj* 1 directed or moving ahead 2 lying or situated in or near the front part of something 3 presumptuous, pert, or impudent 4 well developed or advanced, esp in physical, material, or intellectual growth or development 5 *archaic* (*often postpositive*) ready, eager, or willing 6 a of or relating to the future or favouring change; progressive b (*in combination*): *forward-looking* 7 *NZ* (of an animal) in good condition ▷ *n* 8 a an attacking player in any of various sports, such as soccer, hockey, or basketball b (in American football) a lineman ▷ *adv-* 9 an email that has been sent to one recipient and then forwarded to another 10 a variant of **forwards** 11 (ˈfɔːwəd; *Nautical* ˈforəd) towards the front or bow of an aircraft or ship 12 into prominence or a position of being subject to public scrutiny; out; forth ▷ *vb* (*tr*) 13 to send forward or pass on to an ultimate destination 14 to advance, help, or promote 15 *bookbinding* to prepare (a book) for the finisher [Old English *foreweard*] ▷ 'forwardly *adv*

forward bias *or* **voltage** *n* a voltage applied to a circuit or device, esp a semiconductor device, in the direction that produces the larger current

forward delivery *n* (in commerce) delivery at a future date

forwarder (ˈfɔːwədə) *n* 1 a person or thing that forwards 2 a person engaged in the bookbinding process of forwarding 3 See **forwarding agent**

forwarding (ˈfɔːwədɪŋ) *n* all the processes involved in the binding of a book subsequent to cutting and up to the fitting of its cover

forwarding agent *n* a person, agency, or enterprise engaged in the collection, shipment, and delivery of goods

forward market *n* a market in which contracts are made to buy or sell currencies, commodities, etc, at some future date at a price fixed at the date of the contract. Compare **spot market**

forwardness (ˈfɔːwədnɪs) *n* 1 lack of modesty; presumption; boldness 2 willing readiness; eagerness 3 a state or condition of advanced progress or development

forward pass *n rugby* an illegal pass towards the opponent's dead-ball line. Also called: **throw-forward**

forward quotation *n* (in commerce) the price quoted for goods sent on forward delivery

forward roll *n* a gymnastic movement in which the body is turned heels over head with the back of the neck resting on the ground

forwards (ˈfɔːwədz) *or* **forward** *adv* 1 towards or at a place ahead or in advance, esp in space but also in time 2 towards the front

forwent (fɔːˈwɛnt) *vb* the past tense of **forgo**

forwhy (fɔːˈwaɪ) *archaic* ▷ *adv* 1 for what reason; why ▷ *conj* 2 (*subordinating*) because [Old English *for hwī*]

forworn *or* **foreworn** (fɔːˈwɔːn) *adj archaic* weary [c16 past participle of obsolete *forwear* to wear out, from Middle English *forweren* to hollow out]

forza (ˈfɔːtsə) *n music* force [c19 Italian, literally: force]

forzando (fɔːˈtsændəʊ) *adj, adv, n* another word for **sforzando**

FOS *abbreviation for* fructooligosaccharide: a chain polymer of fructose found in a variety of plants, vegetables, and fruits and used as a sweetener

Fosbury flop (ˈfɒzbərɪ, -brɪ) *n athletics* a modern high-jumping technique whereby the jumper clears the bar headfirst and backwards [c20 named after Dick *Fosbury*, US winner of men's high jump at Mexico Olympics in 1968, who perfected the technique]

Foshan (ˈfɔːˈʃɑːn) *or* **Fatshan** *n* a city in SE China, in W Guangdong province. Pop: 483 000 (2005 est). Also called: **Namhoi**

fossa[1] (ˈfɒsə) *n, pl* -sae (-siː) an anatomical depression, trench, or hollow area [c19 from Latin: ditch, from *fossus* dug up, from *fodere* to dig up]

fossa[2] (ˈfɒsə) *n* a large primitive catlike viverrine mammal, *Cryptoprocta ferox*, inhabiting the forests of Madagascar: order Carnivora (carnivores). It has thick reddish-brown fur and preys on lemurs, poultry, etc [from Malagasy]

fosse *or* **foss** (fɒs) *n* a ditch or moat, esp one dug as a fortification [c14 from Old French, from Latin *fossa*; see FOSSA[1]]

fossette (fɒˈsɛt) *n* 1 *anatomy* a small depression or fossa, as in a bone 2 *pathol* a small deep ulcer of the cornea [c19 from French: dimple, from *fosse* ditch]

Fosse Way (fɒs) *n* a Roman road in Britain between Lincoln and Exeter, with a fosse on each side

fossick (ˈfɒsɪk) *vb Austral and NZ* 1 (*intr*) to search for gold or precious stones in abandoned workings, rivers, etc 2 to rummage or search for (something) [c19 Australian, probably from English dialect *fussock* to bustle about, from FUSS] ▷ 'fossicker *n*

fossil (ˈfɒsəl) *n* 1 a a relic, remnant, or representation of an organism that existed in a past geological age, or of the activity of such an organism, occurring in the form of mineralized bones, shells, etc, as casts, impressions, and moulds, and as frozen perfectly preserved organisms b (*as modifier*): *fossil insects* 2 *informal derogatory* a a person, idea, thing, etc, that is outdated or incapable of change b (*as modifier*): *fossil politicians* 3 *linguistics* a form once current but now appearing only in one or two special contexts, as for example *stead*, which is found now only in *instead* (*of*) and in phrases like *in his stead* 4 *obsolete* any rock or mineral dug out of the earth [c17 from Latin *fossilis* dug up, from *fodere* to dig]

fossil energy *n* heat energy released by burning fossil fuel

fossil fuel *n* any naturally occurring carbon or hydrocarbon fuel, such as coal, petroleum, peat, and natural gas, formed by the decomposition of prehistoric organisms

fossiliferous (ˌfɒsɪˈlɪfərəs) *adj* (of sedimentary rocks) containing fossils

fossilize *or* **fossilise** (ˈfɒsɪˌlaɪz) *vb* 1 to convert or be converted into a fossil 2 to become or cause to become antiquated or inflexible ▷ 'fossil,izable *or* 'fossil,isable *adj* ▷ ,fossili'zation *or* ,fossili'sation *n*

fossorial (fɒˈsɔːrɪəl) *adj* 1 (of the forelimbs and skeleton of burrowing animals) adapted for digging 2 (of burrowing animals, such as the mole and armadillo) having limbs of this type [c19 from Medieval Latin *fossōrius* from Latin *fossor* digger, from *fodere* to dig]

foster (ˈfɒstə) *vb* (*tr*) 1 to promote the growth or development of 2 to bring up (a child, etc); rear 3 to cherish (a plan, hope, etc) in one's mind 4 *chiefly Brit* a to place (a child) in the care of foster parents b to bring up under fosterage ▷ *adj* 5 (*in combination*) of or involved in the rearing of a child by persons other than his natural or adopted parents [Old English *fōstrian* to feed, from *fōstor* FOOD] ▷ 'fosterer *n* ▷ 'fosteringly *adv*

fosterage (ˈfɒstərɪdʒ) *n* 1 the act of caring for or bringing up a foster child 2 the condition or state of being a foster child 3 the act of encouraging or promoting

foster child *n* a child looked after temporarily or brought up by people other than its natural or adoptive parents

foster father *n* a man who looks after or brings up a child or children as a father, in place of the natural or adoptive father

fosterling (ˈfɒstəlɪŋ) *n* a less common word for **foster child**

foster mother *n* a woman who looks after or brings up a child or children as a mother, in place of the natural or adoptive mother

Fotheringhay (ˈfɒðərɪŋˌgeɪ) *n* a village in E England, in NE Northamptonshire: ruined castle, scene of the imprisonment and execution of Mary Queen of Scots (1587)

fou (fuː) *adj Scot* 1 full 2 drunk [perhaps a Scot

variant of *full*]

Foucault current (*French* fuko) *n* another name for **eddy current** [named after J. B. L. *Foucault* (1819–68), French physicist]

foudroyant (fuːˈdrɔɪənt) *adj* 1 (of a disease) occurring suddenly and with great severity 2 *rare* stunning, dazzling, or overwhelming [c19 from French, from *foudroyer* to strike with lightning, from Old French *foudre* lightning, from Latin *fulgur*]

fouetté *French* (fwete) *n* a step in ballet in which the dancer stands on one foot and makes a whiplike movement with the other [c19 French, past participle of *fouetter* to whip, from *fouet* a whip]

fought (fɔːt) *vb* the past tense and past participle of **fight**

foul (faʊl) *adj* 1 offensive to the senses; revolting 2 offensive in odour; stinking 3 charged with or full of dirt or offensive matter; filthy 4 (of food) putrid; rotten 5 morally or spiritually offensive; wicked; vile 6 obscene; vulgar 7 not in accordance with accepted standards or established rules; unfair 8 (esp of weather) unpleasant or adverse 9 blocked or obstructed with dirt or foreign matter 10 entangled or impeded 11 (of the bottom of a vessel) covered with barnacles and other growth that slow forward motion 12 *informal* unsatisfactory or uninteresting; bad 13 *archaic* ugly ▷ *n* 14 *sport* a a violation of the rules b (*as modifier*): *a foul shot; a foul blow* 15 something foul 16 an entanglement or collision, esp in sailing or fishing ▷ *vb* 17 to make or become dirty or polluted 18 to become or cause to become entangled or snarled 19 (*tr*) to disgrace or dishonour 20 to become or cause to become clogged or choked 21 (*tr*) *nautical* (of underwater growth) to cling to (the bottom of a vessel) so as to slow its motion 22 (*tr*) *sport* to commit a foul against (an opponent) 23 (*tr*) *baseball* to hit (a ball) in an illegal manner 24 (*intr*) *sport* to infringe the rules 25 (*tr*) (of an animal, especially a dog) to defecate on 26 to collide with (a boat, etc) ▷ *adv* 27 in a foul or unfair manner 28 **fall foul of** a to come into conflict with b *nautical* to come into collision with ▷ See also **foul up** [Old English *fūl*; related to Old Norse *fūll*, Gothic *fūls* smelling offensively, Latin *pūs* PUS, Greek *puol* pus] > **ˈfoully** *adv*

foulard (fuːˈlɑːd, ˈfuːlɑː) *n* 1 a soft light fabric of plain-weave or twill-weave silk or rayon, usually with a printed design 2 something made of this fabric, esp a scarf or handkerchief [c19 from French, of unknown origin]

foulie (ˈfaʊlɪ) *n Austral informal* a bad mood [c20 from FOUL]

foul marten *n* another name for the **polecat** (sense 1) See also **sweet marten**

foul-mouthed *adj* given to using obscene, abusive, or blasphemous language

foulness (ˈfaʊlnɪs) *n* 1 the state or quality of being foul 2 obscenity; vulgarity 3 viciousness or inhumanity 4 foul matter; filth

Foulness (ˈfaʊlnɛs) *n* a flat marshy island in SE England, in Essex north of the Thames estuary

foul play *n* 1 unfair or treacherous conduct esp with violence 2 a violation of the rules in a game or sport

foul shot *n basketball* an unimpeded shot at the basket from the **free-throw line** given for a technical fault (one free shot) or a foul (two free shots). Also called: **free throw**

foul up *vb* (*adverb*) 1 (*tr*) to bungle; mismanage 2 (*tr*) to make dirty; contaminate 3 to be or cause to be blocked, choked, or entangled ▷ *n* **foul-up** 4 a state of confusion or muddle caused by bungling

foumart (ˈfuːmɑːt, -mət) *n* a former name for the **polecat** (sense 1) [c15 *folmarde*: from Old English *fūl* foul + *mearth* a marten]

found¹ (faʊnd) *vb* 1 the past tense and past participle of **find** ▷ *adj* 2 furnished, or fitted out: *the boat is well found* 3 *Brit* with meals, heating, bed

linen, etc, provided without extra charge (esp in the phrase **all found**)

found² (faʊnd) *vb* 1 (*tr*) to bring into being, set up, or establish (something, such as an institution, society, etc) 2 (*tr*) to build or establish the foundation or basis of 3 (*also intr;* foll by *on* or *upon*) to have a basis (in); depend (on) [c13 from Old French *fonder*, from Latin *fundāre*, from *fundus* bottom]

found³ (faʊnd) *vb* (*tr*) 1 to cast (a material, such as metal or glass) by melting and pouring into a mould 2 to shape or make (articles) in this way; cast [c14 from Old French *fondre*, from Latin *fundere* to melt]

foundation (faʊnˈdeɪʃən) *n* 1 that on which something is founded; basis 2 (*often plural*) a construction below the ground that distributes the load of a building, wall, etc 3 the base on which something stands 4 the act of founding or establishing or the state of being founded or established 5 a an endowment or legacy for the perpetual support of an institution such as a school or hospital b on the foundation entitled to benefit from the funds of a foundation 6 an institution supported by an endowment, often one that provides funds for charities, research, etc 7 the charter incorporating or establishing a society or institution and the statutes or rules governing its affairs 8 a cosmetic in cream or cake form used as a base for make-up 9 See **foundation garment** 10 *cards* a card on which a sequence may be built > **founˈdational** *adj* > **founˈdationally** *adv* > **founˈdationary** *adj*

foundation garment *n* a woman's undergarment worn to shape and support the figure; brassiere or corset

foundation stone *n* a stone laid at a ceremony to mark the foundation of a new building

foundation subjects *pl n Brit education* the subjects studied as part of the National Curriculum, including the compulsory core subjects

founder¹ (ˈfaʊndə) *n* a person who establishes an institution, company, society, etc [c14 see FOUND²]

founder² (ˈfaʊndə) *vb* (*intr*) 1 (of a ship) to sink 2 to break down or fail 3 to sink into or become stuck in soft ground 4 to fall in or give way; collapse 5 (of a horse) to stumble or go lame 6 *archaic* (of animals, esp livestock) to become ill from overeating ▷ *n* 7 *vet science* another name for **laminitis** [c13 from Old French *fondrer* to submerge, from Latin *fundus* bottom; see FOUND²]

> **USAGE** *Founder* is sometimes wrongly used where *flounder* is meant: *this unexpected turn of events left him floundering* (not *foundering*)

founder³ (ˈfaʊndə) *n* a a person who makes metal castings b (*in combination*): *an iron founder* [c15 see FOUND³]

founders' shares *pl n* shares awarded to the founders of a company and often granting special privileges

founder's type *n printing* special type cast by a type founder for hand composition, as opposed to type cast in a mechanical composing machine

founding father *n* (*often capitals*) a person who founds or establishes an important institution, esp a member of the US Constitutional Convention (1787)

foundling (ˈfaʊndlɪŋ) *n* an abandoned infant whose parents are not known [c13 *foundeling;* see FIND]

found object *n* another name for *objet trouvé*

foundry (ˈfaʊndrɪ) *n, pl* **-ries** 1 a place in which metal castings are produced 2 the science or practice of casting metal 3 cast-metal articles collectively [c17 from Old French *fonderie*, from *fondre;* see FOUND³]

foundry proof *n printing* a proof taken from a forme before duplicate plates are made from it

foundry sand *n* silica-based sand mixed with clay, oil, etc, to improve its cohesive strength,

used in moulding

fount¹ (faʊnt) *n* 1 *poetic* a spring or fountain 2 source or origin [c16 back formation from FOUNTAIN]

fount² (faʊnt, fɒnt) *n printing* another word for **font²** [c16 from Old French *fonte* a founding, casting, from Vulgar Latin *funditus* (unattested) a casting, from Latin *fundere* to melt; see FOUND³]

fountain (ˈfaʊntɪn) *n* 1 a jet or spray of water or some other liquid 2 a structure from which such a jet or a number of such jets spurt, often incorporating figures, basins, etc 3 a natural spring of water, esp the source of a stream 4 a stream, jet, or cascade of sparks, lava, etc 5 a principal source or origin 6 a reservoir or supply chamber, as for oil in a lamp 7 short for **drinking fountain** or **soda fountain** [c15 from Old French *fontaine*, from Late Latin *fontāna*, from Latin *fons* spring, source] > **ˈfountained** *adj* > **ˈfountainless** *adj* > **ˈfountain-ˌlike** *adj*

fountainhead (ˈfaʊntɪnˌhɛd) *n* 1 a spring that is the source of a stream 2 a principal or original source

fountain pen *n* a pen the nib of which is supplied with ink from a cartridge or a reservoir in its barrel

Fountains Abbey (ˈfaʊntɪns) *n* a ruined Cistercian abbey near Ripon in Yorkshire: founded 1132, dissolved 1539; landscaped 1720

four (fɔː) *n* 1 the cardinal number that is the sum of three and one 2 a numeral, 4, IV, etc, representing this number 3 something representing, represented by, or consisting of four units, such as a playing card with four symbols on it 4 Also called: **four o'clock** four hours after noon or midnight 5 *cricket* a a shot that crosses the boundary after hitting the ground b the four runs scored for such a shot 6 *rowing* a a racing shell propelled by four oarsmen pulling one oar each, with or without a cox b the crew of such a shell ▷ *determiner* 7 a amounting to four: *four thousand eggs; four times* b (*as pronoun*): *four are ready* ▷ Related prefixes: **quadri-, tetra-** [Old English *fēower;* related to Old Frisian *fiūwer*, Old Norse *fjórir*, Old High German *fior*, Latin *quattuor*, Greek *tessares*, Sanskrit *catur*]

fourball (ˈfɔːbɔːl) *n golf* a match for two pairs in which each player uses his own ball, the better score of each pair being counted at every hole. Compare **foursome** (sense 2), **greensome**

four-by-four *n* a vehicle equipped with four-wheel drive

four-by-two *n Austral and NZ* a piece of timber with a cross section that measures 4 inches by 2 inches

fourchette (fʊəˈʃɛt) *n* 1 *anatomy* the bandlike fold of skin, about one inch from the anus, forming the posterior margin of the vulva 2 a less common name for **furcula** or **frog³** [c18 from French: a little fork, from Old French *forche*, from Latin *furca* FORK]

four-colour *n* (*modifier*) (of a print or photographic process) using the principle in which four colours (magenta, cyan, yellow, and black) are used in combination to produce almost any other colour

four-cycle *adj US and Canadian* relating to or designating an internal-combustion engine in which the piston makes four strokes for every explosion. Equivalent term (in Britain and certain other countries): four-stroke Compare **two-stroke**

four-deal bridge *n* a version of bridge in which four hands only are played, the players then cutting for new partners

four-dimensional *adj* having or specified by four dimensions, esp the three spatial dimensions and the dimension of time: *a four-dimensional continuum*

Fourdrinier (fʊəˈdrɪnɪə) *n* a particular type of paper-making machine that forms the paper in a continuous web [c19 named after Henry (died 1854) and Sealy (died 1847) *Fourdrinier*, English paper makers]

four-eyed fish *n* either of two viviparous tropical

f

American freshwater cyprinodont fishes, *Anableps anableps* or *A. microlepis*, that swim at the surface of the water and have half of each eye specialized for seeing in air, the other half for seeing in water

four-eyes *n* a disparaging term of address for a person wearing spectacles > **'four-,eyed** *adj*

four flush *n* **1** a useless poker hand, containing four of a suit and one odd card ▷ *vb* **four-flush** (*intr*) **2** to bid confidently on a poor hand such as a four flush **3** *US and Canadian* a slang word for **bluff**[1]

four-flusher ('fɔː,flʌʃə) *n* *US and Canadian slang* a person who bluffs or attempts to deceive

fourfold ('fɔː,fəʊld) *adj* **1** equal to or having four times as many or as much **2** composed of four parts ▷ *adv* **3** by or up to four times as many or as much

four-four time *n* *music* a form of simple quadruple time in which there are four crotchets to the bar, indicated by the time signature ⁴⁄₄. Often shortened to: **four-four** Also called: **common time**

fourgon *French* (furgɔ̃) *n* a long covered wagon, used mainly for carrying baggage, supplies, etc [C19 from French: from Old French *forgon* poker, from *furgier* to search, ultimately from Latin *fūr* thief]

four-handed *adj* **1** (of a card game) arranged for four players **2** (of a musical composition) written for two performers at the same piano > **four-'handedly** *adv*

Four Hundred *n* the *US* the most exclusive or affluent social clique in a particular place

Fourier analysis ('fʊərɪ,eɪ) *n* the analysis of a periodic function into its simple sinusoidal or harmonic components, whose sum forms a Fourier series [C19 named after Baron Jean Baptiste Joseph *Fourier* (1768–1830), French mathematician, Egyptologist, and administrator]

Fourierism ('fʊərɪə,rɪzəm) *n* the system of Charles Fourier (1772–1837), the French social reformer, under which society was to be organized into self-sufficient cooperatives > **'Fourierist** or **Fourierite** ('fʊərɪə,raɪt) *n, adj* > **,Fourier'istic** *adj*

Fourier series *n* an infinite trigonometric series of the form $\frac{1}{2}a_0 + a_1\cos x + b_1\sin x + a_2\cos 2x + b_2\sin 2x + ...$, where $a_0, a_1, b_1, a_2, b_2 ...$ are the **Fourier coefficients**. It is used, esp in mathematics and physics, to represent or approximate any periodic function by assigning suitable values to the coefficients

Fourier transform *n* an integral transform, used in many branches of science, of the form $F(x) = [1/\sqrt{(2\pi)}]\int e^{ixy}f(y)dy$, where the limits of integration are from −∞ to +∞ and the function F is the transform of the function f

four-in-hand *n* **1** Also called: **tally-ho** a road vehicle drawn by four horses and driven by one driver **2** a four-horse team in a coach or carriage **3** a long narrow tie formerly worn tied in a flat slipknot with the ends dangling

four-leaf clover or **four-leaved clover** *n* **1** a clover with four leaves rather than three, supposed to bring good luck **2** another name for **cloverleaf** (sense 1)

four-letter word *n* any of several short English words referring to sex or excrement: often used as swearwords and regarded generally as offensive or obscene

four-o'clock *n* **1** Also called: **marvel-of-Peru** a tropical American nyctaginaceous plant, *Mirabilis jalapa*, cultivated for its tubular yellow, red, or white flowers that open in late afternoon **2** *Austral* another name for **friarbird**, esp the noisy friarbird (*Philemon corniculatus*): so called because of its cry

404 (,fɔːrəʊ'fɔː) *n* *slang* a stupid or ineffectual person [C21 from the World Wide Web error message '404 Not Found']

four-part *adj* *music* arranged for four voices or instruments

fourpence ('fɔːpəns) *n* a former English silver

coin then worth four pennies

fourpenny ('fɔːpənɪ) *adj* fourpenny one *Brit slang* a blow, esp with the fist

four-poster *n* a bed with posts at each corner supporting a canopy and curtains. Also called: **four-poster bed**

fourragère ('fʊərə,ʒɛə; *French* furaʒɛr) *n* an ornamental cord worn on the shoulder of a uniform for identification or as an award, esp in the US and French Armies [French, feminine adj of *fourrager* relating to forage, from *fourrage* FORAGE]

fourscore (,fɔː'skɔː) *determiner* an archaic word for **eighty**

foursome ('fɔːsəm) *n* **1** a set or company of four **2** *sport* a game between two pairs of players, esp a form of golf in which each partner in a pair takes alternate strokes at the same ball. Compare **fourball, greensome 3** (*modifier*) of or performed by a company of four: *a foursome competition*

foursquare (,fɔː'skwɛə) *adv* **1** squarely; firmly ▷ *adj* **2** solid and strong **3** forthright; honest **4** a rare word for **square**. > **four'squarely** *adv* > **,four'squareness** *n*

four-stroke *adj* relating to or designating an internal-combustion engine in which the piston makes four strokes for every explosion. US and Canadian name: **four-cycle** Compare **two-stroke**

fourteen ('fɔː'tiːn) *n* **1** the cardinal number that is the sum of ten and four **2** a numeral, 14, XIV, etc, representing this number **3** something represented by, representing, or consisting of 14 units ▷ *determiner* **4 a** amounting to fourteen: *fourteen cats* **b** (*as pronoun*): *the fourteen who remained* [Old English *fēowertīene*]

Fourteen Points *pl n* the principles expounded by President Wilson in 1918 as war aims of the US

fourteenth ('fɔː'tiːnθ) *adj* **1 a** coming after the thirteenth in order, position, time etc. Often written: 14th **b** (*as noun*): *the fourteenth in succession* ▷ *n* **2 a** one of 14 equal or nearly equal parts of something **b** (*as modifier*): *a fourteenth part* **3** the fraction equal to one divided by 14 (1/14)

fourth (fɔːθ) *adj* (*usually prenominal*) **1 a** coming after the third in order, position, time, etc. Often written: 4th **b** (*as noun*): *the fourth in succession* **2** denoting the fourth forward ratio of a gearbox in motor vehicles ▷ *n* **3** *music* **a** the interval between one note and another four notes away from it counting inclusively along the diatonic scale **b** one of two notes constituting such an interval in relation to the other. See also **perfect** (sense 9), **interval** (sense 5), **diminished** (sense 2) **4** the fourth forward ratio of a gearbox in a motor vehicle **5** a less common word for **quarter** (sense 2) ▷ *adv also* **fourthly 6** after the third person, position, event, etc ▷ *sentence connector also*

fourthly 7 as the fourth point: linking what follows with the previous statements, as in a speech or argument

fourth-class *US* ▷ *adj* **1** of or relating to mail that is carried at the lowest rate ▷ *adv* **2** by fourth-class mail

fourth dimension *n* **1** the dimension of time, which is necessary in addition to three spatial dimensions to specify fully the position and behaviour of a point or particle **2** the concept in science fiction of a dimension in addition to three spatial dimensions, used to explain supranatural phenomena, events, etc > **,fourth-di'mensional** *adj*

fourth estate *n* (*sometimes capitals*) journalists or their profession; the press. See **estate** (sense 4)

Fourth International *n* another name for any of the Trotskyist Internationals

Fourth of July *n* (preceded by *the*) a holiday in the United States, traditionally celebrated with fireworks: the day of the adoption of the Declaration of Independence in 1776. Official name: **Independence Day**

Fourth Republic *n* the fourth period of republican government in France or the republic itself (1945–58)

Fourth World *n* **1** the poorest countries in the

most undeveloped parts of the world in Africa, Asia, and Latin America **2** the poorest people in developed countries

four-way *adj* (*usually prenominal*) **1** giving passage in four directions **2** made up of four elements

four-wheel drive *n* a system used in motor vehicles in which all four wheels are connected to the source of power

fovea ('fəʊvɪə) *n, pl* **-veae** (-vɪ,iː) **1** *anatomy* any small pit or depression in the surface of a bodily organ or part **2** See **fovea centralis** [C19 from Latin: a small pit] > **'foveal** *adj* > **'foveate** or **'fove,ated** *adj*

fovea centralis (sɛn'traːlɪs) *n* a small depression in the centre of the retina that contains only cone cells and is therefore the area of sharpest vision [C19 from New Latin: central fovea]

foveola (fəʊ'viːələ) *n, pl* **-lae** (-,liː) *biology* a small fovea [C19 from New Latin, diminutive of FOVEA] > **fo'veolar** *adj* > **foveolate** ('fəʊvɪə,leɪt) *or* **'foveo,lated** *adj*

Fowey (fɔɪ) *n* a resort and fishing village in SW England, in Cornwall, linked administratively with St Austell from 1968 to 1974. Pop: 2064 (2001)

fowl (faʊl) *n* **1** See **domestic fowl 2** any other bird, esp any gallinaceous bird, that is used as food or hunted as game. See also **waterfowl, wildfowl 3** the flesh or meat of fowl, esp of chicken **4** an archaic word for any **bird** ▷ *vb* **5** (*intr*) to hunt or snare wildfowl [Old English *fugol*; related to Old Frisian *fugel*, Old Norse *fogl*, Gothic *fugls*, Old High German *fogal*]

fowl cholera *n* *vet science* a contagious disease of poultry and other fowl, usually resulting in sudden death; caused by the organism *Pasteurella multocida*

Fowliang or **Fou-liang** ('fuː'ljæn) *n* a variant transliteration of the Chinese name for **Jingdezhen**

fowling ('faʊlɪŋ) *n* the shooting or trapping of birds for sport or as a livelihood > **'fowler** *n*

fowl mite *n* any of various mites parasitic in birds, usually bloodsucking and including the **red fowl mite** (*Dermanyssus gallinae*) and the **northern fowl mite** (*Ornithonyssus sylviarum*), both pests of poultry

fowl pest *n* **1** an acute and usually fatal viral disease of domestic fowl, characterized by refusal to eat, high temperature, and discoloration of the comb and wattles **2** another name for **Newcastle disease**

fox (fɒks) *n, pl* **foxes** *or* **fox 1** any canine mammal of the genus *Vulpes* and related genera. They are mostly predators that do not hunt in packs and typically have large pointed ears, a pointed muzzle, and a bushy tail. Related adj: **vulpine 2** the fur of any of these animals, usually reddish-brown or grey in colour **3** a person who is cunning and sly **4** *slang, chiefly US* a sexually attractive woman **5** *Bible* **a** a jackal **b** an image of a false prophet **6** *nautical* small stuff made from yarns twisted together and then tarred ▷ *vb* **7** (*tr*) to perplex or confound **8** to cause (paper, wood, etc) to become discoloured with spots, or (of paper, etc) to become discoloured, as through mildew **9** (*tr*) to trick; deceive **10** (*intr*) to act deceitfully or craftily **11** (*tr*) *Austral informal* to pursue stealthily; tail **12** (*tr*) *Austral informal* to chase and retrieve (a ball) **13** (*tr*) *obsolete* to befuddle with alcoholic drink [Old English; related to Old High German *fuhs*, Old Norse *fōa* fox, Sanskrit *puccha* tail; see VIXEN] > **'fox,like** *adj*

Fox (fɒks) *n* **1** (*pl* Fox *or* Foxes) a member of a North American Indian people formerly living west of Lake Michigan along the Fox River **2** the language of this people, belonging to the Algonquian family

Foxe Basin (fɒks) *n* an arm of the Atlantic in NE Canada, between Melville Peninsula and Baffin Island

foxfire ('fɒks,faɪə) *n* a luminescent glow emitted by certain fungi on rotting wood. See also bioluminescence

foxglove ('fɒks,glʌv) *n* any Eurasian scrophulariaceous plant of the genus *Digitalis*, esp *D. purpurea*, having spikes of purple or white thimble-like flowers. The soft wrinkled leaves are a source of digitalis

fox grape *n* a common wild grape, *Vitis labrusca* of the northern US, having purplish-black fruit and woolly leaves: the source of many cultivated grapes, including the catawba

foxhole ('fɒks,həʊl) *n military* a small pit dug during an action to provide individual shelter against hostile fire

foxhound ('fɒks,haʊnd) *n* either of two breeds (the English and the American) of dog having a short smooth coat and pendent ears. Though not large (height about 60 cm or 23 in) they have great stamina and are usually kept for hunting foxes

fox hunt *n* 1 a the hunting of foxes with hounds b an instance of this 2 an organization for fox-hunting within a particular area

fox-hunting *n* a sport in which hunters follow a pack of hounds in pursuit of a fox > **'fox-,hunter** *n*

foxie ('fɒksɪ) *n Austral* an informal name for **fox terrier**

foxing ('fɒksɪŋ) *n* a piece of leather used to reinforce or trim part of the upper of a shoe

fox moth *n* a coppery-brown European eggar moth, *Macrothylacia rubi*, whose black-and-yellow woolly larvae are commonly found on heather and bramble

fox squirrel *n* a large squirrel, *Sciurus niger*, occurring in E North America

foxtail ('fɒks,teɪl) *n* 1 any grass of the genus *Alopecurus*, esp *A. pratensis*, of Europe, Asia, and South America, having soft cylindrical spikes of flowers: cultivated as a pasture grass 2 any of various similar and related grasses, esp any of the genus *Setaria*

fox terrier *n* either of two breeds of small terrier, the wire-haired and the smooth, having a white coat with markings of black or tan or both

foxtrot ('fɒks,trɒt) *n* 1 a ballroom dance in quadruple time, combining short and long steps in various sequences ▷ *vb* -trots, -trotting, -trotted 2 (*intr*) to perform this dance

Foxtrot ('fɒks,trɒt) *n communications* a code word for the letter f

foxy ('fɒksɪ) *adj* foxier, foxiest 1 of or resembling a fox, esp in craftiness 2 smelling strongly like a fox 3 of a reddish-brown colour 4 (of paper, wood, etc) spotted, esp by mildew 5 (of wine) having the flavour of fox grapes 6 (of oats) having a musty smell as a result of getting wet, fermenting, and drying out 7 *slang* sexy; sexually attractive > **'foxily** *adv* > **'foxiness** *n*

foyboat ('fɔɪ,bəʊt) *n Tyneside dialect* a small rowing boat b (*in combination*): *a foyboatman* [C19 from *foy* to provide aid for ships, esp those in distress]

foyer ('fɔɪeɪ, 'fɔɪə) *n* 1 a hall, lobby, or anteroom, used for reception and as a meeting place, as in a hotel, theatre, cinema, etc 2 (in Britain) a centre providing accommodation and employment training, etc for homeless young people [C19 from French: fireplace, from Medieval Latin *focārius*, from Latin *focus* fire]

fp 1 *abbreviation for* fine point 2 *music symbol for* fortepiano

FP *or* **fp** *abbreviation for* 1 freezing point 2 fully paid

FPA *abbreviation for* Family Planning Association

FPO *abbreviation for* field post office

fps *abbreviation for* 1 feet per second 2 foot-pound-second 3 *photog* frames per second

fps units *pl n* an Imperial system of units based on the foot, pound, and second as the units of length, mass, and time. For scientific and most technical purposes these units have been replaced by SI units

fr *the internet domain name for* France

f.r. franc *abbreviation for* 1 *Christianity* Father 2

France 3 French 4 the German equivalent of **Mrs** [from German *Frau*]

Fr 1 *Christianity abbreviation for* a Frater b Father 2 *the chemical symbol for* francium [(for sense 1) Latin: brother]

FR ▷ *international car registration for* Faeroes

Fra (frɑː) *n* brother: a title given to an Italian monk or friar [Italian, short for *frate* brother (in either natural or religious sense), from Latin *frater* BROTHER]

fracas ('frækɑː) *n* a noisy quarrel; brawl [C18 from French, from *fracasser* to shatter, from Latin *frangere* to break, influenced by *quassāre* to shatter]

FRACP *abbreviation for* Fellow of the Royal Australasian College of Physicians

FRACS *abbreviation for* Fellow of the Royal Australasian College of Surgeons

fractal ('fræktəl) *maths* ▷ *n* 1 a figure or surface generated by successive subdivisions of a simpler polygon or polyhedron, according to some iterative process ▷ *adj* 2 of, relating to, or involving such a process: *fractal geometry; fractal curve* [C20 from Latin *frāctus* past participle of *frangere* to break]

fraction ('frækʃən) *n* 1 *maths* a a ratio of two expressions or numbers other than zero b any rational number that is not an integer 2 any part or subdivision 3 a small piece 4 *chem* a component of a mixture separated by a fractional process, such as fractional distillation 5 *Christianity* the formal breaking of the bread in Communion 6 the act of breaking ▷ *vb* 7 (*tr*) to divide [C14 from Late Latin *fractiō* a breaking into pieces, from Latin *fractus* broken, from *frangere* to break]

fractional ('frækʃənəl) *adj* 1 relating to, containing, or constituting one or more fractions 2 of or denoting a process in which components of a mixture are separated by exploiting differences in their physical properties, such as boiling points, solubility, etc 3 very small or insignificant 4 broken up; fragmented. Also: fractionary ('frækʃənərɪ) > **'fractionally** *adv*

fractional crystallization *n chem* the process of separating the components of a solution on the basis of their different solubilities, by means of evaporating the solution until the least soluble component crystallizes out

fractional currency *n* paper or metal money of smaller denomination than the standard monetary unit

fractional distillation *n* 1 the process of separating the constituents of a liquid mixture by heating it and condensing separately the components according to their different boiling points 2 a distillation in which the vapour is brought into contact with a countercurrent of condensed liquid to increase the purity of the final products ▷ Sometimes shortened to: distillation

fractionate ('frækʃə,neɪt) *vb* 1 to separate or cause to separate into constituents or into fractions containing concentrated constituents 2 (*tr*) *chem* to obtain (a constituent of a mixture) by a fractional process > ,fraction'ation *n* > 'fraction,ator *n*

fractionating column *n chem* a long vertical cylinder used in fractional distillation, in which internal reflux enables separation of high and low boiling fractions to take place

fractionize *or* **fractionise** ('frækʃə,naɪz) *vb* to divide (a number or quantity) into fractions > ,fractioni'zation *or* ,fractioni'sation *n*

fractious ('frækʃəs) *adj* 1 irritable 2 unruly [C18 from (obsolete) *fraction* discord + -OUS] > 'fractiously *adv* > 'fractiousness *n*

> USAGE *Fractious* is sometimes wrongly used where *factious* is meant: *this factious (not fractious) dispute has split the party still further*

fractocumulus (,fræktəʊ'kjuː:mjʊləs) *n, pl* -li (-,laɪ) low ragged slightly bulbous cloud, often

appearing below nimbostratus clouds during rain. Also called: fractocumulus cloud [C19 from Latin *fractus* broken + CUMULUS]

fractostratus (,fræktəʊ'strɑːtəs, -'stræt-) *n, pl* -ti (-taɪ) low ragged layered cloud often appearing below nimbostratus clouds during rain [C19 from Latin *fractus* broken + STRATUS]

fracture ('fræktʃə) *n* 1 the act of breaking or the state of being broken 2 a the breaking or cracking of a bone or the tearing of a cartilage b the resulting condition. See also **Colles' fracture, comminuted fracture, compound fracture, greenstick fracture, impacted** (sense 2) 3 a division, split, or breach 4 *mineralogy* a the characteristic appearance of the surface of a freshly broken mineral or rock b the way in which a mineral or rock naturally breaks ▷ *vb* 5 to break or cause to break; split 6 to break or crack (a bone) or (of a bone) to become broken or cracked 7 to tear (a cartilage) or (of a cartilage) to become torn [C15 from Old French, from Latin *fractūra*, from *frangere* to break] > 'fracturable *adj* > 'fractural *adj*

frae (freɪ) *prep* a Scot word for **from**

fraenum *or* **frenum** ('friːnəm) *n, pl* -na (-nə) a fold of membrane or skin, such as the fold beneath the tongue, that supports an organ [C18 from Latin: bridle]

frag (fræg) *vb* frags, fragging, fragged (*tr*) US *military slang* to kill or wound (a fellow soldier or superior officer) deliberately with an explosive device [C20 short for *fragmentation grenade*, as used in Vietnam] > 'fragging *n*

fragile ('frædʒaɪl) *adj* 1 able to be broken easily 2 in a weakened physical state 3 delicate; light 4 slight; tenuous [C17 from Latin *fragilis*, from *frangere* to break] > 'fragilely *adv* > fragility (frə'dʒɪlɪtɪ) *or* fragileness *n*

fragile-X syndrome *n* an inherited condition characterized by mental subnormality: affected individuals have an X-chromosome that is easily damaged under certain conditions

fragment *n* ('frægmənt) 1 a piece broken off or detached: *fragments of rock* 2 an incomplete piece; portion: *fragments of a novel* 3 a scrap; morsel; bit ▷ *vb* (fræg'ment) *also or US* fragmentize ('frægmən,taɪz) 4 to break or cause to break into fragments [C15 from Latin *fragmentum*, from *frangere* to break]

fragmental (fræg'mentəl) *adj* 1 (of rocks or deposits) composed of fragments of pre-existing rocks and minerals 2 another word for **fragmentary**. > frag'mentally *adv*

fragmentary ('frægməntərɪ, -trɪ) *adj* made up of fragments; disconnected; incomplete. Also: fragmental > 'fragmentarily *adv* > 'fragmentariness *n*

fragmentation (,frægmen'teɪʃən) *n* 1 the act of fragmenting or the state of being fragmented 2 the disintegration of norms regulating behaviour, thought, and social relationships 3 the steel particles of an exploded projectile 4 (*modifier*) of or relating to a weapon designed to explode into many small pieces, esp as an antipersonnel weapon: *a fragmentation bomb*

fragrance ('freɪgrəns) *or* **fragrancy** *n, pl* -grances *or* -grancies 1 a pleasant or sweet odour; scent; perfume 2 the state of being fragrant

fragrant ('freɪgrənt) *adj* having a pleasant or sweet smell [C15 from Latin *frāgrāns*, from *frāgrāre* to emit a smell] > 'fragrantly *adv*

fragrant orchid *n* another name for **scented orchid**

frail¹ (freɪl) *adj* 1 physically weak and delicate 2 fragile: *a frail craft* 3 easily corrupted or tempted [C13 from Old French *frele*, from Latin *fragilis*, FRAGILE] > 'frailly *adv* > 'frailness *n*

frail² (freɪl) *n* 1 a rush basket for figs or raisins 2 a quantity of raisins or figs equal to between 50 and 75 pounds [C13 from Old French *fraiel*, of uncertain origin]

frailty ('freɪltɪ) *n, pl* -ties 1 physical or moral

f

weakness **2** (*often plural*) a fault symptomatic of moral weakness

fraise (freɪz) *n* **1** a neck ruff worn during the 16th century **2** a sloping or horizontal rampart of pointed stakes **3 a** a tool for enlarging a drill hole **b** a tool for cutting teeth on watch wheels [c18 from French: mesentery of a calf, from Old French *fraiser* to remove a shell, from Latin *frendere* to crush]

Fraktur (*German* frak'tuːr) *n* a style of typeface, formerly used in German typesetting for many printed works [German, from Latin *fractūra* a breaking, FRACTURE; from the curlicues that seem to interrupt the continuous line of a word]

framboesia or US **frambesia** (fræm'biːzɪə) *n* *pathol* another name for **yaws** [c19 from New Latin, from French *framboise* raspberry; see FRAMBOISE; so called because of its raspberry-like excrescences]

framboise *French* (frɑ̃bwaz) *n* a brandy distilled from raspberries in the Alsace-Lorraine region [c16 from Old French: raspberry, probably of Germanic origin]

frame (freɪm) *n* **1** an open structure that gives shape and support to something, such as the transverse stiffening ribs of a ship's hull or an aircraft's fuselage or the skeletal beams and uprights of a building **2** an enclosing case or border into which something is fitted **3** the system around which something is built up **4** the structure of the human body **5** a condition; state (esp in the phrase **frame of mind**) **6 a** one of a series of individual exposures on a strip of film used in making motion pictures **b** an individual exposure on a film used in still photography **c** an individual picture in a comic strip **7 a** a television picture scanned by one or more electron beams at a particular frequency **b** the area of the picture so formed **8** *billiards, snooker* **a** the wooden triangle used to set up the balls **b** the balls when set up **c** a single game finished when all the balls have been potted. US and Canadian equivalent (for senses 8a, 8b): **rack 9** *computing* (on a website) a self-contained section that functions independently from other parts; by using frames, a website designer can make some areas of a website remain constant while others change according to the choices made by the internet user **10** short for **cold frame 11** one of the sections of which a beehive is composed, esp one designed to hold a honeycomb **12** a machine or part of a machine over which yarn is stretched in the production of textiles **13** (in language teaching, etc) a syntactic construction with a gap in it, used for assigning words to syntactic classes by seeing which words may fill the gap **14** *statistics* an enumeration of a population for the purposes of sampling, esp as the basis of a stratified sample **15** (in telecommunications, computers, etc) one cycle of a regularly recurring number of pulses in a pulse train **16** *slang* another word for **frame-up 17** *obsolete* shape; form **18 in the frame** likely to be awarded or to achieve ▷ *vb* (*mainly tr*) **19** to construct by fitting parts together **20** to draw up the plans or basic details for; outline **21** to compose, contrive, or conceive **22** to provide, support, or enclose with a frame **23** to form (words) with the lips, esp silently **24** *slang* to conspire to incriminate (someone) on a false charge **25** *slang* to contrive the dishonest outcome of (a contest, match, etc); rig **26** (*intr*) *Yorkshire and Northeastern English dialect* **a** (*usually imperative or dependent imperative*) to make an effort **b** to have ability [Old English *framie* to avail; related to Old Frisian *framia* to carry out, Old Norse *frama*] > 'framable *or* 'frameable *adj* > 'frameless *adj* > 'framer *n*

frame aerial *n* another name for **loop aerial**

frame house *n* a house that has a timber framework and cladding

frame line *n* *films* a black horizontal bar appearing between successive picture images

frame of reference *n* **1** a set of basic assumptions or standards that determines and sanctions behaviour **2** any set of planes or curves, such as the three coordinate axes, used to locate or measure movement of a point in space

frame saw *n* a saw with a thin blade held in a specially shaped frame. Also called: **span saw**

frame-up *n* *slang* **1** a conspiracy to incriminate someone on a false charge **2** a plot to bring about a dishonest result, as in a contest

framework ('freɪm,wɜːk) *n* **1** a structural plan or basis of a project **2** a structure or frame supporting or containing something **3** frames collectively **4** work such as embroidery or weaving done in or on a frame

framing ('freɪmɪŋ) *n* **1** a frame, framework, or system of frames **2** the way in which something is framed **3** adjustment of the longitudinal position of the film in a projector gate to secure proper vertical positioning of the picture on the screen

franc (fræŋk; *French* frɑ̃) *n* **1** the former standard monetary unit of France, most French dependencies, Andorra, and Monaco, divided into 100 centimes; replaced by the euro in 2002. Also called: **French franc 2** the former standard monetary unit of Belgium (**Belgian franc**) and Luxembourg (**Luxembourg franc**), divided into 100 centimes; replaced by the euro in 2002 **3** the standard monetary unit of Switzerland and Liechtenstein, divided into 100 centimes. Also called: **Swiss franc 4** the standard monetary unit, comprising 100 centimes, of the following countries: Benin, Burkina-Faso, Cameroon, the Central African Republic, Chad, Congo-Brazzaville, Côte d'Ivoire, Equatorial Guinea, Gabon, Guinea-Bissau, Mali, Niger, Senegal, and Togo. Also called: **franc CFA, CFA franc, franc of the African financial community 5** the standard monetary unit of Burundi (**Burundi franc**), Comoros (**Comorian franc**), Democratic Republic of Congo (formerly Zaïre; **Congolese franc**), Djibouti (**Djibouti franc**), Guinea (**Guinea franc**), Madagascar (**franc malgache**), Rwanda (**Rwanda franc**), and French Polynesia and New Caledonia (**French Pacific franc**)

France (frɑːns) *n* a republic in W Europe, between the English Channel, the Mediterranean, and the Atlantic: the largest country wholly in Europe; became a republic in 1793 after the French Revolution and an empire in 1804 under Napoleon; reverted to a monarchy (1815–48), followed by the Second Republic (1848–52), the Second Empire (1852–70), the Third Republic (1870–1940), and the Fourth and Fifth Republics (1946 and 1958); a member of the European Union. It is generally flat or undulating in the north and west and mountainous in the south and east. Official language: French. Religion: Roman Catholic majority. Currency: euro. Capital: Paris. Pop: 60 434 000 (2004 est). Area: (including Corsica) 551 600 sq km (212 973 sq miles). Related adjs: **French, Gallic**

Franche-Comté (*French* frɑ̃ʃkɔ̃te) *n* a region of E France, covering the Jura and the low country east of the Saône: part of the Kingdom of Burgundy (6th cent. AD–1137); autonomous as the Free County of Burgundy (1137–1384); under Burgundian rule again (1384–1477) and Hapsburg rule (1493–1674); annexed by France (1678)

franchise ('fræntʃaɪz) *n* **1** (usually preceded by *the*) the right to vote, esp for representatives in a legislative body; suffrage **2** any exemption, privilege, or right granted to an individual or group by a public authority, such as the right to use public property for a business **3** *commerce* authorization granted by a manufacturing enterprise to a distributor to market the manufacturer's products **4** the full rights of citizenship **5** *films* a film that is or has the potential to be part of a series and lends itself to merchandising **6** (in marine insurance) a sum or percentage stated in a policy, below which the insurer disclaims all liability ▷ *vb* **7** (*tr*) *commerce, chiefly US and Canadian* to grant (a person, firm, etc) a franchise **8** an obsolete word for **enfranchise** [c13 from Old French, from *franchir* to set free, from *franc* free; see FRANK] > 'franchi,see *n* > 'franchiser *n* > franchisement ('fræntʃɪzmənt) *n*

Franciscan (fræn'sɪskən) *n* **a** a member of any of several Christian religious orders of mendicant friars or nuns tracing their origins back to Saint Francis of Assisi; a Grey Friar **b** (*as modifier*): *a Franciscan friar*

Francis turbine (fra:nsɪs) *n* a water turbine designed to produce high flow from a low head of pressure: used esp in hydroelectric power generation [named after J. B. *Francis* (1815–92), English-born hydraulic engineer, who invented it]

francium ('frænsɪəm) *n* an unstable radioactive element of the alkali-metal group, occurring in minute amounts in uranium ores. Symbol: Fr; atomic no: 87; half-life of most stable isotope, ^{223}Fr: 22 minutes; valency: 1; melting pt: 27°C; boiling pt: 677°C [c20 from New Latin, from FRANCE + -IUM; so-called because first found in France]

Franco- ('fræŋkəʊ-) *combining form* indicating France or French: *Franco-Prussian* [from Medieval Latin *Francus*, from Late Latin: FRANK]

francolin ('fræŋkəʊlɪn) *n* any African or Asian partridge of the genus *Francolinus* [c17 from French, from Old Italian *francolino*, of unknown origin]

Franconia (fræn'kəʊnɪə) *n* a medieval duchy of Germany, inhabited by the Franks from the 7th century, now chiefly in Bavaria, Hesse, and Baden-Württemberg

Franconian (fræn'kəʊnɪən) *n* **1** a group of medieval Germanic dialects spoken by the Franks in an area from N Bavaria and Alsace to the mouth of the Rhine. **Low Franconian** developed into Dutch, while **Upper Franconian** contributed to High German, of which it remains a recognizable dialect. See also **Old Low German, Old High German, Frankish** ▷ *adj* **2** of or relating to Franconia, the Franks, or their languages

Francophile ('fræŋkəʊ,faɪl) *or* **Francophil** ('fræŋkəʊfɪl) (*sometimes not capital*) *n* **1** a person who admires France and the French ▷ *adj* **2** marked by or possessing admiration of France and the French

Francophobe ('fræŋkəʊ,fəʊb) *n* (*sometimes not capital*) **1** a person who hates or despises France or its people **2** *Canadian* a person who hates or fears Canadian Francophones

Francophone ('fræŋkəʊ,fəʊn) (*often not capital*) *n* **1** a person who speaks French, esp a native speaker ▷ *adj* **2** speaking French as a native language **3** using French as a lingua franca ▷ Compare **Anglophone**

Franco-Prussian War *n* the war of 1870–71 between France and Prussia culminating in the fall of the French Second Empire and the founding of the German empire

franc-tireur *French* (frɑ̃tirœr) *n* **1** a sniper **2** a guerrilla or irregular soldier [c19 from *franc* free + *tireur* shooter, from *tirer* to shoot, of unknown origin]

franger ('fræŋə) *n* *Austral slang* a condom [c20 perhaps related to FRENCH LETTER]

frangible ('frændʒɪbᵊl) *adj* breakable or fragile [c15 from Old French, ultimately from Latin *frangere* to break] > ,frangi'bility *or* 'frangibleness *n*

frangipane ('frændʒɪ,peɪn) *n* **1 a** a pastry filled with cream and flavoured with almonds **b** a rich cake mixture containing ground almonds **2** a variant of **frangipani** (the perfume)

frangipani (,frændʒɪ'pɑːnɪ) *n, pl* **-panis, -pani 1** any tropical American apocynaceous shrub of the genus *Plumeria*, esp *P. rubra*, cultivated for its waxy typically white or pink flowers, which have a sweet overpowering scent **2** a perfume prepared from this plant or resembling the odour of its flowers **3** native frangipani *Austral* an Australian evergreen tree, *Hymenosporum flavum*, with large fragrant yellow flowers: family *Pittosporaceae* [C17 via French from Italian: perfume for scenting gloves, named after the Marquis Muzio *Frangipani*, 16th-century Roman nobleman who invented it]

Franglais (*French* frɑ̃glɛ) *n* informal French containing a high proportion of words of English origin [C20 from French *français* French + *anglais* English]

frank (fræŋk) *adj* **1** honest and straightforward in speech or attitude: *a frank person* **2** outspoken or blunt **3** open and avowed; undisguised: *frank interest* **4** an obsolete word for **free** or **generous** ▷ *vb* (*tr*) **5** *chiefly Brit* to put a mark on (a letter, parcel, etc), either cancelling the postage stamp or in place of a stamp, ensuring free carriage. See also **postmark 6** to mark (a letter, parcel, etc) with an official mark or signature, indicating the right of free delivery **7** to facilitate or assist (a person) to come and go, pass, or enter easily **8** to obtain immunity for or exempt (a person) ▷ *n* **9** an official mark or signature affixed to a letter, parcel, etc, ensuring free delivery or delivery without stamps **10** the privilege, issued to certain people and establishments, entitling them to delivery without postage stamps [C13 from Old French *franc*, from Medieval Latin *francus* free; identical with FRANK (in Frankish Gaul only members of this people enjoyed full freedom)] > '**frankable** *adj* > '**franker** *n* > '**frankness** *n*

Frank (fræŋk) *n* a member of a group of West Germanic peoples who spread from the east bank of the middle Rhine into the Roman Empire in the late 4th century AD, gradually conquering most of Gaul and Germany. The Franks achieved their greatest power under Charlemagne [Old English *Franca*; related to Old High German *Franko*; perhaps from the name of a typical Frankish weapon (compare Old English *franca* javelin)]

frankalmoign (ˈfræŋkəlˌmɔɪn) *n English legal history* a form of tenure by which religious bodies held lands, esp on condition of praying for the soul of the donor [C16 from Anglo-French *fraunke almoigne*, from *fraunke* FRANK + *almoign* church treasury, alms chest]

franked investment income *n* (formerly) dividends from one UK company received by another on which the paying company had paid corporation tax so that the receiving company had no corporation tax to pay: discontinued from 1999

Frankenstein (ˈfræŋkɪnˌstaɪn) *n* **1** a person who creates something that brings about his ruin **2** Also called: **Frankenstein's monster** a thing that destroys its creator [C19 after Baron *Frankenstein*, who created a destructive monster from parts of corpses in the novel by Mary Shelley (1818)] > ˌFranken'steinian *adj*

Frankenstein food *or* **Frankenfood** (ˈfræŋkənˌfuːd) *n facetious* any foodstuff that has been genetically modified [C20 from FRANKENSTEIN, alluding to its unnatural origin]

Frankfort (ˈfræŋkfət) *n* **1** a city in N Kentucky: the state capital. Pop: 27 408 (2003 est) **2** *now rare* an English spelling of **Frankfurt**

Frankfurt (am Main) (*German* ˈfraŋkfʊrt ˌam ˈmain,) *n* a city in central Germany, in Hesse on the Main River: a Roman settlement in the 1st century; a free imperial city (1372–1806); seat of the federal assembly (1815–66); university (1914); trade fairs since the 13th century. Pop: 643 432 (2003 est)

Frankfurt (an der Oder) (*German* ˈfraŋkfʊrt ˌan der ˈoːdər,) *n* a city in E Germany on the Polish border: member of the Hanseatic League (1368–1450). Pop: 67 014 (2003 est)

frankfurter (ˈfræŋkˌfɜːtə) *n* a light brown smoked sausage, made of finely minced pork or beef, often served in a bread roll [C20 short for German *Frankfurter Wurst* sausage from FRANKFURT (AM MAIN)]

Frankfurter (ˈfræŋkˌfɜːtə) *n* an inhabitant or native of Frankfurt

Frankfurt School *n philosophy* a school of thought, founded at the University of Frankfurt in 1923 by Theodor Adorno, Herbert Marcuse and others, derived from Marxist, Freudian, and Hegelian theory

frankincense (ˈfræŋkɪnˌsɛns) *n* an aromatic gum resin obtained from trees of the burseraceous genus *Boswellia*, which occur in Asia and Africa. Also called: **olibanum** [C14 from Old French *franc* free, pure + *encens* INCENSE¹; see FRANK]

Frankish (ˈfræŋkɪʃ) *n* **1** the ancient West Germanic language of the Franks, esp the dialect that contributed to the vocabulary of modern French. See also **Franconian, Old High German** ▷ *adj* **2** of or relating to the Franks or their language

franklin (ˈfræŋklɪn) *n* (in 14th- and 15th-century England) a substantial landholder of free but not noble birth [C13 from Anglo-French *fraunclein*, from Old French *franc* free, on the model of CHAMBERLAIN]

franklinite (ˈfræŋklɪˌnaɪt) *n* a black mineral consisting of an oxide of iron, manganese, and zinc: a source of iron and zinc. Formula: $(Fe,Mn,Zn) (Fe,Mn)_2O_4$ [C19 from *Franklin*, New Jersey, where it is found, + -ITE¹]

frankly (ˈfræŋklɪ) *adv* **1** (*sentence modifier*) in truth; to be honest **2** in a frank manner

frankpledge (ˈfræŋkˌplɛdʒ) *n* (in medieval England) **1** the corporate responsibility of members of a tithing for the good behaviour of each other **2** a member of a tithing **3** a tithing itself [C15 via Anglo-French from Old French *franc* free (see FRANK) + *plege* PLEDGE]

frantic (ˈfræntɪk) *adj* **1** distracted with fear, pain, joy, etc **2** marked by or showing frenzy: *frantic efforts* **3** *archaic* insane [C14 from Old French *frenetique*, from Latin *phreneticus* mad, FRENETIC] > '**frantically** *or* '**franticly** *adv* > '**franticness** *n*

Franz Josef Land (*German* frants ˈjoːzɛf) *n* an archipelago of over 100 islands in the Arctic Ocean, administratively part of Russia. Area: about 21 000 sq km (8000 sq miles). Russian name: **Zemlya Frantsa Iosifa** (zjiˈmlja ˈfrantsə ˈjɔsifa)

frap (fræp) *vb* **fraps, frapping, frapped** (*tr*) *nautical* to lash down or together [C14 from Old French *fraper* to hit, probably of imitative origin]

frape (freɪp) *adj Southwest English dialect* tightly bound [see FRAP]

frappé (ˈfræpeɪ; *French* frape) *n* **1** a drink consisting of a liqueur, poured over crushed ice ▷ *adj* **2** (*postpositive*) (esp of drinks) chilled; iced [C19 from French, from *frapper* to strike, hence, chill; see FRAP]

Frascati (fræˈskɑːtɪ) *n* a dry or semisweet white wine from the Lazio region of Italy

Fraser (ˈfreɪzə) *n* a river in SW Canada, in S central British Columbia, flowing northwest, south, and west through spectacular canyons in the Coast Mountains to the Strait of Georgia. Length: 1370 km (850 miles)

frass (fræs) *n* excrement or other refuse left by insects and insect larvae [C19 from German, from *fressen* to devour]

frat (fræt) *n US slang* **a** a member of a fraternity **b** (*as modifier*): *the frat kid*

fratch (frætʃ) *n English dialect* a quarrel [C19 from obsolete *fratch* to make a harsh noise; perhaps of imitative origin] > '**fratchy** *adj*

frater¹ (ˈfreɪtə) *n* a mendicant friar or a lay brother in a monastery or priory [C16 from Latin: BROTHER]

frater² (ˈfreɪtə) *n archaic* a refectory [C13 from Old French *fraiteur*, apheptic variant of *refreitor*, from Late Latin *refectōrium* REFECTORY]

fraternal (frəˈtɜːnªl) *adj* **1** of or suitable to a brother; brotherly **2** of or relating to a fraternity **3** designating either or both of a pair of twins of the same or opposite sex that developed from two separate fertilized ova. Compare **identical** (sense 3) [C15 from Latin *frāternus*, from *frāter* brother] > fra'ternalism *n* > fra'ternally *adv*

fraternity (frəˈtɜːnɪtɪ) *n, pl* **-ties 1** a body of people united in interests, aims, etc: *the teaching fraternity* **2** brotherhood **3** *US and Canadian* a secret society joined by male students, usually functioning as a social club

fraternize *or* **fraternise** (ˈfrætəˌnaɪz) *vb* (*intr*; often foll by *with*) to associate on friendly terms > ˌfraterni'zation *or* ˌfraterni'sation *n* > '**frater,nizer** *or* '**frater,niser** *n*

fratricide (ˈfrætrɪˌsaɪd, ˈfreɪ-) *n* **1** the act of killing one's brother **2** a person who kills his brother **3** *military* the destruction of or interference with a nuclear missile before it can strike its target caused by the earlier explosion of a warhead at a nearby target [C15 from Latin *frātricīda*; see FRATER¹, -CIDE] > ˌfratri'cidal *adj*

Frau (frau) *n, pl* **Frauen** (ˈfrauən) *or* **Fraus** a married German woman: usually used as a title equivalent to *Mrs* and sometimes extended to older unmarried women [from Old High German *frouwa*; related to Dutch *vrouw*]

fraud (frɔːd) *n* **1** deliberate deception, trickery, or cheating intended to gain an advantage **2** an act or instance of such deception **3** something false or spurious: *his explanation was a fraud* **4** *informal* a person who acts in a false or deceitful way [C14 from Old French *fraude*, from Latin *fraus* deception]

Fraud Squad *n* (in Britain) the department of a police force that is concerned with criminal fraud

fraudster (ˈfrɔːdstə) *n* a swindler

fraudulent (ˈfrɔːdjʊlənt) *adj* **1** acting with or having the intent to deceive **2** relating to or proceeding from fraud or dishonest action [C15 from Latin *fraudulentus* deceitful] > '**fraudulence** *or* '**fraudulency** *n* > '**fraudulently** *adv*

Frauenfeld (*German* ˈfrauənfɛlt) *n* a town in NE Switzerland, capital of Thurgau canton. Pop: 21 954 (2000)

fraughan (ˈfrɒhən) *n* an Irish word for **whortleberry** (senses 1, 2) [from Irish Gaelic *fraochán*, diminutive of *fraoch* heather]

fraught (frɔːt) *adj* **1** (*usually postpositive* and foll by *with*) filled or charged; attended: *a venture fraught with peril* **2** *informal* showing or producing tension or anxiety **3** *archaic* (*usually postpositive* and foll by *with*) freighted ▷ *n* **4** an obsolete word for **freight** [C14 from Middle Dutch *vrachten*, from *vracht* FREIGHT]

Fräulein (*German* ˈfrɔylain; *English* ˈfrɔːlaɪn, ˈfrau-) *n, pl* **-lein** *or English* **-leins** an unmarried German woman: formerly used as a title equivalent to *Miss*. Abbreviation: Frl [from Middle High German *vrouwelīn*, diminutive of *vrouwe* lady]

Fraunhofer lines (*German* ˈfraunhoːfər) *pl n* a set of dark lines appearing in the continuous emission spectrum of the sun. It is caused by the absorption of light of certain wavelengths coming from the hotter region of the sun by elements in the cooler outer atmosphere [named after J. von *Fraunhofer* (1787–1826), German physicist]

frawzey (ˈfrɔːzɪ) *n Southwest English dialect* a celebration; treat

fraxinella (ˌfræksɪˈnɛlə) *n* another name for **gas plant** [C17 from New Latin: a little ash tree, from Latin *frāxinus* ash]

fray¹ (freɪ) *n* **1** a noisy quarrel **2** a fight or brawl **3** an archaic word for **fright** ▷ *vb archaic* **4** (*tr*) to frighten [C14 short for AFFRAY]

fray² (freɪ) *vb* **1** to wear or cause to wear away into tatters or loose threads, esp at an edge or end **2** to make or become strained or irritated **3** to rub or chafe (another object) or (of two objects) to rub against one another ▷ *n* **4** a frayed place, as in cloth [C14 from French *frayer* to rub, from Latin *fricāre*; see FRICTION, FRIABLE]

Fray Bentos (ˌfreɪ ˈbɛntɒs) *n* a port in W Uruguay, on the River Uruguay: noted for meat-packing. Pop: 21 400 (1995 est)

frazil (ˈfreɪzɪl) *n* small pieces of ice that form in

water moving turbulently enough to prevent the formation of a sheet of ice [C19 from Canadian French *frasil*, from French *fraisil* cinders, ultimately from Latin *fax* torch]

frazzle ('fræzªl) *vb* **1** *informal* to make or become exhausted or weary; tire out **2** a less common word for **fray²** (sense 1) ▷ *n* **3** *informal* the state of being frazzled or exhausted **4** a frayed end or remnant **5** **to a frazzle** *informal* absolutely; completely (esp in the phrase **burnt to a frazzle**) [C19 probably from Middle English *faselen* to fray, from *fasel* fringe; influenced by FRAY²]

FRCM (in Britain) *abbreviation for* Fellow of the Royal College of Music

FRCO (in Britain) *abbreviation for* Fellow of the Royal College of Organists

FRCP (in Britain) *abbreviation for* Fellow of the Royal College of Physicians

FRCS (in Britain) *abbreviation for* Fellow of the Royal College of Surgeons

FRCVS (in Britain) *abbreviation for* Fellow of the Royal College of Veterinary Surgeons

freak¹ (fri:k) *n* **1** a person, animal, or plant that is abnormal or deformed; monstrosity **2 a** an object, event, etc, that is abnormal or extremely unusual **b** (*as modifier*): *a freak storm* **3** a personal whim or caprice **4** *informal* a person who acts or dresses in a markedly unconventional or strange way **5** *informal* a person who is obsessed with something specified: *a jazz freak* ▷ *vb* **6** See **freak out** [C16 of obscure origin]

freak² (fri:k) *rare* ▷ *n* **1** a fleck or streak of colour ▷ *vb* **2** (*tr*) to streak with colour; variegate [C17 from earlier *freaked*, probably coined by Milton, based on STREAK¹ + obsolete *freckt* freckled; see FRECKLE]

freaking ('fri:kɪŋ) *adj* (*prenominal*), *adv slang, chiefly US* (intensifier): *his freaking mother; this is freaking weird* [C20 euphemism for FUCKING]

freakish ('fri:kɪʃ) *adj* **1** of, related to, or characteristic of a freak; abnormal or unusual **2** unpredictable or changeable: *freakish weather* ▷ '**freakishly** *adv* ▷ '**freakishness** *n*

freak out *vb* (*adverb*) *informal* to be or cause to be in a heightened emotional state, such as that of fear, anger, or excitement

freaky ('fri:kɪ) *adj* **freakier, freakiest 1** *slang* strange; unconventional; bizarre **2** another word for **freakish**. ▷ '**freakily** *adv* ▷ '**freakiness** *n*

freckle ('frekªl) *n* **1** a small brownish spot on the skin: a localized deposit of the pigment melanin, developed by exposure to sunlight. Technical name: **lentigo 2** any small area of discoloration; a spot **3** *Austral slang* the anus ▷ *vb* **4** to mark or become marked with freckles or spots [C14 from Old Norse *freknur* freckles; related to Swedish *fräkne*, Danish *fregne*] ▷ '**freckled** or '**freckly** *adj*

Fredericia (Danish frɛðəˈrɛdʃæ) *n* a port in Denmark, in E Jutland at the N end of the Little Belt. Pop: 37 054 (2004 est)

Fredericton ('frɛdrɪktən) *n* a city in SE Canada, capital of New Brunswick, on the St John River. Pop: 54 068 (2001)

Frederiksberg (Danish frɛðregsˈbɛr) *n* a city in E Denmark, within the area of greater Copenhagen: founded in 1651 by King Frederick III. Pop: 91 721 (2004 est)

Fredrikstad (Norwegian 'frɛdrikstad) *n* a port in SE Norway at the entrance to Oslo Fjord. Pop: 69 867 (2004 est)

free (fri:) *adj* **freer, freest 1** able to act at will; not under compulsion or restraint **2 a** having personal rights or liberty; not enslaved or confined **b** (*as noun*): *land of the free* **3** (*often postpositive* and foll by *from*) not subject (to) or restricted (by some regulation, constraint, etc); exempt **4** (of a country, etc) autonomous or independent **5** exempt from external direction or restriction; not forced or induced: *free will* **6** not subject to conventional constraints: *free verse* **7** (of jazz) totally improvised, with no preset melodic, harmonic, or rhythmic basis **8** not exact or literal

9 costing nothing; provided without charge **10** *law* (of property) **a** not subject to payment of rent or performance of services; freehold **b** not subject to any burden or charge, such as a mortgage or lien; unencumbered **11** (*postpositive; often foll by of* or *with*) ready or generous in using or giving; liberal; lavish: *free with advice* **12** unrestrained by propriety or good manners; licentious **13** not occupied or in use; available: *a free cubicle* **14** not occupied or busy; without previous engagements: *I'm not free until Wednesday* **15** open or available to all; public **16** without charge to the subscriber or user: *free post; freephone* **17** not fixed or joined; loose: *the free end of a chain* **18** without obstruction or impediment **19** *chem* chemically uncombined: *free nitrogen* **20** *phonetics* denoting a vowel that can occur in an open syllable, such as the vowel in *see* as opposed to the vowel in *cat* **21** *grammar* denoting a morpheme that can occur as a separate word. Compare **bound¹** (sense 8a) **22** *logic* denoting an occurrence of a variable not bound by a quantifier. Compare **bound¹** (sense 9) **23** (of some materials, such as certain kinds of stone) easily worked **24** *nautical* (of the wind) blowing from the quarter **25 for free** *not standard* without charge or cost **26 free and easy** casual or tolerant; easy-going **27 feel free** (*usually imperative*) to regard oneself as having permission to perform a specified action **28 make free with** to take liberties with; behave too familiarly towards ▷ *adv* **29** in a free manner; freely **30** without charge or cost **31** *nautical* with the wind blowing from the quarter: *a yacht sailing free* ▷ *vb* **frees, freeing, freed** (*tr*) **32** (sometimes foll by *up*) to set at liberty; release **33** to remove obstructions, attachments, or impediments from; disengage **34** (often foll by *of* or *from*) to relieve or rid (of obstacles, pain, etc) ▷ *n* **35** *informal* a freesheet [Old English *frēo*; related to Old Saxon, Old High German *frī*, Gothic *freis* free, Sanskrit *priya* dear] ▷ '**freer** *n* ▷ '**freely** *adv* ▷ '**freeness** *n*

-free *adj combining form* free from: *trouble-free; lead-free petrol*

free agent *n* a person whose actions are not constrained by others

free alongside ship *adj* (of a shipment of goods) delivered to the dock without charge to the buyer, but excluding the cost of loading onto the vessel. Compare **free on board** Abbreviations: **FAS, f.a.s** Also: **free alongside vessel**

free association *n* **1** *psychoanal* a method of exploring a person's unconscious by eliciting words and thoughts that are associated with key words provided by a psychoanalyst **2** a spontaneous mental process whereby ideas, words, or images suggest other ideas, etc, in a nonlogical chain reaction

freebase ('fri:ˌbeɪs) *n* **1** *slang* cocaine that has been refined by heating it in either or some other solvent ▷ *vb* **freebases, freebasing, freebased 2** to refine (cocaine) in this way **3** to smoke or inhale the fumes from (refined cocaine)

freebie ('fri:bɪ) *slang* ▷ *n* **1** something provided without charge ▷ *adj* **2** without charge; free

freeboard ('fri:ˌbɔːd) *n* the space or distance between the deck of a vessel and the waterline

freeboot ('fri:ˌbuːt) *vb* (*intr*) to act as a freebooter; pillage

freebooter ('fri:ˌbuːtə) *n* **1** a person, such as a pirate, living from plunder **2** *informal* a person, esp an itinerant, who seeks pleasure, wealth, etc, without responsibility [C16 from Dutch *vrijbuiter*, from *vrijbuit* booty; see FILIBUSTER]

freeborn ('fri:ˌbɔːn) *adj* **1** not born in slavery **2** of, relating to, or suitable for people not born in slavery

Free Church *n chiefly Brit* **a** any Protestant Church, esp the Presbyterian, other than the Established Church **b** (*as modifier*): *Free-Church attitudes*

free city *n* a sovereign or autonomous city; city-state

free climbing *n mountaineering* climbing without using pitons, étriers, etc, as direct aids to ascent, but using ropes, belays, etc, at discretion for security. Compare **aid climbing**

free coinage *n US* coinage of bullion brought to the mint by any individual

free companion *n* (in medieval Europe) a member of a company of mercenary soldiers

free company *n European history* a band of mercenary soldiers during the Middle Ages

freediving ('fri:daɪvɪŋ) *n* the sport or activity of diving without the aid of breathing aparatus ▷ **free diver** *n*

freedman ('fri:d,mæn) *n, pl* **-men** a man who has been freed from slavery ▷ '**freed,woman** *fem n*

freedom ('fri:dəm) *n* **1** personal liberty, as from slavery, bondage, serfdom, etc **2** liberation or deliverance, as from confinement or bondage **3** the quality or state of being free, esp to enjoy political and civil liberties **4** (usually foll by *from*) the state of being without something unpleasant or bad; exemption or immunity **5** the right or privilege of unrestricted use or access **6** autonomy, self-government, or independence **7** the power or liberty to order one's own actions **8** *philosophy* the quality, esp of the will or the individual, of not being totally constrained; able to choose between alternative actions in identical circumstances **9** ease or frankness of manner; candour **10** excessive familiarity of manner; boldness **11** ease and grace, as of movement; lack of effort [Old English *frēodōm*]

freedom fighter *n* a militant revolutionary

Freedom Food *n* (in Britain) food that is produced by farmers conforming to the guidelines for humane farming set by the Freedom Food programme set up by the RSPCA in conjunction with some major supermarkets

Freedomites ('fri:də,maɪts) *pl n* another name for **Sons of Freedom**

freedom of the seas *n international law* **1** the right of ships of all nations to sail the high seas in peacetime **2** (in wartime) the immunity accorded to neutral ships from attack **3** the exclusive jurisdiction possessed by a state over its own ships sailing the high seas in peacetime

freedom rider *n US* a person who participated, esp in the 1960s, in an organized tour, usually by public transport in the South, in order to protest against racism and put federal laws on integration to the test

free electron *n* any electron that is not attached to an ion, atom, or molecule and is free to move under the influence of an applied electric or magnetic field

free energy *n* a thermodynamic property that expresses the capacity of a system to perform work under certain conditions. See **Gibbs function, Helmholtz function**

free enterprise *n* an economic system in which commercial organizations compete for profit with little state control

free fall *n* **1** free descent of a body in which the gravitational force is the only force acting on it **2** the part of a parachute descent before the parachute opens

free flight *n* the flight of a rocket, missile, etc, when its engine has ceased to produce thrust

free-floating *adj* unattached or uncommitted, as to a cause, a party, etc ▷ '**free-'floater** *n*

free-floating anxiety *n psychiatry* chronic anxiety occurring for no identifiable cause

Freefone ('fri:ˌfəʊn) *n Brit trademark* a system of telephone use in which the cost of calls in response to an advertisement is borne by the advertiser

free-for-all *n informal* a disorganized brawl or argument, usually involving all those present

free form *arts* ▷ *n* **1** an irregular flowing shape, often used in industrial or fabric design ▷ *adj* **free-form 2** freely flowing, spontaneous

freegan ('fri:gən) *n* a person who, through

opposition to capitalism and consumerism, attempts to live without buying consumer goods, recycling discarded goods instead [C21 from FREE + (VE)GAN]

free gift *n* something given away, esp as an incentive to a purchaser

free gold *n* **1** gold, uncombined with other minerals, found in a pure state **2** *US* the excess of gold held by the Federal Reserve Banks over the legal reserve

free hand *n* **1** unrestricted freedom to act (esp in the phrase **give (someone) a free hand**) ▷ *adj, adv* **freehand 2** (done) by hand without the use of guiding instruments: *a freehand drawing*

free-handed *adj* generous or liberal; unstinting > ˌfree-ˈhandedly *adv* > ˌfree-ˈhandedness *n*

free-hearted *adj* frank and spontaneous; open; generous > ˌfree-ˈheartedly *adv* > ˌfree-ˈheartedness *n*

freehold (ˈfriːˌhəʊld) *property law* ▷ *n* **1 a** tenure by which land is held in fee simple, fee tail, or for life **b** an estate held by such tenure ▷ *adj* **2** relating to or having the nature of freehold

freeholder (ˈfriːˌhəʊldə) *n property law* a person in possession of a freehold building or estate in land

free house *n Brit* a public house not bound to sell only one brewer's products

free kick *n soccer* a place kick awarded for a foul or infringement, either direct, from which a goal may be scored, or indirect, from which the ball must be touched by at least one other player for a goal to be allowed

free labour *n* **1** the labour of workers who are not members of trade unions **2** such workers collectively

freelance (ˈfriːˌlɑːns) *n* **1 a** Also called: **freelancer** a self-employed person, esp a writer or artist, who is not employed continuously but hired to do specific assignments **b** (*as modifier*): *a freelance journalist* **2** a person, esp a politician, who supports several causes or parties without total commitment to any one **3** (in medieval Europe) a mercenary soldier or adventurer ▷ *vb* **4** to work as a freelance on (an assignment, etc) ▷ *adv* **5** as a freelance [C19 (in sense 3): later applied to politicians, writers, etc]

free list *n* **1** *commerce, chiefly US* a list of commodities not subject to tariffs **2** a list of people admitted free

free-living *adj* **1** given to ready indulgence of the appetites **2** (of animals and plants) not parasitic; existing independently > ˌfree-ˈliver *n*

freeload (ˈfriːˌləʊd) *vb* (*intr*) *slang* to act as a freeloader; sponge

freeloader (ˈfriːˌləʊdə) *n slang* a person who habitually depends on the charity of others for food, shelter, etc > ˈfreeˌloading *n*

free love *n* the practice of sexual relationships without fidelity to a single partner or without formal or legal ties

freeman (ˈfriːmən) *n, pl* -men **1** a person who is not a slave or in bondage **2** a person who enjoys political and civil liberties; citizen **3** a person who enjoys a privilege or franchise, such as the freedom of a city

free market *n* **a** an economic system that allows supply and demand to regulate prices, wages, etc, rather than government policy **b** (*as modifier*): *a free-market economy*

freemartin (ˈfriːˌmɑːtɪn) *n* the female of a pair of twin calves of unlike sex that is imperfectly developed and sterile, probably due to the influence of the male hormones of its twin during development in the uterus [C17 of uncertain origin]

freemason (ˈfriːˌmeɪsᵊn) *n medieval history* a member of a guild of itinerant skilled stonemasons, who had a system of secret signs and passwords with which they recognized each other > **freemasonic** (ˌfriːməˈsɒnɪk) *adj*

Freemason (ˈfriːˌmeɪsᵊn) *n* a member of the widespread secret order, constituted in London in

1717, of **Free and Accepted Masons**, pledged to brotherly love, faith, and charity. Sometimes shortened to: **Mason** > **Freemasonic** (ˌfriːməˈsɒnɪk) *adj*

freemasonry (ˈfriːˌmeɪsᵊnrɪ) *n* natural or tacit sympathy and understanding

Freemasonry (ˈfriːˌmeɪsᵊnrɪ) *n* **1** the institutions, rites, practices, etc, of Freemasons **2** Freemasons collectively

free on board *adj* (of a shipment of goods) delivered on board ship or other carrier without charge to the buyer. Compare **free alongside ship** Abbreviations: **FOB, f.o.b**

free on rail *adj* (of a consignment of goods) delivered to a railway station and loaded onto a train without charge to the buyer. Abbreviations: **FOR, f.o.r**

freephone (ˈfriːˌfəʊn) *n* a common spelling of **Freefone**

free port *n* **1** a port open to all commercial vessels on equal terms **2** Also called: **free zone** a zone adjoining a port that permits the duty-free entry of foreign goods intended for re-export

Freepost (ˈfriːˌpəʊst) *n Brit trademark* a method of postage by which the cost of replies to an advertisement is borne by the advertiser

free radical *n* an atom or group of atoms containing at least one unpaired electron and existing for a brief period of time before reacting to produce a stable molecule. Sometimes shortened to: **radical** Compare **group** (sense 10)

free-range *adj chiefly Brit* kept or produced in natural nonintensive conditions: *free-range eggs*

free recall *n psychol* the recollection of the members of a list of items without regard to their serial order

free running *n* another name for **parkour**

free-running *adj* **1** (of a mechanism, material, etc) moving smoothly and uninterruptedly **2** *electronics* of or relating to a periodic signal that is not synchronized to a timing source: *free-running interference produces moving patterns on a television screen*

free-select *vb* (*tr*) *Austral history* to select (areas of crown land) and acquire the freehold by a series of annual payments > ˌfree-seˈlection *n* > ˌfree-seˈlector *n*

freesheet (ˈfriːˌʃiːt) *n* a newspaper that is distributed free, paid for by its advertisers. Also called: **giveaway**

freesia (ˈfriːzɪə, ˈfriːʒə) *n* any iridaceous plant of the genus *Freesia*, of southern Africa, cultivated for their white, yellow, or pink tubular fragrant flowers [C19 New Latin, named after F. H. T. *Freese* (died 1876), German physician]

free silver *n* the unlimited minting of silver coins, esp when at a fixed ratio to gold

free skating *n* either the short programme of specified movements or the long programme chosen by a skater in a figure-skating competition

Free Soil Party *n* a former US political party opposing slavery from 1848 until 1854 when it merged with the Republican party

free space *n* a region that has no gravitational and electromagnetic fields: used as an absolute standard. Also called (no longer in technical usage): **vacuum**

free speech *n* the right to express one's opinions publicly

free-spoken *adj* speaking frankly or without restraint > ˌfree-ˈspokenly *adv* > ˌfree-ˈspokenness *n*

freestanding (ˌfriːˈstændɪŋ) *adj* **1** standing apart; not attached to or supported by another object **2** (in systemic grammar) denoting a clause that can stand alone as a sentence; denoting or being a main clause. Compare **bound¹** (sense 8b)

Free State *n* **1** a province of central South Africa; replaced the former province of Orange Free State in 1994: gold and uranium mining. Capital: Bloemfontein. Pop: 2 950 661 (2004 est). Area: 129 480 sq km (49 992 sq miles) **2** *US history* (before the Civil War) any state prohibiting slavery **3** short for the **Irish Free State**

freestone (ˈfriːˌstəʊn) *n* **1 a** any fine-grained stone, esp sandstone or limestone, that can be cut and worked in any direction without breaking **b** (*as modifier*): *a freestone house* **2** *botany* **a** a fruit, such as a peach, in which the flesh separates readily from the stone **b** (*as modifier*): *a freestone peach*. Compare **clingstone**

freestyle (ˈfriːˌstaɪl) *n* **1** a competition or race, as in swimming, in which each participant may use a style of his or her choice instead of a specified style **2 a** an amateur style of wrestling with an agreed set of rules **b** Also called: **all-in wrestling** a style of professional wrestling with no internationally agreed set of rules **3** a series of acrobatics performed in skiing, etc **4** (*as modifier*): *a freestyle event*

freestyling (ˈfriːˌstaɪlɪŋ) *n* the practice of improvising scenes when making a film or performing a play

free-swimming *adj* (of aquatic animals or larvae) not sessile or attached to any object and therefore able to swim freely in the water > ˌfree-ˈswimmer *n*

freethinker (ˌfriːˈθɪŋkə) *n* a person who forms his ideas and opinions independently of authority or accepted views, esp in matters of religion > ˌfreeˈthinking *n, adj*

free thought *n* thought unrestrained and uninfluenced by dogma or authority, esp in religious matters

free throw *n basketball* an unimpeded shot at the basket from the **free-throw line** given for a technical fault (one free shot) or a foul (two free shots)

free-to-air *n* **a** a system of television for which viewers do not have to subscribe or pay **b** (*as modifier*): *free-to-air networks* ▷ Compare **pay-per-view, pay television**

Freetown (ˈfriːˌtaʊn) *n* the capital and chief port of Sierra Leone: founded in 1787 for slaves freed and destitute in England. Pop: 1 007 000 (2005 est)

free trade *n* **1** international trade that is free of such government interference as import quotas, export subsidies, protective tariffs, etc. Compare **protection** (sense 3) **2** *archaic* illicit trade; smuggling

free-trader *n* **1** a person who supports or advocates free trade **2** *archaic* a smuggler or smuggling vessel

free verse *n* unrhymed verse without a metrical pattern

free vibration *n* the vibration of a structure that occurs at its natural frequency, as opposed to a forced vibration

free vote *n chiefly Brit* a parliamentary division in which members are not constrained by a party whip

freeware (ˈfriːˌwɛə) *n* computer software that may be distributed and used without payment

freeway (ˈfriːˌweɪ) *n US* **1** another name for **expressway 2** a major road that can be used without paying a toll

freewheel (ˌfriːˈwiːl) *n* **1** a ratchet device in the rear hub of a bicycle wheel that permits the wheel to rotate freely while the pedals are stationary **2** a device in the transmission of some vehicles that automatically disengages the drive shaft when it rotates more rapidly than the engine shaft, so that the drive shaft can turn freely ▷ *vb* **3** (*intr*) to coast in a vehicle or on a bicycle using the freewheel

freewheeling (ˌfriːˈwiːlɪŋ) *adj* **1** relating to, operating as, or having a freewheel; coasting **2** *informal* free of restraints; carefree or uninhibited

free will *n* **1 a** the apparent human ability to make choices that are not externally determined **b** the doctrine that such human freedom of choice is not illusory. Compare **determinism** (sense 1) **c** (*as modifier*): *a free-will decision* **2** the ability to make a choice without coercion

Free World *n* **the** the non-Communist countries collectively, esp those that are actively anti-Communist

f

freeze (friːz) *vb* freezes, freezing, froze (frəʊz) frozen ('frəʊzᵊn) **1** to change (a liquid) into a solid as a result of a reduction in temperature, or (of a liquid) to solidify in this way, esp to convert or be converted into ice **2** (when *intr*, sometimes foll by *over* or *up*) to cover, clog, or harden with ice, or become so covered, clogged, or hardened **3** to fix fast or become fixed (to something) because of the action of frost **4** (*tr*) to preserve (food) by subjection to extreme cold, as in a freezer **5** to feel or cause to feel the sensation or effects of extreme cold **6** to die or cause to die of frost or extreme cold **7** to become or cause to become paralysed, fixed, or motionless, esp through fear, shock, etc **8** (*tr*) to cause (moving film) to stop at a particular frame **9** to decrease or cause to decrease in animation or vigour **10** to make or become formal, haughty, etc, in manner **11** (*tr*) to fix (prices, incomes, etc) at a particular level, usually by government direction **12** (*tr*) to forbid by law the exchange, liquidation, or collection of (loans, assets, etc) **13** (*tr*) to prohibit the manufacture, sale, or use of (something specified) **14** (*tr*) to stop (a process) at a particular stage of development **15** (*tr*) *informal* to render (tissue or a part of the body) insensitive, as by the application or injection of a local anaesthetic **16** (*intr*; foll by *onto*) *informal, chiefly US* to cling ▷ *n* **17** the act of freezing or state of being frozen **18** *meteorol* a spell of temperatures below freezing point, usually over a wide area **19** the fixing of incomes, prices, etc, by legislation **20** another word for **frost** ▷ *sentence substitute* **21** *chiefly US* a command to stop still instantly or risk being shot [Old English *frēosan*; related to Old Norse *frjōsa*, Old High German *friosan*, Latin *prūrīre* to itch; see FROST] > 'freezable *adj*

freeze-dry *vb* -dries, -drying, -dried (*tr*) to preserve (a substance) by rapid freezing and subsequently drying in a vacuum

freeze-frame *n* **1** *films, television* a single frame of a film repeated to give an effect like a still photograph **2** a single frame of a video recording viewed as a still by stopping the tape ▷ *vb* (*tr*) **3** to make a freeze-frame of (an image)

freeze out *vb* (*tr, adverb*) *informal* to force out or exclude, as by unfriendly behaviour, boycotting, etc

freezer ('friːzə) *n* **1** Also called: **deepfreeze** a device that freezes or chills, esp an insulated cold-storage cabinet for long-term storage of perishable foodstuffs **2** a former name for a **refrigerator**

freeze-up *n informal* **1** a period of freezing or extremely cold weather **2** *US, Canadian* **a** the freezing of lakes, rivers, and topsoil in autumn or early winter **b** the time of year when this occurs

freezing ('friːzɪŋ) *adj informal* extremely cold

freezing injunction *n law* an order enabling the court to freeze the assets of a defendant, esp to prevent him or her taking them abroad. Formerly called **Mareva injunction**

freezing mixture *n* a mixture of two substances, usually salt and ice, to give a temperature below 0°C

freezing point *n* the temperature below which a liquid turns into a solid. It is equal to the melting point

freezing works *n Austral and NZ* a slaughterhouse at which animal carcasses are frozen for export. See also **chamber** (sense 10)

free zone *n* an area at a port where certain customs restrictions are not implemented. See also **free port**

F region *n* the highest region of the ionosphere, extending from a height of about 150 kilometres to about 1000 kilometres. It contains the highest proportion of free electrons and is the most useful region for long-range radio transmission. Also called: **Appleton layer** See also **ionosphere**

Freiburg (German 'fraɪbʊrk) *n* **1** a city in SW Germany, in SW Baden-Württemberg: under Austrian rule (1368–1805); university (1457). Pop: 212 495 (2003 est). Official name: **Freiburg im Breisgau** (ɪm 'braɪsgaʊ) **2** the German name for **Fribourg**

freight (freɪt) *n* **1 a** commercial transport that is slower and cheaper than express **b** the price charged for such transport **c** goods transported by this means **d** (*as modifier*): *freight transport* **2** *chiefly Brit* a ship's cargo or part of it ▷ *vb* (*tr*) **3** to load with goods for transport **4** *chiefly US and Canadian* to convey commercially as or by freight **5** to load or burden; charge [C16 from Middle Dutch *vrecht*; related to French *fret*, Spanish *flete*, Portuguese *frete*] > 'freightless *adj*

freightage ('freɪtɪdʒ) *n* **1** the commercial conveyance of goods **2** the goods so transported **3** the price charged for such conveyance

freighter ('freɪtə) *n* **1** a ship or aircraft designed for transporting cargo **2** a person concerned with the loading or chartering of a ship

Freightliner ('freɪt,laɪnə) *n trademark* **1** a goods train carrying containers that can be transferred onto lorries or ships **2** (in Britain) a containerized transportation service involving both rail and road

freight ton *n* the full name for **ton'** (sense 4)

Fremantle ('friː,mæntᵊl) *n* a port in SW Western Australia, on the Indian Ocean. Pop: 25 197 (2001)

fremd (fremd, freɪmd) *adj archaic* alien or strange [Old English *fremde*; related to Old High German *fremidi*]

fremitus ('fremɪtəs) *n, pl* -tus a vibration felt by the hand when placed on a part of the body, esp the chest, when the patient is speaking or coughing [C19 from Latin: a roaring sound, a humming, from *fremere* to make a low roaring, murmur]

French (frentʃ) *n* **1** the official language of France: also an official language of Switzerland, Belgium, Canada, and certain other countries. It is the native language of approximately 70 million people; also used for diplomacy. Historically, French is an Indo-European language belonging to the Romance group. See also **Old French, Anglo-French 2** the French (*functioning as plural*) the natives, citizens, or inhabitants of France collectively **3** See **French vermouth** ▷ *adj* **4** relating to, denoting, or characteristic of France, the French, or their language ▷ Related prefixes: **Franco-, Gallo- 5** (in Canada) of or relating to French Canadians [Old English *Frencisc* French, Frankish; see FRANK] > 'Frenchness *n*

French Academy *n* an association of 40 French scholars and writers, founded by Cardinal Richelieu in 1635, devoted chiefly to preserving the purity of the French language

French and Indian War *n* the war (1755–60) between the French and British, each aided by different Indian tribes, that formed part of the North American Seven Years' War

French bean *n* **1** a small twining bushy or annual bean plant, *Phaseolus vulgaris*, with white or lilac flowers and slender green edible pods **2** the pod of this plant. See also **haricot** Also called: **dwarf bean, kidney bean**

French bread *n* white bread in a long slender loaf that is made from a water dough and has a crisp brown crust

French bulldog *n* a small stocky breed of dog with a sleek coat, usually brindled or pied, a large square head, and large erect rounded ears

French Cameroons *pl n* the part of Cameroon formerly administered by France (1919–60)

French Canada *n* the areas of Canada, esp in the province of Quebec, where French Canadians predominate

French Canadian *n* **1** a Canadian citizen whose native language is French ▷ *adj* **French-Canadian 2** of or relating to French Canadians or their language

French chalk *n* a compact variety of talc used to mark cloth or remove grease stains from materials

French Community *n* an international association consisting of France and a number of former French colonies: founded in 1958 as a successor to the French Union

French cricket *n* a child's game resembling cricket, in which the batsman's legs are used as the wicket

French cuff *n* a double cuff formed by a backward fold of the material

French curve *n* a thin plastic sheet with profiles of several curves, used by draughtsmen for drawing curves

French doors *pl n US and Canadian* a pair of casement windows extending to floor level and opening onto a balcony, garden, etc. Also called (in Britain and certain other countries): **French windows**

French dressing *n* a salad dressing made from oil and vinegar with seasonings; vinaigrette

French Equatorial Africa *n* the former French overseas territories of Chad, Gabon, Middle Congo, and Ubangi-Shari (1910–58)

French fact *n* (in Canada) the presence of French Canada as a distinct cultural force within Confederation

French Foreign Legion *n* a unit of the French Army formerly serving esp in French North African colonies. It is largely recruited from foreigners, with French senior officers

French fried potatoes *pl n* a more formal name for **chips** Also called (US and Canadian): **French fries**

French Guiana *n* a French overseas region in NE South America, on the Atlantic: colonized by the French in about 1637; tropical forests. Capital: Cayenne. Pop: 183 000 (2004 est). Area: about 91 000 sq km (23 000 sq miles)

French Guianese or **Guianan** *adj* **1** of or relating to French Guiana or its inhabitants ▷ *n* **2** a native or inhabitant of French Guiana

French Guinea *n* a former French territory of French West Africa: became independent as Guinea in 1958

French heel *n* a fairly high and narrow-waisted heel on women's shoes > ,French-'heeled *adj*

French horn *n music* a valved brass instrument with a funnel-shaped mouthpiece and a tube of conical bore coiled into a spiral. It is a transposing instrument in F Range: about three and a half octaves upwards from B on the second leger line below the bass staff. See **horn**

Frenchify ('frentʃɪ,faɪ) *vb* -fies, -fying, -fied *informal* to make or become French in appearance, behaviour, etc > ,Frenchifi'cation *n*

French India *n* a former French overseas territory in India, including Chandernagore and Pondicherry: restored to India between 1949 and 1954

French Indochina *n* the territories of SE Asia that were colonized by France and held mostly until 1954: included Cochin China, Annam, and Tonkin (now largely Vietnam), Cambodia, Laos, and Kuang-Chou Wan (returned to China in 1945, now Zhanjiang)

French kiss *n* a kiss involving insertion of the tongue into the partner's mouth

French knickers *pl n* women's wide-legged underpants

French knot *n* an ornamental stitch made by looping the thread three or four times around the needle before putting it into the fabric

French leave *n* an unauthorized or unannounced absence or departure [C18 alluding to a custom in France of leaving without saying goodbye to one's host or hostess]

French letter *n Brit* a slang term for **condom**

French lilac *n* another name for **goat's-rue** (sense 1)

Frenchman ('frentʃmən) *n, pl* -men a native, citizen, or inhabitant of France > 'French,woman *fem n*

French Morocco *n* a former French protectorate in NW Africa, united in 1956 with Spanish Morocco and Tangier to form the kingdom of Morocco

French mustard *n* a mild mustard paste made with vinegar rather than water

French navy *n* **a** a dark dull navy blue **b** (*as adjective*): *a French-navy dress*

French North Africa *n* the former French possessions of Algeria, French Morocco, and Tunisia

French Oceania *n* a former name (until 1958) of **French Polynesia**

French paradox *n* the theory that the lower incidence of heart disease in Mediterranean countries compared to that in the US is a consequence of the larger intake of flavonoids from red wine in these countries

French pastry *n* a rich pastry made esp from puff pastry and filled with cream, fruit, etc

French pleat *or* **roll** *n* a woman's hair style with the hair gathered at the back into a cylindrical roll

French polish *n* **1** a varnish for wood consisting of shellac dissolved in alcohol **2** the gloss finish produced by repeated applications of this polish

French-polish *vb* to treat with French polish or give a French polish (to)

French Polynesia *n* a French Overseas Country (formerly Territory) in the S Pacific Ocean, including the Society Islands, the Tuamotu group, the Gambier group, the Tubuai Islands, and the Marquesas Islands. Capital: Papeete, on Tahiti. Pop: 248 000 (2004 est). Area: about 4000 sq km (1500 sq miles). Former name (until 1958): French Oceania

French Revolution *n* the anticlerical and republican revolution in France from 1789 until 1799, when Napoleon seized power

French Revolutionary calendar *n* the full name for the **Revolutionary calendar**

French seam *n* a seam in which the edges are not visible

French sixth *n* (in musical harmony) an augmented sixth chord having a major third and an augmented fourth between the root and the augmented sixth

French Somaliland *n* a former name (until 1967) of Djibouti

French Southern and Antarctic Territories *pl n* a French overseas territory, comprising Adélie Land in Antarctica and the islands of Amsterdam and St Paul and the Kerguelen and Crozet archipelagos in the S Indian Ocean. All claims to the mainland of Antarctica are suspended under the Antarctic Treaty of 1959

French stick *n* *Brit* a long straight notched stick loaf. Also called: **French stick loaf**

French Sudan *n* a former name (1898–1959) of **Mali**

French toast *n* **1** *Brit* toast cooked on one side only **2** bread dipped in beaten egg and lightly fried

French Togoland *n* a former United Nations Trust Territory in W Africa, administered by France (1946–60), now the independent republic of Togo

French Union *n* a union of France with its dependencies (1946–58): replaced by the French Community

French vermouth *n* a dry aromatic white wine. Also called: **French**

French West Africa *n* a former group (1895–1958) of French Overseas Territories: consisted of Senegal, Mauritania, French Sudan, Burkina-Faso, Niger, French Guinea, the Ivory Coast, and Dahomey

French West Indies *pl n* **the** a group of islands in the Lesser Antilles, administered by France. Pop: 838 000 (2004 est). Area: 2792 sq km (1077 sq miles)

French windows *pl n* (*sometimes singular*) *Brit* a pair of casement windows extending to floor level and opening onto a balcony, garden, etc. US and Canadian name: **French doors**

Frenchy ('frɛntʃɪ) *adj* **1** *informal* characteristic of or resembling the French ▷ *n, pl* -ies **2** an informal name for a French person

frenetic (frɪ'nɛtɪk) *adj* distracted or frantic; frenzied [c14 via Old French *frenetique* from Latin *phrenēticus*, from Greek *phrenētikos*, from *phrenitis* insanity, from *phrēn* mind] > **fre'netically** *adv* > **fre'neticness** *n*

Frenkel defect ('frɛnkªl) *n physics* a crystal defect in which a lattice ion has moved to an interstitial position leaving a vacant lattice site [c20 named after I. I. *Frenkel* (1894–1952), Russian physicist]

frenulum ('frɛnjʊləm) *n, pl* -la (-lə) **1** a strong bristle or group of bristles on the hind wing of some moths and other insects, by which the forewing and hind wing are united during flight **2** a small fraenum [c18 New Latin, diminutive of Latin *frēnum* bridle]

frenum ('friːnəm) *n, pl* -na (-nə) a variant spelling (esp US) of **fraenum**

frenzied ('frɛnzɪd) *adj* filled with or as if with frenzy; wild; frantic > **'frenziedly** *adv*

frenzy ('frɛnzɪ) *n, pl* -zies **1** violent mental derangement **2** wild excitement or agitation; distraction **3** a bout of wild or agitated activity: *a frenzy of preparations* ▷ *vb* -zies, -zying, -zied **4** (*tr*) to make frantic; drive into a frenzy [c14 from Old French *frenesie*, from Late Latin *phrēnēsis* madness, delirium, from Late Greek, ultimately from Greek *phrēn* mind; compare FRENETIC]

Freon ('friːɒn) *n trademark* any of a group of chemically unreactive chlorofluorocarbons used as aerosol propellants, refrigerants, and solvents

frequency ('friːkwənsɪ) *n, pl* -cies **1** the state of being frequent; frequent occurrence **2** the number of times that an event occurs within a given period; rate of recurrence **3** *physics* the number of times that a periodic function or vibration repeats itself in a specified time, often 1 second. It is usually measured in hertz. Symbol: ν or *f* **4** *statistics* **a** the number of individuals in a class (**absolute frequency**) **b** the ratio of this number to the total number of individuals under survey (**relative frequency**) **5** *ecology* **a** the number of individuals of a species within a given area **b** the percentage of quadrats that contains individuals of a species. Also called (for senses 1, 2): frequence [c16 from Latin *frequentia* a large gathering, from *frequēns* numerous, crowded]

frequency band *n* a continuous range of frequencies, esp in the radio spectrum, between two limiting frequencies

frequency distribution *n statistics* the function of the distribution of a sample corresponding to the probability density function of the underlying population and tending to it as the sample size increases, the set of relative frequencies of sample points falling within given intervals of the range of the random variable

frequency-division multiplex *n* See **multiplex** (sense 1)

frequency modulation *n* a method of transmitting information using a radio-frequency carrier wave. The frequency of the carrier wave is varied in accordance with the amplitude and polarity of the input signal, the amplitude of the carrier remaining unchanged. Abbreviation: **FM** Compare **amplitude modulation**

frequent *adj* ('friːkwənt) **1** recurring at short intervals **2** constant or habitual ▷ *vb* (frɪ'kwɛnt) **3** (*tr*) to visit repeatedly or habitually [c16 from Latin *frequēns* numerous; perhaps related to Latin *farcīre* to stuff] > **fre'quentable** *adj* > **fre'quenter** *n* > **'frequently** *adv* > **'frequentness** *n*

frequentation (ˌfriːkwɛn'teɪʃən) *n* the act or practice of frequenting or visiting often

frequentative (frɪ'kwɛntətɪv) *grammar* ▷ *adj* **1** denoting an aspect of verbs in some languages used to express repeated or habitual action **2** (in English) denoting a verb or an affix having meaning that involves repeated or habitual action, such as the verb *wrestle*, from *wrest* ▷ *n* **3 a** a frequentative verb or affix **b** the frequentative aspect of verbs

fresco ('frɛskəʊ) *n, pl* -coes *or* -cos **1** a very durable method of wall-painting using watercolours on wet plaster or, less properly, dry plaster (**fresco secco**), with a less durable result **2** a painting done in this way [c16 from Italian: fresh plaster, coolness, from *fresco* (adj) fresh, cool, of Germanic origin]

fresh (frɛʃ) *adj* **1** not stale or deteriorated; newly made, harvested, etc **2** newly acquired, created, found, etc **3** novel; original: *a fresh outlook* **4** latest; most recent **5** further; additional; more **6** not canned, frozen, or otherwise preserved: *fresh fruit* **7** (of water) not salt **8** clear **9** chilly or invigorating **10** not tired; alert; refreshed **11** not worn or faded **12** having a healthy or ruddy appearance **13** newly or just arrived; straight **14** youthful or inexperienced **15** *chiefly US* designating a female farm animal, esp a cow, that has recently given birth **16** *informal* presumptuous or disrespectful; forward **17** *Northern English dialect* partially intoxicated; tipsy ▷ *n* **18** the fresh part or time of something **19** another name for **freshet** ▷ *vb* **20** *obsolete* to make or become fresh; freshen ▷ *adv* **21** in a fresh manner; freshly **22** fresh out of *informal* having just run out of supplies of [Old English *fersc* fresh, unsalted; related to Old High German *frisc*, Old French *freis*, Old Norse *ferskr*] > **'freshly** *adv* > **'freshness** *n*

fresh breeze *n* a fairly strong breeze of force five on the Beaufort scale

freshen ('frɛʃən) *vb* **1** to make or become fresh or fresher **2** (*often foll by up*) to refresh (oneself), esp by washing **3** (*intr*) (of the wind) to increase **4** to lose or cause to lose saltiness **5** (*intr*) *chiefly US* **a** (of farm animals) to give birth **b** (of cows) to commence giving milk after calving > **'freshener** *n*

fresher ('frɛʃə) *or* **freshman** ('frɛʃmən) *n, pl* -ers *or* -men a first-year student at college or university

freshet ('frɛʃɪt) *n* **1** the sudden overflowing of a river caused by heavy rain or melting snow **2** a stream of fresh water emptying into the sea

fresh gale *n* a gale of force eight on the Beaufort scale

freshie ('frɛʃɪ) *n Hinglish informal* a new immigrant to the UK from the Asian subcontinent [c21 from *fresh off the* (*banana*) *boat*]

fresh-run *adj* (of fish) newly migrated upstream from the sea, esp to spawn

freshwater ('frɛʃˌwɔːtə) *n* (*modifier*) **1** of, relating to, or living in fresh water **2** (esp of a sailor who has not sailed on the sea) unskilled or inexperienced **3** *US* small and little known

fresnel ('freɪnɛl; *French* frɛnɛl) *n* a unit of frequency equivalent to 10¹² hertz [c20 named after Augustin Jean *Fresnel* (1788–1827), French physicist]

Fresnel lens *n* a lens consisting of a number of smaller lenses arranged to give a flat surface of short focal length [c20 named after Augustin Jean *Fresnel* (1788–1827), French physicist]

Fresno ('frɛznəʊ) *n* a city in central California, in the San Joaquin Valley. Pop: 451 455 (2003 est)

fret¹ (frɛt) *vb* frets, fretting, fretted **1** to distress or be distressed; worry **2** to rub or wear away **3** to irritate or be irritated; feel or give annoyance or vexation **4** to eat away or be eaten away by chemical action; corrode **5** (*intr*) (of a road surface) to become loose so that potholes develop; scab **6** to agitate (water) or (of water) to be agitated **7** (*tr*) to make by wearing away; erode ▷ *n* **8** a state of irritation or anxiety **9** the result of fretting; corrosion **10** a hole or channel caused by fretting [Old English *fretan* to EAT; related to Old High German *frezzan*, Gothic *fraitan*, Latin *peredere*]

fret² (frɛt) *n* **1** a repetitive geometrical figure, esp one used as an ornamental border **2** such a pattern made in relief and with numerous small openings; fretwork **3** *heraldry* a charge on a shield consisting of a mascle crossed by a saltire ▷ *vb* **frets, fretting, fretted 4** (*tr*) to ornament with fret or fretwork [c14 from Old French *frete* interlaced design used on a shield, probably of Germanic origin] > 'fretless *adj*

fret³ (frɛt) *n* any of several small metal bars set across the fingerboard of a musical instrument of the lute, guitar, or viol family at various points along its length so as to produce the desired notes when the strings are stopped by the fingers [c16 of unknown origin] > 'fretless *adj*

fret⁴ (frɛt) *n* short for **sea fret**

fretboard ('frɛtbɔːd) *n* a fingerboard with frets on a stringed musical instrument

fretful ('frɛtful) *adj* peevish, irritable, or upset > 'fretfully *adv* > 'fretfulness *n*

fret saw *n* a fine-toothed saw with a long thin narrow blade, used for cutting designs in thin wood or metal

fretted ('frɛtɪd) *adj* **1** ornamented with angular designs or frets **2** decorated with fretwork

fretwork ('frɛt,wɜːk) *n* **1** decorative geometrical carving or openwork **2** any similar pattern of light and dark **3** ornamental work of three-dimensional frets

Freudian ('frɔɪdɪən) *adj* **1** of or relating to Sigmund Freud (1856–1939), the Austrian psychiatrist, or his ideas ▷ *n* **2** a person who follows or believes in the basic ideas of Sigmund Freud > 'Freudian,ism *n*

Freudian slip *n* any action, such as a slip of the tongue, that may reveal an unconscious thought

Frey (frɛɪ) or **Freyr** (frɛɪə) *n Norse myth* the god of earth's fertility and dispenser of prosperity

Freya or **Freyja** ('frɛɪə) *n Norse myth* the goddess of love and fecundity, sister of Frey

FRG *abbreviation for* Federal Republic of Germany

FRGS (in Britain) *abbreviation for* Fellow of the Royal Geographical Society

Fri. *abbreviation for* Friday

friable ('fraɪəbʳl) *adj* easily broken up; crumbly [c16 from Latin *friābilis*, from *friāre* to crumble; related to Latin *fricāre* to rub down] > ,fria'bility or 'friableness *n*

friar ('fraɪə) *n* a member of any of various chiefly mendicant religious orders of the Roman Catholic Church, the main orders being the **Black Friars** (Dominicans), **Grey Friars** (Franciscans), **White Friars** (Carmelites), and **Austin Friars** (Augustinians) [c13 *frere*, from Old French: brother, from Latin *frāter* BROTHER] > 'friarly *adj*

friarbird ('fraɪə,bɜːd) *n* any of various Australian honeyeaters of the genus *Philemon*, having a naked head

Friar Minor *n, pl* Friars Minor *Christianity* a member of either of two of the three orders into which the order founded by St Francis of Assisi came to be divided, namely the **Order of Friars Minor** and the **Order of Friars Minor Conventual**. Compare **Capuchin**

friar's balsam *n* a compound containing benzoin, mixed with hot water, and used as an inhalant to relieve colds and sore throats

friar's lantern *n* another name for **will-o'-the-wisp**

Friar Tuck *n English legend* a jolly friar who joined Robin Hood's band and aided their exploits

friary ('fraɪərɪ) *n, pl* -aries *Christianity* a convent or house of friars

frib (frɪb) *n Austral and NZ* a short heavy-conditioned piece of wool removed from a fleece during classing [of unknown origin]

fribble ('frɪbʳl) *vb* **1** (*tr*) to fritter away; waste **2** (*intr*) to act frivolously; trifle ▷ *n* **3** a wasteful or frivolous person or action ▷ *adj* **4** frivolous; trifling [c17 of unknown origin] > 'fribbler *n*

Fribourg (*French* fribur) *n* **1** a canton in W Switzerland. Capital: Fribourg. Pop: 242 700 (2002 est). Area: 1676 sq km (645 sq miles) **2** a town in W

Switzerland, capital of Fribourg canton: university (1889). Pop: 35 547 (2000). German name: Freiburg

fricandeau or **fricando** ('frɪkən,dəʊ) *n, pl* -deaus, -deaux or -does (-,dəʊz) a larded and braised veal fillet [c18 from Old French, probably based on FRICASSEE]

fricassee (,frɪkə'siː, 'frɪkəsɪ, 'frɪkə,seɪ) *n* **1** stewed meat, esp chicken or veal, and vegetables, served in a thick white sauce ▷ *vb* -sees, -seeing, -seed **2** (*tr*) to prepare (meat) as a fricassee [c16 from Old French, from *fricasser* to fricassee; probably related to *frire* to FRY¹]

fricative ('frɪkətɪv) *n* **1** a continuant consonant produced by partial occlusion of the airstream, such as (f) or (z) ▷ *adj* **2** relating to or denoting a fricative [c19 from New Latin *fricātivus*, from Latin *fricāre* to rub]

fricking ('frɪkɪŋ) *adj slang* (intensifier): *surrounded by fricking idiots* [c20 euphemism for FUCKING]

FRICS (in Britain) *abbreviation for* Fellow of the Royal Institution of Chartered Surveyors

friction ('frɪkʃən) *n* **1** a resistance encountered when one body moves relative to another body with which it is in contact **2** the act, effect, or an instance of rubbing one object against another **3** disagreement or conflict; discord **4** *phonetics* the hissing element of a speech sound, such as a fricative **5** perfumed alcohol used on the hair to stimulate the scalp [c16 from French, from Latin *frictiō* a rubbing, from *fricāre* to rub, rub down; related to Latin *friāre* to crumble] > 'frictional *adj* > 'frictionless *adj*

frictional soil *n* another term for **cohesionless soil**

frictional unemployment *n* those people who are in the process of moving from one job to another and who therefore appear in the unemployment statistics collected at any given time

friction clutch *n* a mechanical clutch in which the drive is transmitted by the friction between surfaces, lined with cork, asbestos, or other fibrous materials, attached to the driving and driven shafts

friction layer *n* the atmospheric layer extending up to about 600 m, in which the aerodynamic effects of surface friction are appreciable

friction match *n* a match that ignites as a result of the heat produced by friction when it is struck on a rough surface. See also **safety match**

friction rub or **murmur** *n med* the sound, heard through a stethoscope, made by the rubbing together of the two inflamed layers of pericardium in patients with pericarditis or of pleura in patients with pleurisy

friction tape *n US and Canadian* adhesive tape, impregnated with a moisture-repelling substance, used to insulate exposed electrical conductors. Also called (in Britain and certain other countries): **insulating tape**

friction welding *n* a form of welding in which the welding heat is generated by pressure and relative movement at the interface in the area of the weld

Friday ('fraɪdɪ) *n* **1** the sixth day of the week; fifth day of the working week **2** See **girl Friday, man Friday** [Old English *Frīgedæg*, literally: Freya's day; related to Old Frisian *frīadei*, Old High German *frīatag*]

fridge (frɪdʒ) *n informal* short for **refrigerator**

fried (fraɪd) *vb* the past tense and past participle of **fry¹**

friend (frɛnd) *n* **1** a person known well to another and regarded with liking, affection, and loyalty; an intimate **2** an acquaintance or associate **3** an ally in a fight or cause; supporter **4** a fellow member of a party, society, etc **5** a patron or supporter: *a friend of the opera* **6** be friends (with) to be friendly (with) **7** make friends (with) to become friendly (with) ▷ *vb* **8** (*tr*) an archaic word for **befriend** [Old English *frēond*; related to Old

Saxon *friund*, Old Norse *frǣndi*, Gothic *frijōnds*, Old High German *friunt*] > 'friendless *adj* > 'friendlessness *n* > 'friendship *n*

Friend¹ (frɛnd) *n* a member of the Religious Society of Friends; Quaker

Friend² (frɛnd) *n trademark mountaineering* a device consisting of a shaft with double-headed spring-loaded cams that can be wedged in a crack to provide an anchor point

friend at court *n* an influential acquaintance who can promote one's interests

friendly ('frɛndlɪ) *adj* -lier, -liest **1** showing or expressing liking, goodwill, or trust **2** on the same side; not hostile **3** tending or disposed to help or support; favourable ▷ *n, pl* -lies **4** Also called: **friendly match** *sport* a match played for its own sake, and not as part of a competition, etc > 'friendlily *adv* > 'friendliness *n*

-friendly *adj combining form* helpful, easy, or good for the person or thing specified: *ozone-friendly*

friendly fire *n military* firing by one's own side, esp when it harms one's own personnel

Friendly Islands *pl n* another name for **Tonga²**

friendly society *n Brit* an association of people who pay regular dues or other sums in return for old-age pensions, sickness benefits, etc. US term: benefit society

friend of Dorothy ('dɒrəθɪ) *n informal* a male homosexual [c20 after a character in the 1939 film *The Wizard of Oz* played by the US actress Judy Garland (1922–69), who has a large gay following]

Friends of the Earth *n* (*functioning as singular or plural*) an organization of environmentalists and conservationists whose aim is to promote the sustainable use of the earth's resources. Abbrevs: FoE, FOE

frier ('fraɪə) *n* a variant spelling of **fryer**

fries (fraɪz) *pl n* another name for **French fried potatoes**

Friesian¹ ('friːʒən) *n Brit* any of several breeds of black-and-white dairy cattle having a high milk yield. Usual US and Canadian name: Holstein

Friesian² ('friːʒən) *n, adj* a variant of **Frisian**

Friesland ('friːzlənd; *Dutch* 'friːslɑnt) *n* **1** a province of the N Netherlands, on the IJsselmeer and the North Sea: includes four of the West Frisian Islands; flat, with sand dunes and fens, canals, and lakes. Capital: Leeuwarden. Pop: 640 000 (2003 est). Area: 3319 sq km (1294 sq miles). Official and Frisian name: **Fryslân 2** an area comprising the province of Friesland in the Netherlands along with the regions of **East Friesland** and **North Friesland** in Germany

frieze¹ (friːz) *n* **1** *architect* **a** the horizontal band between the architrave and cornice of a classical entablature, esp one that is decorated with sculpture **b** the upper part of the wall of a room, below the cornice, esp one that is decorated **2** any ornamental band or strip on a wall [c16 from French *frise*, perhaps from Medieval Latin *frisium*, changed from Latin *Phrygium* Phrygian (work), from *Phrygia* Phrygia, famous for embroidery in gold]

frieze² (friːz) *n* a heavy woollen fabric with a long nap, used for coats, etc [c15 from Old French *frise*, from Middle Dutch *friese, vriese*, perhaps from *Vriese* Frisian]

frig (frɪg) *vb* frigs, frigging, frigged *taboo slang* **1** to have sexual intercourse (with) **2** to masturbate **3** (*intr*; foll by *around, about,* etc) to behave foolishly or aimlessly [c15 (in the sense: to wriggle): of uncertain origin; perhaps related to obsolete *frike* strong, or to Old English *frīgan* to love]

frigate ('frɪgɪt) *n* **1** a medium-sized square-rigged warship of the 18th and 19th centuries **2 a** *Brit* a warship larger than a corvette and smaller than a destroyer **b** *US* (formerly) a warship larger than a destroyer and smaller than a cruiser **c** *US* a small escort vessel [c16 from French *frégate*, from Italian *fregata*, of unknown origin]

frigate bird *n* any bird of the genus *Fregata* and family *Fregatidae*, of tropical and subtropical seas, having a long bill with a downturned tip, a wide wingspan, and a forked tail: order *Pelecaniformes* (pelicans, cormorants, etc). Also called: **man-of-war bird**

Frigg (frɪɡ) *or* **Frigga** ('frɪɡə) *n Norse myth* the wife of Odin; goddess of the heavens and married love

frigging ('frɪɡɪŋ) *adj (prenominal)* ▷ *adv slang* (intensifier): *it's only a frigging game; frigging hopeless* [C20 euphemism for FUCKING]

fright (fraɪt) *n* **1** sudden intense fear or alarm **2** a sudden alarming shock **3** *informal* a horrifying, grotesque, or ludicrous person or thing: *she looks a fright in that hat* **4** **take fright** to become frightened ▷ *vb* **5** a poetic word for **frighten** [Old English *fryhto*; related to Gothic *faurhtei*, Old Frisian *fruchte*, Old High German *forhta*]

frighten ('fraɪtᵊn) *vb (tr)* **1** to cause fear in; terrify; scare **2** to drive or force to go (away, off, out, in, etc) by making afraid > **'frightened** *adj* > **'frighteningly** *adv*

frightener ('fraɪtᵊnə) *n* **1** a person or thing that causes fear **2** **put the frighteners on** *Brit informal* to intimidate

frightful ('fraɪtfʊl) *adj* **1** very alarming, distressing, or horrifying **2** unpleasant, annoying, or extreme > **'frightfulness** *n*

frightfully ('fraɪtfəlɪ) *adv* (intensifier): *I'm frightfully glad*

fright wig *n* **a** a wig with frizzy hair standing straight up from the surface **b** a hairstyle resembling this

frigid ('frɪdʒɪd) *adj* **1** formal or stiff in behaviour or temperament; lacking in affection or warmth **2** (esp of a woman) **a** lacking sexual responsiveness **b** averse to sexual intercourse or unable to achieve orgasm during intercourse **3** characterized by physical coldness: *a frigid zone* [C15 from Latin *frigidus* cold, from *frīgēre* to be cold, freeze; related to Latin *frīgus* frost] > **fri'gidity** *or* **'frigidness** *n* > **'frigidly** *adv*

Frigid Zone *n archaic* the cold region inside the Arctic or Antarctic Circle where the sun's rays are very oblique

frigorific (ˌfrɪɡə'rɪfɪk) *adj obsolete* causing cold or freezing [C17 from French *frigorifique*, from Latin *frīgorificus*, from *frīgus* cold, coldness + *facere* to make]

frijol ('friːhəʊl; *Spanish* fri'xol) *n, pl* **-joles** (-həʊlz; *Spanish* -'xoles) a variety of bean, esp of the French bean, extensively cultivated for food in Mexico [C16 from Spanish, ultimately from Latin *phaseolus*, diminutive of *phasēlus*, from Greek *phasēlos* bean with edible pod]

frill (frɪl) *n* **1** a gathered, ruched, or pleated strip of cloth sewn on at one edge only, as on garments, as ornament, or to give extra body **2** a ruff of hair or feathers around the neck of a dog or bird or a fold of skin around the neck of a reptile or amphibian **3** Full name: **oriental frill** *(often capital)* a variety of domestic fancy pigeon having a ruff of curled feathers on the chest and crop **4** *photog* a wrinkling or loosening of the emulsion at the edges of a negative or print **5** *(often plural) informal* a superfluous or pretentious thing or manner; ▷ *vb* **6** *(tr)* to adorn or fit with a frill or frills **7** to form into a frill or frills **8** *(intr) photog* (of an emulsion) to develop a frill [C14 perhaps of Flemish origin] > **'frilliness** *n* > **'frilly** *adj*

frill-necked lizard *n* a large arboreal insectivorous Australian lizard, *Chlamydosaurus kingi*, having an erectile fold of skin around the neck: family *Agamidae* (agamas). Also called: **frilled lizard**

Frimaire *French* (frimɛr) *n* the frosty month: the third month of the French Revolutionary calendar, extending from Nov 22 to Dec 21 [C19 from French, from *frimas* hoarfrost, from Old French *frim*, of Germanic origin; related to Old Norse *hrīm* RIME¹]

fringe (frɪndʒ) *n* **1** an edging consisting of hanging threads, tassels, etc **2** **a** an outer edge; periphery **b** *(as modifier)*: *fringe dwellers; a fringe area* **3** *(modifier)* unofficial; not conventional in form: *fringe theatre* **4** *chiefly Brit* a section of the front hair cut short over the forehead **5** an ornamental border or margin **6** *physics* any of the light and dark or coloured bands produced by diffraction or interference of light ▷ *vb (tr)* **7** to adorn or fit with a fringe or fringes **8** to be a fringe for: *fur fringes the satin* [C14 from Old French *frenge*, ultimately from Latin *fimbria* fringe, border; see FIMBRIA] > **'fringeless** *adj*

fringe benefit *n* an incidental or additional advantage, esp a benefit provided by an employer to supplement an employee's regular pay, such as a pension, company car, luncheon vouchers, etc

fringed orchis *n* any orchid of the genus *Habenaria*, having yellow, white, purple, or greenish flowers with fringed petals. See also **purple-fringed orchid**

fringe tree *n* either of two ornamental oleaceous shrubs or small trees of the genus *Chionanthus*, of North America and China, having clusters of white narrow-petalled flowers

fringilline (frɪn'dʒɪlaɪn, -ɪn) *or* **fringillid** (frɪn'dʒɪlɪd) *adj* of, relating to, or belonging to the *Fringillidae*, a family of songbirds that includes the finches [C19 from New Latin *Fringilla* type genus, from Latin *fringilla* a small bird, perhaps a chaffinch]

fringing reef *n* a coral reef close to the shore to which it is attached, having a steep seaward edge

frippery ('frɪpərɪ) *n, pl* **-peries** **1** ornate or showy clothing or adornment **2** showiness; ostentation **3** unimportant considerations; trifles; trivia [C16 from Old French *freperie*, from *frepe* frill, rag, old garment, from Medieval Latin *faluppa* a straw, splinter, of obscure origin]

frippet ('frɪpɪt) *n Brit old-fashioned informal* a frivolous or flamboyant young woman

Frisbee ('frɪzbiː) *n trademark* a light plastic disc, usually 20–25 centimetres in diameter, thrown with a spinning motion for recreation or in competition

Frisches Haff ('frɪʃəs 'haf) *n* the German name for **Vistula** (sense 2)

frisé ('friːzeɪ) *n* a fabric with a long normally uncut nap used for upholstery and rugs [from French, literally: curled]

frisette *or* **frizette** (frɪ'zɛt) *n* a curly or frizzed fringe, often an artificial hairpiece, worn by women on the forehead [C19 from French, literally: little curl, from *friser* to curl, shrivel up, probably from *frire* to FRY¹]

friseur *French* (frizœr) *n* a hairdresser [C18 literally: one who curls (hair); see FRISETTE]

Frisian ('frɪʒən) *or* **Friesian** *n* **1** a language spoken in the NW Netherlands, parts of N Germany, and adjacent islands, belonging to the West Germanic branch of the Indo-European family: the nearest relative of the English language; it has three main dialects **2** a native or inhabitant of Friesland or a speaker of the Frisian language ▷ *adj* **3** **a** of or relating to the Frisian language or its speakers **b** of or relating to Friesland or its peoples and culture [C16 from Latin *Frīsiī* people of northern Germany]

Frisian Islands *pl n* a chain of islands in the North Sea along the coasts of the Netherlands, Germany, and Denmark: separated from the mainland by shallows

frisk (frɪsk) *vb* **1** *(intr)* to leap, move about, or act in a playful manner; frolic **2** *(tr)* (esp of animals) to whisk or wave briskly: *the dog frisked its tail* **3** *(tr) informal* **a** to search (someone) by feeling for concealed weapons, etc **b** to rob by searching in this way ▷ *n* **4** a playful antic or movement; frolic **5** *informal* the act or an instance of frisking a person [C16 from Old French *frisque*, of Germanic origin; related to Old High German *frisc* lively, FRESH] > **'frisker** *n* > **'friskingly** *adv*

frisket ('frɪskɪt) *n printing* a light rectangular frame, attached to the tympan of a hand printing press, that carries a parchment sheet to protect the nonprinting areas [C17 from French *frisquette*, of obscure origin]

frisky ('frɪskɪ) *adj* **friskier, friskiest** lively, high-spirited, or playful > **'friskily** *adv* > **'friskiness** *n*

frisson *French* (frisɔ̃) *n* a shudder or shiver; thrill [C18 (but in common use only from C20): literally: shiver]

frit *or* **fritt** (frɪt) *n* **1** **a** the basic materials, partially or wholly fused, for making glass, glazes for pottery, enamel, etc **b** a glassy substance used in some soft-paste porcelain **2** the material used for making the glaze for artificial teeth ▷ *vb* **frits** *or* **fritts, fritting, fritted** **3** *(tr)* to fuse (materials) in making frit [C17 from Italian *fritta*, literally: fried, from *friggere* to fry, from Latin *frīgere*]

frit fly *n* a small black dipterous fly, *Oscinella frit*, whose larvae are destructive to barley, wheat, rye, oats, etc: family *Chloropidae*

frith (frɪθ) *n* a variant of **firth**

fritillary (frɪ'tɪlərɪ) *n, pl* **-laries** **1** any N temperate liliaceous plant of the genus *Fritillaria*, having purple or white drooping bell-shaped flowers, typically marked in a chequered pattern. See also **snake's head** **2** any of various nymphalid butterflies of the genera *Argynnis, Boloria*, etc, having brownish wings chequered with black and silver [C17 from New Latin *fritillāria*, from Latin *fritillus* dice box; probably with reference to the spotted markings]

frittata (frɪ'tɑːtə) *n* an Italian dish made with eggs and chopped vegetables or meat, resembling a flat thick omelette [C20 Italian, from *fritto*, past participle of *friggere* to fry]

fritter¹ ('frɪtə) *vb (tr)* **1** (usually foll by *away*) to waste or squander **2** to break or tear into small pieces; shred ▷ *n* **3** a small piece [C18 probably from obsolete *fitter* to break into small pieces, ultimately from Old English *fitt* a piece] > **'fritterer** *n*

fritter² ('frɪtə) *n* a piece of food, such as apple or clam, that is dipped in batter and fried in deep fat [C14 from Old French *friture*, from Latin *frictus* fried, roasted, from *frīgere* to fry, parch]

Friuli (*Italian* fri'uːli) *n* a historic region of SW Europe, between the Carnic Alps and the Gulf of Venice: the W part (**Venetian Friuli**) was ceded by Austria to Italy in 1866 and **Eastern Friuli** in 1919; in 1947 Eastern Friuli (except Gorizia) was ceded to Yugoslavia

Friulian (frɪ'uːlɪən) *n* **1** the Rhaetian dialect spoken in parts of Friuli. See also **Ladin, Romansch** **2** an inhabitant of Friuli or a speaker of Friulian ▷ *adj* **3** of or relating to Friuli, its inhabitants, or their language

Friuli-Venezia Giulia (*Italian* 'dʒuːlja) *n* a region of NE Italy, formed in 1947 from **Venetian Friuli** and part of **Eastern Friuli**. Capital: Trieste. Pop: 1 191 588 (2003 est). Area: 7851 sq km (3031 sq miles)

frivol ('frɪvᵊl) *vb* **-ols, -olling, -olled** *or US* **-ols, -oling, -oled** *informal* **1** *(intr)* to behave frivolously; trifle **2** *(tr;* often foll by *away)* to waste on frivolous pursuits [C19 back formation from FRIVOLOUS] > **'frivoller** *or US* **'frivoler** *n*

frivolous ('frɪvələs) *adj* **1** not serious or sensible in content, attitude, or behaviour; silly: *a frivolous remark* **2** unworthy of serious or sensible treatment; unimportant: *frivolous details* [C15 from Latin *frīvolus* silly, worthless] > **'frivolously** *adv* > **'frivolousness** *or* **frivolity** (frɪ'vɒlɪtɪ) *n*

frizette (frɪ'zɛt) *n* a variant spelling of **frisette**

frizz (frɪz) *vb* **1** (of the hair, nap, etc) to form or cause (the hair, etc) to form tight wiry curls or crisp tufts ▷ *n* **2** hair that has been frizzed **3** the state of being frizzed [C19 from French *friser* to curl, shrivel up (see FRISETTE): influenced by FRIZZLE¹] > **'frizzer** *n*

frizzante (frɪ'zæntɪ; *Italian* frid'dzante) *adj* (of wine) slightly effervescent [Italian, from *frizzare* to sparkle]

frizzle¹ ('frɪzᵊl) *vb* **1** to form (the hair) into tight crisp curls; frizz ▷ *n* **2** a tight crisp curl [C16 probably related to Old English *frīs* curly, Old

f

Frisian *frêsle* curl, ringlet] > ˈ**frizzler** *n* > ˈ**frizzly** *adj*
frizzle[2] (ˈfrɪzᵊl) *vb* **1** to scorch or be scorched, esp with a sizzling noise **2** (*tr*) to fry (bacon, etc) until crisp [C16 probably blend of FRY[1] + SIZZLE]
frizzy (ˈfrɪzɪ) *or* **frizzly** (ˈfrɪzlɪ) *adj* **-zier, -ziest** *or* **-zlier, -zliest** (of the hair) in tight crisp wiry curls > ˈ**frizzily** *adv* > ˈ**frizziness** *or* ˈ**frizzliness** *n*
Frl. *abbreviation for* Fräulein [German: Miss]
fro[1] (frəʊ) *adv* back or from. See **to and fro** [C12 from Old Norse *frā*; related to Old English *fram* FROM]
fro[2] *or* **ˈfro** (frəʊ) *n, pl* **fros** *or* **ˈfros** short for **Afro**
Frobisher Bay (ˈfrəʊbɪʃə) *n* **1** an inlet of the Atlantic in NE Canada, in the SE coast of Baffin Island **2** the former name of **Iqaluit**
frock (frɒk) *n* **1** a girl's or woman's dress **2** a loose garment of several types, such as a peasant's smock **3** a coarse wide-sleeved outer garment worn by members of some religious orders ▷ *vb* **4** (*tr*) to invest (a person) with the office or status of a cleric [C14 from Old French *froc*; related to Old Saxon, Old High German *hroc* coat]
frock coat *n* a man's single- or double-breasted skirted coat, as worn in the 19th century
frocking (ˈfrɒkɪŋ) *n* coarse material suitable for making frocks or work clothes
frock tart *n NZ slang* a person who makes or designs costumes for films or television
froe *or* **frow** (frəʊ) *n* a cutting tool with handle and blade at right angles, used for stripping young trees, etc [C16 from *frower*, from *froward* (in the sense: turned away)]
Froebel *or* **Fröbel** (*German* ˈfrøːbəl) *adj* of, denoting, or relating to a system of kindergarten education developed by Friedrich (Wilhelm August) Froebel (1782–1852), German educator and founder of the first kindergarten in 1840, or to the training and qualification of teachers to use this system
frog[1] (frɒg) *n* **1** any insectivorous anuran amphibian of the family *Ranidae*, such as *Rana temporaria* of Europe, having a short squat tailless body with a moist smooth skin and very long hind legs specialized for hopping **2** any of various similar amphibians of related families, such as the tree frog. Related adj: **batrachian** **3** any spiked or perforated object used to support plant stems in a flower arrangement **4** a recess in a brick to reduce its weight **5** **a frog in one's throat** phlegm on the vocal cords that affects one's speech ▷ *vb* **frogs, frogging, frogged** **6** (*intr*) to hunt or catch frogs [Old English *frogga*; related to Old Norse *froskr*, Old High German *forsk*] > ˈ**froggy** *adj*
frog[2] (frɒg) *n* **1** (*often plural*) a decorative fastening of looped braid or cord, as on the front of a 19th-century military uniform **2** a loop or other attachment on a belt to hold the scabbard of a sword, etc **3** *music, US and Canadian* **a** the ledge or ridge at the upper end of the fingerboard of a violin, cello, etc, over which the strings pass to the tuning pegs **b** the end of a violin bow that is held by the player. Also called (in Britain and certain other countries): **nut** [C18 perhaps ultimately from Latin *floccus* tuft of hair, FLOCK[2]]
frog[3] (frɒg) *n* a tough elastic horny material in the centre of the sole of a horse's foot [C17 of uncertain origin]
frog[4] (frɒg) *n* a grooved plate of iron or steel placed to guide train wheels over an intersection of railway lines [C19 of uncertain origin; perhaps a special use of FROG[1]]
Frog (frɒg) *or* **Froggy** (ˈfrɒgɪ) *n, pl* **Frogs** *or* **Froggies** a derogatory word for a French person
frog-bit *n* a floating aquatic Eurasian plant, *Hydrocharis morsus-ranae*, with heart-shaped leaves and white flowers: family *Hydrocharitaceae*
frogfish (ˈfrɒg,fɪʃ) *n, pl* **-fish** *or* **-fishes** any angler (fish) of the family *Antennariidae*, in which the body is covered with fleshy processes, including a fleshy lure on top of the head
frogged (frɒgd) *adj* (of a coat) fitted with ornamental frogs
frogging (ˈfrɒgɪŋ) *n* the ornamental frogs on a coat collectively
froggy (ˈfrɒgɪ) *adj* **-gier, -giest** of, like, or relating to frogs; full of frogs
froghopper (ˈfrɒg,hɒpə) *n* any small leaping herbivorous homopterous insect of the family *Cercopidae*, whose larvae secrete a protective spittle-like substance around themselves. Also called: **spittle insect, spittlebug**
frog kick *n* a type of kick used in swimming, as in the breast stroke, in which the legs are simultaneously drawn towards the body and bent at the knees with the feet together, straightened out with the legs apart, and then brought together again quickly
frogman (ˈfrɒgmən) *n, pl* **-men** a swimmer equipped with a rubber suit, flippers, and breathing equipment for working underwater
frogmarch (ˈfrɒg,mɑːtʃ) *n* **1** a method of carrying a resisting person in which each limb is held by one person and the victim is carried horizontally and face downwards **2** any method of making a resisting person move forward against his will ▷ *vb* **3** (*tr*) to carry in a frogmarch or cause to move forward unwillingly
frogmouth (ˈfrɒg,maʊθ) *n* any nocturnal insectivorous bird of the genera *Podargus* and *Batrachostomus*, of SE Asia and Australia, similar to the nightjars: family *Podargidae*, order *Caprimulgiformes*
frog orchid *n* any of several orchids having greenish flowers thought to resemble small frogs, esp *Coeloglossum viride* of calcareous turf
frog pad *n* a rubber or leather cushion fixed to a leather sole and fitted under a horseshoe to reduce shock to a horse's foot
frogspawn (ˈfrɒg,spɔːn) *n* a mass of fertilized frogs' eggs or developing tadpoles, each egg being surrounded by a protective nutrient jelly
frog spit *or* **spittle** *n* **1** another name for **cuckoo spit** **2** a foamy mass of threadlike green algae floating on ponds
frolic (ˈfrɒlɪk) *n* **1** a light-hearted entertainment or occasion **2** light-hearted activity; gaiety; merriment ▷ *vb* **-ics, -icking, -icked** **3** (*intr*) to caper about; act or behave playfully ▷ *adj* **4** *archaic or literary* full of merriment or fun [C16 from Dutch *vrolijk*, from Middle Dutch *vro* happy, glad; related to Old High German *frō* happy] > ˈ**frolicker** *n*
frolicsome (ˈfrɒlɪksəm) *or* **frolicky** *adj* given to frolicking; merry and playful > ˈ**frolicsomely** *adv* > ˈ**frolicsomeness** *n*
from (frɒm; *unstressed* frəm) *prep* **1** used to indicate the original location, situation, etc: *from Paris to Rome* **2** in a period of time starting at: *he lived from 1910 to 1970* **3** used to indicate the distance between two things or places **4** used to indicate a lower amount: *from five to fifty pounds* **5** showing the model of: *painted from life* **6** used with the gerund to mark prohibition, restraint, etc **7** because of [Old English *fram*; related to Old Norse *frā*, Old Saxon, Old High German, Gothic *fram* from, Greek *promos* foremost]
fromage frais (ˈfrɒmɑːʒ ˈfreɪ) *n* a low-fat soft cheese with a smooth light texture [French, literally: fresh cheese]
Frome (frəʊm) *n* **Lake** a shallow salt lake in NE South Australia: intermittently filled with water. Length: 100 km (60 miles). Width: 48 km (30 miles)
fromenty (ˈfrəʊməntɪ) *n* a variant of **frumenty**
frond (frɒnd) *n* **1** a large compound leaf, esp of a fern **2** the thallus of a seaweed or a lichen [C18 from Latin *frōns*] > ˈ**fronded** *adj* > ˈ**frondless** *adj*
Fronde (frɒnd; *French* frɔ̃d) *n French history* either of two rebellious movements against the ministry of Cardinal Mazarin in the reign of Louis XIV, the first led by the parlement of Paris (1648–49) and the second by the princes (1650–53) [C18 from French, literally: sling, the insurgent parliamentarians being likened to naughty schoolboys using slings]
frondescence (frɒnˈdɛsəns) *n* **1** *now rare* the process or state of producing leaves **2** a less common name for **foliage** [C19 from New Latin *frondēscentia*, from Latin *frondēscere* to put forth leaves, from *frōns* foliage; see FROND] > fronˈ**descent,** ˈ**frondose** *or* ˈ**frondous** *adj*
Frondeur (frɒnˈdɜː; *French* frɔ̃dœr) *n* **1** *French history* a member of the Fronde **2** any malcontent or troublemaker
frons (frɒnz) *n, pl* **frontes** (ˈfrɒntiːz) an anterior cuticular plate on the head of some insects, in front of the clypeus [C19 from Latin: forehead, brow, FRONT]
front (frʌnt) *n* **1** that part or side that is forward, prominent, or most often seen or used **2** a position or place directly before or ahead **3** the beginning, opening, or first part **4** the position of leadership; forefront; vanguard **5** land bordering a lake, street, etc **6** land along a seashore or large lake, esp a promenade **7** *military* **a** the total area in which opposing armies face each other **b** the lateral space in which a military unit or formation is operating **c** the direction in which troops are facing when in a formed line **8** *meteorol* the dividing line or plane between two air masses or water masses of different origins and having different characteristics. See also **warm front, cold front** **9** outward aspect or bearing, as when dealing with a situation: *a bold front* **10** assurance, overconfidence, or effrontery **11** *informal* a business or other activity serving as a respectable cover for another, usually criminal, organization **12** *chiefly US* a nominal leader of an organization, etc, who lacks real power or authority; figurehead **13** *informal* outward appearance of rank or wealth **14** a particular field of activity involving some kind of struggle: *on the wages front* **15** a group of people with a common goal: *a national liberation front* **16** a false shirt front; a dicky **17** *archaic* the forehead or the face ▷ *adj* (*prenominal*) **18** of, at, or in the front: *a front seat* **19** *phonetics* of, relating to, or denoting a vowel articulated with the blade of the tongue brought forward and raised towards the hard palate, as for the sound of *ee* in English *see* or *a* in English *hat* **20** **on the front foot** at an advantage, outclassing and outmanoeuvring one's opponents ▷ *vb* **21** (when *intr*, foll by *on* or *onto*) to be opposite (to); face (onto): *this house fronts the river* **22** (*tr*) to be a front of or for **23** (*tr*) *informal* to appear as a presenter in (a television show) **24** (*tr*) to be the lead singer or player in (a band) **25** (*tr*) to confront, esp in hostility or opposition **26** (*tr*) to supply a front for **27** (*intr; often foll by* up) *Austral and NZ informal* to appear (at): *to front up at the police station* [C13 (in the sense: forehead, face): from Latin *frōns* forehead, foremost part] > ˈ**frontless** *adj*
front. *abbreviation for* frontispiece
frontage (ˈfrʌntɪdʒ) *n* **1** the façade of a building or the front of a plot of ground **2** the extent of the front of a shop, plot of land, etc, esp along a street, river, etc **3** the direction in which a building faces: *a frontage on the river*
frontal (ˈfrʌntᵊl) *adj* **1** of, at, or in the front **2** of or relating to the forehead: *frontal artery* **3** of or relating to the anterior part of a body or organ **4** *meteorol* of, relating to, or resulting from a front or its passage: *frontal rainfall* ▷ *n* **5** a decorative hanging for the front of an altar **6** See **frontal lobe, frontal bone** **7** another name for **frontlet** (sense 1) [C14 (in the sense: adornment for forehead, altar cloth): via Old French *frontel*, from Latin *frontālia* (pl) ornament worn on forehead, *frontellum* altar cloth, both from *frōns* forehead, FRONT] > ˈ**frontally** *adv*
frontal bone *n* the bone forming the forehead and the upper parts of the orbits. It contains several air spaces
frontality (frənˈtælɪtɪ) *n fine arts* a frontal view, as in a painting or other work of art

frontal lobe *n anatomy* the anterior portion of each cerebral hemisphere, situated in front of the central sulcus

front bench *n Brit* **a** the foremost bench of either the Government or Opposition in the House of Commons **b** the leadership (**frontbenchers**) of either group, who occupy this bench **c** (*as modifier*): *a front-bench decision*

front bottom *n Brit informal* the female genitals [C20]

front door *n* **1** the main entrance to a house **2** an open legitimate means of obtaining a job, position, etc: *to get in by the front door*

front-end *adj* (of money, credit, etc) required or incurred in advance of a project in order to get it under way

front-end load *n* commission and other expenses paid for as a large proportion of the early payments made by an investor in an insurance policy or a long-term investment plan > **front-end loading** *n*

front-end processor *n* a small computer that receives data from input devices and performs some initial processing tasks on it before passing it to a more powerful computer for final processing

frontier ('frʌntɪə, frʌn'tɪə) *n* **1 a** the region of a country bordering on another or a line, barrier, etc, marking such a boundary **b** (*as modifier*): *a frontier post* **2** *US and Canadian* **a** the edge of the settled area of a country **b** (*as modifier*): *the frontier spirit* **3** (*often plural*) the limit of knowledge in a particular field: *the frontiers of physics have been pushed back* [C14 from Old French *frontiere*, from *front* (in the sense: part which is opposite); see FRONT]

frontier orbital *n chem* the highest-energy occupied orbital or lowest-energy unoccupied orbital in a molecule. Such orbitals have a large influence on chemical properties

frontiersman ('frʌntɪəzmən, frʌn'tɪəz-) *n, pl* **-men** (formerly) a man living on a frontier, esp in a newly pioneered territory of the US

frontierswoman ('frʌntɪəzwʊmən, frʌn'tɪəz-) *n, pl* **-women** (formerly) a woman living on a frontier, esp in a newly pioneered territory of the US

frontispiece ('frʌntɪsˌpiːs) *n* **1** an illustration facing the title page of a book **2** the principal façade of a building; front **3** a pediment, esp an ornamented one, over a door, window, etc [C16 *frontispice*, from French, from Late Latin *frontispicium* façade, inspection of the forehead, from Latin *frōns* forehead + *specere* to look at; influenced by PIECE]

frontlet ('frʌntlɪt) *n* **1** Also called: **frontal** a small decorative loop worn on a woman's forehead, projecting from under her headdress, in the 15th century **2** the forehead of an animal, esp of a bird when it is a different colour from the rest of the head **3** the decorated border of an altar frontal **4** *Judaism* a phylactery worn on the forehead. See also **tefillah** [C15 from Old French *frontelet* a little FRONTAL]

front line *n* **1** *military* the most advanced military units or elements in a battle **2** the most advanced, exposed, or conspicuous element in any activity or situation **3 frontline** (*modifier*) **a** of, relating to, or suitable for the front line of a military formation: *frontline troops* **b** *Brit esp journalistic* of, relating to, or suitable for public service and business employees who are in direct contact with the public: *frontline staff* **c** to the fore; advanced, conspicuous, etc: *frontline news* **d** of or relating to a country bordering on or close to a hostile country or scene of armed conflict

front list *n* **a** a publisher's list of forthcoming books **b** (*as modifier*): *a front-list writer*. See also **backlist, mid-list**

front loader *n* a washing machine with a door at the front which opens one side of the drum into which washing is placed

front man *n informal* **1** a nominal leader of an organization, etc, who lacks real power or authority, esp one who lends respectability to some nefarious activity **2** the leader or visual focus of a group of musicians, usually the singer. Also called: **front person**

front matter *n* another name for **prelims** (sense 1)

front of house *n* the areas of a theatre, opera house, etc, used by the audience

frontogenesis (ˌfrʌntəʊ'dʒɛnɪsɪs) *n meteorol* the formation or development of a front through the meeting of air or water masses from different origins > **frontogenetic** (ˌfrʌntəʊdʒə'nɛtɪk) *adj* > **fronto'ge'netically** *adv*

frontolysis (frʌn'tɒlɪsɪs) *n meteorol* the weakening or dissipation of a front

fronton ('frʌntɒn, frɒn'tɒn) *n* a wall against which pelota or jai alai is played [C17 from Spanish *frontón*, from *frente* forehead, from Latin *frōns*]

front-page *n* (*modifier*) important or newsworthy enough to be put on the front page of a newspaper

front row *n* (*functioning as singular or plural*) *rugby Union* **a** the forwards at the front of a scrum **b** (*as modifier*): *perhaps the finest front-row forward in the world*

frontrunner ('frʌntˌrʌnə) *n informal* the leader or a favoured contestant in a race, election, etc

frontrunning ('frʌntˌrʌnɪŋ) *n stock exchange* the practice by market makers of using advance information provided by their own investment analysts before it has been given to clients

frontwards ('frʌntwədz) or **frontward** *adv* towards the front

frore (frɔː) *adj archaic* very cold or frosty [C13 *froren*, past participle of Old English *frēosan* to FREEZE]

frosh (frɒʃ) *n US and Canadian slang* a freshman [C20 altered from FRESHMAN]

frost (frɒst) *n* **1** a white deposit of ice particles, esp one formed on objects out of doors at night. See also **hoarfrost 2** an atmospheric temperature of below freezing point, characterized by the production of this deposit **3** degrees below freezing point: *eight degrees of frost indicates a temperature of either −8°C or 24°F* **4** *informal* something given a cold reception; failure **5** *informal* coolness of manner **6** the act of freezing ▷ *vb* **7** to cover or be covered with frost **8** (*tr*) to give a frostlike appearance to (glass, etc), as by means of a fine-grained surface **9** (*tr*) *chiefly US and Canadian* to decorate (cakes, etc) with icing or frosting **10** (*tr*) to kill or damage (crops, etc) with frost [Old English *frost*; related to Old Norse, Old Saxon, Old High German *frost*; see FREEZE] > **'frost,like** *adj*

frostbite ('frɒst,baɪt) *n* **1** destruction of tissues, esp those of the fingers, ears, toes, and nose, by freezing, characterized by tingling, blister formation, and gangrene **2** *NZ* a type of small sailing dinghy

frostbitten ('frɒst,bɪtᵊn) *adj* of or affected with frostbite

frosted ('frɒstɪd) *adj* **1** covered or injured by frost **2** covered with icing, as a cake **3** (of glass, etc) having a surface roughened, as if covered with frost, to prevent clear vision through it

frost heave *n* the upthrust and cracking of a ground surface through the freezing and expansion of water underneath. Also called: **frost heaving**

frost hollow *n* a depression in a hilly area in which cold air collects, becoming very cold at night

frosting ('frɒstɪŋ) *n* **1** a soft icing based on sugar and egg whites **2** a sugar preparation, variously flavoured and coloured, for coating and decorating cakes, biscuits, etc. Also called: **icing 3** a rough or matt finish on glass, silver, etc **4** *slang* the practice of stealing a car while the owner has left it idling in order to defrost the windows and heat the engine

frost line *n* **1** the deepest point in the ground to which frost will penetrate **2** the limit towards the equator beyond which frosts do not occur

frost stud *n* an antislip device fitted to a horse's shoe. Also called: **frost cog**

frostwork ('frɒst,wɜːk) *n* **1** the patterns made by frost on glass, metal, etc **2** similar artificial ornamentation

frosty ('frɒstɪ) *adj* **frostier, frostiest 1** characterized by frost: *a frosty night* **2** covered by or decorated with frost **3** lacking warmth or enthusiasm **4** like frost in appearance or colour; hoary > **'frostily** *adv* > **'frostiness** *n*

froth (frɒθ) *n* **1** a mass of small bubbles of air or a gas in a liquid, produced by fermentation, detergent, etc **2** a mixture of saliva and air bubbles formed at the lips in certain diseases, such as rabies **3** trivial ideas, talk, or entertainment ▷ *vb* **4** to produce or cause to produce froth **5** (*tr*) to give out in the form of froth **6** (*tr*) to cover with froth [C14 from Old Norse *frotha* or *frauth*; related to Old English *āfrēothan* to foam, Sanskrit *prothati* he snorts] > **'frothy** *adj* > **'frothily** *adv* > **'frothiness** *n*

froth flotation *n* another name for **flotation** (in metallurgy)

frottage ('frɒtɑːʒ, *French* frɔtaʒ) *n* **1** the act or process of taking a rubbing from a rough surface, such as wood, for a work of art **2** sexual excitement obtained by rubbing against another person's clothed body [French, from *frotter* to rub]

Froude number (fraʊd) *n* a dimensionless number used in hydrodynamics for model simulation of actual conditions [named after William *Froude* (1810–79), English civil engineer]

froufrou ('fruːˌfruː) *n* **1** a swishing sound, as made by a long silk dress **2** elaborate dress or ornamentation, esp worn by women [C19 from French, of imitative origin]

frow (fraʊ) *n* a variant spelling of **froe**

froward ('frəʊəd) *adj archaic* obstinate; contrary [C14 see FRO, -WARD] > **'frowardly** *adv* > **'frowardness** *n*

frown (fraʊn) *vb* **1** (*intr*) to draw the brows together and wrinkle the forehead, esp in worry, anger, or concentration **2** (*intr; foll by on or upon*) to have a dislike (of); look disapprovingly (upon) **3** (*tr*) to express (worry, etc) by frowning **4** (*tr; often foll by down*) to force, silence, etc, by a frowning look ▷ *n* **5** the act of frowning **6** a show of dislike or displeasure [C14 from Old French *froigner*, of Celtic origin; compare Welsh *ffroen* nostril, Middle Breton *froan*] > **'frowner** *n* > **'frowningly** *adv*

frowst (fraʊst) *n Brit informal* a hot and stale atmosphere; fug [C19 back formation from *frowsty* musty, stuffy, variant of FROWZY]

frowsty ('fraʊstɪ) *adj* **-stier, -stiest** ill-smelling; stale; musty > **'frowstiness** *n*

frowzy, frouzy or **frowsy** ('fraʊzɪ) *adj* **frowzier, frowziest; frouzier, frouziest; frowsier, frowsiest 1** untidy or unkempt in appearance; shabby **2** ill-smelling; frowsty [C17 of unknown origin] > **'frowziness, 'frouziness** or **'frowsiness** *n*

froze (frəʊz) *vb* the past tense of **freeze**

frozen ('frəʊzᵊn) *vb* **1** the past participle of **freeze** ▷ *adj* **2** turned into or covered with ice **3** obstructed or blocked by ice **4** killed, injured, or stiffened by extreme cold **5** (of a region or climate) icy or snowy **6** (of food) preserved by a freezing process **7 a** (of prices, wages, etc) arbitrarily pegged at a certain level **b** (of business assets) not convertible into cash, as by government direction or business conditions **8** frigid, unfeeling, or disdainful in manner **9** motionless or unyielding: *he was frozen with horror* > **'frozenly** *adv* > **'frozenness** *n*

frozen shoulder *n pathol* a painful stiffness in a shoulder joint

FRPS (in Britain) *abbreviation for* Fellow of the Royal Photographic Society

FRS (in Britain) *abbreviation for* Fellow of the Royal Society

FRSC (in Britain) *abbreviation for* Fellow of the

f

Royal Society of Chemistry

FRSNZ *abbreviation for* Fellow of the Royal Society of New Zealand

frt *abbreviation for* freight

fructan ('frʌktən) *n* a type of polymer of fructose, present in certain fruits

Fructidor *French* (fryktidɔr) *n* the month of fruit: the twelfth month of the French Revolutionary calendar, extending from Aug 19 to Sept 22 [c18 from Latin *frūctus* fruit + Greek *dōron* gift]

fructiferous (frʌk'tɪfərəs, frʊk-) *adj* (of plants or trees) bearing or yielding fruit > fruc'tiferously *adv*

fructification (ˌfrʌktɪfɪ'keɪʃən, ˌfrʊk-) *n* **1** the act or state of fructifying **2** the product of a seed-bearing plant **3** any spore-bearing structure in ferns, mosses, fungi, etc

fructify ('frʌktɪˌfaɪ, 'frʊk-) *vb* -fies, -fying, -fied **1** to bear or cause to bear fruit **2** to make or become productive or fruitful [c14 from Old French *fructifier*, from Late Latin *frūctificāre* to bear fruit, from Latin *frūctus* fruit + *facere* to make, produce] > 'fructiˌfier *n*

fructose ('frʌktəʊs, -təʊz, 'frʊk-) *n* a white crystalline water-soluble sugar occurring in honey and many fruits. Formula: $C_6H_{12}O_6$. Also called: laevulose, fruit sugar [c19 from Latin *frūctus* fruit + -OSE²]

fructuous ('frʌktjʊəs, 'frʊk-) *adj* productive or fruitful; fertile [c14 from Latin *frūctuōsus*, from *frūctus* fruit + -OUS] > 'fructuously *adv* > 'fructuousness *n*

frugal ('fruːg²l) *adj* **1** practising economy; living without waste; thrifty **2** not costly; meagre [c16 from Latin *frūgālis*, from *frūgī* useful, temperate, from *frux* fruit] > fru'gality *or* 'frugalness *n* > 'frugally *adv*

frugivorous (fruː'dʒɪvərəs) *adj* feeding on fruit; fruit-eating [c18 from *frugi-* (as in FRUGAL) + -VOROUS]

fruit (fruːt) *n* **1** *botany* the ripened ovary of a flowering plant, containing one or more seeds. It may be dry, as in the poppy, or fleshy, as in the peach **2** any fleshy part of a plant, other than the above structure, that supports the seeds and is edible, such as the strawberry **3** the specialized spore-producing structure of plants that do not bear seeds **4** any plant product useful to man, including grain, vegetables, etc **5** (often plural) the result or consequence of an action or effort **6** *Brit old-fashioned slang* fellow: used as a term of address **7** *slang, chiefly Brit* a person considered to be eccentric or insane **8** *slang, chiefly US and Canadian* a male homosexual **9** *archaic* offspring of man or animals; progeny ▷ *vb* **10** to bear or cause to bear fruit [c12 from Old French, from Latin *frūctus* enjoyment, profit, fruit, from *fruī* to enjoy] > 'fruitˌlike *adj*

fruitage ('fruːtɪdʒ) *n* **1** the process, state, or season of producing fruit **2** fruit collectively

fruitarian (fruː'tɛərɪən) *n* a person who eats only fruit ▷ *adj* **2** of or relating to a fruitarian: *a fruitarian diet* > frui'tarianˌism *n*

fruit bat *n* any large Old World bat of the suborder *Megachiroptera*, occurring in tropical and subtropical regions and feeding on fruit. Compare **insectivorous bat**

fruit body *n* a variant of **fruiting body**

fruitcake ('fruːtˌkeɪk) *n* **1** a rich cake containing mixed dried fruit, lemon peel, nuts, etc **2** *slang, chiefly Brit* a person considered to be eccentric or insane

fruit cocktail *n* fruit salad consisting of small or diced fruits

fruit cup *n* a variety of fruits served in a cup or glass as an appetizer or dessert

fruit drop *n* **1** the premature shedding of fruit from a tree before fully ripe **2** a boiled sweet with a fruity flavour

fruiter ('fruːtə) *n* **1** a fruit grower **2** any tree that bears fruit, esp edible fruit

fruiterer ('fruːtərə) *n* *chiefly Brit* a fruit dealer or seller

fruit fly *n* **1** any small dipterous fly of the family *Trypetidae*, which feed on and lay their eggs in plant tissues. See also **gallfly 2** any dipterous fly of the genus *Drosophila*. See **drosophila**

fruitful ('fruːtfʊl) *adj* **1** bearing fruit in abundance **2** productive or prolific, esp in bearing offspring **3** causing or assisting prolific growth **4** producing results or profits: *a fruitful discussion* > 'fruitfully *adv* > 'fruitfulness *n*

fruiting body *n* the part of a fungus in which the spores are produced. Also: fruit body

fruition (fruː'ɪʃən) *n* **1** the attainment or realization of something worked for or desired; fulfilment **2** enjoyment of this **3** the act or condition of bearing fruit [c15 from Late Latin *fruitiō* enjoyment, from Latin *fruī* to enjoy]

fruit knife *n* a small stainless knife for cutting fruit

fruitless ('fruːtlɪs) *adj* **1** yielding nothing or nothing of value; unproductive; ineffectual **2** without fruit > 'fruitlessly *adv* > 'fruitlessness *n*

fruit machine *n* *Brit* a gambling machine that pays out when certain combinations of diagrams, usually of fruit, are displayed

fruit salad *n* a dish consisting of sweet fruits cut up and served in a syrup: often sold canned

fruit sugar *n* another name for **fructose**

fruit tree *n* any tree that bears edible fruit

fruity ('fruːtɪ) *adj* fruitier, fruitiest **1** of or resembling fruit **2** (of a voice) mellow or rich **3** ingratiating or unctuous **4** *informal, chiefly Brit* erotically stimulating; salacious **5** *slang* eccentric or insane **6** *chiefly US and Canadian* a slang word for **homosexual**. > 'fruitiness *n* > 'fruitily *adv*

frumentaceous (ˌfruːmɛn'teɪʃəs) *adj* resembling or made of wheat or similar grain [c17 from Late Latin *frūmentāceus*, from Latin *frūmentum* corn, grain]

frumenty ('fruːməntɪ), **fromenty, furmenty** *or* **furmity** *n* *Brit* a kind of porridge made from hulled wheat boiled with milk, sweetened, and spiced [c14 from Old French *frumentee*, from *frument* grain, from Latin *frūmentum*]

frump (frʌmp) *n* a woman who is dowdy, drab, or unattractive [c16 (in the sense: to be sullen; c19 dowdy woman): from Middle Dutch *verrompelen* to wrinkle, RUMPLE]

frumpy ('frʌmpɪ) *or* **frumpish** ('frʌmpɪʃ) *adj* (of a woman, clothes, etc) dowdy, drab, or unattractive > 'frumpily *or* 'frumpishly *adv* > 'frumpiness *or* 'frumpishness *n*

Frunze (*Russian* 'frʊnzɪ) *n* the former name (until 1991) of **Bishkek**

frusemide ('frʌsəˌmaɪd) *or* **furosemide** ('fjʊərˌəʊsəˌmaɪd) *n* a diuretic used to relieve oedema, for example caused by heart or kidney disease

frustrate (frʌ'streɪt) *vb* (*tr*) **1** to hinder or prevent (the efforts, plans, or desires) of; thwart **2** to upset, agitate, or tire ▷ *adj* **3** *archaic* frustrated or thwarted; baffled [c15 from Latin *frustrāre* to cheat, from *frustrā* in error] > frus'trater *n*

frustrated (frʌ'streɪtɪd) *adj* having feelings of dissatisfaction or lack of fulfilment

frustration (frʌ'streɪʃən) *n* **1** the condition of being frustrated **2** something that frustrates **3** *psychol* **a** the prevention or hindering of a potentially satisfying activity **b** the emotional reaction to such prevention that may involve aggression

frustule ('frʌstjuːl) *n* *botany* the hard siliceous cell wall of a diatom [c19 from French, from Late Latin *frustulum* a small piece, from *frustum* a bit]

frustum ('frʌstəm) *n*, *pl* -tums *or* -ta (-tə) **1** *geometry* **a** the part of a solid, such as a cone or pyramid, contained between the base and a plane parallel to the base that intersects the solid **b** the part of such a solid contained between two parallel planes intersecting the solid **2** *architect* a single drum of a column or a single stone used to construct a pier [c17 from Latin: piece; probably related to Old English *brȳsan* to crush, BRUISE]

frutescent (fruː'tɛsᵊnt) *or* **fruticose** ('fruːtɪˌkəʊs, -ˌkəʊz) *adj* having the appearance or habit of a shrub; shrubby [c18 from Latin *frutex* shrub, bush] > fru'tescence *n*

fry¹ (fraɪ) *vb* fries, frying, fried **1** (when *tr*, sometimes foll by *up*) to cook or be cooked in fat, oil, etc, usually over direct heat **2** (*intr*) *informal* to be excessively hot **3** *slang, chiefly US* to kill or be killed by electrocution, esp in the electric chair ▷ *n, pl* fries **4** a dish of something fried, esp the offal of a specified animal: *pig's fry* **5** *US and Canadian* a social occasion, often outdoors, at which the chief food is fried **6** *Brit informal* the act of preparing a mixed fried dish or the dish itself [c13 from Old French *frire*, from Latin *frīgere* to roast, fry]

fry² (fraɪ) *pl n* **1** the young of various species of fish **2** the young of certain other animals, such as frogs **3** young children See also **small fry** [c14 (in the sense: young, offspring): perhaps via Norman French from Old French *freier* to spawn, rub, from Latin *fricāre* to rub]

fryer *or* **frier** ('fraɪə) *n* **1** a person or thing that fries **2** a young chicken suitable for frying

frying pan *or esp US* **fry-pan** *n* **1** a long-handled shallow pan used for frying **2** out of the frying pan into the fire from a bad situation to a worse one

f.s. *abbreviation for* foot-second

FSA *abbreviation for* **1** Fellow of the Society of Antiquaries **2** Financial Services Authority **3** (in Britain) Food Standards Association

FSB *abbreviation for* the Russian Federal Security Service, founded in 1995 [c20 Russian *Federalnaya sluzhba bezopasnosti*]

FSH *abbreviation for* follicle-stimulating hormone

f-stop *n* any of the settings for the f-number of a camera

ft *abbreviation for* fort

FT (in Britain) *abbreviation for* Financial Times

ft *abbreviation for* **1** foot *or* feet **2** fortification

fth. *or* **fthm.** *abbreviation for* fathom

ft-l *abbreviation for* foot-lambert

ft-lb *abbreviation for* foot-pound

FTP *or* **ftp** **1** *n* file transfer protocol; the standard protocol used to transfer files across the internet, or a similar network, between computer systems **2** the program implementing this ▷ *vb* (*tr*) **3** to transfer (a file) in this way

FT-SE 100 Index *abbreviation for* Financial Times Stock Exchange 100 Index

FT Share Indexes *pl n* any of a number of share indexes published by the *Financial Times* to reflect various aspects of stock exchange prices. See **Financial Times Industrial Ordinary Share Index, Financial Times Stock Exchange 100 Index**

fubar *or* **foobar** ('fuːbɑː) *adj slang* irreparably damaged or bungled [c20 acronym for *f(ucked) u(p) b(eyond) a(ll) r(epair)*]

fubsy ('fʌbzɪ) *adj* -sier, -siest *archaic or dialect* short and stout; squat [c18 from obsolete *fubs* plump person]

Fu-chou ('fuː'tʃəʊ) *n* a variant transliteration of the Chinese name for **Fuzhou**

fuchsia ('fjuːʃə) *n* **1** any onagraceous shrub of the mostly tropical genus *Fuchsia*, widely cultivated for their showy drooping purple, red, or white flowers **2** Also called: **California fuchsia** a North American onagraceous plant, *Zauschneria californica*, with tubular scarlet flowers **3 a** a reddish-purple to purplish-pink colour **b** (*as adjective*): *a fuchsia dress* [c18 from New Latin, named after Leonhard Fuchs (1501–66), German botanist]

fuchsin ('fuːksɪn) *or* **fuchsine** ('fuːksiːn, -sɪn) *n* a greenish crystalline substance, the quaternary chloride of rosaniline, forming a red solution in water: used as a textile dye and a biological stain. Formula: $C_{20}H_{19}N_3HCl$. Also called: **magenta** [c19 from FUCHS(IA) + -IN; from its similarity in colour to the flower]

fucivorous (fjuː'kɪvərəs) *adj zoology* feeding on seaweed [c19 from Greek *phukos* seaweed +

-VOROUS]

fuck (fʌk) *taboo* ▷ *vb* **1** to have sexual intercourse with (someone) ▷ *n* **2** an act of sexual intercourse **3** *slang* a partner in sexual intercourse, esp one of specified competence or experience **4 not care** *or* **give a fuck** not to care at all ▷ *interj* **5** *offensive* an expression of strong disgust or anger (often in exclamatory phrases such as **fuck you! fuck it!** etc) [C16 of Germanic origin; related to Middle Dutch *fokken* to strike]

USAGE The use and overuse of *fuck* in the everyday speech of many people has led, to some extent, to a lessening of its impact as an expletive. However, the word still retains its shock value, although it is less now than it was when the critic Kenneth Tynan caused controversy by saying it on British television in 1965

fuck about *or* **around** *vb* (*adverb*) *offensive taboo slang* **1** (*intr*) to act in a stupid or aimless manner **2** (*tr*) to treat (someone) in an inconsiderate or selfish way

fucker ('fʌkə) *n taboo* **1** *slang* a despicable or obnoxious person **2** *slang* a person; fellow **3** a person who fucks

fucking ('fʌkɪŋ) *adj* (*prenominal*) ▷ *adv taboo slang* (intensifier): *turn off that fucking phone*

fucking A *interj taboo slang*, *US* an emphatic exclamation of approval

fuck off *offensive taboo slang* ▷ *interj* **1** a forceful expression of dismissal or contempt ▷ *vb* (*adverb*) **2** (*intr*) to go away **3** (*tr*) to irritate or annoy (a person) ▷ *adj* **4** (*prenominal*) very large or impressive: *a huge fuck-off cigar*

fuck up *offensive taboo slang* ▷ *vb* (*tr, adverb*) **1** to damage or bungle **2** to make confused ▷ *n* **fuck-up 3** an act or an instance of bungling

fuckwit ('fʌkwɪt) *n taboo slang* a fool or idiot

fucoid ('fjuːkɔɪd) *adj also* **fucoidal fucous** ('fjuːkəs) **1** of, relating to, or resembling seaweeds of the genus *Fucus* ▷ *n* **2** any seaweed of the genus *Fucus*

fucoxanthin (,fjuːkəʊ'zænθɪn) *n* a carotenoid pigment that gives brown algae and diatoms their colour: functions in photosynthesis. Formula: $C_{40}H_{56}O_6$ or $C_{40}H_{60}O_6$

fucus ('fjuːkəs) *n, pl* **-ci** (-saɪ) *or* **-cuses** any seaweed of the genus *Fucus*, common in the intertidal regions of many shores and typically having greenish-brown slimy fronds. See also **wrack²** (sense 2) [C16 from Latin: rock lichen, from Greek *phukos* seaweed, dye, of Semitic origin]

fuddle ('fʌdᵊl) *vb* **1** (*tr; often passive*) to cause to be confused or intoxicated **2** (*intr*) to drink excessively; tipple ▷ *n* **3** a muddled or confused state [C16 of unknown origin]

fuddy-duddy ('fʌdɪ,dʌdɪ) *n, pl* **-dies** *informal* a person, esp an elderly man, who is extremely conservative or dull [C20 of uncertain origin]

fudge¹ (fʌdʒ) *n* a soft variously flavoured sweet made from sugar, butter, cream, etc [C19 of unknown origin]

fudge² (fʌdʒ) *n* **1** foolishness; nonsense ▷ *interj* **2** a mild exclamation of annoyance ▷ *vb* **3** (*intr*) to talk foolishly or emptily [C18 of uncertain origin]

fudge³ (fʌdʒ) *n* **1** a small section of type matter in a box in a newspaper allowing late news to be included without the whole page having to be remade **2** the box in which such type matter is placed **3** the late news so inserted **4** a machine attached to a newspaper press for printing this **5** an unsatisfactory compromise reached to evade a difficult problem or controversial issue ▷ *vb* **6** (*tr*) to make or adjust in a false or clumsy way **7** (*tr*) to misrepresent; falsify **8** to evade (a problem, issue, etc); dodge; avoid [C19 see FADGE]

Fuegian (fjuː'iːdʒɪən, 'fweɪdʒ-) *adj* **1** of or relating to Tierra del Fuego or its indigenous Indians ▷ *n* **2** an Indian of Tierra del Fuego

fuel (fjʊəl) *n* **1** any substance burned as a source of heat or power, such as coal or petrol **2 a** the material, containing a fissile substance, such as uranium-235, that produces energy in a nuclear reactor **b** a substance that releases energy in a fusion reactor **3** something that nourishes or builds up emotion, action, etc ▷ *vb* **fuels, fuelling, fuelled** *or US* **fuels, fueling, fueled 4** to supply with or receive fuel [C14 from Old French *feuaile*, from *feu* fire, ultimately from Latin *focus* fireplace, hearth] > **'fueller** *or US* **'fueler** *n*

fuel air bomb *n* a type of bomb that spreads a cloud of gas, which is then detonated, over the target area, causing extensive destruction

fuel cell *n* a cell in which the energy produced by oxidation of a fuel is converted directly into electrical energy

fuel element *n* a can containing nuclear fuel for use in a fission reactor

fuel injection *n* a system for introducing atomized liquid fuel under pressure directly into the combustion chambers of an internal-combustion engine without the use of a carburetor

fuel oil *n* a liquid petroleum product having a flash point above 37.8°C: used as a substitute for coal in industrial furnaces, domestic heaters, ships, and locomotives

fuel rod *n* a long tube, often made of a zirconium alloy and containing uranium-oxide pellets, that is stacked in bundles of about 200 to provide the fuel in certain types of nuclear reactor

fug (fʌg) *n chiefly Brit* a hot, stale, or suffocating atmosphere [C19 perhaps variant of FOG¹] > **'fuggy** *adj*

fugacious (fjuː'geɪʃəs) *adj* **1** passing quickly away; transitory; fleeting **2** *botany* lasting for only a short time: *fugacious petals* [C17 from Latin *fugax* inclined to flee, swift, from *fugere* to flee; see FUGITIVE] > **fu'gaciously** *adv* > **fu'gaciousness** *n*

fugacity (fjuː'gæsɪtɪ) *n* **1** Also called: **escaping tendency** *thermodynamics* a property of a gas, related to its partial pressure, that expresses its tendency to escape or expand, given by d(log$_e f$) = dμ/RT, where μ is the chemical potential, R the gas constant, and T the thermodynamic temperature. Symbol: *f* **2** the state or quality of being fugacious

fugal ('fjuːgᵊl) *adj* of, relating to, or in the style of a fugue > **'fugally** *adv*

fugato (fʊ'gɑːtəʊ) *music* ▷ *adv* ▷ *adj* **1** in the manner or style of a fugue ▷ *n* **2** a movement, section, or piece in this style [C19 from Italian, from *fugare* to compose in the style of a FUGUE]

-fuge *n combining form* indicating an agent or substance that expels or drives away: *vermifuge* [from Latin *fugāre* to expel, put to flight] > **-fugal** *adj combining form*

fugio ('fjuːdʒɪəʊ) *n, pl* **-gios** a former US copper coin worth one dollar, the first authorized by Congress (1787) [C18 Latin: I flee; one of the words inscribed on the coin]

fugitive ('fjuːdʒɪtɪv) *n* **1** a person who flees **2** a thing that is elusive or fleeting ▷ *adj* **3** fleeing, esp from arrest or pursuit **4** not permanent; fleeting; transient **5** moving or roving about [C14 from Latin *fugitīvus* fleeing away, from *fugere* to take flight, run away] > **'fugitively** *adv* > **'fugitiveness** *n*

fugitometer (,fjuːdʒɪ'tɒmɪtə) *n* an instrument used for measuring the fastness to light of dyed materials

fugleman ('fjuːgᵊlmən) *n, pl* **-men 1** (*formerly*) a soldier used as an example for those learning drill **2** any person who acts as a leader or example [C19 from German *Flügelmann*, from *Flügel* wing, flank + *Mann* MAN]

fugly ('fʌglɪ) *adj* **-lier, -liest** *chiefly US and Austral offensive* extremely ugly [C20 FUCKING + UGLY]

fugu ('fuːguː) *n* any of various marine pufferfish of the genus *Tetraodontidae*, eaten as a delicacy in Japan once certain poisonous and potentially lethal parts have been removed [Japanese]

fugue (fjuːg) *n* **1** a musical form consisting essentially of a theme repeated a fifth above or a fourth below the continuing first statement **2** *psychiatry* a dreamlike altered state of consciousness, lasting from a few hours to several days, during which a person loses his memory for his previous life and often wanders away from home [C16 from French, from Italian *fuga*, from Latin: a running away, flight] > **'fugue,like** *adj*

fuguist ('fjuːgɪst) *n* a composer of fugues

Führer *or* **Fuehrer** *German* ('fyːrər; *English* 'fjʊərə) *n* a leader: applied esp to Adolf Hitler (**der Führer**) while he was Chancellor [German, from *führen* to lead]

Fuji ('fuːdʒɪ) *n* **Mount** an extinct volcano in central Japan, in S central Honshu: the highest mountain in Japan, famous for its symmetrical snow-capped cone. Height: 3776 m (12 388 ft). Also called: Fujiyama, Fuji-san

Fujian *or* **Fukien** ('fuːˈkjɛn) *n* **1** a province of SE China: mountainous and forested, drained chiefly by the Min River; noted for the production of flower-scented teas. Capital: Fuzhou. Pop: 34 880 000 (2003 est). Area: 123 000 sq km (47 970 sq miles) **2** any of the Chinese dialects of this province. See also **Min**

Fukuoka (,fuːkuːˈəʊkə) *n* an industrial city and port in SW Japan, in N Kyushu: an important port in ancient times; site of Kyushu university. Pop: 1 302 454 (2002 est)

Fukushima (,fuːkuːˈʃiːmə) *n* a city in Japan, in N Honshu: noted for production of silk. Pop: 288 926 (2002 est)

Fukuyama (,fuːkuːˈjɑːmə) *n* a city in Japan, in SW Honshu: industrial and commercial centre. Pop: 381 098 (2002 est)

-ful *suffix* **1** (*forming adjectives*) full of or characterized by: *painful* **2** (*forming adjectives*) able or tending to: *helpful* **3** (*forming nouns*) indicating as much as will fill the thing specified: *mouthful* [Old English *-ful, -full*, from FULL¹]

USAGE Where the amount held by a spoon, etc, is used as a rough unit of measurement, the correct form is *spoonful*, etc: *take a spoonful of this medicine every day. Spoon full* is used in a sentence such as *he held out a spoon full of dark liquid*, where *full of* describes the spoon. A plural form such as *spoonfuls* is preferred by many speakers and writers to *spoonsful*

Fula ('fuːlə) *or* **Fulah** ('fuːlɑː) *n* **1** (*pl* **-la, -las** *or* **-lah, -lahs**) a member of a pastoral nomadic people of W and central Africa, living chiefly in the sub-Sahara region from Senegal to N Cameroon: a racial mixture of light-skinned Berber peoples of the North and darker-skinned W Africans **2** the language of this people; Fulani

Fulani (fuː'lɑːnɪ, 'fuːlənɪ) *n* **1** the language of the Fula, belonging to the West Atlantic branch of the Niger-Congo family, widely used as a trade pidgin in W Africa **2** (*pl* **-nis, -ni**) another name for **Fula** (the people) **3** (*pl* **-nis, -ni**) a humped breed of cattle from W Africa ▷ *adj* **4** of or relating to the Fula or their language

fulcrum ('fʊlkrəm, 'fʌl-) *n, pl* **-crums** *or* **-cra** (-krə) **1** the pivot about which a lever turns **2** something that supports or sustains; prop **3** a spinelike scale occurring in rows along the anterior edge of the fins in primitive bony fishes such as the sturgeon [C17 from Latin: foot of a couch, bedpost, from *fulcire* to prop up]

fulfil *or US* **fulfill** (fʊl'fɪl) *vb* **-fils** *or US* **-fills, -filling, -filled** (*tr*) **1** to bring about the completion or achievement of (a desire, promise, etc) **2** to carry out or execute (a request, etc) **3** to conform with or satisfy (regulations, demands, etc) **4** to finish or reach the end of: *he fulfilled his prison sentence* **5** **fulfil oneself** to achieve one's potential or desires [Old English *fulfyllan*] > **ful'filler** *or US* **ful'fillment** *n*

fulgent ('fʌldʒənt) *or* **fulgid** ('fʌldʒɪd) *adj poetic* shining brilliantly; resplendent; gleaming [C15

f

from Latin *fulgēre* to shine, flash] > ˈful**gently** *adv*

fulgurate (ˈfʌlgjʊˌreɪt) *vb* (*intr*) *rare* to flash like lightning [c17 from Latin *fulgurāre*, from *fulgur* lightning] > **fulgurant** (ˈfʌlgjʊrənt) *adj*

fulgurating (ˈfʌlgjʊˌreɪtɪŋ) *adj* **1** *pathol* (of pain) sudden and sharp; piercing **2** *surgery* of or relating to fulguration

fulguration (ˌfʌlgjʊˈreɪʃən) *n surgery* destruction of tissue by means of high-frequency (more than 10 000 per second) electric sparks

fulgurite (ˈfʌlgjʊˌraɪt) *n* a tube of glassy mineral matter found in sand and rock, formed by the action of lightning [c19 from Latin *fulgur* lightning]

fulgurous (ˈfʌlgjʊrəs) *adj rare* flashing like or resembling lightning; fulgurant [c17 from Latin *fulgur* lightning]

Fulham (ˈfʊləm) *n* a district of the Greater London borough of Hammersmith and Fulham (since 1965): contains **Fulham Palace** (16th century), residence of the Bishop of London

fuliginous (fjuːˈlɪdʒɪnəs) *adj* **1** sooty or smoky **2** of the colour of soot; dull greyish-black or brown [c16 from Late Latin *fūlīginōsus* full of soot, from Latin *fūlīgō* soot] > fu'**liginously** *adv* > fu'**liginousness** *n*

full¹ (fʊl) *adj* **1** holding or containing as much as possible; filled to capacity or near capacity **2** abundant in supply, quantity, number, etc **3** having consumed enough food or drink **4** (esp of the face or figure) rounded or plump; not thin **5** (*prenominal*) with no part lacking; complete: *a full dozen* **6** (*prenominal*) with all privileges, rights, etc; not restricted: *a full member* **7** (*prenominal*) of, relating to, or designating a relationship established by descent from the same parents: *full brother* **8** filled with emotion or sentiment: *a full heart* **9** (*postpositive*; foll by *of*) occupied or engrossed (with) **10** *music* **a** powerful or rich in volume and sound **b** completing a piece or section; concluding: *a full close* **11** (of a garment, esp a skirt) containing a large amount of fabric; of ample cut **12** (of sails, etc) distended by wind **13** (of wine, such as a burgundy) having a heavy body **14** (of a colour) containing a large quantity of pure hue as opposed to white or grey; rich; saturated **15** *informal* drunk **16 full and by** *nautical* another term for **close-hauled 17 full of oneself** full of pride or conceit; egoistic **18 full up** filled to capacity **19 in full cry** (esp of a pack of hounds) in hot pursuit of quarry **20 in full swing** at the height of activity: *the party was in full swing* ▷ *adv* **21 a** completely; entirely **b** (*in combination*): *full-grown; full-fledged* **22** exactly; directly; right **23** very; extremely (esp in the phrase **full well**) **24 full out** with maximum effort or speed ▷ *n* **25** the greatest degree, extent, etc **26** *Brit* a ridge of sand or shingle along a seashore **27 in full** without omitting, decreasing, or shortening **28 to the full** to the greatest extent; thoroughly; fully ▷ *vb* **29** (*tr*) *needlework* to gather or tuck **30** (*intr*) (of the moon) to be fully illuminated [Old English; related to Old Norse *fullr*, Old High German *foll*, Latin *plēnus*, Greek *plērēs*; see FILL] > ˈ**fullness** *or esp US* ˈ**fulness** *n*

full² (fʊl) *vb* (of cloth, yarn, etc) to become or to make (cloth, yarn, etc) heavier and more compact during manufacture through shrinking and beating or pressing [c14 from Old French *fouler*, ultimately from Latin *fullō* a FULLER¹]

fullback (ˈfʊlˌbæk) *n* **1** *soccer, hockey* one of two defensive players positioned in front of the goalkeeper **2** *rugby* a defensive player positioned close to his own line **3** the position held by any of these players

full blood *n* **1** an individual, esp a horse or similar domestic animal, of unmixed race or breed **2** the relationship between individuals having the same parents

full-blooded *adj* **1** (esp of horses) of unmixed ancestry; thoroughbred **2** having great vigour or health; hearty; virile > ,full-ˈ**bloodedness** *n*

full-blown *adj* **1** characterized by the fullest, strongest, or best development **2** in full bloom

full board *n* **a** the provision by a hotel of a bed and all meals **b** (*as modifier*): *full board accommodation*

full-bodied *adj* having a full rich flavour or quality

full-bottomed *adj* (of a wig) long at the back

full-court press *n basketball* the tactic of harrying the opposing team in all areas of the court, as opposed to the more usual practice of trying to defend one's own basket

full-cream *adj* denoting or made with whole unskimmed milk

full dress *n* **a** a formal or ceremonial style of dress, such as white tie and tails for a man and a full-length evening dress for a woman **b** (*as modifier*): *full-dress uniform*

full employment *n* a state in which the labour force and other economic resources of a country are utilized to their maximum

fuller¹ (ˈfʊlə) *n* a person who fulls cloth for his living [Old English *fullere*, from Latin *fullō*]

fuller² (ˈfʊlə) *n* **1** Also called: **fulling tool** a tool for forging a groove **2** a tool for caulking a riveted joint ▷ *vb* **3** (*tr*) to forge (a groove) or caulk (a riveted joint) with a fuller [c19 perhaps from the name *Fuller*]

fullerene (ˈfʊləˌriːn) *n* **1** short for **buckminsterfullerene 2** any of various carbon molecules with a polyhedral structure similar to that of buckminsterfullerene, such as C_{70}, C_{76}, and C_{84}

fulleride (ˈfʊləˌraɪd) *n* a compound of a fullerene in which atoms are trapped inside the cage of carbon atoms

fullerite (ˈfʊləˌraɪt) *n* a crystalline form of a fullerene

fuller's earth *n* a natural absorbent clay used, after heating, for decolorizing oils and fats, fulling cloth, etc

fuller's teasel *n* **1** a Eurasian teasel plant, *Dipsacus fullonum*, whose prickly flower heads are used for raising the nap on woollen cloth **2** a similar and related plant, *Dipsacus sativum*

full-faced *adj* **1** having a round full face **2** Also: **full face** facing towards the viewer, with the entire face visible **3** another name for **bold face** > ˈfull**ˈface** *n*, *adv*

full-fledged *adj* See **fully fledged**

full forward *n Australian Rules Football* an attacking player who plays in the centre of the forward line

full-frontal *adj* **1** *informal* (of a nude person or a photograph of a nude person) exposing the genitals to full view **2** all-out; unrestrained ▷ *n* **full frontal 3** a full-frontal photograph

full house *n* **1** *poker* a hand with three cards of the same value and another pair **2** a theatre, etc, filled to capacity **3** (in bingo, etc) the set of numbers needed to win

full-length *n* (*modifier*) **1** extending to or showing the complete length: *a full-length mirror* **2** of the original length; not abridged

full monty (ˈmɒntɪ) *n* **the** *informal* something in its entirety [of unknown origin]

full moon *n* **1** one of the four phases of the moon, occurring when the earth lies between the sun and the moon so that the moon is visible as a fully illuminated disc **2** the moon in this phase **3** the time at which this occurs

full-mouthed *adj* **1** (of livestock) having a full adult set of teeth **2** uttered loudly

full nelson *n* a wrestling hold, illegal in amateur wrestling, in which a wrestler places both arms under his opponent's arms from behind and exerts pressure with both palms on the back of the neck. Compare **half-nelson**

full-on *adj informal* complete; unrestrained

full pitch *n cricket* another term for **full toss**

full professor *n US and Canadian* a university teacher of the highest academic rank

full radiator *n physics* another name for **black body**

full-rigged *adj* (of a sailing vessel) having three or

more masts rigged square

full sail *adv* **1** at top speed ▷ *adj* (*postpositive*), *adv* **2** with all sails set > ,full-ˈ**sailed** *adj*

full-scale *n* (*modifier*) **1** (of a plan, etc) of actual size; having the same dimensions as the original **2** done with thoroughness or urgency; using all resources; all-out

full score *n* the entire score of a musical composition, showing each part separately

full stop *or* **full point** *n* the punctuation mark (.) used at the end of a sentence that is not a question or exclamation, after abbreviations, etc. Also called (*esp US and Canadian*): **period**

full time *n* the end of a football or other match. Compare **half-time**

full-time *adj* **1** for the entire time appropriate to an activity: *a full-time job; a full-time student* ▷ *adv* **full time 2** on a full-time basis: *he works full time* ▷ Compare **part-time**. > ,full-ˈ**timer** *n*

full toss *or* **full pitch** *n cricket* a bowled ball that reaches the batsman without bouncing

full-wave rectifier *n* an electronic circuit in which both half-cycles of incoming alternating current furnish the direct current output

fully (ˈfʊlɪ) *adv* **1** to the greatest degree or extent; totally; entirely **2** amply; sufficiently; adequately **3** at least

fully fashioned *adj* (of stockings, knitwear, etc) shaped and seamed so as to fit closely

fully fledged *or* **full-fledged** *adj* **1** (of a young bird) having acquired its adult feathers and thus able to fly **2** developed or matured to the fullest degree **3** of full rank or status

fulmar (ˈfʊlmə) *n* any heavily built short-tailed oceanic bird of the genus *Fulmarus* and related genera, of polar regions: family *Procellariidae*, order *Procellariiformes* (petrels) [c17 of Scandinavian origin; related to Old Norse *fūlmār*, from *fūll* foul + *mār* gull]

fulminant (ˈfʌlmɪnənt, ˈfʊl-) *adj* **1** sudden and violent **2** *pathol* (of pain) sudden and sharp; piercing [c17 from Latin *fulmināre* to cause lightning, from *fulmen* lightning that strikes]

fulminate (ˈfʌlmɪˌneɪt, ˈfʊl-) *vb* **1** (*intr*; often foll by *against*) to make criticisms or denunciations; rail **2** to explode with noise and violence **3** (*intr*) *archaic* to thunder and lighten ▷ *n* **4** any salt or ester of fulminic acid, esp the mercury salt, which is used as a detonator [c15 from Medieval Latin *fulmināre*; see FULMINANT] > ,fulmi'**nation** *n* > ˈ**fulmi**,**nator** *n* > ˈ**fulmi**,**natory** *adj*

fulminating powder *n* powder that detonates by percussion

fulminic acid (fʌlˈmɪnɪk, fʊl-) *n* an unstable volatile acid known only in solution and in the form of its salts and esters. Formula: HONC. Compare **cyanic acid** [c19 from Latin *fulmen* lightning]

fulminous (ˈfʌlmɪnəs, ˈfʊl-) *adj rare* **1** harshly critical **2** of, involving, or resembling thunder and lightning

fulsome (ˈfʊlsəm) *adj* **1** excessive or insincere, esp in an offensive or distasteful way: *fulsome compliments* **2** *not standard* extremely complimentary **3** *informal* full, rich or abundant **4** *archaic* disgusting; loathsome > ˈ**fulsomely** *adv* > ˈ**fulsomeness** *n*

> **USAGE** The use of *fulsome* to mean *extremely complimentary* or *full, rich or abundant* is common in journalism, but should be avoided in other kinds of writing

fulvous (ˈfʌlvəs, ˈfʊl-) *adj* of a dull brownish-yellow colour; tawny [c17 from Latin *fulvus* reddish yellow, gold-coloured, tawny; probably related to *fulgēre* to shine]

fumaric acid (fjuːˈmærɪk) *n* a colourless crystalline acid with a fruity taste, found in some plants and manufactured from benzene; *trans*-butenedioic acid: used esp in synthetic resins. Formula: HCOOCH:CHCOOH [c19 from New Latin *Fumāria* name of genus, from Late Latin: fumitory, from Latin *fūmus* smoke]

fumarole ('fjuːməˌrəʊl) *n* a vent in or near a volcano from which hot gases, esp steam, are emitted [c19 from French *fumerolle*, from Late Latin *fūmāriolum* smoke hole, from Latin *fūmus* smoke] > **fumarolic** (ˌfjuːməˈrɒlɪk) *adj*

fumatorium (ˌfjuːməˈtɔːrɪəm) *n, pl* -riums *or* -ria (-rɪə) an airtight chamber in which insects and fungi on organic matter or plants are destroyed by fumigation. Also called: **fumatory** [New Latin, from Latin *fūmāre* to smoke]

fumatory ('fjuːmətərɪ, -trɪ) *adj* **1** of or relating to smoking or fumigation ▷ *n, pl* -ries **2** another name for a **fumatorium**

fumble ('fʌmbᵊl) *vb* **1** (*intr; often foll by for or with*) to grope about clumsily or blindly, esp in searching **2** (*intr; foll by at or with*) to finger or play with, esp in an absent-minded way **3** to say or do hesitantly or awkwardly **4** to fail to catch or grasp (a ball, etc) cleanly ▷ *n* **5** the act of fumbling [c16 probably of Scandinavian origin; related to Swedish *fumla*] > **fumbler** *n* > **fumblingly** *adv* > **fumblingness** *n*

fume (fjuːm) *vb* **1** (*intr*) to be overcome with anger or fury; rage **2** to give off (fumes) or (of fumes) to be given off, esp during a chemical reaction **3** (*tr*) to subject to or treat with fumes; fumigate ▷ *n* **4** (*often plural*) a pungent or toxic vapour **5** a sharp or pungent odour **6** a condition of anger [c14 from Old French *fum*, from Latin *fūmus* smoke, vapour] > **fumeless** *adj* > **fumeˌlike** *adj* > **fumer** *n* > **fumingly** *adv* > **fumy** *adj*

fume cupboard *n* a ventilated enclosure for storing or experimenting with chemicals with harmful vapours

fumed (fjuːmd) *adj* (of wood, esp oak) having a dark colour and distinctive grain from exposure to ammonia fumes

fumet¹ (fjuːˈmet) *n* a strong-flavoured liquor from cooking fish, meat, or game: used to flavour sauces [French, literally: aroma]

fumet² ('fjuːmət) *n* (*often plural*) *archaic* the dropping of a deer [c16 *fewmet*: probably via Old French from Latin *fimāre* to spread dung on, from *fimus* dung]

fumigant ('fjuːmɪɡənt) *n* a substance used for fumigating

fumigate ('fjuːmɪˌɡeɪt) *vb* to treat (something contaminated or infected) with fumes or smoke [c16 from Latin *fūmigāre* to smoke, steam, from *fūmus* smoke + *agere* to drive, produce] > ˌfumiˈgation *n* > ˈfumiˌgator *n*

fuming sulphuric acid *n* a mixture of pyrosulphuric acid, $H_2S_2O_7$, and other condensed acids, made by dissolving sulphur trioxide in concentrated sulphuric acid. Also called: oleum, Nordhausen acid ('nɔːdhaʊzᵊn)

fumitory ('fjuːmɪtərɪ, -trɪ) *n, pl* -ries any plant of the chiefly European genus *Fumaria*, esp *F. officinalis*, having spurred flowers and formerly used medicinally: family *Fumariaceae* [c14 from Old French *fumetere*, from Medieval Latin *fūmus terrae*, literally: smoke of the earth; see FUME]

fun (fʌn) *n* **1** a source of enjoyment, amusement, diversion, etc **2** pleasure, gaiety, or merriment **3** jest or sport (esp in the phrases **in** or **for fun**) **4** **fun and games** *ironic or facetious* amusement; frivolous activity **5** **like fun** *informal* **a** (*adverb*) quickly; vigorously **b** (*interjection*) not at all! certainly not! **6** **make fun of** or **poke fun at** to ridicule or deride **7** (*modifier*) full of amusement, diversion, gaiety, etc: *a fun sport* ▷ *vb* **funs**, **funning**, **funned 8** (*intr*) *informal* to act in a joking or sporting manner [c17 perhaps from obsolete *fon* to make a fool of; see FOND¹]

funambulist (fjuːˈnæmbjʊlɪst) *n* a tightrope walker [c18 from Latin *fūnambulus* rope dancer, from *fūnis* rope + *ambulāre* to walk] > fuˈnambulism *n*

Funchal (Portuguese fũˈʃal) *n* the capital and chief port of the Madeira Islands, on the S coast of Madeira. Pop: 103 962 (2001)

function ('fʌŋkʃən) *n* **1** the natural action or intended purpose of a person or thing in a specific role **2** an official or formal social gathering or ceremony **3** a factor dependent upon another or other factors **4** Also called: map, mapping *maths, logic* a relation between two sets that associates a unique element (the value) of the second (the range) with each element (the argument) of the first (the domain): a many-one relation. Symbol: f(x) The value of f(x) for x = 2 is f(2) ▷ *vb* (*intr*) **5** to operate or perform as specified; work properly **6** (foll by *as*) to perform the action or role (of something or someone else) [c16 from Latin *functiō*, from *fungī* to perform, discharge] > **functionless** *adj*

functional ('fʌŋkʃənᵊl) *adj* **1** of, involving, or containing a function or functions **2** practical rather than decorative **3** capable of functioning; working **4** *psychol* **a** relating to the purpose or context of a behaviour **b** denoting a psychosis such as schizophrenia assumed not to have a direct organic cause, like deterioration or poisoning of the brain Compare **organic psychosis** ▷ *n* **5** *maths* a function whose domain is a set of functions and whose range is a set of functions or a set of numbers > **functionally** *adv*

functional calculus *n* another name for predicate calculus

functional disease *n* a disease in which there is no observable change in the structure of an organ or part. Compare **organic disease**

functional food *n* a food containing additives which provide extra nutritional value. Also called: nutraceutical

functional group *n* *chem* the group of atoms in a compound, such as the hydroxyl group in an alcohol, that determines the chemical behaviour of the compound

functional illiterate *n* a person whose literacy is insufficient for most work and normal daily situations > functional illiteracy *n*

functionalism ('fʌŋkʃənəˌlɪzəm) *n* **1** the theory of design that the form of a thing should be determined by its use **2** any doctrine that stresses utility or purpose **3** *psychol* a system of thought based on the premise that all mental processes derive from their usefulness to the organism in adapting to the environment > **functionalist** *n, adj*

functionality (ˌfʌŋkʃənˈalɪtɪ) *n* **1** the quality of being functional **2** *computing* a function or range of functions in a computer, program, package, etc

functional water *n* water containing additives that provide extra nutritional value. Also called: aquaceutical

functionary ('fʌŋkʃənərɪ) *n, pl* -aries **1** a person acting in an official capacity, as for a government; an official ▷ *adj* **2** a less common word for **functional** or **official**

function creep *n* the gradual widening of the use of a technology or system beyond the purpose for which it was originally intended, esp when this leads to potential invasion of privacy

function key *n* *computing* a key on the keyboard of a microcomputer, etc that gives special commands to the computer

function shift or **change** *n* **1** *grammar* a change in the syntactic function of a word, as when the noun *mushroom* is used as an intransitive verb **2** *linguistics* sound change involving a realignment of the phonemic system of a language

function word *n* *grammar* a word, such as *the*, with a particular grammatical role but little identifiable meaning. Compare **content word, grammatical meaning**

fund (fʌnd) *n* **1** a reserve of money, etc, set aside for a certain purpose **2** a supply or store of something; stock ▷ *vb* (*tr*) **3** to furnish money to in the form of a fund **4** to place or store up in a fund **5** to convert (short-term floating debt) into long-term debt bearing fixed interest and represented by bonds **6** to provide a fund for the redemption of principal or payment of interest of

7 to accumulate a fund for the discharge of (a recurrent liability): *to fund a pension plan* **8** to invest (money) in government securities. See also **funds** [c17 from Latin *fundus* the bottom, piece of land, estate; compare FOND²] > **funder** *n*

fundament ('fʌndəmənt) *n* **1** *euphemistic or facetious* the buttocks **2** the natural features of the earth's surface, unaltered by man **3** a base or foundation, esp of a building **4** a theory, principle, or underlying basis [c13 from Latin *fundāmentum* foundation, from *fundāre* to FOUND²]

fundamental (ˌfʌndəˈmentᵊl) *adj* **1** of, involving, or comprising a foundation; basic **2** of, involving, or comprising a source; primary **3** *music* denoting or relating to the principal or lowest note of a harmonic series **4** of or concerned with the component of lowest frequency in a complex vibration ▷ *n* **5** a principle, law, etc, that serves as the basis of an idea or system **6** **a** the principal or lowest note of a harmonic series **b** the bass note of a chord in root position **7** Also called: fundamental frequency, first harmonic *physics* **a** the component of lowest frequency in a complex vibration **b** the frequency of this component > ˌfundamenˈtality *or* fundaˈmentalness *n*

fundamental constant *n* a physical constant, such as the gravitational constant or speed of light, that plays a fundamental role in physics and chemistry and usually has an accurately known value

fundamental interaction *n* any of the four basic interactions that occur in nature: the gravitational, electromagnetic, strong, and weak interactions

fundamentalism (ˌfʌndəˈmentəˌlɪzəm) *n* **1** *Christianity* (esp among certain Protestant sects) the belief that every word of the Bible is divinely inspired and therefore true **2** *Islam* a movement favouring strict observance of the teachings of the Koran and Islamic law **3** strict adherence to the fundamental principles of any set of beliefs > ˌfundaˈmentalist *n, adj* > ˌfundaˌmentalˈistic *adj*

fundamental law *n* the law determining the constitution of the government of a state; organic law

fundamentally (ˌfʌndəˈmentᵊlɪ) *adv* **1** in a way that affects the basis or essentials; utterly **2** (*sentence modifier*) in essence; at heart

fundamental particle *n* another name for **elementary particle**

fundamental unit *n* one of a set of unrelated units that form the basis of a system of units. For example, the metre, kilogram, and second are fundamental units of the SI system

funded debt *n* the part of the national debt, consisting mostly of consols, that the government has no obligation to repay by a specified date

fundholding ('fʌndˌhəʊldɪŋ) *n* (formerly, in the National Health Service in Britain) the system enabling general practitioners to receive a fixed budget from which to pay for primary care, drugs, and nonurgent hospital treatment for patients > ˈfundˌholder *n*

fundi¹ ('fʊndiː) *n* *E African* a person skilled in repairing or maintaining machinery; mechanic [c20 from Swahili]

fundi² ('fʊndiː) *n* *South African* an expert [c20 from Nguni *umfindisi* a teacher]

fundie ('fʌndɪ) *n* *Austral derogatory slang* a fundamentalist Christian

funding operations *pl n* *finance* the conversion of government floating stock or short-term debt into holdings of long-term bonds

fund manager *n* an employee of an insurance company, pension fund, investment trust, etc, who manages its fund of investments

fundraise ('fʌndˌreɪz) *vb* (*intr*) to raise money for a cause

fundraiser ('fʌndˌreɪzə) *n* **1** a person who raises money for a cause **2** an event held to raise money for a cause

funds (fʌndz) *pl n* **1** money that is readily

f

available **2** British government securities representing national debt

fund supermarket *n* an online facility offering discounted investment opportunities and advice

fundus ('fʌndəs) *n, pl* -di (-daɪ) *anatomy* the base of an organ or the part farthest away from its opening [c18 from Latin, literally: the bottom, a farm, estate] > 'fundic *adj*

Fundy ('fʌndɪ) *n* **Bay of** an inlet of the Atlantic in SE Canada, between S New Brunswick and W Nova Scotia: remarkable for its swift tides of up to 21 m (70 ft)

Funen ('fuːnən) *n* the second largest island of Denmark, between the Jutland peninsula and the island of Zealand. Pop: 441 795 (2003 est). Area: 3481 sq km (1344 sq miles). Danish name: **Fyn** German name: **Fünen**

funeral ('fjuːnərəl) *n* **1 a** a ceremony at which a dead person is buried or cremated **b** (*as modifier*): *a funeral service* **2** a procession of people escorting a corpse to burial **3** *informal* worry; concern; affair: *that's your funeral* [c14 from Medieval Latin *fūnerālia*, from Late Latin *fūnerālis* (adj), from Latin *fūnus* funeral]

funeral director *n* an undertaker

funeral parlour *n* a place where the dead are prepared for burial or cremation. Usual US name: **funeral home**

funerary ('fjuːnərərɪ) *adj* of, relating to, or for a funeral

funereal (fjuːˈnɪərɪəl) *adj* suggestive of a funeral; gloomy or mournful. Also: **funebrial** (fjuːˈniːbrɪəl) [c18 from Latin *fūnereus*] > fuˈnereally *adv*

funfair ('fʌnˌfɛə) *n* Brit an amusement park or fairground

fun fur *n* a relatively inexpensive synthetic fur garment

fungal ('fʌŋɡəl) *adj* of, derived from, or caused by a fungus or fungi: *fungal spores; a fungal disease*

fungi ('fʌŋɡaɪ, 'fʌndʒaɪ, 'fʌndʒiː) *n* a plural of **fungus**

fungi- or before a vowel **fung-** combining form fungus: *fungicide; fungoid*

fungible ('fʌndʒɪbəl) *law ⊳ n* **1** (*often plural*) moveable perishable goods of a sort that may be estimated by number or weight, such as grain, wine, etc *⊳ adj* **2** having the nature or quality of fungibles [c18 from Medieval Latin *fungibilis*, from Latin *fungī* to perform; see FUNCTION] > ˌfungiˈbility *n*

fungible issue *n* *finance* a bond issued by a company on the same terms as a bond previously issued by that company, although the redemption yield will probably be different

fungicide ('fʌndʒɪˌsaɪd) *n* a substance or agent that destroys or is capable of destroying fungi > ˌfungiˈcidal *adj*

fungiform ('fʌndʒɪˌfɔːm) *adj* shaped like a mushroom or similar fungus

fungistat ('fʌndʒɪˌstæt) *n* a substance that inhibits the growth of fungi > ˌfungiˈstatic *adj*

fungoid ('fʌŋɡɔɪd) *adj* resembling a fungus or fungi: *a fungoid growth*

fungous ('fʌŋɡəs) *adj* **1** appearing suddenly and spreading quickly like a fungus, but not lasting **2** a less common word for **fungal**

fungus ('fʌŋɡəs) *n, pl* fungi ('fʌŋɡaɪ, 'fʌndʒaɪ, 'fʌndʒiː) or funguses **1** any member of a kingdom of organisms (Fungi) that lack chlorophyll, leaves, true stems, and roots, reproduce by spores, and live as saprotrophs or parasites. The group includes moulds, mildews, rusts, yeasts, and mushrooms **2** something resembling a fungus, esp in suddenly growing and spreading rapidly **3** *pathol* any soft tumorous growth [c16 from Latin: mushroom, fungus; probably related to Greek *spongos* SPONGE] > fungic ('fʌndʒɪk) *adj* > 'fungusˌlike *adj*

funicle ('fjuːnɪkəl) *n* botany the stalk that attaches an ovule or seed to the wall of the ovary. Also called: **funiculus** [c17 from Latin *fūniculus* a thin rope, from *fūnis* rope] > **funiculate** (fjʊˈnɪkjʊlɪt,

-ˌleɪt) *adj*

funicular (fjuːˈnɪkjʊlə) *n* **1** Also called: **funicular railway** a railway up the side of a mountain, consisting of two counterbalanced cars at either end of a cable passing round a driving wheel at the summit *⊳ adj* **2** relating to or operated by a rope, cable, etc **3** of or relating to a funicle

funiculus (fjuːˈnɪkjʊləs) *n, pl* -li (-ˌlaɪ) **1** *anatomy* a cordlike part or structure, esp a small bundle of nerve fibres in the spinal cord **2** a variant of **funicle** [c17 from Latin; see FUNICLE]

funk¹ (fʌŋk) *informal, chiefly Brit ⊳ n* **1** Also called: **blue funk** a state of nervousness, fear, or depression (esp in the phrase **in a funk**) **2** a coward *⊳ vb* **3** to flinch from (responsibility) through fear **4** (*tr; usually passive*) to make afraid [c18 university slang, perhaps related to FUNK²] > 'funker *n*

funk² (fʌŋk) *n* US slang a strong foul odour [C17 (in the sense: tobacco smoke): from *funk* (vb) to smoke (tobacco), probably of French dialect origin; compare Old French *funkier* to smoke, from Latin *fūmigāre*]

funk³ (fʌŋk) *n* informal a type of polyrhythmic Black dance music with heavy syncopation [c20 back formation from FUNKY¹]

funk hole *n* informal **1** military a dugout **2** a job that affords exemption from military service

funkster ('fʌŋkstə) *n* **1** a performer or fan of funk music **2** someone who follows the latest trends in music, ideas, or fashion

funky¹ ('fʌŋkɪ) *adj* funkier, funkiest *informal* **1** (of music) passionate, soulful; of or pertaining to funk **2** authentic; earthy **3** stylish and exciting; cool: *funky jeans* [c20 from FUNK², perhaps alluding to music that was smelly, that is, earthy (like the early blues)]

funky² ('fʌŋkɪ) *adj* funkier, funkiest *slang, chiefly US* evil-smelling; foul [c18 from FUNK²]

funnel ('fʌnəl) *n* **1** a hollow utensil with a wide mouth tapering to a small hole, used for pouring liquids, powders, etc, into a narrow-necked vessel **2** something resembling this in shape or function **3** a smokestack for smoke and exhaust gases, as on a steamship or steam locomotive **4** a shaft or tube, as in a building, for ventilation *⊳ vb* -nels, nelling, -nelled or US -nels, -neling, -neled **5** to move or cause to move or pour through or as if through a funnel **6** to concentrate or focus or be concentrated or focused in a particular direction **7** (*intr*) to take on a funnel-like shape [c15 from Old Provençal *fonilh*, ultimately from Latin *infundibulum* funnel, hopper (in a mill), from *infundere* to pour in] > 'funnel-ˌlike *adj*

funnel cap *n* any of various basidiomycetous fungi of the genus *Clitocybe*, characterized by the funnel-shaped caps and, usually, markedly decurrent gills

funnel cloud *n* a whirling column of cloud extending downwards from the base of a cumulonimbus cloud: part of a waterspout or tornado

funnel-web *n* Austral any large poisonous black spider of the family *Dipluridae*, constructing funnel-shaped webs

funnies ('fʌnɪz) *pl n* US and Canadian informal comic strips in a newspaper

funny ('fʌnɪ) *adj* -nier, -niest **1** causing amusement or laughter; humorous; comical **2** peculiar; odd **3** suspicious or dubious (esp in the phrase **funny business**) **4** informal faint or ill: *to feel funny ⊳ n, pl* -nies **5** informal a joke or witticism > 'funnily *adv* > 'funniness *n*

funny bone *n* the area near the elbow where the ulnar nerve is close to the surface of the skin: when it is struck, a sharp tingling sensation is experienced along the forearm and hand. Also called (US): **crazy bone**

funny farm *n* facetious a mental institution

funny money *n* **1** a sum of money so large as to be considered unreal **2** counterfeit money **3** *derogatory* foreign currency

funny paper *n* US and Canadian a section or separate supplement of a newspaper, etc, containing comic strips

fun run *n* a long run or part-marathon run for exercise and pleasure, often by large numbers of people

fur (fɜː) *n* **1** the dense coat of fine silky hairs on such mammals as the cat, seal, and mink **2 a** the dressed skin of certain fur-bearing animals, with the hair left on **b** (*as modifier*): *a fur coat* **3** a garment made of fur, such as a coat or stole **4 a** a pile fabric made in imitation of animal fur **b** a garment made from such a fabric **5** *heraldry* any of various stylized representations of animal pelts or their tinctures, esp ermine or vair, used in coats of arms **6 make the fur fly** to cause a scene or disturbance **7** *informal* a whitish coating of cellular debris on the tongue, caused by excessive smoking, an upset stomach, etc **8** *Brit* a whitish-grey deposit consisting chiefly of calcium carbonate precipitated from hard water onto the insides of pipes, boilers, and kettles *⊳ vb* **furs, furring, furred 9** (*tr*) to line or trim a garment, etc, with fur **10** (*often foll by up*) to cover or become covered with a furlike lining or deposit **11** (*tr*) to clothe (a person) in a fur garment or garments [c14 from Old French *forrer* to line a garment, from *fuerre* sheath, of Germanic origin; related to Old English *fōdder* case, Old Frisian *fōder* coat lining] > 'furless *adj*

fur. *abbreviation for* furlong

furaldehyde (fjʊəˈrældəˌhaɪd) *n* either of two aldehydes derived from furan, esp **2-furaldehyde** (see furfuraldehyde) [c20 shortened from *furfuraldehyde*, from *furfurol* (see FURFUR, -OL¹) + ALDEHYDE]

furan ('fjʊəræn, fjʊəˈræn) *n* a colourless flammable toxic liquid heterocyclic compound, used in the manufacture of cotton textiles and in the synthesis of nylon. Formula: C₄H₄O. Also called: **furfuran** [c19 shortened form of *furfuran*, from FURFUR]

furbelow ('fɜːbɪˌləʊ) *n* **1** a flounce, ruffle, or other ornamental trim **2** (*often plural*) showy ornamentation *⊳ vb* **3** (*tr*) to put a furbelow on (a garment) [c18 by folk etymology from French dialect *farbella*; see FALBALA]

furbish ('fɜːbɪʃ) *vb* (*tr*) **1** to make bright by polishing; burnish **2** (*often foll by up*) to improve the appearance or condition of; renovate; restore [c14 from Old French *fourbir* to polish, of Germanic origin] > 'furbisher *n*

fur brigade *n* Canadian (formerly) a convoy of canoes, horses, or dog sleighs that transported furs and other goods between trading posts and towns or factories

furca ('fɜːkə) *n, pl* -cae (-kiː) *zoology* any forklike structure, esp in insects [Latin: fork] > 'furcal *adj*

furcate *vb* ('fɜːkeɪt) **1** to divide into two parts; fork *⊳ adj* ('fɜːkeɪt, -kɪt) or **furcated 2** forked; divided: *furcate branches* [c19 from Late Latin *furcātus* forked, from Latin *furca* a fork] > fur'cation *n*

furcula ('fɜːkjʊlə) or **furculum** ('fɜːkjʊləm) *n, pl* -lae (-ˌliː) -la (-lə) any forklike part or organ, esp the fused clavicles (wishbone) of birds [c19 from Latin: a forked support for a wall, diminutive of *furca* fork]

furfur ('fɜːfə) *n, pl* furfures ('fɜːfjʊˌriːz, -fəˌriːz) **1** a scaling of the skin; dandruff **2** any scale of the epidermis [c17 from Latin: bran, scurf]

furfuraceous (ˌfɜːfjʊˈreɪʃəs, -fəˈreɪ-) *adj* **1** relating to or resembling bran **2** *med* resembling dandruff; scaly > ˌfurfuˈraceously *adv*

furfuraldehyde (ˌfɜːfjəˈrældəˌhaɪd) *n* a colourless flammable soluble mobile liquid with a penetrating odour, present in oat and rice hulls; 2-furaldehyde: used as a solvent and in the manufacture of resins. Formula: C₅H₄O₂. Also called: **furfural**

furfuran ('fɜːfəˌræn, 'fɜːfjʊ-) *n* another name for furan

Furies ('fjʊərɪz) *pl n, sing* Fury *classical myth* the snake-haired goddesses of vengeance, usually three in number, who pursued unpunished criminals. Also called: **Erinyes, Eumenides**

furioso (ˌfjʊərɪˈəʊsəʊ) *music* ▷ *adj, adv* **1** in a frantically rushing manner ▷ *n* **2** a passage or piece to be performed in this way [C19 Italian, literally: furious; see FURY]

furious (ˈfjʊərɪəs) *adj* **1** extremely angry or annoyed; raging **2** violent, wild, or unrestrained, as in speed, vigour, energy, etc > ˈ**furiously** *adv* > ˈ**furiousness** *n*

furkid (ˈfɜːkɪd) *n chiefly US* an animal kept for companionship [C20 from FUR + KID[1] (child)]

> USAGE This term is considered by some people concerned with the rights of animals to be more acceptable than *pet*

furl (fɜːl) *vb* **1** to roll up (an umbrella, a flag, etc) neatly and securely or (of an umbrella, flag, etc) to be rolled up in this way **2** (*tr*) *nautical* to gather in (a square sail) ▷ *n* **3** the act or an instance of furling **4** a single rolled-up section [C16 from Old French *ferlier* to bind tightly, from *ferm* tight (from Latin *firmus* FIRM[1]) + *lier* to tie, bind, from Latin *ligāre*] > ˈ**furlable** *adj* > ˈ**furler** *n*

furlong (ˈfɜːˌlɒŋ) *n* a unit of length equal to 220 yards (201.168 metres) [Old English *furlang*, from *furh* FURROW + *lang* LONG[1]]

furlough (ˈfɜːləʊ) *n* **1** leave of absence from military duty **2** *US* a temporary laying-off of employees, usually because there is insufficient work to occupy them ▷ *vb* (*tr*) **3** to grant a furlough to **4** *US* to lay off (staff) temporarily [C17 from Dutch *verlof*, from *ver-* FOR- + *lof* leave, permission; related to Swedish *förlof*]

furmenty (ˈfɜːməntɪ) *or* **furmity** (ˈfɜːmɪtɪ) *n* variants of **frumenty**

furnace (ˈfɜːnɪs) *n* **1** an enclosed chamber in which heat is produced to generate steam, destroy refuse, smelt or refine ores, etc **2** a very hot or stifling place [C13 from Old French *fornais*, from Latin *fornax* oven, furnace; related to Latin *formus* warm] > ˈ**furnace-ˌlike** *adj*

Furness (ˈfɜːnɪs) *n* a region in NW England in Cumbria, forming a peninsula between the Irish Sea and Morecambe Bay

furnish (ˈfɜːnɪʃ) *vb* (*tr*) **1** to provide (a house, room, etc) with furniture, carpets, etc **2** to equip with what is necessary; fit out **3** to give; supply: *the records furnished the information required* [C15 from Old French *fournir*, of Germanic origin; related to Old High German *frummen* to carry out] > ˈ**furnisher** *n*

furnishings (ˈfɜːnɪʃɪŋz) *pl n* **1** furniture and accessories, including carpets and curtains, with which a room, house, etc, is furnished **2** *US and Canadian* articles of dress and accessories

furniture (ˈfɜːnɪtʃə) *n* **1** the movable, generally functional, articles that equip a room, house, etc **2** the equipment necessary for a ship, factory, etc **3** *printing* lengths of wood, plastic, or metal, used in assembling formes to create the blank areas and to surround the type **4** the wooden parts of a rifle **5** *obsolete* the full armour, trappings, etc, for a man and horse **6** the attitudes or characteristics that are typical of a person or thing **7** **part of the furniture** *informal* someone or something that is so long established in an environment as to be accepted as an integral part of it **8** See **door furniture, street furniture** [C16 from French *fourniture*, from *fournir* to equip, FURNISH]

furniture beetle *n* See **anobiid**

furore (fjʊˈrɔːrɪ) *or esp US* **furor** (ˈfjʊərɔː) *n* **1** a public outburst, esp of protest; uproar **2** a sudden widespread enthusiasm for something; craze **3** frenzy; rage; madness [C15 from Latin: frenzy, rage, from *furere* to rave]

furphy (ˈfɜːfɪ) *n, pl* **-phies** *Austral slang* a rumour or fictitious story [C20 from *Furphy* carts (used for water or sewage in World War I), made at a foundry established by the Furphy family]

furred (fɜːd) *adj* **1** made of, lined with, or covered in fur **2** wearing fur **3** (of animals) having fur **4** another word for **furry** (sense 4) **5** Also: **furry** provided with furring strips **6** (of a pipe, kettle, etc) lined with hard lime or other salts deposited from water

furrier (ˈfʌrɪə) *n* a person whose occupation is selling, making, dressing, or repairing fur garments [C14 *furour*, from Old French *fourrer* to trim or line with FUR]

furriery (ˈfʌrɪərɪ) *n, pl* **-eries** **1** the occupation of a furrier **2** furs worn as a garment or trim collectively

furring (ˈfɜːrɪŋ) *n* **1 a** a short for **furring strip** **b** the fixing of furring strips **c** furring strips collectively **2** the formation of fur on the tongue **3** trimming of animal fur, as on a coat or other garment, or furs collectively

furring strip *n* a strip of wood or metal fixed to a wall, floor, or ceiling to provide a surface for the fixing of plasterboard, floorboards, etc. Sometimes shortened to: **furring**

furrow (ˈfʌrəʊ) *n* **1** a long narrow trench made in the ground by a plough or a trench resembling this **2** any long deep groove, esp a deep wrinkle on the forehead ▷ *vb* **3** to develop or cause to develop furrows or wrinkles **4** to make a furrow or furrows in (land) [Old English *furh*; related to Old Frisian *furch*, Old Norse *for*, Old High German *furuh* furrow, Latin *porca* ridge between furrows] > ˈ**furrower** *n* > ˈ**furrowless** *adj* > ˈ**furrow-ˌlike** *or* ˈ**furrowy** *adj*

furry (ˈfɜːrɪ) *adj* **-rier, -riest** **1** covered with fur or something furlike **2** of, relating to, or resembling fur **3** another word for **furred** (sense 5) **4** Also: **furred** (of the tongue) coated with whitish cellular debris > ˈ**furrily** *adv* > ˈ**furriness** *n*

fur seal *n* any of various eared seals, esp of the genus *Arctocephalus*, that have a fine dense underfur and are hunted as a source of sealskin

Fur Seal Islands *pl n* another name for the **Pribilof Islands**

furshlugginer (ˌfɜːˈʃlʌɡɪnə) *adj US informal* crazy; foolish [C20 from Yiddish]

furth (fʌrθ) *adv Scot* out; outside; to the outside [a Scot variant of FORTH]

Fürth (*German* fyːrt) *n* a city in S central Germany, in Bavaria northwest of Nuremberg: Pop: 111 892 (2003 est)

further (ˈfɜːðə) *adv* **1** in addition; furthermore **2** to a greater degree or extent **3** to or at a more advanced point **4** to or at a greater distance in time or space; farther ▷ *adj* **5** additional; more **6** more distant or remote in time or space; farther ▷ *vb* **7** (*tr*) to assist the progress of; promote ▷ See also **far, furthest** [Old English *furthor*; related to Old Frisian *further*, Old Saxon *furthor*, Old High German *furdar*; see FORTH] > ˈ**furtherer** *n*

> USAGE See at **farther**

furtherance (ˈfɜːðərəns) *n* **1** the act of furthering; advancement **2** something that furthers or advances

further education *n* (in Britain) formal education beyond school

furthermore (ˈfɜːðəˌmɔː) *adv* in addition

furthermost (ˈfɜːðəˌməʊst) *adj* most distant; furthest

furthest (ˈfɜːðɪst) *adv* **1** to the greatest degree or extent **2** to or at the greatest distance in time or space; farthest ▷ *adj* **3** most distant or remote in time or space; farthest

furtive (ˈfɜːtɪv) *adj* characterized by stealth; sly and secretive [C15 from Latin *furtīvus* stolen, clandestine, from *furtum* a theft, from *fūr* a thief; related to Greek *phōr* thief] > ˈ**furtively** *adv* > ˈ**furtiveness** *n*

furuncle (ˈfjʊərʌŋkᵊl) *n pathol* the technical name for **boil** [C17 from Latin *fūrunculus* pilferer, petty thief, sore on the body, from *fūr* thief] > **furuncular** (fjʊˈrʌŋkjʊlə) *or* **fuˈrunculous** *adj*

furunculosis (fjʊˌrʌŋkjʊˈləʊsɪs) *n* **1** a skin condition characterized by the presence of multiple boils **2** an infectious ulcerative disease of salmon and trout caused by the bacterium *Aeromonas salmonicida*

fury (ˈfjʊərɪ) *n, pl* **-ries** **1** violent or uncontrolled anger; wild rage **2** an outburst of such anger **3** uncontrolled violence: *the fury of the storm* **4** a person, esp a woman, with a violent temper **5** See **Furies** **6** **like fury** *informal* violently; furiously: *they rode like fury* [C14 from Latin *furia* rage, from *furere* to be furious]

furze (fɜːz) *n* another name for **gorse** [Old English *fyrs*] > ˈ**furzy** *adj*

fusain (fjuːˈzeɪn; *French* fyzɛ̃) *n* **1** a fine charcoal pencil or stick made from the spindle tree **2** a drawing done with such a pencil **3** a dull black brittle form of carbon resembling charcoal, found in certain coals [C19 from French: spindle tree or charcoal made from it, from Vulgar Latin *fūsāgō* (unattested) a spindle (generally made from the spindle tree), from Latin *fūsus*]

fuscous (ˈfʌskəs) *adj* of a brownish-grey colour [C17 from Latin *fuscus* dark, swarthy, tawny]

fuse[1] *or US* **fuze** (fjuːz) *n* **1** a lead of combustible black powder in a waterproof covering (**safety fuse**), or a lead containing an explosive (**detonating fuse**), used to fire an explosive charge **2** any device by which an explosive charge is ignited **3** **blow a fuse** See **blow[1]** (sense 12) ▷ *vb* **4** (*tr*) to provide or equip with such a fuse [C17 from Italian *fuso* spindle, from Latin *fūsus*] > ˈ**fuseless** *adj*

fuse[2] (fjuːz) *vb* **1** to unite or become united by melting, esp by the action of heat **2** to become or cause to become liquid, esp by the action of heat; melt **3** to join or become combined; integrate **4** (*tr*) to equip (an electric circuit, plug, etc) with a fuse **5** *Brit* to fail or cause to fail as a result of the blowing of a fuse ▷ *n* **6** a protective device for safeguarding electric circuits, etc, containing a wire that melts and breaks the circuit when the current exceeds a certain value [C17 from Latin *fūsus* melted, cast, poured out, from *fundere* to pour out, shed; sense 5 influenced by FUSE[1]]

f

fuse box *n* a housing for electric fuses

fusee *or* **fuzee** (fjuːˈziː) *n* **1** (in early clocks and watches) a spirally grooved spindle, functioning as an equalizing force on the unwinding of the mainspring **2** a friction match with a large head, capable of remaining alight in a wind **3** an explosive fuse [C16 from French *fusée* spindleful of thread, from Old French *fus* spindle, from Latin *fūsus*]

fuselage (ˈfjuːzɪˌlɑːʒ) *n* the main body of an aircraft, excluding the wings, tailplane, and fin [C20 from French, from *fuseler* to shape like a spindle, from Old French *fusel* spindle; see FUSEE]

fusel oil *or* **fusel** (ˈfjuːzᵊl) *n* a mixture of amyl alcohols, propanol, and butanol: a by-product in the distillation of fermented liquors used as a source of amyl alcohols [C19 from German *Fusel* bad spirits]

Fushih *or* **Fu-shih** (ˈfuːˈʃiː) *n* another name for **Yanan**

Fushun (ˈfuːˈʃʌn) *n* a city in NE China, in central Liaoning province near Shenyang: situated on one of the richest coalfields in the world; site of the largest thermal power plant in NE Asia. Pop: 1 425 000 (2005 est)

fusible (ˈfjuːzəbᵊl) *adj* capable of being fused or melted > ˌ**fusiˈbility** *or* ˈ**fusibleness** *n* > ˈ**fusibly** *adv*

fusible metal *or* **alloy** *n* any of various alloys with low melting points that contain bismuth, lead, and tin. They are used as solders and in safety devices

fusiform (ˈfjuːzɪˌfɔːm) *adj* elongated and tapering at both ends; spindle-shaped [C18 from Latin *fūsus* spindle]

fusil[1] (ˈfjuːzɪl) *n* a light flintlock musket [C16 (in the sense: steel for a tinderbox): from Old French *fuisil*, from Vulgar Latin *focīlis* (unattested), from Latin *focus* fire]

fusil[2] (ˈfjuːzɪl) *n heraldry* a charge shaped like a lengthened lozenge [C15 from Old French *fusel*, ultimately from Latin *fūsus* spindle, FUSE[1] (the heraldic lozenge originally represented a spindle covered with tow for spinning)]

fusile ('fju:zaɪl) *or* **fusil** *adj* **1** easily melted; fusible **2** formed by casting or melting; founded [c14 from Latin *fūsilis* molten, from *fundere* to pour out, melt]

fusilier (ˌfju:zɪ'lɪə) *n* **1** (formerly) an infantryman armed with a light musket Also: **fusileer a** a soldier, esp a private, serving in any of certain British or other infantry regiments **b** (*pl; cap when part of a name*): *the Royal Welch Fusiliers* [c17 from French; see FUSIL[1]]

fusillade (ˌfju:zɪ'leɪd, -'lɑːd) *n* **1** a simultaneous or rapid continual discharge of firearms **2** a sudden outburst, as of criticism ▷ *vb* **3** (*tr*) to attack with a fusillade [c19 from French, from *fusiller* to shoot; see FUSIL[1]]

fusion ('fju:ʒən) *n* **1** the act or process of fusing or melting together; union **2** the state of being fused **3** something produced by fusing **4** See **nuclear fusion 5** the merging of juxtaposed speech sounds, morphemes, or words **6** a coalition of political parties or other groups, esp to support common candidates at an election **7** a kind of popular music that is a blend of two or more styles, such as jazz and funk **8** *psychol* the processing by the mind of elements falling on the two eyes so that they yield a single percept **9** (*modifier*) relating to a style of cooking which combines traditional Western techniques and ingredients with those used in Eastern cuisine [c16 from Latin *fūsiō* a pouring out, melting, casting, from *fundere* to pour out, FOUND[3]]

fusion bomb *n* a type of bomb in which most of the energy is provided by nuclear fusion, esp the fusion of hydrogen isotopes. Also called: **thermonuclear bomb**, **fission-fusion bomb** See also **hydrogen bomb**

fusionism ('fju:ʒəˌnɪzəm) *n* the favouring of coalitions among political groups > **'fusionist** *n, adj*

fusion reactor *n* a nuclear reactor in which a thermonuclear fusion reaction takes place

fuss (fʌs) *n* **1** nervous activity or agitation, esp when disproportionate or unnecessary **2** complaint or objection **3** an exhibition of affection or admiration, esp if excessive **4** a quarrel; dispute ▷ *vb* **5** (*intr*) to worry unnecessarily **6** (*intr*) to be excessively concerned over trifles **7** (when *intr*, usually foll by *over*) to show great or excessive concern, affection, etc (for) **8** (*intr*; foll by *with*) Jamaican to quarrel violently **9** (*tr*) to bother (a person) [c18 of uncertain origin] > **'fusser** *n*

fusspot ('fʌsˌpɒt) *n Brit informal* a person who fusses unnecessarily. Also called (US): **fuss-budget**

fussy ('fʌsɪ) *adj* **fussier, fussiest 1** inclined to fuss over minor points **2** very particular about detail **3** characterized by overelaborate detail: *the furniture was too fussy to be elegant* > **'fussily** *adv* > **'fussiness** *n*

fustanella (ˌfʌstə'nɛlə) *or* **fustanelle** *n* a white knee-length pleated skirt worn by men in Greece and Albania [c19 from Italian, from Modern Greek *phoustani*, probably from Italian *fustagno* FUSTIAN]

fustian ('fʌstɪən) *n* **1 a** a hard-wearing fabric of cotton mixed with flax or wool with a slight nap **b** (*as modifier*): *a fustian jacket* **2** pompous or pretentious talk or writing ▷ *adj* **3** cheap; worthless **4** pompous; bombastic [c12 from Old French *fustaigne*, from Medieval Latin *fustāneum*, from Latin *fustis* cudgel]

fustic ('fʌstɪk) *n* **1** Also called: **old fustic** a large tropical American moraceous tree, *Chlorophora tinctoria* **2** the yellow dye obtained from the wood of this tree **3** any of various trees or shrubs that yield a similar dye, esp *Rhus cotinus* (**young fustic**), a European sumach [c15 from French *fustoc*, from Spanish, from Arabic *fustuq*, from Greek *pistakē* pistachio tree]

fustigate ('fʌstɪˌgeɪt) *vb* (*tr*) *archaic* to beat; cudgel [c17 from Late Latin *fūstīgāre* to cudgel to death, from Latin *fūstis* cudgel] > ˌfusti'gation *n* > 'fustiˌgator *n* > 'fustiˌgatory *adj*

fusty ('fʌstɪ) *adj* **-tier, -tiest 1** smelling of damp or mould; musty **2** old-fashioned in attitude [c14 from *fust* wine cask, from Old French: cask, tree trunk, from Latin *fūstis* cudgel, club] > 'fustily *adv* > 'fustiness *n*

futhark, futharc ('fu:θɑːk) *or* **futhorc, futhork** ('fu:θɔːk) *n* a phonetic alphabet consisting of runes [c19 from the first six letters: *f, u, th, a, r, k*; compare ALPHABET]

futile ('fju:taɪl) *adj* **1** having no effective result; unsuccessful **2** pointless; unimportant; trifling **3** inane or foolish: *don't be so futile!* [c16 from Latin *futtilis* pouring out easily, worthless, from *fundere* to pour out] > 'futilely *adv* > 'futileness *n*

futilitarian (fju:ˌtɪlɪ'tɛərɪən) *adj* **1** of or relating to the belief that human endeavour can serve no useful purpose ▷ *n* **2** one who holds this belief [c19 facetious coinage from FUTILE + UTILITARIAN] > fuˌtili'tarianˌism *n*

futility (fju:'tɪlɪtɪ) *n, pl* **-ties 1** lack of effectiveness or success **2** lack of purpose or meaning **3** something futile

futon ('fu:tɒn) *n* a Japanese padded quilt, laid on the floor for use as a bed [c19 from Japanese]

futsal ('fʊtˌsæl) *n* a form of association football, played indoors with five players on each side [c20 Spanish from *futbol* football + *sala* indoor]

futtock ('fʌtək) *n nautical* one of the ribs in the frame of a wooden vessel [c13 perhaps variant of *foothook*]

futtock plate *n nautical* a horizontal metal disc fixed at the top of a lower mast for holding the futtock shrouds

futtock shroud *n nautical* any of several metal rods serving as a brace between the futtock plate on a lower mast and the topmast

future ('fju:tʃə) *n* **1** the time yet to come **2** undetermined events that will occur in that time **3** the condition of a person or thing at a later date **4** likelihood of later improvement or advancement: *he has a future as a singer* **5** *grammar* **a** a tense of verbs used when the action or event described is to occur after the time of utterance **b** a verb in this tense **6 in future** from now on; henceforth ▷ *adj* **7** that is yet to come or be **8** of or expressing time yet to come **9** (*prenominal*) destined to become **10** *grammar* in or denoting the future as a tense of verbs ▷ See also **futures** [c14 from Latin *fūtūrus* about to be, from *esse* to be] > 'futureless *adj*

future life *n* a life after death; afterlife

future perfect *grammar* ▷ *adj* **1** denoting a tense of verbs describing an action that will have been performed by a certain time. In English this is formed with *will have* or *shall have* plus the past participle ▷ *n* **2 a** the future perfect tense **b** a verb in this tense

future-proof *adj* (of a system, computer, program, etc) guaranteed not to be superseded by future versions, developments, etc

futures ('fju:tʃəz) *pl n* **a** commodities or other financial products bought or sold at an agreed price for delivery at a specified future date. See also **financial futures b** (*as modifier*): *futures contract*

future value *n* the value that a sum of money invested at compound interest will have after a specified period

futurism ('fju:tʃəˌrɪzəm) *n* an artistic movement that arose in Italy in 1909 to replace traditional aesthetic values with the characteristics of the machine age > 'futurist *n, adj*

futuristic (ˌfju:tʃə'rɪstɪk) *adj* **1** denoting or relating to design, technology, etc, that is thought likely to be current or fashionable at some future time; ultramodern **2** of or relating to futurism > ˌfutur'istically *adv*

futurity (fju:'tjʊərɪtɪ) *n, pl* **-ties 1** a less common word for **future 2** the quality of being in the future **3** a future event

futurology (ˌfju:tʃə'rɒlədʒɪ) *n* the study or prediction of the future of mankind > ˌfutur'ologist *n*

fuze (fju:z) *n chiefly US* a variant spelling of **fuse**

fuzee (fju:'zi:) *n* a variant spelling of **fusee**

Fuzhou ('fu:'dʒəʊ), **Foochow** *or* **Fuchou** *n* a port in SE China, capital of Fujian province on the Min Jiang: one of the original five treaty ports (1842). Pop: 1 398 000 (2005 est)

fuzz[1] (fʌz) *n* **1** a mass or covering of fine or curly hairs, fibres, etc **2** a blur ▷ *vb* **3** to make or become fuzzy **4** to make or become indistinct; blur [c17 perhaps from Low German *fussig* loose]

fuzz[2] (fʌz) *n* a slang word for **police** *or* **policeman** [c20 of uncertain origin]

fuzz box *n music* an electronic device that breaks up the sound passing through it, used esp by guitarists

fuzzy ('fʌzɪ) *adj* **fuzzier, fuzziest 1** of, resembling, or covered with fuzz **2** indistinct; unclear or distorted **3** not clearly thought out or expressed **4** (of the hair) tightly curled or very wavy **5** *maths* of or relating to a form of set theory in which set membership depends on a likelihood function: *fuzzy set; fuzzy logic* **6** (of a computer program or system) designed to operate according to the principles of fuzzy logic, so as to be able to deal with data which is imprecise or has uncertain boundaries > 'fuzzily *adv* > 'fuzziness *n*

fuzzy logic *n* a branch of logic designed to allow degrees of imprecision in reasoning and knowledge, typified by terms such as 'very', 'quite possibly', and 'unlikely', to be represented in such a way that the information can be processed by computer

fuzzy-wuzzy ('fʌzɪˌwʌzɪ) *n, pl* **-wuzzies** *or* **-wuzzy** *archaic, offensive slang* a Black fuzzy-haired native of any of various countries

fuzzy-wuzzy angel *n Austral informal* any native of Papua New Guinea who assisted as a stretcher-bearer in World War II

fv *abbreviation for* folio verso [Latin: on the reverse (that is left-hand) page]

FWA *abbreviation for* flexible working arrangement: an agreement between an employer and employee that the employee's working hours may be adapted to suit his or her particular needs

fwd *abbreviation for* forward

FWD *text messaging abbreviation for* forward

f.w.d. *abbreviation for* **1** four-wheel drive **2** front-wheel drive

FWIW *text messaging abbreviation for* for what it's worth

f-word *n* (*sometimes capital; preceded by the*) a euphemistic way of referring to the word **fuck**

FX *n* **1** *films informal* short for **special effects 2** *US and Canadian abbreviation for* foreign exchange

-fy *suffix forming verbs* to make or become: *beautify; simplify; liquefy* [from Old French *-fier*, from Latin *-ficāre*, verbal ending formed from *-ficus* -FIC]

FYI *text messaging abbreviation for* for your information

fyke (faɪk) *n US* a fish trap consisting of a net suspended over a series of hoops, laid horizontally in the water [c19 from Middle Dutch *fuycke*]

Fylde (faɪld) *n* a region in NW England in Lancashire between the Wyre and Ribble estuaries

fylfot ('faɪlfɒt) *n* a rare word for **swastika** [c16 (apparently meaning: a sign or device for the lower part or foot of a painted window): from *fillen* to FILL + *fot* FOOT]

Fyn (*Danish* fy:n) *n* the Danish name for **Funen**

fynbos ('feɪnbɒs) *n* a type of vegetation unique to the Mediterranean-climate region of southern and southwestern South Africa, characterized by evergreen hard-leaved shrubs and almost no trees [Afrikaans: fine bush]

fyrd (fɪəd, faɪəd) *n history* the local militia of an Anglo-Saxon shire, in which all freemen had to serve

FYROM *abbreviation for* Former Yugoslav Republic of Macedonia

FZS *abbreviation for* Fellow of the Zoological Society

Gg

2G *abbreviation for* second-generation; a system for mobile phones, characterized by digital technology, internet access, and a short-message service

3G *abbreviation for* third-generation; a system for mobile phones allowing fast connection, internet access, digital photography, graphics transmission and display, and other advanced features

4G *abbreviation for* fourth generation: a stage in mobile phone technology when data can be provided more quickly and on broader bandwidths than previously

g *or* **G** (dʒiː) *n, pl* **g's, G's** *or* **Gs 1** the seventh letter and fifth consonant of the modern English alphabet **2** a speech sound represented by this letter, in English usually either a voiced velar stop, as in *grass*, or a voiced palato-alveolar affricate, as in *page*

g *symbol for* **1** gallon(s) **2** gram(s) **3** acceleration of free fall (due to gravity) near the surface of the earth **4** grav **5** *chess* See **algebraic notation**

G *symbol for* **1** *music* **a** a note having a frequency of 392 hertz (**G above middle C**) or this value multiplied or divided by any power of 2; the fifth note of the scale of C major **b** a key, string, or pipe producing this note **c** the major or minor key having this note as its tonic **2** gauss **3** gravitational constant **4** *physics* conductance **5** *biochem* guanine **6** German **7** Gibbs function **8** giga **9** good **10** *slang, chiefly US* grand (a thousand dollars or pounds) **11** (in Australia) **a** general exhibition (used to describe a category of film certified as suitable for viewing by anyone) **b** (*as modifier*): *a G film*

G. *or* **g.** *abbreviation for* **1** Gulf **2** guilder(s) **3** guinea(s)

G3 *abbreviation for* Group of Three
G5 *abbreviation for* Group of Five
G7 *abbreviation for* Group of Seven
G8 *abbreviation for* Group of Eight
G9 *text messaging abbreviation for* genius
G10 *abbreviation for* Group of Ten
G24 *abbreviation for* Group of Twenty-Four
G77 *abbreviation for* Group of Seventy-Seven
ga *the internet domain name for* Gabon
Ga¹ *the chemical symbol for* gallium
Ga² *or* **Gā** (gɑː) *n* **1** (*pl* **Ga, Gas** *or* **Gā, Gās**) a member of a Negroid people of W Africa living chiefly in S Ghana **2** the language of this people, belonging to the Kwa branch of the Niger-Congo family

GA *abbreviation for* **1** General Assembly (of the United Nations) **2 general average 3** Georgia
Ga *abbreviation for* Georgia
GAA (in Ireland) *abbreviation for* Gaelic Athletic Association

gab¹ (gæb) *informal* ▷ *vb* **gabs, gabbing, gabbed 1** (*intr*) to talk excessively or idly, esp about trivial matters; gossip; chatter ▷ *n* **2** idle or trivial talk **3 gift of the gab** ability to speak effortlessly, glibly,

or persuasively [c18 variant of Northern dialect *gob* mouth, probably from Irish Gaelic *gob* beak, mouth] > 'gabber *n*

gab² (gæb) *n* **1** a hook or open notch in a rod or lever that drops over the spindle of a valve to form a temporary connection for operating the valve **2** a pointed tool used in masonry [c18 probably from Flemish *gabbe* notch, gash]

GAB *international car registration for* Gabon

GABA ('gæbə) *n acronym for* gamma-aminobutyric acid: a biologically active substance found in plants and in brain and other animal tissues; it is a neurotransmitter that inhibits activation of neurones

gabapentin (ˌgæbəˈpɛntɪn) *n* an antiepileptic drug that is also used to control neurological pain

Gabar ('gɑːbə), **Gheber** *or* **Ghebre** *n* **1** a member of an Iranian religious sect practising a modern version of Zoroastrianism ▷ *adj* **2** of, relating to, or characterizing the Gabar sect or its beliefs

gabardine *or* **gaberdine** (ˈgæbəˌdiːn, ˌgæbəˈdiːn) *n* **1** a twill-weave worsted, cotton, or spun-rayon fabric **2** an ankle-length loose coat or frock worn by men, esp by Jews, in the Middle Ages **3** any of various other garments made of gabardine, esp a child's raincoat [c16 from Old French *gauvardine* pilgrim's garment, from Middle High German *wallewart* pilgrimage; related to Spanish *gabardina*]

gabble ('gæbᵊl) *vb* **1** to utter (words, etc) rapidly and indistinctly; jabber **2** (*intr*) (of geese and some other birds or animals) to utter rapid cackling noises ▷ *n* **3** rapid and indistinct speech or noises [c17 from Middle Dutch *gabbelen*, of imitative origin] > 'gabbler *n*

gabbro ('gæbrəʊ) *n, pl* **-bros** a dark coarse-grained basic plutonic igneous rock consisting of plagioclase feldspar, pyroxene, and often olivine [c19 from Italian, probably from Latin *glaber* smooth, bald] > gab'broic *or* ˌgabbro'itic *adj*

gabby ('gæbɪ) *adj* **-bier, -biest** *informal* inclined to chatter; talkative

gabelle (gæ'bɛl) *n French history* a salt tax levied until 1790 [c15 from Old Italian *gabella*, from Arabic *qabālah* tribute, from *qabala* he received] > ga'belled *adj*

gaberdine (ˈgæbəˌdiːn, ˌgæbəˈdiːn) *n* a variant spelling of **gabardine**

gaberlunzie (ˌgæbəˈlʌnzɪ, -ˈluːnjɪ) *n Scot archaic or literary* a wandering beggar. Also called: **gaberlunzie-man** [c16 variant of earlier *gaberlungy*]

Gaberones (ˌgæbəˈrəʊnɛs) *n* the former name for **Gaborone**

Gabès ('gɑːbɛs; *French* gabɛs) *n* **1** a port in E Tunisia. Pop: 116 000 (2005 est) **2 Gulf of** an inlet of the Mediterranean on the E coast of Tunisia. Ancient name: **Syrtis Minor** Arabic name: **Qabis**

gabfest ('gæbfɛst) *n informal, chiefly US and Canadian* **1** prolonged gossiping or conversation **2** an informal gathering for conversation [c19 from GAB¹ + FEST]

gabion ('geɪbɪən) *n* **1** a cylindrical metal

container filled with stones, used in the construction of underwater foundations **2** a wickerwork basket filled with stones or earth, used (esp formerly) as part of a fortification [c16 from French: basket, from Italian *gabbione*, from *gabbia* cage, from Latin *cavea*; see CAGE]

gabionade *or* **gabionnade** (ˌgeɪbɪəˈneɪd) *n* **1** a row of gabions submerged in a waterway, stream, river, etc, to control the flow of water **2** a fortification constructed of gabions [c18 from French; see GABION]

gable ('geɪbᵊl) *n* **1** the triangular upper part of a wall between the sloping ends of a pitched roof (**gable roof**) **2** a triangular ornamental feature in the form of a gable, esp as used over a door or window **3** the triangular wall on both ends of a gambrel roof [c14 Old French *gable*, probably from Old Norse *gafl*; related to Old English *geafol* fork, Old High German *gibil* gable] > 'gabled *adj* > 'gable-ˌlike *adj*

gable end *n* the end wall of a building on the side which is topped by a gable

gablet ('geɪblɪt) *n* a small gable

gable window *n* a window positioned in a gable or having a small gable over it

Gabon (gəˈbɒn; *French* gabɔ̃) *n* a republic in W central Africa, on the Atlantic: settled by the French in 1839; made part of the French Congo in 1888; became independent in 1960; almost wholly forested. Official language: French. Religion: Christian majority; significant animist minority. Currency: franc. Capital: Libreville. Pop: 1 352 000 (2004 est). Area: 267 675 sq km (103 350 sq miles)

Gabonese (ˌgæbəˈniːz) *adj* **1** of or relating to Gabon or its inhabitants ▷ *n* **2** a native or inhabitant of Gabon

gaboon (gəˈbuːn) *n* the dark mahogany-like wood from a western and central African burseraceous tree, *Aucoumea klaineana*, used in plywood, for furniture, and as a veneer [c20 altered from GABON]

gaboon viper *n* a large venomous viper, *Bitis gabonica*, that occurs in African rainforests. It has brown and purple markings and hornlike projections on its snout

Gaborone (ˌhæbəˈrəʊnɪ) *n* the capital of Botswana (since 1964), in the extreme southeast. Pop: 186 007 (2001). Former name: **Gaberones**

Gabriel ('geɪbrɪəl) *n Bible* one of the archangels, the messenger of good news (Daniel 8:16–26; Luke 1:11–20, 26–38)

gaby ('geɪbɪ) *n, pl* **-bies** *archaic or dialect* a simpleton [c18 of unknown origin]

gad¹ (gæd) *vb* **gads, gadding, gadded 1** (*intr; often foll by* about *or* around) to go out in search of pleasure, esp in an aimless manner; gallivant ▷ *n* **2** carefree adventure (esp in the phrase **on** *or* **upon the gad**) [c15 back formation from obsolete *gadling* companion, from Old English, from *gæd* fellowship; related to Old High German *gatuling*] > 'gadder *n*

gad² (gæd) *n* **1** *mining* a short chisel-like instrument for breaking rock or coal from the face **2** a goad for driving cattle **3** a western US word for **spur** (sense 1) ▷ *vb* **gads, gadding, gadded 4** (*tr*) *mining* to break up or loosen with a gad [C13 from Old Norse *gaddr* spike; related to Old High German *gart*, Gothic *gazds* spike]

Gad¹ (gæd) *n, interj* an archaic euphemism for **God**: used as or in an oath

Gad² (gæd) *n Old Testament* **1 a** Jacob's sixth son, whose mother was Zilpah, Leah's maid **b** the Israelite tribe descended from him **c** the territory of this tribe, lying to the east of the Jordan and extending southwards from the Sea of Galilee **2** a prophet and admonisher of David (I Samuel 22; II Samuel 24)

gadabout ('gædə,baʊt) *n informal* a person who restlessly seeks amusement

Gadarene ('gædə,riːn) *adj* relating to or engaged in a headlong rush [C19 via Late Latin from Greek *Gadarēnos*, of Gadara (Palestine), alluding to the Biblical Gadarene swine (Matthew 8:28ff.)]

gadfly ('gæd,flaɪ) *n, pl* **-flies 1** any of various large dipterous flies, esp the horsefly, that annoy livestock by sucking their blood **2** a constantly irritating or harassing person [C16 from GAD² (sting) + FLY¹]

gadget ('gædʒɪt) *n* **1** a small mechanical device or appliance **2** any object that is interesting for its ingenuity or novelty rather than for its practical use [C19 perhaps from French *gâchette* lock catch, trigger, diminutive of *gâche* staple] > 'gadgety *adj*

gadgeteer (,gædʒɪ'tɪə) *n* a person who delights in gadgetry

gadgetry ('gædʒɪtrɪ) *n* **1** gadgets collectively **2** use of or preoccupation with gadgets and their design

gadgie ('gædʒɪ) *or* **gadge** (gædʒ) *n Brit dialect* a fellow [from Romany]

Gadhelic (gæd'hɛlɪk) *n, adj* another term for **Goidelic** [C19 from Old Irish *Gaídelc, Goídelc* the Gaelic language]

gadid ('geɪdɪd) *n* **1** any marine teleost fish of the family *Gadidae*, which includes the cod, haddock, whiting, and pollack ▷ *adj* **2** of, relating to, or belonging to the *Gadidae* [C19 see GADOID]

gado-gado ('gɑːdəʊ'gɑːdəʊ) *n* an Indonesian dish of cooked mixed vegetables and hard-boiled eggs served with a peanut sauce [Bahasa Indonesia]

gadoid ('geɪdɔɪd) *adj* **1** of, relating to, or belonging to the *Anacanthini*, an order of marine soft-finned fishes typically having the pectoral and pelvic fins close together and small cycloid scales. The group includes gadid fishes and hake ▷ *n* **2** any gadoid fish [C19 from New Latin *Gadidae*, from *gadus* cod; see -OID]

gadolinite ('gædəlɪ,naɪt) *n* a rare brown or black mineral consisting of a silicate of iron, beryllium, and yttrium in monoclinic crystalline form. Formula: 2BeO.FeO.Y₂O₃.2SiO₂. Also called: **ytterbite** [C19 named after Johan *Gadolin* (1760–1852), Finnish mineralogist]

gadolinium (,gædə'lɪnɪəm) *n* a ductile malleable silvery-white ferromagnetic element of the lanthanide series of metals: occurs principally in monazite and bastnaesite. Symbol: Gd; atomic no.: 64; atomic wt.: 157.25; valency: 3; relative density: 7.901; melting pt.: 1313±°C; boiling pt.: 3273°C (approx) [C19 New Latin, from GADOLINITE] > ,gado'linic *adj*

gadroon *or* **godroon** (gə'druːn) *n* **1** a moulding composed of a series of convex flutes and curves joined to form a decorative pattern, used esp as an edge to silver articles **2** *architect* a carved ornamental moulding having a convex cross section [C18 from French *godron*, perhaps from Old French *godet* cup, goblet, drinking vessel] > ga'drooned *or* go'drooned *adj*

Gadsden Purchase ('gædzdən) *n* an area of about 77 000 sq km (30 000 sq miles) in present-day Arizona and New Mexico, bought by the US from Mexico for 10 million dollars in 1853. The purchase was negotiated by James Gadsden (1788–1858), US diplomat

gadwall ('gæd,wɔːl) *n, pl* **-walls** *or* **-wall** a duck, *Anas strepera*, related to the mallard. The male has a grey body and black tail [C17 of unknown origin]

gadzooks (gæd'zuːks) *interj archaic* a mild oath [C17 perhaps from *God's hooks* (the nails of the cross); see GAD¹]

gae (ge) *vb* **gaes, gaun, gaed, gane** a Scot word for **go¹**

Gaea ('dʒiːə) *n Greek myth* a variant of **Gaia**

Gaekwar *or* **Gaikwar** ('gaɪkwɑː) *n history* the title of the ruler of the former native state of Baroda in India [C19 from Marathi *Gaekvād*, literally: Guardian of the Cows, from Sanskrit *gauh* cow + *-vad* guardian]

Gael (geɪl) *n* a person who speaks a Gaelic language, esp a Highland Scot or an Irishman [C19 from Gaelic *Gaidheal*; related to Old Irish *goidel*, Old Welsh *gwyddel* Irishman] > 'Gaeldom *n*

Gaelic ('geɪlɪk, 'gæl-) *n* **1** any of the closely related languages of the Celts in Ireland, Scotland, or (formerly) the Isle of Man. Compare **Goidelic** ▷ *adj* **2** of, denoting, or relating to the Celtic people of Ireland, Scotland, or the Isle of Man or their language or customs

Gaelic coffee *n* another name for **Irish coffee**

Gaelic football *n* an Irish game played with 15 players on each side and goals resembling rugby posts with a net on the bottom part. Players are allowed to kick, punch, and bounce the ball and attempt to get it over the bar or in the net

Gaeltacht ('geːltəxt) *or* **Gaedhealtacht** ('geɪl,tæxt, 'gæl-) *n* any of the regions in Ireland in which Irish Gaelic is the vernacular speech. The form *Gaeltacht* is sometimes also used to mean the region of Scotland in which Scottish Gaelic is spoken. See also **Gaidhealtachd** [C20 from Irish Gaelic]

gaff¹ (gæf) *n* **1** *angling* a stiff pole with a stout prong or hook attached for landing large fish **2** *nautical* a boom hoisted aft of a mast to support a gaffsail **3** a metal spur fixed to the leg of a gamecock ▷ *vb* (*tr*) **4** *angling* to hook or land (a fish) with a gaff **5** *slang* to cheat; hoax [C13 from French *gaffe*, from Provençal *gaf* boathook]

gaff² (gæf) *n* **1** *slang* foolish talk; nonsense **2 blow the gaff** *Brit slang* to divulge a secret **3 stand the gaff** *slang, chiefly US and Canadian* to endure ridicule, difficulties, etc [C19 of unknown origin]

gaff³ (gæf) *n Brit slang archaic* **1** a person's home, esp a flat **2** Also called: **penny-gaff** a cheap or low-class place of entertainment, esp a cheap theatre or music hall in Victorian England [C18 of unknown origin]

gaffe (gæf) *n* a social blunder, esp a tactless remark [C19 from French]

gaffer ('gæfə) *n* **1** an old man, esp one living in the country: often used affectionately or patronizingly. Compare **gammer 2** *informal, chiefly Brit* a boss, foreman, or owner of a factory, mine, etc **3** the senior electrician on a television or film set [C16 alteration of GODFATHER]

gaffer tape *n Brit* strong adhesive tape used in electrical repairs

gaff-rigged *adj* (of a sailing vessel) rigged with one or more gaffsails

gaffsail ('gæf,seɪl, -səl) *n* a quadrilateral fore-and-aft sail on a sailing vessel

gaff-topsail *n* a sail set above a gaffsail

gag¹ (gæg) *vb* **gags, gagging, gagged 1** (*tr*) to stop up (a person's mouth), esp with a piece of cloth, etc, to prevent him or her from speaking or crying out **2** (*tr*) to suppress or censor (free expression, information, etc) **3** to retch or cause to retch **4** (*intr*) to struggle for breath; choke **5** (*tr*) to hold (the jaws) of (a person or animal) apart with a surgical gag **6** (*tr*) to apply a gag-bit to (a horse) **7 be gagging for** *or to slang* to be very eager to have or do something ▷ *n* **8** a piece of cloth, rope, etc, stuffed into or tied across the mouth **9** any restraint on or suppression of information, free speech, etc **10** a surgical device for keeping the jaws apart, as during a tonsillectomy **11** *parliamentary procedure* another word for **closure** (sense 4) [C15 *gaggen*; perhaps imitative of a gasping sound]

gag² (gæg) *informal* ▷ *n* **1** a joke or humorous story, esp one told by a professional comedian **2** a hoax, practical joke, etc: *he did it for a gag* ▷ *vb* **gags, gagging, gagged 3** (*intr*) to tell jokes or funny stories, as comedians in nightclubs, etc **4** (often foll by *up*) *theatre* **a** to interpolate lines or business not in the actor's stage part, usually comic and improvised **b** to perform a stage jest, either spoken or based on movement [C19 perhaps special use of GAG¹]

gaga ('gɑːgɑː) *adj informal* **1** senile; doting **2** slightly crazy [C20 from French, of imitative origin]

Gagauzi (gə'gɔːzɪ) *n* a language spoken chiefly in Ukraine, on the NW coast of the Black Sea, belonging to the Turkic branch of the Altaic family

gag-bit *n* a powerful type of bit used in breaking horses

gage¹ (geɪdʒ) *n* **1** something deposited as security against the fulfilment of an obligation; pledge **2** (formerly) a glove or other object thrown down to indicate a challenge to combat ▷ *vb* **3** (*tr*) *archaic* to stake, pledge, or wager [C14 from Old French *gage*, of Germanic origin; compare Gothic *wadi* pledge]

gage² (geɪdʒ) *n* short for **greengage**

gage³ (geɪdʒ) *n US dated slang* marijuana [C20 of uncertain origin; compare GANJA]

gage⁴ (geɪdʒ) *n, vb US* a variant spelling (esp in technical senses) of **gauge**

gager ('geɪdʒə) *n* a variant spelling of **gauger**

gagger ('gægə) *n* **1** a person or thing that gags **2** a wedge for a core in a casting mould

gaggery ('gægərɪ) *n* the practice of telling jokes

gaggle ('gægəl) *vb* **1** (*intr*) (of geese) to cackle ▷ *n* **2** a flock of geese **3** *informal* a disorderly group of people **4** a gabbling or cackling sound [C14 of Germanic origin; compare Old Norse *gagl* gosling, Dutch *gaggelen* to cackle, all of imitative origin]

gag rule *or* **resolution** *n US* any closure regulation adopted by a deliberative body

gahnite ('gɑːnaɪt) *n* a dark green mineral of the spinel group consisting of zinc aluminium oxide. Formula: ZnAl₂O₄ [C19 named after J. G. *Gahn* (1745–1818), Swedish chemist; see -ITE²]

GAI (geɪn) *n* (in Canada) ▷ *abbreviation for* Guaranteed Annual Income

Gaia ('geɪə), **Gaea** *or* **Ge** *n* the goddess of the earth, who bore Uranus and by him Oceanus, Cronus, and the Titans [from Greek *gaia* earth]

Gaia hypothesis *or* **theory** ('gaɪə) *n* the theory that the earth and everything on it constitutes a single self-regulating living entity

Gaidhealtachd ('geɪl,tæxt, 'gæl,tæxg) *n* **1** the area of Scotland in which Scottish Gaelic is the vernacular speech. See also **Gaeltacht 2** the culture and traditions of the Scottish Gaels [Scottish Gaelic]

gaiety ('geɪətɪ) *n, pl* **-ties 1** the state or condition of being merry, bright, or lively **2** festivity; merrymaking ▷ Also (esp US): **gayety**

▷ USAGE See at **gay**

gaijin (gaɪ'dʒɪn) *n* (*pl* **-jin**) (in Japan) a foreigner [C20 Japanese, a contraction of *gaikoku-jin*, from *gaikoku* foreign country + *jin* person]

Gaikwar ('gaɪkwɑː) *n* a variant spelling of **Gaekwar**

Gaillard Cut (gɪl'jɑːd, geɪlɑːd) *n* the SE section of the Panama Canal, cut through Culebra Mountain. Length: about 13 km (8 miles). Former name: Culebra Cut [C19 named after David Du Bose *Gaillard* (1859–1913), US army engineer in charge of the work]

gaillardia (geɪ'lɑːdɪə) *n* any plant of the North American genus *Gaillardia*, having ornamental flower heads with yellow or red rays and purple discs: family *Asteraceae* (composites) [C19 from New Latin, named after *Gaillard* de Marentonneau, 18th-century French amateur botanist]

gaily ('geɪlɪ) *adv* 1 in a lively manner; cheerfully 2 with bright colours; showily

gain¹ (geɪn) *vb* 1 (*tr*) to acquire (something desirable); obtain 2 (*tr*) to win in competition: *to gain the victory* 3 to increase, improve, or advance: *the car gained speed; the shares gained in value* 4 (*tr*) to earn (a wage, living, etc) 5 (*intr*; usually foll by *on* or *upon*) **a** to get nearer (to) or catch up (on) **b** to get farther away (from) 6 (*tr*) (esp of ships) to get to; reach: *the steamer gained port* 7 (of a timepiece) to operate too fast, so as to indicate a time ahead of the true time or to run fast by a specified amount: *this watch gains; it gains ten minutes a day* 8 **gain ground** to make progress or obtain an advantage 9 **gain time** **a** to obtain extra time by a delay or postponement **b** (of a timepiece) to operate too fast ▷ *n* 10 something won, acquired, earned, etc; profit; advantage 11 an increase in size, amount, etc 12 the act of gaining; attainment; acquisition 13 Also called: **amplification** *electronics* the ratio of the output signal of an amplifier to the input signal, usually measured in decibels ▷ See also **gains** [C15 from Old French *gaaignier*, of Germanic origin; related to Old High German *weidenen* to forage, hunt] ▷ **'gainable** *adj*

gain² (geɪn) *n* 1 a notch, mortise, or groove, esp one cut to take the flap of a butt hinge ▷ *vb* 2 (*tr*) to cut a gain or gains in [C17 of obscure origin]

GAIN (geɪn) *n* (in Canada) ▷ *abbreviation or acronym for* Guaranteed Annual Income

gainer ('geɪnə) *n* 1 a person or thing that gains 2 Also called: **full gainer** a type of dive in which the diver leaves the board facing forward and completes a full backward somersault to enter the water feet first with his back to the diving board. Compare **half gainer**

gainful ('geɪnfʊl) *adj* profitable; lucrative: *gainful employment* ▷ **'gainfully** *adv* ▷ **'gainfulness** *n*

gainings ('geɪnɪŋz) *pl n* profits or earnings

gainly ('geɪnlɪ) *obsolete or dialect* ▷ *adj* 1 graceful or well-formed; shapely ▷ *adv* 2 conveniently or suitably ▷ **'gainliness** *n*

gains (geɪnz) *pl n* profits or winnings: *ill-gotten gains*

gainsay (geɪn'seɪ) *vb* -says, -saying, -said (*tr*) *archaic or literary* to deny (an allegation, a statement, etc); contradict [C13 *gainsaien*, from *gain-* AGAINST + *saien* to SAY¹] ▷ **gain'sayer** *n*

'gainst or **gainst** (gɛnst, geɪnst) *prep poetic* short for **against**

gait (geɪt) *n* 1 manner of walking or running; bearing 2 (used esp of horses and dogs) the pattern of footsteps at various speeds, as the walk, trot, canter, etc, each pattern being distinguished by a particular rhythm and footfall ▷ *vb* 3 (*tr*) to teach (a horse) a particular gait [C16 variant of GATE¹]

-gaited ('geɪtɪd) *adj* (*in combination*) having a gait as specified: *slow-gaited*

gaiter ('geɪtə) *n* (*often plural*) 1 a cloth or leather covering for the leg or ankle buttoned on one side and usually strapped under the foot 2 Also called: **spat** a similar covering extending from the ankle to the instep 3 a waterproof covering for the ankle worn by climbers and walkers to prevent snow, mud, or gravel entering over the top of the boot [C18 from French *guêtre*, probably of Germanic origin and related to WRIST] ▷ **'gaiterless** *adj*

gal¹ (gæl) *n slang* a girl

gal² (gæl) *n* a unit of acceleration equal to 1 centimetre per second per second [C20 named after Galileo Galilei (1564–1642), Italian mathematician, astronomer, and physicist]

GAL *text messaging abbreviation for* get a life

gal. or **gall.** *abbreviation for* gallon

Gal. *Bible abbreviation for* Galatians

gala ('gɑːlə, 'geɪlə) *n* 1 **a** a celebration; festive occasion **b** (*as modifier*): *a gala occasion* 2 *chiefly Brit* a sporting occasion involving competitions in several events: *a swimming gala* [C17 from French or Italian, from Old French *gale* pleasure, from Old French *galer* to make merry, probably of Germanic origin; compare GALLANT]

galactagogue (gə'læktəgɒg) *adj* 1 inducing milk secretion ▷ *n* 2 a galactagogue agent [C19 from Greek *gala, galaktos*, milk + -AGOGUE]

galactic (gə'læktɪk) *adj* 1 *astronomy* of or relating to a galaxy, esp the Galaxy: *the galactic plane* 2 *med* of or relating to milk [C19 from Greek *galaktikos*; see GALAXY]

galactic equator or **circle** *n* the great circle on the celestial sphere containing the galactic plane

galactic halo *n astronomy* a spheroidal aggregation of globular clusters, individual stars, dust, and gas that surrounds the Galaxy

Galactico (gə'læktɪ,kəʊ) *n informal* a famous and highly paid footballer [C20 from Spanish *Los Galacticos* the nickname of the expensively assembled Real Madrid team of the early years of the 21st century; *galactico* someone from another galaxy, denoting their superstar status]

galactic plane *n* the plane passing through the spiral arms of the Galaxy

galactic poles *pl n* the two points on the celestial sphere, diametrically opposite each other, that can be joined by an imaginary line perpendicular to the galactic plane

galacto- or before a vowel **galact-** *combining form* milk or milky: *galactometer* [from Greek *galakt-, gala*]

galactometer (,gælək'tɒmɪtə) *n* an instrument, similar to a hydrometer, for measuring the relative density of milk. It is used to determine the fat content ▷ ,galac'tometry *n*

galactopoietic (gə,læktəʊpɔɪ'ɛtɪk) *adj* 1 inducing or increasing the secretion of milk ▷ *n* 2 a galactopoietic agent ▷ **galactopoiesis** (gə,læktəʊpɔɪ'iːsɪs) *n*

galactose (gə'læktəʊz, -əʊs) *n* a white water-soluble monosaccharide found in lactose. Formula: $C_6H_{12}O_6$

galago (gə'lɑːgəʊ) *n, pl* -gos another name for **bushbaby** [C19 from New Latin, perhaps from Wolof *golokh* monkey]

galah (gə'lɑː) *n* 1 an Australian cockatoo, *Kakatoe roseicapilla*, having grey wings, back, and crest and a pink body 2 *Austral slang* a fool or simpleton [C19 from a native Australian language]

Galahad ('gælə,hæd) *n* 1 **Sir** (in Arthurian legend) the most virtuous knight of the Round Table, destined to regain the Holy Grail; son of Lancelot and Elaine 2 a pure or noble man

galah session *n Austral informal* an occasion on which people from remote areas converse with each other by radio

galangal (gə'læŋgəl) *n* another name for **galingale** 2 a zingiberaceous plant, *Alpinia officinarum*, of China and the East Indies 3 the pungent aromatic root of this plant, dried and used as a seasoning and in medicine

galant (gə'lɑːnt) *n* an 18th-century style of music characterized by homophony and elaborate ornamentation [C17 from Old French *galant*, from *galer* to make merry, from *gale* enjoyment, pleasure]

galantamine (gə'læntə,miːn) *n* a drug that, by blocking the action of the enzyme acetylcholinesterase in the cortex of the brain, has been used to slow down the cognitive decline that characterizes Alzheimer's disease

galantine ('gælən,tiːn) *n* a cold dish of meat or poultry, which is boned, cooked, stuffed, then pressed into a neat shape and glazed [C14 from Old French, from Medieval Latin *galatina*, probably from Latin *gelātus* frozen, set; see GELATINE]

galanty show (gə'læntɪ) *n* (formerly) a pantomime shadow play, esp one in miniature using figures cut from paper [C19 perhaps from Italian *galante* GALLANT]

Galápagos Islands (gə'læpəgəs; *Spanish* ga'lapaɣos) *pl n* a group of 15 islands in the Pacific west of Ecuador, of which they form a province: discovered (1535) by the Spanish; main settlement on San Cristóbal. Pop: 18 640 (2001). Area: 7844 sq km (3028 sq miles). Official Spanish name: Archipiélago de Colón

Galashiels (,gælə'ʃiːlz) *n* a town in SE Scotland, in central Scottish Borders. Pop: 14 361 (2001)

Galata ('gælətə) *n* a port in NW Turkey, a suburb and the chief business section of Istanbul

galatea (,gælə'tɪə) *n* a strong twill-weave cotton fabric, striped or plain, for clothing [C19 named after the man-of-war HMS *Galatea* (the fabric was at one time in demand for children's sailor suits)]

Galatea (,gælə'tɪə) *n Greek myth* a statue of a maiden brought to life by Aphrodite in response to the prayers of the sculptor Pygmalion, who had fallen in love with his creation

Galați (*Romanian* ga'latsj) *n* an inland port in SE Romania, on the River Danube. Pop: 251 000 (2005 est)

Galatia (gə'leɪʃə, -ʃɪə) *n* an ancient region in central Asia Minor, conquered by Gauls 278–277 BC: later a Roman province

Galatian (gə'leɪʃən, -ʃɪən) *adj* 1 of or relating to Galatia or its inhabitants ▷ *n* 2 a native or inhabitant of Galatia

Galatians (gə'leɪʃənz, -ʃɪənz) *n* (*functioning as singular*) a book of the New Testament (in full **The Epistle of Paul the Apostle to the Galatians**)

galaxy ('gæləksɪ) *n, pl* -axies 1 any of a vast number of star systems held together by gravitational attraction in an asymmetric shape (an **irregular galaxy**) or, more usually, in a symmetrical shape (a **regular galaxy**), which is either a spiral or an ellipse. Former names: island universe, extragalactic nebula ▷ Related adjective: **galactic** 2 a splendid gathering, esp one of famous or distinguished people [C14 (in the sense: the Milky Way), from Medieval Latin *galaxia*, from Latin *galaxias*, from Greek, from *gala* milk; related to Latin *lac* milk]

Galaxy ('gæləksɪ) *n* **the** the spiral galaxy, approximately 100 000 light years in diameter, that contains the solar system about three fifths of the distance from its centre. Also called: **the Milky Way System** See also **Magellanic Cloud**

galbanum ('gælbənəm) *n* a bitter aromatic gum resin extracted from any of several Asian umbelliferous plants of the genus *Ferula*, esp *F. galbaniflua*, and used in incense and medicinally as a counterirritant [C14 from Latin, from Greek *khalbanē*, from Hebrew *helbenāh*]

gale¹ (geɪl) *n* 1 a strong wind, specifically one of force seven to ten on the Beaufort scale or from 45 to 90 kilometres per hour 2 (*often plural*) a loud outburst, esp of laughter 3 *archaic and poetic* a gentle breeze [C16 of unknown origin]

gale² (geɪl) *n* short for **sweet gale** [Old English *gagel*; related to Middle Low German *gagel*]

galea ('geɪlɪə) *n, pl* -leae (-lɪ,iː) a part or organ shaped like a helmet or hood, such as the petals of certain flowers [C18 from Latin: helmet] ▷ **'galeˌate** or **'galeˌated** *adj* ▷ **'galeiˌform** *adj*

galena (gə'liːnə) or **galenite** (gə'liːnaɪt) *n* a grey mineral, found in hydrothermal veins. It is the chief source of lead. Composition: lead sulphide. Formula: PbS. Crystal structure: cubic [C17 from Latin: lead ore, dross left after melting lead]

Galenic (geɪ'lɛnɪk, gə-) *adj* of or relating to Galen (Latin name *Claudius Galenus* ?130–?200 AD), the Greek physician, anatomist, and physiologist, or his teachings or methods

galenical (geɪ'lɛnɪkəl, gə-) *pharmacol* ▷ *n* 1 any drug prepared from plant or animal tissue, esp vegetables, rather than being chemically synthesized ▷ *adj* 2 denoting or belonging to this group of drugs [C17 after *Galen* (?130–?200 AD), Greek physician, anatomist, and physiologist]

Galenism ('geɪlɪ,nɪzəm) *n* a system of medicine based on the 84 surviving technical treatises of

Galen (Latin name *Claudius Galenus* ?130–?200 AD), Greek physician, anatomist, and physiologist, including the theory of the four bodily humours ▷ 'Galenist *adj*, *n*

galère *French* (galɛr) *n* **1** a group of people having a common interest, esp a coterie of undesirable people **2** an unpleasant situation [c18 literally: a galley]

Galibi (gɑːˈliːbɪ) *n* (*pl* **-bi** *or* **-bis**) a member of an American Indian people of French Guiana **2** the language of this people, belonging to the Carib family

Galicia *n* **1** (gəˈlɪʃɪə, -ˈlɪʃə) a region of E central Europe on the N side of the Carpathians, now in SE Poland and Ukraine **2** (*Spanish* gaˈliθja) an autonomous region and former kingdom of NW Spain, on the Bay of Biscay and the Atlantic. Pop: 1 969 000 (2003 est)

Galician (gəˈlɪʃɪən, -ʃən) *adj* **1** of or relating to Galicia in E central Europe **2** of or relating to Galicia in NW Spain ▷ *n* **3** a native or inhabitant of either Galicia **4** the Romance language or dialect of Spanish Galicia, sometimes regarded as a dialect of Spanish, although historically it is more closely related to Portuguese

Galilean¹ (ˌɡælɪˈliːən) *n* **1** a native or inhabitant of Galilee **2 a** **the** an epithet of Jesus Christ (?4 BC–?29 AD), the founder of Christianity **b** (*often plural*) a Christian ▷ *adj* **3** of Galilee

Galilean² (ˌɡælɪˈleɪən) *adj* of or relating to Galileo Galilei (1564–1642), the Italian mathematician, astronomer, and physicist

Galilean satellite (ˌɡælɪˈleɪən) *n* any of the four large satellites of the planet Jupiter – Io, Europa, Ganymede, or Callisto – discovered in 1610 by Galileo

Galilean telescope (ˌɡælɪˈleɪən) *n* a type of telescope with a convex objective lens and a concave eyepiece; it produces an erect image and is suitable for terrestrial use

galilee (ˈɡælɪˌliː) *n* a porch or chapel at the entrance to some medieval churches and cathedrals in England

Galilee (ˈɡælɪˌliː) *n* **1 Sea of** Also called: **Lake Tiberias**, **Lake Kinneret**. a lake in NE Israel, 209 m (686 ft) below sea level, through which the River Jordan flows. Area: 165 sq km (64 sq miles) **2** a northern region of Israel: scene of Christ's early ministry

Galileo (ˌɡælɪˈleɪəʊ) *n* a US spacecraft, launched 1989, that entered orbit around Jupiter in late 1995 to study the planet and its major satellites

galimatias (ˌɡælɪˈmeɪʃɪəs, -ˈmætɪəs) *n rare* confused talk; gibberish [c17 from French, of unknown origin]

galingale (ˈɡælɪŋˌɡeɪl) *or* **galangal** *n* a European cyperaceous plant, *Cyperus longus*, with rough-edged leaves, reddish spikelets of flowers, and aromatic roots [c13 from Old French *galingal*, from Arabic *khalanjān*, from Chinese *kaoliang-chiang*, from *Kaoliang* district in Guangdong province + *chiang* ginger]

galiot *or* **galliot** (ˈɡælɪət) *n* **1** a small swift galley formerly sailed on the Mediterranean **2** a shallow-draught ketch formerly used along the coasts of Germany and the Netherlands [c14 from Old French *galiote*, from Italian *galeotta*, from Medieval Latin *galea* GALLEY]

galipot *or* **gallipot** (ˈɡælɪˌpɒt) *n* a resin obtained from several species of pine, esp from the S European *Pinus pinaster* [c18 from French, of unknown origin]

gall¹ (ɡɔːl) *n* **1** *informal* impudence **2** bitterness; rancour **3** something bitter or disagreeable **4** *physiol* an obsolete term for **bile** **5** an obsolete term for **gall bladder** [from Old Norse, replacing Old English *gealla*; related to Old High German *galla*, Greek *kholē*]

gall² (ɡɔːl) *n* **1** a sore on the skin caused by chafing **2** something that causes vexation or annoyance: *a gall to the spirits* **3** irritation; exasperation ▷ *vb* **4** *pathol* to abrade (the skin,

etc) as by rubbing **5** (*tr*) to irritate or annoy; vex [c14 of Germanic origin; related to Old English *gealla* sore on a horse, and perhaps to GALL¹]

gall³ (ɡɔːl) *n* an abnormal outgrowth in plant tissue caused by certain parasitic insects, fungi, bacteria, or mechanical injury [c14 from Old French *galle*, from Latin *galla*]

gall. *or* **gal.** *abbreviation for* gallon

Galla (ˈɡælə) *n* **1** (*pl* **-las** *or* **-la**) a member of a tall dark-skinned people inhabiting Somalia and SE Ethiopia **2** the language of this people, belonging to the Cushitic subfamily of the Afro-Asiatic family of languages

gallant *adj* (ˈɡælənt) **1** brave and high-spirited; courageous and honourable; dashing: *a gallant warrior* **2** (ɡəˈlænt, ˈɡælənt) (of a man) attentive to women; chivalrous **3** imposing; dignified; stately: *a gallant ship* **4** *archaic* showy in dress ▷ *n* (ˈɡælənt, ɡəˈlænt) *archaic* **5** a woman's lover or suitor **6** a dashing or fashionable young man, esp one who pursues women **7** a brave, high-spirited, or adventurous man ▷ *vb* (ɡəˈlænt, ˈɡælənt) *rare* **8** (when *intr*, usually foll by *with*) to court or flirt (with) **9** (*tr*) to attend or escort (a woman) [c15 from Old French *galant*, from *galer* to make merry, from *gale* enjoyment, pleasure, of Germanic origin; related to Old English *wela* WEAL²] > '**gallantly** *adv* > '**gallantness** *n*

gallantry (ˈɡæləntrɪ) *n*, *pl* **-ries** **1** conspicuous courage, esp in war **2** polite attentiveness to women **3** a gallant action, speech, etc

gallant soldier *n* a South American plant, *Galinsoga parviflora*, widely distributed as a weed, having small daisy-like flowers surrounded by silvery scales: family *Asteraceae* (composites). Also called: **Joey Hooker** [c20 by folk etymology from New Latin *Galinsoga*]

gall bladder *n* a muscular pear-shaped sac, lying underneath the right lobe of the liver, that stores bile and ejects it into the duodenum through the common bile duct

Galle (ˈɡɔːl) ▷ *n* a port in SW Sri Lanka; along with other coastal settlements, it suffered badly in the Indian Ocean tsunami of December 2004. Pop: 123 616 (1997 est). Former name: **Point de Galle**

galleass *or* **galliass** (ˈɡælɪˌæs) *n nautical* a three-masted lateen-rigged galley used as a warship in the Mediterranean from the 15th to the 18th centuries [c16 from French *galleasse*, from Italian *galeazza*, from *galea* GALLEY]

galleon (ˈɡælɪən) *n nautical* a large sailing ship having three or more masts, lateen-rigged on the after masts and square-rigged on the foremast and mainmast, used as a warship or trader from the 15th to the 18th centuries [c16 from Spanish *galeón*, from French *galion*, from Old French *galie* GALLEY]

galleria (ˌɡæləˈriːə) *n* a central court through several storeys of a shopping centre or department store onto which shops or departments open at each level [c20 from Italian; see GALLERY]

galleried (ˈɡælərɪd) *adj* having a gallery or galleries

gallerist (ˈɡæləˌrɪst) *n* a person who owns or runs an art gallery

gallery (ˈɡælərɪ) *n*, *pl* **-leries** **1** a room or building for exhibiting works of art **2** a covered passageway open on one side or on both sides. See also **colonnade** (sense 1) **3 a** a balcony running along or around the inside wall of a church, hall, etc **b** a covered balcony, sometimes with columns on the outside **4** *theatre* **a** an upper floor that projects from the rear over the main floor and contains the cheapest seats **b** the seats there **c** the audience seated there **5** a long narrow room, esp one used for a specific purpose: *a shooting gallery* **6** *chiefly US* a building or room where articles are sold at auction **7** an underground passage, as in a mine, the burrow of an animal, etc **8** *theatre* a narrow raised platform at the side or along the back of the stage for the use of technicians and

stagehands **9** (in a TV studio) a glass-fronted soundproof room high up to one side of the studio looking into it. One gallery is used by the director and an assistant and one is for lighting, etc **10** *nautical* a balcony or platform at the quarter or stern of a ship, sometimes used as a gun emplacement **11** a small ornamental metal or wooden balustrade or railing on a piece of furniture, esp one surrounding the top of a desk, table, etc **12** any group of spectators, as at a golf match **13 play to the gallery** to try to gain popular favour, esp by crude appeals [c15 from Old French *galerie*, from Medieval Latin *galeria*, probably from *galilea* GALILEE]

gallery forest *n* a stretch of forest along a river in an area of otherwise open country

gallery tray *n* a tray usually of silver with a raised rim, used for serving drinks

galley (ˈɡælɪ) *n* **1** any of various kinds of ship propelled by oars or sails used in ancient or medieval times as a warship or as a trader **2** the kitchen of a ship, boat, or aircraft **3** any of various long rowing boats **4** *printing* **a** (in hot-metal composition) a tray open at one end for holding composed type **b** short for **galley proof** [c13 from Old French *galie*, from Medieval Latin *galea*, from Greek *galaia*, of unknown origin; the sense development apparently is due to the association of a galley or slave ship with a ship's kitchen and hence with a hot furnace, trough, printer's tray, etc]

galley proof *n* a printer's proof, esp one taken on a long strip of paper from type in a galley, used to make corrections before the matter has been split into pages. Often shortened to: **galley**

galley slave *n* **1** a criminal or slave condemned to row in a galley **2** *informal* a drudge

galley-west *adv slang*, *chiefly US* into confusion, inaction, or unconsciousness (esp in the phrase **knock (someone** *or* **something) galley-west**) [c19 from English dialect *colly-west* awry, perhaps from *Collyweston*, a village in Northamptonshire]

gallfly (ˈɡɔːlˌflaɪ) *n*, *pl* **-flies** any of several small insects that produce galls in plant tissues, such as the gall wasp and gall midge

Gallia (ˈɡælɪə) *n* the Latin name for **Gaul**

galliambic (ˌɡælɪˈæmbɪk) *prosody* ▷ *adj* **1** of or relating to a metre consisting of four lesser Ionics, used by Callimachus and Catullus and imitated by Tennyson in *Boadicea* ▷ *n* **2** a verse in this metre [c19 from Latin *galliambus* song of the *Galli* (priests of Cybele)]

galliard (ˈɡæljəd) *n* **1** a spirited dance in triple time for two persons, popular in the 16th and 17th centuries **2** a piece of music composed for this dance ▷ *adj* **3** *archaic* lively; spirited [c14 from Old French *gaillard* valiant, perhaps of Celtic origin]

gallic¹ (ˈɡælɪk) *adj* of or containing gallium in the trivalent state [c18 from GALL(IUM) + -IC]

gallic² (ˈɡælɪk) *adj* of, relating to, or derived from plant galls [c18 from French *gallique*; see GALL³]

Gallic (ˈɡælɪk) *adj* **1** of or relating to France **2** of or relating to ancient Gaul or the Gauls

gallic acid *n* a colourless crystalline compound obtained from tannin: used as a tanning agent and in making inks, paper, and pyrogallol; 3,4,5-trihydroxybenzoic acid. Formula: $C_6H_2(OH)_3COOH$

Gallican (ˈɡælɪkən) *adj* **1** of or relating to Gallicanism ▷ *n* **2** an upholder of Gallicanism

Gallicanism (ˈɡælɪkəˌnɪzəm) *n* a movement among French Roman Catholic clergy that favoured the restriction of papal control and greater autonomy for the French church. Compare ultramontanism

Gallice (ˈɡælɪsɪ) *adv* in French [c19 from Latin]

Gallicism (ˈɡælɪˌsɪzəm) *n* a word or idiom borrowed from French

Gallicize *or* **Gallicise** (ˈɡælɪˌsaɪz) *vb* to make or become French in attitude, language, etc > ˌGallici'zation *or* ˌGallici'sation *n* > 'Galliˌcizer *or* 'Galliˌciser *n*

galligaskins or **gallygaskins** (ˌgælɪˈgæskɪnz) pl n **1** loose wide breeches or hose, esp as worn by men in the 17th century **2** leather leggings, as worn in the 19th century [C16 from obsolete French *garguesques,* from Italian *grechesco* Greek, from Latin *Graecus*]

gallimaufry (ˌgælɪˈmɔːfrɪ) n, pl -fries a jumble; hotchpotch [C16 from French *galimafrée* ragout, hash, of unknown origin]

gallinacean (ˌgælɪˈneɪʃən) n any gallinaceous bird

gallinaceous (ˌgælɪˈneɪʃəs) adj **1** of, relating to, or belonging to the *Galliformes,* an order of birds, including domestic fowl, pheasants, grouse, etc, having a heavy rounded body, short bill, and strong legs **2** of, relating to, or resembling the domestic fowl [C18 from Latin *gallīnāceus,* from *gallīna* hen]

Gallinas Point (gɑːˈjiːnəs) n a cape in NE Colombia: the northernmost point of South America. Spanish name: **Punta Gallinas** (ˈpunta gaˈʎinas)

galling (ˈgɔːlɪŋ) adj **1** irritating, exasperating, or bitterly humiliating **2** obsolete rubbing painfully; chafing > **gallingly** adv

gallinule (ˈgælɪˌnjuːl) n **1** any of various aquatic birds of the genera *Porphyrio* and *Porphyrula,* typically having a dark plumage, red bill, and a red shield above the bill: family *Rallidae* (rails) **2** common gallinule the US name for **moorhen** (sense 1) [C18 from New Latin *Gallīnula* genus name, from Late Latin: pullet, chicken, from Latin *gallīna* hen]

galliot (ˈgælɪət) n a variant spelling of **galiot**

Gallipoli (gəˈlɪpəlɪ) n **1** a peninsula in NW Turkey, between the Dardanelles and the Gulf of Saros: scene of a costly but unsuccessful Allied campaign in 1915 **2** a port in NW Turkey, at the entrance to the Sea of Marmara: historically important for its strategic position. Pop: 16 751 (latest est). Turkish name: **Gelibolu**

gallipot[1] (ˈgælɪˌpɒt) n a small earthenware pot used by pharmacists as a container for ointments, etc [C16 probably from GALLEY + POT[1]; so called because imported in galleys]

gallipot[2] (ˈgælɪˌpɒt) n a variant spelling of **galipot**

gallium (ˈgælɪəm) n a silvery metallic element that is liquid for a wide temperature range. It occurs in trace amounts in some ores and is used in high-temperature thermometers and low-melting alloys. **Gallium arsenide** is a semiconductor. Symbol: Ga; atomic no.: 31; atomic wt.: 69.723; valency: 2 or 3; relative density: 5.904; melting pt.: 29.77°C; boiling pt.: 2205°C [C19 from New Latin, from Latin *gallus* cock, translation of French *coq* in the name of its discoverer, Lecoq de Boisbaudran, 19th-century French chemist]

gallivant, galivant or **galavant** (ˈgælɪˌvænt) vb (intr) to go about in search of pleasure; gad about [C19 perhaps whimsical modification of GALLANT]

Gällivare (Swedish ˈjɛliːvaːrə) n a town in N Sweden, within the Arctic Circle: iron mines. Pop: 19 191 (2004 est)

galliwasp (ˈgælɪˌwɒsp) n any lizard of the Central American genus *Diploglossus,* esp *D. monotropis* of the Caribbean: family *Anguidae* [C18 of unknown origin]

gall midge n any of various small fragile mosquito-like dipterous flies constituting the widely distributed family *Cecidomyidae,* many of which have larvae that produce galls on plants. Also called: **gallfly, gall gnat** See also **Hessian fly**

gall mite n any of various plant-feeding mites of the family *Phytoptidae* that cause galls or blisters on buds, leaves, or fruit

gallnut (ˈgɔːlˌnʌt) or **gall-apple** n a type of plant gall that resembles a nut

Gallo- (ˈgæləʊ) combining form indicating Gaul or France: *Gallo-Roman* [from Latin *Gallus* a Gaul]

gallock (ˈgælək) adj Northern English dialect **1** left-handed **2** left-handed

galloglass or **gallowglass** (ˈgæləʊˌglɑːs) n a heavily armed mercenary soldier, originally Hebridean (Gaelic-Norse), maintained by Irish and some other Celtic chiefs from about 1235 to the 16th century [C16 from Irish Gaelic *gallóglach,* from *gall* foreigner + *óglach,* young warrior-servant, from *og* young + *-lach* a noun suffix]

gallon (ˈgælən) n Also called: **imperial gallon** Brit a unit of capacity equal to 277.42 cubic inches. 1 Brit gallon is equivalent to 1.20 US gallons or 4.55 litres **2** US a unit of capacity equal to 231 cubic inches. 1 US gallon is equivalent to 0.83 imperial gallon or 3.79 litres [C13 from Old Northern French *galon* (Old French *jalon*), perhaps of Celtic origin]

gallonage (ˈgælənɪdʒ) n **1** a capacity measured in gallons **2** the rate of pumping, transmission, or consumption of a fluid in gallons per unit of time

galloon (gəˈluːn) n a narrow band of cord, embroidery, silver or gold braid, etc, used on clothes and furniture [C17 from French *galon,* from Old French *galonner* to trim with braid, of unknown origin] > **gal'looned** adj

galloot (gəˈluːt) n a variant spelling of **galoot**

gallop (ˈgæləp) vb **-lops, -loping, -loped 1** (intr) (of a horse or other quadruped) to run fast with a two-beat stride in which all four legs are off the ground at once **2** to ride (a horse, etc) at a gallop **3** (intr) to move, read, talk, etc, rapidly; hurry ▷ n **4** the fast two-beat gait of horses and other quadrupeds **5** an instance of galloping [C16 from Old French *galoper,* of uncertain origin] > **'galloper** n

gallopade or **galopade** (ˌgæləˈpeɪd) n another word for **galop**

galloping (ˈgæləpɪŋ) adj (prenominal) progressing at or as if at a gallop: *galloping consumption*

Gallo-Romance or **Gallo-Roman** n **1** the vernacular language or group of dialects, of which few records survive, spoken in France between about 600 AD and 900 AD; the intermediate stage between Vulgar Latin and Old French ▷ adj **2** denoting or relating to this language or the period during which it was spoken

gallous (ˈgæləs) adj of or containing gallium in the divalent state

Gallovidian (ˌgæləʊˈvɪdɪən) n **1** a native or inhabitant of Galloway ▷ adj **2** of or relating to Galloway ▷ Also: **Galwegian**

Galloway (ˈgæləˌweɪ) n **1** an area of SW Scotland, on the Solway Firth: consists of the former counties of Kirkcudbright and Wigtown, now part of Dumfries and Galloway, in the west is a large peninsula, the **Rhinns of Galloway,** with the **Mull of Galloway,** a promontory, at the south end of it (the southernmost point of Scotland). Related adjs: **Gallovidian, Galwegian 2** a breed of hardy beef cattle, usually black, originally bred in Galloway

gallows (ˈgæləʊz) n, pl **-lowses** or **-lows 1** a wooden structure usually consisting of two upright posts with a crossbeam from which a rope is suspended, used for hanging criminals **2** any timber structure resembling this, such as (in Australia and New Zealand) a frame for hoisting up the bodies of slaughtered cattle **3** the gallows execution by hanging [C13 from Old Norse *galgi,* replacing Old English *gealga;* related to Old High German *galgo*]

gallows bird n informal a person considered deserving of hanging

gallows humour n sinister and ironic humour

gallows tree or **gallow tree** n another name for **gallows** (sense 1)

gallsickness (ˈgɔːlˌsɪknɪs) n a disease of cattle and sheep, caused by infection with rickettsiae of the genus *Anaplasma,* resulting in anaemia and jaundice. Also called: **anaplasmosis**

gallstone (ˈgɔːlˌstəʊn) n pathol a small hard concretion of cholesterol, bile pigments, and lime salts, formed in the gall bladder or its ducts. Also called: **bilestone**

Gallup Poll (ˈgæləp) n a sampling by the American Institute of Public Opinion or its British counterpart of the views of a representative cross section of the population, used esp as a means of forecasting voting [C20 named after George Horace Gallop (1901–84), US statistician]

gallus (ˈgæləs) adj Scot bold; daring; reckless [a variant of *gallows* used as an adjective, meaning fit for the gallows]

galluses (ˈgæləsɪz) pl n dialect braces for trousers [C18 variant spelling of *gallowses,* from GALLOWS (in the obsolete sense: braces)]

gall wasp n any small solitary wasp of the family *Cynipidae* and related families that produces galls in plant tissue, which provide shelter and food for the larvae

Galois theory (ˈgælwɑː) n maths the theory applying group theory to solving algebraic equations [C19 named after Évariste *Galois* (1811–32), French mathematician]

galoot or **galloot** (gəˈluːt) n slang, chiefly US a clumsy or uncouth person [C19 of unknown origin]

galop (ˈgæləp) n **1** a 19th-century couple dance in quick duple time **2** a piece of music composed for this dance ▷ Also called: **gallopade** [C19 from French; see GALLOP]

galore (gəˈlɔː) determiner (immediately postpositive) in great numbers or quantity: *there were daffodils galore in the park* [C17 from Irish Gaelic *go leór* to sufficiency]

galoshes or **goloshes** (gəˈlɒʃɪz) pl n (sometimes singular) a pair of waterproof overshoes [C14 (in the sense: wooden shoe): from Old French *galoche,* from Late Latin *gallicula* Gallic shoe]

gal pal n informal **1** a female friend **2** a lesbian lover

galtonia (gɔːlˈtəʊnɪə) n any plant of the bulbous genus *Galtonia,* esp *G. candicans,* with lanceolate leaves, drooping racemes of waxy white flowers, and a fragrant scent: family *Liliaceae* [named after Sir Francis *Galton* (1822–1911), English explorer and scientist]

galumph (gəˈlʌmpf, -ˈlʌmf) vb (intr) informal to leap or move about clumsily or joyfully [C19 (coined by Lewis Carroll): probably a blend of GALLOP + TRIUMPH]

galvanic (gælˈvænɪk) or **galvanical** adj **1** Also: **voltaic** of, producing, or concerned with an electric current, esp a direct current produced chemically: *a galvanic cell* **2** informal resembling the effect of an electric shock; convulsive, startling, or energetic: *galvanic reflexes* > **gal'vanically** adv

galvanic pile n another name for **voltaic pile**

galvanic skin response n a change in the electrical resistance of the skin occurring in moments of strong emotion; measurements of this change are used in lie detector tests. Abbreviation: **GSR**

galvanism (ˈgælvəˌnɪzəm) n **1** obsolete electricity, esp when produced by chemical means as in a cell or battery **2** med treatment involving the application of electric currents to tissues [C18 via French from Italian *galvanismo,* after Luigi Galvani (1737–98), Italian physiologist]

galvanize or **galvanise** (ˈgælvəˌnaɪz) vb (tr) **1** to stimulate to action; excite; startle **2** to cover (iron, steel, etc) with a protective zinc coating by dipping into molten zinc or by electrodeposition **3** to stimulate by application of an electric current ▷ n **4** Caribbean galvanized iron, usually in the form of corrugated sheets as used in roofing > ˌgalvani'zation or ˌgalvani'sation n > 'galvaˌnizer or 'galvaˌniser n

galvanized iron or **galvanised iron** n building trades iron, esp a sheet of corrugated iron, covered with a protective coating of zinc

galvano- combining form indicating a galvanic current: *galvanometer*

galvanometer (ˌgælvəˈnɒmɪtə) n any sensitive instrument for detecting or measuring small electric currents > galvanometric (ˌgælvənəʊˈmɛtrɪk, gæl,vænə-) or ˌgalvano'metrical adj > ˌgalvano'metrically adv > ˌgalva'nometry n

g

galvanoscope ('gælvənə,skəup, gæl'vænə-) *n* a galvanometer that depends for its action on the deflection of a magnetic needle in a magnetic field produced by the electric current that is to be detected > **galvanoscopic** (,gælvənə'skɒpɪk, gæl,vænə-) *adj* > **galva'noscopy** *n*

galvanotropism (,gælvə'nɒtrə,pɪzəm) *n* the directional growth of an organism, esp a plant, in response to an electrical stimulus > **galvanotropic** (,gælvənəu'trɒpɪk, gæl,vænəu-) *adj*

Galveston plan ('gælvɪstən) *n* another term for **commission plan**

galvo ('gælvəu) *n, pl* **-vos** an informal name for a galvanometer

Galway ('gɔːlweɪ) *n* **1** a county of W Republic of Ireland, in S Connacht, on **Galway Bay** and the Atlantic: it has a deeply indented coastline and many offshore islands, including the Aran Islands. County town: Galway. Pop: 209 077 (2002). Area: 5939 sq km (2293 sq miles) **2** a port in W Republic of Ireland, county town of Co Galway, on Galway Bay: important fisheries (esp for salmon). Pop: 66 163 (2002) **3** *Former name:* Roscommon a breed of sheep with long wool, originally from W Ireland

Galwegian (gæl'wiːdʒən) *n* **1** another word for **Gallovidian** (sense 1) **2** a native or inhabitant of the town or county of Galway in W Republic of Ireland ▷ *adj* **3** another word for **Gallovidian** (sense 2) [c18 influenced by *Norway, Norwegian*]

galyak *or* **galyac** ('gæljæk, gæl'jæk) *n* a smooth glossy fur obtained from the skins of newborn or premature lambs and kids [from Russian (Uzbek dialect)]

gam¹ (gæm) *n* **1** a school of whales **2** *nautical* an informal visit between crew members of whalers **3** *NZ* a flock of large sea birds ▷ *vb* **gams, gamming, gammed 4** (*intr*) (of whales) to form a school **5** *nautical* (of members of the crews of whalers) to visit (each other) informally **6** (*tr*) *US* to visit or exchange visits with [c19 perhaps dialect variant of GAME¹]

gam² (gæm) *n* *slang* a leg, esp a woman's shapely leg [c18 probably from Old Northern French *gambe* or Lingua Franca *gambe*; see JAMB]

gama grass ('gɑːmə) *n* a tall perennial grass, *Tripsacum dactyloides*, of SE North America: cultivated for fodder [c19 *gama*, probably changed from GRAMA]

gamahuche ('gæmə,huːʃ) *or* **gamaruche** ('gæmə,ruːʃ) *taboo* ▷ *vb* (*tr*) **1** to practise cunnilingus or fellatio on ▷ *n* **2** cunnilingus or fellatio [c19 from French *gamahucher*]

gamba ('gæmbə) *n* short for **viola da gamba**

gambado¹ (gæm'beɪdəu) *n, pl* **-dos** *or* **-does 1** either of two leather holders for the feet attached to a horse's saddle like stirrups **2** either of a pair of leggings [c17 from Italian *gamba* leg, from Late Latin: leg, hoof; see JAMB]

gambado² (gæm'beɪdəu), **gambade** (gæm'beɪd, -'bɑːd) *n, pl* **-bados, -badoes** *or* **-bades 1** *dressage* another word for **curvet 2** a leap or gambol; caper [c19 from French *gambade* spring (of a horse), ultimately from Spanish or Italian *gamba* leg]

gamba stop *n* an organ stop with a tone resembling that of stringed instruments

gambeson ('gæmbɪsᵊn) *n* a quilted and padded or stuffed leather or cloth garment worn under chain mail in the Middle Ages and later as a doublet by men and women [c13 from Old French, of Germanic origin; related to Old High German *wamba* belly; see WOMB]

Gambia ('gæmbɪə) *n* **The** a republic in W Africa, entirely surrounded by Senegal except for an outlet to the Atlantic: sold to English merchants by the Portuguese in 1588; became a British colony in 1843; gained independence and became a member of the Commonwealth in 1965; joined with Senegal to form the Confederation of Senegambia (1982–89); consists of a strip of land about 16 km (10 miles) wide, on both banks of the **Gambia River**, extending inland for about 480 km

(300 miles). Official language: English. Religion: Muslim majority. Currency: dalasi. Capital: Banjul. Pop: 1 462 000 (2004 est). Area: 11 295 sq km (4361 sq miles)

Gambian ('gæmbɪən) *adj* **1** of or relating to Gambia or its inhabitants ▷ *n* **2** a native or inhabitant of Gambia

gambier *or* **gambir** ('gæmbɪə) *n* an astringent resinous substance obtained from a rubiaceous tropical Asian woody climbing plant, *Uncaria gambir* (or *U. gambier*): used as an astringent and tonic and in tanning [c19 from Malay]

Gambier Islands ('gæmbɪə) *pl n* a group of islands in the S Pacific Ocean, in French Polynesia. Chief settlement: Rikitéa. Pop: 1097 (2002). Area: 30 sq km (11 sq miles)

gambit ('gæmbɪt) *n* **1** *chess* an opening move in which a chessman, usually a pawn, is sacrificed to secure an advantageous position **2** an opening comment, manoeuvre, etc, intended to secure an advantage or promote a point of view [c17 from French, from Italian *gambetto* a tripping up, from *gamba* leg]

gamble ('gæmbᵊl) *vb* **1** (*intr*) to play games of chance to win money **2** to risk or bet (money) on the outcome of an event, sport, etc **3** (*intr; often foll by on*) to act with the expectation of: *to gamble on its being a sunny day* **4** (*often foll by away*) to lose by or as if by betting; squander ▷ *n* **5** a risky act or venture **6** a bet, wager, or other risk or chance taken for possible monetary gain [c18 probably variant of GAME¹] > **gambler** *n* > **gambling** *n*

gamblers' fallacy *n* *psychol* the fallacy that in a series of chance events the probability of one event occurring increases with the number of times another event has occurred in succession

gamboge (gæm'bəudʒ, -'buːʒ) *n* **1 a** a gum resin used as the source of a yellow pigment and as a purgative **b** the pigment made from this resin **2 gamboge tree** any of several tropical Asian trees of the genus *Garcinia*, esp *G. hanburyi*, that yield this resin: family *Clusiaceae* **3** a strong yellow colour ▷ *Also called (for senses 1, 2):* **cambogia** [c18 from New Latin *gambaugium*, from CAMBODIA] > **gam'bogian** *adj*

gambol ('gæmbᵊl) *vb* **-bols, -bolling, -bolled** *or US* **-bols, -boling, -boled 1** (*intr*) to skip or jump about in a playful manner; frolic ▷ *n* **2** a playful antic; frolic [c16 from French *gambade*; see GAMBADO², JAMB]

gambrel ('gæmbrəl) *n* **1** the hock of a horse or similar animal **2** a frame of wood or metal shaped like a horse's hind leg, used by butchers for suspending carcasses of meat **3** short for **gambrel roof** [c16 from Old Northern French *gamberel*, from *gambe* leg]

gambrel roof *n* **1** *chiefly Brit* a hipped roof having a small gable at both ends **2** *chiefly US and Canadian* a roof having two slopes on both sides, the lower slopes being steeper than the upper. Compare **mansard** (sense 1) ▷ *Sometimes shortened to:* **gambrel** > **'gambrel-,roofed** *adj*

Gambrinus (gæm'braɪnəs) *n* a legendary Flemish king who was said to have invented beer

game¹ (geɪm) *n* **1** an amusement or pastime; diversion **2** a contest with rules, the result being determined by skill, strength, or chance **3** a single period of play in such a contest, sport, etc **4** the score needed to win a contest **5** a single contest in a series; match **6** (*plural; often capital*) an event consisting of various sporting contests, esp in athletics: *Olympic Games; Highland Games* **7** equipment needed for playing certain games **8** short for **computer game 9** style or ability in playing a game: *he is a keen player but his game is not good* **10** a scheme, proceeding, etc, practised like a game: *the game of politics* **11** an activity undertaken in a spirit of levity; joke: *marriage is just a game to him* **12 a** wild animals, including birds and fish, hunted for sport, food, or profit **b** (*as modifier*): *game laws* **13** the flesh of such animals, used as food: generally taken not to include fish **14** an

object of pursuit; quarry; prey (esp in the phrase **fair game**) **15** *informal* work or occupation **16** *informal* a trick, strategy, or device: *I can see through your little game* **17** *obsolete* pluck or courage; bravery **18** *slang, chiefly Brit* prostitution (esp in the phrase **on the game**) **19 give the game away** to reveal one's intentions or a secret **20 make (a) game of** to make fun of; ridicule; mock **21 on (or off) one's game** playing well (or badly) **22 play the game** to behave fairly or in accordance with rules **23 the game is up** there is no longer a chance of success ▷ *adj* **24** *informal* full of fighting spirit; plucky; brave **25 (as) game as Ned Kelly** *Austral informal* extremely brave; indomitable **26** (usually foll by *for*) *informal* prepared or ready; willing: *I'm game for a try* ▷ *vb* **27** (*intr*) to play games of chance for money, stakes, etc; gamble [Old English *gamen*; related to Old Norse *gaman*, Old High German *gaman* amusement] > **'game,like** *adj*

game² (geɪm) *adj* a less common word for **lame¹** (esp in the phrase **game leg**) [c18 probably from Irish *cam* crooked]

game-ball *adj* *Irish* **1** (of a person) in perfect health **2** (of an arrangement, plan, etc) excellent

game bird *n* a bird of any species hunted as game

gamebreaker ('geɪm,breɪkə) *n* a person who makes a significant contribution to a team's sporting success

game chips *pl n* round thin potato chips served with game

gamecock ('geɪm,kɒk) *n* a cock bred and trained for fighting. Also called: **fighting cock**

game fish *n* any fish providing sport for the angler

game fowl *n* any of several breeds of domestic fowl reared for cockfighting

gamekeeper ('geɪm,kiːpə) *n* a person employed to take care of game and wildlife, as on an estate > **'game,keeping** *n*

gamelan ('gæmɪ,læn) *n* a type of percussion orchestra common in the East Indies [from Javanese]

game laws *pl n* laws governing the hunting and preservation of game

gamely ('geɪmlɪ) *adv* in a brave or sporting manner

gameness ('geɪmnɪs) *n* courage or bravery; pluck

game park *n* (esp in Africa) a large area of country set aside as a reserve for wild animals

game plan *n* **1** a strategy **2** a plan of campaign, esp in politics

gameplay ('geɪm,pleɪ) *n* the plot of a computer or video game or the way that it is played

game point *n* *tennis, squash, badminton* a stage at which winning one further point would enable one player or side to win a game

gamer ('geɪmə) *n* a person who plays computer games or participates in a role-playing game

games console *n* an electronic device used in playing computer games on the screen of a television to which it is connected

gamesmanship ('geɪmzmən,ʃɪp) *n* *informal* the art of winning games or defeating opponents by clever or cunning practices without actually cheating > **'gamesman** *n*

gamesome ('geɪmsəm) *adj* full of merriment; sportive > **'gamesomely** *adv* > **'gamesomeness** *n*

gamester ('geɪmstə) *n* a person who habitually plays games for money; gambler

gametangium (,gæmɪ'tændʒɪəm) *n, pl* **-gia** (-dʒɪə) *biology* an organ or cell in which gametes are produced, esp in algae and fungi [c19 New Latin, from GAMETO- + Greek *angeion* vessel] > **,game'tangial** *adj*

gamete ('gæmiːt, gə'miːt) *n* a haploid germ cell, such as a spermatozoon or ovum, that fuses with another germ cell during fertilization [c19 from New Latin, from Greek *gametē* wife, from *gamos* marriage] > **ga'metal** *or* **gametic** (gə'mɛtɪk) *adj*

gamete intrafallopian transfer (,ɪntrəfə'ləupɪən) *n* the full name for GIFT

game theory *n* mathematical theory concerned

with the optimum choice of strategy in situations involving a conflict of interest. Also called: theory of games ▷ ˌgame-ˌtheoˈretic *adj*

gameto- *or sometimes before a vowel* **gamet-** *combining form* gamete: *gametocyte*

gametocyte (gəˈmiːtəʊˌsaɪt) *n* an animal or plant cell that develops into gametes by meiosis. See also **oocyte, spermatocyte**

gametogenesis (ˌgæmɪtəʊˈdʒɛnɪsɪs) *or* **gametogeny** (ˌgæmɪˈtɒdʒɪnɪ) *n* the formation and maturation of gametes. See also **spermatogenesis, oogenesis.** ▷ ˌgametoˈgenic *or* ˌgameˈtogenous *adj*

gametophore (gəˈmiːtəʊˌfɔː) *n* the part of a plant that bears the reproductive organs ▷ gaˌmetoˈphoric *adj*

gametophyte (gəˈmiːtəʊˌfaɪt) *n* the plant body, in species showing alternation of generations, that produces the gametes. Compare **sporophyte** ▷ gametophytic (ˌgæmɪtəʊˈfɪtɪk) *adj*

game warden *n* a person who looks after game, as in a game reserve

gamey *or* **gamy** (ˈgeɪmɪ) *adj* gamier, gamiest **1** having the smell or flavour of game, esp high game **2** *informal* spirited; plucky; brave ▷ ˈgamily *adv* ▷ ˈgaminess *n*

gamic (ˈgæmɪk) *adj* (esp of reproduction) requiring the fusion of gametes; sexual [C19 from Greek *gamikos* of marriage; see GAMETE]

gamin (ˈgæmɪn; *French* gamɛ̃) *n* a street urchin; waif [from French]

gamine (ˈgæmiːn; *French* gamin) *n* **a** a slim and boyish girl or young woman; an elfish tomboy **b** (*as modifier*): *a gamine style of haircut* [from French]

gaming (ˈgeɪmɪŋ) *n* **a** gambling on games of chance **b** (*as modifier*): *gaming house; gaming losses*

gamma (ˈgæmə) *n* **1** the third letter in the Greek alphabet (Γ, γ), a consonant, transliterated as *g*. When double, it is transcribed and pronounced as *ng* **2** the third highest grade or mark, as in an examination **3** a unit of magnetic field strength equal to 10^{-5} oersted. 1 gamma is equivalent to $0.795\,775 \times 10^{-3}$ ampere per metre **4** *photog, television* the numerical value of the slope of the characteristic curve of a photographic emulsion or television camera; a measure of the contrast reproduced in a photographic or television image **5** (*modifier*) **a** involving or relating to photons of very high energy: *a gamma detector* **b** relating to one of two or more allotropes or crystal structures of a solid: *gamma iron* **c** relating to one of two or more isomeric forms of a chemical compound, esp one in which a group is attached to the carbon atom next but one to the atom to which the principal group is attached [C14 from Greek; related to Hebrew *gīmel* third letter of the Hebrew alphabet (probably: camel)]

Gamma (ˈgæmə) *n* (*foll by the genitive case of a specified constellation*) the third brightest star in a constellation: *Gamma Leonis*

gamma-aminobutyric acid (ˌgæməəˌmiːnəʊbjuːˈtɪrɪk) *n* the full name for **GABA**

gamma camera *n* a medical apparatus that detects gamma rays emitted from a person's body after the administration of a radioactive drug and so produces images of the organ being investigated

gammadion (gæˈmeɪdɪən) *n, pl* -dia (-dɪə) a decorative figure composed of a number of Greek capital gammas, esp radiating from a centre, as in a swastika [C19 from Late Greek, literally: little GAMMA]

gamma distribution *n statistics* a continuous two-parameter distribution from which the chi-square and exponential distributions are derived, written Gamma (α. β), where α and β are greater than zero, and defined in terms of the gamma function

gamma function *n maths* a function defined by $\Gamma(x) = \int_0^\infty t^{x-1}e^{-t}dt$, where *x* is real and greater than zero

gamma globulin *n* any of a group of proteins in blood plasma that includes most known antibodies

gamma hydroxybutyrate (ˌgæməhaɪˌdrɒksɪˈbjuːtɪreɪt) *n* a substance that occurs naturally in the brain, used medically as a sedative but also as a recreational drug and alleged aphrodisiac: known as 'liquid ecstasy' when mixed with alcohol. Abbreviation: **GHB**

gamma iron *n* an allotrope of iron that is nonmagnetic and exists between 910°C and 1400°C

gamma knife *n* an machine that uses radiation with extreme accuracy to destroy abnormal tissue, esp in the brain

gamma radiation *n* **1** electromagnetic radiation emitted by atomic nuclei; the wavelength is generally in the range 1×10^{-10} to 2×10^{-13} metres **2** electromagnetic radiation of very short wavelength emitted by any source, esp the portion of the electromagnetic spectrum with a wavelength less than about 1×10^{-11} metres

gamma-ray astronomy *n* the investigation of cosmic gamma rays, such as those from quasars

gamma-ray burst *n astronomy* an intense but short-lived burst of gamma rays from an unknown celestial source. First detected in 1970, they have since been found to be widely distributed in the sky

gamma rays *pl n* streams of gamma radiation

gamma stock *n* any of the third rank of active securities on the London Stock Exchange. Prices displayed by market makers are given as an indication rather than an offer to buy or sell

gammat (xamat) *n South African derogatory* a reference to the accent of Cape Coloured people [C20 corruption of *Achmet*, a common Arabic name]

gammer (ˈgæmə) *n rare, chiefly Brit* a dialect word for an old woman: now chiefly humorous or contemptuous. Compare **gaffer** (sense 1) [C16 probably alteration of GODMOTHER or GRANDMOTHER]

gammon¹ (ˈgæmən) *n* **1** a cured or smoked ham **2** the hindquarter of a side of bacon, cooked either whole or cut into large rashers [C15 from Old Northern French *gambon*, from *gambe* leg; see GAMBREL]

gammon² (ˈgæmən) *n* **1** a double victory in backgammon in which one player throws off all his pieces before his opponent throws any **2** *archaic* the game of backgammon ▷ *vb* **3** (*tr*) to score a gammon over [C18 probably special use of Middle English *gamen* GAME¹]

gammon³ (ˈgæmən) *Brit informal* ▷ *n* **1** deceitful nonsense; humbug ▷ *vb* **2** to deceive (a person) [C18 perhaps special use of GAMMON²] ▷ ˈgammoner *n*

gammon⁴ (ˈgæmən) *vb* (*tr*) *nautical* to fix (a bowsprit) to the stemhead of a vessel [C18 perhaps related to GAMMON¹, with reference to the tying up of a ham]

gammy (ˈgæmɪ) *adj* -mier, -miest *Brit slang* (esp of the leg) malfunctioning, injured, or lame; game. US equivalent: **gimpy** [C19 from Shelta *gyamyath* bad, altered form of Irish *cam* crooked; see GAME²]

gamo- *or before a vowel* **gam-** *combining form* **1** indicating sexual union or reproduction: *gamogenesis* **2** united or fused: *gamopetalous* [from Greek *gamos* marriage]

gamogenesis (ˌgæməʊˈdʒɛnɪsɪs) *n* another name for **sexual reproduction.** ▷ gamogenetic (ˌgæməʊdʒɪˈnɛtɪk) *or* ˌgamoˈgenetical *adj* ▷ ˌgamoˈgenetically *adv*

gamone (ˈgæməʊn) *n botany* any chemical substance secreted by a gamete that attracts another gamete during sexual reproduction

gamopetalous (ˌgæməʊˈpɛtələs) *adj* (of flowers) having petals that are united or partly united, as the primrose. Also: **sympetalous** Compare **polypetalous**

gamophyllous (ˌgæməʊˈfɪləs) *adj* (of flowers) having united leaves or perianth segments

gamosepalous (ˌgæməʊˈsɛpələs) *adj* (of flowers) having united or partly united sepals, as the primrose. Compare **polysepalous**

-gamous *adj combining form* denoting marrying or uniting sexually: *monogamous* [from Greek *gamos*; see -GAMY]

gamp (gæmp) *n Brit informal* an umbrella [C19 after Mrs Sarah *Gamp*, a nurse in Dickens' *Martin Chuzzlewit*, who carried a faded cotton umbrella]

gamut (ˈgæmət) *n* **1** entire range or scale, as of emotions **2** *music* **a** a scale, esp (in medieval theory) one starting on the G on the bottom line of the bass staff **b** the whole range of notes **3** *physics* the range of chromaticities that can be obtained by mixing three colours [C15 from Medieval Latin, changed from *gamma ut*, from *gamma*, the lowest note of the hexachord as established by Guido d'Arezzo + *ut* (now, *doh*), the first of the notes of the scale *ut, re, mi, fa, sol, la, si,* derived from a Latin hymn to St John: *Ut queant laxis resonare fibris, Mira gestorum famuli tuorum, Solve polluti labi reatum, Sancte Iohannes*]

-gamy *n combining form* denoting marriage or sexual union: *bigamy* [from Greek -*gamia*, from *gamos* marriage]

gan¹ (gæn) *vb archaic or poetic* the past tense of **gin³**

gan² (gæn) *vb* **gans, ganning, ganned** (*intr*) *Northeast English dialect* to go [from Old English *gangan*; related to Old Norse *ganga*. See GANG¹]

ganache (gəˈnæʃ) *n* a smooth mixture of chocolate and cream, used in cakes, truffles, and chocolates [C20 from French]

Gäncä (ˈganʒə) *n* a variant transliteration of the Azerbaijani name for **Gandzha**

Gand (gɑ̃) *n* the French name for **Ghent**

Ganda (ˈgændə) *n* **1** (*pl* -das *or* -da) a member of the Buganda people of Uganda, whose kingdom was formerly the largest in E Africa. See also **Luganda 2** the Luganda language of this people

gander (ˈgændə) *n* **1** a male goose **2** *informal* a quick look (esp in the phrase **take** (*or* **have**) **a gander**) **3** *informal* a simpleton [Old English *gandra, ganra*; related to Low German and Dutch *gander* and to GANNET]

Gandhian (ˈgændɪən) *adj* **1** of or relating to Mohandas Karamchand Gandhi (1869–1948), the Indian political and spiritual leader and social reformer, or his ideas ▷ *n* **2** a follower of Gandhi or his ideas

Gandhi cap *n* a cap made with white hand-woven cloth worn by some men in India

Gandhiism (ˈgændɪˌɪzəm) *or* **Gandhism** (ˈgændɪzəm) *n* the political principles of M. K. Gandhi, the Indian political and spiritual leader and social reformer (1869–1948), esp civil disobedience and passive resistance as means of achieving reform

gandy dancer (ˈgændɪ) *n slang* a railway track maintenance worker [C20 of uncertain origin]

Gandzha (*Russian* gan'dʒa) *or* **Gäncä** *n* a city in NW Azerbaijan: annexed by the Russians in 1804; centre of a cotton-growing region. Pop: 314 000 (2005 est). Former names: Yelisavetpol (1813–1920), Kirovabad (1936–91)

gane (gen) *vb* the past participle of **gae**

ganef, ganev, ganof (ˈgɑːnəf) *or* **gonif, gonof** *n slang* an unscrupulous opportunist who stoops to sharp practice [from Yiddish, from Hebrew *gannābh* thief, from *gānnabh* he stole]

Ganesh (gæˈniːʃ) *n* the Hindu god of prophecy, represented as having an elephant's head

gang¹ (gæŋ) *n* **1** a group of people who associate together or act as an organized body, esp for criminal or illegal purposes **2** an organized group of workmen **3** a herd of buffaloes or elks or a pack of wild dogs **4** *NZ* a group of shearers who travel to different shearing sheds, shearing, classing, and baling wool **5 a** a series of similar tools arranged to work simultaneously in parallel **b** (*as modifier*): *a gang saw* ▷ *vb* **6** to form into, become part of, or act as a gang **7** (*tr*) *electronics* to mount

g

(two or more components, such as variable capacitors) on the same shaft, permitting adjustment by a single control ▷ See also **gang up** [Old English *gang* journey; related to Old Norse *gangr*, Old High German *gang*, Sanskrit *jangha* foot] > **ganged** *adj*

gang² (gæŋ) *vb Scot* to go [Old English *gangan* to GO¹]

gang³ (gæŋ) *n* a variant spelling of **gangue**

Ganga jal ('gʌŋgə 'dʒʌl) *n* sacred water from the River Ganges in India [Hindi, from *Ganga* GANGES + *jal* water]

gangbang ('gæŋ,bæŋ) *slang* ▷ *n* **1** an instance of sexual intercourse between one woman and several men one after the other, esp against her will ▷ *vb* **2** (*tr*) to force (a woman) to take part in a gangbang **3** (*intr*) to take part in a gangbang ▷ Also called: **gangshag** ('gæŋ,ʃæg)

gang-banger *n US slang* a member of a street gang > **'gang-,banging** *n*

ganger ('gæŋə) *n chiefly Brit* the foreman of a gang of labourers

Ganges ('gændʒi:z) *n* the great river of N India and central Bangladesh: rises in two headstreams in the Himalayas and flows southeast to Allahabad, where it is joined by the Jumna; continues southeast into Bangladesh, where it enters the Bay of Bengal in a great delta; the most sacred river to Hindus, with many places of pilgrimage, esp Varanasi. Length: 2507 km (1557 miles). Hindi name: **Ganga** ('gʌŋgə, 'gɑːŋ-)

Gangetic (gæn'dʒɛtɪk) *adj* of or relating to the river Ganges

gang-gang ('gæŋ,gæŋ) *n* a small black cockatoo, *Callocephalon fimbriatum*, of SE Australia, the male of which has a scarlet head [c19 from a native Australian language]

gangland ('gæŋ,lænd, -lənd) *n* the criminal underworld

gangling ('gæŋglɪŋ) *or* **gangly** ('gæŋglɪ) *adj* tall, lanky, and awkward in movement [perhaps related to GANGREL; see GANG²]

ganglion ('gæŋglɪən) *n, pl* -glia (-glɪə) *or* -glions **1** an encapsulated collection of nerve-cell bodies, usually located outside the brain and spinal cord **2** any concentration of energy, activity, or strength **3** a cystic tumour on a tendon sheath or joint capsule [c17 from Late Latin: swelling, from Greek: cystic tumour] > **'ganglial** *or* **'gangliar** *adj* > ,**gangli'onic** *or* **'gangli,ated** *adj*

Gangnail ('gæŋ,neɪl) *n trademark* a particular arrangement of nails on a metal plate, used as a connecting piece in strong timber joints

Gang of Four *n* **the** a radical faction within the Chinese Communist Party that emerged as a political force in the spring of 1976 and was suppressed later that year. Its members, Zhang Chunqiao, Wang Hongwen, Yao Wenyuan, and Jiang Qing, were tried and imprisoned (1981)

gangplank ('gæŋ,plæŋk) *or* **gangway** *n nautical* a portable bridge for boarding and leaving a vessel at dockside

gang plough *n* a plough having two or more shares, coulters, and mouldboards designed to work simultaneously

gangrel ('gæŋgrəl, 'gæŋrəl) *n Scot archaic or literary* **1** a wandering beggar **2** a child just able to walk; toddler [c16 from Old English *gangan* to GO¹]

gangrene ('gæŋgri:n) *n* **1** death and decay of tissue as the result of interrupted blood supply, disease, or injury **2** moral decay or corruption ▷ *vb* **3** to become or cause to become affected with gangrene [c16 from Latin *gangraena*, from Greek *gangraina* an eating sore; related to Greek *gran* to gnaw] > **gangrenous** ('gæŋgrɪnəs) *adj*

gang saw *n* a saw having several parallel blades making simultaneous cuts > **gang sawyer** *n*

gangsta rap ('gæŋstə) *n* a style of rap music, usually characterized by lyrics about Black street gangs in the US, often with violent, nihilistic, and misogynistic themes [c20 phonetic rendering of GANGSTER] > **gangsta rapper** *n*

gangster ('gæŋstə) *n* a member of an organized gang of criminals, esp one who resorts to violence

gangster chic *n* a cinematic or literary genre which seeks to glamorize the criminal underworld

gangsterism ('gæŋstə,rɪzəm) *n* the culture of belonging to organized gangs of criminals, esp involving violence

Gangtok ('gʌŋtɒk) *n* a town in NE India: capital of Sikkim state. Pop: 29 162 (2001)

gangue *or* **gang** (gæŋ) *n* valueless and undesirable material, such as quartz in small quantities, in an ore [c19 from French *gangue*, from German *Gang* vein of metal, course; see GANG¹]

gang up *vb* (often foll by *on* or *against*) *informal* to combine in a group (against)

gangway ('gæŋ,weɪ) *n* **1** an opening in a ship's side to take a gangplank **2** another word for **gangplank 3** *Brit* an aisle between rows of seats **4** Also called: **logway** *chiefly US* a ramp for logs leading into a sawmill **5** a main passage in a mine **6** temporary planks over mud or earth, as on a building site ▷ *sentence substitute* **7** clear a path!

ganister *or* **gannister** ('gænɪstə) *n* **1** a highly refractory siliceous sedimentary rock occurring beneath coal seams: used for lining furnaces **2** a similar material synthesized from ground quartz and fireclay [c19 of unknown origin]

ganja ('gɑːndʒə) *n* a highly potent form of cannabis, usually used for smoking [from Hindi *gājā*, from Sanskrit *grñja*]

gannet ('gænɪt) *n* **1** any of several heavily built marine birds of the genus *Morus* (or *Sula*), having a long stout bill and typically white plumage with dark markings: family *Sulidae*, order *Pelecaniformes* (pelicans, cormorants, etc). See also **booby** (sense 3) **2** *slang* a gluttonous or greedy person [Old English *ganot*; related to Old High German *gannazzo* gander]

ganof ('gɑːnəf) *n* a variant spelling of **ganef**

ganoid ('gænɔɪd) *adj* **1** (of the scales of certain fishes) consisting of an inner bony layer and an outer layer of an enamel-like substance (ganoin) **2** denoting fishes, including the sturgeon and bowfin, having such scales ▷ *n* **3** a ganoid fish [c19 from French *ganoïde*, from Greek *ganos* brightness + -OID]

gansey ('gænzɪ) *n dialect* a jersey or pullover [from the island of GUERNSEY]

Gansu ('gæn'su:) *or* **Kansu** *n* a province of NW China, between Tibet and Inner Mongolia: mountainous, with desert regions; forms a corridor, the Old Silk Road, much used in early and medieval times for trade with Turkestan, India, and Persia. Capital: Lanzhou. Pop: 26 030 000 (2003 est). Area: 366 500 sq km (141 500 sq miles)

gantlet¹ ('gæntlɪt, 'gɔːnt-) *n* **1** a section of a railway where two tracks overlap **2** *US* a variant spelling of **gauntlet²** [c17 *gantlope* (modern spelling influenced by GAUNTLET¹), from Swedish *gatlopp*, literally: passageway, from *gata* way (related to GATE³) + *lop* course]

gantlet² ('gæntlɪt, 'gɔːnt-) *n* a variant of **gauntlet¹**

gantline ('gænt,laɪn, -lɪn) *n nautical* a line rove through a sheave for hoisting men or gear [c19 variant of *girtline*; see GIRT¹, LINE]

gantry ('gæntrɪ) *or* **gauntry** *n, pl* -tries **1** a bridgelike framework used to support a travelling crane, signals over a railway track, etc **2** Also called: **gantry scaffold** the framework tower used to attend to a large rocket on its launching pad **3** a supporting framework for a barrel or cask **4 a** the area behind a bar where bottles, esp spirit bottles are kept for use or display **b** the range or quality of the spirits on view: *this pub's got a good gantry* [c16 (in the sense: wooden platform for barrels): from Old French *chantier*, from Medieval Latin *cantārius*, changed from Latin *canthērius* supporting frame, pack ass; related to Greek *kanthēlios* pack ass]

Gantt chart (gænt) *n* a chart showing, in horizontal lines, activity planned to take place during specified periods, which are indicated in vertical bands [c20 named after Henry L. *Gantt* (1861–1919), US management consultant]

Ganymede¹ ('gænɪ,mi:d) *n classical myth* a beautiful Trojan youth who was abducted by Zeus to Olympus and made the cupbearer of the gods

Ganymede² ('gænɪ,mi:d) *n* the brightest and largest of the four Galilean satellites of Jupiter, and the largest in the solar system. Diameter: 5262 km; orbital radius: 1 070 000 km

Gao (gɑːɔ) *n* a town in E Mali, on the River Niger: a small river port. Pop: 54 903 (1998 est)

gaol (dʒeɪl) *n, vb Brit* a variant spelling of **jail** > **'gaoler** *n*

Gaoxiong (,jauə'ʃɒŋ) *n* a variant transliteration of the Chinese name for **Kaohsiung**

gap (gæp) *n* **1** a break or opening in a wall, fence, etc **2** a break in continuity; interruption; hiatus: *there is a serious gap in the accounts* **3** a break in a line of hills or mountains affording a route through **4** *chiefly US* a gorge or ravine **5** a divergence or difference; disparity: *there is a gap between his version of the event and hers; the generation gap* **6** *electronics* **a** a break in a magnetic circuit that increases the inductance and saturation point of the circuit **b** See **spark gap 7** bridge, close, fill, *or* stop a gap to remedy a deficiency ▷ *vb* gaps, gapping, gapped **8** (*tr*) to make a breach or opening in [c14 from Old Norse *gap* chasm; related to *gapa* to GAPE, Swedish *gap*, Danish *gab* open mouth, opening] > **'gapless** *adj* > **'gappy** *adj*

gape (geɪp) *vb* (*intr*) **1** to stare in wonder or amazement, esp with the mouth open **2** to open the mouth wide, esp involuntarily, as in yawning or hunger **3** to be or become wide open: *the crater gaped under his feet* ▷ *n* **4** the act of gaping **5** a wide opening; breach **6** the width of the widely opened mouth of a vertebrate **7** a stare or expression of astonishment ▷ See also **gapes** [c13 from Old Norse *gapa*; related to Middle Dutch *gapen*, Danish *gabe*]

gaper ('geɪpə) *n* **1** a person or thing that gapes **2** any of various large marine bivalve molluscs of the genera *Mya* and *Lutraria* that burrow in muddy sand. *M. arenaria* is the American soft-shelled clam and the two species of *Lutraria* are the otter shells. The valves have a permanent gap at the hind end

gapes (geɪps) *n* (functioning as singular) **1** a disease of young domestic fowl, characterized by gaping or gasping for breath and caused by gapeworms **2** *informal* a fit of yawning > **'gapy** *adj*

gapeworm ('geɪp,wɜːm) *n* a parasitic nematode worm, *Syngamus trachea*, that lives in the trachea of birds and causes gapes in domestic fowl: family *Syngamidae*

gaping ('geɪpɪŋ) *adj* wide open; extremely wide: *a gaping hole* > **'gapingly** *adv*

gapped scale *n music* a scale, such as a pentatonic scale, containing fewer than seven notes

gapper ('gæpə) *n Brit* a person who is taking a gap year

gapping ('gæpɪŋ) *n* **1** (in transformational grammar) a rule that deletes repetitions of a verb, as in the sentence *Bill voted for Smith, Sam for McKay, and Dave for Harris* **2** the act or practice of taking a gap year

gap-toothed *adj* having wide spaces between the teeth

gap year *n Brit* a year's break taken by a student between leaving school and starting further education

gar¹ (gɑː) *n, pl* gar *or* gars short for **garpike** *or* **garfish**

gar² (gɑːr) *vb* (*tr*) *Scot* to cause or compel [from Old Norse]

garage ('gærɑːʒ, -rɪdʒ) *n* **1** a building or part of a building used to house a motor vehicle **2** a commercial establishment in which motor vehicles are repaired, serviced, bought, and sold, and which usually also sells motor fuels **3 a** a rough-and-ready style of rock music **b** a type of disco music based on soul ▷ *vb* **4** (*tr*) to put into, keep in, or take to a garage [C20 from French, from *garer* to dock (a ship), from Old French: to protect, from Old High German *warōn*; see BEWARE]

garage band *n* a rough-and-ready amateurish rock group [perhaps from the practice of such bands rehearsing in a garage]

garage sale *n* a sale of personal belongings or household effects held at a person's home, usually in the garage

garaging ('gærədʒɪŋ) *n* accommodation for housing a motor vehicle: *there is garaging for two cars*

garam masala ('gɑːrəm mɑː'sɑːlə) *n* an aromatic mixture of spices, extensively used in curries [from Hindi]

Garamond ('gærəmɒnd) *n* a typeface, designed by Claude Garamond (?1480–1561), French type founder

Garand rifle ('gærənd, gə'rænd) *n* another name for M-1 rifle [C20 named after John C. *Garand* (1888–1974), US gun designer]

garb (gɑːb) *n* **1** clothes, esp the distinctive attire of an occupation or profession: *clerical garb* **2** style of dress; fashion **3** external appearance, covering, or attire ▷ *vb* **4** (*tr*) to clothe or cover; attire [C16 from Old French *garbe* graceful contour, from Old Italian *garbo* grace, probably of Germanic origin] ▷ 'garbless *adj*

garbage ('gɑːbɪdʒ) *n* **1** worthless, useless, or unwanted matter **2** discarded or waste matter; refuse. Also called: rubbish **3** *computing* invalid data **4** *informal* nonsense [C15 probably from Anglo-French *garbelage* removal of discarded matter, of uncertain origin; compare Old Italian *garbuglio* confusion]

garbage can *n* *US and Canadian* a large, usually cylindrical container for refuse, esp one used by a household. Also called: ash bin, ash can, trash can, (in Britain (and certain other countries)) dustbin

garbage collection *n* *computing* a systems routine for eliminating invalid or out-of-date data and releasing storage locations

garbage truck *n* *US and Canadian* a road vehicle for collecting domestic refuse. Also called (in Britain) (dated): dustcart

garbanzo (gɑː'bænzəʊ) *n*, *pl* -zos another name for chickpea [C18 from Spanish, from *arvanço*, probably of Germanic origin; compare Old High German *arawiz* pea]

garble ('gɑːbəl) *vb* (*tr*) **1** to jumble (a story, quotation, etc), esp unintentionally **2** to distort the meaning of (an account, text, etc), as by making misleading omissions; corrupt **3** *rare* to select the best part of ▷ *n* **4 a** the act of garbling **b** garbled matter [C15 from Old Italian *garbellare* to strain, sift, from Arabic *gharbala*, from *ghirbāl* sieve, from Late Latin *crībellum* small sieve, from *crībrum* sieve] ▷ 'garbler *n*

garbled ('gɑːbəld) *adj* jumbled or unclear because of distortion or omissions

garbo ('gɑːbəʊ) *n*, *pl* -bos *Austral informal* a dustman [C20 from GARBAGE]

garboard ('gɑːbɔːd) *n* *nautical* the bottommost plank of a vessel's hull. Also called: garboard plank, garboard strake [C17 from Dutch *gaarboord*, probably from Middle Dutch *gaderen* to GATHER + *boord* BOARD]

garboil ('gɑːbɔɪl) *n* *archaic* confusion or disturbance; uproar [C16 from Old French *garbouil*, from Old Italian *garbuglio*, ultimately from Latin *bullīre* to boil, hence, seethe with indignation]

garbology (gɑː'bɒlədʒɪ) *n* the study of the contents of domestic dustbins to analyse the consumption patterns of households [C20 from GARB(AGE) + OLOGY] ▷ gar'bologist *n*

garçon ('gɑːsɒn; *French* garsɔ̃) *n* a waiter or male servant, esp if French [C19 from Old French *gars* lad, probably of Germanic origin]

Gard (*French* gar) *n* a department of S France, in

Languedoc-Roussillon region. Capital: Nîmes. Pop: 648 522 (2003 est). Area: 5881 sq km (2294 miles)

garda ('gɑːrdə) *n*, *pl* gardaí ('gɑːrdiː) a member of the Garda Síochána

Garda ('gɑːdə) *n* Lake a lake in N Italy: the largest lake in the country. Area: 370 sq km (143 sq miles)

gardant ('gɑːdənt) *adj* a less common spelling of guardant

Garda Síochána ('gɑːrdə ʃɪə'xɑːnə) *n* the police force of the Republic of Ireland [C20 from Irish Gaelic *garda* guard + *síochána* of the peace, from *síocháin* peace]

garden ('gɑːdən) *n* **1** *Brit* **a** an area of land, usually planted with grass, trees, flowerbeds, etc, adjoining a house. US and Canadian word: yard **b** (*as modifier*): *a garden chair* **2 a** an area of land used for the cultivation of ornamental plants, herbs, fruit, vegetables, trees, etc **b** (*as modifier*): *garden tools*. Related adj: horticultural **3** (*often plural*) such an area of land that is open to the public, sometimes part of a park: *botanical gardens* **4 a** a fertile and beautiful region **b** (*as modifier*): *a garden paradise* **5** (*modifier*) provided with or surrounded by a garden or gardens: *a garden flat* **6** lead (a person) up the garden path *informal* to mislead or deceive (a person) ▷ *adj* **7** common or garden *informal* ordinary; unexceptional ▷ *vb* **8** to work in, cultivate, or take care of (a garden, plot of land, etc) [C14 from Old French *gardin*, of Germanic origin; compare Old High German *gart* enclosure; see YARD² (sense 1)] ▷ 'gardenless *adj* ▷ 'garden-,like *adj*

garden centre *n* a place where gardening tools and equipment, plants, seeds, etc, are sold

garden city *n* *Brit* a planned town of limited size with broad streets and spacious layout, containing trees and open spaces and surrounded by a rural belt. See also garden suburb

garden cress *n* a pungent-tasting plant, *Lepidium sativum*, with white or reddish flowers: cultivated for salads, as a garnish, etc: family Brassicaceae (crucifers)

gardener ('gɑːdnə) *n* **1** a person who works in or takes care of a garden as an occupation or pastime **2** any bowerbird of the genus *Amblyornis*

garden flat *n* a flat with direct access to a garden: typically, a garden flat consists of basement accommodation in prewar property, but some are in purpose-built blocks in urban areas

garden frame *n* another name for a cold frame

gardenia (gɑː'diːnɪə) *n* **1** any evergreen shrub or tree of the Old World tropical rubiaceous genus *Gardenia*, cultivated for their large fragrant waxlike typically white flowers **2** the flower of any of these shrubs [C18 New Latin, named after Dr Alexander *Garden* (1730–91), American botanist]

gardening ('gɑːdənɪŋ) *n* **a** the planning and cultivation of a garden **b** (*as modifier*): *gardening gloves*

gardening leave *or* **garden leave** *n* *Brit informal* a period during which an employee who is about to leave a company continues to receive a salary but does not work

Garden of Eden *n* the full name for Eden

garden party *n* a social gathering held in the grounds of a house, school, etc, usually with light refreshments

garden snail *n* any of several land snails common in gardens, where they may become pests, esp *Helix aspersa*, and sometimes including *Cepaea nemoralis*, common in woods and hedgerows

garden suburb *n* *Brit* a suburb of a large established town or city, planned along the lines of a garden city

garden warbler *n* any of several small brownish-grey European songbirds of the genus *Sylvia* (warblers), esp *S. borin*, common in woods and hedges: in some parts of Europe they are esteemed as a delicacy

garderobe ('gɑːd,rəʊb) *n* *archaic* **1** a wardrobe or the contents of a wardrobe **2** a bedroom or

private room **3** a privy [C14 from French, from *garder* to keep + *robe* dress, clothing; see WARDROBE]

garfish ('gɑːfɪʃ) *n*, *pl* -fish *or* -fishes **1** another name for garpike (sense 1) **2** an elongated European marine teleost fish, *Belone belone*, with long toothed jaws: related to the flying fishes **3** any of various marine or estuarine fish with a long needle-like lower jaw [Old English *gār* spear + FISH]

garganey ('gɑːgənɪ) *n* a small Eurasian duck, *Anas querquedula*, closely related to the mallard. The male has a white stripe over each eye [C17 from Italian dialect *garganei*, of imitative origin]

Gargantua (gɑː'gæntjʊə) *n* a gigantic king noted for his great capacity for food and drink, in Rabelais' satire *Gargantua and Pantagruel* (1534)

gargantuan (gɑː'gæntjʊən) *adj* (*sometimes capital*) huge; enormous

> USAGE Some people think that *gargantuan* should only be used to describe things connected with food: *a gargantuan meal*; *his gargantuan appetite*

garget ('gɑːgɪt) *n* *archaic* inflammation of the mammary gland of domestic animals, esp cattle [C16 (in the sense: throat): from Old French *gargate*, perhaps from Latin *gurges* gulf] ▷ 'gargety *adj*

gargle ('gɑːgəl) *vb* **1** to rinse (the mouth and throat) with a liquid, esp a medicinal fluid by slowly breathing out through the liquid **2** to utter (words, sounds, etc) with the throaty bubbling noise of gargling ▷ *n* **3** the liquid used for gargling **4** the sound produced by gargling [C16 from Old French *gargouiller* to gargle, make a gurgling sound, from *gargouille* throat, perhaps of imitative origin] **5** *Brit informal* an alcoholic drink: *what was her favourite gargle?* ▷ 'gargler *n*

gargoyle ('gɑːgɔɪl) *n* **1** a waterspout carved in the form of a grotesque face or creature and projecting from a roof gutter, esp of a Gothic church **2** any grotesque ornament or projection, esp on a building **3** a person with a grotesque appearance [C15 from Old French *gargouille* gargoyle, throat; see GARGLE] ▷ 'gargoyled *adj*

gari ('gɑːrɪ) *n* thinly sliced pickled ginger, often served with sushi [C20 Japanese]

garibaldi (,gærɪ'bɔːldɪ) *n* **1** a woman's loose blouse with long sleeves popular in the 1860s, copied from the red flannel shirt worn by Garibaldi's soldiers **2** *Brit* a type of biscuit having a layer of currants in the centre

garigue *or* **garrigue** (*French* garig) *n* open shrubby vegetation of dry Mediterranean regions, consisting of spiny or aromatic dwarf shrubs interspersed with colourful ephemeral species

garish ('gɛərɪʃ) *adj* gay or colourful in a crude or vulgar manner; gaudy [C16 from earlier *gaure* to stare + -ISH] ▷ 'garishly *adv* ▷ 'garishness *n*

garland ('gɑːlənd) *n* **1** a wreath or festoon of flowers, leaves, etc, worn round the head or neck or hung up **2** a representation of such a wreath, as in painting, sculpture, etc **3** a collection of short literary pieces, such as ballads or poems; miscellany or anthology **4** *nautical* a ring or grommet of rope ▷ *vb* **5** (*tr*) to deck or adorn with a garland or garlands [C14 from Old French *garlande*, perhaps of Germanic origin]

garlic ('gɑːlɪk) *n* **1** a hardy widely cultivated Asian alliaceous plant, *Allium sativum*, having a stem bearing whitish flowers and bulbils **2 a** the bulb of this plant, made up of small segments (cloves) that have a strong odour and pungent taste and are used in cooking **b** (*as modifier*): *a garlic taste* **3** any of various other plants of the genus *Allium* [Old English *gārlēac*, from *gār* spear + *lēac* LEEK]

garlicky ('gɑːlɪkɪ) *adj* containing or resembling the taste or odour of garlic

garlic mustard *n* a plant, *Alliaria petiolata*, of N temperate regions, with small white flowers and an odour of garlic: family Brassicaceae (crucifers). Also called: jack-by-the-hedge, hedge garlic Compare garlic

g

garment ('gɑːmənt) *n* **1** (*often plural*) an article of clothing **2** outer covering ▷ *vb* **3** (*tr; usually passive*) to cover or clothe [c14 from Old French *garniment*, from *garnir* to equip; see CARNISH] > 'garmentless *adj*

garner ('gɑːnə) *vb* (*tr*) **1** to gather or store in or as if in a granary ▷ *n* **2** an archaic word for **granary 3** *archaic* a place for storage or safekeeping [c12 from Old French *gernier* granary, from Latin *grānārium*, from *grānum* grain]

garnet[1] ('gɑːnɪt) *n* any of a group of hard glassy red, yellow, or green minerals consisting of the silicates of calcium, iron, manganese, chromium, magnesium, and aluminium in cubic crystalline form: used as a gemstone and abrasive. Formula: $A_3B_2(SiO_4)_3$ where A is a divalent metal and B is a trivalent metal [c13 from Old French *grenat*, from *grenat* (adj) red, from *pome grenate* POMEGRANATE] > 'garnet-,like *adj*

garnet[2] ('gɑːnɪt) *n nautical* a tackle used for lifting cargo [c15 probably from Middle Dutch *garnaat*]

garnet paper *n* sandpaper having powdered garnet as the abrasive

garnierite ('gɑːnɪə,raɪt) *n* a green amorphous mineral consisting of hydrated nickel magnesium silicate: a source of nickel [c19 named after Jules Garnier (died 1904), French geologist]

garnish ('gɑːnɪʃ) *vb* (*tr*) **1** to decorate; trim **2** to add something to (food) in order to improve its appearance or flavour **3** *law* **a** to serve with notice of proceedings; warn **b** *obsolete* to summon to proceedings already in progress **c** to attach (a debt) **4** *slang* to extort money from ▷ *n* **5** a decoration; trimming **6** something, such as parsley, added to a dish for its flavour or decorative effect **7** *obsolete slang* a payment illegally extorted, as from a prisoner by his jailer [c14 from Old French *garnir* to adorn, equip, of Germanic origin; compare Old High German *warnōn* to pay heed] > 'garnisher *n*

garnishee (,gɑːnɪ'fiː) *law* ▷ *n* **1** a person upon whom a garnishment has been served ▷ *vb* -nishees, -nisheeing, -nisheed (*tr*) **2** to attach (a debt or other property) by garnishment **3** to serve (a person) with a garnishment

garnishment ('gɑːnɪʃmənt) *n* **1** the act of garnishing **2** decoration or embellishment; garnish **3** *law* **a** a notice or warning **b** *obsolete* a summons to court proceedings already in progress **c** a notice warning a person holding money or property belonging to a debtor whose debt has been attached to hold such property until directed by the court to apply it

garniture ('gɑːnɪtʃə) *n* decoration or embellishment [c16 from French, from *garnir* to CARNISH]

Garonne (*French* garɔn) *n* a river in SW France, rising in the central Pyrenees in Spain and flowing northeast then northwest into the Gironde estuary. Length: 580 km (360 miles)

garotte (gə'rɒt) *n, vb* a variant spelling of **garrotte**. > gə'rotter *n*

garoupa (gə'ruːpə) *n* (in Chinese and SE Asian cookery) another name for **groper**

garpike ('gɑː,paɪk) *n* **1** Also called: garfish, gar any primitive freshwater elongated bony fish of the genus *Lepisosteus*, of North and Central America, having very long toothed jaws and a body covering of thick scales **2** another name for **garfish** (sense 2)

garret ('gærɪt) *n* another word for **attic** (sense 1) [c14 from Old French *garite* watchtower, from *garir* to protect, of Germanic origin; see WARY]

garret window *n* a skylight that lies along the slope of the roof

garrigue French (garig) *n* a variant spelling of **garigue**

garrison ('gærɪsⁿn) *n* **1** the troops who maintain and guard a base or fortified place **2 a** the place itself **b** (*as modifier*): *a garrison town* ▷ *vb* **3** (*tr*) to station (troops) in (a fort) [c13 from Old French *garison*, from *garir* to defend, of Germanic origin;

compare Old Norse *verja* to defend, Old English, Old High German *werian*]

garron ('gærən) *n* a small sturdy pony bred and used chiefly in Scotland and Ireland [c16 from Gaelic *gearran*]

garrotte, garrote *or* **garotte** (gə'rɒt) *n* **1** a Spanish method of execution by strangulation or by breaking the neck **2** the device, usually an iron collar, used in such executions **3** *obsolete* strangulation of one's victim while committing robbery ▷ *vb* (*tr*) **4** to execute by means of the garrotte **5** to strangle, esp in order to commit robbery [c17 from Spanish *garrote*, perhaps from Old French *garrot* cudgel; of obscure origin] > gar'rotter, gar'roter *or* ga'rotter *n*

garrulous ('gærʊləs) *adj* **1** given to constant and frivolous chatter; loquacious; talkative **2** wordy or diffuse; prolix [c17 from Latin *garrulus*, from *garrīre* to chatter] > 'garrulously *adv* > 'garrulousness *or* garrulity (gæ'ruːlɪtɪ) *n*

garrya ('gærɪə) *n* any ornamental catkin-bearing evergreen shrub of the North American genus *Garrya*: family Garryaceae [c19 named after Nicholas Garry (1781–1856), an officer of the Hudson's Bay Company]

garryowen (,gærɪ'əʊɪn) *n* (in rugby union) another term for **up-and-under** [c20 named after *Garryowen* RFC, Ireland]

garter ('gɑːtə) *n* **1** a band, usually of elastic, worn round the arm or leg to hold up a shirtsleeve, sock, or stocking **2** *US and Canadian* **a** an elastic strap attached to a belt or corset having a fastener at the end, for holding up women's stockings **b** a similar fastener attached to a garter belt worn by men in order to support socks. Also called (in Britain and certain other countries): **suspender 3** have someone's guts for garters See **gut** (sense 10) ▷ *vb* **4** (*tr*) to fasten, support, or secure with or as if with a garter [c14 from Old Northern French *gartier*, from *garet* bend of the knee, probably of Celtic origin]

Garter ('gɑːtə) *n* the **1** See **Order of the Garter** (*sometimes not capital*) **a** the badge of this Order **b** membership of this Order

garter snake *n* any nonvenomous North American colubrid snake of the genus *Thamnophis*, typically marked with longitudinal stripes

garter stitch *n* knitting in which all the rows are knitted in plain stitch instead of alternating with purl rows

garth[1] (gɑːθ) *n* **1** a courtyard surrounded by a cloister **2** *archaic* a yard or garden [c14 from Old Norse *garthr*; related to Old English *geard* YARD[2]]

garth[2] (gɑːθ) *n Northern English dialect* a child's hoop, often the rim of a bicycle wheel [dialect variant of GIRTH]

Gary ('gærɪ) *n* a port in NW Indiana, on Lake Michigan: a major world steel producer. Pop: 99 961 (2003 est)

gas (gæs) *n, pl* **gases** *or* **gasses 1** a substance in a physical state in which it does not resist change of shape and will expand indefinitely to fill any container. If very high pressure is applied a gas may become liquid or solid, otherwise its density tends towards that of the condensed phase. Compare **liquid** (sense 1), **solid** (sense 1) **2** any substance that is gaseous at room temperature and atmospheric pressure **3** any gaseous substance that is above its critical temperature and therefore not liquefiable by pressure alone. Compare **vapour** (sense 2) **4 a** a fossil fuel in the form of a gas, used as a source of domestic and industrial heat. See also **coal gas, natural gas b** (*as modifier*): *a gas cooker; gas fire* **5** a gaseous anaesthetic, such as nitrous oxide **6** *mining* firedamp or the explosive mixture of firedamp and air **7** the usual US, Canadian, and New Zealand word for **petrol**, a shortened form of **gasoline 8 step on the gas** *informal* **a** to increase the speed of a motor vehicle; accelerate **b** to hurry **9** a toxic or suffocating substance in suspension in air used against an enemy **10**

informal idle talk or boasting **11** *slang* a delightful or successful person or thing: *his latest record is a gas* **12** *US* an informal name for **flatus** ▷ *vb* **gases** *or* **gasses, gassing, gassed 13** (*tr*) to provide or fill with gas **14** (*tr*) to subject to gas fumes, esp so as to asphyxiate or render unconscious **15** (*intr*) to give off gas, as in the charging of a battery **16** (*tr*) (in textiles) to singe (fabric) with a flame from a gas burner to remove unwanted fibres **17** (*intr; foll by to*) *informal* to talk in an idle or boastful way to a person) **18** (*tr*) *slang, chiefly US and Canadian* to thrill or delight [c17 (coined by J. B. van Helmont (1577–1644), Flemish chemist): modification of Greek *khaos* atmosphere] > 'gasless *adj*

gasbag ('gæs,bæg) *informal* ▷ *n* **1** a person who talks in a voluble way, esp about unimportant matters ▷ *vb* -bags, -bagging, -bagged **2** (*intr*) *Irish* to talk in a voluble way, esp about unimportant matters

gas black *n* finely powdered carbon produced by burning natural gas. It is used as a pigment in paints, etc

gas burner *n* **1** Also called: **gas jet** a jet or nozzle from which a combustible gas issues in order to form a stable flame **2** an assembly of such jets or nozzles, used esp in cooking

gas chamber *or* **oven** *n* an airtight room into which poison gas is introduced to kill people or animals

gas chromatography *n* a technique for analysing a mixture of volatile substances in which the mixture is carried by an inert gas through a column packed with a selective adsorbent and a detector records on a moving strip the conductivity of the gas leaving the tube. Peaks on the resulting graph indicate the presence of a particular component. Also called: **gas-liquid chromatography**

gas coal *n* coal that is rich in volatile hydrocarbons, making it a suitable source of domestic gas

gascon ('gæskən) *n rare* a boaster; braggart [c14 from Old French *gascoun*; compare Latin *Vascōnēs* Basque]

Gascon ('gæskən) *n* **1** a native or inhabitant of Gascony **2** the dialect of French spoken in Gascony ▷ *adj* **3** of or relating to Gascony, its inhabitants, or their dialect of French

gasconade (,gæskə'neɪd) *rare* ▷ *n* **1** boastful talk, bragging, or bluster ▷ *vb* **2** (*intr*) to boast, brag, or bluster [c18 from French *gasconnade*, from *gasconner* to chatter, boast like a GASCON] > ,gascon'ader *n*

gas constant *n* the constant in the gas equation. It is equal to 8.31472 joules per kelvin per mole. Symbol: *R* Also called: universal gas constant

Gascony ('gæskənɪ) *n* a former province of SW France. French name: Gascogne (gaskɔɲ)

gas-cooled reactor *n* a nuclear reactor using a gas as the coolant. In the Mark I type the coolant is carbon dioxide, the moderator is graphite, and the fuel is uranium cased in magnox. See also **advanced gas-cooled reactor**

gas-discharge tube *n electronics* any tube in which an electric discharge takes place through a gas

gaselier (,gæsə'lɪə) *n* a variant spelling of **gasolier**

gas engine *n* a type of internal-combustion engine using a flammable gas, such as coal gas or natural gas, as fuel

gaseous ('gæsɪəs, -ʃəs, -ʃɪəs, 'geɪ-) *adj* of, concerned with, or having the characteristics of a gas > 'gaseousness *n*

gas equation *n* an equation that equates the product of the pressure and the volume of one mole of a gas to the product of its thermodynamic temperature and the **gas constant**. The equation is exact for an ideal gas and is a good approximation for real gases at low pressures. Also called: ideal gas equation *or* law

gas gangrene *n* gangrene resulting from infection of a wound by anaerobic bacteria (esp *Clostridium welchii*) that cause gas bubbles and swelling in the surrounding tissues

gas giant *n* one of the four planets in our solar system that are composed chiefly of hydrogen and helium, namely Jupiter, Saturn, Uranus, and Neptune [C20 coined by James Blish (1921–75), US science fiction writer]

gas guzzler *n informal* a large car with very high petrol consumption

gash[1] (gæʃ) *vb* **1** (*tr*) to make a long deep cut or wound in; slash ▷ *n* **2** a long deep cut or wound [C16 from Old French *garser* to scratch, wound, from Vulgar Latin *charissāre* (unattested), from Greek *kharassein* to scratch]

gash[2] (gæʃ) *adj slang* surplus to requirements; unnecessary, extra, or spare [C20 of unknown origin]

gasholder ('gæs,həʊldə) *n* **1** Also called: **gasometer** a large tank for storing coal gas or natural gas prior to distribution to users **2** any vessel for storing or measuring a gas

gasiform ('gæsɪ,fɔːm) *adj* in a gaseous form

gasify ('gæsɪ,faɪ) *vb* -fies, -fying, -fied **1** to make into or become a gas **2** to subject (coal, etc) to destructive distillation to produce gas, esp for use as a fuel > ˌgasiˈfiable *adj* > ˌgasifiˈcation *n* > ˈgasiˌfier *n*

gasket ('gæskɪt) *n* **1** a compressible packing piece of paper, rubber, asbestos, etc, sandwiched between the faces or flanges of a joint to provide a seal **2** *nautical* a piece of line used as a sail stop **3 blow a gasket** *slang* to burst out in anger [C17 (in the sense: rope lashing a furled sail): probably from French *garcette* rope's end, literally: little girl, from Old French *garce* girl, feminine of *gars* boy, servant]

gaskin ('gæskɪn) *n* the lower part of a horse's thigh, between the hock and the stifle [C16 perhaps shortened from GALLIGASKINS]

gas laws *pl n* the physical laws obeyed by gases, esp Boyle's law and Charles' law. See also **gas equation**

gaslight ('gæs,laɪt) *n* **1** a type of lamp in which the illumination is produced by an incandescent mantle heated by a jet of gas **2** the light produced by such a lamp

gas lighter *n* **1** a device for igniting a jet of gas **2** a cigarette lighter using a gas as fuel

gas-liquid chromatography *n* another name for **gas chromatography**

gas main *n* a large pipeline in which gas is carried for distribution through smaller pipes to consumers

gasman ('gæs,mæn) *n, pl* -men a man employed to read household gas meters, supervise gas fittings, etc

gas mantle *n* a mantle for use in a gaslight. See **mantle** (sense 4)

gas mask *n* a mask fitted with a chemical filter to enable the wearer to breathe air free of poisonous or corrosive gases: used for military or industrial purposes. Also called (in Britain): **respirator**

gas meter *n* an apparatus for measuring and recording the amount of gas passed through it

gasohol ('gæsə,hɒl) *n* a mixture of 80% or 90% petrol with 20% or 10% ethyl alcohol, for use as a fuel in internal-combustion engines

gas oil *n* a fuel oil obtained in the distillation of petroleum, intermediate in viscosity and boiling point between paraffin and lubricating oils. It boils above about 250°C

gasolier or **gaselier** (ˌgæsə'lɪə) *n* a branched hanging fitting for gaslights [C19 from GAS + (CHAND)ELIER]

gasoline or **gasolene** ('gæsə,liːn) *n US and Canadian* any one of various volatile flammable liquid mixtures of hydrocarbons, mainly hexane, heptane, and octane, obtained from petroleum and used as a solvent and a fuel for internal-combustion engines. Usually petrol also contains additives such as antiknock compounds and corrosion inhibitors. Also called (esp in Britain): petrol > **gasolinic** (ˌgæsə'lɪnɪk) *adj*

gasometer (gæs'ɒmɪtə) *n* a nontechnical name for **gasholder**

gasometry (gæs'ɒmɪtrɪ) *n* the measurement of quantities of gases > **gasometric** (ˌgæsə'mɛtrɪk) or ˌgaso'metrical *adj*

gas oven *n* **1** a domestic oven heated by gas **2** a gas-fuelled cremation chamber **3** another name for **gas chamber**

gasp (gɑːsp) *vb* **1** (*intr*) to draw in the breath sharply, convulsively, or with effort, esp in expressing awe, horror, etc **2** (*intr*; foll by *after* or *for*) to crave **3** (*tr*; often foll by *out*) to utter or emit breathlessly ▷ *n* **4** a short convulsive intake of breath **5** a short convulsive burst of speech **6** at the last gasp **a** at the point of death **b** at the last moment [C14 from Old Norse *geispa* to yawn; related to Swedish dialect *gispa*, Danish *gispe*] > 'gaspingly *adv*

Gaspar ('gæspə, 'gæspɑː) *n* a variant of **Caspar**

Gaspé Peninsula (gæ'speɪ; *French* gaspe) *n* a peninsula in E Canada, in SE Quebec between the St Lawrence River and New Brunswick: mountainous and wooded with many lakes and rivers. Area: about 29 500 sq km (11 400 sq miles). Also called: the Gaspé

gasper ('gɑːspə) *n* **1** a person who gasps **2** *Brit dated slang* a cheap cigarette **3** *informal* something that shocks one or causes one to gasp in astonishment

gaspereau ('gæspərəʊ) *n Canadian* another name for **alewife** [from Canadian French]

gas-permeable lens *n* a contact lens made of rigid plastic that is more permeable to air than a standard hard lens. Abbreviation: GP Compare **hard lens, soft lens**

gas plant *n* an aromatic white-flowered Eurasian rutaceous plant, *Dictamnus albus*, that emits a vapour capable of being ignited. Also called: **burning bush, dittany, fraxinella**

gas poker *n* a long tubular gas burner used to kindle a fire

gas ring *n* a circular assembly of gas jets, used esp for cooking

gassed (gæst) *adj slang* drunk

gasser ('gæsə) *n* a drilling or well that yields natural gas

gassing ('gæsɪŋ) *n* **1** the act or process of supplying or treating with gas **2** the affecting or poisoning of persons with gas or fumes **3** the evolution of a gas, esp in electrolysis

gas station *n chiefly US and Canadian* another term for **filling station**

gassy ('gæsɪ) *adj* -sier, -siest **1** filled with, containing, or resembling gas **2** *informal* full of idle or vapid talk > 'gassiness *n*

gasteropod ('gæstərə,pɒd) *n, adj* a variant of **gastropod**

gas thermometer *n* a device for measuring temperature by observing the pressure of gas at a constant volume or the volume of a gas kept at a constant pressure

gastight ('gæs,taɪt) *adj* not allowing gas to enter or escape

gastralgia (gæs'trældʒɪə) *n* pain in the stomach > gas'tralgic *adj*

gastrectomy (gæs'trɛktəmɪ) *n, pl* -mies surgical removal of all or part of the stomach

gastric ('gæstrɪk) *adj* of, relating to, near, or involving the stomach: *gastric pains*

gastric juice *n* a digestive fluid secreted by the stomach, containing hydrochloric acid, pepsin, rennin, etc

gastric ulcer *n* an ulcer of the mucous membrane lining the stomach. Compare **peptic ulcer**

gastrin ('gæstrɪn) *n* a polypeptide hormone secreted by the stomach: stimulates secretion of gastric juice

gastritis (gæs'traɪtɪs) *n* inflammation of the lining of the stomach > gastritic (gæs'trɪtɪk) *adj*

gastro- or often before a vowel **gastr-** *combining form* stomach: *gastroenteritis; gastritis* [from Greek *gastēr*]

gastrocolic (ˌgæstrəʊ'kɒlɪk) *adj* of or relating to the stomach and colon: *gastrocolic reflex*

gastroduodenostomy (ˌgæstrəʊˌdjuːəʊdiː'nɒstəmɪ) *n* a surgical operation in which the duodenum is joined to a new opening in the stomach, esp to bypass an obstruction

gastroenteric (ˌgæstrəʊɛn'tɛrɪk) *adj* another word for **gastrointestinal**

gastroenteritis (ˌgæstrəʊˌɛntə'raɪtɪs) *n* inflammation of the stomach and intestines > gastroenteritic (ˌgæstrəʊˌɛntə'rɪtɪk) *adj*

gastroenterology (ˌgæstrəʊˌɛntə'rɒlədʒɪ) *n* the branch of medical science concerned with diseases of the stomach and intestines > ˌgastroˌenterˈologist *n*

gastroenterostomy (ˌgæstrəʊˌɛntə'rɒstəmɪ) *n, pl* -mies surgical formation of an artificial opening between the stomach and the small intestine

gastrointestinal (ˌgæstrəʊɪn'tɛstɪn°l) *adj* of or relating to the stomach and intestinal tract

gastrolith ('gæstrəlɪθ) *n pathol* a stone in the stomach; gastric calculus

gastrology (gæs'trɒlədʒɪ) *n* a former name for **gastroenterology**. > gastrological (ˌgæstrə'lɒdʒɪk°l) *adj* > gas'trologist *n*

gastronome ('gæstrə,nəʊm), **gastronomer** (gæs'trɒnəmə) or **gastronomist** *n* less common words for **gourmet**

gastronomic (ˌgæstrə'nɒmɪk) or **gastronomical** *adj* of or relating to food and cookery, esp the art of good eating > ˌgastro'nomically *adv*

gastronomy (gæs'trɒnəmɪ) *n* **1** the art of good eating **2** the type of cookery of a particular region: *the gastronomy of Provence* [C19 from French *gastronomie*, from Greek *gastronomia*, from *gastēr* stomach; see -NOMY]

gastropod ('gæstrə,pɒd) or **gasteropod** *n* **1** any mollusc of the class *Gastropoda*, typically having a flattened muscular foot for locomotion and a head that bears stalked eyes. The class includes the snails, whelks, limpets, and slugs ▷ *adj* **2** of, relating to, or belonging to the *Gastropoda* > gastropodan (gæs'trɒpəd°n) *adj, n* > gas'tropodous *adj*

gastro-pub *n* a pub serving restaurant-quality food

gastroscope ('gæstrə,skəʊp) *n* a medical instrument for examining the interior of the stomach > gastroscopic (ˌgæstrə'skɒpɪk) *adj* > gastroscopist (gæs'trɒskəpɪst) *n* > gas'troscopy *n*

gastrostomy (gæs'trɒstəmɪ) *n, pl* -mies surgical formation of an artificial opening into the stomach from the skin surface: used for feeding

gastrotomy (gæs'trɒtəmɪ) *n, pl* -mies surgical incision into the stomach

gastrotrich ('gæstrətrɪk) *n* any minute aquatic multicellular animal of the phylum *Gastrotricha*, having a wormlike body covered with cilia and bristles [from New Latin *gastrotricha*, from GASTRO- + Greek -*trichos* -haired: see TRICHO-]

gastrovascular (ˌgæstrəʊ'væskjʊlə) *adj* (esp of the body cavities of coelenterates) functioning in digestion and circulation

gastrula ('gæstrʊlə) *n, pl* -las or -lae (-ˌliː) a saclike animal embryo consisting of three layers of cells (see **ectoderm, mesoderm**, and **endoderm**) surrounding a central cavity (archenteron) with a small opening (blastopore) to the exterior [C19 New Latin: little stomach, from Greek *gastēr* belly] > 'gastrular *adj*

gastrulation (ˌgæstrʊ'leɪʃən) *n embryol* the process in which a gastrula is formed from a blastula by the inward migration of cells

gas turbine *n* an internal-combustion engine in which the expanding gases emerging from one or more combustion chambers drive a turbine. A rotary compressor driven by the turbine compresses the air used for combustion, power being taken either as torque from the turbine or thrust from the expanding gases

g

gas vacuole *n biology* a gas-filled structure that provides buoyancy in some aquatic bacteria

gas welding *n* a method of welding in which a combination of gases, usually oxyacetylene, is used to provide a hot flame

gas well *n* a well for obtaining natural gas

gasworks ('gæs,wɜːks) *n* (*functioning as singular*) a plant in which gas, esp coal gas, is made

gat¹ (gæt) *vb archaic* a past tense of **get**

gat² (gæt) *n slang, chiefly US* a pistol or revolver [C20 shortened from GATLING GUN]

gat³ (gæt) *n* a narrow channel of water [C18 probably from Old Norse *gat* passage; related to GATE¹]

gate¹ (geɪt) *n* **1** a movable barrier, usually hinged, for closing an opening in a wall, fence, etc **2** an opening to allow passage into or out of an enclosed place **3** any means of entrance or access **4** a mountain pass or gap, esp one providing entry into another country or region **5 a** the number of people admitted to a sporting event or entertainment **b** the total entrance money received from them **6** (in a large airport) any of the numbered exits leading to the airfield or aircraft: *passengers for Paris should proceed to gate 14* **7** *horse racing* short for **starting gate 8** *electronics* **a** a logic circuit having one or more input terminals and one output terminal, the output being switched between two voltage levels determined by the combination of input signals **b** a circuit used in radar that allows only a fraction of the input signal to pass **9** the electrode region or regions in a field-effect transistor that is biased to control the conductivity of the channel between the source and drain **10** a component in a motion-picture camera or projector that holds each frame flat and momentarily stationary behind the lens **11** a slotted metal frame that controls the positions of the gear lever in a motor vehicle **12** *rowing* a hinged clasp to prevent the oar from jumping out of a rowlock **13** a frame surrounding the blade or blades of a saw ▷ *vb* (*tr*) **14** to provide with a gate or gates **15** *Brit* to restrict (a student) to the school or college grounds as a punishment **16** to select (part of a waveform) in terms of amplitude or time [Old English *geat*; related to Old Frisian *jet* opening, Old Norse *gat* opening, passage] > 'gateless *adj* > 'gate,like *adj*

gate² (geɪt) *n dialect* **1** the channels by which molten metal is poured into a mould **2** the metal that solidifies in such channels [C17 probably related to Old English *gyte* a pouring out, *geotan* to pour]

gate³ (geɪt) *n Scot and northern English dialect* **1** a way, road, street, or path **2** a way or method of doing something [C13 from Old Norse *gata* path; related to Old High German *gazza* road, street]

-gate *n combining form* indicating a person or thing that has been the cause of, or is associated with, a public scandal [C20 on the analogy of WATERGATE]

gateau *or* **gâteau** ('gætəu) *n, pl* **-teaux** (-təuz) any of various elaborate cakes, usually layered with cream and richly decorated [French: cake]

gate-crash *vb* to gain entry to (a party, concert, etc) without invitation or payment > 'gate-,crasher *n*

gatefold ('geɪt,fəuld) *n* an oversize page in a book or magazine that is folded in. Also called: **foldout**

gatefold sleeve *n* a record sleeve that opens out like a book

gatehouse ('geɪt,haus) *n* **1** a building above or beside an entrance gate to a city, university, etc, often housing a porter or guard, or (formerly) used as a fortification **2** a small house at the entrance to the grounds of a country mansion **3** a structure that houses the controls operating lock gates or dam sluices

gatekeeper ('geɪt,kiːpə) *n* **1** a person who has charge of a gate and controls who may pass through it **2** any of several Eurasian butterflies of the genus *Pyronia*, esp *P. tithonus*, having brown-bordered orange wings with a black-and-white eyespot on each forewing: family *Satyridae* **3** a manager in a large organization who controls the flow of information, esp to parent and subsidiary companies

gate-leg table *or* **gate-legged table** *n* a table with one or two drop leaves that are supported when in use by a hinged leg swung out from the frame

gate money *n* the total receipts taken for admission to a sporting event or other entertainment

gatepost ('geɪt,pəust) *n* **1 a** the post on which a gate is hung **b** the post to which a gate is fastened when closed **2 between you, me, and the gatepost** confidentially **3** *logic* another name for **turnstile** (sense 3)

gater ('geɪtə) *n* a variant of **gator**

Gateshead ('geɪts,hɛd) *n* **1** a port in NE England, in Gateshead unitary authority, Tyne and Wear: engineering works, cultural centre. Pop: 78 403 (2001) **2** a unitary authority in NE England, in Tyne and Wear. Pop: 191 000 (2003 est). Area: 142 sq km (55 sq miles)

gate valve *n* a valve in a pipe or channel having a sliding plate that controls the flow

gateway ('geɪt,weɪ) *n* **1** an entrance that may be closed by or as by a gate **2** a means of entry or access: *Bombay, gateway to India* **3** *computing* hardware and software that connect incompatible computer networks, allowing information to be passed from one to another **4** a software utility that enables text messages to be sent and received over digital cellular telephone networks

gateway drug *n* a recreational drug such as cannabis, the use of which is believed by some to encourage the user to try stronger drugs

Gath (gæθ) *n Old Testament* one of the five cities of the Philistines, from which Goliath came (I Samuel 17:4) and near which Saul fell in battle (II Samuel 1:20). Douay spelling: **Geth** (gɛθ)

Gatha ('gɑːtə) *n Zoroastrianism* any of a number of versified sermons in the Avesta that are in a more ancient dialect than the rest [from Avestan *gāthā-*; related to Sanskrit *gāthā* song]

gather ('gæðə) *vb* **1** to assemble or cause to assemble **2** to collect or be collected gradually; muster **3** (*tr*) to learn from information given; conclude or assume **4** (*tr*) to pick or harvest (flowers, fruit, etc) **5** (*tr*; foll by *to* or *into*) to clasp or embrace: *the mother gathered the child into her arms* **6** (*tr*) to bring close (to) or wrap (around): *she gathered her shawl about her shoulders* **7** to increase or cause to increase gradually, as in force, speed, intensity, etc **8** to contract (the brow) or (of the brow) to become contracted into wrinkles; knit **9** (*tr*) to assemble (sections of a book) in the correct sequence for binding **10** (*tr*) to collect by making a selection **11** (*tr*) to prepare or make ready: *to gather one's wits* **12** to draw (material) into a series of small tucks or folds by passing a thread through it and then pulling it tight **13** (*intr*) (of a boil or other sore) to come to a head; form pus ▷ *n* **14 a** the act of gathering **b** the amount gathered **15** a small fold in material, as made by a tightly pulled stitch; tuck **16** *printing* an informal name for **section** (sense 17) [Old English *gadrian*; related to Old Frisian *gaderia*, Middle Low German *gaderen*] > 'gatherable *adj* > 'gatherer *n*

gathering ('gæðərɪŋ) *n* **1** a group of people, things, etc, that are gathered together; assembly **2** *sewing* a gather or series of gathers in material **3 a** the formation of pus in a boil **b** the pus so formed **4** *printing* an informal name for **section** (sense 17)

Gatling gun ('gætlɪŋ) *n* a hand-cranked automatic machine gun equipped with a rotating cluster of barrels that are fired in succession using brass cartridges [C19 named after R. J. *Gatling* (1818–1903), its US inventor]

gator *or* **gater** ('geɪtə) *n chiefly US informal* an alligator [C19]

GATT (gæt) *n acronym for* General Agreement on Tariffs and Trade: a multilateral international treaty signed in 1947 to promote trade, esp by means of the reduction and elimination of tariffs and import quotas; replaced in 1995 by the World Trade Organization

Gatún Lake (*Spanish* ga'tun) *n* a lake in Panama, part of the Panama Canal: formed in 1912 on the completion of the **Gatún Dam** across the Chagres River. Area: 424 sq km (164 sq miles)

gatvol ('xʌt,fɒl) *adj South African* annoyed; fed up [Afrikaans, literally: completely full]

gauche (gəuʃ) *adj* lacking tact or ease of manner; tactless [C18 French: awkward, left, from Old French *gauchir* to swerve, ultimately of Germanic origin; related to Old High German *wankōn* to stagger] > 'gauchely *adv* > 'gaucheness *n*

gaucherie (,gəuʃə'riː, 'gəuʃərɪ; *French* goʃri) *n* **1** the quality of being gauche **2** a gauche act

gaucho ('gautʃəu) *n, pl* **-chos** a cowboy of the South American pampas, usually one of mixed Spanish and Indian descent [C19 from American Spanish, probably from Quechuan *wáhcha* orphan, vagabond]

gaud (gɔːd) *n* an article of cheap finery; trinket; bauble [C14 probably from Old French *gaudir* to be joyful, from Latin *gaudēre*]

gaudeamus igitur *Latin* (,gaudɪ'ɑːmus 'ɪgɪ,tuə, ,gɔːdɪ'eɪməs 'ɪdʒɪtə) *interj* let us therefore rejoice [from a medieval student song]

gaudery ('gɔːdərɪ) *n, pl* **-eries** cheap finery or display

gaudy¹ ('gɔːdɪ) *adj* **gaudier, gaudiest** gay, bright, or colourful in a crude or vulgar manner; garish [C16 from GAUD] > 'gaudily *adv* > 'gaudiness *n*

gaudy² ('gɔːdɪ) *n, pl* **gaudies** a celebratory festival or feast held at some schools and colleges [C16 from Latin *gaudium* joy, from *gaudēre* to rejoice]

gauffer ('gəufə) *n, vb* a less common spelling of **goffer**

gauge *or* **gage** (geɪdʒ) *vb* (*tr*) **1** to measure or determine the amount, quantity, size, condition, etc, of **2** to estimate or appraise; judge **3** to check for conformity or bring into conformity with a standard measurement, dimension, etc ▷ *n* **4** a standard measurement, dimension, capacity, or quantity **5** any of various instruments for measuring a quantity: *a pressure gauge* **6** any of various devices used to check for conformity with a standard measurement **7** a standard or means for assessing; test; criterion **8** scope, capacity, or extent **9** the diameter of the barrel of a gun, esp a shotgun **10** the thickness of sheet metal or the diameter of wire **11** the distance between the rails of a railway track: in Britain 4 ft 8½ in. (1.435 m) **12** the distance between two wheels on the same axle of a vehicle, truck, etc **13** *nautical* the position of a vessel in relation to the wind and another vessel. One vessel may be windward (**weather gauge**) or leeward (**lee gauge**) of the other **14** the proportion of plaster of Paris added to mortar to accelerate its setting **15** the distance between the nails securing the slates, tiles, etc, of a roof **16** a measure of the fineness of woven or knitted fabric, usually expressed as the number of needles used per inch **17** the width of motion-picture film or magnetic tape ▷ *adj* **18** (of a pressure measurement) measured on a pressure gauge that registers zero at atmospheric pressure; above or below atmospheric pressure: *5 bar gauge*. See also **absolute** (sense 10) [C15 from Old Northern French, probably of Germanic origin] > 'gaugeable *or* 'gageable *adj* > 'gaugeably *or* 'gageably *adv*

gauge boson *n physics* a boson that mediates the interaction between elementary particles. There are several types: photons for electromagnetic interactions, W and Z intermediate vector bosons for weak interactions, and gravitons for gravitational interactions

gauger *or* **gager** ('geɪdʒə) *n* **1** a person or thing that gauges **2** *chiefly Brit* a customs officer who inspects bulk merchandise, esp liquor casks, for excise duty purposes **3** a collector of excise taxes

gauge theory *n physics* a type of theory of elementary particles designed to explain the strong, weak, and electromagnetic interactions in terms of exchange of virtual particles

Gauhati (gaʊˈhɑːtɪ) *n* a city in NE India, in Assam on the River Brahmaputra: centre of British administration in Assam (1826–74). Pop: 808 021 (2001)

Gaul (gɔːl) *n* **1** an ancient region of W Europe corresponding to N Italy, France, Belgium, part of Germany, and the S Netherlands: divided into Cisalpine Gaul, which became a Roman province before 100 BC, and Transalpine Gaul, which was conquered by Julius Caesar (58–51 BC). Latin name: Gallia **2** a native of ancient Gaul **3** a Frenchman

Gauleiter (ˈgaʊˌlaɪtə) *n* **1** a provincial governor in Germany under Hitler **2** (*sometimes not capital*) *informal* a person in a position of petty or local authority who behaves in an overbearing authoritarian manner [from German, from *Gau* district + *Leiter* LEADER]

Gaulish (ˈgɔːlɪʃ) *n* **1** the extinct language of the pre-Roman Gauls, belonging to the Celtic branch of the Indo-European family ▷ *adj* **2** of or relating to ancient Gaul, the Gauls, or their language

Gaullism (ˈgəʊlɪzəm, ˈgɔː-) *n* the conservative French nationalist policies and principles associated with General Charles de Gaulle (1890–1970), the French general and statesman **2** a political movement founded on and supporting General de Gaulle's principles and policies

Gaullist (ˈgəʊlɪst, ˈgɔː-) *n* **1** a supporter of Gaullism ▷ *adj* **2** of, characteristic of, supporting, or relating to Gaullism

gault (gɔːlt) *n* a stiff compact clay or thick heavy clayey soil [c16 of obscure origin]

Gault (gɔːlt) *n* **the** the Lower Cretaceous clay formation in eastern England

gaultheria (gɔːlˈθɪərɪə) *n* any aromatic evergreen shrub of the ericaceous genus *Gaultheria*, of America, Asia, Australia, and New Zealand, esp the wintergreen [c19 New Latin, after Jean-François *Gaultier*, 18th-century Canadian physician and botanist]

gaumless (ˈgɔːmlɪs) *adj* a variant spelling of **gormless**

gaun (gɔːn) *vb* the present participle of **gae**

gaunt (gɔːnt) *adj* **1** bony and emaciated in appearance **2** (of places) bleak or desolate [c15 perhaps of Scandinavian origin; compare Norwegian dialect *gand* tall lean person] ▷ ˈgauntly *adv* ▷ ˈgauntness *n*

gauntlet¹ (ˈgɔːntlɪt) *or* **gantlet** *n* **1** a medieval armoured leather glove **2** a heavy glove with a long cuff **3** take up (*or* throw down) the gauntlet to accept (or offer) a challenge [c15 from Old French *gantelet*, diminutive of *gant* glove, of Germanic origin]

gauntlet² (ˈgɔːntlɪt) *n* **1** a punishment in which the victim is forced to run between two rows of men who strike at him as he passes: formerly a military punishment **2** run the gauntlet **a** to suffer this punishment **b** to endure an onslaught or ordeal, as of criticism **3** a testing ordeal; trial **4** a variant spelling of **gantlet¹** (sense 1) [c15 changed (through influence of GAUNTLET¹) from earlier *gantlope*; see GANTLET¹]

gauntry (ˈgɔːntrɪ) *n, pl* -tries a variant of **gantry**

gaup (gɔːp) *vb* a variant spelling of **gawp**

gaur (gaʊə) *n* a large wild member of the cattle tribe, *Bos gaurus*, inhabiting mountainous regions of S Asia [c19 from Hindi, from Sanskrit *gāura*]

Gause's principle (ˈgaʊzəz) *n ecology* the principle that similar species cannot coexist for long in the same ecological niche [named after G. F. *Gause*, 20th-century Soviet biologist]

gauss (gaʊs) *n, pl* gauss the cgs unit of magnetic flux density; the flux density that will induce an emf of 1 abvolt (10⁻⁸ volt) per centimetre in a wire moving across the field at a velocity of 1 centimetre per second. 1 gauss is equivalent to 10^{-4} tesla [after Karl Friedrich *Gauss* (1777–1855), German mathematician]

Gaussian (ˈgaʊsɪən) *adj* of or relating to Karl Friedrich Gauss, the German mathematician (1777–1855)

Gaussian distribution *n* another name for **normal distribution**

gaussmeter (ˈgaʊsˌmiːtə) *n* an instrument for measuring the intensity of a magnetic field

Gautama (ˈgaʊtəmə) *n* the Sanskrit form of the family name of Siddhartha, the historical Buddha

Gauteng (xaʊˈtɛŋ) *n* a province of N South Africa; formed in 1994 from part of the former Transvaal: service industries, mining, and manufacturing. Capital: Johannesburg. Pop: 8 847 740 (2004 est). Area: 18 810 sq km (7262 sq miles)

gauze (gɔːz) *n* **1 a** a transparent cloth of loose plain or leno weave **b** (*as modifier*): *a gauze veil* **2** a surgical dressing of muslin or similar material **3** any thin openwork material, such as wire **4** a fine mist or haze [c16 from French *gaze*, perhaps from GAZA, where it was believed to originate]

gauzy (ˈgɔːzɪ) *adj* gauzier, gauziest resembling gauze; thin and transparent ▷ ˈgauzily *adv* ▷ ˈgauziness *n*

gavage (ˈgævɑːʒ) *n* forced feeding by means of a tube inserted into the stomach through the mouth [c19 from French, from *gaver*, from Old French (dialect) *gave* throat]

gave (geɪv) *vb* the past tense of **give**

gavel (ˈgævəl) *n* **1** a small hammer used by a chairman, auctioneer, etc, to call for order or attention **2** a hammer used by masons to trim rough edges off stones [c19 of unknown origin]

gavelkind (ˈgævəlˌkaɪnd) *n* **1** a former system of land tenure peculiar to Kent based on the payment of rent to the lord instead of the performance of services by the tenant **2** the land subject to such tenure **3** *English law* (formerly) land held under this system [c13 from Old English *gafol* tribute + *gecynd* KIND²]

gavial (ˈgeɪvɪəl) *or* **gharial, garial** (ˈgærɪəl) *n* **1** a large fish-eating Indian crocodilian, *Gavialis gangeticus*, with a very long slender snout: family *Gavialidae* **2** false gavial a SE Asian crocodile, *Tomistoma schlegeli*, similar to but smaller than the gavial [c19 from French, from Hindi *ghariyāl*]

Gävle (Swedish ˈjɛːvlə) *n* a port in E Sweden, on an inlet of the Gulf of Bothnia. Pop: 92 025 (2004 est)

gavotte *or* **gavot** (gəˈvɒt) *n* **1** an old formal dance in quadruple time **2** a piece of music composed for or in the rhythm of this dance [c17 from French, from Provençal *gavoto*, from *gavot* mountaineer, dweller in the Alps (where the dance originated), from *gava* goitre (widespread in the Alps), from Old Latin *gaba* (unattested) throat]

gawk (gɔːk) *n* **1** a clumsy stupid person; lout ▷ *vb* **2** (*intr*) to stare in a stupid way; gape [c18 from Old Danish *gaukr*; probably related to GAPE]

gawky (ˈgɔːkɪ) *or* **gawkish** *adj* gawkier, gawkiest **1** clumsy or ungainly; awkward **2** *West Yorkshire dialect* left-handed ▷ ˈgawkily *or* ˈgawkishly *adv* ▷ ˈgawkiness *or* ˈgawkishness *n*

gawp *or* **gaup** (gɔːp) *vb* (*intr; often foll by at*) *Brit slang* to stare stupidly; gape [c14 *galpen*; probably related to Old English *gielpan* to boast, YELP. Compare Dutch *galpen* to yelp]

gay (geɪ) *adj* **1 a** homosexual **b** (*as noun*): *a group of gays* **2** carefree and merry: *a gay temperament* **b** brightly coloured; brilliant: *a gay hat* **c** given to pleasure, esp in social entertainment: *a gay life* [c13 from Old French *gai*, from Old Provençal, of Germanic origin] ▷ ˈgayness *n*

▪ USAGE *Gayness* is the state of being homosexual. The noun which refers to the state of being carefree and merry is *gaiety*.

Gaya (ˈgɑːjə, ˈgaɪə) *n* a city in NE India, in Bihar: Hindu place of pilgrimage and one of the holiest sites of Buddhism. Pop: 383 197 (2001)

gayal (gəˈjæl) *n, pl* gayal *or* gayals an ox of India

and Myanmar, *Bibos frontalis*, possibly a semidomesticated variety of gaur, black or brown with white stockings [c19 from Bengali *gayal*, from Sanskrit *gāura*; compare GAUR]

gaydar (ˈgeɪdɑː) *n informal* the ability of a homosexual person to recognize whether another person is homosexual [c20 from GAY + (RA)DAR]

Gay Gordons (ˈgɔːdənz) *n* (*functioning as singular*) *Brit* an energetic old time dance

Gay-Lussac's law (ˈgeɪˈluːsæks) *n* **1** the principle that gases react together in volumes (measured at the same temperature and pressure) that bear a simple ratio to each other and to the gaseous products **2** another name for **Charles's law** [c19 named after Joseph Louis *Gay-Lussac* (1778–1850), French physicist and chemist]

Gayomart (ˈgɑːjəʊmɑːt) *n Zoroastrianism* the first man, whose seed was buried in the earth for 40 years and then produced the first human couple

Gaza (ˈgɑːzə) *n* a city in the Gaza Strip: a Philistine city in biblical times. It was under Egyptian administration from 1949 until occupied by Israel (1967). Pop: 787 000 (2005 est). Arabic name: Ghazzah

gazania (gəˈzeɪnɪə) *n* any plant of the S. African genus *Gazania*, grown for their rayed flowers in variegated colours; the flowers close in the afternoon: family *Asteraceae*. Also called: **treasure flower** [named after Theodore of *Gaza*, 1398–1478, translator of the botanical treatises of Theophrastus]

Gazankulu (ˌgazanˈkuːluː) *n* (formerly) a Bantu homeland in South Africa; abolished in 1993. Capital: Giyani

Gaza Strip *n* a coastal region on the SE corner of the Mediterranean: administered by Egypt from 1949; occupied by Israel from 1967; granted autonomy in 1993 and administered by the Palestinian National Authority from 1994. Pop: 1 406 423 (2004 est)

gaze (geɪz) *vb* **1** (*intr*) to look long and fixedly, esp in wonder or admiration ▷ *n* **2** a fixed look; stare [c14 from Swedish dialect *gasa* to gape at] ▷ ˈgazer *n*

gazebo (gəˈziːbəʊ) *n, pl* -bos *or* -boes a summerhouse, garden pavilion, or belvedere, sited to command a view [c18 perhaps a pseudo-Latin coinage based on GAZE]

gazehound (ˈgeɪzˌhaʊnd) *n* **1** a hound such as a greyhound that hunts by sight rather than by scent **2** another name for a **Saluki**

gazelle (gəˈzɛl) *n, pl* -zelles *or* -zelle any small graceful usually fawn-coloured antelope of the genera *Gazella* and *Procapra*, of Africa and Asia, such as *G. thomsoni* (**Thomson's gazelle**) [c17 from Old French, from Arabic *ghazāl*] ▷ gaˈzelle-ˌlike *adj*

gazelle hound *n* another name for **Saluki**

gazette (gəˈzɛt) *n* **1 a** a newspaper or official journal **b** (*capital when part of the name of a newspaper*): *the Thame Gazette* **2** *Brit* an official document containing public notices, appointments, etc. Abbreviation: **gaz** ▷ *vb* **3** (*tr*) *Brit* to announce or report (facts or an event) in a gazette [c17 from French, from Italian *gazzetta*, from Venetian dialect *gazeta* news-sheet, from Venetian dialect *gazeta* news-sheet costing one *gazet*, small copper coin, perhaps from *gaza* magpie, from Latin *gaia, gaius* jay]

gazetted officer *n* (in India) a senior official whose appointment is published in the government gazette

gazetteer (ˌgæzɪˈtɪə) *n* **1** a book or section of a book that lists and describes places. Abbreviation: **gaz 2** *archaic* a writer for a gazette or newspaper; journalist

Gaziantep (ˌgɑːziːɑːnˈtɛp) *n* a city in S Turkey: base for Ibrahim Pasha's campaign against the Turks (1839) and centre of Turkish resistance to French forces (1921). Pop: 1 004 000 (2005 est). Former name (until 1921): Aintab

gazillion (gəˈzɪljən) *informal* ▷ *n, pl* -lions *or* -lion **1** (*often pl*) an extremely large but unspecified number, quantity, or amount: *gazillions of people turned up* ▷ *determiner* **2 a** amounting to a

g

gazillion: *a gazillion types to choose from* **b** (*as pronoun*): *I found a gazillion under the sink* [C20 on the model of *million*]

gazillionaire (gə'zɪljə,nɛə) *n informal* a person who is enormously rich

gazpacho (gəz'pɑ:tʃəʊ, gæs-) *n* a Spanish soup made from tomatoes, peppers, etc, and served cold [from Spanish]

gazump (gə'zʌmp) *Brit* ▷ *vb* **1** to raise the price of something, esp a house, after agreeing a price verbally with (an intending buyer) **2** (*tr*) to swindle or overcharge ▷ *n* **3** the act or an instance of gazumping [C20 of uncertain origin] > ga'zumper *n*

gazunder (gə'zʌndə) *Brit* ▷ *vb* **1** to reduce an offer on a property immediately before exchanging contracts, having previously agreed a higher price with (the seller) ▷ *n* **2** an act or instance of gazundering [C20 modelled on GAZUMP] > ga'zunderer *n*

Gb 1 *symbol for* gilbert **2** Also: **GB** ▷ *abbreviation for* gigabyte

GB *abbreviation for* **1** Great Britain **2** Also: **Gb** gigabyte **3** ▷ *international car registration for* Great Britain

GBA *international car registration for* Alderney

GBE *abbreviation for* (Knight or Dame) Grand Cross of the British Empire (a Brit title)

GBG *international car registration for* Guernsey

GBH *abbreviation for* **grievous bodily harm** **gamma-hydroxybentyrate**

GBJ *international car registration for* Jersey

GBL *abbreviation for* gamma butyrolactone: a dangerous chemical which may illegally be contained in some dietary supplements and which the body converts to GHB

GBM *international car registration for* Isle of Man

GBS *abbreviation for* George Bernard Shaw

GBZ *international car registration for* Gibraltar

GC *abbreviation for* George Cross (a Brit award for bravery)

GCA 1 *aeronautics abbreviation for* ground control approach **2** ▷ *international car registration for* Guatemala

GCB *abbreviation for* (Knight) Grand Cross of the Bath (a Brit title)

GCE *abbreviation for* General Certificate of Education: a public examination in specified subjects taken in English and Welsh schools at the ages of 17 and 18. The GCSE has replaced the former GCE O-level for 16-year-olds. See also **AS level, S level**

GCF *or* **gcf** *abbreviation for* greatest common factor

GCHQ (in Britain) *abbreviation for* Government Communications Headquarters

G clef *n* another name for **treble clef**

GCMG *abbreviation for* (Knight or Dame) Grand Cross of the Order of St Michael and St George (a Brit title)

G-cramp *n* another name for **cramp²** (sense 2)

GCSE (in Britain) *abbreviation for* General Certificate of Secondary Education: a public examination in specified subjects for 16-year-old schoolchildren. It replaced the GCE O-level and CSE

GCVO *abbreviation for* (Knight or Dame) Grand Cross of the Royal Victorian Order (a Brit title)

gd *the internet domain name for* Grenada

Gd *the chemical symbol for* gadolinium

Gdańsk (*Polish* gdajinsk) *n* **1** the chief port of Poland, on the Baltic: a member of the Hanseatic league; under Prussian rule (1793–1807 and 1814–1919); a free city under the League of Nations from 1919 until annexed by Germany in 1939; returned to Poland in 1945. Pop: 851 000 (2005 est). German name: Danzig **2** **Bay of** a wide inlet of the Baltic Sea on the N coast of Poland

g'day *or* **gidday** (gə'daɪ) *sentence substitute* an Austral and NZ *informal* variant of **good day**

Gdns *abbreviation for* Gardens

GDP *or* **gdp** *abbreviation for* gross domestic product

GDR *abbreviation for* German Democratic Republic (East Germany; DDR)

gds *abbreviation for* goods

Gdynia (*Polish* 'gdinja) *n* a port in N Poland, near Gdańsk: developed 1924–39 as the outlet for trade through the Polish Corridor; naval base. Pop: 253 521 (1999 est)

ge *the internet domain name for* Georgia

Ge¹ (dʒi:) *n* another name for **Gaia**

Ge² *the chemical symbol for* germanium

GE *international car registration for* Georgia

gean (gi:n) *n* **1** Also called: **wild cherry** a white-flowered rosaceous tree, *Prunus avium*, of Europe, W Asia, and N Africa, the ancestor of the cultivated sweet cherries **2** See **sweet cherry** (sense 1)

geanticline (dʒi:'æntɪ,klaɪn) *n* a gently sloping anticline covering a large area [C19 from Greek *gē* earth, land + ANTICLINE] > ge,anti'clinal *adj*

gear (gɪə) *n* **1** a toothed wheel that engages with another toothed wheel or with a rack in order to change the speed or direction of transmitted motion **2** a mechanism for transmitting motion by gears, esp for a specific purpose: *the steering gear of a boat* **3** the engagement or specific ratio of a system of gears: *in gear; high gear* **4** personal equipment and accoutrements; belongings **5** equipment and supplies for a particular operation, sport, etc: *fishing gear* **6** *nautical* all equipment or appurtenances belonging to a certain vessel, sailor, etc **7** short for **landing gear** **8** *informal* up-to-date clothes and accessories, esp those bought by young people **9** *slang* **a** stolen goods **b** illegal drugs **10** a less common word for **harness** (sense 1) **11** **in gear** working or performing effectively or properly **12** **out of gear** out of order; not functioning properly ▷ *vb* **13** (*tr*) to adjust or adapt (one thing) so as to fit in or work with another: *to gear our output to current demand* **14** (*tr*) to equip with or connect by gears **15** (*intr*) to be in or come into gear **16** (*tr*) to equip with harness [C13 from Old Norse *gervi*; related to Old High German *garawī* equipment, Old English *gearwe*] > 'gearless *adj*

gearbox ('gɪə,bɒks) *n* **1** the metal casing within which a train of gears is sealed **2** this metal casing and its contents, esp in a motor vehicle

gear cluster *n engineering* an assembly of gears permanently attached to a shaft

gear down *vb* (*tr, adverb*) to adapt to a new situation by decreasing output, intensity of operations, etc

gearing ('gɪərɪŋ) *n* **1** an assembly of gears designed to transmit motion **2** the act or technique of providing gears to transmit motion **3** Also called: **capital gearing** *accounting, Brit* the ratio of a company's debt capital to its equity capital. US word: **leverage**

gear knob *n Brit* a gear lever

gear lever *or US and Canadian* **gearshift** ('gɪə,ʃɪft) *n* a lever used to move gearwheels relative to each other, esp in a motor vehicle

gear train *n engineering* a system of gears that transmits power from one shaft to another

gear up *vb* (*adverb*) **1** (*tr*) to equip with gears **2** to prepare, esp for greater efficiency: *is our industry geared up for these new challenges?*

gearwheel ('gɪə,wi:l) *n* another name for **gear** (sense 1)

gecko ('gɛkəʊ) *n, pl -os or -oes* any small insectivorous terrestrial lizard of the family *Gekkonidae*, of warm regions. The digits have adhesive pads, which enable these animals to climb on smooth surfaces [C18 from Malay *ge'kok*, of imitative origin]

gedact (gə'dɑ:kt, -'dækt) *or* **gedeckt** (gə'dɛkt) *n music* a flutelike stopped metal diapason organ pipe [(*gedeckt*) from German: covered, from *decken* to cover]

geddit ('gɛdɪt) *interj slang* an exclamation meaning *do you understand it?*: *they nicknamed him 'Treasure', because of his sunken chest, geddit?* [C20 from *Do you get it?* from GET understand]

gee¹ (dʒi:) *interj* **1** Also: **gee up!** an exclamation, as to a horse or draught animal, to encourage it to turn to the right, go on, or go faster ▷ *vb* **gees, geeing, geed 2** (usually foll by *up*) to move (an animal, esp a horse) ahead; urge on **3** (foll by *up*) to encourage (someone) to greater effort or activity ▷ *n* **4** *slang* See **gee-gee** [C17 origin uncertain]

gee² (dʒi:) *interj US and Canadian informal* a mild exclamation of surprise, admiration, etc. Also: **gee whizz** [C20 euphemism for JESUS]

geebag ('gi:,bæg) *n Irish slang* a disagreeable woman

geebung ('dʒi:bʌŋ) *n* **1** any of various trees and shrubs of the genus *Persoonia* of Australia having an edible but tasteless fruit **2** the fruit of these trees **3** (in the 19th century) an uncultivated Australian from the country districts [from a native Australian language]

gee-gee ('dʒi:,dʒi:) *n slang* a horse [C19 reduplication of GEE¹]

geek (gi:k) *n slang* **1** a person who is preoccupied with or very knowledgeable about computing **2** a boring and unattractive social misfit **3** a degenerate [C19 probably variant of Scottish *geck* fool, from Middle Low German *geck*] > 'geeky *adj*

geekspeak ('gi:k,spi:k) *n slang* jargon used by geeks, esp computer enthusiasts

geelbek ('xɪəl,bɛk) *n South African* a yellow-jawed edible marine fish [from Afrikaans *geel* yellow + *bek* mouth]

Geelong (dʒə'lɒŋ) *n* a port in SE Australia, in S Victoria on Port Phillip Bay. Pop: 130 194 (2001)

geepound ('dʒi:,paʊnd) *n* another name for **slug²** (sense 1) [C20 from *gee*, representing G(RAVITY) + POUND²]

geese (gi:s) *n* the plural of **goose**

geest (gi:st) *n* an area of sandy heathland in N Germany and adjacent areas [C19 Low German *Geest* dry soil]

gee-whiz *adj informal* impressive or amazing: *gee-whiz special effects* [C20 from GEE²]

Ge'ez ('gi:ɛz) *n* the classical form of the ancient Ethiopic language, having an extensive Christian literature and still used in Ethiopia as a liturgical language

geezah ('gi:zə) *n* a variant spelling of **geezer**

geezer ('gi:zə) *n informal* a man [C19 probably from dialect pronunciation of *guiser*, from GUISE + -ER¹]

gefilte fish *or* **gefüllte fish** (gə'fɪltə) *n Jewish cookery* a dish consisting of fish and matzo meal rolled into balls and poached, formerly served stuffed into the skin of a fish [Yiddish, literally: filled fish]

gegenschein ('geɪgən,ʃaɪn) *n* a faint glow in the sky, just visible at a position opposite to that of the sun and having a similar origin to zodiacal light. Also called: **counterglow** [German, from *gegen* against, opposite + *Schein* light; see SHINE]

geggie ('gɛgɪ) *n* a Scottish, esp Glaswegian, slang word for the **mouth**

Gehenna (gɪ'hɛnə) *n* **1** *Old Testament* the valley below Jerusalem, where children were sacrificed and where idolatry was practised (II Kings 23:10; Jeremiah 19:6) and where later offal and refuse were slowly burned **2** *New Testament, Judaism* a place where the wicked are punished after death **3** a place or state of pain and torment [C16 from Late Latin, from Greek *Geena*, from Hebrew *Gê' Hinnōm*, literally: valley of Hinnom, symbolic of hell]

gehlenite ('geɪlə,naɪt) *n* a green mineral consisting of calcium aluminium silicate in tetragonal crystalline form. Formula: $Ca_2Al_2SiO_7$ [named after A. F. Gehlen (1775–1815), German chemist; see -ITE¹]

Geiger counter *or* **Geiger-Müller counter** ('gaɪgə'mʊlə) *n* an instrument for detecting and measuring the intensity of ionizing radiation. It consists of a gas-filled tube containing a fine wire anode along the axis of a cylindrical cathode with a potential difference of several hundred volts.

Any particle or photon which ionizes any number of gas molecules in the tube causes a discharge which is registered by electronic equipment. The magnitude of the discharge does not depend upon the nature or the energy of the ionizing particle. Compare **proportional counter** [c20 named after Hans *Geiger* (1882–1945), German physicist and W. *Müller*, 20th-century German physicist]

geisha ('geɪʃə) *n*, *pl* -sha or -shas a professional female companion for men in Japan, trained in music, dancing, and the art of conversation [c19 from Japanese, from *gei* art + *sha* person, from Ancient Chinese *ngi* and *che*]

Geissler tube ('gaɪslə) *n* a glass or quartz vessel, usually having two bulbs containing electrodes separated by a capillary tube, for maintaining an electric discharge in a low-pressure gas as a source of visible or ultraviolet light for spectroscopy [c19 named after Heinrich *Geissler* (1814–79), German mechanic]

geitonogamy (,gaɪtə'nɒgəmɪ) *n botany* the transfer of pollen to a stigma of a different flower on the same plant [c19 from Greek *geitōn* neighbour + -GAMY]

gel (dʒel) *n* **1** a semirigid jelly-like colloid in which a liquid is dispersed in a solid: *nondrip paint is a gel* See **hair gel 3** *theatre informal* See **gelatine** (sense 4) ▷ *vb* **gels, gelling, gelled 4** to become or cause to become a gel **5** a variant spelling of **jell** [c19 by shortening from GELATINE]

gelada ('dʒelədə, 'gel-, dʒɪ'lɑːdə, gɪ-) *n* a NE African baboon, *Theropithecus gelada*, with dark brown hair forming a mane over the shoulders, a bare red chest, and a ridged muzzle: family *Cercopithecidae*. Also called: **gelada baboon** [probably from Arabic *qilādah* mane]

Geländesprung (gə'lendə,ʃprʊŋ) or **gelände jump** (gə'lendə) *n skiing* a jump made in downhill skiing, usually over an obstacle [German, from *Gelände* terrain + *Sprung* jump]

gelatine ('dʒelə,tiːn) or **gelatin** (dʒelətɪn) *n* **1** a colourless or yellowish water-soluble protein prepared by boiling animal hides and bones: used in foods, glue, photographic emulsions, etc **2** an edible jelly made of this substance, sweetened and flavoured **3** any of various substances that resemble gelatine **4** Also called (informal): **gel** a translucent substance used for colour effects in theatrical lighting [c19 from French *gélatine*, from Medieval Latin *gelātīna*, from Latin *gelāre* to freeze]

gelatinize or **gelatinise** (dʒɪ'lætɪ,naɪz) *vb* **1** to make or become gelatinous **2** (*tr*) *photog* to coat (glass, paper, etc) with gelatine > ge,latini'zation or ge,latini'sation *n* > ge'lati,nizer or ge'lati,niser *n*

gelatinoid (dʒɪ'lætɪ,nɔɪd) *adj* **1** resembling gelatine ▷ *n* **2** a gelatinoid substance, such as collagen

gelatinous (dʒɪ'lætɪnəs) *adj* **1** consisting of or resembling jelly; viscous **2** of, containing, or resembling gelatine > ge'latinously *adv* > ge'latinousness *n*

gelation¹ (dʒɪ'leɪʃən) *n* the act or process of freezing a liquid [c19 from Latin *gelātiō* a freezing; see GELATINE]

gelation² (dʒɪ'leɪʃən) *n* the act or process of forming into a gel [c20 from GEL]

gelcap ('dʒel,kæp) *n* a dose of medicine enclosed in a soluble case of gelatine [c20 from GEL(ATINE) + CAP(SULE)]

geld¹ (geld) *vb* **gelds, gelding, gelded** or **gelt** (*tr*) **1** to castrate (a horse or other animal) **2** to deprive of virility or vitality; emasculate; weaken [c13 from Old Norse *gelda*, from *geldr* barren] > 'gelder *n*

geld² (geld) *n* a tax on land levied in late Anglo-Saxon and Norman England [Old English *gield* service, tax; related to Old Norse *gjald* tribute, Old Frisian *jeld*, Old High German *gelt* retribution, income]

Gelderland or **Guelderland** ('geldə,lænd; *Dutch* 'xeldərlɑnt) *n* a province of the E Netherlands: formerly a duchy, belonging successively to several different European powers. Capital:

Arnhem. Pop: 1 960 000 (2003 est). Area: 5014 sq km (1955 sq miles). Also called: **Guelders**

gelding ('geldɪŋ) *n* a castrated male horse [c14 from Old Norse *geldingr*; see GELD¹, -ING¹]

Gelibolu (ge'libɔlu) *n* the Turkish name for **Gallipoli**

gelid ('dʒelɪd) *adj* very cold, icy, or frosty [c17 from Latin *gelidus* icy cold, from *gelu* frost] > ge'lidity or 'gelidness *n* > 'gelidly *adv*

gelignite ('dʒelɪg,naɪt) *n* a type of dynamite in which the nitrogelatine is absorbed in a base of wood pulp and potassium or sodium nitrate. Also called (informal): **gelly** ('dʒelɪ) [c19 from GEL(ATINE) + Latin *ignis* fire + -ITE¹]

Gelligaer (*Welsh* ,gehli:'gaɪr) *n* a town in S Wales, in Caerphilly county borough. Pop (including Ystrad Mynach): 17 185 (2001)

gelsemium (dʒel'siːmɪəm) *n*, *pl* -miums or -mia (-mɪə) **1** any climbing shrub of the loganiaceous genus *Gelsemium*, of SE Asia and North America, esp the yellow jasmine, having fragrant yellow flowers **2** the powdered root of the yellow jasmine, formerly used as a sedative [c19 New Latin, from Italian *gelsomino* JASMINE]

Gelsenkirchen (*German* gelzən'kɪrçən) *n* an industrial city in W Germany, in North Rhine-Westphalia. Pop: 272 445 (2003 est)

gelt¹ (gelt) *vb archaic* or *dialect* a past tense and past participle of **geld**¹

gelt² (gelt) *n slang, chiefly US* cash or funds; money [c19 from Yiddish, from Old High German *gelt* reward]

gem (dʒem) *n* **1** a precious or semiprecious stone used in jewellery as a decoration; jewel **2** a person or thing held to be a perfect example; treasure **3** a size of printer's type, approximately equal to 4 point **4** *NZ* a type of small sweet cake ▷ *vb* **gems, gemming, gemmed 5** (*tr*) to set or ornament with gems [c14 from Old French *gemme*, from Latin *gemma* bud, precious stone] > 'gem,like *adj* > 'gemmy *adj*

Gemara (ge'mɔrə; *Hebrew* gema'ra) *n Judaism* the main body of the Talmud, consisting of a record of ancient rabbinical debates about the interpretation of the Mishna and constituting the primary source of Jewish religious law. See also **Talmud** [c17 from Aramaic *gemārā* completion, from *gemār* to complete] > Ge'maric *adj* > Ge'marist *n*

gemclip ('dʒem,klɪp) *n South African* a paperclip

gemeinschaft (*German* gə'maɪnʃaft) *n*, *pl* -schaften (*German* -ʃaftən) (*often capital*) a social group united by common beliefs, family ties, etc. Compare **gesellschaft** [German, literally: community]

gemfibrozil (dʒem'faɪbrəʊzɪl) *n* a drug that lowers the concentration of low-density lipoproteins in the blood and is therefore used to treat patients with hyperlipoproteinaemia

gemfish ('dʒem,fɪʃ) *n*, *pl* -fish or -fishes a food fish, *Rexea solandri*, of Australia, having a delicate flavour

geminate *adj* ('dʒemɪnɪt, -,neɪt) *also* geminated **1** combined in pairs; doubled: *a geminate leaf; a geminate consonant* ▷ *vb* ('dʒemɪ,neɪt) **2** to arrange or be arranged in pairs: *the "t"s in "fitted" are geminated* [c17 from Latin *gemināre* to double, from *geminus* born at the same time, twin] > 'geminately *adv*

gemination (,dʒemɪ'neɪʃən) *n* **1** the act or state of being doubled or paired **2** the doubling of a consonant **3** the immediate repetition of a word, phrase, or clause for rhetorical effect

Geminga *n astronomy* one of the brightest and nearest gamma-ray sources, situated in the constellation Gemini. A pulsar, it is believed to be a spinning neutron star [c20 from GEMINI + *gamma ray*]

Gemini ('dʒemɪ,naɪ, -,niː) *n, Latin genitive* **Geminorum** (,dʒemɪ'nɔːrəm) **1** *astronomy* a zodiacal constellation in the N hemisphere lying between Taurus and Cancer on the ecliptic and containing

the stars Castor and Pollux **2** *classical myth* another name for **Castor and Pollux 3** *astronautics* any of a series of manned US spacecraft launched between the Mercury and Apollo projects to improve orbital rendezvous and docking techniques **4** *astrology* **a** Also called: **the Twins** the third sign of the zodiac, symbol ♊, having a mutable air classification and ruled by the planet Mercury. The sun is in this sign between about May 21 and June 20 **b** a person born when the sun is in this sign ▷ *adj* **5** *astrology* born under or characteristic of Gemini ▷ Also (for senses 4b, 5): **Geminian** (,dʒemɪ'naɪən)

Geminid ('dʒemɪ,nɪd) *n* a member of a shower of meteors (the *Geminids*) occurring annually around December 13

Gemini telescope *n* either of two identical 8-metre telescopes for optical and near-infrared observations built by an international consortium. **Gemini North** is in Hawaii at an altitude of 4200 m on Mauna Kea and **Gemini South** is in Chile at 2715 m on Cerro Pachón

gem iron *n NZ* a heavy, usually cast-iron oven dish used for baking small cakes (gems)

gemma ('dʒemə) *n*, *pl* -mae (-mi:) **1** a small asexual reproductive structure in liverworts, mosses, etc, that becomes detached from the parent and develops into a new individual **2** *zoology* another name for **gemmule** (sense 1) [c18 from Latin: bud, GEM] > gemmaceous (dʒe'meɪʃəs) *adj*

gemmate ('dʒemeɪt) *adj* **1** (of some plants and animals) having or reproducing by gemmae ▷ *vb* **2** (*intr*) to produce or reproduce by gemmae > gem'mation *n*

gemmiparous (dʒe'mɪpərəs) *adj* (of plants and animals) reproducing by gemmae or buds. Also: **gemmiferous** (dʒe'mɪfərəs) > gem'miparously *adv*

gemmulation (,dʒemjʊ'leɪʃən) *n* the process of reproducing by or bearing gemmules

gemmule ('dʒemjuːl) *n* **1** *zoology* a cell or mass of cells produced asexually by sponges and developing into a new individual; bud **2** *botany* a small gemma **3** a small hereditary particle postulated by Darwin in his theory of pangenesis [c19 from French, from Latin *gemmula* a little bud; see GEM]

gemology or **gemmology** (dʒe'mɒlədʒɪ) *n* the branch of mineralogy that is concerned with gems and gemstones > gemological or gemmological (,dʒemə'lɒdʒɪkˀl) *adj* > gem'ologist or gem'mologist *n*

gemot or **gemote** (gɪ'məʊt) *n* (in Anglo-Saxon England) a legal or administrative assembly of a community, such as a shire or hundred [Old English *gemōt* MOOT]

gemsbok or **gemsbuck** ('gemz,bʌk) *n*, *pl* -bok, -boks or -buck, -bucks *South African* another word for **oryx** [c18 from Afrikaans, from German *Gemsbock*, from *Gemse* chamois + *Bock* BUCK¹]

gemstone ('dʒem,stəʊn) *n* a precious or semiprecious stone, esp one cut and polished for setting in jewellery. Related adj: **lapidary**

gemütlich *German* (gə'myːtlɪç) *adj* having a feeling or atmosphere of warmth and friendliness; cosy

gen (dʒen) *n informal* information. See also **gen up** [c20 from *gen*(eral information)]

Gen. *abbreviation for* **1** General **2** *Bible* Genesis

-gen *suffix forming nouns* **1** producing or that which produces: *hydrogen* **2** something produced: *carcinogen* [via French -*gène*, from Greek -*genēs* born]

genappe (dʒə'næp) *n* a smooth worsted yarn used for braid, etc [c19 from *Genappe*, Belgium, where originally manufactured]

Genck (*Flemish* xeŋk) *n* a variant spelling of **Genk**

gendarme ('ʒɒndɑːm; *French* ʒɑ̃darm) *n* **1** a member of the police force in France or in countries formerly influenced or controlled by France **2** a slang word for a **policeman 3** a sharp pinnacle of rock on a mountain ridge, esp in the Alps [c16 from French, from *gens d'armes* people of arms]

g

gendarmerie *or* **gendarmery** (ʒɒn'dɑːmərɪ; *French* ʒɑ̃darməri) *n* **1** the whole corps of gendarmes **2** the headquarters or barracks of a body of gendarmes

gender ('dʒɛndə) *n* **1** a set of two or more grammatical categories into which the nouns of certain languages are divided, sometimes but not necessarily corresponding to the sex of the referent when animate. See also **natural gender 2** any of the categories, such as masculine, feminine, neuter, or common, within such a set **3** *informal* the state of being male, female, or neuter **4** *informal* all the members of one sex: *the female gender* [C14 from Old French *gendre*, from Latin *genus* kind] > **'genderless** *adj*

gender-bender *n* **1** *informal* a person who adopts an androgynous style of dress, hair, make-up, etc **2** a male-male or female-female adaptor, used esp for computer hardware

gender-blind *adj* not discriminating on the basis of gender, or not making a distinction between the sexes

gender dysphoria *n* a condition in which a person feels uncertainty or anxiety about his or her birth gender

gender reassignment *n* male-to-female or female-to-male transformation involving surgery and hormone treatment

gene (dʒiːn) *n* a unit of heredity composed of DNA occupying a fixed position on a chromosome (some viral genes are composed of RNA). A gene may determine a characteristic of an individual by specifying a polypeptide chain that forms a protein or part of a protein (**structural gene**); or encode an RNA molecule; or regulate the operation of other genes or repress such operation. See also **operon** [C20 from German *Gen*, shortened from *Pangen*; see PAN-, -GEN]

-gene *suffix forming nouns* a variant of **-gen**

geneal. *abbreviation for* genealogy

genealogical tree *n* another name for a **family tree**

genealogy (ˌdʒiːnɪ'ælədʒɪ) *n, pl* **-gies 1** the direct descent of an individual or group from an ancestor **2** the study of the evolutionary development of animals and plants from earlier forms **3** a chart showing the relationships and descent of an individual, group, genes, etc [C13 from Old French *genealogie*, from Late Latin *geneālogia*, from Greek, from *genea* race] > **genealogical** (ˌdʒiːnɪə'lɒdʒɪkəl) *or* ˌgenea'logic *adj* > ˌgenea'logically *adv* > ˌgene'alogist *n*

gene bank *n botany* **1** a collection of seeds, plants, tissue cultures, etc, of potentially useful species, esp species containing genes of significance to the breeding of crops **2** another name for **gene library**

gene clone *n* See **clone** (sense 2)

genecology (ˌdʒiːnɪ'kɒlədʒɪ) *n* the study of the gene frequency of a species in relation to its population distribution within a particular environment

gene flow *n* the movement and exchange of genes between interbreeding populations

gene frequency *n* the frequency of occurrence of a particular allele in a population

gene library *n* a collection of gene clones that represents the genetic material of an organism: used in genetic engineering. Also called: **gene bank**

gene pool *n* the sum of all the genes in an interbreeding population

genera ('dʒɛnərə) *n* a plural of **genus**

generable ('dʒɛnərəbəl) *adj* able to be generated [C15 from Late Latin *generābilis*, from Latin *generāre* to beget]

general ('dʒɛnərəl, 'dʒɛnrəl) *adj* **1** common; widespread: *a general feeling of horror at the crime* **2** of, including, applying to, or participated in by all or most of the members of a group, category, or community **3** relating to various branches of an activity, profession, etc; not specialized: *general*

office work **4** including various or miscellaneous items: *general knowledge; a general store* **5** not specific as to detail; overall: *a general description of the merchandise* **6** not definite; vague: *give me a general idea of when you will finish* **7** applicable or true in most cases; usual **8** (*prenominal or immediately postpositive*) having superior or extended authority or rank: *general manager; consul general* **9** Also: **pass** designating a degree awarded at some universities, studied at a lower academic standard than an honours degree. See **honours** (sense 2) **10** *med* relating to or involving the entire body or many of its parts; systemic **11** *logic* (of a statement) not specifying an individual subject but quantifying over a domain ▷ *n* **12** an officer of a rank senior to lieutenant general, esp one who commands a large military formation **13** any person acting as a leader and applying strategy or tactics **14** a general condition or principle: opposed to *particular* **15** a title for the head of a religious order, congregation, etc **16** *med* short for **general anaesthetic 17** *archaic* the people; public **18** **in general** generally; mostly or usually [C13 from Latin *generālis* of a particular kind, from *genus* kind] > **'generalness** *n*

general anaesthetic *n* a drug producing anaesthesia of the entire body, with loss of consciousness

General Assembly *n* **1** the deliberative assembly of the United Nations. Abbreviation: **GA 2** the former name for the parliament of New Zealand **3** the supreme governing body of certain religious denominations, esp of the Presbyterian Church

general average *n insurance* loss or damage to a ship or its cargo that is shared among the shipowners and all the cargo owners. Abbreviation: **GA** Compare **particular average**

General Certificate of Education *n* See **GCE**

General Certificate of Secondary Education *n* See **GCSE**

general delivery *n US and Canadian* **1** an address on mail indicating that it should be kept at a specified post office until collected by the addressee **2** the mail-delivery service or post-office department that handles mail having this address. Also called (not in the US or Canada): **poste restante**

general election *n* **1** an election in which representatives are chosen in all constituencies of a state **2** *US* a final election from which successful candidates are sent to a legislative body. Compare **primary 3** *US and Canadian* (in the US) a national or state election or (in Canada) a federal or provincial election in contrast to a local election

general hospital *n* a hospital not specializing in the treatment of particular illnesses or of patients of a particular sex or age group

generalissimo (ˌdʒɛnərə'lɪsɪˌməʊ, ˌdʒɛnrə-) *n, pl* **-mos** a supreme commander of combined military, naval, and air forces, esp one who wields political as well as military power [C17 from Italian, superlative of *generale* GENERAL]

generalist ('dʒɛnərəlɪst, 'dʒɛnrə-) *n* **1 a** a person who is knowledgeable in many fields of study **b** (*as modifier*): *a generalist profession* **2** *ecology* an organism able to utilize many food sources and therefore able to flourish in many habitats. Compare **specialist** (sense 3)

generality (ˌdʒɛnə'rælɪtɪ) *n, pl* **-ties 1** a principle or observation having general application, esp when imprecise or unable to be proved **2** the state or quality of being general **3** *archaic* the majority

generalization *or* **generalisation** (ˌdʒɛnrəlaɪ'zeɪʃən) *n* **1** a principle, theory, etc, with general application **2** the act or an instance of generalizing **3** *psychol* the evoking of a response learned to one stimulus by a different but similar stimulus. See also **conditioning 4** *logic* the derivation of a general statement from a particular one, formally by prefixing a quantifier

and replacing a subject term by a bound variable. If the quantifier is universal (**universal generalization**) the argument is not in general valid; if it is existential (**existential generalization**) it is valid **5** *logic* any statement ascribing a property to every member of a class (**universal generalization**) or to one or more members (**existential generalization**)

generalize *or* **generalise** ('dʒɛnrəˌlaɪz) *vb* **1** to form (general principles or conclusions) from (detailed facts, experience, etc); infer **2** (*intr*) to think or speak in generalities, esp in a prejudiced way **3** (*tr; usually passive*) to cause to become widely used or known **4** (*intr*) (of a disease) **a** to spread throughout the body **b** to change from a localized infection or condition to a systemic one: *generalized infection* > **'general,izer** *or* **'general,iser** *n*

generalized other *n psychol* an individual's concept of other people

generally ('dʒɛnrəlɪ) *adv* **1** usually; as a rule **2** commonly or widely **3** without reference to specific details or facts; broadly

general officer *n* an officer holding a commission of brigadier's rank or above in the army, air force, or marine corps

general paralysis of the insane *n* a disease of the central nervous system: a late manifestation of syphilis, often occurring up to 15 years after the original infection, characterized by mental deterioration, speech defects, and progressive paralysis. Abbreviation: **GPI** Also called: **general paresis, dementia paralytica**

General Post Office *n* **1** (in Britain until 1969) the department of the central Government that provided postal and telephone services **2** the main post office in a locality

general practitioner *n* a physician who does not specialize but has a medical practice (**general practice**) in which he deals with all illnesses. Informal name: **family doctor** Abbreviation: **GP**

general-purpose *adj* having a range of uses or applications; not restricted to one function

general semantics *n* (*functioning as singular*) a school of thought, founded by Alfred Korzybski, that stresses the arbitrary nature of language and other symbols and the problems that result from misunderstanding their nature

generalship ('dʒɛnrəlˌʃɪp) *n* **1** the art or duties of exercising command of a major military formation or formations **2** tactical or administrative skill

general staff *n* officers assigned to advise commanders in the planning and execution of military operations

general strike *n* a strike by all or most of the workers of a country, province, city, etc, esp (*caps.*) such a strike that took place in Britain in 1926

General Synod *n* the governing body, under Parliament, of the Church of England, made up of the bishops and elected clerical and lay representatives

general theory of relativity *n* the theory of gravitation, developed by Einstein in 1916, extending the special theory of relativity to include acceleration and leading to the conclusion that gravitational forces are equivalent to forces caused by acceleration

general will *n* (in the philosophy of Rousseau) the source of legitimate authority residing in the collective will as contrasted with individual interests

generate ('dʒɛnəˌreɪt) *vb* (*mainly tr*) **1** to produce or bring into being; create **2** (*also intr*) to produce (electricity), esp in a power station **3** to produce (a substance) by a chemical process **4** *maths, linguistics* to provide a precise criterion or specification for membership in (a set): *these rules will generate all the noun phrases in English* **5** *geometry* to trace or form by moving a point, line, or plane in a specific way: *circular motion of a line generates a cylinder* [C16 from Latin *generāre* to beget, from *genus* kind]

generation (ˌdʒɛnəˈreɪʃən) n **1** the act or process of bringing into being; production or reproduction, esp of offspring **2 a** a successive stage in natural descent of organisms: the time between when an organism comes into being and when it reproduces **b** the individuals produced at each stage **3** the normal or average time between two such generations of a species: about 35 years for humans **4** a phase or form in the life cycle of a plant or animal characterized by a particular type of reproduction: *the gametophyte generation* **5** all the people of approximately the same age, esp when considered as sharing certain attitudes, etc **6** production of electricity, heat, etc **7** *physics* a set of nuclei formed directly from a preceding set in a chain reaction **8** (*modifier, in combination*) **a** belonging to a generation specified as having been born in or as having parents, grandparents, etc, born in a given country: *a third-generation American* **b** belonging to a specified stage of development in manufacture, usually implying improvement: *a second-generation computer* > ˌgenerˈational adj

generation gap n the years separating one generation from the generation that precedes or follows it, esp when regarded as representing the difference in outlook and the lack of understanding between them

Generation X n members of the generation of people born between the mid-1960s and the mid-1970s who are highly educated and underemployed, reject consumer culture, and have little hope for the future [c20 from the novel *Generation X: Tales for an Accelerated Culture* by Douglas Coupland] > ˌGeneration ˈXer n

Generation XL n *informal facetious* overweight children or young adults of the generation that spends a great deal of time on sedentary pursuits such as surfing the internet and playing computer games

Generation Y n members of the generation of people born since the early 1980s who are seen as being discerning consumers with a high disposable income

generative (ˈdʒɛnərətɪv) adj **1** of or relating to the production of offspring, parts, etc: *a generative cell* **2** capable of producing or originating

generative grammar n a description of a language in terms of explicit rules that ideally generate all and only the grammatical sentences of the language. Compare **transformational grammar**

generative semantics n (*functioning as singular*) a school of semantic theory based on the doctrine that syntactic and semantic structure are of the same formal nature and that there is a single system of rules that relates surface structure to meaning. Compare **interpretive semantics**

generator (ˈdʒɛnəˌreɪtə) n **1** *physics* **a** any device for converting mechanical energy into electrical energy by electromagnetic induction, esp a large one as in a power station **b** a device for producing a voltage electrostatically **c** any device that converts one form of energy into another form: *an acoustic generator* **2** an apparatus for producing a gas **3** a person or thing that generates

generatrix (ˈdʒɛnəˌreɪtrɪks) n, pl **generatrices** (ˈdʒɛnəˌreɪtrɪˌsiːz) a point, line, or plane that is moved in a specific way to produce a geometric figure

generic (dʒɪˈnɛrɪk) or **generical** adj **1** applicable or referring to a whole class or group; general **2** *biology* of, relating to, or belonging to a genus: *the generic name* **3** denoting the nonproprietary name of a drug, food product, etc ▷ n **4** a drug, food product, etc that does not have a trademark [c17 from French; see GENUS] > geˈnerically adv

generosity (ˌdʒɛnəˈrɒsɪtɪ) n, pl **-ties 1** willingness and liberality in giving away one's money, time, etc; magnanimity **2** freedom from pettiness in character and mind **3** a generous act **4** abundance; plenty

generous (ˈdʒɛnərəs, ˈdʒɛnrəs) adj **1** willing and liberal in giving away one's money, time, etc; munificent **2** free from pettiness in character and mind **3** full or plentiful: *a generous portion* **4** (of wine) rich in alcohol **5** (of a soil type) fertile [c16 via Old French from Latin *generōsus* nobly born, from *genus* race; see GENUS] > ˈgenerously adv > ˈgenerousness n

genesis (ˈdʒɛnɪsɪs) n, pl **-ses** (-ˌsiːz) a beginning or origin of anything [Old English: via Latin from Greek; related to Greek *gignesthai* to be born]

Genesis (ˈdʒɛnɪsɪs) n the first book of the Old Testament recounting the events from the Creation of the world to the sojourning of the Israelites in Egypt

-genesis n combining form indicating genesis, development, or generation: *biogenesis*; *parthenogenesis* [New Latin, from Latin: GENESIS] > **-genetic** or **-genic** adj combining form

genet¹ (ˈdʒɛnɪt), **genette** (dʒɪˈnɛt) n **1** any agile catlike viverrine mammal of the genus *Genetta*, inhabiting wooded regions of Africa and S Europe, having an elongated head, thick spotted or blotched fur, and a very long tail **2** the fur of such an animal [c15 from Old French *genette*, from Arabic *jarnayt*]

genet² (ˈdʒɛnɪt) n an obsolete spelling of **jennet**

gene therapy n the replacement or alteration of defective genes in order to prevent the occurrence of such inherited diseases as haemophilia. Effected by genetic engineering techniques, it is still at the experimental stage

genetic (dʒɪˈnɛtɪk) or **genetical** adj of or relating to genetics, genes, or the origin of something [c19 from GENESIS] > geˈnetically adv

genetically modified adj denoting or derived from an organism whose DNA has been altered for the purpose of improvement or correction of defects: *genetically modified food*. Abbreviation: **GM** > **genetic modification** n

genetic code n *biochem* the order in which the nitrogenous bases of DNA are arranged in the molecule, which determines the type and amount of protein synthesized in the cell. The four bases are arranged in groups of three in a specific order, each group acting as a unit (codon), which specifies a particular amino acid. See also **messenger RNA, transfer RNA**

genetic counselling n the provision of advice for couples with a history of inherited disorders who wish to have children, including the likelihood of having affected children and the course and management of the disorder, etc

genetic engineering n alteration of the DNA of a cell for purposes of research, as a means of manufacturing animal proteins, correcting genetic defects, or making improvements to plants and animals bred by man

genetic fingerprint n the pattern of DNA unique to each individual that can be analysed in a sample of blood, saliva, or tissue: used as a means of identification

geneticist (dʒɪˈnɛtɪsɪst) n a person who studies or specializes in genetics

genetic map n a graphic representation of the order of genes within chromosomes by means of detailed analysis of the DNA. See also **chromosome map**. > **genetic mapping** n

genetic marker n a gene with two or more alternative forms, producing readily identifiable variations in a particular character, used in studies of linkage, genetic mapping, and identification of the presence of other genes that are closely linked to, and therefore usually inherited with, it

genetics (dʒɪˈnɛtɪks) n **1** (*functioning as singular*) the branch of biology concerned with the study of heredity and variation in organisms **2** the genetic features and constitution of a single organism, species, or group

Geneva (dʒɪˈniːvə) n **1** a city in SW Switzerland, in the Rhône valley on Lake Geneva: centre of Calvinism; headquarters of the International Red Cross (1864), the International Labour Office (1925), the League of Nations (1929–46), the World Health Organization, and the European office of the United Nations; banking centre. Pop: 177 500 (2002 est) **2** a canton in SW Switzerland. Capital: Geneva. Pop: 419 300 (2002 est). Area: 282 sq km (109 sq miles) ▷ French name: **Genève** German name: **Genf 3 Lake a** lake between SW Switzerland and E France: fed and drained by the River Rhône, it is the largest of the Alpine lakes; the surface is subject to considerable changes of level. Area: 580 sq km (224 sq miles). French name: **Lac Léman** German name: **Genfersee**

Geneva bands pl n a pair of white lawn or linen strips hanging from the front of the neck or collar of some ecclesiastical and academic robes [c19 named after GENEVA, where originally worn by Swiss Calvinist clergy]

Geneva Convention n the international agreement, first formulated in 1864 at Geneva, establishing a code for wartime treatment of the sick or wounded: revised and extended on several occasions to cover maritime warfare and prisoners of war

Geneva gown n a long loose black gown with very wide sleeves worn by academics or Protestant clerics [c19 named after GENEVA; see GENEVA BANDS]

Genevan (dʒɪˈniːvᵊn) or **Genevese** (ˌdʒɛnɪˈviːz) adj **1** of, relating to, or characteristic of Geneva **2** of, adhering to, or relating to the teachings of Calvin or the Calvinists ▷ n, pl **-vans** or **-vese 3** a native or inhabitant of Geneva **4** a less common name for a **Calvinist**

Geneva protocol n the agreement in 1925 to ban the use of asphyxiating, poisonous, or other gases in war. It does not ban the development or manufacture of such gases

Genève (ʒəˈnɛv) n the French name for **Geneva**

Genf (ɡɛnf) n the German name for **Geneva** (senses 1, 2)

Genfersee (ˈɡɛnfərzeː) n the German name for (Lake) **Geneva**

genial¹ (ˈdʒiːnjəl, -nɪəl) adj **1** cheerful, easy-going, and warm in manner or behaviour **2** pleasantly warm, so as to give life, growth, or health: *the genial sunshine* [c16 from Latin *geniālis* relating to birth or marriage, from *genius* tutelary deity; see GENIUS] > **geniality** (ˌdʒiːnɪˈælɪtɪ) or **genialness** n > ˈgenially adv

genial² (dʒɪˈniːəl) adj *anatomy* of or relating to the chin [c19 from Greek *geneion*, from *genus* jaw]

genic (ˈdʒiːnɪk) adj of or relating to a gene or genes

-genic adj combining form **1** relating to production or generation: *carcinogenic* **2** well suited to or suitable for: *photogenic* [from -GEN + -IC]

genicular (dʒɪˈnɪkjʊlə) adj of or relating to the knee [c19 from Latin *genu* knee]

geniculate (dʒɪˈnɪkjʊlɪt, -ˌleɪt) adj **1** *biology* bent at a sharp angle: *geniculate antennae* **2** having a joint or joints capable of bending sharply [c17 from Latin *geniculātus* jointed, from *geniculum* a little knee, small joint, from *genu* knee] > geˈniculately adv > geˌnicuˈlation n

genie (ˈdʒiːnɪ) n **1** (in fairy tales and stories) a servant who appears by magic and fulfils a person's wishes **2** another word for **jinni** [c18 from French *génie*, from Arabic *jinni* demon, influenced by Latin *genius* attendant spirit; see GENIUS]

Genie (ˈdʒiːnɪ) n *Canadian* an award given by the Academy of Canadian Cinema and Television in recognition of Canadian cinematic achievements

genii (ˈdʒiːnɪˌaɪ) n the plural of **genius** (senses 5, 6)

genip (ˈdʒɛnɪp) n another word for **genipap** [c18 from Spanish *genipa*, from French, from Guarani]

genipap (ˈdʒɛnɪˌpæp) or **genip** n **1** an evergreen Caribbean rubiaceous tree, *Genipa americana*, with reddish-brown edible orange-like fruits **2** the fruit of this tree [c17 from Portuguese *genipapo*, from Tupi]

g

677

genit. *abbreviation for* genitive

genital (ˈdʒɛnɪtᵊl) *adj* **1** of or relating to the sexual organs or to reproduction **2** *psychoanal* relating to the mature stage of psychosexual development in which an affectionate relationship with one's sex partner is established. Compare **anal** (sense 2), **oral** (sense 7), **phallic** (sense 2) [C14 from Latin *genitālis* concerning birth, from *gignere* to beget]

genital herpes *n* a sexually transmitted disease caused by a variety of the herpes simplex virus in which painful blisters occur in the genital region

genitals (ˈdʒɛnɪtᵊlz) *or* **genitalia** (ˌdʒɛnɪˈteɪlɪə, -ˈteɪljə) *pl n* the sexual organs; the testicles and penis of a male or the labia, clitoris, and vagina of a female. Related adj: **venereal.** > **genitalic** (ˌdʒɛnɪˈtælɪk) *adj*

genitive (ˈdʒɛnɪtɪv) *grammar* ▷ *adj* **1** denoting a case of nouns, pronouns, and adjectives in inflected languages used to indicate a relation of ownership or association, usually translated by English *of* ▷ *n* **2 a** the genitive case **b** a word or speech element in this case [C14 from Latin *genetīvus* relating to birth, from *gignere* to produce] > **genitival** (ˌdʒɛnɪˈtaɪvᵊl) *adj* > ˌ**geni'tivally** *adv*

genitor (ˈdʒɛnɪtə, -tɔː) *n* the biological father as distinguished from the pater or legal father [C15 from Latin, from *gignere* to beget]

genitourinary (ˌdʒɛnɪtəʊˈjʊərɪnərɪ) *adj* of or relating to both the reproductive and excretory organs; urogenital

genitourinary medicine *n* the branch of medical science concerned with the study and treatment of diseases of the genital and urinary organs, esp sexually transmitted diseases. Abbreviation: **GUM**

genius (ˈdʒiːnɪəs, -njəs) *n, pl* **-uses** *or for senses 5, 6* **genii** (ˈdʒiːnɪˌaɪ) **1** a person with exceptional ability, esp of a highly original kind **2** such ability or capacity: *Mozart's musical genius* **3** the distinctive spirit or creative nature of a nation, era, language, etc **4** a person considered as exerting great influence of a certain sort: *an evil genius* **5** *Roman myth* **a** the guiding spirit who attends a person from birth to death **b** the guardian spirit of a place, group of people, or institution **6** *Arabic myth* (*usually plural*) a demon; jinn [C16 from Latin, from *gignere* to beget]

genius loci *Latin* (ˈdʒiːnɪəs ˈləʊsaɪ) *n* **1** the guardian spirit of a place **2** the special atmosphere of a particular place [genius of the place]

genizah (ɡeˈniːzə) *n Judaism* a repository (usually in a synagogue) for books and other sacred objects which can no longer be used but which may not be destroyed [C19 from Hebrew, literally: a hiding place, from *gānaz* to hide, set aside]

Genk *or* **Genck** (*Flemish* xɛŋk) *n* a town in NE Belgium, in Limburg province: coal-mining. Pop: 106 213 (2004 est)

Genl *or* **genl** *abbreviation for* General *or* general

genoa (ˈdʒɛnəʊə) *n yachting* a large triangular jib sail, often with a foot that extends as far aft as the clew of the mainsail. Also called: **genoa jib** Sometimes shortened to: **genny, jenny**

Genoa (ˈdʒɛnəʊə) *n* a port in NW Italy, capital of Liguria, on the **Gulf of Genoa**: Italy's main port; an independent commercial city with many colonies in the Middle Ages; university (1243); heavy industries. Pop: 610 307 (2001). Italian name: **Genova**

Genoa cake *n* a rich fruit cake, usually decorated with almonds

genocide (ˈdʒɛnəʊˌsaɪd) *n* the policy of deliberately killing a nationality or ethnic group [C20 from *geno-*, from Greek *genos* race + -CIDE] > ˌ**geno'cidal** *adj*

Genoese (ˌdʒɛnəʊˈiːz) *or* **Genovese** (ˌdʒɛnəˈviːz) *n, pl* **-ese** *or* **-vese** **1** a native or inhabitant of Genoa ▷ *adj* **2** of or relating to Genoa or its inhabitants

genome *or* **genom** (ˈdʒiːnəʊm) *n* **1** the full complement of genetic material within an organism **2** all the genes comprising a haploid set of chromosomes [C20 from German *Genom*, from *Gen* GENE + (CHROMOS)OME] > **genomic** (dʒɪˈnɒmɪk) *adj*

genomics (dʒɪˈnɒmɪks) *n* (*functioning as singular*) the branch of molecular genetics concerned with the study of genomes, specifically the identification and sequencing of their constituent genes and the application of this knowledge in medicine, pharmacy, agriculture, etc

genotype (ˈdʒɛnəʊˌtaɪp) *n* **1** the genetic constitution of an organism **2** a group of organisms with the same genetic constitution ▷ Compare **phenotype.** > **genotypic** (ˌdʒɛnəʊˈtɪpɪk) *or* ˌ**geno'typical** *adj* > ˌ**geno'typically** *adv* > **genotypicity** (ˌdʒɛnəʊtɪˈpɪsɪtɪ) *n*

-genous *adj combining form* **1** yielding or generating: *androgenous; erogenous* **2** generated by or issuing from: *endogenous* [from -GEN + -OUS]

Genova (ˈdʒɛːnova) *n* the Italian name for **Genoa**

genre (ˈʒɑːnrə) *n* **1 a** kind, category, or sort, esp of literary or artistic work **b** (*as modifier*): *genre fiction* **2** a category of painting in which domestic scenes or incidents from everyday life are depicted [C19 from French, from Old French *gendre*; see GENDER]

genre-busting *adj* not conforming to established patterns, styles, etc

genro (ˈɡɛnˈrəʊ) *n* **1** (*functioning as singular or plural*) a group of highly respected elder statesmen in late 19th- and early 20th-century Japan **2** a member of this group [C20 from Japanese, from Ancient Chinese *nguan lao*, from *nguan* first + *lao* elder]

gens (dʒɛnz) *n, pl* **gentes** (ˈdʒɛntiːz) **1** (in ancient Rome) any of a group of aristocratic families, having a common name and claiming descent from a common ancestor in the male line **2** *anthropol* a group based on descent in the male line [C19 from Latin: race; compare GENUS, GENDER]

gent (dʒɛnt) *n informal* short for **gentleman**

Gent (xɛnt) *n* the Flemish name for **Ghent**

gentamicin (ˌdʒɛntəˈmaɪsɪn) *n* a broad-spectrum antibiotic used in the treatment of serious infections [C20 from *genta* (of unknown origin) + -MYCIN]

genteel (dʒɛnˈtiːl) *adj* **1** affectedly proper or refined; excessively polite **2** respectable, polite, and well-bred: *a genteel old lady* **3** appropriate to polite or fashionable society: *genteel behaviour* [C16 from French *gentil* well-born; see GENTLE] > **gen'teelly** *adv* > **gen'teelness** *n*

genteelism (dʒɛnˈtiːlɪzəm) *n* a word or phrase used in place of a less genteel one

gentian (ˈdʒɛnʃən) *n* **1** any gentianaceous plant of the genera *Gentiana* or *Gentianella*, having blue, yellow, white, or red showy flowers **2** the bitter-tasting dried rhizome and roots of *Gentiana lutea* (**European** or **yellow gentian**), which can be used as a tonic **3** any of several similar plants, such as the horse gentian [C14 from Latin *gentiāna*; perhaps named after *Gentius*, a second-century BC Illyrian king, reputedly the first to use it medicinally]

gentianaceous (ˌdʒɛnʃɪəˈneɪʃəs) *adj* of, relating to, or belonging to the *Gentianaceae*, a family of flowering plants that includes centaury, felwort, and gentian

gentian blue *n* **a** a purplish-blue colour **b** (*as adjective*): *gentian-blue shoes*

gentianella (ˌdʒɛnʃəˈnɛlə, -ʃɪə-) *n* **1** any of various gentianaceous plants, esp the alpine species *Gentiana acaulis*, which has showy blue flowers **2** any of several related plants of the genus *Gentianella* [C17 from New Latin, literally: a little GENTIAN]

gentian violet *n* a greenish crystalline substance, obtained from rosaniline, that forms a violet solution in water, used as an indicator, antiseptic, and in the treatment of burns. Also called: **crystal violet**

gentile (ˈdʒɛntaɪl) *adj* **1** denoting an adjective or proper noun used to designate a place or the inhabitants of a place, as *Spanish* and *Spaniard* **2** of or relating to a tribe or people [C14 from Late Latin *gentīlis*, from Latin: one belonging to the same tribe or family; see GENS]

Gentile (ˈdʒɛntaɪl) *n* **1** a person who is not a Jew **2** a Christian, as contrasted with a Jew **3** a person who is not a member of one's own church: used esp by Mormons **4** a heathen or pagan ▷ *adj* **5** of or relating to a race or religion that is not Jewish **6** Christian, as contrasted with Jewish **7** not being a member of one's own church: used esp by Mormons **8** pagan or heathen

gentilesse (ˈdʒɛntᵊˌlɛs) *n archaic* politeness or good breeding [C14 from Old French *gentillesse*; see GENTEEL]

gentility (dʒɛnˈtɪlɪtɪ) *n, pl* **-ties** **1** respectability and polite good breeding **2** affected politeness **3** noble birth or ancestry **4** people of noble birth [C14 from Old French *gentilite*, from Latin *gentīlitās* relationship of those belonging to the same tribe or family; see GENS]

gentle (ˈdʒɛntᵊl) *adj* **1** having a mild or kindly nature or character **2** soft or temperate; mild; moderate: *a gentle scolding* **3** gradual: *a gentle slope* **4** easily controlled; tame: *a gentle horse* **5** *archaic* of good breeding; noble: *gentle blood* **6** *archaic* gallant; chivalrous ▷ *vb* (*tr*) **7** to tame or subdue (a horse) **8** to appease or mollify **9** *obsolete* to ennoble or dignify ▷ *n* **10** a maggot, esp when used as bait in fishing **11** *archaic* a person who is of good breeding [C13 from Old French *gentil* noble, from Latin *gentīlis* belonging to the same family; see GENS] > **'gently** *adv*

gentle breeze *n meteorol* a light breeze of force three on the Beaufort scale, blowing at 8–12 mph

gentlefolk (ˈdʒɛntᵊlˌfəʊk) *or* **gentlefolks** *pl n* persons regarded as being of good breeding

gentleman (ˈdʒɛntᵊlmən) *n, pl* **-men** **1** a man regarded as having qualities of refinement associated with a good family **2** a man who is cultured, courteous, and well-educated **3** a polite name for a man **4** the personal servant of a gentleman (esp in the phrase **gentleman's gentleman**) **5** *Brit history* a man of gentle birth, who was entitled to bear arms, ranking above a yeoman in social position **6** (formerly) a euphemistic word for a **smuggler.** > **'gentlemanly** *adj* > **'gentlemanliness** *n*

gentleman-at-arms *n, pl* **gentlemen-at-arms** a member of the guard who attend the British sovereign on ceremonial and state occasions

gentleman-farmer *n, pl* **gentlemen-farmers** **1** a person who engages in farming but does not depend on it for his living **2** a person who owns farmland but does not farm it personally

gentlemen's agreement *or* **gentleman's agreement** *n* a personal understanding or arrangement based on honour and not legally binding

gentleness (ˈdʒɛntᵊlnɪs) *n* **1** the quality of being gentle **2** *physics* a property of elementary particles, conserved in certain strong interactions. See also **charm** (sense 7)

gentlewoman (ˈdʒɛntᵊlˌwʊmən) *n, pl* **-women** **1** *archaic* a woman regarded as being of good family or breeding; lady **2** *rare* a woman who is cultured, courteous, and well-educated **3** *history* a woman in personal attendance on a high-ranking lady > **'gentleˌwomanly** *adj* > **'gentleˌwomanliness** *n*

Gentoo (ˈdʒɛntuː) *n, pl* **-toos** (*sometimes not capital*) *archaic* a Hindu, esp as distinguished from a Muslim [C17 from Portuguese *gentio* pagan (literally: GENTILE)]

gentrification (ˌdʒɛntrɪfɪˈkeɪʃən) *n Brit* a process by which middle-class people take up residence in a traditionally working-class area of a city, changing the character of the area [C20 from *gentrify* (to become GENTRY)] > **'gentriˌfier** *n*

gentry (ˈdʒɛntrɪ) *n* **1** persons of high birth or social standing; aristocracy **2** *Brit* persons just below the nobility in social rank **3** *informal, often derogatory* people, esp of a particular group or kind [C14 from Old French *genterie*, from *gentil* GENTLE]

gents (dʒɛnts) *n* (*functioning as singular*) *Brit informal* a men's public lavatory

genu ('dʒɛnjuː) *n, pl* **genua** ('dʒɛnjʊə) *anatomy* **1** the technical name for the **knee 2** any kneelike bend in a structure or part [Latin: knee]

genuflect ('dʒɛnjʊ,flɛkt) *vb* (*intr*) **1** to act in a servile or deferential manner **2** *RC Church* to bend one or both knees as a sign of reverence, esp when passing before the Blessed Sacrament [c17 from Medieval Latin *genūflectere*, from Latin *genu* knee + *flectere* to bend] > ,genu'flection *or esp Brit* ,genu'flexion *n* > ,genu'flector *n*

genuine ('dʒɛnjʊɪn) *adj* **1** not fake or counterfeit; original; real; authentic **2** not pretending; frank; sincere **3** being of authentic or original stock [c16 from Latin *genuīnus* inborn, hence (in Late Latin) authentic, from *gignere* to produce] > 'genuinely *adv* > 'genuineness *n*

gen up *vb* gens up, genning up, genned up (*adverb; often passive; when intr*, usually foll by *on*) *Brit informal* to brief (someone) or study (something) in detail; make or become fully conversant with: *I can only take over this job if I am properly genned up*

genus ('dʒiːnəs) *n, pl* **genera** ('dʒɛnərə) **1** *biology* any of the taxonomic groups into which a family is divided and which contains one or more species. For example, *Vulpes* (foxes) is a genus of the dog family (*Canidae*) **2** *logic* a class of objects or individuals that can be divided into two or more groups or species **3** a class, group, etc, with common characteristics **4** *maths* a number characterizing a closed surface in topology equal to the number of handles added to a sphere to form the surface. A sphere has genus 0, a torus, genus 1, etc [c16 from Latin: race]

-geny *n combining form* indicating origin or manner of development: *phylogeny* [from Greek *-geneia*, from *-genēs* born] > **-genic** *adj combining form*

geo *or* **gio** ('dʒiːəʊ) *n, pl* **geos** *or* **gios** (esp in Shetland) a small fjord or gully [c18 from Old Norse *gjā* ravine; related to Old English *gionian* to YAWN]

geo- *combining form* indicating earth: *geomorphology* [from Greek, from *gē* earth]

geocaching ('dʒiːəʊ,kæʃɪŋ) *n* a game in which the object is to identify and find items deposited by other players, using GPS navigation [c20 from GEO(GRAPHY) + *caching*]

geocarpy ('dʒiːəʊ,kɑːpɪ) *n botany* the ripening of fruits below ground, as occurs in the peanut

geocentric (,dʒiːəʊ'sɛntrɪk) *adj* **1** having the earth at its centre: *the Ptolemaic system postulated a geocentric universe* **2** measured from or relating to the centre of the earth > ,geo'centrically *adv*

geocentric parallax *n* See **parallax** (sense 2)

geochemistry (,dʒiːəʊ'kɛmɪstrɪ) *n* the geology and chemistry concerned with the chemical composition of, and chemical reactions taking place within, the earth's crust > geochemical (,dʒiːəʊ'kɛmɪkəl) *adj* > ,geo'chemist *n*

geochronology (,dʒiːəʊkrə'nɒlədʒɪ) *n* the branch of geology concerned with ordering and dating of events in the earth's history, including the origin of the earth itself > geochronological (,dʒiːəʊ,krɒnə'lɒdʒɪkəl) *adj*

geod. *abbreviation for* **1** geodesy **2** geodetic

geode ('dʒiːəʊd) *n* a cavity, usually lined with crystals, within a rock mass or nodule [c17 from Latin *geōdēs* a precious stone, from Greek: earthlike; see GEO-, -ODE[1]] > **geodic** (dʒɪ'ɒdɪk) *adj*

geodemographics (,dʒiːəʊdɛmə'græfɪks) *pl n* (*functioning as singular*) the study and grouping of the people in a geographical area according to socioeconomic criteria, esp for market research

geodesic (,dʒiːəʊ'dɛsɪk, -'diː-) *adj* **1** Also: **geodetic, geodesical** relating to or involving the geometry of curved surfaces ▷ *n* **2** Also called: **geodesic line** the shortest line between two points on a curved or plane surface

geodesic dome *n* a light structural framework arranged as a set of polygons in the form of a shell and covered with sheeting made of plastic, plywood, metal, etc; developed by Buckminster Fuller

geodesy (dʒɪ'ɒdɪsɪ) *or* **geodetics** (,dʒiːəʊ'dɛtɪks) *n* the branch of science concerned with determining the exact position of geographical points and the shape and size of the earth [c16 from French *géodésie*, from Greek *geōdaisia*, from GEO- + *daiein* to divide] > ge'odesist *n*

geodetic (,dʒiːəʊ'dɛtɪk) *adj* **1** of or relating to geodesy **2** another word for **geodesic** > ,geo'detically *adv*

geodetic surveying *n* the surveying of the earth's surface, making allowance for its curvature and giving an accurate framework for smaller-scale surveys

geodynamics (,dʒiːəʊdaɪ'næmɪks) *n* (*functioning as singular*) the branch of geology concerned with the forces and processes, esp large-scale, of the earth's interior, particularly as regards their effects on the crust or lithosphere > ,geody'namic *adj* > ,geody'namicist *n*

geog. *abbreviation for* **1** geographic(al) **2** geography

geognosy (dʒɪ'ɒgnəsɪ) *n* the study of the origin and distribution of minerals and rocks in the earth's crust: superseded generally by the term **geology** [c18 from French *géognosie*, from GEO- + Greek *gnōsis* a seeking to know, knowledge] > geognostic (,dʒiːɒg'nɒstɪk) *adj*

geographical determinism *n sociol* the theory that human activity is determined by geographical conditions

geographical mile *n* a former name for **nautical mile**

geographic north *n* another name for **true north**

geography (dʒɪ'ɒgrəfɪ) *n, pl* **-phies 1** the study of the natural features of the earth's surface, including topography, climate, soil, vegetation, etc, and man's response to them **2** the natural features of a region **3** an arrangement of constituent parts; plan; layout > ge'ographer *n* > geographical (,dʒiːə'græfɪkəl) *or* ,geo'graphic *adj* > ,geo'graphically *adv*

geoid ('dʒiːɔɪd) *n* **1** a hypothetical surface that corresponds to mean sea level and extends at the same level under the continents **2** the shape of the earth

geol. *abbreviation for* **1** geologic(al) **2** geology

geological cycle *n* the series of events in which a rock of one type is converted to one or more other types and then back to the original type. Also called: **rock cycle**

Geological Survey *n* a government-sponsored organization working in the field of geology, such as the US Geological Survey, the Geological Survey of India, or the Institute of Geological Sciences (UK)

geological timescale *n* any division of geological time into chronological units, whether relative (with units in the correct temporal sequence) or absolute (with numerical ages attached)

geologize *or* **geologise** (dʒɪ'ɒlə,dʒaɪz) *vb* to study the geological features of (an area)

geology (dʒɪ'ɒlədʒɪ) *n* **1** the scientific study of the origin, history, structure, and composition of the earth **2** the geological features of a district or country > geological (,dʒiːə'lɒdʒɪkəl) *or* ,geo'logic *adj* > ,geo'logically *adv* > ge'ologist *or* ge'ologer *n*

geom. *abbreviation for* **1** geometric(al) **2** geometry

geomagnetism (,dʒiːəʊ'mægnɪ,tɪzəm) *n* **1** the magnetic field of the earth **2** the branch of physics concerned with this > geomagnetic (,dʒiːəʊmæg'nɛtɪk) *adj*

geomancy ('dʒiːəʊ,mænsɪ) *n* prophecy from the pattern made when a handful of earth is cast down or dots are drawn at random and connected with lines > 'geo,mancer *n* > ,geo'mantic *adj*

geomechanics (,dʒiːəʊmɪ'kænɪks) *n* (*functioning as singular*) the study and application of rock and soil mechanics

geometer (dʒɪ'ɒmɪtə) *or* **geometrician** (dʒɪ,ɒmɪ'trɪʃən, ,dʒiːəʊmɪ-) *n* a person who is practised in or who studies geometry

geometric (,dʒiːə'mɛtrɪk) *or* **geometrical** *adj* **1** of, relating to, or following the methods and principles of geometry **2** consisting of, formed by, or characterized by points, lines, curves, or surfaces: *a geometric figure* **3** (of design or ornamentation) composed predominantly of simple geometric forms, such as circles, rectangles, triangles, etc > ,geo'metrically *adv*

geometric distribution *n statistics* the distribution of the number, x, of independent trials required to obtain a first success: where the probability in each is p, the probability that $x = r$ is $p(1-p)^{r-1}$, where $r = 1, 2, 3, ...$, with mean $1/p$. See also **Bernoulli trial**

geometric mean *n* the average value of a set of n integers, terms, or quantities, expressed as the nth root of their product. Compare **arithmetic mean**

geometric pace *n* a modern form of a Roman pace, a measure of length taken as 5 feet

geometric progression *n* a sequence of numbers, each of which differs from the succeeding one by a constant ratio, as 1, 2, 4, 8, ... Compare **arithmetic progression**

geometric series *n* a geometric progression written as a sum, as in $1 + 2 + 4 + 8$

geometrid (dʒɪ'ɒmɪtrɪd) *n* **1** any moth of the family *Geometridae*, the larvae of which are called measuring worms, inchworms, or loopers ▷ *adj* **2** of, relating to, or belonging to the *Geometridae* [c19 from New Latin *Geōmetridae*, from Latin, from Greek *geōmetrēs*: land measurer, from the looping gait of the larvae]

geometrize *or* **geometrise** (dʒɪ'ɒmɪ,traɪz) *vb* **1** to use or apply geometric methods or principles (to) **2** (*tr*) to represent in geometric form

geometry (dʒɪ'ɒmɪtrɪ) *n* **1** the branch of mathematics concerned with the properties, relationships, and measurement of points, lines, curves, and surfaces. See also **analytical geometry, non-Euclidean geometry 2 a** any branch of geometry using a particular notation or set of assumptions: *analytical geometry* **b** any branch of geometry referring to a particular set of objects: *solid geometry* **3** a shape, configuration, or arrangement **4** *arts* the shape of a solid or a surface [c14 from Latin *geōmetria*, from Greek, from *geōmetrein* to measure the land]

geomorphic (,dʒiːəʊ'mɔːfɪk) *adj* of, relating to, or resembling the earth's surface

geomorphology (,dʒiːəʊmɔː'fɒlədʒɪ) *or* **geomorphogeny** (,dʒiːəʊmɔː'fɒdʒənɪ) *n* the branch of geology that is concerned with the structure, origin, and development of the topographical features of the earth's surface > geomorphological (,dʒiːəʊ,mɔːfə'lɒdʒɪkəl) *or* ,geo,morpho'logic *adj* > ,geo,morpho'logically *adv*

geophagy (dʒɪ'ɒfədʒɪ), **geophagia** (,dʒiːə'feɪdʒə, -dʒɪə) *or* **geophagism** (dʒɪ'ɒfədʒɪzəm) *n* **1** the practice of eating earth, clay, chalk, etc, found in some primitive tribes **2** *zoology* the habit of some animals, esp earthworms, of eating soil > ge'ophagist *n* > geophagous (dʒɪ'ɒfəgəs) *adj*

geophysical (,dʒiːə'fɪzɪkəl) *adj* of or relating to geophysics

geophysics (,dʒiːə'fɪzɪks) *n* (*functioning as singular*) the study of the earth's physical properties and of the physical processes acting upon, above, and within the earth. It includes seismology, geomagnetism, meteorology, and oceanography > ,geo'physicist *n*

geophyte ('dʒiːəʊ,faɪt) *n* a perennial plant that propagates by means of buds below the soil surface > geophytic (,dʒiːəʊ'fɪtɪk) *adj*

geopolitical (,dʒiːəʊpə'lɪtɪkəl) *adj* of or relating to geopolitics; involving geographical and political elements

geopolitics (,dʒiːəʊ'pɒlɪtɪks) *n* **1** (*functioning as singular*) the study of the effect of geographical factors on politics, esp international politics; political geography **2** (*functioning as plural*) the

g

combination of geographical and political factors affecting a country or area > **geo,poli'tician** n

geoponic (,dʒiːəʊ'pɒnɪk) adj **1** of or relating to agriculture, esp as a science **2** rural; rustic [c17 from Greek *geōponikos* concerning land cultivation, from *geōponein* to till the soil, from GEO- + *ponein* to labour]

geoponics (,dʒiːəʊ'pɒnɪks) n (functioning as singular) the science of agriculture

Geordie ('dʒɔːdɪ) Brit ▷ n **1** a person who comes from or lives in Tyneside **2** the dialect spoken by these people ▷ adj **3** of or relating to these people or their dialect [c19 a diminutive of *George*]

George (dʒɔːdʒ) n Brit informal the automatic pilot in an aircraft [c20 originally a slang name for an airman]

George Cross n a British award for bravery, esp of civilians: instituted 1940. Abbreviation: **GC**

Georgetown ('dʒɔːdʒ,taʊn) n **1** the capital and chief port of Guyana, at the mouth of the Demerara River: became capital of the Dutch colonies of Essequibo and Demerara in 1784; seat of the University of Guyana. Pop: 237 000 (2005 est). Former name (until 1812): **Stabroek 2** the capital of the Cayman Islands: a port on Grand Cayman Island. Pop: 20 626 (1999)

George Town n a port in NW Malaysia, capital of Penang state, in NE Penang Island: the first chartered city of the Malayan federation. Pop: 162 000 (2005 est). Also called: **Penang**

georgette or **georgette crepe** (dʒɔː'dʒɛt) n **a** a thin silk or cotton crepe fabric with a mat finish **b** (as modifier): a georgette blouse [c20 from the name Mme *Georgette*, a French modiste]

Georgia ('dʒɔːdʒə) n **1** a republic in NW Asia, on the Black Sea: an independent kingdom during the middle ages, it was divided by Turkey and Persia in 1555; became part of Russia in 1918 and a separate Soviet republic in 1936; its independence was recognized internationally in 1992. It is rich in minerals and has hydroelectric resources. Official language: Georgian. Religion: believers are mainly Christian or Muslim. Currency: lari. Capital: Tbilisi. Pop: 5 074 000 (2004 est). Area: 69 493 sq km (26 831 sq miles) **2** a state of the southeastern US, on the Atlantic: consists of coastal plains with forests and swamps, rising to the Cumberland Plateau and the Appalachians in the northwest. Capital: Atlanta. Pop: 8 684 715 (2003 est). Area: 152 489 sq km (58 876 sq miles). Abbreviations: **Ga**, (with zip code) **GA**

Georgian ('dʒɔːdʒən) adj **1** of, characteristic of, or relating to any or all of the four kings who ruled Great Britain and Ireland from 1714 to 1830, or to their reigns **2** of or relating to George V of Great Britain and Northern Ireland or his reign (1910–36): the Georgian poets **3** of or relating to the republic of Georgia, its people, or their language **4** of or relating to the American State of Georgia or its inhabitants **5** in or imitative of the style prevalent in England during the 18th century (reigns of George I, II, and III); in architecture, dominated by the ideas of Palladio, and in furniture represented typically by the designs of Sheraton ▷ n **6** the official language of Georgia, belonging to the South Caucasian family **7** a native or inhabitant of Georgia **8** an aboriginal inhabitant of the Caucasus **9** a native or inhabitant of the American State of Georgia **10** a person belonging to or imitating the styles of either of the Georgian periods in England

Georgian Bay n a bay in S central Canada, in Ontario, containing many small islands: the NE part of Lake Huron. Area: 15 000 sq km (5800 sq miles)

georgic ('dʒɔːdʒɪk) adj **1** literary agricultural ▷ n **2** a poem about rural or agricultural life [c16 from Latin *geōrgicus*, from Greek *geōrgikos*, from *geōrgos* farmer, from *gē* land, earth + *-ourgos*, from *ergon* work]

geoscience (,dʒiːəʊ'saɪəns) n **1** any science, such as geology, geophysics, geochemistry, or geodesy,

concerned with the earth; an earth science **2** these sciences collectively

geosphere ('dʒiːəʊ,sfɪə) n another name for **lithosphere**

geostatic (,dʒiːəʊ'stætɪk) adj **1** denoting or relating to the pressure exerted by a mass of rock or a similar substance. also: **lithostatic 2** (of a construction) able to resist the pressure of a mass of earth or similar material

geostatics (,dʒiːəʊ'stætɪks) n (functioning as singular) the branch of physics concerned with the statics of rigid bodies, esp the balance of forces within the earth

geostationary (,dʒiːəʊ'steɪʃənərɪ) adj (of a satellite) in a circular equatorial orbit in which it circles the earth once per sidereal day so that it appears stationary in relation to the earth's surface. Also: **geosynchronous**

geostrategy (,dʒiːəʊ'strætədʒɪ) n the study of geopolitics and strategics, esp as they affect the analysis of a region

geostrophic (,dʒiːəʊ'strɒfɪk) adj of, relating to, or caused by the force produced by the rotation of the earth: geostrophic wind

geosynchronous (,dʒiːəʊ'sɪŋkrənəs) adj another word for **geostationary**

geosyncline (,dʒiːəʊ'sɪŋklaɪn) n a broad elongated depression in the earth's crust containing great thicknesses of sediment > **,geosyn'clinal** adj

geotaxis (,dʒiːəʊ'tæksɪs) n movement of an organism in response to the stimulus of gravity > **geo'tactic** adj > **geo'tactically** adv

geotectonic (,dʒiːəʊtɛk'tɒnɪk) adj of or relating to the formation, arrangement, and structure of the rocks of the earth's crust

geotextile (,dʒiːəʊ'tɛkstaɪl) n any strong synthetic fabric used in civil engineering, as to retain an embankment

geotherm ('dʒiːəʊ,θɜːm) n **1** a line or surface within or on the earth connecting points of equal temperature **2** the representation of such a line or surface on a map or diagram

geothermal (,dʒiːəʊ'θɜːməl) or **geothermic** adj of or relating to the heat in the interior of the earth

geothermal power n power generated using steam produced by heat emanating from the molten core of the earth

geotropism (dʒɪ'ɒtrə,pɪzəm) n the response of a plant part to the stimulus of gravity. Plant stems, which grow upwards irrespective of the position in which they are placed, show **negative geotropism** > **geotropic** (,dʒiːəʊ'trɒpɪk) adj > **,geo'tropically** adv

ger. abbreviation for **1** gerund **2** gerundive

Ger. abbreviation for **1** German **2** Germany

Gera (German 'geːra) n an industrial city in E central Germany, in Thuringia. Pop: 106 365 (2003 est)

gerah ('ɡɪərə) n **1** an ancient Hebrew unit of weight **2** an ancient Hebrew coin equal to one twentieth of a shekel [c16 from Hebrew *gērāh* bean]

Geraldton waxflower ('dʒɛrəldtən 'wæks,flaʊə) n an evergreen shrub, Chamelaucium uncinatum, native to W Australia, cultivated for its pale pink flowers. Also called: **Geraldton wax** [named after *Geraldton*, a port in W Australia]

geraniaceous (dʒɪ,reɪnɪ'eɪʃəs) adj of, relating to, or belonging to the Geraniaceae, a family of plants with typically hairy stems and beaklike fruits: includes the geranium, pelargonium, storksbill, and cranesbill [c19 from New Latin *Geraniāceae*; see GERANIUM]

geranial (dʒɪ'reɪnɪəl) n the cis- isomer of citral [c19 from GERANI(UM) + AL(DEHYDE)]

geraniol (dʒɪ'reɪnɪ,ɒl, dʒɪ'rɑː-) n a colourless or pale yellow terpine alcohol with an odour of roses, found in many essential oils: used in perfumery. Formula: $C_{10}H_{18}O$ [c19 from GERANI(UM + ALCOH)OL]

geranium (dʒɪ'reɪnɪəm) n **1** any cultivated

geraniaceous plant of the genus Pelargonium, having scarlet, pink, or white showy flowers. See also **pelargonium, rose geranium, lemon geranium 2** any geraniaceous plant of the genus Geranium, such as cranesbill and herb Robert, having divided leaves and pink or purplish flowers **3** a strong red to a moderate or strong pink colour [c16 from Latin: cranesbill, from Greek *geranion*, from *geranos* CRANE]

geratology (,dʒɛrə'tɒlədʒɪ) n the branch of medicine concerned with the elderly and the phenomena associated with ageing; geriatrics and gerontology [c19 from *gerato-*, from Greek *gēras* old age + -LOGY] > **geratological** (,dʒɛrətə'lɒdʒɪkəl) adj > **,gera'tologist** n

gerbera ('dʒɜːbərə) n any plant of the perennial genus Gerbera, esp the Barberton daisy from S. Africa, G. jamesonii, grown, usually as a greenhouse plant, for its large brightly coloured daisy-like flowers: family Asteraceae [named after Traugott Gerber (died 1743), German naturalist]

gerbil or **gerbille** ('dʒɜːbɪl) n any burrowing rodent of the subfamily Gerbillinae, inhabiting hot dry regions of Asia and Africa and having soft pale fur: family Cricetidae [c19 from French *gerbille*, from New Latin *gerbillus* a little JERBOA]

gerent ('dʒɛrənt) n rare a person who rules or manages [c16 from Latin *gerēns* managing, from *gerere* to bear]

gerenuk ('ɡɛrɪ,nʊk) n a slender E African antelope, Litocranius walleri, with a long thin neck and backward-curving horns [from Somali *garanug*]

gerfalcon ('dʒɜː,fɔːlkən, -,fɔːkən) n a variant spelling of **gyrfalcon**

geriatric (,dʒɛrɪ'ætrɪk) adj **1** of or relating to geriatrics or to elderly people **2** facetious, derogatory, or offensive (of people or machines) old, obsolescent, worn out, or useless ▷ n **3** an elderly person **4** derogatory an older person considered as one who may be disregarded as senile or irresponsible ▷ See also **psychogeriatric** [c20 from Greek *gēras* old age + IATRIC]

geriatrician (,dʒɛrɪə'trɪʃən) or **geriatrist** (,dʒɛrɪ'ætrɪst) n a physician who specializes in geriatrics

geriatrics (,dʒɛrɪ'ætrɪks) n (functioning as singular) the branch of medical science concerned with the diagnosis and treatment of diseases affecting elderly people. Compare **gerontology**

Gerlachovka (Slovak 'ɡɛrlaxɔfka) n a mountain in N Slovakia, in the Tatra Mountains: the highest peak of the Carpathian Mountains. Height: 2663 m (8737 ft)

germ (dʒɜːm) n **1** a microorganism, esp one that produces disease in animals or plants **2** (often plural) the rudimentary or initial form of something: the germs of revolution **3** a simple structure, such as a fertilized egg, that is capable of developing into a complete organism [c17 from French *germe*, from Latin *germen* sprig, bud, sprout, seed]

german¹ ('dʒɜːmən) n US a dance consisting of complicated figures and changes of partners [c19 shortened from *German cotillion*]

german² ('dʒɜːmən) adj **1** (used in combination) **a** having the same parents as oneself: a brother-german **b** having a parent that is a brother or sister of either of one's own parents: cousin-german **2** a less common word for **germane** [c14 via Old French *germain*, from Latin *germānus* of the same race, from *germen* sprout, offshoot]

German ('dʒɜːmən) n **1** the official language of Germany and Austria and one of the official languages of Switzerland; the native language of approximately 100 million people. It is an Indo-European language belonging to the West Germanic branch, closely related to English and Dutch. There is considerable diversity of dialects; modern standard German is a development of Old High German, influenced by Martin Luther's translation of the Bible. See also **High German,**

Low German **2** a native, inhabitant, or citizen of Germany **3** a person whose native language is German: *Swiss Germans; Volga Germans* ▷ *adj* **4** denoting, relating to, or using the German language **5** relating to, denoting, or characteristic of any German state or its people ▷ Related prefixes: **Germano-, Teuto-**

German Baptist Brethren *pl n* a Protestant sect founded in 1708 in Germany but who migrated to the US in 1719–29, the members of which (Dunkers) insist on adult baptism by total immersion. Also called: **Church of the Brethren**

German cockroach *n* a small cockroach, *Blattella germanica*: a common household pest. Also called (US): **Croton bug**

German Democratic Republic *n* (formerly) the official name of **East Germany** Abbreviations: **GDR, DDR**

germander (dʒɜː'mændə) *n* any of several plants of the genus *Teucrium*, esp *T. chamaedrys* (**wall germander**) of Europe, having two-lipped flowers with a very small upper lip: family *Lamiaceae* (labiates) [C15 from Medieval Latin *germandrea*, from Late Greek *khamandrua*, from Greek *khamaidrus*, from *khamai* on the ground + *drus* oak tree]

germander speedwell *n* a creeping scrophulariaceous Eurasian plant, *Veronica chamaedrys*, naturalized in North America, having small bright blue flowers with white centres. Usual US name: **bird's-eye speedwell**

germane (dʒɜː'meɪn) *adj* (*postpositive*; usually foll by *to*) related (to the topic being considered); akin; relevant: *an idea germane to the conversation* [variant of GERMAN²] > **ger'manely** *adv* > **ger'maneness** *n*

German East Africa *n* a former German territory in E Africa, consisting of Tanganyika and Ruanda-Urundi: divided in 1919 between Great Britain and Belgium; now in Tanzania, Rwanda, and Burundi

germanic (dʒɜː'mænɪk) *adj* of or containing germanium in the tetravalent state

Germanic (dʒɜː'mænɪk) *n* **1** a branch of the Indo-European family of languages that includes English, Dutch, German, the Scandinavian languages, and Gothic. See **East Germanic, West Germanic, North Germanic** Abbreviation: Gmc **2** the unrecorded language from which all of these languages developed; Proto-Germanic ▷ *adj* **3** of, denoting, or relating to this group of languages **4** of, relating to, or characteristic of Germany, the German language, or any people that speaks a Germanic language

Germanism (dʒɜː'mə,nɪzəm) *n* **1** a word or idiom borrowed from or modelled on German **2** a German custom, trait, practice, etc **3** attachment to or high regard for German customs, institutions, etc

germanite (dʒɜː'mə,naɪt) *n* a mineral consisting of a complex copper arsenic sulphide containing germanium, gallium, iron, zinc, and lead: an ore of germanium and gallium [from GERMANIUM + -ITE¹]

germanium (dʒɜː'meɪnɪəm) *n* a brittle crystalline grey element that is a semiconducting metalloid, occurring principally in zinc ores and argyrodite: used in transistors, as a catalyst, and to strengthen and harden alloys. Symbol: Ge; atomic no.: 32; atomic wt.: 72.61; valency: 2 or 4; relative density: 5.323; melting pt.: 938.35°C; boiling pt.: 2834°C [C19 New Latin, named after GERMANY]

Germanize or **Germanise** (dʒɜː'mə,naɪz) *vb* to adopt or cause to adopt German customs, speech, institutions, etc > ,Germani'zation or ,Germani'sation *n* > 'German,izer or 'German,iser *n*

German measles *n* (*functioning as singular*) a nontechnical name for **rubella**

German Ocean *n* a former name for the **North Sea**

Germanophile (dʒɜː'mænə,faɪl) or **Germanophil** *n* a person having admiration for or devotion to Germany and the Germans > Germanophilia (dʒɜː,mænə'fɪlɪə) *n*

Germanophobe (dʒɜː'mænə,fəʊb) *n* a person who hates Germany or its people > Ger,mano'phobia *n*

germanous (dʒɜː'mænəs) *adj* of or containing germanium in the divalent state

German shepherd or **German shepherd dog** *n* another name for **Alsatian** (sense 1)

German short-haired pointer *n* a medium-sized short-haired variety of pointer having a liver-coloured or black coat, sometimes with white markings

German silver *n* another name for **nickel silver**

German sixth *n* (in musical harmony) an augmented sixth chord having a major third and a perfect fifth between the root and the augmented sixth. Compare **Italian sixth, French sixth**

German wire-haired pointer *n* a medium-sized powerfully-built variety of pointer with a wiry coat in liver, liver and white, or black and white, and a short beard

Germany ('dʒɜː:mənɪ) *n* a country in central Europe: in the Middle Ages the centre of the Holy Roman Empire; dissolved into numerous principalities; united under the leadership of Prussia in 1871 after the Franco-Prussian War; became a republic with reduced size in 1919 after being defeated in World War I; under the dictatorship of Hitler from 1933 to 1945; defeated in World War II and divided by the Allied Powers into four zones, which became established as East and West Germany in the late 1940s; reunified in 1990: a member of the European Union. It is flat and low-lying in the north with plateaus and uplands (including the Black Forest and the Bavarian Alps) in the centre and south. Official language: German. Religion: Christianity, Protestant majority. Currency: euro. Capital: Berlin. Pop: 82 526 000 (2004 est.). Area: 357 041 sq km (137 825 sq miles). German name: Deutschland Official name: **Federal Republic of Germany** See also **East Germany, West Germany** Related adj: **Teutonic**

germ cell *n* a sexual reproductive cell; gamete. Compare **somatic cell**

germen ('dʒɜː:mən) *n*, *pl* **-mens** or **-mina** (-mɪnə) *biology, now rare* the mass of undifferentiated cells that gives rise to the germ cells [C17 from Latin; see GERM]

germicide ('dʒɜː:mɪ,saɪd) *n* any substance that kills germs or other microorganisms > ,germi'cidal *adj*

germinal ('dʒɜː:mɪnəl) *adj* **1** of, relating to, or like germs or a germ cell **2** of, or in the earliest stage of development; embryonic [C19 from New Latin *germinālis*, from Latin *germen* bud; see GERM] > 'germinally *adv*

Germinal French (ʒɛrminal) *n* the month of buds: the seventh month of the French revolutionary calendar, from March 22 to April 20

germinal vesicle *n* biology the large nucleus of an oocyte before it develops into an ovum

germinant ('dʒɜː:mɪnənt) *adj* in the process of germinating; sprouting

germinate ('dʒɜː:mɪ,neɪt) *vb* **1** to cause (seeds or spores) to sprout or (of seeds or spores) to sprout or form new tissue following increased metabolism **2** to grow or cause to grow; develop **3** to come or bring into existence; originate: *the idea germinated with me* [C17 from Latin *germināre* to sprout; see GERM] > 'germinable or 'germinative *adj* > ,germi'nation *n* > 'germi,nator *n*

Germiston ('dʒɜː:mɪstən) *n* a city in South Africa, southeast of Johannesburg: industrial centre, with the world's largest gold refinery, serving the Witwatersrand mines. Pop: 139 721 (2001)

germ layer *n* embryol any of the three layers of cells formed during gastrulation. See **ectoderm, mesoderm, endoderm**

germ line *n* the lineage of cells culminating in the germ cells

germ plasm *n* **a** the part of a germ cell that contains hereditary material; the chromosomes and genes **b** the germ cells collectively. Compare **somatoplasm**

germ theory *n* **1** the theory that all infectious diseases are caused by microorganisms **2** the theory that living organisms develop from other living organisms by the growth and differentiation of germ cells

germ tube *n* botany a tube produced by a germinating spore, such as the pollen tube produced by a pollen grain

germ warfare *n* the military use of disease-spreading bacteria against an enemy. Also called: **bacteriological warfare**

Gerona (Spanish xe'rona) *n* a city in NE Spain: city walls and 14th-century cathedral; often besieged, in particular by the French (1809). Pop: 81 220 (2003 est). Catalan name: Girona Ancient name: Gerunda (dʒə'ru:ndə)

geronimo (dʒə'rɒnɪ,məʊ) *interj* **1** US a shout given by paratroopers as they jump into battle **2** an exclamation expressing exhilaration, esp when jumping from a great height [from *Geronimo* (1829–1909), Apache Indian chieftain]

gerontic (dʒɛ'rɒntɪk) *adj* biology of or relating to the senescence of an organism

geronto- or before a vowel **geront-** combining form indicating old age: *gerontology; gerontophilia* [from Greek *gerōn, geront-* old man]

gerontocracy (,dʒɛrɒn'tɒkrəsɪ) *n*, *pl* **-cies** **1** government by old people **2** a governing body of old people > gerontocratic (dʒɛ,rɒntə'krætɪk) *adj* > ge'ronto,crat *n*

gerontology (,dʒɛrɒn'tɒlədʒɪ) *n* the scientific study of ageing and the problems associated with elderly people. Compare **geriatrics** > gerontological (,dʒɛrɒntə'lɒdʒɪkᵊl) *adj* > ,geron'tologist *n*

-gerous *adj combining form* bearing or producing: *armigerous*. Compare **-ferous** [from Latin *-ger* bearing + -OUS]

gerrymander ('dʒɛrɪ,mændə) *vb* **1** to divide the constituencies of (a voting area) so as to give one party an unfair advantage **2** to manipulate or adapt to one's advantage ▷ *n* **3** an act or result of gerrymandering [C19 from Elbridge *Gerry*, US politician + (SALA)MANDER; from the salamander-like outline of an electoral district reshaped (1812) for political purposes while Gerry was governor of Massachusetts] > ,gerry'mandering *n*

Gers (French ʒɛr) *n* a department of SW France, in Midi-Pyrénées region. Capital: Auch. Pop: 175 055 (2003 est). Area: 6291 sq km (2453 sq miles)

gert (gɜːt) *adv* English dialect great or very big

gerund ('dʒɛrənd) *n* a noun formed from a verb, denoting an action or state. In English, the gerund, like the present participle, is formed in *-ing*: *the living is easy* [C16 from Late Latin *gerundium*, from Latin *gerundum* something to be carried on, from *gerere* to wage] > gerundial (dʒɪ'rʌndɪəl) *adj*

gerundive (dʒɪ'rʌndɪv) *n* **1** (in Latin grammar) an adjective formed from a verb, expressing the desirability of the activity denoted by the verb ▷ *adj* **2** of or relating to the gerund or gerundive [C17 from Late Latin *gerundīvus*, from *gerundium* GERUND] > gerundival (,dʒɛrən'daɪvᵊl) *adj* > ge'rundively *adv*

Geryon ('gɛrɪən) *n* Greek myth a winged monster with three bodies joined at the waist, killed by Hercules, who stole the monster's cattle as his tenth labour

gesellschaft (German gə'zɛlʃaft) *n*, *pl* **-schaften** (German -ʃaftən) (often capital) a social group held together by practical concerns, formal and impersonal relationships, etc. Compare **gemeinschaft** [German, literally: society]

gesneria (gɛs'nɪərɪə) *n* any plant of the mostly tuberous-rooted S. American genus *Gesneria*, grown as a greenhouse plant for its large leaves and showy tubular flowers in a range of bright colours: family *Gesneriaceae* [named after Conrad Gesner, 1516–65, Swiss naturalist]

g

gesso ('dʒɛsəʊ) *n* **1** a white ground of plaster and size, used esp in the Middle Ages and Renaissance to prepare panels or canvas for painting or gilding **2** any white substance, esp plaster of Paris, that forms a ground when mixed with water [c16 from Italian: chalk, GYPSUM]

gest *or* **geste** (dʒɛst) *n archaic* **1** a notable deed or exploit **2** a tale of adventure or romance, esp in verse. See also **chanson de geste** [c14 from Old French, from Latin *gesta* deeds, from *gerere* to carry out]

Gestalt (gə'ʃtælt) *n, pl* **-stalts** *or* **-stalten** (-'ʃtæltən) (*sometimes not capital*) a perceptual pattern or structure possessing qualities as a whole that cannot be described merely as a sum of its parts. See also **Gestalt psychology** [c20 German: form, from Old High German *stellen* to shape]

Gestalt psychology *n* a system of thought, derived from experiments carried out by German psychologists, that regards all mental phenomena as being arranged in gestalts

Gestalt psychotherapy *n* a therapy devised in the US in the 1960s in which patients are encouraged to concentrate on the immediate present and to express their true feelings

Gestapo (gɛ'stɑːpəʊ; *German* ge'ʃtaːpo) *n* the secret state police in Nazi Germany, noted for its brutal methods of interrogation [from German *Ge(heime) Sta(ats)po(lizei)*, literally: secret state police]

Gesta Romanorum ('dʒɛstə ˌrəʊmə'nɔːrəm) *n* a popular collection of tales in Latin with moral applications, compiled in the late 13th century as a manual for preachers [Latin: deeds of the Romans]

gestate ('dʒɛsteɪt) *vb* **1** (*tr*) to carry (developing young) in the uterus during pregnancy **2** (*tr*) to develop (a plan or idea) in the mind **3** (*intr*) to be in the process of gestating [c19 back formation from GESTATION]

gestation (dʒɛ'steɪʃən) *n* **1 a** the development of the embryo of a viviparous mammal, between conception and birth: about 266 days in humans, 624 days in elephants, and 63 days in cats **b** (*as modifier*): *gestation period* **2** the development of an idea or plan in the mind **3** the period of such a development [c16 from Latin *gestātiō* a bearing, from *gestāre* to bear, frequentative of *gerere* to carry] > **ges'tational** *or* **gestative** ('dʒɛstətɪv, dʒɛ'steɪ-) *adj* > **'gestatory** *adj*

gestatorial chair (ˌdʒɛstə'tɔːrɪəl) *n* a ceremonial chair on which the pope is carried

gesticulate (dʒɛ'stɪkjʊˌleɪt) *vb* to express by or make gestures [c17 from Latin *gesticulārī*, from Latin *gesticulus* (unattested except in Late Latin) gesture, diminutive of *gestus* gesture, from *gerere* to bear, conduct] > **ges'ticulative** *adj* > **ges'ticuˌlator** *n*

gesticulation (dʒɛˌstɪkjʊ'leɪʃən) *n* **1** the act of gesticulating **2** an animated or expressive gesture > **ges'ticulatory** *adj*

gesture ('dʒɛstʃə) *n* **1** a motion of the hands, head, or body to emphasize an idea or emotion, esp while speaking **2** something said or done as a formality or as an indication of intention: *a political gesture* **3** *obsolete* the manner in which a person bears himself; posture ▷ *vb* **4** to express by or make gestures; gesticulate [c15 from Medieval Latin *gestūra* bearing, from Latin *gestus*, past participle of *gerere* to bear] > **'gestural** *adj* > **'gesturer** *n*

gesundheit *German* (gə'zʊnthait) *sentence substitute* an expression used to wish good health to someone who has just sneezed [from *gesund* healthy + *-heit* -HOOD; see SOUND²]

get (gɛt) *vb* **gets, getting, got** (gɒt) (*mainly tr*) **1** to come into possession of; receive or earn **2** to bring or fetch **3** to contract or be affected by: *he got a chill at the picnic* **4** to capture or seize: *the police finally got him* **5** (*also intr*) to become or cause to become or act as specified: *to get a window open; get one's hair cut; get wet* **6** (*intr;* foll by a preposition or adverbial particle) to succeed in going, coming, leaving, etc: *get off the bus* **7** (*takes an infinitive*) to manage or contrive: *how did you get to be captain?* **8** to make ready or prepare: *to get a meal* **9** to hear, notice, or understand: *I didn't get your meaning* **10** *US and Canadian informal* to learn or master by study **11** (*intr; often foll by to*) to come (to) or arrive (at): *we got home safely; to get to London* **12** to catch or enter: *to get a train* **13** to induce or persuade: *get him to leave at once* **14** to reach by calculation: *add 2 and 2 and you will get 4* **15** to receive (a broadcast signal) **16** to communicate with (a person or place), as by telephone **17** (*also intr;* foll by *to*) *informal* to have an emotional effect (on): *that music really gets me* **18** *informal* to annoy or irritate: *her high voice gets me* **19** *informal* to bring a person into a difficult position from which he or she cannot escape **20** *informal* to puzzle; baffle **21** *informal* to hit: *the blow got him in the back* **22** *informal* to be revenged on, esp by killing **23** *US slang* **a** (foll by *to*) to gain access (to a person) with the purpose of bribing him **b** (often foll by *to*) to obtain access (to someone) and kill or silence him **24** *informal* to have the better of: *your extravagant habits will get you in the end* **25** (*intr;* foll by present participle) *informal* to begin: *get moving* **26** (used as a command) *informal* go! leave now! **27** *archaic* to beget or conceive **28 get even with** See **even¹** (sense 15) **29 get it (in the neck)** *informal* to be reprimanded or punished severely **30 get with it** *slang* to allow oneself to respond to new ideas, styles, etc **31 get with child** *archaic* to make pregnant ▷ *n* **32** *rare* the act of begetting **33** *rare* something begotten; offspring **34** *Brit slang* a variant of **git 35** *informal* (in tennis) a successful return of a shot that was difficult to reach ▷ See also **get about, get across, get ahead, get along, get at, get away, get back, get by, get down, get in, get into, get off, get on, get onto, get out, get over, get round, get through, get-together, get up, got, gotten** [Old English *gietan;* related to Old Norse *geta* to get, learn, Old High German *bigezzan* to obtain] > **'getable** *or* **'gettable** *adj*

USAGE The use of *off* after *get* as in *I got this chair off an antique dealer* is acceptable in conversation, but should not be used in formal writing

GeT *abbreviation for* Greenwich Electronic Time

get about *or* **around** *vb* (*intr, adverb*) **1** to move around, as when recovering from an illness **2** to be socially active **3** (of news, rumour, etc) to become known; spread

get across *vb* **1** to cross or cause or help to cross **2** (*adverb*) to be or cause to be readily understood **3** (*intr, preposition*) *informal* to annoy: *her constant interference really got across him*

get ahead *vb* (*intr, adverb*) **1** to be successful; prosper **2** (foll by *of*) to surpass or excel

get along *vb* (*intr, adverb*) **1** (often foll by *with*) to be friendly or compatible: *my brother gets along well with everybody* **2** to manage, cope, or fare: *how are you getting along in your job?* **3** (*also preposition; often imperative*) to go or move away; leave ▷ *interj* **4** *Brit informal* an exclamation indicating mild disbelief

get around *vb* See **get about, get round**

get at *vb* (*intr, preposition*) **1** to gain access to: *the dog could not get at the meat on the high shelf* **2** to mean or intend: *what are you getting at when you look at me like that?* **3** to irritate or annoy persistently; criticize: *she is always getting at him* **4** to influence or seek to influence, esp illegally by bribery, intimidation, etc: *someone had got at the witness before the trial*

get-at-able *adj informal* accessible

get away *vb* (*adverb, mainly intr*) **1** to make an escape; leave **2** to make a start **3 get away with a** to steal and escape (with money, goods, etc) **b** to do (something wrong, illegal, etc) without being discovered or punished or with only a minor punishment ▷ *interj* **4** an exclamation indicating mild disbelief ▷ *n* **getaway 5** the act of escaping, esp by criminals **6** a start or acceleration **7** (*modifier*) used for escaping: *a getaway car*

get back *vb* (*adverb*) **1** (*tr*) to recover or retrieve **2** (*intr; often foll by to*) to return, esp to a former position or activity: *let's get back to the original question* **3** (*intr;* foll by *at*) to retaliate (against); wreak vengeance (on) **4 get one's own back** *informal* to obtain one's revenge

get by *vb* **1** to pass; go past or overtake **2** (*intr, adverb*) *informal* to manage, esp in spite of difficulties: *I can get by with little money* **3** (*intr*) to be accepted or permitted: *that book will never get by the authorities*

get down *vb* (*mainly adverb*) **1** (*intr; also preposition*) to dismount or descend **2** (*tr; also preposition*) to bring down: *we could not get the wardrobe down the stairs* **3** (*tr*) to write down **4** (*tr*) to make depressed: *your nagging gets me down* **5** (*tr*) to swallow: *he couldn't get the meal down* **6** (*intr;* foll by *to*) to attend seriously (to); concentrate (on) (esp in the phrases **get down to business** *or* **brass tacks**) **7** (*intr*) *informal, chiefly US* to enjoy oneself uninhibitedly, esp by dancing

get-go *n* **from the get-go** *informal* from the beginning: *I've been your friend from the get-go*

Gethsemane (gɛθ'sɛmənɪ) *n New Testament* the garden in Jerusalem where Christ was betrayed on the night before his Crucifixion (Matthew 26:36–56)

get in *vb* (*mainly adverb*) **1** (*intr*) to enter a car, train, etc **2** (*intr*) to arrive, esp at one's home or place of work: *I got in at midnight* **3** (*tr*) to bring in or inside: *get the milk in* **4** (*tr*) to insert or slip in: *he got his suggestion in before anyone else* **5** (*tr*) to gather or collect (crops, debts, etc) **6** (*tr*) to ask (a person, esp a specialist) to give a service: *shall I get the doctor in?* **7** to be elected or cause to be elected: *he got in by 400 votes* **8** (*tr*) to succeed in doing (something), esp during a specified period: *I doubt if I can get this task in today* **9** (*intr*) to obtain a place at university, college, etc **10** (foll by *on*) to join or cause to join (an activity or organization) **11 get in with** to be or cause to be on friendly terms with (a person) **12** (*preposition*) See **get into** ▷ *n* **get-in 13** *theatre* the process of moving into a theatre the scenery, props, and costumes for a production

get into *vb* (*preposition*) **1** (*intr*) to enter **2** (*intr*) to reach (a destination): *the train got into London at noon* **3** to get dressed in (clothes) **4** (*intr*) to preoccupy or obsess (a person's emotions or thoughts): *what's got into him tonight?* **5** to assume or cause to assume (a specified condition, habit, etc): *to get into debt; get a person into a mess* **6** to be elected to or cause to be elected to: *to get into Parliament* **7** (*usually intr*) *informal* to become or cause to become familiar with (a skill): *once you get into driving you'll enjoy it* **8** (*usually intr*) *informal* to develop or cause to develop an absorbing interest in (a hobby, subject, or book)

get off *vb* **1** (*intr, adverb*) to escape the consequences of an action: *he got off very lightly in the accident* **2** (*adverb*) to be or cause to be acquitted: *a good lawyer got him off* **3** (*adverb*) to depart or cause to depart: *to get the children off to school* **4** (*intr*) to descend (from a bus, train, etc); dismount: *she got off at the terminus* **5** to move or cause to move to a distance (from): *get off the field* **6** (*tr, adverb*) to remove; take off: *get your coat off* **7** (*adverb*) to go or send to sleep **8** (*adverb*) to send (letters) or (of letters) to be sent **9** (*intr, adverb*) *slang* to become high on or as on heroin or some other drug **10 get off with** *Brit informal* to establish an amorous or sexual relationship with **11 tell (someone) where to get off** *informal* to rebuke or criticize harshly

get on *vb* (*mainly adverb*) **1** Also (when *preposition*): **get onto** to board or cause or help to board (a bus, train, etc) **2** (*tr*) to dress in (clothes as specified) **3** (*intr*) to grow late or (of time) to elapse: *it's getting on and I must go* **4** (*intr*) (of a person) to grow old **5** (*intr;* foll by *for*) to approach (a time, age, amount, etc): *she is getting on for seventy* **6** (*intr*) to make progress, manage, or fare: *how did you get on in your exam?* **7** (*intr; often foll by with*) to establish a friendly relationship: *he gets on well with other people* **8** (*intr;* foll by *with*) to continue to do: *get on with your homework!* ▷ *interj* **9** I don't believe you!

get onto vb (preposition) **1** Also: **get on** to board or cause or help to board (a bus, train, etc) **2** (intr) to make contact with; communicate with **3** (intr) to become aware of (something illicit or secret): *the boss will get onto their pilfering unless they're careful* **4** (intr) to deliver a demand, request, or rebuke to: *I'll get onto the manufacturers to replace these damaged goods* ▷ See usage note at **onto**

get out vb (adverb) **1** to leave or escape or cause to leave or escape: used in the imperative when dismissing a person **2** to make or become known; publish or be published **3** (tr) to express with difficulty **4** (tr; often foll by of) to extract (information or money) (from a person): *to get a confession out of a criminal* **5** (tr) to gain or receive something, esp something of significance or value: *you get out of life what you put into it* **6** (foll by of) to avoid or cause to avoid: *she always gets out of swimming* **7** (tr) to solve (a puzzle or problem) successfully **8** cricket to dismiss or be dismissed ▷ n **get-out 9** an escape, as from a difficult situation **10** theatre the process of moving out of a theatre the scenery, props, and costumes after a production

get over vb **1** to cross or surmount (something): *the children got over the fence* **2** (intr, preposition) to recover from (an illness, shock, etc) **3** (intr, preposition) to overcome or master (a problem): *you'll soon get over your shyness* **4** (intr, preposition) to appreciate fully: *I just can't get over seeing you again* **5** (tr, adverb) to communicate effectively: *he had difficulty getting the message over* **6** (tr, adverb; sometimes foll by with) to bring (something necessary but unpleasant) to an end: *let's get this job over with quickly*

get round or **around** vb (intr) **1** (preposition) to circumvent or overcome: *he got round the problem by an ingenious trick* **2** (preposition) informal to have one's way with; cajole: *that girl can get round anyone* **3** (preposition) to evade (a law or rules) **4** (adverb; foll by to) to reach or come to at length: *I'll get round to that job in an hour*

getter ('gɛtə) n **1** a person or thing that gets **2** a substance, usually a metal such as titanium, evaporated onto the walls of a vacuum tube, vessel, etc, to adsorb the residual gas and lower the pressure ▷ vb **3** (tr) to remove (a gas) by the action of a getter

get through vb **1** to succeed or cause or help to succeed in an examination, test, etc **2** to bring or come to a destination, esp after overcoming problems: *we got through the blizzards to the survivors* **3** (intr, adverb) to contact, as by telephone **4** (intr, preposition) to use, spend, or consume (money, supplies, etc) **5** to complete or cause to complete (a task, process, etc) **6** (adverb; foll by to) to reach the awareness and understanding (of a person): *I just can't get the message through to him* **7** (intr, adverb) US slang to obtain drugs

get-together n **1** informal a small informal meeting or social gathering ▷ vb **get together** (adverb) **2** (tr) to gather or collect **3** (intr) (of people) to meet socially **4** (intr) to discuss, esp in order to reach an agreement **5 get it together** informal **a** to achieve one's full potential, either generally as a person or in a particular field of activity **b** to achieve a harmonious frame of mind

Gettysburg ('gɛtɪz,bɜːg) n a small town in S Pennsylvania, southwest of Harrisburg: scene of a crucial battle (1863) during the American Civil War, in which Meade's Union forces defeated Lee's Confederate army; site of the national cemetery dedicated by President Lincoln. Pop: 7825 (2003 est)

Gettysburg Address n US history the speech made by President Lincoln at the dedication of the national cemetery on the Civil War battlefield at Gettysburg in Nov 1863

get up vb (mainly adverb) **1** to wake and rise from one's bed or cause to wake and rise from bed **2** (intr) to rise to one's feet; stand up **3** (also

preposition) to ascend or cause to ascend: *the old van couldn't get up the hill* **4** to mount or help to mount (a bicycle, horse, etc) **5** to increase or cause to increase in strength: *the wind got up at noon* **6** (tr) informal to dress (oneself) in a particular way, esp showily or elaborately **7** (tr) informal to devise or create: *to get up an entertainment for Christmas* **8** (tr) informal to study or improve one's knowledge of: *I must get up my history* **9** (intr; foll by to) informal to be involved in: *he's always getting up to mischief* **10** (intr) Austral informal to win, esp in a sporting event ▷ n **get-up 11** informal a costume or outfit, esp one that is striking or bizarre **12** informal the arrangement or production of a book, etc

get-up-and-go n informal energy, drive, or ambition

geum ('dʒiːəm) n any herbaceous plant of the rosaceous genus *Geum*, having compound leaves and red, orange, or white flowers. See also **avens** [c19 New Latin, from Latin: herb bennet, avens]

GeV abbreviation for giga-electronvolts (10^9 electronvolts). Sometimes written (esp US and Canadian) **BeV** (billion electronvolts)

gewgaw ('gjuːgɔː, 'guː-) n **1** a showy but valueless trinket ▷ adj **2** showy and valueless; gaudy [c15 of unknown origin]

Gewürztraminer (gə,vɜːts'træmɪnə; German gə,vyrts'traminər) n **1** a white grape grown in Alsace, Germany, and elsewhere, used for making wine **2** any of various fragrant white wines made from this grape [German, from *Gewürz* spice, seasoning + *Traminer* a variety of grape first grown in the *Tramin* area of the South Tyrol]

gey (gaɪ; Scot gəɪ) adv Scot and Northumberland dialect (intensifier): *it's gey cold* [variant of GAY]

geyser ('giːzə; US 'gaɪzər) n **1** a spring that discharges steam and hot water **2** Brit a domestic gas water heater [c18 from Icelandic *Geysir*, from Old Norse *geysa* to gush]

geyserite ('giːzə,raɪt) n a mineral form of hydrated silica resembling opal, deposited from the waters of geysers and hot springs. Formula: $SiO_2.nH_2O$

Gezira (dʒə'zɪərə) n a region of the E central Sudan between the Blue and White Niles: site of a large-scale irrigation system

gf the internet domain name for French Guiana

G-force n the force of gravity

gg the internet domain name for Guernsey

GG abbreviation for **1** Girl Guides **2** Governor General **3** text messaging good game

gh the internet domain name for Ghana

GH international car registration for Ghana

Ghan (gæn) n Austral **1** short for **Afghan** (sense 3) **2 the** the train connecting Adelaide and Alice Springs [from the number of Afghan camelmen at the Oodnadatta railhead]

Ghana ('gɑːnə) n a republic in W Africa, on the Gulf of Guinea: a powerful empire from the 4th to the 13th centuries; a major source of gold and slaves for Europeans after 1471; British colony of the Gold Coast established in 1874; united with British Togoland in 1957 and became a republic and a member of the Commonwealth in 1960. Official language: English. Religions: Christian, Muslim, and animist. Currency: cedi. Capital: Accra. Pop: 21 377 000 (2004 est). Area: 238 539 sq km (92 100 sq miles)

Ghanaian (gɑː'neɪən) or **Ghanian** ('gɑːnɪən) adj **1** of or relating to Ghana or its inhabitants ▷ n **2** a native or inhabitant of Ghana

gharial ('gæriəl) n another name for for **gavial**

gharry or **gharri** ('gærɪ) n, pl -ries (in India) a horse-drawn vehicle available for hire [c19 from Hindi *gārī*]

ghastly ('gɑːstlɪ) adj -lier, -liest **1** informal very bad or unpleasant **2** deathly pale; wan **3** informal extremely unwell; ill: *they felt ghastly after the party* **4** terrifying; horrible ▷ adv **5** unhealthily; sickly: *ghastly pale* **6** archaic in a horrible or hideous manner [Old English *gāstlīc* spiritual; see CHOSTLY] ▷ 'ghastliness n

ghat (gɔːt) n (in India) **1** stairs or a passage leading down to a river **2** a mountain pass or mountain range **3** a place of cremation [c17 from Hindi *ghāt*, from Sanskrit *ghatta*]

Ghats (gɔːts) pl n See **Eastern Ghats** and **Western Ghats**

ghaut (gʌt) n Caribbean a small cleft in a hill through which a rivulet runs down to the sea [c17 *gaot*, a mountain **pass**, from Hindi: GHAT]

ghazi ('gɑːzɪ) n, pl -zis **1** a Muslim fighter against infidels **2** (often capital) a Turkish warrior of high rank [c18 from Arabic, from *ghazā* he made war]

Ghazzah ('gɑːzə, 'gʌzə) n transliteration of the Arabic name for **Gaza**

GHB abbreviation for gamma hydroxybutyrate. Also called: liquid ecstasy

Gheber or **Ghebre** ('geɪbə, 'giː-) n other words for **Gabar**

ghee (giː) n butter, clarified by boiling, used in Indian cookery [c17 from Hindi *ghī*, from Sanskrit *ghri* sprinkle]

Ghent (gent) n an industrial city and port in NW Belgium, capital of East Flanders province, at the confluence of the Rivers Lys and Scheldt: formerly famous for its cloth industry; university (1816). Pop: 229 344 (2004 est). Flemish name: Gent French name: Gand

gherao (ge'rau) n a form of industrial action in India in which workers imprison their employers on the premises until their demands are met [from Hindi *gherna* to besiege]

gherkin ('gɜːkɪn) n **1** the immature fruit of any of various cucumbers, used for pickling **2 a** a tropical American cucurbitaceous climbing plant, *Cucumis anguria* **b** the small edible fruit of this plant [c17 from early modern Dutch *agurkkijn*, diminutive of *gurk*, from Slavonic, ultimately from Greek *angourion*]

Gherkin ('gɜːkɪn) n **the** an informal name for **Swiss Re Tower**

ghetto ('gɛtəʊ) n, pl -tos or -toes **1** sociol a densely populated slum area of a city inhabited by a socially and economically deprived minority **2** an area in a European city in which Jews were formerly required to live **3** a group or class of people that is segregated in some way [c17 from Italian, perhaps shortened from *borghetto*, diminutive of *borgo* settlement outside a walled city; or from the Venetian *ghetto* the medieval iron-founding district, largely inhabited by Jews]

ghetto blaster n informal a large portable cassette recorder or CD player with built-in speakers

ghetto fabulous adj (of fashion) characterized by gaudy, extravagant, and often sexually alluring clothes

ghettoize or **ghettoise** ('gɛtəʊ,aɪz) vb (tr) to confine or restrict to a particular area, activity, or category: *to ghettoize women as housewives* > ,ghettoi'zation or ,ghettoi'sation n

Ghibelline ('gɪbɪ,laɪn, -,liːn) n **1** a member of the political faction in medieval Italy originally based on support for the German emperor **2** (modifier) of or relating to the Ghibellines. Compare **Guelph[1]** [c16 from Italian *Ghibellino*, probably from Middle High German *Waiblingen*, a Hohenstaufen estate] > 'Ghibel,linism n

ghibli or **gibli** ('gɪblɪ) n a fiercely hot wind of North Africa [c20 from Arabic *gibliy* south wind]

ghillie ('gɪlɪ) n **1** a type of tongueless shoe with lacing up the instep, originally worn by the Scots **2** a variant spelling of **gillie** [from Scottish Gaelic *gille* boy]

ghost (gəʊst) n **1** the disembodied spirit of a dead person, supposed to haunt the living as a pale or shadowy vision; phantom. Related adj: **spectral 2** a haunting memory: *the ghost of his former life rose up before him* **3** a faint trace or possibility of something; glimmer: *a ghost of a smile* **4** the spirit; soul (archaic, except in the phrase **the Holy Ghost**) **5** physics **a** a faint secondary image produced by an optical system **b** a similar image on a television screen, formed by reflection of the

g

transmitting waves or by a defect in the receiver **6** See **ghost word 7** Also called: **ghost edition** an entry recorded in a bibliography of which no actual proof exists **8** Another name for **ghostwriter 9** (*modifier*) falsely recorded as doing a particular job or fulfilling a particular function in order that some benefit, esp money, may be obtained: *a ghost worker* **10** **give up the ghost a** to die **b** (of a machine) to stop working ▷ *vb* **11** See **ghostwrite 12** (*tr*) to haunt **13** (*intr*) to move effortlessly and smoothly, esp unnoticed: *he ghosted into the penalty area* [Old English *gāst*; related to Old Frisian *jēst*, Old High German *geist* spirit, Sanskrit *hēda* fury, anger] > 'ghost,like *adj*

ghost car *n* *Canadian* an unmarked police car

ghost dance *n* a religious dance of certain North American Indians, connected with a political movement (from about 1888) that looked to reunion with the dead and a return to an idealized state of affairs before Europeans came

ghost gum *n* *Austral* a eucalyptus tree with white trunk and branches

ghostly ('gəʊstlɪ) *adj* **-lier, -liest 1** of or resembling a ghost; spectral: *a ghostly face appeared at the window* **2** suggesting the presence of ghosts; eerie **3** *archaic* of or relating to the soul or spirit > 'ghostliness *n*

ghost moth *n* any of various large pale moths of the family *Hepialidae* that are active at dusk

ghost town *n* a deserted town, esp one in the western US that was formerly a boom town

ghost word *n* a word that has entered the language through the perpetuation, in dictionaries, etc, of an error

ghostwrite ('gəʊst,raɪt) *vb* **-writes, -writing, -wrote, -written** to write (an autobiographical or other article) on behalf of a person who is then credited as author. Often shortened to: **ghost** > 'ghost,writer *n*

ghoul (guːl) *n* **1** a malevolent spirit or ghost **2** a person interested in morbid or disgusting things **3** a person who robs graves **4** (in Muslim legend) an evil demon thought to eat human bodies, either stolen corpses or children [c18 from Arabic *ghūl*, from *ghāla* he seized]

ghoulish ('guːlɪʃ) *adj* of or relating to ghouls; morbid or disgusting; unhealthily interested in death > 'ghoulishly *adv* > 'ghoulishness *n*

GHQ *military abbreviation for* General Headquarters

ghyll (gɪl) *n* a variant spelling of **gill³**

gi¹ (giː) *n* a loose-fitting white suit worn in judo, karate, and other martial arts: *a karate gi* [from Japanese *-gi* costume, from *ki* to wear]

gi² *the internet domain name for* Gibraltar

Gi *electronics abbreviation for* gilbert

GI¹ *n* *US informal* **1** (*pl* **GIs** or **GI's**) a soldier in the US Army, esp an enlisted man ▷ *adj* **2** conforming to US Army regulations; of standard government issue [c20 abbrev of *government issue*]

GI² or **g.i.** *abbreviation for* **1** gastrointestinal **2** glycaemic index

giant ('dʒaɪənt) *n* **1** Also (feminine): **giantess** ('dʒaɪəntɪs) a mythical figure of superhuman size and strength, esp in folklore or fairy tales **2** a person or thing of exceptional size, reputation, etc: *a giant in nuclear physics* **3** *Greek myth* any of the large and powerful offspring of Uranus (sky) and Gaea (earth) who rebelled against the Olympian gods but were defeated in battle **4** *pathol* a person suffering from gigantism **5** *astronomy* See **giant star 6** *mining* another word for **monitor** (sense 8) ▷ *adj* **7** remarkably or supernaturally large **8** *architect* another word for **colossal** [c13 from Old French *geant*, from Vulgar Latin *gagās* (unattested), from Latin *gigās*, *gigant-*, from Greek] > 'giant-,like *adj*

giant cell *n* *histology* an exceptionally large cell, often possessing several nuclei, such as an osteoclast

giant hogweed *n* an umbelliferous garden escape, *Heracleum mantegazzianum*, a tall species of cow parsley that grows up to 3½ metres (10 ft) and

whose irritant hairs and sap can cause a severe reaction if handled. Also called: **cartwheel flower**

giantism ('dʒaɪən,tɪzəm) *n* another term for **gigantism**

giant killer *n* a person, sports team, etc, that defeats an apparently superior opponent

giant panda *n* See **panda** (sense 1)

giant peacock moth *n* the largest European moth, an emperor, *Saturnia pyri*, reaching 15 cm (6 in.) in wingspan. It is mottled brown with a prominent ocellus on each wing and being night-flying can be mistaken for a bat

giant planet *n* any of the planets Jupiter, Saturn, Uranus, and Neptune, characterized by large mass, low density, and an extensive atmosphere

giant powder *n* dynamite composed of trinitroglycerine absorbed in kieselguhr

Giant's Causeway *n* a promontory of columnar basalt on the N coast of Northern Ireland, in Antrim: consists of several thousand pillars, mostly hexagonal, that were formed by the rapid cooling of lava and the inward contraction of the lava flow

giant slalom *n* *skiing* a type of slalom in which the course is longer and the obstacles are further apart than in a standard slalom

giant star *n* any of a class of stars, such as Capella and Arcturus, that have swelled and brightened considerably as they approach the end of their life, their energy supply having changed. Sometimes shortened to: **giant** Compare **supergiant**

giant tortoise *n* any of various very large tortoises of the genus *Testudo*, of the Galápagos, Seychelles, and certain other islands, weighing up to 225 kilograms (495 lbs.)

giaour ('dʒaʊə) *n* a derogatory term for a non-Muslim, esp a Christian, used esp by the Turks [c16 from Turkish *giaur* unbeliever, from Persian *gaur*, variant of *gäbr*]

giardiasis (,dʒaɪə'daɪəsɪs) *n* infection with the parasitic protozoan *Giardia lamblia*, which can cause severe diarrhoea

gib¹ (gɪb) *n* **1** a metal wedge, pad, or thrust bearing, esp a brass plate let into a steam engine crosshead ▷ *vb* **gibs, gibbing, gibbed 2** (*tr*) to fasten or supply with a gib [c18 of unknown origin]

gib² (gɪb) *n* a male cat, esp a castrated one [c14 probably a shortening and alteration of the proper name *Gilbert*]

Gib (dʒɪb) *n* an informal name for **Gibraltar**

gibber¹ ('dʒɪbə) *vb* **1** to utter rapidly and unintelligibly; prattle **2** (*intr*) (of monkeys and related animals) to make characteristic chattering sounds ▷ *n* **3** a less common word for **gibberish** [c17 of imitative origin]

gibber² ('dʒɪbə) *n* *Austral* **1** a stone or boulder **2** (*modifier*) of or relating to a dry flat area of land covered with wind-polished stones: *gibber plains* [c19 from a native Australian language]

gibberellic acid (,dʒɪbə'rɛlɪk) *n* a slightly soluble crystalline plant hormone first isolated from the fungus *Gibberella fujikuroi*: a gibberellin. Formula: $C_{19}H_{22}O_6$ [c20 from New Latin *Gibberella*, literally: a little hump, from Latin *gibber* hump + -ic]

gibberellin (,dʒɪbə'rɛlɪn) *n* any of several plant hormones, including gibberellic acid, whose main action is to cause elongation of the stem: used in promoting the growth of plants, in the malting of barley, etc

gibberish ('dʒɪbərɪʃ) *n* **1** rapid chatter like that of monkeys **2** incomprehensible talk; nonsense

gibbet ('dʒɪbɪt) *n* **1 a** a wooden structure resembling a gallows, from which the bodies of executed criminals were formerly hung to public view **b** a gallows ▷ *vb* (*tr*) **2** to put to death by hanging on a gibbet **3** to hang (a corpse) on a gibbet **4** to expose to public ridicule [c13 from Old French *gibet* gallows, literally: little cudgel, from *gibe* cudgel; of uncertain origin]

Gib board *n* *NZ informal* short for **Gibraltar board**

gibbon ('gɪbʳn) *n* any small agile arboreal anthropoid ape of the genus *Hylobates*, inhabiting forests in S Asia [c18 from French, probably from an Indian dialect word]

gibbosity (gɪ'bɒsɪtɪ) *n, pl* **-ties** *rare* **1** the state of being gibbous **2** *biology* a bulge or protuberance

gibbous ('gɪbəs) or **gibbose** ('gɪbəʊs) *adj* **1** (of the moon or a planet) more than half but less than fully illuminated **2** having a hunchback; hunchbacked **3** bulging [c17 from Late Latin *gibbōsus* humpbacked, from Latin *gibba* hump] > 'gibbously *adv* > 'gibbousness *n*

Gibbs function (gɪbz) *n* a thermodynamic property of a system equal to the difference between its enthalpy and the product of its temperature and its entropy. It is usually measured in joules. Symbol: *G*, (esp US) *F* Also called: **Gibbs free energy, free enthalpy** Compare **Helmholtz function** [c19 named after Josiah Willard *Gibbs* (1839–1903), US physicist and mathematician]

gibbsite ('gɪbzaɪt) *n* a mineral consisting of hydrated aluminium oxide: a constituent of bauxite and a source of alumina. Formula: $Al(OH)_3$ [c19 named after George *Gibbs* (died 1833), American mineralogist]

gibe¹ or **jibe** (dʒaɪb) *vb* **1** to make jeering or scoffing remarks (at); taunt ▷ *n* **2** a derisive or provoking remark [c16 perhaps from Old French *giber* to treat roughly, of uncertain origin] > 'giber or 'jiber *n* > 'gibingly or 'jibingly *adv*

gibe² (dʒaɪb) *vb, n* *nautical* a variant spelling of **gybe**

Gibeon ('gɪbɪən) *n* an ancient town of Palestine: the excavated site thought to be its remains lies about 9 kilometres (6 miles) northwest of Jerusalem

Gibeonite ('gɪbɪə,naɪt) *n* *Old Testament* one of the inhabitants of the town of Gibeon, who were compelled by Joshua to serve the Hebrews (Joshua 9)

giblets ('dʒɪblɪts) *pl n* (*sometimes singular*) the gizzard, liver, heart, and neck of a fowl [c14 from Old French *gibelet* stew of game birds, probably from *gibier* game, of Germanic origin]

gibli ('gɪblɪ) *n* a variant spelling of **ghibli**

Gibraltar (dʒɪ'brɔːltə) *n* **1 City of** a city on the **Rock of Gibraltar,** a limestone promontory at the tip of S Spain: settled by Moors in 711 and taken by Spain in 1462; ceded to Britain in 1713; a British crown colony (1830–1969), still politically associated with Britain; a naval and air base of strategic importance. Pop: 27 000 (2003 est). Area: 6.5 sq km (2.5 sq miles). Ancient name: **Calpe 2 Strait of** a narrow strait between the S tip of Spain and the NW tip of Africa, linking the Mediterranean with the Atlantic

Gibraltar board *n* *trademark* *NZ* a type of lining board with a cardboard surface and a gypsum core

Gibraltarian (,dʒɪbrɔːl'tɛərɪən) *adj* **1** of or relating to Gibraltar or its inhabitants ▷ *n* **2** a native or inhabitant of Gibraltar

Gibson ('gɪbsʳn) *n* *chiefly US* a cocktail consisting of four or more parts dry gin and one part dry vermouth, iced and served with a pickled pearl onion

Gibson Desert *n* a desert in W central Australia, between the Great Sandy Desert and the Victoria Desert: salt marshes, salt lakes, and scrub. Area: about 220 000 sq km (85 000 sq miles)

Gibson girl *n* the ideal fashionable American girl of the late 1890s and early 1900s, as portrayed in the drawings of Charles Dana Gibson, 1867–1944, US illustrator

gibus ('dʒaɪbəs) *n* another name for **opera hat** [c19 named after *Gibus*, 19th-century Frenchman who invented it]

GIC (in Canada) *abbreviation for* Guaranteed Investment Certificate: a form of investment that earns interest but is guaranteed not to incur loss

gid (gɪd) *n* a disease of sheep characterized by an unsteady gait and staggering, caused by infestation of the brain with tapeworms (*Taenia caenuris*) [c17 back formation from GIDDY]

giddap (gɪˈdæp) *or* **giddy-up** (ˌgɪdɪˈʌp) *interj* an exclamation used to make a horse go faster [c20 colloquial form of *get up*]

giddy (ˈgɪdɪ) *adj* **-dier, -diest 1** affected with a reeling sensation and feeling as if about to fall; dizzy **2** causing or tending to cause vertigo **3** impulsive; scatterbrained **4** *my giddy aunt* an exclamation of surprise ▷ *vb* **-dies, -dying, -died 5** to make or become giddy [Old English *gydig* mad, frenzied, possessed by God; related to GOD]
> **ˈgiddily** *adv* > **ˈgiddiness** *n*

Gideon (ˈgɪdɪən) *n Old Testament* a Hebrew judge who led the Israelites to victory over their Midianite oppressors (Judges 6:11–8:35)

Gideon Bible *n* a Bible purchased by members of a Christian organization (**Gideons**) and placed in a hotel room, hospital ward, etc

gidgee *or* **gidjee** (ˈgɪdʒiː) *n Austral* any of various small acacia trees, *Acacia cambagei*, which at times emits an unpleasant smell [c19 from a native Australian language]

gie (giː) *vb* a Scot word for **give**

Giessen (*German* ˈgiːsən) *n* a city in central Germany, in Hesse: university (1607). Pop: 74 001 (2003 est)

GIF (gɪf) *n computing* **a** a standard compressed file format used for pictures **b** a picture held in this format [c20 from *g(raphic) i(nterchange) f(ormat)*]

gift (gɪft) *n* **1** something given; a present **2** a special aptitude, ability, or power; talent **3** the power or right to give or bestow (esp in the phrases **in the gift of, in (someone's) gift**) **4** the act or process of giving **5** *look a gift-horse in the mouth* (*usually negative*) to find fault with a free gift or chance benefit ▷ *vb* (*tr*) **6** to present (something) as a gift to (a person) **7** (*often foll by with*) to present (someone) with a gift **8** *rare* to endow with; bestow [Old English *gift* payment for a wife, dowry; related to Old Norse *gipt*, Old High German *gift*, Gothic *fragifts* endowment, engagement; see GIVE] > **ˈgiftless** *adj*

GIFT (gɪft) *n acronym for* gamete intrafallopian transfer: a technique, similar to in vitro fertilization, that enables some women who are unable to conceive to bear children. Egg cells are removed from the woman's ovary, mixed with sperm, and introduced into one of her Fallopian tubes

gifted (ˈgɪftɪd) *adj* having or showing natural talent or aptitude: *a gifted musician; a gifted performance* > **ˈgiftedly** *adv* > **ˈgiftedness** *n*

gift of tongues *n* an utterance, partly or wholly unintelligible, believed by some to be produced under the influence of ecstatic religious emotion and conceived to be a manifestation of the Holy Ghost: practised in certain Christian churches, usually called Pentecostal. Also called: **glossolalia**

gift tax *n* another name for (the former) **capital transfer tax**

giftwrap (ˈgɪftˌræp) *vb* **-wraps, -wrapping, -wrapped** to wrap (an article intended as a gift) attractively

Gifu (ˈgiːfuː) *n* a city in Japan, on central Honshu: hot springs, textile and paper lantern manufacturing. Pop: 401 269 (2002 est)

gig¹ (gɪg) *n* **1** a light two-wheeled one-horse carriage without a hood **2** *nautical* a light tender for a vessel, often for the personal use of the captain **3** a long light rowing boat, used esp for racing **4** a machine for raising the nap of a fabric ▷ *vb* **gigs, gigging, gigged 5** (*intr*) to travel in a gig **6** (*tr*) to raise the nap of (fabric) [c13 (in the sense: flighty girl, spinning top): perhaps of Scandinavian origin: compare Danish *gig* top, Norwegian *giga* to shake about]

gig² (gɪg) *n* **1** a cluster of barbless hooks drawn through a shoal of fish to try to impale them **2** short for **fishgig** ▷ *vb* **gigs, gigging, gigged 3** to catch (fish) with a gig [c18 shortened from FISHGIG]

gig³ (gɪg) *informal* ▷ *n* **1** a job, esp a single booking for jazz or pop musicians to play at a concert or club **2** the performance itself ▷ *vb* **gigs, gigging, gigged 3** (*intr*) to perform at a gig or gigs [c20 of unknown origin]

gig⁴ (gɪg) *n informal* short for **gigabyte**

giga- (ˈgɪgə) *ˈgaɪgə, combining form* **1** denoting 10^9: *gigavolt*. Symbol: **G 2** (in computer technology) denoting 2^{30}: *gigabyte* [from Greek *gigas* GIANT]

gigabit (ˈgɪgəˌbɪt, ˈgaɪgəˌbɪt) *n Computing* one million bits

gigabyte (ˈgɪgəˌbaɪt, ˈgaɪgəˌbaɪt) *n computing* one thousand and twenty-four megabytes. See also **giga-** (sense 2)

gigaflop (ˈgɪgəˌflɒp, ˈgaɪgəˌflɒp) *n computing* a measure of processing speed, consisting of a thousand million floating-point operations a second [c20 from GIGA- + *flo(ating) p(oint)*]

gigahertz (ˈgɪgəˌhɜːts, ˈgaɪgə-) *n, pl* **-hertz** a unit of frequency equal to 10^9 hertz. Symbol: **GHz**

gigantic (dʒaɪˈgæntɪk) *adj* **1** very large; enormous: *a gigantic error* **2** Also: **gigantesque** (ˌdʒaɪgænˈtɛsk) of or suitable for giants [c17 from Greek *gigantikos*, from *gigas* GIANT] > **giˈgantically** *adv* > **giˈganticness** *n*

gigantism (ˈdʒaɪgænˌtɪzəm, dʒaɪˈgæntɪzəm) *n* **1** Also called: **giantism** excessive growth of the entire body, caused by over-production of growth hormone by the pituitary gland during childhood or adolescence. Compare **acromegaly 2** the state or quality of being gigantic

gigantomachy (ˌdʒaɪgænˈtɒmək ɪ) *or* **gigantomachia** (dʒaɪˌgæntəʊˈmeɪkɪə) *n, pl* **-chies** *or* **-chias 1** *Greek myth* the war fought between the gods of Olympus and the rebelling giants. See **giant** (sense 3) **2** any battle fought between or as if between giants [c17 from Greek *gigantomakhia*, from *gigas* giant + *makhē* battle]

giggle (ˈgɪgəl) *vb* **1** (*intr*) to laugh nervously or foolishly ▷ *n* **2** such a laugh **3** *informal* something or someone that provokes amusement **4** **the giggles** a fit of prolonged and uncontrollable giggling **5** **for a giggle** *informal* as a joke or prank; not seriously [c16 of imitative origin] > **ˈgiggler** *n* > **ˈgiggling** *n, adj* > **ˈgigglingly** *adv* > **ˈgiggly** *adj*

gig-lamps *pl n* an old-fashioned slang term for **spectacles**

GIGO (ˈgaɪgəʊ) *n computing slang acronym for* garbage in, garbage out

gigolo (ˈʒɪgəˌləʊ) *n, pl* **-los 1** a man who is kept by a woman, esp an older woman **2** a man who is paid to dance with or escort women [c20 from French, back formation from *gigolette* girl for hire as a dancing partner, prostitute, from *giguer* to dance, from *gigue* a fiddle; compare GIGOT, GIGUE, JIG]

gigot (ˈʒiːgəʊ, ˈdʒɪgət) *n* **1** a leg of lamb or mutton **2** a leg-of-mutton sleeve [c16 from Old French: leg, a small fiddle, from *gigue* a fiddle, of Germanic origin]

gigue (ʒiːg) *n* **1** a piece of music, usually in six-eight time and often fugal, incorporated into the classical suite **2** a formal couple dance of the 16th and 17th centuries, derived from the jig [c17 from French, from Italian *giga*, literally: a fiddle; see GIGOT]

GI Joe *n US informal* a US enlisted soldier; a GI

Gijón (giːˈhɔːn; *Spanish* xiˈxɔn) *n* a port in NW Spain, on the Bay of Biscay: capital of the kingdom of Asturias until 791. Pop: 270 875 (2003 est). Asturian name: Xixón Ancient name: Gigia

Gila monster (ˈhiːlə) *n* a large venomous brightly coloured lizard, *Heloderma suspectum*, inhabiting deserts of the southwestern US and Mexico and feeding mostly on eggs and small mammals; family Helodermatidae [c19 after the *Gila*, a river in New Mexico and Arizona]

gilbert (ˈgɪlbət) *n* a unit of magnetomotive force; the magnetomotive force resulting from the passage of 4π abamperes through one turn of a coil. 1 gilbert is equivalent to $10/4\pi = 0.795\,775$

ampere-turn. Symbols: **Gb** or **Gi** [c19 named after William *Gilbert* (1540–1603), English physician and physicist]

Gilbertian (gɪlˈbɜːtɪən) *adj* characteristic of or resembling the style or whimsical humour of Sir W S Gilbert (1836–1911), English librettist famous for his comic operettas written with Arthur Sullivan

Gilbertine (ˈgɪlbətaɪn, -tiːn) *n* a member of a Christian order founded in approximately 1135 by St Gilbert of Sempringham, composed of nuns who followed the Cistercian rule and Augustinian canons who ministered to them. It was the only religious order of English origin and never spread to Europe ▷ *adj* **2** of, relating to, or belonging to this order

Gilbert Islands *pl n* a group of islands in the W Pacific: with Banaba, the Phoenix Islands, and three of the Line Islands they constitute the independent state of Kiribati; until 1975 they formed part of the British colony of **Gilbert and Ellice Islands**; achieved full independence in 1979. Pop: 71 757 (1995). Area: 295 sq km (114 sq miles)

gild¹ (gɪld) *vb* **gilds, gilding, gilded** *or* **gilt** (gɪlt) (*tr*) **1** to cover with or as if with gold **2** **gild the lily a** to adorn unnecessarily something already beautiful **b** to praise someone inordinately **3** to give a falsely attractive or valuable appearance to **4** *archaic* to smear with blood [Old English *gyldan*, from *gold* GOLD; related to Old Norse *gylla*, Middle High German *vergülden*] > **ˈgilder** *n*

gild² (gɪld) *n* a variant spelling of **guild** (sense 2) > **ˈgildsman** *n*

gilder (ˈgɪldə) *n* a variant spelling of **guilder**

gilding (ˈgɪldɪŋ) *n* **1** the act or art of applying gilt to a surface **2** the surface so produced **3** another word for **gilt¹** (sense 2)

Gilead¹ (ˈgɪlɪˌæd) *n* a historic mountainous region east of the River Jordan, rising over 1200 m (4000 ft)

Gilead² (ˈgɪlɪˌæd) *n Old Testament* a grandson of Manasseh; ancestor of the Coileadites (Numbers 26: 29–30)

Gileadite (ˈgɪlɪəˌdaɪt) *n* **1** an inhabitant of the region of Gilead **2** a descendant of Gilead (the man)

gilet (dʒɪˈleɪ) *n* **1** a waist- or hip-length garment, usually sleeveless, fastening up the front; sometimes made from a quilted fabric, and designed to be worn over a blouse, shirt, etc **2** a bodice resembling a waistcoat in a woman's dress **3** such a bodice as part of a ballet dancer's costume [c19 French, literally: waistcoat]

gilgai (ˈgɪlgaɪ) *n Austral* a natural water hole [c19 from a native Australian language]

Gilgamesh (ˈgɪlgəˌmɛʃ) *n* a legendary Sumerian king

gill¹ (gɪl) *n* **1** the respiratory organ in many aquatic animals, consisting of a membrane or outgrowth well supplied with blood vessels. **External gills** occur in tadpoles, some molluscs, etc; **internal gills**, within gill slits, occur in most fishes. Related adj: **branchial 2** any of the radiating leaflike spore-producing structures on the undersurface of the cap of a mushroom ▷ *vb* **3** to catch (fish) or (of fish) to be caught in a gill net **4** (*tr*) to gut (fish) ▷ See also **gills** [c14 of Scandinavian origin; compare Swedish *gäl*, Danish *gjælle*, Greek *khelunē* lip] > **gilled** *adj* > **ˈgill-less** *adj* > **ˈgill-ˌlike** *adj*

gill² (dʒɪl) *n* **1** a unit of liquid measure equal to one quarter of a pint **2** *Northern English dialect* half a pint, esp of beer [c14 from Old French *gille* vat, tub, from Late Latin *gillō* cooling vessel for liquids, of obscure origin]

gill³ *or* **ghyll** (gɪl) *n dialect* **1** a narrow stream; rivulet **2** a wooded ravine **3** (*capital when part of place name*) a deep natural hole in rock; pothole: *Gaping Gill* [c11 from Old Norse *gil* steep-sided valley]

gill⁴ (dʒɪl) *n* **1** *archaic* a girl or sweetheart **2** *dialect* Also spelt: **jill** a female ferret **3** an archaic or

g

dialect name for **ground ivy** [c15 special use of *Gill*, short for *Gillian*, girl's name]

Gilles de la Tourette syndrome (dʒi:l də læ tʊəˈrɛt) *n* another name for **Tourette syndrome**

gill fungus (gɪl) *n* any fungus of the basidiomycetous family *Agaricaceae*, in which the spores are produced on gills underneath a cap. See also **agaric**

gillie, ghillie or **gilly** ('gɪlɪ) *n, pl* -lies *Scot* **1** an attendant or guide for hunting or fishing **2** (formerly) a Highland chieftain's male attendant or personal servant [c17 from Scottish Gaelic *gille* boy, servant]

Gillingham ('dʒɪlɪŋəm) *n* a town in SE England, in Medway unitary authority, Kent, on the Medway estuary: former dockyards. Pop: 98 403 (2001)

gillion ('dʒɪljən) *n Brit* (no longer in technical use) one thousand million. US and Canadian equivalent: billion [c20 from G(IGA-) + (M)ILLION]

gill net (gɪl) *n fishing* a net suspended vertically in the water to trap fish by their gills in its meshes

gill pouch (gɪl) *n* any of a series of paired linear pouches in chordate embryos, arising as outgrowths of the wall of the pharynx. In fish and some amphibians they become the gill slits

gills (gɪlz) *pl n* **1** (*sometimes singular*) the wattle of birds such as domestic fowl **2 green around** or **about the gills** *informal* looking or feeling nauseated

gill slit (gɪl) *n* any of a series of paired linear openings to the exterior from the sides of the pharynx in fishes and some amphibians. They contain the gills

gillyflower or **gilliflower** ('dʒɪlɪˌflaʊə) *n* **1** any of several plants with fragrant flowers, such as the stock and wallflower **2** an archaic name for **carnation** [c14 changed (through influence of *flower*) from *gilofre*, from Old French *girofle*, from Medieval Latin, from Greek *karuophullon* clove tree, from *karuon* nut + *phullon* leaf]

Gilolo (dʒaɪˈləʊləʊ, dʒɪ-) *n* See **Halmahera**

Gilsonite ('gɪlsəˌnaɪt) *n trademark* a very pure form of asphalt found in Utah and Colorado; used for making paints, varnishes, and linoleum [c19 named after S. H. *Gilson* of Salt Lake City, Utah, who discovered it]

gilt¹ (gɪlt) *vb* **1** a past tense and past participle of **gild¹** ▷ *n* **2** gold or a substance simulating it, applied in gilding **3** another word for **gilding** (senses 1, 2) **4** superficial or false appearance of excellence; glamour **5** a gilt-edged security **6 take the gilt off the gingerbread** to destroy the part of something that gives it its appeal ▷ *adj* **7** covered with or as if with gold or gilt; gilded

gilt² (gɪlt) *n* a young female pig, esp one that has not had a litter [c15 from Old Norse *gyltr*; related to Old English *gelte*, Old High German *gelza*, Middle Low German *gelte*]

gilt-edged *adj* **1** *stock exchange* denoting government securities on which interest payments will certainly be met and that will certainly be repaid at par on the due date **2** of the highest quality: *the last track on the album is a gilt-edged classic* **3** (of books, papers, etc) having gilded edges

gilthead ('gɪltˌhɛd) *n* **1** a sparid fish, *Sparus aurata*, of Mediterranean and European Atlantic waters, having a gold-coloured band between the eyes **2** any similar or related fish

gimbals ('dʒɪmbᵊlz, 'gɪm-) *pl n* a device, consisting of two or three pivoted rings at right angles to each other, that provides free suspension in all planes for an object such as a gyroscope, compass, chronometer, etc. Also called: **gimbal ring** [c16 variant of earlier *gimmal* finger ring, from Old French *gemel*, from Latin *gemellus*, diminutive of *geminus* twin]

gimcrack ('dʒɪmˌkræk) *adj* **1** cheap; shoddy ▷ *n* **2** a cheap showy trifle or gadget [c18 changed from C14 *gibecrake* little ornament, of unknown origin] > 'gim,crackery *n*

gimel ('gɪməl; *Hebrew* 'gi:mɛl) *n* the third letter of the Hebrew alphabet (ג) transliterated as *g* or, when final, *gh* [literally: camel]

gimlet ('gɪmlɪt) *n* **1** a small hand tool consisting of a pointed spiral tip attached at right angles to a handle, used for boring small holes in wood **2** *US* a cocktail consisting of half gin or vodka and half lime juice **3** a eucalyptus of W Australia having a twisted bole ▷ *vb* **4** (*tr*) to make holes in (wood) using a gimlet ▷ *adj* **5** penetrating; piercing (esp in the phrase **gimlet-eyed**) [c15 from Old French *guimbelet*, of Germanic origin, see WIMBLE]

gimme ('gɪmi:) *interj* **1** *slang* give me! ▷ *n* **2** *golf* a short putt that one is excused by one's opponent from playing because it is considered too easy to miss

gimmick ('gɪmɪk) *n* **1** something designed to attract extra attention, interest, or publicity **2** any clever device, gadget, or stratagem, esp one used to deceive **3** *chiefly US* a device or trick of legerdemain that enables a magician to deceive the audience [c20 originally US slang, of unknown origin] > 'gimmickry *n* > 'gimmicky *adj*

gimp¹ or **guimpe** (gɪmp) *n* a tapelike trimming of silk, wool, or cotton, often stiffened with wire [c17 probably from Dutch *gimp*, of unknown origin]

gimp² (gɪmp) *n* **1** *US and Canadian offensive slang* a physically disabled person, esp one who is lame **2** *slang* a sexual fetishist who likes to be dominated and who dresses in a leather or rubber body suit with mask, zips, and chains [c20 of unknown origin]

gimpy ('gɪmpɪ) *adj* the US equivalent of **gammy**

gin¹ (dʒɪn) *n* **1** an alcoholic drink obtained by distillation and rectification of the grain of malted barley, rye, or maize, flavoured with juniper berries **2** any of various grain spirits flavoured with other fruit or aromatic essences: *sloe gin* **3** an alcoholic drink made from any rectified spirit [c18 shortened from Dutch *genever* juniper, via Old French from Latin *jūniperus* JUNIPER]

gin² (dʒɪn) *n* **1** a primitive engine in which a vertical shaft is turned by horses driving a horizontal beam or yoke in a circle **2** Also called: **cotton gin** a machine of this type used for separating seeds from raw cotton **3** a trap for catching small mammals, consisting of a noose of thin strong wire **4** a hand-operated hoist that consists of a drum winder turned by a crank ▷ *vb* **gins, ginning, ginned** (*tr*) **5** to free (cotton) of seeds with a gin **6** to trap or snare (game) with a gin [c13 *gyn*, shortened from ENGINE] > 'ginner *n*

gin³ (dʒɪn) *vb* **gins, ginning, gan, gun** an archaic word for **begin**

gin⁴ (gɪn) *conj Scot* if [perhaps related to *gif*, an earlier form of *if*]

gin⁵ (dʒɪn) *n Austral offensive slang* an Aboriginal woman [c19 from a native Australian language]

ging (gɪŋ) *n Austral slang* a child's catapult [of unknown origin]

ginge (dʒɪndʒ) *n informal* a person with ginger hair

ginger ('dʒɪndʒə) *n* **1** any of several zingiberaceous plants of the genus *Zingiber*, esp *Z. officinale* of the East Indies, cultivated throughout the tropics for its spicy hot-tasting underground stem. See also **galangal** Compare **wild ginger 2** the underground stem of this plant, which is used fresh or powdered as a flavouring or crystallized as a sweetmeat **3** any of certain related plants **4 a** a reddish-brown or yellowish-brown colour **b** (*as adjective*): *ginger hair* **5** *informal* liveliness; vigour ▷ *vb* **6** (*tr*) to add the spice ginger to (a dish) ▷ See also **ginger up** [c13 from Old French *gingivre*, from Medieval Latin *gingiber*, from Latin *zinziberi*, from Greek *zingiberis*, probably from Sanskrit *śṛṅgaveram*, from *śṛṅga-* horn + *vera-* body, referring to its shape]

ginger ale *n* a sweetened effervescent nonalcoholic drink flavoured with ginger extract

ginger beer *n* a slightly alcoholic drink made by fermenting a mixture of syrup and root ginger

gingerbread ('dʒɪndʒəˌbrɛd) *n* **1** a moist brown cake, flavoured with ginger and treacle or syrup **2 a** a rolled biscuit, similarly flavoured, cut into various shapes and sometimes covered with icing **b** (*as modifier*): *gingerbread man* **3 a** an elaborate but unsubstantial ornamentation **b** (*as modifier*): *gingerbread style of architecture*

gingerbread tree *n* a W African tree, *Parinari macrophyllum*, with large mealy edible fruits (**gingerbread plums**): family *Chrysobalanaceae*

ginger group *n chiefly Brit* a group within a party, association, etc, that enlivens or radicalizes its parent body

gingerly ('dʒɪndʒəlɪ) *adv* **1** in a cautious, reluctant, or timid manner ▷ *adj* **2** cautious, reluctant, or timid [c16 perhaps from Old French *gensor* dainty, from *gent* of noble birth; see GENTLE] > 'gingerliness *n*

ginger nut or **snap** *n* a crisp biscuit flavoured with ginger

ginger up *vb* (*tr, adverb*) to enliven (an activity, group, etc)

ginger wine *n* an alcoholic drink made from fermented bruised ginger, sugar, and water

gingery ('dʒɪndʒərɪ) *adj* **1** like or tasting of ginger **2** of or like the colour ginger **3** full of vigour; high-spirited **4** pointed; biting: *a gingery remark*

gingham ('gɪŋəm) *n textiles* **a** a cotton fabric, usually woven of two coloured yarns in a checked or striped design **b** (*as modifier*): *a gingham dress* [c17 from French *guingan*, from Malay *ginggang* striped cloth]

gingili, gingelli or **gingelly** ('dʒɪndʒɪlɪ) *n* **1** the oil obtained from sesame seeds **2** another name for **sesame** [c18 from Hindi *jingalī*]

gingiva ('dʒɪndʒɪvə, dʒɪn'dʒaɪvə) *n, pl* -givae (-dʒɪ,vi:, -'dʒaɪvi:) *anatomy* the technical name for the **gum²** [from Latin] > 'gingival *adj*

gingivitis (ˌdʒɪndʒɪ'vaɪtɪs) *n* inflammation of the gums

ginglymus ('dʒɪŋglɪməs, 'gɪŋ-) *n, pl* -mi (-ˌmaɪ) *anatomy* a hinge joint. See **hinge** (sense 2) [c17 New Latin, from Greek *ginglumos* hinge]

gink (gɪŋk) *n slang* a man or boy, esp one considered to be odd [c20 of unknown origin]

ginkgo ('gɪŋkgəʊ) or **gingko** ('gɪŋkəʊ) *n, pl* -goes or -koes a widely planted ornamental Chinese gymnosperm tree, *Ginkgo biloba*, with fan-shaped deciduous leaves and fleshy yellow fruit: phylum *Ginkgophyta*. It is used in herbal remedies and as a food supplement. Also called: maidenhair tree [c18 from Japanese *ginkyō*, from Ancient Chinese *yin* silver + *hang* apricot]

ginnel ('gɪnᵊl, 'dʒɪn-) *n Northern English dialect* a narrow passageway between buildings [c17 perhaps a corruption of CHANNEL¹]

ginormous (dʒaɪ'nɔːməs) *adj informal* very large [c20 blend of *giant* or *gigantic* and *enormous*]

gin palace (dʒɪn) *n* (formerly) a gaudy drinking house

gin rummy (dʒɪn) *n* a version of rummy in which a player may go out if the odd cards outside his sequences total less than ten points. Often shortened to: gin [c20 from GIN¹ + RUMMY¹, apparently from a humorous allusion to gin and rum]

ginseng ('dʒɪnsɛŋ) *n* **1** either of two araliaceous plants, *Panax schinseng* of China or *P. quinquefolius* of North America, whose forked aromatic roots are used medicinally **2** the root of either of these plants or a substance obtained from the roots, believed to possess stimulant, tonic, and energy-giving properties [c17 from Mandarin Chinese *jen shen*, from *jen* man (from a resemblance of the roots to human legs) + *shen* ginseng]

gin sling (dʒɪn) *n* an iced drink made from gin and water, sweetened, and flavoured with lemon or lime juice

gio ('dʒi:əʊ) *n* an older variant of **geo**

Gioconda (*Italian* dʒo'konda) *n* **La** See **Mona Lisa**

[Italian: the smiling (lady)]
Giorgi system (ˈdʒɔːdʒɪ) *n* a system of units based on the metre, kilogram, second, and ampere, in which the magnetic constant has the value $4\pi \times 10^{-7}$ henries per metre. It was used as a basis for SI units. Also called: **MKSA system** [C20 named after Giovanni *Giorgi* (1871–1950), Italian physicist]
Giotto (ˈdʒɒtəʊ) *n* a European spacecraft that intercepted the path of Halley's comet in March 1986, gathering data and recording images, esp of the comet's nucleus
gip (dʒɪp) *vb* **gips, gipping, gipped 1** a variant spelling of **gyp¹ 2** *Northern English informal* to vomit or feel like vomiting ▷ *n* **3** a variant spelling of **gyp²**
gipon (dʒɪˈpɒn, ˈdʒɪpɒn) *n* another word for **jupon**
Gippsland (ˈɡɪpsˌlænd) *n* a fertile region of SE Australia, in SE Victoria, extending east along the coast from Melbourne to the New South Wales border. Area: 35 200 sq km (13 600 sq miles)
gippy (ˈdʒɪpɪ) *slang* ▷ *n, pl* **-pies 1** an Egyptian person or thing **2** Also called: **gippo** *pl* **-poes** a Gypsy ▷ *adj* **3** Egyptian **4** **gippy tummy** diarrhoea, esp as experienced by visitors to hot climates [C19 from GYPSY and EGYPTIAN]
gippy (ˈɡɪpɪ) *n, pl* **-ies** *Northern English dialect* a starling
Gipsy (ˈdʒɪpsɪ) *n, pl* **-sies** (*sometimes not capital*) a variant spelling of **Gypsy**. > ˈ**Gipsyish** *adj* > ˈ**Gipsydom** *n* > ˈ**Gipsyˌhood** *n* > ˈ**Gipsy-ˌlike** *adj*
gipsy moth *n* a European moth, *Lymantria dispar*, introduced into North America, where it is a serious pest of shade trees: family *Lymantriidae* (or *Liparidae*). See also **tussock moth**
gipsywort (ˈdʒɪpsɪˌwɜːt) *n* a hairy Eurasian plant, *Lycopus europaeus*, having two-lipped white flowers with purple dots on the lower lip: family *Lamiaceae* (labiates). See also **bugleweed** (sense 1)
giraffe (dʒɪˈrɑːf, -ˈræf) *n, pl* **-raffes** *or* **-raffe** a large ruminant mammal, *Giraffa camelopardalis*, inhabiting savannas of tropical Africa: the tallest mammal, with very long legs and neck and a colouring of regular reddish-brown patches on a beige ground: family *Giraffidae* [C17 from Italian *giraffa*, from Arabic *zarāfah*, probably of African origin]
girandole (ˈdʒɪrənˌdəʊl) *or* **girandola** (dʒɪˈrændələ) *n* **1** an ornamental branched wall candleholder, usually incorporating a mirror **2** an earring or pendant having a central gem surrounded by smaller ones **3** a kind of revolving firework **4** *artillery* a group of connected mines [C17 from French, from Italian *girandola*, from *girare* to revolve, from Latin *gȳrāre* to GYRATE]
girasol, girosol *or* **girasole** (ˈdʒɪrəˌsɒl, -ˌsəʊl) *n* a type of opal that has a red or pink glow in bright light; fire opal [C16 from Italian, from *girare* to revolve (see GYRATE) + *sole* the sun, from Latin *sōl*]
gird¹ (ɡɜːd) *vb* **girds, girding, girded** *or* **girt** (*tr*) **1** to put a belt, girdle, etc, around (the waist or hips) **2** to bind or secure with or as if with a belt **3** to surround **4** to prepare (oneself) for action (esp in the phrase **gird** (**up**) **one's loins**) **5** to endow with a rank, attribute, etc, esp knighthood [Old English *gyrdan*, of Germanic origin; related to Old Norse *gyrtha*, Old High German *gurten*]
gird² (ɡɜːd) *Northern English dialect* ▷ *vb* **1** (when *intr*, foll by *at*) to jeer (at someone); mock **2** (*tr*) to strike (a blow at someone) **3** (*intr*) to move at high speed ▷ *n* **4 a** a blow or stroke **b** a taunt; gibe **5** a display of bad temper or anger (esp in the phrases **in a gird; throw a gird**) [C13 *girden* to strike, cut, of unknown origin]
gird³ (ɡɪrd) *n Scot* a hoop, esp a child's hoop. Also: **girr** [a Scot variant of GIRTH]
girder (ˈɡɜːdə) *n* **1** a large beam, esp one made of steel, used in the construction of bridges, buildings, etc **2** *botany* the structure composed of tissue providing mechanical support for a stem or leaf
girdle¹ (ˈɡɜːdᵊl) *n* **1** a woman's elastic corset covering the waist to the thigh **2** anything that surrounds or encircles **3** a belt or sash **4** *jewellery* the outer edge of a gem **5** *anatomy* any encircling structure or part. See **pectoral girdle, pelvic girdle 6** the mark left on a tree trunk after the removal of a ring of bark ▷ *vb* (*tr*) **7** to put a girdle on or around **8** to surround or encircle **9** to remove a ring of bark from (a tree or branch), thus causing it to die [Old English *gyrdel*, of Germanic origin, related to Old Norse *gyrthill*, Old Frisian *gerdel*, Old High German *gurtila*; see GIRD¹] > ˈ**girdle-ˌlike** *adj*
girdle² (ˈɡɜːdᵊl) *n Scot and northern English dialect* another word for **griddle**
girdler (ˈɡɜːdlə) *n* **1** a person or thing that girdles **2** a maker of girdles **3** any insect, such as the twig girdler, that bores circular grooves around the stems or twigs in which it lays its eggs
girdlescone (ˈɡɜːdᵊlˌskəʊn, -ˌskɒn) *or* **girdle scone, girdlecake** (ˈɡɜːdᵊlˌkeɪk) *n* less common names for **drop scone**
girdle traverse *n mountaineering* a climb that consists of a complete traverse of a face or crag
Girgenti (*Italian* dʒirˈdʒɛnti) *n* a former name (until 1927) of **Agrigento**
girl (ɡɜːl) *n* **1** a female child from birth to young womanhood **2** a young unmarried woman; lass; maid **3** *informal* a sweetheart or girlfriend **4** *informal* a woman of any age **5** an informal word for **daughter 6** a female employee, esp a female servant **7** *South African derogatory* a Black female servant of any age **8** (*usually plural* and preceded by *the*) *informal* a group of women, esp acquaintances [C13 of uncertain origin; perhaps related to Low German *Göre* boy, girl]
girl band *n* an all-female vocal pop group created to appeal to a young audience
girl Friday *n* a female employee who has a wide range of duties, usually including secretarial and clerical work [C20 coined on the pattern of MAN FRIDAY]
girlfriend (ˈɡɜːlˌfrɛnd) *n* **1** a female friend with whom a man or boy is romantically or sexually involved; sweetheart **2** any female friend
Girl Guide *n* See **Guide**
girlhood (ˈɡɜːlˌhʊd) *n* the state or time of being a girl
girlie (ˈɡɜːlɪ) *or* **girly** *n* **1** a little girl ▷ *adj* **2** displaying or featuring nude or scantily dressed women: *a girlie magazine* **3** suited to or designed to appeal to young women: *a girlie night out*
girlish (ˈɡɜːlɪʃ) *adj* of or like a girl in looks, behaviour, innocence, etc > ˈ**girlishly** *adv* > ˈ**girlishness** *n*
Girls' Brigade *n* (in Britain) an organization for girls, founded in 1893, with the aim of promoting self-discipline and self-respect
Girl Scout *n US* a member of the equivalent organization for girls to the Scouts. Brit equivalent: **Guide**
girn (ɡərn, ɡɜːn) *vb* (*intr*) *Scot and northern English dialect* **1** to snarl **2** to grimace; pull grotesque faces **3** to complain fretfully or peevishly [C14 a variant of GRIN]
giro (ˈdʒaɪrəʊ) *n, pl* **-ros 1** a system of transferring money within the financial institutions of a country, such as banks and post offices, by which bills, etc may be paid by filling in a giro form authorizing the debit of a specified sum from one's own account to the credit of the payee's account **2** *Brit informal* an unemployment or income support payment by giro cheque, posted fortnightly [C20 ultimately from Greek *guros* circuit]
girolle (ʒiːˈrɒl) *n* another word for **chanterelle** [C20 French]
giron *or* **gyron** (ˈdʒaɪrɒn) *n heraldry* a charge consisting of the lower half of a diagonally divided quarter, usually in the top left corner of the shield [C16 from Old French *giron* a triangular piece of material, of Germanic origin; related to Old High German *gēro* triangular object; compare GORE³]
Girona (dʒiˈrona) *n* the Catalan name for **Gerona**
Gironde (*French* ʒirɔ̃d) *n* **1** a department of SW France, in Aquitaine region. Capital: Bordeaux. Pop: 1 330 683 (2003 est). Area: 10 726 sq km (4183 sq miles) **2** an estuary in SW France, formed by the confluence of the Rivers Garonne and Dordogne. Length: 72 km (45 miles)
Girondist (dʒɪˈrɒndɪst) *n* **1** a member of a party of moderate republicans during the French Revolution, many of whom came from Gironde: overthrown (1793) by their rivals the Jacobins. See also **Jacobin** (sense 1) ▷ *adj* **2** of or relating to the Girondists or their principles > **Giˈrondism** *n*
gironny *or* **gyronny** (dʒaɪˈrɒnɪ) *adj* (*usually postpositive*) *heraldry* divided into segments from the fesse point
girosol (ˈdʒɪrəˌsɒl, -ˌsəʊl) *n* a variant spelling of **girasol**
girr (ɡɪr) *n Scot* a variant of **gird³**
girt¹ (ɡɜːt) *vb* **1** a past tense and past participle of **gird¹** ▷ *adj* **2** *nautical* moored securely to prevent swinging
girt² (ɡɜːt) *vb* **1** (*tr*) to bind or encircle; gird **2** to measure the girth of (something)
girth (ɡɜːθ) *n* **1** the distance around something; circumference **2** size or bulk: *a man of great girth* **3** a band around a horse's belly to keep the saddle in position ▷ *vb* **4** (usually foll by *up*) to fasten a girth on (a horse) **5** (*tr*) to encircle or surround [C14 from Old Norse *gjörth* belt; related to Gothic *gairda* GIRDLE¹; see GIRD¹]
GIS (in Canada) *abbreviation for* guaranteed income supplement
gisarme (ɡɪˈzɑːm) *n* a long-shafted battle-axe with a sharp point on the back of the axe head [C13 from Old French *guisarme*, probably from Old High German *getīsarn* weeding tool, from *getan* to weed + *īsarn* IRON]
Gisborne (ˈɡɪzbən) *n* a port in N New Zealand, on E North Island on Poverty Bay. Pop: 44 900 (2004 est)
gist (dʒɪst) *n* **1** the point or substance of an argument, speech, etc **2** *law* the essential point of an action [C18 from Anglo-French, as in *cest action gist en* this action consists in, literally: lies in, from Old French *gésir* to lie, from Latin *jacēre*, from *jacere* to throw]
git (ɡɪt) *n Brit slang* **1** a contemptible person, often a fool **2** a bastard [C20 from GET (in the sense: *to beget*, hence a bastard, fool)]
gîte (ʒiːt) *n* a self-catering holiday cottage for let in France [C20 French]
gittarone (ˌɡɪtəˈrəʊnɪ) *n music* an acoustic bass guitar
gittern (ˈɡɪtɜːn) *n music* an obsolete medieval stringed instrument resembling the guitar. Compare **cittern** [C14 from Old French *guiterne*, ultimately from Old Spanish *guitarra* GUITAR; see CITTERN]
giusto (ˈdʒuːstəʊ) *adv music* (of a tempo marking) **a** to be observed strictly **b** to be observed appropriately: *allegro giusto* [Italian: just, proper]
give (ɡɪv) *vb* **gives, giving, gave** (ɡeɪv) **given** (ˈɡɪvᵊn) (*mainly tr*) **1** (*also intr*) to present or deliver voluntarily (something that is one's own) to the permanent possession of another or others **2** (often foll by *for*) to transfer (something that is one's own, esp money) to the possession of another as part of an exchange: *to give fifty pounds for a painting* **3** to place in the temporary possession of another: *I gave him my watch while I went swimming* **4** (when *intr*, foll by *of*) to grant, provide, or bestow: *give me some advice* **5** to administer: *to give a reprimand* **6** to award or attribute: *to give blame, praise, etc* **7** to be a source of: *he gives no trouble* **8** to impart or communicate: *to give news; give a person a cold* **9** to utter or emit: *to give a shout* **10** to perform, make, or do: *the car gave a jolt and stopped* **11** to sacrifice or devote: *he gave his life for his country* **12** to surrender: *to give place to others* **13** to concede or yield: *I will give you this game* **14** (*intr*) *informal* to happen: *what gives?* **15** (often

g

foll by *to*) to cause; lead: *she gave me to believe that she would come* 16 (foll by *for*) to value (something) at: *I don't give anything for his promises* 17 to perform or present as an entertainment: *to give a play* 18 to propose as a toast: *I give you the Queen* 19 (*intr*) to yield or break under force or pressure: *this surface will give if you sit on it; his courage will never give* 20 **give as good as one gets** to respond to verbal or bodily blows to at least an equal extent as those received 21 **give battle** to commence fighting 22 **give birth** (often foll by *to*) **a** to bear (offspring) **b** to produce, originate, or create (an idea, plan, etc) 23 **give (a person) five** *or* **some skin** *slang* to greet or congratulate (someone) by slapping raised hands 24 **give ground** to draw back or retreat 25 **give it up for (someone)** *slang* to applaud (someone) 26 **give (someone) one** *Brit slang* to have sex with someone 27 **give rise to** to be the cause of 28 **give me** *informal* I prefer: *give me hot weather any day!* 29 **give or take** plus or minus: *three thousand people came, give or take a few hundred* 30 **give way** See **way** (sense 24) 31 **give (a person) what for** *informal* to punish or reprimand (a person) severely ▷ *n* 32 a tendency to yield under pressure; resilience: *there's bound to be some give in a long plank; there is no give in his moral views* ▷ See also **give away, give in, give off, give onto, give out, give over, give up** [Old English *giefan;* related to Old Norse *gefa,* Gothic *giban,* Old High German *geban,* Swedish *giva*] > '**givable** *or* '**giveable** *adj* > '**giver** *n*

give-and-take *n* 1 mutual concessions, shared benefits, and cooperation 2 a smoothly flowing exchange of ideas and talk ▷ *vb* **give and take** (*intr*) 3 to make mutual concessions

give away *vb* (*tr, adverb*) 1 to donate or bestow as a gift, prize, etc 2 to sell very cheaply 3 to reveal or betray (esp in the phrases **give the game** *or* **show away**) 4 to fail to use (an opportunity) through folly or neglect 5 to present (a bride) formally to her husband in a marriage ceremony 6 *Austral and NZ informal* to give up or abandon (something) ▷ *n* **giveaway** 7 a betrayal or disclosure of information, esp when unintentional 8 *chiefly US and Canadian* something given, esp with articles on sale, at little or no charge to increase sales, attract publicity, etc 9 *journalism* another name for **freesheet** 10 *chiefly US and Canadian* a radio or television programme characterized by the award of money and prizes 11 (*modifier*) **a** very cheap (esp in the phrase **giveaway prices**) **b** free of charge: *a giveaway property magazine*

give in *vb* (*adverb*) 1 (*intr*) to yield; admit defeat 2 (*tr*) to submit or deliver (a document)

given ('gɪvᵊn) *vb* 1 the past participle of **give** ▷ *adj* 2 (*postpositive;* foll by *to*) tending (to); inclined or addicted (to) 3 specific or previously stated 4 assumed as a premise 5 *maths* known or determined independently: *a given volume* 6 (on official documents) issued or executed, as on a stated date ▷ *n* 7 an assumed fact 8 *philosophy* the supposed raw data of experience. See also **sense datum**

given name *n* another term for **first name**

give off *vb* (*tr, adverb*) to emit or discharge: *the mothballs gave off an acrid odour*

give onto *vb* (*intr; preposition*) to afford a view or prospect of: *their new house gives onto the sea*

give out *vb* (*adverb*) 1 (*tr*) to emit or discharge 2 (*tr*) to publish or make known: *the chairman gave out that he would resign* 3 (*tr*) to hand out or distribute: *they gave out free chewing gum on the street* 4 (*intr*) to become exhausted; fail: *the supply of candles gave out* 5 (*intr;* foll by *to*) *Irish informal* to reprimand (someone) at length 6 (*tr*) *cricket* (of an umpire) to declare (a batsman) dismissed

give over *vb* (*adverb*) 1 (*tr*) to transfer, esp to the care or custody of another 2 (*tr*) to assign or resign to a specific purpose or function: *the day was given over to pleasure* 3 *informal* to cease (an activity): *give over fighting, will you!*

give up *vb* (*adverb*) 1 to abandon hope (for) 2 (*tr*) to renounce (an activity, belief, etc): *I have given up smoking* 3 (*tr*) to relinquish or resign from: *he gave up the presidency* 4 (*tr; usually reflexive*) to surrender: *the escaped convict gave himself up* 5 (*tr*) to reveal or disclose (information) 6 (*intr*) to admit one's defeat or inability to do something 7 (*tr; often passive or reflexive*) to devote completely (to): *she gave herself up to caring for the sick*

Gîza ('gi:zə) *n* See **El Gîza**

gizmo *or* **gismo** ('gɪzməʊ) *n, pl* **-mos** *slang* a device; gadget [C20 of unknown origin]

gizzard ('gɪzəd) *n* 1 the thick-walled part of a bird's stomach, in which hard food is broken up by muscular action and contact with grit and small stones 2 a similar structure in many invertebrates 3 *informal* the stomach and entrails generally [C14 from Old North French *guisier* fowl's liver, alteration of Latin *gigēria* entrails of poultry when cooked, of uncertain origin]

Gk *abbreviation for* Greek

gl *the internet domain name for* Greenland

GL *abbreviation for* glycaemic load

GLA *abbreviation for* Greater London Assembly, established in 2000

glabella (glə'bɛlə) *n, pl* **-lae** (-li:) *anatomy* a smooth elevation of the frontal bone just above the bridge of the nose: a reference point in physical anthropology or craniometry [C19 New Latin, from Latin *glabellus* smooth, from *glaber bald, smooth*] > **gla'bellar** *adj*

glabrescent (gleɪ'brɛsənt) *adj botany* 1 becoming hairless at maturity: *glabrescent stems* 2 nearly hairless [C19 from Latin *glabrescere* to become smooth]

glabrous ('gleɪbrəs) *or* **glabrate** ('gleɪbreɪt, -brɪt) *adj biology* without hair or a similar growth; smooth: *a glabrous stem* [C17 *glabrous,* from Latin *glaber*] > '**glabrousness** *n*

glacé ('glæseɪ) *adj* 1 crystallized or candied: *glacé cherries* 2 covered in icing 3 (of leather, silk, etc) having a glossy finish 4 *chiefly US* frozen or iced ▷ *vb* **-cés, -céing, -céed** 5 (*tr*) to ice or candy (cakes, fruits, etc) [C19 from French *glacé,* literally: iced, from *glacer* to freeze, from *glace* ice, from Latin *glaciēs*]

glacial ('gleɪsɪəl, -ʃəl) *adj* 1 characterized by the presence of masses of ice 2 relating to, caused by, or deposited by a glacier 3 extremely cold; icy 4 cold or hostile in manner: *a glacial look* 5 (of a chemical compound) of or tending to form crystals that resemble ice: *glacial acetic acid* 6 very slow in progress: *a glacial pace* > '**glacially** *adv*

glacial acetic acid *n* pure acetic acid (more than 99.8 per cent)

glacial period *n* 1 any period of time during which a large part of the earth's surface was covered with ice, due to the advance of glaciers, as in the late Carboniferous period, and during most of the Pleistocene; glaciation 2 (*often capitals*) the Pleistocene epoch ▷ Also called: **glacial epoch, ice age**

glaciate ('gleɪsɪˌeɪt) *vb* 1 to cover or become covered with glaciers or masses of ice 2 (*tr*) to subject to the effects of glaciers, such as denudation and erosion > ˌ**glaci'ation** *n*

glacier ('glæsɪə, 'gleɪs-) *n* a slowly moving mass of ice originating from an accumulation of snow. It can either spread out from a central mass (**continental glacier**) or descend from a high valley (**alpine glacier**) [C18 from French (Savoy dialect), from Old French *glace* ice, from Late Latin *glacia,* from Latin *glaciēs* ice]

glacier cream *n mountaineering* a barrier cream, esp against ultraviolet radiation, used when climbing above the snow line

glacier milk *n* water flowing in a stream from the snout of a glacier and containing particles of rock

glacier table *n* a rock sitting on a pillar of ice on top of a glacier, as a result of the ice immediately beneath the rock being protected from the heat of the sun and not melting

glaciology (ˌglæsɪ'ɒlədʒɪ, ˌgleɪ-) *n* the study of the distribution, character, and effects of glaciers > **glaciological** (ˌglæsɪə'lɒdʒɪkᵊl, ˌgleɪ-) *or* ˌ**glacio'logic** *adj* > ˌ**glaci'ologist** *or* '**glacialist** *n*

glacis ('glæsɪs, 'glæsɪ, 'gleɪ-) *n, pl* **-ises** *or* **-is** (-i:z, -ɪz) 1 a slight incline; slope 2 an open slope in front of a fortified place 3 short for **glacis plate** [C17 from French, from Old French *glacier* to freeze, slip, from Latin *glaciāre,* from *glaciēs* ice]

glacis plate *n* 1 the frontal plate armour on a tank 2 a section of armour plate shielding an opening on a naval vessel

glad[1] (glæd) *adj* **gladder, gladdest** 1 happy and pleased; contented 2 causing happiness or contentment 3 (*postpositive;* foll by *to*) very willing: *he was glad to help* 4 (*postpositive;* foll by *of*) happy or pleased to have: *glad of her help* ▷ *vb* **glads, gladding, gladded** 5 an archaic word for **gladden** [Old English *glæd;* related to Old Norse *glathr,* Old High German *glat* smooth, shining, Latin *glaber* smooth, Lithuanian *glodùs* fitting closely] > '**gladly** *adv* > '**gladness** *n*

glad[2] (glæd) *n informal* short for **gladiolus** Also called (Austral): **gladdie** ('glædɪ)

Gladbeck (*German* 'glatbɛk) *n* a city in NW Germany, in North Rhine-Westphalia. Pop: Pop: 77 166 (2003 est)

gladden ('glædᵊn) *vb* to make or become glad and joyful > '**gladdener** *n*

gladdon ('glædᵊn) *n* another name for the **stinking iris** [Old English, of uncertain origin]

glade (gleɪd) *n* an open place in a forest; clearing [C16 of uncertain origin; perhaps related to GLAD[1] (in obsolete sense: bright); see GLEAM] > '**glade**ˌ**like** *adj*

glad eye *n informal* an inviting or seductive glance (esp in the phrase **give (someone) the glad eye**)

glad hand *n* 1 **a** a welcoming hand **b** a welcome ▷ *vb* **glad-hand** 2 (*tr*) to welcome by or as if by offering a hand

gladiate ('glædɪɪt, -ˌeɪt, 'gleɪ-) *adj botany* shaped like a sword: *gladiate leaves* [C18 from Latin *gladius* sword]

gladiator ('glædɪˌeɪtə) *n* 1 (in ancient Rome and Etruria) a man trained to fight in arenas to provide entertainment 2 a person who supports and fights publicly for a cause [C16 from Latin: swordsman, from *gladius* sword]

gladiatorial (ˌglædɪə'tɔ:rɪəl) *adj* of, characteristic of, or relating to gladiators, combat, etc

gladiolus (ˌglædɪ'əʊləs) *n, pl* **-lus, -li** (-laɪ) *or* **-luses** 1 Also called: **sword lily, gladiola** any iridaceous plant of the widely cultivated genus *Gladiolus,* having sword-shaped leaves and spikes of funnel-shaped brightly coloured flowers 2 *anatomy* the large central part of the breastbone [C16 from Latin: a small sword, sword lily, from *gladius* a sword]

glad rags *pl n informal* best clothes or clothes used on special occasions

gladsome ('glædsəm) *adj* an archaic word for **glad**[1] > '**gladsomely** *adv* > '**gladsomeness** *n*

Gladstone ('glædstən) *n* a light four-wheeled horse-drawn vehicle [C19 named after William Ewart *Gladstone* (1809–98), British Liberal statesman]

Gladstone bag *n* a piece of hand luggage consisting of two equal-sized hinged compartments [C19 named after William Ewart *Gladstone* (1809–98), British Liberal statesman]

gladwrap ('glædˌræp) *n trademark NZ* 1 a thin polythene material that clings closely to any surface around which it is placed: used for wrapping food ▷ *vb* **-wraps, -wrapping, -wrapped** 2 (*tr*) to cover (food) with gladwrap

Glagolitic (ˌglægə'lɪtɪk) *adj* of, relating to, or denoting a Slavic alphabet whose invention is attributed to Saint Cyril, preserved only in certain Roman Catholic liturgical books found in Dalmatia [C19 from New Latin *glagoliticus,* from Serbo-Croat *glagolica* the Glagolitic alphabet; related to Old Church Slavonic *glagolŭ* word]

glaikit *or* **glaiket** ('gleɪkɪt) *adj Scot* foolish; silly; thoughtless: *a glaiket expression* [C15 of obscure origin] > 'glaikitness *or* 'glaiketness *n*

glair (glɛə) *n* **1** white of egg, esp when used as a size, glaze, or adhesive, usually in bookbinding **2** any substance resembling this ▷ *vb* **3** (*tr*) to apply glair to (something) [c14 from Old French *glaire*, from Vulgar Latin *clāria* (unattested) CLEAR, from Latin *clārus*] > 'glairy *or* 'glaireous *adj* > 'glairiness *n*

glaive (gleɪv) *n* an archaic word for **sword** [c13 from Old French: javelin, from Latin *gladius* sword] > 'glaived *adj*

glam (glæm) *adj slang* short for **glamorous**

Glamis Castle (glɑːmz) *n* a castle near Glamis in Angus, Scotland: ancestral seat of the Lyons family, forebears of Elizabeth, the Queen Mother; famous for its legend of a secret chamber

Glamorgan (ɡləˈmɔːɡən) *or* **Glamorganshire** (ɡləˈmɔːɡənʃɪə, -ʃə) *n* a former county of SE Wales: divided into West Glamorgan, Mid Glamorgan, and South Glamorgan in 1974; since 1996 administered by the county of Swansea and the county boroughs of Neath Port Talbot, Bridgend, Rhondda Cynon Taff, Vale of Glamorgan, Merthyr Tydfil, and part of Caerphilly

glamorize, glamorise *or sometimes US* **glamourize** (ˈɡlæməˌraɪz) *vb* (*tr*) to cause to be or seem glamorous; romanticize or beautify > ˌglamoriˈzation *or* ˌglamoriˈsation *n* > 'glamorˌizer *or* 'glamourˌiser *n*

glamorous *or* **glamourous** (ˈɡlæmərəs) *adj* **1** possessing glamour; alluring and fascinating: *a glamorous career* **2** beautiful and smart, esp in a showy way: *a glamorous woman* > 'glamorously *or* 'glamourously *adv* > 'glamorousness *or* 'glamourousness *n*

glamour *or sometimes US* **glamor** (ˈɡlæmə) *n* **1** charm and allure; fascination **2 a** fascinating or voluptuous beauty, often dependent on artifice **b** (*as modifier*): *a glamour girl* **3** *archaic* a magic spell; charm [c18 Scottish variant of GRAMMAR (hence a magic spell, because occult practices were popularly associated with learning)]

glam rock *n* a style of rock music of the early 1970s, characterized by the glittery flamboyance and androgynous image of its performers

glance¹ (ɡlɑːns) *vb* **1** (*intr*) to look hastily or briefly **2** (*intr*; foll by *over, through,* etc) to look over briefly: *to glance through a report* **3** (*intr*) to reflect, glint, or gleam: *the sun glanced on the water* **4** (*intr*; usually foll by *off*) to depart (from an object struck) at an oblique angle: *the arrow glanced off the tree* **5** (*tr*) to strike at an oblique angle: *the arrow glanced the tree* ▷ *n* **6** a hasty or brief look; peep **7** at a glance from one's first look; immediately **8** a flash or glint of light; gleam **9** the act or an instance of an object glancing or glancing off another **10** a brief allusion or reference **11** *cricket* a stroke in which the ball is deflected off the bat to the leg side; glide [c15 modification of *glacen* to strike obliquely, from Old French *glacier* to slide (see GLACIS); compare Middle English *glenten* to make a rapid sideways movement, GLINT] > 'glancingly *adv*

▌ USAGE *Glance* is sometimes wrongly used where *glimpse* is meant: *he caught a glimpse* (not *glance*) *of her making her way through the crowd*

glance² (ɡlɑːns) *n* any mineral having a metallic lustre, esp a simple sulphide: *copper glance* [c19 from German *Glanz* brightness, lustre]

gland¹ (glænd) *n* **1** a cell or organ in man and other animals that synthesizes chemical substances and secretes them for the body to use or eliminate, either through a duct (see **exocrine gland**) or directly into the bloodstream (see **endocrine gland**) **2** a structure, such as a lymph node, that resembles a gland in form **3** a cell or organ in plants that synthesizes and secretes a particular substance ▷ Related adjective: **adenoid** [c17 from Latin *glāns* acorn] > 'gland,like *adj*

gland² (glænd) *n* a device that prevents leakage of fluid along a rotating shaft or reciprocating rod passing through a boundary between areas of high and low pressure. It often consists of a

flanged metal sleeve bedding into a stuffing box [c19 of unknown origin]

glanders (ˈɡlændəz) *n* (*functioning as singular*) a highly infectious bacterial disease of horses, sometimes transmitted to man, caused by *Actinobacillus mallei* and characterized by inflammation and ulceration of the mucous membranes of the air passages, skin, and lymph glands [c16 from Old French *glandres* enlarged glands, from Latin *glandulae*, literally: little acorns, from *glāns* acorn; see GLAND¹] > 'glandered *adj* > 'glanderous *adj*

glandular (ˈɡlændjʊlə) *or* **glandulous** (ˈɡlændjʊləs) *adj* of, relating to, containing, functioning as, or affecting a gland: *glandular tissue* [c18 from Latin *glandula*, literally: a little acorn; see GLANDERS] > 'glandularly *or* 'glandulously *adv*

glandular fever *n* another name for **infectious mononucleosis**

glandule (ˈɡlændjuːl) *n* a small gland

glans (glænz) *n, pl* **glandes** (ˈɡlændiːz) *anatomy* any small rounded body or glandlike mass, such as the head of the penis (**glans penis**) [c17 from Latin: acorn; see GLAND¹]

glare¹ (ɡlɛə) *vb* **1** (*intr*) to stare angrily; glower **2** (*tr*) to express by glowering **3** (*intr*) (of light, colour, etc) to be very bright and intense **4** (*intr*) to be dazzlingly ornamented or garish ▷ *n* **5** an angry stare **6** a dazzling light or brilliance **7** garish ornamentation or appearance; gaudiness [c13 probably from Middle Low German, Middle Dutch *glaren* to gleam; probably related to Old English *glæren* glassy; see GLASS] > 'glareless *adj* > 'glary *adj*

glare² (ɡlɛə) *adj chiefly US and Canadian* smooth and glassy: *glare ice* [c16 special use of GLARE¹]

glaring (ˈɡlɛərɪŋ) *adj* **1** conspicuous: *a glaring omission* **2** dazzling or garish > 'glaringly *adv* > 'glaringness *n*

Glarus (German ˈɡlɑːrʊs) *n* **1** an Alpine canton of E central Switzerland. Capital: Glarus. Pop: 38 400 (2002 est). Area 684 sq km (264 sq miles) **2** a town in E central Switzerland, the capital of Glarus canton. Pop: 5556 (2000) ▷ French name: Glaris (glari)

Glasgow (ˈɡlɑːzɡəʊ, ˈɡlæz-) *n* **1** a city in W central Scotland, in City of Glasgow council area on the River Clyde: the largest city in Scotland; centre of a major industrial region, formerly an important port; universities (1451, 1964, 1992). Pop: 629 501 (2001). Related adj: **Glaswegian 2 City of** a council area in W central Scotland. Pop: 577 090 (2003 est). Area: 175 sq km (68 sq miles)

glasnost (ˈɡlæsˌnɒst) *n* the policy of public frankness and accountability developed in the former Soviet Union under the leadership of Mikhail Gorbachov [c20 Russian, literally: openness]

glass (ɡlɑːs) *n* **1 a** a hard brittle transparent or translucent noncrystalline solid, consisting of metal silicates or similar compounds. It is made from a fused mixture of oxides, such as lime, silicon dioxide, etc, and is used for making windows, mirrors, bottles, etc ▷ (*as modifier*): *a glass bottle*. Related adjs: **vitreous, vitric 2** any compound that has solidified from a molten state into a noncrystalline form **3** something made of glass, esp a drinking vessel, a barometer, or a mirror **4** Also called: **glassful** the amount contained in a drinking glass **5** glassware collectively **6** See **volcanic glass 7** See **fibreglass** ▷ *vb* (*tr*) **8** to cover with, enclose in, or fit with glass **9** *informal* to hit (someone) in the face with a glass or a bottle [Old English *glæs*; related to Old Norse *gler*, Old High German *glas*, Middle High German *glast* brightness; see GLARE¹] > 'glassless *adj* > 'glass,like *adj*

glass-blowing *n* the process of shaping a mass of molten or softened glass into a vessel, shape, etc, by blowing air into it through a tube > 'glass-,blower *n*

glass can *n Austral slang* a short squat beer bottle

glass ceiling *n* a situation in which progress, esp promotion, appears to be possible but restrictions or discrimination create a barrier that prevents it

glasses (ˈɡlɑːsɪz) *pl n* a pair of lenses for correcting faulty vision, in a frame that rests on the bridge of the nose and hooks behind the ears. Also called: **spectacles, eyeglasses**

glass eye *n* an artificial eye made of glass

glass fibre *n* another name for **fibreglass**

glass harmonica *n* a musical instrument of the 18th century consisting of a set of glass bowls of graduated pitches, played by rubbing the fingers over the moistened rims or by a keyboard mechanism. Sometimes shortened to: **harmonica** Also called: **musical glasses**

glasshouse (ˈɡlɑːsˌhaʊs) *n* **1** *Brit* a glass building, esp a greenhouse, used for growing plants in protected or controlled conditions **2** *obsolete informal, chiefly Brit* a military detention centre **3** *US* another word for **glassworks**

glassine (ɡlæˈsiːn) *n* a glazed translucent paper used for book jackets

glass jaw *n boxing informal* a jaw that is excessively fragile or susceptible to punches

glass-maker *n* a person who makes glass or glass objects > 'glass-,making *n*

glassman (ˈɡlɑːsmən) *n, pl* -men **1** a man whose work is making or selling glassware **2** a less common word for **glazier**

glasspaper (ˈɡlɑːsˌpeɪpə) *n* **1** strong paper coated with powdered glass or other abrasive material for smoothing and polishing ▷ *vb* **2** to smooth or polish with glasspaper

glass snake *n* any snakelike lizard of the genus *Ophisaurus*, of Europe, Asia, and North America, with vestigial hind limbs and a tail that breaks off easily: family Anguidae

glass string *n* (in Malaysia) the string of a kite used in kite fighting that has an abrasive coating of glue and crushed glass

glassware (ˈɡlɑːsˌwɛə) *n* articles made of glass

glass wool *n* fine spun glass massed into a wool-like bulk, used in insulation, filtering, etc

glasswork (ˈɡlɑːsˌwɜːk) *n* **1** the production of glassware **2** the fitting of glass **3** articles of glass > 'glass-,worker *n*

glassworks (ˈɡlɑːsˌwɜːks) *n* (*functioning as singular*) a factory for the moulding of glass

glasswort (ˈɡlɑːsˌwɜːt) *n* **1** Also called: **marsh samphire** any plant of the chenopodiaceous genus *Salicornia*, of salt marshes, having fleshy stems and scalelike leaves: formerly used as a source of soda for glass-making **2** another name for **saltwort** (sense 1)

glassy (ˈɡlɑːsɪ) *adj* **glassier, glassiest 1** resembling glass, esp in smoothness, slipperiness, or transparency **2** void of expression, life, or warmth: *a glassy stare* > 'glassily *adv* > 'glassiness *n*

Glastonbury (ˈɡlæstənbərɪ, -brɪ) *n* a town in SW England, in Somerset: remains of prehistoric lake villages; the reputed burial place of King Arthur; site of a ruined Benedictine abbey, probably the oldest in England. Pop: 8429 (2001)

Glaswegian (ɡlæzˈwiːdʒən) *adj* **1** of or relating to Glasgow or its inhabitants ▷ *n* **2** a native or inhabitant of Glasgow [c19 influenced by *Norway, Norwegian*]

Glauber's salt (ˈɡlaʊbəz) *or* **Glauber salt** (ˈɡlaʊbə) *n* the crystalline decahydrate of sodium sulphate [c18 named after J. R. Glauber (1604–68), German chemist]

Glauce (ˈɡlɔːsɪ) *n Greek myth* **1** the second bride of Jason, murdered on her wedding day by Medea, whom Jason had deserted **2** a sea nymph, one of the Nereids

glaucoma (ɡlɔːˈkəʊmə) *n* a disease of the eye in which pressure within the eyeball damages the optic disc, impairing vision, sometimes progressing to blindness [c17 from Latin, from Greek *glaukōma*, from *glaukos*; see GLAUCOUS] > glau'comatous *adj*

g

glauconite ('glɔːkəˌnaɪt) *n* a green mineral consisting of the hydrated silicate of iron, potassium, aluminium, and magnesium: found in greensand and other similar rocks. Formula: $(K,Na,Ca)_{0.5-1}(Fe,Al,Mg)_2(Si,Al)_4O_{10}(OH)_2.nH_2O$ [C19 from Greek *glaukon*, neuter of *glaukos* bluish-green + -ITE¹; see GLAUCOUS] > **glauconitic** (ˌglɔːkəˈnɪtɪk) *adj*

glaucous ('glɔːkəs) *adj* 1 *botany* covered with a bluish waxy or powdery bloom 2 bluish-green [C17 from Latin *glaucus* silvery, bluish-green, from Greek *glaukos*] > **glaucously** *adv*

glaucous gull *n* a gull, *Larus hyperboreus*, of northern and arctic regions, with a white head and tail and pale grey back and wings

glaur (glɔːr) *n Scot* mud or mire [C16 of unknown origin] > **glaury** *adj*

glaze (gleɪz) *vb* 1 (*tr*) to fit or cover with glass 2 (*tr*) *ceramics* to cover with a vitreous solution, rendering impervious to liquid and smooth to the touch 3 (*tr*) to cover (a painting) with a layer of semitransparent colour to modify the tones 4 (*tr*) to cover (foods) with a shiny coating by applying beaten egg, sugar, etc 5 (*tr*) to make glossy or shiny 6 (when *intr*, often foll by *over*) to become or cause to become glassy: *his eyes were glazing over* ▷ *n* 7 *ceramics* a a vitreous or glossy coating b the substance used to produce such a coating 8 a semitransparent coating applied to a painting to modify the tones 9 a smooth lustrous finish on a fabric produced by applying various chemicals 10 something used to give a glossy surface to foods: *a syrup glaze* [C14 *glasen*, from *glas* GLASS] > **glazed** *adj* > **glazer** *n* > **glazy** *adj*

glaze ice *or* **glazed frost** *n Brit* a thin clear layer of ice caused by the freezing of rain or water droplets in the air on impact with a cool surface or by refreezing after a thaw. Also called: **silver frost** US term: **glaze**

glazier ('gleɪzɪə) *n* a person who glazes windows, etc > **glaziery** *n*

glazing ('gleɪzɪŋ) *n* 1 the surface of a glazed object 2 glass fitted, or to be fitted, in a door, frame, etc

glazing-bar *n* a supporting or strengthening bar for a glass window, door, etc. Usual US word: **muntin**

GLC *abbreviation for* Greater London Council, abolished 1986

gld *abbreviation for* guilder

gleam (gliːm) *n* 1 a small beam or glow of light, esp reflected light 2 a brief or dim indication: *a gleam of hope* ▷ *vb* 3 (*intr*) to send forth or reflect a beam of light 4 to appear, esp briefly: *intelligence gleamed in his eyes* [Old English *glǣm*; related to Old Norse *gljā* to flicker, Old High German *gleimo* glow-worm, *glīmo* brightness, Old Irish *glē* bright] > **gleaming** *adj* > **gleamy** *adj*

glean (gliːn) *vb* 1 to gather (something) slowly and carefully in small pieces: *to glean information from the newspapers* 2 to gather (the useful remnants of a crop) from the field after harvesting [C14 from Old French *glener*, from Late Latin *glennāre*, probably of Celtic origin] > **gleanable** *adj* > **gleaner** *n*

gleanings ('gliːnɪŋz) *pl n* the useful remnants of a crop that can be gathered from the field after harvesting

glebe (gliːb) *n* 1 *Brit* land granted to a clergyman as part of his benefice 2 *poetic* land, esp when regarded as the source of growing things [C14 from Latin *glaeba*]

glede (gliːd) *or* **gled** (glɛd) *n* a former Brit name for the **red kite** See **kite** (sense 4) [Old English *glida*; related to Old Norse *gletha*, Middle Low German *glede*]

glee (gliː) *n* 1 great merriment or delight, often caused by someone else's misfortune 2 a type of song originating in 18th-century England, sung by three or more unaccompanied voices. Compare **madrigal** (sense 1) [Old English *glēo*; related to Old Norse *glȳ*]

glee club *n Now chiefly US and Canadian* a club or society organized for the singing of choral music

gleed (gliːd) *n archaic or dialect* a burning ember or hot coal [Old English *glēd*; related to German *Glut*, Dutch *gloed*, Swedish *glöd*]

gleeful ('gliːfʊl) *adj* full of glee; merry > **gleefully** *adv* > **gleefulness** *n*

gleeman ('gliːmən) *n*, *pl* **-men** *obsolete* a minstrel

gleenie ('gliːnɪ) *n Southwest English dialect* a guinea fowl

gleet (gliːt) *n* 1 inflammation of the urethra with a slight discharge of thin pus and mucus: a stage of chronic gonorrhoea 2 the pus and mucus discharged [C14 from Old French *glette* slime, from Latin *glittus* sticky] > **gleety** *adj*

Gleichschaltung ('glaɪkˌʃæltʊŋ) *n* the enforcement of standardization and the elimination of all opposition within the political, economic, and cultural institutions of a state [C20 German]

Gleiwitz ('glaɪvɪts) *n* the German name for **Gliwice**

glen (glɛn) *n* a narrow and deep mountain valley, esp in Scotland or Ireland [C15 from Scottish Gaelic *gleann*, from Old Irish *glend*] > **'glen,like** *adj*

Glen Albyn ('ælbɪn, ˌɔːl-) *n* another name for the **Great Glen**

Glencoe (glɛnˈkəʊ) *n* a glen in W Scotland, in S Highland: site of a massacre of Macdonalds by Campbells and English troops (1692)

glengarry (glɛnˈgærɪ) *n*, *pl* **-ries** a brimless Scottish woollen cap with a crease down the crown, often with ribbons dangling at the back. Also called: **glengarry bonnet** [C19 after *Glengarry*, Scotland]

Glen More (mɔː) *n* another name for the **Great Glen**

Glen of Imaal terrier (ɪˈmɑːl) *n* a strongly-built medium-sized variety of terrier with a medium-length coat and short forelegs

glenoid ('gliːnɔɪd) *adj anatomy* 1 resembling or having a shallow cavity 2 denoting the cavity in the shoulder blade into which the head of the upper arm bone fits [C18 from Greek *glēnoeidēs*, from *glēnē* socket of a joint]

Glenrothes (glɛnˈrɒθɪs) *n* a new town in E central Scotland, the administrative centre of Fife: founded in 1948. Pop: 38 679 (2001)

gley *or* **glei** (gleɪ) *n* a bluish-grey compact sticky soil occurring in certain humid regions [C20 from Russian *glei* clay]

glia ('gliːə) *n* the delicate web of connective tissue that surrounds and supports nerve cells. Also called: **neuroglia** > **'glial** *adj*

gliadin ('glaɪədɪn) *or* **gliadine** ('glaɪəˌdiːn, -dɪn) *n* a protein of cereals, esp wheat, with a high proline content: forms a sticky mass with water that binds flour into dough. Compare **glutelin** [C19 from Italian *gliadina*, from Greek *glia* glue]

glib (glɪb) *adj* **glibber**, **glibbest** fluent and easy, often in an insincere or deceptive way [C16 probably from Middle Low German *glibberich* slippery] > **'glibly** *adv* > **'glibness** *n*

glib ice *n Canadian* ice that is particularly smooth and slippery

glide (glaɪd) *vb* 1 to move or cause to move easily without jerks or hesitations: *to glide in a boat down the river* 2 (*intr*) to pass slowly or without perceptible change: *to glide into sleep* 3 to cause (an aircraft) to come into land without engine power, or (of an aircraft) to land in this way 4 (*intr*) to fly a glider 5 (*intr*) *music* to execute a portamento from one note to another 6 (*intr*) *phonetics* to produce a glide ▷ *n* 7 a smooth easy movement 8 a any of various dances featuring gliding steps b a step in such a dance 9 a manoeuvre in which an aircraft makes a gentle descent without engine power. See also **glide path** 10 the act or process of gliding 11 *music* a a long portion of tubing slipped in and out of a trombone to increase its length for the production of lower harmonic series. See also **valve** (sense 5) b a portamento or slur 12 *phonetics* a a transitional sound as the speech organs pass from the articulatory position of one speech sound to that of the next, as the (w) sound in some pronunciations of the word *doing* b another word for **semivowel** 13 *crystallog* another name for **slip¹** (sense 33) 14 *cricket* another word for **glance¹** (sense 11) [Old English *glīdan*; related to Old High German *glītan*] > **'glidingly** *adv*

glide path *or* **glide slope** *n* the approach path of an aircraft when landing, usually defined by a radar beam

glider ('glaɪdə) *n* 1 an aircraft capable of gliding and soaring in air currents without the use of an engine. See also **sailplane** 2 a person or thing that glides 3 another name for **flying phalanger**

glide time *n NZ* a system permitting flexibility of working hours at the beginning or end of the day, provided an agreed period of each day (**core time**) is spent at work. Also called (in Britain and certain other countries): **flexitime**

gliding ('glaɪdɪŋ) *n* the sport of flying in a glider

glim (glɪm) *n slang* 1 a light or lamp 2 an eye [C17 probably short for GLIMMER; compare GLIMPSE]

glimmer ('glɪmə) *vb* (*intr*) 1 (of a light, candle, etc) to glow faintly or flickeringly 2 to be indicated faintly: *hope glimmered in his face* ▷ *n* 3 a glow or twinkle of light 4 a faint indication [C14 compare Middle High German *glimmern*, Swedish *glimra*, Danish *glimre*] > **'glimmeringly** *adv*

glimpse (glɪmps) *n* 1 a brief or incomplete view: *to catch a glimpse of the sea* 2 a vague indication: *he had a glimpse of what the lecturer meant* 3 *archaic* a glimmer of light ▷ *vb* 4 (*tr*) to catch sight of briefly or momentarily 5 (*intr*; usually foll by *at*) *chiefly US* to look (at) briefly or cursorily; glance (at) 6 (*intr*) *archaic* to shine faintly; glimmer [C14 of Germanic origin; compare Middle High German *glimsen* to glimmer] > **'glimpser** *n*

USAGE *Glimpse* is sometimes wrongly used where *glance* is meant: *he gave a quick glance* (not *glimpse*) *at his watch*

glint (glɪnt) *vb* 1 to gleam or cause to gleam brightly ▷ *n* 2 a bright gleam or flash 3 brightness or gloss 4 a brief indication [C15 probably from Scandinavian origin; compare Swedish dialect *glänta*, *glinta* to gleam]

glioma (glaɪˈəʊmə) *n*, *pl* **-mata** (-ˈmətə) *or* **-mas** a tumour of the brain and spinal cord, composed of neuroglia cells and fibres [C19 from New Latin, from Greek *glia* glue + -OMA] > **gli'omatous** *adj*

glissade (glɪˈsɑːd, -ˈseɪd) *n* 1 a gliding step in ballet, in which one foot slides forwards, sideways, or backwards 2 a controlled slide down a snow slope ▷ *vb* 3 (*intr*) to perform a glissade [C19 from French, from *glisser* to slip, from Old French *glicier*, of Frankish origin; compare Old High German *glītan* to GLIDE] > **glis'sader** *n*

glissando (glɪˈsændəʊ) *n*, *pl* **-di** (-diː) *or* **-dos** 1 a rapidly executed series of notes on the harp or piano, each note of which is discretely audible 2 a portamento, esp as executed on the violin, viola, etc [C19 probably Italianized variant of GLISSADE]

glisten ('glɪsⁿn) *vb* (*intr*) 1 (of a wet or glossy surface) to gleam by reflecting light: *wet leaves glisten in the sunlight* 2 (of light) to reflect with brightness: *the sunlight glistens on wet leaves* ▷ *n* 3 *rare* a gleam or gloss [Old English *glisnian*; related to *glisian* to glitter, Middle High German *glistern*] > **'glisteningly** *adv*

glister ('glɪstə) *vb, n* an archaic word for **glitter** [C14 probably from Middle Dutch *glisteren*] > **'glisteringly** *adv*

glitch (glɪtʃ) *n* 1 a sudden instance of malfunctioning or irregularity in an electronic system 2 a change in the rotation rate of a pulsar [C20 of unknown origin]

glitter ('glɪtə) *vb* (*intr*) 1 (of a hard, wet, or polished surface) to reflect light in bright flashes 2 (of light) to be reflected in bright flashes 3 (usually foll by *with*) to be decorated or enhanced by the glamour (of) ▷ *n* 4 sparkle or brilliance 5 show and glamour 6 tiny pieces of shiny decorative material used for ornamentation, as on the skin **7** *Canadian* Also called: **silver thaw** ice formed from freezing rain [c14 from Old Norse *glitra*; related to Old High German *glīzan* to shine] > **'glitteringly** *adv* > **'glittery** *adj*

glitterati (ˌɡlɪtəˈrɑːtiː) *pl n informal* the leaders of society, esp the rich and beautiful; fashionable celebrities [c20 from GLITTER + *-ati* as in LITERATI]

glitz (ɡlɪts) *n slang* ostentatious showiness, gaudiness or glitter [c20 back formation from GLITZY]

glitzy (ˈɡlɪtsɪ) *adj* glitzier, glitziest *slang* showily attractive; flashy or glittery [c20 originally US, probably via Yiddish from German *glitzern* to glitter]

Gliwice (*Polish* ɡliˈvitsɛ) *n* an industrial city in S Poland. Pop: 212 164 (1999 est). German name: Gleiwitz

gloaming (ˈɡləʊmɪŋ) *n poetic* twilight or dusk [Old English *glōmung*, from *glōm*; related to Old Norse *glāmr* moon]

gloat (ɡləʊt) *vb* **1** (*intr*; often foll by *over*) to dwell (on) with malevolent smugness or exultation ▷ *n* **2** the act of gloating [c16 probably of Scandinavian origin; compare Old Norse *glotta* to grin, Middle High German *glotzen* to stare] > **'gloater** *n* > **'gloatingly** *adv*

glob (ɡlɒb) *n informal* a rounded mass of some thick fluid or pliable substance: *a glob of cream* [c20 probably from GLOBE, influenced by BLOB]

global (ˈɡləʊbəl) *adj* **1** covering, influencing, or relating to the whole world **2** comprehensive > **'globally** *adv*

global community *n* the people or nations of the world, considered as being closely connected by modern telecommunications and as being economically, socially, and politically interdependent

global dimming *n* a decrease in the amount of sunlight reaching the surface of the earth, believed to be caused by pollution in the atmosphere

globalization *or* **globalisation** (ˌɡləʊbəlaɪˈzeɪʃən) *n* **1** the process enabling financial and investment markets to operate internationally, largely as a result of deregulation and improved communications **2** the emergence since the 1980s of a single world market dominated by multinational companies, leading to a diminishing capacity for national governments to control their economies **3** the process by which a company, etc, expands to operate internationally

globalize *or* **globalise** (ˈɡləʊbəˌlaɪz) *vb* (*tr*) to put into effect or spread worldwide

global positioning system *n* a system of earth-orbiting satellites, transmitting signals continuously towards the earth, that enables the position of a receiving device on or near the earth's surface to be accurately estimated from the difference in arrival times of the signals. Abbreviation: **GPS**

global product *n* a commercial product, such as Coca Cola, that is marketed throughout the world under the same brand name

global rule *n* (in transformational grammar) a rule that makes reference to nonconsecutive stages of a derivation

global search *n* a word-processing operation in which a complete computer file or set of files is searched for every occurrence of a particular word or other sequence of characters

global village *n* the whole world considered as being closely connected by modern telecommunications and as being interdependent economically, socially, and politically [c20 coined by Marshall McLuhan (1911–80), Canadian author of works analysing the mass media]

global warming *n* an increase in the average temperature worldwide believed to be caused by the greenhouse effect

globate (ˈɡləʊbeɪt) *or* **globated** *adj* shaped like a globe

globe (ɡləʊb) *n* **1** a sphere on which a map of the world or the heavens is drawn or represented **2 the** the world; the earth **3** a planet or some other astronomical body **4** an object shaped like a sphere, such as a glass lampshade or fish-bowl **5** *Austral, NZ, and South African* an electric light bulb **6** an orb, usually of gold, symbolic of authority or sovereignty ▷ *vb* **7** to form or cause to form into a globe [c16 from Old French, from Latin *globus*] > **'globe,like** *adj*

globe artichoke *n* See **artichoke** (senses 1, 2)

globefish (ˈɡləʊb,fɪʃ) *n, pl* **-fish** *or* **-fishes** another name for **puffer** (sense 2) *or* **porcupine fish**

globeflower (ˈɡləʊb,flaʊə) *n* any ranunculaceous plant of the genus *Trollius*, having pale yellow, white, or orange globe-shaped flowers

globesity (ˌɡləʊˈbiːsɪtɪ) *n informal* obesity seen as a worldwide social problem [c21 from GLOBAL + OBESITY]

globetrotter (ˈɡləʊb,trɒtə) *n* a habitual worldwide traveller, esp a tourist or businessman > **'globe,trotting** *n, adj*

globigerina (ɡləʊ,bɪdʒəˈraɪnə) *n, pl* **-nas** *or* **-nae** (-niː) **1** any marine protozoan of the genus *Globigerina*, having a rounded shell with spiny processes: phylum *Foraminifera* (foraminifers) **2** globigerina ooze a deposit on the ocean floor consisting of the shells of these protozoans [c19 from New Latin, from Latin *globus* GLOBE + *gerere* to carry, bear]

globin (ˈɡləʊbɪn) *n biochem* the protein component of the pigments myoglobin and haemoglobin [c19 from Latin *globus* ball, sphere + -IN]

globoid (ˈɡləʊbɔɪd) *adj* **1** shaped approximately like a globe ▷ *n* **2** a globoid body, such as any of those occurring in certain plant granules

globose (ˈɡləʊbəʊs, ɡləʊˈbəʊs) *or* **globous** (ˈɡləʊbəs) *adj* spherical or approximately spherical [c15 from Latin *globōsus*; see GLOBE] > **'globosely** *adv* > **globosity** (ɡləʊˈbɒsɪtɪ) *or* **globoseness** *n*

globular (ˈɡlɒbjʊlə) *or* **globulous** *adj* **1** shaped like a globe or globule **2** having or consisting of globules > **globularity** (ˌɡlɒbjʊˈlærɪtɪ) *or* **'globularness** *n* > **'globularly** *adv*

globular cluster *n astronomy* a densely populated spheroidal star cluster with the highest concentration of stars near its centre, found in the galactic halo and in other galaxies

globule (ˈɡlɒbjuːl) *n* **1** a small globe, esp a drop of liquid **2** *astronomy* a small dark nebula thought to be a site of star formation [c17 from Latin *globulus*, diminutive of *globus* GLOBE]

globuliferous (ˌɡlɒbjʊˈlɪfərəs) *adj* producing, containing, or having globules

globulin (ˈɡlɒbjʊlɪn) *n* any of a group of simple proteins, including gamma globulin, that are generally insoluble in water but soluble in salt solutions and coagulated by heat [c19 from GLOBULE + -IN]

globus (ˈɡləʊbəs) *n anatomy* any spherelike structure

globus hystericus (hɪˈstɛrɪkəs) *n* the technical name for a **lump in the throat** See **lump** (sense 8)

glochidium (ɡləʊˈkɪdɪəm) *n, pl* **-chidia** (-ˈkɪdɪə) **1** a barbed hair, esp among the spore masses of water ferns and on certain other plants **2** a parasitic larva of certain freshwater mussels that attaches itself to the fins or gills of fish by hooks or suckers [c19 from New Latin, from Greek *glōkhis* projecting point] > **glo'chidiate** *adj*

glockenspiel (ˈɡlɒkən,spiːl, -,ʃpiːl) *n* a percussion instrument consisting of a set of tuned metal plates played with a pair of small hammers [c19 German, from *Glocken* bells + *Spiel* play]

glogg (ɡlɒɡ) *n* a hot alcoholic mixed drink, originally from Sweden, consisting of sweetened brandy, red wine, bitters or other flavourings, and blanched almonds [from Swedish *glögg*, from *glödga* to burn]

glom (ɡlɒm) *vb slang* **1** (*tr*; foll by *on to*) to attach

oneself to or associate oneself with **2** *US* to acquire, esp without paying

glomerate (ˈɡlɒmərɪt) *adj* **1** gathered into a compact rounded mass **2** wound up like a ball of thread **3** *anatomy* (esp of glands) conglomerate in structure [c18 from Latin *glomerāre* to wind into a ball, from *glomus* ball]

glomeration (ˌɡlɒməˈreɪʃən) *n* a conglomeration or cluster

glomerule (ˈɡlɒmə,ruːl) *n botany* **1** a cymose inflorescence in the form of a ball-like cluster of flowers **2** a ball-like cluster of spores [c18 from New Latin GLOMERULUS] > **glomerulate** (ɡlɒˈmɛrʊlɪt, -,leɪt) *adj*

glomerulonephritis (ɡlɒ,mɛrʊləʊnɪˈfraɪtɪs) *n* any of various kidney diseases in which the glomeruli are affected

glomerulus (ɡlɒˈmɛrʊləs) *n, pl* **-li** (-,laɪ) **1** a knot of blood vessels in the kidney projecting into the capsular end of a urine-secreting tubule **2** any cluster or coil of blood vessels, nerve fibres, etc, in the body [c18 from New Latin, diminutive of *glomus* ball] > **glo'merular** *adj*

Glomma (*Norwegian* ˈɡlɒma) *n* a river in SE Norway, rising near the border with Sweden and flowing generally south to the Skagerrak: the largest river in Scandinavia; important for hydroelectric power and floating timber. Length: 588 km (365 miles)

gloom (ɡluːm) *n* **1** partial or total darkness **2** a state of depression or melancholy **3** an appearance or expression of despondency or melancholy **4** *poetic* a dim or dark place ▷ *vb* **5** (*intr*) to look sullen or depressed **6** to make or become dark or gloomy [c14 *gloumben* to look sullen; related to Norwegian dialect *glome* to eye suspiciously] > **'gloomful** *adj* > **'gloomfully** *adv* > **'gloomless** *adj*

gloomy (ˈɡluːmɪ) *adj* gloomier, gloomiest **1** dark or dismal **2** causing depression, dejection, or gloom: *gloomy news* **3** despairing; sad > **'gloomily** *adv* > **'gloominess** *n*

Glooscap, Gluscap *or* **Gluskap** (ˈɡluːskæp) *n* (among the Micmac and other Native North American peoples) a traditional trickster hero [of Algonquian origin]

gloria (ˈɡlɔːrɪə) *n* **1** a silk, wool, cotton, or nylon fabric used esp for umbrellas **2** a halo or nimbus, esp as represented in art [c16 from Latin: GLORY]

Gloria (ˈɡlɔːrɪə, -ˌɑː) *n* **1** any of several doxologies beginning with the word *Gloria*, esp the Greater and the Lesser Doxologies **2** a musical setting of one of these

Gloria in Excelsis Deo (ˈɡlɔːrɪə ɪn ɛkˈsɛlsɪsˈdeɪəʊ, ˈɡlɔːrɪ,ɑː, ˌɛksˈtʃɛlsɪs) *n* **1** the Greater Doxology (see **doxology**), beginning in Latin with these words **2** a musical setting of this, usually incorporated into the Ordinary of the Mass. Often shortened to: Gloria [literally: glory to God in the highest]

Gloria Patri (ˈɡlɔːrɪə ˈpɑːtrɪ, ˈɡlɔːrɪ,ɑː, ˈpæt-) *n* **1** the Lesser Doxology (see **doxology**), beginning in Latin with these words **2** a musical setting of this [literally: glory to the father]

glorification (ˌɡlɔːrɪfɪˈkeɪʃən) *n* **1** the act of glorifying or state of being glorified **2** *informal* an enhanced or favourably exaggerated version or account **3** *Brit informal* a celebration

glorify (ˈɡlɔːrɪ,faɪ) *vb* **-fies, -fying, -fied** (*tr*) **1** to make glorious **2** to make more splendid; adorn **3** to worship, exalt, or adore **4** to extol **5** to cause to seem more splendid or imposing than reality > **'glori,fiable** *adj* > **'glori,fier** *n*

gloriole (ˈɡlɔːrɪ,əʊl) *n* another name for a **halo** *or* **nimbus** (senses 2, 3) [c19 from Latin *glōriola*, literally: a small GLORY]

gloriosa (ˌɡlɔːrɪˈəʊsə) *n* any plant of the bulbous tropical African genus *Gloriosa*, some species of which are grown as ornamental greenhouse climbers for their showy flowers of yellow, orange, and red: family *Liliaceae*. Also called: **glory lily** [New Latin, from Latin *gloriosus* glorious]

glorious (ˈɡlɔːrɪəs) *adj* **1** having or full of glory;

g

illustrious **2** conferring glory or renown: *a glorious victory* **3** brilliantly beautiful **4** delightful or enjoyable **5** *informal* drunk ▷ '**gloriously** *adv* ▷ '**gloriousness** *n*

Glorious Revolution *n* the events of 1688–89 in England that resulted in the ousting of James II and the establishment of William III and Mary II as joint monarchs. Also called: **Bloodless Revolution**

glory ('glɔːrɪ) *n, pl* -ries **1** exaltation, praise, or honour, as that accorded by general consent: *the glory for the exploit went to the captain* **2** something that brings or is worthy of glory (esp in the phrase **crowning glory**) **3** thanksgiving, adoration, or worship: *glory be to God* **4** pomp; splendour: *the glory of the king's reign* **5** radiant beauty; resplendence: *the glory of the sunset* **6** the beauty and bliss of heaven **7** a state of extreme happiness or prosperity **8** another word for **halo** or **nimbus** ▷ *vb* -ries, -rying, -ried **9** (*intr*; often foll by *in*) to triumph or exult **10** (*intr*) *obsolete* to brag ▷ *interj* **11** *informal* a mild interjection to express pleasure or surprise (often in the exclamatory phrase **glory be!**) [C13 from Old French *glorie*, from Latin *glōria*, of obscure origin]

glory box *n* *Austral and NZ informal* a box in which a young woman stores clothes, etc, in preparation for marriage

glory hole *n* **1** *informal* a room, cupboard, or other storage space that contains an untidy and miscellaneous collection of objects **2** *nautical* another term for **lazaretto** (sense 1)

glory-of-the-snow *n* a small W Asian liliaceous plant, *Chionodoxa luciliae*, cultivated for its early-blooming blue flowers

Glos *abbreviation for* Gloucestershire

gloss¹ (glɒs) *n* **1** lustre or sheen, as of a smooth surface **2** a superficially attractive appearance **3** See **gloss paint** **4** a cosmetic preparation applied to the skin to give it a faint sheen: *lip gloss* ▷ *vb* **5** to give a gloss to or obtain a gloss ▷ See also **gloss over** [C16 probably of Scandinavian origin; compare Icelandic *glossi* flame, Middle High German *glosen* to glow] ▷ '**glosser** *n* ▷ '**glossless** *adj*

gloss² (glɒs) *n* **1** a short or expanded explanation or interpretation of a word, expression, or foreign phrase in the margin or text of a manuscript, etc **2** an intentionally misleading explanation or interpretation **3** short for **glossary** ▷ *vb* (*tr*) **4** to add glosses to [C16 from Latin *glōssa* unusual word requiring explanatory note, from Ionic Greek] ▷ '**glosser** *n* ▷ '**glossingly** *adv*

gloss. *abbreviation for* glossary

glossa ('glɒsə) *n, pl* -sae (-siː) *or* -sas **1** *anatomy* a technical word for the **tongue 2** a paired tonguelike lobe in the labium of an insect ▷ '**glossal** *adj*

glossary ('glɒsərɪ) *n, pl* -ries an alphabetical list of terms peculiar to a field of knowledge with definitions or explanations. Sometimes called: **gloss** [C14 from Late Latin *glossārium*; see GLOSS²] ▷ **glossarial** (glɒ'sɛərɪəl) *adj* ▷ **glos'sarially** *adv* ▷ '**glossarist** *n*

glossator (glɒ'seɪtə) *n* **1** Also called: **glossarist, glossist, glossographer** a writer of glosses and commentaries, esp (in the Middle Ages) an interpreter of Roman and Canon Law **2** a compiler of a glossary

glossectomy (glɒ'sɛktəmɪ) *n, pl* -mies surgical removal of all or part of the tongue

glosseme ('glɒsiːm) *n* the smallest meaningful unit of a language, such as stress, form, etc [C20 from Greek *glōssēma*; see GLOSS², -EME]

glossitis (glɒ'saɪtɪs) *n* inflammation of the tongue ▷ **glossitic** (glɒ'sɪtɪk) *adj*

glosso- *or before a vowel* **gloss-** *combining form* indicating a tongue or language: *glossolaryngeal* [from Greek *glossa* tongue]

glossography (glɒ'sɒɡrəfɪ) *n* the art of writing textual glosses or commentaries ▷ **glos'sographer** *n*

glossolalia (,glɒsə'leɪlɪə) *n* **1** another term for **gift**

of tongues **2** *psychol* babbling in a nonexistent language [C19 New Latin, from GLOSSO- + Greek *lalein* to speak, babble]

glossology (glɒ'sɒlədʒɪ) *n* an obsolete term for **linguistics.** ▷ **glossological** (,glɒsə'lɒdʒɪk°l) *adj* ▷ **glos'sologist** *n*

glossopharyngeal nerve (,glɒsəʊˌfærɪn'dʒiːəl) *n* the ninth cranial nerve, which supplies the muscles of the pharynx, the tongue, the middle ear, and the parotid gland

gloss over *vb* (*tr, adverb*) **1** to hide under a deceptively attractive surface or appearance **2** to deal with (unpleasant facts) rapidly and cursorily, or to omit them altogether from an account of something

gloss paint *n* a type of paint composed of pigments ground up in a varnish medium, which produces a hard, shiny, and usually durable finish. Also called: **gloss**

glossy ('glɒsɪ) *adj* glossier, glossiest **1** smooth and shiny; lustrous **2** superficially attractive; plausible **3** (of a magazine) lavishly produced on shiny paper and usually with many colour photographs ▷ *n, pl* glossies **4** Also called (US): **slick** an expensively produced magazine, typically a sophisticated fashion or glamour magazine, printed on shiny paper and containing high quality colour photography. Compare **pulp** (sense 3) **5** a photograph printed on paper that has a smooth shiny surface ▷ '**glossily** *adv* ▷ '**glossiness** *n*

glottal ('glɒt°l) *adj* **1** of or relating to the glottis **2** *phonetics* articulated or pronounced at or with the glottis

glottal stop *n* a plosive speech sound produced as the sudden onset of a vowel in several languages, such as German, by first tightly closing the glottis and then allowing the air pressure to build up in the trachea before opening the glottis, causing the air to escape with force

glottic ('glɒtɪk) *adj* of or relating to the tongue or the glottis

glottis ('glɒtɪs) *n, pl* -tises *or* -tides (-tɪˌdiːz) the vocal apparatus of the larynx, consisting of the two true vocal cords and the opening between them [C16 from New Latin, from Greek *glōttis*, from *glōtta*, Attic form of Ionic *glōssa* tongue; see GLOSS²] ▷ **glottidean** (glɒ'tɪdɪən) *adj*

glottochronology (,glɒtəʊkrə'nɒlədʒɪ) *n* the use of lexicostatistics to establish that languages are historically related [C20 *glotto-*, from Greek *glōtta* tongue]

Gloucester ('glɒstə) *n* a city in SW England, administrative centre of Gloucestershire, on the River Severn; cathedral (founded 1100). Pop: 123 205 (2001). Latin name: **Glevum** ('gliːvʊm)

Gloucester Old Spot *n* a hardy rare breed of pig, white with a few black markings, that originally lived off windfalls in orchards in the Severn valley

Gloucestershire ('glɒstəˌʃɪə, -ʃə) *n* a county of SW England, situated around the lower Severn valley: contains the Forest of Dean and the main part of the Cotswold Hills: the geographical and ceremonial county includes the unitary authority of South Gloucestershire (part of Avon county from 1974 to 1996). Administrative centre: Gloucester. Pop (excluding South Gloucestershire): 568 500 (2003 est). Area (excluding South Gloucestershire): 2643 sq km (1020 sq miles). Abbreviation: **Glos**

glove (glʌv) *n* **1** (*often plural*) a shaped covering for the hand with individual sheaths for the fingers and thumb, made of leather, fabric, etc. See also **gauntlet¹** (sense 2) **2** any of various large protective hand covers worn in sports, such as a boxing glove **3** **hand in glove** *informal* in an intimate relationship or close association **4** **handle with kid gloves** *informal* to treat with extreme care **5** **with the gloves off** *informal* (of a dispute, argument, etc) conducted mercilessly and in earnest, with no reservations ▷ *vb* **6** (*tr; usually passive*) to cover or provide with or as if with gloves [Old English *glōfe*; related to Old Norse *glōfi*]

▷ '**gloved** *adj* ▷ '**gloveless** *adj*

glove box *n* a closed box in which toxic or radioactive substances can be handled by an operator who places his hands through protective gloves sealed to the box

glove compartment *n* a small compartment in a car dashboard for the storage of miscellaneous articles

glove puppet *n* a small figure of a person or animal that fits over and is manipulated by the hand

glover ('glʌvə) *n* a person who makes or sells gloves

glow (gləʊ) *n* **1** light emitted by a substance or object at a high temperature **2** a steady even light without flames **3** brilliance or vividness of colour **4** brightness or ruddiness of complexion **5** a feeling of wellbeing or satisfaction **6** intensity of emotion; ardour ▷ *vb* (*intr*) **7** to emit a steady even light without flames **8** to shine intensely, as if from great heat **9** to be exuberant or high-spirited, as from excellent health or intense emotion **10** to experience a feeling of wellbeing or satisfaction: *to glow with pride* **11** (esp of the complexion) to show a strong bright colour, esp a shade of red **12** to be very hot [Old English *glōwan*; related to Old Norse *glōa*, Old High German *gluoen*, Icelandic *glōra* to sparkle]

glow discharge *n* a silent luminous discharge of electricity through a low-pressure gas

glower ('glaʊə) *vb* **1** (*intr*) to stare hard and angrily ▷ *n* **2** a sullen or angry stare [C16 probably of Scandinavian origin; related to Middle Low German *glüren* to watch] ▷ '**gloweringly** *adv*

glowing ('gləʊɪŋ) *adj* **1** emitting a steady bright light without flames: *glowing embers* **2** warm and rich in colour: *the room was decorated in glowing shades of gold and orange* **3** flushed and rosy, as from exercise or excitement: *glowing cheeks* **4** displaying or indicative of extreme satisfaction, pride, or emotion: *he gave a glowing account of his son's achievements* ▷ '**glowingly** *adv*

glow lamp *n* a small light consisting of two or more electrodes in an inert gas, such as neon, at low pressure, across which an electrical discharge occurs when the voltage applied to the electrodes exceeds the ionization potential

glow plug *n* one of usually four plugs fitted to the cylinder block of a diesel engine that warms the engine chamber to facilitate starting in cold weather. Also called: **heater plug**

glowstick ('gləʊˌstɪk) *n* a plastic tube containing a luminescent material, waved or held aloft esp at gigs, raves, etc

glow-worm *n* **1** a European beetle, *Lampyris noctiluca*, the females and larvae of which bear luminescent organs producing a greenish light: family *Lampyridae* **2** any of various other beetles or larvae of the family *Lampyridae* ▷ See also **firefly** (sense 1)

gloxinia (glɒk'sɪnɪə) *n* any of several tropical plants of the genus *Sinningia*, esp the South American *S. speciosa*, cultivated for its large white, red, or purple bell-shaped flowers: family *Gesneriaceae* [C19 named after Benjamin P. *Gloxin*, 18th-century German physician and botanist who first described it]

gloze (gləʊz) *archaic* ▷ *vb* **1** (*tr*; often foll by *over*) to explain away; minimize the effect or importance of **2** to make explanatory notes or glosses on (a text) **3** to use flattery (on) ▷ *n* **4** flattery or deceit **5** an explanatory note or gloss **6** specious or deceptive talk or action [C13 from Old French *glosser* to comment; see GLOSS²]

glucagon ('gluːkəˌɡɒn, -ɡən) *n* a polypeptide hormone, produced in the pancreas by the islets of Langerhans, that stimulates the release of glucose into the blood. Compare **insulin** [C20 from GLUC(OSE) + -*agon*, perhaps from Greek *agein* to lead]

glucan ('gluːˌkæn) *n* any polysaccharide consisting of a polymer of glucose, such as cellulose or starch

glucinum (gluːˈsaɪnəm) *or* **glucinium** (gluːˈsɪnɪəm) *n* a former name for **beryllium** [C19 New Latin *glucina* beryllium oxide, from Greek *glukus* sweet + -IN; alluding to the sweet taste of some of the salts]

glucocorticoid (ˌgluːkəʊˈkɔːtɪˌkɔɪd) *n* any of a class of corticosteroids that control carbohydrate, protein, and fat metabolism and have anti-inflammatory activity

gluconeogenesis (ˌgluːkəʊˌniːəʊˈdʒɛnɪsɪs) *n biochem* the sequence of metabolic reactions by which glucose is synthesized, esp in the liver, from noncarbohydrate sources, such as amino acids, pyruvic acid, or glycerol. Also called: **glyconeogenesis**

glucophore (ˈgluːkəˌfɔː) *n* a chemical group responsible for sweetness of taste

glucoprotein (ˌgluːkəʊˈprəʊtiːn) *n* another name for **glycoprotein**

glucosamine (gluːˈkəʊzəˌmiːn) *n* the amino derivative of glucose that occurs in chitin. It has been used in some herbal remedies

glucosamine sulphate *n* a compound used in some herbal remedies and dietary supplements, esp to strengthen joint cartilage

glucose (ˈgluːkəʊz, -kəʊs) *n* **1** a white crystalline monosaccharide sugar that has several optically active forms, the most abundant being dextrose: a major energy source in metabolism. Formula: $C_6H_{12}O_6$ **2** a yellowish syrup (or, after desiccation, a solid) containing dextrose, maltose, and dextrin, obtained by incomplete hydrolysis of starch: used in confectionery, fermentation, etc [C19 from French, from Greek *gleukos* sweet wine; related to Greek *glukus* sweet] > **glucosic** (gluːˈkɒsɪk) *adj*

glucoside (ˈgluːkəʊˌsaɪd) *n biochem* any of a large group of glycosides that yield glucose on hydrolysis > **gluco'sidal** *or* **glucosidic** (ˌgluːkəʊˈsɪdɪk) *adj*

glucosuria (ˌgluːkəʊˈsjʊərɪə) *n pathol* a less common word for **glycosuria**. > **gluco'suric** *adj*

glue (gluː) *n* **1** any natural or synthetic adhesive, esp a sticky gelatinous substance prepared by boiling animal products such as bones, skin, and horns **2** any other sticky or adhesive substance ▷ *vb* **glues**, **gluing** *or* **glueing**, **glued** **3** (*tr*) to join or stick together with or as if with glue [C14 from Old French *glu*, from Late Latin *glūs*; compare Greek *gloios*] > **'glue,like** *adj* > **'gluer** *n* > **'gluey** *adj*

glue ear *n* accumulation of fluid in the middle ear in children, caused by infection and sometimes resulting in deafness

glue-sniffing *n* the practice of inhaling the fumes of certain types of glue to produce intoxicating or hallucinatory effects > **'glue-,sniffer** *n*

glug (glʌg) *n* a word representing a gurgling sound, as of liquid being poured from a bottle or swallowed [C19 of imitative origin]

gluggable (ˈglʌgəbəl) *adj informal* (of wine) easy and pleasant to drink

gluhwein (ˈgluːˌvaɪn) *n* mulled wine [German]

glum (glʌm) *adj* **glummer**, **glummest** silent or sullen, as from gloom [C16 variant of GLOOM] > **'glumly** *adv* > **'glumness** *n*

glum bum *n Austral slang* a pessimistic person

glume (gluːm) *n* **1** *botany* one of a pair of dry membranous bracts at the base of the spikelet of grasses **2** the bract beneath each flower in a sedge or related plant [C18 from Latin *glūma* husk of corn; related to Latin *glūbere* to remove the bark from] > **glu'maceous** *adj* > **'glume,like** *adj*

gluon (ˈgluːɒn) *n* a hypothetical particle believed to be exchanged between quarks in order to bind them together to form particles [C20 from GLUE + -ON]

glurge (glɜːdʒ) *n* stories, often sent by email, that are supposed to be true and uplifting, but which are often fabricated and sentimental [C20 of unknown origin]

glut (glʌt) *n* **1** an excessive amount, as in the production of a crop, often leading to a fall in price **2** the act of glutting or state of being glutted ▷ *vb* **gluts**, **glutting**, **glutted** (*tr*) **3** to feed or supply beyond capacity **4** to supply (a market) with a commodity in excess of the demand for it **5** to cram full or choke up: *to glut a passage* [C14 probably from Old French *gloutir*, from Latin *gluttīre*; see GLUTTON¹] > **'gluttingly** *adv*

glutamate (ˈgluːtəˌmeɪt) *n* any salt of glutamic acid, esp its sodium salt (see **monosodium glutamate**) [C19 from GLUTAM(IC ACID) + -ATE¹]

glutamic acid (gluːˈtæmɪk) *or* **glutaminic acid** (ˌgluːtəˈmɪnɪk) *n* a nonessential amino acid, occurring in proteins, that acts as a neurotransmitter and plays a part in nitrogen metabolism

glutamine (ˈgluːtəˌmiːn, -mɪn) *n* a nonessential amino acid occurring in proteins: plays an important role in protein metabolism [C19 from GLUT(EN) + -AMINE]

glutaraldehyde (ˌgluːtəˈrældɪˌhaɪd) *n* a water-soluble oil used as a disinfectant, tanning agent, and in resins. Formula: $C_5H_8O_2$

glutathione (ˌgluːtəˈθaɪəʊn, -aɪˈəʊn) *n biochem* a tripeptide consisting of glutamic acid, cysteine, and glycine: important in biological oxidations and the activation of some enzymes. Formula: $C_{10}H_{17}N_3O_6S$ [C20 from GLUTA(MIC ACID) + THI- + -ONE]

glute (gluːt) *n informal* short for **gluteus** [C20]

glutelin (ˈgluːtɪlɪn) *n* any of a group of water-insoluble plant proteins found in cereals. They are precipitated by alcohol and are not coagulated by heat. Compare **gliadin** [C20 See GLUTEN, -IN]

gluten (ˈgluːtᵊn) *n* a protein consisting of a mixture of glutelin and gliadin, present in cereal grains, esp wheat. A gluten-free diet is necessary in cases of coeliac disease [C16 from Latin: GLUE] > **'gluteneous** *adj*

gluten bread *n* bread made from flour containing a high proportion of gluten

gluteus *or* **glutaeus** (gluˈtiːəs) *n, pl* **-tei** *or* **-taei** (-ˈtiːaɪ) any one of the three large muscles that form the human buttock and move the thigh, esp the **gluteus maximus** [C17 from New Latin, from Greek *gloutos* buttock, rump] > **glu'teal** *or* **glu'taeal** *adj*

glutinous (ˈgluːtɪnəs) *adj* resembling glue in texture; sticky > **'glutinously** *adv* > **'glutinousness** *or* **glutinosity** (ˌgluːtɪˈnɒsɪtɪ) *n*

glutton¹ (ˈglʌtᵊn) *n* **1** a person devoted to eating and drinking to excess; greedy person **2** *often ironic* a person who has or appears to have a voracious appetite for something: *a glutton for punishment* [C13 from Old French *glouton*, from Latin *glutto*, *gluttīre* to swallow] > **'gluttonous** *adj* > **'gluttonously** *adv*

glutton² (ˈglʌtᵊn) *n* another name for **wolverine** [C17 from GLUTTON¹, apparently translating German *Vielfrass* great eater]

gluttony (ˈglʌtᵊnɪ) *n* the act or practice of eating to excess

glycaemia *or US* **glycemia** (ˌglaɪˈsiːmɪə) *n* the presence of glucose in blood [C20 from GLYCO- + -AEMIA] > **glycaemic** *or US* **glycemic** (ˌglaɪˈsiːmɪk) *adj*

glycaemic index *or US* **glycemic index** *n* an index indicating the effects of various foods on blood sugar. Fast-releasing foods that raise blood sugar levels quickly are high on the index, while slow-releasing foods, at the bottom of the index, give a slow but sustained release of sugar. Abbreviation: **GI**

glycaemic load *or US* **glycemic load** *n* an index indicating the amount of carbohydrate contained in a specified serving of a particular food. It is calculated by multiplying the food's glycaemic index by its carbohydrate content in grams and then dividing by 100. Abbreviation: **GL**

glyceric (glɪˈsɛrɪk) *adj* of, containing, or derived from glycerol

glyceric acid *n* a viscous liquid carboxylic acid

produced by the oxidation of glycerol; 2,3-dihydroxypropanoic acid. Formula: $C_3H_6O_4$

glyceride (ˈglɪsəˌraɪd) *n* any fatty-acid ester of glycerol

glycerine (ˈglɪsərɪn, ˌglɪsəˈriːn) *or* **glycerin** (ˈglɪsərɪn) *n* another name (not in technical usage) for **glycerol** [C19 from French *glycérine*, from Greek *glukeros* sweet + -ine -IN; related to Greek *glukus* sweet]

glycerol (ˈglɪsəˌrɒl) *n* a colourless or pale yellow odourless sweet-tasting syrupy liquid; 1,2,3-propanetriol: a by-product of soap manufacture, used as a solvent, antifreeze, plasticizer, and sweetener (**E422**). Formula: $C_3H_8O_3$. Also called (not in technical usage): **glycerine**, **glycerin** [C19 from GLYCER(INE) + -OL¹]

glyceryl (ˈglɪsərɪl) *n* (*modifier*) derived from glycerol by replacing or removing one or more of its hydroxyl groups: *a glyceryl group or radical*

glyceryl trinitrate *n* another name for **nitroglycerine**

glycine (ˈglaɪsiːn, glaɪˈsiːn) *n* a nonessential amino acid occurring in most proteins that acts as a neurotransmitter; aminoacetic acid [C19 GLYCO- + -INE²]

glyco- *or before a vowel* **glyc-** *combining form* indicating sugar: *glycogen* [from Greek *glukus* sweet]

glycogen (ˈglaɪkəʊdʒᵊn, -dʒɛn) *n* a polysaccharide consisting of glucose units: the form in which carbohydrate is stored in the liver and muscles in man and animals. It can easily be hydrolysed to glucose. Also called: **animal starch** > **glycogenic** (ˌglaɪkəʊˈdʒɛnɪk) *adj*

glycogenesis (ˌglaɪkəʊˈdʒɛnɪsɪs) *n* the formation of sugar, esp (in animals) from glycogen > **glycogenetic** (ˌglaɪkəʊdʒɪˈnɛtɪk) *adj*

glycol (ˈglaɪkɒl) *n* another name (not in technical usage) for **ethanediol** or a **diol** > **glycolic** *or* **glycollic** (glaɪˈkɒlɪk) *adj*

glycolic acid *n* a colourless crystalline soluble hygroscopic compound found in sugar cane and sugar beet: used in tanning and in the manufacture of pharmaceuticals, pesticides, adhesives, and plasticizers; hydroxyacetic acid. Formula: $CH_2(OH)COOH$

glycolipid (ˌglaɪkəʊˈlɪpɪd) *n* any of a group of lipids containing a carbohydrate group, commonly glucose or galactose

glycolysis (glaɪˈkɒlɪsɪs) *n biochem* the breakdown of glucose by enzymes into pyruvic and lactic acids with the liberation of energy

glyconeogenesis (ˌglaɪkəʊˌniːəʊˈdʒɛnɪsɪs) *n* another name for **gluconeogenesis**

glycophyte (ˈglaɪkəʊˌfaɪt) *n* any plant that will only grow healthily in soils with a low content of sodium salts > **glycophytic** (ˌglaɪkəʊˈfɪtɪk) *adj*

glycoprotein (ˌglaɪkəʊˈprəʊtiːn) *or* **glucoprotein, glycopeptide** (ˌglaɪkəʊˈpɛptaɪd) *n* any of a group of conjugated proteins containing small amounts of carbohydrates as prosthetic groups. See also **mucoprotein**

glycose (ˈglaɪkəʊz, -kəʊs) *n* **1** an older word for **glucose** **2** any of various monosaccharides

glycoside (ˈglaɪkəʊˌsaɪd) *n* any of a group of substances, such as digitoxin, derived from monosaccharides by replacing the hydroxyl group by another group. Many are important medicinal drugs. See also **glucoside**. > **glycosidic** (ˌglaɪkəʊˈsɪdɪk) *adj*

glycosuria (ˌglaɪkəʊˈsjʊərɪə) *or* **glucosuria** *n* the presence of excess sugar in the urine, as in diabetes [C19 from New Latin, from French *glycose* GLUCOSE + -URIA] > **glyco'suric** *or* **gluco'suric** *adj*

glycosylation (ˌglaɪkəʊsəˈleɪʃən) *n* the process by which sugars are chemically attached to proteins to form glycoproteins [from *glycosyl* radical derived from *glycose* + -ATION]

Glyndebourne (ˈglaɪndˌbɔːn) *n* an estate in SE England, in East Sussex: site of a famous annual festival of opera founded in 1934 by John Christie

glyoxaline (glaɪˈɒksəlɪn) *n* another name (not in technical usage) for **imidazole**

glyph (glɪf) *n* **1** a carved channel or groove, esp a vertical one as used on a Doric frieze **2** *now rare* another word for **hieroglyphic** **3** any computer-generated character regarded in terms of its shape and bit pattern [C18 from French *glyphe,* from Greek *gluphē* carving, from *gluphein* to carve] ▷ **'glyphic** *adj*

glyphography (glɪ'fɒɡrəfɪ) *n* a plate-making process in which an electrotype is made from an engraved copper plate [C19 from Greek *gluphē* carving + -GRAPHY] ▷ **glyphograph** ('glɪfə,ɡrɑːf, -,ɡræf) *n* ▷ **gly'phographer** *n* ▷ **glyphographic** (,glɪfə'ɡræfɪk) *or* **,glypho'graphical** *adj*

glyptal ('glɪptəl) *n* an alkyd resin obtained from polyhydric alcohols and polybasic organic acids or their anhydrides; used for surface coatings [C20 a trademark, perhaps from GLY(CEROL) + P(H)T(H)AL(IC)]

glyptic ('glɪptɪk) *adj* of or relating to engraving or carving, esp on precious stones [C19 from French *glyptique,* from Greek *gluptikos,* from *gluptos,* from *gluphein* to carve]

glyptics ('glɪptɪks) *n* (*functioning as singular*) the art of engraving precious stones

glyptodont ('glɪptə,dɒnt) *n* any extinct late Cenozoic edentate mammal of the genus *Glyptodon* and related genera, of South America, which resembled giant armadillos [C19 from Greek *gluptos* carved + -ODONT]

glyptography (glɪp'tɒɡrəfɪ) *n* the art of carving or engraving upon gemstones ▷ **glyp'tographer** *n* ▷ **glyptographic** (,glɪptə'ɡræfɪk) *or* **,glypto'graphical** *adj*

gm *the internet domain name for* Gambia

GM *abbreviation for* **1** general manager **2** genetically modified **3** (in Britain) George Medal **4** Grand Master **5** grant-maintained

G-man *n, pl* **G-men 1** *US slang* an FBI agent **2** *Irish* a political detective

GMB *abbreviation for* **1** Grand Master Bowman; the highest standard of archer **2** General, Municipal, and Boilermakers (trades union)

GmbH (in Germany) *abbreviation for* Gesellschaft mit beschränkter Haftung; a limited company [German: company with limited liabilities]

Gmc *abbreviation for* Germanic

GMC *abbreviation for* **1** general management committee **2** General Medical Council

GMDSS *abbreviation for* Global Marine Distress and Safety System: a worldwide satellite communication system used for transmitting messages (esp distress messages) at sea; officially superseded Morse code in 1999

GMO *abbreviation for* genetically modified organism

GMT *abbreviation for* **Greenwich Mean Time**

GMTA *text messaging abbreviation for* great minds think alike

gn *the internet domain name for* Guinea

gnamma hole ('næmə) *n* a variant spelling of **namma hole**

gnarl¹ (nɑːl) *n* **1** any knotty protuberance or swelling on a tree ▷ *vb* **2** (*tr*) to knot or cause to knot [C19 back formation from *gnarled,* probably variant of *knurled;* see KNURL]

gnarl² (nɑːl), **gnar** (nɑː) *vb* (*intr*) *obsolete* to growl or snarl [C16 of imitative origin]

gnarled (nɑːld) *adj* **1** having gnarls **2** (esp of hands) rough, twisted, and weather-beaten in appearance **3** perverse or ill-tempered

gnarly ('nɑːlɪ) *adj* **1** another word for **gnarled 2** *NZ informal* good; great **3** *surfing slang* difficult and dangerous

gnash (næʃ) *vb* **1** to grind (the teeth) together, as in pain or anger **2** (*tr*) to bite or chew as by grinding the teeth ▷ *n* **3** the act of gnashing the teeth [C15 probably of Scandinavian origin; compare Old Norse *gnastan* gnashing of teeth, *gnesta* to clatter] ▷ **'gnashingly** *adv*

gnashers ('næʃəz) *pl n slang* teeth, esp false ones

gnat (næt) *n* any of various small fragile biting dipterous insects of the suborder *Nematocera,* esp *Culex pipiens* (**common gnat**), which abounds near stagnant water [Old English *gnætt;* related to Middle High German *gnaz* scurf, German dialect *Gnitze* gnat] ▷ **'gnat,like** *adj*

gnatcatcher ('næt,kætʃə) *n* any of various small American songbirds of the genus *Polioptila* and related genera, typically having a long tail and a pale bluish-grey plumage: family *Muscicapidae* (Old World flycatchers, etc)

gnathic ('næθɪk) *or* **gnathal** *adj anatomy* of or relating to the jaw [C19 from Greek *gnathos* jaw]

gnathion ('neɪθɪ,ɒn, 'næθ-) *n* the lowest point of the midline of the lower jaw: a reference point in craniometry [C19 from New Latin, from Greek *gnathos* jaw]

gnathite ('neɪθaɪt, 'næθ-) *n zoology* an appendage of an arthropod that is specialized for grasping or chewing; mouthpart [C19 from Greek *gnathos* jaw]

gnathonic (næ'θɒnɪk) *adj literary* deceitfully flattering; sycophantic [C17 from Latin *gnathōnicus,* from *Gnathō,* such a character in the *Eunuchus,* Roman comedy by Terence] ▷ **gna'thonically** *adv*

gnathostome ('neɪθəʊ,stəʊm) *n* any vertebrate of the superclass *Gnathostomata,* having a mouth with jaws, including all vertebrates except the agnathans [from New Latin *Gnathostomata,* from Greek *gnathos* jaw + *stoma* mouth] ▷ **,gnatho'stomatous** *adj*

-gnathous *adj combining form* indicating or having a jaw of a specified kind: *prognathous* [from New Latin *-gnathus,* from Greek *gnathos* jaw]

gnaw (nɔː) *vb* **gnaws, gnawing, gnawed; gnawed** *or* **gnawn** (nɔːn) **1** (when *intr,* often foll by *at* or *upon*) to bite (at) or chew (upon) constantly so as to wear away little by little **2** (*tr*) to form by gnawing: *to gnaw a hole* **3** to cause erosion of (something) **4** (when *intr,* often foll by *at*) to cause constant distress or anxiety (to) ▷ *n* **5** the act or an instance of gnawing [Old English *gnagan;* related to Old Norse *gnaga,* Old High German *gnagan*] ▷ **'gnawable** *adj* ▷ **'gnawer** *n* ▷ **'gnawing** *adj, n* ▷ **'gnawingly** *adv*

GNC (in Britain) *abbreviation for* General Nursing Council

gneiss (naɪs) *n* any coarse-grained metamorphic rock that is banded and foliated: represents the last stage in the metamorphism of rocks before melting [C18 from German *Gneis,* probably from Middle High German *ganeist* spark; related to Old Norse *gneista* to give off sparks] ▷ **'gneissic, 'gneissoid** *or* **'gneissose** *adj*

gnetophyte ('niːtəʊ,faɪt) *n* any gymnosperm plant of the phylum *Genetophyta,* which includes three genera: *Gnetum,* consisting of small tropical trees and vines, *Ephedra* (see **ephedra**), and *Welwitschia* (see **welwitschia**)

gnocchi ('nɒkɪ, gə'nɒkɪ, 'gnɒkɪ) *pl n* dumplings made of pieces of semolina pasta, or sometimes potato, used to garnish soup or served alone with sauce [Italian, plural of *gnocco* lump, probably of Germanic origin; compare Middle High German *knoche* bone]

gnome¹ (nəʊm) *n* **1** one of a species of legendary creatures, usually resembling small misshapen old men, said to live in the depths of the earth and guard buried treasure **2** the statue of a gnome, esp in a garden **3** a very small or ugly person **4** *facetious or derogatory* an international banker or financier (esp in the phrase **gnomes of Zürich**) [C18 from French, from New Latin *gnomus,* coined by Paracelsus, of obscure origin] ▷ **'gnomish** *adj*

gnome² (nəʊm) *n* a short pithy saying or maxim expressing a general truth or principle [C16 from Greek *gnōmē,* from *gignōskein* to know]

gnomic ('nəʊmɪk, 'nɒm-) *or* **gnomical** *adj* **1** consisting of, containing, or relating to gnomes or aphorisms **2** of or relating to a writer of such sayings ▷ **'gnomically** *adv*

gnomon ('nəʊmɒn) *n* **1** the stationary arm that projects the shadow on a sundial **2** a geometric figure remaining after a parallelogram has been removed from one corner of a larger parallelogram [C16 from Latin, from Greek: interpreter, from *gignōskein* to know] ▷ **gno'monic** *adj* ▷ **gno'monically** *adv*

gnosis ('nəʊsɪs) *n, pl* **-ses** (-siːz) supposedly revealed knowledge of various spiritual truths, esp that said to have been possessed by ancient Gnostics [C18 ultimately from Greek: knowledge, from *gignōskein* to know]

-gnosis *n combining form* (esp in medicine) recognition or knowledge: *prognosis; diagnosis* [via Latin from Greek: GNOSIS] ▷ **-gnostic** *adj combining form*

gnostic ('nɒstɪk) *or* **gnostical** *adj* of, relating to, or possessing knowledge, esp esoteric spiritual knowledge ▷ **'gnostically** *adv*

Gnostic ('nɒstɪk) *n* **1** an adherent of Gnosticism ▷ *adj* **2** of or relating to Gnostics or Gnosticism [C16 from Late Latin *Gnosticī* the Gnostics, from Greek *gnōstikos* relating to knowledge, from *gnōstos* known, from *gignōskein* to know]

Gnosticism ('nɒstɪ,sɪzəm) *n* a religious movement characterized by a belief in gnosis, through which the spiritual element in man could be released from its bondage in matter: regarded as a heresy by the Christian Church

Gnosticize *or* **Gnosticise** ('nɒstɪ,saɪz) *vb* **1** (*intr*) to maintain or profess Gnostic views **2** to put a Gnostic interpretation upon (something) ▷ **'Gnosti,cizer** *or* **'Gnosti,ciser** *n*

gnotobiotics (,nəʊtəʊbaɪ'ɒtɪks) *n* (*functioning as singular*) the study of organisms living in germ-free conditions or when inoculated with known microorganisms [C20 from Greek, from *gnōtos,* from *gignōskein* to know + *bios* known life] ▷ **,gnotobi'otic** *adj* ▷ **,gnotobi'otically** *adv*

gnow (naʊ) *n W Austral* another name for **mallee fowl**

GNP *abbreviation for* **gross national product**

GnRH *biochem abbreviation for* gonadotrophin-releasing hormone: a peptide that is released from the brain and stimulates the pituitary gland to secrete gonadotrophic hormones that act in turn on the sex glands

gns. *abbreviation for* guineas

gnu (nuː) *n, pl* **gnus** *or* **gnu** either of two sturdy antelopes, *Connochaetes taurinus* (**brindled gnu**) or the much rarer *C. gnou* (**white-tailed gnu**), inhabiting the savannas of Africa, having an oxlike head and a long tufted tail. Also called: **wildebeest** [C18 from Xhosa *nqu*]

GNVQ (in Britain) *abbreviation for* general national vocational qualification: a qualification which rewards the development of skills which are likely to be of use to employers

go¹ (ɡəʊ) *vb* **goes, going, went, gone** (*mainly intr*) **1** to move or proceed, esp to or from a point or in a certain direction: *to go to London; to go home* **2** (*tr; takes an infinitive,* often with *to* omitted or replaced by *and*) to proceed towards a particular person or place with some specified intention or purpose: *I must go and get that book* **3** to depart: *we'll have to go at eleven* **4** to start, as in a race: often used in commands **5** to make regular journeys: *this train service goes to the east coast* **6** to operate or function effectively: *the radio won't go* **7** (*copula*) to become: *his face went red with embarrassment* **8** to make a noise as specified: *the gun went bang* **9** to enter into a specified state or condition: *to go into hysterics; to go into action* **10** to be or continue to be in a specified state or condition: *to go in rags; to go in poverty* **11** to lead, extend, or afford access: *this route goes to the north* **12** to proceed towards an activity: *to go to supper; to go to sleep* **13** (*tr; takes an infinitive*) to serve or contribute: *this letter goes to prove my point* **14** to follow a course as specified; fare: *the lecture went badly* **15** to be applied or allotted to a particular purpose or recipient: *her wealth went to her son; his money went on drink* **16** to be sold or otherwise transferred to a recipient: *the necklace went for three thousand pounds* **17** to be ranked; compare: *this meal is good as my meals go* **18** to blend or harmonize:

these chairs won't go with the rest of your furniture **19** (foll by *by* or *under*) to be known (by a name or disguise) **20** to fit or extend: *that skirt won't go round your waist* **21** to have a usual or proper place: *those books go on this shelf* **22** (of music, poetry, etc) to be sounded; expressed, etc: *how does that song go?* **23** to fail or give way: *my eyesight is going* **24** to break down or collapse abruptly: *the ladder went at the critical moment* **25** to die: *the old man went at 2 a.m* **26** (often foll by *by*) **a** (of time) to elapse: *the hours go by so slowly at the office* **b** to travel past: *the train goes by her house at four* **c** to be guided (by) **27** to occur: *happiness does not always go with riches* **28** to be eliminated, abolished, or given up: *this entry must go to save space* **29** to be spent or finished: *all his money has gone* **30** to circulate or be transmitted: *the infection went around the whole community* **31** to attend: *go to school; go to church* **32** to join a stated profession: *go to the bar; go on the stage* **33** (foll by *to*) to have recourse (to); turn: *to go to arbitration* **34** (foll by *to*) to subject or put oneself (to): *she goes to great pains to please him* **35** to proceed, esp up to or beyond certain limits: *you will go too far one day and then you will be punished* **36** to be acceptable or tolerated: *anything goes in this place* **37** to carry the weight of final authority: *what the boss says goes* **38** (foll by *into*) to be contained in: *four goes into twelve three times* **39** (often foll by *for*) to endure or last out: *we can't go for much longer without water in this heat* **40** (*tr*) *cards* to bet or bid: *I go two hearts* **41** (*tr*) *informal, chiefly US* to have as one's weight: *I went 112 pounds a year ago* **42** *US and Canadian* (*usually used in commands*; takes an infinitive without *to*) **a** to start to act so as to: *go shut the door* **b** to leave so as to: *go blow your brains out* **43** *informal* to perform well; be successful: *that group can really go* **44** (*tr*) *not standard* to say: widely used, esp in the historic present, in reporting dialogue: *Then she goes, "Give it to me!" and she just snatched it* **45** **go and** *informal* to be so foolish or unlucky as to: *then she had to go and lose her hat* **46** **be going** to intend or be about to start (to do or be doing something): often used as an alternative future construction: *what's going to happen to us?* **47** **go ape** *slang* to become crazy, enraged, or out of control **48** **go ape over** *slang* to become crazy or extremely enthusiastic about **49** **go astray** to be mislaid; go missing **50** **go bail** to act as surety **51** **go bush** See **bush** (sense 13) **52** **go halves** See **half** (sense 15) **53** **go hard** (often foll by *with*) to cause trouble or unhappiness (to) **54** **go it** *slang* to do something or move energetically **55** **go it alone** *informal* to act or proceed without allies or help **56** **go much on** *informal* to approve of or be in agreement with (something): usually used in the negative: *I don't go much on the idea* **57** **go one better** *informal* to surpass or outdo (someone) **58** **go the whole hog** *informal* See **hog** (sense 9) **59** **let go** **a** to relax one's hold (on); release **b** *euphemistic* to dismiss (from employment) **c** to discuss or consider no further **60** **let oneself go** **a** to act in an uninhibited manner **b** to lose interest in one's appearance, manners, etc **61** **to go** **a** remaining **b** *US and Canadian informal* (of food served by a restaurant) for taking away ▷ *n, pl* **goes** **62** the act of going **63** *informal* **a** an attempt or try: *he had a go at the stamp business* **b** an attempt at stopping a person suspected of a crime: *the police are not always in favour of the public having a go* **c** an attack, esp verbal: *she had a real go at them* **64** a turn: *it's my go next* **65** *informal* the quality of being active and energetic: *she has much more go than I* **66** *informal* hard or energetic work: *it's all go* **67** *informal* a successful venture or achievement: *he made a go of it* **68** *informal* a bout or attack (of an illness): *he had a bad go of flu last winter* **69** *informal* an unforeseen, usually embarrassing or awkward, turn of events: *here's a rum go* **70** *informal* a bargain or agreement **71** **all the go** *informal* very popular; in fashion **72** **from the word go** *informal* from the very beginning **73** See **get-up-and-go** **74** **no go** *informal* impossible; abortive or futile: *it's no go, I'm afraid* **75** **on the go** *informal* active and energetic ▷ *adj* **76** (*postpositive*) *informal* functioning properly and ready for action: esp used in astronautics: *all systems are go* ▷ See also **go about, go against, go ahead, go along, go around, go at, go away, go back, go by, go down, go for, go forth, go in, going, go into, gone, go off, go on, go out, go over, go through, go to, go together, go under, go up, go with, go without** [Old English *gān*; related to Old High German *gēn*, Greek *kikhanein* to reach, Sanskrit *jahāti* he forsakes]

go[2] (gəʊ) *or* **I-go** *n* a game for two players in which stones are placed on a board marked with a grid, the object being to capture territory on the board [from Japanese]

GO *military abbreviation for* general order

goa (ˈgəʊə) *n* a gazelle, *Procapra picticaudata*, inhabiting the plains of the Tibetan plateau, having a brownish-grey coat and backward-curving horns [C19 from Tibetan *dgoba*]

Goa (ˈgəʊə) *n* a state on the W coast of India: a Portuguese overseas territory from 1510 until annexed by India in 1961. Pop: 1 343 998 (2001). Area: 3702 sq km (1430 sq miles)

go about *vb* (*intr*) **1** (*adverb*) to move from place to place **2** (*preposition*) to busy oneself with: *to go about one's duties* **3** (*preposition*) to tackle (a problem or task) **4** (*preposition*) to be actively and constantly engaged in (doing something): *he went about doing good* **5** to circulate (in): *there's a lot of flu going about* **6** (*adverb*) (of a sailing ship) to change from one tack to another

goad (gəʊd) *n* **1** a sharp pointed stick for urging on cattle, etc **2** anything that acts as a spur or incitement ▷ *vb* **3** (*tr*) to drive with or as if with a goad; spur; incite [Old English *gād*, of Germanic origin, related to Old English *gār*, Old Norse *geirr* spear] > **ˈgoadˌlike** *adj*

Goa, Daman, and Diu *n* a former Union Territory of India consisting of the widely separated districts of Goa and Daman and the island of Diu. Capital: Panjim (or Panaji). Area: 3814 sq km (1472 sq miles)

go against *vb* (*intr, preposition*) **1** to be contrary to (principles or beliefs) **2** to be unfavourable to (a person): *the case went against him*

go ahead *vb* **1** (*intr, adverb*) to start or continue, often after obtaining permission ▷ *n* **go-ahead** **2** (usually preceded by *the*) *informal* permission to proceed ▷ *adj* **go-ahead** **3** enterprising or ambitious

goal (gəʊl) *n* **1** the aim or object towards which an endeavour is directed **2** the terminal point of a journey or race **3** (in various sports) the net, basket, etc into or over which players try to propel the ball, puck, etc, to score **4** *sport* **a** a successful attempt at scoring **b** the score so made **5** (in soccer, hockey, etc) the position of goalkeeper [C16 perhaps related to Middle English *gol* boundary, Old English *gǣlan* to hinder, impede] > **ˈgoalless** *adj*

goal area *n* *soccer* a rectangular area to the sides and front of the goal, measuring 20 × 6 yards on a full-sized pitch, from which goal kicks are taken. Also called: **six-yard area**

goalball (ˈgəʊlˌbɔːl) *n* **1** a game played by two teams who compete to score goals by throwing a ball that emits audible sound when in motion. Players, who may be blind or sighted, are blindfolded during play **2** the ball used in this game

goalie (ˈgəʊlɪ) *n* *informal* short for **goalkeeper**

goalkeeper (ˈgəʊlˌkiːpə) *n* *sport* a player in the goal whose duty is to prevent the ball, puck, etc, from entering or crossing it > **ˈgoalˌkeeping** *n*

goal kick *n* *soccer* a kick taken from the six-yard line by the defending team after the ball has been put out of play by an opposing player

goal line *n* *sport* the line marking each end of the pitch, on which the goals stand

goalmouth (ˈgəʊlˌmaʊθ) *n* *sport* the area in front of the goal

go along *vb* (*intr, adverb*; often foll by *with*) to refrain from disagreement; assent

goalpost (ˈgəʊlˌpəʊst) *n* **1** either of two upright posts supporting the crossbar of a goal **2** **move the goalposts** to change the aims of an activity to ensure the desired results

goanna (gəʊˈænə) *n* **1** any of various Australian monitor lizards **2** *Austral slang* a piano [C19 sense 1 changed from IGUANA; sense 2 from rhyming slang *pianna*]

Goa powder *n* another name for **araroba** (sense 2)

go around *or* **round** *vb* (*intr*) **1** (*adverb*) to move about **2** (*adverb*; foll by *with*) to frequent the society (of a person or group of people): *she went around with older men* **3** (*adverb*) to be sufficient: *are there enough sweets to go round?* **4** to circulate (in): *measles is going round the school* **5** (*preposition*) to be actively and constantly engaged in (doing something): *she went around caring for the sick* **6** to be long enough to encircle: *will that belt go round you?*

goat (gəʊt) *n* **1** any sure-footed agile bovid mammal of the genus *Capra*, naturally inhabiting rough stony ground in Europe, Asia, and N Africa, typically having a brown-grey colouring and a beard. Domesticated varieties (*C. hircus*) are reared for milk, meat, and wool. Related adjs: **caprine, hircine** **2** short for **Rocky Mountain goat** **3** *informal* a lecherous man **4** a bad or inferior member of any group (esp in the phrase **separate the sheep from the goats**) **5** short for **scapegoat** **6** **act** (*or* **play**) **the (giddy) goat** to fool around **7** **get (someone's) goat** *slang* to cause annoyance to (someone) [Old English *gāt*; related to Old Norse *geit*, Old High German *geiz*, Latin *haedus* kid] > **ˈgoatˌlike** *adj*

Goat (gəʊt) *n* **the** the constellation Capricorn, the tenth sign of the zodiac

go at *vb* (*intr, preposition*) **1** to make an energetic attempt at (something) **2** to attack vehemently

goat antelope *n* any bovid mammal of the tribe *Rupicaprini*, including the chamois, goral, serow, and Rocky Mountain goat, having characteristics of both goats and antelopes

goatee (gəʊˈtiː) *n* a pointed tuftlike beard on the chin [C19 from GOAT + *-ee* (see -Y[2])] > **goatˈeed** *adj*

goatfish (ˈgəʊtˌfɪʃ) *n, pl* **-fish** *or* **-fishes** the US name for the **red mullet**

goatherd (ˈgəʊtˌhɜːd) *n* a person employed to tend or herd goats

goatish (ˈgəʊtɪʃ) *adj* **1** of, like, or relating to a goat **2** *archaic or literary* lustful or lecherous > **ˈgoatishly** *adv* > **ˈgoatishness** *n*

goat moth *n* a large European moth, *Cossus cossus*, with pale brownish-grey variably marked wings: family *Cossidae*

goatsbeard *or* **goat's-beard** (ˈgəʊtsˌbɪəd) *n* **1** Also called: **Jack-go-to-bed-at-noon** a Eurasian plant, *Tragopogon pratensis*, with woolly stems and large heads of yellow rayed flowers surrounded by large green bracts: family *Asteraceae* (composites) **2** an American rosaceous plant, *Aruncus sylvester*, with long spikes of small white flowers

goatskin (ˈgəʊtˌskɪn) *n* **1** the hide of a goat **2** **a** something made from the hide of a goat, such as leather or a container for wine **b** (*as modifier*): *a goatskin rug*

goat's-rue *n* **1** Also called: **French lilac** a Eurasian leguminous plant, *Galega officinalis*, cultivated for its white, mauve, or pinkish flowers: formerly used medicinally **2** a North American leguminous plant, *Tephrosia virginiana*, with pink-and-yellow flowers

goatsucker (ˈgəʊtˌsʌkə) *n* *US and Canadian* any nocturnal bird of the family *Caprimulgidae*, esp *Caprimulgus europaeus* (**European nightjar**): order *Caprimulgiformes*. Also called (in Britain and certain other countries): **nightjar**

go away *vb* (*intr, adverb*) to leave, as when starting from home on holiday

go-away bird *n* *South African* a common name for a grey-plumaged **lourie** of the genus *Corythaixoides* [C19 imitative of its call]

g

gob[1] (gɒb) *n* **1** a lump or chunk, esp of a soft substance **2** (*often plural*) *informal* a great quantity or amount **3** *mining* **a** waste material such as clay, shale, etc **b** a worked-out area in a mine often packed with this **4** a lump of molten glass used to make a piece of glassware **5** *informal* a globule of spittle or saliva ▷ *vb* **gobs, gobbing, gobbed 6** (*intr*) *Brit informal* to spit [C14 from Old French *gobe* lump, from *gober* to gulp down; see GOBBET]

gob[2] (gɒb) *n US slang* an enlisted ordinary seaman in the US Navy [C20 of unknown origin]

gob[3] (gɒb) *n* a slang word (esp *Brit*) for the **mouth** [C16 perhaps from Gaelic *gob*]

go back *vb* (*intr, adverb*) **1** to return **2** (*often foll by to*) to originate (in): *the links with France go back to the Norman Conquest* **3** (*foll by on*) to change one's mind about; repudiate (esp in the phrase **go back on one's word**) **4** (of clocks and watches) to be set to an earlier time, as during British Summer Time: *when do the clocks go back this year?*

gobbet (ˈgɒbɪt) *n* a chunk, lump, or fragment, esp of raw meat [C14 from Old French *gobet*, from *gober* to gulp down]

gobble[1] (ˈgɒbᵊl) *vb* **1** (when *tr*, often foll by *up*) to eat or swallow (food) hastily and in large mouthfuls **2** (*tr*; often foll by *up*) *informal* to snatch [C17 probably from GOB[1]]

gobble[2] (ˈgɒbᵊl) *n* **1** the loud rapid gurgling sound made by male turkeys ▷ *interj* **2** an imitation of this sound ▷ *vb* **3** (*intr*) (of a turkey) to make this sound [C17 probably of imitative origin]

gobbledegook *or* **gobbledygook** (ˈgɒbᵊldɪˌguːk) *n* pretentious or unintelligible jargon, such as that used by officials [C20 whimsical formation from GOBBLE[2]]

gobbler (ˈgɒblə) *n informal* a male turkey

gobby (ˈgɒbɪ) *adj* -**bier**, -**biest** *informal* loudmouthed and offensive

Gobelin (ˈgəʊbᵊlɪn; *French* gɔblɛ̃) *adj* **1** of or resembling tapestry made at the Gobelins' factory in Paris, having vivid pictorial scenes ▷ *n* **2** a tapestry of this kind [C19 from the *Gobelin* family, who founded the factory]

go-between *n* a person who acts as agent or intermediary for two people or groups in a transaction or dealing

Gobi (ˈgəʊbɪ) *n* a desert in E Asia, mostly in Mongolia and the Inner Mongolian Autonomous Region of China: sometimes considered to include all the arid regions east of the Pamirs and north of the plateau of Tibet and the Great Wall of China: one of the largest deserts in the world. Length: about 1600 km (1000 miles). Width: about 1000 km (625 miles). Average height: 900 m (3000 ft). Chinese name: **Shamo**

Gobian (ˈgəʊbɪən) *adj* of or relating to the Gobi desert

gobioid (ˈgəʊbɪˌɔɪd) *adj* **1** of or relating to the *Gobioidea*, a suborder of spiny-finned teleost fishes that includes gobies and mudskippers (family *Gobiidae*) and sleepers (family *Eleotridae*) ▷ *n* **2** any gobioid fish [C19 from New Latin *Gobioidea*, from Latin *gōbius* gudgeon]

goblet (ˈgɒblɪt) *n* **1** a vessel for drinking, usually of glass or metal, with a base and stem but without handles **2** *archaic* a large drinking cup shaped like a bowl [C14 from Old French *gobelet* a little cup, from *gobel* ultimately of Celtic origin]

goblin (ˈgɒblɪn) *n* (in folklore) a small grotesque supernatural creature, regarded as malevolent towards human beings [C14 from Old French, from Middle High German *kobolt*; compare COBALT]

gobo (ˈgəʊbəʊ) *n, pl* -**bos** *or* -**boes 1** a shield placed around a microphone to exclude unwanted sounds **2** a black screen placed around a camera lens, television lens, etc, to reduce the incident light [C20 of unknown origin]

gobshite (ˈgɒbʃaɪt) *n slang* a stupid person [C20 from GOB[3] + *shite* excrement; see SHIT]

▶ **USAGE** This word was formerly considered to be taboo, and it was labelled as such in previous editions of *Collins English Dictionary*. However, it has now become acceptable in speech, although some older or more conservative people may object to its use

gobsmacked (ˈgɒbˌsmækt) *adj Brit slang* astounded; astonished [C20 from GOB[3] + SMACK[2]]

gobstopper (ˈgɒbˌstɒpə) *n Brit* a large hard sweet consisting of different coloured concentric layers that are revealed as it is sucked

goby (ˈgəʊbɪ) *n, pl* -**by** *or* -**bies 1** any small spiny-finned fish of the family *Gobiidae*, of coastal or brackish waters, having a large head, an elongated tapering body, and the ventral fins modified as a sucker **2** any other gobioid fish [C18 from Latin *gōbius* gudgeon, fish of little value, from Greek *kōbios*]

go-by *n slang* a deliberate snub or slight (esp in the phrase **give** (**a person**) **the go-by**)

go by *vb* (*intr*) **1** to pass: *the cars went by; as the years go by we all get older; don't let those opportunities go by!* **2** (*preposition*) to be guided by: *in the darkness we could only go by the stars* **3** (*preposition*) to use as a basis for forming an opinion or judgment: *it's wise not to go only by appearances*

go-cart *n* **1** *chiefly US and Canadian* a small wagon for young children to ride in or pull **2** *chiefly US and Canadian* a light frame on casters or wheels that supports a baby learning to walk. *Brit* word: **baby-walker 3** *motor racing* See **kart 4** another word for **handcart**

GOC(-in-C) *abbreviation for* General Officer Commanding(-in-Chief)

god (gɒd) *n* **1** a supernatural being, who is worshipped as the controller of some part of the universe or some aspect of life in the world or is the personification of some force. Related adj: **divine 2** an image, idol, or symbolic representation of such a deity **3** any person or thing to which excessive attention is given: *money was his god* **4** a man who has qualities regarded as making him superior to other men **5** (*in plural*) the gallery of a theatre [Old English *god*; related to Old Norse *goth*, Old High German *got*, Old Irish *guth* voice]

God (gɒd) *n* **1** *theol* the sole Supreme Being, eternal, spiritual, and transcendent, who is the Creator and ruler of all and is infinite in all attributes; the object of worship in monotheistic religions **2 play God** to behave in an imperious or superior manner ▷ *interj* **3** an oath or exclamation used to indicate surprise, annoyance, etc (and in such expressions as **My God!** or **God Almighty!**)

Godavari (gəʊˈdɑːvərɪ) *n* a river in central India, rising in the Western Ghats and flowing southeast to the Bay of Bengal: extensive delta, linked by canal with the Krishna delta; a sacred river to Hindus. Length: about 1500 km (900 miles)

God-botherer (ˈgɒdˌbɒðərə) *n informal* an over-zealous Christian

godchild (ˈgɒdˌtʃaɪld) *n, pl* -**children** (-ˌtʃɪldrən) a person, usually an infant, who is sponsored by adults at baptism

goddamn (ˈgɒdˈdæm) *informal, chiefly US and Canadian* ▷ *interj also* **God damn 1** an oath expressing anger, surprise, etc ▷ *adv also* **goddam** ▷ *adj also* **goddam** *or* **goddamned 2** (intensifier): *a goddamn fool*

goddaughter (ˈgɒdˌdɔːtə) *n* a female godchild

goddess (ˈgɒdɪs) *n* **1** a female divinity **2** a woman who is adored or idealized, esp by a man ▷ **ˈgoddess,hood** *or* **ˈgoddess-,ship** *n*

Gödel's proof (ˈgɜːdᵊl) *n* a proof that in a formal axiomatic system such as logic or mathematics it is possible to prove consistency without using methods from outside the system, demonstrated by Kurt Gödel (1906–78)

Godesberg (*German* ˈgoːdəsbɛrk) *n* a town and spa in W Germany, in North Rhine-Westphalia on the Rhine: a SE suburb of Bonn. Official name: **Bad Godesberg**

godet (ˈgəʊdeɪ, gəʊˈdɛt) *n* a triangular piece of material inserted into a garment, such as into a skirt to create a flare [C19 from French]

godetia (gəʊˈdiːʃə) *n* any plant of the American onagraceous genus *Godetia*, esp one grown as a showy-flowered annual garden plant [C19 named after C. H. *Godet* (died 1879), Swiss botanist]

godfather (ˈgɒdˌfɑːðə) *n* **1** a male godparent **2** the head of a Mafia family or other organized criminal ring **3** an originator or leading exponent: *the godfather of South African pop*

godfather offer *n informal* a takeover bid pitched so high that the management of the target company is unable to dissuade shareholders from accepting it [C20 from the 1972 film *The Godfather*, in which a character was made an offer he could not refuse by a threatening mafioso]

God-fearing *adj* pious; devout: *a God-fearing people*

godforsaken (ˈgɒdfəˌseɪkən, ˌgɒdfəˈseɪkən) *adj* (*sometimes capital*) **1** (*usually prenominal*) desolate; dreary; forlorn **2** wicked

Godhead (ˈgɒdˌhɛd) *n* (*sometimes not capital*) **1** the essential nature and condition of being God **2 the Godhead** God

godhood (ˈgɒdˌhʊd) *n* the state of being divine

godless (ˈgɒdlɪs) *adj* **1** wicked or unprincipled **2** lacking a god **3** refusing to acknowledge God ▷ **ˈgodlessly** *adv* ▷ **ˈgodlessness** *n*

godlike (ˈgɒdˌlaɪk) *adj* resembling or befitting a god or God; divine

godly (ˈgɒdlɪ) *adj* -**lier**, -**liest** having a religious character; pious; devout: *a godly man* ▷ **ˈgodliness** *n*

God man *n* a person, such as Jesus Christ, who unites humanity with God

godmother (ˈgɒdˌmʌðə) *n* a female godparent

godown (ˈgɒdˌdaʊn) *n* (in East Asia and India) a warehouse [C16 from Malay *godong*]

go down *vb* (*intr, mainly adverb*) **1** (*also preposition*) to move or lead to or as if to a lower place or level; sink, decline, decrease, etc: *the sun went down this morning; prices are going down; the path goes down to the sea* **2** to be defeated; lose **3** to be remembered or recorded (esp in the phrase **go down in history**) **4** to be received: *his speech went down well* **5** (of food) to be swallowed **6** *bridge* to fail to make the number of tricks previously contracted for **7** *Brit* to leave a college or university at the end of a term or the academic year **8** (*usually foll by with*) to fall ill; be infected **9** (of a celestial body) to sink or set: *the sun went down before we arrived* **10** *Brit slang* to go to prison, esp for a specified period: *he went down for six months* **11** *slang, chiefly US* to happen

godparent (ˈgɒdˌpɛərənt) *n* a person who stands sponsor to another at baptism

God particle *n* an informal name for **Higgs boson**

godroon (gəˈdruːn) *n* a variant spelling of **gadroon**. ▷ **goˈdrooned** *adj*

God's acre *n literary* a churchyard or burial ground [C17 translation of German *Gottesacker*]

godsend (ˈgɒdˌsɛnd) *n* a person or thing that comes unexpectedly but is particularly welcome [C19 changed from C17 *God's send*, alteration of *goddes sand* God's message, from Old English *sand*; see SEND[1]]

godslot (ˈgɒdˌslɒt) *n informal* a time in a television or radio schedule traditionally reserved for religious broadcasts

godson (ˈgɒdˌsʌn) *n* a male godchild

Godspeed (ˈgɒdˈspiːd) *interj, n* an expression of one's good wishes for a person's success and safety [C15 from *God spede* may God prosper (you)]

godsquad (ˈgɒdˌskwɒd) *n informal, derogatory* any group of evangelical Christians, members of which are regarded as intrusive and exuberantly pious

Godthaab *or* **Godthåb** (ˈgɒdhɔːb) *n* the Danish and former official name for **Nuuk**

Godwin-Austen *n* another name for **K2**

godwit (ˈgɒdwɪt) *n* any large shore bird of the genus *Limosa*, of northern and arctic regions, having long legs and a long upturned bill: family

Scolopacidae (sandpipers, etc), order *Charadriiformes* [C16 of unknown origin]

Godzone (ˈgɒdzəʊn) *n Austral informal* one's home country [from *God's own country*]

goer (ˈgəʊə) *n* **1 a** a person who attends something regularly **b** (*in combination*): *filmgoer* **2** an energetic person **3** *informal* an acceptable or feasible idea, proposal, etc **4** *Austral and NZ informal* a person trying to succeed

goethite *or* **göthite** (ˈgəʊθaɪt; *German* ˈgøːtiːt) *n* a black, brown, or yellow mineral consisting of hydrated iron oxide in the form of orthorhombic crystals or fibrous masses. Formula: FeO(OH) [C19 named after Johann Wolfgang von *Goethe* (1749–1832), German poet, novelist, and dramatist]

go-faster stripe *n informal* a decorative line, often suggestive of high speed, on the bodywork of a car

gofer (ˈgəʊfə) *n slang, chiefly US and Canadian* an employee or assistant whose duties include menial tasks such as running errands [C20 originally US: alteration of *go for*]

goffer *or* **gauffer** (ˈgəʊfə) *vb* (*tr*) **1** to press pleats into (a frill) **2** to decorate (the gilt edges of a book) with a repeating pattern ▷ *n* **3** an ornamental frill made by pressing pleats **4** the decoration formed by goffering books **5** the iron or tool used in making goffers [C18 from French *gaufrer* to impress a pattern, from *gaufre*, from Middle Low German *wāfel*; see WAFFLE[1], WAFER]

go for *vb* (*intr, preposition*) **1** to go somewhere in order to have or fetch: *he went for a drink; shall I go for a doctor?* **2** to seek to obtain: *I'd go for that job if I were you* **3** to apply to: *what I told him goes for you too* **4** to prefer or choose; like: *I really go for that new idea of yours* **5** to be to the advantage of: *you'll have great things going for you in the New Year* **6** to make a physical or verbal attack on **7** to be considered to be of a stated importance or value: *his twenty years went for nothing when he was made redundant* **8 go for it** *informal* to make the maximum effort to achieve a particular goal

go forth *vb* (*intr, adverb*) *archaic or formal* **1** to be issued: *the command went forth that taxes should be collected* **2** to go out: *the army went forth to battle*

Gog and Magog (gɒg, ˈmeɪgɒg) *n* **1** *Old Testament* a hostile prince and the land from which he comes to attack Israel (Ezekiel 38) **2** *New Testament* two kings, who are to attack the Church in a climactic battle, but are then to be destroyed by God (Revelation 20:8–10) **3** *Brit folklore* two giants, the only survivors of a race of giants destroyed by Brutus, the legendary founder of Britain

go-getter *n informal* an ambitious enterprising person > ˈ**go-ˌgetting** *adj*

gogga (ˈxɒxə) *n South African informal* any small animal that crawls or flies, esp an insect [C20 from Khoikhoi *xoxon* insects collectively]

goggle (ˈgɒgᵊl) *vb* **1** (*intr*) to stare stupidly or fixedly, as in astonishment **2** to cause (the eyes) to roll or bulge or (of the eyes) to roll or bulge ▷ *n* **3** a fixed or bulging stare **4** (*plural*) spectacles, often of coloured glass or covered with gauze: used to protect the eyes [C14 from *gogelen* to look aside, of uncertain origin; see AGOG] > ˈ**goggly** *adj*

gogglebox (ˈgɒgᵊlˌbɒks) *n Brit slang* a television set

goggle-eyed *adj* (*often postpositive*) with a surprised, staring, or fixed expression

goglet (ˈgɒglɪt) *or* **gurglet** *n* a long-necked water-cooling vessel of porous earthenware, used esp in India. Also called: **guglet** (ˈgʌglɪt) [C17 from Portuguese *gorgoleta* a little throat, from *gorja* throat; related to French *gargoule*; see GARGLE]

go-go *adj informal, chiefly US and Canadian* **1** of or relating to discos or the lively music and dancing performed in them **2** dynamic or forceful [C20 altered from French *à-gogo* aplenty, ad lib: sense influenced by English verb *go*]

go-go dancer *n* a dancer, usually scantily dressed, who performs rhythmic and often erotic modern dance routines, esp in a nightclub

Gogolian (ˌgəʊˈgɒlɪən) *adj* of, relating to, or like the Russian writer Gogol (1809–52) or his works

Gogra (ˈgɒgrə) *n* a river in N India, rising in Tibet, in the Himalayas, and flowing southeast through Nepal as the Karnali, then through Uttar Pradesh to join the Ganges. Length: about 1000 km (600 miles)

gohonzon (gəʊˈhɒnzɒn) *n* (in Nichiren Buddhism) the paper scroll to which devotional chanting is directed [from Japanese *go* an honorific prefix + *honzon* object of respect]

Goiânia (gɔɪˈɑːnɪə; *Portuguese* goˈjənja) *n* a city in central Brazil, capital of Goiás state: planned in 1933 to replace the old capital, Goiás; two universities. Pop: 1 878 000 (2005 est)

Goiás (*Portuguese* gɔˈjas) *n* a state of central Brazil, in the Brazilian Highlands: contains Brasília, the capital of Brazil. Capital: Goiânia. Pop: 5 210 335 (2002). Area: 341 289 sq km (131 772 sq miles)

Goidel (ˈgɔɪdᵊl) *n* a Celt who speaks a Goidelic language; Gael. Compare **Brython**

Goidelic, Goidhelic (gɔɪˈdɛlɪk) *or* **Gadhelic** *n* **1** the N group of Celtic languages, consisting of Irish Gaelic, Scottish Gaelic, and Manx. Compare **Brythonic** ▷ *adj* **2** of, relating to, or characteristic of this group of languages [C19 from Old Irish *Goidel* a Celt, from Old Welsh *gwyddel*, from *gwydd* savage]

go in *vb* (*intr, mainly adverb*) **1** to enter **2** (*preposition*) See **go into 3** (of the sun) to become hidden behind a cloud **4** to be assimilated or grasped: *nothing much goes in if I try to read in the evenings* **5** *cricket* to begin an innings **6 go in for a** to enter as a competitor or contestant **b** to adopt as an activity, interest, or guiding principle: *she went in for nursing; some men go in for football in a big way*

going (ˈgəʊɪŋ) *n* **1** a departure or farewell **2** the condition of a surface such as a road or field with regard to walking, riding, etc: *muddy going* **3** *informal* speed, progress, etc: *we made good going on the trip* ▷ *adj* **4** thriving (esp in the phrase **a going concern**) **5** current or accepted, as from past negotiations or commercial operation: *the going rate for electricians; the going value of the firm* **6** (*postpositive*) available: *the best going* **7 going, going, gone!** a statement by an auctioneer that the bidding has finished

going-over *n, pl* **goings-over** *informal* **1** a check, examination, or investigation **2** a castigation or thrashing

goings-on *pl n informal* **1** actions or conduct, esp when regarded with disapproval **2** happenings or events, esp when mysterious or suspicious: *there were strange goings-on up at the Hall*

go into *vb* (*intr, preposition*) **1** to enter **2** to start a career in: *to go into publishing* **3** to investigate or examine: *to go into the problem of price increases* **4** to discuss: *we won't go into that now* **5** to dress oneself differently in: *to go into mourning* **6** to hit: *the car had gone into a lamppost* **7** to go to live in or be admitted to, esp temporarily: *she went into hospital on Tuesday* **8** to enter a specified state: *she went into fits of laughter*

goitre *or US* **goiter** (ˈgɔɪtə) *n pathol* a swelling of the thyroid gland, in some cases nearly doubling the size of the neck, usually caused by under- or overproduction of hormone by the gland [C17 from French *goitre*, from Old French *goitron*, ultimately from Latin *guttur* throat] > ˈ**goitred** *or US* ˈ**goitered** *adj* > ˈ**goitrous** *adj*

go-juice *n informal* fuel for an engine, esp petrol

go-kart *or* **go-cart** *n* See **kart**

Golan Heights (ˈgəʊˌlæn) *pl n* a range of hills in the Middle East, possession of which is disputed between Israel and Syria: under Syrian control until 1967 when they were stormed by Israeli forces; Jewish settlements have since been established. Highest peak: 2224 m (7297 ft)

Golconda (gɒlˈkɒndə) *n* **1** a ruined town and fortress in S central India, in W Andhra Pradesh near Hyderabad city: capital of one of the five Muslim kingdoms of the Deccan from 1512 to 1687, then annexed to the Mogul empire; renowned for its diamonds **2** (*sometimes not capital*) a source of wealth or riches, esp a mine

gold (gəʊld) *n* **1 a** a dense inert bright yellow element that is the most malleable and ductile metal, occurring in rocks and alluvial deposits: used as a monetary standard and in jewellery, dentistry, and plating. The radioisotope gold-198 (**radiogold**), with a half-life of 2.69 days, is used in radiotherapy. Symbol: Au; atomic no.: 79; atomic wt.: 196.96654; valency: 1 or 3; relative density: 19.3; melting pt.: 1064.43°C; boiling pt.: 2857°C. Related adjs: **aurous, auric b** (*as modifier*): *a gold mine* **2** a coin or coins made of this metal **3** money; wealth **4** something precious, beautiful, etc, such as a noble nature (esp in the phrase **heart of gold**) **5 a** a deep yellow colour, sometimes with a brownish tinge **b** (*as adjective*): *a gold carpet* **6** *archery* the bull's eye of a target, scoring nine points **7** short for **gold medal** [Old English *gold*; related to Old Norse *gull*, Gothic *gulth*, Old High German *gold*]

goldarn (gɒlˈdɑːn) *interj, adv US and Canadian slang* a euphemistic variant of **goddamn**

Goldbach's conjecture (ˈgəʊldˌbɑːxs) *n* the conjecture that every even number greater than two is the sum of two prime numbers [named after C. *Goldbach* (1690–1764), German mathematician]

gold basis *n* the gold standard as a criterion for the determination of prices

goldbeater's skin (ˈgəʊldˌbiːtəz) *n* animal membrane used to separate sheets of gold that are being hammered into gold leaf

gold-beating *n* the act, process, or skill of hammering sheets of gold into gold leaf > ˈ**gold-ˌbeater** *n*

gold beetle *or* **goldbug** (ˈgəʊldˌbʌg) *n* any American beetle of the family *Chrysomelidae* having a bright metallic lustre

gold brick *n* **1** something with only a superficial appearance of value **2** *US slang* an idler or shirker

gold card *n* a credit card issued by credit-card companies to favoured clients, entitling them to high unsecured overdrafts, some insurance cover, etc

gold certificate *n* (in the US) **1** a currency note issued exclusively to the Federal Reserve Banks by the US Treasury. It forms a claim on gold reserves deposited by the Federal Reserve Banks at the Treasury and is used to transfer interbank balances within the Federal Reserve System **2** Also called: **gold note** (formerly) a banknote issued by the US Treasury to the public and redeemable in gold

Gold Coast *n* **1** the former name (until 1957) of **Ghana 2** a line of resort towns and beaches in E Australia, extending for over 30 km (20 miles) along the SE coast of Queensland and the NE coast of New South Wales

goldcrest (ˈgəʊldˌkrɛst) *n* a small Old World warbler, *Regulus regulus*, having a greenish plumage and a bright yellow-and-black crown

gold-digger *n* **1** a person who prospects or digs for gold **2** *informal* a woman who uses her sexual attractions to accumulate gifts and wealth or advance her social position > ˈ**gold-ˌdigging** *n*

gold disc *n* **a** (in Britain) an LP record certified to have sold 250 000 copies or a single certified to have sold 500 000 copies **b** (in the US) an LP record or single certified to have sold 1 000 000 copies or a single certified to have sold 500 000 copies. Compare **silver disc, platinum disc**

gold dust *n* **1** gold in the form of small particles or powder, as found in placer-mining **2** a valuable or rare thing: *tickets for this match are gold dust*

golden (ˈgəʊldən) *adj* **1** of the yellowish or brownish-yellow metallic colour of gold: *golden hair* **2** made from or largely consisting of gold: *a golden statue* **3** happy or prosperous: *golden days* **4** (*sometimes capital*) (of anniversaries) the 50th in a series: *Golden Jubilee; golden wedding* **5** *informal* very successful or destined for success: *the golden girl of tennis* **6** extremely valuable or advantageous: *a golden opportunity* > **'goldenly** *adv* > **'goldenness** *n*

golden age *n* **1** *classical myth* the first and best age of mankind, when existence was happy, prosperous, and innocent **2** the most flourishing and outstanding period, esp in the history of an art or nation: *the golden age of poetry* **3** the great classical period of Latin literature, occupying approximately the 1st century BC and represented by such writers as Cicero and Virgil

golden aster *n* any North American plant of the genus *Chrysopsis,* esp *C. mariana* of the eastern US, having yellow rayed flowers: family *Asteraceae* (composites)

golden calf *n* **1** *Old Testament* **a** an idol made by Aaron and set up for the Israelites to worship (Exodus 32) **b** either of two similar idols set up by Jeroboam I at Dan and Bethel in the northern kingdom (I Kings 12:28–30) **2** *informal* the pursuit or idolization of material wealth

golden chain *n* another name for **laburnum**

Golden Delicious *n* a variety of eating apple having sweet flesh and greenish-yellow skin

golden eagle *n* a large eagle, *Aquila chrysaetos,* of mountainous regions of the N hemisphere, having a plumage that is golden brown on the back and brown elsewhere

goldeneye (ˈɡəʊldənˌaɪ) *n, pl* **-eyes** or **-eye** **1** either of two black-and-white diving ducks, *Bucephala clangula* or *B. islandica,* of northern regions **2** any lacewing of the family *Chrysopidae* that has a greenish body and eyes of a metallic lustre

Golden Fleece *n Greek myth* the fleece of a winged ram that rescued Phrixus and brought him to Colchis, where he sacrificed it to Zeus. Phrixus gave the fleece to King Aeëtes who kept it in a sacred grove, whence Jason and the Argonauts stole it with the help of Aeëtes' daughter. See also **Phrixus**

Golden Gate *n* a strait between the Pacific and San Francisco Bay: crossed by the **Golden Gate Bridge**, with a central span of 1280 m (4200 ft)

golden goal *n* *soccer* (in certain matches) the first goal scored in extra time, which wins the match for the side scoring it

golden goose *n* a goose in folklore that laid a golden egg a day until its greedy owner killed it in an attempt to get all the gold at once

golden handcuffs *pl n* *informal* payments deferred over a number of years that induce a person to stay with a particular company or in a particular job

golden handshake *n* *informal* a sum of money, usually large, given to an employee, either on retirement in recognition of long or excellent service or as compensation for loss of employment

Goldenhar's syndrome (ˈɡəʊldənˌhaːz) *n* a congenital disorder in which one side of the face is malformed, often with an enlargement of one side of the mouth. There may also be hearing loss, curvature of the spine, and mild retardation. Technical name **oculoauriculovertebral displasia** [c20 named after Maurice *Goldenhar,* Swiss physician]

golden hello *n* *informal* a payment made to a sought-after recruit on signing a contract of employment with a company

Golden Horde *n* the Mongol horde that devastated E Europe in the early 13th century. It established the westernmost Mongol khanate, which at its height ruled most of European Russia. Defeated by the power of Muscovy (1380), the realm split into four smaller khanates in 1405

Golden Horn *n* an inlet of the Bosporus in NW Turkey, forming the harbour of Istanbul. Turkish name: **Haliç**

golden hour *n* the first hour after a serious accident, when it is crucial that the victim receives medical treatment in order to have a chance of surviving

golden mean *n* **1** the middle course between extremes **2** another term for **golden section**

golden number *n* a number between 1 and 19, used to indicate the position of any year in the Metonic cycle, calculated as the remainder when 1 is added to the given year and the sum is divided by 19. If the remainder is zero the number is 19: *the golden number of 1984 is 9*

golden oldie *n* something old or long-established, esp a hit record or song that has remained popular or is enjoying a revival. Also called: **oldie**

golden oriole *n* a European oriole, *Oriolus oriolus,* the male of which has a bright yellow head and body with black wings and tail

golden parachute *n* *informal* a clause in the employment contract of a senior executive providing for special benefits if the executive's employment is terminated as a result of a takeover

golden perch *n* another name for **callop**

golden pheasant *n* a brightly coloured pheasant, *Chrysolophus pictus,* of the mountainous regions of W and central Asia, the males of which have a crest and ruff

golden plover *n* any of several plovers of the genus *Pluvialis,* such as *P. apricaria* of Europe and Asia, that have golden brown back, head, and wings

golden ratio *n* the ratio of two lengths, equal in value to $(1 + \sqrt{5})/2$, and given by $b/a = (b + a)/b$; it is the reciprocal of the **golden section** and also equal to (1 + golden section). Symbol: Φ

golden retriever *n* a compact large breed of dog having a silky coat of flat or wavy hair of a gold or dark-cream colour, well-feathered on the legs and tail

goldenrod (ˌɡəʊldənˈrɒd) *n* **1** any plant of the genus *Solidago,* of North America, Europe, and Asia, having spikes made up of inflorescences of minute yellow florets: family *Asteraceae* (composites). See also **yellowweed** **2** any of various similar related plants, such as *Brachychaeta sphacelata* (**false goldenrod**) of the southern US

golden rule *n* **1** any of a number of rules of fair conduct, such as *Whatsoever ye would that men should do to you, do ye even so to them* (Matthew 7:12) or *thou shalt love thy neighbour as thyself* (Leviticus 19:28) **2** any important principle: *a golden rule of sailing is to wear a life jacket* **3** *Brit* the principle adopted by Chancellor of the Exchequer Gordon Brown (in office from 1997) that a government should only borrow to invest **4** another name for **rule of three**

goldenseal (ˌɡəʊldənˈsiːl) *n* a ranunculaceous woodland plant, *Hydrastis canadensis,* of E North America, whose thick yellow rootstock contains such alkaloids as berberine and hydrastine and was formerly used medicinally

golden section *or* **mean** *n* the proportion of the two divisions of a straight line or the two dimensions of a plane figure such that the smaller is to the larger as the larger is to the sum of the two. If the sides of a rectangle are in this proportion and a square is constructed internally on the shorter side, the rectangle that remains will also have sides in the same proportion. Compare **golden ratio**

golden share *n* a share in a company that controls at least 51% of the voting rights, esp one retained by the UK government in some privatization issues

Golden Spaniard *n* another name for **taramea** Also called: **golden speargrass**

Golden Starfish *n* an award given to a bathing beach that meets EU standards of cleanliness

golden syrup *n Brit* a light golden-coloured treacle produced by the evaporation of cane sugar juice, used to sweeten and flavour cakes, puddings, etc

golden triangle *n* **the** an opium-producing area of SE Asia, comprising parts of Myanmar, Laos, and Thailand **2** any more or less triangular area

or region noted for its success, prosperity, influence, etc **3** *maths* a triangle which has two 72-degree angles and one 36-degree angle

golden wattle *n* **1** an Australian yellow-flowered leguminous plant, *Acacia pycnantha,* that yields a useful gum and bark **2** any of several similar and related plants, esp *Acacia longifolia* of Australia

gold-exchange standard *n* a monetary system by which one country's currency, which is not itself based on the gold standard, is kept at a par with another currency that is based on the gold standard

goldeye (ˈɡəʊldˌaɪ) *n, pl* **-eyes** or **-eye** a North American clupeoid fish, *Hiodon alosoides,* with yellowish eyes, silvery sides, and a dark blue back: family *Hiodontidae* (mooneyes)

goldfinch (ˈɡəʊldˌfɪntʃ) *n* **1** a common European finch, *Carduelis carduelis,* the adult of which has a red-and-white face and yellow-and-black wings **2** any of several North American finches of the genus *Spinus,* esp the yellow-and-black species *S. tristis*

goldfinny (ˈɡəʊldˌfɪnɪ) *n, pl* **-nies** another name for **goldsinny**

goldfish (ˈɡəʊldˌfɪʃ) *n, pl* **-fish** or **-fishes** **1** a freshwater cyprinid fish, *Carassius auratus,* of E Europe and Asia, esp China, widely introduced as a pond or aquarium fish. It resembles the carp and has a typically golden or orange-red coloration **2** any of certain similar ornamental fishes, esp the golden orfe (see **orfe**)

goldfish bowl *n* Also called: **fishbowl** a glass bowl, typically spherical, in which fish are kept as pets **2** a place or situation open to observation by onlookers

gold foil *n* thin gold sheet that is thicker than gold leaf

goldilocks (ˈɡəʊldɪˌlɒks) *n* (*functioning as singular*) **1** a Eurasian plant, *Aster linosyris* (or *Linosyris vulgaris*), with clusters of small yellow flowers: family *Asteraceae* (composites) **2** a Eurasian ranunculaceous woodland plant, *Ranunculus auricomus,* with yellow flowers. See also **buttercup** **3** (*sometimes capital*) a person, esp a girl, with light blond hair **4** (*modifier; sometimes capital*) not prone to extremes of temperature, volatility, etc: *a goldilocks planet; a goldilocks economy* [(for sense 4): c20 from the fairy tale *Goldilocks and the Three Bears,* in which the heroine prefers the porridge that is neither too hot nor too cold]

gold leaf *n* very thin gold sheet with a thickness usually between 0.076 and 0.127 micrometre, produced by rolling or hammering gold and used for gilding woodwork, etc

gold medal *n* a medal of gold, awarded to the winner of a competition or race. Compare **silver medal, bronze medal**

gold mine *n* **1** a place where gold ore is mined **2** a source of great wealth, profit, etc > **'gold-ˌminer** *n* > **'gold-ˌmining** *n*

gold note *n* (in the US) another name for **gold certificate**

gold-of-pleasure *n* a yellow-flowered Eurasian plant, *Camelina sativa,* widespread as a weed, esp in flax fields, and formerly cultivated for its oil-rich seeds: family *Brassicaceae* (crucifers)

gold-plate *vb* (*tr*) to coat (other metal) with gold, usually by electroplating

gold plate *n* **1** a thin coating of gold, usually produced by electroplating **2** vessels or utensils made of gold

gold point *n* *finance* either of two exchange rates (the **gold export point** and the **gold import point**) at which it is as cheap to settle international accounts by exporting or importing gold bullion as by selling or buying bills of exchange. Also called: **specie point**

gold record *n* a former name for **gold disc**

gold reserve *n* the gold reserved by a central bank to support domestic credit expansion, to cover balance of payments deficits, and to protect currency

gold rush n a large-scale migration of people to a territory where gold has been found

goldsinny ('gəʊld,sɪnɪ) n, pl -nies any of various small European wrasses, esp the brightly coloured *Ctenolabrus rupestris*. Also called: goldfinny [origin obscure, but probably has reference to the colour of the fins and tail]

goldsmith ('gəʊld,smɪθ) n 1 a a dealer in articles made of gold b an artisan who makes such articles 2 (formerly) a dealer or manufacturer of gold articles who also engaged in banking or other financial business 3 (in Malaysia) a Chinese jeweller

goldsmith beetle n any of various scarabaeid beetles that have a metallic golden lustre, esp the rose chafer

gold standard n 1 a monetary system in which the unit of currency is defined with reference to gold 2 the supreme example of something against which others are judged or measured: *the current gold standard for breast cancer detection*

Gold Stick n (sometimes not capitals) 1 a gilt rod carried by the colonel of the Life Guards or the captain of the gentlemen-at-arms 2 the bearer of this rod

goldstone ('gəʊld,stəʊn) n another name for **aventurine** (senses 2, 3)

goldtail moth ('gəʊld,teɪl) n a European moth, *Euproctis chrysorrhoea* (or *similis*), having white wings and a soft white furry body with a yellow tail tuft: its hairy caterpillars are known as palmer worms: family *Lymantriidae*. Also called: yellowtail, yellowtail moth

goldthread ('gəʊld,θrɛd) n 1 a North American woodland ranunculaceous plant, *Coptis trifolia* (or *C. groenlandica*), with slender yellow roots 2 the root of this plant, which yields a medicinal tonic and a dye

gold tranche n former name for **reserve tranche**

golem ('gəʊlɛm) n (in Jewish legend) an artificially created human being brought to life by supernatural means [from Yiddish *goylem*, from Hebrew *gōlem* formless thing]

golf (gɒlf) n 1 a a game played on a large open course, the object of which is to hit a ball using clubs, with as few strokes as possible, into each of usually 18 holes b (as modifier): *a golf bag* ▷ vb 2 (intr) to play golf [c15 perhaps from Middle Dutch *colf* CLUB]

Golf (gɒlf) n communications a code word for the letter g

golf ball n 1 a small resilient, usually white, ball of either two-piece or three-piece construction, the former consisting of a solid inner core with a thick covering of toughened material, the latter consisting of a liquid centre, rubber-wound core, and a thin layer of balata 2 (in some electric typewriters) a small detachable metal sphere, around the surface of which type characters are arranged

golf cart n 1 a small motorized vehicle for transporting golfers and their equipment round a golf course 2 a two-wheeled trolley with a long handle used for carrying golf clubs

golf club n 1 any of various long-shafted clubs with wood or metal heads used to strike a golf ball 2 a an association of golf players, usually having its own course and facilities b the premises of such an association

golf course n a general term for an area of ground, either inland or beside the sea, laid out for the playing of golf

golfer ('gɒlfə) n 1 a person who plays golf 2 a type of cardigan

golfer's elbow n a painful inflammation of the muscles on the inside of the forearm caused by exertion in playing golf

golf links pl n a large open undulating stretch of land beside the sea laid out for the playing of golf. See also **links**

Golgi body, apparatus or **complex** n a membranous complex of vesicles, vacuoles, and flattened sacs in the cytoplasm of most cells: involved in intracellular secretion and transport [c20 named after Camillo *Golgi* (1844–1926), Italian neurologist and histologist]

Golgotha ('gɒlgəθə) n 1 another name for **Calvary** 2 (sometimes not capital) now rare a place of burial [c17 from Late Latin, from Greek, from Aramaic, based on Hebrew *gulgōleth* skull]

goliard ('gəʊljəd) n one of a number of wandering scholars in 12th- and 13th-century Europe famed for their riotous behaviour, intemperance, and composition of satirical and ribald Latin verse [c15 from Old French *goliart* glutton, from Latin *gula* gluttony] > goliardic (gəʊl'jɑːdɪk) adj

goliardery (gəʊl'jɑːdərɪ) n the poems of the goliards

Goliath (gə'laɪəθ) n Old Testament a Philistine giant from Gath who terrorized the Hebrews until he was killed by David with a stone from his sling (I Samuel 17)

Goliathan (gə'laɪəθən) adj huge; gigantic

goliath beetle n any very large tropical scarabaeid beetle of the genus *Goliathus*, esp *G. giganteus* of Africa, which may grow to a length of 20 centimetres

goliath frog n the largest living frog, *Rana goliath*, which occurs in the Congo region of Africa and can grow to a length of 30 centimetres

golliwog or **golliwogg** ('gɒlɪ,wɒg) n a soft doll with a black face, usually made of cloth or rags [c19 from the name of a doll character in children's books by Bertha Upton (died 1912), US writer, and Florence Upton (died 1922), US illustrator]

gollop ('gɒləp) vb to eat or drink (something) quickly or greedily [dialect variant of GULP] > 'golloper n

golly[1] ('gɒlɪ) interj an exclamation of mild surprise or wonder [c19 originally a euphemism for GOD]

golly[2] ('gɒlɪ) n, pl -lies Brit informal short for **golliwog**: used chiefly by children

golly[3] ('gɒlɪ) Austral slang ▷ vb -lies, -lying, -lied 1 to spit ▷ n, pl -lies 2 a gob of spit [c20 altered from *gollion* a gob of phlegm, probably of imitative origin]

goloshes (gə'lɒʃɪz) pl n a less common spelling of **galoshes**

GOM abbreviation for Grand Old Man: used to describe an old and respected person or institution

gombeenism ('gɒmbiːnɪzəm) n Irish the practice of usury [c19 from Irish Gaelic *gaimbín* interest on a loan, from Middle English *cambie* exchange, barter, from Latin *cambium*]

gombeen-man ('gɒmbiːn,mæn) n Irish a shopkeeper who practises usury

gombroon (gɒm'bruːn) n Persian and Chinese pottery and porcelain wares [c17 named after *Gombroon*, Iran, from which it was originally exported]

Gomel (Russian 'gɔmɪlj) n an industrial city in SE Belarus, on the River Sozh; an industrial centre. Pop: 480 000 (2005 est)

gomeril ('gɒmərɪl) n Scot a slow-witted or stupid person [c19 of uncertain origin]

Gomorrah or **Gomorrha** (gə'mɒrə) n 1 Old Testament one of two ancient cities near the Dead Sea, the other being Sodom, that were destroyed by God as a punishment for the wickedness of their inhabitants (Genesis 19:24) 2 any place notorious for vice and depravity > Go'morrean or Go'morrhean adj

gomphosis (gɒm'fəʊsɪs) n, pl -ses (-siːz) anatomy a form of immovable articulation in which a peglike part fits into a cavity, as in the setting of a tooth in its socket [c16 from New Latin, from Greek *gomphoein* to bolt together, from *gomphos* tooth, peg]

gomuti or **gomuti palm** (gə'muːtɪ) n, pl gomutis or gomuti palms 1 an East Indian feather palm, *Arenga pinnata*, whose sweet sap is a source of sugar 2 a black wiry fibre obtained from the leafstalks of this plant, used for making rope, etc 3 a Malaysian sago palm, *Metroxylon sagu* [from Malay *gĕmuti*]

gon- combining form a variant of **gono-** before a vowel: *gonidium*

-gon n combining form indicating a figure having a specified number of angles: *pentagon* [from Greek *-gōnon*, from *gōnia* angle]

gonad ('gɒnæd) n an animal organ in which gametes are produced, such as a testis or an ovary 2 slang a foolish or stupid person [c19 from New Latin *gonas*, from Greek *gonos* seed] > 'gonadal, gonadial (gɒ'neɪdɪəl) or go'nadic adj

gonadotrophin (,gɒnədəʊ'trəʊfɪn) or **gonadotropin** (,gɒnədəʊ'trəʊpɪn) n any of several glycoprotein hormones secreted by the pituitary gland and placenta that stimulate the gonads and control reproductive activity. See chorionic gonadotrophin, follicle-stimulating hormone, luteinizing hormone, prolactin > ,gonado'trophic or ,gonado'tropic adj

Gonaïves (French gɔnaiv) n a port in W Haiti, on the Gulf of Gonaïves; scene of the proclamation of Haiti's independence (1804). Pop: 63 291 (1992)

Gond (gɒnd) n a member of a formerly tribal people now living in scattered enclaves throughout S central India

Gondar ('gɒndɑː) n a city in NW Ethiopia: capital of Ethiopia from the 17th century until 1868. Pop: 191 000 (2005 est)

Gondi ('gɒndɪ) n the language or group of languages spoken by the Gonds, belonging to the Dravidian family of languages

gondola ('gɒndələ) n 1 a long narrow flat-bottomed boat with a high ornamented stem and a platform at the stern where an oarsman stands and propels the boat by sculling or punting: traditionally used on the canals of Venice 2 a a car or cabin suspended from an airship or balloon b a moving cabin suspended from a cable across a valley, etc 3 a flat-bottomed barge used on canals and rivers of the US as far west as the Mississippi 4 US and Canadian a low open flat-bottomed railway goods wagon 5 a set of island shelves in a self-service shop: used for displaying goods 6 Canadian a broadcasting booth built close to the roof over an ice-hockey arena, used by commentators [c16 from Italian (Venetian dialect), from Medieval Latin *gondula*, perhaps ultimately from Greek *kondu* drinking vessel]

gondolier (,gɒndə'lɪə) n a man who propels a gondola

Gondwanaland (gɒnd'wɑːnə,lænd) or **Gondwana** n one of the two ancient supercontinents produced by the first split of the even larger supercontinent Pangaea about 200 million years ago, comprising chiefly what are now Africa, South America, Australia, Antarctica, and the Indian subcontinent [c19 from *Gondwana* region in central north India, where the rock series was originally found]

gone (gɒn) vb 1 the past participle of GO[1] ▷ adj (usually postpositive) 2 ended; past 3 lost; ruined (esp in the phrases gone goose or gosling) 4 dead or near to death 5 spent; consumed; used up 6 informal faint or weak 7 informal having been pregnant (for a specified time): *six months gone* 8 (usually foll by on) slang in love (with) 9 slang in an exhilarated state, as through music or the use of drugs 10 gone out informal blank and without comprehension, as if stupefied in surprise ▷ adv 11 past: *it's gone midnight*

goner ('gɒnə) n slang a person or thing beyond help or recovery, esp a person who is dead or about to die

gonfalon ('gɒnfələn) or **gonfanon** ('gɒnfanən) n 1 a banner hanging from a crossbar, used esp by certain medieval Italian republics or in ecclesiastical processions 2 a battle flag suspended crosswise on a staff, usually having a serrated edge to give the appearance of streamers [c16 from Old Italian *gonfalone*, from Old French

g

gonfalon, of Germanic origin; compare Old English *gūthfana* war banner, Old Norse *gunnfani*]

gonfalonier (ˌɡɒnfələˈnɪə) *n* the chief magistrate or other official of a medieval Italian republic, esp the bearer of the republic's gonfalon

gong (ɡɒŋ) *n* **1** Also called: **tam-tam** a percussion instrument of indefinite pitch, consisting of a metal platelike disc struck with a soft-headed drumstick **2** a rimmed metal disc, hollow metal hemisphere, or metal strip, tube, or wire that produces a note when struck. It may be used to give alarm signals when operated electromagnetically **3** a fixed saucer-shaped bell, as on an alarm clock, struck by a mechanically operated hammer **4** *Brit slang* a medal, esp a military one ▷ *vb* **5** (*intr*) to sound a gong **6** (*tr*) (of traffic police) to summon (a driver) to stop by sounding a gong [c17 from Malay, of imitative origin] > ˈgongˌlike *adj*

Gongorism (ˈɡɒŋɡəˌrɪzəm) *n* **1** an affected literary style characterized by intricate language and obscurity **2** an example of this [c19 from Spanish *gongorismo*; named after Luis de Góngora y Argote (1561–1627), Spanish lyric poet, noted for his exaggerated pedantic style] > **Gongorist** *n* > ˌGongoˈristic *adj*

gongyo (ˈɡɒŋjəʊ) *n* (in Nichiren Buddhism) a ceremony, performed twice a day, involving reciting parts of the Lotus Sutra and chanting the Daimoku to the Gohonzon [from Japanese, literally: assiduous practice]

goniatite (ˈɡɒnɪəˌtaɪt) *n* any extinct cephalopod mollusc of the genus *Goniatites* and related genera, similar to ammonites: a common fossil of Devonian and Carboniferous rocks [c19 from Greek *gōnia* angle, referring to the angular sutures in some species + -ITE[1]]

gonidium (ɡəˈnɪdɪəm) *n, pl* **-ia** (-ɪə) **1** a green algal cell in the thallus of a lichen **2** an asexual reproductive cell in some colonial algae [c19 from New Latin, diminutive from GONO-] > **goˈnidial** or **goˈnidic** *adj*

goniometer (ˌɡəʊnɪˈɒmɪtə) *n* **1** an instrument for measuring the angles between the faces of a crystal **2** an instrument consisting of a transformer circuit connected to two directional aerials, used to determine the bearing of a distant radio station [c18 via French from Greek *gōnia* angle] > **goniometric** (ˌɡəʊnɪəˈmɛtrɪk) or ˌgonioˈmetrical *adj* > ˌgonioˈmetrically *adv* > ˌgoniˈometry *n*

gonion (ˈɡəʊnɪən) *n, pl* **-nia** (-nɪə) *anatomy* the point or apex of the angle of the lower jaw [c19 from New Latin, from Greek *gōnia* angle]

gonioscope (ˈɡəʊnɪəʊˌskəʊp) *n* an instrument used for examining the structures of the eye between the cornea and the lens that are not directly visible

-gonium *n combining form* indicating a seed or reproductive cell: *archegonium* [from New Latin *gonium*, from Greek *gonos* seed]

gonk (ɡɒŋk) *n* a stuffed toy, often used as a mascot

gonna (ˈɡɒnə) *vb slang* ▷ *contraction of* going to

gono- or before a vowel **gon-** *combining form* sexual or reproductive: *gonorrhoea* [New Latin, from Greek *gonos* seed]

gonococcus (ˌɡɒnəʊˈkɒkəs) *n, pl* **-cocci** (-ˈkɒksaɪ) a spherical Gram-negative bacterium, *Neisseria gonorrhoeae*, that causes gonorrhoea: family *Neisseriaceae* > ˌgonoˈcoccal or ˌgonoˈcoccic *adj* > ˌgonoˈcoccoid *adj*

gonocyte (ˈɡɒnəʊˌsaɪt) *n* an oocyte or spermatocyte

gonoduct (ˈɡɒnəʊˌdʌkt) *n zoology* a duct leading from a gonad to the exterior, through which gametes pass

gonof or **gonif** (ˈɡɒnəf) *n* a variant of **ganef**

gonophore (ˈɡɒnəʊˌfɔː) *n* **1** *zoology* a polyp in certain coelenterates that bears gonads **2** *botany* an elongated structure in certain flowers that bears the stamens and pistil above the level of the

other flower parts > **gonophoric** (ˌɡɒnəʊˈfɒrɪk) or **gonophorous** (ɡəʊˈnɒfərəs) *adj*

gonopod (ˈɡɒnəʊˌpɒd) *n zoology* either member of a pair of appendages that are the external reproductive organs of insects and some other arthropods

gonopore (ˈɡɒnəˌpɔː) *n* an external pore in insects, earthworms, etc, through which the gametes are extruded

gonorrhoea or *esp US* **gonorrhea** (ˌɡɒnəˈrɪə) *n* an infectious venereal disease caused by a gonococcus, characterized by a burning sensation when urinating and a mucopurulent discharge from the urethra or vagina [c16 from Late Latin, from Greek, from *gonos* seed + *rhoia* flux, flow] > ˌgonorˈrhoeal, ˌgonorˈrhoeic or *esp US* ˌgonorˈrheal, ˌgonorˈrheic *adj*

gonosome (ˈɡɒnəʊˌsəʊm) *n zoology* the individuals, collectively, in a colonial animal that are involved with reproduction

-gony *n combining form* genesis, origin, or production: *cosmogony* [from Latin *-gonia*, from Greek, *-goneia*, from *gonos* seed, procreation]

gonzo (ˈɡɒnzəʊ) *adj slang* **1** wild or crazy **2** (of journalism) explicitly including the writer's feelings at the time of witnessing the events or undergoing the experiences written about [c20 perhaps from Italian, literally: fool, or Spanish *ganso* idiot, bumpkin (literally: goose)]

goo (ɡuː) *n informal* **1** a sticky or viscous substance **2** coy or sentimental language or ideas [c20 of uncertain origin]

goober or **goober pea** (ˈɡuːbə) *n* another name for **peanut** [c19 of African (Angolan) origin; related to Kongo *nguba*]

gooby (ˈɡuːbɪ) *n, pl* **goobies** *NZ informal* spittle

good (ɡʊd) *adj* **better, best 1** having admirable, pleasing, superior, or positive qualities; not negative, bad or mediocre: *a good idea; a good teacher* **2 a** morally excellent or admirable; virtuous; righteous: *a good man* **b** (*as collective noun; preceded by the*): *the good* **3** suitable or efficient for a purpose: *a good secretary; a good winter coat* **4** beneficial or advantageous: *vegetables are good for you* **5** not ruined or decayed; sound or whole: *the meat is still good* **6** kindly, generous, or approving: *you are good to him* **7** right or acceptable: *your qualifications are good for the job* **8** rich and fertile: *good land* **9** valid or genuine: *I would not do this without good reason* **10** honourable or held in high esteem: *a good family* **11** commercially or financially secure, sound, or safe: *good securities; a good investment* **12** (of a draft) drawn for a stated sum **13** (of debts) expected to be fully paid **14** clever, competent, or talented: *he's good at science* **15** obedient or well-behaved: *a good dog* **16** reliable, safe, or recommended: *a good make of clothes* **17** affording material pleasure or indulgence: *the good things in life; the good life* **18** having a well-proportioned, beautiful, or generally fine appearance: *a good figure; a good complexion* **19** complete; full: *I took a good look round the house* **20** propitious; opportune: *a good time to ask the manager for a rise* **21** satisfying or gratifying: *a good rest* **22** comfortable: *did you have a good night?* **23** newest or of the best quality: *to keep the good plates for important guests* **24** fairly large, extensive, or long: *a good distance away* **25** sufficient; ample: *we have a good supply of food* **26** *US* (of meat) of the third government grade, above *standard* and below *choice* **27** serious or intellectual: *good music* **28** used in a traditional description: *the good ship "America"* **29** used in polite or patronizing phrases or to express anger (often intended ironically): *how is your good lady?; look here, my good man!* **30 a good one a** an unbelievable assertion **b** a very funny joke **31** as good as virtually; practically: *it's as good as finished* **32** as good as gold excellent; very good indeed **33** be as or so good as to would you please **34** come good to recover and perform well after a bad start or setback **35** good and *informal* (intensifier): *good and mad* **36** (intensifier; used in mild oaths): *good*

grief!; good heavens! ▷ *interj* **37** an exclamation of approval, agreement, pleasure, etc ▷ *n* **38** moral or material advantage or use; benefit or profit: *for the good of our workers; what is the good of worrying?* **39** positive moral qualities; goodness; virtue; righteousness; piety **40** (*sometimes capital*) moral qualities seen as a single abstract entity: *we must pursue the Good* **41** a good thing **42** *economics* a commodity or service that satisfies a human need **43 for good (and all)** forever; permanently: *I have left them for good* **44 make good a** to recompense or repair damage or injury **b** to be successful **c** to demonstrate or prove the truth of (a statement or accusation) **d** to secure and retain (a position) **e** to effect or fulfil (something intended or promised) **45 good on** or **for you (him, etc)** well done, well said, etc: a term of congratulation **46 get any** (or **some**) **good of** *Irish* **a** to handle or use to good effect: *I never got any good of this machine* **b** to understand properly: *I could never get any good of him* **c** to receive cooperation from ▷ See also **goods** [Old English *gōd*; related to Old Norse *gōthr*, Old High German *guot* good] > ˈgoodish *adj*

good afternoon *sentence substitute* a conventional expression of greeting or farewell used in the afternoon

Good Book *n* a name for the **Bible** Also called: the **Book**

goodbye (ˌɡʊdˈbaɪ) *sentence substitute* **1** farewell: a conventional expression used at leave-taking or parting with people and at the loss or rejection of things or ideas ▷ *n* **2** a leave-taking; parting: *they prolonged their goodbyes for a few more minutes* **3** a farewell: *they said goodbyes to each other* [c16 contraction of *God be with ye*]

good cholesterol *n* a nontechnical name for **high-density lipoprotein**

good day *sentence substitute* a conventional expression of greeting or farewell used during the day

good evening *sentence substitute* a conventional expression of greeting or farewell used in the evening

good-for-nothing *n* **1** an irresponsible or worthless person ▷ *adj* **2** irresponsible; worthless

Good Friday *n* the Friday before Easter, observed as a commemoration of the Crucifixion of Jesus

good hair *n Caribbean* hair showing evidence of some European strain in a person's blood

Good Hope *n* **Cape** ▷ See **Cape of Good Hope**

good-humoured *adj* being in or expressing a pleasant, tolerant, and kindly state of mind > ˌgood-ˈhumouredly *adv* > ˌgood-ˈhumouredness *n*

goodies (ˈɡʊdɪz) *pl n* any objects, rewards, prizes, etc, considered particularly desirable, attractive, or pleasurable

Good King Henry *n* a weedy edible chenopodiaceous plant, *Chenopodium bonus-henricus*, of N Europe, W Asia, and North America, having arrow-shaped leaves and clusters of small green flowers

good-looker *n* a handsome or pretty person

good-looking *adj* handsome or pretty

good looks *pl n* personal attractiveness or beauty

goodly (ˈɡʊdlɪ) *adj* **-lier, -liest 1** considerable: *a goodly amount of money* **2** *obsolete* attractive, pleasing, or fine: *a goodly man* > ˈgoodliness *n*

goodman (ˈɡʊdmən) *n, pl* **-men** *archaic* **1** a husband **2** a man not of gentle birth: used as a title **3** a master of a household

good morning *sentence substitute* a conventional expression of greeting or farewell used in the morning

good-natured *adj* of a tolerant and kindly disposition > ˌgood-ˈnaturedly *adv* > ˌgood-ˈnaturedness *n*

goodness (ˈɡʊdnɪs) *n* **1** the state or quality of being good **2** generosity; kindness **3** moral excellence; piety; virtue ▷ *interj* **4** a euphemism for **God**: used as an exclamation of surprise (often in phrases such as **goodness knows!, thank goodness!**)

goodness of fit *n statistics* the extent to which observed sample values of a variable approximate to values derived from a theoretical density, often measured by a chi square test

good night *sentence substitute* a conventional expression of farewell, or, rarely, of greeting, used in the late afternoon, the evening, or at night, esp when departing to bed

good-oh *or* **good-o** ('gʊd'əʊ) *informal* ▷ *interj* **1** *Brit and Austral* an exclamation of pleasure, agreement, approval, etc ▷ *adj, adv* **2** *Austral* all right: *it was good-oh; I was getting on good-oh*

good oil *n* (usually preceded by *the*) *Austral slang* true or reliable facts, information, etc

good ol' boy *n US informal* **a** a man considered as being trustworthy and dependable because of his ordinary and down-to-earth background and upbringing **b** (*as modifier*): *he was expected to bring some good-ol'-boy informality to the White House*

good people *pl n* **the** *folklore* fairies

good question *n* a question that is hard to answer immediately

goods (gʊdz) *pl n* **1** possessions and personal property **2** (*sometimes singular*) *economics* commodities that are tangible, usually movable, and generally not consumed at the same time as they are produced. Compare **services** **3** articles of commerce; merchandise **4** *chiefly Brit* **a** merchandise when transported, esp by rail; freight **b** (*as modifier*): *a goods train* **5** **the goods** **a** *informal* that which is expected or promised: *to deliver the goods* **b** *slang* the real thing **c** *US and Canadian slang* incriminating evidence (esp in the phrase **have the goods on someone**) **6** **a piece of goods** *slang* a person, esp a woman

Good Samaritan *n* **1** *New Testament* a figure in one of Christ's parables (Luke 10:30–37) who is an example of compassion towards those in distress **2** a kindly person who helps another in difficulty or distress

goods and chattels *pl n* any property that is not freehold, usually limited to include only moveable property

Good Shepherd *n New Testament* a title given to Jesus Christ in John 10:11–12

good-sized *adj* quite large

good sort *n informal* **1** a person of a kindly and likable disposition **2** *Austral* an agreeable or attractive woman

good-tempered *adj* of a kindly and generous disposition

good-time *adj* (of a person) wildly seeking pleasure

good turn *n* a helpful and friendly act; good deed; favour

goodwife ('gʊd,waɪf) *n, pl* **-wives** *archaic* **1** the mistress of a household **2** a woman not of gentle birth: used as a title

goodwill (,gʊd'wɪl) *n* **1** a feeling of benevolence, approval, and kindly interest **2** (*modifier*) resulting from, showing, or designed to show goodwill: *the government sent a goodwill mission to Moscow; a goodwill ambassador for UNICEF* **3** willingness or acquiescence **4** *accounting* an intangible asset taken into account in assessing the value of an enterprise and reflecting its commercial reputation, customer connections, etc

Goodwin Sands ('gʊdwɪn) *pl n* a dangerous stretch of shoals at the entrance to the Strait of Dover: separated from the E coast of Kent by the Downs roadstead

Goodwood ('gʊd,wʊd) *n* an area in SE England, in Sussex: site of a famous racecourse and of **Goodwood House**, built 1780–1800

goody[1] ('gʊdɪ) *interj* **1** a child's exclamation of pleasure and approval ▷ *n, pl* **goodies** **2** short for **goody-goody** **3** *informal* the hero in a film, book, etc **4** something particularly pleasant to have or (often) to eat. See also **goodies**

goody[2] ('gʊdɪ) *n, pl* **goodies** *archaic or literary* a married woman of low rank: used as a title: *Goody Two-Shoes* [C16 shortened from GOODWIFE]

goody-goody *n, pl* **-goodies** **1** a smugly virtuous or sanctimonious person ▷ *adj* **2** smug and sanctimonious

gooey ('guːɪ) *adj* **gooier, gooiest** *informal* **1** sticky, soft, and often sweet **2** oversweet and sentimental > **'gooily** *adv*

goof (guːf) *informal* ▷ *n* **1** a foolish error or mistake **2** a stupid person ▷ *vb* **3** to bungle (something); botch **4** (*intr;* often foll by *about* or *around*) to fool (around); mess (about) **5** (*tr*) to dope with drugs **6** (*intr;* often foll by *off*) *US and Canadian* to waste time; idle [C20 probably from (dialect) *goff* simpleton, from Old French *goffe* clumsy, from Italian *goffo*, of obscure origin]

goofball ('guːf,bɔːl) *n US and Canadian slang* **1** a barbiturate sleeping pill **2** a fool

go off *vb* (*intr*) **1** (*adverb*) (of power, a water supply, etc) to cease to be available, running, or functioning: *the lights suddenly went off* **2** (*adverb*) to be discharged or activated; explode **3** (*adverb*) to occur as specified: *the meeting went off well* **4** to leave (a place): *the actors went off stage* **5** (*adverb*) (of a sensation) to gradually cease to be felt or perceived **6** (*adverb*) to fall asleep **7** (*adverb*) to enter a specified state or condition: *she went off into hysterics* **8** (*adverb;* foll by *with*) to abscond (with) **9** (*adverb*) (of concrete, mortar, etc) to harden **10** (*adverb*) *Brit informal* (of food, milk, etc) to become stale or rotten **11** (*preposition*) *Brit informal* to cease to like: *she went off him after their marriage* **12** (*adverb*) *informal* to become bad-tempered **13** (*adverb*) *slang* to have an orgasm **14** (*adverb*) *Austral slang* (of premises) to be raided by the police **15** (*adverb*) *Austral slang* (of a racehorse) to win a fixed race **16** (*adverb*) *Austral slang* to be stolen

goofy ('guːfɪ) *adj* **goofier, goofiest** *informal* **1** foolish; silly; stupid **2** *Brit* (of teeth) sticking out; protruding > **'goofily** *adv* > **'goofiness** *n*

goofy-footer *n Austral informal* a surfboard rider who stands with his right foot forward instead of his left foot forward

goog (gʊg) *n Austral informal* **1** an egg **2** **full as a goog** drunk

google ('guːgᵊl) *vb* (*tr*) **1** to search for (something on the internet) using a search engine **2** to check (the credentials of someone) by searching for websites containing his or her name [C20 from *Google*, a popular search engine on the World Wide Web]

googlewhack ('guːgᵊl,wæk) *n* a search of the internet, using the Google search engine and without using quote marks, for a combination of two legitimate words that yields only one result [C21 from *Google* + *whack* attempt]

googly ('guːglɪ) *n, pl* **-lies** *cricket* an off break bowled with a leg break action [C20 Australian, of unknown origin]

googol ('guːgɒl, -gᵊl) *n* the number represented as one followed by 100 zeros (10^{100}) [C20 coined by E. Kasner (1878–1955), American mathematician]

googolplex ('guːgɒl,plɛks, -gᵊl-) *n* the number represented as one followed by a googol (10^{100}) of zeros [C20 from GOOGOL + (DU)PLEX]

gook (gʊk, guːk) *n US* **1** *slang* a derogatory word for a person from a Far Eastern country **2** *informal* a messy sticky substance; muck [C20 of uncertain origin]

Goole (guːl) *n* an inland port in NE England, in the East Riding of Yorkshire at the confluence of the Ouse and Don Rivers, 75 km (47 miles) from the North Sea. Pop: 18 741 (2001)

goolie *or* **gooly** ('guːlɪ) *n, pl* **-lies** **1** (*usually plural*) *slang* a testicle **2** *Austral slang* a stone or pebble [from Hindustani *goli* a ball, bullet]

> USAGE This word was formerly considered to be taboo, and it was labelled as such in previous editions of *Collins English Dictionary*. However, it has now become acceptable in speech, although some older or more conservative people may object to its use

goon (guːn) *n* **1** a stupid or deliberately foolish person **2** *US informal* a thug hired to commit acts of violence or intimidation, esp in an industrial dispute [C20 partly from dialect *gooney* fool, partly after the character Alice the *Goon*, created by E. C. Segar (1894–1938), American cartoonist]

go on *vb* (*intr, mainly adverb*) **1** to continue or proceed **2** to happen or take place: *there's something peculiar going on here* **3** (of power, water supply, etc) to start running or functioning **4** (*preposition*) to mount or board and ride on, esp as a treat: *children love to go on donkeys at the seaside* **5** *theatre* to make an entrance on stage **6** to act or behave: *he goes on as though he's rich* **7** to talk excessively; chatter **8** to continue talking, esp after a short pause: *"When I am Prime Minister," he went on, "we shall abolish taxes."* **9** (foll by *at*) to criticize or nag: *stop going on at me all the time!* **10** (*preposition*) to use as a basis for further thought or action: *the police had no evidence at all to go on in the murder case* **11** (foll by *for*) *Brit* to approach (a time, age, amount, etc): *he's going on for his hundredth birthday* **12** *cricket* to start to bowl **13** to take one's turn **14** (of clothes) to be capable of being put on **15** **go much on** (*used with a negative*) *Brit* to care for; like **16** **something to go on** *or* **to be going on with** something that is adequate for the present time ▷ *interj* **17** I don't believe what you're saying

gooney bird ('guːnɪ) *n* an informal name for **albatross,** esp the black-footed albatross (*Diomedea nigripes*) [C19 *gony* (originally sailors' slang), probably from dialect *gooney* fool, of obscure origin; compare GOON]

goop (guːp) *n US and Canadian slang* **1** a rude or ill-mannered person **2** any sticky or semiliquid substance [C20 coined by G. Burgess (1866–1951), American humorist] > **'goopy** *adj*

goorie *or* **goory** ('guːrɪ) *n, pl* **-ries** See **kuri**

goosander (guː'sændə) *n* a common merganser (a duck), *Mergus merganser*, of Europe and North America, having a dark head and white body in the male [C17 probably from GOOSE[1] + Old Norse *önd* (genitive *andar*) duck]

goose[1] (guːs) *n, pl* **geese** (giːs) **1** any of various web-footed long-necked birds of the family *Anatidae*: order *Anseriformes*. They are typically larger and less aquatic than ducks and are gregarious and migratory. Related adj: **anserine** See also **brent goose, barnacle goose, greylag, snow goose** **2** the female of such a bird, as opposed to the male (gander) **3** *informal* a silly person **4** (*pl* **gooses**) a pressing iron with a long curving handle, used esp by tailors **5** the flesh of the goose, used as food **6** **all his geese are swans** he constantly exaggerates the importance of a person or thing **7** **cook someone's goose** *informal* **a** to spoil someone's plans **b** to bring about someone's ruin, downfall, etc **8** **kill the goose that lays the golden eggs** to sacrifice future benefits for the sake of momentary present needs. See also **golden goose** [Old English *gōs*; related to Old Norse *gās*, Old High German *gans*, Old Irish *gēiss* swan, Greek *khēn*, Sanskrit *hainsas*]

goose[2] (guːs) *slang* ▷ *vb* **1** (*tr*) to prod (a person) playfully in the behind ▷ *n, pl* **gooses** **2** a playful prod in the behind [C19 from GOOSE[1], probably from a comparison with the jabbing of a goose's bill]

goose barnacle *n* any barnacle of the genus *Lepas*, living attached by a stalk to pieces of wood, having long feathery appendages (cirri) and flattened shells

gooseberry ('gʊzbərɪ, -brɪ) *n, pl* **-ries** **1** a Eurasian shrub, *Ribes uva-crispa* (or *R. grossularia*), having greenish, purple-tinged flowers and ovoid yellow-green or red-purple berries: family *Grossulariaceae*. See also **currant** (sense 2) **2** **a** the berry of this plant **b** (*as modifier*): *gooseberry jam* **3** *Brit informal* an unwanted single person in a group of couples, esp a third person with a couple (often in the phrase **play gooseberry**) **4** **Cape gooseberry** a tropical American solanaceous plant, *Physalis*

g

peruviana, naturalized in southern Africa, having yellow flowers and edible yellow berries. See also **ground cherry**

gooseberry bush *n* **1** See **gooseberry** (sense 1) **2** under a gooseberry bush used humorously in answering children's questions regarding their birth

gooseberry stone *n* another name for **grossularite**

goosefish ('gu:s,fɪʃ) *n, pl* -fish *or* -fishes US another name for **monkfish** (sense 1)

goose flesh *n* the bumpy condition of the skin induced by cold, fear, etc, caused by contraction of the muscles at the base of the hair follicles with consequent erection of papillae: so called because of the resemblance to the skin of a freshly-plucked fowl. Also called: **goose bumps, goose pimples, goose skin**

goosefoot ('gu:s,fʊt) *n, pl* -foots any typically weedy chenopodiaceous plant of the genus *Chenopodium*, having small greenish flowers and leaves shaped like a goose's foot. See also **Good King Henry, fat hen**

goosegog ('gʊzgɒg) *or* **goosegob** *n* Brit a dialect or informal word for **gooseberry** [from *goose* in GOOSEBERRY + *gog*, variant of GOB[1]]

goosegrass ('gu:s,grɑ:s) *n* another name for **cleavers**

gooseneck ('gu:s,nɛk) *n* **1** nautical a pivot between the forward end of a boom and a mast, to allow the boom to swing freely **2** something in the form of a neck of a goose > 'goose,necked *adj*

goose step *n* **1** a military march step in which the leg is swung rigidly to an exaggerated height, esp as in the German army in the Third Reich **2** an abnormal gait in animals ▷ *vb* **goose-step** -steps, -stepping, -stepped **3** (*intr*) to march in goose step

goosy *or* **goosey** ('gu:sɪ) *adj* goosier, goosiest **1** of or like a goose **2** having goose flesh **3** silly and foolish > 'goosiness *n*

go out *vb* (*intr, adverb*) **1** to depart from a room, house, country, etc **2** to cease to illuminate, burn, or function: *the fire has gone out* **3** to cease to be fashionable or popular: *that style went out ages ago!* **4** to become unconscious or fall asleep: *she went out like a light* **5** (of a broadcast) to be transmitted **6** to go to entertainments, social functions, etc **7** (usually foll by *with* or *together*) to associate (with a person of the opposite sex) regularly; date **8** (of workers) to begin to strike **9** (foll by *to*) to be extended (to): *our sympathy went out to her on the death of her sister* **10** cards to get rid of the last card, token, etc, in one's hand **11** go all out to make a great effort to achieve or obtain something: *he went all out to pass the exam*

go over *vb* (*intr*) **1** to be received in a specified manner: *the concert went over very well* **2** (*preposition*) Also: **go through** to examine and revise as necessary: *he went over the accounts* **3** (*preposition*) Also: **go through** to clean: *she went over the room before her mother came* **4** (*preposition*) to check or repair: *can you go over my car please?* **5** (*preposition*) Also: **go through** to rehearse: *I'll go over my lines before the play* **6** (*adverb*; foll by *to*) **a** to change (to a different practice or system): *will Britain ever go over to driving on the right?* **b** to change one's allegiances **7** (*preposition*) slang to do physical violence to: *they went over him with an iron bar*

GOP (in the US) abbreviation for **Grand Old Party**

gopak ('gəʊ,pæk) *n* a spectacular high-leaping Russian peasant dance for men [from Russian, from Ukrainian *hopak*, from *hop!* a cry in the dance, from German *hopp!*]

Go-Ped ('gəʊ,pɛd) *n* trademark a motorized vehicle consisting of a low footboard on wheels, steered by handlebars

gopher ('gəʊfə) *n* **1** Also called: pocket gopher any burrowing rodent of the family *Geomyidae*, of North and Central America, having a thickset body, short legs, and cheek pouches **2** another name for **ground squirrel 3** any burrowing

tortoise of the genus *Gopherus*, of SE North America **4** gopher snake another name for **bull snake** [C19 shortened from earlier *megopher* or *magopher*, of obscure origin]

gopherwood ('gəʊfə,wʊd) *n* US another name for **yellowwood** (sense 1)

gopher wood *n* the wood used in the construction of Noah's ark, thought to be a type of cypress (Genesis 6:14) [from Hebrew *gōpher*]

gora ('gɔːrə) *n* Hinglish informal a White or fair-skinned male [C21 from Hindi]

Gorakhpur ('gɔːrək,pʊə) *n* a city in N India, in SE Uttar Pradesh: formerly an important Muslim garrison. Pop: 624 570 (2001)

goral ('gɔːrəl) *n* a small goat antelope, *Naemorhedus goral*, inhabiting mountainous regions of S Asia. It has a yellowish-grey and black coat and small conical horns [C19 from Hindi, probably of Sanskrit origin]

Gorbals ('gɔːbəlz) *n* the a district of Glasgow, formerly known for its slums

gorblimey (gɔːˈblaɪmɪ) *interj* a variant of **cor blimey**

gorcock ('gɔː,kɒk) *n* the male of the red grouse [C17 gor- (of unknown origin) + COCK[1]]

Gordian knot ('gɔːdɪən) *n* **1** (in Greek legend) a complicated knot, tied by King Gordius of Phrygia, that Alexander the Great cut with a sword **2** a complicated and intricate problem (esp in the phrase **cut the Gordian knot**)

Gordon setter *n* a breed of large setter originating in Scotland, with a black-and-tan coat [C19 named after Alexander *Gordon* (1743–1827), Scottish nobleman who promoted this breed]

gore[1] (gɔː) *n* **1** blood shed from a wound, esp when coagulated **2** informal killing, fighting, etc [Old English *gor* dirt; related to Old Norse *gor* half-digested food, Middle Low German *göre*, Dutch *goor*]

gore[2] (gɔː) *vb* (*tr*) (of an animal, such as a bull) to pierce or stab (a person or another animal) with a horn or tusk [C16 probably from Old English *gār* spear]

gore[3] (gɔː) *n* **1** a tapering or triangular piece of material used in making a shaped skirt, umbrella, etc **2** a similarly shaped piece, esp of land ▷ *vb* **3** (*tr*) to make into or with a gore or gores [Old English *gāra*; related to Old Norse *geiri* gore, Old High German *gēro*] > **gored** *adj*

gorehound ('gɔː,haʊnd) *n* an enthusiast of gory horror films

Gore-Tex ('gɔː,tɛks) *n* trademark a type of synthetic fabric which is waterproof yet allows the wearer's skin to breathe; used for sportswear

gorge (gɔːdʒ) *n* **1** a deep ravine, esp one through which a river runs **2** the contents of the stomach **3** feelings of disgust or resentment (esp in the phrase **one's gorge rises**) **4** an obstructing mass: *an ice gorge* **5** fortifications **a** a narrow rear entrance to a work **b** the narrow part of a bastion or outwork **6** archaic the throat or gullet ▷ *vb* also **engorge 7** (*intr*) falconry (of hawks) to eat until the crop is completely full **8** to swallow (food) ravenously **9** (*tr*) to stuff (oneself) with food [C14 from Old French *gorger* to stuff, from *gorge* throat, from Late Latin *gurga*, modification of Latin *gurges* whirlpool] > 'gorgeable *adj* > 'gorger *n*

gorgeous ('gɔːdʒəs) *adj* **1** strikingly beautiful or magnificent: *gorgeous array; a gorgeous girl* **2** informal extremely pleasing, fine, or good: *gorgeous weather* [C15 from Old French *gorgias* elegant, from *gorgias* wimple, from *gorge*; see GORGE] > 'gorgeously *adv* > 'gorgeousness *n*

gorgerin ('gɔːdʒərɪn) *n* architect another name for **necking** [C17 from French, from *gorge* throat; see GORGE]

gorget ('gɔːdʒɪt) *n* **1** a collar-like piece of armour worn to protect the throat **2** a part of a wimple worn by women to cover the throat and chest, esp in the 14th century **3** a band of distinctive colour on the throat of an animal, esp a bird [C15 from Old French, from *gorge*; see GORGE] > 'gorgeted *adj*

Gorgio (gɔːˈdʒəʊ, -dʒɪəʊ) *n, pl* -gios (*sometimes not capital*) a word used by Gypsies for a non-Gypsy [from Romany]

Gorgon ('gɔːɡən) *n* **1** Greek myth any of three winged monstrous sisters, Stheno, Euryale, and Medusa, who had live snakes for hair, huge teeth, and brazen claws **2** (*often not capital*) informal a fierce or unpleasant woman [via Latin *Gorgō* from Greek, from *gorgos* terrible]

gorgoneion (,gɔːɡəˈniːɒn) *n, pl* -neia (-'niːə) a representation of a Gorgon's head, esp Medusa's [C19 from Greek, from *gorgoneios* of a GORGON]

gorgonian (gɔːˈɡəʊnɪən) *n* **1** any coral of the order *Gorgonacea*, having a horny or calcareous branching skeleton: includes the sea fans and red corals ▷ *adj* **2** of, relating to, or belonging to the *Gorgonacea*

Gorgonian (gɔːˈɡəʊnɪən) *adj* of or resembling a Gorgon

Gorgonzola *or* **Gorgonzola cheese** (,gɔːɡənˈzəʊlə) *n* a semihard blue-veined cheese of sharp flavour, made from pressed milk [C19 named after *Gorgonzola*, Italian town where it originated]

gori ('gɔːriː) *n* Hinglish informal a White or fair-skinned female [C21 Hindi]

Gorica ('ɡɒritsa) *n* the Serbo-Croat name for **Gorizia**

gorilla (ɡəˈrɪlə) *n* **1** the largest anthropoid ape, *Gorilla gorilla*, inhabiting the forests of central W Africa. It is stocky and massive, with a short muzzle and coarse dark hair **2** informal a large, strong, and brutal-looking man [C19 New Latin, from Greek *Gorillai*, an African tribe renowned for their hirsute appearance] > go'rilla-,like *adj* > go'rillian *or* gorilline (ɡəˈrɪlaɪn) *adj* > go'rilloid *adj*

gorillagram (ɡəˈrɪlə,ɡræm) *n* informal a jocular greetings message delivered to someone celebrating a birthday, engagement, etc, by a person dressed as a gorilla [C20 from GORILLA + (TELE)GRAM]

Gorizia (*Italian* goˈrittsja) *n* a city in NE Italy, in Friuli-Venezia Giulia, on the Isonzo River: cultural centre under the Hapsburgs. Pop: 35 667 (2001). German name: **Görz** Serbo-Croat name: **Gorica**

Gorki *or* **Gorky** (*Russian* ˈɡɔrjkij) *n* the former name (until 1991) of **Nizhni Novgorod**

Gorlin syndrome ('gɔːlɪn) *n* a rare congenital disorder in which cancer destroys the facial skin and causes blindness; skeletal anomalies and some mental retardation can also occur [C20 named after R. J. *Gorlin* (born 1923), US oral pathologist]

Görlitz (*German* ˈɡœrlɪts) *n* a city in E Germany, in Saxony on the Neisse River: divided in 1945, the area on the E bank of the river becoming the Polish town of **Zgorzelec**. Pop: 58 518 (2003 est)

Gorlovka (*Russian* ˈɡɔrləfkə) *n* a city in SE Ukraine in the centre of the Donets Basin: a major coal-mining centre. Pop: 280 000 (2005 est)

gorm ('gɔːm) *n* Northern English dialect a foolish person

gormand ('gɔːmənd) *n* a less common variant of **gourmand**

gormandize *or* **gormandise** *vb* ('gɔːmən,daɪz) **1** to eat (food) greedily and voraciously ▷ *n* ('gɔːmən,diːz) **2** a less common variant of **gourmandise**. > 'gormand,izer *or* 'gormand,iser *n*

gormless ('gɔːmlɪs) *adj* Brit informal stupid; dull [C19 variant of C18 *gaumless*, from dialect *gome*, from Old English *gom*, *gome*, from Old Norse *gaumr* heed]

Gorno-Altai Republic ('gɔːnəʊæl'taɪ, -'æltaɪ) *n* a constituent republic of S Russia: mountainous, rising over 4350 m (14 500 ft) in the Altai Mountains of the south. Capital: Gorno-Altaisk. Pop: 202 900 (2002). Area: 92 600 sq km (35 740 sq miles). Also called: Altai Republic

Gorno-Badakhshan Autonomous Republic (-bəˈdækʃɑːn) *n* an administrative division of Tajikistan: generally mountainous and inaccessible. Capital: Khorog. Pop: 206 000 (2000

est). Area: 63 700 sq km (24 590 sq miles). Also called: **Badakhshan**

gorse (gɔːs) *n* any evergreen shrub of the leguminous genus *Ulex*, esp the European species *U. europeaus*, which has yellow flowers and thick green spines instead of leaves. Also called: **furze**, **whin** [Old English *gors*; related to Old Irish *garb* rough, Latin *horrēre* to bristle, Old High German *gersta* barley, Greek *khēr* hedgehog] > **'gorsy** *adj*

Gorsedd ('gɔːsɛð) *n* (in Wales) the bardic institution associated with the eisteddfod, esp a meeting of bards and druids held daily before the eisteddfod [from Welsh, literally: throne]

gory ('gɔːrɪ) *adj* **gorier, goriest** 1 horrific or bloodthirsty: *a gory story* 2 involving bloodshed and killing: *a gory battle* 3 covered in gore > **'gorily** *adv* > **'goriness** *n*

Görz (gœrts) *n* the German name for **Gorizia**

gosh (gɒʃ) *interj* an exclamation of mild surprise or wonder [C18 euphemistic for *God*, as in *by gosh!*]

goshawk ('gɒsˌhɔːk) *n* a large hawk, *Accipiter gentilis*, of Europe, Asia, and North America, having a bluish-grey back and wings and paler underparts: used in falconry [Old English *gōshafoc*; see GOOSE[1], HAWK[1]]

Goshen ('gəʊʃən) *n* 1 a region of ancient Egypt, east of the Nile delta: granted to Jacob and his descendants by the king of Egypt and inhabited by them until the Exodus (Genesis 45:10) 2 a place of comfort and plenty

Goslar ('gɒslaː) *n* a city in N central Germany, in Lower Saxony: imperial palace and other medieval buildings, silver mines. Pop: 43 727 (2003 est)

gosling ('gɒzlɪŋ) *n* 1 a young goose 2 an inexperienced or youthful person [C15 from Old Norse *gæslingr*; related to Danish *gäsling*; see GOOSE[1], -LING[1]]

go-slow *n* 1 *Brit* **a** a deliberate slackening of the rate of production by organized labour as a tactic in industrial conflict **b** (*as modifier*): *go-slow tactics*. US and Canadian equivalent: **slowdown** ▷ *vb* **go slow** 2 (*intr*) to work deliberately slowly as a tactic in industrial conflict

gospel ('gɒspᵊl) *n* 1 Also called: **gospel truth** an unquestionable truth: *to take someone's word as gospel* 2 a doctrine maintained to be of great importance 3 Black religious music originating in the churches of the Southern states of the United States 4 the message or doctrine of a religious teacher 5 **a** the story of Christ's life and teachings as narrated in the Gospels **b** the good news of salvation in Jesus Christ **c** (*as modifier*): *the gospel story* [Old English *gōdspell*, from *gōd* GOOD + *spell* message; see SPELL[2]; compare Old Norse *guthspjall*, Old High German *guotspell*]

Gospel ('gɒspᵊl) *n* 1 any of the first four books of the New Testament, namely Matthew, Mark, Luke, and John 2 a reading from one of these in a religious service

gospeller ('gɒspələ) *n* 1 a person who reads or chants the Gospel in a religious service 2 a person who professes to preach a gospel held exclusively by him and others of a like mind

gospel oath *n* an oath sworn on the Gospels

Gosplan ('gɒsˌplæn) *n* the state planning commission of the former Soviet Union or any of its constituent republics: it was responsible for coordination and development of the economy, social services, etc [C20 from Russian *Gos(udarstvennaya) Plan(ovaya Comissiya)* State Planning Committee]

gospodin *Russian* (gəspa'din) *n, pl* ***-poda*** (-pa'da) a Russian title of address, often indicating respect, equivalent to *sir* when used alone or to *Mr* when before a name [literally: lord]

Gosport ('gɒsˌpɔːt) *n* a town in S England, in Hampshire on Portsmouth harbour: naval base since the 16th century. Pop: 69 348 (2001)

goss[1] (gɒs) *vb* (*intr*) *English dialect* to spit

goss[2] (gɒs) *n informal* short for **gossip**

gossamer ('gɒsəmə) *n* 1 a gauze or silk fabric of the very finest texture 2 a filmy cobweb often seen on foliage or floating in the air 3 anything resembling gossamer in fineness or filminess 4 (*modifier*) made of or resembling gossamer: *gossamer wings* [C14 (in the sense: a filmy cobweb): probably from *gos* GOOSE[1] + *somer* SUMMER[1]; the phrase refers to *St Martin's summer*, a period in November when goose was traditionally eaten; from the prevalence of the cobweb in the autumn; compare German *Gänsemonat*, literally: goosemonth, used for November] > **'gossamery** *adj*

gossip ('gɒsɪp) *n* 1 casual and idle chat: *to have a gossip with a friend* 2 a conversation involving malicious chatter or rumours about other people: *a gossip about the neighbours* 3 Also called: **gossipmonger** a person who habitually talks about others, esp maliciously 4 light easy communication: *to write a letter full of gossip* 5 *archaic* a close woman friend ▷ *vb* **-sips, -siping, -siped** 6 (*intr*; often foll by *about*) to talk casually or maliciously (about other people) [Old English *godsibb* godparent, from GOD + SIB; the term came to be applied to familiar friends, esp a woman's female friends at the birth of a child, hence a person, esp a woman, fond of light talk] > **'gossiper** *n* > **'gossiping** *n, adj* > **'gossipingly** *adv* > **'gossipy** *adj*

gossipmonger ('gɒsɪpˌmʌŋgə) *n* another word for **gossip** (sense 3)

gossoon (gɒ'suːn) *n Irish* a boy, esp a servant boy [C17 from Old French *garçon*]

gossypol ('gɒsɪˌpɒl) *n* a toxic crystalline pigment that is a constituent of cottonseed oil [C19 from Modern Latin *gossypium* cotton plant + -OL[1]]

goster ('gɒstə) *vb* (*intr*) *Northern English dialect* 1 to laugh uncontrollably 2 to gossip [C18 from earlier *gauster*, from Middle English *galstre*, of obscure origin]

got (gɒt) *vb* 1 the past tense and past participle of **get** 2 **have got** **a** to possess: *he has got three apples* **b** (*takes an infinitive*) used as an auxiliary to express compulsion felt to be imposed by or upon the speaker: *I've got to get a new coat* 3 **have got it bad** *or* **badly** *informal* to be infatuated

Göta (*Swedish* 'jøːta) *n* a river in S Sweden, draining Lake Vänern and flowing south-southwest to the Kattegat: forms part of the **Göta Canal,** which links Göteborg in the west with Stockholm in the east. Length: 93 km (58 miles)

Gotama ('gəʊtəmə) *n* the Pali form of the name **Gautama**

gotcha lizard ('gɒtʃə) *n Austral* another name for **crocodile**

Göteborg (*Swedish* jœtə'bɔrj) *or* **Gothenburg** *n* a port in SW Sweden, at the mouth of the Göta River: the largest port and second largest city in the country; developed through the Swedish East India Company and grew through Napoleon's continental blockade and with the opening of the Göta Canal (1832); university (1891). Pop: 481 523 (2004 est)

Goth (gɒθ) *n* 1 a member of an East Germanic people from Scandinavia who settled south of the Baltic early in the first millennium AD. They moved on to the Ukrainian steppes and raided and later invaded many parts of the Roman Empire from the 3rd to the 5th century. See also **Ostrogoth, Visigoth** 2 a rude or barbaric person 3 (*sometimes not capital*) Also called: **Gothic** an aficionado of Goth music and fashion ▷ *adj* 4 (*sometimes not capital*) Also: **Gothic** **a** (of music) in a style of guitar-based rock with some similarities to heavy metal and punk and usually characterized by depressing or mournful lyrics **b** (of fashion) characterized by black clothes and heavy make-up, often creating a ghostly appearance

Gotha ('gəʊθə; *German* 'goːta) *n* a town in central Germany, in Thuringia on the N edge of the Thuringian forest: capital of Saxe-Coburg-Gotha (1826–1918); noted for the *Almanach de Gotha* (a record of the royal and noble houses of Europe, first published in 1764). Pop: 47 158 (2003 est)

Gothamite ('gɒθəˌmaɪt) *n US* a native or inhabitant of New York City [C20 from *Gotham*, a nickname for New York City]

Gothenburg ('gɒθənˌbɜːg) *n* the English name for **Göteborg**

Gothic ('gɒθɪk) *adj* 1 denoting, relating to, or resembling the style of architecture that was used in W Europe from the 12th to the 16th centuries, characterized by the lancet arch, the ribbed vault, and the flying buttress. See also **Gothic Revival** 2 of or relating to the style of sculpture, painting, or other arts as practised in W Europe from the 12th to the 16th centuries 3 (*sometimes not capital*) of or relating to a literary style characterized by gloom, the grotesque, and the supernatural, popular esp in the late 18th century: when used of modern literature, films, etc, sometimes spelt: **Gothick** 4 of, relating to, or characteristic of the Goths or their language 5 (*sometimes not capital*) primitive and barbarous in style, behaviour, etc 6 of or relating to the Middle Ages 7 another word for **Goth** (sense 4) ▷ *n* 8 Gothic architecture or art 9 the extinct language of the ancient Goths, known mainly from fragments of a translation of the Bible made in the 4th century by Bishop Wulfila. See also **East Germanic** 10 Also called (esp Brit): **black letter** the family of heavy script typefaces 11 another word for **Goth** (sense 3) > **'Gothically** *adv*

Gothic arch *n* another name for **lancet arch**

Gothicism ('gɒθɪˌsɪzəm) *n* 1 conformity to, use of, or imitation of the Gothic style, esp in architecture 2 crudeness of manner or style

Gothicize *or* **Gothicise** ('gɒθɪˌsaɪz) *vb* (*tr*) to make Gothic in style > **'Gothiˌcizer** *or* **'Gothiˌciser** *n*

Gothic Revival *n* a Gothic style of architecture popular between the late 18th and late 19th centuries, exemplified by the Houses of Parliament in London (1840). Also called: **neogothic**

go through *vb* (*intr*) 1 (*adverb*) to be approved or accepted: *the amendment went through* 2 (*preposition*) to consume; exhaust: *we went through our supplies in a day; some men go through a pair of socks in no time* 3 (*preposition*) Also: **go over** to examine and revise as necessary: *he went through the figures* 4 (*preposition*) to suffer: *she went through tremendous pain* 5 (*preposition*) Also: **go over** to rehearse: *let's just go through the details again* 6 (*preposition*) Also: **go over** to clean: *she went through the cupboards in the spring-cleaning* 7 (*preposition*) to participate in: *she went through the degree ceremony without getting too nervous* 8 (*adverb*; foll by *with*) to bring to a successful conclusion, often by persistence 9 (*preposition*) (of a book) to be published in: *that book has gone through three printings this year alone* 10 to proceed to the next round of a competition

Gotland ('gɒtlənd; *Swedish* 'gɔtlant), **Gothland** ('gɒθlənd) *or* **Gottland** ('gɒtlənd) *n* an island in the Baltic Sea, off the SE coast of Sweden: important trading centre since the Bronze Age; long disputed between Sweden and Denmark, finally becoming Swedish in 1645; tourism and agriculture now important. Capital: Visby. Pop: (including associated islands) 57 677 (2004 est). Area: 3140 sq km (1212 sq miles)

go to *vb* (*intr, preposition*) 1 to be awarded to: *the Nobel prize last year went to a Scot* 2 **go to it** to tackle a task vigorously ▷ *interj* 3 *archaic* an exclamation expressing surprise, encouragement, etc

go together *vb* (*intr, adverb*) 1 to be mutually suited; harmonize: *the colours go well together* 2 *informal* (of two people) to have a romantic or sexual relationship: *they had been going together for two years*

gotta ('gɒtə) *vb slang* ▷ *contraction of* got to

gotten ('gɒtᵊn) *vb US* 1 a past participle of **get** 2 **have gotten** (*not usually in the infinitive*) **a** to have obtained: *he had gotten a car for his 21st birthday* **b** to have become: *I've gotten sick of your constant bickering*

Götterdämmerung (ˌgɒtə'dɛməˌrʊŋ; *German* gœtər'dɛmərʊŋ) *n german myth* the twilight of the gods; their ultimate destruction in a battle with the forces of evil. Norse equivalent: **Ragnarök**

Göttingen ('gœtɪŋən) *n* a city in central Germany, in Lower Saxony: important member of the Hanseatic League (14th century); university, founded in 1734 by George II of England. Pop: 122 883 (2003 est)

gouache (gʊ'ɑːʃ) *n* 1 Also called: **body colour** a painting technique using opaque watercolour paint in which the pigments are bound with glue and the lighter tones contain white 2 the paint used in this technique 3 a painting done by this method [c19 from French, from Italian *guazzo* puddle, from Latin *aquātiō* a watering place, from *aqua* water]

Gouda ('gaʊdə; *Dutch* 'xɔʊdɑ:) *n* 1 a town in the W Netherlands, in South Holland province: important medieval cloth trade; famous for its cheese. Pop: 72 000 (2003 est) 2 a large round Dutch cheese, mild and similar in taste to Edam

gouge (gaʊdʒ) *vb* (*mainly tr*) 1 (usually foll by *out*) to scoop or force (something) out of its position, esp with the fingers or a pointed instrument 2 (sometimes foll by *out*) to cut (a hole or groove) in (something) with a sharp instrument or tool 3 *US and Canadian informal* to extort from 4 (*also intr*) *Austral* to dig for (opal) ▷ *n* 5 a type of chisel with a blade that has a concavo-convex section 6 a mark or groove made with, or as if with, a gouge 7 *geology* a fine deposit of rock fragments, esp clay, occurring between the walls of a fault or mineral vein 8 *US and Canadian informal* extortion; swindling [c15 from French, from Late Latin *gulbia* a chisel, of Celtic origin]

gouger ('gaʊdʒə) *n* 1 a person or tool that gouges 2 *Irish dialect* a low-class city lout

goujon ('guːʒɒn) *n* a small strip of fish or chicken, coated in breadcrumbs and deep-fried [French, literally: gudgeon]

goulash ('guːlæʃ) *n* 1 Also called: **Hungarian goulash** a rich stew, originating in Hungary, made of beef, lamb, or veal highly seasoned with paprika 2 *bridge* a method of dealing in threes and fours without first shuffling the cards, to produce freak hands [c19 from Hungarian *gulyás hus* herdsman's meat, from *gulya* herd]

Gouldian finch ('guːldɪən) *n* a multicoloured finch, *Chloebia gouldiae*, of tropical N Australia [named after Elizabeth *Gould* (1804–41), British natural history artist]

go under *vb* (*intr, mainly adverb*) 1 (*also preposition*) to sink below (a surface) 2 to founder or drown 3 to be conquered or overwhelmed: *the firm went under in the economic crisis*

go up *vb* (*intr, mainly adverb*) 1 (*also preposition*) to move or lead to or as if to a higher place or level; rise; increase: *prices are always going up; the curtain goes up at eight o'clock; new buildings are going up all around us* 2 to be destroyed: *the house went up in flames* 3 *Brit* to go or return (to college or university) at the beginning of a term or academic year

gourami ('gʊərəmɪ) *n, pl* **-mi** or **-mis** 1 a large SE Asian labyrinth fish, *Osphronemus goramy*, used for food and (when young) as an aquarium fish 2 any of various other labyrinth fishes, such as *Helostoma temmincki* (**kissing gourami**), many of which are brightly coloured and popular aquarium fishes [from Malay *gurami*]

gourd (gʊəd) *n* 1 the fruit of any of various cucurbitaceous or similar plants, esp the bottle gourd and some squashes, whose dried shells are used for ornament, drinking cups, etc 2 any plant that bears this fruit. See also **sour gourd, dishcloth gourd, calabash** 3 a bottle or flask made from the dried shell of the bottle gourd 4 a small bottle shaped like a gourd [c14 from Old French *gourde*, ultimately from Latin *cucurbita*] > 'gourd,like *adj* > 'gourd-,shaped *adj*

gourde (gʊəd) *n* the standard monetary unit of Haiti, divided into 100 centimes [c19 from French, feminine of *gourd* heavy, from Latin *gurdus* a stupid person]

gourmand ('gʊəmənd; *French* gurmɑ̃) or **gormand** *n* a person devoted to eating and drinking, esp to excess [c15 from Old French *gourmant*, of uncertain origin] > 'gourmand,ism *n*

gourmandise (,gʊəmən'diːz) or **gormandize** *n* a love of and taste for good food

gourmet ('gʊəmei; *French* gurmɛ) *n* a person who cultivates a discriminating palate for the enjoyment of good food and drink [c19 from French, from Old French *gromet* serving boy]

gout (gaʊt) *n* 1 a metabolic disease characterized by painful inflammation of certain joints, esp of the big toe and foot, caused by deposits of sodium urate in them 2 *archaic* a drop or splash, esp of blood [c13 from Old French *goute* gout (thought to result from drops of humours), from Latin *gutta* a drop] > 'gouty *adj* > 'goutily *adv* > 'goutiness *n*

goût *French* (gu) *n* taste or good taste

goutweed ('gaʊt,wiːd) *n* a widely naturalized Eurasian umbelliferous plant, *Aegopodium podagraria*, with white flowers and creeping underground stems. Also called: **bishop's weed, ground elder, herb Gerard**

gov *an internet domain name for* a US government organization

Gov. or **gov.** *abbreviation for* governor

govern ('gʌvən) *vb* (*mainly tr*) 1 (*also intr*) to direct and control the actions, affairs, policies, functions, etc, of (a political unit, organization, nation, etc); rule 2 to exercise restraint over; regulate or direct: *to govern one's temper* 3 to be a predominant influence on (something); decide or determine (something): *his injury governed his decision to avoid sports* 4 to control the speed of (an engine, machine, etc) using a governor 5 to control the rate of flow of (a fluid) by using an automatic valve 6 (of a word) to determine the inflection of (another word): *Latin nouns govern adjectives that modify them* [c13 from Old French *gouverner*, from Latin *gubernāre* to steer, from Greek *kubernan*] > 'governable *adj* > ,governa'bility or 'governableness *n*

governance ('gʌvənəns) *n* 1 government, control, or authority 2 the action, manner, or system of governing

governess ('gʌvənɪs) *n* a woman teacher employed in a private household to teach and train the children

government ('gʌvənmənt, 'gʌvəmənt) *n* 1 the exercise of political authority over the actions, affairs, etc, of a political unit, people, etc, as well as the performance of certain functions for this unit or body; the action of governing; political rule and administration 2 the system or form by which a community, etc, is ruled: *tyrannical government* 3 a the executive policy-making body of a political unit, community, etc; ministry or administration: *yesterday we got a new government* b (*capital when of a specific country*): *the British Government* 4 a the state and its administration: *blame it on the government* b (*as modifier*): *a government agency* 5 regulation; direction 6 *grammar* the determination of the form of one word by another word > **governmental** (,gʌvən'mɛntəl, ,gʌvə'mɛntəl) *adj* > ,govern'mentally *adv*

Government House *n* the official residence of a representative of the British Crown (such as a Canadian Lieutenant-Governor or an Australian Governor General) in a state or province that recognizes the British sovereign as Head of the Commonwealth

government issue *adj* supplied by a government or government agency

government man *n Austral* (in the 19th century) a convict

governor ('gʌvənə) *n* 1 a person who governs 2 the ruler or chief magistrate of a colony, province, etc 3 the representative of the Crown in a British colony 4 *Brit* the senior administrator or head of a society, prison, etc 5 the chief executive of any state in the US 6 a device that controls the speed of an engine, esp by regulating the supply of fuel, etc, either to limit the maximum speed or to maintain a constant speed 7 *grammar* Also called: **head** a a word in a phrase or clause that is the principal item and gives the function of the whole, as *hat* in *the big red hat* b (*as modifier*): *a governor noun* 8 *Brit informal* a name or title of respect for a father, employer, etc ▷ Related adjective: **gubernatorial**

governor general *n, pl* **governors general** or **governor generals** 1 the representative of the Crown in a dominion of the Commonwealth or a British colony; vicegerent 2 *Brit* a governor with jurisdiction or precedence over other governors > ,governor-'general,ship *n*

governorship ('gʌvənəʃɪp) *n* the office, jurisdiction, or term of a governor

Govt or **govt** *abbreviation for* government

gowan ('gaʊən) *n Scot* any of various yellow or white flowers growing in fields, esp the common daisy [c16 variant of *gollan*, probably of Scandinavian origin; compare Old Norse *gullin* golden] > 'gowaned *adj* > 'gowany *adj*

Gower ('gaʊə) *n* **the** a peninsula in S Wales, in Swansea county on the Bristol Channel: mainly agricultural with several resorts

go with *vb* (*intr, preposition*) 1 to accompany 2 to blend or harmonize: *that new wallpaper goes well with the furniture* 3 to be a normal part of: *three acres of land go with the house* 4 to be of the same opinion as: *I'm sorry I can't go with you on your new plan* 5 (of two people) to associate frequently with (each other)

go without *vb* (*intr*) 1 *chiefly Brit* to be denied or deprived of (something, esp food): *if you don't like your tea you can go without* 2 **that goes without saying** that is obvious or self-evident

gowk (gaʊk) *n Scot and northern English dialect* 1 a stupid person; fool 2 a cuckoo [from Old Norse *gaukr* cuckoo; related to Old High German *gouh*]

gowl (gaʊl) *n Midland English dialect* the substance often found in the corner of the eyes after sleep

gown (gaʊn) *n* 1 any of various outer garments, such as a woman's elegant or formal dress, a dressing robe, or a protective garment, esp one worn by surgeons during operations 2 a loose wide garment indicating status, such as worn by academics 3 the members of a university as opposed to the other residents of the university town. Compare **town** (sense 7) ▷ *vb* 4 (*tr*) to supply with or dress in a gown [c14 from Old French *goune*, from Late Latin *gunna* garment made of leather or fur, of Celtic origin]

goy (gɔɪ) *n, pl* **goyim** ('gɔɪɪm) or **goys** a Jewish word for a gentile [from Yiddish, from Hebrew *goi* people] > 'goyish *adj*

gp *the internet domain name for* Guadeloupe

GP *abbreviation for* 1 general practitioner 2 Gallup Poll 3 (in Britain) graduated pension 4 Grand Prix 5 gas-permeable (contact lens) 6 *music* general pause

GPI *abbreviation for* general paralysis of the insane (general paresis)

GPMU (in Britain) *abbreviation for* Graphical, Paper and Media Union

GPO *abbreviation for* general post office

GPRS *abbreviation for* general packet radio service: a telecommunications system providing very fast internet connections for mobile phones

GPS *abbreviation for* 1 **global positioning system** 2 (in Australia) Great Public Schools; used of a group of mainly nonstate schools, and of sporting competitions between them

GPU *abbreviation for* State Political Administration; the Soviet police and secret police from 1922 to 1923 [from Russian *Gosudarstvennoye politicheskoye upravlenie*]

gq *the internet domain name for* Equatorial Guinea

GQ *military abbreviation for* general quarters

gr *the internet domain name for* Greece

GR *international car registration for* Greece

Gr. *abbreviation for* 1 Grecian 2 Greece 3 Greek

GR8 *text messaging abbreviation for* great

Graafian follicle ('grɑːfɪən) *n* a fluid-filled vesicle in the mammalian ovary containing a developing egg cell [C17 named after R. de Graaf (1641–73), Dutch anatomist]

grab (græb) *vb* **grabs, grabbing, grabbed** **1** to seize hold of (something) **2** (*tr*) to seize illegally or unscrupulously **3** (*tr*) to arrest; catch **4** (*intr*) (of a brake or clutch in a vehicle) to grip and release intermittently causing juddering **5** (*tr*) *informal* to catch the attention or interest of; impress ▷ *n* **6** the act or an instance of grabbing **7** a mechanical device for gripping objects, esp the hinged jaws of a mechanical excavator **8** something that is grabbed **9** **up for grabs** *informal* available to be bought, claimed, or won [C16 probably from Middle Low German or Middle Dutch *grabben;* related to Swedish *grabba,* Sanskrit *grbhnāti* he seizes] > **'grabber** *n*

grab bag *n* **1** a collection of miscellaneous things **2** *US, Canadian, and Austral* a bag or other container from which gifts are drawn at random

grabble ('græb^{ə}l) *vb* **1** (*intr*) to scratch or feel about with the hands **2** (*intr*) to fall to the ground; sprawl **3** (*tr*) *Caribbean* to seize rashly [C16 probably from Dutch *grabbelen,* from *grabben* to GRAB] > **'grabbler** *n*

grabby ('græbɪ) *adj* **-bier, -biest** **1** greedy or selfish **2** direct, stimulating, or attention-grabbing: *grabbier opening paragraphs*

graben ('grɑːb^{ə}n) *n* an elongated trough of land produced by subsidence of the earth's crust between two faults [C19 from German, from Old High German *graban* to dig]

grace (greɪs) *n* **1** elegance and beauty of movement, form, expression, or proportion **2** a pleasing or charming quality **3** goodwill or favour **4** the granting of a favour or the manifestation of goodwill, esp by a superior **5** a sense of propriety and consideration for others **6** (*plural*) **a** affectation of manner (esp in the phrase **airs and graces**) **b** **in (someone's) good graces** regarded favourably and with kindness by (someone) **7** mercy; clemency **8** *Christianity* **a** the free and unmerited favour of God shown towards man **b** the divine assistance and power given to man in spiritual rebirth and sanctification **c** the condition of being favoured or sanctified by God **d** an unmerited gift, favour, etc, granted by God **9** a short prayer recited before or after a meal to invoke a blessing upon the food or give thanks for it **10** *music* a melodic ornament or decoration **11** See **days of grace** **12** **with (a) bad grace** unwillingly or grudgingly **13** **with (a) good grace** willingly or cheerfully ▷ *vb* **14** (*tr*) to add elegance and beauty to: *flowers graced the room* **15** (*tr*) to honour or favour: *to grace a party with one's presence* **16** to ornament or decorate (a melody, part, etc) with nonessential notes [C12 from Old French, from Latin *grātia,* from *grātus* pleasing]

Grace (greɪs) *n* (preceded by *your, his,* or *her*) a title used to address or refer to a duke, duchess, or archbishop

grace-and-favour *n* (*modifier*) *Brit* (of a house, flat, etc) owned by the sovereign and granted free of rent to a person to whom the sovereign wishes to express gratitude

grace cup *n* a cup, as of wine, passed around at the end of the meal for the final toast

graceful ('greɪsfʊl) *adj* characterized by beauty of movement, style, form, etc > **'gracefully** *adv* > **'gracefulness** *n*

graceless ('greɪslɪs) *adj* **1** lacking any sense of right and wrong; depraved **2** lacking grace or excellence > **'gracelessly** *adv* > **'gracelessness** *n*

grace note *n* *music* a note printed in small type to indicate that it is melodically and harmonically nonessential

Graces ('greɪsɪz) *pl n* *Greek myth* three sisters, the goddesses Aglaia, Euphrosyne, and Thalia, givers of charm and beauty

gracile ('græsaɪl) *adj* **1** gracefully thin or slender **2** a less common word for **graceful** [C17 from Latin *gracilis* slender] > **gracility** (græ'sɪlɪtɪ) *or* **'gracileness** *n*

gracioso (ˌgræsɪ'əʊsəʊ; *Spanish* gra'θjoso) *n, pl* **-sos** a clown in Spanish comedy [C17 from Spanish: GRACIOUS]

gracious ('greɪʃəs) *adj* **1** characterized by or showing kindness and courtesy **2** condescendingly courteous, benevolent, or indulgent **3** characterized by or suitable for a life of elegance, ease, and indulgence: *gracious living; gracious furnishings* **4** merciful or compassionate **5** *obsolete* fortunate, prosperous, or happy ▷ *interj* **6** an expression of mild surprise or wonder (often in exclamatory phrases such as **good gracious!, gracious me!**) > **'graciously** *adv* > **'graciousness** *n*

grackle ('græk^{ə}l) *n* **1** Also called: **crow blackbird** any American songbird of the genera *Quiscalus* and *Cassidix,* having a dark iridescent plumage: family *Icteridae* (American orioles) **2** any of various starlings of the genus *Gracula,* such as *G. religiosa* (**Indian grackle** or **hill mynah**) [C18 from New Latin *Grācula,* from Latin *grāculus* jackdaw]

grad (græd) *n* *informal* a graduate

grad. *abbreviation for* **1** *maths* gradient **2** *education* graduate(d)

gradable ('greɪdəb^{ə}l) *adj* **1** capable of being graded **2** *linguistics* denoting or relating to a word in whose meaning there is some implicit relationship to a standard: *"big" and "small" are gradable adjectives* ▷ *n* **3** *linguistics* a word of this kind > **ˌgrada'bility** *or* **'gradableness** *n*

gradate (grə'deɪt) *vb* **1** to change or cause to change imperceptibly, as from one colour, tone, or degree to another **2** (*tr*) to arrange in grades or ranks

gradation (grə'deɪʃən) *n* **1** a series of systematic stages; gradual progression **2** (*often plural*) a stage or degree in such a series or progression **3** the act or process of arranging or forming in stages, grades, etc, or of progressing evenly **4** (in painting, drawing, or sculpture) transition from one colour, tone, or surface to another through a series of very slight changes **5** *linguistics* any change in the quality or length of a vowel within a word indicating certain distinctions, such as inflectional or tense differentiations. See **ablaut** **6** *geology* the natural levelling of land as a result of the building up or wearing down of pre-existing formations > **gra'dational** *adj* > **gra'dationally** *adv*

grade (greɪd) *n* **1** a position or degree in a scale, as of quality, rank, size, or progression: *small-grade eggs; high-grade timber* **2** a group of people or things of the same category **3** *chiefly US* a military or other rank **4** a stage in a course of progression **5** a mark or rating indicating achievement or the worth of work done, as at school **6** *US and Canadian* a unit of pupils of similar age or ability taught together at school **7** *US and Canadian* **a** a part of a railway, road, etc, that slopes upwards or downwards; inclination **b** a measure of such a slope, esp the ratio of the vertical distance between two points on the slope to the horizontal distance between them. Also called: **gradient** **8** a unit of angle equal to one hundredth of a right angle or 0.9 degree **9** *stockbreeding* **a** an animal with one purebred parent and one of unknown or unimproved breeding **b** (*as modifier*): *a grade sheep.* Compare **crossbred** (sense 2), **purebred** (sense 2) **10** *linguistics* one of the forms of the vowel in a morpheme when this vowel varies because of gradation **11** **at grade** **a** on the same level **b** (of a river profile or land surface) at an equilibrium level and slope, because there is a balance between erosion and deposition **12** **make the grade** *informal* **a** to reach the required standard **b** to succeed ▷ *vb* **13** (*tr*) to arrange according to quality, rank, etc **14** (*tr*) to determine the grade of or assign a grade to **15** (*intr*) to achieve or deserve a grade or rank **16** to change or blend (something) gradually; merge **17** (*tr*) to level (ground, a road, etc) to a suitable gradient **18** (*tr*) *stockbreeding* to cross (one animal) with another to produce a grade animal [C16 from French, from Latin *gradus* step, from *gradī* to step]

-grade *adj combining form* indicating a kind or manner of movement or progression: *plantigrade; retrograde* [via French from Latin *-gradus,* from *gradus* a step, from *gradī* to walk]

grade cricket *n* *Austral* competitive cricket, in which cricket club teams are arranged in grades

grade crossing *n* *US and Canadian* a point at which a railway and a road cross, esp one with barriers that close the road when a train is scheduled to pass. Also called (in Britain and certain other countries): **level crossing**

graded post *n* *Brit* a position in a school having special responsibility for which additional payment is given

grade inflation *n* an apparently continual increase in numbers of students attaining high examination grades, or the practice of awarding grades in this way

gradely ('greɪdlɪ) *adj* **-lier, -liest** *Midland English dialect* fine; excellent [C13 *greithlic, greithli,* from Old Norse *greidhligr,* from *greidhr* ready]

grader ('greɪdə) *n* **1** a person or thing that grades **2** a machine, either self-powered or towed by a tractor, that levels earth, rubble, etc, as in road construction

grade school *n* *US* another name for **elementary school**

gradient ('greɪdɪənt) *n* **1** Also called (esp US): **grade** a part of a railway, road, etc, that slopes upwards or downwards; inclination **2** Also called (esp US and Canadian): **grade** a measure of such a slope, esp the ratio of the vertical distance between two points on the slope to the horizontal distance between them **3** *physics* a measure of the change of some physical quantity, such as temperature or electric potential, over a specified distance **4** *maths* **a** (of a curve) the slope of the tangent at any point on a curve with respect to the horizontal axis **b** (of a function, $f(x, y, z)$) the vector whose components along the axes are the partial derivatives of the function with respect to each variable, and whose direction is that in which the derivative of the function has its maximum value. Usually written: grad **f**, ∇f or ∇**f**. Compare **curl** (sense 11), **divergence** (sense 4) ▷ *adj* **5** sloping uniformly [C19 from Latin *gradiēns* stepping, from *gradī* to go]

g

gradient post *n* a small white post beside a railway line at a point where the gradient changes having arms set at angles representing the gradients

gradin ('greɪdɪn) *or* **gradine** (grə'diːn) *n* **1** a ledge above or behind an altar on which candles, a cross, or other ornaments stand **2** one of a set of steps or seats arranged on a slope, as in an amphitheatre [C19 from French, from Italian *gradino,* a little step, from *grado* step; see GRADE]

gradiometer (ˌgrædɪ'ɒmɪtə) *n* **1** *physics* an instrument for measuring the gradient of a magnetic field **2** *surveying* an instrument used to ensure that a long gradient remains constant

gradual ('grædjʊəl) *adj* **1** occurring, developing, moving, etc, in small stages: *a gradual improvement in health* **2** not steep or abrupt: *a gradual slope* ▷ *n* **3** (*often capital*) *Christianity* **a** an antiphon or group of several antiphons, usually from the Psalms, sung or recited immediately after the epistle at Mass **b** a book of plainsong containing the words and music of the parts of the Mass that are sung by the cantors and choir [C16 from Medieval Latin *graduālis* relating to steps, from Latin *gradus* a step] > **'gradually** *adv* > **'gradualness** *n*

gradualism ('grædjʊəˌlɪzəm) *n* **1** the policy of seeking to change something or achieve a goal gradually rather than quickly or violently, esp in politics **2** the theory that explains major changes in rock strata, fossils, etc in terms of gradual evolutionary processes rather than sudden violent catastrophes. Compare **catastrophism** > **'gradualist** *n, adj* > **ˌgradual'istic** *adj*

graduand ('grædjʊˌænd) *n chiefly Brit* a person who is about to graduate [C15 from Medieval Latin *graduandus,* gerundive of *graduārī* to GRADUATE]

graduate *n* ('grædjʊɪt) **1 a** a person who has been awarded a first degree from a university or college **b** (*as modifier*): *a graduate profession* **2** *US and Canadian* a student who has completed a course of studies at a high school and received a diploma **3** *US* a container, such as a flask, marked to indicate its capacity ▷ *vb* ('grædjʊˌeɪt) **4** to receive or cause to receive a degree or diploma **5** (*tr*) *chiefly US and Canadian* to confer a degree, diploma, etc upon **6** (*tr*) to mark (a thermometer, flask, etc) with units of measurement; calibrate **7** (*tr*) to arrange or sort into groups according to type, quality, etc **8** (*intr; often foll by to*) to change by degrees (from something to something else) [C15 from Medieval Latin *graduārī* to take a degree, from Latin *gradus* a step] > **'graduˌator** *n*

graduation (ˌgrædjʊ'eɪʃən) *n* **1** the act of graduating or the state of being graduated **2** the ceremony at which school or college degrees and diplomas are conferred **3** a mark or division or all the marks or divisions that indicate measure on an instrument or vessel

gradus ('greɪdəs) *n, pl* **-duses 1** a book of études or other musical exercises arranged in order of increasing difficulty **2** *prosody* a dictionary or textbook of prosody for use in writing Latin or Greek verse [C18 shortened from Latin *Gradus ad Parnassum* a step towards Parnassus, a dictionary of prosody used in the 18th and 19th centuries]

Graeae ('griːiː) *or* **Graiae** *pl n Greek myth* three aged sea deities, having only one eye and one tooth among them, guardians of their sisters, the Gorgons

Graecism *or esp US* **Grecism** ('griːsɪzəm) *n* **1** Greek characteristics or style **2** admiration for or imitation of these, as in sculpture or architecture **3** a form of words characteristic or imitative of the idiom of the Greek language

Graecize, Graecise *or esp US* **Grecize** ('griːsaɪz) *vb* another word for **Hellenize** [C17 from Latin *graecizāre* to imitate the Greeks, from Greek *graikizein*]

Graeco- *or esp US* **Greco-** ('griːkəʊ, 'grɛkəʊ) *combining form* Greek: *Graeco-Roman*

Graeco-Roman *or esp US* **Greco-Roman** *adj* **1** of, characteristic of, or relating to Greek and Roman influences, as found in Roman sculpture **2** denoting a style of wrestling in which the legs may not be used to obtain a fall and no hold may be applied below the waist

Graf *German* (graːf) *n, pl* *Grafen* ('graːfən) a German count: often used as a title [German, from Old High German *grāvo*]

graffiti (græ'fiːtiː) *pl n, sing* **-to** (-təʊ) **1** (*sometimes with singular verb*) drawings, messages, etc, often obscene, scribbled on the walls of public lavatories, advertising posters, etc **2** *archaeol* inscriptions or drawings scratched or carved onto a surface, esp rock or pottery [C19 *graffito* from Italian: a little scratch, from *graffio,* from Latin *graphium* stylus, from Greek *grapheion;* see GRAFT[1]] > **graffitist** *n*

graft[1] (grɑːft) *n* **1** *horticulture* **a** a piece of plant tissue (the scion), normally a stem, that is made to unite with an established plant (the stock), which supports and nourishes it **b** the plant resulting from the union of scion and stock **c** the point of union between the scion and the stock **2** *surgery* a piece of tissue or an organ transplanted from a donor or from the patient's own body to an area of the body in need of the tissue **3** the act of joining one thing to another by or as if by grafting ▷ *vb* **4** *horticulture* **a** to induce (a plant or part of a plant) to unite with another part or (of a plant or part of a plant) to unite in this way **b** to produce (fruit, flowers, etc) by this means or (of fruit, flowers, etc) to grow by this means **5** to transplant (tissue) or (of tissue) to be transplanted **6** to attach or incorporate or become attached or incorporated: *to graft a happy ending onto a sad tale* [C15 from Old French *graffe,* from Medieval Latin *graphium,* from Latin: stylus, from Greek *grapheion,* from *graphein* to write] > **'grafter** *n* > **'grafting** *n*

graft[2] (grɑːft) *informal* ▷ *n* **1** work (esp in the phrase **hard graft**) **2 a** the acquisition of money, power, etc, by dishonest or unfair means, esp by taking advantage of a position of trust **b** something gained in this way, such as profit from government business **c** a payment made to a person profiting by such a practice ▷ *vb* **3** (*intr*) to work **4** to acquire by or practise graft [C19 of uncertain origin] > **'grafter** *n*

graft hybrid *n* a plant produced by grafting a scion and stock from dissimilar plants such that cells of both stock and scion are mixed in the visible parts, giving an intermediate appearance in at least some parts; chimera

graham ('greɪəm) *n* (*modifier*) *chiefly US and Canadian* made of graham flour: *graham crackers* [C19 named after S. *Graham* (1794–1851), American dietetic reformer]

graham flour *n chiefly US and Canadian* unbolted wheat flour ground from whole-wheat grain, similar to whole-wheat flour

Graham Land *n* the N part of the Antarctic Peninsula: became part of the British Antarctic Territory in 1962 (formerly part of the Falkland Islands Dependencies; Claims are suspended under the Antarctic Treaty)

Graham's Law *n* the principle that the rates of diffusion and effusion of a gas are inversely proportional to the square root of its density, proposed by Thomas Graham (1805-69) in 1831

Graiae ('greɪiː, 'graɪiː) *pl n* a variant of **Graeae**

Graian Alps ('greɪən, 'graɪ-) *pl n* the N part of the Western Alps, in France and NW Piedmont, Italy. Highest peak: Gran Paradiso, 4061 m (13 323 ft)

Grail (greɪl) *n* See **Holy Grail**

grain (greɪn) *n* **1** the small hard seedlike fruit of a grass, esp a cereal plant **2** a mass of such fruits, esp when gathered for food **3** the plants, collectively, from which such fruits are harvested **4** a small hard particle: *a grain of sand* **5 a** the general direction or arrangement of the fibrous elements in paper or wood: *to saw across the grain* **b** the pattern or texture of wood resulting from such an arrangement: *the attractive grain of the table* **6** the relative size of the particles of a substance: *sugar of fine grain* **7 a** the granular texture of a rock, mineral, etc **b** the appearance of a rock, mineral, etc, determined by the size and arrangement of its constituents **8 a** the outer (hair-side) layer of a hide or skin from which the hair or wool has been removed **b** the pattern on the outer surface of such a hide or skin **9** a surface artificially imitating the grain of wood, leather, stone, etc; graining **10** the smallest unit of weight in the avoirdupois, Troy, and apothecaries' systems, based on the average weight of a grain of wheat: in the avoirdupois system it equals 1/7000 of a pound, and in the Troy and apothecaries' systems it equals 1/5760 of a pound. 1 grain is equal to 0.0648 gram. Abbreviation: **gr** **11** Also called: **metric grain** a metric unit of weight used for pearls or diamonds, equal to 50 milligrams or one quarter of a carat **12** the threads or direction of threads in a woven fabric **13** *photog* any of a large number of particles in a photographic emulsion, the size of which limit the extent to which an image can be enlarged without serious loss of definition **14** *television* a granular effect in a television picture caused by electrical noise **15** cleavage lines in crystalline material, parallel to growth planes **16** *chem* any of a large number of small crystals forming a polycrystalline solid, each having a regular array of atoms that differs in orientation from that of the surrounding crystallites **17** a state of crystallization: *to boil syrup to the grain* **18** a very small amount: *a grain of truth* **19** natural disposition, inclination, or character (esp in the phrase **go against the grain**) **20** *astronautics* a homogenous mass of solid propellant in a form designed to give the required combustion characteristics for a particular rocket **21** (*not in technical usage*) kermes or a red dye made from this insect **22** *dyeing* an obsolete word for **colour** **23** **with a grain** *or* **pinch of salt** without wholly believing: sceptically ▷ *vb* (*mainly tr*) **24** (*also intr*) to form grains or cause to form into grains; granulate; crystallize **25** to give a granular or roughened appearance or texture to **26** to paint, stain, etc, in imitation of the grain of wood or leather **27 a** to remove the hair or wool from (a hide or skin) before tanning **b** to raise the grain pattern on (leather) [C13 from Old French, from Latin *grānum*] > **'grainer** *n* > **'grainless** *adj*

grain alcohol *n* ethanol containing about 10 per cent of water, made by the fermentation of grain

grain elevator *n* a machine for raising grain to a higher level, esp one having an endless belt fitted with scoops

graining ('greɪnɪŋ) *n* **1** the pattern or texture of the grain of wood, leather, etc **2** the process of painting, printing, staining, etc, a surface in imitation of a grain **3** a surface produced by such a process

grains of paradise *pl n* the peppery seeds of either of two African zingiberaceous plants, *Aframomum melegueta* or *A. granum-paradisi,* used as stimulants, diuretics, etc. Also called: **guinea grains**

grainy ('greɪnɪ) *adj* **grainier, grainiest 1** resembling, full of, or composed of grain; granular **2** resembling the grain of wood, leather, etc **3** *photog* having poor definition because of large grain size > **'graininess** *n*

grallatorial (ˌgrælə'tɔːrɪəl) *adj* of or relating to long-legged wading birds, such as cranes, herons, and storks [C19 from New Latin *grallātōrius,* from Latin *grallātor* one who walks on stilts, from *grallae* stilts]

gralloch ('grælək; *Scot* 'grælɒx) *Brit* ▷ *n* **1** the entrails of a deer **2** the act or an instance of disembowelling a deer killed in a hunt ▷ *vb* (*tr*) **3** to disembowel (a deer killed in a hunt) [C19 from Scottish Gaelic *grealach* intestines]

gram[1] (græm) *n* a metric unit of mass equal to one thousandth of a kilogram. It is equivalent to 15.432 grains or 0.002 205 pounds. Symbol: **g** [C18 from French *gramme,* from Late Latin *gramma,* from Greek: small weight, from *graphein* to write]

gram[2] (græm) *n* **1** any of several leguminous plants, such as the beans *Phaseolus mungo* (**black gram** or **urd**) and *P. aureus* (**green gram**), whose seeds are used as food in India **2** the seed of any of these plants [C18 from Portuguese *gram* (modern spelling *grão*), from Latin *grānum* GRAIN]

gram[3] (grɑːm) *n* (in India) a village [Hindi]

gram. *abbreviation for* **1** grammar **2** grammatical

-gram *n combining form* indicating a drawing or something written or recorded: *hexagram; telegram* [from Latin *-gramma,* from Greek, from *gramma* letter and *grammē* line]

grama *or* **grama grass** ('grɑːmə) *n* any of various grasses of the genus *Bouteloua,* of W North America and South America: often used as pasture grasses [C19 from Spanish, ultimately from Latin *grāmen* grass]

gramarye *or* **gramary** ('græmərɪ) *n archaic* magic, necromancy, or occult learning [C14 from Old French *gramaire* GRAMMAR]

gram atom *or* **gram-atomic weight** *n* an amount of an element equal to its atomic weight expressed in grams: now replaced by the mole. See **mole[3]**

gram calorie *n* another name for **calorie**

gram equivalent *or* **gram-equivalent weight** *n* an amount of a substance equal to its equivalent weight expressed in grams

gramercy (grə'mɜːsɪ) *interj archaic* **1** many thanks **2** an expression of surprise, wonder, etc [C13 from Old French *grand merci* great thanks]

gramicidin or **gramicidin D** (ˌgræmɪˈsaɪdɪn) n an antibiotic used in treating local Gram-positive bacterial infections: obtained from the soil bacterium *Bacillus brevis* [c20 from GRAM(-POSITIVE) + -CID(E) + -IN]

gramineous (grəˈmɪnɪəs) adj resembling a grass; grasslike. Also: graminaceous (ˌgræmɪˈneɪʃəs) [c17 from Latin *grāmineus* of grass, grassy, from *grāmen* grass]

graminicolous (ˌgræmɪˈnɪkələs) adj (esp of parasitic fungi) living on grass

graminivorous (ˌgræmɪˈnɪvərəs) adj (of animals) feeding on grass [c18 from Latin *grāmen* grass + -VOROUS]

graminology (ˌgræmɪˈnɒlədʒɪ) n the branch of botany concerned with the study of grasses

grammage (ˈgræmɪdʒ) n the weight of paper expressed as grams per square metre

grammalogue (ˈgræməˌlɒg) n (in shorthand) a sign or symbol representing a word [c19 from Greek, *gramma* letter + *logos* word]

grammar (ˈgræmə) n **1** the branch of linguistics that deals with syntax and morphology, sometimes also phonology and semantics **2** the abstract system of rules in terms of which a person's mastery of his native language can be explained **3** a systematic description of the grammatical facts of a language **4** a book containing an account of the grammatical facts of a language or recommendations as to rules for the proper use of a language **5 a** the use of language with regard to its correctness or social propriety, esp in syntax: *the teacher told him to watch his grammar* **b** (*as modifier*): *a grammar book* **6** the elementary principles of a science or art: *the grammar of drawing* [c14 from Old French *gramaire*, from Latin *grammatica*, from Greek *grammatikē (tekhnē)* the grammatical (art), from *grammatikos* concerning letters, from *gramma* letter] > ˈgrammarless adj

grammarian (grəˈmɛərɪən) n **1** a person whose occupation is the study of grammar **2** the author of a grammar

grammar school n **1** Brit (esp formerly) a state-maintained secondary school providing an education with an academic bias for children who are selected by the eleven-plus examination, teachers' reports, or other means. Compare **secondary modern school, comprehensive school 2** US another term for **elementary school 3** NZ a secondary school forming part of the public education system

grammatical (grəˈmætɪkᵊl) adj **1** of or relating to grammar **2** (of a sentence) well formed; regarded as correct and acceptable by native speakers of the language > gramˈmatically adv > gramˈmaticalness n

grammatical meaning n the meaning of a word by reference to its function within a sentence rather than to a world outside the sentence. Compare **lexical meaning, function word**

grammatology (ˌgræməˈtɒlədʒɪ) n the scientific study of writing systems > ˌgrammaˈtologist n

gram molecule or **gram-molecular weight** n an amount of a compound equal to its molecular weight expressed in grams: now replaced by the mole. See **mole³** > ˌgram-moˈlecular or gram-molar (ˌgræmˈməʊlə) adj

Grammy (ˈgræmɪ) n, pl -mys or -mies (in the US) one of the gold-plated discs awarded annually for outstanding achievement in the record industry [c20 from GRAM(OPHONE) + my as in EMMY]

Gram-negative adj designating bacteria that fail to retain the violet stain in Gram's method

gramophone (ˈgræməˌfəʊn) n **1** Also called: acoustic gramophone a device for reproducing the sounds stored on a record: now usually applied to the nearly obsolete type that uses a clockwork motor and acoustic horn. US and Canadian name: phonograph **b** (*as modifier*): *a gramophone record* **2** the technique and practice of recording sound on disc: *the gramophone has made music widely available* [c19 originally a trademark,

perhaps based on an inversion of *phonogram*; see PHONO-, -GRAM] > gramophonic (ˌgræməˈfɒnɪk) adj

Grampian Mountains (ˈgræmpɪən) pl n **1** a mountain system of central Scotland, extending from the southwest to the northeast and separating the Highlands from the Lowlands. Highest peak: Ben Nevis, 1344 m (4408 ft) **2** a mountain range in SE Australia, in W Victoria ▷ Also called: the Grampians

Grampian Region n a former local government region in NE Scotland, formed in 1975 from Aberdeenshire, Kincardineshire, and most of Banffshire and Morayshire; replaced in 1996 by the council areas of Aberdeenshire, City of Aberdeen, and Moray

Gram-positive adj designating bacteria that retain the violet stain in Gram's method

grampus (ˈgræmpəs) n, pl -puses **1** a widely distributed slaty-grey dolphin, *Grampus griseus*, with a blunt snout **2** another name for **killer whale** [c16 from Old French *graspois*, from *gras* fat (from Latin *crassus*) + *pois* fish (from Latin *piscis*)]

Gram's method n bacteriol a staining technique used to classify bacteria, based on their ability to retain or lose a violet colour, produced by crystal violet and iodine, after treatment with a decolorizing agent. See also **Gram-negative, Gram-positive** [c19 named after Hans Christian Joachim Gram (1853–1938), Danish physician]

gran (græn) n an informal word for **grandmother**

Granada (grəˈnɑːdə) n **1** a former kingdom of S Spain, in Andalusia: founded in the 13th century and divided in 1833 into the present-day provinces of Granada, Almería, and Málaga **2** a city in S Spain, in Andalusia: capital of the Moorish kingdom of Granada from 1238 to 1492 and a great commercial and cultural centre, containing the Alhambra palace (13th and 14th centuries); university (1531). Pop: 237 663 (2003 est) **3** a city in SW Nicaragua, on the NW shore of Lake Nicaragua: the oldest city in the country, founded in 1523 by Córdoba; attacked frequently by pirates in the 17th century. Pop: 95 000 (2005 est)

granadilla (ˌgrænəˈdɪlə) n **1** any of various passionflowers, such as *Passiflora quadrangularis* (**giant granadilla**), that have edible egg-shaped fleshy fruit **2** Also called: passion fruit the fruit of such a plant [c18 from Spanish, diminutive of *granada* pomegranate, from Late Latin *grānātum*]

Grana Padano (ˌgrɑːnə pəˈdɑːnəʊ) n a rich semifat hard cheese with a granular texture, often used grated, esp on pasta dishes and soups [c21 from Italian *grana* grain + *Padano* from the Po Valley]

granary (ˈgrænərɪ; US ˈgreɪnərɪ) n, pl -ries **1** a building or store room for storing threshed grain, farm feed, etc **2** a region that produces a large amount of grain [c16 from Latin *grānārium*, from *grānum* GRAIN]

Granary (ˈgrænərɪ) adj trademark (of bread, flour, etc) containing malted wheat grain

Gran Canaria (graŋ kaˈnarja) n the Spanish name for **Grand Canary**

gran cassa (Italian gran ˈkassa) n music another name for **bass drum** [Italian: great drum]

Gran Chaco (Spanish gran ˈtʃako) n a plain of S central South America, between the Andes and the Paraguay River in SE Bolivia, E Paraguay, and N Argentina: huge swamps and scrub forest. Area: about 780 000 sq km (300 000 sq miles). Often shortened to: Chaco

grand (grænd) adj **1** large or impressive in size, extent, or consequence: *grand mountain scenery* **2** characterized by or attended with magnificence or display; sumptuous: *a grand feast* **3** of great distinction or pretension; dignified or haughty **4** designed to impress: *he punctuated his story with grand gestures* **5** very good; wonderful **6** comprehensive; complete: *a grand total* **7** worthy of respect; fine: *a grand old man* **8** large or impressive in conception or execution: *grand ideas* **9** most important; chief: *the grand arena* ▷ n **10** short for **grand piano 11** pl

grand *slang* a thousand pounds or dollars [c16 from Old French, from Latin *grandis*] > ˈgrandly adv > ˈgrandness n

grand- prefix (in designations of kinship) one generation removed in ascent or descent: *grandson; grandfather* [from French *grand-*, on the model of Latin *magnus* in such phrases as *avunculus magnus* great-uncle]

grandad, granddad (ˈgrænˌdæd) or **grandaddy, granddaddy** (ˈgrænˌdædɪ) n, pl -dads or -daddies informal words for **grandfather**

grandad shirt n a long-sleeved collarless shirt

grandam (ˈgrændəm, -dæm) or **grandame** (ˈgrændeɪm, -dəm) n an archaic word for **grandmother** [c13 from Anglo-French *grandame*, from Old French GRAND- + *dame* lady, mother]

grandaunt (ˈgrændˌɑːnt) n another name for **great-aunt**

Grand Bahama n an island in the Atlantic, in the W Bahamas. Pop: 46 994 (2000). Area: 1114 sq km (430 sq miles)

Grand Banks pl n a part of the continental shelf in the Atlantic, extending for about 560 km (350 miles) off the SE coast of Newfoundland: meeting place of the cold Labrador Current and the warm Gulf Stream, producing frequent fogs and formerly rich fishing grounds

Grand Canal n **1** a canal in E China, extending north from Hangzhou to Tianjin: the longest canal in China, now partly silted up; central section, linking the Yangtze and Yellow Rivers, finished in 486 BC; north section finished by Kublai Khan between 1282 and 1292. Length: about 1600 km (1000 miles). Chinese name: Da Yunhe **2** a canal in Venice, forming the main water thoroughfare: noted for its bridges, the Rialto, and the fine palaces along its banks

Grand Canary n an island in the Atlantic, in the Canary Islands: part of the Spanish province of Las Palmas. Capital: Las Palmas. Pop: 771 333 (2002 est). Area: 1533 sq km (592 sq miles). Spanish name: Gran Canaria

Grand Canyon n a gorge of the Colorado River in N Arizona, extending from its junction with the Little Colorado River to Lake Mead; cut by vertical river erosion through the multicoloured strata of a high plateau; partly contained in the **Grand Canyon National Park**, covering 2610 sq km (1008 sq miles). Length: 451 km (280 miles). Width: 6 km (4 miles) to 29 km (18 miles). Greatest depth: over 1.5 km (1 mile)

grand chain n a figure in formation dances, such as the lancers and Scottish reels, in which couples split up and move around in a circle in opposite directions, passing all other dancers until reaching their original partners

grandchild (ˈgrænˌtʃaɪld) n, pl -children (-ˌtʃɪldrən) the son or daughter of one's child

Grand Coulee (ˈkuːlɪ) n a canyon in central Washington State, over 120 m (400 ft) deep, at the N end of which is situated the **Grand Coulee Dam**, on the Columbia River. Height of dam: 168 m (550 ft). Length of dam: 1310 m (4300 ft)

granddaughter (ˈgrænˌdɔːtə) n a daughter of one's son or daughter

grand duchess n **1** the wife or a widow of a grand duke **2** a woman who holds the rank of grand duke in her own right

grand duchy n the territory, state, or principality of a grand duke or grand duchess

grand duke n **1** a prince or nobleman who rules a territory, state, or principality **2** a son or a male descendant in the male line of a Russian tsar **3** a medieval Russian prince who ruled over other princes

grande dame French (grɑ̃d dam) n a woman regarded as the most experienced, prominent, or venerable member of her profession, etc: *the grande dame of fashion*

grandee (grænˈdiː) n **1** a Spanish or Portuguese prince or nobleman of the highest rank **2** a man of great rank or eminence [c16 from Spanish

g

grande] > gran'deeship *n*

Grande-Terre (*French* grɑ̃dtɛr) *n* a French island in the Caribbean, in the Lesser Antilles: one of the two main islands which constitute Guadeloupe. Chief town: Pointe-à-Pitre

grandeur ('grænd͡ʒə) *n* 1 personal greatness, esp when based on dignity, character, or accomplishments 2 magnificence; splendour 3 pretentious or bombastic behaviour

Grand Falls *pl n* the former name (until 1965) of **Churchill Falls**

grandfather ('græn,fɑːðə, 'grænd-) *n* 1 the father of one's father or mother 2 (*often plural*) a male ancestor 3 (*often capital*) a familiar term of address for an old man 4 *dialect* a caterpillar or woodlouse

grandfather clause *n* 1 *US history* a clause in the constitutions of several Southern states that waived electoral literacy requirements for lineal descendants of people voting before 1867, thus ensuring the franchise for illiterate Whites: declared unconstitutional in 1915 2 a clause in legislation that forbids or regulates an activity so that those engaged in it are exempted from the ban

grandfather clock *n* any of various types of long-pendulum clocks in tall standing wooden cases, usually between six and eight feet tall. Also called: **longcase clock**

grandfatherly ('græn,fɑːðəlɪ, 'grænd-) *adj* of, resembling, or suitable to a grandfather, esp in being kindly

grand final *n Austral* the final game of the season in any of various sports, esp football

Grand Guignol French (grɑ̃ giɲɔl) *n* **a** a brief sensational play intended to horrify **b** (*modifier*) of, relating to, or like plays of this kind [c20 after *Le Grand Guignol*, a small theatre in Montmartre, Paris]

grandiloquent (græn'dɪləkwənt) *adj* inflated, pompous, or bombastic in style or expression [c16 from Latin *grandiloquus*, from *grandis* great + *loquī* to speak] > gran'diloquence *n* > gran'diloquently *adv*

grandiose ('grændɪ,əʊs) *adj* 1 pretentiously grand or stately 2 imposing in conception or execution [c19 from French, from Italian *grandioso*, from *grande* great; see GRAND] > 'grandi,osely *adv* > grandiosity (,grændɪ'ɒsɪtɪ) *n*

grandioso (,grændɪ'əʊsəʊ) *adj, adv music* (to be played) in a grand manner

grand jury *n law* (esp in the US and, now rarely, in Canada) a jury of between 12 and 23 persons summoned to inquire into accusations of crime and ascertain whether the evidence is adequate to found an indictment. Abolished in Britain in 1948. Compare **petit jury**

Grand Lama *n* either of two high priests of Lamaism, the Dalai Lama or the Panchen Lama

grand larceny *n* 1 (formerly in England) the theft of property valued at over 12 pence. Abolished in 1827 2 (in some states of the US) the theft of property of which the value is above a specified figure, varying from state to state but usually being between $25 and $60 ▷ Compare **petit larceny**

grandma ('græn,mɑː, 'grænd-, 'græm-) or **grandmama, grandmamma** ('grænmə,mɑː, 'grænd-) *n* informal words for **grandmother**

grand mal (grɒn mæl; *French* grɑ̃ mal) *n* a form of epilepsy characterized by loss of consciousness for up to five minutes and violent convulsions. Compare **petit mal** [French: great illness]

Grand Manan (mə'næn) *n* a Canadian island, off the SW coast of New Brunswick: separated from the coast of Maine by the **Grand Manan Channel**. Area: 147 sq km (57 sq miles)

Grand Marnier (grɒn 'mɑːnɪeɪ; *French* grɑ̃ marnje) *n trademark* a French cognac-based liqueur with an orange flavour

grandmaster ('grænd,mɑːstə) *n* 1 *chess* **a** one of the top chess players of a particular country **b** (*capital as part of title*): *Grandmaster of the USSR* 2 *chess* Also called: **International Grandmaster** a player

who has been awarded the highest title by the Fédération Internationale des Échecs 3 a leading exponent of any of various arts

Grand Master *n* the title borne by the head of any of various societies, orders, and other organizations, such as the Templars or Freemasons, or the various martial arts

grandmother ('græn,mʌðə, 'grænd-) *n* 1 the mother of one's father or mother 2 (*often plural*) a female ancestor 3 (*often capital*) a familiar term of address for an old woman 4 **teach one's grandmother to suck eggs** See **egg¹** (sense 8)

grandmother clock *n* a longcase clock with a pendulum, about two thirds the size of a grandfather clock

grandmotherly ('græn,mʌðəlɪ, 'grænd-) *adj* of, resembling, or suitable to a grandmother, esp in being protective, indulgent, or solicitous

Grand Mufti *n* 1 the titular head of the Muslim community in Jerusalem and formerly the chief constitutional administrator there 2 (in Turkey) the former official head of the state religion

Grand National *n* the an annual steeplechase run at Aintree, Liverpool, since 1839

grandnephew ('græn,nɛvjuː, -,nɛfjuː, 'grænd-) *n* another name for **great-nephew**

grandniece ('græn,niːs, 'grænd-) *n* another name for **great-niece**

Grand Old Party *n* (in the US) a nickname for the Republican Party since 1880. Abbreviation: **GOP**

grand opera *n* an opera that has a serious plot and is entirely in musical form, with no spoken dialogue

grandpa ('græn,pɑː, 'grænd-, 'græm-) or **grandpapa** ('grænpə,pɑː, 'grænd-) *n* informal words for **grandfather**

grandparent ('græn,pɛərənt, 'grænd-) *n* the father or mother of either of one's parents

grand piano *n* a form of piano in which the strings are arranged horizontally. Grand pianos exist in three sizes (see **baby grand, boudoir grand, concert grand**). Compare **upright piano**

Grand Pré (grɒn preɪ; *French* grɑ̃ pre) *n* a village in SE Canada, in W Nova Scotia: setting of Longfellow's *Evangeline*

Grand Prix (*French* grɑ̃ pri) *n* 1 **a** any of a series of formula motor races held to determine the annual Drivers' World Championship **b** (*as modifier*): *a Grand Prix car* 2 *horse racing* a race for three-year-old horses run at Maisons Lafitte near Paris 3 a very important competitive event in various other sports, such as athletics, snooker, or powerboating [French: great prize]

Grand Rapids *n* (*functioning as singular*) a city in SW Michigan: electronics, car parts. Pop: 195 601 (2003 est)

Grand Remonstrance *n* the *English history* the document prepared by the Long Parliament in 1640 listing the evils of the king's government, the abuses already rectified, and the reforms Parliament advocated

grand seigneur French (grɑ̃ sɛɲœr) *n*, *pl grands seigneurs* (grɑ̃ sɛɲœr) *often ironic* a dignified or aristocratic man [literally: great lord]

grand siècle French (grɑ̃ sjɛklə) *n*, *pl grands siècles* (grɑ̃ sjɛklə) the 17th century in French art and literature, esp the classical period of Louis XIV [literally: great century]

grandsire¹ ('græn,saɪə, 'grænd-) *n* an archaic word for **grandfather**

grandsire² ('grændsə, -,saɪə) *n bell-ringing* a well-established method used in change-ringing. See **method** (sense 4)

grand slam *n* 1 *bridge* the winning of 13 tricks by one player or side or the contract to do so 2 the winning of all major competitions in a season, esp in tennis and golf 3 (*often capital*) *rugby Union* the winning of all five games in the annual Six Nations Championship involving England, Scotland, Wales, Ireland, France, and Italy. Compare **triple crown** (sense 3)

grandson ('græns˄n, 'grænd-) *n* a son of one's son or daughter

grandstand ('græn,stænd, 'grænd-) *n* 1 **a** a terraced block of seats, usually under a roof, commanding the best view at racecourses, football pitches, etc **b** (*as modifier*): *grandstand tickets* 2 the spectators in a grandstand 3 (*modifier*) as if from a grandstand; unimpeded (esp in the phrase **grandstand view**) ▷ *vb* 4 (*intr*) *informal, chiefly US and Canadian* to behave ostentatiously in an attempt to impress onlookers > 'grand,stander *n*

grandstand finish *n* a close or exciting ending to a sports match or competition

grand tour *n* 1 (*formerly*) an extended tour through the major cities of Europe, esp one undertaken by a rich or aristocratic Englishman to complete his education 2 *informal* an extended sightseeing trip, tour of inspection, etc

granduncle ('grænd,˄ŋkᵊl) *n* another name for **great-uncle**

grand unified theory *n physics* any of a number of theories of elementary particles and fundamental interactions designed to explain the gravitational, electromagnetic, strong, and weak interactions in terms of a single mathematical formalism. Abbreviation: **GUT**

Grand Union Canal *n* a canal in S England linking London and the Midlands: opened in 1801

grand vizier *n* (*formerly*) the chief officer or minister of state in the Ottoman Empire and other Muslim countries

grange (greɪnd͡ʒ) *n* 1 *chiefly Brit* a farm, esp a farmhouse or country house with its various outbuildings 2 *history* an outlying farmhouse in which a religious establishment or feudal lord stored crops and tithes in kind 3 *archaic* a granary or barn [c13 from Anglo-French *graunge*, from Medieval Latin *grānica*, from Latin *grānum* GRAIN]

Grange (greɪnd͡ʒ) *n* (in the US) 1 **the** an association of farmers that strongly influenced state legislatures in the late 19th century 2 a lodge of this association

Grangemouth ('greɪnd͡ʒməʊθ, -məθ) *n* a port in Scotland, in Falkirk council area: now Scotland's second port, with oil refineries, shipyards, and chemical industries. Pop: 17 771 (2001)

grangerize or **grangerise** ('greɪnd͡ʒə,raɪz) *vb* (*tr*) 1 to illustrate (a book) by inserting prints, drawings, etc, taken from other works 2 to raid (books) to acquire material for illustrating another book [c19 named after Joseph Granger, 18th-century English writer, whose *Biographical History of England* (1769) included blank pages for illustrations to be supplied by the reader] > 'grangerism *n* > ,granger'ization or ,granger'isation *n* > 'granger,izer or 'granger,iser *n*

grani- *combining form* indicating grain: *graniform* [from Latin, from *grānum* GRAIN]

Granicus (grə'naɪkəs) *n* an ancient river in NW Asia Minor where Alexander the Great won his first major battle against the Persians (334 BC)

granita (grə'niːtə) *n* a type of Italian dessert, similar to a sorbet [from Italian *granito* grainy]

granite ('grænɪt) *n* 1 a light-coloured coarse-grained acid plutonic igneous rock consisting of quartz, feldspars, and such ferromagnesian minerals as biotite or hornblende: widely used for building 2 great hardness, endurance, or resolution 3 another name for a **stone** (sense 9) [c17 from Italian *granito* grained, from *granire* to grain, from *grano* grain, from Latin *grānum*] > 'granite-,like *adj* > granitic (grə'nɪtɪk) or 'granit,oid *adj*

graniteware ('grænɪt,wɛə) *n* 1 iron vessels coated with enamel of a granite like appearance 2 a type of very durable white semivitreous pottery 3 a type of pottery with a speckled glaze

granitite ('grænɪ,taɪt) *n* any granite with a high content of biotite

granitization or **granitisation** (,grænɪtaɪ'zeɪʃən) *n* the metamorphic conversion of a rock into granite

granivorous (græ'nɪvərəs) *adj* (of animals) feeding on seeds and grain > **granivore** ('grænɪ,vɔː) *n*

grannies ('grænɪz) *pl n NZ informal* Granny Smith apples

grannom ('grænəm) *n* a widespread caddis fly, *Brachycentrus subnubilus,* the larvae of which attach their cases to vegetation under running water and are esteemed as a bait by anglers [c18 altered from *green tail*]

granny *or* **grannie** ('grænɪ) *n, pl* -nies 1 *informal* words for **grandmother** 2 *informal* an irritatingly fussy person 3 a revolving cap on a chimneypot that keeps out rain, etc 4 *Southern US* a midwife or nurse 5 See **granny knot**

granny bond *n* (in Britain) an informal name for **retirement issue certificate,** an index-linked savings certificate, originally available only to people over retirement age

granny flat *n* self-contained accommodation within or built onto a house, suitable for an elderly parent. Also called: **granny annexe**

grannyish ('grænɪɪʃ) *adj* typical of or suitable for an elderly woman; old-fashioned

granny knot *or* **granny's knot** *n* a reef knot with the ends crossed the wrong way, making it liable to slip or jam

Granny Smith *n* a variety of hard green-skinned apple eaten raw or cooked [c19 named after Maria Ann Smith, known as *Granny Smith* (died 1870), who first produced them at Eastwood, Sydney]

grano- *combining form* of or resembling granite: *granolith* [from German, from *Granit* GRANITE]

granodiorite (,grænəʊ'daɪə,raɪt) *n* a coarse-grained acid igneous rock containing almost twice as much plagioclase as orthoclase: intermediate in composition between granite and diorite [c19 from *grano* + DIORITE]

granola (grə'nəʊlə) *n US and Canadian* a mixture of rolled oats, brown sugar, nuts, fruit, etc, eaten with milk [c20 originally *Granola* a trademark]

granolith ('grænəʊ,lɪθ) *n* a paving material consisting of a mixture of cement and crushed granite or granite chippings > ,grano'lithic *adj, n*

granophyre ('grænəʊ,faɪə) *n* a fine-grained granitic rock in which irregular crystals of intergrown quartz and feldspar are embedded in a groundmass of these minerals [c19 from GRAN(ITE) + -*phyre* after *porphyry*] > **granophyric** (,grænəʊ'fɪrɪk) *adj*

Gran Paradiso (Italian gram para'diːzo) *n* a mountain in NW Italy, in NW Piedmont: the highest peak of the Graian Alps. Height: 4061 m (13 323 ft)

grant (grɑːnt) *vb* (tr) 1 to consent to perform or fulfil: *to grant a wish* 2 (may take a clause as object) to permit as a favour, indulgence, etc: *to grant an interview* 3 (may take a clause as object) to acknowledge the validity of; concede: *I grant what you say is true* 4 to bestow, esp in a formal manner 5 to transfer (property) to another, esp by deed; convey 6 **take for granted a** to accept or assume without question **b** to fail to appreciate the value, merit, etc, of (a person) ▷ *n* 7 a sum of money provided by a government, local authority, or public fund to finance educational study, overseas aid, building repairs, etc 8 a privilege, right, etc, that has been granted 9 the act of granting 10 a transfer of property by deed or other written instrument; conveyance 11 *US* a territorial unit in Maine, New Hampshire, and Vermont, originally granted to an individual or organization [c13 from Old French *graunter,* from Vulgar Latin *credentāre* (unattested), from Latin *crēdere* to believe] > 'grantable *adj* > 'granter *n*

Granta ('grænta, 'grɑːntə) *n* the original name, still in use locally, for the River Cam

grantee (grɑːn'tiː) *n law* a person to whom a grant is made

Grantham ('grænθəm) *n* a town in E England, in Lincolnshire: birthplace of Sir Isaac Newton and Margaret Thatcher. Pop: 34 592 (2001)

Granthi ('grʌn,tiː) *n* the caretaker of a gurdwara and the reader of the Guru Granth, who officiates at Sikh ceremonies [from Punjabi: keeper of the (GURU) GRANTH]

grant-in-aid *n, pl* grants-in-aid 1 a sum of money granted by one government to a lower level of government or to a dependency for a programme, etc 2 *education* a grant provided by the central government or local education authority to ensure consistent standards in buildings and other facilities

grant-maintained *adj* (grant maintained *when postpostive*) (of schools or educational institutions) funded directly by central government

grant of probate *n law* a certificate stating that a will is valid

grantor (grɑːn'tɔː, 'grɑːntə) *n law* a person who makes a grant

gran turismo ('græn tʊə'rizməʊ) *n, pl* gran turismos the full form of **GT** [c20 Italian, literally: great touring (i.e., touring on a grand scale)]

granular ('grænjʊlə) *adj* 1 of, like, containing, or resembling a granule or granules 2 having a grainy or granulated surface > 'granularly *adv*

granularity (,grænjʊ'lærɪtɪ) *n* 1 the state or quality of being grainy or granular 2 the state or quality of being composed of many individual pieces or elements

granulate ('grænjʊ,leɪt) *vb* 1 (tr) to make into grains 2 to make or become roughened in surface texture 3 (intr) (of a wound, ulcer, etc) to form granulation tissue > 'granulative *adj* > 'granu,lator *or* 'granu,later *n*

granulated sugar *n* a coarsely ground white sugar

granulation (,grænjʊ'leɪʃən) *n* 1 the act or process of granulating 2 a granulated texture or surface 3 a single bump or grain in such a surface 4 See **granulation tissue** 5 Also called: **granule** *astronomy* any of numerous bright regions (approximate diameter 900 km) having a fine granular structure that can appear briefly on any part of the sun's surface

granulation tissue *n* a mass of new connective tissue and capillaries formed on the surface of a healing ulcer or wound, usually leaving a scar. Nontechnical name: **proud flesh**

granule ('grænjuːl) *n* 1 a small grain 2 *geology* a single rock fragment in gravel, smaller than a pebble but larger than a sand grain 3 *astronomy* another name for **granulation** (sense 5) [c17 from Late Latin *grānulum* a small GRAIN]

granulite ('grænjʊ,laɪt) *n* a granular foliated metamorphic rock in which the minerals form a mosaic of equal-sized granules > **granulitic** (,grænjʊ'lɪtɪk) *adj*

granulocyte ('grænjʊlə,saɪt) *n* any of a group of phagocytic leucocytes having cytoplasmic granules that take up various dyes. See also **eosinophil, neutrophil** (sense 1), **basophil** (sense 2) > **granulocytic** (,grænjʊlə'sɪtɪk) *adj*

granulocytopenia (,grænjʊləʊ,saɪtəʊ'piːnɪə) *n* a diminished number of granulocytes in the blood, which occurs in certain forms of anaemia

granuloma (,grænjʊ'ləʊmə) *n, pl* -mas *or* -mata (-mətə) a tumour composed of granulation tissue produced in response to chronic infection, inflammation, a foreign body, or to unknown causes > **granulomatous** (,grænjʊ'lɒmətəs) *adj*

granulose ('grænjʊ,ləʊs, -,ləʊz) *adj* a less common word for **granular**

grape (greɪp) *n* 1 the fruit of the grapevine, which has a purple or green skin and sweet flesh: eaten raw, dried to make raisins, currants, or sultanas, or used for making wine 2 any of various plants that bear grapelike fruit, such as the Oregon grape 3 See **grapevine** (sense 1) 4 **the** an informal term for **wine** 5 See **grapeshot** [c13 from Old French *grape* bunch of grapes, of Germanic origin; compare Old High German *krāpfo;* related to CRAMP², GRAPPLE] > 'grapeless *adj* > 'grape,like *adj* > 'grapey *or* 'grapy *adj*

grapefruit ('greɪp,fruːt) *n, pl* -fruit *or* -fruits 1 a tropical or subtropical cultivated evergreen rutaceous tree, *Citrus paradisi* 2 the large round edible fruit of this tree, which has yellow rind and juicy slightly bitter pulp

grape hyacinth *n* any of various Eurasian liliaceous plants of the genus *Muscari,* esp *M. botryoides,* with clusters of rounded blue flowers resembling tiny grapes

grape ivy *n* See **rhoicissus**

grapes (greɪps) *n* (functioning as singular) *vet science archaic* an abnormal growth, resembling a bunch of grapes, on the fetlock of a horse

grapeshot ('greɪp,ʃɒt) *n* ammunition for cannons consisting of a canvas tube containing a cluster of small iron or lead balls that scatter after firing

grape sugar *n* another name for **dextrose**

grapevine ('greɪp,vaɪn) *n* 1 any of several vitaceous vines of the genus *Vitis,* esp *V. vinifera* of E Asia, widely cultivated for its fruit (grapes): family Vitaceae 2 *informal* an unofficial means of relaying information, esp from person to person 3 a wrestling hold in which a wrestler entwines his own leg around his opponent's and exerts pressure against various joints

grapey *or* **grapy** ('greɪpɪ) *adj* -pier, -piest tasting or smelling of grapes

graph (grɑːf, græf) *n* 1 Also called: **chart** a drawing depicting the relation between certain sets of numbers or quantities by means of a series of dots, lines, etc, plotted with reference to a set of axes. See also **bar graph** 2 *maths* a drawing depicting a functional relation between two or three variables by means of a curve or surface containing only those points whose coordinates satisfy the relation 3 *maths* a structure represented by a diagram consisting of points (vertices) joined by lines (edges) 4 *linguistics* a symbol in a writing system not further subdivisible into other such symbols ▷ *vb* 5 (tr) to draw or represent in a graph [c19 short for *graphic formula*]

-graph *n combining form* 1 an instrument that writes or records: *telegraph* 2 a writing, record, or drawing: *autograph; lithograph* [via Latin from Greek *-graphos,* from *graphein* to write] > **-graphic** *or* **-graphical** *adj combining form* > **-graphically** *adv combining form*

grapheme ('græfiːm) *n linguistics* one of a set of orthographic symbols (letters or combinations of letters) in a given language that serve to distinguish one word from another and usually correspond to or represent phonemes, eg the *f* in *fun,* the *ph* in *phantom,* and the *gh* in *laugh* [c20 from Greek *graphēma* a letter] > **gra'phemically** *adv*

-grapher *n combining form* 1 indicating a person who writes about or is skilled in a subject: *geographer; photographer* 2 indicating a person who writes, records, or draws in a specified way: *stenographer; lithographer*

graphic ('græfɪk) *or* **graphical** *adj* 1 vividly or clearly described 2 sexually explicit 3 of or relating to writing or other inscribed representations: *graphic symbols* 4 *maths* using, relating to, or determined by a graph 5 of or relating to the graphic arts 6 *geology* having or denoting a texture formed by intergrowth of the crystals to resemble writing: *graphic granite* [c17 from Latin *graphicus,* from Greek *graphikos,* from *graphein* to write; see CARVE] > 'graphically *or* 'graphicly *adv* > 'graphicalness *or* 'graphicness *n*

graphicacy ('græfɪkəsɪ) *n* the ability to understand and use maps, plans, symbols, etc [c20 formed on the model of *literacy*]

graphical user interface *n* an interface between a user and a computer system that involves the use of a mouse-controlled screen cursor to select options from menus, make choices with buttons, start programs by clicking icons, etc. Abbreviation: **GUI**

graphic arts *pl n* any of the fine or applied visual arts based on drawing or the use of line, as

g

opposed to colour or relief, on a plane surface, esp illustration and printmaking of all kinds

graphic equalizer *n* an electronic device for cutting or boosting selected frequencies, using small linear faders. Compare **parametric equalizer**

graphic novel *n* a novel in the form of a comic strip

graphics ('græfɪks) *n* **1** (*functioning as singular*) the process or art of drawing in accordance with mathematical principles **2** (*functioning as singular*) the study of writing systems **3** (*functioning as plural*) the drawings, photographs, etc, in the layout of a magazine or book, or in a television or film production **4** (*functioning as plural*) the information displayed on a visual display unit or on a computer printout in the form of diagrams, graphs, pictures, and symbols

graphics adapter *n computing* (on a computer) the hardware that controls the way graphics appear on the monitor

graphite ('græfaɪt) *n* a blackish soft allotropic form of carbon in hexagonal crystalline form: used in pencils, crucibles, and electrodes, as a lubricant, as a moderator in nuclear reactors, and, in a carbon fibre form, as a tough lightweight material for sporting equipment. Also called: **plumbago** [c18 from German *Graphit*; from Greek *graphein* to write + -ITE[1]] > **graphitic** (græ'fɪtɪk) *adj*

graphitize *or* **graphitise** ('græfɪ,taɪz) *vb* (*tr*) **1** to convert (a substance) into graphite, usually by heating **2** to coat or impregnate with graphite > ,graphiti'zation *or* ,graphiti'sation *n*

graphology (græ'fɒlədʒɪ) *n* **1** the study of handwriting, esp to analyse the writer's character **2** *linguistics* the study of writing systems > **graphologic** (,græfə'lɒdʒɪk) *or* ,grapho'logical *adj* > gra'phologist *n*

graphomotor (,græfə,məʊtə) *adj* of or relating to the muscular movements used or required in writing

graph paper *n* paper printed with intersecting lines, usually horizontal and vertical and equally spaced, for drawing graphs, diagrams etc

-graphy *n combining form* **1** indicating a form or process of writing, representing, etc: *calligraphy; photography* **2** indicating an art or descriptive science: *choreography; oceanography* [via Latin from Greek *-graphia*, from *graphein* to write]

grapnel ('græpnəl) *n* **1** a device with a multiple hook at one end and attached to a rope, which is thrown or hooked over a firm mooring to secure an object attached to the other end of the rope **2** a light anchor for small boats [c14 from Old French *grapin* a little hook, from *grape* a hook; see GRAPE]

grappa ('græpə) *n* a spirit distilled from the fermented remains of grapes after pressing [Italian: grape stalk, of Germanic origin; see GRAPE]

grapple ('græpəl) *vb* **1** to come to grips with (one or more persons), esp to struggle in hand-to-hand combat **2** (*intr; foll by with*) to cope or contend **3** (*tr*) to secure with a grapple ⊳ *n* **4** any form of hook or metal instrument by which something is secured, such as a grapnel **5 a** the act of gripping or seizing, as in wrestling **b** a grip or hold **6** a contest of grappling, esp a wrestling match [c16 from Old French *grappelle* a little hook, from *grape* hook; see GRAPNEL] > 'grappler *n*

grapple plant *n* a herbaceous plant, *Harpagophytum procumbens*, of southern Africa, whose fruits are covered with large woody barbed hooks: family *Pedaliaceae*. Also called: **wait-a-bit**

grappling ('græplɪŋ) *n* **1** the act of gripping or seizing, as in wrestling **2** a hook used for securing something

grappling iron *or* **hook** *n* a grapnel, esp one used for securing ships

graptolite ('græptə,laɪt) *n* any extinct Palaeozoic colonial animal of the class *Graptolithina*, usually regarded as related to either the hemichordates or the coelenterates: a common fossil, used to

determine the age of sedimentary rocks [c19 from Greek *graptos* written, from *graphein* to write + -LITE]

Grasmere ('grɑːs,mɪə) *n* a village in NW England, in Cumbria at the head of **Lake Grasmere**: home of William Wordsworth and of Thomas de Quincey

grasp (grɑːsp) *vb* **1** to grip (something) firmly with or as if with the hands **2** (when *intr*, often foll by *at*) to struggle, snatch, or grope (for) **3** (*tr*) to understand, esp with effort ⊳ *n* **4** the act of grasping **5** a grip or clasp, as of a hand **6** the capacity to accomplish (esp in the phrase **within one's grasp**) **7** total rule or possession **8** understanding; comprehension [c14 from Low German *grapsen*; related to Old English *græppian* to seize, Old Norse *grāpa* to steal] > 'graspable *adj* > 'grasper *n*

grasping ('grɑːspɪŋ) *adj* greedy; avaricious; rapacious > 'graspingly *adv*

grass (grɑːs) *n* **1** any monocotyledonous plant of the family *Poaceae* (formerly *Gramineae*), having jointed stems sheathed by long narrow leaves, flowers in spikes, and seedlike fruits. The family includes cereals, bamboo, etc **2** such plants collectively, in a lawn, meadow, etc. Related adjs: **gramineous, verdant 3** any similar plant, such as knotgrass, deergrass, or scurvy grass **4** ground on which such plants grow; a lawn, field, etc **5** ground on which animals are grazed; pasture **6** a slang word for **marijuana 7** *Brit slang* a person who informs, esp on criminals **8** short for **sparrowgrass 9** get off the grass NZ *informal* an exclamation of disbelief **10** let the grass grow under one's feet to squander time or opportunity **11** put out to grass **a** to retire (a racehorse) **b** *informal* to retire (a person) ⊳ *vb* **12** to cover or become covered with grass **13** to feed or be fed with grass **14** (*tr*) to spread (cloth) out on grass for drying or bleaching in the sun **15** (*tr*) *sport* to knock or bring down (an opponent) **16** (*tr*) to shoot down (a bird) **17** (*tr*) to land (a fish) on a river bank **18** (*intr; usually foll by on*) *Brit slang* to inform, esp to the police ⊳ See also **grass up** [Old English *græs*; related to Old Norse, Gothic, Old High German *gras*, Middle High German *gruose* sap] > 'grassless *adj* > 'grass,like *adj*

grass box *n* a container attached to a lawn mower that receives grass after it has been cut

grass cloth *n* a cloth made from plant fibres, such as jute or hemp

grass court *n* a tennis court covered with grass. See also **hard court**

grassfinch ('grɑːs,fɪntʃ) *n* any Australian weaverbird of the genus *Poephila* and related genera, many of which are brightly coloured and kept as cagebirds

grass hockey *n* *Canadian* field hockey, as contrasted with ice hockey

grasshook ('grɑːs,hʊk) *n* another name for **sickle**

grasshopper ('grɑːs,hɒpə) *n* **1** any orthopterous insect of the families *Acrididae* (**short-horned grasshoppers**) and *Tettigoniidae* (**long-horned grasshoppers**), typically terrestrial, feeding on plants, and producing a ticking sound by rubbing the hind legs against the leathery forewings. See also **locust** (sense 1), **katydid 2** knee-high to a **grasshopper** *informal* very young or very small **3** an iced cocktail of equal parts of crème de menthe, crème de cacao, and cream **4** (*modifier*) unable to concentrate on any one subject for long

grassland ('grɑːs,lænd) *n* **1** land, such as a prairie, on which grass predominates **2** land reserved for natural grass pasture

grass moth *n* any of a large subfamily of small night-flying pyralid moths, esp *Crambus pratellus*, that during the day cling to grass stems

grass-of-Parnassus *n* a herbaceous perennial N temperate marsh plant, *Parnassia palustris*, with solitary whitish flowers: family *Parnassiaceae*

grassquit ('grɑːs,kwɪt) *n* any tropical American finch of the genus *Tiaris* and related genera, such

as *T. olivacea* (**yellow-faced grassquit**) [from GRASS + *quit*, a bird name in Jamaica]

grass roots *pl n* **1 a** the ordinary people as distinct from the active leadership of a party or organization: used esp of the rank-and-file members of a political party, or of the voters themselves **b** (*as modifier*): *the newly elected MP expressed a wish for greater contact with people at grass-roots level* **2** the origin or essentials [c20 sense 1 originally US, with reference to rural areas in contrast to the towns]

grass snake *n* **1** a harmless nonvenomous European colubrid snake, *Natrix natrix*, having a brownish-green body with variable markings **2** any of several similar related European snakes, such as *Natrix maura* (**viperine grass snake**)

grass tree *n* **1** Also called: **black boy** any plant of the Australian genus *Xanthorrhoea*, having a woody stem, stiff grasslike leaves, and a spike of small white flowers: family *Xanthorrhoeaceae*. Some species produce fragrant resins. Also called: **yacca, yacka** See also **acaroid gum 2** any of several similar Australasian plants

grass up *vb* (*tr, adverb*) *slang* to inform on (someone), esp to the police

grass widow *n* **1** a woman divorced, separated, or living away from her spouse **2** a woman whose spouse is regularly away for short periods [c16, meaning a discarded mistress: perhaps an allusion to a grass bed as representing an illicit relationship; compare BASTARD; C19 in the modern sense]

grass widower *n* **1** a man divorced, separated, or living away from his spouse **2** a man whose spouse is regularly away for short periods

grassy ('grɑːsɪ) *adj* grassier, grassiest covered with, containing, or resembling grass > 'grassiness *n*

grate[1] (greɪt) *vb* **1** (*tr*) to reduce to small shreds by rubbing against a rough or sharp perforated surface: *to grate carrots* **2** to scrape (an object) against something or (objects) together, producing a harsh rasping sound, or (of objects) to scrape with such a sound **3** (*intr; foll by on or upon*) to annoy ⊳ *n* **4** a harsh rasping sound [c15 from Old French *grater* to scrape, of Germanic origin; compare Old High German *krazzōn*]

grate[2] (greɪt) *n* **1** a framework of metal bars for holding fuel in a fireplace, stove, or furnace **2** a less common word for **fireplace 3** another name for **grating**[1] (sense 1) **4** *mining* a perforated metal screen for grading crushed ore ⊳ *vb* **5** (*tr*) to provide with a grate or grates [c14 from Old French *grate*, from Latin *crātis* hurdle]

grateful ('greɪtfʊl) *adj* **1** thankful for gifts, favours, etc; appreciative **2** showing gratitude: *a grateful letter* **3** favourable or pleasant: *a grateful rest* [c16 from obsolete *grate*, from Latin *grātus* + -FUL] > 'gratefully *adv* > 'gratefulness *n*

grater ('greɪtə) *n* **1** a kitchen utensil with sharp-edged perforations for grating carrots, cheese, etc **2** a person or thing that grates

graticule ('grætɪ,kjuːl) *n* **1** the grid of intersecting lines, esp of latitude and longitude on which a map is drawn **2** another name for **reticle 3** a transparent scale in front of a cathode-ray oscilloscope or other measuring instrument [c19 from French, from Latin *crāticula*, from *crātis* wickerwork]

gratification (,grætɪfɪ'keɪʃən) *n* **1** the act of gratifying or the state of being gratified **2** something that gratifies **3** an obsolete word for **gratuity**

gratify ('grætɪ,faɪ) *vb* -fies, -fying, -fied (*tr*) **1** to satisfy or please **2** to yield to or indulge (a desire, whim, etc) **3** *obsolete* to reward [c16 from Latin *grātificārī* to do a favour to, from *grātus* grateful + *facere* to make] > 'grati,fier *n*

gratifying ('grætɪ,faɪɪŋ) *adj* giving one satisfaction or pleasure > 'grati,fyingly *adv*

gratin (French gratɛ̃) *adj* See **au gratin**

gratinated ('grætɪ,neɪtɪd) *adj* another term for **au**

gratin

grating¹ ('greɪtɪŋ) n **1** Also called: **grate** a framework of metal bars in the form of a grille set into a wall, pavement, etc, serving as a cover or guard but admitting air and sometimes light **2** short for **diffraction grating**

grating² ('greɪtɪŋ) adj **1** (of sounds) harsh and rasping **2** annoying; irritating ▷ n **3** (often plural) something produced by grating > **'gratingly** adv

gratis ('greɪtɪs, 'grætɪs, 'grɑːtɪs) adv, adj (postpositive) without payment; free of charge [C15 from Latin: out of kindness, from grātiīs, ablative pl of grātia favour]

gratitude ('grætɪˌtjuːd) n a feeling of thankfulness or appreciation, as for gifts or favours [C16 from Medieval Latin grātitūdō, from Latin grātus GRATEFUL]

gratuitous (grə'tjuːɪtəs) adj **1** given or received without payment or obligation **2** without cause; unjustified **3** law given or made without receiving any value in return: a gratuitous agreement [C17 from Latin grātuītus, from grātia favour] > gra'tuitously adv > gra'tuitousness n

gratuity (grə'tjuːɪtɪ) n, pl -ties **1** a gift or reward, usually of money, for services rendered; tip **2** something given without claim or obligation **3** military a financial award granted for long or meritorious service

gratulate ('grætjʊˌleɪt) vb (tr) archaic **1** to greet joyously **2** to congratulate [C16 from Latin grātulārī, from grātus pleasing] > 'gratulant adj > ,gratu'lation n > 'gratulatory adj

Graubünden (German grau'byndən) n an Alpine canton of E Switzerland: the largest of the cantons, but sparsely populated. Capital: Chur. Pop: 186 100 (2002 est). Area: 7109 sq km (2773 sq miles). Italian name: **Grigioni** Romansch name: **Grishun** French name: **Grisons**

graunch (grɔːntʃ) vb **1** (tr) NZ to crush or destroy **2** South African to kiss and cuddle (someone) passionately [C19 from English dialect word, of imitative origin]

graupel ('graʊpˀl) n soft hail or snow pellets [German, from Graupe, probably from Serbo-Croat krupa; related to Russian krupá peeled grain]

grav (græv) n a unit of acceleration equal to the standard acceleration of free fall. 1 grav is equivalent to 9.806 65 metres per second per second. Symbol: **g**

gravadlax ('grævədˌlæks) n another name for **gravlax**

gravamen (grə'veɪmɛn) n, pl -vamina (-'væmɪnə) **1** law that part of an accusation weighing most heavily against an accused **2** law the substance or material grounds of a complaint **3** a rare word for **grievance** [C17 from Late Latin: trouble, from Latin gravāre to load, from gravis heavy; see GRAVE²]

grave¹ (greɪv) n **1** a place for the burial of a corpse, esp beneath the ground and usually marked by a tombstone. Related adj: **sepulchral 2** something resembling a grave or resting place: the ship went to its grave **3** (often preceded by the) a poetic term for **death 4 have one foot in the grave** informal to be near death **5 to make (someone) turn (over) in his grave** to do something that would have shocked or distressed (someone now dead) [Old English græf; related to Old Frisian gref, Old High German grab, Old Slavonic grobǔ; see GRAVE³]

grave² (greɪv) adj **1** serious and solemn **2** full of or suggesting danger **3** important; crucial **4** (of colours) sober or dull **5** (also grɑːv) phonetics **a** (of a vowel or syllable in some languages with a pitch accent, such as ancient Greek) spoken on a lower or falling musical pitch relative to neighbouring syllables or vowels **b** of or relating to an accent (`) over vowels, denoting a pronunciation with lower or falling musical pitch (as in ancient Greek), with certain special quality (as in French), or in a manner that gives the vowel status as a syllable nucleus not usually possessed by it in that position (as in English agèd). Compare **acute**

(sense 8), **circumflex** ▷ n **6** (also grɑːv) a grave accent [C16 from Old French, from Latin gravis; related to Greek barus heavy; see GRAVAMEN] > 'gravely adv > 'graveness n

grave³ (greɪv) vb graves, graving, graved; graved or graven (tr) archaic **1** to cut, carve, sculpt, or engrave **2** to fix firmly in the mind [Old English grafan; related to Old Norse grafa, Old High German graban to dig]

grave⁴ (greɪv) vb (tr) nautical to clean and apply a coating of pitch to (the bottom of a vessel) [C15 perhaps from Old French grave GRAVEL]

grave⁵ ('grɑːvɪ) adj, adv music to be performed in a solemn manner [C17 from Italian: heavy, from Latin gravis]

grave clothes pl n the wrappings in which a dead body is interred

gravel ('grævˀl) n **1** an unconsolidated mixture of rock fragments that is coarser than sand **2** geology a mixture of rock fragments with diameters in the range 4–76 mm **3** pathol small rough calculi in the kidneys or bladder ▷ vb -els, -elling, -elled or US -els, -eling, -eled (tr) **4** to cover with gravel **5** to confound or confuse **6** US informal to annoy or disturb [C13 from Old French gravele, diminutive of grave gravel, perhaps of Celtic origin] > 'gravelish adj

gravel-blind adj literary almost entirely blind [C16 from GRAVEL + BLIND, formed on the model of SAND-BLIND]

gravelly ('grævəlɪ) adj **1** consisting of or abounding in gravel **2** of or like gravel **3** (esp of a voice) harsh and grating

gravel-voiced adj speaking in a rough and rasping tone

graven ('greɪvˀn) vb **1** a past participle of **grave³** ▷ adj **2** strongly fixed

Gravenhage (xra:vən'ha:xə) n **'s** a Dutch name for (The) **Hague**

graven image n chiefly Bible a carved image used as an idol

graveolent ('grævɪələnt) adj (of plants) having a strong fetid smell [C17 from Latin gravis heavy + olēre to smell]

graver ('greɪvə) n any of various engraving, chasing, or sculpting tools, such as a burin

Graves (grɑːv) n (sometimes not capital) a white or red wine from the district around Bordeaux, France

Graves' disease (greɪvz) n another name for exophthalmic goitre [C19 named after R. J. Graves (1796–1853), Irish physician]

Gravesend (ˌgreɪvz'ɛnd) n a river port in SE England, in NW Kent on the Thames. Pop: 53 045 (2001)

gravestone ('greɪvˌstəʊn) n a stone marking a grave and usually inscribed with the name and dates of the person buried

Gravettian (grə'vɛtɪən) adj of, referring to, or characteristic of an Upper Palaeolithic culture, characterized esp by small pointed blades with blunt backs [C20 from La Gravette on the Dordogne, France]

grave-wax n the nontechnical name for **adipocere**

graveyard ('greɪvˌjɑːd) n a place for graves; a burial ground, esp a small one or one in a churchyard

graveyard orbit n another name for **dump orbit**

graveyard shift n US the working shift between midnight and morning

graveyard slot n television the hours from late night until early morning when the number of people watching television is at its lowest

gravid ('grævɪd) adj the technical word for **pregnant** [C16 from Latin gravidus, from gravis heavy] > gra'vidity or 'gravidness n > 'gravidly adv

gravimeter (grə'vɪmɪtə) n **1** an instrument for measuring the earth's gravitational field at points on its surface **2** an instrument for measuring relative density [C18 from French gravimètre, from Latin gravis heavy] > gra'vimetry n

gravimetric (ˌgrævɪ'mɛtrɪk) or **gravimetrical** adj of, concerned with, or using measurement by weight. Compare **volumetric**. > ,gravi'metrically adv

gravimetric analysis n chem quantitative analysis by weight, usually involving the precipitation, filtration, drying, and weighing of the precipitate. Compare **volumetric analysis**

graving dock n another term for **dry dock**

graviperception (ˌgrævɪpə'sɛpʃən) n the perception of gravity by plants

gravitas ('grævɪˌtæs) n seriousness, solemnity, or importance [C20 from Latin gravitās weight, from gravis heavy]

gravitate ('grævɪˌteɪt) vb (intr) **1** physics to move under the influence of gravity **2** (usually foll by to or towards) to be influenced or drawn, as by strong impulses **3** to sink or settle > 'gravi,tater n

gravitation (ˌgrævɪ'teɪʃən) n **1** the force of attraction that bodies exert on one another as a result of their mass **2** any process or result caused by this interaction, such as the fall of a body to the surface of the earth ▷ Also called: **gravity** See also **Newton's law of gravitation**

gravitational (ˌgrævɪ'teɪʃənəl) adj of, relating to, or involving gravitation > ,gravi'tationally adv

gravitational constant n the factor relating force to mass and distance in Newton's law of gravitation. It is a universal constant with the value 6.673×10^{-11} N m² kg⁻². Symbol: G

gravitational field n the field of force surrounding a body of finite mass in which another body would experience an attractive force that is proportional to the product of the masses and inversely proportional to the square of the distance between them

gravitational interaction or **force** n an interaction between particles or bodies resulting from their mass. It is very weak and occurs at all distances. See **interaction** (sense 2)

gravitational lens n astronomy a lenslike effect in which light rays are bent when passing through the gravitational field of such massive objects as galaxies or black holes

gravitational mass n the mass of a body determined by its response to the force of gravity. Compare **inertial mass**

gravitational wave n physics another name for **gravity wave**

gravitative ('grævɪˌteɪtɪv) adj **1** of, involving, or produced by gravitation **2** tending or causing to gravitate

graviton ('grævɪˌtɒn) n a postulated quantum of gravitational energy, usually considered to be a particle with zero charge and rest mass and a spin of 2. Compare **photon**

gravity ('grævɪtɪ) n, pl -ties **1** the force of attraction that moves or tends to move bodies towards the centre of a celestial body, such as the earth or moon **2** the property of being heavy or having weight. See also **specific gravity, centre of gravity 3** another name for **gravitation 4** seriousness or importance, esp as a consequence of an action or opinion **5** manner or conduct that is solemn or dignified **6** lowness of pitch **7** (modifier) of or relating to gravity or gravitation or their effects: gravity wave; gravity feed [C16 from Latin gravitās weight, from gravis heavy]

gravity cell n an electrolytic cell in which the electrodes lie in two different electrolytes, which are separated into two layers by the difference in their relative densities

gravity dam n a dam whose weight alone is great enough to prevent it from tipping over

gravity fault n a fault in which the rocks on the upper side of an inclined fault plane have been displaced downwards; normal fault

gravity platform n (in the oil industry) a drilling platform that rests directly on the sea bed and is kept in position by its own weight; it is usually made of reinforced concrete

gravity scale n a scale giving the relative density

g

of fluids. See **API gravity scale**

gravity wave *n physics* **1** a wave propagated in a gravitational field, predicted to occur as a result of an accelerating mass **2** a surface wave on water or other liquid propagated because of the weight of liquid in the crests ▷ Also called: **gravitational wave**

gravlax ('græv,læks) *or* **gravadlax** *n* dry-cured salmon, marinated in salt, sugar, and spices, as served in Scandinavia [c20 from Norwegian, from *grav* grave (because the salmon is left to ferment) + *laks* or Swedish *lax* salmon]

gravure (grə'vjʊə) *n* **1** a method of intaglio printing using a plate with many small etched recesses. See also **rotogravure 2** See **photogravure 3** matter printed by this process [c19 from French, from *graver* to engrave, of Germanic origin; see GRAVE³]

gravy ('greɪvɪ) *n, pl* **-vies 1 a** the juices that exude from meat during cooking **b** the sauce made by thickening and flavouring such juices **2** *slang* money or gain acquired with little effort, esp above that needed for ordinary living **3** *slang* wonderful; excellent: *it's all gravy* [c14 from Old French *gravé*, of uncertain origin]

gravy boat *n* a small often boat-shaped vessel for serving gravy or other sauces

gravy train *n slang* a job requiring comparatively little work for good pay, benefits, etc

gray¹ (greɪ) *adj, n, vb* a variant spelling (now esp US) of **grey**. > 'grayish *adj* > 'grayly *adv* > 'grayness *n*

gray² (greɪ) *n* the derived SI unit of absorbed ionizing radiation dose or kerma equivalent to an absorption per unit mass of one joule per kilogram of irradiated material. 1 gray is equivalent to 100 rads. Symbol: Gy [c20 named after Louis Harold Gray (1905–65), English physicist]

Gray code *n* a modification of a number system, esp a binary code, in which any adjacent pair of numbers, in counting order, differ in their digits at one position only, the absolute difference being the value 1 [named after Frank Gray, 20th-century American physicist]

grayling ('greɪlɪŋ) *n, pl* **-ling** *or* **-lings 1** any freshwater salmonoid food fish of the genus *Thymallus* and family *Thymallidae,* of the N hemisphere, having a long spiny dorsal fin, a silvery back, and greyish-green sides **2** any butterfly of the satyrid genus *Hipparchia* and related genera, esp *H. semele* of Europe, having grey or greyish-brown wings

Gray's Inn *n* (in England) one of the four legal societies in London that together form the Inns of Court

Graz (*German* gra:ts) *n* an industrial city in SE Austria, capital of Styria province: the second largest city in the country. Pop: 226 244 (2001)

graze¹ (greɪz) *vb* **1** to allow (animals) to consume the vegetation on (an area of land), or (of animals, esp cows and sheep) to feed thus **2** (*tr*) to tend (livestock) while at pasture **3** *informal* to eat snacks throughout the day rather than formal meals **4** *South African informal* to eat **5** (*intr*) *informal* to switch between television channels while viewing without watching any channel for long **6** *US* to pilfer and eat sweets, vegetables, etc, from supermarket shelves while shopping ▷ *n* **7** *South African informal* a snack; something to eat [Old English *grasian*, from *græs* GRASS; related to Old High German *grasōn*, Dutch *grazen*, Norwegian *grasa*]

graze² (greɪz) *vb* **1** (when *intr*, often foll by *against* or *along*) to brush or scrape (against) gently, esp in passing **2** (*tr*) to break the skin of (a part of the body) by scraping ▷ *n* **3** the act of grazing **4** a scrape or abrasion made by grazing [c17 probably special use of GRAZE¹; related to Swedish *gräsa*] > 'grazer *n* > 'grazingly *adv*

grazier ('greɪzɪə) *n* a rancher or farmer who rears or fattens cattle or sheep on grazing land

grazing ('greɪzɪŋ) *n* **1** the vegetation on pastures that is available for livestock to feed upon **2** the land on which this is growing

grease *n* (gri:s, gri:z) **1** animal fat in a soft or melted condition **2** any thick fatty oil, esp one used as a lubricant for machinery, etc **3** Also called: **grease wool** shorn fleece before it has been cleaned **4** Also called: **seborrhoea** *vet science* inflammation of the skin of horses around the fetlocks, usually covered with an oily secretion ▷ *vb* (gri:z, gri:s) (*tr*) **5** to soil, coat, or lubricate with grease **6** to ease the course of **7** **grease the palm** (*or* **hand**) **of** *slang* to bribe; influence by giving money to [c13 from Old French *craisse,* from Latin *crassus* thick] > 'greaseless *adj*

grease cup *n* a container that stores grease and feeds it through a small hole into a bearing

grease gun *n* a device for forcing grease through nipples into bearings, usually consisting of a cylinder with a plunger and nozzle fitted to it

grease monkey *n informal* a mechanic, esp one who works on cars or aircraft

grease nipple *n* a metal nipple designed to engage with a grease gun for injecting grease into a bearing, etc

greasepaint ('gri:s,peɪnt) *n* **1** a waxy or greasy substance used as make-up by actors **2** theatrical make-up

greaseproof paper ('gri:s,pru:f) *n* any paper that is resistant to penetration by greases and oils

greaser ('gri:zə, 'gri:sə) *n Brit slang* **1** a mechanic, esp of motor vehicles **2** a semiskilled engine attendant aboard a merchant ship **3** a young long-haired motorcyclist, usually one of a gang **4** an unpleasant person, esp one who ingratiates himself with superiors

greasewood ('gri:s,wʊd) *or* **greasebush** ('gri:s,bʊʃ) *n* **1** Also called: **chico** a spiny chenopodiaceous shrub, *Sarcobatus vermiculatus* of W North America, that yields an oil used as a fuel **2** any of various similar or related plants, such as the creosote bush

greasies ('gri:sɪz) *pl n NZ informal* fish and chips

greasy ('gri:zɪ, -sɪ) *adj* **greasier, greasiest 1** coated or soiled with or as if with grease **2** composed of or full of grease **3** resembling grease **4** unctuous or oily in manner ▷ *n, pl* **greasies** *Austral slang* **5** a shearer **6** an outback cook, esp cooking for a number of men > 'greasily *adv* > 'greasiness *n*

greasy spoon *n slang* a small, cheap, and often unsanitary restaurant, usually specializing in fried foods

greasy wool *n* untreated wool, still retaining the lanolin, which is used for waterproof clothing

great (greɪt) *adj* **1** relatively large in size or extent; big **2** relatively large in number; having many parts or members: *a great assembly* **3** of relatively long duration: *a great wait* **4** of larger size or more importance than others of its kind: *the great auk* **5** extreme or more than usual: *great worry* **6** of significant importance or consequence: *a great decision* **7 a** of exceptional talents or achievements; remarkable: *a great writer* **b** (*as noun*): *the great; one of the greats* **8** arising from or possessing idealism in thought, action, etc; heroic: *great deeds* **9** illustrious or eminent: *a great history* **10** impressive or striking: *a great show of wealth* **11** much in use; favoured **12** active or enthusiastic: *a great walker* **13** doing or exemplifying (a characteristic or pursuit) on a large scale: *what a great buffoon* **14** (often foll by *at*) skilful or adroit: *a great carpenter* **15** *informal* excellent; fantastic **16** *Brit informal* (intensifier): *a dirty great smack in the face* **17** (postpositive) *archaic* **a** pregnant: *great with child* **b** full (of): *great with hope* **18** (intensifier, used in mild oaths): *Great Scott!* **19** **be great on** *informal* **a** to be informed about **b** to be enthusiastic about or for ▷ *adv* **20** *informal* very well; excellently ▷ *n* **21** Also called: **great organ** the principal manual on an organ. Compare **choir** (sense 4), **swell** (sense 16) [Old English *grēat;* related to Old Frisian *grāt,* Old High German *grōz;* see GRIT, GROAT] > 'greatly *adv* > 'greatness *n*

great- *prefix* **1** being the parent of a person's grandparent (in the combinations **great-grandfather, great-grandmother, great-grandparent**) **2** being the child of a person's grandchild (in the combinations **great-grandson, great-granddaughter, great-grandchild**)

great ape *n* any of the larger anthropoid apes, such as the chimpanzee, orang-utan, or gorilla

Great Attractor *n astronomy* a large mass, possibly a gigantic cluster of galaxies, postulated to explain the fact that many galaxies appear to be moving towards a particular point in the sky

great auk *n* a large flightless auk, *Pinguinus impennis,* extinct since the middle of the 19th century

great-aunt *or* **grandaunt** *n* an aunt of one's father or mother; sister of one's grandfather or grandmother

Great Australian Bight *n* a wide bay of the Indian Ocean, in S Australia, extending from Cape Pasley to the Eyre Peninsula: notorious for storms

Great Barrier Reef *n* a coral reef in the Coral Sea, off the NE coast of Australia, extending for about 2000 km (1250 miles) from the Torres Strait along the coast of Queensland; the largest coral reef in the world

Great Basin *n* a semiarid region of the western US, between the Wasatch and the Sierra Nevada Mountains, having no drainage to the ocean: includes Nevada, W Utah, and parts of E California, S Oregon, and Idaho. Area: about 490 000 sq km (189 000 sq miles)

Great Bear *n* **the** the English name for **Ursa Major**

Great Bear Lake *n* a lake in NW Canada, in the Northwest Territories: the largest freshwater lake entirely in Canada; drained by the **Great Bear River,** which flows to the Mackenzie River. Area: 31 792 sq km (12 275 sq miles)

Great Belt *n* a strait in Denmark, between Zealand and Funen islands, linking the Kattegat with the Baltic. Danish name: **Store Bælt**

Great Britain *n* England, Wales, and Scotland including those adjacent islands governed from the mainland (i.e. excluding the Isle of Man and the Channel Islands). The United Kingdom of Great Britain was formed by the Act of Union (1707), although the term Great Britain had been in use since 1603, when James VI of Scotland became James I of England (including Wales). Later unions created the United Kingdom of Great Britain and Ireland (1801) and the United Kingdom of Great Britain and Northern Ireland (1922). Pop: 57 851 100 (2003 est). Area: 229 523 sq km (88 619 sq miles). See also **United Kingdom**

great circle *n* a circular section of a sphere that has a radius equal to that of the sphere. Compare **small circle**

greatcoat ('greɪt,kəʊt) *n* a heavy overcoat, now worn esp by men in the armed forces > 'great,coated *adj*

great council *n* (in medieval England) an assembly of the great nobles and prelates to advise the king

great crested grebe *n* a European grebe, *Podiceps cristatus,* having blackish ear tufts and, in the breeding season, a dark brown frill around the head

Great Dane *n* one of a very large powerful yet graceful breed of dog with a short smooth coat

Great Divide *n* another name for the **continental divide**

Great Dividing Range *pl n* a series of mountain ranges and plateaus roughly parallel to the E coast of Australia, in Queensland, New South Wales, and Victoria; the highest range is the Australian Alps, in the south

Great Dog *n* **the** the English name for **Canis Major**

greaten (ˈɡreɪtᵊn) *vb archaic* to make or become great

Greater (ˈɡreɪtə) *adj* (of a city) considered with the inclusion of the outer suburbs: *Greater London*

Greater Antilles *pl n* **the** a group of islands in the Caribbean, including Cuba, Jamaica, Hispaniola, and Puerto Rico

greater celandine *n* a Eurasian papaveraceous plant, *Chelidonium majus,* with yellow flowers and deeply divided leaves. Also called: **swallowwort** Compare **lesser celandine**

Greater London *n* See **London** (sense 2)

Greater Manchester *n* a metropolitan county of NW England, administered since 1986 by the unitary authorities of Wigan, Bolton, Bury, Rochdale, Salford, Manchester, Oldham, Trafford, Stockport, and Tameside. Area: 1286 sq km (496 sq miles)

Greater Sunda Islands *pl n* a group of islands in the W Malay Archipelago, forming the larger part of the Sunda Islands: consists of Borneo, Sumatra, Java, and Sulawesi

greatest (ˈɡreɪtɪst) *adj* **1** the superlative of **great** ▷ *n* **2 the greatest** *slang* an exceptional person

greatest common divisor *n* another name for **highest common factor**

greatest happiness principle *n* the ethical principle that an action is right in so far as it promotes the greatest happiness of the greatest number of those affected. See **utilitarianism**

Great Glen *n* **the** a fault valley across the whole of Scotland, extending southwest from the Moray Firth in the east to Loch Linnhe and containing Loch Ness and Loch Lochy. Also called: **Glen More, Glen Albyn**

great gross *n* a unit of quantity equal to one dozen gross (or 1728)

great-hearted *adj* benevolent or noble; magnanimous > ˌgreat-ˈheartedness *n*

Great Indian Desert *n* another name for the **Thar Desert**

Great Lakes *pl n* a group of five lakes in central North America with connecting waterways: the largest group of lakes in the world: consists of Lakes Superior, Huron, Erie, and Ontario, which are divided by the border between the US and Canada and Lake Michigan, which is wholly in the US; constitutes the most important system of inland waterways in the world, discharging through the St Lawrence into the Atlantic. Total length: 3767 km (2340 miles). Area: 246 490 sq km (95 170 sq miles)

Great Leap Forward *n* **the** the attempt by the People's Republic of China in 1959–60 to solve the country's economic problems by labour-intensive industrialization

Great Mogul *n* any of the Muslim emperors of India (1526–1857)

great mountain buttercup *n* NZ See **Mount Cook lily**

great-nephew or **grandnephew** *n* a son of one's nephew or niece; grandson of one's brother or sister

great-niece or **grandniece** *n* a daughter of one's nephew or niece; granddaughter of one's brother or sister

great northern diver *n* a large northern bird, *Gavia immer,* with a black-and-white chequered back and a black head and neck in summer: family *Gaviidae* (divers)

great organ *n* the full name for **great** (sense 21)

Great Ouse *n* See **Ouse** (sense 1)

Great Plains *pl n* a vast region of North America east of the Rocky Mountains, extending from the lowlands of the Mackenzie River (Canada), south to the Big Bend of the Rio Grande

Great Power *n* a nation that has exceptional political influence, resources, and military strength

great primer *n* (formerly) a size of printer's type approximately equal to 18 point

Great Rebellion *n* **the** another name for the English **Civil War**

Great Red Spot *n* a large long-lived oval feature, south of Jupiter's equator, that is an anticyclonic disturbance in the atmosphere

Great Rift Valley *n* **the** the most extensive rift in the earth's surface, extending from the Jordan valley in Syria to Mozambique; marked by a chain of steep-sided lakes, volcanoes, and escarpments

Great Russian *n* **1** *linguistics* the technical name for **Russian**. Compare **Belarussian, Ukrainian 2** a member of the chief East Slavonic people of Russia ▷ *adj* **3** of or relating to this people or their language

Greats (ɡreɪts) *pl n* (at Oxford University) **1** the Honour School of Literae Humaniores, involving the study of Greek and Roman history and literature and philosophy **2** the final examinations at the end of this course

Great Salt Lake *n* a shallow salt lake in NW Utah, in the Great Basin at an altitude of 1260 m (4200 ft): the area has fluctuated from less than 2500 sq km (1000 sq miles) to over 5000 sq km (2000 sq miles)

Great Sandy Desert *n* **1** a desert in NW Australia. Area: about 415 000 sq km (160 000 sq miles) **2** an English name for the **Rub' al Khali**

Great Satan *n* any force, person, organization, or country that is regarded as evil, used esp of the United States by radical Islamists

Great Schism *n* **1** the breach between the Eastern and Western churches, usually dated from 1054 **2** the division within the Roman Catholic Church from 1378 to 1429, during which rival popes reigned at Rome and Avignon

great seal *n* (*often capitals*) the principal seal of a nation, sovereign, etc, used to authenticate signatures and documents of the highest importance

Great Slave Lake *n* a lake in NW Canada, in the Northwest Territories: drained by the Mackenzie River into the Arctic Ocean. Area: 28 440 sq km (10 980 sq miles)

Great Slave River *n* another name for the **Slave River**

Great Smoky Mountains or **Great Smokies** *pl n* the W part of the Appalachians, in W North Carolina and E Tennessee. Highest peak: Clingman's Dome, 2024 m (6642 ft)

Great St Bernard Pass *n* a pass over the W Alps, between SW central Switzerland and N Italy: noted for the hospice at the summit, founded in the 11th century. Height: 2469 m (8100 ft)

Great Stour *n* another name for **Stour** (sense 1)

great tit *n* a large common Eurasian tit, *Parus major,* with yellow-and-black underparts and a black-and-white head

Great Trek *n* **the** *South African history* the migration of Boer farmers with their slaves and African servants from the Cape Colony to the north and east from about 1836 to 1845 to escape British authority

great-uncle or **granduncle** *n* an uncle of one's father or mother; brother of one's grandfather or grandmother

Great Victoria Desert *n* a desert in S Australia, in SE Western Australia and W South Australia. Area: 323 750 sq km (125 000 sq miles)

Great Vowel Shift *n* *linguistics* a phonetic change that took place during the transition from Middle to Modern English, whereby the long vowels were raised (e: became i:, o: became u:, etc). The vowels (i:) and (u:) underwent breaking and became the diphthongs (aɪ) and (aʊ)

Great Wall *n* *astronomy* a vast sheet of many thousands of gravitationally associated galaxies detected in the universe

Great Wall of China *n* a defensive wall in N China, extending from W Gansu to the Gulf of Liaodong: constructed in the 3rd century BC as a defence against the Mongols; substantially rebuilt in the 15th century. Length: over 2400 km (1500 miles). Average height: 6 m (20 ft). Average width: 6 m (20 ft)

Great War *n* another name for **World War I**

Great Week *n* *Eastern Church* the week preceding Easter, the equivalent of Holy Week in the Western Church

great white heron *n* **1** a large white heron, *Ardea occidentalis,* of S North America **2** a widely distributed white egret, *Egretta* (or *Casmerodius*) *albus*

Great White Way *n* the theatre district on Broadway in New York City

Great Yarmouth (ˈjɑːməθ) *n* a port and resort in E England, in E Norfolk. Pop: 58 032 (2001)

great year *n* one complete cycle of the precession of the equinoxes; about 25 800 years

greave (ɡriːv) *n* (*often plural*) a piece of armour worn to protect the shin from the ankle to the knee [C14 from Old French *greve,* perhaps from *graver* to part the hair, of Germanic origin] > **greaved** *adj*

greaves (ɡriːvz) *pl n* the residue left after the rendering of tallow [C17 from Low German *greven;* related to Old High German *griubo*]

grebe (ɡriːb) *n* any aquatic bird, such as *Podiceps cristatus* (**great crested grebe**), of the order *Podicipediformes,* similar to the divers but with lobate rather than webbed toes and a vestigial tail [C18 from French *grèbe,* of unknown origin]

Grecian (ˈɡriːʃən) *adj* **1** (esp of beauty or architecture) conforming to Greek ideals, esp in being classically simple ▷ *n* **2** a scholar of or expert in the Greek language or literature ▷ *adj* ▷ *n* **3** another word for **Greek**

Grecism (ˈɡriːˌsɪzəm) *n* a variant spelling (esp US) of **Graecism**

Grecize (ˈɡriːsaɪz) *vb* a variant spelling (esp US) of **Graecize**

Greco- (ˈɡriːkəʊ, ˈɡrɛkəʊ) *combining form* a variant (esp US) of **Graeco-**

gree¹ (ɡriː) *n Scot archaic* **1** superiority or victory **2** the prize for a victory [C14 from Old French *gré,* from Latin *gradus* step]

gree² (ɡriː) *n obsolete* **1** goodwill; favour **2** satisfaction for an insult or injury [C14 from Old French *gré,* from Latin *grātum* what is pleasing; see GRATEFUL]

gree³ (ɡriː) *vb* **grees, greeing, greed** *archaic or dialect* to come or cause to come to agreement or harmony [C14 variant of AGREE]

greebo (ˈɡriːbəʊ) *n, pl* **greeboes** an unkempt or dirty-looking young man

Greece (ɡriːs) *n* a republic in SE Europe, occupying the S part of the Balkan Peninsula and many islands in the Ionian and Aegean Seas; site of two of Europe's earliest civilizations (the Minoan and Mycenaean); in the classical era divided into many small independent city-states, the most important being Athens and Sparta; part of the Roman and Byzantine Empires; passed under Turkish rule in the late Middle Ages; became an independent kingdom in 1827; taken over by a military junta (1967–74); the monarchy was abolished in 1973; became a republic in 1975; a member of the European Union. Official language: Greek. Official religion: Eastern (Greek) Orthodox. Currency: euro. Capital: Athens. Pop: 10 977 000 (2004 est). Area: 131 944 sq km (50 944 sq miles). Modern Greek name: Ellás Related adj: **Hellenic**

greed (ɡriːd) *n* **1** excessive consumption of or desire for food; gluttony **2** excessive desire, as for wealth or power [C17 back formation from GREEDY] > **ˈgreedless** *adj*

greedy (ˈɡriːdɪ) *adj* **greedier, greediest 1** excessively desirous of food or wealth, esp in large amounts; voracious **2** (*postpositive; foll by for*) **eager** (for): *a man greedy for success* [Old English *grǣdig;* related to Old Norse *grāthugr,* Gothic *grēdags* hungry, Old High German *grātac*] > **ˈgreedily** *adv* > **ˈgreediness** *n*

greedy guts *n* (*functioning as singular*) *slang* a glutton

g

greegree ('gri:gri:) *n* a variant spelling of **grigri**

Greek (gri:k) *n* **1** the official language of Greece, constituting the Hellenic branch of the Indo-European family of languages. See **Ancient Greek, Late Greek, Medieval Greek, Modern Greek 2** a native or inhabitant of Greece or a descendant of such a native **3** a member of the Greek Orthodox Church **4** *informal* anything incomprehensible (esp in the phrase **it's (all) Greek to me**) **5** **Greek meets Greek equals meet** ▷ *adj* **6** denoting, relating to, or characteristic of Greece, the Greeks, or the Greek language; Hellenic **7** of, relating to, or designating the Greek Orthodox Church [from Old English *Grēcas* (plural), or Latin *Graecus,* from Greek *Graikos*] > **'Greekness** *n*

Greek Catholic *n* **1** a member of an Eastern Church in communion with the Greek patriarchal see of Constantinople **2** a member of one of the Uniat Greek Churches, which acknowledge the Pope's authority while retaining their own institutions, discipline, and liturgy

Greek Church *n* another name for the **Greek Orthodox Church**

Greek cross *n* a cross with each of the four arms of the same length

greeked text (gri:kt) *n* *computing* words which appear on screen as grey lines when the type size is too small for actual letters to be shown

Greek fire *n* **1** a Byzantine weapon employed in naval warfare from 670 AD. It consisted of an unknown mixture that, when wetted, exploded and was projected, burning, from tubes **2** any of several other inflammable mixtures used in warfare up to the 19th century

Greek gift *n* a gift given with the intention of tricking and causing harm to the recipient [c19 in allusion to Virgil's *Aeneid* ii 49; see also TROJAN HORSE]

Greek mallow *n* See **sidalcea**

Greek Orthodox Church *n* **1** Also called: **Greek Church** the established Church of Greece, governed by the holy synod of Greece, in which the Metropolitan of Athens has primacy of honour **2** another name for **Orthodox Church**

Greek Revival *n* (*modifier*) denoting, relating to, or having the style of architecture used in Western Europe in the late 18th and early 19th centuries, based upon ancient Greek classical examples > **Greek Revivalism** *n* > **Greek Revivalist** *adj, n*

green (gri:n) *n* **1** any of a group of colours, such as that of fresh grass, that lie between yellow and blue in the visible spectrum in the wavelength range 575–500 nanometres. Green is the complementary colour of magenta and with red and blue forms a set of primary colours. Related adj: **verdant 2** a dye or pigment of or producing these colours **3** something of the colour green **4** a small area of grassland, esp in the centre of a village **5** an area of ground used for a purpose: *a putting green* **6** (*plural*) **a** the edible leaves and stems of certain plants, eaten as a vegetable **b** freshly cut branches of ornamental trees, shrubs, etc, used as a decoration **7** (*sometimes capital*) a person, esp a politician, who supports environmentalist issues (see sense 13) **8** *slang* money **9** *slang* marijuana of low quality **10** (*plural*) *slang* sexual intercourse ▷ *adj* **11** of the colour green **12** greenish in colour or having parts or marks that are greenish: *a green monkey* **13** (*sometimes capital*) concerned with or relating to conservation of the world's natural resources and improvement of the environment: *green policies* **14** vigorous; not faded: *a green old age* **15** envious or jealous **16** immature, unsophisticated, or gullible **17** characterized by foliage or green plants: *a green wood* **18** fresh, raw, or unripe: *green bananas* **19** unhealthily pale in appearance **20** denoting a unit of account that is adjusted in accordance with fluctuations between the currencies of the EU nations and is used to make payments to agricultural producers within the EU: *green pound; green franc* **21** (of pottery) not fired **22** (of meat) not smoked or cured; unprocessed: *green bacon* **23** *metallurgy* (of a product, such as a sand mould or cermet) compacted but not yet fired; ready for firing **24** (of timber) freshly felled; not dried or seasoned **25** (of concrete) not having matured to design strength ▷ *vb* **26** to make or become green [Old English *grēne;* related to Old High German *gruoni;* see GROW] > **'greenish** *adj* > **'greenly** *adv* > **'greenness** *n* > **'greeny** *adj*

green algae *pl n* the algae of the phylum *Chlorophyta,* which possess the green pigment chlorophyll. The group includes sea lettuce and spirogyra

greenback ('gri:n,bæk) *n* **1** US *informal* an inconvertible legal-tender US currency note originally issued during the Civil War in 1862 **2** US *slang* a dollar bill

Greenback Party *n* US *history* a political party formed after the Civil War advocating the use of fiat money and opposing the reduction of paper currency > **'Green,backer** *n* > **'Green,backism** *n*

green ban *n* *Austral* a trade union ban on any development that might be considered harmful to the environment

green bean *n* any bean plant, such as the French bean, having narrow green edible pods when unripe

green belt *n* a zone of farmland, parks, and open country surrounding a town or city: usually officially designated as such and preserved from urban development

Green Beret *n* an informal name for a member of the US Army Special Forces

greenbone ('gri:n,bəʊn) *n* NZ another name for **butterfish** (sense 2)

greenbottle ('gri:n,bɒtᵊl) *n* a common dipterous fly, *Lucilia caesar,* that has a dark greenish body with a metallic lustre and lays its eggs in carrion: family *Calliphoridae*

greenbrier ('gri:n,braɪə) *n* any of several prickly climbing plants of the liliaceous genus *Smilax,* esp *S. rotundifolia* of the eastern US, which has small green flowers and blackish berries. Also called: **cat brier**

green card *n* **1** an official permit allowing the holder permanent residence and employment, issued to foreign nationals in the US **2** an insurance document covering motorists against accidents abroad **3** *social welfare* (in Britain) an identification card issued by the Manpower Services Commission to a disabled person, to show registration for employment purposes and eligibility for special services. See also **handicap register, registered disabled**

green corn *n* another name for **sweet corn** (sense 1)

Green Cross Code *n* (in Britain) a code for children giving rules for road safety: first issued in 1971

green dragon *n* a North American aroid plant, *Arisaema dracontium,* with a long slender spadix projecting from a green or white long narrow spathe. Also called: **dragonroot**

greenery ('gri:nərɪ) *n* green foliage or vegetation, esp when used for decoration

green-eyed *adj* **1** jealous or envious **2** **the green-eyed monster** jealousy or envy

greenfield ('gri:n,fi:ld) *n* (*modifier*) denoting or located in a rural area which has not previously been built on

greenfinch ('gri:n,fɪntʃ) *n* a common European finch, *Carduelis chloris,* the male of which has a dull green plumage with yellow patches on the wings and tail

green fingers *pl n* considerable talent or ability to grow plants. US and Canadian equivalent: **green thumb**

Green Flag *n* an award given to a bathing beach that meets EU standards of cleanliness

green flash *n* *astronomy* a flash of bright green light sometimes seen as the sun passes below the horizon, caused by a combination of the dispersion, scattering, and refraction of light

greenfly ('gri:n,flaɪ) *n, pl* -**flies** a greenish aphid commonly occurring as a pest on garden and crop plants

green footprint *n* the impact of a building on the environment

greengage ('gri:n,geɪdʒ) *n* **1** a cultivated variety of plum tree, *Prunus domestica italica,* with edible green plumlike fruits **2** the fruit of this tree [c18 GREEN + -*gage,* after Sir W. *Gage* (1777–1864), English botanist who brought it from France]

green gland *n* one of a pair of excretory organs in some crustaceans that open at the base of each antenna

green glass *n* glass in its natural colour, usually greenish as a result of metallic substances in the raw materials

Green Goddess *n* Brit an army fire engine [c20 so-called because of its green livery]

greengrocer ('gri:n,grəʊsə) *n* chiefly Brit a retail trader in fruit and vegetables > **'green,grocery** *n*

Greenham Common ('gri:nəm) *n* a village in West Berkshire unitary authority, Berkshire; site of a US cruise missile base, and, from 1981, a camp of women protesters against nuclear weapons; although the base had closed by 1991 a small number of women remained until 2000

greenhead ('gri:n,hed) *n* a male mallard

greenheart ('gri:n,hɑːt) *n* **1** Also called: **bebeeru** a tropical American lauraceous tree, *Ocotea* (or *Nectandra*) *rodiaei,* that has dark green durable wood and bark that yields the alkaloid bebeerine **2** any of various similar trees **3** the wood of any of these trees

green heron *n* a small heron, *Butorides virescens,* of subtropical North America, with dark greenish wings and back

greenhorn ('gri:n,hɔːn) *n* **1** an inexperienced person, esp one who is extremely gullible **2** chiefly US a newcomer or immigrant [c17 originally an animal with *green* (that is, young) horns]

greenhouse ('gri:n,haʊs) *n* **1** a building with transparent walls and roof, usually of glass, for the cultivation and exhibition of plants under controlled conditions ▷ *adj* **2** relating to or contributing to the greenhouse effect: *greenhouse gases such as carbon dioxide*

greenhouse effect *n* **1** an effect occurring in greenhouses, etc, in which radiant heat from the sun passes through the glass warming the contents, the radiant heat from inside being trapped by the glass **2** the application of this effect to a planet's atmosphere; carbon dioxide and some other gases in the planet's atmosphere can absorb the infrared radiation emitted by the planet's surface as a result of exposure to solar radiation, thus increasing the mean temperature of the planet

greenie ('gri:nɪ) *n* Austral *informal* a conservationist

greening ('gri:nɪŋ) *n* the process of making or becoming more aware of environmental considerations [c20 from GREEN (sense 13)]

green keeper *n* a person in charge of a golf course or bowling green

Greenland ('gri:nlənd) *n* a large island, lying mostly within the Arctic Circle off the NE coast of North America: first settled by Icelanders in 986; resettled by Danes from 1721 onwards; integral part of Denmark (1953–79); granted internal autonomy 1979; mostly covered by an icecap up to 3300 m (11 000 ft) thick, with ice-free coastal strips and coastal mountains; the population is largely Inuit, with a European minority; fishing, hunting, and mining. Capital: Nuuk. Pop: 57 000 (2003 est). Area: 175 600 sq km (840 000 sq miles). Danish name: **Grønland** Greenlandic name: **Kalaallit Nunaat**

Greenlander ('gri:nləndə) *n* a native or inhabitant of Greenland

Greenlandic (gri:n'lændɪk) *adj* **1** of, relating to, or characteristic of Greenland, the Greenlanders, or the Inuit dialect spoken in Greenland ▷ *n* **2** the dialect of Inuktitut spoken in Greenland

Greenland Sea *n* the S part of the Arctic Ocean, off the NE coast of Greenland

Greenland whale *n* an arctic right whale, *Balaena mysticetus*, that is black with a cream-coloured throat

green leek *n* any of several Australian parrots with a green or mostly green plumage

greenlet ('gri:nlɪt) *n* a vireo, esp one of the genus *Hylophilus*

green light *n* **1** a signal to go, esp a green traffic light **2** permission to proceed with a project ▷ *vb* **greenlight** -lights, -lighting, -lighted (*tr*) **3** to permit (a project, etc) to proceed

green light district *n* an area in which prostitution is officially tolerated [C21 from GREEN LIGHT, modelled on *red-light district*]

green line *n* (*sometimes capitals*) a line of demarcation between two hostile communities

greenling ('gri:nlɪŋ) *n* any scorpaenoid food fish of the family *Hexagrammidae* of the North Pacific Ocean

green lung *n* an area of parkland within a town or city, considered in terms of the healthier environment it provides

greenmail ('gri:n,meɪl) *n* (*esp in the US*) the practice of a company buying sufficient shares in another company to threaten takeover and making a quick profit as a result of the threatened company buying back its shares at a higher price

green manure *n* **1** a growing crop that is ploughed under to enrich the soil **2** manure that has not yet decomposed

green monkey *n* a W African variety of a common guenon monkey, *Cercopithecus aethiops*, having greenish-brown fur and a dark face. Compare **grivet, vervet**

green monkey disease *n* another name for **Marburg disease**

green mould *n* another name for **blue mould** (sense 1)

Green Mountain Boys *pl n* the members of the armed bands of Vermont organized in 1770 to oppose New York's territorial claims. Under Ethan Allen they won fame in the War of American Independence

Green Mountains *pl n* a mountain range in E North America, extending from Canada through Vermont into W Massachusetts: part of the Appalachian system. Highest peak: Mount Mansfield, 1338 m (4393 ft)

Greenock ('gri:nək) *n* a port in SW Scotland, in Inverclyde on the Firth of Clyde: shipbuilding and other marine industries. Pop: 45 467 (2001)

greenockite ('gri:nə,kaɪt) *n* a rare yellowish mineral consisting of cadmium sulphide in hexagonal crystalline form: the only ore of cadmium. Formula: CdS [C19 named after Lord C. C. *Greenock*, 19th-century English soldier]

green paper *n* (*often capitals*) (in Britain) a command paper containing policy proposals to be discussed, esp by Parliament

Green Party *n* a political party whose policies are based on concern for the environment

Greenpeace ('gri:n,pi:s) *n* an organization founded in 1971 that stresses the need to maintain a balance between human progress and environmental conservation. Members take active but nonviolent measures against what are regarded as threats to environmental safety, such as the dumping of nuclear waste in the sea

green pepper *n* **1** the green unripe fruit of the sweet pepper, eaten raw or cooked **2** the unripe fruit of various other pepper plants, eaten as a green vegetable

green plover *n* another name for **lapwing**

green pound *n* a unit of account used in calculating Britain's contributions to and payments from the Community Agricultural Fund of the EU

green revolution *n* the introduction of high-yielding seeds and modern agricultural techniques in developing countries

Green River *n* a river in the western US, rising in W central Wyoming and flowing south into Utah, east through NW Colorado, re-entering Utah before joining the Colorado River. Length: 1175 km (730 miles)

green roof *n* a roof covered with vegetation, designed for its aesthetic value and to optimize energy conservation

greenroom ('gri:n,ru:m, -,rʊm) *n* (*esp formerly*) a backstage room in a theatre where performers may rest or receive visitors [C18 probably from its original colour]

green run *n* *skiing* a very easy run, suitable for complete beginners

greensand ('gri:n,sænd) *n* an olive-green sandstone consisting mainly of quartz and glauconite

Greensboro ('gri:nzbərə, -brə) *n* a city in N central North Carolina. Pop: 229 110 (2003 est)

greenshank ('gri:n,ʃæŋk) *n* a large European sandpiper, *Tringa nebularia*, with greenish legs and a slightly upturned bill

greensickness ('gri:n,sɪknɪs) *n* another name for **chlorosis**. ▷ '**green,sick** *adj*

green soap *n* *med* a soft or liquid alkaline soap made from vegetable oils, used in treating certain chronic skin diseases. Also called: **soft soap**

greensome ('gri:nsəm) *n* *golf* a match for two pairs in which each of the four players tees off and after selecting the better drive the partners of each pair play that ball alternately. Compare **fourball, foursome** (sense 2)

greenstick fracture ('gri:n,stɪk) *n* a fracture in children in which the bone is partly bent and splinters only on the convex side of the bend [C20 alluding to the similar way in which a green stick splinters]

greenstone ('gri:n,stəʊn) *n* **1** any basic igneous rock that is dark green because of the presence of chlorite, actinolite, or epidote **2** a variety of jade used in New Zealand for ornaments and tools

greenstuff ('gri:n,stʌf) *n* green vegetables, such as cabbage or lettuce

greensward ('gri:n,swɔːd) *n* *archaic or literary* fresh green turf or an area of such turf

green tea *n* a sharp tea made from tea leaves that have been steamed and dried quickly without fermenting

green thumb *n* *US and Canadian* considerable talent or ability to grow plants. Also called (in Britain and certain other countries): **green fingers**

green turtle *n* a mainly tropical edible turtle, *Chelonia mydas*, with greenish flesh used to prepare turtle soup: family *Chelonidae*

green vitriol *n* another name for **ferrous sulphate**

greenwash ('gri:n,wɒʃ) *n* a superficial or insincere display of concern for the environment that is shown by an organization

greenway ('gri:n,weɪ) *n* *US* a corridor of protected open space that is maintained for conservation, recreation, and non-motorized transportation

green-wellie *n* (*modifier*) characterizing or belonging to the upper-class set devoted to hunting, shooting, and fishing

Greenwich ('grɪnɪdʒ, -ɪtʃ, 'grɛn-) *n* a Greater London borough on the Thames: site of a Royal Naval College and of the original Royal Observatory designed by Christopher Wren (1675), accepted internationally as the prime meridian of longitude since 1884, and the basis of Greenwich Mean Time; also site of the Millennium Dome. Pop: 223 700 (2003 est). Area: 46 sq km (18 sq miles)

Greenwich Mean Time *or* **Greenwich Time** *n* mean solar time on the 0° meridian passing through Greenwich, England, measured from midnight: formerly a standard time in Britain and a basis for calculating times throughout most of the world, it has been replaced by an atomic timescale. See **universal time** Abbreviation: **GMT**

▬ USAGE The name **Greenwich mean** time is ambiguous, having been measured from mean midday in astronomy up to 1925, and is not used for scientific purposes. It is generally and incorrectly used in the sense of **universal coordinated time**, an atomic timescale available since 1972 from broadcast signals, in addition to the earliest sense of **universal time**, adopted internationally in 1928 as the name for GMT measured from midnight

Greenwich Village ('grɛnɪtʃ, 'grɪn-) *n* a part of New York City in the lower west side of Manhattan; traditionally the home of many artists and writers

greenwood ('gri:n,wʊd) *n* a forest or wood when the leaves are green: the traditional setting of stories about English outlaws, esp Robin Hood

green woodpecker *n* a European woodpecker, *Picus viridis*, with a dull green back and wings and a red crown

greet¹ (gri:t) *vb* (*tr*) **1** to meet or receive with expressions of gladness or welcome **2** to send a message of friendship to **3** to receive in a specified manner **4** to become apparent to [Old English *grētan*; related to Old High German *gruozzen* to address]

greet² (gri:t) *Scot* ▷ *vb* **1** (*intr*) to weep; lament ▷ *n* **2** weeping; lamentation [from Old English *grētan*, northern dialect variant of *grætan*; compare Old Norse *grāta*, Middle High German *grazen*]

greeter ('gri:tə) *n* a person who greets people at the entrance of a shop, restaurant, casino, etc

greeting ('gri:tɪŋ) *n* **1** the act or an instance of welcoming or saluting on meeting **2** (*often plural*) **a** an expression of friendly salutation **b** (*as modifier*): *a greetings card*

gregarine ('grɛgə,ri:n, -rɪn) *n* **1** any parasitic protozoan of the order *Gregarinida*, typically occurring in the digestive tract and body cavity of other invertebrates: phylum *Apicomplexa* (sporozoans) ▷ *adj also* **gregarinian** (,grɛgə'rɪnɪən) **2** of, relating to, or belonging to the *Gregarinida* [C19 from New Latin *Gregarīna* genus name, from Latin *gregārius*; see GREGARIOUS]

gregarious (grɪ'gɛərɪəs) *adj* **1** enjoying the company of others **2** (of animals) living together in herds or flocks. Compare **solitary** (sense 6) **3** (of plants) growing close together but not in dense clusters **4** of, relating to, or characteristic of crowds or communities [C17 from Latin *gregārius* belonging to a flock, from *grex* flock] ▷ gre'gariously *adv* ▷ gre'gariousness *n*

Gregorian (grɪ'gɔːrɪən) *adj* relating to, associated with, or introduced by any of the popes named Gregory, esp Gregory I (?540–604 AD, pope (590–604)), or Gregory XIII (1502–85, pope (1572–85))

Gregorian calendar *n* the revision of the Julian calendar introduced in 1582 by Pope Gregory XIII and still in force, whereby the ordinary year is made to consist of 365 days and a leap year occurs in every year whose number is divisible by four, except those centenary years, such as 1900, whose numbers are not divisible by 400

Gregorian chant *n* another name for **plainsong**

Gregorian telescope *n* a form of reflecting astronomical telescope with a concave ellipsoidal secondary mirror and the eyepiece set behind the centre of the parabolic primary mirror [C18 named after J. *Gregory* (died 1675), Scottish mathematician who invented it]

Gregorian tone *n* a plainsong melody. See **tone** (sense 6)

Gregory's powder *n* a formulation of rhubarb powder used as a laxative or purgative [C19 named after Dr James *Gregory* (1753–1821), who first made it]

greige (greɪʒ) *chiefly US* ▷ *adj* **1** (of a fabric or material) not yet dyed ▷ *n* **2** an unbleached or undyed cloth or yarn [C20 from French *grège* raw]

greisen ('graɪzᵊn) *n* a light-coloured

g

metamorphic rock consisting mainly of quartz, white mica, and topaz formed by the pneumatolysis of granite [c19 from German, from *greissen* to split]

gremial ('gri:mɪəl) *n RC Church* a cloth spread upon the lap of a bishop when seated during Mass [c17 from Latin *gremium* lap]

gremlin ('grɛmlɪn) *n* **1** an imaginary imp jokingly said to be responsible for malfunctions in machinery **2** any mischievous troublemaker [c20 of unknown origin]

Grenache (grɪ'nɑːʃ) *n* (*sometimes not capital*) **1** a black grape originally grown in the Languedoc-Roussillon region of France and now in other wine-producing areas **2** any of various red wines made from this grape [French]

Grenada (grɛ'neɪdə) *n* an island state in the Caribbean, in the Windward Islands: formerly a British colony (1783–1967); since 1974 an independent state within the Commonwealth; occupied by US troops (1983–85); mainly agricultural. Official language: English. Religion: Christian majority. Currency: East Caribbean dollar. Capital: St George's. Pop: 80 000 (2003 est). Area: 344 sq km (133 sq miles)

grenade (grɪ'neɪd) *n* **1** a small container filled with explosive thrown by hand or fired from a rifle **2** a sealed glass vessel that is thrown and shatters to release chemicals, such as tear gas or a fire extinguishing agent [c16 from French, from Spanish *granada* pomegranate, from Late Latin *grānāta*, from Latin *grānātus* seedy; see GRAIN]

Grenadian (grɛ'neɪdɪən) *adj* **1** of or relating to Grenada or its inhabitants ▷ *n* **2** a native or inhabitant of Grenada

grenadier (,grɛnə'dɪə) *n* **1** *military* **a** (in the British Army) a member of the senior regiment of infantry in the Household Brigade **b** (formerly) a member of a special formation, usually selected for strength and height **c** (formerly) a soldier trained to throw grenades **2** *Also called:* rat-tail any deep-sea gadoid fish of the family *Macrouridae,* typically having a large head and trunk and a long tapering tail **3** any of various African weaverbirds of the genus *Estrilda*. See **waxbill** [c17 from French; see GRENADE]

grenadine[1] (,grɛnə'di:n) *n* a light thin leno-weave fabric of silk, wool, rayon, or nylon, used esp for dresses [c19 from French, from earlier *grenade* silk with a grained texture, from *grenu* grained; see GRAIN]

grenadine[2] (,grɛnə'di:n, 'grɛnə,di:n) *n* **1** a syrup made from pomegranate juice, used as a sweetening and colouring agent in various drinks **2 a** a moderate reddish-orange colour **b** (*as adjective*): *a grenadine coat* [c19 from French: a little pomegranate, from *grenade* pomegranate; see GRENADE]

Grenadines (,grɛnə'di:nz, 'grɛnə,di:nz) *pl n* **the** a chain of about 600 islets in the Caribbean, part of the Windward Islands, extending for about 100 km (60 miles) between St Vincent and Grenada and divided administratively between the two states. Largest island: Carriacou

Grendel ('grɛndᵊl) *n* (in Old English legend) a man-eating monster defeated by the hero Beowulf

Grenoble (grə'nəʊbᵊl; *French* grənɔblə) *n* a city in SE France, on the Isère River: university (1339). Pop: 153 317 (1999)

grenz rays (grɛnz) *n physics* X-rays of long wavelength produced in a device when electrons are accelerated through 25 kilovolts or less [c20 from *grenz* from German *Grenze* boundary]

Gresham's law *or* **theorem** (grɛʃəmz) *n* the economic hypothesis that bad money drives good money out of circulation; the superior currency will tend to be hoarded and the inferior thus dominate the circulation [c16 named after Sir Thomas *Gresham* (?1519–79), English financier]

gressorial (grɛ'sɔːrɪəl) *or* **gressorious** *adj* **1** (of the feet of certain birds) specialized for walking **2**

(of birds, such as the ostrich) having such feet [c19 from New Latin *gressōrius,* from *gressus* having walked, from *gradī* to step]

Gretna Green ('grɛtnə) *n* a village in S Scotland, in Dumfries and Galloway on the border with England: famous smithy where eloping couples were married by the blacksmith from 1754 until 1940, when such marriages became illegal. Pop: 2705 (2001)

grevillea (grə'vɪljə) *n* any of a large variety of evergreen trees and shrubs that comprise the genus *Grevillea*, native to Australia, Tasmania, and New Caledonia: family *Proteaceae* [named after C. F. *Greville* (1749–1809), a founder of the Royal Horticultural Society]

grew (gruː) *vb* the past tense of **grow**

grewsome ('gruːsəm) *adj* an archaic or US spelling of **gruesome**

grex (grɛks) *n* a group of plants that has arisen from the same hybrid parent group [c20 from Latin *grex* flock]

grey *or now esp US* **gray** (greɪ) *adj* **1** of a neutral tone, intermediate between black and white, that has no hue and reflects and transmits only a little light **2** greyish in colour or having parts or marks that are greyish **3** dismal or dark, esp from lack of light; gloomy **4** neutral or dull, esp in character or opinion **5** having grey hair **6** of or relating to people of middle age or above: *grey power* **7** ancient; venerable **8** (of textiles) natural, unbleached, undyed, and untreated ▷ *n* **9** any of a group of grey tones **10** grey cloth or clothing: *dressed in grey* **11** an animal, esp a horse, that is grey or whitish ▷ *vb* **12** to become or make grey [Old English *grǣg*; related to Old High German *grāo*, Old Norse *grar*] > 'greyish *or now esp US* 'grayish *adj* > 'greyly *or now esp US* 'grayly *adv* > 'greyness *or now esp US* 'grayness *n*

grey area *n* **1** (in Britain) a region in which unemployment is relatively high **2** an area or part of something existing between two extremes and having mixed characteristics of both **3** an area, situation, etc, lacking clearly defined characteristics

greyback *or US* **grayback** ('greɪ,bæk) *n* any of various animals having a grey back, such as the grey whale and the hooded crow

greybeard *or US* **graybeard** ('greɪ,bɪəd) *n* **1** an old man, esp a sage **2** a large stoneware or earthenware jar or jug for spirits > 'grey,bearded *or US* 'gray,bearded *adj*

grey body *n physics* a body that emits radiation in constant proportion to the corresponding black-body radiation

grey-crowned babbler *n* an insect-eating Australian bird, *Pomatostomus temporalis* of the family *Timaliidae*

grey duck *n* another name for **parera**

greyed out *adj* (of a navigation button, menu item, etc on a computer screen) not highlighted, indicating that the function is unavailable at a given time

grey eminence *n* the English equivalent of *éminence grise*

grey-faced petrel *n* a dark-coloured New Zealand petrel, *Pterodroma macroptera gouldi*. *Also called:* North Island muttonbird, oi

grey fox *n* **1** a greyish American fox, *Urocyon cinereoargenteus,* inhabiting arid and woody regions from S North America to N South America **2** island grey fox a similar and related animal, *U. littoralis,* inhabiting islands off North America

Grey Friar *n* a Franciscan friar

grey gum *n* any of various eucalyptus trees of New South Wales having dull grey bark, esp *Eucalyptus punctata*

greyhen ('greɪ,hɛn) *n* the female of the black grouse. Compare **blackcock**

grey heron *n* a large European heron, *Ardea cinerea,* with grey wings and back and a long black drooping crest

greyhound ('greɪ,haʊnd) *n* a tall slender fast-

moving dog of an ancient breed originally used for coursing

greyhound racing *n* a sport in which a mechanically propelled dummy hare is pursued by greyhounds around a race track

grey import *n* an imported vehicle that does not have an exact model equivalent in the receiving country

grey knight *n informal* an ambiguous intervener in a takeover battle, who makes a counterbid for the shares of the target company without having made his intentions clear. Compare **black knight, white knight**

greylag *or* **greylag goose** ('greɪ,læg) *n* a large grey Eurasian goose, *Anser anser*: the ancestor of many domestic breeds of goose. US spelling: graylag [c18 from GREY + LAG[1], from its migrating later than other species]

greylist ('greɪ,lɪst) *vb* (*tr*) to hold (someone) in suspicion, without actually excluding him or her from a particular activity

grey market *n* **1** a system involving the secret but not illegal sale of goods at excessive prices. Compare **black market 2** *stock exchange* a market in the shares of a new issue, in which market makers deal with investors who have applied for shares but not yet received an allotment **3** the market for goods and services created by older people with a comfortable disposable income and increased opportunities for spending it

grey matter *n* **1** the greyish tissue of the brain and spinal cord, containing nerve cell bodies, dendrites, and bare (unmyelinated) axons. Technical name: **substantia grisea**. Compare **white matter 2** *informal* brains or intellect

grey mullet *n* any teleost food fish of the family *Mugilidae,* mostly occurring in coastal regions, having a spindle-shaped body and a broad fleshy mouth. US name: mullet. Compare **red mullet**

grey nurse shark *n* a common greyish Australian shark, *Odontaspis arenarius*

grey panther *n* a member of the generation of affluent older consumers, who regard themselves as young, active, and sociable

grey power *n* the political, financial, or social influence of elderly people

grey propaganda *n* propaganda that does not identify its source. Compare **black propaganda, white propaganda**

Greys *pl n* **the** another name for (the) **Royal Scots Greys**

grey sedge *n Brit* an angler's name for a greyish caddis fly, *Odontocerum albicorne,* that frequents running water, in which its larvae make cases from grains of sand

grey squirrel *n* a grey-furred squirrel, *Sciurus carolinensis,* native to E North America but now widely established

grey-state *n* (*modifier*) (of a fabric or material) not yet dyed

grey vote *n* the body of elderly people's votes, or elderly people regarded collectively as voters

greywacke *or US* **graywacke** ('greɪ,wækə) *n* any dark sandstone or grit having a matrix of clay minerals [c19 partial translation of German *Grauwacke*; see WACKE]

grey warbler *n NZ* a small bush bird that hatches the eggs of the shining cuckoo. Also called: riroriro

grey water *n* water that has been used for one purpose but can be used again without repurification, eg bath water, which can be used to water plants

grey-wave *adj informal* denoting a company or an investment that is potentially profitable but is unlikely to fulfil expectations before the investor has grey hair

greywether ('greɪ,wɛðə) *n geology* another name for **sarsen** [from its resemblance to a grey sheep; see WETHER]

grey whale *n* a large N Pacific whalebone whale, *Eschrichtius glaucus,* that is grey or black with white spots and patches: family *Eschrichtidae*

grey wolf *n* another name for **timber wolf**

GRF *biochem abbreviation for* growth hormone-releasing factor: a peptide that is released from the brain and stimulates the pituitary gland to secrete growth hormone

gribble ('grɪbᵊl) *n* any small marine isopod crustacean of the genus *Limnoria*, which bores into and damages wharves and other submerged wooden structures [C19 perhaps related to GRUB]

grice ('graɪs) *vb* **1** (*intr*) (of a railway enthusiast) to collect objects or visit places connected with trains and railways ▷ *n* **2** an object collected or place visited by a railway enthusiast [C20 origin obscure] > '**gricer** *n* > '**gricing** *n*

grid (grɪd) *n* **1** See **gridiron** **2** a network of horizontal and vertical lines superimposed over a map, building plan, etc, for locating points **3** a grating consisting of parallel bars **4** **the grid** the national network of transmission lines, pipes, etc, by which electricity, gas, or water is distributed **5** NZ short for **national grid** **6** Also called: **control grid** *electronics* **a** an electrode situated between the cathode and anode of a valve usually consisting of a cylindrical mesh of wires, that controls the flow of electrons between cathode and anode. See also **screen grid, suppressor grid** **b** (*as modifier*): *the grid bias* **7** See **starting grid** **8** a plate in an accumulator that carries the active substance **9** any interconnecting system of links **10** Northern English dialect word for **face** [C19 back formation from GRIDIRON] > '**gridded** *adj*

grid bias *n* the fixed voltage applied between the control grid and cathode of a valve

grid declination *n* the angular difference between true north and grid north on a map

griddle ('grɪdᵊl) *n* **1** Also called: **girdle** *Brit* a thick round iron plate with a half hoop handle over the top, for making scones, etc **2** any flat heated surface, esp on the top of a stove, for cooking food ▷ *vb* **3** (*tr*) to cook (food) on a griddle [C13 from Old French *gridil*, from Late Latin *crātīculum* (unattested) fine wickerwork; see GRILL[1]]

griddlebread ('grɪdᵊl,brɛd) *or* **griddlecake** ('grɪdᵊl,keɪk) *n* bread or cake made on a griddle

gride (graɪd) *vb* **1** (*intr*) *literary* to grate or scrape harshly **2** *obsolete* to pierce or wound ▷ *n* **3** *literary* a harsh or piercing sound [C14 variant of *girde* GIRD[2]]

gridiron ('grɪd,aɪən) *n* **1** a utensil of parallel metal bars, used to grill meat, fish, etc **2** any framework resembling this utensil **3** a framework above the stage in a theatre from which suspended scenery, lights, etc, are manipulated **4** **a** the field of play in American football **b** an informal name for American football **c** (*as modifier*): *a gridiron hero* ▷ Often shortened to: **grid** [C13 *gredire*, perhaps variant (through influence of *ire* IRON) of *gredile* GRIDDLE]

gridlock ('grɪd,lɒk) *chiefly US* ▷ *n* **1** obstruction of urban traffic caused by queues of vehicles forming across junctions and causing further queues to form in the intersecting streets **2** a point in a dispute at which no agreement can be reached; deadlock: *political gridlock* ▷ *vb* **3** (*tr*) (of traffic) to block or obstruct (an area)

grid networking *n* a type of computer networking that harnesses unused processing cycles of ordinary desktop computers to create a virtual supercomputer

grid reference *n* a method of locating a point on a map or plan by a number referring to the lines of a grid drawn upon the map or plan and to subdivisions of the space between the lines

grid road *n* (in Canada) a road that follows a surveyed division between areas of a township, municipality, etc

grid variation *n* *navigation* the angle between grid north and magnetic north at a point on a map or chart. Also called: **grivation**

grief (gri:f) *n* **1** deep or intense sorrow or distress, esp at the death of someone **2** something that causes keen distress or suffering **3** *informal* trouble or annoyance **4** **come to grief** *informal* to end unsuccessfully or disastrously **5** **tune someone grief** See **tune** (sense 17) [C13 from Anglo-French *gref*, from *grever* to GRIEVE[1]] > '**griefless** *adj*

griefer ('gri:fə) *or* **grief player** *n* an online game player who intentionally spoils the game for other players

grief-stricken *adj* deeply affected by sorrow or distress

grievance ('gri:vᵊns) *n* **1** a real or imaginary wrong causing resentment and regarded as grounds for complaint **2** a feeling of resentment or injustice at having been unfairly treated **3** *obsolete* affliction or hardship [C15 *grevance*, from Old French, from *grever* to GRIEVE[1]]

grieve[1] (gri:v) *vb* **1** to feel or cause to feel great sorrow or distress, esp at the death of someone **2** (*tr*) *obsolete* to inflict injury, hardship, or sorrow on [C13 from Old French *grever*, from Latin *gravāre* to burden, from *gravis* heavy] > '**griever** *n* > '**grieving** *n, adj* > '**grievingly** *adv*

grieve[2] (gri:v) *n* *Scot* a farm manager or overseer [C15 from Old English (Northumbrian) *grǣfa* reeve]

grievous ('gri:vəs) *adj* **1** very severe or painful: *a grievous injury* **2** very serious; heinous: *a grievous sin* **3** showing or marked by grief: *a grievous cry* **4** causing great pain or suffering: *a grievous attack* > '**grievously** *adv* > '**grievousness** *n*

grievous bodily harm *n* *criminal law* really serious injury caused by one person to another. Abbreviation: **GBH**

griff (grɪf) *n* *slang* information; news [C20 from GRIFFIN[2]]

griffe (grɪf) *n* *architect* a carved ornament at the base of a column, often in the form of a claw [C19 from French: claw, of Germanic origin]

griffin[1] ('grɪfɪn), **griffon** *or* **gryphon** *n* a winged monster with an eagle-like head and the body of a lion [C14 from Old French *grifon*, from Latin *grȳphus*, from Greek *grups*, from *grupos* hooked]

griffin[2] ('grɪfɪn) *n* a newcomer to the Orient, esp one from W Europe [C18 of unknown origin]

griffon[1] ('grɪfᵊn) *n* **1** any of various small wire-haired breeds of dog, originally from Belgium **2** any large vulture of the genus *Gyps*, of Africa, S Europe, and SW Asia, having a pale plumage with black wings: family *Accipitridae* (hawks) [C19 from French: GRIFFIN[1]]

griffon[2] ('grɪfᵊn) *n* a variant of **griffin[1]**

grig (grɪg) *n* *dialect* **1** a lively person **2** a short-legged hen **3** a young eel [C14 dwarf, perhaps of Scandinavian origin; compare Swedish *krik* a little creature]

Grigioni (gri'dʒo:ni) *n* the Italian name for **Graubünden**

Grignard reagent ('gri:njɑ:; *French* griɲar) *n* *chem* any of a class of organometallic reagents, having the general formula RMgX, where R is an organic group and X is a halogen atom: used in the synthesis of organic compounds [C20 named after Victor *Grignard* (1871–1934), French chemist]

grigri, gris-gris *or* **greegree** ('gri:gri:) *n, pl* **-gris** (-gri:z) *or* **-grees** an African talisman, amulet, or charm [of African origin]

grike *or* **gryke** (graɪk) *n* a solution fissure, a vertical crack about 0.5 m wide formed by the dissolving of limestone by water, that divides an exposed limestone surface into sections or clints [C20 in geological sense: from northern dialect]

Grikwa ('gri:kwə, 'grɪk-) *n, pl* **-kwa** *or* **-kwas** a variant spelling of **Griqua**

grill[1] (grɪl) *vb* **1** to cook (meat, fish, etc) by direct heat, as under a grill or over a hot fire, or (of meat, fish, etc) to be cooked in this way. Usual US and Canadian word: **broil** **2** (*tr; usually passive*) to torment with or as if with extreme heat **3** (*tr*) *informal* to subject to insistent or prolonged questioning ▷ *n* **4** a device with parallel bars of thin metal on which meat, fish, etc, may be cooked by a fire; gridiron **5** a device on a cooker that radiates heat downwards for grilling meat, fish, etc **6** food cooked by grilling **7** See **grillroom** [C17 from French *gril* gridiron, from Latin *crātīcula* fine wickerwork; see GRILLE] > '**griller** *n*

grill[2] (grɪl) *n* a variant spelling of **grille** [C17 see GRILLE]

grillage ('grɪlɪdʒ) *n* an arrangement of beams and crossbeams used as a foundation on soft ground [C18 from French, from *griller* to furnish with a grille]

grille *or* **grill** (grɪl) *n* **1** Also called: **grillwork** a framework, esp of metal bars arranged to form an ornamental pattern, used as a screen or partition **2** Also called: **radiator grille** a grating, often chromium-plated, that admits cooling air to the radiator of a motor vehicle **3** a metal or wooden openwork grating used as a screen or divider **4** a protective screen, usually plastic or metal, in front of the loudspeaker in a radio, record player, etc **5** *real tennis* the opening in one corner of the receiver's end of the court **6** a group of small pyramidal marks impressed in parallel rows into a stamp to prevent reuse [C17 from Old French, from Latin *crātīcula* fine hurdlework, from *crātis* a hurdle]

grilled (grɪld) *adj* **1** cooked on a grill or gridiron **2** having a grille

grillion ('grɪljən) *n, pl* **-lions** *or* **-lion** *informal* **1** (*often plural*) an extremely large but unspecified number, quantity, or amount: *he had grillions more goes than me* ▷ *determiner* **2** amounting to a grillion: *a grillion years old* [C20 on the model of *million*]

grillroom ('grɪl,ru:m, -,rʊm) *n* a restaurant or room in a restaurant, etc, where grilled steaks and other meat are served

grilse (grɪls) *n, pl* **grilses** *or* **grilse** a young salmon that returns to fresh water after one winter in the sea [C15 *grilles* (plural), of uncertain origin]

grim (grɪm) *adj* **grimmer, grimmest** **1** stern; resolute **2** harsh or formidable in manner or appearance **3** harshly ironic or sinister **4** cruel, severe, or ghastly **5** *archaic or poetic* fierce: *a grim warrior* **6** *informal* unpleasant; disagreeable **7** **hold on like grim death** to hold very firmly or resolutely [Old English *grimm*; related to Old Norse *grimmr*, Old High German *grimm* savage, Greek *khremizein* to neigh] > '**grimly** *adv* > '**grimness** *n*

grimace (grɪ'meɪs) *n* **1** an ugly or distorted facial expression, as of wry humour, disgust, etc ▷ *vb* **2** (*intr*) to contort the face [C17 from French *grimace*, of Germanic origin; related to Spanish *grimazo* caricature; see GRIM] > **gri'macer** *n* > **gri'macingly** *adv*

Grimaldi (grɪ'mɔ:ldɪ) *n* a large crater in the SE quadrant of the moon, about 190 km in diameter, which is conspicuous because of its dark floor [named after Francesco Maria *Grimaldi* (1618–63), Italian physicist]

Grimaldi man *n* *anthropol* a type of Aurignacian man having a negroid appearance, thought to be a race of Cro-Magnon man [C20 named after the *Grimaldi* caves, Italy, where skeletons of this type were found]

grimalkin (grɪ'mælkɪn, -'mɔ:l-) *n* **1** an old cat, esp an old female cat **2** a crotchety or shrewish old woman [C17 from GREY + MALKIN]

grim dig *n* *NZ informal obsolete* an obdurate soldier

grime (graɪm) *n* **1** dirt, soot, or filth, esp when thickly accumulated or ingrained **2** a genre of music originating in the East End of London and combining elements of garage, hip-hop, rap, and jungle ▷ *vb* **3** (*tr*) to make dirty or coat with filth [C15 from Middle Dutch *grime*; compare Flemish *grijm*, Old English *grīma* mask] > '**grimy** *adj* > '**griminess** *n*

Grimm's law (grɪmz) *n* the rules accounting for systematic correspondences between consonants in the Germanic languages and consonants in other Indo-European languages; it states that Proto-Indo-European voiced aspirated stops, voiced unaspirated stops, and voiceless stops became voiced unaspirated stops, voiceless stops, and voiceless fricatives respectively [formulated by Jakob Ludwig Karl Grimm (1785–1863), German philologist and folklorist]

grimoire (griːmˈwɑː) *n* a textbook of sorcery and magic [c19 from French, altered from *grammaire* GRAMMAR; compare GLAMOUR]

Grimsby (ˈɡrɪmzbɪ) *n* a port in E England, in North East Lincolnshire unitary authority, Lincolnshire, formerly important for fishing. Pop: 87 574 (2001)

grin (ɡrɪn) *vb* **grins, grinning, grinned 1** to smile with the lips drawn back revealing the teeth or express (something) by such a smile: *to grin a welcome* **2** (*intr*) to draw back the lips revealing the teeth, as in a snarl or grimace **3 grin and bear it** *informal* to suffer trouble or hardship without complaint ▷ *n* **4** a broad smile **5** a snarl or grimace [Old English *grennian;* related to Old High German *grennen* to snarl, Old Norse *grenja* to howl; see GRUNT] > ˈ**grinner** *n* > ˈ**grinning** *adj, n*

grinch (ɡrɪntʃ) *n* *US informal* a person whose lack of enthusiasm or bad temper has a depressing effect on others [c20 from a character in the 1957 children's book *How the Grinch stole Christmas* by Dr Seuss (1904–91), US writer and illustrator, whose full name was Theodor Seuss Geisel]

grind (ɡraɪnd) *vb* **grinds, grinding, ground 1** to reduce or be reduced to small particles by pounding or abrading: *to grind corn* **2** (*tr*) to smooth, sharpen, or polish by friction or abrasion: *to grind a knife* **3** to scrape or grate together (two things, esp the teeth) with a harsh rasping sound or (of such objects) to be scraped together **4** (*tr;* foll by *out*) to speak or say (something) in a rough voice **5** (*tr;* often foll by *down*) to hold down; oppress; tyrannize **6** (*tr*) to operate (a machine) by turning a handle **7** (*tr;* foll by *out*) to produce in a routine or uninspired manner **8** (*tr;* foll by *out*) to continue to play in a dull or insipid manner: *the band only ground out old tunes all evening* **9** (*tr;* often foll by *into*) to instil (facts, information, etc) by persistent effort **10** (*intr*) *informal* to study or work laboriously **11** (*intr*) *chiefly US* to dance erotically by rotating the pelvis (esp in the phrase **bump and grind**) ▷ *n* **12** *informal* laborious or routine work or study **13** *slang, chiefly US* a person, esp a student, who works excessively hard **14** a specific grade of pulverization, as of coffee beans: *coarse grind* **15** *Brit slang* the act of sexual intercourse **16** *chiefly US* a dance movement involving an erotic rotation of the pelvis **17** the act or sound of grinding ▷ See also **grind in, grind on** [Old English *grindan;* related to Latin *frendere,* Lithuanian *grendu* I rub, Low German *grand* sand] > ˈ**grindingly** *adv*

grindelia (ɡrɪnˈdiːlɪə) *n* **1** any coarse plant of the American genus *Grindelia,* having yellow daisy-like flower heads: family *Asteraceae* (composites). See also **gum plant 2** the dried leaves and tops of certain species of these plants, used in tonics and sedatives [c19 named after David Hieronymus *Grindel* (1777–1836), Russian botanist]

Grindelwald (*German* ˈɡrɪndəlvalt) *n* a valley and resort in central Switzerland, in the Bernese Oberland: mountaineering centre, with the Wetterhorn and the Eiger nearby

grinder (ˈɡraɪndə) *n* **1** a person who grinds, esp one who grinds cutting tools **2** a machine for grinding **3** a molar tooth

grindery (ˈɡraɪndərɪ) *n, pl* **-eries 1** a place in which tools and cutlery are sharpened **2** the equipment of a shoemaker

grindhouse (ˈɡraɪndˌhaʊs) *n* *chiefly US* **a** a cinema specializing in violent or exploitative films such as martial arts movies from Japan and Hong Kong **b** (*as modifier*): *a grindhouse film*

grind in *vb* (*tr, adverb*) *engineering* to make (a conical valve) fit its seating by grinding them together in the presence of an abrasive paste

grinding wheel *n* an abrasive wheel, usually a composite of hard particles in a resin filler, used for grinding

grind on *vb* (*intr, adverb*) to move further relentlessly: *the enemy's invasion ground slowly on*

grindstone (ˈɡraɪndˌstəʊn) *n* **1 a** a machine having a circular block of stone or composite abrasive rotated for sharpening tools or grinding metal **b** the stone used in this machine **c** any stone used for sharpening; whetstone **2** another name for **millstone 3 keep** *or* **have one's nose to the grindstone** to work hard and perseveringly

gringo (ˈɡrɪŋɡəʊ) *n, pl* **-gos** a person from an English-speaking country: used as a derogatory term by Latin Americans [c19 from Spanish: foreigner, probably from *griego* Greek, hence an alien]

griot (ˈɡriːəʊ, ɡriːˈɒt) *n* (in Western Africa) a member of a caste responsible for maintaining an oral record of tribal history in the form of music, poetry, and storytelling [c20 from French *guirot,* perhaps from Portuguese *criado* domestic servant]

grip[1] (ɡrɪp) *n* **1** the act or an instance of grasping and holding firmly **2** Also called: **handgrip** the strength or pressure of such a grasp, as in a handshake **3** the style or manner of grasping an object, such as a tennis racket **4** understanding, control, or mastery of a subject, problem, etc (esp in such phrases as **get** *or* **have a grip on**) **5** Also called: **handgrip** a part by which an object is grasped; handle **6** Also called: **handgrip** a travelling bag or holdall **7** See **hairgrip 8** any device that holds by friction, such as certain types of brake **9** a method of clasping or shaking hands used by members of secret societies to greet or identify one another **10** a spasm of pain **11** a worker in a camera crew or a stagehand who shifts sets and props, etc **12** a small drainage channel cut above an excavation to conduct surface water away from the excavation **13 get** *or* **come to grips** (often foll by *with*) **a** to deal with (a problem or subject) **b** to tackle (an assailant) ▷ *vb* **grips, gripping, gripped 14** to take hold of firmly or tightly, as by a clutch **15** to hold the interest or attention of: *to grip an audience* [Old English *gripe* grasp; related to Old Norse *gripr* property, Old High German *grif*] > ˈ**gripper** *n* > ˈ**grippingly** *adv*

grip[2] (ɡrɪp) *n* *med* a variant spelling of **grippe**

gripe (ɡraɪp) *vb* **1** (*intr*) *informal* to complain, esp in a persistent nagging manner **2** to cause sudden intense pain in the intestines of (a person) or (of a person) to experience this pain **3** (*intr*) *nautical* (of a ship) to tend to come up into the wind in spite of the helm **4** *archaic* to clutch; grasp **5** (*tr*) *archaic* to afflict ▷ *n* **6** (*usually plural*) a sudden intense pain in the intestines; colic **7** *informal* a complaint or grievance **8** *now rare* **a** the act of gripping **b** a firm grip **c** a device that grips **9** (*in plural*) *nautical* the lashings that secure a boat [Old English *grīpan;* related to Gothic *greipan,* Old High German *grīfan* to seize, Lithuanian *greibiu*] > ˈ**griper** *n* > ˈ**gripingly** *adv*

gripe water *n* *Brit* a solution given to infants to relieve colic

grippe *or* **grip** (ɡrɪp) *n* a former name for **influenza** [c18 from French *grippe,* from *gripper* to seize, of Germanic origin; see GRIP[1]]

grip tape *n* a rough tape for sticking to a surface to provide a greater grip

Griqua *or* **Grikwa** (ˈɡriːkwə, ˈɡrɪk-) *n* **1** (*pl* **-qua, -quas** *or* **-kwa, -kwas**) a member of a people of mixed European and Khoikhoi ancestry, living chiefly in Griqualand **2** the language or dialect of Khoikhoi spoken by this people, belonging to the Khoisan family

Griqualand East (ˈɡriːkwəˌlænd, ˈɡrɪk-) *n* an area of central South Africa: settled in 1861 by Griquas led by Adam Kok III; annexed to the Cape Colony in 1879; part of the Transkei in 1903–94. Chief town: Kokstad. Area: 17 100 sq km (6602 sq miles)

Griqualand West *n* an area of N South Africa, north of the Orange river: settled after 1803 by the Griquas; annexed by the British in 1871 following a dispute with the Orange Free State; became part of the Cape Colony in 1880. Chief town: Kimberley. Area: 39 360 sq km (15 197 sq miles)

grisaille (ɡrɪˈzeɪl; *French* ɡrizɑj) *n* **1** a technique of monochrome painting in shades of grey, as in an oil painting or a wall decoration, imitating the effect of relief **2** a painting, stained glass window, etc, in this manner [c19 from French, from *gris* grey]

griseofulvin (ˌɡrɪzɪəʊˈfʊlvɪn) *n* an antibiotic used to treat fungal infections [c20 from New Latin, from *Penicillium griseofulvum dierckx* (fungus from which it was isolated), from Medieval Latin *griseus* grey + Latin *fulvus* reddish yellow]

griseous (ˈɡrɪsɪəs, ˈɡrɪz-) *adj* streaked or mixed with grey; somewhat grey [c19 from Medieval Latin *griseus,* of Germanic origin]

grisette (ɡrɪˈzɛt) *n* **1** (esp formerly) a French working-class girl, esp a pretty or flirtatious one **2** an edible toadstool of the genus *Amanita* of broad-leaved and birch woods [c18 from French, from *grisette* grey fabric used for dresses, from *gris* grey]

gris-gris (ˈɡriːɡriː) *n, pl* **-gris** (-ɡriːz) a variant spelling of **grigri**

Grishun (ɡriːˈʃʊn) *n* the Romansch name for **Graubünden**

griskin (ˈɡrɪskɪn) *n* *Brit* the lean part of a loin of pork [c17 probably from dialect *gris* pig, from Old Norse *griss*]

grisly[1] (ˈɡrɪzlɪ) *adj* **-lier, -liest** causing horror or dread; gruesome [Old English *grislic;* related to Old Frisian *grislik,* Old High German *grīsenlīh*] > ˈ**grisliness** *n*

USAGE See at **grizzly**

grisly[2] (ˈɡrɪzlɪ) *n, pl* **-lies** *obsolete* a variant spelling of **grizzly**

grison (ˈɡraɪsᵊn, ˈɡrɪzᵊn) *n* either of two musteline mammals, *Grison* (or *Galictis*) *cuja* or *G. vittata,* of Central and South America, having a greyish back and black face and underparts [c18 from French, from *grison* grey animal, from Old French *gris* grey]

Grisons (ɡrizɔ̃) *n* the French name for **Graubünden**

grissini (ɡrɪˈsiːnɪ) *pl n* thin crisp breadsticks [c20 from Italian]

grist (ɡrɪst) *n* **1 a** grain intended to be or that has been ground **b** the quantity of such grain processed in one grinding **2** *brewing* malt grains that have been cleaned and cracked **3 grist to** (*or* **for**) **the** (*or* **one's**) **mill** anything that can be turned to profit or advantage [Old English *grīst;* related to Old Saxon *grist-grimmo* gnashing of teeth, Old High German *grist-grimmōn*]

gristle (ˈɡrɪsᵊl) *n* cartilage, esp when in meat [Old English *gristle;* related to Old Frisian, Middle Low German *gristel*] > ˈ**gristly** *adj* > ˈ**gristliness** *n*

gristmill (ˈɡrɪstˌmɪl) *n* a mill, esp one equipped with large grinding stones for grinding grain

grit (ɡrɪt) *n* **1** small hard particles of sand, earth, stone, etc **2** Also called: **gritstone** any coarse sandstone that can be used as a grindstone or millstone **3** the texture or grain of stone **4** indomitable courage, toughness, or resolution **5** *engineering* an arbitrary measure of the size of abrasive particles used in a grinding wheel or other abrasive process ▷ *vb* **grits, gritting, gritted 6** to clench or grind together (two objects, esp the teeth) **7** to cover (a surface, such as icy roads) with grit [Old English *grēot;* related to Old Norse *grjōt* pebble, Old High German *grioz;* see GREAT, GROATS, GRUEL] > ˈ**gritless** *adj*

Grit (ɡrɪt) *n, adj* *Canadian* an informal word for **Liberal**

grith (ɡrɪθ) *n* **1** *English legal history* security, peace, or protection, guaranteed either in a certain place, such as a church, or for a period of time **2** a place of safety or protection [Old English *grith;* related to Old Norse *grith* home]

grits (ɡrɪts) *pl n* **1** hulled and coarsely ground grain **2** *US* See **hominy grits** [Old English *grytt;* related to Old High German *gruzzi;* see GREAT, GRIT]

gritter (ˈɡrɪtə) *n* *Brit* a vehicle which spreads grit on roads during icy weather, or when icy conditions are expected

gritting ('grɪtɪŋ) *n Brit* **a** the spreading of grit on road surfaces to render them less slippery for vehicles during icy weather **b** (*as modifier*): *gritting lorries*

gritty ('grɪtɪ) *adj* **-tier, -tiest** **1** courageous; hardy; resolute **2** of, like, or containing grit > 'grittily *adv* > 'grittiness *n*

grivation (grɪ'veɪʃən) *n navigation* short for **grid variation**

grivet ('grɪvɪt) *n* an E African variety of a common guenon monkey, *Cercopithecus aethiops*, having long white tufts of hair on either side of the face. Compare **green monkey, vervet** [c19 from French, of unknown origin]

grizzle[1] ('grɪzᵊl) *vb* **1** to make or become grey ▷ *n* **2** a grey colour **3** grey or partly grey hair **4** a grey wig [c15 from Old French *grisel*, from *gris*, of Germanic origin; compare Middle High German *grīs* grey]

grizzle[2] ('grɪzᵊl) *vb* (*intr*) *informal, chiefly Brit* **1** (esp of a child) to fret; whine **2** to sulk or grumble [c18 of Germanic origin; compare Old High German *grist-grimmōn* gnashing of teeth, German *Griesgram* unpleasant person] > 'grizzler *n*

grizzled ('grɪzᵊld) *adj* **1** streaked or mixed with grey; grizzly; griseous **2** having grey or partly grey hair

grizzly ('grɪzlɪ) *adj* **-zlier, -zliest** **1** somewhat grey; grizzled ▷ *n, pl* **-zlies** **2** See **grizzly bear**

> USAGE *Grizzly* is sometimes wrongly used where *grisly* is meant: *a grisly* (not *grizzly*) *murder*

grizzly bear *n* a variety of the brown bear, *Ursus arctos horribilis*, formerly widespread in W North America; its brown fur has cream or white hair tips on the back, giving a grizzled appearance. Often shortened to: **grizzly**

gro. *abbreviation for* gross (unit of quantity)

groan (grəʊn) *n* **1** a prolonged stressed dull cry expressive of agony, pain, or disapproval **2** a loud harsh creaking sound, as of a tree bending in the wind **3** *informal* a grumble or complaint, esp a persistent one ▷ *vb* **4** to utter (low inarticulate sounds) expressive of pain, grief, disapproval, etc: *they all groaned at Larry's puns* **5** (*intr*) to make a sound like a groan **6** (*intr*, usually foll by *beneath* or *under*) to be weighed down (by) or suffer greatly (under) **7** (*intr*) *informal* to complain or grumble [Old English *grānian*; related to Old Norse *grīna*, Old High German *grīnan*; see GRIN] > 'groaning *n, adj* > 'groaningly *adv*

groaner ('grəʊnə) *n* **1** a person or thing that groans **2** *informal* an bad or corny joke or pun

groat (grəʊt) *n* an English silver coin worth four pennies, taken out of circulation in the 17th century [c14 from Middle Dutch *groot*, from Middle Low German *gros*, from Medieval Latin (*denarius*) *grossus* thick (coin); see GROSCHEN]

groats (grəʊts) *pl n* **1** the hulled and crushed grain of oats, wheat, or certain other cereals **2** the parts of oat kernels used as food [Old English *grot* particle; related to *grota* fragment, as in *meregrota* pearl; see GRIT, GROUT]

grocer ('grəʊsə) *n* a dealer in foodstuffs and other household supplies [c15 from Old French *grossier*, from *gros* large; see GROSS]

groceries ('grəʊsərɪz) *pl n* merchandise, esp foodstuffs, sold by a grocer

grocery ('grəʊsərɪ) *n, pl* **-ceries** the business or premises of a grocer

grockle ('grɒkᵊl) *n Southwest English dialect* a tourist, esp one from the Midlands or the North of England [c20 of unknown origin]

Grodno (*Russian* 'grɔdnə) *n* a city in W Belarus on the Neman River: part of Poland (1921–39); an industrial centre. Pop: 318 000 (2005 est)

grog (grɒg) *n* **1** diluted spirit, usually rum, as an alcoholic drink **2** *informal, chiefly Austral and NZ* alcoholic drink in general, esp spirits [c18 from Old *Grog*, nickname of Edward Vernon (1684–1757), British admiral, who in 1740 issued naval rum diluted with water; his nickname arose from his grogram cloak]

groggy ('grɒgɪ) *adj* **-gier, -giest** *informal* **1** dazed or staggering, as from exhaustion, blows, or drunkenness **2** faint or weak > 'groggily *adv* > 'grogginess *n*

grogram ('grɒgrəm) *n* a coarse fabric of silk, wool, or silk mixed with wool or mohair, often stiffened with gum, formerly used for clothing [c16 from French *gros grain* coarse grain; see GROSGRAIN]

grogshop ('grɒgʃɒp) *n* **1** *rare* a drinking place, esp one of disreputable character **2** *Austral and NZ informal* a shop where liquor can be bought for drinking off the premises

groin (grɔɪn) *n* **1** the depression or fold where the legs join the abdomen. Related adj: **inguinal** **2** *euphemistic* the genitals, esp the testicles **3** a variant spelling (esp US) of **groyne** **4** *architect* a curved arris formed where two intersecting vaults meet ▷ *vb* **5** (*tr*) *architect* to provide or construct with groins [c15 perhaps from English *grynde* abyss; related to GROUND[1]]

Grolier ('grəʊlɪə; *French* grɔlje) *adj* relating to or denoting a decorative style of bookbinding using interlaced leather straps, gilded ornamental scrolls, etc [c19 named after Jean *Grolier de Servières* (1479–1565), French bibliophile]

grommet ('grɒmɪt) *or* **grummet** *n* **1** a ring of rubber or plastic or a metal eyelet designed to line a hole to prevent a cable or pipe passed through it from chafing **2** a ring of rope hemp used to stuff the gland of a pipe joint **3** *med* a small tube inserted into the eardrum in cases of glue ear in order to allow air to enter the middle ear **4** *Austral informal* a young or inexperienced surfer [c15 from obsolete French *gourmette* chain linking the ends of a bit, from *gourmer* bridle, of unknown origin]

gromwell ('grɒmwəl) *n* any of various hairy plants of the boraginaceous genus *Lithospermum*, esp *L. officinale*, having small greenish-white, yellow, or blue flowers, and smooth nutlike fruits. See also **puccoon** (sense 1) [c13 from Old French *gromil*, from *gres* sandstone + *mil* millet, from Latin *milium*]

Groningen ('grəʊnɪŋən; *Dutch* 'xro:nɪŋə) *n* **1** a province in the NE Netherlands: mainly agricultural. Capital: Groningen. Pop: 573 000 (2003 est). Area: 2336 sq km (902 sq miles) **2** a city in the NE Netherlands, capital of Groningen province. Pop: 177 000 (2003 est)

Grønland ('grœnlan) *n* the Danish name for **Greenland**

groom (gru:m, grʊm) *n* **1** a person employed to clean and look after horses **2** See **bridegroom** **3** any of various officers of a royal or noble household **4** *archaic* a male servant or attendant **5** *archaic and poetic* a young man ▷ *vb* (*tr*) **6** to make or keep (clothes, appearance, etc) clean and tidy **7** to rub down, clean, and smarten (a horse, dog, etc) **8** to train or prepare for a particular task, occupation, etc **9** to win the confidence of (a victim) in order to a commit sexual assault on him or her [C13 *grom* manservant; perhaps related to Old English *grōwan* to GROW] > 'groomer *n* > 'grooming *n*

groomsman ('gru:mzmən, 'grʊmz-) *n, pl* **-men** a man who attends the bridegroom at a wedding, usually the best man

groove (gru:v) *n* **1** a long narrow channel or furrow, esp one cut into wood by a tool **2** the spiral channel, usually V-shaped, in a gramophone record. See also **microgroove** **3** one of the spiral cuts in the bore of a gun **4** *anatomy* any furrow or channel on a bodily structure or part; sulcus **5** *mountaineering* a shallow fissure in a rock face or between two rock faces, forming an angle of more than 120° **6** a settled existence, routine, etc, to which one is suited or accustomed, esp one from which it is difficult to escape **7** *slang* an experience, event, etc, that is groovy **8** **in the groove** **a** *jazz* playing well and apparently effortlessly, with a good beat, etc **b** *US* fashionable ▷ *vb* **9** (*tr*) to form or cut a groove in **10** (*intr*) *dated slang* to enjoy oneself or feel in rapport with one's surroundings **11** (*intr*) *jazz* to play well, with a good beat, etc [c15 from obsolete Dutch *groeve*, of Germanic origin; compare Old High German *gruoba* pit, Old Norse *grof*] > 'grooveless *adj* > 'groove,like *adj*

grooving saw *n* a circular saw used for making grooves

groovy ('gru:vɪ) *adj* **groovier, grooviest** *slang, often jocular* attractive, fashionable, or exciting

grope (grəʊp) *vb* **1** (*intr*; usually foll by *for*) to feel or search about uncertainly (for something) with the hands **2** (*intr*; usually foll by *for* or *after*) to search uncertainly or with difficulty (for a solution, answer, etc) **3** (*tr*) to find or make (one's way) by groping **4** (*tr*) *slang* to feel or fondle the body of (someone) for sexual gratification ▷ *n* **5** the act of groping [Old English *grāpian*; related to Old High German *greifōn*, Norwegian *greipa*; compare GRIPE] > 'gropingly *adv*

groper ('grəʊpə) *or* **grouper** *n, pl* **-er** *or* **-ers** any large marine serranid fish of the genus *Epinephelus* and related genera, of warm and tropical seas also called: **garoupa** [c17 from Portuguese *garupa*, probably from a South American Indian word]

grosbeak ('grəʊs,bi:k, 'grɒs-) *n* **1** any of various finches, such as *Pinicola enucleator* (**pine grosbeak**), that have a massive powerful bill **2** **cardinal grosbeak** any of various mostly tropical American buntings, such as the cardinal and pyrrhuloxia, the males of which have brightly coloured plumage [c17 from French *grosbec*, from Old French *gros* large, thick + *bec* BEAK[1]]

groschen ('grəʊʃən; *German* 'grɔʃən) *n, pl* **-schen** **1** a former Austrian monetary unit worth one hundredth of a schilling **2** a former German coin worth ten pfennigs **3** a former German silver coin [c17 from German: Bohemian dialect alteration of Middle High German *grosse*, from Medieval Latin (*denarius*) *grossus* thick (penny); see GROSS, GROAT]

gros de Londres *French* (gro də lɔ̃drə) *n* a lightweight shiny ribbed silk fabric, the ribs alternating between wide and narrow between different colours or between different textures of yarn [literally: heavy (fabric) from London]

grosgrain ('grəʊ,greɪn) *n* a heavy ribbed silk or rayon fabric or tape for trimming clothes, etc [c19 from French *gros grain* coarse grain; see GROSS, GRAIN]

gros point ('grəʊ 'pɔɪnt; *French* gro pwɛ̃) *n* **1** a needlepoint stitch covering two horizontal and two vertical threads **2** work done in this stitch ▷ Compare **petit point**

gross (grəʊs) *adj* **1** repellently or excessively fat or bulky **2** with no deductions for expenses, tax, etc; total: *gross sales; gross income*. Compare **net**[2] (sense 1) **3** (of personal qualities, tastes, etc) conspicuously coarse or vulgar **4** obviously or exceptionally culpable or wrong; flagrant: *gross inefficiency* **5** lacking in perception, sensitivity, or discrimination: *gross judgments* **6** (esp of vegetation) dense; thick; luxuriant **7** *obsolete* coarse in texture or quality **8** *rare* rude; uneducated; ignorant ▷ *interj slang* **9** an exclamation indicating disgust ▷ *n* **10** (*pl* **gross**) a unit of quantity equal to 12 dozen **11** *pl* **grosses** **a** the entire amount **b** the great majority ▷ *vb* (*tr*) **12** to earn as total revenue, before deductions for expenses, tax, etc ▷ See also **gross out, gross up** [c14 from Old French *gros* large, from Late Latin *grossus* thick] > 'grossly *adv* > 'grossness *n*

gross domestic product *n* the total value of all goods and services produced domestically by a nation during a year. It is equivalent to gross national product minus net investment incomes from foreign nations. Abbreviation: **GDP**

gross national product *n* the total value of all final goods and services produced annually by a nation. Abbreviation: **GNP**

gross out *US slang* ▷ *vb* (*tr, adverb*) **1** to cause (a person) to feel distaste or strong dislike for

g

(something) ▷ *n* **gross-out 2** a person or thing regarded as disgusting or objectionable ▷ *adj* **gross-out 3** disgusting, boring, or objectionable

gross profit *n accounting* the difference between total revenue from sales and the total cost of purchases or materials, with an adjustment for stock

gross ton *n* another name for **long ton**: see **ton**¹ (sense 1)

grossularite (ˈɡrɒsjʊləˌraɪt) *n* a green or greenish-grey garnet, used as a gemstone. Formula: Ca₃Al₂(SiO₄)₃. Also called: **gooseberry stone** [C19 from New Latin *grossulāria* gooseberry, from Old French *grosele* + -ITE¹]

gross up *vb* (*tr, adverb*) to increase (net income) to its pretax value

Grosswardein (groːsvarˈdaɪn) *n* the German name for **Oradea**

gross weight *n* total weight of an article inclusive of the weight of the container and packaging

grosz (grɔːʃ) *n, pl* **groszy** (ˈgrɔːʃɪ) a Polish monetary unit worth one hundredth of a zloty [from Polish, from Czech *grosh; see* GROSCHEN]

grot¹ (grɒt) *n slang* rubbish; dirt [C20 from GROTTY]

grot² (grɒt) *n* a poetic word for **grotto** [C16 from French *grotte*, from Old Italian *grotta; see* GROTTO]

grotesque (grəʊˈtɛsk) *adj* **1** strangely or fantastically distorted; bizarre **2** of or characteristic of the grotesque in art **3** absurdly incongruous; in a ludicrous context ▷ *n* **4** a 16th-century decorative style in which parts of human, animal, and plant forms are distorted and mixed **5** a decorative device, as in painting or sculpture, in this style **6** *printing* the family of 19th-century sans serif display types **7** any grotesque person or thing [C16 from French, from Old Italian (*pittura*) *grottesca* cave painting, from *grottesco* of a cave, from *grotta* cave; see GROTTO] ▷ **groˈtesquely** *adv* ▷ **groˈtesqueness** *n*

grotesquery or **grotesquerie** (grəʊˈtɛskərɪ) *n, pl* **-queries 1** the state of being grotesque **2** something that is grotesque, esp an object such as a sculpture

grotto (ˈgrɒtəʊ) *n, pl* **-toes** *or* **-tos 1** a small cave, esp one with attractive features **2** a construction in the form of a cave, esp as in landscaped gardens during the 18th century [C17 from Old Italian *grotta*, from Late Latin *crypta* vault; see CRYPT]

grotty (ˈgrɒtɪ) *adj* **-tier, -tiest** *Brit slang* **1** unpleasant, nasty, or unattractive **2** of poor quality or in bad condition; unsatisfactory or useless [C20 from GROTESQUE]

grouch (graʊtʃ) *informal* ▷ *vb* (*intr*) **1** to complain; grumble ▷ *n* **2** a complaint, esp a persistent one **3** a person who is always grumbling [C20 from obsolete *grutch*, from Old French *grouchier* to complain; see GRUDGE]

grouchy (ˈgraʊtʃɪ) *adj* **grouchier, grouchiest** *informal* bad-tempered; tending to complain; peevish ▷ **ˈgrouchily** *adv* ▷ **ˈgrouchiness** *n*

grough (grʌf) *n mountaineering* a natural channel or fissure in a peat moor; a peat hag [C20 possibly the same as *grough*, an obsolete variant of GRUFF in the obsolete sense: "rough" (of terrain)]

ground¹ (graʊnd) *n* **1** the land surface **2** earth or soil **3** (*plural*) the land around a dwelling house or other building **4** (*sometimes plural*) an area of land given over to a purpose: *football ground* **5** land having a particular characteristic: *level ground* **6** matter for consideration or debate; field of research or inquiry: *the lecture was familiar ground to him* **7** a position or viewpoint, as in an argument or controversy (esp in the phrases **give ground, hold, stand,** *or* **shift one's ground**) **8** position or advantage, as in a subject or competition (esp in the phrases **gain ground, lose ground,** etc) **9** (*often plural*) reason; justification: *grounds for complaint* **10** *arts* **a** the prepared surface applied to the support of a painting, such as a wall, canvas, etc, to

prevent it reacting with or absorbing the paint **b** the support of a painting **c** the background of a painting or main surface against which the other parts of a work of art appear superimposed **11 a** the first coat of paint applied to a surface **b** (*as modifier*): *ground colour* **12** the bottom of a river or the sea **13** (*plural*) sediment or dregs, esp from coffee **14** *chiefly Brit* the floor of a room **15** *cricket* **a** the area from the popping crease back past the stumps, in which a batsman may legally stand **b** ground staff **16** See **ground bass 17** a mesh or network supporting the main pattern of a piece of lace **18** *electrical, US and Canadian* **a** a connection between an electrical circuit or device and the earth, which is at zero potential **b** a terminal to which this connection is made. Also called: **earth** (sense 8) **19 above ground** alive **20 below ground** dead and buried **21 break new ground** to do something that has not been done before **22 cut the ground from under someone's feet** to anticipate someone's action or argument and thus make it irrelevant or meaningless **23** (*down*) **to the ground** *Brit informal* completely; absolutely: *it suited him down to the ground* **24 get off the ground** *informal* to make a beginning, esp one that is successful **25 go to ground** to go into hiding **26 into the ground** beyond what is requisite or can be endured; to exhaustion **27 meet someone on his own ground** to meet someone according to terms he has laid down himself **28 the (moral) high ground** a position of moral or ethical superiority in a dispute **29 touch ground a** (of a ship) to strike the sea bed **b** to arrive at something solid or stable after discussing or dealing with topics that are abstract or inconclusive **30** (*modifier*) situated on, living on, or used on the ground: *ground frost* **31** (*modifier*) concerned with or operating on the ground, esp as distinct from in the air: *ground crew* **32** (*modifier*) (used in names of plants) low-growing and often trailing or spreading ▷ *vb* **33** (*tr*) to put or place on the ground **34** (*tr*) to instruct in fundamentals **35** (*tr*) to provide a basis or foundation for; establish **36** (*tr*) to confine (an aircraft, pilot, etc) to the ground **37** (*tr*) *informal* to confine (a child) to the house as a punishment **38** the usual US word for **earth** (sense 16) **39** (*tr*) *nautical* to run (a vessel) aground **40** (*tr*) to cover (a surface) with a preparatory coat of paint **41** (*intr*) to hit or reach the ground [Old English *grund*; related to Old Norse *grunn* shallow, *grunnr, grund* plain, Old High German *grunt*]

ground² (graʊnd) *vb* **1** the past tense and past participle of **grind** ▷ *adj* **2** having the surface finished, thickness reduced, or an edge sharpened by grinding **3** reduced to fine particles by grinding

groundage (ˈgraʊndɪdʒ) *n Brit* a fee levied on a vessel entering a port or anchored off a shore

groundbait (ˈgraʊndˌbeɪt) *angling* ▷ *n* **1** bait, such as scraps of bread, maggots, etc, thrown into an area of water to attract fish. See **chum**² ▷ *vb* **2** (*tr*) to prepare (an area of water) with groundbait

ground bass *or* **ground** (beɪs) *n music* a short melodic bass line that is repeated over and over again

ground beetle *n* **1** any beetle of the family *Carabidae*, often found under logs, stones, etc, having long legs and a dark coloration **2** any beetle of the family *Tenebrionidae*, feeding on plants and plant products **3** any of various other beetles that live close to or beneath the ground

ground-breaking *adj* innovative

ground bug *n* any member of a family (*Lygaeidae*) of hemipterous plant-eating insects, having generally dark bodies, sometimes marked with red, and lighter, yellowish wings

ground cherry *n* any of various American solanaceous plants of the genus *Physalis*, esp *P. pubescens*, having round fleshy fruit enclosed in a bladder-like husk. See also **winter cherry, gooseberry** (sense 4)

ground control *n* **1** the personnel, radar, computers, etc, on the ground that monitor the progress of aircraft or spacecraft **2** a system for feeding continuous radio messages to an aircraft pilot to enable him to make a blind landing

ground cover *n* **a** dense low herbaceous plants and shrubs that grow over the surface of the ground, esp, in a forest, preventing soil erosion or, in a garden, stifling weeds **b** (*as modifier*): *ground-cover plants*

grounded (ˈgraʊndɪd) *adj* sensible and down-to-earth; having one's feet on the ground

ground effect *n* the improvement to the aerodynamic qualities of a low-slung motor vehicle resulting from a cushion of air beneath it

ground elder *n* another name for **goutweed**

ground engineer *n* an engineer qualified and licensed to certify the airworthiness of an aircraft. Official name: **licensed aircraft engineer**

ground floor *n* **1** the floor of a building level or almost level with the ground **2 get in on** (*or* **start from**) **the ground floor** *informal* **a** to enter a business, organization, etc, at the lowest level **b** to be in a project, undertaking, etc, from its inception

ground frost *n* the condition resulting from a temperature reading of 0°C or below on a thermometer in contact with a grass surface

ground game *n Brit* game animals, such as hares or deer, found on the earth's surface: distinguished from game birds

ground glass *n* **1** glass that has a rough surface produced by grinding, used for diffusing light **2** glass in the form of fine particles produced by grinding, used as an abrasive

groundhog (ˈgraʊndˌhɒg) *n* another name for **woodchuck**

Groundhog Day *n* **1** (in the US and Canada) February 2nd, when, according to tradition, the groundhog emerges from hibernation; if it sees its shadow, it returns to its burrow for six weeks as a sunny day indicates a late spring, while a cloudy day would mean an early spring **2** a situation in which events are or appear to be continually repeated [C20 sense 2 from the 1993 film *Groundhog Day*, in which the lead character experiences the same day repeatedly]

ground ice *n* sea ice that is in contact with the coast or sea bed and thus not floating freely

grounding (ˈgraʊndɪŋ) *n* a basic knowledge of or training in a subject

ground ivy *n* a creeping or trailing Eurasian aromatic herbaceous plant, *Glechoma* (or *Nepeta*) *hederacea*, with scalloped leaves and purplish-blue flowers: family *Lamiaceae* (labiates)

ground layer *n* See **layer** (sense 2)

groundless (ˈgraʊndlɪs) *adj* without reason or justification: *his suspicions were groundless* ▷ **ˈgroundlessly** *adv* ▷ **ˈgroundlessness** *n*

groundling (ˈgraʊndlɪŋ) *n* **1** any animal or plant that lives close to the ground or at the bottom of a lake, river, etc **2 a** (in Elizabethan theatre) a spectator standing in the yard in front of the stage and paying least **b** a spectator in the cheapest section of any theatre **3** a person on the ground as distinguished from one in an aircraft

ground loop *n* a sudden uncontrolled turn by an aircraft on the ground, while moving under its own power

groundmass (ˈgraʊndˌmæs) *n* the matrix of igneous rocks, such as porphyry, in which larger crystals (phenocrysts) are embedded

groundnut (ˈgraʊndˌnʌt) *n* **1** a North American climbing leguminous plant, *Apios tuberosa*, with fragrant brown flowers and small edible underground tubers **2** the tuber of this plant **3** any of several other plants having underground nutlike parts **4** *Brit* another name for **peanut**

groundnut oil *n* a mild-tasting oil extracted from peanuts and used in cooking

ground pine *n* **1** a hairy plant, *Ajuga chamaepitys*, of Europe and N Africa, having two-lipped yellow flowers marked with red spots: family *Lamiaceae* (labiates). It smells of pine when crushed. See also **bugle²** **2** any of certain North American club mosses, esp *Lycopodium obscurum*

ground plan *n* **1** a drawing of the ground floor of a building, esp one to scale. See also **plan** (sense 3). Compare **elevation** (sense 5) **2** a preliminary or basic outline

ground-plane aerial *n electronics* a quarter-wave vertical dipole aerial in which the electrical image forming the other quarter-wave section is formed by reflection in a system of radially disposed metal rods or in a conductive sheet

ground plate *n* a joist forming the lowest member of a timber frame. Also called: **groundsill**, **soleplate**

ground plum *n* **1** a North American leguminous plant, *Astragalus caryocarpus*, with purple or white flowers and green thick-walled plumlike edible pods **2** the pod of this plant

ground provisions *pl n Caribbean* starchy vegetables, esp root crops and plantains

ground rent *n law* the rent reserved by a lessor on granting a lease, esp one for a long period of years

ground rule *n* a procedural rule or principle

ground run *n* the distance taken by an aircraft to brake from its landing speed to its taxiing speed or a stop

groundsel ('graʊnsəl) *n* **1** any of certain plants of the genus *Senecio*, esp *S. vulgaris*, a Eurasian weed with heads of small yellow flowers: family *Asteraceae* (composites). See also **ragwort 2 groundsel tree** a shrub, *Baccharis halimifolia*, of E North America, with white plumelike fruits: family *Asteraceae* [Old English *grundeswelge*, changed from *gundeswilge*, from *gund* pus + *swelgan* to swallow; after its use in poultices on abscesses]

groundshare ('graʊndˌʃɛə) *vb* **1** (*intr*) to share the facilities and running costs of a single stadium with another team ▷ *n* **2** an arrangement, often temporary, whereby two sporting clubs share one stadium

groundsheet ('graʊndˌʃiːt) *or* **ground cloth** *n* **1** a waterproof rubber, plastic, or polythene sheet placed on the ground in a tent, etc, to keep out damp **2** a similar sheet put over a sports field to protect it against rain

groundsill ('graʊndˌsɪl) *n* another name for **ground plate**

groundsman ('graʊndzmən) *n, pl* **-men** a person employed to maintain a sports ground, park, etc

groundspeed ('graʊndˌspiːd) *n* the speed of an aircraft relative to the ground. Compare **airspeed**

ground squirrel *n* any burrowing sciurine rodent of the genus *Citellus* and related genera, resembling chipmunks and occurring in North America, E Europe, and Asia. Also called: **gopher**

ground state *or* **level** *n* the lowest energy state of an atom, molecule, particle, etc. Compare **excited** (sense 4)

ground stroke *n tennis* any return made to a ball that has touched the ground, as opposed to a volley

groundswell ('graʊndˌswɛl) *n* **1** a considerable swell of the sea, often caused by a distant storm or earthquake or by the passage of waves into shallow water **2** a strong public feeling or opinion that is detectable even though not openly expressed: *a groundswell of discontent*

ground water *n* underground water that has come mainly from the seepage of surface water and is held in pervious rocks

ground wave *or* **ray** *n* a radio wave that travels directly between a transmitting and a receiving aerial. Compare **sky wave**

groundwork ('graʊndˌwɜːk) *n* **1** preliminary work as a foundation or basis **2** the ground or background of a painting, etc

ground zero *n* **1** a point on the surface of land or water at or directly above or below the centre of a nuclear explosion **2** a scene of great devastation **3**

(*sometimes capitals*) the name given to the devastated site of the collapsed World Trade Center towers in New York after September 11 2001

group (gruːp) *n* **1** a number of persons or things considered as a collective unit **2 a** a number of persons bound together by common social standards, interests, etc **b** (*as modifier*): *group behaviour* **3** a small band of players or singers, esp of pop music **4** a number of animals or plants considered as a unit because of common characteristics, habits, etc **5** *grammar* another word, esp in systemic grammar, for **phrase** (sense 1) **6** an association of companies under a single ownership and control, consisting of a holding company, subsidiary companies, and sometimes associated companies **7** two or more figures or objects forming a design or unit in a design, in a painting or sculpture **8** a military formation comprising complementary arms and services, usually for a purpose **9** an air force organization of higher level than a squadron **10** Also called: **radical** *chem* two or more atoms that are bound together in a molecule and behave as a single unit: *a methyl group* $-CH_3$. Compare **free radical 11** a vertical column of elements in the periodic table that all have similar electronic structures, properties, and valencies. Compare **period** (sense 8) **12** *geology* any stratigraphical unit, esp the unit for two or more formations **13** *maths* a set that has an associated operation that combines any two members of the set to give another member and that also contains an identity element and an inverse for each element **14** See **blood group** ▷ *vb* **15** to arrange or place (things, people, etc) in or into a group or (of things, etc) to form into a group [c17 from French *groupe*, of Germanic origin; compare Italian *gruppo*; see CROP]

group captain *n* an officer holding commissioned rank senior to a wing commander but junior to an air commodore in the RAF and certain other air forces

group dynamics *n* (*functioning as singular*) *psychol* a field of social psychology concerned with the nature of human groups, their development, and their interactions with individuals, other groups, and larger organizations

grouper ('gruːpə) *n* a variant of **groper**

groupie ('gruːpɪ) *n slang* an ardent fan of a celebrity, esp a pop star: originally, often a girl who followed the members of a pop group on tour in order to have sexual relations with them

grouping ('gruːpɪŋ) *n* a planned arrangement of things, people, etc, within a group

group insurance *n chiefly US and Canadian* insurance relating to life, health, or accident and covering several persons, esp the employees of a firm, under a single contract at reduced premiums

group marriage *n* an arrangement in which several males live together with several females, forming a conjugal unit

Group of Eight *n* the Group of Seven nations and Russia, whose heads of government meet to discuss economic matters and international relations. Abbreviation: **G8**

Group of Five *n* France, Japan, UK, US, and Germany acting as a group to stabilize their currency exchange rates. Abbreviation: **G5**

Group of Seven *n* the seven leading industrial nations, Canada, France, Germany, Italy, Japan, UK, and the US, whose heads of government and finance ministers meet regularly to coordinate economic policy. Abbreviation: **G7**

Group of Seventy-Seven *n* the developing countries of the world. Abbreviation: **G77**

Group of Ten *n* the ten nations who met in Paris in 1961 to arrange the special drawing rights of the IMF; Belgium, Canada, France, Italy, Japan, Netherlands, Sweden, UK, US, and West Germany. Abbreviation: **G10**

Group of Three *n* Japan, US, and Germany (formerly West Germany), regarded as the largest

western industrialized nations

Group of Twenty-Four *n* the twenty-four richest and most industrialized countries of the world. Abbreviation: **G24**

group practice *n* a medical practice undertaken by a group of associated doctors who work together as partners or as specialists in different areas

group speed *or* **velocity** *n physics* the speed at which energy is propagated in a wave. This is the quantity determined when one measures the distance which the radiation travels in a given time. In a medium in which the speed increases with wavelength the group speed is less than the phase speed, and vice versa

group therapy *n psychol* the simultaneous treatment of a number of individuals who are members of a natural group or who are brought together to share their problems in group discussion

groupthink ('gruːpˌθɪŋk) *n* a tendency within organizations or society to promote or establish the view of the predominant group

groupuscule ('gruːpəˌskjuːl) *n usually derogatory* a small group within a political party or movement [c20 from French: small group]

groupware ('gruːpˌwɛə) *n* software that enables computers within a group or organization to work together, allowing users to exchange electronic-mail messages, access shared files and databases, use video conferencing, etc

grouse¹ (graʊs) *n, pl* **grouse** *or* **grouses 1** any gallinaceous bird of the family *Tetraonidae*, occurring mainly in the N hemisphere, having a stocky body and feathered legs and feet. They are popular game birds. See also **black grouse, red grouse** ▷ *adj* **2** *Austral and NZ slang* excellent [c16 of unknown origin] ▷ '**grouse**ˌ**like** *adj*

grouse² (graʊs) *vb* **1** (*intr*) to grumble; complain ▷ *n* **2** a persistent complaint [c19 of unknown origin] ▷ '**grouser** *n*

grout (graʊt) *n* **1** a thin mortar for filling joints between tiles, masonry, etc **2** a fine plaster used as a finishing coat **3** coarse meal or porridge ▷ *vb* **4** (*tr*) to fill (joints) or finish (walls, etc) with grout [Old English *grūt*; related to Old Frisian *grēt* sand, Middle High German *grūz*, Middle Dutch *grūte* coarse meal; see GRIT, GROATS] ▷ '**grouter** *n*

grouts (graʊts) *pl n chiefly Brit* sediment or grounds, as from making coffee **2** a variant of **groats**

grove (grəʊv) *n* **1** a small wooded area or plantation **2 a** a road lined with houses and often trees, esp in a suburban area **b** (*capital as part of a street name*): *Ladbroke Grove* [Old English *grāf*; related to *grǣfa* thicket, GREAVE, Norwegian *greivla* to intertwine]

grovel ('grɒvᵊl) *vb* **-els, -elling, -elled** *or US* **-els, -eling, -eled** (*intr*) **1** to humble or abase oneself, as in making apologies or showing respect **2** to lie or crawl face downwards, as in fear or humility **3** (*often foll by in*) to indulge or take pleasure (in sensuality or vice) [c16 back formation from obsolete *groveling* (adv), from Middle English *on grufe* on the face, of Scandinavian origin; compare Old Norse *ā grūfu*, from *grūfa* prone position; see -LING²] ▷ '**groveller** *n* ▷ '**grovelling** *n, adj* ▷ '**grovellingly** *adv*

grovet ('grɒvət) *n* a wrestling hold in which a wrestler in a kneeling position grips the head of his kneeling opponent with one arm and forces his shoulders down with the other

grow (grəʊ) *vb* **grows, growing, grew** (gruː) **grown** (grəʊn) **1** (of an organism or part of an organism) to increase in size or develop (hair, leaves, or other structures) **2** (*intr; usually foll by out of or from*) to originate, as from an initial cause or source **3** (*intr*) to increase in size, number, degree, etc: *the population is growing rapidly* **4** (*intr*) to change in length or amount in a specified direction: *some plants grow downwards* **5** (*copula; may take an infinitive*) (esp of emotions, physical states, etc) to develop or

g

come into existence or being gradually: *to grow cold; to grow morose; he grew to like her* **6** (*intr; usually foll by up*) to come into existence **7** (*intr; foll by together*) to be joined gradually by or as by growth: *the branches on the tree grew together* **8** (*intr; foll by away, together, etc*) to develop a specified state of friendship: *the lovers grew together gradually* **9** (when *intr*, foll by *with*) to become covered with a growth: *the path grew with weeds* **10** to produce (plants) by controlling or encouraging their growth, esp for home consumption or on a commercial basis ▷ See also **grow into, grow on, grow out of, grow up** [Old English *grōwan*; related to Old Norse *grōa*, Old Frisian *grōia*, Old High German *gruoen*; see GREEN, GRASS]

grow bag *n* a plastic bag containing a sufficient amount of a sterile growing medium and nutrients to enable a plant, such as a tomato or pepper, to be grown to full size in it, usually for one season only [C20 from *Gro-bag*, trademark for the first ones marketed]

grower ('grəʊə) *n* **1** a person who grows plants: *a vegetable grower* **2** a plant that grows in a specified way: *a fast grower* **3** a piece of music that is initially unimpressive but becomes more enjoyable after further hearings

growing pains *pl n* **1** pains in muscles or joints sometimes experienced by children during a period of unusually rapid growth **2** difficulties besetting a new enterprise in its early stages

grow into *vb* (*intr, preposition*) to become big or mature enough for

growl (graʊl) *vb* **1** (of animals, esp when hostile) to utter (sounds) in a low inarticulate manner **2** to utter (words) in a gruff or angry manner: *he growled an apology* **3** (*intr*) to make sounds suggestive of an animal growling: *the thunder growled around the lake* ▷ *n* **4** the act or sound of growling **5** *jazz* an effect resembling a growl, produced at the back of the throat when playing a wind instrument [C18 from earlier *grolle*, from Old French *grouller* to grumble] > **'growlingly** *adv*

growler ('graʊlə) *n* **1** a person, animal, or thing that growls **2** *Brit slang, obsolete* a four-wheeled hansom cab **3** *Canadian* a small iceberg that has broken off from a larger iceberg or from a glacier, often hazardous to shipping **4** *US slang* any container, such as a can, for draught beer **5** *derogatory slang* a woman, esp one who is considered physically unattractive

grown (grəʊn) *adj* **a** developed or advanced: *fully grown* **b** (*in combination*): *half-grown*

grown-up *adj* **1** having reached maturity; adult **2** suitable for or characteristic of an adult ▷ *n* **3** an adult

grow on *vb* (*intr, preposition*) to become progressively more acceptable or pleasant to

grow out of *vb* (*intr, adverb + preposition*) to become too big or mature for

growth (grəʊθ) *n* **1** the process or act of growing, esp in organisms following assimilation of food **2** an increase in size, number, significance, etc **3** something grown or growing: *a new growth of hair* **4** a stage of development **5** any abnormal tissue, such as a tumour **6** (*modifier*) of, relating to, causing or characterized by growth

growth curve *n* a curve on a graph in which a variable is plotted against time to illustrate the growth of the variable

growth factor *n* any of several substances present in serum that induce growth of cells. Excessive amounts of growth factor may be associated with the production of cancer cells

growth hormone *n* a hormone synthesized in and secreted by the anterior lobe of the pituitary gland that promotes growth of the long bones in the limbs and increases the synthesis of protein essential for growth. Also called: **somatotrophin, human growth hormone**

growth ring *n* another name for **annual ring**

growth shares *pl n finance* ordinary shares with good prospects of appreciation in yield and value

growth substance *n botany* any substance, produced naturally by a plant or manufactured commercially, that, in very low concentrations, affects plant growth; a plant hormone

grow up *vb* (*intr, adverb*) **1** to reach maturity; become adult **2** to come into existence; develop

groyne *or esp US* **groin** (grɔɪn) *n* a wall or jetty built out from a riverbank or seashore to control erosion. Also called: **spur, breakwater** [C16 origin uncertain: perhaps altered from GROIN]

grozing iron ('grəʊzɪŋ) *n* an iron for smoothing joints between lead pipes [C17 part translation of Dutch *gruisijzer*, from *gruizen* to crush, from *gruis* gravel + *yzer* iron]

Grozny (*Russian* 'grɔznij) *n* a city in S Russia, capital of the Chechen Republic: a major oil centre: it was badly damaged during fighting between separatists and Russian troops (1994–95, 1999–2000). Pop: 199 000 (2005 est)

GRU *abbrev* (formerly) the Soviet military intelligence service; the military counterpart of the **KGB** [from Russian *Glavnoye Razvedyvatelnoye Upravleniye* Main Intelligence Directorate]

grub (grʌb) *vb* **grubs, grubbing, grubbed** **1** (when *tr*, often foll by *up* or *out*) to search for and pull up (roots, stumps, etc) by digging in the ground **2** to dig up the surface of (ground, soil, etc), esp to clear away roots, stumps, etc **3** (*intr; often foll by in* or *among*) to search carefully **4** (*intr*) to work unceasingly, esp at a dull task or research **5** *slang* to provide (a person) with food or (of a person) to take food **6** (*tr*) *slang, chiefly US* to scrounge: *to grub a cigarette* ▷ *n* **7** the short legless larva of certain insects, esp beetles **8** *slang* food; victuals **9** a person who works hard, esp in a dull plodding way **10** *Brit informal* a dirty child [C13 of Germanic origin; compare Old High German *grubilōn* to dig, German *grübeln* to rack one's brain, Middle Dutch *grobben* to scrape together; see GRAVE[3], GROOVE]

grubber ('grʌbə) *n* **1** a person who grubs **2** another name for **grub hoe** **3** *rugby* a kick of the ball along the ground **4** *cricket* a delivery which keeps very low upon bouncing

grubby ('grʌbɪ) *adj* **-bier, -biest** **1** dirty; slovenly **2** mean; beggarly **3** infested with grubs > **'grubbily** *adv* > **'grubbiness** *n*

grub hoe *or* **grubbing hoe** *n* a heavy hoe for grubbing up roots. Also called: **grubber**

grub screw *n* a small headless screw having a slot cut for a screwdriver or a socket for a hexagon key and used to secure a sliding component in a determined position

grubstake ('grʌbˌsteɪk) *n* **1** *US and Canadian informal* supplies provided for a prospector on the condition that the donor has a stake in any finds ▷ *vb* (*tr*) **2** *US informal* to furnish with such supplies **3** *chiefly US and Canadian* to supply (a person) with a stake in a gambling game > **'grubˌstaker** *n*

Grub Street *n* **1** a former street in London frequented by literary hacks and needy authors **2** the world or class of literary hacks, etc ▷ *adj also* **'Grub"street** **3** (*sometimes not capital*) relating to or characteristic of hack literature

grudge (grʌdʒ) *n* **1** a persistent feeling of resentment, esp one due to some cause, such as an insult or injury **2** (*modifier*) planned or carried out in order to settle a grudge: *a grudge fight* ▷ *vb* **3** (*tr*) to give or allow unwillingly **4** to feel resentful or envious about (someone else's success, possessions, etc) [C15 from Old French *grouchier* to grumble, probably of Germanic origin; compare Old High German *grunnizōn* to grunt] > **'grudgeless** *adj* > **'grudger** *n* > **'grudging** *adj* > **'grudgingly** *adv*

grue (gruː) *Scot* ▷ *n* **1** a shiver or shudder; a creeping of the flesh ▷ *vb* (*intr*) **2** to shiver or shudder **3** to feel strong aversion [C14 of Scandinavian origin; compare Old Swedish *grua*, Old Danish *grue*; related to German *graven*, Dutch *gruwen* to abhor]

gruel ('gruːəl) *n* a drink or thin porridge, made by boiling meal, esp oatmeal, in water or milk [C14 from Old French, of Germanic origin; see GROUT]

gruelling *or US* **grueling** ('gruːəlɪŋ) *adj* **1** severe or tiring: *a gruelling interview* ▷ *n* **2** *informal* a severe experience, esp punishment [C19 from now obsolete vb *gruel* to exhaust, punish]

gruesome ('gruːsəm) *adj* inspiring repugnance and horror; ghastly [C16 originally Northern English and Scottish; see GRUE, -SOME[1]] > **'gruesomely** *adv* > **'gruesomeness** *n*

gruff (grʌf) *adj* **1** rough or surly in manner, speech, etc: *a gruff reply* **2** (of a voice, bark, etc) low and throaty [C16 originally Scottish, from Dutch *grof*, of Germanic origin; compare Old High German *girob*; related to Old English *hrēof*, Lithuanian *kraupùs*] > **'gruffish** *adj* > **'gruffly** *adv* > **'gruffness** *n*

grugru ('gruːgruː) *n* **1** any of several tropical American palms, esp *Acrocomia sclerocarpa*, which has a spiny trunk and leaves and edible nuts **2** the large edible wormlike larva of a weevil, *Rhynchophorus palmarum*, that infests this palm [C18 from American Spanish (Puerto Rican dialect) *grugrú*, of Cariban origin]

grumble ('grʌmbᵊl) *vb* **1** to utter (complaints) in a nagging or discontented way **2** (*intr*) to make low dull rumbling sounds ▷ *n* **3** a complaint; grouse **4** a low rumbling sound [C16 from Middle Low German *grommelen*, of Germanic origin; see GRIM] > **'grumbler** *n* > **'grumblingly** *adv* > **'grumbly** *adj*

grumbling appendix *n informal* a condition in which the appendix causes intermittent pain but appendicitis has not developed

grummet ('grʌmɪt) *n* another word for **grommet**

grumous ('gruːməs) *or* **grumose** ('gruːməʊs) *adj* (esp of plant parts) consisting of granular tissue [C17 from *grume* a clot of blood, from Latin *grumus* a little heap; related to CRUMB]

grump (grʌmp) *informal* ▷ *n* **1** a surly or bad-tempered person **2** (*plural*) a sulky or morose mood (esp in the phrase **have the grumps**) ▷ *vb* **3** (*intr*) to complain or grumble [C18 dialect *grump* surly remark, probably of imitative origin]

grumpy ('grʌmpɪ) *or* **grumpish** ('grʌmpɪʃ) *adj* **grumpier, grumpiest** peevish; sulky [C18 from GRUMP + -Y[1]] > **'grumpily** *or* **'grumpishly** *adv* > **'grumpiness** *or* **'grumpishness** *n*

grundies ('grʌndɪz) *pl n NZ informal* men's underpants

Grundy ('grʌndɪ) *n* a narrow-minded person who keeps critical watch on the propriety of others [C18 named after Mrs *Grundy*, the character in T. Morton's play *Speed the Plough* (1798)] > **'Grundyˌism** *n* > **'Grundyist** *or* **'Grundyite** *n*

grunge (grʌndʒ) *n* **1** *US slang* dirt or rubbish **2** a style of rock music originating in the US in the late 1980s, featuring a distorted guitar sound **3** a deliberately untidy and uncoordinated fashion style [C20 possibly a coinage imitating GRIME + SLUDGE]

grungy ('grʌndʒɪ) *adj* **-gier, -giest** *slang* **1** *chiefly US and Canadian* squalid or seedy **2** (of pop music) characterized by a loud fuzzy guitar sound

grunion ('grʌnjən) *n* a Californian marine teleost fish, *Leuresthes tenuis*, that spawns on beaches: family *Atherinidae* (silversides) [C20 probably from Spanish *gruñón* a grunter]

grunt (grʌnt) *vb* **1** (*intr*) (esp of pigs and some other animals) to emit a low short gruff noise **2** (when *tr, may take a clause as object*) to express something gruffly: *he grunted his answer* ▷ *n* **3** the characteristic low short gruff noise of pigs, etc, or a similar sound, as of disgust **4** any of various mainly tropical marine sciaenid fishes, such as *Haemulon macrostomum* (**Spanish grunt**), that utter a grunting sound when caught **5** *US slang* an infantry soldier or US Marine, esp in the Vietnam War [Old English *grunnettan*, probably of imitative origin; compare Old High German *grunnizōn*, *grunni* moaning, Latin *grunnīre*] > **'gruntingly** *adv*

grunter ('grʌntə) *n* **1** a person or animal that grunts, esp a pig **2** another name for **grunt** (sense 4)

gruntled ('grʌnt^əld) *adj informal* happy or contented; satisfied [c20 back formation from DISGRUNTLED]

gruppetto (grʊ'pɛtəʊ) *n, pl* -ti (-tiː) *music* a turn [c19 from Italian, diminutive of *gruppo* a group, a turn]

Grus (grʊs) *n, Latin genitive* Gruis ('gruːis) a constellation in the S hemisphere lying near Phoenix and Piscis Austrinus and containing a first and a second magnitude star [via New Latin from Latin: crane]

Gruyère or **Gruyère cheese** ('gruːjɛə; *French* gryjɛr) *n* a hard flat whole-milk cheese, pale yellow in colour and with holes [c19 after *Gruyère*, Switzerland where it originated]

gr. wt. *abbreviation for* gross weight

gryke (graɪk) *n* a variant spelling of **grike**

gryphon ('grɪf^ən) *n* a variant of **griffin¹**

grysbok ('graɪsˌbɒk) *n* either of two small antelopes, *Raphicerus melanotis* or *R. sharpei*, of central and southern Africa, having small straight horns [c18 Afrikaans, from Dutch *grijs* grey + *bok* BUCK¹]

gs *the internet domain name for* South Georgia and the South Sandwich Islands

GS *abbreviation for* 1 General Secretary 2 General Staff

gsm *abbreviation for* grams per square metre: the term used to specify the weight of paper

GSM *abbreviation for* Global System for Mobile Communications

GSOH *abbreviation for* good sense of humour: used in lonely hearts columns and personal advertisements

G-spot *n* an area in the front wall of the vagina which is alleged to produce an extremely intense orgasm when stimulated [c20 short for *Gräfenberg spot*, named after Ernst *Gräfenberg* (1881–1957), German gynaecologist]

GSR *abbreviation for* **galvanic skin response**

GST (in Australia, New Zealand, and Canada) *abbreviation for* goods and services tax

G-string *n* 1 a piece of cloth attached to a narrow waistband covering the pubic area, worn esp by strippers 2 a strip of cloth attached to the front and back of a waistband and covering the loins 3 *music* a string tuned to G, such as the lowest string of a violin

G-suit *n* a close-fitting garment covering the legs and abdomen that is worn by the crew of high-speed aircraft and can be pressurized to prevent blackout during certain manoeuvres. Also called: **anti-G suit** [c20 from *g(ravity) suit*]

GSVQ (in Britain) *abbreviation for* General Scottish Vocational Qualification. Compare **GNVQ**

gt *the internet domain name for* Guatemala

GT *abbreviation for* gran turismo: a high-performance luxury sports car with a hard fixed roof, designed for covering long distances

GTC *abbreviation for* 1 Also: **gtc** (on a commercial order for goods) good till cancelled (*or* countermanded) 2 (in Scotland) General Teaching Council

gtd *abbreviation for* guaranteed

gu *the internet domain name for* Guam

g.u. or **GU** *abbreviation for* genitourinary

guacamole or **guachamole** (ˌgwɑːkəˈməʊlɪ) *n* 1 a spread of mashed avocado, tomato pulp, mayonnaise, and seasoning 2 any of various Mexican or South American salads containing avocado [from American Spanish, from Nahuatl *ahuacamolli*, from *ahuacatl* avocado + *molli* sauce]

guacharo (ˈgwɑːtʃəˌrəʊ) *n, pl* -ros another name for **oilbird** [c19 from Spanish *guácharo*]

guaco (ˈgwɑːkəʊ) *n, pl* -cos 1 any of several tropical American plants whose leaves are used as an antidote to snakebite, esp the climbers *Mikania guaco*, family *Asteraceae* (composites), or *Aristolochia maxima* (*A. serpentina*), family *Aristolochiaceae* 2 the leaves of any of these plants [c19 from American Spanish]

Guadalajara (ˌgwɑːdələˈhɑːrə; *Spanish* gwaðalaˈxara) *n* 1 a city in W Mexico, capital of Jalisco state: the second largest city of Mexico: centre of the Indian slave trade until its abolition, declared here in 1810; two universities (1792 and 1935). Pop: 3 905 000 (2005 est) 2 a city in central Spain, in New Castile. Pop: 70 732 (2003 est)

Guadalcanal (ˌgwɑːd^əlkəˈnæl; *Spanish* gwaðalkaˈnal) *n* a mountainous island in the SW Pacific, the largest of the Solomon Islands: under British protection until 1978; occupied by the Japanese (1942–43). Pop: 60 275 (1999). Area: 6475 sq km (2500 sq miles)

Guadalquivir (ˌgwɑːd^əlkwɪˈvɪə; *Spanish* gwaðalkiˈβir) *n* the chief river of S Spain, rising in the Sierra de Segura and flowing west and southwest to the Gulf of Cádiz: navigable by ocean-going vessels to Seville. Length: 560 km (348 miles)

Guadalupe Hidalgo (ˌgwɑːd^əˈluːp hɪˈdælgəʊ; *Spanish* gwaðaˈlupe iˈðalɣo) *n* the former name (until 1931) of **Gustavo A. Madero**

Guadeloupe (ˌgwɑːd^əˈluːp) *n* an overseas region of France in the E Caribbean, in the Leeward Islands, formed by the islands of Basse-Terre and Grande-Terre and five dependencies. Capital: Basse-Terre. Pop: 443 000 (2004 est). Area: 1780 sq km (687 sq miles)

Guadiana (*Spanish* gwaˈðjana; *Portuguese* gwəˈðjənə) *n* a river in SW Europe, rising in S central Spain and flowing west, then south as part of the border between Spain and Portugal, to the Gulf of Cádiz. Length: 578 km (359 miles)

guaiacol (ˈgwaɪəˌkɒl) *n* a yellowish oily creosote-like liquid extracted from guaiacum resin and hardwood tar, used medicinally as an expectorant. Formula: $C_7H_8O_2$ [from GUAIAC(UM) + -OL²]

guaiacum or **guaiocum** (ˈgwaɪəkəm) *n* 1 any tropical American evergreen tree of the zygophyllaceous genus *Guaiacum*, such as the lignum vitae 2 the hard heavy wood of any of these trees 3 Also called: **guaiac** (ˈgwaɪæk) a brownish resin obtained from the lignum vitae, used medicinally and in making varnishes [c16 New Latin, from Spanish *guayaco*, of Taino origin]

Guam (gwɑːm) *n* an island in the N Pacific, the largest and southernmost of the Marianas: belonged to Spain from the 17th century until 1898, when it was ceded to the US; site of naval and air force bases. Capital: Agaña. Pop: 165 000 (2004 est). Area: 541 sq km (209 sq miles)

Guamanian (gwɑːˈmeɪnɪən) *adj* 1 of or relating to Guam or its inhabitants ▷ *n* 2 a native or inhabitant of Guam

guan (gwɑːn) *n* any gallinaceous bird of the genera *Penelope, Pipile*, etc, of Central and South America: family *Cracidae* (curassows) [c18 from American Spanish]

Guanabara (*Portuguese* gwənaˈbara) *n* (until 1975) a state of SE Brazil, on the Atlantic and **Guanabara Bay**, now amalgamated with the state of Rio de Janeiro

guanaco (gwaˈnɑːkəʊ) *n, pl* -cos a cud-chewing South American artiodactyl mammal, *Lama guanicoe*, closely related to the domesticated llama: family *Camelidae* [c17 from Spanish, from Quechuan *huanacu*]

Guanajuato (*Spanish* gwanaˈxwato) *n* 1 a state of central Mexico, on the great central plateau: mountainous in the north, with fertile plains in the south; important mineral resources. Capital: Guanajuato. Pop: 4 656 761 (2000). Area: 30 588 sq km (11 810 sq miles) 2 a city in central Mexico, capital of Guanajuato state: founded in 1554, it became one of the world's richest silver-mining centres. Pop: 80 000 (2005 est)

guanase (ˈgwɑːneɪz) *n* an enzyme that converts guanine to xanthine by removal of an amino group [c20 from GUAN(INE) + -ASE]

Guangdong (ˈgwænˈdʊŋ) or **Kwangtung** *n* a province of SE China, on the South China Sea: includes the Leizhou Peninsula, with densely populated river valleys; traditionally also including Macao and Hong Kong; the only true tropical climate in China. Capital: Canton. Pop: 79 540 000 (2003 est). Area: 197 100 sq km (76 100 sq miles)

Guangxi Zhuang Autonomous Region (ˈgwænˈsiː ˈdʒwæŋ) or **Kwangsi-Chuang Autonomous Region** *n* an administrative division of S China. Capital: Nanning. Pop: 48 570 000 (2003 est). Area: 220 400 sq km (85 100 sq miles)

Guangzhou (ˈgwænˈdzəʊ) *n* the Pinyin transliteration of the Chinese name for **Canton**

guanidine (ˈgwɑːnɪˌdiːn, -dɪn, ˈgwænɪ-) or **guanidin** (ˈgwɑːnɪdɪn, ˈgwænɪ-) *n* a strongly alkaline crystalline substance, soluble in water and found in plant and animal tissues. It is used in organic synthesis. Formula: $HNC(NH_2)_2$. Also called: carbamidine, iminourea [c19 from GUANO + -ID³ + -INE²]

guanine (ˈgwɑːniːn, ˈguːəˌniːn) *n* a white almost insoluble compound: one of the purine bases in nucleic acids. Formula: $C_5H_5N_5O$ [c19 from GUANO + -INE²]

guano (ˈgwɑːnəʊ) *n, pl* -nos 1 a the dried excrement of fish-eating sea birds, deposited in rocky coastal regions of South America: contains the urates, oxalates, and phosphates of ammonium and calcium; used as a fertilizer b the accumulated droppings of bats and seals 2 any similar but artificial substance used as a fertilizer [c17 from Spanish, from Quechuan *huano* dung]

guanosine (ˈgwɑːnəˌsiːn, -ˌziːn) *n biochem* a nucleoside consisting of guanine and ribose

Guantánamo (*Spanish* gwanˈtanamo) *n* a city in SE Cuba, on **Guantánamo Bay**: site of a US naval base. Pop: 214 000 (2005 est)

guanxi (ˌgwænˈsiː) *n* a Chinese social concept based on the exchange of favours, in which personal relationships are considered more important than laws and written agreements [c20 Chinese: relationships]

guanylic acid (gwəˈnɪlɪk) *n* a nucleotide consisting of guanine, ribose or deoxyribose, and a phosphate group. It is a constituent of DNA or RNA. Also called: guanosine monophosphate

Guaporé (*Portuguese* gwapoˈrɛ) *n* 1 a river in W central South America, rising in SW Brazil and flowing northwest as part of the border between Brazil and Bolivia, to join the Mamoré River. Length: 1750 km (1087 miles). Spanish name: Iténez 2 the former name (until 1956) of **Rondônia**

guar (gwɑː) *n* 1 a leguminous Indian plant, *Cyamopsis tetragonolobus*, grown as a fodder crop and for the gum obtained from its seeds 2 Also called: **guar gum** a gum obtained from the seeds of this plant, used as a stabilizer and thickening agent in food (E412) and as sizing for paper [c19 from Hindi]

guaraní (ˈgwɑːrənɪ) *n, pl* -ní or -nís the standard monetary unit of Paraguay, divided into 100 céntimos

Guarani (ˌgwɑːrəˈniː) *n* 1 (*pl* -ni or -nis) a member of a South American Indian people of Paraguay, S Brazil, and Bolivia 2 the language of this people, belonging to the Tupi-Guarani family; one of the official languages of Paraguay, along with Spanish

guarantee (ˌgærənˈtiː) *n* 1 a formal assurance, esp in writing, that a product, service, etc, will meet certain standards or specifications 2 *law* a promise, esp a collateral agreement, to answer for the debt, default, or miscarriage of another 3 a a person, company, etc, to whom a guarantee is made b a person, company, etc, who gives a guarantee 4 a person who acts as a guarantor 5 something that makes a specified condition or outcome certain 6 a variant spelling of **guaranty** ▷ *vb* -tees, -teeing, -teed (*mainly tr*) 7 (*also tr*) to take responsibility for (someone else's debts,

g

obligations, etc) **8** to serve as a guarantee for **9** to secure or furnish security for **10** (usually foll by *from* or *against*) to undertake to protect or keep secure, as against injury, loss, etc **11** to ensure **12** (*may take a clause as object or an infinitive*) to promise or make certain [c17 perhaps from Spanish *garante* or French *garant*, of Germanic origin; compare WARRANT]

guarantor (ˌgærənˈtɔː) *n* a person who gives or is bound by a guarantee or guaranty; surety

guaranty (ˈgærəntɪ) *n*, *pl* -ties **1** a pledge of responsibility for fulfilling another person's obligations in case of that person's default **2** a thing given or taken as security for a guaranty **3** the act of providing security **4** a person who acts as a guarantor ▷ *vb* -ties, -tying, -tied **5** a variant of **guarantee** [c16 from Old French *garantie*, variant of *warantie*, of Germanic origin; see WARRANTY]

guard (ɡɑːd) *vb* **1** to watch over or shield (a person or thing) from danger or harm; protect **2** to keep watch over (a prisoner or other potentially dangerous person or thing), as to prevent escape **3** (*tr*) to control: *to guard one's tongue* **4** (*intr*; usually foll by *against*) to take precautions **5** to control entrance and exit through (a gate, door, etc) **6** (*tr*) to provide (machinery, etc) with a device to protect the operator **7** (*tr*) **a** *chess*, *cards* to protect or cover (a chess man or card) with another **b** *curling*, *bowling* to protect or cover (a stone or bowl) by placing one's own stone or bowl between it and another player **8** (*tr*) *archaic* to accompany as a guard ▷ *n* **9** a person or group who keeps a protecting, supervising, or restraining watch or control over people, such as prisoners, things, etc. Related adj: **custodial** **10** a person or group of people, such as soldiers, who form a ceremonial escort: *guard of honour* **11** *Brit* the official in charge of a train **12 a** the act or duty of protecting, restraining, or supervising **b** (*as modifier*): *guard duty* **13** *Irish* another word for **garda** **14** a device, part, or attachment on an object, such as a weapon or machine tool, designed to protect the user against injury, as on the hilt of a sword or the trigger of a firearm **15** anything that provides or is intended to provide protection **16 a** another name for **safety chain** **b** a long neck chain often holding a chatelaine **17** See **guard ring** **18** *sport* an article of light tough material worn to protect any of various parts of the body **19** *basketball* **a** the position of the two players in a team who play furthest from the basket **b** a player in this position **20** the posture of defence or readiness in fencing, boxing, cricket, etc **21** **take guard** *cricket* (of a batsman) to choose a position in front of the wicket to receive the bowling, esp by requesting the umpire to indicate his position relative to the stumps **22** **give guard** *cricket* (of an umpire) to indicate such a position to a batsman **23** **off** (one's) **guard** having one's defences down; unprepared **24** **on** (one's) **guard** prepared to face danger, difficulties, etc **25** **stand guard** (of a military sentry, etc) to keep watch **26** **mount guard a** (of a sentry) to begin to keep watch **b** (with *over*) to take up a protective or defensive stance (over something) [c15 from Old French *garde*, from *garder* to protect, of Germanic origin; compare Spanish *guardar*; see WARD] > ˈguardable *adj* > ˈguarder *n* > ˈguardless *adj* > ˈguard,like *adj*

Guardafui (ˌgwɑːdəˈfuːɪ) *n* **Cape** a cape at the NE tip of Somalia, extending into the Indian Ocean

guardant or **gardant** (ˈgɑːdᵊnt) *adj* (*usually postpositive*) *heraldry* (of a beast) shown full face [c16 from French *gardant* guarding, from *garder* to GUARD]

guard band *n* a space left vacant between two radio frequency bands, or between two tracks on a magnetic tape recording, to avoid mutual interference

guard cell *n* *botany* one of a pair of crescent-shaped cells that surround a pore (stoma) in the epidermis. Changes in the turgidity of the cells cause the opening and closing of the stoma

guarded (ˈgɑːdɪd) *adj* **1** protected or kept under surveillance **2** prudent, restrained, or noncommittal: *a guarded reply* > ˈguardedly *adv* > ˈguardedness *n*

guardee (ˌgɑːˈdiː) *n* *Brit informal* a guardsman, esp considered as representing smartness and dash

guard hair *n* any of the coarse hairs that form the outer fur in certain mammals, rising above the underfur

guardhouse (ˈgɑːdˌhaʊs) *n* *military* a building serving as the headquarters or a post for military police and in which military prisoners are detained

guardian (ˈgɑːdɪən) *n* **1** one who looks after, protects, or defends: *the guardian of public morals* **2 a** *law* someone legally appointed to manage the affairs of a person incapable of acting for himself, as a minor or person of unsound mind **b** *social welfare* (in England) a local authority, or person accepted by it, named under the Mental Health Act 1983 as having the powers to require a mentally disordered person to live at a specified place, attend for treatment, and be accessible to a doctor or social worker **3** (*often capital*) (in England) another word for **custos** ▷ *adj* **4** protecting or safeguarding > ˈguardian,ship *n*

Guardian Angels *pl n* vigilante volunteers who patrol the underground railway in New York, London, and elsewhere, wearing red berets, to deter violent crime

Guardianista (ˈgɑːdɪənˈiːstə) *n* *Brit informal* a reader of the *Guardian* newspaper, seen as being typically left-wing, liberal, and politically correct [c20 from the *Guardian* newspaper + (SANDIN)ISTA]

guardrail (ˈgɑːdˌreɪl) *n* **1** a railing at the side of a staircase, road, etc, as a safety barrier **2** Also called (Brit): **checkrail** *railways* a short metal rail fitted to the inside of the main rail to provide additional support in keeping a train's wheels on the track

guard ring *n* **1** Also called: **guard, keeper ring** *jewellery* an extra ring worn to prevent another from slipping off the finger **2** an electrode used to counteract distortion of the electric fields at the edges of other electrodes in a capacitor or electron lens

guardroom (ˈgɑːdˌruːm, -ˌrʊm) *n* **1** a room used by guards **2** a room in which prisoners are confined under guard

Guards (ɡɑːdz) *pl n* **a** (esp in European armies) any of various regiments responsible for ceremonial duties and, formerly, the protection of the head of state **b** (*as modifier*): *a Guards regiment*

guardsman (ˈgɑːdzmən) *n*, *pl* -men **1** (in Britain) a member of a Guards battalion or regiment **2** (in the US) a member of the National Guard **3** a guard

guard's van *n* *railways*, *Brit and NZ* the van in which the guard travels, usually attached to the rear of a train. US and Canadian equivalent: **caboose**

Guarneri (gwɑːˈnɪərɪ; *Italian* gwarˈnɛːri), **Guarnieri** (*Italian* gwarˈnjɛːri) or **Guarnerius** (gwɑːˈnɛərɪəs) *n*, *pl* **Guarneris, Guarnieris** or **Guarneriuses** any violin made by a member of the Guarneri family (active in Italy in the 17th and 18th centuries)

Guat. *abbreviation for* Guatemala

Guatemala (ˌgwɑːtəˈmɑːlə) *n* a republic in Central America: original Maya Indians conquered by the Spanish in 1523; became the centre of Spanish administration in Central America; gained independence and was annexed to Mexico in 1821, becoming an independent republic in 1839. Official language: Spanish. Religion: Roman Catholic majority. Currency: quetzal and US dollar. Capital: Guatemala City. Pop: 12 661 000 (2004 est). Area: 108 889 sq km (42 042 sq miles)

Guatemala City *n* the capital of Guatemala, in the southeast: founded in 1776 to replace the former capital, Antigua Guatemala, after an

earthquake; university (1676). Pop: 982 000 (2005 est)

Guatemalan (ˌgwɑːtəˈmɑːlən) *adj* **1** of or relating to Guatemala or its inhabitants ▷ *n* **2** a native or inhabitant of Guatemala

guava (ˈgwɑːvə) *n* **1** any of various tropical American trees of the myrtaceous genus *Psidium*, esp *P. guajava*, grown in tropical regions for their edible fruit **2** the fruit of such a tree, having yellow skin and pink pulp: used to make jellies, jams, etc [c16 from Spanish *guayaba*, from a South American Indian word]

Guayaquil (*Spanish* gwajaˈkil) *n* a port in W Ecuador: the largest city in the country and its chief port; university (1867). Pop: 2 387 000 (2005 est)

guayule (gwəˈjuːlɪ) *n* **1** a bushy shrub, *Parthenium argentatum*, of the southwestern US: family *Asteraceae* (composites) **2** rubber derived from the sap of this plant [from American Spanish, from Nahuatl *cuauhuli*, from *cuahuitl* tree + *uli* gum]

gubbins (ˈgʌbɪnz) *n informal* **1** an object of little or no value **2** a small device or gadget **3** odds and ends; litter or rubbish **4** a silly person [c16 (meaning: fragments): from obsolete *gobbon*, probably related to GOBBET]

gubernatorial (ˌgjuːbənəˈtɔːrɪəl, ˌguː-) *adj chiefly US* of or relating to a governor [c18 from Latin *gubernātor* governor]

guberniya *Russian* (guˈbjɛrnɪjə) *n* **1** a territorial division of imperial Russia **2** a territorial and administrative subdivision in the former Soviet Union [from Russian: government, ultimately from Latin *gubernāre* to GOVERN]

guck (ɡʌk, ɡʊk) *n* slimy matter; gunk [c20 perhaps a blend of GOO and MUCK]

guddle (ˈgʌdᵊl) *Scot* ▷ *vb* **1** to catch (fish) by groping with the hands under the banks or stones of a stream ▷ *n* **2** a muddle; confusion [c19 of unknown origin]

gudgeon¹ (ˈgʌdʒən) *n* **1** a small slender European freshwater cyprinid fish, *Gobio gobio*, with a barbel on each side of the mouth: used as bait by anglers **2** any of various other fishes, such as the goby **3** bait or enticement **4** *slang* a person who is easy to trick or cheat ▷ *vb* **5** (*tr*) *slang* to trick or cheat [c15 from Old French *gougon*, probably from Latin *gōbius*; see GOBY]

gudgeon² (ˈgʌdʒən) *n* **1 a** a pivot at the end of a beam or axle **b** the female or socket portion of a pinned hinge **2** *nautical* one of two or more looplike sockets, fixed to the transom of a boat, into which the pintles of a rudder are fitted [c14 from Old French *goujon*, perhaps from Late Latin *gulbia* chisel]

gudgeon pin *n* *Brit* the pin through the skirt of a piston in an internal-combustion engine, to which the little end of the connecting rod is attached. US and Canadian name: **wrist pin**

Gudrun (ˈgʊdruːn), **Guthrun** (ˈgʊθruːn) or **Kudrun** (ˈkʊdruːn) *n* *Norse myth* the wife of Sigurd and, after his death, of Atli, whom she slew for his murder of her brother Gunnar. She corresponds to Kriemhild in the *Nibelungenlied*

guelder-rose (ˈgɛldəˌrəʊz) *n* a Eurasian caprifoliaceous shrub, *Viburnum opulus*, with clusters of white flowers and small red fruits [c16 from Dutch *geldersche roos*, from *Gelderland* or *Gelders*, province of Holland]

Guelders (ˈgɛldəz) *n* another name for **Gelderland**

Guelph¹ or **Guelf** (gwɛlf) *n* **1** a member of the political faction in medieval Italy that supported the power of the pope against the German emperors. Compare **Ghibelline** **2** a member of a secret society in 19th-century Italy opposed to foreign rule > ˈGuelphic or ˈGuelfic *adj* > ˈGuelphism or ˈGuelfism *n*

Guelph² (gwɛlf) *n* a city in Canada, in SE Ontario. Pop: 106 920 (2001)

guenon (gəˈnɒn) *n* any slender agile Old World monkey of the genus *Cercopithecus*, inhabiting wooded regions of Africa and having long hind limbs and tail and long hair surrounding the face [c19 from French, of unknown origin]

guerdon ('gɜːd°n) *poetic* ▷ *n* **1** a reward or payment ▷ *vb* **2** (*tr*) to give a guerdon to [c14 from Old French *gueredon*, of Germanic origin; compare Old High German *widarlōn*, Old English *witherlēan*; final element influenced by Latin *dōnum* gift] > 'guerdoner *n*

guereza (gə'rɛzə) *n* a handsome colobus monkey of the mountain forests of Ethiopia [c19 its native name]

Guernica (gɜː'niːkə, 'gɜːnɪkə; *Spanish* gɛr'nika) *n* a town in N Spain: formerly the seat of a Basque parliament; destroyed in 1937 by German bombers during the Spanish Civil War, an event depicted in one of Picasso's most famous paintings. Pop: 15 454 (2003 est). Basque name: **Gernika**

Guernsey ('gɜːnzɪ) *n* **1** an island in the English Channel: the second largest of the Channel Islands, which, with Alderney and Sark, Herm, Jethou, and some islets, forms the bailiwick of Guernsey; finance, market gardening, dairy farming, and tourism. Capital: St Peter Port. Pop: 59 710 (2001). Area: 63 sq km (24.5 sq miles) **2** a breed of dairy cattle producing rich creamy milk, originating from the island of Guernsey **3** (*sometimes not capital*) a seaman's knitted woollen sweater **4** (*not capital*) *Austral* a sleeveless woollen shirt or jumper worn by a football player **5 get a guernsey** *Austral* to be selected or gain recognition for something

Guernsey lily *n* See **nerine**

Guerrero (*Spanish* gɛ'rrɛro) *n* a mountainous state of S Mexico, on the Pacific: rich mineral resources. Capital: Chilpancingo. Pop: 3 075 083 (2000 est). Area: 63 794 sq km (24 631 sq miles)

guerrilla *or* **guerilla** (gə'rɪlə) *n* **1 a** a member of an irregular usually politically motivated armed force that combats stronger regular forces, such as the army or police **b** (*as modifier*): *guerrilla warfare* **2** a form of vegetative spread in which the advance is from several individual rhizomes or stolons growing rapidly away from the centre, as in some clovers ▷ Compare **phalanx** [c19 from Spanish, diminutive of *guerra* WAR] > **guer'rillaism** *or* **gue'rillaism** *n*

guess (gɛs) *vb* (when *tr*, may take a clause as object) **1** (when *intr*, often foll by *at* or *about*) to form or express an uncertain estimate or conclusion (about something), based on insufficient information **2** to arrive at a correct estimate of (something) by guessing: *he guessed my age* **3** *informal, chiefly US and Canadian* to believe, think, or suppose (something) **4 keep a person guessing** to let a person remain in a state of uncertainty ▷ *n* **5** an estimate or conclusion arrived at by guessing **6** the act of guessing **7 anyone's guess** something difficult to predict [c13 probably of Scandinavian origin; compare Old Swedish *gissa*, Old Danish *gitse*, Middle Dutch *gissen*; see GET] > 'guessable *adj* > 'guesser *n* > 'guessingly *adv*

guesstimate *or* **guestimate** *informal* ▷ *n* ('gɛstɪmɪt) **1** an estimate calculated mainly or only by guesswork ▷ *vb* ('gɛstɪˌmeɪt) **2** to form a guesstimate of

guesswork ('gɛsˌwɜːk) *n* **1** a set of conclusions, estimates, etc, arrived at by guessing **2** the process of making guesses

guest (gɛst) *n* **1** a person who is entertained, taken out to eat, etc, and paid for by another **2 a** a person who receives hospitality at the home of another: *a weekend guest* **b** (*as modifier*): *the guest room* **3 a** a person who receives the hospitality of a government, establishment, or organization **b** (*as modifier*): *a guest speaker* **4 a** an actor, contestant, entertainer, etc, taking part as a visitor in a programme in which there are also regular participants **b** (*as modifier*): *a guest appearance* **5** a patron of a hotel, boarding house, restaurant, etc **6** *zoology* a nontechnical name for **inquiline 7 be my guest** *informal* do as you like ▷ *vb* **8** (*intr*) (in theatre and broadcasting) to be a guest: *to guest on*

a show [Old English *giest* guest, stranger, enemy; related to Old Norse *gestr*, Gothic *gasts*, Old High German *gast*, Old Slavonic *gostĭ*, Latin *hostis* enemy]

guest beer *n* a draught beer stocked by a bar, often for a limited period, in addition to its usual range

guesthouse ('gɛstˌhaʊs) *n* a private home or boarding house offering accommodation, esp to travellers

guest rope *n nautical* any line sent or trailed over the side of a vessel as a convenience for boats drawing alongside, as an aid in warping or towing, etc

guff (gʌf) *n slang* ridiculous or insolent talk [c19 imitative of empty talk; compare dialect Norwegian *gufs* puff of wind]

guffaw (gʌ'fɔː) *n* **1** a crude and boisterous laugh ▷ *vb* **2** to laugh crudely and boisterously or express (something) in this way [c18 of imitative origin]

Guggenheim Museum ('gʊgən,haɪm) *n* an international chain of art museums, some of which are architecturally important buildings in their own right, most notably one in New York, designed by Frank Lloyd Wright (1956–59), and one in Bilbao, desgned by Frank O Gehry (1997)

GUI ('guːi) *n acronym for* graphical user interface

Guiana (gaɪ'ænə, gɪ'ɑːnə) *or* **The Guianas** *n* a region of NE South America, including Guyana, Surinam, French Guiana, and the **Guiana Highlands** (largely in SE Venezuela and partly in N Brazil). Area: about 1 787 000 sq km (690 000 sq miles) > **Guianese** (ˌgaɪə'niːz, ˌgɪə-) *or* **Guianan** (gaɪ'ænən, gɪ'ɑːnən) *adj, n*

Guianese (ˌgaɪə'niːz, ˌgɪə-) *or* **Guianan** (gaɪ'ænən, gɪ'ɑːnən) *adj* **1** of or relating to the South American region of Guiana or its inhabitants ▷ *n* **2** a native or inhabitant of Guiana

guichet ('giːʃeɪ) *n* a grating, hatch, or small opening in a wall, esp a ticket-office window [c19 from French]

guid (gʌd, gɪd) *adj* a Scot word for **good**

guidance ('gaɪd°ns) *n* **1** leadership, instruction, or direction **2 a** counselling or advice on educational, vocational, or psychological matters **b** (*as modifier*): *the marriage-guidance counsellor* **3** something that guides **4** any process by which the flight path of a missile is controlled in flight. See also **guided missile**

guide (gaɪd) *vb* **1** to lead the way for (a person) **2** to control the movement or course of (an animal, vehicle, etc) by physical action; steer **3** to supervise or instruct (a person) **4** (*tr*) to direct the affairs of (a person, company, nation, etc) **5** (*tr*) to advise or influence (a person) in his standards or opinions: *let truth guide you always* ▷ *n* **6 a** a person, animal, or thing that guides **b** (*as modifier*): *a guide dog* **7** a person, usually paid, who conducts tour expeditions, etc **8** a model or criterion, as in moral standards or accuracy **9** See **guidebook 10** a book that instructs or explains the fundamentals of a subject or skill **11** any device that directs the motion of a tool or machine part **12 a** a mark, sign, etc, that points the way **b** (*in combination*): *guidepost* **13** *spiritualism* a spirit believed to influence a medium so as to direct what he utters and convey messages through him **14 a** *naval* a ship in a formation used as a reference for manoeuvres, esp with relation to maintaining the correct formation and disposition **b** *military* a soldier stationed to one side of a column or line to regulate alignment, show the way, etc [c14 from (Old) French *guider*, of Germanic origin; compare Old English *wītan* to observe] > 'guidable *adj* > 'guideless *adj* > 'guider *n* > 'guiding *adj, n*

Guide (gaɪd) *n* (*sometimes not capital*) a member of an organization for girls equivalent to the Scouts. US equivalent: **Girl Scout**

guidebook ('gaɪd,bʊk) *n* a handbook with information for visitors to a place, as a historic building, museum, or foreign country. Also called:

guide

guided missile *n* a missile, esp one that is rocket-propelled, having a flight path controlled during flight either by radio signals or by internal preset or self-actuating homing devices. See also **command guidance, field guidance, homing guidance, inertial guidance, terrestrial guidance**

guide dog *n* a dog that has been specially trained to live with and accompany someone who is blind, enabling the blind person to move about safely

guideline ('gaɪd,laɪn) *n* a principle put forward to set standards or determine a course of action

guidepost ('gaɪd,paʊst) *n* **1** a sign on a post by a road indicating directions **2** a principle or guideline

Guider ('gaɪdə) *n* (*sometimes not capital*) **1** In full: **Guide Guider** a woman leader of a company of Guides **2 Brownie Guider** a woman leader of a pack of Brownie Guides

guide rope *n* **1** a stay or rope attached to another rope that is lifting a load, either to steady the load or guide the rope **2** another name for **dragrope** (sense 2)

guide vanes *pl n* fixed aerofoils that direct air, gas, or water into the moving blades of a turbine or into or around bends in ducts with minimum loss of energy

guidon ('gaɪd°n) *n* **1** a small pennant, used as a marker or standard, esp by cavalry regiments **2** the man or vehicle that carries this [c16 from French, from Old Provençal *guidoo*, from *guida* GUIDE]

Guienne *or* **Guyenne** (*French* gɥijɛn) *n* a former province of SW France: formed, with Gascony, the duchy of Aquitaine during the 12th century

guild *or* **gild** (gɪld) *n* **1** an organization, club, or fellowship **2** (esp in medieval Europe) an association of men sharing the same interests, such as merchants or artisans: formed for mutual aid and protection and to maintain craft standards or pursue some other purpose such as communal worship **3** *ecology* a group of plants, such as a group of epiphytes, that share certain habits or characteristics [c14 of Scandinavian origin; compare Old Norse *gjald* payment, *gildi* guild; related to Old English *gield* offering, Old High German *gelt* money]

guilder, gilder ('gɪldə) *or* **gulden** *n*, *pl* -ders, -der *or* -dens, -den **1** the former standard monetary unit of the Netherlands, divided into 100 cents; replaced by the euro in 2002. Also called: **florin 2** the standard monetary unit of the Netherlands Antilles and Surinam, divided into 100 cents **3** any of various former gold or silver coins of Germany, Austria, or the Netherlands [c15 changed from Middle Dutch *gulden*, literally: GOLDEN]

Guildford ('gɪlfəd) *n* a city in S England, in Surrey: cathedral (1936–68); seat of the University of Surrey (1966). Pop: 69 400 (2001)

guildhall ('gɪld,hɔːl) *n* **1** *Brit* **a** the hall of a guild or corporation **b** a town hall **2** Also: **gildhall** the meeting place of a medieval guild

guildsman *or* **gildsman** ('gɪldzmən) *n*, *pl* -men a man who is a member of a guild

guild socialism *n* a form of socialism advocated in Britain in the early 20th century. Industry was to be owned by the state but managed and controlled by worker-controlled guilds > **guild socialist** *n*

guildswoman *or* **gildswoman** ('gɪldzwʊmən) *n*, *pl* -women a woman who is a member of a guild

guile (gaɪl) *n* clever or crafty character or behaviour [c18 from Old French *guile*, of Germanic origin; see WILE] > 'guileful *adj* > 'guilefully *adv* > 'guilefulness *n*

guileless ('gaɪllɪs) *adj* free from guile; ingenuous > 'guilelessly *adv* > 'guilelessness *n*

Guilin ('gweɪ'lɪn), **Kweilin** *or* **Kuei-lin** *n* a city in S China, in Guangxi Zhuang AR on the Li River: noted for the unusual caves and formations of the surrounding karst scenery; trade and manufacturing centre. Pop: 631 000 (2005 est)

Guillain-Barré syndrome (French ˌɡije ˈbareɪ) n an acute neurological disorder, usually following a virus or bacterial infection, that causes progressive muscle weakness and partial paralysis [c20 named after Georges *Guillain* (1876–1961) and Jean Alexandre *Barré* (1880–1967), French neurologists]

guillemet (ˈɡɪlɪˌmɛt) n *printing* another name for **duckfoot quote**

guillemot (ˈɡɪlɪˌmɒt) n any northern oceanic diving bird of the genera *Uria* and *Cepphus*, having a black-and-white plumage and long narrow bill: family *Alcidae* (auks, etc), order *Charadriiformes* [c17 from French, diminutive of *Guillaume* William]

guilloche (ɡɪˈlɒʃ) n an ornamental band or border with a repeating pattern of two or more interwoven wavy lines, as in architecture [c19 from French: tool used in ornamental work, perhaps from *Guillaume* William]

guillotine n (ˈɡɪləˌtiːn) **1 a** a device for beheading persons, consisting of a weighted blade set between two upright posts **b** **the guillotine** execution by this instrument **2** a device for cutting or trimming sheet material, such as paper or sheet metal, consisting of a blade inclined at a small angle that descends onto the sheet **3** a surgical instrument for removing tonsils, growths in the throat, etc **4** Also called: **closure by compartment** (in Parliament, etc) a form of closure under which a bill is divided into compartments, groups of which must be completely dealt with each day ▷ vb (ˌɡɪləˈtiːn) (tr) **5** to behead (a person) by guillotine **6** (in Parliament, etc) to limit debate on (a bill, motion, etc) by the guillotine [c18 from French, named after Joseph Ignace *Guillotin* (1738–1814), French physician, who advocated its use in 1789] ▷ ˌguilloˈtiner n

guilt (ɡɪlt) n **1** the fact or state of having done wrong or committed an offence **2** responsibility for a criminal or moral offence deserving punishment or a penalty **3** remorse or self-reproach caused by feeling that one is responsible for a wrong or offence **4** *archaic* sin or crime [Old English *gylt*, of obscure origin]

guiltless (ˈɡɪltlɪs) adj free of all responsibility for wrongdoing or crime; innocent ▷ ˈguiltlessly adv ▷ ˈguiltlessness n

guilty (ˈɡɪltɪ) adj **guiltier, guiltiest 1** responsible for an offence or misdeed **2** *law* having committed an offence or adjudged to have done so: *the accused was found guilty* **3** **plead guilty** *law* (of a person charged with an offence) to admit responsibility; confess **4** of, showing, or characterized by guilt ▷ ˈguiltily adv ▷ ˈguiltiness n

guimpe (ɡɪmp, ɡæmp) n **1** a short blouse with sleeves worn under a pinafore dress **2** a fill-in for a low-cut dress **3** a piece of starched cloth covering the chest and shoulders of a nun's habit **4** a variant spelling of **gimp** [c19 variant of GIMP]

Guin. *abbreviation for* Guinea

guinea (ˈɡɪnɪ) n **1 a** a British gold coin taken out of circulation in 1813, worth 21 shillings **b** the sum of 21 shillings (£1.05), still used in some contexts, as in quoting professional fees **2** See **guinea fowl 3** *US slang, derogatory* an Italian or a person of Italian descent [c16 the coin was originally made of gold from Guinea]

Guinea (ˈɡɪnɪ) n **1** a republic in West Africa, on the Atlantic: established as the colony of French Guinea in 1890 and became an independent republic in 1958. Official language: French. Religion: Muslim majority and animist. Currency: franc. Capital: Conakry. Pop: 8 620 000 (2004 est). Area: 245 855 sq km (94 925 sq miles) **2** (formerly) the coastal region of West Africa, between Cape Verde and Namibe (formerly Moçâmedes; Angola): divided by a line of volcanic peaks into **Upper Guinea** (between The Gambia and Cameroon) and **Lower Guinea** (between

Cameroon and S Angola) **3 Gulf of** a large inlet of the S Atlantic on the W coast of Africa, extending from Cape Palmas, Liberia, to Cape Lopez, Gabon: contains two large bays, the Bight of Bonny and the Bight of Benin, separated by the Niger delta

Guinea-Bissau n a republic in West Africa, on the Atlantic: first discovered by the Portuguese in 1446 and of subsequent importance in the slave trade; made a colony in 1879; became an independent republic in 1974. Official language: Portuguese; Cape Verde creole is widely spoken. Religion: animist majority and Muslim. Currency: franc. Capital: Bissau. Pop: 1 537 000 (2004 est). Area: 36 125 sq km (13 948 sq miles). Former name (until 1974): **Portuguese Guinea**

Guinea corn n another name for **durra**

guinea fowl or **guinea** n any gallinaceous bird, esp *Numida meleagris*, of the family *Numididae* of Africa and SW Asia, having a dark plumage mottled with white, a naked head and neck, and a heavy rounded body

guinea grains pl n another name for **grains of paradise**

guinea hen n a guinea fowl, esp a female

Guinean (ˈɡɪnɪən) adj **1** of or relating to Guinea or its inhabitants ▷ n **2** a native or inhabitant of Guinea

Guinea pepper n a variety of the pepper plant *Capsicum frutescens*, from which cayenne pepper is obtained

guinea pig n **1** a domesticated cavy, probably descended from *Cavia porcellus*, commonly kept as a pet and used in scientific experiments **2** a person or thing used for experimentation [c17 origin uncertain: perhaps from old use of the name *Guinea* to mean any remote unknown land]

Guinea worm n a parasitic nematode worm, *Dracunculus medinensis*, that lives beneath the skin in man and other vertebrates and is common in India and Africa

Guinevere (ˈɡwɪnɪˌvɪə), **Guenevere** (ˈɡwɛnɪˌvɪə) or **Guinever** (ˈɡwɪnɪvə) n (in Arthurian legend) the wife of King Arthur and paramour of Lancelot

guipure (ɡɪˈpjʊə) n **1** Also called: **guipure lace** any of many types of heavy lace that have their pattern connected by brides, rather than supported on a net mesh **2** a heavy corded trimming; gimp [c19 from Old French *guipure*, from *guiper* to cover with cloth, of Germanic origin; see WIPE, WHIP]

guise (ɡaɪz) n **1** semblance or pretence: *under the guise of friendship* **2** external appearance in general **3** *archaic* manner or style of dress **4** *obsolete* customary behaviour or manner ▷ vb **5** *dialect* to disguise or be disguised in fancy dress **6** (tr) *archaic* to dress or dress up [c13 from Old French *guise*, of Germanic origin; see WISE²]

guiser (ˈɡaɪzə) n a mummer, esp at Christmas or Halloween revels

guitar (ɡɪˈtɑː) n *music* a plucked stringed instrument originating in Spain, usually having six strings, a flat sounding board with a circular sound hole in the centre, a flat back, and a fretted fingerboard. Range: more than three octaves upwards from E on the first leger line below the bass staff. See also **electric guitar, bass guitar, Hawaiian guitar** [c17 from Spanish *guitarra*, from Arabic *qītār*, from Greek *kithara* CITHARA] ▷ guiˈtarist n ▷ guiˈtar-ˌlike adj

guitarfish (ɡɪˈtɑːˌfɪʃ) n, pl **-fish** or **-fishes** any marine sharklike ray of the family *Rhinobatidae*, having a guitar-shaped body with a stout tail and occurring at the bottom of the sea

Guiyang (ˈɡweɪˈjæŋ), **Kweiyang** or **Kuei-yang** n a city in S China, capital of Guizhou province: reached by rail in 1959, with subsequent industrial growth. Pop: 2 467 000 (2005 est)

Guizhou (ˈɡweɪˈdʒəʊ), **Kweichow** or **Kueichou** n a province of SW China, between the Yangtze and Xi Rivers: a high plateau. Capital: Guiyang. Pop: 38 700 000 (2003 est). Area: 174 000 sq km (69 278 sq miles)

Gujarat or **Gujerat** (ˌɡʊdʒəˈrɑːt) n **1** a state of W India: formed in 1960 from the N and W parts of Bombay State; one of India's most industrialized states. Capital: Gandhinagar. Pop: 50 596 992 (2001). Area: 196 024 sq km (75 268 sq miles) **2** a region of W India, north of the Narmada River: generally includes the areas north of Bombay city where Gujarati is spoken

Gujarati or **Gujerati** (ˌɡʊdʒəˈrɑːtɪ) n **1** (pl **-ti**) a member of a people of India living chiefly in Gujarat **2** the state language of Gujarat, belonging to the Indic branch of the Indo-European family ▷ adj **3** of or relating to Gujarat, its people, or their language

Gujju (ˈɡʊdʒuː) *Hinglish informal* ▷ n **1** a Gujarati person ▷ adj **2** Gujarati: *Gujju food* [c21 Gujarati]

Gujranwala (ɡuːdʒˈrɑːnˌwʌlə) n a city in NE Pakistan: textile manufacturing. Pop: 1 466 000 (2005 est)

Gulag (ˈɡuːlæɡ) n (formerly) the central administrative department of the Soviet security service, established in 1930, responsible for maintaining prisons and forced labour camps [c20 from Russian G(lavnoye) U(pravleniye Ispravitelno-Trudovykh) Lag(erei) Main Administration for Corrective Labour Camps]

gular (ˈɡuːlə, ˈɡjuː-) adj *anatomy* of, relating to, or situated in the throat or oesophagus [c19 from Latin *gula* throat]

gulch (ɡʌltʃ) n *US and Canadian* a narrow ravine cut by a fast stream [c19 of obscure origin]

gulden (ˈɡʊldᵊn) n, pl **-dens** or **-den** a variant of **guilder**

Gülek Bogaz (ɡuːˈlɛk bəʊˈɡɑːz) n the Turkish name for the **Cilician Gates**

gules (ɡjuːlz) adj (usually postpositive) ▷ n *heraldry* red [c14 from Old French *gueules* red fur worn around the neck, from *gole* throat, from Latin *gula* GULLET]

gulf (ɡʌlf) n **1** a large deep bay **2** a deep chasm **3** something that divides or separates, such as a lack of understanding **4** something that engulfs, such as a whirlpool ▷ vb **5** (tr) to swallow up; engulf [c14 from Old French *golfe*, from Italian *golfo*, from Greek *kolpos*] ▷ ˈgulf,like adj ▷ ˈgulfy adj

Gulf (ɡʌlf) n **the 1** the Persian Gulf **2** *Austral* **a** the Gulf of Carpentaria **b** (modifier) of, relating to, or adjoining the Gulf: *Gulf country* **3** NZ the Hauraki Gulf

Gulf States pl n **the 1** the oil-producing states around the Persian Gulf: Iran, Iraq, Kuwait, Saudi Arabia, Bahrain, Qatar, the United Arab Emirates, and Oman **2** the states of the US that border on the Gulf of Mexico: Alabama, Florida, Louisiana, Mississippi, and Texas

Gulf Stream n **1** a relatively warm ocean current flowing northeastwards off the Atlantic coast of the US from the Gulf of Mexico **2** another name for **North Atlantic Drift**

Gulf War n **1** the war (1991) between US-led UN forces and Iraq, following Iraq's invasion of Kuwait **2** See **Iran-Iraq War**

Gulf War syndrome n a group of various debilitating symptoms experienced by many soldiers who served in the Gulf War of 1991. It is claimed to be associated with damage to the central nervous system, caused by exposure to pesticides containing organophosphates

gulfweed (ˈɡʌlfˌwiːd) n any brown seaweed of the genus *Sargassum*, esp *S. bacciferum*, having air bladders and forming dense floating masses in tropical Atlantic waters, esp the Gulf Stream. Also called: **sargasso, sargasso weed**

gull¹ (ɡʌl) n any aquatic bird of the genus *Larus* and related genera, such as *L. canus* (**common gull** or **mew**) having long pointed wings, short legs, and a mostly white plumage: family *Laridae*, order *Charadriiformes*. Related adj: **larine** [c15 of Celtic origin; compare Welsh *gwylan*] ▷ ˈgull-ˌlike adj

gull² (ɡʌl) *archaic* ▷ n **1** a person who is easily fooled or cheated ▷ vb **2** (tr) to fool, cheat, or hoax [c16 perhaps from dialect *gull* unfledged bird, probably from *gul*, from Old Norse *gulr* yellow]

Gullah ('gʌlə) *n* **1** (*pl* -lahs *or* -lah) a member of a Negroid people living on the Sea Islands or in the coastal regions of South Carolina, Georgia, and NE Florida **2** the creolized English spoken by these people

gullet ('gʌlɪt) *n* **1** a less formal name for the **oesophagus** Related adj: **oesophageal 2** the throat or pharynx **3** *mining, quarrying* a preliminary cut in excavating, wide enough to take the vehicle that removes the earth [c14 from Old French *goulet*, diminutive of *goule* throat, from Latin *gula* throat]

gullible ('gʌləbᵊl) *adj* easily taken in or tricked ▷ ˌgulliˈbility *n* ▷ 'gullibly *adv*

gull-wing ('gʌlˌwɪŋ) *adj* **1** (of a car door) opening upwards **2** (of an aircraft wing) having a short upward-sloping inner section and a longer horizontal outer section

gully¹ *or* **gulley** ('gʌlɪ) *n, pl* -lies *or* -leys **1** a channel or small valley, esp one cut by heavy rainwater **2** NZ a small bush-clad valley **3** a deep, wide fissure between two buttresses in a mountain face, sometimes containing a stream or scree **4** *cricket* **a** a fielding position between the slips and point **b** a fielder in this position **5** either of the two channels at the side of a tenpin bowling lane ▷ *vb* -lies, -lying, -lied **6** (*tr*) to make (channels) in (the ground, sand, etc) [c16 from French *goulet* neck of a bottle; see GULLET]

gully² ('gʌlɪ) *n, pl* -lies *Scot* a large knife, such as a butcher's knife [c16 of obscure origin]

gulosity (gjʊ'lɒsɪtɪ) *n archaic* greed or gluttony [c16 from Late Latin *gulōsitās*, from Latin *gulōsus* gluttonous, from *gula* gullet]

gulp (gʌlp) *vb* **1** (*tr*; often foll by *down*) to swallow rapidly, esp in large mouthfuls **2** (*tr*; often foll by *back*) to stifle or choke **3** (*intr*) to swallow air convulsively, as while drinking, because of nervousness, surprise, etc **4** (*intr*) to make a noise, as when swallowing too quickly ▷ *n* **5** the act of gulping **6** the quantity taken in a gulp [c15 from Middle Dutch *gulpen*, of imitative origin] ▷ 'gulper *n* ▷ 'gulpingly *adv* ▷ 'gulpy *adj*

gulper eel *or* **fish** *n* any deep-sea eel-like fish of the genera *Eurypharynx* and *Saccopharynx* and order *Lyomeri*, having the ability to swallow large prey

gum¹ (gʌm) *n* **1** any of various sticky substances that exude from certain plants, hardening on exposure to air and dissolving or forming viscous masses in water **2** any of various products, such as adhesives, that are made from such exudates **3** any sticky substance used as an adhesive; mucilage; glue **4** NZ short for **kauri gum 5** See **chewing gum, bubble gum,** and **gumtree 6** *chiefly Brit* a gumdrop ▷ *vb* **gums, gumming, gummed 7** to cover or become covered, clogged, or stiffened with or as if with gum **8** (*tr*) to stick together or in place with gum **9** (*intr*) to emit or form gum ▷ See also **gum up** [c14 from Old French *gomme*, from Latin *gummi*, from Greek *kommi*, from Egyptian *kemai*] ▷ 'gumless *adj* ▷ 'gum‚like *adj*

gum² (gʌm) *n* the fleshy tissue that covers the jawbones around the bases of the teeth. Technical name: **gingiva** Related adj: **gingival** [Old English *gōma* jaw; related to Old Norse *gōmr*, Middle High German *gūme*, Lithuanian *gomurĩs*]

gum³ (gʌm) *n* used in the mild oath *by gum!* [c19 euphemism for GOD]

GUM *abbreviation for* genitourinary medicine

gum accroides (ə'krɔɪdiːz) *n* another name for **acaroid gum**

gum ammoniac *n* another name for **ammoniac²**

gum arabic *n* a gum exuded by certain acacia trees, esp *Acacia senegal*: used in the manufacture of ink, food thickeners, pills, emulsifiers, etc. Also called: **acacia, gum acacia**

gum benzoin *n* another name for **benzoin**

gumbo *or* **gombo** ('gʌmbəʊ) *n, pl* -bos *US and Canadian* **1** the mucilaginous pods of okra **2** another name for **okra 3** a soup or stew thickened with okra pods **4** a fine soil in the W

prairies that becomes muddy when wet [c19 from Louisiana French *gombo*, of Bantu origin]

Gumbo ('gʌmbəʊ) *n* (*sometimes not capital*) a French patois spoken by Creoles in Louisiana and the Caribbean [see GUMBO]

gumboil ('gʌmˌbɔɪl) *n* an abscess on the gums, often at the root of a decayed tooth. Also called: parulis

gumboots ('gʌmˌbuːts) *pl n* another name for **Wellington boots** (sense 1)

gumbotil ('gʌmbətɪl) *n* a sticky clay formed by the weathering of glacial drift [c20 from GUMBO + TIL(L)⁴]

gum digger *n* NZ a person who digs for fossilized kauri gum in a gum field

gum digger's spear *n* NZ a long steel probe used by gum diggers digging for kauri gum

gumdrop ('gʌmˌdrɒp) *n* a small jelly-like sweet containing gum arabic and various colourings and flavourings. Also called (esp Brit): **gum**

gum elastic *n* another name for **rubber¹** (sense 1)

gum elemi *n* another name for **elemi**

gum field *n* NZ an area of land containing buried fossilized kauri gum

gumlands ('gʌmˌlændz) *pl n* NZ infertile land from which the original kauri bush has been removed or burnt producing only kauri gum

gumma ('gʌmə) *n, pl* -mas *or* -mata (-mətə) *pathol* a rubbery tumour characteristic of advanced syphilis, occurring esp on the skin, liver, brain or heart [c18 from New Latin, from Latin *gummi* GUM¹] ▷ 'gummatous *adj*

gummite ('gʌmaɪt) *n* an orange or yellowish amorphous secondary mineral consisting of hydrated uranium oxides

gummosis (gʌ'məʊsɪs) *n* the abnormal production of excessive gum in certain trees, esp fruit trees, as a result of wounding, infection, adverse weather conditions, severe pruning, etc [c19 from New Latin; see GUMMA]

gummous ('gʌməs) *or* **gummose** ('gʌməʊs) *adj rare* resembling or consisting of gum

gummy¹ ('gʌmɪ) *adj* -mier, -miest **1** sticky or tacky **2** consisting of, coated with, or clogged by gum or a similar substance **3** producing gum [c14 from GUM¹ + -Y¹] ▷ 'gumminess *n*

gummy² ('gʌmɪ) *adj* -mier, -miest **1** toothless; not showing one's teeth ▷ *n, pl* -mies **2** *Austral* a small crustacean-eating shark, *Mustelus antarcticus*, with bony ridges resembling gums in its mouth **3** NZ an old ewe that has lost its incisor teeth [c20 from GUM² + -Y¹] ▷ 'gummily *adv*

gummy shark *n Austral* another term for **gummy²** (sense 2)

Gum Nebula *n astronomy* a large, almost circular, emission nebula in the constellation Vela and Puppis. Thought to be the remains of a supernova explosion 1 million years ago, it is estimated to lie 1300 light years away [c20 discovered by C. S. *Gum* (1924–60), Australian astronomer]

gum nut *n Austral* the hardened seed container of the gum tree *Eucalyptus gummifera*

gum plant *or* **gumweed** ('gʌmˌwiːd) *n* any of several American yellow-flowered plants of the genus *Grindelia*, esp *G. robusta*, that have sticky flower heads: family *Asteraceae* (composites)

gumption ('gʌmpʃən) *n informal* **1** *Brit* common sense or resourcefulness **2** initiative or courage: *you haven't the gumption to try* [c18 originally Scottish, of unknown origin]

gum resin *n* a mixture of resin and gum obtained from various plants and trees. See also **bdellium, gamboge**

gumshield ('gʌmˌʃiːld) *n* a plate or strip of soft waxy substance used by boxers to protect the teeth and gums. Also called: mouthpiece

gumshoe ('gʌmˌʃuː) *n* **1** a waterproof overshoe **2** *US and Canadian* a rubber-soled shoe **3** *US and Canadian slang* a detective or one who moves about stealthily **4** *US and Canadian slang* a stealthy action or movement ▷ *vb* -shoes, -shoeing, -shoed **5** (*intr*) *US and Canadian slang* to act stealthily

gumsucker ('gʌmˌsʌkə) *n Austral informal* (in the 19th century) **a** a native-born Australian **b** a native of Victoria

gumtree ('gʌmˌtriː) *n* **1** any of various trees that yield gum, such as the eucalyptus, sweet gum, and sour gum. Sometimes shortened to: **gum 2** Also called: **gumwood** the wood of the eucalyptus tree **3** up a gumtree *informal* in a very awkward position; in difficulties

gum up *vb* (*tr, adverb*) **1** to cover, dab, or stiffen with gum **2** *informal* to make a mess of; bungle (often in the phrase **gum up the works**)

gun (gʌn) *n* **1 a** a weapon with a metallic tube or barrel from which a missile is discharged, usually by force of an explosion. It may be portable or mounted. In a military context the term applies specifically to a flat-trajectory artillery piece **b** (*as modifier*): *a gun barrel* **2** the firing of a gun as a salute or signal, as in military ceremonial **3** a member of or a place in a shooting party or syndicate **4** any device used to project something under pressure *a spray gun* **5** *US slang* an armed criminal; gunman **6** *Austral and NZ slang* **a** an expert **b** (*as modifier*): *a gun shearer;* **7** go great guns *slang* to act or function with great speed, intensity, etc **8** jump *or* beat the gun **a** (of a runner, etc) to set off before the starting signal is given **b** *informal* to act prematurely **9** spike someone's guns See **spike¹** (sense 15) **10** stick to one's guns *informal* to maintain one's opinions or intentions in spite of opposition ▷ *vb* **guns, gunning, gunned 11** (when *tr*, often foll by *down*) to shoot (someone) with a gun **12** (*tr*) to press hard on the accelerator of (an engine) **13** (*intr*) to hunt with a gun ▷ See also **gun for** [c14 probably from a female pet name shortened from the Scandinavian name *Gunnhildr* (from Old Norse *gunnr* war + *hildr* war)]

gunboat ('gʌnˌbəʊt) *n* a small shallow-draft vessel carrying mounted guns and used by coastal patrols, etc

gunboat diplomacy *n* diplomacy conducted by threats of military intervention, esp by a major power against a militarily weak state

gun carriage *n* a mechanical frame on which a gun is mounted for adjustment and firing or for transportation

guncotton ('gʌnˌkɒtᵊn) *n* cellulose nitrate containing a relatively large amount of nitrogen: used as an explosive

gun dog *n* **1** a dog trained to work with a hunter or gamekeeper, esp in retrieving, pointing at, or flushing game **2** a dog belonging to any breed adapted to these activities

gunfight ('gʌnˌfaɪt) *n chiefly US* a fight between persons using firearms ▷ 'gunˌfighter *n* ▷ 'gunˌfighting *n*

gunfire ('gʌnˌfaɪə) *n* **1** the firing of one or more guns, esp when done repeatedly **2** the use of firearms, as contrasted with other military tactics

gunflint ('gʌnˌflɪnt) *n* a piece of flint in a flintlock's hammer used to strike the spark that ignites the charge

gun for *vb* (*intr, preposition*) **1** to search for in order to reprimand, punish, or kill **2** to try earnestly for: *he was gunning for promotion*

gunge (gʌndʒ) *informal* ▷ *n* **1** sticky, rubbery, or congealed matter ▷ *vb* **2** (*tr; usually passive;* foll by *up*) to block or encrust with gunge; clog [c20 of imitative origin, perhaps influenced by GOO and SPONGE] ▷ 'gungy *adj*

gung ho (gʌŋ həʊ) *adj* **1** extremely enthusiastic and enterprising, sometimes to excess **2** extremely keen to participate in military combat [c20 pidgin English, from Mandarin Chinese *kung* work + *ho* together]

gunite ('gʌnˌaɪt) *n civil engineering* a cement-sand mortar that is sprayed onto formwork, walls, or rock by a compressed air ejector giving a very dense strong concrete layer: used to repair reinforced concrete, to line tunnel walls or mine airways, etc [c20 from GUN + -ITE¹]

g

gunk (gʌŋk) *n informal* slimy, oily, or filthy matter [c20 perhaps of imitative origin]

gunlock ('gʌn,lɒk) *n* the mechanism in some firearms that causes the charge to be exploded

gunman ('gʌnmən) *n, pl* -men **1** a man who is armed with a gun, esp unlawfully **2** a man who is skilled with a gun **3** *US* a person who makes, repairs, or has expert knowledge of guns > 'gunman,ship *n*

gunmetal ('gʌn,mɛtəl) *n* **1** a type of bronze containing copper (88 per cent), tin (8–10 per cent), and zinc (2–4 per cent): used for parts that are subject to wear or to corrosion, esp by sea water **2** any of various dark grey metals used for toys, belt buckles, etc **3** a dark grey colour with a purplish or bluish tinge

gun moll *n slang* a female criminal or a woman who associates with criminals

Gunnar ('gʊnɑ:) *n Norse myth* brother of Gudrun and husband of Brynhild, won for him by Sigurd. He corresponds to Gunther in the *Nibelungenlied*

gunned (gʌnd) *adj* **a** having a gun or guns as specified **b** (*in combination*): three-gunned

Gunn effect (gʌn) *n* a phenomenon observed in some semiconductors in which a steady electric field of magnitude greater than a threshold value generates electrical oscillations with microwave frequencies [c20 named after John Battiscombe *Gunn* (born 1928), British physicist]

gunnel¹ ('gʌnəl) *n* any eel-like blennioid fish of the family *Pholidae*, occurring in coastal regions of northern seas. See also **butterfish** [c17 of unknown origin]

gunnel² ('gʌnəl) *n* a variant spelling of **gunwale**

gunner ('gʌnə) *n* **1** a serviceman who works with, uses, or specializes in guns **2** *naval* (formerly) a warrant officer responsible for the training of gun crews, their performance in action, and accounting for ammunition **3** (in the British Army) an artilleryman, esp a private. Abbreviation: **gnr 4** a person who hunts with a rifle or shotgun > 'gunner,ship *n*

gunnera ('gʌnərə) *n* any herbaceous perennial plant of the genus *Gunnera,* found throughout the S hemisphere and cultivated for its large leaves [c18 named after J. E. *Gunnerus* (1718–73), Norwegian bishop and botanist]

gunnery ('gʌnərɪ) *n* **1** the art and science of the efficient design and use of ordnance, esp artillery **2** guns collectively **3** the use and firing of guns **4** (*modifier*) of, relating to, or concerned with heavy guns, as in warfare: *a gunnery officer*

gunning ('gʌnɪŋ) *n* **1** the act or an instance of shooting with guns **2** the art, practice, or act of hunting game with guns

gunny ('gʌnɪ) *n, pl* -nies *chiefly US* **1** a coarse hardwearing fabric usually made from jute and used for sacks, etc **2** Also called: **gunny sack** a sack made from this fabric [c18 from Hindi *gōnī,* from Sanskrit *gonī* sack, probably of Dravidian origin]

gunpaper ('gʌn,peɪpə) *n* a cellulose nitrate explosive made by treating paper with nitric acid

gunplay ('gʌn,pleɪ) *n chiefly US* the use of firearms, as by criminals

gunpoint ('gʌn,pɔɪnt) *n* **1** the muzzle of a gun **2 at gunpoint** being under or using the threat of being shot

gunpowder ('gʌn,paʊdə) *n* an explosive mixture of potassium nitrate, charcoal, and sulphur (typical proportions are 75:15:10): used in time fuses, blasting, and fireworks. Also called: **black powder** > 'gun,powdery *adj*

Gunpowder Plot *n* the unsuccessful conspiracy to blow up James I and Parliament at Westminster on Nov 5, 1605. See also **Guy Fawkes Day**

gunpowder tea *n* a fine variety of green tea, each leaf of which is rolled into a pellet

gun room *n* **1** (esp in the Royal Navy) the mess allocated to subordinate or junior officers **2** a room where guns are stored

gunrunning ('gʌn,rʌnɪŋ) *n* the smuggling of guns and ammunition or other weapons of war

into a country > 'gun,runner *n*

gunsel ('gʌnsəl) *n US slang* **1** a catamite **2** a stupid or inexperienced person, esp a youth **3** a criminal who carries a gun [c20 probably from Yiddish *genzel;* compare German *ganslein* gosling, from *gans* GOOSE¹]

gunshot ('gʌn,ʃɒt) *n* **1 a** a shot fired from a gun **b** (*as modifier*): gunshot wounds **2** the range of a gun **3** the shooting of a gun

gun-shy *adj* afraid of a gun or the sound it makes

gunslinger ('gʌn,slɪŋə) *n slang* a gunfighter or gunman, esp in the Old West > 'gun,slinging *n*

gunsmith ('gʌn,smɪθ) *n* a person who manufactures or repairs firearms, esp portable guns > 'gun,smithing *n*

gunstock ('gʌn,stɒk) *n* the wooden or metallic handle or support to which is attached the barrel of a rifle

gunter rig ('gʌntə) *n nautical* a type of gaffing in which the gaff is hoisted parallel to the mast [c18 named after Edmund *Gunter* (1581–1626), English mathematician and astronomer] > 'gunter-,rigged *adj*

Gunter's chain *n surveying* a measuring chain 22 yards in length, or this length as a unit. See **chain** (sense 7) [c17 named after Edmund *Gunter* (1581–1626), English mathematician and astronomer]

Gunther ('gʊntə) *n* (in the *Nibelungenlied*) a king of Burgundy, allied with Siegfried, who won for him his wife Brunhild. He corresponds to Gunnar in Norse mythology

Guntur (gʊn'tʊə) *n* a city in E India, in central Andhra Pradesh: founded by the French in the 18th century; ceded to Britain in 1788. Pop: 514 707 (2001)

gunwale *or* **gunnel** ('gʌnəl) *n* **1** *nautical* the top of the side of a boat or the topmost plank of a wooden vessel **2 full to the gunwales** completely full; full to overflowing

gunyah ('gʌnjə) *n Austral* a bush hut or shelter [c19 from a native Australian language]

Günz (gʊnts) *n* the first major Pleistocene glaciation of the Alps. See also **Mindel, Riss, Würm** [named after the river *Günz* in Germany]

guppy ('gʌpɪ) *n, pl* -pies a small brightly coloured freshwater viviparous cyprinodont fish, *Lebistes reticulatus,* of N South America and the Caribbean: a popular aquarium fish [c20 named after R. J. L. *Guppy,* 19th-century clergyman of Trinidad who first presented specimens to the British Museum]

Gupta ('gʌptə) *n* the dynasty ruling northern India from the early 4th century to the late 6th century AD: the period is famous for achievements in art, science, and mathematics

Gur (gʊə) *n* a small group of languages of W Africa, spoken chiefly in Burkina-Faso and Ghana, forming a branch of the Niger-Congo family. Also called: **Voltaic**

gurdwara ('gɜ:dwɑ:rə) *n* a Sikh place of worship [c20 from Punjabi *gurduārā,* from Sanskrit *guru* teacher + *dvārā* DOOR]

gurgitation (,gɜ:dʒɪ'teɪʃən) *n* surging or swirling motion, esp of water [c16 from Late Latin *gurgitātus* engulfed, from *gurgitāre* to engulf, from Latin *gurges* whirlpool]

gurgle ('gɜ:gəl) *vb* (*intr*) **1** (of liquids, esp of rivers, streams, etc) to make low bubbling noises when flowing **2** to utter low throaty bubbling noises, esp as a sign of contentment ▷ *n* **3** the act or sound of gurgling [c16 perhaps from Vulgar Latin *gurgulāre,* from Latin *gurguliō* gullet] > 'gurgling *adj*

gurglet ('gɜ:glɪt) *n* another word for **goglet**

Gurindji (gʊ'rɪndʒɪ) *n* **1** an Aboriginal people of N central Australia **2** the language of this people

gurjun ('gɜ:dʒən) *n* **1** any of several S or SE Asian dipterocarpaceous trees of the genus *Dipterocarpus* that yield a resin **2** Also called: **gurjun balsam** the resin from any of these trees, used as a varnish [c19 from Bengali *garjon*]

Gurkha ('gʊəkɑ:, 'gɜ:kə) *n, pl* -khas *or* -kha **1** a member of a Hindu people, descended from

Brahmins and Rajputs, living chiefly in Nepal, where they achieved dominance after being driven from India by the Muslims **2** a member of this people serving as a soldier in the Indian or British army

Gurkhali (,gʊə'kɑ:lɪ, ,gɜ:-) *n* the language of the Gurkhas, belonging to the Indic branch of the Indo-European family

Gurmukhi ('gʊəmʊkɪ) *n* the script used for writing the Punjabi language [Sanskrit, from *guru* teacher + *mukh* mouth]

gurn (gɜrn, gɜ:n) *vb* (*intr*) a variant spelling of **girn**

gurnard ('gɜ:nəd) *or* **gurnet** ('gɜ:nɪt) *n, pl* -nard, -nards *or* -net, -nets any European marine scorpaenoid fish of the family *Triglidae,* such as *Trigla lucerna* (**tub** or **yellow gurnard**), having a heavily armoured head and finger-like pectoral fins [c14 from Old French *gornard* grunter, from *grognier* to grunt, from Latin *grunnīre*]

gurney ('gɜ:nɪ) *n US* a wheeled stretcher for transporting hospital patients [c20 of unknown origin]

gurrier ('gʌrɪər) *n Dublin dialect* a low-class tough ill-mannered person [perhaps from CURRIER]

guru ('gʊru:, 'gu:ru:) *n* **1** a Hindu or Sikh religious teacher or leader, giving personal spiritual guidance to his disciples **2** often derogatory a leader or chief theoretician of a movement, esp a spiritual or religious cult **3** often facetious a leading authority in a particular field: *a cricketing guru* [c17 from Hindi *gurū,* from Sanskrit *guruh* weighty] > 'guru,ship *n*

Guru Granth *or* **Guru Granth Sahib** (grʌnt) *n* the sacred scripture of the Sikhs, believed by them to be the embodiment of the gurus. Also called: **Adi Granth** [from Punjabi, from Sanskrit *grantha* a book]

gush (gʌʃ) *vb* **1** to pour out or cause to pour out suddenly and profusely, usually with a rushing sound **2** to act or utter in an overeffusive, affected, or sentimental manner ▷ *n* **3** a sudden copious flow or emission, esp of liquid **4** something that flows out or is emitted **5** an extravagant and insincere expression of admiration, sentiment, etc [c14 probably of imitative origin; compare Old Norse *gjósa,* Icelandic *gusa*] > 'gushing *adj* > 'gushingly *adv*

gusher ('gʌʃə) *n* **1** a person who gushes, as in being unusually effusive or sentimental **2** something, such as a spurting oil well, that gushes

gushy ('gʌʃɪ) *adj* gushier, gushiest *informal* displaying excessive admiration or sentimentality > 'gushily *adv* > 'gushiness *n*

gusset ('gʌsɪt) *n* **1** an inset piece of material used esp to strengthen or enlarge a garment **2** a triangular metal plate for strengthening a corner joint between two structural members **3** a piece of mail fitted between armour plates or into the leather or cloth underclothes worn with armour, to give added protection ▷ *vb* **4** (*tr*) to put a gusset in (a garment) [c15 from Old French *gousset* a piece of mail, a diminutive of *gousse* pod, of unknown origin] > 'gusseted *adj*

gussy up ('gʌsɪ) *vb* (*tr, adverb*) -sies, -sying, -sied *slang, chiefly US* to give (a person or thing) a smarter or more interesting appearance [c20 probably from the name *Gussie,* diminutive of *Augusta*]

gust (gʌst) *n* **1** a sudden blast of wind **2** a sudden rush of smoke, sound, etc **3** an outburst of emotion ▷ *vb* (*intr*) **4** to blow in gusts [c16 from Old Norse *gustr;* related to *gjósa* to GUSH; see GEYSER]

gustation (gʌ'steɪʃən) *n* the act of tasting or the faculty of taste [c16 from Latin *gustātiō,* from *gustāre* to taste] > **gustatory** ('gʌstətərɪ, -trɪ) *or* 'gustative *adj*

Gustavo A. Madero (*Spanish* gus'taβo a ma'ðero) *n* a city in central Mexico, northeast of Mexico City: became a pilgrimage centre after an Indian convert had a vision of the Virgin Mary here in

1531. Pop: 668 500 (2000 est). Former name (until 1931): Guadalupe Hidalgo

gusto ('gʌstəʊ) *n* vigorous enjoyment, zest, or relish, esp in the performance of an action: *the aria was sung with great gusto* [C17 from Spanish: taste, from Latin *gustus* a tasting; see GUSTATION]

gusty ('gʌstɪ) *adj* **gustier, gustiest 1** blowing or occurring in gusts or characterized by blustery weather: *a gusty wind* **2** given to sudden outbursts, as of emotion or temperament > **'gustily** *adv* > **'gustiness** *n*

gut (gʌt) *n* **1 a** the lower part of the alimentary canal; intestine **b** the entire alimentary canal. Related adj: **visceral 2** (*often plural*) the bowels or entrails, esp of an animal **3** *slang* the belly; paunch **4** See **catgut 5** a silky fibrous substance extracted from silkworms, used in the manufacture of fishing tackle **6** a narrow channel or passage **7** (*plural*) *informal* courage, willpower, or daring; forcefulness **8** (*plural*) *informal* the essential part: *the guts of a problem* **9** bust a gut *informal* to make an intense effort **10** have someone's guts for garters *informal* to be extremely angry with someone **11** hate a person's guts *informal* to dislike a person very strongly **12** sweat *or* work one's guts out *informal* to work very hard ▷ *vb* **guts, gutting, gutted** (*tr*) **13** to remove the entrails from (fish, etc) **14** (esp of fire) to destroy the inside of (a building) **15** to plunder; despoil **16** to take out the central points of (an article), esp in summary form ▷ *adj* **17** (*informal*) arising from or characterized by what is basic, essential, or natural: *a gut problem* [Old English *gutt;* related to *gēotan* to flow; see FUSION] > **'gut,like** *adj*

GUT (gʌt) *n acronym for* grand unified theory

gutbucket ('gʌt,bʌkɪt) *n* a highly emotional style of jazz playing [C20 from US *gutbucket* a cheap gambling saloon where musicians could play for hand-outs]

gut check *n US and Canadian informal* a pause to assess the state, progress, or condition of something such as an enterprise or institution

Gütersloh (German 'gy:tərslo:) *n* a town in NW Germany, in North Rhine-Westphalia. Pop: 95 928 (2003 est)

Guthrun ('gʊðruːn) *n* a variant of **Gudrun**

gutless ('gʌtlɪs) *adj informal* lacking courage or determination

gut reaction *n* a reaction to a situation derived from a person's instinct and experience

gutser ('gʌtsə) *n* come a gutser *Austral and NZ slang* **1** to fall heavily to the ground **2** to fail through error or misfortune [C20 from *guts* + -ER¹]

gutsy ('gʌtsɪ) *adj* **gutsier, gutsiest** *slang* **1** gluttonous; greedy **2** full of courage, determination, or boldness

gutta ('gʌtə) *n, pl* **-tae** (-ti:) **1** *architect* one of a set of small droplike ornaments, esp as used on the architrave of a Doric entablature **2** *med* (formerly used in writing prescriptions) a technical name for a **drop**. Abbreviation: **gt** [C16 from Latin: a drop]

gutta-percha ('gʌtə'pɜ:tʃə) *n* **1** any of several tropical trees of the sapotaceous genera *Palaquium* and *Payena,* esp *Palaquium gutta* **2** a whitish rubber substance derived from the coagulated milky latex of any of these trees: used in electrical insulation and dentistry [C19 from Malay *getah* gum + *percha* name of a tree that produces it]

guttate ('gʌteɪt) *or* **guttated** *adj biology* **1** (esp of plants) covered with small drops or droplike markings, esp oil glands **2** resembling a drop or drops [C19 from Latin *guttātus* dappled, from *gutta* a drop] > **gut'tation** *n*

gutted ('gʌtɪd) *adj informal* disappointed and upset

gutter ('gʌtə) *n* **1** a channel along the eaves or on the roof of a building, used to collect and carry away rainwater **2** a channel running along the kerb or the centre of a road to collect and carry away rainwater **3** a trench running beside a

canal lined with clay puddle **4** either of the two channels running parallel to a tenpin bowling lane **5** *printing* **a** the space between two pages in a forme **b** the white space between the facing pages of an open book **c** the space between two columns of type **6** the space left between stamps on a sheet in order to separate them **7** *surfing* a dangerous deep channel formed by currents and waves **8** *Austral* (in gold-mining) the channel of a former watercourse that is now a vein of gold **9** the gutter a poverty-stricken, degraded, or criminal environment ▷ *vb* **10** (*tr*) to make gutters in **11** (*intr*) to flow in a stream or rivulet **12** (*intr*) (of a candle) to melt away by the wax forming channels and running down in drops **13** (*intr*) (of a flame) to flicker and be about to go out [C13 from Anglo-French *goutiere,* from Old French *goute* a drop, from Latin *gutta*] > **'gutter-,like** *adj*

guttering ('gʌtərɪŋ) *n* **1** the gutters, downpipes, etc, that make up the rainwater disposal system on the outside of a building **2** the materials used in this system

gutter press *n* the section of the popular press that seeks sensationalism in its coverage

guttersnipe ('gʌtə,snaɪp) *n* **1** a child who spends most of his time in the streets, esp in a slum area **2** a person regarded as having the behaviour, morals, etc, of one brought up in squalor [C19 originally a name applied to the common snipe (the bird), then to a person who gathered refuse from gutters in city streets] > **'gutter,snipish** *adj*

guttural ('gʌtərəl) *adj* **1** *anatomy* of or relating to the throat **2** *phonetics* pronounced in the throat or the back of the mouth; velar or uvular **3** raucous ▷ *n* **4** *phonetics* a guttural consonant [C16 from New Latin *gutturālis* concerning the throat, from Latin *guttur* gullet] > **'gutturally** *adv* > **'gutturalness, ,guttur'ality** *or* **'gutturalism** *n*

gutturalize *or* **gutturalise** ('gʌtərə,laɪz) *vb* **1** (*tr*) *phonetics* to change into a guttural speech sound or pronounce with guttural articulation or pharyngeal constriction **2** to speak or utter in harsh raucous tones > **,gutturali'zation** *or* **,gutturali'sation** *n*

gutty ('gʌtɪ) *n, pl* **-ties** *Irish dialect* **1** an urchin or delinquent **2** a low-class person [probably from GUTTER, perhaps from the compound GUTTERSNIPE]

gut-wrenching *adj informal* causing great distress or suffering: *gut-wrenching scenes*

guv (gʌv) *or* **guv'nor** ('gʌvnə) *n Brit* an informal name for **governor**

guy¹ (gaɪ) *n* **1** *informal* a man or youth **2** *Brit* a crude effigy of Guy Fawkes, usually made of old clothes stuffed with straw or rags, that is burnt on top of a bonfire on Guy Fawkes Day **3** *Brit* a person in shabby or ludicrously odd clothes **4** (*plural*) *informal* persons of either sex ▷ *vb* **5** (*tr*) to make fun of; ridicule [C19 short for *Guy* Fawkes (1570–1606), English conspirator in the Gunpowder Plot]

guy² (gaɪ) *n* **1** a rope, chain, wire, etc, for anchoring an object, such as a radio mast, in position or for steadying or guiding it while being hoisted or lowered ▷ *vb* **2** (*tr*) to anchor, steady, or guide with a guy or guys [C14 probably from Low German; compare Dutch *gei* brail, *geiblok* pulley, Old French *guie* guide, from *guier* to GUIDE]

GUY *international car registration for* Guyana

Guyana (gaɪ'ænə) *n* a republic in NE South America, on the Atlantic: colonized chiefly by the Dutch in the 17th and 18th centuries; became a British colony in 1831 and an independent republic within the Commonwealth in 1966. Official language: English. Religions: Christian and Hindu. Currency: dollar. Capital: Georgetown. Pop: 767 000 (2004 est). Area: about 215 000 sq km (83 000 sq miles). Former name (until 1966): British Guiana

Guyanese (,gaɪə'niːz) *or* **Guyanan** (gaɪ'ænən) *adj* **1** of or relating to Guyana or its inhabitants ▷ *adj* **2** a native or inhabitant of Guyana

Guyenne (French gɥijɛn) *n* a variant spelling of Guienne

Guy Fawkes Day *n* the anniversary of the discovery of the Gunpowder Plot, celebrated on Nov 5 in Britain with fireworks and bonfires

guyot ('giːəʊ) *n* a flat-topped submarine mountain, common in the Pacific Ocean, usually an extinct volcano whose summit did not reach above the sea surface. Compare **seamount** [C20 named after A. H. *Guyot* (1807–84), Swiss geographer and geologist]

guzzle ('gʌzəl) *vb* to consume (food or drink) excessively or greedily [C16 of unknown origin]

guzzler ('gʌzlə) *n* **a** a person or thing that guzzles **b** (*in combination*) a gas-guzzler

gv *abbreviation for* gravimetric volume

gw *the internet domain name for* Guinea-Bissau

Gwalior ('gwɑːlɪɔː) *n* **1** a city in N central India, in Madhya Pradesh: built around the fort, which dates from before 525; industrial and commercial centre. Pop: 826 919 (2001) **2** a former princely state of central India, established in the 18th century: merged with Madhya Bharat in 1948, which in turn merged with Madhya Pradesh in 1956

Gwent (gwɛnt) *n* a former county of SE Wales: formed in 1974 from most of Monmouthshire and part of Breconshire; replaced in 1996 by Monmouthshire and the county boroughs of Newport, Torfaen, Blaenau Gwent, and part of Caerphilly

Gweru ('gweɪruː) *n* a city in central Zimbabwe. Pop: 140 000 (2005 est). Former name (until 1982): Gwelo ('gwiːləʊ)

Gwich'in ('gwɪtʃɪn) *n* **1** a member of a North American Indian people from northwest Canada and northeast Alaska **2** the languge of these people

Gwynedd ('gwɪnɛð) *n* a county of NW Wales, formed in 1974 from Anglesey, Caernarvonshire, part of Denbighshire, and most of Merionethshire; lost Anglesey and part of the NE in 1996: generally mountainous with many lakes, much of it lying in Snowdonia National Park. Administrative centre: Caernarfon. Pop: 117 500 (2003 est). Area: 2550 sq km (869 sq miles)

gwyniad ('gwɪnɪˌæd) *n* a freshwater white fish, *Coregonus pennantii,* occurring in Lake Bala in Wales: related to the powan [C17 Welsh, from *gwyn* white, related to Scottish Gaelic *fionn;* see FINNOCK]

gy *the internet domain name for* Guyana

Gyani ('gjɑːnɪ) *n* (in India) a title placed before the name of a Punjabi scholar [Hindi, from Sanskrit *gyan* knowledge]

gybe *or* **jibe** (dʒaɪb) *nautical* ▷ *vb* **1** (*intr*) (of a fore-and-aft sail) to shift suddenly from one side of the vessel to the other when running before the wind, as the result of allowing the wind to catch the leech **2** to cause (a sailing vessel) to gybe or (of a sailing vessel) to undergo gybing ▷ *n* **3** an instance of gybing [C17 from obsolete Dutch *gijben* (now *gijpen*), of obscure origin]

gym (dʒɪm) *n, adj* short for **gymnasium, gymnastics, gymnastic**

gym bunny *n informal* a person who spends a lot of time exercising at a gymnasium

gymkhana (dʒɪm'kɑːnə) *n* **1** *chiefly Brit* an event in which horses and riders display skill and aptitude in various races and contests **2** (esp in Anglo-India) a place providing sporting and athletic facilities [C19 from Hindi *gend-khānā,* literally: ball house, from *khāna* house; influenced by GYMNASIUM]

gymnasiarch (dʒɪm'neɪzɪˌɑːk) *n* **1** (in ancient Greece) an official who supervised athletic schools and contests **2** *obsolete* the governor or chief tutor of an academy or college [C17 from Latin, from Greek *gymnasiarchos,* from *gymnasion* gymnasium + *-archos* ruling]

gymnasiast (dʒɪm'neɪzɪˌæst) *n* a student in a gymnasium

gymnasium (dʒɪm'neɪzɪəm) *n, pl* **-siums** *or* **-sia**

(-zɪə) **1** a large room or hall equipped with bars, weights, ropes, etc, for games or physical training **2** (in various European countries) a secondary school that prepares pupils for university [c16 from Latin: school for gymnastics, from Greek *gumnasion,* from *gumnazein* to exercise naked, from *gumnos* naked]

gymnast ('dʒɪmnæst) *n* a person who is skilled or trained in gymnastics

gymnastic (dʒɪm'næstɪk) *adj* of, relating to, like, or involving gymnastics > gym'nastically *adv*

gymnastics (dʒɪm'næstɪks) *n* **1** (*functioning as singular*) practice or training in exercises that develop physical strength and agility or mental capacity **2** (*functioning as plural*) gymnastic exercises

gymno- *combining form* naked, bare, or exposed: *gymnosperm* [from Greek *gumnos* naked]

gymnosophist (dʒɪm'nɒsəfɪst) *n* one of a sect of naked Indian ascetics who regarded food or clothing as detrimental to purity of thought [c16 from Latin *gymnosophistae,* from Greek *gumnosophistai* naked philosophers] > gym'nosophy *n*

gymnosperm ('dʒɪmnəʊˌspɜːm, 'gɪm-) *n* any seed-bearing plant in which the ovules are borne naked on the surface of the megasporophylls, which are often arranged in cones. Gymnosperms, which include conifers and cycads, are traditionally classified in the division *Gymnospermae* but in modern classifications are split into separate phyla. Compare **angiosperm** > ˌgymno'spermous *adj*

gympie ('gɪmpɪ) *n Austral* **1** a tall tree with stinging hairs on its leaves **2** a hammer [c19 from a native Australian language]

gym shoe *n* another name for **plimsoll**

gymslip ('dʒɪmˌslɪp) *n* a tunic or pinafore dress worn by schoolgirls, often part of a school uniform

gyn. *abbreviation for* **1** gynaecological **2** gynaecology

gyn- *combining form* variant of **gyno-** before a vowel

gynae ('gaɪnɪ) *adj informal* gynaecological

gynaeceum (ˌdʒaɪnɪ'siːəm) *n, pl* -cea (-'siːə) **1** (in ancient Greece and Rome) the inner section of a house, used as women's quarters **2** (dʒaɪ'niːsɪəm, gaɪ-) a variant spelling of **gynoecium** [c17 from Latin: women's apartments, from Greek *gunaikeion,* from *gunē* a woman]

gynaeco- *or US* **gyneco-** *combining form* relating to women; female: *gynaecology* [from Greek, from *gunē, gunaik-* woman, female]

gynaecocracy *or US* **gynecocracy** (ˌdʒaɪnɪ'kɒkrəsɪ, ˌgaɪ-) *n, pl* -cies government by women or by a single woman. Also called: *gynarchy* > gynaecocratic *or US* gynecocratic (dʒaɪˌniːkə'krætɪk, gaɪ-) *adj*

gynaecoid *or US* **gynecoid** ('dʒaɪnɪˌkɔɪd, 'gaɪ-) *adj* resembling, relating to, or like a woman

gynaecology *or US* **gynecology** (ˌgaɪnɪ'kɒlədʒɪ) *n* the branch of medicine concerned with diseases in women, esp those of the genitourinary tract > gynaecological (ˌgaɪnɪkə'lɒdʒɪkᵊl), gynaeco'logic, *US* ˌgyneco'logical, ˌgyneco'logic *adj* > ˌgynae'cologist *or US* ˌgyne'cologist *n*

gynaecomastia *or US* **gynecomastia** (ˌgaɪnɪkəʊ'mæstɪə) *n* abnormal overdevelopment of the breasts in a man [c19 from GYNAECO- + Greek *mastos* breast]

gynandromorph (dʒɪ'nændrəʊˌmɔːf, gaɪ-, dʒaɪ-) *n* an organism, esp an insect, that has both male and female physical characteristics. Compare **hermaphrodite** (sense 1) > gyˌnandro'morphic *or* gyˌnandro'morphous *adj* > gyˌnandro'morphism *or* gy'nandromorphy *n*

gynandrous (dʒaɪ'nændrəs, dʒɪ-, gaɪ-) *adj* **1** (of flowers such as the orchid) having the stamens and styles united in a column **2** hermaphroditic [c19 from Greek *gunandros* of uncertain sex, from

gunē woman + *anēr* man] > gy'nandry *or* gy'nandrism *n*

gynarchy ('dʒaɪˌnɑːkɪ, 'gaɪ-) *n, pl* -chies another word for **gynaecocracy**

gynecium (dʒaɪ'niːsɪəm, gaɪ-) *n, pl* -cia (-sɪə) a variant spelling (esp US) of **gynoecium**

gyneco- *combining form* a variant (esp US) of **gynaeco-**

gyniatrics (ˌdʒaɪnɪ'ætrɪks, ˌgaɪ-) *or* **gyniatry** (dʒaɪ'naɪətrɪ, gaɪ-) *n med* less common words for **gynaecology**

gyno- *or before a vowel* **gyn-** *combining form* **1** relating to women; female: *gynarchy* **2** denoting a female reproductive organ: *gynophore* [from Greek, from *gunē* woman]

gynodioecious (ˌgaɪnəʊdaɪ'iːʃəs) *adj* (of a plant species) having some individuals bearing female flowers only and others bearing hermaphrodite flowers only

gynoecium, gynaeceum, gynaecium *or esp US* **gynecium** (dʒaɪ'niːsɪəm, gaɪ-) *n, pl* -cia *or* -cea (-sɪə) the carpels of a flowering plant collectively [c18 New Latin, from Greek *gunaikeion* women's quarters, from *gunaik-, gunē* woman + -*eion,* suffix indicating place]

gynomonoecious (ˌgaɪnəʊmɒ'niːʃəs) *adj* (of a plant species) having each individual bearing both female and hermaphrodite flowers

gynophore ('dʒaɪnəʊˌfɔː, 'gaɪ-) *n* a stalk in some plants that bears the gynoecium above the level of the other flower parts > gynophoric (ˌdʒaɪnəʊ'fɒrɪk, ˌgaɪ-) *adj*

-gynous *adj combining form* **1** of or relating to women or females: *androgynous; misogynous* **2** relating to female organs: *epigynous* [from New Latin -*gynus,* from Greek -*gunos,* from *gunē* woman] > -gyny *n combining form*

Győr (Hungarian djøːr) *n* an industrial town in NW Hungary: medieval Benedictine abbey. Pop: 128 913 (2003 est)

gyoza (giː'əʊzə) *n* a Japanese fried dumpling [Japanese]

gyp¹ *or* **gip** (dʒɪp) *slang* ▷ *vb* gyps, gypping, gypped *or* gips, gipping, gipped **1** (*tr*) to swindle, cheat, or defraud ▷ *n* **2** an act of cheating **3** a person who gyps [c18 back formation from GYPSY]

gyp² (dʒɪp) *n Brit and NZ slang* severe pain; torture [c19 probably a contraction of *gee up!;* see GEE¹]

gyp³ (dʒɪp) *n* a college servant at the universities of Cambridge and Durham. Compare **scout¹** (sense 5) [c18 perhaps from GYPSY, or from obsolete *gippo* a scullion]

gyppo ('dʒɪpəʊ) *n, pl* -pos *slang* a derogatory term for **Gypsy**

Gyprock ('dʒɪprɒk) *n trademark Austral* the brand name of a type of plasterboard [from GYPSUM + ROCK]

gypsophila (dʒɪp'sɒfɪlə) *n* any caryophyllaceous plant of the mainly Eurasian genus *Gypsophila,* such as baby's-breath, having small white or pink flowers [c18 New Latin, from Greek *gupsos* chalk + *philos* loving]

gypsum ('dʒɪpsəm) *n* a colourless or white mineral sometimes tinted by impurities, found in beds as an evaporite. It is used in the manufacture of plaster of Paris, cement, paint, school chalk, glass, and fertilizer. Composition: hydrated calcium sulphate. Formula: $CaSO_4.2H_2O$. Crystal structure: monoclinic [c17 from Latin, from Greek *gupsos* chalk, plaster, cement, of Semitic origin] > gypseous ('dʒɪpsɪəs) *adj* > gypsiferous (dʒɪp'sɪfərəs) *adj*

Gypsy *or* **Gipsy** ('dʒɪpsɪ) *n, pl* -sies (*sometimes not capital*) **1 a** a member of a people scattered throughout Europe and North America, who maintain a nomadic way of life in industrialized societies. They migrated from NW India from about the 9th century onwards **b** (*as modifier*): *a Gypsy fortune-teller* **2** the language of the Gypsies; Romany **3** a person who looks or behaves like a

Gypsy [c16 from EGYPTIAN, since they were thought to have come originally from Egypt] > 'Gypsydom *or* 'Gipsydom *n* > 'Gypsyˌhood *or* 'Gipsyˌhood *n* > 'Gypsyish *or* 'Gipsyish *adj* > 'Gypsy-ˌlike *or* 'Gipsy-ˌlike *adj*

gypsy moth *n* a variant spelling of **gipsy moth**

gyral ('dʒaɪrəl) *adj* **1** having a circular, spiral, or rotating motion; gyratory **2** *anatomy* of or relating to a convolution (gyrus) of the brain > 'gyrally *adv*

gyrate *vb* (dʒɪ'reɪt, dʒaɪ-) **1** (*intr*) to rotate or spiral, esp about a fixed point or axis ▷ *adj* ('dʒaɪrɪt, -reɪt) **2** *biology* curved or coiled into a circle; circinate [c19 from Late Latin *gӯrāre,* from Latin *gӯrus* circle, from Greek *guros*] > gyratory ('dʒaɪrətərɪ, -trɪ, dʒaɪ'reɪtərɪ) *adj*

gyration (dʒaɪ'reɪʃən) *n* **1** the act or process of gyrating; rotation **2** any one of the whorls of a spiral-shaped shell

gyrator (dʒaɪ'reɪtə) *n* an electronic circuit that inverts the impedance

gyre (dʒaɪə) *chiefly literary* ▷ *n* **1** a circular or spiral movement or path **2** a ring, circle, or spiral ▷ *vb* **3** (*intr*) to whirl [c16 from Latin *gӯrus* circle, from Greek *guros*]

gyrfalcon *or* **gerfalcon** ('dʒɜːˌfɔːlkən, -ˌfɔːkən) *n* a very large rare falcon, *Falco rusticolus,* of northern and arctic regions: often used for hunting [c14 from Old French *gerfaucon,* perhaps from Old Norse *geirfalki,* from *geirr* spear + *falki* falcon]

gyro ('dʒaɪrəʊ) *n, pl* -ros **1** See **gyrocompass 2** See **gyroscope**

gyro- *or before a vowel* **gyr-** *combining form* **1** indicating rotating or gyrating motion: *gyroscope* **2** indicating a spiral **3** indicating a gyroscope: *gyrocompass* [via Latin from Greek *guro-,* from *guros* circle]

gyrocompass ('dʒaɪrəʊˌkʌmpəs) *n navigation* a nonmagnetic compass that uses a motor-driven gyroscope to indicate true north. Sometimes shortened to: gyro

gyrodyne ('dʒaɪrəʊˌdaɪn) *n* an aircraft that uses a powered rotor to take off and manoeuvre, but uses autorotation when cruising

gyro horizon *n* another name for **artificial horizon** (sense 1)

gyromagnetic (ˌdʒaɪrəʊmæg'nɛtɪk) *adj* of or caused by magnetic properties resulting from the spin of a charged particle, such as an electron

gyromagnetic ratio *n physics* the ratio of the magnetic moment of a rotating charged particle, such as an electron, to its angular momentum

gyron ('dʒaɪrɒn) *n* a variant spelling of **giron**

gyronny (dʒaɪ'rɒnɪ) *adj* a variant spelling of **gironny**

gyroplane ('dʒaɪrəˌpleɪn) *n* another name for **autogiro**

gyroscope ('dʒaɪrəˌskəʊp) *or* **gyrostat** *n* a device containing a disc rotating on an axis that can turn freely in any direction so that the disc resists the action of an applied couple and tends to maintain the same orientation in space irrespective of the movement of the surrounding structure. Sometimes shortened to: gyro > gyroscopic (ˌdʒaɪrə'skɒpɪk) *adj* > ˌgyro'scopically *adv* > ˌgyro'scopics *n*

gyrose ('dʒaɪrəʊz) *adj botany* marked with sinuous lines

gyrostabilizer *or* **gyrostabiliser** (ˌdʒaɪrəʊ'steɪbɪˌlaɪzə) *n* a gyroscopic device used to stabilize the rolling motion of a ship

gyrostatic (ˌdʒaɪrəʊ'stætɪk) *adj* of or concerned with the gyroscope or with gyrostatics > ˌgyro'statically *adv*

gyrostatics (ˌdʒaɪrəʊ'stætɪks) *n* (*functioning as singular*) the science of rotating bodies

gyrus ('dʒaɪrəs) *n, pl* gyri ('dʒaɪraɪ) another name for **convolution** (sense 3) [c19 from Latin; see GYRE]

gyve (dʒaɪv) *archaic* ▷ *vb* **1** (*tr*) to shackle or fetter ▷ *n* **2** (*usually plural*) fetters [c13 of unknown origin]

H h

h *or* **H** (eɪtʃ) *n, pl* **h's, H's** *or* **Hs 1** the eighth letter and sixth consonant of the modern English alphabet **2** a speech sound represented by this letter, in English usually a voiceless glottal fricative, as in *hat* **3 a** something shaped like an H **b** (*in combination*): *an H-beam*

h *symbol for* **1** *physics* Planck constant **2** hecto- **3** *chess* See **algebraic notation**

H *symbol for* **1** *chem* hydrogen **2** *physics* **a** magnetic field strength **b** Hamiltonian **3** *electronics* henry or henries **4** *thermodynamics* enthalpy **5** (on Brit pencils, signifying degree of hardness of lead) hard: *H; 2H; 3H*. Compare **B** (sense 9) **6** *slang* heroin **7** ▷ *international car registration for* Hungary

h. *or* **H.** *abbreviation for* **1** harbour **2** height **3** hour **4** husband

H8 *text messaging abbreviation for* hate

ha¹ *or* **hah** (hɑː) *interj* **1** an exclamation expressing derision, triumph, surprise, etc, according to the intonation of the speaker **2** (*reiterated*) a representation of the sound of laughter

ha² *symbol for* hectare

Ha *abbreviation for* Hawaii

h.a. *abbreviation for* hoc anno [Latin: in this year]

HAA *abbreviation for* hepatitis-associated antigen; an antigen that occurs in the blood serum of some people, esp those with serum hepatitis

haaf (hɑːf) *n* a deep-sea fishing ground off the Shetland and Orkney Islands [Old English *hæf* sea; related to Old Norse *haf*; see HEAVE]

haar (hɑː) *n Eastern Brit* a cold sea mist or fog off the North Sea [c17 related to Dutch dialect *harig* damp]

Haarlem (*Dutch* ˈhaːrlɛm) *n* a city in the W Netherlands, capital of North Holland province. Pop: 147 000 (2003 est)

Hab. *Bible abbreviation for* Habakkuk

Habakkuk (ˈhæbəkək) *n Old Testament* **1** a Hebrew prophet **2** the book containing his oracles and canticle. Douay spelling: Habacuc

Habana (aˈβana) *n* the Spanish name for **Havana**

habanera (ˌhæbəˈnɛərə) *n* **1** a slow Cuban dance in duple time **2** a piece of music composed for or in the rhythm of this dance [from Spanish *danza habanera* dance from Havana]

Habanero (*Spanish* aβaˈnero) *n, pl* -ros (-ros) a native or inhabitant of Havana

habeas corpus (ˈheɪbɪəs ˈkɔːpəs) *n law* a writ ordering a person to be brought before a court or judge, esp so that the court may ascertain whether his detention is lawful [c15 from the opening of the Latin writ, literally: you may have the body]

haberdasher (ˈhæbəˌdæʃə) *n* **1** *Brit* a dealer in small articles for sewing, such as buttons, zips, and ribbons **2** *US* a men's outfitter [c14 from Anglo-French *hapertas* small items of merchandise, of obscure origin]

haberdashery (ˈhæbəˌdæʃərɪ) *n, pl* -eries the goods or business kept by a haberdasher

habergeon (ˈhæbədʒən) *or* **haubergeon** *n* a light sleeveless coat of mail worn in the 14th century under the plated hauberk [c14 from Old French *haubergeon* a little HAUBERK]

Haber process (ˈhɑːbə) *n* an industrial process for producing ammonia by reacting atmospheric nitrogen with hydrogen at about 200 atmospheres (2×10^7 pascals) and 500°C in the presence of a catalyst, usually iron [named after Fritz *Haber* (1868–1934), German chemist]

habile (ˈhæbiːl) *adj* **1** *rare* skilful **2** *obsolete* fit [c14 from Latin *habilis*, from *habēre* to have; see ABLE]

habiliment (həˈbɪlɪmənt) *n* (*often plural*) dress or attire [c15 from Old French *habillement*, from *habiller* to dress, from *bille* log; see BILLET²]

habilitate (həˈbɪlɪˌteɪt) *vb* **1** (*tr*) *US, chiefly Western* to equip and finance (a mine) **2** (*intr*) to qualify for office **3** (*tr*) *archaic* to clothe [c17 from Medieval Latin *habilitāre* to make fit, from Latin *habilitās* aptness, readiness; see ABILITY] ▷ haˌbiliˈtation *n* ▷ haˈbiliˌtator *n*

habit (ˈhæbɪt) *n* **1** a tendency or disposition to act in a particular way **2** established custom, usual practice, etc **3** *psychol* a learned behavioural response that has become associated with a particular situation, esp one frequently repeated **4** mental disposition or attitude: *a good working habit of mind* **5 a** a practice or substance to which a person is addicted: *drink has become a habit with him* **b** the state of being dependent on something, esp a drug **6** *botany, zoology* the method of growth, type of existence, behaviour, or general appearance of a plant or animal: *a climbing habit; a burrowing habit* **7** the customary apparel of a particular occupation, rank, etc, now esp the costume of a nun or monk **8** Also called: **riding habit** a woman's riding dress **9** *crystallog* short for **crystal habit** ▷ *vb* (*tr*) **10** to clothe **11** an archaic word for **inhabit** *or* **habituate** [c13 from Latin *habitus* custom, from *habēre* to have]

habitable (ˈhæbɪtəbˀl) *adj* able to be lived in ▷ ˌhabitaˈbility *or* ˈhabitableness *n* ▷ ˈhabitably *adv*

habitant (ˈhæbɪtˀnt) *n* **1** a less common word for **inhabitant 2** (ˈhæbɪtˀnt; *French* abitɑ̃) **a** an early French settler in Canada or Louisiana, esp a small farmer **b** a descendant of these settlers, esp a farmer

habitat (ˈhæbɪˌtæt) *n* **1** the environment in which an animal or plant normally lives or grows **2** the place in which a person, group, class, etc, is normally found [c18 from Latin: it inhabits, from *habitāre* to dwell, from *habēre* to have]

habitation (ˌhæbɪˈteɪʃən) *n* **1** a dwelling place **2** occupation of a dwelling place ▷ ˌhabiˈtational *adj*

habited (ˈhæbɪtɪd) *adj* **1** dressed in a habit **2** clothed

habit-forming *adj* (of an activity, indulgence, etc) tending to become a habit or addiction

habitual (həˈbɪtjʊəl) *adj* **1** (*usually prenominal*) done or experienced regularly and repeatedly: *the habitual Sunday walk* **2** (*usually prenominal*) by habit: *a*

habitual drinker 3 customary; usual: *his habitual comment* ▷ haˈbitually *adv* ▷ haˈbitualness *n*

habituate (həˈbɪtjʊˌeɪt) *vb* **1** to accustom; make used (to) **2** *US and Canadian archaic* to frequent

habituation (həˌbɪtjʊˈeɪʃən) *n* **1** the act or process of habituating **2** *psychol* the temporary waning of an innate response that occurs when it is elicited many times in succession. Compare **extinction** (sense 6)

habitude (ˈhæbɪˌtjuːd) *n rare* habit or tendency ▷ ˌhabiˈtudinal *adj*

habitué (həˈbɪtjʊˌeɪ) *n* a frequent visitor to a place [c19 from French, from *habituer* to frequent]

habitus (ˈhæbɪtəs) *n, pl* -tus **1** *med* general physical state, esp with regard to susceptibility to disease **2** tendency or inclination, esp of plant or animal growth; habit [c19 from Latin: state, HABIT]

habu (ˈhɑːbuː) *n* a large venomous snake, *Trimeresurus flavoviridis*, of Okinawa and other Ryukyu Islands: family *Crotalidae* (pit vipers) [from the native name originally used in the Ryukyu Islands]

HAC *abbreviation for* Honourable Artillery Company

háček (ˈhɑːtʃɛk) *n* a diacritic mark (ˇ) placed over certain letters in order to modify their sounds, esp used in Slavonic languages to indicate various forms of palatal articulation, as in the affricate *č* and the fricative trill *ř* used in Czech [from Czech]

hachure (hæˈfjʊə) *n* **1** another word for **hatching** (**see hatch³**) **2** shading of short lines drawn on a relief map to indicate gradients ▷ *vb* **3** (*tr*) to mark or show by hachures [c19 from French, from *hacher* to chop up, HATCH³]

hacienda (ˌhæsɪˈɛndə) *n* (in Spain or Spanish-speaking countries) **1 a** a ranch or large estate **b** any substantial stock-raising, mining, or manufacturing establishment in the country **2** the main house on such a ranch or plantation [c18 from Spanish, from Latin *facienda* things to be done, from *facere* to do]

hack¹ (hæk) *vb* **1** (when *intr*, usually foll by *at* or *away*) to cut or chop (at) irregularly, roughly, or violently **2** to cut and clear (a way, path, etc), as through undergrowth **3** (in sport, esp rugby) to foul (an opposing player) by kicking or striking his shins **4** *basketball* to commit the foul of striking (an opposing player) on the arm **5** (*intr*) to cough in short dry spasmodic bursts **6** (*tr*) to reduce or cut (a story, article, etc) in a damaging way **7** to manipulate a computer program skilfully, esp, to gain unauthorized access to another computer system **8** (*tr*) *slang* to tolerate; cope with: *I joined the army but I couldn't hack it* **9** hack to bits to damage severely: *his reputation was hacked to bits* ▷ *n* **10** a cut, chop, notch, or gash, esp as made by a knife or axe **11** any tool used for shallow digging, such as a mattock or pick **12** a chopping blow **13** a dry spasmodic cough **14** a kick on the shins, as in rugby **15** a wound from a sharp kick ▷ See also **hack off** [Old English *haccian;* related to Old Frisian *hackia,* Middle High German *hacken*]

hack² ('hæk) *n* **1** a horse kept for riding or (more rarely) for driving **2** an old, ill-bred, or overworked horse **3** a horse kept for hire **4** *Brit* a country ride on horseback **5** a drudge **6** a person who produces mediocre literary or journalistic work **7** Also called: **hackney** *US* a coach or carriage that is for hire **8** Also called: **hackie** *US informal* **a** a cab driver **b** a taxi ▷ *vb* **9** *Brit* to ride (a horse) cross-country for pleasure **10** (*tr*) to let (a horse) out for hire **11** (*tr*) *informal* to write (an article) as or in the manner of a hack **12** (*intr*) *US informal* to drive a taxi ▷ *adj* **13** (*prenominal*) banal, mediocre, or unoriginal: *hack writing* [c17 short for HACKNEY]

hack³ (hæk) *n* **1** a rack used for fodder for livestock **2** a board on which meat is placed for a hawk **3** a pile or row of unfired bricks stacked to dry ▷ *vb* (*tr*) **4** to place (fodder) in a hack **5** to place (bricks) in a hack [c16 variant of HATCH²]

hackamore ('hækə,mɔː) *n US and NZ* a rope or rawhide halter used for unbroken foals [c19 by folk etymology from Spanish *jáquima* headstall, from Old Spanish *xaquima,* from Arabic *shaqīmah*]

hackberry ('hæk,bɛrɪ) *n, pl* **-ries 1** any American tree or shrub of the ulmaceous genus *Celtis,* having edible cherry-like fruits **2** the fruit or soft yellowish wood of such a tree [c18 variant of C16 *hagberry,* of Scandinavian origin; compare Old Norse *heggr* hackberry]

hackbut ('hækbʌt) *or* **hagbut** *n* another word for **arquebus.** > ,hackbut'eer, 'hackbutter, ,hagbut'eer *or* 'hagbutter *n*

hacker ('hækə) *n* **1** a person that hacks **2** *slang* a computer fanatic, esp one who through a personal computer breaks into the computer system of a company, government, etc

hackery ('hækərɪ) *n* **1** *ironic* journalism; hackwork

hackette (,hæ'kɛt) *n informal, derogatory* a female journalist [c20 from HACK² (sense 6) + -ETTE]

hack hammer *n* an adzelike tool, used for dressing stone

hacking ('hækɪŋ) *adj* (of a cough) harsh, dry, and spasmodic

hacking jacket *or* **coat** *n chiefly Brit* a riding jacket with side or back vents and slanting pockets

hackle ('hækəl) *n* **1** any of the long slender feathers on the necks of poultry and other birds **2** *angling* **a** parts of an artificial fly made from hackle feathers, representing the legs and sometimes the wings of a real fly **b** short for **hackle fly 3** a feathered ornament worn in the headdress of some British regiments **4** a steel flax comb ▷ *vb* (*tr*) **5** to comb (flax) using a hackle ▷ See also **hackles** [c15 *hakell,* probably from Old English; variant of HECKLE; see HATCHEL] > 'hackler *n*

hackle fly *n angling* an artificial fly in which the legs and wings are represented by hackle feathers

hackles ('hækəlz) *pl n* **1** the hairs on the back of the neck and the back of a dog, cat, etc, which rise when the animal is angry or afraid **2** anger or resentment (esp in the phrases **get one's hackles up, make one's hackles rise**)

hackney ('hæknɪ) *n* **1** a compact breed of harness horse with a high-stepping trot **2 a** a coach or carriage that is for hire **b** (*as modifier*): *a hackney carriage* **3** a popular term for **hack²** (sense 1) ▷ *vb* **4** (*tr; usually passive*) to make commonplace and banal by too frequent use [c14 probably after HACKNEY, where horses were formerly raised; sense 4 meaning derives from the allusion to a weakened hired horse] > 'hackneyism *n*

Hackney ('hæknɪ) *n* a borough of NE Greater London: formed in 1965 from the former boroughs of Shoreditch, Stoke Newington, and Hackney; nearby are **Hackney Marshes,** the largest recreation ground in London. Pop: 208 400 (2003 est). Area: 19 sq km (8 sq miles)

hackneyed ('hæknɪd) *adj* (of phrases, fashions, etc) used so often as to be trite, dull, and stereotyped

hack off *vb* (*adv*) *informal* (*tr; often passive*) to annoy, irritate, or disappoint

hacksaw ('hæk,sɔː) *n* **1** a handsaw for cutting metal, with a hard-steel blade in a frame under tension ▷ *vb* **-saws, -sawing, -sawed,** *or* **-sawn** (-,sɔːn) **2** (*tr*) to cut with a hacksaw

hackwork ('hæk,wɜːk) *n* undistinguished literary work produced to order

had (hæd) *vb* the past tense and past participle of **have**

hadal ('heɪdəl) *adj* of, relating to, or constituting the zones of the oceans deeper than **abyssal:** below about 6000 metres (18 000 ft) [c20 from French, from *Hadés* HADES]

hadaway (,hædə'weɪ) *sentence substitute Northeastern English dialect* an exclamation urging the hearer to refrain from delay in the execution of a task [perhaps from HOLD¹ + AWAY]

haddock ('hædək) *n, pl* **-docks** *or* **-dock** a North Atlantic gadoid food fish, *Melanogrammus aeglefinus:* similar to but smaller than the cod [c14 of uncertain origin]

hade (heɪd) *geology* ▷ *n* **1** the angle made to the vertical by the plane of a fault or vein ▷ *obsolete vb* **2** (*intr*) (of faults or veins) to incline from the vertical [c18 of unknown origin]

hadedah ('hɑːdɪ,dɑː) *n South African* a large greyish-green ibis, *Hagedeshia hagedash,* having a greenish metallic sheen on the wing coverts and shoulders [probably imitative of the bird's call]

Hades ('heɪdiːz) *n* **1** *Greek myth* **a** the underworld abode of the souls of the dead **b** Pluto, the god of the underworld, brother of Zeus and husband of Persephone **2** *New Testament* the abode or state of the dead **3** (*often not capital*) *informal* hell > **Hadean** (heɪ'diːən, 'heɪdɪən) *adj*

Hadhramaut *or* **Hadramaut** (,hɑːdrə'mɔːt) *n* a plateau region of the S Arabian Peninsula, in SE Yemen on the Indian Ocean; formerly in South Yemen: corresponds roughly to the former East Aden Protectorate. Area: about 151 500 sq km (58 500 sq miles)

Hadith ('hædɪθ, hɑː'diːθ) *n* the body of tradition and legend about Mohammed and his followers, used as a basis of Islamic law [Arabic]

hadj (hædʒ) *n, pl* **hadjes** a variant spelling of **hajj**

hadji ('hædʒɪ) *n, pl* **hadjis** a variant spelling of **hajji**

hadn't ('hædənt) *vb contraction of* had not

Hadrian's Wall *n* a fortified Roman wall, of which substantial parts remain, extending across N England from the Solway Firth in the west to the mouth of the River Tyne in the east. It was built in 120–123 AD on the orders of the emperor Hadrian as a defence against the N British tribes

hadron ('hædrɒn) *n* any elementary particle capable of taking part in a strong nuclear interaction and therefore excluding leptons and photons [c20 from Greek *hadros* heavy, from *hadēn* enough + -ON] > had'ronic *adj*

hadrosaur ('hædrə,sɔː) *or* **hadrosaurus** (,hædrə'sɔːrəs) *n* any one of a large group of bipedal Upper Cretaceous dinosaurs of the genus *Anatosaurus, Maiasaura, Edmontosaurus,* and related genera: partly aquatic, with a duck-billed skull and webbed feet. Also called: **duck-billed dinosaur** [c19 from Greek *hadros* thick, fat + -SAUR]

hadst (hædst) *vb archaic or dialect* (used with the pronoun *thou*) a singular form of the past tense (indicative mood) of **have**

hae (heɪ, hæ) *vb* a *Scot* variant of **have**

haecceity (hɛk'siːɪtɪ, hiːk-) *n, pl* **-ties** *philosophy* the property that uniquely identifies an object. Compare **quiddity** [c17 from Medieval Latin *haecceitas,* literally: thisness, from *haec,* feminine of *hic* his]

haem *or US* **heme** (hiːm) *n biochem* a complex red organic pigment containing ferrous iron, present in haemoglobin [c20 shortened from HAEMATIN]

haem- *combining form* a variant of **haemo-** before a vowel. Also (*US*): **hem-**

haema- *combining form* a variant of **haemo-** Also (*US*): **hema-**

haemachrome *or US* **hemachrome** ('hiːmə,krəʊm, 'hɛm-) *n* variants of **haemochrome**

haemacytometer *or US* **hemacytometer** (,hiːməsaɪ'tɒmɪtə) *n med* variants of **haemocytometer**

haemagglutinate *or US* **hemagglutinate** (,hiːmə'gluːtɪ,neɪt, ,hɛm-) *vb* (*tr*) to cause the clumping of red blood cells (in a blood sample)

haemagglutinin *or US* **hemagglutinin** (,hiːmə'gluːtɪnɪn, ,hɛm-) *n* an antibody that causes the clumping of red blood cells

haemagogue *or US* **hemagogue, hemagog** ('hiːmə,gɒg) *adj* **1** promoting the flow of blood ▷ *n* **2** a drug or agent that promotes the flow of blood, esp the menstrual flow [c18 from HAEMO- + Greek *agōgos* leading]

haemal *or US* **hemal** ('hiːməl) *adj* **1** of or relating to the blood or the blood vessels **2** denoting or relating to the region of the body containing the heart

haemangioma *or esp US* **hemangioma** (hɪ,mændʒɪ'əʊmə) *n, pl* **-mas** *or* **-mata** (-mətə) a nonmalignant tumour of blood vessels, esp affecting those of the skin. See **strawberry mark** [from HAEM(O)- + ANGI(O)- + -OMA]

haematein *or US* **hematein** (,hiːmə'tiːɪn, ,hɛm-) *n* a dark purple water-insoluble crystalline substance obtained from logwood and used as an indicator and biological stain. Formula: $C_{16}H_{12}O_6$

haematemesis *or US* **hematemesis** (,hiːmə'tɛmɪsɪs, ,hɛm-) *n* vomiting of blood, esp as the result of a bleeding ulcer. Compare **haemoptysis** [c19 from HAEMATO- + Greek *emesis* vomiting]

haematic *or US* **hematic** (hiː'mætɪk) *adj* **1** Also: **haemic** relating to, acting on, having the colour of, or containing blood ▷ *n* **2** *med* another name for a **haematinic**

haematin *or US* **hematin** ('hɛmətɪn, 'hiː-) *n biochem* a dark bluish or brownish pigment containing iron in the ferric state, obtained by the oxidation of haem

haematinic *or US* **hematinic** (,hɛmə'tɪnɪk, ,hiː-) *n* **1** Also called: **haematic** an agent that stimulates the production of red blood cells or increases the amount of haemoglobin in the blood ▷ *adj* **2** having the effect of enriching the blood

haematite ('hiːmə,taɪt, 'hɛm-) *n* a variant spelling of **hematite.** > **haematitic** (,hiːmə'tɪtɪk, ,hɛm-) *adj*

haemato- *or before a vowel* **haemat-** *combining form* indicating blood: *haematolysis.* Also: **haemo-,** (*US*) **hemato-,** (*US*) **hemat-** [from Greek *haima, haimat-* blood]

haematoblast *or US* **hematoblast** (hiː'mætəʊ,blæst) *n* any of the undifferentiated cells in the bone marrow that develop into blood cells > **hae,mato'blastic** *adj*

haematocele *or US* **hematocele** ('hɛmətəʊ,siːl, 'hiː-) *n pathol* a collection of blood in a body cavity, as in the space surrounding the testis; blood cyst

haematocrit *or US* **hematocrit** ('hɛmətəʊkrɪt, 'hiː-) *n* **1** a centrifuge for separating blood cells from plasma **2** Also called: **packed cell volume** the ratio of the volume occupied by these cells, esp the red cells, to the total volume of blood, expressed as a percentage [c20 from HAEMATO- + Greek *kritēs* judge, from *krinein* to separate]

haematocryal *or US* **hematocryal** (,hɛmətəʊ'kraɪəl, ,hiː-) *adj zoology* another word for **poikilothermic**

haematogenesis *or US* **hematogenesis** (,hɛmətəʊ'dʒɛnɪsɪs, ,hiː-) *n* another name for **haematopoiesis.** > **,haemato'genic** > **haematogenetic** (,haemətəʊdʒɪ'nɛtɪk, ,hiː-) *or US* **,hemato'genic** *or* ,hematoge'netic *adj*

haematogenous or US **hematogenous** (ˌhɛmə'tɒdʒɪnəs, ˌhiː-) adj **1** producing blood **2** produced by, derived from, or originating in the blood **3** (of bacteria, cancer cells, etc) borne by or distributed by the blood

haematoid ('hiːmə,tɔɪd, 'hɛm-), **haemoid** or US **hematoid, hemoid** adj resembling blood

haematology or US **hematology** (ˌhiːmə'tɒlədʒɪ) n the branch of medical science concerned with diseases of the blood and blood-forming tissues > haematologic (ˌhiːmətə'lɒdʒɪk), ˌhaemato'logical, US ˌhemato'logic, ˌhemato'logical adj > ˌhaema'tologist or US ˌhema'tologist n

haematolysis or US **hematolysis** (ˌhiːmə'tɒlɪsɪs) n, pl **-ses** (-ˌsiːz) another name for **haemolysis**

haematoma or US **hematoma** (ˌhiːmə'təʊmə, ˌhɛm-) n, pl **-mas** or **-mata** (-mətə) pathol a tumour of clotted or partially clotted blood

haematophagous or US **hematophagous** (ˌhiːmə'tɒfəgəs) adj (of certain animals) feeding on blood

haematopoiesis (ˌhɛmətəʊpɔɪ'iːsɪs, ˌhiː-), **haemopoiesis** or US **hematopoiesis, hemopoiesis** n physiol the formation of blood. Also called: haematosis, haematogenesis > haematopoietic (ˌhɛmətəʊpɔɪ'ɛtɪk, ˌhiː-) or haemopoietic (ˌhiːməpɔɪ'ɛtɪk, ˌhɛm-) or US ˌhematopoi'etic or ˌhemopoi'etic adj

haematosis or US **hematosis** (ˌhiːmə'təʊsɪs, ˌhɛm-) n physiol **1** another word for **haematopoiesis 2** the oxygenation of venous blood in the lungs

haematothermal or US **hematothermal** (ˌhɛmətəʊ'θɜːməl, ˌhiː-) adj zoology another word for **homoiothermic**

haematoxylin or US **hematoxylin** (ˌhiːmə'tɒksɪlɪn, ˌhɛm-) n **1** a colourless or yellowish crystalline compound that turns red on exposure to light: obtained from logwood and used in dyes and as a biological stain. Formula: $C_{16}H_{14}O_6.3H_2O$ **2** a variant spelling of **haematoxylon** [C19 from New Latin *Haematoxylon* genus name of logwood, from HAEMATO- + Greek *xulon* wood + -IN] > haematoxylic (ˌhiːmətɒk'sɪlɪk) adj

haematoxylon (ˌhiːmə'tɒksɪlɒn) or **haematoxylin** n any thorny leguminous tree of the genus *Haematoxylon,* esp the logwood, of tropical America and SW Africa. The heartwood yields the dye haematoxylin [C19 see HAEMATOXYLIN]

haematozoon or US **hematozoon** (ˌhiːmətəʊ'zəʊɒn, ˌhɛm-) n, pl **-zoa** (-'zəʊə) any microorganism, esp a protozoan, that is parasitic in the blood

haematuria or esp US **hematuria** (ˌhiːmə'tjʊərɪə, ˌhɛm-) n pathol the presence of blood or red blood cells in the urine > ˌhaema'turic or US ˌhema'turic adj

haemia or esp US **-hemia** n combining form variants of **-aemia**

haemic or US **hemic** ('hiːmɪk, 'hɛm-) adj another word for **haematic**

haemin or US **hemin** ('hiːmɪn) n biochem haematin chloride; insoluble reddish-brown crystals formed by the action of hydrochloric acid on haematin in a test for the presence of blood [C20 from HAEMO- + -IN]

haemo-, haema- or before a vowel **haem-** combining form denoting blood: *haemophobia.* Also: haemato-, (US) hemo-, (US) hema-, (US) hem- [from Greek *haima* blood]

haemochrome or US **hemochrome** ('hiːmə,krəʊm, 'hɛm-) n a blood pigment, such as haemoglobin, that carries oxygen

haemocoel or US **hemocoel** ('hiːmə,siːl) n the body cavity of many invertebrates, including arthropods and molluscs, developed from part of the blood system [C19 from HAEMO- + New Latin *coel,* from Greek *koilos* hollow]

haemocyanin or US **hemocyanin**
(ˌhiːməʊ'saɪənɪn) n a blue copper-containing respiratory pigment in crustaceans and molluscs that functions as haemoglobin

haemocyte or US **hemocyte** ('hiːməʊ,saɪt, 'hɛm-) n any blood cell, esp a red blood cell

haemocytometer (ˌhiːməʊsaɪ'tɒmɪtə), **haemacytometer,** US **hemocytometer, hemacytometer** n med an apparatus for counting the number of cells in a quantity of blood, typically consisting of a graduated pipette for drawing and diluting the blood and a ruled glass slide on which the cells are counted under a microscope

haemodialysis or US **hemodialysis** (ˌhiːməʊdaɪ'ælɪsɪs) n, pl **-ses** (-ˌsiːz) med the filtering of circulating blood through a semipermeable membrane in an apparatus (**haemodialyser** or **artificial kidney**) to remove waste products: performed in cases of kidney failure. Also called: **extracorporeal dialysis** See also **dialysis** [C20 from HAEMO- + DIALYSIS]

haemoflagellate or US **hemoflagellate** (ˌhiːmə'flædʒə,leɪt) n a flagellate protozoan, such as a trypanosome, that is parasitic in the blood

haemoglobin or US **hemoglobin** (ˌhiːməʊ'gləʊbɪn, ˌhɛm-) n a conjugated protein, consisting of haem and the protein globin, that gives red blood cells their characteristic colour. It combines reversibly with oxygen and is thus very important in the transportation of oxygen to tissues. See also **oxyhaemoglobin** [C19 shortened from *haematoglobulin,* from HAEMATIN + GLOBULIN the two components]

haemoglobinometer or US **hemoglobinometer** (ˌhiːməʊgləʊbɪ'nɒmɪtə) n an instrument used to determine the haemoglobin content of blood

haemoglobinopathy or US **hemoglobinopathy** (ˌhiːməʊgləʊbɪ'nɒpəθɪ) n any of various inherited diseases, including sickle-cell anaemia and thalassaemia, characterized by abnormal haemoglobin

haemoglobinuria or US **hemoglobinuria** (ˌhiːməʊgləʊbɪ'njʊərɪə, ˌhɛm-) n pathol the presence of haemoglobin in the urine

haemoid or US **hemoid** ('hiːmɔɪd) adj a former word for **haematoid**

haemolysin or US **hemolysin** (ˌhiːməʊ'laɪsɪn, ˌhɛmə-, hɪ'mɒlɪsɪn) n biochem any substance, esp an antibody, that causes the breakdown of red blood cells

haemolysis (hɪ'mɒlɪsɪs), **haematolysis,** US **hemolysis, hematolysis** n, pl **-ses** (-ˌsiːz) the disintegration of red blood cells, with the release of haemoglobin, occurring in the living organism or in a blood sample

haemolytic or US **hemolytic** (ˌhiːməʊ'lɪtɪk, ˌhɛm-) adj of or relating to the disintegration of red blood cells

haemophile or US **hemophile** ('hiːməʊ,faɪl, 'hɛm-) n **1** another name for **haemophiliac 2** a haemophilic bacterium

haemophilia or US **hemophilia** (ˌhiːməʊ'fɪlɪə, ˌhɛm-) n an inheritable disease, usually affecting only males but transmitted by women to their male children, characterized by loss or impairment of the normal clotting ability of blood so that a minor wound may result in fatal bleeding > ˌhaemo'phili,oid or US ˌhemo'phili,oid adj

haemophiliac or US **hemophiliac** (ˌhiːməʊ'fɪlɪ,æk, ˌhɛm-) n a person having haemophilia. Nontechnical name: **bleeder** Also called: haemophile

haemophilic or US **hemophilic** (ˌhiːməʊ'fɪlɪk, ˌhɛm-) adj **1** of, relating to, or affected by haemophilia **2** (of bacteria) growing well in a culture medium containing blood

haemopoiesis or US **hemopoiesis** (ˌhiːməʊpɔɪ'iːsɪs, ˌhɛm-) n physiol another name for **haematopoiesis** > haemopoietic or US hemopoietic (ˌhiːməʊpɔɪ'ɛtɪk, ˌhɛm-) adj

haemoptysis or US **hemoptysis** (hɪ'mɒptɪsɪs) n, pl **-ses** (-ˌsiːz) spitting or coughing up of blood or blood-streaked mucus, as in tuberculosis. Compare **haematemesis** [C17 from HAEMO- + -ptysis, from Greek *ptyein* to spit]

haemorrhage or US **hemorrhage** ('hɛmərɪdʒ) n **1** profuse bleeding from ruptured blood vessels **2** a steady or severe loss or depletion of resources, staff, etc ▷ vb **3** (intr) to bleed profusely **4** (tr) to undergo a steady or severe loss or depletion of (resources, staff, etc) [C17 from Latin *haemorrhagia;* see HAEMO-, -RRHAGIA] > haemorrhagic or US hemorrhagic (ˌhɛmə'rædʒɪk) adj

haemorrhagic fever n any of a group of fevers, such as Ebola virus disease and yellow fever, characterized by internal bleeding or bleeding into the skin

haemorrhoidectomy or US **hemorrhoidectomy** (ˌhɛmərɔɪ'dɛktəmɪ) n, pl **-mies** surgical removal of haemorrhoids

haemorrhoids or US **hemorrhoids** ('hɛmə,rɔɪdz) pl n pathol swollen and twisted veins in the region of the anus and lower rectum, often painful and bleeding. Nontechnical name: **piles** [C14 from Latin *haemorrhoidae* (plural), from Greek, from *haimorrhoos* discharging blood, from *haimo-* HAEMO- + *rhein* to flow] > haemor'rhoidal or US ˌhemor'rhoidal adj

haemostasis (ˌhiːməʊ'steɪsɪs, ˌhɛm-), **haemostasia** (ˌhiːməʊ'steɪʒɪə, -ʒə, ˌhɛm-) or US **hemostasis, hemostasia** n **1** the stopping of bleeding or arrest of blood circulation in an organ or part, as during a surgical operation **2** stagnation of the blood [C18 from New Latin, from HAEMO- + Greek *stasis* a standing still]

haemostat or US **hemostat** ('hiːməʊ,stæt, 'hɛm-) n **1** a surgical instrument that stops bleeding by compression of a blood vessel **2** a chemical agent that retards or stops bleeding

haemostatic or US **hemostatic** (ˌhiːməʊ'stætɪk, ˌhɛm-) adj **1** retarding or stopping the flow of blood within the blood vessels **2** retarding or stopping bleeding ▷ n **3** a drug or agent that retards or stops bleeding

haeremai ('haɪrə,maɪ) interj NZ a Māori expression of welcome [C18 Māori, literally: come hither]

haere ra (ha:ərə 'ra:) sentence substitute goodbye! [from Māori, literally: go away]

haeres ('hɪəriːz) n, pl **haeredes** (hɪ'riːdiːz) a variant spelling of **heres**

Ha-erh-pin ('ha:'ɛə'pɪn) n a transliteration of the Chinese name for **Harbin**

haet (het) n Scot a whit; iota; the least amount [C16 originally in the phrase *deil hae'* it devil have it]

hafiz ('ha:fɪz) n Islam a title for a person who knows the Koran by heart [from Persian, from Arabic *hāfiz,* from *hafiza* to guard]

hafnium ('hæfnɪəm) n a bright metallic element found in zirconium ores: used in tungsten filaments and as a neutron absorber in nuclear reactors. Symbol: Hf; atomic no.: 72; atomic wt.: 178.49; valency: 4; relative density: 13.31; melting pt.: 2231±20°C; boiling pt.: 4603°C [C20 New Latin, named after *Hafnia,* Latin name of Copenhagen + -IUM]

haft (ha:ft) n **1** the handle of an axe, knife, etc ▷ vb **2** (tr) to provide with a haft [Old English *hæft;* related to Old Norse *hapt,* Old High German *haft* fetter, *hefti* handle] > 'hafter n

Haftarah or **Haphtarah** (ha:f'təʊrə; Hebrew hafta'ra:) n, pl **-taroth** (-'təʊrəʊt; Hebrew -ta'ro:t) Judaism a short reading from the Prophets which follows the reading from the Torah on Sabbaths and festivals, and relates either to the theme of the Torah reading or to the observances of the day. See also **maftir**

hag¹ (hæg) n **1** an unpleasant or ugly old woman **2** a witch **3** short for **hagfish 4** obsolete a female demon [Old English *hægtesse* witch; related to Old High German *hagazussa,* Middle Dutch *haghetisse*]

h

> 'haggish *adj* > 'haggishly *adv* > 'haggishness *n*
> 'hag,like *adj*

hag² (hæg, hɑːg) *n Scot and northern English dialect* **1** a firm spot in a bog **2** a soft place in a moor [c13 of Scandinavian origin; compare Old Norse *högg* gap; see HEW]

Hag. *Bible* abbreviation for Haggai

Hagar ('heɪɡɑː, -ɡə) *n Old Testament* an Egyptian maid of Sarah, who bore Ishmael to Abraham, Sarah's husband

hagbut ('hæɡbʌt) *n* another word for **arquebus** > 'hagbut,eer *or* 'hagbutter *n*

Hagen¹ ('hɑːɡən) *n* (in the *Nibelungenlied*) Siegfried's killer, who in turn is killed by Siegfried's wife, Kriemhild

Hagen² (*German* 'haːɡən) *n* an industrial city in NW Germany, in North Rhine-Westphalia. Pop: 200 039 (2003 est)

hagfish ('hæɡ,fɪʃ) *n, pl* **-fish** *or* **-fishes** any eel-like marine cyclostome vertebrate of the family *Myxinidae,* having a round sucking mouth and feeding on the tissues of other animals and on dead organic material. Often shortened to: **hag**

Haggadah *or* **Haggodoh** (hə'ɡɑːdə; *Hebrew* haɡa'daː, -ɡɔ'dɔ) *n, pl* **-dahs, -das** *or* **-doth** (*Hebrew* -'doːt) *Judaism* **1 a** a book containing the order of service of the traditional Passover meal **b** the narrative of the Exodus from Egypt that constitutes the main part of that service. See also **Seder 2** another word for **Aggadah** [c19 from Hebrew *haggādāh* a story, from *hagged* to tell] > **haggadic** (hə'ɡædɪk, -'ɡɑː-) *or* **hag'gadical** *adj*

haggadist (hə'ɡɑːdɪst) *n Judaism* **1** a writer of Aggadoth **2** an expert in or a student of haggadic literature > **haggadistic** (,hæɡə'dɪstɪk) *adj*

Haggai ('hæɡeɪ,aɪ) *n Old Testament* **1** a Hebrew prophet, whose oracles are usually dated between August and December of 520 BC **2** the book in which these oracles are contained, chiefly concerned with the rebuilding of the Temple after the Exile. Douay spelling: **Aggeus** (ə'dʒiːəs)

haggard¹ ('hæɡəd) *adj* **1** careworn or gaunt, as from lack of sleep, anxiety, or starvation **2** wild or unruly **3** (of a hawk) having reached maturity in the wild before being caught ▷ *n* **4** *falconry* a hawk that has reached maturity before being caught. Compare **eyas, passage hawk** [c16 from Old French *hagard* wild; perhaps related to HEDGE] > 'haggardly *adv* > 'haggardness *n*

haggard² ('hæɡəd) *n* (in Ireland and the Isle of Man) an enclosure beside a farmhouse in which crops are stored [c16 related to Old Norse *heygarthr,* from *hey* hay + *garthr* yard]

haggis ('hæɡɪs) *n* a Scottish dish made from sheep's or calf's offal, oatmeal, suet, and seasonings boiled in a skin made from the animal's stomach [c15 perhaps from *haggen* to HACK¹]

haggle ('hæɡ³l) *vb* **1** (*intr*; often foll by *over*) to bargain or wrangle (over a price, terms of an agreement, etc); barter **2** (*tr*) *rare* to hack [c16 of Scandinavian origin; compare Old Norse *haggva* to HEW] > 'haggler *n*

hagiarchy ('hæɡɪ,ɑːkɪ) *n, pl* **-archies 1** government by saints, holy men, or men in holy orders **2** an order of saints

hagio- *or before a vowel* **hagi-** *combining form* indicating a saint, saints, or holiness: *hagiography* [via Late Latin from Greek, from *hagios* holy]

hagiocracy (,hæɡɪ'ɒkrəsɪ) *n, pl* **-cies 1** government by holy men **2** a state, community, etc, governed by holy men

Hagiographa (,hæɡɪ'ɒɡrəfə) *n* the third of the three main parts into which the books of the Old Testament are divided in Jewish tradition (the other two parts being the Law and the Prophets), comprising Psalms, Proverbs, Job, the Song of Solomon, Ruth, Lamentations, Ecclesiastes, Esther, Daniel, Ezra, Nehemiah, and Chronicles. Also called: **Writings**

hagiographer (,hæɡɪ'ɒɡrəfə) *or* **hagiographist** *n* **1** a person who writes about the lives of the saints

2 one of the writers of the Hagiographa

hagiography (,hæɡɪ'ɒɡrəfɪ) *n, pl* **-phies 1** the writing of the lives of the saints **2** biography of the saints **3** any biography that idealizes or idolizes its subject > **hagiographic** (,hæɡɪə'ɡræfɪk) *or* ,hagio'graphical *adj*

hagiolatry (,hæɡɪ'ɒlətrɪ) *n* worship or veneration of saints > ,hagi'olater *n* > ,hagi'olatrous *adj*

hagiology (,hæɡɪ'ɒlədʒɪ) *n, pl* **-gies 1** literature concerned with the lives and legends of saints **2 a** a biography of a saint **b** a collection of such biographies **3** an authoritative canon of saints **4** a history of sacred writings > hagiologic (,hæɡɪə'lɒdʒɪk) *or* ,hagio'logical *adj* > ,hagi'ologist *n*

hagioscope ('hæɡɪə,skəʊp) *n architect* another name for **squint** (sense 6) > hagioscopic (,hæɡɪə'skɒpɪk) *adj*

hag-ridden *adj* **1** tormented or worried, as if by a witch **2** *facetious* (of a man) harassed by women

Hague (heɪɡ) *n* **The** the seat of government of the Netherlands and capital of South Holland province, situated about 3 km (2 miles) from the North Sea. Pop: 464 000 (2003 est). Dutch names: 's Gravenhage, Den Haag

Hague Tribunal *n* a tribunal of judges at The Hague, founded in 1899 to provide a panel of arbitrators for international disputes. It also chooses nominees for election by the United Nations to the International Court of Justice. Official name: **Permanent Court of Arbitration**

hah (hɑː) *interj* a variant spelling of **ha**

ha-ha¹ ('hɑː 'hɑː) *or* **haw-haw** *interj* **1** a representation of the sound of laughter **2** an exclamation expressing derision, mockery, surprise, etc

ha-ha² ('hɑː 'hɑː) *or* **haw-haw** *n* a wall or other boundary marker that is set in a ditch so as not to interrupt the landscape [c18 from French *haha,* probably based on *ha!* ejaculation denoting surprise]

hahnium ('hɑːnɪəm) *n* a name once advanced by the American Chemical Society for a transuranic element, artificially produced from californium, atomic no.: 105; half-life of most stable isotope, ²⁶²Ha: 40 seconds. now called **dubnium** [c20 named after Otto Hahn (1879–1968), German physicist]

Haida ('haɪdə) *n* **1** (*pl* **-das** *or* **-da**) a member of a seafaring group of North American Indian peoples inhabiting the coast of British Columbia and SW Alaska **2** the language of these peoples, belonging to the Na-Dene phylum > 'Haidan *adj*

Haiduk, Heyduck *or* **Heiduc** ('haɪdʊk) *n* a rural brigand in the European part of the Ottoman Empire [c17 from Hungarian *hajdúk* brigands]

Haifa ('haɪfə) *n* a port in NW Israel, near Mount Carmel, on the Bay of Acre: Israel's chief port, with an oil refinery and other heavy industry. Pop: 269 400 (2003 est)

haik *or* **haick** (haɪk, heɪk) *n* an Arab's outer garment of cotton, wool, or silk, for the head and body [c18 from Arabic *hā'ik*]

haiku *or* **hokku** ('haɪkuː) *n, pl* **-ku** an epigrammatic Japanese verse form in 17 syllables [from Japanese, from *hai* amusement + *ku* verse]

hail¹ (heɪl) *n* **1** small pellets of ice falling from cumulonimbus clouds when there are very strong rising air currents **2** a shower or storm of such pellets **3** words, ideas, etc, directed with force and in great quantity: *a hail of abuse* **4** a collection of objects, esp bullets, spears, etc, directed at someone with violent force ▷ *vb* **5** (*intr*; with *it* as subject) to be the case that hail is falling **6** (often with *it* as subject) to fall or cause to fall as or like hail: *to hail criticism; bad language hailed about him* [Old English *hægl*; related to Old Frisian *heil,* Old High German *hagal* hail, Greek *kakhlēx* pebble]

hail² (heɪl) *vb* (mainly *tr*) **1** to greet, esp enthusiastically: *the crowd hailed the actress with joy* **2** to acclaim or acknowledge: *they hailed him as their hero* **3** to attract the attention of by shouting or gesturing: *to hail a taxi; to hail a passing ship* **4** (*intr*;

foll by *from*) to be a native (of); originate (in): *she hails from India* ▷ *n* **5** the act or an instance of hailing **6** a shout or greeting **7** distance across which one can attract attention (esp in the phrase **within hail**) ▷ *sentence substitute* **8** *poetic* an exclamation of greeting [c12 from Old Norse *heill* WHOLE; see HALE¹, WASSAIL] > 'hailer *n*

hail-fellow-well-met *adj* genial and familiar, esp in an offensive or ingratiating way

Hail Mary *n* **1** *RC Church* a prayer to the Virgin Mary, based on the salutations of the angel Gabriel (Luke 1:28) and Elizabeth (Luke 1:42) to her. Also called: **Ave Maria 2** *American football slang* a very long high pass into the end zone, made in the final seconds of a half or of a game

hailstone ('heɪl,stəʊn) *n* a pellet of hail

hailstorm ('heɪl,stɔːm) *n* a storm during which hail falls

Hainan ('haɪ'næn) *or* **Hainan Tao** (taʊ) *n* an island and province in the South China Sea, separated from the mainland of S China by the **Hainan Strait**: part of Guangdong province until 1988; mainland China's largest island. Pop: 8 110 000 (2003 est). Area: 33 572 sq km (12 962 sq miles)

Hainaut *or* **Hainault** (*French* ɛno) *n* a province of SW Belgium: stretches from the Flanders Plain in the north to the Ardennes in the south. Capital: Mons. Pop: 1 283 200 (2004 est). Area: 3797 sq km (1466 sq miles)

hain't (heɪnt) *archaic or dialect* ▷ contraction of has not, have not, or is not

Haiphong ('haɪ'fɒŋ) *n* a port in N Vietnam, on the Red River delta: a major industrial centre. Pop: 1 817 000 (2005 est)

hair (hɛə) *n* **1** any of the threadlike pigmented structures that grow from follicles beneath the skin of mammals and consist of layers of dead keratinized cells **2** a growth of such structures, as on the human head or animal body, which helps prevent heat loss from the body **3** *botany* any threadlike outgrowth from the epidermis, such as a root hair **4 a** a fabric or material made from the hair of some animals **b** (*as modifier*): *a hair carpet; a hair shirt* **5** another word for **hair's-breadth** *to lose by a hair* **6** get in someone's hair *informal* to annoy someone persistently **7** hair of the dog (that bit one) an alcoholic drink taken as an antidote to a hangover **8** keep your hair on! *Brit informal* keep calm **9** let one's hair down to behave without reserve **10** not turn a hair to show no surprise, anger, fear, etc **11** split hairs to make petty and unnecessary distinctions [Old English *hær;* related to Old Norse *hār,* Old High German *hār* hair, Norwegian *herren* stiff, hard, Lettish *sari* bristles, Latin *crescere* to grow] > 'hair,like *adj*

hairball ('hɛə,bɔːl) *n* a compact mass of hair that forms in the stomach of cats, calves, etc, as a result of licking and swallowing the fur, and causes vomiting, coughing, bloat, weight loss, and depression

hairbrush ('hɛə,brʌʃ) *n* a brush for grooming the hair

haircloth ('hɛə,klɒθ) *n* a cloth woven from horsehair, used in upholstery

haircut ('hɛə,kʌt) *n* **1** the act or an instance of cutting the hair **2** the style in which hair has been cut

hairdo ('hɛə,duː) *n, pl* **-dos** the arrangement of a person's hair, esp after styling and setting

hairdresser ('hɛə,drɛsə) *n* **1** a person whose business is cutting, curling, colouring and arranging hair, esp that of women **2** a hairdresser's establishment ▷ Related adjective. **tonsorial.** > 'hair,dressing *n*

hairdryer *or* **hairdrier** ('hɛə,draɪə) *n* **1** a hand-held electric device that blows out hot air and is used to dry and, sometimes, assist in styling the hair, as in blow-drying **2** a device for drying the hair in which hot air is blown into a hood that surrounds the head of a seated person

-haired _adj_ having hair as specified: _long-haired_

hair follicle _n_ a narrow tubular cavity that contains the root of a hair, formed by an infolding of the epidermis and corium of the skin

hair gel _n_ a jelly-like substance applied to the hair before styling in order to retain the shape of the style

hair grass _n_ any grass of the genera _Aira, Deschampsia_, etc, having very narrow stems and leaves

hairgrip ('hɛə,grɪp) _n chiefly Brit_ a small tightly bent metal hair clip. Also called (esp US, Canadian, and NZ): **bobby pin**

hairif ('hɛərɪf) _n_ another name for **cleavers**

hair lacquer _n_ another name for **hairspray**

hairless ('hɛəlɪs) _adj_ **1** having little or no hair **2** _Brit slang_ very angry; raging

hairline ('hɛə,laɪn) _n_ **1** the natural margin formed by hair on the head **2 a** a very narrow line **b** (_as modifier_): _a hairline crack_ **3** _printing_ **a** a thin stroke in a typeface **b** any typeface consisting of such strokes **c** thin lines beside a character, produced by worn or poorly cast type **4** a rope or line of hair

hairline fracture _n_ a very fine crack in a bone

hairnet ('hɛə,nɛt) _n_ any of several kinds of light netting worn over the hair to keep it in place

hairpiece ('hɛə,piːs) _n_ **1** a wig or toupee **2** Also called: **postiche** a section of extra hair attached to a woman's real hair to give it greater bulk or length

hairpin ('hɛə,pɪn) _n_ **1** a thin double-pronged pin used by women to fasten the hair **2** (_modifier_) (esp of a bend in a road) curving very sharply

hair-raising _adj_ inspiring horror; terrifying: _a hair-raising drop of 600 feet_ > **hair-,raiser** _n_

hair restorer _n_ a lotion claimed to promote hair growth

hair's-breadth _n_ **a** a very short or imperceptible margin or distance **b** (_as modifier_): _a hair's-breadth escape_

hair seal _n_ any earless seal, esp the harbour seal, having a coat of stiff hair with no underfur

hair sheep _n_ any variety of sheep growing hair instead of wool, yielding hides with a finer and tougher grain than those of wool sheep

hair shirt _n_ **1** a shirt made of haircloth worn next to the skin as a penance **2** a secret trouble or affliction

hair slide _n_ a hinged clip with a tortoiseshell, bone, or similar back, used to fasten the hair

hair space _n printing_ the thinnest of the metal spaces used in setting type to separate letters or words

hairsplitting ('hɛə,splɪtɪŋ) _n_ **1** the making of petty distinctions ▷ _adj_ **2** occupied with or based on petty distinctions > **hair,splitter** _n_

hairspray ('hɛə,spreɪ) _n_ a fixative solution sprayed onto the hair to keep a hairstyle in shape. Also called: **hair lacquer**

hairspring ('hɛə,sprɪŋ) _n horology_ a very fine spiral spring in some timepieces, which, in combination with the balance wheel, controls the timekeeping

hairstreak ('hɛə,striːk) _n_ any small butterfly of the genus _Callophrys_ and related genera, having fringed wings marked with narrow white streaks: family _Lycaenidae_

hair stroke _n_ a very fine line in a written character

hairstyle ('hɛə,staɪl) _n_ a particular mode of arranging, cutting, or setting the hair > **hair,stylist** _n_

hairtail ('hɛə,teɪl) _n_ any marine spiny-finned fish of the family _Trichiuridae_, most common in warm seas, having a long whiplike scaleless body and long sharp teeth. Usual US name: **cutlass fish**

hair trigger _n_ **1** a trigger of a firearm that responds to very slight pressure **2** _informal_ **a** any mechanism, reaction, etc, set in operation by slight provocation **b** (_as modifier_): _a hair-trigger temper_

hairweaving ('hɛə,wiːvɪŋ) _n_ the interweaving of false hair with the hair on a balding person's head

hairworm ('hɛə,wɜːm) _n_ **1** any hairlike nematode worm of the family _Trichostrongylidae_, such as the stomach worm, parasitic in the intestines of vertebrates **2** Also called: **horsehair worm** any very thin long worm of the phylum (or class) _Nematomorpha_, the larvae of which are parasitic in arthropods

hairy ('hɛərɪ) _adj_ **hairier, hairiest 1** having or covered with hair **2** _slang_ **a** difficult or problematic **b** scaring, dangerous, or exciting > 'hairiness _n_

hairyback ('hɛərɪbæk) _n South African slang_ an offensive word for **Afrikaner**

hairy frog _n_ a W African frog, _Astylosternus robustus_, the males of which have glandular hairlike processes on the flanks

hairy willowherb _n_ another name for **codlins-and-cream**

Haiti ('heɪtɪ, hɑːˈiːtɪ) _n_ **1** a republic occupying the W part of the island of Hispaniola in the Caribbean, the E part consisting of the Dominican Republic: ceded by Spain to France in 1697 and became one of the richest colonial possessions in the world, with numerous plantations; slaves rebelled under Toussaint L'Ouverture in 1793 and defeated the French; taken over by the US (1915–41) after long political and economic chaos; under the authoritarian regimes of François Duvalier ("Papa Doc") (1957–71) and his son Jean-Claude Duvalier ("Baby Doc") (1971–86); returned to civilian rule in 1990, but another coup in 1991 brought military rule, which was ended in 1994 with US intervention. Official languages: French and Haitian creole. Religions: Roman Catholic and voodoo. Currency: gourde. Capital: Port-au-Prince. Pop: 8 437 000 (2004 est). Area: 27 749 sq km (10 714 sq miles) **2** a former name for **Hispaniola**

Haitian _or_ **Haytian** ('heɪʃən, hɑːˈiːʃən) _adj_ **1** relating to or characteristic of Haiti, its inhabitants, or their language ▷ _n_ **2** a native, citizen, or inhabitant of Haiti **3** the creolized French spoken in Haiti

hajj _or_ **hadj** (hædʒ) _n, pl_ **hajjes** _or_ **hadjes** the pilgrimage to Mecca that every Muslim is required to make at least once in his life, provided he has enough money and the health to do so [from Arabic _hajj_ pilgrimage]

hajji, hadji _or_ **haji** ('hædʒɪ) _n, pl_ **hajis, hadjis** _or_ **hajis 1** a Muslim who has made a pilgrimage to Mecca: also used as a title **2** a Christian of the Greek Orthodox or Armenian Churches who has visited Jerusalem > 'hajjah _fem n_

haka ('hɑːkə) _n NZ_ **1** a Māori war chant accompanied by gestures **2** a similar performance by a rugby team [Māori]

hakari (hɑːkɑːriː) _n, pl_ **hakari** _NZ_ a feast which follows a ceremonial funeral or other important occasion [Māori]

hake¹ (heɪk) _n, pl_ **hake** _or_ **hakes 1** any gadoid food fish of the genus _Merluccius_, such as M. _merluccius_ (European hake), of the N hemisphere, having an elongated body with a large head and two dorsal fins **2** any North American fish of the genus _Urophycis_, similar and related to _Merluccius_ species **3** _Austral_ another name for **barracouta** [C15 perhaps from Old Norse _haki_ hook; compare Old English _hacod_ pike; see HOOK]

hake² (heɪk) _n_ a wooden frame for drying cheese or fish [C18 variant of HECK²]

hakea ('hɑːkɪə, 'heɪkɪə) _n_ any shrub or tree of the Australian genus _Hakea_, having a hard woody fruit and often yielding a useful wood: family _Proteaceae_ [C19 New Latin, named after C. L. von _Hake_ (died 1818), German botanist]

Hakenkreuz _German_ ('hɑːkən,krɔʏts) _n_ the swastika [literally: hooked cross]

hakim _or_ **hakeem** (hɑːˈkiːm, 'hɑːkiːm) _n_ **1** a Muslim judge, ruler, or administrator **2** a Muslim physician [C17 from Arabic, from _hakama_ to rule]

Hakodate (,hɑːkəʊˈdɑːteɪ) _n_ a port in N Japan, on S Hokkaido: fishing industry and shipbuilding. Pop: 284 690 (2002 est)

haku (hɑːkuː) _n, pl_ **haku** _NZ_ another name for **kingfish** (sense 4) [Māori]

hakuna matata (,hɑːˈkuːnə ,mɑːˈtɑːtə) _sentence substitute_ no problem [from Swahili, there is no difficulty]

hal- _combining form_ a variant of **halo-** before a vowel

Halabja (həˈlæbdʒə) _n_ a Kurdish town in NE Iraq; in March 1998 Iraqi forces used poison gas on the population, killing hundreds of civilians. Pop: 80 000 (latest est)

Halacha, Halaka _or_ **Halakha** (_Hebrew_ hɑlɑˈxɑː; _Yiddish_ hɑˈlɔxə) _n_ **1 a** a Jewish religious law **b** a ruling on some specific matter **2 a** that part of the Talmud which is concerned with legal matters as distinct from homiletics **b** Jewish legal literature in general ▷ Compare **Aggadah** (sense 1) [from Hebrew _hălākhāh_ way]

Halafian (həˈlɑːfɪən) _adj_ of or relating to the Neolithic culture extending from Iran to the Mediterranean

halal _or_ **hallal** (hɑːˈlɑːl) _n_ **1** meat from animals that have been killed according to Muslim law ▷ _adj_ **2** of or relating to such meat: _a halal butcher_ ▷ _vb_ **-als, -alling, -alled** (_tr_) **3** to kill (animals) in this way [from Arabic: lawful]

halation (həˈleɪʃən) _n photog_ fogging usually seen as a bright ring surrounding a source of light: caused by reflection from the back of the film [C19 from HALO + -ATION]

halberd ('hælbəd) _or_ **halbert** ('hælbət) _n_ a weapon consisting of a long shaft with an axe blade and a pick, topped by a spearhead: used in 15th- and 16th-century warfare [C15 from Old French _hallebarde_, from Middle High German _helm_ handle, HELM¹ + _barde_ axe, from Old High German _bart_ BEARD] > ,halber'dier _n_

Halberstadt ('hælbəʃtæt) _n_ a town in central Germany, in Saxony-Anhalt: industrial centre noted for its historic buildings. Pop: 40 014 (2003 est)

halcyon ('hælsɪən) _adj also_ **halcyonian** (,hælsɪ'əʊnɪən) _or_ **halcyonic** (,hælsɪ'ɒnɪk) **1** peaceful, gentle, and calm **2** happy and carefree ▷ _n_ **3** _Greek myth_ a fabulous bird associated with the winter solstice **4** a poetic name for the **kingfisher 5 halcyon days a** a fortnight of calm weather during the winter solstice **b** a period of peace and happiness [C14 from Latin _alcyon_, from Greek _alkuōn_ kingfisher, of uncertain origin]

Halcyone (hælˈsaɪənɪ) _n_ a variant of **Alcyone**

hale¹ (heɪl) _adj_ **1** healthy and robust (esp in the phrase **hale and hearty**) **2** _Scot and northern English dialect_ whole [Old English _hæl_ WHOLE] > 'haleness _n_

hale² (heɪl) _vb_ (_tr_) to pull or drag; haul [C13 from Old French _haler_, of Germanic origin; compare Old High German _halōn_ to fetch, Old English _geholian_ to acquire] > 'haler _n_

Haleakala (,hɑːliː,ɑːkɑːˈlɑː) _n_ a volcano in Hawaii, on E Maui Island. Height: 3057 m (10 032 ft). Area of crater: 49 sq km (19 sq miles). Depth of crater: 829 m (2720 ft)

haler ('hɑːlə) _n, pl_ **-lers** _or_ **-leru** (-ləˌruː) a variant of **heller¹** (sense 1)

Halesowen (,heɪlz'əʊɪn) _n_ a town in W central England, in Dudley unitary authority, West Midlands. Pop: 55 273 (2001)

half (hɑːf) _n, pl_ **halves** (hɑːvz) **1 a** either of two equal or corresponding parts that together comprise a whole **b** a quantity equalling such a part: _half a dozen_ **2** half a pint, esp of beer **3** _Scot_ a small drink of spirits, esp whisky **4** _sport_ the half of the pitch regarded as belonging to one team **5** _golf_ an equal score on a hole or round with an opponent **6** (in various games) either of two periods of play separated by an interval (the **first half** and **second half**) **7** a half-price ticket on a bus, train, etc **8** short for **half-hour 9** short for **halfpenny** (sense 1) **10** _sport_ short for **halfback 11** _obsolete_ a half-year period **12** better half _humorous_

h

735

a person's wife or husband **13 by half** by an excessive amount or to an excessive degree: *he's too arrogant by half* **14 by halves** (used with a negative) without being thorough or exhaustive: *we don't do things by halves* **15 go halves** (often foll by *on*, *in*, etc) **a** to share the expenses (of something with one other person) **b** to share the whole amount (of something with another person): *to go halves on an orange* ▷ *determiner* **16 a** being a half or approximately a half: *half the kingdom* **b** (as pronoun; functioning as sing or plural): *half of them came* ▷ *adj* **17** not perfect or complete; partial: *he only did a half job on it* ▷ *adv* **18** to the amount or extent of a half **19** to a great amount or extent **20** partially; to an extent **21 half two**, etc *informal* 30 minutes after two o'clock **22 have half a mind to** to have the intention of **23 not half** *informal* **a** not in any way: *he's not half clever enough* **b** *Brit* really; very; indeed: *he isn't half stupid* **c** certainly; yes, indeed ▷ Related prefixes: **bi-, demi-, hemi-, semi-** [Old English *healf*; related to Old Norse *halfr*, Old High German *halb*, Dutch *half*]

half-a-crown *n* another name for a **half-crown**

half-a-dollar *n Brit slang* another name for a **half-crown**

half-and-half *n* **1** a mixture of half one thing and half another thing **2** a drink consisting of equal parts of beer and stout, or equal parts of bitter and mild ▷ *adj* **3** of half one thing and half another thing ▷ *adv* **4** in two equal parts

half-arsed *adj slang* incompetent; inept; badly organized

half-asleep *adj* neither fully asleep nor awake

half-assed *adj US and Canadian slang* **1** incompetent; inept **2** lacking efficiency or organization

half-awake *adj* not fully awake

halfback ('hɑːfˌbæk) *n* **1** *rugby* either the scrum half or the stand-off half **2** *soccer old-fashioned* any of three players positioned behind the line of forwards and in front of the fullbacks **3** any of certain similar players in other team sports **4** the position of a player who is halfback

half-baked *adj* **1** insufficiently baked **2** *informal* foolish; stupid **3** *informal* poorly planned or conceived

half-ball *n* **a** a contact in billiards, etc, in which the player aims through the centre of the cue ball to the edge of the object ball, so that half the object ball is covered **b** (as modifier): *a half-ball stroke*

halfbeak ('hɑːfˌbiːk) *n* any marine and freshwater teleost fish of the tropical and subtropical family *Hemiramphidae,* having an elongated body with a short upper jaw and a long protruding lower jaw

half-binding *n* a type of hardback bookbinding in which the spine and corners are bound in one material, such as leather, and the sides in another, such as cloth

half-blind *adj* having a limited capacity to see

half-blood *n* **1 a** the relationship between individuals having only one parent in common **b** an individual having such a relationship **2** a less common name for a **half-breed 3** a half-blooded domestic animal

half-blooded *adj* **1** being related to another individual through only one parent **2** having parents of different races **3** (of a domestic animal) having only one parent of known pedigree

half-blue *n* (at Oxford and Cambridge universities) a sportsman who substitutes for a full blue or who represents the university in a minor sport. Compare **blue** (sense 4)

half board *n* **a** the daily provision by a hotel of bed, breakfast, and one main meal **b** (as modifier): *half-board accommodation.* Also called: **demi-pension**

half-board *n* a manoeuvre by a sailing ship enabling it to gain distance to windward by luffing up into the wind

half-boot *n* a boot reaching to the midcalf

half-bottle *n* a bottle half the size of a standard bottle of wine, spirits, etc

half-bound *adj* (of a book) having a half-binding

half-breed *n* **1** *offensive* a person whose parents are of different races, esp the offspring of a White person and an American Indian ▷ *adj* also **half-bred 2** of, relating to, or designating offspring of people or animals of different races or breeds

half-brother *n* the son of either of one's parents by another partner

half-buried *adj* partially buried: *a ring half-buried in the mud*

half-butt *n* a snooker cue longer than an ordinary cue, usually used with a long rest

half-caste *n* **1** *offensive* a person having parents of different races, esp the offspring of a European and an Indian ▷ *adj* **2** of, relating to, or designating such a person

half-century *n, pl* **-ies 1** a period of 50 years: *during the past half-century* **2 a** a score or grouping of 50: *a half-century of points* **b** (as modifier): *as I near the half-century mark*

half-circle *n* **1 a** one half of a circle **b** half the circumference of a circle **2** anything having the shape or form of half a circle

half-closed *adj* partially closed: *with half-closed eyes*

half-cock *n* **1** on a single-action firearm, a halfway position in which the hammer can be set for safety; in this position the trigger is cocked by the hammer which cannot reach the primer to fire the weapon **2 go off at half-cock** or **half-cocked a** to fail as a result of inadequate preparation or premature starting **b** to act or function prematurely

half-cocked *adj* (of a firearm) at half-cock

half-completed *adj* (of a job, task, project, etc) only partially completed

half-concealed *adj* partially hidden: *little half-concealed paths*

half-conscious *adj* only partially alert and awake

half-convinced *adj* not entirely convinced

half-cooked *adj* not cooked thoroughly

half-covered *adj* partially covered or concealed

half-crown *n* a British silver or cupronickel coin worth two shillings and sixpence (now equivalent to 12½p), taken out of circulation in 1970. Also called: **half-a-crown**

half-cut *adj* **1** partially severed or divided: *half-cut citrus fruits lying around* **2** *informal* intoxicated with alcohol: *he looks half-cut already*

half-day *n* a day when one works only in the morning or only in the afternoon

half-dead *adj Brit informal* very tired

half-deserted *adj* (of a place) not having many inhabitants, visitors, etc

half-digested *adj* **1** (of food, drink, etc) partially digested **2** (of ideas, beliefs, etc) not entirely assimilated mentally: *half-digested tenets of the latest intellectual fads*

half-dollar *n* (in the US) a 50-cent piece

half-done *adj* (of a job, task, project, etc) only partially completed

half-dozen *determiner* (preceded by *a*) **a** six or a group of six: *a half-dozen roses* **b** (as pronoun; functioning as singular or plural) at least a half-dozen

half-dressed *adj* partially clothed

half-drowned *adj* nearly dead or killed by immersion in liquid: *half-drowned crewmen lay on the planks*

half-drunk *adj* partially intoxicated with alcohol

half eagle *n* a former US gold coin worth five dollars

half-eaten *adj* (of food, a meal, etc) partially consumed: *he pushed his half-eaten meal away*

half-educated *adj* not having benefited from a comprehensive education

half-empty *adj* (of a vessel, place, etc) holding or containing half its capacity

half-English *adj* having partial English citizenship through the nationality of one parent

half-filled *adj* (of a vessel, place, etc) holding or containing half its capacity

half-finished *adj* only partially completed: *a half-finished jigsaw puzzle*

half-forgotten *adj* having been nearly forgotten: *a half-forgotten dream*

half-formed *adj* not or not having been fully formed

half-forward *n Australian rules football* any of three forwards positioned between the centre line and the forward line

half frame *n* **a** a photograph taking up half the normal area of a frame on a particular film, taken esp on 35-millimetre film **b** (as modifier): *a half-frame camera*

half-frozen *adj* **1** extremely cold: *the half-frozen, but still conscious boy* **2** (of food, ice, etc) partially defrosted

half-full *adj* (of a vessel, place, etc) holding or containing half its capacity

half gainer *n* a type of dive in which the diver completes a half backward somersault to enter the water headfirst facing the diving board. Compare **gainer**

half-grown *adj* not yet fully grown

half-hardy *adj* (of a cultivated plant) able to survive out of doors except during severe frost

half-hearted *adj* without enthusiasm or determination > ˌhalf-'heartedly *adv* > ˌhalf-'heartedness *n*

half-hitch *n* a knot made by passing the end of a piece of rope around itself and through the loop thus made

half holiday *n* a day of which either the morning or the afternoon is a holiday

half-hoping *adj* having or expressing some hope

half-hour *n* **1 a** a period of 30 minutes **b** (as modifier): *a half-hour stint on the treadmill* **2 a** the point of time 30 minutes after the beginning of an hour **b** (as modifier): *a half-hour chime* > ˌhalf-'hourly *adv, adj*

half-human *adj* having half the properties of, characterizing, or relating to man and mankind

half-hunter *n* a watch with a hinged lid in which a small circular opening or crystal allows the approximate time to be read. See **hunter** (sense 5)

half-inch *n* **1** a measure of length approximately equivalent to 13 millimetres ▷ *vb* **2** *slang, old-fashioned* to steal [sense 2: from rhyming slang for PINCH to steal]

half-jack *n South African informal* a flat pocket-sized bottle of alcohol [C20 *jack*, probably from C16 *jack* a leather-covered vessel, from Old French *jaque*, of uncertain origin]

half-joking *adj* said, done, or acting in a seemingly jokey manner, but with some serious intent > ˌhalf-'jokingly *adv*

half landing *n* a landing halfway up a flight of stairs

half-leather *n* a type of half-binding in which the backs and corners of a book are bound in leather

half-length *adj* **1** (of a portrait) showing only the body from the waist up and including the hands **2** of half the entire or original length ▷ *n* **3** a half-length portrait

half-life *n* **1** the time taken for half of the atoms in a radioactive material to undergo decay. Symbol: τ **2** the time required for half of a quantity of radioactive material absorbed by a living tissue or organism to be naturally eliminated (**biological half-life**) or removed by both elimination and decay (**effective half-life**)

half-light *n* a dim light, as at dawn or dusk

half-mad *adj* **1** not entirely sane **2** extremely upset or distracted: *half-mad with fear*

half-marathon *n* a race on foot of 13 miles 352 yards (21.243 kilometres)

half-mast *n* **1** the lower than normal position to which a flag is lowered on a mast as a sign of mourning or distress ▷ *vb* **2** (tr) to put (a flag) in this position

half measure *n* (often plural) an inadequate measure

half-mile *n* **a** half a mile **b** (as modifier): *a half-mile stretch of the river*

half-miler *n* a runner who specializes in running races over half a mile or a similar metric distance

half-minute *n* **1 a** 30 seconds **b** (*as modifier*): *a half-minute lead* **2** a short period of time; moment: *I'll be a half-minute*

half-moon *n* **1** the moon at first or last quarter when half its face is illuminated **2** the time at which a half-moon occurs **3 a** something shaped like a half-moon **b** (*as modifier*): *half-moon spectacles* **4** *anatomy* a nontechnical name for **lunula**

half-mourning *n* dark grey clothes worn by some during a period after full formal mourning

half-naked *adj* partially clothed: *a half-naked body*

half-nelson *n* a wrestling hold in which a wrestler places an arm under one of his opponent's arms from behind and exerts pressure with his palm on the back of his opponent's neck. Compare **full nelson**

half-note *n* *US and Canadian* a note having the time value of half a semibreve. Also called: **minim**

half-open *adj* *chess* (of a file) having a pawn or pawns of only one colour on it

half-p *n*, *pl* **-ps** an informal name for a **halfpenny** (sense 1)

half-pedalling *n* a technique of piano playing in which the sustaining pedal is raised and immediately depressed thus allowing the lower strings to continue sounding

halfpenny *or* **ha'penny** ('heɪpnɪ; *for sense 1* 'hɑːfˌpɛnɪ) *n* **1** (*pl* **-pennies** Also called: **half** a small British coin worth half a new penny, withdrawn from circulation in 1985 **2** (*pl* **-pennies**) an old British coin worth half an old penny **3** (*pl* **-pence**) the sum represented by half a penny **4** (*pl* **-pence**) something of negligible value **5** (*modifier*) having the value or price of a halfpenny **6** (*modifier*) of negligible value

halfpennyworth *or* **ha'p'orth** ('heɪpəθ) *n* **1** an amount that may be bought for a halfpenny **2** a trifling or very small amount

half-pie *adj* *NZ informal* poorly planned or conceived. Equivalent expression (in certain other countries): **half-baked** [from Māori *pai* good]

half-pipe *n* a structure with a U-shaped cross-section, used in performing stunts in skateboarding, snowboarding, rollerblading, etc

half-plate *n* *photog* a size of plate measuring $6\frac{1}{2} \times 4\frac{3}{4}$ inches

half-price *adj*, *adv* for half the normal price: *children go half-price*

half-quartern *n* *Brit* a loaf having a weight, when baked, of 800 g

half-remembered *adj* (of a memory, idea, etc) partially remembered or recalled

half-rhyme *n* a rhyme in which the vowel sounds are not identical, such as *years* and *yours*. See **consonance** (sense 2)

half-right *adj* not entirely correct: *they were only half-right*

half-round chisel *n* a cold chisel with a semicircular cutting edge used for making narrow channels

half-round file *n* *engineering* a file having a semicircular cross-section

half-ruined *adj* badly damaged, decayed, or ruined

half seas over *adj* *Brit informal* drunk

half-second *n* **1 a** 1/120 of a minute of time **b** (*as modifier*): *a half-second lead over the Finn* **2** a very short period of time; moment

half-section *n* *engineering* a scale drawing of a section through a symmetrical object that shows only half the object

half-serious *adj* not entirely serious > ˌhalf'seriously *adv*

half silvered *adj* (of a mirror) having an incomplete reflective coating, so that half the incident light is reflected and half transmitted: used in optical instruments and two-way mirrors

half-sister *n* the daughter of either of one's parents by another partner

half-size *n* any size, esp in clothing, that is halfway between two sizes

half-slip *n* a woman's topless slip that hangs from the waist. Also called: **waist-slip**

half-smile *n* a smile that is uncertain or short-lived

half-sole *n* **1** a sole from the shank of a shoe to the toe ▷ *vb* **2** (*tr*) to replace the half-sole of (a shoe)

half-starved *adj* having been deprived of food; malnourished

half-step *n* *music, US and Canadian* another word for **semitone**

half term *n* *Brit education* **a** a short holiday midway through an academic term **b** (*as modifier*): *a half-term holiday*

half-tide *n* the state of the tide between flood and ebb

half tiger *n* *South African slang* a five-rand coin

half-timbered *or* **half-timber** *adj* (of a building, wall, etc) having an exposed timber framework filled with brick, stone, or plastered laths, as in Tudor architecture > ˌhalf-'timbering *n*

half-time *n* *sport* **a** a rest period between the two halves of a game **b** (*as modifier*): *the half-time score*

half-title *n* **1** the short title of a book as printed on the right-hand page preceding the title page **2** a title on a separate page preceding a section of a book

halftone ('hɑːfˌtəʊn) *n* **1 a** a process used to reproduce an illustration by photographing it through a fine screen to break it up into dots **b** the etched plate thus obtained **c** the print obtained from such a plate **2** *art* a tonal value midway between highlight and dark shading ▷ *adj* **3** relating to, used in, or made by halftone

half-track *n* a vehicle with caterpillar tracks on the wheels that supply motive power only > ˌhalf-ˌtracked *adj*

half-truth *n* a partially true statement intended to mislead > ˌhalf-'true *adj*

half-used *adj* having been partially used: *half-used tubes of toothpaste*

half volley *sport* ▷ *n* **1** a stroke or shot in which the ball is hit immediately after it bounces ▷ *vb* **half-volley 2** to hit or kick (a ball) immediately after it bounces

halfway (ˌhɑːf'weɪ) *adv*, *adj* **1** at or to half the distance; at or to the middle **2** in or of an incomplete manner or nature **3 meet halfway** to compromise with

halfway house *n* **1** a place to rest midway on a journey **2** the halfway point in any progression **3** a centre or hostel designed to facilitate the readjustment to private life of released prisoners, mental patients, etc **4** *Brit* a compromise: *a halfway house between fixed and floating exchange rates*

halfwit ('hɑːfˌwɪt) *n* **1** a feeble-minded person **2** a foolish or inane person > ˌhalf'witted *adj* > ˌhalf'wittedly *adv* > ˌhalf'wittedness *n*

half-year *n* **a** a period of 6 months: *the campaign lasted nearly a half-year* **b** (*as modifier*): *a half-year break*

hali- *combining form* a variant of **halo-**

halibut ('hælɪbət) *or* **holibut** ('hɒlɪbət) *n*, *pl* **-buts** *or* **-but 1** the largest flatfish, a dark green North Atlantic species, *Hippoglossus hippoglossus*, that is a very important food fish: family *Pleuronectidae* **2** any of several similar and related flatfishes, such as *Reinhardtius hippoglossoides* (**Greenland halibut**) [C15 from *hali* HOLY (because it was eaten on holy days) + *butte* flat fish, from Middle Dutch *butte*]

Haliç (ha'liːtʃ) *n* the Turkish name for the **Golden Horn**

Halicarnassian (ˌhælɪkɑː'næsɪən) *adj* of or relating to the ancient Greek city of Halicarnassus

Halicarnassus (ˌhælɪkɑː'næsəs) *n* a Greek colony on the SW coast of Asia Minor: one of the major Hellenistic cities

halide ('hælaɪd) *or* **halid** ('hælɪd) *n* **1** a binary compound containing a halogen atom or ion in combination with a more electropositive element **2** any organic compound containing halogen atoms in its molecules

halidom ('hælɪdəm) *n* *archaic* a holy place or thing [Old English *hāligdōm*; see HOLY, -DOM]

Halifax ('hælɪˌfæks) *n* **1** a port in SE Canada, capital of Nova Scotia, on the Atlantic: founded in 1749 as a British stronghold. Pop: 276 221 (2001) **2** a town in N England, in Calderdale unitary authority, West Yorkshire: textiles. Pop: 83 570 (2001)

haliplankton ('hælɪˌplæŋktən) *n* plankton living in sea water

halite ('hælaɪt) *n* a colourless or white mineral sometimes tinted by impurities, found in beds as an evaporite. It is used to produce common salt and chlorine. Composition: sodium chloride. Formula: NaCl. Crystal structure: cubic. Also called: **rock salt** [C19 from New Latin *halītes*; see HALO-, -ITE²]

halitosis (ˌhælɪ'təʊsɪs) *n* the state or condition of having bad breath [C19 New Latin, from Latin *hālitus* breath, from *hālāre* to breathe]

hall (hɔːl) *n* **1** a room serving as an entry area within a house or building **2** (*sometimes capital*) a building for public meetings **3** (*often capital*) the great house of an estate; manor **4** a large building or room used for assemblies, worship, concerts, dances, etc **5** a residential building, esp in a university; hall of residence **6 a** a large room, esp for dining, in a college or university **b** a meal eaten in this room **7** the large room of a house, castle, etc **8** *US and Canadian* a passage or corridor into which rooms open **9** (*often plural*) *informal* short for **music hall** [Old English *heall*; related to Old Norse *höll*, Old High German *halla* hall, Latin *cela* CELL¹, Old Irish *cuile* cellar, Sanskrit *śālā* hut; see HELL]

hallah (ˈxɑːlə; *Hebrew* xa'la) *n*, *pl* **-lahs** *or* **-lot** (*Hebrew* -'lɔt) a variant spelling of **challah**

Halle (*German* 'halə) *n* a city in E central Germany, in Saxony-Anhalt, on the River Saale: early saltworks; a Hanseatic city in the late Middle Ages; university (1694). Pop: 240 119 (2003 est). Official name: **Halle an der Saale** (an der 'zaːlə)

Hall effect *n* the production of a potential difference across a conductor carrying an electric current when a magnetic field is applied in a direction perpendicular to that of the current flow [named after Edwin Herbert Hall (1855–1938), American physicist who discovered it]

Hallel (*Hebrew* ha'lel; *Yiddish* hɑː'leɪl) *n* *Judaism* a section of the liturgy consisting of Psalms 113–18, read during the morning service on festivals, Chanukah, and Rosh Chodesh [C18 from Hebrew *hallēl*, from *hellēl* to praise]

hallelujah, halleluiah (ˌhælɪ'luːjə) *or* **alleluia** (ˌælɪ'luːjə) *interj* **1** an exclamation of praise to God **2** an expression of relief or a similar emotion ▷ *n* **3** an exclamation of "Hallelujah!" **4** a musical composition that uses the word *Hallelujah* as its text [C16 from Hebrew *hallelūyāh* praise the Lord, from *hellēl* to praise + *yāh* the Lord, YAHWEH]

Halley's Comet ('hælɪz) *n* a comet revolving around the sun in a period of about 76 years, last seen in 1985–86, whose return was predicted by Edmund Halley (1656–1742)

halliard ('hæljəd) *n* a variant spelling of **halyard**

hallmark ('hɔːlˌmɑːk) *n* **1** *Brit* an official series of marks, instituted by statute in 1300, and subsequently modified, stamped by the Guild of Goldsmiths at one of its assay offices on gold, silver, or platinum (since 1975) articles to guarantee purity, date of manufacture, etc **2** a mark or sign of authenticity or excellence **3** an outstanding or distinguishing feature ▷ *vb* **4** (*tr*) to stamp with or as if with a hallmark ▷ Also (for senses 1, 4): **platemark** [C18 named after Goldsmiths' Hall in London, where items were graded and stamped]

hallo (hə'ləʊ) *sentence substitute*, *n* **1** a variant spelling of **hello** ▷ *sentence substitute*, *n*, *vb* **2** a variant spelling of **halloo**

Hall of Fame *n* *chiefly US and Canadian* (*sometimes not capitals*) **1** a building containing plaques or

h

busts honouring famous people **2** a group of famous people

hall of residence *n* a residential block in or attached to a university, college, etc

halloo (həˈluː) *or* **hallo, halloa** (həˈləʊ) *sentence substitute* **1** a shout to attract attention, esp to call hounds at a hunt ▷ *n*, *pl* **-loos, -los** *or* **-loas 2** a shout of "halloo" ▷ *vb* **-loos, -looing, -looed; -los, -loing, -loed** *or* **-loas, -loaing, -loaed 3** to shout (something) to (someone) **4** (*tr*) to urge on or incite (dogs) with shouts [C16 perhaps variant of *hallow* to encourage hounds by shouting]

halloumi *or* **haloumi** (həˈluːmɪ) *n* a salty white sheep's-milk cheese from Greece or Turkey, usually eaten grilled [probably from Arabic *haluma* be mild]

hallow (ˈhæləʊ) *vb* (*tr*) **1** to consecrate or set apart as being holy **2** to venerate as being holy [Old English *hālgian*, from *hālig* HOLY] > **ˈhallower** *n*

hallowed (ˈhæləʊd; *liturgical* ˈhæləʊɪd) *adj* **1** set apart as sacred **2** consecrated or holy > **ˈhallowedness** *n*

Halloween *or* **Hallowe'en** (ˌhæləʊˈiːn) *n* the eve of All Saints' Day celebrated on Oct 31 by masquerading; Allhallows Eve [C18 see ALLHALLOWS, EVEN²]

Hallowmas *or* **Hallowmass** (ˈhæləʊˌmæs) *n archaic* the feast celebrating All Saints' Day [C14 see ALLHALLOWS, Mass]

hall stand *or esp US* **hall tree** *n* a piece of furniture on which are hung coats, hats, etc

Hallstatt (ˈhælstæt) *or* **Hallstattian** (hælˈstætɪən) *adj* of or relating to a late Bronze Age culture extending from central Europe to Britain and lasting from the 9th to the 5th century BC, characterized by distinctive burial customs, bronze and iron tools, etc [C19 named after *Hallstatt*, Austrian village where remains were found]

hallucinate (həˈluːsɪˌneɪt) *vb* (*intr*) to experience hallucinations [C17 from Latin *ālūcinārī* to wander in mind; compare Greek *aluein* to be distraught] > **halˈluciˌnator** *n*

hallucination (həˌluːsɪˈneɪʃən) *n* the alleged perception of an object when no object is present, occurring under hypnosis, in some mental disorders, etc > **halˌluciˈnational, halˈlucinative** *or* **halˈlucinatory** *adj*

hallucinogen (həˈluːsɪnəˌdʒɛn) *n* any drug, such as LSD or mescaline, that induces hallucinations

hallucinogenic (həˌluːsɪnəʊˈdʒɛnɪk) *adj* **1** (of drugs, plants, substances, etc) inducing hallucinations **2** having qualities suggestive of hallucination or hallucinogens: *strange, hallucinogenic scenes*

hallucinosis (həˌluːsɪˈnəʊsɪs) *n psychiatry* a mental disorder the symptom of which is hallucinations, commonly associated with the ingestion of alcohol or other drugs

hallux (ˈhæləks) *n* the first digit on the hind foot of a mammal, bird, reptile, or amphibian; the big toe of man [C19 New Latin, from Late Latin *allex* big toe]

hallux valgus *n* an abnormal bending or deviation of the big toe towards the other toes of the same foot

hallway (ˈhɔːlˌweɪ) *n* a hall or corridor

halm (hɔːm) *n* a variant spelling of **haulm**

halma (ˈhælmə) *n* a board game in which players attempt to transfer their pieces from their own to their opponents' bases [C19 from Greek *halma* leap, from *hallesthai* to leap]

Halmahera (ˌhælməˈhɪərə) *n* an island in NE Indonesia, the largest of the Moluccas: consists of four peninsulas enclosing three bays; mountainous and forested. Area: 17 780 sq km (6865 sq miles). Dutch name: **Djailolo, Gilolo** *or* **Jilolo**

Halmstad (*Swedish* ˈhalmstaːd) *n* a port in SW Sweden, on the Kattegat. Pop: 88 032 (2004 est)

halo (ˈheɪləʊ) *n, pl* **-loes** *or* **-los 1** a disc or ring of light around the head of an angel, saint, etc, as in

painting or sculpture **2** the aura surrounding an idealized, famous, or admired person, thing, or event **3** a circle of light around the sun or moon, caused by the refraction of light by particles of ice **4** *astronomy* a spherical cloud of stars surrounding the Galaxy and other spiral galaxies ▷ *vb* **-loes** *or* **-los, -loing, -loed 5** to surround with or form a halo [C16 from Medieval Latin, from Latin *halōs* circular threshing floor, from Greek] > **ˈhaloˌlike** *adj*

halo-, hali- *or before a vowel* **hal-** *combining form* **1** indicating salt or the sea: *halophyte* **2** relating to or containing a halogen: *halothane* [from Greek *hals, hal-* sea, salt]

halobiont (ˌhæləʊˈbaɪɒnt) *n* a plant or animal that lives in a salty environment such as the sea [C20 from HALO- + -*biont* from Greek *bios* life] > **ˌhalobiˈontic** *adj*

halo effect *n* **1** See **horns and halo effect 2** the beneficial effect on sales of a company's range of products produced by the popularity or high profile of one particular product

halogen (ˈhæləˌdʒɛn) *n* any of the chemical elements fluorine, chlorine, bromine, iodine, and astatine. They are all monovalent and readily form negative ions [C19 from Swedish; see HALO-, -GEN] > **ˈhalogenˌoid** *adj* > **halogenous** (həˈlɒdʒɪnəs) *adj*

halogenate (ˈhælədʒəˌneɪt) *vb chem* to treat or combine with a halogen > **ˌhalogenˈation** *n*

haloid (ˈhælɔɪd) *chem* ▷ *adj* **1** resembling or derived from a halogen: *a haloid salt* ▷ *n* **2** a compound containing halogen atoms in its molecules; halide

halon (ˈhælɒn) *n* any of a class of chemical compounds derived from hydrocarbons by replacing one or more hydrogen atoms by bromine atoms and other hydrogen atoms by other halogen atoms (chlorine, fluorine, or iodine). Halons are stable compounds that are used in fire extinguishers, although they may contribute to depletion of the ozone layer

halophile (ˈhæləʊˌfaɪl) *n* an organism that thrives in an extremely salty environment, such as the Dead Sea > **ˌhaloˈphilic** *adj*

halophyte (ˈhæləʊˌfaɪt) *n* a plant that grows in very salty soil, as in a salt marsh > **halophytic** (ˌhæləˈfɪtɪk) *adj* > **ˈhaloˌphytism** *n*

halosere (ˈhæləʊˌsɪə) *n ecology* a plant community that originates and develops in conditions of high salinity

halothane (ˈhæləˌθeɪn) *n* a colourless volatile slightly soluble liquid with an odour resembling that of chloroform; 2-bromo-2-chloro-1,1,1-trifluoroethane: a general anaesthetic. Formula: $CF_3CHBrCl$ [C20 from HALO- + -*thane*, as in METHANE]

haloumi (həˈluːmɪ) *n* a variant spelling of **halloumi**

Hälsingborg (*Swedish* hɛlsɪŋˈbɔrj) *n* the former name (until 1971) of **Helsingborg**

halt¹ (hɔːlt) *n* **1** an interruption or end to activity, movement, or progress **2** *chiefly Brit* a minor railway station, without permanent buildings **3 call a halt (to)** to put an end (to something); stop ▷ *n* ▷ *sentence substitute* **4** a command to halt, esp as an order when marching ▷ *vb* **5** to come or bring to a halt [C17 from the phrase *to make halt*, translation of German *halt machen*, from *halten* to HOLD¹, STOP]

halt² (hɔːlt) *vb* (*intr*) **1** (esp of logic or verse) to falter or be defective **2** to waver or be unsure **3** *archaic* to be lame ▷ *adj* **4** *archaic* **a** lame **b** (*as collective noun; preceded by the*): *the halt* ▷ *n* **5** *archaic* lameness [Old English *healt* lame; related to Old Norse *haltr*, Old High German *halz* lame, Greek *kólos* maimed, Old Slavonic *kladivo* hammer]

halter (ˈhɔːltə) *n* **1** a rope or canvas headgear for a horse, usually with a rope for leading **2** Also called: **halterneck** a style of woman's top fastened behind the neck and waist, leaving the back and arms bare **3** a rope having a noose for hanging a

person **4** death by hanging ▷ *vb* (*tr*) **5** to secure with a halter or put a halter on **6** to hang (someone) [Old English *hælfter*; related to Old High German *halftra*, Middle Dutch *heliftra*]

haltere (ˈhæltɪə) *or* **halter** (ˈhæltə) *n*, *pl* **halteres** (hælˈtɪəriːz) one of a pair of short projections in dipterous insects that are modified hind wings, used for maintaining equilibrium during flight. Also called: **balancer** [C18 from Greek *haltēres* (plural) hand-held weights used as balancers or to give impetus in leaping, from *hallesthai* to leap]

halting (ˈhɔːltɪŋ) *adj* **1** hesitant: *halting speech* **2** lame > **ˈhaltingly** *adv* > **ˈhaltingness** *n*

Halton (ˈhɔːltən) *n* a unitary authority in NW England, in N Cheshire. Pop: 118 400 (2003 est). Area: 75 sq km (29 sq miles)

halutz *Hebrew* (xaˈluts; *English* haːˈluts) *n* a variant spelling of **chalutz**

halvah, halva (ˈhælvaː) *or* **halavah** (ˈhæləvaː) *n* an Eastern Mediterranean, Middle Eastern, or Indian sweetmeat made of honey and containing sesame seeds, nuts, rose water, saffron, etc [from Yiddish *halva*, from Romanian, from Turkish *helve*, from Arabic *halwā* sweetmeat]

halve (haːv) *vb* (*tr*) **1** to divide into two approximately equal parts **2** to share equally **3** to reduce by half, as by cutting **4** *golf* to take the same number of strokes on (a hole or round) as one's opponent [Old English *hielfan*; related to Middle High German *helben*; see HALF]

halyard *or* **halliard** (ˈhæljəd) *n nautical* a line for hoisting or lowering a sail, flag, or spar [C14 *halier*, influenced by YARD¹; see HALE²]

ham¹ (hæm) *n* **1** the part of the hindquarters of a pig or similar animal between the hock and the hip **2** the meat of this part, esp when salted or smoked **3** *informal* **a** the back of the leg above the knee **b** the space or area behind the knee **4** *needlework* a cushion used for moulding curves [Old English *hamm*; related to Old High German *hamma* haunch, Old Irish *cnáim* bone, *camm* bent, Latin *camur* bent]

ham² (hæm) *n* **1** *theatre informal* **a** an actor who overacts or relies on stock gestures or mannerisms **b** overacting or clumsy acting **c** (*as modifier*): *a ham actor* **2** *informal* **a** a licensed amateur radio operator **b** (*as modifier*): *a ham licence* ▷ *vb* **hams, hamming, hammed 3** *informal* to overact [C19 special use of HAM¹; in some senses probably influenced by AMATEUR]

Hama (ˈhaːmaː) *n* a city in W Syria, on the Orontes River: an early Hittite settlement; famous for its huge water wheels, used for irrigation since the Middle Ages. Pop: 439 000 (2005 est). Biblical name: **Hamath**

Hamadān *or* **Hamedān** (ˈhæməˌdæn) *n* city in W central Iran, at an altitude of over 1830 m (6000 ft): changed hands several times from the 17th century between Iraq, Persia, and Turkey; trading centre. Pop: 508 000 (2005 est)

hamadryad (ˌhæməˈdraɪəd, -æd) *n* **1** *classical myth* one of a class of nymphs, each of which inhabits a tree and dies with it **2** another name for **king cobra** [C14 from Latin *Hamādryas*, from Greek *Hamadruas*, from *hama* together with + *drus* tree; see DRYAD]

hamadryas (ˌhæməˈdraɪəs) *n* a baboon, *Papio* (or *Comopithecus*) *hamadryas*, of Arabia and NE Africa, having long silvery hair on the head, neck, and chest: regarded as sacred by the ancient Egyptians: family *Cercopithecidae*. Also called: **hamadryas baboon, sacred baboon** [C19 via New Latin from Latin; see HAMADRYAD]

hamal, hammal *or* **hamaul** (həˈmaːl) *n* (in Middle Eastern countries) a porter, bearer, or servant [from Arabic *hamala* to carry]

Hamamatsu (ˌhæməˈmætsuː) *n* a city in central Japan, in S central Honshu: cotton textiles and musical instruments. Pop: 573 504 (2002 est)

hamamelidaceous (ˌhæməˌmiːlɪˈdeɪʃəs, -ˌmɛlɪ-) *adj* of, relating to, or belonging to the *Hamamelidaceae*, a chiefly subtropical family of trees and shrubs that includes the witch hazel [c19 from New Latin *Hamamelis* type genus, from Greek: medlar, from *hama* together with + *mēlon* fruit]

hamamelis (ˌhæməˈmiːlɪs) *n* any of several trees or shrubs constituting the hamameliaceous genus *Hamamelis*, native to E Asia and North America and cultivated as ornamentals ▷ See **witch hazel**

hamartia (həˈmɑːtɪə) *n literature* the flaw in character which leads to the downfall of the protagonist in a tragedy [c19 from Greek]

hamartiology (həˌmɑːtɪˈɒlədʒɪ) *n* the doctrine of sin in Christian theology [c19 from Greek *hamartia* sin + -LOGY]

Hamas (ˈhæmæs) *n* an organization founded in 1987 with the aim of establishing an Islamic state in Palestine [c20 Arabic: zeal; also an acronym for *haraka muqawama islamya* Islamic Armed Movement]

hamate (ˈheɪmeɪt) *adj rare* hook-shaped [c18 from Latin *hāmātus*, from *hāmus* hook]

hamba (ˈhæmbə) *interj South African usually offensive* go away; be off [from Nguni *ukuttamba* to go]

hamba kahle (ˈhæmbə ˈɡɑːʃlɪ) *sentence substitute* goodbye, farewell (esp to the dead) [from Xhosa, literally: go well]

Hambletonian (ˌhæmbᵊlˈtəʊnɪən) *n* one of a breed of trotting horses descended from a stallion of that name

Hamburg (ˈhæmbɜːɡ) *n* a city-state and port in NW Germany, on the River Elbe: the largest port in Germany; a founder member of the Hanseatic League; became a free imperial city in 1510 and a state of the German empire in 1871; university (1919); extensive shipyards. Pop: 1 734 083 (2003 est)

hamburger (ˈhæmˌbɜːɡə) *or* **hamburg** *n* a flat fried cake of minced beef, often served in a bread roll. Also called: Hamburger steak, beefburger [c20 shortened from *Hamburger steak* (that is, steak in the fashion of HAMBURG)]

hame[1] (heɪm) *n* either of the two curved bars holding the traces of the harness, attached to the collar of a draught animal [c14 from Middle Dutch *hame*; related to Middle High German *hame* fishing rod]

hame[2] (hem) *n, adv* a Scot word for **home**

Hameln (German ˈhaːməln) *n* an industrial town in N Germany, in Lower Saxony on the Weser River: famous for the legend of the Pied Piper (supposedly took place in 1284). Pop: 58 902 (2003 est). English name: Hamelin (ˈhæməlɪn, ˈhæmlɪn)

Hamersley Range (ˈhæməzlɪ) *n* a mountain range in N Western Australia: iron-ore deposits. Highest peak: 1236 m (4056 ft)

hames (heɪmz) *n* make a hames of *Irish informal* to spoil through clumsiness or ineptitude [of unknown origin]

ham-fisted *or* **ham-handed** *adj informal* lacking dexterity or elegance; clumsy

Hamhung *or* **Hamheung** (ˈhɑːmˈhʊŋ) *n* an industrial city in central North Korea: commercial and governmental centre of NE Korea during the Yi dynasty (1392–1910). Pop: 753 000 (2005 est)

Hamilton (ˈhæməltən) *n* **1** a port in central Canada, in S Ontario on Lake Ontario: iron and steel industry. Pop: 618 820 (2001) **2** a city in New Zealand, on central North Island. Pop: 129 300 (2004 est) **3** a town in S Scotland, in South Lanarkshire near Glasgow. Pop: 48 546 (2001) **4** the capital and chief port of Bermuda. Pop: 3461 (2000) **5** the former name of the **Churchill** River in Labrador

Hamiltonian (ˌhæməlˈtəʊnɪən) *physics, maths* ▷ *n* **1** a mathematical function of the coordinates and momenta of a system of particles used to express their equations of motion **2** a mathematical operator that generates such a function. Symbol: H ▷ *adj* **3** denoting or relating to the Irish mathematician Sir William Rowan Hamilton (1805–65), or to the theory of mechanics or

mathematical operator devised by him

Hamiltonstovare (ˌhæmɪltənˌstəˈvɑːrɪ) *n* a large strong short-haired breed of hound with a black, brown, and white coat [c20 named after Count Adolf Patrik *Hamilton*, the founder of the Swedish Kennel Club, who created the breed in the 1880s]

Hamite (ˈhæmaɪt) *n* a member of a group of peoples of N Africa supposedly descended from Noah's son Ham (Genesis 5:32, 10:6), including the ancient Egyptians, the Berbers, etc

Hamitic (hæˈmɪtɪk, hə-) *n* **1** a group of N African languages related to Semitic. They are now classified in four separate subfamilies of the Afro-Asiatic family: Egyptian, Berber, Cushitic, and Chadic ▷ *adj* **2** denoting, relating to, or belonging to this group of languages **3** denoting, belonging to, or characteristic of the Hamites

Hamito-Semitic *n* **1** a former name for the **Afro-Asiatic** family of languages ▷ *adj* **2** denoting or belonging to this family of languages

hamlet (ˈhæmlɪt) *n* **1** a small village or group of houses **2** (in Britain) a village without its own church [c14 from Old French *hamelet*, diminutive of *hamel*, from *ham*, of Germanic origin; compare Old English *hamm* plot of pasture, Low German *hamm* enclosed land; see HOME]

Hamm (German ham) *n* an industrial city in NW Germany, in North Rhine-Westphalia: a Hanse town from 1417; severely damaged in World War II. Pop: 184 961 (2003 est)

hammam (hʌmˈɑːm) *n* a bathing establishment, such as a Turkish bath [Arabic: literally, bath]

hammer (ˈhæmə) *n* **1** a hand tool consisting of a heavy usually steel head held transversely on the end of a handle, used for driving in nails, beating metal, etc **2** any tool or device with a similar function, such as the moving part of a door knocker, the striking head on a bell, etc **3** a power-driven striking tool, esp one used in forging. A **pneumatic hammer** delivers a repeated blow from a pneumatic ram, a **drop hammer** uses the energy of a falling weight **4** a part of a gunlock that rotates about a fulcrum to strike the primer or percussion cap, either directly or via a firing pin **5** *athletics* **a** a heavy metal ball attached to a flexible wire: thrown in competitions **b** the event or sport of throwing the hammer **6** an auctioneer's gavel **7** a device on a piano that is made to strike a string or group of strings causing them to vibrate **8** *anatomy* the nontechnical name for **malleus** **9** *curling* the last stone thrown in an end **10** go (*or* come) under the hammer to be offered for sale by an auctioneer **11** hammer and tongs with great effort or energy: *fighting hammer and tongs* **12** on someone's hammer *Austral and NZ slang* **a** persistently demanding and critical of someone **b** in hot pursuit of someone ▷ *vb* **13** to strike or beat (a nail, wood, etc) with or as if with a hammer **14** (*tr*) to shape or fashion with or as if with a hammer **15** (*tr*; foll by *in* or *into*) to impress or force (facts, ideas, etc) into (someone) through constant repetition **16** (*intr*) to feel or sound like hammering: *his pulse was hammering* **17** (*intr*; often foll by *away*) to work at constantly **18** (*tr*) *Brit* **a** to question in a relentless manner **b** to criticize severely **19** *informal* to inflict a defeat on **20** (*tr*) *slang* to beat, punish, or chastise **21** (*tr*) *stock exchange* **a** to announce the default of (a member) **b** to cause prices of (securities, the market, etc) to fall by bearish selling ▷ See also **hammer out** [Old English *hamor*; related to Old Norse *hamarr* crag, Old High German *hamar* hammer, Old Slavonic *kamy* stone]
> ˈhammerer *n* > ˈhammer-ˌlike *adj*

hammer and sickle *n* **1** the emblem on the flag of the former Soviet Union, representing the industrial workers and the peasants respectively **2** a symbolic representation of the former Soviet Union or of Communism in general

hammer beam *n* either of a pair of short horizontal beams that project from opposite walls to support arched braces and struts

hammer blow *n* **1** a blow from a hammer **2** a severe shock or setback: *Liam's death was a hammer blow*

hammer drill *n* **1** a rock drill operated by compressed air in which the boring bit is not attached to the reciprocating piston **2** an electric hand drill providing hammering in addition to rotating action

Hammerfest (Norwegian ˈhamərfest) *n* a port in N Norway, on the W coast of Kvalöy Island: the northernmost town in Europe, with uninterrupted daylight from May 17 to July 29 and no sun between Nov 21 and Jan 21; fishing and tourist centre. Pop: 9157 (2004 est)

hammerhead (ˈhæməˌhed) *n* **1** any shark of the genus *Sphyrna* and family *Sphyrnidae*, having a flattened hammer-shaped head **2** a heavily built tropical African wading bird, *Scopus umbretta*, related to the herons, having a dark plumage and a long backward-pointing crest: family *Scopidae*, order *Ciconiiformes* **3** a large African fruit bat, *Hypsignathus monstrosus*, with a large square head and hammer-shaped muzzle
> ˈhammerˌheaded *adj*

hammerless (ˈhæməlɪs) *adj* (of a firearm) having the hammer enclosed so that it is not visible

hammerlock (ˈhæməˌlɒk) *n* a wrestling hold in which a wrestler twists his opponent's arm upwards behind his back

hammer out *vb* (*tr, adverb*) **1** to shape or remove with or as if with a hammer **2** to form or produce (an agreement, plan, etc) after much discussion or dispute

hammer price *n* the price offered as the winning bid in a public auction

Hammersmith and Fulham (ˈhæməˌsmɪθ) *n* a borough of Greater London on the River Thames: established in 1965 by the amalgamation of Fulham and Hammersmith. Pop: 174 200 (2003 est). Area: 16 sq km (6 sq miles)

hammerstone (ˈhæməˌstəʊn) *n* a stone used as a hammer in the production of tools during the Acheulian period

hammertoe (ˈhæməˌtəʊ) *n* **1** a deformity of the bones of a toe causing the toe to be bent in a clawlike arch **2** such a toe

hammock[1] (ˈhæmək) *n* a length of canvas, net, etc, suspended at the ends and used as a bed [c16 from Spanish *hamaca*, of Taino origin]
> ˈhammock-ˌlike *adj*

hammock[2] (ˈhæmək) *n* a variant of **hummock** (sense 3)

Hammond (ˈhæmənd) *n* a city in NW Indiana, adjacent to Chicago. Pop: 80 547 (2003 est)

Hammond organ *n trademark* an electric organ with two keyboards, electronic tone generation, and a wide variety of tone colours: invented in 1934 [c20 named after Laurens *Hammond* (1895–1973), US mechanical engineer]

hammy (ˈhæmɪ) *adj* -mier, -miest *informal* **1** (of an actor) overacting or tending to overact **2** (of a play, performance, etc) overacted or exaggerated

hamper[1] (ˈhæmpə) *vb* **1** (*tr*) to prevent the progress or free movement of **2** *nautical* gear aboard a vessel that, though essential, is often in the way [c14 of obscure origin; perhaps related to Old English *hamm* enclosure, *hemm* HEM[1]]
> ˈhamperedness *n* > ˈhamperer *n*

hamper[2] (ˈhæmpə) *n* **1** a large basket, usually with a cover **2** *Brit* such a basket and its contents, usually food **3** *US* a laundry basket [c14 variant of HANAPER]

Hampshire (ˈhæmpʃɪə, -ʃə) *n* a county of S England, on the English Channel: crossed by the Hampshire Downs and the South Downs, with the New Forest in the southwest and many prehistoric and Roman remains: the geographical and ceremonial county includes Portsmouth and Southampton, which became independent unitary authorities in 1997. Administrative centre: Winchester. Pop (excluding unitary authorities): 1 251 000 (2003 est). Area (excluding unitary

h

authorities): 3679 sq km (1420 sq miles). Abbreviation: **Hants**

Hampshire Down *n* a breed of stocky sheep having a dark face and dense close wool, originating from Hampshire, S England

Hampstead ('hæmpstɪd) *n* a residential district in N London: part of the Greater London borough of Camden since 1965; nearby is **Hampstead Heath**, a popular recreation area

Hampton ('hæmptən) *n* **1** a city in SE Virginia, on the harbour of **Hampton Roads** on Chesapeake Bay. Pop: 146 878 (2003 est) **2** a district of the Greater London borough of Richmond-upon-Thames, on the River Thames: famous for **Hampton Court Palace** (built in 1515 by Cardinal Wolsey)

hamshackle ('hæmˌʃækᵊl) *vb* (*tr*) to hobble (a cow, horse, etc) by tying a rope around the head and one of the legs

hamster ('hæmstə) *n* any Eurasian burrowing rodent of the tribe *Cricetini*, such as *Mesocricetus auratus* (**golden hamster**), having a stocky body, short tail, and cheek pouches: family *Cricetidae*. They are popular pets [C17 from German, from Old High German *hamustro*, of Slavic origin]

hamstring ('hæmˌstrɪŋ) *n* **1** *anatomy* any of the tendons at the back of the knee. Related adj: **popliteal 2** the large tendon at the back of the hock in the hind leg of a horse, etc ▷ *vb* -**strings**, -**stringing**, -**strung** (*tr*) **3** to cripple by cutting the hamstring of **4** to ruin or thwart [C16 HAM¹ + STRING]

hamulus ('hæmjʊləs) *n, pl* -**li** (-ˌlaɪ) *biology* a hook or hooklike process at the end of some bones or between the fore and hind wings of a bee or similar insect [C18 from Latin: a little hook, from *hāmus* hook] > 'hamular, 'hamuˌlate, 'hamuˌlose or 'hamulous *adj*

hamza or **hamzah** ('hɑːmzɑː, -zə) *n* the sign used in Arabic to represent the glottal stop [from Arabic *hamzah*, literally: a compression]

Han¹ (hæn) *n* a river in E central China, rising in S Shaanxi and flowing southeast through Hubei to the Yangtze River at Wuhan. Length: about 1450 km (900 miles)

Han² (hæn) *n* the Chinese people as contrasted to Mongols, Manchus, etc

hanaper ('hænəpə) *n* a small wickerwork basket, often used to hold official papers [C15 from Old French *hanapier*, from *hanap* cup, of Germanic origin; compare Old High German *hnapf* bowl, Old English *hnæp*]

Hanau (German 'haːnau) *n* a city in central Germany, in Hesse east of Frankfurt am Main: a centre of the jewellery industry. Pop: 88 897 (2003 est)

hance (hæns) *n* a variant of **haunch** (sense 3)

Han Cities *pl n* a group of three cities in E central China, in SE Hubei at the confluence of the Han and Yangtze Rivers: Hanyang, Hankow, and Wuchang; united in 1950 to form the conurbation of Wuhan, the capital of Hubei province

hand (hænd) *n* **1 a** the prehensile part of the body at the end of the arm, consisting of a thumb, four fingers, and a palm **b** the bones of this part. Related adj: **manual 2** the corresponding or similar part in animals **3** something resembling this in shape or function **4 a** the cards dealt to one or all players in one round of a card game **b** a player holding such cards **c** one round of a card game **5** agency or influence: *the hand of God* **6** a part in something done: *he had a hand in the victory* **7** assistance: *to give someone a hand with his work* **8** a pointer on a dial, indicator, or gauge, esp on a clock: *the minute hand* **9** acceptance or pledge of partnership, as in marriage: *he asked for her hand; he gave me his hand on the merger* **10** a position or direction indicated by its location to the side of an object or the observer: *on the right hand; on every hand* **11** a contrastive aspect, condition, etc (in the phrases **on the one hand, on the other hand**) **12** (preceded by an ordinal number) source or origin:

a story heard at third hand **13** a person, esp one who creates something: *a good hand at painting* **14** a labourer or manual worker: *we've just taken on a new hand at the farm* **15** a member of a ship's crew: *all hands on deck* **16** *printing* another name for **index** (sense 9) **17** a person's handwriting: *the letter was in his own hand* **18** a round of applause: *give him a hand* **19** ability or skill: *a hand for woodwork* **20** a manner or characteristic way of doing something: *the hand of a master* **21** a unit of length measurement equalling four inches, used for measuring the height of horses, usually from the front hoof to the withers **22** a cluster or bundle, esp of bananas **23** a shoulder of pork **24** one of the two possible mirror-image forms of an asymmetric object, such as the direction of the helix in a screw thread **25 a free hand** freedom to do as desired **26 a hand's turn** (*usually used with a negative*) a small amount of work: *he hasn't done a hand's turn* **27 a heavy hand** tyranny, persecution, or oppression: *he ruled with a heavy hand* **28 a high hand** an oppressive or dictatorial manner **29** (*near*) **at hand** very near or close, esp in time **30 at someone's hand(s)** from: *the acts of kindness received at their hands* **31 by hand a** by manual rather than mechanical means **b** by messenger or personally: *the letter was delivered by hand* **32 come to hand** to become available; be received **33 force someone's hand** to force someone to act **34 from hand to hand** from one person to another **35 from hand to mouth a** in poverty: *living from hand to mouth* **b** without preparation or planning **36 hand and foot** in all ways possible; completely: *they waited on him hand and foot* **37 hand in glove** in an intimate relationship or close association **38 hand in hand a** together; jointly **b** clasping each other's hands **39 hand over fist** steadily and quickly; with rapid progress: *he makes money hand over fist* **40 hold one's hand** to stop or postpone a planned action or punishment **41 hold someone's hand** to support, help, or guide someone, esp by giving sympathy or moral support **42 in hand a** in possession **b** under control **c** receiving attention or being acted on **d** available for use; in reserve **e** with deferred payment: *he works a week in hand* **43 keep one's hand in** to continue or practise **44 lend a hand** to help **45 on hand** close by; present: *I'll be on hand to help you* **46 out of hand a** beyond control **b** without reservation or deeper examination: *he condemned him out of hand* **47 set one's hand to a** to sign (a document) **b** to start (a task or undertaking) **48 show one's hand** to reveal one's stand, opinion, or plans **49 take in hand** to discipline; control **50 throw one's hand in** See **throw in** (sense 3) **51 to hand** accessible **52 try one's hand** to attempt to do something **53** (*modifier*) **a** of or involving the hand: *a hand grenade* **b** made to be carried in or worn on the hand: *hand luggage* **c** operated by hand: *a hand drill* **54** (*in combination*) made by hand rather than by a machine: *hand-sewn* ▷ *vb* (*tr*) **55** to transmit or offer by the hand or hands **56** to help or lead with the hand **57** *nautical* to furl (a sail) **58 hand it to someone** to give credit to someone ▷ See also **hand down, hand in, hand-off, hand on, hand-out, hand over, hands** [Old English *hand*; related to Old Norse *hönd*, Gothic *handus*, Old High German *hant*] > 'handless *adj* > 'handˌlike *adj*

HAND *text messaging abbreviation for* have a nice day

handba' ('handbɔː, -baː) *n Scot* another name for **ba'** (sense 2)

handbag ('hændˌbæg) *n* **1** Also called: **bag, purse** (US and Canadian), **pocketbook** (chiefly US) a woman's small bag carried to contain personal articles **2** a small suitcase that can be carried by hand **3** a commercial style of House music [(for sense 3) C20 humorous allusion to the trend for groups of women to dance round their handbags in discos, nightclubs, etc]

handbags ('hændˌbægz) *pl n facetious* an incident in which people, esp sportsmen, fight or threaten to fight, but without real intent to inflict harm

(esp in the phrases **handbags at dawn, handbags at twenty paces,** etc)

handball ('hændˌbɔːl) *n* **1** a game in which two teams of seven players try to throw a ball into their opponent's goal **2** a game in which two or four people strike a ball against a wall or walls with the hand, usually gloved **3** the small hard rubber ball used in this game **4** *soccer* the offence committed when a player other than a goalkeeper in his own penalty area touches the ball with a hand ▷ *vb* **5** *Australian rules football* to pass (the ball) with a blow of the fist > 'handˌballer *n*

handbarrow ('hændˌbærəʊ) *n* a flat tray for transporting loads, usually carried by two men

handbell ('hændˌbel) *n* a bell rung by hand, esp one of a tuned set used in musical performance

handbill ('hændˌbɪl) *n* a small printed notice for distribution by hand

handbook ('hændˌbʊk) *n* a reference book listing brief facts on a subject or place or directions for maintenance or repair, as of a car: *a tourists' handbook*

handbrake ('hændˌbreɪk) *n* **1** a brake operated by a hand lever **2** the lever that operates the handbrake

handbrake turn *n* a turn sharply reversing the direction of a vehicle by speedily applying the handbrake while turning the steering wheel

handbreadth ('hændˌbretθ, -ˌbredθ) or **hand's-breadth** *n* the width of a hand used as an indication of length

h and c *abbreviation for* hot and cold (water)

handcart ('hændˌkɑːt) *n* a simple cart, usually with one or two wheels, pushed or drawn by hand

handclasp ('hændˌklɑːsp) *n US* another word for **handshake**

handcraft ('hændˌkrɑːft) *n* **1** another word for **handicraft** ▷ *vb* **2** (*tr*) to make by handicraft

handcrafted ('hændˌkrɑːftɪd) *adj* made by handicraft

handcuff ('hændˌkʌf) *vb* **1** (*tr*) to put handcuffs on (a person); manacle ▷ *n* **2** (*plural*) a pair of locking metal rings joined by a short bar or chain for securing prisoners, etc

hand down *vb* (*tr, adverb*) **1** to leave to a later period or generation; bequeath **2** to pass (an outgrown garment) on from one member of a family to a younger one **3** *law* to announce or deliver (a verdict)

-handed *adj* **1** having a hand or hands as specified: *broad-handed; a four-handed game of cards* **2** made as specified for either left- or right-hand operation or positioning

handedness ('hændɪdnɪs) *n* **1** the tendency to use one hand more skilfully or in preference to the other **2** the property of some chemical substances of rotating the plane of polarized light in one direction rather than another. See also **dextrorotation, laevorotation 3** the relation between the vectors of spin and momentum of neutrinos and certain other elementary particles. See also **helicity**

handfast ('hændˌfɑːst) *archaic* ▷ *n* **1** an agreement, esp of marriage, confirmed by a handshake **2** a firm grip ▷ *vb* (*tr*) **3** to betroth or marry (two persons or another person) by joining the hands **4** to grip with the hand

handfasting ('hændˌfɑːstɪŋ) *n* **1** an archaic word for **betrothal 2** (formerly) a kind of trial marriage marked by the formal joining of hands

handfeed ('hændˌfiːd) *vb* -**feeds**, -**feeding**, -**fed** (-ˌfed) (*tr*) **1** to feed (a person or an animal) by hand **2** *agriculture* to give food to (poultry or livestock) in fixed amounts and at fixed times, rather than use a self-feeding system

hand, foot, and mouth disease *n* a usually mild disease, mainly affecting children under seven, in which the sufferers develop mouth ulcers accompanied by blisters or rashes on their hands and feet. Caused by the Coxsackie virus A16, it has no known cure. Abbreviation: HFMD

handful ('hændfʊl) *n, pl* -**fuls 1** the amount or

number that can be held in the hand **2** a small number or quantity **3** *informal* a person or thing difficult to manage or control

hand glass *n* **1** a magnifying glass with a handle **2** a small mirror with a handle **3** a small glazed frame for seedlings or plants

hand grenade *n* a small metal or plastic canister containing explosives, usually activated by a short fuse and used in close combat

handgrip ('hænd,grɪp) *n* **1** another word for **grip¹** (senses 2, 5, 6) **2** *sport* a covering, usually of towelling or rubber, that makes the handle of a racket or club easier to hold

handgun ('hænd,gʌn) *n* a firearm that can be held, carried, and fired with one hand, such as a pistol

hand-held *adj* **1** held in position by the hand **2** (of a film camera) held rather than mounted, as in close-up action shots **3** (of a computer) able to be held in the hand and not requiring connection to a fixed power source ▷ *n* **4** a computer that can be held in the hand

handhold ('hænd,həʊld) *n* **1** an object, crevice, etc, that can be used as a grip or support, as in climbing **2** a grip with the hand or hands

handicap ('hændɪ,kæp) *n* **1** something that hampers or hinders **2 a** a contest, esp a race, in which competitors are given advantages or disadvantages of weight, distance, time, etc, in an attempt to equalize their chances of winning **b** the advantage or disadvantage prescribed **3** *golf* the number of strokes by which a player's averaged score exceeds the standard scratch score for the particular course: used as the basis for handicapping in competitive play **4** any physical disability or disadvantage resulting from physical, mental, or social impairment or abnormality ▷ *vb* **-caps, -capping, -capped** (*tr*) **5** to be a hindrance or disadvantage to **6** to assign a handicap or handicaps to **7** to organize (a contest) by handicapping **8** *US and Canadian* **a** to attempt to forecast the winner of (a contest, esp a horse race) **b** to assign odds for or against (a contestant) [c17 probably from *hand in cap*, a lottery game in which players drew forfeits from a cap or deposited money in it] > '**handi,capper** *n*

handicapped ('hændɪ,kæpt) *adj* **1** physically disabled **2** *psychol* denoting a person whose social behaviour or emotional reactions are in some way impaired **3** (of a competitor) assigned a handicap

USAGE Many disabled people find the use of the word *handicapped* to describe them, or their condition, offensive. See at **disabled**

handicapper ('hændɪ,kæpə) *n* **1** an official appointed to assign handicaps to competitors in such sports as golf and horse racing **2** a newspaper columnist employed to estimate the chances that horses have of winning races

handicap register *n social welfare* (in Britain) **1** a list of the disabled people in its area that a local authority has a duty to compile under the Chronically Sick and Disabled Persons Act 1970. Eligibility for certain welfare benefits may depend on registration **2** a different list of disabled people, kept by the Manpower Services Commission for employment purposes. See also **green card, registered disabled**

handicraft ('hændɪ,krɑːft) *n* **1** skill or dexterity in working with the hands **2** a particular skill or art performed with the hands, such as weaving, pottery, etc **3** the work produced by such a skill or art: *local handicraft is on sale.* Also called: **handcraft** [c15 changed from HANDCRAFT through the influence of HANDIWORK, which was analysed as if HANDY + WORK] > '**handi,craftsman** *n*

handily ('hændɪlɪ) *adv* **1** in a handy way or manner **2** conveniently or suitably: *handily nearby* **3** *US and Canadian* easily: *the horse won handily*

hand in *vb* (*tr, adverb*) to return or submit (something, such as an examination paper)

handism ('hænd,ɪzəm) *n* discriminination

against people on the grounds of whether they are left-handed or right-handed

handiwork ('hændɪ,wɜːk) *n* **1** work performed or produced by hand, such as embroidery or pottery **2** the result of the action or endeavours of a person or thing [Old English *handgeweorc*, from HAND + *geweorc*, from *ge-* (collective prefix) + *weorc* WORK]

handkerchief ('hæŋkətʃɪf, -tʃiːf) *n* a small square of soft absorbent material, such as linen, silk, or soft paper, carried and used to wipe the nose, etc

hand-knit *adj also* **hand-knitted 1** knitted by hand, not on a machine ▷ *vb* **-knits, -knitting, -knitted** *or* **-knit 2** to knit (garments) by hand

handlanger ('hænd,læŋə) *n South African* **1** an unskilled assistant to a tradesman **2** *informal* a friend; sidekick [from Dutch]

handle ('hændəl) *n* **1** the part of a utensil, drawer, etc, designed to be held in order to move, use, or pick up the object **2** NZ a glass beer mug with a handle **3** *slang* a person's name or title **4** a CB radio slang name for **call sign 5** an opportunity, reason, or excuse for doing something: *his background served as a handle for their mockery* **6** the quality, as of textiles, perceived by touching or feeling **7** the total amount of a bet on a horse race or similar event **8 fly off the handle** *informal* to become suddenly extremely angry ▷ *vb* (*mainly tr*) **9** to pick up and hold, move, or touch with the hands **10** to operate or employ using the hands: *the boy handled the reins well* **11** to have power or control over: *my wife handles my investments* **12** to manage successfully: *a secretary must be able to handle clients* **13** to discuss (a theme, subject, etc) **14** to deal with or treat in a specified way: *I was handled with great tact* **15** to trade or deal in (specified merchandise) **16** (*intr*) to react or respond in a specified way to operation or control: *the car handles well on bends* [Old English; related to Old Saxon *handlon* (vb), Old High German *hantilla* towel] > '**handleable** *adj* > '**handled** *adj* > '**handleless** *adj*

handlebar moustache *n* a bushy extended moustache with curled ends that resembles handlebars

handlebars ('hændəl,bɑːz) *pl n* (*sometimes singular*) a metal tube having its ends curved to form handles, used for steering a bicycle, motorcycle, etc

handler ('hændlə) *n* **1** a person, esp a police officer, in charge of a specially trained dog **2** a person who handles some specified thing: *a baggage handler* **3** a person who holds or incites a dog, gamecock, etc, esp in a race or contest **4** the trainer or second of a boxer

handling ('hændlɪŋ) *n* **1** the act or an instance of picking up, turning over, or touching something **2** treatment, as of a theme in literature **3 a** the process by which a commodity is packaged, transported, etc **b** (*as modifier*): *handling charges* **4** *law* the act of receiving property that one knows or believes to be stolen

hand-loomed *adj* (of a garment) made on a hand loom

handmade (,hænd'meɪd) *adj* made by hand, not by machine, esp with care or craftsmanship

handmaiden ('hænd,meɪdən) *or* **handmaid** *n* **1** a person or thing that serves a useful but subordinate purpose: *logic is the handmaid of philosophy* **2** *archaic* a female servant or attendant

hand-me-down *n informal* **1 a** something, esp an outgrown garment, passed down from one person to another **b** (*as modifier*): *a hand-me-down dress* **2 a** anything that has already been used by another **b** (*as modifier*): *hand-me-down ideas*

hand-me-up *n informal* **a** something, such as an item of electronic equipment, that is passed from a younger to an older member of a family **b** (*as modifier*): *a hand-me-up computer*

hand-off *rugby* ▷ *n* **1** the act of warding off an opposing player with the open hand ▷ *vb* **hand off 2** (*tr, adverb*) to ward off (an opponent) using a hand-off

hand on *vb* (*tr, adverb*) to pass to the next in a succession

hand organ *n* another name for **barrel organ**

hand-out *n, pl* **hand-outs 1** clothing, food, or money given to a needy person **2** a leaflet, free sample, etc, given out to publicize something **3** a statement or other document distributed to the press or an audience to confirm, supplement, or replace an oral presentation ▷ *vb* **hand out** (*tr, adverb*) **4** to distribute

hand over *vb* (*tr, adverb*) **1** to surrender possession of; transfer ▷ *n* **handover 2** a transfer or surrender

handphone ('hænd,fəʊn) *n SE Asian English* a mobile phone

hand-pick *vb* (*tr*) to choose or select with great care, as for a special job or purpose

hand-picked *adj* selected with great care, as for a special job or purpose; chosen

hand-piece *n Austral and NZ* hand-held, power-operated shears used by a shearer. See also **comb** (sense 3)

handrail ('hænd,reɪl) *n* a rail alongside a stairway, etc, at a convenient height to be grasped to provide support

handroll ('hænd,rəʊl) *n* a Japanese dish consisting of a large cone of dried seaweed filled with cold rice and other ingredients, eaten with the fingers rather than chopsticks

hands (hændz) *pl n* **1** power or keeping: *your welfare is in his hands* **2** Also called: **handling** *soccer* the infringement of touching the ball with any part of the hand or arm **3 change hands** to pass from the possession of one person or group to another **4 clean hands** freedom from guilt **5 hands down** without effort; easily **6 hands off** do not touch or interfere **7 hands up!** raise the hands above the level of the shoulders, an order usually given by an armed robber to a victim, etc **8 have one's hands full a** to be completely occupied **b** to be beset with problems **9 have one's hands tied** to be wholly unable to act **10 in good hands** in protective care **11 join hands** See **join** (sense 12) **12 lay hands on** *or* **upon a** to seize or get possession of **b** to beat up; assault **c** to find: *I just can't lay my hands on it anywhere* **d** *Christianity* to confirm or ordain by the imposition of hands **13 off one's hands** for which one is no longer responsible **14 on one's hands a** for which one is responsible: *I've got too much on my hands to help* **b** to spare: *time on my hands* **15 out of one's hands** no longer one's responsibility **16 throw up one's hands** to give up in despair **17 wash one's hands of** to have nothing more to do with

handsaw ('hænd,sɔː) *n* any saw for use in one hand only

hand's-breadth *n* another name for **handbreadth**

handsel *or* **hansel** ('hænsəl) *archaic or dialect* ▷ *n* **1** a gift for good luck at the beginning of a new year, new venture, etc ▷ *vb* **-sels, -selling, -selled** *or US* **-sels, -seling, -seled** (*tr*) **2** to give a handsel to (a person) **3** to begin (a venture) with ceremony; inaugurate [Old English *handselen* delivery into the hand; related to Old Norse *handsal* promise sealed with a handshake, Swedish *handsöl* gratuity; see HAND, SELL]

handset ('hænd,set) *n* a telephone mouthpiece and earpiece mounted so that they can be held simultaneously to mouth and ear

hand setting *n printing* text matter composed in metal type by hand, rather than by machine

handshake ('hænd,ʃeɪk) *n* the act of grasping and shaking a person's hand, as when being introduced or agreeing on a deal

handshaking ('hænd,ʃeɪkɪŋ) *n computing* communication between a computer system and an external device, by which each tells the other that data is ready to be transferred, and that the receiver is ready to accept it

hands-off *adj* (of a machine, device, etc) without need of manual operation

h

741

handsome ('hændsəm) *adj* **1** (of a man) good-looking, esp in having regular, pleasing, and well-defined features **2** (of a woman) fine-looking in a dignified way **3** well-proportioned, stately, or comely: *a handsome room* **4** liberal or ample: *a handsome allowance* **5** gracious or generous: *a handsome action* **6** *Southwest English* pleasant: *handsome weather* ▷ *n* **7** *Southwest English* a term of endearment for a beloved person, esp in **my handsome** [C15 *handsom* easily handled; compare Dutch *handzaam*; see HAND, -SOME¹] ▷ '**handsomely** *adv* ▷ '**handsomeness** *n*

hands-on *adj* involving practical experience of equipment, etc: *hands-on training in the use of computers*

handspike ('hænd,spaɪk) *n* a bar or length of pipe used as a lever

handspring ('hænd,sprɪŋ) *n* a gymnastic feat in which a person starts from a standing position and leaps forwards or backwards into a handstand and then onto his feet

handstand ('hænd,stænd) *n* the act or instance of supporting the body on the hands alone in an upside down position

handstroke ('hænd,strəʊk) *n* *bell-ringing* the downward movement of the bell rope as the bell swings around allowing the ringer to grasp and pull it. Compare **backstroke** (sense 4)

hand-to-hand *adj, adv* at close quarters: *they fought hand-to-hand*

hand-to-mouth *adj, adv* with barely enough money or food to satisfy immediate needs: *a hand-to-mouth existence*

handwork ('hænd,wɜːk) *n* work done by hand rather than by machine ▷ '**hand,worked** *adj*

hand-wringing *n* *informal* an extended debate over the correct course of action in a situation

handwriting ('hænd,raɪtɪŋ) *n* **1** writing by hand rather than by typing or printing **2** a person's characteristic writing style: *that signature is in my handwriting*

handwritten ('hænd,rɪtᵊn) *adj* written by hand; not printed or typed

handy ('hændɪ) *adj* **handier**, **handiest 1** conveniently or easily within reach **2** easy to manoeuvre, handle, or use: *a handy tool* **3** skilful with one's hands ▷ '**handiness** *n*

handyman ('hændɪ,mæn) *n, pl* **-men 1** a man employed to do various tasks **2** a man skilled in odd jobs, etc

Hanepoot ('hɑːnə,pʊət) *n* *South African* a variety of muscat grape used as a dessert fruit and in making wine [from Afrikaans *hane* cock + *poot* claw]

hang (hæŋ) *vb* **hangs, hanging, hung** (hʌŋ) **1** to fasten or be fastened from above, esp by a cord, chain, etc; suspend: *the picture hung on the wall; to hang laundry* **2** to place or be placed in position as by a hinge so as to allow free movement around or at the place of suspension: *to hang a door* **3** (*intr*; sometimes foll by *over*) to be suspended or poised; hover: *a pall of smoke hung over the city* **4** (*intr*; sometimes foll by *over*) to be imminent; threaten **5** (*intr*) to be or remain doubtful or unresolved (esp in the phrase **hang in the balance**) **6** (*past tense and past participle* **hanged**) to suspend or be suspended by the neck until dead **7** (*tr*) to fasten, fix, or attach in position or at an appropriate angle: *to hang a scythe to its handle* **8** (*tr*) to decorate, furnish, or cover with something suspended or fastened: *to hang a wall with tapestry* **9** (*tr*) to fasten to or suspend from a wall: *to hang wallpaper* **10** to exhibit (a picture or pictures) by (a particular painter, printmaker, etc) or (of a picture or a painter, etc) to be exhibited in an art gallery, etc **11** to fall or droop or allow to fall or droop: *to hang one's head in shame* **12** (of cloth, clothing, etc) to drape, fall, or flow, esp in a specified manner: *her skirt hangs well* **13** (*tr*) to suspend (game such as pheasant) so that it becomes slightly decomposed and therefore more tender and tasty **14** (of a jury) to prevent or be prevented from reaching a verdict

15 (*past tense and past participle* **hanged**) *slang* to damn or be damned: used in mild curses or interjections: *I'll be hanged before I'll go out in that storm* **16** (*intr*) to pass slowly (esp in the phrase **time hangs heavily**) **17** hang fire **a** to be delayed **b** to procrastinate. See also **fire** (sense 16) **18** hang tough See **tough** (sense 10) ▷ *n* **19** the way in which something hangs **20** (*usually used with a negative*) *slang* a damn: *I don't care a hang for what you say* **21** get the hang of *informal* **a** to understand the technique of doing something **b** to perceive the meaning or significance of ▷ See also **hang about, hang back, hang behind, hang in, hang on, hang out, hang together, hang up, hang with** [Old English *hangian*; related to Old Norse *hanga*, Old High German *hangēn*]

hang about or **around** *vb* (*intr*) **1** to waste time; loiter **2** (*adverb*; foll by *with*) to frequent the company (of someone) ▷ *interj* **3** wait a moment! stop!

hangar ('hæŋə) *n* a large workshop or building for storing and maintaining aircraft [C19 from French: shed, perhaps from Medieval Latin *angārium* shed used as a smithy, of obscure origin]

hang back *vb* (*intr, adverb*; often foll by *from*) to be reluctant to go forward or carry on (with some activity)

hang behind *vb* (*intr, adverb*) to remain in a place after others have left; linger

hangbird ('hæŋ,bɜːd) *n* *US and Canadian* any bird, esp the Baltimore oriole, that builds a hanging nest

Hangchow *n* a variant transliteration of the Chinese name for **Hangzhou**

hangdog ('hæŋ,dɒg) *adj* **1** downcast, furtive, or guilty in appearance or manner ▷ *n* **2** a furtive or sneaky person

hanger ('hæŋə) *n* **1 a** any support, such as a hook, strap, peg, or loop, on or by which something may be hung **b** See **coat hanger 2 a** a person who hangs something **b** (*in combination*): *paperhanger* **3** a bracket designed to attach one part of a mechanical structure to another, such as the one that attaches the spring shackle of a motor car to the chassis **4** a wood on a steep hillside, characteristically beech growing on chalk in southern England **5 a** a loop or strap on a sword belt from which a short sword or dagger was hung **b** the weapon itself

hanger-on *n, pl* **hangers-on** a sycophantic follower or dependant, esp one hoping for personal gain

hang-glider *n* an unpowered aircraft consisting of a large cloth wing stretched over a light framework from which the pilot hangs in a harness, using a horizontal bar to control the flight ▷ '**hang-gliding** *n*

hangi ('hʌŋiː) *n NZ* **1** Also called: **Māori oven, umu** an open-air cooking pit **2** the food cooked in it **3** the social gathering at the resultant meal [Māori]

hang in *vb* (*intr, preposition*) *informal* to persist: *just hang in there for a bit longer*

hanging ('hæŋɪŋ) *n* **1 a** the putting of a person to death by suspending the body by the neck from a noose **b** (*as modifier*): *a hanging offence* **2** (*often plural*) a decorative textile such as a tapestry or drapery hung on a wall or over a window **3** the act of a person or thing that hangs ▷ *adj* **4** not supported from below; suspended **5** undecided; still under discussion **6** inclining or projecting downwards; overhanging **7** situated on a steep slope or in a high place **8** (*prenominal*) given to issuing harsh sentences, esp death sentences: *a hanging judge* **9** *Northern English informal* unpleasant **10** *chess* See **hanging pawn**

Hanging Gardens of Babylon *n* (in ancient Babylon) gardens, probably planted on terraces of a ziggurat: one of the Seven Wonders of the World

hanging glacier *n* a glacier situated on a shelf above a valley or another glacier; it may be joined to the lower level by an icefall or separate from it

hanging indentation *n* *printing* a style of text-setting in which the first line of a paragraph is set to the full measure and subsequent lines are indented at the left-hand side

hanging pawn *n* *chess* one of two or more adjacent pawns on central half-open files with no pawns of the same colour on the files immediately to left and right of them

hanging valley *n* *geography* a tributary valley entering a main valley at a much higher level because of overdeepening of the main valley, esp by glacial erosion

hanging wall *n* the rocks on the upper side of an inclined fault plane or mineral vein. Compare **footwall**

hangman ('hæŋmən) *n, pl* **-men** an official who carries out a sentence of hanging on condemned criminals

hangnail ('hæŋ,neɪl) *n* a piece of skin torn away from, but still attached to, the base or side of a fingernail [C17 from Old English *angnægl*, from *enge* tight + *nægl* NAIL; influenced by HANG]

hang on *vb* (*intr*) **1** (*adverb*) to continue or persist in an activity, esp with effort or difficulty: *hang on at your present job until you can get another* **2** (*adverb*) to cling, grasp, or hold: *she hangs on to her mother's arm* **3** (*preposition*) to be conditioned or contingent on; depend on: *everything hangs on this business deal* **4** (*preposition*) Also: **hang onto, hang upon** to listen attentively to: *she hung on his every word* **5** (*adverb*) *informal* to wait or remain: *hang on for a few minutes*

hang out *vb* (*adverb*) **1** to suspend, be suspended, or lean, esp from an opening, as for display or airing: *to hang out the washing* **2** (*intr*) *informal* to live at or frequent a place: *the police know where the thieves hang out* **3** (*intr*; foll by *with*) *informal* to frequent the company (of someone) **4** *slang* to relax completely in an unassuming way (esp in the phrase **let it all hang out**) **5** (*intr*) *US informal* to act or speak freely, in an open, cooperative, or indiscreet manner ▷ *n* **hang-out 6** *informal* a place where one lives or that one frequently visits

hangover ('hæŋ,əʊvə) *n* **1** the delayed aftereffects of drinking too much alcohol in a relatively short period of time, characterized by headache and sometimes nausea and dizziness **2** a person or thing left over from or influenced by a past age

Hang Seng Index (hæŋ sɛŋ) *n* an index of share prices based on an average of 33 stocks quoted on the Hong Kong Stock Exchange [name of a Hong Kong bank]

hang together *vb* (*intr, adverb*) **1** to be cohesive or united **2** to be consistent: *your statements don't quite hang together*

Hanguk ('hæn'gʊk) *n* the Korean name for **South Korea**

hang up *vb* (*adverb*) **1** (*tr*) to put on a hook, hanger, etc: *please hang up your coat* **2** to replace (a telephone receiver) on its cradle at the end of a conversation, often breaking a conversation off abruptly **3** (*tr; usually passive*; usually foll by *on*) *informal* to cause to have an emotional or psychological preoccupation or problem: *he's really hung up on his mother* ▷ *n* **hang-up** *informal* **4** an emotional or psychological preoccupation or problem **5** a persistent cause of annoyance

hang with *vb* (*intr, preposition*) *US informal* to frequent the company of (someone)

Hangzhou ('hæŋ'dʒəʊ) or **Hangchow** *n* a port in E China, capital of Zhejiang province, on **Hangzhou Bay** (an inlet of the East China Sea), at the foot of the Eye of Heaven Mountains: regarded by Marco Polo as the finest city in the world; seat of two universities (1927, 1959). Pop: 1 955 000 (2005 est)

Hania ('hɑːnɪə) *n* a variant spelling of **Chania**

hank (hæŋk) *n* **1** a loop, coil, or skein, as of rope, wool, or yarn **2** *nautical* a ringlike fitting that can be opened to admit a stay for attaching the luff of a sail **3** a unit of measurement of cloth, yarn, etc, such as a length of 840 yards (767 m) of cotton or 560 yards (512 m) of worsted yarn ▷ *vb* **4** (*tr*) *nautical* to attach (a sail) to a stay by hanks [c13 of Scandinavian origin; compare Old Norse *hanka* to coil, Swedish *hank* string]

hanker ('hæŋkə) *vb* (foll by *for, after,* or an infinitive) to have a yearning (for something or to do something) [c17 probably from Dutch dialect *hankeren*] > **'hankering** *n*

Hankow *or* **Han-k'ou** ('hæn'kaʊ) *n* a former city in SE China, in SE Hubei at the confluence of the Han and Yangtze Rivers: one of the Han Cities; merged with Hanyang and Wuchang in 1950 to form the conurbation of Wuhan

hanky *or* **hankie** ('hæŋkɪ) *n, pl* **hankies** *informal* short for **handkerchief**

hanky-panky ('hæŋkɪ'pæŋkɪ) *n informal* **1** dubious or suspicious behaviour **2** foolish behaviour or talk **3** illicit sexual relations [c19 variant of HOCUS-POCUS]

Hannah ('hænə) *n Old Testament* the woman who gave birth to Samuel (I Samuel 1–2)

Hannover (*German* ha'noːfər) *n* a city in N Germany, capital of Lower Saxony: capital of the kingdom of Hannover (1815–66); situated on the Mittelland canal. Pop: 516 160 (2003 est). English spelling: **Hanover**

Hanoi (hæ'nɔɪ) *n* the capital of Vietnam, on the Red River: became capital of Tonkin in 1802, of French Indochina in 1887, of Vietnam in 1945, and of North Vietnam (1954–75); university (1917); industrial centre. Pop: 4 147 000 (2005 est)

Hanover ('hænəʊvə) *n* the English spelling of **Hannover**

Hanoverian (,hænə'vɪərɪən) *adj* **1** of, relating to, or situated in Hannover **2** of or relating to the princely house of Hanover or to the monarchs of England or their reigns from 1714 to 1901 ▷ *n* **3** a member or supporter of the house of Hanover

Hansard ('hænsɑːd) *n* **1** the official report of the proceedings of the British Parliament **2** a similar report kept by other legislative bodies [c19 named after T.C. *Hansard* (1752–1828) and his son, who compiled the reports until 1889]

Hanse (hæns) *or* **Hansa** ('hænsə, -zə) *n* **1** a medieval guild of merchants **2** a fee paid by the new members of a medieval trading guild **3** a another name for the **Hanseatic League** **b** (*as modifier*): *a Hanse town* [c12 of Germanic origin; compare Old High German *hansa,* Old English *hōs* troop]

Hanseatic (,hænsɪ'ætɪk) *adj* **1** of or relating to the Hanseatic League ▷ *n* **2** a member of the Hanseatic League

Hanseatic League *n* a commercial association of towns in N Germany formed in the mid-14th century to protect and control trade. It was at its most powerful in the 15th century. Also called: **Hansa, Hanse**

hansel ('hænsᵊl) *n, vb* a variant spelling of **handsel**

Hansen's disease ('hænsənz) *n pathol* another name for **leprosy** [c20 named after G. H. *Hansen* (1841–1912), Norwegian physician]

hansom ('hænsəm) *n* (*sometimes capital*) a two-wheeled one-horse carriage with a fixed hood. The driver sits on a high outside seat at the rear. Also called: **hansom cab** [c19 short for *hansom cab,* named after its designer J. A. *Hansom* (1803–82)]

hantavirus ('hæntə,vaɪrəs) *n* any one of a group of viruses that are transmitted to humans by rodents and cause disease of varying severity, ranging from a mild form of influenza to respiratory or kidney failure [c20 from *Hanta*(an), river in North and South Korea where the disease was first reported + VIRUS]

Hants (hænts) *abbreviation for* Hampshire

hanukiah *or* **chanukiah** ('hɑːnukɪə, 'hɑːnəkiːə; *Hebrew* xanuˈkiːa) *n* a candelabrum having nine branches that is lit during the festival of Hanukkah [from Hebrew]

Hanukkah, Hanukah *or* **Chanukah** ('hɑːnəkə, -nʊ,kaː; *Hebrew* xanuˈka) *n* the eight-day Jewish festival of lights beginning on the 25th of Kislev

and commemorating the rededication of the temple by Judas Maccabaeus in 165 BC. Also called: **Feast of Dedication, Feast of Lights** [from Hebrew, literally: a dedication]

Hanuman (,hʌnʊ'mɑːn) *n* **1** another word for **entellus** (the monkey) **2** the monkey chief of Hindu mythology and devoted helper of Rama [from Hindi *Hanumān,* from Sanskrit *hanumant* having (conspicuous) jaws, from *hanu* jaw]

Hanyang *or* **Han-yang** ('hæn'jæŋ) *n* a former city in SE China, in SE Hubei at the confluence of the Han and Yangtze Rivers: one of the Han Cities; merged with Hankow and Wuchang in 1950 to form the conurbation of Wuhan

hào (haʊ) *n* a monetary unit of Vietnam, worth one tenth of a dông

hap¹ (hæp) *n archaic* **1** luck; chance **2** an occurrence ▷ *vb* **haps, happing, happed** **3** (*intr*) an archaic word for **happen** [c13 from Old Norse *happ* good luck; related to Old English *gehæplic* convenient, Old Slavonic *kobŭ* fate]

hap² (hæp) *Scot and eastern English dialect* ▷ *vb* (*tr*) **1** to cover up; wrap up warmly ▷ *n* **2** a covering of any kind [c14 perhaps of Norse origin]

hapaxanthic (,hæpə'zænθɪk) *or* **hapaxanthous** (,hæpə'zænθəs) *adj botany* another word for **semelparous** [from Greek: fruiting only once]

hapax legomenon ('hæpæks lɪ'ɡɒmɪ,nɒn) *n, pl* **hapax legomena** (lə'ɡɒmɪnə) another term for **nonce word** [Greek: thing said only once]

ha'penny ('heɪpnɪ) *n, pl* **-nies** *Brit* a variant spelling of **halfpenny**

haphazard (hæp'hæzəd) *adv, adj* **1** at random ▷ *adj* **2** careless; slipshod ▷ *n* **3** *rare* chance > **hap'hazardly** *adv* > **hap'hazardness** *n*

Haphtarah (hɑːf'tɑːrə; *Hebrew* hafta'ra:) *n, pl* **-taroth** (-'taʊraʊt; *Hebrew* -ta'roːt) *or* **-tarahs** a variant spelling of **Haftarah**

hapless ('hæplɪs) *adj* unfortunate; wretched > **'haplessly** *adv* > **'haplessness** *n*

haplite ('hæplaɪt) *n* a variant of **aplite**. > **haplitic** (hæp'lɪtɪk) *adj*

haplo- *or before a vowel* **hapl-** *combining form* single or simple: *haplology; haplosis* [from Greek *haplous* simple]

haplobiont (,hæpləʊ'baɪɒnt) *n biology* an organism, esp a plant, that exists in either the diploid form or the haploid form (but never alternates between these forms) during its life cycle > ,haplobi'ontic *adj*

haplography (hæp'lɒɡrəfɪ) *n, pl* **-phies** the accidental writing of only one letter or syllable where there should be two similar letters or syllables, as in spelling *endodontics* as *endontics* [c19 from Greek, from *haplous* single + -GRAPHY]

haploid ('hæplɔɪd) *biology* ▷ *adj also* **haploidic** **1** (esp of gametes) having a single set of unpaired chromosomes ▷ *n* **2** a haploid cell or organism. Compare **diploid** [c20 from Greek *haploeidēs* single, from *haplous* single] > **'haploidy** *n*

haplology (hæp'lɒlədʒɪ) *n* omission of a repeated occurrence of a sound or syllable in fluent speech, as for example in the pronunciation of *library* as ('laɪbrɪ) > **haplologic** (,hæplə'lɒdʒɪk) *adj*

haplont ('hæplɒnt) *n biology* an organism, esp a plant, that has the haploid number of chromosomes in its somatic cells > **ha'plontic** *adj*

haplosis (hæp'ləʊsɪs) *n biology* the production of a haploid number of chromosomes during meiosis

haplostemonous (,hæpləʊ'stiːmənəs, -'stɛm-) *adj* (of plants) having the stamens arranged in a single whorl [c19 from New Latin, from HAPLO- + -*stemonous* relating to a STAMEN]

haply ('hæplɪ) *adv* (*sentence modifier*) an archaic word for **perhaps**

ha'p'orth ('heɪpəθ) *n Brit* **1** a variant spelling of **halfpennyworth** **2** *informal* a person considered as specified: *daft ha'p'orth*

happen ('hæpᵊn) *vb* **1** (*intr*) (of an event in time) to come about or take place; occur **2** (*intr;* foll by *to*) (of some unforeseen circumstance or event, esp death), to fall to the lot (of); be a source of good or

bad fortune (to): *if anything happens to me it'll be your fault* **3** (*tr*) to chance (to be or do something): *I happen to know him* **4** (*tr; takes a clause as object*) to be the case, esp if by chance, that: *it happens that I know him* **5** *sentence substitute* **5** *Northern English dialect* **a** another word for **perhaps** **b** (*as sentence modifier*): *happen I'll see thee tomorrow* [c14 see HAP¹, -EN¹]

■ USAGE See at **occur**

happen by, past, along *or* **in** *vb* (*intr, adverb*) *informal, chiefly US* to appear, arrive, or come casually or by chance

happening ('hæpənɪŋ, 'hæpnɪŋ) *n* **1** an occurrence; event **2** an improvised or spontaneous display or performance consisting of bizarre and haphazard events ▷ *adj* **3** *informal* fashionable and up-to-the-minute

happen on *or* **upon** *vb* (*intr, preposition*) to find by chance: *I happened upon a five-pound note lying in the street*

happenstance ('hæpən,stæns) *n* **1** chance **2** a chance occurrence

happy ('hæpɪ) *adj* **-pier, -piest** **1** feeling, showing, or expressing joy; pleased **2** willing: *I'd be happy to show you around* **3** causing joy or gladness **4** fortunate; lucky: *the happy position of not having to work* **5** aptly expressed; appropriate: *a happy turn of phrase* **6** (*postpositive*) *informal* slightly intoxicated ▷ *interj* **7** (*in combination*): *happy birthday; happy Christmas* ▷ See also **trigger-happy** [c14 see HAP¹, -Y¹] > **'happily** *adv* > **'happiness** *n*

-happy *adj combining form* denoting excessive enthusiasm for or devotion to: *gun-happy*

happy camper *n informal* a happy, satisfied person (esp in the phrase **not a happy camper**)

happy-clappy ('hæpɪ'klæpɪ) *derogatory* ▷ *adj* **1** of or denoting a form of evangelical Christianity in which members of the congregation sing and clap enthusiastically during acts of worship ▷ *n, pl* **-pies** **2** Also called: **happy clapper** an enthusiastic evangelical Christian

happy event *n informal* the birth of a child

happy family *or* **happy family bird** *n Austral* **1** another name for **grey-crowned babbler** **2** another name for **apostle bird**

happy-go-lucky *adj* carefree or easy-going

happy hour *n* a time, usually in the early evening, when some pubs or bars sell drinks at reduced prices

happy hunting ground *n* **1** (in American Indian legend) the paradise to which a person passes after death **2** a productive or profitable area for a person with a particular interest or requirement: *jumble sales proved happy hunting grounds in her search for old stone jars*

Happy Jack *n Austral* another name for **grey-crowned babbler**

happy medium *n* a course or state that avoids extremes

happy release *n* liberation, esp by death, from an unpleasant condition

hapten ('hæptən) *or* **haptene** ('hæptiːn) *n immunol* an incomplete antigen that can stimulate antibody production only when it is chemically combined with a particular protein [c20 from German, from Greek *haptein* to fasten]

hapteron ('hæptərɒn) *n* a cell or group of cells that occurs in certain plants, esp seaweeds, and attaches the plant to its substratum; holdfast [c20 from Greek *haptein* to make fast]

haptic ('hæptɪk) *adj* relating to or based on the sense of touch [c19 from Greek, from *haptein* to touch]

haptotropism (,hæptəʊ'trəʊpɪzəm) *n* another name for **thigmotropism**

hapu ('hɑːpuː) *n NZ* a subtribe [Māori]

hapuka *or* **hapuku** (hə'puːkə, 'hɑːpʊkə) *n NZ* another name for **groper** [Māori]

harakeke (hɑːrə'kiːkiː) *n NZ* another name for **flax** (sense 4) [Māori]

hara-kiri (,hærə'kɪrɪ) *or* **hari-kari** (,hærɪ'kɑːrɪ) *n* (formerly, in Japan) ritual suicide by

h

disembowelment with a sword when disgraced or under sentence of death. Also called: **seppuku** [c19 from Japanese taboo slang, from *hara* belly + *kiri* cutting]

haram ('hɑːˌrɑːm) *n* anything that is forbidden by Islamic law [from Arabic, literally: forbidden]

harambee (ˌhɑːrɑːm'beɪ) *n* **1** a work chant used on the E African coast **2** a rallying cry used in Kenya ▷ *interj* **3** a cry of harambee [Swahili: pull together]

haramzada (ˌhʌrəm'zɑːdə) *or* **haramda** (hʌ'rɑːmdə) *n Indian slang* **1** a male born of unmarried parents **2** an obnoxious or despicable male [from Urdu *haraam* forbidden]

haramzadi (ˌhʌrəm'zɑːdiː) *or* **haramdi** (hʌ'rɑːmdiː) *n Indian slang* **1** a female born of unmarried parents **2** an obnoxious or despicable female

harangue (hə'ræŋ) *vb* **1** to address (a person or crowd) in an angry, vehement, or forcefully persuasive way ▷ *n* **2** a loud, forceful, or angry speech [c15 from Old French, from Old Italian *aringa* public speech, probably of Germanic origin; related to Medieval Latin *harenga;* see HARRY, RING[1]] > **ha'ranguer** *n*

Harappa (hə'ræpə) *n* an ancient city in the Punjab in NW Pakistan: one of the centres of the Indus civilization that flourished from 2500 to 1700 BC; probably destroyed by Indo-European invaders

Harappan (hə'ræpən) *adj* **1** of or relating to Harappa (an ancient city in the Punjab) or its inhabitants ▷ *n* **2** a native or inhabitant of Harappa

Harar *or* **Harrer** ('hɑːrə) *n* a city in E Ethiopia: former capital of the Muslim state of Adal. Pop: 96 000 (2005 est)

Harare (hə'rɑːrɪ) *n* the capital of Zimbabwe, in the northeast: University of Zimbabwe (1957); industrial and commercial centre. Pop: 1 527 000 (2005 est). Former name (until 1982): **Salisbury**

harass ('hærəs, hə'ræs) *vb* (*tr*) to trouble, torment, or confuse by continual persistent attacks, questions, etc [c17 from French *harasser,* variant of Old French *harer* to set a dog on, of Germanic origin; compare Old High German *harēn* to cry out] > **'harassed** *adj* > **'harassing** *adj, n* > **'harassment** *n*

Harbin (hɑː'biːn, -'bɪn) *n* a city in NE China, capital of Heilongjiang province on the Songhua River: founded by the Russians in 1897; centre of tsarist activities after the October Revolution in Russia (1917). Pop: 2 989 000 (2005 est). Also called: **Ha-erh-pin**

harbinger ('hɑːbɪndʒə) *n* **1** a person or thing that announces or indicates the approach of something; forerunner **2** *obsolete* a person sent in advance of a royal party or army to obtain lodgings for them ▷ *vb* **3** (*tr*) to announce the approach or arrival of [c12 from Old French *herbergere,* from *herberge* lodging, from Old Saxon *heriberga;* compare Old High German *heriberga* army shelter; see HARRY, BOROUGH]

harbour *or US* **harbor** ('hɑːbə) *n* **1** a sheltered port **2** a place of refuge or safety ▷ *vb* **3** (*tr*) to give shelter to: *to harbour a criminal* **4** (*tr*) to maintain secretly: *to harbour a grudge* **5** to shelter (a vessel) in a harbour or (of a vessel) to seek shelter [Old English *herebeorg,* from *here* troop, army + *beorg* shelter; related to Old High German *heriberga* hostelry, Old Norse *herbergi*] > **'harbourer** *or US* **'harborer** *n* > **'harbourless** *or US* **'harborless** *adj*

harbourage *or US* **harborage** ('hɑːbərɪdʒ) *n* shelter or refuge, as for a ship, or a place providing shelter

harbour master *n* an official in charge of a harbour

harbour seal *n* a common earless seal, *Phoca vitulina,* that is greyish-black with paler markings: occurs off the coasts of North America, N Europe, and NE Asia

hard (hɑːd) *adj* **1** firm or rigid; not easily dented, crushed, or pierced **2** toughened by or as if by physical labour; not soft or smooth: *hard hands* **3** difficult to do or accomplish; arduous: *a hard task* **4** difficult to understand or perceive: *a hard question* **5** showing or requiring considerable physical or mental energy, effort, or application: *hard work; a hard drinker* **6** stern, cold, or intractable: *a hard judge* **7** exacting; demanding: *a hard master* **8** harsh; cruel: *a hard fate* **9** inflicting pain, sorrow, distress, or hardship: *hard times* **10** tough or adamant: *a hard man* **11** forceful or violent: *a hard knock* **12** cool or uncompromising: *we took a long hard look at our profit factor* **13** indisputable; real: *hard facts* **14** *chem* (of water) impairing the formation of a lather by soap. See **hardness** (sense 3) **15** practical, shrewd, or calculating: *he is a hard man in business* **16** too harsh to be pleasant: *hard light* **17 a** (of cash, money, etc) in coin and paper rather than cheques **b** (of currency) in strong demand, esp as a result of a good balance of payments situation **c** (of credit) difficult to obtain; tight **18** (of alcoholic drink) being a spirit rather than a wine, beer, etc: *the hard stuff* **19** (of a drug such as heroin, morphine, or cocaine) highly addictive. Compare **soft** (sense 20) **20** *physics* (of radiation, such as gamma rays and X-rays) having high energy and the ability to penetrate solids **21** *physics* (of a vacuum) almost complete **22** *chiefly US* (of goods) durable **23** short for **hard-core**. See **hardcore** (senses 3, 4) **24** (of news coverage) concentrating on serious stories **25** *phonetics* **a** an older word for **fortis b** (not in modern technical usage) denoting the consonants *c* and *g* in English when they are pronounced as velar stops (k, g) **c** (of consonants in the Slavonic languages) not palatalized **26 a** being heavily fortified and protected **b** (of nuclear missiles) located underground in massively reinforced silos **27** politically extreme: *the hard left* **28** *Brit and NZ informal* incorrigible or disreputable (esp in the phrase **a hard case**) **29** (of bread, etc) stale and old **30 a hard nut to crack a** a person not easily persuaded or won over **b** a thing not easily understood **31 hard by** near; close by **32 hard doer** *NZ* a tough worker at anything **33 hard done by** unfairly or badly treated **34 hard up** *informal* **a** in need of money; poor **b** (foll by *for*) in great need (of): *hard up for suggestions* **35 put the hard word on** *Austral and NZ informal* to ask or demand something from ▷ *adv* **36** with great energy, force, or vigour: *the team always played hard* **37** as far as possible; all the way: *hard left* **38** with application; earnestly or intently: *she thought hard about the formula* **39** with great intensity, force, or violence: *his son's death hit him hard* **40** (foll by *on, upon, by,* or *after*) close; near: *hard on his heels* **41** (foll by *at*) assiduously; devotedly **42 a** with effort or difficulty: *their victory was hard won* **b** (*in combination*): *hard-earned* **43** slowly and reluctantly: *prejudice dies hard* **44 go hard with** to cause pain or difficulty to (someone): *it will go hard with you if you don't tell the truth* **45 hard at it** working hard **46 hard put (to it)** scarcely having the capacity (to do something): *he's hard put to get to work by 9:30* ▷ *n* **47** any colorant that produces a harsh coarse appearance **48** *Brit* a roadway across a foreshore **49** *slang* hard labour **50** *slang* an erection of the penis (esp in the phrase **get** or **have a hard on**) [Old English *heard;* related to Old Norse *harthr,* Old Frisian *herd,* Old High German *herti,* Gothic *hardus* hard, Greek *kratus* strong]

hard and fast *adj* (**hard-and-fast** *when prenominal*) (esp of rules) invariable or strict

hardback ('hɑːdˌbæk) *n* **1** a book or edition with covers of cloth, cardboard, or leather. Compare **paperback** ▷ *adj* **2** Also: **casebound, hardbound** ('hɑːdˌbaʊnd), **hardcover** ('hɑːdˌkʌvə) of or denoting a hardback or the publication of hardbacks

hardbake ('hɑːdˌbeɪk) *n* almond toffee

hardball ('hɑːdbɔːl) *n* **1** *US and Canadian* baseball as distinct from softball **2 play hardball** *informal, chiefly US and Canadian* to act in a ruthless or uncompromising way

hard-bitten *adj* tough and realistic

hardboard ('hɑːdˌbɔːd) *n* a thin stiff sheet made of compressed sawdust and wood pulp bound together with plastic adhesive or resin under heat and pressure

hard-boiled *adj* **1** (of an egg) boiled until the yolk and white are solid **2** *informal* **a** tough, realistic **b** cynical

hard bop *n* a form of jazz originating in the late 1950s that is rhythmically less complex than bop

hard cash *n* money or payment in the form of coins or notes rather than cheques or credit

hard cheese *sentence substitute, n Brit slang* bad luck

hard cider *n US and Canadian* fermented apple juice. Compare **sweet cider**

hard coal *n* another name for **anthracite** Compare **soft coal**

hard copy *n* computer output printed on paper, as contrasted with machine-readable output such as magnetic tape

hardcore ('hɑːdˌkɔː) *n* **1** a style of rock music characterized by short fast numbers with minimal melody and aggressive delivery **2** a type of dance music with a very fast beat

hard core *n* **1** the members of a group or movement who form an intransigent nucleus resisting change **2** material, such as broken bricks, stones, etc, used to form a foundation for a road, paving, building, etc ▷ *adj* **hard-core 3** (of pornography) describing or depicting sexual acts in explicit detail **4** extremely committed or fanatical: *a hard-core Communist*

hard court *n* a tennis court made of asphalt, concrete, etc. See also **grass court**

hard disk *n* a disk of rigid magnetizable material that is used to store data for computers: it is permanently mounted in its disk drive and usually has a storage capacity of a few gigabytes

hard drive *or* **hard disk drive** *n computing* (on a computer) the mechanism that handles the reading, writing, and storage of data on the hard disk

hard-edge *adj* of, relating to, or denoting a style of painting in which vividly coloured subjects are clearly delineated

harden[1] ('hɑːdᵊn) *vb* **1** to make or become hard or harder; freeze, stiffen, or set **2** to make or become more hardy, tough, or unfeeling **3** to make or become stronger or firmer: *they hardened defences* **4** to make or become more resolute or set: *hardened in his resolve* **5** (*intr*) *commerce* **a** (of prices, a market, etc) to cease to fluctuate **b** (of price) to rise higher ▷ See also **harden off, harden up**

harden[2] ('hɑːdᵊn) *n* a rough fabric made from hards

hardened ('hɑːdᵊnd) *adj* **1** rigidly set, as in a mode of behaviour **2** toughened, as by custom; seasoned **3** (of a nuclear missile site) constructed to withstand a nuclear attack

hardener ('hɑːdᵊnə) *n* **1** a person or thing that hardens **2** a substance added to paint or varnish to increase durability **3** an ingredient of certain adhesives and synthetic resins that accelerates or promotes setting

hardening ('hɑːdᵊnɪŋ) *n* **1** the act or process of becoming or making hard **2** a substance added to another substance or material to make it harder

hardening of the arteries *n* a nontechnical name for **arteriosclerosis**

harden off *vb* (*adverb*) to accustom (a cultivated plant) or (of such a plant) to become accustomed to outdoor conditions by repeated exposure

harden up *vb* (*intr*) *nautical* to tighten the sheets of a sailing vessel so as to prevent luffing

hard-faced *adj Northern English dialect* cheeky

hard feeling *n* (*often plural; often used with a negative*) resentment; ill will: *no hard feelings?*

hard fern *n* a common tufted erect fern of the polypody family, *Blechnum spicant,* having dark-green lanceolate leaves: it prefers acid soils, and in the US is sometimes grown as deer feed. US name: **deer fern**

hardhack ('hɑːˌhæk) *n* a woody North American rosaceous plant, *Spiraea tomentosa*, with downy leaves and tapering clusters of small pink or white flowers. Also called: **steeplebush**

hard hat *n* **1** a hat made of a hard material for protection, worn esp by construction workers, equestrians, etc **2** *informal, chiefly US and Canadian* a construction worker ▷ *adj* **hard-hat 3** *informal, chiefly US* characteristic of the presumed conservative attitudes and prejudices typified by construction workers

hard-headed *adj* **1** tough, realistic, or shrewd; not moved by sentiment **2** *chiefly US and Canadian* stubborn; obstinate > **hard-'headedly** *adv* > ˌhard-'headedness *n*

hardheads ('hɑːˌhɛdz) *n* (*functioning as singular*) a thistle-like plant, *Centaurea nigra*, native to Europe and introduced into North America and New Zealand, that has reddish-purple flower heads: family *Asteraceae* (composites). Also called: **knapweed** See also **centaury** (sense 2)

hardhearted (ˌhɑːd'hɑːtɪd) *adj* unkind or intolerant > ˌhard'heartedly *adv* > ˌhard'heartedness *n*

hard-hit *adj* seriously affected or hurt: *hard-hit by taxation*

hard hitter *n* NZ *informal* a bowler hat

hard-hitting *adj* uncompromising; tough: *a hard-hitting report on urban deprivation*

hardihood ('hɑːdɪˌhʊd) *n* courage, daring, or audacity

hardily ('hɑːdɪlɪ) *adv* in a hardy manner; toughly or boldly

hardiness ('hɑːdɪnɪs) *n* the condition or quality of being hardy, robust, or bold

hard labour *n criminal law* (formerly) the penalty of compulsory physical labour imposed in addition to a sentence of imprisonment: abolished in England in 1948

hard landing *n* **1** a landing by a rocket or spacecraft in which the vehicle is destroyed on impact **2** a sharp fall into recession following a sustained period of economic growth ▷ Compare **soft landing**

hard lens *n* a rigid plastic lens which floats on the layer of tears in front of the cornea, worn to correct defects of vision. Compare **gas-permeable lens, soft lens**

hard line *n* **a** an uncompromising course or policy **b** **hardline** (*as modifier*): *a hardline policy* > ˌhard'liner *n*

hard lines *sentence substitute, n Brit informal* bad luck. Also: **hard cheese**

hardly ('hɑːdlɪ) *adv* **1** scarcely; barely: *we hardly knew the family* **2** just; only just: *he could hardly hold the cup* **3** *often used ironically* almost or probably not or not at all: *he will hardly incriminate himself* **4** with difficulty or effort **5** *rare* harshly or cruelly

USAGE Since *hardly, scarcely,* and *barely* already have negative force, it is redundant to use another negative in the same clause: *he had hardly had* (not *he hadn't hardly had*) *time to think; there was scarcely any* (not *scarcely no*) *bread left*

hardman ('hɑːdˌmæn) *n* a tough, ruthless, or violent man

hard money *n politics* (in the US) money given directly to a candidate in an election to assist his or her campaign. Compare **soft money**

hard-mouthed *adj* **1** (of a horse) not responding satisfactorily to a pull on the bit **2** stubborn; obstinate

hard neck *n Irish informal* audacity; nerve

hardness ('hɑːdnɪs) *n* **1** the quality or condition of being hard **2** one of several measures of resistance to indentation, deformation, or abrasion. See **Mohs scale, Brinell hardness number 3** the quality of water that causes it to impair the lathering of soap: caused by the presence of certain calcium salts. **Temporary**

hardness can be removed by boiling whereas **permanent hardness** cannot

hard-nosed *adj informal* tough, shrewd, and practical

hard of hearing *adj* **a** deaf or partly deaf **b** (*as collective noun; preceded by the*): *the hard of hearing*

hard pad *n* (in dogs) an abnormal increase in the thickness of the foot pads: one of the clinical signs of canine distemper. See **distemper¹** (sense 1)

hard palate *n* the anterior bony portion of the roof of the mouth, extending backwards to the soft palate

hardpan ('hɑːˌpæn) *n* a hard impervious layer of clay below the soil, resistant to drainage and root growth

hard paste *n* **a** porcelain made with kaolin and petuntse, of Chinese origin and made in Europe from the early 18th century **b** (*as modifier*): *hard-paste porcelain*

hard-pressed *adj* **1** in difficulties: *the swimmer was hard-pressed* **2** subject to severe competition **3** subject to severe attack **4** closely pursued

hardrock ('hɑːˌrɒk) *Canadian* ▷ *adj* **1** (of mining) concerned with extracting minerals other than coal, usually from solid rock ▷ *n* **2** *slang* a tough uncompromising man

hard rock *n music* a rhythmically simple and usually highly amplified style of rock and roll

hard rubber *n* a hard fairly inelastic material made by vulcanizing natural rubber. See **vulcanite**

hards (hɑːdz) *or* **hurds** *pl n* coarse fibres and other refuse from flax and hemp [Old English *heordan* (plural); related to Middle Dutch *hēde*, Greek *keskeon* tow]

hard sauce *n* another name for **brandy butter**

hard science *n* **a** one of the natural or physical sciences, such as physics, chemistry, biology, geology, or astronomy **b** (*as modifier*): *a hard-science lecture* > **hard scientist** *n*

hardscrabble ('hɑːdˌskræbəl) *n US informal* **1** (*modifier*) (of a place) difficult to make a living in; barren **2** great effort made in the face of difficulties

hard sell *n* an aggressive insistent technique of selling or advertising. Compare **soft sell**

hard-shell *adj also* **hard-shelled 1** *zoology* having a shell or carapace that is thick, heavy, or hard **2** *US* strictly orthodox ▷ *n* **3** another name for the **quahog**

hard-shell clam *n* another name for the **quahog**

hard-shell crab *n* a crab, esp of the edible species *Cancer pagurus*, that has not recently moulted and therefore has a hard shell. Compare **soft-shell crab**

hardship ('hɑːdʃɪp) *n* **1** conditions of life difficult to endure **2** something that causes suffering or privation

hard shoulder *n Brit* a surfaced verge running along the edge of a motorway for emergency stops

hard-spun *adj* (of yarn) spun with a firm close twist

hard standing *n* a hard surface on which vehicles, such as cars or aircraft, may be parked

hardtack ('hɑːdˌtæk) *n* a kind of hard saltless biscuit, formerly eaten esp by sailors as a staple aboard ship. Also called: **pilot biscuit, ship's biscuit, sea biscuit**

hard tack *n Irish informal* whisky

hardtop ('hɑːdˌtɒp) *n* **1** a car equipped with a metal or plastic roof that is sometimes detachable **2** the detachable hard roof of some sports cars

hardware ('hɑːdˌwɛə) *n* **1** metal tools, implements, etc, esp cutlery or cooking utensils **2** *computing* the physical equipment used in a computer system, such as the central processing unit, peripheral devices, and memory. Compare **software 3** mechanical equipment, components, etc **4** heavy military equipment, such as tanks and missiles or their parts **5** *informal* a gun or guns collectively

hard-wearing *adj* resilient, durable, and tough

hard wheat *n* a type of wheat with hard kernels,

yielding a strong flour and used for bread, macaroni, etc

Hardwick Hall ('hɑːdwɪk) *n* an Elizabethan mansion near Chesterfield in Derbyshire: built 1591–97 for Elizabeth, Countess of Shrewsbury (Bess of Hardwick)

hard-wired *adj* **1** (of a circuit or instruction) permanently wired into a computer, replacing separate software **2** (of human behaviour) innate; not learned: *humans have a hard-wired ability for acquiring language*

hardwood ('hɑːdˌwʊd) *n* **1** the wood of any of numerous broad-leaved dicotyledonous trees, such as oak, beech, ash, etc, as distinguished from the wood of a conifer **2** any tree from which this wood is obtained ▷ Compare **softwood**

hard-working *adj* (of a person) industrious; diligent

hardy¹ ('hɑːdɪ) *adj* **-dier, -diest 1** having or demanding a tough constitution; robust **2** bold; courageous **3** foolhardy; rash **4** (of plants) able to live out of doors throughout the winter [c13 from Old French *hardi* bold, past participle of *hardir* to become bold, of Germanic origin; compare Old English *hierdan* to HARDEN¹, Old Norse *hertha*, Old High German *herten*]

hardy² ('hɑːdɪ) *n, pl* **-dies** any blacksmith's tool made with a square shank so that it can be lodged in a square hole in an anvil [c19 probably from HARD]

hard yards *pl n* a great deal of effort or hard work, esp in playing a sport: *Dallaglio's ability to make the hard yards and cross the gain line*

hare (hɛə) *n, pl* **hares** *or* **hare 1** any solitary leporid mammal of the genus *Lepus*, such as L. *europaeus* (**European hare**). Hares are larger than rabbits, having longer ears and legs, and live in shallow nests (forms). Related adj: **leporine 2** **make a hare of (someone)** *Irish informal* to defeat (someone) completely **3** **run with the hare and hunt with the hounds** to be on good terms with both sides > *vb* **4** (*intr*; often foll by *off, after,* etc) *Brit informal* to go or run fast or wildly [Old English *hara*; related to Old Norse *heri*, Old High German *haso*, Swedish *hare*, Sanskrit *śaśá*] > **'hareˌlike** *adj*

Hare (hɛə) *n* a member of a Dene Native Canadian people of northern Canada [of Athaspascan origin]

hare and hounds *n* (*functioning as singular*) a game in which certain players (**hares**) run across country scattering pieces of paper that the other players (**hounds**) follow in an attempt to catch the hares

harebell ('hɛəˌbɛl) *n* a N temperate campanulaceous plant, *Campanula rotundifolia*, having slender stems and leaves, and bell-shaped pale blue flowers. Also called (in Scotland): **bluebell**

harebrained *or* **hairbrained** ('hɛəˌbreɪnd) *adj* rash, foolish, or badly thought out: *harebrained schemes*

Hare Krishna ('hɑːrɪ 'krɪʃnə) *n* **1** a Hindu sect devoted to a form of Hinduism (**Krishna Consciousness**) based on the worship of the god Krishna **2** (*pl* **Hare Krishnas**) a member or follower of this sect [c20 from Hindi, literally: Lord Krishna (vocative): the opening words of a sacred verse often chanted in public by adherents of the movement]

harelip ('hɛəˌlɪp) *n* a congenital cleft or fissure in the midline of the upper lip, resembling the cleft upper lip of a hare, often occurring with cleft palate > 'hareˌlipped *adj*

harem ('hɛərəm, hɑːˈriːm) *or* **hareem** (hɑːˈriːm) *n* **1** the part of an Oriental house reserved strictly for wives, concubines, etc **2** a Muslim's wives and concubines collectively **3** a group of female animals of the same species that are the mates of a single male [c17 from Arabic *harīm* forbidden (place)]

hare's-foot *n* a leguminous annual plant,

h

Trifolium arvense, that grows on sandy soils in Europe and NW Asia and has downy heads of white or pink flowers. Also called: hare's-foot clover

harestail ('hɛəsˌteɪl) *n* a species of cotton grass, *Eriophorum vaginatum,* more tussocky than common cotton grass and having only a single flower head

Harewood House ('hɛəwʊd) *n* a mansion near Harrogate in Yorkshire: built 1759–71 by John Carr for the Lascelles family; interior decoration by Robert Adam

Harfleur ('hɑːfləːr, *French* arflœr) *n* a port in N France, in Seine-Maritime department: important centre in the Middle Ages. Pop: 8517 (1999)

Hargeisa (hɑːˈɡeɪsə) *n* a city in NW Somalia: former capital of British Somaliland (1941–60); trading centre for nomadic herders. Pop: 400 000 (latest est)

haricot ('hærɪkəʊ) *n* **1** a variety of French bean with light-coloured edible seeds, which can be dried and stored **2** another name for **French bean 3** the seed or pod of any of these plants, eaten as a vegetable [c17 from French, perhaps from Nahuatl *ayecotli*]

Harijan ('hʌrɪdʒən) *n* a member of certain classes in India, formerly considered inferior and untouchable. See **scheduled castes** [Hindi, literally: man of God (so called by Mahatma Gandhi), from *Hari* god + *jan* man]

hari-kari (ˌhærɪˈkɑːrɪ) *n* a non-Japanese variant of **hara-kiri**

Haringey ('hærɪŋˌɡeɪ) *n* a borough of N Greater London. Pop: 224 700 (2003 est). Area: 30 sq km (12 sq miles)

harira (həˈrɪərə) *n* a Moroccan soup made from a variety of vegetables with lentils, chickpeas, and coriander [Arabic]

harissa (həˈrɪsə) *n* (in Tunisian cookery) a hot paste or sauce made from chilli peppers, tomatoes, spices, and olive oil, often served with couscous [c20 from Arabic]

hark (hɑːk) *vb* (*intr; usually imperative*) to listen; pay attention [Old English *heorcnian* to HEARKEN; related to Old Frisian *herkia,* Old High German *hōrechen*; see HEAR]

hark back *vb* (*intr, adverb*) to return to an earlier subject, point, or position, as in speech or thought

harken ('hɑːkən) *vb* a variant spelling (esp US) of **hearken.** > **'harkener** *n*

harl¹ (hærl, hɑːl) *Scot* ▷ *vb* **1** (*tr*) to drag (something) along the ground **2** (*intr*) to drag oneself; trail along **3** (*tr*) to cover (a building) with a mixture of lime and gravel; roughcast **4** (*intr*) to troll for fish ▷ *n* **5** the act of harling or dragging **6** a small quantity; a scraping **7** a mixture of lime and gravel; roughcast [c18 of unknown origin] > **'harling** *n*

harl² (hɑːl) *n angling* a variant of **herl**

Harlech ('hɑːˌlɪk) *n* a town in N Wales, in Gwynedd: noted for its ruined 13th-century castle overlooking Cardigan Bay: tourism. Pop: 1233 (2001)

Harlem ('hɑːləm) *n* a district of New York City, in NE Manhattan: now largely a Black ghetto

harlequin ('hɑːlɪkwɪn) *n* **1** (*sometimes capital*) *theatre* a stock comic character originating in the commedia dell'arte, the foppish lover of Columbine in the English harlequinade. He is usually represented in diamond-patterned multicoloured tights, wearing a black mask **2** a clown or buffoon ▷ *adj* **3** varied in colour or decoration **4** (of certain animals) having a white coat with irregular patches of black or other dark colour. *harlequin Great Dane* **5** comic; ludicrous [c16 from Old French *Herlequin, Hellequin* leader of band of demon horsemen, perhaps from Middle English *Herle king* (unattested) King Herle, mythical being identified with Woden]

harlequinade (ˌhɑːlɪkwɪˈneɪd) *n* **1** (*sometimes capital*) *theatre* a play or part of a pantomime in which harlequin has a leading role **2** buffoonery

harlequin bug *n* a brightly coloured heteropterous insect, *Murgantia histrionica,* of the US and Central America: a pest of cabbages and related plants: family *Pentatomidae*

harlequin duck *n* a northern sea duck, *Histrionicus histrionicus,* the male of which has a blue and red plumage with black and white markings

Harley Street ('hɑːlɪ) *n* a street in central London famous for its large number of medical specialists' consulting rooms

harlot ('hɑːlət) *n* **1** a prostitute or promiscuous woman ▷ *adj* **2** *archaic* of or like a harlot [c13 from Old French *herlot* rascal, of obscure origin] > **'harlotry** *n*

Harlow ('hɑːləʊ) *n* a town in SE England, in W Essex: designated a new town in 1947. Pop: 78 389 (2001 est)

harm (hɑːm) *n* **1** physical or mental injury or damage **2** moral evil or wrongdoing ▷ *vb* **3** (*tr*) to injure physically, morally, or mentally [Old English *hearm*; related to Old Norse *harmr* grief, Old High German *harm* injury, Old Slavonic *sramŭ* disgrace] > **'harmer** *n*

harmattan (hɑːˈmætən) *n* a dry dusty wind from the Sahara blowing towards the W African coast, esp from November to March [c17 from Twi *haramata,* perhaps from Arabic *harām* forbidden thing; see HAREM]

harmful ('hɑːmfʊl) *adj* causing or tending to cause harm; injurious > **'harmfully** *adv* > **'harmfulness** *n*

harmless ('hɑːmlɪs) *adj* **1** not causing any physical or mental damage or injury **2** unlikely to annoy or worry people: *a harmless sort of man* > **'harmlessly** *adv* > **'harmlessness** *n*

harmolodics (ˌhɑːməˈlɒdɪks) *n* (*functioning as singular*) *jazz* the technique of each musician in a group simultaneously improvising around the melodic and rhythmic patterns in a tune, rather than one musician improvising on its underlying harmonic pattern while the others play an accompaniment [c20 of unknown origin] > **ˌharmoˈlodic** *adj*

harmonic (hɑːˈmɒnɪk) *adj* **1** of, involving, producing, or characterized by harmony; harmonious **2** *music* of, relating to, or belonging to harmony **3** *maths* **a** capable of expression in the form of sine and cosine functions **b** of or relating to numbers whose reciprocals form an arithmetic progression **4** *physics* of or concerned with an oscillation that has a frequency that is an integral multiple of a fundamental frequency **5** *physics* of or concerned with harmonics ▷ *n* **6** *physics, music* a component of a periodic quantity, such as a musical tone, with a frequency that is an integral multiple of the fundamental frequency. The **first harmonic** is the fundamental, the **second harmonic** (twice the fundamental frequency) is the **first overtone,** the **third harmonic** (three times the fundamental frequency) is the **second overtone,** etc **7** *music* (not in technical use) overtone: in this case, the first overtone is the first harmonic, etc ▷ See also **harmonics** [c16 from Latin *harmonicus* relating to HARMONY] > **harˈmonically** *adv*

harmonica (hɑːˈmɒnɪkə) *n* **1** a small wind instrument of the reed organ family in which reeds of graduated lengths set into a metal plate enclosed in a narrow oblong box are made to vibrate by blowing and sucking. Also called: **mouth organ 2** See **glass harmonica** [c18 from Latin *harmonicus* relating to HARMONY]

harmonic analysis *n* **1** the representation of a periodic function by means of the summation and integration of simple trigonometric functions **2** the study of this means of representation

harmonic distortion *n electronics* distortion caused by nonlinear characteristics of electronic apparatus, esp of audio amplifiers, that generate unwanted harmonics of the input frequencies

harmonic mean *n* the reciprocal of the arithmetic mean of the reciprocals of a set of specified numbers: the harmonic mean of 2, 3, and 4 is $3(\frac{1}{2} + \frac{1}{3} + \frac{1}{4})^{-1} = 36/13$

harmonic minor scale *n music* a minor scale modified from the state of being natural by the sharpening of the seventh degree. See **minor** Compare **melodic minor scale**

harmonic motion *n* a periodic motion in which the displacement is symmetrical about a point or a periodic motion that is composed of such motions. See also **simple harmonic motion**

harmonic progression *n* a sequence of numbers whose reciprocals form an arithmetic progression, as 1, $\frac{1}{2}$, $\frac{1}{3}$, ...

harmonics (hɑːˈmɒnɪks) *n* **1** (*functioning as singular*) the science of musical sounds and their acoustic properties **2** (*functioning as plural*) the overtones of a fundamental note, as produced by lightly touching the string of a stringed instrument at one of its node points while playing. See **harmonic** (sense 6)

harmonic series *n* **1** *maths* a series whose terms are in harmonic progression, as in $1 + \frac{1}{2} + \frac{1}{3} + ...$ **2** *acoustics* the series of tones with frequencies strictly related to one another and to the fundamental tone, as obtained by touching lightly the node points of a string while playing it. Its most important application is in the playing of brass instruments

harmonious (hɑːˈməʊnɪəs) *adj* **1** (esp of colours or sounds) fitting together well **2** having agreement or consensus **3** tuneful, consonant, or melodious > **harˈmoniously** *adv*

harmonist ('hɑːmənɪst) *n* **1** a person skilled in the art and techniques of harmony **2** a person who combines and collates parallel narratives > **harmoˈnistic** *adj* > **ˌharmoˈnistically** *adv*

harmonium (hɑːˈməʊnɪəm) *n* a musical keyboard instrument of the reed organ family, in which air from pedal-operated bellows causes the reeds to vibrate [c19 from French, from *harmonie* HARMONY]

harmonization *or* **harmonisation** (ˌhɑːmənaɪˈzeɪʃən) *n* **1** the act of harmonizing **2** a system, particularly used in the EU, whereby the blue-collar workers and the white-collar workers in an organization have similar status and any former differences in terms and conditions of employment are levelled up

harmonize *or* **harmonise** ('hɑːməˌnaɪz) *vb* **1** to make or become harmonious **2** (*tr*) *music* to provide a harmony for (a melody, tune, etc) **3** (*intr*) to sing in harmony, as with other singers **4** to collate parallel narratives > **'harmoˌnizable** *or* **'harmoˌnisable** *adj*

harmonizer *or* **harmoniser** ('hɑːməˌnaɪzə) *n music* **1** a person skilled in the theory of composition of harmony **2** a device that electronically duplicates a signal at a different pitch or different pitches

harmony ('hɑːmənɪ) *n, pl* **-nies 1** agreement in action, opinion, feeling, etc; accord **2** order or congruity of parts to their whole or to one another **3** agreeable sounds **4** *music* **a** any combination of notes sounded simultaneously **b** the vertically represented structure of a piece of music. Compare **melody** (sense 1b), **rhythm** (sense 1) **c** the art or science concerned with the structure and combinations of chords **5** a collation of the material of parallel narratives, esp of the four Gospels [c14 from Latin *harmonia* concord of sounds, from Greek: harmony, from *harmos* a joint]

harmotome ('hɑːməˌtəʊm) *n* a mineral of the zeolite group consisting of hydrated aluminium barium silicate in the form of monoclinic twinned crystals. Formula: $Ba(Al_2Si_6O_{16}).6H_2O$ [c19 from French, from Greek *harmos* a joint + *tomē* a slice, from *temnein* to cut]

harness ('hɑːnɪs) *n* **1** an arrangement of leather straps buckled or looped together, fitted to a draught animal in order that the animal can be attached to and pull a cart **2** something resembling this, esp for attaching something to the body: *a parachute harness* **3** *mountaineering* an arrangement of webbing straps that enables a climber to attach himself to the rope so that the impact of a fall is minimized **4** the total system of electrical leads for a vehicle or aircraft **5** *weaving* the part of a loom that raises and lowers the warp threads, creating the shed **6** *archaic* armour collectively **7 in harness** at one's routine work ▷ *vb* (*tr*) **8** to put harness on (a horse) **9** (usually foll by *to*) to attach (a draught animal) by means of harness to (a cart, etc) **10** to control so as to employ the energy or potential power of: *to harness the atom* **11** to equip or clothe with armour [c13 from Old French *harneis* baggage, probably from Old Norse *hernest* (unattested) provisions, from *herr* army + *nest* provisions] > 'harnesser *n* > 'harnessless *adj* > 'harness-,like *adj*

harnessed antelope *n* any of various antelopes with vertical white stripes on the back, esp the bushbuck

harness hitch *n* a knot forming a loop with no free ends

harness race *n* *horse racing* a trotting or pacing race for standard-bred horses driven in sulkies and harnessed in a special way to cause them to use the correct gait

Harney Peak ('hɑːnɪ) *n* a mountain in SW South Dakota: the highest peak in the Black Hills. Height: 2207 m (7242 ft)

harp (hɑːp) *n* **1** a large triangular plucked stringed instrument consisting of a soundboard connected to an upright pillar by means of a curved crossbar from which the strings extend downwards. The strings are tuned diatonically and may be raised in pitch either one or two semitones by the use of pedals (**double-action harp**). Basic key: B major; range: nearly seven octaves **2** something resembling this, esp in shape **3** an informal name (esp in pop music) for **harmonica** ▷ *vb* **4** (*intr*) to play the harp **5** (*tr*) *archaic* to speak; utter; express **6** (*intr*; foll by *on* or *upon*) to speak or write in a persistent and tedious manner [Old English *hearpe*; related to Old Norse *harpa*, Old High German *harfa*, Latin *corbis* basket, Russian *korobit* to warp] > 'harper *or* 'harpist *n*

Harper's Ferry ('hɑːpəz) *n* a village in NE West Virginia, at the confluence of the Potomac and Shenandoah Rivers: site of an arsenal seized by John Brown (1859). Pop: 302 (2003 est)

harpings ('hɑːpɪŋz) *or* **harpins** ('hɑːpɪnz) *pl n* **1** *nautical* wooden members used for strengthening the bow of a vessel **2** *shipbuilding* wooden supports used in construction [c17 perhaps related to French *harpe* cramp iron]

harpoon (hɑː'puːn) *n* **1 a** a barbed missile attached to a long cord and hurled or fired from a gun when hunting whales, etc **b** (*as modifier*): *a harpoon gun* ▷ *vb* **2** (*tr*) to spear with or as if with a harpoon [c17 probably from Dutch *harpoen*, from Old French *harpon* clasp, from *harper* to seize, perhaps of Scandinavian origin] > har'pooner *or* ,harpoon'eer *n* > har'poon-,like *adj*

harp seal *n* a brownish-grey earless seal, *Pagophilus groenlandicus*, of the North Atlantic and Arctic Oceans

harpsichord ('hɑːpsɪˌkɔːd) *n* a horizontally strung stringed keyboard instrument, triangular in shape, consisting usually of two manuals controlling various sets of strings plucked by pivoted plectrums mounted on jacks. Some harpsichords have a pedal keyboard and stops by which the tone colour may be varied [c17 from New Latin *harpichordium*, from Late Latin *harpa* HARP + Latin *chorda* CHORD] > 'harpsi,chordist *n*

harpy ('hɑːpɪ) *n, pl* **-pies** a cruel grasping woman [c16 from Latin *Harpyia*, from Greek *Harpuiai* the Harpies, literally: snatchers, from *harpazein* to seize]

Harpy ('hɑːpɪ) *n, pl* **-pies** *Greek myth* a ravenous creature with a woman's head and trunk and a bird's wings and claws

harpy eagle *n* a very large tropical American eagle, *Harpia harpyja*, with a black-and-white plumage and a head crest

harquebus ('hɑːkwɪbəs) *n, pl* **-buses** a variant of **arquebus**

harquebusier (,hɑːkwɪbə'sɪə) *n* (formerly) a soldier armed with an arquebus. Also called: **arquebusier**

Harrer ('hɑːrə) *n* a variant spelling of **Harar**

harridan ('hærɪdªn) *n* a scolding old woman; nag [c17 of uncertain origin; perhaps related to French *haridelle*, literally: broken-down horse; of obscure origin]

harrier¹ ('hærɪə) *n* **1** a person or thing that harries **2** any diurnal bird of prey of the genus *Circus*, having broad wings and long legs and tail and typically preying on small terrestrial animals: family *Accipitridae* (hawks, etc). See also **marsh harrier, Montagu's harrier**

harrier² ('hærɪə) *n* **1** a smallish breed of hound used originally for hare-hunting **2** a cross-country runner [c16 from HARE + -ER¹; influenced by HARRIER¹]

Harrier ('hærɪə) *n* a British subsonic multipurpose military jet plane capable of vertical takeoff and landing by means of vectoring the engine thrust

Harris ('hærɪs) *n* the S part of the island of Lewis with Harris, in the Outer Hebrides. Pop: (including Lewis) 23 390 (latest est). Area: 500 sq km (190 sq miles)

Harrisburg ('hærɪsˌbɜːg) *n* a city in S Pennsylvania, on the Susquehanna River: the state capital. Pop: 48 322 (2003 est)

Harris Tweed *n trademark* a loose-woven tweed made in the Outer Hebrides, esp Lewis and Harris

Harrogate ('hærəgɪt) *n* a town in N England, in North Yorkshire: a former spa, now a centre for tourism and conferences. Pop: 70 811 (2001 est)

Harrovian (hə'rəʊvɪən) *n* **1** a person educated at Harrow School ▷ *adj* **2** of or concerning Harrow [c19 from New Latin *Harrōvia* HARROW + -AN]

harrow¹ ('hærəʊ) *n* **1** any of various implements used to level the ground, stir the soil, break up clods, destroy weeds, etc, in soil ▷ *vb* **2** (*tr*) to draw a harrow over (land) **3** (*intr*) (of soil) to become broken up through harrowing **4** (*tr*) to distress; vex [c13 of Scandinavian origin; compare Danish *harv*, Swedish *harf*; related to Middle Dutch *harke* rake] > 'harrower *n* > 'harrowing *adj, n*

harrow² ('hærəʊ) *vb* (*tr*) *archaic* **1** to plunder or ravish **2** (of Christ) to descend into (hell) to rescue righteous souls [c13 variant of Old English *hergian* to HARRY] > 'harrowment *n*

Harrow ('hærəʊ) *n* a borough of NW Greater London; site of an English boys' public school founded in 1571 at **Harrow-on-the-Hill,** a part of this borough. Pop: 210 700 (2003 est). Area: 51 sq km (20 sq miles)

harrumph (hə'rʌmf) *vb* (*intr*) to clear or make the noise of clearing the throat

harry ('hærɪ) *vb* **-ries, -rying, -ried 1** (*tr*) to harass; worry **2** to ravage (a town, etc), esp in war [Old English *hergian*; related to *here* army, Old Norse *herja* to lay waste, Old High German *heriōn*]

harsh (hɑːʃ) *adj* **1** rough or grating to the senses **2** stern, severe, or cruel [c16 probably of Scandinavian origin; compare Middle Low German *harsch*, Norwegian *harsk* rancid] > 'harshly *adv* > 'harshness *n*

harslet ('hɑːzlɪt, 'hɑːs-) *n* a variant of **haslet**

hart (hɑːt) *n, pl* **harts** *or* **hart** the male of the deer, esp the red deer aged five years or more [Old English *heorot*; related to Old Norse *hjörtr*, Old High German *hiruz* hart, Latin *cervus* stag, Lithuanian *kárve* cow; see HORN]

hartal (hɑː'tɑːl) *n* (in India) the act of closing shops or suspending work, esp in political protest [c20 from Hindi *hartāl*, from *hāt* shop (from Sanskrit *hatta*) + *tāla* bolt for a door (from Sanskrit: latch)]

hartebeest ('hɑːtɪˌbiːst) *or* **hartbeest** ('hɑːtˌbiːst)

n **1** either of two large African antelopes, *Alcelaphus buselaphus* or *A. lichtensteini*, having an elongated muzzle, lyre-shaped horns, and a fawn-coloured coat **2** any similar and related animal, such as *Damaliscus hunteri* (**Hunter's hartebeest**) [c18 via Afrikaans from Dutch; see HART, BEAST]

Hartford ('hɑːtfəd) *n* a port in central Connecticut, on the Connecticut River: the state capital. Pop: 124 387 (2003 est)

Hartlepool ('hɑːtlɪˌpuːl) *n* **1** a port in NE England, in Hartlepool unitary authority, Co Durham, on the North Sea: greatly enlarged in 1967 by its amalgamation with West Hartlepool; engineering, clothing, food processing. Pop: 86 075 (2001) **2** a unitary authority in NE England, in Co Durham: formerly (1974–96) part of the county of Cleveland. Pop: 90 200 (2003 est). Area: 93 sq km (36 sq miles)

hartshorn ('hɑːtsˌhɔːn) *n* an obsolete name for **sal volatile** (sense 2) [Old English *heortes horn* hart's horn (formerly a chief source of ammonia)]

hart's-tongue *n* an evergreen Eurasian fern, *Asplenium scolopendrium*, with narrow undivided fronds bearing rows of sori: family *Polypodiaceae*

harum-scarum (ˌhɛərəm'skɛərəm) *adj, adv* **1** in a reckless way or of a reckless nature ▷ *n* **2** a person who is impetuous or rash [c17 perhaps from *hare* (in obsolete sense: harass) + *scare*, variant of STARE¹; compare HELTER-SKELTER]

haruspex (hə'rʌspɛks) *n, pl* **haruspices** (hə'rʌspɪˌsiːz) (in ancient Rome) a priest who practised divination, esp by examining the entrails of animals [c16 from Latin, probably from *hīra* gut + *specere* to look] > haruspical (hə'rʌspɪkªl) *adj* > haruspicy (hə'rʌspɪsɪ) *n*

Harvard classification ('hɑːvəd) *n* a classification of stars based on the characteristic spectral absorption lines and bands of the chemical elements present. See **spectral type** [c20 named after the observatory at *Harvard*, Massachusetts, where it was prepared and published as part of *The Henry Draper Catalogue* (1924)]

harvest ('hɑːvɪst) *n* **1** the gathering of a ripened crop **2** the crop itself or the yield from it in a single growing season **3** the season for gathering crops **4** the product of an effort, action, etc: *a harvest of love* ▷ *vb* **5** to gather or reap (a ripened crop) from (the place where it has been growing) **6** (*tr*) to receive or reap (benefits, consequences, etc) **7** (*tr*) *chiefly US* to remove (an organ) from the body for transplantation [Old English *hærfest*; related to Old Norse *harfr* harrow, Old High German *herbist* autumn, Latin *carpere* to pluck, Greek *karpos* fruit, Sanskrit *krpāna* shears] > 'harvesting *n* > 'harvestless *adj*

harvester ('hɑːvɪstə) *n* **1** a person who harvests **2** a harvesting machine, esp a combine harvester

harvest home *n* **1** the bringing in of the harvest **2** *chiefly Brit* a harvest supper

harvestman ('hɑːvɪstmən) *n, pl* **-men 1** a person engaged in harvesting **2** Also called (US and Canadian): **daddy-longlegs** any arachnid of the order *Opiliones* (or *Phalangida*), having a small rounded body and very long thin legs

harvest mite *or* **tick** *n* the bright red parasitic larva of any of various free-living mites of the genus *Trombicula* and related genera, which causes intense itching of human skin

harvest moon *n* the full moon occurring nearest to the autumnal equinox

harvest mouse *n* **1** a very small reddish-brown Eurasian mouse, *Micromys minutus*, inhabiting cornfields, hedgerows, etc, and feeding on grain and seeds: family *Muridae* **2 American harvest mouse** any small greyish mouse of the American genus *Reithrodontomys*: family *Cricetidae*

Harwell ('hɑːwɛl) *n* a village in S England, in Oxfordshire: atomic research station (1947)

Harwich ('hærɪtʃ) *n* a port in SE England, in NE Essex on the North Sea. Pop: 20 130 (2001)

Haryana (hər'jɑːnə) *n* a state of NE India, formed

h

in 1966 from the Hindi-speaking parts of the state of Punjab. Capital: Chandigarh (shared with Punjab). Pop: 21 082 989 (2001 est). Area: 44 506 sq km (17 182 sq miles)

Harz or **Harz Mountains** (hɑːts) *pl n* a range of wooded hills in central Germany, between the Rivers Weser and Elbe: source of many legends. Highest peak: Brocken, 1142 m (3746 ft)

has (hæz) *vb* (used with *he, she, it,* or a singular noun) a form of the present tense (indicative mood) of **have**

has-been *n informal* a person or thing that is no longer popular, successful, effective, etc

hasbian ('hæzbɪən) *n* a former lesbian who has become heterosexual or bisexual [C20 HAS-BEEN + LESBIAN]

hash[1] (hæʃ) *n* **1** a dish of diced cooked meat, vegetables, etc, reheated in a sauce **2** something mixed up **3** a reuse or rework of old material **4** **make a hash of** *informal* **a** to mix or mess up **b** to defeat or destroy **5** **settle** (*or* **fix**) **someone's hash** *informal* to subdue or silence someone ▷ *vb* (*tr*) **6** to chop into small pieces **7** to mix or mess up [C17 from Old French *hacher* to chop up, from *hache* HATCHET]

hash[2] (hæʃ) *n slang* short for **hashish**

hash[3] (hæʃ) or **hash mark** *n* **1** the character (#) used to precede a number **2** this sign used in printing or writing to indicate that a space should be inserted

hash browns *pl n* diced boiled potatoes mixed with chopped onion, shaped and fried until brown

HaShem (ha'ʃem) *n Judaism* a periphrastic way of referring to God in contexts other than prayer, scriptural reading, etc because the name itself is considered too holy for such use [from Hebrew, literally: The Name]

Hashemite Kingdom of Jordan ('hæʃɪˌmaɪt) *n* the official name of **Jordan**

hash house *n US slang* a cheap café or restaurant

hashish ('hæʃiːʃ, -ɪʃ) or **hasheesh** ('hæʃiːʃ) *n* **1** a purified resinous extract of the dried flower tops of the female hemp plant, used as a hallucinogenic. See also **cannabis 2** any hallucinogenic substance prepared from this resin [C16 from Arabic *hashish* hemp, dried herbage]

haslet ('hæzlɪt) or **harslet** *n* a loaf of cooked minced pig's offal, eaten cold [C14 from Old French *hastelet* piece of spit roasted meat, from *haste* spit, of Germanic origin; compare Old High German *harsta* frying pan]

hasn't ('hæzᵊnt) *vb contraction of* has not

hasp (hɑːsp) *n* **1** a metal fastening consisting of a hinged strap with a slot that fits over a staple and is secured by a pin, bolt, or padlock ▷ *vb* **2** (*tr*) to secure (a door, etc) with a hasp [Old English *hæpse*; related to Old Norse *hespa*, Old High German *haspa* hasp, Dutch *haspel* reel, Sanskrit *capa* bow]

Hasselt (*Flemish* 'hɑsəlt; *French* asɛlt) *n* a market town in E Belgium, capital of Limburg province. Pop: 69 127 (2004 est)

Hassid or **Hasid** ('hæsɪd; *Hebrew* xa'sid) *n* variant spellings of **Chassid**

hassium ('hæsɪəm) *n* a synthetic element produced in small quantities by high-energy ion bombardment. Symbol: Hs; atomic no. 108 [C20 from Latin, from Hesse, German state where it was discovered]

hassle ('hæsᵊl) *informal* ▷ *n* **1** a prolonged argument; wrangle **2** a great deal of trouble; difficulty; nuisance ▷ *vb* **3** (*intr*) to quarrel or wrangle **4** (*tr*) to cause annoyance or trouble to (someone); harass [C20 of unknown origin]

hassock ('hæsək) *n* **1** a firm upholstered cushion used for kneeling on, esp in church **2** a thick clump of grass [Old English *hassuc* matted grass]

hast (hæst) *vb archaic* or *dialect* (used with the pronoun *thou* or its relative equivalent) a singular form of the present tense (indicative mood) of **have**

hastate ('hæsteɪt) *adj* (of a leaf) having a pointed tip and two outward-pointing lobes at the base [C18 from Latin *hastātus* with a spear, from *hasta* spear]

haste (heɪst) *n* **1** speed, esp in an action; swiftness; rapidity **2** the act of hurrying in a careless or rash manner **3** a necessity for hurrying; urgency **4** **make haste** to hurry; rush ▷ *vb* **5** a poetic word for **hasten** [C14 from Old French *haste*, of Germanic origin; compare Old Norse *heifst* hate, Old English *hǣst* strife, Old High German *heisti* powerful] > **'hasteful** *adj* > **'hastefully** *adv*

hasten ('heɪsᵊn) *vb* **1** (*may take an infinitive*) to hurry or cause to hurry; rush **2** (*tr*) to be anxious (to say something): *I hasten to add that we are just good friends* > **'hastener** *n*

Hastings ('heɪstɪŋz) *n* **1** a port in SE England, in East Sussex on the English Channel: near the site of the **Battle of Hastings** (1066), in which William the Conqueror defeated King Harold; chief of the Cinque Ports. Pop: 85 828 (2001) **2** a town in New Zealand, on E North Island: centre of a rich agricultural and fruit-growing region. Pop: 71 100 (2004 est)

hasty ('heɪstɪ) *adj* **-tier, -tiest 1** rapid; swift; quick **2** excessively or rashly quick **3** short-tempered **4** showing irritation or anger: *hasty words* > **'hastily** *adv* > **'hastiness** *n*

hasty pudding *n* **1** *Brit* a simple pudding made from milk thickened with tapioca, semolina, etc, and sweetened **2** *US* a mush of cornmeal, served with treacle sugar

hat (hæt) *n* **1 a** any of various head coverings, esp one with a brim and a shaped crown **b** (*in combination*): *hatrack* **2** *informal* a role or capacity **3** **at the drop of a hat** without hesitation or delay **4** **I'll eat my hat** *informal* I will be greatly surprised if (something that proves me wrong) happens: *I'll eat my hat if this book comes out late* **5** **hat in hand** humbly or servilely **6** **keep (something) under one's hat** to keep (something) secret **7** **my hat** (*interjection*) *Brit informal* **a** my word! my goodness! **b** nonsense! **8** **old hat** something stale or old-fashioned **9** **out of a hat a** as if by magic **b** at random **10** **pass** (*or* **send**) **the hat round** to collect money, as for a cause **11** **take off one's hat to** to admire or congratulate **12** **talk through one's hat a** to talk foolishly **b** to deceive or bluff **13** **throw one's hat at (it)** *Irish* to give up all hope of getting or achieving (something): *you can throw your hat at it now* **14** **throw** (*or* **toss**) **one's hat in the ring** to announce one's intentions to be a candidate or contestant ▷ *vb* **hats, hatting, hatted 15** (*tr*) to supply (a person, etc) with a hat or to put a hat on (someone) [Old English *hætt*; related to Old Norse *höttr* cap, Latin *cassis* helmet; see HOOD[1]] > **'hatless** *adj* > **'hat,like** *adj*

hatband ('hæt,bænd) *n* a band or ribbon around the base of the crown of a hat

hatbox ('hæt,bɒks) *n* a box or case for a hat or hats

hatch[1] (hætʃ) *vb* **1** to cause (the young of various animals, esp birds) to emerge from the egg or (of young birds, etc) to emerge from the egg **2** to cause (eggs) to break and release the fully developed young or (of eggs) to break and release the young animal within **3** (*tr*) to contrive or devise (a scheme, plot, etc) ▷ *n* **4** the act or process of hatching **5** a group of newly hatched animals [C13 of Germanic origin; compare Middle High German *hecken* to mate (used of birds), Swedish *häcka* to hatch, Danish *hække*] > **'hatchable** *adj* > **'hatcher** *n*

hatch[2] (hætʃ) *n* **1** a covering for a hatchway **2** short for **hatchway 3** Also called: **serving hatch** an opening in a wall between a kitchen and a dining area **4** the lower half of a divided door **5** a sluice or sliding gate in a dam, dyke, or weir **6** **down the hatch** *slang* (used as a toast) drink up! **7** **under hatches a** below decks **b** out of sight **c** brought low; dead [Old English *hæcc*; related to

Middle High German *heck*, Dutch *hek* gate]

hatch[3] (hætʃ) *vb art* to mark (a figure, shade, etc) with fine parallel or crossed lines to indicate shading. Compare **hachure** [C15 from Old French *hacher* to chop, from *hache* HATCHET] > **'hatching** *n*

hatch[4] (hætʃ) *n informal* short for **hatchback**

hatchback ('hætʃ,bæk) *n* **1 a** a sloping rear end of a car having a single door that is lifted to open **b** (*as modifier*): *a hatchback model* **2** a car having such a rear end

hatchel ('hætʃəl) *vb* **-els, -elling, -elled** or *US* **-els, -eling, -eled,** *n* another word for **heckle** (senses 2, 3) [C13 *hechele*, of Germanic origin; related to Old High German *hāko* hook, Middle Dutch *hekele* HACKLE] > **'hatcheller** *n*

hatchery ('hætʃərɪ) *n, pl* **-eries** a place where eggs are hatched under artificial conditions

hatchet ('hætʃɪt) *n* **1** a short axe used for chopping wood, etc **2** a tomahawk **3** (*modifier*) of narrow dimensions and sharp features: *a hatchet face* **4** **bury the hatchet** to cease hostilities and become reconciled [C14 from Old French *hachette*, from *hache* axe, of Germanic origin; compare Old High German *happa* knife] > **'hatchet-,like** *adj*

hatchet job *n informal* a malicious or devastating verbal or written attack

hatchet man *n informal* **1** a person carrying out unpleasant assignments for an employer or superior **2** *US and Canadian* a hired murderer **3** a severe or malicious critic

hatchling ('hætʃlɪŋ) *n* a young animal that has newly emerged from an egg [C19 from HATCH[1] + -LING]

hatchment ('hætʃmənt) *n heraldry* a diamond-shaped tablet displaying the coat of arms of a dead person. Also called: **achievement** [C16 changed from ACHIEVEMENT]

hatchway ('hætʃ,weɪ) *n* **1** an opening in the deck of a vessel to provide access below **2** a similar opening in a wall, floor, ceiling, or roof, usually fitted with a lid or door ▷ Often shortened to: **hatch**

hate (heɪt) *vb* **1** to dislike (something) intensely; detest **2** (*intr*) to be unwilling (to be or do something) ▷ *n* **3** intense dislike **4** *informal* a person or thing that is hated (esp in the phrase **pet hate**) **5** (*modifier*) expressing or arousing feelings of hatred: *hate mail* [Old English *hatian*; related to Old Norse *hata*, Old Saxon *hatōn*, Old High German *hazzēn*] > **'hateable** or **'hatable** *adj*

hate crime *n* a crime, esp of violence, in which the victim is targeted because of his or her race, religion, sexuality, etc

hateful ('heɪtfʊl) *adj* **1** causing or deserving hate; loathsome; detestable **2** full of or showing hate > **'hatefully** *adv* > **'hatefulness** *n*

hate speech *n* speech disparaging a racial, sexual, or ethnic group or a member of such a group

Hatfield ('hæt,fiːld) *n* a market town in S central England, in Hertfordshire, with a new town of the same name built on the outskirts: university (1992); site of **Hatfield House** (1607–11), the seat of the Cecil family. Pop: 32 281 (2001)

hath (hæθ) *vb archaic* or *dialect* (used with the pronouns *he, she,* or *it* or a singular noun) a form of the present tense (indicative mood) of **have**

hatha yoga ('hʌtə, 'hæθə) *n* (*sometimes capitals*) a form of yoga concerned chiefly with the regulation of breathing by exercises consisting of various postures designed to maintain healthy functioning of the body and to induce mental calm. Compare **raja yoga** [C20 from Sanskrit *hatha* force + YOGA]

Hathor ('hæθɔː) *n* (in ancient Egyptian religion) the mother of Horus and goddess of creation > **Hathoric** (hæ'θɔːrɪk, -'θɒr-) *adj*

hatpin ('hæt,pɪn) *n* a sturdy pin used to secure a woman's hat to her hair, often having a decorative head

hatred ('heɪtrɪd) *n* a feeling of intense dislike; enmity

hat stand or esp US **hat tree** n a frame or pole equipped with hooks or arms for hanging up hats, coats, etc

hatter ('hætə) n **1** a person who makes and sells hats **2** mad as a hatter crazily eccentric

Hatteras ('hætərəs) n Cape a promontory off the E coast of North Carolina, on Hatteras Island, which is situated between Pamlico Sound and the Atlantic: known as the "Graveyard of the Atlantic" for its danger to shipping

hat-trick n **1** cricket the achievement of a bowler in taking three wickets with three successive balls **2** any achievement of three points, victories, awards, etc within a given period, esp three goals scored by the same player in a soccer match

haubergeon ('hɔːbədʒən) n a variant of **habergeon**

hauberk ('hɔːbɜːk) n a long coat of mail, often sleeveless [c13 from Old French hauberc, of Germanic origin; compare Old High German halsberc, Old English healsbeorg, from heals neck + beorg protection, shelter]

haud (hɔːd, hud) vb, n a Scot word for **hold**

hauf (hɔːf) n, determiner, adj, adv a Scot word for **half**

haugh (hɑːk, hɑːf; Scot hɒx) n Scot and northern English dialect a low-lying often alluvial riverside meadow [Old English healh corner of land; see HOLLOW]

haughty ('hɔːtɪ) adj -tier, -tiest **1** having or showing arrogance **2** archaic noble or exalted [c16 from Old French haut, literally: lofty, from Latin altus high] > 'haughtily adv > 'haughtiness n

Hauhau ('hauhau) n NZ history a 19th-century Māori religious sect [Māori]

haul (hɔːl) vb **1** to drag or draw (something) with effort **2** (tr) to transport, as in a lorry **3** nautical to alter the course of (a vessel), esp so as to sail closer to the wind **4** (tr) nautical to draw or hoist (a vessel) out of the water onto land or a dock for repair, storage, etc **5** (intr) nautical (of the wind) to blow from a direction nearer the bow. Compare **veer¹** (sense 3b) **6** (intr) to change one's opinion or action ▷ n **7** the act of dragging with effort **8** (esp of fish) the amount caught at a single time **9** something that is hauled **10** the goods obtained from a robbery **11** a distance of hauling: a three-mile haul **12** the amount of a contraband seizure: arms haul; drugs haul **13** in (or over) the long haul **a** in a future time **b** over a lengthy period of time [c16 from Old French haler, of Germanic origin; see HALE²]

haulage ('hɔːlɪdʒ) n **1** the act or labour of hauling **2** a rate or charge levied for the transportation of goods, esp by rail

haulier ('hɔːljə) or US **hauler** ('hɔːlə) n **1** a person or firm that transports goods by lorry; one engaged in road haulage **2** a person that hauls, esp a mine worker who conveys coal from the workings to the foot of the shaft

haulm or **halm** (hɔːm) n **1** the stems or stalks of beans, peas, potatoes, grasses, etc, collectively, as used for thatching, bedding, etc **2** a single stem of such a plant [Old English healm; related to Old Norse halmr, Old High German halm stem, straw, Latin culmus stalk, Greek kalamos reed, Old Slavonic slama straw]

haul off vb (intr, adverb) **1** (foll by and) US and Canadian informal to draw back in preparation (esp to strike or fight): I hauled off and slugged him **2** nautical to alter the course of a vessel so as to avoid an obstruction, shallow waters, etc

haul up vb (adverb) **1** (tr) informal to call to account or criticize **2** nautical to sail (a vessel) closer to the wind

haunch (hɔːntʃ) n **1** the human hip or fleshy hindquarter of an animal, esp a horse or similar quadruped **2** the leg and loin of an animal, used for food: a haunch of venison **3** Also called: hance architect the part of an arch between the impost and the apex [c13 from Old French hanche; related to Spanish, Italian anca, of Germanic origin;

compare Low German hanke] > haunched adj

haunch bone n a nontechnical name for the **ilium** or **hipbone**

haunt (hɔːnt) vb **1** to visit (a person or place) in the form of a ghost **2** (tr) to intrude upon or recur to (the memory, thoughts, etc): he was haunted by the fear of insanity **3** to visit (a place) frequently **4** to associate with (someone) frequently ▷ n **5** (often plural) a place visited frequently: an old haunt of hers **6** a place to which animals habitually resort for food, drink, shelter, etc [c13 from Old French hanter, of Germanic origin; compare Old Norse heimta to bring home, Old English hāmettan to give a home to; see HOME] > 'haunter n

haunted ('hɔːntɪd) adj **1** frequented or visited by ghosts **2** (postpositive) obsessed or worried

haunting ('hɔːntɪŋ) adj **1** (of memories) poignant or persistent **2** poignantly sentimental; enchantingly or eerily evocative > 'hauntingly adv

Hauraki Gulf (hau'rækɪ) n an inlet of the Pacific in New Zealand, on the N coast of North Island

Hausa ('hausə) n **1** (pl -sas or -sa) a member of a Negroid people of W Africa, living chiefly in N Nigeria **2** the language of this people: the chief member of the Chadic subfamily of the Afro-Asiatic family of languages. It is widely used as a trading language throughout W Africa and the S Sahara

hausfrau ('haus,frau) n a German housewife [German, from Haus HOUSE + Frau woman, wife]

haustellum (hɔː'stɛləm) n, pl -la (-lə) the tip of the proboscis of a housefly or similar insect, specialized for sucking food [c19 New Latin, diminutive of Latin haustrum device for drawing water, from haurīre to draw up; see EXHAUST] > haus'tellate adj

haustorium (hɔː'stɔːrɪəm) n, pl -ria (-rɪə) the organ of a parasitic plant that penetrates the host tissues and absorbs food and water from them [c19 from New Latin, from Late Latin haustor a water-drawer; see HAUSTELLUM] > haus'torial adj

hautboy ('əubɔɪ) n **1** Also called: hautbois strawberry, haubois ('əubɔɪ) a strawberry, Fragaria moschata, of central Europe and Asia, with large fruit **2** an archaic word for **oboe** [c16 from French hautbois, from haut high + bois wood, of Germanic origin; see BUSH¹]

haute couture French (ot kutyr) n high fashion [literally: high dressmaking]

haute cuisine French (ot kwizin) n high-class cooking [literally: high cookery]

haute école French (ot ekɔl) n the classical art of riding [literally: high school]

Haute-Garonne (French otgarɔn) n a department of SW France, in Midi-Pyrénées region. Capital: Toulouse. Pop: 1 102 919 (2003 est). Area: 6367 sq km (2483 sq miles)

Haute-Loire (French otlwar) n a department of S central France, in Auvergne region. Capital: Le Puy. Pop: 213 993 (2003 est). Area: 5001 sq km (1950 sq miles)

Haute-Marne (French otmarn) n a department of NE France, in Champagne-Ardenne region. Capital: Chaumont. Pop: 190 983 (2003 est). Area: 6257 sq km (2440 sq miles)

Haute-Normandie (French otnɔrmɑ̃di) n a region of NW France, on the English Channel: generally fertile and flat

Hautes-Alpes (French otzalp) n a department of SE France in Provence-Alpes-Côte d'Azur region. Capital: Gap. Pop: 126 810 (2003 est). Area: 5643 sq km (2201 sq miles)

Haute-Saône (French otson) n a department of E France, in Franche-Comté region. Capital: Vesoul. Pop: 232 283 (2003 est). Area: 5375 sq km (2096 sq miles)

Haute-Savoie (French otsavwa) n a department of E France, in Rhône-Alpes region. Capital: Annecy. Pop: 663 810 (2003 est). Area: 4958 sq km (1934 sq miles)

Hautes-Pyrénées (French otpirene) n a department of SW France, in Midi-Pyrénées

region. Capital: Tarbes. Pop: 224 053 (2003 est). Area: 4534 sq km (1768 sq miles)

hauteur (əʊ'tɜː) n pride; haughtiness [c17 from French, from haut high; see HAUGHTY]

Haute-Vienne (French otvjɛn) n a department of W central France, in Limousin region. Capital: Limoges. Pop: 353 788 (2003 est). Area: 5555 sq km (2166 sq miles)

haut monde French (o mɔ̃d) n high society [literally: high world]

Haut-Rhin (French orɛ̃) n a department of E France in Alsace region. Capital: Colmar. Pop: 722 692 (2003 est). Area: 3566 sq km (1377 sq miles)

Hauts-de-Seine (French odəsɛn) n a department of N central France, in Île-de-France region just west of Paris: formed in 1964. Capital: Nanterre. Pop: 1 470 706 (2003 est). Area: 175 sq km (68 sq miles)

Havana (hə'vænə) n the capital of Cuba, a port in the northwest on the Gulf of Mexico: the largest city in the Caribbean; founded in 1514 as San Cristóbal de la Habana by Diego Velásquez. Pop: 2 192 000 (2005 est). Spanish name: Habana Related adjective: Habanero

Havana Brown n a breed of medium-sized cat with large eyes, large ears, and a sleek brown coat

Havana cigar n any of various cigars hand rolled in Cuba, known esp for their high quality. Also called: Havana

Havant ('hævnt) n a market town in S England, in SE Hampshire. Pop: 45 435 (2001)

havdalah or **havdoloh** Hebrew (havdɑ'la; Yiddish hav'dɔlə) n Judaism the ceremony marking the end of the sabbath or of a festival, including the blessings over wine, candles, and spices [literally: separation]

have (hæv) vb has, having, had (mainly tr) **1** to be in material possession of; own: he has two cars **2** to possess as a characteristic quality or attribute: he has dark hair **3** to receive, take, or obtain: she had a present from him; have a look **4** to hold or entertain in the mind: to have an idea **5** to possess a knowledge or understanding of: I have no German **6** to experience or undergo: to have a shock **7** to be infected with or suffer from: to have a cold **8** to gain control of or advantage over: you have me on that point **9** (usually passive) slang to cheat or outwit: he was had by that dishonest salesman **10** (foll by on) to exhibit (mercy, compassion, etc, towards): have mercy on us, Lord **11** to engage or take part in: to have a conversation **12** to arrange, carry out, or hold: to have a party **13** to cause, compel, or require to (be, do, or be done): have my shoes mended **14** (takes an infinitive with to) used as an auxiliary to express compulsion or necessity: I had to run quickly to escape him **15** to eat, drink, or partake of: to have a good meal **16** slang to have sexual intercourse with: he had her on the sofa **17** (used with a negative) to tolerate or allow: I won't have all this noise **18** to declare, state, or assert: rumour has it that they will marry **19** to put or place: I'll have the sofa in this room **20** to receive as a guest: to have three people to stay **21** to beget or bear (offspring): she had three children **22** (takes a past participle) used as an auxiliary to form compound tenses expressing completed action: I have gone; I shall have gone; I would have gone; I had gone **23** had better or best ought to: used to express compulsion, obligation, etc: you had better go **24** had rather or sooner to consider or find preferable that: I had rather you left at once **25** have done See done (sense 3) **26** have had it informal **a** to be exhausted, defeated, or killed **b** to have lost one's last chance **c** to become unfashionable **27** have it in a victory **28** have it away (or off) Brit slang to have sexual intercourse **29** have it coming informal to be about to receive or to merit punishment or retribution **30** have it in for informal to wish or intend harm towards **31** have it so good to have so many benefits, esp material benefits **32** have to do with **a** to have dealings or associate with: I have nothing to do with her **b** to be of relevance to: this has nothing to do with you **33** I have

h

it *informal* I know the answer **34 let (someone) have it** *slang* to launch or deliver an attack on, esp to discharge a firearm at (someone) **35 not having any** (foll by *of*) *informal* refusing to take part or be involved (in) ▷ *n* **36** (*usually plural*) a person or group of people in possession of wealth, security, etc: *the haves and the have-nots* ▷ See also **have at, have in, have on, have out, have up** [Old English *habban*; related to Old Norse *hafa*, Old Saxon *hebbian*, Old High German *habēn*, Latin *habēre*]

have-a-go *adj informal* (of people attempting arduous or dangerous tasks) brave or spirited: *a have-a-go pensioner*

have at *vb* (*intr, preposition*) *archaic* to make an opening attack on, esp in fencing

have in *vb* (*tr, adverb*) **1** to ask (a person) to give a service: *we must have the electrician in to mend the fire* **2** to invite to one's home

Havel (*German* 'haːfəl) *n* a river in E Germany, flowing south to Berlin, then west and north to join the River Elbe. Length: about 362 km (225 miles)

havelock ('hævlɒk) *n* a light-coloured cover for a service cap with a flap extending over the back of the neck to protect the head and neck from the sun [c19 named after Sir H. *Havelock* (1795–1857), English general in India]

haven ('heɪvᵊn) *n* **1** a port, harbour, or other sheltered place for shipping **2** a place of safety or sanctuary; shelter ▷ *vb* **3** (*tr*) to secure or shelter in or as if in a haven [Old English *hæfen*, from Old Norse *höfn*; related to Middle Dutch *havene*, Old Irish *cuan* to bend] > **ˈhavenless** *adj*

have-not *n* (*usually plural*) a person or group of people in possession of relatively little material wealth

haven't ('hævᵊnt) *vb contraction of* have not

have on *vb* (*tr*) **1** (*usually adverb*) to wear **2** (*usually adverb*) to have (a meeting or engagement) arranged as a commitment: *what does your boss have on this afternoon?* **3** (*adverb*) *informal* to trick or tease (a person) **4** (*preposition*) to have available (information or evidence, esp when incriminating) about (a person): *the police had nothing on him, so they let him go*

have out *vb* (*tr, adverb*) **1** to settle (a matter) or come to (a final decision), esp by fighting or by frank discussion (often in the phrase **have it out**) **2** to have extracted or removed: *I had a tooth out*

haver ('heɪvə) *vb* (*intr*) *Brit* **1** *Scot and northern English dialect* to talk nonsense; babble ▷ *n* **3** (*usually plural*) *Scot* nonsense [c18 of unknown origin]

Havering ('heɪvərɪŋ) *n* a borough of NE Greater London, formed in 1965 from Romford and Hornchurch (both previously in Essex). Pop: 224 600 (2003 est). Area: 120 sq km (46 sq miles)

haversack ('hævəˌsæk) *n* a canvas bag for provisions or equipment, carried on the back or shoulder [c18 from French *havresac*, from German *Habersack* oat bag, from Old High German *habaro* oats + *Sack* SACK¹]

Haversian canal (hæˈvɜːʃən) *n histology* any of the channels that form a network in bone and contain blood vessels and nerves [c19 named after C. *Havers* (died 1702), English anatomist who discovered them]

haversine ('hævəˌsaɪn) *n obsolete* half the value of the versed sine [c19 combination of *half* + *versed* + SINE¹]

have up *vb* (*tr, adverb; usually passive*) to cause to appear for trial: *he was had up for breaking and entering*

havildar ('hævɪlˌdɑː) *n* a noncommissioned officer in the Indian army, equivalent in rank to sergeant [c17 from Hindi, from Persian *hawāldār* one in charge]

havoc ('hævək) *n* **1** destruction; devastation; ruin **2** *informal* confusion; chaos **3 cry havoc** *archaic* to give the signal for pillage and destruction **4 play havoc** (often foll by *with*) to cause a great deal of damage, distress, or confusion (to) ▷ *vb* -ocs,

-ocking, -ocked **5** (*tr*) *archaic* to lay waste [c15 from Old French *havot* pillage, probably of Germanic origin]

Havre ('hɑːvrə; *French* ɑvrə) *n* See Le Havre

haw¹ (hɔː) *n* **1** the round or oval fruit (a pome) of the hawthorn, usually red or yellow, containing one to five seeds **2** another name for **hawthorn** [Old English *haga*, identical with *haga* HEDGE; related to Old Norse *hagi* pasture]

haw² (hɔː) *n, interj* **1** an inarticulate utterance, as of hesitation, embarrassment, etc; hem ▷ *vb* **2** (*intr*) to make this sound **3 hem** (*or* **hum**) **and haw** See **hem²** (sense 3) [c17 of imitative origin]

haw³ (hɔː) *n archaic* a yard or close [of unknown origin]

haw⁴ (hɔː) *n* the nictitating membrane of a horse or other domestic animal [c15 of unknown origin]

Hawaii (həˈwaɪɪ) *n* a state of the US in the central Pacific, consisting of over 20 volcanic islands and atolls, including Hawaii, Maui, Oahu, Kauai, and Molokai: discovered by Captain Cook in 1778; annexed by the US in 1898; naval base at Pearl Harbor attacked by the Japanese in 1941, a major cause of US entry into World War II; became a state in 1959. Capital: Honolulu. Pop: 1 257 608 (2003 est). Area: 16 640 sq km (6425 sq miles). Former name: **Sandwich Islands**. Abbreviations: **Ha**, (with zip code) **HI**

Hawaiian (həˈwaɪən) *adj* **1** of or relating to Hawaii, its people, or their language ▷ *n* **2** a native or inhabitant of Hawaii, esp one descended from Melanesian or Tahitian immigrants **3** a language of Hawaii belonging to the Malayo-Polynesian family

Hawaiian guitar *n* a lap-held steel-strung guitar with a wood or metal body, tuned to an open chord and played with a slide. Compare **Dobro**, **pedal steel guitar**

Hawaiki ('hɑːwaɪkiː) *n NZ* a legendary Pacific island from which the Māoris migrated to New Zealand by canoe [Māori]

Hawes Water (hɔːz) *n* a lake in NW England, in the Lake District: provides part of Manchester's water supply; extended by damming from 4 km (2.5 miles) to 6 km (4 miles)

hawfinch ('hɔːˌfɪntʃ) *n* an uncommon European finch, *Coccothraustes coccothraustes*, having a very stout bill and brown plumage with black-and-white wings

haw-haw¹ ('hɔːˈhɔː) *interj* a variant of **ha-ha¹**

haw-haw² ('hɔːˈhɔː) *n* a variant of **ha-ha²**

Hawick ('hɔːɪk) *n* a town in SE Scotland, in S central Scottish Borders: knitwear industry. Pop: 14 573 (2001)

hawk¹ (hɔːk) *n* **1** any of various diurnal birds of prey of the family *Accipitridae*, such as the goshawk and Cooper's hawk, typically having short rounded wings and a long tail. Related adj: **accipitrine 2** *US and Canadian* any of various other falconiform birds, including the falcons but not the eagles or vultures **3** a person who advocates or supports war or warlike policies. Compare **dove¹** (sense 2) **4** a ruthless or rapacious person **5 know a hawk from a handsaw** to be able to judge things; be discerning [from Shakespeare (*Hamlet* II:2:375)]; *handsaw* is probably a corruption of dialect *heronshaw* heron] ▷ *vb* **6** (*intr*) to hunt with falcons, hawks, etc **7** (*intr*) (of falcons or hawks) to fly in quest of prey **8** to pursue or attack on the wing, as a hawk [Old English *hafoc*; related to Old Norse *haukr*, Old Frisian *havek*, Old High German *habuh*, Polish *kobuz*] > **ˈhawkˌlike** *adj*

hawk² (hɔːk) *vb* **1** to offer (goods) for sale, as in the street **2** (*tr; often foll by *about*) to spread (news, gossip, etc) [c16 back formation from HAWKER¹]

hawk³ (hɔːk) *vb* **1** (*intr*) to clear the throat noisily **2** (*tr*) to force (phlegm) up from the throat **3** *Brit* a slang word for **spit** ▷ *n* **4** a noisy clearing of the throat [c16 of imitative origin; see HAW²]

hawk⁴ (hɔːk) *n* a small square board with a handle underneath, used for carrying wet plaster

or mortar. Also called: **mortar board** [of unknown origin]

hawkbill ('hɔːkˌbɪl) *n* another name for **hawksbill turtle**

hawkbit ('hɔːkˌbɪt) *n* any of three composite perennial plants of the genus *Leontodon*, with yellow dandelion-like flowers and lobed leaves in a rosette, erect or prostrate: found in grassland [c18 from HAWK(WEED) + (DEVIL'S) BIT]

hawker¹ ('hɔːkə) *n* a person who travels from place to place selling goods [c16 probably from Middle Low German *hōker*, from *hōken* to peddle; see HUCKSTER]

hawker² ('hɔːkə) *n* a person who hunts with hawks, falcons, etc [Old English *hafecere*; see HAWK¹, -ER¹]

Hawk-Eye *n trademark cricket* a machine, employed by TV commentators, that uses a missile tracking system to spot legitimate leg before wickets by determining whether the ball would have hit the stumps

hawk-eyed *adj* **1** having extremely keen sight **2** vigilant, watchful, or observant: *hawk-eyed scrutiny*

hawking ('hɔːkɪŋ) *n* another name for **falconry**

Hawking radiation *n astronomy* the emission of particles by a black hole. Pairs of virtual particles in the intense gravitational field around a black hole may live long enough for one to move outward when the other is pulled into the black hole, making it appear that the black hole is emitting radiation [c20 discovered by Stephen *Hawking* (born 1942), British physicist]

hawkish ('hɔːkɪʃ) *adj* favouring the use or display of force rather than diplomacy to achieve foreign policy goals

hawk moth *n* any of various moths of the family *Sphingidae*, having long narrow wings and powerful flight, with the ability to hover over flowers when feeding from the nectar. Also called: **sphinx moth, hummingbird moth**. See also **death's-head moth**

hawk owl *n* a hawklike northern owl, *Surnia ulula*, with a long slender tail and brownish speckled plumage

hawk's-beard *n* any plant of the genus *Crepis*, having a ring of fine hairs surrounding the fruit and clusters of small dandelion-like flowers: family *Asteraceae* (composites)

hawksbill turtle *or* **hawksbill** ('hɔːksˌbɪl) *n* a small tropical turtle, *Eretmochelys imbricata*, with a hooked beaklike mouth: a source of tortoiseshell: family *Chelonidae*. Also called: **hawkbill, tortoiseshell turtle**

hawk's-eye *n* a dark blue variety of the mineral crocidolite: a semiprecious gemstone

hawkweed ('hɔːkˌwiːd) *n* any typically hairy plant of the genus *Hieracium*, with clusters of dandelion-like flowers: family *Asteraceae* (composites)

Haworth ('hauəθ) *n* a village in N England, in Bradford unitary authority, West Yorkshire: home of Charlotte, Emily, and Anne Brontë. Pop: 6078 (2001)

hawse (hɔːz) *nautical* ▷ *n* **1** the part of the bows of a vessel where the hawseholes are **2** short for **hawsehole** *or* **hawsepipe 3** the distance from the bow of an anchored vessel to the anchor **4** the arrangement of port and starboard anchor ropes when a vessel is riding on both anchors ▷ *vb* **5** (*intr*) (of a vessel) to pitch violently when at anchor [c14 from earlier *halse*, probably from Old Norse *háls*; related to Old English *heals* neck]

hawsehole ('hɔːzˌhəʊl) *n nautical* one of the holes in the upper part of the bows of a vessel through which the anchor ropes pass. Often shortened to: **hawse**

hawsepipe ('hɔːzˌpaɪp) *n nautical* a strong metal pipe through which an anchor rope passes. Often shortened to: **hawse**

hawser ('hɔːzə) *n nautical* a large heavy rope [c14 from Anglo-French *hauceour*, from Old French *haucier* to hoist, ultimately from Latin *altus* high]

hawser bend *n* a knot for tying two ropes together

hawser-laid *adj* (of a rope) made up of three strands, the fibres (or yarns) of which have been twisted together in a left-handed direction. These three strands are then twisted together in a right-handed direction to make the rope

hawthorn ('hɔːˌθɔːn) *n* any of various thorny trees or shrubs of the N temperate rosaceous genus *Crataegus*, esp *C. oxyacantha*, having white or pink flowers and reddish fruits (haws). Also called (in Britain): **may, may tree, mayflower** [Old English *haguthorn* from *haga* hedge + *thorn* thorn; related to Old Norse *hagthorn*, Middle High German *hagendorn*, Dutch *haagdoorn*]

Hawthorne effect ('hɔːˌθɔːn) *n* improvement in the performance of employees, students, etc, brought about by making changes in working methods, resulting from research into means of improving performance. Compare **iatrogenic, placebo effect** [from the Western Electric Company's *Hawthorne* works in Chicago, USA, where it was discovered during experiments in the 1920s]

hay¹ (heɪ) *n* **1 a** grass, clover, etc, cut and dried as fodder **b** (*in combination*): *a hayfield; a hayloft* **2 hit the hay** *slang* to go to bed **3 make hay of** to throw into confusion **4 make hay while the sun shines** to take full advantage of an opportunity **5 roll in the hay** *informal* sexual intercourse or heavy petting ▷ *vb* **6** to cut, dry, and store (grass, clover, etc) as fodder **7** (*tr*) to feed with hay [Old English *hieg*; related to Old Norse *hey*, Gothic *hawi*, Old Frisian *hē*, Old High German *houwi*; see HEW]

hay² *or* **hey** (heɪ) *n* **1** a circular figure in country dancing **2** a former country dance in which the dancers wove in and out of a circle [c16 of uncertain origin]

haybox ('heɪˌbɒks) *n* an airtight box full of hay or other insulating material used to keep partially cooked food warm and allow cooking by retained heat

haycock ('heɪˌkɒk) *n* a small cone-shaped pile of hay left in the field until dry enough to carry to the rick or barn

hay fever *n* an allergic reaction to pollen, dust, etc, characterized by sneezing, runny nose, and watery eyes due to inflammation of the mucous membranes of the eyes and nose. Technical names **allergic rhinitis, pollinosis**

hayfork ('heɪˌfɔːk) *n* a long-handled fork with two long curved prongs, used for moving or turning hay; pitchfork

haylage ('heɪˌlɪdʒ) *n* silage made from partially dried grass [c20 from HAY¹ + (SI)LAGE]

haymaker ('heɪˌmeɪkə) *n* **1** a person who helps to cut, turn, toss, spread, or carry hay **2** Also called: **hay conditioner** either of two machines, one designed to crush stems of hay, the other to break and bend them, in order to cause more rapid and even drying **3** *boxing slang* a wild swinging punch ▷ **'hayˌmaking** *adj, n*

haymow ('heɪˌmaʊ) *n* **1** a part of a barn where hay is stored **2** a quantity of hay stored in a barn or loft

hayrack ('heɪˌræk) *n* **1** a rack for holding hay for feeding to animals **2** a rack fixed to a cart or wagon to increase the quantity of hay or straw that it can carry

hayseed ('heɪˌsiːd) *n* **1** seeds or fragments of grass or straw **2** *US and Canadian informal, derogatory* a yokel

haystack ('heɪˌstæk) *or* **hayrick** ('heɪˌrɪk) *n* a large pile of hay, esp one built in the open air and covered with thatch

hayward ('heɪˌwɔːd) *n* *Brit obsolete* a parish officer in charge of enclosures and fences

haywire ('heɪˌwaɪə) *adj* (*postpositive*) *informal* **1** (of things) not functioning properly; disorganized (esp in the phrase **go haywire**) **2** (of people) erratic or crazy [c20 alluding to the disorderly tangle of wire removed from bales of hay]

hazan *or* **hazzan** *Hebrew* (xaˈzan; *English* 'hɑːzəⁿn) *n* variant spellings of **chazan**

hazard ('hæzəd) *n* **1** exposure or vulnerability to injury, loss, evil, etc **2 at hazard** at risk; in danger **3** a thing likely to cause injury, etc **4** *golf* an obstacle such as a bunker, a road, rough, water, etc **5** chance; accident (esp in the phrase **by hazard**) **6** a gambling game played with two dice **7** *real Tennis* **a** the receiver's side of the court **b** one of the winning openings **8** *billiards* a scoring stroke made either when a ball other than the striker's is pocketed (**winning hazard**) or the striker's cue ball itself (**losing hazard**) ▷ *vb* (*tr*) **9** to chance or risk **10** to venture (an opinion, guess, etc) **11** to expose to danger [c13 from Old French *hasard*, from Arabic *az-zahr* the die] ▷ **'hazardable** *adj* ▷ **'hazard-ˌfree** *adj*

hazard lights *adj, pl n* the indicator lights of a motor vehicle when flashing simultaneously to indicate that the vehicle is stationary and temporarily obstructing the traffic. Also called: **hazard warning lights, hazards**

hazardous ('hæzədəs) *adj* **1** involving great risk **2** depending on chance ▷ **'hazardously** *adv* ▷ **'hazardousness** *n*

hazard warning device *n* an appliance fitted to a motor vehicle that operates the hazard lights

Hazchem ('hæzˌkɛm) *n* a word used on warning signs to indicate the presence of hazardous chemicals

haze¹ (heɪz) *n* **1** *meteorol* **a** reduced visibility in the air as a result of condensed water vapour, dust, etc, in the atmosphere **b** the moisture or dust causing this **2** obscurity of perception, feeling, etc ▷ *vb* **3** (when *intr*, often foll by *over*) to make or become hazy [c18 back formation from HAZY]

haze² (heɪz) *vb* (*tr*) **1** *chiefly US and Canadian* to subject (fellow students) to ridicule or abuse **2** *nautical* to harass with humiliating tasks [c17 of uncertain origin] ▷ **'hazer** *n*

hazel ('heɪzəl) *n* **1** Also called: **cob** any of several shrubs of the N temperate genus *Corylus*, esp *C. avellana*, having oval serrated leaves and edible rounded brown nuts: family *Corylaceae* **2** the wood of any of these trees **3** short for **hazelnut 4 a** a light yellowish-brown colour **b** (*as adjective*): *hazel eyes* [Old English *hæsel*; related to Old Norse *hasl*, Old High German *hasala*, Latin *corylus*, Old Irish *coll*]

hazelhen ('heɪzəlˌhɛn) *n* a European woodland gallinaceous bird, *Tetrastes bonasia*, with a speckled brown plumage and slightly crested crown: family *Tetraonidae* (grouse)

hazelnut ('heɪzəlˌnʌt) *n* the nut of a hazel shrub, having a smooth shiny hard shell. Also called: **filbert**, (*Brit*) **cobnut**, (*Brit*) **cob**

hazelnut oil *n* an oil extracted from hazelnuts and used mostly in cooking

hazy ('heɪzɪ) *adj* **-zier, -ziest 1** characterized by reduced visibility; misty **2** indistinct; vague [c17 of unknown origin] ▷ **'hazily** *adv* ▷ **'haziness** *n*

hazzan *Hebrew* (xaˈzan; *English* 'hɑːzəⁿn) *n* a variant spelling of **chazan**

Hb *symbol for* haemoglobin

HB (*on Brit pencils*) *symbol for* hard-black: denoting a medium-hard lead. Compare **H** (sense 5), **B** (sense 9)

H.B.C. (*in Canada*) *abbreviation for* **Hudson's Bay Company**

H-beam *n* a rolled steel joist or girder with a cross section in the form of a capital letter H. Compare **I-beam**

HBM (*in Britain*) *abbreviation for* His (or Her) Britannic Majesty

H-bomb *n* short for **hydrogen bomb**

HC *abbreviation for* **1** Holy Communion **2** (in Britain) House of Commons

HCF *or* **hcf** *abbreviation for* **highest common factor**

HCG *abbreviation for* human chorionic gonadotrophin. See **gonadotrophin**

hcp *abbreviation for* handicap

hd *abbreviation for* **1** hand **2** head

hdbk *abbreviation for* handbook

HDD *abbreviation for* *computing* hard disk drive

HD-DVD *abbreviation for* High Definition DVD: a DVD capable of storing between two and four times as much data as a standard DVD

HDL *abbreviation for* high-density lipoprotein

hdqrs *abbreviation for* headquarters: replaced in military use by **HQ**

HDR energy *n* hot dry rock energy; energy extracted from hot rocks below the earth's surface by pumping water around a circuit in the hot region and back to the surface

HDTV *abbreviation for* **high definition television**

he¹ (hiː; *unstressed* iː) *pron* (*subjective*) **1** refers to a male person or animal: *he looks interesting; he's a fine stallion* **2** refers to an indefinite antecedent such as *one, whoever*, or *anybody*: *everybody can do as he likes in this country* **3** refers to a person or animal of unknown or unspecified sex: *a member of the party may vote as he sees fit* ▷ *n* **4 a** a male person or animal **b** (*in combination*): *he-goat* **5 a** a children's game in which one player chases the others in an attempt to touch one of them, who then becomes the chaser. Compare **tag² b** the person chasing. Compare **it** (sense 7) [Old English *hē*; related to Old Saxon *hie*, Old High German *her* he, Old Slavonic *sī* this, Latin *cis* on this side]

he² (heɪ; *Hebrew* he) *n* the fifth letter of the Hebrew alphabet (ה), transliterated as *h*

he³ (hiː, heɪ) *interj* an expression of amusement or derision. Also: **he-he!** *or* **hee-hee!**

He *the chemical symbol for* helium

HE *abbreviation for* **1** high explosive **2** His Eminence **3** His (or Her) Excellency

head (hɛd) *n* **1** the upper or front part of the body in vertebrates, including man, that contains and protects the brain, eyes, mouth, and nose and ears when present. Related adj: **cephalic 2** the corresponding part of an invertebrate animal **3** something resembling a head in form or function, such as the top of a tool **4 a** the person commanding most authority within a group, organization, etc **b** (*as modifier*): *head buyer* **c** (*in combination*): *headmaster* **5** the position of leadership or command: *at the head of his class* **6 a** the most forward part of a thing; a part that juts out; front: *the head of a queue* **b** (*as modifier*): *head point* **7** the highest part of a thing; upper end: *the head of the pass* **8** the froth on the top of a glass of beer **9** aptitude, intelligence, and emotions (esp in the phrases **above** or **over one's head, have a head for, keep one's head, lose one's head**, etc): *she has a good head for figures; a wise old head* **10** (*pl* **head**) a person or animal considered as a unit: *the show was two pounds per head; six hundred head of cattle* **11** the head considered as a measure of length or height: *he's a head taller than his mother* **12** *botany* **a** a dense inflorescence such as that of the daisy and other composite plants **b** any other compact terminal part of a plant, such as the leaves of a cabbage or lettuce **13** a culmination or crisis (esp in the phrase **bring** or **come to a head**) **14** the pus-filled tip or central part of a pimple, boil, etc **15** the head considered as the part of the body on which hair grows densely: *a fine head of hair* **16** the source or origin of a river or stream **17** (*capital when part of name*) a headland or promontory, esp a high one **18** the obverse of a coin, usually bearing a portrait of the head or a full figure of a monarch, deity, etc. Compare **tail¹ 19** a main point or division of an argument, discourse, etc **20** (*often plural*) the headline at the top of a newspaper article or the heading of a section within an article **21** *nautical* **a** the front part of a ship or boat **b** (in sailing ships) the upper corner or edge of a sail **c** the top of any spar or derrick **d** any vertical timber cut to shape **e** (*often plural*) a slang word for **lavatory 22** *grammar* another word for **governor** (sense 7) **23** the taut membrane of a drum, tambourine, etc **24 a** the height of the surface of liquid above a specific point, esp when

h

considered or used as a measure of the pressure at that point: *a head of four feet* **b** pressure of water, caused by height or velocity, measured in terms of a vertical column of water **c** any pressure: *a head of steam in the boiler* **25** *slang* **a** a person who regularly takes drugs, esp LSD or cannabis **b** (*in combination*): *an acidhead; a pothead* **26** *mining* a road driven into the coal face **27** **a** the terminal point of a route **b** (*in combination*): *railhead* **28** a device on a turning or boring machine, such as a lathe, that is equipped with one or more cutting tools held to the work by this device **29** See **cylinder head** **30** an electromagnet that can read, write, or erase information on a magnetic medium such as a magnetic tape, disk, or drum, used in computers, tape recorders, etc **31** *informal* short for **headmaster** *or* **headmistress** **32** **a** the head of a horse considered as a narrow margin in the outcome of a race (in the phrase **win by a head**) **b** any narrow margin of victory (in the phrase (**win**) **by a head**) **33** *informal* short for **headache** **34** *curling* the stones lying in the house after all 16 have been played **35** *bowls* the jack and the bowls that have been played considered together as a target area **36** **against the head** *rugby* from the opposing side's put-in to the scrum **37** **bite** *or* **or snap someone's head off** to speak sharply and angrily to someone **38** **bring** *or* **come to a head** **a** to bring or be brought to a crisis: *matters came to a head* **b** (of a boil) to cause to be or be about to burst **39** **get it into one's head** to come to believe (an idea, esp a whimsical one): *he got it into his head that the earth was flat* **40** **give head** *slang* to perform fellatio **41** **give someone** (*or* **something**) **his** (*or* **its**) **head** **a** to allow a person greater freedom or responsibility **b** to allow a horse to gallop by lengthening the reins **42** **go to one's head** **a** to make one dizzy or confused, as might an alcoholic drink **b** to make one conceited: *his success has gone to his head* **43** **head and shoulders above** greatly superior to **44** **head over heels** **a** turning a complete somersault **b** completely; utterly (esp in the phrase **head over heels in love**) **45** **hold up one's head** to be unashamed **46** **keep one's head** to remain calm **47** **keep one's head above water** to manage to survive a difficult experience **48** **make head** to make progress **49** **make head or tail of** (*used with a negative*) to attempt to understand (a problem, etc): *he couldn't make head or tail of the case* **50** **off** (*or* **out of**) **one's head** *slang* insane or delirious **51** **off the top of one's head** without previous thought; impromptu **52** **on one's (own) head** at one's (own) risk or responsibility **53** **one's head off** *slang* loudly or excessively: *the baby cried its head off* **54** **over someone's head** **a** without a person in the obvious position being considered, esp for promotion: *the graduate was promoted over the heads of several of his seniors* **b** without consulting a person in the obvious position but referring to a higher authority: *in making his complaint he went straight to the director, over the head of his immediate boss* **c** beyond a person's comprehension **55** **put (our, their, etc) heads together** *informal* to consult together **56** **take it into one's head** to conceive a notion, desire, or wish (to do something) **57** **turn heads** to be so beautiful, unusual, or impressive as to attract a lot of attention **58** **turn** *or* **stand (something) on its head** to treat or present (something) in a completely new and different way: *health care which has turned orthodox medicine on its head* **59** **turn someone's head** to make someone vain, conceited, etc ▷ *vb* **60** (*tr*) to be at the front or top of: *to head the field* **61** (*tr*; often foll by *up*) to be in the commanding or most important position **62** (often foll by *for*) to go or cause to go (towards): *where are you heading?* **63** to turn or steer (a vessel) as specified: *to head into the wind* **64** *soccer* to propel (the ball) by striking it with the head **65** (*tr*) to provide with or be a head or heading: *to head a letter; the quotation which heads chapter 6* **66** (*tr*) to cut the top branches or shoots off (a tree or plant) **67** (*intr*) to form a head, as a boil or plant **68** (*intr*; often foll by *in*) (of streams, rivers, etc) to originate or rise in **69** **head them** *Austral* to toss the coins in a game of two-up ▷ See also **head for, head off, heads** [Old English *hēafod*; related to Old Norse *haufuth*, Old Frisian *hāved*, Old Saxon *hōbid*, Old High German *houbit*] > ˈ**headˌlike** *adj*

-head *combining form* indicating a person having a preoccupation as specified: *breadhead*

headache (ˈhɛdˌeɪk) *n* **1** pain in the head, caused by dilation of cerebral arteries, muscle contraction, insufficient oxygen in the cerebral blood, reaction to drugs, etc. Technical name: **cephalalgia** **2** *informal* any cause of worry, difficulty, or annoyance

headachy *or* **headachey** (ˈhɛdˌeɪkɪ) *adj* suffering from, caused by, or likely to cause a headache

head arrangement *n jazz* a spontaneous orchestration

headband (ˈhɛdˌbænd) *n* **1** a ribbon or band worn around the head **2** a narrow cloth band attached to the top of the spine of a book for protection or decoration

headbang (ˈhɛdˌbæŋ) *vb* (*intr*) *slang* to nod one's head violently to the beat of loud rock music

head-banger *n slang* **1** a heavy-metal rock fan **2** a crazy or stupid person

headboard (ˈhɛdˌbɔːd) *n* a vertical board or terminal at the head of a bed

head-butt *vb* (*tr*) **1** to deliberately strike (someone) with the head ▷ *n* **head butt** **2** an act or an instance of deliberately striking someone with the head

headcase (ˈhɛdˌkeɪs) *n informal* an insane person

headcheese (ˈhɛdˌtʃiːz) *n US and Canadian* a seasoned jellied loaf made from the head and sometimes the feet of a pig or calf. Also called (in Britain and certain other countries): **brawn**

head collar *n* the part of a bridle that fits round a horse's head. Also called (esp US): **headstall**

headdress (ˈhɛdˌdrɛs) *n* any head covering, esp an ornate one or one denoting a rank or occupation

headed (ˈhɛdɪd) *adj* **1** **a** having a head or heads **b** (*in combination*): *two-headed; bullet-headed* **2** having a heading: *headed notepaper* **3** (*in combination*) having a mind or intellect as specified: *thickheaded*

header (ˈhɛdə) *n* **1** Also called: **header tank** a reservoir, tank, or hopper that maintains a gravity feed or a static fluid pressure in an apparatus **2** a manifold for distributing a fluid supply amongst a number of passages **3** a machine that trims the heads from castings, forgings, etc, or one that forms heads, as in wire, to make nails **4** a person who operates such a machine **5** a brick or stone laid across a wall so that its end is flush with the outer surface. Compare **stretcher** (sense 5) **6** the action of striking a ball with the head **7** *informal* a headlong fall or dive **8** *computing* **a** a block of data on a tape or disk providing information about the size, location, etc, of a file **b** (*as modifier*): *header card; header label* **9** *dialect* a mentally unbalanced person

headfast (ˈhɛdfɑːst) *n* a mooring rope at the bows of a ship [C16 from HEAD (in the sense: front) + *fast* a mooring rope, from Middle English *fest*, from Old Norse *festr*; related to FAST[1]]

headfirst (ˈhɛdˈfɜːst) *adj, adv* **1** with the head foremost; headlong: *he fell headfirst* ▷ *adv* **2** rashly or carelessly

head for *vb* (*preposition*) **1** to go or cause to go (towards) **2** to be destined for: *to head for trouble*

headfuck (ˈhɛdfʌk) *n taboo slang* an experience that is wildly exciting or impressive

head gate *n* **1** a gate that is used to control the flow of water at the upper end of a lock or conduit. Compare **tail gate** **2** another name for **floodgate** (sense 1)

headgear (ˈhɛdˌɡɪə) *n* **1** any head covering, esp a hat **2** any part of a horse's harness that is worn on the head **3** the hoisting mechanism at the pithead of a mine

headguard (ˈhɛdˌɡɑːd) *n* a padded helmet worn to protect the head in contact sports such as rugby and boxing

head-hunting *n* **1** the practice among certain peoples of removing the heads of slain enemies and preserving them as trophies **2** the recruitment, esp through an agency, of executives from one company to another, often rival, company **3** *US slang* the destruction or neutralization of political opponents > ˈ**head-ˌhunter** *n*

heading (ˈhɛdɪŋ) *n* **1** a title for a page, paragraph, chapter, etc **2** a main division, as of a lecture, speech, essay, etc **3** *mining* **a** a horizontal tunnel **b** the end of such a tunnel **4** the angle between the direction of an aircraft and a specified meridian, often due north **5** the compass direction parallel to the keel of a vessel **6** the act of heading **7** anything that serves as a head

heading dog *n NZ* a dog that heads off a flock of sheep or a single sheep

headland *n* **1** (ˈhɛdlənd) a narrow area of land jutting out into a sea, lake, etc **2** (ˈhɛdˌlænd) a strip of land along the edge of an arable field left unploughed to allow space for machines

headless (ˈhɛdlɪs) *adj* **1** without a head **2** without a leader **3** foolish or stupid **4** *prosody* another word for **catalectic**

headlight (ˈhɛdˌlaɪt) *or* **headlamp** *n* a powerful light, equipped with a reflector and attached to the front of a motor vehicle, locomotive, etc. See also **quartz-iodine lamp**

headline (ˈhɛdˌlaɪn) *n* **1** Also called: **head, heading** **a** a phrase at the top of a newspaper or magazine article indicating the subject of the article, usually in larger and heavier type **b** a line at the top of a page indicating the title, page number, etc **2** (*usually plural*) the main points of a television or radio news broadcast, read out before the full broadcast and summarized at the end **3** **hit the headlines** to become prominent in the news ▷ *vb* **4** (*tr*) to furnish (a story or page) with a headline **5** to have top billing (in)

headliner (ˈhɛdˌlaɪnə) *n* a performer given prominent billing; star

headline rate *n* a basic rate of inflation, taxation, etc, before distorting factors have been removed: *the headline rate of inflation*

head-load *African* ▷ *n* **1** baggage or goods arranged so as to be carried on the heads of African porters ▷ *vb* **2** (*tr*) to convey or carry (goods) on the head

headlock (ˈhɛdˌlɒk) *n* a wrestling hold in which a wrestler locks his opponent's head between the crook of his elbow and the side of his body

headlong (ˈhɛdˌlɒŋ) *adv, adj* **1** with the head foremost; headfirst **2** with great haste ▷ *adj* **3** *archaic* (of slopes, etc) very steep; precipitous

headman (ˈhɛdmən) *n, pl* **-men** **1** *anthropol* a chief or leader **2** a foreman or overseer

headmaster (ˌhɛdˈmɑːstə) *n* a male principal of a school > ˌ**headˈmasterˌship** *n*

headmasterly (ˌhɛdˈmæstəlɪ) *adj* typical of the duties and behaviour of a headmaster

headmistress (ˌhɛdˈmɪstrəs) *n* a female principal of a school > ˌ**headˈmistressˌship** *n*

headmistressy (ˌhɛdˈmɪstrɪsɪ) *adj* typical of the duties and behaviour of a headmistress

head money *n* **1** a reward paid for the capture or slaying of a fugitive, outlaw, etc **2** an archaic term for **poll tax**

headmost (ˈhɛdˌməʊst) *adj* a less common word for **foremost**

head off *vb* (*tr, adverb*) **1** to intercept and force to change direction: *to head off the stampede* **2** to prevent or forestall (something that is likely to happen) **3** to depart or set out: *to head off to school*

head of the river *n* **a** any of various annual rowing regattas held on particular rivers **b** the boat or team winning such a regatta: *Eton are head of the river again this year*

head-on *adv* ▷ *adj* **1** with the front or fronts foremost: *a head-on collision* **2** with directness or without compromise: *in his usual head-on fashion*

headphones ('hɛd,fəʊnz) *pl n* an electrical device consisting of two earphones held in position by a flexible metallic strap passing over the head. Informal name: **cans**

headpiece ('hɛd,piːs) *n* **1** *printing* a decorative band at the top of a page, chapter, etc **2** any covering for the head, esp a helmet **3** *archaic* the intellect **4** a less common word for **crownpiece** (sense 2)

headpin ('hɛd,pɪn) *n tenpin bowling* another word for **kingpin**

headquarter (,hɛd'kwɔːtə) *vb informal, chiefly US* to place in or establish as headquarters

headquarters (,hɛd'kwɔːtəz) *pl n* (*sometimes functioning as singular*) **1** any centre or building from which operations are directed, as in the military, the police, etc **2** a military formation comprising the commander, his staff, and supporting echelons ▷ Abbreviations: **HQ, h.q**

headrace ('hɛd,reɪs) *n* a channel that carries water to a water wheel, turbine, etc. Compare **tailrace**

headrail ('hɛd,reɪl) *n billiards, snooker* the end of the table from which play is started, nearest the baulkline

headreach ('hɛd,riːtʃ) *nautical* ▷ *n* **1** the distance made to windward while tacking ▷ *vb* **2** (*tr*) to gain distance over (another boat) when tacking

headrest ('hɛd,rɛst) *n* a support for the head, as on a dentist's chair or car seat

head restraint *n* an adjustable support for the head, attached to a car seat, to prevent the neck from being jolted backwards sharply in the event of a crash or sudden stop

headroom ('hɛd,rʊm, -,ruːm) *or* **headway** *n* the height of a bridge, room, etc; clearance

heads (hɛdz) *interj, adv* **1** with the obverse side of a coin uppermost, esp if it has a head on it: used as a call before tossing a coin. Compare **tails 2** the *Austral informal* people in authority

headsail ('hɛd,seɪl; *Nautical* 'hɛdsəl) *n* any sail set forward of the foremast

headscarf ('hɛd,skɑːf) *n, pl* **-scarves** (-,skɑːvz) a scarf for the head, often worn tied under the chin

head sea *n* a sea in which the waves run directly against the course of a ship

headset ('hɛd,sɛt) *n* a pair of headphones, esp with a microphone attached

headship ('hɛdʃɪp) *n* **1** the position or state of being a leader; command; leadership **2** *education, Brit* the position of headmaster or headmistress of a school

headshrinker ('hɛd,ʃrɪŋkə) *n* **1** a slang name for **psychiatrist**. Often shortened to: **shrink 2** a head-hunter who shrinks the heads of his victims

headsman ('hɛdzmən) *n, pl* **-men** (formerly) an executioner who beheaded condemned persons

headspring ('hɛd,sprɪŋ) *n* **1** a spring that is the source of a stream **2** a spring using the head as a lever from a position lying on the ground **3** *rare* a source

headsquare ('hɛd,skwɛə) *n* a scarf worn on the head

headstall ('hɛd,stɔːl) *n* another word (esp US) for **head collar**

headstand ('hɛd,stænd) *n* the act or an instance of balancing on the head, usually with the hands as support

head start *n* an initial advantage in a competitive situation [originally referring to a horse's having its head in front of others at the start of a race]

head station *n Austral* the main buildings on a large sheep or cattle farm

headstock ('hɛd,stɒk) *n* **1** the part of a machine that supports and transmits the drive to the chuck. Compare **tailstock 2** the wooden or metal block on which a church bell is hung

headstone ('hɛd,stəʊn) *n* **1** a memorial stone at the head of a grave **2** *architect* another name for **keystone**

headstream ('hɛd,striːm) *n* a stream that is the source or a source of a river

headstrong ('hɛd,strɒŋ) *adj* **1** self-willed; obstinate **2** (of an action) heedless; rash > 'head,strongly *adv* > 'head,strongness *n*

heads up *n US and Canadian* a tip-off or small amount of information given in advance

head teacher *n* a headmaster or headmistress

head-to-head *informal* ▷ *adj* **1** in direct competition ▷ *n* **2** a competition involving two people, teams, etc

head-up display *n* the projection of readings from instruments onto a windscreen, enabling an aircraft pilot or car driver to see them without looking down

head voice *or* **register** *n* the high register of the human voice, in which the vibrations of sung notes are felt in the head

head waiter *n* a waiter who supervises the activities of other waiters and arranges the seating of guests

headward ('hɛdwəd) *adj* **1** (of river erosion) cutting backwards or upstream above the original source, which recedes ▷ *adv* **2** a variant of **headwards**

headwards ('hɛdwədz) *or* **headward** *adv* backwards beyond the original source: *a river erodes headwards*

headwaters ('hɛd,wɔːtəz) *pl n* the tributary streams of a river in the area in which it rises; headstreams

headway ('hɛd,weɪ) *n* **1** motion in a forward direction: *the vessel made no headway* **2** progress or rate of progress: *he made no headway with the problem* **3** another name for **headroom 4** the distance or time between consecutive trains, buses, etc, on the same route

headwind ('hɛd,wɪnd) *n* a wind blowing directly against the course of an aircraft or ship. Compare **tailwind**

headword ('hɛd,wɜːd) *n* a key word placed at the beginning of a line, paragraph, etc, as in a dictionary entry

headwork ('hɛd,wɜːk) *n* **1** mental work **2** the ornamentation of the keystone of an arch > 'head,worker *n*

heady ('hɛdɪ) *adj* **headier, headiest 1** (of alcoholic drink) intoxicating **2** strongly affecting the mind or senses; extremely exciting **3** rash; impetuous > 'headily *adv* > 'headiness *n*

heal (hiːl) *vb* **1** to restore or be restored to health **2** (*intr*; often foll by *over* or *up*) (of a wound, burn, etc) to repair by natural processes, as by scar formation **3** (*tr*) **a** to treat (a wound, etc) by assisting in its natural repair **b** to cure (a disease or disorder) **4** to restore or be restored to friendly relations, harmony, etc [Old English *hælan*; related to Old Norse *heila*, Gothic *hailjan*, Old High German *heilen*; see HALE[1], WHOLE] > 'healable *adj* > 'healer *n* > 'healing *n, adj*

heal-all *n* another name for **selfheal**

healee (hiːˈliː) *n* a person who is being healed

health (hɛlθ) *n* **1** the state of being bodily and mentally vigorous and free from disease **2** the general condition of body and mind: *in poor health* **3** the condition of any unit, society, etc: *the economic health of a nation* **4** a toast to a person, wishing him or her good health, happiness, etc **5** (*modifier*) of or relating to food or other goods reputed to be beneficial to the health: *health food; a health store* **6** (*modifier*) of or relating to health, esp to the administration of health: *a health committee; health resort; health service* ▷ *interj* **7** an exclamation wishing someone good health as part of a toast (in the phrases **your health, good health**, etc) [Old English *hǣlth*, related to *hāl* HALE[1]]

health camp *n NZ* a camp, usually at the seaside, for children requiring health care

health card *n Canadian* an identity card required to obtain public health insurance services

health centre *n* (in Britain) premises, owned by a local authority, providing health care for the local community and usually housing a group practice, nursing staff, a child-health clinic, X-ray facilities, etc

health check *n* **1** a medical checkup **2** *Brit* any examination carried out to verify the physical condition of an appliance or machine **3** *Brit* any examination carried out to verify the financial success or security of a company or person

health farm *n* a residential establishment, often in the country, visited by those who wish to improve their health by losing weight, eating healthy foods, taking exercise, etc

health food *n* **a** vegetarian food organically grown and with no additives, eaten for its dietary value and benefit to health **b** (*as modifier*): *a health-food shop*

healthful ('hɛlθfʊl) *adj* a less common word for **healthy** (senses 1–3) > 'healthfully *adv* > 'healthfulness *n*

healthism ('hɛlθɪzəm) *n* a lifestyle that prioritizes health and fitness over anything else

health physics *n* (*functioning as singular*) the branch of physics concerned with the health and safety of people in medical, scientific, and industrial work, esp with protection from the biological effects of ionizing radiation

health salts *pl n* magnesium sulphate or similar salts taken as a mild laxative

Health Service Commissioner *n* (in Britain) the official name for an ombudsman who investigates personal complaints of injustice or hardship resulting from the failure, absence, or maladministration of a service for which a Regional or District Health Authority or Family Practitioner Committee is responsible, after other attempts to obtain redress have failed. See also **Commissioner for Local Administration, Parliamentary Commissioner**

health stamp *n NZ* a postage stamp with a surcharge that is used to support a health camp

health visitor *n* (in Britain) a nurse employed by a district health authority to visit people in their homes and give help and advice on health and social welfare, esp to mothers of preschool children, to the handicapped, and to elderly people

healthy ('hɛlθɪ) *adj* **healthier, healthiest 1** enjoying good health **2** functioning well or being sound: *the company's finances are not very healthy* **3** conducive to health; salutary **4** indicating soundness of body or mind: *a healthy appetite* **5** *informal* considerable in size or amount: *a healthy sum* > 'healthily *adv* > 'healthiness *n*

heap (hiːp) *n* **1** a collection of articles or mass of material gathered together in one place **2** (*often plural; usually foll by of*) *informal* a large number or quantity **3** **give them heaps** *Austral slang* to contend strenuously with an opposing sporting team **4** **give it heaps** *NZ slang* to try very hard **5** *informal* a place or thing that is very old, untidy, unreliable, etc: *the car was a heap* ▷ *adv* **6** **heaps** (intensifier): *he said he was feeling heaps better* ▷ *vb* **7** (often foll by *up* or *together*) to collect or be collected into or as if into a heap or pile: *to heap up wealth* **8** (*tr*; often foll by *with, on,* or *upon*) to load or supply (with) abundantly: *to heap with riches* [Old English *héap*; related to Old Frisian *hāp*, Old Saxon *hōp*, Old High German *houf*] > 'heaper *n*

heaping ('hiːpɪŋ) *adj US and Canadian* (of a spoonful) heaped

hear (hɪə) *vb* **hears, hearing, heard** (hɜːd) **1** (*tr*) to perceive (a sound) with the sense of hearing **2** (*tr; may take a clause as object*) to listen to: *did you hear what I said?* **3** (when *intr*, sometimes foll by *of* or *about*; when *tr*, may take a clause as object) to be informed (of), receive information (about): *to hear of his success; have you heard?* **4** *law* to give a hearing to (a case) **5** (when *intr*, usually foll by *of* and used with a negative) to listen (to) with favour, assent, etc: *she wouldn't hear of it* **6** (*intr*; foll by *from*) to receive a letter, news, etc (from) **7** **hear! hear!** an exclamation used to show approval of something

h

said **8** hear tell (of) *dialect* to be told (about); learn (of) [Old English *hieran*; related to Old Norse *heyra*, Gothic *hausjan*, Old High German *hōren*, Greek *akouein*] ⊳ '**hearable** *adj* ⊳ '**hearer** *n*

Heard and McDonald Islands (hɜːd, mək'dɒnəld) *pl n* a group of islands in the S Indian Ocean: an external territory of Australia from 1947. Area: 412 sq km (159 sq miles)

hearing ('hɪərɪŋ) *n* **1** the faculty or sense by which sound is perceived. Related adj: **audio 2** an opportunity to be listened to **3** the range within which sound can be heard; earshot **4** the investigation of a matter by a court of law, esp the preliminary inquiry into an indictable crime by magistrates **5** a formal or official trial of an action or lawsuit

hearing aid *n* a device for assisting the hearing of partially deaf people, typically consisting of a small battery-powered electronic amplifier with microphone and earphone, worn by a deaf person in or behind the ear. Also called: **deaf aid**

hearing dog *n* a dog that has been specially trained to help deaf or partially deaf people by alerting them to sounds such as a ringing doorbell, an alarm, etc

hearing loss *n* an increase in the threshold of audibility caused by age, infirmity, or prolonged exposure to intense noise

hearken *or sometimes US* **harken** ('hɑːkən) *vb archaic* to listen to (something) [Old English *heorcnian*; see HARK] ⊳ '**hearkener** *n*

hear out *vb* (*tr, adverb*) to listen in regard to every detail and give a proper or full hearing to

hearsay ('hɪəˌseɪ) *n* gossip; rumour

hearsay evidence *n law* evidence based on what has been reported to a witness by others rather than what he has himself observed or experienced (not generally admissible as evidence)

hearse (hɜːs) *n* a vehicle, such as a specially designed car or carriage, used to carry a coffin to a place of worship and ultimately to a cemetery or crematorium [c14 from Old French *herce*, from Latin *hirpex* harrow]

heart (hɑːt) *n* **1** the hollow muscular organ in vertebrates whose contractions propel the blood through the circulatory system. In mammals it consists of a right and left atrium and a right and left ventricle. Related adj: **cardiac 2** the corresponding organ or part in invertebrates **3** this organ considered as the seat of life and emotions, esp love **4** emotional mood or disposition: *a happy heart; a change of heart* **5** tenderness or pity: *you have no heart* **6** courage or spirit; bravery **7** the inmost or most central part of a thing: *the heart of the city* **8** the most important or vital part: *the heart of the matter* **9** (of vegetables such as cabbage) the inner compact part **10** the core of a tree **11** the part nearest the heart of a person; breast: *she held him to her heart* **12** a dearly loved person: usually used as a term of address: *dearest heart* **13** a conventionalized representation of the heart, having two rounded lobes at the top meeting in a point at the bottom **14 a** a red heart-shaped symbol on a playing card **b** a card with one or more of these symbols or (*when pl.*) the suit of cards so marked **15** a fertile condition in land, conducive to vigorous growth in crops or herbage (esp in the phrase **in good heart**) **16** after one's own heart appealing to one's own disposition, taste, or tendencies **17** at heart in reality or fundamentally **18** break one's (*or* someone's) heart to grieve (*or* cause to grieve) very deeply, esp through love **19** by heart by committing to memory **20** cross my heart (and hope to die)! I promise! **21** eat one's heart out to brood or pine with grief or longing **22** from (the bottom of) one's heart very sincerely or deeply **23** have a heart! be kind or merciful **24** have one's heart in it (*usually used with a negative*) to have enthusiasm for something **25** have one's heart in one's boots to be depressed or down-hearted **26**

have one's heart in one's mouth (*or* throat) to be full of apprehension, excitement, or fear **27** have one's heart in the right place **a** to be kind, thoughtful, or generous **b** to mean well **28** have the heart (*usually used with a negative*) to have the necessary will, callousness, etc, (to do something): *I didn't have the heart to tell him* **29** heart and soul absolutely; completely **30** heart of hearts the depths of one's conscience or emotions **31** heart of oak a brave person **32** in one's heart secretly; fundamentally **33** lose heart to become despondent or disillusioned (over something) **34** lose one's heart to to fall in love with **35** near *or* close to one's heart cherished or important **36** set one's heart on to have as one's ambition to obtain; covet **37** take heart to become encouraged **38** take to heart to take seriously or be upset about **39** to one's heart's content as much as one wishes **40** wear one's heart on one's sleeve to show one's feelings openly **41** with all one's (*or* one's whole) heart very willingly ⊳ *vb* **42** (*intr*) (of vegetables) to form a heart **43** an archaic word for **hearten** ⊳ See also **hearts** [Old English *heorte*; related to Old Norse *hjarta*, Gothic *hairtō*, Old High German *herza*, Latin *cor*, Greek *kardia*, Old Irish *cride*]

heartache ('hɑːtˌeɪk) *n* intense anguish or mental suffering

heart attack *n* any sudden severe instance of abnormal heart functioning, esp coronary thrombosis

heartbeat ('hɑːtˌbiːt) *n* one complete pulsation of the heart. See **diastole, systole**

heart block *n* impaired conduction or blocking of the impulse that regulates the heartbeat, resulting in a lack of coordination between the beating of the atria and the ventricles. Also called: **Adams-Stokes syndrome, atrioventricular block**

heartbreak ('hɑːtˌbreɪk) *n* intense and overwhelming grief, esp through disappointment in love

heartbreaker ('hɑːtˌbreɪkə) *n* a person or thing that causes intense sadness or disappointment

heartbreaking ('hɑːtˌbreɪkɪŋ) *adj* extremely sad, disappointing, or pitiful ⊳ '**heartˌbreakingly** *adv*

heartbroken ('hɑːtˌbrəʊkən) *adj* suffering from intense grief ⊳ '**heartˌbrokenly** *adv* ⊳ '**heartˌbrokenness** *n*

heartburn ('hɑːtˌbɜːn) *n* a burning sensation beneath the breastbone caused by irritation of the oesophagus, as from regurgitation of the contents of the stomach. Technical names: **cardialgia, pyrosis**

heart cherry *n* a heart-shaped variety of sweet cherry

-hearted *adj* having a heart or disposition as specified: *good-hearted; cold-hearted; great-hearted; heavy-hearted*

hearten ('hɑːtᵊn) *vb* to make or become cheerful

heartening ('hɑːtᵊnɪŋ) *adj* causing cheerfulness; encouraging

heart failure *n* **1** a condition in which the heart is unable to pump an adequate amount of blood to the tissues, usually resulting in breathlessness, swollen ankles, etc **2** sudden and permanent cessation of the heartbeat, resulting in death

heartfelt ('hɑːtˌfɛlt) *adj* sincerely and strongly felt

hearth (hɑːθ) *n* **1 a** the floor of a fireplace, esp one that extends outwards into the room **b** (*as modifier*): *hearth rug* **2** this part of a fireplace as a symbol of the home, etc **3** the bottom part of a metallurgical furnace in which the molten metal is produced or contained [Old English *heorth*; related to Old High German *herd* hearth, Latin *carbō* charcoal]

hearthstone ('hɑːθˌstəʊn) *n* **1** a stone that forms a hearth **2** a less common word for **hearth** (sense 1) **3** soft stone used to clean and whiten floors, steps, etc

heartily ('hɑːtɪlɪ) *adv* **1** thoroughly or vigorously: *to eat heartily* **2** in a sincere manner: *he congratulated*

me heartily on my promotion

heartland ('hɑːtˌlænd) *n* **1** the central region of a country or continent **2** the core or most vital area: *the industrial heartland of England*

heartless ('hɑːtlɪs) *adj* unkind or cruel; hard-hearted ⊳ '**heartlessly** *adv* ⊳ '**heartlessness** *n*

heart-lung machine *n* a machine used to maintain the circulation and oxygenation of the blood during heart surgery

heart murmur *n* an abnormal sound heard through a stethoscope over the region of the heart

heart-rending *adj* causing great mental pain and sorrow ⊳ '**heart-ˌrendingly** *adv*

hearts (hɑːts) *n* (*functioning as singular*) a card game in which players must avoid winning tricks containing hearts or the queen of spades. Also called: **Black Maria**

heart-searching *n* examination of one's feelings or conscience

heartsease *or* **heart's-ease** ('hɑːtsˌiːz) *n* **1** another name for the **wild pansy 2** peace of mind

heartsick ('hɑːtˌsɪk) *adj* deeply dejected or despondent ⊳ '**heartˌsickness** *n*

heartsome ('hɑːtsəm) *adj chiefly Scot* **1** cheering or encouraging: *heartsome news* **2** gay; cheerful ⊳ '**heartsomely** *adv* ⊳ '**heartsomeness** *n*

heart starter *n Austral slang* the first drink of the day

heartstrings ('hɑːtˌstrɪŋz) *pl n often facetious* deep emotions or feelings [c15 originally referring to the tendons supposed to support the heart]

heart-throb *n* **1** an object of infatuation **2** a heart beat

heart-to-heart *adj* **1** (esp of a conversation or discussion) concerned with personal problems or intimate feelings ⊳ *n* **2** an intimate conversation or discussion

heart urchin *n* any echinoderm of the genus *Echinocardium*, having a heart-shaped body enclosed in a rigid spiny test: class *Echinoidea* (sea urchins)

heart-warming *adj* **1** pleasing; gratifying **2** emotionally moving

heart-water *n vet science* a tick-borne disease of cattle, sheep, and goats characterized by fluid accumulation in the pericardial sac. It is caused by the organism *Rickettsia ruminantium*

heart-whole *adj rare* **1** not in love **2** sincere **3** stout-hearted ⊳ ˌheart-'wholeness *n*

heartwood ('hɑːtˌwʊd) *n* the central core of dark hard wood in tree trunks, consisting of nonfunctioning xylem tissue that has become blocked with resins, tannins, and oils. Compare **sapwood**

heartworm ('hɑːtˌwɜːm) *n* a parasitic nematode worm, *Dirofilaria immitis*, that lives in the heart and bloodstream of vertebrates

hearty ('hɑːtɪ) *adj* **heartier, heartiest 1** warm and unreserved in manner or behaviour **2** vigorous and enthusiastic: *a hearty slap on the back* **3** sincere and heartfelt: *hearty dislike* **4** healthy and strong (esp in the phrase **hale and hearty**) **5** substantial and nourishing ⊳ *n informal* **6** a comrade, esp a sailor **7** a vigorous sporting man: *a rugby hearty* ⊳ '**heartiness** *n*

heat (hiːt) *n* **1 a** the energy transferred as a result of a difference in temperature **b** the random kinetic energy of the atoms, molecules, or ions in a substance or body. Related adjs: **thermal, calorific 2** the sensation caused in the body by heat energy; warmth **3** the state or quality of being hot **4** hot weather: *the heat of summer* **5** intensity of feeling; passion: *the heat of rage* **6** pressure: *the political heat on the government over the economy* **7** the most intense or active part: *the heat of the battle* **8** a period or condition of sexual excitement in female mammals that occurs at oestrus **9** *sport* **a** a preliminary eliminating contest in a competition **b** a single section of a contest **10** *slang* police activity after a crime: *the heat is off* **11** *chiefly US slang* criticism or abuse: *he took a lot of heat for that mistake* **12** in the heat of the

moment without pausing to think **13** *on* or *in* **heat a** *Also*: **in season** (of some female mammals) sexually receptive **b** in a state of sexual excitement **14 the heat** *slang* the police **15 turn up** or **on the heat** *informal* to increase the intensity of activity, coercion, etc ▷ *vb* **16** to make or become hot or warm **17** to make or become excited or intense [Old English *hǣtu*; related to *hāt* HOT, Old Frisian *hēte* heat, Old High German *heiʒī*] > **'heatless** *adj*

heat barrier *n* another name for **thermal barrier**

heat capacity *n* the heat required to raise the temperature of a substance by unit temperature interval under specified conditions, usually measured in joules per kelvin. Symbol: C_p (for constant pressure) or C_v (for constant volume)

heat content *n* another name for **enthalpy**

heat death *n thermodynamics* the condition of any closed system when its total entropy is a maximum and it has no available energy. If the universe is a closed system it should eventually reach this state

heated ('hi:tɪd) *adj* **1** made hot; warmed **2** impassioned or highly emotional > **'heatedly** *adv* > **'heatedness** *n*

heat engine *n* an engine that converts heat energy into mechanical energy

heater ('hi:tə) *n* **1** any device for supplying heat, such as a hot-air blower, radiator, convector, etc **2** *US slang* a pistol **3** *electronics* a conductor carrying a current that indirectly heats the cathode in some types of valve

heat exchanger *n* a device for transferring heat from one fluid to another without allowing them to mix

heat exhaustion *n* a condition resulting from exposure to intense heat, characterized by dizziness, abdominal cramp, and prostration. Also called: **heat prostration**. Compare **heatstroke**

heath (hi:θ) *n* **1** *Brit* a large open area, usually with sandy soil and scrubby vegetation, esp heather **2** *Also called*: **heather** any low-growing evergreen ericaceous shrub of the Old World genus *Erica* and related genera, having small bell-shaped typically pink or purple flowers **3** any of several nonericaceous heathlike plants, such as sea heath **4** *Austral* any of various heathlike plants of the genus *Epacris*: family *Epacridaceae* **5** any of various small brown satyrid butterflies of the genus *Coenonympha*, with coppery-brown wings, esp the **large heath** (*C. tullia*) [Old English *hǣth*; related to Old Norse *heithr* field, Old High German *heida* heather] > **'heath,like** *adj* > **'heathy** *adj*

heathberry ('hi:θ,bɛrɪ) *n*, *pl* -ries any of various plants that have berry-like fruits and grow on heaths, such as the bilberry and crowberry

heath cock *n* another name for **blackcock**

heathen ('hi:ðən) *n*, *pl* -thens or -then **1** a person who does not acknowledge the God of Christianity, Judaism, or Islam; pagan **2** an uncivilized or barbaric person **3 the heathen** (*functioning as plural*) heathens collectively ▷ *adj* **4** irreligious; pagan **5** unenlightened; uncivilized; barbaric **6** of or relating to heathen peoples or their religious, moral, and other customs, practices, and beliefs [Old English *hǣthen*; related to Old Norse *heithinn*, Old Frisian *hēthin*, Old High German *heidan*] > **'heathenism** or **'heathenry** *n* > **'heathenness** *n*

heathendom ('hi:ðəndəm) *n* heathen lands, peoples, or beliefs

heathenish ('hi:ðənɪʃ) *adj* of, relating to, or resembling a heathen or heathen culture > **'heathenishly** *adv* > **'heathenishness** *n*

heathenize or **heathenise** ('hi:ðə,naɪz) *vb* **1** to render or become heathen, or bring or come under heathen influence **2** (*intr*) to engage in heathen practices

heather ('hɛðə) *n* **1** *Also called*: **ling, heath** a low-growing evergreen Eurasian ericaceous shrub, *Calluna vulgaris*, that grows in dense masses on

open ground and has clusters of small bell-shaped typically pinkish-purple flowers **2** any of certain similar plants **3** a purplish-red to pinkish-purple colour ▷ *adj* **4** of a heather colour **5** of or relating to interwoven yarns of mixed colours: *heather mixture* [C14 originally Scottish and Northern English, probably from HEATH] > **'heathered** *adj* > **'heathery** *adj*

heathfowl ('hi:θ,faʊl) *n* (in British game laws) an archaic name for the **black grouse**. Compare **moorfowl**

heath grass or **heather grass** *n* a perennial European grass, *Danthonia decumbens*, with flat hairless leaves

heath hen *n* **1** another name for **greyhen 2** a recently extinct variety of the prairie chicken

Heath Robinson ('rɒbɪnsən) *adj* (of a mechanical device) absurdly complicated in design and having a simple function [C20 named after William *Heath Robinson* (1872–1944), British cartoonist]

heath wren *n* either of two ground-nesting warblers of southern Australia, *Hylacola pyrrhopygia* or *H. cauta*, noted for their song and their powers of mimicry

heating ('hi:tɪŋ) *n* **1** a device or system for supplying heat, esp central heating, to a building **2** the heat supplied

heating element *n* a coil or other arrangement of wire in which heat is produced by an electric current

heat-island *n meteorol* the mass of air over a large city, characteristically having a slightly higher average temperature than that of the surrounding air

heat lightning *n* flashes of light seen near the horizon, esp on hot evenings: reflections of more distant lightning

heat of combustion *n chem* the heat evolved when one mole of a substance is burnt in oxygen at constant volume

heat of formation *n chem* the heat evolved or absorbed when one mole of a compound is formed from its constituent atoms

heat of reaction *n chem* the heat evolved or absorbed when one mole of a product is formed at constant pressure

heat of solution *n chem* the heat evolved or absorbed when one mole of a substance dissolves completely in a large volume of solvent

heat prostration *n* another name for **heat exhaustion**

heat pump *n* a device, as used in a refrigerator, for extracting heat from a source and delivering it elsewhere at a much higher temperature

heat rash *n* a nontechnical name for **miliaria**

heat-seeking *adj* **1** (of a detecting device) able to detect sources of infrared radiation: *a heat-seeking camera* **2** (of a missile) able to detect and follow a source of heat, as from an aircraft engine: *a heat-seeking missile* > **heat seeker** *n*

heat shield *n* a coating or barrier for shielding from excessive heat, such as that experienced by a spacecraft on re-entry into the earth's atmosphere

heat sink *n* **1** a metal plate specially designed to conduct and radiate heat from an electrical component **2** a layer of material placed within the outer skin of high-speed aircraft to absorb heat

heatstroke ('hi:t,strəʊk) *n* a condition resulting from prolonged exposure to intense heat, characterized by high fever and in severe cases convulsions and coma. See **sunstroke**

heat-treat *vb* (*tr*) to apply heat to (a metal or alloy) in one or more temperature cycles to give it desirable properties > **heat treatment** *n*

heat wave *n* **1** a continuous spell of abnormally hot weather **2** (*not in technical use*) an extensive slow-moving air mass at a relatively high temperature

heaume (həʊm) *n* (in the 12th and 13th centuries)

a large helmet reaching and supported by the shoulders [C16 from Old French *helme*; see HELMET]

heave (hi:v) *vb* **heaves, heaving, heaved** or *chiefly nautical* **hove 1** (*tr*) to lift or move with a great effort **2** (*tr*) to throw (something heavy) with effort **3** to utter (sounds, sighs, etc) or breathe noisily or unhappily: *to heave a sigh* **4** to rise and fall or cause to rise and fall heavily **5** (*past tense and past participle* **hove**) *nautical* **a** to move or cause to move in a specified way, direction, or position: *to heave in sight* **b** (*intr*) (of a vessel) to pitch or roll **6** (*tr*) to displace (rock strata, mineral veins, etc) in a horizontal direction **7** (*intr*) to retch ▷ *n* **8** the act or an instance of heaving ▷ a fling **9** the horizontal displacement of rock strata at a fault ▷ See also **heave down, heaves, heave to** [Old English *hebban*; related to Old Norse *hefja*, Old Saxon *hebbian*, Old High German *heffen* to raise, Latin *capere* to take, Sanskrit *kapatī* two hands full] > **'heaver** *n*

heave down *vb* (*intr, adverb*) *nautical* to turn a vessel on its side for cleaning

heave-ho *sentence substitute* **1** a sailors' cry, as when hoisting anchor ▷ *n* **2** *informal* dismissal, as from employment

heaven ('hɛvən) *n* **1** (*sometimes capital*) Christianity **a** the abode of God and the angels **b** a place or state of communion with God after death. Compare **hell 2** (*usually plural*) the sky, firmament or space surrounding the earth **3** (in any of various mythologies) a place, such as Elysium or Valhalla, to which those who have died in the gods' favour are brought to dwell in happiness **4** a place or state of joy and happiness **5** (*singular* or *plural*; *sometimes capital*) God or the gods, used in exclamatory phrases of surprise, exasperation, etc: *for heaven's sake*; *heavens above* **6 in seventh heaven** ecstatically happy **7 move heaven and earth** to do everything possible (to achieve something) [Old English *heofon*; related to Old Saxon *heban*]

heavenly ('hɛvənlɪ) *adj* **1** *informal* alluring, wonderful, or sublime **2** of or occurring in space: *a heavenly body* **3** divine; holy > **'heavenliness** *n*

heaven-sent *adj* providential; fortunate: *a heaven-sent opportunity*

heavenward ('hɛvənwəd) *adj* **1** directed towards heaven or the sky ▷ *adv* **2** a variant of **heavenwards**

heavenwards ('hɛvənwədz) or **heavenward** *adv* towards heaven or the sky

heaves (hi:vz) *n* (*functioning as singular or plural*) **1** *Also called*: **broken wind** a chronic respiratory disorder of animals of the horse family caused by allergies and dust **2 the heaves** *slang* an attack of vomiting or retching

heave to *vb* (*adverb*) to stop (a vessel) or (of a vessel) to stop, as by trimming the sails, etc. Also: lay to

heavier-than-air *adj* **1** having a density greater than that of air **2** of or relating to an aircraft that does not depend on buoyancy for support but gains lift from aerodynamic forces

Heaviside layer ('hɛvɪ,saɪd) *n* another name for **E region** (of the ionosphere), predicted by English physicist Oliver Heaviside (1850–1925) in 1902

heavy ('hɛvɪ) *adj* **heavier, heaviest 1** of comparatively great weight: *a heavy stone* **2** having a relatively high density: *lead is a heavy metal* **3** great in yield, quality, or quantity: *heavy rain*; *heavy traffic* **4** great or considerable: *heavy emphasis* **5** hard to bear, accomplish, or fulfil: *heavy demands* **6** sad or dejected in spirit or mood: *heavy at heart* **7** coarse or broad: *a heavy line*; *heavy features* **8** (of soil) having a high clay content; cloggy **9** solid or fat: *heavy legs* **10** (of an industry) engaged in the large-scale complex manufacture of capital goods or extraction of raw materials. Compare **light²** (sense 19) **11** serious; grave **12** *military* **a** armed or equipped with large weapons, armour, etc **b** (of guns, etc) of a large and powerful type **13** (of a syllable) having stress or accentuation. Compare

h

light² (sense 24) **14** dull and uninteresting: *a heavy style* **15** prodigious: *a heavy drinker* **16** (of cakes, bread, etc) insufficiently leavened **17** deep and loud: *a heavy thud* **18** (of music, literature, etc) **a** dramatic and powerful; grandiose **b** not immediately comprehensible or appealing **19** *slang* **a** unpleasant or tedious **b** wonderful **c** (of rock music) having a powerful beat; hard **20** weighted; burdened: *heavy with child* **21** clumsy and slow: *heavy going* **22** permeating: *a heavy smell* **23** cloudy or overcast, esp threatening rain: *heavy skies* **24** not easily digestible: *a heavy meal* **25** (of an element or compound) being or containing an isotope with greater atomic weight than that of the naturally occurring element: *heavy hydrogen; heavy water* **26** *horse racing* (of the going on a racecourse) soft and muddy **27** *slang* using, or prepared to use, violence or brutality: *the heavy mob* **28** heavy on *informal* using large quantities of: *this car is heavy on petrol* ▷ *n, pl* heavies **29 a a** villainous role **b** an actor who plays such a part **30** *military* **a** a large fleet unit, esp an aircraft carrier or battleship **b** a large calibre or weighty piece of artillery **31** *informal* (*usually plural*, often preceded by *the*) a serious newspaper: *the Sunday heavies* **32** *informal* a heavyweight boxer, wrestler, etc **33** *slang* a man hired to threaten violence or deter others by his presence **34** *Scot* strong bitter beer ▷ *adv* **35 a** in a heavy manner; heavily: *time hangs heavy* **b** (*in combination*): *heavy-laden* [Old English *hefig*; related to *hebban* to HEAVE, Old High German *hebīg*] ▷ **'heavily** *adv* ▷ **'heaviness** *n*

heavy breather *n* **1** a person who breathes stertorously or with difficulty **2** an anonymous telephone caller who imitates such sounds, as being suggestive of sexual excitement

heavy chain *n immunol* a type of polypeptide chain present in an immunoglobulin molecule

heavy-duty *n* (*modifier*) **1** made to withstand hard wear, bad weather, etc: *heavy-duty uniforms* **2** subject to high import or export taxes

heavy earth *n* another name for **barium oxide**

heavy-footed *adj* having a heavy or clumsy tread

heavy-handed *adj* **1** clumsy **2** harsh and oppressive ▷ **,heavy-'handedly** *adv* ▷ **,heavy-'handedness** *n*

heavy-hearted *adj* sad; melancholy

heavy hitter *n informal* another term for **big hitter** (sense 2)

heavy hydrogen *n* another name for **deuterium**

heavy metal *n* **1 a** a type of rock music characterized by a strong beat and amplified instrumental effects, often with violent, nihilistic, and misogynistic lyrics **b** (*as modifier*): *a heavy-metal band* **2** a metal with a high specific gravity **3** *military* large guns or shot

heavy oil *n* a hydrocarbon mixture, heavier than water, distilled from coal tar

heavy spar *n* another name for **barytes**

heavy water *n* water that has been electrolytically decomposed to enrich it in the deuterium isotope in the form HDO or D_2O

heavy-water reactor *n* a nuclear reactor that uses heavy water as moderator

heavyweight ('hɛvɪ,weɪt) *n* **1** a person or thing that is heavier than average **2 a** a professional boxer weighing more than 175 pounds (79 kg) **b** an amateur boxer weighing more than 81 kg (179 pounds) **c** (*as modifier*): *the world heavyweight championship* **3** a wrestler in a similar weight category (usually over 214 pounds (97 kg)) **4** *informal* an important or highly influential person

Heb. or **Hebr.** *abbreviation for* **1** Hebrew (language) **2** *Bible* Hebrews

hebdomad ('hɛbdə,mæd) *n* **1** *obsolete* the number seven or a group of seven **2** a rare word for **week** [c16 from Greek, from *hebdomos* seventh, from *heptas* seven]

hebdomadal (hɛb'dɒmədªl) or **hebdomadary** (hɛb'dɒmədərɪ, -drɪ) *adj* a rare word for **weekly** ▷ heb'domadally *adv*

Hebdomadal Council *n* the governing council or senate of Oxford University

Hebe ('hi:bɪ) *n Greek myth* the goddess of youth and spring, daughter of Zeus and Hera and wife of Hercules

Hebei ('hʌ'beɪ), **Hopeh** or **Hopei** *n* a province of NE China, on the Gulf of Chihli: important for the production of winter wheat, cotton, and coal. Capital: Shijiazhuang. Pop: 67 690 000 (2003 est.). Area: 202 700 sq km (79 053 sq miles)

hebephrenia (,hi:bɪ'fri:nɪə) *n* a form of pubertal schizophrenia, characterized by hallucinations, delusions, foolish behaviour, and senseless laughter [c20 New Latin, from Greek *hēbē* youth + -*phrenia* mental disorder, from *phrēn* mind] ▷ hebephrenic (,hi:bɪ'frɛnɪk) *adj*

hebetate ('hɛbɪ,teɪt) *adj* **1** (of plant parts) having a blunt or soft point ▷ *vb* **2** *rare* to make or become blunted [c16 from Latin *hebetāre* to make blunt, from *hebes* blunt] ▷ ,hebe'tation *n* ▷ 'hebe,tative *adj*

hebetic (hɪ'bɛtɪk) *adj* of or relating to puberty [c19 from Greek *hēbētikos* youth, from *hēbē* youth]

hebetude ('hɛbɪ,tju:d) *n rare* mental dullness or lethargy [c17 from Late Latin *hebetūdō*, from Latin *hebes* blunt] ▷ ,hebe'tudinous *adj*

Hebraic (hɪ'breɪɪk), **Hebraical** or **Hebrew** *adj* of, relating to, or characteristic of the Hebrews or their language or culture ▷ He'braically *adv*

Hebraism ('hi:breɪ,ɪzəm) *n* a linguistic usage, custom, or other feature borrowed from or particular to the Hebrew language, or to the Jewish people or their culture

Hebraist ('hi:breɪɪst) *n* a person who studies the Hebrew language and culture ▷ ,Hebra'istic or ,Hebra'istical *adj* ▷ ,Hebra'istically *adv*

Hebraize or **Hebraise** ('hi:breɪ,aɪz) *vb* to become or cause to become Hebrew or Hebraic ▷ ,Hebrai'zation or ,Hebrai'sation *n* ▷ 'Hebra,izer or 'Hebra,iser *n*

Hebrew ('hi:bru:) *n* **1** the ancient language of the Hebrews, revived as the official language of Israel. It belongs to the Canaanitic branch of the Semitic subfamily of the Afro-Asiatic family of languages **2** a member of an ancient Semitic people claiming descent from Abraham; an Israelite **3** *archaic or offensive* a Jew ▷ *adj* **4** of or relating to the Hebrews or their language **5** *archaic or offensive* Jewish [c13 from Old French *Ebreu*, from Latin *Hebraeus*, from Greek *Hebraios*, from Aramaic '*ibhray*, from Hebrew '*ibhrī* one from beyond (the river)]

Hebrew calendar *n* another term for the **Jewish calendar**

Hebrews ('hi:bru:z) *n* (*functioning as singular*) a book of the New Testament

Hebridean (,hɛbrɪ'di:ən) or **Hebridian** (hɛ'brɪdɪən) *adj* **1** of or relating to the Hebrides or their inhabitants ▷ *n* **2** a native or inhabitant of the Hebrides

Hebrides ('hɛbrɪ,di:z) *pl n* **the** a group of over 500 islands off the W coast of Scotland: separated by the North Minch, Little Minch, and the Sea of the Hebrides: the chief islands are Skye, Raasay, Rum, Eigg, Coll, Tiree, Mull, Jura, Colonsay, and Islay (**Inner Hebrides**), and Lewis with Harris, North Uist, Benbecula, South Uist, and Barra (**Outer Hebrides**). Also called: Western Isles

Hebron ('hɛbrɒn, 'hi:-) *n* a city in the West Bank: famous for the Haram, which includes the cenotaphs of Abraham and Sarah, Isaac and Rebecca, and Jacob and Leah. Pop: 168 000 (2005 est.). Arabic name: El Khalil

Hecate or **Hekate** ('hɛkətɪ) *n Greek myth* a goddess of the underworld

hecatomb ('hɛkə,təʊm, -,tu:m) *n* **1** (in ancient Greece or Rome) any great public sacrifice and feast, originally one in which 100 oxen were sacrificed **2** a great sacrifice [c16 from Latin *hecatombē*, from Greek *hekatombē*, from *hekaton* hundred + *bous* ox]

heck¹ (hɛk) *interj* a mild exclamation of surprise, irritation, etc [c19 euphemistic for *hell*]

heck² (hɛk) *n Northern English dialect* a frame for obstructing the passage of fish in a river [c14 variant of HATCH²]

heckelphone ('hɛkəl,fəʊn) *n music* a type of bass oboe [c20 named after W. *Heckel* (1856–1909), German inventor]

heckle ('hɛkªl) *vb* **1** to interrupt (a public speaker, performer, etc) by comments, questions, or taunts **2** (*tr*) Also: hackle, hatchel to comb (hemp or flax) ▷ *n* **3** an instrument for combing flax or hemp [c15 Northern and East Anglian form of HACKLE] ▷ 'heckler *n*

hectare ('hɛktɑ:) *n* one hundred ares. 1 hectare is equivalent to 10 000 square metres or 2.471 acres. Symbol: ha [c19 from French; see HECTO-, ARE²]

hectic ('hɛktɪk) *adj* **1** characterized by extreme activity or excitement **2** associated with, peculiar to, or symptomatic of tuberculosis (esp in the phrases **hectic fever, hectic flush**) ▷ *n* **3** a hectic fever or flush **4** *rare* a person who is consumptive or who experiences a hectic fever or flush [c14 from Late Latin *hecticus*, from Greek *hektikos* habitual, from *hexis* state, from *ekhein* to have] ▷ 'hectically *adv*

hecto- or before a vowel **hect-** *prefix* denoting 100: *hectogram*. Symbol: h [via French from Greek *hekaton* hundred]

hectocotylus (,hɛktəʊ'kɒtɪləs) *n, pl* -li (-,laɪ) a tentacle in certain male cephalopod molluscs, such as the octopus, that is specialized for transferring spermatozoa to the female [c19 New Latin, from HECTO- + Greek *kotulē* cup]

hectogram or **hectogramme** ('hɛktəʊ,græm) *n* one hundred grams. 1 hectogram is equivalent to 3.527 ounces. Symbol: hg

hectograph ('hɛktəʊ,grɑ:f, -,græf) *n* **1** Also called: copygraph a process for copying type or manuscript from a glycerine-coated gelatine master to which the original has been transferred **2** a machine using this process ▷ hectographic (,hɛktəʊ'græfɪk) *adj* ▷ ,hecto'graphically *adv* ▷ hectography (hɛk'tɒgrəfɪ) *n*

hectolitre or US **hectoliter** ('hɛktəʊ,li:tə) *n* one hundred litres. A measure of capacity equivalent to 3.531 cubic feet. Symbol: hl

hectometre or US **hectometer** ('hɛktəʊ,mi:tə) *n* one hundred metres: 1 hectometre is equivalent to 328.089 feet. Symbol: hm

hector ('hɛktə) *vb* **1** to bully or torment ▷ *n* **2** a blustering bully [c17 after HECTOR (the son of Priam), in the sense: a bully]

Hector ('hɛktə) *n classical myth* a son of King Priam of Troy, who was killed by Achilles

Hecuba ('hɛkjʊbə) *n classical myth* the wife of King Priam of Troy, and mother of Hector and Paris

he'd (hi:d; *unstressed* i:d, hɪd, ɪd) *contraction of* he had *or* he would

heddle ('hɛdªl) *n* one of a set of frames of vertical wires on a loom, each wire having an eye through which a warp thread can be passed [Old English *hefeld* loom; related to Old Norse *hafald*, Middle Low German *hevelte*]

heder *Hebrew* ('xɛdɛr; *English* 'heɪdə) *n, pl* hadarim (xada'ri:m) a variant spelling of **cheder**

hedera ('hɛdərə) *n* See ivy (sense 1) [Latin: ivy]

hedge (hɛdʒ) *n* **1** a row of shrubs, bushes, or trees forming a boundary to a field, garden, etc **2** a barrier or protection against something **3** the act or a method of reducing the risk of financial loss on an investment, bet, etc **4** a cautious or evasive statement **5** (*modifier; often in combination*) low, inferior, or illiterate: *a hedge lawyer* ▷ *vb* **6** (*tr*) to enclose or separate with or as if with a hedge **7** (*intr*) to make or maintain a hedge, as by cutting and laying **8** (*tr*; often foll by *in, about,* or *around*) to hinder, obstruct, or restrict **9** (*intr*) to evade decision or action, esp by making noncommittal statements **10** (*tr*) to guard against the risk of loss in (a bet, the paying out of a win, etc), esp by laying bets with other bookmakers **11** (*intr*) to protect against financial loss through future price fluctuations, as by investing in futures [Old English *hecg*; related to Old High German *heckia*,

Middle Dutch *hegge*; see HAW¹] > ˈhedger *n* > ˈhedging *n* > ˈhedgy *adj*

hedge fund *n* a largely unregulated speculative fund which offers substantial returns for high-risk investments

hedge garlic *n* another name for **garlic mustard**

hedgehog (ˈhɛdʒ,hɒg) *n* **1** any small nocturnal Old World mammal of the genus *Erinaceus,* such as *E. europaeus,* and related genera, having a protective covering of spines on the back: family *Erinaceidae,* order *Insectivora* (insectivores). Related adj: **erinaceous 2** any other insectivore of the family *Erinaceidae,* such as the moon rat **3** *US* any of various other spiny animals, esp the porcupine

hedgehop (ˈhɛdʒ,hɒp) *vb* **-hops, -hopping, -hopped** (*intr*) (of an aircraft) to fly close to the ground, as in crop spraying > ˈhedge,hopper *n* > ˈhedge,hopping *n, adj*

hedge hyssop *n* any of several North American scrophulariaceous plants of the genus *Gratiola,* esp *G. aurea,* having small yellow or white flowers

hedge laying *n* the art or practice of making or maintaining a hedge by cutting branches partway through, laying them horizontally, and pegging them in position in order to create a strong thick hedge

hedgerow (ˈhɛdʒ,rəʊ) *n* a hedge of shrubs or low trees growing along a bank, esp one bordering a field or lane

hedge-school *n Irish history* a school held out of doors in favourable weather, indoors in winter > ˈhedge-schoolˌmaster *n*

hedge sparrow *n* a small brownish European songbird, *Prunella modularis:* family *Prunellidae* (accentors). Also called: **dunnock**

Hedjaz (hiːˈdʒæz) *n* a variant spelling of **Hejaz**

hedonic damages (hiːˈdɒnɪk) *pl n law* compensation based on what the victim of a crime might have earnt in the future

hedonics (hiːˈdɒnɪks) *n* (*functioning as singular*) **1** the branch of psychology concerned with the study of pleasant and unpleasant sensations **2** (in philosophy) the study of pleasure, esp in its relation to duty

hedonism (ˈhiːd°,nɪzəm, ˈhɛd-) *n* **1** *ethics* **a** the doctrine that moral value can be defined in terms of pleasure. See **utilitarianism b** the doctrine that the pursuit of pleasure is the highest good **2** the pursuit of pleasure as a matter of principle **3** indulgence in sensual pleasures [c19 from Greek *hēdonē* pleasure] > heˈdonic *or* ,hedonˈistic *adj* > ˈhedonist *n*

-hedron *n combining form* indicating a geometric solid having a specified number of faces or surfaces: *tetrahedron* [from Greek *-edron* -sided, from *hedra* seat, base] > **-hedral** *adj combining form*

heebie-jeebies (ˈhiːbɪˈdʒiːbɪz) *pl n the slang* apprehension and nervousness [c20 coined by W. De Beck (1890–1942), American cartoonist]

heed (hiːd) *n* **1** close and careful attention; notice (often in the phrases **give, pay,** *or* **take heed**) > *vb* **2** to pay close attention to (someone or something) [Old English *hēdan*; related to Old Saxon *hōdian,* Old High German *huoten*] > ˈheeder *n* > ˈheedful *adj* > ˈheedfully *adv* > ˈheedfulness *n*

heedless (ˈhiːdlɪs) *adj* taking little or no notice; careless or thoughtless > ˈheedlessly *adv* > ˈheedlessness *n*

heehaw (ˌhiːˈhɔː) *interj* an imitation or representation of the braying sound of a donkey

heel¹ (hiːl) *n* **1** the back part of the human foot from the instep to the lower part of the ankle. Compare **calcaneus 2** the corresponding part in other vertebrates **3** the part of a shoe, stocking, etc, designed to fit the heel **4** the outer part of a shoe underneath the heel **5** the part of the palm of a glove nearest the wrist **6** the lower, end, or back section of something: *the heel of a loaf* **7** *horticulture* the small part of the parent plant that remains attached to a young shoot cut for propagation and that ensures more successful rooting **8** *nautical* **a** the bottom of a mast **b** the

after end of a ship's keel **9** the back part of a golf club head where it bends to join the shaft **10** *rugby* possession of the ball as obtained from a scrum (esp in the phrase **get the heel**) **11** *slang* a contemptible person **12 at** (*or* **on**) **one's heels** just behind or following closely **13 dig one's heels in** See **dig in** (sense 5) **14 down at heel a** shabby or worn **b** slovenly or careless **15 kick** (*or* **cool**) **one's heels** to wait or be kept waiting **16 rock back on one's heels** to astonish or be astonished **17 show a clean pair of heels** to run off **18 take to one's heels** to run off **19 to heel** disciplined or under control, as a dog walking by a person's heel > *vb* **20** (*tr*) to repair or replace the heel of (shoes, boots, etc) **21** to perform (a dance) with the heels **22** (*tr*) *golf* to strike (the ball) with the heel of the club **23** *rugby* to kick (the ball) backwards using the sole and heel of the boot **24** to follow at the heels of (a person) **25** (*tr*) to arm (a gamecock) with spurs **26** (*tr*) *NZ* (of a cattle dog) to drive (cattle) by biting their heels [Old English *hēla*; related to Old Norse *hæll,* Old Frisian *hēl*] > ˈheelless *adj*

heel² (hiːl) *vb* **1** (of a vessel) to lean over; list > *n* **2** inclined position from the vertical: *the boat is at ten degrees of heel* [Old English *hieldan*; related to Old Norse *hallr* inclined, Old High German *helden* to bow]

heel-and-toe *adj* **1** of or denoting a style of walking in which the heel of the front foot touches the ground before the toes of the rear one leave it > *vb* **2** (*intr*) (esp in motor racing) to use the heel and toe of the same foot to operate the brake and accelerator

heelball (ˈhiːl,bɔːl) *n* **a** a black waxy substance used by shoemakers to blacken the edges of heels and soles **b** a similar substance used to take rubbings, esp brass rubbings

heel bar *n* a small shop or a counter in a department store where shoes are mended while the customer waits

heel bone *n* the nontechnical name for **calcaneus**

heeled (hiːld) *adj* **1 a** having a heel or heels **b** (*in combination*): *high-heeled* **2 well-heeled** wealthy

heeler (ˈhiːlə) *n* **1** *US* See **ward heeler 2** a person or thing that heels **3** *Austral and NZ* a dog that herds cattle by biting at their heels

heel in *or dialect* **hele in** *vb* (*tr, adverb*) to insert (cuttings, shoots, etc) into the soil before planting to keep them moist

heelpiece (ˈhiːl,piːs) *n* the piece of a shoe, stocking, etc, designed to fit the heel

heelpost (ˈhiːl,pəʊst) *n* a post for carrying the hinges of a door or gate

heeltap (ˈhiːl,tæp) *n* **1** Also called: **lift** a layer of leather, etc, in the heel of a shoe **2** a small amount of alcoholic drink left at the bottom of a glass after drinking

Heerlen (ˈhɪələn; *Dutch* ˈheːrlə) *n* a city in the SE Netherlands, in Limburg province: industrial centre of a coal-mining region. Pop: 94 000 (2003 est)

Hefei (ˈhʌˈfeɪ) *or* **Hofei** *n* a city in SE China, capital of Anhui province: administrative and commercial centre in a rice- and cotton-growing region. Pop: 1 320 000 (2005 est)

heft (hɛft) *vb* (*tr*) **1** to assess the weight of (something) by lifting **2** to lift > *n* **3** *US* weight **4** *US* the main part [c19 probably from HEAVE, by analogy with *thieve, theft, cleave, cleft*] > ˈhefter *n*

hefty (ˈhɛftɪ) *adj* **heftier, heftiest** *informal* **1** big and strong **2** characterized by vigour or force: *a hefty blow* **3** large, bulky, or heavy **4** sizable; involving a large amount of money: *a hefty bill; a hefty wage* > ˈheftily *adv* > ˈheftiness *n*

Hegelian (hɪˈgeɪlɪən, heɪˈgiː-) *adj* of or relating to Georg Wilhelm Friedrich Hegel, the German philosopher (1770–1831) > Heˈgelianˌism *n*

Hegelian dialectic *n philosophy* an interpretive method in which the contradiction between a proposition (thesis) and its antithesis is resolved at a higher level of truth (synthesis)

hegemony (hɪˈgɛmənɪ) *n, pl* **-nies** ascendancy or domination of one power or state within a league, confederation, etc, or of one social class over others [c16 from Greek *hēgemonia* authority, from *hēgemōn* leader, from *hēgeisthai* to lead] > hegemonic (ˌhɛgəˈmɒnɪk) *adj*

Hegira *or* **Hejira** (ˈhɛdʒɪrə) *n* **1** the departure of Mohammed from Mecca to Medina in 622 AD; the starting point of the Muslim era **2** the Muslim era itself. See also AH **3** (*often not capital*) an emigration escape or flight > Also called: **Hijrah** [c16 from Medieval Latin, from Arabic *hijrah* emigration or flight]

hegumen (hɪˈgjuːmɛn) *or* **hegumenos** (hɪˈgjuːmɪ,nəʊs) *n* the head of a monastery of the Eastern Church [c16 from Medieval Latin *hēgūmenus,* from Late Greek *hēgoumenos* leader, from Greek *hēgeisthai* to lead]

heh (heɪ) *interj* an exclamation of surprise or inquiry

heid (hiːd) *n* a Scot word for **head**

Heidelberg (ˈhaɪd°l,bɜːg; *German* ˈhaɪdəlbɛrk) *n* a city in SW Germany, in NW Baden-Württemberg on the River Neckar: capital of the Palatinate from the 13th century until 1719; famous castle (begun in the 12th century) and university (1386), the oldest in Germany. Pop: 142 959 (2003 est)

Heidelberg man *n* a type of primitive man, *Homo heidelbergensis,* occurring in Europe in the middle Palaeolithic age, known only from a single fossil lower jaw [c20 referring to the site where remains were found, at Mauer, near *Heidelberg,* Germany (1907)]

Heiduc (ˈhaɪdʊk) *n* a variant spelling of **Haiduk**

heifer (ˈhɛfə) *n* a young cow [Old English *heahfore;* related to Greek *poris* calf; see HIGH]

heigh-ho (ˈheɪˈhəʊ) *interj* an exclamation of weariness, disappointment, surprise, or happiness

height (haɪt) *n* **1** the vertical distance from the bottom or lowest part of something to the top or apex **2** the vertical distance of an object or place above the ground or above sea level; altitude **3** relatively great altitude or distance from the bottom to the top **4** the topmost point; summit **5** *astronomy* the angular distance of a celestial body above the horizon **6** the period of greatest activity or intensity: *the height of the battle* **7** an extreme example of its kind: *the height of rudeness* **8** (*often plural*) an area of high ground **9** (*often plural*) the state of being far above the ground: *I don't like heights* **10** (*often plural*) a position of influence, fame, or power: *the giddy heights they occupied in the 1980s* [Old English *hīehthu*; related to Old Norse *hæthe,* Gothic *hauhitha,* Old High German *hōhida*; see HIGH]

heighten (ˈhaɪt°n) *vb* **1** to make or become high or higher **2** to make or become more extreme or intense > ˈheightened *adj* > ˈheightener *n*

height of land *n US and Canadian* a watershed

height-to-paper *n* the overall height of printing plates and type, standardized as 0.9175 inch (Brit) and 0.9186 inch (US)

Heilbronn (*German* haɪlˈbrɔn) *n* a city in SW Germany, in N Baden-Württemberg on the River Neckar. Pop: 120 705 (2003 est)

Heilongjiang (ˈheɪˈlʊŋˈdʒɑːˈæn) *or* **Heilungkiang** (ˈheɪˈlʊŋˈkjæŋ, -kaɪˈæŋ) *n* a province of NE China, in Manchuria: coal-mining, with placer gold in some rivers. Capital: Harbin. Pop: 38 150 000 (2003 est). Area: 464 000 sq km (179 000 sq miles)

Heilong Jiang (ˈheɪˈlʊŋ ˈdʒɑːˈæn) *n* the Pinyin transliteration of the Chinese name for the **Amur**

Heiltsuk (ˈhaɪlˌstʊk) *n* a member of a coastal Native Canadian people living in British Columbia. Formerly called: **Bella Bella** [of Wakashan origin]

Heimdall, Heimdal (ˈheɪmˌdɑːl) *or* **Heimdallr** (ˈheɪmˌdɑːlə) *n Norse myth* the god of light and the dawn, and the guardian of the rainbow bridge Bifrost

Heimlich manoeuvre (ˈhaɪmlɪk) *n* a technique

h

in first aid to dislodge a foreign body in a person's windpipe by applying sudden upward pressure on the upper abdomen. Also called: **abdominal thrust** [c20 named after Henry J. Heimlich (born 1920), American surgeon]

heinous ('heɪnəs, 'hiː-) *adj* evil; atrocious [c14 from Old French *haineus*, from *haine* hatred, from *hair* to hate, of Germanic origin; see HATE]
> '**heinously** *adv* > '**heinousness** *n*

heir (ɛə) *n* **1** *civil law* the person legally succeeding to all property of a deceased person, irrespective of whether such person died testate or intestate, and upon whom devolves as well as the rights the duties and liabilities attached to the estate **2** any person or thing that carries on some tradition, circumstance, etc, from a forerunner **3** an archaic word for **offspring** [c13 from Old French, from Latin *hērēs*; related to Greek *khēros* bereaved]
> '**heirless** *adj*

heir apparent *n, pl* **heirs apparent** *property law* a person whose right to succeed to certain property cannot be defeated, provided such person survives his ancestor. Compare **heir presumptive**

heir-at-law *n, pl* **heirs-at-law** *property law* the person entitled to succeed to the real property of a person who dies intestate

heirdom ('ɛədəm) *n property law* succession by right of blood; inheritance

heiress ('ɛərɪs) *n* **1** a woman who inherits or expects to inherit great wealth **2** *property law* a female heir

heirloom ('ɛə,luːm) *n* **1** an object that has been in a family for generations **2** *property law* a chattel inherited by special custom or in accordance with the terms of a will [c15 from HEIR + *lome* tool; see LOOM¹]

heir presumptive *n property law* a person who expects to succeed to an estate but whose right may be defeated by the birth of one nearer in blood to the ancestor. Compare **heir apparent**

heirship ('ɛəʃɪp) *n law* **1** the state or condition of being an heir **2** the right to inherit; inheritance

Heisenberg uncertainty principle ('haɪz°n,bɜːg) *n* a more formal name for **uncertainty principle**

heist (haɪst) *slang, chiefly US and Canadian* ▷ *n* **1** a robbery ▷ *vb* **2** (*tr*) to steal or burgle [variant of HOIST] > '**heister** *n*

heitiki (heɪ'tiːkiː) *n NZ* a Māori neck ornament of greenstone [c19 from Māori, from *hei* to hang + TIKI]

hejab (hɛ'dʒɑːb) *n* a variant of **hijab**

Hejaz, Hedjaz or **Hijaz** (hiː'dʒæz) *n* a region of W Saudi Arabia, along the Red Sea and the Gulf of Aqaba: formerly an independent kingdom; united with Nejd in 1932 to form Saudi Arabia. Area: about 348 600 sq km (134 600 sq miles)

Hejira ('hedʒɪrə) *n* a variant spelling of **Hegira**

Hekate ('hɛkətɪ) *n* a variant spelling of **Hecate**

heketara (hɛkɛtɑːrə) *n* a small shrub, *Olearia rani*, which has flowers with white petals and yellow centres [Māori]

Hekla ('hɛklə) *n* a volcano in SW Iceland: several craters, subject to fairly frequent eruptions in recent times. Height: 1491 m (4892 ft)

Hel (hɛl) or **Hela** ('hɛlɑː) *n* **1** *Norse myth* the goddess of the dead **2** the underworld realm of the dead

held (hɛld) *vb* the past tense and past participle of **hold**¹

Heldentenor *German* ('hɛldənteno:r) *n, pl* **-tenöre** (-te'nɜːrə) a tenor with a powerful voice suited to singing heroic roles, esp in Wagner [literally: hero tenor]

hele (hiː) *vb* (*tr, adverb*) a dialect variant of **heel in** [Old English *helian* hide]

Helen ('hɛlɪn) *n Greek myth* the beautiful daughter of Zeus and Leda, whose abduction by Paris from her husband Menelaus caused the Trojan War

Helena ('hɛlənə) *n* a city in W Montana: the state capital. Pop: 26 718 (2003 est)

helenium (hə'liːnɪəm) *n* any plant of the American genus *Helenium*, up to 1.6 m (5 ft) tall,

some species of which are grown as border plants for their daisy-like yellow or variegated flowers: family *Asteraceae* [New Latin, from Greek *helenion*, a plant name]

Helgoland ('hɛlgolant) *n* the German name for **Heligoland**

heli- *combining form* helicopter: *helipad* [c20 shortened from HELICOPTER]

heliacal rising (hɪ'laɪək°l) *n* **1** the rising of a celestial object at approximately the same time as the rising of the sun **2** the date at which such a celestial object first becomes visible in the dawn sky [c17 from Late Latin *hēliacus* relating to the sun, from Greek *hēliakos*, from *hēlios* sun]

helianthemum (hiːlɪ'ænθəməm) *n* any plant of the dwarf evergreen genus *Helianthemum*, some species of which are grown as rock-garden plants for their numerous papery yellow or orange flowers; related to the rockrose, which they resemble: family *Cistaceae*. Also called: **Cape primrose** [New Latin, from Greek *hēlios* sun + *anthemon* flower]

helianthus (hiːlɪ'ænθəs) *n, pl* **-thuses** any plant of the genus *Helianthus*, such as the sunflower and Jerusalem artichoke, typically having large yellow daisy-like flowers with yellow, brown, or purple centres: family *Asteraceae* (composites) [c18 New Latin, from Greek *hēlios* sun + *anthos* flower]

heli-boarding *n NZ* the sport of snowboarding on mountains or glaciers accessible only by helicopter or skiplane

helical ('hɛlɪk°l) *adj* of or shaped like a helix; spiral > '**helically** *adv*

helical gear *n* a cylindrical gearwheel having the tooth form generated on a helical path about the axis of the wheel

helical scan *n* (*modifier*) denoting a recording technique used with video tapes in which the recorded tracks on the tape are segments of a helix: *a helical-scan tape*

helices ('hɛlɪˌsiːz) *n* a plural of **helix**

helichrysum (ˌhɛlɪ'kraɪzəm) *n* any plant of the widely cultivated genus *Helichrysum*, whose flowers retain their shape and colour when dried: family *Asteraceae* (composites) [c16 from Latin, from Greek *helikhrusos*, from *helix* spiral + *khrusos* gold]

helicity (hɪ'lɪsɪtɪ) *n, pl* **-ties** *physics* the projection of the spin of an elementary particle on the direction of propagation [c20 from HELIX + -ITY]

helicline ('hɛlɪˌklaɪn) *n architect* a spiral-shaped ramp [from HELICO- + -CLINE]

helico- *or before a vowel* **helic-** *combining form* spiral or helical: *helicograph* [from Latin, from Greek *helix* spiral]

helicograph ('hɛlɪkəʊˌɡrɑːf, -ˌgræf) *n* an instrument for drawing spiral curves

helicoid ('hɛlɪˌkɔɪd) *adj also* **helicoidal 1** *biology* shaped like a spiral: *a helicoid shell* ▷ *n* **2** *geometry* any surface resembling that of a screw thread > '**helico'idally** *adv*

helicon ('hɛlɪkən) *n* a bass tuba made to coil over the shoulder of a band musician [c19 probably from HELICON, associated with Greek *helix* spiral]

Helicon ('hɛlɪkən) *n* a mountain in Greece, in Boeotia: location of the springs of Hippocrene and Aganippe, believed by the Ancient Greeks to be the source of poetic inspiration and the home of the Muses. Height: 1749 m (5738 ft). Modern Greek name: Elikón

helicopter ('hɛlɪˌkɒptə) *n* **1** an aircraft capable of hover, vertical flight, and horizontal flight in any direction. Most get all of their lift and propulsion from the rotation of overhead blades. See also **autogiro** ▷ *vb* **2** to transport (people or things) or (of people or things) to be transported by helicopter [c19 from French *hélicoptère*, from HELICO- + Greek *pteron* wing]

helicopter gunship *n* a large heavily armed helicopter used for ground attack

helicopter view *n* an overview of a situation without any details

helideck ('hɛlɪˌdɛk) *n* a landing deck for

helicopters on ships, oil platforms, etc [c20 from HELI- + DECK]

Heligoland ('hɛlɪɡəʊˌlænd) *n* a small island in the North Sea, one of the North Frisian Islands, separated from the coast of NW Germany by the **Heligoland Bight**: administratively part of the German state of Schleswig-Holstein: a large island in early medieval times, now eroded to an area of about 150 hectares (380 acres); ceded by Britain to Germany in 1890 in exchange for Zanzibar. German name: **Helgoland**

helio- *or before a vowel* **heli-** *combining form* indicating the sun: *heliocentric; heliolithic* [from Greek, from *hēlios* sun]

heliocentric (ˌhiːlɪəʊ'sɛntrɪk) *adj* **1** having the sun at its centre **2** measured from or in relation to the centre of the sun > ˌhelio'centrically *adv* > ˌheliocen'tricity or ˌhelio'centriˌcism *n*

heliocentric parallax *n* See **parallax** (sense 2)

Heliochrome ('hiːlɪəʊˌkrəʊm) *n trademark* a photograph that reproduces the natural colours of the subject > ˌhelio'chromic *adj*

heliodor (ˌhiːlɪəʊˌdɔː) *n* a clear yellow form of beryl used as a gemstone

heliograph ('hiːlɪəʊˌɡrɑːf, -ˌgræf) *n* **1** an instrument with mirrors and a shutter used for sending messages in Morse code by reflecting the sun's rays **2** a device used to photograph the sun > **heliographer** (ˌhiːlɪ'ɒɡrəfə) *n* > heliographic (ˌhiːlɪəʊ'ɡræfɪk) or ˌhelio'graphical *adj* > ˌheli'ography *n*

heliolatry (ˌhiːlɪ'ɒlətrɪ) *n* worship of the sun > ˌheli'olater *n* > ˌheli'olatrous *adj*

heliolithic (ˌhiːlɪəʊ'lɪθɪk) *adj* of or relating to a civilization characterized by sun worship and megaliths

heliometer (ˌhiːlɪ'ɒmɪtə) *n* a refracting telescope having a split objective lens that is used to determine very small angular distances between celestial bodies > **heliometric** (ˌhiːlɪəʊ'mɛtrɪk) or ˌhelio'metrical *adj* > ˌhelio'metrically *adv* > ˌheli'ometry *n*

heliopause ('hiːlɪəʊˌpɔːz) *n* the boundary between the region of space dominated by the solar wind and the interstellar medium

heliophyte ('hiːlɪəʊˌfaɪt) *n* any plant that grows best in direct sunlight

Heliopolis (ˌhiːlɪ'ɒpəlɪs) *n* **1** (in ancient Egypt) a city near the apex of the Nile delta: a centre of sun worship. Ancient Egyptian name: On **2** the Ancient Greek name for **Baalbek**

Helios ('hiːlɪˌɒs) *n Greek myth* the god of the sun, who drove his chariot daily across the sky. Roman counterpart: Sol

heliosphere ('hiːlɪəʊˌsfɪə) *n* the region around the sun outside of which the sun's influence is negligible and interstellar space begins

heliostat ('hiːlɪəʊˌstæt) *n* an astronomical instrument used to reflect the light of the sun in a constant direction > 'helio'static *adj*

heliotaxis (ˌhiːlɪəʊ'tæksɪs) *n* movement of an entire organism in response to the stimulus of sunlight > heliotactic (ˌhiːlɪəʊ'tæktɪk) *adj*

heliotherapy (ˌhiːlɪəʊ'θɛrəpɪ) *n* the therapeutic use of sunlight

heliotrope ('hiːlɪəˌtrəʊp, 'hɛljə-) *n* **1** any boraginaceous plant of the genus *Heliotropium*, esp the South American *H. arborescens*, cultivated for its small fragrant purple flowers **2** garden heliotrope a widely cultivated valerian, *Valeriana officinalis*, with clusters of small pink, purple, or white flowers **3** any of various plants that turn towards the sun **4 a** a bluish-violet to purple colour **b** (*as adjective*): *a heliotrope dress* **5** an instrument used in geodetic surveying employing the sun's rays reflected by a mirror as a signal for the sighting of stations over long distances **6** another name for **bloodstone** [c17 from Latin *hēliotropium*, from Greek *hēliotropion*, from *hēlios* sun + *trepein* to turn]

heliotropin (ˌhiːlɪ'ɒtrəpɪn) *n* another term for **piperonal**

heliotropism (ˌhiːlɪˈɒtrəˌpɪzəm) *n* the growth of plants or plant parts (esp flowers) in response to the stimulus of sunlight, so that they turn to face the sun > **heliotropic** (ˌhiːlɪəʊˈtrɒpɪk) *adj* > ˌ**helioˈtropically** *adv*

heliotype (ˈhiːlɪəʊˌtaɪp) *n* **1** a printing process in which an impression is taken in ink from a gelatine surface that has been exposed under a negative and prepared for printing. Also called: **heliotypy** **2** the gelatine plate produced by such a process **3** a print produced from such a plate > **heliotypic** (ˌhiːlɪəʊˈtɪpɪk) *adj*

heliozoan (ˌhiːlɪəʊˈzəʊən) *n* any protozoan of the mostly freshwater group *Heliozoa*, typically having a siliceous shell and stiff radiating cytoplasmic projections: phylum *Actinopoda* (actinopods)

helipad (ˈhɛlɪˌpæd) *n* a place for helicopters to land and take off [C20 from HELI- + PAD[1]]

heliport (ˈhɛlɪˌpɔːt) *n* an airport for helicopters [C20 from HELI- + PORT[1]]

heli-skiing *n* skiing in which skiers are transported by helicopter to remote slopes > ˈ**heli-ˌskier** *n*

helium (ˈhiːlɪəm) *n* a very light nonflammable colourless odourless element that is an inert gas, occurring in certain natural gases: used in balloons and in cryogenic research. Symbol: He; atomic no.: 2; atomic wt.: 4.002602; density: 0.1785 kg/m³; at normal pressures it is liquid down to absolute zero; melting pt.: below –272.2°C; boiling pt.: –268.90°C. See also **alpha particle** [C19 New Latin, from HELIO- + -IUM; named from its having first been detected in the solar spectrum]

helium flash *n astronomy* the explosive burning of helium in the case of a star of low mass that occurs when the core is so dense that the matter has become degenerate. The burning causes a rapid rise in temperature until it is so high that the gas ceases to be degenerate, after which there is a rapid expansion

helix (ˈhiːlɪks) *n, pl* **helices** (ˈhɛlɪˌsiːz) *or* **helixes** **1** a curve that lies on a cylinder or cone, at a constant angle to the line segments making up the surface; spiral **2** a spiral shape or form **3** the incurving fold that forms the margin of the external ear **4** another name for **volute** (sense 2) **5** any terrestrial gastropod mollusc of the genus *Helix*, which includes the garden snail (*H. aspersa*) [C16 from Latin, from Greek: spiral; probably related to Greek *helissein* to twist]

hell (hɛl) *n* **1** *Christianity* (*sometimes capital*) **a** the place or state of eternal punishment of the wicked after death, with Satan as its ruler **b** forces of evil regarded as residing there **2** (*sometimes capital*) (in various religions and cultures) the abode of the spirits of the dead. See also **Hel, Hades, Sheol** **3** pain, extreme difficulty, etc **4** *informal* a cause of such difficulty or suffering: *war is hell* **5** *US and Canadian* high spirits or mischievousness: *there's hell in that boy* **6** a box used by a tailor for discarded material **7** *now rare* a gambling house, booth, etc **8** **as hell** (intensifier): *tired as hell* **9** **for the hell of it** *informal* for the fun of it **10** **from hell** *informal* denoting a person or thing that is particularly bad or alarming: *neighbour from hell; hangover from hell* **11** **give someone hell** *informal* **a** to give someone a severe reprimand or punishment **b** to be a source of annoyance or torment to someone **12** **hell of a** *or* **helluva** *informal* (intensifier): *a hell of a good performance* **13** **hell for leather** at great speed **14** (**come**) **hell or high water** *informal* whatever difficulties may arise **15** **hell to pay** *informal* serious consequences, as of a foolish action **16** **like hell** *informal* **a** (*adverb*) (intensifier): *he works like hell* **b** an expression of strong disagreement with a previous statement, request, order, etc **17** **play (merry) hell with** *informal* to throw into confusion and disorder; disrupt **18** **raise hell** **a** to create a noisy disturbance, as in fun **b** to react strongly and unfavourably **19** **the hell** *informal* **a** (intensifier) used in such phrases as **what the hell, who the hell,** etc **b** an expression of strong disagreement or disfavour: *the hell I will.* ▷ *interj* **20** *informal* an exclamation of anger, annoyance, surprise, etc (Also in exclamations such as **hell's bells, hell's teeth,** etc) [Old English *hell*; related to *helan* to cover, Old Norse *hel*, Gothic *halja* hell, Old High German *hella*]

he'll (hiːl; *unstressed* iːl, hɪl, ɪl) *contraction of* he will *or* he shall

hellacious (hɛˈleɪʃəs) *adj US slang* **1** remarkable; horrifying **2** wonderful; excellent [C20 from HELL + *-acious* as in AUDACIOUS]

Helladic (hɛˈlædɪk) *adj* of, characteristic of, or related to the Bronze Age civilization that flourished about 2900 to 1100 BC on the Greek mainland and islands

Hellas (ˈhɛləs) *n* transliteration of the Ancient Greek name for **Greece**

hellbender (ˈhɛlˌbɛndə) *n* a very large dark grey aquatic salamander, *Cryptobranchus alleganiensis*, with internal gills: inhabits rivers in E and central US: family *Cryptobranchidae*

hellbent (ˌhɛlˈbɛnt) *adj* (*postpositive* and foll by *on*) *informal* strongly or rashly intent

hellcat (ˈhɛlˌkæt) *n* a spiteful fierce-tempered woman

helldiver (ˈhɛlˌdaɪvə) *n US informal* a small greyish-brown North American grebe, *Podilymbus podiceps*, with a small bill. Also called: **pied-billed grebe, dabchick**

Helle (ˈhɛlɪ) *n Greek myth* a daughter of King Athamas, who was borne away with her brother Phrixus on the golden winged ram. She fell from its back and was drowned in the Hellespont. See also **Phrixus, Golden Fleece**

hellebore (ˈhɛlɪˌbɔː) *n* **1** any plant of the Eurasian ranunculaceous genus *Helleborus*, esp *H. niger* (black hellebore), typically having showy flowers and poisonous parts. See also **Christmas rose** **2** any of various liliaceous plants of the N temperate genus *Veratrum*, esp *V. album*, that have greenish flowers and yield alkaloids used in the treatment of heart disease [C14 from Greek *helleboros*, of uncertain origin]

helleborine (ˌhɛlɪˈbɔːriːn) *n* any of various N temperate orchids of the genera *Cephalanthera* and *Epipactis* [C16 ultimately from Greek *helleborinē* a plant resembling hellebore]

Hellen (ˈhɛlɪn) *n* (in Greek legend) a Thessalian king and eponymous ancestor of the Hellenes

Hellene (ˈhɛliːn) *or* **Hellenian** (hɛˈliːnɪən) *n* another name for a **Greek**

Hellenic (hɛˈlɛnɪk, -ˈliː-) *adj* **1** of or relating to the ancient or modern Greeks or their language **2** of or relating to ancient Greece or the Greeks of the classical period (776–323 BC). Compare **Hellenistic** **3** another word for **Greek** ▷ *n* **4** a branch of the Indo-European family of languages consisting of Greek in its various ancient and modern dialects > **Helˈlenically** *adv*

Hellenism (ˈhɛlɪˌnɪzəm) *n* **1** the principles, ideals, and pursuits associated with classical Greek civilization **2** the spirit or national character of the Greeks **3** conformity to, imitation of, or devotion to the culture of ancient Greece **4** the cosmopolitan civilization of the Hellenistic world

Hellenist (ˈhɛlɪnɪst) *n* **1** Also called: **Hellenizer** (in the Hellenistic world) a non-Greek, esp a Jew, who adopted Greek culture **2** a student of the Greek civilization or language

Hellenistic (ˌhɛlɪˈnɪstɪk) *or* **Hellenistical** *adj* **1** characteristic of or relating to Greek civilization in the Mediterranean world, esp from the death of Alexander the Great (323 BC) to the defeat of Antony and Cleopatra (30 BC) **2** of or relating to the Greeks or to Hellenism > ˌ**Hellenˈistically** *adv*

Hellenize *or* **Hellenise** (ˈhɛlɪˌnaɪz) *vb* to make or become like the ancient Greeks > ˌ**Helleniˈzation** *or* ˌ**Helleniˈsation** *n* > ˈ**Hellenˌizer** *or* ˈ**Hellenˌiser** *n*

heller[1] (ˈhɛlə) *n, pl* **-ler** **1** a monetary unit of the Czech Republic and Slovakia, worth one hundredth of a koruna **2** any of various old German or Austrian coins of low denomination [from German *haller* a silver coin, after *Hall*, town in Swabia where the coins were minted]

heller[2] (ˈhɛlə) *n* another word for **hellion**

Hellerwork (ˈhɛləˌwɜːk) *n* a form of deep tissue massage intended to release the build-up of physical and emotional traumas in the body

hellery (ˈhɛlərɪ) *n Canadian slang, rare* wild or mischievous behaviour

Helles (ˈhɛlɪs) *n* **Cape** a cape in NW Turkey, at the S end of the Gallipoli Peninsula

Hellespont (ˈhɛlɪˌspɒnt) *n* the ancient name for the **Dardanelles**

hellfire (ˈhɛlˌfaɪə) *n* **1** the torment and punishment of hell, envisaged as eternal fire **2** (*modifier*) characterizing sermons or preachers that emphasize this aspect of Christian belief: *hellfire evangelism*

hellgrammite (ˈhɛlgrəˌmaɪt) *n US* the larva of the dobsonfly, about 10 cm long with biting mouthparts: used as bait for bass. Also called: **dobson** [C19 of unknown origin]

hellhole (ˈhɛlˌhəʊl) *n* an unpleasant or evil place

hellhound (ˈhɛlˌhaʊnd) *n* **1** a hound of hell **2** a fiend

hellion (ˈhɛljən) *n US informal* a rough or rowdy person, esp a child; troublemaker. Also called: **heller** [C19 probably from dialect *hallion* rogue, of unknown origin]

hellish (ˈhɛlɪʃ) *adj* **1** of or resembling hell **2** wicked; cruel **3** *informal* very difficult or unpleasant ▷ *adv* **4** *Brit informal* (intensifier): *a hellish good idea* > ˈ**hellishly** *adv* > ˈ**hellishness** *n*

hello, hallo *or* **hullo** (hɛˈləʊ, hə-, ˈhɛləʊ) *sentence substitute* **1** an expression of greeting used on meeting a person or at the start of a telephone call **2** a call used to attract attention **3** an expression of surprise **4** an expression used to indicate that the speaker thinks his or her listener is naive or slow to realize something: *Hello? Have you been on Mars for the past two weeks or something?* ▷ *n, pl* **-los** **5** the act of saying or calling "hello" [C19 see HALLO]

hello money *n* a charge made by a retailer to a supplier for introducing the supplier's goods to its stores

Hell's Angel *n* a member of a motorcycle gang of a kind originating in the US in the 1950s, who typically dress in denim and Nazi-style paraphernalia and are noted for their initiation rites, lawless behaviour, etc

helluva (ˈhɛləvə) *adv, adj informal* (intensifier): *a helluva difficult job; he's a helluva guy*

helm[1] (hɛlm) *n* **1** *nautical* **a** the wheel, tiller, or entire apparatus by which a vessel is steered **b** the position of the helm: that is, on the side of the keel opposite from that of the rudder **2** a position of leadership or control (esp in the phrase **at the helm**) ▷ *vb* **3** (*tr*) to direct or steer [Old English *helma*; related to Old Norse *hjalm* rudder, Old High German *halmo*] > ˈ**helmless** *adj*

helm[2] (hɛlm) *n* **1** an archaic or poetic word for **helmet** ▷ *vb* **2** (*tr*) *archaic or poetic* to supply with a helmet [Old English *helm*; related to *helan* to cover, Old Norse *hjalmr*, Gothic *hilms*, Old High German *helm* helmet, Sanskrit *śárman* protection]

Helmand (ˈhɛlmənd) *n* a river in S Asia, rising in E Afghanistan and flowing generally southwest to a marshy lake, Hamun Helmand, on the border with Iran. Length: 1400 km (870 miles)

helmer (ˈhɛlmə) *n informal* a film director

helmet (ˈhɛlmɪt) *n* **1** a piece of protective or defensive armour for the head worn by soldiers, policemen, firemen, divers, etc **2** *biology* a part or structure resembling a helmet, esp the upper part of the calyx of certain flowers [C15 from Old French, diminutive of *helme*, of Germanic origin] > ˈ**helmeted** *adj*

Helmholtz function (*German* ˈhɛlmhɔlts) *n* a thermodynamic property of a system equal to the difference between its internal energy and the product of its temperature and its entropy. Symbol: *A* or *F* Also called: **Helmholtz free energy** [C20 named after Baron Hermann Ludwig

h

Ferdinand von *Helmholtz* (1821–94), German physiologist, physicist, and mathematician]

helminth ('hɛlmɪnθ) *n* any parasitic worm, esp a nematode or fluke [c19 from Greek *helmins* parasitic worm] > **helminthoid** ('hɛlmɪnˌθɔɪd, hɛlˈmɪnθɔɪd) *adj*

helminthiasis (ˌhɛlmɪnˈθaɪəsɪs) *n* infestation of the body with parasitic worms [c19 from New Latin, from Greek *helminthian* to be infested with worms]

helminthic (hɛlˈmɪnθɪk) *adj* **1** of, relating to, or caused by parasitic worms ▷ *n, adj* **2** another word for **vermifuge**

helminthology (ˌhɛlmɪnˈθɒlədʒɪ) *n* the study of parasitic worms > **helminthological** (ˌhɛlmɪnθəˈlɒdʒɪkᵊl) *adj* > **helminˈthologist** *n*

helmsman ('hɛlmzmən) *n, pl* **-men** the person at the helm who steers the ship; steersman

helophyte ('hɛləfaɪt) *n* any perennial marsh plant that bears its overwintering buds in the mud below the surface [c20 from Modern Greek *helos* marsh + -PHYTE]

Helot ('hɛlət, 'hiː-) *n* **1** (in ancient Greece, esp Sparta) a member of the class of unfree men above slaves owned by the state **2** (*usually not capital*) a serf or slave [c16 from Latin *Hēlōtēs*, from Greek *Heilōtes*, alleged to have meant originally: inhabitants of Helos, who, after its conquest, were serfs of the Spartans]

helotism ('hɛləˌtɪzəm, 'hiː-) *n* **1** the condition or quality of being a Helot **2** a sociopolitical system in which a class, minority, nation, etc, is held in a state of subjection **3** *zoology* another name for **dulosis** ▷ Also called (for senses 1, 2): **helotage**

helotry ('hɛlətrɪ, 'hiː-) *n* **1** serfdom or slavery **2** serfs or slaves as a class

help (hɛlp) *vb* **1** to assist or aid (someone to do something), esp by sharing the work, cost, or burden of something: *he helped his friend to escape; she helped him climb out of the boat* **2** to alleviate the burden of (someone else) by giving assistance **3** (*tr*) to assist (a person) to go in a specified direction: *help the old lady up from the chair* **4** to promote or contribute to: *to help the relief operations* **5** to cause improvement in (a situation, person, etc): *crying won't help* **6** (*tr*; preceded by *can, could,* etc; *usually used with a negative*) **a** to avoid or refrain from: *we can't help wondering who he is* **b** (usually foll by *it*) to prevent or be responsible for: *I can't help it if it rains* **7** to alleviate (an illness, etc) **8** (*tr*) to serve (a customer): *can I help you, madam?* **9** (*tr*; foll by *to*) **a** to serve (someone with food, etc) (usually in the phrase **help oneself**): *may I help you to some more vegetables?; help yourself to peas* **b** to provide (oneself) with) without permission: *he's been helping himself to money out of the petty cash* **10** cannot help but to be unable to do anything else except: *I cannot help but laugh* **11** help a person on *or* off with to assist a person in the putting on or removal of (clothes) **12** so help me on my honour **b** no matter what: *so help me, I'll get revenge* ▷ *n* **13** the act of helping, or being helped, or a person or thing that helps: *she's a great help* **14** a helping **15 a** a person hired for a job; employee, esp a farm worker or domestic servant **b** (*functioning as singular*) several employees collectively **16** a means of remedy: *there's no help for it* ▷ *interj* **17** used to ask for assistance ▷ See also **help out** [Old English *helpan*; related to Old Norse *hjalpa*, Gothic *hilpan*, Old High German *helfan*] > **'helpable** *adj* > **'helper** *n*

helpful ('hɛlpfʊl) *adj* serving a useful function; giving help > **'helpfully** *adv* > **'helpfulness** *n*

helping ('hɛlpɪŋ) *n* a single portion of food taken at a meal

helping hand *n* assistance: *many people lent a helping hand in making arrangements for the party*

helpless ('hɛlplɪs) *adj* **1** unable to manage independently **2** made powerless or weak: *they were helpless from so much giggling* **3** without help > **'helplessly** *adv* > **'helplessness** *n*

helpline ('hɛlpˌlaɪn) *n* **1** a telephone line operated by a charitable organization for people in distress

2 a telephone line operated by a commercial organization to provide information

helpmate ('hɛlpˌmeɪt) *n* a companion and helper, esp a wife

helpmeet ('hɛlpˌmiːt) *n* a less common word for **helpmate** [c17 from the phrase *an helpe meet* (suitable) *for him* Genesis 2:18]

help out *vb* (*adverb*) **1** to assist or aid (someone), esp by sharing the burden **2** to share the burden or cost of something with (another person)

help screens *pl n* computer instructions displayed on a visual display unit

Helsingborg (*Swedish* hɛlsɪŋˈbɔrj) *n* a port in SW Sweden, on the Sound opposite Helsingør, Denmark: changed hands several times between Denmark and Sweden, finally becoming Swedish in 1710; shipbuilding. Pop: 121 097 (2004 est). Former name (until 1971): **Hälsingborg**

Helsingør (*Danish* hɛlsenˈøːr) *n* a port in NE Denmark, in NE Zealand: site of Kronborg Castle (16th century), famous as the scene of Shakespeare's *Hamlet*. Pop: 35 002 (2004 est). English name: **Elsinore**

Helsinki ('hɛlsɪŋkɪ, hɛlˈsɪŋ-) *n* the capital of Finland, a port in the south on the Gulf of Finland: founded by Gustavus I of Sweden in 1550; replaced Turku as capital in 1812, while under Russian rule; university. Pop: 559 330 (2003 est). Swedish name: **Helsingfors** (hɛlsɪŋˈfɔrs)

helter-skelter ('hɛltəˈskɛltə) *adj* **1** haphazard or carelessly hurried ▷ *adv* **2** in a helter-skelter manner ▷ *n* **3** *Brit* a high spiral slide, as at a fairground **4** disorder or haste [c16 probably of imitative origin]

helve (hɛlv) *n* **1** the handle of a hand tool such as an axe or pick ▷ *vb* **2** (*tr*) to fit a helve to (a tool) [Old English *hielfe*; related to Old Saxon *hĕlvi*, Old High German *halb*, Lithuanian *kìlpa* stirrup; see HALTER]

Helvellyn (hɛlˈvɛlɪn) *n* a mountain in NW England, in the Lake District. Height: 949 m (3114 ft)

Helvetia (hɛlˈviːʃə) *n* **1** the Latin name for Switzerland **2** a Roman province in central Europe (1st century BC to the 5th century AD), corresponding to part of S Germany and parts of W and N Switzerland

Helvetian (hɛlˈviːʃən) *adj* **1** of or relating to the Helvetii **2** another word for **Swiss** ▷ *n* **3** a native or citizen of Switzerland **4** a member of the Helvetii

Helvetic (hɛlˈvɛtɪk) *adj* **1** Helvetian or Swiss **2** of or relating to the Helvetic Confessions or to Swiss Protestantism ▷ *n* **3** a Swiss Protestant or reformed Calvinist who subscribes to one of the two **Helvetic Confessions** (of faith) formulated in 1536 and 1566

Helvetii (hɛlˈviːʃɪˌaɪ) *pl n* a Celtic tribe from SW Germany who settled in Helvetia from about 200 BC

hem¹ (hɛm) *n* **1** an edge to a piece of cloth, made by folding the raw edge under and stitching it down **2** short for **hemline** ▷ *vb* **hems, hemming, hemmed** (*tr*) **3** to provide with a hem **4** (*usually foll by* *in, around, or about*) to enclose or confine [Old English *hemm*; related to Old Frisian *hemme* enclosed land]

hem² (hɛm) *n, interj* **1** a representation of the sound of clearing the throat, used to gain attention, express hesitation, etc ▷ *vb* **hems, hemming, hemmed 2** (*intr*) to utter this sound **3** hem (*or* hum) and haw to hesitate in speaking or in making a decision

hem- *combining form* a US variant of **haemo-** before a vowel

hema- *combining form* a US variant of **haemo-**

he-man *n, pl* **-men** *informal* a strongly built muscular man

hematite ('hɛmətaɪt) *or* **haematite** ('hɛmətaɪt, 'hiːm-) *n* a red, grey, or black mineral, found as massive beds and in veins and igneous rocks. It is the chief source of iron. Composition: iron (ferric)

oxide. Formula: Fe_2O_3. Crystal structure: hexagonal (rhombohedral). Also called: **iron glance** [c16 via Latin from Greek *haimatitēs* resembling blood, from *haima* blood] > **hematitic** *or* **haematitic** (ˌhɛməˈtɪtɪk) *adj*

hemato- *or before a vowel* **hemat-** *combining form* US variants of **haemato-**

Hemel Hempstead ('hɛməl 'hɛmstɪd) *n* a town in SE England, in W Hertfordshire: designated a new town in 1947. Pop: 83 118 (2001)

hemelytron (hɛˈmɛlɪˌtrɒn) *or* **hemielytron** (ˌhɛmɪˈɛlɪˌtrɒn) *n, pl* **-tra** (-trə) the forewing of plant bugs and related insects, having a thickened base and a membranous apex [c19 from New Latin *hemielytron*, from HEMI- + Greek *elutron* a covering] > **hem'elytral** *or* **ˌhemi'elytral** *adj*

hemeralopia (ˌhɛmərəˈləʊpɪə) *n* inability to see clearly in bright light. Nontechnical name: **day blindness**. Compare **nyctalopia** [c19 New Latin, from Greek *hēmeralōps*, from *hēmera* day + *alaos* blind + *ōps* eye] > **hemeralopic** (ˌhɛmərəˈlɒpɪk) *adj*

hemerocallis (ˌhɛmərəʊˈkælɪs) *n* See **day lily** [from Greek *hemera* day + *kallos* beautiful]

hemi- *prefix* half: *hemicycle; hemisphere*. Compare **demi-** (sense 1), **semi-** (sense 1) [from Latin, from Greek *hēmi-*]

-hemia *n combining form* US variant of **-aemia**

hemialgia (ˌhɛmɪˈældʒɪə) *n* pain limited to one side of the body

hemianopia (ˌhɛmɪænˈəʊpɪə) *n* loss of vision in either the whole left or the whole right half of the field of vision. Also called: **hemianopsia** (ˌhɛmɪænˈɒpsɪə) [c19 from HEMI- + AN- + Greek *opsis* sight]

hemicellulose (ˌhɛmɪˈsɛljʊˌləʊz) *n* any of a group of plant polysaccharides that occur chiefly in the cell wall

hemichordate (ˌhɛmɪˈkɔːˌdeɪt) *n* **1** any small wormlike marine animal of the subphylum *Hemichordata* (or *Hemichorda*), having numerous gill slits in the pharynx: phylum *Chordata* (chordates) ▷ *adj* **2** of, relating to, or belonging to the subphylum *Hemichordata* ▷ See also **acorn worm**

hemicryptophyte (ˌhɛmɪˈkrɪptəfaɪt) *n* any perennial plant that bears its overwintering buds at soil level, where they are often partly covered by surface debris [c20 HEMI- + CRYPTOPHYTE]

hemicrystalline (ˌhɛmɪˈkrɪstəˌlaɪn) *adj* a former name for **hypocrystalline**. Compare **holocrystalline**

hemicycle ('hɛmɪˌsaɪkᵊl) *n* **1** a semicircular structure, room, arena, wall, etc **2** a rare word for **semicircle**. > **hemicyclic** (ˌhɛmɪˈsaɪklɪk, -'sɪk-) *adj*

hemidemisemiquaver (ˌhɛmɪˌdɛmɪˈsɛmɪˌkweɪvə) *n music* a note having the time value of one sixty-fourth of a semibreve. Usual US and Canadian name: **sixty-fourth note**

hemielytron (ˌhɛmɪˈɛlɪˌtrɒn) *n, pl* **-tra** (-trə) a variant of **hemelytron**. > **ˌhemi'elytral** *adj*

hemihedral (ˌhɛmɪˈhiːdrəl) *adj* (of a crystal) exhibiting only half the number of planes necessary for complete symmetry

hemihydrate (ˌhɛmɪˈhaɪdreɪt) *n chem* a hydrate in which there are two molecules of substance to every molecule of water > **'hemiˌhydrated** *adj*

hemimorphic (ˌhɛmɪˈmɔːfɪk) *adj* (of a crystal) having different forms at each end of an axis > **ˌhemi'morphism** *or* **'hemiˌmorphy** *n*

hemimorphite (ˌhɛmɪˈmɔːfaɪt) *n* a white mineral consisting of hydrated zinc silicate in orthorhombic crystalline form: a common ore of zinc. Formula: $Zn_4Si_2O_7(OH)_2.H_2O$. Also called (US) **calamine**

Hemingwayesque (ˌhɛmɪŋˈweɪˈɛsk) *adj* of, relating to, or like Ernest Hemingway (1899–1961), the US novelist and short-story writer, his works, ideas, etc

hemiola (ˌhɛmɪˈəʊlə) *or* **hemiolia** *n music* a rhythmic device involving the superimposition of, for example, two notes in the time of three. Also called: **sesquialtera** [New Latin, from Greek *hēmiolia* ratio of one to one and a half, from HEMI-

+ (h)olos whole] > **hemiolic** (ˌhɛmɪˈɒlɪk) adj

hemiparasite (ˌhɛmɪˈpærɪˌsaɪt) or **semiparasite** n **1** a parasitic plant, such as mistletoe, that carries out photosynthesis but also obtains food from its host **2** an organism that can live independently or parasitically > **hemiparasitic** (ˌhɛmɪˌpærəˈsɪtɪk) adj

hemiplegia (ˌhɛmɪˈpliːdʒɪə) n paralysis of one side of the body, usually as the result of injury to the brain. Compare **paraplegia, quadriplegia** > ˌhemiˈplegic adj

hemipode (ˈhɛmɪˌpəʊd) or **hemipod** (ˈhɛmɪˌpɒd) n other names for **button quail**

hemipteran (hɪˈmɪptərən) n **1** Also called: **hemipteron** (hɪˈmɪptəˌrɒn) any hemipterous insect ▷ adj **2** another word for **hemipterous** [C19 from HEMI- + Greek pteron wing]

hemipterous (hɪˈmɪptərəs) or **hemipteran** adj of, relating to, or belonging to the Hemiptera, a large order of insects having sucking or piercing mouthparts specialized as a beak (rostrum). The group is divided into the suborders Homoptera (aphids, cicadas, etc) and Heteroptera (water bugs, bedbugs, etc)

hemisphere (ˈhɛmɪˌsfɪə) n **1** one half of a sphere **2 a** half of the terrestrial globe, divided into **northern** and **southern hemispheres** by the equator or into **eastern** and **western hemispheres** by some meridians, usually 0° and 180° **b** a map or projection of one of the hemispheres **3** either of the two halves of the celestial sphere that lie north or south of the celestial equator **4** anatomy short for **cerebral hemisphere.** > **hemispheric** (ˌhɛmɪˈsfɛrɪk) or ˌhemiˈspherical adj

hemispheroid (ˌhɛmɪˈsfɪərɔɪd) n half of a spheroid > ˌhemisphe'roidal adj

hemistich (ˈhɛmɪˌstɪk) n prosody a half line of verse

hemiterpene (ˌhɛmɪˈtɜːpiːn) n any of a class of simple unsaturated hydrocarbons, such as isoprene, having the formula C_5H_8

hemitrope (ˈhɛmɪˌtrəʊp) n chem another name for **twin** (sense 3) > **hemitropic** (ˌhɛmɪˈtrɒpɪk) > ˌhemi'tropism or hemitropy (hiːˈmɪtrəpɪ) n

hemizygous (ˌhɛmɪˈzaɪɡəs) adj genetics (of a chromosome or gene) not having a homologue; not paired in a diploid cell

hemline (ˈhɛmˌlaɪn) n the level to which the hem of a skirt or dress hangs; hem: knee-length hemlines

hemlock (ˈhɛmˌlɒk) n **1** an umbelliferous poisonous Eurasian plant, Conium maculatum, having finely divided leaves, spotted stems, and small white flowers. US name: **poison hemlock**. See also **water hemlock 2** a poisonous drug derived from this plant Also called: **hemlock spruce** any coniferous tree of the genus Tsuga, of North America and E Asia, having short flat needles: family Pinaceae. See also **western hemlock 4** the wood of any of these trees, used for lumber and as a source of wood pulp [Old English hymlic; perhaps related to hymele hop plant, Middle Low German homele, Old Norwegian humli, Old Slavonic chŭmelĭ]

hemmer (ˈhɛmə) n an attachment on a sewing machine for hemming

hemo- combining form a US variant of **haemo-**

hemp (hɛmp) n **1** Also called: **cannabis, marijuana** an annual strong-smelling Asian plant, Cannabis sativa, having tough clothes, deeply lobed leaves, and small greenish flowers: family Cannabidaeceae. See also **Indian hemp 2** the fibre of this plant, used to make canvas, rope, etc **3** any of several narcotic drugs obtained from some varieties of this plant, esp from Indian hemp. See **bhang, cannabis, hashish, marijuana** ▷ See also **bowstring hemp** [Old English hænep; related to Old Norse hampr, Old High German hanuf, Greek kannabis, Dutch hennep] > 'hemp,like adj

hemp agrimony n a Eurasian plant, Eupatorium cannabinum, with clusters of small pink flower heads: family Asteraceae (composites)

hemp nettle n **1** a hairy weedy plant, Galeopsis

---

tetrahit, of northern regions, having helmet-shaped pink, purple, and white flowers and toothed leaves: family Lamiaceae (labiates) **2** any of various other plants of the genus Galeopsis

hemstitch (ˈhɛmˌstɪtʃ) n **1** a decorative edging stitch, usually for a hem, in which the cross threads are stitched in groups ▷ vb **2** to decorate (a hem, etc) with hemstitches > 'hem,stitcher n

hen (hɛn) n **1** the female of any bird, esp the adult female of the domestic fowl **2** the female of certain other animals, such as the lobster **3** informal a woman regarded as gossipy or foolish **4** Scot dialect a term of address (often affectionate), used to women and girls **5** scarce as hen's teeth extremely rare [Old English henn; related to Old High German henna, Old Frisian henne]

Henan (ˈhʌˈnæn) or **Honan** n a province of N central China: the chief centre of early Chinese culture; mainly agricultural (the largest wheat-producing province in China). Capital: Zhengzhou. Pop: 96 670 000 (2003 est)

hen-and-chickens n, pl hens-and-chickens (functioning as singular or plural) any of several plants, such as the houseleek and ground ivy, that produce many offsets or runners

henbane (ˈhɛnˌbeɪn) n a poisonous solanaceous European plant, Hyoscyamus niger, with sticky hairy leaves and funnel-shaped greenish flowers: yields the drug hyoscyamine

henbit (ˈhɛnˌbɪt) n a plant, Lamium amplexicaule, that is native to Europe and has toothed opposite leaves and small dark red flowers: family Lamiaceae (labiates)

hence (hɛns) sentence connector **1** for this reason; following from this; therefore ▷ adv **2** from this time: a year hence **3** archaic **a** from here or from this world; away **b** from this origin or source ▷ interj **4** archaic begone! away! [Old English hionane; related to Old High German hinana away from here, Old Irish cen on this side]

henceforth (ˈhɛnsˈfɔːθ), **henceforwards** or **henceforward** adv from this time forward; from now on

henchman (ˈhɛntʃmən) n, pl -men **1** a faithful attendant or supporter **2** archaic a squire; page [C14 hengestman, from Old English hengest stallion + MAN; related to Old Norse hestr horse, Old High German hengist gelding]

hencoop (ˈhɛnˌkuːp) n a cage for poultry

hendeca- combining form eleven: hendecagon; hendecahedron; hendecasyllable [from Greek hendeka, from hen, neuter of heis one + deka ten]

hendecagon (hɛnˈdɛkəgən) n a polygon having 11 sides > **hendecagonal** (ˌhɛndɪˈkæɡənl) adj

hendecahedron (ˌhɛndɛkəˈhɛdrən, -ˈhiːdrən) n, pl -drons or -dra (-drə) a solid figure having 11 plane faces. See also **polyhedron**

hendecasyllable (ˈhɛndɛkəˌsɪləbəl) n prosody a verse line of 11 syllables [C18 via Latin from Greek hendekasullabos] > **hendecasyllabic** (ˌhɛnˌdɛkəsɪˈlæbɪk) adj

hendiadys (hɛnˈdaɪədɪs) n a rhetorical device by which two nouns joined by a conjunction, usually and, are used instead of a noun and a modifier, as in to run with fear and haste instead of to run with fearful haste [C16 from Medieval Latin, changed from Greek phrase hen dia duoin, literally: one through two]

Hendra (ˈhɛndrə) n a virus that affects humans and horses, causing a fatal, influenza-like illness [C20 after the suburb of Brisbane, the location of the outbreak during which the virus was first isolated]

henequen, henequin or **heniquen** (ˈhɛnɪkɪn) n **1** an agave plant, Agave fourcroydes, that is native to Yucatán **2** the fibre of this plant, used in making rope, twine, and coarse fabrics [C19 from American Spanish henequén, probably of Taino origin]

henge (hɛndʒ) n a circular area, often containing a circle of stones or sometimes wooden posts, dating from the Neolithic and Bronze Ages [back

---

formation from STONEHENGE]

Hengelo (Dutch ˈhɛŋələ:) n a city in the E Netherlands, in Overijssel province on the Twente Canal: industrial centre, esp for textiles. Pop: 81 000 (2003 est)

Hengyang (ˈhɛŋˈjæn) n a city in SE central China, in Hunan province on the Xiang River. Pop: 853 000 (2005 est)

hen harrier n a common harrier, Circus cyaneus, that flies over fields and marshes and nests in marshes and open land. US and Canadian names: **marsh hawk, marsh harrier**

henhouse (ˈhɛnˌhaʊs) n a coop for hens

Henle's loop (ˈhɛnlɪz) n anatomy See **loop¹** (sense 10b) [C19 named after F. G. J. Henle (1809–85), German anatomist]

Henley-on-Thames (ˈhɛnlɪ-) n a town in S England, in SE Oxfordshire on the River Thames: a riverside resort with an annual regatta. Pop: 10 513 (2001). Often shortened to: **Henley**

henna (ˈhɛnə) n **1** a lythraceous shrub or tree, Lawsonia inermis, of Asia and N Africa, with white or reddish fragrant flowers **2** a reddish dye obtained from the powdered leaves of this plant, used as a cosmetic and industrial dye **3** a reddish-brown or brown colour ▷ vb **4** (tr) to dye with henna ▷ Archaic name (for senses 1, 2): **camphire** [C16 from Arabic hinnā'; see ALKANET]

hennery (ˈhɛnərɪ) n, pl -neries a place or farm for keeping poultry

hen night n informal a party for women only, esp held for a woman shortly before she is married. Compare **hen party, stag night**

henotheism (ˈhɛnəʊθiːˌɪzəm) n the worship of one deity (of several) as the special god of one's family, clan, or tribe [C19 from Greek heis one + theos god] > 'henotheist n, henothe'istic adj

hen party n informal a party at which only women are present. Compare **hen night, stag night**

henpeck (ˈhɛnˌpɛk) vb (tr) (of a woman) to harass or torment (a man, esp her husband) by persistent nagging

henpecked (ˈhɛnˌpɛkt) adj (of a man) continually harassed or tormented by the persistent nagging of a woman (esp his wife)

hen run n an enclosure for hens, esp one made of chicken wire

henry (ˈhɛnrɪ) n, pl -ry, -ries or -rys the derived SI unit of electric inductance; the inductance of a closed circuit in which an emf of 1 volt is produced when the current varies uniformly at the rate of 1 ampere per second. Symbol: H [C19 named after Joseph Henry (1797–1878), US physicist]

Henry's law n chem the principle that the amount of a gas dissolved at equilibrium in a given quantity of a liquid is proportional to the pressure of the gas in contact with the liquid [C19 named after William Henry (1774–1836), English chemist]

hent¹ (hɛnt) archaic ▷ vb **1** (tr) to seize; grasp ▷ n **2** anything that has been grasped, esp by the mind [Old English hentan to pursue; related to huntian to HUNT]

hent² (hɛnt) vb (tr) Southwestern English dialect to empty: I'll hent the water out in the garden

hep¹ (hɛp) adj hepper, heppest slang an earlier word for **hip⁴**

hep² (hɛp) n informal short for **hepatitis**

heparin (ˈhɛpərɪn) n a polysaccharide, containing sulphate groups, present in most body tissues: an anticoagulant used in the treatment of thrombosis [C20 from Greek hēpar the liver + -IN] > 'heparin,oid adj

hepatic (hɪˈpætɪk) adj **1** of or relating to the liver **2** botany of or relating to the liverworts **3** having the colour of liver ▷ n **4** obsolete any of various drugs for use in treating diseases of the liver **5** a less common name for a **liverwort** [C15 from Latin hēpaticus, from Greek hēpar liver]

hepatica (hɪˈpætɪkə) n any ranunculaceous woodland plant of the N temperate genus Hepatica, having three-lobed leaves and white, mauve, or pink flowers [C16 from Medieval Latin: liverwort, from Latin *hēpaticus* of the liver]

hepatitis (ˌhɛpəˈtaɪtɪs) *n* inflammation of the liver, characterized by fever, jaundice, and weakness. See **hepatitis A, hepatitis B, hepatitis C**

hepatitis A *n* a form of hepatitis caused by a virus transmitted in contaminated food or drink

hepatitis B *n* a form of hepatitis caused by a virus transmitted by infected blood (as in transfusions), contaminated hypodermic needles, sexual contact, or by contact with any other body fluid. Former name: **serum hepatitis**

hepatitis C *n* a form of hepatitis caused by a virus that is transmitted in the same ways as that responsible for hepatitis B. Former name: **non-A, non-B hepatitis**

hepato- *or before a vowel* **hepat-** *combining form* denoting the liver: *hepatitis* [from Greek *hēpat-, hēpar*]

hepatogenous (ˌhɛpəˈtɒdʒɪnəs) *adj* originating in the liver

hepatomegaly (ˌhɛpətəʊˈmɛgəlɪ) *n* an abnormal enlargement of the liver, caused by congestion, inflammation, or a tumour [C20 from HEPATO- + New Latin *megalia*, from Greek *megas* great]

hepcat (ˈhɛpˌkæt) *n obsolete slang* a person who is hep, esp a player or admirer of jazz and swing in the 1940s

Hephaestus (hɪˈfiːstəs) *or* **Hephaistos** (hɪˈfaɪstɒs) *n Greek myth* the lame god of fire and metal-working. Roman counterpart: Vulcan

Hepplewhite (ˈhɛpəlˌwaɪt) *adj* of, denoting, or made in a style of ornamental and carved 18th-century English furniture, of which oval or shield-shaped open chairbacks are characteristic [C18 named after George *Hepplewhite* (1727–86), English cabinetmaker]

hepta- *or before a vowel* **hept-** *combining form* seven: *heptameter* [from Greek]

heptad (ˈhɛptæd) *n* 1 a group or series of seven 2 the number or sum of seven 3 an atom or element with a valency of seven [C17 from Greek *heptas* seven]

heptadecanoic acid (ˌhɛptəˌdɛkəˈnəʊɪk) *n* a colourless crystalline water-insoluble carboxylic acid used in organic synthesis. Formula: $CH_3(CH_2)_{15}COOH$. Also called: **margaric acid**

heptagon (ˈhɛptəgən) *n* a polygon having seven sides > **heptagonal** (hɛpˈtægənəl) *adj*

heptahedron (ˌhɛptəˈhiːdrən) *n* a solid figure having seven plane faces. See also **polyhedron** > ˌhepta'hedral *adj*

heptamerous (hɛpˈtæmərəs) *adj* (esp of plant parts such as petals or sepals) arranged in groups of seven

heptameter (hɛpˈtæmɪtə) *n prosody* a verse line of seven metrical feet > **heptametrical** (ˌhɛptəˈmɛtrɪkəl) *adj*

heptane (ˈhɛpteɪn) *n* an alkane existing in nine isomeric forms, esp the isomer with a straight chain of carbon atoms (*n*-heptane), which is found in petroleum and used as an anaesthetic. Formula: C_7H_{16} [C19 from HEPTA- + -ANE, so called because it has seven carbon atoms]

heptangular (hɛpˈtæŋgjʊlə) *adj* having seven angles

heptarchy (ˈhɛptɑːkɪ) *n, pl* -chies 1 government by seven rulers 2 a state divided into seven regions each under its own ruler 3 a the seven kingdoms into which Anglo-Saxon England is thought to have been divided from about the 7th to the 9th centuries AD: Kent, East Anglia, Essex, Sussex, Wessex, Mercia, and Northumbria b the period when this grouping existed > ˈheptarch *n* > hepˈtarchic *or* hepˈtarchal *adj*

heptastich (ˈhɛptəˌstɪk) *n prosody* a poem, strophe, or stanza that consists of seven lines

Heptateuch (ˈhɛptəˌtjuːk) *n* the first seven books of the Old Testament [C17 from Late Latin *Heptateuchos*, from Greek HEPTA- + *teukhos* book]

heptathlon (hɛpˈtæθlɒn) *n* an athletic contest for

women in which each athlete competes in seven different events [C20 from HEPTA- + Greek *athlon* contest] > hep'tathlete *n*

heptavalent (hɛpˈtævələnt, ˌhɛptəˈveɪlənt) *adj chem* having a valency of seven. Also: **septivalent**

heptose (ˈhɛptəʊs, -təʊz) *n* any monosaccharide that has seven carbon atoms per molecule

her (hɜː; *unstressed* hə, ə) *pron (objective)* 1 refers to a female person or animal: *he loves her; they sold her a bag; something odd about her; lucky her!* 2 refers to things personified as feminine or traditionally to ships and nations 3 *chiefly US* a dialect word for **herself** when used as an indirect object: *she needs to get her a better job* ▷ *determiner* 4 of, belonging to, or associated with her: *her silly ideas; her hair; her smoking annoys me* [Old English *hire*, genitive and dative of *hēo* SHE, feminine of *hēo* HE[1]; related to Old High German *ira*, Gothic *izōs*, Middle Dutch *hare*]

▪ USAGE See at **me**[1]

her. *abbreviation for* 1 heraldic 2 heraldry

Hera *or* **Here** (ˈhɪərə) *n Greek myth* the queen of the Olympian gods and sister and wife of Zeus. Roman counterpart: Juno

Heraclea (ˌhɛrəˈkliːə) *n* any of several ancient Greek colonies. The most famous is the S Italian site where Pyrrhus of Epirus defeated the Romans (280 BC)

Heracles *or* **Herakles** (ˈhɛrəˌkliːz) *n* the usual name (in Greek) for **Hercules**. > ˌHera'clean *or* ˌHera'klean *adj*

Heraclid *or* **Heraklid** (ˈhɛrəklɪd) *n, pl* Heraclidae *or* Heraklidae (ˌhɛrəˈklaɪdiː) any person claiming descent from Hercules, esp one of the Dorian aristocrats of Sparta > **Heraclidan** *or* **Heraklidan** (ˌhɛrəˈklaɪdən) *adj*

Herakleion *or* **Heraklion** (*Greek* heˈraːkliɔn) *n* variants of **Iráklion**

herald (ˈhɛrəld) *n* 1 a a person who announces important news b (*as modifier*): *herald angels* 2 *often literary* a forerunner; harbinger 3 the intermediate rank of heraldic officer, between king-of-arms and pursuivant 4 (in the Middle Ages) an official at a tournament ▷ *vb* (*tr*) 5 to announce publicly 6 to precede or usher in [C14 from Old French *herault*, of Germanic origin; compare Old English *here* war; see WIELD]

heraldic (hɛˈrældɪk) *adj* 1 of or relating to heraldry 2 of or relating to heralds > her'aldically *adv*

herald moth *n* a noctuid moth, *Scoliopteryx libatrix*, having brownish cryptically mottled forewings and plain dull hind wings. The adult hibernates and has a prolonged life

heraldry (ˈhɛrəldrɪ) *n, pl* -ries 1 the occupation or study concerned with the classification of armorial bearings, the allocation of rights to bear arms, the tracing of genealogies, etc 2 the duties and pursuit of a herald 3 armorial bearings, insignia, devices, etc 4 heraldic symbols or symbolism 5 the show and ceremony of heraldry > 'heraldist *n*

heralds' college *n* another name for **college of arms**

Herat (hɛˈræt) *n* a city in NW Afghanistan, on the Hari Rud River: on the site of several ancient cities; at its height as a cultural centre in the 15th century. Pop: 344 000 (2005 est)

Hérault (*French* ero) *n* a department of S France, in Languedoc-Roussillon region. Capital: Montpellier. Pop: 945 901 (2003 est). Area: 6224 sq km (2427 sq miles)

herb (hɜːb; *US* ɜːrb) *n* 1 a seed-bearing plant whose aerial parts do not persist above ground at the end of the growing season; herbaceous plant 2 a any of various usually aromatic plants, such as parsley, rue, and rosemary, that are used in cookery and medicine b (*as modifier*): *a herb garden* 3 *Caribbean* a slang term for **marijuana** [C13 from Old French *herbe*, from Latin *herba* grass, green plants] > 'herb,like *adj*

herbaceous (hɜːˈbeɪʃəs) *adj* 1 designating or

relating to plants or plant parts that are fleshy as opposed to woody: *a herbaceous plant* 2 (of petals and sepals) green and leaflike 3 of or relating to herbs > her'baceously *adv*

herbaceous border *n* a flower bed that primarily contains nonwoody perennials rather than annuals

herbage (ˈhɜːbɪdʒ) *n* 1 herbaceous plants collectively, esp the edible parts on which cattle, sheep, etc, graze 2 the vegetation of pasture land; pasturage

herbal (ˈhɜːbəl) *adj* 1 of or relating to herbs, usually culinary or medicinal herbs 2 *Austral informal* interested or participating in activities relating to esoteric philosophies, traditional remedies, etc ▷ *n* 3 a book describing and listing the properties of plants

herbalism (ˈhɜːbəlɪzəm) *n* the study or use of the medicinal properties of plants

herbalist (ˈhɜːbəlɪst) *n* 1 a person who grows, collects, sells, or specializes in the use of herbs, esp medicinal herbs 2 (formerly) a descriptive botanist

herbarium (hɜːˈbɛərɪəm) *n, pl* -iums *or* -ia (-ɪə) 1 a collection of dried plants that are mounted and classified systematically 2 a building, room, etc, in which such a collection is kept > her'barial *adj*

herb bennet *n* a Eurasian and N African rosaceous plant, *Geum urbanum*, with yellow flowers. Also called: **wood avens, bennet** [C13 *herbe beneit*, from Old French *herbe benoite*, literally: blessed herb, from Medieval Latin *herba benedicta*]

herb Christopher *n, pl* herbs Christopher another name for **baneberry** [C16 named after St *Christopher*]

herb Gerard (ˈdʒɛˌrɑːd) *n, pl* herbs Gerard another name for **goutweed** [C16 named after St *Gerard* (feast day April 23), who was invoked by those suffering from gout]

herbicide (ˈhɜːbɪˌsaɪd) *n* a chemical that destroys plants, esp one used to control weeds > ˌherbi'cidal *adj*

herbivore (ˈhɜːbɪˌvɔː) *n* 1 an animal that feeds on grass and other plants 2 *informal* a liberal, idealistic, or nonmaterialistic person [C19 from New Latin *herbivora* grass-eaters]

herbivorous (hɜːˈbɪvərəs) *adj* 1 (of animals) feeding on grass and other plants 2 *informal* liberal, idealistic, or nonmaterialistic > her'bivorously *adv* > her'bivorousness *n*

herb layer *n* See **layer** (sense 2)

herb of grace *n* an archaic name for **rue** (the plant)

herb Paris *n, pl* herbs Paris a Eurasian woodland plant, *Paris quadrifolia*, with a whorl of four leaves and a solitary yellow flower: formerly used medicinally: family *Trilliaceae* [C16 from Medieval Latin *herba paris*, literally: herb of a pair: so called because the four leaves on the stalk look like a true lovers' knot; associated in folk etymology with *Paris*, France]

herb Robert *n, pl* herbs Robert a low-growing N temperate geraniaceous plant, *Geranium robertianum*, with strongly scented divided leaves and small pink flowers [C13 from Medieval Latin *herba Roberti* herb of Robert, probably named after St *Robert*, 11th-century French ecclesiastic]

herby (ˈhɜːbɪ) *adj* herbier, herbiest 1 abounding in herbs 2 of or relating to medicinal or culinary herbs

Hercegovina (*Serbo-Croat* ˈhɛrtsɛgɔvina) *n* a variant of **Herzegovina**

Herculaneum (ˌhɜːkjʊˈleɪnɪəm) *n* an ancient city in SW Italy, of marked Greek character, on the S slope of Vesuvius: buried along with Pompeii by an eruption of the volcano (79 AD). Excavation has uncovered well preserved streets, houses, etc

herculean (ˌhɜːkjʊˈliːən) *adj* 1 requiring tremendous effort, strength, etc: *a herculean task* 2 (*sometimes capital*) resembling Hercules in strength, courage, etc

Hercules[1] (ˈhɜːkjʊˌliːz), **Heracles** *or* **Herakles** *n* 1

Also called: **Alcides** *classical myth* a hero noted for his great strength, courage, and for the performance of twelve immense labours **2** a man of outstanding strength or size > ˌHercu'lean, ˌHera'clean *or* ˌHera'klean *adj*

Hercules² ('hɜːkjʊˌliːz) *n, Latin genitive* **Herculeis** (ˌhɜːkjʊ'liːɪs) **1** a large constellation in the N hemisphere lying between Lyra and Corona Borealis **2** a conspicuous crater in the NW quadrant of the moon, about 70 kilometres in diameter

hercules beetle *n* a very large tropical American scarabaeid beetle, *Dynastes hercules*: the male has two large anterior curved horns

Hercules'-club *n* **1** a prickly North American araliaceous shrub, *Aralia spinosa*, with medicinal bark and leaves **2** a prickly North American rutaceous tree, *Zanthoxylum clava-herculis*, with medicinal bark and berries

Hercynian (hɜː'sɪnɪən) *adj* denoting a period of mountain building in Europe in the late Palaeozoic [c16 from Latin *Hercynia silva* the Hercynian forest (i.e., the wooded mountains of central Germany, esp the Erzgebirge)]

herd¹ (hɜːd) *n* **1** a large group of mammals living and feeding together, esp a group of cattle, sheep, etc **2** *often disparaging* a large group of people **3** *derogatory* the large mass of ordinary people ▷ *vb* **4** to collect or be collected into or as if into a herd [Old English *heord*; related to Old Norse *hjörth*, Gothic *hairda*, Old High German *herta*, Greek *kórthus* troop]

herd² (hɜːd) *n* **1 a** *archaic or dialect* a man or boy who tends livestock; herdsman **b** (*in combination*): *goatherd; swineherd* ▷ *vb* (*tr*) **2** to drive forwards in a large group **3** to look after (livestock) [Old English *hirde*; related to Old Norse *hirthir*, Gothic *hairdeis*, Old High German *hirti*, Old Saxon *hirdi, herdi*; see HERD¹]

herd-book *n* a book containing the pedigrees of breeds of pigs, cattle, etc

herder ('hɜːdə) *n chiefly US* a person who cares for or drives herds of cattle or flocks of sheep, esp on an open range. Brit equivalent: herdsman

herdic ('hɜːdɪk) *n US* a small horse-drawn carriage with a rear entrance and side seats [c19 named after P. Herdic, 19th-century American inventor]

herd instinct *n psychol* the inborn tendency to associate with others and follow the group's behaviour

herdsman ('hɜːdzmən) *n, pl* **-men** *chiefly Brit* a person who breeds, rears, or cares for cattle or (rarely) other livestock in the herd. US equivalent: herder

herd tester *n NZ* a technician trained to test the health and production of milk and butterfat of dairy cows > herd testing *n*

Herdwick ('hɜːdwɪk) *n* a hardy breed of coarse-woolled sheep from NW England [c19 from obsolete *herdwick* pasture, sheep farm (see HERD² (sense 1), WICK²); the breed is thought to have originated on the herdwicks of Furness Abbey]

here (hɪə) *adv* **1** in, at, or to this place, point, case, or respect: *we come here every summer; here, the policeman do not usually carry guns; here comes Roy* **2** **here and there** at several places in or throughout an area **3 here goes** an exclamation indicating that the speaker is about to perform an action **4 here's to** a formula used in proposing a toast to someone or something **5 here today, gone tomorrow** short-lived; transitory **6 here we go again** an event or process is about to repeat itself **7 neither here nor there** of no relevance or importance **8 this here** See **this** (senses 1–3) ▷ *n* **9** this place: *they leave here tonight* **10** (the) here and now the present time [Old English *hēr*; related to Old Norse *hēr*, Old High German *hiar*, Old Saxon *hīr*]

hereabouts (ˈhɪərəˌbaʊts) *or* **hereabout** *adv* in this region or neighbourhood; near this place

hereafter (ˌhɪər'ɑːftə) *adv* **1** *formal* in a subsequent part of this document, matter, case, etc **2** a less common word for **henceforth 3** at

some time in the future **4** in a future life after death ▷ *n* (usually preceded by *the*) **5** life after death **6** the future

hereat (ˌhɪər'æt) *adv archaic* because of this

hereby (ˌhɪə'baɪ) *adv* **1** (used in official statements, proclamations, etc) by means of or as a result of this **2** *archaic* nearby

heredes (hɪ'riːdiːz) *n* the plural of **heres**

hereditable (hɪ'rɛdɪtəbəl) *adj* a less common word for **heritable**. > heˌredita'bility > he'reditably *adv*

hereditament (ˌhɛrɪ'dɪtəmənt) *n property law* **1** any kind of property capable of being inherited **2** property that before 1926 passed to an heir if not otherwise disposed of by will

hereditarianism (həˌrɛdɪ'tɛərɪəˌnɪzəm) *n psychol* a school of thought that emphasizes the influence of heredity in the determination of human behaviour. Compare **environmentalism**

hereditary (hɪ'rɛdɪtərɪ, -trɪ) *adj* **1** of, relating to, or denoting factors that can be transmitted genetically from one generation to another **2** *law* **a** descending or capable of descending to succeeding generations by inheritance **b** transmitted or transmissible according to established rules of descent **3** derived from one's ancestors; traditional: *hereditary feuds* **4** *maths, logic* **a** (of a set) containing all those elements which have a given relation to any element of the set **b** (of a property) transferred by the given relation, so that if *x* has the property *P* and *xRy*, then *y* also has the property *P* > he'reditarily *adv* > he'reditariness *n*

hereditist (hə'rɛdɪtɪst) *n* any person who places the role of heredity above that of the environment as the determining factor in human or animal behaviour

heredity (hɪ'rɛdɪtɪ) *n, pl* **-ties 1** the transmission from one generation to another of genetic factors that determine individual characteristics: responsible for the resemblances between parents and offspring **2** the sum total of the inherited factors or their characteristics in an organism [c16 from Old French *heredite*, from Latin *hērēditās* inheritance; see HEIR]

heredo-familial (həˌrɛdəʊfə'mɪlɪəl) *adj* denoting a condition or disease that may be passed from generation to generation and to several members of one family

Hereford ('hɛrɪfəd) *n* **1** a city in W England, in Herefordshire on the River Wye: trading centre for agricultural produce; cathedral (begun 1079). Pop: 56 373 (2001) **2** a hardy breed of beef cattle characterized by a red body, red and white head, and white markings

Hereford and Worcester *n* a former county of the W Midlands of England, created in 1974 from the historic counties of Herefordshire and (most of) Worcestershire: abolished in 1998 when Herefordshire became an independent unitary authority

Herefordshire ('hɛrɪfədˌʃɪə, -ʃə) *n* a county of W England: from 1974 to 1998 part of Hereford and Worcester: drained chiefly by the River Wye; agricultural (esp fruit and cattle). Administrative centre: Hereford. Pop: 176 900 (2003 est). Area: 2180 sq km (842 sq miles)

herein (ˌhɪər'ɪn) *adv* **1** *formal* in or into this place, thing, document, etc **2** *rare* in this respect, circumstance, etc

hereinafter (ˌhɪərɪn'ɑːftə) *adv formal* in a subsequent part or from this point on in this document, statement, etc

hereinbefore (ˌhɪərɪnbɪ'fɔː) *adv formal* in a previous part of or previously in this document, statement, etc

hereinto (ˌhɪər'ɪntuː) *adv formal* into this place, circumstance, etc

hereof (ˌhɪər'ɒv) *adv formal* of or concerning this

hereon (ˌhɪər'ɒn) *adv* an archaic word for **hereupon**

Herero (hə'rɛərəʊ, 'hɛərəˌrəʊ) *n* **1** (*pl* **-ro** *or* **-ros**) a member of a formerly rich cattle-keeping Negroid

people of southern Africa, living chiefly in central Namibia **2** the language of this people, belonging to the Bantu group of the Niger-Congo family

heres *or* **haeres** ('hɪəriːz) *n, pl* **heredes** *or* **haeredes** (hɪ'riːdiːz) *civil law* an heir [from Latin]

heresiarch (hɪ'riːzɪˌɑːk) *n* the leader or originator of a heretical movement or sect

heresthetic (ˌhɛrəs'θɛtɪk) *n* a political strategy by which a person or group sets or manipulates the context and structure of a decision-making process in order to win or be more likely to win [c20 coined, originally in the form *heresthetics*, by the US political scientist William Riker (1921–93), from Greek *hairein* to choose] > heres'thetical *adj* > heresthetician (ˌhɛrəsθə'tɪʃən) *n*

heresy ('hɛrəsɪ) *n, pl* **-sies 1 a** an opinion or doctrine contrary to the orthodox tenets of a religious body or church **b** the act of maintaining such an opinion or doctrine **2** any opinion or belief that is or is thought to be contrary to official or established theory **3** belief in or adherence to unorthodox opinion [c13 from Old French *eresie*, from Late Latin *haeresis*, from Latin: sect, from Greek *hairesis* a choosing, from *hairein* to choose]

heretic ('hɛrətɪk) *n* **1** *now chiefly RC Church* a person who maintains beliefs contrary to the established teachings of the Church **2** a person who holds unorthodox opinions in any field > **heretical** (hɪ'rɛtɪkəl) *adj* > he'retically *adv*

hereto (ˌhɪə'tuː) *adv* **1** *formal* to this place, thing, matter, document, etc **2** an obsolete word for **hitherto**

heretofore (ˌhɪətʊ'fɔː) *adv* **1** *formal* until now; before this time ▷ *adj* **2** *obsolete* previous; former ▷ *n* **3** (preceded by *the*) *archaic* the past

hereunder (ˌhɪər'ʌndə) *adv formal* **1** (in documents, etc) below this; subsequently; hereafter **2** under the terms or authority of this

hereunto (ˌhɪərʌn'tuː) *adv* an archaic word for **hereto** (sense 1)

hereupon (ˌhɪərə'pɒn) *adv* **1** following immediately after this; at this stage **2** *formal* upon this thing, point, subject, etc

herewith (ˌhɪə'wɪð, -'wɪθ) *adv* **1** *formal* together with this: *we send you herewith your statement of account* **2** a less common word for **hereby** (sense 1)

heriot ('hɛrɪət) *n* (in medieval England) a death duty paid by villeins and free tenants to their lord, often consisting of the dead man's best beast or chattel [Old English *heregeatwa*, from *here* army + *geatwa* equipment]

Herisau (German 'heːrizau) *n* a town in NE Switzerland, capital of Appenzell Outer Rhodes demicanton. Pop: 15 882 (2000)

heritable ('hɛrɪtəbəl) *adj* **1** capable of being inherited; inheritable **2** *chiefly law* capable of inheriting [c14 from Old French, from *heriter* to INHERIT] > ˌherita'bility *n* > 'heritably *adv*

heritage ('hɛrɪtɪdʒ) *n* **1** something inherited at birth, such as personal characteristics, status, and possessions **2** anything that has been transmitted from the past or handed down by tradition **3 a** the evidence of the past, such as historical sites, buildings, and the unspoilt natural environment, considered collectively as the inheritance of present-day society **b** (*as modifier; cap. as part of name*): *Bannockburn Heritage Centre* **4** something that is reserved for a particular person or group or the outcome of an action, way of life, etc: *the sea was their heritage; the heritage of violence* **5** *law* any property, esp land, that by law has descended or may descend to an heir **6** *Bible* **a** the Israelites regarded as belonging inalienably to God **b** the land of Canaan regarded as God's gift to the Israelites [c13 from Old French; see HEIR]

heritor ('hɛrɪtə) *n Scots law* a person who inherits; inheritor > **heritress** ('hɛrɪtrɪs) *or* 'heritrix *fem n*

herl (hɜːl) *or* **harl** *n angling* **1** the barb or barbs of a feather, used to dress fishing flies **2** an artificial fly dressed with such barbs [c15 from Middle Low

h

German *herle*, of obscure origin]

herm (hɜːm) *or* **herma** (ˈhɜːmə) *n, pl* **herms**, **hermae** (ˈhɜːmiː) *or* **hermai** (ˈhɜːmaɪ) (in ancient Greece) a stone head of Hermes surmounting a square stone pillar [c16 from Latin *herma*, from Greek *hermēs* HERMES¹]

Hermannstadt (ˈhɛrmanʃtat) *n* the German name for **Sibiu**

hermaphrodite (hɜːˈmæfrəˌdaɪt) *n* 1 *biology* an individual animal or flower that has both male and female reproductive organs 2 a person having both male and female sexual characteristics and genital tissues 3 a person or thing in which two opposite forces or qualities are combined ▷ *adj* 4 having the characteristics of a hermaphrodite [c15 from Latin *hermaphrodītus*, from Greek, after HERMAPHRODITUS]
> herˌmaphroˈditic *or* herˌmaphroˈditical *adj*
> herˌmaphroˈditically *adv* > herˈmaphrodiˌtism *n*

hermaphrodite brig *n* a sailing vessel with two masts, rigged square on the foremast and fore-and-aft on the aftermast. Also called: **brigantine**

Hermaphroditus (hɜːˌmæfrəˈdaɪtəs) *n Greek myth* a son of Hermes and Aphrodite who merged with the nymph Salmacis to form one body

hermeneutic (ˌhɜːmɪˈnjuːtɪk) *or* **hermeneutical** *adj* 1 of or relating to the interpretation of Scripture; using or relating to hermeneutics 2 interpretive > ˌhermeˈneutically *adv*
> ˌhermeˈneutist *n*

hermeneutics (ˌhɜːmɪˈnjuːtɪks) *n (functioning as singular)* 1 the science of interpretation, esp of Scripture 2 the branch of theology that deals with the principles and methodology of exegesis 3 *philosophy* a the study and interpretation of human behaviour and social institutions b (in existentialist thought) discussion of the purpose of life [c18 from Greek *hermēneutikos* expert in interpretation, from *hermēneuein* to interpret, from *hermēneus* interpreter, of uncertain origin]

Hermes¹ (ˈhɜːmiːz) *n Greek myth* the messenger and herald of the gods; the divinity of commerce, cunning, theft, travellers, and rascals. He was represented as wearing winged sandals. Roman counterpart: **Mercury**

Hermes² (ˈhɜːmiːz) *n* a small asteroid some 800 m in diameter that passed within 670 000 kilometres of the earth in 1937, and is now lost

Hermes Trismegistus (ˌtrɪsməˈdʒɪstəs) *n* a Greek name for the Egyptian god Thoth, credited with various works on mysticism and magic [Greek: Hermes thrice-greatest]

hermetic (hɜːˈmɛtɪk) *or* **hermetical** *adj* sealed so as to be airtight [c17 from Medieval Latin *hermēticus* belonging to HERMES TRISMEGISTUS, traditionally the inventor of a magic seal]
> herˈmetically *adv*

Hermetic (hɜːˈmɛtɪk) *adj* of or relating to ancient science, esp alchemy [see HERMETIC]

hermit (ˈhɜːmɪt) *n* 1 one of the early Christian recluses 2 any person living in solitude [c13 from Old French *hermite*, from Late Latin *erēmīta*, from Greek *erēmītēs* living in the desert, from *erēmia* desert, from *erēmos* lonely] > herˈmitic *or* herˈmitical *adj* > herˈmitically *adv* > ˈhermit-ˌlike *adj*

hermitage (ˈhɜːmɪtɪdʒ) *n* 1 the abode of a hermit 2 any place where a person may live in seclusion; retreat

Hermitage¹ (ˈhɜːmɪtɪdʒ) *n* **the** an art museum in Leningrad, originally a palace built by Catherine the Great

Hermitage² (ˈhɜːmɪtɪdʒ) *n* a full-bodied red or white wine from the Rhône valley at Tain-l'Ermitage, in SE France

hermit crab *n* any small soft-bodied decapod crustacean of the genus *Pagurus* and related genera, living in and carrying about the empty shells of whelks or similar molluscs

Hermitian conjugate (hɜːˈmɪtɪən) *n maths* a matrix that is the transpose of the matrix of the complex conjugates of the entries of a given matrix. Also called: **adjoint** [c19 named after

Charles *Hermite* (1822–1901), French mathematician]

Hermitian matrix *n maths* a matrix whose transpose is equal to the matrix of the complex conjugates of its entries [c20 named after Charles *Hermite* (1822–1901), French mathematician]

Hermon (ˈhɜːmən) *n* **Mount** a mountain on the border between Lebanon and SW Syria, in the Anti-Lebanon Range: represented as the NE limits of Israeli conquests under Moses and Joshua. Height: 2814 m (9232 ft)

Hermosillo (*Spanish* ɛrmoˈsiʎo) *n* a city in NW Mexico, capital of Sonora state, on the Sonora River: university (1938); winter resort and commercial centre for an agricultural and mining region. Pop: 668 000 (2005 est)

Hermoupolis (hɜːˈmuːpəlɪs) *n* a port in Greece, capital of Cyclades department, on the E coast of Syros Island. Pop: 14 115 (latest est)

hern (hɜːn) *n* an archaic or dialect word for **heron**

Herne (*German* ˈhɛrnə) *n* an industrial city in W Germany, in North Rhine-Westphalia, in the Ruhr on the Rhine-Herne Canal. Pop: 172 870 (2003 est)

hernia (ˈhɜːnɪə) *n, pl* **-nias** *or* **-niae** (-nɪˌiː) the projection of an organ or part through the lining of the cavity in which it is normally situated, esp the protrusion of intestine through the front wall of the abdominal cavity. It is caused by muscular strain, injury, etc. Also called: **rupture** [c14 from Latin] > ˈhernial *adj* > ˈherniˌated *adj*

herniorrhaphy (ˌhɜːnɪˈɒrəfɪ) *n, pl* **-phies** surgical repair of a hernia by means of a suturing operation

hero (ˈhɪərəʊ) *n, pl* **-roes** 1 a man distinguished by exceptional courage, nobility, fortitude, etc 2 a man who is idealized for possessing superior qualities in any field 3 *classical myth* a being of extraordinary strength and courage, often the offspring of a mortal and a god, who is celebrated for his exploits 4 the principal male character in a novel, play, etc [c14 from Latin *hērōs*, from Greek]

Hero (ˈhɪərəʊ) *n Greek myth* a priestess of Aphrodite, who killed herself when her lover Leander drowned while swimming the Hellespont to visit her

heroic (hɪˈrəʊɪk) *or* **heroical** *adj* 1 of, like, or befitting a hero 2 courageous but desperate 3 relating to or treating of heroes and their deeds 4 of, relating to, or resembling the heroes of classical mythology 5 (of language, manner, etc) extravagant 6 *prosody* of, relating to, or resembling heroic verse 7 (of the arts, esp sculpture) larger than life-size; smaller than colossal 8 *RC Church* held to such a degree as to enable a person to perform virtuous actions with exceptional promptness, ease and pleasure, and with self-abnegation and self-control: *heroic virtue* b performed or undergone by such a person: *the heroic witness of martyrdom* > See also **heroics**
> heˈroically *adv* > heˈroicalness *or* heˈroicness *n*

heroic age *n* the period in an ancient culture, when legendary heroes are said to have lived

heroic couplet *n prosody* a verse form consisting of two rhyming lines in iambic pentameter

heroics (hɪˈrəʊɪks) *pl n* 1 *prosody* short for **heroic verse** 2 extravagant or melodramatic language, behaviour, etc

heroic stanza *n poetry* a quatrain having the rhyme scheme a b a b

heroic tenor *n* a tenor with a dramatic voice

heroic verse *n prosody* a type of verse suitable for epic or heroic subjects, such as the classical hexameter, the French Alexandrine, or the English iambic pentameter

heroin (ˈhɛrəʊɪn) *n* a white odourless bitter-tasting crystalline powder related to morphine: a highly addictive narcotic. Formula: $C_{21}H_{23}NO_5$. Technical names: **diamorphine, diacetylmorphine** [c19 coined in German as a trademark, probably from HERO, referring to its aggrandizing effect on the personality]

heroin chic *n* the perceived glamorization of heroin and the characteristics associated with heroin addicts, such as gauntness and hollow eyes

heroine (ˈhɛrəʊɪn) *n* 1 a woman possessing heroic qualities 2 a woman idealized for possessing superior qualities 3 the main female character in a novel, play, film, etc

heroism (ˈhɛrəʊˌɪzəm) *n* the state or quality of being a hero

heron (ˈhɛrən) *n* any of various wading birds of the genera *Butorides*, *Ardea*, etc, having a long neck, slim body, and a plumage that is commonly grey or white: family *Ardeidae*, order *Ciconiiformes* [c14 from Old French *hairon*, of Germanic origin; compare Old High German *heigaro*, Old Norse *hegri*]

heronry (ˈhɛrənrɪ) *n, pl* **-ries** a colony of breeding herons

hero worship *n* 1 admiration for heroes or idealized persons 2 worship by the ancient Greeks and Romans of heroes ▷ *vb* **hero-worship, -ships, -shipping, -shipped** *or US* **-ships, -shiping, -shiped** 3 (*tr*) to feel admiration and adulation for > ˈhero-ˌworshipper *n*

herpes (ˈhɜːpiːz) *n* any of several inflammatory diseases of the skin, esp herpes simplex, characterized by the formation of small watery blisters. See also **genital herpes** [c17 via Latin from Greek: a creeping, from *herpein* to creep]

herpes labialis (ˌleɪbɪˈælɪs) *n* a technical name for **cold sore** [New Latin: herpes of the lip]

herpes simplex (ˈsɪmplɛks) *n* an acute viral disease characterized by formation of clusters of watery blisters, esp on the margins of the lips and nostrils or on the genitals. It can be sexually transmitted and may recur fitfully [New Latin: simple herpes]

herpesvirus (ˈhɜːpiːzˌvaɪrəs) *n* any one of a family of DNA-containing viruses that includes the agents causing herpes, the Epstein-Barr virus, and the cytomegalovirus

herpes zoster (ˈzɒstə) *n* a technical name for **shingles** [New Latin: girdle herpes, from HERPES + Greek *zōstēr* girdle]

herpetic (hɜːˈpɛtɪk) *adj* 1 of or relating to any of the herpes diseases ▷ *n* 2 a person suffering from any of the herpes diseases

herpetology (ˌhɜːpɪˈtɒlədʒɪ) *n* the study of reptiles and amphibians [c19 from Greek *herpeton* creeping animal, from *herpein* to creep]
> herpetologic (ˌhɜːpɪtəˈlɒdʒɪk) *or* ˌherpetoˈlogical *adj* > ˌherpetoˈlogically *adv* > ˌherpeˈtologist *n*

herptile (ˈhɜːpˌtaɪl) *adj chiefly US* denoting, relating to, or characterizing both reptiles and amphibians [from Greek *herp(eton)* (see HERPETOLOGY) + (REP)TILE]

Herr (*German* hɛr) *n, pl* **Herren** (ˈhɛrən) a German man: used before a name as a title equivalent to *Mr* [German, from Old High German *herro* lord]

Herrenvolk *German* (ˈhɛrənfɔlk) *n* See **master race**

herring (ˈhɛrɪŋ) *n, pl* **-rings** *or* **-ring** any marine soft-finned teleost fish of the family *Clupeidae*, esp *Clupea harengus*, an important food fish of northern seas, having an elongated body covered, except in the head region, with large fragile silvery scales [Old English *hæring*; related to Old High German *hāring*, Old Frisian *hēring*, Dutch *haring*]

herringbone (ˈhɛrɪŋˌbəʊn) *n* 1 a a pattern used in textiles, brickwork, etc, consisting of two or more rows of short parallel strokes slanting in alternate directions to form a series of parallel Vs or zigzags b (*as modifier*): *a herringbone jacket; a herringbone pattern of very long, narrow bricks* 2 *skiing* a method of ascending a slope by walking with the skis pointing outwards and one's weight on the inside edges ▷ *vb* 3 to decorate (textiles, brickwork, etc) with herringbone 4 (*intr*) *skiing* to ascend a slope in herringbone fashion

herringbone bond *n* a type of bricklaying in which the bricks are laid on the slant to form a herringbone pattern

herringbone gear *n* a gearwheel having two sets

of helical teeth, one set inclined at an acute angle to the other so that V-shaped teeth are formed. Also called: double-helical gear

herring gull *n* a common gull, *Larus argentatus*, that has a white plumage with black-tipped wings and pink legs

hers (h3:z) *pron* **1** something or someone belonging to or associated with her: *hers is the nicest dress; that cat is hers* **2** of hers belonging to or associated with her [C14 *hires*; see HER]

herself (hə'sɛlf) *pron* **1 a** the reflexive form of *she* or *her* **b** (intensifier): *the queen herself signed the letter* **2** (*preceded by a copula*) her normal or usual self: *she looks herself again after the operation* **3** *Irish and Scot* the wife or woman of the house: *is herself at home?*

Herstmonceux *or* **Hurstmonceux** ('h3:stmən,sju:, -,səʊ) *n* a village in S England, in E Sussex north of Eastbourne: 15th-century castle, site of the Royal Observatory, which was transferred from Greenwich between 1948 and 1958, until 1990

herstory ('h3:stəri) *n* history from a female point of view or as it relates to women [C20 from changing the initial *his* in HISTORY to *her*, as if HISTORY were derived from *his* + *story* rather than from Latin *historia*]

Hertford ('ha:tfəd) *n* a town in SE England, administrative centre of Hertfordshire. Pop: 24 460 (2001)

Hertfordshire ('ha:tfəd,ʃɪə, -ʃə) *n* a county of S England, bordering on Greater London in the south: mainly low-lying, with the Chiltern Hills in the northwest; largely agricultural; expanding light industries, esp in the new towns. Administrative centre: Hertford. Pop: 1 040 900 (2003 est). Area: 1634 sq km (631 sq miles)

Hertogenbosch (*Dutch* hɛrtoːxən'bɔs) *n* 's See 's Hertogenbosch

Herts (ha:ts) *abbreviation for* Hertfordshire

hertz (h3:ts) *n, pl* **hertz** the derived SI unit of frequency; the frequency of a periodic phenomenon that has a periodic time of 1 second; 1 cycle per second. Symbol: Hz [C20 named after Heinrich Rudolph *Hertz* (1857–94), German physicist]

Hertzian wave *n* an electromagnetic wave with a frequency in the range from about 3×10^{10} hertz to about 1.5×10^5 hertz [C19 named after Heinrich Rudolph *Hertz* (1857–94), German physicist]

Hertzsprung-Russell diagram ('h3:tsspraŋ'rʌsəl) *n* a graph in which the spectral types of stars are plotted against their absolute magnitudes. Stars fall into different groupings in different parts of the graph. See also **main sequence** [C20 named after Ejnar *Hertzsprung* (1873–1967), Danish astronomer, and Henry Norris *Russell* (1877–1957), US astronomer and astrophysicist]

Herzegovina (,h3:tsəgəʊ'vi:nə) *or* **Hercegovina** *n* a region in Bosnia-Herzegovina: originally under Austro-Hungarian rule; became part of the province of Bosnia-Herzegovina (1878), which was a constituent republic of Yugoslavia (1946–92)

he's (hi:z) *contraction of* he is *or* he has

Heshvan (xɜʃˈvan) *n* a variant spelling of Cheshvan

Hesione (hɪˈsaɪənɪ) *n Greek myth* daughter of King Laomedon, rescued by Hercules from a sea monster

hesitant ('hɛzɪtənt) *adj* wavering, hesitating, or irresolute > 'hesitance *or* 'hesitancy *n* > 'hesitantly *adv*

hesitate ('hɛzɪ,teɪt) *vb* (*intr*) **1** to hold back or be slow in acting; be uncertain **2** to be unwilling or reluctant (to do something) **3** to stammer or pause in speaking [C17 from Latin *haesitāre*, from *haerēre* to cling to] > 'hesi,tater *or* 'hesi,tator *n* > 'hesi,tatingly *adv* > ,hesi'tation *n* > 'hesi,tative *adj*

Hesperia (hɛˈspɪərɪə) *n* a poetic name used by the ancient Greeks for Italy and by the Romans for Spain or beyond [Latin, from Greek: land of the west, from *hesperos* western]

Hesperian (hɛˈspɪərɪən) *adj* **1** *poetic* western **2** of

or relating to the Hesperides ▷ *n* **3** a native or inhabitant of a western land

Hesperides (hɛˈspɛrɪ,di:z) *pl n Greek myth* **1** the daughters of Hesperus, nymphs who kept watch with a dragon over the garden of the golden apples in the Islands of the Blessed **2** (*functioning as singular*) the gardens themselves **3** another name for the **Islands of the Blessed**. > Hesperidian (,hɛspəˈrɪdɪən) *or* ,Hesperˈidean *adj*

hesperidin (hɛˈspɛrɪdɪn) *n* a glycoside extracted from orange peel or other citrus fruits and used to treat capillary fragility [C19 from New Latin HESPERIDIUM + -IN]

hesperidium (,hɛspəˈrɪdɪəm) *n botany* the fruit of citrus plants, in which the flesh consists of fluid-filled hairs and is protected by a tough rind [C19 New Latin; alluding to the fruit in the garden of the HESPERIDES]

Hesperus ('hɛspərəs) *n* an evening star, esp Venus [from Latin, from Greek *Hesperos*, from *hesperos* western]

Hesse (hɛs) *n* a state of central Germany, formed in 1945 from the former Prussian province of Hesse-Nassau and part of the former state of Hesse; part of West Germany until 1990. Capital: Wiesbaden. Pop: 6 089 000 (2003 est). Area: 21 111 sq km (8151 sq miles). German name: Hessen ('hɛsʰn)

Hesse-Nassau *n* a former province of Prussia, now part of the state of Hesse, Germany

hessian ('hɛsɪən) *n* a coarse jute fabric similar to sacking, used for bags, upholstery, etc [C18 from HESSE + -IAN]

Hessian ('hɛsɪən) *n* **1** a native or inhabitant of Hesse **2 a** a Hessian soldier in any of the mercenary units of the British Army in the War of American Independence or the Napoleonic Wars **b** *US* any German mercenary in the British Army during the War of American Independence **3** *chiefly US* a mercenary or ruffian ▷ *adj* **4** of or relating to Hesse or its inhabitants

Hessian boots *pl n* men's high boots with tassels around the top, fashionable in England in the early 19th century

Hessian fly *n* a small dipterous fly, *Mayetiola destructor*, whose larvae damage wheat, barley, and rye: family *Cecidomyidae* (gall midges) [C18 so called because it was thought to have been introduced into America by Hessian soldiers]

hessite ('hɛsaɪt) *n* a black or grey metallic mineral consisting of silver telluride in cubic crystalline form. Formula: Ag_2Te [C19 from German *Hessit*; named after Henry *Hess*, 19th-century chemist of Swiss origin who worked in Russia; see -ITE[1]]

hessonite ('hɛsə,naɪt) *n* an orange-brown variety of grossularite garnet. Also called: **essonite**, cinnamon stone [C19 from French, from Greek *hēssōn* less, inferior + -ITE[1]; so called because it is less hard than genuine hyacinth]

hest (hɛst) *n* an archaic word for **behest** [Old English *hǣs*; related to *hātan* to promise, command]

Hestia ('hɛstɪə) *n Greek myth* the goddess of the hearth. Roman counterpart: **Vesta**

Hesychast ('hɛsɪ,kæst) *n Greek Orthodox Church* a member of a school of mysticism developed by the monks of Mount Athos in the 14th century [C18: from Medieval Latin *hesychasta* mystic, from Greek *hēsukhastēs*, from *hēsukhazein* to be tranquil, from *hēsukhos* quiet] > ,Hesy'chastic *adj*

het[1] (hɛt) *n slang* short for **heterosexual**

het[2] (hɛt) *vb* **1** *archaic or dialect* a past tense and past participle of **heat** ▷ *adj* **2** a Scot word for **hot** ▷ See also **het up**

hetaera (hɪˈtɪərə) *or* **hetaira** (hɪˈtaɪrə) *n, pl* -taerae (-ˈtɪəri:) *or* -tairai (-ˈtaɪraɪ) (esp in ancient Greece) a female prostitute, esp an educated courtesan [C19 from Greek *hetaira* concubine] > he'taeric *or* he'tairic *adj*

hetaerism (hɪˈtɪərɪzəm) *or* **hetairism** (hɪˈtaɪrɪzəm) *n* **1** the state of being a concubine **2**

sociol, anthropol a social system attributed to some primitive societies, in which women are communally shared > he'taerist *or* he'tairist *n* > ,hetae'ristic *or* ,hetai'ristic *adj*

heterarchy ('hɛtəra:kɪ) *n linguistics* a formal structure, usually represented by a diagram of connected nodes, without any single permanent uppermost node. Compare **hierarchy** (sense 5), **tree** (sense 6) [from Greek *heteros* other, different + *archē* sovereignty]

hetero ('hɛtərəʊ) *n, pl* -os, *adj informal* short for **heterosexual**

hetero- *combining form* other, another, or different: *heterodyne; heterophony; heterosexual*. Compare **homo-** [from Greek *heteros* other]

heteroblastic (,hɛtərəʊˈblæstɪk) *adj botany* (of a plant or plant part) showing a marked difference in form between the juvenile and the adult structures. Compare **homoblastic**

heterocercal (,hɛtərəʊˈsɜːkʰl) *adj ichthyol* of or possessing a tail in which the vertebral column turns upwards and extends into the upper, usually larger, lobe, as in sharks. Compare **homocercal** [C19 from HETERO- + Greek *kerkos* tail]

heterochlamydeous (,hɛtərəʊkləˈmɪdɪəs) *adj* (of a plant) having a perianth consisting of distinct sepals and petals. Compare **homochlamydeous**

heterochromatic (,hɛtərəʊkrəʊˈmætɪk) *adj* **1** of or involving many different colours **2** *physics* consisting of or concerned with different frequencies or wavelengths > ,hetero'chromatism *n*

heterochromatin (,hɛtərəʊˈkrəʊmətɪn) *n* the condensed part of a chromosome that stains strongly with basic dyes in nondividing cells and has little genetic activity. Compare **euchromatin**

heterochromosome (,hɛtərəʊˈkrəʊməsəʊm) *n* **1** an atypical chromosome, esp a sex chromosome **2** a chromosome composed mainly of heterochromatin

heterochromous (,hɛtərəʊˈkrəʊməs) *adj* (esp of plant parts) of different colours: *the heterochromous florets of a daisy flower*

heteroclite ('hɛtərə,klaɪt) *adj also* **heteroclitic** (,hɛtərəˈklɪtɪk) **1** (esp of the form of a word) irregular or unusual ▷ *n* **2** an irregularly formed word [C16 from Late Latin *heteroclitus* declining irregularly, from Greek *heteroklitos*, from HETERO- + *klinein* to bend, inflect]

heterocyclic (,hɛtərəʊˈsaɪklɪk, -ˈsɪk-) *adj* (of an organic compound) containing a closed ring of atoms, at least one of which is not a carbon atom. Compare **homocyclic**

heterodactyl (,hɛtərəʊˈdæktɪl) *adj* **1** (of the feet of certain birds) having the first and second toes directed backwards and the third and fourth forwards ▷ *n* **2** a bird with heterodactyl feet ▷ Compare **zygodactyl**

heterodont ('hɛtərə,dɒnt) *adj* (of most mammals) having teeth of different types. Compare **homodont**

heterodox ('hɛtərəʊ,dɒks) *adj* **1** at variance with established, orthodox, or accepted doctrines or beliefs **2** holding unorthodox opinions [C17 from Greek *heterodoxos* holding another opinion, from HETERO- + *doxa* opinion] > 'hetero,doxy *n*

heterodyne ('hɛtərəʊ,daɪn) *vb* **1** *electronics* to combine by intermodulation (two alternating signals, esp radio signals) to produce two signals having frequencies corresponding to the sum and the difference of the original frequencies. See also **superheterodyne receiver** ▷ *adj* **2** produced by, operating by, or involved in heterodyning two signals

heteroecious (,hɛtəˈri:ʃəs) *adj* (of parasites, esp rust fungi) undergoing different stages of the life cycle on different host species. Compare **autoecious** [from HETERO- + -oecious, from Greek *oikia* house] > ,heter'oecism *n*

heteroflexible (,hɛtərəʊˈflɛksɪbʰl) *adj* **1** (of a person) predominantly heterosexual but not exclusively so ▷ *n* **2** such a person [C20 from

h

HETERO(SEXUAL) + FLEXIBLE]

heterogamete (ˌhɛtərəʊgæˈmiːt) n a gamete that differs in size and form from the one with which it unites in fertilization. Compare **isogamete**

heterogametic (ˌhɛtərəʊgæˈmɛɒɡɪk) adj genetics denoting the sex that possesses dissimilar sex chromosomes. In humans and many other mammals it is the male sex, possessing one X-chromosome and one Y-chromosome. Compare **homogametic**

heterogamy (ˌhɛtəˈrɒɡəmɪ) n **1** a type of sexual reproduction in which the gametes differ in both size and form. Compare **isogamy 2** a condition in which different types of reproduction occur in successive generations of an organism **3** the presence of both male and female flowers in one inflorescence. Compare **homogamy** (sense 1) > ˌheterˈogamous adj

heterogeneous (ˌhɛtərəʊˈdʒiːnɪəs) adj **1** composed of unrelated or differing parts or elements **2** not of the same kind or type **3** chem of, composed of, or concerned with two or more different phases. Compare **homogeneous** [C17 from Medieval Latin heterogeneus, from Greek heterogenēs, from HETERO- + genos sort] > heterogeneity (ˌhɛtərəʊdʒɪˈniːɪtɪ) or ˌheteroˈgeneousness n > ˌheteroˈgeneously adv

heterogenesis (ˌhɛtərəʊˈdʒɛnɪsɪs) n another name for **alternation of generations** or **abiogenesis** > heterogenetic (ˌhɛtərəʊdʒɪˈnɛtɪk) or ˌheteroˈgenic adj > ˌheterogeˈnetically adv

heterogenous (ˌhɛtəˈrɒdʒɪnəs) adj biology, med not originating within the body; of foreign origin: a heterogenous skin graft. Compare **autogenous**

heterogony (ˌhɛtəˈrɒɡənɪ) n **1** biology the alternation of parthenogenetic and sexual generations in rotifers and similar animals **2** the condition in plants, such as the primrose, of having flowers that differ from each other in the length of their stamens and styles. Compare **homogony**. > ˌheterˈogonous adj > ˌheterˈogonously adv

heterograft (ˈhɛtərəʊˌgrɑːft) n a tissue graft obtained from a donor of a different species from the recipient

heterography (ˌhɛtəˈrɒɡrəfɪ) n **1** the phenomenon of different letters or sequences of letters representing the same sound in different words, as for example -ight and -ite in blight and bite **2** any writing system in which this phenomenon occurs > heterographic (ˌhɛtərəʊˈgræfɪk) or ˌheteroˌgraphical adj

heterogynous (ˌhɛtəˈrɒdʒɪnəs) adj (of ants, bees, etc) having two types of female, one fertile and the other infertile

heterokaryon (ˌhɛtərəʊˈkærɪɒn) n biology a fungal cell or mycelium containing two or more nuclei of different genetic constitution [from HETERO- + karyon, from Greek karuon kernel]

heterokont (ˈhɛtərəʊˌkɒnt) n **1** any organism that possesses two flagella of unequal length. Heterokonts include diatoms and some other algae ▷ adj **2** possessing two flagella of unequal length

heterolecithal (ˌhɛtərəʊˈlɛsɪθəl) adj (of the eggs of birds) having an unequally distributed yolk. Compare **isolecithal** [C19 HETERO- + Greek lekithos egg yolk]

heterologous (ˌhɛtəˈrɒləɡəs) adj **1** pathol of, relating to, or designating cells or tissues not normally present in a particular part of the body **2** (esp of parts of an organism or of different organisms) differing in structure or origin > ˌheterˈology n

heterolysis (ˌhɛtəˈrɒlɪsɪs) n **1** the dissolution of the cells of one organism by the lysins of another. Compare **autolysis 2** Also called: **heterolytic fission** chem the dissociation of a molecule into two ions with opposite charges. Compare **homolysis**. > heterolytic (ˌhɛtərəʊˈlɪtɪk) adj

heteromerous (ˌhɛtəˈrɒmərəs) adj biology having or consisting of parts that differ, esp in number

heteromorphic (ˌhɛtərəʊˈmɔːfɪk) or **heteromorphous** adj biology **1** differing from the normal form in size, shape, and function **2** (of pairs of homologous chromosomes) differing from each other in size or form **3** (esp of insects) having different forms at different stages of the life cycle > ˌheteroˈmorphism or ˌheteroˈmorphy n

heteronomous (ˌhɛtəˈrɒnɪməs) adj **1** subject to an external law, rule, or authority. Compare **autonomous 2** (of the parts of an organism) differing in the manner of growth, development, or specialization **3** (in Kant's philosophy) directed to an end other than duty for its own sake. Compare **autonomous** (sense 4b) > ˌheterˈonomously adv > ˌheterˈonomy n

heteronym (ˈhɛtərəʊˌnɪm) n one of two or more words pronounced differently but spelt alike: the two English words spelt "bow" are heteronyms. Compare **homograph** [C17 from Late Greek heteronumos, from Greek HETERO- + onoma name] > heteronymous (ˌhɛtəˈrɒnɪməs) adj > ˌheterˈonymously adv

Heteroousian (ˌhɛtərəʊˈuːsɪən, -ˈaʊsɪən) n **1** a Christian who maintains that God the Father and God the Son are different in substance ▷ adj **2** of or relating to this belief [C17 from Late Greek heteroousios, from Greek HETERO- + ousia nature]

heterophony (ˌhɛtəˈrɒfənɪ) n the simultaneous performance of different versions of the same melody by different voices or instruments

heterophyllous (ˌhɛtərəʊˈfɪləs, ˌhɛtəˈrɒfɪləs) adj (of plants such as arrowhead) having more than one type of leaf on the same plant. Also: **anisophyllous** > ˌheteroˈphylly n

heteroplasty (ˈhɛtərəʊˌplæstɪ) n, pl -ties the surgical transplantation of tissue obtained from another person or animal > ˌheteroˈplastic adj

heteroploid (ˈhɛtərəʊˌplɔɪd) adj **1** of a chromosome number that is neither the haploid nor diploid number characteristic of the species ▷ n **2** such a chromosome number

heteropolar (ˌhɛtərəʊˈpəʊlə) adj a less common word for **polar** (sense 5a) > heteropolarity (ˌhɛtərəʊpəʊˈlærɪtɪ)

heteropterous (ˌhɛtəˈrɒptərəs) or **heteropteran** adj of, relating to, or belonging to the Heteroptera, a suborder of hemipterous insects, including bedbugs, water bugs, etc, in which the forewings are membranous but have leathery tips. Compare **homopterous** [C19 from New Latin Heteroptera, from HETERO- + Greek pteron wing]

heteroscedastic (ˌhɛtərəʊskɪˈdæstɪk) adj statistics **1** (of several distributions) having different variances **2** (of a bivariate or multivariate distribution) not having any variable whose variance is the same for all values of the other or others **3** (of a random variable) having different variances for different values of the others in a multivariate distribution ▷ Compare **homoscedastic** [C20 from HETERO- + scedastic, from Greek skedasis a scattering, dispersal] > heteroscedasticity (ˌhɛtərəʊskɪdæsˈtɪsɪtɪ) n

heterosexism (ˌhɛtərəʊˈsɛkˌsɪzəm) n discrimination on the basis of sexual orientation, practised by heterosexuals against homosexuals > ˌheteroˈsexist adj, n

heterosexual (ˌhɛtərəʊˈsɛksjʊəl) n **1** a person who is sexually attracted to the opposite sex ▷ adj **2** of or relating to heterosexuality ▷ Compare **homosexual**

heterosexuality (ˌhɛtərəʊˌsɛksjʊˈælɪtɪ) n sexual attraction to or sexual relations with a person or persons of the opposite sex. Compare **homosexuality**

heterosis (ˌhɛtəˈrəʊsɪs) n biology another name for **hybrid vigour** [C19 from Late Greek: alteration, from Greek heteroioun to alter, from heteros other, different]

heterosocial (ˌhɛtərəʊˈsəʊʃəl) adj relating to or denoting mixed-sex social relationships > heterosociality (ˌhɛtərəʊˌsəʊʃɪˈælɪtɪ) n ▷ Compare **homosocial**

heterosporous (ˌhɛtəˈrɒspərəs) adj (of seed plants and some ferns and club mosses) producing megaspores and microspores. Compare **homosporous**. > ˌheterˈospory n

heterostyly (ˈhɛtərəˌstaɪlɪ) n the condition in certain plants, such as primroses, of having styles of different lengths, each type of style in flowers on different plants, which promotes cross-pollination [C20 from Greek, from heteros different + stylos pillar] > ˌheterˈostylous adj

heterotaxis (ˌhɛtərəʊˈtæksɪs), **heterotaxy** or **heterotaxia** n an abnormal or asymmetrical arrangement of parts, as of the organs of the body or the constituents of a rock > ˌheterˈotactic, ˌheteroˈtactous or ˌheterˈotaxic adj

heterothallic (ˌhɛtərəʊˈθælɪk) adj **1** (of some algae and fungi) having male and female reproductive organs on different thalli **2** (of some fungi) having sexual reproduction that occurs only between two self-sterile mycelia ▷ Compare **homothallic** [C20 from HETERO- + Greek thallos green shoot, young twig] > ˌheterˈothallism n

heterotopia (ˌhɛtərəʊˈtəʊpɪə) or **heterotopy** (ˌhɛtəˈrɒtəpɪ) n abnormal displacement of a bodily organ or part [C19 from New Latin, from HETERO- + Greek topos place] > ˌheterˈotopic or ˌheterˈotopous adj

heterotrophic (ˌhɛtərəʊˈtrɒfɪk) adj (of organisms, such as animals) obtaining carbon for growth and energy from complex organic compounds. Compare **autotrophic** [C20 from HETERO- + Greek trophikos concerning food, from trophē nourishment] > ˈheterˌotroph n

heterotypic (ˌhɛtərəʊˈtɪpɪk) or **heterotypical** adj denoting or relating to the first nuclear division of meiosis, in which the chromosome number is halved. Compare **homeotypic**

heterozygote (ˌhɛtərəʊˈzaɪgəʊt, -ˈzɪgəʊt) n an animal or plant that is heterozygous; a hybrid. Compare **homozygote**. > ˌheterozyˈgosis n

heterozygous (ˌhɛtərəʊˈzaɪgəs) adj genetics (of an organism) having different alleles for any one gene: heterozygous for eye colour Compare **homozygous**

heth or **cheth** (hɛt; Hebrew xɛt) n the eighth letter of the Hebrew alphabet (ח), transliterated as h and pronounced as a pharyngeal fricative [from Hebrew]

hetman (ˈhɛtmən) n, pl -mans another word for **ataman** [C18 from Polish, from German Hauptmann headman]

het up adj angry; excited: too many people are getting het up about money in rugby

HEU abbreviation for highly enriched uranium

heuchera (ˈhjuːkərə) n any plant of the N. American genus Heuchera, with low-growing heart-shaped leaves and mostly red flowers carried in sprays on slender graceful stems: family Saxifragaceae. See also **alumroot** [named after J. H. Heucher (1677–1747), German doctor and botanist]

heulandite (ˈhjuːlənˌdaɪt) n a white, grey, red, or brown zeolite mineral that consists essentially of hydrated calcium aluminium silicate in the form of elongated tabular crystals. Formula: $CaAl_2Si_7O_{18}.6H_2O$ [C19 named after H. Heuland, 19th-century English mineral collector; see -ITE[1]]

heuristic (hjʊəˈrɪstɪk) adj **1** helping to learn; guiding in discovery or investigation **2** (of a method of teaching) allowing pupils to learn things for themselves **3 a** maths, science, philosophy using or obtained by exploration of possibilities rather than by following set rules **b** computing denoting a rule of thumb for solving a problem without the exhaustive application of an algorithm: a heuristic solution ▷ n **4** (plural) the science of heuristic procedure [C19 from New Latin heuristicus, from Greek heuriskein to discover] > heuˈristically adv

heuristics (hjʊəˈrɪstɪks) n (functioning as singular) maths, logic a method or set of rules for solving problems other than by algorithm. See also **algorithm** (sense 1), **artificial intelligence**

hevea ('hiːvjə) *n* any tree of the South American euphorbiaceous genus *Hevea*, having a milky sap which provides rubber [C19 New Latin from native name *hevé*]

Hever Castle ('hiːvə) *n* a Tudor mansion near Edenbridge in Kent: home of Anne Boleyn before her marriage; Italian garden added in the 20th century by the Astor family

hew (hjuː) *vb* hews, hewing, hewed, hewed *or* hewn (hjuːn) **1** to strike (something, esp wood) with cutting blows, as with an axe **2** (*tr*; often foll by *out*) to shape or carve from a substance **3** (*tr*; often foll by *away, down, from, off*, etc) to sever from a larger or another portion **4** (*intr*; often foll by *to*) *US and Canadian* to conform (to a code, principle, etc) [Old English *hēawan*; related to Old Norse *heggva*, Old Saxon *hāwa*, Old High German *houwan*, Latin *cūdere* to beat] > 'hewer *n*

HEW (in the US) *abbreviation for* Department of Health, Education, and Welfare

hex¹ (hɛks) *n* **a** short for **hexadecimal notation** *or* **hexadecimal** **b** (*as modifier*): hex code

hex² (hɛks) *informal* ▷ *vb* **1** (*tr*) to bewitch ▷ *n* **2** an evil spell or symbol of bad luck **3** a witch [C19 via Pennsylvania Dutch from German *Hexe* witch, from Middle High German *hecse*, perhaps from Old High German *hagzissa*; see HAG¹] > 'hexer *n*

hexa- *or before a vowel* **hex-** *combining form* six: *hexachord; hexameter* [from Greek, from *hex* SIX]

hexachlorocyclohexane (,hɛksə,klɔːrəˌsaɪkləʊ'hɛksɛɪn) *n* a white or yellowish powder existing in many isomeric forms. A mixture of isomers, including lindane, is used as an insecticide. Formula: $C_6H_6Cl_6$

hexachloroethane (,hɛksə,klɔːrəʊ'εθɛɪn) *or* **hexachlorethane** *n* a colourless crystalline insoluble compound with a camphor-like odour: used in pyrotechnics and explosives. Formula: C_2Cl_6

hexachlorophene (,hɛksə'klɔːrəfiːn) *n* an insoluble almost odourless white bactericidal substance used in antiseptic soaps, deodorants, etc Formula: $(C_6HCl_3OH)_2CH_2$

hexachord ('hɛksəˌkɔːd) *n* (in medieval musical theory) any of three diatonic scales based upon C, F, and G, each consisting of six notes, from which solmization was developed

hexacosanoic acid (,hɛksəkəʊsə'nəʊɪk) *n* a white insoluble odourless wax present in beeswax, carnauba, and Chinese wax. Formula: $CH_3(CH_2)_{24}COOH$. Also called: cerotic acid

hexad ('hɛksæd) *n* **1** a group or series of six **2** the number or sum of six [C17 from Greek *hexas*, from *hex* six] > hex'adic *adj*

hexadecane ('hɛksədɛˌkeɪn, ,hɛksə'dɛkeɪn) *n* the systematic name for **cetane** [C19 from HEXA- + DECA- + -ANE]

hexadecanoic acid ('hɛksə,dɛkənəʊɪk) *n* the systematic name for **palmitic acid**

hexadecimal notation *or* **hexadecimal** (,hɛksə'dɛsɪməl) *n* a number system having a base 16; the symbols for the numbers 0–9 are the same as those used in the decimal system, and the numbers 10–15 are usually represented by the letters A–F. The system is used as a convenient way of representing the internal binary code of a computer

hexaemeron (,hɛksə'ɛmərɒn) *or* **hexahemeron** *n* **a** the period of six days in which God created the world **b** the account of the Creation in Genesis 1 [C16 via Late Latin from Greek, from *hexaēmeros* (adj) of six days, from HEXA- + *hēmera* day] > ,hexa'emeric *or* ,hexa'hemeric *adj*

hexagon ('hɛksəgən) *n* a polygon having six sides

hexagonal (hɛk'sægənəl) *adj* **1** having six sides and six angles **2** of or relating to a hexagon **3** *crystallog* relating or belonging to the crystal system characterized by three equal coplanar axes inclined at 60° to each other and a fourth longer or shorter axis at right angles to their plane. See also **trigonal**. > hex'agonally *adv*

hexagram ('hɛksəˌgræm) *n* **1** a star-shaped figure formed by extending the sides of a regular hexagon to meet at six points **2** a group of six broken or unbroken lines which may be combined into 64 different patterns, as used in the *I Ching* > ,hexa'grammoid *adj, n*

hexahedron (,hɛksə'hiːdrən) *n* a solid figure having six plane faces. A regular hexahedron (cube) has square faces. See also **polyhedron** > ,hexa'hedral *adj*

hexahydrate (,hɛksə'haɪdreɪt) *n* a hydrate, such as magnesium chloride, $MgCl_2.6H_2O$, with six molecules of water per molecule of substance > ,hexa'hydrated *adj*

hexahydropiridine (,hɛksəhaɪdrəʊ'pɪrɪˌdiːn) *n* the systematic name for **piperidine**

hexahydropyrazine (,hɛksəhaɪdrəʊ'paɪrəˌziːn) *n* the systematic name for **piperazine**

hexamerous (hɛk'sæmərəs) *or* **hexameral** *adj* (esp of the parts of a plant) arranged in groups of six > hex'amerism *n*

hexameter (hɛk'sæmɪtə) *n prosody* **1** a verse line consisting of six metrical feet **2** (in Greek and Latin epic poetry) a verse line of six metrical feet, of which the first four are usually dactyls or spondees, the fifth almost always a dactyl, and the sixth a spondee or trochee > hexametric (,hɛksə'mɛtrɪk), hex'ametral *or* ,hexa'metrical *adj*

hexamethylenetetramine (,hɛksə,mɛθɪliːn'tɛtrəˌmiːn) *n* a colourless crystalline organic compound used as a urinary antiseptic. Formula: $C_6H_{12}N_4$. Also called: hexamine, methenamine

hexamine ('hɛksəmiːn) *n* **1** another name for **hexamethylenetetramine** **2** a type of fuel produced in small solid blocks or tablets for use in miniature camping stoves

hexane ('hɛkseɪn) *n* a liquid alkane existing in five isomeric forms that are found in petroleum and used as solvents, esp the isomer with a straight chain of carbon atoms (*n*-hexane). Formula: C_6H_{14} [C19 from HEXA- + -ANE]

hexangular (hɛk'sæŋgjʊlə) *adj* having six angles

hexanoic acid (,hɛksə'nəʊɪk) *n* an insoluble oily carboxylic acid found in coconut and palm oils and in milk. Formula: $C_5H_{11}COOH$ [C20 from HEXANE + -*oic*]

hexapla ('hɛksəplə) *n* an edition of the Old Testament compiled by Origen, containing six versions of the text [C17 from Greek *hexaploos* sixfold] > 'hexaplar, hexaplaric (,hɛksə'plærɪk) *or* hexaplarian (,hɛksə'plɛərɪən) *adj*

hexapod ('hɛksəˌpɒd) *n* any arthropod of the class *Hexapoda* (or *Insecta*); an insect

hexapody (hɛk'sæpədɪ) *n, pl* -dies *prosody* a verse measure consisting of six metrical feet > hexapodic (,hɛksə'pɒdɪk) *adj*

hexastich ('hɛksəˌstɪk) *or* **hexastichon** (hɛk'sæstɪˌkɒn) *n prosody* a poem, stanza, or strophe that consists of six lines > ,hexa'stichic *adj*

hexastyle ('hɛksəˌstaɪl) *architect* ▷ *n* **1** a portico or façade with six columns ▷ *adj* **2** having six columns

Hexateuch ('hɛksəˌtjuːk) *n* the first six books of the Old Testament [C19 from HEXA- + Greek *teukhos* a book] > 'Hexa,teuchal *adj*

hexavalent (,hɛksə'veɪlənt) *adj chem* having a valency of six. Also: sexivalent

hexone ('hɛksəʊn) *n* another name for **methyl isobutyl ketone**

hexosan ('hɛksəˌsæn) *n* any of a group of polysaccharides that yield hexose on hydrolysis

hexose ('hɛksəʊs, -əʊz) *n* a monosaccharide, such as glucose, that contains six carbon atoms per molecule

hexyl ('hɛksɪl) *n* (*modifier*) of, consisting of, or containing the group of atoms C_6H_{13}, esp the isomeric form of this group, $CH_3(CH_2)_4CH_2$-: *a hexyl group or radical*

hexylresorcinol (,hɛksɪlrɪ'zɔːsɪˌnɒl) *n* a yellowish-white crystalline phenol that has a fatty odour and sharp taste; 2,4- dihydroxy-1-hexylbenzene: used for treating bacterial infections of the urinary tract. Formula: $C_{12}H_{18}O_2$

hey (heɪ) *interj* **1** an expression indicating surprise, dismay, discovery, etc, or calling for another's attention **2** *South African* an exclamation used for emphasis at the end of a statement, or alone to seek repetition or confirmation of another person's statement **3** hey presto an exclamation used by conjurors to herald the climax of a trick [C13 compare Old French *hay*, German *hei*, Swedish *hej*]

heyday ('heɪˌdeɪ) *n* the time of most power, popularity, vigour, etc; prime [C16 probably based on HEY]

Heyduck ('haɪdʊk) *n* a variant spelling of **Haiduk**

Heysham ('hiːʃəm) *n* a port in NW England, in NW Lancashire. Pop (with Morecambe): 46 657 (1991)

Heywood ('heɪˌwʊd) *n* a town in NW England, in Rochdale unitary authority, Greater Manchester, near Bury. Pop: 28 024 (2001)

Hezbollah (,hɛzbə'lɑː) *or* **Hizbollah** *n* an organization of militant Shiite Muslims based in Lebanon [C20 Arabic, literally: party of God]

Hezekiah (,hɛzə'kaɪə) *n* a king of Judah ?715–?687 BC, noted for his religious reforms (II Kings 18–19). Douay spelling: Ezechias [from Hebrew *hizqīyyāh ū* God has strengthened]

hf *abbreviation for* half

Hf *the chemical symbol for* hafnium

HF *or* **h.f.** *abbreviations. for* high frequency

HFEA (in Britain) *abbreviation for* Human Fertilization and Embryology Authority

HFMD *abbreviation for* hand, foot, and mouth disease

hg *abbreviation for* hectogram

Hg *the chemical symbol for* mercury [from New Latin HYDRARGYRUM]

HG *abbreviation for* **1** High German **2** His (*or* Her) Grace **3** (formerly, in Britain) Home Guard

HGH *abbreviation for* human growth hormone

hgt *abbreviation for* height

HGV (formerly, in Britain) *abbreviation for* heavy goods vehicle

HH *abbreviation for* **1** His (*or* Her) Highness **2** His Holiness (title of the Pope) **3** (on Brit pencils) ▷ *symbol for* double hard

hhd *abbreviation for* hogshead

H-hour *n military* the specific hour at which any operation commences. Also called: zero hour

hi¹ (haɪ) *sentence substitute* an informal word for **hello** [C20 originally US, from HIYA]

hi² (haɪ) *interj* an expression used to attract attention [C15 *hy*; compare HEY]

HI *abbreviation for* **1** Hawaii (state) **2** Hawaiian Islands

Hialeah (,haɪə'liːə) *n* a city in SE Florida, near Miami: racetrack. Pop: 226 401 (2003 est)

hiatus (haɪ'eɪtəs) *n, pl* -tuses *or* -tus **1** (esp in manuscripts) a break or gap where something is missing **2** a break or interruption in continuity **3** a break between adjacent vowels in the pronunciation of a word **4** *anatomy* a natural opening or aperture; foramen **5** *anatomy* a less common word for **vulva** [C16 from Latin: gap, cleft, aperture, from *hiāre* to gape, yawn] > hi'atal *adj*

hiatus hernia *or* **hiatal hernia** *n* protrusion of part of the stomach through the diaphragm at the oesophageal opening

Hib (hɪb) *n acronym for Haemophilus influenzae* type b: a vaccine against a type of bacterial meningitis, administered to children

hibachi (hɪ'bɑːtʃɪ) *n* a portable brazier for heating and cooking food [from Japanese, from *hi* fire + *bachi* bowl]

hibakusha (hɪ'bɑːkʊʃə) *n, pl* -sha *or* -shas a survivor of either of the atomic-bomb attacks on Hiroshima and Nagasaki in 1945 [C20 from Japanese, from *hibaku* exposed + -*sha* -person]

hibernaculum (,haɪbə'nækjʊləm) *or* **hibernacle** ('haɪbə,nækəl) *n, pl* -ula (-jʊlə) *or* -les *rare* **1** the winter quarters of a hibernating animal **2** the protective case or covering of a plant bud or animal [C17 from Latin: winter residence; see HIBERNATE]

hibernal (haɪˈbɜːnəl) *adj* of or occurring in winter [C17 from Latin *hībernālis*, from *hiems* winter]

hibernate (ˈhaɪbəˌneɪt) *vb* (*intr*) **1** (of some mammals, reptiles, and amphibians) to pass the winter in a dormant condition with metabolism greatly slowed down. Compare **aestivate 2** to cease from activity [C19 from Latin *hībernāre* to spend the winter, from *hībernus* of winter, from *hiems* winter] > ˌhiberˈnation *n* > ˈhiberˌnator *n*

Hibernia (haɪˈbɜːnɪə, hɪˈbɜːnɪə) *n* the Roman name for **Ireland**: used poetically in later times

Hibernian (haɪˈbɜːnɪən) *adj* **1** of or relating to Ireland or its inhabitants ▷ *n* **2** a native or inhabitant of Ireland [from *Hibernia*, the Roman name for Ireland]

Hibernicism (haɪˈbɜːnɪˌsɪzəm) or **Hibernianism** (haɪˈbɜːnɪəˌnɪzəm) *n* an Irish expression, idiom, trait, custom, etc

Hiberno- (haɪˈbɜːnəʊ) *combining form* denoting Irish or Ireland: *Hiberno-English*

hibiscus (haɪˈbɪskəs) *n, pl* **-cuses** any plant of the chiefly tropical and subtropical malvaceous genus *Hibiscus*, esp *H. rosa-sinensis*, cultivated for its large brightly coloured flowers [C18 from Latin, from Greek *hibiskos* marsh mallow]

hic (hɪk) *interj* a representation of the sound of a hiccup

hiccup (ˈhɪkʌp) *n* **1** a spasm of the diaphragm producing a sudden breathing in followed by a closing of the glottis, resulting in a sharp sound. Technical name: **singultus 2** the state or condition of having such spasms **3** *informal* a minor difficulty or problem ▷ *vb* **-cups, -cuping, -cuped** or **-cups, -cupping, -cupped 4** (*intr*) to make a hiccup or hiccups **5** (*tr*) to utter with a hiccup or hiccups Also: **hiccough** (ˈhɪkʌp) [C16 of imitative origin]

hic jacet Latin (hɪk ˈjækɛt) (on gravestones) here lies

hick (hɪk) *n informal* **a** a country person; bumpkin **b** (*as modifier*): *hick ideas* [C16 after *Hick*, familiar form of *Richard*]

hickey (ˈhɪkɪ) *n* **1** *US and Canadian informal* an object or gadget: used as a name when the correct name is forgotten, etc; doodah **2** *US and Canadian informal* a mark on the skin, esp a lovebite **3** *printing* a spot on a printed sheet caused by an imperfection or a speck on the printing plate [C20 of unknown origin]

hickory (ˈhɪkərɪ) *n, pl* **-ries 1** any juglandaceous tree of the chiefly North American genus *Carya*, having nuts with edible kernels and hard smooth shells. See also **pecan, pignut** (sense 1), **bitternut** (sense 1), **shagbark 2** the hard tough wood of any of these trees **3** the nut of any of these trees **4** a switch or cane made of hickory wood [C17 from earlier *pohickery*, from Algonquian *pawcohiccora* food made from ground hickory nuts]

hickymal (ˈhɪkɪməl) *n Southwest English dialect* a titmouse

hid (hɪd) *vb* the past tense and a past participle of **hide¹**

hidalgo (hɪˈdælɡəʊ; *Spanish* iˈðalɣo) *n, pl* **-gos** (-ɡəʊz; *Spanish* -ɣos) a member of the lower nobility in Spain [C16 from Spanish, from Old Spanish *fijo dalgo* nobleman, from Latin *filius* son + *dē* of + *aliquid* something]

Hidalgo (hɪˈdælɡəʊ; *Spanish* iˈðalɣo) *n* a state of central Mexico: consists of a high plateau, with the Sierra Madre Oriental in the north and east; ancient remains of Teltec culture (at Tula); rich mineral resources. Capital: Pachuca. Pop: 2 231 392 (2000). Area: 20 987 sq km (8103 sq miles)

hidden (ˈhɪdən) *vb* **1** a past participle of **hide¹** ▷ *adj* **2** concealed or obscured: *a hidden cave; a hidden meaning* > ˈhiddenly *adv* > ˈhiddenness *n*

hidden agenda *n* a hidden motive or intention behind an overt action, policy, etc

hidden hand *n* an unknown force or influence believed to be the cause of certain, often unfortunate, events

hiddenite (ˈhɪdəˌnaɪt) *n* a green transparent variety of the mineral spodumene, used as a gemstone [C19 named after W. E. *Hidden* (1853–1918), American mineralogist who discovered it]

hide¹ (haɪd) *vb* **hides, hiding, hid** (hɪd) **hidden** (ˈhɪdən) or **hid 1** to put or keep (oneself or an object) in a secret place; conceal (oneself or an object) from view or discovery: *to hide a pencil; to hide from the police* **2** (*tr*) to conceal or obscure: *the clouds hid the sun* **3** (*tr*) to keep secret **4** (*tr*) to turn (one's head, eyes, etc) away ▷ *n* **5** *Brit* a place of concealment, usually disguised to appear as part of the natural environment, used by hunters, birdwatchers, etc. US and Canadian equivalent: **blind** ▷ See also **hide-out** [Old English *hȳdan*; related to Old Frisian *hēda*, Middle Low German *hüden*, Greek *keuthein*] > ˈhidable *adj* > ˈhider *n*

hide² (haɪd) *n* **1** the skin of an animal, esp the tough thick skin of a large mammal, either tanned or raw **2** *informal* the human skin **3** *Austral and NZ informal* impudence ▷ *vb* **hides, hiding, hided 4** (*tr*) *informal* to flog [Old English *hȳd*; related to Old Norse *hūth*, Old Frisian *hēd*, Old High German *hūt*, Latin *cutis* skin, Greek *kutos*; see CUTICLE] > ˈhideless *adj*

hide³ (haɪd) *n* an obsolete Brit unit of land measure, varying in magnitude from about 60 to 120 acres [Old English *hīgid*; related to *hīw* family, household, Latin *cīvis* citizen]

hide-and-seek or *US and Canadian* **hide-and-go-seek** *n* a game in which one player covers his eyes and waits while the others hide, and then he tries to find them

hideaway (ˈhaɪdəˌweɪ) *n* a hiding place or secluded spot

hidebound (ˈhaɪdˌbaʊnd) *adj* **1** restricted by petty rules, a conservative attitude, etc **2** (of cattle, etc) having the skin closely attached to the flesh as a result of poor feeding **3** (of trees) having a very tight bark that impairs growth

hideous (ˈhɪdɪəs) *adj* **1** extremely ugly; repulsive: *a hideous person* **2** terrifying and horrific [C13 from Old French *hisdos*, from *hisde* fear; of uncertain origin] > ˈhideously *adv* > ˈhideousness or hideosity (ˌhɪdɪˈɒsɪtɪ) *n*

hide-out *n* **1** a hiding place, esp a remote place used by outlaws, etc; hideaway ▷ *vb* **hide out** (*intr*) **2** to remain deliberately concealed, esp for a prolonged period of time

hiding¹ (ˈhaɪdɪŋ) *n* **1** the state of concealment (esp in the phrase **in hiding**) **2 hiding place** a place of concealment

hiding² (ˈhaɪdɪŋ) *n* **1** *informal* a flogging; beating **2 be on a hiding to nothing** to be bound to fail; to face impossible odds

hidrosis (hɪˈdrəʊsɪs) *n* **1** a technical word for **sweating** or **sweat 2** any skin disease affecting the sweat glands **3** Also called: hyperhidrosis (ˌhaɪpəhɪˈdrəʊsɪs, -haɪˈdrəʊsɪs) *pathol* excessive perspiration [C18 via New Latin from Greek: sweating, from *hidrōs* sweat] > hidrotic (hɪˈdrɒtɪk) *adj*

hidy-hole or **hidey-hole** (ˈhaɪdɪˌhəʊl) *n informal* a hiding place

hie (haɪ) *vb* **hies, hieing** or **hying, hied** *archaic* or *poetic* to hurry; hasten; speed [Old English *hīgian* to strive]

HIE *abbreviation for* (in Scotland) Highlands and Islands Enterprise

hieland (ˈhiːlənd) *adj Scot dialect* **1** a variant of **Highland 2** characteristic of Highlanders, esp alluding to their supposed gullibility or foolishness in towns or cities

hiemal (ˈhaɪəməl) *adj* a less common word for **hibernal** [C16 from Latin *hiems* winter; see HIBERNATE]

hieracosphinx (ˌhaɪəˈreɪkəʊˌsfɪŋks) *n, pl* **-sphinxes** or **-sphinges** (-ˌsfɪndʒiːz) (in ancient Egyptian myth) a hawk-headed sphinx [C18 from Greek *hierax* hawk + SPHINX]

hierarch (ˈhaɪəˌrɑːk) *n* **1 a** a person in a position

of high priestly authority **b** a person holding high rank in a religious hierarchy **2** a person at a high level in a hierarchy > ˌhierˈarchal *adj*

hierarchy (ˈhaɪəˌrɑːkɪ) *n, pl* **-chies 1** a system of persons or things arranged in a graded order **2** a body of persons in holy orders organized into graded ranks **3** the collective body of those so organized **4** a series of ordered groupings within a system, such as the arrangement of plants and animals into classes, orders, families, etc **5** *linguistics, maths* a formal structure, usually represented by a diagram of connected nodes, with a single uppermost element. Compare **ordering, heterarchy, tree** (sense 6) **6** government by an organized priesthood [C14 from Medieval Latin *hierarchia*, from Late Greek *hierarkhia*, from *hierarkhēs* high priest; see HIERO-, -ARCHY] > ˌhierˈarchical or ˌhierˈarchic *adj* > ˌhierˈarchically *adv* > ˈhierˌarchism *n*

hieratic (ˌhaɪəˈrætɪk) *adj also* **hieratical 1** of or relating to priests **2** of or relating to a cursive form of hieroglyphics used by priests in ancient Egypt **3** of or relating to styles in art that adhere to certain fixed types or methods, as in ancient Egypt ▷ *n* **4** the hieratic script of ancient Egypt [C17 from Latin *hierāticus*, from Greek *hieratikos*, from *hiereus* a priest, from *hieros* holy] > ˌhierˈatically *adv*

hiero- or before a vowel **hier-** *combining form* holy or divine: *hierocracy; hierarchy* [from Greek, from *hieros*]

hierocracy (ˌhaɪəˈrɒkrəsɪ) *n, pl* **-cies** government by priests or ecclesiastics > hierocratic (ˌhaɪərəʊˈkrætɪk) or ˌhieroˈcratical *adj*

hierodule (ˈhaɪərəˌdjuːl) *n* (in ancient Greece) a temple slave, esp a sacral prostitute [C19 from Greek *hierodoulos*, from HIERO- + *doulos* slave] > ˌhieroˈdulic *adj*

hieroglyphic (ˌhaɪərəˈɡlɪfɪk) *adj also* **hieroglyphical 1** of or relating to a form of writing using picture symbols, esp as used in ancient Egypt **2** written with hieroglyphic symbols **3** difficult to read or decipher ▷ *n also* **hieroglyph 4** a picture or symbol representing an object, concept, or sound **5** a symbol or picture that is difficult to read or decipher [C16 from Late Latin *hieroglyphicus*, from Greek *hierogluphikos*, from HIERO- + *gluphē* carving, from *gluphein* to carve] > ˌhieroˈglyphically *adv* > hieroglyphist (ˌhaɪərəˈɡlɪfɪst, ˌhaɪəˈrɒɡ-) *n*

hieroglyphics (ˌhaɪərəˈɡlɪfɪks) *n* (*functioning as singular or plural*) **1** a form of writing, esp as used in ancient Egypt, in which pictures or symbols are used to represent objects, concepts, or sounds **2** difficult or undecipherable writing

hierogram (ˈhaɪərəˌɡræm) *n* a sacred symbol

hierology (ˌhaɪəˈrɒlədʒɪ) *n, pl* **-gies 1** sacred literature **2** a biography of a saint > hierologic (ˌhaɪərəˈlɒdʒɪk) or ˌhieroˈlogical *adj* > ˌhierˈologist *n*

hierophant (ˈhaɪərəˌfænt) *n* **1** (in ancient Greece) an official high priest of religious mysteries, esp those of Eleusis **2** a person who interprets and explains esoteric mysteries [C17 from Late Latin *hierophanta*, from Greek *hierophantēs*, from HIERO- + *phainein* to reveal] > ˌhieroˈphantic *adj* > ˌhieroˈphantically *adv*

hifalutin (ˌhaɪfəˈluːtɪn) *adj* a variant spelling of **highfalutin**

hi-fi (ˈhaɪˌfaɪ) *n informal* **1 a** short for **high fidelity b** (*as modifier*): *hi-fi equipment* **2** a set of high-quality sound-reproducing equipment

higgle (ˈhɪɡəl) *vb* a less common word for **haggle** > ˈhiggler *n*

higgledy-piggledy (ˈhɪɡəldɪˈpɪɡəldɪ) *informal* ▷ *adj* ▷ *adv* **1** in a jumble ▷ *n* **2** a muddle

Higgs boson or **Higgs particle** (hɪɡs) *n physics* an elementary particle with zero spin and mass greater than zero, predicted to exist by electroweak theory and other gauge theories. Also called (*Informal*): **God particle** [C20 named after Peter *Higgs* (born 1929), British theoretical physicist]

high (haɪ) *adj* **1** being a relatively great distance from top to bottom; tall: *a high building* **2** situated at or extending to a relatively great distance above the ground or above sea level: *a high plateau* **3 a** (*postpositive*) being a specified distance from top to bottom: *three feet high* **b** (*in combination*): *a seven-foot-high wall* **4** extending from an elevation: *a high dive* **5** (*in combination*) coming up to a specified level: *knee-high* **6** being at its peak or point of culmination: *high noon* **7** of greater than average height: *a high collar* **8** greater than normal in degree, intensity, or amount: *high prices; a high temperature; a high wind* **9** of large or relatively large numerical value: *high frequency; high voltage; high mileage* **10** (of sound) acute in pitch; having a high frequency **11** (of latitudes) situated relatively far north or south from the equator **12** (of meat) slightly decomposed or tainted, regarded as enhancing the flavour of game **13** of great eminence; very important: *the high priestess* **14** exalted in style or character; elevated: *high drama* **15** expressing or feeling contempt or arrogance: *high words* **16** elated; cheerful: *high spirits* **17** (*predicative*) *informal* overexcited: *by the end of term the children are really high* **18** *informal* being in a state of altered consciousness, characterized esp by euphoria and often induced by the use of alcohol, narcotics, etc **19** luxurious or extravagant: *high life* **20** advanced in complexity or development: *high finance* **21** (of a gear) providing a relatively great forward speed for a given engine speed. Compare **low¹** (sense 21) **22** *phonetics* of, relating to, or denoting a vowel whose articulation is produced by raising the back of the tongue towards the soft palate or the blade towards the hard palate, such as for the *ee* in English *see* or *oo* in English *moon*. Compare **low¹** (sense 20) **23** (*capital when part of name*) formal and elaborate in style: *High Mass* **24** (*usually capital*) of or relating to the High Church **25** remote, esp in time **26** *cards* **a** having a relatively great value in a suit **b** able to win a trick **27 high and dry** stranded; helpless; destitute **28 high and low** in all places; everywhere **29 high and mighty** *informal* arrogant **30 high as a kite** *informal* **a** very drunk **b** overexcited **c** euphoric from drugs **31 high opinion** a favourable opinion ▷ *adv* **32** at or to a height: *he jumped high* **33** in a high manner **34** *nautical* close to the wind with sails full ▷ *n* **35** a high place or level **36** *informal* a state of altered consciousness, often induced by alcohol, narcotics, etc **37** another word for **anticyclone 38** short for **high school 39** (*capital*) (esp in Oxford) the High Street **40** *electronics* the voltage level in a logic circuit corresponding to logical one. Compare **low¹** (sense 30) **41** on **high a** at a height **b** in heaven [Old English *hēah*; related to Old Norse *hār*, Gothic *hauhs*, Old High German *hōh* high, Lithuanian *kaũkas* bump, Russian *kúcha* heap, Sanskrit *kuča* bosom]

high altar *n* the principal altar of a church

High Arctic *n* the regions of Canada, esp the northern islands, within the Arctic Circle

highball (ˈhaɪˌbɔːl) *chiefly US* ▷ *n* **1** a long iced drink consisting of a spirit base with water, soda water, etc **2** (originally in railway use) a signal that the way ahead is clear and one may proceed ▷ *vb* **3** (*intr*) to move at great speed **4** (*tr*) to drive (a vehicle) at great speed [c19 (in sense 2) from the early railway signal consisting of a ball hoisted to the top of a pole]

highbinder (ˈhaɪˌbaɪndə) *n US informal* **1** a gangster **2** a corrupt politician **3** (formerly) a member of a Chinese-American secret society that engaged in blackmail, murder, etc [c19 named after the *High-binders*, a New York city gang]

highborn (ˈhaɪˌbɔːn) *adj* of noble or aristocratic birth

highboy (ˈhaɪˌbɔɪ) *n US and Canadian* a tall chest of drawers in two sections, the lower section being a lowboy. Brit equivalent: **tallboy**

high brass *n* brass containing 65 per cent copper and 35 per cent zinc, used for most applications

highbrow (ˈhaɪˌbraʊ) *often disparaging* ▷ *n* **1** a

person of scholarly and erudite tastes ▷ *adj also* **highbrowed 2** appealing to highbrows: *highbrow literature*

high camp *n* a sophisticated form of **camp²** (the style)

high-carb *n* (*modifier*) having a high carbohydrate content: *high-carb foods*

high-carbon steel *n* steel containing between 0.5 and 1.5 per cent carbon

highchair (ˈhaɪˌtʃɛə) *n* a long-legged chair for a child, esp one with a table-like tray used at meal times

High Church *n* **1** the party or movement within the Church of England stressing continuity with Catholic Christendom, the authority of bishops, and the importance of sacraments, rituals, and ceremonies. Compare **Broad Church, Low Church** ▷ *adj* **High-Church 2** of or relating to this party or movement > ˈHigh-ˈChurchman *n*

high-class *adj* **1** of very good quality; superior: *a high-class grocer* **2** belonging to, associated with, or exhibiting the characteristics of an upper social class: *a high-class lady; a high-class prostitute*

high-coloured *adj* (of the complexion) deep red or purplish; florid

high comedy *n* comedy set largely among cultured and articulate people and featuring witty dialogue. Compare **low comedy** > high comedian *n*

high command *n* the commander-in-chief and senior officers of a nation's armed forces

high commissioner *n* **1** the senior diplomatic representative sent by one Commonwealth country to another instead of an ambassador **2** the head of an international commission **3** the chief officer in a colony or other dependency

high concept *n* **a** popular appeal **b** high-concept (*as modifier*): *Baz Luhrmann's high-concept Romeo and Juliet*

high-context *adj* preferring to communicate in person, rather than by electronic methods such as email. Compare **low-context**

high country *n* (often preceded by *the*) sheep pastures in the foothills of the Southern Alps, New Zealand

High Court *n* **1 a** (in England and Wales) a shortened form of High Court of Justice **b** (in Scotland) a shortened form of High Court of Justiciary **2** (in New Zealand) a court of law inferior to the Court of Appeal. Formerly called: Supreme Court

High Court of Justice *n* (in England and Wales) one of the two divisions of the Supreme Court of Judicature. See also **Court of Appeal**

High Court of Justiciary *n* the senior criminal court in Scotland, to which all cases of murder and rape and all cases involving heavy penalties are referred

high day *n* a day of celebration; festival (esp in the phrase **high days and holidays**)

high definition television *n* a television system offering a picture with superior definition, using 1000 or more scanning lines, and possibly a higher field repetition rate to reduce flicker effects. Abbreviation: HDTV

high-density *adj computing* (of a floppy disk) having a relatively high storage capacity, usually of 1.44 megabytes

high-density lipoprotein *n* a lipoprotein that is the form in which cholesterol is transported in the bloodstream from the tissues to the liver. Abbreviation: HDL

high-dependency *adj* needing or providing a more than usually high level of healthcare: *a shortage of high-dependency beds*

high-end *adj* (*prenominal*) (esp of computers, electronic equipment, etc) of the greatest power or sophistication

high-energy physics *n* another name for **particle physics**

higher (ˈhaɪə) *adj* **1** the comparative of **high** ▷ *n* (*usually capital*) (in Scotland) **2 a** the advanced level of the Scottish Certificate of Education **b** (*as*

modifier): Higher Latin **3** a pass in a particular subject at Higher level: *she has four Highers*

higher criticism *n* the use of scientific techniques of literary criticism to establish the sources of the books of the Bible. Compare **lower criticism**

higher education *n* education and training at colleges, universities, polytechnics, etc

higher mathematics *n* (*functioning as singular*) abstract mathematics, including number theory and topology, that is more advanced than basic arithmetic, algebra, geometry, and trigonometry

higher rate *n* (in Britain) a rate of income tax that is higher than the basic rate and becomes payable on taxable income in excess of a specified limit

higher self *n* a person's spiritual self, as the focus of many meditation techniques, as opposed to the physical body

Higher Still *n* (in Scotland) **a** a system of post-Standard Grade qualifications offered at five levels including Higher and Advanced Higher **b** (*as modifier*): *Higher Still courses*

higher-up *n informal* a person of higher rank or in a superior position

highest common factor *n* the largest number or quantity that is a factor of each member of a group of numbers or quantities. Abbreviation: HCF, h.c.f Also called: **greatest common divisor**

high explosive *n* an extremely powerful chemical explosive, such as TNT or gelignite

highfalutin, hifalutin (ˌhaɪfəˈluːtɪn) *or* **highfaluting** *adj informal* pompous or pretentious [c19 from HIGH + -*falutin*, perhaps variant of *fluting*, from FLUTE]

high fashion *n* another name for **haute couture**

high fidelity *n* **a** the reproduction of sound using electronic equipment that gives faithful reproduction with little or no distortion **b** (*as modifier*): *a high-fidelity amplifier* ▷ Often shortened to: hi-fi

high-five *slang* ▷ *n* **1** a gesture of greeting or congratulation in which two people slap raised right palms together ▷ *vb* **2** to greet or congratulate (a person) in this way

high-flown *adj* extravagant or pretentious in conception or intention: *high-flown ideas*

high-flyer *or* **high-flier** *n* **1** a person who is extreme in aims, ambition, etc **2** a person of great ability, esp in a career

high-flying *adj* having great ambition or ability

high frequency *n* a radio-frequency band or radio frequency lying between 3 and 30 megahertz. Abbreviation: HF

High German *n* **1** the standard German language, historically developed from the form of West Germanic spoken in S Germany. Abbreviation: HG See also **German, Low German 2** any of the German dialects of S Germany, Austria, or Switzerland

high-handed *adj* tactlessly overbearing and inconsiderate > ˌhigh-ˈhandedly *adv* > ˌhigh-ˈhandedness *n*

high hat *n* another name for **top hat**

high-hat *adj* **1** *informal* snobbish and arrogant ▷ *vb* -hats, -hatting, -hatted (*tr*) **2** *informal, chiefly US and Canadian* to treat in a snobbish or offhand way ▷ *n* **3** *informal* a snobbish person **4** two facing brass cymbals triggered by means of a foot pedal

High Holidays *pl n Judaism* the festivals of Rosh Hashanah and Yom Kippur, the period of repentance in the first ten days of the Jewish new year. Also called: **Days of Awe, Yamim Nora'im**

high hurdles *n* (*functioning as singular*) a race in which competitors leap over hurdles 42 inches (107 cm) high

high-impact *adj* (*prenominal*) **1** (of a plastic or other material) able to withstand great force **2** (of aerobic or other exercise) placing great stress on various areas of the body **3** *informal* having great effect: *high-impact sound*

h

highjack (ˈhaɪˌdʒæk) *vb, n* a less common spelling of **hijack**. > ˈ**high**ˌ**jacker** *n*

high jinks *or* **hijinks** (ˈhaɪˌdʒɪŋks) *n* lively enjoyment

high jump *n* **1 a** (usually preceded by *the*) an athletic event in which a competitor has to jump over a high bar set between two vertical supports **b** (*as modifier*): *high-jump techniques* **2** be for the high jump *Brit informal* to be liable to receive a severe reprimand or punishment > **high jumper** *n* > **high jumping** *n*

high-key *adj* (of a photograph, painting, etc) having a predominance of light grey tones or light colours. Compare **low-key** (sense 3)

high-keyed *adj* **1** having a high pitch; shrill **2** *US* highly strung **3** bright in colour

highland (ˈhaɪlənd) *n* **1** relatively high ground **2** (*modifier*) of or relating to a highland > ˈ**highlander** *n*

Highland (ˈhaɪlənd) *n* **1** a council area in N Scotland, formed in 1975 (as Highland Region) from Caithness, Sutherland, Nairnshire, most of Inverness-shire, and Ross and Cromarty except for the Outer Hebrides. Administrative centre: Inverness. Pop: 209 080 (2003 est). Area: 25 149 sq km (9710 sq miles) **2** (*modifier*) of, relating to, or denoting the Highlands of Scotland

Highland cattle *n* a breed of cattle with shaggy hair, usually reddish-brown in colour, and long horns

Highland Clearances *pl n* in Scotland, the removal, often by force, of the people from some parts of the Highlands to make way for sheep, during the eighteenth and nineteenth centuries. Also called: **the Clearances**

Highland dress *n* **1** the historical costume, including the plaid, kilt or filibeg, and bonnet, as worn by Highland clansmen and soldiers **2** a modern version of this worn for formal occasions

Highlander (ˈhaɪləndə) *n* **1** a native of the Highlands of Scotland **2** a member of a Scottish Highland regiment

Highland fling *n* a vigorous Scottish solo dance

Highland Games *n* (*functioning as singular or plural*) a meeting in which competitions in sport, piping, and dancing are held: originating in the Highlands of Scotland

Highlands (ˈhaɪləndz) *n* the **1 a** the part of Scotland that lies to the northwest of the great fault that runs from Dumbarton to Stonehaven **b** a smaller area consisting of the mountainous north of Scotland: distinguished by Gaelic culture **2** (*often not capital*) the highland region of any country

high-level *adj* (of conferences, talks, etc) involving very important people

high-level language *n* a computer programming language that resembles natural language or mathematical notation and is designed to reflect the requirements of a problem; examples include Ada, BASIC, C, COBOL, FORTRAN, Pascal. See also **machine code**

high-level waste *n* radioactive waste material, such as spent nuclear fuel initially having a high activity and thus needing constant cooling for several decades by its producers before it can be reprocessed or treated. Compare **intermediate-level waste, low-level waste**

highlife (ˈhaɪˌlaɪf) *n* **a** a style of music combining West African elements with US jazz forms, found esp in the cities of West Africa **b** (*as modifier*): *a highlife band*

highlight (ˈhaɪˌlaɪt) *n* **1** an area of the lightest tone in a painting, drawing, photograph, etc **2** the most exciting or memorable part of an event or period of time **3** (*often plural*) a bleached blond streak in the hair ▷ *vb* (*tr*) **4** *painting, drawing, photog* to mark (any brightly illuminated or prominent part of a form or figure) with light tone **5** to bring notice or emphasis to **6** to be the highlight of **7** to produce blond streaks in (the hair) by bleaching

highlighter (ˈhaɪˌlaɪtə) *n* **1** a cosmetic cream or powder applied to the face to highlight the cheekbones, eyes, etc **2** a fluorescent felt-tip pen used as a marker to emphasize a section of text without obscuring it

highly (ˈhaɪlɪ) *adv* **1** (*intensifier*): *highly pleased; highly disappointed* **2** with great approbation or favour: *we spoke highly of it* **3** in a high position: *placed highly in class* **4** at or for a high price or cost

highly strung *or US and Canadian* **high-strung** *adj* tense and easily upset; excitable; nervous

high-maintenance *adj* **1** (of a piece of equipment, motor vehicle, etc) requiring regular maintenance to keep it in working order **2** *informal* (of a person) requiring a high level of care and attention

High Mass *n* a solemn and elaborate sung Mass. Compare **Low Mass**

high-minded *adj* **1** having or characterized by high moral principles **2** *archaic* arrogant; haughty > ˌ**high-ˈmindedly** *adv* > ˌ**high-ˈmindedness** *n*

high-muck-a-muck *n* a conceited or haughty person [c19 from Chinook Jargon *hiu muckamuck*, literally: plenty (of) food]

highness (ˈhaɪnɪs) *n* the condition of being high or lofty

Highness (ˈhaɪnɪs) *n* (preceded by *Your, His,* or *Her*) a title used to address or refer to a royal person

high-octane *adj* **1** (of petrol) having a high octane number **2** *informal* dynamic, forceful, or intense: *high-octane drive and efficiency*

high-pass filter *n* *electronics* a filter that transmits all frequencies above a specified value, substantially attenuating frequencies below this value. Compare **low-pass filter, band-pass filter**

high-pitched *adj* **1** pitched high in volume or tone. See **high** (sense 10) **2** (of a roof) having steeply sloping sides **3** (of an argument, style, etc) lofty or intense

high place *n Old Testament* a place of idolatrous worship, esp a hilltop

high places *pl n* positions and offices of influence and importance: *a scandal in high places*

high point *n* a moment or occasion of great intensity, interest, happiness, etc: *the award marked a high point in his life*

high-powered *adj* **1** (of an optical instrument or lens) having a high magnification: *a high-powered telescope* **2** dynamic and energetic; highly capable **3** possessing great strength, power, etc: *a high-powered engine*

high-pressure *adj* **1** having, using, involving, or designed to withstand a pressure above normal pressure: *a high-pressure gas; a high-pressure cylinder* **2** *informal* (of selling) persuasive in an aggressive and persistent manner

high priest *n* **1** *Judaism* the priest of highest rank who alone was permitted to enter the holy of holies of the tabernacle and Temple **2** *Mormon Church* a priest of the order of Melchizedek priesthood **3** Also (feminine): **high priestess** the head of a group or cult > **high priesthood** *n*

high profile *n* **a** a position or approach characterized by a deliberate seeking of prominence or publicity **b** (*as modifier*): *a high-profile campaign*. Compare **low profile**

high relief *n* relief in which forms and figures stand out from the background to half or more than half of their natural depth. Also called: **alto-relievo**

High Renaissance *n* **a** the the period from about the 1490s to the 1520s in painting, sculpture, and architecture in Europe, esp in Italy, when the Renaissance ideals were considered to have been attained through the mastery of Leonardo, Michelangelo, and Raphael **b** (*as modifier*): *High Renaissance art*

high-rise *adj* **a** (*prenominal*) of or relating to a building that has many storeys, esp one used for flats or offices: *a high-rise block*. Compare **low-rise b** (*as noun*): *a high-rise in Atlanta*

high-risk *adj* denoting a group, part, etc, that is particularly subject or exposed to a danger

highroad (ˈhaɪˌrəʊd) *n* **1** a main road; highway **2** (usually preceded by *the*) the sure way: *the highroad to fame*

high roller *n slang, chiefly US and Canadian* a person who spends money extravagantly or gambles recklessly > **high rolling** *n, adj*

high school *n* **1** *Brit* another term for **grammar school** **2** *US and NZ* a secondary school from grade 7 to grade 12 **3** *Canadian* a secondary school, the grades covered depending on the province

high seas *pl n* (*sometimes singular*) the open seas of the world, outside the jurisdiction of any one nation

high season *n* the most popular time of year at a holiday resort, etc

high society *n* **a** the upper classes, esp when fashionable **b** (*as modifier*): *her high-society image*

high-sounding *adj* another term for **high-flown**

high-speed *adj photog* **1** employing or requiring a very short exposure time: *high-speed film* **2** recording or making exposures at a rate usually exceeding 50 and up to several million frames per second **3** moving or operating at a high speed

high-speed steel *n* any of various steels that retain their hardness at high temperatures and are thus suitable for making tools used on lathes and other high-speed machines

high-spirited *adj* vivacious, bold, or lively > ˌ**high-ˈspiritedly** *adv* > ˌ**high-ˈspiritedness** *n*

high spot *n informal* another word for **highlight** (sense 2)

high-stepper *n* a horse trained to lift its feet high off the ground when walking or trotting

High Street (*often not capitals*) *n* (usually preceded by *the*) **1** *Brit* the main street of a town, usually where the principal shops are situated **2** the market constituted by the general public **3** (*modifier*) geared to meet the requirements of, and readily available for purchase by, the general public: *High-Street fashion*

hight (haɪt) *vb* (*tr; used only as a past tense in the passive or as a past participle*) *archaic and poetic* to name; call: *a maid hight Mary* [Old English *heht*, from *hatan* to call; related to Old Norse *heita*, Old Frisian *hēta*, Old High German *heizzan*]

high table *n* (*sometimes capitals*) the table, sometimes elevated, in the dining hall of a school, college, etc, at which the principal teachers, fellows, etc, sit

hightail (ˈhaɪˌteɪl) *vb* (*intr*) *informal, chiefly US and Canadian* to go or move in a great hurry. Also: **hightail it**

High Tatra *n* another name for the **Tatra Mountains**

high tea *n Brit* See **tea** (sense 4c)

high tech (tɛk) *n* a variant spelling of **hi tech**

high technology *n* highly sophisticated, often electronic, techniques used in manufacturing and other processes

high-tension *n* (*modifier*) subjected to, carrying, or capable of operating at a relatively high voltage: *a high-tension wire*. Abbreviation: **HT**

high tide *n* **1 a** the tide at its highest level **b** the time at which it reaches this **2** a culminating point

high time *informal* ▷ *adv* **1** the latest possible time; a time that is almost too late: *it's high time you mended this shelf* ▷ *n* **2** Also called: **high old time** an enjoyable and exciting time

high-toned *adj* **1** having a superior social, moral, or intellectual quality **2** affectedly superior **3** high in tone

high tops *pl n* training shoes that reach above the ankles

high treason *n* an act of treason directly affecting a sovereign or state

high-up *n informal* a person who holds an important or influential position

highveld (ˈhaɪˌfɛlt, -ˌvɛlt) *n* the the high-altitude grassland region of E South Africa

high water *n* **1** another name for **high tide** (sense 1) **2** the state of any stretch of water at its highest level, as during a flood Abbreviation: HW

high-water mark *n* **1 a** the level reached by sea water at high tide or by other stretches of water in flood **b** the mark indicating this level **2** the highest point

highway ('haɪ,weɪ) *n* **1** a public road that all may use **2** *Now chiefly US and Canadian except in legal contexts* a main road, esp one that connects towns or cities **3** a main route for any form of transport **4** a direct path or course

Highway Code *n* (in Britain) an official government booklet giving guidance to users of public roads

highwayman ('haɪ,weɪmən) *n*, *pl* -men (formerly) a robber, usually on horseback, who held up travellers

highway robbery *n informal* blatant overcharging

high wire *n* a tightrope stretched high in the air for balancing acts

High Wycombe ('wɪkəm) *n* a town in S central England, in S Buckinghamshire: furniture industry. Pop: 77 178 (2001)

HIH *abbreviation for* His (or Her) Imperial Highness

hi-hat *n* a variant spelling of **high-hat** (sense 4)

hijab (hɪ'dʒæb, hɛ'dʒɑːb) *or* **hejab** *n* a covering for the head and face, worn by Muslim women [from Arabic, literally: curtain]

hijack *or* **highjack** ('haɪ,dʒæk) *vb* **1** (*tr*) to seize, divert, or appropriate (a vehicle or the goods it carries) while in transit: *to hijack an aircraft* **2** to rob (a person or vehicle) by force: *to hijack a traveller* **3** (esp in the US during Prohibition) to rob (a bootlegger or smuggler) of his illicit goods or to steal (illicit goods) in transit ▷ *n* **4** the act or an instance of hijacking [C20 from unknown origin] > 'hi,jacker *or* 'high,jacker *n*

Hijaz (hiː'dʒæz) *n* a variant spelling of **Hejaz**

Hijrah ('hɪdʒrə) *n* a variant spelling of **Hegira**

hike (haɪk) *vb* **1** (*intr*) to walk a long way, usually for pleasure or exercise, esp in the country **2** (usually foll by *up*) to pull or be pulled; hitch **3** (*tr*) to increase (a price) ▷ *n* **4** a long walk **5** a rise in prices, wages, etc [C18 of uncertain origin] > 'hiker *n*

hike out *vb* (*intr, adverb*) *nautical, US and Canadian* to lean backwards over the side of a light sailing boat in order to carry the centre of gravity as far to windward as possible to reduce heeling. equivalent term (in Britain and certain other countries): sit out

hikoi ('hiː,kɔɪ) *NZ* ▷ *n* **1** a walk or march, esp a Māori protest march ▷ *vb* **2** (*intr*) to take part in such a march [Māori]

hilarious (hɪ'lɛərɪəs) *adj* very funny or merry [C19 from Latin *hilaris* glad, from Greek *hilaros*] > hi'lariously *adv* > hi'lariousness *n*

hilarity (hɪ'lærɪtɪ) *n* mirth and merriment; cheerfulness

Hilary term ('hɪlərɪ) *n* the spring term at Oxford University, the Inns of Court, and some other educational establishments [C16 named after Saint *Hilary* of Poitiers (?315–?367 AD), French bishop, whose feast day is Jan. 13 or 14]

Hildesheim (*German* 'hɪldəshaɪm) *n* a city in N central Germany, in Lower Saxony: a member of the Hanseatic League. Pop: 103 245 (2003 est)

hill (hɪl) *n* **1 a** a conspicuous and often rounded natural elevation of the earth's surface, less high or craggy than a mountain **b** (*in combination*): *a hillside; a hilltop* **2 a** a heap or mound made by a person or animal **b** (*in combination*): *a dunghill* **3** an incline; slope **4** *over the hill* **a** *informal* beyond one's prime **b** *military slang* absent without leave or deserting **5** *up hill and down dale* strenuously and persistently ▷ *vb* (*tr*) **6** to form into a hill or mound **7** to cover or surround with a mound or heap of earth ▷ See also **hills** [Old English *hyll*; related to Old Frisian *holla* head, Latin *collis* hill, Low German *hull* hill] > 'hiller *n* > 'hilly *adj*

Hilla ('hɪlə) *n* a market town in central Iraq, on a branch of the Euphrates: built partly of bricks from the nearby site of Babylon. Pop: 364 000 (2005 est). Also called: Al Hillah

hillbilly ('hɪl,bɪlɪ) *n*, *pl* -lies **1** *usually disparaging* an unsophisticated person, esp from the mountainous areas in the southeastern US **2** another name for **country and western** [C20 from HILL + Billy (the nickname)]

hill climb *n* a competition in which motor vehicles attempt singly to ascend a steep slope as fast as possible

hill country *n NZ* (in North Island) elevated pasture land for sheep or cattle

hillfort ('hɪl,fɔːt) *n archaeol* a hilltop fortified with ramparts and ditches, dating from the second millennium BC

Hillingdon ('hɪlɪŋdən) *n* a residential borough of W Greater London. Pop: 247 600 (2003 est). Area: 110 sq km (43 sq miles)

hill mynah *n* a starling, *Gracula religiosa*, of S and SE Asia: a popular cage bird because of its ability to talk. Also called: Indian grackle

hillock ('hɪlək) *n* a small hill or mound [C14 *hilloc*, from HILL + -OCK] > 'hillocked *or* 'hillocky *adj*

hills (hɪlz) *pl n* **1** *the* a hilly and often remote region **2** *as old as the hills* very old

hill station *n* (in northern India) a settlement or resort at a high altitude

hilt (hɪlt) *n* **1** the handle or shaft of a sword, dagger, etc **2** *to the hilt* to the full ▷ *vb* **3** (*tr*) to supply with a hilt [Old English; related to Old Norse *hjalt*, Old Saxon *helta* oar handle, Old High German *helza*]

hilum ('haɪləm) *n*, *pl* -la (-lə) **1** *botany* **a** a scar on the surface of a seed marking its point of attachment to the seed stalk (funicle) **b** the nucleus of a starch grain **2** a deep fissure or depression on the surface of a bodily organ around the point of entrance or exit of vessels, nerves, or ducts [C17 from Latin: trifle; see NIHIL]

hilus ('haɪləs) *n* a rare word for **hilum** (sense 2) [C19 via New Latin from Latin: a trifle] > 'hilar *adj*

Hilversum ('hɪlvəsəm; *Dutch* 'hɪlvərsym) *n* a city in the central Netherlands, in North Holland province: Dutch radio and television centre. Pop: 83 000 (2003 est))

him (hɪm; *unstressed* ɪm) *pron* (*objective*) **1** refers to a male person or animal: *they needed him; she baked him a cake; not him again!* **2** *chiefly US* a dialect word for **himself** when used as an indirect object: *he ought to find him a wife* [Old English *him*, dative of *hē* HE[1]]

▣ USAGE See at me[1]

HIM *abbreviation for* His (or Her) Imperial Majesty

Himachal Pradesh (hɪ'mɑːtʃəl prɑː'dɛʃ) *n* a state of N India, in the W Himalayas: rises to about 6700 m (22 000 ft) and is densely forested. Capital: Simla. Pop: 6 077 248 (2001). Area: 55 658 sq km (21 707 sq miles)

Himalayan (,hɪmə'leɪən) *adj* of or relating to the Himalayas or their inhabitants

Himalayan cat *n* the US name for **colourpoint cat**

Himalayan guinea pig *n* a variety of short-haired guinea pig with markings on its nose, ears, and feet

Himalayas (,hɪmə'leɪəz, hɪ'mɑːljəz) *or* **Himalaya** *pl n the* a vast mountain system in S Asia, extending 2400 km (1500 miles) from Kashmir (west) to Assam (east), between the valleys of the Rivers Indus and Brahmaputra: covers most of Nepal, Sikkim, Bhutan, and the S edge of Tibet; the highest range in the world, with several peaks over 7500 m (25 000 ft). Highest peak: Mount Everest, 8848 m (29 028 ft)

Himalia (hɪ'mɑːlɪə) *n astronomy* a satellite of Jupiter in an intermediate orbit

himation (hɪ'mætɪˌɒn) *n*, *pl* -ia (-ɪə) (in ancient Greece) a cloak draped around the body [C19 from Greek: a little garment, from *heima* dress, from *hennunai* to clothe]

himbo ('hɪmbəʊ) *n*, *pl* -bos *slang, usually derogatory* an attractive, but empty-headed man [C20 from HIM + (BIM)BO]

Himeji ('hiː'mɛ,dʒiː) *n* a city in central Japan, on W Honshu: cotton textile centre. Pop: 475 892 (2002 est)

Hims (hɪmz) *n* a former name of **Homs**

himself (hɪm'sɛlf; *medially often* ɪm'sɛlf) *pron* **1 a** the reflexive form of *he* or *him* **b** (*intensifier*): *the king himself waved to me* **2** (*preceded by a copula*) his normal or usual self: *he seems himself once more* **3** *Irish and Scot* the man of the house: *how is himself?* [Old English *him selfum*, dative singular of *hē self*; see HE[1], SELF]

Himyarite ('hɪmjəˌraɪt) *n* **1** a member of an ancient people of SW Arabia, sometimes regarded as including the Sabeans ▷ *adj* **2** of or relating to this people or their culture [C19 named after *Himyar* legendary king in ancient Yemen]

Himyaritic (,hɪmjə'rɪtɪk) *n* **1** the extinct language of the Himyarites, belonging to the SE Semitic subfamily of the Afro-Asiatic family ▷ *adj* **2** of, relating to, or using this language

hin (hɪn) *n* a Hebrew unit of capacity equal to about 12 pints or 3.5 litres [from Late Latin, from Greek, from Hebrew *hīn*, from Egyptian *hnw*]

hinahina ('hiːnə'hiːnə) *n*, *pl* hinahina another name for **mahoe** [Māori]

hinau ('hiːnaʊ:) *n*, *pl* hinau a tall New Zealand tree, *Elaeocarpus dentatus*, with white flowers and purple fruit [Māori]

Hinayana (,hiːnə'jɑːnə) *n* **a** any of various early forms of Buddhism **b** (*as modifier*): *Hinayana Buddhism* [from Sanskrit *hīnayāna*, from *hīna* lesser + *yāna* vehicle] > ,Hina'yanist *n* > ,Hinaya'nistic *adj*

Hinckley ('hɪŋklɪ) *n* a town in central England, in Leicestershire. Pop: 43 246 (2001)

hind[1] (haɪnd) *adj* hinder, hindmost *or* hindermost (*prenominal*) (esp of parts of the body) situated at the back or rear: *a hind leg* [Old English *hindan* at the back, related to German *hinten*; see BEHIND, HINDER[2]]

hind[2] (haɪnd) *n*, *pl* hinds *or* hind **1** the female of the deer, esp the red deer when aged three years or more **2** any of several marine serranid fishes of the genus *Epinephelus*, closely related and similar to the gropers [Old English *hind*; related to Old High German *hinta*, Greek *kemas* young deer, Lithuanian *szmúlas* hornless]

hind[3] (haɪnd) *n* (formerly) **1** a simple peasant **2** (in N Britain) a skilled farm worker **3** a steward [Old English *hīne*, from *hīgna*, genitive plural of *hīgan* servants]

Hind. *abbreviation for* **1** Hindi **2** Hindu **3** Hindustan **4** Hindustani

hindbrain ('haɪnd,breɪn) *n* the nontechnical name for **rhombencephalon**

Hindenburg ('hɪndənbʊrk) *n* the German name for **Zabrze**

Hindenburg line ('hɪndən,bɜːɡ) *n* a line of strong fortifications built by the German army near the Franco-Belgian border in 1916–17: breached by the Allies in August 1918 [C20 named after Paul von Beneckendorff und von *Hindenburg* (1847–1934), German field marshal and statesman]

hinder[1] ('hɪndə) *vb* **1** to be or get in the way of (someone or something); hamper **2** (*tr*) to prevent [Old English *hindrian*; related to Old Norse *hindra*, Old High German *hintarōn*] > 'hinderer *n* > 'hindering *adj, n*

hinder[2] ('haɪndə) *adj* (*prenominal*) situated at or further towards the back or rear; posterior: *the hinder parts* [Old English; related to Old Norse *hindri* latter, Gothic *hindar* beyond, Old High German *hintar* behind]

hindgut ('haɪnd,ɡʌt) *n* **1** the part of the vertebrate digestive tract comprising the colon and rectum **2** the posterior part of the digestive tract of arthropods ▷ See also **foregut, midgut**

Hindi ('hɪndɪ) *n* **1** a language or group of dialects of N central India. It belongs to the Indic branch of the Indo-European family and is closely related

h

to Urdu. See also **Hindustani 2** a formal literary dialect of this language, the official language of India, usually written in Nagari script **3** a person whose native language is Hindi [c18 from Hindi *hindī*, from *Hind* India, from Old Persian *Hindu* the river Indus]

hindmost ('haɪnd,məʊst) *or* **hindermost** ('haɪndə,məʊst) *adj* furthest back; last

Hindoo ('hɪndu:, hɪn'du:) *n, pl* **-doos**, *adj* an older spelling of **Hindu**. ▷ **Hindooism** ('hɪndʊ,ɪzəm) *n*

hindquarter ('haɪnd,kwɔːtə) *n* **1** one of the two back quarters of a carcass of beef, lamb, etc **2** (*plural*) the rear, esp of a four-legged animal

hindrance ('hɪndrəns) *n* **1** an obstruction or snag; impediment **2** the act of hindering; prevention

hindsight ('haɪnd,saɪt) *n* **1** the ability to understand, after something has happened, what should have been done or what caused the event **2** a firearm's rear sight

Hindu *or* **Hindoo** ('hɪndu:, hɪn'du:) *n, pl* **-dus**, **-doos 1** a person who adheres to Hinduism **2** an inhabitant or native of Hindustan or India, esp one adhering to Hinduism ▷ *adj* **3** relating to Hinduism, Hindus, or India [c17 from Persian *Hindū*, from *Hind* India; see HINDI]

Hinduism *or* **Hindooism** ('hɪndʊ,ɪzəm) *n* the complex of beliefs, values, and customs comprising the dominant religion of India, characterized by the worship of many gods, including Brahma as supreme being, a caste system, belief in reincarnation, etc

Hindu Kush (kʊʃ, ku:ʃ) *pl n* a mountain range in central Asia, extending over 800 km (500 miles) east from the Koh-i-Baba Mountains of central Afghanistan to the Pamirs. Highest peak: Tirich Mir, 7690 m (25 230 ft)

Hindustan (,hɪndʊ'stɑːn) *n* **1** the land of the Hindus, esp India north of the Deccan and excluding Bengal **2** the general area around the Ganges where Hindi is the predominant language **3** the areas of India where Hinduism predominates, as contrasted with those areas where Islam predominates

Hindustani, Hindoostani (,hɪndʊ'stɑːnɪ) *or* **Hindostani** (,hɪndəʊ'stɑːnɪ) *n* **1** the dialect of Hindi spoken in Delhi: used as a lingua franca throughout India **2** a group of languages or dialects consisting of all spoken forms of Hindi and Urdu considered together ▷ *adj* **3** of or relating to these languages or Hindustan

Hindutva (hɪn'dʊtvə) *n* (in India) a political movement advocating Hindu nationalism and the establishment of a Hindu state [c21 Hindi, literally: Hinduness]

hinge (hɪndʒ) *n* **1** a device for holding together two parts such that one can swing relative to the other, typically having two interlocking metal leaves held by a pin about which they pivot **2** *anatomy* a type of joint, such as the knee joint, that moves only backwards and forwards; a joint that functions in only one plane. Technical name: ginglymus **3** a similar structure in invertebrate animals, such as the joint between the two halves of a bivalve shell **4** something on which events, opinions, etc, turn **5** Also called: mount *philately* a small thin transparent strip of gummed paper for affixing a stamp to a page ▷ *vb* **6** (*tr*) to attach or fit a hinge to (something) **7** (*intr*; usually foll by *on* or *upon*) to depend (on) **8** (*intr*) to hang or turn on or as if on a hinge [c13 probably of Germanic origin; compare Middle Dutch *henge*; see HANG] ▷ **hinged** *adj* ▷ **'hingeless** *adj* ▷ **'hinge,like** *adj*

Hinglish ('hɪŋglɪʃ) *n* a variety of English incorporating elements of Hindi [c20 a blend of HINDI + ENGLISH]

hinny¹ ('hɪnɪ) *n, pl* **-nies** the sterile hybrid offspring of a male horse and a female donkey or ass. Compare **mule¹** (sense 1) [c17 from Latin *hinnus*, from Greek *hinnos*]

hinny² ('hɪnɪ) *vb* **-nies, -nying, -nied** a less common word for **whinny**

hinny³ ('hɪnɪ) *n Scot and northern English dialect* a

term of endearment, esp for a woman or child [variant of HONEY]

hint (hɪnt) *n* **1** a suggestion or implication given in an indirect or subtle manner: *he dropped a hint* **2** a helpful piece of advice or practical suggestion **3** a small amount; trace ▷ *vb* **4** (when *intr*, often foll by *at*; when *tr*, takes a clause as object) to suggest or imply indirectly [c17 of uncertain origin] ▷ **'hinter** *n* ▷ **'hinting** *n* ▷ **'hintingly** *adv*

hinterland ('hɪntə,lænd) *n* **1** land lying behind something, esp a coast or the shore of a river **2** remote or undeveloped areas of a country **3** an area located near and dependent on a large city, esp a port [c19 from German, from *hinter* behind + *land* LAND; see HINDER²]

hioi ('hi:ɒi:) *n* a New Zealand plant, *Mentha cunninghamii*, of the mint family. Also called: Māori mint [Māori]

hip¹ (hɪp) *n* **1** (*often plural*) either side of the body below the waist and above the thigh, overlying the lateral part of the pelvis and its articulation with the thighbones **2** another name for **pelvis** (sense 1) **3** short for **hip joint 4** the angle formed where two sloping sides of a roof meet or where a sloping side meets a sloping end [Old English *hype*; related to Old High German *huf*, Gothic *hups*, Dutch *heup*] ▷ **'hipless** *adj* ▷ **'hip,like** *adj*

hip² (hɪp) *n* the berry-like brightly coloured fruit of a rose plant: a swollen receptacle, rich in vitamin C, containing several small hairy achenes. Also called: rosehip [Old English *héopa*; related to Old Saxon *hiopo*, Old High German *hiufo*, Dutch *joop*, Norwegian dialect *hjūpa*]

hip³ (hɪp) *interj* an exclamation used to introduce cheers (in the phrase **hip, hip, hurrah**) [c18 of unknown origin]

hip⁴ (hɪp) *or* **hep** *adj* **hipper, hippest** *or* **hepper, heppest** *slang* **1** aware of or following the latest trends in music, ideas, fashion, etc **2** (*often postpositive*; foll by *to*) informed (about) [c20 variant of earlier *hep*]

hip bath *n* a portable bath in which the bather sits

hipbone ('hɪp,bəʊn) *n* the nontechnical name for **innominate bone**

hip dysplasia *n vet science* a common disorder of large and giant-breed dogs, as well as other species, in which the femoral head does not sit properly in the socket of the hip joint

hip flask *n* a small metal flask for spirits, etc, often carried in a hip pocket

hip-hop ('hɪp,hɒp) *n* a US pop culture movement originating in the 1980s comprising rap music, graffiti, and break dancing

hip-huggers *pl n chiefly US* trousers that begin at the hips instead of the waist. Usual Brit word: hipsters

hip joint *n* the ball-and-socket joint that connects each leg to the trunk of the body, in which the head of the femur articulates with the socket (acetabulum) of the pelvis

hipparch ('hɪpɑːk) *n* (in ancient Greece) a cavalry commander [c17 from Greek *hippos* horse + -ARCH]

Hipparchus (hɪ'pɑːkəs) *n* a large crater in the SW quadrant of the moon, about 130 kilometres in diameter

Hipparchus satellite (hɪ'pɑːkəs) *n* an astrometric satellite launched in 1989 by the European Space Agency that measured the position, proper motion, and brightness of 118 218 stars down to 12th magnitude and the magnitude and colour of a million stars down to 10th magnitude [after *Hipparchus*, Greek astronomer (2nd century BC)]

hippeastrum (hɪpɪ'æstrəm) *n* any plant of the South American amaryllidaceous genus *Hippeastrum*: cultivated for their large funnel-shaped typically red flowers [c19 New Latin, from Greek *hippeus* knight + *astron* star]

hipped¹ (hɪpt) *adj* **1 a** having a hip or hips **b** (*in combination*): *broad-hipped; low-hipped* **2** (esp of cows, sheep, reindeer, elk, etc) having an injury to the

hip, such as a dislocation of the bones **3** *architect* having a hip or hips. See also **hipped roof**

hipped² (hɪpt) *adj* (*often postpositive*; foll by *on*) *US and Canadian dated slang* very enthusiastic (about) [c20 from HIP⁴]

hipped roof *n* a roof having sloping ends and sides

hippie ('hɪpɪ) *n* a variant spelling of **hippy¹**

hippo ('hɪpəʊ) *n, pl* **-pos** *informal* **1** short for **hippopotamus 2** *South African* an armoured police car

hippocampus (,hɪpəʊ'kæmpəs) *n, pl* **-pi** (-paɪ) **1** a mythological sea creature with the forelegs of a horse and the tail of a fish **2** any marine teleost fish of the genus *Hippocampus*, having a horselike head. See **sea horse 3** an area of cerebral cortex that forms a ridge in the floor of the lateral ventricle of the brain, which in cross section has the shape of a sea horse. It functions as part of the limbic system [c16 from Latin, from Greek *hippos* horse + *kampos* a sea monster] ▷ ,hippo'campal *adj*

hip pocket *n* a pocket at the back of a pair of trousers

hippocras ('hɪpəʊ,kræs) *n* an old English drink of wine flavoured with spices [c14 *ypocras*, from Old French: Hippocrates (?460–?377 BC), Greek physician, probably referring to a filter called *Hippocrates' sleeve*]

Hippocratic (,hɪpə'krætɪk) *or* **Hippocratical** (,hɪpə'krætɪkəl) *adj* of or relating to Hippocrates, the Greek physician (?460–?377 BC)

Hippocratic facies (,hɪpə'krætɪk) *n* the sallow facial expression, with listless staring eyes, often regarded as denoting approaching death

Hippocratic oath (,hɪpəʊ'krætɪk) *n* an oath taken by a doctor to observe a code of medical ethics supposedly derived from that of Hippocrates (?460–?337), Greek physician commonly regarded as the father of medicine

Hippocrene ('hɪpəʊ,kriːn, ,hɪpəʊ'kriːnɪ) *n* a spring on Mount Helicon in Greece, said to engender poetic inspiration [c17 via Latin from Greek *hippos* horse + *krēnē* spring] ▷ ,Hippo'crenian *adj*

hippodrome ('hɪpə,drəʊm) *n* **1** a music hall, variety theatre, or circus **2** (in ancient Greece or Rome) an open-air course for horse and chariot races [c16 from Latin *hippodromos*, from Greek *hippos* horse + *dromos* a race]

hippogriff *or* **hippogryph** ('hɪpəʊ,grɪf) *n* a monster of Greek mythology with a griffin's head, wings, and claws and a horse's body [c17 from Italian *ippogrifo*, from *ippo-* horse (from Greek *hippos*) + *grifo* GRIFFIN¹]

Hippolyta (hɪ'pɒlɪtə) *or* **Hippolyte** (hɪ'pɒlɪ,tiː) *n Greek myth* a queen of the Amazons, slain by Hercules in battle for her belt, which he obtained as his ninth labour

Hippolytus (hɪ'pɒlɪtəs) *n Greek myth* a son of Theseus, killed after his stepmother Phaedra falsely accused him of raping her ▷ Hip'polytan *adj*

Hippomenes (hɪ'pɒmɪ,niːz) *n Greek myth* the husband, in some traditions, of Atalanta

hippopotamus (,hɪpə'pɒtəməs) *n, pl* **-muses** *or* **-mi** (-,maɪ) **1** a very large massive gregarious artiodactyl mammal, *Hippopotamus amphibius*, living in or around the rivers of tropical Africa: family *Hippopotamidae*. It has short legs and a thick skin sparsely covered with hair **2** pigmy hippopotamus a related but smaller animal, *Choeropsis liberiensis* [c16 from Latin, from Greek *hippopotamos* river horse, from *hippos* horse + *potamos* river]

Hippo Regius ('hɪpəʊ 'riːdʒɪəs) *n* an ancient Numidian city, adjoining present-day Annaba, Algeria. Often shortened to: Hippo

hippuric acid (hɪ'pjʊərɪk) *n* a crystalline solid excreted in the urine of mammals. Formula: $C_9H_9NO_3$

hippy¹ *or* **hippie** ('hɪpɪ) *n, pl* **-pies a** (esp during the 1960s) a person whose behaviour, dress, use of drugs, etc, implied a rejection of conventional values **b** (*as modifier*): *hippy language* [c20 see HIP⁴]

hippy² ('hɪpɪ) *adj* -pier, -piest *informal* (esp of a woman) having large hips

hip roof *n* a roof having sloping ends and sides

hipster ('hɪpstə) *n* **1** *slang, now rare* **a** an enthusiast of modern jazz **b** an outmoded word for **hippy¹ 2** (*modifier*) (of trousers) cut so that the top encircles the hips

hipsters ('hɪpstəz) *pl n Brit* trousers cut so that the top encircles the hips. Usual US word: hip-huggers

hiragana (ˌhɪərə'gɑːnə) *n* one of the Japanese systems of syllabic writing based on Chinese cursive ideograms. The more widely used of the two current systems, it is employed in newspapers and general literature. Compare **katakana** [from Japanese: flat kana]

hircine ('hɜːsaɪn, -sɪn) *adj* **1** *archaic* of or like a goat, esp in smell **2** *literary* lustful; lascivious [c17 from Latin *hircīnus*, from *hircus* goat]

hire ('haɪə) *vb* (*tr*) **1** to acquire the temporary use of (a thing) or the services of (a person) in exchange for payment **2** to employ (a person) for wages **3** (often foll by *out*) to provide (something) or the services of (oneself or others) for an agreed payment, usually for an agreed period **4** (*tr*; foll by *out*) *chiefly Brit* to pay independent contractors for (work to be done) ▷ *n* **5 a** the act of hiring or the state of being hired **b** (*as modifier*): *a hire car* **6 a** the price paid or payable for a person's services or the temporary use of something **b** (*as modifier*): *the hire charge* **7 for** *or* **on hire** available for service or temporary use in exchange for payment [Old English *hȳrian*; related to Old Frisian *hēra* to lease, Middle Dutch *hūren*] > '**hirable** *or* '**hireable** *adj* > '**hirer** *n*

hireling ('haɪəlɪŋ) *n derogatory* a person who works only for money, esp one paid to do something unpleasant [Old English *hȳrling*; related to Dutch *huurling*; see HIRE, -LING¹]

hire-purchase *n Brit, Austral, NZ, and South African* **a** a system for purchasing merchandise, such as cars or furniture, in which the buyer takes possession of the merchandise on payment of a deposit and completes the purchase by paying a series of regular instalments while the seller retains ownership until the final instalment is paid **b** (*as modifier*): *hire-purchase legislation*. Abbreviation: HP, h.p US and Canadian equivalents: **installment plan, instalment plan**

Hiri Motu ('hɪərɪ 'məʊtuː) *n* another name for **Motu** (the language)

hiring-fair *n* (formerly, in rural areas) a fair or market at which agricultural labourers were hired

Hiroshima (ˌhɪrɒ'ʃiːmə, hɪ'rɒʃɪmə) *n* a port in SW Japan, on SW Honshu on the delta of the Ota River: largely destroyed on August 6, 1945, by the first atomic bomb to be used in warfare, dropped by the US, which killed over 75 000 of its inhabitants. Pop: 1 113 786 (2002 est)

hirple ('hɪrpəl) *Scot* ▷ *vb* (*intr*) **1** to limp ▷ *n* **2** a limping gait [c15 of unknown origin]

hirsute ('hɜːsjuːt) *adj* **1** covered with hair **2** (of plants or their parts) covered with long but not stiff hairs **3** (of a person) having long, thick, or untrimmed hair [c17 from Latin *hirsūtus* shaggy; related to Latin *horrēre* to bristle, *hirtus* hairy; see HORRID] > **hirsuteness** *n*

hirudin (hɪ'ruːdɪn) *n med* an anticoagulant extracted from the mouth glands of leeches [c20 from Latin *hirudin-, hirudo* leech + -IN]

hirundine (hɪ'rʌndɪn, -daɪn) *adj* **1** of or resembling a swallow **2** belonging to the bird family *Hirundinidae*, which includes swallows and martins [c19 from Late Latin *hirundineus*, from Latin *hirundō* a swallow]

his (hɪz; *unstressed* ɪz) *determiner* **1 a** of, belonging to, or associated with him: *his own fault; his knee; I don't like his being out so late* **b** as pronoun: *his is on the left; that book is his* **2 his and hers** (of paired objects) for a man and woman respectively ▷ *pron* **3** of his belonging to or associated with him [Old

English *his*, genitive of *hē* HE¹ and of *hit* IT]

Hispania (hɪ'spæniə) *n* the Iberian peninsula in the Roman world

Hispanic (hɪ'spænɪk) *adj* **1** relating to, characteristic of, or derived from Spain or the Spanish ▷ *n* **2** *US* a US citizen of Spanish or Latin-American descent

Hispanicism (hɪ'spænɪˌsɪzəm) *n* a word or expression borrowed from Spanish or modelled on the form of a Spanish word or expression

Hispanicize *or* **Hispanicise** (hɪ'spænɪˌsaɪz) *vb* (*tr*) to make Spanish, as in custom or culture; bring under Spanish control or influence > His'panicist *n* > His,panici'zation *or* His,panici'sation *n*

Hispaniola (ˌhɪspən'jəʊlə; *Spanish* ispa'ɲola) *n* the second largest island in the Caribbean, in the Greater Antilles: divided politically into Haiti and the Dominican Republic; discovered in 1492 by Christopher Columbus, who named it La Isla Española. Area: 18 703 sq km (29 418 sq miles). Former name: **Santo Domingo**

hispid ('hɪspɪd) *adj biology* covered with stiff hairs or bristles [c17 from Latin *hispidus* bristly] > his'pidity *n*

hiss (hɪs) *n* **1** a voiceless fricative sound like that of a prolonged *s* **2** such a sound uttered as an exclamation of derision, contempt, etc, esp by an audience or crowd **3** *electronics* receiver noise with a continuous spectrum, caused by thermal agitation, shot noise, etc ▷ *interj* **4** an exclamation of derision or disapproval ▷ *vb* **5** (*intr*) to produce or utter a hiss **6** (*tr*) to express with a hiss, usually to indicate derision or anger **7** (*tr*) to show derision or anger towards (a speaker, performer, etc) by hissing [c14 of imitative origin] > 'hisser *n*

hissy fit ('hɪsɪ) *n informal* a childish temper tantrum

hist (hɪst) *interj* an exclamation used to attract attention or as a warning to be silent

histaminase (hɪ'stæmɪˌneɪs) *n* an enzyme, occurring in the digestive system, that inactivates histamine by removal of its amino group. Also called: **diamine oxidase**

histamine ('hɪstəˌmiːn, -mɪn) *n* an amine formed from histidine and released by the body tissues in allergic reactions, causing irritation. It also stimulates gastric secretions, dilates blood vessels, and contracts smooth muscle. Formula: $C_5H_9N_3$. See also **antihistamine** [c20 from HIST(IDINE) + -AMINE] > **histaminic** (ˌhɪstə'mɪnɪk) *adj*

histidine ('hɪstɪˌdiːn, -dɪn) *n* a nonessential amino acid that occurs in most proteins: a precursor of histamine

histiocyte ('hɪstɪəˌsaɪt) *n physiol* a macrophage that occurs in connective tissue [c20 alteration of German *histiozyt*, from Greek *histion* a little web, from *histos* web + -CYTE] > **histiocytic** (ˌhɪstɪə'sɪtɪk) *adj*

histo- *or before a vowel* **hist-** *combining form* indicating animal or plant tissue: *histology; histamine* [from Greek, from *histos* web]

histochemistry (ˌhɪstəʊ'kemɪstrɪ) *n* the chemistry of tissues, such as liver and bone, often studied with the aid of a microscope > ˌhisto'chemical *adj*

histocompatibility (ˌhɪstəʊkəmˌpætɪ'bɪlɪtɪ) *n* the degree of similarity between the histocompatibility antigens of two individuals. Histocompatibility determines whether an organ transplant will be tolerated > ˌhistocom'patible *adj*

histocompatibility antigen *n* a molecule occurring on the surface of tissue cells that can take several different forms. The differences between histocompatibility antigens are inherited and determine organ transplant rejection

histogen ('hɪstəˌdʒen) *n* (formerly) any of three layers in an apical meristem that were thought to give rise to the different parts of the plant: the apical meristem is now regarded as comprising

two layers ▷ See **corpus, tunica**

histogenesis (ˌhɪstəʊ'dʒenɪsɪs) *or* **histogeny** (hɪ'stɒdʒənɪ) *n* the formation of tissues and organs from undifferentiated cells > **histogenetic** (ˌhɪstəʊdʒə'netɪk) *or* ˌhisto'genic *adj* > ˌhistoge'netically *or* ˌhisto'genically *adv*

histogram ('hɪstəˌgræm) *n* a statistical graph that represents the frequency of values of a quantity by vertical rectangles of varying heights and widths. The width of the rectangles is in proportion to the class interval under consideration, and their areas represent the relative frequency of the phenomenon in question. See also **stem-and-leaf diagram** [c20 perhaps from HISTO(RY) + -GRAM]

histoid ('hɪstɔɪd) *adj* (esp of a tumour) **1** resembling normal tissue **2** composed of one kind of tissue

histology (hɪ'stɒlədʒɪ) *n* **1** the study, esp the microscopic study, of the tissues of an animal or plant **2** the structure of a tissue or organ > **histological** (ˌhɪstə'lɒdʒɪkəl) *or* ˌhisto'logic *adj* > ˌhisto'logically *adv* > his'tologist *n*

histolysis (hɪ'stɒlɪsɪs) *n* the disintegration of organic tissues > **histolytic** (ˌhɪstə'lɪtɪk) *adj* > ˌhisto'lytically *adv*

histone ('hɪstəʊn) *n* any of a group of basic proteins present in cell nuclei and implicated in the spatial organization of DNA

histopathology (ˌhɪstəʊpə'θɒlədʒɪ) *n* the study of the microscopic structure of diseased tissues > **histopathological** (ˌhɪstəʊˌpæθə'lɒdʒɪkəl) *adj*

histoplasmosis (ˌhɪstəʊplæz'məʊsɪs) *n* a severe fungal disease of the lungs caused by *Histoplasma capsulatum*

historian (hɪ'stɔːrɪən) *n* a person who writes or studies history, esp one who is an authority on it

historiated (hɪ'stɔːrɪˌeɪtɪd) *adj* decorated with flowers or animals. Also: **storiated** [c19 from Medieval Latin *historiāre* to tell a story in pictures, from Latin *historia* story]

historic (hɪ'stɒrɪk) *adj* **1** famous or likely to become famous in history; significant **2** a less common word for **historical** (senses 1–5) **3** Also: **secondary** *linguistics* (of Latin, Greek, or Sanskrit verb tenses) referring to past time

> **USAGE** A distinction is usually made between *historic* (important, significant) and *historical* (pertaining to history): *a historic decision; a historical perspective*

historical (hɪ'stɒrɪkəl) *adj* **1** belonging to or typical of the study of history: *historical methods* **2** concerned with or treating of events of the past: *historical accounts* **3** based on or constituting factual material as distinct from legend or supposition **4** based on or inspired by history: *a historical novel* **5** occurring or prominent in history **6** a less common word for **historic** (sense 1) > his'torically *adv* > his'toricalness *n*

historical-cost accounting *n* a method of accounting that values assets at the original cost. In times of high inflation profits can be overstated. Compare **current-cost accounting**

historical geology *n* the branch of geology concerned with the evolution of the earth and its life forms from its origins to the present

historical linguistics *n* (*functioning as singular*) the study of language as it changes in the course of time, with a view either to discovering general principles of linguistic change or to establishing the correct genealogical classification of particular languages. Also called: diachronic linguistics. Compare **descriptive linguistics**

historical materialism *n* the part of Marxist theory maintaining that social structures derive from economic structures and that these are transformed as a result of class struggles, each ruling class producing another, which will overcome and destroy it, the final phase being the emergence of a communist society

historical method *n* a means of learning about

h

something by considering its origins and development
historical present *n* the present tense used to narrate past events, usually employed in English for special effect or in informal use, as in *a week ago I'm walking down the street and I see this accident*
historical school *n* **1** a group of 19th-century German economists who maintained that modern economies evolved from historical institutions **2** the school of jurists maintaining that laws are based on social and historical circumstances rather than made by a sovereign power
historic episcopate *n Christian Church* the derivation of the episcopate of a Church in historic succession from the apostles
historicism (hɪˈstɒrɪˌsɪzəm) *n* **1** the belief that natural laws govern historical events which in turn determine social and cultural phenomena **2** the doctrine that each period of history has its own beliefs and values inapplicable to any other, so that nothing can be understood independently of its historical context **3** the conduct of any enquiry in accordance with these views **4** excessive emphasis on history, historicism, past styles, etc > **hisˈtoricist** *n, adj*
historicity (ˌhɪstəˈrɪsɪtɪ) *n* historical authenticity
Historic Places Trust *n* (in New Zealand) the statutory body concerned with the conservation of historic buildings, esp with ancient Māori sites
historiographer (hɪˌstɔːrɪˈɒɡrəfə) *n* **1** a historian, esp one concerned with historical method and the writings of other historians **2** a historian employed to write the history of a group or public institution
historiography (ˌhɪstɔːrɪˈɒɡrəfɪ) *n* **1** the writing of history **2** the study of the development of historical method, historical research, and writing **3** any body of historical literature > **historiographic** (hɪˌstɔːrɪəˈɡræfɪk) *or* **hisˌtorioˈgraphical** *adj*
history (ˈhɪstərɪ, ˈhɪstrɪ) *n, pl* **-ries** **1 a** a record or account, often chronological in approach, of past events, developments, etc **b** (*as modifier*): *a history book; a history play* **2** all that is preserved or remembered of the past, esp in written form **3** the discipline of recording and interpreting past events involving human beings **4** past events, esp when considered as an aggregate **5** an event in the past, esp one that has been forgotten or reduced in importance: *their quarrel was just history* **6** the past, background, previous experiences, etc, of a thing or person: *the house had a strange history* **7** *computing* a stored list of the websites that a user has recently visited **8** a play that depicts or is based on historical events **9** a narrative relating the events of a character's life: *the history of Joseph Andrews*. Abbreviation (for senses 1–3): **hist** [C15 from Latin *historia*, from Greek: enquiry, from *historein* to narrate, from *histōr* judge]
histrionic (ˌhɪstrɪˈɒnɪk) *or* **histrionical** *adj* **1** excessively dramatic, insincere, or artificial: *histrionic gestures* **2** *now rare* dramatic ▷ *n* **3** (*plural*) melodramatic displays of temperament **4** *rare* (*plural, functioning as singular*) dramatics [C17 from Late Latin *histriōnicus* of a player, from *histriō* actor] > **ˌhistriˈonically** *adv*
hit (hɪt) *vb* **hits, hitting, hit** (*mainly tr*) **1** (*also intr*) to deal (a blow or stroke) to (a person or thing); strike: *the man hit the child* **2** to come into violent contact with: *the car hit the tree* **3** to reach or strike with a missile, thrown object, etc: *to hit a target* **4** to make or cause to make forceful contact; knock or bump: *I hit my arm on the table* **5** to propel or cause to move by striking: *to hit a ball* **6** *cricket* to score (runs) **7** to affect (a person, place, or thing) suddenly or adversely: *his illness hit his wife very hard* **8** to become suddenly apparent to (a person): *the reason for his behaviour hit me and made the whole episode clear* **9** to achieve or reach: *to hit the jackpot; unemployment hit a new high* **10** to experience or encounter: *I've hit a slight snag here* **11** *slang* to murder (a rival criminal) in fulfilment of an underworld contract or vendetta **12** to accord or suit (esp in the phrase **hit one's fancy**) **13** to guess correctly or find out by accident: *you have hit the answer* **14** *informal* to set out on (a road, path, etc): *let's hit the road* **15** *informal* to arrive or appear in: *he will hit town tomorrow night* **16** *informal, chiefly US and Canadian* to demand or request from: *he hit me for a pound* **17** *slang* to drink an excessive amount of (alcohol): *to hit the bottle* **18** **hit it** *music slang* start playing **19** **hit skins** *US slang* to have sexual intercourse **20** **hit the sack** (*or* **hay**) *slang* to go to bed **21** **not know what has hit one** to be completely taken by surprise ▷ *n* **22** an impact or collision **23** a shot, blow, etc, that reaches its object **24** an apt, witty, or telling remark **25** *informal* **a** a person or thing that gains wide appeal: *she's a hit with everyone* **b** (*as modifier*): *a hit record* **26** *informal* a stroke of luck **27** *slang* **a** a murder carried out as the result of an underworld vendetta or rivalry **b** (*as modifier*): *a hit squad* **28** *slang* a drag on a cigarette, a swig from a bottle, a line of a drug, or an injection of heroin **29** *computing* a single visit to a website **30** **make** (*or* **score**) **a hit with** *informal* to make a favourable impression on ▷ See also **hit off, hit on, hit out** [Old English *hittan*, from Old Norse *hitta*]
Hitachi (hɪˈtætʃɪ) *n* a city in Japan, in E Honshu: a centre of the electronics industry. Pop: 193 080 (2002 est)
hit-and-miss *adj informal* random; haphazard: *a hit-and-miss affair; the technique is very hit and miss*. Also: **hit or miss**
hit-and-run *adj* (*prenominal*) **1 a** involved in or denoting a motor-vehicle accident in which the driver leaves the scene without stopping to give assistance, inform the police, etc **b** (*as noun*): *a hit-and-run* **2** (of an attack, raid, etc) relying on surprise allied to a rapid departure from the scene of operations for the desired effect: *hit-and-run tactics* **3** *baseball* denoting a play in which a base runner begins to run as the pitcher throws the ball to the batter
hitch (hɪtʃ) *vb* **1** to fasten or become fastened with a knot or tie, esp temporarily **2** (often foll by *up*) to connect (a horse, team, etc); harness **3** (*tr*; often foll by *up*) to pull up (the trousers, a skirt, etc) with a quick jerk **4** (*intr*) *chiefly US* to move in a halting manner: *to hitch along* **5** to entangle or become entangled: *the thread was hitched on the reel* **6** (*tr; passive*) *slang* to marry (esp in the phrase **get hitched**) **7** *informal* to obtain (a ride or rides) by hitchhiking ▷ *n* **8** an impediment or obstacle, esp one that is temporary or minor: *a hitch in the proceedings* **9** a knot for fastening a rope to posts, other ropes, etc, that can be undone by pulling against the direction of the strain that holds it **10** a sudden jerk; tug; pull: *he gave it a hitch and it came loose* **11** *chiefly US* a hobbling gait: *to walk with a hitch* **12** a device used for fastening **13** *informal* a ride obtained by hitchhiking **14** *US and Canadian slang* a period of time spent in prison, in the army, etc [C15 of uncertain origin] > **ˈhitcher** *n*
hitchhike (ˈhɪtʃˌhaɪk) *vb* (*intr*) to travel by obtaining free lifts in motor vehicles > **ˈhitchˌhiker** *n*
hitching post *n* a post or rail to which the reins of a horse, etc, are tied
hi tech *or* **high tech** (tɛk) *n* **1** short for **high technology** **2** a style of interior design using features of industrial equipment ▷ *adj* **hi-tech** *or* **high-tech** **3** designed for or using high technology **4** of or in the interior design style. Compare **low tech**
hither (ˈhɪðə) *adv* **1** Also (archaic): **hitherward, hitherwards** to or towards this place (esp in the phrase **come hither**) **2** **hither and thither** this way and that, as in a state of confusion ▷ *adj* **3** *archaic or dialect* (of a side or part, esp of a hill or valley) nearer; closer [Old English *hider*; related to Old Norse *hethra* here, Gothic *hidrē*, Latin *citrā* on this side, *citrō*]
hithermost (ˈhɪðəˌməʊst) *adj now rare* nearest to this place or in this direction
hitherto (ˈhɪðəˈtuː) *adv* **1** until this time: *hitherto, there have been no problems* **2** *archaic* to this place or point
Hitler (ˈhɪtlə) *n* a person who displays dictatorial characteristics [from Adolf *Hitler* (1889–1945), president of the National Socialist German Workers' Party (Nazi party) and German dictator]
Hitlerism (ˈhɪtləˌrɪzəm) *n* the policies, principles, and methods of the Nazi party as developed by its leader Adolf Hitler (1889–1945)
hit list *n informal* **1** a list of people to be murdered: *a terrorist hit list* **2** a list of targets to be eliminated in some way: *a hit list of pits to be closed*
hit man *n slang* a hired assassin, esp one employed by gangsters
hit off *vb* **1** (*tr, adverb*) to represent or mimic accurately **2** **hit it off** *informal* to have a good relationship with
hit on *vb* (*tr, preposition*) **1** to strike **2** Also: **hit upon** to discover unexpectedly or guess correctly **3** *US and Canadian slang* to make sexual advances to (a person)
hit out *vb* (*intr, adverb*; often foll by *at*) **1** to direct blows forcefully and vigorously **2** to make a verbal attack (upon someone)
hit parade *n old-fashioned* a listing or playing of the current most popular songs
hitter (ˈhɪtə) *n* **1** *informal* a boxer who has a hard punch rather than skill or finesse **2** a person who hits something
Hittite (ˈhɪtaɪt) *n* **1** a member of an ancient people of Anatolia, who built a great empire in N Syria and Asia Minor in the second millennium BC **2** the extinct language of this people, deciphered from cuneiform inscriptions found at Boğazköy and elsewhere. It is clearly related to the Indo-European family of languages, although the precise relationship is disputed ▷ *adj* **3** of or relating to this people, their civilization, or their language
hit wicket *n cricket* an instance of a batsman breaking the wicket with the bat or a part of the body while playing a stroke and so being out
HIV *abbreviation for* human immunodeficiency virus; the cause of AIDS. Two strains have been identified: HIV-1 and HIV-2
hive (haɪv) *n* **1** a structure in which social bees live and rear their young **2** a colony of social bees **3** a place showing signs of great industry (esp in the phrase **a hive of activity**) **4** a teeming crowd; multitude **5** an object in the form of a hive ▷ *vb* **6** to cause (bees) to collect or (of bees) to collect inside a hive **7** to live or cause to live in or as if in a hive **8** (*tr*) (of bees) to store (honey, pollen, etc) in the hive **9** (*tr*; often foll by *up* or *away*) to store, esp for future use: *he used to hive away a small sum every week* [Old English *hȳf*; related to Westphalian *hüwe*, Old Norse *hūfr* ship's hull, Latin *cūpa* barrel, Greek *kupē*, Sanskrit *kūpa* cave] > **ˈhiveˌlike** *adj*
hive bee *n* another name for a **honeybee**
hive dross *n* another name for **propolis**
hive off *vb* (*adverb*) **1** to transfer or be transferred from a larger group or unit **2** (*usually tr*) to transfer (profitable activities of a nationalized industry) back to private ownership
hives (haɪvz) *n* (*functioning as singular or plural*) *pathol* a nontechnical name for **urticaria** [C16 of uncertain origin]
hiya (ˈhaɪjə, ˌhaɪˈjɑː) *sentence substitute* an informal term of greeting [C20 shortened from *how are you?*]
Hizbollah (ˌhɪzbəˈlɑː) *n* a variant spelling of **Hezbollah**
HJ (on gravestones) *abbreviation for* hic jacet [Latin: here lies]
HJS (on gravestones) *abbreviation for* hic jacet sepultus [Latin: here lies buried]
hk *the internet domain name for* Hong Kong
HK **1** *abbreviation for* House of Keys (Manx Parliament) **2** ▷ *international car registration for* Hong Kong

HKJ *international car registration for* (Hashemite Kingdom of) Jordan

hl *symbol for* hectolitre

HL (in Britain) *abbreviation for* House of Lords

HLA system *n* human leucocyte antigen system; a group of the most important antigens responsible for tissue compatibility, together with the genes that encode them. For tissue and organ transplantation to be successful there needs to be a minimum number of HLA differences between the donor's and recipient's tissue

hm¹ *symbol for* hectometre

hm² *the internet domain name for* Heard and McDonald Islands

HM *abbreviation for* **1** His (or Her) Majesty **2** heavy metal (sense 1) **3** headmaster; headmistress

h'm (*spelling pron* hmmm) *interj* used to indicate hesitation, doubt, assent, pleasure, etc

HMAS *abbreviation for* His (or Her) Majesty's Australian Ship

HMCS *abbreviation for* His (or Her) Majesty's Canadian Ship

HMG *abbreviation for* His (or Her) Majesty's Government

HMI (in Britain) *abbreviation for* Her Majesty's Inspector; a government official who examines and supervises schools

H.M.S. *or* **HMS** *abbreviation for* **1** His (or Her) Majesty's Service **2** His (or Her) Majesty's Ship

HMSO (formerly, in Britain) *abbreviation for* His (or Her) Majesty's Stationery Office, now The Stationery Office (TSO)

hn *the internet domain name for* Honduras

HNC (in Britain) *abbreviation for* Higher National Certificate; a qualification recognized by many national technical and professional institutions

HND (in Britain) *abbreviation for* Higher National Diploma; a qualification in technical subjects equivalent to an ordinary degree

ho¹ (həʊ) *interj* **1** Also: **ho-ho** an imitation or representation of the sound of a deep laugh **2** an exclamation used to attract attention, announce a destination, etc: *what ho! land ho! westward ho!* [C13 of imitative origin; compare Old Norse *hó*, Old French *ho!* halt!]

ho² (həʊ) *n US Black slang* a derogatory term for a woman [C20 from Black or Southern US pronunciation of WHORE]

Ho *the chemical symbol for* holmium

HO *or* **H.O.** *abbreviation for* **1** head office **2** *Brit government* Home Office

ho. *abbreviation for* house

hoactzin (həʊˈæktsɪn) *n* a variant of **hoatzin**

hoar (hɔː) *n* **1** short for **hoarfrost** ▷ *adj* **2** *rare* covered with hoarfrost **3** *archaic* a poetic variant of **hoary** [Old English *hār*; related to Old Norse *hārr*, Old High German *hēr*, Old Slavonic *sěrŭ* grey]

hoard (hɔːd) *n* **1** an accumulated store hidden away for future use **2** a cache of ancient coins, treasure, etc ▷ *vb* **3** to gather or accumulate (a hoard) [Old English *hord*; related to Old Norse *hodd*, Gothic *huzd*, German *Hort*, Swedish *hydda* hut] ▷ **'hoarder** *n*

> **USAGE** *Hoard* is sometimes wrongly written where *horde* is meant: *hordes* (not *hoards*) *of tourists*

hoarding (ˈhɔːdɪŋ) *n* **1** a large board used for displaying advertising posters, as by a road. Also called (esp US and Canadian): billboard **2** a temporary wooden fence erected round a building or demolition site [C19 from C15 *hoard* fence, from Old French *hourd* palisade, of Germanic origin, related to Gothic *haurds*, Old Norse *hurth* door]

hoarfrost (ˈhɔːˌfrɒst) *n* a deposit of needle-like ice crystals formed on the ground by direct condensation at temperatures below freezing point. Also called: white frost

hoarhound (ˈhɔːˌhaʊnd) *n* a variant spelling of **horehound**

hoarse (hɔːs) *adj* **1** gratingly harsh or raucous in tone **2** low, harsh, and lacking in intensity: *a hoarse whisper* **3** having a husky voice, as through

illness, shouting, etc [C14 of Scandinavian origin; related to Old Norse *hās*, Old Saxon *hēs*] ▷ **'hoarsely** *adv* ▷ **'hoarseness** *n*

hoarsen (ˈhɔːsən) *vb* to make or become hoarse

hoary (ˈhɔːrɪ) *adj* **hoarier**, **hoariest** **1** having grey or white hair **2** white or whitish-grey in colour **3** ancient or venerable ▷ **'hoarily** *adv* ▷ **'hoariness** *n*

hoary cress *n* a perennial Mediterranean plant, *Cardaria* (or *Lepidium*) *draba*, with small white flowers: a widespread troublesome weed: family *Brassicaceae* (crucifers)

hoast (host) *Scot* ▷ *n* **1** a cough ▷ *vb* (*intr*) **2** to cough [from Old Norse]

hoatching (ˈhəʊtʃɪŋ) *adj Scot* infested; swarming: *this food's hoatching with flies* [of unknown origin]

hoatzin (həʊˈætsɪn) *or* **hoactzin** *n* a unique South American gallinaceous bird, *Opisthocomus hoazin*, with a brownish plumage, a very small crested head, and clawed wing digits in the young: family *Opisthocomidae* [C17 from American Spanish, from Nahuatl *uatzin* pheasant]

hoax (həʊks) *n* **1** a deception, esp a practical joke ▷ *vb* **2** to deceive or play a joke on (someone) [C18 probably from HOCUS] ▷ **'hoaxer** *n*

hob¹ (hɒb) *n* **1** the flat top part of a cooking stove, or a separate flat surface, containing hotplates or burners **2** a shelf beside an open fire, for keeping kettles, etc, hot **3** a steel pattern used in forming a mould or die in cold metal **4** a hard steel rotating cutting tool used in machines for cutting gears ▷ *vb* **hobs**, **hobbing**, **hobbed** **5** (*tr*) to cut or form with a hob [C16 variant of obsolete *hubbe*, of unknown origin; perhaps related to HUB]

hob² (hɒb) *n* **1** a hobgoblin or elf **2** **raise** *or* **play hob** *US informal* to cause mischief or disturbance **3** a male ferret [C14 variant of *Rob*, short for *Robin* or *Robert*] ▷ **'hob,like** *adj*

Hobart (ˈhəʊbɑːt) *n* a port in Australia, capital of the island state of Tasmania on the estuary of the Derwent: excellent natural harbour; University of Tasmania (1890). Pop: 126 048 (2001)

Hobbesian (ˈhɒbzɪən) *adj* of or relating to Thomas Hobbes, the English political philosopher (1588–1679)

Hobbism (ˈhɒbɪzəm) *n* the mechanistic political philosophy of Thomas Hobbes, the English political philosopher (1588–1679), which stresses the necessity for a powerful sovereign to control human beings ▷ **'Hobbist** *n*

hobbit (ˈhɒbɪt) *n* **1** one of an imaginary race of half-size people living in holes **2** a nickname used for a very small type of primitive human, *Homo floresiensis*, following the discovery of remains of eight such people on the Island of Flores, Indonesia, in 2004 [C20 coined by British writer J. R. R. Tolkien (1892–1973), with the meaning "hole-builder"] ▷ **'hobbitry** *n*

hobble (ˈhɒbəl) *vb* **1** (*intr*) to walk with a lame awkward movement **2** (*tr*) to fetter the legs of (a horse) in order to restrict movement **3** to progress unevenly or with difficulty **4** (*tr*) to hamper or restrict (the actions or scope of a person, organization, etc) ▷ *n* **5** a strap, rope, etc, used to hobble a horse **6** a limping gait **7** *Brit dialect* a difficult or embarrassing situation **8** a castrated ferret ▷ Also (for senses 2, 5): **hopple** [C14 probably from Low German; compare Flemish *hoppelen*, Middle Dutch *hobbelen* to stammer] ▷ **'hobbler** *n*

hobbledehoy (ˌhɒbəldɪˈhɔɪ) *n archaic* or *dialect* a clumsy or bad-mannered youth [C16 from earlier *hobbard de hoy*, of uncertain origin]

hobble skirt *n* a long skirt, popular between 1910 and 1914, cut so narrow at the ankles that it hindered walking

hobby¹ (ˈhɒbɪ) *n, pl* **-bies** **1** an activity pursued in spare time for pleasure or relaxation **2** *archaic or dialect* a small horse or pony **3** short for **hobbyhorse** (sense 1) **4** an early form of bicycle, without pedals [C14 *hobyn*, probably variant of proper name *Robin*; compare DOBBIN] ▷ **'hobbyist** *n*

hobby² (ˈhɒbɪ) *n, pl* **-bies** any of several small Old World falcons, esp the European *Falco subbuteo*,

formerly used in falconry [C15 from Old French *hobet*, from *hobe* falcon; probably related to Middle Dutch *hobbelen* to roll, turn]

hobby farmer *n* a person who runs a farm as a hobby rather than a means of making a living

hobbyhorse (ˈhɒbɪˌhɔːs) *n* **1** a toy consisting of a stick with a figure of a horse's head at one end **2** another word for **rocking horse** **3** a figure of a horse attached to a performer's waist in a pantomime, morris dance, etc **4** a favourite topic or obsessive fixed idea (esp in the phrase **on one's hobbyhorse**) ▷ *vb* **5** (*intr*) *nautical* (of a vessel) to pitch violently [C16 from HOBBY¹, originally a small horse, hence sense 3; then generalized to apply to any pastime]

hobday (ˈhɒbˌdeɪ) *vb* (*tr*) to alleviate (a breathing problem in certain horses) by the surgical operation of removing soft tissue ventricles to pull back the vocal fold [C20 named after F. T. *Hobday* (1869–1939), English veterinary surgeon, who devised the operation] ▷ **'hob,dayed** *adj*

hobgoblin (ˌhɒbˈɡɒblɪn) *n* **1** an evil or mischievous goblin **2** a bogey; bugbear [C16 from HOB² + GOBLIN]

hobnail (ˈhɒbˌneɪl) *n* **a** a short nail with a large head for protecting the soles of heavy footwear **b** (*as modifier*): *hobnail boots* [C16 from HOB¹ (in the archaic sense: peg) + NAIL] ▷ **'hob,nailed** *adj*

hobnob (ˈhɒbˌnɒb) *vb* **-nobs**, **-nobbing**, **-nobbed** (*intr; often foll by* with) **1** to socialize or talk informally **2** *obsolete* to drink (with) [C18 from *hob or nob* to drink to one another in turns, hence, to be familiar, ultimately from Old English *habban* to HAVE + *nabban* not to have]

hobo (ˈhəʊbəʊ) *n, pl* **-bos** *or* **-boes** *chiefly US and Canadian* **1** a tramp; vagrant **2** a migratory worker, esp an unskilled labourer [C19 (US): origin unknown] ▷ **'hoboism** *n*

Hoboken (ˈhəʊbəʊkən) *n* a city in N Belgium, in Antwerp province, on the River Scheldt. Pop: 33 476 (2002 est)

hobson-jobson (ˌhɒbsən'dʒɒbsən) *n* another word for **folk etymology** [C19 Anglo-Indian folk-etymological variant of Arabic *yā Hasan! yā Husayn!* O Hasan! O Husain! (ritual lament for the grandsons of Mohammed); influenced by the surnames *Hobson* and *Jobson*]

Hobson's choice (ˈhɒbsənz) *n* the choice of taking what is offered or nothing at all [C16 named after Thomas *Hobson* (1544–1631), English liveryman who gave his customers no choice but had them take the nearest horse]

Hochheimer (ˈhɒkˌhaɪmə; *German* ˈhoːxhaimər) *n* a German white wine from the area around Hochheim near Mainz. Also called: **Hochheim**

Ho Chi Minh City (ˈhəʊ ˈtʃiː ˈmɪn) *n* a port in S Vietnam, 97 km (60 miles) from the South China Sea, on the Saigon River: captured by the French in 1859; merged with adjoining Cholon in 1932; capital of the former Republic of Vietnam (South Vietnam) from 1954 to 1976; university (1917); US headquarters during the Vietnam War. Pop: 5 030 000 (2005 est). Former name (until 1976): Saigon

hochmagandy *or* **houghmagandie** (ˌhɒxməˈɡændɪ) *n Scot* a mainly jocular or literary word for **sexual intercourse** [of uncertain origin]

hock¹ (hɒk) *n* **1** the joint at the tarsus of a horse or similar animal, pointing backwards and corresponding to the human ankle **2** the corresponding joint in domestic fowl ▷ *vb* **3** another word for **hamstring** [C16 short for *hockshin*, from Old English *hōhsinu* heel sinew]

hock² (hɒk) *n* **1** any of several white wines from the German Rhine **2** (not in technical usage) any dry white wine [C17 short for obsolete *hockamore* HOCHHEIMER]

hock³ (hɒk) *informal, chiefly US and Canadian* ▷ *vb* **1** (*tr*) to pawn or pledge ▷ *n* **2** the state of being in pawn (esp in the phrase **in hock**) **3** **in hock** **a** in prison **b** in debt [C19 from Dutch *hok* prison, debt] ▷ **'hocker** *n*

h

775

hockey[1] ('hɒkɪ) *n* **1** Also called (esp US and Canadian): **field hockey a** a game played on a field by two opposing teams of 11 players each, who try to hit a ball into their opponents' goal using long sticks curved at the end **b** (*as modifier*): *hockey stick; hockey ball* **2** See **ice hockey** [C19 from earlier *hawkey*, of unknown origin]

hockey[2] ('hɒkɪ) *n East Anglian dialect* **a** the feast at harvest home; harvest supper **b** (*as modifier*): *the hockey cart.* Also: **hawkey, horkey** [C16 of unknown origin]

hockle ('hɒk°l) *vb* **hockles, hockled, hockling** (*intr*) *Northumbrian English dialect* to spit

Hocktide ('hɒk,taɪd) *n Brit history* a former festival celebrated on the second Monday and Tuesday after Easter [C15 from *hock-, hoke-* (of unknown origin) + TIDE[1]]

hocus ('həʊkəs) *vb* **-cuses, -cusing, -cused** *or* **-cuses, -cussing, -cussed** (*tr*) *now rare* **1** to take in; trick **2** to stupefy, esp with a drug **3** to add a drug to (a drink)

hocus-pocus ('həʊkəs'pəʊkəs) *n* **1** trickery or chicanery **2** mystifying jargon **3** an incantation used by conjurors or magicians when performing tricks **4** conjuring skill or practice ▷ *vb* **-cuses, -cusing, -cused** *or* **-cuses, -cussing, -cussed** **5** to deceive or trick (someone) [C17 perhaps a dog-Latin formation invented by jugglers]

hod (hɒd) *n* **1** an open metal or plastic box fitted with a handle, for carrying bricks, mortar, etc **2** a tall narrow coal scuttle [C14 perhaps alteration of C13 dialect *hot*, from Old French *hotte* pannier, creel, probably from Germanic]

hod carrier *n* a labourer who carries the materials in a hod for a plasterer, bricklayer, etc. Also called: **hodman**

hodden ('hɒd°n) *or* **hoddin** ('hɒdɪn) *n* a coarse homespun cloth produced in Scotland: **hodden grey** is made by mixing black and white wools [C18 Scottish, of obscure origin]

Hodeida (hɒ'deɪdə) *n* a port in N Yemen, on the Red Sea. Pop: 547 000 (2005 est)

Hodge (hɒdʒ) *n* a typical name for a farm labourer; rustic [C14 *hogge*, from familiar form of *Roger*]

hodgepodge ('hɒdʒ,pɒdʒ) *n US and Canadian* **1** a jumbled mixture **2** a thick soup or stew made from meat and vegetables. Also called (in Britain and certain other countries): **hotchpotch** [C15 variant of HOTCHPOT]

Hodgkin's disease ('hɒdʒkɪnz) *n* a malignant disease, a form of lymphoma, characterized by painless enlargement of the lymph nodes, spleen, and liver. Also called: **lymphoadenoma, lymphogranulomatosis** [C19 named after Thomas *Hodgkin* (1798–1866), London physician, who first described it]

hodman ('hɒdmən) *n, pl* **-men** *Brit* another name for **hod carrier**

hodograph ('hɒdə,grɑːf, -,græf) *n* a curve of which the radius vector represents the velocity of a moving particle [C19 from Greek *hodos* way + -GRAPH] ▷ ,hodo'graphic *adj*

hodometer (hɒ'dɒmɪtə) *n US* another name for **odometer**. ▷ ho'dometry *n*

hodoscope ('hɒdə,skəʊp) *n physics* any device for tracing the path of a charged particle, esp a particle found in cosmic rays [C20 from Greek *hodos* way, path + -SCOPE]

hoe (həʊ) *n* **1** any of several kinds of long-handled hand implement equipped with a light blade and used to till the soil, eradicate weeds, etc ▷ *vb* **hoes, hoeing, hoed 2** to dig, scrape, weed, or till (surface soil) with or as if with a hoe [C14 via Old French *houe* from Germanic: compare Old High German *houwā, houwan* to HEW, German *Haue* hoe] ▷ 'hoer *n* ▷ 'hoe,like *adj*

hoedown ('həʊ,daʊn) *n US and Canadian* **1** a boisterous square dance **2** a party at which hoedowns are danced

hoe in *vb* (*intr, adverb*) *Austral and NZ informal* to eat food heartily

hoe into *vb* (*intr, preposition*) *Austral and NZ informal* to eat (food) heartily

Hoek van Holland ('huːk fən 'hɒlɑnt) *n* the Dutch name for the **Hook of Holland**

Hofei ('həʊ'feɪ) *n* a variant transliteration of the Chinese name for **Hefei**

Hofuf (hʊ'fuːf) *n* another name for **Al Hufuf**

hog (hɒg) *n* **1** a domesticated pig, esp a castrated male weighing more than 102 kg **2** *US and Canadian* any artiodactyl mammal of the family *Suidae*; pig **3** Also: **hogg** *Brit dialect, Austral, and NZ* another name for **hogget 4** *informal* a selfish, greedy or slovenly person **5** *nautical* a stiff brush, for scraping a vessel's bottom **6** *nautical* the amount or extent to which a vessel is hogged. Compare **sag** (sense 6) **7** another word for **camber** (sense 4) **8** *slang, chiefly US* a large powerful motorcycle **9 go the whole hog** *informal* to do something thoroughly or unreservedly: *if you are redecorating one room, why not go the whole hog and paint the entire house?* **10 live high on the hog** *informal, chiefly US* to have an extravagant lifestyle ▷ *vb* **hogs, hogging, hogged** (*tr*) **11** *slang* to take more than one's share of **12** to arch (the back) like a hog **13** to cut (the mane) of (a horse) very short [Old English *hogg*, from Celtic; compare Cornish *hoch*] ▷ 'hogger *n* ▷ 'hog,like *adj*

hogan ('həʊgən) *n* a wooden dwelling covered with earth, typical of the Navaho Indians of N America [from Navaho]

Hogarthian (,həʊ'gɑːθɪən) *adj* reminiscent of the engravings of William Hogarth, the English engraver and painter (1697–1764), in which he satirized contemporary vices and affectations

hogback ('hɒg,bæk) *n* **1** Also called: **hog's back** a narrow ridge that consists of steeply inclined rock strata **2** *archaeol* a Saxon or Scandinavian tomb with sloping sides

hog badger *n* a SE Asian badger, *Arctonyx collaris,* with a piglike mobile snout. Also called: **sand badger**

hog cholera *n* the US term for **swine fever**

hogfish ('hɒg,fɪʃ) *n, pl* **-fish** *or* **-fishes 1** a wrasse, *Lachnolaimus maximus,* that occurs in the Atlantic off the SE coast of North America. The head of the male resembles a pig's snout **2** another name for **pigfish** (sense 1)

hogg (hɒg) *n* **1** an uncastrated male pig **2** a sheep of either sex aged between birth and second shearing

hogged (hɒgd) *adj nautical* (of a vessel) having a keel that droops at both ends. Compare **sag** (sense 6)

hogget ('hɒgɪt) *n Brit dialect, Austral, and NZ* **1** a sheep up to the age of one year that has yet to be sheared **2** the meat of this sheep

hoggin ('hɒgɪn) *or* **hogging** ('hɒgɪŋ) *n* a finely sifted gravel containing enough clay binder for it to be used in its natural form for making paths or roads [C19 perhaps the same as *hogging* from HOG in the sense of arching the back, from the shape given to a road to facilitate drainage]

hogging moment *n* a bending moment that produces convex bending at the supports of a continuously supported beam. Also called: **negative bending moment**

hoggish ('hɒgɪʃ) *adj* selfish, gluttonous, or dirty ▷ 'hoggishly *adv* ▷ 'hoggishness *n*

Hogmanay (,hɒgmə'neɪ) *n* (*sometimes not capital*) **a** New Year's Eve in Scotland **b** (*as modifier*): *a Hogmanay party.* See also **first-foot** [C17 Scottish and Northern English, perhaps from Norman French *hoguinane,* from Old French *aguillanneuf* the last day of the year; also, a New Year's eve gift]

hognose skunk ('hɒg,nəʊz) *n* any of several American skunks of the genus *Conepatus,* esp *C. leuconotus,* having a broad snoutlike nose

hognose snake ('hɒg,nəʊz) *n* any North American nonvenomous colubrid snake of the genus *Heterodon,* having a trowel-shaped snout and inflating the body when alarmed. Also called: **puff adder**

hognut ('hɒg,nʌt) *n* another name for **pignut**

hog peanut *n* a North American leguminous climbing plant, *Amphicarpa bracteata,* having fleshy curved one-seeded pods, which ripen in or on the ground

hog's fennel *n* any of several Eurasian umbelliferous marsh plants of the genus *Peucedanum,* esp *P. officinale,* having clusters of small whitish flowers

hogshead ('hɒgz,hed) *n* **1** a unit of capacity, used esp for alcoholic beverages. It has several values, being 54 imperial gallons in the case of beer and 52.5 imperial gallons in the case of wine **2** a large cask used for shipment of wines and spirits [C14 of obscure origin]

hogtie ('hɒg,taɪ) *vb* **-ties, -tying, -tied** (*tr*) *chiefly US* **1** to tie together the legs or the arms and legs of **2** to impede, hamper, or thwart

Hogtown ('hɒg,taʊn) *n Canadian* a slang name for **Toronto**

Hogue (French ɔg) *n* See **La Hogue**

hogwash ('hɒg,wɒʃ) *n* **1** nonsense **2** pigswill

hogweed ('hɒg,wiːd) *n* any of several coarse weedy umbelliferous plants, esp cow parsnip. See also **giant hogweed**

hoha ('hɒhɑː) *adj NZ* bored or annoyed [Māori]

Hohenlinden (German hoːən'lɪndən) *n* a village in S Germany, in Bavaria east of Munich: scene of the defeat of the Austrians by the French during the Napoleonic Wars (1800)

Hohhot ('hɒ'hɒt), **Huhehot** *or* **Hu-ho-hao-t'e** *n* a city in N China, capital of Inner Mongolia Autonomous Region (since 1954); previously capital of the former Suiyüan province; Inner Mongolia University (1957). Pop: 998 000 (2005 est)

ho-hum ('həʊ'hʌm) *adj informal* lacking interest or inspiration; dull; mediocre: *a ho-hum album*

hoick (hɔɪk) *vb* **1** *informal* to rise or raise abruptly and sharply: *She hoicked her dress above her knees* **2** *NZ informal* to clear the throat and spit [C20 perhaps a variant of *hike*]

hoicks (hɔɪks) *interj* a cry used to encourage hounds to hunt. Also: **yoicks**

hoiden ('hɔɪd°n) *n* a variant spelling of **hoyden** ▷ 'hoidenish *adj* ▷ 'hoidenishness *n*

hoi polloi (,hɔɪ pə'lɔɪ) *pl n often derogatory* the masses; common people [Greek, literally: the many]

hoisin (,hɔɪ'sɪn) *n* (in Chinese cookery) a sweet spicy reddish-brown sauce made from soya beans, sugar, vinegar, and garlic. Also called: **Peking sauce** [C20 from Cantonese]

hoist (hɔɪst) *vb* **1** (*tr*) to raise or lift up, esp by mechanical means **2 hoist with one's own petard** See **petard** (sense 2) ▷ *n* **3** any apparatus or device for hoisting **4** the act of hoisting **5** See **rotary clothesline 6** *nautical* **a** the amidships height of a sail bent to the yard with which it is hoisted. Compare **drop** (sense 15) **b** the difference between the set and lowered positions of this yard **7** *nautical* the length of the luff of a fore-and-aft sail **8** *nautical* a group of signal flags **9** the inner edge of a flag next to the staff. Compare **fly**[1] (sense 25) [C16 variant of *hoise,* probably from Low German; compare Dutch *hijschen,* German *hissen*] ▷ 'hoister *n*

hoity-toity (,hɔɪtɪ'tɔɪtɪ) *adj informal* arrogant or haughty: *we have had enough of her hoity-toity manner* [C17 rhyming compound based on C16 *hoit* to romp, of obscure origin]

hoka ('hɒkɑː) *n, pl* **hoka** *NZ* another name for **red cod** [Māori]

hoke (həʊk) *vb* (*tr; usually foll by up*) to overplay (a part, etc) [C20 perhaps from HOKUM]

hokey ('həʊkɪ) *adj slang, chiefly US and Canadian* **1** corny; sentimental **2** contrived; phoney [C20 from HOKUM]

hokey cokey ('həʊkɪ 'kəʊkɪ) *n* a Cockney song with a traditional dance routine to match the words

hokey-pokey (,həʊkɪ'pəʊkɪ) *n* **1** another word for **hocus-pocus** (senses 1, 2) **2** *NZ* a brittle toffee sold in lumps

hoki ('hɒkiː) *n, pl* **hoki** an edible saltwater fish, *Macruronus novaezeelandiae*, of southern New Zealand waters [Māori]
Hokkaido (hɒ'kaɪdəʊ) *n* the second largest and northernmost of the four main islands of Japan, separated from Honshu by the Tsugaru Strait and from the island of Sakhalin, Russia, by La Pérouse Strait: constitutes an autonomous administrative division. Capital: Sapporo. Pop: 5 670 000 (2002 est). Area: 78 508 sq km (30 312 sq miles)
hokku ('hɒkuː) *n, pl* **-ku** *prosody* another word for **haiku** [from Japanese, from *hok* beginning + *ku* hemistich]
hokonui (həʊkə'nuːiː) *n NZ obsolete* illicit whisky [from *Hokonui*, district of Southland region, NZ]
hokum ('həʊkəm) *n slang* **1** claptrap; bunk **2** obvious or hackneyed material of a sentimental nature in a play, film, etc [c20 probably a blend of HOCUS-POCUS and BUNKUM]
hol- *combining form* a variant of **holo-** before a vowel
holarchy ('həʊl,ɑːkɪ) N a system composed of interacting holons [c20 from HOLO- + -ARCHY]
Holarctic (həʊ'lɑːktɪk) *adj* of or denoting a zoogeographical region consisting of the Palaearctic and Nearctic regions [c19 from HOLO- + ARCTIC]
hold¹ (həʊld) *vb* **holds, holding, held** (hɛld) **1** to have or keep (an object) with or within the hands, arms, etc; clasp **2** (*tr*) to support or bear: *to hold a drowning man's head above water* **3** to maintain or be maintained in a specified state or condition: *to hold one's emotions in check; hold firm* **4** (*tr*) to set aside or reserve: *they will hold our tickets until tomorrow* **5** (when *intr, usually used in commands*) to restrain or be restrained from motion, action, departure, etc: *hold that man until the police come* **6** (*intr*) to remain fast or unbroken: *that cable won't hold much longer* **7** (*intr*) (of the weather) to remain dry and bright: *how long will the weather hold?* **8** (*tr*) to keep the attention of: *her singing held the audience* **9** (*tr*) to engage in or carry on: *to hold a meeting* **10** (*tr*) to have the ownership, possession, etc, of: *he holds a law degree from London; who's holding the ace of spades?* **11** (*tr*) to have the use of or responsibility for: *to hold the office of director* **12** (*tr*) to have the space or capacity for: *the carton will hold only eight books* **13** (*tr*) to be able to control the outward effects of drinking beer, spirits, etc: *he can hold his drink well* **14** (often foll by *to* or *by*) to remain or cause to remain committed to: *hold him to his promise; he held by his views in spite of opposition* **15** (*tr; takes a clause as object*) to claim: *he holds that the theory is incorrect* **16** (*intr*) to remain relevant, valid, or true: *the old philosophies don't hold nowadays* **17** (*tr*) to keep in the mind: *to hold affection for someone* **18** (*tr*) to regard or consider in a specified manner: *I hold him very dear* **19** (*tr*) to guard or defend successfully: *hold the fort against the attack* **20** (*intr*) to continue to go: *hold on one's way* **21** (sometimes foll by *on*) *music* to sustain the sound of (a note) throughout its specified duration: *to hold on a semibreve for its full value* **22** (*tr*) *computing* to retain (data) in a storage device after copying onto another storage device or onto another location in the same device. Compare **clear** (sense 49) **23** (*tr*) to be in possession of illegal drugs **24** **hold (good) for** to apply or be relevant to: *the same rules hold for everyone* **25** **holding thumbs** *South African* holding the thumb of one hand with the other, in the hope of bringing good luck **26** **hold it!** **a** stop! wait! **b** stay in the same position! as when being photographed **27** **hold one's head high** to conduct oneself in a proud and confident manner **28** **hold one's own** to maintain one's situation or position esp in spite of opposition or difficulty **29** **hold one's peace** *or* **tongue** to keep silent **30** **hold water** to prove credible, logical, or consistent **31** **there is no holding him** he is so spirited or resolute that he cannot be restrained ▷ *n* **32** the act or method of holding fast or grasping, as with the hands **33** something to hold onto, as for support or control **34** an object or device that holds fast or grips something else so as to hold it fast **35** controlling force or influence: *she has a hold on him* **36** a short delay or pause **37** **on hold** in a state of temporary postponement or delay **38** a prison or a cell in a prison **39** *wrestling* a way of seizing one's opponent: *a wrist hold* **40** *music* a pause or fermata **41** **a** a tenure or holding, esp of land **b** (*in combination*): *leasehold; freehold; copyhold* **42** a container **43** *archaic* a fortified place **44** **get hold of** **a** to obtain **b** to come into contact with **45** **no holds barred** all limitations removed ▷ See also **hold back, hold down, hold forth, hold in, hold off, hold on, hold out, hold over, hold together, hold-up, hold with** [Old English *healdan*; related to Old Norse *halla*, Gothic *haldan*, German *halten*] > 'holdable *adj*
hold² (həʊld) *n* the space in a ship or aircraft for storing cargo [c16 variant of HOLE]
holdall ('həʊld,ɔːl) *n Brit* a large strong bag with handles. Usual US and Canadian name: **carryall**
hold back *vb* (*adverb*) **1** to restrain or be restrained **2** (*tr*) to withhold: *he held back part of the payment* ▷ *n* **holdback** **3** a strap of the harness joining the breeching to the shaft, so that the horse can hold back the vehicle **4** something that restrains or hinders
hold down *vb* (*tr, adverb*) **1** to restrain or control **2** *informal* to manage to retain or keep possession of
holden ('həʊldən) *vb archaic or dialect* a past participle of **hold¹**
holder ('həʊldə) *n* **1** a person or thing that holds **2** **a** a person, such as an owner, who has possession or control of something **b** (*in combination*): *householder* **3** *law* a person who has possession of a bill of exchange, cheque, or promissory note that he is legally entitled to enforce > 'holder,ship *n*
holdfast ('həʊld,fɑːst) *n* **1** **a** the act of gripping strongly **b** such a grip **2** any device used to secure an object, such as a hook, clamp, etc **3** the organ of attachment of a seaweed or related plant
hold forth *vb* (*adverb*) **1** (*intr*) to speak for a long time or in public **2** (*tr*) to offer (an attraction or enticement)
hold in *vb* (*tr, adverb*) **1** to curb, control, or keep in check **2** to conceal or restrain (feelings)
holding ('həʊldɪŋ) *n* **1** land held under a lease and used for agriculture or similar purposes **2** (*often plural*) property to which the holder has legal title, such as land, stocks, shares, and other investments **3** *sport* the obstruction of an opponent with the hands or arms, esp in boxing ▷ *adj* **4** *Austral informal* in funds; having money
holding company *n* a company with controlling shareholdings in one or more other companies
holding operation *n* a plan or procedure devised to prolong the existing situation
holding paddock *n Austral and NZ* a paddock in which cattle or sheep are kept temporarily, as before shearing, etc
holding pattern *n* the oval or circular path of an aircraft flying around an airport awaiting permission to land
hold off *vb* (*adverb*) **1** (*tr*) to keep apart or at a distance **2** (*intr; often foll by from*) to refrain (from doing something): *he held off buying the house until prices fell slightly*
hold on *vb* (*intr, adverb*) **1** to maintain a firm grasp: *she held on with all her strength* **2** to continue or persist **3** (foll by *to*) to keep or retain: *hold on to those stamps as they'll soon be valuable* **4** to keep a telephone line open ▷ *interj* **5** *informal* stop! wait!
hold out *vb* (*adverb*) **1** (*tr*) to offer or present **2** (*intr*) to last or endure **3** (*intr*) to continue to resist or stand firm, as a city under siege or a person refusing to succumb to persuasion **4** *chiefly US* to withhold (something due or expected) **5** **hold out for** to wait patiently or uncompromisingly for (the fulfilment of one's demands) **6** **hold out on** *informal* to delay in or keep from telling (a person) some new or important information ▷ *n* **holdout** *US* **7** a person, country, organization, etc, that continues to resist or refuses to change: *Honecker was one of the staunchest holdouts against reform* **8** a person, country, organization, etc, that declines to cooperate or participate: *they remain the only holdouts to signing the accord*
hold over *vb* (*tr, mainly adverb*) **1** to defer consideration of or action on **2** to postpone for a further period **3** to prolong (a note, chord, etc) from one bar to the next **4** (*preposition*) to intimidate (a person) with (a threat) ▷ *n* **holdover** *US and Canadian informal* **5** an elected official who continues in office after his term has expired **6** a performer or performance continuing beyond the original engagement
hold together *vb* (*adverb*) **1** to cohere or remain or cause to cohere or remain in one piece: *your old coat holds together very well* **2** to stay or cause to stay united: *the children held the family together*
hold-up *n* **1** a robbery, esp an armed one **2** a delay; stoppage **3** *US* an excessive charge; extortion **4** (*usually plural*) a stocking that is held up by an elasticated top without suspenders ▷ *vb* **hold up** (*adverb*) **5** (*tr*) to delay; hinder: *we were held up by traffic* **6** (*tr*) to keep from falling; support **7** (*tr*) to stop forcibly or waylay in order to rob, esp using a weapon **8** (*tr*) to exhibit or present: *he held up his achievements for our admiration* **9** (*intr*) to survive or last: *how are your shoes holding up?* **10** *bridge* to refrain from playing a high card, so delaying the establishment of (a suit) **11** **hold up one's hands** to confess a mistake or misdeed
hold with *vb* (*intr, preposition*) to support; approve of
hole (həʊl) *n* **1** an area hollowed out in a solid **2** an opening made in or through something **3** an animal's hiding place or burrow **4** *informal* an unattractive place, such as a town or a dwelling **5** *informal* a cell or dungeon **6** *US informal* a small anchorage **7** a fault (esp in the phrase **pick holes in**) **8** *slang* a difficult and embarrassing situation **9** the cavity in various games into which the ball must be thrust **10** (on a golf course) **a** the cup on each of the greens **b** each of the divisions of a course (usually 18) represented by the distance between the tee and a green **c** the score made in striking the ball from the tee into the hole **11** *physics* **a** a vacancy in a nearly full band of quantum states of electrons in a semiconductor or an insulator. Under the action of an electric field holes behave as carriers of positive charge **b** (*as modifier*): *hole current* **c** a vacancy in the nearly full continuum of quantum states of negative energy of fermions. A hole appears as the antiparticle of the fermion **12** **in holes** so worn as to be full of holes: *his socks were in holes* **13** **in the hole** *chiefly US* **a** in debt **b** (of a card, the **hole card**, in stud poker) dealt face down in the first round **14** **make a hole in** to consume or use a great amount of (food, drink, money, etc): *to make a hole in a bottle of brandy* ▷ *vb* **15** to make a hole or holes in (something) **16** (when *intr*, often foll by *out*) *golf* to hit (the ball) into the hole [Old English *hol*; related to Gothic *hulundi*, German *Höhle*, Old Norse *hylr* pool, Latin *caulis* hollow stem; see HOLLOW]
hole-and-corner *adj* (*usually prenominal*) *informal* furtive or secretive
hole in one *golf* ▷ *n* **1** a shot from the tee that finishes in the hole ▷ *vb* **2** (*intr*) to score a hole in one ▷ Also (esp US): **ace**
hole in the heart *n* **a** a defect of the heart in which there is an abnormal opening in any of the walls dividing the four heart chambers **b** (*as modifier*): *a hole-in-the-heart operation*
hole in the wall *n informal* **1** *chiefly Brit* another name for **cash dispenser** **2** a small dingy place, esp one difficult to find
hole up *vb* (*intr, adverb*) **1** (of an animal) to hibernate, esp in a cave **2** *informal* to hide or remain secluded
holey ('həʊlɪ) *adj* **holeyer, holeyest** full of holes
Holguín (*Spanish* ɔl'ɣin) *n* a city in NE Cuba, in Holguín province: trading centre. Pop: 278 000 (2005 est)

h

Holi ('hɒˌliː) *n* a Hindu spring festival, celebrated for two to five days, commemorating Krishna's dalliance with the cowgirls. Bonfires are lit and coloured powder and water thrown over celebrants [named after *Holika*, legendary female demon]

-holic *suffix forming nouns* indicating a person having an abnormal desire for or dependence on: *workaholic; chocoholic* [C20 on the pattern of *alcoholic*]

holiday ('hɒlɪˌdeɪ, -dɪ) *n* **1** (*often plural*) *chiefly Brit* **a** a period in which a break is taken from work or studies for rest, travel, or recreation. US and Canadian word is (*as modifier*): *a holiday mood* **2** a day on which work is suspended by law or custom, such as a religious festival, bank holiday, etc. Related adj: **ferial** ▷ *vb* **3** (*intr*) *chiefly Brit* to spend a holiday [Old English *hāligdæg*, literally: holy day]

holiday camp *n Brit* a place, esp one at the seaside, providing accommodation, recreational facilities, etc, for holiday-makers

holiday-maker *n Brit* a person who goes on holiday. US and Canadian equivalents: **vacationer, vacationist**

holily ('həʊlɪlɪ) *adv* in a holy, devout, or sacred manner

holiness ('həʊlɪnɪs) *n* the state or quality of being holy

Holiness ('həʊlɪnɪs) *n* (*preceded by his or your*) a title once given to all bishops, but now reserved for the pope

holism ('həʊlɪzəm) *n* **1** any doctrine that a system may have properties over and above those of its parts and their organization **2** the treatment of any subject as a whole integrated system, esp in medicine, the consideration of the complete person, physically and psychologically, in the treatment of a disease. See also **alternative medicine 3** *philosophy* one of a number of methodological theses holding that the significance of the parts can only be understood in terms of their contribution to the significance of the whole and that the latter must therefore be epistemologically prior. Compare **reductionism, atomism** (sense 2) [C20 from HOLO- + -ISM]

holistic (həʊˈlɪstɪk) *adj* **1** of or relating to a doctrine of holism **2** of or relating to the the medical consideration of the complete person, physically and psychologically, in the treatment of a disease ▷ **ho'listically** *adv*

Holkar State (hɒlˈkɑː) *n* a former state of central India, ruled by the Holkar dynasty of Maratha rulers of Indore (18th century until 1947)

Holkham Hall ('həʊkəm, 'hɒlkəm) *n* a Palladian mansion near Wells in Norfolk: built 1734–59 by William Kent for Thomas Coke

holland ('hɒlənd) *n* a coarse linen cloth, used esp for furnishing [C15 after HOLLAND, where it was made]

Holland ('hɒlənd) *n* **1** another name for the **Netherlands 2** a county of the Holy Roman Empire, corresponding to the present-day North and South Holland provinces of the Netherlands **3 Parts of** an area in E England constituting a former administrative division of Lincolnshire

hollandaise sauce (ˌhɒlənˈdeɪz, 'hɒlənˌdeɪz) *n* a rich sauce of egg yolks, butter, vinegar, etc, served esp with fish [C19 from French *sauce hollandaise* Dutch sauce]

Hollander ('hɒləndə) *n* another name for a **Dutchman**

Hollandia (hɒˈlændɪə) *n* a former name of **Jayapura**

Hollands ('hɒləndz) *n* Dutch gin, often sold in stone bottles [C18 from Dutch *hollandsch genever*]

holler ('hɒlə) *informal* ▷ *vb* **1** to shout or yell (something) ▷ *n* **2** a shout; call [variant of C16 *hollow*, from *holla*, from French *holà* stop! (literally: ho there!)]

hollo ('hɒləʊ), **holla** ('hɒlə) *or* **holloa** (hə'ləʊ) *n, pl* **-los, -las** *or* **-loas** (-'ləʊz) ▷ *interj* **1** a cry for attention, or of encouragement ▷ *vb* **2** (*intr*) to

shout [C16 from French *holà* ho there!]

hollow ('hɒləʊ) *adj* **1** having a hole, cavity, or space within; not solid **2** having a sunken area; concave **3** recessed or deeply set: *hollow cheeks* **4** (of sounds) as if resounding in a hollow place **5** without substance or validity **6** hungry or empty **7** insincere; cynical **8** **a hollow leg** *or* **hollow legs** the capacity to eat or drink a lot without ill effects ▷ *adv* **9 beat (someone) hollow** *Brit informal* to defeat (someone) thoroughly and convincingly ▷ *n* **10** a cavity, opening, or space in or within something **11** a depression or dip in the land ▷ *vb* (*often foll by out*, usually when *tr*) **12** to make or become hollow **13** to form (a hole, cavity, etc) or (of a hole, etc) to be formed [C12 from *holu*, inflected form of Old English *holh* cave; related to Old Norse *holr*, German *hohl*; see HOLE] ▷ **'hollowly** *adv* ▷ **'hollowness** *n*

hollow-back *n pathol* the nontechnical name for **lordosis** Compare **hunchback**

hollow-eyed *adj* with the eyes appearing to be sunk into the face, as from excessive fatigue

hollowware ('hɒləʊˌwɛə) *n* hollow articles made of metal, china, etc, such as pots, jugs, and kettles. Compare **flatware** (sense 2)

holly ('hɒlɪ) *n, pl* **-lies 1** any tree or shrub of the genus *Ilex*, such as the Eurasian *I. aquifolium*, having bright red berries and shiny evergreen leaves with prickly edges **2** branches of any of these trees, used for Christmas decorations **3 holly oak** another name for **holm oak** ▷ See also **sea holly** [Old English *holegn*; related to Old Norse *hulfr*, Old High German *hulis*, German *Hulst*, Old Slavonic *kolja* prick]

hollyhock ('hɒlɪˌhɒk) *n* a tall widely cultivated malvaceous plant, *Althaea rosea*, with stout hairy stems and spikes of white, yellow, red, or purple flowers. Also called (US): **rose mallow** [C16 from HOLY + *hock*, from Old English *hoc* mallow]

Hollywood ('hɒlɪˌwʊd) *n* **1** a NW suburb of Los Angeles, California: centre of the American film industry. Pop: 250 000 (latest est) **2 a** the American film industry **b** (*as modifier*): *a Hollywood star*

holm[1] (həʊm) *n dialect, chiefly Northwestern English* **1** an island in a river, lake, or estuary **2** low flat land near a river [Old English *holm* sea, island; related to Old Saxon *holm* hill, Old Norse *holmr* island, Latin *culmen* tip]

holm[2] (həʊm) *n* **1** short for **holm oak 2** *chiefly Brit* a dialect word for **holly** [C14 variant of obsolete *holin*, from Old English *holegn* HOLLY]

holmic ('hɒlmɪk) *adj* of or containing holmium

holmium ('hɒlmɪəm) *n* a malleable silver-white metallic element of the lanthanide series. Symbol: Ho; atomic no.: 67; atomic wt.: 164.93032; valency: 3; relative density: 8.795; melting pt.: 1474°C; boiling pt.: 2700°C [C19 from New Latin *Holmia* Stockholm]

holm oak *n* an evergreen Mediterranean oak tree, *Quercus ilex*, widely planted for ornament: the leaves are holly-like when young but become smooth-edged with age. Also called: **holm, holly oak, ilex**

holo- *or before a vowel* **hol-** *combining form* whole or wholly: *holograph; holotype; Holarctic* [from Greek *holos*]

holobenthic (ˌhɒləˈbɛnθɪk) *adj* (of an animal) completing its life cycle in the ocean depths

holoblastic (ˌhɒləˈblæstɪk) *adj embryol* of or showing cleavage of the entire zygote into blastomeres, as in eggs with little yolk. Compare **meroblastic**. ▷ ˌholo'blastically *adv*

Holocaine ('hɒləˌkeɪn) *n* a trademark for **phenacaine**

holocaust ('hɒləˌkɔːst) *n* **1** great destruction or loss of life or the source of such destruction, esp fire **2** (*usually capital*) **the** Also called: **Churban, Shoah**. the mass murder by the Nazis of the Jews of continental Europe between 1940 and 1945 **3** a rare word for **burnt offering** [C13 from Late Latin *holocaustum* whole burnt offering, from Greek

holokauston, from HOLO- + *kaustos*, from *kaiein* to burn] ▷ ˌholo'caustal *or* ˌholo'caustic *adj*

Holocene ('hɒləˌsiːn) *adj* **1** of, denoting, or formed in the second and most recent epoch of the Quaternary period, which began 10 000 years ago at the end of the Pleistocene ▷ *n* **2 the** the Holocene epoch or rock series ▷ Also: **Recent**

holocrine ('hɒləkrɪn) *adj* (of the secretion of glands) characterized by disintegration of the entire glandular cell in releasing its product, as in sebaceous glands. Compare **merocrine, apocrine** [C20 from HOLO- + Greek *krinein* to separate, decide]

holocrystalline (ˌhɒləˈkrɪstəˌlaɪn) *adj* (of igneous rocks) having only crystalline components and no glass. Compare **hemicrystalline**

holoenzyme (ˌhɒləʊˈɛnzaɪm) *n* an active enzyme consisting of a protein component (apoenzyme) and its coenzyme

Holofernes (ˌhɒləˈfɜːniːz, həˈlɒfəˌniːz) *n* the Assyrian general, who was killed by the biblical heroine Judith

hologram ('hɒləˌgræm) *n* a photographic record produced by illuminating the object with coherent light (as from a laser) and, without using lenses, exposing a film to light reflected from this object and to a direct beam of coherent light. When interference patterns on the film are illuminated by the coherent light a three-dimensional image is produced

holograph ('hɒləˌgræf, -ˌgrɑːf) *n* **a** a book or document handwritten by its author; original manuscript; autograph **b** (*as modifier*): *a holograph document*

holographic (ˌhɒləˈgræfɪk) *adj* of, relating to, or produced using holograms; three-dimensional ▷ ˌholo'graphically *adv*

holography (hɒˈlɒgrəfɪ) *n* the science or practice of producing holograms

holohedral (ˌhɒləˈhiːdrəl) *adj* (of a crystal) exhibiting all the planes required for the symmetry of the crystal system ▷ ˌholo'hedrism *n*

holomorphic (ˌhɒləˈmɔːfɪk) *adj maths* another word for **analytic** (sense 5)

holon ('həʊlən) *N* an autonomous self-reliant unit, esp in manufacturing [C20 from HOLO- + -ON] ▷ ho'Ionic *adj*

holophrastic (ˌhɒləˈfræstɪk) *adj* **1** denoting the stage in a child's acquisition of syntax when most utterances are single words **2** (of languages) tending to express in one word what would be expressed in several words in other languages; polysynthetic [C19 from HOLO- + Greek *phrastikos* expressive, from *phrazein* to express]

holophytic (ˌhɒləˈfɪtɪk) *adj* (of plants) capable of synthesizing their food from inorganic molecules, esp by photosynthesis ▷ **holophyte** ('hɒləˌfaɪt) *n*

holoplankton (ˌhɒləˈplæŋktən) *n* organisms, such as diatoms and algae, that spend all stages of their life cycle as plankton. Compare **meroplankton**

holothurian (ˌhɒləˈθjʊərɪən) *n* **1** any echinoderm of the class *Holothuroidea*, including the sea cucumbers, having a leathery elongated body with a ring of tentacles around the mouth ▷ *adj* **2** of, relating to, or belonging to the *Holothuroidea* [C19 from New Latin *Holothūria* name of type genus, from Latin: water polyp, from Greek *holothourion*, of obscure origin]

holotype ('hɒləˌtaɪp) *n biology* another name for **type specimen**. ▷ **holotypic** (ˌhɒləˈtɪpɪk) *adj*

holozoic (ˌhɒləˈzəʊɪk) *adj* (of animals) obtaining nourishment by feeding on plants or other animals

holp (həʊlp) *vb archaic or dialect* a past tense of **help**

holpen ('həʊlpən) *vb archaic* a past participle of **help**

hols (hɒlz) *pl n Brit school slang* holidays

Holstein[1] ('həʊlstaɪn) *n* the usual US and Canadian name for **Friesian** (the cattle)

Holstein[2] (*German* 'hɔlʃtaɪn) *n* a region of N Germany, in S Schleswig-Holstein: in early times a German duchy of Saxony; became a duchy of

Denmark in 1474; finally incorporated into Prussia in 1866

holster ('həʊlstə) *n* **1** a sheathlike leather case for a pistol, attached to a belt or saddle **2** *mountaineering* a similar case for an ice axe or piton hammer [c17 via Dutch *holster* from Germanic; compare Old Norse *hulstr* sheath, Old English *heolstor* darkness, Gothic *hulistr* cover]
▷ ˈholstered *adj*

holt¹ ('həʊlt) *n archaic or poetic* a wood or wooded hill [Old English *holt;* related to Old Norse *holt,* Old High German *holz,* Old Slavonic *kladŭ* log, Greek *klados* twig]

holt² (həʊlt) *n* the burrowed lair of an animal, esp an otter [c16 a phonetic variant of HOLD²]

holus-bolus ('həʊləsˈbəʊləs) *adv informal* all at once [c19 pseudo-Latin based on *whole bolus;* see BOLUS]

holy ('həʊlɪ) *adj* holier, holiest **1** of, relating to, or associated with God or a deity; sacred **2** endowed or invested with extreme purity or sublimity **3** devout, godly, or virtuous **4** holier-than-thou offensively sanctimonious or self-righteous: *a holier-than-thou attitude* **5** holy terror **a** a difficult or frightening person **b** *Irish informal* a person who is an active gambler, womanizer, etc ▷ *n, pl* -lies **6 a** a sacred place **b** the holy *(functioning as plural)* persons or things invested with holiness [Old English *hālig, hǣlig;* related to Old Saxon *hēlag,* Gothic *hailags,* German *heilig;* see HALLOW]

Holy Alliance *n* **1** a document advocating government according to Christian principles that was signed in 1815 by the rulers of Russia, Prussia, and Austria **2** the informal alliance that resulted from this agreement

Holy Bible *n* another name for the **Bible**

Holy City *n* the **1** Jerusalem, esp when regarded as the focal point of the religions of Judaism, Christianity, or Islam **2** *Christianity* heaven regarded as the perfect counterpart of Jerusalem **3** any city regarded as especially sacred by a particular religion

Holy Communion *n* **1** the celebration of the Eucharist **2** the consecrated elements of the Eucharist ▷ Often shortened to: Communion

holy day *n* a day on which a religious festival is observed

holy day of obligation *n* a major feastday of the Roman Catholic Church on which Catholics are bound to attend Mass and refrain from servile work

Holy Family *n* the *Christianity* the infant Jesus, Mary, and St Joseph

Holy Father *n RC Church* a title of the pope

Holy Ghost *n* another name for the **Holy Spirit**

Holy Grail *n* **1 a** Also called: Grail, Sangraal (in medieval legend) the bowl used by Jesus at the Last Supper. It was allegedly brought to Britain by Joseph of Arimathea, where it became the quest of many knights **b** (in modern spirituality) a symbol of the spiritual wholeness that leads a person to union with the divine **2** *informal* any desired ambition or goal: *the Holy Grail of infrared astronomy* [c14 *grail* from Old French *graal,* from Medieval Latin *gradālis* bowl, of unknown origin]

Holyhead ('hɒlɪˌhed) *n* a town in NW Wales, in Anglesey, the chief town of Holy Island: a port on the N coast. Pop: 11 237 (2001)

Holy Hour *n* **1** *RC Church* an hour set aside for prayer and reflection **2** *(not capitals) Irish informal* a period during the afternoon when public houses are obliged to close by law

Holy Innocents' Day *n* Dec 28, a day commemorating the massacre of male children at Bethlehem by Herod's order (Matthew 2:16); Childermas

Holy Island *n* **1** an island off the NE coast of Northumberland, linked to the mainland by road but accessible only at low water: site of a monastery founded by St Aidan in 635. Also called: Lindisfarne **2** an island off the NW coast of Anglesey. Area: about 62 sq km (24 sq miles)

Holy Joe *n informal* **1** a minister or chaplain **2** any sanctimonious or self-righteous person

Holy Land *n* the another name for **Palestine** (sense 1)

holy Mary *n Irish* a pietistic person: *he's a real holy Mary*

Holy Office *n RC Church* a congregation established in 1542 as the final court of appeal in heresy trials; it now deals with matters of doctrine

holy of holies *n* **1** any place of special sanctity **2** *(capitals)* the innermost compartment of the Jewish tabernacle, and later of the Temple, where the Ark was enshrined

holy orders *pl n* **1** the sacrament or rite whereby a person is admitted to the Christian ministry **2** the grades of the Christian ministry **3** the rank or status of an ordained Christian minister ▷ See also **orders**

holy place *n* **1** the outer chamber of a Jewish sanctuary **2** a place of pilgrimage

Holy Roller *n derogatory* a member of a sect that expresses religious fervour in an ecstatic or frenzied way

Holy Roman Empire *n* the complex of European territories under the rule of the Frankish or German king who bore the title of Roman emperor, beginning with the coronation of Charlemagne in 800 AD The last emperor, Francis II, relinquished his crown in 1806

holy rood *n* **1** a cross or crucifix, esp one placed upon the rood screen in a church **2** *(often capital)* the cross on which Christ was crucified

Holyroodhouse (ˌhɒlɪruːˈdhaʊs) *n* a royal palace in Edinburgh in Scotland: official residence of the Queen when in Scotland; begun in 1501 by James IV of Scotland; scene of the murder of David Rizzio in 1566

Holy Saturday *n* the Saturday before Easter Sunday

Holy Scripture *n* another term for **Scripture**

Holy See *n RC Church* **1** the see of the pope as bishop of Rome and head of the Church **2** the Roman curia

Holy Sepulchre *n New Testament* the tomb in which the body of Christ was laid after the Crucifixion

Holy Spirit *or* **Ghost** *n Christianity* the third person of the Trinity

holystone ('həʊlɪˌstəʊn) *n* **1** a soft sandstone used for scrubbing the decks of a vessel ▷ *vb* **2** *(tr)* to scrub (a vessel's decks) with a holystone [c19 perhaps so named from its being used in a kneeling position]

holy synod *n* the governing body of any of the Orthodox Churches

Holy Thursday *n RC Church* **1** another name for **Maundy Thursday 2** a rare name for **Ascension Day**

holy war *n* a war waged in the cause of a religion

holy water *n* water that has been blessed by a priest for use in symbolic rituals of purification

Holy Week *n* the week preceding Easter Sunday

Holy Willie ('wɪlɪ) *n* a person who is hypocritically pious [c18 from Burns' *Holy Willie's Prayer*]

Holy Writ *n* another term for **Scripture**

Holy Year *n RC Church* a period of remission from sin, esp one granted every 25 years

hom (hɒm) *or* **homa** ('hɒmə) *n* **1** a sacred plant of the Parsees and ancient Persians **2** a drink made from this plant [from Persian, from Avestan *haoma*]

homage ('hɒmɪdʒ) *n* **1** a public show of respect or honour towards someone or something (esp in the phrases pay *or* do homage to) **2** (in feudal society) **a** the act of respect and allegiance made by a vassal to his lord. See also **fealty b** something done in acknowledgment of vassalage ▷ *vb (tr)* **3** *archaic or poetic* to render homage to [c13 from Old French, from *homme* man, from Latin *homo*]

hombre¹ ('ɒmbreɪ, -brɪ) *n Western US* a slang word for **man** [c19 from Spanish: man]

hombre² ('hɒmbə) *n* a variant of **ombre**

homburg ('hɒmbɜːg) *n* a man's hat of soft felt with a dented crown and a stiff upturned brim [c20 named after *Homburg,* in Germany, town where it was originally made]

home (həʊm) *n* **1** the place or a place where one lives: *have you no home to go to?* **2** a house or other dwelling **3** a family or other group living in a house or other place **4** a person's country, city, etc, esp viewed as a birthplace, a residence during one's early years, or a place dear to one **5** the environment or habitat of a person or animal **6** the place where something is invented, founded, or developed: *the US is the home of baseball* **7 a** a building or organization set up to care for orphans, the aged, etc **b** an informal name for a **mental home 8** *sport* one's own ground: *the match is at home* **9 a** the objective towards which a player strives in certain sports **b** an area where a player is safe from attack **10** *lacrosse* **a** one of two positions of play nearest the opponents' goal **b** a player assigned to such a position: *inside home* **11** *baseball* another name for **home plate 12** *NZ informal, obsolete* Britain, esp England **13** a home from home a place other than one's own home where one can be at ease **14** at home **a** in one's own home or country **b** at ease, as if at one's own home **c** giving an informal party at one's own home **d** *Brit* such a party **15** at home in, on, *or* with familiar or conversant with **16** home and dry *Brit informal* definitely safe or successful: *we will not be home and dry until the votes have been counted.* Austral and NZ equivalent: home and hosed **17** near home concerning one deeply ▷ *adj (usually prenominal)* **18** of, relating to, or involving one's home, country, etc; domestic **19** (of an activity) done in one's house: *home taping* **20** effective or deadly: *a home thrust* **21** *sport* relating to one's own ground: *a home game* **22** *US* central; principal: *the company's home office* ▷ *adv* **23** to or at home: *I'll be home tomorrow* **24** to or on the point **25** to the fullest extent: *hammer the nail home* **26** (of nautical gear) into or in the best or proper position: *the boom is home* **27** bring home to **a** to make clear to **b** to place the blame on **28** come home *nautical* (of an anchor) to fail to hold **29** come home to to become absolutely clear to **30** nothing to write home about *informal* to be of no particular interest: *the film was nothing to write home about* ▷ *vb* **31** *(intr)* (of birds and other animals) to return home accurately from a distance **32** (often foll by *on* or *onto*) to direct or be directed onto a point or target, esp by automatic navigational aids **33** to send or go home **34** to furnish with or have a home **35** *(intr;* often foll by *in* or *in on*) to be directed towards a goal, target, etc [Old English *hām;* related to Old Norse *heimr,* Gothic *haims,* Old High German *heim,* Dutch *heem,* Greek *kōmi* village]
▷ ˈhomeˌlike *adj*

home aid *n NZ* another name for **home help**

home-alone *adj informal* (esp of a young child) left in a house, flat, etc unattended

home banking *n* a system whereby a person at home or in an office can use a computer with a modem to call up information from a bank or to transfer funds electronically

homebirth ('həʊmˌbɜːθ) *n* **1** the act of giving birth to a child in one's own home **2** an instance of a woman giving birth to a child at home: *a large increase in homebirths*

homebody ('həʊmˌbɒdɪ) *n, pl* -bodies a person whose life and interests are centred on the home

homeboy ('həʊmˌbɔɪ) *n slang, chiefly US* **1** a close friend **2** a person from one's home town or neighbourhood [c20 US rap-music usage]
▷ ˈhomeˌgirl *fem n*

home brand *n Austral* **a** an item packaged and marketed under the brand name of a particular retailer, usually a large supermarket chain, rather than that of the manufacturer **b** (as modifier):

h

home-brand products. Also called (in certain other countries): **own brand**

homebred ('həʊm,brɛd) *adj* **1** raised or bred at home **2** lacking sophistication or cultivation; crude

home-brew *n* a beer or other alcoholic drink brewed at home rather than commercially > 'home-'brewed *adj*

homecoming ('həʊm,kʌmɪŋ) *n* **1** the act of coming home **2** *US* an annual celebration held by a university, college, or school, for former students

Home Counties *pl n* the counties surrounding London

home economics *n* (*functioning as singular or plural*) the study of diet, budgeting, child care, textiles, and other subjects concerned with running a home > **home economist** *n*

home farm *n Brit* (*esp formerly*) a farm belonging to and providing food for a large country house

home ground *n* a familiar area or topic

home-grown *adj* (*esp of fruit and vegetables*) produced in one's own country, district, estate, or garden

Home Guard *n* **1** a volunteer part-time military force recruited for the defence of the United Kingdom in World War II **2** (in various countries) a civil defence and reserve militia organization

home help *n social welfare* (in Britain and New Zealand) **1** a person who is paid to do domestic chores for persons unable to look after themselves adequately **2** Also called: **home care** such a service provided by a local authority social services department to those whom it judges most need it ▷ Also called (NZ): **home aid**

home invasion *n Austral and NZ* aggravated burglary

homeland ('həʊm,lænd) *n* **1** the country in which one lives or was born **2** the official name for a **Bantustan**

homelands movement *n Austral* the programme to resettle native Australians on their tribal lands

homeless ('həʊmlɪs) *adj* **a** having nowhere to live **b** (*as collective noun; preceded by the*): *the homeless* > 'homelessness *n*

home loan *n* an informal name for **mortgage** (sense 1)

homely ('həʊmlɪ) *adj* **-lier, -liest 1** characteristic of or suited to the ordinary home; unpretentious **2** (of a person) **a** *Brit* warm and domesticated in manner or appearance **b** *chiefly US and Canadian* plain or ugly > 'homeliness *n*

home-made *adj* **1** (*esp of cakes, jam, and other foods*) made at home or on the premises, esp of high-quality ingredients **2** crudely fashioned

homemaker ('həʊm,meɪkə) *n* **1** *chiefly US and Canadian* a person, esp a housewife, who manages a home **2** *US and Canadian* a social worker who manages a household during the incapacity of the housewife > 'home,making *n, adj*

homeo-, homoeo- *or* **homoio-** *combining form* like or similar: *homeomorphism* [from Latin *homoeo-*, from Greek *homoio-*, from *homos* same]

Home Office *n Brit government* the national department responsible for the maintenance of law and order, immigration control, and all other domestic affairs not specifically assigned to another department

homeomorphism *or* **homoeomorphism** (,həʊmɪə'mɔ:fɪzəm) *n* **1** the property, shown by certain chemical compounds, of having the same crystal form but different chemical composition **2** *maths* a one-to-one correspondence, continuous in both directions, between the points of two geometric figures or between two topological spaces > ,homeo'morphic, ,homeo'morphous, ,homoeo'morphic *or* ,homoeo'morphous *adj*

homeopathy *or* **homoeopathy** (,həʊmɪ'ɒpəθɪ) *n* a method of treating disease by the use of small amounts of a drug that, in healthy persons, produces symptoms similar to those of the disease being treated. Compare **allopathy** > homeopathic *or* homoeopathic (,həʊmɪə'pæθɪk) *adj* > ,homeo'pathically *or* ,homoeo'pathically *adv* > homeopathist, homoeopathist (,həʊmɪ'ɒpəθɪst) *or* homeopath, homoeopath ('həʊmɪə,pæθ) *n*

homeostasis *or* **homoeostasis** (,həʊmɪəʊ'steɪsɪs) *n* **1** the maintenance of metabolic equilibrium within an animal by a tendency to compensate for disrupting changes **2** the maintenance of equilibrium within a social group, person, etc > homeostatic *or* homoeostatic (,həʊmɪəʊ'stætɪk) *adj*

homeotypic (,həʊmɪəʊ'tɪpɪk), **homeotypical, homoeotypic** *or* **homoeotypical** *adj* denoting or relating to the second nuclear division of meiosis, which resembles mitosis. Compare **heterotypic**

homeowner ('həʊm,əʊnə) *n* a person who owns the house in which he or she lives > ,home'ownership *n*

home page *n computing* (on a website) the main document relating to an individual or institution that provides introductory information about a website with links to the actual details of services or information provided

home plate *n baseball* a flat often five-sided piece of hard rubber or other material that serves to define the area over which the pitcher must throw the ball for a strike and that a base runner must safely reach on his way from third base to score a run. Also called: **plate, home, home base**

homer ('həʊmə) *n* **1** another word for **homing pigeon 2** *US and Canadian* an informal word for **home run**

home range *n ecology* the area in which an animal normally ranges

Homeric (həʊ'mɛrɪk) *or* **Homerian** (həʊ'mɪərɪən) *adj* **1** of, relating to, or resembling Homer (c. 800 BC), the Greek poet to whom are attributed the *Iliad* and the *Odyssey*, or his poems **2** imposing or heroic **3** of or relating to the archaic form of Greek used by Homer. See **epic**. > Ho'merically *adv*

Homeric laughter *n* loud unrestrained laughter, as that of the gods

homeroom ('həʊm,ru:m, -,rʊm) *n US* **1** a room in a school used by a particular group of students as a base for registration, notices, etc **2** a group of students who use the same room as a base in school

home rule *n* **1** self-government, esp in domestic affairs **2** *US government* the partial autonomy of cities and (in some states) counties, under which they manage their own affairs, with their own charters, etc, within the limits set by the state constitution and laws **3** the partial autonomy sometimes granted to a national minority or a colony

Home Rule *n* self-government for Ireland: the goal of the Irish Nationalists from about 1870 to 1920

home run *n baseball* a hit that enables the batter to run round all four bases, usually by hitting the ball out of the playing area

home-school *vb* **1 a** to teach one's child at home instead of sending him or her to school ▷ *adj* **2 a** being educated at home rather than in school: *home-school kids* **b** relating to the education of children in their own homes instead of in school: *home-school parents*

home-schooler *n* **1** a child who is educated at home, esp by his or her parents **2** a parent who educates a child at home

homescreetch ('həʊm,skri:tʃ) *n Southwest English dialect* a mistle thrush

Home Secretary *n Brit government* short for **Secretary of State for the Home Department**; the head of the Home Office

homesick ('həʊm,sɪk) *adj* depressed or melancholy at being away from home and family > 'home,sickness *n*

homespun ('həʊm,spʌn) *adj* **1** having plain or unsophisticated character **2** woven or spun at home ▷ *n* **3** cloth made at home or made of yarn spun at home **4** a cloth resembling this but made on a power loom

homestead ('həʊm,stɛd, -stɪd) *n* **1** a house or estate and the adjoining land, buildings, etc, esp a farm **2** (in the US) a house and adjoining land designated by the owner as his fixed residence and exempt under the homestead laws from seizure and forced sale for debts **3** (in western Canada) a piece of land, usually 160 acres, granted to a settler by the federal government **4** *Austral and NZ* the owner's or manager's residence on a sheep or cattle station; in New Zealand the term includes all outbuildings

Homestead Act *n* **1** an act passed by the US Congress in 1862 making available to settlers 160-acre tracts of public land for cultivation **2** (in Canada) a similar act passed by the Canadian Parliament in 1872

homesteader ('həʊm,stɛdə) *n* **1** a person owning a homestead **2** *US and Canadian* a person who acquires or possesses land under a homestead law **3** a person taking part in a homesteading scheme

homesteading ('həʊm,stɛdɪŋ) *n* (in Britain) **a** a scheme whereby council tenants are enabled to buy derelict property from the council and renovate it with the aid of Government grants **b** (*as modifier*): *a homesteading scheme*

homestead law *n* (in the US and Canada) any of various laws conferring certain privileges on owners of homesteads

home straight *n* **1** *horse racing* the section of a racecourse forming the approach to the finish **2** the final stage of an undertaking or journey ▷ Also (chiefly US): **home stretch**

home teacher *n Brit* a teacher who educates ill or disabled children in their homes

home truth *n* (*often plural*) an unpleasant fact told to a person about himself

home unit *n Austral and NZ* a self-contained residence which is part of a series of similar residences. Often shortened to: **unit**

homeward ('həʊmwəd) *adj* **1** directed or going home **2** (of a ship, part of a voyage, etc) returning to the home port ▷ *adv also* **homewards 3** towards home

homeware ('həʊmwɛə) *n* crockery, furniture, and furnishings with which a house, room, etc, is furnished [C20 HOME + WARE]

homework ('həʊm,wɜ:k) *n* **1** school work done out of lessons, esp at home **2** any preparatory study **3** work done at home for pay

homeworker ('həʊm,wɜ:kə) *n* a person who does paid work at home, rather than in an office

homey ('həʊmɪ) *adj* **homier, homiest 1** a variant spelling (esp US) of **homy** ▷ *n* **2** *NZ informal* a British person > 'homeyness *n*

homicidal (,hɒmɪ'saɪd°l) *adj* **1** of, involving, or characterized by homicide **2** likely to commit homicide: *a homicidal maniac* > ,homi'cidally *adv*

homicide ('hɒmɪ,saɪd) *n* **1** the killing of a human being by another person **2** a person who kills another [C14 from Old French, from Latin *homo* man + *caedere* to slay]

homicide bomber *n* another name for **suicide bomber**

homie ('həʊmɪ) *n slang, chiefly US* short for **homeboy** or **homegirl**

homiletic (,hɒmɪ'lɛtɪk) *or* **homiletical** *adj* **1** of or relating to a homily or sermon **2** of, relating to, or characteristic of homiletics > ,homi'letically *adv*

homiletics (,hɒmɪ'lɛtɪks) *n* (*functioning as singular*) the art of preaching or writing sermons [C17 from Greek *homilētikos* cordial, from *homilein* to converse with; see HOMILY]

homily ('hɒmɪlɪ) *n, pl* **-lies 1** a sermon or discourse on a moral or religious topic **2** moralizing talk or writing [C14 from Church Latin *homīlia*, from Greek: discourse, from *homilein* to converse with, from *homilos* crowd, from *homou* together + *ilē* crowd] > 'homilist *n*

homing ('həʊmɪŋ) *n (modifier)* **1** *zoology* relating to the ability to return home after travelling great distances: *homing instinct* **2** (of an aircraft, a missile, etc) capable of guiding itself onto a target or to a specified point

homing guidance *n* a method of missile guidance in which internal equipment enables it to steer itself onto the target, as by sensing the target's heat radiation

homing pigeon *n* any breed of pigeon developed for its homing instinct, used for carrying messages or for racing. Also called: **homer**

hominid ('hɒmɪnɪd) *n* **1** any primate of the family *Hominidae*, which includes modern man (*Homo sapiens*) and the extinct precursors of man ▷ *adj* **2** of, relating to, or belonging to the *Hominidae*. [C19 via New Latin from Latin *homo* man + -ID²]

hominoid ('hɒmɪ,nɔɪd) *adj* **1** of or like man; manlike **2** of, relating to, or belonging to the primate superfamily *Hominoidea*, which includes the anthropoid apes and man ▷ *n* **3** a hominoid animal [C20 from Latin *homin-*, *homo* man + -OID]

hominy ('hɒmɪnɪ) *n chiefly US* coarsely ground maize prepared as a food by boiling in milk or water [C17 probably of Algonquian origin]

hominy grits *pl n US* finely ground hominy. Often shortened to: **grits**

homo¹ ('həʊməʊ) *n, pl* -mos *informal* short for **homosexual**

homo² ('həʊməʊ) *n Canadian informal* short for **homogenized milk**

Homo ('həʊməʊ) *n* a genus of hominids including modern man (see *Homo sapiens*) and several extinct species of primitive man, including *H. habilis* and *H. erectus* [Latin: man]

homo- *combining form* being the same or like: *homologous*; *homosexual*. Compare **hetero-** [via Latin from Greek, from *homos* same]

homoblastic (,həʊmə'blæstɪk) *adj* (of a plant or plant part) showing no difference in form between the juvenile and the adult structures. Compare **heteroblastic**

homocentric (,həʊməʊ'sɛntrɪk, ,hɒm-) *adj* having the same centre; concentric
> ,homo'centrically *adv*

homocercal (,həʊməʊ'sɜːk²l, ,hɒm-) *adj ichthyol* of or possessing a symmetrical tail that extends beyond the end of the vertebral column, as in most bony fishes. Compare **heterocercal** [C19 from HOMO- + Greek *kerkos* tail]

homochlamydeous (,həʊmə klə'mɪdɪəs) *adj* (of a plant) having a perianth in which the sepals and petals are fused together and indistinguishable. Compare **heterochlamydeous**

homochromatic (,həʊməʊkrəʊ'mætɪk, ,hɒm-) *adj* a less common word for **monochromatic** (sense 1)
> homochromatism (,həʊməʊ'krəʊmə,tɪzəm, ,hɒm-) *n*

homochromous (,həʊmə'krəʊməs, ,hɒm-) *adj* (esp of plant parts) of only one colour

homocyclic (,həʊməʊ'saɪklɪk, -'sɪk-, ,hɒm-) *adj* (of an organic compound) containing a closed ring of atoms of the same kind, esp carbon atoms. Compare **heterocyclic**

homocysteine (,həʊməʊ'sɪsti:n) *n* an amino acid occurring as an intermediate in the metabolism of methionine. Elevated levels in the blood may indicate increased risk of cardiovascular disease

homodont ('həʊmə,dɒnt) *adj* (of most nonmammalian vertebrates) having teeth that are all of the same type. Compare **heterodont** [C19 from HOMO- + -ODONT]

homoeo- *combining form* a variant of **homeo-**

homoerotic (,həʊməʊɪ'rɒtɪk) *adj* of, concerning, or arousing sexual desire for persons of one's own sex

homoeroticism (,həʊməʊɪ'rɒtɪ,sɪzəm) or **homoerotism** (,həʊməʊ'ɛrə,tɪzəm) *n* eroticism centred on or aroused by persons of one's own sex

homogametic (,həʊməmə'mɛtɪk) *adj genetics* denoting the sex that possesses two similar sex chromosomes. In humans and many other mammals it is the female sex, possessing two X-chromosomes. Compare **heterogametic**

homogamy (hɒ'mɒɡəmɪ) *n* **1** a condition in which all the flowers of an inflorescence are either of the same sex or hermaphrodite. Compare **heterogamy** (sense 3) **2** the maturation of the anthers and stigmas of a flower at the same time, ensuring self-pollination. Compare **dichogamy.** > ho'mogamous *adj*

homogenate (hɒ'mɒdʒɪnɪt, -,neɪt) *n* a substance produced by homogenizing [C20 from HOMOGENIZE + -ATE¹]

homogeneous (,həʊmə'dʒi:nɪəs, ,hɒm-) *adj* **1** composed of similar or identical parts or elements **2** of uniform nature **3** similar in kind or nature **4** having a constant property, such as density, throughout **5** *maths* **a** (of a polynomial) containing terms of the same degree with respect to all the variables, as in $x^2 + 2xy + y^2$ **b** (of a function) containing a set of variables such that when each is multiplied by a constant, this constant can be eliminated without altering the value of the function, as in $\cos x/y + x/y$ **c** (of an equation) containing a homogeneous function made equal to 0 **6** *chem* of, composed of, or concerned with a single phase. Compare **heterogeneous** ▷ Also (for senses 1–4): **homogenous** > homogeneity (,həʊməʊdʒɪ'ni:ɪtɪ, ,hɒm-) *n* > ,homo'geneously *adv* > ,homo'geneousness *n*

homogenize *or* **homogenise** (hɒ'mɒdʒɪ,naɪz) *vb* **1** (*tr*) to break up the fat globules in (milk or cream) so that they are evenly distributed **2** to make or become homogeneous
> ho,mogeni'zation *or* ho,mogeni'sation *n*
> ho'moge,nizer *or* ho'moge,niser *n*

homogenous (hə'mɒdʒɪnəs) *adj* **1** another word for **homogeneous** (senses 1–4) **2** of, relating to, or exhibiting homogeny

homogeny (hɒ'mɒdʒɪnɪ) *n biology* similarity in structure of individuals or parts because of common ancestry [C19 from Greek *homogeneia* community of origin, from *homogenēs* of the same kind]

homogony (hɒ'mɒɡənɪ) *n* the condition in a plant of having stamens and styles of the same length in all the flowers. Compare **heterogony** (sense 2) > ho'mogonous *adj* > ho'mogonously *adv*

homograft ('hɒmə,ɡrɑ:ft) *n* a tissue graft obtained from an organism of the same species as the recipient

homograph ('hɒmə,ɡræf, -,ɡrɑ:f) *n* one of a group of words spelt in the same way but having different meanings. Compare **heteronym**
> ,homo'graphic *adj*

homoio- *combining form* a variant of **homeo-**

homoiothermic (həʊ,mɔɪə'θɜːmɪk) *or* **homothermal** *adj* (of birds and mammals) having a constant body temperature, usually higher than the temperature of the surroundings; warm-blooded. Compare **poikilothermic**
> ho'moio,thermy *or* 'homo,thermy *n*

Homoiousian (,həʊmɔɪ'u:sɪən, -'aʊ-, ,hɒm-) *n* **1** a Christian who believes that the Son is of like (and not identical) substance with the Father. Compare **Homoousian** ▷ *adj* **2** of or relating to the Homoiousians [C18 from Late Greek *homoiousios* of like substance, from Greek *homoio-* like + *ousia* nature] > ,Homoi'ousianism *n*

homologate (hɒ'mɒlə,ɡeɪt) *vb* (*tr*) **1** *law, chiefly Scots* to approve or ratify (a deed or contract, esp one that is defective) **2** *law* to confirm (a proceeding, etc) **3** to recognize (a particular type of car or car component) as a production model or component rather than a prototype, as in making it eligible for a motor race [C17 from Medieval Latin *homologāre* to agree, from Greek *homologein* to approve, from *homologos* agreeing, from HOMO- + *legein* to speak] > ho,molo'gation *n*

homologize *or* **homologise** (hɒ'mɒlə,dʒaɪz) *vb* to be, show to be, or make homologous
> ho'molo,gizer *or* ho'molo,giser *n*

homologous (həʊ'mɒləɡəs, hɒ-), **homological** (,həʊmə'lɒdʒɪk²l, ,hɒm-) *or* **homologic** *adj* **1** having a related or similar position, structure, etc **2** *chem* (of a series of organic compounds) having similar characteristics and structure but differing by a number of CH_2 groups **3** *med* **a** (of two or more tissues) identical in structure **b** (of a vaccine) prepared from the infecting microorganism **4** *biology* (of organs and parts) having the same evolutionary origin but different functions: *the wing of a bat and the paddle of a whale are homologous*. Compare **analogous** (sense 2) **5** *maths* (of elements) playing a similar role in distinct figures or functions > ,homo'logically *adv*

homologous chromosomes *pl n* two chromosomes, one of paternal origin, the other of maternal origin, that are identical in appearance and pair during meiosis

homolographic (həʊ,mɒlə'ɡræfɪk) *or* **homalographic** *adj cartography* another term for **equal-area**

homologue *or sometimes US* **homolog** ('hɒmə,lɒɡ) *n* **1** *biology* a homologous part or organ **2** *chem* any homologous compound

homology (həʊ'mɒlədʒɪ) *n, pl* -gies **1** the condition of being homologous **2** *chem* the similarities in chemical behaviour shown by members of a homologous series **3** *zoology* the measurable likenesses between animals, as used in grouping them according to the theory of cladistics [C17 from Greek *homologia* agreement, from *homologos* agreeing; see HOMOLOGATE]

homolosine projection (hɒ'mɒlə,saɪn) *n* a map projection of the world on which the oceans are distorted to allow for greater accuracy in representing the continents, combining the sinusoidal and equal-area projections [C20 from HOMOLOGRAPHIC + SINE¹]

homolysis (hɒ'mɒlɪsɪs) *n* the dissociation of a molecule into two neutral fragments. Also called: **homolytic fission** Compare **heterolysis** (sense 2)
> homolytic (,həʊməʊ'lɪtɪk, ,hɒm-) *adj*

homomorphism (,həʊməʊ'mɔ:fɪzəm, ,hɒm-) *or* **homomorphy** *n biology* similarity in form
> ,homo'morphic *or* ,homo'morphous *adj*

homonym ('hɒmənɪm) *n* **1** one of a group of words pronounced or spelt in the same way but having different meanings. Compare **homograph, homophone 2** a person with the same name as another **3** *biology* a name for a species or genus that should be unique but has been used for two or more different organisms [C17 from Latin *homōnymum*, from Greek *homōnumon*, from *homōnumos* of the same name; see HOMO-, -ONYM]
> ,homo'nymic *or* ho'monymous *adj*
> ,homo'nymity *or* ho'monymy *n*

Homoousian (,həʊməʊ'u:sɪən, -'aʊ-, ,hɒm-) *n* **1** a Christian who believes that the Son is of the same substance as the Father. Compare **Homoiousian** ▷ *adj* **2** of or relating to the Homoousians [C16 from Late Greek *homoousios* of the same substance, from Greek HOMO- + *ousia* nature] > ,Homo'ousianism *n*

homophile ('həʊmə,faɪl, 'hɒm-) *n* a rare word for **homosexual**

homophobia (,həʊməʊ'fəʊbɪə) *n* intense hatred or fear of homosexuals or homosexuality [C20 from HOMO(SEXUAL) + -PHOBIA] > 'homo,phobe *n*
> ,homo'phobic *adj*

homophone ('hɒmə,fəʊn) *n* **1** one of a group of words pronounced in the same way but differing in meaning or spelling or both, as for example *bear* and *bare* **2** a written letter or combination of letters that represents the same speech sound as another: *"ph" is a homophone of "f" in English*

homophonic (,hɒmə'fɒnɪk) *adj* **1** of or relating to homophony **2** of or relating to music in which the parts move together rather than independently > ,homo'phonically *adv*

homophonous (hɒ'mɒfənəs) *adj* of, relating to, or denoting a homophone

h

homophony (hɒˈmɒfənɪ) *n* **1** the linguistic phenomenon whereby words of different origins become identical in pronunciation **2** part music composed in a homophonic style

homophyly (hɒˈmɒfəlɪ) *n* resemblance due to common ancestry [C19 from Greek, from HOMO- + PHYLUM] > homophyllic (ˌhəʊməˈfɪlɪk, ˌhɒm-) *adj*

homoplastic (ˌhəʊməʊˈplæstɪk, ˌhɒm-) *adj* **1** (of a tissue graft) derived from an individual of the same species as the recipient **2** another word for **analogous** (sense 2) > ˌhomoˈplastically *adv* > ˈhomoˌplasty *n* > homoplasy (ˈhəʊməʊˌpleɪsɪ, ˈhɒm-) *n*

homopolar (ˌhəʊməʊˈpəʊlə) *adj chem* of uniform charge; not ionic; covalent: *a homopolar bond* > homopolarity (ˌhəʊməʊpəʊˈlærɪtɪ, ˌhɒm-) *n*

homopterous (həʊˈmɒptərəs) *or* **homopteran** *adj* of, relating to, or belonging to the *Homoptera*, a suborder of hemipterous insects, including cicadas, aphids, and scale insects, having wings of a uniform texture held over the back at rest. Compare **heteropterous** [C19 from Greek *homopteros*, from HOMO- + *pteron* wing]

homorganic (ˌhəʊmɔːˈgænɪk, ˌhɒm-) *adj phonetics* (of a consonant) articulated at the same point in the vocal tract as a consonant in a different class. Thus ŋ is the homorganic nasal of *k*

Homo sapiens (ˈsæpɪˌɛnz) *n* the specific name of modern man; the only extant species of the genus *Homo*. This species also includes extinct types of primitive man such as Cro-Magnon man. See also **man** (sense 5) [New Latin, from Latin *homo* man + *sapiens* wise]

homoscedastic (ˌhəʊməʊskɪˈdæstɪk) *adj statistics* **1** (of several distributions) having equal variance **2** (of a bivariate or multivariate distribution) having one variable whose variance is the same for all values of the other or others **3** (of a random variable) having this property ▷ Compare **heteroscedastic** [C20 from HOMO- + *scedastic*, from Greek *skedasis* a scattering, dispersal] > homoscedasticity (ˌhəʊməʊˌskɪdæsˈtɪsɪtɪ) *n*

homosexual (ˌhəʊməʊˈsɛksjʊəl, ˌhɒm-) *n* **1** a person who is sexually attracted to members of the same sex ▷ *adj* **2** of or relating to homosexuals or homosexuality **3** of or relating to the same sex ▷ Compare **heterosexual**

homosexuality (ˌhəʊməʊˌsɛksjʊˈælɪtɪ, ˌhɒm-) *n* sexual attraction to or sexual relations with members of the same sex. Compare **heterosexuality**

homosocial (ˌhəʊməʊˈsəʊʃəl) *adj* relating to or denoting same-sex social relationships ▷ Compare **heterosocial**. > homosociality (ˌhəʊməʊˌsəʊʃɪˈælɪtɪ) *n*

homosporous (hɒˈmɒspərəs, ˌhəʊməʊˈspɔːrəs) *adj* (of most ferns and some other spore-bearing plants) producing spores of one kind only, which develop into hermaphrodite gametophytes. Compare **heterosporous**. > homospory (həʊˈmɒspərɪ) *n*

homotaxis (ˌhəʊməʊˈtæksɪs, ˌhɒm-) *n* similarity of composition and arrangement in rock strata of different ages or in different regions > ˌhomoˈtaxic *or* ˌhomoˈtaxial *adj* > ˌhomoˈtaxially *adv*

homothallic (ˌhəʊməʊˈθælɪk) *adj* (of some algae and fungi) having both male and female reproductive organs on the same thallus, which can be self-fertilizing. Compare **heterothallic** [C20 from HOMO- + Greek *thallos* green shoot] > ˌhomoˈthallism *n*

homothermal (ˌhəʊməʊˈθɜːməl, ˌhɒm-) *adj* another word for **homoiothermic**

homozygote (ˌhəʊməʊˈzaɪɡəʊt, -ˈzɪɡ-, ˌhɒm-) *n* an animal or plant that is homozygous and breeds true to type. Compare **heterozygote** > ˌhomozyˈgosis *n* > homozygotic (ˌhəʊməʊzaɪˈɡɒtɪk, -zɪ-, ˌhɒm-) *adj*

homozygous (ˌhəʊməʊˈzaɪɡəs, -ˈzɪɡ-, ˌhɒm-) *adj genetics* (of an organism) having identical alleles for any one gene: *these two fruit flies are homozygous for red eye colour*. Compare **heterozygous**

> ˌhomoˈzygously *adv*

Homs (hɒms) *or* **Hums** (hʊms) *n* a city in W Syria, near the Orontes River: important in Roman times as the capital of Phoenicia-Lebanesia. Pop: 915 000 (2005 est). Ancient name: Emesa (ˈɛmɛsə) Former name: Hims

homunculus (hɒˈmʌŋkjʊləs) *n, pl* -li (-ˌlaɪ) **1** a miniature man; midget **2** (in early biological theory) a fully-formed miniature human being existing in a spermatozoon or egg ▷ Also called: homuncule (həʊˈmʌŋkjuːl) [C17 from Latin, diminutive of *homo* man] > ho'muncular *adj*

homy *or esp US* **homey** (ˈhəʊmɪ) *adj* homier, homiest like a home, esp in comfort or informality; cosy > ˈhominess *or esp US* ˈhomeyness *n*

hon. *abbreviation for* **1** honorary **2** honourable

Hon. *abbreviation for* Honourable (title)

honan (ˈhəʊnæn) *n* (*sometimes capital*) a silk fabric of rough weave [C20 from *Honan*, former name of HENAN, where it is made]

Honan (ˈhəʊnæn) *n* a variant transliteration of the Chinese name for **Henan**

honcho (ˈhɒntʃəʊ) *informal, chiefly US* ▷ *n, pl* -chos **1** the person in charge; the boss ▷ *vb* **2** to supervise or be in charge of [C20 from Japanese *han'chō* group leader]

Hond. *abbreviation for* Honduras

Hondo (ˈhɒndəʊ) *n* another name for **Honshu**

Honduran (hɒnˈdjʊərən) *adj* **1** of or relating to Honduras or its inhabitants ▷ *n* **2** a native or inhabitant of Honduras

Honduras (hɒnˈdjʊərəs) *n* **1** a republic in Central America: an early centre of Mayan civilization; colonized by the Spanish from 1524 onwards; gained independence in 1821. Official language: Spanish; English is also widely spoken. Religion: Roman Catholic majority. Currency: lempira. Capital: Tegucigalpa. Pop: 7 100 000 (2004 est). Area: 112 088 sq km (43 277 sq miles) **2 Gulf of** an inlet of the Caribbean, on the coasts of Honduras, Guatemala, and Belize

hone¹ (həʊn) *n* **1** a fine whetstone, esp for sharpening razors **2** a tool consisting of a number of fine abrasive slips held in a machine head, rotated and reciprocated to impart a smooth finish to cylinder bores, etc ▷ *vb* **3** (tr) to sharpen or polish with or as if with a hone [Old English *hān* stone; related to Old Norse *hein*]

USAGE *Hone* is sometimes wrongly used where *home* is meant: *this device makes it easier to home in on* (not *hone in on*) *the target*

hone² (həʊn) *vb* (intr) *dialect* **1** (often foll by *for* or *after*) to yearn or pine **2** to moan or grieve [C17 from Old French *hogner* to growl, probably of Germanic origin; compare Old High German *hōnen* to revile]

honest (ˈɒnɪst) *adj* **1** not given to lying, cheating, stealing, etc; trustworthy **2** not false or misleading; genuine **3** just or fair: *honest wages* **4** characterized by sincerity and candour: *an honest appraisal* **5** without pretensions or artificial traits: *honest farmers* **6** *archaic* (of a woman) respectable **7** honest broker a mediator in disputes, esp international ones **8** make an honest woman of to marry (a woman, esp one who is pregnant) to prevent scandal **9** honest Injun (*interjection*) *school slang* genuinely, really **10** honest to God (*or* goodness) **a** (*adjective*) completely authentic **b** (*interjection*) an expression of affirmation or surprise [C13 from Old French *honeste*, from Latin *honestus* distinguished, from *honōs* HONOUR] > ˈhonestness *n*

honestly (ˈɒnɪstlɪ) *adv* **1** in an honest manner **2** (intensifier): *I honestly don't believe it* ▷ *interj* **3** an expression of disgust, surprise, etc

honesty (ˈɒnɪstɪ) *n, pl* -ties **1** the condition of being honest **2** sincerity or fairness **3** *archaic* virtue or respect **4** a purple-flowered SE European plant, *Lunaria annua*, cultivated for its flattened silvery pods, which are used for indoor

decoration: family *Brassicaceae* (crucifers). Also called: moonwort, satinpod

honesty box *n* a container into which members of the public are trusted to place payments when there is no attendant to collect them

honewort (ˈhəʊnˌwɜːt) *n* **1** a European umbelliferous plant, *Trinia glauca*, with clusters of small white flowers **2** any of several similar and related plants [C17 apparently from obsolete dialect *hone* a swelling, of obscure origin; the plant was believed to relieve swellings]

honey (ˈhʌnɪ) *n* **1** a sweet viscid substance made by bees from nectar and stored in their nests or hives as food. It is spread on bread or used as a sweetening agent **2** any similar sweet substance, esp the nectar of flowers **3** anything that is sweet or delightful **4** (often capital) chiefly US and Canadian a term of endearment **5** informal, chiefly US and Canadian something considered to be very good of its kind: *a honey of a car* **6** (modifier) of, concerned with, or resembling honey ▷ *vb* honeys, honeying, honeyed *or* honied **7** (tr) to sweeten with or as if with honey **8** (often foll by *up*) to talk to (someone) in a fond or flattering way [Old English *huneg*; related to Old Norse *hunang*, Old Saxon *hanig*, German *Honig*, Greek *knēkos* yellowish, Sanskrit *kánaka-* gold] > ˈhoney-ˌlike *adj*

honey badger *n* another name for **ratel**

honey bear *n* another name for **kinkajou** *or* **sun bear**

honeybee (ˈhʌnɪˌbiː) *n* any of various social honey-producing bees of the genus *Apis*, esp *A. mellifera*, which has been widely domesticated as a source of honey and beeswax. Also called: hive bee

honeybunch (ˈhʌnɪˌbʌntʃ) *or* **honeybun** (ˈhʌnɪˌbʌn) *n* informal, chiefly US honey; darling: a term of endearment

honey buzzard *n* a common European bird of prey, *Pernis apivorus*, having broad wings and a typically dull brown plumage with white-streaked underparts: family *Accipitridae* (hawks, buzzards, etc). It feeds on grubs and honey from bees' nests

honeycomb (ˈhʌnɪˌkəʊm) *n* **1** a waxy structure, constructed by bees in a hive, that consists of adjacent hexagonal cells in which honey is stored, eggs are laid, and larvae develop **2** something resembling this in structure and appearance **3** *zoology* another name for **reticulum** (sense 2) ▷ *vb* (tr) **4** to pierce or fill with holes, cavities, etc **5** to permeate: *honeycombed with spies*

honeycomb moth *n* another name for the **wax moth**

honey creeper *n* **1** any small tropical American songbird of the genus *Dacnis* and related genera, closely related to the tanagers and buntings, having a slender downward-curving bill and feeding on nectar **2** any bird of the family *Drepanididae* of Hawaii

honeydew (ˈhʌnɪˌdjuː) *n* **1** a sugary substance excreted by aphids and similar insects **2** a similar substance exuded by certain plants **3** short for **honeydew melon**. > ˈhoneyˌdewed *adj*

honeydew melon *n* a variety of muskmelon with a smooth greenish-white rind and sweet greenish flesh

honey-eater (ˈhʌnɪˌiːtə) *n* any small arboreal songbird of the Australasian family *Meliphagidae*, having a downward-curving bill and a brushlike tongue specialized for extracting nectar from flowers

honeyed *or* **honied** (ˈhʌnɪd) *adj poetic* **1** flattering or soothing **2** made sweet or agreeable: *honeyed words* **3** of, full of, or resembling honey > ˈhoneyedly *or* ˈhoniedly *adv*

honey fungus *n* an edible basidiomycetous fungus, *Armillaria mellea*, having a yellow-spotted cap and wrinkled stems, parasitic on the roots of woody plants, which it may kill by root rot. It spreads by thin black underground strands. Also called: bootlace fungus

honey guide *n* any small bird of the family

Indicatoridae, inhabiting tropical forests of Africa and Asia and feeding on beeswax, honey, and insects: order *Piciformes* (woodpeckers, etc)

honey locust *n* **1** a thorny leguminous tree, *Gleditsia triacanthos* of E North America, that has long pods containing a sweet-tasting pulp **2** another name for **mesquite**

honey mesquite *n* another name for **mesquite**

honeymoon ('hʌnɪˌmuːn) *n* **1 a** a holiday taken by a newly married couple **b** (*as modifier*): *a honeymoon cottage* **2** a holiday considered to resemble a honeymoon: *a second honeymoon* **3** the early, usually calm period of a relationship, such as a political or business one ▷ *vb* **4** (*intr*) to take a honeymoon [c16 traditionally explained as an allusion to the feelings of married couples as changing with the phases of the moon] > 'honey,mooner *n*

honey mouse *or* **phalanger** *n* a small agile Australian marsupial, *Tarsipes spenserae*, having dark-striped pale brown fur, a long prehensile tail, and a very long snout and tongue with which it feeds on honey, pollen, and insects: family *Phalangeridae*. Also called: **honeysucker**

honey plant *n* any of various plants that are particularly useful in providing bees with nectar

honeypot ('hʌnɪˌpɒt) *n* **1** a container for honey **2** something which attracts people in great numbers: *Cornwall is a honeypot for tourists*

honeysucker ('hʌnɪˌsʌkə) *n* **1** any bird, esp a honey-eater, that feeds on nectar **2** another name for **honey mouse**

honeysuckle ('hʌnɪˌsʌkⁿl) *n* **1** any temperate caprifoliaceous shrub or vine of the genus *Lonicera*: cultivated for their fragrant white, yellow, or pink tubular flowers **2** any of several similar plants **3** any of various Australian trees or shrubs of the genus *Banksia*, having flowers in dense spikes: family *Proteaceae* [Old English *hunigsūce*, from HONEY + SUCK; see SUCKLE] > 'honey,suckled *adj*

honeysuckle ornament *n arts* another term for **anthemion**

honey-sweet *adj* sweet or endearing

honeytrap ('hʌnɪˌtræp) *n informal* a scheme in which a victim is lured into a compromising sexual situation to provide an opportunity for blackmail

hong (hɒŋ) *n* **1** (in China) a factory, warehouse, etc **2** (formerly, in Canton) a foreign commercial establishment [c18 from Chinese (Cantonese dialect)]

hongi ('hɒŋi:) *n* NZ a form of salutation expressed by touching noses [Māori]

Hong Kong (ˌhɒŋ 'kɒŋ) *n* **1** a Special Administrative Region of S China, with some autonomy; formerly a British Crown Colony: consists of Hong Kong Island, leased by China to Britain from 1842 until 1997, Kowloon Peninsula, Stonecutters Island, the New Territories (mainland), leased by China in 1898 for a 99-year period, and over 230 small islands; important entrepôt trade and manufacturing centre, esp for textiles and other consumer goods; university (1912). It retains its own currency, the Hong Kong dollar. Administrative centre: Victoria. Pop: 7 182 000 (2005 est). Area: 1046 sq km (404 sq miles) **2** an island in Hong Kong region, south of Kowloon Peninsula: contains the capital, Victoria. Pop: 1 337 800 (2001). Area: 75 sq km (29 sq miles)

Hong Kongese ('kɒŋiːz) *adj* **1** of, relating to, or characteristic of Hong Kong, its people, or their languages ▷ *n* **2** (*pl* -**nese**) a native or inhabitant of Hong Kong or a descendant of one

Honiara (ˌhəʊnɪ'ɑːrə) *n* the capital of the Solomon Islands, on NW Guadalcanal Island. Pop: 61 000 (2005 est)

honled ('hʌnld) *adj* a variant spelling of **honeyed** > 'honiedly *adv*

honi soit qui mal y pense French (ɔni swa ki mal i pās) shamed be he who thinks evil of it: the motto of the Order of the Garter

Honiton ('hɒnɪtⁿn, 'hʌn-) *or* **Honiton lace** *n* a

type of lace with a floral sprig pattern [c19 named after *Honiton*, Devon, where it was first made]

honk (hɒŋk) *n* **1** a representation of the sound made by a goose **2** any sound resembling this, esp a motor horn ▷ *vb* **3** to make or cause (something) to make such a sound **4** (*intr*) Brit a slang word for **vomit**

honker ('hɒŋkə) *n* **1** a person or thing that honks **2** Canadian an informal name for the **Canada goose** **3** slang a nose, esp a large nose

honky ('hɒŋkɪ) *n, pl* **honkies** derogatory slang, chiefly US a White man or White men collectively [c20 of unknown origin]

honky-tonk ('hɒŋkɪˌtɒŋk) *n* **1** US and Canadian slang **a** a cheap disreputable nightclub, bar, etc **b** (*as modifier*): *a honky-tonk district* **2** a style of ragtime piano-playing, esp on a tinny-sounding piano **3** a type of country music, usually performed by a small band with electric and steel guitars **4** (*as modifier*): *honky-tonk music* [c19 rhyming compound based on HONK]

Honolulu (ˌhɒnə'luːluː) *n* a port in Hawaii, on S Oahu Island: the state capital. Pop: 380 149 (2003 est)

honor ('ɒnə) *n, vb* the US spelling of **honour**

honorarium (ˌɒnə'rɛərɪəm) *n, pl* -**iums** *or* -**ia** (-ɪə) a fee paid for a nominally free service [c17 from Latin: something presented on being admitted to a post of HONOUR]

honorary ('ɒnərərɪ, 'ɒnrərɪ) *adj* (*usually prenominal*) **1 a** (esp of a position, title, etc) held or given only as an honour, without the normal privileges or duties: *an honorary degree* **b** (of a secretary, treasurer, etc) unpaid **2** having such a position or title **3** depending on honour rather than legal agreement

honorific (ˌɒnə'rɪfɪk) *adj* **1** showing or conferring honour or respect **2 a** (of a pronoun, verb inflection, etc) indicating the speaker's respect for the addressee or his acknowledgment of inferior status **b** (*as noun*): *a Japanese honorific* > ˌhonor'ifically *adv*

honoris causa Latin (hɒ'nɔːrɪs 'kaʊzaː) for the sake of honour

honour *or US* **honor** ('ɒnə) *n* **1** personal integrity; allegiance to moral principles **2 a** fame or glory **b** a person or thing that wins this for another: *he is an honour to the school* **3** (*often plural*) great respect, regard, esteem, etc, or an outward sign of this **4** (*often plural*) high or noble rank **5** a privilege or pleasure: *it is an honour to serve you* **6** a woman's virtue or chastity **7 a** *bridge, poker* any of the top five cards in a suit or any of the four aces at no trumps **b** *whist* any of the top four cards **8** *golf* the right to tee off first **9** do honour to **a** to pay homage to **b** to be a credit to **10** do the honours **a** to serve as host or hostess **b** to perform a social act, such as carving meat, proposing a toast, etc **11** honour bright *Brit school slang* an exclamation pledging honour **12** in honour bound under a moral obligation **13** in honour of out of respect for **14** on (*or* upon) one's honour on the pledge of one's word or good name ▷ *vb* **15** to hold in respect or esteem **16** to show courteous behaviour towards **17** to worship **18** to confer a distinction upon **19** to accept and then pay when due (a cheque, draft, etc) **20** to keep (one's promise); fulfil (a previous agreement) **21** to bow or curtsy to (one's dancing partner) ▷ See also **honours** [c12 from Old French *onor*, from Latin *honor* esteem] > 'honourer *or US* 'honorer *n* > 'honourless *or US* 'honorless *adj*

Honour ('ɒnə) *n* (preceded by *Your*, *His*, or *Her*) **a** a title used to or of certain judges **b** (in Ireland) a form of address in general use

honourable *or US* **honorable** ('ɒnərəbⁿl, 'ɒnrəbⁿl) *adj* **1** possessing or characterized by high principles: *honourable intentions* **2** worthy of or entitled to honour or esteem **3** consistent with or bestowing honour > 'honourableness *or US* 'honorableness *n* > 'honourably *or US* 'honorably *adv*

Honourable *or US* **Honorable** ('ɒnərəbⁿl, 'ɒnrəbⁿl) *adj* (*prenominal*) **the**. a title of respect placed before a name: employed before the names of various officials in the English-speaking world, as a courtesy title in Britain for the children of viscounts and barons and the younger sons of earls, and in Parliament by one member speaking of another. Abbreviation: **Hon**.

honourable discharge *n* See **discharge** (sense 15)

honour killing *n* a murder committed by a male on a female relative considered to have brought dishonour to the family, usually through sexual activity forbidden by religion or tradition

Honour Moderations *pl n* (at Oxford University) the first public examination, in which candidates are placed into one of three classes of honours. Sometimes shortened to: **Moderations** *or* **Mods**

honours *or US* **honors** ('ɒnəz) *pl n* **1** observances of respect **2** (*often capital*) **a** (in a university degree or degree course) a rank of the highest academic standard **b** (*as modifier*): *an honours degree*. Abbreviation: **Hons** Compare **general** (sense 9), **pass** (sense 35) **3** a high mark awarded for an examination; distinction **4** last (*or* funeral) honours observances of respect at a funeral **5** military honours ceremonies performed by troops in honour of royalty, at the burial of an officer, etc

honour school *n* (at Oxford University) one of the courses of study leading to an honours degree

honours list *n* Brit a list of those who have had or are having an honour, esp a peerage or membership of an order of chivalry, conferred on them

honours of war *pl n military* the honours granted by the victorious to the defeated, esp as of marching out with all arms and flags flying

Hons (ɒnz) *n* short for **honours** (sense 2)

Hon. Sec. *abbreviation for* Honorary Secretary

Honshu ('hɒnʃuː) *n* the largest of the four main islands of Japan, between the Pacific and the Sea of Japan; regarded as the Japanese mainland; includes a number of offshore islands and contains most of the main cities. Pop: 102 324 961 (2000). Area: 230 448 sq km (88 976 sq miles). Also called: Hondo

hoo (huː) *pron West Yorkshire and South Lancashire dialect* she [from Old English *heo*]

hooch *or* **hootch** (huːtʃ) *n informal, chiefly US and Canadian* alcoholic drink, esp illicitly distilled spirits [c20 shortened from Tlingit *Hootchinoo*, name of a tribe that distilled a type of liquor]

hood[1] (hʊd) *n* **1** a loose head covering either attached to a cloak or coat or made as a separate garment **2** something resembling this in shape or use **3** the US and Canadian name for **bonnet** (of a car) **4** the folding roof of a convertible car **5** a hoodlike garment worn over an academic gown, indicating its wearer's degree and university **6** *falconry* a close-fitting cover, placed over the head and eyes of a falcon to keep it quiet when not hunting **7** *biology* a structure or marking, such as the fold of skin on the head of a cobra, that covers or appears to cover the head or some similar part ▷ *vb* **8** (*tr*) to cover or provide with or as if with a hood [Old English *hōd*; related to Old High German *huot* hat, Middle Dutch *hoet*, Latin *cassis* helmet; see HAT] > 'hoodless *adj* > 'hood,like *adj*

hood[2] (hʊd) *n slang* short for **hoodlum** (gangster)

-hood *suffix forming nouns* **1** indicating state or condition of being: *manhood*; *adulthood* **2** indicating a body of persons: *knighthood*; *priesthood* [Old English *-hād*]

'hood (hʊd) *n slang, chiefly US* short for **neighbourhood**

hooded ('hʊdɪd) *adj* **1** covered with, having, or shaped like a hood **2** (of eyes) having heavy eyelids that appear to be half closed

hooded crow *n* a subspecies of the carrion crow, *Corvus corone cornix*, that has a grey body and black head, wings, and tail. Also called (Scot): hoodie ('hʊdɪ), hoodie crow

hooded seal *n* a large greyish earless seal,

h

Cystophora cristata, of the N Atlantic and Arctic Oceans, having an inflatable hoodlike sac over the nasal region. Also called: **bladdernose**

hoodia (ˈhʊdɪə) *n* any of several succulent asclepiadaceous plants of the genus *Hoodia*, of southern Africa, the sap of which suppresses appetite

hoodie (ˈhʊdɪ) *n informal* a hooded sweatshirt

hoodlum (ˈhuːdləm) *n* **1** a petty gangster or ruffian **2** a lawless youth [C19 perhaps from Southern German dialect *Haderlump* ragged good-for-nothing] > ˈ**hoodlumism** *n*

hoodman-blind *n Brit archaic* blind man's buff

hood mould *n* another name for **dripstone** (sense 2)

hoodoo (ˈhuːduː) *n, pl* **-doos** **1** a variant of **voodoo** **2** *informal* a person or thing that brings bad luck **3** *informal* bad luck **4** (in the western US and Canada) a strangely shaped column of rock ▷ *vb* **-doos, -dooing, -dooed** **5** (*tr*) *informal* to bring bad luck to [C19 variant of VOODOO] > ˈ**hoodooism** *n*

hood rat *n US slang derogatory* a young promiscuous woman from an impoverished urban area [C20 from ʼHOOD; influenced by MALL RAT]

hoodwink (ˈhʊdˌwɪŋk) *vb* (*tr*) **1** to dupe; trick **2** *obsolete* to cover or hide [C16 originally, to cover the eyes with a hood, blindfold] > ˈ**hoodˌwinker** *n*

hooey (ˈhuːɪ) *n, interj slang* nonsense; rubbish [C20 of unknown origin]

hoof (huːf) *n, pl* **hooves** (huːvz) *or* **hoofs** **1 a** the horny covering of the end of the foot in the horse, deer, and all other ungulate mammals **b** (*in combination*): *a hoofbeat*. Related adj: **ungular** **2** the foot of an ungulate mammal **3** a hoofed animal **4** *facetious* a person's foot **5** **on the hoof a** (of livestock) alive **b** in an impromptu manner: *he did his thinking on the hoof* ▷ *vb* **6** (*tr*) to kick or trample with the hoofs **7** **hoof it** *slang* **a** to walk **b** to dance [Old English *hōf*; related to Old Norse *hōfr*, Old High German *huof* (German *Huf*), Sanskrit *saphás*] > ˈ**hoofless** *adj* > ˈ**hoofˌlike** *adj*

hoofbound (ˈhuːfˌbaʊnd) *adj vet science* (of a horse) having dry contracted hooves, with resultant pain and lameness

hoofed (huːft) *adj* **a** having a hoof or hoofs **b** (*in combination*): *four-hoofed; cloven-hoofed*

hoofer (ˈhuːfə) *n slang* a professional dancer, esp a tap-dancer

Hooghly (ˈhuːglɪ) *n* a river in NE India, in West Bengal: the westernmost and commercially most important channel by which the River Ganges enters the Bay of Bengal. Length: 232 km (144 miles)

hoo-ha (ˈhuːˌhɑː) *n* a noisy commotion or fuss [C20 of unknown origin]

hook (hʊk) *n* **1** a piece of material, usually metal, curved or bent and used to suspend, catch, hold, or pull something **2** short for **fish-hook** **3** a trap or snare **4** *chiefly US* something that attracts or is intended to be an attraction **5** something resembling a hook in design or use **6 a** a sharp bend or angle in a geological formation, esp a river **b** a sharply curved spit of land **7** *boxing* a short swinging blow delivered from the side with the elbow bent **8** *cricket* a shot in which the ball is hit square on the leg side with the bat held horizontally **9** *golf* a shot that causes the ball to swerve sharply from right to left **10** *surfing* the top of a breaking wave **11** Also called: **hookcheck** *ice hockey* the act of hooking an opposing player **12** *music* a stroke added to the stem of a written or printed note to indicate time values shorter than a crotchet **13** a catchy musical phrase in a pop song **14** another name for a **sickle** **15** a nautical word for **anchor** **16** **by hook or (by) crook** by any means **17** **get the hook** *US and Canadian slang* to be dismissed from employment **18** **hook, line, and sinker** *informal* completely: *he fell for it hook, line, and sinker* **19** **off the hook a** *slang* out of danger; free from obligation or guilt **b** (of a telephone receiver) not on the support, so that incoming calls cannot be received **20** **on one's own hook** *slang, chiefly US* on one's own initiative **21** **on the hook** *slang* **a** waiting **b** in a dangerous or difficult situation **22** **sling one's hook** *Brit slang* to leave ▷ *vb* **23** (often foll by *up*) to fasten or be fastened with or as if with a hook or hooks **24** (*tr*) to catch (something, such as a fish) on a hook **25** to curve like or into the shape of a hook **26** (*tr*) (of bulls, elks, etc) to catch or gore with the horns **27** (*tr*) to make (a rug) by hooking yarn through a stiff fabric backing with a special instrument **28** (*tr;* often foll by *down*) to cut (grass or herbage) with a sickle: *to hook down weeds* **29** *boxing* to hit (an opponent) with a hook **30** *ice hockey* to impede (an opposing player) by catching hold of him with the stick **31** *golf* to play (a ball) with a hook **32** *rugby* to obtain and pass (the ball) backwards from a scrum to a member of one's team, using the feet **33** *cricket* to play (a ball) with a hook **34** (*tr*) *informal* to trick **35** (*tr*) a slang word for **steal** **36** **hook it** *slang* to run or go quickly away ▷ See also **hook-up** [Old English *hōc*; related to Middle Dutch *hōk*, Old Norse *haki*] > ˈ**hookless** *adj* > ˈ**hookˌlike** *adj*

hookah *or* **hooka** (ˈhʊkə) *n* an oriental pipe for smoking marijuana, tobacco, etc, consisting of one or more long flexible stems connected to a container of water or other liquid through which smoke is drawn and cooled. Also called: **hubble-bubble, kalian, narghile, water pipe** [C18 from Arabic *huqqah*]

hook and eye *n* a fastening for clothes consisting of a small hook hooked onto a small metal or thread loop

hooked (hʊkt) *adj* **1** bent like a hook **2** having a hook or hooks **3** caught or trapped **4** a slang word for **married** **5** *slang* addicted to a drug **6** (often foll by *on*) obsessed (with) > **hookedness** (ˈhʊkɪdnɪs) *n*

hooker¹ (ˈhʊkə) *n* **1** a commercial fishing boat using hooks and lines instead of nets **2** a sailing boat of the west of Ireland formerly used for cargo and now for pleasure sailing and racing [C17 from Dutch *hoeker*]

hooker² (ˈhʊkə) *n* **1** a person or thing that hooks **2** *US and Canadian slang* **a** a draught of alcoholic drink, esp of spirits **b** a prostitute **3** *rugby* the central forward in the front row of a scrum whose main job is to hook the ball

Hooke's law (hʊks) *n* the principle that the stress imposed on a solid is directly proportional to the strain produced, within the elastic limit [C18 named after Robert *Hooke* (1635–1703), English physicist, chemist, and inventor]

hooknose (ˈhʊkˌnəʊz) *n* a nose with a pronounced outward and downward curve; aquiline nose > ˈ**hookˌnosed** *adj*

Hook of Holland *n* **the** **1** a cape on the SW coast of the Netherlands, in South Holland province **2** a port on this cape ▷ Dutch name: **Hoek van Holland**

hook-tip *n* **1** any of several moths of the genus *Daepana*, characterized by the hooked point on each forewing **2** **beautiful hook-tip** a similar but unrelated species, *Laspeyria flexula*

hook-up *n* **1** the contact of an aircraft in flight with the refuelling hose of a tanker aircraft **2** an alliance or relationship, esp an unlikely one, between people, countries, etc **3** the linking of broadcasting equipment or stations to transmit a special programme ▷ *vb* **hook up** (*adverb*) **4** to connect (two or more people or things) **5** (often foll by *with*) *slang* to get married (to)

hookworm (ˈhʊkˌwɜːm) *n* any parasitic blood-sucking nematode worm of the family *Ancylostomatidae*, esp *Ancylostoma duodenale* or *Necator americanus*, both of which cause disease. They have hooked mouthparts and enter their hosts by boring through the skin

hookworm disease *n* the nontechnical name for **ancylostomiasis**

hooky *or* **hookey** (ˈhʊkɪ) *n informal, chiefly US, Canadian, and NZ* truancy, usually from school (esp in the phrase **play hooky**) [C20 perhaps from *hook it* to escape]

hooley *or* **hoolie** (ˈhuːlɪ) *n, pl* **-leys** *or* **-lies** *chiefly Irish and NZ* a lively party [C19 of unknown origin]

hoolie (ˈhuːlɪ) *n slang* a hooligan

hooligan (ˈhuːlɪgən) *n slang* a rough lawless young person [C19 perhaps variant of *Houlihan*, Irish surname] > ˈ**hooliganism** *n*

hoon (huːn) *n Austral and NZ informal* a hooligan [of unknown origin]

hoop¹ (huːp) *n* **1** a rigid circular band of metal or wood **2** something resembling this **3 a** a band of iron that holds the staves of a barrel or cask together **b** (*as modifier*): *hoop iron* **4** a child's toy shaped like a hoop and rolled on the ground or whirled around the body **5** *croquet* any of the iron arches through which the ball is driven **6 a** a light curved frame to spread out a skirt **b** (*as modifier*): *a hoop skirt; a hoop petticoat* **7** *basketball* the round metal frame to which the net is attached to form the basket **8** a large ring through which performers or animals jump **9** *jewellery* **a** an earring consisting of one or more circles of metal, plastic, etc **b** the part of a finger ring through which the finger fits **10** *Austral informal* a jockey **11** **go** *or* **be put through the hoop** to be subjected to an ordeal ▷ *vb* **12** (*tr*) to surround with or as if with a hoop [Old English *hōp*; related to Dutch *hoep*, Old Norse *hōp* bay, Lithuanian *kabē* hook] > **hooped** *adj* > ˈ**hoopˌlike** *adj*

hoop² (huːp) *n, vb* a variant spelling of **whoop**

hooper (ˈhuːpə) *n* a rare word for **cooper**

hoopla (ˈhuːplɑː) *n* **1** *Brit* a fairground game in which a player tries to throw a hoop over an object and so win it **2** *US and Canadian slang* noise; bustle **3** *US slang* nonsense; ballyhoo [C20 see WHOOP, LA²]

hoopoe (ˈhuːpuː) *n* an Old World bird, *Upupa epops*, having a pinkish-brown plumage with black-and-white wings and an erectile crest: family *Upupidae*, order *Coraciiformes* (kingfishers, etc) [C17 from earlier *hoopoop*, of imitative origin; compare Latin *upupa*]

hoop pine *n* a fast-growing timber tree of Australia, *Araucaria cunninghamii*, having rough bark with hoop-like cracks around the trunk and branches: family *Araucariaceae*

hoop snake *n* any of various North American snakes, such as the mud snake (*Farancia abacura*), that were formerly thought to hold the tail in the mouth and roll along like a hoop

hooray (huːˈreɪ) *interj, n, vb* **1** a variant of **hurrah** ▷ *interj* **2** Also: **hooroo** (huːˈruː) *Austral and NZ* goodbye; cheerio

Hooray Henry (ˈhuːˌreɪ) *n, pl* **Hooray Henries** *or* **-rys** a young upper-class man, often with affectedly hearty voice and manners. Sometimes shortened to: **Hooray**

hoosegow *or* **hoosgow** (ˈhuːsgaʊ) *n US* a slang word for **jail** [C20 from Mexican Spanish *jusgado* prison, from Spanish: court of justice, from *juzgar* to judge, from Latin *jūdicāre*, from *judex* a JUDGE; compare JUG]

Hoosier (ˈhuːʒɪə) *n US* a native or inhabitant of Indiana [C19 origin unknown]

hoot¹ (huːt) *n* **1** the mournful wavering cry of some owls **2** a similar sound, such as that of a train whistle **3** a jeer of derision **4** *informal* an amusing person or thing: *the weekend was a hoot* **5** **not give a hoot** not to care at all ▷ *vb* **6** (often foll by *at*) to jeer or yell (something) contemptuously (at someone) **7** (*tr*) to drive (political speakers, actors on stage, etc) off or away by hooting **8** (*intr*) to make a hoot **9** (*intr*) *Brit* to blow a horn [C13 *hoten*, of imitative origin]

hoot² (huːt), *or* **hoots** (huːts) *interj* an exclamation of impatience or dissatisfaction: a supposed Scotticism [C17 of unknown origin]

hoot³ (huːt) *n Austral and NZ* a slang word for **money** [from Māori *utu* price]

hootch (huːtʃ) *n* a variant spelling of **hooch**

hootenanny ('hu:tⁿˌnænɪ) or **hootnanny** ('hu:tˌnænɪ) *n, pl* -nies **1** an informal performance by folk singers **2** *chiefly US* something the name of which is unspecified or forgotten [c20 of unknown origin]

hooter ('hu:tə) *n chiefly Brit* **1** a person or thing that hoots, esp a car horn **2** *slang* a nose

hoot owl *n* any owl that utters a hooting cry, as distinct from a screech owl

Hoover ('hu:və) *n* **1** *trademark* a type of vacuum cleaner ▷ *vb* (*usually not capital*) **2** to vacuum-clean (a carpet, furniture, etc) **3** (*tr; often foll by up*) to consume or dispose of (something) quickly and completely: *he hoovered up his grilled fish*

Hoover Dam *n* a dam in the western US, on the Colorado River on the border between Nevada and Arizona; forms Lake Mead. Height: 222 m (727 ft). Length: 354 m (1180 ft). Former name (1933–47): Boulder Dam

hooves (hu:vz) *n* a plural of **hoof**

hop¹ (hɒp) *vb* hops, hopping, hopped **1** (*intr*) to make a jump forwards or upwards, esp on one foot **2** (*intr*) (esp of frogs, birds, rabbits, etc) to move forwards in short jumps **3** (*tr*) to jump over: *he hopped the hedge* **4** (*intr*) *informal* to move or proceed quickly (in, on, out of, etc): *hop on a bus* **5** (*tr*) *informal* to cross (an ocean) in an aircraft: *they hopped the Atlantic in seven hours* **6** (*tr*) *US and Canadian informal* to travel by means of (an aircraft, bus, etc): *he hopped a train to Chicago* **7** *US and Canadian* to bounce or cause to bounce: *he hopped the flat stone over the lake's surface* **8** (*intr*) *US and Canadian informal* to begin intense activity, esp work **9** (*intr*) another word for **limp¹ 10** **hop it** (or **off**) *Brit slang* to go away ▷ *n* **11** the act or an instance of hopping **12** *old-fashioned informal* a dance, esp one at which popular music is played: *we're all going to the school hop tonight* **13** *informal* a trip, esp in an aircraft **14** *US* a bounce, as of a ball **15** **on the hop** *informal* **a** active or busy **b** *Brit* unawares or unprepared: *the new ruling caught me on the hop* ▷ See also **hop into** [Old English *hoppian*; related to Old Norse *hoppa* to hop, Middle Low German *hupfen*]

hop² (hɒp) *n* **1** any climbing plant of the N temperate genus *Humulus*, esp *H. lupulus*, which has green conelike female flowers and clusters of small male flowers: family *Cannabiaceae* (or *Cannabidaceae*). See also **hops 2 hop garden** a field of hops **3** *obsolete slang* opium or any other narcotic drug [c15 from Middle Dutch *hoppe*; related to Old High German *hopfo*, Norwegian *hupp* tassel]

hop clover *n* the US name for **hop trefoil**

hope (həʊp) *n* **1** (*sometimes plural*) a feeling of desire for something and confidence in the possibility of its fulfilment: *his hope for peace was justified; their hopes were dashed* **2** a reasonable ground for this feeling: *there is still hope* **3** a person or thing that gives cause for hope **4** a thing, situation, or event that is desired: *my hope is that prices will fall* **5** **not a hope** or **some hope** used ironically to express little confidence that expectations will be fulfilled ▷ *vb* **6** (*tr; takes a clause as object or an infinitive*) to desire (something) with some possibility of fulfilment: *we hope you can come; I hope to tell you* **7** (*intr; often foll by for*) to have a wish (for a future event, situation, etc) **8** (*tr; takes a clause as object*) to trust, expect, or believe: *we hope that this is satisfactory* [Old English *hopa*; related to Old Frisian *hope*, Dutch *hoop*, Middle High German *hoffe*] > 'hoper *n*

hope chest *n US and Canadian* a young woman's collection of clothes, linen, cutlery, etc, in anticipation of marriage. Also called (esp in Britain): bottom drawer

hopeful ('həʊpfʊl) *adj* **1** having or expressing hope **2** giving or inspiring hope; promising ▷ *n* **3** a person considered to be on the brink of success (esp in the phrase **a young hopeful**) > 'hopefulness *n*

hopefully ('həʊpfʊlɪ) *adv* **1** in a hopeful manner **2** *informal* it is hoped: *hopefully they will be here soon*

USAGE The use of *hopefully* to mean *it is hoped* used to be considered incorrect by some people but has now become acceptable in informal contexts

Hopeh or **Hopei** ('həʊ'peɪ) *n* a variant transliteration of the Chinese name for **Hebei**

hopeless ('həʊplɪs) *adj* **1** having or offering no hope **2** impossible to analyse or solve **3** unable to learn, function, etc **4** *informal* without skill or ability > 'hopelessly *adv* > 'hopelessness *n*

hophead ('hɒpˌhɛd) *n slang, chiefly US* a heroin or opium addict [c20 from obsolete slang *hop* opium; see HOP²]

Hopi ('həʊpɪ) *n* **1** (*pl* -pis or -pi) a member of a North American Indian people of NE Arizona **2** the language of this people, belonging to the Shoshonean subfamily of the Uto-Aztecan family [from Hopi *Hópi* peaceful]

hop into *vb* (*intr, preposition*) *Austral and NZ slang* **1** to attack (a person) **2** to start or set about (a task)

hoplite ('hɒplaɪt) *n* (in ancient Greece) a heavily armed infantryman [c18 from Greek *hoplitēs*, from *hoplon* weapon, from *hepein* to prepare] > hoplitic (hɒp'lɪtɪk) *adj*

hoplology (hɒp'lɒlədʒɪ) *n* the study of weapons or armour [c19 from Greek, from *hoplon* weapon + -LOGY] > hop'lologist *n*

hopper ('hɒpə) *n* **1** a person or thing that hops **2** a funnel-shaped chamber or reservoir from which solid materials can be discharged under gravity into a receptacle below, esp for feeding fuel to a furnace, loading a railway truck with grain, etc **3** a machine used for picking hops **4** any of various long-legged hopping insects, esp the grasshopper, leaf hopper, and immature locust **5** Also called: **hoppercar** an open-topped railway truck for bulk transport of loose minerals, etc, unloaded through doors on the underside **6** *computing* a device formerly used for holding punched cards and feeding them to a card punch or card reader

hop-picker *n* a person employed or a machine used to pick hops

hopping ('hɒpɪŋ) *n* **1** the action of a person or animal that hops **2** *Tyneside dialect* a fair, esp (**the Hoppings**) an annual fair in Newcastle ▷ *adj* **3** **hopping mad** in a terrible rage

hopple ('hɒpᵊl) *vb, n* a less common word for **hobble** (senses 2, 5) > 'hoppler *n*

Hoppus foot ('hɒpəs) *n* a unit of volume equal to 1.27 cubic feet, applied to timber in the round, the cross-sectional area being taken as the square of one quarter of the circumference [c20 named after Edward *Hoppus*, 18th-century English surveyor]

hops (hɒps) *pl n* the dried ripe flowers, esp the female flowers, of the hop plant, used to give a bitter taste to beer

hopsack ('hɒpˌsæk) *n* **1** a roughly woven fabric of wool, cotton, etc, used for clothing **2** Also called: **hopsacking** a coarse fabric used for bags, etc, made generally of hemp or jute

hopscotch ('hɒpˌskɒtʃ) *n* a children's game in which a player throws a small stone or other object to land in one of a pattern of squares marked on the ground and then hops over to it to pick it up [c19 HOP¹ + SCOTCH¹]

hop, step, and jump *n* **1** an older term for **triple jump 2** Also called: **hop, skip, and jump** a short distance

hop trefoil *n* a leguminous plant, *Trifolium campestre*, of N temperate grasslands, with globular yellow flower heads and trifoliate leaves. US and Canadian name: hop clover

hora ('hɔːrə) *n* a traditional Israeli or Romanian circle dance [from Modern Hebrew *hōrāh*, from Romanian *horă*, from Turkish]

Horae ('hɔːriː) *pl n classical myth* the goddesses of the seasons. Also called: the Hours [Latin: hours]

horal ('hɔːrəl) *adj* a less common word for **hourly** [c18 from Late Latin *hōrālis* of an HOUR]

horary ('hɔːrərɪ) *adj archaic* **1** relating to the hours **2** hourly [c17 from Medieval Latin *hōrārius*; see HOUR]

Horatian (hə'reɪʃən) *adj* of, relating to, or characteristic of the Roman poet Horace (Latin name *Quintus Horatius Flaccus*; 65–8 BC) or his poetry

Horatian ode *n* an ode of several stanzas, each of the same metrical pattern. Also: Sapphic ode

horde (hɔːd) *n* **1** a vast crowd; throng; mob **2** a local group of people in a nomadic society **3** a nomadic group of people, esp an Asiatic group **4** a large moving mass of animals, esp insects ▷ *vb* **5** (*intr*) to form, move in, or live in a horde [c16 from Polish *horda*, from Turkish *ordū* camp; compare *Urdu*]

USAGE *Horde* is sometimes wrongly written where *hoard* is meant: *a hoard* (not *horde*) *of gold coins*

hordein ('hɔːdiːɪn) *n* a simple protein, rich in proline, that occurs in barley [c19 from French *hordéine*, from Latin *hordeum* barley + French -*ine* -IN]

hordeolum (ˌhɔːdɪ'əʊləm) *n* medical name for a **stye** (of the eye)

Horeb ('hɔːrɛb) *n Bible* a mountain, probably Mount Sinai

horehound or **hoarhound** ('hɔːˌhaʊnd) *n* **1** Also called: **white horehound** a downy perennial herbaceous Old World plant, *Marrubium vulgare*, with small white flowers that contain a bitter juice formerly used as a cough medicine and flavouring: family *Lamiaceae* (labiates). See also **black horehound 2 water horehound** another name for **bugleweed** (sense 1) [Old English *hārhūne*, from *hār* grey + *hūne* horehound, of obscure origin]

hori ('hɒriː) *NZ informal derogatory* ▷ *n, pl* horis **1** a Māori **2** falsehood ▷ *adj* **3** of or relating to the Māori [Māori]

horiatiki (ˌhɒrɪə'tiːkɪ) *n* a traditional Greek salad consisting of tomatoes, cucumber, onion, olives, and feta cheese [c21 from Modern Greek]

horizon (hə'raɪzⁿn) *n* **1** Also called: **visible horizon, apparent horizon** the apparent line that divides the earth and the sky **2** *astronomy* **a** Also called: **sensible horizon** the circular intersection with the celestial sphere of the plane tangential to the earth at the position of the observer **b** Also called: **celestial horizon** the great circle on the celestial sphere, the plane of which passes through the centre of the earth and is parallel to the sensible horizon **3** the range or limit of scope, interest, knowledge, etc **4** a thin layer of rock within a stratum that has a distinct composition, esp of fossils, by which the stratum may be dated **5** a layer in a soil profile having particular characteristics. See **A horizon, B horizon, C horizon 6** **on the horizon** likely or about to happen or appear [c14 from Latin, from Greek *horizōn kuklos* limiting circle, from *horizein* to limit, from *horos* limit] > ho'rizonless *adj*

horizontal (ˌhɒrɪ'zɒntᵊl) *adj* **1** parallel to the plane of the horizon; level; flat. Compare **vertical** (sense 1) **2** of or relating to the horizon **3** measured or contained in a plane parallel to that of the horizon **4** applied uniformly or equally to all members of a group **5** *economics* relating to identical stages of commercial activity: *horizontal integration* ▷ *n* **6** a horizontal plane, position, line, etc > 'hori'zontalness or ˌhorizon'tality *n* > ˌhori'zontally *adv*

horizontal bar *n gymnastics* a raised bar on which swinging and vaulting exercises are performed. Also called: high bar

horizontal mobility *n sociol* the movement of groups or individuals to positions that differ from those previously held but do not involve any change in class, status, or power. Compare **vertical mobility**. See also **upward mobility, downward mobility**

horizontal stabilizer *n* the US name for **tailplane**

horizontal union *n* another name (esp US) for **craft union**

h

horlicks ('hɔːlɪks) *n* **make a horlicks** *Brit informal* to make a mistake or a mess: *his boss is making a horlicks of his job* [c20 from *Horlicks*, a drink meant to induce sleep]
horme ('hɔːmɪ) *n* (in the psychology of C. G. Jung) fundamental vital energy [c20 from Greek *hormē* impulse] > '**hormic** *adj*
hormone ('hɔːməʊn) *n* **1** a chemical substance produced in an endocrine gland and transported in the blood to a certain tissue, on which it exerts a specific effect **2** an organic compound produced by a plant that is essential for growth **3** any synthetic substance having the same effects [c20 from Greek *hormōn*, from *horman* to stir up, urge on, from *hormē* impulse, assault] > **hor'monal** *adj*
hormone replacement therapy *n* a form of oestrogen treatment used to control menopausal symptoms and in the prevention of osteoporosis. Abbreviation: **HRT**
Hormuz (hɔː'muːz, 'hɔːmʌz) *or* **Ormuz** *n* an island off the SE coast of Iran, in the **Strait of Hormuz**: ruins of the ancient city of Hormuz, a major trading centre in the Middle Ages. Area: about 41 sq km (16 sq miles)
horn (hɔːn) *n* **1** either of a pair of permanent outgrowths on the heads of cattle, antelopes, sheep, etc, consisting of a central bony core covered with layers of keratin. Related adjs: **corneous, keratoid 2** the outgrowth from the nasal bone of a rhinoceros, consisting of a mass of fused hairs **3** any hornlike projection or process, such as the eyestalk of a snail **4** the antler of a deer **5 a** the constituent substance, mainly keratin, of horns, hooves, etc **b** (*in combination*): *horn-rimmed spectacles* **6** a container or device made from this substance or an artificial substitute: *a shoe horn; a drinking horn* **7** an object or part resembling a horn in shape, such as the points at either end of a crescent, the point of an anvil, the pommel of a saddle, or a cornucopia **8** a primitive musical wind instrument made from the horn of an animal **9** any musical instrument consisting of a pipe or tube of brass fitted with a mouthpiece, with or without valves. See **hunting horn, French horn, cor anglais 10** *jazz slang* any wind instrument **11 a** a device for producing a warning or signalling noise **b** (*in combination*): *a foghorn* **12** (*usually plural*) the hornlike projection attributed to certain devils, deities, etc **13** (*usually plural*) the imaginary hornlike parts formerly supposed to appear on the forehead of a cuckold **14** Also called: **horn balance** an extension of an aircraft control surface that projects in front of the hinge providing aerodynamic assistance in moving the control **15 a** Also called: **acoustic horn, exponential horn** a hollow conical device coupled to the diaphragm of a gramophone to control the direction and quality of the sound **b** any such device used to spread or focus sound, such as the device attached to an electrical loudspeaker in a public address system **c** Also called: **horn antenna** a microwave aerial, formed by flaring out the end of a waveguide **16** *geology* another name for **pyramidal peak 17** a stretch of land or water shaped like a horn **18** *Brit slang* an erection of the penis **19** *Bible* a symbol of power, victory, or success: *in my name shall his horn be exalted* **20 blow one's horn** *US and Canadian* to boast about oneself; brag. Brit equivalent: **blow one's own trumpet 21 draw** (*or* **pull**) **in one's horns a** to suppress or control one's feelings, esp of anger, enthusiasm, or passion **b** to withdraw a previous statement **c** to economize **22 on the horns of a dilemma a** in a situation involving a choice between two equally unpalatable alternatives **b** in an awkward situation ▷ *vb* (*tr*) **23** to provide with a horn or horns **24** to gore or butt with a horn ▷ See also **horn in** [Old English; related to Old Norse *horn*, Gothic *haurn*, Latin *cornu* horn] > '**hornless** *adj* > '**horn,like** *adj*
Horn (hɔːn) *n* **Cape** See **Cape Horn**
hornbag ('hɔːn,bæg) *n Austral slang* a promiscuous woman [c20 from HORNY]
hornbeam ('hɔːn,biːm) *n* **1** any tree of the betulaceous genus *Carpinus*, such as *C. betulus* of Europe and Asia, having smooth grey bark and hard white wood **2** the wood of any of these trees ▷ Also called: **ironwood** [c14 from HORN + BEAM, referring to its tough wood]
hornbill ('hɔːn,bɪl) *n* any bird of the family *Bucerotidae* of tropical Africa and Asia, having a very large bill with a basal bony protuberance: order *Coraciiformes* (kingfishers, etc)
hornblende ('hɔːn,blɛnd) *n* a black or greenish-black mineral of the amphibole group, found in igneous and metamorphic rocks. Composition: calcium magnesium iron sodium aluminium aluminosilicate. General formula: $(Ca,Na)_{2\text{-}3}(Mg,Fe,Al)_5Si_6(Si,Al)_2O_{22}(OH)_2$ [c18 from German *Horn* horn + BLENDE] > ,**horn'blendic** *adj*
hornbook ('hɔːn,bʊk) *n* **1** a page bearing a religious text or the alphabet, held in a frame with a thin window of flattened cattle horn over it **2** any elementary primer
horned (hɔːnd) *adj* having a horn, horns, or hornlike parts > **hornedness** ('hɔːnɪdnɪs) *n*
horned owl *n* any large owl of the genus *Bubo*, having prominent ear tufts: family *Strigidae*
horned poppy *n* any of several Eurasian papaveraceous plants of the genera *Glaucium* and *Roemeria*, having large brightly coloured flowers and long curved seed capsules
horned pout *n* a North American catfish, *Ameiurus* (or *Ictalurus*) *nebulosus*, with a sharp spine on the dorsal and pectoral fins and eight long barbels around the mouth: family *Ameiuridae* Also called: **brown bullhead**
horned toad *or* **lizard** *n* any small insectivorous burrowing lizard of the genus *Phrynosoma*, inhabiting desert regions of America, having a flattened toadlike body covered with spines: family *Iguanidae* (iguanas)
horned viper *n* a venomous snake, *Cerastes cornutus*, that occurs in desert regions of N Africa and SW Asia and has a small horny spine above each eye: family *Viperidae* (vipers). Also called: **sand viper**
hornet ('hɔːnɪt) *n* **1** any of various large social wasps of the family *Vespidae*, esp *Vespa crabro* of Europe, that can inflict a severe sting **2 hornet's nest** a strongly unfavourable reaction (often in the phrase **stir up a hornet's nest**) [Old English *hyrnetu*; related to Old Saxon *hornut*, Old High German *hornuz*]
hornet clearwing *n* See **clearwing**
hornfels ('hɔːnfɛlz) *n* a hard compact fine-grained metamorphic rock formed by the action of heat from a magmatic intrusion on neighbouring sedimentary rocks. Also called: **hornstone** [German: literally, horn rock]
horn in *vb* (*intr, adverb*; often foll by *on*) *slang* to interrupt or intrude: *don't horn in on our conversation*
Horn of Africa *n* a region of NE Africa, comprising Somalia and adjacent territories
horn of plenty *n* **1** another term for **cornucopia 2** an edible basidiomycetous fungus, *Craterellus cornucopioides*, related to the chanterelle and like it funnel shaped but dark brown inside and dark grey outside: found in broad-leaved woodland
hornpipe ('hɔːn,paɪp) *n* **1** an obsolete reed instrument with a mouthpiece made of horn **2** an old British solo dance to a hornpipe accompaniment, traditionally performed by sailors **3** a piece of music for such a dance
horns and halo effect *n* a tendency to allow one's judgement of another person, esp in a job interview, to be unduly influenced by an unfavourable (horns) or favourable (halo) first impression based on appearances
horn silver *n* another name for **chlorargyrite**
hornstone ('hɔːn,stəʊn) *n* another name for **chert** *or* **hornfels** [c17 translation of German *Hornstein*; so called from its appearance]
hornswoggle ('hɔːn,swɒgᵊl) *vb* (*tr*) *slang* to cheat or trick; bamboozle [c19 of unknown origin]
horntail ('hɔːn,teɪl) *n* any of various large wasplike insects of the hymenopterous family *Siricidae*, the females of which have a strong stout ovipositor and lay their eggs in the wood of felled trees. Also called: **wood wasp**
hornwort ('hɔːn,wɜːt) *n* **1** any aquatic plant of the genus *Ceratophyllum*, forming submerged branching masses in ponds and slow-flowing streams: family *Ceratophyllaceae* **2** any of a group of bryophytes belonging to the phylum *Anthocerophyta*, resembling liverworts but with hornlike sporophytes
hornwrack ('hɔːn,ræk) *n* a yellowish bryozoan or sea mat sometimes found on beaches after a storm
horny ('hɔːnɪ) *adj* **hornier, horniest 1** of, like, or hard as horn **2** having a horn or horns **3** *slang* **a** sexually aroused **b** provoking or intended to provoke sexual arousal **c** sexually eager or lustful > '**hornily** *adv* > '**horniness** *n*
hornywink ('hɔːnɪ,wɪŋk) *n Southwest English dialect* a lapwing
horoeka (hɒrɒ'kiːkə) *n, pl* **horoeka** NZ another name for **lancewood** (sense 3) [Māori]
horokaka (hɒrɒ'kɑːkə) *n, pl* **horokaka** a New Zealand low-growing plant, *Disphyma australe* with fleshy leaves and pink or white flowers [Māori]
horol. *abbreviation for* horology
horologe ('hɒrə,lɒdʒ) *n* a rare word for **timepiece** [c14 from Latin *hōrologium*, from Greek *hōrologion*, from *hōra* HOUR + *-logos* from *legein* to tell]
horologist (hɒ'rɒlədʒɪst) *or* **horologer** (hɒ'rɒlədʒə) *n* a person skilled in horology, esp an expert maker of timepieces
horologium (,hɒrə'ləʊdʒɪəm) *n, pl* **-gia** (-dʒɪə) **1** a clocktower **2** Also called: **horologion** (in the Eastern Church) a liturgical book of the offices for the canonical hours, corresponding to the Western breviary [c17 from Latin; see HOROLOGE]
Horologium (,hɒrə'ləʊdʒɪəm) *n, Latin genitive* **Horologii** (,hɒrə'ləʊdʒɪaɪ) a faint constellation in the S hemisphere lying near Eridanus and Hydrus
horology (hɒ'rɒlədʒɪ) *n* the art or science of making timepieces or of measuring time > **horologic** (,hɒrə'lɒdʒɪk) *or* ,**horo'logical** *adj*
horopito ('hɔːrɔːpiːtɔː) *n* a bushy New Zealand shrub, *Pseudowintera colorata*, with red aromatic peppery leaves. It possesses antifungal and antibacterial properties. Also called: **New Zealand pepper tree** [Māori]
horopter (hɒ'rɒptə) *n optics* the locus of all points in space that stimulate points on each eye that yield the same visual direction as each other [c18 from Greek *horos* boundary + *optēr*, from *ops* eye]
horoscope ('hɒrə,skəʊp) *n* **1** the prediction of a person's future based on a comparison of the zodiacal data for the time of birth with the data from the period under consideration **2** the configuration of the planets, the sun, and the moon in the sky at a particular moment **3** Also called: **chart** a diagram showing the positions of the planets, sun, moon, etc, at a particular time and place [Old English *horoscopus*, from Latin, from Greek *hōroskopos* ascendant birth sign, from *hōra* HOUR + -SCOPE] > **horoscopic** (,hɒrə'skɒpɪk) *adj*
horoscopy (hɒ'rɒskəpɪ) *n, pl* **-pies** the casting and interpretation of horoscopes
horrendous (hɒ'rɛndəs) *adj* another word for **horrific** [c17 from Latin *horrendus* fearful, from *horrēre* to bristle, shudder, tremble; see HORROR] > **hor'rendously** *adv*
horrible ('hɒrəbᵊl) *adj* **1** causing horror; dreadful **2** disagreeable; unpleasant **3** *informal* cruel or unkind [c14 via Old French from Latin *horribilis*, from *horrēre* to tremble] > '**horribleness** *n*
horribly ('hɒrɪblɪ) *adv* **1** in a horrible manner **2** (intensifier): *I'm horribly bored*
horrid ('hɒrɪd) *adj* **1** disagreeable; unpleasant: *a horrid meal* **2** repulsive or frightening **3** *informal* unkind [C16 (in the sense: bristling, shaggy): from Latin *horridus* prickly, rough, from *horrēre* to bristle]

> 'horridly *adv* > 'horridness *n*

horrific (hɒ'rɪfɪk, hə-) *adj* provoking horror; horrible > hor'rifically *adv*

horrified ('hɒrɪ,faɪd) *adj* **1** terrified; frightened **2** dismayed or shocked

horrify ('hɒrɪ,faɪ) *vb* -fies, -fying, -fied (*tr*) **1** to cause feelings of horror in; terrify; frighten **2** to dismay or shock greatly > ,horrifi'cation *n*

horrifying ('hɒrɪ,faɪɪŋ) *adj* **1** causing feelings of horror in; awful; terrifying; **2** dismaying or greatly shocking; dreadful > 'horri,fyingly *adv*

horripilation (hɒ,rɪpɪ'leɪʃən) *n physiol* **1** a technical name for **goose flesh 2** the erection of any short bodily hairs [c17 from Late Latin *horripilātiō* a bristling, from Latin *horrēre* to stand on end + *pilus* hair]

horror ('hɒrə) *n* **1** extreme fear; terror; dread **2** intense loathing; hatred **3** (*often plural*) a thing or person causing fear, loathing, etc **4** (*modifier*) having a frightening subject, esp a supernatural one: *a horror film* [c14 from Latin: a trembling with fear; compare HIRSUTE]

horrors ('hɒrəz) *pl n* **1** *slang* a fit of depression or anxiety **2** *informal* See **delirium tremens** ▷ *interj* **3** an expression of dismay, sometimes facetious

horror-struck or **horror-stricken** *adj* shocked; horrified

hors concours French (or kōkur) *adj* (*postpositive,*) ▷ *adv* **1** (of an artist, exhibitor, etc) excluded from competing **2** without equal; unrivalled [literally: out of the competition]

hors de combat French (or də kōba) *adj* (*postpositive,*) ▷ *adv* disabled or injured [literally: out of (the) fight]

hors d'oeuvre (ɔː'dɜːvr; *French* ɔr dœvrə) *n, pl* hors d'oeuvre or hors d'oeuvres ('dɜːvr; *French* dœvrə) an additional dish served as an appetizer, usually before the main meal [c18 from French, literally: outside the work, not part of the main course]

horse (hɔːs) *n* **1** a domesticated perissodactyl mammal, *Equus caballus*, used for draught work and riding: family *Equidae*. Related adj: **equine 2** the adult male of this species; stallion **3** wild horse **a** a horse (*Equus caballus*) that has become feral **b** another name for **Przewalski's horse 4 a** any other member of the family *Equidae*, such as the zebra or ass **b** (*as modifier*): *the horse family* **5** (*functioning as plural*) horsemen, esp cavalry: *a regiment of horse* **6** Also called: **buck** *gymnastics* a padded apparatus on legs, used for vaulting, etc **7** a narrow board supported by a pair of legs at each end, used as a frame for sawing or as a trestle, barrier, etc **8** a contrivance on which a person may ride and exercise **9** a slang word for **heroin 10** *mining* a mass of rock within a vein of ore **11** *nautical* a rod, rope, or cable, fixed at the ends, along which something may slide by means of a thimble, shackle, or other fitting; traveller **12** *chess* an informal name for **knight 13** *informal* short for **horsepower 14** (*modifier*) drawn by a horse or horses: *a horse cart* **15** be (*or* get) on one's high horse *informal* to be disdainfully aloof **16** flog a dead horse See **flog** (sense 6) **17** hold one's horses to hold back; restrain oneself **18** a horse of another *or* a different colour a completely different topic, argument, etc **19** horses for courses a policy, course of action, etc modified slightly to take account of specific circumstances without departing in essentials from the original **20** the horse's mouth the most reliable source **21** to horse! an order to mount horses ▷ *vb* **22** (*tr*) to provide with a horse or horses **23** to put or be put on horseback **24** (*tr*) to move (something heavy) into position by sheer physical strength [Old English *hors*; related to Old Frisian *hors*, Old High German *hros*, Old Norse *hross*] > 'horseless *adj* > 'horse,like *adj*

horse around or **about** *vb* (*intr, adverb*) *informal* to indulge in horseplay

horseback ('hɔːs,bæk) *n* **a** a horse's back (esp in the phrase **on horseback**) **b** (*as modifier*): *horseback riding*

horse bean *n* another name for **broad bean**

horsebox ('hɔːs,bɒks) *n* *Brit* a van or trailer used for carrying horses

horse brass *n* a decorative brass ornament, usually circular, originally attached to a horse's harness

horse chestnut *n* **1** any of several trees of the genus *Aesculus*, esp the Eurasian *A. hippocastanum*, having palmate leaves, erect clusters of white, pink, or red flowers, and brown shiny inedible nuts enclosed in a spiky bur: family *Hippocastanaceae* **2** Also called: **conker** the nut of this tree [c16 so called from its having been used in the treatment of respiratory disease in horses]

horseflesh ('hɔːs,flɛʃ) *n* **1** horses collectively **2** the flesh of a horse, esp edible horse meat

horsefly ('hɔːs,flaɪ) *n, pl* -flies any large stout-bodied dipterous fly of the family *Tabanidae*, the females of which suck the blood of mammals, esp horses, cattle, and man. Also called: **gadfly, cleg**

horse gentian *n* any caprifoliaceous plant of the genus *Triosteum*, of Asia and North America, having small purplish-brown flowers. Also called: feverwort

Horse Guards *pl n* **1** the cavalry regiment that, together with the Life Guards, comprises the cavalry part of the British sovereign's Household Brigade **2** their headquarters in Whitehall, London: also the headquarters of the British Army

horsehair ('hɔːs,hɛə) *n* **a** hair taken chiefly from the tail or mane of a horse, used in upholstery and for fabric, etc **b** (*as modifier*): *a horsehair mattress*

horsehair toadstool or **fungus** *n* a small basidiomycetous fungus, *Marasmius androsaceus*, having a rusty coloured cap and very slender black stems. It is related to the fairy ring mushroom, but is commonly found among conifers and heather

horsehair worm *n* another name for **hairworm** (sense 2)

Horsehead nebula ('hɔːs,hɛd) *n* *astronomy* a dark nebula lying in the constellation of Orion and resembling the head of a horse

horsehide ('hɔːs,haɪd) *n* **1** the hide of a horse **2** leather made from this hide **3** (*modifier*) made of horsehide

horse latitudes *pl n* *nautical* the latitudes near 30°N or 30°S at sea, characterized by baffling winds, calms, and high barometric pressure [c18 referring either to the high mortality of horses on board ship in these latitudes or to *dead horse* (nautical slang: advance pay), which sailors expected to work off by this stage of a voyage]

horse laugh *n* a coarse, mocking, or raucous laugh; guffaw

horseleech ('hɔːs,liːtʃ) *n* **1** any of several large carnivorous freshwater leeches of the genus *Haemopis*, esp *H. sanguisuga* **2** an archaic name for a **veterinary surgeon**

horse mackerel *n* **1** Also called: **scad** a mackerel-like carangid fish, *Trachurus* of European Atlantic waters, with a row of bony scales along the lateral line. Sometimes called (US): **saurel 2** any of various large tunnies or related fishes

horseman ('hɔːsmən) *n, pl* -men **1** a person who is skilled in riding or horsemanship **2** a person who rides a horse > 'horse,woman *fem n*

horsemanship ('hɔːsmən,ʃɪp) *n* **1** the art of riding on horseback **2** skill in riding horses

horse marine *n* *US* **1** (formerly) a mounted marine or cavalryman serving in a ship **2** someone out of his natural element, as if a member of an imaginary body of marine cavalry

horsemint ('hɔːs,mɪnt) *n* **1** a hairy European mint plant, *Mentha longifolia*, with small mauve flowers: family *Lamiaceae* (labiates) **2** any of several similar and related plants, such as *Monarda punctata* of North America

horse mushroom *n* a large edible agaricaceous field mushroom, *Agaricus arvensis*, with a white cap and greyish gills

horse nettle *n* a weedy solanaceous North

American plant, *Solanum carolinense*, with yellow prickles, white or blue flowers, and yellow berries

Horsens (*Danish* 'hɔrsəns) *n* a port in Denmark, in E Jutland at the head of **Horsens Fjord**. Pop: 49 652 (2004 est)

horse opera *n* *informal* another term for **Western** (sense 4)

horse pistol *n* a large holstered pistol formerly carried by horsemen

horseplay ('hɔːs,pleɪ) *n* rough, boisterous, or rowdy play

horsepower ('hɔːs,paʊə) *n* **1** an fps unit of power, equal to 550 foot-pounds per second (equivalent to 745.7 watts) **2** a US standard unit of power, equal to 746 watts ▷ Abbreviations: HP, h.p

horsepower-hour *n* an fps unit of work or energy equal to the work done by 1 horsepower in 1 hour. 1 horsepower-hour is equivalent to 2.686×10^6 joules

horse racing *n* an organized sport, closely associated with gambling, in which riders race horses over dedicated courses, often incorporating hurdles.

horseradish ('hɔːs,rædɪʃ) *n* **1** a coarse Eurasian plant, *Armoracia rusticana*, cultivated for its thick white pungent root: family *Brassicaceae* (crucifers) **2** the root of this plant, which is ground and combined with vinegar, etc, to make a sauce

horse sense *n* another term for **common sense**

horseshit ('hɔːs,ʃɪt) *n* *slang* rubbish; nonsense

USAGE This word was formerly considered to be taboo, and it was labelled as such in previous editions of *Collins English Dictionary*. However, it has now become acceptable in speech, although some older or more conservative people may object to its use

horseshoe ('hɔːs,ʃuː) *n* **1** a piece of iron shaped like a U with the ends curving inwards that is nailed to the underside of the hoof of a horse to protect the soft part of the foot from hard surfaces: commonly thought to be a token of good luck **2** an object of similar shape ▷ *vb* -shoes, -shoeing, -shoed **3** (*tr*) to fit with a horseshoe; shoe

horseshoe arch *n* an arch formed in the shape of a horseshoe, esp as used in Moorish architecture

horseshoe bat *n* any of numerous large-eared Old World insectivorous bats, mostly of the genus *Rhinolophus*, with a fleshy growth around the nostrils, used in echolocation: family *Rhinolophidae*

horseshoe crab *n* any marine chelicerate arthropod of the genus *Limulus*, of North America and Asia, having a rounded heavily armoured body with a long pointed tail: class *Merostomata*. Also called: king crab

horseshoe fern *n* another name for **para³**

horseshoes ('hɔːs,ʃuːz) *n* (*functioning as singular*) a game in which the players try to throw horseshoes so that they encircle a stake in the ground some distance away

horsetail ('hɔːs,teɪl) *n* **1** any tracheophyte plant of the genus *Equisetum*, having jointed stems with whorls of small dark toothlike leaves and producing spores within conelike structures at the tips of the stems: phylum *Sphenophyta* **2** a stylized horse's tail formerly used as the emblem of a pasha, the number of tails increasing with rank

horse trading *n* hard bargaining to obtain equal concessions by both sides in a dispute

horseweed ('hɔːs,wiːd) *n* the US name for **Canadian fleabane** (see **fleabane** (sense 3))

horsewhip ('hɔːs,wɪp) *n* **1** a whip, usually with a long thong, used for managing horses ▷ *vb* -whips, -whipping, -whipped **2** (*tr*) to flog with such a whip > 'horse,whipper *n*

horsey or **horsy** ('hɔːsɪ) *adj* horsier, horsiest **1** of or relating to horses: *a horsey smell* **2** dealing with or devoted to horses **3** like a horse: *a horsey face* > 'horsily *adv* > 'horsiness *n*

h

horst (hɔːst) *n* a ridge of land that has been forced upwards between two parallel faults [c20 from German: thicket]

Horta (Portuguese 'ɔrtɐ) *n* a port in the Azores, on the SE coast of Fayal Island

hortatory ('hɔːtətərɪ, -trɪ) or **hortative** ('hɔːtətɪv) *adj* tending to exhort; encouraging [c16 from Late Latin hortātōrius, from Latin hortārī to EXHORT] > hor'tation *n* > 'hortatorily or 'hortatively *adv*

horticultural (ˌhɔːtɪ'kʌltʃərəl) *adj* of or relating to horticulture > ˌhorti'culturally *adv* > ˌhorti'culturalist *n*

horticulture ('hɔːtɪˌkʌltʃə) *n* the art or science of cultivating gardens [c17 from Latin hortus garden + CULTURE, on the model of AGRICULTURE] > ˌhorti'culturist *n*

hortus siccus ('hɔːtəs 'sɪkəs) *n* a less common name for **herbarium** [c17 Latin, literally: dry garden]

Horus ('hɔːrəs) *n* a solar god of Egyptian mythology, usually depicted with a falcon's head [via Late Latin from Greek Hōros, from Egyptian Hur hawk]

Hos. *Bible* abbreviation for Hosea

hosanna (həʊ'zænə) *interj* **1** an exclamation of praise, esp one to God ▷ *n* **2** the act of crying "hosanna" [Old English osanna, via Late Latin from Greek, from Hebrew hōshī 'āh nnā save now, we pray]

hose¹ (həʊz) *n* **1** a flexible pipe, for conveying a liquid or gas ▷ *vb* **2** (sometimes foll by down) to wash, water, or sprinkle (a person or thing) with or as if with a hose [c15 later use of HOSE²]

hose² (həʊz) *n, pl* **hose** or **hosen** **1** stockings, socks, and tights collectively **2** *history* a man's garment covering the legs and reaching up to the waist; worn with a doublet **3** half-hose socks [Old English hosa; related to Old High German hosa, Dutch hoos, Old Norse hosa]

Hosea (həʊ'zɪə) *n Old Testament* **1** a Hebrew prophet of the 8th century BC **2** the book containing his oracles

hoser ('həʊzə) *n* **1** *US slang* a person who swindles or deceives others **2** *Canadian slang* an unsophisticated, esp rural, person

hosier ('həʊzɪə) *n* a person who sells stockings, etc

hosiery ('həʊzɪərɪ) *n* stockings, socks, and knitted underclothing collectively

hospice ('hɒspɪs) *n, pl* **hospices 1** a nursing home that specializes in caring for the terminally ill **2** Also called: **hospitium** (hɒ'spɪtɪəm) *pl* **hospitia** (hɒ'spɪtɪə) *archaic* a place of shelter for travellers, esp one kept by a monastic order [c19 from French, from Latin hospitium hospitality, from hospes guest, HOST¹]

hospitable ('hɒspɪtəb³l, hɒ'spɪt-) *adj* **1** welcoming to guests or strangers **2** fond of entertaining **3** receptive: hospitable to new ideas [c16 from Medieval Latin hospitāre to receive as a guest, from Latin hospes guest, HOST¹] > 'hospitableness *n* > 'hospitably *adv*

hospital ('hɒspɪt³l) *n* **1** an institution for the medical, surgical, obstetric, or psychiatric care and treatment of patients **2** (modifier) having the function of a hospital: a hospital ship **3** a repair shop for something specified: a dolls' hospital **4** archaic a charitable home, hospice, or school [c13 from Medieval Latin hospitāle hospice, from Latin hospitālis relating to a guest, from hospes, hospit- guest, HOST¹]

hospital corner *n* a corner of a made-up bed in which the bedclothes have been neatly and securely folded, esp as in hospitals

Hospitalet (Spanish ɔspita'let) *n* a city in NE Spain, a SW suburb of Barcelona. Pop: 246 415 (2003 est)

hospitality (ˌhɒspɪ'tælɪtɪ) *n, pl* **-ties 1** kindness in welcoming strangers or guests **2** receptiveness

hospitality suite *n* a room or suite, as at a conference, where free drinks are offered

hospitalization or **hospitalisation**

(ˌhɒspɪtəlaɪ'zeɪʃən) *n* **1** the act or an instance of being hospitalized **2** the duration of a stay in a hospital

hospitalize or **hospitalise** ('hɒspɪtəˌlaɪz) *vb* (tr) to admit or send (a person) into a hospital

hospitaller or US **hospitaler** ('hɒspɪtələ) *n* a person, esp a member of certain religious orders, dedicated to hospital work, ambulance services, etc [c14 from Old French hospitalier, from Medieval Latin hospitālārius, from hospitāle hospice; see HOSPITAL]

Hospitaller or US **Hospitaler** ('hɒspɪtələ) *n* a member of the order of the Knights Hospitallers

hospital pass *n informal* **1** *sport* a pass made to a team-mate who will be tackled heavily as soon as the ball is received **2** a task or project that will inevitably bring heavy criticism on the person to whom it has been assigned

hospodar ('hɒspəˌdɑː) *n* (formerly) the governor or prince of Moldavia or Wallachia under Ottoman rule [c17 via Romanian from Ukrainian, from hospod' lord; related to Russian gospodin courtesy title, Old Slavonic gospodĭ lord]

host¹ (həʊst) *n* **1** a person who receives or entertains guests, esp in his own home **2 a** a country or organization which provides facilities for and receives visitors to an event **b** (as modifier): the host nation **3** the compere of a show or television programme **4** *biology* **a** an animal or plant that nourishes and supports a parasite **b** an animal, esp an embryo, into which tissue is experimentally grafted **5** *computing* a computer connected to a network and providing facilities to other computers and their users **6** the owner or manager of an inn ▷ *vb* **7** to be the host of (a party, programme, etc): to host one's own show **8** (tr) *US informal* to leave (a restaurant) without paying the bill [c13 from French hoste, from Latin hospes guest, foreigner, from hostis enemy]

host² (həʊst) *n* **1** a great number; multitude **2** an archaic word for **army** [c13 from Old French hoste, from Latin hostis stranger, enemy]

Host (həʊst) *n* the bread consecrated in the Eucharist [c14 from Old French oiste, from Latin hostia victim]

hosta ('hɒstə) *n* any plant of the liliaceous genus Hosta, of China and Japan: cultivated esp for their ornamental foliage [c19 New Latin, named after N. T. Host (1761–1834), Austrian physician]

hostage ('hɒstɪdʒ) *n* **1** a person given to or held by a person, organization, etc, as a security or pledge or for ransom, release, exchange for prisoners, etc **2** the state of being held as a hostage **3** any security or pledge **4 give hostages to fortune** to place oneself in a position in which misfortune may strike through the loss of what one values most [c13 from Old French, from hoste guest, HOST¹]

hostel ('hɒst³l) *n* **1** a building providing overnight accommodation, as for the homeless, etc **2** See **youth hostel 3** *Brit* a supervised lodging house for nurses, workers, etc **4** *archaic* another word for **hostelry** [c13 from Old French, from Medieval Latin hospitāle hospice; see HOSPITAL]

hosteller or US **hosteler** ('hɒstələ) *n* **1** a person who stays at youth hostels **2** an archaic word for **innkeeper**

hostelling or US **hosteling** ('hɒstəlɪŋ) *n* the practice of staying at youth hostels when travelling

hostelry ('hɒstəlrɪ) *n, pl* **-ries** *archaic or facetious* an inn

hostel school *n* (in N Canada) a government boarding school for Native American and Inuit students

hostess ('həʊstɪs) *n* **1** a woman acting as host **2** a woman who receives and entertains patrons of a club, restaurant, etc **3** See **air hostess**

hostie ('həʊstɪ) *n Austral informal* short for **air hostess**

hostile ('hɒstaɪl) *adj* **1** antagonistic; opposed **2** of or relating to an enemy **3** unfriendly ▷ *n* **4** a

hostile person; enemy [c16 from Latin hostīlis, from hostis enemy] > 'hostilely *adv*

hostile witness *n* a witness who gives evidence against the party calling him

hostility (hɒ'stɪlɪtɪ) *n, pl* **-ties 1** enmity or antagonism **2** an act expressing enmity or opposition **3** (plural) fighting; warfare

hostler ('ɒslə) *n* another name (esp in Brit) for **ostler**

hot (hɒt) *adj* **hotter, hottest 1** having a relatively high temperature **2** having a temperature higher than desirable **3** causing or having a sensation of bodily heat **4** causing a burning sensation on the tongue: hot mustard; a hot curry **5** expressing or feeling intense emotion, such as embarrassment, anger, or lust **6** intense or vehement: a hot argument **7** recent; fresh; new: a hot trial; hot from the press **8** *ball games* (of a ball) thrown or struck hard, and so difficult to respond to **9** much favoured or approved: a hot tip; a hot favourite **10** *informal* having a dangerously high level of radioactivity: a hot laboratory **11** *slang* (of goods or money) stolen, smuggled, or otherwise illegally obtained **12** *slang* (of people) being sought by the police **13** *informal* sexually attractive **14** (of a colour) intense; striking: hot pink **15** close or following closely: hot on the scent **16** *informal* at a dangerously high electric potential: a hot terminal **17** *physics* having an energy level higher than that of the ground state: a hot atom **18** *slang* impressive or good of its kind (esp in the phrase **not so hot**) **19** *jazz slang* arousing great excitement or enthusiasm by inspired improvisation, strong rhythms, etc **20** *informal* dangerous or unpleasant (esp in the phrase **make it hot for someone**) **21** (in various searching or guessing games) very near the answer or object to be found **22** *metallurgy* (of a process) at a sufficiently high temperature for metal to be in a soft workable state **23** *Austral and NZ informal* (of a price, charge, etc) excessive **24 give it (to someone) hot** to punish or thrash (someone) **25 hot on** *informal* **a** very severe: the police are hot on drunk drivers **b** particularly skilled at or knowledgeable about: he's hot on vintage cars **26 hot under the collar** *informal* aroused with anger, annoyance, etc **27 in hot water** *informal* in trouble, esp with those in authority ▷ *adv* **28** in a hot manner; hotly ▷ See also **hots, hot up** [Old English hāt; related to Old High German heiz, Old Norse heitr, Gothic heito fever] > 'hotly *adv* > 'hotness *n*

hot air *n informal* empty and usually boastful talk

hot-air balloon *n* a lighter-than-air craft in which air heated by a flame is trapped in a large fabric bag

Hotan ('həʊ'tæn) or **Hotien, Ho-t'ien** ('həʊ'tjɛn) *n* **1** an oasis in W China, in the Taklimakan Shamo desert of central Xinjiang Uygur Autonomous Region, around the seasonal Hotan River **2** the chief town of this oasis, situated at the foot of the Kunlun Mountains. Pop: 71 600 (latest est). Also called: **Khotan, Hetian**

hotbed ('hɒtˌbɛd) *n* **1** a glass-covered bed of soil, usually heated by fermenting material, used for propagating plants, forcing early vegetables, etc **2** a place offering ideal conditions for the growth of an idea, activity, etc, esp one considered bad: a hotbed of insurrection

hot-blooded *adj* **1** passionate or excitable **2** (of a horse) being of thoroughbred stock > ˌhot-'bloodedness *n*

hot button *n informal* **a** a controversial subject or issue that is likely to arouse strong emotions **b** (as modifier): the hot-button issue of abortion

hotchpot ('hɒtʃˌpɒt) *n property law* the collecting of property so that it may be redistributed in equal shares, esp on the intestacy of a parent who has given property to his children in his lifetime [c14 from Old French hochepot, from hocher to shake, of Germanic origin + POT¹]

hotchpotch ('hɒtʃˌpɒtʃ) or esp US and Canadian **hodgepodge** *n* **1** a jumbled mixture **2** a thick soup or stew made from meat and vegetables [c15 a variant of HOTCHPOT]

hot cockles n (functioning as singular) (formerly) a children's game in which one blindfolded player has to guess which other player has hit him

hot cross bun n a yeast bun with spices, currants, and sometimes candied peel, marked with a cross and traditionally eaten on Good Friday

hot-desking ('dɛskɪŋ) n the practice of not assigning permanent desks in a workplace, so that employees may work at any available desk

hot dog¹ n a sausage, esp a frankfurter, served hot in a long roll split lengthways [c20 from the supposed resemblance of the sausage to a dachshund]

hot dog² n 1 chiefly US a person who performs showy acrobatic manoeuvres when skiing or surfing ▷ vb hot-dog, -dogs, -dogging, -dogged 2 (intr) to perform a series of manoeuvres in skiing, surfing, etc, esp in a showy manner [c20 from US hot dog!, exclamation of pleasure, approval, etc]

hotel (həʊ'tɛl) n a commercially run establishment providing lodging and usually meals for guests, and often containing a public bar [c17 from French hôtel, from Old French hostel; see HOSTEL]

Hotel (həʊ'tɛl) n communications a code word for the letter h

hotelier (həʊ'tɛljeɪ) n an owner or manager of one or more hotels

hot fence n NZ an electric fence surrounding a farm

hot flush or US **hot flash** n a sudden unpleasant hot feeling in the skin, caused by endocrine imbalance, esp experienced by women at menopause

hotfoot ('hɒt,fʊt) adv 1 with all possible speed; quickly ▷ vb 2 to move quickly

hothead ('hɒt,hɛd) n an excitable or fiery person

hot-headed adj impetuous, rash, or hot-tempered > ˌhot-'headedly adv > ˌhot-'headedness n

hothouse ('hɒt,haʊs) n 1 a a greenhouse in which the temperature is maintained at a fixed level above that of the surroundings b (as modifier): a hothouse plant 2 a place offering ideal conditions for the growth of an idea, activity, etc: the cultural hothouse of Europe and America 3 an environment where there is great pressure: showjumping is a tough, hothouse world

Hotien or **Ho-t'ien** ('həʊ'tjɛn) n a variant transliteration of the Chinese name for **Hotan**

hot key n computing a single key or combination of keys on the keyboard of a computer that carries out a series of commands

hotline ('hɒt,laɪn) n 1 a direct telephone, teletype, or other communications link between heads of government, for emergency use 2 any such direct line kept for urgent use

hot link n a word or phrase in a hypertext document that when selected by mouse or keyboard causes information that has been associated with that word or phrase to be displayed. See **hypertext**

hot metal n a metallic type cast into shape in the molten state b (as modifier): hot-metal printing

hot money n capital transferred from one financial centre to another seeking the highest interest rates or the best opportunity for short-term gain, esp from changes in exchange rates

hot pants pl n 1 very brief skin-tight shorts, worn by young women 2 slang a feeling of sexual arousal: he has hot pants for her

hot pepper n 1 any of several varieties of the pepper Capsicum frutescens, esp chilli pepper 2 the pungent usually small fruit of any of these plants

hotplate ('hɒt,pleɪt) n 1 an electrically heated plate on a cooker 2 a portable device, heated electrically or by spirit lamps, etc, on which food can be kept warm

hot pool n a pool or spring that is heated geothermally

hotpot ('hɒt,pɒt) n 1 Brit a baked stew or casserole made with meat or fish and covered with a layer of potatoes 2 Austral slang a heavily backed horse

hot potato n slang an awkward or delicate matter

hot-press n 1 a machine for applying a combination of heat and pressure to give a smooth surface to paper, to express oil from it, etc ▷ vb 2 (tr) to subject (paper, cloth, etc) to heat and pressure to give it a smooth surface or extract oil

hot rod n a car with an engine that has been radically modified to produce increased power

hots (hɒts) pl n **the** slang intense sexual desire; lust (esp in the phrase **have the hots for someone**)

hot seat n 1 informal a precarious, difficult, or dangerous position 2 US a slang term for **electric chair**

hot shoe n photog an accessory shoe on a camera through which electrical contact is made to an electronic flash device

hotshot ('hɒt,ʃɒt) n informal an important person or expert, esp when showy

hot spot n 1 an area of potential violence or political unrest 2 a lively nightclub or other place of entertainment 3 an area of great activity of a specific type: the world's economic hot spots 4 a any local area of high temperature in a part of an engine, etc b part of the inlet manifold of a paraffin engine that is heated by exhaust gases to vaporize the fuel 5 computing a company that provides wireless access to the internet for users of portable computers or a place from which the internet can be accessed in this manner 6 med a small area on the surface of or within a body with an exceptionally high concentration of radioactivity or of some chemical or mineral considered harmful b a similar area that generates an abnormal amount of heat, as revealed by thermography 7 genetics a part of a chromosome that has a tendency for mutation or recombination

hotspot ('hɒt,spɒt) n a place where wireless broadband services are provided to users through a wireless local area network, such as in an airport, railway station, or library

hot spring n a natural spring of mineral water at a temperature of 21°C (70°F) or above, found in areas of volcanic activity. Also called: **thermal spring**

hotspur ('hɒt,spɜː) n an impetuous or fiery person [c15 from Hotspur, nickname of Sir Henry Percy (1364–1403), English rebel]

hot stuff n informal 1 a person, object, etc, considered important, attractive, sexually exciting, etc 2 a pornographic or erotic book, play, film, etc

hot-swappable adj computing (of devices, disks, etc) capable of being inserted or removed from a computer system that is running, without causing damage or affecting performance

hot swapping n computing the insertion or removal of peripheral devices, disks, etc while a computer is still running without either causing damage to the system or affecting performance

Hottentot ('hɒtⁿ,tɒt) n offensive 1 (pl -tot or -tots) another name for the **Khoikhoi** people 2 any of the languages of this people, belonging to the Khoisan family [c17 from Afrikaans, of uncertain origin]

Hottentot fig n a perennial plant, Mesembryanthemum (or Carpobrotus) edule, originally South African, having fleshy prostrate leaves, showy yellow or purple flowers, and edible fruits

hottie or **hotty** ('hɒtɪ) n, pl -ties informal 1 US a sexually attractive person 2 a hot-water bottle

hotting ('hɒtɪŋ) n informal the practice of stealing fast cars and putting on a show of skilful but dangerous driving > 'hotter n

hottish ('hɒtɪʃ) adj fairly hot

hot up vb (adverb) informal 1 to make or become more exciting, active, or intense: the chase was hotting up 2 (tr) another term for **soup up**

hot-water bottle n a receptacle, now usually made of rubber, designed to be filled with hot water, used for warming a bed or parts of the body

hot-wire vb (tr) slang to start the engine of (a motor vehicle) by bypassing the ignition switch

hot-work vb (tr) to shape (metal) when hot

hot zone n computing a variable area towards the end of a line of text that informs the operator that a decision must be taken as to whether to hyphenate or begin a new line

houdah ('haʊdə) n a variant spelling of **howdah**

Houdan ('huːdæn) n a breed of light domestic fowl originally from France, with a distinctive full crest [c19 named after Houdan, village near Paris where the breed originated]

hough (hɒk) Brit ▷ n 1 another word for **hock¹** 2 (hɒx) in Scotland, a cut of meat corresponding to shin ▷ vb (tr) 3 to hamstring (cattle, horses, etc) [c14 from Old English hōh heel]

houghmagandie (ˌhɒxmə'gændɪ) n Scot a variant spelling of **hochmagandy**

Houghton-le-Spring ('haʊtⁿlə'sprɪŋ) n a town in N England, in Sunderland unitary authority, Tyne and Wear: coal-mining. Pop: 36 746 (2001)

houhere ('hoʊ:hɛrɛ) n, pl houhere NZ another name for **ribbonwood** [Māori]

hommos, **houmous** or **houmus** ('huːməs) n variant spellings of **hummus**

hound¹ (haʊnd) n 1 a any of several breeds of dog used for hunting b (in combination): an otterhound; a deerhound 2 **the hounds** a pack of foxhounds, etc 3 a dog, esp one regarded as annoying 4 a despicable person 5 (in hare and hounds) a runner who pursues a hare 6 slang, chiefly US and Canadian an enthusiast: an autograph hound 7 short for **houndfish** See also **nursehound** 8 **ride to hounds** or **follow the hounds** to take part in a fox hunt with hounds ▷ vb (tr) 9 to pursue or chase relentlessly 10 to urge on [Old English hund; related to Old High German hunt, Old Norse hundr, Gothic hunds] > 'hounder n

hound² (haʊnd) n 1 either of a pair of horizontal bars that reinforce the running gear of a horse-drawn vehicle 2 nautical either of a pair of fore-and-aft braces that serve as supports for a topmast [c15 of Scandinavian origin; related to Old Norse hūnn knob, cube]

houndfish ('haʊnd,fɪʃ) n, pl -fish or -fishes a name given to various small sharks or dogfish. See also **nursehound**

hound's-tongue n any boraginaceous weedy plant of the genus Cynoglossum, esp the Eurasian C. officinale, which has small reddish-purple flowers and spiny fruits. Also called: **dog's-tongue** [Old English hundestunge, translation of Latin cynoglōssos, from Greek kunoglōssos, from kuōn dog + glōssa tongue; referring to the shape of its leaves]

hound's-tooth check n a pattern of broken or jagged checks, esp one printed on or woven into cloth. Also called: **dog's-tooth check, dogtooth check**

houngan or **hungan** ('huːŋgᵃn, 'uːŋgᵃn) n a voodoo priest [c20 from Haitian Creole, from Fon hun deity + ga chief]

Hounslow ('haʊnzloʊ) n a borough of Greater London, on the River Thames: site of London's first civil airport (1919). Pop: 212 900 (2003 est). Area: 59 sq km (23 sq miles)

hour (aʊə) n 1 a period of time equal to 3600 seconds; 1/24th of a calendar day. Related adjs: **horal, horary** 2 any of the points on the face of a timepiece that indicate intervals of 60 minutes 3 **the hour** an exact number of complete hours: the bus leaves on the hour 4 the time of day as indicated by a watch, clock, etc 5 the period of time allowed for or used for something: the lunch hour; the hour of prayer 6 a special moment or period: our finest hour 7 **the hour** the present time: the man of the hour 8 the distance covered in an hour: we live an hour from the city 9 astronomy an angular measurement of right ascension equal to 15° or a 24th part of the celestial equator 10 one's hour a

h

a time of success, fame, etc **b** *Also:* **one's last hour** the time of one's death: *his hour had come* **11** **take one's hour** *Irish informal* to do something in a leisurely manner ▷ See also **hours** [c13 from Old French *hore*, from Latin *hōra*, from Greek: season]

hour angle *n* the angular distance along the celestial equator from the meridian of the observer to the hour circle of a particular celestial body

hour circle *n* a great circle on the celestial sphere passing through the celestial poles and a specified point, such as a star

hourglass ('aʊəˌglɑːs) *n* **1** a device consisting of two transparent chambers linked by a narrow channel, containing a quantity of sand that takes a specified time to trickle to one chamber from the other **2** (*modifier*) well-proportioned with a small waist: *an hourglass figure*

hour hand *n* the pointer on a timepiece that indicates the hour. Compare **minute hand, second hand**

houri ('hʊərɪ) *n, pl* **-ris** **1** (in Muslim belief) any of the nymphs of Paradise **2** any alluring woman [c18 from French, from Persian *hūri*, from Arabic *hūr*, plural of *haurā'* woman with dark eyes]

hourlong ('aʊəˌlɒŋ) *adj, adv* lasting an hour

hourly ('aʊəlɪ) *adj* **1** of, occurring, or done every hour **2** done in or measured by the hour: *we are paid an hourly rate* **3** continual or frequent ▷ *adv* **4** every hour **5** at any moment or time

hours (aʊəz) *pl n* **1** a period regularly or customarily appointed for work, business, etc **2** one's times of rising and going to bed (esp in the phrases **keep regular, irregular,** or **late hours**) **3** **the small hours** the hours just after midnight **4** **till all hours** until very late **5** an indefinite period of time **6** *Also called* (in the Roman Catholic Church): **canonical hours a** the seven times of the day laid down for the recitation of the prayers of the divine office **b** the prayers recited at these times

Hours (aʊəz) *pl n* another word for the **Horae**

house *n* (haʊs) *pl* **houses** ('haʊzɪz) **1 a** a building used as a home; dwelling **b** (*as modifier*): *house dog* **2** the people present in a house, esp its usual occupants **3 a** a building used for some specific purpose **b** (*in combination*): *a schoolhouse* **4** (*often capital*) a family line including ancestors and relatives, esp a noble one: *the House of York* **5 a** a commercial company; firm: *a publishing house* **b** (*as modifier*): *house style; a house journal* **6** an official deliberative or legislative body, such as one chamber of a bicameral legislature **7** a quorum in such a body (esp in the phrase **make a house**) **8** a dwelling for a religious community **9** *astrology* any of the 12 divisions of the zodiac. See also **planet** (sense 3) **10 a** any of several divisions, esp residential, of a large school **b** (*as modifier*): *house spirit* **11 a** a hotel, restaurant, bar, inn, club, etc, or the management of such an establishment **b** (*as modifier*): *house rules* **c** (*in combination*): *steakhouse* **12** (*modifier*) (of wine) sold unnamed by a restaurant, at a lower price than wines specified on the wine list: *the house red* **13** the audience in a theatre or cinema **14** an informal word for **brothel** **15** a hall in which an official deliberative or legislative body meets **16** See **full house** **17** *curling* the 12-foot target circle around the tee **18** *nautical* any structure or shelter on the weather deck of a vessel **19 bring the house down** *theatre* to win great applause **20 house and home** an emphatic form of **home** **21 keep open house** to be always ready to provide hospitality **22 like a house on fire** *informal* very well, quickly, or intensely **23 on the house** (usually of drinks) paid for by the management of the hotel, bar, etc **24 put one's house in order** to settle or organize one's affairs **25 safe as houses** *Brit* very secure ▷ *vb* (haʊz) **26** (*tr*) to provide with or serve as accommodation **27** to give or receive shelter or lodging **28** (*tr*) to contain or cover, esp in order to protect **29** (*tr*) to fit (a piece of wood) into a mortise, joint, etc **30**

(*tr*) *nautical* **a** to secure or stow **b** to secure (a topmast) **c** to secure and stow (an anchor) [Old English *hūs*; related to Old High German *hūs*, Gothic *gudhūs* temple, Old Norse *hūs* house] ▷ **'houseless** *adj*

House (haʊs) *n* **the 1** See **House of Commons 2** *Brit informal* the Stock Exchange

house agent *n Brit* another name for **estate agent**

house arrest *n* confinement to one's own home

houseboat ('haʊsˌbəʊt) *n* a stationary boat or barge used as a home

housebound ('haʊsˌbaʊnd) *adj* unable to leave one's house because of illness, injury, etc

houseboy ('haʊsˌbɔɪ) *n* a male domestic servant

housebreaking ('haʊsˌbreɪkɪŋ) *n criminal law* the act of entering a building as a trespasser for an unlawful purpose. Assimilated with burglary, 1968 > '**house,breaker** *n*

house-broken *adj* another word for **house-trained**

housecarl ('haʊsˌkɑːl) *n* (in medieval Europe) a household warrior of Danish kings and noblemen [Old English *hūscarl*, from Old Norse *hūskarl* manservant, from *hūs* HOUSE + *karl* man; see CHURL]

house church *n* **1** a group of Christians meeting for worship in a private house **2** a nondenominational charismatic Church movement

housecoat ('haʊsˌkəʊt) *n* a woman's loose robelike informal garment

house-craft *n* skill in domestic management

house factor *n* a Scot term for **estate agent**

housefather ('haʊsˌfɑːðə) *n* a man in charge of the welfare of a particular group of children in an institution such as a children's home or approved school > '**house,mother** *fem n*

housefly ('haʊsˌflaɪ) *n, pl* **-flies** a common dipterous fly, *Musca domestica*, that frequents human habitations, spreads disease, and lays its eggs in carrion, decaying vegetables, etc: family *Muscidae*

houseful ('haʊsfʊl) *n* the full amount or number that can be accommodated in a particular house

house group *or* **church** *n* a group of Christians who regularly meet to worship, study the Bible, etc, in someone's house

house guest *n* a guest at a house, esp one who stays for a comparatively long time

household ('haʊsˌhəʊld) *n* **1** the people living together in one house collectively **2** (*modifier*) of, relating to, or used in the running of a household; domestic: *household management*

householder ('haʊsˌhəʊldə) *n* a person who owns or rents a house > '**house,holder,ship** *n*

household gods *pl n* **1** (in ancient Rome) deities of the home; lares and penates **2** *Brit informal* the essentials of domestic life

household name *or* **word** *n* a person or thing that is very well known

household troops *pl n* the infantry and cavalry regiments that carry out escort and guard duties for a head of state

househusband ('haʊsˌhʌzbənd) *n* a married man who keeps house, usually without having paid employment

housekeeper ('haʊsˌkiːpə) *n* **1** a person, esp a woman, employed to run a household **2** a good (*or* bad) housekeeper a person who is (or is not) an efficient and thrifty domestic manager

housekeeping ('haʊsˌkiːpɪŋ) *n* **1** the running of a household **2** money allocated for the running of a household **3** organization and tidiness in general, as of an office, shop, etc **4** the general maintenance of a computer storage system, including removal of obsolete files, documentation, security copying, etc

housel ('haʊz²l) *n* a medieval name for **Eucharist** ▷ *vb* **-sels, -selling, -selled** *or US* **-sels, -seling, -seled 2** (*tr*) to give the Eucharist to (someone) [Old English *hūsl*; related to Gothic *hunsl*

sacrifice, Old Norse *hūsl*]

houseleek ('haʊsˌliːk) *n* any Old World crassulaceous plant of the genus *Sempervivum*, esp *S. tectorum*, which has a rosette of succulent leaves and pinkish flowers: grows on walls. Also called: hen-and-chickens

house lights *pl n* the lights in the auditorium of a theatre, cinema, etc

houseline ('haʊsˌlaɪn) *n nautical* tarred marline. Also called: housing

housemaid ('haʊsˌmeɪd) *n* a girl or woman employed to do housework, esp one who is resident in the household

housemaid's knee *n* inflammation and swelling of the bursa in front of the kneecap, caused esp by constant kneeling on a hard surface. Technical name: prepatellar bursitis

houseman ('haʊsmən) *n, pl* **-men** *med* a junior doctor who is a member of the medical staff of a hospital. US and Canadian equivalent: **intern**

house martin *n* a Eurasian swallow, *Delichon urbica*, with a slightly forked tail and a white and bluish-black plumage

housemaster ('haʊsˌmɑːstə) *n* a teacher, esp in a boarding school, responsible for the pupils in his house > **housemistress** ('haʊsˌmɪstrɪs) *fem n*

housemate ('haʊsˌmeɪt) *n* a person who is not part of the same family, but with whom one shares a house

house moth *n* either of two species of micro moth, esp the **brown house moth** (*Hofmannophila pseudospretella*) which, although it usually inhabits birds' nests, sometimes enters houses where its larvae can be very destructive of stored fabrics and foodstuffs

house mouse *n* any of various greyish mice of the Old World genus *Mus*, esp *M. musculus*, a common household pest in most parts of the world: family *Muridae*

House music *or* **House** *n* a type of disco music originating in the late 1980s, based on funk, with fragments of other recordings edited in electronically

House of Assembly *n* a legislative assembly or the lower chamber of such an assembly, esp in various British colonies and countries of the Commonwealth

house of cards *n* **1** a tiered structure created by balancing playing cards on their edges **2** an unstable situation, plan, etc

House of Commons *n* (in Britain, Canada, etc) the lower chamber of Parliament

house of correction *n* (formerly) a place of confinement for persons convicted of minor offences

house officer *or* **houseman** ('haʊsmən) *n, pl* **-men** *med* a doctor who is the most junior member of the medical staff of a hospital, usually resident in the hospital. US and Canadian equivalent: intern

house of God *n* a church, temple, or chapel

house of ill repute *or* **ill fame** *n* a euphemistic name for **brothel**

House of Keys *n* the lower chamber of the legislature of the Isle of Man

House of Lords *n* (in Britain) the upper chamber of Parliament, composed of the peers of the realm

House of Representatives *n* **1** (in the US) the lower chamber of Congress **2** (in Australia) the lower chamber of Parliament **3** the sole chamber of New Zealand's Parliament: formerly the lower chamber **4** (in the US) the lower chamber in many state legislatures

House of the People *n* another name for **Lok Sabha**

house organ *n* a periodical published by an organization for its employees or clients

house party *n* **1** a party, usually in a country house, at which guests are invited to stay for several days **2** the guests who are invited

house physician *or* **doctor** *n* **1** a house officer working in a medical as opposed to a surgical discipline. Compare **house surgeon 2** a physician who lives in a hospital or other institution in which he is employed. Also called: **house doctor** Compare **resident** (sense 7)

house plant *n* a plant that can be grown indoors

house-proud *adj* proud of the appearance, cleanliness, etc, of one's house, sometimes excessively so

houseroom ('haʊs͵rʊm, -͵ruːm) *n* **1** room for storage or lodging **2** give (something) houseroom (*used with a negative*) to have or keep (something) in one's house: *I wouldn't give that vase houseroom*

house-sit *vb* -sits, -sitting, -sat (*intr*) to live in and look after a house during the absence of its owner or owners > **'house-͵sitter** *n*

Houses of Parliament *n* (in Britain) **1** the building in which the House of Commons and the House of Lords assemble **2** these two chambers considered together

house sparrow *n* a small Eurasian weaverbird, *Passer domesticus,* now established in North America and Australia. It has a brown streaked plumage with grey underparts. Also called (US): **English sparrow**

house spider *n* any largish dark spider of the genus *Tegenaria* that is common in houses, such as the cardinal spider

house style *n* a set of rules concerning spellings, typography, etc, observed by editorial and printing staff in a particular publishing or printing company

house surgeon *n* a house officer working in a surgical as opposed to a medical discipline. Compare **house physician**

house-train *vb* (*tr*) *Brit* to train (pets) to urinate and defecate outside the house or in a special place, such as a litter tray > **'house-͵trained** *adj*

House Un-American Activities Committee *n* the former name of the **Internal Security Committee** of the US House of Representatives: notorious for its anti-Communist investigations in the late 1940s and 1950s

housewares ('haʊs͵wɛəz) *pl n* *US and Canadian* kitchenware and other utensils for use in the home

house-warming *n* **a** a party given after moving into a new home **b** (*as modifier*): *a house-warming party*

housewife ('haʊs͵waɪf) *n, pl* -wives **1** a woman, typically a married woman, who keeps house, usually without having paid employment **2** ('hʌzɪf) Also called: **hussy, huswife** *chiefly Brit* a small sewing kit issued to soldiers > **housewifery** ('haʊs͵wɪfərɪ, -͵wɪfrɪ) *n*

housewifely ('haʊs͵waɪflɪ) *adj* prudent and neat; domestic: *housewifely virtues* > **'house͵wifeliness** *n*

housewifey ('haʊs͵waɪfɪ) *adj* suitable for or typical of a housewife

housework ('haʊs͵wɜːk) *n* the work of running a home, such as cleaning, cooking, etc > **'house͵worker** *n*

housey-housey ('haʊzɪ'haʊzɪ) *n* another name for **bingo** *or* **lotto** [c20 so called from the cry of "house!" shouted by the winner of a game, probably from FULL HOUSE]

housing¹ ('haʊzɪŋ) *n* **1 a** houses or dwellings collectively **b** (*as modifier*): *a housing problem* **2** the act of providing with accommodation **3** a hole, recess, groove, or slot made in one wooden member to receive another **4** a part designed to shelter, cover, contain, or support a component, such as a bearing, or a mechanism, such as a pump or wheel: *a bearing housing; a motor housing; a wheel housing* **5** another word for **houseline**

housing² ('haʊzɪŋ) *n* (*often plural*) *archaic* another word for **trappings** (sense 2) [c14 from Old French *houce* covering, of Germanic origin]

housing association *n* *social welfare* (in Britain) a non-profit-making body whose purpose is to build, convert, or improve houses for letting at fair rents

housing benefit *n* *social welfare* (in Britain) a

payment made by a local authority in the form of a rent rebate to a council tenant or a rent allowance to a private tenant

housing estate *n* a planned area of housing, often with its own shops and other amenities

housing project *n* *US* a housing development built and maintained by a local authority, usually intended for people with a low or moderate income

housing scheme *n* *Brit* **1** a local-authority housing plan **2** the houses built according to such a plan; housing estate ▷ Often shortened to: **scheme**

Houston ('hjuːstən) *n* an inland port in SE Texas, linked by the **Houston Ship Canal** to the Gulf of Mexico and the Gulf Intracoastal Waterway: capital of the Republic of Texas (1837–39; 1842–45); site of the Manned Spacecraft Center (1964). Pop: 2 009 690 (2003 est)

houstonia (huːˈstəʊnɪə) *n* any small North American rubiaceous plant of the genus *Houstonia,* having blue, white or purple flowers [c19 named after Dr. William *Houston* (died 1733), Scottish botanist]

houting ('haʊtɪŋ) *n* a European whitefish, *Coregonus oxyrhynchus,* that lives in salt water but spawns in freshwater lakes: a valued food fish [c19 from Dutch, from Middle Dutch *houtic,* of uncertain origin]

Hovawart ('həʊfə͵vaːt) *n* a medium-sized strongly-built dog of a breed with a long thick coat, a thick tuft of hair round the neck, and a long bushy tail [from Middle High German *hova* yard + *wart* watchman]

hove (həʊv) *vb chiefly nautical* a past tense and past participle of **heave**

Hove (həʊv) *n* a town and coastal resort in S England, in Brighton and Hove unitary authority, East Sussex. Pop: 72 335 (2001)

hovea ('həʊvɪə) *n* any of various plants of the Australian genus *Hovea,* having clusters of small purple flowers

hovel ('hʌvᵊl, 'hɒv-) *n* **1** a ramshackle dwelling place **2** an open shed for livestock, carts, etc **3** the conical building enclosing a kiln ▷ *vb* -els, -elling, -elled *or US* -els, -eled **4** to shelter or be sheltered in a hovel [c15 of unknown origin]

hover ('hɒvə) *vb* **1** (*intr*) to remain suspended in one place **2** (*intr*) (of certain birds, esp hawks) to remain in one place in the air by rapidly beating the wings **3** (*intr*) to linger uncertainly in a nervous or solicitous way **4** (*intr*) to be in a state of indecision: *she was hovering between the two suitors* **5** (*tr*) *computing* to hold (the mouse pointer) over a defined area on a web page without clicking, in order to cause a menu, information box, etc to appear ▷ *n* **6** the act of hovering [c14 *hoveren,* variant of *hoven,* of obscure origin] > **'hoverer** *n* > **'hoveringly** *adv*

hovercraft ('hɒvə͵kraːft) *n* a vehicle that is able to travel across both land and water on a cushion of air. The cushion is produced by a fan continuously forcing air under the vehicle

hover fly *n* any dipterous fly of the family *Syrphidae,* with a typically hovering flight, esp *Syrphus ribesii,* which mimics a wasp

hoverport ('hɒvə͵pɔːt) *n* a port for hovercraft

hovertrain ('hɒvə͵treɪn) *n* a train that moves over a concrete track and is supported while in motion by a cushion of air supplied by powerful fans

how¹ (haʊ) *adv* **1** in what way? in what manner? by what means?: *how did it happen?* Also used in indirect questions: *tell me how he did it* **2** to what extent?: *how tall is he?* **3** how good? how well? what...like?: *how did she sing?; how was the holiday?* **4** how about? used to suggest something: *how about asking her?; how about a cup of tea?* **5** how are you? what is your state of health? **6** how come? *informal* what is the reason (that)?: *how come you told him?* **7** how's that for...? **a** is this satisfactory as regards...?: *how's that for size?* **b** an exclamation used to draw attention to a quality, deed, etc: *how*

is that for endurance? **8** how's that? **a** what is your opinion? **b** *cricket* Also written: howzat (haʊˈzæt) (an appeal to the umpire) is the batsman out? **9** how now? *or* how so? *archaic* what is the meaning of this? **10** Also: as how *not standard* that: *he told me as how the shop was closed* **11** in whatever way: *do it how you wish* **12** used in exclamations to emphasize extent: *how happy I was!* **13** and how! (*intensifier*) very much so! **14** here's how! (as a toast) good health! ▷ *n* **15** the way a thing is done: *the how of it* [Old English *hu;* related to Old Frisian *hū,* Old High German *hweo*]

how² (haʊ) *sentence substitute* a greeting supposed to be or have been used by American Indians and often used humorously [c19 of Siouan origin; related to Dakota *háo*]

howbeit (haʊˈbiːɪt) *archaic* ▷ *sentence connector* **1** however ▷ *conj* **2** (*subordinating*) though; although

howdah *or* **houdah** ('haʊdə) *n* a seat for riding on an elephant's back, esp one with a canopy [c18 from Hindi *haudah,* from Arabic *haudaj* load carried by elephant or camel]

how do you do *sentence substitute* **1** Also: how do?, how d'ye do? a formal greeting said by people who are being introduced to each other or are meeting for the first time ▷ *n* how-do-you-do **2** *informal* a difficult situation

howdy ('haʊdɪ) *sentence substitute chiefly US* an informal word for **hello** [c16 from the phrase *how d'ye do*]

howe (haʊ) *n Scot and northern English dialect* a depression in the earth's surface, such as a basin or valley [c16 from HOLE]

howe'er (haʊˈɛə) *sentence connector, adv* a poetic contraction of **however**

however (haʊˈɛvə) *sentence connector* **1** still; nevertheless **2** on the other hand; yet ▷ *adv* **3** by whatever means; in whatever manner **4** (*used with adjectives expressing or admitting of quantity or degree*) no matter how: *however long it takes, finish it* **5** an emphatic form of **how¹** (sense 1)

howf *or* **howff** (haʊf, hʌʊf) *n Scot* a haunt, esp a public house [c16 of uncertain origin]

howitzer ('haʊɪtsə) *n* a cannon having a short or medium barrel with a low muzzle velocity and a steep angle of fire [c16 from Dutch *houwitser,* from German *Haubitze,* from Czech *houfnice* stone-sling]

howk (haʊk) *vb Scot* to dig (out or up) [c17 from earlier *holk*]

howl (haʊl) *n* **1** a long plaintive cry or wail characteristic of a wolf or hound **2** a similar cry of pain or sorrow **3** *slang* **a** a person or thing that is very funny **b** a prolonged outburst of laughter **4** *electronics* an unwanted prolonged high-pitched sound produced by a sound-producing system as a result of feedback ▷ *vb* **5** to express in a howl or utter such cries **6** (*intr*) (of the wind, etc) to make a wailing noise **7** (*intr*) *informal* to shout or laugh [c14 *houlen;* related to Middle High German *hiuweln,* Middle Dutch *hūlen,* Danish *hyle*]

Howland Island ('haʊlənd) *n* a small island in the central Pacific, near the equator northwest of Phoenix Island: US airfield. Area: 2.6 sq km (1 sq mile)

howl down *vb* (*tr, adverb*) to prevent (a speaker) from being heard by shouting disapprovingly

howler ('haʊlə) *n* **1** Also called: howler monkey any large New World monkey of the genus *Alouatta,* inhabiting tropical forests in South America and having a loud howling cry **2** *informal* a glaring mistake **3** *Brit* (formerly) a device that produces a loud tone in a telephone receiver to attract attention when the receiver is incorrectly replaced **4** a person or thing that howls

howlet ('haʊlɪt) *n archaic, poetic* another word for **owl** [c15 diminutive of *howle* OWL]

howling ('haʊlɪŋ) *adj* (*prenominal*) *informal* (*intensifier*): *a howling success; a howling error* > **'howlingly** *adv*

howlround ('haʊl͵raʊnd) *n* the condition, resulting in a howling noise, when sound from a loudspeaker is fed back into the microphone of a

h

public-address or recording system. Also called: **howlback**

Howrah ('haʊrə) *n* an industrial city in E India, in West Bengal on the Hooghly River opposite Calcutta. Pop: 1 008 704 (2001)

howsoever (,haʊsəʊ'ɛvə) *sentence connector, adv* a less common word for **however**

how-to *adj* (of a book or guide) giving basic instructions to the lay person on how to do or make something, esp as a hobby or for practical purposes: *a how-to book on carpentry*

howtowdie (haʊ'taʊdɪ) *n* a Scottish dish of boiled chicken with poached eggs and spinach [c18 from Old French *hétoudeau, estaudeau* a fat young chicken for cooking]

howzit ('haʊzɪt) *sentence substitute South African* an informal word for **hello** [c20 from the phrase *how is it?*]

hoy¹ (hɔɪ) *n nautical* **1** a freight barge **2** a coastal fishing and trading vessel, usually sloop-rigged, used during the 17th and 18th centuries [c15 from Middle Dutch *hoei*]

hoy² (hɔɪ) *interj* a cry used to attract attention or drive animals [c14 variant of HEY]

hoya ('hɔɪə) *n* any plant of the asclepiadaceous genus *Hoya*, of E Asia and Australia, esp the waxplant popular as a house plant [c19 named after Thomas Hoy (died 1821), English gardener]

hoyden or **hoiden** ('hɔɪd⁰n) *n* a wild boisterous girl; tomboy [c16 perhaps from Middle Dutch *heidijn* heathen] > **'hoydenish** or **'hoidenish** *adj* > **'hoydenishness** or **'hoidenishness** *n*

Hoylake ('hɔɪ,leɪk) *n* a town and resort in NW England, in Wirral unitary authority, Merseyside, on the Irish Sea. Pop: 25 524 (2001)

Hoyle (hɔɪl) *n* an authoritative book of rules for card games [after Edmond *Hoyle* (1672–1769), English authority on games, its compiler]

HP or **h.p.** *abbreviation for* **1** *Brit* hire-purchase **2** horsepower **3** high pressure **4** (in Britain) Houses of Parliament

HPV *abbreviation for* **human papilloma virus**

HQ or **h.q.** *abbreviation for* headquarters

hr¹ *abbreviation for* **1** hour **2** *Baseball.* home run

hr² *the internet domain name for* Croatia

HR *abbreviation for* **1** *US* House of Representatives **2** human resources **3** human rights **4** ▷ *international car registration for* Croatia [(for sense 4) from Serbo-Croat *Hrvatska*]

Hradec Králové (*Czech* 'hradɛts 'kra:lɔvɛ:) *n* a town in the N Czech Republic, on the Elbe River. Pop: 97 000 (2005 est). German name: **Königgrätz**

HRE *abbreviation for* Holy Roman Emperor *or* Empire

HRH *abbreviation for* His (*or* Her) Royal Highness

HRT *abbreviation for* **hormone replacement therapy**

Hrvatska ('hrva:tska:) *n* the Serbo-Croat name for **Croatia**

hryvna ('hrʌvnə) or **hryvnya** ('hrʌvnjə) *n* the standard monetary unit of Ukraine, divided into 100 kopiykas

HS *abbreviation for* **1** High School **2** (in Britain) Home Secretary

HSE (in Britain) *abbreviation for* Health and Safety Executive

HSH *abbreviation for* His (*or* Her) Serene Highness

Hsi (ʃiː) *n* a variant spelling of **Xi**

Hsia-men ('ʃjɑː'mɛn) *n* a transliteration of the modern Chinese name for **Amoy**

Hsian (ʃjɑːn) *n* a variant transliteration of the Chinese name for **Xi'an**

Hsiang (ʃjɑːŋ) *n* a variant transliteration of the Chinese name for **Xiang**

Hsin-hai-lien ('ʃɪn 'haɪ 'ljɛn) *n* a variant transliteration of the alternative name of **Lianyungang**

Hsining ('ʃiː'nɪŋ) *n* a variant transliteration of the Chinese name for **Xining**

Hsinking ('ʃɪn'kɪŋ) *n* the former name (1932–45) of **Changchun**

HSM *abbreviation for* His (*or* Her) Serene Majesty

HSRC *abbreviation for* Human Sciences Research Council

HST *abbreviation for* **1** (in Britain) high speed train **2** Hubble Space Telescope

Hsü-chou ('ʃuː'tʃaʊ) *n* a variant transliteration of the Chinese name for **Xuzhou**

ht¹ *abbreviation for* height

ht² *the internet domain name for* Haiti

HT *physics abbreviation for* high tension

HTLV *abbreviation for* human T-cell lymphotrophic virus: any one of a small family of viruses that cause certain rare diseases in the T-cells of human beings; for instance, HTLV I causes a form of leukaemia

HTML *abbreviation for* hypertext markup language: a text description language that is used for electronic publishing, esp on the World Wide Web

Hts (in place names) *abbreviation for* Heights

HTTP *abbreviation for* hypertext transfer protocol, used esp on the World Wide Web. See also **hypertext**

hu *the internet domain name for* Hungary

Huainan ('hwaɪ'næn) *n* a city in E China, in Anhui province north of Hefei. Pop: 1 422 000 (2005 est)

Huambo (*Portuguese* 'wambu) *n* a town in central Angola: designated at one time by the Portuguese as the future capital of the country. Pop: 756 000 (2005 est). Former name (1928–73): **Nova Lisboa**

Huang Hai ('hwæŋ 'haɪ) *n* the Pinyin transliteration of the Chinese name for the **Yellow Sea**

Huang He ('hwæŋ 'hiː) *n* the Pinyin transliteration of the Chinese name (Huang Ho) for the **Yellow River**

Huascarán (*Spanish* uaska'ran) or **Huascán** (*Spanish* uas'kan) *n* an extinct volcano in W Peru, in the Peruvian Andes: the highest peak in Peru; avalanche in 1962 killed over 3000 people. Height: 6768 m (22 205 ft)

hub (hʌb) *n* **1** the central portion of a wheel, propeller, fan, etc, through which the axle passes **2** the focal point **3** *computing* a device for connecting computers in a network [c17 probably variant of HOB¹]

hub-and-spoke *n* (*modifier*) denoting a method of organizing intercontinental air traffic in which one major airport is used as a feeder for local airports. Sometimes shortened to: **hub**

hubble-bubble ('hʌb⁰l'bʌb⁰l) *n* **1** another name for **hookah** **2** hubbub; turmoil **3** a bubbling or gargling sound [c17 rhyming jingle based on BUBBLE]

Hubble classification *n* a method of classifying galaxies depending on whether they are elliptical, spiral, barred spiral, or irregular [c20 named after Edwin Powell *Hubble* (1889–1953), US astronomer]

Hubble constant *n* the rate at which the expansion velocity of the universe depends on distance away. It is currently estimated to lie in the range 60–80 km s⁻¹ megaparsec⁻¹. Also called: Hubble parameter

Hubble's law *n astronomy* a law stating that the velocity of recession of a galaxy is proportional to its distance from the observer

Hubble telescope *n* a telescope launched into orbit around the earth in 1990 to provide information about the universe in the visible, infrared, and ultraviolet ranges. Also called: Hubble space telescope

hubbub ('hʌbʌb) *n* **1** a confused noise of many voices **2** uproar [c16 probably from Irish *hooboobbes*; compare Scottish Gaelic *ubub!* an exclamation of contempt]

hubby ('hʌbɪ) *n, pl* **-bies** an informal word for **husband** [c17 by shortening and altering]

hubcap ('hʌb,kæp) *n* a metal cap fitting onto the hub of a wheel, esp a stainless steel or chromium-plated one

Hubei ('huː'beɪ), **Hupeh** or **Hupei** *n* a province of central China: largely low-lying with many lakes. Capital: Wuhan. Pop: 60 020 000 (2003 est). Area: 187 500 sq km (72 394 sq miles)

Hubli ('huː'blɪ) *n* a city in W India, in W Mysore:

incorporated with Dharwar in 1961; educational and trading centre. Pop (with Dharwar): 786 018 (2001)

hubris ('hjuːbrɪs) or **hybris** *n* **1** pride or arrogance **2** (in Greek tragedy) an excess of ambition, pride, etc, ultimately causing the transgressor's ruin [c19 from Greek] > **hu'bristic** or **hy'bristic** *adj*

huckaback ('hʌkə,bæk) *n* a coarse absorbent linen or cotton fabric used for towels and informal shirts, etc. Also called: **huck** (hʌk) [c17 of unknown origin]

huckery ('hʌkərɪ) *adj NZ informal* ugly

huckle ('hʌk⁰l) *n rare* **1** the hip or haunch **2** a projecting or humped part [c16 diminutive of Middle English *huck* hip, haunch; perhaps related to Old Norse *hūka* to squat]

huckleberry ('hʌk⁰l,bɛrɪ) *n, pl* **-ries** **1** any American ericaceous shrub of the genus *Gaylussacia*, having edible dark blue berries with large seeds **2** the fruit of any of these shrubs **3** another name for **blueberry** **4** a Brit name for **whortleberry** (sense 1) [c17 probably a variant of *hurtleberry*, of unknown origin]

hucklebone ('hʌk⁰l,bəʊn) *n archaic* **1** the anklebone; talus **2** the hipbone; innominate bone

huckster ('hʌkstə) *n* **1** a person who uses aggressive or questionable methods of selling **2** *now rare* a person who sells small articles or fruit in the street **3** *US* a person who writes for radio or television advertisements ▷ *vb* **4** (*tr*) to peddle **5** (*tr*) to sell or advertise aggressively or questionably **6** to haggle (over) [c12 perhaps from Middle Dutch *hoekster*, from *hoeken* to carry on the back] > **'hucksterism** *n*

HUD *abbreviation for* **head-up display**

Huddersfield ('hʌdəz,fiːld) *n* a town in N England, in Kirklees unitary authority, West Yorkshire, on the River Colne: former textile centre, now with varied manufacturing and services; university 1992. Pop: 146 234 (2001)

huddle ('hʌd⁰l) *n* **1** a heaped or crowded mass of people or things **2** *informal* a private or impromptu conference (esp in the phrase **go into a huddle**) ▷ *vb* **3** to crowd or cause to crowd or nestle closely together **4** (often foll by *up*) to draw or hunch (oneself), as through cold **5** (*intr*) *informal* to meet and confer privately **6** (*tr*) *chiefly Brit* to do (something) in a careless way **7** (*tr*) *rare* to put on (clothes) hurriedly [c16 of uncertain origin; compare Middle English *hoderen* to wrap up] > **'huddler** *n*

hudibrastic (,hjuːdɪ'bræstɪk) *adj* mock-heroic in style [c18 after *Hudibras*, poem (1663–68) by Samuel Butler]

hudna ('hʊdnə) *n Islam* a truce or ceasefire for a fixed duration [c21 Arabic]

Hudson Bay *n* an inland sea in NE Canada: linked with the Atlantic by **Hudson Strait**; the S extension forms James Bay; discovered in 1610 by Henry Hudson. Area (excluding James Bay): 647 500 sq km (250 000 sq miles)

Hudson River *n* a river in E New York State, flowing generally south into Upper New York Bay: linked to the Great Lakes, the St Lawrence Seaway, and Lake Champlain by the New York State Barge Canal and the canalized Mohawk River. Length: 492 km (306 miles)

Hudson's Bay blanket *n Canadian* a woollen blanket with wide stripes [c19 from a type of blanket originally sold by the Hudson's Bay Company]

Hudson's Bay Company *n* an English company chartered in 1670 to trade in all parts of North America drained by rivers flowing into Hudson Bay

Hudson seal *n* muskrat fur that has been dressed and dyed to resemble sealskin

hudud ('hʌdʌd) *n* the set of laws and punishments specified by Allah in the Koran [from Arabic, literally: boundaries, limits]

hue (hjuː) *n* **1** the attribute of colour that enables an observer to classify it as red, green, blue, purple, etc, and excludes white, black, and shades of grey. See also **colour 2** a shade of a colour **3** aspect; complexion: *a different hue on matters* [Old English *hīw* beauty; related to Old Norse *hȳ* fine hair, Gothic *hiwi* form]

Hué (*French* ɥe) *n* a port in central Vietnam, on the delta of the **Hué River** near the South China Sea: former capital of the kingdom of Annam, of French Indochina (1883–1946), and of Central Vietnam (1946–54). Pop: 377 000 (2005 est)

hue and cry *n* **1** (formerly) the pursuit of a suspected criminal with loud cries in order to raise the alarm **2** any loud public outcry [c16 from Anglo-French *hu et cri*, from Old French *hue* outcry, from *huer* to shout, from *hu!* shout of warning + *cri* CRY]

hued (hjuːd) *adj archaic or poetic* **a** having a hue or colour as specified **b** (*in combination*): *rosy-hued dawn*

Huelva (*Spanish* ˈuɛlβa) *n* a port in SW Spain, between the estuaries of the Odiel and Tinto Rivers: exports copper and other ores. Pop: 144 831 (2003 est)

Huesca (*Spanish* ˈueska) *n* a city in NE Spain: Roman town, site of Quintus Sertorius' school (76 BC); 15th-century cathedral and ancient palace of Aragonese kings. Pop: 47 609 (2003 est). Latin name: *Osca* (ˈɒska)

huff (hʌf) *n* **1** a passing mood of anger or pique (esp in the phrase **in a huff**) ▷ *vb* **2** to make or become angry or resentful **3** (*intr*) to blow or puff heavily **4** *Also*: **blow** *draughts* to remove (an opponent's draught) from the board for failure to make a capture **5** (*tr*) *obsolete* to bully **6 huffing and puffing** empty threats or objections; bluster [c16 of imitative origin; compare PUFF] > **ˈhuffish** *or* **ˈhuffy** *adj* > **ˈhuffily** *or* **ˈhuffishly** *adv* > **ˈhuffiness** *or* **ˈhuffishness** *n*

huffing (ˈhʌfɪŋ) *n slang* the practice of inhaling toxic fumes from glue and other household products for their intoxicating effects > **ˈhuffer** *n*

Hufuf (hʊˈfuːf) *n* See **Al Hufuf**

hug (hʌɡ) *vb* **hugs**, **hugging**, **hugged** (*mainly tr*) **1** (*also intr*) to clasp (another person or thing) tightly or (of two people) to cling close together; embrace **2** to keep close to a shore, kerb, etc **3** to cling to (beliefs, etc); cherish **4** to congratulate (oneself); be delighted with (oneself) ▷ *n* **5** a tight or fond embrace [c16 probably of Scandinavian origin; related to Old Norse *hugga* to comfort, Old English *hogian* to take care of] > **ˈhuggable** *adj* > **ˈhugger** *n*

huge (hjuːdʒ) *adj* extremely large in size, amount, or scope. Archaic form: **hugeous** [c13 from Old French *ahuge*, of uncertain origin] > **ˈhugeness** *n*

hugely (ˈhjuːdʒlɪ) *adv* very much; enormously

hugger-mugger (ˈhʌɡəˌmʌɡə) *n* **1** confusion **2** *rare* secrecy ▷ *adj* ▷ *adv archaic* **3** with secrecy **4** in confusion ▷ *vb obsolete* **5** (*tr*) to keep secret **6** (*intr*) to act secretly [c16 of uncertain origin]

huggy (ˈhʌɡɪ) *adj informal* sensitive and caring: *a soft, lovely, huggy person*

Hughes syndrome (hjuːz) *n* a condition of the autoimmune system caused by antibodies reacting against phospholipids, leading to thrombosis [c20 after Graham *Hughes*, British rheumatologist who described it in 1983]

hug-me-tight *n* a woman's knitted jacket

Huguenot (ˈhjuːɡəˌnəʊ, -ˌnɒt) *n* **1** a French Calvinist, esp of the 16th or 17th centuries ▷ *adj* **2** designating the French Protestant Church [c16 from French, from Genevan dialect *eyguenot* one who opposed annexation by Savoy, ultimately from Swiss German *Eidgenoss* confederate; influenced by *Hugues*, surname of 16th-century Genevan burgomaster] > ˌHugueˈnotic *adj* > ˈHugueˌnotism *n*

huh (*spelling pron* hʌ) *interj* an exclamation of derision, bewilderment, inquiry, etc

Huhehot (ˌhuːhɪˈhɒt ˌhuːɪ-) *or* **Hu-ho-hao-t'e** (ˌhuːhəʊ-haʊˈtei) *n* a variant transliteration of the Chinese name for **Hohhot**

huhu (ˈhuːhuː) *n* a New Zealand beetle, *Prionoplus*

reticularis, with a hairy body [Māori]

hui (ˈhuːɪ) *n, pl* **huies** *NZ* **1** a conference, meeting, or other gathering **2** *informal* a party [Māori]

huia (ˈhʊɪə) *n* an extinct bird of New Zealand, *Heteralocha acutirostris*, prized by early Māoris for its distinctive tail feathers [Māori]

hula (ˈhuːlə) *or* **hula-hula** *n* a Hawaiian dance performed by a woman [from Hawaiian]

Hula Hoop *n trademark* a light hoop that is whirled around the body by movements of the waist and hips

hula skirt *n* a skirt made of long grass attached to a waistband and worn by hula dancers

hulk (hʌlk) *n* **1** the body of an abandoned vessel **2** *disparaging* a large or unwieldy vessel **3** *disparaging* a large ungainly person or thing **4** (*often plural*) the frame or hull of a ship, used as a storehouse, etc, or (esp in 19th-century Britain) as a prison ▷ *vb* **5** (*intr*) *Brit informal* to move clumsily **6** (*intr*; often foll by *up*) to rise massively [Old English *hulc*, from Medieval Latin *hulca*, from Greek *holkas* barge, from *helkein* to tow]

hulking (ˈhʌlkɪŋ) *adj* big and ungainly. *Also*: **hulky**

hull (hʌl) *n* **1** the main body of a vessel, tank, flying boat, etc **2** the shell or pod of peas or beans; the outer covering of any fruit or seed; husk **3** the persistent calyx at the base of a strawberry, raspberry, or similar fruit **4** the outer casing of a missile, rocket, etc ▷ *vb* **5** to remove the hulls from (fruit or seeds) **6** (*tr*) to pierce the hull of (a vessel, tank, etc) [Old English *hulu*; related to Old High German *helawa*, Old English *helan* to hide] > **ˈhuller** *n* > **ˈhull-less** *adj*

Hull (hʌl) *n* **1** a city and port in NE England, in Kingston upon Hull unitary authority, East Riding of Yorkshire: fishing, food processing; two universities. Pop: 301 416 (2001). Official name: **Kingston upon Hull 2** a city in SE Canada, in SW Quebec on the River Ottawa: a centre of the timber trade and associated industries. Pop: 66 246 (2001)

hullabaloo *or* **hullaballoo** (ˌhʌləbəˈluː) *n, pl* **-loos** loud confused noise, esp of protest; commotion [c18 perhaps from interjection HALLO + Scottish *baloo* lullaby]

hull down *adj* **1** (of a ship) having its hull concealed by the horizon **2** (of a tank) having only its turret visible

hullo (hʌˈləʊ) *sentence substitute, n* a variant of **hello**

hum (hʌm) *vb* **hums**, **humming**, **hummed 1** (*intr*) to make a low continuous vibrating sound like that of a prolonged *m* **2** (*intr*) (of a person) to sing with the lips closed **3** (*intr*) to utter an indistinct sound, as in hesitation; hem **4** (*intr*) *informal* to be in a state of feverish activity **5** (*intr*) *Brit and Irish slang* to smell unpleasant **6** (*intr*) *Austral slang* to scrounge **7 hum and haw** See **hem²** (sense 3) ▷ *n* **8** a low continuous murmuring sound **9** *electronics* an undesired low-frequency noise in the output of an amplifier or receiver, esp one caused by the power supply **10** *Austral slang* a scrounger; cadger **11** *Brit and Irish slang* an unpleasant odour ▷ *interj, n* **12** an indistinct sound of hesitation, embarrassment, etc; hem [c16 of imitative origin; compare Dutch *hommelen*, Old High German *humbal* bumblebee] > **ˈhummer** *n*

human (ˈhjuːmən) *adj* **1** of, characterizing, or relating to man and mankind: *human nature* **2** consisting of people: *the human race; a human chain* **3** having the attributes of man as opposed to animals, divine beings, or machines: *human failings* **4 a** kind or considerate **b** natural ▷ *n* **5** a human being; person. Related prefix: **anthropo-** [c14 from Latin *hūmānus*; related to Latin *homō* man] > **ˈhuman-ˌlike** *adj* > **ˈhumanness** *n*

human being *n* a member of any of the races of *Homo sapiens*; person; man, woman, or child

human capital *n economics* the abilities and skills of any individual, esp those acquired through investment in education and training, that enhance potential income earning

humane (hjuːˈmein) *adj* **1** characterized by

kindness, mercy, sympathy, etc **2** inflicting as little pain as possible: *a humane killing* **3** civilizing or liberal (esp in the phrases **humane studies, humane education**) [c16 variant of HUMAN] > **huˈmanely** *adv* > **huˈmaneness** *n*

humane society *n* an organization for promotion of humane ideals, esp in dealing with animals

Human Fertilization and Embryology Authority *n* an organization set up by act of Parliament (1990) to control and review research involving embryos. It maintains a register of persons whose gametes are used for assisted conception. Abbreviation: HFEA

human growth hormone *n* another name for **growth hormone** Abbreviation: HGH

human immunodeficiency virus *n* the full name for HIV

human interest *n* (in a newspaper story, news broadcasting, etc) reference to individuals and their emotions

humanism (ˈhjuːməˌnɪzəm) *n* **1** the denial of any power or moral value superior to that of humanity; the rejection of religion in favour of a belief in the advancement of humanity by its own efforts **2** a philosophical position that stresses the autonomy of human reason in contradistinction to the authority of the Church **3** (*often capital*) a cultural movement of the Renaissance, based on classical studies **4** interest in the welfare of people > ˈhumanist *n* > ˌhumanˈistic *adj*

humanistic psychology *n* approach to psychology advocated by some that emphasizes feelings and emotions and the better understanding of the self in terms of observation of oneself and one's relations with others

humanitarian (hjuːˌmænɪˈtɛərɪən) *adj* **1** having the interests of mankind at heart **2** of or relating to ethical or theological humanitarianism ▷ *n* **3** a philanthropist **4** an adherent of humanitarianism

humanitarianism (hjuːˌmænɪˈtɛərɪəˌnɪzəm) *n* **1** humanitarian principles **2** *ethics* **a** the doctrine that man's duty is to strive to promote the welfare of mankind **b** the doctrine that man can achieve perfection through his own resources **3** *theol* the belief that Jesus Christ was only a mortal man > huˌmaniˈtarianist *n*

humanity (hjuːˈmænɪtɪ) *n, pl* **-ties 1** the human race **2** the quality of being human **3** kindness or mercy **4** (*plural; usually preceded by the*) the study of literature, philosophy, and the arts **5** the study of Ancient Greek and Roman language, literature, etc

humanize *or* **humanise** (ˈhjuːməˌnaɪz) *vb* **1** to make or become human **2** to make or become humane > ˌhumaniˈzation *or* ˌhumaniˈsation *n* > ˈhumanˌizer *or* ˈhumanˌiser *n*

humankind (ˌhjuːmənˈkaɪnd) *n* the human race; humanity

⬛ USAGE See at **mankind**

humanly (ˈhjuːmənlɪ) *adv* **1** by human powers or means **2** in a human or humane manner

human nature *n* **1** the qualities common to humanity **2** ordinary human behaviour, esp considered as less than perfect **3** *sociol* the unique elements that form a basic part of human life and distinguish it from other animal life

humanoid (ˈhjuːməˌnɔɪd) *adj* **1** like a human being in appearance ▷ *n* **2** a being with human rather than anthropoid characteristics **3** (in science fiction) a robot or creature resembling a human being

human papilloma virus *n* any one of a class of viruses that cause tumours, including warts, in humans. Certain strains infect the cervix and have been implicated as a cause of cervical cancer. Abbreviation: HPV

human resources *pl n* **1 a** the workforce of an organization **b** (*as modifier*): *human-resources management; human-resources officer* **2 a** the office or

h

department in an organization that interviews, appoints, or keeps records of employees **b** (*as modifier*): *a human-resources consultancy* **3** the contribution to an employing organization which its workforce could provide in effort, skills, knowledge, etc

human rights *pl n* the rights of individuals to liberty, justice, etc

Humber ('hʌmbə) *n* an estuary in NE England, into which flow the Rivers Ouse and Trent: flows east into the North Sea; navigable for large ocean-going ships as far as Hull; crossed by the **Humber Bridge** (1981), a single-span suspension bridge with a main span of 1410 m (4626 ft). Length: 64 km (40 miles)

Humberside ('hʌmbə,saɪd) *n* a former county of N England around the Humber estuary, formed in 1974 from parts of the East and West Ridings of Yorkshire and N Lincolnshire: replaced in 1996 by the unitary authorities of East Riding of Yorkshire, Kingston upon Hull, North Lincolnshire, and North East Lincolnshire

humble ('hʌmbəl) *adj* **1** conscious of one's failings **2** unpretentious; lowly: *a humble cottage; my humble opinion* **3** deferential or servile ▷ *vb* (*tr*) **4** to cause to become humble; humiliate **5** to lower in status [C13 from Old French, from Latin *humilis* low, from *humus* the ground] > **'humbled** *adj* > **'humbleness** *n* > **'humbler** *n* > **'humbling** *adj* > **'humblingly** *adv* > **'humbly** *adv*

humblebee ('hʌmbəl,biː) *n* another name for the **bumblebee** [C15 related to Middle Dutch *hommel* bumblebee, Old High German *humbal; see* HUM]

humble pie *n* **1** (formerly) a pie made from the heart, entrails, etc, of a deer **2 eat humble pie** to behave or be forced to behave humbly; be humiliated [C17 earlier *an umble pie*, by mistaken word division from *a numble pie*, from *numbles* offal of a deer, from Old French *nombles*, ultimately from Latin *lumbulus* a little loin, from *lumbus* loin]

Humboldt Current ('hʌmbəʊlt) *n* a cold ocean current of the S Pacific, flowing north along the coasts of Chile and Peru. Also called: **Peru Current**

humbucker ('hʌm,bʌkə) *n* a twin-coil guitar pick-up

humbug ('hʌm,bʌg) *n* **1** a person or thing that tricks or deceives **2** nonsense; rubbish **3** *Brit* a hard boiled sweet, usually flavoured with peppermint and often having a striped pattern ▷ *vb* **-bugs, -bugging, -bugged 4** to cheat or deceive (someone) [C18 of unknown origin] > **'hum,bugger** *n* > **'hum,buggery** *n*

humdinger ('hʌm,dɪŋə) *n slang* **1** something unusually large: *a humdinger of a recession* **2** an excellent person or thing: *a humdinger of a party* [C20 of unknown origin]

humdrum ('hʌm,drʌm) *adj* **1** ordinary; dull ▷ *n* **2** a monotonous routine, task, or person [C16 rhyming compound, probably based on HUM] > **'hum,drumness** *n*

humectant (hjuː'mɛktənt) *adj* **1** producing moisture ▷ *n* **2** a substance added to another substance to keep it moist [C17 from Latin *ūmectāre* to wet, from *ūmēre* to be moist, from *ūmor* moisture; see HUMOUR]

humeral ('hjuːmərəl) *adj* **1** anatomy of or relating to the humerus **2** of or near the shoulder

humeral veil *n RC Church* a silk shawl worn by a priest at High Mass, used to: veil

humerus ('hjuːmərəs) *n, pl* **-meri** (-mə,raɪ) **1** the bone that extends from the shoulder to the elbow **2** the corresponding bone in other vertebrates [C17 from Latin *umerus*; related to Gothic *ams* shoulder, Greek *ōmos*]

Hume's law (hjuːmz) *n* the philosophical doctrine that an evaluative statement cannot be derived from purely factual premises, often formulated as: *one cannot derive an "ought" from an "is"*. See also **naturalistic fallacy** [named after David Hume (1711–76), Scottish empiricist philosopher, economist, and historian]

humic ('hjuːmɪk) *adj* of, relating to, derived from,

or resembling humus: *humic acids* [C19 from Latin *humus* ground + -IC]

humicole ('hjuːmɪ,kəʊl) *n now rare* any plant that thrives on humus > **humicolous** (hjuː'mɪkələs) *adj*

humid ('hjuːmɪd) *adj* moist; damp: *a humid day* [C16 from Latin *ūmidus*, from *ūmēre* to be wet; see HUMECTANT, HUMOUR] > **'humidly** *adv* > **'humidness** *n*

humidex ('hjuːmɪ,dɛks) *n Canadian* a scale indicating the levels of heat and humidity in current weather conditions [C20 from HUMID + (IN)DEX]

humidifier (hjuː'mɪdɪ,faɪə) *n* a device for increasing or controlling the water vapour in a room, building, etc

humidify (hjuː'mɪdɪ,faɪ) *vb* **-fies, -fying, -fied** (*tr*) to make (air) humid or damp > **hu,midifi'cation** *n*

humidistat (hjuː'mɪdɪ,stæt) *n* a device for maintaining constant humidity. Also called: **hygrostat**

humidity (hjuː'mɪdɪtɪ) *n* **1** the state of being humid; dampness **2** a measure of the amount of moisture in the air. See **relative humidity, absolute humidity**

humidor ('hjuːmɪ,dɔː) *n* a humid place or container for storing cigars, tobacco, etc

humify ('hjuːmɪ,faɪ) *vb* **-fies, -fying, -fied** to convert or be converted into humus > **,humifi'cation** *n*

humiliate (hjuː'mɪlɪ,eɪt) *vb* (*tr*) to lower or hurt the dignity or pride of [C16 from Late Latin *humiliāre*, from Latin *humilis* HUMBLE] > **hu'mili,ated** *adj* > **hu'mili,ating** *adj* > **hu'mili,atingly** *adv* > **hu,mili'ation** *n* > **humiliative** (hjuː'mɪlɪətɪv) *adj* > **hu'mili,ator** *n* > **hu'miliatory** *adj*

humility (hjuː'mɪlɪtɪ) *n, pl* **-ties** the state or quality of being humble

humint ('hjuːmɪnt) *n* human intelligence: military intelligence gained from human sources with knowledge of the target area

hummel ('hʌməl) *adj Scot* **1** (of cattle) hornless **2** (of grain) awnless [C15 of Germanic origin; compare Low German *hummel* hornless animal]

hummingbird ('hʌmɪŋ,bɜːd) *n* any very small American bird of the family *Trochilidae*, having a brilliant iridescent plumage, long slender bill, and wings specialized for very powerful vibrating flight: order *Apodiformes*

hummingbird moth *n US* another name for the **hawk moth**

humming top *n* a top that hums as it spins

hummock ('hʌmək) *n* **1** a hillock; knoll **2** a ridge or mound of ice in an ice field **3** Also called: **hammock** *chiefly Southern US* a wooded area lying above the level of an adjacent marsh [C16 of uncertain origin; compare HUMP, HAMMOCK] > **'hummocky** *adj*

hummus, hoummos or **houmous** ('hʊməs) *n* a creamy dip originating in the Middle East, made from puréed chickpeas, tahina, etc [from Turkish *humus*]

▪ USAGE Avoid confusion with **humus**

humoral ('hjuːmərəl) *adj* **1** *immunol* denoting or relating to a type of immunity caused by free antibodies circulating in the blood **2** *obsolete* of or relating to the four bodily fluids (humours)

humoresque (,hjuːmə'rɛsk) *n* a short lively piece of music [C19 from German *Humoreske*, ultimately from English HUMOUR]

humorist ('hjuːmərɪst) *n* a person who acts, speaks, or writes in a humorous way > **,humor'istic** *adj*

humorous ('hjuːmərəs) *adj* **1** funny; comical; amusing **2** displaying or creating humour **3** *archaic* another word for **capricious**. > **'humorously** *adv* > **'humorousness** *n*

humour or *US* **humor** ('hjuːmə) *n* **1** the quality of being funny **2** Also called: **sense of humour** the ability to appreciate or express that which is humorous **3** situations, speech, or writings that are thought to be humorous **4 a** a state of mind; temper; mood **b** (*in combination*): *ill humour; good*

humour **5** temperament or disposition **6** a caprice or whim **7** any of various fluids in the body, esp the aqueous humour and vitreous humour **8** Also called: **cardinal humour** *archaic* any of the four bodily fluids (blood, phlegm, choler or yellow bile, melancholy or black bile) formerly thought to determine emotional and physical disposition **9 out of humour** in a bad mood ▷ *vb* (*tr*) **10** to attempt to gratify; indulge: *he humoured the boy's whims* **11** to adapt oneself to: *to humour someone's fantasies* [C14 from Latin *humor* liquid; related to Latin *ūmēre* to be wet, Old Norse *vökr* moist, Greek *hugros* wet] > **'humourful** or *US* **'humorful** *adj* > **'humourless** or *US* **'humorless** *adj* > **'humourlessness** or *US* **'humorlessness** *n*

humoursome or *US* **humorsome** ('hjuːməsəm) *adj* **1** capricious; fanciful **2** inclined to humour (someone)

hump (hʌmp) *n* **1** a rounded protuberance or projection, as of earth, sand, etc **2** *pathol* a rounded deformity of the back in persons with kyphosis, consisting of a convex spinal curvature **3** a rounded protuberance on the back of a camel or related animal **4 the hump** *Brit informal* a fit of depression or sulking (esp in the phrase **it gives me the hump**) **5 over the hump** past the largest or most difficult portion of work, time, etc ▷ *vb* **6** to form or become a hump; hunch; arch **7** (*tr*) *Brit slang* to carry or heave **8** *slang* to have sexual intercourse with (someone) **9 hump one's swag** *Austral and NZ informal* (of a tramp) to carry one's belongings from place to place on one's back [C18 probably from earlier HUMPBACKED] > **'hump,like** *adj*

humpback ('hʌmp,bæk) *n* **1** another word for **hunchback 2** Also called: **humpback whale** a large whalebone whale, *Megaptera novaeangliae*, closely related and similar to the rorquals but with a humped back and long flippers: family *Balaenopteridae* **3** a Pacific salmon, *Oncorhynchus gorbuscha*, the male of which has a humped back and hooked jaws **4** Also called: **humpback bridge** *Brit* a road bridge having a sharp incline and decline and usually a narrow roadway [C17 alteration of earlier *crumpbacked*, perhaps influenced by HUNCHBACK; perhaps related to Dutch *homp* lump] > **'hump,backed** *adj*

humph (*spelling pron* hʌmf) *interj* an exclamation of annoyance, dissatisfaction, scepticism, etc

Humphreys Peak ('hʌmfrɪz) *n* a mountain in N central Arizona, in the San Francisco Peaks: the highest peak in the state. Height: 3862 m (12 670 ft)

humpty ('hʌmptɪ) *n Brit* a low padded seat; pouffe [C20 from *humpty* hunchbacked, perhaps influenced by Humpty Dumpty (nursery rhyme)]

humpty dumpty ('hʌmptɪ 'dʌmptɪ) *n chiefly Brit* **1** a short fat person **2** a person or thing that once overthrown or broken cannot be restored or mended [C18 after the nursery rhyme *Humpty Dumpty*]

humpy¹ ('hʌmpɪ) *adj* **humpier, humpiest 1** full of humps **2** *Brit informal* angry or gloomy > **'humpiness** *n*

humpy² ('hʌmpɪ) *n, pl* **humpies** *Austral* a primitive hut [C19 from a native Australian language]

Hums (hʊms) *n* a variant of **Homs**

hum tone *n* a note produced by a bell when struck, lying an octave or (in many English bells) a sixth or seventh below the strike tone. Also called (esp Brit): **hum note**

humus ('hjuːməs) *n* a dark brown or black colloidal mass of partially decomposed organic matter in the soil. It improves the fertility and water retention of the soil and is therefore important for plant growth [C18 from Latin: soil, earth]

▪ USAGE Avoid confusion with **hummus**

humvee ('hʌm,viː) *n* a four-wheel drive military vehicle [from *h(igh-mobility)* + *m(ulti-purpose)* *v(ehicle)* + -EE]

Hun (hʌn) *n* **1** a member of any of several Asiatic

nomadic peoples speaking Mongoloid or Turkic languages who dominated much of Asia and E Europe from before 300 BC, invading the Roman Empire in the 4th and 5th centuries A.D **2** *informal* (esp in World War I) a derogatory name for a German **3** *informal* a vandal [Old English *Hūnas*, from Late Latin *Hūnī*, from Turkish *Hun-yü*] > 'Hun,like *adj*

Hunan ('huːˈnæn) *n* a province of S China, between the Yangtze River and the Nan Ling Mountains: drained chiefly by the Xiang and Yüan Rivers; valuable mineral resources. Capital: Changsha. Pop: 66 630 000 (2003 est). Area: 210 500 sq km (82 095 sq miles)

hunch (hʌntʃ) *n* **1** an intuitive guess or feeling **2** another word for **hump 3** a lump or large piece ▷ *vb* **4** to bend or draw (oneself or a part of the body) up or together **5** (*intr*; usually foll by *up*) to sit in a hunched position [C16 of unknown origin]

hunchback ('hʌntʃ,bæk) *n* **1** a person having an abnormal convex curvature of the thoracic spine **2** such a curvature Also called: **humpback** See **kyphosis** Compare **hollow-back** [C18 from earlier *hunchbacked*, *huckbacked* humpbacked, influenced by *bunchbacked*, from *bunch* (in obsolete sense of *hump*) + BACKED] > 'hunch,backed *adj*

hundred ('hʌndrəd) *n, pl* **-dreds** *or* **-dred 1** the cardinal number that is the product of ten and ten; five score. See also **number** (sense 1) **2** a numeral, 100, C, etc, representing this number **3** (*often plural*) a large but unspecified number, amount, or quantity: *there will be hundreds of people there* **4** the hundreds **a** the numbers 100 to 109: *the temperature was in the hundreds* **b** the numbers 100 to 199: *his score went into the hundreds* **c** the numbers 100 to 999: *the price was in the hundreds* **5** (*plural*) the 100 years of a specified century: *in the sixteen hundreds* **6** something representing, represented by, or consisting of 100 units **7** *maths* the position containing a digit representing that number followed by two zeros: *in 4376, 3 is in the hundred's place* **8** an ancient division of a county in England, Ireland, and parts of the US ▷ *determiner* **9 a** amounting to or approximately a hundred: *a hundred reasons for that* **b** (*as pronoun*): *the hundred I chose* **10** amounting to 100 times a particular scientific quantity: *a hundred volts*. Related prefix: **hecto-** [Old English; related to Old Frisian *hunderd*, Old Norse *hundrath*, German *hundert*, Gothic *hund*, Latin *centum*, Greek *hekaton*]

hundred days *pl n French history* the period between Napoleon Bonaparte's arrival in Paris from Elba on March 20, 1815, and his abdication on June 29, 1815

hundred-percenter *n US* an extreme or unjustified nationalist > 'hundred-per'centism *n*

hundreds and thousands *pl n* tiny beads of brightly coloured sugar, used in decorating cakes, sweets, etc

hundredth ('hʌndrədθ) *adj* **1** (*usually prenominal*) **a** being the ordinal number of 100 in numbering or counting order, position, time, etc **b** (*as noun*): *the hundredth in line* ▷ *n* **2 a** one of 100 approximately equal parts of something **b** (*as modifier*): *a hundredth part* **3** one of 100 equal divisions of a particular scientific quantity. Related prefix: **centi-** *centimetre* **4** the fraction equal to one divided by 100 (1/100)

hundredweight ('hʌndrəd,weɪt) *n, pl* **-weights** *or* **-weight 1** Also called: **long hundredweight** *Brit* a unit of weight equal to 112 pounds or 50.802 35 kilograms **2** Also called: **short hundredweight** *US and Canadian* a unit of weight equal to 100 pounds or 45.359 24 kilograms **3** Also called: **metric hundredweight** a metric unit of weight equal to 50 kilograms ▷ Abbreviation (for senses 1, 2): **cwt**

Hundred Years' War *n* the series of wars fought intermittently between England and France from 1337–1453: after early victories the English were expelled from all of France except Calais

hung (hʌŋ) *vb* **1** the past tense and past participle of **hang** (except in the sense of *to execute* or in the idiom *I'll be hanged*.) ▷ *adj* **2 a** (of a legislative

assembly) not having a party with a working majority: *a hung parliament* **b** unable to reach a decision: *a hung jury* **c** (of a situation) unable to be resolved **3** hung over *informal* suffering from the effects of a hangover **4** hung up *slang* **a** impeded by some difficulty or delay **b** in a state of confusion; emotionally disturbed **5** hung up on *slang* obsessively or exclusively interested in: *he's hung up on modern art these days*

Hung. *abbreviation for* **1** Hungarian **2** Hungary

Hungarian (hʌŋˈgɛərɪən) *n* **1** the official language of Hungary, also spoken in Romania and elsewhere, belonging to the Finno-Ugric family and most closely related to the Ostyak and Vogul languages of NW Siberia **2** a native, inhabitant, or citizen of Hungary **3** a Hungarian-speaking person who is not a citizen of Hungary ▷ *adj* **4** of or relating to Hungary, its people, or their language ▷ Compare **Magyar**

Hungarian goulash *n* the full name of **goulash**

Hungary ('hʌŋgərɪ) *n* a republic in central Europe: Magyars first unified under Saint Stephen, the first Hungarian king (1001–38); taken by the Hapsburgs from the Turks at the end of the 17th century; gained autonomy with the establishment of the dual monarchy of Austria-Hungary (1867) and became a republic in 1918; passed under Communist control in 1949; a popular rising in 1956 was suppressed by Soviet troops; a multi-party democracy replaced Communism in 1989 after mass protests; joined the EU in 2004. It consists chiefly of the Middle Danube basin and plains. Official language: Hungarian. Religion: Christian majority. Currency: forint. Capital: Budapest. Pop: 9 831 000 (2004 est). Area: 93 030 sq km (35 919 sq miles). Hungarian name: **Magyarország**

hunger ('hʌŋgə) *n* **1** a feeling of pain, emptiness, or weakness induced by lack of food **2** an appetite, desire, need, or craving: *hunger for a woman* ▷ *vb* **3** to have or cause to have a need or craving for food **4** (*intr*; usually foll by *for* or *after*) to have a great appetite or desire (for) [Old English *hungor*; related to Old High German *hungar*, Old Norse *hungr*, Gothic *hūhrus*]

hunger march *n* a procession of protest or demonstration by the unemployed

hunger strike *n* a voluntary fast undertaken, usually by a prisoner, as a means of protest > hunger striker *n*

Hungnam (,huŋˈnæm) *n* a port in E North Korea, on the Sea of Japan southeast of Hamhung. Pop: 260 000 (latest est)

hungry ('hʌŋgrɪ) *adj* **-grier, -griest 1** desiring food **2** experiencing pain, weakness, or nausea through lack of food **3** (*postpositive*; foll by *for*) having a craving, desire, or need (for) **4** expressing or appearing to express greed, craving, or desire **5** lacking fertility; poor **6** NZ (of timber) dry and bare > 'hungrily *or* 'hungeringly *adv* > 'hungriness *n*

hunk (hʌŋk) *n* **1** a large piece **2** Also called: **hunk of a man** *slang* a well-built, sexually attractive man [C19 probably related to Flemish *hunke*; compare Dutch *homp* lump]

hunker ('hʌŋkə) *vb* (*intr*: often foll by *down*) to squat; crouch

hunkers ('hʌŋkəz) *pl n* haunches [C18 of uncertain origin]

hunks (hʌŋks) *n* (*functioning as singular*) *rare* **1** a crotchety old person **2** a miserly person [C17 of unknown origin]

hunky-dory (,hʌŋkɪˈdɔːrɪ) *adj informal* very satisfactory; fine [C20 of uncertain origin]

Hunnish ('hʌnɪʃ) *adj* **1** of, relating to, or characteristic of the Huns **2** barbarously destructive; vandalistic > 'Hunnishly *adv* > 'Hunnishness *n*

hunt (hʌnt) *vb* **1** to seek out and kill or capture (game or wild animals) for food or sport **2** (*intr*; often foll by *for*) to look (for); search (for): *to hunt for a book; to hunt up a friend* **3** (*tr*) to use (hounds,

horses, etc) in the pursuit of wild animals, game, etc: *to hunt a pack of hounds* **4** (*tr*) to search or draw (country) to hunt wild animals, game, etc: *to hunt the parkland* **5** (*tr*; often foll by *down*) to track or chase diligently, esp so as to capture: *to hunt down a criminal* **6** (*tr*; usually passive) to persecute; hound **7** (*intr*) (of a gauge indicator, engine speed, etc) to oscillate about a mean value or position **8** (*intr*) (of an aircraft, rocket, etc) to oscillate about a flight path ▷ *n* **9** the act or an instance of hunting **10** chase or search, esp of animals or game **11** the area of a hunt **12** a party or institution organized for the pursuit of wild animals or game, esp for sport **13** the participants in or members of such a party or institution **14** in the hunt *informal* having a chance of success: *that result keeps us in the hunt*. See also **hunt down, hunt up** [Old English *huntian*; related to Old English *hentan*, Old Norse *henda* to grasp] > 'huntedly *adv*

huntaway ('hʌntə,weɪ) *n* NZ a dog trained to drive sheep at a long distance from the shepherd

hunt down *vb* (*adverb*) **1** (*tr*) to pursue successfully by diligent searching and chasing: *they finally hunted down the killer in Mexico* **2** (*intr*) (of a bell) to be rung progressively later during a set of changes

hunted ('hʌntɪd) *adj* harassed and worn: *he has a hunted look*

hunter ('hʌntə) *n* **1** a person or animal that seeks out and kills or captures game. Female equivalent: **huntress** ('hʌntrɪs) **2 a** a person who looks diligently for something **b** (*in combination*): *a fortune-hunter* **3** a specially bred horse used in hunting, usually characterized by strength and stamina **4** a specially bred dog used to hunt game **5** a watch with a hinged metal lid or case (**hunting case**) to protect the crystal. Also called: **hunting watch**. See also **half-hunter**

hunter-gatherer *anthropol* ▷ *adj* **1** (of a society, lifestyle, etc) surviving by hunting animals and gathering plants for subsistence ▷ *n* **2** a member of such a society

hunter-killer *adj* denoting a type of naval vessel, esp a submarine, designed and equipped to pursue and destroy enemy craft

hunter's moon *n* the full moon following the harvest moon

hunting ('hʌntɪŋ) *n* **a** the pursuit and killing or capture of game and wild animals, regarded as a sport **b** (*as modifier*): *hunting boots; hunting lodge*. Related adj: **venatic**

hunting cat *or* **leopard** *n* another name for **cheetah**

Huntingdon ('hʌntɪŋdən) *n* a town in E central England, in Cambridgeshire: birthplace of Oliver Cromwell. Pop (with Godmanchester): 20 600 (2001)

Huntingdonshire ('hʌntɪŋdən,ʃɪə, -ʃə) *n* (until 1974) a former county of E England, now part of Cambridgeshire

hunting ground *n* **1** the area of a hunt **2** Also called: **happy hunting ground** any place containing a supply of what is wanted or in which a search is conducted: *some resorts are a happy hunting ground for souvenirs*

hunting horn *n* **1** a long straight metal tube with a flared end and a cylindrical bore, used in giving signals in hunting. See **horn** (sense 9) **2** an obsolete brass instrument from which the modern French horn was developed

hunting knife *n* a knife used for flaying and cutting up game and sometimes for killing it

hunting spider *n* another name for **wolf spider**

Huntington's disease ('hʌntɪŋtənz) *n* a rare hereditary type of chorea, marked by involuntary jerky movements, impaired speech, and increasing dementia. Former name: Huntington's chorea [C19 named after George *Huntington* (1850–1916), US neurologist]

huntsman ('hʌntsmən) *n, pl* **-men 1** a person who hunts **2** a person who looks after and trains hounds, and manages them during a hunt

huntsman's-cup *n* US any of various pitcher

h

plants of the genus *Sarracenia*, whose leaves are modified to form tubular pitchers

Huntsville ('hʌntsvɪl) *n* a city in NE Alabama: space-flight and guided-missile research centre. Pop: 164 237 (2003 est)

hunt the slipper *n* a children's game in which the players look for a hidden slipper or other object, such as a thimble (**hunt the thimble**)

hunt up *vb (adverb)* **1** *(tr)* to search for, esp successfully: *I couldn't hunt up a copy of it anywhere* **2** *(intr)* (of a bell) to be rung progressively earlier during a set of changes

Huon pine ('hjuːɒn) *n* a Tasmanian coniferous tree, *Dacrydium franklinii*, with scalelike leaves and cup-shaped berry-like fruits: family *Podocarpaceae*. It is among the oldest living individual plants, thought to be up to 10 000 years old [named after the *Huon* River, Tasmania]

Hupeh *or* **Hupei** ('xuː'peɪ) *n* a variant transliteration of the Chinese name for **Hubei**

hupiro ('huːpiːrəʊ) *n, pl* **hupiro** NZ another name for **stinkwood** (sense 3) [Māori]

huppah ('hʊpə) *n* a variant spelling of **chuppah**

Hurban *Hebrew* (xʊːr'bɑn; *Yiddish* 'xʊːrbᵊn) *n* a variant spelling of **Churban**

hurdies ('hʌrdɪz) *pl n Scot* the buttocks or haunches [c16 of unknown origin]

hurdle ('hɜːdᵊl) *n* **1 a** *athletics* one of a number of light barriers over which runners leap in certain events **b** a low barrier used in certain horse races **2** an obstacle to be overcome **3** a light framework of interlaced osiers, wattle, etc, used as a temporary fence **4** *Brit* a sledge on which criminals were dragged to their executions ▷ *vb* **5** to jump (a hurdle, etc), as in racing **6** *(tr)* to surround with hurdles **7** *(tr)* to overcome [Old English *hyrdel;* related to Gothic *haurds* door, Old Norse *hurth* door, Old High German *hurd,* Latin *crātis,* Greek *kurtos* basket] > '**hurdler** *n*

hurdle rate *n finance* the rate of return that a proposed project must provide if it is to be worth considering: usually calculated as the cost of the capital involved adjusted by a risk factor

hurds (hɜːdz) *pl n* another word for **hards**

hurdy-gurdy ('hɜːdɪ'gɜːdɪ) *n, pl* **-dies 1** any mechanical musical instrument, such as a barrel organ **2** a medieval instrument shaped like a viol in which a rosined wheel rotated by a handle sounds the strings [c18 rhyming compound, probably of imitative origin]

hurl (hɜːl) *vb* **1** *(tr)* to throw or propel with great force **2** *(tr)* to utter with force; yell: *to hurl insults* **3** (hʌrl) *Scot* to transport or be transported in a driven vehicle ▷ *n* **4** the act or an instance of hurling **5** (hʌrl) *Scot* a ride in a driven vehicle [c13 probably of imitative origin] > '**hurler** *n*

hurley ('hɜːlɪ) *n* **1** *chiefly Brit* another word for **hurling** (the game) **2** Also called: **hurley stick** the stick used in playing hurling

hurling ('hɜːlɪŋ) *n* a traditional Irish game resembling hockey and lacrosse, played with sticks and a ball between two teams of 15 players each

hurly-burly ('hɜːlɪ'bɜːlɪ) *n, pl* **hurly-burlies 1** confusion or commotion ▷ *adj* **2** turbulent [c16 from earlier *hurling and burling,* rhyming phrase based on *hurling* in obsolete sense of uproar]

Huron ('hjʊərən) *n* **1 Lake** a lake in North America, between the US and Canada: the second largest of the Great Lakes. Area: 59 570 sq km (23 000 sq miles) **2** *(pl* **-rons** *or* **-ron)** a member of a North American Indian people formerly living in the region east of Lake Huron **3** the Iroquoian language of this people

hurrah (hʊ'rɑː), **hooray** (huː'reɪ) *or* **hurray** (hʊ'reɪ) *interj, n* **1** a cheer of joy, victory, etc ▷ *vb* **2** to shout "hurrah" [c17 probably from German *hurra;* compare HUZZAH]

hurricane ('hʌrɪkᵊn, -keɪn) *n* **1** a severe, often destructive storm, esp a tropical cyclone **2 a** a wind of force 12 or above on the Beaufort scale **b** *(as modifier): a wind of hurricane force* **3** anything acting like such a wind [c16 from Spanish *huracán,* from Taino *hurakán,* from *hura* wind]

hurricane deck *n* a ship's deck that is covered by a light deck as a sunshade

hurricane lamp *n* a paraffin lamp, with a glass covering to prevent the flame from being blown out. Also called: **storm lantern**

hurried ('hʌrɪd) *adj* performed with great or excessive haste: *a hurried visit* > '**hurriedly** *adv* > '**hurriedness** *n*

hurry ('hʌrɪ) *vb* **-ries, -rying, -ried 1** *(intr; often foll by up)* to hasten (to do something); rush **2** *(tr; often foll by along)* to speed up the completion, progress, etc, of ▷ *n* **3** haste **4** urgency or eagerness **5 in a hurry** *informal* **a** easily: *you won't beat him in a hurry* **b** willingly: *we won't go there again in a hurry* [C16 *horyen,* probably of imitative origin; compare Middle High German *hurren;* see SCURRY] > '**hurrying** *n, adj* > '**hurryingly** *adv*

hurry-scurry *adv* **1** in frantic haste ▷ *adj* **2** hasty and disorderly ▷ *n* **3** disordered haste ▷ *vb (intr)* **4** to rush about in confusion [c18 reduplication of HURRY; compare HELTER-SKELTER]

hurst (hɜːst) *n archaic* **1** a wood **2** a sandbank [Old English *hyrst;* related to Old High German *hurst*]

Hurstmonceux ('hɜːstmən,suː, -,səʊ) *n* a variant spelling of **Herstmonceux**

hurt[1] (hɜːt) *vb* **hurts, hurting, hurt 1** to cause physical pain to (someone or something) **2** to cause emotional pain or distress to (someone) **3** to produce a painful sensation in (someone): *the bruise hurts* **4** *(intr) informal* to feel pain ▷ *n* **5** physical, moral, or mental pain or suffering **6** a wound, cut, or sore **7** damage or injury; harm ▷ *adj* **8** injured or pained physically or emotionally: *a hurt knee; a hurt look* [C12 *hurten* to hit, from Old French *hurter* to knock against, probably of Germanic origin; compare Old Norse *hrūtr* ram, Middle High German *hurt* a collision] > '**hurter** *n*

hurt[2] (hɜːt), **whort** (hwɜːt) *n Southern English dialect* another name for **whortleberry**

hurter ('hɜːtə) *n* an object or part that gives protection, such as a concrete block that protects a building from traffic or the shoulder of an axle against which the hub strikes [C14 *hurtour,* from Old French *hurtoir* something that knocks or strikes, from *hurter* to HURT[1]]

hurtful ('hɜːtfʊl) *adj* causing distress or injury: *to say hurtful things* > '**hurtfully** *adv* > '**hurtfulness** *n*

hurtle ('hɜːtᵊl) *vb* **1** to project or be projected very quickly, noisily, or violently **2** *(intr) rare* to collide or crash [C13 *hurtlen,* from *hurten* to strike; see HURT[1]]

husband ('hʌzbənd) *n* **1** a woman's partner in marriage **2** *archaic* **a** a manager of an estate **b** a frugal person ▷ *vb* **3** to manage or use (resources, finances, etc) thriftily **4** *archaic* **a** *(tr)* to find a husband for **b** (of a woman) to marry (a man) **5** *(tr) obsolete* to till (the soil) [Old English *hūsbonda,* from Old Norse *hūsbōndi,* from *hūs* house + *bōndi* one who has a household, from *bōa* to dwell] > '**husbander** *n* > '**husbandless** *adj*

husbandman ('hʌzbəndmən) *n, pl* **-men** a farmer

husbandry ('hʌzbəndrɪ) *n* **1** farming, esp when regarded as a science, skill, or art **2** management of affairs and resources

hush[1] (hʌʃ) *vb* **1** to make or become silent; quieten **2** to soothe or be soothed ▷ *n* **3** stillness; silence **4** an act of hushing ▷ *interj* **5** a plea or demand for silence [c16 probably from earlier *husht* quiet!, the *-t* being thought to indicate a past participle] > **hushed** *adj*

hush[2] (hʌʃ) *mining Northern English* ▷ *vb (tr)* **1** to run water over the ground to erode (surface soil), revealing the underlying strata and any valuable minerals present **2** to wash (an ore) by removing particles of earth with rushing water ▷ *n* **3** a gush of water, esp when artificially produced [c18 of imitative origin]

hushaby ('hʌʃə,baɪ) *interj* **1** used in quietening a baby or child to sleep ▷ *n* **2** a lullaby [c18 from HUSH[1] + *by,* as in BYE-BYE]

hush-hush *adj informal* (esp of official work, documents, etc) secret; confidential

hush money *n slang* money given to a person, such as an accomplice, to ensure that something is kept secret

hush up *vb (tr, adverb)* to suppress information or rumours about

husk[1] (hʌsk) *n* **1** the external green or membranous covering of certain fruits and seeds **2** any worthless outer covering ▷ *vb* **3** *(tr)* to remove the husk from [c14 probably based on Middle Dutch *huusken* little house, from *hūs* house; related to Old English *hosu* husk, *hūs* HOUSE] > '**husker** *n* > '**husk,like** *adj*

husk[2] *n* bronchitis in cattle, sheep, and goats, usually caused by lungworm infestation

husky[1] ('hʌskɪ) *adj* **huskier, huskiest 1** (of a voice, an utterance, etc) slightly hoarse or rasping **2** of, like, or containing husks **3** *informal* big, strong, and well-built [c19 probably from HUSK, from the toughness of a corn husk] > '**huskily** *adv* > '**huskiness** *n*

husky[2] ('hʌskɪ) *n, pl* **huskies** a breed of Arctic sled dog with a thick dense coat, pricked ears, and a curled tail [c19 probably based on ESKIMO]

huss (hʌs) *n* the flesh of the European dogfish, when used as food [C15 *husk, huske,* C16 *huss*: of obscure origin]

hussar (hʊ'zɑː) *n* **1 a** a member of any of various light cavalry regiments in European armies, renowned for their elegant dress **b** *(pl; cap when part of a name): the Queen's own Hussars* **2** a Hungarian horseman of the 15th century [c15 from Hungarian *huszár* hussar, formerly freebooter, from Old Serbian *husar,* from Old Italian *corsaro* CORSAIR]

Hussite ('hʌsaɪt) *n* **1** an adherent of the religious ideas of John Huss (?1372–1415), the Bohemian religious reformer, or a member of the movement initiated by him ▷ *adj* **2** of or relating to John Huss, his teachings, followers, etc > '**Hussism** *or* '**Hussitism** *n*

hussy ('hʌsɪ, -zɪ) *n, pl* **-sies 1** a shameless or promiscuous woman **2** *dialect* a folder for needles, thread, etc [C16 (in the sense: housewife): from *hussif* HOUSEWIFE]

hustings ('hʌstɪŋz) *n (functioning as plural or singular)* **1** *Brit* (before 1872) the platform on which candidates were nominated for Parliament and from which they addressed the electors **2** the proceedings at a parliamentary election **3** political campaigning [c11 from Old Norse *hūsthing,* from *hūs* HOUSE + *thing* assembly]

hustle ('hʌsᵊl) *vb* **1** to shove or crowd (someone) roughly **2** to move or cause to move hurriedly or furtively: *he hustled her out of sight* **3** *(tr)* to deal with or cause to proceed hurriedly: *to hustle legislation through* **4** *slang* to earn or obtain (something) forcefully **5** *US and Canadian slang* (of procurers and prostitutes) to solicit ▷ *n* **6** an instance of hustling **7** undue activity **8** a disco dance of the 1970s [c17 from Dutch *husselen* to shake, from Middle Dutch *hutsen*] > '**hustler** *n*

hustle up *vb (tr) informal, chiefly US and Canadian* to prepare quickly

hut (hʌt) *n* **1** a small house or shelter, usually made of wood or metal **2 the** *Austral* (on a sheep or cattle station) accommodation for the shearers, stockmen, etc **3** *NZ* a shelter for mountaineers, skiers, etc ▷ *vb* **4** to furnish with or live in a hut [c17 from French *hutte,* of Germanic origin; related to Old High German *hutta* a crude dwelling] > '**hut,like** *adj*

hutch (hʌtʃ) *n* **1** a cage, usually of wood and wire mesh, for small animals **2** *informal, derogatory* a small house **3** a cart for carrying ore **4** a trough, esp one used for kneading dough or (in mining) for washing ore ▷ *vb* **5** *(tr)* to store or keep in or as if in a hutch [C14 *hucche,* from Old French *huche,* from Medieval Latin *hutica,* of obscure origin]

hutchie ('hʌtʃɪ) *n Austral* a groundsheet draped

over an upright stick, used as a temporary shelter [C20 from HUTCH]

hut circle *n archaeol* a circle of earth or stones representing the site of a prehistoric hut

hutment ('hʌtmənt) *n chiefly military* a number or group of huts

Hutterite ('hʌtəˌraɪt) *n* a member of an Anabaptist Christian sect founded in Moravia, branches of which established farming communities in western Canada and the northwest US [C19 after Jacob *Hutter* (died 1536), Moravian Anabaptist]

Hutu ('huːtuː) *n, pl* -tu *or* -tus a member of a Negroid people of Rwanda and Burundi

hutzpah ('xʊtspə) *n* a variant of **chutzpah**

Huygens' eyepiece ('haɪɡənz) *n physics* a telescope eyepiece consisting of two planoconvex lenses separated by a distance equal to half the sum of their focal lengths, which are in the ratio of three to one, and oriented so that their curved surfaces face the incident light [C19 named after Christiaan *Huygens* (1629–95), Dutch physicist]

huzzah (hə'zɑː) *interj, n, vb* an archaic word for **hurrah** [C16 of unknown origin]

HV *or* **h.v.** *abbreviation for* high voltage

HW *or* **h.w.** *abbreviation for* **1** high water **2** *cricket* hit wicket

hwan (hwɑːn, wɑːn) *n* another name for **won²** (senses 1, 2) [Korean]

Hwange ('hwæŋɡeɪ) *n* a town in W Zimbabwe: coal mines. Pop: 40 000 (latest est). Former name (until 1982): Wankie

Hwang Hai ('wæŋ 'haɪ) *n* a variant transliteration of the Chinese name for the **Yellow Sea**

Hwang Ho ('wæŋ 'həʊ) *n* a variant transliteration of the Chinese name for the **Yellow River**

HWM *abbreviation for* high-water mark

hwyl ('huːɪl) *n* emotional fervour, as in the recitation of poetry [C19 Welsh]

hyacinth ('haɪəsɪnθ) *n* **1** any liliaceous plant of the Mediterranean genus *Hyacinthus*, esp any cultivated variety of *H. orientalis*, having a thick flower stalk bearing white, blue, or pink fragrant flowers **2** the flower or bulb of such a plant **3** any similar or related plant, such as the grape hyacinth **4** Also called: **jacinth** a red or reddish-brown transparent variety of the mineral zircon, used as a gemstone **5** *Greek myth* a flower which sprang from the blood of the dead Hyacinthus **6** any of the varying colours of the hyacinth flower or stone [C16 from Latin *hyacinthus*, from Greek *huakinthos*] > **hyacinthine** (ˌhaɪə'sɪnθaɪn) *adj*

Hyacinthus (ˌhaɪə'sɪnθəs) *n Greek myth* a youth beloved of Apollo and inadvertently killed by him. At the spot where the youth died, Apollo caused a flower to grow

Hyades¹ ('haɪəˌdiːz), **Hyads** ('haɪædz) *pl n* an open cluster of stars in the constellation Taurus. Compare **Pleiades** [C16 via Latin from Greek *huades*, perhaps from *huein* to rain]

Hyades² ('haɪəˌdiːz) *pl n Greek myth* seven nymphs, daughters of Atlas, whom Zeus placed among the stars after death

hyaena (haɪ'iːnə) *n* a variant spelling of **hyena** > **hy'aenic** *adj*

hyalin ('haɪəlɪn) *n* glassy translucent substance, such as occurs in certain degenerative skin conditions or in hyaline cartilage

hyaline ('haɪəlɪn) *adj* **1** *biology* clear and translucent, with no fibres or granules **2** *archaic* transparent ▷ *n* **3** *archaic* a glassy transparent surface [C17 from Late Latin *hyalinus*, from Greek *hualinos* of glass, from *hualos* glass]

hyaline cartilage *n* a common type of cartilage with a translucent matrix containing little fibrous tissue

hyalite ('haɪəˌlaɪt) *n* a clear and colourless variety of opal in globular form

hyalo- *or before a vowel* **hyal-** *combining form* of, relating to, or resembling glass: *hyaloplasm* [from Greek *hualos* glass]

hyaloid ('haɪəˌlɔɪd) *adj anatomy, zoology* clear and transparent; glassy; hyaline [C19 from Greek *hualoeidēs*]

hyaloid membrane *n* the delicate transparent membrane enclosing the vitreous humour of the eye

hyaloplasm ('haɪələʊˌplæzəm) *n* the clear nongranular constituent of cell cytoplasm > ˌhyalo'plasmic *adj*

hyaluronic acid (ˌhaɪəlʊ'rɒnɪk) *n* a viscous polysaccharide with important lubricating properties, present, for example, in the synovial fluid in joints [C20 HYALO- + Greek *ouron* urine + -IC] > ˌhyalu'ronic *adj*

hyaluronidase (ˌhaɪəlʊ'rɒnɪˌdeɪs, -ˌdeɪz) *n* an enzyme that breaks down hyaluronic acid, thus decreasing the viscosity of the medium containing the acid [C20 HYALO- + Greek *ouron* urine + -ID³ + -ASE]

hybrid ('haɪbrɪd) *n* **1** an animal or plant resulting from a cross between genetically unlike individuals. Hybrids between different species are usually sterile **2** anything of mixed ancestry **3** a vehicle that is powered by an internal-combustion engine and another source of power such as a battery **4** a word, part of which is derived from one language and part from another, such as *monolingual*, which has a prefix of Greek origin and a root of Latin origin ▷ *adj* **5** (of a vehicle) powered by more than one source **6** denoting or being a hybrid; of mixed origin **7** *physics* (of an electromagnetic wave) having components of both electric and magnetic field vectors in the direction of propagation **8** *electronics* **a** (of a circuit) consisting of transistors and valves **b** (of an integrated circuit) consisting of one or more fully integrated circuits and other components, attached to a ceramic substrate. Compare **monolithic** (sense 3) [C17 from Latin *hibrida* offspring of a mixed union (human or animal)] > 'hybridism *n* > hy'bridity *n*

hybrid antibody *n* a synthetic antibody that is able to combine with two different antigens

hybrid bill *n* (in Parliament) a public bill to which the standing orders for private business apply; a bill having a general application as well as affecting certain private interests

hybrid car *n* a car which uses electrical power to enhance the efficiency of the engine

hybrid computer *n* a computer that uses both analogue and digital techniques

hybridize *or* **hybridise** ('haɪbrɪˌdaɪz) *vb* to produce or cause to produce hybrids; crossbreed > 'hybrid,izable *or* 'hybrid,isable *adj* > ˌhybridi'zation *or* ˌhybridi'sation *n* > 'hybrid,izer *or* 'hybrid,iser *n*

hybridoma (ˌhaɪbrə'dəʊmə) *n* a hybrid cell formed by the fusion of two different types of cell, esp one capable of producing antibodies, but of limited lifespan, fused with an immortal tumour cell [C20 from HYBRID + -OMA]

hybrid rock *n* an igneous rock formed by molten magma incorporating pre-existing rock through which it passes

hybrid vigour *n biology* the increased size, strength, etc, of a hybrid as compared to either of its parents. Also called: **heterosis**

hybris ('haɪbrɪs) *n* a variant of **hubris** > hy'bristic *adj*

hydantoin (haɪ'dæntəʊɪn) *n* a colourless odourless crystalline compound present in beet molasses: used in the manufacture of pharmaceuticals and synthetic resins. Formula: $C_3H_4N_2O_2$ [C20 from HYD(ROGEN + *all*)*antoin* product occurring in allantoic fluid]

hydathode ('haɪdəˌθəʊd) *n* a pore in plants, esp on the leaves, specialized for excreting water [C19 from Greek, from *hudor* water + *hodos* way]

hydatid ('haɪdətɪd) *n* **1** a large bladder containing encysted larvae of the tapeworm *Echinococcus*: causes serious disease in man **2** sterile fluid-filled cyst produced in man and animals during infestation by *Echinococcus* larval forms. Also

called: **hydatid cyst** [C17 from Greek *hudatis* watery vesicle, from *hudōr, hudat-* water]

Hyde (haɪd) *n* a town in NW England, in Tameside unitary authority, Greater Manchester; textiles, footwear, engineering. Pop: 31 253 (2001)

Hyde Park *n* a park in W central London: popular for open-air meetings

Hyderabad ('haɪdərəˌbɑːd, -ˌbæd, ˌhaɪdrə-) *n* **1** a city in S central India, capital of Andhra Pradesh state and capital of former Hyderabad state; university (1918). Pop: 3 449 878 (2001) **2** a former state of S India: divided in 1956 between the states of Andhra Pradesh, Mysore, and Maharashtra **3** a city in SW Pakistan, on the River Indus: seat of the University of Sind (1947). Pop: 1 392 000 (2005 est)

hydnocarpate (ˌhɪdnəʊ'kɑːpeɪt) *n* any salt or ester of hydnocarpic acid

hydnocarpic acid (ˌhɪdnəʊ'kɑːpɪk) *n* a cyclic fatty acid occurring in the form of its glycerides in chaulmoogra oil. Formula: $C_{16}H_{28}O_2$ [C20 from Greek *hudnon* truffle + *karpos* fruit + -IC]

hydr- *combining form* a variant of **hydro-** before a vowel

hydra ('haɪdrə) *n, pl* -dras, -drae (-driː) **1** any solitary freshwater hydroid coelenterate of the genus *Hydra*, in which the body is a slender polyp with tentacles around the mouth **2** a persistent trouble or evil: *the hydra of the Irish problem* [C16 from Latin, from Greek *hudra* water serpent; compare OTTER]

Hydra¹ ('haɪdrə) *n Greek myth* a monster with nine heads, each of which, when struck off, was replaced by two new ones

Hydra² ('haɪdrə) *n, Latin genitive* **Hydrae** ('haɪdriː) a very long faint constellation lying mainly in the S hemisphere and extending from near Virgo to Cancer

hydracid (haɪ'dræsɪd) *n* an acid, such as hydrochloric acid, that does not contain oxygen

hydragogue ('haɪdrəˌɡɒɡ) *n med* any purgative that causes evacuation of water from the bowels

hydrangea (haɪ'dreɪndʒə) *n* any shrub or tree of the Asian and American genus *Hydrangea*, cultivated for their large clusters of white, pink, or blue flowers: family *Hydrangeaceae* [C18 from New Latin, from Greek *hudōr* water + *angeion* vessel: probably from the cup-shaped fruit]

hydrant ('haɪdrənt) *n* an outlet from a water main, usually consisting of an upright pipe with a valve attached, from which water can be tapped for fighting fires. See also **fire hydrant** [C19 from HYDRO- + -ANT]

hydranth ('haɪdrænθ) *n* a polyp in a colony of hydrozoan coelenterates that is specialized for feeding rather than reproduction [C19 from HYDRA + Greek *anthos* flower]

hydrargyria (ˌhaɪdrɑː'dʒɪrɪə) *or* **hydrargyrism** (haɪ'drɑːdʒɪrɪzəm) *n med* mercury poisoning [C17 see HYDRARGYRUM]

hydrargyrum (haɪ'drɑːdʒɪrəm) *n* an obsolete name for **mercury** (sense 1) [C16 from New Latin, from Latin *hydrargyrus* from Greek *hydrarguros*, from HYDRO- + *arguros* silver] > **hydrargyric** (ˌhaɪdrɑː'dʒɪrɪk) *adj*

hydrastine (haɪ'dræstiːn, -tɪn) *n* a white poisonous alkaloid extracted from the roots of the goldenseal: has been used in medicine (in the form of one of its water-soluble salts) to contract the uterus and arrest haemorrhage. Formula: $C_{21}H_{21}NO_6$ [C19 from HYDRAST(IS) + -INE²]

hydrastinine (haɪ'dræstɪˌniːn) *n* a colourless crystalline water-soluble compound whose pharmacological action resembles that of hydrastine. Formula: $C_{11}H_{13}NO_3$

hydrastis (haɪ'dræstɪs) *n* any ranunculaceous plant of the genus *Hydrastis*, of Japan and E North America, such as goldenseal, having showy foliage and ornamental red fruits [C18 New Latin, from Greek HYDRO- + -astis, of unknown origin]

hydrate ('haɪdreɪt) *n* **1** a chemical compound containing water that is chemically combined with a substance and can usually be expelled without changing the constitution of the substance **2** a chemical compound that can dissociate reversibly into water and another compound. For example sulphuric acid (H_2SO_4) dissociates into sulphur trioxide (SO_3) and water (H_2O) **3** (*not in technical usage*) a chemical compound, such as a carbohydrate, that contains hydrogen and oxygen atoms in the ratio two to one ▷ *vb* **4** to undergo or cause to undergo treatment or impregnation with water [C19 from HYDRO- + -ATE¹] > hy'dration *n* > 'hydrator *n*

hydrated ('haɪdreɪtd) *adj* (of a compound) chemically bonded to water molecules

hydraulic (haɪ'drɒlɪk) *adj* **1** operated by pressure transmitted through a pipe by a liquid, such as water or oil **2** of, concerned with, or employing liquids in motion **3** of or concerned with hydraulics **4** hardening under water: *hydraulic cement* [C17 from Latin *hydraulicus* of a water organ, from Greek *hudraulikos*, from *hudraulos* water organ, from HYDRO- + *aulos* pipe, reed instrument] > hy'draulically *adv*

hydraulic brake *n* a type of brake, used in motor vehicles, in which the braking force is transmitted from the brake pedal to the brakes by a liquid under pressure

hydraulic coupling *n* another name for **torque converter**

hydraulic press *n* a press that utilizes liquid pressure to enable a small force applied to a small piston to produce a large force on a larger piston. The small piston moves through a proportionately greater distance than the larger

hydraulic ram *n* **1** any large device involving the displacement of a piston or plunger driven by fluid pressure **2** a form of water pump utilizing the kinetic energy of running water to provide static pressure to raise water to a reservoir higher than the source

hydraulics (haɪ'drɒlɪks) *n* (*functioning as singular*) another name for **fluid mechanics**

hydraulic suspension *n* a system of motor-vehicle suspension using hydraulic members, often with hydraulic compensation between front and rear systems (**hydroelastic suspension**)

hydrazide ('haɪdrə,zaɪd) *n* any of a class of chemical compounds that result when hydrogen in hydrazine or any of its derivatives is replaced by an acid radical

hydrazine ('haɪdrə,ziːn, -zɪn) *n* a colourless basic liquid made from sodium hypochlorite and ammonia: a strong reducing agent, used chiefly as a rocket fuel. Formula: N_2H_4 [C19 from HYDRO- + AZO- + -INE²]

hydrazoic acid (,haɪdrə'zəʊɪk) *n* a colourless highly explosive liquid. Formula: HN_3. See also **azide**

hydria ('haɪdrɪə) *n* (in ancient Greece and Rome) a large water jar [C19 from Latin, from Greek *hudria*, from *hudōr* water]

hydric ('haɪdrɪk) *adj* **1** of or containing hydrogen **2** containing or using moisture

hydride ('haɪdraɪd) *n* any compound of hydrogen with another element, including ionic compounds such as sodium hydride (NaH), covalent compounds such as borane (B_2H_6), and the transition metal hydrides formed when certain metals, such as palladium, absorb hydrogen

hydrilla (haɪ'drɪlə) *n* any aquatic plant of the Eurasian genus *Hydrilla*, growing underwater and forming large masses: used as an oxygenator in aquaria and pools. It was introduced in the S US where it has become a serious problem, choking fish and hindering navigation [C20 New Latin, probably from HYDRA]

hydriodic acid (,haɪdrɪ'ɒdɪk) *n* the colourless or pale yellow aqueous solution of hydrogen iodide: a strong acid [C19 from HYDRO- + IODIC]

hydro¹ ('haɪdrəʊ) *n, pl* -dros *Brit* (esp formerly) a hotel or resort, often near a spa, offering facilities for hydropathic treatment

hydro² ('haɪdrəʊ) *adj* **1** short for **hydroelectric** ▷ *n* **2** a Canadian name for **electricity** as supplied to a residence, business, institution, etc

hydro- or sometimes before a vowel **hydr-** combining form **1** indicating or denoting water, liquid, or fluid: *hydrolysis; hydrodynamics* **2** indicating the presence of hydrogen in a chemical compound: *hydrochloric acid* **3** indicating a hydroid: *hydrozoan* [from Greek *hudōr* water]

hydroacoustics (,haɪdrəʊə'kuːstɪks) *n* (*functioning as singular*) *physics* the study of sound travelling through water

hydrobromic acid (,haɪdrəʊ'brəʊmɪk) *n* the colourless or faintly yellow aqueous solution of hydrogen bromide: a strong acid

hydrocarbon (,haɪdrəʊ'kɑːbɒn) *n* any organic compound containing only carbon and hydrogen, such as the alkanes, alkenes, alkynes, terpenes, and arenes

hydrocele ('haɪdrəʊ,siːl) *n* an abnormal collection of fluid in any saclike space, esp around the testicles [C16 from HYDRO- + -CELE]

hydrocellulose (,haɪdrəʊ'sɛljʊ,ləʊs, -,ləʊz) *n* a gelatinous material consisting of hydrated cellulose, made by treating cellulose with water, acids, or alkalis: used in making paper, viscose rayon, and mercerized cotton

hydrocephalus (,haɪdrəʊ'sɛfələs) or **hydrocephaly** (,haɪdrəʊ'sɛfəlɪ) *n* accumulation of cerebrospinal fluid within the ventricles of the brain because its normal outlet has been blocked by congenital malformation or disease. In infancy it usually results in great enlargement of the head. Nontechnical name: **water on the brain** > hydrocephalic (,haɪdrəʊsɪ'fælɪk), ,hydro'cephaloid or ,hydro'cephalous *adj*

hydrochloric acid (,haɪdrə'klɒrɪk) *n* the colourless or slightly yellow aqueous solution of hydrogen chloride: a strong acid used in many industrial and laboratory processes. Formerly called: **muriatic acid**

hydrochloride (,haɪdrə'klɔːraɪd) *n* a quaternary salt formed by the addition of hydrochloric acid to an organic base, such as aniline hydrochloride, $[C_6H_5NH_3]^+Cl^-$

hydrocoral (,haɪdrə'kɒrəl) or **hydrocoralline** *n* any hydrozoan coelenterate of the order *Milleporina* (or *Hydrocorallinae*), which includes the millepores [C20 from HYDRO- + CORAL]

hydrocortisone (,haɪdrəʊ'kɔːtɪ,zəʊn) *n* the principal glucocorticoid secreted by the adrenal cortex; 17-hydroxycorticosterone. The synthesized form is used mainly in treating rheumatic, allergic, and inflammatory disorders. Formula: $C_{21}H_{30}O_5$. Also called: **cortisol**

hydrocyanic acid (,haɪdrəʊsaɪ'ænɪk) *n* another name for **hydrogen cyanide**, esp when in aqueous solution

hydrodynamic (,haɪdrəʊdaɪ'næmɪk, -dɪ-) or **hydrodynamical** *adj* **1** of or concerned with the mechanical properties of fluids **2** of or concerned with hydrodynamics > ,hydrody'namically *adv*

hydrodynamics (,haɪdrəʊdaɪ'næmɪks, -dɪ-) *n* **1** (*functioning as singular*) the branch of science concerned with the mechanical properties of fluids, esp liquids. Also called: **hydromechanics**. See also **hydrokinetics, hydrostatics** **2** another name for **hydrokinetics**

hydroelastic suspension (,haɪdrəʊɪ'læstɪk) *n* See **hydraulic suspension**

hydroelectric (,haɪdrəʊɪ'lɛktrɪk) *adj* **1** generated by the pressure of falling water: *hydroelectric power* **2** of or concerned with the generation of electricity by water pressure: *a hydroelectric scheme* > hydroelectricity (,haɪdrəʊɪlɛk'trɪsɪtɪ, -,iːlɛk-) *n*

hydrofluoric acid (,haɪdrəʊfluː'ɒrɪk) *n* the colourless aqueous solution of hydrogen fluoride: a strong acid that attacks glass

hydrofoil ('haɪdrə,fɔɪl) *n* **1** a fast light vessel the hull of which is raised out of the water on one or more pairs of fixed vanes **2** any of these vanes

hydroforming ('haɪdrəʊ,fɔːmɪŋ) *n* chem **1** the catalytic reforming of petroleum to increase the proportion of aromatic and branched-chain hydrocarbons **2** engineering a forming process in which a metal component is shaped by a metal punch forced against a die, consisting of a flexible bag containing a fluid

hydrogel ('haɪdrə,dʒɛl) *n* a gel in which the liquid constituent is water

hydrogen ('haɪdrɪdʒən) *n* **a** a flammable colourless gas that is the lightest and most abundant element in the universe. It occurs mainly in water and in most organic compounds and is used in the production of ammonia and other chemicals, in the hydrogenation of fats and oils, and in welding. Symbol: H; atomic no.: 1; atomic wt.: 1.00794; valency: 1; density: 0.08988 kg/m³; melting pt.: −259.34°C; boiling pt.: −252.87°C. See also **deuterium, tritium** **b** (as modifier): *hydrogen bomb* [C18 from French *hydrogène*, from HYDRO- + -GEN; so called because its combustion produces water]

hydrogenate ('haɪdrədʒɪ,neɪt, haɪ'drɒdʒɪ,neɪt) or **hydrogenize, hydrogenise** ('haɪdrədʒɪ,naɪz, haɪ'drɒdʒɪ,naɪz) *vb* to undergo or cause to undergo a reaction with hydrogen: *to hydrogenate ethylene* > ,hydrogen'ation, ,hydrogeni'zation or ,hydrogeni'sation *n* > 'hydrogen,ator *n*

hydrogen bomb *n* a type of bomb in which energy is released by fusion of hydrogen nuclei to give helium nuclei. The energy required to initiate the fusion is provided by the detonation of an atomic bomb, which is surrounded by a hydrogen-containing substance such as lithium deuteride. Also called: **H-bomb** See also **fusion bomb**

hydrogen bond *n* a weak chemical bond between an electronegative atom, such as fluorine, oxygen, or nitrogen, and a hydrogen atom bound to another electronegative atom. Hydrogen bonds are responsible for the properties of water and many biological molecules

hydrogen bromide *n* **1** a colourless pungent gas used in organic synthesis. Formula: HBr **2** an aqueous solution of hydrogen bromide; hydrobromic acid

hydrogen carbonate *n* another name for **bicarbonate**

hydrogen chloride *n* **1** a colourless pungent corrosive gas obtained by the action of sulphuric acid on sodium chloride: used in making vinyl chloride and other organic chemicals. Formula: HCl **2** an aqueous solution of hydrogen chloride; hydrochloric acid

hydrogen cyanide *n* a colourless poisonous liquid with a faint odour of bitter almonds, usually made by a catalysed reaction between ammonia, oxygen, and methane. It forms prussic acid in aqueous solution and is used for making plastics and dyes and as a war gas. Formula: HCN. Also called: **hydrocyanic acid**

hydrogen embrittlement (ɪm'brɪtəlmənt) *n* engineering the weakening of metal by the sorption of hydrogen during a pickling process, such as that used in plating

hydrogen fluoride *n* **1** a colourless poisonous corrosive gas or liquid made by reaction between calcium fluoride and sulphuric acid: used as a fluorinating agent and catalyst. Formula: HF **2** an aqueous solution of hydrogen fluoride; hydrofluoric acid

hydrogen iodide *n* **1** a colourless poisonous corrosive gas obtained by a catalysed reaction between hydrogen and iodine vapour: used in making iodides. Formula: HI **2** an aqueous solution of this gas; hydriodic acid

hydrogen ion *n* **1** an ionized hydrogen atom, occurring in plasmas and in aqueous solutions of acids, in which it is solvated by one or more water molecules; proton. Formula: H^+ **2** an ionized hydrogen molecule; hydrogen molecular ion. Formula: H_2^+

hydrogenize *or* **hydrogenise** (ˈhaɪdrədʒɪˌnaɪz, haɪˈdrɒdʒɪˌnaɪz) *vb* variants of **hydrogenate** > ˌhydrogeniˈzation *or* ˌhydrogeniˈsation *n*

hydrogenolysis (ˌhaɪdrəʊdʒɪˈnɒlɪsɪs) *n* a chemical reaction in which a compound is decomposed by hydrogen

hydrogenous (haɪˈdrɒdʒɪnəs) *adj* of or containing hydrogen

hydrogen peroxide *n* a colourless oily unstable liquid, usually used in aqueous solution. It is a strong oxidizing agent used as a bleach for textiles, wood pulp, hair, etc, and as an oxidizer in rocket fuels. Formula: H_2O_2

hydrogen sulphate *n* another name for **bisulphate**

hydrogen sulphide *n* a colourless poisonous soluble flammable gas with an odour of rotten eggs: used as a reagent in chemical analysis. Formula: H_2S. Also called: **sulphuretted hydrogen**

hydrogen sulphite *n* another name for **bisulphite**

hydrogen tartrate *n* another name for **bitartrate**

hydrogeology (ˌhaɪdrədʒɪˈɒlədʒɪ) *n* the branch of geology dealing with the waters below the earth's surface and with the geological aspects of surface waters > ˌhydrogeoˈlogical *adj* > ˌhydrogeˈologist *n*

hydrograph (ˈhaɪdrəˌɡrɑːf, -ˌɡræf) *n* a graph showing the seasonal variation in the level of a body of water, from which its velocity and discharge can be calculated

hydrographic (ˌhaɪdrəˈɡræfɪk) *adj* of or relating to hydrographics > ˌhydroˈgraphical *adj* > ˌhydroˈgraphically *adv*

hydrography (haɪˈdrɒɡrəfɪ) *n* **1** the study, surveying, and mapping of the oceans, seas, and rivers. Compare **hydrology** **2** the oceans, seas, and rivers as represented on a chart > hyˈdrographer *n*

hydroid (ˈhaɪdrɔɪd) *adj* **1** of or relating to the *Hydroida*, an order of colonial hydrozoan coelenterates that have the polyp phase dominant **2** (of coelenterate colonies or individuals) having or consisting of hydra-like polyps ▷ *n* **3** a hydroid colony or individual [c19 from HYDRA + -OID]

hydrokinetic (ˌhaɪdrəʊkɪˈnɛtɪk, -kaɪ-) *or* **hydrokinetical** *adj* **1** of or concerned with fluids that are in motion **2** of or concerned with hydrokinetics

hydrokinetics (ˌhaɪdrəʊkɪˈnɛtɪks, -kaɪ-) *n* (*functioning as singular*) the branch of science concerned with the mechanical behaviour and properties of fluids in motion, esp of liquids. Also called: **hydrodynamics**

hydrolase (ˈhaɪdrəˌleɪz) *n* an enzyme, such as an esterase, that controls hydrolysis

hydrologic cycle *n* another name for **water cycle**

hydrology (haɪˈdrɒlədʒɪ) *n* the study of the distribution, conservation, use, etc, of the water of the earth and its atmosphere, particularly at the land surface > hydrologic (ˌhaɪdrəˈlɒdʒɪk) *or* ˌhydroˈlogical *adj* > ˌhydroˈlogically *adv* > hyˈdrologist *n*

hydrolysate (haɪˈdrɒlɪˌseɪt) *n* a substance or mixture produced by hydrolysis [c20 from HYDROLYSIS + -ATE¹]

hydrolyse *or US* **hydrolyze** (ˈhaɪdrəˌlaɪz) *vb* to subject to or undergo hydrolysis > ˈhydroˌlysable *or US* ˈhydroˌlyzable *adj* > ˌhydrolyˈsation *or US* ˌhydrolyˈzation *n* > ˈhydroˌlyser *or US* ˈhydroˌlyzer *n*

hydrolysis (haɪˈdrɒlɪsɪs) *n* a chemical reaction in which a compound reacts with water to produce other compounds

hydrolyte (ˈhaɪdrəˌlaɪt) *n* a substance subjected to hydrolysis

hydrolytic (ˌhaɪdrəˈlɪtɪk) *adj* of, concerned with, producing, or produced by hydrolysis

hydromagnetics (ˌhaɪdrəʊmæɡˈnɛtɪks) *n* another name for **magnetohydrodynamics** > ˌhydromagˈnetic *adj*

hydromancy (ˈhaɪdrəʊˌmænsɪ) *n* divination by water > ˈhydroˌmancer *n* > ˌhydroˈmantic *adj*

hydromechanics (ˌhaɪdrəʊmɪˈkænɪks) *n* another name for **hydrodynamics**. > ˌhydromeˈchanical *adj*

hydromedusa (ˌhaɪdrəʊmɪˈdjuːsə) *n*, *pl* -sas *or* -sae (-siː) the medusa form of hydrozoan coelenterates > ˌhydromeˈdusan *adj*

hydromel (ˈhaɪdrəʊˌmɛl) *n archaic* another word for **mead** (the drink) [c15 from Latin, from Greek *hudromeli*, from HYDRO- + *meli* honey]

hydrometallurgy (ˌhaɪdrəʊˈmɛtəˌlɜːdʒɪ, -mɛˈtælədʒɪ) *n* a technique for the recovery of a metal from an aqueous medium in which the metal or the gangue is preferentially dissolved > ˌhydroˌmetalˈlurgical *adj*

hydrometeor (ˌhaɪdrəʊˈmiːtɪə) *n* any weather condition produced by water or water vapour in the atmosphere, such as rain, snow, or cloud > ˌhydroˌmeteoroˈlogical *adj* > ˌhydroˌmeteorˈology *n*

hydrometer (haɪˈdrɒmɪtə) *n* an instrument for measuring the relative density of a liquid, usually consisting of a sealed graduated tube with a weighted bulb on one end, the relative density being indicated by the length of the unsubmerged stem > hydrometric (ˌhaɪdrəʊˈmɛtrɪk) *or* ˌhydroˈmetrical *adj* > ˌhydroˈmetrically *adv* > hyˈdrometry *n*

hydronaut (ˈhaɪdrəʊˌnɔːt) *n US navy* a person trained to operate deep submergence vessels [c20 from Greek, from HYDRO- + -*naut*, as in aeronaut, astronaut]

hydronium ion (haɪˈdrəʊnɪəm) *n chem* another name for **hydroxonium ion** [c20 from HYDRO- + (AMM)ONIUM]

hydropathy (haɪˈdrɒpəθɪ) *n* a pseudoscientific method of treating disease by the use of large quantities of water both internally and externally. Also called: **water cure**. Compare **hydrotherapy** > hydropathic (ˌhaɪdrəʊˈpæθɪk) *or* ˌhydroˈpathical *adj* > hyˈdropathist *or* ˈhydroˌpath *n*

hydrophane (ˈhaɪdrəʊˌfeɪn) *n* a white partially opaque variety of opal that becomes translucent in water > hydrophanous (haɪˈdrɒfənəs) *adj*

hydrophilic (ˌhaɪdrəʊˈfɪlɪk) *adj chem* tending to dissolve in, mix with, or be wetted by water: *a hydrophilic colloid*. Compare **hydrophobic** > ˈhydroˌphile *n*

hydrophilous (haɪˈdrɒfɪləs) *adj botany* growing in or pollinated by water > hyˈdrophily *n*

hydrophobia (ˌhaɪdrəˈfəʊbɪə) *n* **1** another name for **rabies** **2** a fear of drinking fluids, esp that of a person with rabies, because of painful spasms when trying to swallow. Compare **aquaphobia**

hydrophobic (ˌhaɪdrəˈfəʊbɪk) *adj* **1** of or relating to hydrophobia **2** *chem* tending not to dissolve in, mix with, or be wetted by water: *a hydrophobic colloid*. Compare **hydrophilic**

hydrophone (ˈhaɪdrəˌfəʊn) *n* an electroacoustic transducer that converts sound or ultrasonic waves travelling through water into electrical oscillations

hydrophyte (ˈhaɪdrəʊˌfaɪt) *n* a plant that grows only in water or very moist soil > hydrophytic (ˌhaɪdrəʊˈfɪtɪk) *adj*

hydroplane (ˈhaɪdrəʊˌpleɪn) *n* **1** a motorboat equipped with hydrofoils or with a shaped bottom that raises its hull out of the water at high speeds **2** an attachment to an aircraft to enable it to glide along the surface of water **3** another name (esp US) for **seaplane** **4** a horizontal vane on the hull of a submarine for controlling its vertical motion ▷ *vb* **5** (*intr*) (of a boat) to rise out of the water in the manner of a hydroplane

hydroponics (ˌhaɪdrəʊˈpɒnɪks) *n* (*functioning as singular*) a method of cultivating plants by growing them in gravel, etc, through which water containing dissolved inorganic nutrient salts is pumped. Also called: **aquiculture** [c20 from HYDRO- + (GEO)PONICS] > ˌhydroˈponic *adj* > ˌhydroˈponically *adv*

hydropower (ˈhaɪdrəʊˌpaʊə) *n* hydroelectric power

hydroquinone (ˌhaɪdrəʊkwɪˈnəʊn) *or* **hydroquinol** (ˌhaɪdrəʊˈkwɪnɒl) *n* a white crystalline soluble phenol used as a photographic developer; 1,4-dihydroxybenzene. Formula: $C_6H_4(OH)_2$. Also called: **quinol**

hydroscope (ˈhaɪdrəˌskəʊp) *n* any instrument for making observations of underwater objects > hydroscopic (ˌhaɪdrəˈskɒpɪk) *or* ˌhydroˈscopical *adj*

hydrosere (ˈhaɪdrəʊsɪə) *n* a sere that begins in an aquatic environment

hydroski (ˈhaɪdrəʊˌskiː) *n* a hydrofoil used on some seaplanes to provide extra lift when taking off

hydrosol (ˈhaɪdrəˌsɒl) *n chem* a sol that has water as its liquid phase

hydrosome (ˈhaɪdrəˌsəʊm) *or* **hydrosoma** (ˌhaɪdrəˈsəʊmə) *n zoology* the body of a colonial hydrozoan [c19 from *hydro*-, from HYDRA + -SOME³]

hydrosphere (ˈhaɪdrəˌsfɪə) *n* the watery part of the earth's surface, including oceans, lakes, water vapour in the atmosphere, etc > ˌhydroˈspheric *adj*

hydrostat (ˈhaɪdrəʊˌstæt) *n* a device that detects the presence of water as a prevention against drying out, overflow, etc, esp one used as a warning in a steam boiler

hydrostatic (ˌhaɪdrəʊˈstætɪk) *or* **hydrostatical** *adj* **1** of or concerned with fluids that are not in motion: *hydrostatic pressure* **2** of or concerned with hydrostatics > ˌhydroˈstatically *adv*

hydrostatic balance *n* a balance for finding the weight of an object submerged in water in order to determine the upthrust on it and thus determine its relative density

hydrostatics (ˌhaɪdrəʊˈstætɪks) *n* (*functioning as singular*) the branch of science concerned with the mechanical properties and behaviour of fluids that are not in motion. See also **hydrodynamics**

hydrosulphate (ˌhaɪdrəʊˈsʌlfeɪt) *n* any quaternary acid salt formed by addition of an organic base to sulphuric acid, such as aniline hydrosulphate, $C_6H_5NH_3HSO_4$

hydrosulphide (ˌhaɪdrəʊˈsʌlfaɪd) *n* any salt derived from hydrogen sulphide by replacing one of its hydrogen atoms with a metal atom. Technical name: **hydrogen sulphide**

hydrosulphite (ˌhaɪdrəʊˈsʌlfaɪt) *n* another name (not in technical usage) for **dithionite** [c20 from HYDROSULPH(UROUS) + -ITE²]

hydrosulphurous acid (ˌhaɪdrəʊˈsʌlfərəs) *n* another name (not in technical usage) for **dithionous acid**

hydrotaxis (ˌhaɪdrəʊˈtæksɪs) *n* the directional movement of an organism or cell in response to the stimulus of water > ˌhydroˈtactic *adj*

hydrotherapeutics (ˌhaɪdrəʊˌθɛrəˈpjuːtɪks) *n* (*functioning as singular*) the branch of medical science concerned with hydrotherapy > ˌhydroˌtheraˈpeutic *adj*

hydrotherapy (ˌhaɪdrəʊˈθɛrəpɪ) *n med* the treatment of certain diseases by the external use of water, esp by exercising in water in order to mobilize stiff joints or strengthen weakened muscles. Also called: water cure Compare **hydropathy**. > hydrotherapic (ˌhaɪdrəʊθɪˈræpɪk) *adj* > ˌhydroˈtherapist *n*

hydrothermal (ˌhaɪdrəʊˈθɜːməl) *adj* of or relating to the action of water under conditions of high temperature, esp in forming rocks and minerals > ˌhydroˈthermally *adv*

hydrothorax (ˌhaɪdrəʊˈθɔːræks) *n pathol* an accumulation of fluid in one or both pleural cavities, often resulting from disease of the heart or kidneys > hydrothoracic (ˌhaɪdrəʊθɔːˈræsɪk) *adj*

hydrotropism (haɪˈdrɒtrəˌpɪzəm) *n* the directional growth of plants in response to the stimulus of water > hydrotropic (ˌhaɪdrəʊˈtrɒpɪk) *adj* > ˌhydroˈtropically *adv*

hydrous (ˈhaɪdrəs) *adj* **1** containing water **2** (of a chemical compound) combined with water molecules: *hydrous copper sulphate, CuSO₄.5H₂O*

hydrovane (ˈhaɪdrəʊˌveɪn) *n* a vane on a seaplane conferring stability on water (a sponson) or facilitating take off (a hydrofoil)

hydroxide (haɪˈdrɒksaɪd) *n* **1** a base or alkali

h

containing the ion OH⁻ **2** any compound containing an -OH group

hydroxonium ion (ˌhaɪdrɒkˈsəʊnɪəm) *n* a positive ion, H₃O⁺, formed by the attachment of a proton to a water molecule: occurs in solutions of acids and behaves like a hydrogen ion. Also called: hydronium ion

hydroxy (haɪˈdrɒksɪ) *adj* (of a chemical compound) containing one or more hydroxyl groups [C19 HYDRO- + OXY(GEN)]

hydroxy- *combining form* (in chemical compounds) indicating the presence of one or more hydroxyl groups or ions [from HYDRO- + OXY(GEN)]

hydroxy acid *n* **1** any acid, such as sulphuric acid, containing hydroxyl groups in its molecules **2** any of a class of carboxylic acids that contain both a hydroxyl group and a carboxyl group in their molecules

hydroxyl (haɪˈdrɒksɪl) *n* (*modifier*) of, consisting of, or containing the monovalent group -OH or the ion OH⁻: *a hydroxyl group or radical* > ˌhydroxˈylic *adj*

hydroxylamine (haɪˌdrɒksɪləˈmiːn, -ˈæmɪn, -ˈsaɪləˌmiːn) *n* a colourless crystalline compound that explodes when heated: a reducing agent. Formula: NH₂OH

hydroxyproline (haɪˌdrɒksɪˈprəʊliːn, -lɪn) *n* an amino acid occurring in some proteins, esp collagen. Formula: (OH)C₄H₇N(COOH)

hydroxytryptamine (haɪˌdrɒksɪˈtrɪptəmiːn) *n* 5-hydroxytryptamine: another name for **serotonin**. Abbreviation: 5HT

hydrozoan (ˌhaɪdrəʊˈzəʊən) *n* **1** any colonial or solitary coelenterate of the class *Hydrozoa*, which includes the hydra, Portuguese man-of-war, and the sertularians ▷ *adj* **2** of, relating to, or belonging to the *Hydrozoa*

Hydrus (ˈhaɪdrəs) *n, Latin genitive* Hydri (ˈhaɪdraɪ) a constellation near the S celestial pole lying close to Eridanus and Tucana and containing part of the Small Magellanic cloud [C17 from Latin, from Greek *hudros* water serpent, from *hudōr* water]

hyena *or* **hyaena** (haɪˈiːnə) *n* any of several long-legged carnivorous doglike mammals of the genera *Hyaena* and *Crocuta*, such as *C. crocuta* (**spotted** *or* **laughing hyena**), of Africa and S Asia: family *Hyaenidae*, order *Carnivora* (carnivores). See also **strandwolf** [C16 from Medieval Latin, from Latin *hyaena*, from Greek *huaina*, from *hus* hog] > hyˈenic *or* hyˈaenic *adj*

hyetal (ˈhaɪɪtˀl) *adj* of or relating to rain, rainfall, or rainy regions [C19 from Greek *huetos* rain + -AL¹]

hyeto- *or before a vowel* **hyet-** *combining form* indicating rain [from Greek *huetos*]

hyetograph (ˈhaɪɪtəˌɡrɑːf, -ˌɡræf) *n* **1** a chart showing the distribution of rainfall of a particular area, usually throughout a year **2** a self-recording rain gauge

hyetography (ˌhaɪɪˈtɒɡrəfɪ) *n* the study of the distribution and recording of rainfall > hyetographic (ˌhaɪɪtəˈɡræfɪk) *or* ˌhyetoˈgraphical *adj* > ˌhyetoˈgraphically *adv*

Hygeia (haɪˈdʒiːə) *n* the Greek goddess of health > Hyˈgeian *adj*

hygiene (ˈhaɪdʒiːn) *n* **1** Also called: hygienics the science concerned with the maintenance of health **2** clean or healthy practices or thinking: *personal hygiene* [C18 from New Latin *hygiēna*, from Greek *hugieinē*, from *hugiēs* healthy]

hygienic (haɪˈdʒiːnɪk) *adj* promoting health or cleanliness; sanitary > hyˈgienically *adv*

hygienics (haɪˈdʒiːnɪks) *n* (*functioning as singular*) another word for **hygiene** (sense 1)

hygienist (ˈhaɪdʒiːnɪst) *or* **hygeist, hygieist** (ˈhaɪdʒiː.ɪst) *n* a person skilled in the practice of hygiene. See also **dental hygienist**

hygristor (haɪˈɡrɪstə) *n* an electronic component the resistance of which varies with humidity [C20 from HYGRO- + (RES)ISTOR]

hygro- *or before a vowel* **hygr-** *combining form* indicating moisture: *hygrometer* [from Greek *hugros* wet]

hygrograph (ˈhaɪɡrəˌɡrɑː.f, -ˌɡræf) *n* an automatic

hygrometer that produces a graphic record of the humidity of the air

hygroma (haɪˈɡrəʊmə) *or* **hydroma** (haɪˌdrəʊmə) *n pathol* a swelling in the soft tissue that occurs over a joint, usually caused by repeated injury [C20 from HYGRO- + -OMA]

hygrometer (haɪˈɡrɒmɪtə) *n* any of various instruments for measuring humidity > hygrometric (ˌhaɪɡrəˈmɛtrɪk) *adj* > ˌhygroˈmetrically *adv* > hyˈgrometry *n*

hygrophilous (haɪˈɡrɒfɪləs) *adj* (of a plant) growing in moist places > hygrophile (ˈhaɪɡrəʊˌfaɪl) *n*

hygrophyte (ˈhaɪɡrəˌfaɪt) *n* any plant that grows in wet or waterlogged soil > hygrophytic (ˌhaɪɡrəˈfɪtɪk) *adj*

hygroscope (ˈhaɪɡrəˌskəʊp) *n* any device that indicates the humidity of the air without necessarily measuring it

hygroscopic (ˌhaɪɡrəˈskɒpɪk) *adj* (of a substance) tending to absorb water from the air > ˌhygroˈscopically *adv* > ˌhygroscoˈpicity *n*

hygrostat (ˈhaɪɡrəˌstæt) *n* another name for **humidistat**

hying (ˈhaɪɪŋ) *vb* a present participle of **hie**

Hyksos (ˈhɪksɒs) *n, pl* -sos a member of a nomadic Asian people, probably Semites, who controlled Egypt from 1720 BC until 1560 BC [from Greek *Huksōs* name of ruling dynasty in Egypt, from Egyptian *hq's'sw* ruler of the lands of the nomads]

hyla (ˈhaɪlə) *n* any tree frog of the genus *Hyla*, such as *H. leucophyllata* (**white-spotted hyla**) of tropical America [C19 from New Latin, from Greek *hulē* forest, wood]

hylo- *or before a vowel* **hyl-** *combining form* **1** indicating matter (as distinguished from spirit): *hylozoism* **2** indicating wood: *hylophagous* [from Greek *hulē* wood]

hylomorphism (ˌhaɪləˈmɔːfɪzəm) *n* the philosophical doctrine that identifies matter with the first cause of the universe

hylophagous (haɪˈlɒfəɡəs) *adj* (esp of insects) feeding on wood [C19 from Greek *hulophagos*, from *hulē* wood + *phagein* to devour]

hylotheism (ˌhaɪləˈθiːɪzəm) *n* the doctrine that God is identical to matter

hylozoism (ˌhaɪləˈzəʊɪzəm) *n* the philosophical doctrine that life is one of the properties of matter [C17 HYLO- + Greek *zōē* life] > ˌhyloˈzoic *adj* > ˌhyloˈzoist *n* > ˌhylozoˈistic *adj* > ˌhylozoˈistically *adv*

hymen (ˈhaɪmɛn) *n anatomy* a fold of mucous membrane that partly covers the entrance to the vagina and is usually ruptured when sexual intercourse takes place for the first time [C17 from Greek: membrane] > ˈhymenal *adj*

Hymen (ˈhaɪmɛn) *n* the Greek and Roman god of marriage

hymeneal (ˌhaɪmɛˈniːəl) *adj* **1** *chiefly poetic* of or relating to marriage ▷ *n* **2** a wedding song or poem

hymenium (haɪˈmiːnɪəm) *n, pl* -nia (-nɪə) *or* -niums (in basidiomycetous and ascomycetous fungi) a layer of cells some of which produce the spores

hymenophore (haɪˈmiːnəʊˌfɔː) *n botany* the fruiting body of some basidiomycetous fungi [from HYMENIUM + -PHORE]

hymenopteran (ˌhaɪmɪˈnɒptərən) *or* **hymenopteron** *n, pl* -terans *or* -tera (-tərə) *or* -terons any hymenopterous insect

hymenopterous (ˌhaɪmɪˈnɒptərəs) *or* **hymenopteran** *adj* of, relating to, or belonging to the *Hymenoptera*, an order of insects, including bees, wasps, ants, and sawflies, having two pairs of membranous wings and an ovipositor specialized for stinging, sawing, or piercing [C19 from Greek *humenopteros* membrane wing; see HYMEN, -PTEROUS]

Hymettian (haɪˈmɛtɪən) *or* **Hymettic** (haɪˈmɛtɪk) *adj* of or relating to Hymettus, a mountain in SE Greece

Hymettus (haɪˈmɛtəs) *n* a mountain in SE Greece, in Attica east of Athens: famous for its marble and for honey. Height: 1032 m (3386 ft). Modern Greek name: Imittós

hymn (hɪm) *n* **1** a Christian song of praise sung to God or a saint **2** a similar song praising other gods, a nation, etc ▷ *vb* **3** to express (praises, thanks, etc) by singing hymns [C13 from Latin *hymnus*, from Greek *humnos*] > hymnic (ˈhɪmnɪk) *adj* > ˈhymnˌlike *adj*

hymnal (ˈhɪmnˀl) *n* **1** a book of hymns ▷ *adj* **2** of, relating to, or characteristic of hymns

hymn book *n* a book containing the words and music of hymns

hymnist (ˈhɪmnɪst), **hymnodist** (ˈhɪmnədɪst) *or* **hymnographer** (hɪmˈnɒɡrəfə) *n* a person who composes hymns

hymnody (ˈhɪmnədɪ) *n* **1** the composition or singing of hymns **2** hymns collectively Also called: hymnology [C18 from Medieval Latin *hymnōdia*, from Greek *humnōidia*, from *humnōidein* to chant a hymn, from HYMN + *aeidein* to sing] > hymnodical (hɪmˈnɒdɪkˀl) *adj*

hymnology (hɪmˈnɒlədʒɪ) *n* **1** the study of hymn composition **2** another word for **hymnody** > hymnologic (ˌhɪmnəˈlɒdʒɪk) *or* ˌhymnoˈlogical *adj* > hymˈnologist *n*

hyoid (ˈhaɪɔɪd) *adj also* hyoidal *or* hyoidean **1** of or relating to the hyoid bone ▷ *n also* hyoid bone **2** the horseshoe-shaped bone that lies at the base of the tongue and above the thyroid cartilage **3** a corresponding bone or group of bones in other vertebrates [C19 from New Latin *hyoides*, from Greek *huoeidēs* having the shape of the letter UPSILON, from *hu* upsilon + -OID]

hyoscine (ˈhaɪəˌsiːn) *n* another name for **scopolamine** [C19 from HYOSC(YAMUS) + -INE²]

hyoscyamine (ˌhaɪəˈsaɪəˌmiːn, -mɪn) *n* a poisonous alkaloid occurring in henbane and related plants: an optically active isomer of atropine, used in medicine in a similar way. Formula: C₁₇H₂₃NO₃

hyoscyamus (ˌhaɪəˈsaɪəməs) *n* any plant of the solanaceous genus *Hyoscyamus*, of Europe, Asia, and N Africa, including henbane [C18 from New Latin, from Greek *huoskuamos*, from *hus* pig + *kuamos* bean; the plant was thought to be poisonous to pigs]

hyp. *abbreviation for* hypotenuse **3** hypothetical

hyp- *prefix* a variant of **hypo-** before a vowel: *hypabyssal*

hypabyssal (ˌhɪpəˈbɪsˀl) *adj* (of igneous rocks) derived from magma that has solidified at shallow depth in the form of dykes, sills, etc [C19 from HYP- + -ABYSSAL]

hypaesthesia *or US* **hypesthesia** (ˌhɪpiːsˈθiːzɪə, ˌhaɪ-) *n pathol* a reduced sensibility to touch > hypaesthesic *or US* hypesthesic (ˌhɪpiːsˈθiːsɪk, ˌhaɪ-) *adj*

hypaethral *or US* **hypethral** (hɪˈpiːθrəl, haɪ-) *adj* (esp of a classical temple) having no roof [C18 from Latin *hypaethrus* uncovered, from Greek *hupaithros*, from HYPO- + *aithros* clear sky]

hypalgesia (ˌhaɪpælˈdʒiːzɪə, -sɪə) *n pathol* diminished sensitivity to pain > ˌhypalˈgesic *adj*

hypallage (haɪˈpælədʒiː) *n rhetoric* a figure of speech in which the natural relations of two words in a statement are interchanged, as in *the fire spread the wind* [C16 via Late Latin from Greek *hupallagē* interchange, from HYPO- + *allassein* to exchange]

hypanthium (haɪˈpænθɪəm) *n, pl* -thia (-θɪə) *botany* the cup-shaped or flat receptacle of perigynous or epigynous flowers [C19 from New Latin, from HYPO- + Greek *anthion* a little flower, from *anthos* flower] > hyˈpanthial *adj*

hype¹ (haɪp) *slang* ▷ *n* **1** a hypodermic needle or injection ▷ *vb* **2** (*intr; usually foll by up*) to inject oneself with a drug **3** (*tr*) to stimulate artificially or excite [C20 shortened from HYPODERMIC]

hype² (haɪp) *n* **1** a deception or racket **2** intensive or exaggerated publicity or sales promotion: *media* *hype* **3** the person or thing so publicized ▷ *vb* (*tr*) **4** to market or promote (a product) using exaggerated or intensive publicity **5** to falsify or rig (something) **6** (in the pop-music business) to buy (copies of a particular record) in such quantity as to increase its ratings in the charts [c20 of unknown origin] > 'hyper *n* > 'hyping *n*

hyped up *adj slang* stimulated or excited by or as if by the effect of a stimulating drug

hyper ('haɪpə) *adj informal* overactive; overexcited [c20 probably independent use of HYPER-]

hyper- *prefix* **1** above, over, or in excess: *hypercritical* **2** (in medicine) denoting an abnormal excess: *hyperacidity* **3** indicating that a chemical compound contains a greater than usual amount of an element: *hyperoxide* [from Greek *huper* over]

hyperaccumulator (,haɪpərə'kjuːmjʊˌleɪtə) *n* a plant that absorbs toxins, such as heavy metals, to a greater concentration than that in the soil in which it is growing

hyperacidity (,haɪpərə'sɪdɪtɪ) *n* excess acidity of the gastrointestinal tract, esp the stomach, producing a burning sensation > ,hyper'acid *adj*

hyperactive (,haɪpər'æktɪv) *adj* abnormally active > ,hyper'action > ,hyperac'tivity *n*

hyperaemia *or US* **hyperemia** (,haɪpər'iːmɪə) *n pathol* an excessive amount of blood in an organ or part > ,hyper'aemic *or US* ,hyper'emic *adj*

hyperaesthesia *or US* **hyperesthesia** (,haɪpəriː'sθiːzɪə) *n pathol* increased sensitivity of any of the sense organs, esp of the skin to cold, heat, pain, etc > hyperaesthetic *or US* hyperesthetic (,haɪpəriː'sθɛtɪk) *adj*

hyperbaric (,haɪpə'bærɪk) *adj* of, concerned with, or operating at pressures higher than normal

hyperbaton (haɪ'pɜːbəˌtɒn) *n rhetoric* a figure of speech in which the normal order of words is reversed, as in *cheese I love* [c16 via Latin from Greek, literally: an overstepping, from HYPER- + *bainein* to step]

hyperbola (haɪ'pɜːbələ) *n, pl* **-las, -le** (-ˌliː) a conic section formed by a plane that cuts both bases of a cone; it consists of two branches asymptotic to two intersecting fixed lines and has two foci. Standard equation: $x^2/a^2 - y^2/b^2 = 1$ where $2a$ is the distance between the two intersections with the *x*-axis and $b = a\sqrt{(e^2 - 1)}$, where *e* is the eccentricity [c17 from Greek *huperbolē*, literally: excess, extravagance, from HYPER- + *ballein* to throw]

hyperbole (haɪ'pɜːbəlɪ) *n* a deliberate exaggeration used for effect: *he embraced her a thousand times* [c16 from Greek: from HYPER- + *bolē* a throw, from *ballein* to throw] > hy'perbolism *n*

hyperbolic (,haɪpə'bɒlɪk) *or* **hyperbolical** *adj* **1** of or relating to a hyperbola **2** *rhetoric* of or relating to a hyperbole > ,hyper'bolically *adv*

hyperbolic function *n* any of a group of functions of an angle expressed as a relationship between the distances of a point on a hyperbola to the origin and to the coordinate axes. The group includes sinh (**hyperbolic sine**), cosh (**hyperbolic cosine**), tanh (**hyperbolic tangent**), sech (**hyperbolic secant**), cosech (**hyperbolic cosecant**), and coth (**hyperbolic cotangent**)

hyperbolize *or* **hyperbolise** (haɪ'pɜːbəˌlaɪz) *vb* to express (something) by means of hyperbole

hyperboloid (haɪ'pɜːbəˌlɔɪd) *n* a geometric surface consisting of one sheet, or of two sheets separated by a finite distance, whose sections parallel to the three coordinate planes are hyperbolas or ellipses. Equations $x^2/a^2 + y^2/b^2 - z^2/c^2 = 1$ (one sheet) or $x^2/a^2 - y^2/b^2 - z^2/c^2 = 1$ (two sheets) where *a*, *b*, and *c* are constants

Hyperborean (,haɪpəbɔː'rɪən) *n* **1** *Greek myth* one of a people believed to have lived beyond the North wind in a sunny land **2** an inhabitant of the extreme north ▷ *adj* **3** (*sometimes not capital*) of or relating to the extreme north **4** of or relating to the Hyperboreans [c16 from Latin *hyperboreus*, from Greek *huperboreos*, from HYPER- + *Boreas* north wind]

hypercapnia (,haɪpə'kæpnɪə) *n* an excess of

carbon dioxide in the blood. Also: **hypercarbia** [from HYPER- + Greek *kapnos* smoke] > ,hyper'capnic *adj*

hypercatalectic (,haɪpəˌkætə'lɛktɪk) *adj prosody* (of a line of verse) having extra syllables after the last foot

hypercharge ('haɪpəˌtʃɑːdʒ) *n* a property of baryons that is used to account for the absence of certain strong interaction decays

hypercholesterolaemia *or US* **hypercholesterolemia** (,haɪpəkəˌlɛstərɒl'iːmɪə) *n* the condition of having a high concentration of cholesterol in the blood. See **hyperlipidaemia**

hypercorrect (,haɪpəkə'rɛkt) *adj* **1** excessively correct or fastidious **2** resulting from or characterized by hypercorrection > ,hypercor'rectness *n*

hypercorrection (,haɪpəkə'rɛkʃən) *n* a mistaken correction to text or speech made through a desire to avoid nonstandard pronunciation or grammar: *"between you and I" is a hypercorrection of "between you and me"*

hypercritical (,haɪpə'krɪtɪk³l) *adj* excessively or severely critical; carping; captious > ,hyper'critic *n* > ,hyper'critically *adv* > ,hyper'criti,cism *n*

hypercube ('haɪpəˌkjuːb) *n maths* a figure in a space of four or more dimensions having all its sides equal and all its angles right angles

hyperdulia (,haɪpədjʊ'lɪə) *n RC Church* special veneration accorded to the Virgin Mary. Compare **dulia, latria** [c16 from Latin HYPER- + Medieval Latin *dulia* service] > ,hyper'dulic *or* ,hyper'dulical *adj*

hyperemia (,haɪpər'iːmɪə) *n pathol* the usual US spelling of **hyperaemia**. > ,hyper'emic *adj*

hyperesthesia (,haɪpəriː'sθiːzɪə) *n pathol* the usual US spelling of **hyperaesthesia** > ,hyperes'thetic *adj*

hypereutectic (,haɪpəjuː'tɛktɪk) *or* **hypereutectoid** *adj* (of a mixture or alloy with two components) containing more of the minor component than a eutectic mixture. Compare **hypoeutectic**

hyperextension (,haɪpərɪk'stɛnʃən) *n* extension of an arm or leg beyond its normal limits

hyperfine structure ('haɪpəˌfaɪn) *n* the splitting of a spectral line of an atom or molecule into two or more closely spaced components as a result of interaction of the electrons with the magnetic moments of the nuclei. Compare **fine structure**. See also **Zeeman effect**

hyperfocal distance (,haɪpə'fəʊk³l) *n* the distance from a camera lens to the point beyond which all objects appear sharp and clearly defined

hypergamy (haɪ'pɜːgəmɪ) *n* **1** *anthropol* a custom that forbids a woman to marry a man of lower social status **2** any marriage with a partner of higher social status [c19 from HYPER- + -GAMY] > ,hyper'gamous *adj*

hypergeometric (,haɪpədʒɪə'mɛtrɪk) *adj* of or relating to operations or series that transcend ordinary geometrical operations or series

hyperglycaemia *or US* **hyperglycemia** (,haɪpəglaɪ'siːmɪə) *n pathol* an abnormally large amount of sugar in the blood [c20 from HYPER- + GLYCO- + -AEMIA] > ,hypergly'caemic *or US* ,hypergly'cemic *adj*

hypergolic (,haɪpə'gɒlɪk) *adj* (of a rocket fuel) able to ignite spontaneously on contact with an oxidizer [c20 from German *Hypergol* (perhaps from HYP(ER-) + ERG¹ + -OL²) + -IC]

hypericum (haɪ'pɛrɪkəm) *n* any herbaceous plant or shrub of the temperate genus *Hypericum*: family *Hypericaceae*. See **rose of Sharon** (sense 1), **Saint John's wort** [c16 via Latin from Greek *hupereikon*, from HYPER- + *ereikē* heath]

hyperinflation (,haɪpərɪn'fleɪʃən) *n* extremely high inflation, usually over 50 per cent per month, often involving social disorder. Also called: **galloping inflation**

hyperinsulinism (,haɪpər'ɪnsjʊlɪˌnɪzəm) *n pathol* an excessive amount of insulin in the blood, producing hypoglycaemia, caused by

oversecretion of insulin by the pancreas or overdosage of insulin in treating diabetes. See **insulin reaction**

Hyperion¹ (haɪ'pɪərɪən) *n Greek myth* a Titan, son of Uranus and Gaea, father of Helios (sun), Selene (moon), and Eos (dawn)

Hyperion² (haɪ'pɪərɪən) *n* an irregular-shaped outer satellite of the planet Saturn that tumbles chaotically

hyperkeratosis (,haɪpəˌkɛrə'təʊsɪs) *n pathol* overgrowth and thickening of the outer layer of the skin > hyperkeratotic (,haɪpəˌkɛrə'tɒtɪk) *adj*

hyperkinesia (,haɪpəkɪ'niːzɪə, -kaɪ-) *or* **hyperkinesis** (,haɪpəkɪ'niːsɪs, -kaɪ-) *n pathol* **1** excessive movement, as in a muscle spasm **2** extreme overactivity in children [c20 from HYPER- + -*kinesia* from Greek *kinēsis* movement, from *kinein* to move] > hyperkinetic (,haɪpəkɪ'nɛtɪk, -kaɪ-) *adj*

hyperlink ('haɪpəˌlɪŋk) *n* **1** a word, phrase, picture, icon, etc, in a computer document on which a user may click to move to another part of the document or to another document ▷ *vb* **2** (*tr*) to link (files) in this way ▷ Often shortened to: **link**

hyperlipidaemia *or US* **hyperlipidemia** (,haɪpəˌlɪpɪ'diːmɪə) *n* an abnormally high level of lipids, esp cholesterol, in the blood, predisposing to atherosclerosis and other arterial diseases

hypermania (,haɪpə'meɪnɪə) *n psychol* a condition of extreme mania

hypermarket ('haɪpəˌmɑːkɪt) *n Brit* a huge self-service store, usually built on the outskirts of a town [c20 translation of French *hypermarché*]

hypermedia ('haɪpəˌmiːdɪə) *n* computer software and hardware that allows users to interact with text, graphics, sound, and video, each of which can be accessed from within any of the others. Compare **hypertext**

hypermeter (haɪ'pɜːmɪtə) *n prosody* a verse line containing one or more additional syllables > hypermetric (,haɪpə'mɛtrɪk) *or* ,hyper'metrical *adj*

hypermetropia (,haɪpəmɪ'trəʊpɪə) *or* **hypermetropy** (,haɪpə'mɛtrəpɪ) *n pathol* variants of **hyperopia** [c19 from Greek *hupermetros* beyond measure (from HYPER- + *metron* measure) + -OPIA] > hypermetropic (,haɪpəmɪ'trɒpɪk) *or* ,hyperme'tropical *adj*

hypermnesia (,haɪpəm'niːzɪə) *n psychol* an unusually good ability to remember, found in some mental disorders and possibly in hypnosis [c20 New Latin, from HYPER- + -*mnesia*, formed on the model of AMNESIA]

hypermodern school (,haɪpə'mɒdən) *n* a name given by S. G. Tartakower to a style of chess typified by Richard Reti and A. I. Nimzowitsch and characterized by control of the centre from the flanks

hypernova ('haɪpəˌnəʊvə) *n* an exploding star that produces even more energy and light than a supernova

hypernym ('haɪpəˌnɪm) *n* another name for **superordinate** (sense 3) [c20 HYPER- + Greek *onoma* name]

hyperon ('haɪpəˌrɒn) *n physics* any baryon that is not a nucleon [c20 from HYPER- + -ON]

hyperopia (,haɪpə'rəʊpɪə) *n* inability to see near objects clearly because the images received by the eye are focused behind the retina; long-sightedness. Also called: hypermetropia, hypermetropy Compare **myopia, presbyopia** > hyperopic (,haɪpə'rɒpɪk) *adj*

hyperorexia (,haɪpərɒ'rɛksɪə) *n* compulsive overeating [c20 from HYPER- + Greek *orexis* appetite]

hyperosmia (,haɪpə'ɒzmɪə) *n* an abnormally acute sense of smell [c20 from HYPER- + Greek *osmē* odour]

hyperostosis (,haɪpərɒ'stəʊsɪs) *n, pl* **-ses** (-siːz) *pathol* **1** an abnormal enlargement of the outer layer of a bone **2** a bony growth arising from the root of a tooth or from the surface of a bone > hyperostotic (,haɪpərɒ'stɒtɪk) *adj*

h

hyperparasite (ˌhaɪpəˈpærəˌsaɪt) *n* an organism that is parasitic on another parasite

hyperphagia (ˌhaɪpəˈfeɪdʒɪə) *n psychol* compulsive overeating over a prolonged period

hyperphysical (ˌhaɪpəˈfɪzɪkəl) *adj* beyond the physical; supernatural or immaterial > ˌhyperˈphysically *adv*

hyperpituitarism (ˌhaɪpəpɪˈtjuːɪtəˌrɪzəm) *n pathol* overactivity of the pituitary gland, sometimes resulting in acromegaly or gigantism > ˌhyperpiˈtuitary *adj*

hyperplane (ˈhaɪpəˌpleɪn) *n maths* a higher dimensional analogue of a plane in three dimensions. It can be represented by one linear equation

hyperplasia (ˌhaɪpəˈpleɪzɪə) *n* enlargement of a bodily organ or part resulting from an increase in the total number of cells. Compare **hypertrophy** > hyperplastic (ˌhaɪpəˈplæstɪk) *adj*

hyperploid (ˈhaɪpəˌplɔɪd) *adj biology* having or relating to a chromosome number that exceeds an exact multiple of the haploid number > ˈhyperˌploidy *n*

hyperpnoea *or US* **hyperpnea** (ˌhaɪpəpˈniːə, ˌhaɪpəˈniːə) *n* an increase in the breathing rate or in the depth of breathing, as after strenuous exercise [C20 from New Latin, from HYPER- + Greek *pnoia* breath, from *pnein* to breathe]

hyperpower (ˈhaɪpəˌpaʊə) *n* 1 an extremely powerful state that dominates all other states in every sphere of activity 2 the power wielded by such a state

hyperprosexia (ˌhaɪpəprɒˈsɛksɪə) *n psychol* a condition in which the whole attention is occupied by one object or idea to the exclusion of others [C20 from HYPER- + Greek *prosexein* to heed]

hyperpyrexia (ˌhaɪpəpaɪˈrɛksɪə) *n pathol* an extremely high fever, with a temperature of 41°C (106°F) or above. Also called: hyperthermia, hyperthermy > hyperpyretic (ˌhaɪpəpaɪˈrɛtɪk) *or* ˌhyperpyˈrexial *adj*

hyperreal (ˌhaɪpəˈrɪəl) *adj* 1 involving or characterized by particularly realistic graphic representation 2 distorting or exaggerating reality 3 pertaining to or creating a hyperreality ▷ *n* 4 the hyperreal that which constitutes hyperreality 5 short for **hyperreal number**

hyperrealism (ˌhaɪpəˈrɪəlɪzəm) *n* another word for **photorealism**. > ˌhyperˈrealist *n*, *adj* > ˌhyperˌrealˈistic *adj*

hyperreality (ˌhaɪpərɪˈælɪtɪ) *n*, *pl* -ties an image or simulation, or an aggregate of images and simulations, that either distorts the reality it purports to depict or does not in fact depict anything with a real existence at all, but which nonetheless comes to constitute reality

hyperreal number *n* any of the set of numbers formed by the addition of infinite numbers and infinitesimal numbers to the set of real numbers

hypersensitive (ˌhaɪpəˈsɛnsɪtɪv) *adj* 1 having unduly vulnerable feelings 2 abnormally sensitive to an allergen, a drug, or other agent > ˌhyperˈsensitiveness *or* ˌhyperˌsensiˈtivity *n*

hypersensitize *or* **hypersensitise** (ˌhaɪpəˈsɛnsɪˌtaɪz) *vb* (tr) to treat (a photographic emulsion), usually after manufacture and shortly before exposure, to increase its speed > ˌhyperˌsensitiˈzation *or* ˌhyperˌsensitiˈsation *n*

hypersonic (ˌhaɪpəˈsɒnɪk) *adj* concerned with or having a velocity of at least five times that of sound in the same medium under the same conditions > ˌhyperˈsonics *n*

hyperspace (ˌhaɪpəˈspeɪs) *n* 1 *maths* space having more than three dimensions: often used to describe a multi-dimensional environment 2 (in science fiction) a theoretical dimension within which conventional space-time relationship does not apply > hyperspatial (ˌhaɪpəˈspeɪʃəl) *adj*

hypersthene (ˈhaɪpəsˌθiːn) *n* a green, brown, or black pyroxene mineral consisting of magnesium iron silicate in orthorhombic crystalline form. Formula: $(Mg,Fe)_2Si_2O_6$ [C19 from HYPER- + Greek

sthenos strength] > **hypersthenic** (ˌhaɪpəsˈθɛnɪk) *adj*

hypertension (ˌhaɪpəˈtɛnʃən) *n pathol* abnormally high blood pressure > **hypertensive** (ˌhaɪpəˈtɛnsɪv) *adj*, *n*

hypertext (ˈhaɪpəˌtɛkst) *n* computer software and hardware that allows users to create, store, and view text and move between related items easily and in a nonsequential way; a word or phrase can be selected to link users to another part of the same document or to a different document

hypertext markup language *n* the full name for HTML

hyperthermia (ˌhaɪpəˈθɜːmɪə) *or* **hyperthermy** (ˌhaɪpəˈθɜːmɪ) *n pathol* variants of **hyperpyrexia** > ˌhyperˈthermal *adj*

hyperthermophile (ˌhaɪpəˈθɜːməʊˌfaɪl) *n* an organism, esp a bacterium, that lives at high temperatures (above 80°C), found in some hot springs [C20 from HYPER- + -THERMOPHILE]

hyperthymia (ˌhaɪpəˈθaɪmɪə) *n* excessive emotionalism [C20 from HYPER- + Greek *thymos* spirit]

hyperthyroidism (ˌhaɪpəˈθaɪrɔɪˌdɪzəm) *n* overproduction of thyroid hormone by the thyroid gland, causing nervousness, insomnia, sweating, palpitation, and sensitivity to heat. Also called: **thyrotoxicosis**. See **exophthalmic goitre** > ˌhyperˈthyroid *adj*, *n*

hypertonic (ˌhaɪpəˈtɒnɪk) *adj* 1 (esp of muscles) being in a state of abnormally high tension 2 (of a solution) having a higher osmotic pressure than that of a specified, generally physiological, solution. Compare **hypotonic, isotonic** > hypertonicity (ˌhaɪpətəʊˈnɪsɪtɪ) *n*

hypertrophy (haɪˈpɜːtrəfɪ) *n*, *pl* -phies 1 enlargement of an organ or part resulting from an increase in the size of the cells. Compare **atrophy, hyperplasia** ▷ *vb* -phies, -phying, -phied 2 to undergo or cause to undergo this condition > hypertrophic (ˌhaɪpəˈtrɒfɪk) *adj*

hyperventilate (ˌhaɪpəˈvɛntɪleɪt) *vb* (intr) to breathe in an abnormally deep, long, and rapid manner, sometimes resulting in cramp and dizziness

hyperventilation (ˌhaɪpəˌvɛntɪˈleɪʃən) *n* an increase in the depth, duration, and rate of breathing, sometimes resulting in cramp and dizziness

hypervitaminosis (ˌhaɪpəˌvɪtəmɪˈnəʊsɪs, -vaɪ-) *n pathol* the condition resulting from the chronic excessive intake of vitamins [C20 from HYPER- + VITAMIN + -OSIS]

hypester (ˈhaɪpstə) *n* a person or organization that gives an idea or product intense publicity in order to promote it

hypesthesia (ˌhɪpiːsˈθiːzɪə, ˌhaɪ-) *n* the usual US spelling of **hypaesthesia**. > hypesthesic (ˌhɪpiːsˈθiːsɪk, ˌhaɪ-) *adj*

hypethral (hɪˈpiːθrəl, haɪ-) *adj* the usual US spelling of **hypaethral**

hypha (ˈhaɪfə) *n*, *pl* -phae (-fiː) any of the filaments that constitute the body (mycelium) of a fungus [C19 from New Latin, from Greek *huphē* web] > ˈhyphal *adj*

hyphen (ˈhaɪfən) *n* 1 the punctuation mark (-), used to separate the parts of some compound words, to link the words of a phrase, and between syllables of a word split between two consecutive lines of writing or printing ▷ *vb* 2 (tr) another word for **hyphenate** [C17 from Late Latin (meaning: the combining of two words), from Greek *huphen* (adv) together, from HYPO- + *heis* one]

hyphenate (ˈhaɪfəˌneɪt) *or* **hyphen** *vb* (tr) to separate (syllables, words, etc) with a hyphen > ˌhyphenˈation *n*

hyphenated (ˈhaɪfəˌneɪtɪd) *adj* 1 containing or linked with a hyphen 2 *chiefly US* having a nationality denoted by a hyphenated word, as in *American-Irish* 3 *chiefly US* denoting something, such as a professional career, that consists of two elements, as in *singer-songwriter*

hyphen help *n* a word processing function that

assists the operator to identify automatically those words that can be hyphenated at the end of a line of text

hypnagogic *or* **hypnogogic** (ˌhɪpnəˈgɒdʒɪk) *adj psychol* of or relating to the state just before one is fully asleep. See also **hypnagogic image, hypnopompic** [C19 from French *hypnagogique*; see HYPNO-, -AGOGIC]

hypnagogic image *n psychol* an image experienced by a person just before falling asleep, which often resembles a hallucination

hypno- *or before a vowel* **hypn-** *combining form* 1 indicating sleep: *hypnophobia* 2 relating to hypnosis: *hypnotherapy* [from Greek *hupnos* sleep]

hypnoanalysis (ˌhɪpnəʊəˈnælɪsɪs) *n psychol* psychoanalysis conducted on a hypnotized person > hypnoanalytic (ˌhɪpnəʊˌænəˈlɪtɪk) *adj*

hypnogenesis (ˌhɪpnəʊˈdʒɛnɪsɪs) *n psychol* the induction of sleep or hypnosis > hypnogenetic (ˌhɪpnəʊdʒɪˈnɛtɪk) *adj* > ˌhypnogeˈnetically *adv*

hypnoid[1] (ˈhɪpˌnɔɪd), **hypnoidal** (hɪpˈnɔɪdəl) *adj psychol* of or relating to a state resembling sleep or hypnosis

hypnoid[2] (ˈhɪpˌnɔɪd) *adj* resembling a moss, specifically a moss of the genus *Hypnum* [from New Latin *hypnum*, from Greek *hupnon* a type of lichen, + -OID]

hypnology (hɪpˈnɒlədʒɪ) *n psychol* the study of sleep and hypnosis > hypnologic (ˌhɪpnəˈlɒdʒɪk) *or* ˌhypnoˈlogical *adj* > hypˈnologist *n*

hypnopaedia (ˌhɪpnəʊˈpiːdɪə) *n* the learning of lessons heard during sleep [C20 from HYPNO- + Greek *paideia* education]

hypnopompic (ˌhɪpnəʊˈpɒmpɪk) *adj psychol* relating to the state existing between sleep and full waking, characterized by the persistence of dreamlike imagery. See also **hypnagogic** [C20 from HYPNO- + Greek *pompē* a sending forth, escort + -IC; see POMP]

Hypnos (ˈhɪpnɒs) *n Greek myth* the god of sleep. Roman counterpart: **Somnus**. Compare **Morpheus** [Greek: sleep]

hypnosis (hɪpˈnəʊsɪs) *n*, *pl* -ses (-siːz) an artificially induced state of relaxation and concentration in which deeper parts of the mind become more accessible: used clinically to reduce reaction to pain, to encourage free association, etc. See also **autohypnosis**

hypnotherapy (ˌhɪpnəʊˈθɛrəpɪ) *n* the use of hypnosis in the treatment of emotional and psychogenic problems > ˌhypnoˈtherapist *n*

hypnotic (hɪpˈnɒtɪk) *adj* 1 of, relating to, or producing hypnosis or sleep 2 (of a person) susceptible to hypnotism ▷ *n* 3 a drug or agent that induces sleep 4 a person susceptible to hypnosis [C17 from Late Latin *hypnōticus*, from Greek *hupnōtikos*, from *hupnoun* to put to sleep, from *hupnos* sleep] > hypˈnotically *adv*

hypnotism (ˈhɪpnəˌtɪzəm) *n* 1 the scientific study and practice of hypnosis 2 the process of inducing hypnosis

hypnotist (ˈhɪpnətɪst) *n* a person skilled in the theory and practice of hypnosis

hypnotize *or* **hypnotise** (ˈhɪpnəˌtaɪz) *vb* (tr) 1 to induce hypnosis in (a person) 2 to charm or beguile; fascinate > ˈhypnoˌtizable *or* ˈhypnoˌtisable *adj* > ˌhypnoˌtizaˈbility *or* ˌhypnoˌtisaˈbility *n* > ˌhypnotiˈzation *or* ˌhypnotiˈsation *n* > ˈhypnoˌtizer *or* ˈhypnoˌtiser *n*

hypo[1] (ˈhaɪpəʊ) *n* another name for **sodium thiosulphate**, esp when used as a fixer in photographic developing [C19 shortened from HYPOSULPHITE]

hypo[2] (ˈhaɪpəʊ) *n*, *pl* -pos *informal* short for **hypodermic syringe**

hypo- *or before a vowel* **hyp-** *prefix* 1 under, beneath, or below: *hypodermic* 2 lower; at a lower point: *hypogastrium* 3 less than: *hypoploid* 4 (in medicine) denoting a deficiency or an abnormally low level: *hypothyroid*; *hypoglycaemia* 5 incomplete or partial: *hypoplasia* 6 indicating that a chemical compound contains an element in a lower oxidation state than usual: *hypochlorous acid* [from Greek, from *hupo* under]

Hypo- *prefix* indicating a plagal mode in music: *Hypodorian* [from Greek: beneath (it lies a fourth below the corresponding authentic mode)]

hypoacidity (ˌhaɪpəʊəˈsɪdɪtɪ) *n med* abnormally low acidity, as of the contents of the stomach

hypoallergenic ('haɪpəʊˌæləˈdʒɛnɪk) *adj* (of cosmetics, earrings, etc) not likely to cause an allergic reaction

hypoblast ('haɪpəˌblæst) *n* **1** Also called: endoblast *embryol* the inner layer of an embryo at an early stage of development that becomes the endoderm at gastrulation **2** a less common name for **endoderm**. > ˌhypo'blastic *adj*

hypocaust ('haɪpəˌkɔːst) *n* an ancient Roman heating system in which hot air circulated under the floor and between double walls [C17 from Latin *hypocaustum*, from Greek *hupokauston* room heated from below, from *hupokaiein* to light a fire beneath, from HYPO- + *kaiein* to burn]

hypocentre ('haɪpəʊˌsɛntə) *n* **1** Also called: ground zero the point on the ground immediately below the centre of explosion of a nuclear bomb in the atmosphere **2** another term for **focus** (sense 6)

hypochlorite (ˌhaɪpəˈklɔːraɪt) *n* any salt or ester of hypochlorous acid

hypochlorous acid (ˌhaɪpəˈklɔːrəs) *n* an unstable acid known only in solution and in the form of its salts, formed when chlorine dissolves in water: a strong oxidizing and bleaching agent. Formula: HOCl

hypochondria (ˌhaɪpəˈkɒndrɪə) *n* chronic abnormal anxiety concerning the state of one's health, even in the absence of any evidence of disease on medical examination. Also called: hypochondriasis (ˌhaɪpəʊkɒnˈdraɪəsɪs) [C18 from Late Latin: the abdomen, supposedly the seat of melancholy, from Greek *hupokhondria*, from *hupokhondrios* of the upper abdomen, from HYPO- + *khondros* cartilage]

hypochondriac (ˌhaɪpəˈkɒndrɪˌæk) *n* **1** a person suffering from hypochondria ▷ *adj also* hypochondriacal (ˌhaɪpəkɒnˈdraɪəkᵊl) **2** relating to or suffering from hypochondria **3** *anatomy* of or relating to the hypochondrium > ˌhypochon'driacally *adv*

hypochondrium (ˌhaɪpəˈkɒndrɪəm) *n, pl* -dria (-drɪə) *anatomy* the upper region of the abdomen on each side of the epigastrium, just below the lowest ribs [C17 from New Latin, from Greek *hupokhondrion*; see HYPOCHONDRIA]

hypocorism (haɪˈpɒkəˌrɪzəm) *n* **1** a pet name, esp one using a diminutive affix: *"Sally" is a hypocorism for "Sarah"* **2** another word for **euphemism** (sense 1) [C19 from Greek *hupokorisma*, from *hupokorizesthai* to use pet names, from *hypo-* beneath + *korizesthai*, from *korē* girl, *koros* boy] > hypocoristic (ˌhaɪpəkɒˈrɪstɪk) *adj* > ˌhypoco'ristically *adv*

hypocotyl (ˌhaɪpəˈkɒtɪl) *n* the part of an embryo plant between the cotyledons and the radicle [C19 from HYPO- + COTYL(EDON)] > ˌhypo'cotylous *adj*

hypocrisy (hɪˈpɒkrəsɪ) *n, pl* -sies **1** the practice of professing standards, beliefs, etc, contrary to one's real character or actual behaviour, esp the pretence of virtue and piety **2** an act or instance of this

hypocrite ('hɪpəkrɪt) *n* a person who pretends to be what he is not [C13 from Old French *ipocrite*, via Late Latin, from Greek *hupokritēs* one who plays a part, from *hupokrinein* to feign, from *krinein* to judge] > ˌhypo'critical *adj* > ˌhypo'critically *adv*

hypocrystalline (ˌhaɪpəʊˈkrɪstəˌlaɪn) *adj* (of igneous rocks) having both glass and crystalline components. Former word **hemicrystalline** compare **holocrystalline**

hypocycloid (ˌhaɪpəˈsaɪklɔɪd) *n* a curve described by a point on the circumference of a circle as the circle rolls around the inside of a fixed coplanar circle. Compare **epicycloid, cycloid** (sense 4) > ˌhypocy'cloidal *adj*

hypoderm ('haɪpəˌdɜːm) *n* a variant of hypodermis. > ˌhypo'dermal *adj*

hypodermic (ˌhaɪpəˈdɜːmɪk) *adj* **1** of or relating to the region of the skin beneath the epidermis **2** injected beneath the skin ▷ *n* **3** a hypodermic syringe or needle **4** a hypodermic injection > ˌhypo'dermically *adv*

hypodermic syringe *n med* a type of syringe consisting of a hollow cylinder, usually of glass or plastic, a tightly fitting piston, and a hollow needle (**hypodermic needle**), used for withdrawing blood samples, injecting medicine, etc

hypodermis (ˌhaɪpəˈdɜːmɪs) or **hypoderm** *n* **1** *botany* a layer of thick-walled supportive or water-storing cells beneath the epidermis in some plants **2** *zoology* the epidermis of arthropods, annelids, etc, which secretes and is covered by a cuticle [C19 from HYPO- + EPIDERMIS]

Hypodorian (ˌhaɪpəˈdɔːrɪən) *adj music* denoting a plagal mode represented by the ascending diatonic scale from A to A. Compare **Dorian** (sense 3). See **Hypo-**

hypoeutectic (ˌhaɪpəʊjuːˈtɛktɪk) or **hypoeutectoid** *adj* (of a mixture or alloy with two components) containing less of the minor component than a eutectic mixture. Compare **hypereutectic**

hypogastrium (ˌhaɪpəˈgæstrɪəm) *n, pl* -tria (-trɪə) *anatomy* the lower front central region of the abdomen, below the navel [C17 from New Latin, from Greek *hupogastrion*, from HYPO- + *gastrion*, diminutive of *gastēr* stomach, belly] > ˌhypo'gastric *adj*

hypogeal (ˌhaɪpəˈdʒiːəl) or **hypogeous** *adj* **1** occurring or living below the surface of the ground **2** *botany* of or relating to seed germination in which the cotyledons remain below the ground, because of the growth of the epicotyl [C19 from Latin *hypogēus*, from Greek *hupogeios*, from HYPO- + *gē* earth]

hypogene ('haɪpəˌdʒiːn) *adj* formed, taking place, or originating beneath the surface of the earth. Compare **epigene**. > hypogenic (ˌhaɪpəˈdʒɛnɪk) *adj*

hypogenous (haɪˈpɒdʒɪnəs) *adj botany* produced or growing on the undersurface, esp (of fern spores) growing on the undersurface of the leaves

hypogeous (ˌhaɪpəˈdʒiːəs) *adj* another word for **hypogeal**

hypogeum (ˌhaɪpəˈdʒiːəm) *n, pl* -gea (-ˈdʒiːə) an underground vault, esp one used for burials [C18 from Latin, from Greek *hupogeion*; see HYPOGEAL]

hypoglossal (ˌhaɪpəˈglɒsᵊl) *adj* **1** situated beneath the tongue ▷ *n* **2** short for **hypoglossal nerve**

hypoglossal nerve *n* the twelfth cranial nerve, which supplies the muscles of the tongue

hypoglycaemia or US **hypoglycemia** (ˌhaɪpəʊglaɪˈsiːmɪə) *n pathol* an abnormally small amount of sugar in the blood [C20 from HYPO- + GLYCO- + -AEMIA] > ˌhypogly'caemic or US ˌhypogly'cemic *adj*

hypognathous (haɪˈpɒgnəθəs) *adj* **1** having a lower jaw that protrudes beyond the upper jaw **2** (of insects) having downturned mouthparts > hy'pognathism *n*

hypogynous (haɪˈpɒdʒɪnəs) *adj* **1** (of a flower) having the gynoecium situated above the other floral parts, as in the buttercup **2** of or relating to the parts of a flower arranged in this way > hy'pogyny *n*

hypoid gear ('haɪpɔɪd) *n* a gear having a tooth form generated by a hypocycloidal curve; used extensively in motor vehicle transmissions to withstand a high surface loading [C20 *hypoid*, shortened from HYPOCYCLOID]

hypolimnion (ˌhaɪpəʊˈlɪmnɪən) *n* the lower and colder layer of water in a lake [C20 from HYPO- + Greek *limnion*, diminutive of *limnē* lake]

Hypolydian (ˌhaɪpəˈlɪdɪən) *adj music* denoting a plagal mode represented by the diatonic scale from D to D. Compare **Lydian** (sense 2). See **Hypo-**

hypomagnesaemia or US **hypomagnesemia** (ˌhaɪpəʊˌmægnəˈsiːmɪə) *n vet science* too little magnesium in the blood, particularly in cattle, in which it is also known as **lactation tetany**

hypomania (ˌhaɪpəʊˈmeɪnɪə) *n psychiatry* an abnormal condition of extreme excitement, milder than mania but characterized by great optimism and overactivity and often by reckless spending of money > hypomanic (ˌhaɪpəʊˈmænɪk) *adj*

hyponasty ('haɪpəˌnæstɪ) *n* increased growth of the lower surface of a plant part, resulting in an upward bending of the part. Compare **epinasty** > ˌhypo'nastic *adj* > ˌhypo'nastically *adv*

hyponatraemia (ˌhaɪpɒnəˈtriːmɪə) *n* a condition in which there is a low concentration of sodium in the blood. Also called: **water intoxication** [C20 from HYPO- + Latin *natrium* sodium + -AEMIA]

hyponitrite (ˌhaɪpəˈnaɪtraɪt) *n* any salt or ester of hyponitrous acid

hyponitrous acid (ˌhaɪpəˈnaɪtrəs) *n* a white soluble unstable crystalline acid: an oxidizing and reducing agent. Formula: $H_2N_2O_2$

hyponym ('haɪpəʊnɪm) *n* a word whose meaning is included in that of another word: *'scarlet', 'vermilion', and 'crimson' are hyponyms of 'red'.* Compare **superordinate** (sense 3), **synonym, antonym** [C20 from HYPO- + Greek *onoma* name] > hyponymy (haɪˈpɒnɪmɪ) *n*

hypophosphate (ˌhaɪpəˈfɒsfeɪt) *n* any salt or ester of hypophosphoric acid

hypophosphite (ˌhaɪpəˈfɒsfaɪt) *n* any salt of hypophosphorous acid

hypophosphoric acid (ˌhaɪpəfɒsˈfɒrɪk) *n* a crystalline odourless deliquescent solid: a tetrabasic acid produced by the slow oxidation of phosphorus in moist air. Formula: $H_4P_2O_6$

hypophosphorous acid (ˌhaɪpəˈfɒsfərəs) *n* a colourless or yellowish oily liquid or white deliquescent solid: a monobasic acid and a reducing agent. Formula: H_3PO_2

hypophyge (haɪˈpɒfɪdʒɪ) *n architect* another name for **apophyge**

hypophysis (haɪˈpɒfɪsɪs) *n, pl* -ses (-ˌsiːz) the technical name for **pituitary gland** [C18 from Greek: outgrowth, from HYPO- + *phuein* to grow] > hypophyseal or hypophysial (ˌhaɪpəˈfɪzɪəl, haɪˌpɒfɪˈsɪəl) *adj*

hypopituitarism (ˌhaɪpəpɪˈtjuːɪtəˌrɪzəm) *n pathol* underactivity of the pituitary gland > ˌhypopi'tuitary *adj*

hypoplasia (ˌhaɪpəʊˈpleɪzɪə) or **hypoplasty** ('haɪpəʊˌplæstɪ) *n pathol* incomplete development of an organ or part > hypoplastic (ˌhaɪpəʊˈplæstɪk) *adj*

hypoploid ('haɪpəˌplɔɪd) *adj* having or designating a chromosome number that is less than a multiple of the haploid number > 'hypo,ploidy *n*

hypopnoea or US **hypopnea** (haɪˈpɒpnɪə, ˌhaɪpəˈniːə) *n pathol* abnormally shallow breathing, usually accompanied by a decrease in the breathing rate [C20 New Latin, from HYPO- + Greek *pnoia* breath, from *pnein* to breathe]

hyposensitize or **hyposensitise** (ˌhaɪpəˈsɛnsɪˌtaɪz) *vb* (tr) to desensitize; render less sensitive > ˌhypo,sensiti'zation or ˌhypo,sensiti'sation *n*

hypospadias (ˌhaɪpəˈspeɪdɪəs) *n pathol* a congenital condition in which the opening of the urethra is situated on the underside of the penis instead of at its tip [C19 from Greek *hupospadias* man with hypospadia, from HYPO- + *spadias*, prob. from *spadōn* eunuch]

hypostasis (haɪˈpɒstəsɪs) *n, pl* -ses (-ˌsiːz) **1** *metaphysics* the essential nature of a substance as opposed to its attributes **2** *Christianity* **a** any of the three persons of the Godhead, together constituting the Trinity **b** the one person of Christ in which the divine and human natures are united **3** the accumulation of blood in an organ or part, under the influence of gravity as the result of poor circulation **4** another name for

h

epistasis (sense 3) [C16 from Late Latin: substance, from Greek *hupostasis* foundation, from *huphistasthai* to stand under, from HYPO- + *histanai* to cause to stand] > **hypostatic** (ˌhaɪpəˈstætɪk) or ˌhypoˈstatical *adj* > ˌhypoˈstatically *adv*

hypostasize or **hypostasise** (haɪˈpɒstəˌsaɪz) *vb* another word for **hypostatize**. > hyˌpostasiˈzation or hyˌpostasiˈsation *n*

hypostatize or **hypostatise** (haɪˈpɒstəˌtaɪz) *vb* (*tr*) **1** to regard or treat as real **2** to embody or personify > hyˌpostatiˈzation or hyˌpostatiˈsation *n*

hyposthenia (ˌhaɪpɒsˈθiːnɪə) *n pathol* a weakened condition; lack of strength [C19 from HYPO- + Greek *sthenos* strength] > **hyposthenic** (ˌhaɪpɒsˈθɛnɪk) *adj*

hypostyle (ˈhaɪpəʊˌstaɪl) *adj* **1** having a roof supported by columns ▷ *n* **2** a building constructed in this way

hyposulphite (ˌhaɪpəˈsʌlfaɪt) *n* **1** another name for **sodium thiosulphate**, esp when used as a photographic fixer. Often shortened to: **hypo 2** another name for **dithionite**

hyposulphurous acid (ˌhaɪpəˈsʌlfərəs) *n* another name for **dithionous acid**

hypotaxis (ˌhaɪpəʊˈtæksɪs) *n grammar* the subordination of one clause to another by a conjunction. Compare **parataxis**. > **hypotactic** (ˌhaɪpəʊˈtæktɪk) *adj*

hypotension (ˌhaɪpəʊˈtɛnʃən) *n pathol* abnormally low blood pressure > **hypotensive** (ˌhaɪpəʊˈtɛnsɪv) *adj*

hypotenuse (haɪˈpɒtɪˌnjuːz) *n* the side in a right-angled triangle that is opposite the right angle. Abbreviation: **hyp** [C16 from Latin *hypotēnūsa*, from Greek *hupoteinousa grammē* subtending line, from *hupoteinein* to subtend, from HYPO- + *teinein* to stretch]

hypothalamus (ˌhaɪpəˈθæləməs) *n, pl* -mi (-ˌmaɪ) a neural control centre at the base of the brain, concerned with hunger, thirst, satiety, and other autonomic functions > **hypothalamic** (ˌhaɪpəθəˈlæmɪk) *adj*

hypothec (haɪˈpɒθɪk) *n Roman and Scots law* a charge on property in favour of a creditor [C16 from Late Latin *hypotheca* a security, from Greek *hupothēkē* deposit, pledge, from *hupotithenai* to deposit as a security, place under, from HYPO- + *tithenai* to place]

hypotheca (ˌhaɪpəʊˈθiːkə) *n, pl* -cae (-siː) the inner and younger layer of the cell wall of a diatom. Compare **epitheca** [from HYPO- + THECA]

hypothecate (haɪˈpɒθɪˌkeɪt) *vb* **1** (*tr*) *law* to pledge (personal property or a ship) as security for a debt without transferring possession or title **2** to allocate the revenue raised by a tax for a specified purpose. See also **bottomry** [C17 *hypothēcātus*, past participle of *hypothēcāre*; see HYPOTHEC, -ATE¹] > hyˌpotheˈcation *n* > hyˈpotheˌcator *n*

hypothermal (ˌhaɪpəʊˈθɜːməl) *adj* **1** of, relating to, or characterized by hypothermia. Also: **hypothermic 2** (of rocks and minerals) formed at great depth under conditions of high temperature

hypothermia (ˌhaɪpəʊˈθɜːmɪə) *n* **1** *pathol* an abnormally low body temperature, as induced in the elderly by exposure to cold weather **2** *med* the intentional reduction of normal body temperature, as by ice packs, to reduce the patient's metabolic rate: performed esp in heart and brain surgery

hypothesis (haɪˈpɒθɪsɪs) *n, pl* -ses (-ˌsiːz) **1** a suggested explanation for a group of facts or phenomena, either accepted as a basis for further verification (**working hypothesis**) or accepted as likely to be true. Compare **theory** (sense 5) **2** an assumption used in an argument without its being endorsed; a supposition **3** an unproved theory; a conjecture [C16 from Greek, from *hupotithenai* to propose, suppose, literally: put under; see HYPO-, THESIS] > hyˈpothesist *n*

hypothesis testing *n statistics* the theory, methods, and practice of testing a hypothesis concerning the parameters of a population

distribution (the **null hypothesis**) against another (the **alternative hypothesis**) which will be accepted only if its probability exceeds a predetermined significance level, generally on the basis of statistics derived from random sampling from the given population. Compare **statistical inference**

hypothesize or **hypothesise** (haɪˈpɒθɪˌsaɪz) *vb* to form or assume as a hypothesis > hyˈpotheˌsizer or hyˈpotheˌsiser *n*

hypothetical (ˌhaɪpəˈθɛtɪkᵊl) or **hypothetic** *adj* **1** having the nature of a hypothesis **2** assumed or thought to exist **3** *logic* another word for **conditional** (sense 4) **4** existing only as an idea or concept: *a time machine is a hypothetical device* > ˌhypoˈthetically *adv*

hypothetical imperative *n* (esp in the moral philosophy of Kant) any conditional rule of action, concerned with means and ends rather than with duty for its own sake. Compare **categorical imperative**

hypothetico-deductive (ˌhaɪpəˈθɛtɪkəʊdɪˈdʌktɪv) *adj* pertaining to or governed by the supposed method of scientific progress whereby a general hypothesis is tested by deducing predictions that may be experimentally tested. When such a prediction is falsified the theory is rejected and a new hypothesis is required

hypothymia (haɪpəˈθaɪmɪə) *n* **1** a state of depression **2** a diminished emotional response [C20 from HYPO- + Greek *thymos* spirit]

hypothyroidism (ˌhaɪpəʊˈθaɪrɔɪˌdɪzəm) *n pathol* **1** insufficient production of thyroid hormones by the thyroid gland **2** any disorder, such as cretinism or myxoedema, resulting from this > ˌhypoˈthyroid *n, adj*

hypotonic (ˌhaɪpəˈtɒnɪk) *adj* **1** *pathol* (of muscles) lacking normal tone or tension **2** (of a solution) having a lower osmotic pressure than that of a specified, generally physiological, solution. Compare **hypertonic, isotonic**. > **hypotonicity** (ˌhaɪpətəˈnɪsɪtɪ) *n*

hypoxanthine (ˌhaɪpəˈzænθiːn, -θɪn) *n* a white or colourless crystalline compound that is a breakdown product of nucleoproteins. Formula: $C_5H_4N_4O$

hypoxia (haɪˈpɒksɪə) *n* deficiency in the amount of oxygen delivered to the body tissues [C20 from HYPO- + OXY-² +-IA] > **hypoxic** (haɪˈpɒksɪk) *adj*

hypso- or before a vowel **hyps-** *combining form* indicating height: *hypsometry* [from Greek *hupsos*]

hypsochromic (ˌhɪpsəˈkrəʊmɪk) *adj chem* denoting or relating to a shift to a shorter wavelength in the absorption spectrum of a compound > ˈhypsoˌchrome *n*

hypsography (hɪpˈsɒɡrəfɪ) *n* **1** the study and mapping of the earth's topography above sea level **2** topography or relief, or a map showing this **3** another name for **hypsometry**. > **hypsographic** (ˌhɪpsəˈɡræfɪk) or ˌhypsoˈgraphical *adj*

hypsometer (hɪpˈsɒmɪtə) *n* **1** an instrument for measuring altitudes by determining the boiling point of water at a given altitude **2** any instrument used to calculate the heights of trees by triangulation

hypsometry (hɪpˈsɒmɪtrɪ) *n* (in mapping) the establishment of height above sea level. Also called: **hypsography** > **hypsometric** (ˌhɪpsəˈmɛtrɪk) or ˌhypsoˈmetrical *adj* > ˌhypsoˈmetrically *adv* > hypˈsometrist *n*

hyracoid (ˈhaɪrəˌkɔɪd) *adj* **1** of, relating to, or belonging to the mammalian order *Hyracoidea*, which contains the hyraxes ▷ *n* **2** a hyrax > ˌhyraˈcoidean *adj, n*

hyrax (ˈhaɪræks) *n, pl* hyraxes or hyraces (ˈhaɪrəˌsiːz) any agile herbivorous mammal of the family *Procaviidae* and order *Hyracoidea*, of Africa and SW Asia, such as *Procavia capensis* (**rock hyrax**). They resemble rodents but have feet with hooflike toes. Also called: **dassie** (South African) **rock rabbit** [C19 from New Latin, from Greek *hurax* shrewmouse; probably related to Latin *sōrex*]

Hyrcania (hɜːˈkeɪnɪə) *n* an ancient district of Asia, southeast of the Caspian Sea

Hyrcanian (hɜːˈkeɪnɪən) *adj* of or relating to Hyrcania, an ancient district of Asia

hyson (ˈhaɪsᵊn) *n* a Chinese green tea, the early crop of which is known as **young hyson** and the inferior leaves as **hyson skin** [C18 from Chinese (Cantonese) *hei-ch'un* bright spring]

hyssop (ˈhɪsəp) *n* **1** a widely cultivated Asian plant, *Hyssopus officinalis*, with spikes of small blue flowers and aromatic leaves, used as a condiment and in perfumery and folk medicine: family *Lamiaceae* (labiates) **2** any of several similar or related plants such as the hedge hyssop **3** a Biblical plant, used for sprinkling in the ritual practices of the Hebrews [Old English *ysope*, from Latin *hyssōpus*, from Greek *hussōpos*, of Semitic origin; compare Hebrew *ēzōv*]

hysterectomize or **hysterectomise** (ˌhɪstəˈrɛktəˌmaɪz) *vb* (*tr*) to perform a hysterectomy on (someone)

hysterectomy (ˌhɪstəˈrɛktəmɪ) *n, pl* -mies surgical removal of the uterus

hysteresis (ˌhɪstəˈriːsɪs) *n physics* the lag in a variable property of a system with respect to the effect producing it as this effect varies, esp the phenomenon in which the magnetic flux density of a ferromagnetic material lags behind the changing external magnetic field strength [C19 from Greek *husterēsis* coming late, from *husteros* coming after] > **hysteretic** (ˌhɪstəˈrɛtɪk) *adj* > ˌhysterˈetically *adv*

hysteresis loop *n* a closed curve showing the variation of the magnetic flux density of a ferromagnetic material with the external magnetic field producing it, when this field is changed through a complete cycle

hysteria (hɪˈstɪərɪə) *n* **1** a mental disorder characterized by emotional outbursts, susceptibility to autosuggestion, and, often, symptoms such as paralysis that mimic the effects of physical disorders ▷ See also **conversion disorder 2** any frenzied emotional state, esp of laughter or crying [C19 from New Latin, from Latin *hystericus* HYSTERIC]

hysteric (hɪˈstɛrɪk) *n* **1** a hysterical person ▷ *adj* **2** hysterical ▷ See also **hysterics** [C17 from Latin *hystericus* literally: of the womb, from Greek *husterikos*, from *hustera* the womb; from the belief that hysteria in women originated in disorders of the womb]

hysterical (hɪˈstɛrɪkᵊl) or **hysteric** *adj* **1** of or suggesting hysteria: *hysterical cries* **2** suffering from hysteria **3** *informal* wildly funny > hysˈterically *adv*

hysterics (hɪˈstɛrɪks) *n* (functioning as plural or singular) **1** an attack of hysteria **2** *informal* wild uncontrollable bursts of laughter

hystero- or before a vowel **hyster-** *combining form* **1** indicating the uterus: *hysterotomy* **2** hysteria: *hysterogenic* [from Greek *hustera* womb]

hysterogenic (ˌhɪstərəˈdʒɛnɪk) *adj* inducing hysteria [C20 from HYSTERIA + -GENIC] > **hysterogeny** (ˌhɪstəˈrɒdʒənɪ) *n*

hysteroid (ˈhɪstəˌrɔɪd) or **hysteroidal** *adj* resembling hysteria

hysteron proteron (ˈhɪstəˌrɒn ˈprɒtəˌrɒn) *n* **1** *logic* a fallacious argument in which the proposition to be proved is assumed as a premise **2** *rhetoric* a figure of speech in which the normal order of two sentences, clauses, etc, is reversed, as in *bred and born* (for *born and bred*) [C16 from Late Latin, from Greek *husteron proteron* the latter (placed as) former]

hysterotomy (ˌhɪstəˈrɒtəmɪ) *n, pl* -mies surgical incision into the uterus

hystricomorph (hɪˈstraɪkəʊˌmɔːf) *n* **1** any rodent of the suborder *Hystricomorpha*, which includes porcupines, cavies, agoutis, and chinchillas ▷ *adj* also **hystricomorphic** (hɪˌstraɪkəʊˈmɔːfɪk) **2** of, relating to, or belonging to the *Hystricomorpha* [C19 from Latin *hystrix* porcupine, from Greek *hustrix*]

Hz *symbol for* hertz

I i

i or **I** (aɪ) n, pl **i's, I's** or **Is** **1** the ninth letter and third vowel of the modern English alphabet **2** any of several speech sounds represented by this letter, in English as in *bite* or *hit* **3 a** something shaped like an I **b** (*in combination*): *an I-beam* **4 dot the i's and cross the t's** to pay meticulous attention to detail

i *symbol for* the imaginary number √–1. Also called: **j**

I¹ (aɪ) *pron* (*subjective*) refers to the speaker or writer [c12 reduced form of Old English *ic*; compare Old Saxon *ik*, Old High German *ih*, Sanskrit *ahám*]

I² *symbol for* **1** *chem* iodine **2** *physics* current **3** *physics* isospin **4** *logic* a particular affirmative categorial statement, such as *some men are married*, often symbolized as **SiP**. Compare **A, E, O¹ 5** the Roman numeral for one. See **Roman numerals 6** international car registration for Italy [(for sense4) from Latin (*aff*)i(*rmo*) I affirm]

I. *abbreviation for* **1** International **2** Island *or* Isle

-i *suffix forming adjectives* of or relating to a region or people, esp of the Middle East: *Iraqi; Bangladeshi* [from an adjectival suffix in Semitic and in Indo-Iranian languages]

-i- *connective vowel* used between elements in a compound word: *cuneiform; coniferous.* Compare **-o-** [from Latin, stem vowel of nouns and adjectives in combination]

Ia. or **IA** *abbreviation for* Iowa

-ia *suffix forming nouns* **1** occurring in place names: *Albania; Columbia* **2** occurring in names of diseases and pathological disorders: *pneumonia; aphasia* **3** occurring in words denoting condition or quality: *utopia* **4** occurring in names of botanical genera: *acacia; poinsettia* **5** occurring in names of zoological classes: *Reptilia* **6** occurring in collective nouns borrowed from Latin: *marginalia; memorabilia; regalia* [(for senses 1–4) New Latin, from Latin and Greek, suffix of feminine nouns; (for senses 5–6) from Latin, neuter plural suffix]

IAA *abbreviation for* **indoleacetic acid**

IAAF *abbreviation for* International Amateur Athletic Federation

IAEA *abbreviation for* International Atomic Energy Agency

IAF *abbreviation for* Indian Air Force

-ial *suffix forming adjectives* of; relating to; connected with: *managerial* [from Latin -*iālis*, adj suffix; compare -AL¹]

iamb ('aɪæm, 'aɪæmb) *or* **iambus** (aɪˈæmbəs) *n, pl* **iambs, iambi** (aɪˈæmbaɪ) *or* **iambuses** *prosody* **1** a metrical foot consisting of two syllables, a short one followed by a long one (‿–) **2** a line of verse of such feet [C19 *iamb*, from C16 *iambus*, from Latin, from Greek *iambos*]

iambic (aɪˈæmbɪk) *prosody* ▷ *adj* **1** of, relating to, consisting of, or using an iamb or iambs **2** (in Greek literature) denoting a type of satirical verse written in iambs ▷ *n* **3** a metrical foot, line, or stanza of verse consisting of iambs **4** a type of ancient Greek satirical verse written in iambs ▷ i**'ambically** *adv*

-ian *suffix* a variant of **-an**: *Etonian; Johnsonian* [from Latin -*iānus*]

-iana *suffix forming nouns* a variant of **-ana**

IAP *abbreviation for* internet access provider: a company that provides organizations or individuals with access to the internet

Iapetus (aɪˈæpɪtəs) *n* a large outer satellite of the planet Saturn

IARU *abbreviation for* International Amateur Radio Union

IAS *aeronautics abbreviation for* indicated air speed

Iaşi (Romanian 'iaʃj) *n* a city in NE Romania: capital of Moldavia (1565–1859); university (1860). Pop: 280 000 (2005 est). German name: **Jassy**

-iasis *or* **-asis** *n combining form* (in medicine) indicating a diseased condition: *psoriasis.* Compare **-osis** (sense 2) [from New Latin, from Greek, suffix of action]

IATA (aɪˈɑːtə, iːˈɑːtə) *n acronym for* International Air Transport Association

iatric (aɪˈætrɪk) *or* **iatrical** *adj* relating to medicine or physicians; medical [C19 from Greek *iatrikos* of healing, from *iasthai* to heal]

-iatrics *n combining form* indicating medical care or treatment: *paediatrics.* Compare **-iatry** [from IATRIC]

iatrogenic (aɪˌætrəʊˈdʒɛnɪk) *adj* **1** *med* (of an illness or symptoms) induced in a patient as the result of a physician's words or actions, esp as a consequence of taking a drug prescribed by the physician **2** *social welfare* (of a problem) induced by the means of treating a problem but ascribed to the continuing natural development of the problem being treated ▷ **iatrogenicity** (aɪˌætrəʊdʒɪˈnɪsɪtɪ) *n*

-iatry *n combining form* indicating healing or medical treatment: *psychiatry.* Compare **-iatrics** [from New Latin -*iatria*, from Greek *iatreia* the healing art, from *iatros* healer, physician] ▷ -**iatric** *adj combining form*

ib. See **ibid.**

IBA (in Britain) *abbreviation for* Independent Broadcasting Authority

Ibadan (ɪˈbædᵊn) *n* a city in SW Nigeria, capital of Oyo state: university (1948). Pop: 2 375 000 (2005 est)

Ibagué (Spanish iβaˈɣe) *n* a city in W central Colombia. Pop: 440 000 (2005 est)

I-beam *n* a rolled steel joist or a girder with a cross section in the form of a capital letter I. Compare **H-beam**

Iberia (aɪˈbɪərɪə) *n* **1** the Iberian Peninsula **2** an ancient region in central Asia, south of the Caucasus corresponding approximately to present-day Georgia

Iberian (aɪˈbɪərɪən) *n* **1** a member of a group of ancient Caucasoid peoples who inhabited the Iberian Peninsula in preclassical and classical times. See also **Celtiberian 2** a native or inhabitant of the Iberian Peninsula; a Spaniard or Portuguese **3** a native or inhabitant of ancient Iberia in the Caucasus ▷ *adj* **4** denoting, or relating to the pre-Roman peoples of the Iberian Peninsula or of Caucasian Iberia **5** of or relating to the Iberian Peninsula, its inhabitants, or any of their languages

Iberian Peninsula *n* a peninsula of SW Europe, occupied by Spain and Portugal

iberis (aɪˈbɪərɪs) *n* any plant of the annual or perennial Eurasian genus *Iberis*, 12 to 25 cm (6–12 in.) in height, with white or purple flowers. *I. amara* and *I. umbellata* are the garden candytuft. Family *Brassicaceae* (crucifers) [New Latin, from *Iberia* Spain, where many species are common]

Ibero- ('aɪbərəʊ) *combining form* indicating Iberia or Iberian: *Ibero-Caucasian*

ibex ('aɪbɛks) *n, pl* **ibexes, ibices** ('ɪbɪˌsiːz, 'aɪ-) *or* **ibex** any of three wild goats, *Capra ibex, C. caucasica,* or *C. pyrenaica,* of mountainous regions of Europe, Asia, and North Africa, having large backward-curving horns [c17 from Latin: chamois]

IBF *abbreviation for* International Boxing Federation

Ibibio (ɪˈbɪbɪəʊ) *n* **1** (pl **-os** or **-o**) a member of a Negroid people of SE Nigeria, living esp in and around Calabar **2** Also called: **Efik** the language of this people

ibid. or **ib.** (in annotations, bibliographies, etc, when referring to a book, article, chapter, or page previously cited) *abbreviation for* ibidem [Latin: in the same place]

ibis ('aɪbɪs) *n, pl* **ibises** or **ibis** any of various wading birds of the family *Threskiornithidae*, such as *Threskiornis aethiopica* (**sacred ibis**), that occur in warm regions and have a long thin down-curved bill: order *Ciconiiformes* (herons, storks, etc). Compare **wood ibis** [c14 via Latin from Greek, from Egyptian *hby*]

Ibiza, Iviza (Spanish iˈβiθa) *or* **Eivissa** *n* **1** a Spanish island in the W Mediterranean, one of the Balearic Islands: hilly, with a rugged coast; tourism. Pop: 40 175 (2003 est). Area: 541 sq km (209 sq miles) **2** the capital of Ibiza, a port on the south of the island. Pop: 16 000 (latest est)

Ibizan hound (ɪˈbiːθən) *n* a tall slender short-haired breed of hound with large erect ears and a coat of white, chestnut, or tan, or of a combination of these colours

-ible *suffix forming adjectives* a variant of **-able**. ▷ -**ibly** *suffix forming adverbs* ▷ -**ibility** *suffix forming nouns*

Ibo or **Igbo** ('iːbəʊ) *n* **1** (pl **-bos** or **-bo**) a member of a Negroid people of W Africa, living chiefly in S Nigeria **2** the language of this people, belonging to the Kwa branch of the Niger-Congo family: one of the chief literary and cultural languages of S Nigeria

IBRD *abbreviation for* International Bank for Reconstruction and Development (the World Bank)

ibuprofen (aɪˈbjuːprəʊfən) *n* a drug, isobutylphenylpropionic acid, that relieves pain and reduces inflammation: used to treat arthritis and muscular strains. Formula: $C_{13}H_{18}O_2$

IC *abbreviation for* **1** internal-combustion

2 *electronics* **integrated circuit 3** *text messaging* I see **4** (in transformational grammar) **immediate constituent 5** *astrology* Imum Coeli: the point on the ecliptic lying directly opposite the Midheaven

i/c *abbreviation for* in charge (of)

-ic *suffix forming adjectives* **1** of, relating to, or resembling: *allergic; Germanic; periodic.* See also **-ical 2** (in chemistry) indicating that an element is chemically combined in the higher of two possible valence states: *ferric; stannic.* Compare **-ous** (sense 2) [from Latin *-icus* or Greek *-ikos; -ic* also occurs in nouns that represent a substantive use of adjectives (*magic*) and in nouns borrowed directly from Latin or Greek (*critic, music*)]

Içá (ˈiːsaː; *Portuguese* iˈsa) *n* the Brazilian part of the **Putumayo River**

ICA *abbreviation for* **1** (in Britain) Institute of Contemporary Arts **2** International Cooperation Administration

-ical *suffix forming adjectives* a variant of **-ic**, but in some words having a less literal application than corresponding adjectives ending in *-ic: economical; fanatical* [from Latin *-icālis*] ▷ **-ically** *suffix forming adverbs*

ICAO *abbreviation for* International Civil Aviation Organization

Icaria (aɪˈkɛərɪə, ɪ-) *n* a Greek island in the Aegean Sea, in the Southern Sporades group. Area: 256 sq km (99 sq miles). Modern Greek name: **Ikaría** Also called: **Nikaria**

Icarian¹ (aɪˈkɛərɪən, ɪ-) *adj* of or relating to Icarus

Icarian² (aɪˈkɛərɪən, ɪ-) *adj* **1** of or relating to Icaria or its inhabitants ▷ *n* **2** an inhabitant of Icaria

Icarian Sea *n* the part of the Aegean Sea between the islands of Patmos and Leros and the coast of Asia Minor, where, according to legend, Icarus fell into the sea

Icarus (ˈɪkərəs, ˈaɪ-) *n Greek myth* the son of Daedalus, with whom he escaped from Crete, flying with wings made of wax and feathers. Heedless of his father's warning he flew too near the sun, causing the wax to melt, and fell into the Aegean and drowned

ICBM *abbreviation for* intercontinental ballistic missile: a missile with a range greater than 5500 km

ICC *abbreviation for* International Cricket Council

ice (aɪs) *n* **1** water in the solid state, formed by freezing liquid water. Related adj: **glacial 2** a portion of ice cream **3** *slang* a diamond or diamonds **4** the field of play in ice hockey **5** *slang* a concentrated and highly potent form of methamphetamine with dangerous side effects **6** **break the ice a** to relieve shyness, etc, esp between strangers **b** to be the first of a group to do something **7** **cut no ice** *informal* to fail to make an impression **8** **on ice** in abeyance; pending **9** **on thin ice** unsafe or unsafely; vulnerable or vulnerably **10** **the Ice** *NZ informal* Antarctica ▷ *vb* **11** (often foll by *up, over,* etc) to form or cause to form ice; freeze **12** (*tr*) to mix with ice or chill (a drink, etc) **13** (*tr*) to cover (a cake, etc) with icing **14** (*tr*) *US slang* to kill [Old English *īs*; compare Old High German *īs*, Old Norse *īss*] ▷ **ˈiceless** *adj* ▷ **ˈice₁like** *adj*

ICE (in Britain) *abbreviation for* Institution of Civil Engineers

Ice. *abbreviation for* Iceland(ic)

ice age *n* another name for **glacial period**

ice axe *n* a light axe used by mountaineers for cutting footholds in snow or ice, to provide an anchor point, or to control a slide on snow; it has a spiked tip and a head consisting of a pick and an adze

ice bag *n* **1** a waterproof bag used as an ice pack **2** a strong bag, usually made of canvas and equipped with two handles, used for carrying blocks of ice

ice beer *n* a beer that is chilled after brewing so that any water is turned to ice and then removed

iceberg (ˈaɪsbɜːɡ) *n* **1** a large mass of ice floating in the sea, esp a mass that has broken off a polar glacier **2** **tip of the iceberg** the small visible part of something, esp a problem or difficulty, that is much larger **3** *slang, chiefly US* a person considered to have a cold or reserved manner [c18 probably part translation of Middle Dutch *ijsberg* ice mountain; compare Norwegian *isberg*]

iceberg lettuce *n* a type of lettuce with very crisp pale leaves tightly enfolded

Ice Blacks *pl n* **the** the international ice hockey team of New Zealand

iceblink (ˈaɪsˌblɪŋk) *n* **1** Also called: **blink** a yellowish-white reflected glare in the sky over an ice field **2** a coastal ice cliff

ice block *n Scot, Austral, and NZ* a flavoured frozen water ice: in Australia and New Zealand, sometimes on a stick

iceboat (ˈaɪsˌbəʊt) *n* another name for **icebreaker** (sense 1) or **ice yacht**

icebound (ˈaɪsˌbaʊnd) *adj* covered or made immobile by ice; frozen in: *an icebound ship*

icebox (ˈaɪsˌbɒks) *n* **1** a compartment in a refrigerator for storing or making ice **2** an insulated cabinet packed with ice for storing food

icebreaker (ˈaɪsˌbreɪkə) *n* **1** Also called: **iceboat** a vessel with a reinforced bow for breaking up the ice in bodies of water to keep channels open for navigation **2** any tool or device for breaking ice into smaller lumps **3** something intended to relieve mutual shyness at a gathering of strangers

ice bridge *n Canadian* a body of ice that forms across the width of a river and is strong enough to bear traffic

icecap (ˈaɪsˌkæp) *n* a thick mass of glacial ice and snow that permanently covers an area of land, such as either of the polar regions or the peak of a mountain

ice cream *n* a kind of sweetened frozen liquid, properly made from cream and egg yolks but often made from milk or a custard base, flavoured in various ways

ice-cream cone *or* **cornet** *n* **1** a conical edible wafer for holding ice cream **2** such a cone containing ice cream

ice-cream soda *n chiefly US* ice cream served in a tall glass of carbonated water and a little milk, usually flavoured in various ways

iced (aɪst) *adj* **1** covered, coated, or chilled with ice **2** covered with icing: *iced cakes*

ice dance *n* any of a number of dances, mostly based on ballroom dancing, performed by a couple skating on ice ▷ **ice dancer** *n* ▷ **ice dancing** *n*

icefall (ˈaɪsˌfɔːl) *n* a very steep part of a glacier that has deep crevasses and resembles a frozen waterfall

ice field *n* **1** a very large flat expanse of ice floating in the sea; large ice floe **2** a large mass of ice permanently covering an extensive area of land

ice fish *n* any percoid fish of the family *Chaenichthyidae*, of Antarctic seas, having a semitransparent scaleless body

ice floe *n* a sheet of ice, of variable size, floating in the sea. See also **ice field** (sense 1)

ice foot *n* a narrow belt of ice permanently attached to the coast in polar regions

ice hockey *n* a game played on ice by two opposing teams of six players each, who wear skates and try to propel a flat puck into their opponents' goal with long sticks having an offset flat blade at the end

ice house *n* a building for storing ice

Içel (iːˈtʃɛl) *n* another name for **Mersin**

Iceland (ˈaɪslənd) *n* an island republic in the N Atlantic, regarded as part of Europe: settled by Norsemen, who established a legislative assembly in 930; under Danish rule (1380–1918); gained independence in 1918 and became a republic in 1944; contains large areas of glaciers, snowfields, and lava beds with many volcanoes and hot springs (the chief source of domestic heat); inhabited chiefly along the SW coast. The economy is based largely on fishing and tourism. Official language: Icelandic. Official religion: Evangelical Lutheran. Currency: króna. Capital: Reykjavik. Pop: 291 000 (2004 est). Area: 102 828 sq km (39 702 sq miles)

Iceland agate *n* another name for **obsidian**

Icelander (ˈaɪsˌlændə, ˈaɪsləndə) *n* a native, citizen, or inhabitant of Iceland

Icelandic (aɪsˈlændɪk) *adj* **1** of, relating to, or characteristic of Iceland, its people, or their language ▷ *n* **2** the official language of Iceland, belonging to the North Germanic branch of the Indo-European family. See also **Old Icelandic**

Iceland moss *n* a lichen, *Cetraria islandica,* of arctic regions and N Europe, with brownish edible fronds

Iceland poppy *n* any of various widely cultivated arctic poppies, esp *Papaver nudicaule,* with white or yellow nodding flowers

Iceland spar *n* a pure transparent variety of calcite with double-refracting crystals used in making polarizing microscopes

ice lolly *n Brit informal* an ice cream or water ice on a stick. Also called: **lolly** US and Canadian equivalent (trademark): **Popsicle**

ice machine *n* a machine that automatically produces ice for use in drinks, etc

ice maiden *n* a beautiful but aloof woman

ice man *n chiefly US* a man who sells or delivers ice

ice needle *n meteorol* one of many needle-like ice crystals that form cirrus clouds in clear cold weather

Iceni (aɪˈsiːnaɪ) *pl n* an ancient British tribe that rebelled against the Romans in 61 AD under Queen Boudicca

ice pack *n* **1** a bag or folded cloth containing ice, applied to a part of the body, esp the head, to cool, reduce swelling, etc **2** another name for **pack ice 3** a sachet containing a gel that can be frozen or heated and that retains its temperature for an extended period of time, used esp in cool bags

ice pick *n* a pointed tool used for breaking ice

ice plant *n* a low-growing plant, *Mesembryanthemum* (or *Cryophytum*) *crystallinum,* of southern Africa, with fleshy leaves covered with icelike hairs and pink or white rayed flowers: family *Aizoaceae*

ice point *n* the temperature at which a mixture of ice and water are in equilibrium at a pressure of one atmosphere. It is 0° on the Celsius scale and 32° on the Fahrenheit scale. Compare **steam point**

ice screw *n mountaineering* a screwed tubular or solid steel rod with a ring at one end for inserting into ice as an anchor point

ice sheet *n* a thick layer of ice covering a large area of land for a long time, esp those in Antarctica and Greenland

ice shelf *n* a thick mass of ice that is permanently attached to the land but projects into and floats on the sea

ice show *n* any entertainment performed by ice-skaters

ice skate *n* **1** a boot having a steel blade fitted to the sole to enable the wearer to glide swiftly over ice **2** the steel blade on such a boot or shoe ▷ *vb* **ice-skate 3** (*intr*) to glide swiftly over ice on ice skates ▷ **ˈice-ˌskater** *n*

ice station *n* a scientific research station in polar regions, where ice movement, weather, and environmental conditions are monitored

ice storm *n chiefly US* a storm of freezing rain that deposits a glaze of ice on the ground

ice water *n* **1** water formed from ice **2** Also called: **iced water** drinking water cooled by refrigeration or the addition of ice

icewine (ˈaɪswaɪn) *n Canadian* a dessert wine made from grapes that have frozen before being harvested

ice yacht *n* a sailing craft having a cross-shaped frame with a cockpit and runners for travelling over ice. Also called: **iceboat**

ICF *abbreviation for* **intermediate care facility**

ICFTU *abbreviation for* International Confederation of Free Trade Unions

Ichang *or* **I-ch'ang** (ˈiːˈtʃæŋ) *n* a variant transliteration of the Chinese name of **Yichang**

I.Chem.E. *abbreviation for* Institution of Chemical Engineers

I Ching (ˈiː ˈtʃɪŋ) *n* an ancient Chinese book of divination and a source of Confucian and Taoist philosophy. Answers to questions and advice may be obtained by referring to the text accompanying one of 64 hexagrams, selected at random. Also called: Book of Changes

ich-laut (ˈɪçˌlaʊt, ˈɪk-) *n* (*sometimes capital*) *phonetics* the voiceless palatal fricative sound that is written as *ch* in German *ich*, often allophonic with the ach-laut. See also **ach-laut** [from German, from *ich* I + *Laut* sound]

ichneumon (ɪkˈnjuːmən) *n* a mongoose, *Herpestes ichneumon*, of Africa and S Europe, having greyish-brown speckled fur [c16 via Latin from Greek, literally: tracker, hunter, from *ikhneuein* to track, from *ikhnos* a footprint; so named from the animal's alleged ability to locate the eggs of crocodiles]

ichneumon fly *or* **wasp** *n* any hymenopterous insect of the family *Ichneumonidae*, whose larvae are parasitic in caterpillars and other insect larvae

ichnite (ˈɪknaɪt) *or* **ichnolite** (ˈɪknəˌlaɪt) *n* a less common name for **trace fossil** [c19 from Greek *ikhnos* footprint, track + -ITE[1]]

ichnofossil (ˈɪknəʊˌfɒsəl) *n* another name for **trace fossil** [c19 from Greek *ikhnos* footprint, track + -ITE[1]]

ichnography (ɪkˈnɒɡrəfɪ) *n* **1** the art of drawing ground plans **2** the ground plan of a building, factory, etc [c16 from Latin *ichnographia*, from Greek *ikhnographia*, from *ikhnos* trace, track] > ichnographic (ˌɪknəˈɡræfɪk) *or* ˌichnoˈgraphical *adj* > ˌichnoˈgraphically *adv*

ichnology (ɪkˈnɒlədʒɪ) *n* the study of trace fossils [c19 from Greek *ikhnos* footprint, track] > ichnological (ˌɪknəˈlɒdʒɪkəl) *adj*

ichor (ˈaɪkɔː) *n* **1** *Greek myth* the fluid said to flow in the veins of the gods **2** *pathol* a foul-smelling watery discharge from a wound or ulcer [c17 from Greek *ikhōr*, of obscure origin] > ˈichorous *adj*

ichth. *abbreviation for* ichthyology

ichthyic (ˈɪkθɪɪk) *adj* of, relating to, or characteristic of fishes [c19 from Greek, from *ikhthus* fish]

ichthyo- *or before a vowel* **ichthy-** *combining form* indicating or relating to fishes: *ichthyology* [from Latin, from Greek *ikhthus* fish]

ichthyoid (ˈɪkθɪˌɔɪd) *adj also* ichthyoidal **1** resembling a fish ▷ *n* **2** a fishlike vertebrate

ichthyolite (ˈɪkθɪəˌlaɪt) *n rare* any fossil fish > ichthyolitic (ˌɪkθɪəˈlɪtɪk) *adj*

ichthyology (ˌɪkθɪˈɒlədʒɪ) *n* the study of the physiology, history, economic importance, etc, of fishes > ichthyologic (ˌɪkθɪəˈlɒdʒɪk) *or* ˌichthyoˈlogical *adj* > ˌichthyoˈlogically *adv* > ˌichthyˈologist *n*

ichthyophagous (ˌɪkθɪˈɒfəɡəs) *adj* feeding on fish > ichthyophagy (ˌɪkθɪˈɒfədʒɪ) *n*

ichthyornis (ˌɪkθɪˈɔːnɪs) *n* an extinct Cretaceous sea bird of the genus *Ichthyornis*, thought to have resembled a tern [c19 New Latin, from ICHTHY- + Greek *ornis* bird]

ichthyosaur (ˈɪkθɪəˌsɔː) *or* **ichthyosaurus** (ˌɪkθɪəˈsɔːrəs) *n, pl* -saurs, -sauruses *or* -sauri (-ˌsɔːraɪ) any extinct marine Mesozoic reptile of the order *Ichthyosauria*, which had a porpoise-like body with dorsal and tail fins and paddle-like limbs. See also **plesiosaur**

ichthyosis (ˌɪkθɪˈəʊsɪs) *n* a congenital disease in which the skin is coarse, dry, and scaly. Also called: xeroderma Nontechnical name: fishskin disease > ichthyotic (ˌɪkθɪˈɒtɪk) *adj*

ICI *abbreviation for* Imperial Chemical Industries

-ician *suffix forming nouns* indicating a person skilled or involved in a subject or activity: *physician; beautician* [from French *-icien; see* -IC, -IAN]

icicle (ˈaɪsɪkəl) *n* a hanging spike of ice formed by the freezing of dripping water [c14 from ICE + *ickel*, from Old English *gicel* icicle, related to Old Norse *jökull* large piece of ice, glacier] > ˈicicled *adj*

icily (ˈaɪsɪlɪ) *adv* in an icy or reserved manner

iciness (ˈaɪsɪnɪs) *n* **1** the condition of being icy or very cold **2** a manner that is cold or reserved; aloofness

icing (ˈaɪsɪŋ) *n* **1** Also called (*esp US and Canadian*): frosting a sugar preparation, variously flavoured and coloured, for coating and decorating cakes, biscuits, etc **2** the formation of ice, as on a ship or aircraft, due to the freezing of moisture in the atmosphere **3** any unexpected extra or bonus (esp in **icing on the cake**)

icing sugar *n Brit* a very finely ground sugar used for icings, confections, etc. US term: confectioners' sugar

ICJ *abbreviation for* International Court of Justice

ickle (ˈɪkəl) *adj Brit informal* an ironically childish word for **little**

icky (ˈɪkɪ) *adj* ickier, ickiest **1** sticky **2** excessively sentimental or emotional > ˈickiness *n*

icon *or* **ikon** (ˈaɪkɒn) *n* **1** a representation of Christ, the Virgin Mary, or a saint, esp one painted in oil on a wooden panel, depicted in a traditional Byzantine style and venerated in the Eastern Church **2** an image, picture, representation, etc **3** a symbol resembling or analogous to the thing it represents **4** a person regarded as a sex symbol or as a symbol of a belief or cultural movement **5** a pictorial representation of a facility available on a computer system, that enables the facility to be activated by means of a screen cursor rather than by a textual instruction [c16 from Latin, from Greek *eikōn* image, from *eikenai* to be like]

iconic (aɪˈkɒnɪk) *or* **iconical** *adj* **1** relating to, resembling, or having the character of an icon **2** (of memorial sculptures, esp those depicting athletes of ancient Greece) having a fixed conventional style

iconic memory *n psychol* the temporary persistence of visual impressions after the stimulus has been removed. Compare **echoic memory**

Iconium (aɪˈkəʊnɪəm) *n* the ancient name for **Konya**

icono- *or before a vowel* **icon-** *combining form* indicating an image or likeness: *iconology* [from Greek: ICON]

iconoclasm (aɪˈkɒnəˌklæzəm) *n* the acts or beliefs of an iconoclast

iconoclast (aɪˈkɒnəˌklæst) *n* **1** a person who attacks established or traditional concepts, principles, laws, etc **2 a** a destroyer of religious images or sacred objects **b** an adherent of the heretical movement within the Greek Orthodox Church from 725 to 842 AD, which aimed at the destruction of icons and religious images [c16 from Late Latin *iconoclastes*, from Late Greek *eikonoklastes*, from *eikōn* icon + *klastēs* breaker] > iˌconoˈclastic *adj* > iˌconoˈclastically *adv*

iconography (ˌaɪkɒˈnɒɡrəfɪ) *n, pl* -phies **1 a** the symbols used in a work of art or art movement **b** the conventional significance attached to such symbols **2** a collection of pictures of a particular subject, such as Christ **3** the representation of the subjects of icons or portraits, esp on coins > iˈcoˈnographer *n* > iconographic (aɪˌkɒnəˈɡræfɪk) *or* iˌconoˈgraphical *adj*

iconolatry (ˌaɪkɒˈnɒlətrɪ) *n* the worship or adoration of icons as idols > ˌicoˈnolater *n* > ˌicoˈnolatrous *adj*

iconology (ˌaɪkɒˈnɒlədʒɪ) *n* **1** the study or field of art history concerning icons **2** icons collectively **3** the symbolic representation or symbolism of icons > iconological (aɪˌkɒnəˈlɒdʒɪkəl) *adj* > ˌicoˈnologist *n*

iconomatic (aɪˌkɒnəˈmætɪk) *adj* employing pictures to represent not objects themselves but the sound of their names [c19 from Greek, from

eikon image + *onoma* name] > iconomaticism (aɪˌkɒnəˈmætɪˌsɪzəm) *n*

iconoscope (aɪˈkɒnəˌskəʊp) *n* a television camera tube in which an electron beam scans a photoemissive surface, converting an optical image into electrical pulses

iconostasis (ˌaɪkəʊˈnɒstəsɪs) *or* **iconostas** (aɪˈkɒnəˌstæs) *n, pl* iconostases (ˌaɪkəʊˈnɒstəˌsiːz, aɪˈkɒnəˌstɛsiːz) *Eastern Church* a screen with doors and icons set in tiers, which separates the bema (sanctuary) from the nave [c19 Church Latin, from Late Greek *eikonostasion* shrine, literally: area where images are placed, from ICONO- + *histanai* to stand]

icosahedron (ˌaɪkəsəˈhiːdrən) *n, pl* -drons *or* -dra (-drə) a solid figure having 20 faces. The faces of a **regular icosahedron** are equilateral triangles [c16 from Greek *eikosaedron*, from *eikosi* twenty + -*edron* -HEDRON] > ˌicosaˈhedral *adj*

icositetrahedron (ˌaɪkəsɪˌtɛtrəˈhiːdrən) *n, pl* -drons *or* -dra (-drə) a solid figure having 24 trapezoid faces, as occurring in some crystals

ICS *abbreviation for* Indian Civil Service

-ics *suffix forming nouns (functioning as singular)* **1** indicating a science, art, or matters relating to a particular subject: *aeronautics; politics* **2** indicating certain activities or practices: *acrobatics* [plural of -*ic*, representing Latin -*ica*, from Greek -*ika*, as in *mathēmatika* mathematics]

ICSH *abbreviation for* interstitial-cell-stimulating hormone

ICSI *abbreviation for* intracytoplasmic sperm injection: a method of in vitro fertilization in which a spermatozoon is injected into an ovum for implantation within the womb

ICT *abbreviation for* Information and Communications Technology

icterus (ˈɪktərəs) *n* **1** *pathol* another name for **jaundice** **2** a yellowing of plant leaves, caused by excessive cold or moisture [c18 from Latin: yellow bird, the sight of which reputedly cured jaundice, from Greek *ikteros*] > icteric (ɪkˈtɛrɪk) *adj*

ictus (ˈɪktəs) *n, pl* -tuses *or* -tus **1** *prosody* metrical or rhythmic stress in verse feet, as contrasted with the stress accent on words **2** *med* a sudden attack or stroke [c18 from Latin *icere* to strike] > ˈictal *adj*

ICTZ *abbreviation for* Intertropical Convergence Zone

ICU *abbreviation for* **1** intensive care unit **2** *text messaging* I see you

icy (ˈaɪsɪ) *adj* icier, iciest **1** made of, covered with, or containing ice **2** resembling ice **3** freezing or very cold **4** cold or reserved in manner; aloof

icy pole *n Austral* an ice cream or water ice on a stick. Also called (esp in Britain): ice lolly US and Canadian (Trademark): Popsicle

id[1] (ɪd) *n psychoanal* the mass of primitive instincts and energies in the unconscious mind that, modified by the ego and the superego, underlies all psychic activity [c20 New Latin, from Latin: it; used to render German *Es*]

id[2] *the internet domain name for* Indonesia

ID *abbreviation for* **1** Idaho **2** identification (document) **3** Also: i.d. inside diameter **4** Intelligence Department **5** Also: i.d. intradermal

id. *abbreviation for* idem

Id. *abbreviation for* Idaho

I'd (aɪd) *contraction of* I had *or* I would

-id[1] *suffix forming nouns* **1** indicating the names of meteor showers that appear to radiate from a specified constellation: *Orionids* (from Orion) **2** indicating a particle, body, or structure of a specified kind: *energid* [from Latin -*id-*, -*is*, from Greek, feminine suffix of origin]

-id[2] *suffix forming nouns and adjectives* **1** indicating members of a zoological family: *cyprinid* **2** indicating members of a dynasty: *Seleucid; Fatimid* [from New Latin -*idae* or -*ida*, from Greek -*idēs* suffix indicating offspring]

-id[3] *suffix forming nouns* a variant of **-ide**

Ida (ˈaɪdə) *n* Mount **1** a mountain in central Crete: the highest on the island; in ancient times associated with the worship of Zeus. Height: 2456 m (8057 ft). Modern Greek name: **Idhi 2** a mountain in NW Turkey, southeast of the site of ancient Troy. Height: 1767 m (5797 ft). Turkish name: **Kaz Dağı**

IDA *abbreviation for* **International Development Association**

Ida. *abbreviation for* Idaho

-idae *suffix forming nouns* indicating names of zoological families: *Felidae; Hominidae* [New Latin, from Latin, from Greek *-idai*, suffix indicating offspring]

Idaho ('aɪdəˌhəʊ) *n* a state of the northwestern US: consists chiefly of ranges of the Rocky Mountains, with the Snake River basin in the south; important for agriculture (**Idaho potatoes**), livestock, and silver-mining. Capital: Boise. Pop: 1 366 332 (2003 est). Area: 216 413 sq km (83 557 sq miles). Abbreviations: **Id, Ida,** (with zip code) **ID**

Idahoan ('aɪdəˌhəʊn) *n* **1** a native or inhabitant of Idaho ▷ *adj* **2** of or relating to Idaho or its inhabitants

IDASA (ɪ'dɑːzə) *n acronym for* Institute for a Democratic South Africa

IDB *chiefly South African abbreviation for* illicit diamond buying

IDC *abbreviation for* **industrial development certificate**

ID card *n* a card or document that serves to identify a person, or to prove his age, membership, etc

IDD *abbreviation for* international direct dialling

IDDM *abbreviation for* insulin-dependent diabetes mellitus; a form of diabetes in which patients have little or no ability to produce insulin and are therefore entirely dependent on insulin injections

ide (aɪd) *n* another name for the **silver orfe**. See **orfe** [C19 from New Latin *idus*, from Swedish *id*]

-ide *or* **-id** *suffix forming nouns* **1** (*added to the combining form of the nonmetallic or electronegative elements*) indicating a binary compound: *sodium chloride* **2** indicating an organic compound derived from another: *acetanilide* **3** indicating one of a class of compounds or elements: *peptide; lanthanide* [from German *-id*, from French *oxide* OXIDE, based on the suffix of *acide* ACID]

idea (aɪ'dɪə) *n* **1** any content of the mind, esp the conscious mind **2** the thought of something: *the very idea appals me* **3** a mental representation of something: *she's got a good idea of the layout of the factory* **4** the characterization of something in general terms; concept: *the idea of a square circle is self-contradictory* **5** an individual's conception of something: *his idea of honesty is not the same as yours and mine* **6** the belief that something is the case: *he has the idea that what he's doing is right* **7** a scheme, intention, plan, etc: *here's my idea for the sales campaign* **8** a vague notion or indication; inkling: *he had no idea of what life would be like in Africa* **9** significance or purpose: *the idea of the game is to discover the murderer* **10** *philosophy* **a** a private mental object, regarded as the immediate object of thought or perception **b** a Platonic Idea or Form **11** *music* a thematic phrase or figure; motif **12** *obsolete* a mental image **13 get ideas** to become ambitious, restless, etc **14 not one's idea of** not what one regards as (hard work, a holiday, etc) **15 that's an idea** that is worth considering **16 the very idea!** that is preposterous, unreasonable, etc [C16 via Late Latin from Greek: model, pattern, notion, from *idein* to see] > **i'dealess** *adj*

USAGE It is usually considered correct to say that someone has the *idea of* doing something, rather than the *idea to do* it: *he had the idea of taking* (not *the idea to take*) *a short holiday*

Idea (aɪ'dɪə) *n* another name for **Form**

idea hamster *or* **ideas hamster** *n slang* a person who is employed as a source of new ideas

ideal (aɪ'dɪəl) *n* **1** a conception of something that is perfect, esp that which one seeks to attain **2** a person or thing considered to represent

perfection: *he's her ideal* **3** something existing only as an idea **4** a pattern or model, esp of ethical behaviour ▷ *adj* **5** conforming to an ideal **6** of, involving, or existing in the form of an idea **7** *philosophy* **a** of or relating to a highly desirable and possible state of affairs **b** of or relating to idealism > **ideality** (ˌaɪdɪ'ælɪtɪ) *n* > **i'deally** *adv* > **i'dealness** *n*

ideal crystal *n chem* a crystal in which there are no defects or impurities

ideal element *n* any element added to a mathematical theory in order to eliminate special cases. The ideal element i = √−1 allows all algebraic equations to be solved and the point at infinity (**ideal point**) ensures that any two lines in projective geometry intersect

ideal gas *n* a hypothetical gas which obeys Boyle's law exactly at all temperatures and pressures, and which has internal energy that depends only upon the temperature. Measurements upon real gases are extrapolated to zero pressure to obtain results in agreement with theories relating to an ideal gas, especially in thermometry. Also called: **perfect gas**

idealism (aɪ'dɪəˌlɪzəm) *n* **1** belief in or pursuance of ideals **2** the tendency to represent things in their ideal forms, rather than as they are **3** any of a group of philosophical doctrines that share the monistic view that material objects and the external world do not exist in reality independently of the human mind but are variously creations of the mind or constructs of ideas. Compare **materialism** (sense 2), **dualism** (sense 2) > **i'dealist** *n* > **i,deal'istic** *adj* > **i,deal'istically** *adv*

idealization *or* **idealisation** (aɪˌdɪəlaɪ'zeɪʃən) *n* **1** the representation of something as ideal **2** a conception of something that dwells on its advantages and ignores its deficiencies **3** a general theoretical account of natural phenomena that ignores features that are difficult to accommodate within a theory

idealize *or* **idealise** (aɪ'dɪəˌlaɪz) *vb* **1** to consider or represent (something) as ideal **2** (*tr*) to portray as ideal; glorify **3** (*intr*) to form an ideal or ideals > **i'dealˌizer** *or* **i'dealˌiser** *n*

ideas of reference *pl n* a schizophrenic symptom in which the patient thinks that things completely disconnected from him are influencing him or conveying messages to him

ideate ('aɪdɪˌeɪt) *vb* (*tr*) to form an idea of; to imagine or conceive [C17 from Medieval Latin *ideat-* formed as an idea, from *ideare*, from Greek *idea* model, pattern, notion]

ideatum (ˌaɪdɪ'eɪtəm) *n, pl* **-ata** (-'eɪtə) *philosophy* the objective reality with which human ideas are supposed to correspond [C18 New Latin, from Latin: IDEA]

idée fixe *French* (ide fiks) *n, pl* **idées fixes** (ide fiks) a fixed idea; obsession

idée reçue *French* (ide rəsy) *n, pl* **idées reçues** (ide rəsy) a generally held opinion or concept [literally: received idea]

idem *Latin* ('aɪdɛm, 'ɪdɛm) *the same*: used to refer to an article, chapter, etc, previously cited

idempotent ('aɪdəmˌpəʊtənt, 'ɪd-) *adj maths* (of a matrix, transformation, etc) not changed in value following multiplication by itself [C20 from Latin *idem* same + POTENT[1]]

ident ('aɪdɛnt) *n* a short visual image employed between television programmes that works as a logo to locate the viewer to the channel

identic (aɪ'dɛntɪk) *adj* **1** *diplomacy* (esp of opinions expressed by two or more governments) having the same wording or intention regarding another power: *identic notes* **2** an obsolete word for **identical**

identical (aɪ'dɛntɪkˀl) *adj* **1** Also called: **numerically identical** being one and the same individual: *Cicero and Tully are identical* **2** Also called: **quantitatively identical** exactly alike, equal, or agreeing **3** designating either or both of a pair of

twins of the same sex who developed from a single fertilized ovum that split into two. Compare **fraternal** (sense 3) > **i'dentically** *adv* > **i'denticalness** *n*

identical proposition *n logic* a necessary truth, esp a categorial identity, such as *whatever is triangular has three sides*

identification (aɪˌdɛntɪfɪ'keɪʃən) *n* **1** the act of identifying or the state of being identified **2 a** something that identifies a person or thing **b** (*as modifier*): *an identification card* **3** *psychol* **a** the process of recognizing specific objects as the result of remembering **b** the process by which one incorporates aspects of another person's personality. See also: **empathy c** the transferring of a response from one situation to another because the two bear similar features. See also **generalization** (sense 3)

identification parade *n* a group of persons including one suspected of having committed a crime assembled for the purpose of discovering whether a witness can identify the suspect

identifier (aɪ'dɛntɪˌfaɪ) *n* a person or thing that establishes the identity of someone or something

identify (aɪ'dɛntɪˌfaɪ) *vb* **-fies, -fying, -fied** (*mainly tr*) **1** to prove or recognize as being a certain person or thing; determine the identity of **2** to consider as the same or equivalent **3** (*also intr; often foll by with*) to consider (oneself) as similar to another **4** to determine the taxonomic classification of (a plant or animal) **5** (*intr; usually foll by with*) *psychol* to engage in identification > **i'denti,fiable** *adj* > **i'denti,fiably** *adv*

Identikit (aɪ'dɛntɪˌkɪt) *n trademark* **1 a** a set of transparencies of various typical facial characteristics that can be superimposed on one another to build up, on the basis of a description, a picture of a person sought by the police (*as modifier*): *an Identikit picture* **2** (*modifier*) artificially created by copying different elements in an attempt to form a whole: *an identikit pop group*

identity (aɪ'dɛntɪtɪ) *n, pl* **-ties 1** the state of having unique identifying characteristics held by no other person or thing **2** the individual characteristics by which a person or thing is recognized **3** Also called: **numerical identity** the property of being one and the same individual: *his loss of memory did not affect his identity* **4** Also called: **qualitative identity** the state of being the same in nature, quality, etc: *they were linked by the identity of their tastes* **5** the state of being the same as a person or thing described or claimed: *the identity of the stolen goods has not yet been established* **6** identification of oneself as: *moving to London destroyed his Welsh identity* **7** *logic* **a** that relation that holds only between any entity and itself **b** an assertion that that relation holds, as *Cicero is Tully* **8** *maths* **a** an equation that is valid for all values of its variables, as in $(x − y)(x + y) = x^2 − y^2$. Often denoted by the symbol ≡ **b** Also called: **identity element** a member of a set that when operating on another member, *x*, produces that member *x*: the identity for multiplication of numbers is 1 since $x.1 = 1.x = x$. See also **inverse** (sense 2b) **9** *Austral and NZ informal* a well-known person, esp in a specified locality; figure (esp in the phrase **an old identity**) [C16 from Late Latin *identitās*, from Latin *idem* the same]

identity card *n* a card that establishes a person's identity, esp one issued to all members of the population in wartime, to the staff of an organization, etc

identity theft *n* the crime of setting up and using bank accounts and credit facilities fraudulently in another person's name without his or her knowledge

identity theory *n philosophy* a form of materialism which holds mental states to be identical with certain states of the brain and so to have no separate existence, but regards this identity as contingent so that mentalistic and physicalistic language are not held to be synonymous. See also **anomalous monism, materialism** (sense 2)

ideo- *combining form* of or indicating idea or ideas: *ideology* [from French *idéo-*, from Greek *idea* IDEA]

ideogram ('ɪdɪəʊˌgræm) *or* **ideograph** ('ɪdɪəʊˌgrɑːf, -ˌgræf) *n* **1** a sign or symbol, used in such writing systems as those of China or Japan, that directly represents a concept, idea, or thing rather than a word or set of words for it **2** any graphic sign or symbol, such as %, @, &, etc

ideography (ˌɪdɪˈɒgrəfɪ) *n* the use of ideograms to communicate ideas

ideologist (ˌaɪdɪˈɒlədʒɪst) *n* **1** a person who supports a particular ideology, esp a political theorist **2** a person who studies an ideology or ideologies **3** a theorist or visionary ▷ Also called: **ideologue** ('aɪdɪəˌlɒg)

ideology (ˌaɪdɪˈɒlədʒɪ) *n, pl* **-gies 1** a body of ideas that reflects the beliefs and interests of a nation, political system, etc and underlies political action **2** *philosophy, sociol* the set of beliefs by which a group or society orders reality so as to render it intelligible **3** speculation that is imaginary or visionary **4** the study of the nature and origin of ideas > **ideological** (ˌaɪdɪəˈlɒdʒɪkəl) *or* ˌideoˈlogic *adj* > ˌideoˈlogically *adv*

ideomotor (ˌaɪdɪəˈməʊtə) *adj physiol* designating automatic muscular movements stimulated by ideas, as in absent-minded acts

ides (aɪdz) *n (functioning as singular)* (in the Roman calendar) the 15th day in March, May, July, and October and the 13th day of each other month. See also **calends, nones** [C15 from Old French, from Latin *īdūs* (plural), of uncertain origin]

id est Latin ('ɪd 'ɛst) the full form of **i.e.**

Idhi ('ɪðɪ) *n* a transliteration of the Modern Greek name for (Mount) **Ida** (sense 1)

idio- *combining form* indicating peculiarity, isolation, or that which pertains to an individual person or thing: *idiolect* [from Greek *idios* private, separate]

idioblast ('ɪdɪəʊˌblæst) *n* a plant cell that differs from those around it in the same tissue > ˌidioˈblastic *adj*

idiocy ('ɪdɪəsɪ) *n, pl* **-cies 1** *(not in technical usage)* severe mental retardation **2** foolishness or senselessness; stupidity **3** a foolish act or remark

idioglossia (ˌɪdɪəʊˈglɒsɪə) *n* **1** a private language, as invented by a child or between two children, esp twins **2** a pathological condition in which a person's speech is so severely distorted that it is unintelligible [C19 from Greek *idios* private, separate + *glossa* tongue]

idiogram ('ɪdɪəʊˌgræm) *n* another name for **karyogram**

idiographic (ˌɪdɪəʊˈgræfɪk) *adj psychol* of or relating to the study of individuals. Compare **nomothetic**

idiolect ('ɪdɪəˌlɛkt) *n* the variety or form of a language used by an individual > ˌidioˈlectal *or* ˌidioˈlectic *adj*

idiom ('ɪdɪəm) *n* **1** a group of words whose meaning cannot be predicted from the meanings of the constituent words, as for example (*It was raining*) *cats and dogs* **2** linguistic usage that is grammatical and natural to native speakers of a language **3** the characteristic vocabulary or usage of a specific human group or subject **4** the characteristic artistic style of an individual, school, period, etc [C16 from Latin *idiōma* peculiarity of language, from Greek; see IDIO-] > **idiomatic** (ˌɪdɪəˈmætɪk) *or* ˌidioˈmatical *adj* > ˌidioˈmatically *adv* > ˌidioˈmaticalness *n*

idiomorphic (ˌɪdɪəʊˈmɔːfɪk) *adj* (of minerals) occurring naturally in the form of well-developed crystals > ˌidioˈmorphically *adv* > ˌidioˈmorphism *n*

idiopathy (ˌɪdɪˈɒpəθɪ) *n, pl* **-thies** any disease of unknown cause > **idiopathic** (ˌɪdɪəʊˈpæθɪk) *adj*

idiophone ('ɪdɪəˌfəʊn) *n music* a percussion instrument, such as a cymbal or xylophone, made of naturally sonorous material > **idiophonic** (ˌɪdɪəˈfɒnɪk) *adj*

idioplasm ('ɪdɪəʊˌplæzəm) *n* another name for **germ plasm**. > ˌidioˈplasmic *or* idioplasmatic (ˌɪdɪəʊplæzˈmætɪk) *adj*

idiosyncrasy (ˌɪdɪəʊˈsɪŋkrəsɪ) *n, pl* **-sies 1** a tendency, type of behaviour, mannerism, etc, of a specific person; quirk **2** the composite physical or psychological make-up of a specific person **3** an abnormal reaction of an individual to specific foods, drugs, or other agents [C17 from Greek *idiosunkrasia*, from IDIO- + *sunkrasis* mixture, temperament, from *sun-* SYN- + *kerannunai* to mingle]

idiosyncratic (ˌɪdɪəʊsɪŋˈkrætɪk) *adj* of or relating to idiosyncrasy; characteristic of a specific person > ˌidiosynˈcratically *adv*

idiot ('ɪdɪət) *n* **1** a person with severe mental retardation **2** a foolish or senseless person [C13 from Latin *idiōta* ignorant person, from Greek *idiōtēs* private person, one who lacks professional knowledge, ignoramus; see IDIO-]

idiot board *n* a slang name for **Autocue**

idiot box *n slang* a television set

idiotic (ˌɪdɪˈɒtɪk) *adj* of or resembling an idiot; foolish; senseless > ˌidiˈotically *adv* > ˌidiˈoticalness *n*

idiotism ('ɪdɪəˌtɪzəm) *n* **1** an archaic word for **idiocy 2** an obsolete word for **idiom**

idiot savant ('iːdjəʊ sæˈvɑ̃, 'ɪdɪət 'sævənt) *n, pl* **idiots savants** ('iːdjəʊ sæˈvɑ̃) *or* **idiot savants** a person with learning difficulties who performs brilliantly at some specialized intellectual task, such as giving the day of the week for any calendar date past or present [C19 from French: knowledgeable idiot]

idiot strings *pl n Canadian informal* strings attached to children's mittens to prevent the wearer from losing them

idiot tape *n printing* an input tape for a typesetting machine that contains text only, the typographical instructions being supplied by the typesetting machine itself

idle ('aɪdəl) *adj* **1** unemployed or unoccupied; inactive **2** not operating or being used **3** (of money) not being used to earn interest or dividends **4** not wanting to work; lazy **5** *(usually prenominal)* frivolous or trivial: *idle pleasures* **6** ineffective or powerless; fruitless; vain **7** without basis; unfounded ▷ *vb* **8** (when *tr*, often foll by *away*) to waste or pass (time) fruitlessly or inactively: *he idled the hours away* **9** (*intr*) to loiter or move aimlessly **10** (*intr*) (of a shaft, engine, etc) to turn without doing useful work **11** (*intr*) Also (Brit): **tick over** (of an engine) to run at low speed with the transmission disengaged **12** (*tr*) *US and Canadian* to cause to be inactive or unemployed [Old English *īdel*; compare Old High German *ītal* empty, vain] > **idleness** *n* > **idly** *adv*

idle pulley *or* **idler pulley** *n* a freely rotating trolley used to control the tension or direction of a belt. Also called: **idler**

idler ('aɪdlə) *n* **1** a person who idles **2** another name for **idle pulley** *or* **idle wheel 3** *nautical* a ship's crew member, such as a carpenter, sailmaker, etc, whose duties do not include standing regular watches

idler shaft *n* a shaft carrying one or more gearwheels that idles between a driver shaft and a driven shaft, usually to reverse the direction of rotation or provide different spacing of gearwheels, esp in a gearbox

idle time *n commerce* time during which a machine or a worker could be working but is not, as when one job has been completed and tooling or materials for the next are not complete or available. Compare **downtime**

idle wheel *n* a gearwheel interposed between two others to transmit torque without changing the direction of rotation to the velocity ratio. Also called: **idler**

IDN *abbreviation for* in Dei nomine. Also: **IND** [Latin: in the name of God]

Ido ('iːdəʊ) *n* an artificial language; a

modification of Esperanto [C20 offspring, from Greek *-id* daughter of]

idocrase ('aɪdəˌkreɪs, 'ɪd-) *n* another name for **vesuvianite** [C19 from French, from Greek *eidos* form + *krasis* a mingling]

idol ('aɪdəl) *n* **1** a material object, esp a carved image, that is worshipped as a god **2** *Christianity, Judaism* any being (other than the one God) to which divine honour is paid **3** a person who is revered, admired, or highly loved [C13 from Late Latin *īdōlum*, from Latin: image, from Greek *eidōlon*, from *eidos* shape, form]

idolatrise *or* **idolatrize** (aɪˈdɒləˌtraɪz) *vb* **1** (*tr*) a less common word for **idolize 2** (*intr*) to indulge in the worship of idols > iˈdolaˌtrizer *or* iˈdolaˌtriser *n*

idolatry (aɪˈdɒlətrɪ) *n* **1** the worship of idols **2** great devotion or reverence > iˈdolater *n or* iˈdolatress *fem n* > iˈdolatrous *adj* > iˈdolatrously *adv* > iˈdolatrousness *n*

idolize *or* **idolise** ('aɪdəˌlaɪz) *vb* **1** (*tr*) to admire or revere greatly **2** (*tr*) to worship as an idol **3** (*intr*) to worship idols > iˈdolism, ˌidoliˈzation *or* ˌidoliˈsation *n* > iˈdolist, ˌidolˈizer *or* ˌidolˈiser *n*

idolum (ɪˈdəʊləm) *n* **1** a mental picture; idea **2** a false idea, fallacy [C17 from Latin: IDOL]

Idomeneus (aɪˈdɒmɪˌnjuːs) *n Greek myth* a king of Crete who fought on the Greek side in the Trojan War

IDP *abbreviation for* integrated data processing

Id-ul-Adha ('iːdʊlˌɑːdə) *n* a variant spelling of **Eid-ul-Adha**

Id-ul-Fitr ('iːdʊlˌfɪːtə) *n* a variant spelling of **Eid-ul-Fitr**

Idun ('iːdʊn) *or* **Ithunn** *n Norse myth* the goddess of spring who guarded the apples that kept the gods eternally young; wife of Bragi

idyll *or sometimes US* **idyl** ('ɪdɪl) *n* **1** a poem or prose work describing an idealized rural life, pastoral scenes, etc **2** any simple narrative or descriptive piece in poetry or prose **3** a charming or picturesque scene or event **4** a piece of music with a calm or pastoral character [C17 from Latin *īdyllium*, from Greek *eidullion*, from *eidos* shape, (literary) form]

idyllic (ɪˈdɪlɪk, aɪ-) *adj* **1** of or relating to an idyll **2** charming; picturesque > iˈdyllically *adv*

idyllist *or US* **idylist** ('ɪdɪlɪst) *n* a writer of idylls

ie the internet domain name for Ireland

IE *abbreviation for* Indo-European (languages)

i.e. *abbreviation for* id est [Latin: that is (to say); in other words]

-ie *suffix forming nouns* a variant of **-y²**

IEA *abbreviation for* International Energy Agency

iechyd da (ˌjækɪˈdɑː; *Welsh* ˈjɛxəd dɑː) *interj Welsh* a drinking toast; good health; cheers [Welsh: good health]

IED *abbreviation for* improvised explosive device

IEE *abbreviation for* Institution of Electrical Engineers

Ieper ('iːpər) *n* the Flemish name for **Ypres**

-ier *suffix forming nouns* a variant of **-eer** *brigadier* [from Old English *-ere* -ER¹ or (in some words) from Old French *-ier*, from Latin *-ārius* -ARY]

if (ɪf) *conj (subordinating)* **1** in case that, or on condition that: *if you try hard it might work; if he were poor, would you marry him?* **2** used to introduce an indirect question. In this sense, *if* approaches the meaning of *whether* **3** even though: *an attractive if awkward girl* **4 a** used to introduce expressions of desire, with *only*: *if I had only known* **b** used to introduce exclamations of surprise, dismay, etc: *if this doesn't top everything!* **5 as if** as it would be if; as though: *he treats me as if I were junior to him* > *n* **6** an uncertainty or doubt: *the big if is whether our plan will work at all* **7** a condition or stipulation: *I won't have any ifs or buts* [Old English *gif*; related to Old Saxon *ef, if*, Old High German *iba* whether, if]

IF *or* **i.f.** *electronics abbreviation for* intermediate frequency

IFA *abbreviation for* independent financial adviser

IFAD *abbreviation for* International Fund for Agricultural Development

i

IFC *abbreviation for* **International Finance Corporation**

Ife ('iːfɪ) *n* a town in W central Nigeria: one of the largest and oldest Yoruba towns; university (1961); centre of the cocoa trade. Pop: 229 000 (2005 est)

-iferous *suffix forming adjectives* containing or yielding: *carboniferous*

iff (ɪf) *conj logic* a shortened form of *if and only if*: it indicates that the two sentences so connected are necessary and sufficient conditions for one another. Usually *iff* is used for equivalence in the metalanguage, rather than as the biconditional in the object language

IFF *military abbreviation for* Identification, Friend or Foe: a system using radar transmissions to which equipment carried by friendly forces automatically responds with a precoded signal

iffy ('ɪfɪ) *adj* **iffier, iffiest** *informal* uncertain or subject to contingency: *this scheme sounds a bit iffy* [c20 from IF + -Y[1]]

Ifni (*Spanish* 'ifni) *n* a former Spanish province in S Morocco, on the Atlantic: returned to Morocco in 1969

IFP *abbreviation for* Inkatha Freedom Party

IFR *aeronautics abbreviation for* instrument flying regulations

IFS *abbreviation for* Irish Free State (now called Republic of Ireland)

iftar *or* **Iftar** ('ɪftɑː) *n* the meal eaten by Muslims to break their fast after sunset every day during Ramadan [from Arabic *iftar* the breaking of the fast; compare ID-UL-FITR]

-ify *suffix forming verbs* a variant of **-fy**: *intensify* > **-ification** *suffix forming nouns*

IG *abbreviation for* **1** Indo-Germanic (languages) **2** Inspector General

Igbo ('iːbəʊ) *n, pl* **-bo** *or* **-bos** a variant spelling of **Ibo**

IGBP *abbreviation for* International Geosphere-Biosphere Programme

IGC *abbreviation for* inter-governmental conference (esp in the European Union)

Igdrasil ('ɪgdrəsɪl) *n* a variant spelling of **Yggdrasil**

IGFET ('ɪgfɛt) *n* insulated-gate field-effect transistor; a type of field-effect transistor having one or more semiconductor gate electrodes. Compare **JFET**

igloo *or* **iglu** ('ɪgluː) *n, pl* **-loos** *or* **-lus** **1** a dome-shaped Inuit house, usually built of blocks of solid snow **2** a hollow made by a seal in the snow over its breathing hole in the ice [c19 from Inuktitut *igdlu* house]

IGM *chess abbreviation for* **International Grandmaster**

igneous ('ɪgnɪəs) *adj* **1** (of rocks) derived by solidification of magma or molten lava emplaced on or below the earth's surface. Compare **sedimentary, metamorphic** (sense 2) **2** of or relating to fire [c17 from Latin *igneus* fiery, from *ignis* fire]

ignescent (ɪg'nɛsᵊnt) *adj* **1** giving off sparks when struck, as a flint **2** capable of bursting into flame ▷ *n* **3** an ignescent substance [c19 from Latin *ignescere* to become inflamed]

ignimbrite ('ɪgnɪm,braɪt) *n* a rock formed by the deposition at high temperature and the consolidation of a nuée ardente or other type of ash flow, being a complicated mixture of volcanic materials welded together by heat, hot gases, and pressure. Also called: **welded tuft** See **tuft** [c20 from Latin *ign(is)* fire + *imbr(is)*, *imber* shower of rain + -ITE[1]]

ignis fatuus ('ɪgnɪs 'fætjʊəs) *n, pl* **ignes fatui** ('ɪgniːz 'fætjʊ,aɪ) another name for **will-o'-the-wisp** [c16 from Medieval Latin, literally: foolish fire]

ignite (ɪg'naɪt) *vb* **1** to catch fire or set fire to; burn or cause to burn **2** (*tr*) *chem* to heat strongly **3** (*tr*) to stimulate or provoke: *the case has ignited a nationwide debate* [c17 from Latin *ignīre* to set alight, from *ignis* fire] > **ig'nitable** *or* **ig'nitible** *adj* > **ig,nita'bility** *or* **ig,niti'bility** *n*

igniter (ɪg'naɪtə) *n* **1** a person or thing that ignites **2** a fuse to fire explosive charges **3** an electrical device for lighting a gas turbine **4** a subsidiary electrode in an ignitron

ignition (ɪg'nɪʃən) *n* **1** the act or process of initiating combustion **2** the process of igniting the fuel in an internal-combustion engine **3** (usually preceded by *the*) the devices used to ignite the fuel in an internal-combustion engine

ignition coil *n* an induction coil that supplies the high voltage to the sparking plugs of an internal-combustion engine

ignition key *n* the key used in a motor vehicle to turn the switch that connects the battery to the ignition system and other electrical devices

ignitron (ɪg'naɪtrɒn, 'ɪgnɪ,trɒn) *n* a mercury-arc rectifier controlled by a subsidiary electrode, the igniter, partially immersed in a mercury cathode. A current passed between igniter and cathode forms a hot spot sufficient to strike an arc between cathode and anode [c20 from IGNITER + ELECTRON]

ignoble (ɪg'nəʊbᵊl) *adj* **1** dishonourable; base; despicable **2** of low birth or origins; humble; common **3** of low quality; inferior **4** *falconry* **a** designating short-winged hawks that capture their quarry by swiftness and adroitness of flight. Compare **noble** (sense 7) **b** designating quarry which is inferior or unworthy of pursuit by a particular species of hawk or falcon [c16 from Latin *ignōbilis*, from IN-[1] + Old Latin *gnōbilis* NOBLE] > **,igno'bility** *or* **ig'nobleness** *n* > **ig'nobly** *adv*

ignominy ('ɪgnə,mɪnɪ) *n, pl* **-minies** **1** disgrace or public shame; dishonour **2** a cause of disgrace; a shameful act [c16 from Latin *ignōminia* disgrace, from *ig-* (see IN-[2]) + *nōmen* name, reputation] > **,igno'minious** *adj* > **,igno'miniously** *adv* > **,igno'miniousness** *n*

ignoramus (,ɪgnə'reɪməs) *n, pl* **-muses** an ignorant person; fool [c16 from legal Latin, literally: we have no knowledge of, from Latin *ignōrāre* to be ignorant of; see IGNORE; modern usage originated from the use of *Ignoramus* as the name of an unlettered lawyer in a play by G. Ruggle, 17th-century English dramatist]

ignorance ('ɪgnərəns) *n* lack of knowledge, information, or education; the state of being ignorant

ignorant ('ɪgnərənt) *adj* **1** lacking in knowledge or education; unenlightened **2** (*postpositive; often foll by of*) lacking in awareness or knowledge (of): *ignorant of the law* **3** resulting from or showing lack of knowledge or awareness: *an ignorant remark* > **'ignorantly** *adv*

ignoratio elenchi (,ɪgnə'reɪʃɪəʊ ɪ'lɛŋkaɪ) *n logic* **1** a purported refutation of a proposition that does not in fact prove it false but merely establishes a related but strictly irrelevant proposition **2** the fallacy of arguing in this way [Latin: an ignorance of proof, translating Greek *elenchou agnoia*]

ignore (ɪg'nɔː) *vb* (*tr*) **1** to fail or refuse to notice; disregard ▷ *n* **2** *Austral informal* disregard: *to treat someone with ignore* [c17 from Latin *ignōrāre* not to know, from *ignārus* ignorant of, from *i-* IN-[1] + *gnārus* knowing; related to Latin *noscere* to know] > **ig'norable** *adj* > **ig'norer** *n*

ignotum per ignotius *Latin* (ɪg'nəʊtʊm pər ɪg'nəʊtɪʊs) *n* an explanation that is obscurer than the thing to be explained [literally: the unknown by means of the more unknown]

Igorot (,ɪgə'rəʊt, ,iːgə-) *or* **Igorrote** (,ɪgə'rəʊtɪ, ,iːgə-) *n, pl* **-rot, -rots** *or* **-rote, -rotes** a member of a Negrito people of the mountains of N Luzon in the Philippines: noted as early exponents of mining

Igraine (ɪ'greɪn) *or* **Ygerne** *n* the mother of King Arthur

Iguaçú *or* **Iguassú** (*Portuguese* igua'su) *n* a river in SE South America, rising in S Brazil and flowing west to join the Paraná River, forming part of the border between Brazil and Argentina. Length: 1200 km (745 miles)

Iguaçú Falls *n* a waterfall on the border between Brazil and Argentina, on the Iguaçú River: divided into hundreds of separate falls by forested rocky islands. Width: about 4 km (2.5 miles). Height: 82 m (269 ft)

iguana (ɪ'gwɑːnə) *n* **1** either of two large tropical American arboreal herbivorous lizards of the genus *Iguana*, esp *I. iguana* (**common iguana**), having a greyish-green body with a row of spines along the back: family *Iguanidae* **2** Also called: **iguanid** (ɪ'gwɑːnɪd) any other lizard of the tropical American family *Iguanidae* **3** another name for **leguaan** [c16 from Spanish, from Arawak *iwana*] > **i'guanian** *n, adj*

iguanodon (ɪ'gwɑːnə,dɒn) *n* a massive herbivorous long-tailed bipedal dinosaur of the genus *Iguanodon*, common in Europe and N Africa in Jurassic and Cretaceous times: suborder *Ornithopoda* (ornithopods) [c19 New Latin, from IGUANA + Greek *odōn* tooth]

IGY *abbreviation for* **International Geophysical Year**

IHC (in New Zealand) *abbreviation for* Intellectually Handicapped Children

ihram (ɪ'rɑːm) *n* the customary white robes worn by Muslim pilgrims to Mecca, symbolizing a sacred or consecrated state [c18 from Arabic *ihrām*, from *harama* he forbade]

IHS *n* the first three letters of the name Jesus in Greek (ΙΗΣΟΥΣ), often used as a Christian emblem

iid *statistics abbreviation for* independent identically distributed (of random variables)

IJC (in the US and Canada) *abbreviation for* **International Joint Commission**

IJssel *or* **Yssel** ('aɪsᵊl; *Dutch* 'ɛisəl) *n* a river in the central Netherlands: a distributary of the Rhine, flowing north to the IJsselmeer. Length: 116 km (72 miles)

IJsselmeer *or* **Ysselmeer** (*Dutch* ɛisəl'meːr) *n* a shallow lake in the NW Netherlands; formed from the S part of the Zuider Zee by the construction of the **IJsselmeer Dam** in 1932; salt water gradually replaced by fresh water from the IJssel River; fisheries (formerly marine fish, now esp eels). Area: (before reclamation) 3690 sq km (1425 sq miles). Estimated final area: 1243 sq km (480 sq miles). English name: **Ijssel Lake**

ikan ('iːkan) *n* (in Malaysia) fish used esp in names of cooked dishes: *assam ikan* [from Malay]

Ikaría (ika'ria) *n* a transliteration of the Modern Greek name for **Icaria**

ikat ('aɪkæt) *n* a method of creating patterns in fabric by tie-dyeing the yarn before weaving [c20 from Malay, literally: to tie, bind]

IKBS *abbreviation for* **intelligent knowledge-based system**

ikebana (,iːkə'bɑːnə) *n* the Japanese decorative art of flower arrangement

Ikeja (ɪ'keɪjə) *n* a town in SW Nigeria, capital of Lagos state: residential and industrial suburb of Lagos. Pop: 63 870 (latest est)

Ikey ('aɪkɪ) *n South African informal* a student at the University of Cape Town, esp one representing the University in a sport [from the name *Isaac*]

ikon ('aɪkɒn) *n* a variant spelling of **icon**

il *the internet domain name for* Israel

IL *abbreviation for* **1** Illinois **2** *international car registration for* Israel

il- *prefix* variant of **in-**[1] and **in-**[2] before *l*

ilang-ilang ('iːlæŋ'iːlæŋ) *n* a variant spelling of **ylang-ylang**

-ile *suffix forming adjectives and nouns* indicating capability, liability, or a relationship with something: *agile; fragile; juvenile* [via French from Latin or directly from Latin *-ilis*]

ILEA ('ɪlɪə) *n* (formerly) ▷ *abbreviation or acronym for* Inner London Education Authority

ileac ('ɪlɪ,æk) *or* **ileal** ('ɪlɪəl) *adj* **1** *anatomy* of or relating to the ileum **2** *pathol* of or relating to ileus

Île-de-France (*French* ildəfrɑ̃s) *n* **1** a region of N France, in the Paris Basin: part of the duchy of France in the 10th century **2** a former name (1715–1810) for **Mauritius**

Île du Diable (il dy djɑblə) *n* the French name for **Devil's Island**

ileitis (ˌɪlɪˈaɪtɪs) *n* inflammation of the ileum

ileo- *or before a vowel* **ile-** *combining form* indicating the ileum: *ileostomy*

ileostomy (ˌɪlɪˈɒstəmɪ) *n*, *pl* -mies the surgical formation of a permanent opening through the abdominal wall into the ileum

Îles Comores (il kɔmɔr) *plural n* the French name for the **Comoros**

Îles du Salut (il dy saly) *plural n* the French name for the **Safety Islands**

Ilesha (ɪˈleɪʃə) *n* a town in W Nigeria. Pop: 500 000 (2005 est)

Îles Mascareignes (il maskarɛɲ) *plural n* the French name for the **Mascarene Islands**

Îles sous le Vent (il su lə vã) *plural n* the French name for the **Leeward Islands** (sense 3)

ileum (ˈɪlɪəm) *n* **1** the part of the small intestine between the jejunum and the caecum **2** the corresponding part in insects [C17 New Latin, from Latin *īlium, īleum* flank, groin, of obscure origin]

ileus (ˈɪlɪəs) *n* obstruction of the intestine, esp the ileum, by mechanical occlusion or as the result of distension of the bowel following loss of muscular action [C18 from Latin *īleos* severe colic, from Greek *eileos* a rolling, twisting, from *eilein* to roll]

ilex (ˈaɪlɛks) *n* **1** any of various trees or shrubs of the widely distributed genus *Ilex*, such as the holly and inkberry: family *Aquifoliaceae* **2** another name for the **holm oak** [C16 from Latin]

ilia (ˈɪlɪə) *n* the plural of **ilium**

Ilia (ˈɪlɪə) *n* (in Roman legend) the daughter of Aeneas and Lavinia, who, according to some traditions, was the mother of Romulus and Remus. See also **Rhea Silvia**

Ilía (iˈlia) *n* a transliteration of the Modern Greek name for **Elia¹**

iliac (ˈɪlɪˌæk) *adj anatomy* of or relating to the ilium

Iliad (ˈɪlɪəd) *n* a Greek epic poem describing the siege of Troy, attributed to Homer (c. 800 BC) and probably composed before 700 BC ▷ **Iliadic** (ˌɪlɪˈædɪk) *adj*

Iliamna (ˌɪlɪˈæmnə) *n* **1** a lake in SW Alaska: the largest lake in Alaska. Length: about 130 km (80 miles). Width: 40 km (25 miles) **2** a volcano in SW Alaska, northwest of Iliamna Lake. Height: 3076 m (10 092 ft)

Iligan (ɪˈliːgən) *n* a city in the Philippines, a port on the N coast of Mindanao. Pop: 306 000 (2005 est)

Ilion (ˈɪlɪən) *n* a transliteration of the Greek name for ancient **Troy**

ilium (ˈɪlɪəm) *n*, *pl* -ia (-ɪə) the uppermost and widest of the three sections of the hipbone

Ilium (ˈɪlɪəm) *n* the Latin name for ancient **Troy**

ilk¹ (ɪlk) *n* **1** a type; class; sort (esp in the phrase **of that, his, her,** etc, **ilk**): *people of that ilk should not be allowed here* **2** of that ilk *Scot* the place of the same name: used to indicate that the person named is proprietor or laird of the place named: *Moncrieff of that ilk* [Old English *ilca* the same family, same kind; related to Gothic *is* he, Latin *is*, Old English *gelīc* like]

> USAGE Although the use of *ilk* in the sense of sense 1 is sometimes condemned as being the result of a misunderstanding of the original Scottish expression *of that ilk*, it is nevertheless well established and generally acceptable

ilk² (ɪlk), **ilka** (ˈɪlkə) *determiner Scot* each; every [Old English *ǣlc* each (+ A¹)]

Ilkeston (ˈɪlkɪstən) *n* a town in N central England, in SE Derbyshire. Pop: 37 270 (2001)

Ilkley (ˈɪlklɪ) *n* a town in N England, in Bradford unitary authority, West Yorkshire: nearby is **Ilkley Moor** (to the south). Pop: 13 472 (2001)

ill (ɪl) *adj* worse, worst **1** (*usually postpositive*) not in good health; sick **2** characterized by or intending evil, harm, etc; hostile: *ill deeds* **3** causing or resulting in pain, harm, adversity, etc: *ill effects* **4** ascribing or imputing evil to something referred to: *ill repute* **5** promising an unfavourable outcome; unpropitious: *an ill omen* **6** harsh; lacking kindness: *ill will* **7** not up to an acceptable standard; faulty: *ill manners* **8** ill at ease unable to relax; uncomfortable ▷ *n* **9** evil or harm: *to wish a person ill* **10** a mild disease **11** misfortune; trouble ▷ *adv* **12** badly: *the title ill befits him* **13** with difficulty; hardly: *he can ill afford the money* **14** not rightly: *she ill deserves such good fortune* [C11 (in the sense: evil): from Old Norse *illr* bad]

Ill. *abbreviation for* Illinois

I'll (aɪl) *contraction of* I will or I shall

ill-advised *adj* **1** acting without reasonable care or thought: *you would be ill-advised to sell your house now* **2** badly thought out; not or insufficiently considered: *an ill-advised plan of action* > ˌill-adˈvisedly *adv*

ill-affected *adj* (often foll by *towards*) not well disposed; disaffected

Illampu (*Spanish* iʎamˈpu) *n* one of the two peaks of Mount **Sorata**

ill-assorted *adj* badly matched; incompatible

illation (ɪˈleɪʃən) *n* a rare word for **inference** [C16 from Late Latin *illātiō* a bringing in, from Latin *illātus* brought in, from *inferre* to bring in, from IN-² + *ferre* to bear, carry]

illative (ɪˈleɪtɪv) *adj* **1** of or relating to illation; inferential **2** *grammar* denoting a word or morpheme used to signal inference, for example *so* or *therefore* **3** (in the grammar of Finnish and other languages) denoting a case of nouns expressing a relation of motion or direction, usually translated by the English prepositions *into* or *towards*. Compare **elative** (sense 1) ▷ *n* **4** *grammar* **a** the illative case **b** an illative word or speech element [C16 from Late Latin *illātīvus* inferring, concluding] > ilˈlatively *adv*

Illawarra (ˌɪləˈwɒrə) *n* **1** a coastal district of E Australia, in S New South Wales. Pop: 404 626 (2002 est) **2** an Australian breed of shorthorn dairy cattle noted for its high milk yield and ability to survive on poor pastures

ill-behaved *adj* poorly behaved; lacking good manners

ill-bred *adj* badly brought up; lacking good manners > ˌill-ˈbreeding *n*

ill-considered *adj* done without due consideration; not thought out: *an ill-considered decision*

ill-defined *adj* imperfectly defined; having no clear outline

ill-disposed *adj* (often foll by *towards*) not kindly disposed

Ille-et-Vilaine (*French* ilevilɛn) *n* a department of NW France, in E Brittany. Capital: Rennes. Pop: 894 625 (2003 est). Area: 6992 sq km (2727 sq miles)

illegal (ɪˈliːgəl) *adj* **1** forbidden by law; unlawful; illicit **2** unauthorized or prohibited by a code of official or accepted rules ▷ *n* **3** a person who has entered or attempted to enter a country illegally > ilˈlegally *adv* > ˌille'gality *n*

illegalize *or* **illegalise** (ɪˈliːgəˌlaɪz) *vb* (*tr*) to make illegal > ilˌlegaliˈzation *or* ilˌlegaliˈsation *n*

illegible (ɪˈlɛdʒɪbəl) *adj* unable to be read or deciphered > ilˌlegiˈbility *or* ilˈlegibleness *n* > ilˈlegibly *adv*

illegitimate (ˌɪlɪˈdʒɪtɪmɪt) *adj* **1** born of parents who were not married to each other at the time of birth; bastard **2** forbidden by law; illegal; unlawful **3** contrary to logic; incorrectly reasoned ▷ *n* **4** an illegitimate person; bastard > ˌilleˈgitimacy *or* ˌilleˈgitimateness *n* > ˌilleˈgitimately *adv*

ill-fated *adj* doomed or unlucky: *an ill-fated marriage*

ill-favoured *or US* **ill-favored** *adj* **1** unattractive or repulsive in appearance; ugly **2** offensive, disagreeable, or objectionable > ˌill-ˈfavouredly *or US* ˌill-ˈfavoredly *adv* > ˌill-ˈfavouredness *or US* ˌill-ˈfavoredness *n*

ill feeling *n* hostile feeling; animosity

ill-founded *adj* not founded on true or reliable premises; unsubstantiated: *an ill-founded rumour*

ill-gotten *adj* obtained dishonestly or illegally (esp in the phrase **ill-gotten gains**)

ill humour *n* a disagreeable or sullen mood; bad temper > ill-ˈhumoured *adj* > ˌill-ˈhumouredly *adv*

illiberal (ɪˈlɪbərəl) *adj* **1** narrow-minded; prejudiced; bigoted; intolerant **2** not generous; mean **3** lacking in culture or refinement > ilˌliberˈality, ilˈliberalness *or* ilˈliberalism *n* > ilˈliberally *adv*

illicit (ɪˈlɪsɪt) *adj* **1** another word for **illegal** **2** not allowed or approved by common custom, rule, or standard: *illicit sexual relations* > ilˈlicitly *adv* > ilˈlicitness *n*

Illimani (*Spanish* iʎiˈmani) *n* a mountain in W Bolivia, in the Andes near La Paz. Height: 6882 m (22 580 ft)

illimitable (ɪˈlɪmɪtəbəl) *adj* limitless; boundless > ilˌlimitaˈbility *or* ilˈlimitableness *n* > ilˈlimitably *adv*

illinium (ɪˈlɪnɪəm) *n chem* the former name for **promethium** [C20 New Latin, from ILLINOIS + -IUM]

Illinois (ˌɪlɪˈnɔɪ) *n* **1** a state of the N central US, in the Midwest: consists of level prairie crossed by the Illinois and Kaskaskia Rivers; mainly agricultural. Capital: Springfield. Pop: 12 653 544 (2003 est). Area: 144 858 sq km (55 930 sq miles). Abbreviations: Ill, (with zip code) IL **2** a river in Illinois, flowing SW to the Mississippi. Length: 439 km (273 miles)

Illinoisan (ˌɪlɪˈnɔɪən), **Illinoian** (ˌɪlɪˈnɔɪən) *or* **Illinoisian** (ˌɪlɪˈnɔɪzɪən) *n* **1** a native or inhabitant of Illinois ▷ *adj* **2** of or relating to Illinois or its inhabitants

illiquid (ɪˈlɪkwɪd) *adj* **1** (of an asset) not easily convertible into cash **2** (of an enterprise, organization, etc) deficient in liquid assets

illite (ˈɪlaɪt) *n* a clay mineral of the mica group, found in shales and mudstones. Crystal structure: monoclinic. Formula: $K_{1-1.5}Al_4(Si_{6.5-7}Al_{1-1.5}O_{20})(OH)_4$ [C20 named after ILLINOIS, where it was first found]

illiterate (ɪˈlɪtərɪt) *adj* **1** unable to read and write **2** violating accepted standards in reading and writing: *an illiterate scrawl* **3** uneducated, ignorant, or uncultured: *scientifically illiterate* ▷ *n* **4** an illiterate person > ilˈliteracy *or* ilˈliterateness *n* > ilˈliterately *adv*

ill-judged *adj* rash; ill-advised

ill-mannered *adj* having bad manners; rude; impolite > ˌill-ˈmanneredly *adv*

ill-natured *adj* naturally unpleasant and mean > ˌill-ˈnaturedly *adv* > ˌill-ˈnaturedness *n*

illness (ˈɪlnɪs) *n* **1** a disease or indisposition; sickness **2** a state of ill health **3** *obsolete* wickedness

illocution (ˌɪləˈkjuːʃən) *n philosophy* an act performed by a speaker by virtue of uttering certain words, as for example the acts of promising or of threatening. Also called: illocutionary act See also **performative** Compare **perlocution** [C20 from IL- + LOCUTION] > ˌilloˈcutionary *adj*

illogic (ɪˈlɒdʒɪk) *n* reasoning characterized by lack of logic; illogicality

illogical (ɪˈlɒdʒɪkəl) *adj* **1** characterized by lack of logic; senseless or unreasonable **2** disregarding logical principles > illogicality (ɪˌlɒdʒɪˈkælɪtɪ) *or* ilˈlogicalness *n* > ilˈlogically *adv*

ill-omened *adj* doomed to be unlucky; ill-fated

ill-sorted *adj* badly arranged or matched; ill-assorted

ill-starred *adj* unlucky; unfortunate; ill-fated

ill temper *n* bad temper; irritability

ill-tempered *adj* showing bad temper; irritable > ˌill-ˈtemperedly *adv*

ill-timed *adj* occurring at or planned for an unsuitable time

ill-treat *vb* (*tr*) to behave cruelly or harshly towards; misuse; maltreat > ˌill-ˈtreatment *n*

illude (ɪ'lu:d) *vb literary* to trick or deceive [c15 from Latin *illūdere* to sport with, from *lūdus* game]

illume (ɪ'lu:m) *vb* (*tr*) a poetic word for **illuminate** [c17 shortened from ILLUMINE]

illuminance (ɪ'lu:mɪnəns) *n* the luminous flux incident on unit area of a surface. It is measured in lux. Symbol: E^v Sometimes called: **illumination** Compare **irradiance**

illuminant (ɪ'lu:mɪnənt) *n* **1** something that provides or gives off light ▷ *adj* **2** giving off light; illuminating

illuminate *vb* (ɪ'lu:mɪ,neɪt) **1** (*tr*) to throw light in or into; light up: *to illuminate a room* **2** (*tr*) to make easily understood; clarify **3** to adorn, decorate, or be decorated with lights **4** (*tr*) to decorate (a letter, page, etc) by the application of colours, gold, or silver **5** (*intr*) to become lighted up ▷ *adj* (ɪ'lu:mɪnɪt, -,neɪt) **6** *archaic* made clear or bright with light; illuminated ▷ *n* (ɪ'lu:mɪnɪt, -,neɪt) **7** a person who has or claims to have special enlightenment [c16 from Latin *illūmināre* to light up, from *lūmen* light] > il'lumi,native *adj* > il'lumi,nator *n*

illuminati (ɪ,lu:mɪ'nɑ:ti:) *pl n, sing* **-to** (-təʊ) a group of persons claiming exceptional enlightenment on some subject, esp religion [c16 from Latin, literally: the enlightened ones, from *illūmināre* to ILLUMINATE]

Illuminati (ɪ,lu:mɪ'nɑ:ti:) *pl n, sing* **-to** (-təʊ) **1** any of several groups of illuminati, esp in 18th-century France **2** a group of religious enthusiasts of 16th-century Spain who were persecuted by the Inquisition **3** a masonic sect founded in Bavaria in 1778 claiming that the illuminating grace of Christ resided in it alone **4** a rare name for the Rosicrucians

illuminating (ɪ'lu:mɪ,neɪtɪŋ) *adj* serving to inform or clarify; instructive > il'lumi,natingly *adv*

illumination (ɪ,lu:mɪ'neɪʃən) *n* **1** the act of illuminating or the state of being illuminated **2** a source of light **3** (*often plural*) *chiefly Brit* a light or lights, esp coloured lights, used as decoration in streets, parks, etc **4** spiritual or intellectual enlightenment; insight or understanding **5** the act of making understood; clarification **6** decoration in colours, gold, or silver used on some manuscripts or printed works **7** *physics* another name (not in technical usage) for **illuminance** > il,lumi'national *adj*

illumine (ɪ'lu:mɪn) *vb* a literary word for **illuminate** [c14 from Latin *illūmināre* to make light; see ILLUMINATE] > il'luminable *adj*

illuminism (ɪ'lu:mɪ,nɪzəm) *n* **1** belief in and advocation of special enlightenment **2** the tenets and principles of the Illuminati or of any of several religious or political movements initiated by them > il'luminist *n*

ill-use *vb* ('ɪl'ju:z) **1** to use badly or cruelly; abuse; maltreat ▷ *n* ('ɪl'ju:s) *also* **ill-usage 2** harsh or cruel treatment; abuse

illusion (ɪ'lu:ʒən) *n* **1** a false appearance or deceptive impression of reality: *the mirror gives an illusion of depth* **2** a false or misleading perception or belief; delusion: *he has the illusion that he is really clever* **3** *psychol* a perception that is not true to reality, having been altered subjectively in some way in the mind of the perceiver. See also **hallucination 4** a very fine gauze or tulle used for trimmings, veils, etc [c14 from Latin *illūsiō* deceit, from *illūdere*; see ILLUDE] > il'lusionary *or* il'lusional *adj* > il'lusioned *adj*

illusionism (ɪ'lu:ʒə,nɪzəm) *n* **1** *philosophy* the doctrine that the external world exists only in illusory sense perceptions **2** the use of highly illusory effects in art or decoration, esp the use of perspective in painting to create an impression of three-dimensional reality

illusionist (ɪ'lu:ʒənɪst) *n* **1** a person given to illusions; visionary; dreamer **2** *philosophy* a person who believes in illusionism **3** an artist who practises illusionism **4** a conjuror; magician > il,lusion'istic *adj*

illusory (ɪ'lu:sərɪ) *or* **illusive** (ɪ'lu:sɪv) *adj* producing, produced by, or based on illusion; deceptive or unreal > il'lusorily *or* il'lusively *adv* > il'lusoriness *or* il'lusiveness *n*

▊ USAGE *Illusive* is sometimes wrongly used where *elusive* is meant: *they fought hard, but victory remained elusive* (not *illusive*)

illust. *or* **illus.** *abbreviation for* **1** illustrated **2** illustration

illustrate ('ɪlə,streɪt) *vb* **1** to clarify or explain by use of examples, analogy, etc **2** (*tr*) to be an example or demonstration of **3** (*tr*) to explain or decorate (a book, text, etc) with pictures **4** (*tr*) an archaic word for **enlighten** [c16 from Latin *illustrāre* to make light, explain, from *lustrāre* to purify, brighten; see LUSTRUM] > 'illus,tratable *adj* > 'illus,trative *adj* > 'illus,tratively *adv* > 'illus,trator *n*

illustration (,ɪlə'streɪʃən) *n* **1** pictorial matter used to explain or decorate a text **2** an example or demonstration: *an illustration of his ability* **3** the act of illustrating or the state of being illustrated > ,illus'trational *adj*

illustrious (ɪ'lʌstrɪəs) *adj* **1** of great renown; famous and distinguished **2** glorious or great: *illustrious deeds* **3** *obsolete* shining [c16 from Latin *illustris* bright, distinguished, famous, from *illustrāre* to make light; see ILLUSTRATE] > il'lustriously *adv* > il'lustriousness *n*

illuviation (ɪ,lu:vɪ'eɪʃən) *n* the process by which a material (**illuvium**), which includes colloids and mineral salts, is washed down from one layer of soil to a lower layer [c20 from Latin *illuviēs* dirt, mud, from IL- + -*luviēs*, from *lavere* to wash] > il'luvial *adj*

ill will *n* hostile feeling; enmity; antagonism

Illyria (ɪ'lɪərɪə) *n* an ancient region of uncertain boundaries on the E shore of the Adriatic Sea, including parts of present-day Croatia, Montenegro, and Albania

Illyrian (ɪ'lɪərɪən) *n* **1** a member of the group of related Indo-European peoples who occupied Illyria from the late third millennium to the early first millennium BC **2** the extinct and almost unrecorded language of these peoples: of uncertain relationship within the Indo-European family, but thought by some to be the ancestor of modern Albanian ▷ *adj* **3** of, characteristic of, or relating to Illyria, its people, or their language

Illyricum (ɪ'lɪərɪkəm) *n* a Roman province founded after 168 BC, based on the coastal area of Illyria

Ilmen ('ɪlmən) *n* **Lake** a lake in NW Russia, in the Novgorod Region: drains through the Volkhov River into Lake Ladoga. Area: between 780 sq km (300 sq miles) and 2200 sq km (850 sq miles), according to the season

ilmenite ('ɪlmɪ,naɪt) *n* a black mineral found in igneous rocks as layered deposits and in veins. It is the chief source of titanium. Composition: iron titanium oxide. Formula: $FeTiO_3$. Crystal structure: hexagonal (rhombohedral) [c19 from *Ilmen*, mountain range in the southern Urals, Russia, + -ITE[1]]

ILO *abbreviation for* **International Labour Organisation**

Iloilo (,i:ləʊ'i:ləʊ) *n* a port in the W central Philippines, on SE Panay Island. Pop: 408 000 (2005 est)

Ilorin (ɪ'lɒrɪn) *n* a city in W Nigeria, capital of Kwara state: agricultural trade centre. Pop: 714 000 (2005 est)

ILR (in Britain) *abbreviation for* Independent Local Radio

ILS *aeronautics abbreviation for* instrument landing system

ILU *text messaging abbreviation for* I love you

im *the internet domain name for* Isle of Man

IM *abbreviation for* **1** Also: i.m. intramuscular **2** *chess* **International Master 3** *computing* instant messaging

I'm (aɪm) *contraction of* I am

im- *prefix* a variant of **in-**[1] and **in-**[2] before *b, m,* and *p*

image ('ɪmɪdʒ) *n* **1** a representation or likeness of a person or thing, esp in sculpture **2** an optically formed reproduction of an object, such as one formed by a lens or mirror **3** a person or thing that resembles another closely; double or copy **4** a mental representation or picture; idea produced by the imagination **5** the personality presented to the public by a person, organization, etc: *a criminal charge is not good for a politician's image*. See also **corporate image 6** the pattern of light that is focused on to the retina of the eye **7** *psychol* the mental experience of something that is not immediately present to the senses, often involving memory. See also **imagery, body image, hypnagogic image 8** a personification of a specified quality; epitome: *the image of good breeding* **9** a mental picture or association of ideas evoked in a literary work, esp in poetry **10** a figure of speech, such as a simile or metaphor **11** *maths* **a** (of a point) the value of a function, f(*x*), corresponding to the point *x* **b** the range of a function **12** an obsolete word for **apparition** ▷ *vb* (*tr*) **13** to picture in the mind; imagine **14** to make or reflect an image of **15** *computing* to project or display on a screen or visual display unit **16** to portray or describe **17** to be an example or epitome of; typify [c13 from Old French *imagene,* from Latin *imāgō* copy, representation; related to Latin *imitārī* to IMITATE] > 'imageable *adj* > 'imageless *adj*

image converter *or* **tube** *n* a device for producing a visual image formed by other electromagnetic radiation such as infrared or ultraviolet radiation or X-rays

image enhancement *n* a method of improving the definition of a video picture by a computer program, which reduces the lowest grey values to black and the highest to white: used for pictures from microscopes, surveillance cameras, and scanners

image intensifier *or* **tube** *n* any of various devices for amplifying the intensity of an optical image, sometimes used in conjunction with an image converter

image orthicon *n* a television camera tube in which electrons, emitted from a photoemissive surface in proportion to the intensity of the incident light, are focused onto the target causing secondary emission of electrons

image printer *n computing* a printer which uses optical technology to produce an image of a complete page from digital input

image processing *n* the manipulation or modification of a digitized image, esp in order to enhance its quality

imager ('ɪmɪdʒə) *n* an electronic device that records images: *a thermal imager*

imagery ('ɪmɪdʒrɪ, -dʒərɪ) *n, pl* **-ries 1** figurative or descriptive language in a literary work **2** images collectively **3** *psychol* **a** the materials or general processes of the imagination **b** the characteristic kind of mental images formed by a particular individual. See also **image** (sense 7), **imagination** (sense 1) **4** *military* the presentation of objects reproduced photographically (by infrared or electronic means) as prints or electronic displays

image tube *n* another name for **image converter** *or* **image intensifier**

imaginal (ɪ'mædʒɪnªl) *adj* **1** of, relating to, or resembling an imago **2** of or relating to an image

imaginary (ɪ'mædʒɪnərɪ, -dʒɪnrɪ) *adj* **1** existing in the imagination; unreal; illusory **2** *maths* involving or containing imaginary numbers. The imaginary part of a complex number, *z*, is usually written Imz > im'aginarily *adv* > im'aginariness *n*

imaginary number *n* any complex number of the form i*b*, where i = √−1

imaginary part *n* the coefficient *b* in a complex number *a* + i*b*, where i = √−1

imagination (ɪˌmædʒɪˈneɪʃən) *n* **1** the faculty or action of producing ideas, esp mental images of what is not present or has not been experienced **2** mental creative ability **3** the ability to deal resourcefully with unexpected or unusual problems, circumstances, etc **4** (in romantic literary criticism, esp that of S. T. Coleridge) a creative act of perception that joins passive and active elements in thinking and imposes unity on the poetic material. Compare **fancy** (sense 9) ▷ imˌagiˈnational *adj*

imaginative (ɪˈmædʒɪnətɪv) *adj* **1** produced by or indicative of a vivid or creative imagination: *an imaginative story* **2** having a vivid imagination ▷ imˈaginatively *adv* ▷ imˈaginativeness *n*

imagine (ɪˈmædʒɪn) *vb* **1** (when *tr, may take a clause as object*) to form a mental image of **2** (when *tr, may take a clause as object*) to think, believe, or guess **3** (*tr; takes a clause as object*) to suppose; assume: *I imagine he'll come* **4** (*tr; takes a clause as object*) to believe or assume without foundation: *he imagines he knows the whole story* **5** an archaic word for **plot¹** ▷ *sentence substitute* **6** Also: **imagine that!** an exclamation of surprise [c14 from Latin *imāginārī* to fancy, picture mentally, from *imāgō* likeness; see IMAGE] ▷ imˈaginable *adj* ▷ imˈaginably *adv* ▷ imˈaginer *n*

imagism (ˈɪmɪˌdʒɪzəm) *n* a poetic movement in England and America between 1912 and 1917, initiated chiefly by Ezra Pound, the US poet, translator, and critic (1885–1972), advocating the use of ordinary speech and the precise presentation of images ▷ ˈimagist *n, adj* ▷ ˌimagˈistic *adj* ▷ ˌimagˈistically *adv*

imago (ɪˈmeɪɡəʊ) *n, pl* **imagoes** *or* **imagines** (ɪˈmædʒəˌniːz) **1** an adult sexually mature insect produced after metamorphosis **2** *psychoanal* an idealized image of another person, usually a parent, acquired in childhood and carried in the unconscious in later life [c18 New Latin, from Latin: likeness; see IMAGE]

imam (ɪˈmɑːm) *or* **imaum** (ɪˈmɑːm, ɪˈmɔːm) *n Islam* **1** a leader of congregational prayer in a mosque **2** a caliph, as leader of a Muslim community **3** an honorific title applied to eminent doctors of Islam, such as the founders of the orthodox schools **4** any of a succession of either seven or twelve religious leaders of the Shiites, regarded by their followers as divinely inspired [c17 from Arabic: leader, from *amma* he guided]

imamate (ɪˈmɑːmeɪt) *n Islam* **1** the region or territory governed by an imam **2** the office, rank, or period of office of an imam

IMAP (ˈaɪˌmæp) *abbreviation for* **a** Internet Message Access Protocol: a way of accessing e-mail messages which are held on an internet server, rather than on an individual's computer **b** (*as modifier*): *an IMAP account/server*

IMarE *abbreviation for* Institute of Marine Engineers

imaret (ɪˈmɑːrɛt) *n* (in Turkey) a hospice for pilgrims or travellers [c17 from Turkish, from Arabic *ʿimārah* hospice, building, from *amara* he built]

IMAX (ˈaɪmæks) *n trademark* a process of film projection using a giant screen on which an image approximately ten times larger than standard is projected [c20 from IMAGE + MAXIMUM]

imbalance (ɪmˈbæləns) *n* a lack of balance, as in emphasis, proportion, etc: *the political imbalance of the programme*

imbecile (ˈɪmbɪˌsiːl, -ˌsaɪl) *n* **1** *psychol* a person of very low intelligence (IQ of 25 to 50), usually capable only of guarding himself against danger and of performing simple mechanical tasks under supervision **2** *informal* an extremely stupid person; dolt ▷ *adj also* **imbecilic** (ˌɪmbɪˈsɪlɪk) **3** of or like an imbecile; mentally deficient; feeble-minded **4** stupid or senseless: *an imbecile thing to do* [c16 from Latin *imbēcillus* feeble (physically or mentally)] ▷ ˈimbeˌcilely *or* ˌimbeˈcilically *adv* ▷ ˌimbeˈcility *n*

imbed (ɪmˈbɛd) *vb* -beds, -bedding, -bedded a less common spelling of **embed**

imbibe (ɪmˈbaɪb) *vb* **1** to drink (esp alcoholic drinks) **2** *literary* to take in or assimilate (ideas, facts, etc): *to imbibe the spirit of the Renaissance* **3** (*tr*) to take in as if by drinking: *to imbibe fresh air* **4** to absorb or cause to absorb liquid or moisture; assimilate or saturate [c14 from Latin *imbibere*, from *bibere* to drink] ▷ imˈbiber *n*

imbibition (ˌɪmbɪˈbɪʃən) *n* **1** *chem* the absorption or adsorption of a liquid by a gel or solid **2** *photog* the absorption of dyes by gelatine, used in some colour printing processes **3** *obsolete* the act of imbibing

imbizo (ɪmˈbiːzɒ) *n, pl* -zos *South African* a meeting, esp a gathering of the Zulu people called by the king or a traditional leader [from Zulu *biza* to call or summon]

Imbolc *or* **Imbolg** (ˈɪmbəlk, ˈɪmbəʊlk, ˈɪmmələk) *n* an ancient Celtic festival associated with the goddess Brigit, held on Feb 1 or 2 to mark the beginning of spring. It is also celebrated by modern pagans [c15 from Old Irish *oimelc* ewe's milk]

imbricate *adj* (ˈɪmbrɪkɪt, -ˌkeɪt) *also* **imbricated 1** *architect* relating to or having tiles, shingles, or slates that overlap **2** *botany* (of leaves, scales, etc) overlapping each other ▷ *vb* (ˈɪmbrɪˌkeɪt) **3** (*tr*) to decorate with a repeating pattern resembling scales or overlapping tiles [c17 from Latin *imbricāre* to cover with overlapping tiles, from *imbrex* pantile] ▷ ˈimbricately *adv* ▷ ˌimbriˈcation *n*

imbroglio (ɪmˈbrəʊlɪˌəʊ) *n, pl* -glios **1** a confused or perplexing political or interpersonal situation **2** *obsolete* a confused heap; jumble [c18 from Italian, from *imbrogliare* to confuse, EMBROIL]

Imbros (ˈɪmbrɒs) *n* a Turkish island in the NE Aegean Sea, west of the Gallipoli Peninsula: occupied by Greece (1912–14) and Britain (1914–23). Area: 280 sq km (108 sq miles). Turkish name: Imroz

imbrue *or* **embrue** (ɪmˈbruː) *vb* -brues, -bruing, -brued (*tr*) *rare* **1** to stain, esp with blood **2** to permeate or impregnate [c15 from Old French *embreuver*, from Latin *imbibere* IMBIBE] ▷ imˈbruement *or* emˈbruement *n*

imbue (ɪmˈbjuː) *vb* -bues, -buing, -bued (*tr; usually foll by with*) **1** to instil or inspire (with ideals, principles, etc): *his sermons were imbued with the spirit of the Reformation* **2** *rare* to soak, esp with moisture, dye, etc [c16 from Latin *imbuere* to stain, accustom] ▷ imˈbuement *n*

IMCO *abbreviation for* Intergovernmental Maritime Consultative Organization: the department of the United Nations concerned with international maritime safety, antipollution regulations, etc

IMechE *abbreviation for* Institution of Mechanical Engineers

IMF *abbreviation for* **International Monetary Fund**

IMHO *text messaging abbreviation for* in my humble or honest opinion

imidazole (ˌɪmɪdˈæzəʊl, -ɪdəˈzəʊl) *n* **1** Also called: glyoxaline, iminazole a white crystalline basic heterocyclic compound; 1,3-diazole. Formula: $C_3H_4N_2$ **2** any substituted derivative of this compound [c19 from IMIDE + AZOLE]

imide (ˈɪmaɪd) *n* any of a class of organic compounds whose molecules contain the divalent group -CONHCO- [c19 alteration of AMIDE] ▷ imidic (ɪˈmɪdɪk) *adj*

imine (ɪˈmiːn, ˈɪmiːn) *n* any of a class of organic compounds in which a nitrogen atom is bound to one hydrogen atom and to two alkyl or aryl groups. They contain the divalent group NH [c19 alteration of AMINE]

IMinE *abbreviation for* Institution of Mining Engineers

iminourea (ɪˌmiːnəʊjʊəˈrɪə) *n* another name for **guanidine**

imipramine (ɪˈmɪprəˌmiːn) *n* a tricyclic antidepressant drug. Formula: $C_{19}H_{24}N_2$ [c20 from IMI(DE) + PR(OPYL) + AMINE]

imitate (ˈɪmɪˌteɪt) *vb* (*tr*) **1** to try to follow the manner, style, character, etc, of or take as a model: *many writers imitated the language of Shakespeare* **2** to pretend to be or to impersonate, esp for humour; mimic **3** to make a copy or reproduction of; duplicate; counterfeit **4** to make or be like; resemble or simulate: *her achievements in politics imitated her earlier successes in business* [c16 from Latin *imitārī*; see IMAGE] ▷ ˈimitable *adj* ▷ ˌimitaˈbility *or* ˈimitableness *n* ▷ ˈimiˌtator *n*

imitation (ˌɪmɪˈteɪʃən) *n* **1** the act, practice, or art of imitating; mimicry **2** an instance or product of imitating, such as a copy of the manner of a person; impression **3 a** a copy or reproduction of a genuine article; counterfeit **b** (*as modifier*): *imitation jewellery* **4** (in contrapuntal or polyphonic music) the repetition of a phrase or figure in one part after its appearance in another, as in a fugue **5** a literary composition that adapts the style of an older work to the writer's own purposes ▷ ˌimiˈtational *adj*

imitative (ˈɪmɪtətɪv) *adj* **1** imitating or tending to imitate or copy **2** characterized by imitation **3** copying or reproducing the features of an original, esp in an inferior manner: *imitative painting* **4** another word for **onomatopoeic** ▷ ˈimitatively *adv* ▷ ˈimitativeness *n*

Imittós (ˌɪmiˈtɒs) *n* a transliteration of the Modern Greek name for **Hymettus**

immaculate (ɪˈmækjʊlɪt) *adj* **1** completely clean; extremely tidy: *his clothes were immaculate* **2** completely flawless, etc: *an immaculate rendering of the symphony* **3** morally pure; free from sin or corruption **4** *biology* of only one colour, with no spots or markings [c15 from Latin *immaculātus*, from IM- (not) + *macula* blemish] ▷ imˈmaculacy *or* imˈmaculateness *n* ▷ imˈmaculately *adv*

Immaculate Conception *n Christian theol, RC Church* the doctrine that the Virgin Mary was conceived without any stain of original sin

immanent (ˈɪmənənt) *adj* **1** existing, operating, or remaining within; inherent **2** of or relating to the pantheistic conception of God, as being present throughout the universe. Compare **transcendent** (sense 3) [c16 from Latin *immanēre* to remain in, from IM- (in) + *manēre* to stay] ▷ ˈimmanence *or* ˈimmanency *n* ▷ ˈimmanently *adv*

immanentism (ˈɪmənənˌtɪzəm) *n* belief in the immanence of God ▷ ˈimmanentist *n*

Immanuel *or* **Emmanuel** (ɪˈmænjʊəl) *n Bible* the child whose birth was foretold by Isaiah (Isaiah 7:14) and who in Christian tradition is identified with Jesus [from Hebrew *ʿimmānūʾel*, literally: God with us]

immaterial (ˌɪməˈtɪərɪəl) *adj* **1** of no real importance; inconsequential **2** not formed of matter; incorporeal; spiritual ▷ ˌimmaˌteriˈality *or* ˌimmaˈterialness *n* ▷ ˌimmaˈterially *adv*

immaterialism (ˌɪməˈtɪərɪəˌlɪzəm) *n philosophy* **1** the doctrine that the material world exists only in the mind **2** the doctrine that only immaterial substances or spiritual beings exist. See also **idealism** (sense 3) ▷ ˌimmaˈterialist *n*

immaterialize *or* **immaterialise** (ˌɪməˈtɪərɪəˌlaɪz) *vb* (*tr*) to make immaterial

immature (ˌɪməˈtjʊə, -ˈtʃʊə) *adj* **1** not fully grown or developed **2** deficient in maturity; lacking wisdom, insight, emotional stability, etc **3** *geography* another common term for **youthful** (sense 4) ▷ ˌimmaˈturity *or* ˌimmaˈtureness *n* ▷ ˌimmaˈturely *adv*

immeasurable (ɪˈmɛʒərəbᵊl) *adj* incapable of being measured, esp by virtue of great size; limitless ▷ imˌmeasuraˈbility *or* imˈmeasurableness *n* ▷ imˈmeasurably *adv*

immediate (ɪˈmiːdɪət) *adj* (*usually prenominal*) **1** taking place or accomplished without delay: *an immediate reaction* **2** closest or most direct in effect or relationship: *the immediate cause of his downfall* **3** having no intervening medium; direct in effect: *an immediate influence* **4** contiguous in space, time, or relationship: *our immediate neighbour* **5** present;

i

current: *the immediate problem is food* **6** *philosophy* of or relating to an object or concept that is directly known or intuited **7** *logic* (of an inference) deriving its conclusion from a single premise, esp by conversion or obversion of a categorial statement [c16 from Medieval Latin *immediātus*, from Latin IM- (not) + *mediāre* to be in the middle; see MEDIATE] > im'mediacy *or* im'mediateness *n*

immediate annuity *n* an annuity that starts less than a year after its purchase. Compare **deferred annuity**

immediate constituent *n* a constituent of a linguistic construction at the first step in an analysis; for example, the immediate constituents of a sentence are the subject and the predicate

immediately (ɪ'miːdɪətlɪ) *adv* **1** without delay or intervention; at once; instantly: *it happened immediately* **2** very closely or directly: *this immediately concerns you* **3** near or close by: *he's somewhere immediately in this area* ▷ *conj* **4** (*subordinating*) *chiefly Brit* at the same time as; as soon as: *immediately he opened the door, there was a gust of wind*

immedicable (ɪ'mɛdɪkəbəl) *adj* (of wounds) unresponsive to treatment > im'medicableness *n* > im'medicably *adv*

Immelmann turn *or* **Immelmann** ('ɪməl,mɑːn, -mən) *n* an aircraft manoeuvre used to gain height while reversing the direction of flight. It consists of a half loop followed by a half roll [c20 named after Max *Immelmann* (1890–1916), German aviator]

immemorial (,ɪmɪ'mɔːrɪəl) *adj* originating in the distant past; ancient (postpositive in the phrase **time immemorial**) [c17 from Medieval Latin *immemoriālis*, from Latin IM- (not) + *memoria* MEMORY] > ,imme'morially *adv*

immense (ɪ'mɛns) *adj* **1** unusually large; huge; vast **2** without limits; immeasurable **3** *informal* very good; excellent [c15 from Latin *immensus*, literally: unmeasured, from IM- (not) + *mensus* measured, from *mētīrī* to measure] > im'mensely *adv* > im'menseness *n*

immensity (ɪ'mɛnsɪtɪ) *n, pl* -ties **1** the state or quality of being immense; vastness; enormity **2** enormous expanse, distance, or volume: *the immensity of space* **3** *informal* a huge amount: *an immensity of wealth*

immensurable (ɪ'mɛnʃərəbəl) *adj* a less common word for **immeasurable**

immerge (ɪ'mɜːdʒ) *vb* an archaic word for **immerse** [c17 from Latin *immergere* to IMMERSE] > im'mergence *n*

immerse (ɪ'mɜːs) *vb* (*tr*) **1** (often foll by *in*) to plunge or dip into liquid **2** (often foll by *in*) to involve deeply; engross: *to immerse oneself in a problem* **3** to baptize by immersion [c17 from Latin *immergere*, from IM- (in) + *mergere* to dip] > im'mersible *adj*

immersed (ɪ'mɜːst) *adj* **1** sunk or submerged **2** (of plants) growing completely submerged in water **3** (of a plant or animal organ) embedded in another organ or part **4** involved deeply; engrossed

immerser (ɪ'mɜːsə) *n* an informal term for **immersion heater**

immersion (ɪ'mɜːʃən) *n* **1** a form of baptism in which part or the whole of a person's body is submerged in the water **2** Also called: ingress *astronomy* the disappearance of a celestial body prior to an eclipse or occultation **3** the act of immersing or state of being immersed

immersion heater *n* an electrical device, usually thermostatically controlled, for heating the liquid in which it is immersed, esp as a fixture in a domestic hot-water tank

immersionism (ɪ'mɜːʃə,nɪzəm) *n* the doctrine that immersion is the only true and valid form of Christian baptism > im'mersionist *n*

immersive (ɪ'mɜːsɪv) *adj* providing information or stimulation for a number of senses, not only

sight and sound: *immersive television sets*

immesh (ɪ'mɛʃ) *vb* a variant of **enmesh**

immethodical (,ɪmɪ'θɒdɪkəl) *adj* lacking in method or planning; disorganized > ,imme'thodically *adv* > ,imme'thodicalness *n*

immigrant ('ɪmɪɡrənt) *n* **1 a** a person who immigrates. Compare **emigrant b** (*as modifier*): *an immigrant community* **2** *Brit* a person who has been settled in a country of which he is not a native for less than ten years **3** an animal or plant that lives or grows in a region to which it has recently migrated

immigrate ('ɪmɪ,ɡreɪt) *vb* **1** (*intr*) to come to a place or country of which one is not a native in order to settle there. Compare **emigrate 2** (*intr*) (of an animal or plant) to migrate to a new geographical area **3** (*tr*) to introduce or bring in as an immigrant [c17 from Latin *immigrāre* to go into, from IM- + *migrāre* to move] > 'immi,gratory *adj* > 'immi,grator *n*

immigration (,ɪmɪ'ɡreɪʃən) *n* **1** the movement of non-native people into a country in order to settle there **2** the part of a port, airport, etc where government employees examine the passports, visas, etc of foreign nationals entering the country > ,immi'grational *adj*

imminent ('ɪmɪnənt) *adj* **1** liable to happen soon; impending **2** *obsolete* jutting out or overhanging [c16 from Latin *imminēre* to project over, from IM- (in) + *-minēre* to project; related to *mons* mountain] > 'imminence *or* 'imminentness *n* > 'imminently *adv*

Immingham ('ɪmɪŋəm) *n* a port in NE England, in North East Lincolnshire unitary authority, Lincolnshire: docks opened in 1912, principally for the exporting of coal; now handles chiefly bulk materials, esp imported iron ore. Pop: 11 090 (2001)

immingle (ɪ'mɪŋɡəl) *vb archaic* to blend or mix together; intermingle

immiscible (ɪ'mɪsɪbəl) *adj* (of two or more liquids) incapable of being mixed to form a homogeneous substance: *oil and water are immiscible* > im,misci'bility *n* > im'miscibly *adv*

immitigable (ɪ'mɪtɪɡəbəl) *adj rare* unable to be mitigated; relentless; unappeasable > im'mitigably *adv* > im,mitiga'bility *n*

immix (ɪ'mɪks) *vb* (*tr*) *archaic* to mix in; commix > im'mixture *n*

immobile (ɪ'məʊbaɪl) *adj* **1** not moving; motionless **2** not able to move or be moved; fixed > immobility (,ɪməʊ'bɪlɪtɪ) *n*

immobilism (ɪ'məʊbɪ,lɪzəm) *n* a political policy characterized by inertia and antipathy to change

immobilize *or* **immobilise** (ɪ'məʊbɪ,laɪz) *vb* (*tr*) **1** to make or become immobile: *to immobilize a car* **2** *finance* **a** to remove (specie) from circulation and hold it as a reserve **b** to convert (circulating capital) into fixed capital > im,mobili'zation *or* im,mobili'sation *n* > im'mobi,lizer *or* im'mobi,liser *n*

immoderate (ɪ'mɒdərɪt, ɪ'mɒdrɪt) *adj* **1** lacking in moderation; excessive: *immoderate demands* **2** *obsolete* venial; intemperate: *immoderate habits* > im'moderately *adv* > im,moder'ation *or* im'moderateness *n*

immodest (ɪ'mɒdɪst) *adj* **1** indecent, esp with regard to sexual propriety; improper **2** bold, impudent, or shameless > im'modestly *adv* > im'modesty *n*

immolate ('ɪməʊ,leɪt) *vb* (*tr*) **1** to kill or offer as a sacrifice, esp by fire **2** *literary* to sacrifice (something highly valued) [c16 from Latin *immolāre* to sprinkle an offering with sacrificial meal, sacrifice, from IM- (in) + *mola* spelt grain; see MILL[1]] > immo'lation *n* > 'immo,lator *n*

immoral (ɪ'mɒrəl) *adj* **1** transgressing accepted moral rules; corrupt **2** sexually dissolute; profligate or promiscuous **3** unscrupulous or unethical: *immoral trading* **4** tending to corrupt or resulting from corruption: *an immoral film; immoral earnings* > im'morally *adv*

immoralist (ɪ'mɒrəlɪst) *n* a person who advocates

or practises immorality

immorality (,ɪmə'rælɪtɪ) *n, pl* -ties **1** the quality, character, or state of being immoral **2** immoral behaviour, esp in sexual matters; licentiousness; profligacy or promiscuity **3** an immoral act

immortal (ɪ'mɔːtəl) *adj* **1** not subject to death or decay; having perpetual life **2** having everlasting fame; remembered throughout time **3** everlasting; perpetual; constant **4** of or relating to immortal beings or concepts ▷ *n* **5** an immortal being **6** (*often plural*) a person who is remembered enduringly, esp an author: *Dante is one of the immortals* > ,immor'tality *n* > im'mortally *adv*

immortalize *or* **immortalise** (ɪ'mɔːtə,laɪz) *vb* (*tr*) **1** to give everlasting fame to, as by treating in a literary work: *Macbeth was immortalized by Shakespeare* **2** to give immortality to **3** *biology* to cause (cells) to reproduce indefinitely > im,mortali'zation *or* im,mortali'sation *n* > im'mortal,izer *or* im'mortal,iser *n*

Immortals (ɪ'mɔːtəlz) *pl n* **1** (*sometimes not capital*) the gods of ancient Greece and Rome **2** (in ancient Persia) the royal bodyguard or a larger elite unit of 10 000 men **3** the members of the French Academy

immortelle (,ɪmɔː'tɛl) *n* any of various plants, mostly of the family *Asteraceae* (composites), that retain their colour when dried, esp *Xeranthemum annuum*. Also called: everlasting, everlasting flower [c19 from French (*fleur*) *immortelle* everlasting (flower)]

immotile (ɪ'məʊtaɪl) *adj* (esp of living organisms or their parts) not capable of moving spontaneously and independently > immotility (,ɪməʊ'tɪlɪtɪ) *n*

immovable *or* **immoveable** (ɪ'muːvəbəl) *adj* **1** unable to move or be moved; fixed; immobile **2** unable to be diverted from one's intentions; steadfast **3** unaffected by feeling; impassive **4** unchanging; unalterable **5** (of feasts, holidays, etc) occurring on the same date every year **6** *law* **a** (of property) not liable to be removed; fixed **b** of or relating to immoveables. Compare **movable** > im,mova'bility, im,movea'bility, im'movableness *or* im'moveableness *n* > im'movably *or* im'moveably *adv*

immoveables (ɪ'muːvəbəlz) *pl n* (in most foreign legal systems) real property

immune (ɪ'mjuːn) *adj* **1** protected against a specific disease by inoculation or as the result of innate or acquired resistance **2** relating to or conferring immunity: *an immune body*. See **antibody** **3** (*usually postpositive; foll by to*) unsusceptible (to) or secure (against): *immune to inflation* **4** exempt from obligation, penalty, etc ▷ *n* **5** an immune person or animal [c15 from Latin *immūnis* exempt from a public service, from IM- (not) + *mūnus* duty]

immune complex *or* **immunocomplex** ('ɪmjʊnəʊ,kɒmplɛks) *n* a complex formed between an antibody and an antigen

immune response *n* the reaction of an organism's body to foreign materials (antigens), including the production of antibodies

immunity (ɪ'mjuːnɪtɪ) *n, pl* -ties **1** the ability of an organism to resist disease, either through the activities of specialized blood cells or antibodies produced by them in response to natural exposure or inoculation (**active immunity**) or by the injection of antiserum or the transfer of antibodies from a mother to her baby via the placenta or breast milk (**passive immunity**). See also **acquired immunity, natural immunity 2** freedom from obligation or duty, esp exemption from tax, duty, legal liability, etc **3** any special privilege granting immunity **4** the exemption of ecclesiastical persons or property from various civil obligations or liabilities

immunize *or* **immunise** ('ɪmjʊ,naɪz) *vb* to make immune, esp by inoculation > ,immuni'zation *or* ,immuni'sation *n* > 'immu,nizer *or* 'immu,niser *n*

immuno- *or before a vowel* **immun-** *combining form*

indicating immunity or immune: *immunology*

immunoassay (ˌɪmjʊnəʊˈæseɪ) *n immunol* a technique of identifying a substance by its ability to bind to an antibody > ˈimmunoˌassayist *n*

immunochemistry (ˌɪmjʊnəʊˈkemɪstrɪ) *n* **1** the study of the chemical reactions of immunity **2** a method for the detection and localization of proteins and other cellular components using antibodies that specifically label the materials

immunocompetence (ˌɪmjʊnəʊˈkɒmpɪtəns) *n* the capacity of the immune system to carry out its function of distinguishing alien from endogenous material; ability of the body to resist disease

immunocompromised (ˌɪmjʊnəʊˈkɒmprəmaɪzd) *adj* having an impaired immune system and therefore incapable of an effective immune response, usually as a result of disease, such as AIDS, that damages the immune system

immunocytochemistry (ˌɪmjʊnəʊˌsaɪtəʊˈkemɪstrɪ) *n* the use of immunochemistry to study cells

immunodeficiency (ˌɪmjʊnəʊdɪˈfɪʃənsɪ) *n* a deficiency in or breakdown of a person's immune system

immunoelectrophoresis (ˌɪmjʊnəʊɪˌlektrəʊfəˈriːsɪs) *n* a technique for identifying the antigens in a blood serum, which are separated into fractions by electrophoresis

immunofluorescence (ˌɪmjʊnəʊfluəˈresəns) *n* a method used to determine the location of antibodies or antigens in which the antibodies or antigens are labelled with a fluorescent dye

immunogen (ɪˈmjuːnəʊdʒən) *n* **1** any substance that evokes an immune response **2** any substance that stimulates immunity

immunogenetics (ˌɪmjʊnəʊdʒɪˈnetɪks) *n* (*functioning as singular*) the study of the relationship between immunity and genetics > ˌimmunogeˈnetic *or* ˌimmunogeˈnetical *adj*

immunogenic (ˌɪmjʊnəʊˈdʒenɪk) *adj* causing or producing immunity or an immune response > ˌimmunoˈgenically *adv*

immunoglobulin (ˌɪmjʊnəʊˈglɒbjʊlɪn) *n* any of five classes of proteins, all of which show antibody activity. The most abundant ones are **immunoglobulin G** (**IgG**) and **immunoglobulin A** (**IgA**)

immunohistochemistry (ˌɪmjʊnəʊˌhɪstəʊˈkemɪstrɪ) *n* the use of immunochemistry to study tissues

immunological tolerance *n* the absence of antibody production in response to the presence of antigens, usually as a result of previous exposure to the antigens

immunology (ˌɪmjʊˈnɒlədʒɪ) *n* the branch of biological science concerned with the study of immunity > immunologic (ˌɪmjʊnəˈlɒdʒɪk) *or* ˌimmunoˈlogical *adj* > ˌimmunoˈlogically *adv* > ˌimmuˈnologist *n*

immunopharmacology (ˌɪmjʊnəʊsəˌfɑːməˈkɒlədʒɪ) *n* the branch of pharmacology concerned with the immune system > ˌimmunoˌpharmaˈcologist *n*

immunoreaction (ˌɪˌmjuːnəʊrɪˈækʃən) *n* the reaction between an antigen and its antibody

immunosuppression (ˌɪmjʊnəʊsəˈpreʃən) *n* medical suppression of the body's immune system, esp in order to reduce the likelihood of rejection of a transplanted organ

immunosuppressive (ˌɪmjʊnəʊsəˈpresɪv) *n* **1** any drug used for immunosuppression ▷ *adj* **2** of or relating to such a drug > ˌimmunosupˈpressant *n, adj*

immunotherapy (ˌɪmjʊnəʊˈθerəpɪ) *n med* the treatment of disease by stimulating the body's production of antibodies > immunotherapeutic (ˌɪmjʊnəʊˌθerəˈpjuːtɪk) *adj*

immure (ɪˈmjʊə) *vb* (*tr*) **1** *archaic or literary* to enclose within or as if within walls; imprison **2** to shut (oneself) away from society **3** *obsolete* to build into or enclose within a wall [c16 from Medieval Latin *immūrāre*, from Latin ɪᴍ- (in) + *mūrus* a wall] > imˈmurement *n*

immutable (ɪˈmjuːtəbəl) *adj* unchanging through time; unalterable; ageless: *immutable laws* > imˌmutaˈbility *or* imˈmutableness *n* > imˈmutably *adv*

IMNSHO *text messaging abbreviation for* in my not so humble opinion

Imo (ˈiːməʊ) *n* **a state of SE Nigeria**, formed in 1976 from part of East-Central State. Capital: Owerri. Pop: 2 779 028 (1995 est). Area: 5530 sq km (2135 sq miles)

IMO *abbreviation for* **1** *text messaging* in my opinion **2** International Maritime Organization

imp (ɪmp) *n* **1** a small demon or devil; mischievous sprite **2** a mischievous child ▷ *vb* **3** (*tr*) *falconry* to insert (new feathers) into the stumps of broken feathers in order to repair the wing of a hawk or falcon [Old English *impa* bud, graft, hence offspring, child, from *impian* to graft, ultimately from Greek *emphutos* implanted, from *emphuein* to implant, from *phuein* to plant]

imp. *abbreviation for* **1** imperative **2** imperfect **3** imperial **4** imprimatur

Imp. *abbreviation for* **1** Imperator **2** Imperatrix **3** Imperial [(for sense 1) Latin: Emperor; (for sense 2) Latin: Empress]

impact *n* (ˈɪmpækt) **1** the act of one body, object, etc, striking another; collision **2** the force with which one thing hits another or with which two objects collide **3** the impression made by an idea, cultural movement, social group, etc: *the impact of the Renaissance on Medieval Europe* ▷ *vb* (ɪmˈpækt) **4** to drive or press (an object) firmly into (another object, thing, etc) or (of two objects) to be driven or pressed firmly together **5** to have an impact or strong effect (on) [c18 from Latin *impactus* pushed against, fastened on, from *impingere* to thrust at, from *pangere* to drive in] > imˈpaction *n*

impact adhesive *n* a glue designed to give adhesion when two coated surfaces are pressed together

impacted (ɪmˈpæktɪd) *adj* **1** (of a tooth) unable to erupt, esp because of being wedged against another tooth below the gum **2** (of a fracture) having the jagged broken ends wedged into each other

impactive (ɪmˈpæktɪv) *adj* **1** of or relating to a physical impact **2** making a strong impression

impact printer *n* any printing device in which the printing surface strikes the paper, such as a traditional typewriter or a line printer. See also **non-impact printer**

impair (ɪmˈpeə) *vb* (*tr*) to reduce or weaken in strength, quality, etc: *his hearing was impaired by an accident* [c14 from Old French *empeirer* to make worse, from Late Latin *pejorāre*, from Latin *pejor* worse; see ᴘᴇᴊᴏʀᴀᴛɪᴠᴇ] > imˈpairable *adj* > imˈpairer *n* > imˈpairment *n*

impala (ɪmˈpɑːlə) *n, pl* -las *or* -la an antelope, *Aepyceros melampus*, of southern and eastern Africa, having lyre-shaped horns and able to move with enormous leaps when disturbed [from Zulu]

impale *or* **empale** (ɪmˈpeɪl) *vb* (*tr*) **1** (often foll by *on*, *upon*, or *with*) to pierce with a sharp instrument: *they impaled his severed head on a spear* **2** *archaic* to enclose with pales or fencing; fence in **3** *heraldry* to charge (a shield) with two coats of arms placed side by side [c16 from Medieval Latin *impālāre*, from Latin ɪᴍ- (in) + *pālus* ᴘᴀʟᴇ²] > imˈpalement *or* emˈpalement *n* > imˈpaler *or* emˈpaler *n*

impalpable (ɪmˈpælpəbəl) *adj* **1** imperceptible, esp to the touch: *impalpable shadows* **2** difficult to understand; abstruse > imˌpalpaˈbility *n* > imˈpalpably *adv*

impanation (ˌɪmpæˈneɪʃən) *n Christianity* the embodiment of Christ in the consecrated bread and wine of the Eucharist [c16 from Medieval Latin *impanātiō*, from *impanātus* embodied in bread, from Latin ɪᴍ- (in) + *panis* bread]

impanel (ɪmˈpænəl) *vb* -els, -elling, -elled *or US*

-els, -eling, -eled a variant spelling (esp US) of **empanel.** > imˈpanelment *n*

imparadise (ɪmˈpærədaɪs) *vb* (*tr*) **1** to make blissfully happy; enrapture **2** to make into or like paradise

imparipinnate (ˌɪmpærɪˈpɪneɪt, -ˈpɪnɪt) *adj* (of pinnate leaves) having a terminal unpaired leaflet. Compare **paripinnate**

imparisyllabic (ɪmˌpærɪsɪˈlæbɪk) *adj* (of a noun or verb in inflected languages) having inflected forms with different numbers of syllables. Compare **parisyllabic**

imparity (ɪmˈpærɪtɪ) *n, pl* -ties a less common word for **disparity** (sense 1) [c16 from Late Latin *imparitās*, from Latin *impar* unequal]

impart (ɪmˈpɑːt) *vb* (*tr*) **1** to communicate (information); relate **2** to give or bestow (something, esp an abstract quality): *to impart wisdom* [c15 from Old French *impartir*, from Latin *impertīre*, from ɪᴍ- (in) + *partīre* to share, from *pars* part] > imˈpartable *adj* > ˌimparˈtation *or* imˈpartment *n* > imˈparter *n*

impartial (ɪmˈpɑːʃəl) *adj* not prejudiced towards or against any particular side or party; fair; unbiased > imˌpartiˈality *or* imˈpartialness *n* > imˈpartially *adv*

impartible (ɪmˈpɑːtəbəl) *adj* **1** *law* (of land, an estate, etc) incapable of partition; indivisible **2** capable of being imparted > imˌpartiˈbility *n* > imˈpartibly *adv*

impassable (ɪmˈpɑːsəbəl) *adj* (of terrain, roads, etc) not able to be travelled through or over > imˌpassaˈbility *or* imˈpassableness *n* > imˈpassably *adv*

impasse (æmˈpɑːs, ˈæmpɑːs, ɪmˈpɑːs, ˈɪmpɑːs) *n* a situation in which progress is blocked; an insurmountable difficulty; stalemate; deadlock [c19 from French; see ɪᴍ-, ᴘᴀꜱꜱ]

impassible (ɪmˈpæsəbəl) *adj rare* **1** not susceptible to pain or injury **2** impassive or unmoved > imˌpassiˈbility *or* imˈpassibleness *n* > imˈpassibly *adv*

impassion (ɪmˈpæʃən) *vb* (*tr*) to arouse the passions of; inflame

impassioned (ɪmˈpæʃənd) *adj* filled with passion; fiery; inflamed: *an impassioned appeal* > imˈpassionedly *adv* > imˈpassionedness *n*

impassive (ɪmˈpæsɪv) *adj* **1** not revealing or affected by emotion; reserved **2** calm; serene; imperturbable **3** *rare* unconscious or insensible > imˈpassively *adv* > impassivity (ˌɪmpæˈsɪvɪtɪ) *n*

impaste (ɪmˈpeɪst) *vb* (*tr*) to apply paint thickly to [c16 from Italian *impastare*, from *pasta* ᴘᴀꜱᴛᴇ¹] > impastation (ˌɪmpæsˈteɪʃən) *n*

impasto (ɪmˈpæstəʊ) *n* **1** paint applied thickly, so that brush and palette knife marks are evident **2** the technique of applying paint in this way [c18 from Italian, from *impastare*; see ɪᴍᴘᴀꜱᴛᴇ]

impatience (ɪmˈpeɪʃəns) *n* **1** lack of patience; intolerance of or irritability with anything that impedes or delays **2** restless desire for change and excitement

impatiens (ɪmˈpeɪʃɪˌenz) *n, pl* -ens any balsaminaceous plant of the genus *Impatiens*, such as balsam, touch-me-not, busy Lizzie, and policeman's helmet [c18 New Latin from Latin: impatient; from the fact that the ripe pods burst open when touched]

impatient (ɪmˈpeɪʃənt) *adj* **1** lacking patience; easily irritated at delay, opposition, etc **2** exhibiting lack of patience: *an impatient retort* **3** (*postpositive*; foll by *of*) intolerant (of) or indignant (at): *impatient of indecision* **4** (*postpositive*; often foll by *for*) restlessly eager (for something or to do something) > imˈpatiently *adv*

impeach (ɪmˈpiːtʃ) *vb* (*tr*) **1** *criminal law* to bring a charge or accusation against **2** *Brit criminal law* to accuse of a crime, esp of treason or some other offence against the state **3** *chiefly US* to charge (a public official) with an offence committed in office **4** to challenge or question (a person's honesty, integrity, etc) [C14 from Old French *empeechier*, from Late Latin *impedicāre* to entangle, catch, from Latin IM- (in) + *pedica* a fetter, from *pēs* foot] > **im'peacher** *n*

impeachable (ɪm'piːtʃəbᵊl) *adj* **1** capable of being impeached or accused **2** (of an offence) making a person liable to impeachment > **im,peacha'bility** *n*

impeachment (ɪm'piːtʃmənt) *n* **1** *rare* (in England) committal by the House of Commons, esp of a minister of the Crown, for trial by the House of Lords. The last instance occurred in 1805 **2** (in the US) a proceeding brought against a federal government official **3** an accusation or charge **4** *obsolete* discredit; reproach

impearl (ɪm'pɜːl) *vb (tr) archaic or poetic* **1** to adorn with pearls **2** to form into pearl-like shapes or drops

impeccable (ɪm'pɛkəbᵊl) *adj* **1** without flaw or error; faultless: *an impeccable record* **2** *rare* incapable of sinning [C16 from Late Latin *impeccābilis* sinless, from Latin IM- (not) + *peccāre* to sin] > **im,pecca'bility** *n* > **im'peccably** *adv*

impeccant (ɪm'pɛkənt) *adj* not sinning; free from sin [C18 from IM- (not) + Latin *peccant-*, from *peccāre* to sin] > **im'peccancy** *n*

impecunious (,ɪmpɪ'kjuːnɪəs) *adj* without money; penniless [C16 from IM- (not) + *-pecunious*, from Latin *pecūniōsus* wealthy, from *pecūnia* money] > **,impe'cuniously** *adv* > **,impe'cuniousness** *or* **impecuniosity** (,ɪmpɪkjuːnɪ'ɒsɪtɪ) *n*

impedance (ɪm'piːdᵊns) *n* **1** a measure of the opposition to the flow of an alternating current equal to the square root of the sum of the squares of the resistance and the reactance, expressed in ohms. Symbol: Z **2** a component that offers impedance **3** Also called: **acoustic impedance** the ratio of the sound pressure in a medium to the rate of alternating flow of the medium through a specified surface due to the sound wave. Symbol: Z_a **4** Also called: **mechanical impedance** the ratio of the mechanical force, acting in the direction of motion, to the velocity of the resulting vibration. Symbol: Z_m

impede (ɪm'piːd) *vb (tr)* to restrict or retard in action, progress, etc; hinder; obstruct [C17 from Latin *impedīre* to hinder, literally: shackle the feet, from *pēs* foot] > **im'peder** *n* > **im'pedingly** *adv*

impediment (ɪm'pɛdɪmənt) *n* **1** a hindrance or obstruction **2** a physical defect, esp one of speech, such as a stammer **3** *pl* **-ments** *or* **-menta** (-'mɛntə) *law* an obstruction to the making of a contract, esp a contract of marriage by reason of closeness of blood or affinity > **im,pedi'mental** *or* **im,pedi'mentary** *adj*

impedimenta (ɪm,pɛdɪ'mɛntə) *pl n* **1** the baggage and equipment carried by an army **2** any objects or circumstances that impede progress **3** a plural of **impediment** (sense 3) [C16 from Latin, plural of *impedīmentum* hindrance; see IMPEDE]

impedor (ɪm'piːdə) *n physics* a component, such as an inductor or resistor, that offers impedance

impel (ɪm'pɛl) *vb* **-pels, -pelling, -pelled** *(tr)* **1** to urge or force (a person) to an action; constrain or motivate **2** to push, drive, or force into motion [C15 from Latin *impellere* to push against, drive forward, from IM- (in) + *pellere* to drive, push, strike] > **im'pellent** *n, adj*

impeller (ɪm'pɛlə) *n* **1** the vaned rotating disc of a centrifugal pump, compressor, etc **2** a compressor or centrifugal pump having such an impeller

impend (ɪm'pɛnd) *vb (intr)* **1** (esp of something threatening) to be about to happen; be imminent **2** (foll by *over*) *rare* to be suspended; hang [C16 from Latin *impendēre* to overhang, from *pendēre* to hang] > **im'pendence** *or* **im'pendency** *n* > **im'pending** *adj*

impending (ɪm'pɛndɪŋ) *adj* about to happen; imminent

impenetrable (ɪm'pɛnɪtrəbᵊl) *adj* **1** incapable of being pierced through or penetrated: *an impenetrable forest* **2** incapable of being understood; incomprehensible: *impenetrable jargon* **3** incapable of being seen through: *impenetrable gloom* **4** not susceptible to ideas, influence, etc: *impenetrable ignorance* **5** *physics* (of a body) incapable of occupying the same space as another body > **im,penetra'bility** *n* > **im'penetrableness** *n* > **im'penetrably** *adv*

impenitent (ɪm'pɛnɪtənt) *adj* not sorry or penitent; unrepentant > **im'penitence, im'penitence** *or* **im'penitentness** *n* > **im'penitently** *adv*

impennate (ɪm'pɛneɪt) *adj rare* (of birds) lacking true functional wings or feathers

imperative (ɪm'pɛrətɪv) *adj* **1** extremely urgent or important; essential **2** peremptory or authoritative: *an imperative tone of voice* **3** Also: **imperatival** (ɪm,pɛrə'taɪvᵊl) *grammar* denoting a mood of verbs used in giving orders, making requests, etc. In English the verb root without any inflections is the usual form, as for example *leave* in *Leave me alone* ▷ *n* **4** something that is urgent or essential **5** an order or command **6** *grammar* **a** the imperative mood **b** a verb in this mood [C16 from Late Latin *imperātīvus*, from Latin *imperāre* to command] > **im'peratively** *adv* > **im'perativeness** *n*

imperator (,ɪmpə'rɑːtɔː) *n* **1 a** (in imperial Rome) a title of the emperor **b** (in republican Rome) a temporary title of honour bestowed upon a victorious general **2** a less common word for **emperor** [C16 from Latin: commander, from *imperāre* to command] > **imperatorial** (ɪm,pɛrə'tɔːrɪəl) *adj* > **im,pera'torially** *adv* > **,impe'rator,ship** *n*

imperceptible (,ɪmpə'sɛptɪbᵊl) *adj* too slight, subtle, gradual, etc, to be perceived > **,imper,cepti'bility** *or* **,imper'ceptibleness** *n* > **,imper'ceptibly** *adv*

imperceptive (,ɪmpə'sɛptɪv) *adj also* **impercipient** (,ɪmpə-'sɪpɪənt) lacking in perception; obtuse > **,imper'ception** *n* > **,imper'ceptively** *adv* > **,impercep'tivity, ,imper'ceptiveness** *or* **,imper'cipience** *n*

imperf. *abbreviation for* **1** Also: **impf** imperfect **2** (of stamps) imperforate

imperfect (ɪm'pɜːfɪkt) *adj* **1** exhibiting or characterized by faults, mistakes, etc; defective **2** not complete or finished; deficient **3** *botany* **a** (of flowers) lacking functional stamens or pistils **b** (of fungi) not undergoing sexual reproduction **4** *grammar* denoting a tense of verbs used most commonly in describing continuous or repeated past actions or events, as for example *was walking* as opposed to *walked* **5** *law* (of a trust, an obligation, etc) lacking some necessary formality to make effective or binding; incomplete; legally unenforceable. See also **executory** (sense 1) **6** *music* **a** (of a cadence) proceeding to the dominant from the tonic, subdominant, or any chord other than the dominant **b** of or relating to all intervals other than the fourth, fifth, and octave. Compare **perfect** (sense 9) ▷ *n* **7** *grammar* **a** the imperfect tense **b** a verb in this tense > **im'perfectly** *adv* > **im'perfectness** *n*

imperfect competition *n economics* the market situation that exists when one or more of the necessary conditions for perfect competition do not hold

imperfection (,ɪmpə'fɛkʃən) *n* **1** the condition or quality of being imperfect **2** a fault or defect

imperfective (,ɪmpə'fɛktɪv) *grammar* ▷ *adj* **1** denoting an aspect of the verb in some languages, including English, used to indicate that the action is in progress without regard to its completion. Compare **perfective** ▷ *n* **2 a** the imperfective aspect of a verb **b** a verb in this aspect > **,imper'fectively** *adv*

imperforate (ɪm'pɜːfərɪt, -,reɪt) *adj* **1** not perforated **2** (of a postage stamp) not provided with perforation or any other means of separation. Abbreviation: **imperf** Compare **perforate 3** *anatomy* (of a bodily part, such as the anus) without the normal opening > **im,perfo'ration** *n*

imperia (ɪm'pɪərɪə) *n* the plural of **imperium**

imperial (ɪm'pɪərɪəl) *adj* **1** of or relating to an empire, emperor, or empress **2** characteristic of or befitting an emperor; majestic; commanding **3** characteristic of or exercising supreme authority; imperious **4** (esp of products and commodities) of a superior size or quality **5** *(usually prenominal)* (of weights, measures, etc) conforming to standards or definitions legally established in Britain: *an imperial gallon* ▷ *n* **6** any of various book sizes, esp 7½ by 11 inches (**imperial octavo**) or (chiefly Brit) 11 by 15 inches (**imperial quarto**) **7** a size of writing or printing paper, 23 by 31 inches (US and Canadian) or 22 by 30 inches (Brit) **8** (formerly) a Russian gold coin originally worth ten roubles **9** *US* **a** the top of a carriage, such as a diligence **b** a luggage case carried there **10** *architect* a dome that has a point at the top **11** a small tufted beard popularized by the emperor Napoleon III **12** a member of an imperial family, esp an emperor or empress **13** a red deer having antlers with fourteen points [C14 from Late Latin *imperiālis*, from Latin *imperium* command, authority, empire] > **im'perially** *adv* > **im'perialness** *n*

Imperial (ɪm'pɪərɪəl) *adj* **1** *(sometimes not capital)* of or relating to a specified empire, such as the British Empire ▷ *n* **2** a supporter or soldier of the Holy Roman Empire

imperial gallon *n* a formal name for **gallon** (sense 1)

imperialism (ɪm'pɪərɪə,lɪzəm) *n* **1** the policy or practice of extending a state's rule over other territories **2** an instance or policy of aggressive behaviour by one state against another **3** the extension or attempted extension of authority, influence, power, etc, by any person, country, institution, etc: *cultural imperialism* **4** a system of imperial government or rule by an emperor **5** the spirit, character, authority, etc, of an empire **6** advocacy of or support for any form of imperialism > **im'perialist** *adj, n* > **im,perial'istic** *adj* > **im,perial'istically** *adv*

Imperial War Museum *n* a museum in London, founded in 1920, containing material related to military operations involving British and Commonwealth forces since 1914

imperil (ɪm'pɛrɪl) *vb* **-rils, -rilling, -rilled** *or US* **-rils, -riling, -riled** *(tr)* to place in danger or jeopardy; endanger > **im'perilment** *n*

imperious (ɪm'pɪərɪəs) *adj* **1** domineering; arrogant; overbearing **2** *rare* urgent; imperative [C16 from Latin *imperiōsus* from *imperium* command, power] > **im'periously** *adv* > **im'periousness** *n*

imperishable (ɪm'pɛrɪʃəbᵊl) *adj* **1** not subject to decay or deterioration: *imperishable goods* **2** not likely to be forgotten: *imperishable truths* > **im,perisha'bility** *or* **im'perishableness** *n* > **im'perishably** *adv*

imperium (ɪm'pɪərɪəm) *n, pl* **-ria** (-rɪə) **1** (in ancient Rome) the supreme power, held esp by consuls and emperors, to command and administer in military, judicial, and civil affairs **2** the right to command; supreme power **3** a less common word for **empire** [C17 from Latin: command, empire, from *imperāre* to command; see EMPEROR]

impermanent (ɪm'pɜːmənənt) *adj* not permanent; fleeting; transitory > **im'permanence** *or* **im'permanency** *n* > **im'permanently** *adv*

impermeable (ɪm'pɜːmɪəbᵊl) *adj* (of a substance) not allowing the passage of a fluid through interstices; not permeable > **im,permea'bility** *or* **im'permeableness** *n* > **im'permeably** *adv*

impermissible (,ɪmpə'mɪsɪbᵊl) *adj* not permissible; not allowed > **,imper,missi'bility** *n* > **,imper'missibly** *adv*

imperscriptible (,ɪmpə'skrɪptɪbᵊl) *adj* not supported by written authority [C19 from IM- (not) + Latin *perscribere* to write down]

impersonal (ɪm'pɜːsənᵊl) *adj* **1** without reference to any individual person; objective: *an impersonal* *assessment* **2** devoid of human warmth or sympathy; cold: *an impersonal manner* **3** not having human characteristics: *an impersonal God* **4** *grammar* (of a verb) having no logical subject. Usually in English the pronoun *it* is used in such cases as a grammatical subject, as for example in *It is raining* **5** *grammar* (of a pronoun) not denoting a person > **imˌpersonˈality** *n* > **imˈpersonally** *adv*

impersonalize *or* **impersonalise** (ɪmˈpɜːsənəˌlaɪz) *vb* (*tr*) to make impersonal, esp to rid of such human characteristics as sympathy, warmth, etc; dehumanize > **imˌpersonaliˈzation** *or* **imˌpersonaliˈsation** *n*

impersonate (ɪmˈpɜːsəˌneɪt) *vb* (*tr*) **1** to pretend to be (another person) **2** to imitate the character, mannerisms, etc, of (another person) **3** *rare* to play the part or character of **4** an archaic word for **personify**. > **imˌpersonˈation** *n* > **imˈpersonˌator** *n*

impertinence (ɪmˈpɜːtɪnəns) *or* **impertinency** *n* **1** disrespectful behaviour or language; rudeness; insolence **2** an impertinent act, gesture, etc **3** *rare* lack of pertinence; irrelevance; inappropriateness

impertinent (ɪmˈpɜːtɪnənt) *adj* **1** rude; insolent; impudent **2** irrelevant or inappropriate [C14 from Latin *impertinēns* not belonging, from Latin IM- (not) + *pertinēre* to be relevant; see PERTAIN] > **imˈpertinently** *adv*

imperturbable (ˌɪmpɜːˈtɜːbəb^{ə}l) *adj* not easily perturbed; calm; unruffled > **ˌimperˌturbaˈbility** *or* **ˌimperˈturbableness** *n* > **ˌimperˈturbably** *adv* > **imperturbation** (ˌɪmpɜːtɜːˈbeɪʃən) *n*

impervious (ɪmˈpɜːvɪəs) *or* **imperviable** *adj* **1** not able to be penetrated, as by water, light, etc; impermeable **2** (*often postpositive*; foll by *to*) not able to be influenced (by) or not receptive (to): *impervious to argument* > **imˈperviously** *adv* > **imˈperviousness** *n*

impetigo (ˌɪmpɪˈtaɪɡəʊ) *n* a contagious bacterial skin disease characterized by the formation of pustules that develop into yellowish crusty sores [C16 from Latin: scabby eruption, from *impetere* to assail; see IMPETUS; for form, compare VERTIGO] > **impetiginous** (ˌɪmpɪˈtɪdʒɪnəs) *adj*

impetrate (ˈɪmpɪˌtreɪt) *vb* (*tr*) **1** to supplicate or entreat for, esp by prayer **2** to obtain by prayer [C16 from Latin *impetrāre* to procure by entreaty, from *-petrāre*, from *patrāre* to bring to pass, of uncertain origin; perhaps related to Latin *pater* a father] > **ˌimpeˈtration** *n* > **ˈimpetrative** *adj* > **ˈimpeˌtrator** *n*

impetuous (ɪmˈpɛtjʊəs) *adj* **1** liable to act without consideration; rash; impulsive **2** resulting from or characterized by rashness or haste **3** *poetic* moving with great force or violence; rushing: *the impetuous stream hurtled down the valley* [C14 from Late Latin *impetuōsus* violent; see IMPETUS] > **imˈpetuously** *adv* > **imˈpetuousness** *or* **impetuosity** (ɪmˌpɛtjʊˈɒsɪtɪ) *n*

impetus (ˈɪmpɪtəs) *n, pl* **-tuses** **1** an impelling movement or force; incentive or impulse; stimulus **2** *physics* the force that sets a body in motion or that tends to resist changes in a body's motion [C17 from Latin: attack, from *impetere* to assail, from IM- (in) + *petere* to make for, seek out]

imp. gal. *or* **imp. gall.** *abbreviation for* imperial gallon

Imphal (ɪmˈfɑːl, ˈɪmfəl) *n* a city in NE India, capital of Manipur Territory, on the Manipur River: formerly the seat of the Manipur kings: site of a major Anglo-Indian victory over the Japanese (1944), which was a turning point in the British recovery of Burma (now called Myanmar). Pop: 217 275 (2001)

impi (ˈɪmpɪ) *n, pl* **-pi** *or* **-pies** a group of Bantu warriors [C19 Nguni: regiment, army]

impiety (ɪmˈpaɪɪtɪ) *n, pl* **-ties** **1** lack of reverence or proper respect for a god **2** any lack of proper respect **3** an impious act

impinge (ɪmˈpɪndʒ) *vb* **1** (*intr*; usually foll by *on* or *upon*) to encroach or infringe; trespass: *to impinge on someone's time* **2** (*intr*; usually foll by *on*, *against*, or *upon*) to collide (with); strike [C16 from Latin *impingere* to drive at, dash against, from *pangere* to fasten, drive in] > **imˈpingement** *n* > **imˈpinger** *n*

impingement attack *n* *metallurgy* a form of corrosion of metals caused by erosion of the oxide layer by a moving fluid in which there are suspended particles or air bubbles

impious (ˈɪmpɪəs) *adj* **1** lacking piety or reverence for a god; ungodly **2** lacking respect; undutiful > **ˈimpiously** *adv* > **ˈimpiousness** *n*

impish (ˈɪmpɪʃ) *adj* of or resembling an imp; mischievous > **ˈimpishly** *adv* > **ˈimpishness** *n*

implacable (ɪmˈplækəb^{ə}l) *adj* **1** incapable of being placated or pacified; unappeasable **2** inflexible; intractable > **imˌplacaˈbility** *or* **imˈplacableness** *n* > **imˈplacably** *adv*

implacental (ˌɪmpləˈsɛnt^{ə}l) *adj* another word for **aplacental**

implant *vb* (ɪmˈplɑːnt) (*tr*) **1** to establish firmly; inculcate; instil: *to implant sound moral principles* **2** to plant or embed; infix; entrench **3** *surgery* **a** to graft (a tissue) into the body **b** to insert (a radioactive substance, hormone, etc) into the tissues ▷ *n* (ˈɪmˌplɑːnt) **4** anything implanted, esp surgically, such as a tissue graft or hormone > **imˈplanter** *n*

implantation (ˌɪmplɑːnˈteɪʃən) *n* **1** the act of implanting or the state of being implanted **2** Also called: **nidation** the attachment of the blastocyst of a mammalian embryo to the wall of the uterus of the mother

implausible (ɪmˈplɔːzəb^{ə}l) *adj* not plausible; provoking disbelief; unlikely > **imˌplausiˈbility** *or* **imˈplausibleness** *n* > **imˈplausibly** *adv*

implead (ɪmˈpliːd) *vb* (*tr*) *law rare* **1** **a** to sue or prosecute **b** to bring an action against **2** to accuse [C13 from Anglo-French *empleder*; see IM-, PLEAD] > **imˈpleadable** *adj* > **imˈpleader** *n*

implement *n* (ˈɪmplɪmənt) **1** a piece of equipment; tool or utensil: *gardening implements* **2** something used to achieve a purpose; agent ▷ *vb* (ˈɪmplɪˌmɛnt) (*tr*) **3** to carry out; put into action; perform: *to implement a plan* **4** *archaic* to complete, satisfy, or fulfil [C17 from Late Latin *implēmentum*, literally: a filling up, from Latin *implēre* to fill up, satisfy, fulfil] > **ˌimpleˈmental** *adj* > **ˌimplemenˈtation** *n* > **ˈimpleˌmenter** *or* **ˈimpleˌmentor** *n*

implicate (ˈɪmplɪˌkeɪt) *vb* (*tr*) **1** to show to be involved, esp in a crime **2** to involve as a necessary inference; imply: *his protest implicated censure by the authorities* **3** to affect intimately: *this news implicates my decision* **4** *rare* to intertwine or entangle [C16 from Latin *implicāre* to involve, from IM- + *plicāre* to fold] > **implicative** (ɪmˈplɪkətɪv) *adj* > **imˈplicatively** *adv*

implication (ˌɪmplɪˈkeɪʃən) *n* **1** the act of implicating or the state of being implicated **2** something that is implied; suggestion: *the implication of your silence is that you're bored* **3** *logic* **a** the operator that forms a sentence from two given sentences and corresponds to the English *if … then …* **b** a sentence so formed. Usually written p→q or p⊃q, where p,q are the component sentences, it is true except when p (the antecedent) is true and q (the consequent) is false **c** the relation between such sentences > **ˌimpliˈcational** *adj*

implicature (ɪmˈplɪkətʃə) *n* *logic, philosophy* **1** a proposition inferred from the circumstances of utterances of another proposition rather than from its literal meaning, as when an academic referee writes *the candidate's handwriting is excellent* to convey that he has nothing relevant to commend **2** the relation between the uttered and the inferred statement

implicit (ɪmˈplɪsɪt) *adj* **1** not explicit; implied; indirect: *there was implicit criticism in his voice* **2** absolute and unreserved; unquestioning: *you have implicit trust in him* **3** (*when postpositive*, foll by *in*) contained or inherent: *to bring out the anger implicit in the argument* **4** *maths* (of a function) having an equation of the form f(x,y) = 0, in which y cannot be directly expressed in terms of x, as in $xy + x^2 + y^3x^2 = 0$. Compare **explicit**[1] (sense 4) **5** *obsolete* intertwined [C16 from Latin *implicitus*, variant of *implicātus* interwoven; see IMPLICATE] > **imˈplicitly** *adv* > **imˈplicitness** *or* **imˈplicity** *n*

implied (ɪmˈplaɪd) *adj* hinted at or suggested; not directly expressed: *an implied criticism* > **impliedly** (ɪmˈplaɪɪdlɪ) *adv*

implode (ɪmˈpləʊd) *vb* **1** to collapse or cause to collapse inwards in a violent manner as a result of external pressure: *the vacuum flask imploded* **2** (*tr*) to pronounce (a consonant) with or by implosion ▷ Compare **explode** [C19 from IM- + (EX)PLODE]

implore (ɪmˈplɔː) *vb* (*tr*) **1** to beg or ask (someone) earnestly (to do something); plead with; beseech **2** to ask earnestly or piteously for; supplicate; beg: *to implore someone's mercy* [C16 from Latin *implōrāre*, from IM- + *plōrāre* to bewail] > **ˌimploˈration** *n* > **imˈploratory** *adj* > **imˈplorer** *n* > **imˈploringly** *adv*

implosion (ɪmˈpləʊʒən) *n* **1** the act or process of imploding: *the implosion of a light bulb* **2** *phonetics* the suction or inhalation of breath employed in the pronunciation of an ingressive consonant

implosive (ɪmˈpləʊsɪv) *adj* **1** pronounced by or with implosion ▷ *n* **2** an implosive consonant > **imˈplosively** *adv*

imply (ɪmˈplaɪ) *vb* **-plies, -plying, -plied** (*tr*; *may take a clause as object*) **1** to express or indicate by a hint; suggest: *what are you implying by that remark?* **2** to suggest or involve as a necessary consequence **3** *logic* to enable (a conclusion) to be inferred **4** *obsolete* to entangle or enfold [C14 from Old French *emplier*, from Latin *implicāre* to involve; see IMPLICATE]

USAGE See at **infer**

impolder (ɪmˈpəʊldə) *or* **empolder** *vb* *rare* to make into a polder; reclaim (land) from the sea [C19 from Dutch *inpolderen*, see IN-[2], POLDER]

impolicy (ɪmˈpɒlɪsɪ) *n, pl* **-cies** the act or an instance of being unjudicious or impolitic

impolite (ˌɪmpəˈlaɪt) *adj* discourteous; rude; uncivil > **ˌimpoˈlitely** *adv* > **ˌimpoˈliteness** *n*

impolitic (ɪmˈpɒlɪtɪk) *adj* not politic or expedient; unwise > **imˈpoliticly** *adv* > **imˈpoliticness** *n*

imponderabilia (ɪmˌpɒndərəˈbɪlɪə) *pl n* imponderables [C20 New Latin]

imponderable (ɪmˈpɒndərəb^{ə}l, -drəb^{ə}l) *adj* **1** unable to be weighed or assessed ▷ *n* **2** something difficult or impossible to assess > **imˌponderaˈbility** *or* **imˈponderableness** *n* > **imˈponderably** *adv*

imponent (ɪmˈpəʊnənt) *n* a person who imposes a duty, etc

import *vb* (ɪmˈpɔːt, ˈɪmpɔːt) **1** to buy or bring in (goods or services) from a foreign country. Compare **export** **2** (*tr*) to bring in from an outside source: *to import foreign words into the language* **3** *rare* to signify or be significant; mean; convey: *to import doom* ▷ *n* (ˈɪmpɔːt) **4** (*often plural*) **a** goods (**visible imports**) or services (**invisible imports**) that are bought from foreign countries **b** (*as modifier*): *an import licence* **5** significance or importance: *a man of great import* **6** meaning or signification **7** *Canadian informal* a sportsman or -woman who is not native to the country in which he or she plays [C15 from Latin *importāre* to carry in, from IM- + *portāre* to carry] > **imˈportable** *adj* > **imˌportaˈbility** *n* > **imˈporter** *n*

importance (ɪmˈpɔːt^{ə}ns) *n* **1** the state of being important; significance **2** social status; standing; esteem: *a man of importance* **3** *obsolete* **a** meaning or signification **b** an important matter **c** importunity

important (ɪmˈpɔːt^{ə}nt) *adj* **1** of great significance or value; outstanding: *Voltaire is an important writer* **2** of social significance; notable; eminent; esteemed: *an important man in the town* **3** (*when postpositive*, usually foll by *to*) specially relevant or of great concern (to); valued highly (by): *your wishes are important to me* **4** an obsolete word for **importunate** [C16 from Old Italian *importante*, from

Medieval Latin *importāre* to signify, be of consequence, from Latin: to carry in; see IMPORT] > im'portantly *adv*

USAGE The use of *more importantly* as in *more importantly, the local council is opposed to this proposal* has become very common, but many people still prefer to use *more important*

importation (ˌɪmpɔːˈteɪʃən) *n* **1** the act, business, or process of importing goods or services **2** an imported product or service

importunate (ɪmˈpɔːtjʊnɪt) *adj* **1** persistent or demanding; insistent **2** *rare* troublesome; annoying > im'portunately *adv* > im'portunateness *n*

importune (ɪmˈpɔːtjuːn) *vb* (tr) **1** to harass with persistent requests; demand of (someone) insistently **2** to beg for persistently; request with insistence **3** *obsolete* **a** to anger or annoy **b** to force; impel [C16 from Latin *importūnus* tiresome, from *im-* IN-¹ + -*portūnus* as in *opportūnus* OPPORTUNE] > im'portuner *n* > impor'tunity or im'portunacy *n*

impose (ɪmˈpəʊz) *vb* (usually foll by *on* or *upon*) **1** (tr) to establish as something to be obeyed or complied with; enforce: *to impose a tax on the people* **2** to force (oneself, one's presence, etc) on another or others; obtrude **3** (intr) to take advantage, as of a person or quality: *to impose on someone's kindness* **4** (tr) *printing* to arrange pages so that after printing and folding the pages will be in the correct order **5** (tr) to pass off deceptively; foist: *to impose a hoax on someone* **6** (tr) (of a bishop or priest) to lay (the hands) on the head of a candidate for certain sacraments [C15 from Old French *imposer*, from Latin *impōnere* to place upon, from *pōnere* to place, set] > im'posable *adj* > im'poser *n*

imposing (ɪmˈpəʊzɪŋ) *adj* grand or impressive: *an imposing building* > im'posingly *adv* > im'posingness *n*

imposing stone or **table** *n printing* a flat hard surface upon which pages printed from hot metal are imposed

imposition (ˌɪmpəˈzɪʃən) *n* **1** the act of imposing **2** something that is imposed unfairly on someone **3** (in Britain) a task set as a school punishment **4** the arrangement of pages for printing so that the finished work will have its pages in the correct order

impossibility (ɪmˌpɒsəˈbɪlɪtɪ, ˌɪmpɒs-) *n, pl* -ties **1** the state or quality of being impossible **2** something that is impossible

impossible (ɪmˈpɒsəbəl) *adj* **1** incapable of being done, undertaken, or experienced **2** incapable of occurring or happening **3** absurd or inconceivable; unreasonable: *it's impossible to think of him as a bishop* **4** *informal* intolerable; outrageous: *those children are impossible* > im'possibleness *n* > im'possibly *adv*

impossible figure *n* a picture of an object that at first sight looks three-dimensional but cannot be a two-dimensional projection of a real three-dimensional object, for example a picture of a staircase that re-enters itself while appearing to ascend continuously. Also called: **Escher figure**

impost¹ (ˈɪmpəʊst) *n* **1** a tax, esp a customs duty **2** *horse racing* the specific weight that a particular horse must carry in a handicap race ▷ *vb* **3** (tr) US to classify (imported goods) according to the duty payable on them [C16 from Medieval Latin *impostus* tax, from Latin *impositus* imposed; see IMPOSE] > 'imposter *n*

impost² (ˈɪmpəʊst) *n architect* a member at the top of a wall, pier, or column that supports an arch, esp one that has a projecting moulding [C17 from French *imposte*, from Latin *impositus* placed upon; see IMPOSE]

impostor or **imposter** (ɪmˈpɒstə) *n* a person who deceives others, esp by assuming a false identity; charlatan [C16 from Late Latin: deceiver; see IMPOSE]

impostume (ɪmˈpɒstjuːm) or **imposthume** (ɪmˈpɒsθuːm) *n* an archaic word for **abscess** [C15 from Old French *empostume*, from Late Latin *apostēma*, from Greek, literally: separation (of pus), from *aphistanai* to remove, from *histanai* to stand]

imposture (ɪmˈpɒstʃə) *n* the act or an instance of deceiving others, esp by assuming a false identity [C16 from French, from Late Latin *impostūra*, from Latin *impōnere*; see IMPOSE] > im'postrous (ɪmˈpɒstrəs), impostorous (ɪmˈpɒstərəs) or im'posturous *adj*

impotent (ˈɪmpətənt) *adj* **1** (when postpositive, often takes an infinitive) lacking sufficient strength; powerless **2** (esp of males) unable to perform sexual intercourse. See **erectile impotence 3** *obsolete* lacking self-control; unrestrained > 'impotence, 'impotency or 'impotentness *n* > 'impotently *adv*

impound (ɪmˈpaʊnd) *vb* (tr) **1** to confine (stray animals, illegally parked cars, etc) in a pound **2 a** to seize (chattels, etc) by legal right **b** to take possession of (a document, evidence, etc) and hold in legal custody **3** to collect (water) in a reservoir or dam, as for irrigation **4** to seize or appropriate > im'poundable *adj* > im'poundage or im'poundment *n* > im'pounder *n*

impoverish (ɪmˈpɒvərɪʃ) *vb* (tr) **1** to make poor or diminish the quality of: *to impoverish society by cutting the grant to the arts* **2** to deprive (soil, etc) of fertility [C15 from Old French *empovrir*, from *povre* POOR] > im'poverisher *n* > im'poverishment *n*

impower (ɪmˈpaʊə) *vb* a less common spelling of **empower**

impracticable (ɪmˈpræktɪkəbəl) *adj* **1** incapable of being put into practice or accomplished; not feasible **2** unsuitable for a desired use; unfit **3** an archaic word for **intractable**. > im,practica'bility or im'practicableness *n* > im'practicably *adv*

impractical (ɪmˈpræktɪkəl) *adj* **1** not practical or workable: *an impractical solution* **2** not given to practical matters or gifted with practical skills: *he is intelligent but too impractical for commercial work* > im,practi'cality or im'practicalness *n* > im'practically *adv*

imprecate (ˈɪmprɪˌkeɪt) *vb* **1** (intr) to swear, curse, or blaspheme **2** (tr) to invoke or bring down (evil, a curse, etc): *to imprecate disaster on the ship* **3** (tr) to put a curse on [C17 from Latin *imprecārī* to invoke, from *im-* IN-² + *precārī* to PRAY] > 'impre,catory *adj*

imprecation (ˌɪmprɪˈkeɪʃən) *n* **1** the act of imprecating **2** a malediction; curse

imprecise (ˌɪmprɪˈsaɪs) *adj* not precise; inexact or inaccurate > ,impre'cisely *adv* > imprecision (ˌɪmprɪˈsɪʒən) or ,impre'ciseness *n*

impredicative (ˌɪmprəˈdɪkətɪv) *adj logic* (of a definition) given in terms that require quantification over a range that includes that which is to be defined, as *having all the properties of a great general* where one of the properties as ascribed must be that property itself. Compare **predicative** (sense 2)

impregnable¹ (ɪmˈprɛgnəbəl) *adj* **1** unable to be broken into or taken by force: *an impregnable castle* **2** unable to be shaken or overcome: *impregnable self-confidence* **3** incapable of being refuted: *an impregnable argument* [C15 *imprenable*, from Old French, from IM- (not) + *prenable* able to be taken, from *prendre* to take] > im,pregna'bility or im'pregnableness *n* > im'pregnably *adv*

impregnable² (ɪmˈprɛgnəbəl), **impregnatable** (ˌɪmprɛgˈneɪtəbəl) *adj* able to be impregnated; fertile

impregnate *vb* (ˈɪmprɛgˌneɪt) (tr) **1** to saturate, soak, or infuse: *to impregnate a cloth with detergent* **2** to imbue or permeate; pervade **3** to cause to conceive; make pregnant **4** to fertilize (an ovum) **5** to make (land, soil, etc) fruitful ▷ *adj* (ɪmˈprɛgnɪt, -ˌneɪt) **6** pregnant or fertilized [C17 from Late Latin *impraegnāre* to make pregnant, from Latin *im-* IN-² + *praegnans* PREGNANT] > ,impreg'nation *n* > im'pregnator *n*

impresa (ɪmˈpreɪzə) or **imprese** (ɪmˈpriːz) *n* an emblem or device, usually a motto, as on a coat of arms [C16 from Italian, literally: undertaking,

hence deed of chivalry, motto, from *imprendere* to undertake; see EMPRISE]

impresario (ˌɪmprəˈsɑːrɪˌəʊ) *n, pl* -sarios **1** a producer or sponsor of public entertainments, esp musical or theatrical ones **2** the director or manager of an opera, ballet, or other performing company [C18 from Italian, literally: one who undertakes; see IMPRESA]

imprescriptible (ˌɪmprɪˈskrɪptəbəl) *adj law* immune or exempt from prescription > ,impre,scripti'bility *n* > ,impre'scriptibly *adv*

impress¹ *vb* (ɪmˈprɛs) (tr) **1** to make an impression on; have a strong, lasting, or favourable effect on: *I am impressed by your work* **2** to produce (an imprint, etc) by pressure in or on (something): *to impress a seal in wax; to impress wax with a seal* **3** (often foll by *on*) to stress (something to a person); urge; emphasize: *to impress the danger of a situation on someone* **4** to exert pressure on; press **5** *electronics* to apply (a voltage) to a circuit or device ▷ *n* (ˈɪmprɛs) **6** the act or an instance of impressing **7** a mark, imprint, or effect produced by impressing [C14 from Latin *imprimere* to press into, imprint, from *premere* to PRESS¹] > im'presser *n* > im'pressible *adj*

impress² *vb* (ɪmˈprɛs) **1** to commandeer or coerce (men or things) into government service; press-gang ▷ *n* (ˈɪmprɛs) **2** the act of commandeering or coercing into government service; impressment [C16 see IM- IN-², PRESS²]

impression (ɪmˈprɛʃən) *n* **1** an effect produced in the mind by a stimulus; sensation: *he gave the impression of wanting to help* **2** an imprint or mark produced by pressing: *he left the impression of his finger in the mud* **3** a vague idea, consciousness, or belief: *I had the impression we had met before* **4** a strong, favourable, or remarkable effect: *he made an impression on the managers* **5** the act of impressing or the state of being impressed **6** *printing* **a** the act, process, or result of printing from type, plates, etc **b** one of a number of printings of a publication printed from the same setting of type with no or few alterations. Compare **edition** (sense 2) **c** the total number of copies of a publication printed at one time **7** *dentistry* an imprint of the teeth and gums, esp in wax or plaster, for use in preparing crowns, inlays, or dentures **8** an imitation or impersonation: *he did a funny impression of the politician* > im'pressional *adj* > im'pressionally *adv*

impressionable (ɪmˈprɛʃənəbəl, -ˈprɛʃnə-) *adj* easily influenced or characterized by susceptibility to influence: *an impressionable child; an impressionable age* > im,pressiona'bility or im'pressionableness *n*

impressionism (ɪmˈprɛʃəˌnɪzəm) *n* **1** (often capital) a movement in French painting, developed in the 1870s chiefly by Monet, Renoir, Pissarro, and Sisley, having the aim of objectively recording experience by a system of fleeting impressions, esp of natural light effects **2** the technique in art, literature, or music of conveying experience by capturing fleeting impressions of reality or of mood

impressionist (ɪmˈprɛʃənɪst) *n* **1** (usually capital) any of the French painters of the late 19th century who were exponents of impressionism **2** (sometimes capital) any artist, composer, or writer who uses impressionism **3** an entertainer who impersonates famous people ▷ *adj* **4** (often capital) denoting, of, or relating to impressionism or the exponents of this style > im,pression'istic *adj*

impressive (ɪmˈprɛsɪv) *adj* capable of impressing, esp by size, magnificence, etc; awe-inspiring; commanding > im'pressively *adv* > im'pressiveness *n*

impressment (ɪmˈprɛsmənt) *n* the commandeering or conscription of things or men into government service

impressure (ɪmˈprɛʃə) *n* an archaic word for **impression** [C17 see IMPRESS¹, -URE; formed on the model of PRESSURE]

imprest (ɪmˈprɛst) n 1 a fund of cash from which a department or other unit pays incidental expenses, topped up periodically from central funds 2 chiefly Brit an advance from government funds for the performance of some public business or service 3 Brit (formerly) an advance payment of wages to a sailor or soldier [c16 probably from Italian imprestare to lend, from Latin in- towards + praestāre to pay, from praestō at hand; see PREST0]

imprimatur (ˌɪmprɪˈmeɪtə, -ˈmɑː-) n 1 RC Church a licence granted by a bishop certifying the Church's approval of a book to be published 2 sanction, authority, or approval, esp for something to be printed [c17 New Latin, literally: let it be printed]

imprimis (ɪmˈpraɪmɪs) adv archaic in the first place [c15 from Latin phrase in prīmīs, literally: among the first things]

imprint n (ˈɪmprɪnt) 1 a mark or impression produced by pressure, printing, or stamping 2 a characteristic mark or indication; stamp: the imprint of great sadness on his face 3 the publisher's name and address, usually with the date of publication, in a book, pamphlet, etc 4 the printer's name and address on any printed matter ▷ vb (ɪmˈprɪnt) 5 to produce (a mark, impression, etc) on (a surface) by pressure, printing, or stamping: to imprint a seal on wax; to imprint wax with a seal 6 to establish firmly; impress; stamp: to imprint the details on one's mind 7 (of young animals) to undergo the process of imprinting > imˈprinter n

imprinting (ɪmˈprɪntɪŋ) n the development through exceptionally fast learning in young animals of recognition of and attraction to members of their own species or to surrogates

imprison (ɪmˈprɪzən) vb (tr) to confine in or as if in prison > imˈprisoner n > imˈprisonment n

improbable (ɪmˈprɒbəbəl) adj not likely or probable; doubtful; unlikely > imˌprobaˈbility or imˈprobableness n > imˈprobably adv

improbity (ɪmˈprəʊbɪtɪ) n, pl -ties dishonesty, wickedness, or unscrupulousness

impromptu (ɪmˈprɒmptjuː) adj 1 unrehearsed; spontaneous; extempore 2 produced or done without care or planning; improvised ▷ adv 3 in a spontaneous or improvised way: he spoke impromptu ▷ n 4 something that is impromptu 5 a short piece of instrumental music, sometimes improvisatory in character [c17 from French, from Latin in promptū in readiness, from promptus (adj) ready, PROMPT]

improper (ɪmˈprɒpə) adj 1 lacking propriety; not seemly or fitting 2 unsuitable for a certain use or occasion; inappropriate: an improper use for a tool 3 irregular or abnormal > imˈproperly adv > imˈproperness n

improper fraction n a fraction in which the numerator has a greater absolute value or degree than the denominator, as 7/6 or $(x^2 + 3)/(x + 1)$

improper integral n a definite integral having one or both limits infinite or having an integrand that becomes infinite within the limits of integration

impropriate vb (ɪmˈprəʊprɪˌeɪt) 1 (tr) to transfer (property, rights, etc) from the Church into lay hands ▷ adj (ɪmˈprəʊprɪɪt, -ˌeɪt) 2 transferred in this way [c16 from Medieval Latin impropriāre to make one's own, from Latin im- IN-² + propriāre to APPROPRIATE] > imˌpropriˈation n > imˈpropriˌator n

impropriety (ˌɪmprəˈpraɪɪtɪ) n, pl -ties 1 lack of propriety; indecency; indecorum 2 an improper act or use 3 the state of being improper

improv (ˈɪmprɒv) n improvisational comedy

improve (ɪmˈpruːv) vb 1 to make or become better in quality; ameliorate 2 (tr) to make (buildings, land, etc) more valuable by additions or betterment 3 (intr; usually foll by on or upon) to achieve a better standard or quality in comparison (with): to improve on last year's crop ▷ n 4 on the improve Austral informal improving [c16 from

Anglo-French emprouer to turn to profit, from en prou into profit, from prou profit, from Late Latin prōde beneficial, from Latin prōdesse to be advantageous, from PRO-¹ + esse to be] > imˈprovable adj > imˌprovaˈbility or imˈprovableness n > imˈprovably adv > imˈprover n > imˈprovingly adv

improvement (ɪmˈpruːvmənt) n 1 the act of improving or the state of being improved 2 something that improves, esp an addition or alteration 3 alteration of the structure, fixtures, fittings, or decor of a building without changing its function. Compare **conversion** (sense 9) 4 (usually plural) Austral and NZ a building or other works on a piece of land, adding to its value

improvident (ɪmˈprɒvɪdənt) adj 1 not provident; thriftless, imprudent, or prodigal 2 heedless or incautious; rash > imˈprovidence n > imˈprovidently adv

improvisation (ˌɪmprəvaɪˈzeɪʃən) n 1 the act or an instance of improvising 2 a product of improvising; something improvised > ˌimproviˈsational or improvisatory (ˌɪmprəˈvaɪzətərɪ, -ˈvɪz-, ˌɪmprəvaɪˈzeɪtərɪ, -trɪ) adj

improvise (ˈɪmprəˌvaɪz) vb 1 to perform or make quickly from materials and sources available, without previous planning 2 to perform (a poem, play, piece of music, etc), composing as one goes along [c19 from French, from Italian improvvisare, from Latin imprōvīsus unforeseen, from IM- (not) + prōvīsus, from prōvidēre to foresee; see PROVIDE] > ˈimproˌviser n

improvised explosive device n a home-made explosive device designed to maim, harrass, or kill. Abbreviation: IED

imprudent (ɪmˈpruːdᵊnt) adj not prudent; rash, heedless, or indiscreet > imˈprudence n > imˈprudently adv

impudence (ˈɪmpjʊdəns) or **impudency** n 1 the quality of being impudent 2 an impudent act or statement [c14 from Latin impudēns shameless, from IM- (not) + pudēns modest; see PUDENCY]

impudent (ˈɪmpjʊdənt) adj 1 mischievous, impertinent, or disrespectful 2 an obsolete word for **immodest**. > ˈimpudently adv > ˈimpudentness n

impudicity (ˌɪmpjʊˈdɪsɪtɪ) n rare immodesty [c16 from Old French impudicite, from Latin impudīcus shameless, from IN-¹ + pudīcus modest, virtuous]

impugn (ɪmˈpjuːn) vb (tr) to challenge or attack as false; assail; criticize [c14 from Old French impugner, from Latin impugnāre to fight against, attack, from IM- + pugnāre to fight] > imˈpugnable adj > impugnation (ˌɪmpʌgˈneɪʃən) or imˈpugnment n > imˈpugner n

impuissant (ɪmˈpjuːɪsᵊnt, ɪmˈpwiː-) adj powerless, ineffectual, feeble, or impotent [c17 from French: powerless] > imˈpuissance n

impulse (ˈɪmpʌls) n 1 an impelling force or motion; thrust; impetus 2 a sudden desire, whim, or inclination: I bought it on an impulse 3 an instinctive drive; urge 4 tendency; current; trend 5 physics a the product of the average magnitude of a force acting on a body and the time for which it acts b the change in the momentum of a body as a result of a force acting upon it for a short period of time 6 physiol See **nerve impulse** 7 electronics a less common word for **pulse¹** (sense 2) 8 on impulse spontaneously or impulsively [c17 from Latin impulsus a pushing against, incitement, from impellere to strike against; see IMPEL]

impulse buying n the buying of retail merchandise prompted by a whim on seeing the product displayed > impulse buyer n

impulse turbine n a turbine in which the expansion of the fluid, often steam, is completed in a static nozzle, the torque being produced by the change in momentum of the fluid impinging on curved rotor blades. Compare **reaction turbine**

impulsion (ɪmˈpʌlʃən) n 1 the act of impelling or the state of being impelled 2 motion produced by an impulse; propulsion 3 a driving force; compulsion

impulsive (ɪmˈpʌlsɪv) adj 1 characterized by actions based on sudden desires, whims, or inclinations rather than careful thought: an impulsive man 2 based on emotional impulses or whims; spontaneous: an impulsive kiss 3 forceful, inciting, or impelling 4 (of physical forces) acting for a short time; not continuous 5 (of a sound) brief, loud, and having a wide frequency range > imˈpulsively adv > imˈpulsiveness n

impundulu (ɪmˈpʊnˌdʊlʊ) n South African a mythical bird associated with witchcraft, frequently manifested as the secretary bird [from Nguni mpundulu]

impunity (ɪmˈpjuːnɪtɪ) n, pl -ties 1 exemption or immunity from punishment or recrimination 2 exemption or immunity from unpleasant consequences: a successful career marked by impunity from early mistakes 3 with impunity a with no unpleasant consequences b with no care or heed for such consequences [c16 from Latin impūnitās freedom from punishment, from impūnis unpunished, from IM- (not) + poena punishment]

impure (ɪmˈpjʊə) adj 1 not pure; combined with something else; tainted or sullied 2 (in certain religions) a (of persons) ritually unclean and as such debarred from certain religious ceremonies b (of foodstuffs, vessels, etc) debarred from certain religious uses 3 (of a colour) mixed with another colour or with black or white 4 of more than one origin or style, as of architecture or other design > imˈpurely adv > imˈpureness n

impurity (ɪmˈpjʊərɪtɪ) n, pl -ties 1 the quality of being impure 2 an impure thing, constituent, or element: impurities in the water 3 electronics a small quantity of an element added to a pure semiconductor crystal to control its electrical conductivity. See also **acceptor** (sense 2), **donor** (sense 5)

imputable (ɪmˈpjuːtəbᵊl) adj capable of being imputed; attributable; ascribable > imˌputaˈbility or imˈputableness n > imˈputably adv

imputation system n a former taxation system in which some, or all, of the corporation tax on a company was treated as a tax credit on account of the income tax paid by its shareholders on their dividends; discontinued in 1999. See also **advance corporation tax**

impute (ɪmˈpjuːt) vb (tr) 1 to attribute or ascribe (something dishonest or dishonourable, esp a criminal offence) to a person 2 to attribute to a source or cause: I impute your success to nepotism 3 commerce to give (a notional value) to goods or services when the real value is unknown [c14 from Latin imputāre, from IM- + putāre to think, calculate] > impuˈtation n > imˈputative adj > imˈputer n

Imroz (ˈɪmrɒz) n the Turkish name for **Imbros**

IMS abbreviation for Indian Medical Service

IMunE abbreviation for Institution of Municipal Engineers

in¹ (ɪn) prep 1 inside; within: no smoking in the auditorium 2 at a place where there is: lying in the shade; walking in the rain 3 indicating a state, situation, or condition: in a deep sleep; standing in silence 4 before or when (a period of time) has elapsed: come back in one year 5 using (a language, etc) as a means of communication: written in code 6 concerned or involved with, esp as an occupation: in journalism 7 while or by performing the action of; as a consequence of or by means of: in crossing the street he was run over 8 used to indicate goal or purpose: in honour of the president 9 (used of certain animals) about to give birth to; pregnant with (specified offspring): in foal; in calf 10 a variant of **into**: she fell in the water; he tore the paper in two 11 have it in one (often foll by an infinitive) to have the ability (to do something) 12 in it Austral informal joining in; taking part 13 in that or in so far as (conjunction) because or to the extent that; inasmuch as: I regret my remark in that it upset you 14 nothing, very little, quite a bit, etc, in it no, a great, etc, difference or interval between two

819

things ▷ *adv* (*particle*) **15** in or into a particular place; inward or indoors: *come in; bring him in* **16** so as to achieve office, power, or authority: *the Conservatives got in at the last election* **17** so as to enclose: *block in; cover in a hole* **18** (in certain games) so as to take one's turn or one's team's turn at a certain aspect of the play; taking one's innings: *you have to get the other side out before you go in* **19** *Brit* (of a fire) alight: *do you keep the fire in all night?* **20** (*in combination*) indicating an activity or gathering, esp one organized to protest against something: *teach-in; work-in* **21** **in at** present at (the beginning, end, etc) **22** **in between** between **23** **in for** about to be affected by (something, esp something unpleasant): *you're in for a shock* **24** **in on** acquainted with or sharing in: *I was in on all his plans* **25** **in with** associated with; friendly with; regarded highly by **26** **have (got) it in for** *informal* to wish or intend harm towards ▷ *adj* **27** (*stressed*) fashionable; modish: *the in thing to do* **28** *NZ* competing: *you've got to be in to win* ▷ *n* **29** **ins and outs** intricacies or complications; details: *the ins and outs of a computer system* [Old English; compare Old High German *in*, Welsh *yn*, Old Norse *ī*, Latin *in*, Greek *en*]

in² *the internet domain name for* India

In *the chemical symbol for* indium

IN *abbreviation for* Indiana

in. *abbreviation for* inch(es)

in-¹, il-, im- *or* **ir-** *prefix* not; non-: *incredible; insincere; illegal; imperfect; irregular.* Compare **un-¹** [from Latin *in-*; related to *ne-, nōn* not]

in-², il-, im- *or* **ir-** *prefix* **1** in; into; towards; within; on: *infiltrate; immigrate* **2** having an intensive or causative function: *inflame; imperil* [from **IN** (prep, adv)]

-in *suffix forming nouns* **1** indicating a neutral organic compound, including proteins, glucosides, and glycerides: *insulin; digitoxin; tripalmitin* **2** indicating an enzyme in certain nonsystematic names: *pepsin* **3** indicating a pharmaceutical substance: *penicillin; riboflavin; aspirin* **4** indicating a chemical substance in certain nonsystematic names: *coumarin* [from New Latin *-ina*; compare **-INE²**]

inability (ˌɪnəˈbɪlɪtɪ) *n* lack of ability or means; incapacity

in absentia *Latin* (ɪn æbˈsɛntɪə) *adv* in the absence of (someone indicated): *he was condemned in absentia*

inaccessible (ˌɪnækˈsɛsəbəl) *adj* not accessible; unapproachable > ˌinacˌcessiˈbility *or* ˌinacˈcessibleness *n* > ˌinacˈcessibly *adv*

inaccuracy (ɪnˈækjʊrəsɪ) *n, pl* **-cies** **1** lack of accuracy; imprecision **2** an error, a mistake, or a slip

inaccurate (ɪnˈækjʊrɪt) *adj* not accurate; imprecise, inexact, or erroneous > inˈaccurately *adv* > inˈaccurateness *n*

inaction (ɪnˈækʃən) *n* lack of action; idleness; inertia

inactivate (ɪnˈæktɪˌveɪt) *vb* (*tr*) to render inactive > inˌactiˈvation *n*

inactive (ɪnˈæktɪv) *adj* **1** idle or inert; not active **2** sluggish, passive, or indolent **3** *military* of or relating to persons or equipment not in active service **4** *chem* (of a substance) having little or no reactivity **5** (of an element, isotope, etc) having little or no radioactivity > inˈactively *adv* > ˌinacˈtivity *or* inˈactiveness *n*

inadequate (ɪnˈædɪkwɪt) *adj* **1** not adequate; insufficient **2** not capable or competent; lacking > inˈadequacy *n* > inˈadequately *adv*

inadmissible (ˌɪnədˈmɪsəbəl) *adj* not admissible or allowable > ˌinadˌmissiˈbility *n* > ˌinadˈmissibly *adv*

inadvertence (ˌɪnədˈvɜːtəns) *or* **inadvertency** *n* **1** lack of attention; heedlessness **2** an instance or an effect of being inadvertent; oversight; slip

inadvertent (ˌɪnədˈvɜːtənt) *adj* **1** failing to act carefully or considerately; inattentive **2** resulting from heedless action; unintentional > ˌinadˈvertently *adv*

inadvisable (ˌɪnədˈvaɪzəbəl) *adj* **1** not advisable;

not recommended **2** unwise; imprudent > ˌinadˌvisaˈbility *or* ˌinadˈvisableness *n* > ˌinadˈvisably *adv*

-inae *suffix forming plural proper nouns* occurring in names of zoological subfamilies: *Felinae* [New Latin, from Latin, feminine plural of *-īnus* -INE¹]

in aeternum *Latin* (ɪn iːˈtɜːnəm) *adv* forever; eternally

inalienable (ɪnˈeɪljənəbəl) *adj* not able to be transferred to another; not alienable: *the inalienable rights of the citizen* > inˌalienaˈbility *or* inˈalienableness *n* > inˈalienably *adv*

inalterable (ɪnˈɔːltərəbəl) *adj* not alterable; unalterable > inˌalteraˈbility *or* inˈalterableness *n* > inˈalterably *adv*

inamorata (ɪnˌæməˈrɑːtə, ˌɪnæmə-) *n, pl* **-tas** a woman with whom one is in love; a female lover [C17 see INAMORATO]

inamorato (ɪnˌæməˈrɑːtəʊ, ˌɪnæmə-) *n, pl* **-tos** *or* **-ti** (-tɪ) a man with whom one is in love; a male lover [C16 from Italian *innamorato, innamorata,* from *innamorare* to cause to fall in love, from *amore* love, from Latin *amor*]

in-and-in *adj* (of breeding) carried out repeatedly among closely related individuals of the same species to eliminate or intensify certain characteristics

inane (ɪˈneɪn) *adj* senseless, unimaginative, or empty; unintelligent: *inane remarks* [C17 from Latin *inānis* empty] > inˈanely *adv*

inanga (ˈiːnʌŋə) *n* **1** another name for the New Zealand **whitebait** (sense 2) **2** a common type of New Zealand grass tree, *Dracophyllum longifolium* [Māori]

inanimate (ɪnˈænɪmɪt) *adj* **1** lacking the qualities or features of living beings; not animate: *inanimate objects* **2** lacking any sign of life or consciousness; appearing dead **3** lacking vitality; spiritless; dull > inˈanimately *adv* > inˈanimateness *or* inanimation (ɪnˌænɪˈmeɪʃən) *n*

inanition (ˌɪnəˈnɪʃən) *n* **1** exhaustion resulting from lack of food **2** mental, social, or spiritual weakness or lassitude [C14 from Late Latin *inānītio* emptiness, from *inānis* empty; see INANE]

inanity (ɪˈnænɪtɪ) *n, pl* **-ties** **1** lack of intelligence or imagination; senselessness; silliness **2** a senseless action, remark, etc **3** an archaic word for **emptiness**

inappellable (ˌɪnəˈpɛləbəl) *adj* incapable of being appealed against, as a court decision; unchallengeable [C19 from IN-¹ + Latin *appellāre* to APPEAL]

inappetence (ɪnˈæpɪtəns) *or* **inappetency** *n rare* lack of appetite or desire > inˈappetent *adj*

inapplicable (ɪnˈæplɪkəbəl, ˌɪnəˈplɪk-) *adj* not applicable or suitable; irrelevant > inˌapplicaˈbility *or* inˈapplicableness *n* > inˈapplicably *adv*

inapposite (ɪnˈæpəzɪt) *adj* not appropriate or pertinent; unsuitable > inˈappositely *adv* > inˈappositeness *n*

inappreciable (ˌɪnəˈpriːʃəbəl) *adj* **1** incapable of being appreciated **2** imperceptible; negligible > ˌinapˈpreciably *adv*

inappreciative (ˌɪnəˈpriːʃətɪv) *adj* lacking appreciation; unappreciative > ˌinapˈpreciatively *adv* > ˌinapˌpreciˈation *or* ˌinapˈpreciativeness *n*

inapprehensive (ˌɪnæprɪˈhɛnsɪv) *adj* **1** not perceiving or feeling fear or anxiety; untroubled **2** *rare* unable to understand; imperceptive > ˌinappreˈhensively *adv* > ˌinappreˈhensiveness *n*

inapproachable (ˌɪnəˈprəʊtʃəbəl) *adj* not accessible; unapproachable; unfriendly > ˌinapˌproachaˈbility *noun* > ˌinapˈproachably *adv*

inappropriate (ˌɪnəˈprəʊprɪɪt) *adj* not fitting or appropriate; unsuitable or untimely > ˌinapˈpropriately *adv* > ˌinapˈpropriateness *n*

inapt (ɪnˈæpt) *adj* **1** not apt or fitting; inappropriate **2** lacking skill; inept > inˈaptiˌtude *or* inˈaptness *n* > inˈaptly *adv*

inarch (ɪnˈɑːtʃ) *vb* (*tr*) to graft (a plant) by uniting stock and scion while both are still growing independently

inarticulate (ˌɪnɑːˈtɪkjʊlɪt) *adj* **1** unable to express oneself fluently or clearly; incoherent **2** (of speech, language, etc) unclear or incomprehensible; unintelligible: *inarticulate grunts* **3** unable to speak; dumb **4** unable to be expressed; unvoiced: *inarticulate suffering* **5** *biology* having no joints, segments, or articulation > inarˈticulately *adv* > inarˈticulateness *or* inarˈticulacy *n*

inartificial (ˌɪnɑːtɪˈfɪʃəl) *adj archaic* **1** not artificial; real; natural **2** inartistic > ˌinartiˈficially *adv*

inartistic (ˌɪnɑːˈtɪstɪk) *adj* lacking in artistic skill, appreciation, etc; Philistine > ˌinarˈtistically *adv*

inasmuch as (ˌɪnəzˈmʌtʃ) *conj* (*subordinating*) **1** in view of the fact that; seeing that; since **2** to the extent or degree that; in so far as

inattentive (ˌɪnəˈtɛntɪv) *adj* not paying attention; heedless; negligent > ˌinatˈtention *or* ˌinatˈtentiveness *n* > ˌinatˈtentively *adv*

inaudible (ɪnˈɔːdəbəl) *adj* not loud enough to be heard; not audible > inˌaudiˈbility *or* inˈaudibleness *n* > inˈaudibly *adv*

inaugural (ɪnˈɔːgjʊrəl) *adj* **1** characterizing or relating to an inauguration ▷ *n* **2** a speech made at an inauguration, esp by a president of the US

inaugurate (ɪnˈɔːgjʊˌreɪt) *vb* (*tr*) **1** to commence officially or formally; initiate **2** to place in office formally and ceremonially; induct **3** to open ceremonially; dedicate formally: *to inaugurate a factory* [C17 from Latin *inaugurāre,* literally: to take omens, practise augury, hence to install in office after taking auguries; see IN-², AUGUR] > inˈauguˌration *or* inˈauguˌrator *n* > inauguratory (ɪnˈɔːgjʊrətərɪ, -trɪ) *adj*

Inauguration Day *n* the day on which the inauguration of a president of the US takes place, Jan 20

inauspicious (ˌɪnɔːˈspɪʃəs) *adj* not auspicious; unlucky > ˌinausˈpiciously *adv* > ˌinausˈpiciousness *n*

inauthentic (ˌɪnɔːˈθɛntɪk) *adj* not authentic; false

inbd *abbreviation for* inboard (on an aircraft, a boat, etc)

inbeing (ˈɪnˌbiːɪŋ) *n* **1** existence in something else; inherence **2** basic and inward nature; essence

in-between *adj* **1** intermediate: *he's at the in-between stage, neither a child nor an adult* ▷ *n* **2** an intermediate person or thing

in-betweener *n* an intermediate person or thing

inboard (ˈɪnˌbɔːd) *adj* **1** (esp of a boat's motor or engine) situated within the hull. Compare **outboard** (sense 1) **2** situated between the wing tip of an aircraft and its fuselage: *an inboard engine* ▷ *adv* **3** towards the centre line of or within a vessel, aircraft, etc

in-bond shop *n Caribbean* a duty-free shop

inborn (ˈɪnˈbɔːn) *adj* existing from birth; congenital; innate

inbound (ˈɪnˌbaʊnd) *adj* coming in; inward bound: *an inbound ship*

inbreathe (ɪnˈbriːð) *vb* (*tr*) *rare* to infuse or imbue

inbred (ˈɪnˈbrɛd) *adj* **1** produced as a result of inbreeding **2** deeply ingrained; innate: *inbred good manners*

inbreed (ˈɪnˈbriːd) *vb* **-breeds, -breeding, -bred** **1** to breed from unions between closely related individuals, esp over several generations **2** (*tr*) to develop within; engender > ˈinˈbreeding *n, adj*

in-built *adj* built-in, integral

inby (ɪnˈbaɪ) *adv* **1** *Scot* into the house or an inner room; inside; within **2** *Scot and Northern English dialect* towards or near the house ▷ *adj* **3** *Scot and Northern English dialect* located near or nearest to the house: *the inby field* [C18 from IN (adv) + BY (adv)]

inc. *abbreviation for* **1** included **2** including. **Inc.** *abbreviation for* incorporated. Brit equivalent: **Ltd**

Inca (ˈɪŋkə) *n, pl* **-ca** *or* **-cas** **1** a member of a South American Indian people whose great empire centred on Peru lasted from about 1100 AD to the Spanish conquest in the early 1530s and is famed for its complex culture **2** the ruler or king of this empire or any member of his family **3** the language of the Incas. See also **Quechua** [C16 from Spanish, from Quechua *inka* king] > '**Incan** *adj*

incalculable (ɪnˈkælkjʊləbᵊl) *adj* beyond calculation; unable to be predicted or determined > in,calcula'bility *or* in'calculableness *n* > in'calculably *adv*

incalescent (,ɪnkəˈlɛsᵊnt) *adj chem* increasing in temperature [C17 from Latin *incalescere,* from IN-² + *calescere* to grow warm, from *calēre* to be warm] > ,inca'lescence *n*

in camera (ɪn ˈkæmərə) *adv, adj* **1** in a private or secret session; not in public **2** *law* (formerly) **a** in the privacy of a judge's chambers **b** in a court not open to the public. Official name for sense 2: **in chambers** [Latin: in the chamber]

incandesce (,ɪnkænˈdɛs) *vb* (*intr*) to exhibit incandescence

incandescence (,ɪnkænˈdɛsəns) *or* **incandescency** *n* **1** the emission of light by a body as a consequence of raising its temperature. Compare **luminescence 2** the light produced by raising the temperature of a body

incandescent (,ɪnkænˈdɛsᵊnt) *adj* **1** emitting light as a result of being heated to a high temperature; red-hot or white-hot **2** *informal* extremely angry; raging [C18 from Latin *incandescere* to become hot, glow, from IN-² + *candescere* to grow bright, from *candēre* to be white; see CANDID] > ,incan'descently *adv*

incandescent lamp *n* a source of light that contains a heated solid, such as an electrically heated filament

incantation (,ɪnkænˈteɪʃən) *n* **1** ritual recitation of magic words or sounds **2** the formulaic words or sounds used; a magic spell [C14 from Late Latin *incantātiō* an enchanting, from *incantāre* to repeat magic formulas, from Latin, from IN-² + *cantāre* to sing; see ENCHANT] > ,incan'tational *adj*

incantatory (ɪnˈkæntətrɪ) *adj* relating to or having the characteristics of an incantation

incapable (ɪnˈkeɪpəbᵊl) *adj* **1** (when *postpositive,* often foll by *of*) not capable (of); lacking the ability (to) **2** powerless or helpless, as through injury or intoxication **3** (*postpositive;* foll by *of*) not susceptible (to); not admitting (of): *a problem incapable of solution* > in,capa'bility *or* in'capableness *n* > in'capably *adv*

incapacitant (,ɪnkəˈpæsɪtᵊnt) *n* a substance that can temporarily incapacitate a person, used esp as a weapon in chemical warfare

incapacitate (,ɪnkəˈpæsɪ,teɪt) *vb* (*tr*) **1** to deprive of power, strength, or capacity; disable **2** to deprive of legal capacity or eligibility > ,inca,paci'tation *n*

incapacity (,ɪnkəˈpæsɪtɪ) *n, pl* **-ties 1** lack of power, strength, or capacity; inability **2** *law* **a** legal disqualification or ineligibility **b** a circumstance causing this

incapacity benefit *n* (in Britain) a regular government payment made to people who are unable to work for an extended period through disability

Incaparina (ɪn,kæpəˈriːnə) *n* a cheap high-protein food made of cottonseed, sorghum flours, maize, yeast, etc, used, esp in Latin America, to prevent protein-deficiency diseases [C20 from *Institute of Nutrition in Central America and Panama* + (F)ARINA]

incapsulate (ɪnˈkæpsjʊ,leɪt) *vb* a less common spelling of **encapsulate.** > in,capsu'lation *n*

in-car *adj* installed or provided within a car: *an in-car hi-fi system*

incarcerate (ɪnˈkɑːsə,reɪt) *vb* (*tr*) to confine or imprison [C16 from Medieval Latin *incarcerāre,* from Latin IN-³ + *carcer* prison] > in,carcer'ation *n* > in'carcer,ator *n*

incardinate (ɪnˈkɑːdɪ,neɪt) *vb* (*tr*) *RC Church* to transfer (a cleric) to the jurisdiction of a new bishop [C17 from Late Latin *incardināre,* from IN-² + *cardinālis* CARDINAL]

incardination (ɪn,kɑːdɪˈneɪʃən) *n* **1** the official acceptance by one diocese of a clergyman from another diocese **2** the promotion of a clergyman to the status of a cardinal

incarnadine (ɪnˈkɑːnə,daɪn) *archaic or literary* ⊳ *vb* **1** (*tr*) to tinge or stain with red ⊳ *adj* **2** of a pinkish or reddish colour similar to that of flesh or blood [C16 from French *incarnadin* flesh-coloured, from Italian, from Late Latin *incarnātus* made flesh, INCARNATE]

incarnate *adj* (ɪnˈkɑːnɪt, -neɪt) (*usually immediately postpositive*) **1** possessing bodily form, esp the human form: *a devil incarnate* **2** personified or typified: *stupidity incarnate* **3** (esp of plant parts) flesh-coloured or pink ⊳ *vb* (ɪnˈkɑːneɪt) (*tr*) **4** to give a bodily or concrete form to **5** to be representative or typical of [C14 from Late Latin *incarnāre* to make flesh, from Latin IN-² + *carō* flesh]

incarnation (,ɪnkɑːˈneɪʃən) *n* **1** the act of manifesting or state of being manifested in bodily form, esp human form **2** a bodily form assumed by a god, etc **3** a person or thing that typifies or represents some quality, idea, etc: *the weasel is the incarnation of ferocity*

Incarnation (,ɪnkɑːˈneɪʃən) *n* **1** *Christian theol* the assuming of a human body by the Son of God **2** *Christianity* the presence of God on Earth in the person of Jesus

incarvillea (,ɪnkɑːˈvɪlɪə) *n* any plant of the genus *Incarvillea,* native to China, of which some species are grown as garden or greenhouse plants for their large usually carmine-coloured trumpet-shaped flowers, esp *I. delavayi:* family *Bignoniaceae* [named after Pierre d'*Incarville* (1706–57), French missionary]

incase (ɪnˈkeɪs) *vb* a variant spelling of **encase** > in'casement *n*

incautious (ɪnˈkɔːʃəs) *adj* not careful or cautious > in'cautiously *adv* > in'cautiousness *or* in'caution *n*

incendiarism (ɪnˈsɛndɪə,rɪzəm) *n* **1** the act or practice of illegal burning; arson **2** (esp formerly) the creation of civil strife or violence for political reasons

incendiary (ɪnˈsɛndɪərɪ) *adj* **1** of or relating to the illegal burning of property, goods, etc **2** tending to create strife, violence, etc; inflammatory **3** (of a substance) capable of catching fire, causing fires, or burning readily ⊳ *n, pl* **-aries 4** a person who illegally sets fire to property, goods, etc; arsonist **5** (esp formerly) a person who stirs up civil strife, violence, etc, for political reasons; agitator **6** Also called: **incendiary bomb** a bomb that is designed to start fires **7** an incendiary substance, such as phosphorus [C17 from Latin *incendiārius* setting alight, from *incendium* fire, from *incendere* to kindle]

incense¹ (ˈɪnsɛns) *n* **1** any of various aromatic substances burnt for their fragrant odour, esp in religious ceremonies **2** the odour or smoke so produced **3** any pleasant fragrant odour; aroma **4** *rare* homage or adulation ⊳ *vb* **5** to burn incense in honour of (a deity) **6** (*tr*) to perfume or fumigate with incense [C13 from Old French *encens,* from Church Latin *incensum,* from Latin *incendere* to kindle] > ,incen'sation *n*

incense² (ɪnˈsɛns) *vb* (*tr*) to enrage greatly [C15 from Latin *incensus* set on fire, from *incendere* to kindle] > in'censement *n*

incensory (ˈɪnsɛnsərɪ) *n, pl* **-ries** a less common name for a **censer** [C17 from Medieval Latin *incensorium*]

incentive (ɪnˈsɛntɪv) *n* **1** a motivating influence; stimulus **2 a** an additional payment made to employees as a means of increasing production **b** (*as modifier*): *an incentive scheme* ⊳ *adj* **3** serving to incite to action [C15 from Late Latin *incentīvus* (adj), from Latin: striking up, setting the tune, from *incinere* to sing, from IN-² + *canere* to sing] > in'centively *adv*

incentivize *or* **incentivise** (ɪnˈsɛntɪ,vaɪz) *vb* (*tr*) **a** to provide (someone) with a good reason for wanting to do something: *why not incentivize*

companies to relocate? **b** to promote (something) with a particular incentive: *an incentivized share option scheme*

incept (ɪnˈsɛpt) *vb* (*tr*) **1** (of organisms) to ingest (food) **2** *Brit* (formerly) to take a master's or doctor's degree at a university ⊳ *n* **3** *botany* a rudimentary organ [C19 from Latin *inceptus* begun, attempted, from *incipere* to begin, take in hand, from IN-² + *capere* to take] > in'ceptor *n*

inception (ɪnˈsɛpʃən) *n* the beginning, as of a project or undertaking

inceptive (ɪnˈsɛptɪv) *adj* **1** beginning; incipient; initial **2** Also called: **inchoative** *grammar* denoting an aspect of verbs in some languages used to indicate the beginning of an action ⊳ *n* **3** *grammar* **a** the inceptive aspect of verbs **b** a verb in this aspect > in'ceptively *adv*

incertitude (ɪnˈsɜːtɪ,tjuːd) *n* **1** uncertainty; doubt **2** a state of mental or emotional insecurity

incessant (ɪnˈsɛsᵊnt) *adj* not ceasing; continual [C16 from Late Latin *incessāns,* from Latin IN-¹ + *cessāre* to CEASE] > in'cessancy *or* in'cessantness *n* > in'cessantly *adv*

incest (ˈɪnsɛst) *n* sexual intercourse between two persons commonly regarded as too closely related to marry [C13 from Latin *incestus* incest (from adj: impure, defiled), from IN-¹ + *castus* CHASTE]

incestuous (ɪnˈsɛstjʊəs) *adj* **1** relating to or involving incest: *an incestuous union* **2** guilty of incest **3** *obsolete* resulting from incest: *an incestuous bastard* **4** resembling incest in excessive or claustrophobic intimacy > in'cestuously *adv* > in'cestuousness *n*

inch¹ (ɪntʃ) *n* **1** a unit of length equal to one twelfth of a foot or 0.0254 metre **2** *meteorol* **a** an amount of precipitation that would cover a surface with water one inch deep: *five inches of rain fell in January* **b** a unit of pressure equal to a mercury column one inch high in a barometer **3** a very small distance, degree, or amount **4** **every inch** in every way; completely: *he was every inch an aristocrat* **5** **inch by inch** gradually; little by little **6** **within an inch of** very close to ⊳ *vb* **7** to move or be moved very slowly or in very small steps: *the car inched forward* **8** (*tr;* foll by *out*) to defeat (someone) by a very small margin [Old English *ynce,* from Latin *uncia* twelfth part; see OUNCE¹]

inch² (ɪntʃ) *n Scot and Irish* a small island [C15 from Gaelic *innis* island; compare Welsh *ynys*]

inchmeal (ˈɪntʃ,miːl) *adv* gradually; inch by inch or little by little [C16 from INCH¹ + *-mele,* from Old English *mælum* quantity taken at one time; compare PIECEMEAL]

inchoate *adj* (ɪnˈkəʊeɪt, -ʊɪt) **1** just beginning; incipient **2** undeveloped; immature; rudimentary **3** (of a legal document, promissory note, etc) in an uncompleted state; not yet made specific or valid ⊳ *vb* (ɪnˈkəʊeɪt) (*tr*) **4** to begin [C16 from Latin *incohāre* to make a beginning, literally: to hitch up, from IN-² + *cohum* yokestrap] > in'choately *adv* > in'choateness *n* > ,incho'ation *n* > inchoative (ɪnˈkəʊətɪv) *adj*

Inchon *or* **Incheon** (ˈɪntʃɒn) *n* a port in W South Korea, on the Yellow Sea: the chief port for Seoul: site of a major strategic amphibious assault by UN troops, liberating Seoul (Sept 15, 1950). Pop: 2 642 000 (2005 est). Former name: **Chemulpo**

Inchworm (ˈɪntʃ,wɜːm) *n* another name for a **measuring worm**

incidence (ˈɪnsɪdəns) *n* **1** degree, extent, or frequency of occurrence; amount: *a high incidence of death from pneumonia* **2** the act or manner of impinging on or affecting by proximity or influence **3** *physics* the arrival of a beam of light or particles at a surface. See also **angle of incidence 4** *geometry* the partial coincidence of two configurations, such as a point that lies on a circle

incident (ˈɪnsɪdənt) *n* **1** a distinct or definite occurrence; event **2** a minor, subsidiary, or related event or action **3** a relatively insignificant event that might have serious consequences, esp in international politics **4** a public disturbance: *the police had reports of an incident outside a pub* **5** the occurrence of something interesting or exciting: *the trip was not without incident* ▷ *adj* **6** (*postpositive; foll by to*) related (to) or dependent (on) **7** (*when postpositive, often foll by to*) having a subsidiary or minor relationship (with) **8** (esp of a beam of light or particles) arriving at or striking a surface: *incident electrons* [C15 from Medieval Latin *incidens* an event, from Latin *incidere*, literally: to fall into, hence befall, happen, from IN-² + *cadere* to fall]

incidental (ˌɪnsɪˈdɛntᵊl) *adj* **1** happening in connection with or resulting from something more important; casual or fortuitous **2** (*postpositive; foll by to*) found in connection (with); related (to) **3** (*postpositive; foll by upon*) caused (by) **4** occasional or minor: *incidental expenses* ▷ *n* **5** (*often plural*) an incidental or minor expense, event, or action > ˌinciˈdentalness *n*

incidentally (ˌɪnsɪˈdɛntəlɪ) *adv* **1** as a subordinate or chance occurrence **2** (*sentence modifier*) by the way

incidental music *n* background music for a film, television programme, etc

incinerate (ɪnˈsɪnəˌreɪt) *vb* to burn up completely; reduce to ashes [C16 from Medieval Latin *incinerāre*, from Latin IN-² + *cinis* ashes] > inˌcinerˈation *n*

incinerator (ɪnˈsɪnəˌreɪtə) *n* a furnace or apparatus for incinerating something, esp refuse

incipient (ɪnˈsɪpɪənt) *adj* just starting to be or happen; beginning [C17 from Latin *incipiēns*, from *incipere* to begin, take in hand, from IN-² + *capere* to take] > inˈcipience *or* inˈcipiency *n* > inˈcipiently *adv*

incipit *Latin* (ˈɪnkɪpɪt) here begins: used as an introductory word at the beginning of some medieval manuscripts

incise (ɪnˈsaɪz) *vb* (*tr*) to produce (lines, a design, etc) by cutting into the surface of (something) with a sharp tool [C16 from Latin *incīdere* to cut into, from IN-² + *caedere* to cut]

incised (ɪnˈsaɪzd) *adj* **1** cut into or engraved: *an incised surface* **2** made by cutting or engraving: *an incised design* **3** (of a wound) cleanly cut, as with a surgical knife **4** having margins that are sharply and deeply indented: *an incised leaf*

incisiform (ɪnˈsaɪzɪˌfɔːm) *adj zoology* having the shape of an incisor tooth

incision (ɪnˈsɪʒən) *n* **1** the act of incising **2** a cut, gash, or notch **3** a cut made with a knife during a surgical operation **4** any indentation in an incised leaf **5** *rare* incisiveness

incisive (ɪnˈsaɪsɪv) *adj* **1** keen, penetrating, or acute **2** biting or sarcastic; mordant: *an incisive remark* **3** having a sharp cutting edge: *incisive teeth* > inˈcisively *adv* > inˈcisiveness *n*

incisor (ɪnˈsaɪzə) *n* a chisel-edged tooth at the front of the mouth. In man there are four in each jaw

incisure (ɪnˈsaɪʒə) *n anatomy* an incision or notch in an organ or part > inˈcisural *adj*

incite (ɪnˈsaɪt) *vb* (*tr*) to stir up or provoke to action [C15 from Latin *incitāre*, from IN-² + *citāre* to excite] > ˌinciˈtation *n* > inˈcitement *n* > inˈciter *n* > inˈcitingly *adv*

incivility (ɪnsɪˈvɪlɪtɪ) *n, pl* -ties **1** lack of civility or courtesy; rudeness **2** an impolite or uncivil act or remark

incl. *abbreviation for* **1** including **2** inclusive

inclement (ɪnˈklɛmənt) *adj* **1** (of weather) stormy, severe, or tempestuous **2** harsh, severe, or merciless > inˈclemency *or* inˈclementness *n* > inˈclemently *adv*

inclinable (ɪnˈklaɪnəbᵊl) *adj* **1** (*postpositive; usually foll by to*) having an inclination or tendency (to); disposed (to) **2** capable of being inclined

inclination (ˌɪnklɪˈneɪʃən) *n* **1** (often foll by *for, to, towards*, or an infinitive) a particular disposition, esp a liking or preference; tendency: *I've no inclination for such dull work* **2** the degree of deviation from a particular plane, esp a horizontal or vertical plane **3** a sloping or slanting surface; incline **4** the act of inclining or the state of being inclined **5** the act of bowing or nodding the head **6** *maths* **a** the angle between a line on a graph and the positive limb of the *x*-axis **b** the smaller dihedral angle between one plane and another **7** *astronomy* the angle between the plane of the orbit of a planet or comet and another plane, usually that of the ecliptic **8** *physics* another name for **dip** (sense 28) > ˌincliˈnational *adj*

incline *vb* (ɪnˈklaɪn) **1** to deviate or cause to deviate from a particular plane, esp a vertical or horizontal plane; slope or slant **2** (when *tr*, may take an infinitive) to be disposed or cause to be disposed (towards some attitude or to do something): *he inclines towards levity; that does not incline me to think that you are right* **3** to bend or lower (part of the body, esp the head), as in a bow or in order to listen **4** **incline one's ear** to listen favourably (to) ▷ *n* (ˈɪnklaɪn, ɪnˈklaɪn) **5** an inclined surface or slope; gradient **6** short for **inclined railway** [C13 from Latin *inclīnāre* to cause to lean, from *clīnāre* to bend; see LEAN¹] > inˈcliner *n*

inclined (ɪnˈklaɪnd) *adj* **1** (*postpositive; often foll by to*) having a disposition; tending **2** sloping or slanting

inclined plane *n* a plane whose angle to the horizontal is less than a right angle

inclined railway *n chiefly US* a cable railway used on particularly steep inclines unsuitable for normal adhesion locomotives

inclinometer (ˌɪnklɪˈnɒmɪtə) *n* **1** an aircraft instrument for indicating the angle that an aircraft makes with the horizontal **2** another name for **dip circle**

inclose (ɪnˈkləʊz) *vb* a less common spelling of **enclose.** > inˈclosable *adj* > inˈcloser *n* > inˈclosure *n*

include (ɪnˈkluːd) *vb* (*tr*) **1** to have as contents or part of the contents; be made up of or contain **2** to add as part of something else; put in as part of a set, group, or category **3** to contain as a secondary or minor ingredient or element [C15 (in the sense: to enclose): from Latin *inclūdere* to enclose, from IN-² + *claudere* to close] > inˈcludable *or* inˈcludible *adj*

included (ɪnˈkluːdɪd) *adj* (of the stamens or pistils of a flower) not protruding beyond the corolla > inˈcludedness *n*

include out *vb* (*tr, adverb*) *informal* to exclude: *you can include me out of that deal*

inclusion (ɪnˈkluːʒən) *n* **1** the act of including or the state of being included **2** something included **3** *geology* a solid fragment, liquid globule, or pocket of gas enclosed in a mineral or rock **4** *maths* **a** the relation between two sets that obtains when all the members of the first are members of the second. Symbol: $X \subseteq Y$ **b** **strict** *or* **proper inclusion** the relation that obtains between two sets when the first includes the second but not vice versa. Symbol: $X \subseteq Y$ **5** *engineering* a foreign particle in a metal, such as a particle of metal oxide

inclusion body *n pathol* any of the small particles found in the nucleus and cytoplasm of cells infected with certain viruses

inclusive (ɪnˈkluːsɪv) *adj* **1** (*postpositive; foll by of*) considered together (with): *capital inclusive of profit* **2** (*postpositive*) including the limits specified: *Monday to Friday inclusive is five days* **3** comprehensive **4** not excluding any particular groups of people: *an inclusive society* **5** *logic* (of a disjunction) true if at least one of its component propositions is true. Compare **exclusive** (sense 10) > inˈclusively *adv* > inˈclusiveness *n*

inclusive language *n* language that avoids the use of certain expressions or words that might be considered to exclude particular groups of people, esp gender-specific words, such as "man", "mankind", and masculine pronouns, the use of which might be considered to exclude women

inclusive or *n logic* the connective that gives the value *true* to a disjunction if either or both of the disjuncts are true. Also called: **inclusive disjunction** Compare **exclusive or**

inclusivity (ˌɪnkluːˈsɪvɪtɪ) *n* the fact or policy of not excluding members or participants on the grounds of gender, race, class, sexuality, disability, etc

incoercible (ˌɪnkəʊˈɜːsəbᵊl) *adj* **1** unable to be coerced or compelled **2** (of a gas) not capable of being liquefied by pressure alone

incog. *abbreviation for* incognito

incogitable (ɪnˈkɒdʒɪtəbᵊl) *adj rare* not to be contemplated; unthinkable > inˌcogitaˈbility *n*

incogitant (ɪnˈkɒdʒɪtənt) *adj rare* thoughtless [C17 from Latin *incōgitāns*, from IN-¹ + *cōgitāre* to think]

incognito (ˌɪnkɒgˈniːtəʊ, ɪnˈkɒgnɪtəʊ) *adv* ▷ *adj* (*postpositive*) **1** under an assumed name or appearance; in disguise ▷ *n, pl* -tos **2** a person who is incognito **3** the assumed name or disguise of such a person [C17 from Italian, from Latin *incognitus* unknown, from IN-¹ + *cognitus* known]

incognizant (ɪnˈkɒgnɪzənt) *adj* (*when postpositive, often foll by of*) unaware (of) > inˈcognizance *n*

incoherent (ˌɪnkəʊˈhɪərənt) *adj* **1** lacking in clarity or organization; disordered **2** unable to express oneself clearly; inarticulate **3** *physics* (of two or more waves) having the same frequency but not the same phase: *incoherent light* > ˌincoˈherence, ˌincoˈherency *or* ˌincoˈherentness *n* > ˌincoˈherently *adv*

incombustible (ˌɪnkəmˈbʌstəbᵊl) *adj* **1** not capable of being burnt; fireproof ▷ *n* **2** an incombustible object or material > ˌincomˌbustiˈbility *or* ˌincomˈbustibleness *n* > ˌincomˈbustibly *adv*

income (ˈɪnkʌm, ˈɪnkəm) *n* **1** the amount of monetary or other returns, either earned or unearned, accruing over a given period of time **2** receipts; revenue **3** *rare* an inflow or influx [C13 (in the sense: arrival, entrance): from Old English *incumen* a coming in]

income bond *n* a bond that pays interest at a rate in direct proportion to the issuer's earnings

income group *n* a group in a given population having incomes within a certain range

incomer (ˈɪnkʌmə) *n* a person who comes to live in a place in which he was not born

incomes policy *n* See **prices and incomes policy**

income support *n* (in Britain, formerly) a social security payment for people on very low incomes

income tax *n* a personal tax, usually progressive, levied on annual income subject to certain deductions

incoming (ˈɪnˌkʌmɪŋ) *adj* **1** coming in; entering **2** about to come into office; succeeding **3** (of interest, dividends, etc) being received; accruing ▷ *n* **4** the act of coming in; entrance **5** (*usually plural*) income or revenue

incommensurable (ˌɪnkəˈmɛnʃərəbᵊl) *adj* **1** incapable of being judged, measured, or considered comparatively **2** (*postpositive; foll by with*) not in accordance; incommensurate **3** *maths* **a** (of two numbers) having an irrational ratio **b** not having units of the same dimension **c** unrelated to another measurement by integral multiples ▷ *n* **4** something incommensurable > ˌincomˌmensuraˈbility *or* ˌincomˈmensurableness *n* > ˌincomˈmensurably *adv*

incommensurate (ˌɪnkəˈmɛnʃərɪt) *adj* **1** (*when postpositive, often foll by with*) not commensurate; disproportionate **2** incommensurable > ˌincomˈmensurately *adv* > ˌincomˈmensurateness *n*

incommode (ˌɪnkəˈməʊd) *vb* (*tr*) to bother, disturb, or inconvenience [C16 from Latin *incommodāre* to be troublesome, from *incommodus* inconvenient, from IN-¹ + *commodus* convenient; see COMMODE]

incommodious (ˌɪnkəˈməʊdɪəs) *adj* **1** insufficiently spacious; cramped **2** troublesome or inconvenient > ˌincomˈmodiously *adv* > ˌincomˈmodiousness *n*

incommodity (ˌɪnkəˈmɒdɪtɪ) *n, pl* -ties a less common word for **inconvenience**

incommunicable (ˌɪnkəˈmjuːnɪkəbᵊl) *adj* **1**

incapable of being communicated **2** an obsolete word for **incommunicative**. > ˌincomˌmunicaˈbility or ˌincomˈmunicableness *n* > ˌincomˈmunicably *adv*

incommunicado (ˌɪnkəˌmjuːnɪˈkɑːdəʊ) *adv, adj* (*postpositive*) deprived of communication with other people, as while in solitary confinement [c19 from Spanish *incomunicado,* from *incomunicar* to deprive of communication; see IN-¹, COMMUNICATE]

incommunicative (ˌɪnkəˈmjuːnɪkətɪv) *adj* tending not to communicate with others; taciturn > ˌincomˈmunicatively *adv* > ˌincomˈmunicativeness *n*

incommutable (ˌɪnkəˈmjuːtəbəl) *adj* incapable of being commuted; unalterable > ˌincomˌmutaˈbility or ˌincomˈmutableness *n* > ˌincomˈmutably *adv*

incomparable (ɪnˈkɒmpərəbəl, -prəbəl) *adj* **1** beyond or above comparison; matchless; unequalled **2** lacking a basis for comparison; not having qualities or features that can be compared > inˌcompaˈrability or inˈcomparableness *n* > inˈcomparably *adv*

incompatible (ˌɪnkəmˈpætəbəl) *adj* **1** incapable of living or existing together in peace or harmony; conflicting or antagonistic **2** opposed in nature or quality; inconsistent **3** (of an office, position, etc) only able to be held by one person at a time **4** *med* (esp of two drugs or two types of blood) incapable of being combined or used together; antagonistic **5** *logic* (of two propositions) unable to be both true at the same time **6** (of plants) **a** not capable of forming successful grafts **b** incapable of fertilizing each other **7** *maths* another word for **inconsistent** (sense 4) ▷ *n* **8** (*often plural*) a person or thing that is incompatible with another > ˌincomˌpatiˈbility or ˌincomˈpatibleness *n* > ˌincomˈpatibly *adv*

incompetent (ɪnˈkɒmpɪtənt) *adj* **1** not possessing the necessary ability, skill, etc to do or carry out a task; incapable **2** marked by lack of ability, skill, etc **3** *law* not legally qualified: *an incompetent witness* **4** (of rock strata, folds, etc) yielding readily to pressure so as to undergo structural deformation ▷ *n* **5** an incompetent person > inˈcompetence or inˈcompetency *n* > inˈcompetently *adv*

incomplete (ˌɪnkəmˈpliːt) *adj* **1** not complete or finished **2** not completely developed; imperfect **3** *logic* **a** (of a formal theory) not so constructed that the addition of a non-theorem to the axioms renders it inconsistent **b** (of an expression) not having a reference of its own but requiring completion by another expression > ˌincomˈpletely *adv* > ˌincomˈpleteness or ˌincomˈpletion *n*

incompliant (ˌɪnkəmˈplaɪənt) *adj* not compliant; unyielding or inflexible > ˌincomˈpliance or ˌincomˈpliancy *n* > ˌincomˈpliantly *adv*

incomprehensible (ˌɪnkɒmprɪˈhensəbəl, ɪnˌkɒm-) *adj* **1** incapable of being understood; unintelligible **2** *archaic* limitless; boundless > ˌincompreˌhensiˈbility or ˌincompreˈhensibleness *n* > ˌincompreˈhensibly *adv*

incomprehension (ˌɪnkɒmprɪˈhenʃən, ɪnˌkɒm-) *n* inability or failure to comprehend; lack of understanding

incomprehensive (ˌɪnkɒmprɪˈhensɪv, ɪnˌkɒm-) *adj* not comprehensive; limited in range or scope > ˌincompreˈhensively *adv* > ˌincompreˈhensiveness *n*

incompressible (ˌɪnkəmˈpresəbəl) *adj* incapable of being compressed or condensed > ˌincomˌpressiˈbility or ˌincomˈpressibleness *n* > ˌincomˈpressibly *adv*

incomputable (ˌɪnkəmˈpjuːtəbəl) *adj* incapable of being computed; incalculable > ˌincomˌputaˈbility *n* > ˌincomˈputably *adv*

inconceivable (ˌɪnkənˈsiːvəbəl) *adj* incapable of being conceived, imagined, or considered > ˌinconˌceivaˈbility or ˌinconˈceivableness *n* > ˌinconˈceivably *adv*

inconclusive (ˌɪnkənˈkluːsɪv) *adj* not conclusive or decisive; not finally settled; indeterminate

> ˌinconˈclusively *adv* > ˌinconˈclusiveness *n*

incondensable or **incondensible** (ˌɪnkənˈdensəbəl) *adj* incapable of being condensed > ˌinconˌdensaˈbility or ˌinconˌdensiˈbility *n*

incondite (ɪnˈkɒndɪt, -daɪt) *adj rare* **1** poorly constructed or composed **2** rough or crude [c17 from Latin *inconditus,* from IN-¹ + *conditus,* from *condere* to put together] > inˈconditely *adv*

inconformity (ˌɪnkənˈfɔːmɪtɪ) *n* lack of conformity; irregularity

incongruity (ˌɪnkɒŋˈgruːɪtɪ) *n, pl* -ties **1** something incongruous **2** the state or quality of being incongruous

incongruous (ɪnˈkɒŋgruəs) or **incongruent** *adj* **1** (when *postpositive,* foll by *with* or *to*) incompatible with (what is suitable); inappropriate **2** containing disparate or discordant elements or parts > inˈcongruously or inˈcongruently *adv* > inˈcongruousness or inˈcongruence *n*

inconnu (ˈɪnkənuː) *n* a North American freshwater food and game fish, *Stenodus leucichthys,* related to the salmon [c19 from French, literally: unknown]

inconsecutive (ˌɪnkənˈsekjʊtɪv) *adj* not consecutive; not in sequence > ˌinconˈsecutively *adv* > ˌinconˈsecutiveness *n*

inconsequential (ˌɪnkɒnsɪˈkwenʃəl, ɪnˌkɒn-) or **inconsequent** (ɪnˈkɒnsɪkwənt) *adj* **1** not following logically as a consequence **2** trivial or insignificant **3** not in a logical sequence; haphazard > inˌconse,quentiˈality, ˌinconseˈquentialness, inˈconsequence or inˈconsequentness *n* > ˌinconseˈquentially or inˈconsequently *adv*

inconsiderable (ˌɪnkənˈsɪdərəbəl) *adj* **1** relatively small **2** not worthy of consideration; insignificant > ˌinconˈsiderableness *n* > ˌinconˈsiderably *adv*

inconsiderate (ˌɪnkənˈsɪdərɪt) *adj* **1** lacking in care or thought for others; heedless; thoughtless **2** *rare* insufficiently considered > ˌinconˈsiderately *adv* > ˌinconˈsiderateness or ˌinconˌsiderˈation *n*

inconsistency (ˌɪnkənˈsɪstənsɪ) *n, pl* -cies **1** lack of consistency or agreement; incompatibility **2** an inconsistent feature or quality **3** *logic* **a** the property of being inconsistent **b** a self-contradictory proposition

inconsistent (ˌɪnkənˈsɪstənt) *adj* **1** lacking in consistency, agreement, or compatibility; at variance **2** containing contradictory elements **3** irregular or fickle in behaviour or mood **4** Also: incompatible *maths* (of two or more equations) not having one common set of values of the variables: $x + 2y = 5$ and $x + 2y = 6$ are inconsistent **5** *logic* (of a set of propositions) enabling an explicit contradiction to be validly derived > ˌinconˈsistently *adv*

inconsolable (ˌɪnkənˈsəʊləbəl) *adj* incapable of being consoled or comforted; disconsolate > ˌinconˌsolaˈbility or ˌinconˈsolableness *n* > ˌinconˈsolably *adv*

inconsonant (ɪnˈkɒnsənənt) *adj* lacking in harmony or compatibility; discordant > inˈconsonance *n* > inˈconsonantly *adv*

inconspicuous (ˌɪnkənˈspɪkjʊəs) *adj* not easily noticed or seen; not prominent or striking > ˌinconˈspicuously *adv* > ˌinconˈspicuousness *n*

inconstant (ɪnˈkɒnstənt) *adj* **1** not constant; variable **2** fickle > inˈconstancy *n* > inˈconstantly *adv*

inconsumable (ˌɪnkənˈsjuːməbəl) *adj* **1** incapable of being consumed or used up **2** *economics* providing an economic service without being consumed, as currency > ˌinconˈsumably *adv*

incontestable (ˌɪnkənˈtestəbəl) *adj* incapable of being contested or disputed > ˌinconˌtestaˈbility or ˌinconˈtestableness *n* > ˌinconˈtestably *adv*

incontinent¹ (ɪnˈkɒntɪnənt) *adj* **1** lacking in restraint or control, esp sexually **2** relating to or exhibiting involuntary urination or defecation **3** (foll by *of*) having little or no control (over) **4**

unrestrained; uncontrolled [c14 from Old French, from Latin *incontinens,* from IN-¹ + *continere* to hold, restrain] > inˈcontinence or inˈcontinency *n* > inˈcontinently *adv*

incontinent² (ɪnˈkɒntɪnənt) or **incontinently** *adv* obsolete words for **immediately** [c15 from Late Latin *in continentī tempore,* literally: in continuous time, that is, with no interval]

incontrollable (ˌɪnkənˈtrəʊləbəl) *adj* a less common word for **uncontrollable** > ˌinconˈtrollably *adv*

incontrovertible (ˌɪnkɒntrəˈvɜːtəbəl, ɪnˌkɒn-) *adj* incapable of being contradicted or disputed; undeniable > ˌincontroˌvertiˈbility or ˌincontroˈvertibleness *n* > ˌincontroˈvertibly *adv*

inconvenience (ˌɪnkənˈviːnjəns, -ˈviːnɪəns) *n* **1** the state or quality of being inconvenient **2** something inconvenient; a hindrance, trouble, or difficulty ▷ *vb* **3** (*tr*) to cause inconvenience to; trouble or harass

inconvenient (ˌɪnkənˈviːnjənt, -ˈviːnɪənt) *adj* not convenient; troublesome, awkward, or difficult > ˌinconˈveniently *adv*

inconvertible (ˌɪnkənˈvɜːtəbəl) *adj* **1** incapable of being converted or changed **2** (of paper currency) **a** not redeemable for gold or silver specie **b** not exchangeable for another currency > ˌinconˌvertiˈbility or ˌinconˈvertibleness *n* > ˌinconˈvertibly *adv*

inconvincible (ˌɪnkənˈvɪnsəbəl) *adj* refusing or not able to be convinced > ˌinconˌvinciˈbility or ˌinconˈvincibleness *n* > ˌinconˈvincibly *adv*

incoordinate (ˌɪnkəʊˈɔːdɪnɪt) *adj* **1** not coordinate; unequal in rank, order, or importance **2** uncoordinated

incoordination (ˌɪnkəʊˌɔːdɪˈneɪʃən) *n* **1** lack of coordination or organization **2** *pathol* a lack of muscular control when making a voluntary movement

incorporable (ɪnˈkɔːpərəbəl) *adj* capable of being incorporated or included

incorporate¹ *vb* (ɪnˈkɔːpəˌreɪt) **1** to include or be included as a part or member of a united whole **2** to form or cause to form a united whole or mass; merge or blend **3** to form (individuals, an unincorporated enterprise, etc) into a corporation or other organization with a separate legal identity from that of its owners or members ▷ *adj* (ɪnˈkɔːpərɪt, -prɪt) **4** combined into a whole; incorporated **5** formed into or constituted as a corporation [c14 (in the sense: put into the body of something else): from Late Latin *incorporāre* to embody, from Latin IN-² + *corpus* body] > inˈcorporative *adj* > inˌcorpoˈration *n*

incorporate² (ɪnˈkɔːpərɪt, -prɪt) *adj* an archaic word for **incorporeal** [c16 from Late Latin *incorporātus,* from Latin IN-¹ + *corporātus* furnished with a body]

incorporated (ɪnˈkɔːpəˌreɪtɪd) *adj* **1** united or combined into a whole **2** organized as a legal corporation, esp in commerce. Abbreviation: Inc. or inc. > inˈcorpoˌratedness *n*

incorporating (ɪnˈkɔːpəˌreɪtɪŋ) *adj linguistics* another word for **polysynthetic**

incorporator (ɪnˈkɔːpəˌreɪtə) *n* **1** a person who incorporates **2** *US commerce* **a** any of the signatories of a certificate of incorporation **b** any of the original members of a corporation

incorporeal (ˌɪnkɔːˈpɔːrɪəl) *adj* **1** without material form, body, or substance **2** spiritual or metaphysical **3** *law* having no material existence but existing by reason of its annexation of something material, such as an easement, touchline, copyright, etc: *an incorporeal hereditament* > ˌincorˈporeally *adv* > incorporeity (ɪnˌkɔːpəˈriːɪtɪ) or ˌincorporeˈality *n*

incorrect (ˌɪnkəˈrekt) *adj* **1** false; wrong: *an incorrect calculation* **2** not fitting or proper: *incorrect behaviour* > ˌincorˈrectly *adv* > ˌincorˈrectness *n*

incorrigible (ɪnˈkɒrɪdʒəbəl) *adj* **1** beyond correction, reform, or alteration **2** firmly rooted; ineradicable **3** *philosophy* (of a belief) having the

i

property that whoever honestly believes it cannot be mistaken. Compare **defeasible** ▷ *n* **4** a person or animal that is incorrigible > in,corri'bility or in'corrigibleness *n* > in'corrigibly *adv*

incorrupt (,ɪnkə'rʌpt) *adj* **1** free from corruption; pure **2** free from decay; fresh or untainted **3** (of a manuscript, text, etc) relatively free from error or alteration > ,incor'ruptly *adv* > ,incor'ruption or ,incor'ruptness *n*

incorruptible (,ɪnkə'rʌptəb°l) *adj* **1** incapable of being corrupted; honest; just **2** not subject to decay or decomposition > ,incor,rupti'bility or ,incor'ruptibleness *n* > ,incor'ruptibly *adv*

Incoterms ('ɪnkəʊ,tɜ:mz) *n* a glossary of terms used in international commerce and trade, published by the International Chamber of Commerce

incrassate *adj* (ɪn'kræsɪt, -eɪt) *also* **incrassated 1** *biology* thickened or swollen: *incrassate cell walls* **2** *obsolete* fattened or swollen ▷ *vb* (ɪn'kræseɪt) **3** *obsolete* to make or become thicker [c17 from Late Latin *incrassāre,* from Latin *crassus* thick, dense] > ,incras'sation *n*

increase *vb* (ɪn'kri:s) **1** to make or become greater in size, degree, frequency, etc; grow or expand ▷ *n* ('ɪnkri:s) **2** the act of increasing; augmentation **3** the amount by which something increases **4 on the increase** increasing, esp becoming more frequent [c14 from Old French *encreistre,* from Latin *incrēscere,* from IN-² + *crēscere* to grow] > in'creasable *adj* > increasedly (ɪn'kri:sɪdlɪ) or in'creasingly *adv* > in'creaser *n*

increate (,ɪnkrɪ'eɪt, 'ɪnkrɪ,eɪt) *adj archaic, poetic* (esp of gods) never having been created > ,incre'ately *adv*

incredible (ɪn'krɛdəb°l) *adj* **1** beyond belief or understanding; unbelievable **2** *informal* marvellous; amazing > in,credi'bility or in'credibleness *n* > in'credibly *adv*

incredulity (,ɪnkrɪ'dju:lɪtɪ) *n* lack of belief; scepticism

incredulous (ɪn'krɛdjʊləs) *adj* (often foll by *of*) not prepared or willing to believe (something); unbelieving > in'credulously *adv* > in'credulousness *n*

increment ('ɪnkrɪmənt) *n* **1** an increase or addition, esp one of a series **2** the act of increasing; augmentation **3** *maths* a small positive or negative change in a variable or function. Symbol: Δ, as in Δ*x* or Δ*f* [c15 from Latin *incrēmentum* growth, INCREASE]

incremental (,ɪnkrɪ'mɛnt°l) *adj* of, relating to, using, or rising by increments

incremental plotter *n* a device that plots graphs on paper from computer-generated instructions. See also **microfilm plotter**

incremental recorder *n* *computing* a device for recording data as it is generated, usually on paper tape or magnetic tape, and feeding it into a computer

increscent (ɪn'krɛs°nt) *adj* (esp of the moon) increasing in size; waxing [c16 from Latin *incrēscēns*]

incretion (ɪn'kri:ʃən) *n physiol* **1** direct secretion into the bloodstream, esp of a hormone from an endocrine gland **2** the substance so secreted [c20 from IN-² + (SE)CRETION] > in'cretionary or incretory ('ɪnkrɪtərɪ, -trɪ) *adj*

incriminate (ɪn'krɪmɪ,neɪt) *vb* (*tr*) **1** to imply or suggest the guilt or error of (someone) **2** to charge with a crime or fault [c18 from Late Latin *incrīmināre* to accuse, from Latin *crīmen* accusation; see CRIME] > in,crimi'nation *n* > in'crimi,nator *n* > in'criminatory *adj*

incross ('ɪnkrɒs) *n* **1** a plant or animal produced by continued inbreeding ▷ *vb* **2** to inbreed or produce by inbreeding

incrust (ɪn'krʌst) *vb* a variant spelling of **encrust** > in'crustant *n, adj* > ,incrus'tation *n*

incubate ('ɪnkjʊ,beɪt) *vb* **1** (of birds) to supply (eggs) with heat for their development, esp by sitting on them **2** to cause (eggs, embryos,

bacteria, etc) to develop, esp in an incubator or culture medium **3** (*intr*) (of eggs, embryos, bacteria, etc) to develop in favourable conditions, esp in an incubator **4** (*intr*) (of disease germs) to remain inactive in an animal or human before causing disease **5** to develop or cause to develop gradually; foment or be fomented [c18 from Latin *incubāre* to lie upon, hatch, from IN-² + *cubāre* to lie down] > ,incu'bation *n* > ,incu'bational *adj* > 'incu,bative or 'incu,batory *adj*

incubation period *n med* the time between exposure to an infectious disease and the appearance of the first signs or symptoms. Sometimes shortened to: **incubation**

incubator ('ɪnkjʊ,beɪtə) *n* **1** *med* an enclosed transparent boxlike apparatus for housing prematurely born babies under optimum conditions until they are strong enough to survive in the normal environment **2** a container kept at a constant temperature in which birds' eggs can be artificially hatched or bacterial cultures grown **3** a person, animal, or thing that incubates **4** a commercial property, divided into small work units, which provides equipment and support to new businesses

incubous ('ɪnkjʊbəs) *adj* (of a liverwort) having the leaves arranged so that the upper margin of each leaf lies above the lower margin of the next leaf along. Compare **succubous** [c19 from Latin *incubare* INCUBATE]

incubus ('ɪnkjʊbəs) *n, pl* -**bi** (-,baɪ) *or* -**buses 1** a demon believed in folklore to lie upon sleeping persons, esp to have sexual intercourse with sleeping women. Compare **succubus 2** something that oppresses, worries, or disturbs greatly, esp a nightmare or obsession [c14 from Late Latin, from *incubāre* to lie upon; see INCUBATE]

incudes (ɪn'kju:di:z) *n* the plural of **incus**

inculcate ('ɪnkʌl,keɪt, ɪn'kʌlkeɪt) *vb* (*tr*) to instil by forceful or insistent repetition [c16 from Latin *inculcāre* to tread upon, ram down, from IN-² + *calcāre* to trample, from *calx* heel] > ,incul'cation *n* > 'incul,cator *n*

inculpable (ɪn'kʌlpəb°l) *adj* incapable of being blamed or accused; guiltless > in,culpa'bility or in'culpableness *n* > in'culpably *adv*

inculpate ('ɪnkʌl,peɪt, ɪn'kʌlpeɪt) *vb* (*tr*) to incriminate; cause blame to be imputed to [c18 from Late Latin *inculpāre,* from Latin *culpāre* to blame, from *culpa* fault, blame] > ,incul'pation *n* > inculpative (ɪn'kʌlpətɪv) or inculpatory (ɪn'kʌlpətərɪ, -trɪ) *adj*

incult (ɪn'kʌlt) *adj rare* **1** (of land) uncultivated; untilled; naturally wild **2** lacking refinement and culture [c16 from Latin *incultus,* from IN-¹ + *colere* to till]

incumbency (ɪn'kʌmbənsɪ) *n, pl* -**cies 1** the state or quality of being incumbent **2** the office, duty, or tenure of an incumbent

incumbent (ɪn'kʌmbənt) *adj* **1** *formal* (often *postpositive* and foll by *on* or *upon* and an infinitive) morally binding or necessary; obligatory **2** (usually *postpositive* and foll by *on*) resting or lying (on) ▷ *n* **3** a person who holds an office, esp a clergyman holding a benefice [c16 from Latin *incumbere* to lie upon, devote one's attention to, from IN-² + *-cumbere,* related to Latin *cubāre* to lie down] > in'cumbently *adv*

incumber (ɪn'kʌmbə) *vb* a less common spelling of **encumber.** > in'cumberingly *adv* > in'cumbrance *n*

incunabula (,ɪnkjʊ'næbjʊlə) *pl n, sing or* -**lum** (-ləm) **1** any book printed before 1501 **2** the infancy or earliest stages of something; beginnings [c19 from Latin, originally: swaddling clothes, hence beginnings, from IN-² + *cūnabula* cradle] > ,incu'nabular *adj*

incur (ɪn'kɜ:) *vb* -**curs,** -**curring,** -**curred** (*tr*) **1** to make oneself subject to (something undesirable); bring upon oneself **2** to run into or encounter [c16 from Latin *incurrere* to run into, from *currere* to run] > in'currable *adj*

incurable (ɪn'kjʊərəb°l) *adj* **1** (esp of a disease) not curable; unresponsive to treatment ▷ *n* **2** a person having an incurable disease > in,cura'bility or in'curableness *n* > in'curably *adv*

incurious (ɪn'kjʊərɪəs) *adj* not curious; indifferent or uninterested > incuriosity (ɪn,kjʊərɪ'ɒsɪtɪ) or in'curiousness *n* > in'curiously *adv*

incurrence (ɪn'kʌrəns) *n* the act or state of incurring

incurrent (ɪn'kʌrənt) *adj* **1** (of anatomical ducts, tubes, channels, etc) having an inward flow **2** flowing or running in an inward direction [c16 from Latin *incurrēns* running into; see INCUR]

incursion (ɪn'kɜ:ʃən) *n* **1** a sudden invasion, attack, or raid **2** the act of running or leaking into; penetration [c15 from Latin *incursiō* onset, attack, from *incurrere* to run into; see INCUR] > in'cursive *adj*

incurvate *vb* ('ɪnkɜ:,veɪt) *also* **incurve** (ɪn'kɜ:v) **1** to curve or cause to curve inwards ▷ *adj* (ɪn'kɜ:vɪt, -veɪt) **2** curved inwards [c16 from Latin *incurvāre* (*vb*)] > ,incur'vation *n* > incurvature (ɪn'kɜ:vətʃə) *n*

incus ('ɪnkəs) *n, pl* **incudes** (ɪn'kju:di:z) the central of the three small bones in the middle ear of mammals. Nontechnical name: **anvil** Compare **malleus, stapes** [c17 from Latin: anvil, from *incūdere* to forge] > **incudate** ('ɪnkjʊ,deɪt) or **incudal** ('ɪnkjʊd°l)

incuse (ɪn'kju:z) *n* **1** a design stamped or hammered onto a coin ▷ *vb* **2** to impress (a design) in a coin or to impress (a coin) with a design by hammering or stamping ▷ *adj* **3** stamped or hammered onto a coin [c19 from Latin *incūsus* hammered; see INCUS]

Ind (ɪnd) *n* **1** a poetic name for **India 2** an obsolete name for the **Indies**

IND 1 Also: **IDN** *abbreviation for* **in nomine Dei 2** *international car registration for* India [(for sense 1) Latin: in the name of God]

Ind. *abbreviation for* **1** Independent **2** India **3** Indian **4** Indiana

Indaba (ɪn'dɑ:bə) *n* **1** *anthropol, history* (among Bantu peoples of southern Africa) a meeting to discuss a serious topic **2** *South African informal* a matter of concern or for discussion [c19 from Zulu: topic]

indamine ('ɪndə,mi:n, -mɪn) *n* **1** an organic base used in the production of the dye safranine. Formula: $NH_2C_6H_4N:C_6H_4:NH$ **2** any of a class of organic bases with a similar structure to this compound. Their salts are unstable blue and green dyes [c20 from INDIGO + AMINE]

indebted (ɪn'dɛtɪd) *adj* (*postpositive*) **1** owing gratitude for help, favours, etc; obligated **2** owing money

indebtedness (ɪn'dɛtɪdnɪs) *n* **1** the state of being indebted **2** the total of a person's debts

indecency (ɪn'di:sənsɪ) *n, pl* -**cies 1** the state or quality of being indecent **2** an indecent act, etc

indecent (ɪn'di:s°nt) *adj* **1** offensive to standards of decency, esp in sexual matters **2** unseemly or improper (esp in the phrase **indecent haste**) > in'decently *adv*

indecent assault *n* the act of taking indecent liberties with a person without his or her consent

indecent exposure *n* the offence of indecently exposing parts of one's body in public, esp the genitals

indeciduous (,ɪndɪ'sɪdjʊəs) *adj* **1** (of leaves) not deciduous **2** a less common term for **evergreen**

indecipherable (,ɪndɪ'saɪfərəb°l, -frəb°l) *adj* not decipherable; illegible > ,inde,cipher'ability or ,inde'cipherableness *n* > ,inde'cipherably *adv*

indecisive (,ɪndɪ'saɪsɪv) *adj* **1** (of a person) vacillating; irresolute **2** not decisive or conclusive > ,inde'cision or ,inde'cisiveness *n* > ,inde'cisively *adv*

indeclinable (,ɪndɪ'klaɪnəb°l) *adj* (of a noun or pronoun) having only one form; not declined for case or number > ,inde'clinableness *n* > ,inde'clinably *adv*

indecorous (ɪnˈdɛkərəs) *adj* improper or ungraceful; unseemly > **inˈdecorously** *adv* > **inˈdecorousness** *n*

indecorum (ˌɪndɪˈkɔːrəm) *n* indecorous behaviour or speech; unseemliness

indeed (ɪnˈdiːd) *sentence connector* **1** certainly; actually: *indeed, it may never happen* ▷ *adv* **2** (intensifier): *that is indeed amazing* **3** or rather; what is more: *a comfortable, indeed extremely wealthy family* ▷ *interj* **4** an expression of doubt, surprise, etc

indef. *abbreviation for* indefinite

indefatigable (ˌɪndɪˈfætɪgəbᵊl) *adj* unable to be tired out; unflagging [C16 from Latin *indēfatīgābilis*, from IN-¹ + *dēfatīgāre*, from *fatīgāre* to tire] > **ˌindeˌfatigaˈbility** *or* **ˌindeˈfatigableness** *n* > **ˌindeˈfatigably** *adv*

indefeasible (ˌɪndɪˈfiːzəbᵊl) *adj law* not liable to be annulled or forfeited > **ˌindeˌfeasiˈbility** *or* **ˌindeˈfeasibleness** *n* > **ˌindeˈfeasibly** *adv*

indefectible (ˌɪndɪˈfɛktɪbᵊl) *adj* **1** not subject to decay or failure **2** flawless > **ˌindeˌfectiˈbility** *n* > **ˌindeˈfectibly** *adv*

indefensible (ˌɪndɪˈfɛnsəbᵊl) *adj* **1** not justifiable or excusable **2** capable of being disagreed with; untenable **3** incapable of defence against attack > **ˌindeˌfensiˈbility** *or* **ˌindeˈfensibleness** *n* > **ˌindeˈfensibly** *adv*

indefinable (ˌɪndɪˈfaɪnəbᵊl) *adj* incapable of being defined or analysed: *there was an indefinable sense of terror* > **ˌindeˈfinableness** *n* > **ˌindeˈfinably** *adv*

indefinite (ɪnˈdɛfɪnɪt) *adj* **1** not certain or determined; unsettled **2** without exact limits; indeterminate: *an indefinite number* **3** vague, evasive, or unclear **4** Also: **indeterminate** *botany* **a** too numerous to count: *indefinite stamens* **b** capable of continued growth at the tip of the stem, which does not terminate in a flower: *an indefinite inflorescence* > **inˈdefiniteness** *n*

indefinite article *n grammar* a determiner that expresses nonspecificity of reference, such as *a*, *an*, or *some*. Compare **definite article**

indefinite integral *n maths* **a** any function whose derivative is the given function, as x^2, $x^2 + 3$, $x^2–5$, etc of $2x$ **b** the schema representing all such functions, here $x^2 + k$ **c** the symbolic representation of this as a function of the given function, written $\int f(x)dx$ where $f(x)$ is the given function **d** the symbol ∫

indefinitely (ɪnˈdɛfɪnɪtlɪ) *adv* without any limit of time or number

indefinite pronoun *n grammar* a pronoun having no specific referent, such as *someone*, *anybody*, or *nothing*

indehiscent (ˌɪndɪˈhɪsᵊnt) *adj* (of fruits) not dehiscent; not opening to release seeds > **ˌindeˈhiscence** *n*

indelible (ɪnˈdɛlɪbᵊl) *adj* **1** incapable of being erased or obliterated **2** making indelible marks: *indelible ink* [C16 from Latin *indēlēbilis* indestructible, from IN-¹ + *delēre* to destroy] > **inˌdeliˈbility** *or* **inˈdelibleness** *n* > **inˈdelibly** *adv*

indelicate (ɪnˈdɛlɪkɪt) *adj* **1** coarse, crude, or rough **2** offensive, embarrassing, or tasteless > **inˈdelicacy** *or* **inˈdelicateness** *n* > **inˈdelicately** *adv*

indemnify (ɪnˈdɛmnɪˌfaɪ) *vb* **-fies, -fying, -fied** (*tr*) **1** to secure against future loss, damage, or liability; give security for; insure **2** to compensate for loss, injury, expense, etc; reimburse > **inˌdemnifiˈcation** *n* > **inˈdemniˌfier** *n*

indemnity (ɪnˈdɛmnɪtɪ) *n, pl* **-ties 1** compensation for loss or damage; reimbursement **2** protection or insurance against future loss or damage **3** legal exemption from penalties or liabilities incurred through one's acts or defaults **4** (in Canada) the salary paid to a member of Parliament or of a legislature **5** **act of indemnity** an act of Parliament granting exemption to public officers from technical penalties that they may have been compelled to incur [C15 from Late Latin *indemnitās*, from *indemnis* uninjured, from Latin IN-¹ + *damnum* damage]

indemonstrable (ˌɪndɪˈmɒnstrəbᵊl) *adj* incapable of being demonstrated or proved > **ˌindeˌmonstraˈbility** *n* > **ˌindeˈmonstrably** *adv*

indene (ˈɪndiːn) *n* a colourless liquid hydrocarbon extracted from petroleum and coal tar and used in making synthetic resins. Formula: C_9H_8 [C20 from INDOLE + -ENE]

indent¹ *vb* (ɪnˈdɛnt) (*mainly tr*) **1** to place (written or printed matter, etc) in from the margin, as at the beginning of a paragraph **2** to cut or tear (a document, esp a contract or deed in duplicate) so that the irregular lines may be matched to confirm its authenticity **3** *chiefly Brit* (in foreign trade) to place an order for (foreign goods), usually through an agent **4** (when *intr*, foll by *for*, *on*, or *upon*) *chiefly Brit* to make an order on (a source or supply) or for (something) **5** to notch (an edge, border, etc); make jagged **6** to bind (an apprentice, etc) by indenture ▷ *n* (ˈɪnˌdɛnt) **7** *chiefly Brit* (in foreign trade) an order for foreign merchandise, esp one placed with an agent **8** *chiefly Brit* an official order for goods **9** (in the late 18th-century US) a certificate issued by federal and state governments for the principal or interest due on the public debt **10** another word for **indenture** **11** another word for **indentation** (sense 4) [C14 from Old French *endenter*, from EN-¹ + *dent* tooth, from Latin *dēns*] > **inˈdenter** *or* **inˈdentor** *n*

indent² *vb* (ɪnˈdɛnt) **1** (*tr*) to make a dent or depression in ▷ *n* (ˈɪnˌdɛnt) **2** a dent or depression [C15 from IN-² + DENT¹]

indentation (ˌɪndɛnˈteɪʃən) *n* **1** a hollowed, notched, or cut place, as on an edge or on a coastline **2** a series of hollows, notches, or cuts **3** the act of indenting or the condition of being indented **4** Also called: **indention, indent** the leaving of space or the amount of space left between a margin and the start of an indented line

indention (ɪnˈdɛnʃən) *n* another word for **indentation** (sense 4)

indenture (ɪnˈdɛntʃə) *n* **1** any deed, contract, or sealed agreement between two or more parties **2** (formerly) a deed drawn up in duplicate, each part having correspondingly indented edges for identification and security **3** (*often plural*) a contract between an apprentice and his master **4** a formal or official list or certificate authenticated for use as a voucher, etc **5** a less common word for **indentation** ▷ *vb* **6** (*intr*) to enter into an agreement by indenture **7** (*tr*) to bind (an apprentice, servant, etc) by indenture **8** (*tr*) *obsolete* to indent or wrinkle > **inˈdentureˌship** *n*

independence (ˌɪndɪˈpɛndəns) *n* the state or quality of being independent. Also called: **independency**

Independence (ˌɪndɪˈpɛndəns) *n* a city in W Missouri, near Kansas City: starting point for the Santa Fe, Oregon, and California Trails (1831–44). Pop: 112 079 (2003 est)

Independence Day *n* the official name for the **Fourth of July**

independency (ˌɪndɪˈpɛndənsɪ) *n, pl* **-cies 1** a territory or state free from the control of any other power **2** another word for **independence**

Independency (ˌɪndɪˈpɛndənsɪ) *n* (esp in the Congregational Church) the principle upholding the independence of each local church or congregation

independent (ˌɪndɪˈpɛndənt) *adj* **1** free from control in action, judgment, etc; autonomous **2** not dependent on anything else for function, validity, etc; separate: *two independent units make up this sofa* **3** not reliant on the support, esp financial support, of others **4** capable of acting for oneself or on one's own: *a very independent little girl* **5** providing a large unearned sum towards one's support (esp in the phrases **independent income, independent means**) **6** living on an unearned income **7** *maths* (of a system of equations) not linearly dependent. See also **independent variable** **8** *statistics* **a** (of two or more variables) distributed so that the value taken by one variable will have no effect on that taken by another or others **b** (of two or more events) such that the probability of all occurring equals the product of their individual probabilities. Compare **statistical dependence** **9** *logic* (of a set of propositions) **a** not validly derivable from one another, so that if the propositions are the axioms of some theory none can be dispensed with **b** not logically related, so that in no case can the truth value of one be inferred from those of the others ▷ *n* **10** an independent person or thing **11** a person who is not affiliated to or who acts independently of a political party > **ˌindeˈpendently** *adv*

Independent (ˌɪndɪˈpɛndənt) *n* **1** (in England) a member of the Congregational Church ▷ *adj* **2** of or relating to Independency

independent clause *n grammar* a main or coordinate clause. Compare **dependent clause**

independent school *n* **1** (in Britain) a school that is neither financed nor controlled by the government or local authorities **2** (in Australia) a school that is not part of the state system

independent variable *n* **1** Also called: **argument** a variable in a mathematical equation or statement whose value determines that of the dependent variable: in $y = f(x)$, x is the independent variable **2** *statistics* Also called: **predictor** the variable which an experimenter deliberately manipulates in order to observe its relationship with some other quantity, or which defines the distinct conditions in an experiment. See also **experimental condition**

in-depth *adj* carefully worked out, detailed and thorough: *an in-depth study*

indescribable (ˌɪndɪˈskraɪbəbᵊl) *adj* beyond description; too intense, extreme, etc, for words > **ˌindeˌscribaˈbility** *or* **ˌindeˈscribableness** *n* > **ˌindeˈscribably** *adv*

indestructible (ˌɪndɪˈstrʌktəbᵊl) *adj* incapable of being destroyed; very durable > **ˌindeˌstructiˈbility** *or* **ˌindeˈstructibleness** *n* > **ˌindeˈstructibly** *adv*

indeterminable (ˌɪndɪˈtɜːmɪnəbᵊl) *adj* **1** incapable of being ascertained **2** incapable of being settled > **ˌindeˈterminableness** *n* > **ˌindeˈterminably** *adv*

indeterminacy principle (ˌɪndɪˈtɜːmɪnəsɪ) *n* another name for **uncertainty principle**

indeterminate (ˌɪndɪˈtɜːmɪnɪt) *adj* **1** uncertain in extent, amount, or nature **2** not definite; inconclusive: *an indeterminate reply* **3** unable to be predicted, calculated, or deduced **4** *physics* (of an effect) not obeying the law of causality; noncausal **5** *maths* **a** having no numerical meaning, as 0.00 or 0/0 **b** (of an equation) having more than one variable and an unlimited number of solutions **6** *botany* another word for **indefinite** (sense 4) **7** (of a structure, framework, etc) comprising forces that cannot be fully analysed, esp by vector analysis > **ˌindeˈterminacy, ˌindeˌtermiˈnation** *or* **ˌindeˈterminateness** *n* > **ˌindeˈterminately** *adv*

indeterminate sentence *n law* a prison sentence the length of which depends on the prisoner's conduct

indeterminism (ˌɪndɪˈtɜːmɪˌnɪzəm) *n* the philosophical doctrine that behaviour is not entirely determined by motives > **ˌindeˈterminist** *n, adj* > **ˌindeˌterminˈistic** *adj*

index (ˈɪndɛks) *n, pl* **-dexes** *or* **-dices** (-dɪˌsiːz) **1** an alphabetical list of persons, places, subjects, etc, mentioned in the text of a printed work, usually at the back, and indicating where in the work they are referred to **2** See **thumb index** **3** *library science* a systematic list of book titles or author's names, giving cross-references and the location of each book; catalogue **4** an indication, sign, or token **5** a pointer, needle, or other indicator, as on an instrument **6** *maths* **a** another name for **exponent** (sense 4) **b** a number or variable placed as a superscript to the left of a radical sign indicating by its value the root to be extracted, as in $\sqrt[3]{8} = 2$ **c** a subscript or superscript to the right of a variable to express a set of variables, as in using x_i for x_1, x_2, x_3, etc **7** a numerical scale by means of which variables, such as levels of the cost of living, can be compared with each other or with some base number **8** a number or ratio indicating a specific characteristic, property, etc: *refractive index* **9** Also called: **fist** a printer's mark (☛) used to indicate notes, paragraphs, etc **10** *obsolete* a table of contents or preface ▷ *vb* (*tr*) **11** to put an index in (a book) **12** to enter (a word, item, etc) in an index **13** to point out; indicate **14** to index-link **15** to move (a machine or a workpiece held in a machine tool) so that one particular operation will be repeated at certain defined intervals [c16 from Latin: pointer, hence forefinger, title, index, from *indicāre* to disclose, show; see INDICATE] ▷ **'indexer** *n* ▷ **'indexless** *adj*

indexation (ˌɪndɛkˈseɪʃən) *or* **index-linking** *n* the act of making wages, interest rates, etc, index-linked

index case *n med* the first case of a disease, or the primary case referred to in a report

index finger *n* the finger next to the thumb. Also called: **forefinger**

index fossil *n* a fossil species that characterizes and is used to delimit a geological zone. Also called: **zone fossil**

index futures *pl n* a form of financial futures based on projected movement of a share price index, such as the Financial Times Stock Exchange 100 Share Index

indexical (ɪnˈdɛksɪkəl) *adj* **1** arranged as or relating to an index or indexes ▷ *n* **2** *logic, linguistics* a term whose reference depends on the context of utterance, such as *I, you, here, now,* or *tomorrow*. Also: **deictic**

indexing head *n* a circular plate mounted to rotate on its centre, inscribed with concentric circles, each accurately divided, the dimensions being marked by drilled holes. The plate can be moved round with a workpiece to facilitate the accurate location of holes or other machining operations on the workpiece

Index Librorum Prohibitorum *Latin* ('ɪndɛks laɪ'brɔːrʊm prəʊˌhɪbɪ'tɔːrʊm) *n RC Church* (formerly) an official list of proscribed books. Often called: **the Index** [c17, literally: list of forbidden books]

index-linked *adj* (of wages, interest rates, etc) directly related to the cost-of-living index and rising or falling accordingly

index number *n statistics* a statistic indicating the relative change occurring in each successive period of time in the price, volume, or value of a commodity or in a general economic variable, such as the price level, national income, or gross output, with reference to a previous base period conventionally given the number 100

Index of Industrial Production *n* (in Britain) an index produced by the Central Statistical Office showing changes in the production of the primary British industries

index of refraction *n* another name for **refractive index**

India ('ɪndɪə) *n* **1** a republic in S Asia: history dates from the Indus Valley civilization (3rd millennium BC); came under British supremacy in 1763 and passed to the British Crown in 1858; nationalist movement arose under Gandhi (1869–1948); Indian subcontinent divided into Pakistan (Muslim) and India (Hindu) in 1947; became a republic within the Commonwealth in 1950. It consists chiefly of the Himalayas, rising over 7500 m (25 000 ft) in the extreme north, the Ganges plain in the north, the Thar Desert in the northwest, the Chota Nagpur plateau in the northeast, and the Deccan Plateau in the south. Official and administrative languages: Hindi and English; each state has its own language. Parts of the SE coast suffered badly in the Indian Ocean tsunami of December 2004. Religion: Hindu majority, Muslim minority. Currency: rupee.

Capital: New Delhi. Pop: 1 081 229 000 (2004 est). Area: 3 268 100 sq km (1 261 813 sq miles). Hindi name: **Bharat 2** *communications* a code word for the letter *i*

Indiaman ('ɪndɪəmən) *n, pl* **-men** (formerly) a large merchant ship engaged in trade with India

Indian ('ɪndɪən) *n* **1** a native, citizen, or inhabitant of the Republic of India **2** an American Indian **3** (*not in scholarly usage*) any of the languages of the American Indians ▷ *adj* **4** of, relating to, or characteristic of India, its inhabitants, or any of their languages **5** of, relating to, or characteristic of the American Indians or any of their languages

Indiana (ˌɪndɪ'ænə) *n* a state of the N central US, in the Midwest: consists of an undulating plain, with sand dunes and lakes in the north and limestone caves in the south. Capital: Indianapolis. Pop: 6 195 643 (2003 est). Area: 93 491 sq km (36 097 sq miles). Abbreviations: **Ind,** (with zip code) **IN**

Indian agent *n* an official who represents the US or Canadian government to a group of North American Indians

Indianapolis (ˌɪndɪə'næpəlɪs) *n* a city in central Indiana: the state capital. Pop: 783 438 (2003 est)

Indian bread *n* another name for **corn bread**

Indian cholera *n* another name for **cholera**

Indian club *n* a bottle-shaped club, usually used in pairs by gymnasts, jugglers, etc

Indian corn *n* another name for **maize** (sense 1)

Indian Desert *n* another name for the **Thar Desert**

Indian Empire *n* British India and the Indian states under indirect British control, which gained independence as India and Pakistan in 1947

Indian file *n* another term for **single file**

Indian giver *n US and Canadian offensive* a person who asks for the return of a present he has given ▷ **Indian giving** *n*

Indian hemp *n* **1** another name for **hemp**, esp the variety *Cannabis indica*, from which several narcotic drugs are obtained **2** Also called: **dogbane** a perennial American apocynaceous plant, *Apocynum cannabinum*, whose fibre was formerly used by the Indians to make rope

Indianian (ˌɪndɪ'ænɪən) *n* **1** a native or inhabitant of Indiana ▷ *adj* **2** of or relating to Indiana or its inhabitants

Indian ink *or esp US and Canadian* **India ink** *n* **1** a black pigment made from a mixture of lampblack and a binding agent such as gelatine or glue: usually formed into solid cakes and sticks **2** a black liquid ink made from this pigment ▷ Also called: **China ink, Chinese ink**

Indian liquorice *n* a woody leguminous climbing plant, *Abrus precatorius*, native to tropical Asia and naturalized elsewhere, having scarlet black-spotted poisonous seeds, used as beads, and roots used as a substitute for liquorice. Also called: **jequirity**

Indian list *n informal* (in Canada) a list of persons to whom spirits may not be sold. Also called: **interdict list**

Indian mallow *n* a tall malvaceous weedy North American plant, *Abutilon theophrasti*, with small yellow flowers and large velvety leaves

Indian meal *n* another name for **corn meal**

Indian millet *n* another name for **durra**

Indian mulberry *n* a small rubiaceous tree, *Morinda citrifolia*, of SE Asia and Australasia, with rounded yellow fruits: yields red and yellow dyes

Indian Mutiny *n* a revolt of Indian troops (1857–59) that led to the transfer of the administration of India from the East India Company to the British Crown

Indian National Congress *n* the official name for **Congress** (the political party)

Indian Ocean *n* an ocean bordered by Africa in the west, Asia in the north, and Australia in the east and merging with the Antarctic Ocean in the

south. Average depth: 3900 m (13 000 ft). Greatest depth (off the Sunda Islands): 7450 m (24 442 ft). In December 2004 a major undersea earthquake off Sumatra triggered a tsunami which affected large areas of the ocean as far away as east Africa, and killed around 275 900 people. Area: about 73 556 000 sq km (28 400 000 sq miles)

Indian pipe *n* a white or pinkish saprophytic woodland plant, *Monotropa uniflora*, of the N hemisphere, with a solitary nodding flower resembling a pipe: family *Monotropaceae*

Indian red *n* **1** a red pigment containing ferric oxide, used in paints and cosmetics and produced by oxidizing iron salts **2** a type of red soil containing ferric oxide, found in S Asia and used as a pigment and metal polish

Indian reserve *or* **reservation** *n* See reservation (sense 4)

Indian rice *n* **1** an annual erect aquatic North American grass, *Zizania aquatica*, with edible purplish-black grain **2** the grain of this plant ▷ Also called: **wild rice**

Indian rope-trick *n* the supposed Indian feat of climbing an unsupported rope

Indian sign *n US* a magic spell designed to place the victim in one's power or bring him bad luck

Indian States and Agencies *pl n* another name for the **Native States**

Indian summer *n* **1** a period of unusually settled warm weather after the end of summer proper **2** a period of ease and tranquillity or of renewed productivity towards the end of a person's life or of an epoch ▷ See also **Saint Martin's summer** [originally US: probably so named because it was first noted in regions occupied by American Indians]

Indian sweater *n* another name for **Cowichan sweater**

Indian Territory *n* the territory established in the early 19th century in present-day Oklahoma, where Indians were forced to settle by the US government. The last remnant was integrated into the new state of Oklahoma in 1907

Indian tobacco *n* a poisonous North American campanulaceous plant, *Lobelia inflata*, with small pale blue flowers and rounded inflated seed capsules

India paper *n* **1** a thin soft opaque printing paper made in the Orient **2** another name (not in technical usage) for **Bible paper**

India print *n* a colourful cotton fabric, with a block-printed pattern, made in India

India rubber *n* another name for **rubber¹** (sense 1)

Indic ('ɪndɪk) *adj* **1** denoting, belonging to, or relating to a branch of Indo-European consisting of the Indo-European languages of India, including Sanskrit, Hindi and Urdu, Punjabi, Gujerati, Bengali, and Sinhalese ▷ *n* **2** this group of languages ▷ Also: **Indo-Aryan**

indic. *abbreviation for* **1** indicating **2** indicative **3** indicator

indican ('ɪndɪkən) *n* a compound secreted in the urine, usually in the form of its potassium salt; indoxylsulphuric acid. Formula: $C_8H_6NOSO_2OH$ [c19 from Latin *indicum* INDIGO + -AN]

indicant ('ɪndɪkənt) *n* something that indicates

indicate ('ɪndɪˌkeɪt) *vb* (*tr*) **1** (*may take a clause as object*) to give a sign or symptom of; imply: *cold hands indicate a warm heart* **2** to point out or show **3** (*may take a clause as object*) to state briefly; suggest: *he indicated what his feelings were* **4** (of instruments) to show a reading of: *the speedometer indicated 50 miles per hour* **5** (*usually passive*) to recommend or require: *surgery seems to be indicated for this patient* [c17 from Latin *indicāre* to point out, from IN-² + *dicāre* to proclaim; compare INDEX] ▷ **'indiˌcatable** *adj* ▷ **indicatory** (ɪn'dɪkətərɪ, -trɪ) *adj*

indicated horsepower *n* the power output of a piston engine calculated from the mean effective pressure in the cylinder as derived from an indicator diagram and the speed of the engine in revolutions per minute

indication (ˌɪndɪˈkeɪʃən) n 1 something that serves to indicate or suggest; sign: *an indication of foul play* 2 the degree or quantity represented on a measuring instrument or device 3 the action of indicating 4 something that is indicated as advisable, necessary, or expedient

indicative (ɪnˈdɪkətɪv) adj 1 *(usually postpositive; foll by of)* serving as a sign; suggestive: *indicative of trouble ahead* 2 *grammar* denoting a mood of verbs used chiefly to make statements. Compare **subjunctive** (sense 1) ▷ n 3 *grammar* **a** the indicative mood **b** a verb in the indicative mood ▷ Abbreviation: **indic.** > in**ˈdicatively** adv

indicator (ˈɪndɪˌkeɪtə) n 1 something that provides an indication, esp of trends. See **economic indicator** 2 a device to attract attention, such as the pointer of a gauge or a warning lamp 3 an instrument that displays certain operating conditions in a machine, such as a gauge showing temperature, speed, pressure, etc 4 **a** a device that records or registers something, such as the movements of a lift, or that shows information, such as arrival and departure times of trains **b** *(as modifier)*: *indicator light* 5 Also called: **blinker** a device for indicating that a motor vehicle is about to turn left or right, esp two pairs of lights that flash when operated or a pair of trafficators 6 Also called: **dial gauge** a delicate measuring instrument used to determine small differences in the height of mechanical components. It consists of a spring-loaded plunger that operates a pointer moving over a circular scale 7 *chem* **a** a substance used in titrations to indicate the completion of a chemical reaction, usually by a change of colour **b** a substance, such as litmus, that indicates the presence of an acid or alkali 8 Also called: **indicator species** *ecology* **a** a plant or animal species that thrives only under particular environmental conditions and therefore indicates these conditions where it is found **b** a species of plant or animal whose well-being confirms the well-being of other species in the area

indicator diagram n a graphical or other representation of the cyclic variations of pressure and volume within the cylinder of a reciprocating engine obtained by using an indicator

indices (ˈɪndɪˌsiːz) n a plural of **index**

indicia (ɪnˈdɪʃɪə) pl n, sing or **-cium** (-ʃɪəm) distinguishing markings or signs; indications [C17 from Latin, plural of *indicium* a notice, from INDEX] > in**ˈdicial** adj

indicolite (ˈɪndɪkəˌlaɪt) or **indigolite** n a form of tourmaline ranging in colour from pale blue to blue-black [C19 from Spanish *indico* INDIGO + -LITE]

indict (ɪnˈdaɪt) vb (tr) to charge (a person) with crime, esp formally in writing; accuse [C14 alteration of *enditen* to INDITE] > in**ˈdictee** n > in**ˈdicter** or in**ˈdictor** n

◼◼◼ USAGE See at **indite**

indictable (ɪnˈdaɪtəbəl) adj *criminal law* 1 (of a person) liable to be indicted 2 (of a crime) that makes a person liable to be indicted > in**ˈdictably** adv

indiction (ɪnˈdɪkʃən) n (in the Roman Empire and later in various medieval kingdoms) 1 a recurring fiscal period of 15 years, often used as a unit for dating events 2 a particular year in this period or the number assigned it 3 (from the reign of Constantine the Great) **a** a valuation of property made every 15 years as a basis for taxation **b** the tax based on this valuation [C14 from Latin *indictiō* declaration, announcement of a tax; see INDITE] > in**ˈdictional** adj

indictment (ɪnˈdaɪtmənt) n *criminal law* 1 a formal written charge of crime formerly referred to and presented on oath by a grand jury 2 any formal accusation of crime 3 *Scot* a charge of crime brought at the instance of the Lord Advocate 4 the act of indicting or the state of being indicted

indie (ˈɪndɪ) n *informal* **a** an independent film or record company **b** *(as modifier)*: *an indie producer; the indie charts*

Indies (ˈɪndɪz) n **the** 1 the territories of S and SE Asia included in the East Indies, India, and Indochina 2 See **East Indies** 3 See **West Indies**

indifference (ɪnˈdɪfrəns, -fərəns) n 1 the fact or state of being indifferent; lack of care or concern 2 lack of quality; mediocrity 3 lack of importance; insignificance 4 See **principle of indifference**

indifferent (ɪnˈdɪfrənt, -fərənt) adj 1 (often foll by *to*) showing no care or concern; uninterested: *he was indifferent to my pleas* 2 unimportant; immaterial 3 **a** of only average or moderate size, extent, quality, etc **b** not at all good; poor 4 showing or having no preferences; impartial 5 *biology* **a** (of cells or tissues) not differentiated or specialized **b** (of a species) not found in any particular community [C14 from Latin *indifferēns* making no distinction] > in**ˈdifferently** adv

indifferentism (ɪnˈdɪfrənˌtɪzəm, -fərən-) n systematic indifference, esp in matters of religion > in**ˈdifferentist** n

indigene (ˈɪndɪˌdʒiːn) or **indigen** (ˈɪndɪdʒən) n an indigenous person, animal, or thing; native

indigenous (ɪnˈdɪdʒɪnəs) adj (when *postpositive*, foll by *to*) 1 originating or occurring naturally (in a country, region, etc); native 2 innate (to); inherent (in) [C17 from Latin *indigenus*, from *indigena* indigene, from *indi-* in + *gignere* to beget] > in**ˈdigenously** adv > in**ˈdigenousness** or indigenity (ˌɪndɪˈdʒɛnɪtɪ) n

indigent (ˈɪndɪdʒənt) adj 1 so poor as to lack even necessities; very needy 2 (usually foll by *of*) *archaic* lacking (in) or destitute (of) ▷ n 3 an impoverished person [C14 from Latin *indigēre* to need, from *egēre* to lack] > **ˈindigence** n > **ˈindigently** adv

indigested (ˌɪndɪˈdʒɛstɪd) adj *archaic* undigested

indigestible (ˌɪndɪˈdʒɛstəbəl) adj 1 incapable of being digested or difficult to digest 2 difficult to understand or absorb mentally: *an indigestible book* > ˌindi**ˌgesti'bility** or ˌindi**ˈgestibleness** n > ˌindi**ˈgestibly** adv

indigestion (ˌɪndɪˈdʒɛstʃən) n difficulty in digesting food, accompanied by abdominal pain, heartburn, and belching. Technical name: **dyspepsia**

indigestive (ˌɪndɪˈdʒɛstɪv) adj relating to or suffering from indigestion; dyspeptic

indign (ɪnˈdaɪn) adj *obsolete* or *poetic* 1 undeserving; unworthy 2 unseemly; disgraceful 3 not deserved [C15 from Old French *indigne*, from Latin *indignus* unworthy, from IN-¹ + *dignus* worthy; see DIGNITY]

indignant (ɪnˈdɪgnənt) adj feeling or showing indignation [C16 from Latin *indignārī* to be displeased with] > in**ˈdignantly** adv

indignation (ˌɪndɪgˈneɪʃən) n anger or scorn aroused by something felt to be unfair, unworthy, or wrong

indignity (ɪnˈdɪgnɪtɪ) n, pl **-ties** 1 injury to one's self-esteem or dignity; humiliation 2 *obsolete* disgrace or disgraceful character or conduct

indigo (ˈɪndɪˌgəʊ) n, pl **-gos** or **-goes** 1 Also called: **indigotin** a blue vat dye originally obtained from plants but now made synthetically 2 any of various tropical plants of the leguminous genus *Indigofera*, such as the anil, that yield this dye. Compare **wild indigo** 3 **a** any of a group of colours that have the same blue-violet hue; a spectral colour **b** *(as adjective)*: *an indigo carpet* [C16 from Spanish *indico*, via Latin from Greek *Indikos* of India] > **indigotic** (ˌɪndɪˈgɒtɪk) adj

indigo blue n ▷ adj (indigo-blue *when prenominal*) the full name for **indigo** (the colour and the dye)

indigo bunting, bird or **finch** n a North American bunting, *Passerina cyanea*, the male of which is bright blue and the female brown

indigoid (ˈɪndɪˌgɔɪd) adj 1 of, concerned with, or resembling indigo or its blue colour ▷ n 2 any of a number of synthetic dyes or pigments related in chemical structure to indigo

indigolite (ˈɪndɪgəˌlaɪt) n a variant spelling of **indicolite**

indigo snake n a dark-blue nonvenomous North American colubrid snake, *Drymarchon corais couperi*

indigotin (ɪnˈdɪgətɪn, ˌɪndɪˈgəʊ-) n another name for **indigo** (the dye) [C19 from INDIGO + -IN]

indirect (ˌɪndɪˈrɛkt) adj 1 deviating from a direct course or line; roundabout; circuitous 2 not coming as a direct effect or consequence; secondary: *indirect benefits* 3 not straightforward, open, or fair; devious or evasive: *an indirect insult* 4 (of a title or an inheritance) not inherited in an unbroken line of succession from father to son > ˌindi**ˈrectly** adv > ˌindi**ˈrectness** n

indirect costs pl n another name for **overheads**

indirection (ˌɪndɪˈrɛkʃən) n 1 indirect procedure, courses, or methods 2 lack of direction or purpose; aimlessness 3 indirect dealing; deceit

indirect labour n *commerce* work done in administration and sales rather than in the manufacturing of a product. Compare **direct labour** (sense 1)

indirect lighting n reflected or diffused light from a concealed source

indirect object n *grammar* a noun, pronoun, or noun phrase indicating the recipient or beneficiary of the action of a verb and its direct object, as *John* in the sentence *I bought John a newspaper*. Compare **direct object**

indirect proof n *logic, maths* proof of a conclusion by showing its negation to be self-contradictory; reductio ad absurdum. Compare **direct** (sense 17)

indirect question n a question reported in indirect speech, as in *She asked why you came*. Compare **direct question**

indirect speech or *esp US* **indirect discourse** n the reporting of something said or written by conveying what was meant rather than repeating the exact words, as in the sentence *He asked me whether I would go* as opposed to *He asked me, "Will you go?"*. Also called: **reported speech**

indirect tax n a tax levied on goods or services rather than on individuals or companies. Compare **direct tax.** > **indirect taxation** n

indiscernible (ˌɪndɪˈsɜːnəbəl) adj 1 incapable of being discerned 2 scarcely discernible or perceptible > ˌindis**ˈcernibleness** or ˌindiscerni**ˈbility** n > ˌindis**ˈcernibly** adv

indiscipline (ɪnˈdɪsɪplɪn) n lack of discipline

indiscreet (ˌɪndɪˈskriːt) adj not discreet; imprudent or tactless > ˌindis**ˈcreetly** adv > ˌindis**ˈcreetness** n

indiscrete (ˌɪndɪˈskriːt) adj not divisible or divided into parts > ˌindis**ˈcretely** adv > ˌindis**ˈcreteness** n

indiscretion (ˌɪndɪˈskrɛʃən) n 1 the characteristic or state of being indiscreet 2 an indiscreet act, remark, etc > ˌindis**ˈcretionary** adj

indiscriminate (ˌɪndɪˈskrɪmɪnɪt) adj 1 lacking discrimination or careful choice; random or promiscuous 2 jumbled; confused > ˌindis**ˈcriminately** adv > ˌindis**ˈcriminateness** n > ˌindis**ˌcrimi'nation** n

indispensable (ˌɪndɪˈspɛnsəbəl) adj 1 absolutely necessary; essential 2 not to be disregarded or escaped: *an indispensable role* ▷ n 3 an indispensable person or thing > ˌindis**ˌpensa'bility** or ˌindis**ˈpensableness** n > ˌindis**ˈpensably** adv

indispose (ˌɪndɪˈspəʊz) vb (tr) 1 to make unwilling or opposed; disincline 2 to cause to feel ill 3 to make unfit (for something or to do something)

indisposed (ˌɪndɪˈspəʊzd) adj 1 sick or ill 2 unwilling [C15 from Latin *indispositus* disordered] > indisposition (ˌɪndɪspəˈzɪʃən) n

indisputable (ˌɪndɪˈspjuːtəbəl) adj beyond doubt; not open to question > ˌindis**ˌputa'bility** or ˌindis**ˈputableness** n > ˌindis**ˈputably** adv

indissoluble (ˌɪndɪˈsɒljʊbəl) adj incapable of being dissolved or broken; permanent > ˌindis**ˌsolu'bility** or ˌindis**ˈsolubleness** n > ˌindis**ˈsolubly** adv

indistinct (ˌɪndɪˈstɪŋkt) adj incapable of being clearly distinguished, as by the eyes, ears, or

i

mind; not distinct > ˌindis'tinctly *adv*
> ˌindis'tinctness *n*

indistinctive (ˌɪndɪ'stɪŋktɪv) *adj* **1** without
distinctive qualities **2** unable to make
distinctions; undiscriminating > ˌindis'tinctively
adv > ˌindis'tinctiveness *n*

indistinguishable (ˌɪndɪ'stɪŋɡwɪʃəb³l) *adj* **1** (*often
postpositive*; foll by *from*) identical or very similar
(to): *twins indistinguishable from one another* **2** not
easily perceptible; indiscernible
> ˌindis,tinguisha'bility *or* ˌindis'tinguishableness *n*
> ˌindis'tinguishably *adv*

indite (ɪn'daɪt) *vb* (*tr*) **1** *archaic* to write **2** *obsolete*
to dictate [C14 from Old French *enditer,* from Latin
indīcere to declare, from IN-² + *dīcere* to say]
> in'ditement *n* > in'diter *n*

> USAGE *Indite* and *inditement* are
> sometimes wrongly used where *indict*
> and *indictment* are meant: *he was*
> *indicted* (not *indited*) *for fraud*

indium ('ɪndɪəm) *n* a rare soft silvery metallic
element associated with zinc ores: used in alloys,
electronics, and electroplating. Symbol: In; atomic
no.: 49; atomic wt.: 114.82; valency: 1, 2, or 3;
relative density: 7.31; melting pt.: 156.63°C; boiling
pt.: 2073°C [C19 New Latin, from INDIGO + -IUM]

indiv. *or* **individ.** *abbreviation for* individual

indivertible (ˌɪndɪ'vɜːtɪb³l) *adj* incapable of being
diverted or turned aside > ˌindi'vertibly *adv*

individual (ˌɪndɪ'vɪdjʊəl) *adj* **1** of, relating to,
characteristic of, or meant for a single person or
thing **2** separate or distinct, esp from others of its
kind; particular: *please mark the individual pages* **3**
characterized by unusual and striking qualities;
distinctive **4** *obsolete* indivisible; inseparable ▷ *n*
5 a single person, esp when regarded as distinct
from others **6** *biology* **a** a single animal or plant,
esp as distinct from a species **b** a single member
of a compound organism or colony **7** *logic* **a** Also
called: **particular** an object as opposed to a
property or class **b** an element of the domain of
discourse of a theory [C15 from Medieval Latin
indīviduālis, from Latin *indīviduus* indivisible, from
IN-¹ + *dīviduus* divisible, from *dīvidere* to DIVIDE]
> ˌindi'vidually *adv*

individualism (ˌɪndɪ'vɪdjʊə,lɪzəm) *n* **1** the action
or principle of asserting one's independence and
individuality; egoism **2** an individual quirk or
peculiarity **3** another word for **laissez faire** (sense
1) **4** *philosophy* the doctrine that only individual
things exist and that therefore classes or
properties have no reality. Compare **Platonism,
realism** (sense 5)

individualist (ˌɪndɪ'vɪdjʊəlɪst) *n* **1** a person who
shows independence and individuality in his
behaviour, opinions, or actions **2** an advocate of
individualism > ˌindi'vidual'istic *adj*
> ˌindi,vidual'istically *adv*

individuality (ˌɪndɪ,vɪdjʊ'ælɪtɪ) *n, pl* **-ties 1**
distinctive or unique character or personality: *a*
work of great individuality **2** the qualities that
distinguish one person or thing from another;
identity **3** the state or quality of being a separate
entity; discreteness

individualize *or* **individualise** (ˌɪndɪ'vɪdjʊə,laɪz)
vb (*tr*) **1** to make or mark as individual or
distinctive in character **2** to consider or treat
individually; particularize **3** to make or modify so
as to meet the special requirements of a person
> ˌindi,viduali'zation *or* ˌindi,viduali'sation *n*
> ˌindi'vidual,izer *or* ˌindi'vidual,iser *n*

individuate (ˌɪndɪ'vɪdjʊ,eɪt) *vb* (*tr*) **1** to give
individuality or an individual form to **2** to
distinguish from others of the same species or
group; individualize > ˌindi'vidu,ator *n*

individuation (ˌɪndɪ,vɪdjʊ'eɪʃən) *n* **1** the act or
process of individuating **2** (in the psychology of
Jung) the process by which the wholeness of the
individual is established through the integration
of consciousness and the collective unconscious **3**
zoology the development of separate but mutually
interdependent units, as in the development of

zooids forming a colony

indivisible (ˌɪndɪ'vɪzəb³l) *adj* **1** unable to be
divided **2** *maths* leaving a remainder when
divided by a given number: *8 is indivisible by 3*
> ˌindi,visi'bility *or* ˌindi'visibleness *n*
> ˌindi'visibly *adv*

Indo- ('ɪndəʊ-) *combining form* denoting India or
Indian: *Indo-European*

Indo-Aryan *adj* **1** another word for **Indic** (sense 1)
▷ *n* **2** another name for **Indic** (sense 2) **3** a native
speaker of an Indo-Aryan language

Indo-Canadian *n* **1** a Canadian of Indian descent
▷ *adj* **2** of or relating to Canadians of Indian
descent

Indochina *or* **Indo-China** *n* ('ɪndəʊ'tʃaɪnə) **1** Also
called: **Farther India** a peninsula in SE Asia,
between India and China: consists of Myanmar,
Thailand, Laos, Cambodia, Vietnam, and Malaysia
2 the former French colonial possessions of
Cochin China, Annam, Tonkin, Laos, and
Cambodia

Indochinese *or* **Indo-Chinese** (ˌɪndəʊtʃaɪ'niːz) *adj*
1 of or relating to Indochina or its inhabitants
▷ *n, pl* **-nese 2** a native or inhabitant of Indochina

indocile (ɪn'dəʊsaɪl) *adj* difficult to discipline or
instruct > **indocility** (ˌɪndəʊ'sɪlɪtɪ) *n*

indoctrinate (ɪn'dɒktrɪ,neɪt) *vb* (*tr*) **1** to teach (a
person or group of people) systematically to accept
doctrines, esp uncritically **2** *rare* to impart
learning to; instruct > in,doctri'nation *n*
> in'doctri,nator *n*

Indo-European *adj* **1** denoting, belonging to, or
relating to a family of languages that includes
English and many other culturally and politically
important languages of the world: a
characteristic feature, esp of the older languages
such as Latin, Greek, and Sanskrit, is inflection
showing gender, number, and case **2** denoting or
relating to the hypothetical parent language of
this family, primitive Indo-European **3** denoting,
belonging to, or relating to any of the peoples
speaking these languages ▷ *n* **4** the Indo-
European family of languages **5** Also called:
primitive Indo-European, Proto-Indo-European
the reconstructed hypothetical parent language
of this family **6** a member of the prehistoric
people who spoke this language **7** a descendant
of this people or a native speaker of an Indo-
European language

Indo-Germanic *adj, n obsolete* another term for
Indo-European

Indo-Hittite *n* the Indo-European family of
languages: used by scholars who regard Hittite
not as a branch of Indo-European but as a related
language

Indo-Iranian *adj* **1** of or relating to the Indic and
Iranian branches of the Indo-European family of
languages ▷ *n* **2** this group of languages,
sometimes considered as forming a single branch
of Indo-European

indole ('ɪndəʊl) *or* **indol** ('ɪndəʊl, -dɒl) *n* a white
or yellowish crystalline heterocyclic compound
extracted from coal tar and used in perfumery,
medicine, and as a flavouring agent:
1-benzopyrrole. Formula: C_8H_7N [C19 from IND(IGO)
+ -OLE¹]

indoleacetic acid (ˌɪndəʊlə'siːtɪk, -'sɛtɪk) *n* an
auxin that causes elongation of the cells of plant
stems. Formula: $C_{10}H_9NO_2$. Abbreviation: **IAA**

indolebutyric acid (ˌɪndəʊlbjuː'tɪrɪk) *n* a
synthetic auxin used for stimulating plant
growth and root formation. Formula: $C_{12}H_{13}NO_2$)

indolent ('ɪndələnt) *adj* **1** disliking work or effort;
lazy; idle **2** *pathol* causing little pain: *an indolent*
tumour **3** (esp of a painless ulcer) slow to heal [C17
from Latin *indolēns* not feeling pain, from IN-¹ +
dolēns, from *dolēre* to grieve, cause distress]
> 'indolence *n* > 'indolently *adv*

Indologist (ɪn'dɒlədʒɪst) *n* a student of Indian
literature, history, philosophy, etc > In'dology *n*

indomethacin (ˌɪndəʊ'mɛθəsɪn) *n* a drug
administered orally to relieve pain, fever, and

inflammation, esp in rheumatoid arthritis.
Formula: $C_{19}H_{16}ClNO_4$ [C20 from INDOLE + METH- +
ACETIC ACID + -IN]

indomitable (ɪn'dɒmɪtəb³l) *adj* (of courage, pride,
etc) difficult or impossible to defeat or subdue [C17
from Late Latin *indomitābilis,* from Latin *indomitus*
untamable, from IN-¹ + *domitus* subdued, from
domāre to tame] > in,domita'bility *or*
in'domitableness *n* > in'domitably *adv*

Indonesia (ˌɪndəʊ'niːzɪə) *n* a republic in SE Asia,
in the Malay Archipelago, consisting of the main
islands of Sumatra, Java and Madura, Bali,
Sulawesi (Celebes), Lombok, Sumbawa, Flores, the
Moluccas, part of Timor, part of Borneo
(Kalimantan), Papua (formerly Irian Jaya), and
over 3000 small islands in the Indian and Pacific
Oceans: became the Dutch East Indies in 1798;
declared independence in 1945; became a republic
in 1950; East Timor (illegally annexed in 1975)
became independent in 2002. Parts of Sumatra
suffered badly in the Indian Ocean tsunami of
December 2004. Official language: Bahasa
Indonesia. Religion: Muslim majority. Currency:
rupiah. Capital: Jakarta. Pop: 222 611 000 (2004
est). Area: 1 919 317 sq km (741 052 sq miles). Former
names (1798–1945): **Dutch East Indies, Netherlands
East Indies**

Indonesian (ˌɪndəʊ'niːzɪən) *adj* **1** of or relating to
Indonesia, its people, or their language ▷ *n* **2** a
native or inhabitant of Indonesia **3** another
name for **Bahasa Indonesia**

indoor ('ɪn,dɔː) *adj* (*prenominal*) of, situated in, or
appropriate to the inside of a house or other
building: *an indoor tennis court; indoor amusements*

indoors (ˌɪn'dɔːz) *adv, adj* (*postpositive*) inside or into
a house or other building

Indo-Pacific *adj* **1** of or relating to the region of
the Indian and W Pacific Oceans off the coast of
SE Asia ▷ *n* **2** a hypothetical family of languages
relating the languages of New Guinea other than
Malayo-Polynesian. Tentative affiliations with
Malayo-Polynesian or Australian languages have
been suggested

Indo-Pak *adj* of or relating to India and Pakistan:
the future of Indo-Pak relations

indophenol (ˌɪndəʊ'fiːnɒl) *n* **1** a derivative of
quinonimine. Formula: $HOC_6H_4NC_6H_4O$ **2** any of
a class of derivatives of this compound, esp one of
the blue or green dyes that are used for wool and
cotton [C19 from INDIGO + PHENOL]

Indore (ɪn'dɔː) *n* **1** a city in central India, in W
Madhya Pradesh. Pop: 1 597 441 (2001) **2** a former
state of central India: became part of Madhya
Bharat in 1948, which in turn became part of
Madhya Pradesh in 1956

indorse (ɪn'dɔːs) *vb* a variant spelling of **endorse**
> in'dorsable *adj* > in'dorsement *n* > in'dorser *or*
in'dorsor *n*

indorsee (ˌɪndɔː'siː, ɪn'dɔːsiː) *n* a variant of
endorsee

indoxyl (ɪn'dɒksɪl) *n* a yellow water-soluble
crystalline compound occurring in woad as its
glucoside and in urine as its ester. Formula:
C_8H_7NO. See also **indican** [C19 from INDIGO +
HYDROXYL]

Indra ('ɪndrə) *n Hinduism* the most celebrated god
of the Rig-Veda, governing the weather and
dispensing rain

indraught *or US* **indraft** ('ɪn,drɑːft) *n* **1** the act of
drawing or pulling in **2** an inward flow, esp of air

indrawn (ˌɪn'drɔːn) *adj* **1** drawn or pulled in **2**
inward-looking or introspective

Indre (*French* ɛ̃dr) *n* a department of central
France in the Centre region. Capital:
Châteauroux. Pop: 230 954 (2003 est). Area: 6906 sq
km (2693 sq miles)

Indre-et-Loire (*French* ɛ̃drelwar) *n* a department
of W central France in the Centre region: contains
many famous châteaux along the Loire. Capital:
Tours. Pop: 563 062 (2003 est). Area: 6158 sq km
(2402 sq miles)

indris ('ɪndrɪs) *or* **indri** ('ɪndrɪ) *n, pl* **-dris 1** a large

Madagascan arboreal lemuroid primate, *Indri indri*, with thick silky fur patterned in black, white, and fawn: family *Indriidae* **2 woolly indris** a related nocturnal Madagascan animal, *Avahi laniger*, with thick grey-brown fur and a long tail [C19 from French: lemur, from Malagasy *indry!* look! mistaken for the animal's name]

indubitable (ɪn'djuːbɪtəbªl) *adj* incapable of being doubted; unquestionable [C18 from Latin *indubitābilis*, from IN-¹ + *dubitāre* to doubt] > in,dubita'bility *or* in'dubitableness *n*

indubitably (ɪn'djuːbɪtəblɪ) *adv* without doubt; certainly

induce (ɪn'djuːs) *vb* (*tr*) **1** (often foll by an infinitive) to persuade or use influence on **2** to cause or bring about **3** *med* to initiate or hasten (labour), as by administering a drug to stimulate uterine contractions **4** *logic obsolete* to assert or establish (a general proposition, hypothesis, etc) by induction **5** to produce (an electromotive force or electrical current) by induction **6** to transmit (magnetism) by induction [C14 from Latin *indūcere* to lead in, from *dūcere* to lead] > in'ducer *n* > in'ducible *adj*

induced drag *n* the former name for **trailing vortex drag**

inducement (ɪn'djuːsmənt) *n* **1** the act of inducing **2** a means of inducing; persuasion; incentive **3** *law* (in pleading) the introductory part that leads up to and explains the matter in dispute

induct (ɪn'dʌkt) *vb* (*tr*) **1** to bring in formally or install in an office, place, etc; invest **2** (foll by *to* or *into*) to initiate in knowledge (of) **3** *US* to enlist for military service; conscript **4** *physics* another word for **induce** (senses 5, 6) [C14 from Latin *inductus* led in, past participle of *indūcere* to introduce; see INDUCE]

inductance (ɪn'dʌktəns) *n* **1** Also called: **induction** the property of an electric circuit as a result of which an electromotive force is created by a change of current in the same circuit (see **self-inductance**) or in a neighbouring circuit (see **mutual inductance**). It is usually measured in henries. Symbol: *L* **2** another name for **inductor**

inductile (,ɪndʌk'tiː:) *n US* a military conscript

inductile (ɪn'dʌktaɪl) *adj* not ductile, pliant, or yielding > ,induc'tility *n*

induction (ɪn'dʌkʃən) *n* **1** the act of inducting or state of being inducted **2** the act of inducing **3** (in an internal-combustion engine) the part of the action of a piston by which mixed air and fuel are drawn from the carburettor to the cylinder **4** *logic* **a** a process of reasoning, used esp in science, by which a general conclusion is drawn from a set of premises, based mainly on experience or experimental evidence. The conclusion goes beyond the information contained in the premises, and does not follow necessarily from them. Thus an inductive argument may be highly probable, yet lead from true premises to a false conclusion **b** a conclusion reached by this process of reasoning. Compare **deduction** (sense 4) **5** the process by which electrical or magnetic properties are transferred, without physical contact, from one circuit or body to another. See also **inductance 6** *biology* the effect of one tissue, esp an embryonic tissue, on the development of an adjacent tissue **7** *biochem* the process by which synthesis of an enzyme is stimulated by the presence of its substrate **8** *maths, logic* **a** a method of proving a proposition that all integers have a property, by first proving that 1 has the property and then that if the integer *n* has it so has *n* + 1 **b** the application of recursive rules **9 a** a formal introduction or entry into an office or position **b** (*as modifier*): *induction course; induction period* **10** *US* the formal enlistment of a civilian into military service **11** an archaic word for **preface**. > in'ductional *adj*

induction coil *n* a transformer for producing a high voltage from a low voltage. It consists of a

cylindrical primary winding of few turns, a concentric secondary winding of many turns, and often a common soft-iron core. Sometimes shortened to: **coil**

induction hardening *n* a process in which the outer surface of a metal component is rapidly heated by means of induced eddy currents. After rapid cooling the resulting phase transformations produce a hard wear-resistant skin

induction heating *n* the heating of a conducting material as a result of the electric currents induced in it by an externally applied alternating magnetic field

induction loop system *n* a system enabling partially deaf people to hear dialogue and sound in theatres, cinemas, etc, consisting of a loop of wire placed round the perimeter of a designated area. This emits an electromagnetic signal which is picked up by a hearing aid. Often shortened to: **induction loop**

induction motor *n* a type of brushless electric motor in which an alternating supply fed to the windings of the stator creates a magnetic field that induces a current in the windings of the rotor. Rotation of the rotor results from the interaction of the magnetic field created by the rotor current with the field of the stator

inductive (ɪn'dʌktɪv) *adj* **1** relating to, involving, or operated by electrical or magnetic induction: *an inductive reactance* **2** *logic, maths* of, relating to, or using induction: *inductive reasoning* **3** serving to induce or cause **4** a rare word for **introductory 5** *biology* producing a reaction within an organism, esp induction in embryonic tissue > in'ductively *adv* > in'ductiveness *n*

inductor (ɪn'dʌktə) *n* **1** a person or thing that inducts **2** a component, such as a coil, in an electrical circuit the main function of which is to produce inductance

indue (ɪn'djuː) *vb* **-dues, -duing, -dued** a variant spelling of **endue**

indulge (ɪn'dʌldʒ) *vb* **1** (when *intr*, often foll by *in*) to yield to or gratify (a whim or desire for): *to indulge a desire for new clothes; to indulge in new clothes* **2** (*tr*) to yield to the wishes of; pamper: *to indulge a child* **3** (*tr*) to allow oneself the pleasure of something: *at Christmas he liked to indulge himself* **4** (*tr*) *commerce* to allow (a debtor) an extension of time for payment of (a bill, etc) **5** (*intr*) *informal* to take alcoholic drink, esp to excess [C17 from Latin *indulgēre* to concede, from *-dulgēre*, probably related to Greek *dolikhos* long, Gothic *tulgus* firm] > in'dulger *n* > in'dulgingly *adv*

indulgence (ɪn'dʌldʒəns) *n* **1** the act of indulging or state of being indulgent **2** a pleasure, habit, etc, indulged in; extravagance: *fur coats are an indulgence* **3** liberal or tolerant treatment **4** something granted as a favour or privilege **5** *RC Church* a remission of the temporal punishment for sin after its guilt has been forgiven **6** *commerce* an extension of time granted as a favour for payment of a debt or as fulfilment of some other obligation **7** Also called: **Declaration of Indulgence** a royal grant during the reigns of Charles II and James II of England giving Nonconformists and Roman Catholics a measure of religious freedom ▷ *vb* (*tr*) **8** *RC Church* to designate as providing indulgence: *indulgenced prayers*

indulgent (ɪn'dʌldʒənt) *adj* showing or characterized by indulgence > in'dulgently *adv*

induline ('ɪndjʊ,laɪn) *or* **indulin** ('ɪndjʊlɪn) *n* any of a class of blue dyes obtained from aniline and aminoazobenzene [C19 from INDIGO + -ULE + -INE²]

indult (ɪn'dʌlt) *n RC Church* a faculty granted by the Holy See allowing a specific deviation from the Church's common law [C16 from Church Latin *indultum* a privilege, from Latin *indulgēre* to INDULGE]

indumentum (,ɪndjʊ'mɛntəm) *n, pl* **-ta** (-tə) *or* **-tums** an outer covering, such as hairs or down on a plant or leaf, feathers, fur, etc [C19 Latin, literally: garment]

induna (ɪn'duːnə) *n* (in South Africa) a Black African overseer in a factory, mine, etc [C20 from Zulu *nduna* an official]

induplicate (ɪn'djuː,plɪkɪt, -,keɪt) *or* **induplicated** *adj* (of the parts of a bud) bent or folded inwards with the edges touching but not overlapping > in,dupli'cation *n*

indurate *rarc* ▷ *vb* ('ɪndjʊ,reɪt) **1** to make or become hard or callous **2** to make or become hardy ▷ *adj* ('ɪndjʊrɪt) **3** hardened, callous, or unfeeling [C16 from Latin *indūrāre* to make hard; see ENDURE] > ,indu'ration *n* > 'indu,rative *adj*

Indus¹ ('ɪndəs) *n* a faint constellation in the S hemisphere lying between Telescopium and Tucano

Indus² ('ɪndəs) *n* a river in S Asia, rising in SW Tibet in the Kailas Range of the Himalayas and flowing northwest through Kashmir, then southwest across Pakistan to the Arabian Sea: important throughout history, esp for the Indus Civilization (about 3000 to 1500 BC), and for irrigation. Length: about 2900 km (1800 miles)

indusium (ɪn'djuːzɪəm) *n, pl* **-sia** (-zɪə) **1** a membranous outgrowth on the undersurface of fern leaves that covers and protects the developing sporangia **2** an enveloping membrane, such as the amnion [C18 New Latin, from Latin: tunic, from *induere* to put on] > in'dusial *adj*

industrial (ɪn'dʌstrɪəl) *adj* **1** of, relating to, derived from, or characteristic of industry **2** employed in industry: *the industrial workforce* **3** relating to or concerned with workers in industry: *industrial conditions* **4** used in industry: *industrial chemicals* > in'dustrially *adv*

industrial action *n Brit* any action, such as a strike or go-slow, taken by employees in industry to protest against working conditions, redundancies, etc

industrial archaeology *n* the study of past industrial machines, works, etc > **industrial archaeologist** *n*

industrial democracy *n* control of an organization by the people who work for it, esp by workers holding positions on its board of directors

industrial design *n* the art or practice of designing any object for manufacture > **industrial designer** *n*

industrial development certificate *n* (in Britain) a certificate issued by the Department of the Environment to an industrial organization wishing to build or extend a factory, which has to accompany an application for planning permission. Abbreviation: **IDC**

industrial diamond *n* a small often synthetic diamond, valueless as a gemstone, used in cutting tools, abrasives, etc

industrial disease *n* any disease to which workers in a particular industry are prone

industrial espionage *n* attempting to obtain trade secrets by dishonest means, as by telephone- or computer-tapping, infiltration of a competitor's workforce, etc

industrial estate *n Brit* another name for **trading estate** US equivalent: **industrial park**

industrialism (ɪn'dʌstrɪə,lɪzəm) *n* an organization of society characterized by large-scale mechanized manufacturing industry rather than trade, farming, etc

industrialist (ɪn'dʌstrɪəlɪst) *n* a person who has a substantial interest in the ownership or control of industrial enterprise

industrialize *or* **industrialise** (ɪn'dʌstrɪə,laɪz) *vb* **1** (*tr*) to develop industry on an extensive scale in (a country, region, etc) **2** (*intr*) (of a country, region, etc) to undergo the development of industry on an extensive scale > in,dustriali'zation *or* in,dustriali'sation *n*

industrial medicine *n* the study and practice of the health care of employees of large organizations, including measures to prevent

i

accidents, industrial diseases, and stress in the workforce and to monitor the health of executives

industrial melanism *n* See **melanism** (sense 1)

industrial misconduct *n* behaviour by an employee that is considered to be negligent or irregular to such an extent that disciplinary action may be taken, usually by agreement between management and the employee's representatives

industrial psychology *n* the scientific study of human behaviour and cognitive processes in relation to the working environment

industrial relations *n* **1** (*functioning as plural*) those aspects of collective relations between management and workers' representatives which are normally covered by collective bargaining **2** (*functioning as singular*) the management of relations between the employers or managers of an enterprise and their employees

Industrial Revolution *n* **the** the transformation in the 18th and 19th centuries of first Britain and then other W European countries and the US into industrial nations

industrials (ɪnˈdʌstrɪəlz) *pl n* stocks, shares, and bonds of industrial enterprises

industrial-strength *adj chiefly humorous* extremely strong or powerful: *industrial-strength tea*

industrial tribunal *n* (in Northern Ireland and formerly elsewhere in the UK) a tribunal that rules on disputes between employers and employees regarding unfair dismissal, redundancy, etc

industrial union *n* a labour organization in which all workers in a given industry are eligible for membership. Compare **craft union**

Industrial Workers of the World *n* **the** an international revolutionary federation of industrial unions founded in Chicago in 1905: banned in the US in 1949. Abbreviation: IWW See also **Wobbly**

industrious (ɪnˈdʌstrɪəs) *adj* **1** hard-working, diligent, or assiduous **2** an obsolete word for **skilful**. > inˈdustriously *adv* > inˈdustriousness *n*

industry (ˈɪndəstrɪ) *n, pl* -tries **1** organized economic activity concerned with manufacture, extraction and processing of raw materials, or construction **2** a branch of commercial enterprise concerned with the output of a specified product or service: *the steel industry* **3** **a** industrial ownership and management interests collectively, as contrasted with labour interests **b** manufacturing enterprise collectively, as opposed to agriculture **4** diligence; assiduity [c15 from Latin *industria* diligence, from *industrius* active, of uncertain origin]

industrywide (ˈɪndəstrɪˌwaɪd) *adv, adj* covering or available to all parts of an industry

indwell (ɪnˈdwɛl) *vb* -dwells, -dwelling, -dwelt **1** (*tr*) (of a spirit, principle, etc) to inhabit; suffuse **2** (*intr*) to dwell; exist > inˈdweller *n*

Indy Car racing (ˈɪndɪ) *n* a US form of professional motor racing around banked oval tracks [c20 named after the *Indianapolis 500* motor race]

-ine¹ *suffix forming adjectives* **1** of, relating to, or belonging to: *saturnine* **2** consisting of or resembling: *crystalline* [from Latin *-īnus*, from Greek *-inos*]

-ine² *suffix forming nouns* **1** indicating a halogen: *chlorine* **2** indicating a nitrogenous organic compound, including amino acids, alkaloids, and certain other bases: *alanine; nicotine; purine* **3** Also: -in indicating a chemical substance in certain nonsystematic names: *glycerine* **4** indicating a mixture of hydrocarbons: *benzine* **5** an obsolete equivalent for **-yne** [via French from Latin *-ina* (from *-inus*) and Greek *-inē*]

inearth (ɪnˈɜːθ) *vb* (*tr*) a poetic word for **bury**

inebriant (ɪˈniːbrɪənt) *adj* **1** causing intoxication, esp drunkenness ▷ *n* **2** something that inebriates

inebriate *vb* (ɪˈniːbrɪˌeɪt) (*tr*) **1** to make drunk; intoxicate **2** to arouse emotionally; make excited

▷ *n* (ɪˈniːbrɪɪt) **3** a person who is drunk, esp habitually ▷ *adj* (ɪˈniːbrɪɪt) *also* **inebriated 4** drunk, esp habitually [c15 from Latin *inēbriāre*, from IN-² + *ēbriāre* to intoxicate, from *ēbrius* drunk] > inˌebriˈation *n* inebriety (ˌɪnɪˈbraɪɪtɪ) *n*

inedible (ɪnˈɛdɪbᵊl) *adj* not fit to be eaten; uneatable > inˌediˈbility *n*

inedited (ɪnˈɛdɪtɪd) *adj* **1** not edited **2** not published

ineducable (ɪnˈɛdjʊkəbᵊl) *adj* incapable of being educated, esp on account of mental retardation > inˌeducaˈbility *n*

ineffable (ɪnˈɛfəbᵊl) *adj* **1** too great or intense to be expressed in words; unutterable **2** too sacred to be uttered **3** indescribable; indefinable [c15 from Latin *ineffābilis* unutterable, from IN-¹ + *effābilis*, from *effārī* to utter, from *fārī* to speak] > inˌeffaˈbility *or* inˈeffableness *n* > inˈeffably *adv*

ineffaceable (ˌɪnɪˈfeɪsəbᵊl) *adj* incapable of being effaced; indelible > ˌinefˌfaceaˈbility *n* > ˌineffaceably *adv*

ineffective (ˌɪnɪˈfɛktɪv) *adj* **1** having no effect **2** incompetent or inefficient > ˌineffectively *adv* > ˌineffectiveness *n*

ineffectual (ˌɪnɪˈfɛktʃʊəl) *adj* **1** having no effect or an inadequate effect **2** lacking in power or forcefulness; impotent: *an ineffectual ruler* > ˌinefˌfectuˈality *or* ˌineffectualness *n* > ˌineffectually *adv*

inefficacious (ˌɪnɛfɪˈkeɪʃəs) *adj* failing to produce the desired effect > ˌineffiˈcaciously *adv* > inefficacy (ɪnˈɛfɪkəsɪ) *or* ˌineffiˈcaciousness, inefficacity (ˌɪnɪfɪˈkæsɪtɪ) *n*

inefficient (ˌɪnɪˈfɪʃənt) *adj* **1** unable to perform a task or function to the best advantage; wasteful or incompetent **2** unable to produce the desired result > ˌineffiˈciency *n* > ˌinefficiently *adv*

inelastic (ˌɪnɪˈlæstɪk) *adj* **1** not elastic; not resilient **2** *physics* (of collisions) involving an overall decrease in translational kinetic energy > ineˈlastically *adv* > inelasticity (ˌɪnɪlæsˈtɪsɪtɪ) *n*

inelegant (ɪnˈɛlɪgənt) *adj* **1** lacking in elegance or refinement; unpolished or graceless **2** coarse or crude > inˈelegance *or* inˈelegancy *n* > inˈelegantly *adv*

ineligible (ɪnˈɛlɪdʒəbᵊl) *adj* **1** (often foll by *for* or an infinitive) not fit or qualified: *ineligible for a grant; ineligible to vote* ▷ *n* **2** an ineligible person > inˌeligiˈbility *or* inˈeligibleness *n* > inˈeligibly *adv*

ineloquent (ɪnˈɛləkwənt) *adj* lacking eloquence or fluency of expression > inˈeloquence *n* > inˈeloquently *adv*

ineluctable (ˌɪnɪˈlʌktəbᵊl) *adj* (esp of fate) incapable of being avoided; inescapable [c17 from Latin *inēluctābilis*, from IN-¹ + *ēluctārī* to escape, from *luctārī* to struggle] > ˌineˌluctaˈbility *n* > ˌineˈluctably *adv*

ineludible (ˌɪnɪˈluːdəbᵊl) *adj* a rare word for **inescapable**. > ˌineˌludiˈbility *n* > ˌineˈludibly *adv*

inept (ɪnˈɛpt) *adj* **1** awkward, clumsy, or incompetent **2** not suitable, appropriate, or fitting; out of place [c17 from Latin *ineptus*, from IN-¹ + *aptus* fitting, suitable] > inˈeptiˌtude *n* > inˈeptly *adv* > inˈeptness *n*

inequable (ɪnˈɛkwəbᵊl) *adj* uneven; not uniform

inequality (ˌɪnɪˈkwɒlɪtɪ) *n, pl* -ties **1** the state or quality of being unequal; disparity **2** an instance of disparity **3** lack of smoothness or regularity **4** social or economic disparity **5** *maths* **a** a statement indicating that the value of one quantity or expression is not equal to another, as in x ≠ y **b** a relationship between real numbers involving inequality: x may be greater than y, denoted by x > y, or less than y, denoted by x < y **6** *astronomy* a departure from uniform orbital motion

inequitable (ɪnˈɛkwɪtəbᵊl) *adj* not equitable; unjust or unfair > inˈequitableness *n* > inˈequitably *adv*

inequity (ɪnˈɛkwɪtɪ) *n, pl* -ties **1** lack of equity; injustice; unfairness **2** an unjust or unfair act, sentence, etc

ineradicable (ˌɪnɪˈrædɪkəbᵊl) *adj* not able to be removed or rooted out; inextirpable: *an ineradicable disease* > ˌineˈradicableness *n* > ˌineˈradicably *adv*

inerrable (ɪnˈɛrəbᵊl) *or* **inerrant** (ɪnˈɛrənt) *adj* less common words for **infallible**. > inˌerraˈbility, inˈerrableness *or* inˈerrancy *n* > inˈerrably *adv*

inert (ɪnˈɜːt) *adj* **1** having no inherent ability to move or to resist motion **2** inactive, lazy, or sluggish **3** having only a limited ability to react chemically; unreactive [c17 from Latin *iners* unskilled, from IN-¹ + *ars* skill; see ART¹] > inˈertly *adv* > inˈertness *n*

inert gas *n* **1** Also called: noble gas, rare gas, argonon any of the unreactive gaseous elements helium, neon, argon, krypton, xenon, and radon **2** (loosely) any gas, such as carbon dioxide, that is nonoxidizing

inertia (ɪnˈɜːʃə, -ʃɪə) *n* **1** the state of being inert; disinclination to move or act **2** *physics* **a** the tendency of a body to preserve its state of rest or uniform motion unless acted upon by an external force **b** an analogous property of other physical quantities that resist change: *thermal inertia* > inˈertial *adj*

inertia force *n* an imaginary force supposed to act upon an accelerated body, equal in magnitude and opposite in direction to the resultant of the real forces

inertial force *n* an imaginary force which an accelerated observer postulates so that he can use the equations appropriate to an inertial observer. See also **Coriolis force**

inertial fusion *or* **inertial confinement fusion** *n physics* a type of nuclear fusion in which the inertia of matter enables it to fuse by impact, as by pulses of laser radiation or high-energy charged particles, rather than by high temperature

inertial guidance *or* **navigation** *n* a method of controlling the flight path of a missile by instruments contained within it. Velocities or distances covered, computed from the acceleration measured by these instruments, are compared with stored data and used to control the speed and direction of the missile. Compare **celestial guidance, terrestrial guidance**

inertial mass *n* the mass of a body as determined by its momentum, as opposed to gravitational mass. The acceleration of a falling body is inversely proportional to its inertial mass but directly proportional to its gravitational mass: as all falling bodies have the same constant acceleration the two types of mass must be equal

inertial observer *n* a hypothetical observer who is not accelerated with respect to an inertial system. Newton's laws of motion and the special theory of relativity apply to the measurements which would be made by such observers

inertial system *n* a frame of reference within which bodies are not accelerated unless acted upon by external forces. Also called: inertial reference frame

inertia-reel seat belt *n* a type of car seat belt in which the belt is free to unwind from a metal drum except when the drum locks as a result of rapid deceleration

inertia selling *n* (in Britain) the illegal practice of sending unrequested goods to householders followed by a bill for the price of the goods if they do not return them

inescapable (ˌɪnɪˈskeɪpəbᵊl) *adj* incapable of being escaped or avoided > ˌinesˈcapably *adv*

inescutcheon (ˌɪnɪˈskʌtʃən) *n heraldry* a small shield-shaped charge in the centre of a shield

in esse (ɪn ˈɛsɪ) *adj* actually existing. Compare **in posse** [Latin, literally: in being]

inessential (ˌɪnɪˈsɛnʃəl) *adj* **1** not necessary ▷ *n* **2** anything that is not essential > ˌinesˌsentiˈality *n*

inessive (ɪnˈɛsɪv) *adj* **1** (in the grammar of Finnish and related languages) denoting a case of nouns, etc, used when indicating the location of the referent ▷ *n* **2** the inessive case [c20 from

Latin *inesse* to be in]

inestimable (ɪnˈɛstɪməbᵊl) *adj* **1** not able to be estimated; immeasurable **2** of immeasurable value > **inˌestimaˈbility** *or* **inˈestimableness** *n* > **inˈestimably** *adv*

inevitable (ɪnˈɛvɪtəbᵊl) *adj* **1** unavoidable **2** sure to happen; certain ▷ *n* **3** (often preceded by *the*) something that is unavoidable [C15 from Latin *inēvītābilis*, from IN-[1] + *ēvītābilis*, from *ēvītāre* to shun, from *vītāre* to avoid] > **inˌevitaˈbility** *or* **inˈevitableness** *n* > **inˈevitably** *adv*

inexact (ˌɪnɪɡˈzækt) *adj* not exact or accurate > **ˌinexˈactiˌtude** *or* **ˌinexˈactness** *n* > **ˌinexˈactly** *adv*

inexcusable (ˌɪnɪkˈskjuːzəbᵊl) *adj* not able to be excused or justified > **ˌinexˌcusaˈbility** *or* **ˌinexˈcusableness** *n* > **ˌinexˈcusably** *adv*

inexhaustible (ˌɪnɪɡˈzɔːstəbᵊl) *adj* **1** incapable of being used up; endless: *inexhaustible patience* **2** incapable or apparently incapable of becoming tired; tireless > **ˌinexˌhaustiˈbility** *or* **ˌinexˈhaustibleness** *n* > **ˌinexˈhaustibly** *adv*

inexistent (ˌɪnɪɡˈzɪstənt) *adj* a rare word for **nonexistent**. > **ˌinexˈistence** *or* **ˌinexˈistency** *n*

inexorable (ɪnˈɛksərəbᵊl) *adj* **1** not able to be moved by entreaty or persuasion **2** relentless [C16 from Latin *inexōrābilis*, from IN-[1] + *exōrābilis*, from *exōrāre* to prevail upon, from *ōrāre* to pray] > **inˌexoraˈbility** *or* **inˈexorableness** *n* > **inˈexorably** *adv*

inexpedient (ˌɪnɪkˈspiːdɪənt) *adj* not suitable, advisable, or judicious > **ˌinexˈpedience** *or* **ˌinexˈpediency** *n* > **ˌinexˈpediently** *adv*

inexpensive (ˌɪnɪkˈspɛnsɪv) *adj* not expensive; cheap > **ˌinexˈpensively** *adv* > **ˌinexˈpensiveness** *n*

inexperience (ˌɪnɪkˈspɪərɪəns) *n* lack of experience or of the knowledge and understanding derived from experience > **ˌinexˈperienced** *adj*

inexpert (ɪnˈɛkspɜːt) *adj* not expert; unskilled or unskilful; inept > **inˈexpertly** *adv* > **inˈexpertness** *n*

inexpiable (ɪnˈɛkspɪəbᵊl) *adj* **1** incapable of being expiated; unpardonable **2** *archaic* implacable > **inˈexpiableness** *n* > **inˈexpiably** *adv*

inexplicable (ˌɪnɪkˈsplɪkəbᵊl, ɪnˈɛksplɪkəbᵊl) *or* **inexplainable** *adj* not capable of explanation; unexplainable > **ˌinexplicaˈbility**, **ˌinexˈplicableness**, **ˌinexˌplainaˈbility** *or* **ˌinexˈplainableness** *n* > **ˌinexˈplicably** *or* **ˌinexˈplainably** *adv*

inexplicit (ˌɪnɪkˈsplɪsɪt) *adj* not explicit, clear, or precise; vague > **ˌinexˈplicitly** *adv* > **ˌinexˈplicitness** *n*

inexpressible (ˌɪnɪkˈsprɛsəbᵊl) *adj* too great, etc, to be expressed or uttered; indescribable > **ˌinexˌpressiˈbility** *or* **ˌinexˈpressibleness** *n* > **ˌinexˈpressibly** *adv*

inexpressive (ˌɪnɪkˈsprɛsɪv) *adj* **1** lacking in expression: *an inexpressive face* **2** an archaic word for **inexpressible**. > **ˌinexˈpressively** *adv* > **ˌinexˈpressiveness** *n*

inexpugnable (ˌɪnɪkˈspʌɡnəbᵊl) *adj* a rare word for **impregnable**[1] > **ˌinexˌpugnaˈbility** *or* **ˌinexˈpugnableness** *n* > **ˌinexˈpugnably** *adv*

inexpungible (ˌɪnɪksˈpʌndʒɪbᵊl) *adj* incapable of being expunged

inextensible (ˌɪnɪkˈstɛnsəbᵊl) *adj* not capable of extension > **ˌinexˌtensiˈbility** *n*

in extenso *Latin* (ɪn ɪkˈstɛnsəʊ) *adv* at full length

inextinguishable (ˌɪnɪkˈstɪŋɡwɪʃəbᵊl) *adj* not able to be extinguished, quenched, or put to an end > **ˌinexˈtinguishableness** *n* > **ˌinexˈtinguishably** *adv*

inextirpable (ˌɪnɪkˈstɜːpəbᵊl) *adj* not able to be extirpated; ineradicable > **ˌinexˈtirpableness** *n*

in extremis *Latin* (ɪn ɪkˈstriːmɪs) *adv* **1** in extremity; in dire straits **2** at the point of death [literally: in the furthest reaches]

inextricable (ˌɪnɛksˈtrɪkəbᵊl) *adj* **1** not able to be escaped from: *an inextricable dilemma* **2** not able to be disentangled, etc: *an inextricable knot* **3** extremely involved or intricate > **ˌinextricaˈbility** *or* **ˌinexˈtricableness** *n* > **ˌinexˈtricably** *adv*

INF *abbreviation for* intermediate-range nuclear forces: land-based missiles and aircraft with a range between 500 and 5000 km

inf. *abbreviation for* **1** infinitive **2** infra [Latin: below; after; later]

infallibilism (ɪnˈfælɪbᵊˌlɪzəm) *n* *RC Church* the principle of papal infallibility > **inˈfallibilist** *n*

infallible (ɪnˈfæləbᵊl) *adj* **1** not fallible; not liable to error **2** not liable to failure; certain; sure: *an infallible cure* **3** completely dependable or trustworthy ▷ *n* **4** a person or thing that is incapable of error or failure > **inˌfalliˈbility** *or* **inˈfallibleness** *n* > **inˈfallibly** *adv*

infamize *or* **infamise** (ˈɪnfəˌmaɪz) *vb* (*tr*) to make infamous

infamous (ˈɪnfəməs) *adj* **1** having a bad reputation; notorious **2** causing or deserving a bad reputation; shocking: *infamous conduct* **3** *Criminal law*, (formerly) **a** (of a person) deprived of certain rights of citizenship on conviction of certain offences **b** (of a crime or punishment) entailing such deprivation > **ˈinfamously** *adv* > **ˈinfamousness** *n*

infamy (ˈɪnfəmɪ) *n*, *pl* **-mies** **1** the state or condition of being infamous **2** an infamous act or event [C15 from Latin *infāmis* of evil repute, from IN-[1] + *fāma* FAME]

infancy (ˈɪnfənsɪ) *n*, *pl* **-cies** **1** the state or period of being an infant; childhood **2** an early stage of growth or development **3** infants collectively **4** the period of life prior to attaining legal majority (reached at 21 under common law, at 18 by statute); minority nonage

infant (ˈɪnfənt) *n* **1** a child at the earliest stage of its life; baby **2** *law* another word for **minor** (sense 10) **3** *Brit* a young schoolchild, usually under the age of seven **4** a person who is beginning or inexperienced in an activity **5** (*modifier*) **a** of or relating to young children or infancy **b** designed or intended for young children ▷ *adj* **6** in an early stage of development; nascent: *an infant science or industry* **7** *law* of or relating to the legal status of infancy [C14 from Latin *infāns*, literally: speechless, from IN-[1] + *fārī* to speak] > **ˈinfantˌhood** *n*

infanta (ɪnˈfæntə) *n* (formerly) **1** a daughter of a king of Spain or Portugal **2** the wife of an infante [C17 from Spanish or Portuguese, feminine of INFANTE]

infante (ɪnˈfæntɪ) *n* (formerly) a son of a king of Spain or Portugal, esp one not heir to the throne [C16 from Spanish or Portuguese, literally: INFANT]

infanticide (ɪnˈfæntɪˌsaɪd) *n* **1** the killing of an infant **2** the practice of killing newborn infants, still prevalent in some primitive tribes **3** a person who kills an infant > **inˌfantiˈcidal** *adj*

infantile (ˈɪnfənˌtaɪl) *adj* **1** like a child in action or behaviour; childishly immature; puerile **2** of, relating to, or characteristic of infants or infancy **3** in an early stage of development > **infantility** (ˌɪnfənˈtɪlɪtɪ) *n*

infantile paralysis *n* a former name for **poliomyelitis**

infantilism (ɪnˈfæntɪˌlɪzəm) *n* **1** *psychol* **a** a condition in which an older child or adult is mentally or physically undeveloped **b** isolated instances of infantile behaviour in mature persons **2** childish speech; baby talk

infant prodigy *n* an exceptionally talented child

infantry (ˈɪnfəntrɪ) *n*, *pl* **-tries** **a** soldiers or units of soldiers who fight on foot with small arms **b** (*as modifier*): *an infantry unit*. Abbreviations: **Inf**, **inf** [C16 from Italian *infanteria*, from *infante* boy, foot soldier; see INFANT]

infantryman (ˈɪnfəntrɪmən) *n*, *pl* **-men** a soldier belonging to the infantry

infant school *n* (in England and Wales) a school for children aged between 5 and 7. Compare **junior school**

infarct (ɪnˈfɑːkt) *n* a localized area of dead tissue (necrosis) resulting from obstruction of the blood supply to that part, esp by an embolus. Also called: **infarction** [C19 via New Latin from Latin *infarctus* stuffed into, from *farcīre* to stuff] > **inˈfarcted** *adj*

infarction (ɪnˈfɑːkʃən) *n* **1** the formation or development of an infarct **2** another word for **infarct**

infatuate *vb* (ɪnˈfætjʊˌeɪt) (*tr*) **1** to inspire or fill with foolish, shallow, or extravagant passion **2** to cause to act foolishly ▷ *adj* (ɪnˈfætjʊɪt, -ˌeɪt) **3** an archaic word for **infatuated** ▷ *n* (ɪnˈfætjʊɪt, -ˌeɪt) **4** *literary* a person who is infatuated [C16 from Latin *infatuāre*, from IN-[2] + *fatuus* FATUOUS]

infatuated (ɪnˈfætjʊˌeɪtɪd) *adj* (often foll by *with*) possessed by a foolish or extravagant passion, esp for another person > **inˈfatuˌatedly** *adv*

infatuation (ɪnˌfætjʊˈeɪʃən) *n* **1** the act of infatuating or state of being infatuated **2** foolish or extravagant passion **3** an object of foolish or extravagant passion

infeasible (ɪnˈfiːzəbᵊl) *adj* a less common word for **impracticable**. > **inˌfeasiˈbility** *or* **inˈfeasibleness** *n*

infect (ɪnˈfɛkt) *vb* (*mainly tr*) **1** to cause infection in; contaminate (an organism, wound, etc) with pathogenic microorganisms **2** (*also intr*) to affect or become affected with a communicable disease **3** to taint, pollute, or contaminate **4** to affect, esp adversely, as if by contagion **5** *computing* to affect with a computer virus **6** *chiefly international law* to taint with crime or illegality; expose to penalty or subject to forfeiture ▷ *adj* **7** *archaic* contaminated or polluted with or as if with a disease; infected [C14 from Latin *inficere* to dip into, stain, from *facere* to make] > **inˈfector** *or* **inˈfecter** *n*

infection (ɪnˈfɛkʃən) *n* **1** invasion of the body by pathogenic microorganisms **2** the resulting condition in the tissues **3** an infectious disease **4** the act of infecting or state of being infected **5** an agent or influence that infects **6** persuasion or corruption, as by ideas, perverse influences, etc

infectious (ɪnˈfɛkʃəs) *adj* **1** (of a disease) capable of being transmitted. Compare **contagious** **2** (of a disease) caused by microorganisms, such as bacteria, viruses, or protozoa **3** causing or transmitting infection **4** tending or apt to spread, as from one person to another: *infectious mirth* **5** *international law* **a** tainting or capable of tainting with illegality **b** rendering liable to seizure or forfeiture > **inˈfectiously** *adv* > **inˈfectiousness** *n*

infectious canine hepatitis *n* *vet science* a disease of dogs caused by an adenovirus and characterized by signs of liver disease

infectious hepatitis *n* any form of hepatitis caused by viruses. See **hepatitis A**, **hepatitis B**

infectious mononucleosis *n* an acute infectious disease, caused by Epstein-Barr virus, characterized by fever, sore throat, swollen and painful lymph nodes, and abnormal lymphocytes in the blood. Also called: **glandular fever**

infective (ɪnˈfɛktɪv) *adj* **1** capable of causing infection **2** a less common word for **infectious** > **inˈfectively** *adv* > **inˈfectiveness** *or* **ˌinfecˈtivity** *n*

infecund (ɪnˈfiːkənd) *adj* a less common word for **infertile**. > **infecundity** (ˌɪnfɪˈkʌndɪtɪ) *n*

infelicitous (ˌɪnfɪˈlɪsɪtəs) *adj* **1** not felicitous; unfortunate **2** inappropriate or unsuitable > **ˌinfeˈlicitously** *adv*

infelicity (ˌɪnfɪˈlɪsɪtɪ) *n*, *pl* **-ties** **1** the state or quality of being unhappy or unfortunate **2** an instance of bad luck or mischance; misfortune **3** something, esp a remark or expression, that is inapt or inappropriate

infer (ɪnˈfɜː) *vb* **-fers**, **-ferring**, **-ferred** (when *tr*, *may take a clause as object*) **1** to conclude (a state of affairs, supposition, etc) by reasoning from evidence; deduce **2** (*tr*) to have or lead to as a necessary or logical consequence; indicate **3** (*tr*) to hint or imply [C16 from Latin *inferre* to bring into, from *ferre* to bear, carry] > **inˈferable**, **inˈferible**, **inˈferrable** *or* **inˈferrible** *adj* > **inˈferably** *adv* > **inˈferrer** *n*

USAGE The use of *infer* to mean *imply* is becoming more and more common in both speech and writing. There is nevertheless a useful distinction between the two which many people would be in favour of maintaining. To *infer* means 'to deduce', and is used in the construction *to infer something from something: I inferred from what she said that she had not been well*. To *imply* (sense 1) means 'to suggest, to insinuate' and is normally followed by a clause: *are you implying that I was responsible for the mistake?*

inference ('ɪnfərəns, -frəns) *n* **1** the act or process of inferring **2** an inferred conclusion, deduction, etc **3** any process of reasoning from premises to a conclusion **4** *logic* the specific mode of reasoning used. See also **deduction** (sense 4), **induction** (sense 4)

inferencing ('ɪnfərənsɪŋ) *n psycholinguistics* the practice of inferring the meaning of an unfamiliar word or expression from the meaning of familiar words occurring with it in a context together with one's knowledge of or beliefs about the world

inferential (ˌɪnfə'rɛnʃəl) *adj* of, relating to, or derived from inference > ˌ**infer'entially** *adv*

inferential statistics *n* (*functioning as singular*) another name for **statistical inference**

inferior (ɪn'fɪərɪə) *adj* **1** lower in value or quality **2** lower in rank, position, or status; subordinate **3** not of the best; mediocre; commonplace **4** lower in position; situated beneath **5** (of a plant ovary) enclosed by and fused with the receptacle so that it is situated below the other floral parts **6** *astronomy* **a** orbiting or occurring between the sun and the earth: *an inferior planet; inferior conjunction* **b** lying below the horizon **7** *printing* (of a character) printed at the foot of an ordinary character, as the 2 in H_2O ▷ *n* **8** an inferior person **9** *printing* an inferior character [C15 from Latin: lower, from *inferus* low] > **inferiority** (ɪnˌfɪərɪ'ɒrɪtɪ) *n* > **in'feriorly** *adv*

inferior court *n* **1** a court of limited jurisdiction **2** any court other than the Supreme Court of Judicature

inferiority complex *n psychiatry* a disorder arising from the conflict between the desire to be noticed and the fear of being humiliated, characterized by aggressiveness or withdrawal into oneself

inferior planet *n* either of the planets Mercury and Venus, whose orbits lie inside that of the earth

infernal (ɪn'fɜːnəl) *adj* **1** of or relating to an underworld of the dead **2** deserving hell or befitting its occupants; diabolic; fiendish **3** *informal* irritating; confounded [C14 from Late Latin *infernālis*, from *infernus* hell, from Latin (adj): lower, hellish; related to Latin *inferus* low] > ˌ**infer'nality** *n* > **in'fernally** *adv*

infernal machine *n archaic* a usually disguised explosive device or booby trap

inferno (ɪn'fɜːnəʊ) *n, pl* **-nos 1** (*sometimes capital; usually preceded by* the) hell; the infernal region **2** any place or state resembling hell, esp a conflagration [C19 from Italian, from Late Latin *infernus* hell]

infertile (ɪn'fɜːtaɪl) *adj* **1** not capable of producing offspring; sterile **2** (of land) not productive; barren > **in'fertilely** *adv* > **infertility** (ˌɪnfə'tɪlɪtɪ) *n*

infest (ɪn'fɛst) *vb* (*tr*) **1** to inhabit or overrun in dangerously or unpleasantly large numbers **2** (of parasites such as lice) to invade and live on or in (a host) [C15 from Latin *infestāre* to molest, from *infestus* hostile] > ˌ**infes'tation** *n* > **in'fester** *n*

infeudation (ˌɪnfjʊ'deɪʃən) *n* **1** (in feudal society) **a** the act of putting a vassal in possession of a fief **b** the deed conferring such possession **c** the consequent relationship of lord and vassal **2** the granting of tithes to laymen

infibulate (ɪn'fɪbjʊˌleɪt) *vb* (*tr*) to enclose (esp the genitals, to prevent sexual intercourse) with a clasp [C17 from Latin *infibulāre*, from IN-[2] + *fibula* clasp, FIBULA] > **inˌfibu'lation** *n*

infidel ('ɪnfɪdəl) *n* **1** a person who has no religious belief; unbeliever ▷ *adj* **2** rejecting a specific religion, esp Christianity or Islam **3** of, characteristic of, or relating to unbelievers or unbelief [C15 from Medieval Latin *infidēlis*, from Latin (adj): unfaithful, from IN-[1] + *fidēlis* faithful; see FEAL]

infidelity (ˌɪnfɪ'dɛlɪtɪ) *n, pl* **-ties 1** lack of faith or constancy, esp sexual faithfulness **2** lack of religious faith; disbelief **3** an act or instance of disloyalty

infield ('ɪnˌfiːld) *n* **1** *cricket* the area of the field near the pitch. Compare **outfield 2** *baseball* **a** the area of the playing field enclosed by the base lines and extending beyond them towards the outfield **b** the positions of the first baseman, second baseman, shortstop, third baseman, and sometimes the pitcher, collectively. Compare **outfield 3** *agriculture* **a** the part of a farm nearest to the farm buildings **b** land from which crops are regularly taken

infielder ('ɪnˌfiːldə) *or* **infieldsman** ('ɪnfiːldzmən) *n* a player positioned in the infield

infighting ('ɪnˌfaɪtɪŋ) *n* **1** *boxing* combat at close quarters in which proper blows are inhibited and the fighters try to wear down each other's strength **2** intense competition, as between members of the same organization, esp when kept secret from outsiders > **'inˌfighter** *n*

infill ('ɪnfɪl) *or* **infilling** ('ɪnfɪlɪŋ) *n* **1** the act of filling or closing gaps, etc, in something, such as a row of buildings **2** material used to fill a cavity, gap, hole, etc **3** an acrylic gel application that fills in the gap between a false nail and the root of the real nail, which is created as the real nail grows

infiltrate ('ɪnfɪlˌtreɪt) *vb* **1** to undergo or cause to undergo the process in which a fluid passes into the pores or interstices of a solid; permeate **2** *military* to pass undetected through (an enemy-held line or position) **3** to gain or cause to gain entrance or access surreptitiously: *they infiltrated the party structure* ▷ *n* **4** something that infiltrates **5** *pathol* any substance that passes into and accumulates within cells, tissues, or organs **6** *pathol* a local anaesthetic solution injected into the tissues to cause local anaesthesia [C18 from IN-[2] + FILTRATE] > ˌ**infil'tration** *n* > **'infilˌtrative** *adj* > **'infilˌtrator** *n*

infimum ('ɪnfɪməm) *n, pl* **-ma** (-mə) the greatest lower bound

infin. *abbreviation for* infinitive

infinite ('ɪnfɪnɪt) *adj* **1 a** having no limits or boundaries in time, space, extent, or magnitude **b** (*as noun; preceded by* the): *the infinite* **2** extremely or immeasurably great or numerous: *infinite wealth* **3** all-embracing, absolute, or total: *God's infinite wisdom* **4** *maths* **a** having an unlimited number of digits, factors, terms, members, etc: *an infinite series* **b** (of a set) able to be put in a one-to-one correspondence with part of itself **c** (of an integral) having infinity as one or both limits of integration. Compare **finite** (sense 2) > **'infinitely** *adv* > **'infiniteness** *n*

infinitesimal (ˌɪnfɪnɪ'tɛsɪməl) *adj* **1** infinitely or immeasurably small **2** *maths* of, relating to, or involving a small change in the value of a variable that approaches zero as a limit ▷ *n* **3** *maths* an infinitesimal quantity > ˌ**infini'tesimally** *adv*

infinitesimal calculus *n* another name for **calculus** (sense 1)

infinitive (ɪn'fɪnɪtɪv) *n grammar* a form of the verb not inflected for grammatical categories such as tense and person and used without an overt subject. In English, the infinitive usually consists of the word *to* followed by the verb > **infinitival** (ˌɪnfɪnɪ'taɪvəl) *adj* > **in'finitively** *or* ˌ**infini'tivally** *adv*

infinitive marker *n grammar* a word or affix occurring with the verb stem in the infinitive, such as *to* in *to make*

infinitude (ɪn'fɪnɪˌtjuːd) *n* **1** the state or quality of being infinite **2** an infinite extent, quantity, etc

infinity (ɪn'fɪnɪtɪ) *n, pl* **-ties 1** the state or quality of being infinite **2** endless time, space, or quantity **3** an infinitely or indefinitely great number or amount **4** *optics, photog* a point that is far enough away from a lens, mirror, etc, for the light emitted by it to fall in parallel rays on the surface of the lens, etc **5** *physics* a dimension or quantity of sufficient size to be unaffected by finite variations **6** *maths* the concept of a value greater than any finite numerical value **7** a distant ideal point at which two parallel lines are assumed to meet ▷ Symbol (for senses 4–7): ∞

infirm (ɪn'fɜːm) *adj* **1 a** weak in health or body, esp from old age **b** (*as collective noun; preceded by* the): *the infirm* **2** lacking moral certainty; indecisive or irresolute **3** not stable, sound, or secure: *an infirm structure; an infirm claim* **4** *law* (of a law, custom, etc) lacking legal force; invalid > **in'firmly** *adv* > **in'firmness** *n*

infirmary (ɪn'fɜːmərɪ) *n, pl* **-ries** a place for the treatment of the sick or injured; dispensary; hospital

infirmity (ɪn'fɜːmɪtɪ) *n, pl* **-ties 1** the state or quality of being infirm **2** physical weakness or debility; frailty **3** a moral flaw or failing

infix *vb* (ɪn'fɪks, 'ɪnˌfɪks) **1** (*tr*) to fix firmly in **2** (*tr*) to instil or inculcate **3** *grammar* to insert (an affix) or (of an affix) to be inserted into the middle of a word ▷ *n* ('ɪnˌfɪks) **4** *grammar* an affix inserted into the middle of a word > ˌ**infix'ation** *or* **infixion** (ɪn'fɪkʃən) *n*

in flagrante delicto (ɪn flə'græntɪ dɪ'lɪktəʊ) *adv chiefly law* while committing the offence; red-handed. Also: **flagrante delicto** [Latin, literally: with the crime still blazing]

inflame (ɪn'fleɪm) *vb* **1** to arouse or become aroused to violent emotion **2** (*tr*) to increase or intensify; aggravate **3** to produce inflammation in (a tissue, organ, or part) or (of a tissue, etc) to become inflamed **4** to set or be set on fire; kindle **5** (*tr*) to cause to redden > **in'flamer** *n* > **in'flamingly** *adv*

inflammable (ɪn'flæməbəl) *adj* **1** liable to catch fire; flammable **2** readily aroused to anger or passion ▷ *n* **3** something that is liable to catch fire > **inˌflamma'bility** *or* **in'flammableness** *n* > **in'flammably** *adv*

USAGE See at **flammable**

inflammation (ˌɪnflə'meɪʃən) *n* **1** the reaction of living tissue to injury or infection, characterized by heat, redness, swelling, and pain **2** the act of inflaming or the state of being inflamed

inflammatory (ɪn'flæmətərɪ, -trɪ) *adj* **1** characterized by or caused by inflammation **2** tending to arouse violence, strong emotion, etc > **in'flammatorily** *adv*

inflatable (ɪn'fleɪtəbəl) *n* **1** any of various large air-filled objects made of strong plastic or rubber, used for children to play on at fairs, carnivals, etc ▷ *adj* **2** capable of being inflated

inflate (ɪn'fleɪt) *vb* **1** to expand or cause to expand by filling with gas or air: *she needed to inflate the tyres* **2** (*tr*) to cause to increase excessively; puff up; swell: *to inflate one's opinion of oneself* **3** (*tr*) to cause inflation of (prices, money, etc) **4** (*tr*) to raise in spirits; elate **5** (*intr*) to undergo economic inflation [C16 from Latin *inflāre* to blow into, from *flāre* to blow] > **in'flatedly** *adv* > **in'flatedness** *n* > **in'flater** *or* **in'flator** *n*

inflation (ɪn'fleɪʃən) *n* **1** the act of inflating or state of being inflated **2** *economics* a progressive increase in the general level of prices brought about by an expansion in demand or the money supply (**demand-pull inflation**) or by autonomous increases in costs (**cost-push inflation**). Compare **deflation 3** *informal* the rate of increase of prices

inflationary (ɪn'fleɪʃənərɪ) *adj* of, relating to, causing, or characterized by inflation: *inflationary wage claims*

inflationary gap *n* the excess of total spending in an economy over the value, at current prices, of the output it can produce

inflationary spiral *n* the situation in which price and income increases may each induce further rises in the other

inflationary universe *n* a variation of the cosmological big-bang theory in which the early stage of the evolution of the universe is postulated to include a period of accelerated expansion

inflationism (ɪnˈfleɪʃəˌnɪzəm) *n* the advocacy or policy of inflation through expansion of the supply of money and credit > inˈflationist *n, adj*

inflect (ɪnˈflɛkt) *vb* 1 (*Grammar*) to change (the form of a word) or (of a word) to change in form by inflection 2 (*tr*) to change (the voice) in tone or pitch; modulate 3 (*tr*) to cause to deviate from a straight or normal line or course; bend [c15 from Latin *inflectere* to curve round, alter, from *flectere* to bend] > inˈflectedness *n* > inˈflective *adj* > inˈflector *n*

inflection *or* **inflexion** (ɪnˈflɛkʃən) *n* 1 modulation of the voice 2 (*Grammar*) a change in the form of a word, usually modification or affixation, signalling change in such grammatical functions as tense, voice, mood, person, gender, number, or case 3 an angle or bend 4 the act of inflecting or the state of being inflected 5 *maths* a change in curvature from concave to convex or vice versa. See also **point of inflection**. > inˈflectional *or* inˈflexional *adj* > inˈflectionally *or* inˈflexionally *adv* > inˈflectionless *or* inˈflexionless *adj*

inflexed (ɪnˈflɛkst) *adj* *biology* curved or bent inwards and downwards towards the axis: *inflexed leaves*

inflexible (ɪnˈflɛksəbəl) *adj* 1 not flexible; rigid; stiff 2 obstinate; unyielding 3 without variation; unalterable; fixed [c14 from Latin *inflexibilis*; see INFLECT] > inˌflexiˈbility *or* inˈflexibleness *n* > inˈflexibly *adv*

inflict (ɪnˈflɪkt) *vb* (*tr*) 1 (often foll by *on* or *upon*) to impose (something unwelcome, such as pain, oneself, etc) 2 *rare* to cause to suffer; afflict (with) 3 to deal out (blows, lashes, etc) [c16 from Latin *infligere* to strike (something) against, dash against, from *fligere* to strike] > inˈflictable *adj* > inˈflicter *or* inˈflictor *n* > inˈfliction *n* > inˈflictive *adj*

in-flight *adj* provided during flight in an aircraft: *in-flight meals*

inflorescence (ˌɪnflɔːˈrɛsəns) *n* 1 the part of a plant that consists of the flower-bearing stalks 2 the arrangement of the flowers on the stalks 3 the process of flowering; blossoming [c16 from New Latin *inflōrēscentia*, from Late Latin *inflōrēscere* to blossom, from *flōrēscere* to bloom] > ˌinfloˈrescent *adj*

inflow (ˈɪnˌfləʊ) *n* 1 something, such as a liquid or gas, that flows in 2 the amount or rate of flowing in 3 Also called: **inflowing** the act of flowing in; influx

influence (ˈɪnflʊəns) *n* 1 an effect of one person or thing on another 2 the power of a person or thing to have such an effect 3 power or sway resulting from ability, wealth, position, etc 4 a person or thing having influence 5 *astrology* an ethereal fluid or occult power regarded as emanating from the stars and affecting a person's actions, future, etc 6 **under the influence** *informal* drunk ▷ *vb* (*tr*) 7 to persuade or induce 8 to have an effect upon (actions, events, etc); affect [c14 from Medieval Latin *influentia* emanation of power from the stars, from Latin *influere* to flow into, from *fluere* to flow] > ˈinfluenceable *adj* > ˈinfluencer *n*

influent (ˈɪnflʊənt) *adj* *also* **inflowing** 1 flowing in ▷ *n* 2 something flowing in, esp a tributary 3 *ecology* an organism that has a major effect on the nature of its community

influential (ˌɪnflʊˈɛnʃəl) *adj* having or exerting influence > ˌinfluˈentially *adv*

influenza (ˌɪnflʊˈɛnzə) *n* a highly contagious and often epidemic viral disease characterized by fever, prostration, muscular aches and pains, and inflammation of the respiratory passages. Also called: **grippe** Informal name: **flu** [c18 from Italian, literally: INFLUENCE, hence, incursion, epidemic (first applied to influenza in 1743)] > ˌinfluˈenzal *adj*

influx (ˈɪnˌflʌks) *n* 1 the arrival or entry of many people or things 2 the act of flowing in; inflow 3 the mouth of a stream or river [c17 from Late Latin *influxus*, from *influere*; see INFLUENCE]

info¹ (ˈɪnfəʊ) *n* *informal* short for **information**

info² *an internet domain name for* an information provider

infold (ɪnˈfəʊld) *vb* a variant spelling of **enfold** > inˈfolder *n* > inˈfoldment *n*

infomercial (ˌɪnfəʊˈmɜːʃəl) *n* a short film, usually for television, which advertises a product or service in an informative way [c20 from INFO + (COM)MERCIAL]

infopreneurial (ˌɪnfəʊprəˈnɜːrɪəl) *adj* of or relating to the manufacture or sales of electronic office or factory equipment designed to distribute information: *an infopreneurial industry* [c20 INFO(RMATION) + (ENTRE)PRENEUR + -IAL]

inform¹ (ɪnˈfɔːm) *vb* 1 (*tr*; often foll by *of* or *about*) to give information to; tell 2 (*tr*; often foll by *of* or *about*) to make conversant (with) 3 (*intr*; often foll by *against* or *on*) to give information regarding criminals, as to the police, etc 4 to give form to 5 to impart some essential or formative characteristic to 6 (*tr*) to animate or inspire 7 (*tr*) *obsolete* **a** to train or educate **b** to report [c14 from Latin *informāre* to give form to, describe, from *formāre* to FORM] > inˈformable *adj* > informedly (ɪnˈfɔːmɪdlɪ) *adv* > inˈformingly *adv*

inform² (ɪnˈfɔːm) *adj* *archaic* without shape; unformed [c16 from Latin *informis* from IN-¹ + *forma* shape]

informal (ɪnˈfɔːməl) *adj* 1 not of a formal, official, or stiffly conventional nature: *an informal luncheon* 2 appropriate to everyday life or use: *informal clothes* 3 denoting or characterized by idiom, vocabulary, etc, appropriate to everyday conversational language rather than to formal written language 4 denoting a second-person pronoun in some languages used when the addressee is regarded as a friend or social inferior: *In French the pronoun "tu" is informal, while "vous" is formal* > inˈformally *adv*

informality (ˌɪnfɔːˈmælɪtɪ) *n, pl* -ties 1 the condition or quality of being informal 2 an informal act

informal settlement *n* *South African euphemistic* a squatter camp

informal vote *n* *Austral and NZ* an invalid vote or ballot

informant (ɪnˈfɔːmənt) *n* a person who gives information about a thing, a subject being studied, etc

informatics (ˌɪnfəˈmætɪks) *n* (*functioning as singular*) another term for **information science**

information (ˌɪnfəˈmeɪʃən) *n* 1 knowledge acquired through experience or study 2 knowledge of specific and timely events or situations; news 3 the act of informing or the condition of being informed 4 **a** an office, agency, etc, providing information **b** (*as modifier*): *information service* 5 **a** a charge or complaint made before justices of the peace, usually on oath, to institute summary criminal proceedings **b** a complaint filed on behalf of the Crown, usually by the attorney general 6 *computing* **a** the meaning given to data by the way in which it is interpreted **b** another word for **data** (sense 2) 7 too much information *informal* I don't want to hear any more > ˌinforˈmational *adj*

information age *n* a time when large amounts of information are widely available to many people, largely through computer technology

information processing *n* *computing* the combined processing of numerical data, graphics, text, etc

information question *n* another term for WH question

information retrieval *n* *computing* the process of recovering specific information from stored data

information science *n* the science of the collection, evaluation, organization, and dissemination of information, often employing computers

information superhighway *n* 1 the concept of a worldwide network of computers capable of transferring all types of digital information at high speed 2 another name for the **internet** ▷ Also called: **information highway**

information technology *n* the technology of the production, storage, and communication of information using computers and microelectronics. Abbreviation: IT

information theory *n* a collection of mathematical theories, based on statistics, concerned with methods of coding, transmitting, storing, retrieving, and decoding information

information warfare *n* the use of electronic communciations and the internet to disrupt a country's telecommunications, power supply, transport system, etc

informative (ɪnˈfɔːmətɪv) *or* **informatory** *adj* providing information; instructive > inˈformatively *adv* > inˈformativeness *n*

informed (ɪnˈfɔːmd) *adj* 1 having much knowledge or education; learned or cultured 2 based on information: *an informed judgment*

informer (ɪnˈfɔːmə) *n* 1 a person who informs against someone, esp a criminal 2 a person who provides information: *he was the President's financial informer*

infotainment (ˌɪnfəʊˈteɪnmənt) *n* (in television) the practice of presenting serious or instructive subjects in a style designed primarily to be entertaining [c20 from INFO + (ENTER)TAINMENT]

infra *Latin* (ˈɪnfrə) *adv* (esp in textual annotation) below; further on

infra- *prefix* below; beneath; after: *infrasonic; infralapsarian* [from Latin *infrā*]

infracostal (ˌɪnfrəˈkɒstəl) *adj* *anatomy* situated beneath the ribs

infract (ɪnˈfrækt) *vb* (*tr*) to violate or break (a law, an agreement, etc) [c18 from Latin *infractus* broken off, from *infringere*; see INFRINGE] > inˈfractor *n*

infra dig (ˈɪnfrə ˈdɪɡ) *adj* (*postpositive*) *informal* beneath one's dignity [c19 from Latin phrase *infrā dignitātem*]

infralapsarian (ˌɪnfrəlæpˈsɛərɪən) *n* *Christian theol, chiefly Calvinist* a person who believes that foreknowledge of the Fall preceded God's decree of who was predestined to salvation and who was not. Compare **supralapsarian** [c18 from INFRA- + *lapsarian* (see SUPRALAPSARIAN)] > ˌinfralapˈsarianism *n*

infrangible (ɪnˈfrændʒɪbəl) *adj* 1 incapable of being broken 2 not capable of being violated or infringed [c16 from Late Latin *infrangibilis*, from Latin IN-¹ + *frangere* to break] > inˌfrangiˈbility *or* inˈfrangibleness *n* > inˈfrangibly *adv*

infrared (ˌɪnfrəˈrɛd) *n* 1 the part of the electromagnetic spectrum with a longer wavelength than light but a shorter wavelength than radio waves; radiation with wavelength between 0.8 micrometres and 1 millimetre ▷ *adj* 2 of, relating to, using, or consisting of radiation lying within the infrared: *infrared radiation*

infrared astronomy *n* the study of radiations from space in the infrared region of the electromagnetic spectrum

infrared photography *n* photography using film with an emulsion that is sensitive to infrared light, enabling it to be used in misty weather, in darkened interiors, or at night. It has applications in aerial surveys, the detection of forgeries, etc

infrasound (ˈɪnfrəˌsaʊnd) *n* soundlike waves having a frequency below the audible range, that is, below about 16Hz > **infrasonic** (ˌɪnfrəˈsɒnɪk) *adj*

infraspecific (ˌɪnfrəspəˈsɪfɪk) *adj biology* occurring within or affecting all members of a species: *infraspecific variation*

infrastructure (ˈɪnfrəˌstrʌktʃə) *n* **1** the basic structure of an organization, system, etc **2** the stock of fixed capital equipment in a country, including factories, roads, schools, etc, considered as a determinant of economic growth

infrequent (ɪnˈfriːkwənt) *adj* rarely happening or present; only occasional > in'frequency or in'frequence *n* > in'frequently *adv*

infringe (ɪnˈfrɪndʒ) *vb* **1** (*tr*) to violate or break (a law, an agreement, etc) **2** (*intr; foll by on or upon*) to encroach or trespass [C16 from Latin *infringere* to break off, from *frangere* to break] > in'fringement *n* > in'fringer *n*

infulae (ˈɪnfjʊliː) *pl n, sing* -la (-lə) the two ribbons hanging from the back of a bishop's mitre [C17 from Latin, plural of *infula*, woollen fillet worn on forehead by ancient Romans during religious rites]

infundibular (ˌɪnfʌnˈdɪbjʊlə) *adj* funnel-shaped [C18 from INFUNDIBULUM]

infundibuliform (ˌɪnfʌnˈdɪbjʊlɪˌfɔːm) *adj* (of plant parts) shaped like a funnel

infundibulum (ˌɪnfʌnˈdɪbjʊləm) *n, pl* -la (-lə) *anatomy* any funnel-shaped part, esp the stalk connecting the pituitary gland to the base of the brain [C18 from Latin: funnel, from *infundere* to INFUSE] > ˌinfunˈdibulate *adj*

infuriate *vb* (ɪnˈfjʊərɪˌeɪt) **1** (*tr*) to anger; annoy ▷ *adj* (ɪnˈfjʊərɪɪt) **2** *archaic* furious; infuriated [C17 from Medieval Latin *infuriāre* (vb); see IN-², FURY] > in'furiately *adv* > in'furiˌating *adj* > in'furiatingly *adv* > inˌfuri'ation *n*

infuscate (ɪnˈfʌskeɪt) or **infuscated** *adj* (esp of the wings of an insect) tinged with brown [C17 from Latin *infuscāre* to darken, from *fuscus* dark]

infuse (ɪnˈfjuːz) *vb* **1** (*tr; often foll by into*) to instil or inculcate **2** (*tr; foll by with*) to inspire; emotionally charge **3** to soak or be soaked in order to extract flavour or other properties **4** *rare* (foll by *into*) to pour [C15 from Latin *infundere* to pour into]

infuser (ɪnˈfjuːzə) *n* any device used to make an infusion, esp a tea maker

infusible[1] (ɪnˈfjuːzəbəl) *adj* not fusible; not easily melted; having a high melting point [C16 from IN-¹ + FUSIBLE] > inˌfusi'bility or in'fusibleness *n*

infusible[2] (ɪnˈfjuːzəbəl) *adj* capable of being infused [C17 from INFUSE + -IBLE] > inˌfusi'bility or in'fusibleness *n*

infusion (ɪnˈfjuːʒən) *n* **1** the act of infusing **2** something infused **3** an extract obtained by soaking **4** *med* introduction of a liquid, such as a saline solution, into a vein or the subcutaneous tissues of the body > infusive (ɪnˈfjuːsɪv) *adj*

infusionism (ɪnˈfjuːʒəˌnɪzəm) *n christian theol* the doctrine that at the birth of each individual a pre-existing soul is implanted in his body, to remain there for the duration of his earthly life > in'fusionist *n, adj*

infusorial earth (ˌɪnfjʊˈzɔːrɪəl) *n* another name for **diatomaceous earth**. See **diatomite**

infusorian (ˌɪnfjʊˈzɔːrɪən) *n obsolete* **1** any of the microscopic organisms, such as protozoans and rotifers, found in infusions of organic material **2** any member of the subclass *Ciliata* (see **ciliate** (sense 3)) ▷ *adj* **3** of or relating to infusorians [C18 from New Latin *Infusoria* former class name; see INFUSE] > ˌinfu'sorial *adj*

-ing[1] *suffix forming nouns* **1** (*from verbs*) the action of, process of, result of, or something connected with the verb: *coming; meeting; a wedding; winnings* **2** (*from other nouns*) something used in, consisting of, involving, etc: *tubing; soldiering* **3** (*from other parts of speech*) *an outing* [Old English *-ing, -ung*]

-ing[2] *suffix* **1** forming the present participle of verbs: *walking; believing* **2** forming participial adjectives: *a growing boy; a sinking ship* **3** forming adjectives not derived from verbs: *swashbuckling*

[Middle English *-ing, -inde,* from Old English *-ende*]

-ing[3] *suffix forming nouns* a person or thing having a certain quality or being of a certain kind: *sweeting; whiting* [Old English *-ing;* related to Old Norse *-ingr*]

ingather (ɪnˈgæðə) *vb* (*tr*) to gather together or in (a harvest) > in'gatherer *n*

ingeminate (ɪnˈdʒɛmɪˌneɪt) *vb* (*tr*) *rare* to repeat; reiterate [C16 from Latin *ingemināre* to redouble, from IN-² + *gemināre* to GEMINATE] > inˌgemiˈnation *n*

ingenerate[1] (ɪnˈdʒɛnərɪt) *adj rare* inherent, intrinsic, or innate [C17 from Late Latin *ingenerātus* not generated; see IN-¹, GENERATE]

ingenerate[2] (ɪnˈdʒɛnəˌreɪt) *vb* (*tr*) *archaic* to produce within; engender [C16 from Latin *ingenerāre*; see IN-², GENERATE] > inˌgenerˈation *n*

ingenious (ɪnˈdʒiːnjəs, -nɪəs) *adj* **1** possessing or done with ingenuity; skilful or clever **2** *obsolete* having great intelligence; displaying genius [C15 from Latin *ingeniōsus,* from *ingenium* natural ability; see ENGINE] > in'geniously *adv* > in'geniousness *n*

ingénue (ˌænʒeɪˈnjuː; *French* ɛ̃ʒeny) *n* an artless, innocent, or inexperienced girl or young woman [C19 from French, feminine of *ingénu* INGENUOUS]

ingenuity (ˌɪndʒɪˈnjuːɪtɪ) *n, pl* -ties **1** inventive talent; cleverness **2** an ingenious device, act, etc **3** *archaic* frankness; candour [C16 from Latin *ingenuitās* a freeborn condition, outlook consistent with such a condition, from *ingenuus* native, freeborn (see INGENUOUS); meaning influenced by INGENIOUS]

ingenuous (ɪnˈdʒɛnjʊəs) *adj* **1** naive, artless, or innocent **2** candid; frank; straightforward [C16 from Latin *ingenuus* freeborn, worthy of a freeman, virtuous, from IN-² + *-genuus,* from *gignere* to beget] > in'genuously *adv* > in'genuousness *n*

Ingerland or **Ingerlund** (ˈɪŋgəˌlænd) *n informal* a jocular spelling of England, as pronounced in the chants of sports, esp football, supporters

ingest (ɪnˈdʒɛst) *vb* (*tr*) **1** to take (food or liquid) into the body **2** (of a jet engine) to suck in (an object, a bird, etc) [C17 from Latin *ingerere* to put into, from IN-² + *gerere* to carry; see GEST] > in'gestible *adj* > in'gestion *n* > in'gestive *adj*

ingesta (ɪnˈdʒɛstə) *pl n* nourishment taken into the body through the mouth

ingle (ˈɪŋgəl) *n archaic or dialect* a fire in a room or a fireplace [C16 probably from Scots Gaelic *aingeal* fire]

Ingleborough (ˈɪŋgəlˌbʌrə, -brə) *n* a mountain in N England, in North Yorkshire: potholes. Height: 723 m (2373 ft)

inglenook (ˈɪŋgəlˌnʊk) *n Brit* a corner by a fireplace; chimney corner

inglorious (ɪnˈglɔːrɪəs) *adj* **1** without courage or glory; dishonourable, shameful, or disgraceful **2** unknown or obscure > in'gloriously *adv* > in'gloriousness *n*

ingo (ˈɪŋgəʊ) *n Scot* a reveal M/L. Also: ingoing

ingoing (ˈɪnˌgəʊɪŋ) *adj* **1** coming or going in; entering ▷ *n* **2** (*often plural*) *English law* the sum paid by a new tenant for fixtures left behind by the outgoing tenant **3** *Scot* another word for **ingo**

Ingolstadt (*German* ˈɪŋɔlʃtat) *n* a city in S central Germany, in Bavaria on the River Danube: oil-refining. Pop: 119 528 (2003 est)

ingot (ˈɪŋgət) *n* **1** a piece of cast metal obtained from a mould in a form suitable for storage, transporting, and further use ▷ *vb* **2** to shape (metal) into ingots [C14 perhaps from IN-² + Old English *goten,* past participle of *geotan* to pour]

ingot iron *n* a type of steel containing a small amount of carbon and very small quantities of other elements

ingraft (ɪnˈgrɑːft) *vb* a variant spelling of **engraft** > in'graftment or ˌingrafˈtation *n*

ingrain or **engrain** *vb* (ɪnˈgreɪn) (*tr*) **1** to impress deeply on the mind or nature; instil **2** *archaic* to dye into the fibre of (a fabric) ▷ *adj* (ˈɪnˌgreɪn) **3** variants of **ingrained 4** (of woven or knitted articles, esp rugs and carpets) made of dyed yarn or of fibre that is dyed before being spun into yarn

▷ *n* (ˈɪnˌgreɪn) **5 a** a carpet made from ingrained yarn **b** such yarn [C18 from the phrase *dyed in grain* dyed with kermes through the fibre]

ingrained or **engrained** (ɪnˈgreɪnd) *adj* **1** deeply impressed or instilled: *his fears are deeply ingrained* **2** (*prenominal*) complete or inveterate; utter: *an ingrained fool* **3** (esp of dirt) worked into or through the fibre, grain, pores, etc > ingrainedly or engrainedly (ɪnˈgreɪnɪdlɪ) *adv* > in'grainedness or en'grainedness *n*

ingrate (ˈɪngreɪt, ɪnˈgreɪt) *archaic* ▷ *n* **1** an ungrateful person ▷ *adj* **2** ungrateful [C14 from Latin *ingrātus* (adj), from IN-¹ + *grātus* GRATEFUL] > 'ingrately *adv*

ingratiate (ɪnˈgreɪʃɪˌeɪt) *vb* (*tr; often foll by with*) to place (oneself) purposely in the favour (of another) [C17 from Latin, from IN-² + *grātia* grace, favour] > in'gratiˌating or in'gratiatory *adj* > in'gratiatingly *adv* > inˌgrati'ation *n*

ingratitude (ɪnˈgrætɪˌtjuːd) *n* lack of gratitude; ungratefulness; thanklessness

ingravescent (ˌɪngrəˈvɛsᵊnt) *adj rare* (esp of a disease) becoming more severe [C19 from Latin *ingravescere* to become heavier, from *gravescere* to grow heavy, from *gravis* heavy] > ˌingra'vescence *n*

ingredient (ɪnˈgriːdɪənt) *n* a component of a mixture, compound, etc, esp in cooking [C15 from Latin *ingrediēns* going into, from *ingredī* to enter; see INGRESS]

ingress (ˈɪngrɛs) *n* **1** the act of going or coming in; an entering **2** a way in; entrance **3** the right or permission to enter **4** *astronomy* another name for **immersion** (sense 2) [C15 from Latin *ingressus,* from *ingredī* to go in, from *gradī* to step, go] > ingression (ɪnˈgrɛʃən) *n*

ingressive (ɪnˈgrɛsɪv) *adj* **1** of or concerning ingress **2** (of a speech sound) pronounced with an inhalation rather than exhalation of breath ▷ *n* **3** an ingressive speech sound, such as a Zulu click > in'gressiveness *n*

in-group *n sociol* a highly cohesive and relatively closed social group characterized by the preferential treatment reserved for its members and the strength of loyalty between them. Compare **out-group**

ingrowing (ˈɪnˌgrəʊɪŋ) *adj* **1** (esp of a toenail) growing abnormally into the flesh **2** growing within or into

ingrown (ˈɪnˌgrəʊn, ɪnˈgrəʊn) *adj* **1** (esp of a toenail) grown abnormally into the flesh; covered by adjacent tissues **2** grown within; native; innate **3** excessively concerned with oneself, one's own particular group, etc **4** ingrained

ingrowth (ˈɪnˌgrəʊθ) *n* **1** the act of growing inwards: *the ingrowth of a toenail* **2** something that grows inwards

inguinal (ˈɪŋgwɪnᵊl) *adj anatomy* of or relating to the groin [C17 from Latin *inguinālis,* from *inguen* groin]

ingulf (ɪnˈgʌlf) *vb* a variant spelling of **engulf** > in'gulfment *n*

ingurgitate (ɪnˈgɜːdʒɪˌteɪt) *vb* to swallow (food) with greed or in excess; gorge [C16 from Latin *ingurgitāre* to flood, from IN-² + *gurges* abyss] > inˌgurgi'tation *n*

Ingush (ɪŋˈgʊʃ) *n, pl* -gushes or -gush a member of a people of S central Russia, speaking a Circassian language and chiefly inhabiting the Ingush Republic

Ingush Republic *n* a constituent republic of S Russia: part of the Checheno-Ingush Autonomous Republic from 1936 until 1992. Capital: Magas (formerly at Nazran). Pop: 468 900 (2002). Area: 3600 sq km (1390 sq miles). Also called: Ingushetia (ˌɪnguˈʃetiə)

inhabit (ɪnˈhæbɪt) *vb* -its, -iting, -ited **1** (*tr*) to live or dwell in; occupy **2** (*intr*) *archaic* to abide or dwell [C14 from Latin *inhabitāre,* from *habitāre* to dwell] > in'habitable *adj* > inˌhabita'bility *n* > inˌhabi'tation *n*

inhabitant (ɪnˈhæbɪtənt) *n* a person or animal that is a permanent resident of a particular place or region > in'habitancy or in'habitance n

inhalant (ɪnˈheɪlənt) adj **1** (esp of a volatile medicinal formulation) inhaled for its soothing or therapeutic effect **2** inhaling ▷ n **3** an inhalant medicinal formulation

inhalation (ˌɪnhəˈleɪʃən) n **1** the act of inhaling; breathing in of air or other vapours **2** an inhalant formulation

inhalator (ˈɪnhəˌleɪtə) n another name for **nebulizer**

inhale (ɪnˈheɪl) vb to draw (breath) into the lungs; breathe in [c18 from IN-² + Latin hālāre to breathe]

inhaler (ɪnˈheɪlə) n **1** a device for breathing in therapeutic vapours through the nose or mouth, esp one for relieving nasal congestion or asthma **2** a person who inhales

Inhambane (ˌɪnjəmˈbɑːnə) n a port in SE Mozambique on an inlet of the Mozambique Channel (**Inhambane Bay**). Pop: 64 274 (latest est)

inharmonious (ˌɪnhɑːˈməʊnɪəs) adj Also: **inharmonic** (ˌɪnhɑːˈmɒnɪk) lacking harmony; discordant **2** lacking accord or agreement > ˌinhar'moniously adv > ˌinhar'moniousness n

inhaul (ˈɪnˌhɔːl) or **inhauler** n nautical a line for hauling in a sail

inhere (ɪnˈhɪə) vb (intr; foll by in) to be an inseparable part (of) [c16 from Latin inhaerēre to stick in, from haerēre to stick]

inherence (ɪnˈhɪərəns, -ˈhɛr-) or **inherency** n **1** the state or condition of being inherent **2** metaphysics the relation of attributes, elements, etc, to the subject of which they are predicated, esp if they are its essential constituents

inherent (ɪnˈhɪərənt, -ˈhɛr-) adj existing as an inseparable part; intrinsic > in'herently adv

inherit (ɪnˈhɛrɪt) vb -its, -iting, -ited **1** to receive (property, a right, title, etc) by succession or under a will **2** (intr) to succeed as heir **3** (tr) to possess (a characteristic) through genetic transmission **4** (tr) to receive (a position, attitude, property, etc) from a predecessor [c14 from Old French enheriter, from Late Latin inhērēditāre to appoint an heir, from Latin hērēs HEIR] > in'herited adj > in'heritor n > in'heritress or in'heritrix fem n

inheritable (ɪnˈhɛrɪtəbəl) adj **1** capable of being transmitted by heredity from one generation to a later one **2** capable of being inherited **3** rare capable of inheriting; having the right to inherit > inˌheritaˈbility or in'heritableness n > in'heritably adv

inheritance (ɪnˈhɛrɪtəns) n **1** law **a** hereditary succession to an estate, title, etc **b** the right of an heir to succeed to property on the death of an ancestor **c** something that may legally be transmitted to an heir **2** the act of inheriting **3** something inherited; heritage **4** the derivation of characteristics of one generation from an earlier one by heredity **5** obsolete hereditary rights

inheritance tax n **1** (in Britain) a tax introduced in 1986 to replace capital transfer tax, consisting of a percentage levied on that part of an inheritance exceeding a specified allowance, and scaled charges on gifts made within seven years of death **2** (in the US) a state tax imposed on an inheritance according to its size and the relationship of the beneficiary to the deceased

inhesion (ɪnˈhiːʒən) n a less common word for **inherence** (sense 1) [c17 from Late Latin inhaesiō, from inhaerēre to INHERE]

inhibit (ɪnˈhɪbɪt) vb -its, -iting, -ited (tr) **1** to restrain or hinder (an impulse, a desire, etc) **2** to prohibit; forbid **3** to stop, prevent, or decrease the rate of (a chemical reaction) **4** electronics **a** to prevent the occurrence of (a particular signal) in a circuit **b** to prevent the performance of (a particular operation) [c15 from Latin inhibēre to restrain, from IN-² + habēre to have] > in'hibitable adj > in'hibitive or in'hibitory adj

inhibition (ˌɪnɪˈbɪʃən, ˌɪnhɪ-) n **1** the act of inhibiting or the condition of being inhibited **2** psychol **a** a mental state or condition in which the

varieties of expression and behaviour of an individual become restricted **b** the weakening of a learned response usually as a result of extinction or because of the presence of a distracting stimulus **c** (in psychoanalytical theory) the unconscious restraining of an impulse. See also **repression 3** the process of stopping or retarding a chemical reaction **4** physiol the suppression of the function or action of an organ or part, as by stimulation of its nerve supply **5** Church of England an episcopal order suspending an incumbent

inhibitor (ɪnˈhɪbɪtə) n **1** Also called: **inhibiter** a person or thing that inhibits **2** Also called: **anticatalyst** a substance that retards or stops a chemical reaction. Compare **catalyst 3** biochem **a** a substance that inhibits the action of an enzyme **b** a substance that inhibits a metabolic or physiological process: a plant growth inhibitor **4** any impurity in a solid that prevents luminescence **5** an inert substance added to some rocket fuels to inhibit ignition on certain surfaces

inhomogeneous (ɪnˌhəʊməˈdʒiːnɪəs, -ˌhɒm-) adj not homogeneous or uniform > inhomogeneity (ɪnˌhəʊmədʒɪˈniːɪtɪ, -ˌhɒm-) n

inhospitable (ɪnˈhɒspɪtəbəl, ˌɪnhɒˈspɪt-) adj **1** not hospitable; unfriendly **2** (of a region, an environment, etc) lacking a favourable climate, terrain, etc > in'hospitableness n > in'hospitably adv

inhospitality (ˌɪnhɒspɪˈtælɪtɪ, ɪnˌhɒs-) n the state or attitude of being inhospitable or unwelcoming

in-house adj, adv within an organization or group: an in-house job; the job was done in-house

inhuman (ɪnˈhjuːmən) adj **1** Also: **inhumane** (ˌɪnhjuːˈmeɪn) lacking humane feelings, such as sympathy, understanding, etc; cruel; brutal **2** not human > ˌinhu'manely adv > in'humanly adv > in'humanness n

inhumanity (ˌɪnhjuːˈmænɪtɪ) n, pl -ties **1** lack of humane qualities **2** an inhumane act, decision, etc

inhume (ɪnˈhjuːm) vb (tr) to inter; bury [c17 from Latin inhumāre, from IN-² + humus ground] > ˌinhu'mation n > in'humer n

inimical (ɪˈnɪmɪkəl) adj **1** adverse or unfavourable **2** not friendly; hostile [c17 from Late Latin inimīcālis, from inimīcus, from IN-¹ + amīcus friendly; see ENEMY] > in'imically adv > in'imicalness or inˌimi'cality n

inimitable (ɪˈnɪmɪtəbəl) adj incapable of being duplicated or imitated; unique > inˌimita'bility or in'imitableness n > in'imitably adv

inion (ˈɪnɪən) n anatomy the most prominent point at the back of the head, used as a point of measurement in craniometry [c19 from Greek: back of the head]

iniquity (ɪˈnɪkwɪtɪ) n, pl -ties **1** lack of justice or righteousness; wickedness; injustice **2** a wicked act; sin [c14 from Latin inīquitās, from inīquus unfair, from IN-¹ + aequus even, level; see EQUAL] > in'iquitous adj > in'iquitously adv > in'iquitousness n

initial (ɪˈnɪʃəl) adj **1** of, at, or concerning the beginning ▷ n **2** the first letter of a word, esp a person's name **3** printing a large sometimes highly decorated letter set at the beginning of a chapter or work **4** botany a cell from which tissues and organs develop by division and differentiation; a meristematic cell ▷ vb -tials, -tialling, -tialled or US -tials, -tialing, -tialed **5** (tr) to sign with one's initials, esp to indicate approval; endorse [c16 from Latin initiālis of the beginning, from initium beginning, literally: an entering upon, from inīre to go in, from IN-² + īre to go] > in'itialer or in'itialler n > in'itially adv

initialize or **initialise** (ɪˈnɪʃəˌlaɪz) vb (tr) to assign an initial value to (a variable or storage location) in a computer program > inˌitiali'zation or inˌitiali'sation n

initiate vb (ɪˈnɪʃɪˌeɪt) (tr) **1** to begin or originate **2** to accept (new members) into an organization

such as a club, through often secret ceremonies **3** to teach fundamentals to: she initiated him into the ballet ▷ adj (ɪˈnɪʃɪɪt, -ˌeɪt) **4** initiated; begun ▷ n (ɪˈnɪʃɪɪt, -ˌeɪt) **5** a person who has been initiated, esp recently **6** a beginner; novice [c17 from Latin initiāre (vb), from initium; see INITIAL]

initiation (ɪˌnɪʃɪˈeɪʃən) n **1** the act of initiating or the condition of being initiated **2** the often secret ceremony initiating new members into an organization

initiative (ɪˈnɪʃɪətɪv, -ˈnɪʃətɪv) n **1** the first step or action of a matter; commencing move: he took the initiative; a peace initiative **2** the right or power to begin or initiate something: he has the initiative **3** the ability or attitude required to begin or initiate something **4** government **a** the right or power to introduce legislation, etc, in a legislative body **b** the procedure by which citizens originate legislation, as in many American states and Switzerland **5** on one's own initiative without being prompted ▷ adj **6** of or concerning initiation or serving to initiate; initiatory > in'itiatively adv

initiator (ɪˈnɪʃɪˌeɪtə) n **1** a person or thing that initiates **2** chem a substance that starts a chain reaction **3** chem an explosive used in detonators > in'itiˌatress or in'itiˌatrix fem n

initiatory (ɪˈnɪʃɪətərɪ) adj of or concerning initiation or serving to initiate; initiative

inject (ɪnˈdʒɛkt) vb (tr) **1** med to introduce (a fluid) into (the body of a person or animal) by means of a syringe or similar instrument **2** (foll by into) to introduce (a new aspect or element): to inject humour into a scene **3** to interject (a comment, idea, etc) **4** to place (a rocket, satellite, etc) in orbit [c17 from Latin injicere to throw in, from jacere to throw] > in'jectable adj

injection (ɪnˈdʒɛkʃən) n **1** fluid injected into the body, esp for medicinal purposes **2** something injected **3** the act of injecting **4 a** the act or process of introducing fluid under pressure, such as fuel into the combustion chamber of an engine **b** (as modifier): injection moulding **5** maths a function or mapping for which f(x) = f(y) only if x = y. See also **surjection, bijection**. > in'jective adj

injector (ɪnˈdʒɛktə) n **1** a person or thing that injects **2** a device for spraying fuel into the combustion chamber of an internal-combustion engine **3** a device for forcing water into a steam boiler. Also called: **inspirator**

injera (ɪnˈdʒɪərə) n a white Ethiopian flatbread, similar to a crepe [Amharic]

injudicious (ˌɪndʒʊˈdɪʃəs) adj not discreet; imprudent > ˌinju'diciously adv > ˌinju'diciousness n

Injun (ˈɪndʒən) n **1** US an informal or dialect word for (American) **Indian 2 honest Injun** (interjection) slang genuinely; really

injunct (ɪnˈdʒʌŋkt) vb (tr) to issue a legal injunction against (a person) [c19 from Late Latin injunctiō; see ENJOIN]

injunction (ɪnˈdʒʌŋkʃən) n **1** law an instruction or order issued by a court to a party to an action, esp to refrain from some act, such as causing a nuisance **2** a command, admonition, etc **3** the act of enjoining [c16 from Late Latin injunctiō, from Latin injungere to ENJOIN] > in'junctive adj > in'junctively adv

injure (ˈɪndʒə) vb (tr) **1** to cause physical or mental harm or suffering to; hurt or wound **2** to offend, esp by an injustice [c16 back formation from INJURY] > 'injurable adj > 'injured adj > 'injurer n

injurious (ɪnˈdʒʊərɪəs) adj **1** causing damage or harm; deleterious; hurtful **2** abusive, slanderous, or libellous > in'juriously adv > in'juriousness n

injury (ˈɪndʒərɪ) n, pl -ries **1** physical damage or hurt **2** a specific instance of this: a leg injury **3** harm done to a reputation **4** law a violation or infringement of another person's rights that causes him harm and is actionable at law **5** an obsolete word for **insult** [c14 from Latin injūria injustice, wrong, from injūriōsus acting unfairly, wrongful, from IN-¹ + jūs right]

injury list *n* the people who are unable to participate in a sport as expected, due to illness or injury

injury time *n sport* extra playing time added on to compensate for time spent attending to injured players during the match. Also called: **stoppage time**

injustice (ɪn'dʒʌstɪs) *n* **1** the condition or practice of being unjust or unfair **2** an unjust act

ink (ɪŋk) *n* **1** a fluid or paste used for printing, writing, and drawing **2** a dark brown fluid ejected into the water for self-concealment by an octopus or related mollusc from a gland (**ink sac**) near the anus ▷ *vb* (*tr*) **3** to mark with ink **4** to coat (a printing surface) with ink ▷ See also **ink in, ink up** [c13 from Old French *enque*, from Late Latin *encaustum* a purplish-red ink, from Greek *enkauston* purple ink, from *enkaustos* burnt in, from *enkaiein* to burn in; see EN-², CAUSTIC] > 'inker *n*

Inkatha (ɪn'kɑːtə) *n* a South African Zulu organization founded by Chief Mangosouthu Buthelezi in 1975 as a paramilitary group seeking nonracial democracy; won four seats in South Africa's first nonracial elections in 1994 [c20 Zulu name for the grass coil used by Zulu women carrying loads on their heads, the many strands of which provide its strength and cohesion]

inkberry ('ɪŋk,bɛrɪ) *n, pl* -ries **1** a North American holly tree, *Ilex glabra*, with black berry-like fruits **2** another name for the **pokeweed 3** the fruit of either of these plants

inkblot ('ɪŋk,blɒt) *n psychol* an abstract patch of ink, one of ten commonly used in the Rorschach test

ink-cap *n* any of several saprotrophic agaricaceous fungi of the genus *Coprinus*, whose caps disintegrate into a black inky fluid after the spores mature. It includes the **shaggy ink-cap** (*Coprinus comatus*), also called **lawyer's wig**, a distinctive fungus having a white cylindrical cap covered with shaggy white or brownish scales

Inkerman ('ɪŋkəmən; *Russian* ɪnkɪr'man) *n* a village in Ukraine, in the S Crimea east of Sevastopol: scene of a battle during the Crimean War in which British and French forces defeated the Russians (1854)

inkhorn ('ɪŋk,hɔːn) *n* (formerly) a small portable container for ink, usually made from horn

inkhorn term *n* an affectedly learned and obscure borrowing from another language, esp Greek or Latin

ink in *vb* (*adverb*) **1** (*tr*) to use ink to go over pencil lines in (a drawing) **2** to apply ink to (a printing surface) in preparing to print from it **3** to arrange or confirm definitely

ink jet *n* a method of printing streams of electrically charged ink

inkle ('ɪŋkᵊl) *n* **1** a kind of linen tape used for trimmings **2** the thread or yarn from which this tape is woven [c16 of unknown origin]

inkling ('ɪŋklɪŋ) *n* a slight intimation or suggestion; suspicion [c14 probably from *inclen* to hint at; related to Old English *inca*]

inkstand ('ɪŋk,stænd) *n* a stand or tray on which are kept writing implements and containers for ink

ink up *vb* (*adverb*) to apply ink to (a printing machine) in preparing it for operation

inkwell ('ɪŋk,wɛl) *n* a small container for pen ink, often let into the surface of a desk

inky ('ɪŋkɪ) *adj* **inkier, inkiest 1** resembling ink, esp in colour; dark or black **2** of, containing, or stained with ink: *inky fingers* > 'inkiness *n*

inky smudge *n Austral slang* a judge [rhyming slang]

INLA *abbreviation for* Irish National Liberation Army; a Republican paramilitary organization in Ireland

inlace (ɪn'leɪs) *vb* a variant spelling of **enlace**

inlaid ('ɪn,leɪd, ɪn'leɪd) *adj* **1** set in the surface, as a design in wood **2** having such a design or inlay:

an inlaid table

inland *adj* ('ɪnlənd) **1** of, concerning, or located in the interior of a country or region away from a sea or border **2** *chiefly Brit* operating within a country or region; domestic; not foreign ▷ *n* ('ɪn,lænd, -lənd) **3** the interior of a country or region ▷ *adv* ('ɪn,lænd, -lənd) **4** towards or into the interior of a country or region > 'inlander *n*

inland bill *n* a bill of exchange that is both drawn and made payable in the same country. Compare **foreign bill**

Inland Revenue *n* (in Britain and New Zealand) a government board that administers and collects major direct taxes, such as income tax, corporation tax, and capital gains tax. Abbreviation: IR

Inland Sea *n* a sea in SW Japan, between the islands of Honshu, Shikoku, and Kyushu. Japanese name: **Seto Naikai**

in-law *n* **1** a relative by marriage ▷ *adj* **2** (*postpositive; in combination*) related by marriage: *a father-in-law* [c19 back formation from *father-in-law*, etc]

inlay *vb* (ɪn'leɪ) **-lays, -laying, -laid** (*tr*) **1** to decorate (an article, esp of furniture, or a surface) by inserting pieces of wood, ivory, etc, into prepared slots in the surface ▷ *n* ('ɪn,leɪ) **2** *dentistry* a filling, made of gold, porcelain, etc, inserted into a cavity and held in position by cement **3** decoration made by inlaying **4** an inlaid article, surface, etc > 'in,laid *adj* > 'in,layer *n*

inlet ('ɪn,lɛt) *n* **1** a narrow inland opening of the coastline **2** an entrance or opening **3** the act of letting someone or something in **4** something let in or inserted **5 a** a passage, valve, or part through which a substance, esp a fluid, enters a device or machine **b** (*as modifier*): *an inlet valve* ▷ *vb* (ɪn'lɛt) **-lets, -letting, -let 6** (*tr*) to insert or inlay

inlier ('ɪn,laɪə) *n* an outcrop of rocks that is entirely surrounded by younger rocks

in-line *adj* **1** denoting a linked sequence of manufacturing processes **2** denoting an internal-combustion engine having its cylinders arranged in a line

in-line skate *n* another name for **Rollerblade**

in loc. cit. (in textual annotation) *abbreviation for* in loco citato [Latin: in the place cited]

in loco parentis Latin (ɪn 'ləʊkəʊ pə'rɛntɪs) in place of a parent: said of a person acting in a parental capacity

inly ('ɪnlɪ) *adv poetic* inwardly; intimately

inlying ('ɪn,laɪɪŋ) *adj* situated within or inside

inmate ('ɪn,meɪt) *n* **1** a person who is confined to an institution such as a prison or hospital. See also **resident** (sense 2) **2** *obsolete* a person who lives with others in a house

in medias res Latin (ɪn 'miːdɪ,æs 'reɪs) in or into the middle of events or a narrative [literally: into the midst of things, taken from a passage in Horace's *Ars Poetica*]

in mem. *abbreviation for* in memoriam

in memoriam (ɪn mɪ'mɔːrɪəm) in memory of; as a memorial to: used in obituaries, epitaphs, etc [Latin]

inmesh (ɪn'mɛʃ) *vb* a variant spelling of **enmesh**

inmigrant ('ɪn,maɪɡrənt) *adj* **1** coming in from another area of the same country: *an inmigrant worker* ▷ *n* **2** an inmigrant person or animal

inmost ('ɪn,məʊst) *adj* another word for **innermost**

inn (ɪn) *n* **1** a pub or small hotel providing food and accommodation **2** (formerly, in England) a college or hall of residence for students, esp of law, now only in the names of such institutions as the b [Old English; compare Old Norse *inni* inn, house, place of refuge]

Inn (ɪn) *n* a river in central Europe, rising in Switzerland in Graubünden and flowing northeast through Austria and Bavaria to join the River Danube at Passau: forms part of the border between Austria and Germany. Length: 514 km (319 miles)

innards ('ɪnədz) *pl n informal* **1** the internal organs of the body, esp the viscera **2** the interior parts or components of anything, esp the working parts [c19 colloquial variant of *inwards*]

innate (ɪ'neɪt, 'ɪneɪt) *adj* **1** existing in a person or animal from birth; congenital; inborn **2** being an essential part of the character of a person or thing **3** instinctive; not learned: *innate capacities* **4** *botany* (of anthers) joined to the filament by the base only **5** (in rationalist philosophy) (of ideas) present in the mind before any experience and knowable by pure reason [c15 from Latin, from *innasci* to be born in, from *nasci* to be born] > in'nately *adv* > in'nateness *n*

innate releasing mechanism *n psychol* the process by which a stimulus evokes a response when the connection between the two is inborn. Abbreviation: IRM

inner ('ɪnə) *adj* (*prenominal*) **1** being or located further inside: *an inner room* **2** happening or occurring inside: *inner movement* **3** relating to the soul, mind, spirit, etc: *inner feelings* **4** more profound or obscure; less apparent: *the inner meaning* **5** exclusive or private: *inner regions of the party* **6** *chem* (of a compound) having a cyclic structure formed or apparently formed by reaction of one functional group in a molecule with another group in the same molecule: *an inner ester* ▷ *n* **7** Also called: **red** *archery* **a** the red innermost ring on a target **b** a shot which hits this ring > 'innerly *adv* > 'innerness *n*

inner bar *n Brit* all Queen's or King's Counsel collectively

inner child *n psychol* the part of the psyche believed to retain feelings as they were experienced in childhood

inner city *n* **a** the parts of a city in or near its centre, esp when they are associated with poverty, unemployment, substandard housing, etc **b** (*as modifier*): *inner-city schools*

inner-directed *adj* guided by one's own conscience and values rather than external pressures to conform. Compare **other-directed** > 'inner-di'rection *n*

inner ear *n* another name for **internal ear, labyrinth**

Inner Hebrides *pl n* See **Hebrides**

Inner Light *or* **Word** *n Quakerism* the presence and inner working of God in the soul acting as a guiding spirit that is superior even to Scripture and unites man to Christ

inner man *n* **1** a man's mind, soul, or nature **2** *jocular* the stomach or appetite

Inner Mongolia *n* an autonomous region of NE China: consists chiefly of the Mongolian plateau, with the Gobi Desert in the north and the Great Wall of China in the south. Capital: Hohhot. Pop: 23 800 000 (2003 est). Area: 1 177 500 sq km (459 225 sq miles)

innermost ('ɪnə,məʊst) *adj* **1** being or located furthest within; central **2** intimate; private: *innermost beliefs*

inner planet *n* any of the planets Mercury, Venus, earth, and Mars, whose orbits lie inside the asteroid belt

inner space *n* **1** the environment beneath the surface of the sea **2** the human mind regarded as being as unknown or as unfathomable as space

Inner Temple *n* (in England) one of the four legal societies in London that together form the Inns of Court

inner tube *n* an inflatable rubber tube that fits inside a pneumatic tyre casing

inner-tubing *n* the sport of floating on rivers, rapids, etc using a large inflated inner tube as a buoyancy device

innervate ('ɪnɜː,veɪt) *vb* (*tr*) **1** to supply nerves to (a bodily organ or part) **2** to stimulate (a bodily organ or part) with nerve impulses > ,inner'vation *n*

innerve (ɪ'nɜːv) *vb* (*tr*) to supply with nervous energy; stimulate

inner woman *n* **1** a woman's mind, soul, or nature **2** *jocular* the stomach or appetite

inning ('ɪnɪŋ) *n* **1** *baseball* a division of the game consisting of a turn at bat and a turn in the field for each side **2** *archaic* the reclamation of land from the sea [Old English *innung* a going in, from *innian* to go in]

innings ('ɪnɪŋz) *n* **1** (*functioning as singular*) *cricket* **a** the batting turn of a player or team **b** the runs scored during such a turn **2** (*sometimes singular*) a period of opportunity or action **3** (*functioning as plural*) land reclaimed from the sea

Inniskilling (ˌɪnɪs'kɪlɪŋ) *n* the former name of Enniskillen

innkeeper ('ɪnˌkiːpə) *n* an owner or manager of an inn

innocence ('ɪnəsəns) *n* the quality or state of being innocent. Archaic word: innocency ('ɪnəsənsɪ) [c14 from Latin *innocentia* harmlessness, from *innocēns* doing no harm, blameless, from IN-¹ + *nocēns* harming, from *nocēre* to hurt, harm; see NOXIOUS]

innocent ('ɪnəsənt) *adj* **1** not corrupted or tainted with evil or unpleasant emotion; sinless; pure **2** not guilty of a particular crime; blameless **3** (*postpositive; foll by of*) free (of); lacking: *innocent of all knowledge of history* **4 a** harmless or innocuous: *an innocent game* **b** not cancerous: *an innocent tumour* **5** credulous, naive, or artless **6** simple-minded; slow-witted ▷ *n* **7** an innocent person, esp a young child or an ingenuous adult **8** a simple-minded person; simpleton > 'innocently *adv*

innocuous (ɪ'nɒkjʊəs) *adj* having little or no adverse or harmful effect; harmless [c16 from Latin *innocuus* harmless, from IN-¹ + *nocēre* to harm] > in'nocuously *adv* > in'nocuousness *or* innocuity (ˌɪnəʊ'kjuːɪtɪ) *n*

innominate (ɪ'nɒmɪnɪt) *adj* **1** having no name; nameless **2** a less common word for **anonymous**

innominate bone *n* either of the two bones that form the sides of the pelvis, consisting of three fused components, the ilium, ischium, and pubis. Nontechnical name: hipbone

in nomine (ɪn 'nɒmɪˌneɪ, -ˌniː) *n music* any of several pieces of music of the 16th or 17th centuries for keyboard or for a consort of viols, based on a cantus firmus derived from the Vespers antiphon *Gloria tibi Trinitas* [from Latin *in nomine Jesu* in the name of Jesus, the first words of an introit for which this type of music was originally composed]

innovate ('ɪnəˌveɪt) *vb* to invent or begin to apply (methods, ideas, etc) [c16 from Latin *innovāre* to renew, from IN-² + *novāre* to make new, from *novus* new] > innovative *or* 'inno,vatory *adj* > 'inno,vator *n*

innovation (ˌɪnə'veɪʃən) *n* **1** something newly introduced, such as a new method or device **2** the act of innovating > ˌinno'vational *adj* > ˌinno'vationist *n*

innovative ('ɪnəˌveɪtɪv) *adj* using or showing new methods, ideas, etc

innoxious (ɪ'nɒkʃəs) *adj* not noxious; harmless > in'noxiously *adv* > in'noxiousness *n*

Innsbruck ('ɪnzbrʊk) *n* a city in W Austria, on the River Inn at the foot of the Brenner Pass: tourist centre. Pop: 113 392 (2001)

Inns of Court *pl n* (in England) the four private unincorporated societies in London that function as a law school and have the exclusive privilege of calling candidates to the English bar. See Lincoln's Inn, Inner Temple, Middle Temple, Gray's Inn

Innu ('ɪnuː) *n* **1** a member of an Algonquian people living in Labrador and northern Quebec **2** the Algonquian language of this people

innuendo (ˌɪnjʊ'ɛndəʊ) *n, pl* -dos *or* -does **1** an indirect or subtle reference, esp one made maliciously or indicating criticism or disapproval; insinuation **2** *law* (in pleading) a word introducing an explanatory phrase, usually in parenthesis **3** *law* (in an action for defamation) **a** an explanation of the construction put upon

words alleged to be defamatory where the defamatory meaning is not apparent **b** the words thus explained [c17 from Latin, literally: by hinting, from *innuendum*, gerund of *innuere* to convey by a nod, from IN-² + *nuere* to nod]

Innuit ('ɪnjuːɪt) *n* a variant spelling of **Inuit**

innumerable (ɪ'njuːmərəbəl, ɪ'njuːmrəbəl) *or* **innumerous** *adj* so many as to be uncountable; extremely numerous > ɪnˌnumera'bility *or* in'numerableness *n* > in'numerably *adv*

innumerate (ɪ'njuːmərɪt) *adj* **1** having neither knowledge nor understanding of mathematics or science ▷ *n* **2** an innumerate person > in'numeracy *n*

innutrition (ˌɪnjuː'trɪʃən) *n* lack or absence of nutrition. Compare **malnutrition** > ˌinnu'tritious *adj*

inobservance (ˌɪnəb'zɜːvəns) *n* **1** heedlessness **2** lack of compliance with or adherence to a law, religious duty, etc > ˌinob'servant *adj* > ˌinob'servantly *adv*

inoculable (ɪ'nɒkjʊləbəl) *adj* capable of being inoculated > inˌocula'bility *n*

inoculate (ɪ'nɒkjʊˌleɪt) *vb* **1** to introduce (the causative agent of a disease) into the body of (a person or animal), in order to induce immunity **2** (*tr*) to introduce (microorganisms, esp bacteria) into (a culture medium) **3** (*tr*) to cause to be influenced or imbued, as with ideas or opinions [c15 from Latin *inoculāre* to implant, from IN-² + *oculus* eye, bud] > inˌocu'lation *n* > in'oculative *adj* > in'ocuˌlator *n*

inoculum (ɪ'nɒkjʊləm) *or* **inoculant** *n, pl* -la (-lə) *or* -lants *med* the substance used in giving an inoculation [c20 New Latin; see INOCULATE]

inodorous (ɪn'əʊdərəs) *adj* odourless; having no odour

in-off *n billiards, snooker* a shot that goes into a pocket after striking another ball

inoffensive (ˌɪnə'fɛnsɪv) *adj* **1** not giving offence; unobjectionable **2** not unpleasant, poisonous, or harmful > ˌinof'fensively *adv* > ˌinof'fensiveness *n*

inofficious (ˌɪnə'fɪʃəs) *adj* contrary to moral obligation, as the disinheritance of a child by his parents: *an inofficious will* > ˌinof'ficiously *adv* > ˌinof'ficiousness *n*

inoperable (ɪn'ɒpərəbəl, -'ɒprə-) *adj* **1** incapable of being implemented or operated; unworkable **2** *surgery* not suitable for operation without risk, esp (of a malignant tumour) because metastasis has rendered surgery useless > inˌopera'bility *or* in'operableness *n* > in'operably *adv*

inoperative (ɪn'ɒpərətɪv, -'ɒprə-) *adj* **1** not operating **2** useless or ineffective > in'operativeness *n*

inopportune (ɪn'ɒpəˌtjuːn) *adj* not opportune; inappropriate or badly timed > in'oppor,tunely *adv* > in'oppor,tuneness *or* in,oppor'tunity *n*

inordinate (ɪn'ɔːdɪnɪt) *adj* **1** exceeding normal limits; immoderate **2** unrestrained, as in behaviour or emotion; intemperate **3** irregular or disordered [c14 from Latin *inordinātus* disordered, from IN-¹ + *ordināre* to put in order] > in'ordinacy *or* in'ordinateness *n* > in'ordinately *adv*

inorg. *abbreviation for* inorganic

inorganic (ˌɪnɔː'gænɪk) *adj* **1** not having the structure or characteristics of living organisms; not organic **2** relating to or denoting chemical compounds that do not contain carbon. Compare organic (sense 4) **3** not having a system, structure, or ordered relation of parts; amorphous **4** not resulting from or produced by growth; artificial **5** *linguistics* denoting or relating to a sound or letter introduced into the pronunciation or spelling of a word at some point in its history > ˌinor'ganically *adv*

inorganic chemistry *n* the branch of chemistry concerned with the elements and all their compounds except those containing carbon. Some simple carbon compounds, such as oxides, carbonates, etc, are treated as inorganic. Compare **organic chemistry**

inosculate (ɪn'ɒskjʊˌleɪt) *vb* **1** *physiol* (of small blood vessels) to communicate by anastomosis **2** to unite or be united so as to be continuous; blend **3** to intertwine or cause to intertwine [c17 from IN-² + Latin *ōsculāre* to equip with an opening, from *ōsculum*, diminutive of *ōs* mouth] > inˌoscu'lation *n*

inositol (ɪ'nəʊsɪˌtɒl) *n* a cyclic alcohol, one isomer of which (l-Inositol) is present in yeast and is a growth factor for some organisms; cyclohexanehexol. Formula: $C_6H_{12}O_6$ [c19 from Greek *in-*, *is* sinew + -OSE² + -ITE¹ + -OL¹]

inotropic (ˌɪnə'trɒpɪk, ˌaɪnə-) *adj* affecting or controlling the contraction of muscles, esp those of the heart: *inotropic drugs* [c20 from Greek, from *is* (stem *in-*) tendon + -TROPIC]

inpatient ('ɪnˌpeɪʃənt) *n* a hospital patient who occupies a bed for at least one night in the course of treatment, examination, or observation. Compare **outpatient**

in perpetuum *Latin* (ɪn pɜː'pɛtjʊəm) *adv* for ever

in personam (ɪn pɜː'səʊnæm) *adj law* (of a judicial act) directed against a specific person or persons. Compare in rem [Latin]

in petto (ɪn 'pɛtəʊ) *adj RC Church* not disclosed: used of the names of cardinals designate [Italian, literally: in the breast]

in posse (ɪn 'pɒsɪ) *adj* possible; potential. Compare in esse [Latin, literally: in possibility]

in propria persona *Latin* (ɪn 'prəʊprɪə pɜː'səʊnə) *adv chiefly law* in person; personally

input ('ɪnˌpʊt) *n* **1** the act of putting in **2** that which is put in **3** (*often plural*) a resource required for industrial production, such as capital goods, labour services, raw materials, etc **4** *electronics* **a** the signal or current fed into a component or circuit **b** the terminals, or some other point, to which the signal is applied **5** *computing* the data fed into a computer from a peripheral device **6** (*modifier*) of or relating to electronic, computer, or other input ▷ *vb* -puts, -putting, -put *or* -putted **7** (*tr*) to insert (data) into a computer

input device *n computing* a peripheral device that accepts data and feeds it into a computer

input/output *n computing* **1** the data or information that is passed into or out of a computer. Abbreviation: I/O **2** (*modifier*) concerned with or relating to such passage of data or information

input-output analysis *n economics* an analysis of production relationships between the industries of an economy involving a study of each industry's inputs and outputs, esp as used in social accounting

inqilab ('ɪnkɪˌlɑːb) *n* (in India, Pakistan, etc) revolution (esp in the phrase **inqilab zindabad** long live the revolution) [Urdu]

inquest ('ɪnˌkwɛst) *n* **1** an inquiry into the cause of an unexplained, sudden, or violent death, or as to whether or not property constitutes treasure trove, held by a coroner, in certain cases with a jury **2** *informal* any inquiry or investigation [c13 from Medieval Latin *inquēsta*, from Latin IN-² + *quaesītus* investigation, from *quaerere* to examine]

inquietude (ɪn'kwaɪɪˌtjuːd) *n* restlessness, uneasiness, or anxiety > inquiet (ɪn'kwaɪət) *adj* > in'quietly *adv*

inquiline ('ɪnkwɪˌlaɪn) *n* **1** an animal that lives in close association with another animal without harming it. See also **commensal** (sense 1) ▷ *adj* **2** of or living as an inquiline [c17 from Latin *inquilīnus* lodger, from IN-² + *colere* to dwell] > inquilinism ('ɪnkwɪlɪˌnɪzəm) *or* inquilinity (ˌɪnkwɪ'lɪnɪtɪ) *n* > inquilinous (ˌɪnkwɪ'laɪnəs) *adj*

inquire *or* **enquire** (ɪn'kwaɪə) *vb* **1 a** to seek information; ask: *she inquired his age; she inquired about rates of pay* **b** (foll by *of*) to ask (a person) for information: *I'll inquire of my aunt when she is coming* **2** (*intr; often foll by into*) to make a search or investigation [c13 from Latin *inquīrere* from IN-² + *quaerere* to seek] > in'quirer *or* en'quirer *n*

inquiring (ɪn'kwaɪərɪŋ) *adj* seeking or tending to

seek answers, information, etc > inˈquiringly *adv*

inquiry *or* **enquiry** (ɪnˈkwaɪərɪ) *n, pl* **-ries** **1** a request for information; a question **2** an investigation, esp a formal one conducted into a matter of public concern by a body constituted for that purpose by a government, local authority, or other organization

inquisition (ˌɪnkwɪˈzɪʃən) *n* **1** the act of inquiring deeply or searchingly; investigation **2** a deep or searching inquiry, esp a ruthless official investigation of individuals in order to suppress revolt or root out the unorthodox **3** an official inquiry, esp one held by a jury before an officer of the Crown **4** another word for **inquest** (sense 2) [c14 from legal Latin *inquīsītiō*, from *inquīrere* to seek for; see INQUIRE] > ˌinquiˈsitional *adj* > ˌinquiˈsitionist *n*

Inquisition (ˌɪnkwɪˈzɪʃən) *n history* a judicial institution of the Roman Catholic Church (1232–1820) founded to discover and suppress heresy. See also **Spanish Inquisition**

inquisitive (ɪnˈkwɪzɪtɪv) *adj* **1** excessively curious, esp about the affairs of others; prying **2** eager to learn; inquiring > inˈquisitively *adv* > inˈquisitiveness *n*

inquisitor (ɪnˈkwɪzɪtə) *n* **1** a person who inquires, esp deeply, searchingly, or ruthlessly **2** (*often capital*) an official of the ecclesiastical court of the Inquisition

Inquisitor-General *n, pl* **Inquisitors-General** the head of the Spanish court of Inquisition

inquisitorial (ɪnˌkwɪzɪˈtɔːrɪəl) *adj* **1** of, relating to, or resembling inquisition or an inquisitor **2** offensively curious; prying **3** *law* denoting criminal procedure in which one party is both prosecutor and judge, or in which the trial is held in secret. Compare **accusatorial** (sense 2) > inˌquisiˈtorially *adv* > inˌquisiˈtorialness *n*

inquorate (ɪnˈkwɔːreɪt) *adj Brit* not consisting of or being a quorum: *this meeting is inquorate*

in re (ɪn ˈreɪ) *prep* in the matter of: used esp in bankruptcy proceedings [c17 from Latin]

in rem (ɪn ˈrɛm) *adj law* (of a judicial act) directed against property rather than against a specific person. Compare **in personam** [Latin, literally: against the matter]

in rerum natura *Latin* (ɪn ˈrɛərʊm næˈtʊərə) in the nature of things

INRI *abbreviation for* Iesus Nazarenus Rex Iudaeorum (the inscription placed over Christ's head during the Crucifixion) [Latin: Jesus of Nazareth, King of the Jews]

inroad (ˈɪnˌrəʊd) *n* **1** an invasion or hostile attack; raid or incursion **2** an encroachment or intrusion

inrush (ˈɪnˌrʌʃ) *n* a sudden usually overwhelming inward flow or rush; influx > ˈinˌrushing *n, adj*

INS *abbreviation for* International News Service

ins. *abbreviation for* inches

insalivate (ɪnˈsælɪˌveɪt) *vb* (*tr*) to mix (food) with saliva during mastication > inˌsaliˈvation *n*

insalubrious (ˌɪnsəˈluːbrɪəs) *adj* not salubrious; unpleasant, unhealthy, or sordid > ˌinsaˈlubriously *adv* > insalubrity (ˌɪnsəˈluːbrɪtɪ) *n*

insane (ɪnˈseɪn) *adj* **1** **a** mentally deranged; crazy; of unsound mind **b** (*as collective noun; preceded by the*): *the insane* **2** characteristic of a person of unsound mind: *an insane stare* **3** irresponsible; very foolish; stupid > inˈsanely *adv* > inˈsaneness *n*

insanitary (ɪnˈsænɪtərɪ, -trɪ) *adj* not sanitary; dirty or infected > inˈsanitariness *or* inˌsaniˈtation *n*

insanity (ɪnˈsænɪtɪ) *n, pl* **-ties** **1** relatively permanent disorder of the mind; state or condition of being insane **2** *law* a defect of reason as a result of mental illness, such that a defendant does not know what he or she is doing or that it is wrong **3** utter folly; stupidity

insatiable (ɪnˈseɪʃəbᵊl, -ʃɪə-) *or* **insatiate** (ɪnˈseɪʃɪɪt) *adj* not able to be satisfied or satiated; greedy or unappeasable > inˌsatiaˈbility, inˈsatiableness *or* inˈsatiateness *n* > inˈsatiably *or* inˈsatiately *adv*

inscape (ˈɪnskeɪp) *n* the essential inner nature of a person, an object, etc [c19 from IN-[2] + *-scape*, as in LANDSCAPE; coined by Gerard Manley Hopkins (1844–89), British poet and Jesuit priest]

inscribe (ɪnˈskraɪb) *vb* (*tr*) **1** to make, carve, or engrave (writing, letters, a design, etc) on (a surface such as wood, stone, or paper) **2** to enter (a name) on a list or in a register **3** to sign one's name on (a book, photograph, etc) before presentation to another person **4** to draw (a geometric construction such as a circle, polygon, etc) inside another construction so that the two are in contact but do not intersect. Compare **circumscribe** (sense 3) [c16 from Latin *inscrībere*; see INSCRIPTION] > inˈscribable *adj* > inˈscribableness *n* > inˈscriber *n*

inscription (ɪnˈskrɪpʃən) *n* **1** something inscribed, esp words carved or engraved on a coin, tomb, etc **2** a signature or brief dedication in a book or on a work of art **3** the act of inscribing **4** *philosophy, linguistics* an element of written language, esp a sentence. Compare **utterance**[1] (sense 3) [c14 from Latin *inscriptiō* a writing upon, from *inscrībere* to write upon, from IN-[2] + *scrībere* to write] > inˈscriptional *or* inˈscriptive *adj* > inˈscriptively *adv*

inscrutable (ɪnˈskruːtəbᵊl) *adj* incomprehensible; mysterious or enigmatic [c15 from Late Latin *inscrūtābilis*, from Latin IN-[1] + *scrūtārī* to examine] > inˌscrutaˈbility *or* inˈscrutableness *n* > inˈscrutably *adv*

insect (ˈɪnsɛkt) *n* **1** any small air-breathing arthropod of the class *Insecta*, having a body divided into head, thorax, and abdomen, three pairs of legs, and (in most species) two pairs of wings. Insects comprise about five sixths of all known animal species, with a total of over one million named species. Related adj: **entomic** **2** (loosely) any similar invertebrate, such as a spider, tick, or centipede **3** a contemptible, loathsome, or insignificant person [c17 from Latin *insectum* (animal that has been) cut into, insect, from *insecāre*, from IN-[2] + *secāre* to cut; translation of Greek *entomon* insect] > inˈsectean, inˈsectan *or* inˈsectile *adj* > ˈinsect-ˌlike *adj*

insectarium (ˌɪnsɛkˈtɛərɪəm) *or* **insectary** (ɪnˈsɛktərɪ) *n, pl* **-tariums, -taria** (-ˈtɛərɪə) *or* **-taries** a place where living insects are kept, bred, and studied

insecticide (ɪnˈsɛktɪˌsaɪd) *n* a substance used to destroy insect pests > inˌsectiˈcidal *adj*

insectivore (ɪnˈsɛktɪˌvɔː) *n* **1** any placental mammal of the order *Insectivora*, being typically small, with simple teeth, and feeding on invertebrates. The group includes shrews, moles, and hedgehogs **2** any animal or plant that derives nourishment from insects

insectivorous (ˌɪnsɛkˈtɪvərəs) *adj* **1** feeding on or adapted for feeding on insects: *insectivorous plants* **2** of or relating to the order *Insectivora*

insectivorous bat *n* any bat of the suborder *Microchiroptera*, typically having large ears and feeding on insects. The group includes common bats (*Myotis* species), vampire bats, etc. Compare **fruit bat**

insecure (ˌɪnsɪˈkjʊə) *adj* **1** anxious or afraid; not confident or certain **2** not adequately protected: *an insecure fortress* **3** unstable or shaky > ˌinseˈcurely *adv* > ˌinseˈcureness *n* > ˌinseˈcurity *n*

inselberg (ˈɪnzᵊlˌbɜːg) *n* an isolated rocky hill rising abruptly from a flat plain [from German, from *Insel* island + *Berg* mountain]

inseminate (ɪnˈsɛmɪˌneɪt) *vb* (*tr*) **1** to impregnate (a female) with semen **2** to introduce (ideas or attitudes) into the mind of (a person or group) [c17 from Latin *insēmināre*, from IN-[2] + *sēmināre* to sow, from *sēmen* seed] > inˌsemiˈnation *n* > inˈsemiˌnator *n*

insensate (ɪnˈsɛnseɪt, -sɪt) *adj* **1** lacking sensation or consciousness **2** insensitive; unfeeling **3** foolish; senseless > inˈsensately *adv* > inˈsensateness *n*

insensible (ɪnˈsɛnsəbᵊl) *adj* **1** lacking sensation or consciousness **2** (foll by *of* or *to*) unaware (of) or indifferent (to) **3** thoughtless or callous **4** a less common word for **imperceptible**. > inˌsensiˈbility *or* inˈsensibleness *n* > inˈsensibly *adv*

insensitive (ɪnˈsɛnsɪtɪv) *adj* **1** lacking sensitivity; unfeeling **2** lacking physical sensation **3** (*postpositive; foll by to*) not sensitive (to) or affected (by): *insensitive to radiation* > inˈsensitively *adv* > inˈsensitiveness *or* inˌsensiˈtivity *n*

insentient (ɪnˈsɛnʃɪənt) *adj rare* lacking consciousness or senses; inanimate > inˈsentience *or* inˈsentiency *n*

inseparable (ɪnˈsɛpərəbᵊl, -ˈsɛprə-) *adj* incapable of being separated or divided > inˌseparaˈbility *or* inˈseparableness *n* > inˈseparably *adv*

insert *vb* (ɪnˈsɜːt) (*tr*) **1** to put in or between; introduce **2** to introduce, as into text, such as a newspaper; interpolate ▷ *n* (ˈɪnsɜːt) **3** something inserted **4** **a** a folded section placed in another for binding in with a book **b** a printed sheet, esp one bearing advertising, placed loose between the leaves of a book, periodical, etc **5** another word for **cut-in** (sense 6) [c16 from Latin *inserere* to plant in, ingraft, from IN-[2] + *serere* to join] > inˈsertable *adj* > inˈserter *n*

inserted (ɪnˈsɜːtɪd) *adj* **1** *anatomy* (of a muscle) attached to the bone that it moves **2** *botany* (of parts of a plant) growing from another part, as stamens from the corolla

insertion (ɪnˈsɜːʃən) *n* **1** the act of inserting or something that is inserted **2** a word, sentence, correction, etc, inserted into text, such as a newspaper **3** a strip of lace, embroidery, etc, between two pieces of material **4** *anatomy* the point or manner of attachment of a muscle to the bone that it moves **5** *botany* the manner or point of attachment of one part to another > inˈsertional *adj*

insertion element *or* **sequence** *n genetics* a section of DNA that is capable of becoming inserted into another chromosome. See **transposon**

in-service *adj* denoting training that is given to employees during the course of employment

insessorial (ˌɪnsɛˈsɔːrɪəl) *adj* **1** (of feet or claws) adapted for perching **2** (of birds) having insessorial feet [c19 from New Latin *Insessōrēs* birds that perch, from Latin: perchers, from *insidēre* to sit upon, from *sedēre* to sit]

inset *vb* (ɪnˈsɛt) **-sets, -setting, -set** **1** (*tr*) to set or place in or within; insert ▷ *n* (ˈɪnˌsɛt) **2** something inserted **3** *printing* **a** a small map or diagram set within the borders of a larger one **b** another name for **insert** (sense 4) **4** a piece of fabric inserted into a garment, as to shape it or for decoration **5** a flowing in, as of the tide > ˈinˌsetter *n*

inshallah (ɪnˈʃælə) *sentence substitute Islam* if Allah wills it [c19 from Arabic]

inshore (ˈɪnˈʃɔː) *adj* **1** in or on the water, but close to the shore: *inshore weather* ▷ *adv* ▷ *adj* **2** towards the shore from the water: *an inshore wind*

inshrine (ɪnˈʃraɪn) *vb* a variant spelling of **enshrine**

inside *n* (ˈɪnˈsaɪd) **1** the interior; inner or enclosed part or surface **2** the side of a path away from the road or adjacent to a wall **3** (*also plural*) *informal* the internal organs of the body, esp the stomach and bowels **4** **inside of** in a period of time less than; within **5** **inside out** with the inside facing outwards **6** **know (something) inside out** to know thoroughly or perfectly ▷ *prep* (ˌɪnˈsaɪd) **7** in or to the interior of; within or to within; on the inside of ▷ *adj* (ˈɪnˌsaɪd) **8** on or of an interior; on the inside: *an inside door* **9** (*prenominal*) arranged or provided by someone within an organization or building, esp illicitly: *the raid was an inside job; inside information* ▷ *adv* (ˌɪnˈsaɪd) **10** within or to within a thing or place; indoors **11** by nature; fundamentally **12** *slang* in or into prison

USAGE See at **outside**

inside forward *n soccer* (esp formerly) one of two

players (the **inside right** and the **inside left**) having mainly midfield and attacking roles

inside job *n informal* a crime committed with the assistance of someone associated with the victim, such as a person employed on the premises burgled

inside lane *n athletics* the inside, and therefore the shortest, route around a circular or oval multi-lane running track

insider (ˌɪnˈsaɪdə) *n* **1** a member of a specified group **2** a person with access to exclusive information

insider dealing *or* **trading** *n* dealing in company securities on a recognized stock exchange, with a view to making a profit or avoiding a loss, by a person who has confidential information about the securities that, if generally known, would affect their price. Its practice by those connected with a company is illegal > **insider dealer** *or* **trader** *n*

inside track *n* **1** the inner and therefore shorter side of a racecourse **2** *informal* a position of advantage

insidious (ɪnˈsɪdɪəs) *adj* **1** stealthy, subtle, cunning, or treacherous **2** working in a subtle or apparently innocuous way, but nevertheless deadly: *an insidious illness* [C16 from Latin *insidiōsus* cunning, from *insidiae* an ambush, from *insidēre* to sit in; see INSESSORIAL] > in'sidiously *adv* > in'sidiousness *n*

insight (ˈɪnˌsaɪt) *n* **1** the ability to perceive clearly or deeply; penetration **2** a penetrating and often sudden understanding, as of a complex situation or problem **3** *psychol* **a** the capacity for understanding one's own or another's mental processes **b** the immediate understanding of the significance of an event or action **4** *psychiatry* the ability to understand one's own problems, sometimes used to distinguish between psychotic and neurotic disorders > 'in,sightful *adj*

insignia (ɪnˈsɪgnɪə) *n, pl* -nias *or* -nia **1** a badge or emblem of membership, office, or dignity **2** a distinguishing sign or mark ▷ Also called (rare): insigne (ɪnˈsɪgniː) [C17 from Latin: marks, badges, from *insignis* distinguished by a mark, prominent, from IN-² + *signum* mark]

insignificant (ˌɪnsɪgˈnɪfɪkənt) *adj* **1** having little or no importance; trifling **2** almost or relatively meaningless **3** small or inadequate: *an insignificant wage* **4** not distinctive in character, etc > ˌinsig'nificance *or* ˌinsig'nificancy *n* > ˌinsig'nificantly *adv*

insincere (ˌɪnsɪnˈsɪə) *adj* lacking sincerity; hypocritical > ˌinsin'cerely *adv* > insincerity (ˌɪnsɪnˈsɛrɪtɪ) *n*

insinuate (ɪnˈsɪnjʊˌeɪt) *vb* **1** (may take a clause as object) to suggest by indirect allusion, hints, innuendo, etc **2** (tr) to introduce subtly or deviously **3** (tr) to cause (someone, esp oneself) to be accepted by gradual approaches or manoeuvres [C16 from Latin *insinuāre* to wind one's way into, from IN-² + *sinus* curve] > in'sinuative *or* in'sinuatory *adj* > in'sinu,ator *n*

insinuation (ɪnˌsɪnjʊˈeɪʃən) *n* **1** an indirect or devious hint or suggestion **2** the act or practice of insinuating

insipid (ɪnˈsɪpɪd) *adj* **1** lacking spirit; boring **2** lacking taste; unpalatable [C17 from Latin *insipidus*, from IN-¹ + *sapidus* full of flavour, SAPID] > ˌinsi'pidity *or* in'sipidness *n* > in'sipidly *adv*

insipience (ɪnˈsɪpɪəns) *n archaic* lack of wisdom [C15 from Latin *insipientia*, from IN-¹ + *sapientia* wisdom; see SAPIENT] > in'sipient *adj* > in'sipiently *adv*

insist (ɪnˈsɪst) *vb* when tr., takes a clause as object; when intr., usually foll by *on* or *upon* **1** to make a determined demand (for) **2** to express a convinced belief (in) or assertion (of): *he insisted that she was mad; he insisted on her madness* [C16 from Latin *insistere* to stand upon, urge, from IN-² + *sistere* to stand] > in'sister *n* > in'sistingly *adv*

insistent (ɪnˈsɪstənt) *adj* **1** making continual and

persistent demands **2** demanding notice or attention; compelling: *the insistent cry of a bird* > in'sistence *or* in'sistency *n* > in'sistently *adv*

in situ *Latin* (ɪn ˈsɪtjuː) *adv, adj* (postpositive) **1** in the natural, original, or appropriate position **2** *pathol* (esp of a cancerous growth or tumour) not seen to be spreading from a localized position

insnare (ɪnˈsnɛə) *vb* a less common spelling of ensnare. > in'snarement *n* > in'snarer *n*

insobriety (ˌɪnsəʊˈbraɪɪtɪ) *n* lack of sobriety; intemperance

in so far as *or* **insofar as** (ˌɪnsəʊˈfɑː) *adv* to the degree or extent that

insolate (ˈɪnsəʊˌleɪt) *vb* (tr) to expose to sunlight, as for bleaching [C17 from Latin *insōlāre* to place in the sun, from IN-² + *sōl* sun]

insolation (ˌɪnsəʊˈleɪʃən) *n* **1** the quantity of solar radiation falling upon a body or planet, esp per unit area **2** exposure to the sun's rays **3** former name for sunstroke

insole (ˈɪnˌsəʊl) *n* **1** the inner sole of a shoe or boot **2** a loose additional inner sole used to give extra warmth, comfort, etc

insolent (ˈɪnsələnt) *adj* offensive, impudent, or disrespectful [C14 from Latin *insolens*, from IN-¹ + *solēre* to be accustomed] > 'insolence *n* > 'insolently *adv*

insoluble (ɪnˈsɒljʊbəl) *adj* **1** incapable of being dissolved; incapable of forming a solution, esp in water **2** incapable of being solved > inˌsolu'bility *or* in'solubleness *n* > in'solubly *adv*

insolvable (ɪnˈsɒlvəbəl) *adj* another word for insoluble (sense 2) > inˌsolva'bility *n* > in'solvably *adv*

insolvency provision *n Brit* the right of employees of a firm that goes bankrupt or into receivership to receive money owed to them as wages, etc

insolvent (ɪnˈsɒlvənt) *adj* **1** (of a person, company, etc) having insufficient assets to meet debts and liabilities; bankrupt **2** of or relating to bankrupts or bankruptcy ▷ *n* **3** a person who is insolvent; bankrupt > in'solvency *n*

insomnia (ɪnˈsɒmnɪə) *n* chronic inability to fall asleep or to enjoy uninterrupted sleep. Related adj: agrypnotic [C18 from Latin, from *insomnis* sleepless, from *somnus* sleep] > in'somnious *adj*

insomniac (ɪnˈsɒmnɪˌæk) *adj* **1** exhibiting or causing insomnia ▷ *n* **2** a person experiencing insomnia

insomuch (ˌɪnsəʊˈmʌtʃ) *adv* **1** (foll by *as* or *that*) to such an extent or degree **2** (foll by *as*) because of the fact (that); inasmuch (as)

insouciant (ɪnˈsuːsɪənt) *adj* carefree or unconcerned; light-hearted [C19 from French, from IN-¹ + *souciant* worrying, from *soucier* to trouble, from Latin *sollicitāre*; compare SOLICITOUS] > in'souciance *n* > in'souciantly *adv*

insoul (ɪnˈsəʊl) *vb* (tr) a variant of ensoul

inspan (ɪnˈspæn) *vb* -spans, -spanning, -spanned (tr) *chiefly South African* to harness (animals) to (a vehicle); yoke [C19 from Afrikaans, from Middle Dutch *inspannen*, from *spannen* to stretch, yoke; see SPAN¹]

inspect (ɪnˈspɛkt) *vb* (tr) **1** to examine closely, esp for faults or errors **2** to scrutinize officially (a document, military personnel on ceremonial parade, etc) [C17 from Latin *inspicere*, from *specere* to look] > in'spectable *adj* > in'spectingly *adv* > in'spection *n* > in'spectional *adj* > in'spective *adj*

inspection chamber *n* a more formal name for manhole (sense 1)

inspection pit *n* a hole in the floor of a garage etc from which the underside of a vehicle can be examined and serviced

inspector (ɪnˈspɛktə) *n* **1** a person who inspects, esp an official who examines for compliance with regulations, standards, etc **2** a police officer ranking below a superintendent or chief inspector and above a sergeant > in'spectoral *or* inspectorial (ˌɪnspɛkˈtɔːrɪəl) *adj* > in'spectorˌship *n*

inspectorate (ɪnˈspɛktərɪt) *n* **1** the office, rank,

or duties of an inspector **2** a body of inspectors **3** a district under an inspector

inspector general *n, pl* inspectors general **1** the head of an inspectorate or inspection system; an officer with wide investigative powers **2** a staff officer of the military, air, or naval service with the responsibility of conducting inspections and investigations

Inspector of Taxes *n* an official of the Inland Revenue whose work is to assess individuals' income tax liability

insphere (ɪnˈsfɪə) *vb* a variant spelling of ensphere

inspiration (ˌɪnspɪˈreɪʃən) *n* **1** stimulation or arousal of the mind, feelings, etc, to special or unusual activity or creativity **2** the state or quality of being so stimulated or aroused **3** someone or something that causes this state **4** an idea or action resulting from such a state **5** the act or process of inhaling; breathing in

inspirational (ˌɪnspɪˈreɪʃənəl) *adj* **1** of, relating to, or tending to arouse inspiration; inspiring **2** resulting from inspiration; inspired > ˌinspi'rationally *adv*

inspirator (ˈɪnspɪˌreɪtə) *n* a device for drawing in or injecting a vapour, liquid, etc. Also called: injector

inspiratory (ɪnˈspaɪərətərɪ, -trɪ) *adj* of or relating to inhalation or the drawing in of air

inspire (ɪnˈspaɪə) *vb* **1** to exert a stimulating or beneficial effect upon (a person); animate or invigorate **2** (tr; foll by *with* or *to*; may take an infinitive) to arouse (with a particular emotion or to a particular action) **3** (tr) to prompt or instigate; give rise to: *her beauty inspired his love* **4** (tr; often passive) to guide or arouse by divine influence or inspiration **5** to take or draw (air, gas, etc) into the lungs; inhale **6** (tr) *archaic* **a** to breathe into or upon **b** to breathe life into [C14 (in the sense: to breathe upon, blow into): from Latin *inspīrāre*, from *spīrāre* to breathe] > in'spirable *adj* > in'spirative *adj* > in'spirer *n* > in'spiringly *adv*

inspired (ɪnˈspaɪəd) *adj* **1** aroused or guided by or as if aroused or guided by divine inspiration **2** extremely accurate or apt but based on intuition rather than knowledge or logical deduction

inspirit (ɪnˈspɪrɪt) *vb* (tr) to fill with vigour; inspire > in'spiriter *n* > in'spiritingly *adv* > in'spiritment *n*

inspissate (ɪnˈspɪseɪt) *vb archaic* to thicken, as by evaporation [C17 from Late Latin *inspissātus* thickened, from Latin *spissāre* to thicken, from *spissus* thick] > ˌinspis'sation *n* > 'inspisˌsator *n*

Inst. *abbreviation for* **1** Institute **2** Institution

insta- *combining form* indicating instant or quickly produced: *insta-thriller* [C21 from *instant*]

instability (ˌɪnstəˈbɪlɪtɪ) *n, pl* -ties **1** lack of stability or steadiness **2** tendency to variable or unpredictable behaviour **3** *physics* a fast growing disturbance or wave in a plasma

instable (ɪnˈsteɪbəl) *adj* a less common word for unstable

install *or* **instal** (ɪnˈstɔːl) *vb* -stalls, -stalling, -stalled *or* -stals, -stalling, -stalled (tr) **1** to place (machinery, equipment, etc) in position and connect and adjust for use **2** to transfer (computer software) from a distribution file to a permanent location on disk, and prepare it for its particular environment and application **3** to put in a position, rank, etc **4** to settle (a person, esp oneself) in a position or state: *she installed herself in an armchair* [C16 from Medieval Latin *installāre*, from IN-² + *stallum* STALL¹] > in'staller *n*

installant (ɪnˈstɔːlənt) *n* **a** a person who installs another in an office, etc **b** (as modifier): *an installant bishop*

installation (ˌɪnstəˈleɪʃən) *n* **1** the act of installing or the state of being installed **2** a large device, system, or piece of equipment that has been installed **3** a military establishment usually serving in a support role **4** an art exhibit often involving video or moving parts where the

i

relation of the parts to the whole is important to the interpretation of the piece

installment plan *or esp Canadian* **instalment plan** *n US and Canadian* a system for purchasing merchandise, such as cars or furniture, in which the buyer takes possession of the merchandise on payment of a deposit and completes the purchase by paying a series of regular instalments while the seller retains ownership until the final instalment is paid. Also called (in Britain and certain other countries): **hire-purchase**

instalment[1] *or US* **installment** (ɪnˈstɔːlmənt) *n* **1** one of the portions, usually equal, into which a debt is divided for payment at specified intervals over a fixed period **2** a portion of something that is issued, broadcast, or published in parts, such as a serial in a magazine [C18 from obsolete *estallment*, probably from Old French *estaler* to fix, hence to agree rate of payment, from *estal* something fixed, place, from Old High German *stal* STALL[1]]

instalment[2] *or US* **installment** (ɪnˈstɔːlmənt) *n* another word for **installation** (sense 1)

instance (ˈɪnstəns) *n* **1** a case or particular example **2 for instance** for or as an example **3** a specified stage in proceedings; step (in the phrases **in the first, second,** etc, **instance**) **4** urgent request or demand (esp in the phrase **at the instance of**) **5** *logic* **a** an expression derived from another by instantiation **b** See **substitution** (sense 4b) **6** *archaic* motive or reason ▷ *vb* (*tr*) **7** to cite as an example [C14 (in the sense: case, example): from Medieval Latin *instantia* example, (in the sense: urgency) from Latin: a being close upon, presence, from *instāns* pressing upon, urgent; see INSTANT]

instancy (ˈɪnstənsɪ) *n rare* **1** the quality of being urgent or imminent **2** instantaneousness; immediateness

instant (ˈɪnstənt) *n* **1** a very brief time; moment **2** a particular moment or point in time: *at the same instant* **3 on the instant** immediately; without delay ▷ *adj* **4** immediate; instantaneous **5** (esp of foods) prepared or designed for preparation with very little time and effort: *instant coffee* **6** urgent or imperative **7** (*postpositive*) *rare except when abbreviated in formal correspondence* **a** of the present month: *a letter of the 7th instant*. Abbreviation: **inst** Compare **proximo, ultimo b** currently under consideration ▷ *adv* **8** a poetic word for **instantly** [C15 from Latin *instāns*, from *instāre* to be present, press closely, from IN-[2] + *stāre* to stand]

instantaneous (ˌɪnstənˈteɪnɪəs) *adj* **1** occurring with almost no delay; immediate **2** happening or completed within a moment: *instantaneous death* **3** *maths* **a** occurring at or associated with a particular instant **b** equal to the limit of the average value of a given variable as the time interval over which the variable is considered approaches zero: *instantaneous velocity* > ˌ**instanˈtaneously** *adv* > ˌ**instanˈtaneousness** *or* **instantaneity** (ɪnˌstæntəˈniːɪtɪ) *n*

instanter (ɪnˈstæntə) *adv law* without delay; (in connection with pleading) the same day or within 24 hours [C17 from Latin: urgently, from *instans* INSTANT]

instantiate (ɪnˈstænʃɪˌeɪt) *vb* (*tr*) to represent by an instance [C20 from Latin *instantia* (see INSTANCE) + -ATE[1]]

instantiation (ɪnˌstænʃɪˈeɪʃən) *n* **1** the act or an instance of instantiating **2** the representation of (an abstraction) by a concrete example **3** *logic* **a** the process of deriving an individual statement from a general one by replacing the variable with a name or other referring expression **b** the valid inference of an instance from a universally quantified statement, as *David is rational* from *all men are rational* **c** a statement so derived

instantly (ˈɪnstəntlɪ) *adv* **1** immediately; at once **2** *archaic* urgently or insistently

instant messaging *n computing* the online facility that allows the instant exchange of written messages between two or more people using different computers or mobile phones. Abbreviation: **IM**

instant replay *n* another name for **action replay**

instar (ˈɪnstɑː) *n* the stage in the development of an insect between any two moults [C19 New Latin from Latin: image]

instate (ɪnˈsteɪt) *vb* (*tr*) to place in a position or office; install > **inˈstatement** *n*

instauration (ˌɪnstɔːˈreɪʃən) *n rare* restoration or renewal [C17 from Latin *instaurātiō*, from *instaurāre* to renew] > ˈ**instauˌrator** *n*

instead (ɪnˈstɛd) *adv* **1** as a replacement, substitute, or alternative **2 instead of** (*preposition*) in place of or as an alternative to [C13 from phrase *in stead* in place]

instep (ˈɪnˌstɛp) *n* **1** the middle section of the human foot, forming the arch between the ankle and toes **2** the part of a shoe, stocking, etc, covering this [C16 probably from IN-[2] + STEP]

instigate (ˈɪnstɪˌɡeɪt) *vb* (*tr*) **1** to bring about, as by incitement or urging: *to instigate rebellion* **2** to urge on to some drastic or inadvisable action [C16 from Latin *instīgāre* to stimulate, incite; compare Greek *stizein* to prick] > ˈ**instiˌgatingly** *adv* > ˌ**instiˈgation** *n* > ˈ**instiˌgative** *adj* > ˈ**instiˌgator** *n*

instil *or US* **instill** (ɪnˈstɪl) *vb* **-stils** *or* **-stills, -stilling, -stilled** (*tr*) **1** to introduce gradually; implant or infuse **2** *rare* to pour in or inject in drops [C16 from Latin *instillāre* to pour in a drop at a time, from *stillāre* to drip] > **inˈstiller** *n* > **inˈstilment** *or U.S* **inˈstillment,** ˌ**instilˈlation** *n*

instinct (ˈɪnstɪŋkt) *n* **1** the innate capacity of an animal to respond to a given stimulus in a relatively fixed way **2** inborn intuitive power **3** a natural and apparently innate aptitude ▷ *adj* (ɪnˈstɪŋkt) **4** *rare* (*postpositive; often foll by with*) **a** animated or impelled (by) **b** imbued or infused (with) [C15 from Latin *instinctus* roused, from *instinguere* to incite; compare INSTIGATE]

instinctive (ɪnˈstɪŋktɪv) *or* **instinctual** *adj* **1** of, relating to, or resulting from instinct **2** conditioned so as to appear innate > **inˈstinctively** *or* **inˈstinctually** *adv*

institute (ˈɪnstɪˌtjuːt) *vb* (*tr*) **1** to organize; establish **2** to initiate: *to institute a practice* **3** to establish in a position or office; induct **4** (foll by *in* or *into*) to install (a clergyman) in a church ▷ *n* **5** an organization founded for particular work, such as education, promotion of the arts, or scientific research **6** the building where such an organization is situated **7** something instituted, esp a rule, custom, or precedent [C16 from Latin *instituere*, from *statuere* to place, stand] > ˈ**instiˌtutor** *or* ˈ**instiˌtuter** *n*

institutes (ˈɪnstɪˌtjuːts) *pl n* a digest or summary, esp of laws

Institutes (ˈɪnstɪˌtjuːts) *pl n* **1** an introduction to legal study in ancient Rome, compiled by order of Justinian and divided into four books forming part of the Corpus Juris Civilis **2** short for **Institutes of the Christian Religion,** the book by Calvin, completed in 1536 and constituting the basic statement of the Reformed faith, that repudiates papal authority and postulates the doctrines of justification by faith alone and predestination

institution (ˌɪnstɪˈtjuːʃən) *n* **1** the act of instituting **2** an organization or establishment founded for a specific purpose, such as a hospital, church, company, or college **3** the building where such an organization is situated **4** an established custom, law, or relationship in a society or community **5** Also called: **institutional investor** a large organization, such as an insurance company, bank, or pension fund, that has substantial sums to invest on a stock exchange **6** *informal* a constant feature or practice: *Jones' drink at the bar was an institution* **7** the appointment or admission of an incumbent to an ecclesiastical office or pastoral charge **8** *Christian theol* the creation of a sacrament by Christ, esp the Eucharist > ˌ**instiˈtutionary** *adj*

institutional (ˌɪnstɪˈtjuːʃənᵊl) *adj* **1** of, relating to, or characteristic of institutions **2** dull, routine, and uniform: *institutional meals* **3** relating to principles or institutes, esp of law > ˌ**instiˈtutionally** *adv*

institutionalism (ˌɪnstɪˈtjuːʃənəˌlɪzəm) *n* the system of or belief in institutions > ˌ**instiˈtutionalist** *n*

institutionalize *or* **institutionalise** (ˌɪnstɪˈtjuːʃənəˌlaɪz) *vb* **1** (*tr; often passive*) to subject to the deleterious effects of confinement in an institution **2** (*tr*) to place in an institution **3** to make or become an institution > ˌ**instiˌtutionaliˈzation** *or* ˌ**instiˌtutionaliˈsation** *n*

institutive (ˈɪnstɪˌtjuːtɪv) *adj* **1** concerned with instituting and establishing **2** established by custom or law > ˈ**instiˌtutively** *adv*

in-store *adj* available or taking place within a supermarket or other large shop: *in-store banking facilities*

instruct (ɪnˈstrʌkt) *vb* (*tr*) **1** to direct to do something; order **2** to teach (someone) how to do (something) **3** to furnish with information; apprise **4** *law, chiefly Brit* **a** (esp of a client to his solicitor or a solicitor to a barrister) to give relevant facts or information to **b** to authorize (a barrister or solicitor) to conduct a case on a person's behalf: *to instruct counsel* [C15 from Latin *instruere* to construct, set in order, equip, teach, from *struere* to build] > **inˈstructible** *adj*

instruction (ɪnˈstrʌkʃən) *n* **1** a direction; order **2** the process or act of imparting knowledge; teaching; education **3** *computing* a part of a program consisting of a coded command to the computer to perform a specified function > **inˈstructional** *adj*

instructions (ɪnˈstrʌkʃənz) *pl n* **1** directions, orders, or recommended rules for guidance, use, etc **2** *law* the facts and details relating to a case given by a client to his solicitor or by a solicitor to a barrister with directions to conduct the case

instructive (ɪnˈstrʌktɪv) *adj* serving to instruct or enlighten; conveying information > **inˈstructively** *adv* > **inˈstructiveness** *n*

instructor (ɪnˈstrʌktə) *n* **1** someone who instructs; teacher **2** *US and Canadian* a university teacher ranking below assistant professor > **inˈstructorˌship** *n* > **instructress** (ɪnˈstrʌktrɪs) *fem n*

instrument *n* (ˈɪnstrəmənt) **1** a mechanical implement or tool, esp one used for precision work: *surgical instrument* **2** *music* any of various contrivances or mechanisms that can be played to produce musical tones or sounds **3** an important factor or agency in something **4** *informal* a person used by another to gain an end; dupe; tool **5** a measuring device, such as a pressure gauge or ammeter **6 a** a device or system for use in navigation or control, esp of aircraft **b** (*as modifier*): *instrument landing* **7** a formal legal document ▷ *vb* (ˈɪnstrəˌmɛnt) (*tr*) **8** another word for **orchestrate** (sense 1) **9** to equip with instruments [C13 from Latin *instrūmentum* tool, equipment, from *instruere* to erect, furnish; see INSTRUCT]

instrumental (ˌɪnstrəˈmɛntᵊl) *adj* **1** serving as a means or influence; helpful **2** of, relating to, or characterized by an instrument or instruments **3** played by or composed for musical instruments **4** *grammar* denoting a case of nouns, etc, in certain inflected languages, indicating the instrument used in performing an action, usually translated into English using the prepositions *with* or *by means of* ▷ *n* **5** a piece of music composed for instruments rather than for voices **6** *grammar* **a** the instrumental case **b** a word or speech element in the instrumental case > ˌ**instrumenˈtality** *n* > ˌ**instruˈmentally** *adv*

instrumentalism (ˌɪnstrəˈmɛntəˌlɪzəm) *n* **1** a system of pragmatic philosophy holding that ideas are instruments, that they should guide our actions and can change the world, and that their value consists not in their truth but in their success **2** an antirealist philosophy of science that holds that theories are not true or false but are merely tools for deriving predictions from observational data

instrumentalist (ˌɪnstrəˈmɛntəlɪst) *n* **1** a person who plays a musical instrument **2** *philosophy* a person who believes in the doctrines of instrumentalism ▷ *adj* **3** of or relating to instrumentalism

instrumental learning *n psychol* a method of training in which the reinforcement is made contingent on the occurrence of the response. Compare **classical conditioning**

instrumentation (ˌɪnstrəmɛnˈteɪʃən) *n* **1** the instruments specified in a musical score or arrangement **2** another word for **orchestration 3** the study of the characteristics of musical instruments **4** the use of instruments or tools **5** means; agency

instrument flying *n* the navigation of an aircraft by the use of instruments only

instrument landing *n* an aircraft landing relying only upon instruments and ground radio devices, usually made when visibility is very poor

instrument panel *or* **board** *n* **1** a panel on which instruments are mounted, as on a car. See also **dashboard 2** an array of instruments, gauges, etc, mounted to display the condition or performance of a machine or process

insubordinate (ˌɪnsəˈbɔːdɪnɪt) *adj* **1** not submissive to authority; disobedient or rebellious **2** not in a subordinate position or rank ▷ *n* **3** an insubordinate person > ˌinsubˈordinately *adv* > ˌinsubˌordiˈnation *n*

insubstantial (ˌɪnsəbˈstænʃəl) *adj* **1** not substantial; flimsy, tenuous, or slight **2** imaginary; unreal > ˌinsubˌstantiˈality *n* > ˌinsubˈstantially *adv*

insufferable (ɪnˈsʌfərəbəl) *adj* intolerable; unendurable > inˈsufferableness *n* > inˈsufferably *adv*

insufficiency (ˌɪnsəˈfɪʃənsɪ) *n* **1** Also called: **insufficience** the state of being insufficient **2** *pathol* failure in the functioning of an organ, tissue, etc: *cardiac insufficiency*

insufficient (ˌɪnsəˈfɪʃənt) *adj* not sufficient; inadequate or deficient > ˌinsufˈficiently *adv*

insufflate (ˈɪnsʌˌfleɪt) *vb* **1** (*tr*) to breathe or blow (something) into (a room, area, etc) **2** *med* to blow (air, medicated powder, etc) into the lungs or into a body cavity **3** (*tr*) to breathe or blow upon (someone or something) as a ritual or sacramental act, esp so as to symbolize the influence of the Holy Spirit > ˌinsufˈflation *n* > ˈinsufˌflator *n*

insula (ˈɪnsjʊlə) *n, pl* **-lae** (-ˌliː) a pyramid-shaped area of the brain within each cerebral hemisphere beneath parts of the frontal and temporal lobes. Also called: **island of Reil** [Latin, literally: island]

insular (ˈɪnsjʊlə) *adj* **1** of, relating to, or resembling an island **2** remote, detached, or aloof **3** illiberal or narrow-minded **4** isolated or separated [C17 from Late Latin *insulāris*, from Latin *insula* island, ISLE] > ˈinsularism *or* **insularity** (ˌɪnsjʊˈlærɪtɪ) *n* > ˈinsularly *adv*

insulate (ˈɪnsjʊˌleɪt) *vb* (*tr*) **1** to prevent or reduce the transmission of electricity, heat, or sound to or from (a body, device, or region) by surrounding with a nonconducting material **2** to isolate or detach [C16 from Late Latin *insulātus*: made into an island]

insulating tape *n Brit* adhesive tape, impregnated with a moisture-repelling substance, used to insulate exposed electrical conductors. US and Canadian name: **friction tape**

insulation (ˌɪnsjʊˈleɪʃən) *n* **1** Also called: **insulant** (ˈɪnsjʊlənt) material used to insulate a body, device, or region **2** the act or process of insulating

insulator (ˈɪnsjʊˌleɪtə) *n* any material or device that insulates, esp a material with a very low

electrical conductivity or thermal conductivity or something made of such a material

insulin (ˈɪnsjʊlɪn) *n* a protein hormone, secreted in the pancreas by the islets of Langerhans, that controls the concentration of glucose in the blood. Insulin deficiency results in diabetes mellitus [C20 from New Latin *insula* islet (of the pancreas) + -IN]

insulin reaction *or* **shock** *n* the condition in a diabetic resulting from an overdose of insulin, causing a sharp drop in the blood sugar level with tremor, profuse sweating, and convulsions. See also **hyperinsulinism**

insult *vb* (ɪnˈsʌlt) (*tr*) **1** to treat, mention, or speak to rudely; offend; affront **2** *obsolete* to assault; attack ▷ *n* (ˈɪnsʌlt) **3** an offensive or contemptuous remark or action; affront; slight **4** a person or thing producing the effect of an affront: *some television is an insult to intelligence* **5** *med* an injury or trauma **6** **add insult to injury** to make an unfair or unacceptable situation even worse [C16 from Latin *insultāre* to jump upon, from IN-² + *saltāre* to jump] > inˈsulter *n*

insuperable (ɪnˈsuːpərəbəl, -prəbəl, -ˈsjuː-) *adj* incapable of being overcome; insurmountable > inˌsuperaˈbility *or* inˈsuperableness *n* > inˈsuperably *adv*

insupportable (ˌɪnsəˈpɔːtəbəl) *adj* **1** incapable of being endured; intolerable; insufferable **2** incapable of being supported or justified; indefensible > ˌinsupˈportableness *n* > ˌinsupˈportably *adv*

insuppressible (ˌɪnsəˈprɛsəbəl) *adj* incapable of being suppressed, overcome, or muffled: *an insuppressible giggle* > ˌinsupˈpressibly *adv*

insurable interest *n law* a financial or other interest in the life or property covered by an insurance contract, without which the contract cannot be enforced

insurance (ɪnˈʃʊərəns, -ˈʃɔː-) *n* **1 a** the act, system, or business of providing financial protection for property, life, health, etc, against specified contingencies, such as death, loss, or damage, and involving payment of regular premiums in return for a policy guaranteeing such protection **b** the state of having such protection **c** Also called: **insurance policy** the policy providing such protection **d** the pecuniary amount of such protection **e** the premium payable in return for such protection **f** (*as modifier*): *insurance agent; insurance broker; insurance company* **2** a means of protecting or safeguarding against risk or injury

insure (ɪnˈʃʊə, -ˈʃɔː) *vb* **1** (*often foll by against*) to guarantee or protect (against risk, loss, etc) **2** (*often foll by against*) to issue (a person) with an insurance policy or take out an insurance policy (on) **3** another word (esp US) for **ensure** (senses 1, 2) ▷ Also (*rare*) (for senses 1, 2): **ensure** > inˈsurable *adj* > inˌsuraˈbility *n*

insured (ɪnˈʃʊəd, -ˈʃɔːd) *adj* **1** covered by insurance: *an insured risk* ▷ *n* **2** the person, persons, or organization covered by an insurance policy

insurer (ɪnˈʃʊərə, -ˈʃɔː-) *n* **1** a person or company offering insurance policies in return for premiums **2** a person or thing that insures

insurgence (ɪnˈsɜːdʒəns) *n* rebellion, uprising, or riot

insurgent (ɪnˈsɜːdʒənt) *adj* **1** rebellious or in revolt, as against a government in power or the civil authorities ▷ *n* **2** a person who takes part in an uprising or rebellion; insurrectionist **3** *international law* a person or group that rises in revolt against an established government or authority but whose conduct does not amount to belligerency [C18 from Latin *insurgēns* rising upon or against, from *insurgere* to rise up, from *surgere* to rise] > inˈsurgency *n*

insurmountable (ˌɪnsəˈmaʊntəbəl) *adj* incapable of being overcome; insuperable > ˌinsurˌmountaˈbility *or* ˌinsurˈmountableness *n* > ˌinsurˈmountably *adv*

insurrection (ˌɪnsəˈrɛkʃən) *n* the act or an

instance of rebelling against a government in power or the civil authorities; insurgency [C15 from Late Latin *insurrectiō*, from *insurgere* to rise up] > ˌinsurˈrectional *adj* > ˌinsurˈrectionary *n, adj* > ˌinsurˈrectionism *n* > ˌinsurˈrectionist *n, adj*

insusceptible (ˌɪnsəˈsɛptəbəl) *adj* (when *postpositive*, usually foll by to) not capable of being affected (by); not susceptible (to) > ˌinsusˌceptiˈbility *n* > ˌinsusˈceptibly *adv*

inswing (ˈɪnˌswɪŋ) *n cricket* the movement of a bowled ball from off to leg through the air. Compare **outswing**

inswinger (ˈɪnˌswɪŋə) *n* **1** *cricket* a ball bowled so as to move from off to leg through the air **2** *soccer* a ball kicked, esp from a corner, so as to move through the air in a curve towards the goal or the centre

int *an internet domain name for* an international organization

intact (ɪnˈtækt) *adj* untouched or unimpaired; left complete or perfect [C15 from Latin *intactus* not touched, from *tangere* to touch] > inˈtactness *n*

intaglio (ɪnˈtɑːlɪˌəʊ) *n, pl* **-lios** *or* **-li** (-ˌliː) **1** a seal, gem, etc, ornamented with a sunken or incised design, as opposed to a design in relief. Compare **cameo 2** the art or process of incised carving **3** a design, figure, or ornamentation carved, engraved, or etched into the surface of the material used **4** any of various printing techniques using an etched or engraved plate. The whole plate is smeared with ink, the surface wiped clean, and the ink in the recesses then transferred to the paper or other material **5** an incised die used to make a design in relief [C17 from Italian, from *intagliare* to engrave, from *tagliare* to cut, from Late Latin *tāliāre*; see TAILOR] > intagliated (ɪnˈtɑːlɪˌeɪtɪd) *adj*

intake (ˈɪnˌteɪk) *n* **1** a thing or a quantity taken in: *an intake of students* **2** the act of taking in **3** the opening through which fluid enters a duct or channel, esp the air inlet of a jet engine **4** a ventilation shaft in a mine **5** a contraction or narrowing: *an intake in a garment*

intangible (ɪnˈtændʒɪbəl) *adj* **1** incapable of being perceived by touch; impalpable **2** imprecise or unclear to the mind: *intangible ideas* **3** (of property or a business asset) saleable though not possessing intrinsic productive value ▷ *n* **4** something that is intangible > inˌtangiˈbility *or* inˈtangibleness *n* > inˈtangibly *adv*

intarsia (ɪnˈtɑːsɪə) *or* **tarsia** *n* **1** a decorative or pictorial mosaic of inlaid wood or sometimes ivory of a style developed in the Italian Renaissance and used esp on wooden wall panels **2** the art or practice of making such mosaics **3** (in knitting) an individually worked motif [C19 changed from Italian *intarsio*]

integer (ˈɪntɪdʒə) *n* **1** any rational number that can be expressed as the sum or difference of a finite number of units, being a member of the set ...−3, −2, −1, 0, 1, 2, 3... **2** an individual entity or whole unit [C16 from Latin: untouched, entire, from *tangere* to touch]

integral *adj* (ˈɪntɪgrəl, ɪnˈtɛgrəl) **1** (*often foll by to*) being an essential part (of); intrinsic (to) **2** intact; entire **3** formed of constituent parts; united **4** *maths* **a** of or involving an integral **b** involving or being an integer ▷ *n* (ˈɪntɪgrəl) **5** *maths* the limit of an increasingly large number of increasingly smaller quantities, related to the function that is being integrated (the integrand). The independent variables may be confined within certain limits (**definite integral**) or in the absence of limits (**indefinite integral**). Symbol: ∫ **6** a complete thing; whole > **integrality** (ˌɪntɪˈɡrælɪtɪ) *n* > ˈintegrally *adv*

integral calculus *n* the branch of calculus concerned with the determination of integrals and their application to the solution of differential equations, the determination of areas and volumes, etc. Compare **differential calculus**

integrand (ˈɪntɪˌɡrænd) *n* a mathematical

i

function to be integrated [c19 from Latin: to be integrated]

integrant ('ɪntəgrənt) *adj* **1** part of a whole; integral; constituent ▷ *n* **2** an integrant thing or part

integrate *vb* ('ɪntɪˌgreɪt) **1** to make or be made into a whole; incorporate or be incorporated **2** (*tr*) to designate (a school, park, etc) for use by all races or groups; desegregate **3** to amalgamate or mix (a racial or religious group) with an existing community **4** *maths* to perform an integration on (a quantity, expression, etc) ▷ *adj* ('ɪntɪgrɪt) **5** made up of parts; integrated [c17 from Latin *integrāre*; see INTEGER] ▷ **integrable** ('ɪntəgrəbʰl) *adj* ▷ ˌintegra'bility *n* ▷ 'inteˌgrative *adj*

integrated ('ɪntɪˌgreɪtɪd) *adj* **1** characterized by integration **2** denoting a works which combines various processes normally carried out at different locations: *an integrated steelworks* **3** *biology* denoting a virus the DNA of which is incorporated into the chromosomes of the host cell

integrated circuit *n* a very small electronic circuit consisting of an assembly of elements made from a chip of semiconducting material, such as crystalline silicon. Abbreviation: IC

integrated school *n* (in New Zealand) a private or church school that has joined the state school system

integration (ˌɪntɪ'greɪʃən) *n* **1** the act of combining or adding parts to make a unified whole **2** the act of amalgamating a racial or religious group with an existing community **3** the combination of previously racially segregated social facilities into a nonsegregated system **4** *psychol* organization into a unified pattern, esp of different aspects of the personality into a hierarchical system of functions **5** the assimilation of nutritive material by the body during the process of anabolism **6** *maths* an operation used in calculus in which the integral of a function or variable is determined; the inverse of differentiation ▷ ˌinte'grationist *n*

integrative bargaining ('ɪntɪˌgreɪtɪv) *n industrial relations* a type of bargaining in which all parties involved recognize that there are common problems requiring mutual resolution

integrator ('ɪntɪˌgreɪtə) *n* **1** a person or thing that integrates, esp a mechanical instrument that determines the value of a definite integral, as the area under a curve. See also **planimeter 2** *computing* **a** an arithmetic component with two input variables, *x* and *y*, whose output variable *z* is proportional to the integral of *y* with respect to *x* **b** an arithmetic component whose output variable is proportional to the integral of the input variable with respect to elapsed time

integrity (ɪn'tɛgrɪtɪ) *n* **1** adherence to moral principles; honesty **2** the quality of being unimpaired; soundness **3** unity; wholeness [c15 from Latin *integritās*; see INTEGER]

integument (ɪn'tɛgjʊmənt) *n* **1** the protective layer around an ovule that becomes the seed coat **2** the outer protective layer or covering of an animal, such as skin or a cuticle [c17 from Latin *integumentum*, from *tegere* to cover] ▷ inˌtegu'mental or inˌtegu'mentary *adj*

intel ('ɪntɛl) *n informal* **a** US military intelligence **b** information in general

intellect ('ɪntɪˌlɛkt) *n* **1** the capacity for understanding, thinking, and reasoning, as distinct from feeling or wishing **2** a mind or intelligence, esp a brilliant one **3** *informal* a person possessing a brilliant mind; brain **4** those possessing the greatest mental power [c14 from Latin *intellectus* comprehension, intellect, from *intellegere* to understand; see INTELLIGENCE] ▷ ˌintel'lective *adj* ▷ ˌintel'lectively *adv*

intellection (ˌɪntɪ'lɛkʃən) *n* **1** mental activity; thought **2** an idea or thought

intellectual (ˌɪntɪ'lɛktʃʊəl) *adj* **1** of or relating to the intellect, as opposed to the emotions **2** appealing to or characteristic of people with a

developed intellect: *intellectual literature* **3** expressing or enjoying mental activity ▷ *n* **4** a person who enjoys mental activity and has highly developed tastes in art, literature, etc **5** a person who uses or works with his intellect **6** a highly intelligent person ▷ ˌintel'lectu'ality or ˌintel'lectualness *n* ▷ ˌintel'lectually *adv*

intellectualism (ˌɪntɪ'lɛktʃʊəˌlɪzəm) *n* **1** development and exercise of the intellect **2** the placing of excessive value on the intellect, esp with disregard for the emotions **3** *philosophy* **a** the doctrine that reason is the ultimate criterion of knowledge **b** the doctrine that deliberate action is consequent on a process of conscious or subconscious reasoning ▷ ˌintel'lectualist *n, adj* ▷ ˌintel'lectual'istic *adj* ▷ ˌintel'lectual'istically *adv*

intellectualize or **intellectualise** (ˌɪntɪ'lɛktʃʊəˌlaɪz) *vb* **1** to make or become intellectual **2** (*tr*) to treat or consider in an intellectual way; rationalize ▷ ˌintel'lectuali'zation or ˌintel'lectuali'sation *n* ▷ ˌintel'lectualˌizer or ˌintel'lectualˌiser *n*

intellectually handicapped *adj Austral* mentally handicapped

intellectual property *n* an intangible asset, such as a copyright or patent

intelligence (ɪn'tɛlɪdʒəns) *n* **1** the capacity for understanding; ability to perceive and comprehend meaning **2** good mental capacity **3** *old-fashioned* news; information **4** military information about enemies, spies, etc **5** a group or department that gathers or deals with such information **6** (*often capital*) an intelligent being, esp one that is not embodied **7** (*modifier*) of or relating to intelligence [c14 from Latin *intellegentia*, from *intellegere* to discern, comprehend, literally: choose between, from INTER- + *legere* to choose] ▷ inˌtelli'gential *adj*

intelligence quotient *n* a measure of the intelligence of an individual derived from results obtained from specially designed tests. The quotient is traditionally derived by dividing an individual's mental age by his chronological age and multiplying the result by 100. Abbreviation: IQ

intelligencer (ɪn'tɛlɪdʒənsə) *n archaic* an informant or spy

intelligence test *n* any of a number of tests designed to measure a person's mental skills. See also **Binet-Simon scale**

intelligent (ɪn'tɛlɪdʒənt) *adj* **1** having or indicating intelligence **2** having high intelligence; clever **3** indicating high intelligence; perceptive **4** guided by reason; rational **5** (of computerized functions) able to modify action in the light of ongoing events **6** (*postpositive; foll by of*) *archaic* having knowledge or information ▷ in'telligently *adv*

intelligent card *n* another name for **smart card**

intelligent knowledge-based system *n* a computer system in which the properties of a database and an expert system are combined to enable the system to store and process data and make deductions from stored data. Abbreviation: IKBS

intelligentsia (ɪnˌtɛlɪ'dʒɛntsɪə) *n* (usually preceded by *the*) the educated or intellectual people in a society or community [c20 from Russian *intelligentsiya*, from Latin *intellegentia* INTELLIGENCE]

intelligent terminal *n* a computer operating terminal that can carry out some data processing, as well as sending data to and receiving it from a central processor

intelligible (ɪn'tɛlɪdʒəbʰl) *adj* **1** able to be understood; comprehensible **2** *philosophy* **a** capable of being apprehended by the mind or intellect alone **b** in metaphysical systems such as those of Plato or Kant denoting that metaphysical realm which is accessible to the intellect as opposed to the world of mere phenomena accessible to the senses [c14 from

Latin *intellegibilis*; see INTELLECT] ▷ inˌtelligi'bility or in'telligibleness *n* ▷ in'telligibly *adv*

Intelsat ('ɪntɛlˌsæt) *n* any of the series of communications satellites operated by the International Telecommunications Satellite Consortium

intemerate (ɪn'tɛmərɪt) *adj rare* not defiled; pure; unsullied [c15 from Latin *intemerātus* undefiled, pure, from IN-¹ + *temerāre* to darken, violate, from *temere* rashly] ▷ in'temerately *adv* ▷ in'temerateness *n*

intemperate (ɪn'tɛmpərɪt, -prɪt) *adj* **1** consuming alcoholic drink habitually or to excess **2** indulging bodily appetites to excess; immoderate **3** unrestrained: *intemperate rage* **4** extreme or severe: *an intemperate climate* ▷ in'temperance or in'temperateness *n* ▷ in'temperately *adv*

intend (ɪn'tɛnd) *vb* **1** (*may take a clause as object*) to propose or plan (something or to do something); have in mind; mean **2** (*tr; often foll by for*) to design or destine (for a certain purpose, person, etc) **3** (*tr*) to mean to express or indicate: *what do his words intend?* **4** (*intr*) to have a purpose as specified; mean **5** (*tr*) *archaic* to direct or turn (the attention, eyes, etc) [c14 from Latin *intendere* to stretch forth, give one's attention to, from *tendere* to stretch] ▷ in'tender *n*

intendance (ɪn'tɛndəns) *n* **1** any of various public departments, esp in France **2** a less common word for **superintendence**

intendancy (ɪn'tɛndənsɪ) *n* **1** the position or work of an intendant **2** intendants collectively **3** *history* the district or area administered by an intendant

intendant (ɪn'tɛndənt) *n* **1** *history* a provincial or colonial official of France, Spain, or Portugal **2** a senior administrator in some countries, esp in Latin America **3** a superintendent or manager

intended (ɪn'tɛndɪd) *adj* **1** planned or future ▷ *n* **2** *informal* a person whom one is to marry; fiancé or fiancée

intendment (ɪn'tɛndmənt) *n* **1** the meaning of something as fixed or understood by the law **2** *obsolete* intention, design, or purpose

intenerate (ɪn'tɛnəˌreɪt) *vb* (*tr*) *rare* to soften or make tender [c16 from IN-² + Latin *tener* delicate, TENDER¹] ▷ inˌtener'ation *n*

intense (ɪn'tɛns) *adj* **1** of extreme force, strength, degree, or amount: *intense heat* **2** characterized by deep or forceful feelings: *an intense person* [c14 from Latin *intensus* stretched, from *intendere* to stretch out; see INTEND] ▷ in'tensely *adv* ▷ in'tenseness *n*

USAGE *Intense* is sometimes wrongly used where *intensive* is meant: *the land is under intensive* (not *intense*) *cultivation. Intensely* is sometimes wrongly used where *intently* is meant: *he listened intently* (not *intensely*)

intensifier (ɪn'tɛnsɪˌfaɪə) *n* **1** a person or thing that intensifies **2** a word, esp an adjective or adverb, that has little semantic content of its own but that serves to intensify the meaning of the word or phrase that it modifies: *awfully* and *up* are intensifiers in the phrases *awfully sorry* and *cluttered up* **3** a substance, esp one containing silver or uranium, used to increase the density of a photographic film or plate. Compare **reducer** (sense 1)

intensify (ɪn'tɛnsɪˌfaɪ) *vb* -fies, -fying, -fied **1** to make or become intense or more intense **2** (*tr*) to increase the density of (a photographic film or plate) ▷ inˌtensifi'cation *n*

intension (ɪn'tɛnʃən) *n* **1** *logic* **a** the set of characteristics or properties by which the referent or referents of a given word are determined: thus, the intension of *marsupial* is the set containing the characteristics *suckling its young* and *having a pouch*. Compare **extension** (sense 11a) **b** See **subjective intension** a rare word for **intensity, determination** or **intensification**

intensional (ɪn'tɛnʃənʰl) *adj logic* (of a predicate) incapable of explanation solely in terms of the set of objects to which it is applicable; requiring explanation in terms of meaning or understanding. Compare **extensional** See also **opaque context, Electra paradox.** > in'tensionally *adv*

intensional object *n logic, philosophy* the object of a propositional attitude that may or may not exist, as in *Robert is dreaming of the pot of gold at the end of the rainbow*. This must be an intensional (or opaque) context, for otherwise, since there is no pot of gold, Robert would be dreaming of nothing

intensity (ɪn'tɛnsɪtɪ) *n, pl* **-ties 1** the state or quality of being intense **2** extreme force, degree, or amount **3** *physics* a measure of field strength or of the energy transmitted by radiation. See **radiant intensity, luminous intensity b** (of sound in a specified direction) the average rate of flow of sound energy, usually in watts, for one period through unit area at right angles to the specified direction. Symbol: *I* **4** Also called: **earthquake intensity** *geology* a measure of the size of an earthquake based on observation of the effects of the shock at the earth's surface. Specified on the Mercalli scale. See **Mercalli scale, Richter scale**

intensive (ɪn'tɛnsɪv) *adj* **1** involving the maximum use of land, time, or some other resource: *intensive agriculture; an intensive course* **2** (*usually in combination*) using one factor of production proportionately more than others, as specified: *capital-intensive; labour-intensive* **3** *agriculture* involving or farmed using large amounts of capital or labour to increase production from a particular area. Compare **extensive** (sense 3) **4** denoting or relating to a grammatical intensifier **5** denoting or belonging to a class of pronouns used to emphasize a noun or personal pronoun, such as *himself* in the sentence *John himself did it*. In English, intensive pronouns are identical in form with reflexive pronouns **6** of or relating to intension **7** *physics* of or relating to a local property, measurement, etc, that is independent of the extent of the system. Compare **extensive** (sense 4) ▷ *n* **8** an intensifier or intensive pronoun or grammatical construction > in'tensively *adv* > in'tensiveness *n*

intensive care *n* extensive and continuous care and treatment provided for an acutely ill patient, usually in a specially designated section (**intensive care unit**) of a hospital

intent (ɪn'tɛnt) *n* **1** something that is intended; aim; purpose; design **2** the act of intending **3** *law* the will or purpose with which one does an act **4** implicit meaning; connotation **5 to all intents and purposes** for all practical purposes; virtually ▷ *adj* **6** firmly fixed; determined; concentrated **7** (*postpositive; usually foll by on or upon*) having the fixed intention (of); directing one's mind or energy (to) [C13 (in the sense: intention): from Late Latin *intentus* aim, intent, from Latin: a stretching out; see INTEND] > in'tently *adv* > in'tentness *n*

intention (ɪn'tɛnʃən) *n* **1** a purpose or goal; aim: *it is his intention to reform* **2** *law* the resolve or design with which a person does or refrains from doing an act, a necessary ingredient of certain offences **3** *med* a natural healing process, as by **first intention**, in which the edges of a wound cling together with no tissue between, or by **second intention**, in which the wound edges adhere with granulation tissue **4** (*usually plural*) design or purpose with respect to a proposal of marriage (esp in the phrase **honourable intentions**) **5** an archaic word for **meaning** or **intentness**

intentional (ɪn'tɛnʃənᵊl) *adj* **1** performed by or expressing intention; deliberate **2** of or relating to intention or purpose **3** *philosophy* **a** of or relating to the capacity of the mind to refer to different kinds of objects **b** (of an object) existing only as the object of some mental attitude rather than in reality, as *a unicorn* in *she hopes to meet a unicorn*. See also **intensional.** > in,tention'ality *n* > in'tentionally *adv*

inter (ɪn'tɜː) *vb* **-ters, -terring, -terred** (*tr*) to place (a body) in the earth; bury, esp with funeral rites [C14 from Old French *enterrer*, from Latin IN-² + *terra* earth]

inter. *abbreviation for* intermediate

inter- *prefix* **1** between or among: *international* **2** together, mutually, or reciprocally: *interdependent; interchange* [from Latin]

interact (ˌɪntər'ækt) *vb* (*intr*) to act on or in close relation with each other

Interact ('ɪntərˌækt) *n Canadian* a system of electronic bank payments or withdrawals

interaction (ˌɪntər'ækʃən) *n* **1** a mutual or reciprocal action or influence **2** *physics* the transfer of energy between elementary particles, between a particle and a field, or between fields. See **strong interaction, electromagnetic interaction, fundamental interaction, gravitational interaction, weak interaction, electroweak interaction.** > ,inter'actional *adj*

interactionism (ˌɪntər'ækʃəˌnɪzəm) *n philosophy* the dualistic doctrine that holds that mind and body have a causal effect upon one another, as when pricking one's finger (physical) causes pain (mental), or an embarrassing memory (mental) causes one to blush (physical). Compare **parallelism** (sense 3)

interactive (ˌɪntər'æktɪv) *adj* **1** allowing or relating to continuous two-way transfer of information between a user and the central point of a communication system, such as a computer or television **2** (of two or more persons, forces, etc) acting upon or in close relation with each other; interacting > ,interac'tivity *n*

interactive engineering *n* another name for **concurrent engineering**

interactive video *n* a computer-optical disk system that displays still or moving video images as determined by computer program and user needs

inter alia *Latin* ('ɪntər 'eɪlɪə) *adv* among other things

inter alios *Latin* ('ɪntər 'eɪlɪəʊs) *adv* among other people

interatomic (ˌɪntərə'tɒmɪk) *adj* existing or occurring between or among atoms. Compare **intra-atomic**

interbank (ɪntə'bæŋk) *adj* conducted between or involving two or more banks

interbedded (ˌɪntə'bɛdɪd) *adj geology* occurring between beds, esp (of lava flows or sills) occurring between strata of a different origin or character

interbrain ('ɪntəˌbreɪn) *n anatomy* a nontechnical word for **diencephalon**

interbreed (ˌɪntə'briːd) *vb* **-breeds, -breeding, -bred 1** (*intr*) to breed within a single family or strain so as to produce particular characteristics in the offspring **2** another term for **crossbreed** (sense 1)

interbroker dealer (ˌɪntə'brəʊkə) *n stock exchange* a specialist who matches the needs of different market makers and facilitates dealings between them

intercalary (ɪn'tɜːkələrɪ) *adj* **1** (of a day, month, etc) inserted in the calendar **2** (of a particular year) having one or more days inserted **3** inserted, introduced, or interpolated **4** *botany* growing between the upper branches and the lower branches or bracts on a stem [C17 from Latin *intercalārius*; see INTERCALATE] > in'tercalarily *adv*

intercalate (ɪn'tɜːkəˌleɪt) *vb* (*tr*) **1** to insert (one or more days) into the calendar **2** to interpolate or insert [C17 from Latin *intercalāre* to insert, proclaim that a day has been inserted, from INTER- + *calāre* to proclaim] > in,terca'lation *n* > in'tercalative *adj*

intercede (ˌɪntə'siːd) *vb* (*intr*) **1** (often foll by *in*) to come between parties or act as mediator or advocate: *to intercede in the strike* **2** *Roman history* (of a tribune or other magistrate) to interpose a veto [C16 from Latin *intercēdere* to intervene, from INTER- + *cēdere* to move] > ,inter'ceder *n*

intercellular (ˌɪntə'sɛljʊlə) *adj biology* between or among cells: *intercellular fluid*

intercensal (ˌɪntə'sɛnsəl) *adj* (of population figures, etc) estimated at a time between official censuses [C19 from INTER- + *censal*, irregularly formed from CENSUS]

intercept *vb* (ˌɪntə'sɛpt) (*tr*) **1** to stop, deflect, or seize on the way from one place to another; prevent from arriving or proceeding **2** *sport* to seize or cut off (a pass) on its way from one opponent to another **3** *maths* to cut off, mark off, or bound (some part of a line, curve, plane, or surface) ▷ *n* ('ɪntəˌsɛpt) **4** *maths* **a** a point at which two figures intersect **b** the distance from the origin to the point at which a line, curve, or surface cuts a coordinate axis **c** an intercepted segment **5** *sport, US and Canadian* the act of intercepting an opponent's pass [C16 from Latin *intercipere* to seize before arrival, from INTER- + *capere* to take] > ,inter'ception *n* > ,inter'ceptive *adj*

interceptor *or* **intercepter** (ˌɪntə'sɛptə) *n* **1** a person or thing that intercepts **2** a fast highly manoeuvrable fighter aircraft used to intercept enemy aircraft

intercession (ˌɪntə'sɛʃən) *n* **1** the act or an instance of interceding **2** the act of interceding or offering petitionary prayer to God on behalf of others **3** such petitionary prayer **4** *Roman history* the interposing of a veto by a tribune or other magistrate [C16 from Latin *intercessio; see* INTERCEDE] > ,inter'cessional *or* ,inter'cessory *adj* > ,inter'cessor *n* > ,interces'sorial *adj*

interchange *vb* (ˌɪntə'tʃeɪndʒ) **1** to change places or cause to change places; alternate; exchange; switch ▷ *n* ('ɪntəˌtʃeɪndʒ) **2** the act of interchanging; exchange or alternation **3** a motorway junction of interconnecting roads and bridges designed to prevent streams of traffic crossing one another > ,inter'changeable *adj* > ,inter,changea'bility *or* ,inter'changeableness *n* > ,inter'changeably *adv*

Intercity (ˌɪntə'sɪtɪ) *adj trademark* (in Britain) denoting a fast train or passenger rail service, esp between main towns

interclavicle (ˌɪntə'klævɪkᵊl) *n* a membrane bone between and beneath the clavicles, present in some fossil amphibians, all reptiles except snakes, and monotremes > **interclavicular** (ˌɪntəklə'vɪkjʊlə) *adj*

interclub (ɪntə'klʌb) *adj* of, relating to, or conducted between two or more clubs

intercollegiate (ˌɪntəkə'liːdʒɪt) *adj* of, relating to, or conducted between two or more colleges or universities

intercolumniation (ˌɪntəkəˌlʌmnɪ'eɪʃən) *n architect* **1** the horizontal distance between two adjacent columns **2** the system of spacing for a set of columns [C17 from Latin *intercolumnium* space between two columns] > ,interco'lumnar *adj*

intercom ('ɪntəˌkɒm) *n informal* an internal telephone system for communicating within a building, an aircraft, etc [C20 short for *intercommunication*]

intercommunicate (ˌɪntəkə'mjuːnɪˌkeɪt) *vb* (*intr*) **1** to communicate mutually **2** to interconnect, as two rooms > ,intercom'municable *adj* > ,intercom,munica'bility *n* > ,intercom,muni'cation *n* > ,intercom'municative *adj* > ,intercom'muni,cator *n*

intercommunion (ˌɪntəkə'mjuːnjən) *n* association between Churches, involving esp mutual reception of Holy Communion

intercompany (ˌɪntə'kʌmpənɪ) *adj* conducted between or involving two or more companies

interconnect (ˌɪntəkə'nɛkt) *vb* (*intr; often foll by with*) **1** to relate well **2** to be meaningfully or complexly related or joined ▷ *n* **3 a** a device that connects things **b** (*as modifier*): *interconnect cable* > ,intercon'nection *n*

intercontinental (ˌɪntəˌkɒntɪ'nɛntᵊl) *adj* relating to travel, commerce, relations, etc, between continents

intercontinental ballistic missile

i

(ˌɪntəˌkɒntɪˈnɛntəl) *n* a missile that follows a ballistic trajectory and has the range to carry a nuclear bomb over 5500 km. Abbreviation: **ICBM**

interconversion (ˌɪntəkənˈvɜːʃən) *n* a process in which two things are each converted into the other, often as the result of chemical or physical activity

intercooler (ˌɪntəˈkuːlə) *n* a heat exchanger used in a supercharger or turbocharger

intercostal (ˌɪntəˈkɒstəl) *adj anatomy* between the ribs: *intercostal muscles* [c16 via New Latin from Latin INTER- + *costa* rib]

intercounty (ˌɪntəˈkaʊntɪ) *adj* conducted between or involving two or more counties: *intercounty football*

intercourse (ˈɪntəˌkɔːs) *n* **1** communication or exchange between individuals; mutual dealings **2** See **sexual intercourse** [c15 from Medieval Latin *intercursus* business, from Latin *intercurrere* to run between, from *currere* to run]

intercrop (ˌɪntəˈkrɒp) *n* **1** a crop grown between the rows of another crop ▷ *vb* **-crops, -cropping, -cropped 2** to grow (one crop) between the rows of (another)

intercross (ˌɪntəˈkrɒs) *vb, n* another word for **crossbreed**

intercurrent (ˌɪntəˈkʌrənt) *adj* **1** occurring during or in between; intervening **2** *pathol* (of a disease) occurring during the course of another disease > ˌinterˈcurrence *n* > ˌinterˈcurrently *adv*

intercut (ˌɪntəˈkʌt) *vb* **-cuts, -cutting, -cut** *films* another word for **crosscut**

interdental (ˌɪntəˈdɛntəl) *adj* **1** situated between teeth **2** *phonetics* (of a consonant) pronounced with the tip of the tongue lying between the upper and lower front teeth, as for the *th* sounds in English *thin* and *then* > ˌinterˈdentally *adv*

interdepartmental (ˌɪntəˌdiːpɑːˈtmɛntəl) *adj* of, relating to, or conducted between two or more departments

interdependence (ˌɪntədɪˈpɛndəns) *n* dependence between two or more people, groups, or things > ˌinterdeˈpendency *n*

interdependent (ˌɪntədɪˈpɛndənt) *adj* relating to two or more people or things dependent on each other

interdict *n* (ˈɪntəˌdɪkt, -ˌdaɪt) **1** *RC Church* the exclusion of a person or all persons in a particular place from certain sacraments and other benefits, although not from communion **2** *civil law* any order made by a court or official prohibiting an act **3** *Scots law* an order having the effect of an injunction **4** *Roman history* **a** an order of a praetor commanding or forbidding an act **b** the procedure by which this order was sought ▷ *vb* (ˌɪntəˈdɪkt, -ˈdaɪt) (*tr*) **5** to place under legal or ecclesiastical sanction; prohibit; forbid **6** *military* to destroy (an enemy's lines of communication) by firepower [c13 from Latin *interdictum* prohibition, from *interdīcere* to forbid, from INTER- + *dīcere* to say] > ˌinterˈdictive *or* ˌinterˈdictory *adj* > ˌinterˈdictively *adv* > ˌinterˈdictor *n*

interdiction (ˌɪntəˈdɪkʃən) *n* **1** the act of interdicting or state of being interdicted **2** an interdict

interdict list *n* another name for **Indian list**

interdigitate (ˌɪntəˈdɪdʒɪˌteɪt) *vb* (*intr*) to interlock like the fingers of clasped hands [c19 from INTER- + Latin *digitus* (see DIGIT) + -ATE[1]]

interdisciplinary (ˌɪntəˈdɪsɪˌplɪnərɪ) *adj* involving two or more academic disciplines

interest (ˈɪntrɪst, -tərɪst) *n* **1** the sense of curiosity about or concern with something or someone **2** the power of stimulating such a sense **3** the quality of such stimulation **4** something in which one is interested; a hobby or pursuit **5** (*often plural*) benefit; advantage **6** (*often plural*) **a** a right, share, or claim, esp in a business or property **b** the business, property, etc, in which a person has such concern **7 a** a charge for the use of credit or borrowed money **b** such a charge expressed as a percentage per time unit of the

sum borrowed or used **8** (*often plural*) a section of a community, etc, whose members have common aims **9 declare an interest** to make known one's connection, esp a prejudicial connection, with an affair ▷ *vb* (*tr*) **10** to arouse or excite the curiosity or concern of **11** to cause to become involved in something; concern [c15 from Latin: it concerns, from *interesse*; from INTER- + *esse* to be]

interested (ˈɪntrɪstɪd, -tərɪs-) *adj* **1** showing or having interest **2** (*usually prenominal*) personally involved or implicated > ˈinterestedly *adv* > ˈinterestedness *n*

interesting (ˈɪntrɪstɪŋ, -tərɪs-) *adj* inspiring interest; absorbing > ˈinterestingly *adv* > ˈinterestingness *n*

interest-rate futures *pl n* financial futures based on projected movements of interest rates

interface *n* (ˈɪntəˌfeɪs) **1** *chem* a surface that forms the boundary between two bodies, liquids, or chemical phases **2** a common point or boundary between two things, subjects, etc **3** an electrical circuit linking one device, esp a computer, with another ▷ *vb* (ˌɪntəˈfeɪs) **4** (*tr*) to design or adapt the input and output configurations of (two electronic devices) so that they may work together compatibly **5** to be or become an interface (with) **6** to become interactive (with) > **interfacial** (ˌɪntəˈfeɪʃəl) *adj* > ˌinterˈfacially *adv*

interfacing (ˈɪntəˌfeɪsɪŋ) *n* **1** a piece of fabric sewn beneath the facing of a garment, usually at the inside of the neck, armholes, etc, to give shape and firmness **2** another name for **interlining**

interfaith (ˌɪntəˈfeɪθ) *adj* relating to, between, or involving different religions

interfascicular (ˌɪntəfəˈsɪkjʊlə) *adj botany* between the vascular bundles of the stem

interfere (ˌɪntəˈfɪə) *vb* (*intr*) **1** (*often foll by in*) to interpose, esp meddlesomely or unwarrantedly; intervene **2** (*often foll by with*) to come between or in opposition; hinder; obstruct **3** (*foll by with*) *euphemistic* to assault sexually **4** to strike one against the other, as a horse's legs **5** *physics* to cause or produce interference [c16 from Old French *s'entreferir* to collide, from *entre-* INTER- + *ferir* to strike, from Latin *ferīre*] > ˌinterˈferer *n* > ˌinterˈfering *adj* > ˌinterˈferingly *adv*

interference (ˌɪntəˈfɪərəns) *n* **1** the act or an instance of interfering **2** *physics* the process in which two or more coherent waves combine to form a resultant wave in which the displacement at any point is the vector sum of the displacements of the individual waves. If the individual waves converge the resultant is a system of fringes. Two waves of equal or nearly equal intensity moving in opposite directions combine to form a standing wave **3** Also called: **radio interference** any undesired signal that tends to interfere with the reception of radio waves **4** *aeronautics* the effect on the flow pattern around a body of objects in the vicinity > **interferential** (ˌɪntəfəˈrɛnʃəl) *adj*

interference fit *n engineering* a match between the size and shape of two parts, such that force is required for assembly as one part is slightly larger than the other

interferometer (ˌɪntəfəˈrɒmɪtə) *n* **1** *physics* any acoustic, optical, or microwave instrument that uses interference patterns or fringes to make accurate measurements of wavelength, wave velocity, distance, etc **2** *astronomy* a radio or optical array consisting of two or more telescopes separated by a known distance and connected so that the radiation from a source in space undergoes interference, enabling the source to be imaged or the position of the source to be accurately determined > **interferometric** (ˌɪntəˌfɛrəˈmɛtrɪk) *adj* > ˌinterˌferoˈmetrically *adv* > ˌinterferˈometry *n*

interferon (ˌɪntəˈfɪərɒn) *n biochem* any of a family of proteins made by cells in response to virus infection that prevent the growth of the virus.

Some interferons can prevent cell growth and have been tested for use in cancer therapy [c20 from INTERFERE + -ON]

interfertile (ˌɪntəˈfɜːtaɪl) *adj* (of plants and animals) able to interbreed > ˌinterferˈtility *n*

interfile (ˌɪntəˈfaɪl) *vb* (*tr*) **1** to place (one or more items) among other items in a file or arrangement **2** to combine (two or more sets of items) in one file or arrangement

interflow (ˌɪntəˈfləʊ) *vb* (*intr*) to flow together; merge

interfluent (ɪnˈtɜːflʊənt) *adj* flowing together; merging [c17 from Latin *interfluere*, from INTER- + *fluere* to flow]

interfluve (ˈɪntəˌfluːv) *n* a ridge or area of land dividing two river valleys [c20 back formation from *interfluvial*, from INTER- + Latin *fluvius* river] > ˌinterˈfluvial *adj*

interfuse (ˌɪntəˈfjuːz) *vb* **1** to diffuse or mix throughout or become so diffused or mixed; intermingle **2** to blend or fuse or become blended or fused > ˌinterˈfusion *n*

intergalactic (ˌɪntəgəˈlæktɪk) *adj* of, relating to, or existing between two or more galaxies

intergenerational mobility (ˌɪntəˌdʒɛnəˈreɪʃənəl) *n sociol* movement within or between social classes and occupations, the change occurring from one generation to the next. Compare **intragenerational mobility**

interglacial (ˌɪntəˈgleɪsɪəl, -ʃəl) *adj* **1** occurring or formed between periods of glacial action ▷ *n* **2** a period of comparatively warm climate between two glaciations, esp of the Pleistocene epoch

intergovernmental (ˌɪntəˌgʌvəˈmɛntəl) *adj* conducted between or involving two or more governments: *an intergovernmental conference*

intergrade *vb* (ˌɪntəˈgreɪd) **1** (*intr*) (esp of biological species, etc) to merge one into another ▷ *n* (ˈɪntəˌgreɪd) **2** an intermediate stage or form > ˌintergraˈdation *n* > ˌintergraˈdational *adj* > ˌinterˈgradient *adj*

interim (ˈɪntərɪm) *adj* **1** (*prenominal*) temporary, provisional, or intervening ▷ *n* **2** (*usually preceded by the*) the intervening time; the meantime (esp in the phrase **in the interim**) ▷ *adv* **3** *rare* meantime [c16 from Latin: meanwhile]

Interim (ˈɪntərɪm) *n* any of three provisional arrangements made during the Reformation by the German emperor and Diet to regulate religious differences between Roman Catholics and Protestants

Interim Standard Atmosphere *n* an agreed theoretical description of the atmosphere for altitudes between 50 and 80 km, pending refinement by further measurements. See **International Standard Atmosphere**

interior (ɪnˈtɪərɪə) *n* **1** a part, surface, or region that is inside or on the inside: *the interior of Africa* **2** inner character or nature **3** a film or scene shot inside a building, studio, etc **4** a picture of the inside of a room or building, as in a painting or stage design **5** the inside of a building or room, with respect to design and decoration ▷ *adj* **6** of, situated on, or suitable for the inside; inner **7** coming or acting from within; internal **8** of or involving a nation's domestic affairs; internal **9** (esp of one's spiritual or mental life) secret or private; not observable [c15 from Latin (adj), comparative of *inter* within] > inˈteriorly *adv*

Interior (ɪnˈtɪərɪə) *n* (*in titles*; usually preceded by *the*) the domestic or internal affairs of any of certain countries: *Department of the Interior*

interior angle *n* **1** an angle of a polygon contained between two adjacent sides **2** any of the four angles made by a transversal that lie inside the region between the two intersected lines

interior decoration *n* **1** the colours, furniture, etc, of the interior of a house, etc **2** Also called: **interior design** the art or business of an interior decorator

interior decorator *n* **1** Also called: **interior**

designer a person whose profession is the planning of the decoration and furnishings of the interior of houses, shops, etc **2** a person whose profession is the painting and wallpapering of houses

interiority (ɪnˌtɪərɪˈɒrɪtɪ) *n* the quality of being focused on one's inner life and identity

interiorize *or* **Interiorise** (ɪnˈtɪərɪəˌraɪz) *vb* (*tr*) another word for **internalize**

interior monologue *n* a literary attempt to present the mental processes of a character before they are formed into regular patterns of speech or logical sequence. See also **stream of consciousness**

interior-sprung *adj* (esp of a mattress) containing springs

interj. *abbreviation for* interjection

interjacent (ˌɪntəˈdʒeɪsⁿnt) *adj* located in between; intervening [c16 from Latin *interjacēnt-*, from INTER- + *jacēre* to lie]

interject (ˌɪntəˈdʒɛkt) *vb* (*tr*) **1** to interpose abruptly or sharply; interrupt with; throw in: *she interjected clever remarks* **2** *archaic* to come between; interpose [c16 from Latin *interjicere* to place between, from *jacere* to throw] > ˌinterˈjector *n*

interjection (ˌɪntəˈdʒɛkʃən) *n* **1** a word or remark expressing emotion; exclamation **2** the act of interjecting **3** a word or phrase that is characteristically used in syntactic isolation and that usually expresses sudden emotion; expletive. Abbreviation: interj. > ˌinterˈjectional, ˌinterˈjectory *or* ˌinterˈjectural *adj* > ˌinterˈjectionally *adv*

interlace (ˌIntəˈleɪs) *vb* **1** to join together (patterns, fingers, etc) by crossing, as if woven; intertwine **2** (*tr*) to mingle or blend in an intricate way **3** (*tr*; usually foll by *with*) to change the pattern of; diversify; intersperse > interlacedly (ˌɪntəˈleɪsɪdlɪ) *adv* > ˌinterˈlacement *n*

interlaced scanning *n* a system of scanning a television picture, first along the even-numbered lines, then along the odd-numbered lines, in one complete scan

Interlaken (ˈɪntəˌlɑːkən) *n* a town and resort in central Switzerland, situated between Lakes Brienz and Thun on the River Aar. Pop: 5119 (2000)

interlaminate (ˌɪntəˈlæmɪˌneɪt) *vb* (*tr*) to place, stick, or insert (a sheet, layer, etc) between (other layers) > ˌinterˈlaminar *adj* > ˌinterˌlamiˈnation *n*

interlap (ˌɪntəˈlæp) *vb* -laps, -lapping, -lapped a less common word for **overlap**

interlard (ˌɪntəˈlɑːd) *vb* (*tr*) **1** to scatter thickly in or between; intersperse **2** to occur frequently in; be scattered in or through

interlay *vb* (ˌɪntəˈleɪ) -lays, -laying, -laid (-ˈleɪd) **1** (*tr*) to insert (layers) between; interpose: *to interlay gold among the silver; to interlay the silver with gold* ▷ *n* (ˈɪntəˌleɪ) **2** material, such as paper, placed between a printing plate and its base, either all over in order to bring it up to type height, or in places in order to achieve the correct printing pressure all over the plate

interleaf (ˈɪntəˌliːf) *n, pl* -leaves a blank leaf inserted between the leaves of a book

interleave (ˌɪntəˈliːv) *vb* (*tr*) **1** (often foll by *with*) to interpose (with), esp alternately, as the illustrations in a book (with protective leaves) **2** to provide (a book) with blank leaves for notes, etc, or to protect illustrations

interleukin (ˌɪntəˈluːkɪn) *n* a substance extracted from white blood cells that stimulates their activity against infection and may be used to combat some forms of cancer

interlibrary loan (ˌɪntəˈlaɪbrərɪ) *n* **1** a system by which libraries borrow publications from other libraries **2 a** an instance of such borrowing **b** a publication so borrowed

interline¹ (ˌɪntəˈlaɪn), **interlineate** (ˌɪntəˈlɪnɪˌeɪt) *vb* (*tr*) to write or print (matter) between the lines of (a text, book, etc) > ˌinterˈlining *or* ˌinterˌlineˈation *n*

interline² (ˌɪntəˈlaɪn) *vb* (*tr*) to provide (a part of a garment, such as a collar or cuff) with a second

lining, esp stiffened material > ˈinterˌliner *n*

interlinear (ˌɪntəˈlɪnɪə) *or* **interlineal** *adj* **1** written or printed between lines of text **2** written or printed with the text in different languages or versions on alternate lines > ˌinterˈlinearly *or* ˌinterˈlineally *adv*

interlinear spacing *adv, n* See **leading²**

interlingua (ˌɪntəˈlɪŋgwə) *n* **1** (*usually capital*) an artificial language based on words common to English and the Romance languages **2** any artificial language used to represent the meaning of natural languages, as for purposes of machine translation [c20 from Italian, from INTER- + *lingua* language]

interlining (ˈɪntəˌlaɪnɪŋ) *n* the material used to interline parts of garments, now often made of reinforced paper

interlock *vb* (ˌɪntəˈlɒk) **1** to join or be joined firmly, as by a mutual interconnection of parts ▷ *n* (ˈɪntəˌlɒk) **2** the act of interlocking or the state of being interlocked **3** a device, esp one operated electromechanically, used in a logic circuit or electrical safety system to prevent an activity being initiated unless preceded by certain events **4** a closely knitted fabric ▷ *adj* (ˈɪntəˌlɒk) **5** (of fabric) closely knitted > ˈinterˌlocker *n*

interlocking directorates *pl n* boards of directors of different companies having sufficient members in common to ensure that the companies involved are under the same control

interlocution (ˌɪntələˈkjuːʃən) *n* conversation, discussion, or dialogue

interlocutor (ˌɪntəˈlɒkjʊtə) *n* **1** a person who takes part in a conversation **2** Also called: **middleman** the man in the centre of a troupe of minstrels who engages the others in talk or acts as announcer **3** *Scots law* a decree by a judge > ˌinterˈlocutress, ˌinterˈlocutrice *or* ˌinterˈlocutrix *fem n*

interlocutory (ˌɪntəˈlɒkjʊtərɪ, -trɪ) *adj* **1** *law* pronounced during the course of proceedings; provisional **2** interposed, as into a conversation, narrative, etc **3** of, relating to, or characteristic of dialogue > ˌinterˈlocutorily *adv*

interloper (ˈɪntəˌləʊpə) *n* **1** an intruder **2** a person who introduces himself into professional or social circles where he does not belong **3** a person who interferes in matters that are not his concern **4** a person who trades unlawfully [c17 from INTER- + *loper*, from Middle Dutch *loopen* to leap]

interlude (ˈɪntəˌluːd) *n* **1** a period of time or different activity between longer periods, processes, or events; episode or interval **2** *theatre* a short dramatic piece played separately or as part of a longer entertainment, common in 16th-century England **3** a brief piece of music, dance, etc, given between the sections of another performance [c14 from Medieval Latin *interlūdium*, from Latin INTER- + *lūdus* play]

interlunation (ˌɪntəlʊˈneɪʃən) *n* the period between the old and new moons during which the moon is invisible. See **new moon** > ˌinterˈlunar *adj*

intermarry (ˌɪntəˈmærɪ) *vb* -ries, -rying, -ried (*intr*) **1** (of different groups, races, religions, creeds, etc) to become connected by marriage **2** to marry within one's own family, clan, group, etc > ˌinterˈmarriage *n*

intermeddle (ˌɪntəˈmɛdəl) *vb* (*intr*) *rare* another word for **meddle** [c14 *entremedle*, from Anglo-Norman *entremedler*, from Old French; see INTER- + MEDDLE]

intermediary (ˌɪntəˈmiːdɪərɪ) *n, pl* -aries **1** a person who acts as a mediator or agent between parties **2** something that acts as a medium or means **3** an intermediate state or period ▷ *adj* **4** acting as an intermediary **5** situated, acting, or coming between; intermediate

intermediate *adj* (ˌɪntəˈmiːdɪɪt) **1** occurring or situated between two points, extremes, places, etc; in between **2** (of a class, course, etc) suitable

for learners with some degree of skill or competence **3** *physics* (of a neutron) having an energy between 100 and 100 000 electronvolts **4** *geology* (of such igneous rocks as syenite) containing between 55 and 66 per cent silica ▷ *n* (ˌɪntəˈmiːdɪɪt) **5** something intermediate **6** a substance formed during one of the stages of a chemical process before the desired product is obtained ▷ *vb* (ˌɪntəˈmiːdɪˌeɪt) **7** (*intr*) to act as an intermediary or mediator [c17 from Medieval Latin *intermediāre* to intervene, from Latin INTER- + *medius* middle] > ˌinterˈmediacy *or* ˌinterˈmediateness *n* > ˌinterˈmediately *adv* > ˌinterˌmediˈation *n* > ˌinterˈmediˌator *n*

intermediate-acting *adj* (of a drug) intermediate in its effects between long- and short-acting drugs. Compare **long-acting, short-acting**

intermediate care facility *n* US a medical facility that provides institutional health care services but not to the degree of those provided by a hospital. Abbreviation: ICF

intermediate frequency *n* *electronics* the frequency to which the signal carrier frequency is changed in a superheterodyne receiver and at which most of the amplification takes place

intermediate host *n* an animal that acts as host to a parasite that has not yet become sexually mature

intermediate-level waste *n* radioactive waste material, such as reactor and processing-plant components, that is solidified before being mixed with concrete and stored in steel drums in deep mines or beneath the seabed in concrete chambers. Compare **high-level waste, low-level waste**

intermediate range ballistic missile *n* a missile that follows a ballistic trajectory with a medium range, normally of the order of 750–1500 miles. Abbreviation: IRBM

intermediate school *n* NZ a school for children aged between 11 and 13

intermediate technology *n* technology which combines sophisticated ideas with cheap and readily available materials, especially for use in developing countries

intermediate treatment *n* *social welfare* a form of child care for young people in trouble that involves neither custody nor punishment and provides opportunities to learn constructive patterns of behaviour to replace potentially criminal ones

intermediate vector boson *n* *physics* a hypothetical particle believed to mediate the weak interaction between elementary particles

interment (ɪnˈtɜːmənt) *n* burial, esp with ceremonial rites

intermezzo (ˌɪntəˈmɛtsəʊ) *n, pl* -zos *or* -zi (-tsiː) **1** a short piece of instrumental music composed for performance between the acts or scenes of an opera, drama, etc **2** an instrumental piece either inserted between two longer movements in an extended composition or intended for independent performance **3** another name for **interlude** (sense 3) [c19 from Italian, from Late Latin *intermedium* interval; see INTERMEDIATE]

intermigration (ˌɪntəmaɪˈgreɪʃən) *n* migration between two groups of people, animals, etc, resulting in an exchange of habitat

interminable (ɪnˈtɜːmɪnəbəl) *adj* endless or seemingly endless because of monotony or tiresome length > inˌterminaˈbility *or* inˈterminableness *n* > inˈterminably *adv*

intermingle (ˌɪntəˈmɪŋgəl) *vb* to mix or cause to mix or mingle together

intermission (ˌɪntəˈmɪʃən) *n* **1** an interval, as between parts of a film **2** a period between events or activities; pause **3** the act of intermitting or the state of being intermitted [c16 from Latin *intermissiō*, from *intermittere* to leave off, INTERMIT] > ˌinterˈmissive *adj*

intermit (ˌɪntəˈmɪt) *vb* -mits, -mitting, -mitted to

i

suspend (activity) or (of activity) to be suspended temporarily or at intervals [c16 from Latin *intermittere* to leave off, from INTER- + *mittere* to send] > ˌinterˈmittingly *adv* > ˌinterˈmittor *n*

intermittent (ˌɪntəˈmɪtᵊnt) *adj* occurring occasionally or at regular or irregular intervals; periodic > ˌinterˈmittence *or* ˌinterˈmittency *n* > ˌinterˈmittently *adv*

intermittent claudication *n pathol* pain and cramp in the calf muscles, aggravated by walking and caused by an insufficient supply of blood

intermittent fever *n* any fever, such as malaria, characterized by intervals of periodic remission

intermixture (ˌɪntəˈmɪkstʃə) *n* **1** the act of intermixing or state of being intermixed **2** another word for **mixture 3** an additional constituent or ingredient

intermodal (ˌɪntəˈməʊdᵊl) *adj* **1** (of a transport system) using different modes of conveyance in conjunction, such as ships, aircraft, road vehicles, etc **2** (of a container) able to be carried by different modes of conveyance without being unpacked **3** *psychol* denoting an interaction between different senses

intermodulation (ˈɪntəˌmɒdjʊˈleɪʃən) *n electronics* **a** interaction between two signals in electronic apparatus such that each affects the amplitude of the other **b** (*as modifier*): *intermodulation distortion*

intermolecular (ˌɪntəməˈlɛkjʊlə) *adj* occurring among or between molecules

intermontane (ˌɪntəmɒnˈteɪn) *adj* occurring or situated between mountain ranges

intern *vb* **1** (ɪnˈtɜːn) (*tr*) to detain or confine (foreign or enemy citizens, ships, etc), esp during wartime **2** (ˈɪntɜːn) (*intr*) *chiefly US* to serve or train as an intern > *n* (ˈɪntɜːn) **3** another word for **internee 4** *Also:* **interne** *med, US and Canadian* a graduate in the first year of practical training after medical school, resident in a hospital and under supervision by senior doctors. British equivalent: house officer **5** *chiefly US* a student teacher **6** *chiefly US* a student or recent graduate receiving practical training in a working environment > *adj* (ɪnˈtɜːn) **7** an archaic word for **internal** [c19 from Latin *internus* internal]

internal (ɪnˈtɜːnᵊl) *adj* **1** of, situated on, or suitable for the inside; inner **2** coming or acting from within; interior **3** involving the spiritual or mental life; subjective **4** of or involving a nation's domestic as opposed to foreign affairs **5** *education* denoting assessment by examiners who are employed at the candidate's place of study **6** situated within, affecting, or relating to the inside of the body > *n* **7** a medical examination of the vagina, uterus, or rectum [c16 from Medieval Latin *internālis*, from Late Latin *internus* inward] > ˌinterˈnality *or* inˈternalness *n* > inˈternally *adv*

internal-combustion engine *n* a heat engine in which heat is supplied by burning the fuel in the working fluid (usually air)

internal ear *n* the part of the ear that consists of the cochlea, vestibule, and semicircular canals. Also called: inner ear, labyrinth

internal energy *n* the thermodynamic property of a system that changes by an amount equal to the work done on the system when it suffers an adiabatic change. It is the sum of the kinetic and potential energies of its constituent atoms, molecules, etc. Symbol: U or E

internalize *or* **internalise** (ɪnˈtɜːnəˌlaɪz) *vb* (*tr*) *psychol, sociol* to make internal, esp to incorporate within oneself (values, attitudes, etc) through learning or socialization. Compare **introject** Also: interiorize > inˌternaliˈzation *or* inˌternaliˈsation *n*

internal market *n* a system in which goods and services are sold by the provider to a range of purchasers within the same organization, who compete to establish the price of the product

internal medicine *n* the branch of medical science concerned with the diagnosis and nonsurgical treatment of disorders of the internal structures of the body

internal rate of return *n* an interest rate giving a net present value of zero when applied to the expected cash flow of a project. Its value, compared to the cost of the capital involved, is used to determine the project's viability

internal resistance *n physics* the resistance of a cell, accumulator, etc, usually given as $(E-V)/I$, where E is the emf of the cell, and V the potential difference between terminals when it is delivering a current I

internal revenue *n US* government income derived from taxes, etc, within the country

internal rhyme *n prosody* rhyme that occurs between words within a verse line

internal secretion *n physiol* a secretion, esp a hormone, that is absorbed directly into the blood

international (ˌɪntəˈnæʃənᵊl) *adj* **1** of, concerning, or involving two or more nations or nationalities **2** established by, controlling, or legislating for several nations: *an international court; international fishing rights* **3** available for use by all nations: *international waters* ▷ *n* **4** *sport* **a** a contest between two national teams **b** a member of these teams > ˌinterˈnationˈality *n* > ˌinterˈnationally *adv*

International (ˌɪntəˈnæʃənᵊl) *n* **1** any of several international socialist organizations. See **Comintern, First International, Labour and Socialist International, Second International, Socialist International, Trotskyist International, Vienna Union 2** a member of any of these organizations

International Atomic Time *n* the scientific standard of time based on the SI unit, the second, used by means of atomic clocks and satellites to synchronize the time standards of the major nations. Abbreviation: TAI

International Bank for Reconstruction and Development *n* the official name for the **World Bank** Abbreviation: IBRD

International Brigade *n* a military force that fought on the Republican side in the Spanish Civil War, consisting of volunteers (predominantly socialists and communists) from many countries

international candle *n* a former international unit of luminous intensity, originally defined in terms of a standard candle and later in terms of a pentane-burning lamp. It has now been replaced by the candela

International Court of Justice *n* a court established in the Hague to settle disputes brought by nations that are parties to the Statute of the Court. Also called: World Court

International Criminal Police Organization *n* See **Interpol**

International Date Line *n* the line approximately following the 180° meridian from Greenwich on the east side of which the date is one day earlier than on the west. Also called: date line

International Development Association *n* an organization set up in 1960 to provide low-interest loans to developing countries. It is part of the World Bank Group. Abbreviation: IDA

Internationale (ˌɪntənæʃəˈnɑːl) *n* **the** a revolutionary socialist hymn, first sung in 1871 in France [c19 shortened from French *chanson internationale* international song]

International Finance Corporation *n* an organization that invests directly in private companies and makes or guarantees loans to private investors. It is affiliated to the World Bank and is part of the World Bank Group. Abbreviation: IFC

International Geophysical Year *n* the 18-month period from July 1, 1957, to Dec 31, 1958, during which a number of nations agreed to cooperate in a geophysical research programme. Abbreviation: IGY

International Gothic *n* a style in art during the late 14th and early 15th centuries characterized by elegant stylization of illuminated manuscripts,

mosaics, stained glass, etc, and by increased interest in secular themes. Major contributors were Simone Martini, Giotto, and Pisanello

International Grandmaster *n chess* See **grandmaster** (sense 2)

internationalism (ˌɪntəˈnæʃənəˌlɪzəm) *n* **1** the ideal or practice of cooperation and understanding between nations **2** the state or quality of being international

internationalist (ˌɪntəˈnæʃənəlɪst) *n* **1** an advocate of internationalism **2** a person versed in international law **3** (*capital*) a member of an International

internationalize *or* **internationalise** (ˌɪntəˈnæʃənəˌlaɪz) *vb* (*tr*) **1** to make international **2** to put under international control > ˌinterˌnationaliˈzation *or* ˌinterˌnationaliˈsation *n*

International Joint Commission *n* a joint US–Canadian federal government agency set up in 1909 to oversee the management of shared water resources (esp the Great Lakes–St Lawrence River system)

International Labour Organisation *n* a special agency of the United Nations responsible for research and recommendations in the field of labour conditions and practices: founded in 1919 in affiliation to the League of Nations. Abbreviation: ILO

international law *n* the body of rules generally recognized by civilized nations as governing their conduct towards each other and towards each other's subjects

International Master *n chess* the second highest title awarded by the FIDE to a player: won by obtaining a certain number of points during specific international chess tournaments. Often shortened to: master Compare **grandmaster** (sense 2)

International Modernism *n* See **International Style**

International Monetary Fund *n* an international financial institution organized in 1945 to promote international trade by increasing the exchange stability of the major currencies. A fund is maintained out of which member nations with temporary balance-of-payments deficits may make withdrawals. Abbreviation: IMF

international Morse code *n* the full name for **Morse code**

international nautical mile *n* the full name for **nautical mile** (sense 1)

International Phonetic Alphabet *n* a series of signs and letters propagated by the Association Phonétique Internationale for the representation of human speech sounds. It is based on the Roman alphabet but supplemented by modified signs or symbols from other writing systems, and is usually employed in its revised form of 1951. Abbreviation: IPA

international pitch *n music* the frequency of 435 hertz assigned to the A above middle C, widely used until 1939. See **pitch**¹ (sense 28b)

International Practical Temperature Scale *n* a temperature scale adopted by international agreement in 1968, and revised in 1990, based on thermodynamic temperature and using experimental values to define 16 fixed points. The lowest is the triple point of an equilibrium mixture of orthohydrogen and parahydrogen (−259.34°C) and the highest the freezing point of copper (1084.62°C)

international screw thread *n engineering* a metric system for screw threads relating the pitch to the diameter

international sea and swell scale *n* another name for the **Douglas scale**

International Standard Atmosphere *n* a theoretical vertical distribution of the physical properties of the atmosphere up to an altitude of 50 km established by international agreement. It permits the standardization of aircraft instruments and performance of all types of flying vehicles

International Style or **Modernism** n a 20th-century architectural style characterized by undecorated rectilinear forms and the use of glass, steel, and reinforced concrete

International Telecommunications Union n a special agency of the United Nations, founded in 1947, that is responsible for the international allocation and registration of frequencies for communications and the regulation of telegraph, telephone, and radio services: originally established in 1865 as the International Telegraph Union

international telegram n a telemessage sent from the UK to a foreign country

interne ('ɪntɜːn) n a variant spelling of **intern** (sense 4)

internecine (ˌɪntəˈniːsaɪn) adj **1** mutually destructive or ruinous; maiming both or all sides: *internecine war* **2** of or relating to slaughter or carnage; bloody **3** of or involving conflict within a group or organization [c17 from Latin *internecīnus*, from *internecāre* to destroy, from *necāre* to kill]

internee (ˌɪntɜːˈniː) n a person who is interned, esp an enemy citizen in wartime or a terrorism suspect

internet ('ɪntəˌnɛt) n **the** (sometimes capital) the single worldwide computer network that interconnects other computer networks, on which end-user services, such as World Wide Web sites or data archives, are located, enabling data and other information to be exchanged. Also called: the Net

internet access provider n See **IAP**

internet service provider n See **ISP**

interneuron (ˌɪntəˈnjʊərɒn) n physiol any neuron that connects afferent and efferent neurons in a reflex arc. Also called: internuncial neuron

internist ('ɪntɜːnɪst, ɪnˈtɜːnɪst) n chiefly US a physician who specializes in internal medicine

internment (ɪnˈtɜːnmənt) n **a** the act of interning or state of being interned, esp of enemy citizens in wartime or of terrorism suspects **b** (as modifier): *an internment camp*

internode ('ɪntəˌnəʊd) n **1** the part of a plant stem between two nodes **2** the part of a nerve fibre between two nodes of Ranvier > ˌinterˈnodal adj

internship ('ɪntɜːnʃɪp) n chiefly US and Canadian the position of being an intern or the period during which a person is an intern

internuncial (ˌɪntəˈnʌnʃəl) adj **1** physiol (esp of neurons) interconnecting. See **internode** **2** of, relating to, or emanating from a papal internuncio

internuncio (ˌɪntəˈnʌnʃɪˌəʊ) n, pl -cios **1** an ambassador of the pope ranking immediately below a nuncio **2** a messenger, agent, or go-between [c17 from Italian *internunzio*, from Latin *internuntius*, from INTER- + *nuntius* messenger]

interoceptor (ˌɪntərəʊˈsɛptə) n physiol a sensory receptor of an internal organ (excluding the muscles). Compare **exteroceptor, proprioceptor** [c20 from INTER(IOR) + (RE)CEPTOR] > ˌinteroˈceptive adj

interoperable (ˌɪntərˈɒprəb'l) adj of or relating to the ability to share data between different computer systems, esp on different machines > ˌinterˌoperaˈbility n

interosculate (ˌɪntərˈɒskjʊˌleɪt) vb now rare (intr) biology (of two different species or groups of organisms) to share certain characteristics > ˌinterˌoscuˈlation n

interpage (ˌɪntəˈpeɪdʒ) vb (tr) **1** to print (matter) on intervening pages **2** to insert (intervening pages) into a book

interpellant (ˌɪntəˈpɛlənt) adj **1** causing an interpellation ▷ n **2** a deputy who interpellates

interpellate (ɪnˈtɜːpɛˌleɪt) vb (tr) parliamentary procedure (in European legislatures) to question (a member of the government) on a point of government policy, often interrupting the business of the day [c16 from Latin *interpellāre* to disturb, from INTER- + *pellere* to push] > ˌinˌterpelˈlation n > inˈterpelˌlator n

interpenetrate (ˌɪntəˈpɛnɪˌtreɪt) vb **1** to penetrate (something) thoroughly; pervade **2** to penetrate each other or one another mutually > ˌinterˈpenetrable adj > ˌinterˈpenetrant adj > ˌinterˌpeneˈtration n > ˌinterˈpenetrative adj > ˌinterˈpenetratively adv

interpersonal (ˌɪntəˈpɜːsənᵊl) adj between persons; involving personal relationships

interphase ('ɪntəˌfeɪz) n biology the period between two successive divisions of a cell

interphone ('ɪntəˌfəʊn) n a telephone system for linking different rooms within a building, ship, etc

interplanetary (ˌɪntəˈplænɪtərɪ, -trɪ) adj of, relating to, or existing between planets

interplay ('ɪntəˌpleɪ) n reciprocal and mutual action and reaction, as in circumstances, events, or personal relations

interplead (ˌɪntəˈpliːd) vb -pleads, -pleading; -pleaded, -plead (-plɛd) or -pled (intr) law to institute interpleader proceedings

interpleader (ˌɪntəˈpliːdə) n law **1** a process by which a person holding money or property claimed by two or more parties and having no interest in it himself can require the claimants to litigate with each other to determine the issue **2** a person who interpleads

Interpol ('ɪntəˌpɒl) n acronym for International Criminal Police Organization, an association of over 100 national police forces, devoted chiefly to fighting international crime

interpolate (ɪnˈtɜːpəˌleɪt) vb **1** to insert or introduce (a comment, passage, etc) into (a conversation, text, etc) **2** to falsify or alter (a text, manuscript, etc) by the later addition of (material, esp spurious or valueless passages) **3** (intr) to make additions, interruptions, or insertions **4** maths to estimate (a value of a function) between the values already known or determined. Compare **extrapolate** (sense 1) [c17 from Latin *interpolāre* to give a new appearance to, from INTER- + *polīre* to POLISH] > inˈterpoˌlater or inˈterpoˌlator n > inˈterpolative adj

interpolation (ɪnˌtɜːpəˈleɪʃən) n **1** the act of interpolating or the state of being interpolated **2** something interpolated

interpose (ˌɪntəˈpəʊz) vb **1** to put or place between or among other things **2** to introduce (comments, questions, etc) into a speech or conversation; interject **3** to exert or use power, influence, or action in order to alter or intervene in (a situation) [c16 from Old French *interposer*, from Latin *interpōnere*, from INTER- + *pōnere* to put] > ˌinterˈposable adj > ˌinterˈposal n > ˌinterˈposer n

interposition (ˌɪntəpəˈzɪʃən) n **1** something interposed **2** the act of interposing or the state of being interposed

interpret (ɪnˈtɜːprɪt) vb **1** (tr) to clarify or explain the meaning of; elucidate **2** (tr) to construe the significance or intention of: *to interpret a smile as an invitation* **3** (tr) to convey or represent the spirit or meaning of (a poem, song, etc) in performance **4** (intr) to act as an interpreter; translate orally [c14 from Latin *interpretārī*, from *interpres* negotiator, one who explains, from INTER- + *-pres*, probably related to *pretium* PRICE] > inˈterpretable adj > inˌterpretaˈbility or inˈterpretableness n > inˈterpretably adv

interpretation (ɪnˌtɜːprɪˈteɪʃən) n **1** the act or process of interpreting or explaining; elucidation **2** the result of interpreting; an explanation **3** a particular view of an artistic work, esp as expressed by stylistic individuality in its performance **4** explanation, as of the environment, a historical site, etc, provided by the use of original objects, personal experience, visual display material, etc **5** logic an allocation of significance to the terms of a purely formal system, by specifying ranges for the variables, denotations for the individual constants, etc; a function from the formal language to such elements of a possible world > inˌterpreˈtational adj

interpretative (ɪnˈtɜːprɪtətɪv) or **interpretive** (ɪnˈtɜːprɪtɪv) adj of, involving, or providing interpretation; expository > inˈterpretatively or inˈterpretively adv

interpretive centre n (at a place of interest, such as a country park, historical site, etc) a building that provides interpretation of the place of interest through a variety of media, such as video displays and exhibitions of material. Also called: visitor centre

interpretive semantics n (functioning as singular) a school of semantic theory based on the doctrine that the rules that relate sentences to their meanings form an autonomous system, separate from the rules that determine what is grammatical in a language. Compare **generative semantics**

interprovincial (ˌɪntəprəˈvɪnʃəl) adj conducted between or involving two or more provinces

interquartile range (ˌɪntəˈkwɔːtaɪl) n statistics the difference between the value of a variable below which lie 25 per cent of the population, and that below which lie 75 per cent: a measure of the spread of the distribution

interracial (ˌɪntəˈreɪʃəl) adj conducted, involving, or existing between different races or ethnic groups

interradial (ˌɪntəˈreɪdɪəl) adj situated between two radii or rays, esp between the radii of a sea urchin or similar animal > ˌinterˈradially adv

interregional (ˌɪntəˈriːdʒənᵊl) adj of, relating to, or conducted between two or more regions

interregnum (ˌɪntəˈrɛgnəm) n, pl -nums or -na (-nə) **1** an interval between two reigns, governments, incumbencies, etc **2** any period in which a state lacks a ruler, government, etc **3** a period of absence of some control, authority, etc **4** a gap in a continuity [c16 from Latin, from INTER- + *regnum* REIGN] > ˌinterˈregnal adj

interrelate (ˌɪntərɪˈleɪt) vb to place in or come into a mutual or reciprocal relationship > ˌinterreˈlation n > ˌinterreˈlationˌship n

interreligious (ˌɪntərɪˈlɪdʒəs) adj conducted, involving, or existing between two or more religious groups or movements

interrex (ˌɪntəˈrɛks) n, pl interreges (ˌɪntəˈriːdʒiːz) a person who governs during an interregnum; provisional ruler [c16 from Latin, from INTER- + *rēx* king]

interrogate (ɪnˈtɛrəˌgeɪt) vb to ask questions (of), esp to question (a witness in court, spy, etc) closely [c15 from Latin *interrogāre* to question, examine, from *rogāre* to ask] > inˈterroˌgatingly adv

interrogation (ɪnˌtɛrəˈgeɪʃən) n **1** the technique, practice, or an instance of interrogating **2** a question or query **3** telecomm the transmission of one or more triggering pulses to a transponder > inˌterroˈgational adj

interrogation mark n a less common term for **question mark**

interrogative (ˌɪntəˈrɒgətɪv) adj **1** asking or having the nature of a question **2** denoting a form or construction used in asking a question **3** denoting or belonging to a class of words, such as *which* and *whom*, that are determiners, adjectives, or pronouns and serve to question which individual referent or referents are intended. Compare **demonstrative, relative** ▷ n **4** an interrogative word, phrase, sentence, or construction **5** a question mark > ˌinterˈrogatively adv

interrogator (ɪnˈtɛrəˌgeɪtə) n **1** a person who interrogates **2** a radio or radar transmitter used to send interrogating signals

interrogatories (ˌɪntəˈrɒgətərɪz, -trɪz) pl n law written questions asked by one party to a suit, to which the other party has to give written answers under oath

interrogatory (ˌɪntəˈrɒgətərɪ, -trɪ) *adj* **1** expressing or involving a question ▷ *n, pl* **-tories 2** a question or interrogation > ˌ**interˈrogatorily** *adv*

interrupt (ˌɪntəˈrʌpt) *vb* **1** to break the continuity of (an action, event, etc) or hinder (a person) by intrusion **2** (*tr*) to cease to perform (some action) **3** (*tr*) to obstruct (a view) **4** to prevent or disturb (a conversation, discussion, etc) by questions, interjections, or comment ▷ *n* **5** the signal to initiate the stopping of the running of one computer program in order to run another, after which the running of the original program is usually continued [C15 from Latin *interrumpere*, from INTER- + *rumpere* to break] > ˌ**interˈruptible** *adj* > ˌ**interˈruptive** *adj* > ˌ**interˈruptively** *adv*

interrupted (ˌɪntəˈrʌptɪd) *adj* **1** broken, discontinued, or hindered **2** (of plant organs, esp leaves) not evenly spaced along an axis **3** Also: **deceptive** *music* (of a cadence) progressing from the dominant chord to any other, such as the subdominant or submediant > ˌ**interˈruptedly** *adv*

interrupted screw *n* a screw with a slot or slots cut into the thread, esp one used in the breech of some guns permitting both engagement and release of the block by a partial turn of the screw

interrupter *or* **interruptor** (ˌɪntəˈrʌptə) *n* **1** a person or thing that interrupts **2** an electromechanical device for opening and closing an electric circuit

interruption (ˌɪntəˈrʌpʃən) *n* **1** something that interrupts, such as a comment, question, or action **2** an interval or intermission **3** the act of interrupting or the state of being interrupted

interscholastic (ˌɪntəskəˈlæstɪk) *adj* **1** (of sports events, competitions, etc) occurring between two or more schools **2** representative of various schools

inter se *Latin* (ˈɪntə ˈseɪ) *adv* among or between themselves

intersect (ˌɪntəˈsɛkt) *vb* **1** to divide, cut, or mark off by passing through or across **2** (esp of roads) to cross (each other) **3** *maths* (often foll by *with*) to have one or more points in common (with another configuration) [C17 from Latin *intersecāre* to divide, from INTER- + *secāre* to cut]

intersection (ˌɪntəˈsɛkʃən, ˈɪntəˌsɛk-) *n* **1** a point at which things intersect, esp a road junction **2** the act of intersecting or the state of being intersected **3** *maths* **a** a point or set of points common to two or more geometric configurations **b** Also called: **product** the set of elements that are common to two sets **c** the operation that yields that set from a pair of given sets. Symbol: ∩, as in $A \cap B$ > ˌ**interˈsectional** *adj*

intersex (ˈɪntəˌsɛks) *n* **1** the condition of having characteristics intermediate between those of a male and a female **2** an individual, exhibiting such physiological characteristics. Compare **gynandromorph, hermaphrodite** (senses 1, 2)

intersexual (ˌɪntəˈsɛksjʊəl) *adj* **1** occurring or existing between the sexes **2** relating to or being an intersex > ˌ**interˌsexuˈality** *or* ˌ**interˈsexualism** *n* > ˌ**interˈsexually** *adv*

interspace *vb* (ˌɪntəˈspeɪs) **1** (*tr*) to make or occupy a space between ▷ *n* (ˈɪntəˌspeɪs) **2** space between or among things > **interspatial** (ˌɪntəˈspeɪʃəl) *adj* > ˌ**interˈspatially** *adv*

interspecific (ˌɪntəspəˈsɪfɪk) *adj* hybridized from, relating to, or occurring between different species: *interspecific competition*

intersperse (ˌɪntəˈspɜːs) *vb* (*tr*) **1** to scatter or distribute among, between, or on **2** to diversify (something) with other things scattered here and there [C16 from Latin *interspargere*, from INTER- + *spargere* to sprinkle] > **interspersedly** (ˌɪntəˈspɜːsɪdlɪ) *adv* > **interspersion** (ˌɪntəˈspɜːʃən) *or* ˌ**interˈspersal** *n*

interstadial (ˌɪntəˈsteɪdɪəl) *adj, n* another word for **interglacial** [C20 from New Latin, from INTER- + *stadium* stage]

interstate (ˈɪntəˌsteɪt) *adj* **1** between or involving two or more of the states of the US, Australia, etc ▷ *adv* **2** *Austral* to or into another state

interstellar (ˌɪntəˈstɛlə) *adj* conducted, or existing between two or more stars

interstellar medium *n* the matter occurring between the stars of our Galaxy, largely in the spiral arms, and consisting mainly of huge clouds of ionized, neutral, or molecular hydrogen. Abbreviation: **ISM**

interstice (ɪnˈtɜːstɪs) *n* (*usually plural*) **1** a minute opening or crevice between things **2** *physics* the space between adjacent atoms in a crystal lattice [C17 from Latin *interstitium* interval, from *intersistere*, from INTER- + *sistere* to stand]

interstitial (ˌɪntəˈstɪʃəl) *adj* **1** of or relating to an interstice or interstices **2** *physics* forming or occurring in an interstice: *an interstitial atom* **3** *chem* containing interstitial atoms or ions: *an interstitial compound* **4** *anatomy, zoology* occurring in the spaces between organs, tissues, etc: *interstitial cells* ▷ *n* **5** *chem* an atom or ion situated in the interstices of a crystal lattice > ˌ**interˈstitially** *adv*

interstitial-cell-stimulating hormone *n* another name for **luteinizing hormone**

interstratify (ˌɪntəˈstrætɪˌfaɪ) *vb* **-fies, -fying, -fied** (*tr; usually passive*) to arrange (a series of rock strata) in alternating beds > ˌ**interˌstratifiˈcation** *n*

intertexture (ˌɪntəˈtɛkstʃə) *n* **1** the act or process of interweaving or the condition of having been interwoven **2** something that has been interwoven

intertidal (ˌɪntəˈtaɪdᵊl) *adj* of or relating to the zone of the shore between the high-water mark and low-water mark

intertribal (ˌɪntəˈtraɪbəl) *adj* conducted between or involving two or more tribes

intertrigo (ˌɪntəˈtraɪgəʊ) *n* chafing between two moist closely opposed skin surfaces, as under the breasts or at the armpit [C18 from INTER- + *-trigo*, from Latin *terere* to rub]

Intertropical Convergence Zone (ˌɪntəˈtrɒpɪkᵊl) *n meteorol* the zone of deep convection and heavy rainfall in the tropics, esp along or near the equator. Abbreviation: **ITCZ**

intertwine (ˌɪntəˈtwaɪn) *vb* to unite or be united by twisting or twining together. Also: **intertwist** > ˌ**interˈtwinement** *n* > ˌ**interˈtwiningly** *adv*

interval (ˈɪntəvəl) *n* **1** the period of time marked off by or between two events, instants, etc **2** the distance between two points, objects, etc **3** a pause or interlude, as between periods of intense activity **4** *Brit* a short period between parts of a play, concert, film, etc; intermission **5** *music* the difference of pitch between two notes, either sounded simultaneously (**harmonic interval**) or in succession as in a musical part (**melodic interval**). An interval is calculated by counting the (inclusive) number of notes of the diatonic scale between the two notes **6** the ratio of the frequencies of two sounds **7** *maths* the set containing all real numbers or points between two given numbers or points, called the endpoints. A **closed interval** includes the endpoints, but an **open interval** does not **8 at intervals a** occasionally or intermittently **b** with spaces between [C13 from Latin *intervallum*, literally: space between two palisades, from INTER- + *vallum* palisade, rampart] > **intervallic** (ˌɪntəˈvælɪk) *adj*

interval estimate *n statistics* an interval within which the true value of a parameter of a population is stated to lie with a predetermined probability on the basis of sampling statistics. Compare **point estimate**

intervalometer (ˌɪntəvəˈlɒmɪtə) *n* an automatic device used to trigger an operation at regular intervals, esp such a device operating the shutter of a camera

interval scale *n statistics* a scale of measurement of data according to which the differences between values can be quantified in absolute but not relative terms and for which any zero is merely arbitrary: for instance, dates are measured on an interval scale since differences can be measured in years, but no sense can be given to a ratio of times. Compare **ordinal scale, ratio scale, nominal scale**

interval signal *n* a characteristic snatch of music, chimes, etc, transmitted as an identifying signal by a radio station between programme items

interval training *n* a method of athletic training using alternate sprinting and jogging. Also called: **fartlek**

intervarsity (ˌɪntəˈvɑːsɪtɪ) *adj* conducted, involving, or existing between two or more universities

intervene (ˌɪntəˈviːn) *vb* (*intr*) **1** (often foll by *in*) to take a decisive or intrusive role (in) in order to modify or determine events or their outcome **2** (foll by *in* or *between*) to come or be (among or between) **3** (of a period of time) to occur between events or points in time **4** (of an event) to disturb or hinder a course of action **5** *economics* to take action to affect the market forces of an economy, esp to maintain the stability of a currency **6** *law* to interpose and become a party to a legal action between others, esp in order to protect one's interests [C16 from Latin *intervenīre* to come between, from INTER- + *venīre* to come] > ˌ**interˈvener** *or* ˌ**interˈvenor** *n*

intervening variable (ˌɪntəˈviːnɪŋ) *n psychol* a hypothetical variable postulated to account for the way in which a set of independent variables control a set of dependent variables

intervention (ˌɪntəˈvɛnʃən) *n* **1** the act of intervening **2** any interference in the affairs of others, esp by one state in the affairs of another **3** *economics* the action of a central bank in supporting the international value of a currency by buying large quantities of the currency to keep the price up **4** *commerce* the action of the EU in buying up surplus produce when the market price drops to a certain value > ˌ**interˈventional** *adj*

interventional radiology *n* an application of radiology that enables minimally invasive surgery to be performed with the aid of simultaneous radiological imaging of the field of operation within the body

interventionist (ˌɪntəˈvɛnʃənɪst) *adj* **1** of, relating to, or advocating intervention, esp in the affairs of a foreign country ▷ *n* **2** an interventionist person or state > ˌ**interˈventionism** *n*

intervention price *n commerce* the price at which the EU intervenes to buy surplus produce

intervertebral disc (ˌɪntəˈvɜːtəbrəl) *n* any of the cartilaginous discs between individual vertebrae, acting as shock absorbers

interview (ˈɪntəˌvjuː) *n* **1** a conversation with or questioning of a person, usually conducted for television, radio, or a newspaper **2** a formal discussion, esp one in which an employer assesses an applicant for a job ▷ *vb* **3** to conduct an interview with (someone) **4** (*intr*) to be interviewed, esp for a job: *he interviewed well and was given the position* [C16 from Old French *entrevue*; see INTER-, VIEW] > ˌ**interviewˈee** *n* > ˈ**interˌviewer** *n*

inter vivos *Latin* (ˈɪntə ˈviːvɒs) *adj law* between living people: *an inter vivos gift*

intervocalic (ˌɪntəvəʊˈkælɪk) *adj* pronounced or situated between vowels > ˌ**intervoˈcalically** *adv*

interwar (ˌɪntəˈwɔː) *adj* of or happening in the period between World War I and World War II

interweave (ˌɪntəˈwiːv) *vb* **-weaves, -weaving, -wove** *or* **-weaved; -woven, -wove** *or* **-weaved** to weave, blend, or twine together; intertwine. Also: **interwork** > ˌ**interˈweavement** *n* > ˈ**interˌweaver** *n*

intestate (ɪnˈtɛsteɪt, -tɪt) *adj* **1 a** (of a person) not having made a will **b** (of property) not disposed of by will ▷ *n* **2** a person who dies without having made a will ▷ Compare **testate** [C14 from Latin *intestātus*, from IN-[1] + *testātus*, from *testārī* to bear witness, make a will, from *testis* a witness] > **inˈtestacy** *n*

intestinal flora *n* microorganisms that normally inhabit the lumen of the intestinal tract

intestine (ɪnˈtɛstɪn) *n* (*usually plural*) the part of the alimentary canal between the stomach and the anus. See **large intestine**, **small intestine** Related adj: **alvine** [C16 from Latin *intestīnum* gut, from *intestīnus* internal, from *intus* within] > **intestinal** (ɪnˈtɛstɪnəl, ˌɪntɛsˈtaɪnəl) *adj* > inˈtestinally *adv*

inti (ˈɪntɪ) *n* a former monetary unit of Peru [C20 from Quechua]

intifada (ˌɪntɪˈfɑːdə) *n* the Palestinian uprising against Israel in the West Bank and Gaza Strip that started at the end of 1987 [C20 Arabic, literally: uprising]

intima (ˈɪntɪmə) *n*, *pl* -**mae** (-ˌmiː) *anatomy*, *zoology* the innermost layer of an organ or part, esp of a blood vessel [C19 from Latin, feminine of *intimus* innermost; see INTIMATE[1]] > ˈintimal *adj*

intimacy (ˈɪntɪməsɪ) *n*, *pl* -**cies** 1 close or warm friendship or understanding; personal relationship 2 (*often plural*) euphemistic sexual relations

intimate[1] (ˈɪntɪmɪt) *adj* 1 characterized by a close or warm personal relationship: *an intimate friend* 2 deeply personal, private, or secret 3 (*often postpositive*; foll by *with*) euphemistic having sexual relations (with) 4 a (*postpositive*; foll by *with*) having a deep or unusual knowledge (of) b (*of knowledge*) deep; extensive 5 having a friendly, warm, or informal atmosphere: *an intimate nightclub* 6 of or relating to the essential part or nature of something; intrinsic 7 denoting the informal second person of verbs and pronouns in French and other languages ▷ *n* 8 a close friend [C17 from Latin *intimus* very close friend, from (adj): innermost, deepest, from *intus* within] > ˈintimately *adv* > ˈintimateness *n*

intimate[2] (ˈɪntɪˌmeɪt) *vb* (*tr*; *may take a clause as object*) 1 to hint; suggest 2 to proclaim; make known [C16 from Late Latin *intimāre* to proclaim, from Latin *intimus* innermost] > ˈintiˌmater *n*

intimation (ˌɪntɪˈmeɪʃən) *n* 1 a hint or suggestion 2 *rare* an announcement or notice

intimidate (ɪnˈtɪmɪˌdeɪt) *vb* (*tr*) 1 to make timid or frightened; scare 2 to discourage, restrain, or silence illegally or unscrupulously, as by threats or blackmail [C17 from Medieval Latin *intimidāre*, from Latin IN-[2] + *timidus* fearful, from *timor* fear] > inˈtimiˌdating *adj* > inˌtimiˈdation *n* > inˈtimiˌdator *n*

intinction (ɪnˈtɪŋkʃən) *n Christianity* the practice of dipping the Eucharistic bread into the wine at Holy Communion [C16 from Late Latin *intinctiō* a dipping in, from Latin *intingere* to dip in, from *tingere* to dip]

intine (ˈɪntɪn, -tiːn, -taɪn) *n* the inner wall of a pollen grain or a spore. Compare **exine** [C19 from Latin *intimus* innermost + -INE[1]]

intitule (ɪnˈtɪtjuːl) *vb* (*tr*) *parliamentary procedure* (in Britain) to entitle (an Act) [C15 from Old French *intituler*, from Latin *titulus* TITLE]

intl *abbreviation for* international

into (ˈɪntuː; *unstressed* ˈɪntə) *prep* 1 to the interior or inner parts of: *to look into a case* 2 to the middle or midst of so as to be surrounded by 3 against; up against 4 used to indicate the result of a transformation or change 5 *maths* used to indicate a dividend 6 *informal* interested or enthusiastically involved in

intolerable (ɪnˈtɒlərəbəl) *adj* 1 more than can be tolerated or endured; insufferable 2 *informal* extremely irritating or annoying > inˌtoleraˈbility *or* inˈtolerableness *n* > inˈtolerably *adv*

intolerant (ɪnˈtɒlərənt) *adj* 1 lacking respect for practices and beliefs other than one's own 2 (*postpositive*; foll by *of*) not able or willing to tolerate or endure: *intolerant of noise* > inˈtolerance *n* > inˈtolerantly *adv*

intonate (ˈɪntəʊˌneɪt) *vb* (*tr*) 1 to pronounce or articulate (continuous connected speech) with a characteristic rise and fall of the voice 2 a less common word for **intone**

intonation (ˌɪntəʊˈneɪʃən) *n* 1 the sound pattern of phrases and sentences produced by pitch variation in the voice 2 the act or manner of intoning 3 an intoned, chanted, or monotonous utterance; incantation 4 *music* the opening of a piece of plainsong, sung by a soloist 5 *music* a the correct or accurate pitching of intervals b the capacity to play or sing in tune. See also **just intonation**. > intoˈnational *adj*

intonation pattern *or* **contour** *n linguistics* a characteristic series of musical pitch levels that serves to distinguish between questions, statements, and other types of utterance in a language

intone (ɪnˈtəʊn) *vb* 1 to utter, recite, or sing (a chant, prayer, etc) in a monotonous or incantatory tone 2 (*intr*) to speak with a particular or characteristic intonation or tone 3 to sing (the opening phrase of a psalm, etc) in plainsong [C15 from Medieval Latin *intonare*, from IN-[2] + TONE] > inˈtoner *n*

intorsion (ɪnˈtɔːʃən) *n botany* a spiral twisting in plant stems or other parts

in toto *Latin* (ɪn ˈtəʊtəʊ) *adv* totally; entirely; completely

intoxicant (ɪnˈtɒksɪkənt) *n* 1 anything that causes intoxication ▷ *adj* 2 causing intoxication

intoxicate (ɪnˈtɒksɪˌkeɪt) *vb* (*tr*) 1 (of an alcoholic drink) to produce in (a person) a state ranging from euphoria to stupor, usually accompanied by loss of inhibitions and control; make drunk; inebriate 2 to stimulate, excite, or elate so as to overwhelm 3 (of a drug) to poison [C16 from Medieval Latin, from *intoxicāre* to poison, from Latin *toxicum* poison; see TOXIC] > inˈtoxicable *adj* > inˈtoxiˌcative *adj* > inˈtoxiˌcator *n*

intoxicating (ɪnˈtɒksɪˌkeɪtɪŋ) *adj* 1 (of an alcoholic drink) producing in a person a state ranging from euphoria to stupor, usually accompanied by loss of inhibitions and control; inebriating 2 stimulating, exciting, or producing great elation > inˈtoxiˌcatingly *adv*

intoxication (ɪnˌtɒksɪˈkeɪʃən) *n* 1 drunkenness; inebriation 2 great elation 3 the act of intoxicating 4 poisoning

intr. *abbreviation for* intransitive

intra- *prefix* within; inside: *intravenous* [from Latin *intrā* on the inside, within, from INTERIOR]

intra-atomic (ˌɪntrəəˈtɒmɪk) *adj* existing or occurring within an atom or atoms. Compare **interatomic**

intracapsular (ˌɪntrəˈkæpsjʊlə) *adj anatomy* within a capsule, esp within the capsule of a joint

intracardiac (ˌɪntrəˈkɑːdɪˌæk) *adj* within the heart

intracellular (ˌɪntrəˈsɛljʊlə) *adj biology* situated or occurring inside a cell or cells > ˌintraˈcellularly *adv*

Intracoastal Waterway (ˌɪntrəˈkəʊstəl) *n* short for **Atlantic Intracoastal Waterway**

intracranial (ˌɪntrəˈkreɪnɪəl) *adj* within the skull

intractable (ɪnˈtræktəbəl) *adj* 1 difficult to influence or direct 2 (of a problem, illness, etc) difficult to solve, alleviate, or cure 3 difficult to shape or mould, esp with the hands > inˌtractaˈbility *or* inˈtractableness *n* > inˈtractably *adv*

intracutaneous (ˌɪntrəkjuːˈteɪnɪəs) *adj anatomy* within the skin. Also: **intradermal** > ˌintracuˈtaneously *adv*

intradermal (ˌɪntrəˈdɜːməl) *or* **intradermic** *adj anatomy* other words for **intracutaneous** Abbreviation (esp of an injection): ID, i.d. > ˌintraˈdermally *or* ˌintraˈdermically *adv*

intrados (ɪnˈtreɪdɒs) *n*, *pl* -**dos** *or* -**doses** *architect* the inner curve or surface of an arch or vault. Compare **extrados** [C18 from French, from INTRA- + *dos* back, from Latin *dorsum*]

intrafascicular (ˌɪntrəfəˈsɪkjʊlə) *adj botany* between the xylem and phloem elements of a vascular bundle: *intrafascicular cambium*

intragenerational mobility (ˌɪntrəˌdʒɛnəˈreɪʃənəl) *n sociol* movement within or between social classes and occupations, the change occurring within an individual's lifetime. Compare **intergenerational mobility**

intramolecular (ˌɪntrəməˈlɛkjʊlə) *adj* occurring within a molecule or molecules

intramural (ˌɪntrəˈmjʊərəl) *adj* 1 *education, chiefly US and Canadian* operating within or involving those in a single establishment 2 *anatomy* within the walls of a cavity or hollow organ > ˌintraˈmurally *adv*

intramuscular (ˌɪntrəˈmʌskjʊlə) *adj anatomy* within a muscle: *an intramuscular injection*. Abbreviation (esp of an injection): IM, i.m. > ˌintraˈmuscularly *adv*

intranational (ˌɪntrəˈnæʃənəl) *adj* within one nation

intranet (ˈɪntrəˌnɛt) *n computing* an internal network that makes use of internet technology [C20 from INTRA- + NET[1] (sense 8), modelled on INTERNET]

intrans. *abbreviation for* intransitive

intransigent (ɪnˈtrænsɪdʒənt) *adj* 1 not willing to compromise; obstinately maintaining an attitude ▷ *n also* inˈtransigentist 2 an intransigent person, esp in politics [C19 from Spanish *los intransigentes* the uncompromising (ones), a name adopted by certain political extremists, from IN-[1] + *transigir* to compromise, from Latin *transigere* to settle; see TRANSACT] > inˈtransigence *or* inˈtransigency *adv*

intransitive (ɪnˈtrænsɪtɪv) *adj* 1 a denoting a verb when it does not require a direct object b denoting a verb that customarily does not require a direct object: *"to faint" is an intransitive verb* c (*as noun*) a verb in either of these categories 2 denoting an adjective or noun that does not require any particular noun phrase as a referent 3 *logic, maths* (of a relation) having the property that if it holds between one argument and a second, and between the second and a third, it must fail to hold between the first and the third: *"being the mother of" is an intransitive relation* ▷ Compare **transitive**, **pseudo-intransitive** > inˈtransitively *adv* > inˌtransiˈtivity *or* inˈtransitiveness *n*

intranuclear (ˌɪntrəˈnjuːklɪə) *adj* situated or occurring within a nucleus

intraocular (ˌɪntrəˈɒkjʊlə) *adj anatomy* within an eyeball

intrapartum (ˌɪntrəˈpɑːtəm) *adj med* of or relating to childbirth or delivery: *intrapartum care* [C20 New Latin, from INTRA- + *partum*, from *partus* birth]

intrapreneur (ˌɪntrəprəˈnɜː) *n* a person who while remaining within a larger organization uses entrepreneurial skills to develop a new product or line of business as a subsidiary of the organization [C20 from INTRA- + (ENTRE)PRENEUR]

intraspecific (ˌɪntrəspəˈsɪfɪk) *adj* relating to or occurring between members of the same species: *intraspecific competition*

intrastate (ˌɪntrəˈsteɪt) *adj chiefly US* of, relating to, or confined within a single state, esp a state of the US

intratelluric (ˌɪntrətəˈljʊərɪk) *adj* 1 (of rocks and their constituents, processes, etc) formed or occurring below the surface of the earth 2 denoting crystals formed at depth before magma erupted at the earth's surface 3 denoting the period during which crystallization took place

intrauterine (ˌɪntrəˈjuːtəraɪn) *adj* within the womb

intrauterine device *n* a metal or plastic device, in the shape of a loop, coil, or ring, inserted into the uterus to prevent conception. Abbreviation: IUD

intravasation (ɪnˌtrævəˈseɪʃən) *n* the passage of extraneous material, such as pus, into a blood or lymph vessel. Compare **extravasation**

intravenous (ˌɪntrəˈviːnəs) *adj anatomy* within a vein: *an intravenous injection*. Abbreviations (esp of an injection): IV, i.v. > ˌintraˈvenously *adv*

in-tray *n* a tray for incoming papers requiring

i

attention

intrazonal soil (ˌɪntrəˈzəʊnᵊl) *n* a soil that has a well-developed profile determined by relief, parent material, age, etc

intreat (ɪnˈtriːt) *vb* an archaic spelling of **entreat** > inˈtreatingly *adv* > inˈtreatment *n*

intrench (ɪnˈtrɛntʃ) *vb* a less common spelling of **entrench.** > inˈtrencher *n* > inˈtrenchment *n*

intrepid (ɪnˈtrɛpɪd) *adj* fearless; daring; bold [C17 from Latin *intrepidus*, from IN-¹ + *trepidus* fearful, timid] > ˌintreˈpidity or inˈtrepidness *n* > inˈtrepidly *adv*

intricate (ˈɪntrɪkɪt) *adj* 1 difficult to understand; obscure; complex; puzzling 2 entangled or involved: *intricate patterns* [C15 from Latin *intrīcāre* to entangle, perplex, from IN-² + *trīcae* trifles, perplexities] > ˈintricacy or ˈintricateness *n* > ˈintricately *adv*

intrigant or **intriguant** (ˈɪntrɪgənt; *French* ɛ̃trigɑ̃) *n archaic* a person who intrigues; intriguer

intrigue *vb* (ɪnˈtriːg) -trigues, -triguing, -trigued 1 (*tr*) to make interested or curious 2 (*intr*) to make secret plots or employ underhand methods; conspire 3 (*intr*; often foll by *with*) to carry on a clandestine love affair ▷ *n* (ɪnˈtriːg, ˈɪntriːg) 4 the act or an instance of secret plotting, etc 5 a clandestine love affair 6 the quality of arousing interest or curiosity; beguilement [C17 from French *intriguer*, from Italian *intrigare*, from Latin *intrīcāre*; see INTRICATE] > inˈtriguer *n*

intriguing (ɪnˈtriːgɪŋ) *adj* arousing great interest or curiosity: *an intriguing mystery* > inˈtriguingly *adv*

intrinsic (ɪnˈtrɪnsɪk) or **intrinsical** *adj* 1 of or relating to the essential nature of a thing; inherent 2 *anatomy* situated within or peculiar to a part: *intrinsic muscles* [C15 from Late Latin *intrinsecus* from Latin, inwardly, from *intrā* within + *secus* alongside; related to *sequī* to follow] > inˈtrinsically *adv*

intrinsic factor *n biochem* a glycoprotein, secreted by the stomach, the presence of which is necessary for the absorption of cyanocobalamin (vitamin B₁₂) in the intestine

intrinsic semiconductor *n* an almost pure semiconductor to which no impurities have been added and in which the electron and hole densities are equal at thermal equilibrium. Also called: i-type semiconductor

intro (ˈɪntrəʊ) *n*, *pl* -tros *informal* short for **introduction**

intro. or **introd.** *abbreviation for* 1 introduction 2 introductory

intro- *prefix* in, into, or inward: *introvert* [from Latin *intrō* towards the inside, inwardly, within]

introduce (ˌɪntrəˈdjuːs) *vb* (*tr*) 1 (often foll by *to*) to present (someone) by name (to another person) or (two or more people to each other) 2 (foll by *to*) to cause to experience for the first time 3 to present for consideration or approval, esp before a legislative body 4 to bring in; establish 5 to present (a radio or television programme, etc) verbally 6 (foll by *with*) to start 7 (often foll by *into*) to insert or inject 8 to place (members of a species of plant or animal) in a new environment with the intention of producing a resident breeding population [C16 from Latin *intrōdūcere* to bring inside, from INTRO- + *dūcere* to lead] > ˌintroˈducer *n* > ˌintroˈducible *adj*

introduction (ˌɪntrəˈdʌkʃən) *n* 1 the act of introducing or fact of being introduced 2 a presentation of one person to another or others 3 a means of presenting a person to another person, group, etc, such as a letter of introduction or reference 4 a preliminary part, as of a book, speech, etc 5 *music* a an instrumental passage preceding the entry of a soloist, choir, etc b an opening passage in a movement or composition that precedes the main material 6 something that has been or is introduced, esp something that is not native to an area, country, etc 7 a basic or elementary work of instruction, reference, etc 8 *logic* (qualified by the name of an operation) a

syntactic rule specifying the conditions under which a formula or statement containing the specified operator may be derived from others: *conjunction-introduction; negation-introduction*

introductory (ˌɪntrəˈdʌktərɪ, -trɪ) *adj* serving as an introduction; preliminary; prefatory > ˌintroˈductorily *adv* > ˌintroˈductoriness *n*

introgression (ˌɪntrəˈgrɛʃən) *n* the introduction of genes from the gene pool of one species into that of another during hybridization

introit (ˈɪntrɔɪt) *n RC Church, Church of England* a short prayer said or sung as the celebrant is entering the sanctuary to celebrate Mass or Holy Communion [C15 from Church Latin *introitus* introit, from Latin: entrance, from *introīre* to go in, from INTRO- + *īre* to go] > inˈtroital *adj*

introject (ˌɪntrəˈdʒɛkt) *vb psychol* 1 (*intr*) (esp of a child) to incorporate ideas of others, or (in fantasy) of objects 2 to turn (feelings for another) towards oneself ▷ Compare **project** See also **internalize**

introjection (ˌɪntrəˈdʒɛkʃən) *n psychol* the act or process of introjecting [C20 from INTRO- + (PRO)JECTION] > ˌintroˈjective *adj*

intromission (ˌɪntrəˈmɪʃən) *n* a less common word for **insertion** or **introduction** > ˌintroˈmissive *adj*

intromit (ˌɪntrəˈmɪt) *vb* -mits, -mitting, -mitted (*tr*) *rare* to enter or insert or allow to enter or be inserted [C15 from Latin *intrōmittere* to send in, from INTRO- + *mittere* to send] > ˌintroˈmissible *adj* > ˌintroˌmissiˈbility *n* > ˌintroˈmittent *adj* > ˌintroˈmitter *n*

intron (ˈɪntrɒn) *n biochem* a stretch of DNA that interrupts a gene and does not contribute to the specification of a protein. Compare **exon²** [C20 from intr(*agenic*) (regi)on]

introrse (ɪnˈtrɔːs) *adj botany* turned inwards or towards the axis, as anthers that shed their pollen towards the centre of the flower [C19 from Latin *introrsus*, contraction of *intrōversus*, from INTRO- + *versus* turned, from *vertere* to turn] > inˈtrorsely *adv*

introspect (ˌɪntrəˈspɛkt) *vb* (*intr*) to examine and analyse one's own thoughts and feelings

introspection (ˌɪntrəˈspɛkʃən) *n* the examination of one's own thoughts, impressions, and feelings, esp for long periods [C17 from Latin *intrōspicere* to look within, from INTRO- + *specere* to look] > ˌintroˈspectional or ˌintroˈspective *adj* > ˌintroˈspectionist *n* > ˌintroˈspectively *adv* > ˌintroˈspectiveness *n*

introversion (ˌɪntrəˈvɜːʃən) *n* 1 *psychol* the directing of interest inwards towards one's own thoughts and feelings rather than towards the external world or making social contacts 2 *pathol* the turning inside out of a hollow organ or part ▷ Compare **extroversion.** > ˌintroˈversive or ˌintroˈvertive *adj*

introvert *n* (ˈɪntrəˌvɜːt) 1 *psychol* a person prone to introversion ▷ *adj* (ˈɪntrəˌvɜːt) 2 Also: introverted characterized by introversion ▷ *vb* (ˌɪntrəˈvɜːt) 3 (*tr*) *pathol* to turn (a hollow organ or part) inside out ▷ Compare **extrovert** [C17 see INTRO-, INVERT]

intrude (ɪnˈtruːd) *vb* 1 (often foll by *into*, *on*, or *upon*) to put forward or interpose (oneself, one's views, something) abruptly or without invitation 2 *geology* to force or thrust (rock material, esp molten magma) or (of rock material) to be thrust between solid rocks [C16 from Latin *intrūdere* to thrust in, from IN-² + *trūdere* to thrust] > inˈtrudingly *adv*

intruder (ɪnˈtruːdə) *n* a person who enters a building, grounds, etc, without permission

intrusion (ɪnˈtruːʒən) *n* 1 the act or an instance of intruding; an unwelcome visit, interjection, etc: *an intrusion on one's privacy* 2 a the movement of magma from within the earth's crust into spaces in the overlying strata to form igneous rock b any igneous rock formed in this way 3 *property law* an unlawful entry onto land by a stranger after determination of a particular estate of freehold

and before the remainderman or reversioner has made entry > inˈtrusional *adj*

intrusive (ɪnˈtruːsɪv) *adj* 1 characterized by intrusion or tending to intrude 2 (of igneous rocks) formed by intrusion. Compare **extrusive** (sense 2) 3 *phonetics* relating to or denoting a speech sound that is introduced into a word or piece of connected speech for a phonetic rather than a historical or grammatical reason, such as the (r) often pronounced between *idea* and *of* in *the idea of it* > inˈtrusively *adv* > inˈtrusiveness *n*

intrust (ɪnˈtrʌst) *vb* a less common spelling of **entrust.** > inˈtrustment *n*

intubate (ˈɪntjʊˌbeɪt) *vb* (*tr*) *med* to insert a tube or cannula into (a hollow organ); cannulate > ˌintuˈbation *n*

INTUC (ˈɪntʌk) *n acronym for* Indian National Trade Union Congress

intuit (ɪnˈtjuːɪt) *vb* to know or discover by intuition > inˈtuitable *adj*

intuition (ˌɪntjʊˈɪʃən) *n* 1 knowledge or belief obtained neither by reason nor by perception 2 instinctive knowledge or belief 3 a hunch or unjustified belief 4 *philosophy* immediate knowledge of a proposition or object such as Kant's account of our knowledge of sensible objects 5 the supposed faculty or process by which we obtain any of these [C15 from Late Latin *intuitiō* a contemplation, from Latin *intuērī* to gaze upon, from *tuērī* to look at] > inˈtuitional *adj* > inˈtuitionally *adv*

intuitionism (ˌɪntjʊˈɪʃəˌnɪzəm) or **intuitionalism** *n* 1 (in ethics) a the doctrine that there are moral truths discoverable by intuition b the doctrine that there is no single principle by which to resolve conflicts between intuited moral rules ▷ See also **deontological** 2 *philosophy* the theory that general terms are used of a variety of objects in accordance with perceived similarities. Compare **nominalism, Platonism** 3 *logic* the doctrine that logical axioms rest on prior intuitions concerning time, negation, and provability 4 a the theory that mathematics cannot intelligibly comprehend the properties of infinite sets, and that only what can be shown to be provable can be justifiably asserted b the reconstruction of mathematics or logic in accordance with this view ▷ Compare **formalism, logicism, finitism** 5 the doctrine that knowledge, esp of the external world, is acquired by intuition > ˌintuˈitionist or ˌintuˈitionalist *n*

intuitive (ɪnˈtjuːɪtɪv) *adj* 1 resulting from intuition: *an intuitive awareness* 2 of, characterized by, or involving intuition > inˈtuitively *adv* > inˈtuitiveness *n*

intumesce (ˌɪntjʊˈmɛs) *vb* (*intr*) to swell or become swollen; undergo intumescence [C18 from Latin *intumescere*, from *tumescere* to begin to swell, from *tumēre* to swell]

intumescence (ˌɪntjʊˈmɛsəns) or **intumescency** *n* 1 *pathol* a swelling up, as with blood or other fluid 2 *pathol* a swollen organ or part 3 *chem* the swelling of certain substances on heating, often accompanied by the escape of water vapour > ˌintuˈmescent *adj*

intussuscept (ˌɪntəssəˈsɛpt) *vb* (*tr; usually passive*) *pathol* to turn or fold (an organ or a part) inwards; invaginate > ˌintussusˈceptive *adj*

intussusception (ˌɪntəssəˈsɛpʃən) *n* 1 *pathol* invagination of a tubular organ or part, esp the telescoping of one section of the intestinal tract into a lower section, causing obstruction 2 *biology* growth in the surface area of a cell by the deposition of new material between the existing components of the cell wall. Compare **apposition** (sense 3) [C18 from Latin *intus* within + *susceptiō* a taking up]

intwine (ɪnˈtwaɪn) *vb* a less common spelling of **entwine.** > inˈtwinement *n*

Inuit or **Innuit** (ˈɪnjuːɪt) *n*, *pl* -it or -its any of several Native peoples of N America or Greenland, as distinguished from those from Asia or the

Aleutian Islands (who are still generally referred to as Eskimos); the preferred term for *Eskimo* in N America. Compare **Yupik** [from Inuktitut *inuit* the people, pl of *inuk* a man]

USAGE see at **Eskimo**

Inuk (ˈɪnʊk) *n* a member of any Inuit people [from Inuktitut *inuk* man]

inukshuk (ɪˈnʊkʃʊk) *n, pl* **inukshuks** *or* **inukshuit** (ɪˈnʊkʃjuːɪt) a stone used by the Inuit to mark a location [from Inuktitut, literally: something in the shape of a man]

Inuktitut (ɪˈnʊktɪˌtʊt) *n Canadian* the language of the Inuit [from Inuktitut *inuk* man + *titut* speech]

inulin (ˈɪnjʊlɪn) *n* a fructose polysaccharide present in the tubers and rhizomes of some plants. Formula: $(C_6H_{10}O_5)_n$ [c19 from Latin *inula* elecampane + -IN]

inunction (ɪnˈʌŋkʃən) *n* **1** the application of an ointment to the skin, esp by rubbing **2** the ointment so used **3** the act of anointing; anointment [c15 from Latin *inunguere* to anoint, from *unguere*; see UNCTION]

inundate (ˈɪnʌnˌdeɪt) *vb (tr)* **1** to cover completely with water; overflow; flood; swamp **2** to overwhelm, as if with a flood [c17 from Latin *inundāre* to flood, from *unda* wave] > ˈ**inundant** *or* inˈ**undatory** *adj* > ˌ**inunˈdation** *n* > ˈ**inunˌdator** *n*

inurbane (ˌɪnɜːˈbeɪn) *adj rare* not urbane; lacking in courtesy or polish > **inurbanity** (ˌɪnɜːˈbænɪtɪ) *n* > ˌ**inurˈbanely** *adv*

inure *or* **enure** (ɪˈnjʊə) *vb* **1** *(tr; often passive;* often foll by *to)* to cause to accept or become hardened to; habituate **2** *(intr)* (esp of a law, etc) to come into operation; take effect [C15 *enuren* to accustom, from *ure* use, from Old French *euvre* custom, work, from Latin *opera* works, plural of *opus*] > **inuredness** *or* **enuredness** (ɪˈnjʊərɪdnɪs) *n* > **inˈurement** *or* **enˈurement** *n*

inurn (ɪnˈɜːn) *vb (tr)* **1** to place (esp cremated ashes) in an urn **2** a less common word for **inter**. > **inˈurnment** *n*

in utero *Latin* (ɪn ˈjuːtəˌrəʊ) *adv* within the womb

inutile (ɪnˈjuːtaɪl) *adj rare* useless; unprofitable > **inˈutilely** *adv* > ˌ**inuˈtility** (ˌɪnjuːˈtɪlɪtɪ) *n*

in vacuo *Latin* (ɪn ˈvækjʊˌəʊ) *adv* **1** in a vacuum **2** in isolation; without reference to facts or evidence

invade (ɪnˈveɪd) *vb* **1** to enter (a country, territory, etc) by military force **2** *(tr)* to occupy in large numbers; overrun; infest **3** *(tr)* to trespass or encroach upon (privacy, etc) **4** *(tr)* to enter and spread throughout, esp harmfully; pervade **5** (of plants, esp weeds) to become established in (a place to which they are not native) [c15 from Latin *invādere*, from *vādere* to go] > **inˈvadable** *adj* > **inˈvader** *n*

invaginate *vb* (ɪnˈvædʒɪˌneɪt) **1** *pathol* to push one section of (a tubular organ or part) back into itself so that it becomes ensheathed; intussuscept **2** *(intr)* (of the outer layer of an organism or part) to undergo invagination ▷ *adj* (ɪnˈvædʒɪnɪt, -ˌneɪt) **3** (of an organ or part) folded back upon itself [c19 from Medieval Latin *invāgināre*, from Latin IN-² + *vāgina* sheath] > **inˈvaginable** *adj*

invagination (ɪnˌvædʒɪˈneɪʃən) *n* **1** *pathol* the process of invaginating or the condition of being invaginated **2** *pathol* an invaginated organ or part **3** an infolding of the outer layer of cells of an organism or part of an organism so as to form a pocket in the surface, as in the embryonic development of a gastrula from a blastula

invalid¹ (ˈɪnvəˌliːd, -lɪd) *n* **1** **a** a person suffering from disablement or chronic ill health **b** *(as modifier)*: *an invalid chair* ▷ *adj* **2** suffering from or disabled by injury, sickness, etc ▷ *vb (tr)* **3** to cause to become an invalid; disable **4** *(usually* foll by *out; often passive) chiefly Brit* to require (a member of the armed forces) to retire from active service through wounds or illness [c17 from Latin *invalidus* infirm, from IN-¹ + *validus* strong] > ˌ**invaˈlidity** *n*

invalid² (ɪnˈvælɪd) *adj* **1** not valid; having no cogency or legal force **2** *logic* (of an argument) having a conclusion that does not follow from the premises: it may be false when the premises are all true; not valid [c16 from Medieval Latin *invalidus* without legal force; see INVALID¹] > **invalidity** (ˌɪnvəˈlɪdɪtɪ) *or* **inˈvalidness** *n* > **inˈvalidly** *adv*

invalidate (ɪnˈvælɪˌdeɪt) *vb (tr)* **1** to render weak or ineffective, as an argument **2** to take away the legal force or effectiveness of; annul, as a contract > **inˌvaliˈdation** *n* > **inˈvaliˌdator** *n*

invalidism (ˈɪnvəlɪˌdɪzəm) *n* **1** the state of being an invalid, esp by reason of ill health **2** a state of being abnormally preoccupied with one's physical health

invalidity benefit *n* (formerly, in the British National Insurance scheme) a weekly payment to a person who had been off work through illness for more than six months: replaced by **incapacity benefit** in 1995. Abbreviation: IVB

invaluable (ɪnˈvæljʊəbᵊl) *adj* having great value that is impossible to calculate; priceless > **inˈvaluableness** *n* > **inˈvaluably** *adv*

Invar (ɪnˈvɑː) *n trademark* an alloy containing iron (63.8 per cent), nickel (36 per cent), and carbon (0.2 per cent). It has a very low coefficient of expansion and is used for the balance springs of watches, etc [c20 shortened from INVARIABLE]

invariable (ɪnˈvɛərɪəbᵊl) *adj* **1** not subject to alteration; unchanging ▷ *n* **2** a mathematical quantity having an unchanging value; a constant > **inˌvariaˈbility** *or* **inˈvariableness** *n*

invariably (ɪnˈvɛərɪəblɪ) *adv* always; without exception

invariant (ɪnˈvɛərɪənt) *n* **1** *maths* an entity, quantity, etc, that is unaltered by a particular transformation of coordinates ▷ *adj* **2** *maths* (of a relationship or a property of a function, configuration, or equation) unaltered by a particular transformation of coordinates **3** a rare word for **invariable**. > **inˈvariance** *or* **inˈvariancy** *n*

invasion (ɪnˈveɪʒən) *n* **1** the act of invading with armed forces **2** any encroachment or intrusion **3** the onset or advent of something harmful, esp of a disease **4** *pathol* the spread of cancer from its point of origin into surrounding tissues **5** the movement of plants to a new area or to an area to which they are not native

invasive (ɪnˈveɪsɪv) *adj* **1** of or relating to an invasion, intrusion, etc **2** relating to or denoting cancer at the stage at which it has spread from its site of origin to other tissues **3** (of surgery) involving making a relatively large incision in the body to gain access to the target of the surgery, as opposed to making a small incision or gaining access endoscopically through a natural orifice

invective (ɪnˈvɛktɪv) *n* **1** vehement accusation or denunciation, esp of a bitterly abusive or sarcastic kind ▷ *adj* **2** characterized by or using abusive language, bitter sarcasm, etc [c15 from Late Latin *invectīvus* reproachful, scolding, from Latin *invectus* carried in; see INVEIGH] > **inˈvectively** *adv* > **inˈvectiveness** *n*

inveigh (ɪnˈveɪ) *vb (intr;* foll by *against)* to speak with violent or invective language; rail [c15 from Latin *invehī*, literally: to be carried in, hence, assail physically or verbally, from IN-² + *vehī* to be carried, ride] > **inˈveigher** *n*

inveigle (ɪnˈviːgᵊl, -ˈveɪ-) *vb (tr;* often foll by *into* or an infinitive) to lead (someone into a situation) or persuade (to do something) by cleverness or trickery; cajole: *to inveigle customers into spending more* [c15 from Old French *avogler* to blind, deceive, from *avogle* blind, from Medieval Latin *ab oculis* without eyes] > **inˈveiglement** *n* > **inˈveigler** *n*

invent (ɪnˈvɛnt) *vb* **1** to create or devise (new ideas, machines, etc) **2** to make up (falsehoods); fabricate [c15 from Latin *invenīre* to find, come upon, from IN-² + *venīre* to come] > **inˈventible** *or* **inˈventable** *adj*

invention (ɪnˈvɛnʃən) *n* **1** the act or process of inventing **2** something that is invented **3** *patent law* the discovery or production of some new or improved process or machine that is both useful and is not obvious to persons skilled in the particular field **4** creative power or ability; inventive skill **5** *euphemistic* a fabrication; lie **6** (in traditional rhetoric) one of the five steps in preparing a speech or discourse: the process of finding suitable topics on which to talk or write **7** *music* a short piece consisting of two or three parts usually in imitative counterpoint **8** *sociol* the creation of a new cultural pattern or trait > **inˈventional** *adj* > **inˈventionless** *adj*

inventive (ɪnˈvɛntɪv) *adj* **1** skilled or quick at contriving; ingenious; resourceful **2** characterized by inventive skill: *an inventive programme of work* **3** of or relating to invention > **inˈventively** *adv* > **inˈventiveness** *n*

inventor (ɪnˈvɛntə) *n* a person who invents, esp as a profession > **inˈventress** *fem n*

inventory (ˈɪnvəntərɪ, -trɪ) *n* **1** a detailed list of articles, goods, property, etc **2** *(often plural) accounting, chiefly US* **a** the amount or value of a firm's current assets that consist of raw materials, work in progress, and finished goods; stock **b** such assets individually ▷ *vb* **-tories, -torying, -toried** **3** *(tr)* to enter (items) in an inventory; make a list of [c16 from Medieval Latin *inventōrium*; see INVENT] > ˈ**inventoriable** *adj* > ˌ**invenˈtorial** *adj* > ˌ**invenˈtorially** *adv*

inveracity (ˌɪnvəˈræsɪtɪ) *n, pl* **-ties** *formal or euphemistic* **1** lying; untruthfulness **2** an untruth; lie

Inveraray (ˌɪnvəˈrɛərɪ) *n* a town in W Scotland, in Argyll and Bute: Inveraray Castle is the seat of the Dukes of Argyll. Pop: 512 (1991)

Invercargill (ˌɪnvəˈkɑːgɪl) *n* a city in New Zealand, on South Island: regional trading centre for sheep and agricultural products. Pop: 51 700 (2004 est)

Inverclyde (ˌɪnvəˈklaɪd) *n* a council area of W central Scotland: created in 1996 from part of Strathclyde region. Administrative centre: Greenock. Pop: 83 050 (2003 est). Area: 162 sq km (63 sq miles)

Inverness (ˌɪnvəˈnɛs) *n* **1** a city in N Scotland, administrative centre of Highland: tourism and specialized engineering. Pop: 40 949 (2001) **2** *(sometimes not capital)* an overcoat with a removable cape

Inverness-shire (ˌɪnvəˈnɛsʃɪə, -ʃə) *n* (until 1975) a county of NW Scotland, now part of Highland

inverse (ɪnˈvɜːs, ˈɪnvɜːs) *adj* **1** opposite or contrary in effect, sequence, direction, etc **2** *maths* **a** (of a relationship) containing two variables such that an increase in one results in a decrease in the other: *the volume of a gas is in inverse ratio to its pressure* **b** (of an element) operating on a specified member of a set to produce the identity of the set: *the additive inverse element of x is –x, the multiplicative inverse element of x is 1/x* **3** *(usually prenominal)* upside-down; inverted: *in an inverse position* ▷ *n* **4** *maths* **a** another name for **reciprocal** (sense 7) **b** an inverse element **5** *logic* a categorial proposition derived from another by changing both the proposition and its subject from affirmative to negative, or vice versa, as *all immortals are angels* from *no mortals are angels* [c17 from Latin *inversus*, from *invertere* to INVERT] > **inˈversely** *adv*

inverse square law *n* any natural law in which the magnitude of a physical quantity varies inversely with the square of the distance from its source

inversion (ɪnˈvɜːʃən) *n* **1** the act of inverting or state of being inverted **2** something inverted, esp a reversal of order, mutual functions, etc: *an inversion of their previous relationship* **3** Also called: **anastrophe** *rhetoric* the reversal of a normal order of words **4** *chem* **a** the conversion of a dextrorotatory solution of sucrose into a laevorotatory solution of glucose and fructose by hydrolysis **b** any similar reaction in which the optical properties of the reactants are opposite to those of the products **5** *music* **a** the process or result of transposing the notes of a chord (esp a triad) such that the root, originally in the bass, is

i

placed in an upper part. When the bass note is the third of the triad, the resulting chord is the **first inversion**; when it is the fifth, the resulting chord is the **second inversion**. See also **root position** **b** (in counterpoint) the modification of a melody or part in which all ascending intervals are replaced by corresponding descending intervals and vice versa **c** the modification of an interval in which the higher note becomes the lower or the lower one the higher. See **complement** (sense 8) **6** *pathol* abnormal positioning of an organ or part, as in being upside down or turned inside out **7** *psychiatry* **a** the adoption of the role or characteristics of the opposite sex **b** another word for **homosexuality** **8** *meteorol* an abnormal condition in which the layer of air next to the earth's surface is cooler than an overlying layer **9** *anatomy, phonetics* another word for **retroflexion** (sense 2) **10** *computing* an operation by which each digit of a binary number is changed to the alternative digit, as *10110* to *01001* **11** *genetics* a type of chromosomal mutation in which a section of a chromosome, and hence the order of its genes, is reversed **12** *logic* the process of deriving the inverse of a categorial proposition **13** *maths* a transformation that takes a point *P* to a point *P′* such that $OP \cdot OP' = a^2$, where *a* is a constant and *P* and *P′* lie on a straight line through a fixed point O and on the same side of it > **in'versive** *adj*

invert *vb* (ɪnˈvɜːt) **1** to turn or cause to turn upside down or inside out **2** *(tr)* to reverse in effect, sequence, direction, etc **3** *(tr) phonetics* **a** to turn (the tip of the tongue) up and back **b** to pronounce (a speech sound) by retroflexion **4** *logic* to form the inverse of a categorial proposition ▷ *n* (ˈɪnvɜːt) **5** *psychiatry* **a** a person who adopts the role of the opposite sex **b** another word for **homosexual** **6** *architect* **a** the lower inner surface of a drain, sewer, etc. Compare **soffit** (sense 2) **b** an arch that is concave upwards, esp one used in foundations [C16 from Latin *invertere*, from IN-² + *vertere* to turn] > **in'vertible** *adj* > **in,verti'bility** *n*

invertase (ɪnˈvɜːteɪz) *n* an enzyme, occurring in the intestinal juice of animals and in yeasts, that hydrolyses sucrose to glucose and fructose. Also called: **saccharase**

invertebrate (ɪnˈvɜːtɪbrɪt, -ˌbreɪt) *n* **1** any animal lacking a backbone, including all species not classified as vertebrates ▷ *adj also* **in'vertebral** **2** of, relating to, or designating invertebrates

inverted comma *n* another term for **quotation mark**

inverted mordent *n music* a melodic ornament consisting of the rapid single or double alternation of a principal note with a note one degree higher. Also called: **upper mordent** See also **pralltriller**

inverted pleat *n dressmaking* a box pleat reversed so that the fullness of the material is turned inwards

inverted snob *n* a person who scorns the conventions or attitudes of his own class or social group by attempting to identify with people of a supposedly lower class

inverter *or* **invertor** (ɪnˈvɜːtə) *n* **1** any device for converting a direct current into an alternating current **2** *computing* another name for **NOT circuit**

invert sugar (ˈɪnvɜːt) *n* a mixture of fructose and glucose obtained by the inversion of sucrose

invest (ɪnˈvɛst) *vb* **1** (often foll by *in*) to lay out (money or capital in an enterprise, esp by purchasing shares) with the expectation of profit **2** *(tr; often foll by in)* to devote (effort, resources, etc, to a project) **3** *(tr; often foll by in or with) archaic or ceremonial* to clothe or adorn (in some garment, esp the robes of an office) **4** *(tr; often foll by in)* to install formally or ceremoniously (in an official position, rank, etc) **5** *(tr; foll by in or with)* to place (power, authority, etc, in) or provide (with power or authority) **6** *(tr; usually passive; foll by in or with)* to provide or endow (a person with qualities, characteristics, etc) **7** *(tr; foll by with) usually poetic* to cover or adorn, as if with a coat or garment **8** *(tr) rare* to surround with military forces; besiege **9** *(intr; foll by in) informal* to purchase; buy [C16 from Medieval Latin *investīre* to clothe, from Latin, from *vestīre*, from *vestis* a garment] > **in'vestable** *or* **in'vestible** *adj* > **in'vestor** *n*

investigate (ɪnˈvɛstɪˌɡeɪt) *vb* to inquire into (a situation or problem, esp a crime or death) thoroughly; examine systematically, esp in order to discover the truth [C16 from Latin *investīgāre* to search after, from IN-² + *vestīgium* track; see VESTIGE] > **in'vestigable** *adj* > **in'vestigative** *or* **in'vestigatory** *adj*

investigation (ɪnˌvɛstɪˈɡeɪʃən) *n* the act or process of investigating; a careful search or examination in order to discover facts, etc > **in,vesti'gational** *adj*

investigator (ɪnˈvɛstɪˌɡeɪtə) *n* a person who investigates, such as a private detective

investiture (ɪnˈvɛstɪtʃə) *n* **1** the act of presenting with a title or with the robes and insignia of an office or rank **2** (in feudal society) the formal bestowal of the possessory right to a fief or other benefice **3** a less common word for **investment** (sense 7) > **in'vestive** *adj*

investment (ɪnˈvɛstmənt) *n* **1** **a** the act of investing money **b** the amount invested **c** an enterprise, asset, etc, in which money is or can be invested **2** **a** the act of investing effort, resources, etc **b** the amount invested **3** *economics* the amount by which the stock of capital (plant, machinery, materials, etc) in an enterprise or economy changes **4** *biology* the outer layer or covering of an organ, part, or organism **5** a less common word for **investiture** (sense 1) **6** the act of investing or state of being invested, as with an official robe, a specific quality, etc **7** *rare* the act of besieging with military forces, works, etc

investment analyst *n* a specialist in forecasting the prices of stocks and shares

investment bond *n* a single-premium life-assurance policy in which a fixed sum is invested in an asset-backed fund

investment trust *n* a financial enterprise that invests its subscribed capital in securities for its investors' benefit

inveterate (ɪnˈvɛtərɪt) *adj* **1** long established, esp so as to be deep-rooted or ingrained **2** *(prenominal)* settled or confirmed in a habit or practice, esp a bad one; hardened **3** *obsolete* full of hatred; hostile [C16 from Latin *inveterātus* of long standing, from *inveterāre* to make old, from IN-² + *vetus* old] > **in'veteracy** *or* **in'veterateness** *n* > **in'veterately** *adv*

inviable (ɪnˈvaɪəbᵊl) *adj* not viable, esp financially; not able to survive: *an inviable company* > **in,via'bility** *or* **in'viableness** *n* > **in'viably** *adv*

invidious (ɪnˈvɪdɪəs) *adj* **1** incurring or tending to arouse resentment, unpopularity, etc: *an invidious task* **2** (of comparisons or distinctions) unfairly or offensively discriminating **3** *obsolete* grudging; envious [C17 from Latin *invidiōsus* full of envy, from *invidia* ENVY] > **in'vidiously** *adv* > **in'vidiousness** *n*

invigilate (ɪnˈvɪdʒɪˌleɪt) *vb (intr)* **1** *Brit* to watch examination candidates, esp to prevent cheating. US word: **proctor** **2** *archaic* to keep watch [C16 from Latin *invigilāre* to watch over, from IN-² + *vigilāre* to keep watch; see VIGIL] > **in,vigi'lation** *n* > **in'vigi,lator** *n*

invigorate (ɪnˈvɪɡəˌreɪt) *vb (tr)* to give vitality and vigour to; animate; brace; refresh: *to be invigorated by fresh air* [C17 from IN-² + Latin *vigor* VIGOUR] > **in'vigor,atingly** *adv* > **in,vigor'ation** *n* > **in'vigorative** *adj* > **in'vigoratively** *adv* > **in'vigor,ator** *n*

invincible (ɪnˈvɪnsəbᵊl) *adj* **1** incapable of being defeated; unconquerable **2** unable to be overcome; insuperable: *invincible prejudices* [C15 from Late Latin *invincibilis*, from Latin IN-¹ + *vincere* to conquer] > **in,vinci'bility** *or* **in'vincibleness** *n* > **in'vincibly** *adv*

in vino veritas *Latin* (ɪn ˈviːnəʊ ˈvɛrɪˌtæs) in wine there is truth; people speak the truth when they are drunk

inviolable (ɪnˈvaɪələbᵊl) *adj* that must not or cannot be transgressed, dishonoured, or broken; to be kept sacred: *an inviolable oath* > **in,viola'bility** *or* **in'violableness** *n* > **in'violably** *adv*

inviolate (ɪnˈvaɪəlɪt, -ˌleɪt) *adj* **1** free from violation, injury, disturbance, etc **2** a less common word for **inviolable**. > **in'violacy** *or* **in'violateness** *n* > **in'violately** *adv*

invisible (ɪnˈvɪzəbᵊl) *adj* **1** not visible; not able to be perceived by the eye **2** concealed from sight; hidden **3** not easily seen or noticed **4** kept hidden from public view; secret; clandestine **5** *economics* of or relating to services rather than goods in relation to the invisible balance ▷ *n* **6** *economics* an invisible item of trade; service > **in,visi'bility** *or* **in'visibleness** *n* > **in'visibly** *adv*

invisible balance *n economics* the difference in value between total exports of services plus payment of property incomes from abroad and total imports of services plus payment abroad of property incomes. Compare **balance of trade**

invisible ink *n* a liquid used for writing that does not become visible until it has been treated with chemicals, heat, ultraviolet light, etc

invitation (ˌɪnvɪˈteɪʃən) *n* **1** **a** the act of inviting, such as an offer of entertainment or hospitality **b** *(as modifier)*: *an invitation dance; an invitation race* **2** the act of enticing or attracting; allurement

invitatory (ɪnˈvaɪtətərɪ, -trɪ) *adj* **1** serving as or conveying an invitation ▷ *n, pl* **-tories** **2** any of various invitations to prayer, such as Psalm 95 in a religious service

invite *vb* (ɪnˈvaɪt) *(tr)* **1** to ask (a person or persons) in a friendly or polite way (to do something, attend an event, etc): *he invited them to dinner* **2** to make a request for, esp publicly or formally: *to invite applications* **3** to bring on or provoke; give occasion for **4** to welcome or tempt ▷ *n* (ˈɪnvaɪt) **5** an informal word for **invitation** [C16 from Latin *invītāre* to invite, entertain, from IN-² + *-vītāre*, probably related to Greek *hiesthai* to be desirous of] > **in'viter** *n*

inviting (ɪnˈvaɪtɪŋ) *adj* tempting; alluring; attractive > **in'vitingly** *adv* > **in'vitingness** *n*

in vitro (ɪn ˈviːtrəʊ) *adv, adj* (of biological processes or reactions) made to occur outside the living organism in an artificial environment, such as a culture medium [New Latin, literally: in glass]

in vitro fertilization *n* a technique enabling some women who are unable to conceive to bear children. Egg cells removed from a woman's ovary are fertilized by sperm in vitro; some of the resulting fertilized egg cells are incubated until the blastocyst stage, which are then implanted into her uterus. Abbreviation: **IVF**

in vivo (ɪn ˈviːvəʊ) *adv, adj* (of biological processes or experiments) occurring or carried out in the living organism [New Latin, literally: in a living (thing)]

invocate (ˈɪnvəˌkeɪt) *vb* an archaic word for **invoke**. > **invocative** (ɪnˈvɒkətɪv) *adj* > **'invo,cator** *n*

invocation (ˌɪnvəˈkeɪʃən) *n* **1** the act of invoking or calling upon some agent for assistance **2** a prayer asking God for help, forgiveness, etc, esp as part of a religious service **3** an appeal for inspiration and guidance from a Muse or deity at the beginning of a poem **4** **a** the act of summoning a spirit or demon from another world by ritual incantation or magic **b** the incantation used in this act > **,invo'cational** *adj* > **invocatory** (ɪnˈvɒkətərɪ, -trɪ) *adj*

invoice (ˈɪnvɔɪs) *n* **1** a document issued by a seller to a buyer listing the goods or services supplied and stating the sum of money due ▷ *vb* **2** *(tr)* **a** to present (a customer) with an invoice **b** to list (merchandise sold) on an invoice [C16 from earlier *invoyes*, from Old French *envois*, plural of *envoi* message; see ENVOY¹]

invoke (ɪnˈvəʊk) *vb (tr)* **1** to call upon (an agent, esp God or another deity) for help, inspiration, etc **2** to put (a law, penalty, etc) into use: *the union invoked the dispute procedure* **3** to appeal to (an outside agent or authority) for confirmation, corroboration, etc **4** to implore or beg (help, etc) **5** to summon (a spirit, demon, etc); conjure up [C15 from Latin *invocāre* to call upon, appeal to, from *vocāre* to call] > **in'vocable** *adj* > **in'voker** *n*

> USAGE *Invoke* is sometimes wrongly used where *evoke* is meant: *this proposal evoked* (not *invoked*) *a strong reaction*

involucel (ɪn'vɒljʊˌsɛl) *or* **involucellum** (ɪnˌvɒljʊ'sɛləm) *n, pl* **-cels** *or* **-cella** (-'sɛlə) a ring of bracts at the base of the florets of a compound umbel [C19 from New Latin *involūcellum* a little cover; see INVOLUCRE] > **inˌvolu'cellate** *or* **inˌvolu'cellated** *adj*

involucre ('ɪnvəˌluːkə) *or* **involucrum** (ˌɪnvə'luːkrəm) *n, pl* **-cres** *or* **-cra** (-krə) a ring of bracts at the base of an inflorescence in such plants as the composites [C16 (in the sense: envelope): from New Latin *involucrum*, from Latin: wrapper, from *involvere* to wrap; see INVOLVE] > ˌ**invo'lucral** *adj* > ˌ**invo'lucrate** *adj*

involuntary (ɪn'vɒləntərɪ, -trɪ) *adj* **1** carried out without one's conscious wishes; not voluntary; unintentional **2** *physiol* (esp of a movement or muscle) performed or acting without conscious control > **in'voluntarily** *adv* > **in'voluntariness** *n*

involute *adj* ('ɪnvəˌluːt) *also* **involuted** **1** complex, intricate, or involved **2** *botany* (esp of petals, leaves, etc, in bud) having margins that are rolled inwards **3** (of certain shells) closely coiled so that the axis is obscured ▷ *n* ('ɪnvəˌluːt) **4** *geometry* the curve described by the free end of a thread as it is wound around another curve, the **evolute**, such that its normals are tangential to the evolute ▷ *vb* (ˌɪnvə'luːt) **5** (*intr*) to become involute [C17 from Latin *involūtus*, from *involvere*; see INVOLVE] > '**invoˌlutely** *adv* > ˌ**invo'lutedly** *adv*

involute gear *n* a gear tooth form that is generated by involute geometry

involution (ˌɪnvə'luːʃən) *n* **1** the act of involving or complicating or the state of being involved or complicated **2** something involved or complicated **3** *zoology* degeneration or structural deformation **4** *biology* an involute formation or structure **5** *physiol* reduction in size of an organ or part, as of the uterus following childbirth or as a result of ageing **6** an algebraic operation in which a number, variable, expression etc, is raised to a specified power. Compare **evolution** (sense 5) **7** *grammar* an involved construction, such as one in which the subject is separated from the predicate by an additional clause > ˌ**invo'lutional** *adj*

involve (ɪn'vɒlv) *vb* (*tr*) **1** to include or contain as a necessary part **2** to have an effect on; spread to **3** (*often passive*; usually foll by *in* or *with*) to concern or associate significantly: *many people were involved in the crime* **4** (*often passive*) to make complicated; tangle **5** *rare, often poetic* to wrap or surround **6** *maths obsolete* to raise to a specified power [C14 from Latin *involvere* to roll in, surround, from IN-² + *volvere* to roll] > **in'volvement** *n* > **in'volver** *n*

involved (ɪn'vɒlvd) *adj* **1** complicated; difficult to comprehend **2** (*usually postpositive*) concerned or implicated **3** (*postpositive*; foll by *with*) *euphemistic* having sexual relations

invulnerable (ɪn'vʌlnərəbᵊl, -'vʌlnrəbᵊl) *adj* **1** incapable of being wounded, hurt, damaged, etc, either physically or emotionally **2** incapable of being damaged or captured > **inˌvulnera'bility** *or* **in'vulnerableness** *n* > **in'vulnerably** *adv*

invultuation (ɪnˌvʌltʃʊ'eɪʃən) *n* the use of or the act of making images of people, animals, etc, for witchcraft [C19 from Medieval Latin *invultuare* to make a likeness, from IN-² + *vultus* likeness]

inward ('ɪnwəd) *adj* **1** going or directed towards the middle of or into something **2** situated within; inside **3** of, relating to, or existing in the mind or spirit: *inward meditation* **4** of one's own country or a specific country: *inward investment* ▷ *adv* **5** a variant of **inwards** (sense 1) ▷ *n* **6** the inward part; inside > '**inwardness** *n*

inwardly ('ɪnwədlɪ) *adv* **1** within the private thoughts or feelings; secretly: *inwardly troubled, he kept smiling* **2** not aloud: *to laugh inwardly* **3** with reference to the inside or inner part; internally **4** *archaic* intimately; essentially

inwards *adv* ('ɪnwədz) *also* **inward** **1** towards the interior or middle of something **2** in, into, or towards the mind or spirit ▷ *pl n* ('ɪnədz) **3** a variant spelling of **innards**

inweave (ɪn'wiːv) *vb* **-weaves, -weaving, -wove** *or* **-weaved; -woven** *or* **-weaved** (*tr*) to weave together into or as if into a design, fabric, etc; interweave

inwrap (ɪn'ræp) *vb* **-wraps, -wrapping, -wrapped** a less common spelling of **enwrap**

inwrought (ˌɪn'rɔːt) *adj* **1** worked or woven into material, esp decoratively **2** *rare* blended with other things

in-your-face *adj slang* aggressive and confrontational: *provocative in-your-face activism*

io *the internet domain name for* British Indian Ocean Territory

Io[1] ('aɪəʊ) *n Greek myth* a maiden loved by Zeus and turned into a white heifer by either Zeus or Hera

Io[2] ('aɪəʊ) *n* the innermost of the four Galilean satellites of Jupiter, displaying intense volcanic activity. Diameter: 3640 km; orbital radius: 422 000 km

Io[3] *the chemical symbol for* ionium

I/O *abbreviation for* input/output

Ioánnina (*Greek* jɔ'anina) *or* **Yanina** *n* a city in NW Greece: belonged to the Serbs (1349–1430) and then the Turks (until 1913); seat of Ali Pasha, the "Lion of Janina", from 1788 to 1822. Pop: 78 000 (2005 est). Serbian name: **Janina**

IOC *abbreviation for* International Olympic Committee

iodate ('aɪəˌdeɪt) *n* **1** a salt of iodic acid ▷ *vb* **2** (*tr*) another word for **iodize.** > ˌ**io'dation** *n*

iodic (aɪ'ɒdɪk) *adj* of or containing iodine, esp in the pentavalent state

iodic acid *n* a colourless or pale yellow soluble crystalline substance that forms acidic aqueous solutions. Used as a reagent and disinfectant. Formula: HIO_3

iodide ('aɪəˌdaɪd) *n* **1** a salt of hydriodic acid, containing the iodide ion, I^- **2** a compound containing an iodine atom, such as methyl iodide, CH_3I

iodine ('aɪəˌdiːn) *n* a bluish-black element of the halogen group that sublimates into a violet irritating gas. Its compounds are used in medicine and photography and in dyes. The radioisotope **iodine-131** (**radioiodine**), with a half-life of 8 days, is used in the diagnosis and treatment of thyroid disease. Symbol: I; atomic no.: 53; atomic wt.: 126.90447; valency: 1, 3, 5, or 7; relative density: 4.93; melting pt.: 113.5°C; boiling pt.: 184.35°C [C19 from French *iode*, from Greek *iōdēs* rust-coloured, but taken to mean violet-coloured, through a mistaken derivation from *ion* violet]

iodism ('aɪəˌdɪzəm) *n* poisoning induced by ingestion of iodine or its compounds

iodize *or* **iodise** ('aɪəˌdaɪz) *vb* (*tr*) to treat or react with iodine or an iodine compound. Also: **iodate** > ˌ**iodi'zation** *or* ˌ**iodi'sation** *n* > '**ioˌdizer** *or* '**ioˌdiser** *n*

iodo- *or before a vowel* **iod-** *combining form* indicating iodine: *iodoform; iodism*

iodoform (aɪ'ɒdəˌfɔːm) *n* a yellow crystalline insoluble volatile solid with a penetrating sweet odour made by heating alcohol with iodine and an alkali: used as an antiseptic. Formula: CHI_3. Systematic name: **triiodomethane**

iodometry (ˌaɪə'dɒmɪtrɪ) *n chem* a procedure used in volumetric analysis for determining the quantity of substance present that contains, liberates, or reacts with iodine > **iodometric** (ˌaɪədəʊ'mɛtrɪk) *or* ˌ**iodo'metrical** *adj* > ˌ**iodo'metrically** *adv*

iodopsin (ˌaɪə'dɒpsɪn) *n* a violet light-sensitive pigment in the cones of the retina of the eye that is responsible for colour vision. Also called: **visual violet** See also **rhodopsin**

iodous (aɪ'ɒdəs) *adj* **1** of or containing iodine, esp in the trivalent state **2** concerned with or resembling iodine

iolite ('aɪəˌlaɪt) *n* another name for **cordierite** [C19 from Greek *ion* a violet + -LITE]

IOM *abbreviation for* Isle of Man

Io moth *n* an American saturniid moth, *Automeris io*, bright yellow with a blue-and-pink eyelike spot on each of the hind wings [C19 after Io (who was tormented by a gadfly), referring to the sting of the larva]

ion ('aɪən, -ɒn) *n* an electrically charged atom or group of atoms formed by the loss or gain of one or more electrons. See also **cation, anion** [C19 from Greek, literally: going, from *ienai* to go]

-ion *suffix forming nouns* indicating an action, process, or state: *creation; objection*. Compare **-ation, -tion** [from Latin *-iōn-*, *-io*]

Iona (aɪ'əʊnə) *n* an island off the W coast of Scotland, in the Inner Hebrides: site of St Columba's monastery (founded in 563) and an important early centre of Christianity. Area: 854 ha (2112 acres)

IONARC *abbreviation for* Indian Ocean National Association for Regional Cooperation

ion engine *n* a type of rocket engine in which thrust is obtained by the electrostatic acceleration of charged positive ions. Compare **plasma engine**

ion exchange *n* the process in which ions are exchanged between a solution and an insoluble solid, usually a resin. It is used to soften water, to separate radioactive isotopes, and to purify certain industrial chemicals

Ionia (aɪ'əʊnɪə) *n* an ancient region of W central Asia Minor, including adjacent Aegean islands: colonized by Greeks in about 1100 BC

Ionian (aɪ'əʊnɪən) *n* **1** a member of a Hellenic people who settled in Attica in about 1100 BC and later colonized the islands and E coast of the Aegean Sea ▷ *adj* **2** of or relating to this people or their dialect of Ancient Greek; Ionic **3** of or relating to Ionia **4** *music* relating to or denoting an authentic mode represented by the ascending natural diatonic scale from C to C and forming the basis of the modern major key. See also **Hypo-**

Ionian Islands *pl n* a group of Greek islands in the Ionian Sea, consisting of Corfu, Cephalonia, Zante, Levkas, Ithaca, Cythera, and Paxos: ceded to Greece in 1864. Pop: 212 984 (2001). Area: 2307 sq km (891 sq miles)

Ionian Sea *n* the part of the Mediterranean Sea between SE Italy, E Sicily, and Greece

ionic (aɪ'ɒnɪk) *adj* of, relating to, or occurring in the form of ions

Ionic (aɪ'ɒnɪk) *adj* **1** of, denoting, or relating to one of the five classical orders of architecture, characterized by fluted columns and capitals with scroll-like ornaments. See also **Doric, Composite, Tuscan, Corinthian** **2** of or relating to Ionia, its inhabitants, or their dialect of Ancient Greek **3** *prosody* of, relating to, designating, or employing Ionics in verse ▷ *n* **4** one of four chief dialects of Ancient Greek; the dialect spoken in Ionia. Compare **Aeolic, Arcadic, Doric** See also **Attic** (sense 3) **5** (in classical prosody) a type of metrical foot having either two long followed by two short syllables (**greater Ionic**), or two short followed by two long syllables (**lesser Ionic**)

ionic bond *n* another name for **electrovalent bond**

ion implantation *n* a technique used in the manufacture of semiconductor devices in which impurities are implanted by means of beams of electrically accelerated ions

ionium (aɪ'əʊnɪəm) *n obsolete* a naturally occurring radioisotope of thorium with a mass number of 230. Symbol: **Io** [C20 from New Latin, from ION + -IUM]

ionization *or* **ionisation** (ˌaɪənaɪ'zeɪʃən) *n* **a** the formation of ions as a result of a chemical reaction, high temperature, electrical discharge, particle collisions, or radiation **b** (*as modifier*): *ionization temperature; ionization current*

ionization chamber *n* a device for detecting and measuring ionizing radiation, consisting of a tube containing a low pressure gas and two electrodes between which a high voltage is maintained. The current between the electrodes is a function of the intensity of the radiation

ionization potential *n* the energy usually required to remove an electron from an atom, molecule, or radical, usually measured in electronvolts. Symbol: *I* Compare **electron affinity**

ionize *or* **ionise** ('aɪəˌnaɪz) *vb* to change or become changed into ions > 'ionˌizable *or* 'ionˌisable *adj*

ionizer *or* **ioniser** ('aɪəˌnaɪzə) *n* a person or thing that ionizes, esp an electrical device used within a room to refresh its atmosphere by restoring negative ions

ionizing radiation *n* electromagnetic or corpuscular radiation that is able to cause ionization

ionone ('aɪəˌnəʊn) *n* **1** a yellowish liquid mixture of two isomers with an odour of violets, extracted from certain plants and used in perfumery **2** either of these two isomers. Formula: $C_{13}H_{20}O$

ionopause (aɪˈɒnəˌpɔːz) *n* the transitional zone in the atmosphere between the ionosphere and the exosphere, about 644 km (400 miles) from the earth's surface

ionophore (aɪˈɒnəˌfɔː) *n* a chemical compound capable of forming a complex with an ion and transporting it through a biological membrane [C20 from ION + -O- + -PHORE]

ionosphere (aɪˈɒnəˌsfɪə) *n* a region of the earth's atmosphere, extending from about 60 kilometres to 1000 km above the earth's surface, in which there is a high concentration of free electrons formed as a result of ionizing radiation entering the atmosphere from space. See also **D region, E region, F region.** > ionospheric (aɪˌɒnəˈsfɛrɪk) *adj*

ionospheric wave *n* another name for **sky wave**

ionotropic receptor *n* *physiology* a receptor that functions directly by opening ion channels that enable specific ions to stream in an out of the cell. Compare **metabotropic receptor**

ionotropy (ˌaɪəˈnɒtrəpɪ) *n* *chem* the reversible interconversion of a pair of organic isomers as a result of the migration of an ionic part of the molecule

ion rocket *n* a rocket propelled by an ion engine

iontophoresis (aɪˌɒntəʊfəˈriːsɪs) *n* *biochem* a technique for studying neurotransmitters in the brain by the application of experimental solutions to the tissues through fine glass electrodes [C20 from Greek *iont-, ion,* from *ienai* to go + -PHORESIS]

IOOF *abbreviation for* Independent Order of Oddfellows

iota (aɪˈəʊtə) *n* **1** the ninth letter in the Greek alphabet (I, ι), a vowel or semivowel, transliterated as *i* or *j* **2** (*usually used with a negative*) a very small amount; jot (esp in the phrase **not one** *or* **an iota**) [C16 via Latin from Greek, of Semitic origin; see JOT]

iotacism (aɪˈəʊtəˌsɪzəm) *n* a tendency of vowels and diphthongs, esp in Modern Greek, to acquire the pronunciation of the vowel iota (i:)

IOU *n* a written promise or reminder to pay a debt [C17 representing *I owe you*]

-ious *suffix forming adjectives from nouns* characterized by or full of: *ambitious; religious; suspicious.* Compare **-eous** [from Latin *-ius* and *-iōsus* full of]

IOW *abbreviation for* **1** Isle of Wight **2** *text messaging* in other words

Iowa ('aɪəʊə) *n* a state of the N central US, in the Midwest: consists of rolling plains crossed by many rivers, with the Missouri forming the western border and the Mississippi the eastern. Capital: Des Moines. Pop: 2 944 062 (2003 est.).

Area: 144 887 sq km (55 941 sq miles). Abbreviations: **Ia.**, (with zip code) **IA**

Iowan ('aɪəʊən) *n* **1** a native or inhabitant of Iowa ▷ *adj* **2** of or relating to Iowa or its inhabitants

IP *abbreviation for* **1** internet protocol: a code used to label packets of data sent across the internet, identifying both the sending and the receiving computers **2** *law* intellectual property

IPA *abbreviation for* International Phonetic Alphabet

IP address *n* *computing* internet protocol address: the numeric code that identifies all computers that are connected to the internet

IPCC *abbreviation for* Intergovernmental Panel on Climate Change

ipecacuanha (ˌɪpɪˌkækjʊˈænə) *or* **ipecac** ('ɪpɪˌkæk) *n* **1** a low-growing South American rubiaceous shrub, *Cephaelis ipecacuanha* **2** a drug prepared from the dried roots of this plant, used as a purgative and emetic [C18 from Portuguese, from Tupi *ipekaaguéne,* from *ipeh* low + *kaa* leaves + *guéne* vomit]

Iphigenia (ˌɪfɪdʒɪˈnaɪə) *n* *Greek myth* the daughter of Agamemnon, taken by him to be sacrificed to Artemis, who saved her life and made her a priestess

I-pin (ɪˈpɪn) *n* a variant transliteration of the Chinese name for **Yibin**

IPO *abbreviation for* **1** independent publicly owned company **2** *stock exchange* initial public offering

iPod, iPOD *or* **iPod** ('aɪˌpɒd) *n* *trademark* a small portable digital audio player capable of storing thousands of tracks downloaded from the internet or transferred from a CD > 'iˌPodder *n*

Ipoh ('iːpəʊ) *n* a city in Malaysia, capital of Perak state: tin-mining centre. Pop: 643 000 (2005 est)

ipomoea (ˌɪpəˈmɪə, ˌaɪ-) *n* **1** any tropical or subtropical convolvulaceous plant of the genus *Ipomoea,* such as the morning-glory, sweet potato, and jalap, having trumpet-shaped flowers **2** the dried root of a Mexican species, *I. orizabensis,* which yields a cathartic resin [C18 New Latin, from Greek *ips* worm + *homoios* like]

ippon ('ɪpɒn) *n* *judo, karate* a winning point awarded in a sparring competition for a perfectly executed technique [C20 Japanese, literally: one point]

Ipsambul (ˌɪpsæmˈbuːl) *n* another name for **Abu Simbel**

ipse dixit Latin ('ɪpseɪ 'dɪksɪt) *n* an arbitrary and unsupported assertion [C16, literally: he himself said it]

ipsilateral (ˌɪpsɪˈlætərəl) *adj* on or affecting the same side of the body [C20 irregularly formed from Latin *ipse* self + LATERAL]

ipsissima verba Latin (ɪpˈsɪsɪmə 'vɜːbə) *pl n* the very words; verbatim

ipso facto ('ɪpsəʊ 'fæktəʊ) *adv* by that very fact or act: *ipso facto his guilt was apparent* [from Latin]

ipso jure ('ɪpsəʊ 'jʊərɪ) *adv* by the law itself; by operation of law [from Latin]

Ipsus ('ɪpsəs) *n* an ancient town in Asia Minor, in S Phrygia: site of a decisive battle (301 BC) in the Wars of the Diadochi in which Lysimachus and Seleucus defeated Antigonus and Demetrius

Ipswich ('ɪpswɪtʃ) *n* a town in E England, administrative centre of Suffolk, a port at the head of the Orwell estuary: financial services, telecommunications. Pop: 138 718 (2001)

iq *the internet domain name for* Iraq

IQ *abbreviation for* intelligence quotient

i.q. *abbreviation for* idem quod [Latin: the same as]

Iqaluit (ɪˈkæluɪt) *n* a town in N Canada, capital of Nunavut. Pop: 5236 (2001). Former name: Frobisher Bay

Iquique (Spanish iˈkike) *n* a port in N Chile: oil refineries. Pop: 243 000 (2005 est)

Iquitos (Spanish iˈkitɔs) *n* an inland port in NE Peru, on the Amazon 3703 km (2300 miles) from the Atlantic: head of navigation for large steamers. Pop: 389 000 (2005 est)

ir *the internet domain name for* Iran

Ir *the chemical symbol for* iridium

IR *abbreviation for* **1** infrared **2** (in Britain) Inland Revenue **3** *international car registration for* Iran

Ir. *abbreviation for* **1** Ireland **2** Irish

ir- *prefix* a variant of **in-¹** and **in-²** before *r*

IRA *abbreviation for* **Irish Republican Army**

iracund ('aɪərəˌkʌnd) *adj rare* easily angered [C19 from Latin *īrācundus,* from *īra* anger] > ˌira'cundity *n*

irade (ɪˈrɑːdɛ) *n* a written edict of a Muslim ruler [C19 from Turkish: will, desire, from Arabic *irādah*]

Iráklion (Greek iˈraklion) *n* a port in Greece, in N Crete: former capital of Crete (until 1841); ruled by Venetians (13th–17th centuries). Pop: 150 000 (2005 est). Italian name: **Candia** Also called: **Heraklion, Herakleion**

Iran (ɪˈrɑːn) *n* a republic in SW Asia, between the Caspian Sea and the Persian Gulf: a monarchy until an Islamic revolution in 1979 headed by the Ayatollah Khomeini when the Shah was obliged to leave the country. Consists chiefly of a high central desert plateau almost completely surrounded by mountains, a semitropical fertile region along the Caspian coast, and a hot and dry area beside the Persian Gulf. Oil is the most important export. Official language: Farsi (Persian). Official religion: Muslim majority. Currency: rial. Capital: Tehran. Pop: 68 789 000 (2004 est). Area: 1 647 050 sq km (635 932 sq miles). Former name (until 1935): **Persia** Official name: **Islamic Republic of Iran** See also **Persian Empire**

Iranian (ɪˈreɪnɪən) *n* **1** a native, citizen, or inhabitant of Iran **2** a branch of the Indo-European family of languages, divided into **West Iranian** (including Old Persian, Pahlavi, modern Persian, Kurdish, Baluchi, and Tajik) and **East Iranian** (including Avestan, Sogdian, Pashto, and Ossetic) **3** the modern Persian language ▷ *adj* **4** relating to, denoting, or characteristic of Iran, its inhabitants, or their language; Persian **5** belonging to or relating to the Iranian branch of Indo-European

Iran-Iraq War *n* the war (1980–88) fought by Iran and Iraq, following the Iraqi invasion of disputed border territory in Iran. It ended indecisively with no important gains on either side: Iraq subsequently (1990) conceded the disputed territory. Also called: **Gulf War**

Iraq (ɪˈrɑːk) *n* a republic in SW Asia, on the Persian Gulf: coextensive with ancient Mesopotamia; became a British mandate in 1920, independent in 1932, and a republic in 1958. The Iraqi invasion of Kuwait (1990) led to their defeat in the first Gulf War (1991) by US-led UN forces. The second Gulf War (2003) took place when Iraq was invaded by a coalition of US, UK and other forces. Iraq consists chiefly of the mountains of Kurdistan in the northeast, part of the Syrian Desert, and the lower basin of the Rivers Tigris and Euphrates. Oil is the major export. Official language: Arabic; Kurdish is official in the Kurdish Autonomous Region only. Official religion: Muslim. Currency: dinar. Capital: Baghdad. Pop: 25 856 000 (2004 est). Area: 438 446 sq km (169 284 sq miles)

Iraqi (ɪˈrɑːkɪ) *adj* **1** of or relating to Iraq or its inhabitants ▷ *n* **2** a native or inhabitant of Iraq

IRAS *abbreviation for* Infrared Astronomical Satellite, a pioneering international earth-orbiting satellite that during 1983 made an all-sky survey at infrared wavelengths

irascible (ɪˈræsɪbᵊl) *adj* **1** easily angered; irritable **2** showing irritability: *an irascible action* [C16 from Late Latin *īrascibilis,* from Latin *īra* anger] > iˌrasci'bility *or* i'rascibleness *n* > i'rascibly *adv*

irate (aɪˈreɪt) *adj* **1** incensed with anger; furious **2** marked by extreme anger [C19 from Latin *īrātus* enraged, from *īrascī* to be angry] > i'rately *adv*

Irbid ('ɪrbɪd) *n* a town in NW Jordan. Pop: 280 000 (2005 est)

Irbil ('ɪəbɪl) *n* a variant of **Erbil**

IRBM *abbreviation for* **intermediate range ballistic missile**

IRC *abbreviation for* **1** International Red Cross **2**

International Red Crescent

IRD (in New Zealand) *abbreviation for* Inland Revenue Department

ire (aɪə) *n literary* anger; wrath [c13 from Old French, from Latin *īra*] > 'ireful *adj* > 'irefully *adv* > 'irefulness *n* > 'ireless *adj*

Ire. *abbreviation for* Ireland

Ireland ('aɪələnd) *n* **1** an island off NW Europe: part of the British Isles, separated from Britain by the North Channel, the Irish Sea, and St George's Channel; contains large areas of peat bog, with mountains that rise over 900 m (3000 ft) in the southwest and several large lakes. It was conquered by England in the 16th and early 17th centuries and ruled as a dependency until 1801, when it was united with Great Britain until its division in 1921 into the Irish Free State and Northern Ireland. Latin name: **Hibernia 2 Republic of Ireland** Also called: **Irish Republic, Southern Ireland** a republic in NW Europe occupying most of Ireland: established as the Irish Free State (a British dominion) in 1921 and declared a republic in 1949; joined the European Community (now the European Union) in 1973. Official languages: Irish (Gaelic) and English. Currency: euro. Capital: Dublin. Pop: 3 999 000 (2004 est). Area: 70 285 sq km (27 137 sqmiles). Gaelic name: **Eire** ▷ See also **Northern Ireland**

Irene (aɪ'riːnɪ) *n Greek myth* the goddess of peace

irenic, eirenic (aɪ'riːnɪk, -'rɛn-) *or* **irenical, eirenical** *adj* tending to conciliate or promote peace [c19 from Greek *eirēnikos*, from *eirēnē* peace] > i'renically *or* ei'renically *adv*

irenicon (aɪ'riːnɪˌkɒn) *n* a variant spelling of **eirenicon**

irenics (aɪ'riːnɪks, -'rɛn-) *n* (*functioning as singular*) that branch of theology that is concerned with unity between Christian sects and denominations

Irian Barat ('ɪərɪən 'bærɑːt) *n* a former Indonesian name for **Papua** (sense 2) **(Irian Jaya)**

Irian Jaya *n* a former Indonesian name (1973–2001) for **Papua** (sense 2)

iridaceous (ˌɪrɪ'deɪʃəs, ˌaɪ-) *adj* of, relating to, or belonging to the *Iridaceae*, a family of monocotyledonous plants, including iris and crocus, having swordlike leaves and showy flowers

iridectomy (ˌɪrɪ'dɛktəmɪ, ˌaɪ-) *n, pl* -mies surgical removal of part of the iris

iridescent (ˌɪrɪ'dɛs³nt) *adj* displaying a spectrum of colours that shimmer and change due to interference and scattering as the observer's position changes [c18 from IRIDO- + -ESCENT] > ˌiri'descence *n* > ˌiri'descently *adv*

iridic (aɪ'rɪdɪk, ɪ'rɪd-) *adj* **1** of or containing iridium, esp in the tetravalent state **2** of or relating to the iris of the eye

iridium (aɪ'rɪdɪəm, ɪ'rɪd-) *n* a very hard inert yellowish-white transition element that is the most corrosion-resistant metal known. It occurs in platinum ores and is used as an alloy with platinum. Symbol: Ir; atomic no.: 77; atomic wt.: 192.22; valency: 3 or 4; relative density: 22.42; melting pt.: 2447°C; boiling pt.: 4428°C [c19 New Latin, from IRIDO- + -IUM; from its colourful appearance when dissolving in certain acids]

irido- *or before a vowel* **irid-** *combining form* **1** denoting the iris of the eye or the genus of plants: *iridectomy; iridaceous* **2** denoting a rainbow: *iridescent* [from Latin *irid-*, IRIS]

iridocyte ('ɪrɪdəʊˌsaɪt) *n zoology* a guanine-containing cell in the skin of fish and some cephalopods, giving these animals their iridescence

iridology (ˌɪrɪ'dɒlədʒɪ) *n* a technique used in complementary medicine to diagnose illness by studying a patient's eyes [c20 from Latin IRIDO- + OLOGY] > ˌiri'dologist *n*

iridosmine (ˌɪrɪ'dɒsmaɪn, ˌaɪrɪ-) *or* **iridosmium** *n* other names for **osmiridium** [c19 from IRIDO- + OSM(IUM) + INE-²]

iridotomy (ˌɪrɪ'dɒtəmɪ, ˌaɪrɪ-) *n, pl* -mies surgical

incision into the iris, esp to create an artificial pupil

iris ('aɪrɪs) *n, pl* **irises** *or* **irides** ('aɪrɪˌdiːz, 'ɪrɪ-) **1** the coloured muscular diaphragm that surrounds and controls the size of the pupil **2** Also called: **fleur-de-lys** any plant of the iridaceous genus *Iris*, having brightly coloured flowers composed of three petals and three drooping sepals. See also **flag², orris¹, stinking iris 3** Also called: **rainbow quartz** a form of quartz that reflects light polychromatically from internal fractures **4** a rare or poetic word for **rainbow 5** something resembling a rainbow; iridescence **6** short for **iris diaphragm** [c14 from Latin: rainbow, iris (flower), crystal, from Greek]

Iris ('aɪrɪs) *n* the goddess of the rainbow along which she travelled to earth as a messenger of the gods

iris diaphragm *n* an adjustable diaphragm that regulates the amount of light entering an optical instrument, esp a camera. It usually consists of a number of thin metal leaves arranged so that they open out into an approximately circular aperture. Sometimes shortened to: **iris**

Irish ('aɪrɪʃ) *adj* **1** of, relating to, or characteristic of Ireland, its people, their Celtic language, or their dialect of English **2** *informal, offensive* ludicrous or illogical ▷ *n* **3** the Irish (*functioning as plural*) the natives or inhabitants of Ireland **4** another name for **Irish Gaelic**

Irish bull *n* a ludicrously illogical statement. See also **bull²**

Irish coffee *n* hot coffee mixed with Irish whiskey and topped with double cream

Irish elk *n* an extinct Eurasian giant deer of the Pleistocene genus *Megaloceros*, which had antlers up to 4 metres across

Irish Free State *n* a former name for the (Republic of) **Ireland** (1921–37)

Irish Gaelic *n* the Goidelic language of the Celts of Ireland, now spoken mainly along the west coast; an official language of the Republic of Ireland since 1921

Irishism ('aɪrɪˌʃɪzəm) *n* an Irish custom or idiom

Irishman ('aɪrɪʃmən) *n, pl* -men a male native, citizen, or inhabitant of Ireland or a male descendant of someone Irish

Irish moss *n* another name for **carrageen**

Irish potato *n chiefly US* another name for **potato**

Irish Republic *n* See **Ireland¹** (sense 2)

Irish Republican Army *n* a militant organization of Irish nationalists founded with the aim of striving for a united independent Ireland by means of guerrilla warfare. Abbreviation: **IRA**

Irish Sea *n* an arm of the North Atlantic Ocean between Great Britain and Ireland

Irish setter *n* a breed of setter developed in Ireland, having a flat soft brownish-red coat. Also called: **red setter**

Irish stew *n* a white stew made of mutton, lamb, or beef, with potatoes, onions, etc

Irish terrier *n* a breed of terrier with a wiry wheaten or reddish coat

Irish water spaniel *n* a breed of dog used to hunt duck and having a dense coat of a purplish-liver colour that falls in tight ringlets covering the whole body except for the face and tail

Irish whiskey *n* any of the whiskeys made in Ireland, usually from malt and subject to three distillations

Irish wolfhound *n* a very large breed of hound with a rough thick coat

Irishwoman ('aɪrɪʃˌwʊmən) *n, pl* -women a female native, citizen, or inhabitant of Ireland or a female descendant of someone Irish

iritis (aɪ'raɪtɪs) *n* inflammation of the iris of the eye > **iritic** (aɪ'rɪtɪk) *adj*

irk (ɜːk) *vb* (*tr*) to irritate, vex, or annoy [c13 *irken* to grow weary; probably related to Old Norse *yrkja* to work]

irksome ('ɜːksəm) *adj* causing vexation, annoyance, or boredom; troublesome or tedious > 'irksomely *adv* > 'irksomeness *n*

Irkutsk (*Russian* ir'kutsk) *n* a city in S Russia; situated on the Trans-Siberian railway; university (1918); one of the largest industrial centres in Siberia, esp for heavy engineering. Pop: 587 000 (2005 est)

IRL *abbreviation for* **1** *text messaging* In real life **2** *international car registration for* Republic of Ireland

IRM *abbreviation for* **innate releasing mechanism**

IRO *abbreviation for* **1** (in Britain) Inland Revenue Office **2** International Refugee Organization

iroko (ɪ'rəʊkəʊ) *n, pl* -kos **1** a tropical African hardwood tree of the genus *Chlorophora* **2** the hard reddish-brown wood of this tree [c19 from Yoruba]

iron ('aɪən) *n* **1 a** a malleable ductile silvery-white ferromagnetic metallic element occurring principally in haematite and magnetite. It is widely used for structural and engineering purposes. See also **steel, cast iron, wrought iron, pig iron**. Symbol: Fe; atomic no.: 26; atomic wt.: 55.847; valency: 2,3,4, or 6; relative density: 7.874; melting pt.: 1538°C; boiling pt.: 2862°C. Related adjs: **ferric, ferrous** Related prefix: **ferro- b** (*as modifier*): *iron railings* **2** any of certain tools or implements made of iron or steel, esp for use when hot **3** an appliance for pressing fabrics using dry heat or steam, esp a small electrically heated device with a handle and a weighted flat bottom **4** any of various golf clubs with narrow metal heads, numbered from 1 to 9 according to the slant of the face, used esp for approach shots: *a No. 6 iron* **5** an informal word for **harpoon** (sense 1) **6** *US slang* a splintlike support for a malformed leg **7** great hardness, strength, or resolve **8** *astronomy* short for **iron meteorite 9** See **shooting iron 10** strike while the iron is hot to act at an opportune moment ▷ *adj* **11** very hard, immovable, or implacable **12** very strong; extremely robust **13** cruel or unyielding **14** an iron fist a cruel and unyielding attitude or approach. See also **velvet** (sense 6) ▷ *vb* **15** to smooth (clothes or fabric) by removing (creases or wrinkles) using a heated iron; press **16** (*tr*) to furnish or clothe with iron **17** (*tr*) *rare* to place (a prisoner) in irons ▷ See also **iron out, irons** [Old English *īren*; related to Old High German *īsan*, Old Norse *jārn*; compare Old Irish *īarn*] > 'ironer *n* > 'ironless *adj* > 'iron,like *adj*

iron age *n classical myth* the last and worst age in the history of the world

Iron Age *n* **a** the period following the Bronze Age characterized by the extremely rapid spread of iron tools and weapons, which began in the Middle East about 1100 BC **b** (*as modifier*): *an Iron-Age weapon*

ironbark ('aɪənˌbɑːk) *n* any of several Australian eucalyptus trees that have hard rough bark

ironbound ('aɪənˌbaʊnd) *adj* **1** bound with iron **2** unyielding; inflexible **3** (of a coast) rocky; rugged

ironclad *adj* (ˌaɪən'klæd) **1** covered or protected with iron: *an ironclad warship* **2** inflexible; rigid: *an ironclad rule* **3** not able to be assailed or contradicted ▷ *n* ('aɪənˌklæd) **4** a large wooden 19th-century warship with armoured plating

Iron Cross *n* the highest decoration for bravery awarded to the German armed forces in wartime: instituted in 1813

Iron Curtain *n* **a** (formerly) the guarded border between the countries of the Soviet bloc and the rest of Europe **b** (*as modifier*): *Iron Curtain countries*

Iron Gate *or* **Iron Gates** *n* a gorge of the River Danube on the border between Romania and Serbia and Montenegro. Length: 3 km (2 miles). Romanian name: **Porţile de Fier**

iron glance *n* another name for **hematite**

iron grey *n* **a** a neutral or dark grey colour **b** (*as adjective*): *iron-grey hair*

Iron Guard *n* a Romanian fascist party that ceased to exist after World War II

iron hand *n* harsh or rigorous control;

i

overbearing or autocratic force: *he ruled with an iron hand*

iron horse *n archaic* a steam-driven railway locomotive

ironic (aɪˈrɒnɪk) *or* **ironical** *adj* of, characterized by, or using irony > i'**ronicalness** *n*

ironically (aɪˈrɒnɪkəlɪ) *adv* **1** (*sentence modifier*) it is ironic that **2** in an ironic manner

ironing (ˈaɪənɪŋ) *n* **1** the act of ironing washed clothes **2** clothes that are to be or that have been ironed

ironing board *n* a board, usually on legs, with a suitable covering on which to iron clothes

ironize *or* **ironise** (ˈaɪrəˌnaɪz) *vb* **1** (*intr*) to use or indulge in irony **2** (*tr*) to make ironic or use ironically > '**ironist** *n*

iron lung *n* **1** an airtight metal cylinder enclosing the entire body up to the neck and providing artificial respiration when the respiratory muscles are paralysed, as by poliomyelitis **2** *Irish informal* a gas container used in dispensing beer

iron maiden *n* a medieval instrument of torture, consisting of a hinged case (often shaped in the form of a woman) lined with iron spikes, which was forcibly closed on the victim

iron man *n Austral* an event at a surf carnival in which contestants compete at swimming, surfing, running, etc

ironmaster (ˈaɪənˌmɑːstə) *n Brit* a manufacturer of iron, esp (formerly) the owner of an ironworks

iron meteorite *n* a meteorite that is composed mainly of iron and nickel

ironmonger (ˈaɪənˌmʌŋɡə) *n Brit* a dealer in metal utensils, hardware, locks, etc. US and Canadian equivalent: **hardware dealer** > '**iron,mongery** *n*

iron out *vb* (*tr, adverb*) **1** to smooth, using a heated iron **2** to put right or settle (a problem or difficulty) as a result of negotiations or discussions **3** *Austral informal* to knock unconscious

iron pan *n geology* a hard layer of precipitated iron salts often found below the surface of sands and gravels

iron pyrites (ˈpaɪraɪts) *n* another name for **pyrite**

iron rations *pl n* emergency food supplies, esp for military personnel in action. See also **C rations, K ration, MRE**

irons (ˈaɪənz) *pl n* **1** fetters or chains (often in the phrase **in** *or* **into irons**) **2 in irons** *nautical* (of a sailing vessel) headed directly into the wind without steerageway **3 have several irons in the fire** to be involved in many projects, activities, etc

ironsides (ˈaɪənˌsaɪdz) *n* **1** a person with great stamina or resistance **2** an ironclad ship **3** (*often capital*) (in the English Civil War) **a** the cavalry regiment trained and commanded by Oliver Cromwell **b** Cromwell's entire army

iron sights *pl n* conventional non-telescopic sights on a rifle

ironstone (ˈaɪənˌstəʊn) *n* **1** any rock consisting mainly of an iron-bearing ore **2** Also called: **ironstone china** a tough durable earthenware

ironware (ˈaɪənˌwɛə) *n* domestic articles made of iron

ironwood (ˈaɪənˌwʊd) *n* **1** any of various betulaceous trees, such as hornbeam, that have very hard wood **2** a Californian rosaceous tree, *Lyonothamnus floribundus*, with very hard wood **3** any of various other trees with hard wood, such as the mopani **4** the wood of any of these trees

ironwork (ˈaɪənˌwɜːk) *n* **1** work done in iron, esp decorative work **2** the craft or practice of working in iron ▷ See also **ironworks**

ironworker (ˈaɪənˌwɜːkə) *n* **1** a person who works in an ironworks **2** a person who makes articles of iron

ironworks (ˈaɪənˌwɜːks) *n* (*sometimes functioning as singular*) a building in which iron is smelted, cast, or wrought

irony¹ (ˈaɪrənɪ) *n, pl* **-nies 1** the humorous or mildly sarcastic use of words to imply the opposite of what they normally mean **2** an instance of this, used to draw attention to some incongruity or irrationality **3** incongruity between what is expected to be and what actually is, or a situation or result showing such incongruity **4** See **dramatic irony 5** *philosophy* See **Socratic irony** [c16 from Latin *ironia*, from Greek *eirōneia*, from *eirōn* dissembler, from *eirein* to speak]

irony² (ˈaɪənɪ) *adj* of, resembling, or containing iron

Iroquoian (ˌɪrəˈkwɔɪən) *n* **1** a family of North American Indian languages including Cherokee, Mohawk, Seneca, Oneida, and Onondaga: probably related to Siouan ▷ *adj* **2** of or relating to the Iroquois, their culture, or their languages

Iroquois (ˈɪrəˌkwɔɪ, -ˌkwɔɪz) *n, pl* **-quois 1** a member of any of a group of North American Indian peoples formerly living between the Hudson River and the St Lawrence and Lake Erie. See also **Five Nations, Six Nations 2** any of the Iroquoian languages ▷ *adj* **3** of or relating to the Iroquois, their language, or their culture

IRQ *international car registration for* Iraq

irradiance (ɪˈreɪdɪəns) *n* the radiant flux incident on unit area of a surface. It is measured in watts per square metre. Symbol: E_e Also called: **irradiation** Compare **illuminance**

irradiant (ɪˈreɪdɪənt) *adj* radiating light; shining brightly

irradiate (ɪˈreɪdɪˌeɪt) *vb* **1** (*tr*) *physics* to subject to or treat with light or other electromagnetic radiation or with beams of particles **2** (*tr*) to expose (food) to electromagnetic radiation to kill bacteria and retard deterioration **3** (*tr*) to make clear or bright intellectually or spiritually; illumine **4** a less common word for **radiate** (sense 1) **5** (*intr*) *obsolete* to become radiant > ir'**radiative** *adj* > ir'**radi,ator** *n*

irradiation (ɪˌreɪdɪˈeɪʃən) *n* **1** the act or process of irradiating or the state of being irradiated **2** the apparent enlargement of a brightly lit object when it is viewed against a dark background **3** a shaft of light; beam or ray **4** *med* **a** the therapeutic or diagnostic use of radiation, esp X-rays **b** exposure of a patient to such radiation **5** another name for **radiation** *or* **irradiance**

irrational (ɪˈræʃənˀl) *adj* **1** inconsistent with reason or logic; illogical; absurd **2** incapable of reasoning **3** *maths* **a** not rational **b** (*as noun*): *an irrational* **4** *prosody* (in Greek or Latin verse) **a** of or relating to a metrical irregularity, usually the occurrence of a long syllable instead of a short one **b** denoting a metrical foot where such an irregularity occurs > ir'**rationally** *adv* > ir'**rationalness** *n*

irrationality (ɪˌræʃəˈnælɪtɪ) *or* **irrationalism** *n* **1** the state or quality of being irrational **2** irrational thought, action, or behaviour

irrational number *n* any real number that cannot be expressed as the ratio of two integers, such as π

Irrawaddy (ˌɪrəˈwɒdɪ) *n* the main river in Myanmar, rising in the north in two headstreams and flowing south through the whole length of Myanmar, to enter the Andaman Sea by nine main mouths. Length: 2100 km (1300 miles)

irreclaimable (ˌɪrɪˈkleɪməbˀl) *adj* not able to be reclaimed > ˌirre,claima'bility *or* ˌirre'claimableness *n* > ˌirre'claimably *adv*

irreconcilable (ɪˈrɛkˀnˌsaɪləbˀl, ɪˌrɛkˀnˈsaɪ-) *adj* **1** not able to be reconciled; uncompromisingly conflicting; incompatible ▷ *n* **2** a person or thing that is implacably hostile or uncompromisingly opposed **3** (*usually plural*) one of various principles, ideas, etc, that are incapable of being brought into agreement > ir,recon,cila'bility *or* ir'recon,cilableness *n* > ir'recon,cilably *adv*

irrecoverable (ˌɪrɪˈkʌvərəbˀl, -ˈkʌvrə-) *adj* **1** not able to be recovered or regained **2** not able to be remedied or rectified > ˌirre'coverableness *n* > ˌirre'coverably *adv*

irrecusable (ˌɪrɪˈkjuːzəbˀl) *adj* not able to be rejected or challenged, as evidence, etc > ˌirre'cusably *adv*

irredeemable (ˌɪrɪˈdiːməbˀl) *adj* **1** (of bonds, debentures, shares, etc) without a date of redemption of capital; incapable of being bought back directly or paid off **2** (of paper money) not convertible into specie **3** (of a sinner) not able to be saved or reformed **4** (of a loss) not able to be recovered; irretrievable **5** not able to be improved or rectified; irreparable > ˌirre,deema'bility *or* ˌirre'deemableness *n* > ˌirre'deemably *adv*

irredentist (ˌɪrɪˈdɛntɪst) *n* **1** a person who favours the acquisition of territory that once was part of his country or is considered to have been ▷ *adj* **2** of, relating to, or advocating this belief [c19 from Italian *irredentista*, from the phrase *Italia irredenta*, literally: Italy unredeemed, from *ir-* IN-¹ + *redento* redeemed, from Latin *redemptus* bought back; see REDEEM] > ˌirre'dentism *n*

Irredentist (ˌɪrɪˈdɛntɪst) *n* (*sometimes not capital*) a member of an Italian association prominent in 1878 that sought to recover for Italy certain neighbouring regions (*Italia irredenta*) with a predominantly Italian population that were under foreign control

irreducible (ˌɪrɪˈdjuːsɪbˀl) *adj* **1** not able to be reduced or lessened **2** not able to be brought to a simpler or reduced form **3** *maths* **a** (of a polynomial) unable to be factorized into polynomials of lower degree, as $(x^2 + 1)$ **b** (of a radical) incapable of being reduced to a rational expression, as $\sqrt{(x + 1)}$ > ˌirre,duci'bility *or* ˌirre'ducibleness *n* > ˌirre'ducibly *adv*

irreflexive (ˌɪrɪˈflɛksɪv) *adj logic* (of a relation) failing to hold between each member of its domain and itself: '... *is distinct from* ...' *is irreflexive.* Compare **reflexive** (sense 4), **nonreflexive**

irrefragable (ɪˈrɛfrəɡəbˀl) *adj* not able to be denied or refuted; indisputable [c16 from Late Latin *irrefrāgābilis*, from Latin IR- + *refrāgārī* to resist, thwart] > ir,refraga'bility *or* ir'refragableness *n* > ir'refragably *adv*

irrefrangible (ˌɪrɪˈfrændʒəbˀl) *adj* **1** not to be broken or transgressed; inviolable **2** *physics* incapable of being refracted > ˌirre,frangi'bility *or* ˌirre'frangibleness *n* > ˌirre'frangibly *adv*

irrefutable (ɪˈrɛfjʊtəbˀl, ˌɪrɪˈfjuːtəbˀl) *adj* impossible to deny or disprove; incontrovertible > ir,refuta'bility *or* ir'refutableness *n* > ir'refutably *adv*

irreg. *abbreviation for* irregular(ly)

irregular (ɪˈrɛɡjʊlə) *adj* **1** lacking uniformity or symmetry; uneven in shape, position, arrangement, etc **2** not occurring at expected or equal intervals: *an irregular pulse* **3** differing from the normal or accepted practice or routine **4** not according to established standards of behaviour; unconventional **5** (of the formation, inflections, or derivations of a word) not following the usual pattern of formation in a language, as English plurals ending other than in *-s* or *-es* **6** of or relating to guerrillas or volunteers not belonging to regular forces: *irregular troops* **7** (of flowers) having any of their parts, esp petals, differing in size, shape, etc; asymmetric **8** *US* (of merchandise) not up to the manufacturer's standards or specifications; flawed; imperfect ▷ *n* **9** a soldier not in a regular army **10** (*often plural*) *US* imperfect or flawed merchandise. Compare **second¹** (sense 15) > ir'regularly *adv*

irregularity (ɪˌrɛɡjʊˈlærɪtɪ) *n, pl* **-ties 1** the state or quality of being irregular **2** something irregular, such as a bump in a smooth surface **3** a breach of a convention or normal procedure

irrelative (ɪˈrɛlətɪv) *adj* **1** unrelated **2** a rare word for **irrelevant**. > ir'relatively *adv* > ir'relativeness *n*

irrelevant (ɪˈrɛləvənt) *adj* not relating or pertinent to the matter at hand; not important > ir'relevance *or* ir'relevancy *n* > ir'relevantly *adv*

irrelievable (ˌɪrɪˈliːvəbˀl) *adj* not able to be relieved

irreligion (ˌɪrɪˈlɪdʒən) *n* **1** lack of religious faith **2**

indifference or opposition to religion
> ˌirreˈligionist n

irreligious (ˌɪrɪˈlɪdʒəs) adj lacking in, indifferent to, or opposed to religious faith > ˌirreˈligiously adv > ˌirreˈligiousness n

irremeable (ɪˈrɛmɪəbᵊl, ɪˈriː-) adj archaic or poetic affording no possibility of return [c16 from Latin irremeābilis, from IR- + remeāre to return, from RE- + meāre to go] > irˈremeably adv

irremediable (ˌɪrɪˈmiːdɪəbᵊl) adj not able to be remedied; incurable or irreparable > ˌirreˈmediableness n > ˌirreˈmediably adv

irremissible (ˌɪrɪˈmɪsəbᵊl) adj 1 unpardonable; inexcusable 2 that must be done, as through duty or obligation > ˌirreˈmissiˈbility or ˌirreˈmissibleness n > ˌirreˈmissibly adv

irremovable (ˌɪrɪˈmuːvəbᵊl) adj not able to be removed > ˌirreˌmovaˈbility or ˌirreˈmovableness n > ˌirreˈmovably adv

irreparable (ɪˈrɛpərəbᵊl, ɪˈrɛprəbᵊl) adj not able to be repaired or remedied; beyond repair > irˌreparaˈbility or irˈreparableness n > irˈreparably adv

irrepealable (ˌɪrɪˈpiːləbᵊl) adj not able to be repealed > ˌirreˌpealaˈbility or ˌirreˈpealableness n > ˌirreˈpealably adv

irreplaceable (ˌɪrɪˈpleɪsəbᵊl) adj not able to be replaced: an irreplaceable antique > ˌirreˈplaceably adv

irrepleviable (ˌɪrɪˈplɛvɪəbᵊl) or **irreplevisable** (ˌɪrɪˈplɛvɪzəbᵊl) adj law archaic not able to be replevied [c16 see ir- IN-¹, REPLEVIN]

irrepressible (ˌɪrɪˈprɛsəbᵊl) adj not capable of being repressed, controlled, or restrained > ˌirreˌpressiˈbility or ˌirreˈpressibleness n > ˌirreˈpressibly adv

irreproachable (ˌɪrɪˈprəʊtʃəbᵊl) adj not deserving reproach; blameless > ˌirreˌproachaˈbility or ˌirreˈproachableness n > ˌirreˈproachably adv

irresistible (ˌɪrɪˈzɪstəbᵊl) adj 1 not able to be resisted or refused; overpowering: an irresistible impulse 2 very fascinating or alluring > ˌirreˌsistiˈbility or ˌirreˈsistibleness n > ˌirreˈsistibly adv

irresoluble (ɪˈrɛzəljʊbᵊl) adj 1 a less common word for **insoluble** 2 archaic not capable of being relieved > irˌresoluˈbility n > irˈresolubly adv

irresolute (ɪˈrɛzəˌluːt) adj lacking resolution; wavering; hesitating > irˈresoˌlutely adv > irˈresoˌluteness or irˌresoˈlution n

irresolvable (ˌɪrɪˈzɒlvəbᵊl) adj 1 not able to be resolved into parts or elements 2 not able to be solved; insoluble > ˌirreˌsolvaˈbility or ˌirreˈsolvableness n > ˌirreˈsolvably adv

irrespective (ˌɪrɪˈspɛktɪv) adj 1 irrespective of (preposition) without taking account of; regardless of ▷ adv 2 informal regardless; without due consideration > ˌirreˈspectively adv

irrespirable (ɪˈrɛspɪrəbᵊl, ˌɪrɪˈspaɪərəbᵊl) adj not fit for breathing or incapable of being breathed

irresponsible (ˌɪrɪˈspɒnsəbᵊl) adj 1 not showing or done with due care for the consequences of one's actions or attitudes; reckless 2 not capable of bearing responsibility 3 archaic not answerable to a higher authority for one's actions > ˌirreˌsponsiˈbility or ˌirreˈsponsibleness n > ˌirreˈsponsibly adv

irresponsive (ˌɪrɪˈspɒnsɪv) adj not responsive > ˌirreˈsponsively adv > ˌirreˈsponsiveness n

irretentive (ˌɪrɪˈtɛntɪv) adj not retentive > ˌirreˈtentiveness n

irretrievable (ˌɪrɪˈtriːvəbᵊl) adj not able to be retrieved, recovered, or repaired > ˌirreˌtrievaˈbility or ˌirreˈtrievableness n > ˌirreˈtrievably adv

irreverence (ɪˈrɛvərəns, ɪˈrɛvrəns) n 1 lack of due respect or veneration; disrespect 2 a disrespectful remark or act

irreverent (ɪˈrɛvərənt, ɪˈrɛvrənt) or **irreverential** (ɪˌrɛvəˈrɛnʃəl) adj without due respect or veneration; disrespectful; flippant > irˈreverently adv

irreversible (ˌɪrɪˈvɜːsəbᵊl) adj 1 not able to be reversed 2 not able to be revoked or repealed;

irrevocable 3 chem, physics capable of changing or producing a change in one direction only 4 thermodynamics (of a change, process, etc) occurring through a number of intermediate states that are not all in thermodynamic equilibrium > ˌirreˌversiˈbility or ˌirreˈversibleness n > ˌirreˈversibly adv

irrevocable (ɪˈrɛvəkəbᵊl) adj not able to be revoked, changed, or undone; unalterable > irˌrevocaˈbility or irˈrevocableness n > irˈrevocably adv

irrigate (ˈɪrɪˌɡeɪt) vb 1 to supply (land) with water by means of artificial canals, ditches, etc, esp to promote the growth of food crops 2 med to bathe or wash out a bodily part, cavity, or wound 3 (tr) to make fertile, fresh, or vital by or as if by watering [c17 from Latin irrigāre, from rigāre to moisten, conduct water] > ˈirrigable adj > ˌirriˈgation n > ˈirriˌgational or ˈirriˌgative adj > ˈirriˌgator n

irriguous (ɪˈrɪɡjʊəs) adj archaic or poetic well-watered; watery [c17 from Latin irriguus supplied with water, from riguus watered; see IRRIGATE]

irritable (ˈɪrɪtəbᵊl) adj 1 quickly irritated; easily annoyed; peevish 2 (of all living organisms) capable of responding to such stimuli as heat, light, and touch 3 pathol abnormally sensitive > ˌirritaˈbility n > ˈirritableness n > ˈirritably adv

irritable bowel syndrome n med a chronic condition of recurring abdominal pain with constipation or diarrhoea or both

irritant (ˈɪrɪtənt) adj 1 causing irritation; irritating ▷ n 2 something irritant > ˈirritancy n

irritate (ˈɪrɪˌteɪt) vb 1 to annoy or anger (someone) 2 (tr) biology to stimulate (an organism or part) to respond in a characteristic manner 3 (tr) pathol to cause (a bodily organ or part) to become excessively stimulated, resulting in inflammation, tenderness, etc [c16 from Latin irrītāre to provoke, exasperate] > ˈirriˌtator n

irritation (ˌɪrɪˈteɪʃən) n 1 something that irritates 2 the act of irritating or the condition of being irritated > ˈirriˌtative adj

irrupt (ɪˈrʌpt) vb (intr) 1 to enter forcibly or suddenly 2 (of a plant or animal population) to enter a region suddenly and in very large numbers 3 (of a population) to increase suddenly and greatly [c19 from Latin irrumpere to rush into, invade, from rumpere to break, burst] > irˈruption n

irruptive (ɪˈrʌptɪv) adj 1 irrupting or tending to irrupt 2 of, involving, or causing irruption 3 obsolete (of igneous rocks) intrusive > irˈruptively adv

IRS (in the US) abbreviation for 1 Internal Revenue Service 2 insulin resistance syndrome: a condition associated with diabetes mellitus in which higher than normal levels of insulin are present in the blood to compensate for the failure of normal insulin levels to perform their function

Irtysh or **Irtish** (ɪəˈtɪʃ) n a river in central Asia, rising in China in the Altai Mountains and flowing west through Kazakhstan, then northwest into Russia to join the Ob River as its chief tributary. Length: 4444 km (2760 miles)

Irvine (ˈɜːvɪn) n a town on the W coast of Scotland, the administrative centre of North Ayrshire: designated a new town in 1966. Pop: 33 090 (2001)

IRW text messaging abbreviation for in the real world

is¹ (ɪz) vb (used with he, she, it, and with singular nouns) a form of the present tense (indicative mood) of **be** [Old English; compare Old Norse es, German ist, Latin est, Greek esti]

is² the internet domain name for Iceland

IS international car registration for Iceland [Icelandic Ísland]

Is. abbreviation for 1 Also: Isa Bible Isaiah 2 Island(s) or Isle(s)

is- combining form variant of **iso-** before a vowel: isentropic

ISA¹ aeronautics abbreviation for 1 International Standard Atmosphere 2 Interim Standard

Atmosphere

ISA² (ˈaɪsə) n acronym for individual savings account: a tax-free savings scheme introduced in Britain in 1999

Isaac (ˈaɪzək) n an Old Testament patriarch, the son of Abraham and Sarah and father of Jacob and Esau (Genesis 17; 21–27)

Isabella¹ (ˌɪzəˈbɛlə), **Isabel** (ˈɪzəˌbɛl) n a a greyish-yellow colour b Also: **Isabelline** (ˌɪzəˈbɛliːn) (as adjective): an Isabella mohair coat [c17 from the name Isabella; original reference uncertain]

isagoge (ˈaɪsəˌɡəʊdʒɪ, ˌaɪsəˈɡəʊ-) n an academic introduction to a specialized subject field or area of research [c17 from Latin, from Greek eisagōgē, from eisagein to introduce, from eis- into + agein to lead]

isagogics (ˌaɪsəˈɡɒdʒɪks) n (usually functioning as singular) introductory studies, esp in the history of the Bible > ˌisaˈgogic adj

Isaiah (aɪˈzaɪə) n Old Testament 1 the first of the major Hebrew prophets, who lived in the 8th century BC 2 the book of his and others' prophecies

isallobar (aɪˈsæləˌbɑː) n meteorol a line on a map running through places experiencing equal pressure changes

Isar (ˈiːzɑː) n a river in central Europe, rising in W Austria and flowing generally northeast through S Germany into the Danube. Length: over 260 km (160 miles)

isatin (ˈaɪsətɪn) or **isatine** (ˈaɪsəˌtiːn) n a yellowish-red crystalline compound soluble in hot water, used for the preparation of vat dyes. Formula: $C_8H_5NO_2$ [c19 from Latin isatis woad + -IN] > isaˈtinic adj

Isauria (aɪˈsɔːrɪə) n an ancient district of S central Asia Minor, chiefly on the N slopes of the W Taurus Mountains > Iˈsaurian adj, n

Isaurian (aɪˈsɔːrɪən) adj 1 of or relating to Isauria, an ancient district of S central Asia Minor, or its inhabitants ▷ n 2 a native or inhabitant of Isauria

ISBN abbreviation for International Standard Book Number

Iscariot (ɪˈskærɪət) n See **Judas** (Iscariot)

ischaemia or **ischemia** (ɪˈskiːmɪə) n pathol an inadequate supply of blood to an organ or part, as from an obstructed blood flow [c19 from Greek iskhein to restrict, + -EMIA] > ischaemic or ischemic (ɪˈskɛmɪk) adj

Ischia (ˈiːskjɑː, ˈɪskɪə) n a volcanic island in the Tyrrhenian Sea, at the N end of the Bay of Naples. Area: 47 sq km (18 sq miles)

ischium (ˈɪskɪəm) n, pl **-chia** (-kɪə) one of the three sections of the hipbone, situated below the ilium [c17 from Latin: hip joint, from Greek iskhion] > ˈischial adj

iSCSI abbreviation for internet Small Computer System Interface: an internet Protocol-based storage networking standard used for linking data storage facilities

ISD abbreviation for international subscriber dialling

ISDN abbreviation for integrated services digital network: a rapid telecommunications network, combining data transfer and telephony

-ise suffix forming verbs a variant of **-ize**
◾ USAGE See at **-ize**

isentropic (ˌaɪsɛnˈtrɒpɪk) adj having or taking place at constant entropy

Isère (French izɛr) n 1 a department of SE France, in Rhône-Alpes region. Capital: Grenoble. Pop: 1 128 755 (2003 est). Area: 7904 sq km (3083 sq miles) 2 a river in SE France, rising in the Graian Alps and flowing west and southwest to join the River Rhône near Valence. Length: 290 km (180 miles)

Iseult, Yseult (ɪˈsuːlt) or **Isolde** (ɪˈzəʊldə) n (in Arthurian legend) 1 an Irish princess wed to Mark, king of Cornwall, but in love with his knight Tristan 2 (in another account) the daughter of the king of Brittany, married to

Tristan

Isfahan (ˌɪsfəˈhɑːn) or **Eṣfahān** n a city in central Iran: the second largest city in the country; capital of Persia in the 11th century and from 1598 to 1722. Pop: 1 547 000 (2005 est). Ancient name: Aspadana (ˌæspəˈdɑːnə)

-ish suffix forming adjectives **1** of or belonging to a nationality or group: *Scottish* **2** often derogatory having the manner or qualities of; resembling: *slavish; prudish* **3** somewhat: *yellowish; sevenish* **4** concerned or preoccupied with: *bookish* [Old English *-isc*; related to German *-isch*, Greek *-iskos*]

Ishmael (ˈɪʃmeɪəl) n **1** the son of Abraham and Hagar, Sarah's handmaid: the ancestor of 12 Arabian tribes (Genesis 21:8–21; 25:12–18) **2** a bandit chieftain, who defied the Babylonian conquerors of Judah and assassinated the governor appointed by Nebuchadnezzar (II Kings 25:25; Jeremiah 40:13–41:18) **3** rare an outcast

Ishmaelite (ˈɪʃmeɪəˌlaɪt) n **1** a supposed descendant of Ishmael; a member of a desert people of Old Testament times **2** rare an outcast > ˈIshmaelˌitism n

Ishtar (ˈɪʃtɑː) n the principal goddess of the Babylonians and Assyrians; divinity of love, fertility, and war

isinglass (ˈaɪzɪŋˌglɑːs) n a gelatine made from the air bladders of freshwater fish, used as a clarifying agent and adhesive

Isis¹ (ˈaɪsɪs) n the local name for the River Thames at Oxford

Isis² (ˈaɪsɪs) n an ancient Egyptian fertility goddess, depicted as a woman with a cow's horns, between which was the disc of the sun; wife and sister of Osiris

isit (ˈɪzɪt) sentence substitute South African an expression used in response to a statement, sometimes to seek conformation, but often merely to show that one is listening

Iskenderun (ɪsˈkɛndəˌruːn) n a port in S Turkey, on the **Gulf of Iskenderun**. Pop: 161 000 (2005 est). Former name: Alexandretta

Isl. abbreviation for **1** Island **2** Isle

Islam (ˈɪzlɑːm) n **1** Also called: Islamism (ɪzˈlɑːmɪzəm, ˈɪzləmɪzəm) the religion of Muslims, having the Koran as its sacred scripture and teaching that there is only one God and that Mohammed is his prophet; Mohammedanism **2 a** Muslims collectively and their civilization **b** the countries where the Muslim religion is predominant [C19 from Arabic: surrender (to God), from *aslama* to surrender] > **Isˈlamic** adj

Islamabad (ɪzˈlɑːməˌbɑːd) n the capital of Pakistan, in the north on the Potwar Plateau: site chosen in 1959; surrounded by the Capital Territory of Islamabad for 909 sq km (351 sq miles). Pop: 770 000 (2005 est)

Islamicist (ɪzˈlæmɪˌsɪst) n **1** a specialist in the study of Islam **2** same as **Islamist** (sense 2)

Islamist (ˈɪzləmɪst) adj **1** supporting or advocating Islamic fundamentalism ▷ n **2** a supporter or advocate of Islamic fundamentalism

Islamize or **Islamise** (ˈɪzləˌmaɪz) vb (tr) to convert or subject to the influence of Islam > ˌIslamiˈzation or ˌIslamiˈsation n

Islamophobia (ˌɪzləməˈfəʊbɪə) n hatred or fear of Muslims or of their politics or culture > ˌIslamoˈphobic adj

island (ˈaɪlənd) n **1** a mass of land that is surrounded by water and is smaller than a continent **2** See **traffic island 3** anatomy a part, structure, or group of cells distinct in constitution from its immediate surroundings ▷ Related adjective: **insular** ▷ vb **4** to cause to become an island **5** to intersperse with islands **6** to place on an island; insulate; isolate [Old English *īgland*, from *īg* island + LAND; *s* inserted through influence of ISLE] > ˈisland-ˌlike adj

island arc n an arc-shaped chain of islands, such as the Aleutian Islands or the Japanese Islands, usually lying at the edge of a Benioff zone, indicating volcanic activity where the oceanic

lithosphere is descending into the earth's interior

islander (ˈaɪləndə) n **1** a native or inhabitant of an island **2** (capital) NZ a native or inhabitant of the Pacific Islands

island of Reil (raɪl) n another name for **insula** [after Johann Reil (died 1813), German physician]

Islands (ˈaɪləndz) pl n **the** NZ the islands of the South Pacific

islands council n (in Scotland since 1975) any of the three divisions (Orkney, Shetland, and the Western Isles) into which the Scottish islands are divided for purposes of local government. See also **region** (sense 6)

Islands of the Blessed pl n Greek myth lands where the souls of heroes and good men were taken after death. Also called: **Hesperides**

island universe n a former name for **galaxy**

Islay (ˈaɪlə, ˈaɪleɪ) n an island off the W coast of Scotland: the southernmost of the Inner Hebrides; separated from the island of Jura by the **Sound of Islay**. Pop: 3457 (2001). Area: 606 sq km (234 sq miles)

isle (aɪl) n poetic except when cap. and part of place name an island, esp a small one [C13 from Old French *isle*, from Latin *insula* island]

Isle of Dogs n See (Isle of) **Dogs**

Isle of Man n See (Isle of) **Man**

Isle of Pines n the former name of the (Isle of) **Youth**

Isle of Sheppey n See (Isle of) **Sheppey**

Isle of Wight n See (Isle of) **Wight**

Isle of Youth n See (Isle of) **Youth**

Isle Royale (ˈrɔɪəl) n an island in the northeast US, in NW Lake Superior: forms, with over 100 surrounding islands, **Isle Royale National Park**. Area: 541 sq km (209 sq miles)

islet (ˈaɪlɪt) n a small island [C16 from Old French *islette*; see ISLE]

islets of Langerhans or **islands of Langerhans** (ˈlæŋəˌhæns) pl n small groups of endocrine cells in the pancreas that secrete the hormones insulin and glucagon [C19 named after Paul *Langerhans* (1847–88), German physician]

Islington (ˈɪzlɪŋtən) n a borough of N Greater London. Pop: 180 100 (2003 est). Area: 16 sq km (6 sq miles)

islomania (ˌaɪləˈmeɪnɪə) n an obsessional enthusiasm or partiality for islands

ism (ˈɪzəm) n informal, often derogatory an unspecified doctrine, system, or practice

ISM abbreviation for **interstellar medium**

-ism suffix forming nouns **1** indicating an action, process, or result: *criticism* **2** indicating a state or condition: *paganism* **3** indicating a doctrine, system, or body of principles and practices: *Leninism* **4** indicating behaviour or a characteristic quality: *heroism* **5** indicating a characteristic usage, esp of a language: *colloquialism; Scotticism* **6** indicating prejudice on the basis specified: *sexism* [from Old French *-isme*, from Latin *-ismus*, from Greek *-ismos*]

Ismaili or **Isma'ili** (ˌɪzmɑːˈiːlɪ) n Islam **1** a Shiah sect whose adherents believe that Ismail, son of the sixth imam, was the rightful seventh imam **2** pl **-lis** Also called: Ismailian (ˌɪzmɑːˈliːən) a member of this sect

Ismailia (ˌɪzmaɪˈlɪə) n a city in NE Egypt, on the Suez Canal: founded in 1863 by the former Suez Canal Company; devastated by Israeli troops in the October War (1973). Pop: 299 000 (2005 est)

isna or **isnae** (ˈɪznɪ) vb Scot is not

isn't (ˈɪzənt) vb contraction of is not

ISO n **1** International Organization for Standardization [Greek *isos* equal; often wrongly thought to be an abbreviation for *International Standards Organization*]

iso- or before a vowel **is-** combining form **1** equal or identical: *isomagnetic* **2** indicating that a chemical compound is an isomer of a specified compound: *isobutane; isocyanic acid* [from Greek *isos* equal]

isoagglutination (ˌaɪsəʊəˌgluːtɪˈneɪʃən) n the agglutination of red blood cells of an organism by

the blood serum of another organism of the same species > ˌisoagˈglutinative adj

isoagglutinin (ˌaɪsəʊəˈgluːtɪnɪn) n an antibody that causes agglutination of red blood cells in animals of the same species from which it was derived

isoamyl acetate (ˌaɪsəʊˈæmɪl) n a colourless volatile compound used as a solvent for cellulose lacquers and as a flavouring. Formula: $(CH_3)_2CHCH_2CH_2OOCCH_3$

isoantigen (ˌaɪsəʊˈæntɪdʒən) n immunol an antigen that stimulates antibody production in different members of the same species

isobar (ˈaɪsəʊˌbɑː) n **1** a line on a map connecting places of equal atmospheric pressure, usually reduced to sea level for purposes of comparison, at a given time or period **2** physics any of two or more atoms that have the same mass number but different atomic numbers: *tin-115 and indium-115 are isobars.* Compare **isotope** [C19 from Greek *isobarēs* of equal weight, from ISO- + *baros* weight] > ˈisobarˌism n

isobaric (ˌaɪsəʊˈbærɪk) adj **1** Also: isopiestic having equal atmospheric pressure **2** of or relating to isobars

isobaric spin n See **isospin**

isobath (ˈaɪsəʊˌbæθ) n a line on a map connecting points of equal underwater depth [C19 from Greek *isobathēs* of equal depth, from ISO- + *bathos* depth] > ˌisoˈbathic adj

isobilateral (ˌaɪsəʊbaɪˈlætərəl) adj botany (esp of a leaf) capable of being divided into symmetrical halves along two different planes

isocheim or **isochime** (ˈaɪsəʊˌkaɪm) n a line on a map connecting places with the same mean winter temperature [C19 from ISO- + Greek *kheima* winter weather] > ˌisoˈcheimal, ˌisoˈcheimenal or ˌisoˈchimal adj

isochor or **isochore** (ˈaɪsəʊˌkɔː) n a line on a graph showing the variation of the temperature of a fluid with its pressure, when the volume is kept constant [C19 from ISO- + Greek *khōros* place, space] > ˌisoˈchoric adj

isochromatic (ˌaɪsəʊkrəʊˈmætɪk) adj **1 a** having the same colour **b** of uniform colour **2** photog (of an early type of emulsion) sensitive to green light in addition to blue light but not to red light

isochron (ˈaɪsəʊˌkrɒn) n **1** a line on an isotope ratio diagram denoting a suite of rock or mineral samples all formed at the same time. The slope of the line is related to the age of the rock or mineral suite **2** a line or curve on a geological map or cross section (esp of oceanic crust) connecting points of identical age

isochronal (aɪˈsɒkrənəl) or **isochronous** adj **1** having the same duration; equal in time **2** occurring at equal time intervals; having a uniform period of vibration or oscillation [C17 from New Latin *isochronus*, from Greek *isokhronos*, from ISO- + *khronos* time] > iˈsochronally or iˈsochronously adv > iˈsochroˌnism n

isochrone (ˈaɪsəʊˌkrəʊn) n a line on a map or diagram connecting places from which it takes the same time to travel to a certain point

isochronize or **isochronise** (aɪˈsɒkrəˌnaɪz) vb (tr) to make isochronal

isochroous (aɪˈsɒkrəʊəs) adj of uniform colour

isoclinal (ˌaɪsəʊˈklaɪnəl) or **isoclinic** (ˌaɪsəʊˈklɪnɪk) adj **1** sloping in the same direction and at the same angle **2** geology (of folds) having limbs that are parallel to each other ▷ n **3** Also called: isocline, isoclinal line an imaginary line connecting points on the earth's surface having equal angles of dip

isocline (ˈaɪsəʊˌklaɪn) n **1** a series of rock strata with isoclinal folds **2** another name for **isoclinal** (sense 3)

isocracy (aɪˈsɒkrəsɪ) n, pl **-cies** **1** a form of government in which all people have equal powers **2** equality of political power > **isocratic** (ˌaɪsəʊˈkrætɪk) adj

isocyanic acid (ˌaɪsəʊsaɪˈænɪk) n a hypothetical

acid known only in the form of its compounds. Formula: HNCO

isocyanide (ˌaɪsəʊˈsaɪəˌnaɪd) n any salt or ester of isocyanic acid. Also called: carbylamine, isonitrile

isodiametric (ˌaɪsəʊˌdaɪəˈmɛtrɪk) adj **1** having diameters of the same length **2** (of a crystal) having three equal axes **3** (of a cell or similar body) having a similar diameter in all planes

isodiaphere (ˌaɪsəʊˈdaɪəˌfɪə) n one of two or more nuclides in which the difference between the number of neutrons and the number of protons is the same: *a nuclide that has emitted an alpha particle, and its decay product, are isodiapheres*

isodimorphism (ˌaɪsəʊdaɪˈmɔːfɪzəm) n a property of a dimorphous substance such that it is isomorphous with another dimorphous substance in both its forms > ˌisodiˈmorphous or ˌisodiˈmorphic adj

isodose (ˈaɪsəʊˌdəʊs) n med a dose of radiation applied to a part of the body in radiotherapy that is equal to the dose applied to a different part

isodynamic (ˌaɪsəʊdaɪˈnæmɪk) adj physics **1** having equal force or strength **2** of or relating to an imaginary line on the earth's surface connecting points of equal horizontal magnetic intensity

isoelectric (ˌaɪsəʊɪˈlɛktrɪk) adj having the same electric potential

isoelectric point n biochem the pH value at which the net electric charge of a molecule, such as a protein or amino acid, is zero

isoelectronic (ˌaɪsəʊɪlɛkˈtrɒnɪk) adj (of atoms, radicals, or ions) having an equal number of electrons or a similar configuration of electrons

isoenzyme (ˌaɪsəʊˈɛnzaɪm) n another name for **isozyme**. > isoenzymic (ˌaɪsəʊɛnˈzaɪmɪk, -ˈzɪm-) adj

isoflavone (ˌaɪsəʊˈfleɪvəʊn) n one of a class of phytoestrogens, found in soya beans and marketed as a health supplement

isogamete (ˌaɪsəʊˈɡæmiːt) n a gamete that is similar in size and form to the one with which it unites in fertilization. Compare **heterogamete** > isogametic (ˌaɪsəʊɡæˈmɛtɪk) adj

isogamy (aɪˈsɒɡəmɪ) n (in some algae and fungi) sexual fusion of gametes of similar size and form. Compare **heterogamy** (sense 2) > iˈsogamous adj

isogenous (aɪˈsɒdʒɪnəs) adj biology **1** of similar origin, as parts derived from the same embryonic tissue **2** Also: isogenic (ˌaɪsəʊˈdʒɛnɪk) genetically uniform > iˈsogeny n

isogeotherm (ˌaɪsəʊˈdʒiːəʊˌθɜːm) n an imaginary line below the surface of the earth connecting points of equal temperature > ˌiso.geoˈthermal or ˌiso.geoˈthermic adj

isogloss (ˈaɪsəʊˌɡlɒs) n a line drawn on a map around the area in which a linguistic feature is to be found, such as a particular pronunciation of a given word > ˌisoˈglossal or ˌisoˈglottic adj

isogon (ˈaɪsəʊˌɡɒn) n an equiangular polygon

isogonic (ˌaɪsəʊˈɡɒnɪk) or **isogonal** (aɪˈsɒɡənəl) adj **1** maths having, making, or involving equal angles ▷ n **2** Also called: isogonic line, isogonal line, isogone physics an imaginary line connecting points on the earth's surface having equal magnetic declination

isogram (ˈaɪsəʊˌɡræm) n another name for **isopleth**

isohel (ˈaɪsəʊˌhɛl) n a line on a map connecting places with an equal period of sunshine [c20 from ISO- + Greek hēlios sun]

isohydric (ˌaɪsəʊˈhaɪdrɪk) adj chem having the same acidity or hydrogen-ion concentration

isohyet (ˌaɪsəʊˈhaɪɪt) n a line on a map connecting places having equal rainfall [c19 from ISO- + -hyet, from Greek huetos rain]

isolate vb (ˈaɪsəˌleɪt) (tr) **1** to place apart; cause to be alone **2** med to quarantine (a person or animal) having or suspected of having a contagious disease **3** to obtain (a compound) in an uncombined form **4** to obtain pure cultures of (bacteria, esp those causing a particular disease) **5** electronics to prevent interaction between

(circuits, components, etc); insulate ▷ n (ˈaɪsəlɪt) **6** an isolated person or group [c19 back formation from *isolated*, via Italian from Latin *insulātus*, literally: made into an island; see INSULATE] > ˈisolable adj > ˌisolaˈbility n > ˈisoˌlator n

isolated pawn n chess a pawn without pawns of the same colour on neighbouring files

ISO Latin-1 or **ISO-8859-1** n computing a standard set of characters for Western European languages put together by the International Organization for Standardization

isolating (ˈaɪsəˌleɪtɪŋ) adj linguistics another word for **analytic**

isolation (ˌaɪsəˈleɪʃən) n **1** the act of isolating or the condition of being isolated **2** (of a country, party, etc) nonparticipation in or withdrawal from international politics **3** med **a** social separation of a person who has or is suspected of having a contagious disease. Compare **quarantine** **b** (as modifier): an isolation hospital **4** sociol a lack of contact between persons, groups, or whole societies **5** social psychol the failure of an individual to maintain contact with others or genuine communication where interaction with others persists **6** in isolation without regard to context, similar matters, etc

isolationism (ˌaɪsəˈleɪʃəˌnɪzəm) n **1** a policy of nonparticipation in or withdrawal from international affairs **2** an attitude favouring such a policy > ˌisoˈlationist n, adj

isolative (ˈaɪsəˌleɪtɪv, ˈaɪsələtɪv) adj **1** (of a sound change) occurring in all linguistic environments, as the change of Middle English /iː/ to Modern English /aɪ/, as in *time*. Compare **combinative** (sense 2) **2** of, relating to, or concerned with isolation

Isolde (ɪˈzɒldə) n the German name of **Iseult**

isolecithal (ˌaɪsəʊˈlɛsɪθəl) adj (of the ova of mammals and certain other vertebrates) having an evenly distributed yolk. Compare **heterolecithal**

isoleucine (ˌaɪsəʊˈluːsiːn, -sɪn) n an essential amino acid that occurs in proteins and is formed by protein hydrolysis

isolex (ˈaɪsəˌlɛks) n linguistics an isogloss marking off the area in which a particular item of vocabulary is found [c20 from ISO(GLOSS) + Greek lex(is) word]

isoline (ˈaɪsəʊˌlaɪn) n another term for **isopleth**

isologous (aɪˈsɒləɡəs) adj (of two or more organic compounds) having a similar structure but containing different atoms of the same valency [c19 from ISO- + (HOMO)LOGOUS] > isologue (ˈaɪsəʊˌlɒɡ) n

isomagnetic (ˌaɪsəʊmæɡˈnɛtɪk) adj **1** having equal magnetic induction or force ▷ n **2** Also called: isomagnetic line an imaginary line connecting points on the earth's surface having equal magnetic intensity

isomer (ˈaɪsəmə) n **1** chem a compound that exhibits isomerism with one or more other compounds **2** physics a nuclide that exhibits isomerism with one or more other nuclides > isomeric (ˌaɪsəˈmɛrɪk) adj

isomerase (aɪˈsɒməreɪs) n any enzyme that catalyses the conversion of one isomeric form of a compound to another

isomerism (aɪˈsɒməˌrɪzəm) n **1** the existence of two or more compounds having the same molecular formula but a different arrangement of atoms within the molecule. See also **stereoisomerism, optical isomerism 2** the existence of two or more nuclides having the same atomic numbers and mass numbers but different energy states

isomerize or **isomerise** (aɪˈsɒməˌraɪz) vb chem change or cause to change from one isomer to another > iˌsomeriˈzation or iˌsomeriˈsation n

isomerous (aɪˈsɒmərəs) adj **1** having an equal number of parts or markings **2** (of flowers) having floral whorls with the same number of parts. Compare **anisomerous**

isometric (ˌaɪsəʊˈmɛtrɪk) adj also isometrical **1** having equal dimensions or measurements **2** physiol of or relating to muscular contraction that does not produce shortening of the muscle **3** (of a crystal or system of crystallization) having three mutually perpendicular equal axes **4** crystallog another word for **cubic** (sense 4) **5** prosody having or made up of regular feet **6** (of a method of projecting a drawing in three dimensions) having the three axes equally inclined and all lines drawn to scale ▷ n **7** Also called: isometric drawing a drawing made in this way **8** Also called: isometric line a line on a graph showing variations of pressure with temperature at constant volume [c19 from Greek isometria (see ISO- + -METRY) + -IC] > ˌisoˈmetrically adv

isometrics (ˌaɪsəʊˈmɛtrɪks) n (functioning as singular) physical exercise involving isometric contraction of muscles

isometropia (ˌaɪsəʊmɪˈtrəʊpɪə) n ophthalmol equal refraction of the two eyes [from Greek isometros of equal measure + -OPIA]

isometry (aɪˈsɒmɪtrɪ) n **1** maths rigid motion of a plane or space such that the distance between any two points before and after this motion is unaltered **2** equality of height above sea level

isomorph (ˈaɪsəʊˌmɔːf) n a substance or organism that exhibits isomorphism

isomorphic (ˌaɪsəʊˈmɔːfɪk) or **isomorphous** (ˌaɪsəʊˈmɔːfəs) adj exhibiting isomorphism

isomorphism (ˌaɪsəʊˈmɔːfɪzəm) n **1** biology similarity of form, as in different generations of the same life cycle **2** chem the existence of two or more substances of different composition in a similar crystalline form **3** maths a one-to-one correspondence between the elements of two or more sets, such as those of Arabic and Roman numerals, and between the sums or products of the elements of one of these sets and those of the equivalent elements of the other set or sets

isoniazid (ˌaɪsəʊˈnaɪəzɪd) n a soluble colourless crystalline compound used to treat tuberculosis. Formula: $C_6H_7N_3O$ [c20 isoni(cotinic acid hydr)azid(e)]

isonome (ˈaɪsəʊˌnəʊm) n botany a line on a chart connecting points of equal abundance values of a plant species sampled in different sections of an area. Isonomes of different species from the same area are compared in studies of plant distribution [c20 from ISO- + Greek nomos rule, law]

isonomy (aɪˈsɒnəmɪ) n **1** the equality before the law of the citizens of a state **2** the equality of civil or political rights > isonomic (ˌaɪsəʊˈnɒmɪk) or iˈsonomous adj

isooctane (ˌaɪsəʊˈɒkteɪn) n a colourless liquid alkane hydrocarbon produced from petroleum and used in standardizing petrol. Formula: $(CH_3)_3CCH_2CH(CH_3)_2$. See also **octane number**

isopach (ˈaɪsəʊˌpæk) or **isopachyte** (ˌaɪsəʊˈpækaɪt) n geology a line on a map connecting points below which a particular rock stratum has the same thickness [c20 from ISO- + Greek pakhus thick, pakhutēs thickness]

isophone (ˈaɪsəˌfəʊn) n linguistics an isogloss marking off an area in which a particular feature of pronunciation is found [c20 from iso- (as in ISOGLOSS) + -phone (as in PHONEME)]

isophote (ˈaɪsəˌfəʊt) n astronomy a line on a diagram or image of a galaxy, nebula, or other celestial object joining points of equal surface brightness

isopiestic (ˌaɪsəʊpaɪˈɛstɪk) adj a line on a map connecting places with equal ground water pressure [c19 from iso- + Greek piestos compressible, from piezein to press] > ˌisopiˈestically adv

isopleth (ˈaɪsəʊˌplɛθ) n a line on a map connecting places registering the same amount or ratio of some geographical or meteorological phenomenon or phenomena. Also called: isogram, isoline [c20 from Greek isoplēthēs equal in number, from iso- + plēthos multitude, great number]

isopod ('aɪsəʊˌpɒd) *n* **1** any crustacean of the order *Isopoda,* including woodlice and pill bugs, in which the body is flattened dorsoventrally ▷ *adj* **2** of, relating to, or belonging to the *Isopoda* > isopodan (aɪ'sɒpədən) *or* i'sopodous *adj*

isoprene ('aɪsəʊˌpriːn) *n* a colourless volatile liquid with a penetrating odour: used in making synthetic rubbers. Formula: CH₂:CHC(CH₃):CH₂. Systematic name: methylbuta-1,3-diene [C20 from ISO- + PR(OPYL) + -ENE]

isopropyl (ˌaɪsəʊ'prəʊpɪl) *n* (*modifier*) of, consisting of, or containing the group of atoms (CH₃)₂CH-, derived from propane: *an isopropyl group or radical*

isopycnal (ˌaɪsəʊ'pɪknəl) *or* **isopycnic** (-'pɪknɪk) *n* a line on a map connecting points of equal atmospheric density [C19 from ISO- + Greek *puknos* thick]

ISO rating *n photog* a classification of film speed in which a doubling of the ISO number represents a doubling in sensitivity; for example, ISO 400 film requires half the exposure of ISO 200 under the same conditions. The system uses identical numbers to the obsolete ASA rating [C20 from *International Standards Organization*]

isorhythmic (ˌaɪsəʊ'rɪðmɪk) *adj music* (of medieval motets) having a cantus firmus that is repeated according to a strict system of internal reiterated note values

isosceles (aɪ'sɒsɪˌliːz) *adj* **1** (of a triangle) having two sides of equal length **2** (of a trapezium) having the two nonparallel sides of equal length [C16 from Late Latin, from Greek *isoskelēs,* from ISO- + *skelos* leg]

isoseismal (ˌaɪsəʊ'saɪzməl) *adj* **1** of or relating to equal intensity of earthquake shock ▷ *n* **2** a line on a map connecting points at which earthquake shocks are of equal intensity ▷ Also: **isoseismic**

isosmotic (ˌaɪsɒz'mɒtɪk) *adj* another word for **isotonic** (sense 3)

isospin ('aɪsəʊˌspɪn) *n* an internal quantum number used in the classification of elementary particles. Particles which have very similar properties except for those associated with their charge are regarded as forms of the same fundamental particle with different components of the isospin in a certain direction in an imaginary space. Also called: **isobaric spin**, **isotopic spin**

isospondylous (ˌaɪsə'spɒndə⁣ləs) *adj* of, relating to, or belonging to the *Isospondyli* (or *Clupeiformes*), an order of soft-finned teleost fishes that includes the herring, salmon, trout, and pike [C20 from ISO- + Greek *spondulos* vertebra]

isostasy (aɪ'sɒstəsɪ) *n* the state of balance, or equilibrium, which sections of the earth's lithosphere (whether continental or oceanic) are thought ultimately to achieve when the vertical forces upon them remain unchanged. The lithosphere floats upon the semifluid asthenosphere below. If a section of lithosphere is loaded, as by ice, it will slowly subside to a new equilibrium position; if a section of lithosphere is reduced in mass, as by erosion, it will slowly rise to a new equilibrium position [C19 ISO- + -*stasy,* from Greek *stasis* a standing] > isostatic (ˌaɪsəʊ'stætɪk) *adj*

isostemonous (ˌaɪsəʊ'stiːmənəs, -'stɛm-) *adj botany* (of a flower) having the stamens arranged in a single whorl and equal to the number of petals [C19 from ISO- + Greek -*stemonus* relating to a STAMEN]

isosteric (ˌaɪsəʊ'stɛrɪk) *adj* (of two different molecules) having the same number of atoms and the same number and configuration of valency electrons, as carbon dioxide and nitrous oxide

isotach ('aɪsəʊˌtæk) *n* a line on a map connecting points of equal wind speed [from ISO- + Greek *takhos* speed]

isotactic (ˌaɪsəʊ'tæktɪk) *adj chem* (of a stereospecific polymer) having identical steric configurations of the groups on each asymmetric carbon atom on the chain. Compare **syndiotactic**

isoteniscope (ˌaɪsəʊ'tɛnɪˌskəʊp) *n chem* an instrument used to measure vapour pressure [C20 from ISO- + TEN(SION) + -I- + -SCOPE]

isothere ('aɪsəʊˌθɪə) *n* a line on a map linking places with the same mean summer temperature. Compare **isocheim** [C19 from ISO- + Greek *theros* summer] > isotheral (aɪ'sɒθərəl) *adj*

isotherm ('aɪsəʊˌθɜːm) *n* **1** a line on a map linking places of equal temperature **2** *physics* a curve on a graph that connects points of equal temperature ▷ Also called: **isothermal**, **isothermal line**

isothermal (ˌaɪsəʊ'θɜːməl) *adj* **1** (of a process or change) taking place at constant temperature **2** of or relating to an isotherm ▷ *n* **3** another word for **isotherm**. > ˌiso'thermally *adv*

isotone ('aɪsəˌtəʊn) *n* one of two or more atoms of different atomic number that contain the same number of neutrons

isotonic (ˌaɪsəʊ'tɒnɪk) *adj* **1** *physiol* (of two or more muscles) having equal tension **2** (of a drink) designed to replace the fluid and salts lost from the body during strenuous exercise **3** Also: **isosmotic** (of two solutions) having the same osmotic pressure, commonly having physiological osmotic pressure. Compare **hypertonic, hypotonic** **4** *music* of, relating to, or characterized by the equal intervals of the well-tempered scale: *isotonic tuning* > isotonicity (ˌaɪsəʊtəʊ'nɪsɪtɪ) *n*

isotope ('aɪsəˌtəʊp) *n* one of two or more atoms with the same atomic number that contain different numbers of neutrons [C20 from ISO- + Greek *topos* place] > isotopic (ˌaɪsə'tɒpɪk) *adj* > ˌiso'topically *adv* > isotopy (aɪ'sɒtəpɪ) *n*

isotope geology *n* the study and application of stable and radioactive isotopes to geological processes and their time scales

isotopic spin *n* See **isospin**

isotretinoin (ˌaɪsəʊtrɛ'tɪnəʊɪn) *n* a drug related to vitamin A, used to treat severe acne that has failed to respond to other treatment

isotron ('aɪsəˌtrɒn) *n physics* a device for separating small quantities of isotopes by ionizing them and separating the ions by a mass spectrometer [C20 from ISOTOPE + -TRON]

isotropic (ˌaɪsəʊ'trɒpɪk) *or* **isotropous** (aɪ'sɒtrəpəs) *adj* **1** having uniform physical properties in all directions **2** *biology* not having predetermined axes: *isotropic eggs* > ˌiso'tropically *adv* > i'sotropy *n*

isozyme ('aɪsəʊˌzaɪm) *n* any of a set of structural variants of an enzyme occurring in different tissues in a single species. Also called: **isoenzyme** [from ISO- + (EN)ZYME] > isozymic (ˌaɪsəʊ'zaɪmɪk, -'zɪm-) *adj*

ISP *abbreviation for* internet service provider, a business providing its customers with connection to the internet and other related services

ispaghula (ˌɪspə'guːlə) *n* dietary fibre derived from the seed husks of *Plantago orata* and used as a thickener or stabilizer in the food industry

I-spy *n* a game in which one player specifies the initial letter of the name of an object that he can see, which the other players then try to guess

Israel ('ɪzreɪəl, -rɪəl) *n* **1** a republic in SW Asia, on the Mediterranean Sea: established in 1948, in the former British mandate of Palestine, as a primarily Jewish state; 8 disputes with Arab neighbours (who did not recognize the state of Israel), erupted into full-scale wars in 1948, 1956, 1967 (the Six Day War), and 1973 (the Yom Kippur War). In 1993 Israel agreed to grant autonomous status to the Gaza Strip and the West Bank, according to the terms of a peace agreement with the P.L.O. Official languages: Hebrew and Arabic. Religion: Jewish majority, Muslim and Christian minorities. Currency: shekel. Capital: Jerusalem (international recognition withheld as East Jerusalem was annexed (1967) by Israel: UN recognized capital: Tel Aviv). Pop: 6 560 000 (2004 est). Area (including Golan Heights and East Jerusalem): 21 946 sq km (8473 sq miles) **2 a** the

ancient kingdom of the 12 Hebrew tribes at the SE end of the Mediterranean **b** the kingdom in the N part of this region formed by the ten northern tribes of Israel in the 10th century BC and destroyed by the Assyrians in 721 BC **3** *informal* the Jewish community throughout the world

Israeli (ɪz'reɪlɪ) *n, pl* -lis *or* -li **1** a citizen or inhabitant of the state of Israel ▷ *adj* **2** of, relating to, or characteristic of the state of Israel or its inhabitants

Israelite ('ɪzrɪəˌlaɪt, -rə-) *n* **1** *Bible* a member of the ethnic group claiming descent from Jacob; a Hebrew **2** *Bible* a citizen of the kingdom of Israel (922 to 721 BC) as opposed to Judah **3** a member of any of various Christian sects who regard themselves as God's chosen people **4** an archaic word for a **Jew**

Israfil ('ɪzrəˌfiːl), **Israfel** ('ɪzrəˌfɛl) *or* **Israfeel** ('ɪzrəˌfiːl) *n Koran* the archangel who will sound the trumpet on the Day of Judgment, heralding the end of the world

Issachar ('ɪsəˌkɑː) *n Old Testament* **1** the fifth son of Jacob by his wife Leah (Genesis 30:17–18) **2** the tribe descended from this patriarch **3** the territory of this tribe

ISSN *abbreviation for* International Standard Serial Number

ISSP *abbreviation for* Intensive Supervision and Surveillance Programme: a method of dealing with persistent young offenders involving electronic tagging and making a digital photograph of the subject available for recognition by CCTV surveillance cameras

issuable ('ɪʃuəb⁣l) *adj* **1** capable of issuing or being issued **2** *chiefly law* open to debate or litigation **3** authorized to be issued > 'issuably *adv*

issuance ('ɪʃuəns) *n* the act of issuing

issuant ('ɪʃuənt) *adj heraldry* emerging or issuing

issue ('ɪʃjuː) *n* **1** the act of sending or giving out something; supply; delivery **2** something issued; an edition of stamps, a magazine, etc **3** the number of identical items, such as banknotes or shares in a company, that become available at a particular time **4** the act of emerging; outflow; discharge **5** something flowing out, such as a river **6** a place of outflow; outlet **7** the descendants of a person; offspring; progeny **8** a topic of interest or discussion **9** an important subject requiring a decision **10** an outcome or consequence; result **11** *pathol* **a** a suppurating sore **b** discharge from a wound **12** *law* the matter remaining in dispute between the parties to an action after the pleadings **13** the yield from or profits arising out of land or other property **14** *military* the allocation of items of government stores, such as food, clothing, and ammunition **15** *library science* **a** the system for recording current loans **b** the number of books loaned in a specified period **16** *obsolete* an act, deed, or proceeding **17 at issue a** under discussion **b** in disagreement **18 force the issue** to compel decision on some matter **19 join issue a** to join in controversy **b** to submit an issue for adjudication **20 take issue** to disagree ▷ *vb* -sues, -suing, -sued **21** to come forth or emerge or cause to come forth or emerge **22** to publish or deliver (a newspaper, magazine, etc) **23** (*tr*) to make known or announce **24** (*intr*) to originate or proceed **25** (*intr*) to be a consequence; result **26** (*intr;* foll by *in*) to end or terminate **27** (*tr*) **a** to give out or allocate (equipment, a certificate, etc) officially to someone **b** (foll by *with*) to supply officially (with) [C13 from Old French *eissue* way out, from *eissir* to go out, from Latin *exīre,* from EX-¹ + *īre* to go] > 'issueless *adj* > 'issuer *n*

issue price *n stock exchange* the price at which a new issue of shares is offered to the public

issuing house *n Brit* a financial institution that engages in finding capital for established companies or for private firms wishing to convert to public companies, by issuing shares on their behalf

Issus (ˈɪsəs) *n* an ancient town in S Asia Minor, in Cilicia north of present-day Iskenderun: scene of a battle (333 BC) in which Alexander the Great defeated the Persians

Issyk-Kul (*Russian* isˈsikˈkulj) *n* a lake in NE Kyrgyzstan in the Tian Shan mountains, at an altitude of 1609 m (5280 ft): one of the largest mountain lakes in the world. Area: 6200 sq km (2390 sq miles)

-ist *suffix* 1 (*forming nouns*) a person who performs a certain action or is concerned with something specified: *motorist; soloist* 2 (*forming nouns*) a person who practises in a specific field: *physicist; typist* 3 (*forming nouns and adjectives*) a person who advocates a particular doctrine, system, etc, or relating to such a person or to the doctrine advocated: *socialist* 4 (*forming nouns and adjectives*) a person characterized by a specified trait, tendency, etc, or relating to such a person or trait: *purist* 5 (*forming nouns and adjectives*) a person who is prejudiced on the basis specified: *sexist; ageist* [via Old French from Latin *-ista, -istēs,* from Greek *-istēs*]

-ista *combining form* indicating a supporter or follower of someone or something: *fashionista; Portillista* [C20 back formation from SANDINISTA]

istana (iˈstaːna) *n* (in Malaysia) a royal palace [from Malay]

Istanbul (ˌɪstænˈbuːl) *n* a port in NW Turkey, on the western (European) shore of the Bosporus: the largest city in Turkey; founded in about 660 BC by Greeks; refounded by Constantine the Great in 330 AD as the capital of the Eastern Roman Empire; taken by the Turks in 1453 and remained capital of the Ottoman Empire until 1922; industrial centre for shipbuilding, textiles, etc Pop: 9 760 000 (2005 est)). Ancient name: **Byzantium** Former name (330–1926): **Constantinople**

Isth. *or* **isth.** *abbreviation for* isthmus

isthmian (ˈɪsθmɪən) *adj* relating to or situated in an isthmus

Isthmian (ˈɪsθmɪən) *adj* relating to or situated in the Isthmus of Corinth or the Isthmus of Panama

Isthmian Games *n* a Panhellenic festival celebrated every other year in ancient Corinth

isthmus (ˈɪsθməs) *n, pl* **-muses** *or* **-mi** (-maɪ) 1 a narrow strip of land connecting two relatively large land areas 2 *anatomy* **a** a narrow band of tissue connecting two larger parts of a structure **b** a narrow passage connecting two cavities [C16 from Latin, from Greek *isthmos*] > **isthmoid** *adj*

-istic *suffix forming adjectives* equivalent to a combination of **-ist** and **-ic** but in some words having a less specific or literal application and sometimes a mildly pejorative force, as compared with corresponding adjectives ending in **-ist**: *communistic; impressionistic* [from Latin *-isticus,* from Greek *istikos*]

istle (ˈɪstlɪ) *or* **ixtle** *n* a fibre obtained from various tropical American agave and yucca trees used in making carpets, cord, etc [C19 from Mexican Spanish *ixtle,* from Nahuatl *ichtli*]

Istria (ˈɪstrɪə) *n* a peninsula in the N Adriatic Sea: passed from Italy to Yugoslavia (except for Trieste) in 1947 and to Croatia in 1991 > **Istrian** *n, adj*

Istrian (ˈɪstrɪən) *adj* 1 of or relating to Istria, a peninsula in the N Adriatic Sea, or its inhabitants ▷ *n* 2 a native or inhabitant of Istria

it¹ (ɪt) *pron* (*subjective or objective*) 1 refers to a nonhuman, animal, plant, or inanimate thing, or sometimes to a small baby: *it looks dangerous* 2 refers to an unspecified or implied antecedent or to a previous or understood clause, phrase, etc: *it is impossible* 3 used to represent human life or experience either in totality or in respect of the present situation: *how's it going?; I've had it* 4 used as a formal subject (or object), referring to a following clause, phrase, or word: *it helps to know the truth* 5 used in the nominative as the formal grammatical subject of impersonal verbs. When it functions absolutely in such sentences, it is not referring to any previous or following clause or phrase, the context is nearly always a description

of the environment or of some physical sensation: *it is raining* 6 (used as complement with *be*) *informal* the crucial or ultimate point: *the steering failed and I thought that was it* ▷ *n* 7 (in children's games) the player whose turn it is to try to touch another. Compare **he¹** (sense 5b) 8 *informal* **a** sexual intercourse **b** sex appeal 9 *informal* a desirable quality or ability: *he's really got it* [Old English *hit*]

it² *the internet domain name for* Italy

IT *abbreviation for* information technology

It. *abbreviation for* 1 Italian 2 Italy

ITA (in Britain) *abbreviation for* Independent Television Authority: now superseded by the IBA

i.t.a. *or* **ITA** *abbreviation for* initial teaching alphabet, a partly phonetic alphabet used to teach reading

itacolumite (ˌɪtəˈkɒljʊˌmaɪt) *n* a fine-grained micaceous sandstone that occurs in thin flexible slabs [C19 named after *Itacolumi* mountain in Brazil where it is found]

itaconic acid (ˌɪtəˈkɒnɪk) *n* a white colourless crystalline carboxylic acid obtained by the fermentation of carbohydrates and used in the manufacture of synthetic resins. Formula: $CH_2:C(COOH)CH_2COOH$

ital. *abbreviation for* italic

Ital. *abbreviation for* 1 Italian 2 Italy

Italia (iˈtaːlja) *n* the Italian name for **Italy**

Italia irredenta Italian (irreˈdɛnta) *n* See **Irredentist**

Italian (ɪˈtæljən) *n* 1 the official language of Italy and one of the official languages of Switzerland: the native language of approximately 60 million people. It belongs to the Romance group of the Indo-European family, and there is a considerable diversity of dialects 2 a native, citizen, or inhabitant of Italy, or a descendant of one 3 See **Italian vermouth** ▷ *adj* 4 relating to, denoting, or characteristic of Italy, its inhabitants, or their language

Italianate (ɪˈtæljənɪt, -ˌneɪt) *or* **Italianesque** (ɪˌtæljəˈnɛsk) *adj* Italian in style or character

Italian East Africa *n* a former Italian territory in E Africa, formed in 1936 from the possessions of Eritrea, Italian Somaliland, and Ethiopia: taken by British forces in 1941

Italian greyhound *n* a breed of dog like a miniature greyhound

Italianism (ɪˈtæljəˌnɪzəm) *or* **Italicism** (ɪˈtælɪˌsɪzəm) *n* 1 an Italian custom or style 2 Italian quality or life, or the cult of either

Italianize *or* **Italianise** (ɪˈtæljəˌnaɪz) *vb* to make or become Italian or like an Italian person or thing > *ˌItaliˈzation* or *ˌItaliˈsation n*

Italian sixth *n* (in musical harmony) an augmented sixth chord, having a major third and an augmented sixth above the root

Italian Somaliland *n* a former Italian colony in E Africa, united with British Somaliland in 1960 to form the independent republic of Somalia

Italian sonnet *n* another term for **Petrarchan sonnet**

Italian spinone (spɪˈnəʊnɪ) *n, pl* **-ni** (-niː) a strongly-built gun dog with a wiry white coat and pendulous ears [C20 Italian]

Italian vermouth *n* sweet vermouth

italic (ɪˈtælɪk) *adj* 1 Also: *Italian* of, relating to, or denoting a style of handwriting with the letters slanting to the right ▷ *n* 2 a style of printing type modelled on this, chiefly used to indicate emphasis, a foreign word, etc. Compare **roman¹** 3 (*often plural*) italic type or print [C16 (after an edition of Virgil (1501) printed in Venice and dedicated to Italy): from Latin *Italicus* of Italy, from Greek *Italikos*]

Italic (ɪˈtælɪk) *n* 1 a branch of the Indo-European family of languages that includes many of the ancient languages of Italy, such as Venetic and the Osco-Umbrian group, Latin, which displaced them, and the Romance languages ▷ *adj* 2 denoting, relating to, or belonging to this group of languages, esp the extinct ones

italicize *or* **italicise** (ɪˈtælɪˌsaɪz) *vb* 1 to print

(textual matter) in italic type 2 (*tr*) to underline (letters, words, etc) with a single line to indicate italics > *ˌitaliciˈzation* or *ˌitaliciˈsation n*

Italo- (ɪˈtæləʊ-) *combining form* indicating Italy or Italian: *Italophobia; Italo-German*

Italy (ˈɪtəlɪ) *n* a republic in S Europe, occupying a peninsula in the Mediterranean between the Tyrrhenian and the Adriatic Seas, with the islands of Sardinia and Sicily to the west. first united under the Romans but became fragmented into numerous political units in the Middle Ages; united kingdom proclaimed in 1861; under the dictatorship of Mussolini (1922–43); became a republic in 1946; a member of the European Union. It is generally mountainous, with the Alps in the north and the Apennines running the length of the peninsula. Official language: Italian. Religion: Roman Catholic majority. Currency: euro. Capital: Rome. Pop: 57 346 000 (2004 est) Area: 301 247 sq km (116 312 sq miles). Italian name: **Italia**

Itar Tass (iˈtɑː tæs) *n* a news agency serving Russia, eastern Europe, and central Asia, created in 1992 to replace the former Soviet news agency Tass [Information Telegraph Agency of Russia, Telegraph Agency of Sovereign States]

ITC (in Britain) *abbreviation for* Independent Television Commission

itch (ɪtʃ) *n* 1 an irritation or tickling sensation of the skin causing a desire to scratch 2 a restless desire 3 any skin disorder, such as scabies, characterized by intense itching ▷ *vb* 4 (*intr*) to feel or produce an irritating or tickling sensation 5 (*intr*) to have a restless desire (to do something) 6 *not standard* to scratch (the skin) 7 **itching palm** a grasping nature; avarice 8 **have itchy feet** to be restless; have a desire to travel [Old English *giccean* to itch, of Germanic origin] > **'itchy** *adj* > **'itchiness** *n*

itch mite *n* any mite of the family *Sarcoptidae,* all of which are skin parasites, esp *Sarcoptes scabei,* which causes scabies

-ite¹ *suffix forming nouns* 1 a native or inhabitant of: *Israelite* 2 a follower or advocate of; a member or supporter of a group: *Luddite; labourite* 3 (in biology) indicating a division of a body or organ: *somite* 4 indicating a mineral or rock: *nephrite; peridotite* 5 indicating a commercial product: *vulcanite* [via Latin *-ita* from Greek *-itēs* or directly from Greek]

-ite² *suffix forming nouns* indicating a salt or ester of an acid having a name ending in *-ous: a nitrite is a salt of nitrous acid* [from French, arbitrary alteration of -ATE¹]

item *n* (ˈaɪtəm) 1 a thing or unit, esp included in a list or collection 2 *book-keeping* an entry in an account 3 a piece of information, detail, or note 4 *informal* two people having a romantic or sexual relationship ▷ *vb* 5 (*tr*) an archaic word for **itemize** ▷ *adv* 6 likewise; also [C14 (adv) from Latin: in like manner]

itemize *or* **itemise** (ˈaɪtəˌmaɪz) *vb* (*tr*) to put on a list or make a list of > *ˌitemiˈzation* or *ˌitemiˈsation n*

item veto *n* (in the US) the power of a state governor to veto items in bills without vetoing the entire measure

Itênez (iˈteneθ) *n* the Spanish name for the **Guaporé**

iterate (ˈɪtəˌreɪt) *vb* (*tr*) to say or do again; repeat [C16 from Latin *iterāre,* from *iterum* again] > **'iterant** *adj* > **iterˈation** *or* **'iterance** *n*

iterative (ˈɪtərətɪv) *adj* 1 repetitive or frequent 2 *maths, logic* another word for **recursive** 3 *grammar* another word for **frequentative**. > **'iteratively** *adv* > **'iterativeness** *n*

iteroparous (ˌɪtərəʊˈpærəs) *adj* 1 Also: **polycarpic** (of a plant) producing flowers and fruit more than once (usually many times) before dying 2 (of an animal) producing offspring more than once during its lifetime > **'itero,parity** *n*

It girl *n* a rich, usually attractive, young woman

who spends most of her time shopping or socializing [C20 from IT, in the sense: sex appeal]

Ithaca ('ıθəkə) *n* a Greek island in the Ionian Sea, the smallest of the Ionian Islands: regarded as the home of Homer's Odysseus. Area: 93 sq km (36 sq miles). Modern Greek name: Itháki (i'θaki)

Ithacan ('ıθəkən) *adj* **1** of or relating to the Greek island of Ithaca or its inhabitants ▷ *n* **2** a native or inhabitant of Ithaca

ither ('ıðər) *determiner* a Scot word for **other**

Ithunn ('ı:ðʊn) *n* a variant of **Idun**

ithyphallic (ˌıθı'fælık) *adj* **1** *prosody* (in classical verse) of or relating to the usual metre in hymns to Bacchus **2** of or relating to the phallus carried in the ancient festivals of Bacchus **3** (of sculpture and graphic art) having or showing an erect penis ▷ *n* **4** *prosody* a poem in ithyphallic metre [C17 from Late Latin, from Greek *ithuphallikos,* from *ithuphallos* erect phallus, from *ithus* straight + *phallos* PHALLUS]

itinerancy (ı'tınərənsı, aı-) *or* **itineracy** *n* **1** the act of itinerating **2** *chiefly Methodist Church* the system of appointing a minister to a circuit of churches or chapels **3** itinerants collectively

itinerant (ı'tınərənt, aı-) *adj* **1** itinerating **2** working for a short time in various places, esp as a casual labourer ▷ *n* **3** an itinerant worker or other person [C16 from Late Latin *itinerārī* to travel, from *iter* a journey] > **i'tinerantly** *adv*

itinerary (aı'tınərərı, ı-) *n, pl* **-aries 1** a plan or line of travel; route **2** a record of a journey **3** a guidebook for travellers ▷ *adj* **4** of or relating to travel or routes of travel **5** a less common word for **itinerant**

itinerate (aı'tınəˌreıt, ı-) *vb (intr)* to travel from place to place > **i,tiner'ation** *n*

-itious *suffix forming adjectives* having the nature of; characterized by: *nutritious; suppositious* [from Latin *-icius, -itious*]

-itis *suffix forming nouns* **1** indicating inflammation of a specified part: *tonsillitis* **2** *informal* indicating a preoccupation with or imaginary condition of illness caused by [New Latin, from Greek, feminine of *-itēs* belonging to; see *-ITE*[1]]

it'll ('ıt^əl) *contraction of* it will *or* it shall

ITN (in Britain) *abbreviation for* Independent Television News

ITO *abbreviation for* International Trade Organization

-itol *suffix forming nouns* indicating that certain chemical compounds are polyhydric alcohols: *inisitol; sorbitol* [from *-ITE*[2] + *-OL*[1]]

its (ıts) *determiner* **a** of, belonging to, or associated in some way with it: *its left rear wheel* **b** *(as pronoun):* *each town claims its is the best*

it's (ıts) *contraction of* it is *or* it has

itself (ıt'sɛlf) *pron* **1 a** the reflexive form of **it b** *(intensifier):* *even the money itself won't convince me* **2** *(preceded by a copula)* its normal or usual self: *my cat isn't itself today*

itsy-bitsy ('ıtsı'bıtsı) *or* **itty-bitty** ('ıtı'bıtı) *adj informal* very small; tiny [C20 baby talk alteration of *little bit*]

ITU *abbreviation for* **1** Intensive Therapy Unit **2** **International Telecommunications Union**

iTunes ('aıˌtju:nz) *n trademark* a computer application enabling users to download music from the internet, create and order playlists, etc

ITV (in Britain) *abbreviation for* Independent Television

-ity *suffix forming nouns* indicating state or condition: *technicality* [from Old French *-ite,* from Latin *-itās*]

i-type semiconductor *n* another name for **intrinsic semiconductor**

IU *abbreviation for* **1** immunizing unit **2** international unit

IU(C)D *abbreviation for* **intrauterine (contraceptive) device**

IUI *abbreviation for* **1** intrauterine insemination: a form of fertility treatment in which sperm are injected directly into the uterus **2** intelligent

user interface: a system enabling and facilitating interaction between humans and computers

Iulus (aı'ju:ləs) *n* **1** *Roman myth* another name for **Ascanius 2** *Roman myth* the son of Ascanius, founder of the Julian gens or clan

-ium *or sometimes* **-um** *suffix forming nouns* **1** indicating a metallic element: *platinum; barium* **2** (in chemistry) indicating groups forming positive ions: *ammonium chloride; hydroxonium ion* **3** indicating a biological structure: *syncytium* [New Latin, from Latin, from Greek *-ion,* diminutive suffix]

IUS *abbreviation for* intrauterine system; a hormonal contraceptive coil, such as Mirena, that carries a supply of progestogen, which is released in small amounts over a period of three to five years

i.v. *or* **IV** *abbreviation for* intravenous(ly)

Ivanovo (*Russian* ı'vanəvə) *n* a city in W central Russia, on the Uvod River: textile centre. Pop: 423 000 (2005 est). Former name (1871–1932): Ivanovo-Voznesensk (-vəznı'sjɛnsk)

I've (aıv) *contraction of* I have

-ive *suffix* **1** *(forming adjectives)* indicating a tendency, inclination, character, or quality: *divisive; prohibitive; festive; massive* **2** *(forming nouns of adjectival origin):* *detective; expletive* [from Latin *-īvus*]

ivermectin (ˌaıvə'mɛktın) *n* a drug that kills parasitic nematode worms, mites, and insects. It is used to treat a variety of parasitic infections in domestic animals and onchocerciasis in humans

IVF *abbreviation for* **in vitro fertilization**

ivied ('aıvıd) *adj* covered with ivy

Iviza (*Spanish* i'βiθa) *n* a variant spelling of **Ibiza**

Ivorian (aı'vɔ:rıən) *n* **1** a native or inhabitant of the Côte d'Ivoire ▷ *adj* **2** of or relating to the Côte d'Ivoire or its inhabitants

ivories ('aıvərız, -vrız) *pl n slang* **1** the keys of a piano **2** another word for **teeth 3** another word for **dice**

ivory ('aıvərı, -vrı) *n, pl* **-ries 1 a** a hard smooth creamy white variety of dentine that makes up a major part of the tusks of elephants, walruses, and similar animals **b** *(as modifier): ivory ornaments* **2** a tusk made of ivory **3 a** a yellowish-white colour; cream **b** *(as adjective): ivory shoes* **4** a substance resembling elephant tusk **5** an ornament, etc, made of ivory **6** black ivory *obsolete* Black slaves collectively ▷ See also **ivories** [C13 from Old French *ivurie,* from Latin *evoreus* made of ivory, from *ebur* ivory; related to Greek *elephas* ivory, ELEPHANT] > **'ivory-ˌlike** *adj*

ivory black *n* a black pigment obtained by grinding charred scraps of ivory in oil

Ivory Coast *n* **the** the former name (until 1986) of **Côte d'Ivoire**

ivory gull *n* a white gull, *Pagophila* (or *Larus*) *eburneus,* mostly confined to arctic regions

ivory nut *n* **1** the seed of the ivory palm, which contains an ivory-like substance used to make buttons, etc **2** any similar seed from other palms ▷ Also called: **vegetable ivory**

ivory palm *n* a low-growing South American palm tree, *Phytelephas macrocarpa,* that yields the ivory nut

ivory tower ('taʊə) *n* **a** seclusion or remoteness of attitude regarding real problems, everyday life, etc **b** *(as modifier): ivory-tower aestheticism* > ˌivory-'towered *adj*

ivorywood ('aıvərıˌwʊd) *n* **1** the yellowish-white wood of an Australian tree, *Siphonodon australe,* used for engraving, inlaying, and turnery **2** the tree itself: family *Celastraceae*

IVR *abbreviation for* International Vehicle Registration

ivy ('aıvı) *n, pl* **ivies 1** any woody climbing or trailing araliaceous plant of the Old World genus *Hedera,* esp *H. helix,* having lobed evergreen leaves and black berry-like fruits **2** any of various other climbing or creeping plants, such as Boston ivy, poison ivy, and ground ivy [Old English *īfig;* related to Old High German *ebah,* perhaps to Greek

iphuon a plant] > **'ivy-ˌlike** *adj*

Ivy League *n US* **a** **the** a group of eight universities (Brown, Columbia, Cornell, Dartmouth College, Harvard, Princeton, the University of Pennsylvania, and Yale) that have similar academic and social prestige in the US to Oxford and Cambridge in Britain **b** *(as modifier):* an *Ivy-League education*

IWC *abbreviation for* International Whaling Commission

iwi ('i:wı) *n NZ* a Māori tribe [Māori, literally: bone(s)]

iwis *or* **ywis** (ı'wıs) *adv* an archaic word for **certainly** [C12 from Old English *gewiss* certain]

Iwo ('i:wəʊ) *n* a city in SW Nigeria. Pop: 479 000 (2005 est)

Iwo Jima ('dʒi:mə) *n* an island in the W Pacific, about 1100 km (700 miles) south of Japan: one of the Volcano Islands; scene of prolonged fighting between US and Japanese forces until taken by the US in 1945; returned to Japan in 1968. Area: 20 sq km (8 sq miles)

IWW *abbreviation for* **Industrial Workers of the World**

ixia ('ıksıə) *n* any plant of the iridaceous genus *Ixia,* of southern Africa, having showy ornamental funnel-shaped flowers [C18 New Latin from Greek *ixos* mistletoe, birdlime prepared from mistletoe berries]

Ixion (ık'saıən) *n Greek myth* a Thessalian king punished by Zeus for his love of Hera by being bound to a perpetually revolving wheel > **Ixionian** (ˌıksı'əʊnıən) *adj*

Ixtaccihuatl *or* **Iztaccihuatl** (ˌi:stək'si:wət^əl) *n* a dormant volcano in central Mexico, southeast of Mexico City. Height: (central peak) 5286 m (17 342 ft)

ixtle ('ıkstlı, 'ıst-) *n* a variant of **istle**

Iyar *or* **Iyyar** (i'jar) *n* (in the Jewish calendar) the second month of the year according to biblical reckoning and the eighth month of the civil year, usually falling within April and May [from Hebrew]

IYKWIMAITYD *text messaging abbreviation for* if you know what I mean and I think you do

izard ('ızəd) *n* (esp in the Pyrenees) another name for **chamois**

-ize *or* **-ise** *suffix forming verbs* **1** to cause to become, resemble, or agree with: *legalize* **2** to become; change into: *crystallize* **3** to affect in a specified way; subject to: *hypnotize* **4** to act according to some practice, principle, policy, etc: *economize* [from Old French *-iser,* from Late Latin *-izāre,* from Greek *-izein*]

USAGE In Britain and the US *-ize* is the preferred ending for many verbs, but *-ise* is equally acceptable in British English. Certain words (chiefly those not formed by adding the suffix to an existing word) are, however, always spelt with *-ise* in both Britain and the US: *advertise, revise*

Izhevsk (*Russian* i'ʒefsk) *n* an industrial city in central Russia, capital of the Udmurt Republic. Pop: 632 000 (2005 est)

Izmir ('ızmıə) *n* a port in W Turkey, on the **Gulf of Izmir**: the third largest city in the country; university (1955). Pop: 2 500 000 (2005 est). Former name: Smyrna

Izmit ('ızmıt) *n* a town in NW Turkey, on the **Gulf of Izmit**. Pop: 306 000 (2005 est)

Iznik (ız'nık) *n* the modern Turkish name of **Nicaea**

Iztaccihuatl (ˌi:stək'si:wət^əl) *n* a variant spelling of **Ixtaccihuatl**

izzard ('ızəd) *n archaic* the letter Z [C18 from earlier *ezed,* probably from Old French *et zède,* literally: and zed]

izzat ('ızət) *n Islam* honour or prestige [Urdu, from Arabic '*izzah* glory]

J j

j or **J** (dʒeɪ) *n, pl* **j's, J's** or **Js 1** the tenth letter and seventh consonant of the modern English alphabet **2** a speech sound represented by this letter, in English usually a voiced palato-alveolar affricate, as in *jam*

j *symbol for* **1** *maths* the unit vector along the *y*-axis **2** *obsolete* the imaginary number √−1. Also called: i

J *symbol for* **1** *cards* jack **2** joule(s) **3** current density **4** *international car registration for* Japan

ja (jɑː) *sentence substitute South African* yes [from Afrikaans]

JA *abbreviation for* **1** Also: **J/A** *banking* joint account **2** Judge Advocate **3** *international car registration for* Jamaica

jaap (jɑːp) *n South African offensive* a simpleton or country bumpkin [from Afrikaans]

jab (dʒæb) *vb* **jabs, jabbing, jabbed 1** to poke or thrust sharply **2** to strike with a quick short blow or blows ▷ *n* **3** a sharp poke or stab **4** a quick short blow, esp (in boxing) a straight punch with the leading hand **5** *informal* an injection: *polio jabs* [c19 originally Scottish variant of JOB] ▷ 'jabbingly *adv*

Jabalpur or **Jubbulpore** (ˌdʒʌbəlˈpʊə) *n* a city in central India, in central Madhya Pradesh. Pop: 951 469 (2001)Pop.: 741 927 (1991)

jabber ('dʒæbə) *vb* **1** to speak or say rapidly, incoherently, and without making sense; chatter ▷ *n* **2** such talk [c15 of imitative origin; compare GIBBER¹] > 'jabberer *n*

jabberwocky ('dʒæbəˌwɒkɪ) *n, pl* **-wockies** nonsense verse [c19 coined by Lewis Carroll as the title of a poem in *Through the Looking Glass* (1871)]

jabiru ('dʒæbɪˌruː) *n* **1** a large white tropical American stork, *Jabiru mycteria*, with a dark naked head and a dark bill **2** Also called: **black-necked stork, policeman bird** a large Australian stork, *Xenorhyncus asiaticus*, having a white plumage, dark green back and tail, and red legs **3** another name for **saddlebill 4** (*not in ornithological usage*) another name for **wood ibis** [c18 via Portuguese from Tupi-Guarani]

jaborandi (ˌdʒæbəˈrændɪ) *n* **1** any of several tropical American rutaceous shrubs of the genus *Pilocarpus*, esp *P. jaborandi* **2** the dried leaves of any of these plants, used to induce sweating [c19 from Portuguese, from Tupi-Guarani *yaborandí*]

jabot ('ʒæbəʊ) *n* a frill or ruffle on the breast or throat of a garment, originally to hide the closure of a shirt [c19 from French: bird's crop, jabot; compare Old French *gave* throat]

jacamar ('dʒækəˌmɑː) *n* any bird of the tropical American family *Galbulidae*, having an iridescent plumage and feeding on insects: order *Piciformes* (woodpeckers, etc) [c19 from French, from Tupi *jacamá-ciri*]

jaçana (ˌʒɑːsəˈnɑː, ˌdʒæ-) *n* any bird of the family *Jacanidae*, of tropical and subtropical marshy regions, having long legs and very long toes that enable walking on floating plants: order *Charadriiformes*. Also called: **lily-trotter** [c18 from Portuguese *jaçanã*, from Tupi-Guarani *jasaná*]

jacaranda (ˌdʒækəˈrændə) *n* **1** any bignoniaceous tree of the tropical American genus *Jacaranda*, having fernlike leaves and pale purple flowers and widely cultivated in temperate areas of Australia **2** the fragrant ornamental wood of any of these trees **3** any of several related or similar trees or their wood [c18 from Portuguese, from Tupi-Guarani *yacarandá*]

jacaré ('dʒækəreɪ) *n* another name for **cayman** [c18 from Portuguese, from Tupi *jacaré*]

jacinth ('dʒæsɪnθ) *n* another name for **hyacinth** (sense 4) [c13 from Medieval Latin *jacinthus*, from Latin *hyacinthus* plant, precious stone; see HYACINTH]

jack¹ (dʒæk) *n* **1** a man or fellow **2** a sailor **3** the male of certain animals, esp of the ass or donkey **4** a mechanical or hydraulic device for exerting a large force, esp to raise a heavy weight such as a motor vehicle **5** any of several mechanical devices that replace manpower, such as a contrivance for rotating meat on a spit **6** one of four playing cards in a pack, one for each suit, bearing the picture of a young prince; knave **7** *bowls* a small usually white bowl at which the players aim with their own bowls **8** *electrical engineering* a female socket with two or more terminals designed to receive a male plug (**jack plug**) that either makes or breaks the circuit or circuits **9** a flag, esp a small flag flown at the bow of a ship indicating the ship's nationality. Compare **Union Jack 10** *nautical* either of a pair of crosstrees at the head of a topgallant mast used as standoffs for the royal shrouds **11** a part of the action of a harpsichord, consisting of a fork-shaped device on the end of a pivoted lever on which a plectrum is mounted **12** any of various tropical and subtropical carangid fishes, esp those of the genus *Caranx*, such as *C. hippos* (**crevalle jack**) **13** Also called: **jackstone** one of the pieces used in the game of jacks **14** short for **applejack, bootjack, jackass, jackfish, jack rabbit,** and **lumberjack 15** *US* a slang word for **money 16 every man jack** everyone without exception ▷ *adj* **17 jack of** *Austral slang* tired or fed up with (something) ▷ *vb* (*tr*) **18** to lift or push (an object) with a jack **19** *electrical engineering* to connect (an electronic device) with another by means of a jack and a jack plug **20** Also: **jacklight** *US and Canadian* to hunt (fish or game) by seeking them out or dazzling them with a flashlight ▷ See also **jack in, jacks, jack up** [c16 *jakke*, variant of *Jankin*, diminutive of *John*]

jack² or **jak** (dʒæk) *n* short for **jackfruit** or **jakfruit** [c17 from Portuguese *jaca*; see JACKFRUIT]

jack³ (dʒæk) *n* **1** a short sleeveless coat of armour of the Middle Ages, consisting usually of a canvas base with metal plates **2** *archaic* a drinking vessel, often of leather [c14 from Old French *jaque*, of uncertain origin]

Jack (dʒæk) *n* **I'm all right, Jack** *Brit informal* **a** a remark indicating smug and complacent selfishness **b** (*as modifier*): *an "I'm all right, Jack" attitude*

jackal ('dʒækɔːl) *n* **1** any of several African or S Asian canine mammals of the genus *Canis*, closely related to the dog, having long legs and pointed ears and muzzle: predators and carrion-eaters **2** a person who does menial tasks for another **3** a villain, esp a swindler [c17 from Turkish *chakāl*, from Persian *shagāl*, from Sanskrit *srgāla*]

jackanapes ('dʒækəˌneɪps) *n* **1** a conceited impertinent person **2** a mischievous child **3** *archaic* a monkey [c16 variant of *Jakken-apes*, literally: Jack of the ape, nickname of William de la Pole (1396–1450), first Duke of Suffolk, whose badge showed an ape's ball and chain]

jackass ('dʒækˌæs) *n* **1** a male donkey **2** a stupid person; fool **3 laughing jackass** another name for **kookaburra** [c18 from JACK¹ (male) + ASS¹]

jack bean *n* a tropical American leguminous plant, *Canavalia ensiformis*, that has clusters of purple flowers and long pods and is grown in the southern US for forage

jackboot ('dʒækˌbuːt) *n* **1** an all-leather military boot, extending up to or above the knee **2 a** arbitrary, cruel, and authoritarian rule or behaviour **b** (*as modifier*): *jackboot tactics* > 'jack,booted *adj*

jack-by-the-hedge *n* another name for **garlic mustard**

jackdaw ('dʒækˌdɔː) *n* a large common Eurasian passerine bird, *Corvus monedula*, in which the plumage is black and dark grey: noted for its thieving habits: family *Corvidae* (crows) [c16 from JACK¹ + DAW]

Jackeen (dʒæˈkiːn) *n Irish* a slick self-assertive lower-class Dubliner [c19 from proper name *Jack* + -*een*, Irish diminutive suffix, from Irish Gaelic -*ín*]

jackeroo or **jackaroo** (ˌdʒækəˈruː) *n, pl* **-roos** *Austral informal* a young male management trainee on a sheep or cattle station [c19 from JACK¹ + (KANG)AROO]

jacket ('dʒækɪt) *n* **1** a short coat, esp one that is hip-length and has a front opening and sleeves **2** something that resembles this or is designed to be worn around the upper part of the body: *a life jacket* **3** any exterior covering or casing, such as the insulating cover of a boiler **4** the part of the cylinder block of an internal-combustion engine that encloses the coolant **5** See **dust jacket 6 a** the skin of a baked potato **b** (*as modifier*): *jacket potatoes* **7** a metal casing used in certain types of ammunition **8** *US* a cover to protect a gramophone record. Brit name: **sleeve 9** *chiefly US* a folder or envelope to hold documents ▷ *vb* **10** (*tr*) to put a jacket on (someone or something) [c15 from Old French *jaquet* short jacket, from *jacque* peasant, from proper name *Jacques* James] > 'jacketed *adj* > 'jacket-ˌlike *adj*

jackfish ('dʒækˌfɪʃ) *n, pl* **-fish** or **-fishes** a popular name for **pike** (the fish), esp when small

Jack Frost *n* a personification of frost or winter

jackfruit *or* **jakfruit** ('dʒækˌfruːt) *n* **1** a tropical Asian moraceous tree, *Artocarpus heterophyllus* **2** the edible fruit of this tree, which resembles breadfruit and can weigh up to 27 kilograms (60 pounds) ▷ Sometimes shortened to: **jack** *or* **jak** [C19 from Portuguese *jaca*, from Malayalam *cakka*]

Jack-go-to-bed-at-noon *n* another name for **goatsbeard** (sense 1)

jackhammer ('dʒækˌhæmə) *n* a hand-held hammer drill, driven by compressed air, for drilling rocks, etc

Jackie *or* **Jacky** ('dʒækɪ) *n, pl* **Jackies** *Austral offensive slang* **1** a native Australian **2** native Australians collectively **3** **sit up like Jackie** to sit bolt upright, *esp* cheekily

jack in *vb* (*tr, adverb*) *slang* to abandon or leave (an attempt or enterprise)

jack-in-office *n* a self-important petty official

jack-in-the-box *n, pl* **jack-in-the-boxes** *or* **jacks-in-the-box** a toy consisting of a figure on a compressed spring in a box, which springs out when the lid is opened

jack-in-the-green *n* (in England, formerly) a man who wore or supported a leaf-covered wooden framework while dancing in May-Day celebrations

jack-in-the-pulpit *n* **1** an E North American aroid plant, *Arisaema triphyllum*, having a leaflike spathe partly arched over a clublike spadix **2** *Brit* another name for **cuckoopint**

Jack Ketch (kɛtʃ) *n Brit archaic* a hangman [C18 after *John Ketch* (died 1686), public executioner in England]

jackknife ('dʒækˌnaɪf) *n, pl* **-knives 1** a knife with the blade pivoted to fold into a recess in the handle **2** a former name for a type of dive in which the diver bends at the waist in midair, with his legs straight and his hands touching his feet, finally straightening out and entering the water headfirst: forward pike dive ▷ *vb* (*intr*) **3** (of an articulated lorry) to go out of control in such a way that the trailer swings round at an angle to the cab **4** to make a jackknife dive

jack ladder *n* another name for **Jacob's ladder** (sense 2)

jack of all trades *n, pl* **jacks of all trades** a person who undertakes many different kinds of work

jack-o'-lantern *n* **1** a lantern made from a hollowed pumpkin, which has holes cut in it to represent a human face **2** a will-o'-the-wisp or similar phenomenon

jack pine *n* a coniferous tree, *Pinus banksiana*, of North America, having paired needle-like leaves and small cones that remain on the branches for many years: family *Pinaceae*

jack plane *n* a carpenter's plane, usually with a wooden body, used for rough planing of timber

jackpot ('dʒækˌpɒt) *n* **1** any large prize, kitty, or accumulated stake that may be won in gambling, such as a pool in poker that accumulates until the betting is opened with a pair of jacks or higher **2** **hit the jackpot a** to win a jackpot **b** *informal* to achieve great success, esp through luck [C20 probably from JACK¹ (playing card) + POT¹]

jack rabbit *n* any of various W North American hares, such as *Lepus townsendi* (**white-tailed jack rabbit**), having long hind legs and large ears [C19 shortened from *jackass-rabbit*, referring to its long ears]

jack rafter *n* a short rafter used in a hip roof

Jack Robinson *n* **before you could** (*or* **can**) **say Jack Robinson** extremely quickly or suddenly

Jack Russell *n* a small short-legged terrier having a white coat with tan, black, or lemon markings: there are rough- and smooth-haired varieties. Also called: **Jack Russell terrier** [named after John *Russell* (1795–1883), English clergyman who developed the breed]

jacks (dʒæks) *n* (*functioning as singular*) a game in which bone, metal, or plastic pieces (**jackstones**) are thrown and then picked up in various groups between bounces or throws of a small ball. Sometimes called: **knucklebones** [C19 shortened from *jackstones*, variant of *checkstones* pebbles]

jackscrew ('dʒækˌskruː) *n* another name for **screw jack**

jackshaft ('dʒækˌʃɑːft) *n* a short length of shafting that transmits power from an engine or motor to a machine

jacksie *or* **jacksy** ('dʒæksɪ) *n Brit slang* the buttocks or anus. Also called: **jaxie** *or* **jaxy** [C19 probably from JACK¹]

jacksmelt ('dʒækˌsmɛlt) *n, pl* **-smelts** *or* **-smelt** a marine teleost food fish, *Atherinopsis californiensis*, of American coastal waters of the North Pacific: family *Atherinidae* (silversides)

jacksnipe ('dʒækˌsnaɪp) *n, pl* **-snipe** *or* **-snipes 1** a small Eurasian short-billed snipe, *Lymnocryptes minima* **2** any of various similar birds, such as the pectoral sandpiper

Jackson ('dʒæksən) *n* a city in and state capital of Mississippi, on the Pearl River. Pop: 179 599 (2003 est)

Jacksonian (dʒæk'səʊnɪən) *adj* of or relating to a person surnamed Jackson, esp Andrew Jackson, the US president, general, and lawyer (1767–1845)

Jacksonville ('dʒæksən,vɪl) *n* a port in NE Florida: the leading commercial centre of the southeast. Pop: 773 781 (2003 est)

jackstay ('dʒækˌsteɪ) *n nautical* **1** a metal rod, wire rope, or wooden batten to which an edge of a sail is fastened along a yard **2** a support for the parrel of a yard

jackstraws ('dʒækˌstrɔːz) *n* (*functioning as singular*) another name for **spillikins**

Jack Tar *n now chiefly literary* a sailor

Jack-the-lad *n slang* a young man who is regarded as a brash, loud show-off

Jack-the-rags *n South Wales dialect* a rag-and-bone man

jack towel *n* another name for **roller towel**

jack up *vb* (*adverb*) **1** (*tr*) to increase (prices, salaries, etc) **2** (*tr*) to raise an object, such as a car, with or as with a jack **3** (*intr*) *slang* to inject oneself with a drug, usually heroin **4** (*intr*) *Austral informal* to refuse to comply; rebel, esp collectively **5** *NZ informal* to initiate, organize, or procure ▷ *n* **jack-up 6** *NZ* something that has been contrived or achieved by dishonest means

Jacky ('dʒækɪ) *n* See **Jackie**

Jacky Howe *n Austral informal* (formerly) a sleeveless flannel shirt worn by shearers [C19 named after *Jacky Howe* (1855–1922) who was the world champion shearer in 1892]

Jacob ('dʒeɪkəb) *n* **1** *Old Testament* the son of Isaac, twin brother of Esau, and father of the twelve patriarchs of Israel **2** Also called: **Jacob sheep** any of an ancient breed of sheep having a fleece with dark brown patches and two or four horns [sense 2 in allusion to Genesis 30:40]

Jacobean (ˌdʒækə'bɪən) *adj* **1** *history* characteristic of or relating to James I (1566–1625) of England or to the period of his rule (1603–25) **2** of or relating to the style of furniture current at this time, characterized by the use of dark brown carved oak **3** denoting, relating to, or having the style of architecture used in England during this period, characterized by a combination of late Gothic and Palladian motifs ▷ *n* **4** any writer or other person who lived in the reign of James I [C18 from New Latin *jacōbaeus*, from *Jacōbus* James]

Jacobian (dʒə'kəʊbɪən) *or* **Jacobian determinant** *n maths* a function from *n* equations in *n* variables whose value at any point is the $n \times n$ determinant of the partial derivatives of those equations evaluated at that point [named after Karl Gustav Jacob *Jacobi* (1804–51), German mathematician.]

Jacobin ('dʒækəbɪn) *n* **1** a member of the most radical club founded during the French Revolution, which overthrew the Girondists in 1793 and, led by Maximilien Robespierre (1758–94), instituted the Reign of Terror **2** a leftist or extreme political radical **3** a French Dominican friar **4** (*sometimes not capital*) a variety of fancy pigeon with a hood of feathers swept up over and around the head ▷ *adj* **5** of, characteristic of, or relating to the Jacobins or their policies [C14 from Old French, from Medieval Latin *Jacōbīnus*, from Late Latin *Jacōbus* James; applied to the Dominicans, from the proximity of the church of *St Jacques* (St James) to their first convent in Paris; the political club originally met in the convent in 1789] > **Jaco'binic** *or* **Jaco'binical** *adj* > **Jaco'binically** *adv* > **'Jacobinism** *n*

Jacobite ('dʒækə,baɪt) *n* **1** *Brit history* an adherent of James II (1633–1701), king of England, Ireland, and, as James VII, of Scotland, 1685–88) after his overthrow in 1688, or of his descendants in their attempts to regain the throne **2** a member of the Monophysite Church of Syria, which became a schismatic church in 451 AD [C17 from Late Latin *Jacōbus* James + -ITE¹] > **Jacobitic** (ˌdʒækə'bɪtɪk) *adj* > **'Jaco,bitism** *n*

Jacobite Rebellion *n* the *Brit history* **1** the unsuccessful Jacobite rising of 1715 led by James Francis Edward Stuart **2** the last Jacobite rising (1745-46) led by Charles Edward Stuart, the Young Pretender, which after initial successes was crushed at Culloden

Jacob sheep *n* See **Jacob** (sense 2)

Jacob's ladder *n* **1** *Old Testament* the ladder reaching up to heaven that Jacob saw in a dream (Genesis 28:12–17) **2** Also called: **jack ladder** a ladder made of wooden or metal steps supported by ropes or chains **3** a North American polemoniaceous plant, *Polemonium caeruleum*, with blue flowers and a ladder-like arrangement of leaves **4** any of several similar or related plants

Jacob's staff *n* a medieval instrument for measuring heights and distances

jacobus (dʒə'kəʊbəs) *n, pl* **-buses** an English gold coin minted in the reign of James I [C17 from Late Latin: James]

jaconet ('dʒækənɪt) *n* a light cotton fabric used for clothing, bandages, etc [C18 from Urdu *jagannāthī*, from *Jagannāthpurī*, India, where it was originally made]

Jacquard ('dʒækɑːd, dʒə'kɑːd; *French* ʒakar) *n* **1** Also called: **Jacquard weave** a fabric in which the design is incorporated into the weave instead of being printed or dyed on **2** Also called: **Jacquard loom** the loom that produces this fabric [C19 named after Joseph M. *Jacquard* (1752–1834), French inventor]

Jacquerie *French* (ʒakri) *n* the revolt of the N French peasants against the nobility in 1358 [C16 from Old French: the peasantry, from *jacque* a peasant, from *Jacques* James, from Late Latin *Jacōbus*]

jactation (dʒæk'teɪʃən) *n* **1** *rare* the act of boasting **2** *pathol* another word for **jactitation** (sense 3) [C16 from Latin *jactātiō* bragging, from *jactāre* to flourish, from *jacere* to throw]

jactitation (ˌdʒæktɪ'teɪʃən) *n* **1** the act of boasting **2** a false boast or claim that tends to harm another person, esp a false assertion that one is married to another, formerly actionable at law **3** Also called: **jactation** *pathol* restless tossing in bed, characteristic of severe fevers and certain mental disorders [C17 from Medieval Latin *jactitātiō*, from Latin *jacitāre* to utter publicly, from *jactitāre* to toss about; see JACTATION]

Jacuzzi (dʒə'kuːzɪ) *n, pl* **-zis** *trademark* **1** a system of underwater jets that keep the water in a bath or pool constantly agitated **2** (*sometimes not capital*) a bath or pool equipped with this [C20 named after Candido and Roy *Jacuzzi*, who developed and marketed it]

jade¹ (dʒeɪd) *n* **1 a** a semiprecious stone consisting of either jadeite or nephrite. It varies in colour from white to green and is used for making ornaments and jewellery **b** (*as modifier*): *jade ornaments* **2** the green colour of jade [C18 from French, from Italian *giada*, from obsolete Spanish *piedra de ijada* colic stone (literally: stone of the flank, because it was believed to cure renal colic);

ijada, from Vulgar Latin *īliata* (unattested) flanks, from Latin *īlia*, plural of *īlium*; see ILEUM]
> 'jade,like *adj*

jade² (dʒeɪd) *n* **1** an old overworked horse; nag; hack **2** *derogatory or facetious* a woman considered to be ill-tempered or disreputable ▷ *vb* **3** to exhaust or make exhausted from work or use [c14 of unknown origin] > 'jadish *adj* > 'jadishly *adv*

jaded (dʒeɪdɪd) *adj* **1** exhausted or dissipated **2** satiated > 'jadedly *adv* > 'jadedness *n*

jade green *n, adj* **a** a colour varying from yellowish-green to bluish-green **b** (*as adjective*): *a jade-green carpet*

jadeite (dʒeɪdaɪt) *n* a usually green or white mineral of the clinopyroxene group, found in igneous and metamorphic rocks. It is used as a gemstone (jade). Composition: sodium aluminium silicate. Formula: NaAlSi₂O₆. Crystal structure: monoclinic

Jadotville (*French* ʒadovil) *n* the former name of **Likasi**

j'adoube *French* (ʒadub) *interj chess* an expression of an intention to touch a piece in order to adjust its placement rather than to make a move [literally: I adjust]

jaeger ('jeɪgə) *n* **1** *military* a marksman in certain units of the German or Austrian armies **2** a member of a light or mountain infantry unit in some European armies **3** *US and Canadian* any of several skuas of the genus *Stercorarius* **4** *rare* a hunter or hunter's attendant ▷ Also (for senses 1, 2, 4): **jager, jäger** [c18 from German *Jäger* hunter, from *jagen* to hunt; see YACHT]

Jael ('dʒeɪəl) *n Old Testament* the woman who killed Sisera when he took refuge in her tent (Judges 4:17–21)

Jaén (xa'en) *n* a city in S Spain. Pop: 115 638 (2003 est)

jafa ('dʒæfə) *n NZ slang* an offensive name for a person from Auckland [from *j(ust) a(nother) f(ucking) A(ucklander)*]

Jaffa ('dʒæfə, 'dʒɑ:-) *n* **1** a port in W Israel, on the Mediterranean: incorporated into Tel Aviv in 1950; an old Canaanite city. Biblical name: Joppa Hebrew name: Yafo **2** a large variety of orange, having a thick skin

Jaffna ('dʒæfnə) *n* a port in N Sri Lanka: for many centuries the capital of a Tamil kingdom. Pop: 149 000 (2005 est)

jag¹ (dʒæg) *vb* jags, jagging, jagged **1** (*tr*) to cut unevenly; make jagged **2** *Austral* to catch (fish) by impaling them on an unbaited hook ▷ *n* ▷ *vb* **3** *Scot* an informal word for **jab** (senses 3, 5) ▷ *n* **4** a jagged notch or projection [c14 of unknown origin]

jag² (dʒæg) *n slang* **1 a** intoxication from drugs or alcohol **b** a bout of drinking or drug taking **2** a period of uncontrolled activity: *a crying jag* [of unknown origin]

Jag (dʒæg) *n informal* a Jaguar car: often understood as a symbol of affluence

JAG *abbreviation for* Judge Advocate General

jaga ('dʒɑgə) (in Malaysia) *n* **1** a guard; sentry ▷ *vb* **2** (*tr*) to guard or watch: *jaga the door* [from Malay]

Jagannath, Jagganath ('dʒʌgənɑ:t, -, -nɔ:t) *or* **Jagannatha** (,dʒʌgə'nɑ:θə) *n Hinduism* other names for **Juggernaut**

jäger ('jeɪgə) *n* See **jaeger**

jagged ('dʒægɪd) *adj* having sharp projecting notches; ragged; serrate > 'jaggedly *adv* > 'jaggedness *n*

jaggery, jaggary *or* **jagghery** ('dʒægərɪ) *n* a coarse brown sugar made in the East Indies from the sap of the date palm [c16 from Hindi *jāgrī*; compare Sanskrit *śárkarā* gritty substance, sugar]

jaggy ('dʒægɪ) *adj* gier, giest **1** a less common word for **jagged 2** *Scot* prickly

jaguar ('dʒægjʊə) *n* a large feline mammal, *Panthera onca*, of S North America, Central America, and N South America, similar to the leopard but with a shorter tail and larger spots on its coat [c17

from Portuguese, from Tupi *jaguara*, Guarani *yaguara*]

jaguarondi (,dʒægwə'rɒndɪ) *or* **jaguarundi** (,dʒægwə'rʌndɪ) *n, pl* -dis a feline mammal, *Felis yagouaroundi*, of Central and South America, with a reddish or grey coat, short legs, and a long tail. See also **eyra** [c19 via Portuguese from Tupi]

Jahveh ('jɑ:veɪ) *or* **Jahweh** ('jɑ:weɪ) *n* variant of **Yahweh**

Jahvist ('jɑ:vɪst) *or* **Jahwist** ('jɑ:wɪst) *n* variant of **Yahwist**

Jahwism ('jɑ:wɪzᵊm) *or* **Jahvism** ('jɑ:vɪzəm) *n* variants of **Yahwism** *or* **Yahvism** > Jah'wistic *or* Jah'vistic *adj*

jai (dʒæ) *n Indian* victory (to) [Hindi *jaya* victory]

jai alai ('haɪ 'laɪ, 'haɪ ə,laɪ, ,haɪ ə'laɪ) *n* a version of pelota played by two or four players [via Spanish from *jai* game, festival + *alai* merry]

Jai Hind ('dʒæ 'hɪnd) *n* victory to India: a political slogan and a form of greeting in Hindi [Hindi, from *jaya* victory + *Hind* India]

jail *or* **gaol** (dʒeɪl) *n* **1** a place for the confinement of persons convicted and sentenced to imprisonment or of persons awaiting trial to whom bail is not granted **2 get out of jail** (free) *informal* to get out of a difficult situation ▷ *vb* **3** (*tr*) to confine in prison [c13 from Old French *jaiole* cage, from Vulgar Latin *caveola* (unattested), from Latin *cavea* enclosure; see CAGE: the two spellings derive from the forms of the word that developed in two different areas of France, and the spelling *gaol* represents a pronunciation in use until the 17th century] > 'jailless *or* 'gaolless *adj* > 'jail-like *or* 'gaol-like *adj*

jailbait ('dʒeɪl,beɪt) *n slang* a young woman, or young women collectively, considered sexually attractive but below the age of consent

jailbird *or* **gaolbird** ('dʒeɪl,bɜ:d) *n* a person who is or has been confined to jail, esp repeatedly

jailbreak *or* **gaolbreak** ('dʒeɪl,breɪk) *n* an escape from jail

jail delivery *n* **1** forcible and illegal liberation of prisoners from jail **2** *English law* (formerly) a commission issued to assize judges when they come to a circuit town authorizing them to try all prisoners and release those acquitted

jailer, jailor *or* **gaoler** ('dʒeɪlə) *n* a person in charge of prisoners in a jail

jail fever *n* a former name for **typhus,** once a common disease in jails

jailhouse ('dʒeɪl,haʊs) *n Southern US* a jail; prison

Jain (dʒaɪn) *or* **Jaina** ('dʒaɪnə) *n* **1** an adherent of Jainism **2** one of the saints believed to be the founders of Jainism ▷ *adj* **3** of or relating to Jainism or the Jains [c19 from Hindi *jaina* saint, literally: overcomer, from Sanskrit]

Jainism ('dʒaɪ,nɪzəm) *n* an ancient Hindu religion, which has its own scriptures and believes that the material world is eternal, progressing endlessly in a series of vast cycles > 'Jainist *n, adj*

Jaipur (dʒaɪ'pʊə) *n* a city of great beauty in N India, capital of Rajasthan state: University of Rajasthan (1947). Pop: 2 324 319 (2001)

Jakarta *or* **Djakarta** (dʒə'kɑ:tə) *n* the capital of Indonesia, in N West Java: founded in 1619 and ruled by the Dutch until 1945; the chief trading centre of the East in the 17th century; University of Indonesia (1947). Pop: 8 347 083 (2000). Former name (until 1949): Batavia

jake (dʒeɪk) *adj Austral and NZ slang* **1** satisfactory; all right **2** she's jake everything is under control [probably from the name *Jake*]

jakes (dʒeɪks) *n* **1** an archaic slang word for **lavatory 2** *Southwestern English dialect* human excrement [c16 probably from French *Jacques* James]

jakey ('dʒeɪkɪ) *n Scot slang derogatory* a homeless alcoholic [c20 from *jake* a tramps' word for a drinker of meths]

Jalalabad (dʒə'læləbæd) *n* a city in NE Afghanistan, capital of Nangarhar province; a

trading, military, and tourist centre on the main route between Kabul and the Khyber Pass. Pop: 140 611 (1991 est)

Jalandhar ('dʒælən,dɑ:) *n* a city in NW India, in central Punjab. Pop: 701 223 (2001)

jalap *or* **jalop** ('dʒæləp) *n* **1** a Mexican convolvulaceous plant, *Exogonium* (or *Ipomoea*) *purga* **2** any of several similar or related plants **3** the dried, powdered root of any of these plants, used as a purgative **4** the resin obtained from any of these plants [c17 from French, from Mexican Spanish *jalapa*, short for *purga de Jalapa* purgative of Jalapa] > jalapic (dʒə'læpɪk) *adj*

Jalapa (*Spanish* xa'lapa) *n* a city in E central Mexico, capital of Veracruz State, at an altitude of 1427 m (4681 ft): resort. Pop: 525 000 (2005 est)

jalapeño (dʒælə'pi:nəʊ; *Spanish* xala'penjo) *n* a very hot type of green chilli pepper, used esp in Mexican cookery. Also: **jalapeño pepper** [Mexican Spanish]

Jalisco (*Spanish* xa'lisko) *n* a state of W Mexico, on the Pacific: crossed by the Sierra Madre; valuable mineral resources. Capital: Guadalajara. Pop: 6 321 278 (2000). Area: 80 137 sq km (30 934 sq miles)

jalopy *or* **jaloppy** (dʒə'lɒpɪ) *n, pl* -lopies *or* -loppies *informal* a dilapidated old car [c20 of unknown origin]

jalouse (dʒə'lu:z) *vb Scot* to suspect; infer [c19 from French *jalouser* to be jealous of]

jalousie ('ʒælʊ,zi:) *n* **1** a window blind or shutter constructed from angled slats of wood, plastic, etc **2** a window made of similarly angled slats of glass [c19 from Old French *gelosie* latticework screen, literally: JEALOUSY, perhaps because one can look through the screen without being seen]

jam¹ (dʒæm) *vb* jams, jamming, jammed **1** (*tr*) to cram or wedge into or against something: *to jam paper into an incinerator* **2** (*tr*) to crowd or pack: *cars jammed the roads* **3** to make or become stuck or locked: *the switch has jammed* **4** (*tr; often foll by on*) to activate suddenly (esp in the phrase **jam on the brakes**) **5** (*tr*) to block; congest: *to jam the drain with rubbish* **6** (*tr*) to crush, bruise, or squeeze; smash **7** *radio* to prevent the clear reception of (radio communications or radar signals) by transmitting other signals on the same frequency **8** (*intr*) *slang* to play in a jam session ▷ *n* **9** a crowd or congestion in a confined space: *a traffic jam* **10** the act of jamming or the state of being jammed **11** *informal* a difficult situation; predicament **12** See **jam session** [c18 probably of imitative origin; compare CHAMP¹] > 'jammer *n*

jam² (dʒæm) *n* **1** a preserve containing fruit, which has been boiled with sugar until the mixture sets **2** *slang* something desirable: *you want jam on it* **3 jam today** the principle of living for the moment [c18 perhaps from JAM¹ (the act of squeezing)]

Jam. *abbreviation for* **1** Jamaica **2** *Bible* James

Jamaica (dʒə'meɪkə) *n* an island and state in the Caribbean: colonized by the Spanish from 1494 onwards, large numbers of Black slaves being imported; captured by the British in 1655 and established as a colony in 1866; gained full independence in 1962; a member of the Commonwealth. Exports: chiefly bauxite and alumina, sugar, and bananas. Official language: English. Religion: Protestant majority. Currency: Jamaican dollar. Capital: Kingston. Pop: 2 676 000 (2004 est). Area: 10 992 sq km (4244 sq miles)

Jamaican (dʒə'meɪkən) *adj* **1** of or relating to Jamaica or its inhabitants ▷ *n* **2** a native or inhabitant of Jamaica

Jamaican ebony *n* another name for **cocuswood**

Jamaica pepper *n* another name for **allspice**

Jamaica rum *n* a highly flavoured rum produced in Jamaica

jamb *or* **jambe** (dʒæm) *n* **1** a vertical side member of a doorframe, window frame, or lining **2** a vertical inside face of an opening in a wall [c14 from Old French *jambe* leg, jamb, from Late Latin *gamba* hoof, hock, from Greek *kampē* joint]

j

jambalaya (ˌdʒʌmbəˈlaɪə) *n* a Creole dish made of shrimps, ham, rice, onions, etc [c19 from Louisiana French, from Provençal *jambalaia* chicken and rice stew]

jambeau (ˈdʒæmbəʊ), **jambart** (ˈdʒæmbaːt) *or* **jamber** (ˈdʒæmbə) *n, pl* -**beaux** (-bəʊz) -**barts** *or* -**bers** (*often plural*) other words for **greave** [c14 from Anglo-French, from *jambe* leg; see JAMB]

Jambi *or* **Djambi** (ˈdʒæmbɪ) *n* a port in W Indonesia, in SE Sumatra on the Hari River. Pop: 417 507 (2000). Also called: Telanaipura

jambo (ˈdʒæmbɔ) *sentence substitute* an E African salutation [c20 from Swahili]

jamboree (ˌdʒæmbəˈriː) *n* **1** a large and often international gathering of Scouts **2** a party or spree [c19 of uncertain origin]

James (dʒeɪmz) *n New Testament* an epistle traditionally ascribed to James, a brother or close relative of Jesus (in full **The Epistle of James**)

James Bay *n* the S arm of Hudson Bay, in central Canada. Area: 108 780 sq km (42 000 sq miles)

Jamesian *or* **Jamesean** (ˈdʒeɪmzɪən) *adj* relating to or characteristic of Henry James (1843–1916), the US-born British novelist, short-story writer, and critic, or his brother William (1842–1910), the US philosopher and psychologist

James-Lange theory (ˈdʒeɪmzˈlɑːŋgə) *n psychol* a theory that emotions are caused by bodily sensations; for example, we are sad because we weep [named after William *James* (1842–1910), US philosopher and psychologist + Carl *Lange* (1834–1900), Danish psychologist]

Jameson Raid (ˈdʒeɪmsᵊn) *n* an expedition into the Transvaal in 1895 led by Sir Leander Starr Jameson (1853–1917) in an unsuccessful attempt to topple its Boer regime

Jamestown (ˈdʒeɪmzˌtaʊn) *n* a ruined village in E Virginia, on **Jamestown Island** (a peninsula in the James River): the first permanent settlement by the English in America (1607); capital of Virginia (1607–98); abandoned in 1699

jamming (ˈdʒæmɪŋ) *n mountaineering* a rock-climbing technique in which holds are got by wedging the hands and feet in suitable cracks

Jammu (ˈdʒʌmuː) *n* a city in N India, winter capital of the state of Jammu and Kashmir. Pop: 378 431 (2001)

Jammu and Kashmir *n* the official name for the part of **Kashmir** under Indian control

jammy (ˈdʒæmɪ) *adj* -**mier**, -**miest 1** covered with or tasting like jam **2** *Brit slang* lucky

Jamnagar (ˌdʒæmnəˈgɑː) *n* a city in India, in Gujarat: noted for its palaces and temples: cement, pottery, textiles. Pop: 447 734 (2001)

jam-packed *adj* crowded, packed, or filled to capacity

jampan (ˈdʒæmˌpæn) *n* a type of sedan chair used in India [c19 from Bengali *jhāmpān*]

jam session *n slang* an unrehearsed or improvised jazz or rock performance [c20 probably from JAM¹]

Jamshedpur (ˌdʒæmʃɛdˈpʊə) *n* a city in NE India, in Jharkhand: large iron and steel works (1907–11); a major industrial centre. Pop: 570 349 (2001)

Jamshid *or* **Jamshyd** (dʒæmˈʃiːd) *n Persian myth* a ruler of the peris who was punished for bragging that he was immortal by being changed into human form. He then became a great king of Persia. See also **peri**

Jan *abbreviation for* January

Jana Sangh (ˈdʒʌnə ˈsʌŋg) *n* a political party in India [Hindi, literally: people's party]

Janata (ˈdʒʌnətaː) *n* **1** (in India) the general public; the people **2** a political party in India: founded in 1976 and came to power in 1977 [Hindi]

Jandal (ˈdʒændᵊl) *n trademark* NZ a type of sandal with a strip of material between the big toe and the other toes and over the foot

jane (dʒeɪn) *n slang, chiefly US* a girl or woman

Janeite (ˈdʒeɪˌnaɪt) *n* a devotee of the works of Jane Austen (1775–1817), English novelist

Jane's (dʒeɪnz) *n* any of several periodical publications such as *Fighting Ships* and *All the World's Aircraft* [c20 named after Frederick Thomas *Jane* (1865–1916), British naval writer and artist]

jangle (ˈdʒæŋgᵊl) *vb* **1** to sound or cause to sound discordantly, harshly, or unpleasantly: *the telephone jangled* **2** (*tr*) to produce a jarring effect on: *the accident jangled his nerves* **3** an archaic word for **wrangle** ▷ *n* **4** a harsh, unpleasant ringing noise **5** an argument or quarrel [c13 from Old French *jangler*, of Germanic origin; compare Middle Dutch *jangelen* to whine, complain] > ˈjangler *n*

Janiculum (dʒəˈnɪkjʊləm) *n* a hill in Rome across the River Tiber from the Seven Hills

Janina (ˈjaniːna) *n* the Serbian name for **Ioánnina**

janissary (ˈdʒænɪsərɪ) *or* **janizary** (ˈdʒænɪzərɪ) *n, pl* -**saries** *or* -**zaries** an infantryman in the Turkish army, originally a member of the sovereign's personal guard, from the 14th to the early 19th century [c16 from French *janissaire*, from Italian *giannizzero*, from Turkish *yeniçeri*, from *yeni* new + *çeri* soldiery]

janitor (ˈdʒænɪtə) *n* **1** *Scot, US, and Canadian* the caretaker of a building, esp a school **2** *chiefly US and Canadian* a person employed to clean and maintain a building, esp the public areas in a block of flats or office building; porter [c17 from Latin: doorkeeper, from *jānua* door, entrance, from *jānus* covered way (compare JANUS¹); related to Latin *īre* to go] > **janitorial** (ˌdʒænɪˈtɔːrɪəl) *adj* > ˈjanitress *fem n*

Janjaweed *or* **Janjawid** (ˈdʒænˌdʒəwɪd) *n* an armed tribal militia group in the Darfur region of Sudan [Arabic: a man with a horse and a gun]

Jan Mayen (ˈjæn ˈmaɪən) *n* an island in the Arctic Ocean, between Greenland and N Norway: volcanic, with large glaciers; former site of Dutch whaling stations; annexed to Norway in 1929. Area: 373 sq km (144 sq miles)

janny (ˈdʒænɪ) *n, pl* -**nies** *Scot informal* a janitor

janola (ˌdʒəˈnəʊlə) *n trademark* NZ household bleach

Jansenism (ˈdʒænsəˌnɪzəm) *n* **1** *RC Church* the doctrine of the Dutch Roman Catholic theologian Cornelis Jansen (1585–1638), and his disciples, who maintained that salvation was limited to those subject to a supernatural determinism, the rest being destined to perdition **2** the religious movement arising from these doctrines > ˈJansenist *n, adj* > Jansenˈistic *or* Jansenˌistical *adj*

jansky (ˈdʒænskɪ) *n, pl* -**skys** a unit of flux density equal to 10^{-26} W m⁻² Hz⁻¹, used predominantly in radio and infrared astronomy. Symbol: Jy [c20 named after Karl Guthe *Jansky* (1905–50), US electrical engineer]

January (ˈdʒænjʊərɪ) *n, pl* -**aries** the first month of the year, consisting of 31 days [c14 from Latin *Jānuārius*, from *adj*: (month) of JANUS¹]

Janus¹ (ˈdʒeɪnəs) *n* the Roman god of doorways, passages, and bridges. In art he is depicted with two heads facing opposite ways [c16 from Latin, from *jānus* archway]

Janus² (ˈdʒeɪnəs) *n* a small inner satellite of Saturn

Janus-faced *adj* two-faced; hypocritical; deceitful

Jap (dʒæp) *n, adj informal, often derogatory* short for **Japanese**

JAP *abbreviation for US slang* **Jewish American Princess**

Jap. *abbreviation for* Japan(ese)

japan (dʒəˈpæn) *n* **1** a glossy durable black lacquer originally from the Orient, used on wood, metal, etc **2** work decorated and varnished in the Japanese manner **3** a liquid used as a paint drier ▷ *adj* **4** relating to or varnished with japan ▷ *vb* -**pans**, -**panning**, -**panned 5** (*tr*) to lacquer with japan or any similar varnish

Japan (dʒəˈpæn) *n* an archipelago and empire in E Asia, extending for 3200 km (2000 miles) between the Sea of Japan and the Pacific and consisting of the main islands of Hokkaido, Honshu, Shikoku, and Kyushu and over 3000 smaller islands: feudalism abolished in 1871, followed by industrialization and expansion of territories, esp during World Wars I and II, when most of SE Asia came under Japanese control; dogma of the emperor's divinity abolished in 1946 under a new democratic constitution; rapid economic growth has made Japan the most industrialized nation in the Far East. Official language: Japanese. Religion: Shintoist majority, large Buddhist minority. Currency: yen. Capital: Tokyo. Pop: 127 799 000 (2004 est). Area: 369 660 sq km (142 726 sq miles). Japanese names: Nippon, Nihon

Japan Current *n* a warm ocean current flowing northeastwards off the E coast of Japan towards the North Pacific. Also called: Kuroshio

Japanese (ˌdʒæpəˈniːz) *adj* **1** of, relating to, or characteristic of Japan, its people, or their language ▷ *n* **2** (*pl* -**nese**) a native or inhabitant of Japan or a descendant of one **3** the official language of Japan: the native language of approximately 100 million people: considered by some scholars to be part of the Altaic family of languages

Japanese andromeda *n* an ericaceous Japanese shrub, *Pieris japonica*, with drooping clusters of small bell-shaped white flowers

Japanese basil *n* another name for **beefsteak plant**

Japanese beetle *n* a scarabaeid beetle, *Popillia japonica*, that eats the leaves and fruits of various plants: accidentally introduced into the US from Japan

Japanese cedar *n* another name for **cryptomeria**

Japanese Chin *n* a small compact dog of a Japanese breed with a long straight silky coat in black and white or red and white and feathered ears, legs, feet, and tail

Japanese ivy *n* another name for **Virginia creeper** (sense 2)

Japanese lantern *n* another name for **Chinese lantern** (sense 1)

Japanese persimmon *n* an Asian persimmon tree, *Diospyros kaki*, with red or orange edible fruit. Also called: kaki

Japanese river fever *n* another name for **scrub typhus**

Japanese slippers *pl n* (in Malaysia) casual sandals; flip-flops

Japanese stranglehold *n* a wrestling hold in which an opponent's wrists are pulled to cross his arms in front of his own neck and exert pressure on his windpipe

Japanese umbrella pine *n* a single aberrant species of pine, *Sciadopitys verticillata*, in which the leaves are fused in pairs and the crown is spire-shaped

Japanglish (dʒəˈpæŋlɪʃ) *n* another name for **Japlish**

Japan wax *or* **tallow** *n* a yellow wax obtained from the berries of plants of the genus *Rhus*. It is used in making matches, soaps, candles, and polishes

jape (dʒeɪp) *n* **1** a jest or joke ▷ *vb* **2** to joke or jest (about) [c14 perhaps from Old French *japper* to bark, yap, of imitative origin] > ˈjaper *n* > ˈjapery *n* > ˈjapingly *adv*

Japheth (ˈdʒeɪfɛθ) *n Old Testament* the second son of Noah, traditionally regarded as the ancestor of a number of non-Semitic nations (Genesis 10:1–5)

Japhetic (dʒeɪˈfɛtɪk) *adj* denoting a discredited grouping of languages that postulated a relationship between Basque, Etruscan, and Georgian among others [c19 from New Latin *Japheti* descendants of JAPHETH + -IC]

Japlish (ˈdʒæplɪʃ) *n* the adoption and adaptation of English words into the Japanese language. Also called: Japanglish [c20 from a blend of JAPANESE + ENGLISH]

japonica (dʒəˈpɒnɪkə) *n* **1** Also called: Japanese quince, flowering quince a Japanese rosaceous shrub, *Chaenomeles japonica*, cultivated for its red flowers and yellowish fruit **2** another name for the **camellia** [c19 from New Latin, feminine of *japonicus* Japanese, from *Japonia* JAPAN]

Japurá (Portuguese ʒapu'ra) *n* a river in NW South America, rising in SW Colombia and flowing southeast across Colombia and Brazil to join the Amazon near Tefé: known as the Caquetá in Colombia. Length: about 2800 km (1750 miles). Spanish name: Yapurá

jar¹ (dʒɑː) *n* **1** a wide-mouthed container that is usually cylindrical, made of glass or earthenware, and without handles **2** Also: **jarful** the contents or quantity contained in a jar **3** *Brit informal* a glass of alcoholic drink, esp beer **4** *obsolete* a measure of electrical capacitance [C16 from Old French *jarre*, from Old Provençal *jarra*, from Arabic *jarrah* large earthen vessel]

jar² (dʒɑ) *vb* **jars, jarring, jarred 1** to vibrate or cause to vibrate **2** to make or cause to make a harsh discordant sound **3** (often foll by *on*) to have a disturbing or painful effect (on the nerves, mind, etc) **4** (*intr*) to disagree; clash ▷ *n* **5** a jolt or shock **6** a harsh discordant sound [C16 probably of imitative origin; compare Old English *cearran* to creak] > **'jarring** *adj* > **'jarringly** *adv*

jar³ (dʒɑ) *n* **on a** (*or* **the**) **jar** (of a door) slightly open; ajar [C17 (in the sense: turn): from earlier *char*, from Old English *cierran* to turn; see AJAR¹]

jardinière (ˌʒɑːdɪ'njɛə) *n* **1** an ornamental pot or trough for plants **2** a garnish of fresh vegetables, cooked, diced, and served around a dish of meat [C19 from French, feminine of *jardinier* gardener, from *jardin* GARDEN]

jargon¹ ('dʒɑːgən) *n* **1** specialized language concerned with a particular subject, culture, or profession **2** language characterized by pretentious syntax, vocabulary, or meaning **3** gibberish **4** another word for **pidgin** ▷ *vb* **5** (*intr*) to use or speak in jargon [C14 from Old French, perhaps of imitative origin; see GARGLE]

jargon² (dʒɑː'gɒn), **jargoon** (dʒɑː'guːn) *n mineralogy rare* a golden yellow, smoky, or colourless variety of zircon [C18 from French, from Italian *giargone*, ultimately from Persian *zargūn* of the golden colour; see ZIRCON]

jargonize *or* **jargonise** ('dʒɑːgəˌnaɪz) *vb* **1** (*tr*) to translate into jargon **2** (*intr*) to talk in jargon > **jargoni'zation** *or* **jargoni'sation** *n*

jarhead ('dʒɑːˌhɛd) *n US military slang* a member of the United States Marine Corps [C20 so called because of their distinctive haircut]

jarl (jɑːl) *n medieval history* a Scandinavian chieftain or noble [C19 from Old Norse; see EARL] > **'jarldom** *n*

Jarlsberg ('jɑːlzbɜːg) *n trademark* a hard mild-tasting yellow-coloured cheese with holes in it [C20 after *Jarlsberg*, Norway, where it originated]

jarosite ('dʒærəˌsaɪt) *n* a yellow to brown secondary mineral consisting of basic hydrated sulphate of iron and potassium in masses or hexagonal crystals. Formula: $KFe_3(SO_4)_2(OH)_6$ [C19 from *Barranco Jaroso*, in Almeria, Spain + -ITE¹]

jarp (dʒɑːp) *or* **jaup** (dʒɔːp) *vb* (*tr*) *Northeast English dialect* to strike or smash, esp to break the shell of (an egg) at Easter [from Scottish *jaup, jawp* to dash or splash like water: perhaps of imitative origin]

jarrah ('dʒærə) *n* a widely planted Australian eucalyptus tree, *Eucalyptus marginata*, that yields a valuable timber [from a native Australian language]

Jarrow ('dʒærəʊ) *n* a port in NE England, in South Tyneside unitary authority, Tyne and Wear: ruined monastery where the Venerable Bede lived and died; its unemployed marched on London in the 1930s; shipyards, oil installations, iron and steel works. Pop: 27 526 (2001)

jarvey *or* **jarvie** ('dʒɑːvɪ) *n Brit informal obsolete* a hackney coachman [C19 from *Jarvey*, familiar form of personal name *Jarvis*]

Jas. *abbreviation for* James

jasmine ('dʒæsmɪn, 'dʒæz-) *n* **1** Also called: **jessamine** any oleaceous shrub or climbing plant of the tropical and subtropical genus *Jasminum*, esp *J. officinalis*: widely cultivated for their white, yellow, or red fragrant flowers, which are used in making perfume and in flavouring tea. See also **winter jasmine 2** any of several other fragrant shrubs such as the Cape jasmine, yellow jasmine, and frangipani (**red jasmine**) **3** a light to moderate yellow colour [C16 from Old French *jasmin*, from Arabic *yāsamīn*, from Persian *yāsmīn*]

Jason ('dʒeɪsᵊn) *n Greek myth* the hero who led the Argonauts in quest of the Golden Fleece. He became the husband of Medea, whom he later abandoned for Glauce

jaspé ('dʒæspeɪ) *adj* resembling jasper; variegated [C19 from French, from *jasper* to marble]

jasper ('dʒæspə) *n* **1** an opaque impure microcrystalline form of quartz, red, yellow, brown, or dark green in colour, used as a gemstone and for ornamental decoration **2** Also called: **jasper ware** a dense hard stoneware, invented in 1775 by Wedgwood, capable of being stained throughout its substance with metallic oxides and used as background for applied classical decoration [C14 from Old French *jaspe*, from Latin *iaspis*, from Greek *iaspis*, of Semitic origin; related to Assyrian *ashpū*, Arabic *yashb*, Hebrew *yāshpheh*]

Jasper National Park ('dʒæspə) *n* a national park in SW Canada, in W Alberta in the Rockies: wildlife sanctuary. Area: 10 900 sq km (4200 sq miles)

Jassy ('jasi) *n* the German name for **Iaşi**

Jat (dʒɑːt) *n, pl* **Jat** *or* **Jats** a member of an Indo-European people widely dispersed throughout N India

Jataka Tales ('dʒɑːtəkə) *pl n* a body of literature comprising accounts of previous lives of the Buddha

jato ('dʒeɪtəʊ) *n, pl* **-tos** *aeronautics* jet-assisted takeoff [C20 *j(et-)a(ssisted) t(ake)o(ff)*]

jaundice ('dʒɔːndɪs) *n* **1** Also called: **icterus** yellowing of the skin and whites of the eyes due to the abnormal presence of bile pigments in the blood, as in hepatitis **2** a mental state of bitterness, jealousy, and ill humour resulting in distorted judgment ▷ *vb* **3** to distort (the judgment, etc) adversely **4** to affect with or as if with jaundice [C14 from Old French *jaunisse*, from *jaune* yellow, from Latin *galbinus* yellowish, from *galbus*] > **'jaundiced** *adj*

jaunt (dʒɔːnt) *n* **1** a short pleasurable excursion; outing ▷ *vb* **2** (*intr*) to go on such an excursion [C16 of unknown origin] > **'jauntingly** *adv*

jaunting car *or* **jaunty car** *n* a light two-wheeled one-horse car, formerly widely used in Ireland

jaunty ('dʒɔːntɪ) *adj* **-tier, -tiest 1** sprightly, self-confident, and cheerful; brisk: *a jaunty step* **2** smart; trim: *a jaunty hat* [C17 from French *gentil* noble; see GENTEEL] > **'jauntily** *adv* > **'jauntiness** *n*

Java¹ ('dʒɑːvə) *n* an island of Indonesia, south of Borneo, from which it is separated by the **Java Sea**: politically the most important island of Indonesia; it consists chiefly of active volcanic mountains and is densely forested. It came under Dutch control in 1596 and became part of Indonesia in 1949. It is one of the most densely populated areas in the world. Capital: Jakarta. Pop (with Madura): 121 193 000 (1999 est). Area: 132 174 sq km (51 032 sq miles)

Java² ('dʒɑːvə) *n trademark* a programming language especially applicable to the World Wide Web [C20 named after *Java* coffee, said to be consumed in large quantities by the language's creators]

Java man *n* a type of primitive man, *Homo erectus* (formerly called *Pithecanthropus erectus*), that lived in the middle Palaeolithic Age in Java. Also called: **Trinil man**

Javan ('dʒɑːvən) *adj* **1** of or relating to Java or its inhabitants ▷ *n* **2** a native or inhabitant of Java

Javanese (ˌdʒɑːvə'niːz) *adj* **1** of, relating to, or characteristic of Java, its people, or the Javanese language ▷ *n* **2** (*pl* **-nese**) a native or inhabitant of Java **3** a Malayo-Polynesian language of Central and Eastern Java

Javari *or* **Javary** (Portuguese ʒava'ri) *n* a river in South America, flowing northeast as part of the border between Peru and Brazil to join the Amazon. Length: about 1050 km (650 miles). Spanish name: Yavarí

Java sparrow *n* a small grey-and-pink finchlike Indonesian weaverbird, *Padda oryzivora*: a popular cage bird

javelin ('dʒævlɪn) *n* **1** a long pointed spear thrown as a weapon or in competitive field events **2** the javelin the event or sport of throwing the javelin [C16 from Old French *javeline*, variant of *javelot*, of Celtic origin]

javelin fish *n* a fish of the genus *Pomadasys* of semitropical Australian seas with a long spine on its anal fin

Javel water *or* **Javelle water** ('dʒævᵊl, dʒə'vɛl) *n* **1** an aqueous solution containing sodium hypochlorite and some sodium chloride, used as a bleach and disinfectant **2** Also called: **eau de Javelle** a similar solution made from potassium carbonate and chlorine [C19 partial translation of French *eau de Javel*, from *Javel*, formerly a town, now part of Paris]

jaw (dʒɔː) *n* **1** the part of the skull of a vertebrate that frames the mouth and holds the teeth. In higher vertebrates it consists of the **upper jaw** (maxilla) fused to the cranium and the **lower jaw** (mandible). Related adjs: **gnathal, gnathic 2** the corresponding part of an invertebrate, esp an insect **3** a pair or either of a pair of hinged or sliding components of a machine or tool designed to grip an object **4** *slang* **a** impudent talk; cheek **b** idle conversation; chat **c** moralizing talk; a lecture ▷ *vb* **5** (*intr*) *slang* **a** to talk idly; chat; gossip **b** to lecture ▷ See also **jaws** [C14 probably from Old French *joue* cheek; related to Italian *gota* cheek] > **'jaw-like** *adj*

Jawan (dʒə'wɑːn) *n* (in India) **1** a soldier **2** a young man [Urdu: young man]

jawbone ('dʒɔːˌbəʊn) *n* **1** a nontechnical name for **mandible** *or* (less commonly) **maxilla** ▷ *vb* **2** *US* to try to persuade or bring pressure to bear (on) by virtue of one's high office or position, esp in urging compliance with official policy

jawbreaker ('dʒɔːˌbreɪkə) *n* **1** Also called: **jawcrusher** a device having hinged jaws for crushing rocks and ores **2** *informal* a word that is hard to pronounce > **'jaw,breaking** *adj* > **'jaw,breakingly** *adv*

jaw-dropping *adj informal* amazing > **'jaw-,droppingly** *adv*

ja well no fine *sentence substitute South African* used to indicate reluctant acceptance

jaws (dʒɔːz) *pl n* **1** the narrow opening of some confined place such as a gorge **2** the jaws a dangerously close position: *the jaws of death*

jaws of life *pl n* (*functioning as singular*) powerful shears used for cutting a vehicle open after a collision

Jaxartes (dʒæk'sɑːtiːz) *n* the ancient name for **Syr Darya**

jay (dʒeɪ) *n* **1** any of various passerine birds of the family *Corvidae* (crows), esp the Eurasian *Garrulus glandarius*, with a pinkish-brown body, blue-and-black wings, and a black-and-white crest. See also **blue jay 2** a foolish or gullible person [C13 from Old French *jai*, from Late Latin *gāius*, perhaps from proper name *Gāius*]

Jaya ('dʒɑːjə) *or* **Djaja** *n* **Mount** a mountain in E Indonesia, in Papua (formerly Irian Jaya) in the Sudirman Range: the highest mountain in New Guinea. Height: 5039 m (16 532 ft). Former names: (Mount) **Carstensz, Sukarno Peak**

Jayapura (ˌdʒɑːjə'pʊərə) *or* **Djajapura** *n* a port in NE Indonesia, capital of Papua (formerly Irian Jaya), on the N coast. Pop: 155 548 (2000). Former names: Sukarnapura, Kotabaru, Hollandia

Jaycee ('dʒeɪsiː) *n Austral, NZ, US, and Canadian* a young person who belongs to a junior chamber of

j

commerce [c20 from the initials of J(unior) C(hamber), short for *United States Junior Chamber of Commerce*]

Jay's Treaty (dʒeɪ) *n* a treaty between the United States and Great Britain that settled outstanding disputes, negotiated by John Jay (1745–1829) in 1794

jaywalk ('dʒeɪ,wɔːk) *vb* (*intr*) to cross or walk in a street recklessly or illegally [c20 from JAY (sense 2)] > 'jay,walker *n* > 'jay,walking *n*

jazz (dʒæz) *n* **1 a** a kind of music of African-American origin, characterized by syncopated rhythms, solo and group improvisation, and a variety of harmonic idioms and instrumental techniques. It exists in a number of styles. Compare **blues** See also **bebop, bop, Dixieland, free** (sense 7), **hard bop, harmolodics, mainstream** (sense 2), **modern jazz, New Orleans jazz, swing** (sense 28), **trad b** (*as modifier*): *a jazz band* **c** (*in combination*): *a jazzman* **2** *informal* enthusiasm or liveliness **3** *slang* rigmarole; paraphernalia: *legal papers and all that jazz* **4** *African-American slang obsolete* sexual intercourse **5** *South African slang* a dance ▷ *vb* **6** (*intr*) to play or dance to jazz music **7** *African-American slang obsolete* to have sexual intercourse with (a person) [c20 of unknown origin] > 'jazzer *n*

jazz age *n* (*often capitals*) **the** (*esp in the US*) the period between the end of World War I and the beginning of the Depression during which jazz became popular [c20 popularized by F. Scott Fitzgerald (1896–1940) US writer, who called a collection of his stories *Tales of the Jazz Age* (1922)]

jazzed (dʒæzd) *adj US and Canadian slang* excited or delighted

jazz mag *n Brit slang* a pornographic magazine

jazz up *vb* (*tr, adverb*) *informal* **1** to imbue (a piece of music) with jazz qualities, esp by improvisation or a quicker tempo **2** to make more lively, gaudy, or appealing

jazzy ('dʒæzɪ) *adj* jazzier, jazziest *informal* **1** of, characteristic of, or resembling jazz music **2** gaudy or flashy: *a jazzy car* > 'jazzily *adv* > 'jazziness *n*

JC *abbreviation for* jurisconsult

JCB *n trademark* a type of construction machine with a hydraulically operated shovel on the front and an excavator arm on the back [named from the initials of J(oseph) C(yril) B(amford) (born 1916), its English manufacturer]

JCD *abbreviation for* **1** Doctor of Canon Law [Latin *Juris Canonici Doctor*] **2** Doctor of Civil Law [Latin *Juris Civilis Doctor*]

JCL *computing abbreviation for* Job Control Language

JCR *abbreviation for* junior common room

JCS *abbreviation for* Joint Chiefs of Staff

JD *abbreviation for* **1** Doctor of Laws [Latin *Jurum Doctor*] **2** juvenile delinquent

je *the internet domain name for* Jersey

jealous ('dʒɛləs) *adj* **1** suspicious or fearful of being displaced by a rival **2** (*often postpositive* and foll by *of*) resentful (of) or vindictive (towards), esp through envy **3** (*often postpositive* and foll by *of*) possessive and watchful in the maintenance or protection (of) **4** characterized by or resulting from jealousy **5** *obsolete except in biblical use* demanding exclusive loyalty: *a jealous God* **6** an obsolete word for **zealous** [c13 from Old French *gelos*, from Medieval Latin *zēlōsus*, from Late Latin *zēlus* emulation, jealousy, from Greek *zēlos* ZEAL] > 'jealously *adv* > 'jealousness *n*

jealousy ('dʒɛləsɪ) *n, pl* -ousies the state or quality of being jealous

jean (dʒiːn) *n* a tough twill-weave cotton fabric used for hard-wearing trousers, overalls, etc. See also **jeans** [c16 short for *jean fustian*, from *Gene* GENOA]

jeans (dʒiːnz) *pl n* informal trousers for casual wear, made esp of denim or corduroy [plural of JEAN]

jebel *or* **djebel** ('dʒɛbᵊl) *n* a hill or mountain in an Arab country

Jebel Musa ('dʒɛbᵊl 'muːsə) *n* a mountain in NW

Morocco, near the Strait of Gibraltar: one of the Pillars of Hercules. Height: 850 m (2790 ft)

Jedda ('dʒɛdə) *n* another name for **Jidda**

jedi *or* **Jedi** ('dʒɛdaɪ) *n* a person who claims to live according to a philosophy based on that of the fictional Jedi, a caste of wizards in the *Star Wars* series of films by George Lucas, US film director

jeelie *or* **jeely** ('dʒiːlɪ) *n Scot* jelly or jam

Jeep (dʒiːp) *n trademark* a small military road vehicle with four-wheel drive [c20 probably from the initials *GP*, for *general purpose* (*vehicle*)]

jeepers *or* **jeepers creepers** ('dʒiːpəz 'kriːpəz) *interj US and Canadian slang* a mild exclamation of surprise [c20 euphemism for *Jesus*]

jeepney ('dʒiːpnɪ) *n* (in the Philippines) a jeep that has been customized and converted into a taxi [c20 from JEEP + JIT(NEY)]

jeer (dʒɪə) *vb* **1** (often foll by *at*) to laugh or scoff (at a person or thing); mock ▷ *n* **2** a remark or cry of derision; gibe; taunt [c16 of unknown origin] > 'jeerer *n* > 'jeering *adj, n* > 'jeeringly *adv*

Jeevesian ('dʒiːvzɪən) *adj* of, relating to, or like the butler Jeeves in the fiction of the English-born US writer P.G. Wodehouse (1881–1975), a master of tact, euphemism, and ingenuity

jefe (*Spanish* 'xefe) *n* (in Spanish-speaking countries) a military or political leader [Spanish, from French *chef* CHIEF]

jeff (dʒɛf) *vb* (*tr*) *Austral slang* **1** to downsize or close down (an organization) **2** to reduce (staff numbers) or dismiss (an employee) **3** to spoil or destroy ruthlessly ▷ Also called: **kennett** [c20 named after *Jeff* Kennett, former premier of the state of Victoria, Australia]

Jefferson City *n* a city in central Missouri, the state capital, on the Missouri River. Pop: 37 550 (2003 est)

Jeffersonian (,dʒɛfə'səʊnɪən) *adj* **1** of or relating to Thomas Jefferson, the US statesman and third president (1743–1826) ▷ *n* **2** a follower or admirer of Jefferson

jehad (dʒɪ'hæd) *n* a variant spelling of **jihad**

Jehol (dʒə'hɒl) *n* **1** a former province of NE China, north of the Great Wall: divided among Hebei, Liaoning, and Inner Mongolia in 1956. Area: 192 380 sq km (74 278 sq miles) **2** a region of NE China, in Hebei and Liaoning provinces: mountainous

Jehoshaphat (dʒɪ'hɒʃə,fæt, -'hɒs-) *n Old Testament* **1** the king of Judah (?873–?849 BC) (I Kings 22:41–50) **2** the site of Jehovah's apocalyptic judgment upon the nations (Joel 4:14)

Jehovah (dʒɪ'həʊvə) *n Old Testament* the personal name of God, revealed to Moses on Mount Horeb (Exodus 3) [c16 from Medieval Latin, from Hebrew YHVH: the original vocalization was considered too sacred to be pronounced and the vowels of Eloah (God) were therefore substituted in the Masoretic text, whence Yetto Vah]

Jehovah's Witness *n* a member of a Christian Church of American origin, the followers of which believe that the end of the present world system of government is near, that all other Churches and religions are false or evil, that all war is unlawful, and that the civil law must be resisted whenever it conflicts with their Church's own religious principles

Jehovist (dʒɪ'həʊvɪst) *n* **1** another name for the **Yahwist 2** a person who maintains that the name YHVH in the Hebrew text of the Old Testament was originally pronounced *Jehovah* ▷ *adj* **3** of or relating to the Yahwist source of the Pentateuch > Je'hovism *n* > Jehovistic (,dʒiː'həʊ'vɪstɪk) *adj*

Jehu ('dʒiːhjuː) *n* **1** *Old Testament* the king of Israel (?842–?815 BC); the slayer of Jezebel (II Kings 9:11–30) **2** a fast driver, esp one who is reckless (from the phrase **to drive like Jehu**. II Kings 9:20)

jejune (dʒɪ'dʒuːn) *adj* **1** simple; naive; unsophisticated **2** insipid; dull; dry **3** lacking nourishment; insubstantial or barren [c17 from Latin *jējūnus* hungry, empty] > je'junely *adv*

> je'juneness *or* je'junity *n*

jejunostomy (dʒiːdʒuː'nɒstəmɪ) *n* the surgical formation of an opening from the jejunum to the surface of the body, through which food may be introduced

jejunum (dʒɪ'dʒuːnəm) *n* the part of the small intestine between the duodenum and the ileum [c16 from Latin, from *jējūnus* empty; from the belief that the jejunum is empty after death] > je'junal *adj*

Jekyll and Hyde ('dʒɛkᵊl, haɪd) *n* **a** a person with two distinct personalities, one good, the other evil **b** (*as modifier*): *a Jekyll-and-Hyde personality* [c19 after the principal character of Robert Louis Stevenson's novel *The Strange Case of Dr Jekyll and Mr Hyde* (1886)]

jell *or* **gel** (dʒɛl) *vb* jells, jelling, jelled *or* gels, gelling, gelled **1** to make or become gelatinous; congeal **2** (*intr*) to assume definite form: *his ideas have jelled* ▷ *n* **3** *US* an informal word for **jelly** [c19 back formation from JELLY¹]

jellaba *or* **jellabah** ('dʒɛləbə) *n* variant spellings of **djellaba** [from Arabic *jallabah*]

jellied ('dʒɛlɪd) *adj* **1** congealed into jelly, esp by cooling **2** containing, set in, or coated with jelly

jellies ('dʒɛlɪz) *pl n* **1** *Brit slang* gelatine capsules of temazepam, dissolved and injected as a recreational drug **2** Also called: **jelly shoes** shoes made from brightly coloured transparent plastic [c20 shortened from GELATINE]

jellify ('dʒɛlɪ,faɪ) *vb* -fies, -fying, -fied to make into or become jelly > jellifi'cation *n*

Jell-o ('dʒɛləʊ) *n trademark* (in US and Canada) jelly

jelly¹ ('dʒɛlɪ) *n, pl* -lies **1** a fruit-flavoured clear dessert set with gelatine. US and Canadian trademark: Jell-o **2** a preserve made from the juice of fruit boiled with sugar and used as jam **3** a savoury food preparation set with gelatine or with a strong gelatinous stock and having a soft elastic consistency: *calf's-foot jelly* **4** anything having the consistency of jelly **5** *informal* a coloured gelatine filter that can be fitted in front of a stage or studio light ▷ *vb* -lies, -lying, -lied **6** to jellify [c14 from Old French *gelee* frost, jelly, from *geler* to set hard, from Latin *gelāre*, from *gelu* frost] > 'jelly-,like *adj*

jelly² ('dʒɛlɪ) *n Brit* a slang name for **gelignite**

jelly baby *n Brit* a small sweet made from a gelatinous substance formed to resemble a baby in shape

jelly bag *n* a muslin bag used to strain off the juice from the fruit in making jelly (the preserve)

jellybean ('dʒɛlɪ,biːn) *n* a bean-shaped sweet with a brightly coloured coating around a gelatinous filling

jellyfish ('dʒɛlɪ,fɪʃ) *n, pl* -fish *or* -fishes **1** any marine medusoid coelenterate of the class *Scyphozoa*, having a gelatinous umbrella-shaped body with trailing tentacles **2** any other medusoid coelenterate **3** *informal* a weak indecisive person

jelly fungus *n* a member of any of three orders (*Auriculariales, Tremellales,* and *Dacrymycetales*) of basidiomycetous fungi that grow on trees and have a jelly-like consistency when wet. They include the conspicuous **yellow brain fungus** (*Tremella mesenterica*), the black **witch's butter** (*Exidia plana*), and the pinky-red **jew's-ear** (*Auricularia auricula-judae*)

jelly mould *n* **1** a mould made of glass, copper, etc, used to make a jelly in a decorative shape **2** *NZ* a member of any of three orders (*Auriculariales, Tremellales,* and *Dacrymycetales*) of basidiomycetous fungi that grow on trees and have a jelly-like consistency when wet. They include the conspicuous **yellow brain fungus** (*Tremella mesenterica*), the black **witch's butter** (*Exidia plana*), and the pinky-red **jew's-ear** (*Auricularia auricula-judae*). Also called (in certain other countries): jelly fungus

jelutong ('dʒɛlə,tɒŋ) *n* **1** a Malaysian apocynaceous tree of the genus *Dyera*, esp *D.*

costulata **2** the latex obtained from this tree, used in the manufacture of chewing gum **3** the wood of this tree [c19 from Malay]

jemadar ('dʒɛmə,dɑː) *n* **1** a native junior officer belonging to a locally raised regiment serving as mercenaries in India, esp with the British Army (until 1947) **2** an officer in the Indian police [c18 from Urdu *jama 'dār*, from Persian *jama 'at* body of men + *dār* having]

Jemappes (*French* ʒəmap) *n* a town in SW Belgium, in Hainaut province west of Mons: scene of a battle (1792) during the French Revolutionary Wars, in which the French defeated the Austrians. Pop: 18 100 (latest date)

jembe ('dʒɛmbɛ) *n* E African a hoe [c19 from Swahili]

jemmy ('dʒɛmɪ) *or US* **jimmy** *n, pl* -mies **1** a short steel crowbar used, esp by burglars, for forcing doors and windows ▷ *vb* -mies, -mying, -mied **2** (*tr*) to prise (something) open with a jemmy [c19 from the pet name for *James*]

Jena (*German* 'jeːna) *n* a city in E central Germany, in Thuringia: university (1558), at which Hegel and Schiller taught; site of the battle (1806) in which Napoleon Bonaparte defeated the Prussians; optical and precision instrument industry. Pop: 102 634 (2003 est)

je ne sais quoi *French* (ʒənsekwa) *n* an indefinable quality, esp of personality [literally: I don't know what]

jennet, genet *or* **gennet** ('dʒɛnɪt) *n* **1** Also called: **jenny** a female donkey or ass **2** a small Spanish riding horse [c15 from Old French *genet*, from Catalan *ginet*, horse of the type used by the *Zenete*, from Arabic *Zanātah* the Zenete, a Moorish people renowned for their horsemanship]

jenny ('dʒɛnɪ) *n, pl* -nies **1** a hand-operated machine for turning up the edge of a piece of sheet metal in preparation for making a joint **2** the female of certain animals or birds, esp a donkey, ass, or wren **3** short for **spinning jenny 4** *billiards, snooker* an in-off. See **long jenny, short jenny** [c17 from the name *Jenny*, diminutive of *Jane*]

jeopardize *or* **jeopardise** ('dʒɛpə,daɪz) *vb* (*tr*) **1** to risk; hazard **2** to put in danger; imperil

jeopardy ('dʒɛpədɪ) *n* (usually preceded by *in*) **1** danger of injury, loss, death, etc; risk; peril; hazard: *his health was in jeopardy* **2** *law* danger of being convicted and punished for a criminal offence. See also **double jeopardy** [c14 from Old French *jeu parti*, literally: divided game, hence uncertain issue, from *jeu* game, from Latin *jocus* joke, game + *partir* to divide, from Latin *partīrī*]

Jephthah ('dʒɛfθə) *n* Old Testament a judge of Israel, who sacrificed his daughter in fulfilment of a vow (Judges 11:12–40). Douay spelling: **Jephte** ('dʒɛftə)

jequirity *or* **jequerity** (dʒɪ'kwɪrɪtɪ) *n, pl* -ties **1** other names for **Indian liquorice 2** the seed of the Indian liquorice [c19 from Portuguese *jequiritĭ*, from Tupi-Guarani *jekiritĭ*]

Jer. *Bible* abbreviation for Jeremiah

Jerba ('dʒɜːbə) *n* a variant spelling of **Djerba**

jerbil ('dʒɜːbɪl) *n* a variant spelling of **gerbil**

jerboa (dʒɜː'bəʊə) *n* any small nocturnal burrowing rodent of the family *Dipodidae*, inhabiting dry regions of Asia and N Africa, having pale sandy fur, large ears, and long hind legs specialized for jumping [c17 from New Latin, from Arabic *yarbū*]

jeremiad (,dʒɛrɪ'maɪəd) *n* a long mournful lamentation or complaint

Jeremiah (,dʒɛrɪ'maɪə) *n* **1** Old Testament **a** a major prophet of Judah from about 626 to 587 bc **b** the book containing his oracles **2** a person who habitually prophesies doom or denounces contemporary society

jerepigo (,dʒɛrə'piːgəʊ) *n* South African a usually red heavy dessert wine [from Portuguese *geropiga*]

Jerez (*Spanish* xe'reθ) *n* a town in SW Spain: famous for the making of sherry. Pop: 191 002 (2003 est). Official name: **Jerez de la Frontera**

(xe'reð ðe la fron'tera) Former name: **Xeres**

Jericho ('dʒɛrɪ,kəʊ) *n* a town in the West Bank near the N end of the Dead Sea, 251 m (825 ft) below sea level: on the site of an ancient city, the first place to be taken by the Israelites under Joshua after entering the Promised Land in the 14th century bc (Joshua 6)

jerid (dʒə'riːd) *n* a wooden javelin used in Muslim countries in military displays on horseback. Also: **jereed** *or* **jerreed**

jerk¹ (dʒɜːk) *vb* **1** to move or cause to move with an irregular or spasmodic motion **2** to throw, twist, pull, or push (something) abruptly or spasmodically **3** (*tr*; often foll by *out*) to utter (words, sounds, etc) in a spasmodic, abrupt, or breathless manner ▷ *n* **4** an abrupt or spasmodic movement **5** an irregular jolting motion: *the car moved with a jerk* **6** (*plural*) Also called: **physical jerks** *Brit informal* physical exercises **7** (*plural*) *US* a slang word for **chorea 8** *slang, chiefly US and Canadian* a person regarded with contempt, esp a stupid or ignorant person [c16 probably variant of *yerk* to pull stitches tight in making a shoe; compare Old English *gearcian* to make ready] > 'jerker *n* > 'jerking *adj, n*

jerk² (dʒɜːk) *vb* (*tr*) **1** to preserve (venison, beef, etc) by cutting into thin strips and curing by drying in the sun ▷ *n* **2** Also called: **jerky** jerked meat, esp beef [c18 back formation from *jerky*, from CHARQUI]

jerkin ('dʒɜːkɪn) *n* **1** a sleeveless and collarless short jacket worn by men or women **2** a man's sleeveless and collarless fitted jacket, often made of leather, worn in the 16th and 17th centuries [c16 of unknown origin]

jerk off *or US* **jack off** *vb* (adverb often reflexive) slang (of a male) to masturbate

> **USAGE** This word was formerly considered to be taboo, and it was labelled as such in previous editions of *Collins English Dictionary*. However, it has now become acceptable in speech, although some older or more conservative people may object to its use

jerkwater ('dʒɜːk,wɔːtə) *adj* US and Canadian slang inferior and insignificant: *a jerkwater town* [c19 originally referring to railway locomotives for which water was taken on in buckets from streams along the route]

jerky¹ ('dʒɜːkɪ) *adj* jerkier, jerkiest characterized by jerks; spasmodic > 'jerkily *adv* > 'jerkiness *n*

jerky² ('dʒɜːkɪ) *n* another word for **jerk²** (sense 2)

jeroboam (,dʒɛrə'bəʊəm) *n* a wine bottle holding the equivalent of four normal bottles (approximately 104 ounces). Also called: **double-magnum** [c19 humorous allusion to JEROBOAM (sense 1), described as a "mighty man of valour" (I Kings 11:28) who "made Israel to sin" (I Kings 14:16)]

Jeroboam (,dʒɛrə'bəʊəm) *n* Old Testament **1** the first king of the northern kingdom of Israel (?922–?901 bc) **2** king of the northern kingdom of Israel (?786–?746 bc)

jerreed (dʒə'riːd) *n* a variant spelling of **jerid**

jerry ('dʒɛrɪ) *n, pl* -ries **1** Brit an informal word for **chamber pot 2** short for **jeroboam**

Jerry ('dʒɛrɪ) *n, pl* -ries Brit slang **1** a German, esp a German soldier **2** the Germans collectively

jerry-build *vb* -builds, -building, -built (*tr*) to build (houses, flats, etc) badly using cheap materials > 'jerry-,builder *n*

jerry can *n* a flat-sided can with a capacity of between 4.5 and 5 gallons used for storing or transporting liquids, esp motor fuel: originally a German design adopted by the British Army during World War II [c20 from JERRY]

jersey ('dʒɜːzɪ) *n* **1** a knitted garment covering the upper part of the body **2 a** a machine-knitted slightly elastic cloth of wool, silk, nylon, etc, used for clothing **b** (*as modifier*): *a jersey suit* **3** a football shirt [c16 from JERSEY, from the woollen sweaters

traditionally worn by the fishermen]

Jersey ('dʒɜːzɪ) *n* **1** an island in the English Channel, the largest of the Channel Islands: forms, with two other islands, the bailiwick of Jersey; colonized from Normandy in the 11th century and still officially French-speaking; noted for finance, market gardening, dairy farming, and tourism. Capital: St Helier. Pop: 87 500 (2003 est). Area: 116 sq km (45 sq miles) **2** a breed of dairy cattle producing milk with a high butterfat content, originating from the island of Jersey

Jersey City *n* an industrial city in NE New Jersey, opposite Manhattan on a peninsula between the Hudson and Hackensack Rivers: part of the Port of New York; site of one of the greatest railway terminals in the world. Pop: 239 097 (2003 est)

Jerusalem (dʒə'ruːsələm) *n* **1** the de facto capital of Israel (recognition of this has been withheld by the United Nations), situated in the Judaean hills: became capital of the Hebrew kingdom after its capture by David around 1000 bc; destroyed by Nebuchadnezzar of Babylon in 586 bc; taken by the Romans in 63 bc; devastated in 70 ad and 135 ad during the Jewish rebellions against Rome; fell to the Arabs in 637 and to the Seljuk Turks in 1071; ruled by Crusaders from 1099 to 1187 and by the Egyptians and Turks until conquered by the British (1917); centre of the British mandate of Palestine from 1920 to 1948, when the Arabs took the old city and the Jews held the new city; unified after the Six Day War (1967) under the Israelis; the holy city of Jews, Christians, and Muslims. Pop: 693 200 (2003 est) **2 a the New Jerusalem** Christianity Heaven **b** any ideal city

Jerusalem artichoke *n* **1** a North American sunflower, *Helianthus tuberosus*, widely cultivated for its underground edible tubers **2** the tuber of this plant, which is cooked and eaten as a vegetable ▷ See also **artichoke** (senses 1, 2) [c17 by folk etymology from Italian *girasole articiocco*; see GIRASOL]

Jerusalem cherry *n* a small South American solanaceous shrub, *Solanum pseudo-capsicum*, cultivated as a house plant for its white flowers and inedible reddish cherry-like fruit

Jerusalem cross *n* a cross the equal arms of which end in a bar. Also called: **cross potent**

Jerusalem oak *n* a weedy North American chenopodiaceous plant, *Chenopodium botrys*, that has lobed leaves and smells of turpentine

Jerusalem syndrome *n* a delusive condition affecting some visitors to Jerusalem in which the sufferer identifies with a major figure from his or her religious background

Jervis Bay ('dʒɑːvɪs) *n* an inlet of the Pacific in SE Australia, on the coast of S New South Wales: part of the Australian Capital Territory (though for some purposes regarded as a separate entity): site of the Royal Australian Naval College

jess (dʒɛs) *falconry* ▷ *n* **1** a short leather strap, one end of which is permanently attached to the leg of a hawk or falcon while the other can be attached to a leash ▷ *vb* **2** (*tr*) to put jesses on (a hawk or falcon) [c14 from Old French *ges*, from Latin *jactus* a throw, from *jacere* to throw] > jessed *adj*

jessamine ('dʒɛsəmɪn) *n* another name for **jasmine** (sense 1)

Jesse ('dʒɛsɪ) *n* Old Testament the father of David (I Samuel 16)

Jesselton ('dʒɛsəltən) *n* the former name of **Kota Kinabalu**

Jesse window *n* a window in a church with a representation of Christ's descent from Jesse, usually in the form of a genealogical tree

jessie ('dʒɛsɪ) *n* slang an effeminate, weak, or cowardly boy or man

jest (dʒɛst) *n* **1** something done or said for amusement; joke **2** a frivolous mood or attitude; playfulness; fun: *to act in jest* **3** a jeer or taunt **4** an object of derision; laughing stock; butt ▷ *vb* **5** to act or speak in an amusing, teasing, or

j

frivolous way; joke **6** to make fun of (a person or thing); scoff or mock [C13 variant of GEST] > 'jestful *adj* > 'jesting *adj, n* > 'jestingly *adv*

jester ('dʒɛstə) *n* a professional clown employed by a king or nobleman, esp at courts during the Middle Ages

Jesuit ('dʒɛzjʊɪt) *n* **1** a member of a Roman Catholic religious order (the **Society of Jesus**) founded by the Spanish ecclesiastic Saint Ignatius Loyola (1491–1556) in 1534 with the aims of defending the papacy and Catholicism against the Reformation and to undertake missionary work among the heathen **2** (*sometimes not capital*) *informal offensive* a person given to subtle and equivocating arguments; casuist [C16 from New Latin *Jēsuita,* from Late Latin *Jēsus* + *-ita* -ITE¹] > Jesu'itic *or* Jesu'itical *adj* > Jesu'itically *adv*

Jesuitism ('dʒɛzjʊɪˌtɪzəm) *or* **Jesuitry** *n* **1** theology or practices of the Jesuits **2** *informal offensive* subtle and equivocating arguments; casuistry

Jesus ('dʒiːzəs) *n* **1** Also called: **Jesus Christ, Jesus of Nazareth** ?4 BC–?29 AD, founder of Christianity, born in Bethlehem and brought up in Nazareth as a Jew. He is believed by Christians to be the Son of God and to have been miraculously conceived by the Virgin Mary, wife of Joseph. With 12 disciples, he undertook two missionary journeys through Galilee, performing miracles, teaching, and proclaiming the coming of the Kingdom of God. After the Last Supper with his disciples, he was betrayed by Judas and crucified. He is believed by Christians to have risen from his tomb after three days, appeared to his disciples several times, and ascended to Heaven after 40 days ▷ *interj also* **Jesus wept 2** *taboo slang* used to express intense surprise, dismay, etc [via Latin from Greek *Iēsous,* from Hebrew *Yeshūa',* shortened from *Yehōshūa'* God is help, JOSHUA]

Jesus freak *n informal* a member of any of various Christian groups that combine a hippy communal way of life with zealous evangelicalism

jet¹ (dʒɛt) *n* **1** a thin stream of liquid or gas forced out of a small aperture or nozzle **2** an outlet or nozzle for emitting such a stream **3** a jet-propelled aircraft **4** *astronomy* a long thin feature extending from an active galaxy and usually observed at radio wavelengths ▷ *vb* **jets, jetting, jetted 5** to issue or cause to issue in a jet: *water jetted from the hose; he jetted them with water* **6** to transport or be transported by jet aircraft [C16 from Old French *jeter* to throw, from Latin *jactāre* to toss about, frequentative of *jacere* to throw]

jet² (dʒɛt) *n* **a** a hard black variety of coal that takes a brilliant polish and is used for jewellery, ornaments, etc **b** (*as modifier*): *jet earrings* [C14 from Old French *jaiet,* from Latin *gagātēs,* from Greek *lithos gagatēs* stone of *Gagai,* a town in Lycia, Asia Minor]

JET (dʒɛt) *n acronym for* Joint European Torus; a tokamak plasma-containment device at Culham, Oxfordshire, for research into energy production by nuclear fusion

jet black *n* **a** a deep black colour **b** (*as adjective*): *jet-black hair*

jet boat *n* NZ a power boat that is powered and steered by a jet of water under pressure

jet condenser *n* a steam condenser in which steam is condensed by jets of water

jeté (ʒə'teɪ) *n ballet* a step in which the dancer springs from one leg and lands on the other [French, literally: thrown, from *jeter; see* JET¹]

jet engine *n* a gas turbine, esp one fitted to an aircraft

jetfoil ('dʒɛtˌfɔɪl) *n* a type of hydrofoil that is propelled by water jets [C20 from a blend of JET¹ + (HYDRO)FOIL]

Jethro ('dʒɛθrəʊ) *n Old Testament* a Midianite priest, the father-in-law of Moses (Exodus 3:1; 4:18)

jet lag *n* a general feeling of fatigue and disorientation often experienced by travellers by jet aircraft who cross several time zones in relatively few hours

jetliner ('dʒɛtˌlaɪnə) *n* a commercial airliner powered by jet engines

jet pipe *n* the duct attached to the rear of a gas turbine through which the exhaust gases are discharged, esp one fitted to an aircraft engine

jet plane *n* an aircraft powered by one or more jet engines

jetport ('dʒɛtˌpɔːt) *n obsolete* an airport for jet planes

jet-propelled *adj* **1** driven by jet propulsion **2** *informal* very fast

jet propulsion *n* **1** propulsion by means of a jet of fluid **2** propulsion by means of a gas turbine, esp when the exhaust gases provide the propulsive thrust

jetsam *or* **jetsom** ('dʒɛtsəm) *n* **1** that portion of the equipment or cargo of a vessel thrown overboard to lighten her, as during a storm. Compare **flotsam** (sense 1), **lagan 2** another word for **flotsam** (sense 2) [C16 shortened from JETTISON]

jet set *n* **a** a rich and fashionable social set the members of which travel widely for pleasure **b** (*as modifier*): *jet-set travellers* > 'jet-ˌsetter *n* > 'jet-ˌsetting *adj*

Jet Ski *n* **1** *trademark* a small self-propelled vehicle for one person resembling a scooter, which skims across water on a flat keel, and is steered by means of handlebars ▷ *vb* **jet-ski -skis, -skiing, -skied** *or* **-ski'd** (*intr; usually not capital*) **2** to ride a Jet Ski > **Jet Skier** *n* > **Jet Skiing** *n*

jet stream *n* **1** *meteorol* a narrow belt of high-altitude winds (about 12 000 metres high) moving east at high speeds and having an important effect on frontogenesis **2** the jet of exhaust gases produced by a jet turbine, rocket motor, etc

jettison ('dʒɛtɪsˀn, -zˀn) *vb* (*tr*) **-sons, -soning, -soned 1** to throw away; abandon **2** to throw overboard ▷ *n* **3** another word for **jetsam** (sense 1) [C15 from Old French *getaison,* ultimately from Latin *jactātiō* a tossing about; see JACTATION]

jetton ('dʒɛtˀn) *n* a counter or token, esp a chip used in such gambling games as roulette [C18 from French *jeton,* from *jeter* to cast up (accounts); see JET¹]

jetty¹ ('dʒɛtɪ) *n, pl* **-ties 1** a structure built from a shore out into the water to direct currents or protect a harbour **2** a landing pier; dock [C15 from Old French *jetee* projecting part, literally: something thrown out, from *jeter* to throw; see JET¹]

jetty² ('dʒɛtɪ) *adj* of or resembling jet, esp in colour or polish > 'jettiness *n*

jeu d'esprit *French* (ʒø dɛspri) *n, pl* **jeux d'esprit** (ʒø dɛspri) a light-hearted display of wit or cleverness, esp in literature [literally: play of spirit]

jeunesse dorée *French* (ʒœnɛs dɔre) *n* rich and fashionable young people [literally: gilded youth]

Jew (dʒuː) *n* **1** a member of the Semitic people who are notionally descended from the ancient Israelites, are spread throughout the world, and are linked by loose cultural or religious ties **2** a person whose religion is Judaism ▷ See also **Hebrew, Israeli, Israelite** [C12 from Old French *juiu,* from Latin *jūdaeus,* from Greek *ioudaios,* from Hebrew *yehūdī,* from *yehūdāh* JUDAH]

Jew-baiting *n* active persecution or harassment of Jews > 'Jew-ˌbaiter *n*

jewel ('dʒuːəl) *n* **1** a precious or semiprecious stone; gem **2** a person or thing resembling a jewel in preciousness, brilliance, etc **3** a gemstone, often synthetically produced, used as a bearing in a watch **4** a piece of jewellery **5** an ornamental glass boss, sometimes faceted, used in stained glasswork **6 jewel in the crown** the most valuable, esteemed, or successful person or thing of a number ▷ *vb* **-els, -elling, -elled** *or US* **-els, -eling, -eled 7** (*tr*) to fit or decorate with a jewel or jewels [C13 from Old French *jouel,* perhaps from *jeu* game, from Latin *jocus*] > 'jewelled *or US* 'jeweled *adj* > 'jewel-ˌlike *adj*

jewel case *or* **box** *n* **1** a box, usually ornamental, in which jewels are kept **2** a plastic case for a compact disc

jewelfish ('dʒuːəlˌfɪʃ) *n, pl* **-fish** *or* **-fishes** an African cichlid, *Hemichromis bimaculatus*: a beautifully coloured and popular aquarium fish

jeweller *or US* **jeweler** ('dʒuːələ) *n* a person whose business is the cutting, polishing, or setting of gemstones or the making, repairing, or selling of jewellery

jeweller's rouge *n* a finely powdered form of ferric oxide used as a metal polish. Also called: **crocus** See also **colcothar**

jewellery *or US* **jewelry** ('dʒuːəlrɪ) *n* **1** objects that are worn for personal adornment, such as bracelets, rings, necklaces, etc, considered collectively **2** the art or business of a jeweller

Jewess ('dʒuːɪs) *n offensive* a Jewish girl or woman

jewfish ('dʒuːˌfɪʃ) *n, pl* **-fish** *or* **-fishes 1** any of various large dark serranid fishes, such as *Mycteroperca bonaci,* of warm or tropical seas **2** *Austral* any of various marine sciaenid food and game fish, esp the mulloway **3** *Austral* a large food fish of W Australian waters *Glaucosama hebraicum* [C17 of uncertain origin]

jewie ('dʒuːɪ) *n Austral informal* a jewfish

Jewish ('dʒuːɪʃ) *adj* **1** of, relating to, or characteristic of Jews ▷ *n* **2** a less common word for **Yiddish**. > 'Jewishly *adv* > 'Jewishness *n*

Jewish American Princess *n US slang* an American Jewish girl of a prosperous family, regarded as being typically pampered and spoilt. Abbreviation: **JAP**

Jewish Autonomous Region *n* an administrative division of SE Russia, in E Siberia: colonized by Jews in 1928; largely agricultural. Capital: Birobidzhan. Pop: 190 900 (2002). Area: 36 000 sq km (13 895 sq miles). Also called: **Birobidzhan, Birobijan**

Jewish calendar *n* the lunisolar calendar used by the Jews, in which time is reckoned from 3761 BC: regarded as the year of the Creation. The months, Nisan, Iyar, Sivan, Tammuz, Av, Elul, Tishri, Cheshvan, Kislev, Tevet, Shevat, and Adar, have either 29 or 30 days. Originally a new month was declared when the new moon was sighted in Jerusalem, but when this became impossible, a complex formula was devised to keep Rosh Chodesh near to the new moon. In addition, to keep the harvest festivals in the right seasons, there is a Metonic cycle of 14 years, in five of which an additional month is added after Shevat (see **Adar**). The year according to biblical reckoning begins with Nisan, and the civil year begins with Tishri; the years are numbered from Tishri. Also called: **Hebrew calendar**

jew lizard *n* another name for **bearded dragon**

Jewry ('dʒʊərɪ) *n, pl* **-ries 1 a** Jews collectively **b** the Jewish religion or culture **2** *archaic* (sometimes found in street names in England) a quarter of a town inhabited by Jews **3 the** (in some anti-semitic literature) the Jews conceived of as an organized force seeking world domination **4** *archaic* the land of Judaea

jew's-ear *n* See **jelly fungus**

jew's-harp *n* a musical instrument consisting of a small lyre-shaped metal frame held between the teeth, with a steel tongue plucked with the finger. Changes in pitch are produced by varying the size of the mouth cavities

Jezebel ('dʒɛzəˌbɛl, -bəl) *n* **1** *Old Testament* the wife of Ahab, king of Israel: she fostered the worship of Baal and tried to destroy the prophets of Israel (I Kings 18:4–13); she was killed by Jehu (II Kings 9:29–37) **2** (*sometimes not capital*) a shameless or scheming woman

Jezreel ('dʒɛzrɪəl) *n* **Plain of** another name for **Esdraelon**

Jezreelite ('dʒɛzrɪəlˌaɪts) *n* a native or inhabitant of Jezreel

JFET ('dʒeɪfɛt) *n acronym for* junction field-effect transistor; a type of field-effect transistor in which the semiconductor gate region or regions form one or more p-n junctions with the conduction channel. Compare IGFET

Jhansi ('dʒɑːnsɪ) *n* a city in central India, in SW Uttar Pradesh: scene of a mutiny against the British in 1857. Pop: 383 248 (2001)

Jharkhand ('dʒɑːkʌnd) *n* a state of NE India, created in 2000 from the S part of Bihar: consists of part of the Chota Nagpur plateau; mineral extraction, including coal and mica. Capital: Ranchi. Pop: 26 909 428 (2001). Area: 74 677 sq km (28 833 sq miles)

jhatka ('dʒætkə) *n* the slaughter of animals for food according to Sikh law [Punjabi]

Jhelum ('dʒiːləm) *n* a river in Pakistan and Kashmir, rising in W central Kashmir and flowing northwest through the Vale of Kashmir, then southwest into NW Punjab to join the Chenab River: important for irrigation, having the Mangla Dam (Pakistan), completed in 1967. Length: about 720 km (450 miles)

JHVH or **JHWH** *n* Old Testament variants of YHVH

-ji (-dʒiː) *suffix* Indian a suffix placed after a person's name or title as a mark of respect [Hindi]

Jiangsu ('dʒjæŋ'suː) or **Kiangsu** *n* a province of E China, on the Yellow Sea: consists mostly of the marshy delta of the Yangtze River, with some of China's largest cities and most densely populated areas. Capital: Nanjing. Pop: 74 060 000 (2003 est). Area: 102 200 sq km (39 860 sq miles)

Jiangxi ('dʒjæŋ'ʃiː) or **Kiangsi** *n* a province of SE central China, in the basins of the Kan River and Poyang Lake: mineral resources include coal and tungsten. Capital: Nanchang. Pop: 42 220 000 (2003 est). Area: 164 800 sq km (64 300 sq miles)

Jiazhou ('dʒjæ'dʒəʊ) or **Kiaochow** *n* a territory of NE China, in SE Shandong province, surrounding **Jiazhou Bay** (an inlet of the Yellow Sea): leased to Germany from 1898 to 1914. Area: about 520 sq km (200 sq miles)

jib¹ (dʒɪb) *n* **1** nautical any triangular sail set forward of the foremast of a vessel **2** **cut of someone's jib** someone's manner, behaviour, style, etc **3** obsolete **a** the lower lip, usually when it protrudes forwards in a grimace **b** the face or nose [C17 of unknown origin]

jib² (dʒɪb) *vb* jibs, jibbing, jibbed (intr) chiefly Brit **1** (often foll by at) to be reluctant (to); hold back (from); balk (at) **2** (of an animal) to stop short and refuse to go forwards: the horse jibbed at the jump **3** nautical variant of gybe [C19 of unknown origin] > **'jibber** n

jib³ (dʒɪb) *n* the projecting arm of a crane or the boom of a derrick, esp one that is pivoted to enable it to be raised or lowered [C18 probably based on GIBBET]

jib⁴ (dʒɪb) *n* (often plural) South Wales dialect a contortion of the face; a face: stop making jibs [special use of JIB¹ in the sense: lower lip, face)]

jibbons ('dʒɪbªnz) pl n Southwest Brit dialect spring onions [from Norman French chiboule, variant of French ciboule onion, ultimately from Latin capulla an onion patch, from caepa an onion]

jib boom *n* nautical a spar forming an extension of the bowsprit

jibe¹ (dʒaɪb), **jib** or **jibb** (dʒɪb) vb, n nautical variants of gybe

jibe² (dʒaɪb) vb a variant spelling of gibe. > **'jiber** n > **'jibingly** adv

jibe³ (dʒaɪb) vb (intr) informal to agree; accord; harmonize [C19 of unknown origin]

jib-headed adj nautical **1** (of a sail) pointed at the top or head **2** (of a sailing vessel or rig) having sails that are triangular

Jibouti or **Jibuti** (dʒɪ'buːtɪ) *n* variant spellings of Djibouti

jicama (dʒɪ'kɑːmə; Spanish xɪkama) *n* a pale brown turnip with crisp sweet flesh, originating in Mexico [C17 from Mexican Spanish jícama, from Nahuatl xicama]

JICTAR ('dʒɪktɑː) *n* acronym for Joint Industry Committee for Television Advertising Research

Jidda ('dʒɪdə) or **Jedda** *n* a port in W Saudi Arabia, on the Red Sea: the diplomatic capital of the country; the port of entry for Mecca, 80 km (50 miles) east. Pop: 3 807 000 (2005 est)

jiffy ('dʒɪfɪ) or **jiff** (dʒɪf) *n, pl* jiffies or jiffs informal a very short time: wait a jiffy [C18 of unknown origin]

Jiffy bag *n* trademark a thickly padded but light envelope in which articles such as books are placed for protection in the post

jig (dʒɪg) *n* **1** any of several old rustic kicking and leaping dances **2** a piece of music composed for or in the rhythm of this dance, usually in six-eight time **3** a mechanical device designed to hold and locate a component during machining and to guide the cutting tool **4** angling any of various spinning lures that wobble when drawn through the water **5** Also called: jigger mining a device for separating ore or coal from waste material by agitation in water **6** obsolete a joke or prank ▷ *vb* jigs, jigging, jigged **7** to dance (a jig) **8** to jerk or cause to jerk up and down rapidly **9** (often foll by up) to fit or be fitted in a jig **10** (tr) to drill or cut (a workpiece) in a jig **11** mining to separate ore or coal from waste material using a jig **12** (intr) to produce a jig **13** Austral slang to play truant from school [C16 (originally: a dance or the music for it; applied to various modern devices because of the verbal sense: to jerk up and down rapidly): of unknown origin]

Jigawa (ˌdʒɪ'gɑːwə) *n* a state of N Nigeria. Capital: Dutse. Pop: 3 164 134 (1995 est). Area (including Kano state): 43 285 sq km (16 712 sq miles)

jigger¹ ('dʒɪgə) *n* **1** a person or thing that jigs **2** golf an iron, now obsolete, with a thin blade, used for hitting long shots from a bare lie **3** any of a number of mechanical devices having a vibratory or jerking motion **4** a light lifting tackle used on ships **5** a small glass, esp for whisky, with a capacity of about one and a half ounces **6** NZ a light hand- or power-propelled vehicle used on railway lines **7** engineering a type of hydraulic lift in which a hydraulic ram operates the lift through a block and tackle which increases the length of the stroke **8** Canadian a device used when setting a gill net beneath ice **9** mining another word for jig (sense 5) **10** nautical short for jiggermast **11** billiards another word for bridge¹ (sense 10) **12** US and Canadian informal a device or thing the name of which is unknown or temporarily forgotten **13** Liverpool dialect an alleyway

jigger² or **jigger flea** ('dʒɪgə) *n* other names for the chigoe (sense 1)

jiggered ('dʒɪgəd) adj (postpositive) **1** informal damned; blowed: I'm jiggered if he'll get away with it **2** (sometimes foll by up) Scot and northern English dialect tired out [C19 probably euphemism for buggered; see BUGGER]

jiggermast ('dʒɪgəˌmɑːst) *n* nautical any small mast on a sailing vessel, esp the mizzenmast of a yawl. Sometimes shortened to: jigger

jiggery-pokery ('dʒɪgərɪ'pəʊkərɪ) *n* informal, chiefly Brit dishonest or deceitful behaviour or business; trickery [C19 from Scottish dialect joukery-pawkery]

jiggle ('dʒɪgªl) vb **1** to move or cause to move up and down or to and fro with a short jerky motion ▷ *n* **2** a short jerky motion [C19 frequentative of JIG; compare JOGGLE] > **'jiggly** adj

jiggy ('dʒɪgɪ) adj get jiggy with slang to have sexual relations with

jigsaw ('dʒɪg,sɔː) *n* **1** a mechanical saw with a fine steel blade for cutting intricate curves in sheets of material **2** See jigsaw puzzle [C19 from JIG (to jerk up and down rapidly) + SAW¹]

jigsaw puzzle *n* a puzzle in which the player has to reassemble a picture that has been mounted on a wooden or cardboard base and cut into a large number of irregularly shaped interlocking pieces

jihad or **jehad** (dʒɪ'hæd) *n* **1** Islam a holy war against infidels undertaken by Muslims in defence of the Islamic faith **2** Islam the personal struggle of the individual believer against evil

and persecution **3** rare a crusade in support of a cause [C19 from Arabic jihād a conflict]

jihadi or **jehadi** (dʒɪ'hædɪ) *n* Islam **a** a person who takes part in a jihad **b** (as modifier): jihadi groups

jihadism or **jehadism** (dʒɪ'hæd,ɪzəm) *n* Islam an Islamic fundamentalist movement that favours the pursuit of jehads in defence of the islamic faith [C21 Arabic] > **ji'hadist** or **je'hadist** adj, n

jilbab (dʒɪl'bɑːb) *n* **1** a long robe worn by Muslim women [from Arabic]

Jilin ('dʒiː'lɪn) or **Kirin** *n* **1** a province of NE China, in central Manchuria. Capital: Changchun. Pop: 27 040 000 (2003 est). Area: 187 000 sq km (72 930 sq miles) **2** Also called: Chi-lin ('tʃiː'lɪn) a river port in NE China, in N central Jilin province on the Songhua River. Pop: 1 496 000 (2005 est)

jill (dʒɪl) *n* dialect a variant spelling of gill⁴ (sense 2)

jillaroo (ˌdʒɪlə'ruː) *n, pl* -roos Austral informal a female jackeroo

jillion ('dʒɪljən) *n* informal an extremely large number or amount: jillions of pounds [C20 fanciful coinage based on MILLION, BILLION, etc] > **'jillionth** adj

Jilolo (dʒaɪ'ləʊləʊ) *n* a variant spelling of Djailolo See Halmahera

Jilong (dʒiː'lʊŋ) *n* the Pinyin transliteration of the Chinese name for Chilung

jilt (dʒɪlt) vb **1** (tr) to leave or reject (a lover), esp without previous warning: she was jilted at the altar ▷ *n* **2** a woman who jilts a lover [C17 from dialect jillet flighty girl, diminutive of proper name Gill] > **'jilter** n

jim crow ('dʒɪm 'krəʊ) *n* (often capitals) US **1** **a** the policy or practice of segregating Blacks **b** (as modifier): jim-crow laws **2** **a** a derogatory term for a Black person **b** (as modifier): a jim-crow saloon **3** an implement for bending iron bars or rails **4** a crowbar fitted with a claw [C19 from Jim Crow, name of song used as the basis of an act by Thomas Rice (1808–60), American entertainer] > **'jim-'crowism** n

jimjams ('dʒɪm,dʒæmz) pl n **1** a slang word for delirium tremens **2** a state of nervous tension, excitement, or unease **3** informal pyjamas [C19 whimsical formation based on JAM¹]

jimmy ('dʒɪmɪ) *n, pl* -mies, vb -mies, -mying, -mied the US word for jemmy

Jimmy ('dʒɪmɪ) *n* Central Scot urban dialect an informal term of address to a male stranger

Jimmy Woodser (ˌdʒɪmɪ 'wʊdzə) *n* Austral informal **1** a man who drinks by himself **2** a drink taken alone

jimson weed ('dʒɪmsªn) *n* US and Canadian a poisonous solanaceous plant, Datura stramonium, of the N hemisphere, having white funnel-shaped flowers and spiny capsule fruits. Also called (in Britain and certain other countries): thorn apple [C17 from earlier Jamestown weed, from Jamestown, Virginia]

Jinan ('dʒiː'næn), **Chinan** or **Tsinan** *n* an industrial city in NE China, capital of Shandong province; probably over 3000 years old. Pop: 2 654 000 (2005 est)

Jingdezhen ('dʒɪŋ'dɛdʒɛn), **Fowliang** or **Fou-liang** *n* a city in SE China, in NE Jiangxi province east of Poyang Lake: famous for its porcelain industry, established in the sixth century. Pop: 416 000 (2005 est)

jingle ('dʒɪŋgªl) vb **1** to ring or cause to ring lightly and repeatedly **2** (intr) to sound in a manner suggestive of jingling: a jingling verse ▷ *n* **3** a sound of metal jingling: the jingle of the keys **4** a catchy and rhythmic verse, song, etc, esp one used in advertising [C16 probably of imitative origin; compare Dutch jengelen] > **'jingler** n > **'jingly** adj

jingo ('dʒɪŋgəʊ) *n, pl* -goes **1** a loud and bellicose patriot; chauvinist **2** jingoism **3** by jingo an exclamation of surprise [C17 originally perhaps a euphemism for Jesus; applied to bellicose patriots after the use of by Jingo! in the refrain of a 19th-

j

century music-hall song] > **'jingoish** adj

jingoism ('dʒɪŋgəʊ,ɪzəm) n the belligerent spirit or foreign policy of jingoes; chauvinism > **'jingoist** n, adj > **jingo'istic** adj > **jingo'istically** adv

Jinja ('dʒɪndʒə) n a town in Uganda, on the N shore of Lake Victoria. Pop: 86 520 (2002 est)

Jinjiang ('dʒɪn'dʒjæŋ), **Chinkiang** or **Chengchiang** n a port in E China, in S Jiangsu at the confluence of the Yangtze River and the Grand Canal. Pop: 620 000 (2005 est)

jink (dʒɪŋk) vb **1** to move swiftly or jerkily or make a quick turn in order to dodge or elude ▷ n **2** a jinking movement [c18 of Scottish origin, imitative of swift movement]

jinker ('dʒɪŋkə) n Austral a vehicle for transporting timber, consisting of a tractor and two sets of wheels for supporting the logs [of unknown origin]

jinks (dʒɪŋks) pl n boisterous or mischievous play (esp in the phrase **high jinks**) [c18 of unknown origin]

jinn (dʒɪn) n (often functioning as singular) the plural of jinni

jinne ('jiːnə) or **jirre** ('jiːrə) interj South African an exclamation expressive of surprise, admiration, shock, etc [from Afrikaans]

jinni, jinnee, djinni or **djinny** (dʒɪ'niː, 'dʒɪnɪ) n, pl **jinn** or **djinn** (dʒɪn) a being or spirit in Muslim belief who could assume human or animal form and influence man by supernatural powers [c17 from Arabic]

jinrikisha, jinricksha, jinrickshaw or **jinriksha** (dʒɪn'rɪkʃɔː, -ʃə) n other names for **rickshaw** [c19 from Japanese, from jin man + riki power + sha carriage]

jinx (dʒɪŋks) n **1** an unlucky or malevolent force, person, or thing ▷ vb **2** (tr) to be or put a jinx on [c20 perhaps from New Latin Jynx genus name of the wryneck, from Greek iunx wryneck, the name of a bird used in magic]

Jinzhou ('dʒɪn'dʒəʊ), **Chin-Chou** or **Chin-chow** n a city in NE China, in SW Liaoning province. Pop: 888 000 (2005 est). Former name (1913–47): **Chin-hsien**

jipijapa (,hiːpiː'hɑːpɑː) n a palmlike plant, Carludovica palmata, of Central and South America, whose fanlike leaves are bleached for making panama hats: family Cyclanthaceae [American Spanish, after Jipijapa, Ecuador]

jism ('dʒɪzəm) or **jissom** ('dʒɪsəm) n taboo informal words for **semen** [of unknown origin]

JIT abbreviation for **just-in-time**

jitney ('dʒɪtnɪ) n US now rare **1** a small bus that carries passengers for a low price, originally five cents **2** slang a nickel; five cents [c20 of unknown origin]

jitter ('dʒɪtə) informal ▷ vb **1** (intr) to be anxious or nervous ▷ n **2** the jitters nervousness and anxiety **3** electronics small rapid variations in the amplitude or timing of a waveform arising from fluctuations in the voltage supply, mechanical vibrations, etc [c20 of unknown origin]

jitterbug ('dʒɪtə,bʌg) n **1** a fast jerky American dance, usually to a jazz accompaniment, that was popular in the 1940s **2** a person who dances the jitterbug **3** a highly nervous or excitable person ▷ vb **-bugs, -bugging, -bugged 4** (intr) to perform such a dance

jittery ('dʒɪtərɪ) adj informal nervous and anxious > **'jitteriness** n

jiujitsu or **jiujutsu** (dʒuː'dʒɪtsuː) n variant spellings of **jujitsu**

Jivaro ('hɪːvərəʊ) n **1 a** a member of a group of sub-tribes native to the Amazonian forests of Peru and Ecuador, formerly noted for their warlike nature and head-shrinking rituals **b** as modifier: Jivaro rituals **2** any of the languages spoken by the Jivaro people [c19 from Spanish jíbaro, from Shuar shuar people]

jive (dʒaɪv) n **1** a style of lively and jerky dance performed to jazz and, later, to rock and roll, popular esp in the 1940s and 1950s **2** Also called:

jive talk a variety of American slang spoken chiefly by Blacks, esp jazz musicians **3 a** slang, chiefly US deliberately misleading or deceptive talk **b** (as modifier): jive talk ▷ vb **4** (intr) to dance the jive **5** slang, chiefly US to mislead; tell lies (to) [c20 of unknown origin] > **'jiver** n

jizz (dʒɪz) n a term for the total combination of characteristics that serve to identify a particular species of bird or plant [origin obscure]

JJ. abbreviation for **1** Judges **2** Justices

jm the internet domain name for Jamaica

jnd abbreviation for just noticeable difference

Jnr abbreviation for junior

jo¹ or **joe** (dʒəʊ) n, pl **joes** a Scot word for **sweetheart** [c16 alteration of JOY]

jo² the internet domain name for Jordan

Joab ('dʒəʊæb) n Old Testament the successful commander of King David's forces and the slayer of Abner and Absalom (II Samuel 2:18–23; 3:24–27; 18:14–15)

joannes (dʒəʊ'æniːz) n, pl **-nes** a variant of **johannes**

João Pessoa (Portuguese 'ʒuəm pe'soa) n a port in NE Brazil, capital of Paraíba state. Pop: 931 000 (2005 est)

job (dʒɒb) n **1** an individual piece of work or task **2** an occupation; post of employment **3** an object worked on or a result produced from working **4** a duty or responsibility: her job was to cook the dinner **5** informal a difficult task or problem: I had a job to contact him **6** a state of affairs it's a good job I saw you **7** informal a damaging piece of work: he really did a job on that **8** informal a crime, esp a robbery or burglary **9** informal an article or specimen: the new car was a nice little job **10** an instance of jobbery **11** computing a unit of work for a computer consisting of a single complete task submitted by a user **12 jobs for the boys** appointments given to or created for allies or favourites **13 on the job a** actively engaged in one's employment **b** Brit taboo engaged in sexual intercourse **14 just the job** exactly what was required ▷ vb **jobs, jobbing, jobbed 15** (intr) to work by the piece or at casual jobs **16** to make a private profit out of (a public office, etc) **17** (intr; usually foll by in) **a** to buy and sell (goods or services) as a middleman: he jobs in government surplus **b** Brit to buy and sell stocks and shares as a stockjobber: he jobs in blue chips **18** (tr; often foll by out) to apportion (a contract, work, etc) among several contractors, workers, etc [c16 of uncertain origin]

Job (dʒəʊb) n **1** Old Testament **a** a Jewish patriarch, who maintained his faith in God in spite of the afflictions sent by God to test him **b** the book containing Job's pleas to God under these afflictions, attempted explanations of them by his friends, and God's reply to him **2** any person who withstands great suffering without despairing

job analysis n the analysis of the contents of a job in order to provide a job description for such purposes as fitting the job into a grading structure or matching individual capabilities to job requirements

jobber ('dʒɒbə) n **1** Brit short for **stockjobber** (sense 1) **2** a person who jobs

jobbery ('dʒɒbərɪ) n the practice of making private profit out of a public office; corruption or graft

jobbing ('dʒɒbɪŋ) adj working on occasional jobs or by the piece rather than in a regular job: a jobbing gardener

jobbing printer n one who prints mainly commercial and display work rather than books or newspapers

Jobcentre ('dʒɒb,sɛntə) n Brit any of a number of government offices having premises usually situated in or near the main shopping area of a town in which people seeking jobs can consult displayed advertisements in informal surroundings

Jobclub ('dʒɒb,klʌb) n a group of unemployed

people organized through a Jobcentre, which meets every day and is given advice on job seeking to increase its members' chances of finding employment

Job Corps (dʒɒb) n US a Federal organization established in 1964 to train unemployed youths in order to make it easier for them to find work

job description n a detailed written account, agreed between management and worker, of all the duties and responsibilities which together make up a particular job

job enlargement n a widening of the range of tasks performed by an employee in order to provide variety in the activities undertaken

job evaluation n the analysis of the relationship between jobs in an organization: often used as a basis for a wages structure

jobless ('dʒɒblɪs) adj **a** unemployed **b** (as collective noun; preceded by the): the jobless > **'joblessness** n

job lot n **1** a miscellaneous collection of articles sold as a lot **2** a collection of cheap or trivial items

job rotation n the practice of transferring an employee from one work station or activity to another during the working day in order to add variety to a job: often used in assembly line work

job satisfaction n the extent to which a person's hopes, desires, and expectations about the employment he is engaged in are fulfilled

Job's comforter n a person who, while purporting to give sympathy, succeeds only in adding to distress

jobseeker's allowance ('dʒɒb,siːkəz) n (in Britain) a National Insurance or social security payment for unemployed people; replaced unemployment benefit in 1996. Abbreviation: **JSA**

job sharing n the division of a job between two or more people such that each covers the same job for complementary parts of the day or week > **job sharer** n

Job's-tears n **1** (functioning as singular) a tropical Asian grass, Coix lacryma-jobi, cultivated for its white beadlike modified leaves, which contain edible seeds **2** (functioning as plural) the beadlike structures of this plant, used as rosary or ornamental beads

jobsworth ('dʒɒbz,wɜːθ) n informal a person in a position of minor authority who invokes the letter of the law in order to avoid any action requiring initiative, cooperation, etc [c20 from it's more than my job's worth to …]

Joburg ('dʒəʊ,bɜːg) n informal Johannesburg. See also **Jozi**

Jocasta (dʒəʊ'kæstə) n Greek myth a queen of Thebes, the wife of Laius, who married Oedipus without either of them knowing he was her son

jock (dʒɒk) n **1** informal short for **disc jockey 2** informal short for **jockstrap 3** US informal an athlete **4** N.Z mining a pointed bar of steel inserted into the wheel of a mine vehicle and used for emergency braking

Jock (dʒɒk) n a slang word or term of address for a Scot

jockey ('dʒɒkɪ) n **1** a person who rides horses in races, esp as a profession or for hire ▷ vb **2 a** (tr) to ride (a horse) in a race **b** (intr) to ride as a jockey **3** (intr; often foll by for) to try to obtain an advantage by manoeuvring, esp literally in a race or metaphorically, as in a struggle for power (esp in the phrase jockey for position) **4** to trick or cheat (a person) [c16 (in the sense: lad): from name Jock + -EY]

jockey cap n a cap with a long peak projecting from the forehead

Jockey Club n Brit the governing body that regulates and controls horse-racing both on the flat and over jumps

jocko ('dʒɒkəʊ) n, pl **-os** a W African name for **chimpanzee** [c19 from French, based on Bantu ngeko]

jockstrap ('dʒɒk,stræp) n an elasticated belt with a pouch worn by men, esp athletes, to support the genitals. Also called: **athletic support** [C20 from slang *jock* penis + STRAP]

jocose (dʒəˈkəʊs) *adj* characterized by humour; merry [C17 from Latin *jocōsus* given to jesting, from *jocus* JOKE] > jo'**cosely** *adv* > jo'**coseness** or **jocosity** (dʒəˈkɒsɪtɪ) *n*

jocular (ˈdʒɒkjʊlə) *adj* **1** characterized by joking and good humour **2** meant lightly or humorously; facetious [C17 from Latin *joculāris*. from *joculus* little JOKE] > **jocularity** (ˌdʒɒkjʊˈlærɪtɪ) *n* > 'jocularly *adv*

jocund (ˈdʒɒkənd) *adj* of a humorous temperament; merry [C14 from Late Latin *jocundus*, from Latin *jūcundus* pleasant, from *juvāre* to please] > **jocundity** (dʒəʊˈkʌndɪtɪ) or 'jocundness *n* > 'jocundly *adv*

Jodhpur (ˌdʒɒdˈpʊə) *n* **1** a former state of NW India, one of the W Rajputana states: now part of Rajasthan **2** a walled city in NW India, in W Rajasthan: university (1962). Pop: 846 408 (2001)

Jodhpuri (ˈdʒɒdpʊrɪ) *adj* of or relating to Jodhpur or its inhabitants

Jodhpuri coat *n* a coat worn by men in India, similar to but shorter than a sherwani [named after JODHPUR]

jodhpurs (ˈdʒɒdpəz) *pl n* **1** riding breeches, loose-fitting around the hips and tight-fitting from the thighs to the ankles **2** Also called: **jodhpur boots** ankle-length leather riding boots [C19 from the town JODHPUR]

Jodo (ˈdʒəʊˌdəʊ) *n* a Japanese Buddhist sect teaching salvation through faith in Buddha [from Japanese]

Jodrell Bank (ˈdʒɒdrəl) *n* an astronomical observatory in NW England, in Cheshire: radio telescope with a steerable parabolic dish, 75 m (250 ft) in diameter

Joe (dʒəʊ) *n* (*sometimes not capital*) *slang* **1** US and Canadian a man or fellow **2** US a GI; soldier

Joe Blake *n* Austral **1** rhyming slang a snake **2** the Joe Blakes the DT's

Joe Bloggs (blɒgz) *n* Brit slang an average or typical man. US, Canadian, and Austral equivalent: Joe Blow See also **Joe Six-Pack**

Joel (ˈdʒəʊəl) *n* Old Testament **1** a Hebrew prophet **2** the book containing his oracles

Joe Public *n* slang the general public

joe-pye weed (ˈdʒəʊˈpaɪ) *n* US and Canadian any of several North American plants of the genus *Eupatorium*, esp *E. purpureum*, having pale purplish clusters of flower heads lacking rays: family *Asteraceae* (composites) [C19 of unknown origin]

joes (dʒəʊz) *pl n* Austral informal **the** a fit of depression [short for *the Joe Blakes*]

Joe Six-Pack (ˈsɪksˌpæk) *n* US slang an average or typical man

Joe Soap *n* **1** Brit slang a person who is regarded as unintelligent and imposed upon as a stooge or scapegoat **2** NZ slang an average or typical man. Also called (Brit): Joe Bloggs, (US and Canadian) Joe Sixpack

joey (ˈdʒəʊɪ) *n* Austral informal **1** a young kangaroo or possum **2** a young animal or child [C19 from a native Australian language]

Joey Hooker (ˈdʒəʊɪ ˈhʊkə) *n* another name for **gallant soldier** (a plant)

jog¹ (dʒɒg) *vb* jogs, jogging, jogged **1** (*intr*) to run or move slowly or at a jog trot, esp for physical exercise **2** (*intr*; foll by *on* or *along*) to continue in a plodding way **3** (*tr*) to jar or nudge slightly; shake lightly **4** (*tr*) to remind; stimulate: *please jog my memory* **5** (*tr*) *printing* to even up the edges of (a stack of paper); square up ▷ *n* **6** the act of jogging **7** a slight jar or nudge **8** a jogging motion; trot [C14 probably variant of *shog* to shake, influenced by dialect *jot* to jolt]

jog² (dʒɒg) *n* US and Canadian **1** a sharp protruding point in a surface; jag **2** a sudden change in course or direction [C18 probably variant of JAG¹]

jogger (ˈdʒɒgə) *n* **1** a person who runs at a jog over some distance for exercise, usually regularly **2** NZ a cart with rubber-tyred wheels used on a farm

jogger's nipple *n* informal painful inflammation of the nipple, caused by friction with a garment when running for long distances

jogging (ˈdʒɒgɪn) *n* running at a slow regular pace usually over a long distance as part of an exercise routine

joggle (ˈdʒɒgᵊl) *vb* **1** to shake or move (someone or something) with a slightly jolting motion **2** (*tr*) to join or fasten (two pieces of building material) by means of a joggle ▷ *n* **3** the act of joggling **4** a slight irregular shake; jolt **5** a joint between two pieces of building material by means of a projection on one piece that fits into a notch in the other; dowel **6** a shoulder designed to take the thrust of a strut or brace [C16 frequentative of JOG¹] > 'joggler *n*

joggle post *n* a post or beam consisting of two timbers joined to each other by joggles

Jogjakarta (ˌdʒɒgjəˈkɑːtɑː, ˌdʒɒg-) *n* a variant spelling of **Yogyakarta**

jog trot *n* **1** an easy bouncy gait, esp of a horse, midway between a walk and a trot **2** a monotonous or regular way of living or doing something ▷ *vb* **jog-trot** -trots, -trotting, -trotted **3** (*intr*) to move at a jog trot

johannes (dʒəʊˈhænɪːz) or **joannes** *n, pl* -nes a Portuguese gold coin minted in the early 18th century [C18 after *Joannes* (King John V) of Portugal, whose name was inscribed on the coin]

Johannesburg (dʒəʊˈhænɪsˌbɜːg) *n* a city in N South Africa: the capital of Gauteng province: South Africa's largest city and chief industrial centre; grew with the establishment in 1886 of the gold-mining industry; University of Witwatersrand (1922). Pop: 1 009 036 (2001)

john (dʒɒn) *n* **1** chiefly US and Canadian a slang word for **lavatory** (sense 1) **2** slang, chiefly US a prostitute's client **3** Austral slang short for **John Hop** [C20 special use of the proper name]

John Barleycorn *n* usually humorous the personification of alcohol, esp of malt spirits

John Birch Society *n* US politics a fanatical right-wing association organized along semisecret lines to fight Communism [C20 named after *John Birch* (killed by Chinese communists 1945), American USAF captain whom its members regarded as the first cold-war casualty]

John Bull *n* **1** a personification of England or the English people **2** a typical Englishman [C18 name of a character intended to be representative of the English nation in *The History of John Bull* (1712) by John Arbuthnot] > John Bullish *adj* > John Bullishness *n* > John Bullism *n*

John Doe *n* See **Doe**

John Dory (ˈdɔːrɪ) *n* **1** a European dory (the fish), *Zeus faber*, having a deep compressed body, spiny dorsal fins, and massive mobile jaws **2** Austral a related fish, *Zeus australis*, which is a valued food fish of Australia [C18 from proper name *John* + DORY¹; on the model of DOE]

Johne's disease (ˈjəʊnəz) *n* an infectious disease of ruminants characterized by chronic inflammation of the bowel and caused by *Mycobacterium paratuberculosis*, a bacterium that can be transmitted in milk [C20 named after H. A. *Johne* (1839–1910), German veterinary surgeon]

John Hancock *n* US and Canadian informal a person's signature: *put your John Hancock on this form.* Also called: John Henry [after *John Hancock* (1737–93), American statesman, from his clear and legible signature on the American Declaration of Independence]

John Hop *n* Austral slang a policeman [rhyming slang for COP¹]

johnny (ˈdʒɒnɪ) *n, pl* -nies Brit **1** (*often capital*) informal a man or boy; chap **2** a slang word for **condom**

johnny cake or **johnny-cake** *n* **1** US a type of thin flat corn bread baked on a griddle **2** Austral a thin cake of flour and water paste cooked in the ashes of a fire or in a pan

Johnny Canuck (kəˈnʌk) *n* Canadian **1** an informal name for a **Canadian 2** a personification of Canada

Johnny-come-lately *n, pl* Johnny-come-latelies or Johnnies-come-lately a brash newcomer, novice, or recruit

Johnny-jump-up *n* US and Canadian any of several violaceous plants, esp the wild pansy [C19 so called from its quick growth]

Johnny raw *n* slang a novice; new recruit

Johnny Reb *n* US informal (in the American Civil War) a Confederate soldier [C19 from REBEL (n)]

John o'Groats (əˈgrəʊts) *n* a village at the northeasternmost tip of the Scottish mainland: considered to be the northernmost point of the mainland of Great Britain although Dunnet Head, slightly to the west, lies further north. See also **Land's End**

Johnson grass *n* a persistent perennial Mediterranean grass, *Sorghum halepense*, cultivated for hay and pasture in the US where it also grows as a weed. See also **sorghum** [C19 named after William *Johnson* (died 1859), American agriculturalist who introduced it]

Johnsonian (dʒɒnˈsəʊnɪən) *adj* of, relating to, or characteristic of the British lexicographer, critic, poet, and conversationalist Samuel *Johnson* (1709–84), his works, or his style of writing

John Thomas *n* a name for **penis**

Johore (dʒəʊˈhɔː) *n* a state of Malaysia, on the S Malay Peninsula: mostly forested, with large swamps; bauxite- and iron-mining. Capital: Johore Bahru. Pop: 2 740 625 (2000). Area: 18 984 sq km (7330 sq miles)

Johore Bahru (ˈbɑːruː) *n* a city in S Malaysia, capital of Johore state: important trading centre, situated at the sole crossing point of **Johore Strait** (between Malaya and Singapore Island). Pop: 719 000 (2005 est)

joie de vivre French (ʒwa də vivrə) *n* joy of living; enjoyment of life; ebullience

j

join (dʒɔɪn) *vb* **1** to come or bring together; connect **2** to become a member of (a club, organization, etc) **3** (*intr*; often foll by *with*) to become associated or allied **4** (*intr*; usually foll by *in*) to take part **5** (*tr*) to meet (someone) as a companion **6** (*tr*) to become part of; take a place in or with **7** (*tr*) to unite (two people) in marriage **8** (*tr*) geometry to connect with a straight line or a curve **9** (*tr*) an informal word for **adjoin 10 join battle** to start fighting **11 join duty** Indian to report for work after a period of leave or a strike **12 join hands a** to hold one's own hands together **b** (of two people) to hold each other's hands **c** (usually foll by *with*) to work together in an enterprise or task ▷ *n* **13** a joint; seam **14** the act of joining **15** maths another name for **union** (sense 9) ▷ See also **join up** [C13 from Old French *joindre* from Latin *jungere* to yoke] > 'joinable *adj*

joinder (ˈdʒɔɪndə) *n* **1** the act of joining, esp in legal contexts **2** law **a** (in pleading) the stage at which the parties join issue (**joinder of issue**) **b** the joining of two or more persons as coplaintiffs or codefendants (**joinder of parties**) **c** the joining of two or more causes in one suit [C17 from French *joindre* to JOIN]

joined-up *adj* **1** with all departments or sections communicating together efficiently with each other and acting together purposefully and effectively: *joined-up government* **2 a** focusing on or producing an integrated and coherent result, strategy, etc: *joined-up thinking* **b** forming an integrated and coherent whole: *joined-up policies*

joiner (ˈdʒɔɪnə) *n* **1** chiefly Brit a person trained and skilled in making finished woodwork, such as windows, doors, and stairs **2** a person or thing that joins **3** informal a person who joins many clubs, causes, etc

joinery (ˈdʒɔɪnərɪ) *n* **1** the skill or craft of a joiner **2** work made by a joiner

joint (dʒɔɪnt) *n* **1** a junction of two or more parts or objects **2** the part or space between two such junctions **3** anatomy the junction between two or more bones, usually formed of connective tissue and cartilage **4** the point of connection between movable parts in invertebrates, esp insects and other arthropods. Related adj: **articular 5** the part of a plant stem from which a branch or leaf grows **6** one of the parts into which a carcass of meat is cut by the butcher, esp for roasting **7** geology a crack in a rock along which no displacement has occurred **8** slang a disreputable establishment, such as a bar or nightclub **b** often facetious a dwelling or meeting place **9** slang a cannabis cigarette **10 out of joint a** dislocated **b** out of order or disorganized **11 put someone's nose out of joint** See **nose** (sense 18) ▷ adj **12** shared by or belonging to two or more: *joint property* **13** created by combined effort **14** sharing with others or with one another: *joint rulers* **15** law (of persons) combined in ownership or obligation; regarded as a single entity in law ▷ vb (tr) **16** to provide with or fasten by a joint or joints **17** to plane the edge of (a board, etc) into the correct shape for a joint **18** to cut or divide (meat, fowl, etc) into joints or at a joint > 'jointly adv

joint account *n* a bank account registered in the name of two or more persons, any of whom may make deposits and withdrawals

joint consultation *n* a formal system of communication between the management of an organization and the employees' representatives used prior to taking decisions affecting the workforce, usually effected through a joint consultative committee

joint density function *n statistics* a function of two or more random variables from which can be obtained a single probability that all the variables in the function will take specified values or fall within specified intervals

jointed ('dʒɔɪntɪd) *adj* **1 a** having a joint or joints **b** (in combination): *large-jointed* **2** (of a plant stem or similar part) marked with constrictions, at which the stem breaks into separate portions > 'jointedly adv > 'jointedness n

jointer ('dʒɔɪntə) *n* **1** a tool for pointing mortar joints, as in brickwork **2** Also called: **jointing plane** a long plane for shaping the edges of planks so that they can be fitted together **3** a person or thing that makes joints

joint resolution *n US* a resolution passed by both houses of a bicameral legislature, signed by the chief executive and legally binding

jointress ('dʒɔɪntrɪs) *n law* a woman entitled to a jointure

joint stock *n* capital funds held in common and usually divided into shares between the owners

joint-stock company *n* **1** *Brit* a business enterprise characterized by its separate legal existence and the sharing of ownership between shareholders, whose liability is limited **2** *US* a business enterprise whose owners are issued shares of transferable stock but do not enjoy limited liability

jointure ('dʒɔɪntʃə) *n* **1** law **a** provision made by a husband for his wife by settling property upon her at marriage for her use after his death **b** the property so settled **2** obsolete the act of joining or the condition of being joined [c14 from Old French, from Latin *junctūra* a joining]

jointworm ('dʒɔɪntˌwɜːm) *n US* the larva of chalcid flies of the genus *Harmolita*, esp *H. tritici*, which form galls on the stems of cereal plants

join up *vb (adverb)* **1** (intr) to become a member of a military or other organization; enlist **2** (often foll by with) to unite or connect

joist (dʒɔɪst) *n* **1** a beam made of timber, steel, or reinforced concrete, used in the construction of floors, roofs, etc. See also **rolled-steel joist** ▷ vb **2** (tr) to construct (a floor, roof, etc) with joists [c14 from Old French *giste* beam supporting a bridge, from Vulgar Latin *jacitum* (unattested) support, from *jacēre* to lie]

jojoba (həʊ'həʊbə) *n* a shrub or small tree of SW North America, *Simmondsia californica*, that has

edible seeds containing a valuable oil used in cosmetics [Mexican Spanish]

joke (dʒəʊk) *n* **1** a humorous anecdote **2** something that is said or done for fun; prank **3** a ridiculous or humorous circumstance **4** a person or thing inspiring ridicule or amusement; butt **5** a matter to be joked about or ignored **6 joking apart** seriously: said to recall a discussion to seriousness after there has been joking **7 no joke** something very serious ▷ vb **8** (intr) to tell jokes **9** (intr) to speak or act facetiously or in fun **10** to make fun of (someone); tease; kid [c17 from Latin *jocus* a jest] > 'jokingly adv

joker ('dʒəʊkə) *n* **1** a person who jokes, esp in an obnoxious manner **2** slang often derogatory a person: *who does that joker think he is?* **3** an extra playing card in a pack, which in many card games can substitute for or rank above any other card **4** chiefly US a clause or phrase inserted in a legislative bill in order to make the bill inoperative or to alter its apparent effect

jokey or **joky** ('dʒəʊkɪ) *adj* **jokier, jokiest** intended as a joke; full of jokes

Jokjakarta (ˌdʒəʊkjɑː'kɑːtɑː, ˌdʒɒk-) *n* a variant spelling of **Yogyakarta**

jol (dʒɒl) *South African slang* ▷ *n* **1** a party ▷ vb jolling, jolled **2** (intr) to have a good time

jolie laide *French* (ʒɔli lɛd) *n, pl* **jolies laides** (ʒɔli lɛd) a woman whose ugliness forms her chief fascination [literally: pretty (attractive) ugly woman]

jollification (ˌdʒɒlɪfɪ'keɪʃən) *n* a merry festivity

jollify ('dʒɒlɪˌfaɪ) *vb* **-fies, -fying, -fied** to be or cause to be jolly

jollities ('dʒɒlɪtɪz) *pl n Brit* a party or celebration

jollity ('dʒɒlɪtɪ) *n, pl* **-ties** the condition of being jolly

jollop ('dʒɒləp) *n Brit informal* a cream or unguent [c20 from French *jalap*, from Spanish *jalapa*, from *purga de Jalapa* purge of Jalapa, Jalapa being a city in Mexico]

jolly ('dʒɒlɪ) *adj* **-lier, -liest 1** full of good humour; jovial **2** having or provoking gaiety and merrymaking; festive **3** greatly enjoyable; pleasing ▷ adv **4** Brit (intensifier): *you're jolly nice* ▷ vb **-lies, -lying, -lied** (tr) informal **5** (often foll by up or along) to try to make or keep (someone) cheerful **6** to make goodnatured fun of ▷ n **7** informal, chiefly Brit a festivity or celebration **8** informal, chiefly Brit a trip, esp one made for pleasure by a public official or committee at public expense **9** Brit slang a Royal Marine [c14 from Old French *jolif*, probably from Old Norse *jōl* YULE] > 'jolliness n

jolly boat *n* **1** a small boat used as a utility tender for a vessel **2** a small sailing boat used for pleasure [c18 *jolly* probably from Danish *jolle* YAWL[1]]

Jolly Jumper *n trademark Canadian* a type of fixed sprung baby harness in which an infant may bounce up and down for exercise

Jolly Roger *n* the traditional pirate flag, consisting of a white skull and crossbones on a black field

Jolo (həʊ'ləʊ) *n* an island in the SW Philippines: the main island of the Sulu Archipelago. Pop: 87 998 (2000). Area: 893 sq km (345 sq miles)

jolt (dʒəʊlt) *vb (tr)* **1** to bump against with a jarring blow; jostle **2** to move in a jolting manner **3** to surprise or shock ▷ n **4** a sudden jar or blow **5** an emotional shock [c16 probably blend of dialect *jot* to jerk and dialect *joll* to bump] > 'jolter n > 'joltingly adv > 'jolty adj

Jon. *Bible abbreviation for* Jonah

Jonah ('dʒəʊnə) or **Jonas** ('dʒəʊnəs) *n* **1** Old Testament **a** a Hebrew prophet who, having been thrown overboard from a ship in which he was fleeing from God, was swallowed by a great fish and vomited onto dry land **b** the book in which his adventures are recounted **2** a person believed to bring bad luck to those around him; a jinx > Jonah'esque adj

Jonathan[1] ('dʒɒnəθən) *n* a variety of red apple

that ripens in early autumn [c19 named after *Jonathan Hasbrouk* (died 1846), American jurist]

Jonathan[2] *n Old Testament* the son of Saul and David's close friend, who was killed in battle (I Samuel 31; II Samuel 1:19–26)

jong (jɒŋ) *n South African informal* a friend, often used in direct address [from Afrikaans]

jongleur (*French* ʒɔ̃glœr) *n* (in medieval France) an itinerant minstrel [c18 from Old French *jogleour*, from Latin *joculātor* joker, jester; see JUGGLE]

Jönköping (*Swedish* 'jœntçøːpiŋ) *n* a city in S Sweden, on the S shore of Lake Vättern: scene of the conclusion of peace between Sweden and Denmark in 1809. Pop: 119 971 (2004 est)

jonnock ('dʒɒnək) or **jannock** ('dʒænək) *dialect* ▷ adj **1** (usually postpositive) genuine; real ▷ adv **2** honestly; truly; genuinely [of uncertain origin]

jonquil ('dʒɒŋkwɪl) *n* **1** a Eurasian amaryllidaceous plant, *Narcissus jonquilla* with long fragrant yellow or white short-tubed flowers **2** any of various other small daffodil-like plants [c17 from French *jonquille*, from Spanish *junquillo*, diminutive of *junco* reed; see JUNCO]

jook (dʒuk) or **chook** *Caribbean informal* ▷ vb **1** (tr) to poke or puncture (the skin) ▷ n **2** a jab or the resulting wound [c20 of uncertain origin]

Joppa ('dʒɒpə) *n* the biblical name of **Jaffa**, the port from which Jonah embarked (Jonah 1:3)

Jordan ('dʒɔːdˀn) *n* **1** a kingdom in SW Asia: coextensive with the biblical Moab, Gilead, and Edom; made a League of Nations mandate and emirate under British control in 1922 and became an independent kingdom in 1946; territories west of the River Jordan and the Jordanian part of Jerusalem (intended to be part of an autonomous Palestine) were occupied by Israel after the war of 1967. It contains part of the Great Rift Valley and consists mostly of desert. Official language: Arabic. Official religion: (Sunni) Muslim. Currency: dinar. Capital: Amman. Pop: 5 613 000 (2004 est). Area: 89 185 sq km (34 434 sq miles). Official name: Hashemite Kingdom of Jordan Former name (1922–49): **Trans-Jordan 2** the chief and only perennial river of Israel and Jordan, rising in several headstreams in Syria and Lebanon, and flowing south through the Sea of Galilee to the Dead Sea: occupies the N end of the Great Rift Valley system and lies mostly below sea level. Length: over 320 km (200 miles)

Jordan almond *n* **1** a large variety of Spanish almond used in confectionery **2** a sugar-coated almond [c15 by folk etymology from earlier *jardyne almaund*, literally: garden almond, from Old French *jardin* GARDEN]

Jordanian (dʒɔː'deɪnɪən) *adj* **1** of or relating to Jordan or its inhabitants ▷ n **2** a native or inhabitant of Jordan

jorum ('dʒɔːrəm) *n* a large drinking bowl or vessel or its contents: *a jorum of punch* [c18 probably named after *Jorum*, who brought vessels of silver, gold, and brass to King David (II Samuel 8:10)]

Jos (dʒɒs) *n* a city in central Nigeria, capital of Plateau state on the **Jos Plateau**: major centre of the tin-mining industry. Pop: 685 000 (2005 est)

joseph ('dʒəʊzɪf) *n* a woman's floor-length riding coat with a small cape, worn esp in the 18th century [perhaps from the story of Joseph and his long coat (Genesis 37:3)]

Joseph ('dʒəʊzɪf) *n* **1** Old Testament **a** the eleventh son of Jacob and one of the 12 patriarchs of Israel (Genesis 30:2–24) **b** either or both of two tribes descended from his sons Ephraim and Manasseh **2 Saint** New Testament the husband of Mary the mother of Jesus (Matthew 1:16–25). Feast day: Mar 19

Joseph Bonaparte Gulf *n* an inlet of the Timor Sea in N Australia. Width: 360 km (225 miles)

Joseph of Arimathea (ˌærɪmə'θɪːə) *n Saint New Testament* a wealthy member of the Sanhedrin, who obtained the body of Jesus after the Crucifixion and laid it in his own tomb (Matthew 27:57–60). Feast day: Mar 17 or July 31

Josephson effect ('dʒəʊzɪfsən) *n physics* any one of the phenomena which occur when an electric current passes through a very thin insulating layer between two superconducting substances. The applications include the very precise standardization of the volt [C20 named after Brian David *Josephson* (born 1940), English physicist; shared the Nobel prize for physics in 1973]

josh (dʒɒʃ) *slang* ▷ *vb* **1** to tease (someone) in a bantering way ▷ *n* **2** a teasing or bantering joke [C19 perhaps from JOKE, influenced by BOSH¹] > ˈjosher *n*

Josh. *Bible abbreviation for* Joshua

Joshua ('dʒɒʃʊə) *n Old Testament* **1** Moses' successor, who led the Israelites in the conquest of Canaan **2** the book recounting his deeds. Douay spelling: Josue ('dʒɒsjuː:)

Joshua tree *n* a treelike desert yucca plant, *Yucca brevifolia*, of the southwestern US, with sword-shaped leaves and greenish-white flowers [named after the prophet *Joshua*, alluding to the extended branches of the tree]

Josiah (dʒəʊˈsaɪə) *n* died ?609 BC, king of Judah (?640–?609). After the discovery of a book of law (probably Deuteronomy) in the Temple he began a programme of religious reform. Douay spelling: Josias (dʒəʊˈsaɪəs)

joss (dʒɒs) *n* a Chinese deity worshipped in the form of an idol [C18 from pidgin English, from Portuguese *deos* god, from Latin *deus*]

josser ('dʒɒsə) *n slang* **1** *Brit* a simpleton; fool **2** *Brit* a fellow; chap **3** *Austral* a clergyman [C19 from JOSS + -ER¹]

joss house *n* a Chinese temple or shrine where an idol or idols are worshipped

joss stick *n* a stick of dried perfumed paste, giving off a fragrant odour when burnt as incense

jostle ('dʒɒsəl) *vb* **1** to bump or push (someone) roughly **2** to come or bring into contact **3** to force (one's way) by pushing ▷ *n* **4** the act of jostling **5** a rough bump or push [C14 see JOUST] > ˈjostlement *n* > ˈjostler *n*

jot (dʒɒt) *vb* jots, jotting, jotted **1** (*tr; usually foll by down*) to write a brief note of ▷ *n* **2** (*used with a negative*) a little bit (in phrases such as **not to care** (*or give*) **a jot**) [C16 from Latin *jota*, from Greek *iōta*, of Semitic origin; see IOTA]

jota (*Spanish* 'xɔta) *n* a Spanish dance with castanets in fast triple time, usually to a guitar and voice accompaniment [Spanish, probably modification of Old Spanish *sota*, from *sotar* to dance, from Latin *saltāre*]

jotter ('dʒɒtə) *n* a small notebook

jotting ('dʒɒtɪŋ) *n* something jotted down

Jotun *or* **Jotunn** ('jɔ:tʊn) *n Norse myth* any of a race of giants [from Old Norse *jötunn* giant; related to EAT]

Jotunheim *or* **Jotunnheim** ('jɔ:tʊn,heɪm) *n Norse myth* the home of the giants in the northeast of Asgard [from Old Norse, from *jötunn* giant + *heimr* world, HOME]

joual (ʒwɑ:l) *n* nonstandard Canadian French dialect, esp as associated with ill-educated speakers [from the pronunciation in this dialect of French *cheval* horse]

jougs (dʒʊgz) *pl n Scot history* an iron ring, fastened by a chain to a wall, post, or tree, in which an offender was held by the neck: common in Scotland from the 16th to 18th century [C16 probably from French *joug* yoke]

jouk (dʒʊk) *Scot* ▷ *vb* **1** to duck or dodge ▷ *n* **2** a sudden evasive movement [C16 of uncertain origin]

joule (dʒu:l) *n* the derived SI unit of work or energy; the work done when the point of application of a force of 1 newton is displaced through a distance of 1 metre in the direction of the force. 1 joule is equivalent to 1 watt-second, 10^7 ergs, 0.2390 calories, or 0.738 foot-pound. Symbol: J [C19 named after James Prescott *Joule* (1818–89), English physicist]

Joule effect *n physics* **1** the production of heat as the result of a current flowing through a conductor. Also called: Joule heating See **Joule's law 2** an increase in length of certain ferromagnetic materials when longitudinally magnetized [C20 named after James Prescott *Joule* (1818–89), English physicist]

Joule's law *n* **1** *physics* the principle that the heat produced by an electric current is equal to the product of the resistance of the conductor, the square of the current, and the time for which it flows **2** *thermodynamics* the principle that at constant temperature the internal energy of an ideal gas is independent of volume. Real gases change their internal energy with volume as a result of intermolecular forces [C19 named after James Prescott *Joule* (1818–89), English physicist]

Joule-Thomson effect *n* a change in temperature of a thermally insulated gas when it is forced through a small hole or a porous material. For each gas there is a temperature of inversion above which the change is positive and below which it is negative. Also called: Joule-Kelvin effect [C20 named after James Prescott *Joule* (1818–89), English physicist, and Sir William Thomson, 1st Baron Kelvin (1824–1907), British physicist]

jounce (dʒaʊns) *vb* **1** to shake or jolt or cause to shake or jolt; bounce ▷ *n* **2** a jolting movement; shake; bump [C15 probably a blend of dialect *joll* to bump + BOUNCE]

journal ('dʒɜ:nəl) *n* **1** a newspaper or periodical **2** a book in which a daily record of happenings, etc, is kept **3** an official record of the proceedings of a legislative body **4** *book-keeping* **a** Also called: Book of Original Entry one of several books in which transactions are initially recorded to facilitate subsequent entry in the ledger **b** another name for **daybook 5** the part of a shaft or axle in contact with or enclosed by a bearing **6** a plain cylindrical bearing to support a shaft or axle [C14 from Old French: daily, from Latin *diurnālis*; see DIURNAL]

journal box *n machinery* a case enclosing or supporting a journal, often used as a means of retaining the lubricant

journalese (,dʒɜ:nəˈli:z) *n derogatory* a superficial cliché-ridden style of writing regarded as typical of newspapers

journalism ('dʒɜ:nə,lɪzəm) *n* **1** the profession or practice of reporting about, photographing, or editing news stories for one of the mass media **2** newspapers and magazines collectively; the press **3** the material published in a newspaper, magazine, etc: *this is badly written journalism* **4** news reports presented factually without analysis

journalist ('dʒɜ:nəlɪst) *n* **1** a person whose occupation is journalism **2** a person who keeps a journal

journalistic (,dʒɜ:nəˈlɪstɪk) *adj* of, relating to, or characteristic of journalism or journalists > journalˈistically *adv*

journalize *or* **journalise** ('dʒɜ:nə,laɪz) *vb* to record (daily events) in a journal > journaliˈzation *or* journaliˈsation *n* > ˈjournal,izer *or* ˈjournal,iser *n*

journey ('dʒɜ:nɪ) *n* **1** a travelling from one place to another; trip or voyage **2 a** the distance travelled in a journey **b** the time taken to make a journey ▷ *vb* **3** (*intr*) to make a journey [C13 from Old French *journee* a day, a day's travelling, from Latin *diurnum* day's portion; see DIURNAL] > ˈjourneyer *n*

journeyman ('dʒɜ:nɪmən) *n, pl* -men **1** a craftsman, artisan, etc, who is qualified to work at his trade in the employment of another **2** a competent workman **3** (formerly) a worker hired on a daily wage [C15 from JOURNEY (in obsolete sense: a day's work) 1 MAN]

journeywork ('dʒɜ:nɪ,wɜ:k) *n rare* **1** necessary, routine, and menial work **2** the work of a journeyman

journo ('dʒɜ:nəʊ) *n, pl* journos a journalist

joust (dʒaʊst) *history* ▷ *n* **1** a combat between two mounted knights tilting against each other with lances. A tournament consisted of a series of such engagements ▷ *vb* **2** (*intr; often foll by against* or *with*) to encounter or engage in such a tournament [C13 from Old French *jouste*, from *jouster* to fight on horseback, from Vulgar Latin *juxtāre* (unattested) to come together, from Latin *juxtā* close] > ˈjouster *n*

j'ouvert ('ʒu:veət) *n chiefly Caribbean* the eve of Mardi gras; the Monday morning on which the festivities begin [from French *jour ouvert* the day having been opened]

Jove (dʒəʊv) *n* **1** another name for **Jupiter¹ 2 by Jove** an exclamation of surprise or excitement [C14 from Old Latin *Jovis* Jupiter]

jovial ('dʒəʊvɪəl) *adj* having or expressing convivial humour; jolly [C16 from Latin *joviālis* of (the planet) Jupiter, considered by astrologers to foster good humour] > joviˈality *or* ˈjovialness *n* > ˈjovially *adv*

Jovian¹ ('dʒəʊvɪən) *adj* **1** of or relating to the god Jove (Jupiter) **2** of, occurring on, or relating to the planet Jupiter **3** of or relating to the giant planets Jupiter, Saturn, Uranus, and Neptune: *the Jovian planets* [C16 from Old Latin *Jovis* Jupiter]

jowl¹ (dʒaʊl) *n* **1** the jaw, esp the lower one **2** (*often plural*) a cheek, esp a prominent one **3** cheek by jowl See **cheek** (sense 7) [Old English *ceafl* jaw; related to Middle High German *kivel*, Old Norse *kjaptr*] > jowled *adj*

jowl² (dʒaʊl) *n* **1** fatty flesh hanging from the lower jaw **2** a similar fleshy part in animals, such as the wattle of a fowl or the dewlap of a bull [Old English *ceole* throat; compare Old High German *kela*]

joy (dʒɔɪ) *n* **1** a deep feeling or condition of happiness or contentment **2** something causing such a feeling **3** an outward show of pleasure or delight; rejoicing **4** *Brit informal* success; satisfaction: *I went to the bank for a loan, but got no joy* ▷ *vb* **5** (*intr*) to feel joy **6** (*tr*) obsolete to make joyful; gladden [C13 from Old French *joie*, from Latin *gaudium* joy, from *gaudēre* to be glad]

joyance ('dʒɔɪəns) *n archaic* a joyous feeling or festivity

Joycean ('dʒɔɪsɪən) *adj* **1** of, relating to, or like the Irish novelist and short-story writer James Joyce (1882–1941) or his works ▷ *n* **2** a student or admirer of Joyce or his works

joyful ('dʒɔɪfʊl) *adj* **1** full of joy; elated **2** expressing or producing joy: *a joyful look; a joyful occasion* > ˈjoyfully *adv* > ˈjoyfulness *n*

joyless ('dʒɔɪlɪs) *adj* having or producing no joy or pleasure > ˈjoylessly *adv* > ˈjoylessness *n*

joyous ('dʒɔɪəs) *adj* **1** having a happy nature or mood **2** joyful > ˈjoyously *adv* > ˈjoyousness *n*

joypop ('dʒɔɪ,pɒp) *vb* -pops, -popping, -popped (*intr*) *slang* to take addictive drugs occasionally without becoming addicted

joyride *n* **1** a ride taken for pleasure in a car, esp in a stolen car driven recklessly ▷ *vb* joy-ride -rides, -riding, -rode, -ridden **2** (*intr*) to take such a ride > ˈjoy,rider *n* > ˈjoy,riding *n*

joystick ('dʒɔɪ,stɪk) *n* **1** *informal* the control stick of an aircraft or of any of various machines **2** *computing* a lever by means of which the display on a screen may be controlled used esp for games, flight simulators, etc

Jozi ('dʒəʊsɪ) *n South African informal* Johannesburg. See also **Joburg**

jp *the internet domain name for* Japan

JP *abbreviation for* Justice of the Peace

JPEG ('dʒeɪ,peg) *n computing* a standard file format for compressing pictures by disposing of redundant pixels [C20 technique devised by the J(oint) P(hotographic) E(xperts) G(roup)]

J/psi particle *n* a type of elementary particle (meson) thought to be formed from charmed quarks. See **charm¹** (sense 7)

Jr *or* **jr** *abbreviation for* junior

JSA (in Britain) *abbreviation for* **jobseeker's allowance**

j

JSD *abbreviation for* Doctor of Juristic Science
jt *abbreviation for* joint
Juan de Fuca (ˈdʒuːən dɪ ˈfjuːkə; *Spanish* xwan de ˈfuka) *n* **Strait of** a strait between Vancouver Island (Canada) and NW Washington (US). Length: about 129 km (80 miles). Width: about 24 km (15 miles)
Juan Fernández Islands (ˈdʒuːən fəˈnændɛz; *Spanish* xwan fɛrˈnandɛθ) *pl n* a group of three islands in the S Pacific Ocean, administered by Chile: volcanic and wooded. Area: about 180 sq km (70 sq miles)
Juárez (*Spanish* ˈxwarɛθ) *n* short for **Ciudad Juárez**
juba (ˈdʒuːbə) *n* a lively African-American dance developed in the southern US [c19 of Zulu origin]
Juba (ˈdʒuːbə) *n* a river in NE Africa, rising in S central Ethiopia and flowing south across Somalia to the Indian Ocean: the chief river of Somalia. Length: about 1660 km (1030 miles)
Jubal (ˈdʒuːbᵊl) *n* *Old Testament* the alleged inventor of musical instruments (Genesis 4:21)
jubbah (ˈdʒʊbə) *n* a long loose outer garment with wide sleeves, worn by Muslim men and women, esp in India [c16 from Arabic]
Jubbulpore (ˌdʒʌbᵊlˈpʊə) *n* a variant spelling of **Jabalpur**
jube¹ (ˈdʒuːbɪ) *n* **1** a gallery or loft over the rood screen in a church or cathedral **2** another name for **rood screen** [c18 from French *jubé*, from opening words of Medieval Latin prayer *Jube, Domine, benedicere* Bid, Lord, a blessing; probably from the deacon's standing by the rood screen or in the rood loft to pronounce this prayer]
jube² (dʒuːb) *n* *Austral and NZ informal* any jelly-like sweet [c20 shortened from JUJUBE]
jubilant (ˈdʒuːbɪlənt) *adj* feeling or expressing great joy [c17 from Latin *jūbilāns* shouting for joy, from *jūbilāre* to give a joyful cry, from *jūbilum* a shout, wild cry] > ˈ**jubilance** *or* ˈ**jubilancy** *n* > ˈ**jubilantly** *adv*
jubilate (ˈdʒuːbɪˌleɪt) *vb* (*intr*) **1** to have or express great joy; rejoice **2** to celebrate a jubilee [c17 from Latin *jūbilāre* to raise a shout of joy; see JUBILANT]
Jubilate (ˌdʒuːbɪˈlɑːtɪ) *n* **1** *RC Church, Church of England* the 100th psalm used as a canticle in the liturgy **2** a musical setting of this psalm [from the opening word (*Jubilate* make a joyful noise) of the Vulgate version]
jubilation (ˌdʒuːbɪˈleɪʃən) *n* a feeling of great joy and celebration
jubilee (ˈdʒuːbɪˌliː, ˌdʒuːbɪˈliː) *n* **1** a time or season for rejoicing **2** a special anniversary, esp a 25th or 50th one **3** *RC Church* a specially appointed period, now ordinarily every 25th year, in which special indulgences are granted **4** *Old Testament* a year that was to be observed every 50th year, during which Hebrew slaves were to be liberated, alienated property was to be restored, etc **5** a less common word for **jubilation** [c14 from Old French *jubile*, from Late Latin *jubilaeus*, from Late Greek *iōbēlaios*, from Hebrew *yōbhēl* ram's horn, used for the proclamation of the year of jubilee; influenced by Latin *jūbilāre* to shout for joy]
JUD *abbreviation for* Doctor of Canon and Civil Law [Latin *Juris Utriusque Doctor*]
Jud. *Bible abbreviation for* **1** Also: **Judg** Judges **2** Judith
Judaea *or* **Judea** (dʒuːˈdɪə) *n* the S division of ancient Palestine, succeeding the kingdom of Judah: a Roman province during the time of Christ
Judaean *or* **Judean** (dʒuːˈdɪən) *adj* **1** of or relating to Judaea, the S division of ancient Palestine, or its inhabitants ▷ *n* **2** a native or inhabitant of Judaea
Judaeo- *or US* **Judeo-** (dʒuːˈdeɪəʊ-, dʒuːˈdiːəʊ-) *combining form* relating to Judaism: *Judaeo-Christian*
Judaeo-German *n* another name for **Yiddish**
Judaeo-Spanish *n* another name for **Ladino**
Judah (ˈdʒuːdə) *n* *Old Testament* **1** the fourth son of Jacob, one of whose descendants was to be the Messiah (Genesis 29:35; 49:8–12) **2** the tribe descended from him **3** the tribal territory of his descendants which became the nucleus of David's kingdom and, after the kingdom had been divided into Israel and Judah, the southern kingdom of Judah, with Jerusalem as its centre. Douay spelling: **Juda**
Judaic (dʒuːˈdeɪɪk) *or* **Judaical** *adj* **1** of or relating to the Jews or Judaism **2** a less common word for **Jewish.** > **Juˈdaically** *adv*
Judaica (dʒuːˈdeɪɪkə) *pl n* **1** the literature, customs, culture, etc, of the Jews **2** books or artefacts of Jewish interest, esp as a collection [Latin, literally: Jewish matters]
Judaism (ˈdʒuːdeɪˌɪzəm) *n* **1** the religion of the Jews, based on the Old Testament and the Talmud and having as its central point a belief in the one God as transcendent creator of all things and the source of all righteousness **2** the religious and cultural traditions, customs, attitudes, and way of life of the Jews > **Judaˈistic** *adj*
Judaize *or* **Judaise** (ˈdʒuːdeɪˌaɪz) *vb* **1** to conform or bring into conformity with Judaism **2** (*tr*) to convert to Judaism **3** (*tr*) to imbue with Jewish principles > **Judaiˈzation** *or* **Judaiˈsation** *n* > ˈ**Judaˌizer** *or* ˈ**Judaˌiser** *n*
judas (ˈdʒuːdəs) *n* (*sometimes capital*) a peephole or a very small window in a door. Also called: **judas window, judas hole** [c19 after *Judas Iscariot*]
Judas (ˈdʒuːdəs) *n* **1** *New Testament* the apostle who betrayed Jesus to his enemies for 30 pieces of silver (Luke 22:3–6, 47–48). Full name: **Judas Iscariot** **2** a person who betrays a friend; traitor **3** a brother or relative of James and also of Jesus (Matthew 13:55). This figure, Thaddaeus, and Jude were probably identical ▷ *adj* **4** denoting an animal or bird used to lure others of its kind or lead them to slaughter
Judas tree *n* small Eurasian leguminous tree, *Cercis siliquastrum*, with pinkish-purple flowers that bloom before the leaves appear: popularly thought to be the tree on which Judas hanged himself. See also **redbud**
judder (ˈdʒʌdə) *informal, chiefly Brit* ▷ *vb* **1** (*intr*) to shake or vibrate ▷ *n* **2** abnormal vibration in a mechanical system, esp due to grabbing between friction surfaces, as in the clutch of a motor vehicle **3** a juddering motion [probably blend of JAR² + SHUDDER]
judder bar *n* *NZ* a bump built across roads, esp in housing estates, to reduce speeding. Also called: **ramp,** (*chiefly Brit*) **sleeping policeman**
Jude (dʒuːd) *n* **1** a book of the New Testament (in full **The Epistle of Jude**) **2** **Saint** Also called: **Judas** the author of this, stated to be the brother of James (Jude 1) and almost certainly identical with Thaddaeus (Matthew 10:2–4). Feast day: Oct 28 or June 19
Judea (dʒuːˈdɪə) *n* a variant spelling of **Judaea**
Judezmo (dʒʊˈdɛzməʊ) *n* another name for **Ladino** [from Ladino: Jewish]
judge (dʒʌdʒ) *n* **1** a public official with authority to hear cases in a court of law and pronounce judgment upon them. Compare **magistrate, justice** (senses 5, 6) Related adj: **judicial** **2** a person who is appointed to determine the result of contests or competitions **3** a person qualified to comment critically: *a good judge of antiques* **4** a leader of the peoples of Israel from Joshua's death to the accession of Saul ▷ *vb* **5** to hear and decide upon (a case at law) **6** (*tr*) to pass judgment on; sentence **7** (*when tr, may take a clause as object or an infinitive*) to decide or deem (something) after inquiry or deliberation **8** to determine the result of (a contest or competition) **9** to appraise (something) critically **10** (*tr; takes a clause as object*) to believe (something) to be the case; suspect [c14 from Old French *jugier*, from Latin *jūdicāre* to pass judgment, from *jūdex* a judge] > ˈ**judgeable** *adj* > ˈ**judgeless** *adj* > ˈ**judgeˌlike** *adj* > ˈ**judger** *n* > ˈ**judgingly** *adv*
judge advocate *n, pl* **judge advocates** an officer who superintends proceedings at a court martial
judge advocate general *n, pl* **judge advocates general** *or* **judge advocate generals** the civil adviser to the Crown on matters relating to courts martial and on military law generally
judge-made *adj* based on a judge's interpretation or decision (esp in the phrase **judge-made law**)
Judges (ˈdʒʌdʒɪz) *n* (*functioning as singular*) the book of the Old Testament recounting the history of Israel under the warrior champions and national leaders known as judges from the death of Joshua to the birth of Samuel
judgeship (ˈdʒʌdʒʃɪp) *n* the position, office, or function of a judge
judges' rules *pl n* (in English law, formerly) a set of rules, not legally binding, governing the behaviour of police towards suspects, as in administering a caution to a person under arrest
judgment *or* **judgement** (ˈdʒʌdʒmənt) *n* **1** the faculty of being able to make critical distinctions and achieve a balanced viewpoint; discernment **2** **a** the decision or verdict pronounced by a court of law **b** an obligation arising as a result of such a decision or verdict, such as a debt **c** the document recording such a decision or verdict **d** (*as modifier*): *a judgment debtor* **3** the formal decision of one or more judges at a contest or competition **4** a particular decision or opinion formed in a case in dispute or doubt **5** an estimation **6** criticism or censure **7** *logic* **a** the act of establishing a relation between two or more terms, esp as an affirmation or denial **b** the expression of such a relation **8** **against one's better judgment** contrary to a more appropriate or preferred course of action **9** **sit in judgment** **a** to preside as judge **b** to assume the position of critic **10** **in someone's judgment** in someone's opinion
Judgment (ˈdʒʌdʒmənt) *n* **1** the estimate by God of the ultimate worthiness or unworthiness of the individual (the **Particular Judgment**) or of all mankind (the **General Judgment** or **Last Judgment**) **2** God's subsequent decision determining the final destinies of all individuals
judgmental *or* **judgemental** (dʒʌdʒˈmɛntᵊl) *adj* of or denoting an attitude in which judgments about other people's conduct are made
Judgment Day *n* the occasion of the Last (or General) Judgment by God at the end of the world. Also called: **Day of Judgment** See **Last Judgment**
judicable (ˈdʒuːdɪkəbᵊl) *adj* capable of being judged, esp in a court of law
judicative (ˈdʒuːdɪkətɪv) *adj* **1** having the function of trying causes **2** competent to judge and pass sentence
judicator (ˈdʒuːdɪˌkeɪtə) *n* a person who acts as a judge
judicatory (ˈdʒuːdɪkətərɪ) *adj* **1** of or relating to the administration of justice ▷ *n* **2** a court of law **3** the administration of justice > **judicaˈtorial** *adj*
judicature (ˈdʒuːdɪkətʃə) *n* **1** the administration of justice **2** the office, function, or power of a judge **3** the extent of authority of a court or judge **4** a body of judges or persons exercising judicial authority; judiciary **5** a court of justice or such courts collectively
judicial (dʒuːˈdɪʃəl) *adj* **1** of or relating to the administration of justice **2** of or relating to judgment in a court of law or to a judge exercising this function **3** inclined to pass judgment; discriminating **4** allowed or enforced by a court of law: *a decree of judicial separation* **5** having qualities appropriate to a judge **6** giving or seeking judgment, esp determining or seeking determination of a contested issue [c14 from Latin *jūdiciālis* belonging to the law courts, from *jūdicium* judgment, from *jūdex* a judge] > **juˈdicially** *adv*
Judicial Committee of the Privy Council *n* the highest appellate court for Britain's dependencies and for some dominions of the Commonwealth
judicial separation *n* *family law* a court decree requiring a man and wife to cease cohabiting but not dissolving the marriage. See also **a mensa et thoro** Compare **divorce**

judiciary (dʒu:ˈdɪʃɪərɪ, -ˈdɪʃərɪ) *adj* **1** of or relating to courts of law, judgment, or judges ▷ *n, pl* -aries **2** the branch of the central authority in a state concerned with the administration of justice. Compare **executive** (sense 2), **legislature 3** the system of courts in a country **4** the judges collectively; bench

judicious (dʒu:ˈdɪʃəs) *adj* having or proceeding from good judgment > ju'**diciously** *adv* > ju'**diciousness** *n*

Judith (ˈdʒu:dɪθ) *n* **1** the heroine of one of the books of the Apocrypha, who saved her native town by decapitating Holofernes **2** the book recounting this episode

judo (ˈdʒu:dəʊ) *n* **a** the modern sport derived from jujitsu, in which the object is to throw, hold to the ground, or otherwise force an opponent to submit, using the minimum of physical effort **b** (*as modifier*): *a judo throw* [Japanese, from *jū* gentleness + *dō* way] > '**judoist** *n*

judogi (dʒʊˈdəʊgɪ) *n* a white two-piece cotton costume worn during judo contests [from Japanese]

judoka (ˈdʒu:dəʊˌkæ) *n* a competitor or expert in judo [Japanese; see JUDO]

Judy (ˈdʒu:dɪ) *n, pl* -dies **1** the wife of Punch in the children's puppet show *Punch and Judy*. See **Punch 2** (*often not capital*) *Brit slang* a girl or woman

jug (dʒʌg) *n* **1** a vessel for holding or pouring liquids, usually having a handle and a spout or lip. US equivalent: **pitcher 2** *Austral and NZ* such a vessel used as a kettle: *an electric jug* **3** *US* a large vessel with a narrow mouth **4** Also called: **jugful** the amount of liquid held by a jug **5** *Brit informal* a glass of alcoholic drink, esp beer **6** a slang word for **jail** ▷ *vb* jugs, jugging, jugged **7** to stew or boil (meat, esp hare) in an earthenware container **8** (*tr*) *slang* to put in jail [c16 probably from *Jug*, nickname from girl's name *Joan*]

jugal (ˈdʒu:gəl) *adj* **1** of or relating to the zygomatic bone ▷ *n* **2** Also called: **jugal bone** other names for **zygomatic bone** [c16 from Latin *jugālis* of a yoke, from *jugum* a yoke]

jugate (ˈdʒu:geɪt, -gɪt) *adj* (*esp of compound leaves*) having parts arranged in pairs [c19 from New Latin *jugātus* (unattested), from Latin *jugum* a yoke]

jug band *n* a small group playing music, using empty jugs that are played by blowing across their openings to produce bass notes

Jugendstil *German* (ˈju:gəntʃtiːl) *n* another name for **Art Nouveau** [from *Jugend* literally: youth, name of illustrated periodical that first appeared in 1896, + *Stil* STYLE]

jugged hare *n* a stew of hare cooked in an earthenware pot or casserole

juggernaut (ˈdʒʌgəˌnɔ:t) *n* **1** any terrible force, esp one that destroys or that demands complete self-sacrifice **2** *Brit* a very large lorry for transporting goods by road, esp one that travels throughout Europe

Juggernaut (ˈdʒʌgəˌnɔ:t) *n Hinduism* **1** a crude idol of Krishna worshipped at Puri and throughout Orissa and Bengal. At an annual festival the idol is wheeled through the town on a gigantic chariot and devotees are supposed to have formerly thrown themselves under the wheels **2** a form of Krishna miraculously raised by Brahma from the state of a crude idol to that of a living god [c17 from Hindi *Jagannath*, from Sanskrit *Jagannātha* lord of the world (that is, Vishnu, chief of the Hindu gods), from *jagat* world + *nātha* lord]

juggins (ˈdʒʌgɪnz) *n Brit informal* a silly person; simpleton [c19 special use of the surname *Juggins*]

juggle (ˈdʒʌgəl) *vb* **1** to throw and catch (several objects) continuously so that most are in the air all the time, as an entertainment **2** to arrange or manipulate (facts, figures, etc) so as to give a false or misleading picture **3** (*tr*) to keep (several activities) in progress, esp with difficulty ▷ *n* **4** an act of juggling [c14 from Old French *jogler* to perform as a jester, from Latin *joculārī* to jest, from

jocus a jest] > '**jugglery** *n*

juggler (ˈdʒʌglə) *n* **1** a person who juggles, esp a professional entertainer **2** a person who fraudulently manipulates facts or figures

juglandaceous (ˌdʒu:glænˈdeɪʃəs) *adj* of, relating to, or belonging to the *Juglandaceae*, a family of trees that includes walnut and hickory [c19 via New Latin from Latin *juglans* walnut, from *ju-*, shortened from *Iovi-* of *Iupiter* + *glans* acorn]

Jugoslav (ˈju:gəʊˌsla:v) or **Jugoslavian** (ˌju:gəʊˈsla:vɪən) *adj, n* a variant spelling of **Yugoslav** or **Yugoslavian**

Jugoslavia (ˌju:gəʊˈsla:vɪə) *n* a variant spelling of **Yugoslavia**

jugular (ˈdʒʌgjʊlə) *adj* **1** of, relating to, or situated near the throat or neck **2** of, having, or denoting pelvic fins situated in front of the pectoral fins: *a jugular fish* ▷ *n* **3** short for **jugular vein 4** go for the jugular to make a savage and destructive attack on an enemy's weakest point [c16 from Late Latin *jugulāris*, from Latin *jugulum* throat]

jugular vein *n* any of three large veins of the neck that return blood to the heart from the head and face

jugulate (ˈdʒʌgjʊˌleɪt) *vb* (*tr*) *rare* to check (a disease) by extreme measures or remedies [c17 (in the obsolete sense: kill by cutting the throat of): from Latin *jugulāre*, from *jugulum* throat, from *jugum* yoke] > jugu'**lation** *n*

jugum (ˈdʒu:gəm) *n* **1** a small process at the base of each forewing in certain insects by which the forewings are united to the hindwings during flight **2** *botany* a pair of opposite leaflets [c19 from Latin, literally: YOKE]

Jugurthine War (dʒu:ˈgɜ:θaɪn) *n* an unsuccessful war waged against the Romans (112–105 BC) by Jugurtha, king of Numidia (died 104)

juice (dʒu:s) *n* **1** any liquid that occurs naturally in or is secreted by plant or animal tissue: *the juice of an orange; digestive juices* **2** *informal* **a** fuel for an engine, esp petrol **b** electricity **c** alcoholic drink **3 a** vigour or vitality **b** essence or fundamental nature **4** stew in one's own juice See **stew¹** (sense 10) ▷ *vb* **5** to extract juice from (fruits or vegetables) in order to drink [c13 from Old French *jus*, from Latin] > '**juiceless** *adj*

juicer *n* a kitchen appliance, usually operated by electricity, for extracting juice from fruits and vegetables. Also called: **juice extractor**

juice up *vb* (*tr, adverb*) **1** *US slang* to make lively: *to juice up a party* **2** (*often passive*) to cause to be drunk: *he got juiced up on Scotch last night*

juicy (ˈdʒu:sɪ) *adj* juicier, juiciest **1** full of juice **2** provocatively interesting; spicy: *juicy gossip* **3** *slang* voluptuous or seductive: *she's a juicy bit* **4** *chiefly US and Canadian* profitable: *a juicy contract* > '**juicily** *adv* > '**juiciness** *n*

Juiz de Fora (Portuguese ʒuˈiʃ di ˈfɔra) *n* a city in SE Brazil, in Minas Gerais state on the Rio de Janeiro–Belo Horizonte railway: textiles. Pop: 502 000 (2005 est)

jujitsu, jujutsu or **jiujutsu** (dʒu:ˈdʒɪtsu:) *n* the traditional Japanese system of unarmed self-defence perfected by the samurai. See also **judo** [c19 from Japanese, from *jū* gentleness + *jutsu* art]

juju (ˈdʒu:dʒu:) *n* **1** an object superstitiously revered by certain W African peoples and used as a charm or fetish **2** the power associated with a juju **3** a taboo effected by a juju **4** any process in which a mystery is exploited to confuse people [c19 probably from Hausa *djudju* evil spirit, fetish] > '**jujuism** *n* > '**jujuist** *n*

jujube (ˈdʒu:dʒu:b) *n* **1** any of several Old World spiny rhamnaceous trees of the genus *Ziziphus*, esp *Z. jujuba*, that have small yellowish flowers and dark red edible fruits. See also **Christ's-thorn 2** the fruit of any of these trees **3** a chewy sweet made of flavoured gelatine and sometimes medicated to soothe sore throats ▷ Also called (for senses 1, 2): **Chinese date** [c14 from Medieval Latin *jujuba*, modification of Latin *zizyphum*, from Greek *zizuphon*]

jukebox (ˈdʒu:kˌbɒks) *n* a coin-operated machine, usually found in pubs, clubs, etc, that contains records, CDs, or videos, which are played when selected by a customer [c20 from Gullah *juke* bawdy (as in *juke house* brothel) + BOX¹]

jukskei (ˈjʊkˌskeɪ) *n South African* a game in which a peg is thrown at a stake driven into the ground [from Afrikaans *juk* yoke + *skei* pin]

Jul *abbreviation for* July

julep (ˈdʒu:lɪp) *n* **1** a sweet drink, variously prepared and sometimes medicated **2** *chiefly US* short for **mint julep** [c14 from Old French, from Arabic *julāb*, from Persian *gulāb* rose water, from *gul* rose + *āb* water]

Julian² (ˈdʒu:lɪən, -lɪən) *adj* **1** of or relating to Julius Caesar (100–44 BC), the Roman general, statesman, and historian **2** denoting or relating to the Julian calendar

Julian Alps *pl n* a mountain range in Slovenia: an E range of the Alps

Julian calendar *n* the calendar introduced by Julius Caesar in 46 BC, identical to the present calendar in all but two aspects: the beginning of the year was not fixed on Jan 1 and leap years occurred every fourth year and in every centenary year. Compare **Gregorian calendar**

julienne (ˌdʒu:lɪˈɛn) *adj* **1** (*of vegetables*) cut into thin shreds ▷ *n* **2** a clear consommé to which a mixture of such vegetables has been added [French, from name *Jules, Julien,* or *Julienne*]

Juliet (ˈdʒu:lɪˈɛt) *n communications* a code word for the letter *j*

Juliet cap (ˈdʒu:lɪɪt) *n* a close-fitting decorative cap, worn esp by brides [c20 after the heroine of Shakespeare's *Romeo and Juliet* (1594)]

Jullundur (ˈdʒʌləndə) *n* the former name of **Jalandhar**

July (dʒu:ˈlaɪ, dʒə-, dʒʊ-) *n, pl* -lies the seventh month of the year, consisting of 31 days [c13 from Anglo-French *julie*, from Latin *Jūlius*, after Gaius Julius Caesar (100–44 BC), Roman statesman in whose honour it was named]

Jumada (dʒʊˈmɑ:də) *n* either the fifth or the sixth month of the Muslim year, known respectively as **Jumada I** and **Jumada II** [Arabic]

jumar (ˈdʒu:mə) *n mountaineering* **1** Also called: **jumar clamp** a clamp with a handle that can move freely up a rope on which it is clipped but locks when downward pressure is applied ▷ *vb* (*intr*) **2** to climb (up a fixed rope) using jumars [c20 Swiss name]

jumble (ˈdʒʌmbəl) *vb* **1** to mingle (objects, papers, etc) in a state of disorder **2** (*tr; usually passive*) to remember in a confused form; muddle ▷ *n* **3** a disordered mass, state, etc **4** *Brit* articles donated for a jumble sale **5** Also called: **jumbal** a small thin cake, usually ring-shaped [c16 of uncertain origin] > '**jumbler** *n* > '**jumbly** *adj*

jumble sale *n* a sale of miscellaneous articles, usually cheap and predominantly secondhand, in aid of charity. US and Canadian equivalent: **rummage sale**

jumbo (ˈdʒʌmbəʊ) *n, pl* -bos **1** *informal* **a** a very large person or thing **b** (*as modifier*): *a jumbo box of detergent* **2** See **jumbo jet** [c19 after the name of a famous elephant exhibited by P. T. Barnum, from Swahili *jumbe* chief]

jumboize or **jumboise** (ˈdʒʌmbəʊˌaɪz) *vb* (*tr*) to extend (a ship, esp a tanker) by cutting out the middle part and inserting a new larger part between the original bow and stern [c20 from JUMBO + -IZE]

jumbo jet *n informal* a type of large jet-propelled airliner that carries several hundred passengers

jumbuck (ˈdʒʌmˌbʌk) *n Austral archaic* an informal word for **sheep** [c19 from a native Australian language]

Jumna (ˈdʒʌmnə) *n* a river in N India, rising in Uttaranchal in the Himalayas and flowing south and southeast to join the Ganges just below Allahabad (a confluence held sacred by Hindus). Length: 1385 km (860 miles)

j

jump (dʒʌmp) *vb* **1** (*intr*) to leap or spring clear of the ground or other surface by using the muscles in the legs and feet **2** (*tr*) to leap over or clear (an obstacle): *to jump a gap* **3** (*tr*) to cause to leap over an obstacle: *to jump a horse over a hedge* **4** (*intr*) to move or proceed hastily (into, onto, out of, etc): *she jumped into a taxi and was off* **5** (*tr*) *informal* to board so as to travel illegally on: *he jumped the train as it was leaving* **6** (*intr*) to parachute from an aircraft **7** (*intr*) to jerk or start, as with astonishment, surprise, etc: *she jumped when she heard the explosion* **8** to rise or cause to rise suddenly or abruptly **9** to pass or skip over (intervening objects or matter): *she jumped a few lines and then continued reading* **10** (*intr*) to change from one thing to another, esp from one subject to another **11** (*tr*) to drill by means of a jumper **12** (*intr*) (of a film) **a** to have sections of a continuous sequence omitted, as through faulty cutting **b** to flicker, as through faulty alignment of the film **13** (*tr*) *US* to promote in rank, esp unexpectedly or to a higher rank than expected **14** (*tr*) to start (a car) using jump leads **15** *draughts* to capture (an opponent's piece) by moving one of one's own pieces over it to an unoccupied square **16** (*intr*) *bridge* to bid in response to one's partner at a higher level than is necessary, to indicate a strong hand **17** (*tr*) to come off (a track, rail, etc): *the locomotive jumped the rails* **18** (*intr*) (of the stylus of a record player) to be jerked out of the groove **19** (*intr*) *slang* to be lively: *the party was jumping when I arrived* **20** (*tr*) *informal* to attack without warning: *thieves jumped the old man as he walked through the park* **21** (*tr*) *informal* (of a driver or a motor vehicle) to pass through (a red traffic light) or move away from (traffic lights) before they change to green **22** (*tr*) *Brit slang* (of a man) to have sexual intercourse with **23 jump bail** to forfeit one's bail by failing to appear in court, esp by absconding **24 jump down someone's throat** *informal* to address or reply to someone with unexpected sharpness **25 jump ship** to desert, esp to leave a ship in which one is legally bound to serve **26 jump the queue** See **queue-jump 27 jump to it** *informal* to begin something quickly and efficiently ▷ *n* **28** an act or instance of jumping **29** a space, distance, or obstacle to be jumped or that has been jumped **30** a descent by parachute from an aircraft **31** *sport* any of several contests involving a jump: *the high jump* **32** a sudden rise: *the jump in prices last month* **33** a sudden or abrupt transition **34** a sudden jerk or involuntary muscular spasm, esp as a reaction of surprise **35** a step or degree: *one jump ahead* **36** *draughts* a move that captures an opponent's piece by jumping over it **37** *films* **a** a break in continuity in the normal sequence of shots **b** (*as modifier*): *a jump cut* **38** *computing* another name for **branch** (sense 7) **39** *Brit slang* an act of sexual intercourse **40 on the jump** *informal, chiefly US and Canadian* **a** in a hurry **b** busy and energetic **41 take a running jump** *Brit informal* a contemptuous expression of dismissal ▷ See also **jump at, jump-off, jump on, jump-up** [c16 probably of imitative origin; compare Swedish *gumpa* to jump] > ˈ**jumpable** *adj* > ˈ**jumpingly** *adv*

jump at *vb* (*intr, preposition*) to be glad to accept: *I would jump at the chance of going*

jump ball *n basketball* a ball thrown high by the referee between two opposing players to put it in play, as after a stoppage in which no foul or violation was committed

jump bid *n bridge* a bid by the responder at a higher level than is necessary

jumped-up *adj informal* suddenly risen in significance, esp when appearing arrogant

jumper¹ (ˈdʒʌmpə) *n* **1** *chiefly Brit* a knitted or crocheted garment covering the upper part of the body **2** *US and Canadian* Also called: **pinafore dress** a sleeveless dress worn over a blouse or sweater [c19 from obsolete *jump* man's loose jacket, variant of *jupe*, from Old French, from Arabic *jubbah* long cloth coat]

jumper² (ˈdʒʌmpə) *n* **1** a boring tool that works by repeated impact, such as a steel bit in a hammer drill used in boring rock **2** Also called: **jumper cable, jumper lead** a short length of wire used to make a connection, usually temporarily, between terminals or to bypass a component **3** a type of sled with a high crosspiece **4** a person or animal that jumps **5** *Irish derogatory slang* a person who changes religion; a convert

jumping bean *n* a seed of any of several Mexican euphorbiaceous plants, esp species of *Sebastiania*, that contains a moth caterpillar whose movements cause it to jerk about

jumping gene *n* a fragment of nucleic acid, such as a plasmid or a transposon, that can become incorporated into the DNA of a cell

jumping jack *n* **1** a firework having a long narrow tube filled with gunpowder, folded like an accordion so that when lit it burns with small explosions causing it to jump along the ground **2** a toy figure of a man with jointed limbs that can be moved by pulling attached strings

jumping mouse *n* any long-tailed small mouselike rodent of the family *Zapodidae*, of North America, E Asia, and N and E Europe, having long hind legs specialized for leaping

jumping-off place *or* **point** *n* **1** a starting point, as in an enterprise **2** a final or extreme condition **3** *Canadian* a place where one leaves civilization to go into the wilderness **4** *US* a very remote spot

jumping spider *n* any spider of the family *Salticidae*, esp *Attulus saltator*, that catch their prey by hunting and can jump considerable distances

jump jet *n* a fixed-wing jet aircraft that is capable of landing and taking off vertically

jump jockey *n Brit* a jockey who rides in steeplechases (as opposed to in flat races)

jump leads (liːdz) *pl n* two heavy cables fitted with crocodile clips used to start a motor vehicle with a discharged battery by connecting the battery to an external battery. US and Canadian name: **jumper cables**

jump-off *n* **1** an extra round in a showjumping contest when two or more horses are equal first, the fastest round deciding the winner ▷ *vb* **jump off 2** (*intr, adverb*) to begin or engage in a jump-off

jump on *vb* (*intr, preposition*) *informal* to reprimand or attack suddenly and forcefully

jump seat *n* **1** a folding seat for temporary use, as on the flight deck of some aircraft for an additional crew member **2** *Brit* a folding seat in a motor vehicle such as in a London taxi

jump shot *n basketball* a shot at the basket made by a player releasing the ball at the highest point of a leap

jump-start *vb* **1** to start the engine of (a car) by pushing or rolling it and then engaging the gears or (of a car) to start in this way ▷ *n* **2** the act of starting a car in this way ▷ Also (Brit): **bump-start**

jump suit *n* a one-piece garment of combined trousers and jacket or shirt

jump-up *n* **1** (in the Caribbean) an occasion of mass dancing and merrymaking, as in a carnival ▷ *vb* **jump up** (*intr, adverb*) **2** to stand up quickly and suddenly **3** (in the Caribbean) to take part in a jump-up

jumpy (ˈdʒʌmpɪ) *adj* **jumpier, jumpiest 1** nervous or apprehensive **2** moving jerkily or fitfully > ˈ**jumpily** *adv* > ˈ**jumpiness** *n*

Jun *abbreviation for* **1** June **2** Also: **jun** junior

Junagadh (ˌdʒuːnəˈgæd) *n* a town in India, in Gujarat: noted for its Buddhist caves and temples. Pop: 168 686 (2001)

junc. *abbreviation for* junction

juncaceous (dʒʌŋˈkeɪʃəs) *adj* of, relating to, or belonging to the *Juncaceae*, a family of grasslike plants with small brown flowers: includes the rushes and woodrushes. Compare **cyperaceous** [c19 via New Latin from Latin *juncus* a rush]

junco (ˈdʒʌŋkəʊ) *n, pl* **-cos** *or* **-coes** any North American bunting of the genus *Junco*, having a greyish plumage with white outer tail feathers [c18 from Spanish: a rush, a marsh bird, from Latin *juncus* rush]

junction (ˈdʒʌŋkʃən) *n* **1** a place where several routes, lines, or roads meet, link, or cross each other: *a railway junction* **2** a point on a motorway where traffic may leave or join it **3** *electronics* **a** a contact between two different metals or other materials: *a thermocouple junction* **b** a transition region between regions of differing electrical properties in a semiconductor: *a p-n junction* **4** a connection between two or more conductors or sections of transmission lines **5** the act of joining or the state of being joined [c18 from Latin *junctiō* a joining, from *junctus* joined, from *jungere* to join] > ˈ**junctional** *adj*

junction box *n* an earthed enclosure within which wires or cables can be safely connected

junction transistor *n* a bipolar transistor consisting of two p-n junctions combined to form either an n-p-n or a p-n-p transistor, having the three electrodes, the emitter, base, and collector

juncture (ˈdʒʌŋktʃə) *n* **1** a point in time, esp a critical one (often in the phrase **at this juncture**) **2** *linguistics* **a** a pause in speech or a feature of pronunciation that introduces, accompanies, or replaces a pause **b** the set of phonological features signalling a division between words, such as those that distinguish *a name* from *an aim* **3** a less common word for **junction**

Jundiaí (*Portuguese* ʒundiaˈi) *n* an industrial city in SE Brazil, in São Paulo state. Pop: 332 000 (2005 est)

June (dʒuːn) *n* the sixth month of the year, consisting of 30 days [Old English *iunius*, from Latin *junius*, probably from *Junius* name of Roman gens]

Juneau (ˈdʒuːnəʊ) *n* a port in SE Alaska: state capital. Pop: 31 187 (2003 est)

Juneberry (ˈdʒuːnˌbɛrɪ) *n, pl* **-ries** another name for **serviceberry** (senses 1, 2)

June bug *or* **beetle** *n* any of various large brown North American scarabaeid beetles that are common in late spring and early summer, esp any of the genus *Polyphylla*. Also called: **May beetle, May bug**

Jungfrau (*German* ˈjʊŋfrau) *n* a mountain in S Switzerland, in the Bernese Alps south of Interlaken. Height: 4158 m (13 642 ft)

Junggar Pendi (ˈdʒʊŋˈgɛər ˈpɛnˈdiː), **Dzungaria** *or* **Zungaria** *n* an arid region of W China, in N Xinjiang Uygur between the Altai Mountains and the Tian Shan

Jungian (ˈjʊŋɪən) *adj* of, following, or relating to the Swiss psychologist Carl Gustav Jung (1875–1961), his system of psychoanalysis, or to analytical psychology

jungle (ˈdʒʌŋgᵊl) *n* **1** an equatorial forest area with luxuriant vegetation, often almost impenetrable **2** any dense or tangled thicket or growth **3** a place of intense competition or ruthless struggle for survival: *the concrete jungle* **4** a type of fast electronic dance music, originating in the early 1990s, which combines elements of techno and ragga **5** *US slang* (esp in the Depression) a gathering place for the unemployed, etc [c18 from Hindi *jangal*, from Sanskrit *jāngala* wilderness] > ˈ**jungly** *adj*

jungle fever *n* a serious malarial fever occurring in the East Indies

jungle fowl *n* **1** any small gallinaceous bird of the genus *Gallus*, of S and SE Asia, the males of which have an arched tail and a combed and wattled head: family *Phasianidae* (pheasants). *G. gallus* (**red jungle fowl**) is thought to be the ancestor of the domestic fowl **2** *Austral* any of several megapodes, esp *Megapodius freycinet*

jungle gym *n* a climbing frame for young children [from a trademark]

jungle juice *n* a slang name for alcoholic liquor, esp home-made liquor

junior (ˈdʒuːnjə) *adj* **1** lower in rank or length of service; subordinate **2** younger in years: *junior* citizens **3** of or relating to youth or childhood: *junior pastimes* **4** *Brit* of or relating to schoolchildren between the ages of 7 and 11 approximately **5** *US* of, relating to, or designating the third year of a four-year course at college or high school ▷ *n* **6** *law* (in England) any barrister below the rank of Queen's Counsel **7** a junior person **8** *Brit* a junior schoolchild **9** *US* a junior student [c17 from Latin: younger, from *juvenis* young]

Junior ('dʒuːnjə) *adj* being the younger: usually used after a name to distinguish the son from the father with the same first name or names: *Charles Parker, Junior* Abbreviations: Jnr, Jr, Jun, Junr

junior college *n US and Canadian* an educational establishment providing a two-year course that either terminates with an associate degree or is the equivalent of the freshman and sophomore years of a four-year undergraduate course **2** the junior section of a college or university

junior common room *n* (in certain universities and colleges) a common room for the use of students. Compare **senior common room, middle common room**

junior lightweight *n* **a** a professional boxer weighing 126–130 pounds (57–59 kg) **b** (*as modifier*): *a junior-lightweight bout*

junior middleweight *n* **a** a professional boxer weighing 147–154 pounds (66.5–70 kg) **b** (*as modifier*): *the junior-middleweight championship*. Compare **light middleweight**

junior school *n* (in England and Wales) a school for children aged between 7 and 11. Compare **infant school**

junior technician *n* a rank in the RAF senior to aircraftman: comparable to that of private in the army

junior welterweight *n* **a** a professional boxer weighing 135–140 pounds (61–63.5 kg) **b** (*as modifier*): *a junior-welterweight fight*. Compare **light welterweight**

juniper ('dʒuːnɪpə) *n* **1** any coniferous shrub or small tree of the genus *Juniperus*, of the N hemisphere, having purple berry-like cones. The cones of *J. communis* (**common** or **dwarf juniper**) are used as a flavouring in making gin. See also **red cedar** (sense 1) **2** any of various similar trees, mainly ornamentals **3** *Old Testament* one of the trees used in the building of Solomon's temple (I Kings 6:15, 34) and for shipbuilding (Ezekiel 27:5) [c14 from Latin *jūniperus*, of obscure origin]

junk¹ (dʒʌŋk) *n* **1** discarded or secondhand objects, etc, collectively **2** *informal* **a** rubbish generally **b** nonsense: *the play was absolute junk* **3** *slang* any narcotic drug, esp heroin ▷ *vb* **4** (*tr*) *informal* to discard as junk; scrap [C15 *jonke* old useless rope]

junk² (dʒʌŋk) *n* a sailing vessel used in Chinese waters and characterized by a very high poop, flat bottom, and square sails supported by battens [c17 from Portuguese *junco*, from Javanese *jon;* related to Dutch *jonk*]

junk bond *n finance* a security that offers a high yield but often involves a high risk of default

junk DNA *n* DNA that consists of repeated sequences of nucleotide and has no apparent function

Junker ('jʊŋkə) *n* **1** *history* any of the aristocratic landowners of Prussia who were devoted to maintaining their identity and extensive social and political privileges **2** an arrogant, narrow-minded, and tyrannical German army officer or official **3** (formerly) a young German nobleman [c16 from German, from Old High German *junchērro* young lord, from *junc* young + *hērro* master, lord] > 'Junkerdom *n* > 'Junkerism *n*

junket ('dʒʌŋkɪt) *n* **1** an excursion, esp one made for pleasure at public expense by a public official or committee **2** a sweet dessert made of flavoured milk set to a curd with rennet **3** a feast or festive occasion ▷ *vb* **4** (*intr*) (of a public official, committee, etc) to go on a junket **5** to have or entertain with a feast or festive gathering [C14 (in

the sense: rush basket, hence custard served on rushes): from Old French (dialect) *jonquette*, from *jonc* rush, from Latin *juncus* reed] > 'junketer, 'junketter *or* junke'teer *n*

junk food *n* food that is low in nutritional value, often highly processed or ready-prepared

junkie *or* **junky** ('dʒʌŋkɪ) *n, pl* **junkies** an informal word for **drug addict**, esp one who injects heroin

junk mail *n* untargeted mail advertising goods or services

junkman ('dʒʌŋk,mæn) *n, pl* -**men** *US and Canadian* a man who buys and sells discarded clothing, furniture, etc. Also called (chiefly *Brit*): **rag-and-bone man**

junk shop *n* **1** a shop selling miscellaneous secondhand goods **2** *derogatory* a shop selling antiques

junkyard ('dʒʌŋk,jɑːd) *n* a place where junk is stored or collected for sale

Juno¹ ('dʒuːnəʊ) *n* **1** (in Roman tradition) the queen of the Olympian gods. Greek counterpart: Hera **2** a woman of stately bearing and beauty

Juno³ *n* an award given for achievements in the Canadian music industry [c20 originally after Pierre *Juneau* (born 1922) Canadian broadcaster]

Juno² ('dʒuː,nəʊ) *n astronomy* the fourth largest known asteroid (approximate diameter 240 kilometres) and one of the four brightest

Junoesque (,dʒuː,nəʊ'ɛsk) *adj* having stately bearing and regal beauty like the goddess Juno

Junr *or* **junr** abbreviation for junior

junta ('dʒʊntə, 'dʒʌn-; *chiefly US* 'hʊntə) *n* **1** a group of military officers holding the power in a country, esp after a coup d'état **2** Also called: junto a small group of men; cabal, faction, or clique **3** a legislative or executive council in some parts of Latin America [c17 from Spanish: council, from Latin *junctus* joined, from *jungere* to JOIN]

junto ('dʒʊntəʊ, 'dʒʌn-) *n, pl* -tos a variant of **junta** (sense 2) [c17 variant of JUNTA]

Jupiter¹ ('dʒuːpɪtə) *n* (in Roman tradition) the king and ruler of the Olympian gods. Greek counterpart: Zeus

Jupiter² ('dʒuːpɪtə) *n* the largest of the planets and the fifth from the sun. It has 16 satellites and is surrounded by a transient planar ring system consisting of dust particles. Mean distance from sun: 778 million km; period of revolution around sun: 11.86 years; period of axial rotation: 9.83 hours; diameter and mass: 11.2 and 317.9 times that of earth respectively. See **Galilean satellite**

jupon ('ʒuːpɒn) *n* a short close-fitting sleeveless padded garment, used in the late 14th and early 15th centuries with armour. Also called: **gipon** [c15 from Old French, from Old French *jupe;* see JUMPER¹]

jura ('dʒʊərə) *n* the plural of **jus**

Jura ('dʒʊərə) *n* **1** a department of E France, in Franche-Comté region. Capital: Lons-le-Saunier. Pop: 253 309 (2003 est). Area: 5055 sq km (1971 sq miles) **2** a canton of Switzerland, bordering the French frontier: formed in 1979 from part of Bern. Capital: Delémont. Pop: 69 200 (2002 est). Area: 838 sq km (323 sq miles) **3** an island off the W coast of Scotland, in the Inner Hebrides, separated from the mainland by the **Sound of Jura**. Pop: 200 (2004 est). Area: 381 sq km (147 sqmiles) **4** a mountain range in W central Europe, between the Rivers Rhine and Rhône: mostly in E France, extending into W Switzerland **5** a range of mountains in the NE quadrant of the moon lying on the N border of the Mare Imbrium

jural ('dʒʊərəl) *adj* **1** of or relating to law or to the administration of justice **2** of or relating to rights and obligations [c17 from Latin *iūs* law + -AL¹] > 'jurally *adv*

Jurassic (dʒʊ'ræsɪk) *adj* **1** of, denoting, or formed in the second period of the Mesozoic era, between the Triassic and Cretaceous periods, lasting for 55 million years during which dinosaurs and ammonites flourished ▷ *n* **2** the Jurassic period or rock system [c19 from French *jurassique*,

after the JURA (Mountains)]

jurat ('dʒʊəræt) *n* **1** *law* a statement at the foot of an affidavit, naming the parties, stating when, where, and before whom it was sworn, etc **2** (in England) a municipal officer of the Cinque Ports, having a similar position to that of an alderman **3** (in France and the Channel Islands) a magistrate [c16 from Medieval Latin *jūrātus* one who has been sworn, from Latin *jūrāre* to swear]

juratory ('dʒʊərətərɪ, -trɪ) *adj law* of, relating to, or expressed in an oath

JurD abbreviation for Doctor of Law [Latin *Juris Doctor*]

jurel (hʊ'rel) *n* any of several carangid food fishes of the genus *Caranx*, of warm American Atlantic waters [c18 from Spanish, from Catalan *sorell*, from Late Latin *saurus* horse mackerel, from Greek *sauros* lizard]

juridical (dʒʊ'rɪdɪkᵊl) *or* **juridic** *adj* of or relating to law, to the administration of justice, or to the office or function of a judge; legal [c16 from Latin *jūridicus*, from *iūs* law + *dicere* to say] > ju'ridically *adv*

juridical days *pl n law* days on which the courts are in session. Compare **dies non**

jurisconsult (,dʒʊərɪs'kɒnsʌlt) *n* **1** a person qualified to advise on legal matters **2** a master of jurisprudence [c17 from Latin *jūris consultus;* see JUS, CONSULT]

jurisdiction (,dʒʊərɪs'dɪkʃən) *n* **1** the right or power to administer justice and to apply laws **2** the exercise or extent of such right or power **3** power or authority in general [c13 from Latin *jūrisdictiō* administration of justice; see JUS, DICTION] > juris'dictional *adj* > juris'dictionally *adv* > juris'dictive *adj*

jurisprudence (,dʒʊərɪs'pruːdᵊns) *n* **1** the science or philosophy of law **2** a system or body of law **3** a branch of law: *medical jurisprudence* [c17 from Latin *jūris prūdentia;* see JUS, PRUDENCE] > jurisprudential (,dʒʊərɪspruː'dɛnʃəl) *adj* > jurispru'dentially *adv*

jurisprudent (,dʒʊərɪs'pruːdᵊnt) *adj* **1** skilled in jurisprudence or versed in the principles of law ▷ *n* **2** a jurisprudent person

jurist ('dʒʊərɪst) *n* **1** a person versed in the science of law, esp Roman or civil law **2** a writer on legal subjects **3** a student or graduate of law **4** (in the US) a lawyer [c15 from French *juriste*, from Medieval Latin *jūrista;* see JUS]

juristic (dʒʊ'rɪstɪk) *or* **juristical** *adj* **1** of or relating to jurists **2** of, relating to, or characteristic of the study of law or the legal profession

juristic act *n* **1** a proceeding designed to have a legal effect **2** an act by an individual aimed at altering, terminating, or otherwise affecting a legal right

juror ('dʒʊərə) *n* **1** a member of a jury **2** a person whose name is included on a panel from which a jury is selected **3** a person who takes an oath [c14 from Anglo-French *jurour*, from Old French *jurer* to take an oath, from Latin *jūrāre*]

Juruá (Portuguese ʒu'rua) *n* a river in South America, rising in E central Peru and flowing northeast across NW Brazil to join the Amazon. Length: 1900 km (1200 miles)

jury¹ ('dʒʊərɪ) *n, pl* -ries **1** a group of, usually twelve, people sworn to deliver a true verdict according to the evidence upon a case presented in a body in a court of law. See also **grand jury, petit jury 2** a body of persons appointed to judge a competition and award prizes **3 the jury is still out** *informal* it has not yet been decided or agreed on [c14 from Old French *juree*, from *jurer* to swear; see JUROR]

jury² ('dʒʊərɪ) *adj chiefly nautical* (in combination) makeshift: *jury-rigged* [c17 of unknown origin]

jury box *n* an enclosure where the jury sit in court

juryman ('dʒʊərɪmən) *n, pl* -**men** a member of a jury, esp a man

jury process *n* the writ used to summon jurors

jury-rigged *adj chiefly nautical* set up in a makeshift manner

jurywoman ('dʒʊərɪ,wʊmən) *n, pl* -**women** a

j

female member of a jury

jus[1] (dʒʌs) *n, pl* **jura** ('dʒʊərə) *law* **1** a right, power, or authority **2** law in the abstract or as a system, as distinguished from specific enactments [Latin: law]

jus[2] (ʒuː; *French* ʒy) *n* a sauce [French: juice]

jus canonicum (kə'nɒnɪkəm) *n* canon law [from Latin]

jus civile (sɪ'viːlɪ) *n* **1** the civil law of the Roman state **2** the body of law derived from the principles of this law. Compare **jus gentium, jus naturale** [from Latin]

jus divinum (dɪ'viːnəm) *n* divine law [from Latin]

jus gentium ('dʒɛntɪəm) *n Roman law* those rules of law common to all nations [from Latin]

jus naturale (ˌnætjʊ'reɪlɪ) *n Roman law* **1** (originally) a system of law based on fundamental ideas of right and wrong; natural law **2** (in later usage) another term for **jus gentium** [from Latin]

jus sanguinis ('sæŋgwɪnɪs) *n law* the principle that a person's nationality at birth is the same as that of his natural parents. Compare **jus soli** [Latin, literally: law of blood]

jussive ('dʒʌsɪv) *adj grammar* another word for **imperative** (sense 3) [C19 from Latin *jūssus* ordered, from *jubēre* to command]

jus soli ('səʊlaɪ) *n law* the principle that a person's nationality at birth is determined by the territory within which he was born. Compare **jus sanguinis** [from Latin, literally: law of soil]

just *adj* (dʒʌst) **1 a** fair or impartial in action or judgment **b** (*as collective noun; preceded by the*): *the just* **2** conforming to high moral standards; honest **3** consistent with justice: *a just action* **4** rightly applied or given; deserved: *a just reward* **5** legally valid; lawful: *a just inheritance* **6** well-founded; reasonable: *just criticism* **7** correct, accurate, or true: *a just account* ▷ *adv* (dʒʌst; *unstressed* dʒəst) **8** used with forms of *have* to indicate an action performed in the very recent past: *I have just closed the door* **9** at this very instant: *he's just coming in to land* **10** no more than; merely; only: *just an ordinary car* **11** exactly; precisely: *that's just what I mean* **12** by a small margin; barely: *he just got there in time* **13** (intensifier): *it's just wonderful to see you* **14** *informal* indeed; with a vengeance: *isn't it just* **15** **just about a** at the point of starting (to do something) **b** very nearly; almost: *I've just about had enough* **16** **just a moment, second,** *or* **minute** an expression requesting the hearer to wait or pause for a brief period of time **17** **just now a** a very short time ago **b** at this moment **c** *South African informal* in a little while **18** **just on** having reached exactly: *it's just on five o'clock* **19** **just so a** an expression of complete agreement or of unwillingness to dissent **b** arranged with precision [C14 from Latin *jūstus* righteous, from *jūs* justice] > **'justly** *adv* > **'justness** *n*

USAGE The use of *just* with *exactly* (*it's just exactly what they want*) is redundant: *it's exactly what they want*

justice ('dʒʌstɪs) *n* **1** the quality or fact of being just **2** *ethics* **a** the principle of fairness that like cases should be treated alike **b** a particular distribution of benefits and burdens fairly in accordance with a particular conception of what are to count as like cases **c** the principle that punishment should be proportionate to the offence **3** the administration of law according to prescribed and accepted principles **4** conformity to the law; legal validity **5** a judge of the Supreme Court of Judicature **6** short for **justice of the peace** **7** good reason (esp in the phrase **with justice**): *he was disgusted by their behaviour, and with justice* **8** **do justice to a** to show to full advantage: *the picture did justice to her beauty* **b** to show full appreciation of by action: *he did justice to the meal* **c** to treat or judge fairly **9** **do oneself justice** to make full use of one's abilities **10** **bring to justice** to capture, try, and usually punish (a criminal, an outlaw, etc) [C12 from Old French, from Latin *jūstitia*, from *justus* JUST]

justice court *n* an inferior court presided over by a justice of the peace

justice of the peace *n* **1** (in Britain) a lay magistrate, appointed by the crown or acting *ex officio*, whose function is to preserve the peace in his area, try summarily such cases as are within his jurisdiction, and perform miscellaneous administrative duties **2** (in Australia and New Zealand) a person authorised to administer oaths, attest instruments, and take declarations

justice of the peace court *n* (in Scotland, formerly) a court with limited criminal jurisdiction held by justices of the peace in counties: replaced in 1975 by the **district court**

justiceship ('dʒʌstɪsʃɪp) *n* the rank or office of a justice

justiciable (dʒʌ'stɪʃɪəbᵊl) *adj* **1** capable of being determined by a court of law **2** liable to be brought before a court for trial > **jusˌticia'bility** *n*

justiciar (dʒʌ'stɪʃɪˌɑː) *n English legal history* the chief political and legal officer from the time of William I to that of Henry III, who deputized for the king in his absence and presided over the kings' courts. Also called: **justiciary** > **jus'ticiarˌship** *n*

justiciary (dʒʌ'stɪʃɪərɪ) *adj* **1** of or relating to the administration of justice ▷ *n, pl* **-aries** **2** an officer or administrator of justice; judge **3** another word for **justiciar**

justifiable ('dʒʌstɪˌfaɪəbᵊl) *adj* capable of being justified; understandable > **justiˌfia'bility** *or* **'justiˌfiableness** *n* > **'justiˌfiably** *adv*

justifiable homicide *n* lawful killing, as in self-defence or to prevent a crime

justification (ˌdʒʌstɪfɪ'keɪʃən) *n* **1** reasonable grounds for complaint, defence, etc **2** the act of justifying; proof, vindication, or exculpation **3** *theol* **a** the act of justifying **b** the process of being justified or the condition of having been justified **4** Also called: **justification by faith** *Protestant theol* the doctrine that God vindicates only those who repent and believe in Jesus **5** *printing, computing* the process of adjusting interword spacing in text or data so that both right and left margins are straight **6** *computing* the process of moving data right or left so that the first or last character occurs in a predefined position

justificatory ('dʒʌstɪfɪˌkeɪtərɪ, -trɪ) *or* **justificative** ('dʒʌstɪfɪˌkeɪtɪv) *adj* serving as justification or capable of justifying; vindicatory

justify ('dʒʌstɪˌfaɪ) *vb* **-fies, -fying, -fied** (*mainly tr*) **1** (*often passive*) to prove or see to be just or valid; vindicate: *he was certainly justified in taking the money* **2** to show to be reasonable; warrant or substantiate: *his behaviour justifies our suspicion* **3** to declare or show to be free from blame or guilt; absolve **4** *law* **a** to show good reason in court for (some action taken) **b** to show adequate grounds for doing (that with which a person is charged): *to justify a libel* **5** (*also intr*) *printing, computing* to adjust the spaces between words in (a line of type or data) so that it is of the required length or (of a line of type or data) to fit exactly **6 a** *Protestant theol* to account or declare righteous by the imputation of Christ's merits to the sinner **b** *RC theol* to change from sinfulness to righteousness by the transforming effects of grace **7** (*also intr*) *law* to prove (a person) to have sufficient means to act as surety, etc, or (of a person) to qualify to provide bail or surety [C14 from Old French *justifier*, from Latin *justificāre*, from *jūstus* JUST + *facere* to make] > **'justiˌfier** *n*

Justinian Code *n* a compilation of Roman imperial law made by order of Justinian I, forming part of the **Corpus Juris Civilis**

just-in-time *adj* denoting or relating to an industrial method in which waste of resources is eliminated or reduced by producing production-line components, etc, as they are required, rather than holding large stocks. Abbreviation: **JIT**

just intonation *n* a form of tuning employing the pitch intervals of the untempered natural scale, sometimes employed in the playing of the violin, cello, etc

justle ('dʒʌsᵊl) *vb* a less common word for **jostle**

just noticeable difference *n psychol* another name for **difference threshold** Abbreviation: **jnd**

jut (dʒʌt) *vb* **juts, jutting, jutted** **1** (*intr; often foll by out*) to stick out or overhang beyond the surface or main part; protrude or project ▷ *n* **2** something that juts out [C16 variant of JET[1]] > **'jutting** *adj*

jute (dʒuːt) *n* **1** either of two Old World tropical yellow-flowered herbaceous plants, *Corchorus capsularis* or *C. olitorius*, cultivated for their strong fibre: family *Tiliaceae* **2** this fibre, used in making sacks, rope, etc [C18 from Bengali *jhuto*, from Sanskrit *jūta* braid of hair, matted hair]

Jute (dʒuːt) *n* a member of one of various Germanic tribes, some of whom invaded England in the 6th century AD, settling in Kent

Jutish ('dʒuːtɪʃ) *adj* **1** of or relating to the Jutes ▷ *n* **2** another name for **Kentish**

Jutland ('dʒʌtlənd) *n* a peninsula of N Europe: forms the continental portion of Denmark and geographically includes the N part of the German province of Schleswig-Holstein, while politically it includes only the mainland of Denmark and the islands north of Limfjorden; a major but inconclusive naval battle was fought off its NW coast in 1916 between the British and German fleets. Danish name: **Jylland**

Jutlander ('dʒʌtləndə) *n* a native or inhabitant of Jutland

juvenal ('dʒuːvɪnᵊl) *adj ornithol* a variant spelling (esp US) of **juvenile** (sense 4)

juvenescence (ˌdʒuːvɪ'nɛsəns) *n* **1** youth or immaturity **2** the act or process of growing from childhood to youth **3** restoration of youth

juvenescent (ˌdʒuːvɪ'nɛsᵊnt) *adj* becoming or being young or youthful [C19 from Latin *juvenēscere* to grow up, regain strength, from *juvenis* youthful]

juvenile ('dʒuːvɪˌnaɪl) *adj* **1** young, youthful, or immature **2** suitable or designed for young people: *juvenile pastimes* **3** (of animals or plants) not yet fully mature **4** of or denoting young birds that have developed their first plumage of adult feathers **5** *geology* occurring at the earth's surface for the first time; new: *juvenile water; juvenile gases* ▷ *n* **6** a juvenile person, animal, or plant **7** an actor who performs youthful roles **8** a book intended for young readers [C17 from Latin *juvenīlis* youthful, from *juvenis* young] > **'juveˌnilely** *adv* > **'juveˌnileness** *n*

juvenile court *n* the former name for **youth court**

juvenile delinquency *n* antisocial or criminal conduct by juvenile delinquents

juvenile delinquent *n* a child or young person guilty of some offence, act of vandalism, or antisocial behaviour or whose conduct is beyond parental control and who may be brought before a juvenile court

juvenile hormone *n* a hormone, secreted by insects from a pair of glands behind the brain, that promotes the growth of larval characteristics and inhibits metamorphosis

juvenilia (ˌdʒuːvɪ'nɪlɪə) *pl n* works of art, literature, or music produced in youth or adolescence, before the artist, author, or composer has formed a mature style [C17 from Latin, literally: youthful things; see JUVENILE]

juvenility (ˌdʒuːvɪ'nɪlɪtɪ) *n, pl* **-ties** **1** the quality or condition of being juvenile, esp of being immature **2** (*often plural*) a juvenile act or manner **3** juveniles collectively

juxtapose (ˌdʒʌkstə'pəʊz) *vb* (*tr*) to place close together or side by side [C19 back formation from *juxtaposition*, from Latin *juxta* next to + POSITION] > **juxtapo'sition** *n* > **juxtapo'sitional** *adj*

JWV *abbreviation for* Jewish War Veterans

Jylland ('jylan) *n* the Danish name for **Jutland**

Kk

k *or* **K** (keɪ) *n, pl* **k's, K's** *or* **Ks 1** the 11th letter and 8th consonant of the modern English alphabet **2** a speech sound represented by this letter, usually a voiceless velar stop, as in *kitten* **3** See **five Ks**

k *symbol for* **1** kilo(s) **2** *maths* the unit vector along the z-axis

K *symbol for* **1** kelvin(s) **2** *chess* king **3** *chem* potassium **4** *physics* kaon **5** *currency* **a** kina **b** kip **c** kopeck **d** kwacha **e** kyat **6** one thousand **7** *computing* **a** a unit of 1024 words, bits, or bytes **b** (not in technical usage) 1000 **8** ▷ *international car registration for* Cambodia [(for sense 3) from New Latin *kalium*; (for sense 6) from KILO-; (for sense 8) from *Kampuchea*]

K *or* **K.** *abbreviation for* Köchel: indicating the serial number in the catalogue (1862) of the works of Mozart made by Ludwig von Köchel (1800–77)

K2 *n* a mountain in the Karakoram Range on the Kashmir-Xinjiang Uygur AR border: the second highest mountain in the world. Height: 8611 m (28 250 ft). Also called: **Godwin-Austen, Dapsang**

ka (kɑː) *n* (in ancient Egypt) an attendant spirit supposedly dwelling as a vital force in a man or statue [from Egyptian]

Kaaba *or* **Caaba** ('kɑːbə) *n* a cube-shaped building in Mecca, the most sacred Muslim pilgrim shrine, into which is built the black stone believed to have been given by Gabriel to Abraham. Muslims turn in its direction when praying [from Arabic *ka'bah*, from *ka'b* cube]

kaal ('kɑːl) *or* **kaal gat** ('kɑːl gæt) *adj South African informal* naked [from Afrikaans, literally: bare (arsed)]

kab (kæb) *n* a variant spelling of **cab²**

kabaddi (kə'bɑːdɪ) *n* a game played between two teams of seven players, in which individuals take turns to chase and try to touch members of the opposing team without being captured [Tamil]

kabaka (kə'bɑːkə) *n* any of the former rulers of the Baganda people of S Uganda [c19 from Luganda]

Kabalega Falls (ˌkɑːbə'leɪgə) *pl n* rapids on the lower Victoria Nile, about 35 km (22 miles) east of Lake Albert, where the Nile drops 120 m (400 ft)

kabaragoya (kəˌbɑːrə'gəʊjə) *n* a very large monitor lizard, *Varanus salvator*, of SE Asia: it grows to a length of three metres. Also called: **Malayan monitor** [perhaps Tagalog]

Kabardian (kə'bɑːdɪən) *n* **1** a member of a Circassian people of the North West Caucasus **2** the Eastern dialect of the Circassian language. Compare **Adygei**

Kabardino-Balkar Republic (ˌkæbə'diˌnəʊˌbælkə) *n* a constituent republic of S Russia, on the N side of the Caucasus Mountains. Capital: Nalchik. Pop: 900 500 (2002). Area: 12 500 sq km (4825 sq miles). Also called: **Kabardino Balkaria** (ˌkæbəˌdiːnəʊbæl'kɑːrɪə)

kabbalah, kabbala, kabala, cabbala, cabala *or* **qabalah** (kə'bɑːlə) *n* **1** an ancient Jewish mystical tradition based on an esoteric interpretation of the Old Testament **2** any secret

or occult doctrine or science [c16 from Medieval Latin, from Hebrew *qabbālāh* tradition, what is received, from *qābal* to receive] > kabbalism, kabalism, cabbalism, cabalism *or* qabalism ('kæbəˌlɪzəm) *n* > 'kabbalist, 'kabalist, 'cabbalist, 'cabalist *or* 'qabalist *n* > ˌkabba'listic, ˌkaba'listic, ˌcabba'listic, ˌcaba'listic *or* ˌqaba'listic *adj*

kabeljou ('kɑːbəlˌjəʊ) *n South African* a large marine sciaenid fish, *Argyrosomus hololepidotus*, that is an important food fish of South African waters [c18 from Afrikaans, from Dutch, cod]

Kabinett (ˌkæbɪ'nɛt) *n* a dry, usually white, wine produced in Germany, made from mature grapes with no added sugar [c20 from German, literally: cabinet]

Kabloona (kə'bluːnə) *n* (in Canada) a person who is not of Inuit ancestry, esp a White person [from Inuktitut]

kabob (kə'bɒb) *n* another name for **kebab**

kabuki (kæ'buːkɪ) *n* a form of Japanese drama based on popular legends and characterized by elaborate costumes, stylized acting, and the use of male actors for all roles. See also **No¹** [Japanese, from *ka* singing + *bu* dancing + *ki* art]

Kabul (kə'bʊl, 'kɑːbʊl) *or* **Kabol** *n* **1** the capital of Afghanistan, in the northeast of the country at an altitude of 1800 m (5900 ft) on the **Kabul River**: over 3000 years old, with a strategic position commanding passes through the Hindu Kush and main routes to the Khyber Pass; destroyed and rebuilt many times; capital of the Mogul Empire from 1504 until 1738 and of Afghanistan from 1773; university (1932). Pop: 3 288 000 (2005 est) **2** a river in Afghanistan and Pakistan, rising in the Hindu Kush and flowing east into the Indus at Attock, Pakistan. Length: 700 km (435 miles)

Kabyle (kə'baɪl) *n* **1** (*pl* -byles *or* -byle) a member of a Berber people inhabiting the E Atlas Mountains in Tunisia and Algeria **2** the dialect of Berber spoken by this people [c19 from Arabic *qabā'il*, plural of *qabīlah* tribe]

kachang puteh ('kɑːtʃaŋ puː'teɪ) *n* (in Malaysia) roasted or fried nuts or beans [from Malay, literally: white beans]

Kachera (kʌ'tʃeɪrə) *or* **Kacha** ('kʌtʃə) *n* short trousers traditionally worn by Sikhs as a symbol of their religious and cultural loyalty: originally worn for ease of horse riding. See also **five Ks** [Punjabi]

kachina (kə'tʃiːnə) *n* any of the supernatural beings believed by the Hopi Indians to be the ancestors of living humans [from Hopi *qačina* supernatural]

kadaitcha (kə'daɪtʃə) *n* a variant spelling of **kurdaitcha**

Kaddish ('kædɪʃ) *n, pl* **Kaddishim** (kæ'dɪʃɪm) *Judaism* **1** an ancient Jewish liturgical prayer largely written in Aramaic and used in various forms to separate sections of the liturgy. Mourners have the right to recite some of these in public prayer during the year after, and on the

anniversary of, a death **2** say Kaddish to be a mourner [c17 from Aramaic *qaddīsh* holy]

kadi ('kɑːdɪ, 'keɪdɪ) *n, pl* -dis a variant spelling of **cadi**

Kaduna (kə'duːnə) *n* **1** a state of N Nigeria. Capital: Kaduna. Pop: 4 438 007 (1995 est). Area: 46 053 sq km (17 781 sq miles). Former name (until 1976): **North-Central State 2** a city in N central Nigeria, capital of Kaduna state on the **Kaduna River** (a principal tributary of the Niger). Pop: 1 329 000 (2005 est)

Kaesŏng (ˌkeɪ'sʌŋ) *n* a city in SW North Korea: former capital of Korea (938–1392). Pop: 621 000 (2005 est)

Kaffir *or* **Kafir** ('kæfə) *n, pl* -firs *or* -fir **1** *offensive* **a** (in southern Africa) any Black African **b** (*as modifier*): *Kaffir farming* **2** a former name for the **Xhosa** language **3** *offensive* (among Muslims) a non-Muslim or infidel [c19 from Arabic *kāfir* infidel, from *kafara* to deny, refuse to believe]

kaffir beer *n South African* beer made from sorghum (kaffir corn) or millet

kaffirboom ('kæfəˌbʊəm) *n South African* a deciduous flowering tree, *Erythrina caffra*, having large clusters of brilliant orange or scarlet flowers [from KAFFIR + Afrikaans *boom* tree]

kaffir corn *or sometimes US* **kafir corn** *n* a Southern African variety of sorghum, cultivated in dry regions for its grain and as fodder. Sometimes shortened to: **kaffir, (US) kafir**

kaffiyeh (kæ'fiːjə) *n* a variant of **keffiyeh**

Kaffraria (kæ'frɛərɪə) *n* a former region of S central South Africa: inhabited chiefly by people then known as the Kaffirs; British Kaffraria was a crown colony established in 1853 in the southwest of the region and annexed to Cape Colony in 1865

Kaffrarian (kæ'frɛərɪən) *adj* **1** of or relating to Kaffraria, a former region of S central South Africa, or its inhabitants ▷ *n* **2** a native or inhabitant of Kaffraria

Kafir ('kæfə) *n, pl* -irs *or* -ir **1** another name for the **Nuri 2** a variant spelling of **Kaffir** [c19 from Arabic; see KAFFIR]

Kafiristan (ˌkæfɪrɪ'stɑːn) *n* the former name of **Nuristan**

Kafkaesque (ˌkæfkə'ɛsk) *adj* reminiscent of the nightmarish dehumanized world portrayed in the novels of Franz Kafka, the Czech novelist (1883–1924)

kaftan *or* **caftan** ('kæftæn, -ˌtɑːn) *n* **1** a long coatlike garment, usually worn with a belt and made of rich fabric, worn in the East **2** an imitation of this, worn esp by women, in the West, consisting of a loose dress with long wide sleeves [c16 from Turkish *qaftān*]

Kagera (kæ'gɛɪə) *n* a river in E Africa, rising in headstreams on the border between Tanzania and Rwanda and flowing east to Lake Victoria: the most remote headstream of the Nile and largest tributary of Lake Victoria. Length: about 480 km (300 miles)

Kagoshima (ˌkæɡɒˈʃiːmə) *n* a port in SW Japan, on S Kyushu. Pop: 544 840 (2002 est)

kagoul *or* **kagoule** (kəˈɡuːl) *n* variant spellings of **cagoule**

kagu (ˈkɑːɡuː) *n* a crested nocturnal bird, *Rhynochetos jubatus*, with a red bill and greyish plumage: occurs only in New Caledonia and is nearly extinct: family *Rhynochetidae*, order *Gruiformes* (cranes, rails, etc) [native name in New Caledonia]

kahawai (ˈkɑːhəˌwaɪ) *n* a large food and game fish of Australian and New Zealand coastal waters, *Arripis trutta*, that is greenish grey to silvery underneath and spotted with brown: resembles a salmon but is in fact a marine perch. Also called: **Australian salmon** [Māori]

kahawai bird (ˈkɑːhəwaːiː) *n* NZ another name for **white-fronted tern** [Māori]

kahikatea (ˌkɑːɪkəˈtɪə) *n* a tall New Zealand coniferous tree, *Podocarpus dacrydioides*, valued for its timber and resin. Also called: **white pine** [Māori]

kahikatoa (kɑːhiːkəˈtəʊə) *n, pl* **kahikatoa** NZ another name for **manuka** [Māori]

kai (kaɪ) *n* NZ food [Māori, from Melanesian pidgin *kaikai*]

kaiak (ˈkaɪæk) *n* a variant of **kayak**

Kaieteur Falls (ˌkaɪəˈtʊə) *pl n* a waterfall in Guyana, on the Potaro River. Height: 226 m (741 ft). Width: about 107 m (350 ft)

kaif (kaɪf) *n* a variant of **kif**

Kaifeng (ˈkaɪˈfɛŋ) *n* a city in E China, in N Henan on the Yellow River: one of the oldest cities in China and its capital (as Pien-liang) from 907 to 1126. Pop: 810 000 (2005 est)

kaik (kaɪk) *or* **kaika** (kɑːiːˈŋɡɑː) *n* NZ the South Island dialect word for **kainga**

kaikawaka (kɑːiːˈkwɑːkə) *n, pl* **kaikawaka** a small pyramid-shaped New Zealand conifer, *Libocedrus bidwillii*, with pinkish bark and red wood. Also called: **pahautea** [Māori]

kaikomako (kɑːiːkɒmɑːˈkɒ) *n, pl* **kaikomako** a small New Zealand tree, *Pennantia corymbosa* with white flowers and black fruit [Māori]

kail (keɪl) *n* a variant spelling of **kale**

kailyard (ˈkeɪlˌjɑːd) *n* a variant spelling of **kaleyard**

kai moana (məʊˈænə) *n* NZ seafood [Māori, from ᴋᴀɪ + *moana* sea]

kain (keɪn) *n history* a variant spelling of **cain**

kainga (ˈkaɪŋə) *n* (in New Zealand) a Māori village or small settlement. Also called (on South Island): **kaik** [Māori]

kainite (ˈkaɪnaɪt) *n* a white mineral consisting of potassium chloride and magnesium sulphate: a fertilizer and source of potassium salts. Formula: $KCl.MgSO_4.3H_2O$ [c19 from German *Kainit*, from Greek *kainos* new + -ɪᴛᴇ[1]]

kainogenesis (ˌkaɪnəʊˈdʒɛnɪsɪs) *n* another name for **caenogenesis**. ▷ **kainogenetic** (ˌkaɪnəʊdʒəˈnɛtɪk) *adj* ▷ ˌkainogeˈnetically *adv*

Kairouan (*French* kɛrwɑ̃) *or* **Kairwan, Qairwan** (kaɪəˈwɑːn) *n* a city in NE Tunisia: one of the holy cities of Islam; pilgrimage and trading centre. Pop: 124 000 (2005 est)

Kaiser (ˈkaɪzə) *n* (*sometimes not capital*) *history* **1** any German emperor, esp Wilhelm II (1888–1918) **2** *obsolete* any Austro-Hungarian emperor [c16 from German, ultimately from Latin *Caesar* emperor, from the cognomen of Gaius Julius Caesar (100–44 ʙᴄ), Roman general, statesman, and historian] ▷ ˈkaiserdom *or* ˈkaiserism *n*

Kaiserslautern (*German* kaɪzərsˈlautərn) *n* a city in W Germany, in S Rhineland-Palatinate. Pop: 999 095 (2003 est)

kaizen *Japanese* (kaɪˈzɛn) *n* a philosophy of continuous improvement of working practices that underlies total quality management and just-in-time business techniques [literally: improvement]

kak (ˈkʌk) *n South African taboo* **1** faeces **2** rubbish [Afrikaans]

kaka (ˈkɑːkə) *n* a New Zealand parrot, *Nestor meridionalis*, with a long compressed bill [c18 from Māori, perhaps imitative of its call]

kaka beak *n* an evergreen climbing shrub, *Clianthus puniceus*, having pinnate leaves and clusters of bright red flowers in the shape of a parrot's beak. It is native to New Zealand but now rare except in cultivation. Also called: **red kowhai**

kakapo (ˈkɑːkəˌpəʊ) *n, pl* **-pos** a ground-living nocturnal parrot, *Strigops habroptilus*, of New Zealand, resembling an owl [c19 from Māori, literally: night kaka]

kakariki (ˈkɑːkəˌriːkiː) *n, pl* **kakariki** any of various green-feathered New Zealand parrots of the genus *Cyanoramphus* [Māori]

kakemono (ˌkækɪˈməʊnəʊ) *n, pl* **-nos** a Japanese paper or silk wall hanging, usually long and narrow, with a picture or inscription on it and a roller at the bottom [c19 from Japanese, from *kake* hanging + *mono* thing]

kaki (ˈkɑːkɪ) *n, pl* **kakis** another name for **Japanese persimmon** [Japanese]

kala-azar (ˌkɑːləəˈzɑː) *n* a tropical infectious disease caused by the protozoan *Leishmania donovani* in the liver, spleen, etc, characterized by fever and weight loss; visceral leishmaniasis [from Assamese *kālā* black + *āzār* disease]

Kalahari (ˌkæləˈhɑːrɪ) *n* **the** an extensive arid plateau of South Africa, Namibia, and Botswana. Area: 260 000 sq km (100 000 sq miles). Also called: **Kalahari Desert**

kalamata olive *or* **calamata olive** (ˌkæləˈmɑːtə) *n* an aubergine-coloured Greek olive [Greek]

Kalamazoo (ˌkæləməˈzuː) *n* a city in SW Michigan, midway between Detroit and Chicago: aircraft, missile parts. Pop: 75 312 (2003 est)

kalanchoe (ˌkælənˈkəʊɪ) *n* any plant of the tropical succulent genus *Kalanchoe*, grown as pot plants for their small brightly coloured flowers, sometimes scented, and their dark shiny leaves: family *Crassulaceae* [New Latin, from the Chinese name of one of the species]

Kalashnikov (kəˈlæʃnɪˌkɒf) *n* a Russian-made automatic rifle. See also **AK-47** [c20 named after Mikhail *Kalashnikov* (born 1919), its designer]

Kalat *or* **Khelat** (kəˈlɑːt) *n* a region of SW Pakistan, in S Baluchistan: formerly a princely state ruled by the Khan of Kalat, which joined Pakistan in 1948

kale[1] *or* **kail** (keɪl) *n* **1** a cultivated variety of cabbage, *Brassica oleracea acephala*, with crinkled leaves: used as a potherb. See also **collard** **2** *Scot* a cabbage **3** *US slang* money ▷ Compare (for senses 1, 2) **sea kale** [Old English *cāl*; see ᴄᴏʟᴇ]

kale[2] (keɪl) *n Northern English dialect* a queue

kaleidoscope (kəˈlaɪdəˌskəʊp) *n* **1** an optical toy for producing symmetrical patterns by multiple reflections in inclined mirrors enclosed in a tube. Loose pieces of coloured glass, paper, etc, are placed between transparent plates at the far end of the tube, which is rotated to change the pattern **2** any complex pattern of frequently changing shapes and colours **3** a complicated set of circumstances [c19 from Greek *kalos* beautiful + *eidos* form + -ꜱᴄᴏᴘᴇ] ▷ **kaleidoscopic** (kəˌlaɪdəˈskɒpɪk) *adj* ▷ kaˌleidoˈscopically *adv*

kalends (ˈkælɪndz) *pl n* a variant spelling of **calends**

Kalevala (ˌkɑːləˈvɑːlə; *Finnish* ˈkɑlɛvɑlɑ) *n Finnish legend* **1** the land of the hero Kaleva, who performed legendary exploits **2** the Finnish national epic in which these exploits are recounted, compiled by Elias Lönnrot from folk poetry in 1835 to 1849 [Finnish, from *kaleva* of a hero + -*la* dwelling place, home]

kaleyard *or* **kailyard** (ˈkeɪlˌjɑːd, *Scot* -ˌjɑːd) *n Scot* a vegetable garden [c19 literally: cabbage garden]

kaleyard school *or* **kailyard school** *n* a group of writers who depicted the sentimental and homely aspects of life in the Scottish Lowlands from about 1880 to 1914. The best known contributor to the school was J. M. Barrie

Kalgan (ˈkɑːlˈɡɑːn) *n* a former name of **Zhangjiakou**

Kalgoorlie (kælˈɡʊəlɪ) *n* a city in Western Australia, adjoining the town of Boulder: a centre of the Coolgardie gold rushes of the early 1890s; declining gold resources superseded by the discovery of nickel ore in 1966. Pop: 28 281 (including Boulder) (2001)

kali (ˈkælɪ, ˈkeɪ-) *n* another name for **saltwort**[1]

Kali (ˈkɑːlɪ) *n* the Hindu goddess of destruction, consort of Siva. Her cult was characterized by savagery and cannibalism

kalian (kælˈjɑːn) *n* another name for **hookah** [c19 from Persian, from Arabic *qalyān*]

kalif (ˈkeɪlɪf, ˈkæl-) *n* a variant spelling of **caliph**

Kalimantan (ˌkælɪˈmæntən) *n* the Indonesian name for Borneo: applied to the Indonesian part of the island only, excluding the Malaysian states of Sabah and Sarawak and the sultanate of Brunei. Pop: 11 341 558 (2000)

Kalinin (*Russian* kaˈlinin) *n* the former name (until 1991) of **Tver**

Kaliningrad (*Russian* kəlininˈɡrat) *n* a port in W Russia, on the Pregolya River: severely damaged in World War II as the chief German naval base on the Baltic; ceded to the Soviet Union in 1945 and is now Russia's chief Baltic naval base. Pop: 436 000 (2005 est). Former name (until 1946): Königsberg

Kalisz (*Polish* ˈkaliʃ) *n* a town in central Poland, on an island in the Prosna River: textile industry. Pop: 110 000 (2005 est). Ancient name: Calissia (kəˈlɪsɪə)

Kaliyuga (ˌkɑːlɪˈjuːɡə) *n* (in Hindu mythology) the fourth (present) age of the world, characterized by total decadence

Kalmar (*Swedish* ˈkalmar) *n* a port in SE Sweden, partly on the mainland and partly on a small island in the **Sound of Kalmar** opposite Öland: scene of the signing of the Union of Kalmar, which united Sweden, Denmark, and Norway into a single monarchy (1397–1523). Pop: 60 734 (2004 est)

kalmia (ˈkælmɪə) *n* any evergreen ericaceous shrub of the North American genus *Kalmia*, having showy clusters of white or pink flowers. See also **mountain laurel** [c18 named after Peter *Kalm* (1715–79), Swedish botanist and pupil of Linnaeus]

Kalmuck (ˈkælmʌk) *or* **Kalmyk** (ˈkælmɪk) *n* **1** (*pl* **-mucks, -muck** *or* **-myks, -myk**) a member of a Mongoloid people of Buddhist tradition, who migrated from W China in the 17th century **2** the language of this people, belonging to the Mongolic branch of the Altaic family

Kalmuck Republic *or* **Kalmyk Republic** *n* a constituent republic of S Russia, on the Caspian Sea: became subject to Russia in 1646. Capital: Elista. Pop: 292 400 (2002). Area: 76 100 sq km (29 382 sq miles). Also called: **Kalmykia**

kalong (ˈkɑːlɒŋ) *n* any fruit bat of the genus *Pteropus*; a flying fox [Javanese]

kalpa (ˈkælpə) *n* (in Hindu cosmology) a period in which the universe experiences a cycle of creation and destruction [c18 Sanskrit]

kalpak (ˈkælpæk) *n* a variant spelling of **calpac**

kalsomine (ˈkælsəˌmaɪn, -mɪn) *n, vb* a variant of **calcimine**

Kaluga (*Russian* kaˈluɡə) *n* a city in central Russia, on the Oka River. Pop: 340 000 (2005 est)

Kama[1] (*Russian* ˈkamə) *n* a river in central Russia, rising in the Ural Mountains and flowing to the River Volga, of which it is the largest tributary. Length: 2030 km (1260 miles)

Kama[2] (ˈkɑːmə) *n* the Hindu god of love [from Sanskrit]

kamacite (ˈkæməˌsaɪt) *n* an alloy of iron and nickel, occurring in meteorites [c19 from (obsolete) German *Kamacit*, from Greek *kamax* shaft, pole + -ɪᴛᴇ[1]]

kamahi (ˈkɑːmɑːhiː) *n, pl* **kamahi** a tall New Zealand hardwood tree, *Weinmannia racemosa*, with pinkish flowers [Māori]

Kamakura (ˌkæməˈkʊərə) *n* a city in central

Japan, on S Honshu: famous for its Great Buddha (Daibutsu), a 13th-century bronze, 15 m (49 ft) high. Pop: 169 714 (2002 est)

kamala (kə'mɑːlə, 'kæmələ) *n* **1** an East Indian euphorbiaceous tree, *Mallotus philippinensis* **2** a powder obtained from the seed capsules of this tree, used as a dye and formerly as a worm powder [C19 from Sanskrit, probably of Dravidian origin; compare Kanarese *kōmale*]

Kama Sutra (ˌkɑːmə 'suːtrə) *n* **the** an ancient Hindu text on erotic pleasure and other topics [Sanskrit: book on love, from *kāma* love + *sūtra* thread]

Kamchatka (*Russian* kam'tʃatkə) *n* a peninsula in E Russia, between the Sea of Okhotsk and the Bering Sea. Length: about 1200 km (750 miles)

Kamchatkan (*Russian* kam'tʃatkən) *adj* **1** of or relating to Kamchatka, a peninsula in E Russia, or its inhabitants ▷ *n* **2** a native or inhabitant of Kamchatka

kame (keɪm) *n* an irregular mound or ridge of gravel, sand, etc, deposited by water derived from melting glaciers [C19 Scottish and northern English variant of COMB]

kameez (kə'miːz) *n* (*pl* **-meez** or **-meezes**) a long tunic worn in the Indian subcontinent, often with shalwar [Urdu *kamis*, from Arabic *qamīs*]

Kamensk-Uralski (*Russian* 'kamınsku'raljskij) *n* an industrial city in S Russia. Pop: 183 000 (2005 est)

Kamerad *German* (kamə'raːt; *English* 'kæmə,rɑːd) *sentence substitute* a shout of surrender, used by German soldiers [German: COMRADE]

Kamerun ('kaməruːn) *n* the German name for **Cameroon**

Kamet ('kɑːmɛt, 'kʌmeɪt) *n* a mountain on the border of China and India, west of Nepal in the Himalayas. Height: 7756 m (25 447 ft)

kami ('kɑːmɪ) *n, pl* **-mi** a divine being or spiritual force in Shinto [C18 from Japanese: god, lord]

kamik ('kɑːmɪk) *n Canadian* a traditional Inuit boot made of caribou hide or sealskin [from Inuktitut]

kamikaze (ˌkæmɪ'kɑːzɪ) *n* (*often capital*) **1** (in World War II) one of a group of Japanese pilots who performed suicidal missions by crashing their aircraft, loaded with explosives, into an enemy target, esp a ship **2** an aircraft used for such a mission **3** (*modifier*) (of an action) undertaken or (of a person) undertaking an action in the knowledge that it will result in the death of the person performing it in order that maximum damage may be inflicted on an enemy: *a kamikaze attack; a kamikaze bomber* **4** (*modifier*) extremely foolhardy and possibly self-defeating: *kamikaze pricing* [C20 from Japanese, from *kami* divine + *kaze* wind, referring to the winds that, according to Japanese tradition, destroyed a Mongol invasion fleet in 1281]

Kamilaroi ('kæmələrɔɪ) *n* an Australian Aboriginal language formerly used in NW New South Wales

Kamloops trout ('kæm,luːps) *n Canadian* a variety of rainbow trout found in Canadian lakes

kamokamo (kɑːməʊkə:məʊ) *n, pl* **kamokamo** a New Zealand marrow of the family *Cucurbitaceae.* Also called: **kumikumi** [Māori]

Kampala (kæm'paːlə) *n* the capital and largest city of Uganda, in Central region on Lake Victoria: Makerere University (1961). Pop: 1 208 544 (2002 est)

kampong ('kæmpɒŋ, kæm'pɒŋ) *n* (in Malaysia) a village [C19 from Malay]

Kampuchea (ˌkæmpʊ'tʃɪə) *n* the name of Cambodia from 1976 until 1989

Kampuchean (ˌkæmpʊ'tʃɪən) *adj* **1** of or relating to Kampuchea, a former name for Cambodia, or its inhabitants ▷ *n* **2** a native or inhabitant of Kampuchea

kamseen (kæm'siːn) *or* **kamsin** ('kæmsɪn) *n* variants of **khamsin**

Kan. *abbreviation for* Kansas

kana ('kɑːnə) *n* the Japanese syllabary, which consists of two written varieties. See **hiragana, katakana** [C18 from Japanese, literally: borrowed or provisional letters; compare KANJI, which are regarded as real letters]

kanae (kɑːnɑːiː) *n, pl* **kanae** *NZ* another name for **grey mullet** [Māori]

Kanak (kə'næk) *n* a native or inhabitant of New Caledonia who seeks independence from France [C20 from Hawaiian: man]

Kanaka (kə'nækə, 'kænəkə) *n* **1** (esp in Hawaii) a native Hawaiian **2** (*often not capital*) *Austral* any native of the South Pacific islands, esp (formerly) one abducted to work in Australia [C19 from Hawaiian: man, human being]

kanamycin (ˌkænə'maɪsɪn) *n* an aminoglycoside antibiotic obtained from the soil bacterium *Streptomyces kanamyceticus,* used in the treatment of various infections, esp those caused by Gram-negative bacteria. Formula: $C_{18}H_{36}N_4O_{11}$ [C20 from New Latin *kanamyceticus*]

Kananga (kə'næŋgə) *n* a city in the SW Democratic Republic of Congo (formerly Zaïre): a commercial centre on the railway from Lubumbashi to Port Francqui. Pop: 424 000 (2005 est). Former name (until 1966): Luluabourg

Kanara *or* **Canara** (kə'nɑːrə) *n* a region of SW India, in Karnataka on the Deccan Plateau and the W Coast. Area: about 155 000 sq km (60 000 sq miles)

Kanarese *or* **Canarese** (ˌkænə'riːz) *n* **1** (*pl* **-rese**) a member of a people of S India living chiefly in Kanara **2** the language of this people; Kannada

Kanazawa (ˌkænə'zɑːwə) *n* a port in central Japan, on W Honshu: textile and porcelain industries. Pop: 439 892 (2002 est)

kanban *Japanese* ('kænbæn) *n* **1** a just-in-time manufacturing process in which the movements of materials through a process are recorded on specially designed cards **2** any of the cards used for ordering materials in such a system [literally: advertisement hoarding]

Kanchenjunga (ˌkænʧən'dʒʌŋgə) *n* a variant spelling of **Kangchenjunga**

Kanchipuram (kɑːn'tʃiːpərəm) *n* a city in SE India, in Tamil Nadu: a sacred Hindu town known as "the Benares of the South"; textile industries. Pop: 152 984 (2001)

Kandahar (ˌkændə'hɑː) *n* a city in S Afghanistan: an important trading centre, built by Ahmad Shah Durrani (1724–73) as his capital on the site of several former cities. Pop: 436 000 (2005 est)

Kandy ('kændɪ) *n* a city in central Sri Lanka: capital of the kingdom of Kandy from 1480 until 1815, when occupied by the British; sacred Buddhist temple; University of Sri Lanka. Pop: 112 000 (2005 est)

kanga *or* **khanga** ('kɑːŋgɑː) *n* a piece of gaily decorated thin cotton cloth used as a garment by women in E Africa [from Swahili]

kanga pirau ('kɑːˀŋgɑː 'piːrɑːuː) *n NZ* fermented corn used as food [Māori]

kangaroo (ˌkæŋgə'ruː) *n, pl* **-roos** **1** any large herbivorous marsupial of the genus *Macropus* and related genera, of Australia and New Guinea, having large powerful hind legs, used for leaping, and a long thick tail: family *Macropodidae.* See also **rat kangaroo, tree kangaroo 2** (*usually plural*) *stock exchange* an Australian share, esp in mining, land, or a tobacco company ▷ *vb* **-roos, -rooing, -rooed 3** *informal* (of a car) to move forward or to cause (a car) to move forward with short sudden jerks, as a result of improper use of the clutch [C18 probably from a native Australian language] ▷ ˌkanga'roo-ˌlike *adj*

kangaroo closure *n parliamentary procedure* a form of closure in which the chairman or speaker selects certain amendments for discussion and excludes others. Compare **guillotine** (sense 4)

kangaroo court *n* an irregular court, esp one set up by prisoners in a jail or by strikers to judge strikebreakers

kangaroo dog *n* an Australian breed of large rough-haired dog that resembles a greyhound and is bred to hunt kangaroos

kangaroo grass *n* a tall widespread Australian grass, *Themeda australis,* which is highly palatable to cattle and is used for fodder

Kangaroo Island *n* an island in the Indian Ocean, off South Australia. Area: 4350 sq km (1680 sq miles)

kangaroo paw *n* any plant of the Australian genus *Anigozanthos,* resembling a kangaroo's paw, esp the red-and-green flowered *A.manglesii,* which is the floral emblem of Western Australia: family *Haemodoraceae*

kangaroo rat *n* **1** any small leaping rodent of the genus *Dipodomys,* related to the squirrels and inhabiting desert regions of North America, having a stocky body and very long hind legs and tails: family *Heteromyidae* **2** Also called: **kangaroo mouse** any of several leaping murine rodents of the Australian genus *Notomys*

kangaroo vine *n* See **cissus**

Kangchenjunga, Kanchenjunga (ˌkæntʃən'dʒʌŋgə) *or* **Kinchinjunga** *n* a mountain on the border between Nepal and Sikkim, in the Himalayas: the third highest mountain in the world. Height: 8598 m (28 208 ft)

Kangha ('kʌŋhə) *n* the comb traditionally worn by Sikhs as a symbol of their religious and cultural loyalty: originally worn to keep the hair clean. See also **five Ks** [Punjabi *kanghā*]

KaNgwane (ˌkɑːˀŋ'gwɑːneɪ) *n* (formerly) a Bantu homeland in South Africa; replaced in 1994. Capital: Schoemansdal. Former name: Swazi Territory

kanji ('kændʒɪ, 'kɑːn-) *n, pl* **-ji** or **-jis 1** a Japanese writing system using characters mainly derived from Chinese ideograms **2** a character in this system [Japanese, from Chinese *han* Chinese + *zi* character]

Kannada ('kɑːnədə, 'kæn-) *n* a language of S India belonging to the Dravidian family of languages: the state language of Karnataka, also spoken in Madras and Maharashtra. Also called: **Kanarese**

Kannon (kɑnon) *n* the Japanese name for **Kuan Yin**

Kano ('kɑːnəʊ, 'keɪnəʊ) *n* **1** a state of N Nigeria: consists of wooded savanna in the south and scrub vegetation in the north. Capital: Kano. Pop: 2 884 000 (2005 est). Area: 20 131 sq km (7773 sq miles) **2** a city in N Nigeria, capital of Kano state: transport and market centre. Pop: 674 100 (1996 est)

Kanpur (kɑːn'pʊə) *n* an industrial city in NE India, in S Uttar Pradesh on the River Ganges: scene of the massacre by Nana Sahib of British soldiers and European families and his later defeat by British forces in 1857. Pop: 2 532 138 (2001). Former name: Cawnpore

Kansan ('kænzən) *n* **1** a native or inhabitant of Kansas ▷ *adj* **2** of or relating to Kansas or its inhabitants

Kansas ('kænzəs) *n* a state of the central US: consists of undulating prairie, drained chiefly by the Arkansas, Kansas, and Missouri Rivers; mainly agricultural. Capital: Topeka. Pop: 2 723 507 (2003 est). Area: 213 096 sq km (82 277 sq miles). Abbreviations: **Kan, Kans,** (with zip code) **KS**

Kansas City *n* **1** a city in W Missouri, at the confluence of the Missouri and Kansas Rivers: important centre of livestock and meat-packing industry. Pop: 442 768 (2003 est) **2** a city in NE Kansas, adjacent to Kansas City, Missouri. Pop: 145 757 (2003 est)

Kansu ('kæn'suː) *n* a variant transliteration of the Chinese name for **Gansu**

kantar (kæn'tɑː) *n* a unit of weight used in E Mediterranean countries, equivalent to 100 pounds or 45 kilograms but varying from place to place [C16 from Arabic *qintār,* from Late Greek *kentēnarion* weight of a hundred pounds, from Late

k

Latin *centēnārium,* from *centum* hundred]

Kantian ('kæntɪən) *adj* (of a philosophical theory) derived from or analogous to a position of the German idealist philosopher Immanuel Kant (1724–1804), esp his doctrines that there are synthetic a priori propositions which order our experience but are not derived from it, that metaphysical conclusions can be inferred from the nature of possible experience, that duty is to be done for its own sake and not as a means to any other end, and that there is a world of things-in-themselves to be distinguished from mere phenomena. See also **transcendental argument, transcendental idealism, categorical imperative, noumenon.** ▷ 'Kantian,ism *or* 'Kantism *n*

KANU ('ka:nu:) *n acronym for* Kenya African National Union

kanuka ('ka:nu:kə) *n, pl* kanuka a New Zealand myrtaceous tree, *Leptospermum Ericoides,* with aromatic leaves. Also called: **white tea tree** [Māori]

kanzu ('kænzʊ) *n* a long garment, usually white, with long sleeves, worn by E African men [c20 from Swahili]

Kaohsiung, Kao-hsiung ('kaʊ'ʃjʊŋ) *or* **Gaoxiong** *n* a port in SW Taiwan, on the South China Sea: the chief port of the island. Pop: 1 506 000 (2005 est). Japanese name: Takao

Kaolack ('ka:əʊ,læk, 'kaʊlæk) *n* a port in SW Senegal, on the Saloum River. Pop: 299 000 (2005 est)

kaoliang (,keɪəʊlɪ'æŋ) *n* any of various E Asian varieties of the sorghum *Sorghum vulgare* [from Chinese *kao* tall + *liang* grain]

kaolin *or* **kaoline** ('keɪəlɪn) *n* a fine white clay used for the manufacture of hard-paste porcelain and bone china and in medicine as a poultice and gastrointestinal absorbent. Also called: **china clay, china stone** [c18 from French, from Chinese *Kaoling* Chinese mountain where supplies for Europe were first obtained, from *kao* high + *ling* hill] ▷ ,kao'linic *adj*

kaolinite ('keɪəlɪ,naɪt) *n* a white or grey clay mineral consisting of hydrated aluminium silicate in triclinic crystalline form, the main constituent of kaolin. Formula: $Al_2Si_2O_5(OH)_4$

kaon ('keɪɒn) *n* a meson that has a positive or negative charge and a rest mass of about 966 electron masses, or no charge and a rest mass of 974 electron masses. Also called: **K-meson** [c20 *ka* representing the letter *k* + (MES)ON]

kapa haka ('ka:pə 'ha:kə) *n* NZ the traditional Māori performing arts, often performed competitively [Māori, literally: traditional dance performed by groups in a line]

ka pai (,kə 'paɪ) *sentence substitute* NZ good! well done! [Māori]

kapellmeister (kæ'pɛl,maɪstə) *n, pl* -ter a variant spelling of **capellmeister**

Kapfenberg (German 'kapfənbɛrk) *n* an industrial town in E Austria, in Styria. Pop: 22 234 (2001)

kaph (kɔːf, ka:f; *Hebrew* kaf) *n* the 11th letter of the Hebrew alphabet (כ or, at the end of a word, ך) transliterated as *k* or, when final, *kh* [Hebrew, literally: palm of the hand]

kapok ('keɪpɒk) *n* a silky fibre obtained from the hairs covering the seeds of a tropical bombacaceous tree, *Ceiba pentandra* (**kapok tree** or **silk-cotton tree**): used for stuffing pillows, etc, and for sound insulation. Also called: **silk cotton** [c18 from Malay]

Kaposi's sarcoma (kæ'pəʊsɪz) *n* a form of skin cancer found in Africans and more recently in victims of AIDS [c20 named after Moritz Kohn *Kaposi* (1837–1902), Austrian dermatologist who first described the sores that characterize the disease]

kappa ('kæpə) *n* the tenth letter in the Greek alphabet (K, κ), a consonant, transliterated as *c* or *k* [Greek, of Semitic origin]

kapuka (ka:pu:kə) *n, pl* kapuka NZ another name for **broadleaf** (sense 2) [Māori]

kaput (kæ'pʊt) *adj* (*postpositive*) *informal* ruined, broken, or not functioning [c20 from German *kaputt* done for, from French *être capot* to have made no tricks (literally: to be hoodwinked), from *capot* hooded cloak]

Kara ('ka:rə) *n* the steel bangle traditionally worn by Sikhs as a symbol of their religious and cultural loyalty, symbolizing unity with God: originally worn as a wristguard by swordsmen. See also **five Ks** [Punjabi *karā*]

karabiner (,kærə'bi:nə) *n mountaineering* a metal clip with a spring for attaching to a piton, belay, etc. Also called: **snaplink, krab** [shortened from German *Karabinerhaken,* literally: carbine hook, that is, one used to attach carbines to a belt]

Karachai-Cherkess Republic (kərʌ'tʃaɪtʃɛə'kɛs) *or* **Karachayevo-Cherkess Republic** (kərʌ'tʃaɪɛvəʊtʃɛə'kɛs) *n* a constituent republic of W Russia, on the N side of the Caucasus Mountains. Capital: Cherkessk. Pop: 439 700 (2002). Area: 14 100 sq km (5440 sq miles). Also called: **Karachai-Cherkessia** (kərʌ,tʃaɪtʃɛə'kɛsɪə)

Karachi (kə'ra:tʃɪ) *n* a port in S Pakistan, on the Arabian Sea: capital of Pakistan (1947–60); university (1950); chief port: commercial and industrial centre. Pop: 11 819 000 (2005 est)

Karafuto (,ka:ra:'fu:tɔ) *n* transliteration of the Japanese name for **Sakhalin**

Karaganda (*Russian* kərəgan'da) *n* a city in E central Kazakhstan, founded in 1857: a major coal-mining and industrial centre. Pop: 412 000 (2005 est). Also called: **Qaraghandy**

Karaite ('kɛərə,aɪt) *n* **1** a member of a Jewish sect originating in the 8th century AD, which rejected the Talmud, favoured strict adherence to and a literal interpretation of the Bible, and attempted to deduce a code of life from it ▷ *adj* **2** of, relating to, or designating the Karaite sect [c18 from Hebrew *qārāīm* members of the sect, scripturalists, from *qārā* to read]

karaka (kə'ra:kə) *n, pl* karaka a common coastal New Zealand tree, *Corynocarpus laevigatus,* with orange fruits and seeds which are poisonous unless cooked [Māori]

Kara-Kalpak (kə'ra:kəl'pa:k) *n* **1** (*pl* -paks *or* -pak) a member of a Mongoloid people of central Asia **2** the language of this people, belonging to the Turkic branch of the Altaic family

Kara-Kalpak Autonomous Republic (kə'ra:kəl'pa:k) *n* an administrative division in NW Uzbekistan, on the Aral Sea: came under Russian rule by stages from 1873 until Uzbekistan became independent in 1991. Capital: Nukus. Pop: 1 633 900 (2002 est). Area: 165 600 sq km (63 900 sq miles). Also called: **Kara-Kalpakia** (kə'ra:kəl'pa:kɪə), **Kara-Kalpakstan** (kə'ra:kəl,pa:k,stæn, -'sta:n)

karakia (,ka:rə'ki:ə) *n* NZ a prayer [Māori]

Karakoram *or* **Karakorum** (,kærə'kɔ:rəm) *n* a mountain system in N Kashmir, extending for about 480 km (300 miles) from northwest to southeast: contains the second highest peak in the world (K2); crossed by several high passes, notably the **Karakoram Pass** 5575 m (18 290 ft)

Karakorum (,kærə'kɔ:rəm) *n* a ruined city in Mongolia: founded in 1220 by Ghenghis Khan; destroyed by Kublai Khan when his brother rebelled against him, after Kublai Khan had moved his capital to Peking (now Beijing)

karakul *or* **caracul** ('kærək°l) *n* **1** a breed of sheep of central Asia having coarse black, grey, or brown hair: the lambs have soft curled usually black hair **2** the fur prepared from these lambs ▷ See also **Persian lamb** [c19 from Russian, from the name of a region in Bukhara where the sheep originated]

Kara Kum (*Russian* kərə 'kuːm) *n* a desert in Turkmenistan, covering most of the country: extensive areas now irrigated. Area: about 300 000 sq km (120 000 sq miles)

karamu (ka:ra:'mu:) *n* a small New Zealand tree, *Coprosma robusta,* with glossy leaves and orange fruit [Māori]

karanga (kə'ræŋə) NZ ▷ *n* **1** a call or chant of welcome, sung by a female elder ▷ *vb* **2** (*intr*) to perform a karanga [Māori]

karaoke (,ka:rə'əʊkɪ) *n* **a** an entertainment of Japanese origin in which people take it in turns to sing well-known songs over a prerecorded backing tape **b** (*as modifier*): *a karaoke bar* [from Japanese, from *kara* empty + *ōkesutora* orchestra]

Kara Sea ('ka:rə) *n* a shallow arm of the Arctic Ocean off the N coast of Russia: ice-free for about three months of the year

karat ('kærət) *n* US and Canadian a measure of the proportion of gold in an alloy, expressed as the number of parts of gold in 24 parts of the alloy. Also spelt (in Britain and certain other countries): **carat** [c16 from Old French, from Medieval Latin *carratus,* from Arabic *qīrāt* weight of four grains, carat, from Greek *keration* a little horn, from *keras* horn]

karate (kə'ra:tɪ) *n* **a** a traditional Japanese system of unarmed combat, employing smashes, chops, kicks, etc, made with the hands, feet, elbows, or legs **b** (*as modifier*): *a karate chop to the head* [Japanese, literally: empty hand, from *kara* empty + *te* hand]

karateka (kə'ra:tɪ,kæ) *n* a competitor or expert in karate [Japanese; see KARATE]

Karbala ('ka:bələ) *or* **Kerbela** *n* a town in central Iraq: the chief holy city of Iraq and centre of Shiah Muslim pilgrimage; burial place of Mohammed's grandson Husain. Pop: 460 000 (2005 est)

karearea (kə'rɛərɛə) *n, pl* karearea a New Zealand falcon, *Falco novaeseelandiae.* Also called: **bush-hawk** [Māori]

Karelia (kə'ri:lɪə; *Russian* ka'reljə) *n* **1** a region of NE Europe comprising areas of both Finland and Russia. Following the Russo-Finnish War (1939–40) a large part of what had been Finnish Karelia was annexed by the former Soviet Union; together with the part of Karelia which already belonged to Russia at that time, it corresponds roughly to the modern Karelian Republic in Russia **2** another name for the **Karelian Republic**

Karelian (kə'ri:lɪən) *adj* **1** of or relating to Karelia, its people, or their language ▷ *n* **2** a native or inhabitant of Karelia **3** the dialect of Finnish spoken in Karelia

Karelian Isthmus *n* a strip of land, now in Russia, between the Gulf of Finland and Lake Ladoga: annexed by the former Soviet Union after the Russo-Finnish War (1939–40)

Karelian Republic *n* a constituent republic of NW Russia between the White Sea and Lakes Onega and Ladoga. Capital: Petrozavodsk. Pop: 716 700 (2002). Area: 172 400 sq km (66 560 sq miles). Also called: **Karelia**

Karen (kə'rɛn) *n* **1** (*pl* -rens *or* -ren) a member of a Thai people of Myanmar **2** the language of this people, probably related to Thai and belonging to the Sino-Tibetan family

karengo ('ka:rə°ŋgəʊ) *n* an edible Pacific seaweed, *Porphyra columbina* [Māori]

Kariba (kə'ri:bə) *n* **Lake** a lake on the Zambia-Zimbabwe border, created by the building of the **Kariba Dam** across the Zambezi for hydroelectric power. Length: 282 km (175 miles)

Karitane (,kærɪ'ta:nɪ) *n* short for **Karitane nurse**

Karitane hospital *n* NZ a hospital for young babies and their mothers [from *Karitane,* a town on South Island, New Zealand, headquarters of the PLUNKET SOCIETY]

Karitane nurse *n* NZ a nurse trained in the care of young babies and their mothers according to the principles of the Plunket Society. Often shortened to: **Karitane**

Karl-Marx Stadt (*German* karl'marksʃtat) *n* the former name (1953–90) of **Chemnitz**

Karlovy Vary (*Czech* 'karlovi 'vari) *n* a city in the W Czech Republic, at the confluence of the Tepla and Ohře Rivers: warm mineral springs. Pop: 56 290 (1991). German name: Karlsbad or Carlsbad ('karlsba:t)

Karlskrona (ˈkɑːlsˌkrəʊnə) *n* a port in S Sweden: Sweden's main naval base since 1680. Pop: 61 097 (2004 est)

Karlsruhe (*German* ˈkɑːlsruːə) *n* a city in SW Germany, in Baden-Württemberg: capital of the former Baden state. Pop: 282 595 (2003 est)

karma (ˈkɑːmə) *n* **1** *Hinduism, Buddhism* the principle of retributive justice determining a person's state of life and the state of his reincarnations as the effect of his past deeds **2** *theosophy* the doctrine of inevitable consequence **3** destiny or fate [c19 from Sanskrit: action, effect, from *karoti* he does] > ˈkarmic *adj*

Kármán vortex street (ˈkɑːmən) *n* a regular stream of vortices shed from a body placed in a fluid stream: investigated by Kármán who advanced a formula for the frequency of the shed vortices in terms of the stream velocity and the dimensions of the body. See also **vortex street** [named after Theodore Von *Kármán* (1881–1963), Hungarian-born engineer]

Karmapa (ˈkɑːməpə) *or* **Karmapa Lama** *n* the head of the Kagyupa, Karma Kagyu or Black Hat sect of Tibetan Buddhism, third in importance in the hierarchy of lamas

Karnak (ˈkɑːnæk) *n* a village in E Egypt, on the Nile: site of the N part of the ruins of ancient Thebes

Karnataka (kəˈnɑːtəkə) *n* a state of S India, on the Arabian Sea: consists of a narrow coastal plain rising to the South Deccan plateau; mainly agricultural. Capital: Bangalore. Pop: 52 733 958 (2001). Area: 191 791 sq km (74 051 sq miles). Former name (1956–73): **Mysore**

Karnatak music (kəˈnɑːtək) *n* the classical music of South India

Kärnten (ˈkɛrntən) *n* the German name for **Carinthia**

karo (ˈkɑːrɒ) *n*, *pl* karo a small New Zealand tree or shrub, *Pittosporum crassifolium* with sweet-smelling brown flowers [Māori]

Karoo *or* **Karroo** (kəˈruː) *n*, *pl* -roos (*often not capital*) **1** any of several high arid plateaus in South Africa, esp the **Central Karoo** and the **Little Karoo**. The highveld, north of the Central Karoo, is sometimes called the **Northern Karoo 2** a period or rock system in Southern Africa equivalent to the period or system extending from the Upper Carboniferous to the Lower Jurassic: divided into **Lower** and **Upper Karoo** ▷ *adj* **3** of, denoting, or formed in the Karoo period [c18 from Afrikaans *karo,* probably from Khoikhoi *garo* desert]

karoro (ˈkɑːrəʊrəʊ) *n*, *pl* karoros a large seagull, *Laris dominicanus,* with black feathers on its back [Māori]

karoshi (kaˈrəʊʃi) *n* (in Japan) death caused by overwork [from Japanese *ka* excess + *ro* labour + *shi* death]

kaross (kəˈrɒs) *n* a garment of skins worn by indigenous peoples in southern Africa [c18 from Afrikaans *karos,* perhaps from Dutch *kuras,* from French *cuirasse* CUIRASS]

karri (ˈkɑːrɪ) *n*, *pl* -ris **1** an Australian eucalyptus tree, *Eucalyptus diversifolia* **2** the durable wood of this tree, used esp for construction [from a native Australian language]

karst (kɑːst) *n* (*modifier*) denoting the characteristic scenery of a limestone region, including underground streams, gorges, etc [c19 German, from *Karst,* limestone plateau near Trieste] > ˈkarstic *adj*

kart (kɑːt) *n* a light low-framed vehicle with small wheels and engine used for recreational racing. Also called: **go-cart, go-kart**

karuhiruhi (kɑːruːhiːruːhiː) *n*, *pl* karuhiruhi another name for **pied shag** [Māori]

karyo- *or* **caryo-** *combining form* indicating the nucleus of a cell: *karyogamy* [from New Latin, from Greek *karuon* kernel, nut]

karyogamy (ˌkærɪˈɒgəmɪ) *n* *biology* the fusion of two gametic nuclei during fertilization

> **karyogamic** (ˌkærɪəˈgæmɪk) *adj*

karyogram (ˈkærɪəʊˌgræm) *n* a diagram or photograph of the chromosomes of a cell, arranged in homologous pairs and in a numbered sequence. Also called: **idiogram**

karyokinesis (ˌkærɪəʊkɪˈniːsɪs, -kaɪ-) *n* the division of a cell nucleus in mitosis or meiosis [c19 from KARYO- + Greek *kinēsis* movement] > **karyokinetic** (ˌkærɪəʊkɪˈnɛtɪk, -kaɪ-) *adj*

karyology (ˌkærɪˈɒlədʒɪ) *n* the study of cell nuclei, esp with reference to the number and shape of the chromosomes > ˌkaryˈologist *n*

karyolymph (ˈkærɪəʊˌlɪmf) *n* the liquid portion of the nucleus of a cell

karyolysis (ˌkærɪˈɒlɪsɪs) *n* *cytology* the disintegration of a cell nucleus, which occurs on death of the cell [c20 from Greek, from *karyon* a nut + -LYSIS] > **karyolytic** (ˌkærɪəˈlɪtɪk) *adj*

karyoplasm (ˈkærɪəʊˌplæzəm) *n* another name for **nucleoplasm**. > ˌkaryoˈplasmic *adj*

karyosome (ˈkærɪəʊˌsəʊm) *n* **1** any of the dense aggregates of chromatin in the nucleus of a cell **2** the nucleus of a cell

karyotin (ˌkærɪˈəʊtɪn) *n* a less common word for **chromatin** [from KARYO- + (CHROMA)TIN]

karyotype (ˈkærɪəˌtaɪp) *n* **1** the appearance of the chromosomes in a somatic cell of an individual or species, with reference to their number, size, shape, etc ▷ *vb* (*tr*) **2** to determine the karyotype of (a cell) > **karyotypic** (ˌkærɪəˈtɪpɪk) *or* ˌkaryoˈtypical *adj*

Kasai (kɑːˈsaɪ) *n* a river in southwestern Africa, rising in central Angola and flowing east then north as part of the border between Angola and the Democratic Republic of Congo (formerly Zaïre), continuing northwest through the Democratic Republic of Congo to the River Congo. Length: 2154 km (1338 miles)

kasbah *or* **casbah** (ˈkæzbɑː) *n* (*sometimes capital*) **1** the citadel of any of various North African cities **2** the quarter in which a kasbah is located. Compare **medina** [from Arabic *qaṣba* citadel]

kasha (ˈkɑːʃə) *n* a dish originating in Eastern Europe, consisting of boiled or baked buckwheat [from Russian]

kasher *Hebrew* (ˈkɑːʃə) *vb* (*tr*) *Judaism* to make fit for use; render kosher: for instance, to remove excess blood from (meat) by the prescribed process of washing and salting, or to remove all trace of previous nonkosher substances from (a utensil) by heating, immersion, etc. See also **kosher** [see KOSHER]

Kashi (ˈkɑːʃiː) *or* **Kashgar** (ˈkɑːʃgɑː) *n* an oasis city in W China, in W Xinjiang Uygur AR. Pop: 318 000 (2005 est)

kashmir (ˈkæʃmɪə) *n* a variant spelling of **cashmere**

Kashmir (kæʃˈmɪə) *n* a region of SW central Asia: from the 16th century ruled by the Moguls, Afghans, Sikhs, and British successively; since 1947 disputed between India, Pakistan, and China; 84 000 sq km (33 000 sq miles) in the northwest are held by Pakistan and in part known as Azad Kashmir (Free Kashmir), part as the Northern Areas; an area of 42 735 sq km (16 496 sq miles) in the east (the Aksai Chin) is held by China; the remainder was in 1956 officially incorporated into India as the state of Jammu and Kashmir; traversed by the Himalaya and Karakoram mountain ranges and the Rivers Jhelum and Indus; a fruit-growing and cattle-grazing region, with a woollen industry. Capitals: (Jammu and Kashmir) Srinagar (summer), Jammu (winter); (Azad Kashmir) Muzaffarabad; (Northern Areas) Gilgit

Kashmir goat *n* a Himalayan breed of goat having an undercoat of silky wool from which cashmere wool is obtained

Kashmiri (kæʃˈmɪərɪ) *adj* **1** of or relating to Kashmir, its people, or their language ▷ *n* **2** (*pl* -miris *or* -miri) a member of the people of Kashmir **3** the state language of Kashmir, belonging to the Dardic group of the Indo-European family of languages

Kashmirian (kæʃˈmɪərɪən) *adj* **1** of or relating to Kashmir, its people, or their language ▷ *n* **2** a member of the people of Kashmir

kashruth *or* **kashrut** *Hebrew* (kaʃˈruːt) *n* **1** the condition of being fit for ritual use in general **2** the system of dietary laws which require ritual slaughter, the removal of excess blood from meat, and the complete separation of milk and meat, and prohibit such foods as pork and shellfish ▷ See also **kosher** (sense 1) [literally: appropriateness, fitness]

kasme (ˈɡʌsmiː) *interj* *Hinglish* I swear! [c21 Hindi *Kasam-se,* Urdu *kasme*]

Kassa (ˈkɒʃʃɒ) *n* the Hungarian name for **Košice**

Kassala (kəˈsɑːlə) *n* a city in the E Sudan: founded as a fort by the Egyptians in 1834. Pop: 430 000 (2005 est)

Kassel *or* **Cassel** (*German* ˈkasəl) *n* a city in central Germany, in Hesse; capital of Westphalia (1807–13) and of the Prussian province of Hesse-Nassau (1866–1945). Pop: 194 322 (2003 est)

Kastrop-Rauxel (*German* ˈkastrɔpˈrauksəl) *n* a variant spelling of **Castrop-Rauxel**

kat (kæt, kɑːt) *n* a variant spelling of **khat**

kata (ˈkætə) *n* an exercise consisting of a sequence of the specific movements of a martial art, used in training and designed to show skill in technique [c20 Japanese, literally: shape, pattern]

kata- *prefix* a variant of **cata-**

katabasis (kəˈtæbəsɪs) *n*, *pl* -ses (-ˌsiːz) **1** the retreat of the Greek mercenaries of Cyrus the Younger, after his death at Cunaxa, from the Euphrates to the Black Sea in 401–400 BC under the leadership of Xenophon: recounted in his *Anabasis*. Compare **anabasis 2** *literary* a retreat [c19 from Greek: a going down, from *katabainein* to go down]

katabatic (ˌkætəˈbætɪk) *adj* (of winds) blowing downhill through having become denser with cooling, esp at night when heat is lost from the earth's surface. Compare **anabatic**

katabolism (kəˈtæbəˌlɪzəm) *n* a variant spelling of **catabolism**. > **katabolic** (ˌkætəˈbɒlɪk) *adj* > ˌkataˈbolically *adv*

katakana (ˌkɑːtəˈkɑːnə) *n* one of the two systems of syllabic writing employed for the representation of Japanese, based on Chinese ideograms. It is used mainly for foreign or foreign-derived words [Japanese, from *kata* side + KANA]

katana (kəˈtɑːnə) *n* a long, curved single-edged sword traditionally used by Japanese samurai [c18 Japanese]

Katanga (kəˈtæŋgə) *n* a region of SE Democratic Republic of Congo (formerly Zaïre): site of a secessionist movement during the 1960s and again in 1993; important for hydroelectric power and rich mineral resources (copper and tin ore). Pop: 4 125 000 (1998 est). Area: 496 964 sq km (191 878 sq miles). Former name (1972–97): **Shaba**

Katar (kæˈtɑː) *n* a variant spelling of **Qatar**

Katari (kæˈtɑːrɪ) *adj, n* a variant spelling of **Qatari**

Kathak (ˈkɑːtək) *n* a form of N Indian classical dancing that tells a story [Bengali: narrator, from Sanskrit *kathayati* he tells]

Kathakali (ˌkɑːtəˈkɑːlɪ) *n*, *pl* -lis a form of dance drama of S India using mime and based on Hindu literature [from Malayalam, from *katha* story + *kali* play]

Katharevusa *or* **Katharevousa** (ˌkɑːθəˈrɛvəˌsɑː) *n* a literary style of Modern Greek, derived from the Attic dialect of Ancient Greek and including many archaic features. Compare **Demotic**

katharometer (ˌkæθəˈrɒmɪtə) *n* *chem* an instrument used for the analysis of gases by measurement of thermal conductivity

Kathiawar (ˌkætɪəˈwɑː) *n* a large peninsula of W India, in Gujarat between the Gulf of Kutch and the Gulf of Cambay. Area: about 60 690 sq km (23 430 sq miles)

k

katipo ('kætɪ,pəʊ, 'kɑːd-) *n, pl* **-pos** a small venomous spider, *Latrodectus katipo*, of New Zealand, commonly black with a red or orange stripe on the abdomen [Māori]

Katmai ('kætmaɪ) *n* **Mount** a volcano in SW Alaska, in the Aleutian Range: erupted in 1912 forming the Valley of Ten Thousand Smokes, a region with numerous fumaroles; established as **Katmai National Monument**, 10 917 sq km (4215 sq miles), in 1918. Height: 2100 m (7000 ft). Depth of crater: 1130 m (3700 ft). Width of crater: about 4 km (2.5 miles)

Katmandu *or* **Kathmandu** (,kætmæn'duː) *n* the capital of Nepal, in the east at the confluence of the Baghmati and Vishnumati Rivers. Pop: 814 000 (2005 est)

Katowice (*Polish* katɔ'vitsɛ) *n* an industrial city in S Poland. Pop: 2 914 000 (2005 est). Former name (1953–56): **Stalinogrod**

Katrine ('kætrɪn) *n* **Loch** a lake in central Scotland, east of Loch Lomond: noted for its associations with Sir Walter Scott's *Lady of the Lake*. Length: about 13 km (8 miles)

Katsina (kæt'siːnə) *n* a city in N Nigeria, in Kaduna state: a major intellectual and cultural centre of the Hausa people (16th–18th centuries). Pop: 530 000 (2005 est)

Kattegat ('kætɪ,gæt) *n* a strait between Denmark and Sweden: linked by the Sound, the Great Belt, and the Little Belt with the Baltic Sea and by the Skagerrak with the North Sea. Former spelling: **Cattegat**

katydid ('keɪtɪ,dɪd) *n* any typically green long-horned grasshopper of the genus *Microcentrum* and related genera, living among the foliage of trees in North America [c18 of imitative origin]

katzenjammer ('kætsən,dʒæmə) *n chiefly US* **1** a confused uproar **2** a hangover [German, literally: hangover, from *Katzen* cats + *jammer* misery, wailing]

Kauai (kɑː'wɑːiː) *n* a volcanic island in NW Hawaii, northwest of Oahu. Chief town: Lihue. Pop (Kauai county): 60 747 (2003 est). Area (island): 1433 sq km (553 sq miles)

kaumatua (kaʊ'mɑːtuːə) *n NZ* a senior member of a tribe; elder [Māori]

Kaunas ('kaʊnəs) *n* a city in central Lithuania at the confluence of the Neman and Viliya Rivers: ceded by Poland to Russia in 1795; became the provisional capital of Lithuania (1920–40); incorporated into the Soviet Union 1944–91; university (1922). Pop: 364 000 (2005 est). Russian name: **Kovno**

kaupapa (kaʊ'pɑːpə) *n NZ* a strategy, policy, or cause [Māori]

Kaur ('kaʊr) *n* a title assumed by a Sikh woman when she becomes a full member of the community [from Punjabi, literally: princess]

kauri ('kaʊrɪ) *n, pl* **-ris** **1** a New Zealand coniferous tree, *Agathis australis*, with oval leaves and round cones: family *Araucariaceae* **2** the wood or resin of this tree [c19 Māori]

kauri gum *n* a hard resin from the kauri tree, found usually as a fossil in the soil where an extinct tree once grew: used chiefly in making varnishes

kauru ('kɑːuːruː) *n, pl* **kauru** *NZ* the edible stem of the cabbage tree [Māori]

kava ('kɑːvə) *n* **1** a Polynesian shrub, *Piper methysticum*: family *Piperaceae* **2** a drink prepared from the aromatic roots of this shrub [c18 from Polynesian (Tongan): bitter]

Kaválla (kə'vælə; *Greek* ka'vala) *n* a port in E Greece, in Macedonia East and Thrace region on the **Bay of Kaválla** an important Macedonian fortress of the Byzantine empire; ceded to Greece by Turkey after the Balkan War (1912–13). Pop: 58 576 (1991). Ancient name: **Neapolis**

Kaveri ('kɔːvərɪ) *n* a variant spelling of **Cauvery**

Kavir Desert (kæ'vɪə) *n* another name for the **Dasht-i-Kavir**

kawa ('kɑːwə) *n NZ* protocol or etiquette, particularly in a Māori tribal meeting place [Māori]

kawakawa ('kɑːwə,kɑːwə) *n* an aromatic shrub or small tree of New Zealand, *Macropiper excelsum*: held to be sacred by the Māoris. Also called: **peppertree** [Māori]

kawanatanga ('kɑːwɑːnɑːtɑːᵊŋgɑː) *n NZ* governing; governorship [Māori]

Kawasaki (,kɑːwə'sɑːkɪ) *n* an industrial port in central Japan, on SE Honshu, between Tokyo and Yokohama. Pop: 1 245 780 (2002 est)

Kawasaki's disease (,kɑːwə'sɑːkɪ) *n* a disease of children that causes a rash, fever, and swelling of the lymph nodes and often damages the heart muscle [c20 named after T. *Kawasaki*, Japanese physician who first described it]

kawau (kɑːwɑːuː) *n, pl* **kawau** *NZ* another name for **black shag** [Māori]

Kay (keɪ) *n* **Sir** (in Arthurian legend) the braggart foster brother and steward of King Arthur

kayak *or* **kaiak** ('kaɪæk) *n* **1** a small light canoe-like boat used by the Inuit, consisting of a light frame covered with watertight animal skins **2** a fibreglass or canvas-covered canoe of similar design [c18 from Inuktitut (Greenland dialect)]

kaylied ('keɪliːd) *adj Brit slang* intoxicated; drunk

kayo *or* **KO** ('keɪ'əʊ) *n, pl* **kayos**, *vb* **kayoes** *or* **kayos, kayoing, kayoed** *boxing slang* another term for **knockout** *or* **knock out** [c20 from the initial letters of *knock out*]

Kayseri (,kaɪsɛ'riː; *Turkish* 'kaiseri) *n* a city in central Turkey: trading centre since ancient times as the chief city of Cappadocia. Pop: 605 000 (2005 est). Ancient name: **Caesarea Mazaca**

kazachok (,kɑːzə'tʃɒk) *n* a Russian folk dance in which the performer executes high kicks from a squatting position [Russian]

Kazakh *or* **Kazak** (kə'zɑːk, kɑː-) *n* **1** (*pl* **-zakhs** *or* **-zaks**) a member of a traditionally Muslim Mongoloid people of Kazakhstan **2** the language of this people, belonging to the Turkic branch of the Altaic family

Kazakhstan *or* **Kazakstan** (,kɑːzɑːk'stæn, -'stɑːn) *n* a republic in central Asia: conquered by Mongols in the 13th century; came under Russian control in the 18th and 19th centuries; was a Soviet republic from 1936 until it gained independence in 1991. It has rich mineral deposits and agriculture is important. Official language: Kazakh. Religion: nonreligious, Muslim, and Christian. Official currency: tenge. Capital: Astana (formerly Akmola); capital functions moved from Almaty (formerly Alma-Ata) in 1997. Pop: 15 403 000 (2004 est). Area: 2 715 100 sq km (1 048 030 sq miles)

Kazan (kə'zæn, -'zɑːn; *Russian* ka'zanj) *n* a city in W Russia, capital of the Tatar Autonomous Republic on the River Volga: capital of an independent khanate in the 15th century; university (1804); a major industrial centre. Pop: 1 108 000 (2005 est)

Kazan Retto (kɑː'zɑːn 'rɛtəʊ) *n* transliteration of the Japanese name for the **Volcano Islands**

Kazbek (kɑː'zʲbɛk) *n* **Mount** an extinct volcano in N Georgia in the central Caucasus Mountains. Height: 5047 m (16 558 ft)

Kaz Daği ('kaz 'daj) *n* the Turkish name for (Mount) **Ida** (sense 2)

kazoo (kə'zuː) *n, pl* **-zoos** a cigar-shaped musical instrument of metal or plastic with a membranous diaphragm of thin paper that vibrates with a nasal sound when the player hums into it [c20 probably imitative of the sound produced]

kb *abbreviation for* kilobar

Kb *or* **kb** *abbreviation for computing* kilobit

KB *abbreviation for* **1** (in Britain) King's Bench **2** (in Britain) Knight Bachelor **3** *computing* kilobyte **4** *chess symbol for* king's bishop

KBE *abbreviation for* Knight (Commander of the Order) of the British Empire

KBP *chess symbol for* king's bishop's pawn

Kbps *or* **kbps** *abbreviation for computing* kilobits per second

kbyte *computing abbreviation for* kilobyte

kc *abbreviation for* kilocycle

KC (in Britain) *abbreviation for* **1** King's Counsel **2** Kennel Club

kcal *abbreviation for* kilocalorie

KCB *abbreviation for* Knight Commander of the Bath (a Brit title)

KCMG *abbreviation for* Knight Commander (of the Order) of St Michael and St George (a Brit title)

Kčs. *abbreviation for* koruna [Czech *koruna československá*]

KCVO *abbreviation for* Knight Commander of the Royal Victorian Order (a Brit title)

KD *or* **k.d.** *commerce abbreviation for* knocked down: indicating furniture, machinery, etc, in separate parts

ke *the internet domain name for* Kenya

KE *abbreviation for* **kinetic energy**

kea ('keɪə) *n* a large New Zealand parrot, *Nestor notabilis*, with brownish-green plumage [c19 from Māori, imitative of its call]

Kea *n, pl* **Kea** (in New Zealand) a member of the junior branch of the Scouts [from KEA]

Kéa ('kɛa) *n* transliteration of the Modern Greek name for **Keos**

kebab (kə'bæb) *n* a dish consisting of small pieces of meat, tomatoes, onions, etc, threaded onto skewers and grilled, generally over charcoal. Also called: **shish kebab, kabob, cabob** [c17 via Urdu from Arabic *kabāb* roast meat]

Kechua ('kɛtʃwə) *n* a variant of **Quechua**

keck¹ (kɛk) *vb (intr) chiefly US* **1** to retch or feel nausea **2** to feel or express disgust [c17 of imitative origin]

keck² (kɛk) *n* another name for **cow parsnip** and **cow parsley** [c17 from KEX, which was mistaken as a plural (as if *kecks*)]

kecks *or* **keks** (kɛks) *pl n* *Northern English dialect* trousers [c19 from obsolete *kicks* breeches]

Kecskemét (*Hungarian* 'kɛtʃkɛmeːt) *n* a city in central Hungary: vineyards and fruit farms. Pop: 107 604 (2003 est)

ked (kɛd) *n* See **sheep ked** [c16 of unknown origin]

Kedah ('kɛdə) *n* a state of NW Malaysia: under Thai control until it came under the British in 1909; the chief exports are rice, tin, and rubber. Capital: Alor Star. Pop: 1 648 756 (2000). Area: 9425 sq km (3639 sq miles)

keddah ('kɛdə) *n* a variant spelling of **kheda**

kedge (kɛdʒ) *nautical* ▷ *vb* **1** to draw (a vessel) along by hauling in on the cable of a light anchor that has been dropped at some distance from it, or (of a vessel) to be drawn in this fashion ▷ *n* **2** a light anchor, used esp for kedging [c15 from *caggen* to fasten]

kedgeree (,kɛdʒə'riː) *n chiefly Brit* a dish consisting of rice, cooked flaked fish, and hard-boiled eggs [c17 from Hindi *khicarī*, from Sanskrit *khiccā*, of obscure origin]

Kediri (kɪ'dɪərɪ) *n* a city in Indonesia, in E Java: commercial centre. Pop: 244 519 (2000)

Kedleston Hall ('kɛdlstən) *n* a mansion near Derby in Derbyshire: rebuilt (1759–65) for the Curzon family by Matthew Brettingham, James Paine, and Robert Adam

Kedron ('kɛdrɒn) *or* **Kidron** *n Bible* a ravine under the eastern wall of Jerusalem

keef (kiːf) *n* a variant spelling of **kif**

keek (kiːk) *n, vb* a Scot word for **peep¹** [c18 probably from Middle Dutch *kīken* to look]

keel¹ (kiːl) *n* **1** one of the main longitudinal structural members of a vessel to which the frames are fastened and that may extend into the water to provide lateral stability **2** on an even keel well-balanced; steady **3** any structure corresponding to or resembling the keel of a ship, such as the central member along the bottom of an aircraft fuselage **4** *biology* a ridgelike part; carina **5** a poetic word for **ship** ▷ *vb* **6** to capsize ▷ See also **keel over** [c14 from Old Norse *kjölr*;

related to Middle Dutch *kiel*, KEEL[2]] > 'keel-less *adj*
keel[2] (kiːl) *n* *Eastern English dialect* **1** a flat-bottomed vessel, esp one used for carrying coal **2** a measure of coal equal to about 21 tons [C14 *kele*, from Middle Dutch *kiel*; compare Old English *cēol* ship]
keel[3] (kiːl) *n* **1** red ochre stain used for marking sheep, timber, etc ▷ *vb* (*tr*) **2** to mark with this stain [Old English *cēlan*, from *cōl* COOL]
keel[4] (kiːl) *vb* an archaic word for **cool** [C15 probably from Scottish Gaelic *cīl*]
keel[5] (kiːl) *n* a fatal disease of young ducks, characterized by intestinal bleeding caused by Salmonella bacteria [C19 from KEEL[1]; see KEEL OVER]
keelage ('kiːlɪdʒ) *n* a fee charged by certain ports to allow a ship to dock
keel arch *n* another name for **ogee arch**
keelboat ('kiːlˌbəʊt) *n* a river boat with a shallow draught and a keel, used for freight and moved by towing, punting, or rowing
keelhaul ('kiːlˌhɔːl) *vb* (*tr*) **1** to drag (a person) by a rope from one side of a vessel to the other through the water under the keel **2** to rebuke harshly [C17 from Dutch *kielhalen*; see KEEL[1], HAUL]
keelie ('kiːlɪ) *n* *Scot* **1** a kestrel **2** an urban ruffian; lower-class town or city dweller, esp Glaswegian [C19 of uncertain origin]
Keeling Islands ('kiːlɪŋ) *pl n* another name for the **Cocos Islands**
keel over *vb* (*adverb*) **1** to turn upside down; capsize **2** (*intr*) *informal* to collapse suddenly
keelson ('kɛlsən, 'kiːl-) *or* **kelson** *n* a longitudinal beam fastened to the keel of a vessel for strength and stiffness [C17 probably from Low German *kielswin*, keel swine, ultimately of Scandinavian origin]
Keelung (kiː'lʊŋ) *n* another name for **Chilung**
keen[1] (kiːn) *adj* **1** eager or enthusiastic **2** (*postpositive*; foll by *on*) fond (of); devoted (to): *keen on a girl; keen on golf* **3** intellectually acute: *a keen wit* **4** (of sight, smell, hearing, etc) capable of recognizing fine distinctions **5** having a sharp cutting edge or point **6** extremely cold and penetrating: *a keen wind* **7** intense or strong: *a keen desire* **8** *chiefly Brit* extremely low so as to be competitive: *keen prices* **9** *slang, chiefly US and Canadian* very good [Old English *cēne*; related to Old High German *kuoni* brave, Old Norse *koenn* wise; see CAN[1], KNOW] > 'keenly *adv* > 'keenness *n*
keen[2] (kiːn) *vb* (*intr*) **1** to lament the dead ▷ *n* **2** a dirge or lament for the dead [C19 from Irish Gaelic *caoine*, from Old Irish *coīnim* I wail] > 'keener *n*
keener ('kiːnə) *n* *Canadian informal* a person, esp a student, who is keen, enthusiastic, or zealous
keep (kiːp) *vb* **keeps, keeping, kept** (kɛpt) **1** (*tr*) to have or retain possession of **2** (*tr*) to have temporary possession or charge of: *keep my watch for me during the game* **3** (*tr*) to store in a customary place: *I keep my books in the desk* **4** to remain or cause to remain in a specified state or condition: *keep the dog quiet; keep ready* **5** to continue or cause to continue: *keep the beat; keep in step* **6** (*tr*) to have or take charge or care of: *keep the shop for me till I return* **7** (*tr*) to look after or maintain for use, pleasure, etc: *to keep chickens; keep two cars* **8** (*tr*) to provide for the upkeep or livelihood of **9** (*tr*) to support financially, esp in return for sexual favours: *he keeps a mistress in the country* **10** to confine or detain or be confined or detained **11** to withhold or reserve or admit of withholding or reserving: *your news will keep till later* **12** (*tr*) to refrain from divulging or violating: *to keep a secret; keep one's word* **13** to preserve or admit of preservation **14** (*tr*; sometimes foll by *up*) to observe with due rites or ceremonies: *to keep Christmas* **15** (*tr*) to maintain by writing regular records in: *to keep a diary* **16** (when *intr*, foll by *in, on, to*, etc) to stay in, on, or at (a place or position): *please keep your seats; keep to the path* **17** (*tr*) to associate with (esp in the phrase **keep bad company**) **18** (*tr*) to maintain in existence: *to keep court in the palace* **19** (*tr*) *chiefly Brit* to have habitually in stock: *this shop keeps all kinds of wool* **20** **how are you keeping?** how are you? **21** **keep tabs on** *informal* to keep a watchful eye on **22** **keep track of** See **track** (sense 15) **23** **keep time** See **time** (sense 42) **24** **keep wicket** to play as wicketkeeper in the game of cricket **25** **you can keep it** *informal* I have no interest in what you are offering ▷ *n* **26** living or support: *he must work for his keep* **27** *archaic* charge or care **28** Also called: **dungeon, donjon** the main tower within the walls of a medieval castle or fortress **29** *informal* **a** completely; permanently **b** for the winner or possessor to keep permanently ▷ See also **keep at, keep away, keep back, keep down, keep from, keep in, keep off, keep on, keep out, keep to, keep under, keep up** [Old English *cēpan* to observe; compare Old Saxon *kapōn* to look, Old Norse *kōpa* to stare]
keep at *vb* (*preposition*) **1** (*intr*) to persevere with or persist in **2** (*tr*) to constrain (a person) to continue doing (a task)
keep away *vb* (*adverb*; often foll by *from*) **1** to refrain or prevent from coming (near) **2** to stop using, touching, etc
keep back *vb* (*adverb*; often foll by *from*) **1** (*tr*) to refuse to reveal or disclose **2** to prevent, be prevented, or refrain from advancing, entering, etc
keep down *vb* (*adverb, mainly tr*) **1** to repress; hold in submission **2** to restrain or control: *he had difficulty keeping his anger down* **3** to cause not to increase or rise: *prices were kept down for six months* **4** (*intr*) not to show oneself to one's opponents; lie low **5** to cause (food) to stay in the stomach; not vomit
keeper ('kiːpə) *n* **1** a person in charge of animals, esp in a zoo **2** a person in charge of a museum, collection, or section of a museum **3** a person in charge of other people, such as a warder in a jail **4** See **goalkeeper, wicketkeeper, gamekeeper** **5** a person who keeps something **6** a device, such as a clip, for keeping something in place **7** a soft iron or steel bar placed across the poles of a permanent magnet to close the magnetic circuit when it is not in use > 'keeperless *adj* > 'keeperˌship *n*
keeper ring *n* another name for **guard ring**
keep fit *n* **a** exercises designed to promote physical fitness if performed regularly **b** (*as modifier*): *keep-fit classes*
keep from *vb* (*preposition*) **1** (*foll by a gerund*) to prevent or restrain (oneself or another); refrain or cause to refrain **2** (*tr*) to protect or preserve from
keep in *vb* (*mainly adverb*) **1** (*intr; also preposition*) to stay indoors **2** (*tr*) to restrain (an emotion); repress **3** (*tr*) to detain (a schoolchild) after hours as a punishment **4** (of a fire) to stay alight or to cause (a fire) to stay alight **5** (*tr, prep*) to allow a constant supply of: *her prize money kept her in new clothes for a year* **6** **keep in with** to maintain good relations with
keeping ('kiːpɪŋ) *n* **1** conformity or harmony (esp in the phrases **in** *or* **out of keeping**) **2** charge or care: *valuables in the keeping of a bank*
keepnet ('kiːpˌnɛt) *n* a cylindrical net strung on wire hoops and sealed at one end, suspended in water by anglers to keep alive the fish they have caught
keep off *vb* **1** to stay or cause to stay at a distance (from) **2** (*preposition*) not to eat or drink or prevent from eating or drinking **3** (*preposition*) to avoid or cause to avoid (a topic) **4** (*intr, adverb*) not to start: *the rain kept off all day*
keep on *vb* (*adverb*) **1** to continue or persist in (doing something): *keep on running* **2** (*tr*) to continue to wear **3** (*tr*) to continue to employ: *the firm kept on only ten men* **4** (*intr*; foll by *about*) to persist in talking (about) **5** (*intr*; foll by *at*) to nag (a person)
keep out *vb* (*adverb*) **1** to remain or cause to remain outside **2** **keep out of** **a** to remain or cause to remain unexposed to: *keep out of the sun* **b** to avoid or cause to avoid: *the boss is in an angry mood, so keep out of her way*
keepsake ('kiːpˌseɪk) *n* a gift that evokes memories of a person or event with which it is associated
keep to *vb* (*preposition*) **1** to adhere to or stand by or cause to adhere to or stand by: *to keep to a promise* **2** to confine or be confined to **3** **keep to oneself** **a** (*intr*) to avoid the society of others **b** (*tr*) to refrain from sharing or disclosing **4** **keep oneself to oneself** to avoid the society of others
keep under *vb* **1** to remain or cause to remain below (a surface) **2** (*tr, adverb*) to cause to remain unconscious **3** (*tr, adverb*) to hold in submission
keep up *vb* (*adverb*) **1** (*tr*) to maintain (prices, one's morale) at the present level **2** (*intr*) to maintain a pace or rate set by another **3** (*intr*; often foll by *with*) to remain informed: *to keep up with technological developments* **4** (*tr*) to maintain in good condition **5** (*tr*) to hinder (a person) from going to bed at night: *the excitement kept the children up well past their bedtime* **6** **keep it up** to continue a good performance **7** **keep one's chin up** to keep cheerful under difficult circumstances **8** **keep one's end up** to maintain one's stance or position against opposition or misfortune **9** **keep up with** to remain in contact with, esp by letter **10** **keep up with (the Joneses)** *informal* to compete with (one's neighbours) in material possessions, etc
keepy-uppy (ˌkiːpɪ'ʌpɪ) *n* *soccer* the act or an instance of keeping a ball off the ground by bouncing it repeatedly on a foot, knee, or head
keeshond ('keɪsˌhɒnd, 'kiːs-) *n, pl* **-honds** *or* **-honden** (-ˌhɒndᵊn) a breed of dog of the spitz type with a shaggy greyish coat and tightly curled tail, originating in Holland [C20 from Dutch, probably from *Kees* nickname for *Cornelis* Cornelius, from Latin + *hond* HOUND[1]]
Keewatin (kiː'weɪtɪn) *n* a former administrative district of the Northwest Territories of Canada stretching from the district of Mackenzie to Hudson Bay; became part of Nunavut in 1999: mostly tundra
kef (kɛf) *n* a variant of **kif**
keffiyeh (kɛ'fiːjə), **kaffiyeh** *or* **kufiyah** *n* a cotton headdress worn by Arabs [C19 from Arabic, perhaps from Late Latin *cofea* COIF]
Keflavík ('kɛfləˌvɪk) *n* a port in SW Iceland: NATO airbase, fishing. Pop: 7963 (2003 est)
keftedes (kɛf'teðɛs) *n* a Greek dish of meatballs cooked with herbs and onions [C20 from Modern Greek]
keg (kɛg) *n* **1** a small barrel with a capacity of between five and ten gallons **2** *Brit* **a** an aluminium container in which beer is transported and stored **b** Also called: **keg beer** beer kept in a keg: it is infused with gas and served under pressure [C17 variant of Middle English *kag*, of Scandinavian origin; related to Old Norse *kaggi* cask]
Kegel exercises ('kɛgəl) *pl n* exercises for rehabilitating the pelvic-floor muscles of women suffering stress incontinence, esp after childbirth. Also called: **pelvic-floor exercises** [C20 named after A. H. *Kegel*, US gynaecologist]
kegler ('kɛglə) *or* **kegeler** ('kɛgələ) *n* *informal, chiefly US* a participant in a game of tenpin bowling [from German, from *Kegel* pin, from Old High German *kegil* peg]
kehua ('kɛhuːə) *n* *NZ* a ghost or spirit [Māori]
Keighley ('kiːθlɪ) *n* a town in N England, in Bradford unitary authority, West Yorkshire, on the River Aire: textile industry. Pop: 49 453 (2001)
Keijo (ˌkeɪ'dʒəʊ) *n* transliteration of the Japanese name for **Seoul**
keister *or* **keester** ('kiːstə) *n* *slang, chiefly US* **1** the rump; buttocks **2** a suitcase, trunk, or box [C20 of uncertain origin]
keitloa ('kaɪtləʊə, 'keɪt-) *n* a southern African variety of the black two-horned rhinoceros, *Diceros bicornis* [C19 from Tswana *khetlwa*]

kekeno ('kɛkɛnəʊ) *n, pl* **kekeno** another name for **New Zealand fur seal** [Māori]

kekerengu (kɛkɛ'rɛn²ŋguː) *n, pl* **kekerengu** another name for **Māori bug** [Māori]

keks (kɛks) *pl n* a variant spelling of **kecks**

Kekulé formula ('kɛkjəˌleɪ) *n* a representation of the benzene molecule as six carbon atoms at the corners of a regular hexagon with alternate double and single bonds joining them and with one hydrogen atom bound to each carbon atom. See **benzene ring** [C19 named after Friedrich August *Kekulé* von Stradonitz (1829–96), German chemist]

Kekulé structure *n* the structure of many molecules, notably benzene, suggested by Friedrich August *Kekulé* von Stradonitz (1829–96), the German chemist

Kelantan (kɛ'læntən, kɪˌlæn'tæn) *n* a state of NE Malaysia: under Thai control until it came under the British in 1909; produces rice and rubber. Capital: Kota Bharu. Pop: 1 313 014 (2000). Area: 14 930 sq km (5765 sq miles)

Kells (kɛlz) *n* a town in the Republic of Ireland, in Co Meath: *The Book of Kells,* an illuminated manuscript of the Gospels, was produced at the monastery here in the 8th century. Pop: 4421 (2002)

Kelly ('kɛlɪ) *n* (**as**) game as Ned Kelly See **game¹** (sense 25) [from Ned *Kelly* (1855–80), Australian horse and cattle thief and bushranger: captured by the police and hanged]

Kelmscott Manor ('kɛlmzˌkɒt) *n* a Tudor house near Lechlade in Oxfordshire: home (1871–96) of William Morris

keloid *or* **cheloid** ('kiːlɔɪd) *n pathol* a hard smooth pinkish raised growth of scar tissue at the site of an injury, tending to occur more frequently in dark-skinned races [C19 from Greek *khēlē* claw] > **ke'loidal** *or* **che'loidal** *adj*

kelp (kɛlp) *n* **1** any large brown seaweed, esp any in the order *Laminariales* **2** the ash of such seaweed, used as a source of iodine and potash [C14 of unknown origin]

kelpie¹ *or* **kelpy** ('kɛlpɪ) *n, pl* **-pies** an Australian breed of sheepdog, originally developed from Scottish collies, having a smooth coat of various colours and erect ears [named after a particular specimen of the breed, c. 1870]

kelpie² ('kɛlpɪ) *n* (in Scottish folklore) a water spirit in the form of a horse that drowned its riders [C18 probably related to Scottish Gaelic *cailpeach* heifer, of obscure origin]

kelson ('kɛlsən) *n* a variant of **keelson**

kelt (kɛlt) *n* a salmon that has recently spawned and is usually in poor condition [C14 of unknown origin]

Kelt (kɛlt) *n* a variant of **Celt**. > '**Keltic** *adj* > '**Keltically** *adv* > '**Kelti**ˌ**cism** *n* > '**Kelticist** *or* '**Keltist** *n*

kelter ('kɛltə) *n* a variant of **kilter**

kelvin ('kɛlvɪn) *n* the basic SI unit of thermodynamic temperature; the fraction 1/273.16 of the thermodynamic temperature of the triple point of water. Symbol: K

Kelvin scale *n* a thermodynamic temperature scale based upon the efficiencies of ideal heat engines. The zero of the scale is absolute zero. Originally the degree was equal to that on the Celsius scale but it is now defined so that the triple point of water is exactly 273.16 kelvins. The International Practical Temperature Scale (1968, revised 1990) realizes the Kelvin scale over a wide range of temperatures. See also **Rankine scale**

kelyphitic rim (ˌkɛlɪ'fɪtɪk) *n geology* a mineral shell enclosing another mineral in an igneous rock, formed by reaction of the interned mineral with the surrounding rock [C19 from Greek *keluphos* pod + *-itic*; see -ITE¹]

Kemalism (kɛ'mɑːlɪzəm) *n* the theory and form of government associated with Kemal Atatürk, the Turkish general and statesman (1881–1938), who founded the Turkish republic and westernized and secularized the country > **Ke'malist** *n, adj*

kembla ('kɛmblə) *n Austral slang* small change [from rhyming slang *Kembla Grange*]

Kemerovo (*Russian* 'kjemɪrəvə) *n* a city in S Russia: a major coal-mining centre of the Kuznetsk Basin, with important chemical plants. Pop: 479 000 (2005 est). Former name (until 1932): Shcheglovsk

kemp (kɛmp) *n* a coarse hair or strand of hair, esp one in a fleece that resists dyeing [C14 from Old Norse *kampr* beard, moustache] > '**kempy** *adj*

kempt (kɛmpt) *adj* (of hair) tidy; combed. See also **unkempt** [C20 back formation from *unkempt*; originally past participle of dialect *kemb* to COMB]

ken (kɛn) *n* **1** range of knowledge or perception (esp in the phrases **beyond** *or* **in one's ken**) ▷ *vb* **kens, kenning, kenned** *or* **kent** (kɛnt) **2** *Scot and northern English dialect* to know **3** *Scot and northern English dialect* to understand; perceive **4** (*tr*) *archaic* to see [Old English *cennan*; related to Old Norse *kenna* to perceive, Old High German *kennen* to make known; see CAN¹]

Ken. *abbreviation for* Kentucky

kenaf (kə'næf) *n* another name for **ambary** [from Persian]

Kendal ('kɛnd³l) *n* a town in NW England, in Cumbria: a gateway town to the Lake District, with an ancient woollen industry. Pop: 28 030 (2001)

Kendal green *n* **1** a green woollen cloth, formerly worn by foresters **2** the colour of this cloth, produced by a dye obtained from the woad plant. See also **dyer's-greenweed** [C14 from *Kendal,* where it originated]

kendo ('kɛndəʊ) *n* the Japanese art of fencing with pliable bamboo staves or, sometimes, real swords: strict conventions are observed [from Japanese]

Kenilworth ('kɛnɪlˌwɜːθ) *n* a town in central England, in Warwickshire: ruined 12th-century castle, subject of Sir Walter Scott's novel *Kenilworth.* Pop: 22 218 (2001)

Kénitra (*French* kenitra) *n* a port in NW Morocco, on the Sebou River 16 km (10 miles) from the Atlantic. Pop: 598 000 (2003). Also called: **Mina Hassan Tani** Former name (1932–56): **Port Lyautey**

Kennedy ('kɛnɪdɪ) *n* **Cape** a former name (1963–73) of (Cape) **Canaveral**

kennel¹ ('kɛn³l) *n* **1** a hutlike shelter for a dog. US name: **doghouse 2** (*usually plural*) an establishment where dogs are bred, trained, boarded, etc **3** the lair of a fox or other animal **4** a ramshackle house; hovel **5** a pack of hounds ▷ *vb* **-nels, -nelling, -nelled** *or* US **-nels, -neling, -neled 6** to put or go into a kennel; keep or stay in a kennel [C14 from Old French *chenil,* from Vulgar Latin *canīle* (unattested), from Latin *canis* dog]

kennel² ('kɛn³l) *n archaic* a sewer or street gutter [C16 variant of *cannel* CHANNEL¹]

Kennelly-Heaviside layer *n* See **E region**

kennett ('kɛnɪt) *vb* (*tr*) *Austral slang* another word for **jeff**

kenning ('kɛnɪŋ) *n* a conventional metaphoric name for something, esp in Old Norse and Old English poetry, such as Old English *bānhūs* (bone house) for "body" [C14 from Old Norse, from *kenna;* see KEN]

Kenny method *or* **treatment** ('kɛnɪ) *n* a method of treating poliomyelitis by applying hot moist packs to the affected muscles alternated by passive and later active movement of the muscles [C20 named after Sister Elizabeth *Kenny,* 1886–1952, Australian nurse who developed it]

keno, keeno, kino *or* **quino** ('kiːnəʊ) *n US and Canadian* a game of chance similar to bingo [C19 of unknown origin]

kenogenesis (ˌkiːnəʊ'dʒɛnɪsɪs) *n* a secondary US spelling of **caenogenesis**. > **kenogenetic** (ˌkiːnəʊdʒə'nɛtɪk) *adj* > ˌkenoge'netically *adv*

kenosis (kɪ'nəʊsɪs) *n Christianity* Christ's voluntary renunciation of certain divine attributes, in order to identify himself with mankind (Philippians 2:6–7) [C19 from Greek: an emptying, from *kenoun* to empty from *kenos* empty] > **kenotic** (kɪ'nɒtɪk) *adj, n*

Kensington and Chelsea ('kɛnzɪŋtən) *n* a borough of Greater London, on the River Thames: **Kensington Palace** (17th century) and gardens. Pop: 174 400 (2003 est). Area: 12 sq km (5 sq miles)

kenspeckle ('kɛnˌspɛk³l) *adj Scot* easily seen or recognized [C18 from dialect *kenspeck,* of Scandinavian origin; compare Old Norse *kennispecki* power of recognition; related to KEN]

kent (kɛnt) *vb* a past tense and past participle of **ken**

Kent (kɛnt) *n* a county of SE England, on the English Channel: the first part of Great Britain to be colonized by the Romans; one of the seven kingdoms of Anglo-Saxon England until absorbed by Wessex in the 9th century AD. Apart from the Downs it is mostly low-lying and agricultural, specializing in fruit and hops. The Medway towns of Rochester and Gillingham became an independent unitary authority in 1998. Administrative centre: Maidstone. Pop (excluding Medway): 1 348 800 (2003 est). Area (excluding Medway): 3526 sq km (1361 sq miles)

kente ('kɛntɪ) *n* **1** Also called: **kente cloth** a brightly coloured handwoven cloth of Ghana, usually with some gold thread **2** the toga made of this cloth [from a Ghanaian language, possibly Akan]

kentia ('kɛntɪə) *n* a plant name formerly used to include palms now allotted to several different genera and still used commercially to denote the feather palm genus *Howea,* native to Lord Howe Island, popular as greenhouse or house plants for their decorative arching foliage: family *Palmaceae* [named after William *Kent* (died 1828), British botanist]

Kentish ('kɛntɪʃ) *adj* **1** of or relating to Kent ▷ *n* **2** Also called: **Jutish** the dialect of Old and Middle English spoken in Kent. See also **Anglian, West Saxon**

Kentish glory *n* a moth, *Endromis versicolora,* common in north and central Europe, having brown variegated front wings and, in the male, orange hindwings

kentledge ('kɛntlɪdʒ) *n nautical* scrap metal used as ballast in a vessel [C17 perhaps from Old French *quintelage* ballast, from *quintal* hundredweight, ultimately from Arabic *qintār;* see KANTAR]

Kentuckian (kɛn'tʌkɪən) *n* **1** a native or inhabitant of Kentucky ▷ *adj* **2** of or relating to Kentucky or its inhabitants

Kentucky (kɛn'tʌkɪ) *n* **1** a state of the S central US: consists of an undulating plain in the west, the Bluegrass region in the centre, the Tennessee and Ohio River basins in the southwest, and the Appalachians in the east. Capital: Frankfort. Pop: 4 117 827 (2003 est). Area: 102 693 sq km (39 650 sq miles). Abbreviations: **Ken, Ky,** (with zip code) **KY 2** a river in central Kentucky, rising in the Cumberland Mountains and flowing northwest to the Ohio River. Length: 417 km (259 miles)

Kentucky bluegrass *n* a Eurasian grass, *Poa pratensis,* grown for forage and naturalized throughout North America

Kentucky coffee tree *n* a North American leguminous tree, *Gymnocladus dioica,* whose seeds, in brown curved pulpy pods, were formerly used as a coffee substitute

Kentucky Derby *n* a race for three-year-old horses run annually since 1875 at Louisville, Kentucky

Kenwood House ('kɛnwʊd) *n* a 17th-century mansion on Hampstead Heath in London: remodelled and decorated by Robert Adam: contains the Iveagh bequest, a noted art collection

Kenya ('kɛnjə, 'kiːnjə) *n* **1** a republic in E Africa, on the Indian Ocean: became a British protectorate in 1895 and a colony in 1920; gained independence in 1963 and is a member of the

Commonwealth. Tea and coffee constitute about a third of the total exports. Official languages: Swahili and English. Religions: Christian majority, animist minority. Currency: shilling. Capital: Nairobi. Pop: 32 420 000 (2004 est). Area: 582 647 sq km (224 960 sq miles) **2 Mount** an extinct volcano in central Kenya: the second highest mountain in Africa; girth at 2400 m (8000 ft) is about 150 km (95 miles). The regions above 3200 m (10 500 ft) constitute **Mount Kenya National Park**. Height: 5199 m (17 058 ft). local name: **Kirinyaga**

Kenyan ('kɛnjən, 'kiːnjən) *adj* **1** of or relating to Kenya or its inhabitants ▷ *n* **2** a native or inhabitant of Kenya

Keos ('keɪɒs) *n* an island in the Aegean Sea, in the NW Cyclades. Pop: 2412 (2001). Area: 174 sq km (67 sq miles). Italian name: **Zea** Modern Greek name: **Kéa**

kep (kɛp) *vb* **keps, kepping, keppit** ('kɛpɪt) (*tr*) *Scot and N English dialect* to catch [from KEEP (in obsolete sense: to put oneself in the way of)]

Kephallinía (ˌkɛfaliˈniːa; *English* ˌkɛfəˈliːnɪə) *n* transliteration of the Modern Greek name for **Cephalonia**

kepi ('keɪpiː) *n, pl* **kepis** a military cap with a circular top and a horizontal peak [c19 from French *képi*, from German (Swiss dialect) *käppi* a little cap, from *kappe* CAP]

Kepler ('kɛplə) *n* a small crater in the NW quadrant of the moon, centre of a large bright ray system

Kepler's laws *pl n* three laws of planetary motion published by Johannes Kepler between 1609 and 1619. The first states that the orbit of a planet describes an ellipse with the sun at one focus. The second states that, during one orbit, the straight line joining the sun and a planet sweeps out equal areas in equal times. The third states that the squares of the periods of any two planets are proportional to the cubes of their orbital major axes

kept (kɛpt) *vb* **1** the past tense and past participle of **keep 2 kept woman** *censorious* a woman maintained by a man as his mistress

Kerala ('kɛrələ, kəˈrɑːlə) *n* a state of SW India, on the Arabian Sea: formed in 1956, it includes the former state of Travancore-Cochin; has the highest population density of any Indian state. Capital: Trivandrum. Pop: 31 838 619 (2001). Area: 38 863 sq km (15 005 sq miles)

keramic (kɪˈræmɪk) *adj* a rare variant of **ceramic**

keramics (kɪˈræmɪks) *n* a rare variant of **ceramics**

keratin ('kɛrətɪn) *or* **ceratin** *n* a fibrous protein that occurs in the outer layer of the skin and in hair, nails, feathers, hooves, etc

keratinize *or* **keratinise** (kɪˈrætɪˌnaɪz, ˈkɛrətɪ-) *vb* to become or cause to become impregnated with keratin > keˌratiniˈzation *or* keˌratiniˈsation *n*

keratitis (ˌkɛrəˈtaɪtɪs) *n* inflammation of the cornea

kerato- *or before a vowel* **kerat-** *combining form* **1** indicating horn or a horny substance: *keratin*; *keratogenous* **2** indicating the cornea: *keratoplasty* [from Greek *kerat-, keras* horn]

keratogenous (ˌkɛrəˈtɒdʒɪnəs) *adj* developing or causing the growth of horny tissue

keratoid ('kɛrəˌtɔɪd) *adj* resembling horn; horny

keratoplasty ('kɛrətəʊˌplæstɪ) *n, pl* **-ties** plastic surgery of the cornea, esp involving corneal grafting > ˌkeratoˈplastic *adj*

keratose ('kɛrəˌtəʊs, -ˌtəʊz) *adj* (esp of certain sponges) having a horny skeleton

keratosis (ˌkɛrəˈtəʊsɪs) *n pathol* **1** any skin condition marked by a horny growth, such as a wart **2** a horny growth

keratotomy (ˌkɛrəˈtɒtəmɪ) *n* surgical incision of the cornea

kerb *or US and Canadian* **curb** (kɜːb) *n* **1** a line of stone or concrete forming an edge between a pavement and a roadway, so that the pavement is some 15 cm above the level of the road ▷ *vb* **2** (*tr*)

to provide with or enclose with a kerb [c17 from Old French *courbe* bent, from Latin *curvus*; see CURVE]

kerb appeal *n Brit* an attractive appearance when viewed in passing from the road

kerbaya ('kɛrbaja) *n* a blouse worn by Malay women [from Malay]

kerb crawling *n* the act of driving slowly along the edge of the pavement seeking to entice someone into the car for sexual purposes > **kerb crawler** *n*

kerb drill *n* a pedestrian's procedure for crossing a road safely, esp as taught to children

Kerbela ('kɜːbələ) *n* a variant of **Karbala**

kerbing *or US and Canadian* **curbing** ('kɜːbɪŋ) *n* **1** material used for a kerb **2** a less common word for **kerb** (sense 1)

kerb market *n stock exchange* **1** an after-hours street market **2** a street market dealing in unquoted securities

kerbside ('kɜːbˌsaɪd) *n* **a** the edge of a pavement where it drops to the level of the road **b** (*as modifier*): *kerbside rubbish collections*

kerbstone *or US and Canadian* **curbstone** ('kɜːbˌstəʊn) *n* one of a series of stones that form a kerb

kerb weight *n* the weight of a motor car without occupants, luggage, etc

Kerch (*Russian* kjɛrtʃ) *n* a port in S Ukraine on the **Kerch Peninsula** and the **Strait of Kerch** (linking the Black Sea with the Sea of Azov): founded as a Greek colony in the 6th century BC; ceded to Russia in 1774; iron-mining, steel production, and fishing. Pop: 153 000 (2005 est)

kerchief ('kɜːtʃɪf) *n* a piece of cloth worn tied over the head or around the neck [c13 from Old French *cuevrechef*, from *covrir* to COVER + *chef* head; see CHIEF] > 'kerchiefed *adj*

kerel ('kɛrəl) *n South African* a chap or fellow [c19 Afrikaans]

kereru (kɛˈrɛruː) *n, pl* **kereru** another name for **New Zealand pigeon** [Māori]

kerf (kɜːf) *n* the cut made by a saw, an axe, etc [Old English *cyrf* a cutting; related to Old English *ceorfan* to CARVE]

kerfuffle, carfuffle *or* **kurfuffle** (kəˈfʌfəl) *n* **1** *informal, chiefly Brit* commotion; disorder; agitation ▷ *vb* **2** (*tr*) *Scot* to put into disorder or disarray; ruffle or disarrange [from Scottish *curfuffle, carfuffle*, from Scottish Gaelic *car* twist, turn + *fuffle* to disarrange]

Kerguelen ('kɜːgɪlɪn) *n* an archipelago in the S Indian Ocean: consists of one large volcanic island (Kerguelen or Desolation Island) and 300 small islands; part of the French Southern and Antarctic Territories

Kerkrade (*Dutch* 'kɛrkraːdə) *n* a town in the SE Netherlands, in Limburg: one of the oldest coal-mining centres in Europe. Pop: 50 000 (2003 est)

kerky ('kɜːkɪ) *adj* **kerkier, kerkiest** *Midland English dialect* stupid

Kérkyra ('kɛrkira) *n* transliteration of the Modern Greek name for **Corfu**

kerma ('kɜːmə) *n physics* the quotient of the sum of the initial kinetic energies of all the charged particles liberated by indirectly ionizing radiation in a volume element of a material divided by the mass of the volume element. The SI unit is the gray [c20 k(inetic) e(nergy) r(eleased per unit) ma(ss)]

Kerman (kəˈmɑːn) *n* a city in SE Iran: carpet-making centre. Pop: 546 000 (2005 est)

Kermanshah (ˌkɜːmænˈʃɑː) *n* the former name (until 1987) of **Bakhtaran**

kermes ('kɜːmɪz) *n* **1** the dried bodies of female scale insects of the genus *Kermes*, esp *K. ilices* of Europe and W Asia, used as a red dyestuff **2** a small evergreen Eurasian oak tree, *Quercus coccifera*, with prickly leaves resembling holly: the host plant of kermes scale insects [c16 from French *kermès*, from Arabic *qirmiz*, from Sanskrit *krmija*- red dye, literally: produced by a worm, from *krmi*

worm + *ja*- produced]

kermis *or* **kirmess** ('kɜːmɪs) *n* **1** (formerly, esp in Holland and Northern Germany) an annual country festival or carnival **2** *US and Canadian* a similar event, esp one held to collect money for charity [c16 from Middle Dutch *kercmisse*, from *kerc* church + *misse* MASS; originally a festival held to celebrate the dedication of a church]

kern¹ *or* **kerne** (kɜːn) *n* **1** the part of the character on a piece of printer's type that projects beyond the body ▷ *vb* **2** (*tr*) to furnish (a typeface) with a kern [c17 from French *carne* corner of type, projecting angle, ultimately from Latin *cardō* hinge]

kern² (kɜːn) *n* **1** a lightly armed foot soldier in medieval Ireland or Scotland **2** a troop of such soldiers **3** *archaic* a loutish peasant [c14 from Middle Irish *cethern* band of foot soldiers, from *cath* battle]

kern³ (kɜːn) *n engineering* the central area of a wall, column, etc, through which all compressive forces pass [from German *Kern* core, heart]

kernel ('kɜːnⁱl) *n* **1** the edible central part of a seed, nut, or fruit within the shell or stone **2** the grain of a cereal, esp wheat, consisting of the seed in a hard husk **3** the central or essential part of something ▷ *vb* -nels, -nelling, *or US or Canadian* -nels, -neling, -neled **4** (*intr*) *rare* to form kernels [Old English *cyrnel* a little seed, from *corn* seed; see CORN¹] > 'kernel-less *adj*

kerning ('kɜːnɪŋ) *n printing* the adjustment of space between the letters of words to improve the appearance of text matter

kernite ('kɜːnaɪt) *n* a light soft colourless or white mineral consisting of a hydrated sodium borate in monoclinic crystalline form: an important source of borax and other boron compounds. Formula: $Na_2B_4O_7.4H_2O$ [c20 from *Kern* County, California, where it was found + -ITE¹]

kernmantel rope ('kɜːnˌmæntⁱl) *n mountaineering* a rope made of many straight nylon fibres within a plaited sheath; used for its tensile strength, freedom from twisting, and elasticity [c20 from German *Kernmantel*, from *Kern* core + *Mantel* coat, casing]

kero ('kɛrəʊ) *n Austral and NZ* short for **kerosene**

kerogen ('kɛrədʒən) *n* the solid organic material found in some rocks, such as oil shales, that produces hydrocarbons similar to petroleum when heated [c20 from Greek *kēro(s)* wax + -GEN]

kerosene *or* **kerosine** ('kɛrəˌsiːn) *n* **1** a liquid mixture consisting mainly of alkane hydrocarbons with boiling points in the range 150°–300°C, used as an aircraft fuel, in domestic heaters, and as a solvent. Also called: **paraffin 2** the general name for paraffin as a fuel for jet aircraft [c19 from Greek *kēros* wax + -ENE]

USAGE The spelling *kerosine* is now the preferred form in technical and industrial usage

Kerr effect *n* **1** Also called: **electro-optical effect** the production of double refraction in certain transparent substances by the application of a strong electric field **2** Also called: **magneto-optical effect** a slight elliptical polarization of plane polarized light when reflected from one of the poles of a strong magnet [c19 named after John *Kerr* (1824–1907), Scottish physicist]

Kerry ('kɛrɪ) *n* **1** a county of SW Republic of Ireland, in W Munster province: mostly mountainous (including the highest peaks in Ireland), with a deeply indented coast and many offshore islands. County town: Tralee. Pop: 132 527 (2002). Area: 4701 sq km (1815 sq miles) **2** a small black breed of dairy cattle, originally from Kerry

Kerry blue terrier *n* an Irish breed of terrier with a soft silky wavy coat of a silvery-grey or smoky blue colour

Kerry Hill *n* a breed of sturdy sheep having black-and-white markings on the head and legs and a dense fleece, originating from Powys, on the English-Welsh borders

k

kersey ('kɜːzɪ) n 1 a smooth woollen cloth used for overcoats, etc 2 a twilled woollen cloth with a cotton warp [c14 probably from *Kersey,* village in Suffolk]

kerseymere ('kɜːzɪˌmɪə) n a fine soft woollen cloth of twill weave [c18 from KERSEY + (CASSI)MERE]

kerygma (ˌke'riːɡmə) n *Christianity* the essential news of Jesus, as preached by the early Christians to elicit faith rather than to educate or instruct [from Greek: preaching, proclamation]

Kesh (keʃ) n the beard and uncut hair, covered by the turban, traditionally worn by Sikhs as a symbol of their religious and cultural loyalty, symbolizing the natural life. See also **five Ks** [Punjabi *keś*]

Kesteven ('kɛstɪvən, kɛ'stiːvən) n **Parts of** an area in E England constituting a former administrative division of Lincolnshire

kestrel ('kɛstrəl) n any of several small falcons, esp the European *Falco tinnunculus,* that tend to hover against the wind and feed on small mammals on the ground [c15 changed from Old French *cresserele,* from *cressele* rattle, from Vulgar Latin *crepicella* (unattested), from Latin *crepitāre* to crackle, from *crepāre* to rustle]

Keswick ('kezɪk) n a market town in NW England, in Cumbria in the Lake District: tourist centre. Pop: 4984 (2001)

ketamine ('kɛtəmiːn) n a drug, chemically related to PCP, that is used in medicine as a general anaesthetic, being administered by injection; cyclohexylamine

ketch (kɛtʃ) n a two-masted sailing vessel, fore-and-aft rigged, with a tall mainmast and a mizzen stepped forward of the rudderpost. Compare **yawl¹** (sense 1) [c15 *cache,* probably from *cacchen* to hunt; see CATCH]

ketchup ('kɛtʃəp), **catchup** or **catsup** n any of various piquant sauces containing vinegar: *tomato ketchup* [c17 from Chinese (Amoy) *kōetsiap* brine of pickled fish, from *kōe* seafood + *tsiap* sauce]

kete ('kɛtɛ) n, pl **kete** NZ a basket woven from flax [Māori]

ketene ('kiːtiːn, 'kɛt-) n a colourless irritating toxic gas used as an acetylating agent in organic synthesis. Formula: CH_2:CO. Also called: ethenone

keto- or before a vowel **ket-** *combining form* indicating that a chemical compound is a ketone or is derived from a ketone: *ketose; ketoxime*

keto-enol tautomerism ('kiːtəʊ'iːnɒl) n *chem* tautomerism in which the tautomers are an enol and a keto form. The change occurs by transfer of a hydrogen atom within the molecule

keto form ('kiːtəʊ) n the form of tautomeric compounds when they are ketones rather than enols. See keto-enol tautomerism

ketogenic (ˌkiːtəʊ'dʒɛnɪk) *adj med* forming or able to stimulate the production of ketone bodies: *a ketogenic diet*

ketonaemia or US **ketonemia** (ˌkiːtəʊ'niːmɪə) n *pathol* an excess of ketone bodies in the blood

ketone ('kiːtəʊn) n any of a class of compounds with the general formula R′COR, where R and R′ are alkyl or aryl groups. See also **acetone** [c19 from German *Keton,* from *Aketon* ACETONE] > **ketonic** (kɪ'tɒnɪk) *adj*

ketone body n *biochem* any of three compounds (acetoacetic acid, 3-hydroxybutanoic acid, and acetone) produced when fatty acids are broken down in the liver to provide a source of energy. Excess ketone bodies are present in the blood and urine of people unable to use glucose as an energy source, as in diabetes and starvation. Also called: acetone body

ketone group n *chem* the functional group of ketones: a carbonyl group attached to the carbon atoms of two other organic groups

ketonuria (ˌkiːtəʊ'njʊərɪə, ˌkiːtə-) n *pathol* the presence of ketone bodies in the urine. Also called: acetonuria

ketose ('kiːtəʊz) n any monosaccharide that

contains a ketone group

ketosis (kɪ'təʊsɪs) n *pathol* a high concentration of ketone bodies in the blood. Also called: acetonaemia

ketoxime (kiː'tɒksiːm) n an oxime formed by reaction between hydroxylamine and a ketone

Kettering ('kɛtərɪŋ) n a town in central England, in Northamptonshire: footwear industry. Pop: 51 063 (2001)

kettle ('kɛt°l) n 1 a metal or plastic container with a handle and spout for boiling water 2 any of various metal containers for heating liquids, cooking fish, etc 3 a large metal vessel designed to withstand high temperatures, used in various industrial processes such as refining and brewing 4 short for **kettle hole** [c13 from Old Norse *ketill;* related to Old English *cietel* kettle, Old High German *kezzil;* all ultimately from Latin *catillus* a little pot, from *catīnus* pot]

kettledrum ('kɛt°lˌdrʌm) n a percussion instrument of definite pitch, consisting of a hollow bowl-like hemisphere covered with a skin or membrane, supported on a tripod or stand. The pitch may be adjusted by means of screws or pedals, which alter the tension of the skin > 'kettleˌdrummer n

kettle hole n a round hollow formed by the melting of a mass of buried ice. Often shortened to: kettle

kettle of fish n 1 a situation; state of affairs (often used ironically in the phrase **a pretty** or **fine kettle of fish**) 2 case; matter for consideration: *that's quite a different kettle of fish*

ketubah (kətu'baː) n *Judaism* the contract that states the obligations within Jewish marriage [from Hebrew, literally: document]

keV *abbreviation for* kilo-electronvolt

kevel ('kɛv°l) n 1 *nautical* a strong bitt or bollard for securing heavy hawsers 2 *building trades* a hammer having an edged end and a pointed end, used for breaking and rough-shaping stone [c14 from Old Northern French *keville,* from Latin *clāvicula* a little key, from *clāvis* key]

Kevlar ('kɛvˌlaː) n *trademark* a synthetic fibre, consisting of long-chain polyamides, having high tensile strength and temperate resistance

Kew (kjuː) n part of the Greater London borough of Richmond-upon-Thames, on the River Thames: famous for **Kew Gardens** (the Royal Botanic Gardens), established in 1759 and given to the nation in 1841

kewl (kuːl) *adj informal* a nonstandard variant spelling of **cool** (sense 11)

Kewpie Doll ('kjuːpɪ) n *US and Canadian* 1 *trademark* a doll having rosy cheeks and a curl of hair on its head 2 *(often not capitals)* any brightly coloured doll, commonly given as a prize at carnivals [C20 *kewpie,* perhaps from *Cupid*]

kex (kɛks) n 1 any of several large hollow-stemmed umbelliferous plants, such as cow parsnip and chervil 2 the dried stalks of any of these plants [c14 of obscure origin]

key¹ (kiː) n 1 a metal instrument, usually of a specifically contoured shape, that is made to fit a lock and, when rotated, operates the lock's mechanism 2 any instrument that is rotated to operate a valve, clock winding mechanism, etc 3 a small metal peg or wedge inserted into keyways 4 any of a set of levers operating a typewriter, computer, etc 5 any of the visible parts of the lever mechanism of a musical keyboard instrument that when depressed set in motion the action that causes the instrument to sound 6 a Also called: tonality any of the 24 major and minor diatonic scales considered as a corpus of notes upon which a piece of music draws for its tonal framework b the main tonal centre in an extended composition: *a symphony in the key of F major* c the tonic of a major or minor scale d See **tuning key** 7 something that is crucial in providing an explanation or interpretation: *the key to adult behaviour lies in childhood* 8 a means of

achieving a desired end: *the key to happiness* 9 a means of access or control: *Gibraltar is the key to the Mediterranean* 10 a list of explanations of symbols, codes, etc 11 a text that explains or gives information about a work of literature, art, or music 12 Also called: **key move** the correct initial move in the solution of a set problem 13 *biology* a systematic list of taxonomic characteristics, used to identify animals or plants 14 *photog, painting* the dominant tonal value and colour intensity of a picture. See also **low-key** (sense 3), **high-key** 15 *electrical engineering* **a** a hand-operated device for opening or closing a circuit or for switching circuits **b** a hand-operated switch that is pressed to transmit coded signals, esp Morse code 16 the grooving or scratching of a surface or the application of a rough coat of plaster, etc, to provide a bond for a subsequent finish 17 *pitch: he spoke in a low key* 18 a characteristic mood or style: *a poem in a melancholic key* 19 level of intensity: *she worked herself up to a high key* 20 *railways* a wooden wedge placed between a rail and a chair to keep the rail firmly in place 21 a wedge for tightening a joint or for splitting stone or timber 22 short for **keystone** (sense 1) 23 *botany* any dry winged fruit, esp that of the ash 24 *(modifier)* of great importance: *a key issue* 25 *(modifier) photog* determining the tonal value of a photograph: *flesh colour is an important key tone* ▷ *vb (mainly tr)* 26 (foll by *to*) to harmonize (with): *to key one's actions to the prevailing mood* 27 to adjust or fasten with a key or some similar device 28 to provide with a key or keys 29 to scratch the paintwork of (a car) with a key 30 (often foll by *up*) to locate the position of (a piece of copy, artwork, etc) on a layout by the use of symbols 31 *(also intr)* another word for **keyboard** (sense 3) 32 to include a distinguishing device in (an advertisement, etc), so that responses to it can be identified 33 to provide a keystone for (an arch) ▷ See also **key in, key up** [Old English *cǣg;* related to Old Frisian *kēi,* Middle Low German *keie* spear] > 'keyless *adj*

key² (kiː) n a variant spelling of **cay**

keyboard ('kiːˌbɔːd) n 1 **a** a complete set of keys, usually hand-operated, as on a piano, organ, typewriter, or typesetting machine **b** *(as modifier): a keyboard instrument* 2 *(often plural)* a musical instrument, esp an electronic one, played by means of a keyboard ▷ *vb* 3 to set (a text, etc) in type, onto magnetic tape, or into some other medium, by using a keyboard machine > 'keyˌboarder n

keyboardist ('kiːˌbɔːdɪst) n a person who plays a keyboard instrument, esp an electronic musical instrument

key drive n *computing* a very small, portable storage device that plugs into a computer and facilitates moving data between machines. Also: pen drive

key fruit n another name for **samara**

key grip n *chiefly US* the person in charge of moving and setting up camera tracks and scenery in a film or television studio. See also **grip¹** (sense 11)

keyhole ('kiːˌhəʊl) n 1 an aperture in a door or a lock case through which a key may be passed to engage the lock mechanism 2 any small aperture resembling a keyhole in shape or function 3 a transient column of vapour or plasma formed during the welding or cutting of materials, using high energy beams, such as lasers

keyhole surgery n surgery carried out through a very small incision

key in *vb (tr, adverb)* to enter (information or instructions) in a computer or other device by means of a keyboard or keypad

key light n *television, theatre, photog* the main stage or studio light that gives the required overall intensity of illumination

keylogger ('kiːˌlɒɡə) n a device or software application used for covertly recording and monitoring keystrokes made on a remote computer

key-man assurance *n* an assurance policy taken out, esp by a small company, on the life of a senior executive whose death would create a serious loss

key money *n* a fee payment required from a new tenant of a house or flat before he moves in

Keynesian ('keɪnzɪən) *adj* **1** of or relating to the theories of John Maynard Keynes, 1st Baron Keynes, the English economist (1883–1946) **2** a follower or admirer of Keynes ▷ **'Keynesian,ism** *n*

keynote ('ki:,nəʊt) *n* **1** a central or determining principle in a speech, literary work, etc **b** (*as modifier*): *a keynote speech* **2** the note upon which a scale or key is based; tonic ▷ *vb* (*tr*) **3** to deliver a keynote address to (a political convention, etc) **4** to outline (political issues, policy, etc) in or as in a keynote address

keypad ('ki:,pæd) *n* **1** a small keyboard with push buttons, as on a pocket calculator, remote control unit for a television, etc **2** *computing* a data input device consisting of a limited number of keys, each with nominated functions

keypal ('ki:,pæl) *n* a person with whom one regularly exchanges E-mails for fun [c20 from KEYBOARD + PENPAL]

key punch *n* **1** Also called: **card punch** a device having a keyboard that is operated manually to transfer data onto punched cards, paper tape, etc ▷ *vb* **key-punch 2** to transfer (data) onto punched cards, paper tape, etc, by using a key punch

keyring drive *n* *computing* another name for **pocket drive**

keys (ki:z) *interj Scot dialect* a children's cry for truce or respite from the rules of a game [origin uncertain]

key signature *n music* a group of sharps or flats appearing at the beginning of each stave line to indicate the key in which a piece, section, etc, is to be performed

key stage *n Brit education* any one of four broad age-group divisions (5–7; 7–11; 11–14; 14–16) to which each level of the National Curriculum applies

keystone ('ki:,stəʊn) *n* **1** Also called: **headstone, quoin** the central stone at the top of an arch or the top stone of a dome or vault **2** something that is necessary to connect or support a number of other related things

keystroke ('ki:,strəʊk) *n* a single operation of the mechanism of a typewriter or keyboard-operated typesetting machine by the action of a key

key up *vb* (*tr, adverb*) to raise the intensity, excitement, tension, etc, of

keyway ('ki:,weɪ) *n* a longitudinal slot cut into a component to accept a key that engages with a similar slot on a mating component to prevent relative motion of the two components

keyword ('ki:,wɜːd) *n* **1** a word used as a key to a code **2** any significant word or phrase, esp a word used to describe the contents of a document

key worker *n chiefly Brit* **1** a social worker, mental health worker, or nursery nurse assigned to an individual case, patient, or child **2** (in Britain) a worker in any of a number of public sector professions considered by the government to be essential to society, for example teachers, police officers, NHS health workers etc

kg[1] *abbreviation for* keg **2** ▷ *symbol for* kilogram

kg[2] *the internet domain name for* Kyrgyzstan

KG *abbreviation for* Knight of the Order of the Garter (a Brit title)

KGB *abbreviation for* the former Soviet secret police, founded in 1954. Compare **GRU** [from Russian *Komitet Gosudarstvennoi Bezopasnosti* State Security Committee]

kh *the internet domain name for* Cambodia

Khabarovsk (*Russian* xaˈbarəfsk) *n* a port in E Russia, on the Amur River: it was the administrative centre of the whole Soviet Far Eastern territory until 1938; a major industrial centre. Pop: 579 000 (2005 est)

khaddar ('kɑːdə) *or* **khadi** ('kɑːdɪ) *n* a cotton cloth of plain weave, produced in India [from Hindi *khādar*]

Khakass Republic (kəˈkæs) *n* a constituent republic of S central Russia, formerly in Krasnoyarsk Territory: formed in 1930. Capital: Abakan. Pop: 546 100 (2002). Area: 61 900 sq km (23 855 sq miles). Also called: **Khakassia** (kəˈkæsɪə; *Russian* xəˈkasɪ̈jə)

khaki ('kɑːkɪ) *n, pl* **-kis 1 a** a dull yellowish-brown colour **b** (*as adjective*): *a khaki background* **2 a** a hard-wearing fabric of this colour, used esp for military uniforms **b** (*as modifier*): *a khaki jacket* [c19 from Urdu, from Persian: dusty, from *khāk* dust]

khaki election *n Brit* a general election held during or immediately after a war, esp one in which the war has an effect on how people vote [c20 first used of the 1900 general election, during which the conduct of the Boer war was an election issue]

khalif ('keɪlɪf, 'kæl-) *n* a variant spelling of **caliph**

Khalkha ('kælkə) *n* the dialect of Mongolian that is the official language of Mongolia

Khalkidikí (xalkɪðiˈki) *n* transliteration of the Modern Greek name for **Chalcidice**

Khalkís (xalˈkis) *n* transliteration of the Modern Greek name for **Chalcis**

Khalsa ('kælsə) *n* an order of the Sikh religion, founded (1699) by Guru Gobind Singh. Members vow to wear the five Ks, to eat only ritually killed meat, and to refrain from committing adultery or cutting their hair

khamsin ('kæmsɪn, kæm'si:n), **kamseen** *or* **kamsin** *n* a hot southerly wind blowing from about March to May, esp in Egypt [c17 from Arabic, literally: fifty]

khan[1] (kɑːn) *n* **1 a** (formerly) a title borne by medieval Chinese emperors and Mongol and Turkic rulers: usually added to a name: *Kublai Khan* **b** such a ruler **2** a title of respect borne by important personages in Afghanistan and central Asia [c14 from Old French *caan*, from Medieval Latin *caanus*, from Turkish *khān*, contraction of *khāqān* ruler]

khan[2] (kɑːn) *n* an inn in Turkey, certain Arab countries, etc; caravanserai [c14 via Arabic from Persian]

khanate ('kɑːneɪt, 'kæn-) *n* **1** the territory ruled by a khan **2** the position or rank of a khan

khanda ('kɑːndə) *n* a double-edged sword that appears as the emblem on the Sikh flag and is used in the Amrit ceremony to stir the amrit

khanga ('kæŋgə) *n* a variant spelling of **kanga**

Khaniá (xaˈnja) *n* transliteration of the Modern Greek name for **Chania**

kharif (kəˈriːf) *n* (in Pakistan, India, etc) a crop that is harvested at the beginning of winter. Compare **rabi** [Urdu, ultimately from Arabic *kharafa* to gather]

Kharkov (*Russian* 'xarjkəf) *n* a city in E Ukraine: capital of the Ukrainian Soviet Socialist Republic (1917–34); university (1805). Pop: 1 436 000 (2005 est)

Khartoum *or* **Khartum** (kɑːˈtuːm) *n* the capital of the Sudan, at the junction of the Blue and the White Nile: with adjoining Khartoum North and Omdurman, the largest conurbation in the country; destroyed by the Mahdists in 1885 when General Gordon was killed; seat of the Anglo-Egyptian government of the Sudan until 1954, then capital of the new republic. Pop: 4 495 000 (2005 est)

khat *or* **kat** (kæt, kɑːt) *n* **1** a white-flowered evergreen shrub, *Catha edulis*, of Africa and Arabia, whose leaves have narcotic properties **2** the leaves of this shrub, chewed or prepared as a drink [c19 from Arabic *qāt*]

khayal (kəˈjɑːl) *n* a kind of Indian classical vocal music [Urdu: literally: thought, imagination]

khazi ('kɑːzɪ) *n slang* a lavatory; toilet [c19 from *casa, case* a brothel, from Italian *casa* a house; modern spelling probably influenced by KHAKI]

kheda, khedah *or* **keddah** ('kɛdə) *n* (in India, Myanmar, etc) an enclosure into which wild elephants are driven to be captured [from Hindi]

khedive (kɪˈdiːv) *n* the viceroy of Egypt under Ottoman suzerainty (1867–1914) [c19 from French *khédive*, from Turkish *hidiv*, from Persian *khidīw* prince] ▷ **khe'dival** *or* **khe'divial** *adj* ▷ **khe'divate** *or* **khe'diviate** *n*

Khelat (kəˈlɑːt) *n* a variant spelling of **Kalat**

Kherson (*Russian* xɪrˈson) *n* a port in S Ukraine on the Dnieper River near the Black Sea: shipyards. Pop: 320 000 (2005 est)

Khingan Mountains (ʃɪŋˈɑːn) *pl n* a mountain system of NE China, in W Manchuria. Highest peak: 2034 m (6673 ft)

Khíos ('çios) *n* transliteration of the Modern Greek name for **Chios**

Khirbet Qumran ('kɪəbɛt 'kʊmrɑːn) *n* an archaeological site in NW Jordan, near the NW shore of the Dead Sea: includes the caves where the Dead Sea Scrolls were found

Khiva (*Russian* xiˈva) *n* a former khanate of W Asia, on the Amu Darya River: divided between the former Uzbek and Turkmen Soviet Socialist Republics in 1924

Khmer (kmɛə, kmɜː) *n* **1** a member of a people of Cambodia, noted for a civilization that flourished from about 800 AD to about 1370, remarkable for its architecture **2** the language of this people, belonging to the Mon-Khmer family: the official language of Cambodia ▷ *adj* **3** of or relating to this people or their language ▷ **Kh'merian** *adj*

Khmer Republic *n* the former official name (1970–76) of **Cambodia**

Khmer Rouge (ruːʒ) *n* the Kampuchean communist party, which seized power (1975) in a civil war: in exile since 1979, dispersed in 1999

Khoikhoi (ˈkɔɪˈkɔɪ, ˌxɔɪˈxɔɪ) *n* **1** a member of a race of people of Southern Africa, of short stature and a dark yellowish-brown complexion, who formerly occupied the region near the Cape of Good Hope and are now almost extinct **2** any of the languages of this people, belonging to the Khoisan family

Khoisan ('kɔɪsɑːn, kɔɪ'sɑːn) *n* **1** a family of languages spoken in southern Africa by the Khoikhoi and Bushmen and by two small groups in Tanzania. A characteristic phonological feature of these languages is the use of suction stops (clicks) ▷ *adj* **2** denoting, relating to, or belonging to this family of languages

Khojent, Khodzhent (*Russian* xadˈʒɛnt) *or* **Khujand** (*Russian* xuˈʃænd) *n* a town in Tajikistan on the Syr Darya River: one of the oldest towns in central Asia; textile industries. Pop: 146 000 (2005 est). Former name (1936–91): Leninabad

Khotan ('kəʊˈtɑːn) *n* another name for **Hotan**

Khujand (*Russian* xuˈʃænd) *n* a variant spelling of **Khojent**

Khulna ('kʊlnɑː) *n* a city in S Bangladesh. Pop: 1 497 000 (2005 est)

khurta ('kʊətə) *n* a variant spelling of **kurta**

khuskhus ('kʊskʊs) *n* an aromatic perennial Indian grass, *Vetiveria zizanioides* (or *Andropogon squarrosus*), whose roots are woven into mats, fans, and baskets [Hindi]

khutbah ('kʊtˌbɑː) *n Islam* a Muslim sermon that is delivered on a Friday [c21 from Arabic *khataba* to preach]

Khyber Pass ('kaɪbə) *n* a narrow pass over the Safed Koh Range between Afghanistan and Pakistan, over which came the Persian, Greek, Tatar, Mogul, and Afghan invasions of India; scene of bitter fighting between the British and Afghans (1838–42, 1878–80). Length: about 53 km (33 miles). Highest point: 1072 m (3518 ft)

kHz *symbol for* kilohertz

ki *the internet domain name for* Kiribati

kiaat ('ki:ɑːt) *n* **1** a tropical African leguminous tree, *Pterocarpus angolensis* **2** the wood of this tree, used for furniture, floors, etc [c19 Afrikaans, from Dutch, probably from Malay *kaju* wood]

k

kia kaha (ˌkɪə ˈkɑːhə) *sentence substitute NZ* be strong! [Māori]

kiang (kɪˈæŋ) *n* a variety of the wild ass, *Equus hemionus*, that occurs in Tibet and surrounding regions. Compare **onager** [C19 from Tibetan *rkyan*]

Kiangsi (ˈkjæŋˈsiː) *n* a variant transliteration of the Chinese name for **Jiangxi**

Kiangsu (ˈkjæŋˈsuː) *n* a variant transliteration of the Chinese name for **Jiangsu**

Kiaochow (ˈkjaʊˈtʃaʊ) *n* a variant transliteration of the Chinese name for **Jiazhou**

kia ora (ˌkɪə ˈɔːrə) *sentence substitute NZ* greetings! good luck! [Māori, literally: be well!]

kibble[1] (ˈkɪbᵊl) *n Brit* a bucket used in wells or in mining for hoisting [C17 from German *Kübel*; related to Old English *cyfel*, ultimately from Medieval Latin *cuppa* CUP]

kibble[2] (ˈkɪbᵊl) *vb* **1** (*tr*) to grind into small pieces ▷ *n* **2** *US and Canadian* ground meal formed into pellets and used as pet food [C18 of unknown origin]

kibbutz (kɪˈbʊts) *n, pl* **kibbutzim** (ˌkɪbʊtˈsiːm) a collective agricultural settlement in modern Israel, owned and administered communally by its members and on which children are reared collectively [C20 from Modern Hebrew *qibbūs*: gathering, from Hebrew *qibbūtz*]

kibe (kaɪb) *n* a chilblain, esp an ulcerated one on the heel [C14 probably from Welsh *cibi*, of obscure origin]

kibi- (ˈkɪbɪ) *prefix computing* denoting 2^{10}: *kibibyte*. Symbol: Ki [C20 from KI(LO-) + BI(NARY)]

kibitka (kɪˈbɪtkə) *n* **1** (in Russia) a covered sledge or wagon **2** a felt tent used among the Tatars of central Asia **3** a Tatar family [C18 Russian, from Tatar *kibits*]

kibitz (ˈkɪbɪts) *vb* (*intr*) *US and Canadian informal* to interfere or offer unwanted advice, esp as a spectator at a card game [C20 from Yiddish *kibitzen*, from German *kiebitzen* to be an onlooker, from *Kiebitz* busybody, literally: plover] > ˈ**kibitzer** *n*

kiblah *or* **kibla** (ˈkɪblɑː) *n Islam* the direction of Mecca, to which Muslims turn in prayer, indicated in mosques by a niche (mihrab) in the wall [C18 from Arabic *qiblah* that which is placed opposite; related to *qabala* to be opposite]

kibosh *or* **kybosh** (ˈkaɪˌbɒʃ) *slang* ▷ *n* **1** **put the kibosh on** to put a stop to; halt ▷ *vb* **2** (*tr*) to put a stop to [C19 of unknown origin]

kick (kɪk) *vb* **1** (*tr*) to drive or impel with the foot **2** (*tr*) to hit with the foot or feet **3** (*intr*) to strike out or thrash about with the feet, as in fighting or swimming **4** (*intr*) to raise a leg high, as in dancing **5** (of a gun, etc) to recoil or strike in recoiling when fired **6** (*tr*) *rugby* **a** to make (a conversion or a drop goal) by means of a kick **b** to score (a goal) by means of a kicked conversion **7** (*tr*) *soccer* to score (a goal) by a kick **8** (*intr*) *cricket* (of a ball) to rear up sharply **9** (*intr*; sometimes foll by *against*) *informal* to object or resist **10** (*intr*) *informal* to be active and in good health (esp in the phrase **alive and kicking**) **11** *informal* to change gear in (a car, esp a racing car): *he kicked into third and passed the bigger car* **12** (*tr*) *informal* to free oneself of (an addiction, etc): *to kick heroin; to kick the habit* **13** **kick against the pricks** See **prick** (sense 20) **14** **kick into touch** **a** *rugby, soccer* to kick the ball out of the playing area and into touch. See **touch** (sense 15) **b** *informal* to take some temporizing action so that a problem is shelved or a decision postponed **15** **kick one's heels** to wait or be kept waiting **16** **kick over the traces** See **trace**[2] (sense 3) **17** **kick the bucket** *slang* to die **18** **kick up one's heels** *informal* to enjoy oneself without inhibition ▷ *n* **19** a thrust or blow with the foot **20** any of certain rhythmic leg movements used in swimming **21** the recoil of a gun or other firearm **22** *informal* a stimulating or exciting quality or effect (esp in the phrases **get a kick out of** or **for kicks**) **23** *informal* the sudden stimulating or intoxicating effect of strong alcoholic drink or certain drugs **24** *informal* power or force **25** *slang* a temporary enthusiasm: *he's on a new kick every week* **26** **kick in the pants** *slang* **a** a reprimand or scolding designed to produce greater effort, enthusiasm, etc, in the person receiving it **b** a setback or disappointment **27** **kick in the teeth** *slang* a humiliating rebuff ▷ See also **kick about, kickback, kick in, kick off, kick out, kick up, kick upstairs** [C14 *kiken*, perhaps of Scandinavian origin] > ˈ**kickable** *adj*

kick about *or* **around** *vb* (*mainly adverb*) *informal* **1** (*tr*) to treat harshly **2** (*tr*) to discuss (ideas, etc) informally **3** (*intr*) to wander aimlessly **4** (*intr*) to lie neglected or forgotten **5** (*intr; also preposition*) to be present in (some place) ▷ *n* **kickabout** *or* **kickaround** **6** an informal game of soccer

kick ass *slang* ▷ *vb* (*intr*) **1** to be impressive, esp in a forceful way: *pop music that kicks ass* ▷ *adj* **kick-ass** **2** forceful, aggressive, and impressive

kickback (ˈkɪkˌbæk) *n* **1** a strong reaction **2** part of an income paid to a person having influence over the size or payment of the income, esp by some illegal arrangement ▷ *vb* **kick back** (*adverb*) **3** (*intr*) to have a strong reaction **4** (*intr*) (esp of a gun) to recoil **5** to pay a kickback to (someone)

kick boxing *n* a martial art that resembles boxing but permits blows with the feet as well as punches

kickdown (ˈkɪkˌdaʊn) *n* a method of changing gear in a car with automatic transmission, by fully depressing the accelerator

kicker (ˈkɪkə) *n* **1** a person or thing that kicks **2** *sport* a player in a rugby or occasionally a soccer team whose task is to attempt to kick conversions, penalty goals, etc **3** *US and Canadian slang* a hidden and disadvantageous factor, such as a clause in a contract **4** *informal* any light outboard motor for propelling a boat

kick in *vb* (*adverb*) **1** (*intr*) to start or become activated **2** (*tr*) *chiefly Austral and NZ informal* to contribute

kick off *vb* (*intr, adverb*) **1** to start play in a game of football by kicking the ball from the centre of the field **2** *informal* to commence a discussion, job, etc ▷ *n* **kickoff** **3** **a** a place kick from the centre of the field in a game of football **b** the time at which the first such kick is due to take place: *kickoff is at 2.30 p.m* **4** *informal* **a** the beginning of something **b** **for a kickoff** to begin with

kick on *vb* (*adverb*) *informal* to continue

kick out *vb* (*tr, adverb*) *informal* to eject or dismiss

kick pleat *n* a back pleat at the hem of a straight skirt to allow the wearer greater ease in walking

kickshaw (ˈkɪkʃɔː) *or* **kickshaws** *n* **1** a valueless trinket **2** *archaic* a small elaborate or exotic delicacy [C16 back formation from *kickshaws*, by folk etymology from French *quelque chose* something]

kicksorter (ˈkɪkˌsɔːtə) *n physics* a multichannel pulse-height analyser used esp to distinguish between isotopes by sorting their characteristic pulses (kicks)

kickstand (ˈkɪkˌstænd) *n* a short metal bar attached to and pivoting on the bottom of the frame of a motorcycle or bicycle, which when kicked into a vertical position holds the stationary vehicle upright

kick-start (ˈkɪkˌstɑːt) *vb* (*tr*) **1** to start (a motorcycle engine) by means of a pedal that is kicked downwards **2** *informal* to make (something) active, functional, or productive again ▷ *n* **3** an action or event resulting in the reactivation of something > ˈ**kick-ˌstarter** *n*

kick turn *n skiing* a standing turn performed by swivelling each ski separately through 180°

kick up *vb* (*adverb*) **1** *informal* to cause (trouble, a fuss, etc) **2** **kick up bobsy-die** See **bobsy-die**

kick upstairs *vb* (*tr, adverb*) *informal* to promote to a nominally higher but effectively powerless position

kid[1] (kɪd) *n* **1** the young of a goat or of a related animal, such as an antelope **2** soft smooth leather made from the hide of a kid **3** *informal* **a** a young person; child **b** (*modifier*) younger or being still a child: *kid brother; kid sister* **4** **our kid** *Liverpool dialect* my younger brother or sister ▷ *vb* **kids, kidding, kidded** **5** (of a goat) to give birth to (young) [C12 of Scandinavian origin; compare Old Norse *kith*, Shetland Islands *kidi* lamb] > ˈ**kiddishness** *n* > ˈ**kidˌlike** *adj*

kid[2] (kɪd) *vb* **kids, kidding, kidded** (sometimes foll by *on* or *along*) *informal* **1** (*tr*) to tease or deceive for fun **2** (*intr*) to behave or speak deceptively for fun **3** (*tr*) to delude or fool (oneself) into believing (something): *don't kid yourself that no-one else knows* [C19 probably from KID[1]] > ˈ**kidder** *n* > ˈ**kiddingly** *adv*

kid[3] (kɪd) *n* a small wooden tub [C18 probably variant of KIT[1] (in the sense: barrel)]

kidder (ˈkɪdə) *n* **1** a person who kids **2** *Northern English dialect* a brother or friend

Kidderminster (ˈkɪdəˌmɪnstə) *n* **1** a town in W central England, in N Worcestershire on the River Stour: carpet industry. Pop: 55 610 (2001) **2** a type of ingrain reversible carpet originally made at Kidderminster

kiddle (ˈkɪdᵊl) *n Brit archaic* a device, esp a barrier constructed of nets and stakes, for catching fish in a river or in the sea [C13 from Anglo-French, from Old French *quidel*, of obscure origin]

Kiddush (ˈkɪdəʃ; *Hebrew* kɪˈdʊʃ) *n Judaism* **1** a special blessing said before a meal on sabbaths and festivals, usually including the blessing for wine or bread **2** a reception usually for the congregants after a service at which drinks and snacks are served and this grace is said [from Hebrew *qiddūsh* sanctification]

kiddy *or* **kiddie** (ˈkɪdɪ) *n, pl* **-dies** *informal* an affectionate word for **child**

kid glove *n* **1** a glove made of kidskin **2** **handle with kid gloves** to treat with great tact or caution ▷ *adj* **kidglove** **3** overdelicate or overrefined **4** diplomatic; tactful: *a kidglove approach*

kidnap (ˈkɪdnæp) *vb* **-naps, -napping, -napped** *or US* **-naps, -naping, -naped** (*tr*) to carry off and hold (a person), usually for ransom [C17 KID[1] + obsolete *nap* to steal; see NAB] > ˈ**kidnapper** *or US* ˈ**kidnaper** *n* > ˈ**kidnapping** *or US* ˈ**kidnaping** *n*

kidney (ˈkɪdnɪ) *n* **1** either of two bean-shaped organs at the back of the abdominal cavity in man, one on each side of the spinal column. They maintain water and electrolyte balance and filter waste products from the blood, which are excreted as urine. Related adjs: **nephritic, renal** **2** the corresponding organ in other animals **3** the kidneys of certain animals used as food **4** class, type, or disposition (esp in the phrases **of the same** or **a different kidney**) [C14 of uncertain origin] > ˈ**kidneyˌlike** *adj*

kidney bean *n* **1** any of certain bean plants having kidney-shaped seeds, esp the French bean and scarlet runner **2** the seed of any of these beans

kidney machine *n* another name for **artificial kidney** See **haemodialysis**

kidney ore *n geology* a form of hematite that occurs in kidney-shaped masses

kidney-shaped *adj* shaped like an oval with an inward curve at one side

kidney stone *n* **1** *pathol* a hard mass formed in the kidney, usually composed of oxalates, phosphates, and carbonates. Also called: **renal calculus** **2** *mineralogy* another name for **nephrite**

kidney vetch *n* a silky leguminous perennial plant, *Anthyllis vulneraria*, of Europe and N Africa, with yellow or orange flowers. Also called: **ladies' fingers**

kidology (kɪˈdɒlədʒɪ) *n Brit informal* the art or practice of bluffing or deception [C20 from KID[2] + -OLOGY]

kid-on *adj Brit informal* artificial; make-believe

Kidron (ˈkiːdrən) *n* a variant of **Kedron**

kidskin (ˈkɪdˌskɪn) *n* a soft smooth leather made from the hide of a young goat. Often shortened to: kid

kids' stuff *n slang* **1** something considered fit

only for children **2** something considered simple or easy

kidstakes ('kɪd,steɪks) *pl n Austral informal* pretence; nonsense: *cut the kidstakes!*

kidult ('kɪdʌlt) *informal* ▷ *n* **1** an adult who is interested in forms of entertainment such as computer games, television programmes, etc that are intended for children ▷ *adj* **2** aimed at or suitable for kidults, or both children and adults [C20 from KID¹ + (AD)ULT]

kief (kiːf) *n* a variant spelling of **kif**

kiekie ('kɪəˌkɪə, 'kiːˌkiː) *n* a climbing bush plant, *Freycinetia banksii*, of New Zealand, having elongated leaves and edible berries [Māori]

Kiel (kiːl) *n* a port in N Germany, capital of Schleswig-Holstein state, on the **Kiel Canal** (connecting the North Sea with the Baltic): joined the Hanseatic League in 1284; became part of Denmark in 1773 and passed to Prussia in 1866; an important naval base in World Wars I and II; shipbuilding and engineering industries. Pop: 233 039 (2003 est)

Kielce (*Polish* 'kjɛltsɛ) *n* an industrial city in S Poland. Pop: 212 383 (1999 est)

kier (kɪə) *n* a vat in which cloth is bleached [C16 from Old Norse *ker* tub; related to Old High German *kar*]

Kierkegaardian (,kɪəkə'gɑːdɪən) *adj* of or relating to Søren Aabye Kierkegaard, the Danish philosopher and theologian (1813–55), whose theories anticipated existentialism

kieselguhr ('kiːzəˌlɡʊə) *n* an unconsolidated form of **diatomite** [C19 from German *Kieselgur*, from *Kiesel* flint, pebble + *Gur* loose earthy deposit]

kieserite ('kiːzəˌraɪt) *n* a white mineral consisting of hydrated magnesium sulphate. Formula: $MgSO_4.H_2O$ [C19 named after Dietrich G. *Kieser* (died 1862), German physician; see -ITE¹]

Kiev ('kiːɛf; *Russian* 'kijɪf) *n* the capital of Ukraine, on the Dnieper River: formed the first Russian state by the late 9th century; university (1834). Pop: 2 623 000 (2005 est)

kif (kɪf, kiːf), **kaif**, **keef**, **kef** *or* **kief** *n* **1** another name for **marijuana 2** any drug or agent that when smoked is capable of producing a euphoric condition **3** the euphoric condition produced by smoking marijuana [C20 from Arabic *kayf* pleasure]

kiff (kɪf) *adj South African slang* excellent; cool [perhaps related to KIF]

Kigali (kɪ'ɡɑːlɪ) *n* the capital of Rwanda, in the central part. Pop: 782 000 (2005 est)

Kigoma-Ujiji (kɪ'ɡəʊmə uː'dʒiːdʒiː) *n* a city in W Tanzania, on the shore of Lake Tanganyika; formed by the merger of the towns of Kigoma and Ujiji in the 1960s

kike (kaɪk) *n US and Canadian slang* an offensive word for **Jew** [C20 probably variant of *kiki*, reduplication of *-ki*, common name-ending among Jews from Slavic countries]

Kikládhes (ki'klaðɛs) *n* transliteration of the Modern Greek name for **Cyclades**

kikoi ('kiːkɔɪ) *n* (in E Africa) **a** a piece of cotton cloth with coloured bands, worn wrapped around the body **b** (*as modifier*): *kikoi material* [C20 from Swahili]

kikumon ('kiːkuːˌmɒn) *n* the chrysanthemum emblem of the imperial family of Japan [Japanese]

Kikuyu (kɪ'kuːjuː) *n* **1** (*pl* **-yus** *or* **-yu**) a member of a Negroid people of E Africa, living chiefly in Kenya on the high foothills around Mount Kenya **2** the language of this people, belonging to the Bantu group of the Niger-Congo family

Kilauea (,kiːlɑːuː'eɪə) *n* a crater on the E side of Mauna Loa volcano, on SE Hawaii Island: the world's largest active crater. Height: 1247 m (4090 ft). Width: 3 km (2 miles)

Kildare (kɪl'dɛə) *n* a county of E Republic of Ireland, in Leinster province: mostly low-lying and fertile. County town: Naas. Pop: 163 944 (2002). Area: 1694 sq km (654 sq miles)

kilderkin ('kɪldəkɪn) *n* **1** an obsolete unit of liquid capacity equal to 16 or 18 Imperial gallons or of dry capacity equal to 16 or 18 wine gallons **2** a cask capable of holding a kilderkin [C14 from Middle Dutch *kindekijn*, from *kintal* hundredweight, from Medieval Latin *quintale*; see KENTLEDGE]

kiley ('kaɪlɪ) *n* a variant spelling of **kylie**

kilim (kɪ'liːm, 'kiːlɪm) *n* a pileless woven rug of intricate design made in the Middle East [C19 from Turkish, from Persian *kilīm*]

Kilimanjaro (,kɪlɪmən'dʒɑːrəʊ) *n* a volcanic massif in N Tanzania: the highest peak in Africa; extends from east to west for 80 km (50 miles). Height: 5895 m (19 340 ft)

Kilkenny (kɪl'kɛnɪ) *n* **1** a county of SE Republic of Ireland, in Leinster province: mostly agricultural. County town: Kilkenny. Pop: 80 339 (2002). Area: 2062 sq km (796 sq miles) **2** a market town in SE Republic of Ireland, county town of Co Kilkenny: capital of the ancient kingdom of Ossory. Pop: 9500 (latest est)

kill¹ (kɪl) *vb* (*mainly tr*) **1** (*also intr*; when *tr*, sometimes foll by *off*) to cause the death of (a person or animal) **2** to put an end to; destroy: *to kill someone's interest* **3** to make (time) pass quickly, esp while waiting for something **4** to deaden (sound) **5** *informal* to tire out; exhaust: *the effort killed him* **6** *informal* to cause to suffer pain or discomfort: *my shoes are killing me* **7** *informal* to cancel, cut, or delete: *to kill three lines of text* **8** *informal* to quash, defeat, or veto: *the bill was killed in the House of Lords* **9** *informal* to switch off; stop: *to kill a motor* **10** (*also intr*) *informal* to overcome with attraction, laughter, surprise, etc: *she was dressed to kill; his gags kill me* **11** *slang* to consume (alcoholic drink) entirely: *he killed three bottles of rum* **12** *sport* to hit (a ball) so hard or so accurately that the opponent cannot return it **13** *soccer* to bring (a moving ball) under control; trap **14 kill oneself** *informal* to overexert oneself: *don't kill yourself* **15 kill two birds with one stone** to achieve two results with one action ▷ *n* **16** the act of causing death, esp at the end of a hunt, bullfight, etc **17** the animal or animals killed during a hunt **18** *NZ* the seasonal tally of stock slaughtered at a freezing works **19** the destruction of a battleship, tank, etc **20 in at the kill** present at the end or climax of some undertaking [C13 *cullen*; perhaps related to Old English *cwellan* to kill; compare German (Westphalian dialect) *küllen*; see QUELL]

kill² (kɪl) *n US* a channel, stream, or river (chiefly as part of place names) [C17 from Middle Dutch *kille*; compare Old Norse *kīll* small bay, creek]

Killarney (kɪ'lɑːnɪ) *n* a town in SW Republic of Ireland, in Co Kerry: a tourist centre near the **Lakes of Killarney**. Pop: 13 137 (2002)

killdeer ('kɪl,dɪə) *n, pl* **-deer** *or* **-deers** a large brown-and-white North American plover, *Charadrius vociferus*, with two black breast bands and a noisy cry [C18 of imitative origin]

killer ('kɪlə) *n* **1 a** a person or animal that kills, esp habitually **b** (*as modifier*): *a killer shark* **2** something, esp a task or activity, that is particularly taxing or exhausting **3** *Austral and NZ* an animal selected to be slaughtered for food

killer application *n* a highly innovative, very powerful, or extremely useful computer application; esp one sufficiently important as to justify purchase of the equipment or software

killer bee *n* an African honeybee, or one of its hybrids originating in Brazil, that is extremely aggressive when disturbed

killer cell *n* a type of white blood cell that is able to kill cells, such as cancer cells and cells infected with viruses

killer whale *n* a predatory black-and-white toothed whale, *Orcinus orca*, with a large erect dorsal fin, most common in cold seas: family Delphinidae. Also called: **killer**, **grampus**, **orc**

killick ('kɪlɪk) *or* **killock** ('kɪlək) *n nautical* a small anchor, esp one made of a heavy stone [C17 of unknown origin]

Killiecrankie (,kɪlɪ'kræŋkɪ) *n* a pass in central Scotland, in the Grampians: scene of a battle (1689) in which the Jacobites defeated William III's forces but lost their leader, Viscount Dundee

killifish ('kɪlɪ,fɪʃ) *n, pl* **-fish** *or* **-fishes** any of various chiefly American minnow-like cyprinodont fishes of the genus *Fundulus* and related genera, of fresh and brackish waters: used as aquarium fishes, to control mosquitoes, and as anglers' bait [C19 see KILL², FISH]

killikinick (,kɪlɪkɪ'nɪk) *n* a variant of **kinnikinnick**

killing ('kɪlɪŋ) *adj* **1** *informal* very tiring; exhausting: *a killing pace* **2** *informal* extremely funny; hilarious **3** causing death; fatal ▷ *n* **4** the act of causing death; slaying **5** *informal* a sudden stroke of success, usually financial, as in speculations on the stock market (esp in the phrase **make a killing**) > **'killingly** *adv*

killjoy ('kɪl,dʒɔɪ) *n* a person who spoils other people's pleasure

kill-time *n* **a** an occupation that passes the time **b** (*as modifier*): *kill-time pursuits*

Kilmarnock (kɪl'mɑːnək) *n* a town in SW Scotland, the administrative centre of East Ayrshire: associations with Robert Burns; engineering and textile industries; whisky blending. Pop: 43 588 (2001)

kiln (kɪln) *n* **1** a large oven for burning, drying, or processing something, such as porcelain or bricks ▷ *vb* **2** (*tr*) to fire or process in a kiln [Old English *cylen*, from Late Latin *culīna* kitchen, from Latin *coquere* to COOK]

Kilner jar ('kɪlnə) *n trademark* a glass preserving jar with an airtight lid, used for bottling fruit or vegetables

kilo¹ ('kiːləʊ) *n, pl* **kilos** short for **kilogram** *or* **kilometre**

kilo² ('kiːləʊ) *n communications* a code word for the letter *k*

kilo- *prefix* **1** denoting 10^3 (1000): *kilometre*. Symbol: k **2** (in computer technology) denoting 2^{10} (1024): *kilobyte*: in computer usage, *kilo-* is restricted to sizes of storage (eg *kilobit*) when it means 1024; in other computer contexts it retains its usual meaning of 1000 [from French, from Greek *khilioi* thousand]

kilobit ('kɪlə,bɪt) *n computing* **1** (in general computer contexts, such as data transfer) 1000 bits **2** (in data-storage contexts) 1024 bits ▷ Abbreviations: **Kb**, **kb**

kilobyte ('kɪlə,baɪt) *n computing* 1024 bytes. Abbreviations: **KB**, **kbyte** See also **kilo-** (sense 2)

kilocalorie (,kɪləʊ,kælərɪ) *n* another name for **Calorie**

kilocycle ('kɪləʊ,saɪkəl) *n* short for kilocycle per second: a former unit of frequency equal to 1 kilohertz

kilogram ('kɪləʊ,ɡræm) *n* **1** one thousand grams **2** the basic SI unit of mass, equal to the mass of the international prototype held by the *Bureau International des Poids et Mesures*. One kilogram is equivalent to 2.204 62 pounds. Symbol: **kg**

kilogram calorie *n* another name for **Calorie**

kilohertz ('kɪləʊ,hɜːts) *n* one thousand hertz; one thousand cycles per second. Symbol: **kHz**

kilometre *or US* **kilometer** ('kɪlə,miːtə, kɪ'lɒmɪtə) *n* one thousand metres, equal to 0.621371 miles. Symbol: **km** > **kilometric** (,kɪləʊ'mɛtrɪk) *or* **kilo'metrical** *adj*

kiloton ('kɪləʊ,tʌn) *n* **1** one thousand tons **2** an explosive power, esp of a nuclear weapon, equal to the power of 1000 tons of TNT. Abbreviation: **kt**

kilovolt ('kɪləʊ,vəʊlt) *n* one thousand volts. Symbol: **kV**

kilowatt ('kɪləʊ,wɒt) *n* one thousand watts. Symbol: **kW**

kilowatt-hour *n* a unit of energy equal to the work done by a power of 1000 watts in one hour. Symbol: **kWh**

kilt (kɪlt) *n* **1** a knee-length pleated skirt-like garment, esp one in tartan, as worn by men in Highland dress ▷ *vb* (*tr*) **2** to tuck (a skirt) up around one's body **3** to put pleats in (cloth, a

k

skirt, etc) [c18 of Scandinavian origin; compare Danish *kilte* to tuck up, Old Swedish *kilta* lap] > 'kilted *adj* > 'kilt,like *adj*

kilter ('kɪltə) *or* **kelter** *n* working order or alignment (esp in the phrases **off kilter, out of kilter**) [c17 origin unknown]

Kilung ('kiː'lʊŋ) *n* another name for **Chilung**

Kimberley ('kɪmbəlɪ) *n* **1** a city in central South Africa; the capital of Northern Cape province: besieged (1899–1900) for 126 days during the Boer War; diamond-mining and -marketing centre, with heavy engineering works. Pop: 62 526 (2001) **2** Also called: **the Kimberleys** a plateau region of NW Australia, in N Western Australia: consists of rugged mountains surrounded by grassland. Area: about 360 000 sq km (140 000 sq miles)

kimberlite ('kɪmbə,laɪt) *n* an intrusive igneous rock generated at great depth in the earth's mantle and consisting largely of olivine and phlogopite. It often contains diamonds [c19 from KIMBERLEY + -ITE[1]]

kimono (kɪ'məʊnəʊ) *n*, *pl* -nos **1** a loose sashed ankle-length garment with wide sleeves, worn in Japan **2** any garment copied from this [c19 from Japanese: clothing, from *kiru* to wear + *mono* thing] > ki'monoed *adj*

kin (kɪn) *n* **1** a person's relatives collectively; kindred **2** a class or group with similar characteristics **3** See next of kin ▷ *adj* **4** (*postpositive*) related by blood **5** a less common word for **akin** [Old English *cyn*; related to Old Norse *kyn* family, Old High German *kind* child, Latin *genus* kind]

-kin *suffix forming nouns* small: *lambkin* [from Middle Dutch, of West Germanic origin; compare German *-chen*]

kina[1] ('kiːnə) *n* the standard monetary unit of Papua New Guinea, divided into 100 toea [from a Papuan language]

kina[2] ('kiːnə) *n*, *pl* kina a green sea urchin, *Evichinus chloroticus*, eaten in New Zealand. Also called: **sea egg** [Māori]

Kinabalu (,kɪnəbə'luː) *n* a mountain in Malaysia, on N Borneo in central Sabah: the highest peak in Borneo. Height: 4125 m (13 533 ft)

kinaesthesia (,kɪnɪs'θiːzɪə, ,kaɪn-), **kinaesthesis** *or US* **kinesthesia, kinesthesis** *n* the sensation by which bodily position, weight, muscle tension, and movement are perceived. Also called: **muscle sense** [c19 from New Latin, from Greek *kinein* to move + AESTHESIA] > **kinaesthetic** *or US* **kinesthetic** (,kɪnɪs'θɛtɪk, ,kaɪn-) *adj*

kinase ('kaɪneɪz, 'kɪn-) *n* **1** any enzyme that can convert an inactive zymogen to the corresponding enzyme **2** any enzyme that brings about the phosphorylation of a molecule [c20 from KIN(ETIC) + -ASE]

Kincardineshire (kɪn'kɑːdɪn,ʃɪə, -ʃə) *n* a former county of E Scotland: became part of Grampian region in 1975 and part of Aberdeenshire in 1996. Also called: **the Mearns**

Kinchinjunga (,kɪntʃɪn'dʒʌŋɡə) *n* a variant of **Kangchenjunga**

kincob ('kɪŋkɒb) *n* a fine silk fabric embroidered with threads of gold or silver, of a kind made in India [c18 from Urdu *kimkhāb*]

kind[1] (kaɪnd) *adj* **1** having a friendly or generous nature or attitude **2** helpful to others or to another: *a kind deed* **3** considerate or humane **4** cordial; courteous (esp in the phrase **kind regards**) **5** pleasant; agreeable; mild: *a kind climate* **6** *informal* beneficial or not harmful: *a detergent that is kind to the hands* **7** *archaic* loving [Old English *gecynde* natural, native; see KIND[2]]

kind[2] (kaɪnd) *n* **1** a class or group having characteristics in common; sort; type: *two of a kind; what kind of creature?* **2** an instance or example of a class or group, esp a rudimentary one: *heating of a kind* **3** essential nature or character: *the difference is one of kind rather than degree* **4** *archaic* gender or sex **5** *archaic* nature; the natural order **6** in kind **a** (of payment) in goods or produce rather than in

money **b** with something of the same sort: *to return an insult in kind* **7** kind of (*adverb*) *informal* somewhat; rather: *kind of tired* [Old English *gecynd* nature; compare Old English *cyn* KIN, Gothic *kuni* race, Old High German *kikunt*, Latin *gens*]

▌USAGE The mixture of plural and singular constructions, although often used informally with *kind* and *sort*, should be avoided in serious writing: *children enjoy those kinds* (not *those kind*) *of stories; these sorts* (not *these sort*) *of distinctions are becoming blurred*

kindergarten ('kɪndə,ɡɑːtᵊn) *n* a class or small school for young children, usually between the ages of four and six to prepare them for primary education. Often shortened (in Australia) to **kinder** or (in Australia and New Zealand) to **kindy** or **kindie** [c19 from German, literally: children's garden] > 'kinder,gartener *n*

kind-hearted *adj* characterized by kindness; sympathetic > ,kind-'heartedly *adv* > ,kind-'heartedness *n*

kindle ('kɪndᵊl) *vb* **1** to set alight or start to burn **2** to arouse or be aroused: *the project kindled his interest* **3** to make or become bright [c12 from Old Norse *kynda*, influenced by Old Norse *kyndill* candle] > 'kindler *n*

kindless ('kaɪndlɪs) *adj archaic* **1** heartless **2** against nature; unnatural > 'kindlessly *adv*

kindling ('kɪndlɪŋ) *n* material for starting a fire, such as dry wood, straw, etc

kindly ('kaɪndlɪ) *adj* -lier, -liest **1** having a sympathetic or warm-hearted nature **2** motivated by warm and sympathetic feelings: *a kindly act* **3** pleasant, mild, or agreeable: *a kindly climate* **4** *archaic* natural; normal ▷ *adv* **5** in a considerate or humane way **6** with tolerance or forbearance: *he kindly forgave my rudeness* **7** cordially; pleasantly: *he greeted us kindly* **8** please (often used to express impatience or formality): *will you kindly behave yourself!* **9** *archaic* in accordance with nature; appropriately **10** to react favourably > 'kindliness *n*

kindness ('kaɪndnɪs) *n* **1** the practice or quality of being kind **2** a kind, considerate, or helpful act

kindred ('kɪndrɪd) *adj* **1** having similar or common qualities, origin, etc **2** related by blood or marriage **3** kindred spirit a person with whom one has something in common ▷ *n* **4** relationship by blood **5** similarity in character **6** a person's relatives collectively [c12 *kinred*, from KIN + -red, from Old English *rǣden* rule, from *rǣdan* to rule] > 'kindredness *or* 'kindred,ship *n*

kindy *or* **kindie** ('kɪndɪ) *n Austral and NZ informal* short for **kindergarten**

kine (kaɪn) *n* (*functioning as plural*) an archaic word for **cows** or **cattle** [Old English *cȳna* of cows, from *cū* cow[1]]

kinematics (,kɪnɪ'mætɪks, ,kaɪn-) *n* (*functioning as singular*) the study of the motion of bodies without reference to mass or force. Compare **dynamics** (sense 1) [c19 from Greek *kinēma* movement; see CINEMA, -ICS] > ,kine'matic *adj* > ,kine'matically *adv*

kinematic viscosity *n* a measure of the resistance to flow of a fluid, equal to its absolute viscosity divided by its density. Symbol: v

kinematograph (,kɪnɪ'mætə,ɡrɑːf, ,kaɪnɪ-, -,ɡræf) *n* a variant of **cinematograph**. > **kinematographer** (,kɪnəmə'tɒɡrəfə) *n* > **kinematographic** (,kɪnɪ,mætə'ɡræfɪk, ,kaɪnɪ-) *adj* > ,kinema'tography *n*

kinescope ('kɪnəskəʊp) *n* the US name for **television tube**

kinesics (kɪ'niːsɪks) *n* (*functioning as singular*) the study of the role of body movements, such as winking, shrugging, etc, in communication

kinesiology (kɪ,niːsɪ'ɒlədʒɪ) *n* the study of the mechanics and anatomy of human muscles

kinesis (kɪ'niːsɪs, kaɪ-) *n biology* the nondirectional movement of an organism or cell in response to a stimulus, the rate of movement being dependent on the strength of the stimulus

kinesthesia (,kɪnɪs'θiːzɪə, ,kaɪn-) *or* **kinesthesis** *n* the usual US spelling of **kinaesthesia**

kinetheodolite (,kɪnəθɪ'ɒdə,laɪt) *n* a type of theodolite containing a cine camera instead of a telescope and giving continuous film of a moving target together with a record of its altitude and azimuth: used in tracking a missile, satellite, etc

kinetic (kɪ'nɛtɪk, kaɪ-) *adj* relating to, characterized by, or caused by motion [c19 from Greek *kinētikos*, from *kinein* to move] > ki'netically *adv*

kinetic art *n* art, esp sculpture, that moves or has moving parts

kinetic energy *n* the energy of motion of a body, equal to the work it would do if it were brought to rest. The **translational kinetic energy** depends on motion through space, and for a rigid body of constant mass is equal to the product of half the mass times the square of the speed. The **rotational kinetic energy** depends on rotation about an axis, and for a body of constant moment of inertia is equal to the product of half the moment of inertia times the square of the angular velocity. In relativistic physics kinetic energy is equal to the product of the increase of mass caused by motion times the square of the speed of light. The SI unit is the joule but the electronvolt is often used in atomic physics. Symbol: E_k, K *or* T Abbreviation: **KE**

kinetics (kɪ'nɛtɪks, kaɪ-) *n* (*functioning as singular*) **1** another name for **dynamics** (sense 2) **2** the branch of mechanics, including both dynamics and kinematics, concerned with the study of bodies in motion **3** the branch of dynamics that excludes the study of bodies at rest **4** the branch of chemistry concerned with the rates of chemical reactions

kinetic theory *n* **the** a theory of gases postulating that they consist of particles of negligible size moving at random and undergoing elastic collisions. In full: **kinetic theory of gases**

kinetoplast (kɪ'nɛtə,plæst, -'niː-, -,plɑːst) *n* a small granular cell body close to the nucleus in some flagellate protozoans. Also called: **kinetonucleus** (kɪ,nɛtəʊ'njuːklɪəs) [c20 from Greek; see KINETIC, -PLAST]

kinfolk ('kɪn,fəʊk) *pl n* *chiefly US and Canadian* another word for **kinsfolk**

king (kɪŋ) *n* **1** a male sovereign prince who is the official ruler of an independent state; monarch. Related adjs: **royal, regal, monarchical** **2 a** a ruler or chief: *king of the fairies* **b** (*in combination*): *the pirate king* **3 a** a person, animal, or thing considered as the best or most important of its kind **b** (*as modifier*): *a king bull* **4** any of four playing cards in a pack, one for each suit, bearing the picture of a king **5** the most important chess piece, although theoretically the weakest, being able to move only one square at a time in any direction. See also **check** (sense 30), **checkmate** **6** *draughts* a piece that has moved entirely across the board and has been crowned, after which it may move backwards as well as forwards **7** king of kings **a** God **b** a title of any of various oriental monarchs ▷ *vb* (*tr*) **8** to make (someone) a king **9** king it to act in a superior fashion [Old English *cyning*; related to Old High German *kunig* king, Danish *konge*] > 'king,hood *n* > 'kingless *adj* > 'king,like *adj*

kingbird ('kɪŋ,bɜːd) *n* any of several large American flycatchers of the genus *Tyrannus*, esp *T. tyrannus* (**eastern kingbird** *or* **bee martin**)

kingbolt ('kɪŋ,bəʊlt) *or* **king rod** *n* **a** the pivot bolt that connects the body of a horse-drawn carriage to the front axle and provides the steering joint **b** a similar bolt placed between a railway carriage and the bogies

King Charles spaniel *n* **1** a toy breed of spaniel with a short turned-up nose and a domed skull **2** cavalier King Charles spaniel a similar breed that is slightly larger and has a longer nose [c17 named after Charles II of England, who popularized the breed]

king cobra n a very large venomous tropical Asian elapid snake, *Ophiophagus hannah*, that feeds on snakes and other reptiles and extends its neck into a hood when alarmed. Also called: hamadryad

King Country n **the** an area in the centre of North Island, New Zealand: home of the King Movement, a nineteenth-century Māori separatist movement

king crab n another name for **horseshoe crab**

kingcraft ('kɪŋ,krɑːft) n *archaic* the art of ruling as a king, esp by diplomacy and cunning

kingcup ('kɪŋ,kʌp) n *Brit* any of several yellow-flowered ranunculaceous plants, esp the marsh marigold

kingdom ('kɪŋdəm) n **1** a territory, state, people, or community ruled or reigned over by a king or queen **2** any of the three groups into which natural objects may be divided: the animal, plant, and mineral kingdoms **3** *biology* any of the major categories into which living organisms of the domain *Eukarya* are classified. Modern systems recognize four kingdoms: *Protoctista* (algae, protozoans, etc), *Fungi*, *Plantae*, and *Animalia*. See also **domain** (sense 12) **4** *theol* the eternal sovereignty of God **5** an area of activity, esp mental activity, considered as being the province of something specified: *the kingdom of the mind* > 'kingdomless *adj*

kingdom come n **1** the next world; life after death **2** *informal* the end of the world (esp in the phrase **until kingdom come**) **3** *informal* unconsciousness or death

king fern n another name for **para³**

kingfish ('kɪŋ,fɪʃ) n, *pl* **-fish** or **-fishes 1** any marine sciaenid food and game fish of the genus *Menticirrhus*, occurring in warm American Atlantic coastal waters **2** another name for **opah** (the fish) **3** any of various other large food fishes, esp the Spanish mackerel **4** Also called (NZ): **haku** a large food and game fish, *Seriola lalandi lalandi*, of New Zealand waters

kingfisher ('kɪŋ,fɪʃə) n any coraciiform bird of the family *Alcedinidae*, esp the Eurasian *Alcedo atthis*, which has a greenish-blue and orange plumage. Kingfishers have a large head, short tail, and long sharp bill and tend to live near open water and feed on fish [c15 originally *king's fisher*]

king-hit *Austral informal* ▷ n **1** a knockout blow, esp an unfair one ▷ vb **-hits, -hitting, -hit** (*tr*) **2** to deliver a knockout blow to

King James Version or **Bible** n the another name for **Authorized Version**

kingklip ('kɪŋ,klɪp) n *South African* an edible eel-like marine fish

kinglet ('kɪŋlɪt) n **1** *often derogatory* the king of a small or insignificant territory **2** *US and Canadian* any of various small warblers of the genus *Regulus*, having a black-edged yellow crown: family *Muscicapidae*

kingly ('kɪŋlɪ) *adj* **-lier, -liest 1** appropriate to a king; majestic **2** royal ▷ *adv* **3** *poetic or archaic* in a manner appropriate to a king > 'kingliness *n*

kingmaker ('kɪŋ,meɪkə) n a person who has control over appointments to positions of authority

king-of-arms n, *pl* **kings-of-arms 1** the highest rank of heraldic officer, itself divided into the ranks of Garter, Clarenceaux, and Norroy and Ulster. In Scotland the first is Lyon **2** a person holding this rank

king of the castle n *chiefly Brit* **1** a children's game in which each child attempts to stand alone on a mound, sandcastle, etc, by pushing other children off it **2** *informal* a person who is in a commanding or superior position

king of the herrings n another name for **oarfish** or **rabbitfish** (sense 1)

king penguin n a large penguin, *Aptenodytes patagonica*, found on islands bordering the Antarctic Circle

kingpin ('kɪŋ,pɪn) n **1** the most important person in an organization **2** the crucial or most important feature of a theory, argument, etc **3** Also called (Brit): **swivel pin** a pivot pin that provides a steering joint in a motor vehicle by securing the stub axle to the axle beam **4** *tenpin bowling* the front pin in the triangular arrangement of the ten pins **5** (in ninepins) the central pin in the diamond pattern of the nine pins

king post n a vertical post connecting the apex of a triangular roof truss to the tie beam. Also called: **joggle post** Compare **queen post**

king prawn n any of several large prawns of the genus *Penaeus*, which are fished commercially in Australian waters

Kings (kɪŋz) n (*functioning as singular*) *Old Testament* (in versions based on the Hebrew, including the Authorized Version) either of the two books called I and II Kings recounting the histories of the kings of Judah and Israel

king salmon n another name for **Chinook salmon**

King's Bench n (when the sovereign is male) another name for **Queen's Bench Division**

King's Counsel n (when the sovereign is male) another name for **Queen's Counsel**

King's English n (esp when the British sovereign is male) standard Southern British English

king's evidence n (when the sovereign is male) another name for **queen's evidence**

king's evil n the *pathol* a former name for **scrofula** [c14 from the belief that the king's touch would heal scrofula]

king's highway n (in Britain, esp when the sovereign is male) any public road or right of way

kingship ('kɪŋʃɪp) n **1** the position or authority of a king **2** the skill or practice of ruling as a king

king-size or **king-sized** *adj* larger or longer than a standard size

King's Lynn ('kɪŋz 'lɪn) n a market town in E England, in Norfolk on the estuary of the Great Ouse near the Wash: a leading port in the Middle Ages. Pop: 40 921 (2001). Also called: **Lynn, Lynn Regis**

king snake n any nonvenomous North American colubrid snake of the genus *Lampropeltis*, feeding on other snakes, small mammals, etc

king's peace n **1** (in early medieval England) the protection secured by the king for particular people or places **2** (in medieval England) the general peace secured to the entire realm by the law administered in the king's name

King's proctor n (in England when the sovereign is male) an official empowered to intervene in divorce and certain other cases when it is alleged that facts are being suppressed

King's Regulations *pl* n (in Britain and the Commonwealth when the sovereign is male) the code of conduct for members of the armed forces that deals with discipline, military law, etc

King's Scout n (in Britain and the Commonwealth when the sovereign is male) another name for **Queen's Scout** US equivalent: **Eagle Scout**

king's shilling or when the sovereign was female **queen's shilling** n **1** (until 1879) a shilling paid to new recruits to the British army **2** **take the king's shilling** *Brit archaic* to enlist in the army

King's speech n (in Britain and the Commonwealth when the sovereign is male) another name for the **speech from the throne**

Kingston ('kɪŋstən) n **1** the capital and chief port of Jamaica, on the SE coast: University of the West Indies. Pop: 574 000 (2005 est) **2** a port in SE Canada, in SE Ontario: the chief naval base of Lake Ontario and a large industrial centre; university (1841). Pop: 108 158 (2001) **3** short for **Kingston upon Thames**

Kingston upon Hull n **1** the official name of **Hull¹** **2** a unitary authority in NE England, in the East Riding of Yorkshire: formerly (1974–96) part of the county of Humberside. Pop: 247 900 (2003 est). Area: 71 sq km (27 sq miles)

Kingston upon Thames n a borough of SW Greater London, on the River Thames: formed in 1965 by the amalgamation of several former boroughs of Surrey; administrative centre of Surrey. Pop: 150 400 (2003 est). Area: 38 sq km (15 sq miles)

Kingstown ('kɪŋz,taʊn) n the capital of St Vincent and the Grenadines: a port and resort. p.: 31 000 (2005 est)

Kingwana (kɪŋ'wɑːnə) n a language of the Democratic Republic of Congo (formerly Zaïre) in W Africa, closely related to Swahili and used as a lingua franca

kingwood ('kɪŋ,wʊd) n **1** the hard fine-grained violet-tinted wood of a Brazilian leguminous tree, *Dalbergia cearensis*, used in cabinetwork **2** the tree yielding this wood

kinin ('kaɪnɪn) n **1** any of a group of polypeptides in the blood that cause dilation of the blood vessels and make smooth muscles contract **2** another name for **cytokinin** [c20 from Greek *kin(ēma)* motion + -ɪɴ]

kink (kɪŋk) n **1** a sharp twist or bend in a wire, rope, hair, etc, esp one caused when it is pulled tight **2** a crick in the neck or similar muscular spasm **3** a flaw or minor difficulty in some undertaking or project **4** a flaw or idiosyncrasy of personality; quirk **5** *Brit informal* a sexual deviation **6** *US* a clever or unusual idea ▷ vb **7** to form or cause to form a kink [c17 from Dutch: a curl in a rope; compare Middle Low German *kinke* kink, Old Norse *kinka* to nod]

kinkajou ('kɪŋkə,dʒuː) n Also called: honey bear, potto an arboreal fruit-eating mammal, *Potos flavus*, of Central and South America, with a long prehensile tail: family *Procyonidae* (raccoons) order *Carnivora* (carnivores) [c18 from French *quincajou*, from Algonquian; related to Ojibwa *gwîngwâage* wolverine]

kinky ('kɪŋkɪ) *adj* **kinkier, kinkiest 1** *slang* given to unusual, abnormal, or deviant sexual practices **2** *informal* exhibiting unusual idiosyncrasies of personality; quirky; eccentric **3** *informal* attractive or provocative in a bizarre way: *kinky clothes* **4** tangled or tightly looped, as a wire or rope **5** tightly curled, as hair > 'kinkily *adv* > 'kinkiness *n*

kinnikinnick, kinnikinic (,kɪnɪkɪ'nɪk) or **killikinick** n **1** the dried leaves and bark of certain plants, sometimes with tobacco added, formerly smoked by some North American Indians **2** any of the plants used for such a preparation, such as the sumach *Rhus glabra* [c18 from Algonquian, literally: that which is mixed; related to Natick *kinukkinuk* mixture]

kino ('kiːnəʊ) n a dark red resin obtained from various tropical plants, esp an Indian leguminous tree, *Pterocarpus marsupium*, used as an astringent and in tanning. Also called: kino gum [c18 of West African origin; related to Mandingo *keno*]

Kinross-shire (kɪn'rosʃɪə, -ʃə) n a former county of E central Scotland: became part of Tayside region in 1975 and part of Perth and Kinross in 1996

kin selection n *biology* natural selection resulting from altruistic behaviour by animals towards members of the same species, esp their offspring or other relatives

kinsfolk ('kɪnz,fəʊk) *pl* n one's family or relatives

Kinshasa (kɪn'ʃɑːzə, -'ʃɑːsə) n the capital of the Democratic Republic of Congo (formerly Zaïre), on the River Congo opposite Brazzaville: became capital of the Belgian Congo in 1929 and of Zaïre in 1960; university (1954). Pop: 5 717 000 (2005 est). Former name (until 1966): Léopoldville

kinship ('kɪnʃɪp) n **1** blood relationship **2** the state of having common characteristics or a common origin

kinsman ('kɪnzmən) n, *pl* **-men 1** a blood relation or a relation by marriage **2** a member of the same race, tribe, or ethnic stock > 'kins,woman *fem* n

kiore ('kiːɒrɛ) n, *pl* **kiore** another name for **Māori rat** [Māori]

k

kiosk ('ki:ɒsk) *n* **1** a small sometimes movable booth from which cigarettes, newspapers, light refreshments, etc, are sold **2** *chiefly Brit* a telephone box **3** *chiefly US* a thick post on which advertisements are posted **4** (in Turkey, Iran, etc, esp formerly) a light open-sided pavilion [C17 from French *kiosque* bandstand, from Turkish *kösk*, from Persian *küshk* pavilion]

Kioto (kɪ'əʊtəʊ, 'kjəʊ-) *n* a variant spelling of **Kyoto**

kip[1] (kɪp) *slang* ▷ *n* **1** *Brit* sleep or slumber: *to get some kip* **2** *Brit* a bed or lodging **3** *obsolete (except Irish)* a brothel ▷ *vb* **kips, kipping, kipped** (*intr*) **4** *Brit* to sleep or take a nap **5** *Brit* (foll by *down*) to prepare for sleep [C18 of uncertain origin; apparently related to Danish *kippe* common alehouse]

kip[2], **kipskin** ('kɪp,skɪn) *n* the hide of a young animal, esp a calf or lamb [C16 from Middle Dutch *kipp*; related to Middle Low German *kip*, Old Norse *kippa* bundle]

kip[3] (kɪp) *n* a unit of weight equal to one thousand pounds [C20 from KI(LO)[1] + P(OUND)[2]]

kip[4] (kɪp) *n* the standard monetary unit of Laos, divided into 100 at [from Thai]

kip[5] (kɪp) *n* *Austral* a small board used to spin the coins in two-up [C19 from KEP]

kippa (ki'pa) *n* *Judaism* a skullcap worn by orthodox male Jews at all times and by others for prayer, esp a crocheted one worn by those with a specifically religious Zionist affiliation

kipper[1] ('kɪpə) *n* **1** a fish, esp a herring, that has been cleaned, salted, and smoked **2** a male salmon during the spawning season **3** *Austral archaic derogatory slang* an Englishman ▷ *vb* **4** (*tr*) to cure (a fish, esp a herring) by salting and smoking [Old English *cypera*, perhaps from *coper* COPPER[1]; referring to its colour]

kipper[2] ('kɪpə) *n* a native Australian youth who has completed an initiation rite [from a native Australian language]

kipper[3] ('kɪpə) *n* *informal* an adult who cannot afford to move away from his or her parents' home [C21 from k(ids) i(n) p(arents') p(ockets) e(roding) r(etirement) (savings)]

kippered ('kɪpəd) *adj* **1** (of fish, esp herring) having been cleaned, salted, and smoked **2** *slang* utterly defeated or outwitted

Kipp's apparatus (kɪps) *n* a laboratory apparatus for producing a gas, usually hydrogen sulphide, by the action of a liquid on a solid without heating [C19 named after Petrus Jacobus *Kipp* (1808–84), Dutch chemist]

kir (kɜ:, kir) *n* a drink made from dry white wine and cassis [named after Canon F. *Kir* (1876–1968), mayor of Dijon, who is reputed to have invented it]

kirby grip ('kɜ:bɪ) *n* *Brit* a hairgrip consisting of a piece of metal bent over to form a tight clip and having the upper part ridged to prevent it slipping on the hair [from *Kerbigrip*, trademark for the original such hairgrip]

Kirchhoff's laws *pl n* two laws describing the flow of currents in electric circuits. The first states that the algebraic sum of all the electric currents meeting at any point in a circuit is zero. The second states that in a closed loop of a circuit the algebraic sum of the products of the resistances and the currents flowing through them is equal to the algebraic sum of all the electromotive forces acting in the loop [C19 after G. R. *Kirchhoff* (1824–87), German physicist]

Kirghiz or **Kirgiz** ('kɜ:gɪz) *n* a variant spelling of **Kyrgyz**

Kirghizia or **Kirgizia** (kɜ:'gɪzɪə) *n* the former Russian name for **Kyrgyzstan**

Kirghiz Steppe *n* a variant spelling of **Kyrgyz Steppe**

Kiribati (,kɪrɪ'bætɪ, ,kɪrɪ'bæs) *n* an independent republic in the W Pacific: comprises 33 islands including Banaba (Ocean Island), the Gilbert and Phoenix Islands, and eight of the Line Islands;

part of the British colony of the Gilbert and Ellice Islands until 1975; became self-governing in 1977 and gained full independence in 1979 as the Republic of Kiribati; a member of the Commonwealth. Official languages: English, I-Kiribati (Gilbertese) is widely spoken. Religion: Christian majority. Currency: Australian dollar. Capital: Bairiki islet, in Tarawa atoll. Pop: 88 000 (2003 est). Area: 684 sq km (264 sq miles)

kirigami (,kɪrɪ'ga:mɪ) *n* the art, originally Japanese, of folding and cutting paper into decorative shapes. Compare **origami** [C20 from Japanese]

Kirin ('ki:'rɪn) *n* a variant transliteration of the Chinese name for **Jilin**

Kirinyaga (,kɪrɪn'ja:ga:) *n* the local name of **Mount Kenya**. See **Kenya** (sense 2)

Kiritimati ('kɪrɪtɪ'ma:tɪ) *n* an island in the central Pacific, in Kiribati: one of the Line Islands; the largest atoll in the world. Pop: 3225 (1995). Former name: **Christmas Island**

kirk (kɜ:k; *Scot* kɪrk) *n* **1** a Scot word for **church 2** a Scottish church [C12 from Old Norse *kirkja*, from Old English *cirice* CHURCH]

Kirk (kɜ:k; *Scot* kɪrk) *n* **the** *informal* **the** Presbyterian Church of Scotland

Kirkby ('kɜ:bɪ) *n* a town in NW England, in Knowsley unitary authority, Merseyside. Pop: 40 006 (2001)

Kirkcaldy (kɜ:'kɔ:dɪ) *n* a port in E Scotland, in SE Fife on the Firth of Forth. Pop: 46 912 (2001)

Kirkcudbrightshire (kɜ:'ku:brɪʃɪə, -ʃə) *n* a former county of SW Scotland, part of Dumfries and Galloway since 1975

Kirklees (,kɜ:k'li:z) *n* a unitary authority in N England, in West Yorkshire. Pop: 391 400 (2003 est). Area: 410 sq km (158 sq miles)

kirkman ('kɜ:kmən, 'kɪrk-) *n*, *pl* **-men** *Scot* **1** a member or strong upholder of the Kirk **2** a churchman; clergyman

Kirkpatrick (kɜ:k'pætrɪk) *n* **Mount** a mountain in Antarctica, in S Victoria Land in the Queen Alexandra Range. Height: 4528 m (14 856 ft)

kirk session *n* the lowest court of the Presbyterian Church

Kirkuk (kɜ:'kʊk, 'kɜ:kʊk) *n* a city in NE Iraq: centre of a rich oilfield with pipelines to the Mediterranean. Pop: 548 000 (2005 est)

Kirkwall ('kɜ:k,wɔ:l) *n* a town on the N coast of Mainland in the Orkney Islands: administrative centre of the island authority of Orkney: cathedral built by Norsemen (begun in 1137). Pop: 6206 (2001)

Kirlian photography ('kɜ:lɪən) *n* a process that is said to record directly on photographic film the field radiation of electricity emitted by an object to which an electric charge has been applied [C20 named after Semyan D. and Valentina K. *Kirlian*, Armenian researchers who described the process]

Kirman (kɪə'ma:n) *n*, *pl* **-mans** a Persian carpet or rug [named after KERMAN, Iran]

kirmess ('kɜ:mɪs) *n* a variant spelling of **kermis**

Kirov (*Russian* 'kirəf) *n* a city in NW Russia, on the Vyatka River: an early trading centre; engineering industries. Pop: 454 000 (2005 est). Former name (1780–1934): **Vyatka**

Kirovabad (*Russian* kirəva'bat) *n* the former name (1936–91) of **Gandzha**

Kirovograd (*Russian* kirəva'grat) *n* a city in S central Ukraine on the Ingul River: manufacturing centre of a rich agricultural area. Pop: 250 000 (2005 est). Former names: **Yelisavetgrad** (until 1924), **Zinovievsk** (1924–36)

Kirpan (kɪr'pa:n) *n* the short sword traditionally carried by Sikhs as a symbol of their religious and cultural loyalty, symbolizing protection for the weak. See also **five Ks** [Punjabi *kirpān*]

Kirribilli House ('kɪrɪ,bɪlɪ) *n* the official Sydney residence of the Australian Prime Minister

Kirsch (kɪəʃ) or **Kirschwasser** ('kɪəʃ,va:sə) *n* a brandy distilled from cherries, made chiefly in the Black Forest in Germany and in the Jura and

Vosges districts of France [German *Kirschwasser* cherry water]

kirtan ('kɪrtən) *n* *Hinduism* devotional singing, usually accompanied by musical instruments [from Sanskrit *kīrtanam* praise, eulogy]

kirtle ('kɜ:t[ə]l) *n* *archaic* **1** a woman's skirt or dress **2** a man's coat [Old English *cyrtel*, probably from *cyrtan* to shorten, ultimately from Latin *curtus* cut short]

Kiruna (*Swedish* 'ki:runa) *n* a town in N Sweden: iron-mining centre. Pop: 23 273 (2004 est)

Kirundi (kɪ'rʊndɪ) *n* the official language of Burundi, belonging to the Bantu group of the Niger-Congo family and closely related to Rwanda

Kisangani (,kɪsæŋ'ga:nɪ) *n* a city in the N Democratic Republic of Congo (formerly Zaïre), at the head of navigation of the River Congo below Stanley Falls: Université Libre du Congo (1963). Pop: 475 000 (2005 est). Former name (until 1966): **Stanleyville**

kish (kɪʃ) *n* *metallurgy* graphite formed on the surface of molten iron that contains a large amount of carbon [C19 perhaps changed from German *Kies* gravel; related to Old High German *kisil* pebble]

Kishinev (*Russian* kiʃi'njɔf) *n* the capital of Moldova on the Byk River: manufacturing centre of a rich agricultural region; university (1945). Pop: 662 000 (2005 est). Romanian name: **Chişinău**

kishke ('kɪʃkə) *n* a beef or fowl intestine or skin stuffed with flour, onion, etc, and boiled and roasted [Yiddish: gut, probably from Russian *kishka*]

Kislev (ki'slev) *n* (in the Jewish calendar) the ninth month of the year according to biblical reckoning and the third month of the civil year, usually falling within November and December [from Hebrew]

Kismayu (kɪs'ma:ju:) *n* another name for **Chisimaio**

kismet ('kɪzmɛt, 'kɪs-) *n* **1** *Islam* the will of Allah **2** fate or destiny [C19 from Turkish, from Persian *qismat*, from Arabic *qasama* he divided]

kiss (kɪs) *vb* **1** (*tr*) to touch with the lips or press the lips against as an expression of love, greeting, respect, etc **2** (*intr*) to join lips with another person in an act of love or desire **3** to touch (each other) lightly: *their hands kissed* **4** *billiards* (of balls) to touch (each other) lightly while moving ▷ *n* **5** the act of kissing; a caress with the lips. Related adj: **oscular 6** a light touch **7** a small light sweet or cake, such as one made chiefly of egg white and sugar: *coffee kisses* ▷ See also **kiss off** [Old English *cyssan*, from *coss*; compare Old High German *kussen*, Old Norse *kyssa*] > **kissable** *adj*

KISS *text messaging abbreviation for* keep it simple, stupid

kissagram ('kɪsə,græm) *n* a greetings service in which a person is employed to present greetings by kissing the person celebrating [C20 blend of *kiss* and *telegram*]

kiss-and-tell *modifier* denoting the practice of publicizing one's former sexual relationship with a celebrity, esp in the tabloid press: *a kiss-and-tell interview*

kiss curl *n* *Brit* a circular curl of hair pressed flat against the cheek or forehead. US and Canadian term: **spit curl**

kissel ('kɪs[ə]l) *n* a Russian dessert of sweetened fruit purée thickened with arrowroot [from Russian *kisel*]

kisser ('kɪsə) *n* **1** a person who kisses, esp in a way specified: *a good kisser* **2** a slang word for **mouth** or **face**

kissing bug *n* a North American assassin bug, *Melanolestes picipes*, with a painful bite, usually attacking the lips or cheeks of man

kissing gate *n* a gate set in a U- or V-shaped enclosure, allowing only one person to pass through at a time

kiss of death *n* an act or relationship that has fatal or disastrous consequences [from Judas' kiss that betrayed Jesus in the garden of Gethsemane (Mark 14:44–45)]

kiss off *slang, chiefly US and Canadian* ▷ *vb* **1** (*tr, adverb*) to ignore or dismiss rudely and abruptly ▷ *n* **kiss-off** **2** a rude and abrupt dismissal

kiss of life *n* the **1** mouth-to mouth or mouth-to-nose resuscitation in which a person blows gently into the mouth or nose of an unconscious person, allowing the lungs to deflate after each blow **2** something that revitalizes or reinvigorates

kissy ('kɪsɪ) *or* **kissy-kissy** *adj informal* showing exaggerated affection, esp by frequent touching or kissing

kist¹ (kɪst) *n Scot and northern English dialect* a large chest or coffer [C14 from Old Norse *kista*; see CHEST]

kist² (kɪst) *n archaeol* a variant spelling of **cist²**

kist³ (kɪst) *n South African* a large wooden chest in which linen is stored, esp one used to store a bride's trousseau [from Afrikaans, from Dutch: CHEST]

Kistna ('kɪstnə) *n* another name for the (River) **Krishna**

Kisumu (kɪ'suːmuː) *n* a port in W Kenya, in Nyanza province on the NE shore of Lake Victoria: fishing and trading centre. Pop: 433 000 (2005 est)

kit¹ (kɪt) *n* **1** a set of tools, supplies, construction materials, etc, for use together or for a purpose: *a first-aid kit; a model aircraft kit* **2** the case or container for such a set **3 a** a set of pieces of equipment ready to be assembled **b** (*as modifier*): *kit furniture* **4 a** clothing and other personal effects, esp those of a traveller or soldier: *safari kit; battle kit* **b** *informal* clothing in general (esp in the phrase **get one's kit off**) **5** NZ a flax basket **6** the whole kit *or* kit and caboodle *informal* everything or everybody ▷ See also **kit out** [C14 from Middle Dutch *kitte* tankard]

kit² (kɪt) *n* a kind of small violin, now obsolete, used esp by dancing masters in the 17th–18th centuries [C16 of unknown origin]

kit³ (kɪt) *n* **1** an informal or diminutive name for **kitten 2** a cub of various small mammals, such as the ferret or fox [C16 by shortening]

kit⁴ (kɪt) *n* NZ a plaited flax basket [from Māori *kete*]

KIT *text messaging abbreviation for* keep in touch

Kitakyushu (ˌkiːtə'kjuːʃuː) *n* a port in Japan, on N Kyushu: formed in 1963 by the amalgamation of the cities of Wakamatsu, Yahata, Tobata, Kokura, and Moji; one of Japan's largest industrial centres. Pop: 999 806 (2002 est)

kitbag ('kɪtˌbæg) *n* a canvas or other bag for a serviceman's kit

kitchen ('kɪtʃɪn) *n* **a** a room or part of a building equipped for preparing and cooking food **b** (*as modifier*): *a kitchen table* [Old English *cycene*, ultimately from Late Latin *coquīna*, from Latin *coquere* to COOK; see KILN]

kitchenalia (ˌkɪtʃɪ'neɪlɪə) *n* cooking equipment and other items found in a kitchen

kitchen cabinet *n* a group of unofficial advisers to a political leader, esp when considered to be more influential than the official cabinet

Kitchener ('kɪtʃɪnə) *n* an industrial town in SE Canada, in S Ontario: founded in 1806 as Dutch Sand Hills, it was renamed Berlin in 1830 and Kitchener in 1916. Pop: 190 399 (2001)

kitchenette *or* **kitchenet** (ˌkɪtʃɪ'nɛt) *n* a small kitchen or part of another room equipped for use as a kitchen

kitchen garden *n* a garden where vegetables and sometimes also fruit are grown ▷ **kitchen gardener** *n*

kitchen kaffir *n* a derogatory term for **Fanagalo**

kitchen midden *n archaeol* the site of a large mound of domestic refuse marking a prehistoric settlement: usually including bones, potsherds, seashells, etc

kitchen police *pl n* US soldiers who have been detailed to work in the kitchen, esp as a punishment. Abbreviation: KP

kitchen sink *n* **1** a sink in a kitchen for washing dishes, vegetables, etc **2** everything but the kitchen sink everything that can be conceived of **3** (*modifier*) denoting a type of drama or painting of the 1950s depicting the sordid aspects of domestic reality

kitchen tea *n Austral and NZ* a party held before a wedding to which female guests bring items of kitchen equipment as wedding presents

kitchenware ('kɪtʃɪnˌwɛə) *n* pots and pans, knives, forks, spoons, and other utensils used in the kitchen

kite¹ (kaɪt) *n* **1** a light frame covered with a thin material flown in the wind at the end of a length of string **2** Brit slang an aeroplane **3** (*plural*) *nautical* any of various light sails set in addition to the working sails of a vessel **4** any diurnal bird of prey of the genera *Milvus, Elanus,* etc, typically having a long forked tail and long broad wings and usually preying on small mammals and insects: family *Accipitridae* (hawks, etc) **5** *archaic* a person who preys on others **6** *commerce* a negotiable paper drawn without any actual transaction or assets and designed to obtain money on credit, give an impression of affluence, etc **7** fly a kite See **fly¹** (sense 14) **8** high as a kite See **high** (sense 30) ▷ *vb* **9** to issue (fictitious papers) to obtain credit or money **10** (*tr*) *US and Canadian* to write (a cheque) in anticipation of sufficient funds to cover it **11** (*intr*) to soar and glide [Old English *cȳta*; related to Middle High German *küze* owl, Old Norse *kȳta* to quarrel] ▷ 'kiter *n*

kite² (kəɪt) *n* a variant spelling of **kyte**

kite fighting *n* (in Malaysia) a game in which one player attempts to cut the string of his opponent's kite with the string of his own. See also **glass string**

kite flying *n commerce* the practice of drawing cheques on deposits which are already committed, assuming that the delay in clearing the cheque will allow time to replenish the account. Also called: kiting

Kitemark *n Brit* the official mark of quality and reliability, in the form of a kite, on articles approved by the British Standards Institution

kitenge (ki:'tɛŋgɛ) *n E African* **a** a thick cotton cloth measuring 114 × 213 cm (45 × 84 inches), used in making garments **b** (*as modifier*): *a kitenge dress* [C20 from Swahili]

kitesurfing ('kaɪtˌsɜːfɪŋ) *n* the sport of sailing standing up on a surfboard while being pulled along by a large kite

kit fox *n* another name for **swift fox**

kith (kɪθ) *n* one's friends and acquaintances (esp in the phrase **kith and kin**) [Old English *cȳthth*, from *cūth*; see UNCOUTH]

kithara ('kɪθərə) *n* a variant of **cithara**

Kíthira ('kɪθira) *n* transliteration of the Modern Greek name for **Cythera**

kit out *or* **up** *vb* kits, kitting, kitted **1** (*tr, adverb*) *chiefly Brit* to provide with (a kit of personal effects and necessities) **2** to provide with (an outfit of clothes)

kitsch (kɪtʃ) *n* **a** tawdry, vulgarized, or pretentious art, literature, etc, usually with popular or sentimental appeal **b** (*as modifier*): *a kitsch plaster bust of Beethoven* [C20 from German] ▷ 'kitschy *adj*

kitschness ('kɪtʃnɪs) *n* the quality of being tawdry, vulgarized, or pretentious, and usually with popular or sentimental appeal

kitset ('kɪtˌsɛt) *n* NZ **a** a piece of furniture supplied in pieces for the purchaser to assemble himself or herself **b** (*as modifier*): *a kitset kitchen*

kittel ('kiːtɛl) *n* a white garment used as a shroud or worn by traditional Jews on Yom Kippur [from German *Kittel*, smock]

kitten ('kɪtᵊn) *n* **1** a young cat **2** have kittens Also: **have a canary** *Brit informal* to react with disapproval, anxiety, etc: *she had kittens when she got the bill.* US equivalent: **have a cow** ▷ *vb* **3** (of cats)

to give birth to (young) [C14 from Old Northern French *caton*, from CAT¹; probably influenced by Middle English *kiteling*] ▷ **kitten-ˌlike** *adj*

kitten heel *n* **1** a low stiletto heel on a woman's shoe **2** a woman's shoe with a low stiletto heel

kittenish ('kɪtᵊnɪʃ) *adj* **1** like a kitten; lively **2** (of a woman) flirtatious, esp coyly flirtatious ▷ 'kittenishly *adv* ▷ 'kittenishness *n*

kitten moth *n* any of three prominent moths, notably the **poplar kitten** (*Furcula bifida*), that have larvae like those of the related puss moth

kittiwake ('kɪtɪˌweɪk) *n* either of two oceanic gulls of the genus *Rissa*, esp *R. tridactyla*, having a white plumage with pale grey black-tipped wings and a square-cut tail [C17 of imitative origin]

kittle ('kɪtᵊl) *Scot* ▷ *adj* **1** capricious and unpredictable ▷ *vb* **2** to be troublesome or puzzling to (someone) **3** to tickle [C16 probably from Old Norse *kitla* to TICKLE]

kitty¹ ('kɪtɪ) *n, pl* **-ties** a diminutive or affectionate name for a **kitten** *or* **cat¹** [C18 see KIT³]

kitty² ('kɪtɪ) *n, pl* **-ties 1** the pool of bets in certain gambling games **2** any shared fund of money, etc **3** (in bowls) the jack [C19 see KIT¹]

kitty-cornered *adj* a variant of **cater-cornered**

Kitty Hawk ('kɪtɪ hɔːk) *n* a village in NE North Carolina, near Kill Devil Hill, where the Wright brothers made the world's first aeroplane flight (1903)

Kitwe ('kɪtweɪ) *n* a city in N Zambia: commercial centre of the Copper Belt. Pop: 545 000 (2005 est)

Kitzbühel ('kɪtsbuːəl) *n* a town in W Austria, in the Tirol: centre for winter sports. Pop: 8574 (2001)

Kiushu ('kjuːʃuː) *n* a variant spelling of **Kyushu**

kiva ('kiːvə) *n* a large underground or partly underground room in a Pueblo Indian village, used chiefly for religious ceremonies [from Hopi]

Kivu ('kiːvuː) *n* **Lake** a lake in central Africa, between the Democratic Republic of Congo (formerly Zaïre) and Rwanda at an altitude of 1460 m (4790 ft). Area: 2698 sq km (1042 sq miles). Depth: (maximum) 475 m (1558 ft)

Kiwanis (kɪ'wɑːnɪs) *n* a North American organization of men's clubs founded in 1915 to promote community service [C20 alleged to be from an American Indian language: to make oneself known] ▷ Ki'wanian *n*

kiwi ('kiːwiː) *n, pl* kiwis **1** any nocturnal flightless New Zealand bird of the genus *Apteryx*, having a long beak, stout legs, and weakly barbed feathers: order *Apterygiformes* (see **ratite**) **2** short for kiwi fruit **3** *informal except in New Zealand* a New Zealander [C19 from Māori, of imitative origin]

Kiwiana (ˌkiːwɪ'ɑːnə) *pl n Austral and NZ* collectable objects, ornaments, etc, esp dating from the 1950s or 1960s, relating to the history or popular culture of New Zealand

Kiwi Ferns *pl n* **the** the women's international Rugby League football team of New Zealand

kiwi fruit *n* the edible oval fruit of the kiwi plant, *Actinidia chinensis*, a climbing plant native to Asia but grown extensively in New Zealand; it has a brown fuzzy skin and pale green flesh. Also called: Chinese gooseberry

Kiwis ('kiːwiːs) *pl n* **the** the men's international Rugby League football team of New Zealand

kiwisports ('kiːwiˌspɔːts) *pl n* NZ (*functioning as singular*) a fitness programme developed for schools, involving a selection of sports such as rounders, cricket, and netball

Kizil Irmak (kɪ'zɪl ɪə'mɑːk) *n* a river in Turkey, rising in the Kizil Dag and flowing southwest, northwest, and northeast to the Black Sea: the longest river in Asia Minor. Length: about 1150 km (715 miles). Ancient name: Halys ('heɪlɪs)

KKK *abbreviation for* Ku Klux Klan

KKt *chess symbol for* king's knight

KKtP *chess symbol for* king's knight's pawn

kl *symbol for* kilolitre

Klagenfurt (German 'klɑːɡənfʊrt) *n* a city in S Austria, capital of Carinthia province: tourist centre. Pop: 90 141 (2001)

k

Klaipeda (*Russian* ˈklajpɪdə) *n* a port in Lithuania on the Baltic: shipbuilding and fish canning. Pop: 190 000 (2005 est). German name: Memel

Klan (klæn) *n* (usually preceded by *the*) short for **Ku Klux Klan**. > ˈKlanism *n*

klangfarbe (ˈklɑːŋˌfɑːbə) *n* (*often capital*) instrumental timbre or tone colour [German: tone colour]

Klansman (ˈklænzmən) *n, pl* -men a member of the Ku Klux Klan

klap (klʌp) *South African* ▷ *vb* **1** (*tr*) to slap or spank (a person) ▷ *n* **2** a slap or smack [from Afrikaans]

Klausenburg (ˈklauzənbʊrk) *n* the German name for Cluj

klaxon *or* **claxon** (ˈklæksᵊn) *n* a type of loud horn formerly used on motor vehicles [c20 former trademark, from the name of the manufacturing company]

klebsiella (ˌklɛbzɪˈɛlə) *n* a Gram-negative bacteria found in the respiratory, intestinal, and urinogenital tracts of humans and animals, which can cause pneumonia and urinary infections [c20 after Edwin *Klebs* (1834–913), German bacteriologist]

Klebs-Löffler bacillus (ˈklɛbzˈlʌflə; *German* ˈkleːpsˈlœflər) *n* a rodlike Gram-positive bacterium, *Corynebacterium diphtheriae*, that causes diphtheria: family *Corynebacteriaceae*. [c19 named after Edwin *Klebs* (1834–1913) and Friedrich A. J. *Löffler* (1852–1915), German bacteriologists]

Kleenex (ˈkliːnɛks) *n, pl* -ex *or* -exes *trademark* a kind of soft paper tissue, used esp as a handkerchief

Klein bottle (klaɪn) *n maths* a surface formed by inserting the smaller end of an open tapered tube through the surface of the tube and making this end contiguous with the other end [named after Felix *Klein* (1849–1925) German mathematician]

kleinhuisie (ˈklaɪnˈheɪsɪ) *n South African* an outside lavatory [c20 Afrikaans: literally, little house]

klepht (klɛft) *n* any of the Greeks who fled to the mountains after the 15th-century Turkish conquest of Greece and whose descendants survived as brigands into the 19th century [c19 from Modern Greek *klephtēs*, from Greek *kleptēs* thief] > ˈklephtic *adj*

kleptocracy *or* **cleptocracy** (ˌklɛpˈtɒkrəsɪ) *n, pl* -cies *informal* a government where officials are politically corrupt and financially self-interested [c20 from KLEPTO(MANIA) + -CRACY]

kleptocratic (ˌklɛptəʊˈkrætɪk) *adj* (of a government, state, etc) characterized by corruption amongst those in power

kleptomania (ˌklɛptəʊˈmeɪnɪə) *n psychol* a strong impulse to steal, esp when there is no obvious motivation [c19 *klepto-* from Greek *kleptēs* thief, from *kleptein* to steal + -MANIA] > ˌkleptoˈmaniˌac *n*

kletterschuh (ˈklɛtəʃuː) *n, pl* kletterschuhe (ˈklɛtəˌʃuːə) a lightweight climbing boot with a canvas or suede upper and Vibram (originally felt or cord) sole. Also called: **klett** [c20 from German: climbing shoe]

klezmer (ˈklɛzmə) *n* **1** a Jewish folk musician, usually a member of a small band **2** Also called: **klezmer music** the music performed by such a band [Yiddish]

klieg light (kliːg) *n* an intense carbon-arc light used for illumination in producing films [c20 named after John H. *Kliegl* (1869–1959) and his brother Anton (1872–1927), German-born American inventors in the field of lighting]

klipspringer (ˈklɪpˌsprɪŋə) *n* a small agile antelope, *Oreotragus oreotragus*, inhabiting rocky regions of Africa south of the Sahara [c18 from Afrikaans, from Dutch *klip* rock (see CLIFF) + *springer*, from *springen* to SPRING]

Klondike (ˈklɒndaɪk) *n* **1** a region of NW Canada, in the Yukon in the basin of the Klondike River: site of rich gold deposits, discovered in 1896 but largely exhausted by 1910. Area: about 2100 sq km (800 sq miles) **2** a river in NW Canada, rising in the Yukon and flowing west to the Yukon River.

Length: about 145 km (90 miles)

klondyker *or* **klondiker** (ˈklɒnˌdaɪkə) *n Brit* an East European factory ship [c20 from the gold miners who took part in the 19th-century gold rush to the KLONDIKE]

klong (klɒŋ) *n* a type of canal in Thailand [from Thai]

kloof (kluːf) *n* a mountain pass or gorge in southern Africa [c18 from Afrikaans, from Middle Dutch *clove* a cleft; see CLEAVE¹]

klootchman (ˈkluːtʃmən) *n, pl* -mans *or* -men *Northwestern Canadian* a North American Indian woman. Also called: **klootch, klooch** [c19 from Chinook Jargon, from Nootka *hlotssma* woman, wife]

klutz (klʌts) *n US and Canadian slang* a clumsy or stupid person [from German *Klotz* dolt; compare CLOT] > ˈklutzy *adj*

klystron (ˈklɪstrɒn, ˈklaɪ-) *n* an electron tube for the amplification or generation of microwaves by means of velocity modulation [c20 *klys-*, from Greek *klus-*, *kluzein* to wash over, break over + -TRON]

km¹ *symbol for* kilometre

km² *the internet domain name for* Comoros

K-meson *n* another name for **kaon**

km/h *abbreviation for* kilometres per hour

kn¹ *abbreviation for* **1** *nautical* knot **2** krona **3** krone

kn² *the internet domain name for* Saint Kitts and Nevis

KN *chess symbol for* king's knight

knack (næk) *n* **1** a skilful, ingenious, or resourceful way of doing something **2** a particular talent or aptitude, esp an intuitive one [c14 probably variant of *knak* sharp knock, rap, of imitative origin]

knacked (nækd) *adj Brit slang* **1** broken **2** worn out [c20 from KNACKERED]

knacker (ˈnækə) *Brit* ▷ *n* **1** a person who buys up old horses for slaughter **2** a person who buys up old buildings and breaks them up for scrap **3** (*usually plural*) *slang* another word for **testicle 4** *Irish slang* a despicable person ▷ *vb* **5** (*tr; usually passive*) *slang* to exhaust; tire [c16 probably from *nacker* saddler, probably of Scandinavian origin; compare Old Norse *hnakkur* saddle]

knackered (ˈnækəd) *Brit slang* ▷ *adj* **1** exhausted; tired out **2** worn out; no longer working, esp after long or hard use

knacker's yard *n Brit* **1** a slaughterhouse for horses **2** *informal* destruction because of being beyond all usefulness (esp in the phrase **ready for the knacker's yard**)

knackwurst *or* **knockwurst** (ˈnɒk,wɜːst) *n* a short fat highly seasoned sausage [German, from *knacken* to make a cracking sound + *Wurst* sausage]

knag (næg) *n* **1** a knot in wood **2** a wooden peg [c15 perhaps from Low German *knagge*]

knap¹ (næp) *n dialect* the crest of a hill [Old English *cnæpp* top; compare Old Norse *knappr* knob]

knap² (næp) *vb* knaps, knapping, knapped (*tr*) *dialect* to hit, hammer, or chip [c15 (in the sense: to strike with a sharp sound): of imitative origin; compare Dutch *knappen* to crack] > ˈknapper *n*

knapping hammer *n* a hammer used for breaking and shaping stones

knapsack (ˈnæpˌsæk) *n* a canvas or leather bag carried strapped on the back or shoulder [c17 from Low German *knappsack*, probably from *knappen* to bite, snap + *sack* bag; related to Dutch *knapzak*; see SACK¹]

knapweed (ˈnæpˌwiːd) *n* any of several plants of the genus *Centaurea*, having purplish thistle-like flowers: family *Asteraceae* (composites). See also **centaury** (sense 2), **hardheads** [c15 *knopwed*; see KNOP, WEED¹]

knar (nɑː) *n* a variant of **knur** [c14 *knarre* rough stone, knot on a tree; related to Low German *knarre*] > **knarred** *or* ˈknarry *adj*

knarly (ˈnɑːlɪ) *adj informal* same as **gnarly** (sense 3)

knave (neɪv) *n* **1** *archaic* a dishonest man; rogue **2** another word for **jack** (the playing card) **3** *obsolete*

a male servant [Old English *cnafa*; related to Old High German *knabo* boy] > **knavish** *adj* > **knavishly** *adv* > **knavishness** *n*

knavery (ˈneɪvərɪ) *n, pl* -eries **1** a deceitful or dishonest act **2** dishonest conduct; trickery

knawel (ˈnɔːəl) *n* any of several Old World caryophyllaceous plants of the genus *Scleranthus*, having heads of minute petal-less flowers [c16 from German *Knauel*, literally: ball of yarn, from Old High German *kliuwa* ball]

knead (niːd) *vb* (*tr*) **1** to work and press (a soft substance, such as bread dough) into a uniform mixture with the hands **2** to squeeze, massage, or press with the hands **3** to make by kneading [Old English *cnedan*; related to Old Saxon *knedan*, Old Norse *knotha*] > **kneader** *n*

Knebworth House (ˈnɛbwɜːθ) *n* a Tudor mansion in Knebworth in Hertfordshire: home of Sir Edward Bulwer-Lytton; decorated (1843) in the Gothic style

knee (niː) *n* **1** the joint of the human leg connecting the tibia and fibula with the femur and protected in front by the patella. Technical name: **genu** Related adj: **genicular 2 a** the area surrounding and above this joint **b** (*modifier*) reaching or covering the knee: *knee breeches; knee socks* **3** a corresponding or similar part in other vertebrates **4** the part of a garment that covers the knee **5** the upper surface of a seated person's thigh: *the child sat on her mother's knee* **6** anything resembling a knee in action, such as a device pivoted to allow one member angular movement in relation to another **7** anything resembling a knee in shape, such as an angular bend in a pipe **8** any of the hollow rounded protuberances that project upwards from the roots of the swamp cypress: thought to aid respiration in waterlogged soil **9 bend** *or* **bow the knee** to kneel or submit **10 bring someone to his knees** to force someone into submission **11 bring something to its knees** to cause something to be in a weakened or impoverished state ▷ *vb* **knees, kneeing, kneed 12** (*tr*) to strike, nudge, or push with the knee [Old English *cnēow*; compare Old High German *kneo*, Old Norse *knē*, Latin *genu*]

kneecap (ˈniːˌkæp) *n* **1** *anatomy* a nontechnical name for **patella 2** another word for **poleyn** ▷ *vb* -caps, -capping, -capped (*tr*) **3** (esp of certain terrorist groups) to shoot (a person) in the kneecap, esp as an act of retaliation

knee-deep *adj* **1** so deep as to reach or cover the knees: *knee-deep mud* **2** (*postpositive; often foll by in*) **a** sunk or covered to the knees: *knee-deep in sand* **b** immersed; deeply involved: *knee-deep in work*

knee drop *n* a wrestling attack in which a wrestler lifts his opponent and drops him onto his bent knee

knee-high *adj* **1** another word for **knee-deep** (sense 1) **2** as high as the knee: *a knee-high child*

kneehole (ˈniːˌhəʊl) *n* **a** a space for the knees, esp under a desk **b** (*as modifier*): *a kneehole desk*

knee jerk *n* **1** *physiol* Also called: **patellar reflex** an outward reflex kick of the lower leg caused by a sharp tap on the quadriceps tendon just below the patella ▷ *modifier* **kneejerk 2** made or occurring as a predictable and automatic response, without thought: *kneejerk support*

kneel (niːl) *vb* kneels, kneeling, knelt *or* kneeled **1** (*intr*) to rest, fall, or support oneself on one's knees ▷ *n* **2** the act or position of kneeling [Old English *cnēowlian*; see KNEE] > **kneeler** *n*

knee-length *adj* reaching to the knee: *a knee-length skirt; knee-length boots*

kneepad (ˈniːˌpæd) *n* any of several types of protective covering for the knees. Also called: **kneecap**

kneepan (ˈniːˌpæn) *n anatomy* another word for **patella**

knee spavin *n vet science* chronic inflammation of the carpal joint of a horse

knees-up *n, pl* knees-ups **1** a boisterous dance involving the raising of alternate knees **2** a lively noisy party or celebration, esp one with dancing [c20 from the song "Knees up Mother Brown" to which the dance is performed]

knee-trembling *adj informal* very exciting

kneidel ('kneɪdªl, 'knaɪ-) *n* (in Jewish cookery) a small dumpling, usually served in chicken soup [from Yiddish]

knell (nɛl) *n* **1** the sound of a bell rung to announce a death or a funeral **2** something that precipitates or indicates death or destruction ▷ *vb* **3** (*intr*) to ring a knell **4** (*tr*) to proclaim or announce by or as if by a tolling bell [Old English *cnyll*; related to Middle High German *knüllen* to strike, Dutch *knallen* to bang]

knelt (nɛlt) *vb* a past tense and past participle of **kneel**

Knesset or **Knesseth** ('knɛsɪt) *n* the unicameral parliament of Israel [Hebrew, literally: gathering]

knew (nju:) *vb* the past tense of **know**

knicker ('nɪkə) *noun* (*modifier*) of or relating to knickers: *knicker elastic*

Knickerbocker ('nɪkə,bɒkə) *n* US **1** a descendant of the original Dutch settlers of New York **2** an inhabitant of New York [c19 named after Diedrich *Knickerbocker*, fictitious Dutchman alleged to be the author of Washington Irving's *History of New York* (1809)]

knickerbocker glory *n* a rich confection consisting of layers of ice cream, jelly, cream, and fruit served in a tall glass

knickerbockers ('nɪkə,bɒkəz) *pl n* baggy breeches fastened with a band at the knee or above the ankle. Also called (US): knickers [c19 regarded as the traditional dress of the Dutch settlers in America; see KNICKERBOCKER]

knickers ('nɪkəz) *pl n* **1** an undergarment for women covering the lower trunk and sometimes the thighs and having separate legs or leg-holes **2** a US variant of **knickerbockers 3 get one's knickers in a twist** *slang* to become agitated, flustered, or upset [c19 contraction of KNICKERBOCKERS]

knick-knack or **nick-nack** ('nɪk,næk) *n* **1** a cheap ornament; trinket **2** an ornamental article of furniture, dress, etc [c17 by reduplication from *knack*, in obsolete sense: toy] > 'knick-,knackery or 'nick-,nackery *n*

knickpoint or esp US **nickpoint** ('nɪk,pɔɪnt) *n* a break in the slope of a river profile caused by renewed erosion by a rejuvenated river [c20 partial translation of German *Knickpunkt*, from *knicken* to bend + *Punkt* POINT]

knife (naɪf) *n, pl* **knives** (naɪvz) **1** a cutting instrument consisting of a sharp-edged often pointed blade of metal fitted into a handle or onto a machine **2** a similar instrument used as a weapon **3 have one's knife in someone** to have a grudge against or victimize someone **4 twist the knife** to make a bad situation worse in a deliberately malicious way **5 the knives are out for (someone)** *Brit* people are determined to harm or put a stop to (someone): *the knives are out for Stevens* **6 under the knife** undergoing a surgical operation ▷ *vb* (*tr*) **7** to cut, stab, or kill with a knife **8** to betray, injure, or depose in an underhand way [Old English *cnīf*; related to Old Norse *knífr*, Middle Low German *knīf*] > 'knife,like *adj* > 'knifer *n*

knife edge *n* **1** the sharp cutting edge of a knife **2** any sharp edge **3** a sharp-edged wedge of hard material on which the beam of a balance pivots or about which a pendulum is suspended **4** a critical point in the development of a situation, process of making a decision, etc

knife grinder *n* a person who makes and sharpens knives, esp an itinerant one

knifeman ('naɪfmən) *n, pl* **men** a man who is armed with a knife, esp unlawfully

knife pleat *n* a single pleat turned in one direction

knife-point *n* **1** the tip of a knife blade **2 at knife-point** under threat of being stabbed

kniferest ('naɪf,rɛst) *n* a support on which a carving knife or carving fork is placed at the table

knife switch *n* an electric switch in which a flat metal blade, hinged at one end, is pushed between fixed contacts

knight (naɪt) *n* **1** (in medieval Europe) **a** (originally) a person who served his lord as a mounted and heavily armed soldier **b** (later) a gentleman invested by a king or other lord with the military and social standing of this rank **2** (in modern times) a person invested by a sovereign with a nonhereditary rank and dignity usually in recognition of personal services, achievements, etc. A British knight bears the title *Sir* placed before his name, as in *Sir Winston Churchill* **3** a chess piece, usually shaped like a horse's head, that moves either two squares horizontally and one square vertically or one square horizontally and two squares vertically **4** a heroic champion of a lady or of a cause or principle **5** a member of the Roman class of the equites ▷ *vb* **6** (*tr*) to make (a person) a knight; dub [Old English *cniht* servant; related to Old High German *kneht* boy]

knight bachelor *n, pl* knights bachelors or knights bachelor **1** a person who has been knighted but who does not belong to any of the orders of knights **2** another name for a **bachelor** (sense 3)

knight banneret *n, pl* knights bannerets another name for a **banneret**

knight errant *n, pl* knights errant (esp in medieval romance) a knight who wanders in search of deeds of courage, chivalry, etc

knight errantry *n* **1** the practices of a knight errant **2** quixotic behaviour or practices

knighthead ('naɪt,hɛd) *n nautical* either of a pair of vertical supports for each side of the bowsprit [c18 originally decorated with carvings of knights' heads]

knighthood ('naɪthʊd) *n* **1** the order, dignity, or rank of a knight **2** the qualities of a knight; knightliness **3** knights collectively

knightly ('naɪtlɪ) *adj* of, relating to, resembling, or befitting a knight > 'knightliness *n*

knight marshal *n* another name for **marshal** (sense 5)

knight of the road *n informal or facetious* **1** a tramp **2** a commercial traveller **3** a lorry driver **4** *obsolete* a highwayman

Knights Hospitallers *n* **1** Also called: Knights of St John of Jerusalem a military religious order founded about the time of the first crusade (1096–99) among European crusaders. It took its name from a hospital and hostel in Jerusalem. Full name: Knights of the Hospital of St John of Jerusalem **2** See **Hospitaller**

Knights of St Columba *n* an international, semi-secret fraternal and charitable order for Catholic laymen, which originated in New Haven, Connecticut in 1882 (the **Knights of Columbus**)

Knights of the Round Table *n* (in Arthurian legend) an order of knights created by King Arthur

Knight Templar *n, pl* Knights Templars or Knights Templar another term for **Templar**

kniphofia (nɪ'fəʊfɪə) *n* any plant of the perennial southern African genus *Kniphofia*, some species of which are cultivated for their conical spikes of bright red or yellow drooping tubular flowers: family *Liliaceae*. Also called: red-hot poker [named after J. H. *Kniphof* (1704–1763), German doctor and botanist]

knish (knɪʃ) *n* a piece of dough stuffed with potato, meat, or some other filling and baked or fried [Yiddish, from Russian *knysh* cake; compare Polish *knysz*]

knit (nɪt) *vb* **knits, knitting, knitted** or **knit 1** to make (a garment, etc) by looping and entwining (yarn, esp wool) by hand by means of long eyeless needles (**knitting needles**) or by machine (**knitting machine**) **2** to join or be joined together closely **3**

to draw (the brows) together or (of the brows) to come together, as in frowning or concentrating **4** (of a broken bone) to join together; heal ▷ *n* **5 a** a fabric or garment made by knitting **b** (in combination): *a heavy knit* [Old English *cnyttan* to tie in; related to Middle Low German *knütten* to knot together; see KNOT¹] > 'knittable *adj* > 'knitter *n*

knitting ('nɪtɪŋ) *n* **a** knitted work or the process of producing it **b** (*as modifier*): *a knitting machine*

knitwear ('nɪt,wɛə) *n* knitted clothes, esp sweaters

knives (naɪvz) *n* the plural of **knife**

knob (nɒb) *n* **1** a rounded projection from a surface, such as a lump on a tree trunk **2** a handle of a door, drawer, etc, esp one that is rounded **3** a round hill or knoll or morainic ridge **4** *Brit taboo* a slang word for **penis 5** and the same to you with (brass) knobs on *Brit informal* the same to you but even more so ▷ *vb* knobs, knobbing, knobbed **6** (*tr*) to supply or ornament with knobs **7** (*intr*) to form into a knob; bulge **8** *Brit taboo* to have sexual intercourse with (someone) [c14 from Middle Low German *knobbe* knot in wood; see KNOP] > 'knobby *adj* > 'knob,like *adj*

knobbly ('nɒblɪ) *adj* -blier, -bliest having or covered with small knobs; bumpy

knobby ('nɒbɪ) *adj* -bier, -biest having or covered with small knobs; knobbly

knobhead ('nɒb,hɛd) *n derogatory slang* a stupid person

knobkerrie ('nɒb,kɛrɪ) or **knobstick** ('nɒb,stɪk) *n* a stick with a round knob at the end, used as a club or missile by South African tribesmen [c19 from Afrikaans *knopkierie*, from *knop* knob, from Middle Dutch *cnoppe* + *kierie* stick, from Khoikhoi *kīrri*]

knock (nɒk) *vb* **1** (*tr*) to give a blow or push to; strike **2** (*intr*) to rap sharply with the knuckles, a hard object, etc, esp to capture attention: *to knock at the door* **3** (*tr*) to make or force by striking: *to knock a hole in the wall* **4** (*intr; usually foll by against*) to collide (with) **5** (*tr*) to bring into a certain condition by hitting or pushing: *to knock someone unconscious* **6** (*tr*) *informal* to criticize adversely; belittle: *to knock someone's work* **7** (*intr*) Also: **pink** (of an internal-combustion engine) to emit a characteristic metallic noise as a result of faulty combustion **8** (*intr*) (of a bearing, esp one in an engine) to emit a regular characteristic sound as a result of wear **9** *Brit slang* to have sexual intercourse with (a person) **10 knock (a person) into the middle of next week** *informal* to hit (a person) with a very heavy blow **11 knock one's head against** to have a violent or unpleasant encounter with (adverse facts or circumstances) **12 knock on the head a** to daze or kill (a person) by striking on the head **b** effectively to prevent the further development of (a plan) ▷ *n* **13 a** a blow, push, or rap: *he gave the table a knock* **b** the sound so caused **14** the sound of knocking in an engine or bearing **15** *informal* a misfortune, rebuff, or setback **16** *informal* unfavourable criticism **17** *informal* (in cricket) an innings or a spell of batting ▷ See also **knock about, knock back, knock down, knock off, knock-on, knockout, knock up** [Old English *cnocian*, of imitative origin; related to Old Norse *knoka* to hit]

knock about or **around** *vb* **1** (*intr, adverb*) to wander about aimlessly **2** (*intr, preposition*) to travel about, esp as resulting in varied and exotic experience: *he's knocked about the world a bit* **3** (*intr, adverb; foll by with*) to associate: *to knock about with a gang* **4** (*tr, adverb*) to treat brutally: *he knocks his wife about* **5** (*tr, adverb*) to consider or discuss informally: *to knock an idea about* ▷ *n* **knockabout 6** a sailing vessel, usually sloop rigged, without a bowsprit and with a single jib ▷ *adj* knockabout **7** rough; boisterous: *knockabout farce*

knock back *vb* (*tr, adverb*) **1** *informal* to drink, esp quickly **2** *informal* to cost **3** *slang* to reject or refuse: *you cannot possibly knock back such an offer* **4**

k

slang to come as an unpleasant surprise to; disconcert ▷ *n* **knock-back** **5** *slang* a refusal or rejection **6** *prison slang* failure to obtain parole

knock down *vb (tr, adverb)* **1** to strike to the ground with a blow, as in boxing **2** (in auctions) to declare (an article) sold, as by striking a blow with a gavel **3** to demolish **4** to dismantle, for ease of transport **5** *informal* to reduce (a price, etc) **6** *Austral slang* to spend (a cheque) **7** *Austral slang* to drink ▷ *adj* **knockdown** *(prenominal)* **8** overwhelming; powerful: *a knockdown blow* **9** *chiefly Brit* cheap: *I got the table at a knockdown price* **10** easily dismantled: *knockdown furniture* ▷ *n* **knockdown** **11** *US and Austral slang* an introduction: *will you give me a knockdown to her?*

knocker (ˈnɒkə) *n* **1** an object, usually ornamental and made of metal, attached to a door by a hinge and used for knocking **2** *informal* a person who finds fault or disparages **3** *(usually plural) slang* a female breast **4** a person or thing that knocks **5** **on the knocker** *Austral and NZ informal* promptly; at once: *you pay on the knocker here*

knock-for-knock *adj* designating an agreement between vehicle insurers that in the event of an accident each will pay for the damage to the vehicle insured with him without attempting to establish blame for the accident

knocking copy *n* advertising or publicity material designed to denigrate a competing product

knocking-shop *n Brit* a slang word for **brothel**

knock-knee *n* a condition in which the legs are bent inwards causing the knees to touch when standing. Technical name: **genu valgum** > ˌ**knock-ˈkneed** *adj*

knock off *vb (mainly adverb)* **1** *(intr, also preposition) informal* to finish work: *we knocked off an hour early* **2** *(tr) informal* to make or do hastily or easily: *to knock off a novel in a week* **3** *(tr; also preposition) informal* to reduce the price of (an article) by (a stated amount) **4** *(tr) slang* to kill **5** *(tr) slang* to rob or steal: *to knock off a bank; to knock off a watch* **6** *(tr) slang* to stop doing something, used as a command: *knock it off!* **7** *(tr) slang* to have sexual intercourse with; to seduce

knock-on *adj* **1** resulting inevitably but indirectly from another event or circumstance: *the works closed with the direct loss of 3000 jobs and many more from the knock-on effect on the area* ▷ *n* **2** *rugby* the infringement of playing the ball forward with the hand or arm ▷ *vb* **knock on** *(adverb)* **3** *rugby* to play (the ball) forward with the hand or arm

knockout (ˈnɒkˌaʊt) *n* **1** the act of rendering unconscious **2** a blow that renders an opponent unconscious **3** **a** a competition in which competitors are eliminated progressively **b** *(as modifier)*: *a knockout contest* **4** a series of absurd invented games, esp obstacle races, involving physical effort or skill **5** *informal* a person or thing that is overwhelmingly impressive or attractive: *she's a knockout* ▷ *vb* **knock out** *(tr, adverb)* **6** to render unconscious, esp by a blow **7** *boxing* to defeat (an opponent) by a knockout **8** to destroy, damage, or injure badly **9** to eliminate, esp in a knockout competition **10** *informal* to overwhelm or amaze, esp with admiration or favourable reaction: *I was knocked out by that new song* **11** to remove the ashes from (one's pipe) by tapping

knockout drops *pl n slang* a drug secretly put into someone's drink to cause stupefaction. See also **Mickey Finn**

knock up *vb (adverb, mainly tr)* **1** Also: **knock together** *informal* to assemble quickly; improvise: *to knock up a set of shelves* **2** *Brit informal* to waken; rouse **3** *slang* to make pregnant **4** *Brit informal* to exhaust: *the heavy work knocked him up* **5** *cricket* to score (runs) **6** *(intr) tennis, squash, badminton* to practise or hit the ball about informally, esp before a match ▷ *n* **knock-up** **7** a practice session at tennis, squash, or a similar game

knockwurst (ˈnɒkˌwɜːst) *n* a variant spelling of **knackwurst**

Knole (nəʊl) *n* a mansion in Sevenoaks in Kent: built (1454) for Thomas Bourchier, Archbishop of Canterbury; later granted to the Sackville family, who made major alterations (1603–08)

knoll[1] (nəʊl) *n* a small rounded hill [Old English *cnoll*; compare Old Norse *knollr* hilltop] > ˈ**knolly** *adj*

knoll[2] (nəʊl) *n, vb* an archaic or dialect word for **knell**. > ˈ**knoller** *n*

knop (nɒp) *n archaic* a knob, esp an ornamental one [C14 from Germanic; compare Middle Dutch *cnoppe* bud, Old High German *knopf*]

Knossos *or* **Cnossus** (ˈnɒsəs, ˈknɒs-) *n* a ruined city in N central Crete: remains of the Minoan Bronze Age civilization

knot[1] (nɒt) *n* **1** any of various fastenings formed by looping and tying a piece of rope, cord, etc, in upon itself, to another piece of rope, or to another object **2** a prescribed method of tying a particular knot **3** a tangle, as in hair or string **4** a decorative bow or fastening, as of ribbon or braid **5** a small cluster or huddled group **6** a tie or bond: *the marriage knot* **7** a difficult problem **8** a protuberance or lump of plant tissues, such as that occurring on the trunks of certain trees **9** **a** a hard mass of wood at the point where a branch joins the trunk of a tree **b** a cross section of this, usually roundish and cross-grained, visible in a piece of timber **10** a sensation of constriction, caused by tension or nervousness: *his stomach was tying itself in knots* **11** **a** *pathol* a lump of vessels or fibres formed in a part, as in a muscle **b** *anatomy* a protuberance on an organ or part **12** a unit of speed used by nautical vessels and aircraft, being one nautical mile (about 1.15 statute miles or 1.85 km) per hour **13** one of a number of equally spaced knots on a log line used to indicate the speed of a ship in nautical miles per hour **14** **at a rate of knots** very fast **15** **tie (someone) in knots** to completely perplex or confuse (someone) **16** **tie the knot** *informal* to get married ▷ *vb* **knots, knotting, knotted** **17** *(tr)* to tie or fasten in a knot **18** to form or cause to form into a knot **19** *(tr)* to ravel or entangle or become ravelled or entangled **20** *(tr)* to make (an article or a design) by tying thread in an interlaced pattern of ornamental knots, as in macramé [Old English *cnotta*; related to Old High German *knoto*, Old Norse *knūtr*] > ˈ**knotter** *n* > ˈ**knotless** *adj* > ˈ**knotˌlike** *adj*

knot[2] (nɒt) *n* a small northern sandpiper, *Calidris canutus*, with a short bill and grey plumage [C15 of unknown origin]

knot garden *n* (esp formerly) a formal garden of intricate design

knotgrass (ˈnɒtˌɡrɑːs) *n* **1** Also called: **allseed** a polygonaceous weedy plant, *Polygonum aviculare*, whose small green flowers produce numerous seeds **2** any of several related plants

knothole (ˈnɒtˌhəʊl) *n* a hole in a piece of wood where a knot has been

knotted (ˈnɒtɪd) *adj* **1** (of wood, rope, etc) having knots **2** **get knotted!** *Brit slang* used as a response to express disapproval or rejection

knotting (ˈnɒtɪŋ) *n* **1** a sealer applied over knots in new wood before priming to prevent resin from exuding **2** (esp formerly) a kind of decorative knotted fancywork

knotty (ˈnɒtɪ) *adj* **-tier, -tiest** **1** (of wood, rope, etc) full of or characterized by knots **2** extremely difficult or intricate > ˈ**knottily** *adv* > ˈ**knottiness** *n*

knotweed (ˈnɒtˌwiːd) *n* any of several polygonaceous plants of the genus *Polygonum*, having small flowers and jointed stems

knotwork (ˈnɒtˌwɜːk) *n* ornamentation consisting of a mass of intertwined and knotted cords

knout (naʊt) *n* a stout whip used formerly in Russia as an instrument of punishment [C17 from Russian *knut*, of Scandinavian origin; compare Old Norse *knūtr* knot]

know (nəʊ) *vb* **knows, knowing, knew** (njuː) **known** (nəʊn) *(mainly tr)* **1** *(also intr; may take a clause as object)* to be or feel certain of the truth or accuracy of (a fact, etc) **2** to be acquainted or familiar with: *she's known him five years* **3** to have a familiarity or grasp of, as through study or experience: *he knows French* **4** *(also intr; may take a clause as object)* to understand, be aware of, or perceive (facts, etc): *he knows the answer now* **5** *(foll by how)* to be sure or aware of (how to be or do something) **6** to experience, esp deeply: *to know poverty* **7** to be intelligent, informed, or sensible enough (to do something): *she knew not to go home yet* **8** *(may take a clause as object)* to be able to distinguish or discriminate **9** *archaic* to have sexual intercourse with **10** **I know what** I have an idea **11** **know what's what** to know how one thing or things in general work **12** **you know** *informal* a parenthetical filler phrase used to make a pause in speaking or add slight emphasis to a statement **13** **you never know** things are uncertain ▷ *n* **14** **in the know** *informal* aware or informed [Old English *gecnāwan*; related to Old Norse *knā* I can, Latin *noscere* to come to know] > ˈ**knowable** *adj* > ˈ**knower** *n*

know-all *n informal, disparaging* a person who pretends or appears to know a great deal

know-how *n informal* **1** ingenuity, aptitude, or skill; knack **2** commercial and saleable knowledge of how to do a particular thing; experience

knowing (ˈnəʊɪŋ) *adj* **1** suggesting secret information or knowledge **2** wise, shrewd, or clever **3** deliberate; intentional ▷ *n* **4** **there is no knowing** one cannot tell > ˈ**knowingly** *adv* > ˈ**knowingness** *n*

knowledge (ˈnɒlɪdʒ) *n* **1** the facts, feelings or experiences known by a person or group of people **2** the state of knowing **3** awareness, consciousness, or familiarity gained by experience or learning **4** erudition or informed learning **5** specific information about a subject **6** sexual intercourse (obsolete except in the legal phrase **carnal knowledge**) **7** **come to one's knowledge** to become known to one **8** **to my knowledge** **a** as I understand it **b** as I know **9** **grow out of one's knowledge** *Irish* to behave in a presumptuous or conceited manner

knowledgeable *or* **knowledgable** (ˈnɒlɪdʒəbᵊl) *adj* possessing or indicating much knowledge > ˈ**knowledgeableness** *or* ˈ**knowledgableness** *n* > ˈ**knowledgeably** *or* ˈ**knowledgably** *adv*

knowledge-based system *n computing* an expert system. Abbreviation: **KBS**

knowledge economy *n* an economy in which information services are dominant as an area of growth

knowledge worker *n* a person employed to produce or analyse ideas and information

known (nəʊn) *vb* **1** the past participle of **know** ▷ *adj* **2** specified and identified: *a known criminal* ▷ *n* **3** a fact or entity known

know-nothing *n informal, disparaging* an ignorant person

Knowsley (ˈnəʊzlɪ) *n* a unitary authority of NW England, in Merseyside. Pop: 150 200 (2003 est). Area: 97 sq km (38 sq miles)

Knoxville (ˈnɒksvɪl) *n* an industrial city in E Tennessee, on the Tennessee River: state capital (1796–1812; 1817–19). Pop: 173 278 (2003 est)

KNP *chess symbol for* king's knight's pawn

Knt *abbreviation for* Knight

knuckle (ˈnʌkᵊl) *n* **1** a joint of a finger, esp that connecting a finger to the hand **2** a joint of veal, pork, etc, consisting of the part of the leg below the knee joint, often used in making stews or stock **3** the cylindrical portion of a hinge through which the pin passes **4** an angle joint between two members of a structure **5** **near the knuckle** *informal* approaching indecency ▷ *vb* **6** *(tr)* to rub or press with the knuckles **7** *(intr)* to keep the knuckles on the ground while shooting a marble ▷ See also **knuckle down, knuckle under** [C14 related to Middle High German *knöchel*, Middle Low German *knoke* bone, Dutch *knok*] > ˈ**knuckly** *adj*

knucklebone (ˈnʌkᵊlˌbəʊn) *n* any bone forming part of a knuckle or knuckle joint

knucklebones (ˈnʌkᵊlˌbəʊnz) *n* (*functioning as singular*) a less common name for **jacks** (the game)

knuckle down *vb* (*intr, adverb*) *informal* to apply oneself diligently: *to knuckle down to some work*

knuckle-duster *n* (*often plural*) a metal bar fitted over the knuckles, often with holes for the fingers, for inflicting injury by a blow with the fist

knucklehead (ˈnʌkᵊlˌhɛd) *n* *informal* fool; idiot ⊳ **ˈknuckleˌheaded** *adj*

knuckle joint *n* **1** any of the joints of the fingers **2** *mechanical engineering* a hinged joint between two rods, often a ball and socket joint

knuckle under *vb* (*intr, adverb*) to give way under pressure or authority; yield

knur, knurr (nɜː) *or* **knar** *n* a knot or protuberance in a tree trunk or in wood [C16 *knor*; related to Middle High German *knorre* knot; compare KNAR]

knurl *or* **nurl** (nɜːl) *vb* (*tr*) **1** to impress with a series of fine ridges or serrations ⊳ *n* **2** a small ridge, esp one of a series providing a rough surface that can be gripped [C17 probably from KNUR]

knurly (ˈnɜːlɪ) *adj* **knurlier, knurliest** a rare word for **gnarled**

KO *or* **k.o.** (ˈkeɪˈəʊ) *vb* **KO's, KO'ing, KO'd; k.o.'s, k.o.'ing, k.o.'d,** *n,* *pl* **KO's** *or* **k.o.'s** a slang term for **knock out** *or* **knockout**

koa (ˈkəʊə) *n* **1** a Hawaiian leguminous tree, *Acacia koa,* yielding a hard wood **2** the reddish wood of this tree, used esp for furniture [C19 from Hawaiian]

koala *or* **koala bear** (kəʊˈɑːlə) *n* a slow-moving Australian arboreal marsupial, *Phascolarctus cinereus,* having dense greyish fur and feeding on eucalyptus leaves and bark. Also called (Austral): **native bear** [from a native Australian language]

koan (ˈkəʊæn) *n* (in Zen Buddhism) a problem or riddle that admits no logical solution [from Japanese]

koap (ˈkəʊˌæp) *n* *Papua New Guinean slang* sexual intercourse [Neo-Melanesian]

kob (kɒb) *n* any of several species of African antelope, esp *Kobus kob:* similar to waterbucks [C20 from a Niger-Congo language; compare Wolof *koba,* Fulani *kōba*]

Kobarid (ˈkəʊbaˌriːd; *Serbo-Croat* ˈkɔbaˌrid) *n* a village in Slovenia on the Isonzo River: part of Italy until 1947; scene of the defeat of the Italians by Austro-German forces (1917). Italian name: **Caporetto**

Kobe (ˈkəʊbɪ) *n* a port in S Japan, on S Honshu on Osaka Bay: formed in 1889 by the amalgamation of Hyogo and Kobe; a major industrial complex, producing ships, steel, and rubber goods. Pop: 1 478 380 (2002 est)

Kobe beef *n* a grade of beef from cattle raised in Kobe, Japan, which is extremely tender and full-flavoured as a result of the cattle being massaged with sake and fed a special diet including large quantities of beer

København (købənˈhaun) *n* the Danish name for **Copenhagen**

Koblenz *or* **Coblenz** (*German* ˈkoːblɛnts) *n* a city in W central Germany, in the Rhineland-Palatinate at the confluence of the Rivers Moselle and Rhine: ruled by the archbishop-electors of Trier from 1018 until occupied by the French in 1794; passed to Prussia in 1815, becoming capital of the Rhine Province (1824–1945) and of the Rhineland-Palatinate (1946–50); wine trade centre. Pop: 107 608 (2003 est). Latin name: **Confluentes** (ˌkɒnfluˈɛntiːz)

kobold (ˈkɒbəʊld) *n* *german myth* **1** a mischievous household sprite **2** a spirit that haunts subterranean places, such as mines [C19 from German; see COBALT]

Köchel (*German* ˈkœçəl) *n* See **K**

Kochi (kəʊˈtʃiː) *n* **1** a port in SW Japan, on central Shikoku on Urado Bay. Pop: 326 490 (2002 est) **2** another name for **Cochin** (sense 2)

kochia (ˈkəʊkɪə) *n* any plant of the widely distributed annual genus *Kochia,* esp *K. Scoparia trichophila,* grown for its foliage, which turns dark red in the late summer: family *Chenopodiaceae.* Also called: **burning bush, summer cypress** [named after W. D. J. *Koch* (1771–1849), German botanist]

Kodiak (ˈkəʊdɪˌæk) *n* an island in S Alaska, in the Gulf of Alaska: site of the first European settlement in Alaska, made by Russians in 1784. Pop: 13 466 (2004 est). Area: 8974 sq km (3465 sq miles)

Kodiak bear *or* **Kodiak** *n* a large variety of the brown bear, *Ursus arctos,* inhabiting the west coast of Alaska and neighbouring islands, esp Kodiak

Kodok (ˈkəʊdɒk) *n* the modern name for **Fashoda**

koekoea (kəkəˈɑː) *n,* *pl* **koekoea** a common New Zealand cuckoo, *Eudynamis taitensis,* found in forest areas. Also called: **long-tailed cuckoo** [Māori]

koeksister (ˈkukˌsɪstə) *n* *South African* a plaited doughnut deep-fried and soaked in syrup [Afrikaans, but possibly of Malay origin]

koel (ˈkəʊəl) *n* any of several parasitic cuckoos of the genus *Eudynamys,* esp *E. scolopacea,* of S and SE Asia and Australia [C19 from Hindi, from Sanskrit *kokila*]

kofta (ˈkɒftə) *n* an Indian dish of seasoned minced meat shaped into small balls and cooked [Urdu]

koftgar (ˈkɒftgɑː) *n* (in India) a person skilled in the art of inlaying steel with gold (**koftgari**) [C19 Urdu]

Kofu (ˈkəʊfuː) *n* a city in central Japan, on S Honshu: textiles. Pop: 190 098 (2002 est)

Kogi (ˈkəʊgɪ) *n* a state of W Nigeria. Capital: Lokoja. Pop: 2 346 946 (1995 est)

koha (ˈkəʊhə) *n* *NZ* a gift or donation, esp of cash [Māori]

kohanga reo (kɔːˈhɑːŋa ˈreɪəʊ) *n* *NZ* an infant class in which the lessons are conducted in Māori [Māori, literally: language nest]

kohekohe (kɒhəkɒhə) *n,* *pl* **kohekohe** a New Zealand tree, *Dysoxylum spectabile,* with large glossy leaves and reddish wood [Māori]

Koheleth (kəʊˈhɛlθ) *n* *Old Testament* Ecclesiastes or its author, traditionally believed to be Solomon [from Hebrew *qōheleth*]

Kohen *or* **Cohen** (kɒˈhɛn, kɔɪn) *n* *Judaism* a member of the priestly family of the Tribe of Levi, descended from Aaron, who has certain ritual privileges in the synagogue service [from Hebrew, literally: priest]

Kohima (ˈkəʊhɪˌmɑː) *n* a city in NE India, capital of Nagaland, near the Burmese border: centre of fierce fighting in World War II, when it was surrounded by the Japanese but not captured (1944). Pop: 78 584 (2001)

Koh-i-noor, Kohinor *or* **Kohinur** (ˌkəʊɪˈnʊə) *n* a very large oval Indian diamond, part of the British crown jewels since 1849, weighing 108.8 carats [C19 from Persian *Kōh-i-nūr,* literally: mountain of light, from *kōh* mountain + Arabic *nūr* light]

kohl (kəʊl) *n* a cosmetic powder used, originally esp in Muslim and Asian countries, to darken the area around the eyes. It is usually powdered antimony sulphide [C18 from Arabic *kohl;* see ALCOHOL]

kohlrabi (kəʊlˈrɑːbɪ) *n,* *pl* **-bies** a cultivated variety of cabbage, *Brassica oleracea caulorapa* (or *gongylodes*), whose thickened stem is eaten as a vegetable. Also called: **turnip cabbage** [C19 from German, from Italian *cavoli rape* (pl), from *cavolo* cabbage (from Latin *caulis*) + *rapa* turnip (from Latin); influenced by German *Kohl* cabbage]

Kohoutek (kəˈhuːtɛk) *n* a comet of almost parabolic orbit that reached its closest approach to the sun in Dec 1973 [C20 named after Luboš *Kohoutek,* Czech astronomer working in Germany who discovered it in March, 1973]

kohutuhutu (kɒhuːtuːhuːtuː) *n,* *pl* **kohutuhutu** another name for **kotukutuku**

koi (kɔɪ) *n* any of various ornamental forms of the common carp [Japanese]

koine (ˈkɔɪniː) *n* a common language among speakers of different languages; lingua franca [from Greek *koinē dialektos* common language]

Koine (ˈkɔɪniː) *n* (*sometimes not capital*) **the.** the Ancient Greek dialect that was the lingua franca of the empire of Alexander the Great and was widely throughout the E Mediterranean area in Roman times

kokako (ˈkəʊˌkaːkəʊ) *n,* *pl* **-kos** a dark grey long-tailed wattled crow of New Zealand, *Callaeas cinerea* [Māori]

Kokand (*Russian* kaˈkant) *n* a city in NE Uzbekistan, in the Fergana valley. Pop: 211 000 (2005 est)

kokanee (kəʊˈkænɪ) *n* a landlocked salmon, *Oncorhynchus nerka kennerlyi,* of lakes in W North America: a variety of sockeye [probably from *Kokanee* Creek, in SE British Columbia]

kokiri (kɒkiːriː) *n,* *pl* **kokiri** **1** a rough-skinned New Zealand triggerfish, *Parika scaber,* known also as **leatherjacket** (sense 2) **2** a Māori self-help group providing training and support in the community [Māori]

kokobeh (ˈkʌkʌbeh) *adj* (of certain fruit) having a rough skin: *kokobeh breadfruit* [from Twi: leprosy]

Koko Nor (ˈkəʊˈkəʊ ˈnɔː) *or* **Kuku Nor** *n* a lake in W China, in Qinghai province in the NE Tibetan Highlands at an altitude of about 3000 m (10 000 ft): the largest lake in China. Area: about 4100 sq km (1600 sq miles). Chinese name: Qinghai

kokopu (kɒkɒpuː) *n,* *pl* **kokopu** *NZ* another name for **cockabully** [Māori]

kokowai (ˈkɒkɒˌwaːhiː) *n* *NZ* a type of clay used in decoration because of its red colour [Māori]

Kokura (ˌkəʊkəˈrɑː) *n* a former city in SW Japan, on N Kyushu: merged with adjacent townships in 1963 to form the new city of **Kitakyushu**

kola (ˈkəʊlə) *n* a variant spelling of **cola**

kola nut *n* a variant spelling of **cola nut**

Kola Peninsula (ˈkəʊlə) *n* a peninsula in NW Russia, between the Barents and White Seas: forms most of the Murmansk region. Area: about 130 000 sq km (50 000 sq miles)

Kolar Gold Fields (kəʊˈlɑː) *n* a city in S India, in SE Karnataka: a major gold-mining centre since 1881. Pop: 72 481 (1991)

Kolding (*Danish* ˈkɔlɛŋ) *n* a port in Denmark, in E Jutland at the head of **Kolding Fjord** (an inlet of the Little Belt). Pop: 54 941 (2004 est)

Kolhapur (ˌkəʊlhɑːˈpʊə) *n* a city in W India, in S Maharashtra: university (1963). Pop: 485 183 (2001)

kolinsky (kəˈlɪnskɪ) *n,* *pl* **-skies** **1** any of various Asian minks, esp *Mustela sibirica* of Siberia **2** the rich tawny fur of this animal [C19 from Russian *kolinski* of *Kola:* see KOLA PENINSULA]

Kolkata (ˈkɒlkɑːtə) *n* the official name of **Calcutta**

kolkhoz, kolkhos (kɒlˈhɔːz; *Russian* kalˈxɔs) *or* **kolkoz** (kɒlˈkɔːz) *n* a Russian collective farm [C20 from Russian, short for *kollektivnoe khozyaistvo* collective farm]

Kolmar (ˈkɒlmar) *n* the German name for **Colmar**

Köln (kœln) *n* the German name for **Cologne**

Kol Nidre (kɔːl ˈnɪdreɪ; *Hebrew* kɔl niːˈdre) *n* *Judaism* **1** the evening service with which Yom Kippur begins **2** the opening prayer of that service, declaring null in advance any purely religious vows one may come to make in the coming year [Aramaic *kōl nidhrē* all the vows; the prayer's opening words]

kolo (ˈkəʊləʊ) *n,* *pl* **-los** **1** a Serbian folk dance in which a circle of people dance slowly around one or more dancers in the centre **2** a piece of music composed for or in the rhythm of this dance [Serbo-Croat, from Old Slavonic: wheel; related to Old English wheel WHEEL]

Kolomna (*Russian* kaˈlɔmnə) *n* a city in the W central Russia, at the confluence of the Moskva and Oka Rivers: railway engineering centre. Pop: 151 500 (1999 est)

k

Kolozsvár ('koloʒvaːr) *n* the Hungarian name for **Cluj**

Kolyma (*Russian* kəli'ma) *n* a river in NE Russia, rising in the Kolyma Mountains north of the Sea of Okhotsk and flowing generally north to the East Siberian Sea. Length: 2600 km (1615 miles)

Kolyma Range *n* a mountain range in NE Russia, in NE Siberia, extending about 1100 km (700 miles) between the Kolyma River and the Sea of Okhotsk. Highest peak: 1862 m (6109 ft)

Komati (kə'maːtɪ, 'kəʊmətɪ) *n* a river in southern Africa, rising in E South Africa and flowing east through Swaziland and Mozambique to the Indian Ocean at Delagoa Bay. Length: about 800 km (500 miles)

komatik ('kəʊmætɪk) *n* a sledge having wooden runners and crossbars bound with rawhide, used by the Inuit and other related peoples [c20 from Inuktitut (Labrador)]

kombu ('kombuː) *or* **konbu** *n* a dark brown seaweed of the genus *Laminaria* (class Phaeophyceae) the leaves of which are dried and used esp in Japanese cookery [c19 Japanese]

Komi ('kəʊmɪ) *n* **1** (*pl* **Komi** *or* **Komis**) a member of a Finno-Ugric people living chiefly in the Komi Republic, in the NW Urals **2** the Finno-Ugric language of this people; Zyrian

Komi Republic ('kəʊmɪ) *n* a constituent republic of NW Russia: annexed by the princes of Moscow in the 14th century. Capital: Syktyvkar. Pop: 1 019 000 (2002). Area: 415 900 sq km (160 540 sq miles)

Kommunarsk (*Russian* kəmu'narsk) *n* the former name (until 1992) of **Alchevsk**

Kommunizma Peak (*Russian* kəmu'njizmə) *n* a mountain in SE Tajikistan in the Pamirs: the highest mountain in the former Soviet Union. Height: 7495 m (24 590 ft). Former name: Stalin Peak

Komodo dragon *or* **lizard** (kə'məʊdəʊ) *n* the largest monitor lizard, *Varanus komodoensis,* of Komodo and other East Indian islands: grows to a length of 3 m (about 10 ft) and a weight of 135 kilograms (about 300 lbs.)

komondor ('kɒmənˌdɔː) *n* a large powerful dog of an ancient Hungarian breed, originally used for sheep herding. It has a very long white coat that hangs in woolly or matted locks

Komsomol (ˌkɒmsə'mɒl, 'kɒmsəˌmɒl; *Russian* kəmsa'mɔl) *n* (formerly) the youth association of the Soviet Union for 14- to 26-year-olds [c20 from Russian, from Kom(munisticheski) So(yuz) Mol(odezhi) Communist Union of Youth]

Komsomolsk (*Russian* kəmsa'mɔljsk) *n* an industrial city in W Russia, on the Amur River: built by members of the Komsomol (Communist youth league) in 1932. Pop: 275 000 (2005 est)

Konakry *or* **Konakri** (*French* kɔnakri) *n* variant spellings of **Conakry**

konbu ('kɒnbuː) *n* a variant of **kombu** [c19 Japanese]

kondo ('kɒndəʊ) *n, pl* **-dos** (in Uganda) a thief or armed robber [c20 from Luganda]

koneke ('kɒnˌɛkɪ) *or* **konaki** ('kɒnaːki) *n, pl* **koneke** *or* **konaki** NZ a farm vehicle with runners in front and wheels at the rear [Māori]

Kongo ('kɒŋgəʊ) *n* **1** (*pl* **-gos** *or* **-go**) a member of a Negroid people of Africa living in the tropical forests of the Democratic Republic of Congo (formerly Zaïre), Congo Brazzaville, and Angola **2** the language of this people, belonging to the Bantu group of the Niger-Congo family

kongoni (kəŋ'gəʊnɪ) *n, pl* **-ni** an E African hartebeest, *Alcelaphus buselaphus.* See **hartebeest** (sense 1) [Swahili]

Kongur Shan ('kʊngʊə 'fæn), **Kungur** *or* **Qungur** *n* a mountain in China, in W Xinjiang Uygur: the highest peak in the Pamirs. Height: 7719 m (25 325 ft)

Königgrätz (kø:nɪç'grɛːts) *n* the German name for **Hradec Králové**

Königsberg ('kɜːnɪgzˌbɜːg; *German* 'køːnɪçsbɛrk) *n* the former name (until 1946) of **Kaliningrad**

Königshütte ('køːnɪçshytə) *n* the German name for **Chorzów**

konimeter (kəʊ'nɪmɪtə) *n* a device for measuring airborne dust concentration in which samples are obtained by sucking the air through a hole and allowing it to pass over a glass plate coated with grease on which the particles collect [c20 from Greek *konia* dust + -METER]

konini ('kɒniːniː) *n, pl* **konini** the edible dark purple berry of the kotukutuku (tree fuchsia) [Māori]

koniology *or* **coniology** (ˌkəʊnɪ'ɒlədʒɪ) *n* the study of atmospheric dust and its effects [c20 from Greek *konia* dust + -LOGY]

Konstanz ('kɒnstants) *n* the German name for **Constance**

Konya *or* **Konia** ('kɔːnjaː) *n* a city in SW central Turkey: in ancient times a Phrygian city and capital of Lycaonia. Pop: 883 000 (2005 est). Ancient name: Iconium

koodoo ('kuːduː) *n* a variant spelling of **kudu**

kook (kuːk) *n* US and Canadian informal an eccentric, crazy, or foolish person [c20 probably from CUCKOO]

kookaburra ('kʊkəˌbʌrə) *n* **1** a large arboreal Australian kingfisher, *Dacelo novaeguineae* (or *gigas*), with a cackling cry. Also called: laughing jackass **2** a related smaller bird *D. Leachii,* of tropical Australia and New Guinea. Also called: blue-winged kookaburra [c19 from a native Australian language]

kooky *or* **kookie** ('kuːkɪ) *adj* **kookier, kookiest** informal crazy, eccentric, or foolish

koori ('kʊərɪ) *n, pl* **-ries** a native Australian [c19 from a native Australian language]

Kootenay *or* **Kootenai** ('kuːtᵊniː, 'kuːtneɪ) *n* a river in W North America, rising in SE British Columbia and flowing south into NW Montana, then north into Idaho before re-entering British Columbia, broadening into **Kootenay Lake,** then flowing to the Columbia River. Length: 655 km (407 miles)

kop (kɒp) *n* a prominent isolated hill or mountain in southern Africa. See **inselberg** [from Afrikaans: head, hence high part; compare German *Kopf* head; see COP²]

kopeck, kopek *or* **copeck** ('kəʊpɛk) *n* a monetary unit of Russia and Belarus worth one hundredth of a rouble: coins are still used as tokens for coin-operated machinery although the kopeck itself is virtually valueless [Russian *kopeika,* from *kopye* lance; so called because of the representation of Tsar Ivan IV on the coin with a lance in his hand]

Kopeisk *or* **Kopeysk** (*Russian* ka'pjejsk) *n* a city in SW central Russia, in Chelyabinsk province: lignite mining. Pop: 24 000 (2005 est). Former name: Kopi ('kɒpi)

koph *or* **qoph** (kɒf) *n* the 19th letter in the Hebrew alphabet (ק) transliterated as *q,* and pronounced as a velar or uvular stop [from Hebrew *qoph*; see QOPH]

kopiyka ('kəʊpɪkə) *n* a monetary unit of Ukraine, worth one hundredth of a hryvna

kopje *or* **koppie** ('kɒpɪ) *n* a small isolated hill [c19 from Afrikaans *koppie,* from Dutch *kopje,* literally: a little head, from *kop* head; see KOP]

koppa ('kɒpə) *n* a consonantal letter in the Greek alphabet pronounced like kappa (K) with the point of articulation further back in the throat. It became obsolete in classical (Attic) Greek orthography, but was passed on to the Romans who incorporated it into their alphabet as Q [Greek, of Semitic origin]

kora ('kɔːrə) *n* a West African instrument with twenty-one strings, combining features of the harp and the lute

Koran (kɔː'raːn) *n* the sacred book of Islam, believed by Muslims to be the infallible word of God dictated to Mohammed through the medium of the angel Gabriel. Also: **Qur'an** [c17 from Arabic *qur'ān* reading, book; related to *qara'a* to read, recite] > **Ko'ranic** *adj*

korari ('kɒraːri) *n, pl* **korari** a native New Zealand flax plant, *Phormium tenax.* Also called: **claddie** [Māori]

Korat cat ('kɔːræt) *n* a rare type of cat originating in Thailand that has a blue-grey coat and, in the adult, brilliant green eyes [named after the *Korat* Plateau in Thailand]

Korçë (*Albanian* 'kortʃə) *n* a market town in SE Albania. Pop: 67 100 (1991 est)

Kordofan (ˌkɔːdəʊ'fæn) *n* a region of the central Sudan: consists of a plateau with rugged uplands (the Nuba Mountains). Area: 380 548 sq km (146 930 sq miles)

Kordofanian (ˌkɔːdəʊ'feɪnɪən) *n* **1** a group of languages spoken in the Kordofan and Nuba Hills of the S Sudan: classed as an independent family, probably distantly related to Niger-Congo ▷ *adj* **2** denoting, relating to, or belonging to this group of languages **3** of or relating to Kordofan

Korea (kə'riːə) *n* a former country in E Asia, now divided into two separate countries, North Korea and South Korea. Korea occupied the peninsula between the Sea of Japan and the Yellow Sea: an isolated vassal of Manchu China for three centuries until the opening of ports to Japanese trade in 1876; gained independence in 1895; annexed by Japan in 1910 and divided in 1945 into two occupation zones (Russian in the north, American in the south), which became North Korea and South Korea in 1948. Japanese name (1910–45): Chosen. See **North Korea, South Korea**

Korean (kə'riːən) *adj* **1** of or relating to Korea, its people, or their language ▷ *n* **2** a native or inhabitant of Korea **3** the official language of North and South Korea, considered by some scholars to be part of the Altaic family of languages

Korean War *n* the war (1950–53) fought between North Korea, aided by Communist China, and South Korea, supported by the US and other members of the UN

Korea Strait *n* a strait between South Korea and SW Japan, linking the Sea of Japan with the East China Sea

korero ('kɒrərəʊ) *n, pl* **-ros 1** a talk or discussion; meeting ▷ *vb* **2** (*intr*) to speak or converse [Māori]

korfball ('kɔːfˌbɔːl) *n* a game similar to basketball, in which each team consists of six men and six women [c20 from Dutch *korfbal* basketball]

korimako ('kɒrɪmaːkɒ) *n, pl* **korimako** NZ another name for **bellbird** (sense 2) [Māori]

Kórinthos ('kɒrɪnθɒs) *n* transliteration of the Modern Greek name for **Corinth**

korma *or* **qorma** ('kɔːmə) *n* any of a variety of Indian dishes consisting of meat or vegetables braised with water, stock, yogurt, or cream [Urdu]

koro ('kɒrɒ) *n, pl* **koro a** an elderly Māori man **b** a title of respect for an elderly Māori man [Māori]

koromiko (kɒrɒmi:kɒ) *n, pl* **koromiko** a flowering New Zealand shrub, *Hebe salicifolia* [Māori]

korora (ˌkəʊrəʊ'raː) *n, pl* **korora** NZ another name for **fairy penguin** [Māori]

korowai (kɒrɒwaːi:) *n, pl* **korowai** a decorative woven cloak worn by a Māori chief [Māori]

Korsakoffian (ˌkɔːsə'kɒfɪən) *adj* **1** relating to or suffering from Korsakoff's psychosis ▷ *n* **2** a person suffering from Korsakoff's psychosis

Korsakoff's psychosis *or* **syndrome** ('kɔːsəkɒfs) *n* a mental illness involving severe confusion and inability to retain recent memories, usually caused by alcoholism [c19 named after Sergei *Korsakoff* (1854–1900), Russian neuropsychiatrist, who described it]

Kortrijk ('kɔːtreɪk) *n* the Flemish name for **Courtrai**

koru ('kɒruː) *n* NZ a stylized curved pattern used esp in carving [Māori]

koruna (kɒ'ruːnə) *n* the standard monetary unit of the Czech Republic and Slovakia, divided into 100 hellers

kos (kəʊs) *n, pl* **kos** an Indian unit of distance having different values in different localities. It is usually between 1 and 3 miles or 1 and 5 kilometres. Also called: **coss** [from Hindi *kōs*]

Kos *or* **Cos** (kɒs) *n* an island in the SE Aegean Sea, in the Greek Dodecanese Islands: separated from SW Turkey by the **Kos Channel**; settled in ancient times by Dorians and became famous for literature and medicine. Pop: 30 947 (2001). Area: 282 sq km (109 sq miles)

Kosciuszko (ˌkɒsɪˈʌskəʊ) *n* **Mount** a mountain in Australia, in SE New South Wales in the Australian Alps: the highest peak in Australia. Height: 2230 m (7316 ft)

kosher (ˈkəʊʃə) *adj* **1** *Judaism* conforming to religious law; fit for use: esp, (of food) prepared in accordance with the dietary laws. See also **kasher, kashruth** **2** *informal* **a** genuine or authentic **b** legitimate or proper [c19 from Yiddish, from Hebrew *kāshēr* right, proper]

kosher salt *n* *US* a coarse flaky salt that contains no additives, used in cooking and in preparing kosher meals

Košice (Czech ˈkɔʃitsɛ) *n* a city in E Slovakia: passed from Hungary to Czechoslovakia in 1920 and to Slovakia in 1993. Pop: 236 093 (2001). Hungarian name: **Kassa**

Kosovo (Serbo-Croat ˈkɔsɔvɔ) *or* **Kosova** *n* an autonomous province of Serbia and Montenegro, in SW Serbia: chiefly Albanian in population since the 13th century, it declared independence in 1990; Serb suppression of separatists escalated to a policy of ethnic cleansing in 1998, provoking NATO airstrikes against Serbia in 1999: now under UN administration: mainly a plateau. Capital: Priština. Pop: 2 325 000 (2001 est). Area: 10 887 sq km (4203 sq miles). Full name: **Kosovo-Metohija** (*Serbo-Croat* ˈkɔsɔvɔmɛˌtɔhija)

Kostroma (Russian kəstraˈma) *n* a city in W central Russia, on the River Volga: fought over bitterly by Novgorod, Tver, and Moscow, until annexed by Moscow in 1329; textile centre. Pop: 280 000 (2005 est)

Kota *or* **Kotah** (ˈkəʊtə) *n* a city in NW India, in Rajasthan on the Chambal River: textile industry. op.: 695 899 (2001)

Kotabaru (ˈkəʊtəˈbɑːruː) *n* a former name of **Jayapura**

Kota Bharu *or* **Bahru** (ˈkəʊtə ˈbɑːruː) *n* a port in NE Peninsular Malaysia: capital of Kelantan state on the delta of the Kelantan River. Pop: 263 000 (2005 est)

kotahitanga (kəʊtɑːhiˈtɑːˀŋə) *n* **1** NZ unity or solidarity **2** (*often capital*) (in New Zealand) a Māori political movement which advocates national unity [Māori]

Kota Kinabalu (ˈkəʊtə ˌkɪnəbəˈluː) *n* a port in Malaysia, capital of Sabah state on the South China Sea: exports timber and rubber. Pop: 439 000 (2005 est). Former name: **Jesselton**

kotare (ˈkɒtərɪ) *n, pl* **kotare** a small greenish-blue kingfisher, *Halcyon sanctus*, found in New Zealand, Australia, and some Pacific islands to the north [Māori]

kotch (kɒtʃ) *vb South African slang* (*intr*) to vomit [from Afrikaans *kots*]

koto (ˈkəʊtəʊ) *n, pl* **kotos** a Japanese stringed instrument, consisting of a rectangular wooden body over which are stretched silk strings, which are plucked with plectrums or a nail-like device [Japanese]

kotuku (ˈkəʊtʊkuː) *n, pl* **-ku** the white heron, *Egretta alba*, having brilliant white plumage, black legs and yellow eyes and bill [Māori]

kotukutuku (kɒtuːkuːˈtuːkuː) *n, pl* **kotukutuku** a New Zealand forest tree, *Fuchsia excorticata*, with dark purple fruit called **konini**. Also called: **kohutuhutu, tree fuchsia** [Māori]

koulibiaca *or* **coulibiaca** (ˌkəʊlɪˈbjɑːkə) *n* a Russian baked dish consisting of flaked fish mixed with semolina encased in pastry [from Russian]

koumis (ˈkuːmɪs) *n* a variant spelling of **kumiss**

kouprey (ˈkuːpreɪ) *n* a large wild member of the cattle tribe, *Bos sauveli*, of SE Asia, having a blackish-brown body and white legs: an endangered species [c20 from French, from a Cambodian native name, from Pali *gō* cow + Khmer *brai* forest]

koura (ˈkəʊrɑː) *n, pl* **koura** either of two New Zealand freshwater crayfish of the genus *Paranephrops* [Māori]

Kourou (ˈkuːruː) *n* a town in N central French Guiana; site of the European Space Agency's launch and research base. Pop: 19 107 (1999)

Kovno (ˈkɒvnə) *n* transliteration of the Russian name for **Kaunas**

Kovrov (Russian kavˈrɒf) *n* a city in W central Russia, on the Klyazma River: textiles and heavy engineering. Pop: 155 000 (2005 est)

Kowaiti (kəʊˈweɪtɪ) *adj, n* a variant of **Kuwaiti**

Koweit (kəʊˈweɪt) *n* a variant of **Kuwait**

kowhai (ˈkəʊwaɪ, ˈkəʊfaɪ) *n* NZ a small leguminous tree, *Sophora tetraptera*, of New Zealand and Chile, with clusters of yellow flowers [c19 from Māori]

kowhaiwhai (kɒfaːiːfɑːiː) *n* a type of ornamental Māori art that uses elaborate scroll patterns [Māori]

Kowloon (ˈkaʊˈluːn) *n* **1** a peninsula of SE China, opposite Hong Kong Island: part of the former British colony of Hong Kong. Area: 10 sq km (3.75 sq miles) **2** a port in Hong Kong, on Kowloon Peninsula. Pop: 2 025 800 (2001)

kowtow (ˌkaʊˈtaʊ) *vb* (*intr*) **1** to touch the forehead to the ground as a sign of deference: a former Chinese custom **2** (*often foll by to*) to be servile or obsequious (towards) ▷ *n* **3** the act of kowtowing [c19 from Chinese, from *k'o t'ou*, from *k'o* to strike, knock + *t'ou* head] > ˌkow'tower *n*

Kozhikode (ˌkəʊʒɪˈkəʊd) *n* a port in SW India, in W Kerala on the Malabar coast: important European trading post (1511–1765): formerly calico-manufacturing. Pop: 436 527 (2001). Former name: **Calicut**

kp *the internet domain name for* Democratic Republic of Korea

KP *abbreviation for* **1** Knight (of the Order) of St Patrick **2** *US military* **kitchen police** **3** *chess symbol for* king's pawn

kph *abbreviation for* kilometres per hour

kr *the internet domain name for* Republic of Korea

Kr **1** *currency symbol for* **a** krona **b** krone **2** ▷ *the chemical symbol for* krypton

KR *chess symbol for* king's rook

kr. *abbreviation for* **1** krona **2** krone

Kra (krɑː) *n* **Isthmus of** an isthmus of SW Thailand, between the Bay of Bengal and the Gulf of Siam: the narrowest part of the Malay Peninsula. Width: about 56 km (35 miles)

kraal (krɑːl) *South African* ▷ *n* **1** a hut village in southern Africa, esp one surrounded by a stockade **2** an enclosure for livestock ▷ *adj* **3** denoting or relating to the tribal aspects of the Black African way of life ▷ *vb* **4** (*tr*) to enclose (livestock) in a kraal [c18 from Afrikaans, from Portuguese *curral* pen; see CORRAL]

kraft (krɑːft) *n* strong wrapping paper, made from pulp processed with a sulphate solution [from German: force]

Kragujevac (Serbo-Croat ˈkragujevats) *n* a town in E central Serbia and Montenegro, in Serbia; capital of Serbia (1818–39); automobile industry. Pop: 145 890 (2002)

krait (kraɪt) *n* any nonaggressive brightly coloured venomous elapid snake of the genus *Bungarus*, of S and SE Asia [c19 from Hindi *karait*, of obscure origin]

Krakatoa (ˌkrɑːkəˈtəʊə, ˌkrækəˈtəʊə) *or* **Krakatau** (ˌkrɑːkəˈtaʊ, ˌkrækəˈtaʊ) *n* a volcanic island in Indonesia, in the Sunda Strait between Java and Sumatra: partially destroyed by its eruption in 1883, the greatest in recorded history. Further eruptions 44 years later formed a new island,

Anak Krakatau ("Child of Krakatau"). Also called: Rakata

Krakau (ˈkrɑːkaʊ) *n* the German name for **Cracow**

kraken (ˈkrɑːkən) *n* a legendary sea monster of gigantic size believed to dwell off the coast of Norway [c18 from Norwegian, of obscure origin]

Kraków (ˈkrakuf) *n* the Polish name for **Cracow**

Kramatorsk (Russian krəma'tɔrsk) *n* a city in Ukraine: a major industrial centre of the Donets Basin. Pop: 177 000 (2005 est)

krameria (krəˈmɪərɪə) *n* another name for **rhatany** (plant or drug) [c18 New Latin, named (by Linnaeus) after J. G. H. *Kramer*, an Austrian botanist]

Kranj (kra:nj) *n* the Slovene name for **Carniola**

krans (krɑːns) *n* *South African* a sheer rock face; precipice [c18 from Afrikaans]

Krasnodar (Russian krəsna'dar) *n* an industrial city in SW Russia, on the Kuban River. Pop: 650 000 (2005 est). Former name (until 1920): Yekaterinodar

Krasnoyarsk (Russian krəsna'jarsk) *n* a city in E central Russia, on the Yenisei River: the country's largest hydroelectric power station is nearby. Pop: 912 000 (2005 est)

K ration *n* a small package containing emergency rations used by US and Allied forces in the field in World War II [c20 K, from the initial of the surname of Ancel *Keys* (born 1904), US physiologist who instigated it]

Kraut (kraʊt) *n, adj slang* a derogatory word for **German** [from German (*Sauer*)*kraut*, literally: (pickled) cabbage]

Krav Maga (kræv'mægə) *n* a form of exercise based on unarmed combat movements developed by the Israeli armed forces

Krebs cycle *n* a stage of tissue respiration: a series of biochemical reactions occurring in mitochondria in the presence of oxygen by which acetate, derived from the breakdown of foodstuffs, is converted to carbon dioxide and water, with the release of energy. Also called: **citric acid cycle, tricarboxylic acid cycle** [c20 named after Hans Adolf *Krebs* (1900–81), German-born British biochemist]

Krefeld (ˈkreɪfɛlt; German ˈkreːfɛlt) *n* a city in Germany, in W North Rhine-Westphalia: textile industries. Pop: 238 565 (2003 est)

Kremenchug (Russian krɪmɪn'tʃuk) *n* an industrial city in E central Ukraine on the Dnieper River. Pop: 234 000 (2005 est)

kremlin (ˈkrɛmlɪn) *n* the citadel of any Russian city [c17 from obsolete German *Kremelin*, from Russian *kreml*]

Kremlin (ˈkrɛmlɪn) *n* **1** the 12th-century citadel in Moscow, containing the former Imperial Palace, three Cathedrals, and the offices of the Russian government **2** (formerly) the central government of the Soviet Union

Kremlinology (ˌkrɛmlɪnˈɒlədʒɪ) *n* (formerly) the study and analysis of the policies and practices of the Soviet government > ˌKremlin'ologist *n*

Krems (German krɛms) *n* a town in NE Austria, in Lower Austria on the River Danube. Pop: 23 713 (2001)

kreplach (ˈkrɛplaːk, -laːx) *pl n* small filled dough casings usually served in soup [c20 from Yiddish]

kreutzer *or* **kreuzer** (ˈkrɔɪtsə) *n* any of various former copper and silver coins of Germany or Austria [c16 from German *Kreuzer*, from *Kreuz* cross, from Latin *crux*; referring to the cross originally stamped upon such coins]

kriegspiel (ˈkriːgˌspiːl) *n* **1** (*sometimes capital*) a form of war game in which symbols representing military formations are moved about on maps **2** a variation of chess in which each player has his own board and men and does not see his opponent's board and men. The moves are regulated by an umpire on a third board out of sight of both players [c19 from German *Kriegsspiel* war game]

Kriemhild (ˈkriːmhɪlt) *or* **Kriemhilde**

k

('kri:m,hɪldə) *n* (in the *Nibelungenlied*) the wife of Siegfried. She corresponds to Gudrun in Norse mythology

krill (krɪl) *n, pl* **krill** any small shrimplike marine crustacean of the order *Euphausiacea*: the principal food of whalebone whales [C20 from Norwegian *kril* young fish]

krimmer or **crimmer** ('krɪmə) *n* a tightly curled light grey fur obtained from the skins of lambs from the Crimean region [C20 from German, from *Krim* CRIMEA]

Krio ('kri:əʊ) *n* **1** the English-based creole widely used as a lingua franca in Sierra Leone. Its principal language of admixture is Yoruba **2** (*pl* -**os**) a native speaker of Krio **3** (*modifier*) of or relating to the Krio language or Krios: *Krio poetry* [alteration of CREOLE]

Kriol ('kriɒl) *n* a creole language used by Aboriginal communities in the northern regions of Australia, developed from Northern Territory pidgin

kris (krɪs) *n* a Malayan and Indonesian stabbing or slashing knife with a scalloped edge. Also called: **crease, creese** [C16 from Malay *kris*]

Krishna[1] ('krɪʃnə) *n* a river in S India, rising in the Western Ghats and flowing generally southeast to the Bay of Bengal. Length: 1300 km (800 miles). Also called: **Kistna**

Krishna[2] ('krɪʃnə) *n Hinduism* the most celebrated of the Hindu deities, whose life story is told in the *Mahabharata* [via Hindi from Sanskrit, literally: dark, black] ⊳ 'Krishnaism *n*

Kriss Kringle (,krɪs 'krɪŋgəl) *n chiefly US* another name for **Santa Claus** [changed from German *Christkindl* little Christ child, from CHRIST + *Kindl*, from *Kind* child]

Kristiania (,krɪstɪ'ɑ:nɪə) *n* a former name (1877–1924) of **Oslo**

Kristiansand or **Christiansand** ('krɪstʃən,sænd; *Norwegian* kristian'san) *n* a port in S Norway, on the Skagerrak: shipbuilding. Pop: 75 280 (2004 est)

Kristianstad ('krɪstʃən,stɑ:d; *Swedish* kri'ʃansta:d) *n* a town in S Sweden: founded in 1614 as a Danish fortress, it was finally acquired by Sweden in 1678. Pop: 75 590 (2004 est)

Kríti ('kriti) *n* transliteration of the Modern Greek name for **Crete**

Krivoy Rog (*Russian* kri'vɔj 'rɔk) *n* a city in SE Ukraine: founded in the 17th century by Cossacks; iron-mining centre; iron- and steelworks. Pop: 658 000 (2005 est)

KRL *abbreviation for* knowledge representation language (in artificial intelligence)

kromesky (krə'mɛskɪ) *n, pl* -**kies** a croquette consisting of a piece of bacon wrapped round minced meat or fish [C19 from Russian *kromochka*, diminutive of *kroma* slice of bread]

krona ('krəʊnə) *n, pl* **kronor** ('krəʊnə) the standard monetary unit of Sweden, divided into 100 öre

króna ('krəʊnə) *n, pl* -**nur** (-nə) the standard monetary unit of Iceland, divided into 100 aurar

krone[1] ('krəʊnə) *n, pl* -**ner** (-nə) **1** the standard monetary unit of Denmark, the Faeroe Islands, and Greenland, divided into 100 øre **2** the standard monetary unit of Norway, divided into 100 øre [C19 from Danish or Norwegian, from Middle Low German *krōne*, ultimately from Latin *corōna* CROWN]

krone[2] ('krəʊnə) *n, pl* -**nen** (-nən) **1** a former German gold coin worth ten marks **2** a former Austrian monetary unit [C19 from German, literally: crown; see KRONE[1]]

Kronecker delta ('krɒnɪkə) *n maths* a function of two variables, *i* and *j*, that has a value of zero unless *i* = *j*, when it has a value of unity. Symbol: δ$_{ij}$ [named after Leopold *Kronecker* (1823–91), German mathematician]

Kronos ('krəʊnɒs) *n* a variant of **Cronus**

Kronstadt *n* **1** (*Russian* kran'ʃtat) a port in NW Russia, on Kotlin island in the Gulf of Finland: naval base. Pop: 44 400 (1994 est) **2** ('kro:nʃtat) the German name for **Braşov**

kroon (kru:n) *n, pl* **kroons** or **krooni** ('kru:nɪ) the standard monetary unit of Estonia, divided into 100 senti [Estonian *kron*, from German *Krone* KRONE[2]]

KRP *chess symbol for* king's rook's pawn

Kruger National Park *n* a wildlife sanctuary in NE South Africa: the world's largest game reserve. Area: over 21 700 sq km (8400 sq miles)

Krugerrand ('kru:gə,rænd) *n* a South African coin used for investment only and containing 1 troy ounce of gold [C20 from Stephanus Johannes Paulus *Kruger* (1825–1904), Boer statesman + RAND[1]]

Krugersdorp ('kru:gəz,dɔ:p) *n* a city in NE South Africa, on the Witwatersrand, at an altitude of 1720 m (5650 ft): a gold-, manganese-, and uranium-mining centre. Pop: 86 618 (2001)

kruller ('krʌlə) *n* a variant spelling of **cruller**

krummholz ('krʊm,həʊlts) *n botany* another name for **elfin forest, woodland** [C20 from German *krumm* bent + *Holz* wood]

krummhorn ('krʌm,hɔ:n) *n* a variant spelling of **crumhorn**

Krušné Hory ('kruʃne 'hɔrɪ) *n* the Czech name for the **Erzgebirge**

Krym or **Krim** (krɪm) *n* transliteration of the Russian name for **Crimea**

krypton ('krɪptɒn) *n* an inert gaseous element occurring in trace amounts in air and used in fluorescent lights and lasers. Symbol: Kr; atomic no.: 36; atomic wt.: 83.80; valency: 0; density: 3.733 kg/m³; melting pt.: −157.37°C; boiling pt.: −153.23±0.10°C [C19 from Greek, from *kruptos* hidden; see CRYPT]

krytron ('kraɪtrɒn) *n electronics* a type of fast electronic gas-discharge switch, used as a trigger in nuclear weapons

KS 1 *abbreviation for* Kansas **2** ⊳ *international car registration for* Kyrgyzstan

KSG *abbreviation for* Knight of the Order of St Gregory the Great (a Papal honorary title)

Kshatriya ('kʃætrɪə) *n* a member of the second of the four main Hindu castes, the warrior caste [C18 from Sanskrit, from *kshatra* rule]

KStJ *abbreviation for* Knight of the Order of St John

kt *abbreviation for* **1** karat **2** *nautical* knot

Kt 1 Also: **Knt** *abbreviation for* knight **2** Also: **N** *chess symbol for* knight

KT *abbreviation for* **1** Knight of the Order of the Thistle (a Brit title) **2** Knight Templar

K/T boundary *n geology* **a** Cretaceous/Tertiary boundary: the time zone comprising the end of the Cretaceous and the beginning of the Tertiary periods **b** (*as modifier*): *K/T boundary sediments* [C20 K and T, symbols for Cretaceous and Tertiary, respectively]

Kuala Lumpur ('kwɑ:lə 'lʊmpʊə, -pə) *n* a city in Malaysia, in the SW Malay Peninsula: formerly (until 1999) the capital of Malaysia; became capital of the Federated Malay States in 1895, and of Malaysia in 1963; capital of Selangor state from 1880 to 1973, when it was made a federal territory. Pop: 1 392 000 (2005 est)

Kuan Yin or **Kwan Yin** (kwan jɪn) *n* a female Chinese Bodhisattva of compassion, regarded as the protector of women and children and patron of sailors. Japanese name: **Kannon** [from Chinese: one who hears the sounds of the world]

Kuban (*Russian* ku'banj) *n* a river in SW Russia, rising in the Caucasus Mountains and flowing north and northwest to the Sea of Azov. Length: 906 km (563 miles)

Kuch Bihar ('ku:tʃ bɪ'hɑ:) *n* a variant spelling of **Cooch Behar**

kuchen ('ku:xən) *n* a breadlike cake containing apple, nuts, and sugar, originating from Germany [German: CAKE]

Kuching ('ku:tʃɪŋ) *n* a port in E Malaysia, capital of Sarawak state, on the Sarawak River 24 km (15 miles) from its mouth. Pop: 152 310 (2000)

kudlik ('ku:dlɪk) *n Canadian* an Inuit soapstone seal-oil lamp [Inuktitut]

kudos ('kju:dɒs) *n* (*functioning as singular*) acclaim,

glory, or prestige: *the kudos of playing Carnegie Hall* [C18 from Greek]

kudu or **koodoo** ('ku:du:) *n* either of two spiral-horned antelopes, *Tragelaphus strepsiceros* (**greater kudu**) or *T. imberbis* (**lesser kudu**), which inhabit the bush of Africa [C18 from Afrikaans *koedoe*, probably from Khoi]

kudzu ('kʊdzu:) *n* a hairy leguminous climbing plant, *Pueraria thunbergiana*, of China and Japan, with trifoliate leaves and purple fragrant flowers [from Japanese *kuzu*]

kueh ('kʊeɪ) *n* (*functioning as singular or plural*) (in Malaysia) any cake of Malay, Chinese, or Indian origin [from Malay]

Kuenlun ('kʊn'lʊn) *n* a variant spelling of **Kunlun**

Kufic or **Cufic** ('ku:fɪk, 'kju:-) *adj* **1** of, relating to, or denoting an early form of the Arabic alphabet employed in making copies of the Koran ⊳ *n* **2** the script formed by the letters of this alphabet

kufiyah (kʊ'fi:jə) *n* a variant of **keffiyeh**

kuia ('ku:jə) *n NZ* a Māori female elder or elderly woman [Māori]

Kuibyshev or **Kuybyshev** (*Russian* 'kujbɪʃəf) *n* the former name (until 1991) of **Samara**

Kuiper belt ('kɪpə) *n* a region of the solar system beyond the orbit of Neptune, some 30–1000 astronomical units from the sun, containing up to one thousand million icy planetesimals or comet nuclei. See also **Oort cloud** [C20 named after G. P. *Kuiper* (1905–73), Dutch American astronomer, who proposed it in 1951]

Ku Klux Klan ('ku: 'klʌks 'klæn) *n* **1** a secret organization of White Southerners formed after the US Civil War to fight Black emancipation and Northern domination **2** a secret organization of White Protestant Americans, mainly in the South, who use violence against Blacks, Jews, and other minority groups [C19 *Ku Klux*, probably based on Greek *kuklos* CIRCLE + *Klan* CLAN] ⊳ **Ku Kluxer** or **Ku Klux Klanner** *n* ⊳ **Ku Kluxism** *n*

kukri ('kʊkrɪ) *n, pl* -**ris** a knife with a curved blade that broadens towards the point, esp as used by Gurkhas [from Hindi]

kuku (ku:ku:) *n, pl* **kuku** *NZ* **1** another name for **New Zealand pigeon 2** a mussel [Māori]

Kuku Nor ('ku:'ku: 'nɔ:) *n* a variant of **Koko Nor**

kula ('ku:lə) *n* a ceremonial gift exchange practised among a group of islanders in the W Pacific, used to establish relations between islands [of Melanesian origin]

kulak ('ku:læk) *n* (in Russia after 1906) a member of the class of peasants who became proprietors of their own farms. After the October Revolution the kulaks opposed collectivization of land, but in 1929 Stalin initiated their liquidation [C19 from Russian: fist, hence, tightfisted person; related to Turkish *kol* arm]

kulan ('ku:,lɑ:n) *n* the Asiatic wild ass of the Russian steppes, probably a variety of kiang or onager [C18 from Kirghiz]

kulfi ('kʊlfɪ) *n* an Indian dessert made by freezing milk which has been concentrated by boiling away some of the water in it, and flavoured with nuts and cardamom seeds

Kultur (kʊl'tʊə) *n* (often used ironically) German civilization, esp as characterized by authoritarianism and earnestness [German, from Latin *cultūra* CULTURE]

Kulturkampf (kʊl'tʊə,kæmpf, 'kʊltə-) *n* the struggle of the Prussian state against the Roman Catholic Church (1872–87), which took the form of laws designed to bring education, marriage, etc, under the control of the state [German: culture struggle]

Kulun ('ku:'lu:n) *n* the Chinese name for **Ulan Bator**

Kum (kʊm) *n* a variant spelling of **Qom**

Kumamoto (,kʊmə'məʊtəʊ) *n* a city in SW Japan, on W central Kyushu: Kumamoto Medical University (1949). Pop: 653 835 (2002 est)

kumara or **kumera** ('ku:mərə) *n NZ* **1** a convolvulaceous twining plant, *Ipomoea batatas*, of tropical America, cultivated in the tropics for its edible fleshy yellow root **2** the root of this plant. Also called: **sweet potato** [Māori]

kumarahou (kuˈmɑːrəhəuː) *n* a shrub, *Pomaderris kumeraho*, found in the north of New Zealand's North Island, the flowers of which produce a soap-like lather when rubbed [Māori]

Kumasi (kuːˈmæsɪ) *n* a city in S Ghana: seat of Ashanti kings since 1663; university (1961); market town for a cocoa-producing region. Pop: 862 000 (2005 est)

Kumayri (*Russian* ˌkumaɪˈrɪ) *n* a city in NW Armenia: textile centre. Pop: 144 000 (2005 est). Former names: Aleksandropol (1840–1924), Leninakan (1924–91)

kumbaloi (ˌkumbəˈlɔɪ) *pl n* another name for **worry beads** [c20 Modern Greek]

Kumbh Mela (ˌkum ˈmeɪlə, ˌkum məˈlɑː) *n* a Hindu festival held once every twelve years in one of four sacred sites, where bathing for purification from sin is considered especially efficacious [from Hindi, literally: pitcher festival or Aquarius festival, from Sanskrit *kumbha* pot, Aquarius + *melā* assembly]

kumikumi (kuːmiːkuːmiː) *n*, *pl* kumikumi another name for **kamokamo** [Māori]

kunekune (ˈkuːnɪkuːnɪ) *n*, *pl* kunekune NZ a feral pig [Māori]

kumiss, koumiss, koumis or **koumyss** (ˈkuːmɪs) *n* a drink made from fermented mare's or other milk, drunk by certain Asian tribes, esp in Russia or used for dietetic and medicinal purposes [c17 from Russian *kumys*, from Kazan Tatar *kumyz*]

kumite (ˈkuːmɪˌteɪ) *n* martial Arts freestyle sparring or fighting [c20 Japanese, literally: sparring]

kümmel (ˈkuməl; *German* ˈkyməl) *n* a German liqueur flavoured with aniseed and cumin [c19 from German *Kümmel*, from Old High German *kumil*, probably variant of *kumin* CUMIN]

kummerbund (ˈkuməˌbʌnd) *n* a variant spelling of **cummerbund**

Kumon (ˈkuːmɔːn) or **Kumon Method** *n* **a** a method of teaching mathematics, reading, and languages in which students start at a level of work at which they have a firm grasp of facts and concepts and then, working at their own pace in an individualized study programme of problem-solving on worksheets, progress by small steps to more advanced levels of knowledge **b** (*as modifier*): *Kumon mathematics* [c20 named after its founder, Toru *Kumon* (1914–95), a Japanese mathematics teacher]

kumquat or **cumquat** (ˈkʌmkwɒt) *n* **1** any of several small Chinese trees of the rutaceous genus *Fortunella* **2** the small round orange fruit of such a tree, with a sweet rind, used in preserves and confections [c17 from Chinese (Cantonese) *kam kwat*, representing Mandarin Chinese *chin chü* golden orange]

kuna (ˈkuːnə) *pl* **-ne** (-nɪ) *n* the standard monetary unit of Croatia, divided into 100 lipa

kundalini (ˈkundəˌliːnɪ) *n* (*sometimes capital*) (in yoga) the life force that resides at the base of the spine

kung fu (ˈkʌŋ ˈfuː) *n* any of various Chinese martial arts, some focusing on unarmed combat, others involving the use of weapons [from Chinese: martial art]

Kungur (ˈkunguə) *n* a variant transliteration of the Chinese name for **Kongur Shan**

kunjoos (gʌnˈdʒuːs) *adj* Hinglish mean or stingy [c21 Hindi]

Kunlun (ˈkunˈlun), **Kuenlun** or **Kwenlun** *n* a mountain range in China, between the Tibetan plateau and the Tarim Basin, extending over 1600 km (1000 miles) east from the Pamirs: the largest mountain system of Asia. Highest peak: Ulugh Muztagh, 7723 m (25 338 ft)

Kunming (ˈkunˈmɪŋ) or **K'un-ming** *n* a city in SW China, capital of Yunnan province, near Lake

Tien: important during World War II as a Chinese military centre, American air base, and transport terminus for the Burma Road; Yunnan University (1934). Pop: 1 748 000 (2005 est)

kunzite (ˈkuntsaɪt) *n* a pink-coloured transparent variety of the mineral spodumene: a gemstone [c20 named after George F. *Kunz* (1856–1932), US gem expert]

Kuomintang (ˈkwəʊˈmɪnˈtæŋ) *n* the political party founded by Sun Yat-sen in 1911 and dominant in China from 1928 until 1949 under the leadership of Chiang Kai-shek. Since then it has been the official ruling party of Taiwan [c20 from Chinese (Mandarin): National People's Party, from *kuo* nation + *min* people + *tang* party]

Kuopio (*Finnish* ˈkwɔpjɔ) *n* a city in S central Finland. Pop: 88 250 (2003 est)

Kura (kuˈrɑː) *n* a river in W Asia, rising in NE Turkey and flowing across Georgia and Azerbaijan to the Caspian Sea. Length: 1515 km (941 miles)

kura kaupapa Māori (kuːrə kɑːuːpɑːpɑː) *n*, *pl* kura kaupapa Māori NZ a primary school where teaching is based on Māori language and culture [Māori]

kurchatovium (ˌkɜːtʃəˈtəʊvɪəm) *n* another name for **rutherfordium**, esp as used in the former Soviet Union [c20 from Russian, named after I. V. *Kurchatov* (1903–60), Soviet physicist]

Kurd (kɜːd) *n* a member of a nomadic people living chiefly in E Turkey, N Iraq, and W Iran

kurdaitcha (kəˈdaɪtʃə) *n* (in certain Central Australian Aboriginal tribes) the man with the mission of avenging the death of a tribesman. Also: **kadaitcha**

kurdaitcha shoes *pl n* (in certain Central Australian Aboriginal tribes) the emu-feather shoes worn by the kurdaitcha on his mission so that his footsteps may not be traced. Also: **kadaitcha shoes**

Kurdish (ˈkɜːdɪʃ) *n* **1** the language of the Kurds, belonging to the West Iranian branch of the Indo-European family ▷ *adj* **2** of or relating to the Kurds or their language

Kurdistan, Kurdestan or **Kordestan** (ˌkɜːdɪˈstɑːn) *n* a large plateau and mountainous region, between the Caspian Sea and the Black Sea, south of the Caucasus. Area: over 29 000 sq km (74 000 sq miles)

Kure (kuːˈreɪ) *n* a port in SW Japan, on SW Honshu: a naval base; shipyards. Pop: 202 628 (2002 est)

Kurgan (*Russian* kurˈgan) *n* a city in W Russia, on the Tobol River: industrial centre for an agricultural region. Pop: 344 000 (2005 est)

kuri (ˈkurɪ) *n*, *pl* **-ris** **1** NZ Also called: **goorie** a mongrel dog **2** NZ *slang* an unpleasant or unpopular person [Māori]

Kuril Islands or **Kurile Islands** (kuˈriːl) *pl n* a chain of 56 volcanic islands off the NE coast of Asia, extending for 1200 km (750 miles) from the S tip of the Kamchatka Peninsula to NE Hokkaido. Area: 14 990 sq km (6020 sq miles). Japanese name: **Chishima**

Kurland (ˈkuələnd) *n* a variant spelling of **Courland**

Kuroshio (kəˈrəʊʃɪˌəʊ) *n* another name for **Japan Current**

kurrajong or **currajong** (ˈkʌrəˌdʒɒŋ) *n* any of various Australian trees or shrubs, esp *Brachychiton populneum*, a sterculiaceous tree that yields a tough durable fibre [c19 from a native Australian language]

kursaal (ˈkɜːzᵊl) *n* **1** a public room at a health resort **2** an amusement park at a seaside or other resort [from German, literally: cure room]

Kursk (*Russian* kursk) *n* a city in W Russia: industrial centre of an agricultural region: scene of a major Soviet victory (1943). Pop: 410 000 (2005 est)

kurta or **khurta** (ˈkuətə) *n* a long loose garment like a shirt without a collar worn in India [Hindi]

kurtosis (kəˈtəʊsɪs) *n* *statistics* a measure of the

concentration of a distribution around its mean, esp the statistic $B_2 = m_4/m_2{}^2$ where m_2 and m_4 are respectively the second and fourth moment of the distribution around the mean. In a normal distribution $B_2 = 3$. See also **platykurtic, mesokurtic, leptokurtic** Compare **skewness** [from Greek: curvature, from *kurtos* arched]

kuru (ˈkuruː) *n* a degenerative disease of the nervous system, restricted to certain tribes in New Guinea, marked by loss of muscular control and thought to be caused by a slow virus [c20 from a native name]

kuruş (kuˈruːʃ) *n*, *pl* **-ruş** a Turkish monetary unit worth one hundredth of a lira. Also called: **piastre** [from Turkish]

Kurzeme (ˈkurzɛmɛ) *n* the Latvian name for **Courland**

Kush (kʌʃ, kuʃ) *n* a variant spelling of **Cush**

Kuskokwim (ˈkʌskəˌkwɪm) *n* a river in SW Alaska, rising in the Alaska Range and flowing generally southwest to **Kuskokwim Bay** an inlet of the Bering Sea. Length: about 970 km (600 miles)

kuta (guːˈðɑː) *n* Hinglish **1** a male dog **2** derogatory a man or boy regarded as unpleasant or contemptible [c21 Hindi]

Kutaisi (*Russian* kutaˈisi) *n* an industrial city in W Georgia on the Rioni River: one of the oldest towns of the Caucasus. Pop: 175 000 (2005 est)

Kutch or **Cutch** (kʌtʃ) *n* **1** a former state of W India, on the **Gulf of Kutch** (an inlet of the Arabian Sea): part of Gujarat state since 1960 **2 Rann of** an extensive salt waste in W central India, and S Pakistan: consists of the Great Rann in the north and the Little Rann in the southeast; seasonal alternation between marsh and desert; some saltworks. In 1968 an international tribunal awarded about 10 per cent of the border area to Pakistan. Area: 23 000 sq km (9000 sq miles)

kuti (guːˈðiː) *n* Hinglish **1** a female dog; bitch **2** *derogatory* a woman or girl regarded as unpleasant or contemptible [c21 Hindi]

kutu (ˈkuːtuː) *n* NZ a slang word for **body louse** (see **louse** (sense 1)). Also called: **cootie** [Māori]

Kuwait (kʊˈweɪt) or **Koweit** *n* **1** a state on the NW coast of the Persian Gulf: came under British protection in 1899 and gained independence in 1961; invaded by Iraq in 1990; liberated by US-led UN forces 1991 in the Gulf War: mainly desert. The economy is dependent on oil. Official language: Arabic. Official religion: Muslim. Currency: dinar. Capital: Kuwait. Pop: 2 595 000 (2004 est). Area: 24 280 sq km (9375 sq miles) **2** the capital of Kuwait: a port on the Persian Gulf. Pop: 1 225 000 (2005 est)

Kuwaiti (kʊˈweɪtɪ) or **Koweiti** (kəʊˈweɪtɪ) *adj* **1** of or relating to Kuwait or its inhabitants ▷ *n* **2** a native or inhabitant of Kuwait

Kuznetsk Basin (*Russian* kuzˈnjɛtsk) or **Kuzbass** (*Russian* kuzˈbas) *n* a region of S Russia, in the Kemerovo Region of W Siberia, the richest coalfield in the country, with reserves of iron ore. Chief industrial centre: Novokuznetsk. Area: about 69 900 sq km (27 000 sq miles)

kV *abbreviation for* kilovolt

KV *abbreviation for* Köchel Verzeichnis. See **K** [German, literally: Köchel catalogue]

Kvaløy (*Norwegian* ˈkvɑːlœj) *n* two islands in the Arctic Ocean, off the N coast of Norway: **North Kvaløy**, 329 sq km (127 sq miles), and **South Kvaløy**, 735 sq km (284 sq miles)

kvass, kvas or **quass** (kvɑːs) *n* an alcoholic drink of low strength made in Russia and E Europe from cereals and stale bread [c16 from Russian *kvas*; related to Old Slavic *kvasĭ* yeast, Latin *cāseus* cheese]

kvell (kvɛl) *vb* (*intr*) informal, chiefly US to be happy or show satisfaction [c20 from Yiddish *kveln* to well up]

kvetch (kvɛtʃ) *vb* (*intr*) slang, chiefly US to complain or grumble, esp incessantly [c20 from Yiddish *kvetshn*, literally: to squeeze, press]

kvetchy (ˈkvɛtʃɪ) *adj* slang, chiefly US tending to

k

grumble or complain; complaining > 'kvetchily adv > 'kvetchiness n

kw the internet domain name for Kuwait

kW abbreviation for kilowatt

Kwa (kwɑː) n **1** a group of languages, now generally regarded as a branch of the Niger-Congo family, spoken in an area of W Africa extending from the Ivory Coast to E Nigeria and including Akan, Ewe, Yoruba, and Ibo ▷ adj **2** relating to or belonging to this group of languages

kwacha ('kwɑːtʃə) n **1** the standard monetary unit of Zambia, divided into 100 ngwee **2** the standard monetary unit of Malawi, divided into 100 tambala [from a native word in Zambia]

kwaito ('kwaɪˌtəʊ) n a type of South African pop music with lyrics spoken over an instrumental backing usually consisting of slowed-down house music layered with African percussion and melodies [c20 from Amakwaito, a gang in Sophiatown, South Africa, in the 1950s]

Kwajalein ('kwɑːdʒəˌleɪn) n an atoll in the W Pacific, in the W Marshall Islands, in the central part of the Ralik Chain. Length: about 125 km (78 miles)

Kwakiutl (ˌkwɑːkɪˈuːtəl) n **1** (pl -utl or -utls) a member of a North American Indian people of N Vancouver Island and the adjacent mainland **2** the language of this people, belonging to the Wakashan family

Kwangchow ('kwæŋ'tʃaʊ) n a variant transliteration of the Chinese name for **Canton**

Kwangchowan ('kwæŋ'tʃaʊ'wɑːn) n a territory of SE China, in SW Kwantung province: leased to France as part of French Indochina from 1898 to 1945. Area: 842 sq km (325 sq miles)

Kwangju ('kwæŋ'dʒuː) n a city in SW South Korea: an important military base during the Korean War; cotton textile industry. Pop: 1 448 000 (2005 est)

Kwangsi-Chuang Autonomous Region ('kwæŋ'siː'tʃwæn) a variant transliteration of the Chinese name for **Guangxi Zhuang Autonomous Region**

Kwangtung ('kwæŋ'tʊŋ) n a variant transliteration of the Chinese name for **Guangdong**

Kwantung Leased Territory (ˌkwæn'tʊŋ) n a strategic territory of NE China, at the S tip of the Liaodong Peninsula of Manchuria: leased forcibly by Russia in 1898; taken over by Japan in 1905; occupied by the Soviet Union in 1945 and subsequently returned to China on the condition of shared administration; made part of Liaoning province by China in 1954. Area: about 3400 sq km (1300 sq miles). Also called: Kuan-tung

kwanza ('kwænzə) n the standard monetary unit of Angola, divided into 100 lwei [from a Bantu language]

Kwanzaa ('kwænzɑː) n a seven-day festival beginning on Dec 26 when African-Americans celebrate family, community, and culture [c20 from Swahili (matunda ya) kwanza first (fruits)]

Kwara ('kwɑːrə) n a state of W Nigeria: mainly wooded savanna. Capital: Ilorin. Pop: 1 751 464 (1995 est). Area: 36 825 sq km (14 218 sq miles)

kwashiorkor (ˌkwæʃɪˈɔːkə) n severe malnutrition of infants and young children, esp soon after weaning, resulting from dietary deficiency of protein [c20 from a native word in Ghana]

KwaZulu (kwɑːˈzuːluː) n (formerly) a Bantu homeland in South Africa, in Natal: abolished in 1993 and became part of the new province of KwaZulu/Natal in 1994. Capital: Ulundi

KwaZulu/Natal (kwɑːˌzuːluːnəˈtæl, -'tɑːl) n a province of NE South Africa; replaced the former province of Natal in 1994: service industries. Capital: Pietermaritzburg. Pop: 9 665 875 (2004 est). Area: 92 180 sq km (35 591 sq miles)

Kwedien (kwɪˈdiːn) n a young African boy, esp one who has not yet undergone the rites of initiation [from Xhosa inKwenkwe boy]

Kweichow or **Kueichou** ('kweɪ'tʃaʊ) n a variant transliteration of the Chinese name for **Guizhou**

Kweilin or **Kuei-lin** ('kweɪ'lɪn) n a variant transliteration of the Chinese name for **Guilin**

Kweisui ('kweɪ'sweɪ) n the former name of **Hohhot**

Kweiyang or **Kuei-yang** ('kweɪ'jæŋ) n a variant transliteration of the Chinese name for **Guiyang**

kwela ('kweɪlə, 'kwɛlə) n a type of pop music popular among the Black communities of South Africa [c20 said to be from Zulu or Xhosa: jump up]

kWh abbreviation for kilowatt-hour

KWIC (kwɪk) n acronym for key word in context (esp in the phrase KWIC index)

KWOC (kwɒk) n acronym for key word out of context

KWT international car registration for Kuwait

ky the internet domain name for Cayman Islands

Ky. or **KY** abbreviation for Kentucky

kyanite ('kaɪəˌnaɪt) n a grey, green, or blue mineral consisting of aluminium silicate in triclinic crystalline form. It occurs in metamorphic rocks and is used as a refractory. Formula Al_2SiO_5 > **kyanitic** (ˌkaɪəˈnɪtɪk) adj

kyanize or **kyanise** ('kaɪəˌnaɪz) vb (tr) to treat (timber) with corrosive sublimate to make it resistant to decay [c19 after J. H. Kyan (died 1850), English inventor of the process] > ˌkyani'zation or ˌkyani'sation n

kyat (kɪˈɑːt) n the standard monetary unit of Myanmar, divided into 100 pyas [from Burmese]

kybo ('kaɪˌbəʊ) n Austral slang a temporary lavatory constructed for use when camping [said to be an acronym for k(eep) y(our) b(owels) o(pen)]

kybosh ('kaɪˌbɒʃ) n a variant spelling of **kibosh**

kye (kaɪ) n (functioning as plural) a Scottish and Northern English variant of **kine**

kyle (kaɪl) n Scot (esp in place names) a narrow strait or channel: Kyle of Lochalsh [c16 from Gaelic caol, from caol narrow]

kylie or **kiley** ('kaɪlɪ) n Austral a boomerang that is flat on one side and convex on the other [c19 from a native Australian language]

kylin ('kiː'lɪn) n (in Chinese art) a mythical animal of composite form [c19 from Chinese ch'i-lin, literally: male-female]

kylix or **cylix** ('kaɪlɪks, 'kɪl-) n, pl -likes (-lɪˌkiːz) a shallow two-handled drinking vessel used in ancient Greece [c19 from Greek kulix cup; compare CHALICE]

kyloe ('kaɪləʊ) n a breed of small long-horned long-haired beef cattle from NW Scotland [c19 of uncertain origin]

kymograph ('kaɪməˌgrɑːf, -ˌgræf) or **cymograph** n **1** med a rotatable drum for holding paper on which a tracking stylus continuously records variations in blood pressure, respiratory movements, etc **2** phonetics this device as applied to the measurement of variations in the muscular action of the articulatory organs **3** an instrument for recording the angular oscillations of an aircraft in flight [c20 from Greek kuma wave + -GRAPH] > ˌkymo'graphic or ˌcymo'graphic adj

Kymric ('kɪmrɪk) n, adj a variant spelling of **Cymric**

Kymry ('kɪmrɪ) pl n a variant spelling of **Cymry**

Kyongsong ('kjɔːŋ'sɔːŋ) n another name for **Seoul**

Kyoto or **Kioto** (kɪˈəʊtəʊ, 'kjəʊ-) n a city in central Japan, on S Honshu: the capital of Japan from 794 to 1868; cultural centre, with two universities (1875, 1897). Pop: 1 387 264 (2002 est)

Kyoto protocol n an amendment to the United Nations international treaty on global warming in which participating nations commit to reducing their emissions of carbon dioxide, negotiated in Kyoto, Japan, in 1997

kype (kaɪp) n the hook on the lower jaw of a mature male salmon [from Scot kip, kipp anything beaked or hooked; perhaps related to Low German kippe point, tip]

kyphosis (kaɪˈfəʊsɪs) n pathol backward curvature of the thoracic spine, of congenital origin or resulting from injury or disease; hunchback. See also **Pott's disease**. Compare **lordosis, scoliosis** [c19 from New Latin, from Greek kuphōsis, from kuphos humpbacked] > **kyphotic** (kaɪˈfɒtɪk) adj

Kyrgyz ('kɪəgɪz), **Kirghiz** or **Kirgiz** n **1** (pl -gyz, -ghiz or -giz) a member of a Mongoloid people of central Asia, inhabiting Kyrgyzstan and a vast area of central Siberia **2** the language of this people, belonging to the Turkic branch of the Altaic family

Kyrgyzstan ('kɪəgɪzˌstɑːn, -ˌstæn), **Kirghizstan** or **Kirgizstan** n a republic in central Asia: came under Russian rule in the 19th century, became a Soviet republic in 1936 and gained independence in 1991; it has deposits of minerals, oil, and gas. Official languages: Kyrgyz and Russian. Religion: nonreligious, Muslim. Currency: som. Capital: Bishkek. Pop: 5 208 000 (2004 est). Area: 198 500 sq km (76 460 sq miles)

Kyrgyz Steppe n a vast steppe region in central Kazakhstan. Also called: the Steppes

Kyrie eleison ('kɪrɪɪ əˈleɪsˑən) n **1** a formal invocation used in the liturgies of the Roman Catholic, Greek Orthodox, and Anglican Churches **2** a musical setting of this. Often shortened to: **Kyrie** [c14 via Late Latin from Late Greek kurie, eleēson Lord, have mercy]

kyte or **kite** (kaɪt) n Scot the belly [c16 of uncertain origin]

Kythera ('kɪθɪrə) n a variant spelling of **Cythera**

kyu (kjuː) n judo **1** one of the five student grades for inexperienced competitors **2** a student in the kyu grades. Compare **dan²** [from Japanese]

Kyushu or **Kiushu** ('kjuːʃuː) n an island of SW Japan: the southernmost of Japan's four main islands, with over 300 surrounding small islands; coalfield and chemical industries. Chief cities: Fukuoka, Kitakyushu, and Nagasaki. Pop: 14 786 000 (2002 est). Area: 35 659 sq km (13 768 sq miles)

Kyzyl Kum (Russian kiˈzil ˈkum) n a desert in Kazakhstan and Uzbekistan

kz the internet domain name for Kazakhstan

KZ international car registration for Kazakhstan

KZN (in South Africa) abbreviation for KwaZulu/Natal

L l

l *or* **L** (ɛl) *n, pl* **l's**, **L's** *or* **Ls** **1** the 12th letter and ninth consonant of the modern English alphabet **2** a speech sound represented by this letter, usually a lateral, as in *label* **3 a** something shaped like an L **b** (*in combination*): *an L-shaped room*

l *symbol for* **1** litre **2** *physics* lepton number

L *symbol for* **1** ell (unit) **2** lambert(s) **3** large **4** Latin **5** (on British motor vehicles) learner driver **6** *physics* length **7** live **8** *currency* **a** Usually written **£**. pound **b** lempira **c** lek **d** leu **e** lire **9** *aeronautics* lift **10** *electronics* inductor (in circuit diagrams) **11** *physics* latent heat **12** *physics* self-inductance **13** *chem* the Avogadro constant **14** ▷ *the Roman numeral for* 50. See **Roman numerals 15** ▷ *international car registration for* Luxembourg [(for sense 8a) Latin *libra* pound]

L. *or* **l.** *abbreviation for* **1** lake **2** left **3** length

L8R *text messaging abbreviation for* later

la¹ (lɑː) *n music* a variant spelling of **lah**

la² (lɔː) *interj* an exclamation of surprise or emphasis [Old English *lā* LO]

la³ *the internet domain name for* Lao People's Democratic Republic

La *the chemical symbol for* lanthanum

LA *abbreviation for* **1** Legislative Assembly **2** Library Association **3** local agent **4** Los Angeles **5** Louisiana

La. *abbreviation for* Louisiana

laager *or* **lager** ('lɑːgə) *n* **1** (in Africa) a camp, esp one defended by a circular formation of wagons **2** *military* a place where armoured vehicles are parked ▷ *vb* **3** to form (wagons) into a laager **4** (*tr*) to park (armoured vehicles) in a laager [c19 from Afrikaans *lager*, via German from Old High German *legar* bed, lair]

Laaland (*Danish* 'lɔlan) *n* a variant spelling of **Lolland**

lab (læb) *n informal* **1** short for laboratory **2** short for Labrador retriever

lab. *abbreviation for* **1** laboratory **2** labour

Lab. *abbreviation for* **1** *politics* Labour **2** Labrador

Laban ('leɪbən) *n Old Testament* the father-in-law of Jacob, father of Leah and Rachel (Genesis 29:16)

labarum ('læbərəm) *n, pl* **-ra** (-rə) **1** a standard or banner carried in Christian religious processions **2** the military standard bearing a Christian monogram used by Constantine the Great [c17 from Late Latin, of obscure origin]

labdanum ('læbdənəm) *or* **ladanum** *n* a dark resinous juice obtained from various rockroses of the genus *Cistus*, used in perfumery and in the manufacture of fumigants and medicinal plasters [c16 Latin, from Greek *ladanon*, from *lēdon* rockrose, from Semitic]

Labe ('lɑbɛ) *n* the Czech name for the (River) **Elbe**

labefaction (ˌlæbɪˈfækʃən) *or* **labefactation** (ˌlæbɪfækˈteɪʃən) *n rare* deterioration; weakening [c17 from Late Latin *labefactiō*, from Latin *labefacere* shake, from *lābī* to fall + *facere* to make]

label ('leɪbəl) *n* **1** a piece of paper, card, or other material attached to an object to identify it or give instructions or details concerning its ownership, use, nature, destination, etc; tag **2** a brief descriptive phrase or term given to a person, group, school of thought, etc: *the label "Romantic" is applied to many different kinds of poetry* **3** a word or phrase heading a piece of text to indicate or summarize its contents **4** a trademark or company or brand name on certain goods, esp on gramophone records **5** another name for **dripstone** (sense 2) **6** *heraldry* a charge consisting of a horizontal line across the chief of a shield with three or more pendants: the charge of an eldest son **7** *computing* a group of characters, such as a number or a word, appended to a particular statement in a program to allow its unique identification **8** *chem* a radioactive element used in a compound to trace the mechanism of a chemical reaction ▷ *vb* **-bels**, **-belling**, **-belled** *or US* **-bels**, **-beling**, **-beled** (*tr*) **9** to fasten a label to **10** to mark with a label **11** to describe or classify in a word or phrase: *to label someone a liar* **12** to make (one or more atoms in a compound) radioactive, for use in determining the mechanism of a reaction [c14 from Old French, from Germanic; compare Old High German *lappa* rag] > **'labeller** *n*

labellist ('leɪbəlɪst) *n NZ informal* a person who wears only clothes with fashionable brand names

labellum (lə'bɛləm) *n, pl* **-la** (-lə) **1** the part of the corolla of certain plants, esp orchids, that forms a distinct, often lobed, lip **2** a lobe at the tip of the proboscis of a fly [c19 New Latin, diminutive of Latin *labrum* lip] > **la'belloid** *adj*

labia ('leɪbɪə) *n* the plural of **labium**

labial ('leɪbɪəl) *adj* **1** of, relating to, or near lips or labia **2** *music* producing sounds by the action of an air stream over a narrow liplike fissure, as in a flue pipe of an organ **3** *phonetics* relating to a speech sound whose articulation involves movement or use of the lips: *a labial click* ▷ *n* **4** Also called: **labial pipe** *music* an organ pipe with a liplike fissure **5** *phonetics* a speech sound such as English p or m, whose articulation involves movement or use of the lips [c16 from Medieval Latin *labiālis*, from Latin *labium* lip] > ˌlabi'ality *n* > 'labially *adv*

labialize *or* **labialise** ('leɪbɪəˌlaɪz) *vb* (*tr*) *phonetics* to pronounce with articulation involving rounded lips, such as for (k) before a close back vowel (uː) as in English *cool* > 'labialˌism, ˌlabiali'zation *or* ˌlabiali'sation *n*

labia majora (mə'dʒɔːrə) *pl n* the two elongated outer folds of skin in human females surrounding the vaginal orifice [c18 New Latin: greater lips]

labia minora (mɪ'nɔːrə) *pl n* the two small inner folds of skin in human females forming the margins of the vaginal orifice [c18 New Latin: smaller lips]

labiate ('leɪbɪˌeɪt, -ɪt) *n* **1** any plant of the family *Lamiaceae* (formerly *Labiatae*), having square stems, aromatic leaves, and a two-lipped corolla: includes mint, thyme, sage, rosemary, etc ▷ *adj* **2** of, relating to, or belonging to the family *Lamiaceae* [c18 from New Latin *labiātus*, from Latin *labium* lip]

labile ('leɪbɪl) *adj* **1** *chem* (of a compound) prone to chemical change **2** liable to change or move [c15 via Late Latin *lābilis*, from Latin *lābī* to slide, slip] > **lability** (lə'bɪlɪtɪ) *n*

labio- *or before a vowel* **labi-** *combining form* relating to or formed by the lips and (another organ or part): *labiodental* [from Latin *labium* lip]

labiodental (ˌleɪbɪəʊˈdɛntəl) *phonetics* ▷ *adj* **1** pronounced by bringing the bottom lip into contact or near contact with the upper teeth, as for the fricative (f) in English *fat, puff* ▷ *n* **2** a labiodental consonant

labionasal (ˌleɪbɪəʊ'neɪzəl) *phonetics* ▷ *adj* **1** pronounced by making a complete closure of the air passage at the lips and lowering the soft palate allowing air to escape through the nasal cavity ▷ *n* **2** a labionasal consonant, such as m

labiovelar (ˌleɪbɪəʊ'viːlə) *phonetics* ▷ *adj* **1** relating to or denoting a speech sound pronounced with simultaneous articulation at the soft palate and the lips ▷ *n* **2** a labiovelar speech sound, such as some pronunciations of the consonant spelt q in English

labium ('leɪbɪəm) *n, pl* **-bia** (-bɪə) **1** a lip or liplike structure **2** any one of the four lip-shaped folds of the female vulva. See **labia majora, labia minora 3** the fused pair of appendages forming the lower lip of insects **4** the lower lip of the corolla of labiate flowers [c16 New Latin, from Latin: lip]

lablab ('læbˌlæb) *n* **1** a twining leguminous plant, *Dolichos lablab* (or *Lablab niger*), of tropical Africa but widely cultivated **2** the edible pod or bean of this plant [from Arabic]

labor ('leɪbə) *vb, n* the US spelling of **labour**

laboratory (lə'bɒrətərɪ, -trɪ; *US* 'læbrəˌtɔːrɪ) *n, pl* **-ries 1 a** a building or room equipped for conducting scientific research or for teaching practical science **b** (*as modifier*): *laboratory equipment* **2** a place where chemicals or medicines are manufactured ▷ Often shortened to: **lab** See also **language laboratory** [c17 from Medieval Latin *labōrātōrium* workshop, from Latin *labōrāre* to LABOUR]

Labor Day *n* **1** (in the US and Canada) a public holiday in honour of labour, held on the first Monday in September **2** (in Australia) a public holiday observed on different days in different states

laborious (lə'bɔːrɪəs) *adj* **1** involving great exertion or long effort **2** given to working hard **3** (of literary style, etc) not fluent > **la'boriously** *adv* > **la'boriousness** *n*

Labor Party *n* one of the chief political parties of Australia, generally supporting the interests of organized labour

labour *or US* **labor** ('leɪbə) *n* **1** productive work, esp physical toil done for wages **2 a** the people, class, or workers involved in this, esp in contrast to management, capital, etc **b** (*as modifier*): *a labour*

dispute; labour relations **3 a** difficult or arduous work or effort **b** (*in combination*): *labour-saving* **4** a particular job or task, esp of a difficult nature **5 a** the process or effort of childbirth or the time during which this takes place **b** (*as modifier*): *labour pains* **6 labour of love** something done for pleasure rather than gain ▷ *vb* **7** (*intr*) to perform labour; work **8** (*intr*; foll by *for*, etc) to strive or work hard (for something) **9** (*intr*; usually foll by *under*) to be burdened (by) or be at a disadvantage (because of): *to labour under a misapprehension* **10** (*intr*) to make one's way with difficulty **11** (*tr*) to deal with or treat too persistently **12** (*intr*) (of a woman) to be in labour **13** (*intr*) (of a ship) to pitch and toss [C13 via Old French from Latin *labor*; perhaps related to *lābī* to fall]
> 'labouringly *or US* 'laboringly *adv*

Labour and Socialist International *n* the an international association of socialist parties formed in Hamburg in 1923: destroyed by World War II. Also called: **Second International**

labour camp *n* **1** a penal colony involving forced labour **2** a camp for migratory labourers

Labour Day *n* a public holiday in many countries in honour of labour, usually held on May 1. See also **Labor Day**

laboured *or US* **labored** ('leɪbəd) *adj* **1** (of breathing) performed with difficulty **2** showing effort; contrived; lacking grace or fluency
> 'labouredly *or US* 'laboredly *adv* > 'labouredness *or US* 'laboredness *n*

labourer *or US* **laborer** ('leɪbərə) *n* a person engaged in physical work, esp of an unskilled kind

labour exchange *n Brit* a former name for **employment office**

labour-intensive *adj* of or denoting a task, organization, industry, etc, in which a high proportion of the costs are due to wages, salaries, etc

labourism *or US* **laborism** ('leɪbə,rɪzəm) *n* **1** the dominance of the working classes **2** a political, social, or economic system that favours such dominance **3** support for workers' rights

labourist *or US* **laborist** ('leɪbərɪst) *n* **1** a person who supports workers' rights **2** a supporter of labourism

Labourite ('leɪbə,raɪt) *n* an adherent of the Labour Party

labour law *n* those areas of law which appertain to the relationship between employers and employees and between employers and trade unions

Labour Party *n* **1** a British political party, formed in 1900 as an amalgam of various trade unions and socialist groups, generally supporting the interests of organized labour and advocating democratic socialism and social equality **2** any similar party in any of various other countries

labour relations *pl n* **a** collective relations between the management of an organization and its employees or employees' representatives **b** a set of such relations in a wider context, such as in an industry, or in a national economy

labra ('leɪbrə, 'læb-) *n* the plural of **labrum**

labradoodle ('læbrə,duː dəl) *n* a type of dog that is a cross between a labrador retriever and a poodle

Labrador ('læbrə,dɔː) *n* **1** Also called: **Labrador-Ungava** a large peninsula of NE Canada, on the Atlantic, the Gulf of St Lawrence, Hudson Strait, and Hudson Bay: contains most of Quebec and the mainland part of the province of Newfoundland and Labrador; geologically part of the Canadian Shield. Area: 1 619 000 sq km (625 000 sq miles) **2** Also called: **Coast of Labrador** a region of NE Canada, on the Atlantic and consisting of the mainland part of Newfoundland and Labrador province **3** (*often not capital*) short for **Labrador retriever**

Labrador Current *n* a cold ocean current flowing southwards off the coast of Labrador and meeting the warm Gulf Stream, causing dense fogs off

the coast of Newfoundland

labradorescent (,læbrədɔː'resənt) *adj* (of minerals) displaying a brilliant play of colours, as that shown by some forms of labradorite

labradorite (,læbrə'dɔːraɪt) *n* a blue, green, or reddish-brown feldspar mineral of the plagioclase series: used as a decorative stone. Formula: $CaAl_2Si_2O_8.NaAlSi_3O_8$ [C18 named after LABRADOR, where it was found; see -ITE¹]

Labrador retriever *n* a powerfully-built variety of retriever with a short dense usually black or golden-brown coat. Often shortened to: **Labrador**, (*informal*) **lab**

Labrador tea *n* **1** either of two arctic evergreen ericaceous shrubs, *Ledum groenlandicum* or *L. palustre* var. *decumbens* **2** (in Canada) an infusion brewed from the leaves of either of these plants

labret ('leɪbret) *n* a piece of bone, shell, etc; inserted into the lip as an ornament by certain peoples [C19 from Latin *labrum* lip]

labroid ('læbrɔɪd, 'leɪ-) *or* **labrid** ('læbrɪd) *n* **1** any percoid fish of the family *Labridae* (wrasses) ▷ *adj* **2** of or relating to the *Labridae* [C19 from New Latin *Labroidea*, from Latin *lābrus* a fish, from *labrum* lip]

labrum ('leɪbrəm, 'læb-) *n*, *pl* **-bra** (-brə) a lip or liplike part, such as the cuticular plate forming the upper lip of insects [C19 New Latin, from Latin]

Labuan (lə'buːən) *n* an island in Malaysia, off the NW coast of Borneo: part of the Straits Settlements until 1946, when transferred to North Borneo. Chief town: Victoria (or Labuan). Area: 98 sq km (38 sq miles)

laburnum (lə'bɜːnəm) *n* any leguminous tree or shrub of the Eurasian genus *Laburnum*, having clusters of yellow drooping flowers: all parts of the plant are poisonous [C16 New Latin, from Latin]

labyrinth ('læbərɪnθ) *n* **1** a mazelike network of tunnels, chambers, or paths, either natural or man-made. Compare **maze** (sense 1) **2** any complex or confusing system of streets, passages, etc **3** a complex or intricate situation **4 a** any system of interconnecting cavities, esp those comprising the internal ear **b** another name for **internal ear 5** *electronics* an enclosure behind a high-performance loudspeaker, consisting of a series of air chambers designed to absorb unwanted sound waves [C16 via Latin from Greek *laburinthos*, of obscure origin]

Labyrinth ('læbərɪnθ) *n Greek myth* a huge maze constructed for King Minos in Crete by Daedalus to contain the Minotaur

labyrinth fish *n* any tropical freshwater spiny-finned fish of the family *Anabantidae* of SE Asia and Africa, having a lunglike respiratory organ. See also **anabantid**

labyrinthine (,læbə'rɪnθaɪn), **labyrinthian** (,læbə'rɪnθɪən) *or* **labyrinthic** (,læbə'rɪnθɪk) *adj* **1** of or relating to a labyrinth **2** resembling a labyrinth in complexity > ,laby'rinthically *adv*

labyrinthitis (,læbərɪn'θaɪtɪs) *n* inflammation of the inner ear, causing loss of balance, vertigo, and vomiting. Also called: **otitis interna**

labyrinthodont (,læbə'rɪnθə,dɒnt) *n* any primitive amphibian of the order *Labyrinthodontia*, of late Devonian to Triassic times, having teeth with much-folded dentine [C19 from Greek *laburinthos* LABYRINTH + -ODONT]

lac¹ (læk) *n* a resinous substance secreted by certain lac insects, used in the manufacture of shellac [C16 from Dutch *lak* or French *laque*, from Hindi *lākh* resin, ultimately from Sanskrit *lākshā*]

lac² (lɑːk) *n* a variant spelling of **lakh**

LAC *Brit* ▷ abbreviation for **leading aircraftman**

Laccadive, Minicoy, and Amindivi Islands (ˈlækədɪv, ˈmɪnɪˌkɔɪ, ˌʌmənˈdiːviː) *pl n* the former name (until 1973) of the **Lakshadweep Islands**

laccolith ('lækəlɪθ) *or* **laccolite** ('lækə,laɪt) *n* a dome-shaped body of igneous rock between two layers of older sedimentary rock: formed by the intrusion of magma, forcing the overlying strata

into the shape of a dome [C19 from Greek *lakkos* cistern + -LITH] > ,lacco'lithic *or* **laccolitic** (,lækə'lɪtɪk) *adj*

lace (leɪs) *n* **1** a delicate decorative fabric made from cotton, silk, etc, woven in an open web of different symmetrical patterns and figures **2** a cord or string drawn through holes or eyelets or around hooks to fasten a shoe or garment **3** ornamental braid often used on military uniforms, etc **4** a dash of spirits added to a beverage ▷ *vb* **5** to fasten (shoes, etc) with a lace **6** (*tr*) to draw (a cord or thread) through holes, eyes, etc, as when tying shoes **7** (*tr*) to compress the waist of (someone), as with a corset **8** (*tr*) to add a small amount of alcohol or drugs to (food or drink) **9** (*tr*; *usually passive* and foll by *with*) to streak or mark with lines or colours: *the sky was laced with red* **10** (*tr*) to intertwine; interlace **11** (*tr*) *informal* to give a sound beating to ▷ See also **lace into, lace up** [C13 *las*, from Old French *laz*, from Latin *laqueus* noose] > 'lace,like *adj* > 'lacer *n*

lacebark ('leɪsbɑːk) *n* another name for **ribbonwood**

lace bug *n* a small bug of the family *Tingidae*, having a delicate pattern in the wing venation. They are plant feeders and include the **thistle lace bugs** (*Tingis cardui* and *T. ampliata*) and the **rhododendron bug** (*Stephanitis rhododendri*)

Lacedaemon (,læsɪ'diːmən) *n* another name for **Sparta** *or* **Laconia**

Lacedaemonian (,læsɪdɪ'məʊnɪən) *adj*, *n* another word for **Spartan**

lace into *vb* (*intr*, *preposition*) to attack violently, either verbally or physically

lacerant ('læsərənt) *adj* painfully distressing; harrowing

lacerate *vb* ('læsə,reɪt) (*tr*) **1** to tear (the flesh, etc) jaggedly **2** to hurt or harrow (the feelings, etc) ▷ *adj* ('læsə,reɪt, -rɪt) **3** having edges that are jagged or torn; lacerated: *lacerate leaves* [C16 from Latin *lacerāre* to tear, from *lacer* mangled] > 'lacerable *adj* > ,lacera'bility *n* > ,lacer'ation *n* > 'lacerative *adj*

Lacerta (lə'sɜːtə) *n*, Latin genitive **Lacertae** (lə'sɜːtiː) a small faint constellation in the N hemisphere, part of which is crossed by the Milky Way, lying between Cygnus and Andromeda [Latin: lizard]

lacertilian (,læsə'tɪlɪən) *n* also **lacertian** (lə'sɜːʃən) **1** any reptile of the suborder *Lacertilia* (lizards) ▷ *adj* **2** of, relating to, or belonging to the *Lacertilia* [C19 New Latin, from Latin *lacerta* lizard]

lace up *vb* **1** (*tr*, *adverb*) to tighten or fasten (clothes or footwear) with laces ▷ *adj* **lace-up 2** (of footwear) to be fastened with laces ▷ *n* **lace-up 3** a lace-up shoe or boot

lacewing ('leɪs,wɪŋ) *n* any of various neuropterous insects, esp any of the families *Chrysopidae* (**green lacewings**) and *Hemerobiidae* (**brown lacewings**), having lacy wings and preying on aphids and similar pests

laches ('lætʃɪz) *n law* negligence or unreasonable delay in pursuing a legal remedy [C14 *lachesse*, via Old French *lasche* slack, from Latin *laxus* LAX]

Lachesis ('lækɪsɪs) *n Greek myth* one of the three Fates [via Latin from Greek, from *lakhesis* destiny, from *lakhein* to befall by lot]

Lachlan ('lɒklən) *n* a river in SE Australia, rising in central New South Wales and flowing northwest then southwest to the Murrumbidgee River. Length: about 1450 km (900 miles) [named after Lachlan Macquarie, governor of New South Wales (1809–21)]

lachryma Christi (ˈlækrəmə ˈkrɪstɪ) *n* a red or white wine from the bay of Naples in S Italy [C17 from Latin: Christ's tear]

lachrymal ('lækrɪməl) *adj* a variant spelling of **lacrimal**

lachrymator ('lækrɪ,meɪtə) *n* a variant spelling of **lacrimator**

lachrymatory ('lækrɪmətərɪ, -trɪ) *n*, *pl* **-ries 1** a small vessel found in ancient tombs, formerly thought to hold the tears of mourners ▷ *adj* **2** a variant spelling of **lacrimatory**

lachrymose ('lækrɪ,məʊs, -,məʊz) *adj* **1** given to weeping; tearful **2** mournful; sad [c17 from Latin *lacrimōsus*, from *lacrima* a tear] > **'lachry,mosely** *adv* > **lachrymosity** (,lækrɪ'mɒsɪtɪ) *n*

lacing ('leɪsɪŋ) *n* **1** *chiefly Brit* a course of bricks, stone, etc, for strengthening a rubble or flint wall **2** another word for **lace** (senses 2, 3) **3** *informal* a severe beating (esp in the phrase **give someone a lacing**)

laciniate (lə'sɪnɪ,eɪt, -ɪt) *or* **laciniated** *adj* **1** *biology* jagged: *a laciniate leaf* **2** having a fringe [c17 from Latin *lacinia* flap] > **la,cini'ation** *n*

lac insect (læk) *n* any of various homopterous insects of the family *Lacciferidae*, esp *Laccifer lacca* of India, the females of which secrete lac

lack (læk) *n* **1** an insufficiency, shortage, or absence of something required or desired **2** something that is required but is absent or in short supply ▷ *vb* **3** (when *intr*, often foll by *in* or *for*) to be deficient (in) or have need (of): *to lack purpose* [c12 related to Middle Dutch *laken* to be wanting]

lackadaisical (,lækə'deɪzɪk^əl) *adj* **1** lacking vitality and purpose **2** lazy or idle, esp in a dreamy way [c18 from earlier *lackadaisy*, extended form of LACKADAY] > **,lacka'daisically** *adv* > **,lacka'daisicalness** *n*

lackaday ('lækə,deɪ) *interj archaic* another word for **alas** [c17 from *alack the day*]

lacker ('lækə) *n* a variant spelling of **lacquer**

lackey ('lækɪ) *n* **1** a servile follower; hanger-on **2** a liveried male servant or valet **3** a person who is treated like a servant ▷ *vb* **4** (when *intr*, often foll by *for*) to act as a lackey (to) ▷ Also (rare): **lacquey** [c16 via French *laquais*, from Old French, perhaps from Catalan *lacayo, alacayo*; perhaps related to ALCALDE]

lackey moth *n* a bombycid moth, *Malacosoma neustria*, whose brightly striped larvae live at first in a communal web often on fruit trees, of which they may become a pest

lacklustre *or US* **lackluster** ('læk,lʌstə) *adj* lacking force, brilliance, or vitality

Laconia (lə'kəʊnɪə) *n* an ancient country of S Greece, in the SE Peloponnese, of which Sparta was the capital: corresponds to the present-day department of Lakonia

Laconian (lə'kəʊnɪən) *n* **1** a native or inhabitant of Laconia, the ancient Greek country of which Sparta was the capital ▷ *adj* **2** of or relating to Laconia or its inhabitants

laconic (lə'kɒnɪk) *or* **laconical** *adj* (of a person's speech) using few words; terse [c16 via Latin from Greek *Lakōnikos*, from *Lakōn* Laconian, Spartan; referring to the Spartans' terseness of speech] > **la'conically** *adv*

laconism ('lækə,nɪzəm) *or* **laconicism** (lə'kɒnɪ,sɪzəm) *n rare* **1** economy of expression **2** a terse saying

La Coruña (*Spanish* la ko'ruɲa) *n* a port in NW Spain, on the Atlantic: point of departure for the Spanish Armada (1588); site of the defeat of the French by the British under Sir John Moore in the Peninsular War (1809). Pop: 243 902 (2003 est). Galician name: **A Coruña** English name: **Corunna**

lacquer ('lækə) *n* **1** a hard glossy coating made by dissolving cellulose derivatives or natural resins in a volatile solvent **2** a black resinous substance, obtained from certain trees, used to give a hard glossy finish to wooden furniture **3 lacquer tree** Also called: **varnish tree** an E Asian anacardiaceous tree, *Rhus verniciflua*, whose stem yields a toxic exudation from which black lacquer is obtained **4** Also called: **hair lacquer** a mixture of shellac and alcohol for spraying onto the hair to hold a style in place **5** *art* decorative objects coated with such lacquer, often inlaid ▷ *vb* (*tr*) **6** to apply lacquer to [c16 from obsolete French *lacre* sealing wax, from Portuguese *laca* LAC¹] > **'lacquerer** *n*

lacrimal, lachrymal *or* **lacrymal** ('lækrɪməl) *adj*

of or relating to tears or to the glands that secrete tears [c16 from Medieval Latin *lachrymālis*, from Latin *lacrima* a tear]

lacrimal duct *n* a short tube in the inner corner of the eyelid through which tears drain into the nose. Nontechnical name: **tear duct**

lacrimal gland *n* the compound gland that secretes tears and lubricates the surface of the eye and the conjunctiva of the eyelid

lacrimation (,lækrɪ'meɪʃən) *n* the secretion of tears

lacrimator, lachrymator *or* **lacrymator** ('lækrɪ,meɪtə) *n* a substance causing an increase in the flow of tears. See **tear gas**

lacrimatory, lachrymatory *or* **lacrymatory** ('lækrɪmətərɪ, -trɪ) *adj* of, causing, or producing tears

lacrosse (lə'krɒs) *n* a ball game invented by American Indians, now played by two teams who try to propel a ball into each other's goal by means of long-handled hooked sticks that are loosely strung with a kind of netted pouch [c19 Canadian French: the hooked stick, crosier]

lactalbumin (læk'tælbjʊmɪn) *n* a protein occurring in milk that contains all the amino acids essential to man. See also **caseinogen** [c19 from LACTO- + ALBUMIN]

lactam ('læktæm) *n chem* any of a group of inner amides, derived from amino acids, having the characteristic group -CONH- [c20 from LACT(ONE) + AM(IDE)]

lactase ('lækteɪs, -teɪz) *n* any of a group of enzymes that hydrolyse lactose to glucose and galactose [c20 from LACTO- + -ASE]

lactate¹ ('lækteɪt) *n* an ester or salt of lactic acid [c18 from LACTO- + -ATE¹]

lactate² ('lækteɪt) *vb* (*intr*) (of mammals) to produce or secrete milk

lactation (læk'teɪʃən) *n* **1** the secretion of milk from the mammary glands after parturition **2** the period during which milk is secreted > **lac'tational** *adj* > **lac'tationally** *adv*

lactation tetany *n vet science* another name for **hypomagnesaemia**

lacteal ('læktɪəl) *adj* **1** of, relating to, or resembling milk **2** (of lymphatic vessels) conveying or containing chyle ▷ *n* **3** any of the lymphatic vessels conveying chyle from the small intestine to the thoracic duct [c17 from Latin *lacteus* of milk, from *lac* milk] > **'lacteally** *adv*

lactescent (læk'tɛs^ənt) *adj* **1** (of plants and certain insects) secreting a milky fluid **2** milky or becoming milky [c18 from Latin *lactescēns*, from *lactescēre* to become milky, from *lact-, lac* milk] > **lac'tescence** *n*

lactic ('læktɪk) *adj* relating to or derived from milk [c18 from Latin *lact-, lac* milk]

lactic acid *n* a colourless syrupy carboxylic acid found in sour milk and many fruits and used as a preservative (E270) for foodstuffs, such as soft margarine, and for making pharmaceuticals and adhesives. Formula: $CH_3CH(OH)COOH$. Systematic name: **2-hydroxypropanoic acid**

lactiferous (læk'tɪfərəs) *adj* **1** producing, conveying, or secreting milk or a milky fluid: *lactiferous ducts* **2** *botany* containing latex; laticiferous [c17 from Latin *lactifer*, from *lact-, lac* milk] > **lac'tiferousness** *n*

lacto- *or before a vowel* **lact-** *combining form* indicating milk: *lactobacillus* [from Latin *lact-, lac* milk]

lactobacillus (,læktəʊbə'sɪləs) *n, pl* **-li** (-laɪ) any Gram-positive rod-shaped bacterium of the genus *Lactobacillus*, which ferments carbohydrates to lactic acid, for example in the souring of milk: family *Lactobacillaceae*

lactoflavin (,læktəʊ'fleɪvɪn) *n* a less common name for **riboflavin**

lactogenic (,læktə'dʒɛnɪk) *adj* inducing lactation: *lactogenic hormone*. See also **prolactin**

lactoglobulin (,læktəʊ'glɒbjʊlɪn) *n biochem* any of a number of globular proteins found in milk

lactometer (læk'tɒmɪtə) *n* a hydrometer used to measure the relative density of milk and thus determine its quality. Also called: **galactometer**

lactone ('læktəʊn) *n* any of a class of organic compounds formed from hydroxy acids and containing the group -C(CO)OC-, where the carbon atoms are part of a ring > **lactonic** (læk'tɒnɪk) *adj*

lactoprotein (,læktəʊ'prəʊtiːn) *n* any protein, such as lactalbumin or caseinogen, that is present in milk

lactoscope ('læktə,skəʊp) *n* an instrument for measuring the amount of cream in milk

lactose ('læktəʊs, -təʊz) *n* a white crystalline disaccharide occurring in milk and used in the manufacture of pharmaceuticals and baby foods. Formula: $C_{12}H_{22}O_{11}$. Also called: **milk sugar**

lactosuria (,læktəʊ'sjʊərɪə) *n med* the presence of lactose in the urine

lacto-vegetarian *n* a vegetarian whose diet includes dairy produce and eggs

La Cumbre (la 'kuːmbreɪ) *n* another name for the **Uspallata Pass**

lacuna (lə'kjuːnə) *n, pl* **-nae** (-niː) *or* **-nas 1** a gap or space, esp in a book or manuscript **2** *biology* a cavity or depression, such as any of the spaces in the matrix of bone **3** another name for **coffer** (sense 3) [c17 from Latin *lacūna* pool, cavity, from *lacus* lake] > **la'cunose, la'cunal** *or* **la'cunary** *adj* > **lacunosity** (,lækjʊ'nɒsɪtɪ) *n*

lacunar (lə'kjuːnə) *n, pl* **lacunars** *or* **lacunaria** (,lækjʊ'nɛərɪə) **1** Also called: **lequear** a ceiling, soffit, or vault having coffers **2** another name for **coffer** (sense 3) ▷ *adj* **3** of, relating to, or containing a lacuna or lacunas [c17 from Latin *lacūnar* panelled ceiling, from *lacūna* cavity; see LACUNA]

lacustrine (lə'kʌstraɪn) *adj* **1** of or relating to lakes **2** living or growing in or on the shores of a lake [c19 from Italian *lacustre*, from Latin *lacus* lake]

LACW *Brit* ▷ *abbreviation for* leading aircraftwoman

lacy ('leɪsɪ) *adj* **lacier, laciest** made of or resembling lace > **'lacily** *adv* > **'laciness** *n*

lad (læd) *n* **1** a boy or young man **2** *informal* a familiar form of address for any male **3** a lively or dashing man or youth (esp in the phrase **a bit of a lad**) **4** a young man whose behaviour is characteristic of male adolescents, esp in being rowdy, macho, or immature **5** *Brit* a boy or man who looks after horses [c13 *ladde*; perhaps of Scandinavian origin]

ladanum ('lædənəm) *n* another name for **labdanum**

ladder ('lædə) *n* **1** a portable framework of wood, metal, rope, etc, in the form of two long parallel members connected by several parallel rungs or steps fixed to them at right angles, for climbing up or down **2** any hierarchy conceived of as having a series of ascending stages, levels, etc: *the social ladder* **3 a** anything resembling a ladder **b** (*as modifier*): *ladder stitch* **4** Also called: **run** *chiefly Brit* a line of connected stitches that have come undone in knitted material, esp stockings **5** See **ladder tournament** ▷ *vb* **6** *chiefly Brit* to cause a line of interconnected stitches in (stockings, etc) to undo, as by snagging, or (of a stocking) to come undone in this way [Old English *hlǣdder*; related to Old High German *leitara*]

ladder back *n* a type of chair in which the back is constructed of horizontal slats between two uprights

ladder tournament *n* a tournament in a sport or game in which each contestant in a list attempts to defeat and displace the contestant above him. Also called: **ladder**

laddie ('lædɪ) *n chiefly Scot* a familiar term for a male, esp a young man; lad

laddish ('lædɪʃ) *adj informal, usually derogatory* characteristic of male adolescents or young men, esp by being rowdy, macho, or immature: *laddish behaviour* > **'laddish,ness** *n*

lade¹ (leɪd) *vb* **lades, lading, laded, laden** ('leɪd^ən) *or* **laded 1** to put cargo or freight on board (a ship, etc) or (of a ship, etc) to take on cargo or freight **2** (*tr; usually passive* and foll by *with*) to burden or oppress **3** (*tr; usually passive* and foll by *with*) to fill or load **4** to remove (liquid) with or as if with a ladle [Old English *hladen* to load; related to Dutch *laden*] > **'lader** *n*

lade² (leɪd, leɪd) *n Scot* a watercourse, esp a millstream [of uncertain origin]

laden ('leɪdᵊn) *vb* **1** a past participle of **lade¹** ▷ *adj* **2** weighed down with a load; loaded **3** encumbered; burdened

ladette (ˌlædˈɛt) *n informal* a young woman whose social behaviour is similar to that of male adolescents or young men

la-di-da, lah-di-dah *or* **la-de-da** (ˌlɑːdiːˈdɑː) *adj* **1** *informal* affecting exaggeratedly genteel manners or speech ▷ *n* **2** a la-di-da person [c19 mockingly imitative of affected speech]

ladies *or* **ladies' room** *n* (*functioning as singular*) *informal* a women's public lavatory

ladies' fingers *n* (*functioning as singular or plural*) another name for **kidney vetch** *or* **okra**

ladies' gallery *n* (formerly, in Britain) **1** a gallery in the old House of Commons set aside for women spectators **2** a portion of the strangers' gallery of the new House of Commons similarly reserved

ladies' man *or* **lady's man** *n* a man who is fond of, attentive to, and successful with women

ladies'-tresses *n* (*functioning as singular or plural*) a variant spelling of **lady's-tresses**

Ladin (læˈdiːn) *n* a Rhaetian dialect spoken in parts of South Tyrol. Compare **Friulian, Romansch** [c19 from Italian *ladino,* from Latin *latīnus* Latin]

lading ('leɪdɪŋ) *n* a load; cargo; freight

ladino (ləˈdiːnəʊ) *n, pl* -nos an Italian variety of white clover grown as a forage crop in North America [c20 perhaps from Italian *ladino* (see LADIN), referring to a person or thing from the Italian-speaking area of Switzerland, where the clover is grown]

Ladino (ləˈdiːnəʊ) *n* a language of Sephardic Jews, based on Spanish with some Hebrew elements and usually written in Hebrew characters. Also called: **Judaeo-Spanish, Judezmo** [from Spanish: Latin]

ladle ('leɪdᵊl) *n* **1** a long-handled spoon having a deep bowl for serving or transferring liquids: *a soup ladle* **2** a large bucket-shaped container for transferring molten metal ▷ *vb* **3** (*tr*) to lift or serve out with or as if with a ladle [Old English *hlædel,* from *hladan* to draw out] > **'ladle.ful** *n*

ladle out *vb* (*tr, adverb*) *informal* to distribute (money, gifts, etc) generously

lad lit *n* **a** fiction about young men and their emotional and personal lives **b** (*as modifier*): *lad-lit novels*

lad mag *n* a magazine aimed at or appealing to men, focusing on fashion, gadgets, and often featuring scantily dressed women

Ladoga (*Russian* 'ladəgə) *n* **Lake** a lake in NW Russia, in the SW Karelian Republic: the largest lake in Europe; drains through the River Neva into the Gulf of Finland. Area: about 18 000 sq km (7000 sq miles). Russian name: **Ladozhskoye Ozero** ('ladəʃskəjə 'ɔzırə)

Ladrone Islands (ləˈdrəʊn) *pl n* the former name (1521–1668) of the **Mariana Islands**

lad's love *n* another name for **southernwood**

lady ('leɪdɪ) *n, pl* -dies **1** a woman regarded as having the characteristics of a good family and high social position; female counterpart of **gentleman** (sense 1) **2 a** a polite name for a woman **b** (*as modifier*): *a lady doctor* **3** an informal name for **wife 4 lady of the house** the female head of the household **5** *history* a woman with proprietary rights and authority, as over a manor. Compare **lord** (sense 3) [Old English *hlǣfdīge,* from *hlāf* bread + *dīge* kneader, related to *dāh* dough]

Lady ('leɪdɪ) *n, pl* -dies **1** (in Britain) a title of honour borne by various classes of women of the peerage **2 my lady** a term of address to holders of

the title Lady, used esp by servants **3 Our Lady** a title of the Virgin Mary **4** *archaic* an allegorical prefix for the personifications of certain qualities: *Lady Luck* **5** *chiefly Brit* the term of address by which certain positions of respect are prefaced when held by women: *Lady Chairman*

ladybird ('leɪdɪˌbɜːd) *n* any of various small brightly coloured beetles of the family *Coccinellidae,* such as *Adalia bipunctata* (**two-spotted ladybird**), which has red elytra marked with black spots. Usual US and Canadian name: **ladybug** [c18 named after *Our Lady,* the Virgin Mary]

lady bountiful *n* an ostentatiously charitable woman [after a character in George Farquhar's play *The Beaux' Stratagem* (1707)]

ladyboy ('leɪdɪˌbɔɪ) *n informal* a transvestite or transsexual, esp one from the Far East

Lady Chapel *n* a chapel within a church or cathedral, dedicated to the Virgin Mary

Lady Day *n* March 25, the feast of the Annunciation of the Virgin Mary; one of the four quarter days in England, Wales and Ireland. Also called: **Annunciation Day**

lady fern *n* a large, graceful, but variable fern, *Athyrium filix-femina,* with bipinnate fronds, commonly found on damp acid soils in woods and on hillsides

ladyfinger ('leɪdɪˌfɪŋgə) *or* **lady's finger** *n* a small finger-shaped sponge cake

ladyfy *or* **ladify** ('leɪdɪˌfaɪ) *vb* -fies, -fying, -fied (*tr*) to make a lady of (someone)

lady-in-waiting *n, pl* ladies-in-waiting a lady of a royal household who attends a queen or princess

lady-killer *n informal* a man who is, or thinks he is, irresistibly fascinating to women > **'lady-ˌkilling** *n, adj*

ladylike ('leɪdɪˌlaɪk) *adj* **1** like or befitting a lady in manners and bearing; refined and fastidious **2** *derogatory* (of a man) effeminate > **'lady.likeness** *n*

ladylove ('leɪdɪˌlʌv) *n now rare* a beloved woman

Lady Luck *n* the personification of fortune or chance

Lady Macbeth strategy *n informal* a strategy in a takeover battle in which a third party makes a bid acceptable to the target company, appearing to act as a white knight but subsequently joining forces with the original (unwelcome) bidder [c20 after *Lady Macbeth* in Shakespeare's *Macbeth* (1605)]

lady mayoress *n Brit* the wife of a lord mayor

Lady Muck *n informal, usually derogatory* an ordinary woman behaving or being treated as if she were aristocratic. See also **Lord Muck**

Lady of the Lake *n* (in Arthurian legend) a mysterious supernatural being sometimes identified with **Vivian**

lady orchid *n* a tall graceful orchid, *Orchis purpurea,* with faintly scented purple-brown and green flowers with a pinkish or white lip [c19 named from a fancied resemblance to a lady in regency dress and bonnet]

lady's bedstraw *n* a Eurasian rubiaceous plant, *Galium verum,* with clusters of small yellow flowers

lady's finger *n* another name for **bhindi**

Ladyship ('leɪdɪˌʃɪp) *n* (preceded by *your* or *her*) a title used to address or refer to any peeress except a duchess

lady's maid *n* a personal servant to a woman, esp in matters of dress and toilet

lady's man *n* a variant spelling of **ladies' man**

lady's mantle *n* any of various rosaceous plants of the N temperate genus *Alchemilla,* having small green flowers

Ladysmith ('leɪdɪˌsmɪθ) *n* a city in E South Africa: besieged by Boers for four months (1899–1900) during the Boer War. Pop: 41 427 (2001)

lady's-slipper *n* any of various orchids of the Eurasian genus *Cypripedium,* esp *C. calceolus,* having reddish or purple flowers. See also **moccasin flower, cypripedium**

lady's-smock *n* a N temperate plant, *Cardamine pratensis,* with white or rose-pink flowers: family *Brassicaceae* (crucifers). Also called: **cuckooflower**

lady's-thumb *n* the usual US name for **red shank** (the plant)

lady's-tresses *or* **ladies'-tresses** *n* (*functioning as singular or plural*) any of various orchids of the genera *Spiranthes* or *Goodyera,* having spikes of small white fragrant flowers

Laertes (leɪˈɜːtiːz) *n Greek myth* the father of Odysseus

laetrile ('leɪəˌtraɪl) *n* an extract of peach stones, containing amygdalin, sold as a cure for cancer but judged useless and possibly dangerous by medical scientists [c20 from LAEVOROTATORY + NITRILE]

laevo- *or US* **levo-** *combining form* **1** on or towards the left: *laevorotatory* **2** (in chemistry) denoting a laevorotatory compound: *laevulose* [from Latin *laevus* left]

laevogyrate (ˌliːvəʊˈdʒaɪreɪt) *adj* another word for **laevorotatory**

laevorotation (ˌliːvəʊrəʊˈteɪʃən) *n* **1** a rotation to the left **2** an anticlockwise rotation of the plane of polarization of plane-polarized light as a result of its passage through a crystal, liquid, or solution ▷ Compare **dextrorotation**

laevorotatory (ˌliːvəʊˈrəʊtətərɪ, -trɪ) *or* **laevorotary** *adj* of, having, or causing laevorotation. Also: **laevogyrate**

laevulin ('lɛvjʊlɪn) *n* a polysaccharide occurring in the tubers of certain helianthus plants [c19 from LAEVULOSE + -IN]

laevulose ('lɛvjʊˌləʊs, -ˌləʊz) *n* another name for **fructose** [c19 from LAEVO- + -ULE + -OSE²]

Laffer curve ('læfə) *n economics* a curve on a graph showing government tax revenue plotted against percentage tax rates. It has been used to show that a cut in a high tax rate can increase government revenue [c20 named after Arthur *Laffer* (born 1940), US economist]

LAFTA ('læftə) *n acronym for* Latin American Free Trade Area, the name before 1981 of the Latin American Integration Association. See **LAIA**

lag¹ (læg) *vb* lags, lagging, lagged (*intr*) **1** (often foll by *behind*) to hang (back) or fall (behind) in movement, progress, development, etc **2** to fall away in strength or intensity **3** to determine an order of play in certain games, as by rolling marbles towards a line or, in billiards, hitting cue balls up the table against the top cushion in an attempt to bring them back close to the headrail ▷ *n* **4** the act or state of slowing down or falling behind **5** the interval of time between two events, esp between an action and its effect **6** an act of lagging in a game, such as billiards [c16 of obscure origin]

lag² (læg) *slang* ▷ *n* **1** a convict or ex-convict (esp in the phrase **old lag**) **2** a term of imprisonment ▷ *vb* lags, lagging, lagged **3** (*tr*) to arrest or put in prison [c19 of unknown origin]

lag³ (læg) *vb* lags, lagging, lagged **1** (*tr*) to cover (a pipe, cylinder, etc) with lagging to prevent loss of heat ▷ *n* **2** the insulating casing of a steam cylinder, boiler, etc; lagging **3** a stave or lath [c17 of Scandinavian origin; related to Swedish *lagg* stave]

lagan ('lægᵊn) *or* **ligan** ('laɪgᵊn) *n* goods or wreckage on the sea bed, sometimes attached to a buoy to permit recovery. Compare **flotsam, jetsam** [c16 from Old French *lagan,* probably of Germanic origin; compare Old Norse *lögn* dragnet]

Lag b'Omer *Hebrew* (lag bəˈɔmɛr; *English* læg ˈbəʊmə) *n* a Jewish holiday celebrated on the 18th day of Iyar [Hebrew, literally: 33rd (day) of the Omer]

lag correlation *n statistics* another name for **cross-correlation**

lagena (ləˈdʒiːnə) *n* **1** a bottle with a narrow neck **2** an outgrowth of the sacculus in the ear of fishes and amphibians, thought to be homologous to the cochlea of mammals [c19 Latin, a flask, from Greek *lagēnos*]

lager¹ ('lɑːgə) *n* a light-bodied effervescent beer, fermented in a closed vessel using yeasts that sink to the bottom of the brew. Compare **ale** [c19 from German *Lagerbier* beer for storing, from *Lager* storehouse]

lager² ('lɑːɡə) *n* a variant spelling of **laager**

lagered-up *or* **lagered** ('lɑːɡəd) *adj Brit informal* intoxicated, esp after drinking lager

lager lout *n* a rowdy or aggressive young drunk male

lager top *or* **lager tops** *n Brit* a pint or half-pint of lager with a dash of lemonade

laggard ('læɡəd) *n* **1** a person who lags behind **2** a dawdler or straggler ▷ *adj* **3** *rare* sluggish, slow, or dawdling > 'laggardly *adv* > 'laggardness *n*

lagging ('læɡɪŋ) *n* **1** insulating material wrapped around pipes, boilers, etc, or laid in a roof loft, to prevent loss of heat **2** the act or process of applying lagging **3** a wooden frame used to support an arch during construction

lagniappe *or* **lagnappe** (læn'jæp, 'lænjæp) *n US* **1** a small gift, esp one given to a customer who makes a purchase **2** something given or obtained as a gratuity or bonus [C19 Louisiana French, from American Spanish *la ñapa*, from Quechua *yápa* addition]

lagomorph ('læɡəʊˌmɔːf) *n* any placental mammal of the order *Lagomorpha*, having two pairs of upper incisors specialized for gnawing: includes pikas, rabbits, and hares [C19 via New Latin from Greek *lagōs* hare; see -MORPH] > ˌlago'morphic *or* ˌlago'morphous *adj*

lagoon (lə'ɡuːn) *n* **1** a body of water cut off from the open sea by coral reefs or sand bars **2** any small body of water, esp one adjoining a larger one ▷ Also (rare): **lagune** [C17 from Italian *laguna*, from Latin *lacūna* pool; see LACUNA]

Lagoon Islands *pl n* a former name of **Tuvalu**

Lagos ('leɪɡɒs) *n* **1** the former capital and chief port of Nigeria, on the Bight of Benin: first settled in the sixteenth century; a slave market until the nineteenth century; ceded to Britain (1861); university (1962). Pop: 11 135 000 (2005 est) **2** a state of SW Nigeria. Capital: Ikeja. Pop: 6 357 253 (1995 est). Area: 3345 sq km (1292 sq miles)

Lagrangian (lə'ɡreɪndʒɪən) *adj* of or relating to Comte Joseph Louis Lagrange (1736–1813), the French mathematician and astronomer

Lagrangian point *n astronomy* one of five points in the plane of revolution of two bodies in orbit around their common centre of gravity, at which a third body of negligible mass can remain in equilibrium with respect to the other two bodies [named after Comte Joseph Louis *Lagrange* (1736–1813), French mathematician and astronomer]

La Granja (*Spanish* la 'ɡranxa) *n* another name for **San Ildefonso**

lag screw *n* a woodscrew with a square head [from LAG³; the screw was originally used to fasten barrel staves]

Lagting *or* **Lagthing** ('lɑːɡtɪŋ) *n* the upper chamber of the Norwegian parliament. See also **Storting, Odelsting** [Norwegian, from *lag* law + *ting* parliament]

La Guaira *or* **La Guayra** (*Spanish* la 'ɡwaira) *n* the chief seaport of Venezuela, on the Caribbean. Pop: 26 669 (1990 est)

lah (lɑː) *n music* (in tonic sol-fa) the sixth note of any major scale; submediant [C14 see GAMUT]

lahar ('lɑːhɑː) *n* a landslide of volcanic debris mixed with water down the sides of a volcano, usually precipitated by heavy rainfall [C20 from Javanese: lava]

lah-di-dah (ˌlɑːdiːˈdɑː) *adj, n informal* a variant spelling of **la-di-da**

Lahnda ('lɑːndə) *n* a language or group of dialects of Pakistan, belonging to the Indic branch of the Indo-European family and closely related to Punjabi

La Hogue (*French* la ɔɡ) *n* a roadstead off the NW coast of France: scene of the defeat of the French by the Dutch and English fleet (1692)

Lahore (lə'hɔː) *n* **1** a city in NE Pakistan: capital of the former province of West Pakistan (1955–70);

University of the Punjab (1882). Pop: 6 373 000 (2005 est) **2** a variety of large domestic fancy pigeon having a black-and-white plumage

Lahti (*Finnish* 'lɑhti) *n* a town in S Finland: site of the main Finnish radio and television stations; furniture industry. Pop: 98 253 (2003 est)

LAIA *abbreviation for* Latin American Integration Association (before 1981, known as the Latin American Free Trade Area). An economic group, its members are Argentina, Bolivia, Brazil, Chile, Colombia, Ecuador, Mexico, Paraguay, Peru, Uruguay, and Venezuela

Laibach ('laibax) *n* the German name for **Ljubljana**

laic ('leɪɪk) *adj also* **laical** **1** of or involving the laity; secular ▷ *n* **2** a rare word for **layman** [C15 from Late Latin *lāicus* LAY³] > 'laically *adv* > 'laicism *n*

laicize *or* **laicise** ('leɪɪˌsaɪz) *vb* (*tr*) to withdraw clerical or ecclesiastical character or status from (an institution, building, etc) > ˌlaici'zation *or* ˌlaici'sation *n*

laid (leɪd) *vb* the past tense and past participle of **lay¹**

laid-back *adj informal* relaxed in style, character, or behaviour; easy-going and unhurried

laid paper *n* paper with a regular mesh impressed upon it by the dandy roller on a paper-making machine. Compare **wove paper**

laik (leɪk) *vb Northern English dialect* **1** (when *intr*, often foll by *about*) to play (a game, etc) **2** (*intr*) to be on holiday, esp to take a day off work **3** (*intr*) to be unemployed [C14 *leiken*, from Old Norse *leika*; related to Old English *lacan* to manoeuvre; compare LARK²]

Lailat-ul-Qadr (ˌleɪlætʊlˈkɑːdə) *n* a night of study and prayer observed annually by Muslims to mark the communication of the Koran: it usually follows the 27th day of Ramadan [from Arabic: night of determination]

lain (leɪn) *vb* the past participle of **lie²**

Laingian ('læɪɪən) *adj* **1** of or based on the theory of Scottish psychiatrist R. D. Laing (1927–89) that mental illnesses are understandable as natural responses to stress in family and social situations ▷ *n* **2** a follower or adherent of Laing's teaching

laipse (leɪps) *Northern and Midland English dialect* ▷ *vb* (*tr*) **1** to beat soundly **2** to defeat totally

lair¹ (lɛə) *n* **1** the resting place of a wild animal **2** *informal* a place of seclusion or hiding **3** an enclosure or shed for farm animals **4** *Scot* the ground for a grave in a cemetery ▷ *vb* **5** (*intr*) (esp of a wild animal) to retreat to or rest in a lair **6** (*tr*) to drive or place (an animal) in a lair [Old English *leger*; related to LIE² and Old High German *leger* bed]

lair² (ler) *n, vb* a Scot word for **mire** [from Old Norse *leir* mud]

lair³ (lɛə) *Austral slang* ▷ *n* **1** a flashy man who shows off ▷ *vb* **2** (*intr*; foll by *up* or *around*) to behave or dress like a lair [perhaps from LEER]

lairage ('lɛərɪdʒ) *n* accommodation for farm animals, esp at docks or markets

laird (lɛəd; *Scot* lerd) *n Scot* a landowner, esp of a large estate [C15 Scottish variant of LORD]

lairy ('lɛərɪ) *adj* lairier, lairiest gaudy or flashy [C20 from LEERY]

laissez aller *or* *laisser aller* French (lese ale) *n* lack of constraint; freedom [literally: let go]

laissez faire *or* *laisser faire* (ˌlɛseɪ 'fɛə; *French* lese fɛr) *n* **1** **a** Also called: **individualism** the doctrine of unrestricted freedom in commerce, esp for private interests **b** (*as modifier*): *a laissez-faire economy* **2** indifference or noninterference, esp in the affairs of others [French, literally: let (them) act] > ˌlaissez-'faireism *or* ˌlaisser-'faireism *n*

laissez passer *or* *laisser passer* French (lese pase) *n* a document granting unrestricted access or movement to its holder [literally: let pass]

laity ('leɪɪtɪ) *n* **1** laymen, as distinguished from clergymen **2** all people not of a specific occupation [C16 from LAY³]

Laius ('laɪəs) *n Greek myth* a king of Thebes, killed by his son Oedipus, who did not know of their relationship

lake¹ (leɪk) *n* **1** an expanse of water entirely surrounded by land and unconnected to the sea except by rivers or streams. Related adj: **lacustrine** **2** anything resembling this **3** a surplus of a liquid commodity: *a wine lake* [C13 *lac*, via Old French from Latin *lacus*]

lake² (leɪk) *n* **1** a bright pigment used in textile dyeing and printing inks, produced by the combination of an organic colouring matter with an inorganic compound, usually a metallic salt, oxide, or hydroxide. See also **mordant** **2** a red dye obtained by combining a metallic compound with cochineal [C17 variant of LAC¹]

Lake District *n* a region of lakes and mountains in NW England, in Cumbria: includes England's largest lake (Windermere) and highest mountain (Scafell Pike); national park; literary associations (the Lake Poets); tourist region. Also called: **Lakeland**

lake dwelling *n* a dwelling, esp in prehistoric villages, constructed on platforms supported by wooden piles driven into the bottom of a lake > **lake dweller** *n*

lake herring *n* **1** another name for **cisco** **2** another name for **powan**

Lakeland ('leɪkˌlænd) *n* **1** another name for the **Lake District** ▷ *adj* **2** of or relating to the Lake District

Lakeland terrier *n* a wire-haired breed of terrier, originally from the Lake District and used for hunting

Lake of the Woods *n* a lake in N central North America, mostly in W Northern Ontario, Canada: fed chiefly by the Rainy River; drains into Lake Winnipeg by the Winnipeg River; many islands; tourist region. Area: 3846 sq km (1485 sq miles)

Lake Poets *pl n* the English poets Wordsworth, Coleridge, and Southey, who lived in and drew inspiration from the Lake District at the beginning of the 19th century

laker ('leɪkə) *n* a cargo vessel used on lakes

Lake Success *n* a village in SE New York State, on W Long Island: headquarters of the United Nations Security Council from 1946 to 1951. Pop: 2832 (2003 est)

lakh *or* **lac** (lɑːk) *n* (in India and Pakistan) the number 100 000, esp when referring to this sum of rupees [C17 from Hindi *lākh*, ultimately from Sanskrit *lakshā* a sign]

laksa ('læksa) *n* (in Malaysia) a dish of Chinese origin consisting of rice noodles served in curry or hot soup [from Malay: ten thousand]

Lakshadweep Islands (læk'ʃædwiːp) *pl n* a group of 26 coral islands and reefs in the Arabian Sea, off the SW coast of India: a union territory of India since 1956. Administrative centre: Kavaratti Island. Pop: 60 595 (2001). Area: 28 sq km (11 sq miles). Former name (until 1973): **Laccadive, Minicoy, and Amindivi Islands**

Lakshmi ('lɑːkʃmɪ) *n Hinduism* the goddess of wealth and prosperity, and the consort of the god Vishnu [from Sanskrit *Lākṣmi*, literally: wealth, splendour]

laky ('leɪkɪ) *adj* lakier, lakiest of the reddish colour of the pigment lake

Lala ('lɑːlɑː) *n* a title or form of address, equivalent to *Mr*, used in India [Hindi]

La-La land ('lɑːˌlɑː) *n* **1** *slang* a nickname for **Los Angeles** **2** (*not capitals*) a place that is remote from reality [C20 reduplication of the initials LA]

lalang ('lɑːlɑːŋ) *n* a coarse weedy Malaysian grass, *Imperata arundinacea* [Malay]

lalapalooza (ˌlɒləpə'luːzə) *n* a variant spelling of **lollapalooza**

-lalia *combining form* indicating a speech defect or abnormality: *coprolalia; echolalia* [New Latin, from Greek *lalia* chatter, from *lalein* to babble]

La Línea (*Spanish* la 'linea) *n* a town in SW Spain, on the Bay of Gibraltar. Pop: 61 892 (2003 est).

Official name: La Línea de la Concepción (ðe la ˌkonθepˈθjon)

Lallans (ˈlælənz) *or* **Lallan** (ˈlælən) *n* **1** a literary version of the variety of English spoken and written in the Lowlands of Scotland **2** (*modifier*) of or relating to the Lowlands of Scotland or their dialects [Scottish variant of LOWLANDS]

lallation (læˈleɪʃən) *n phonetics* a defect of speech consisting of the pronunciation of (r) as (l) [c17 from Latin *lallāre* to sing lullaby, of imitative origin]

lallygag (ˈlælɪˌgæg) *or* **lollygag** *vb* -gags, -gagging, -gagged (*intr*) US to loiter aimlessly [c20 of unknown origin]

lam¹ (læm) *vb* lams, lamming, lammed *slang* **1** (*tr*) to thrash or beat **2** (*intr; usually foll by into or out*) to make a sweeping stroke or blow [c16 from Scandinavian; related to Old Norse *lemja*]

lam² (læm) *US and Canadian slang* ▷ *n* **1** a sudden flight or escape, esp to avoid arrest **2** on the lam **a** making an escape **b** in hiding ▷ *vb* lams, lamming, lammed **3** (*intr*) to escape or flee [c19 perhaps from LAM¹ (hence, to be off)]

Lam. *Bible abbreviation for* Lamentations

lama (ˈlɑːmə) *n* a priest or monk of Lamaism [c17 from Tibetan *blama*]

Lamaism (ˈlɑːmɑˌɪzəm) *n* the Mahayana form of Buddhism of Tibet and Mongolia. See also **Dalai Lama**. ▷ ˈLamaist *n, adj* ▷ ˌLamaˈistic *adj*

La Mancha (*Spanish* la ˈmantʃa) *n* a plateau of central Spain, between the mountains of Toledo and the hills of Cuenca: traditionally associated with episodes in *Don Quixote*. Average height: 600 m (2000 ft)

La Manche (*French* la mɑ̃ʃ) *n* See **Manche** (sense 2)

Lamarckian (lɑːˈmɑːkɪən) *adj* **1** of or relating to Jean Baptiste Pierre Antoine de Monet, Chevalier de Lamarck (1744–1829), the French naturalist ▷ *n* **2** a supporter of Lamarckism

Lamarckism (lɑːˈmɑːkɪzəm) *n* the theory of organic evolution proposed by Jean Baptiste Pierre Antoine de Monet, Chevalier de Lamarck (1744–1829), the French naturalist, based on the principle that characteristics of an organism modified during its lifetime are inheritable. See also **acquired characteristic, Neo-Lamarckism**

lamasery (ˈlɑːməsərɪ) *n, pl* -series a monastery of lamas [c19 from French *lamaserie*, from LAMA + French -*serie*, from Persian *serāī* palace]

lamb (læm) *n* **1** the young of a sheep **2** the meat of a young sheep **3** a person, esp a child, who is innocent, meek, good, etc **4** a person easily deceived **5** like a lamb to the slaughter **a** without resistance **b** innocently ▷ *vb* **6** (*intr*) Also: lamb down (of a ewe) to give birth **7** (*tr; used in the passive*) (of a lamb) to be born **8** (*intr*) (of a shepherd) to tend the ewes and newborn lambs at lambing time ▷ See also **lamb down** [Old English *lamb*, from Germanic; compare German *Lamm*, Old High German and Old Norse *lamb*] ▷ ˈlambˌlike *adj*

Lamb¹ (læm) *n* **the** a title given to Christ in the New Testament

lambada (læmˈbɑːdə) *n* **1** an erotic dance, originating in Brazil, performed by two people who hold each other closely and gyrate their hips in synchronized movements **2** the music that accompanies the lambada, combining salsa, calypso, and reggae [c20 from Portuguese, literally: the snapping of a whip]

Lambaréné (*French* lɑbarene) *n* a town in W Gabon on the Ogooué River: site of the hospital built by Albert Schweitzer, who died and was buried there (1965). Pop: 50 000 (latest est)

lambast (læmˈbæst) *or* **lambaste** (læmˈbeɪst) *vb* (*tr*) **1** to beat or whip severely **2** to reprimand or scold [c17 perhaps from LAM¹ + BASTE³]

lambda (ˈlæmdə) *n* the 11th letter of the Greek alphabet (Λ, λ), a consonant transliterated as *l* [c14 from Greek, from Semitic; related to LAMED]

lambda calculus *n logic, computing* a formalized description of functions and the way in which they combine, developed by Alonzo Church and

used in the theory of certain high-level programming languages [c20 from the use of the symbol *lambda* (λ) to represent the mathematical functions]

lambdacism (ˈlæmdəˌsɪzəm) *n phonetics* **1** excessive use or idiosyncratic pronunciation of *l* **2** another word for **lallation** [c17 from Late Latin *labdacismus*, from Greek]

lambdoid (ˈlæmdɔɪd) *or* **lambdoidal** *adj* **1** having the shape of the Greek letter lambda **2** of or denoting the suture near the back of the skull between the occipital and parietal bones [c16 via French from Greek *lambdoeidēs*]

lamb down *vb* (*adverb*) **1** (*intr*) another term for **lamb** (sense 6) **2** (*tr*) Austral informal to persuade (someone) to spend all his money

lambent (ˈlæmbənt) *adj* **1** (*esp of a flame*) flickering softly over a surface **2** glowing with soft radiance **3** (*of wit or humour*) light or brilliant [c17 from the present participle of Latin *lambere* to lick] ▷ ˈlambency *n* ▷ ˈlambently *adv*

lambert (ˈlæmbət) *n* the cgs unit of illumination, equal to 1 lumen per square centimetre. Symbol: L [named after J. H. *Lambert* (1728–77), German mathematician and physicist]

Lambeth (ˈlæmbəθ) *n* **1** a borough of S Greater London, on the Thames: contains **Lambeth Palace** (the London residence of the Archbishop of Canterbury). Pop: 268 500 (2003 est). Area: 27 sq km (11 sq miles) **2** the Archbishop of Canterbury in his official capacity

Lambeth Conference *n* the decennial conference of Anglican bishops, begun in 1867. See also **Lambeth Quadrilateral**

Lambeth Quadrilateral *n* the four essentials agreed upon at the Lambeth Conference of 1888 for a United Christian Church, namely, the Holy Scriptures, the Apostles' Creed, the sacraments of baptism and Holy Communion, and the historic episcopate

Lambeth walk *n chiefly Brit* a line dance popular in the 1930s

lambing (ˈlæmɪŋ) *n* **1 a** the birth of lambs **b** (*as modifier*): *lambing time* **2** the shepherd's work of tending the ewes and newborn lambs at this time

lambkin (ˈlæmkɪn) *or* **lambie** *n* **1** a small or young lamb **2** a term of affection for a small endearing child

Lamb of God *n* a title given to Christ in the New Testament, probably with reference to his sacrificial death

lambrequin (ˈlæmbrɪkɪn, ˈlæmbə-) *n* **1** an ornamental hanging covering the edge of a shelf or the upper part of a window or door **2 a** a border pattern giving a draped effect, used on ceramics, etc **b** (*as modifier*): *a lambrequin pattern* **3** (*often plural*) a scarf worn over a helmet **4** *heraldry* another name for **mantling** [c18 from French, from Dutch *lamperkin* (unattested), diminutive of *lamper* veil]

lamb's ears *n* (*functioning as singular*) a perennial herb, *Stachys lanata*, planted for its foliage, which is covered with white woolly down; the purplish or striped flowers are small. Also called: **lamb's tongue**, (Scot) **lamb's lugs**

lamb's fry *n* **1** Brit lamb's offal, esp lamb's testicles, as food **2** Austral and NZ lamb's liver as food

Lamb shift *n* the small difference in energy between two states of the hydrogen atom detected by Willis Eugene Lamb (born 1913), the US physicist

lambskin (ˈlæmˌskɪn) *n* **1** the skin of a lamb, esp with the wool still on **2 a** a material or garment prepared from this skin **b** (*as modifier*): *a lambskin coat* **3** a cotton or woollen fabric resembling this skin

lamb's lettuce *n* another name for **corn salad**

lamb's-quarters *n, pl* lamb's-quarters a US name for **fat hen**

lamb's tails *pl n* the pendulous catkins of the hazel tree

lamb's wool *n* **a** a fine soft wool obtained from a lamb at its first shearing **b** (*as modifier*): *lamb's-wool jumpers*

LAMDA (ˈlæmdə) *n acronym for* London Academy of Music and Dramatic Art

lame¹ (leɪm) *adj* **1** disabled or crippled in the legs or feet **2** painful or weak: *a lame back* **3** weak; unconvincing: *a lame excuse* **4** not effective or enthusiastic: *a lame try* **5** US slang conventional or uninspiring ▷ *vb* **6** (*tr*) to make lame [Old English *lama*; related to Old Norse *lami*, German *lahm*] ▷ ˈlamely *adv* ▷ ˈlameness *n*

lame² (leɪm) *n* one of the overlapping metal plates used in armour after about 1330; splint [c16 via Old French from Latin *lāmina* a thin plate, LAMINA]

lamé (ˈlɑːmeɪ) *n* **a** a fabric of silk, cotton, or wool interwoven with threads of metal **b** (*as modifier*): *a gold lamé gown* [from French, from Old French *lame* gold or silver thread, thin plate, from Latin *lāmina* thin plate]

lamebrain (ˈleɪmˌbreɪn) *n informal* a stupid or slow-witted person

lamed (ˈlɑːmɪd; *Hebrew* ˈlɑːmɛd) *n* the 12th letter in the Hebrew alphabet (ל), transliterated as *l*. Also: **lamedh** (ˈlɑːmɛd) [from Hebrew, literally: ox goad (from its shape)]

lame duck *n* **1** a person or thing that is disabled or ineffectual **2** *stock exchange* a speculator who cannot discharge his liabilities **3** a company with a large workforce and high prestige that is unable to meet foreign competition without government support **4** US **a** an elected official or body of officials remaining in office in the interval between the election and inauguration of a successor **b** (*as modifier*): *a lame-duck president* **5** (*modifier*) US designating a term of office after which the officeholder will not run for re-election

lamella (ləˈmɛlə) *n, pl* -lae (-liː) *or* -las **1** a thin layer, plate, or membrane, esp any of the calcified layers of which bone is formed **2** *botany* **a** any of the spore-bearing gills of a mushroom **b** any of the membranes in a chloroplast **c** Also called: **middle lamella** a layer of pectin cementing together adjacent cells **3** one of a number of timber, metal, or concrete members connected along a pattern of intersecting diagonal lines to form a framed vaulted roof structure **4** any thin sheet of material or thin layer in a fluid [c17 New Latin, from Latin, diminutive of *lāmina* thin plate] ▷ laˈmellar *or* lamellate (ˈlæmɪˌleɪt, -lɪt, ləˈmɛleɪt, -lɪt) *or* lamellose (ləˈmɛləʊs, ˈlæmɪˌləʊs) *adj* ▷ laˈmellarly *or* lamellately *adv* ▷ ˈlamelˌlated *adj* ▷ ˌlamelˈlation *n* ▷ lamellosity (ˌlæmɛˈlɒsɪtɪ) *n*

lamelli- *combining form* indicating lamella or lamellae: *lamellibranch*

lamellibranch (ləˈmɛlɪˌbræŋk) *n, adj* another word for **bivalve** (senses 1, 2) [c19 from New Latin *lamellibranchia* plate-gilled (animals); see LAMELLA, BRANCHIA] ▷ laˌmelliˈbranchiate *adj, n*

lamellicorn (ləˈmɛlɪˌkɔːn) *n* **1** any beetle of the superfamily *Lamellicornia*, having flattened terminal plates to the antennae: includes the scarabs and stag beetles ▷ *adj* **2** of, relating to, or belonging to the *Lamellicornia* **3** designating antennae with platelike terminal segments [c19 from New Latin *Lamellicornia* plate-horned (animals)]

lamelliform (ləˈmɛlɪˌfɔːm) *adj* shaped like a lamella; platelike: *lamelliform antennae*

lamellirostral (ləˌmɛlɪˈrɒstrəl) *or* **lamellirostrate** (ləˌmɛlɪˈrɒstreɪt) *adj* (of ducks, geese, etc) having a bill fringed with thin plates on the inner edge for straining water from food [c19 from New Latin *lāmellirostris*, from LAMELLA + *rostrum* beak]

lament (ləˈmɛnt) *vb* **1** to feel or express sorrow, remorse, or regret (for or over) ▷ *n* **2** an expression of sorrow **3** a poem or song in which a death is lamented [c16 from Latin *lāmentum*] ▷ laˈmenter *n* ▷ laˈmentingly *adv*

lamentable (ˈlæməntəbᵊl) *adj* **1** wretched, deplorable, or distressing **2** an archaic word for mournful. > ˈlamentableness *n* > ˈlamentably *adv*

lamentation (ˌlæmɛnˈteɪʃən) *n* **1** a lament; expression of sorrow **2** the act of lamenting

Lamentations (ˌlæmɛnˈteɪʃənz) *n (functioning as singular)* **1** a book of the Old Testament, traditionally ascribed to the prophet Jeremiah, lamenting the destruction of Jerusalem **2** a musical setting of these poems

lamented (ləˈmɛntɪd) *adj* grieved for or regretted (often in the phrase **late lamented**): *our late lamented employer* > laˈmentedly *adv*

lamia (ˈleɪmɪə) *n, pl* -mias *or* -miae (-mɪˌiː) **1** *classical myth* one of a class of female monsters depicted with a snake's body and a woman's head and breasts **2** a vampire or sorceress [c14 via Latin from Greek *Lamia*]

lamina (ˈlæmɪnə) *n, pl* -nae (-ˌniː) *or* -nas **1** a thin plate or layer, esp of bone or mineral **2** *botany* the flat blade of a leaf, petal, or thallus [c17 New Latin, from Latin: thin plate] > ˈlaminar *or* laminose (ˈlæmɪˌnəʊs, -ˌnəʊz) *adj*

laminar flow *n* nonturbulent motion of a fluid in which parallel layers have different velocities relative to each other. Compare **turbulent flow** See also **streamline flow**

laminaria (ˌlæmɪˈnɛərɪə) *n* any brown seaweed of the genus *Laminaria*, having large fluted leathery fronds [c19 genus name formed from Latin *lamina* plate]

laminarin (ˌlæmɪˈnɑːrɪn) *n* a carbohydrate, consisting of repeated glucose units, that is the main storage product of brown algae [c20 from LAMINAR(IA) + -IN]

laminate *vb* (ˈlæmɪˌneɪt) **1** *(tr)* to make (material in sheet form) by bonding together two or more thin sheets **2** to split or be split into thin sheets **3** *(tr)* to beat, form, or press (material, esp metal) into thin sheets **4** *(tr)* to cover or overlay with a thin sheet of material ▷ *n* (ˈlæmɪˌneɪt, -nɪt) **5** a material made by bonding together two or more sheets ▷ *adj* (ˈlæmɪˌneɪt, -nɪt) **6** having or composed of lamina; laminated [c17 from New Latin *lāminātus* plated] > laminable (ˈlæmɪnəbᵊl) *adj* > ˈlamiˌnator *n*

laminated (ˈlæmɪˌneɪtɪd) *adj* **1** composed of thin sheets (of plastic, wood, etc) superimposed and bonded together by synthetic resins, usually under heat and pressure **2** covered with a thin protective layer of plastic or synthetic resin **3** another word for **laminate** (sense 6)

lamination (ˌlæmɪˈneɪʃən) *n* **1** the act of laminating or the state of being laminated **2** a layered structure **3** a layer; lamina **4** one of a set of iron plates forming the core of an electrical transformer **5** *geology* laminar stratification, typically shown by shales

laminectomy (ˌlæmɪˈnɛktəmɪ) *n, pl* -mies surgical incision into the backbone to gain access to the spinal cord. Also called: **rachiotomy**

lamington (ˈlæmɪŋtən) *n Austral and NZ* a cube of sponge cake coated in chocolate and dried coconut [c20 (in the earlier sense: a homburg hat): named after Baron *Lamington*, governor of Queensland (1896–1901)]

laminitis (ˌlæmɪˈnaɪtɪs) *n* inflammation of the laminated tissue structure to which the hoof is attached, esp in horses and cattle. Also called: **founder** [c19 from New Latin, from LAMINA + -ITIS]

Lammas (ˈlæməs) *n* **1** *RC Church* Aug 1, held as a feast, commemorating St Peter's miraculous deliverance from prison **2** Also called: **Lammas Day** the same day formerly observed in England as a harvest festival. In Scotland Lammas is a quarter day [Old English *hlāfmæsse* loaf mass]

Lammastide (ˈlæməsˌtaɪd) *n archaic* the season of Lammas

lammergeier *or* **lammergeyer** (ˈlæməˌɡaɪə) *n* a rare vulture, *Gypaetus barbatus*, of S Europe, Africa, and Asia, with dark wings, a pale breast, and black feathers around the bill: family *Accipitridae* (hawks). Also called: **bearded vulture**, (archaic) **ossifrage** [c19 from German *Lämmergeier*, from *Lämmer* lambs + *Geier* vulture]

lamp (læmp) *n* **1 a** any of a number of devices that produce illumination: *an electric lamp; a gas lamp; an oil lamp* **b** *(in combination)*: *lampshade* **2** a device for holding one or more electric light bulbs: *a table lamp* **3** a vessel in which a liquid fuel is burned to supply illumination **4** any of a variety of devices that produce radiation, esp for therapeutic purposes: *an ultraviolet lamp* [c13 *lampe*, via Old French from Latin *lampas*, from Greek, from *lampein* to shine]

lampas¹ (ˈlæmpəs), **lampers** (ˈlæmpəz) *n* a swelling of the mucous membrane of the hard palate of horses [c16 from Old French; origin obscure]

lampas² (ˈlæmpəs) *n* an ornate damask-like cloth of cotton or silk and cotton, used in upholstery [c14 (a kind of crepe): probably from Middle Dutch *lampers*]

lampblack (ˈlæmpˌblæk) *n* a finely divided form of almost pure carbon produced by the incomplete combustion of organic compounds, such as natural gas, used in making carbon electrodes and dynamo brushes and as a pigment

lamp chimney *n* a glass tube that surrounds the wick in an oil lamp

Lampedusa (ˌlæmpɪˈdjuːzə) *n* an island in the Mediterranean, between Malta and Tunisia. Area: about 21 sq km (8 sq miles)

lamper eel (ˈlæmpə) *n* another name for **lamprey** [c19 *lamper*, variant of LAMPREY]

lampern (ˈlæmpən) *n* a migratory European lamprey, *Lampetra fluviatilis*, that spawns in rivers. Also called: **river lamprey** [c14 *laumprun*, from Old French, from *lampreie* LAMPREY]

lampion (ˈlæmpɪən) *n* an oil-burning lamp [c19 from French via Italian *lampione*, from Old French *lampe* LAMP]

lamplighter (ˈlæmpˌlaɪtə) *n* **1** (formerly) a person who lit and extinguished street lamps, esp gas ones **2** *chiefly US and Canadian* any of various devices used to light lamps

lampoon (læmˈpuːn) *n* **1** a satire in prose or verse ridiculing a person, literary work, etc ▷ *vb* **2** *(tr)* to attack or satirize in a lampoon [c17 from French *lampon*, perhaps from *lampons* let us drink (frequently used as a refrain in poems)] > lamˈpooner *or* lamˈpoonist *n* > lamˈpoonery *n*

lamppost (ˈlæmpˌpəʊst) *n* a post supporting a lamp, esp in a street

lamprey (ˈlæmprɪ) *n* any eel-like cyclostome vertebrate of the family *Petromyzonidae*, having a round sucking mouth for clinging to and feeding on the blood of other animals. Also called: **lamper eel** See also **sea lamprey** [c13 from Old French *lamproie*, from Late Latin *lamprēda*; origin obscure]

lamprophyre (ˈlæmprəˌfaɪə) *n* any of a group of basic igneous rocks consisting of feldspathoids and ferromagnesian minerals, esp biotite: occurring as dykes and minor intrusions [c19 from Greek *lampros* bright + -*phyre*, from PORPHYRY]

lamp shell *n* another name for a **brachiopod** [c19 from its likeness in shape to an ancient Roman oil lamp]

lamp standard *n* a tall metal or concrete post supporting a street lamp

LAN *abbreviation for* **local area network**

lanai (lɑːˈnɑːɪ, ləˈnaɪ) *n* a Hawaiian word for veranda

Lanai (lɑːˈnɑːɪ, ləˈnaɪ) *n* an island in central Hawaii, west of Maui Island. Pop: 3193 (2000). Area: 363 sq km (140 sq miles)

Lanarkshire (ˈlænəkˌʃɪə, -ʃə) *n* a historical county of S Scotland: became part of Strathclyde region in 1975; since 1996 administered by the council areas of North Lanarkshire, South Lanarkshire, and Glasgow

lanate (ˈleɪneɪt) *or* **lanose** (ˈleɪnəʊs, -nəʊz) *adj biology* having or consisting of a woolly covering or hairs [c18 from Latin *lānātus*, from *lāna* wool]

Lancashire (ˈlæŋkəˌʃɪə, -ʃə) *n* **1** a county of NW England, on the Irish Sea: became a county

palatine in 1351 and a duchy attached to the Crown; much reduced in size after the 1974 boundary changes, losing the Furness district to Cumbria and much of the south to Greater Manchester, Merseyside, and Cheshire: Blackburn with Darwen and Blackpool became independent unitary authorities in 1998. It was traditionally a cotton textiles manufacturing region. Administrative centre: Preston. Pop (excluding unitary authorities): 1 147 000 (2003 est). Area (excluding unitary authorities): 2889 sq km (1115 sq miles). Abbreviation: **Lancs 2** a mild whitish-coloured cheese with a crumbly texture

Lancashire heeler *n* a small sturdy dog of a breed with a short thick black or liver-coloured coat with tan markings, often used for herding cattle

Lancaster (ˈlæŋkəstə) *n* a city in NW England, former county town of Lancashire, on the River Lune: castle (built on the site of a Roman camp); university (1964). Pop: 45 952 (2001)

Lancastrian (læŋˈkæstrɪən) *n* **1** a native or resident of Lancashire or Lancaster **2** an adherent of the house of Lancaster in the Wars of the Roses. Compare **Yorkist** ▷ *adj* **3** of or relating to Lancashire or Lancaster **4** of or relating to the house of Lancaster

lance (lɑːns) *n* **1** a long weapon with a pointed head used by horsemen to unhorse or injure an opponent **2** a similar weapon used for hunting, whaling, etc **3** *surgery* another name for **lancet 4** short for **sand lance** (another name for **sand eel**) ▷ *vb (tr)* **5** to pierce (an abscess or boil) with a lancet to drain off pus **6** to pierce with or as if with a lance [c13 *launce*, from Old French *lance*, from Latin *lancea*]

lance corporal *n* a noncommissioned officer of the lowest rank in the British Army

lancejack (ˈlɑːnsˌdʒæk) *n Brit military slang* a lance corporal

lancelet (ˈlɑːnslɪt) *n* any of several marine animals of the genus *Branchiostoma* (formerly *Amphioxus*), esp *B. lanceolatus*, that are closely related to the vertebrates: subphylum *Cephalochordata* (cephalochordates). Also called: **amphioxus** [c19 referring to the slender shape]

Lancelot (ˈlɑːnslət) *n* (in Arthurian legend) one of the Knights of the Round Table; the lover of Queen Guinevere

lanceolate (ˈlɑːnsɪəˌleɪt, -lɪt) *adj* narrow and tapering to a point at each end: *lanceolate leaves* [c18 from Late Latin *lanceolātus*, from *lanceola* small LANCE]

lancer (ˈlɑːnsə) *n* **1** (formerly) a cavalryman armed with a lance **2 a** a member of a regiment retaining such a title **b** *(plural; capital when part of a name)* the 21st Lancers ▷ See also **lancers**

lance rest *n* **1** a hinged bracket on the breastplate of a medieval horseman on which the lance was rested in a charge **2** a similar structure on a knight's saddle

lancers (ˈlɑːnsəz) *n (functioning as singular)* **1** a quadrille for eight or sixteen couples **2** a piece of music composed for this dance

lance sergeant *n* a corporal acting as a sergeant, usually on a temporary basis and without additional pay

lancet (ˈlɑːnsɪt) *n* **1** Also called: **lance** a pointed surgical knife with two sharp edges **2** short for **lancet arch** *or* **lancet window** [c15 *lancette*, from Old French: small LANCE]

lancet arch *n* a narrow acutely pointed arch having two centres of equal radii. Sometimes shortened to: **lancet** Also called: **acute arch**, **Gothic arch**, **pointed arch**, **ogive**

lanceted (ˈlɑːnsɪtɪd) *adj architect* having one or more lancet arches or windows

lancet fish *n* either of two deep-sea teleost fishes, *Alepisaurus ferox* or *A. borealis*, having a long body with a long sail-like dorsal fin: family *Alepisauridae*

lancet window *n* a narrow window having a lancet arch. Sometimes shortened to: **lancet**

lancewood ('lɑːnsˌwʊd) *n* **1** any of various tropical trees, esp *Oxandra lanceolata*, yielding a tough elastic wood: family *Annonaceae* **2** the wood of any of these trees **3** Also called: **horoeka** a New Zealand forest tree, *Pseudopanax crassifolius*, with a small round head and a slender trunk

Lanchow or **Lan-chou** ('læn'tʃaʊ) *n* a variant transliteration of the Chinese name for **Lanzhou**

lancinate ('lɑːnsɪˌneɪt) *adj* (esp of pain) sharp or cutting [c17 from Latin *lancinātus* pierced, rent; related to *lacer* mangled] > ˌlanciˈnation *n*

Lancs (læŋks) *abbreviation for* Lancashire

land (lænd) *n* **1** the solid part of the surface of the earth as distinct from seas, lakes, etc. Related adj: **terrestrial 2 a** ground, esp with reference to its use, quality, etc **b** (*in combination*): *land-grabber* **3** rural or agricultural areas as contrasted with urban ones **4** farming as an occupation or way of life **5** *law* **a** any tract of ground capable of being owned as property, together with any buildings on it, extending above and below the surface **b** any hereditament, tenement, or other interest; realty **6 a** a country, region, or area **b** the people of a country, etc **7** a realm, sphere, or domain **8** *economics* the factor of production consisting of all natural resources **9** the unindented part of a grooved surface, esp one of the ridges inside a rifle bore **10** how the land lies the prevailing conditions or state of affairs ▷ *vb* **11** to transfer (something) or go from a ship or boat to the shore: *land the cargo* **12** (*intr*) to come to or touch shore **13** to come down or bring (something) down to earth after a flight or jump **14** to come or bring to some point, condition, or state **15** (*tr*) *angling* to retrieve (a hooked fish) from the water **16** (*tr*) *informal* to win or obtain: *to land a job* **17** (*tr*) *informal* to deliver (a blow) ▷ See also **lands, land up, land with** [Old English; compare Old Norse, Gothic *land*, Old High German *lant*] > ˈlandless *adj* > ˈlandlessness *n*

Land German (lant) *n, pl Länder* ('lɛndər) **a** any of the federal states of Germany **b** any of the provinces of Austria

land agent *n* **1** a person who administers a landed estate and its tenancies **2** a person who acts as an agent for the sale of land > **land agency** *n*

landammann ('lændəmən) *n* (*sometimes capital*) the chairman of the governing council in any of several Swiss cantons [c18 Swiss German, from *Land* country + *Ammann*, from *Amt* office + *Mann* MAN]

landau ('lændɔː) *n* a four-wheeled carriage, usually horse-drawn, with two folding hoods that meet over the middle of the passenger compartment [c18 named after *Landau* (a town in Bavaria), where it was first made]

landaulet or **landaulette** (ˌlændɔːˈlɛt) *n* **1** a small landau **2** *US* an early type of car with a folding hood over the passenger seats and an open driver's seat

land bank *n* a bank that issues banknotes on the security of property

landboard ('lændˌbɔːd) *n* a narrow board, with wheels larger than those on a skateboard, usually ridden while standing > ˈlandˌboarding *n*

land bridge *n* (in zoogeography) a connecting tract of land between two continents, enabling animals to pass from one continent to the other

land crab *n* any of various crabs, esp of the tropical family *Gecarcinidae*, that are adapted to a partly terrestrial life

Landdrost ('lændrɒst) *n South African history* the chief magistrate of a district [c18 Afrikaans, from Dutch *land* country + *drost* sheriff, bailiff]

landed ('lændɪd) *adj* **1** owning land: *landed gentry* **2** consisting of or including land: *a landed estate*

landed immigrant *n Canadian* a former term for **permanent resident**

lander ('lændə) *n* a spacecraft designed to land on a planet or other body. Compare **orbiter**

Landes (*French* lãd) *n* **1** a department of SW France, in Aquitaine region. Capital: Mont-de-Marsan. Pop: 341 254 (2003 est). Area: 9364 sq km (3652 sq miles) **2** a region of SW France, on the Bay of Biscay: occupies most of the Landes department and parts of Gironde and Lot-et-Garonne; consists chiefly of the most extensive forest in France. Area: 14 000 sq km (5400 sq miles)

Landeshauptmann ('lɑːndɪsˌhauptmən) *n* the head of government in an Austrian state [c20 from German, from *Land* country + *Hauptmann* leader]

landfall ('lændˌfɔːl) *n* **1** the act of sighting or nearing land, esp from the sea **2** the land sighted or neared

landfill ('lændˌfɪl) *n* **a** disposal of waste material by burying it under layers of earth **b** (*as modifier*): *landfill sites*

land forces *pl n* armed forces serving on land

landform ('lændˌfɔːm) *n geology* any natural feature of the earth's surface, such as valleys and mountains

land girl *n* a girl or woman who does farm work, esp in wartime

landgrab ('lændˌgræb) *n informal* a sudden attempt to establish ownership of or copyright on something in advance of competitors [c20 from the competition to stake claims to available land in 19th-century America]

land grant *n* **1** *US and Canadian* a grant of public land to a college, railway, etc **2** (*modifier*) *US* designating a state university established with such a grant

landgrave ('lændˌgreɪv) *n german history* **1** (from the 13th century to 1806) a count who ruled over a specified territory **2** (after 1806) the title of any of various sovereign princes in central Germany [c16 via German, from Middle High German *lantgrāve*, from *lant* land + *grāve* count]

landgraviate (lænd'greɪvɪɪt, -ˌeɪt) or **landgravate** ('lændgrəˌveɪt) *n* the domain or position of a landgrave or landgravine

landgravine ('lændgrəˌviːn) *n* **1** the wife or widow of a landgrave **2** a woman who held the rank of landgrave

land-holder *n* a person who owns or occupies land > ˈland-ˌholding *adj, n*

landing ('lændɪŋ) *n* **1 a** the act of coming to land, esp after a flight or sea voyage **b** (*as modifier*): *landing place* **2** a place of disembarkation **3** the floor area at the top of a flight of stairs or between two flights of stairs

landing beacon *n* a radio transmitter that emits a landing beam

landing beam *n* a radio beam transmitted from a landing field to enable aircraft to make an instrument landing

landing craft *n military* any small vessel designed for the landing of troops and equipment on beaches

landing field *n* an area of land on which aircraft land and from which they take off

landing gear *n* another name for **undercarriage** (sense 1)

landing net *n angling* a loose long-handled net on a triangular frame for lifting hooked fish from the water

landing speed *n* the minimum air speed at which an aircraft lands safely

landing stage *n* a platform used for landing goods and passengers from a vessel

landing strip *n* another name for **airstrip**

landlady ('lændˌleɪdɪ) *n, pl* **-dies** **1** a woman who owns and leases property **2** a landlord's wife **3** a woman who owns or runs a lodging house, pub, etc

ländler (*German* 'lɛntlər) *n* **1** an Austrian country dance in which couples spin and clap **2** a piece of music composed for or in the rhythm of this dance, in three-four time [German, from dialect *Landl* Upper Austria]

land line *n* a telecommunications wire or cable laid over land

landlocked ('lændˌlɒkt) *adj* **1** (of a country) completely surrounded by land **2** (esp of lakes) completely or almost completely surrounded by land **3** (esp of certain salmon) living in fresh water that is permanently isolated from the sea

landloper ('lændˌləʊpə) *n Scot* a vagabond or vagrant [c16 from Dutch, from LAND + *loopen* to run, LEAP]

landlord ('lændˌlɔːd) *n* **1** a man who owns and leases property **2** a man who owns or runs a lodging house, pub, etc **3** *Brit archaic* the lord of an estate

landlordism ('lændlɔːˌdɪzəm) *n* the system by which land under private ownership is rented for a fixed sum to tenants

landlubber ('lændˌlʌbə) *n nautical* any person having no experience at sea [c18 LAND + LUBBER]

landmark ('lændˌmɑːk) *n* **1** a prominent or well-known object in or feature of a particular landscape **2** an important or unique decision, event, fact, discovery, etc **3** a boundary marker or signpost

landmass ('lændˌmæs) *n* a large continuous area of land, as opposed to seas or islands

land mine *n military* an explosive charge placed in the ground, usually detonated by stepping or driving on it

land office *n US and Canadian* an office that administers the sale of public land

land-office business *n US and Canadian informal* a booming or thriving business

land of milk and honey *n Old Testament* the land of natural fertility promised to the Israelites by God (Ezekiel 20:6) **2** any fertile land, state, etc

land of Nod *n* **1** *Old Testament* a region to the east of Eden to which Cain went after he had killed Abel (Genesis 4:14) **2** an imaginary land of sleep

Land of the Midnight Sun *n* **1** any land north of the Arctic Circle, which has continuous daylight throughout the short summer, esp N parts of Norway, Sweden, and Finland **2** an informal name for **Lapland**

landowner ('lændˌəʊnə) *n* a person who owns land > ˈlandˌownerˌship *n* > ˈlandˌowning *n, adj*

L & P NZ ▷ *abbreviation for* Lemon and Paeroa: a soda water drink, originally from the town of Paeroa

land-poor *adj* owning much unprofitable land and lacking the money to maintain its fertility or improve it

landrace ('lændˌreɪs) *n* **1** *chiefly Brit* a white very long-bodied lop-eared breed of pork pig **2** a breed of Finnish sheep known for multiple births **3** *botany* an ancient or primitive cultivated variety of a crop plant [from Danish, literally: land race]

land rail *n* another name for **corncrake**

land reform *n* the redistributing of large agricultural holdings among the landless

Landrost ('lændrɒst) *n* a variant spelling of **Landdrost**

lands (lændz) *pl n* **1** holdings in land **2** *South African* the part of a farm on which crops are grown

land sailing *n* the sport or activity of driving wheeled sail-powered vehicles across land, esp beaches or dry lakes

landscape ('lændˌskeɪp) *n* **1** an extensive area of land regarded as being visually distinct: *ugly slagheaps dominated the landscape* **2** a painting, drawing, photograph, etc, depicting natural scenery **3 a** the genre including such pictures **b** (*as modifier*): *landscape painter* **4** the distinctive features of a given area of intellectual activity, regarded as an integrated whole: *the landscape of the European imagination* ▷ *adj* **5** *printing* **a** (of a publication or an illustration in a publication) of greater width than height. Compare **portrait** (sense 3) **b** (of a page) carrying an illustration or table printed at right angles to the normal text ▷ *vb* **6** (*tr*) to improve the natural features of (a garden, park, etc), as by creating contoured features and planting trees **7** (*intr*) to work as a

landscape gardener [C16 *landskip* (originally a term in painting), from Middle Dutch *lantscap* region; related to Old English *landscipe* tract of land, Old High German *lantscaf* region]

landscape gardening *n* the art of laying out grounds in imitation of natural scenery. Also called: **landscape architecture** ▷ **landscape gardener** *n*

landscapist ('lænd,skeɪpɪst) *n* a painter of landscapes

Land's End *n* a granite headland in SW England, on the SW coast of Cornwall: the westernmost point of England

landshark ('lænd,ʃɑːk) *n informal* a person who makes inordinate profits by buying and selling land

Landshut (*German* 'lantshuːt) *n* a city in SE Germany, in Bavaria: Trausnitz castle (13th century); manufacturing centre for machinery and chemicals. Pop: 60 282 (2003 est)

landside ('lænd,saɪd) *n* **1** the part of an airport farthest from the aircraft, the boundary of which is the security check, customs, passport control, etc. Compare **airside 2** the part of a plough that slides along the face of the furrow wall on the opposite side to the mouldboard

landsknecht ('læntskə,nɛkt) *n* a mercenary foot soldier in late 15th-, 16th-, and 17th-century Europe, esp a German pikeman [German, literally: landknight]

landslide ('lænd,slaɪd) *n* **1** Also called: **landslip a** the sliding of a large mass of rock material, soil, etc, down the side of a mountain or cliff **b** the material dislodged in this way **2 a** an overwhelming electoral victory **b** (*as modifier*): *a landslide win*

Landsmål ('lɑːntsmoːl) *n* another name for **Nynorsk**

landsman¹ ('lændzmən) *n, pl* -men **1** a person who works or lives on land, as distinguished from a seaman **2** a person with no experience at sea

landsman² ('lændzmən) *n, pl* -men a Jewish compatriot from the same area of origin as another [from Yiddish]

Landsturm *German* ('lantʃtʊrm) *n* (in German-speaking countries) **1** a reserve force; militia **2** a general levy in wartime [C19 literally: landstorm; originally a summons to arms by means of storm-warning bells]

Landtag ('lɑːnt,tɑːk) *n* **1** the legislative assembly of each state in present-day Germany and Austria **2** the estates of principalities in medieval and modern Germany **3** the assembly of numerous states in 19th-century Germany [C16 German: land assembly]

land tax *n* (formerly) a tax payable annually by virtue of ownership of land, abolished in Britain in 1963

land up *vb* (*adverb, usually intr*) to arrive or cause to arrive at a final point: *after a summer in Europe, he suddenly landed up at home*

landwaiter ('lænd,weɪtə) *n* an officer of the Custom House

landward ('lændwəd) *adj* **1** lying, facing, or moving towards land **2** in the direction of the land ▷ *adv* **3** a variant of **landwards**

landwards ('lændwədz) *or* **landward** *adv* towards land

land with *vb* (*tr, preposition*) to give to, so as to put in difficulties; cause to be burdened with: *why did you land me with this extra work?*

land yacht *n* a three-wheeled recreational vehicle with a sail, used on land and propelled by wind power

lane¹ (leɪn) *n* **1 a** a narrow road or way between buildings, hedges, fences, etc **b** (*capital as part of a street name*). *Drury Lane* **2 a** any of the parallel strips into which the carriageway of a major road or motorway is divided **b** any narrow well-defined route or course for ships or aircraft **3** one of the parallel strips into which a running track or swimming bath is divided for races **4** the long strip of wooden flooring down which balls are bowled in a bowling alley [Old English *lane, lanu,* of Germanic origin; related to Middle Dutch *lāne* lane]

lane² (leɪn) *adj Scot dialect* **1** lone or alone **2** (on) one's lane on one's own

lang (læŋ) *adj* a Scot word for **long**

langar ('lʌŋɑː) *n Sikhism* **a** the dining hall in a gurdwara **b** the food served, given to all regardless of caste or religion as a gesture of equality [Punjabi]

langer ('læŋə) *n Irish slang* **1** another word for **penis 2** *derogatory* a disagreeable person [c20 possibly from LANYARD]

langered ('læŋəd) *adj Irish slang* intoxicated; drunk

Langerhans islets ('læŋə,hæns) *or* **islands** *n anatomy* See **islets of Langerhans**

langlauf ('lɑːŋ,laʊf) *n* cross-country skiing [German, literally: long run] ▷ **langläufer** ('lɑːŋ,lɔɪfə) *n*

Langobard ('læŋgə,bɑːd) *n* a less common name for a **Lombard** [C18 from Late Latin *Langobardicus* Lombard]

Langobardic (,læŋgə'bɑːdɪk) *n* **1** the language of the ancient Lombards: a dialect of Old High German ▷ *adj* **2** of or relating to the Lombards or their language

langouste ('lɒŋguːst, lɒŋ'guːst) *n* another name for the **spiny lobster** [French, from Old Provençal *langosta,* perhaps from Latin *lōcusta* lobster, locust]

langoustine (,lɒŋguːs'tiːn) *n* a large prawn or small lobster [from French, diminutive of LANGOUSTE]

langrage ('læŋgrɪdʒ), **langrel** ('læŋgrəl) *or* **langridge** *n* shot consisting of scrap iron packed into a case, formerly used in naval warfare [c18 of unknown origin]

Langres Plateau (*French* lɑːgrə) *n* a calcareous plateau of E France north of Dijon between the Seine and the Saône, reaching over 580 m (1900 ft): forms a watershed between rivers flowing to the Mediterranean and to the English Channel

langsyne (,læŋ'səɪn, -'saɪn) *Scot* ▷ *adv* **1** long ago; long since ▷ *n* **2** times long past, esp those fondly remembered. See also **auld lang syne** [c16 Scottish: long since]

language ('læŋgwɪdʒ) *n* **1** a system for the expression of thoughts, feelings, etc, by the use of spoken sounds or conventional symbols **2** the faculty for the use of such systems, which is a distinguishing characteristic of man as compared with other animals **3** the language of a particular nation or people: *the French language* **4** any other systematic or nonsystematic means of communicating, such as gesture or animal sounds: *the language of love* **5** the specialized vocabulary used by a particular group: *medical language* **6** a particular manner or style of verbal expression: *your language is disgusting* **7** *computing* See **programming language 8** speak the same language to communicate with understanding because of common background, values, etc [c13 from Old French *langage,* ultimately from Latin *lingua* tongue]

language laboratory *n* a room equipped with tape recorders, etc, for learning foreign languages

language school *n* a school for the teaching of a foreign language or languages

langue (lɑːŋg) *n linguistics* language considered as an abstract system or a social institution, being the common possession of a speech community. Compare **parole** (sense 5) [c19 from French: language]

langue de chat ('lɑːŋ də 'ʃɑː) *n* **1** a flat sweet finger-shaped biscuit **2** a piece of chocolate having the same shape [French: cat's tongue]

Languedoc (*French* lɑːgdɔk) *n* **1** a former province of S France, lying between the foothills of the Pyrenees and the River Rhône: formed around the countship of Toulouse in the 13th century; important production of bulk wines **2** a wine from this region

langue d'oc *French* (lɑːg dɔk) *n* the group of medieval French dialects spoken in S France: often regarded as including Provençal. Compare **langue d'oïl** [literally: language of *oc* (the Provençal form for *yes*), ultimately from Latin *hoc* this]

Languedoc-Roussillon (*French* lɑːgdɔkrusijɔ̃) *n* a region of S France, on the Gulf of Lions: consists of the departments of Lozère, Gard, Hérault, Aude, and Pyrénées-Orientales; mainly mountainous with a coastal plain

langue d'oïl *French* (lɑːg dɔj) *n* the group of medieval French dialects spoken in France north of the Loire; the medieval basis of modern French [literally: language of *oïl* (the northern form for *yes*), ultimately from Latin *hoc ille (fecit)* this he (did)]

languet ('læŋgwɛt) *n rare* anything resembling a tongue in shape or function [c15 from Old French *languette,* diminutive of *langue* tongue]

languid ('læŋgwɪd) *adj* **1** without energy or spirit **2** without interest or enthusiasm **3** sluggish; inactive [c16 from Latin *languidus,* from *languēre* to languish] ▷ **languidly** *adv* ▷ **languidness** *n*

languish ('læŋgwɪʃ) *vb* (*intr*) **1** to lose or diminish in strength or energy **2** (often foll by *for*) to be listless with desire; pine **3** to suffer deprivation, hardship, or neglect: *to languish in prison* **4** to put on a tender, nostalgic, or melancholic expression [C14 *languishen,* from Old French *languiss-,* stem of *languir,* ultimately from Latin *languēre*] ▷ **languishing** *adj* ▷ **languishingly** *adv* ▷ **languishment** *n*

languor ('læŋgə) *n* **1** physical or mental laziness or weariness **2** a feeling of dreaminess and relaxation **3** oppressive silence or stillness [C14 *langour,* via Old French from Latin *languor,* from *languēre* to languish; the modern spelling is directly from Latin]

languorous ('læŋgərəs) *adj* **1** characterized by or producing languor **2** another word for **languid** ▷ **languorously** *adv* ▷ **languorousness** *n*

langur (lʌŋ'gʊə) *n* any of various agile arboreal Old World monkeys of the genus *Presbytis* and related genera, of S and SE Asia having a slender body, long tail and hands, and long hair surrounding the face [Hindi, perhaps related to Sanskrit *lāngūla* tailed]

laniard ('lænjəd) *n* a variant spelling of **lanyard**

laniary ('læniərɪ) *adj* **1** (esp of canine teeth) adapted for tearing ▷ *n, pl* -aries **2** a tooth adapted for tearing [c19 from Latin *lanius* butcher, from *laniāre* to tear]

laniferous (lə'nɪfərəs) *or* **lanigerous** (lə'nɪdʒərəs) *adj* bearing wool or fleecy hairs resembling wool [c17 from Latin *lānifer,* from *lāna* wool]

La Niña (læ 'niːnjə) *n meteorol* a cooling of the eastern tropical Pacific, occurring in certain years [c20 from Spanish: The Little Girl, to distinguish it from El Niño]

lank¹ (læŋk) *adj* **1** long and limp **2** thin or gaunt [Old English *hlanc* loose] ▷ **lankly** *adv* ▷ **lankness** *n*

lank² (læŋk) *adj, adv South African informal* a lot; a great deal [perhaps from Afrikaans *lank* long]

lanky ('læŋkɪ) *adj* **lankier, lankiest** tall, thin, and loose-jointed ▷ **lankily** *adv* ▷ **lankiness** *n*

lanner ('lænə) *n* **1** a large falcon, *Falco biarmicus,* of Mediterranean regions, N Africa, and S Asia **2** *falconry* the female of this falcon. Compare **lanneret** [c15 from Old French *(faucon) lanier* cowardly (falcon), from Latin *lanārius* wool worker, coward; referring to its sluggish flight and timid nature]

lanneret ('lænə,rɛt) *n* the male or tercel of the lanner falcon [c15 diminutive of LANNER]

lanolin ('lænəlɪn) *or* **lanoline** ('lænəlɪn, -,liːn) *n* a yellowish viscous substance extracted from wool, consisting of a mixture of esters of fatty acids: used in some ointments. Also called: **wool fat** [c19 via German from Latin *lāna* wool + *oleum* oil; see -IN] ▷ **lanolated** ('lænə,leɪtɪd) *adj*

lanose ('leɪnəʊs, -nəʊz) *adj* another word for

lanate [C19 from Latin *lānosus*] > **lanosity** (leɪˈnɒsɪtɪ) *n*

Lansing (ˈlænsɪŋ) *n* a city in S Michigan, on the Grand River: the state capital. Pop: 118 379 (2003 est)

Lansker line (ˈlænskə) *n* (in Pembrokeshire) the linguistic and ethnic division between the Welsh-speaking north and the English-speaking south [C19 from Pembrokeshire dialect *lansker* boundary]

lansquenet (ˈlænskəˌnɛt) *n* 1 a gambling game of chance 2 an archaic spelling of **landsknecht** [from French]

lantana (lænˈteɪnə, -ˈtɑː-) *n* any verbenaceous shrub or herbaceous plant of the tropical American genus *Lantana*, esp *L. camara*, having spikes or umbels of yellow or orange flowers. It has been widely introduced and is regarded as a troublesome weed in some places [C18 New Latin, from Italian dialect *lantana* wayfaring tree]

lantern (ˈlæntən) *n* 1 a light with a transparent or translucent protective case 2 a structure on top of a dome or roof having openings or windows to admit light or air 3 the upper part of a lighthouse that houses the light 4 *photog* short for **magic lantern** [C13 from Latin *lanterna*, from Greek *lamptēr* lamp, from *lampein* to shine]

lantern fish *n* any small deep-sea teleost fish of the family *Myctophidae*, having a series of luminescent spots along the body

lantern fly *n* any of various tropical insects of the homopterous family *Fulgoridae*, many species of which have a snoutlike process formerly thought to emit light

lantern jaw *n* (when *plural*, refers to upper and lower jaw; when *singular* usually to lower jaw) a long hollow jaw that gives the face a drawn appearance

lantern-jawed *adj* having a long hollow jaw that gives the face a drawn appearance

lantern pinion *or* **wheel** *n* a type of gearwheel, now used only in clocks, consisting of two parallel circular discs connected by a number of pins running parallel to the axis

lantern slide *n* (formerly) a photographic slide for projection, used in a magic lantern

lanthanide (ˈlænθəˌnaɪd) *or* **lanthanon** (ˈlænθəˌnɒn) *n* any element of the lanthanide series. Also called: rare earth, rare-earth element [C19 from LANTHANUM + -IDE]

lanthanide series *n* a class of 15 chemically related elements with atomic numbers from 57 (lanthanum) to 71 (lutetium)

lanthanum (ˈlænθənəm) *n* a silvery-white ductile metallic element of the lanthanide series, occurring principally in bastnaesite and monazite: used in pyrophoric alloys, electronic devices, and in glass manufacture. Symbol: La; atomic no.: 57; atomic wt.: 138.9055; valency: 3; relative density: 6.145; melting pt.: 918°C; boiling pt.: 3464°C [C19 New Latin, from Greek *lanthanein* to lie unseen]

lanthorn (ˈlænt,hɔːn, ˈlæntən) *n* an archaic word for **lantern**

lanugo (ləˈnjuːɡəʊ) *n*, *pl* -gos a layer of fine hairs, esp the covering of the human fetus before birth [C17 from Latin: down, from *lāna* wool] > **lanuginous** (ləˈnjuːdʒɪnəs) *or* **laˈnugiˌnose** *adj* > **laˈnuginousness** *n*

Lanús (*Spanish* laˈnus) *n* a city in E Argentina: a S suburb of Buenos Aires. Pop: 466 755 (1991)

lanyard *or* **laniard** (ˈlænjəd) *n* 1 a cord worn around the neck, shoulder, etc, to hold something such as a whistle or knife 2 a similar but merely decorative cord worn as part of a military uniform 3 a cord with an attached hook used in firing certain types of cannon 4 *nautical* a line rove through deadeyes for extending or tightening standing rigging [C15 *lanyer*, from French *lanière*, from *lasne* strap, probably of Germanic origin]

Lanzarote (ˌlænzəˈrɒtɪ) *n* the most easterly of the Canary Islands; mountainous, with a volcanic landscape; tourism, fishing. Pop: 109 942 (2002

est). Area: 795 sq km (307 sq miles)

Lanzhou, Lanchow *or* **Lan-chou** (ˈlænˈdʒəʊ) *n* a city in N China, capital of Gansu province, on the Yellow River: situated on the main route between China and the West. op.: 1 788 000 (2005 est)

Lao (laʊ) *adj*, *n* another name for **Laotian**

LAO *international car registration for* Laos

Laoag (lɑːˈwɑːɡ) *n* a city in the N Philippines, on NW Luzon: trade centre for an agricultural region. Pop: 94 466 (2000)

Laocoon (leɪˈɒkəʊˌɒn) *n Greek myth* a priest of Apollo at Troy who warned the Trojans against the wooden horse left by the Greeks; killed with his twin sons by two sea serpents

Laodicea (ˌleɪəʊdɪˈsɪə) *n* the ancient name of several Greek cities in W Asia, notably of **Latakia**

laodicean (ˌleɪəʊdɪˈsɪən) *adj* 1 lukewarm and indifferent, esp in religious matters ▷ *n* 2 a person having a lukewarm attitude towards religious matters [C17 referring to the early Christians of Laodicea (Revelation 3:14–16)]

Laoighis (ˈliː) *n* a variant spelling of **Laois**

Laois (ˈliː) *n* a county of central Republic of Ireland, in Leinster province: formerly boggy but largely reclaimed for agriculture. County town: Portlaoise. Pop: 58 774 (2002). Area: 1719 sq km (664 sq miles). Also called: Laoighis, Leix Former name: Queen's County

Laomedon (leɪˈɒmɪˌdɒn) *n Greek myth* the founder and ruler of Troy, who cheated Apollo and Poseidon of their wage for constructing the city's walls; the father of Priam

Laos (laʊz, laʊs) *n* a republic in SE Asia: first united as the kingdom of Lan Xang ("million elephants") in 1353, after being a province of the Khmer Empire for about four centuries; made part of French Indochina in 1893 and gained independence in 1949; became a republic in 1975. It is generally forested and mountainous, with the Mekong River running almost the whole length of the W border. Official language: Laotian. Religion: Buddhist majority, tribal religions. Currency: kip. Capital: Vientiane. Pop: 5 787 000 (2004 est). Area: 236 800 sq km (91 429 sq miles). Official name: People's Democratic Republic of Laos

Laotian (ˈlaʊʃən) *or* **Lao** (laʊ) *n* 1 (*pl* Laotians, Lao *or* Laos) a member of a Buddhist people of Laos and NE Thailand, related to the Thais 2 the language of this people, closely related to Thai ▷ *adj* 3 of or relating to this people or their language or to Laos

lap¹ (læp) *n* 1 the area formed by the upper surface of the thighs of a seated person 2 Also called: lapful the amount held in one's lap 3 a protected place or environment: *in the lap of luxury* 4 any of various hollow or depressed areas, such as a hollow in the land 5 the part of one's clothing that covers the lap 6 drop in someone's lap give someone the responsibility of 7 in the lap of the gods beyond human control and power [Old English *læppa* flap; see LOBE, LAPPET, LOP²]

lap² (læp) *n* 1 one circuit of a racecourse or track 2 a stage or part of a journey, race, etc 3 a an overlapping part or projection b the extent of overlap 4 the length of material needed to go around an object 5 a rotating disc coated with fine abrasive for polishing gemstones 6 any device for holding a fine abrasive to polish materials 7 *metallurgy* a defect in rolled metals caused by the folding of a fin onto the surface 8 a sheet or band of fibres, such as cotton, prepared for further processing ▷ *vb* laps, lapping, lapped 9 (*tr*) to wrap or fold (around or over): *he lapped a bandage around his wrist* 10 (*tr*) to enclose or envelop in: *he lapped his wrist in a bandage* 11 to place or lie partly or completely over or project beyond 12 (*tr*; *usually passive*) to envelop or surround with comfort, love, etc: *lapped in luxury* 13 (*intr*) to be folded 14 (*tr*) to overtake (an opponent) in a race so as to be one or more circuits ahead 15 (*tr*) to polish or cut (a workpiece, gemstone, etc) with a

fine abrasive, esp to hone (mating metal parts) against each other with an abrasive 16 to form (fibres) into a sheet or band [C13 (in the sense: to wrap): probably from LAP¹] > **lapper** *n*

lap³ (læp) *vb* laps, lapping, lapped 1 (of small waves) to wash against (a shore, boat, etc), usually with light splashing sounds 2 (often foll by *up*) (esp of animals) to scoop (a liquid) into the mouth with the tongue ▷ *n* 3 the act or sound of lapping 4 a thin food for dogs or other animals ▷ See also **lap up** [Old English *lapian*; related to Old High German *laffan*, Latin *lambere*, Greek *laptein*] > **ˈlapper** *n*

La Palma (*Spanish* la ˈpalma) *n* an island in the N Atlantic, in the NW Canary Islands: administratively part of Spain. Chief town: Santa Cruz de la Palma. Pop: 85 547 (2002 est). Area: 725 sq km (280 sq miles)

laparoscope (ˈlæpərəˌskəʊp) *n* a medical instrument consisting of a tube that is inserted through the abdominal wall and illuminated to enable a doctor to view the internal organs [C19 (applied to various instruments used to examine the abdomen) and C20 (in the specific modern sense): from Greek *lapara* (see LAPAROTOMY) + -SCOPE] > ˌlaparoˈscopic *adj* > ˌlapaˈroscopy *n*

laparotomy (ˌlæpəˈrɒtəmɪ) *n*, *pl* -mies 1 surgical incision through the abdominal wall, esp to investigate the cause of an abdominal disorder 2 surgical incision into the loin [C19 from Greek *lapara* flank, from *laparos* soft + -TOMY]

La Paz (læ ˈpæz; *Spanish* la ˈpaθ) *n* a city in W Bolivia, at an altitude of 3600 m (12 000 ft): seat of government since 1898 (though Sucre is still the official capital); the country's largest city; founded in 1548 by the Spaniards; university (1830). Pop: 1 533 000 (2005 est)

lapboard (ˈlæpˌbɔːd) *n* a flat board that can be used on the lap as a makeshift table or desk

lap-chart *n motor racing* a log of every lap covered by each car in a race, showing the exact position throughout

lap dancing *n* a form of entertainment in which scantily dressed women dance erotically for individual members of the audience

lap dissolve *n films* the technique of allowing the end of one scene to overlap the beginning of the next scene by fading out the former while fading in the latter

lapdog (ˈlæpˌdɒg) *n* 1 a pet dog small and docile enough to be cuddled in the lap 2 *informal* a person who attaches himself to someone in admiration or infatuation

lapel (ləˈpɛl) *n* the continuation of the turned or folded back collar on a suit coat, jacket, etc [C18 from LAP¹] > laˈpelled *adj*

LaPerm (ləˈpɜːm) *n* a breed of medium-sized curly-haired cat with large ears

lapheld (ˈlæpˌhɛld) *adj* (esp of a personal computer) small enough to be used on one's lap; portable

lapidary (ˈlæpɪdərɪ) *n*, *pl* -daries 1 a person whose business is to cut, polish, set, or deal in gemstones ▷ *adj* 2 of or relating to gemstones or the work of a lapidary 3 Also: lapidarian (ˌlæpɪˈdɛərɪən) engraved, cut, or inscribed in a stone or gemstone 4 of sufficiently high quality to be engraved on a stone: *a lapidary inscription* [C14 from Latin *lapidārius*, from *lapid-*, *lapis* stone] > ˌlapiˈdarian *adj*

lapidate (ˈlæpɪˌdeɪt) *vb* (*tr*) *literary* 1 to pelt with stones 2 to kill by stoning [C17 from Latin *lapidāre*, from *lapis* stone] > ˌlapiˈdation *n*

lapidicolous (ˌlæpɪˈdɪkələs) *adj zoology* living under stones

lapidify (ləˈpɪdɪˌfaɪ) *vb* -fies, -fying, -fied to change into stone [C17 from French *lapidifier*, from Medieval Latin *lapidificāre*, ultimately from Latin *lapis* stone] > laˌpidifiˈcation *n*

lapillus (ləˈpɪləs) *n*, *pl* -li (-laɪ) a small piece of lava thrown from a volcano [C18 Latin: little stone]

lapis lazuli *or* **lazuli** (ˈlæpɪs) *n* 1 a brilliant blue variety of the mineral lazurite, used as a gemstone **2** the deep blue colour of lapis lazuli ▷ Also called: **lapis** [c14 from Latin *lapis* stone + Medieval Latin *lazulī*, from *lazulum*, from Arabic *lāzaward*, from Persian *lāzhuward*, of obscure origin]

Lapith ('læpıθ) *n, pl* **Lapithae** ('læpı,θi:) *or* **Lapiths** *Greek myth* a member of a people in Thessaly who at the wedding of their king, Pirithoüs, fought the drunken centaurs

lap joint *n* a joint made by placing one member over another and fastening them together. Also called: **lapped joint** ▷ '**lap-,jointed** *adj*

Laplace operator (læ'plɑ:s) *n maths* the operator $\partial^2/\partial x^2 + \partial^2/\partial y^2 + \partial^2/\partial z^2$. Symbol: ∇^2 Also called: **Laplacian** (lə'pleıʃən) [named after Pierre Simon, Marquis de *Laplace* (1749–1827), the French mathematician, physicist, and astronomer]

Lapland ('læp,lænd) *n* an extensive region of N Europe, mainly within the Arctic Circle: consists of the N parts of Norway, Sweden, Finland, and the Kola Peninsula of the extreme NW of Russia. Also called (informal): **Land of the Midnight Sun**

Laplander ('læp,lændə) *n* a native or inhabitant of Lapland

La Plata (*Spanish* la 'plata) *n* **1** a port in E Argentina, near the Río de la Plata estuary: founded in 1882 and modelled on Washington DC; university (1897). Pop: 758 000 (2005 est) **2** See (Río de la) **Plata**

lap of honour *n* a ceremonial circuit of a racing track, etc, by the winner of a race

Lapp (læp) *n* **1** a member of a nomadic people living chiefly in N Scandinavia and the Kola Peninsula of Russia **2** the language of this people, belonging to the Finno-Ugric family ▷ *adj* **3** of or relating to this people or their language

◽ **USAGE** The indigenous people of Lapland prefer to be called *Sami*, although *Lapp* is still in widespread use

lappet ('læpıt) *n* **1** a small hanging flap or piece of lace, etc, such as one dangling from a headdress **2** *zoology* a lobelike hanging structure, such as the wattle on a bird's head [c16 from LAP¹ + -ET] ▷ '**lappeted** *adj*

lappet moth *n* a large purple-brown hairy eggar moth, *Gastropacha quercifolia*, whose grey furry caterpillars have lappets on each flank

Lappish ('læpıʃ) *adj* **1** of or relating to the Lapps, a nomadic people living chiefly in N Scandinavia and the Kola Peninsula of Russia, or their language ▷ *n* **2** the language of this people, belonging to the Finno-Ugric family

Lapsang Souchong ('læpsæn su:'ʃɒn) *n* a large-leafed variety of China tea with a slightly smoky flavour

lapse (læps) *n* **1** a drop in standard of an isolated or temporary nature: *a lapse of justice* **2** a break in occurrence, usage, etc: *a lapse of five weeks between letters* **3** a gradual decline or a drop to a lower degree, condition, or state: *a lapse from high office* **4** a moral fall **5** *law* the termination of some right, interest, or privilege, as by neglecting to exercise it or through failure of some contingency **6** *insurance* the termination of coverage following a failure to pay the premiums ▷ *vb* (*intr*) **7** to drop in standard or fail to maintain a norm **8** to decline gradually or fall in status, condition, etc **9** to be discontinued, esp through negligence or other failure **10** (usually foll by *into*) to drift or slide (into a condition): *to lapse into sleep* **11** (often foll by *from*) to turn away (from beliefs or norms) **12** *law* (of a devise or bequest) to become void, as on the beneficiary's predeceasing the testator **13** (of time) to slip away [c15 from Latin *lāpsus* error, from *lābī* to glide] ▷ '**lapsable** *or* '**lapsible** *adj* ▷ '**lapsed** *adj* ▷ '**lapser** *n*

lapse rate *n* the rate of change of any meteorological factor with altitude, esp atmospheric temperature, which usually decreases at a rate of 0.6°C per 100 metres (**environmental lapse rate**). Unsaturated air loses

about 1°C per 100 m (**dry adiabatic lapse rate**), whereas saturated air loses an average 0.5°C per 100 m (**saturated adiabatic lapse rate**)

lapstrake ('læp,streık) *or* **lapstreak** ('læp,stri:k) *nautical* ▷ *adj* **1** another term for **clinker-built** ▷ *n* **2** a clinker-built boat [c18 from LAP² + STRAKE]

lapsus ('læpsəs) *n, pl* **-sus** *formal* a lapse or error [from Latin: LAPSE]

lapsus linguae ('lıngwi:) *n* a slip of the tongue [Latin]

Laptev Sea ('læptıf) *n* a shallow arm of the Arctic Ocean, along the N coast of Russia between the Taimyr Peninsula and the New Siberian Islands. Former name: **Nordenskjöld Sea**

laptop ('læp,tɒp) *or* **laptop computer** *n* a personal computer that is small and light enough to be operated on the user's lap. Compare **palmtop computer**

laptray ('læp,treı) *n* a tray with a cushioned underside, designed to rest in a person's lap while supporting reading material, a meal eaten while watching television, etc

lap up *vb* (*tr, adverb*) **1** to eat or drink **2** to relish or delight in: *he laps up old horror films* **3** to believe or accept eagerly and uncritically: *he laps up tall stories*

lapwing ('læp,wıŋ) *n* any of several plovers of the genus *Vanellus*, esp *V. vanellus*, typically having a crested head, wattles, and spurs. Also called: **green plover, pewit, peewit** [c17 altered form of Old English *hlēapewince* plover, from *hlēapan* to LEAP + *wincian* to jerk, WINK¹]

lar¹ (lɑː) *n* the singular of **lares** See **lares and penates** [Latin]

lar² (lɑː) *n Northern English dialect* a boy or young man

LAR *international car registration for* Libya(n Arab Republic)

larboard ('lɑːbəd) *n, adj nautical* a former word for **port²** [c14 *laddeborde* (changed to *larboard* by association with *starboard*), from *laden* to load + *borde* BOARD]

larceny ('lɑːsını) *n, pl* **-nies** *law* (formerly) a technical word for **theft** [c15 from Old French *larcin*, from Latin *lātrocinium* robbery, from *latrō* robber] ▷ '**larcenist** *or* '**larcener** *n* ▷ '**larcenous** *adj* ▷ '**larcenously** *adv*

larch (lɑːtʃ) *n* **1** any coniferous tree of the genus *Larix*, having deciduous needle-like leaves and egg-shaped cones: family *Pinaceae* **2** the wood of any of these trees [c16 from German *Lärche*, ultimately from Latin *larix*]

lard (lɑːd) *n* **1** the rendered fat from a pig, esp from the abdomen, used in cooking **2** *informal* excess fat on a person's body ▷ *vb* (*tr*) **3** to prepare (lean meat, poultry, etc) by inserting small strips of bacon or fat before cooking **4** to cover or smear (foods) with lard **5** to add extra material to (speech or writing); embellish [c15 via Old French from Latin *lāridum* bacon fat] ▷ '**lard,like** *adj*

larder ('lɑːdə) *n* a room or cupboard, used as a store for food [c14 from Old French *lardier*, from LARD]

larder beetle *n* See **dermestid**

lardon ('lɑːdən) *or* **lardoon** (lɑː'du:n) *n* a strip or cube of fat or bacon used in larding meat [c15 from Old French, from LARD]

lard pig *n* a large type of pig used principally for lard

lardy ('lɑːdı) *adj* fat; obese

lardy cake ('lɑːdı) *n Brit* a rich sweet cake made of bread dough, lard, sugar, and dried fruit

Laredo (lə'reıdəʊ) *n* a city in the US, in Texas, on the Mexican border: founded by the Spanish in 1755 on the Rio Grande. Pop: 197 488 (2003 est)

lares and penates ('lɛərı:z, 'lɑ:-) *pl n* **1** *Roman myth* **a** household gods **b** statues of these gods kept in the home **2** the valued possessions of a household

Largactil (,lɑː'gæktıl) *n trademark* a brand of chlorpromazine used as a tranquillizer, sedative, and antipsychotic

large (lɑːdʒ) *adj* **1** having a relatively great size,

quantity, extent, etc; big **2** of wide or broad scope, capacity, or range; comprehensive: *a large effect* **3** having or showing great breadth of understanding: *a large heart* **4** *nautical* (of the wind) blowing from a favourable direction **5** *rare* overblown; pretentious **6** generous **7** *obsolete* (of manners and speech) gross; rude ▷ *n* **8 at large a** (esp of a dangerous criminal or wild animal) free; not confined **b** roaming freely, as in a foreign country **c** as a whole; in general **d** in full detail; exhaustively **e** ambassador-at-large See **ambassador** (sense 4) **9** in (the) large as a totality or on a broad scale ▷ *adv* **10** *nautical* with the wind blowing from a favourable direction **11** by and large **a** (*sentence modifier*) generally; as a rule: *by and large, the man is the breadwinner* **b** *nautical* towards and away from the wind **12** loom large to be very prominent or important [c12 (originally: generous): via Old French from Latin *largus* ample, abundant] ▷ '**largeness** *n*

Large Black *n* a heavy black breed of pig with long lop ears: used for crossbreeding

large calorie *n* another name for **Calorie**

large-format *adj* of or relating to a camera with an image area of 5 inches by 4 inches or more

large-handed *adj* generous; profuse

large-hearted *adj* kind; sympathetic. Also: **large-souled**

large intestine *n* the part of the alimentary canal consisting of the caecum, colon, and rectum. It extracts moisture from food residues, which are later excreted as faeces. Compare **small intestine**

large it *vb* (*intr, pron*) *Brit slang* to enjoy oneself or celebrate in an extravagant way

largely ('lɑːdʒlı) *adv* **1** principally; to a great extent **2** on a large scale or in a large manner

large-minded *adj* generous or liberal in attitudes ▷ ,**large-'mindedly** *adv* ▷ ,**large-'mindedness** *n*

largemouth bass ('lɑːdʒ,maʊθ 'bæs) *n* a common North American freshwater black bass, *Micropterus salmoides*: a popular game fish

Large Munsterlander ('mʊnstə,lændə) *n* a strongly built gun dog with a long dense black-and-white coat

largen ('lɑːdʒən) *vb* (*tr*) another word for **enlarge**

large-scale *adj* **1** wide-ranging or extensive **2** (of maps and models) constructed or drawn to a big scale

large-scale integration *n electronics* the process of integrating several thousand circuits on a single silicon chip. Abbreviation: **LSI**

largesse *or* **largess** (lɑː'dʒɛs) *n* **1** the generous bestowal of gifts, favours, or money **2** the things so bestowed **3** generosity of spirit or attitude [c13 from Old French, from LARGE]

large white *n* **1** Also called: **cabbage white** a large white butterfly, *Pieris brassicae*, with scanty black markings, the larvae of which feed on brassica leaves **2** (*often capitals*) a white large-bodied breed of pig commonly kept for pork, bacon, and for fattening

larghetto (lɑː'gɛtəʊ) *music* ▷ *adj, adv* **1** to be performed moderately slowly ▷ *n, pl* **-tos 2** a piece or passage to be performed in this way [Italian: diminutive of LARGO]

largish ('lɑːdʒıʃ) *adj* fairly large

largo ('lɑːgəʊ) *music* ▷ *adj, adv* **1** to be performed slowly and broadly ▷ *n, pl* **-gos 2** a piece or passage to be performed in this way [c17 from Italian, from Latin *largus* LARGE]

lari *or* **laari** (lɑːrı) *n* the standard monetary unit of Georgia, divided into 100 tetri

Lariam ('læriæm) *n trademark* a brand of mefloquine, used in the treatment and prevention of malaria

lariat ('lærıət) *n US and Canadian* **1** another word for **lasso 2** a rope for tethering animals [c19 from Spanish *la reata* the LASSO]

larine ('lærain, -rın) *adj* **1** of, relating to, or resembling a gull **2** of, relating to, or belonging to the suborder *Lari*, which contains the gulls, terns, skuas, and skimmers [C20 via New Latin from *Larus* genus name, from Greek *laros* a kind of gull]

Larisa *or* **Larissa** (lə'rɪsə; *Greek* 'larisa) *n* a city in E Greece, in E Thessaly: fortified by Justinian; annexed to Greece in 1881. Pop: 130 000 (2005 est)

lark[1] (lɑːk) *n* **1** any brown songbird of the predominantly Old World family *Alaudidae*, esp the skylark: noted for their singing **2** short for **titlark** *or* **meadowlark 3** (*often capital*) any of various slender but powerful fancy pigeons, such as the **Coburg Lark 4 up with the lark** up early in the morning [Old English *lāwerce*, *lǣwerce*, of Germanic origin; related to German *Lerche*, Icelandic *lǣvirki*]

lark[2] (lɑːk) *informal* ▷ *n* **1** a carefree adventure or frolic **2** a harmless piece of mischief **3 what a lark!** how amusing! ▷ *vb* (*intr*) **4** (*often foll by about*) to have a good time by frolicking **5** to play a prank [C19 originally slang, perhaps related to LAIK] > 'larker *n* > 'larkish *adj* > 'larkishness *n*

larkspur ('lɑːkˌspɜː) *n* any of various ranunculaceous plants of the genus *Delphinium*, with spikes of blue, pink, or white irregular spurred flowers [C16 LARK[1] + SPUR]

larky ('lɑːkɪ) *adj* larkier, larkiest *informal* frolicsome or mischievous

Larmor precession ('lɑːmɔː) *n* precession of the orbit of an electron in an atom that is subjected to a magnetic field [C20 named after Sir Joseph Larmor (1857–1942), British physicist]

larn (lɑːn) *vb not standard* ▷ *facetious* to learn **2** (*tr*) to teach (someone) a lesson: *that'll larn you!* [C18 from a dialect form of LEARN]

larnax ('lɑːnæks) *n archaeol* a coffin made of terracotta [from Greek; perhaps related to Late Greek *narnax* chest]

Larne (lɒːn) *n* a district of NE Northern Ireland, in Co Antrim. Pop: 30 948 (2003 est). Area: 336 sq km (130 sq miles)

larney ('lɑːnɪ) *South African* ▷ *n* **1** a white person **2** a rich person ▷ *adj* **3** (of clothes) smart [C20 probably from an Indian language]

La Rochelle (*French* la rɔʃɛl) *n* a port in W France, on the Bay of Biscay: a Huguenot stronghold until its submission through famine to Richelieu's forces after a long siege (1627–28). Pop: 76 584 (1999)

larrigan ('lærɪgən) *n* a knee-high oiled leather moccasin boot worn by trappers, etc [C19 of unknown origin]

larrikin ('lærɪkɪn) *n Austral and NZ slang* **a** a mischievous person **b** (*as modifier*): *a larrikin bloke* [C19 from English dialect: a mischievous youth]

larrup ('lærəp) *vb* (*tr*) *dialect* to beat or flog [C19 of unknown origin] > 'larruper *n*

Larry ('lærɪ) *n Brit, Austral, and NZ informal* (*as*) **happy as Larry** extremely happy [of uncertain origin]

larum ('lærəm) *n* an archaic word for **alarm**

larva ('lɑːvə) *n, pl* -vae (-viː) an immature free-living form of many animals that develops into a different adult form by metamorphosis [C18 (C17 in the original Latin sense: ghost): New Latin] > 'larval *adj*

larval therapy *n* the use of maggots that feed on dead tissue to assist in the healing of serious wounds. An ancient practice, it has been revived in rare cases in which healing is hampered by the resistance of bacteria to antibiotics

larvicide ('lɑːvɪˌsaɪd) *n* a chemical used for killing larvae > ˌlarvi'cidal *adj*

laryngeal (ˌlærɪn'dʒiːəl, lə'rɪndʒɪəl) *or* **laryngal** (lə'rɪŋgəl) *adj* **1** of or relating to the larynx **2** *phonetics* articulated at the larynx; glottal [C18 from New Latin *laryngeus* of the LARYNX] > laryn'geally *adv*

laryngitis (ˌlærɪn'dʒaɪtɪs) *n* inflammation of the larynx > **laryngitic** (ˌlærɪn'dʒɪtɪk) *adj*

laryngo- *or before a vowel* **laryng-** *combining form* indicating the larynx: *laryngoscope*

laryngology (ˌlærɪŋ'gɒlədʒɪ) *n* the branch of medicine concerned with the larynx and its

diseases > **laryngological** (lə,rɪŋgə'lɒdʒɪkəl) *or* la,ryngo'logic *adj* > la,ryngo'logically *adv* > ˌlaryn'gologist *n*

laryngoscope (lə'rɪŋgəˌskəʊp) *n* a medical instrument for examining the larynx > **laryngoscopic** (lə,rɪŋgə'skɒpɪk) *adj* > la,ryngo'scopically *adv* > **laryngoscopist** (ˌlærɪŋ'gɒskəpɪst) *n* > ˌlaryn'goscopy *n*

laryngotomy (ˌlærɪŋ'gɒtəmɪ) *n, pl* -mies surgical incision into the larynx

larynx ('lærɪŋks) *n, pl* **larynges** (lə'rɪndʒiːz) a cartilaginous and muscular hollow organ forming part of the air passage to the lungs: in higher vertebrates it contains the vocal cords [C16 from New Latin *larynx*, from Greek *larunx*]

lasagne *or* **lasagna** (lə'zænjə, -'sæn-) *n* **1** a form of pasta consisting of wide flat sheets **2** any of several dishes made from layers of lasagne and meat, cheese, etc [from Italian *lasagna*, from Latin *lasanum* cooking pot]

La Salle (lə 'sæl) *n* a city in SE Canada, in Quebec: a S suburb of Montreal. Pop: 73 804 (1991)

La Scala (la 'skaːla) *n* the chief opera house in Italy, in Milan (opened 1776)

lascar ('læskə) *n* a sailor from the East Indies [C17 from Urdu *lashkar* soldier, from Persian: the army]

Lascaux (*French* lasko) *n* the site of a cave in SW France, in the Dordogne: contains Palaeolithic wall drawings and paintings

lascivious (lə'sɪvɪəs) *adj* **1** lustful; lecherous **2** exciting sexual desire [C15 from Late Latin *lascīviōsus*, from Latin *lascīvia* wantonness, from *lascīvus*] > las'civiously *adv* > las'civiousness *n*

lase (leɪz) *vb* (*intr*) (of a substance, such as carbon dioxide or ruby) to be capable of acting as a laser

laser ('leɪzə) *n* **1** a source of high-intensity optical, infrared, or ultraviolet radiation produced as a result of stimulated emission maintained within a solid, liquid, or gaseous medium. The photons involved in the emission process all have the same energy and phase so that the laser beam is monochromatic and coherent, allowing it to be brought to a fine focus **2** any similar source producing a beam of any electromagnetic radiation, such as infrared or microwave radiation. See also **maser** [C20 from *light amplification by stimulated emission of radiation*]

laser card *n computing* another name for **smart card**

laserdisc *or esp US* **laserdisk** ('leɪzəˌdɪsk) *n* a disk similar in size to a long-playing record, on which data is stored in pits in a similar way to data storage on a compact disk, used esp for storing high-quality video

laser printer *n* a quiet high-quality computer printer that uses a laser beam shining on a photoconductive drum to produce characters, which are then transferred to paper

laser ring gyro *n aeronautics* a system of aerial navigation in which rotation is sensed by the measuring of the frequency shift of laser light in a closed circuit in a horizontal plane

laser treatment *n* any of various medical and surgical techniques using lasers, such as the removal of small growths

lash[1] (læʃ) *n* **1** a sharp cutting blow from a whip or other flexible object: *twenty lashes was his punishment* **2** the flexible end or ends of a whip **3** a cutting or hurtful blow to the feelings, as one caused by ridicule or scolding **4** a forceful beating or impact, as of wind, rain, or waves against something **5** See **eyelash 6 have a lash (at)** *Austral and NZ informal* to make an attempt at or take part in (something) ▷ *vb* (*tr*) **7** to hit (a person or thing) sharply with a whip, rope, etc, esp as a punishment **8** (of rain, waves, etc) to beat forcefully against **9** to attack with words, ridicule, etc **10** to flick or wave sharply to and fro: *the restless panther lashed his tail* **11** to urge or drive with or as if with a whip: *to lash the audience into a violent mood* ▷ See also **lash out** [C14 perhaps imitative] > 'lasher *n* > 'lashingly *adv*

lash[2] (læʃ) *vb* (*tr*) to bind or secure with rope, string, etc [C15 from Old French *lachier*, ultimately from Latin *laqueāre* to ensnare, from *laqueus* noose] > 'lasher *n*

lashed (læʃt) *adj Brit informal* intoxicated; drunk

-lashed *adj* having eyelashes as specified: *long-lashed*

lashing[1] ('læʃɪŋ) *n* **1** a whipping; flogging **2** a scolding **3** (*plural*; *usually foll by of*) *Brit informal* large amounts; lots

lashing[2] ('læʃɪŋ) *n* rope, cord, etc, used for binding or securing

Lashio ('læʃɪˌaʊ) *n* a town in NE central Myanmar: starting point of the Burma Road to Chongqing, China

Lashkar ('lʌʃkə) *n* a former city in N India, in Madhya Pradesh: capital of the former states of Gwalior and Madhya Bharat; now part of the city of Gwalior

lash out *vb* (*intr, adverb*) **1** to burst into or resort to verbal or physical attack **2** *Brit informal* to be extravagant, as in spending

lash-up ('læʃˌʌp) *n* **a** Also called: **hook-up** a temporary connection of equipment for experimental or emergency use **b** (*as modifier*): *lash-up equipment*

LASIK surgery ('leɪsɪk) *n* laser surgery to correct short sight [C20 from *Laser-Assisted In Situ Keratomileusis*]

lasket ('læskɪt) *n* a loop at the foot of a sail onto which an extra sail may be fastened [C18 perhaps an alteration of French *lacet* LATCHET, through the influence of GASKET]

Las Palmas (*Spanish* las 'palmas) *n* a port in the central Canary Islands, on NE Grand Canary: a major fuelling port on the main shipping route between Europe and South America. Pop: 377 600 (2003 est)

La Spezia (*Italian* la 'spɛttsia) *n* a port in NW Italy, in Liguria, on the **Gulf of Spezia**: the chief naval base in Italy. Pop: 91 391 (2001)

lass (læs) *n* a girl or young woman [C13 origin uncertain]

Lassa ('lɑːsə) *n* a variant spelling of **Lhasa**

Lassa fever *n* a serious viral disease of Central West Africa, characterized by high fever and muscular pains [named after *Lassa*, the village in Nigeria where it was first identified]

Lassen Peak ('læsən) *n* a volcano in S California, in the S Cascade Range. An area of 416 sq km (161 sq miles) was established as **Lassen Volcanic National Park** in 1916. Height: 3187 m (10 457 ft)

lassi ('læsɪ) *n* a cold drink made with yoghurt or buttermilk and flavoured with sugar, salt, or a mild spice [from Hindi]

lassie ('læsɪ) *n informal* a little lass; girl

lassitude ('læsɪˌtjuːd) *n* physical or mental weariness [C16 from Latin *lassitūdō*, from *lassus* tired]

lasso (læ'suː, 'læsəʊ) *n, pl* -sos *or* -soes **1** a long rope or thong with a running noose at one end, used (esp in America) for roping horses, cattle, etc; lariat ▷ *vb* -sos *or* -soes; -soing, -soed **2** (*tr*) to catch with or as if with a lasso [C19 from Spanish *lazo*, ultimately from Latin *laqueus* noose] > las'soer *n*

last[1] (lɑːst) *adj* (*often prenominal*) **1** being, happening, or coming at the end or after all others: *the last horse in the race* **2** being or occurring just before the present; most recent: *last Thursday* **3 last but not least** coming last in order but nevertheless important **4 last but one** next to last **5** only remaining: *one's last cigarette* **6** most extreme; utmost **7** least suitable, appropriate, or likely: *he was the last person I would have chosen* **8** (esp relating to the end of a person's life or of the world) **a** final or ultimate: *last rites* **b** (*capital*): *the Last Judgment* **9** (*postpositive*) *Liverpool dialect* inferior, unpleasant, or contemptible: *this ale is last* ▷ *adv* **10** after all others; at or in the end: *he came last* **11 a** most recently: *he was last seen in the mountains* **b** (*in combination*): *last-mentioned* **12**

(*sentence modifier*) as the last or latest item ▷ *n* **13** **the last a** a person or thing that is last **b** the final moment; end **14** one's last moments before death **15** the last thing a person can do (esp in the phrase **breathe one's last**) **16** the final appearance, mention, or occurrence: *we've seen the last of him* **17 at last** in the end; finally **18 at long last** finally, after difficulty, delay, or irritation [variant of Old English *latest, lætest,* superlative of LATE]

> USAGE Since *last* can mean either *after all others* or *most recent,* it is better to avoid using this word where ambiguity might arise as in *her last novel.* Final or *latest* should be used in such contexts to avoid ambiguity

last² (lɑːst) *vb* **1** (when *intr,* often foll by *for*) to remain in being (for a length of time); continue: *his hatred lasted for several years* **2** to be sufficient for the needs of (a person) for (a length of time): *it will last us until Friday* **3** (when *intr,* often foll by *for*) to remain fresh, uninjured, or unaltered (for a certain time or duration): *he lasted for three hours underground* ▷ See also **last out** [Old English *læstan*; related to Gothic *laistjan* to follow] > **'laster** *n*

last³ (lɑːst) *n* **1** the wooden or metal form on which a shoe or boot is fashioned or repaired ▷ *vb* **2** (*tr*) to fit (a shoe or boot) on a last [Old English *læste,* from *lāst* footprint; related to Old Norse *leistr* foot, Gothic *laists*] > **'laster** *n*

last⁴ (lɑːst) *n* a unit of weight or capacity having various values in different places and for different commodities. Commonly used values are 2 tons, 2000 pounds, 80 bushels, or 640 gallons [Old English *hlæst* load; related to *hladan* to LADE¹]

last chance saloon *n* **1** a place frequented by unsavoury or contemptible people **2** a situation considered to be the last opportunity for success

last-cyclic *adj transformational grammar* denoting rules that apply only to main clauses. Compare **cyclic** (sense 6), **post-cyclic**

last-ditch *n* (*modifier*) made or done as a last desperate attempt or effort in the face of opposition

last-gasp *n* (*modifier*) done in desperation at the last minute: *a last-gasp attempt to save the talks*

lasting ('lɑːstɪŋ) *adj* **1** permanent or enduring ▷ *n* **2** a strong durable closely woven fabric used for shoe uppers, etc > **'lastingly** *adv* > **'lastingness** *n*

Last Judgment *n* **the** the occasion, after the resurrection of the dead at the end of the world, when, according to biblical tradition, God will decree the final destinies of all men according to the good and evil in their earthly lives. Also called: **the Last Day, Doomsday, Judgment Day**

lastly ('lɑːstlɪ) *adv* **1** at the end or at the last point ▷ *sentence connector* **2** in the end; finally: *lastly, he put on his jacket*

last-minute *n* (*modifier*) given or done at the latest possible time: *last-minute preparations*

last name *n* another term for **surname** (sense 1)

last out *vb* (*adverb*) **1** (*intr*) to be sufficient for one's needs: *how long will our supplies last out?* **2** (*tr*) to endure or survive: *some old people don't last out the winter*

last post *n* (in the British military services) **1** a bugle call that orders men to retire for sleep **2** a similar call sounded at military funerals

last quarter *n* one of the four principal phases of the moon, occurring between full moon and new moon, when half the lighted surface is visible. Compare **first quarter**

last rites *pl n Christianity* religious rites prescribed for those close to death

last straw *n* **the** the final irritation or problem that stretches one's endurance or patience beyond the limit [from the proverb, "It is the last straw that breaks the camel's back"]

Last Supper *n* **the** the meal eaten by Christ with his disciples on the night before his Crucifixion, during which he is believed to have instituted the Eucharist

last thing *adv* as the final action, esp before retiring to bed at night

Las Vegas (læs 'veɪɡəs) *n* a city in SE Nevada: famous for luxury hotels and casinos. Pop: 517 017 (2003 est)

lat. *abbreviation for* latitude

Lat. *abbreviation for* Latin

latah ('lɑːtə) *n* a psychological condition, observed esp in Malaysian cultures, in which an individual, after experiencing a shock, becomes anxious and suggestible, often imitating the actions of another person [c19 from Malay]

Latakia or **Lattakia** (ˌlætə'kiːə) *n* the chief port of Syria, in the northwest: tobacco industry. Pop: 486 000 (2005 est). Latin name: **Laodicea ad Mare**

Latam ('lætæm) *n* ▷ *adj* short for **Latin America** or **Latin American**

latch (lætʃ) *n* **1** a fastening for a gate or door that consists of a bar that may be slid or lowered into a groove, hole, etc **2** a spring-loaded door lock that can be opened by a key from outside **3** Also called: **latch circuit** *electronics* a logic circuit that transfers the input states to the output states when signalled, the output thereafter remaining insensitive to changes in input status until signalled again ▷ *vb* **4** to fasten, fit, or be fitted with or as if with a latch [Old English *læccan* to seize, of Germanic origin; related to Greek *lazesthai*]

latchet ('lætʃɪt) *n archaic* a shoe fastening, such as a thong or lace [c14 from Old French *lachet,* from *las* LACE]

latchkey ('lætʃˌkiː) *n* **1** a key for an outside door or gate, esp one that lifts a latch **2 a** a supposed freedom from restrictions **b** (*as modifier*): *a latchkey existence*

latchkey child *n* a child who has to let himself in at home on returning from school, as his parents are out at work

latch on *vb* (*intr, adverb*; often foll by *to*) *informal* **1** to attach oneself (to): *to latch on to a new acquaintance* **2** to understand: *he suddenly latched on to what they were up to* **3** *US and Canadian* to obtain; get

latchstring ('lætʃˌstrɪŋ) *n* a length of string fastened to a latch and passed through a hole in the door so that it can be opened from the other side

late (leɪt) *adj* **1** occurring or arriving after the correct or expected time: *the train was late* **2** (*prenominal*) occurring, scheduled for, or being at a relatively advanced time: *a late marriage* **3** (*prenominal*) towards or near the end: *the late evening* **4** at an advanced time in the evening or at night: *it was late* **5** (*prenominal*) occurring or being just previous to the present time: *his late remarks on industry* **6** (*prenominal*) having died, esp recently: *my late grandfather* **7** (*prenominal*) just preceding the present or existing person or thing; former: *the late manager of this firm* **8** of late recently; lately ▷ *adv* **9** after the correct or expected time: *he arrived late* **10** at a relatively advanced age: *she married late* **11** recently; lately: *as late as yesterday he was selling books* **12** late hours rising and going to bed later than is usual **13 late in the day a** at a late or advanced stage **b** too late [Old English *læt*; related to Old Norse *latr,* Gothic *lats*] > **'lateness** *n*

> USAGE Since *late* can mean *deceased,* many people think it is better to avoid using this word to refer to the person who held a post or position before its present holder: *the previous* (not *the late*) *editor of The Times*

latecomer ('leɪtˌkʌmə) *n* a person or thing that comes late

lated ('leɪtɪd) *adj* an archaic word for **belated**

lateen (lə'tiːn) *adj nautical* denoting a rig with a triangular sail (**lateen sail**) bent to a yard hoisted to the head of a low mast, used esp in the Mediterranean [c18 from French *voile latine* Latin sail]

lateenrigged (lə'tiːnˌrɪgd) *adj nautical* rigged with a lateen sail

Late Greek *n* the Greek language from about the 3rd to the 8th centuries A.D. Compare **Medieval Greek, Koine**

Late Latin *n* the form of written Latin used from the 3rd to the 7th centuries A.D. See also **Biblical Latin, Medieval Latin**

lately ('leɪtlɪ) *adv* in recent times; of late

latency period *n psychoanal* a period according to Freud, from the age of about five to puberty, when sexual interest is diminished

La Tène (læ 'tɛn) *adj* of or relating to a Celtic culture in Europe from about the 5th to the 1st centuries BC, characterized by a distinctive type of curvilinear decoration. See also **Hallstatt** [c20 from *La Tène,* a part of Lake Neuchâtel, Switzerland, where remains of this culture were first discovered]

latent ('leɪt³nt) *adj* **1** potential but not obvious or explicit **2** (of buds, spores, etc) dormant **3** *pathol* (esp of an infectious disease) not yet revealed or manifest **4** (of a virus) inactive in the host cell, its nucleic acid being integrated into, and replicated with, the host cell's DNA **5** *psychoanal* relating to that part of a dream expressive of repressed desires: *latent content.* Compare **manifest** (sense 2) [c17 from Latin *latent-,* from *latens* present participle of *latēre* to lie hidden] > **'latency** *n* > **'latently** *adv*

latent heat *n* (*no longer in technical usage*) the heat evolved or absorbed by unit mass (**specific latent heat**) or unit amount of substance (**molar latent heat**) when it changes phase without change of temperature

latent image *n photog* the invisible image produced by the action of light, etc, on silver halide crystals suspended in the emulsion of a photographic material. It becomes visible after development

latent learning *n psychol* learning mediated neither by reward nor by the expectation of reward

latent period *n* **1** the incubation period of an infectious disease, before symptoms appear **2** another name for **latent time**

latent time *n psychol* the time from the onset of a stimulus to that of the response. Also called: **latency, reaction time**

later ('leɪtə) *adj, adv* **1** the comparative of **late** ▷ *adv* **2** afterwards; subsequently **3 see you later** an expression of farewell **4 sooner or later** eventually; inevitably

lateral ('lætərəl) *adj* **1** of or relating to the side or sides: *a lateral blow* **2** *phonetics* (of a speech sound like l) pronounced with the tip of the tongue touching the centre of the alveolar ridge, leaving space on one or both sides for the passage of the airstream ▷ *n* **3** a lateral object, part, passage, or movement **4** *phonetics* a lateral speech sound [c17 from Latin *laterālis,* from *latus* side] > **'laterally** *adv*

laterality (ˌlætə'rælɪtɪ) *n psychol* the difference in the mental functions controlled by the left and right cerebral hemispheres of the brain

lateral line system *n* a system of sensory organs in fishes and aquatic amphibians consisting of a series of cells on the head and along the sides of the body that detect pressure changes and vibrations

lateral thinking *n* a way of solving problems by rejecting traditional methods and employing unorthodox and apparently illogical means

Lateran ('lætərən) *n* **the 1** Also called: **Lateran palace** a palace in Rome, formerly the official residence of the popes **2** any of five ecumenical councils held in this palace between 1123 and 1512 **3** the basilica of Saint John Lateran, the cathedral church of Rome [from Latin: the district is named after the ancient Roman family *Plautii Laterani*]

laterigrade ('lætərɪˌgreɪd) *adj zoology* (of some crabs) having a gait characterized by sideways movement

laterite ('lætəˌraɪt) *n* any of a group of deposits consisting of residual insoluble deposits of ferric and aluminium oxides: formed by weathering of rocks in tropical regions [C19 from Latin *later* brick, tile] > **lateritic** (ˌlætəˈrɪtɪk) *adj*

lateroversion (ˌlætərəʊˈvɜːʃən) *n* abnormal lateral displacement of a bodily organ or part, esp of the uterus [C20 from LATERAL + *-version*, from Latin *versiō* a turning]

latest (ˈleɪtɪst) *adj, adv* **1** the superlative of **late** ▷ *adj* **2** most recent, modern, or new: *the latest fashions* ▷ *n* **3** **at the latest** no later than the time specified **4** **the latest** *informal* the most recent fashion or development

late-type star *n astronomy* any star with a surface temperature below that of the sun, of spectral type K, M, C, or S. Compare: **early-type star**

latex (ˈleɪtɛks) *n, pl* **latexes** or **latices** (ˈlætɪˌsiːz) **1** a whitish milky fluid containing protein, starch, alkaloids, etc, that is produced by many plants. Latex from the rubber tree is used in the manufacture of rubber **2** a suspension of synthetic rubber or plastic in water, used in the manufacture of synthetic rubber products, etc [C19 New Latin, from Latin: liquid, fluid]

lath (lɑːθ) *n, pl* **laths** (lɑːðz, lɑːθs) **1** one of several thin narrow strips of wood used to provide a supporting framework for plaster, tiles, etc **2** expanded sheet metal, wire mesh, etc, used to provide backing for plaster or rendering **3** any thin strip of wood ▷ *vb* **4** (*tr*) to attach laths to (a ceiling, roof, floor, etc) [Old English *lætt*; related to Dutch *lat*, Old High German *latta*] > **lath,like** *adj*

lathe¹ (leɪð) *n* **1** a machine for shaping, boring, facing, or cutting a screw thread in metal, wood, etc, in which the workpiece is turned about a horizontal axis against a fixed tool ▷ *vb* **2** (*tr*) to shape, bore, or cut a screw thread in or on (a workpiece) on a lathe [perhaps C15 *lath* a support, of Scandinavian origin; compare Old Danish *lad* lathe, Old English *hlæd* heap]

lathe² (leɪð) *n Brit history* any of the former administrative divisions of Kent [Old English *læth* district]

lather (ˈlɑːðə, ˈlæ-) *n* **1** foam or froth formed by the action of soap or a detergent in water **2** foam formed by other liquid, such as the sweat of a horse **3** *informal* a state of agitation or excitement ▷ *vb* **4** to coat or become coated with lather **5** (*intr*) to form a lather [Old English *lēathor* soap; related to Old Norse *lauthr* foam] > **lathery** *adj*

lathi (ˈlɑːtɪ) *n* a long heavy wooden stick used as a weapon in India, esp by the police [Hindi]

lathy (ˈlɑːθɪ) *adj* **lathier, lathiest** resembling a lath, esp in being tall and thin

lathyrism (ˈlæθərɪzəm) *n* a neurological disease often resulting in weakness and paralysis of the legs: caused by eating the pealike seeds of the leguminous plant *Lathyrus sativus*

latices (ˈlætɪˌsiːz) *n* a plural of **latex**

laticifer (ləˈtɪsɪfə) *n botany* a cell or group of cells in a plant that contains latex [C19 from New Latin *latic-* LATEX + *-FER*] > **laticiferous** (ˌlætɪˈsɪfərəs) *adj*

latifundium (ˌlætɪˈfʌndɪəm) *n, pl* **-dia** (-dɪə) a large agricultural estate, esp one worked by slaves in ancient Rome [C17 from Latin *lātus* broad + *fundus* farm, estate]

latimeria (ˌlætɪˈmɪərɪə) *n* any coelacanth fish of the genus *Latimeria* [C20 named after Marjorie Courtenay-Latimer (1907–2004), South African museum curator]

Latin (ˈlætɪn) *n* **1** the language of ancient Rome and the Roman Empire and of the educated in medieval Europe, which achieved its classical form during the 1st century BC. Having originally been the language of Latium, belonging to the Italic branch of the Indo-European family, it later formed the basis of the Romance group. See **Late Latin, Low Latin, Medieval Latin, New Latin, Old Latin** See also **Romance 2** a member of any of those peoples whose languages are derived from Latin **3** an inhabitant of ancient Latium ▷ *adj* **4** of or relating to the Latin language, the ancient Latins, or Latium **5** characteristic of or relating to

those peoples in Europe and Latin America whose languages are derived from Latin **6** of or relating to the Roman Catholic Church **7** denoting or relating to the Roman alphabet [Old English *latin* and *læden* Latin, language, from Latin *Latīnus* of Latium]

Latin-1 *n computing* another name for **ISO Latin-1**

Latina (Italian laˈtiːna) *n* a city in W central Italy, in Lazio: built as a planned town in 1932 on reclaimed land of the Pontine Marshes. Pop: 107 898 (2001). Former name (until 1947): **Littoria**

Latin alphabet *n* another term for **Roman alphabet**

Latin America *n* those areas of America whose official languages are Spanish and Portuguese, derived from Latin: South America, Central America, Mexico, and certain islands in the Caribbean

Latin American *n* **1** a native or inhabitant of Latin America ▷ *adj* **2** of or relating to Latin America or its inhabitants

Latinate (ˈlætɪˌneɪt) *adj* (of writing, vocabulary, etc) imitative of or derived from Latin

Latin Church *n* the Roman Catholic Church

Latin cross *n* a cross the lowest arm of which is longer than the other three

Latinism (ˈlætɪˌnɪzəm) *n* a word, idiom, or phrase borrowed from Latin

Latinist (ˈlætɪnɪst) *n* a person who studies or is proficient in Latin

Latinity (ləˈtɪnɪtɪ) *n* **1** facility in the use of Latin **2** Latin style, esp in literature

Latinize or **Latinise** (ˈlætɪˌnaɪz) *vb* (*tr*) **1** to translate into Latin or Latinisms **2** to transliterate into the Latin alphabet **3** to cause to acquire Latin style or customs **4** to bring Roman Catholic influence to bear upon (the form of religious ceremonies, etc) > ˌLatiniˈzation or ˌLatiniˈsation > ˈLatinˌizer or ˈLatinˌiser *n*

Latino (læˈtiːnəʊ) *n, pl* **-nos** US an inhabitant of the US who is of Latin American origin > **Laˈtina** *fem n*

Latin Quarter *n* an area of Paris, on the S bank of the River Seine: contains the city's main educational establishments; centre for students and artists

Latin square *n* (in statistical analysis) one of a set of square arrays of *n* rows and columns, esp as used in statistics and studied in combinatorial analysis, built up from *n* different symbols so that no symbol occurs more than once in any row or column

latish (ˈleɪtɪʃ) *adj* rather late

latitude (ˈlætɪˌtjuːd) *n* **1 a** an angular distance in degrees north or south of the equator (latitude 0°), equal to the angle subtended at the centre of the globe by the meridian between the equator and the point in question **b** (*often plural*) a region considered with regard to its distance from the equator. See **longitude** (sense 1) **2** scope for freedom of action, thought, etc; freedom from restriction: *his parents gave him a great deal of latitude* **3** *photog* the range of exposure over which a photographic emulsion gives an acceptable negative **4** *astronomy* See **celestial latitude** [C14 from Latin *lātitūdō*, from *lātus* broad] > ˌlatiˈtudinal *adj* > ˌlatiˈtudinally *adv*

latitudinarian (ˌlætɪˌtjuːdɪˈnɛərɪən) *adj* **1** permitting or marked by freedom of attitude or behaviour, esp in religious matters **2** (*sometimes capital*) of or relating to a school of thought within the Church of England in the 17th century that minimized the importance of divine authority in matters of doctrine and stressed the importance of reason and personal judgment ▷ *n* **3** a person with latitudinarian views [C17 from Latin *lātitūdō* breadth, LATITUDE, influenced in form by TRINITARIAN] > ˌlatiˌtudiˈnarianism *n*

Latium (ˈleɪʃɪəm) *n* an ancient territory in W central Italy, in modern Lazio, on the Tyrrhenian Sea: inhabited by the Latin people from the 10th century BC until dominated by Rome (4th century

BC). Italian name: **Lazio**

Latona (ləˈtəʊnə) *n* the Roman name of **Leto**

La Trappe (French la trap) *n* a monastery in NW France, in the village of Soligny-la-Trappe northeast of Alençon: founded in about 1140, site of the Trappist reform of Cistercian order in 1664

latria (ləˈtraɪə) *n RC Church, theol* the adoration that may be offered to God alone [C16 via Latin from Greek *latreia* worship]

latrine (ləˈtriːn) *n* a lavatory, as in a barracks, camp, etc [C17 from French, from Latin *lātrīna*, shortened form of *lavātrīna* bath, from *lavāre* to wash]

-latry *n combining form* indicating worship of or excessive veneration of: *idolatry; Mariolatry* [from Greek *-latria*, from *latreia* worship] > **-latrous** *adj combining form*

lats (læts) *n, pl* **lati** (ˈlætiː) the standard monetary unit of Latvia, divided into 100 santimi

latte (ˈlæteɪ, ˈlɑːteɪ) *n* coffee made with hot milk [C20 from Italian (*caffè e*) *latte* (coffee and) milk]

latten (ˈlætⁿn) *n* metal or alloy, esp brass, made in thin sheets [C14 from Old French *laton*, of unknown origin]

latter (ˈlætə) *adj* (*prenominal*) **1 a** denoting the second or second mentioned of two: distinguished from **former b** (as noun; functioning as sing or plural): *the latter is not important* **2** near or nearer the end: *the latter part of a film* **3** more advanced in time or sequence; later

> USAGE *The latter* should only be used to refer to the second of two items: *many people choose to go by hovercraft rather than use the ferry, but I prefer the latter.* The last of three or more items can be referred to as *the last-named*

latter-day *adj* present-day; modern

Latter-day Saint *n* a more formal name for a Mormon

latterly (ˈlætəlɪ) *adv* recently; lately

lattermost (ˈlætəˌməʊst) *adj* a less common word for **last¹**

lattice (ˈlætɪs) *n* **1** Also called: **latticework** an open framework of strips of wood, metal, etc, arranged to form an ornamental pattern **2 a** a gate, screen, etc, formed of such a framework **b** (*as modifier*): *a lattice window* **3** something, such as a decorative or heraldic device, resembling such a framework **4** an array of objects or points in a periodic pattern in two or three dimensions, esp an array of atoms, ions, etc, in a crystal or an array of points indicating their positions in space. See also **Bravais lattice** ▷ *vb* **5** to make, adorn, or supply with a lattice or lattices [C14 from Old French *lattis*, from *latte* LATH] > **latticed** *adj*

lattice energy *n chem* the energy required to separate the ions of a crystal to an infinite distance, usually expressed in joules per mole

latus rectum (ˈlɑːtəs ˈrɛktəm) *n, pl* **latera recta** (ˈlætərə ˈrɛktə) *geometry* a chord that passes through the focus of a conic and is perpendicular to the major axis [C18 New Latin: straight side]

Latvia (ˈlætvɪə) *n* a republic in NE Europe, on the Gulf of Riga and the Baltic Sea: ruled by Poland, Sweden, and Russia since the 13th century, Latvia was independent from 1919 until 1940 and was a Soviet republic (1940–91), gaining its independence after conflict with Soviet forces; it joined the EU in 2004. Latvia is mostly forested. Official language: Latvian. Religion: nonreligious, Christian. Currency: lats. Capital: Riga. Pop: 2 286 000 (2004 est). Area: 63 700 sq km (25 590 sq miles)

Latvian (ˈlætvɪən) *adj* **1** of or relating to Latvia, its people, or their language ▷ *n* **2** Also called: Lettish the official language of Latvia: closely related to Lithuanian and belonging to the Baltic branch of the Indo-European family **3** a native or inhabitant of Latvia

laud (lɔːd) *literary* ▷ *vb* **1** (*tr*) to praise or glorify ▷ *n* **2** praise or glorification [C14 vb from Latin *laudāre*; n from *laudēs*, pl of Latin *laus* praise] > ˈlauder *n*

laudable ('lɔːdəbᵊl) *adj* deserving or worthy of praise; admirable; commendable ▷ 'laudableness *or* ˌlaudaˈbility *n* ▷ 'laudably *adv*

laudanum ('lɔːdᵊnəm) *n* **1** a tincture of opium **2** (formerly) any medicine of which opium was the main ingredient [c16 New Latin, name chosen by Paracelsus for a preparation probably containing opium, perhaps based on LABDANUM]

laudation (lɔːˈdeɪʃən) *n* a formal word for **praise**

laudatory ('lɔːdətərɪ, -trɪ) *or* **laudative** *adj* expressing or containing praise; eulogistic

Laudian ('lɔːdɪən) *adj Church of England* of or relating to the High-Church standards set up for the Church of England by William Laud (1573–1645), English archbishop of Canterbury (1633–45)

lauds (lɔːdz) *n* (*functioning as singular or plural*) *chiefly RC Church* the traditional morning prayer of the Western Church, constituting with matins the first of the seven canonical hours [c14 see LAUD]

laugh (lɑːf) *vb* **1** (*intr*) to express or manifest emotion, esp mirth or amusement, typically by expelling air from the lungs in short bursts to produce an inarticulate voiced noise, with the mouth open **2** (*intr*) (esp of certain mammals or birds) to make a noise resembling a laugh **3** (*tr*) to utter or express with laughter: *he laughed his derision at the play* **4** (*tr*) to bring or force (someone, esp oneself) into a certain condition by laughter: *he laughed himself sick* **5** (*intr*; foll by *at*) to make fun (of); jeer (at) **6** (*intr*; foll by *over*) to read or discuss something with laughter **7 don't make me laugh** *informal* I don't believe you for a moment **8 laugh all the way to the bank** *informal* to be unashamedly pleased at making a lot of money **9 laugh in a person's face** to show open contempt or defiance towards a person **10 laugh like a drain** *informal* to laugh loudly and coarsely **11 laugh up one's sleeve** to laugh or have grounds for amusement, self-satisfaction, etc, secretly **12 laugh on the other side of one's face** to show sudden disappointment or shame after appearing cheerful or confident **13 be laughing** *informal* to be in a favourable situation ▷ *n* **14** the act or an instance of laughing **15** a manner of laughter **16** *informal* a person or thing that causes laughter: *that holiday was a laugh* **17 the last laugh** the final success in an argument, situation, etc, after previous defeat ▷ See also **laugh away, laugh down, laugh off** [Old English *læhan, hliehhen*; related to Gothic *hlahjan*, Dutch *lachen*] ▷ 'laugher *n* ▷ 'laughing *n, adj* ▷ 'laughingly *adv*

laughable ('lɑːfəbᵊl) *adj* **1** producing scorn; ludicrous: *he offered me a laughable sum for the picture* **2** arousing laughter ▷ 'laughableness *n* ▷ 'laughably *adv*

laugh away *vb* (*tr, adverb*) **1** to dismiss or dispel (something unpleasant) by laughter **2** to make (time) pass pleasantly by jesting

laugh down *vb* (*tr, adverb*) to silence by laughing contemptuously

laughing gas *n* another name for **nitrous oxide**

laughing hyena *n* another name for the **spotted hyena** (see **hyena**)

laughing jackass *n* another name for the **kookaburra** (sense 1)

laughing stock *n* an object of humiliating ridicule: *his mistakes have made him a laughing stock*

laugh off *vb* (*tr, adverb*) to treat or dismiss lightly, esp with stoicism: *he laughed off his injuries*

laughter ('lɑːftə) *n* **1** the action of or noise produced by laughing **2** the experience or manifestation of mirth, amusement, scorn, or joy [Old English *hleahtor*; related to Old Norse *hlātr*]

laughter club *n* a group of people who meet regularly to take part in communal laughing for therapeutic effect

launce (lɑːns) *n* another name for the **sand eel**

Launceston ('lɔːnsəstən) *n* a city in Australia, the chief port of the island state of Tasmania on the Tamar River, 64 km (40 miles) from Bass Strait. Pop: 68 443 (2001)

launch¹ (lɔːntʃ) *vb* **1** to move (a vessel) into the water **2** to move (a newly built vessel) into the water for the first time **3** (*tr*) **a** to start off or set in motion: *to launch a scheme* **b** to put (a new product) on the market **4** (*tr*) to propel with force **5** to involve (oneself) totally and enthusiastically: *to launch oneself into work* **6** (*tr*) to set (a missile, spacecraft, etc) into motion **7** (*tr*) to catapult (an aircraft), as from the deck of an aircraft carrier **8** (*intr*; foll by *into*) to start talking or writing (about): *he launched into a story* **9** (*intr*; usually foll by *out*) to start (out) on a fresh course **10** (*intr*; usually foll by *out*) *informal* to spend a lot of money ▷ *n* **11** an act or instance of launching [c14 from Anglo-French *lancher*, from Late Latin *lanceāre* to use a lance, hence, to set in motion. See LANCE]

launch² (lɔːntʃ) *n* **1** a motor driven boat used chiefly as a transport boat **2** the largest of the boats of a man-of-war [c17 via Spanish *lancha* and Portuguese from Malay *lancharan* boat, from *lanchar* speed]

launcher ('lɔːntʃə) *n* any installation, vehicle, or other device for launching rockets, missiles, or other projectiles

launch pad *or* **launching pad** *n* **1** a platform from which a spacecraft, rocket, etc, is launched **2** an effective starting point for a career, enterprise, or campaign

launch shoe *or* **launching shoe** *n* an attachment to an aircraft from which a missile is launched

launch vehicle *or* **launching vehicle** *n* **1** a rocket, without its payload, used to launch a spacecraft **2** another name for **booster** (sense 2)

launch window *n* the limited period during which a spacecraft can be launched on a particular mission

launder ('lɔːndə) *vb* **1** to wash, sometimes starch, and often also iron (clothes, linen, etc) **2** (*intr*) to be capable of being laundered without shrinking, fading, etc **3** (*tr*) to process (something acquired illegally) to make it appear respectable, esp to process illegally acquired funds through a legitimate business or to send them to a foreign bank for subsequent transfer to a home bank ▷ *n* **4** a water trough, esp one used for washing ore in mining [c14 (n, meaning: a person who washes linen): changed from *lavender* washerwoman, from Old French *lavandiere*, ultimately from Latin *lavāre* to wash] ▷ 'launderer *n*

Launderette (ˌlɔːndəˈrɛt, lɔːnˈdrɛt) *n Trademark, Brit and NZ* a commercial establishment where clothes can be washed and dried, using coin-operated machines. Also called (US, Canadian, and NZ): Laundromat

laundress ('lɔːndrɪs) *n* a woman who launders clothes, sheets, etc, for a living

laundrette (lɔːnˈdrɛt) *n* a variant of **Launderette**

Laundromat ('lɔːndrəˌmæt) *n trademark US, Canadian, & NZ* a commercial establishment where clothes can be washed and dried, using coin-operated machines. Also called (in Britain and certain other countries): Launderette, laundrette

laundry ('lɔːndrɪ) *n, pl* **-dries 1** a place where clothes and linen are washed and ironed **2** the clothes or linen washed and ironed **3** the act of laundering [c16 changed from c14 *lavendry*; see LAUNDER]

laundry list *n US and Canadian* a list of items perceived as being long: *a laundry list of complaints*

laundryman ('lɔːndrɪmən) *n, pl* **-men 1** a man who collects or delivers laundry **2** a man who works in a laundry

laundrywoman ('lɔːndrɪˌwʊmən) *n, pl* **-women 1** a woman who collects or delivers laundry **2** a woman who works in a laundry

lauraceous (lɔːˈreɪʃəs) *adj* of, relating to, or belonging to the *Lauraceae*, a family of aromatic trees and shrubs having leathery leaves: includes the laurels and avocado

Laurasia (lɔːˈreɪʃə) *n* one of the two ancient supercontinents produced by the first split of the even larger supercontinent Pangaea about 200 million years ago, comprising what are now North America, Greenland, Europe, and Asia (excluding India). See also **Gondwanaland, Pangaea** [c20 from New Latin *Laur(entia)* (referring to the ancient N American landmass, from *Laurentian* strata of the Canadian Shield) + (*Eur)asia*]

laureate ('lɔːrɪɪt) *adj* (*usually immediately postpositive*) **1** *literary* crowned with laurel leaves as a sign of honour **2** *archaic* made of laurel ▷ *n* **3** short for **poet laureate 4** a person honoured with an award for art or science: *a Nobel laureate* **5** *rare* a person honoured with the laurel crown or wreath [c14 from Latin *laureātus*, from *laurea* LAUREL] ▷ 'laureateˌship *n* ▷ laureation (ˌlɔːrɪˈeɪʃən) *n*

laurel ('lɒrəl) *n* **1** Also called: **bay, true laurel** any lauraceous tree of the genus *Laurus*, such as the bay tree (see **bay⁴**) and *L. canariensis*, of the Canary Islands and Azores **2** any lauraceous plant **3** short for **cherry laurel** *or* **mountain laurel 4** spurge laurel a European thymelaeaceous evergreen shrub, *Daphne laureola*, with glossy leaves and small green flowers **5** spotted *or* Japan laurel an evergreen cornaceous shrub, *Aucuba japonica*, of S and SE Asia, the female of which has yellow-spotted leaves **6** (*plural*) a wreath of true laurel, worn on the head as an emblem of victory or honour in classical times **7** (*plural*) honour, distinction, or fame **8 look to one's laurels** to be on guard against one's rivals **9 rest on one's laurels** to be satisfied with distinction won by past achievements and cease to strive for further achievements ▷ *vb* **-rels, -relling, -relled** *or US* **-rels, -reling, -reled 10** (*tr*) to crown with laurels [c13 *lorer*, from Old French *lorier* laurel tree, ultimately from Latin *laurus*]

Laurentian (lɔːˈrɛnʃən) *adj* **1** Also: **Lawrentian** of or resembling the style of D. H. Lawrence (1885–1930), the British novelist, poet, and short-story writer, or T. E. *Lawrence* "of Arabia" (1885–1935), the British soldier and writer **2** of, relating to, or situated near the St Lawrence River

Laurentian Mountains *pl n* a range of low mountains in E Canada, in Quebec between the St Lawrence River and Hudson Bay. Highest point: 1191 m (3905 ft). Also called: **Laurentides** ('lɔːrənˌtaɪdz)

Laurentian Shield *n* another name for the **Canadian Shield** Also called: Laurentian Plateau

lauric acid ('lɔːrɪk, 'lɒ-) *n* another name for **dodecanoic acid** [c19 from Latin *laurus* laurel; from its occurrence in the berries of the laurel (*Laurus nobilis*)]

laurustinus (ˌlɔːrəˈstaɪnəs) *n* a Mediterranean caprifoliaceous shrub, *Viburnum tinus*, with glossy evergreen leaves and white or pink fragrant flowers [c17 from New Latin, from Latin *laurus* laurel]

lauryl alcohol ('lɔːrɪl, 'lɒ-) *n* a water-insoluble crystalline solid used in the manufacture of detergents; 1-dodecanol. Formula: $CH_3(CH_2)_{10}CH_2OH$ [c20 from LAUR(IC ACID) + -YL]

Lausanne (ləʊˈzæn; *French* lozan) *n* a city in W Switzerland, capital of Vaud canton, on Lake Geneva; cultural and commercial centre; university (1537). Pop: 116 300 (2002 est)

lav (læv) *n Brit informal* short for **lavatory**

lava ('lɑːvə) *n* **1** magma emanating from volcanoes and other vents **2** any extrusive igneous rock formed by the cooling and solidification of molten lava [c18 from Italian (Neapolitan dialect), from Latin *lavāre* to wash]

lavabo (ləˈveɪbəʊ) *n, pl* **-boes** *or* **-bos** *chiefly RC Church* **1 a** the ritual washing of the celebrant's hands after the offertory at Mass **b** (*as modifier*): *lavabo basin; lavabo towel* **2** another name for **washbasin 3** a trough for washing in a convent or monastery [c19 from Latin: I shall wash, the opening of Psalm 26:6]

lavage ('lævɪdʒ, læˈvɑːʒ) *n med* the washing out of a hollow organ by flushing with water [c19 via French, from Latin *lavāre* to wash]

Laval (ləˈvæl) *n* a city in SE Canada, in Quebec: a NW suburb of Montreal. Pop: 343 005 (2001)

lava lamp *n* a decorative type of lamp in which a luminous viscous material moves in constantly changing shapes [c20 from the resemblance of the shapes to molten lava in water]

lava-lava *n* a draped skirtlike garment of printed cotton or calico worn by Polynesians [Samoan]

lavatera (ˌlævəˈtɪərə) *n* any plant of the genus *Lavatera*, closely resembling mallow and grown for their purple, white, or rose-coloured flowers: family *Malvaceae* [named after the two brothers *Lavater*, 18th-century Swiss doctors and naturalists]

lavation (læˈveɪʃən) *n formal or literary* the act or process of washing [c17 from Latin *lavātio*, from *lavāre* to wash] > **laˈvational** *adj*

lavatorial (ˌlævəˈtɔːrɪəl) *adj* **1** of or in the style of decoration supposed to typify public lavatories: *white lavatorial tiling* **2** characterized by excessive mention of lavatories and the excretory functions; vulgar or scatological: *lavatorial humour*

lavatory (ˈlævətərɪ, -trɪ) *n, pl* **-ries 1** Also called: **toilet, water closet, WC a** a sanitary installation for receiving and disposing of urine and faeces, consisting of a bowl fitted with a water-flushing device and connected to a drain **b** a room containing such an installation **2** the washing place in a convent or monastic establishment [c14 from Late Latin *lavātōrium*, from Latin *lavāre* to wash]

lavatory paper *n Brit* another name for **toilet paper**

lave (leɪv) *vb* an archaic word for **wash** [Old English *lafian*, perhaps from Latin *lavāre* to wash]

lavender (ˈlævəndə) *n* **1** any of various perennial shrubs or herbaceous plants of the genus *Lavandula*, esp *L. vera*, cultivated for its mauve or blue flowers and as the source of a fragrant oil (**oil of lavender**): family *Lamiaceae* (labiates). See also **spike lavender** Compare **sea lavender 2** the dried parts of *L. vera*, used to perfume clothes **3 a** a pale or light bluish-purple to a very pale violet colour **b** (*as adjective*): *lavender socks* **4** (*modifier*) perfume scented with lavender **5** (*modifier*) *informal* of or relating to homosexuality: *lavender language* [c13 *lavendre*, via French from Medieval Latin *lavendula*, of obscure origin]

lavender bag *n* a small fabric bag filled with dried lavender flowers and placed amongst clothes or linen to scent them

lavender water *n* a perfume made of essential oils of lavender and alcohol

laver[1] (ˈleɪvə) *n* **1** *Old Testament* a large basin of water used by the priests for ritual ablutions **2** the font or the water of baptism [c14 from Old French *laveoir*, from Late Latin *lavātōrium* washing place]

laver[2] (ˈlɑːvə) *n* any of several seaweeds of the genus *Porphyra* and related genera, with edible fronds: phylum *Rhodophyta* (red algae) [c16 from Latin]

laver bread (ˈlɑːvə) *n* laver seaweed fried as a breakfast food; popular in Wales

laverock (ˈlævərək; *Scot also* ˈlevərək, ˈlevrək) *n* a Scot and northern English dialect word for **skylark** (bird) [Old English *lǣwerce* LARK[1]]

lavish (ˈlævɪʃ) *adj* **1** prolific, abundant, or profuse **2** generous; unstinting; liberal **3** extravagant; prodigal; wasteful: *lavish expenditure* ⊳ *vb* **4** (*tr*) to give, expend, or apply abundantly, generously, or in profusion [c15 adj use of *lavas* profusion, from Old French *lavasse* torrent, from Latin *lavāre* to wash] > **ˈlavisher** *n* > **ˈlavishly** *adv* > **ˈlavishment** *n* > **ˈlavishness** *n*

lavolta (ləˈvɒltə) *n* another word for **volta** [c16 from Italian *la volta* the turn; see VOLTA]

law[1] (lɔː) *n* **1** a rule or set of rules, enforceable by the courts, regulating the government of a state, the relationship between the organs of government and the subjects of the state, and the relationship or conduct of subjects towards each other **2 a** a rule or body of rules made by the legislature. See **statute law b** a rule or body of rules made by a municipal or other authority. See **bylaw 3 a** the condition and control enforced by such rules **b** (*in combination*): *lawcourt* **4** a rule of conduct: *a law of etiquette* **5** one of a set of rules governing a particular field of activity: *the laws of tennis* **6** the law **a** the legal or judicial system **b** the profession or practice of law **c** *informal* the police or a policeman **7** a binding force or statement: *his word is law* **8** Also called: **law of nature** a generalization based on a recurring fact or event **9** the science or knowledge of law; jurisprudence **10** the principles originating and formerly applied only in courts of common law. Compare **equity** (sense 3) **11** a general principle, formula, or rule describing a phenomenon in mathematics, science, philosophy, etc: *the laws of thermodynamics* **12** *Judaism* (*capital*; preceded by *the*) **a** short for **Law of Moses b** the English term for **Torah** ⊳ See also **Oral Law, Written Law 13** a law unto itself (oneself, etc) a person or thing that is outside established laws **14 go to law** to resort to legal proceedings on some matter **15 lay down the law** to speak in an authoritative or dogmatic manner **16 reading (of) the Law** *Judaism* that part of the morning service on Sabbaths, festivals, and Mondays and Thursdays during which a passage is read from the Torah scrolls **17 take the law into one's own hands** to ignore or bypass the law when redressing a grievance ⊳ Related adjectives: **judicial, jural, juridical, legal** [Old English *lagu*, from Scandinavian; compare Icelandic *lög* (pl) things laid down, law]

law[2] (lɔː) *n Scot* a hill, esp one rounded in shape [Old English *hlǣw*]

law[3] (lɔː) *adj* a Scot word for **low**[1]

law-abiding *adj* adhering more or less strictly to the laws: *a law-abiding citizen* > **ˈlaw-aˌbidingness** *n*

law agent *n* (in Scotland) a solicitor holding a certificate from the Law Society of Scotland and thereby entitled to appear for a client in any Sheriff Court

law-and-order *n* (*modifier*) favouring or advocating strong measures to suppress crime and violence: *a law-and-order candidate*

lawbreaker (ˈlɔːˌbreɪkə) *n* **1** a person who breaks the law **2** *informal* something that does not conform with legal standards or requirements > **ˈlawˌbreaking** *n, adj*

law centre *n Brit* an office, usually staffed by professional volunteers, at which free legal advice and information are provided to the general public

Law French *n* a set of Anglo-Norman terms used in English laws and law books

lawful (ˈlɔːfʊl) *adj* allowed, recognized, or sanctioned by law; legal > **ˈlawfully** *adv* > **ˈlawfulness** *n*

lawgiver (ˈlɔːˌgɪvə) *n* **1** the giver of a code of laws **2** Also called: **lawmaker** a maker of laws > **ˈlawˌgiving** *n, adj*

lawin *or* **lawing** (ˈlɔːɪn) *n Scot* a bill or reckoning [c16 from Old Norse *lag* market price]

lawks (lɔːks) *interj Brit* an expression of surprise or dismay [c18 variant of *Lord!*, probably influenced in form by ALACK]

lawless (ˈlɔːlɪs) *adj* **1** without law **2** disobedient to the law **3** contrary to or heedless of the law **4** uncontrolled; unbridled: *lawless rage* > **ˈlawlessly** *adv* > **ˈlawlessness** *n*

Law Lords *pl n* (in Britain) members of the House of Lords who sit as the highest court of appeal, although in theory the full House of Lords has this role

lawman (ˈlɔːmən) *n, pl* **-men** *chiefly US* an officer of the law, such as a policeman or sheriff

law merchant *n mercantile law* the body of rules and principles determining the rights and obligations of the parties to commercial transactions; commercial law

lawn[1] (lɔːn) *n* **1** a flat and usually level area of mown and cultivated grass **2** an archaic or dialect word for **glade** [c16 changed form of c14 *launde*, from Old French *lande*, of Celtic origin; compare Breton *lann* heath; related to LAND] > **ˈlawny** *adj*

lawn[2] (lɔːn) *n* a fine linen or cotton fabric, used for clothing [c15 probably from *Laon*, a town in France where linen was made] > **ˈlawny** *adj*

lawn mower *n* a hand-operated or power-operated machine with rotary blades for cutting grass on lawns

lawn tennis *n* **1** tennis played on a grass court **2** the formal name for **tennis**

law of averages *n* (popularly) the expectation that a possible event is bound to occur regularly with a frequency approximating to its probability, as in the (actually false) example: *after five heads in a row the law of averages makes tails the better bet.* Compare **law of large numbers**

law of effect *n psychol* another name for **Thorndike's Law**

law of large numbers *n* the fundamental statistical result that the average of a sequence of n identically distributed independent random variables tends to their common mean as n tends to infinity, whence the frequency of the occurrence of an event in n independent repetitions of an experiment tends to its probability

Law of Moses *n* **1** the first five books of the Old Testament; Pentateuch **2** *Judaism* a law or body of laws derived from the Torah in accordance with interpretations (the Oral Law) traditionally believed to have been given to Moses on Mount Sinai together with the Written Law

law of nations *n* another term for **international law**

law of nature *n* **1** an empirical truth of great generality, conceived of as a physical (but not a logical) necessity, and consequently licensing counterfactual conditionals **2** a system of morality conceived as grounded in reason. See **natural law** (sense 2), **nomological** (sense 2) **3** See **law** (sense 8)

law of supply and demand *n* the theory that prices are determined by the interaction of supply and demand: an increase in supply will lower prices if not accompanied by increased demand, and an increase in demand will raise prices unless accompanied by increased supply

law of the jungle *n* a state of ruthless competition or self-interest

law of thermodynamics *n* **1** any of three principles governing the relationships between different forms of energy. The **first law of thermodynamics** (law of conservation of energy) states that the change in the internal energy of a system is equal to the sum of the heat added to the system and the work done on it. The **second law of thermodynamics** states that heat cannot be transferred from a colder to a hotter body within a system without net changes occurring in other bodies within that system; in any irreversible process, entropy always increases. The **third law of thermodynamics** (Nernst heat theorem) states that it is impossible to reduce the temperature of a system to absolute zero in a finite number of steps **2** Also called: **zeroth law of thermodynamics** the principle that if two bodies are each in thermal equilibrium with a third body then the first two bodies are in thermal equilibrium with each other

lawrencium (lɒˈrɛnsɪəm, lɔː-) *n* a transuranic element artificially produced from californium. Symbol: Lr; atomic no.: 103; half-life of most stable isotope, ^{256}Lr: 35 seconds; valency: 3 [c20 named after Ernest Orlando Lawrence (1901–58), US physicist]

Lawrentian (lɔːˈrɛnʃən) *adj* relating to or characteristic of D(avid) H(erbert) Lawrence (1885-1930), the British novelist, poet, and short-story writer

Law Society *n* (in England or Scotland) the professional body of solicitors, established in 1825 and entrusted with the registration of solicitors (requiring the passing of certain examinations) and the regulation of professional conduct

law stationer *n* **1** a stationer selling articles used by lawyers **2** *Brit* a person who makes handwritten copies of legal documents

lawsuit (ˈlɔːˌsuːt, -ˌsjuːt) *n* a proceeding in a court of law brought by one party against another, esp a civil action

law term *n* **1** an expression or word used in law **2** any of various periods of time appointed for the sitting of law courts

lawyer (ˈlɔːjə, ˈlɔɪə) *n* **1** a member of the legal profession, esp a solicitor. See also **advocate, barrister, solicitor 2** a popular name for **burbot** (a fish) [C14 from LAW[1]]

lawyer's wig *n* another name for the **shaggy ink-cap**: see **ink-cap**

lawyer vine *n Austral* any of various kinds of entangling and thorny vegetation, such as the rattan palm, esp in tropical areas. Also called: **lawyer cane, lawyer palm**

lax (læks) *adj* **1** lacking firmness; not strict **2** lacking precision or definition **3** not taut **4** *phonetics* (of a speech sound) pronounced with little muscular effort and consequently having relatively imprecise accuracy of articulation and little temporal duration. In English the vowel *i* in *bit* is lax **5** (of flower clusters) having loosely arranged parts [C14 (originally used with reference to the bowels): from Latin *laxus* loose] > ˈ**laxly** *adv* > ˈ**laxity** *or* ˈ**laxness** *n*

laxation (lækˈseɪʃən) *n* **1** the act of making lax or the state of being lax **2** *physiol* another word for **defecation** [C14 from Latin *laxātio*, from *laxāre* to slacken]

laxative (ˈlæksətɪv) *n* **1** an agent stimulating evacuation of faeces ▷ *adj* **2** stimulating evacuation of faeces [C14 (originally: relaxing): from Medieval Latin *laxātīvus*, from Latin *laxāre* to loosen]

lay[1] (leɪ) *vb* **lays, laying, laid** (leɪd) (*mainly tr*) **1** to put in a low or horizontal position; cause to lie: *to lay a cover on a bed* **2** to place, put, or be in a particular state or position: *he laid his finger on his lips* **3** (*intr*) *dialect or not standard* to be in a horizontal position; lie: *he often lays in bed all the morning* **4** (sometimes foll by *down*) to establish as a basis: *to lay a foundation for discussion* **5** to place or dispose in the proper position: *to lay a carpet* **6** to arrange (a table) for eating a meal **7** to prepare (a fire) for lighting by arranging fuel in the grate **8** (*also intr*) (of birds, esp the domestic hen) to produce (eggs) **9** to present or put forward: *he laid his case before the magistrate* **10** to impute or attribute: *all the blame was laid on him* **11** to arrange, devise, or prepare: *to lay a trap* **12** to place, set, or locate: *the scene is laid in London* **13** to apply on or as if on a surface: *to lay a coat of paint* **14** to impose as a penalty or burden: *to lay a fine* **15** to make (a bet) with (someone): *I lay you five to one on Prince* **16** to cause to settle: *to lay the dust* **17** to allay; suppress: *to lay a rumour* **18** to bring down forcefully: *to lay a whip on someone's back* **19** *slang* to have sexual intercourse with **20** *slang* to bet on (a horse) to lose a race **21** to press down or make smooth: *to lay the nap of cloth* **22** to cut (small trunks or branches of shrubs or trees) halfway through and bend them diagonally to form a hedge: *to lay a hedge* **23** to arrange and twist together (strands) in order to form (a rope, cable, etc) **24** *military* to apply settings of elevation and training to (a weapon) prior to firing **25** (foll by *on*) *hunting* to put (hounds or other dogs) onto a scent **26** another word for **inlay 27** (*intr; often foll by to or out*) *dialect or informal* to plan, scheme, or devise **28** (*intr*) *nautical* to move or go, esp into a specified position or direction: *to lay close to the wind* **29 lay aboard** *nautical* (formerly) to move alongside a warship to board it **30 lay a course a** *nautical* to sail on a planned course without tacking **b** to plan an action **31 lay bare** to reveal or explain: *he laid bare his plans* **32 lay hands on** See **hands** (sense 12) **33 lay hold of** to seize or grasp **34 lay oneself open** to make oneself vulnerable (to criticism, attack, etc): *by making such a statement he laid himself open to accusations of favouritism* **35 lay open** to reveal or disclose **36 lay siege to** to besiege (a city, etc) ▷ *n* **37** the manner or position in which something lies or is placed **38** *taboo slang* **a** an act of sexual intercourse **b** a sexual partner **39** a portion of the catch or the profits from a whaling or fishing expedition **40** the amount or direction of hoist in the strands of a rope ▷ See also **layabout, lay aside, lay away, lay-by, lay down, lay in, lay into, lay off, lay on, lay out, lay over, lay to, lay up** [Old English *lecgan*; related to Gothic *lagjan*, Old Norse *leggja*]

> **USAGE** In careful English, the verb *lay* is used with an object and *lie* without one: *the soldier laid down his arms; the Queen laid a wreath; the book was lying on the table; he was lying on the floor.* In informal English, *lay* is frequently used for *lie*: *the book was laying on the table.* All careful writers and speakers observe the distinction even in informal contexts

lay[2] (leɪ) *vb* the past tense of **lie**[2]

lay[3] (leɪ) *adj* **1** of, involving, or belonging to people who are not clergy **2** nonprofessional or nonspecialist; amateur [C14 from Old French *lai*, from Late Latin *lāicus*, ultimately from Greek *laos* people]

lay[4] (leɪ) *n* **1** a ballad or short narrative poem, esp one intended to be sung **2** a song or melody [C13 from Old French *lai*, perhaps of Germanic origin]

layabout (ˈleɪəˌbaʊt) *n* **1** a lazy person; loafer ▷ *vb* **lay about 2** (*preposition, usually intr or reflexive*) *old-fashioned* to hit out with violent and repeated blows in all directions

lay analyst *n* a person without medical qualifications who practises psychoanalysis

lay aside *vb* (*tr, adverb*) **1** to abandon or reject **2** to store or reserve for future use

lay away *vb* (*tr, adverb*) **1** to store or reserve for future use **2** to reserve (merchandise) for future delivery, while payments are being made

layback (ˈleɪˌbæk) *n mountaineering* a technique for climbing cracks by pulling on one side of the crack with the hands and pressing on the other with the feet

lay brother *n* a man who has taken the vows of a religious order but is not ordained and not bound to divine office

lay-by *n* **1** *Brit* a place for drivers to stop at the side of a main road **2** *nautical* an anchorage in a narrow waterway, away from the channel **3** a small railway siding where rolling stock may be stored or parked **4** *Austral and NZ* a system of payment whereby a buyer pays a deposit on an article, which is reserved for him until he has paid the full price ▷ *vb* **lay by** (*adverb*) **5** (*tr*) to set aside or save for future needs **6** Also: **lay to** to cause (a sailing vessel) to stop in open water or (of a sailing vessel) to stop

lay days *pl n* **1** *commerce* the number of days permitted for the loading or unloading of a ship without payment of demurrage **2** *nautical* the time during which a ship is kept from sailing because of loading, bad weather, etc

laydeez (ˈleɪdiːz) *pl n informal* a jocular spelling of ladies, as pronounced in a mid-Atlantic accent

lay down *vb* (*tr, adverb*) **1** to place on the ground, etc **2** to relinquish or discard: *to lay down one's life* **3** to formulate (a rule, principle, etc) **4** to build or begin to build: *the railway was laid down as far as Manchester* **5** to record (plans) on paper **6** to convert (land) into pasture **7** to store or stock: *to lay down wine* **8** *informal* to wager or bet **9** (*tr, adverb*) *informal* to record (tracks) in a studio

layer (ˈleɪə) *n* **1** a thickness of some homogeneous substance, such as a stratum or a coating on a surface **2** one of four or more levels of vegetation defined in ecological studies: the ground or moss layer, the field or herb layer, the shrub layer, and one or more tree layers **3** a laying hen **4** *horticulture* **a** a shoot or branch rooted during layering **b** a plant produced as a result of layering ▷ *vb* **5** to form or make a layer of (something) **6** to take root or cause to take root by layering [C14 *leyer, legger*, from LAY[1] + -ER[1]]

layer cake *n* a cake made in layers with a filling

layering (ˈleɪərɪŋ) *n* **1** *horticulture* a method of propagation that induces a shoot or branch to take root while it is still attached to the parent plant **2** *geology* the banded appearance of certain igneous and metamorphic rocks, each band being of a different mineral composition

layette (leɪˈɛt) *n* a complete set of articles, including clothing, bedclothes, and other accessories, for a newborn baby [C19 from French, from Old French, from *laie*, from Middle Dutch *laege* box]

lay figure *n* **1** an artist's jointed dummy, used in place of a live model, esp for studying effects of drapery **2** a person considered to be subservient or unimportant [C18 from obsolete *layman*, from Dutch *leeman*, literally: joint-man]

lay in *vb* (*tr, adverb*) to accumulate and store: *we must lay in food for the party*

laying on of hands *n* (in Christian ordination, confirmation, faith healing, etc) the act of laying hands on a person's head to confer spiritual blessing

lay into *vb* (*intr, preposition*) *informal* **1** to attack forcefully **2** to berate severely

layman (ˈleɪmən) *n, pl* **-men 1** a man who is not a member of the clergy **2** a person who does not have specialized or professional knowledge of a subject: *science for the layman*

lay off *vb* **1** (*tr, adverb*) to suspend (workers) from employment with the intention of re-employing them at a later date: *the firm had to lay off 100 men* **2** (*intr*) *informal* to leave (a person, thing, or activity) alone: *lay off me, will you!* **3** (*tr, adverb*) to mark off the boundaries of **4** (*tr, adverb*) *soccer* to pass or deflect (the ball) to a team-mate, esp one in a more advantageous position **5** *gambling* another term for **hedge** (sense 10) ▷ *n* **lay-off 6** the act of suspending employees **7** a period of imposed unemployment

lay on *vb* (*tr, adverb*) **1** to provide or supply: *to lay on entertainment* **2** *Brit* to install: *to lay on electricity* **3 lay it on** *informal* **a** to exaggerate, esp when flattering **b** to charge an exorbitant price **c** to punish or strike harshly

lay out *vb* (*tr, adverb*) **1** to arrange or spread out **2** to prepare (a corpse) for burial or cremation **3** to plan or contrive **4** *informal* to spend (money), esp lavishly **5** *informal* to knock unconscious **6** *informal* to exert (oneself) or put (oneself) to an effort: *he laid himself out to please us* ▷ *n* **layout 7** the arrangement or plan of something, such as a building **8** the arrangement of written material, photographs, or other artwork on an advertisement or page in a book, newspaper, etc **9** a preliminary plan indicating this **10** a drawing showing the relative disposition of parts in a machine, etc **11** the act of laying out **12** something laid out **13** the formation of cards on the table in various games, esp in patience **14** *informal, chiefly US* a residence or establishment, esp a large one

lay over *US and Canadian* ▷ *vb* (*adverb*) **1** (*tr*) to postpone for future action **2** (*intr*) to make a temporary stop in a journey ▷ *n* **layover 3** a break in a journey, esp in waiting for a connection

lay person *or* **layperson** *n, pl* **lay persons** *or* **laypersons** *or* **lay people** *or* **laypeople 1** a person who is not a member of the clergy **2** a person who does not have specialized or professional knowledge of a subject: *a lay person's guide to conveyancing*

lay reader n 1 *Church of England* a person licensed by a bishop to conduct religious services other than the Eucharist 2 *RC Church* a layman chosen from among the congregation to read the epistle at Mass and sometimes other prayers

layshaft ('leɪˌʃɑːft) n an auxiliary shaft in a gearbox, running parallel to the main shaft, to and from which drive is transferred to enable varying ratios to be obtained

lay sister n a woman who has taken the vows of a religious order but is not ordained and not bound to divine office

laytime ('leɪˌtaɪm) n *commerce* the period of time allowed by a shipowner to a carrier to carry out cargo loading or discharging operations

lay to vb (intr, adverb) *nautical* 1 to bring a vessel into a haven 2 another term for **heave to**

lay up vb (tr, adverb) 1 to store or reserve for future use 2 (*usually passive*) *informal* to incapacitate or confine through illness

laywoman ('leɪwʊmən) n, pl -women 1 a woman who is not a member of the clergy 2 a woman who does not have specialized or professional knowledge of a subject: *a guide for the laywoman*

lazar ('læzə) n an archaic word for **leper** [c14 via Old French and Medieval Latin, after LAZARUS] > 'lazar-,like adj

lazaretto (ˌlæzə'rɛtəʊ) or **lazaret, lazarette** (ˌlæzə'rɛt) n, pl -rettos, -rets or -rettes 1 Also called: **glory hole** *nautical* a small locker at the stern of a boat or a storeroom between decks of a ship 2 Also called: **lazar house, pesthouse** (formerly) a hospital for persons with infectious diseases, esp leprosy [c16 Italian, from *lazzaro* LAZAR]

Lazarus ('læzərəs) n *New Testament* 1 the brother of Mary and Martha, whom Jesus restored to life (John 11–12) 2 the beggar who lay at the gate of the rich man Dives in Jesus' parable (Luke 16:19–31)

laze (leɪz) vb 1 (intr) to be indolent or lazy 2 (tr; often foll by *away*) to spend (time) in indolence ▷ n 3 the act or an instance of idling [c16 back formation from LAZY]

Lazio ('lattsjo) n 1 a region of W central Italy, on the Tyrrhenian Sea: includes the plain of the lower Tiber, the reclaimed Pontine Marshes, and Campagna. Capital: Rome. Pop: 5 145 805 (2003 est) 2 the Italian name for **Latium**

lazuli ('læzjʊˌlaɪ) n short for **lapis lazuli**

lazulite ('læzjʊˌlaɪt) n a blue mineral, consisting of hydrated magnesium iron phosphate, occurring in metamorphic rocks. Formula: $(Mg,Fe)Al_2(PO_4)_2(OH)_2$ [c19 from Medieval Latin *lāzulum* azure, LAPIS LAZULI]

lazurite ('læzjʊˌraɪt) n a rare blue mineral consisting of a sodium–calcium–aluminium silicate and sulphide: used as the gemstone lapis lazuli. Formula: $(Na,Ca)_8(AlSiO_4)_6(SO_4,S,Cl)_2$ [c19 from Medieval Latin *lāzur* LAPIS LAZULI]

lazy ('leɪzɪ) adj lazier, laziest 1 not inclined to work or exertion 2 conducive to or causing indolence 3 moving in a languid or sluggish manner: *a lazy river* 4 (of a brand letter or mark on livestock) shown as lying on its side [c16 origin uncertain] > 'lazily adv > 'laziness n

lazy bed n (in parts of Scotland and Ireland, formerly) a patch in which potatoes were cultivated by laying them on the surface and covering them with kelp and with soil from a trench on either side of the bed

lazybones ('leɪzɪˌbəʊnz) n *informal* a lazy person

lazy daisy stitch n an embroidery stitch consisting of a long chain stitch, usually used in making flower patterns

lazy Susan n a revolving tray, often divided into sections, for holding condiments, etc

lazy tongs pl n a set of tongs with extensible arms to allow objects to be grasped or handled at a distance

lb¹ abbreviation for 1 *cricket* leg bye 2 Also: **lb** pound (weight) [Latin: *libra*]

lb² the internet domain name for Lebanon

LB international car registration for Liberia

LBD *informal* ▷ abbreviation for little black dress

lbf abbreviation for pound force. See **pound²** (sense 4)

LBO abbreviation for leveraged buyout

lb tr or **lb t** abbreviation for troy pound. See **pound** (sense 2)

LBV abbreviation for Late Bottled Vintage: applied to port wine that has been matured in casks for six years and is then ready for drinking

lbw *cricket* abbreviation for leg before wicket

lc¹ abbreviation for 1 left centre (of a stage, etc) 2 loco citato [Latin: in the place cited] 3 *printing* lower case

lc² the internet domain name for Saint Lucia

LC (in the US) abbreviation for Library of Congress

L/C, l/c or **lc** abbreviation for letter of credit

lcd or **LCD** abbreviation for lowest common denominator

LCD abbreviation for liquid-crystal display

l'chaim (lə'xɑjim) *interj, n* a variant spelling of lechaim

LCJ *Brit* ▷ abbreviation for Lord Chief Justice

LCL or **lcl** *commerce* abbreviation for less than carload lot

lcm or **LCM** abbreviation for lowest common multiple

L/Cpl abbreviation for lance corporal

ld abbreviation for load

Ld abbreviation for Lord (title)

LD abbreviation for 1 lethal dosage: usually used with a subscript numeral showing what percentage of a test group of animals dies as a result of either being given a substance being tested on them or being exposed to ionizing radiation, esp in the median lethal dose: LD_{50} 2 Low Dutch

L-D converter n *metallurgy* a vessel in which steel is made from pig iron by blowing oxygen into the molten metal through a water-cooled tube [c20 L(inz)-D(onawitz), from the Austrian towns of *Linz* and *Donawitz*, where the process was first used successfully]

Ldg abbreviation for leading: *Ldg seaman*

LDL abbreviation for low-density lipoprotein

L-dopa (ɛl'dəʊpə) n a substance occurring naturally in the body and used to treat Parkinson's disease. Formula: $C_9H_{11}NO_4$. Also called: levodopa [c20 from *L-d(ihydr)o(xy)p(henyl)a(lanine)*]

LDR *text messaging* abbreviation for long distance relationship

L-driver n *Brit* a learner-driver: a person who is learning to drive, has not yet passed the official driving test, and must be accompanied by a qualified driver and display L-plates on the car

LDS abbreviation for 1 Latter-day Saints 2 laus Deo semper [Latin: praise be to God for ever] 3 (in Britain) Licentiate in Dental Surgery

LE abbreviation for lupus erythematosus

-le suffix forming verbs denoting repeated or continuous action, often of a diminutive nature: *twiddle; wriggle; wrestle* [from Middle English -len, Old English -lian, with similar significance]

lea¹ (liː) n 1 *poetic* a meadow or field 2 land that has been sown with grass seed [Old English *lēah*; related to German dialect *loh* thicket]

lea² (liː) n 1 a unit for measuring lengths of yarn, usually taken as 80 yards for wool, 120 yards for cotton and silk, and 300 yards for linen 2 a measure of yarn expressed as the length per unit weight, usually the number of leas per pound [c14 of uncertain origin]

LEA (in Britain) abbreviation for Local Education Authority

leach¹ (liːtʃ) vb 1 to remove or be removed from a substance by a percolating liquid 2 to lose or cause to lose soluble substances by the action of a percolating liquid 3 another word for **percolate** (senses 1, 2) ▷ n 4 the act or process of leaching 5 a substance that is leached or the constituents removed by leaching 6 a porous vessel for

leaching [c17 variant of obsolete *letch* to wet, perhaps from Old English *leccan* to water; related to LEAK] > 'leacher n

leach² (liːtʃ) n a variant spelling of leech²

leachate ('liːtʃeɪt) n water that carries salts dissolved out of materials through which it has percolated, esp polluted water from a refuse tip

lead¹ (liːd) vb leads, leading, led (lɛd) 1 to show the way to (an individual or a group) by going with or ahead: *lead the party into the garden* 2 to guide or be guided by holding, pulling, etc: *he led the horse by its reins* 3 (tr) to cause to act, feel, think, or behave in a certain way; induce; influence: *he led me to believe that he would go* 4 (tr) to phrase a question to (a witness) that tends to suggest the desired answer 5 (when intr, foll by *to*) (of a road, route, etc) to serve as the means of reaching a place 6 (tr) to go ahead so as to indicate (esp in the phrase **lead the way**) 7 to guide, control, or direct: *to lead an army* 8 (tr) to direct the course of or conduct (water, a rope or wire, etc) along or as if along a channel 9 to initiate the action of (something); have the principal part in (something): *to lead a discussion* 10 to go at the head of or have the top position in (something): *he leads his class in geography* 11 (intr; foll by *with*) to have as the first or principal item: *the newspaper led with the royal birth* 12 *music* a *Brit* to play first violin in (an orchestra) b (intr) (of an instrument or voice) to be assigned an important entry in a piece of music 13 to direct and guide (one's partner) in a dance 14 (tr) a to pass or spend: *I lead a miserable life* b to cause to pass a life of a particular kind: *to lead a person a dog's life* 15 (intr; foll by *to*) to tend (to) or result (in): *this will only lead to misery* 16 to initiate a round of cards by putting down (the first card) or to have the right to do this: *she led a diamond* 17 (tr) to aim at a point in front of (a moving target) in shooting, etc, in order to allow for the time of flight 18 (intr) *boxing* to make an offensive blow, esp as one's habitual attacking punch: *southpaws lead with their right* 19 **lead astray** to mislead so as to cause error or wrongdoing 20 **lead by the nose** See **nose** (sense 12) ▷ n 21 a the first, foremost, or most prominent place b (as *modifier*): *lead singer* 22 example, precedence, or leadership: *the class followed the teacher's lead* 23 an advance or advantage held over others: *the runner had a lead of twenty yards* 24 anything that guides or directs; indication; clue 25 another name for **leash** 26 the act or prerogative of playing the first card in a round of cards or the card so played 27 the principal role in a play, film, etc, or the person playing such a role 28 a the principal news story in a newspaper: *the scandal was the lead in the papers* b the opening paragraph of a news story c (as *modifier*): *lead story* 29 *music* an important entry assigned to one part usually at the beginning of a movement or section 30 a wire, cable, or other conductor for making an electrical connection 31 *boxing* a one's habitual attacking punch b a blow made with this 32 *nautical* the direction in which a rope runs 33 a deposit of metal or ore; lode 34 the firing of a gun, missile, etc, ahead of a moving target to correct for the time of flight of the projectile ▷ See also **lead off, lead on, lead up to** [Old English *lǣdan*; related to *līthan* to travel, Old High German *līdan* to go]

lead² (lɛd) n 1 a heavy toxic bluish-white metallic element that is highly malleable: occurs principally as galena and used in alloys, accumulators, cable sheaths, paints, and as a radiation shield. Symbol: Pb; atomic no.: 82; atomic wt.: 207.2; valency: 2 or 4; relative density: 11.35; melting pt.: 327.502°C; boiling pt.: 1750°C. Related adjs: plumbic, plumbeous, plumbous 2 a lead weight suspended on a line used to take soundings of the depth of water 3 **swing the lead** to malinger or make up excuses 4 lead weights or shot, as used in cartridges, fishing lines, etc 5 a thin grooved strip of lead for holding small panes of glass or pieces of stained glass 6 (*plural*) a thin sheets or strips of lead used as a roof covering **b** a flat or low-pitched roof covered with such sheets **7** *printing* a thin strip of type metal used for spacing between lines of hot-metal type. Compare **reglet** (sense 2) **8 a** graphite or a mixture containing graphite, clay, etc, used for drawing **b** a thin stick of this material, esp the core of a pencil **9** (*modifier*) of, consisting of, relating to, or containing lead **10** go down like a lead balloon See **balloon** (sense 9) ▷ *vb* (*tr*) **11** to fill or treat with lead **12** to surround, cover, or secure with lead or leads **13** *printing* to space (type) by use of leads [Old English; related to Dutch *lood*, German *Lot*] > 'leadless *adj* > 'leady *adj*

lead acetate (lɛd) *n* a white crystalline toxic solid used in dyeing cotton and in making varnishes and enamels. Formula: $Pb(CH_3CO)_2$. Systematic name: **lead(II) acetate** Also called: **sugar of lead**

lead arsenate (lɛd) *n* a white insoluble toxic crystalline powder used as an insecticide and fungicide. Formula: $Pb_3(AsO_4)_2$.

Leadbeater's cockatoo ('lɛd,biːtəs) *n* another name for **Major Mitchell** [named after Benjamin *Leadbeater*, 19th-century British natural historian]

lead chromate (lɛd) *n chem* a yellow solid used as a pigment, as in chrome yellow. Formula: $PbCrO_4$

lead colic (lɛd) *n* a symptom of lead poisoning characterized by intense abdominal pain. Also called: **painter's colic**

leaded ('lɛdɪd) *adj* **1** (of windows) composed of small panes of glass held in place by thin grooved strips of lead: *leaded lights* **2** (of petrol) containing tetraethyl lead in order to improve combustion

leaden ('lɛdən) *adj* **1** heavy and inert **2** laboured or sluggish: *leaden steps* **3** gloomy, spiritless, or lifeless **4** made partly or wholly of lead **5** of a dull greyish colour: *a leaden sky* > 'leadenly *adv* > 'leadenness *n*

leader ('liːdə) *n* **1** a person who rules, guides, or inspires others; head **2** *music* **a** Also called (esp US and Canadian): **concertmaster** the principal first violinist of an orchestra, who plays solo parts, and acts as the conductor's deputy and spokesman for the orchestra **b** *US* a conductor or director of an orchestra or chorus **3 a** the first man on a climbing rope **b** the leading horse or dog in a team **4** *chiefly US and Canadian* an article offered at a sufficiently low price to attract customers. See also **loss leader 5** a statistic or index that gives an advance indication of the state of the economy **6** *chiefly Brit* Also called: **leading article** the leading editorial in a newspaper **7** *angling* another word for **trace²** (sense 32a) or **cast** (sense 32a) **8** *nautical* another term for **fairlead 9** a strip of blank film or tape used to facilitate threading a projector, developing machine, etc, and to aid identification **10** (*plural*) *printing* rows of dots or hyphens used to guide the reader's eye across a page, as in a table of contents **11** *botany* any of the long slender shoots that grow from the stem or branch of a tree: usually removed during pruning **12** *Brit* a member of the Government having primary authority in initiating legislative business (esp in the phrases **Leader of the House of Commons** and **Leader of the House of Lords**) **13** the senior barrister, usually a Queen's Counsel, in charge of the conduct of a case. Compare **junior** (sense 6) > 'leaderless *adj*

leaderboard ('liːdə,bɔːd) *n* a board displaying the names and current scores of the leading competitors, esp in a golf tournament

leadership ('liːdəʃɪp) *n* **1** the position or function of a leader **2** the period during which a person occupies the position of leader: *during her leadership very little was achieved* **3 a** the ability to lead **b** (*as modifier*): *leadership qualities* **4** the leaders as a group of a party, union, etc: *the union leadership is now very reactionary*

lead glass (lɛd) *n* glass that contains lead oxide as a flux

lead-in ('liːd,ɪn) *n* **1 a** an introduction to a subject **b** (*as modifier*): *a lead-in announcement* **2** the connection between a radio transmitter, receiver, etc, and the aerial or transmission line

leading¹ ('liːdɪŋ) *adj* **1** guiding, directing, or influencing **2** (*prenominal*) principal or primary **3** in the first position: *the leading car in the procession* **4** *maths* (of a coefficient) associated with the term of highest degree in a polynomial containing one variable: *in $5x^2 + 2x + 3$, 5 is the leading coefficient* > 'leadingly *adv*

leading² ('lɛdɪŋ) *n printing* the spacing between lines of photocomposed or digitized type. Also called: **interlinear spacing**

leading aircraftman ('liːdɪŋ) *n Brit air force* the rank above aircraftman > **leading aircraftwoman** *fem n*

leading article ('liːdɪŋ) *n journalism* **1** another term for **leader** (sense 6) **2** *chiefly US* the article given most prominence in a magazine or newspaper

leading dog *n NZ* a dog trained to lead a flock of sheep to prevent them breaking or stampeding

leading edge ('liːdɪŋ) *n* **1** the forward edge of a propeller blade, aerofoil, or wing. Compare **trailing edge 2** *electrical engineering* the part of a pulse signal that has an increasing amplitude ▷ *modifier* **leading-edge 3** advanced; foremost: *leading-edge technology*

leading light ('liːdɪŋ) *n* **1** an important or outstanding person, esp in an organization or cause **2** *nautical* a less common term for **range light**

leading man ('liːdɪŋ) *n* a man who plays the main part in a film, play, etc > **leading lady** *fem n*

leading note ('liːdɪŋ) *n music* **1** another word for **subtonic 2** (esp in cadences) a note, usually the subtonic of a scale, that tends most naturally to resolve to the note lying one semitone above it

leading question ('liːdɪŋ) *n* a question phrased in a manner that tends to suggest the desired answer, such as *What do you think of the horrible effects of pollution?*

leading rating *n* a rank in the Royal Navy comparable but junior to that of a corporal in the army

leading reins or *US and Canadian* **leading strings** ('liːdɪŋ) *pl n* **1** straps or a harness and strap used to assist and control a child who is learning to walk **2** excessive guidance or restraint

lead line (lɛd) *n nautical* a length of line for swinging a lead, marked at various points to indicate multiples of fathoms

lead monoxide (lɛd) *n* a poisonous insoluble oxide of lead existing in red and yellow forms: used in making glass, glazes, and cements, and as a pigment. Formula: PbO. Systematic name: **lead(II) oxide** Also called: **litharge, plumbous oxide**

lead off (liːd) *vb* (*adverb*) **1** to initiate the action of (something); begin ▷ *n* **lead-off 2** an initial move or action **3** a person or thing that begins something

lead on (liːd) *vb* (*tr, adverb*) to lure or entice, esp into trouble or wrongdoing

lead pencil (lɛd) *n* a pencil in which the writing material is a thin stick of a graphite compound

lead poisoning (lɛd) *n* **1** Also called: **plumbism, saturnism** acute or chronic poisoning by lead or its salts, characterized by abdominal pain, vomiting, convulsions, and coma **2** *US slang* death or injury resulting from being shot with bullets

lead screw (liːd) *n* a threaded rod that drives the tool carriage in a lathe when screw cutting, etc

leadsman ('lɛdzmən) *n, pl* -men *nautical* a sailor who takes soundings with a lead line

lead tetraethyl (lɛd) *n* another name for **tetraethyl lead**

lead time (liːd) *n* **1** *manufacturing* the time between the design of a product and its production **2** *commerce* the time from the placing of an order to the delivery of the goods

lead up to (liːd) *vb* (*intr, adverb + preposition*) **1** to act as a preliminary or introduction to **2** to approach (a topic) gradually or cautiously

leadwort ('lɛd,wɜːt) *n* any shrub of the plumbaginaceous genus *Plumbago*, of tropical and subtropical regions, with red, blue, or white flowers

leaf (liːf) *n, pl* leaves (liːvz) **1** the main organ of photosynthesis and transpiration in higher plants, usually consisting of a flat green blade attached to the stem directly or by a stalk. Related adjs: **foliar, foliate 2** foliage collectively **3** in leaf (of shrubs, trees, etc) having a full complement of foliage leaves **4** one of the sheets of paper in a book **5** a hinged, sliding, or detachable part, such as an extension to a table **6** metal in the form of a very thin flexible sheet: *gold leaf* **7** a foil or thin strip of metal in a composite material; lamina **8** short for **leaf spring 9** the inner or outer wall of a cavity wall **10** a crop that is harvested in the form of leaves **11** a metal strip forming one of the laminations in a leaf spring **12** a slang word for **marijuana 13** take a leaf out of (or from) someone's book to imitate someone, esp in one particular course of action **14** turn over a new leaf to begin a new and improved course of behaviour ▷ *vb* **15** (when *intr*, usually foll by *through*) to turn (through pages, sheets, etc) cursorily **16** (*intr*) (of plants) to produce leaves [Old English; related to Gothic *laufs*, Icelandic *lauf*] > 'leafless *adj* > 'leaflessness *n* > 'leaf,like *adj*

leafage ('liːfɪdʒ) *n* a less common word for **foliage**

leaf beet *n* another name for **chard**

leaf beetle *n* any of a large family of beetles (*Chrysomelidae*) that includes more than 25,000 species, mostly leaf feeders and mostly brightly coloured, with a metallic sheen. It includes the notorious **Colorado beetle**, the **bloody-nosed beetle** and the **flea beetles** (*Phyllotreta* species) which attack young cabbage plants

leaf-climber *n* a plant that climbs by using leaves specialized as tendrils

leafcutter ant ('liːf,kʌtə) *n* any of various South American ants of the genus *Atta* that cut pieces of leaves and use them as fertilizer for the fungus on which they feed

leafcutter bee *n* any of various solitary bees of the genus *Megachile* that nest in soil or rotten wood, constructing the cells in which they lay their eggs from pieces of leaf

leaf fat *n* the dense fat that accumulates in layers around the kidneys of certain animals, esp pigs

leaf gap *n botany* a region of parenchyma cells in the vascular tissue of flowering plants and some ferns, situated above a leaf trace

leaf-hopper *n* any homopterous insect of the family *Cicadellidae*, including various pests of crops

leaf insect *n* any of various mostly tropical Asian insects of the genus *Phyllium* and related genera, having a flattened leaflike body: order *Phasmida*. See also **stick insect**

leaf-lard *n* lard prepared from the leaf fat of a pig

leaflet ('liːflɪt) *n* **1** a printed and usually folded sheet of paper for distribution, usually free and containing advertising material or information about a political party, charity, etc **2** any of the subdivisions of a compound leaf such as a fern leaf **3** (*loosely*) any small leaf or leaflike part ▷ *vb* **4** to distribute printed leaflets (to): *they leafleted every flat in the area* > 'leafleter *n*

leaf miner *n* **1** any of various insect larvae that bore into and feed on leaf tissue, esp the larva of dipterous flies of the genus *Philophylla* (family *Trypetidae*) and the caterpillar of moths of the family *Gracillariidae* **2** the adult insect of any of these larvae

leaf monkey *n* another name for **langur**

leaf mould *n* **1** a nitrogen-rich material consisting of decayed leaves, etc, used as a fertilizer **2** any of various fungus diseases affecting the leaves of certain plants

leaf sheath *n botany* the basal part of a grass leaf that encircles the stem

leaf sight *n* a folding rear sight on certain rifles

leaf spot *n* any of various plant diseases, usually caused by fungi: characterized by dark lesions on the leaves

leaf spring *n* 1 one of a number of metal strips bracketed together in length to form a compound spring 2 the compound spring so formed

leafstalk ('liːfˌstɔːk) *n* the stalk attaching a leaf to a stem or branch. Technical name: **petiole**

leaf trace *n botany* a vascular bundle connecting the vascular tissue of the stem with that of a leaf

leafy ('liːfɪ) *adj* **leafier, leafiest** 1 covered with or having leaves 2 resembling a leaf or leaves > **'leafiness** *n*

league¹ (liːg) *n* 1 an association or union of persons, nations, etc, formed to promote the interests of its members 2 an association of sporting clubs that organizes matches between member teams of a similar standard 3 a class, category, or level: *he is not in the same league* 4 **in league (with)** working or planning together with 5 (*modifier*) of, involving, or belonging to a league: *a league game; a league table* ▷ *vb* **leagues, leaguing, leagued** 6 to form or be formed into a league [C15 from Old French *ligue*, from Italian *liga*, ultimately from Latin *ligāre* to bind]

league² (liːg) *n* an obsolete unit of distance of varying length. It is commonly equal to 3 miles [C14 *leuge*, from Late Latin *leuga, leuca*, of Celtic origin]

league football *n* 1 Also called: **league** *chiefly Austral* rugby league football 2 *Austral* an Australian Rules competition conducted within a league rather than a football association

League of Nations *n* an international association of states founded in 1920 with the aim of preserving world peace: dissolved in 1946

leaguer¹ ('liːgə) *n archaic* 1 an encampment, esp of besiegers 2 the siege itself [C16 from Dutch *leger* siege; related to LAIR¹]

leaguer² ('liːgə) *n chiefly US and Canadian* a member of a league

league table *n Brit* 1 a tabulated comparison of clubs or teams competing in a sporting league 2 a set of statistics used to compare the performance of a number of individuals, groups, or institutions: *a league table of examination results*

Leah (lɪə) *n Old Testament* the first wife of Jacob and elder sister of Rachel, his second wife (Genesis 29)

leak (liːk) *n* 1 a a crack, hole, etc, that allows the accidental escape or entrance of fluid, light, etc b such escaping or entering fluid, light, etc 2 **spring a leak** to develop a leak 3 something resembling this in effect: *a leak in the defence system* 4 the loss of current from an electrical conductor because of faulty insulation, etc 5 a disclosure, often intentional, of secret information 6 the act or an instance of leaking 7 a slang word for **urination** ▷ *vb* 8 to enter or escape or allow to enter or escape through a crack, hole, etc 9 (when *intr*, often foll by *out*) to disclose (secret information), often intentionally, or (of secret information) to be disclosed 10 (*intr*) a slang word for **urinate** [C15 from Scandinavian; compare Old Norse *leka* to drip] > **'leaker** *n*

leakage ('liːkɪdʒ) *n* 1 the act or an instance of leaking 2 something that escapes or enters by a leak 3 *commerce* an allowance made for partial loss (of stock, etc) due to leaking 4 *physics* a an undesired flow of electric current, neutrons, etc b (*as modifier*): *leakage current*

leaky ('liːkɪ) *adj* **leakier, leakiest** leaking or tending to leak > **'leakiness** *n*

leal (liːl) *adj Scot* loyal; faithful [C13 from Old French *leial*, from Latin *lēgālis* LEGAL; related to LOYAL] > **'leally** *adv* > **lealty** ('liːəltɪ) *n*

Leamington Spa ('lɛmɪŋtən) *n* a town in central England, in central Warwickshire: saline springs. Pop: 61 595 (2001). Official name: **Royal Leamington Spa**

lean¹ (liːn) *vb* **leans, leaning; leaned** or **leant** 1 (foll by *against, on,* or *upon*) to rest or cause to rest against a support 2 to incline or cause to incline from a vertical position 3 (*intr*; foll by *to* or *towards*) to have or express a tendency or leaning 4 **lean over backwards** *informal* to make a special effort, esp in order to please ▷ *n* 5 the condition of inclining from a vertical position ▷ See also **lean on** [Old English *hleonian, hlinian*; related to Old High German *hlinēn*, Latin *clīnāre* to INCLINE]

lean² (liːn) *adj* 1 (esp of a person or an animal) having no surplus flesh or bulk; not fat or plump 2 not bulky or full 3 (of meat) having little or no fat 4 not rich, abundant, or satisfying 5 (of a mixture of fuel and air) containing insufficient fuel and too much air: *a lean mixture* 6 (of printer's type) having a thin appearance 7 (of a paint) containing relatively little oil 8 (of an ore) not having a high mineral content 9 (of concrete) made with a small amount of cement ▷ *n* 10 the part of meat that contains little or no fat [Old English *hlǣne*, of Germanic origin] > **'leanly** *adv* > **'leanness** *n*

lean-burn *adj* (esp of an internal-combustion engine) designed to use a lean mixture of fuel and air in order to reduce petrol consumption and exhaust emissions

Leander (lɪˈændə) *n* (in Greek legend) a youth of Abydos, who drowned in the Hellespont in a storm on one of his nightly visits to Hero, his beloved. See also **Hero**¹

leaning ('liːnɪŋ) *n* a tendency or inclination

lean on *vb* (*intr, preposition*) 1 Also: **lean upon** to depend on for advice, support, etc 2 *informal* to exert pressure on (someone), as by threats or intimidation

leant (lɛnt) *vb* a past tense and past participle of **lean**¹

lean-to *n, pl* **-tos** 1 a roof that has a single slope with its upper edge adjoining a wall or building 2 a shed or outbuilding with such a roof

leap (liːp) *vb* **leaps, leaping; leapt** or **leaped** 1 (*intr*) to jump suddenly from one place to another 2 (*intr*; often foll by *at*) to move or react quickly 3 (*tr*) to jump over 4 to come into prominence rapidly: *the thought leapt into his mind* 5 (*tr*) to cause (an animal, esp a horse) to jump a barrier ▷ *n* 6 the act of jumping 7 a spot from which a leap was or may be made 8 the distance of a leap 9 an abrupt change or increase 10 Also called (US and Canadian): **skip** *music* a relatively large melodic interval, esp in a solo part 11 **a leap in the dark** an action performed without knowledge of the consequences 12 **by leaps and bounds** with unexpectedly rapid progress [Old English *hlēapan*; related to Gothic *hlaupan*, German *laufen*] > **'leaper** *n*

leapfrog ('liːpˌfrɒg) *n* 1 a children's game in which each player in turn leaps over the others' bent backs, leaning on them with the hands and spreading the legs wide ▷ *vb* **-frogs, -frogging, -frogged** 2 a (*intr*) to play leapfrog b (*tr*) to leap in this way over (something) 3 to advance or cause to advance by jumps or stages

leap second *n* a second added to or removed from a scale for reckoning time on one particular occasion, to synchronize it with another scale

leapt (lɛpt, liːpt) *vb* a past tense and past participle of **leap**

leap year *n* a calendar year of 366 days, February 29 (**leap day**) being the additional day, that occurs every four years (those whose number is divisible by four) except for century years whose number is not divisible by 400. It offsets the difference between the length of the solar year (365.2422 days) and the calendar year of 365 days

lea-rig ('liːˌrɪg) *n Scot* a ridge of unploughed land [Old English *lǣghrycg*]

learn (lɜːn) *vb* **learns, learning; learned** (lɜːnd) or **learnt** 1 (when *tr*, may take a clause as object) to gain knowledge of (something) or acquire skill in (some art or practice) 2 (*tr*) to commit to memory 3 (*tr*) to gain by experience, example, etc 4 (*intr*; often foll by *of* or *about*) to become informed; know 5 *not standard* to teach [Old English *leornian*; related to Old High German *lirnen*] > **'learnable** *adj*

learned ('lɜːnɪd) *adj* 1 having great knowledge or erudition 2 involving or characterized by scholarship 3 (*prenominal*) a title applied in referring to a member of the legal profession, esp to a barrister: *my learned friend* > **'learnedly** *adv* > **'learnedness** *n*

learned helplessness *n* the act of giving up trying as a result of consistent failure to be rewarded in life, thought to be a cause of depression

learner ('lɜːnə) *n* 1 someone who is learning something; beginner 2 (in South Africa) a school pupil

learner's chain *n NZ* an inexperienced team of slaughtermen working in a freezing works

learning ('lɜːnɪŋ) *n* 1 knowledge gained by study; instruction or scholarship 2 the act of gaining knowledge 3 *psychol* any relatively permanent change in behaviour that occurs as a direct result of experience

learning curve *n* a graphical representation of progress in learning: *I'm still only half way up the learning curve*

learning support assistant *n* same as **classroom assistant**

learnt (lɜːnt) *vb* a past tense and past participle of **learn**

leary *adj* **learier, leariest** *Southwest English dialect* empty

lease¹ (liːs) *n* 1 a contract by which property is conveyed to a person for a specified period, usually for rent 2 the instrument by which such property is conveyed 3 the period of time for which it is conveyed 4 a prospect of renewed health, happiness, etc: *a new lease of life* ▷ *vb* (*tr*) 5 to grant possession of (land, buildings, etc) by lease 6 to take a lease of (property); hold under a lease [C15 via Anglo-French from Old French *lais* (n), from *laissier* to let go, from Latin *laxāre* to loosen] > **'leasable** *adj* > **'leaser** *n*

lease² (liːz) *n dialect* open pasture or common [Old English *lǣs*; perhaps related to Old Norse *lāth* property]

leaseback ('liːsˌbæk) *n* a property transaction in which the buyer leases the property to the seller

leasehold ('liːsˌhəʊld) *n* 1 land or property held under a lease 2 the tenure by which such property is held 3 (*modifier*) held under a lease

leaseholder ('liːsˌhəʊldə) *n* 1 a person in possession of leasehold property 2 a tenant under a lease

leash (liːʃ) *n* 1 a line or rope used to walk or control a dog or other animal; lead 2 something resembling this in function: *he kept a tight leash on his emotions* 3 *hunting* three of the same kind of animal, usually hounds, foxes, or hares 4 **straining at the leash** eagerly impatient to begin something ▷ *vb* 5 (*tr*) to control or secure by or as if by a leash [C13 from Old French *laisse*, from *laissier* to loose (hence, to let a dog run on a leash), ultimately from Latin *laxus* LAX]

least (liːst) *determiner* 1 a **the** the superlative of **little** *you have the least talent of anyone* b (*as pronoun; functioning as sing*): *least isn't necessarily worst* 2 **at least** a if nothing else: *you should at least try* b **at the least** 3 **at the least** Also: **at least** at the minimum: *at the least you should earn a hundred pounds* 4 **in the least** (*usually used with a negative*) in the slightest degree; at all: *I don't mind in the least* ▷ *adv* 5 **the least** superlative of **little** *they travel the least of all* ▷ *adj* 6 of very little importance or rank [Old English *lǣst*, superlative of *lǣssa* LESS]

least common denominator *n* another name for **lowest common denominator**

least common multiple *n* another name for **lowest common multiple**

least squares *n* a method for determining the best value of an unknown quantity relating one or more sets of observations or measurements, esp to find a curve that best fits a set of data. It states that the sum of the squares of the deviations of the experimentally determined value from its optimum value should be a minimum

leastways ('liːstˌweɪz) *or US and Canadian* **leastwise** *adv informal* at least; anyway; at any rate

leat (liːt) *n Brit* a trench or ditch that conveys water to a mill wheel [Old English *-gelæt* (as in *wætergelæt* water channel), from LET¹]

leather ('lɛðə) *n* **1 a** a material consisting of the skin of an animal made smooth and flexible by tanning, removing the hair, etc **b** *(as modifier)*: *leather goods.* Related adjs: **coriaceous, leathern 2** *(plural)* leather clothes, esp as worn by motorcyclists **3** the flap of a dog's ear ▷ *vb (tr)* **4** to cover with leather **5** to whip with or as if with a leather strap [Old English *lether-* (in compound words); related to Old High German *leder*, Old Norse *lethr-*]

leatherback ('lɛðəˌbæk) *n* a large turtle, *Dermochelys coriacea*, of warm and tropical seas, having a ridged leathery carapace: family *Dermochelidae*. Also called (in Britain): leathery turtle

leather beetle *n* See dermestid

leatherette (ˌlɛðə'rɛt) *n* an imitation leather made from paper, cloth, etc

leatherhead ('lɛðəˌhɛd) *n* another name for **friarbird**

Leatherhead ('lɛðəˌhɛd) *n* a town in S England, in Surrey. Pop: 42 885 (2001)

leatherjacket ('lɛðəˌdʒækɪt) *n* **1** any of various tropical carangid fishes of the genera *Oligoplites* and *Scomberoides*, having a leathery skin **2** any of various brightly coloured tropical triggerfishes of the genus *Monacanthus* and related genera **3** the greyish-brown tough-skinned larva of certain craneflies, esp of the genus *Tipula*, which destroy the roots of grasses, etc

leathern ('lɛðən) *adj archaic* made of or resembling leather

leatherneck ('lɛðəˌnɛk) *n slang* a member of the US Marine Corps [from the custom of facing the neckband of their uniform with leather]

leatherwood ('lɛðəˌwʊd) *n* **1** Also called: wicopy a North American thymelaeaceous shrub, *Dirca palustris*, with pale yellow flowers and tough flexible branches **2** any of various Australian shrubs of the family *Cunoniaceae*

leathery ('lɛðərɪ) *adj* having the appearance or texture of leather, esp in toughness > 'leatheriness *n*

leave¹ (liːv) *vb* leaves, leaving, left (*mainly tr*) **1** (*also intr*) to go or depart (from a person or place) **2** to cause to remain behind, often by mistake, in a place: *he often leaves his keys in his coat* **3** to cause to be or remain in a specified state: *paying the bill left him penniless* **4** to renounce or abandon: *to leave a political movement* **5** to refrain from consuming or doing something: *the things we have left undone* **6** to result in; cause: *childhood problems often leave emotional scars* **7** to allow to be or remain subject to another person or thing: *leave the past to look after itself* **8** to entrust or commit: *leave the shopping to her* **9** to submit in place of one's personal appearance: *will you leave your name and address?* **10** to pass in a specified direction: *flying out of the country, we left the cliffs on our left* **11** to be survived by (members of one's family): *he leaves a wife and two children* **12** to bequeath or devise: *he left his investments to his children* **13** *(tr)* to have as a remainder: *37 – 14 leaves 23* **14** *not standard* to permit; let **15** leave be *informal* to leave undisturbed **16** leave go *or* hold of *not standard* to stop holding **17** leave it at that *informal* to take a matter no further **18** leave much to be desired to be very unsatisfactory **19** leave (someone) alone **a** Also: let alone See let¹ (sense 7) **b** to permit to stay or be alone **20** leave someone to himself not to control or direct someone ▷ See also **leave behind, leave off, leave out** [Old English *læfan*; related to *belīfan* to be left as a remainder] > 'leaver *n*

leave² (liːv) *n* **1** permission to do something: *he was granted leave to speak* **2** by *or* with your leave with your permission **3** permission to be absent, as from a place of work or duty: *leave of absence* **4** the duration of such absence: *ten days' leave* **5** a farewell or departure (esp in the phrase **take** (**one's**) **leave**) **6** on leave officially excused from work or duty **7** take leave (of) to say farewell (to) **8** take leave of one's senses to go mad or become irrational [Old English *lēaf*; related to *alȳfan* to permit, Middle High German *loube* permission]

leave³ (liːv) *vb* leaves, leaving, leaved (*intr*) to produce or grow leaves

leave behind *vb (tr)* **1** (*adverb*) to forget or neglect to bring or take **2** to cause to remain as a result or sign of something: *the storm left a trail of damage behind* **3** to pass: *once the wind came up, we soon left the land behind us*

leaved (liːvd) *adj* **a** having a leaf or leaves; leafed **b** (*in combination*): *a five-leaved stem*

leaven ('lɛvⁿn) *n also* leavening **1** any substance that produces fermentation in dough or batter, such as yeast, and causes it to rise **2** a piece of such a substance kept to ferment a new batch of dough **3** an agency or influence that produces a gradual change ▷ *vb (tr)* **4** to cause fermentation in (dough or batter) **5** to pervade, causing a gradual change, esp with some moderating or enlivening influence [C14 via Old French ultimately from Latin *levāmen* relief, (hence, raising agent, leaven), from *levāre* to raise]

Leavenworth ('lɛvⁿnˌwɜːθ, -wəθ) *n* a city in NE Kansas, on the Missouri River: the state's oldest city, founded in 1854 by proslavery settlers from Missouri. Pop: 35 211 (2003 est)

leave of absence *n* **1** permission to be absent from work or duty **2** the period of absence

leave off *vb* **1** (*intr*) to stop; cease **2** (*tr, adverb*) to stop wearing or using

leave out *vb (tr, adverb)* **1** to cause to remain in the open: *you can leave your car out tonight* **2** to omit or exclude

leaves (liːvz) *n* the plural of **leaf**

leave-taking *n* the act of departing; a farewell

leavings ('liːvɪŋz) *pl n* something remaining, such as food on a plate, residue, refuse, etc

Leavisite ('liːvɪsˌaɪt) *adj* **1** of or relating to F(rank) R(aymond) Leavis, the English literary critic (1895–1978), ▷ *n* **2** a follower or admirer of Leavis

Lebanese (ˌlɛbə'niːz) *adj* **1** of or relating to Lebanon or its inhabitants ▷ *n* **2** a native or inhabitant of Lebanon

Lebanon ('lɛbənən) *n* (sometimes preceded by *the*) a republic in W Asia, on the Mediterranean: an important centre of the Phoenician civilization in the third millennium BC; part of the Ottoman Empire from 1516 until 1919; gained independence in 1941 (effective by 1945). Official language: Arabic; French and English are also widely spoken. Religion: Muslim and Christian. Currency: Lebanese pound. Capital: Beirut. Pop: 3 708 000 (2004 est). Area: 10 400 sq km (4015 sq miles)

Lebanon Mountains *pl n* a mountain range in central Lebanon, extending across the whole country parallel with the Mediterranean coast. Highest peak: 3104 m (10 184 ft). Arabic name: Jebel Liban ('dʒɛbⁿl 'liːbɑːn)

leben ('lɛbⁿn) *n* a semiliquid food made from curdled milk in N Africa and the Levant [C17 from Arabic *laban*]

Lebensraum ('leɪbənzˌraʊm) *n* territory claimed by a nation or state on the grounds that it is necessary for survival or growth [German, literally: living space]

lebkuchen ('leɪbˌkuːkən) *n, pl* -chen a biscuit, originating from Germany, usually containing honey, spices, etc [German: literally, loaf cake]

Lebowa (lə'bəʊə) *n* a former Bantu homeland in NE South Africa, consisting of three separate

territories with several smaller exclaves: abolished in 1993

LEC (lɛk) *n acronym for* Local Enterprise Company. See **Training Agency**

Le Cateau (*French* lə kato) *n* a town in NE France: site (August 26, 1914) of the largest British battle since Waterloo, which led to the disruption of the German attack on the Allies. Pop: 7460 (1999)

Lecce (*Italian* 'lɛttʃe) *n* a walled city in SE Italy, in Puglia: Greek and Roman remains. Pop: 83 303 (2001)

leccy ('lɛkɪ) *n Brit informal* electricity

lech *or* **letch** (lɛtʃ) *informal* ▷ *vb* **1** (*intr*; usually foll by *after*) to behave lecherously (towards); lust (after) ▷ *n* **2** a lecherous act or indulgence [C19 back formation from LECHER]

Lech (lɛk; *German* lɛç) *n* a river in central Europe, rising in SW Austria and flowing generally north through S Germany to the River Danube. Length: 285 km (177 miles)

lechaim, lehaim *or* **l'chaim** (lə'xajim) *Judaism* ▷ *interj* **1** a drinking toast ▷ *n* **2** a small drink with which to toast something or someone [from Hebrew, literally: to life]

Le Chatelier's principle (lə ʃæ'tɛljeɪz) *n chem* the principle that if a system in chemical equilibrium is subjected to a disturbance it tends to change in a way that opposes this disturbance [C19 named after H. L. *Le Chatelier* (1850–1936), French chemist]

lecher ('lɛtʃə) *n* a promiscuous or lewd man [C12 from Old French *lecheor* lecher, from *lechier* to lick, of Germanic origin; compare Old High German *leccōn* to lick]

lecherous ('lɛtʃərəs) *adj* characterized by or inciting lechery > 'lecherously *adv*

lechery ('lɛtʃərɪ) *n, pl* -eries unrestrained and promiscuous sexuality

lecithin ('lɛsɪθɪn) *n biochem* any of a group of phospholipids that are found in many plant and animal tissues, esp egg yolk: used in making candles, cosmetics, and inks, and as an emulsifier and stabilizer in foods (E322). Systematic name: phosphatidylcholine [C19 from Greek *lekithos* egg yolk]

lecithinase (lə'sɪθɪˌneɪs) *n* any of a group of enzymes that remove the fatty-acid residue from lecithins: present in the venom of many snakes

Leclanché cell (lə'klɑːnʃeɪ) *n electrical engineering* a primary cell with a carbon anode, surrounded by crushed carbon and manganese dioxide in a porous container, immersed in an electrolyte of aqueous ammonium chloride into which the zinc cathode dips. The common dry battery is a form of Leclanché cell [C19 named after Georges *Leclanché* (1839–82), French engineer]

Le Creusot (*French* lə krøzo) *n* a town in E central France: metal, machinery, and armaments industries. Pop: 26 283 (1999)

lectern ('lɛktən) *n* **1** a reading desk or support in a church **2** any similar desk or support [C14 from Old French *lettrun*, from Late Latin *lectrum*, ultimately from *legere* to read]

lectin ('lɛktɪn) *n* a type of protein possessing high affinity for a specific sugar; lectins are often highly toxic [C20 from Latin *lectus*, past participle of *legere* to select + -IN]

lection ('lɛkʃən) *n* a variant reading of a passage in a particular copy or edition of a text [C16 from Latin *lectio* a reading, from *legere* to read, select]

lectionary ('lɛkʃənərɪ) *n, pl* -aries a book containing readings appointed to be read at divine services [C15 from Church Latin *lectiōnārium*, from *lectio* LECTION]

lector ('lɛktɔː) *n* **1** a lecturer or reader in certain universities **2** *RC Church* **a** a person appointed to read lessons at certain services **b** (in convents or monastic establishments) a member of the community appointed to read aloud during meals [C15 from Latin, from *legere* to read] > lectorate ('lɛktərɪt) *or* 'lector,ship *n*

lecture ('lɛktʃə) *n* **1** a discourse on a particular subject given or read to an audience **2** the text of such a discourse **3** a method of teaching by formal discourse **4** a lengthy reprimand or scolding ▷ *vb* **5** to give or read a lecture (to an audience or class) **6** (*tr*) to reprimand at length [C14 from Medieval Latin *lectūra* reading, from *legere* to read]

lecturer (ˈlɛktʃərə) *n* **1** a person who lectures **2** a teacher in higher education without professorial status

lectureship (ˈlɛktʃəˌʃɪp) *n* **1** the office or position of lecturer **2** an endowment financing a series of lectures

lecythus (ˈlɛsɪθəs) *n, pl* **-thi** (-ˌθaɪ) (in ancient Greece) a vase with a narrow neck [from Greek *lēkuthos*]

led (lɛd) *vb* the past tense and past participle of **lead¹**

LED *electronics abbreviation for* **light-emitting diode**

Leda¹ (ˈliːdə) *n Greek myth* a queen of Sparta who was the mother of Helen and Pollux by Zeus, who visited her in the form of a swan

Leda² (ˈliːdə) *n astronomy* a small satellite of Jupiter in an intermediate orbit

LED display *n* a flat-screen device in which an array of light-emitting diodes can be selectively activated to display numerical and alphabetical information, used esp in pocket calculators, digital timepieces, measuring instruments, and in some microcomputers

lederhosen (ˈleɪdəˌhəʊzᵊn) *pl n* leather shorts with H-shaped braces, worn by men in Austria, Bavaria, etc [German: leather trousers]

ledge (lɛdʒ) *n* **1** a narrow horizontal surface resembling a shelf and projecting from a wall, window, etc **2** a layer of rock that contains an ore; vein **3** a ridge of rock that lies beneath the surface of the sea **4** a narrow shelflike rock projection on a cliff or mountain [C14 *legge*, perhaps from *leggen* to LAY¹] > ˈ**ledgy** *or* **ledged** *adj*

ledger (ˈlɛdʒə) *n* **1** *book-keeping* the principal book in which the commercial transactions of a company are recorded **2** a flat horizontal slab of stone **3** a horizontal scaffold pole fixed to two upright poles for supporting the outer ends of putlogs **4** *angling* **a** a wire trace that allows the weight to rest on the bottom and the bait to float freely **b** (*as modifier*): *ledger tackle* ▷ *vb* **5** (*intr*) *angling* to fish using a ledger [C15 *legger* book retained in a specific place, probably from *leggen* to LAY¹]

ledger board *n* **1** a timber board forming the top rail of a fence or balustrade **2** Also called: **ribbon strip** a timber board fixed horizontally to studding to support floor joists

ledger line *n* **1** *music* a short line placed above or below the staff to accommodate notes representing pitches above or below the staff **2** *angling* a line using ledger tackle

lee (liː) *n* **1** a sheltered part or side; the side away from the direction from which the wind is blowing **2** **by the lee** *nautical* so that the wind is blowing on the wrong side of the sail **3** **under the lee** *nautical* towards the lee ▷ *adj* **4** (*prenominal*) *nautical* on, at, or towards the side or part away from the wind: *on a lee shore*. Compare **weather** (sense 5) [Old English *hlēow* shelter; related to Old Norse *hlé*]

Lee (liː) *n* a river in SW Republic of Ireland, flowing east into Cork Harbour. Length: about 80 km (50 miles)

leeboard (ˈliːˌbɔːd) *n nautical* one of a pair of large adjustable paddle-like boards that may be lowered along the lee side to reduce sideways drift or leeway

leech¹ (liːtʃ) *n* **1** any annelid worm of the class *Hirudinea*, which have a sucker at each end of the body and feed on the blood or tissues of other animals. See also **horseleech, medicinal leech** **2** a person who clings to or preys on another person **3** **a** an archaic word for **physician** **b** (*in combination*): *leechcraft* **4** **cling like a leech** to cling or adhere persistently to something ▷ *vb* **5** (*tr*) to use leeches to suck the blood of (a person), as a method of medical treatment [Old English *lǣce*, *lœce*; related to Middle Dutch *lieke*] > ˈ**leechˌlike** *adj*

leech² *or* **leach** (liːtʃ) *n nautical* the after edge of a fore-and-aft sail or either of the vertical edges of a squaresail [C15 of Germanic origin; compare Dutch *lijk*]

Leeds (liːdz) *n* **1** a city in N England, in Leeds unitary authority, West Yorkshire on the River Aire: linked with Liverpool and Goole by canals; a former centre of the clothing industry; two universities (1904, 1992). Pop: 443 247 (2001) **2** a unitary authority in N England, in West Yorkshire. Pop: 715 200 (2003 est). Area 562 sq km (217 sq miles)

Leeds Castle *n* a castle near Maidstone in Kent: the home of several medieval queens of England

leek (liːk) *n* **1** Also called: **scallion** an alliaceous plant, *Allium porrum*, with a slender white bulb, cylindrical stem, and broad flat overlapping leaves: used in cooking **2** any of several related species, such as *A. ampeloprasum* (wild leek) **3** a leek, or a representation of one, as a national emblem of Wales [Old English *lēac*; related to Old Norse *laukr*, Old High German *louh*]

leer (lɪə) *vb* **1** (*intr*) to give an oblique, sneering, or suggestive look or grin ▷ *n* **2** such a look [C16 perhaps verbal use of obsolete *leer* cheek, from Old English *hlēor*] > ˈ**leering** *adj, n* > ˈ**leeringly** *adv*

leery *or* **leary** (ˈlɪərɪ) *adj* **leerier, leeriest** *or* **learier, leariest** **1** *now chiefly dialect* knowing or sly **2** *slang* (foll by *of*) suspicious or wary **3** *slang* rowdy or boisterous [C18 perhaps from obsolete sense (to look askance) of LEER] > ˈ**leeriness** *or* ˈ**leariness** *n*

lees (liːz) *pl n* the sediment from an alcoholic drink [C14 plural of obsolete *lee*, from Old French, probably from Celtic; compare Irish *lige* bed]

leet¹ (liːt) *n English history* **1** Also called: **court-leet** a special kind of manorial court that some lords were entitled to hold **2** the jurisdiction of this court [C15 from Anglo-French, of unknown origin]

leet² (liːt) *n Scot* a list of candidates for an office [C15 perhaps from Anglo-French *litte*, variant of LIST¹]

Leeuwarden (*Dutch* ˈleːwardə) *n* a city in the N Netherlands, capital of Friesland province. Pop: 91 000 (2003 est)

leeward (ˈliːwəd; *Nautical* ˈluːəd) *chiefly nautical* ▷ *adj* **1** of, in, or moving to the quarter towards which the wind blows ▷ *n* **2** the point or quarter towards which the wind blows **3** the side towards the lee ▷ *adv* **4** towards the lee ▷ Compare **windward**

Leeward Islands (ˈliːwəd) *pl n* **1** a group of islands in the Caribbean, in the N Lesser Antilles between Puerto Rico and Martinique **2** a former British colony in the E Caribbean (1871–1956), consisting of Antigua, Barbuda, Redonda, Saint Kitts, Nevis, Anguilla, Montserrat, and the British Virgin Islands **3** a group of islands in the S Pacific, in French Polynesia in the W Society Archipelago: Huahiné, Raiatéa, Tahaa, Bora-Bora, and Maupiti. Pop: 30 221 (2002). French name: **Îles sous le Vent**

lee wave *n meteorol* a stationary wave sometimes formed in an air stream on the leeward side of a hill or mountain range

leeway (ˈliːˌweɪ) *n* **1** room for free movement within limits, as in action or expenditure **2** sideways drift of a boat or aircraft

Lefkoşa (lefˈkoʃə) *n* the Turkish name for **Nicosia**

left¹ (lɛft) *adj* **1** (*usually prenominal*) of or designating the side of something or someone that faces west when the front is turned towards the north **2** (*usually prenominal*) worn on a left hand, foot, etc **3** (*sometimes capital*) of or relating to the political or intellectual left **4** (*sometimes capital*) radical or progressive, esp as compared to less radical or progressive groups, persons, etc ▷ *adv* **5** on or in the direction of the left ▷ *n* **6** a left side, direction, position, area, or part. Related adjs: **sinister, sinistral** **7** (*often capital*) the supporters or advocates of varying degrees of social, political, or economic change, reform, or revolution designed to promote the greater freedom, power, welfare, or comfort of the common people **8** **to the left** radical in the methods, principles, etc, employed in striving to achieve such change **9** *boxing* **a** a blow with the left hand **b** the left hand [Old English *left* idle, weak, variant of *lyft-* (in *lyftādl* palsy, literally: left-disease); related to Middle Dutch *lucht* left]

left² (lɛft) *vb* the past tense and past participle of **leave¹**

Left Bank *n* a district of Paris, on the S bank of the River Seine; frequented by artists, students, etc

left brain *n* **a** the left hemisphere of the human brain, which is believed to control linear and analytical thinking, decision-making, and language **b** (*as modifier*): *a left-brain activity*

left-field *adj informal* regarded as being outside the mainstream; unconventional [C20 from baseball term *left field*, the area of the outfield to the batter's left, regarded as the scene of little action]

left-footer *n informal* (esp in Ireland and Scotland) a Roman Catholic [C20 from the Northern Irish saying that farm workers in Eire use the left foot to push a spade when digging]

left-hand *adj* (*prenominal*) **1** of, relating to, located on, or moving towards the left: *this car is left-hand drive; a left-hand bend* **2** for use by the left hand; left-handed

left-handed *adj* **1** using the left hand with greater ease than the right **2** performed with the left hand **3** designed or adapted for use by the left hand **4** worn on the left hand **5** awkward or clumsy **6** ironically ambiguous: *a left-handed compliment* **7** turning from right to left; anticlockwise **8** *law* another term for **morganatic** ▷ *adv* **9** with the left hand > ˌ**left-ˈhandedly** *adv* > ˌ**left-ˈhandedness** *n*

left-hander *n* **1** a blow with the left hand **2** a left-handed person

leftist (ˈlɛftɪst) *adj* **1** of, tending towards, or relating to the political left or its principles ▷ *n* **2** a person who supports or belongs to the political left > ˈ**leftism** *n*

left-luggage office *n Brit* a place at a railway station, airport, etc, where luggage may be left for a small charge with an attendant for safekeeping. US and Canadian name: **checkroom**

leftover (ˈlɛftˌəʊvə) *n* **1** (*often plural*) an unused portion or remnant, as of material or of cooked food ▷ *adj* **2** left as an unused portion or remnant

leftward (ˈlɛftwəd) *adj* **1** on or towards the left ▷ *adv* **2** a variant of **leftwards**

leftwards (ˈlɛftwədz) *or* **leftward** *adv* towards or on the left

left wing *n* **1** (*often capital*) the leftist faction of an assembly, party, group, etc; the radical or progressive wing **2** the units of an army situated on the left of a battle position **3** *sport* **a** the left-hand side of the field of play from the point of view of either team facing its opponents' goal **b** a player positioned in this area in certain games ▷ *adj* **left-wing** **4** of, belonging to, or relating to the political left wing > ˌ**left-ˈwinger** *n*

lefty (ˈlɛftɪ) *n, pl* **lefties** *informal* **1** a left-winger **2** *chiefly US and Canadian* a left-handed person

leg (lɛg) *n* **1** **a** either of the two lower limbs, including the bones and fleshy covering of the femur, tibia, fibula, and patella **b** (*as modifier*): *leg guard; leg rest*. Related adj: **crural** **2** any similar or analogous structure in animals that is used for locomotion or support **3** this part of an animal, esp the thigh, used for food: *leg of lamb* **4** something similar to a leg in appearance or function, such as one of the four supporting members of a chair **5** a branch, limb, or part of a forked or jointed object **6** the part of a garment that covers the leg **7** a section or part of a journey or course **8** a single stage, lap, length, etc, in a relay race **9** either one of two races on which a cumulative bet has been placed **10** either the opposite or adjacent side of a right-angled triangle **11** *nautical* **a** the distance travelled without tacking **b** (in yacht racing) the course between any two marks **12** one of a series of games, matches, or parts of games **13** *cricket* **a** the side of the field to the left of a right-handed batsman as he faces the bowler **b** (*as modifier*): *a leg slip; leg stump* **14** give (someone) a leg up **a** to help (someone) to climb an obstacle by pushing upwards **b** to help (someone) to advance **15** have legs *informal* to be successful or show the potential to succeed **16** not have a leg to stand on to have no reasonable or logical basis for an opinion or argument **17** on his, its, etc, last legs (of a person or thing) worn out; exhausted **18** pull (someone's) leg *informal* to tease, fool, or make fun of (someone) **19** shake a leg *informal* **a** to hurry up: usually used in the imperative **b** to dance **20** show a leg *informal* to get up in the morning **21** stretch one's legs See **stretch** (sense 17) ▷ *vb* **legs, legging, legged 22** (*tr*) *obsolete* to propel (a canal boat) through a tunnel by lying on one's back and walking one's feet along the tunnel roof **23** leg it *informal* to walk, run, or hurry [C13 from Old Norse *leggr*, of obscure origin] > 'leg,like *adj*

leg. *abbreviation for* legato

legacy ('lɛgəsɪ) *n, pl* -cies **1** a gift by will, esp of money or personal property **2** something handed down or received from an ancestor or predecessor **3** (*modifier*) surviving computer systems, hardware, or software: *legacy network; legacy application* [C14 (meaning: office of a legate), C15 (meaning: bequest): from Medieval Latin *lēgātia* commission; see LEGATE]

legal ('li:gᵊl) *adj* **1** established by or founded upon law; lawful **2** of or relating to law **3** recognized, enforceable, or having a remedy at law rather than in equity **4** relating to or characteristic of the profession of law [C16 from Latin *lēgālis,* from *lēx* law] > 'legally *adv*

legal aid *n* a means-tested benefit in the form of financial assistance for persons to meet the cost of advice and representation in legal proceedings

legal cap *n US* ruled writing paper, about 8 by 13½ inches with the fold at the top, for use by lawyers

legalese (,li:gə'li:z) *n* the conventional language in which legal documents, etc, are written

legal holiday *n US* any of several weekdays which are observed as national holidays. Also called (Canadian): **statutory holiday** Brit equivalent: **bank holiday**

legalism ('li:gə,lɪzəm) *n* strict adherence to the law, esp the stressing of the letter of the law rather than its spirit > 'legalist *n, adj*

legalistic (,li:gə'lɪstɪk) *adj* of, relating to, or exhibiting strict adherence to the law, esp to the letter of the law rather than its spirit > ,legal'istically *adv*

legality (lɪ'gælɪtɪ) *n, pl* -ties **1** the state or quality of being legal or lawful **2** adherence to legal principles

legalize or **legalise** ('li:gə,laɪz) *vb* (*tr*) **1** to make lawful or legal **2** to confirm or validate (something previously unlawful) > ,legali'zation or ,legali'sation *n*

legal medicine *n* another name for **forensic medicine**

legal positivism *n* another name for **positivism** (sense 2)

legal separation *n* another term (esp US) for **judicial separation**

legal tender *n* currency in specified denominations that a creditor must by law accept in redemption of a debt

Legaspi (lɛ'gæspɪ) *n* a port in the Philippines, on SE Luzon on the Gulf of Albay. Pop: 178 000 (2005 est)

legate ('lɛgɪt) *n* **1** a messenger, envoy, or delegate **2** *RC Church* an emissary to a foreign state

representing the Pope [Old English, via Old French from Latin *lēgātus* deputy, from *lēgāre* to delegate; related to *lēx* law] > 'legate,ship *n* > legatine ('lɛgə,taɪn) *adj*

legatee (,lɛgə'ti:) *n* a person to whom a legacy is bequeathed. Compare **devisee**

legation (lɪ'geɪʃən) *n* **1** a diplomatic mission headed by a minister **2** the official residence and office of a diplomatic minister **3** the act of sending forth a diplomatic envoy **4** the mission or business of a diplomatic envoy **5** the rank or office of a legate [C15 from Latin *lēgātiō,* from *lēgātus* LEGATE] > le'gationary *adj*

legato (lɪ'gɑ:təʊ) *music* ▷ *adj, adv* **1** to be performed smoothly and connectedly ▷ *n, pl* -tos **2 a** a style of playing in which no perceptible gaps are left between notes **b** (*as modifier*): *a legato passage* [C19 from Italian, literally: bound]

legator (,lɛgə'tɔ:) *n* a person who gives a legacy or makes a bequest [C17 from Latin, from *lēgāre* to bequeath; see LEGATE] > ,lega'torial *adj*

leg before wicket *n cricket* a manner of dismissal on the grounds that a batsman has been struck on the leg by a bowled ball that otherwise would have hit the wicket. Abbreviation: **lbw**

leg break *n cricket* a bowled ball that spins from leg to off on pitching

leg bye *n cricket* a run scored after the ball has hit the batsman's leg or some other part of his body, except his hand, without touching the bat. Abbreviation: **lb**

Legco ('lɛgkəʊ) *n* the Legislative Council of Hong Kong

legend ('lɛdʒənd) *n* **1** a popular story handed down from earlier times whose truth has not been ascertained **2** a group of such stories: *the Arthurian legend* **3** a modern story that has taken on the characteristics of a traditional legendary tale **4** a person whose fame or notoriety makes him a source of exaggerated or romanticized tales or exploits **5** an inscription or title, as on a coin or beneath a coat of arms **6** explanatory matter accompanying a table, map, chart, etc **7 a** a story of the life of a saint **b** a collection of such stories [C14 (in the sense: a saint's life or a collection of saints' lives): from Medieval Latin *legenda* passages to be read, from Latin *legere* to read] > 'legendry *n*

legendary ('lɛdʒəndərɪ, -drɪ) *adj* **1** of or relating to legend **2** celebrated or described in a legend or legends **3** very famous or notorious

legerdemain (,lɛdʒədə'meɪn) *n* **1** another name for **sleight of hand 2** cunning deception or trickery [C15 from Old French: light of hand] > ,legerde'mainist *n*

leger line ('lɛdʒə) *n* a variant spelling of **ledger line**

leges ('li:dʒi:z) *n* the plural of **lex**

legged ('lɛgɪd, lɛgd) *adj* **a** having a leg or legs **b** (*in combination*): *three-legged; long-legged*

leggings ('lɛgɪŋz) *pl n* **1** an extra outer covering for the lower legs **2** close-fitting trousers worn by women and children > 'legginged *adj*

leggy ('lɛgɪ) *adj* -gier, -giest **1** having unusually long legs **2** (of a woman) having long and shapely legs **3** (of a plant) having an unusually long and weak stem > 'legginess *n*

leghorn ('lɛg,hɔ:n) *n* **1** a type of Italian wheat straw that is woven into hats **2** any hat made from this straw when plaited [C19 named after LEGHORN (Livorno)]

Leghorn *n* **1** ('lɛg,hɔ:n) the English name for **Livorno 2** (lɛ'gɔ:n) a breed of domestic fowl laying white eggs

legible ('lɛdʒəbᵊl) *adj* **1** (of handwriting, print, etc) able to be read or deciphered **2** able to be discovered; discernible [C14 from Late Latin *legibilis,* from Latin *legere* to read] > ,legi'bility or 'legibleness *n* > 'legibly *adv*

legion ('li:dʒən) *n* **1** a military unit of the ancient Roman army made up of infantry with supporting cavalry, numbering some three to six thousand men **2** any large military force: *the*

French Foreign Legion **3** (*usually capital*) an association of ex-servicemen: *the British Legion* **4** (*often plural*) any very large number, esp of people ▷ *adj* **5** (*usually postpositive*) very large or numerous [C13 from Old French, from Latin *legio,* from *legere* to choose]

legionary ('li:dʒənərɪ) *adj* **1** of or relating to a legion ▷ *n, pl* -aries **2** a soldier belonging to a legion

legionary ant *n* another name for the **army ant**

legionella (,li:dʒə'nɛlə) *n, pl* -lae (-,li:) any Gram-negative rod-shaped bacterium of the genus *Legionella,* including *L. pneumophila,* which causes legionnaire's disease [C20 New Latin, diminutive of *legion,* as in LEGIONNAIRE'S DISEASE]

legionnaire (,li:dʒə'nɛə) *n* (*often capital*) a member of certain military forces or associations, such as the French Foreign Legion or the British Legion

legionnaire's or **legionnaires' disease** *n* a serious, sometimes fatal, infection, caused by the bacterium *Legionella pneumophila,* which has symptoms similar to those of pneumonia: believed to be spread by inhalation of contaminated water vapour from showers and air-conditioning plants [C20 after the outbreak at a meeting of the American Legion at Philadelphia in 1976]

Legion of Honour *n* an order for civil or military merit instituted by Napoleon in France in 1802. French name: **Légion d'honneur** (leʒjɔ̃ dɔnœr)

legislate ('lɛdʒɪs,leɪt) *vb* **1** (*intr*) to make or pass laws **2** (*tr*) to bring into effect by legislation [C18 back formation from LEGISLATOR]

legislation (,lɛdʒɪs'leɪʃən) *n* **1** the act or process of making laws; enactment **2** the laws so made

legislative ('lɛdʒɪslətɪv) *adj* **1** of or relating to legislation **2** having the power or function of legislating: *a legislative assembly* **3** of or relating to a legislature ▷ *n* **4** *rare* another word for **legislature** > 'legislatively *adv*

legislative assembly *n* (*often capitals*) **1** the bicameral legislature in 28 states of the US **2** the lower chamber of the bicameral state legislatures in several Commonwealth countries, such as Australia **3** the unicameral legislature in most Canadian provinces **4** any assembly with legislative powers

legislative council *n* (*often capitals*) **1** the upper chamber of certain bicameral legislatures, such as those of the Indian and Australian states **2** the unicameral legislature of certain colonies or dependent territories **3** (in the US) a committee composed of members of both chambers of a state legislature, that meets to discuss problems, construct a legislative programme, etc

legislator ('lɛdʒɪs,leɪtə) *n* **1** a person concerned with the making or enactment of laws **2** a member of a legislature [C17 from Latin *lēgis lātor,* from *lēx* law + *lātor* from *lātus,* past participle of *ferre* to bring] > 'legis,lator,ship *n* > 'legis,latress *fem n*

legislatorial (,lɛdʒɪslə'tɔ:rɪəl) *adj* of or relating to a legislator or legislature

legislature ('lɛdʒɪs,leɪtʃə) *n* a body of persons vested with power to make, amend, and repeal laws. Compare **executive, judiciary**

legist ('li:dʒɪst) *n* a person versed in the law [C15 from Medieval Latin *lēgista,* from *lēx* law]

legit (lɪ'dʒɪt) *slang* ▷ *adj* **1** short for **legitimate** ▷ *n* **2** legitimate or professionally respectable drama

legitimate *adj* (lɪ'dʒɪtɪmɪt) **1** born in lawful wedlock; enjoying full filial rights **2** conforming to established standards of usage, behaviour, etc **3** based on correct or acceptable principles of reasoning **4** reasonable, sensible, or valid: *a legitimate question* **5** authorized, sanctioned by, or in accordance with law **6** of, relating to, or ruling by hereditary right: *a legitimate monarch* **7** of or relating to a body of famous long-established plays as distinct from films, television, vaudeville, etc: *the legitimate theatre* ▷ *vb* (lɪ'dʒɪtɪ,meɪt) **8** (*tr*) to make, pronounce, or show to be legitimate [c15 from Medieval Latin *lēgitimātus* made legal, from *lēx* law] > le'gitimacy *or* le'gitimateness *n* > le'gitimately *adv* > le,giti'mation *n*

legitimist (lɪ'dʒɪtɪmɪst) *n* **1** a monarchist who supports the rule of a legitimate dynasty or of its senior branch **2** (formerly) a supporter of the elder line of the Bourbon family in France **3** a supporter of legitimate authority ▷ *adj also* legitimistic **4** of or relating to legitimists > le'gitimism *n*

legitimize, legitimise (lɪ'dʒɪtɪ,maɪz) *or* **legitimatize, legitimatise** (lɪ'dʒɪtɪmə,taɪz) *vb* (*tr*) to make legitimate; legalize > le,gitimi'zation *or* le,gitimi'sation, le,gitimati'zation *or* le,gitimati'sation *n*

legless ('lɛglɪs) *adj* **1** without legs **2** *informal* very drunk

legman ('lɛgmən) *n, pl* -men *chiefly US and Canadian* **1** a newsman who reports on news stories from the scene of action or original source **2** a person employed to run errands, collect information, etc, outside an office

Legnica (*Polish* lɛg'nitsa) *n* an industrial town in SW Poland. Pop: 109 335 (1999 est). German name: Liegnitz

Lego ('lɛgəʊ) *n* trademark a construction toy consisting of plastic bricks and other standardized components that fit together with studs [c20 from Danish *leg godt* play well]

leg-of-mutton *or* **leg-o'-mutton** *n* (*modifier*) (of a sail, sleeve, etc) tapering sharply or having a triangular profile

leg-pull *n* *Brit informal* a practical joke or mild deception

legroom ('lɛg,ru:m) *n* room to move one's legs comfortably, as in a car

leg rope *Austral and NZ* ▷ *n* **1** a rope used to secure an animal by its hind leg ▷ *vb* **leg-rope** (*tr*) **2** to restrain (an animal) by a leg rope

leguaan ('lɛgjʊən, 'lɛgʊ,ɑːn) *n* *South African* a large amphibious monitor lizard of the genus *Varanus*, esp *V. niloticus* (the **water leguaan**), which can grow up to 2 or 3 m. Also called: **iguana** [c19 Dutch, from French *l'iguane* the iguana]

legume ('lɛgju:m, lɪ'gju:m) *n* **1** the long dry dehiscent fruit produced by leguminous plants; a pod **2** any table vegetable of the family *Fabaceae* (formerly *Leguminosae*), esp beans or peas **3** any leguminous plant [c17 from French *légume*, from Latin *legūmen* bean, from *legere* to pick (a crop)]

legumin (lɪ'gju:mɪn) *n* a protein obtained mainly from the seeds of leguminous plants [c19 from LEGUME]

leguminous (lɪ'gju:mɪnəs) *adj* of, relating to, or belonging to the *Fabaceae* (formerly *Leguminosae*), a family of flowering plants having pods (or legumes) as fruits and root nodules enabling storage of nitrogen-rich material: includes peas, beans, clover, gorse, acacia, and carob [c17 from Latin *legūmen*; see LEGUME]

legwarmer ('lɛg,wɔ:mə) *n* one of a pair of garments resembling stockings without feet, usually knitted and brightly coloured, often worn over jeans, tights, etc or during exercise

legwork ('lɛg,wɜ:k) *n* *informal* work that involves travelling on foot or as if on foot

lehaim (lə'xɑjim) *interj, n* a variant spelling of lehaim

Le Havre (lə 'hɑːvrə; *French* lə avrə) *n* a port in N France, on the English Channel at the mouth of the River Seine: transatlantic trade; oil refining. Pop: 190 905 (1999)

lehr (lɪə) *n* a long tunnel-shaped oven used for annealing glass [from German: pattern, model]

lei¹ (leɪ) *n* (in Hawaii) a garland of flowers, worn around the neck [from Hawaiian]

lei² (leɪ) *n* the plural of leu

Leibnizian *or* **Leibnitzian** (laɪb'nɪtsɪən) *adj* of or relating to Baron Gottfried Wilhelm von Leibniz, the German rationalist philosopher and mathematician (1646–1716)

Leibniz Mountains ('laɪbnɪts) *pl n* a mountain range on the SW limb of the moon, containing the highest peaks (10 000 metres) on the moon

Leibniz's law *n* *logic, philosophy* **1** the principle that two expressions satisfy exactly the same predicates if and only if they both refer to the same subject **2** the weaker principle that if *a=b* whatever is true of *a* is true of *b* [named after Gottfried Wilhelm von *Leibnitz* (1646–1716), German philosopher and mathematician]

Leibniz's rule *n* a rule for finding the derivative of the product of two functions. For a first derivative it is $d(uv)/dx = udv/dx + vdu/dx$

Leicester ('lɛstə) *n* **1** a city in central England, in Leicester unitary authority, on the River Soar: administrative centre of Leicestershire: Roman remains and a ruined Norman castle; two universities (1957, 1992); light engineering, hosiery, and footwear industries. Pop: 283 900 (2003 est) **2** a unitary authority in central England, in Leicestershire. Pop: 330 574 (2001). Area: 73 sq km (28 sq miles) **3** short for **Leicestershire 4** a breed of sheep with long wool, originally from Leicestershire **5** a fairly mild dark orange whole-milk cheese, similar to Cheddar

Leicestershire ('lɛstəʃɪə, -ʃə) *n* a county of central England: absorbed the small historical county of Rutland in 1974; Rutland and Leicester city became independent unitary authorities in 1997; largely agricultural. Administrative centre: Leicester. Pop (excluding Leicester city): 619 200 (2003 est). Area (excluding Leicester city): 2084 sq km (804 sq miles). Shortened form: Leicester Abbreviation: **Leics**

Leics *abbreviation for* Leicestershire

Leiden *or* **Leyden** ('laɪdªn; *Dutch* 'lɛidə) *n* a city in the W Netherlands, in South Holland province: residence of the Pilgrim Fathers for 11 years before they sailed for America in 1620; university (1575). Pop: 118 000 (2003 est)

Leigh (li:) *n* a town in NW England, in Wigan unitary authority, Greater Manchester: engineering industries. Pop: 43 006 (2001)

Leinster ('lɛnstə) *n* a province of E and SE Republic of Ireland: it consists of the counties of Carlow, Dublin, Kildare, Kilkenny, Laois, Longford, Louth, Meath, Offaly, Westmeath, Wexford, and Wicklow. Pop: 2 105 579 (2002). Area: 19 632 sq km (7580 sq miles)

Leipzig ('laɪpsɪg; *German* 'laiptsɪç) *n* a city in E central Germany, in Saxony: famous fairs, begun about 1170; publishing and music centre; university (1409); scene of a decisive defeat for Napoleon Bonaparte in 1813. Pop: 497 531 (2003 est)

Leiria (*Portuguese* lei'riɐ) *n* a city in central Portugal: site of the first printing press in Portugal (1466). Pop: 119 870 (2001)

leishmania (li:ʃ'meɪnɪə) *n* any parasitic flagellate protozoan of the genus *Leishmania*: infects humans and animals and causes diseases ranging from skin lesions to potentially fatal organ damage [c20 New Latin, named after Sir W.B. *Leishman* (1865–1926), Scottish bacteriologist]

leishmaniasis (,li:ʃmə'naɪəsɪs) *or* **leishmaniosis** (li:ʃ,meɪnɪ'əʊsɪs, -,mæn-) *n* any disease, such as kala-azar, caused by protozoa of the genus *Leishmania*

leister ('li:stə) *n* **1** a spear with three or more prongs for spearing fish, esp salmon ▷ *vb* **2** (*tr*) to spear (a fish) with a leister [c16 from Scandinavian; related to Old Norse *ljóstr*, from *ljósta* to stab]

leisure ('lɛʒə; *US also* 'li:ʒər) *n* **1 a** time or opportunity for ease, relaxation, etc **b** (*as modifier*): *leisure activities* **2** ease or leisureliness **3 at leisure a** having free time for ease, relaxation, etc **b** not occupied or engaged **c** without hurrying **4 at one's leisure** when one has free time [c14 from Old French *leisir*; ultimately from Latin *licēre* to be allowed]

leisure centre *n* a building designed to provide facilities for a range of leisure pursuits, such as a sports hall, café, and meeting rooms

leisured ('lɛʒəd) *adj* **1** (*usually prenominal*) having much leisure, as through unearned wealth: *the leisured classes* **2** unhurried or relaxed: *in a leisured manner*

leisurely ('lɛʒəlɪ) *adj* **1** unhurried; relaxed ▷ *adv* **2** without haste; in a relaxed way > 'leisureliness *n*

leisure sickness *n* a medical condition in which people who have been working become ill with symptoms such as fatigue or muscular pains at a weekend or while on holiday

Leith (li:θ) *n* a port in SE Scotland, on the Firth of Forth: part of Edinburgh since 1920

leitmotif *or* **leitmotiv** ('laɪtməʊ,ti:f) *n* **1** *music* a recurring short melodic phrase or theme used, esp in Wagnerian music dramas, to suggest a character, thing, etc **2** an often repeated word, phrase, image, or theme in a literary work [c19 from German *leitmotiv* leading motif]

Leitrim ('li:trɪm) *n* a county of N Republic of Ireland in Connacht province, on Donegal Bay: agricultural. County town: Carrick-on-Shannon. Pop: 25 799 (2002). Area: 1525 sq km (589 sq miles)

Leix (li:ʃ) *n* another name for **Laois**

Leizhou ('leɪ'dʒəʊ) *or* **Luichow Peninsula** *n* a peninsula of SE China, in SW Guangdong province, separated from Hainan Island by Hainan Strait

lek¹ (lɛk) *n* **1** a small area in which birds of certain species, notably the black grouse, gather for sexual display and courtship **2** the act or practice of so gathering [c19 perhaps from dialect *lake* (vb) from Old English *lācan* to frolic, fight, or perhaps from Swedish *leka* to play]

lek² (lɛk) *n* the standard monetary unit of Albania, divided into 100 qindarka [from Albanian]

lekgotla (lɛ'xʊtla) *or* **kgotla** ('xʊtla) *n* *South African* **1** a meeting place for village assemblies, court cases, and meetings of village leaders **2** a conference or business meeting [from Sotho and Tswana *lekgotla* courtyard or court]

lekker ('lɛkə) *adj* *South African slang* **1** pleasing or enjoyable **2** tasty **3** local is lekker popular slogan promoting South African culture, produce, etc [c20 Afrikaans, from Dutch]

LEM (lɛm) *n* acronym for lunar excursion module

leman ('lɛmən, 'li:-) *n* *archaic* **1** a beloved; sweetheart **2** a lover or mistress [c13 *lemman*, *leofman*, from *leof* dear, LIEF + MAN]

Léman (lemã) *n* Lac the French name for (Lake) Geneva

Le Mans (*French* lə mã) *n* a city in NW France: scene of the first experiments in motoring and flying; annual motor race. Pop: 146 105 (1999)

Lemberg ('lɛmbɛrk) *n* the German name for **Lviv**

lemma¹ ('lɛmə) *n, pl* -mas *or* -mata (-mətə) **1** a subsidiary proposition, proved for use in the proof of another proposition **2** *linguistics* a word considered as its citation form together with all the inflected forms. For example, the lemma *go* consists of *go* together with *goes, going, went,* and *gone* **3** an argument or theme, esp when used as the subject or title of a composition [c16 (meaning: proposition), c17 (meaning: title, theme): via Latin from Greek: premise, from *lambanein* to take (for granted)]

lemma² ('lɛmə) *n, pl* -mas *or* -mata (-mətə) the outer of two bracts surrounding each floret in a grass spikelet ▷ Compare **palea** [c19 from Greek: rind, from *lepein* to peel]

lemmatize *or* **lemmatise** ('lɛmə,taɪz) *vb* (*tr*) *linguistics* to group together the inflected forms of (a word) for analysis as a single item > ,lemmati'zation *or* ,lemmati'sation *n*

lemming ('lɛmɪŋ) *n* **1** any of various volelike rodents of the genus *Lemmus* and related genera, of northern and arctic regions of Europe, Asia, and North America: family *Cricetidae*. The Scandinavian variety, *Lemmus lemmus*, migrates periodically when its population reaches a peak **2** a member of any large group following an unthinking course towards mass destruction [C17 from Norwegian; related to Latin *latrāre* to bark] > **'lemming-,like** *adj*

Lemnian ('lɛmnɪən) *adj* **1** of or relating to the Greek island of Lemnos or its inhabitants ▷ *n* **2** a native or inhabitant of Lemnos

lemniscate ('lɛmnɪskɪt) *n* a closed plane curve consisting of two symmetrical loops meeting at a node. Equation: $(x^2 + y^2)^2 = a^2(x^2 - y^2)$, where *a* is the greatest distance from the curve to the origin. The symbol for infinity (∞) is an example

lemniscus (lɛm'nɪskəs) *n, pl* **-nisci** (-'nɪsaɪ, -'nɪskiː) *anatomy* a technical name for **fillet** (sense 9) [C19 New Latin, from Latin, from Greek *lēmniskos* ribbon]

Lemnos ('lɛmnɒs) *n* a Greek island in the N Aegean Sea: famous for its medicinal earth (**Lemnian seal**). Chief town: Kastron. Pop: 18 104 (2001). Area: 477 sq km (184 sq miles). Modern Greek name: **Límnos**

lemon ('lɛmən) *n* **1** a small Asian evergreen tree, *Citrus limon,* widely cultivated in warm and tropical regions, having pale green glossy leaves and edible fruits. Related adjs: **citric, citrine, citrous 2 a** the yellow oval fruit of this tree, having juicy acidic flesh rich in vitamin C **b** (*as modifier*): *a lemon jelly* **3** Also called: **lemon yellow a** a greenish-yellow or strong yellow colour **b** (*as adjective*): *lemon wallpaper* **4** a distinctive tart flavour made from or in imitation of the lemon **5** *slang* a person or thing considered to be useless or defective [C14 from Medieval Latin *lemōn-,* from Arabic *laymūn*] > **'lemonish** *adj* > **'lemon-,like** *adj*

lemonade (,lɛmə'neɪd) *n* a drink made from lemon juice, sugar, and water or from carbonated water, citric acid, etc

lemon balm *n* the full name of **balm** (sense 5)

lemon cheese *or* **curd** *n* a soft paste made from lemons, sugar, eggs, and butter, used as a spread or filling

lemon drop *n* a lemon-flavoured boiled sweet

lemon fish *n* another name for **cobia**

lemon geranium *n* a cultivated geraniaceous plant, *Pelargonium limoneum,* with lemon-scented leaves

lemon grass *n* a perennial grass, *Cymbopogon citratus,* with a large flower spike: used in cooking and grown in tropical regions as the source of an aromatic oil (**lemon grass oil**)

lemon sole *n* a European flatfish, *Microstomus kitt,* with a variegated brown body: highly valued as a food fish: family *Pleuronectidae*

lemon squash *n Brit* a drink made from a sweetened lemon concentrate and water

lemon squeezer *n* **1** any of various devices for extracting the juice from citrus fruit **2** *NZ informal* a peaked hat with four indentations worn by the army on ceremonial occasions

lemon verbena *n* a tropical American verbenaceous shrub, *Lippia citriodora,* with slender lemon-scented leaves yielding an oil used in perfumery

lemonwood ('lɛmən,wʊd) *n* a small tree, *Pittosporum eugenioides,* of New Zealand having a white bark and lemon-scented flowers

lemony ('lɛmənɪ) *adj* **1** having or resembling the taste or colour of a lemon **2** *Austral slang* angry or irritable

lempira (lɛm'pɪərə) *n* the standard monetary unit of Honduras, divided into 100 centavos [American Spanish, after *Lempira,* Indian chief who opposed the Spanish]

lemur ('liːmə) *n* **1** any Madagascan prosimian primate of the family *Lemuridae,* such as *Lemur catta* (the **ring-tailed lemur**). They are typically arboreal, having foxy faces and long tails **2** any similar or closely related animal, such as a loris or indris [C18 New Latin, adapted from Latin *lemurēs* ghosts; so named by Linnaeus for its ghost-like face and nocturnal habits] > **'lemur-,like** *adj*

lemures ('lɛmjʊ,riːz) *pl n Roman myth* the spirits of the dead [Latin: see LEMUR]

lemuroid ('lɛmjʊ,rɔɪd) *or* **lemurine** ('lɛmjʊ,raɪn, -rɪn) *adj* **1** of, relating to, or belonging to the superfamily *Lemuroidea,* which includes the lemurs and indrises **2** resembling or closely related to a lemur ▷ *n* **3** an animal that resembles or is closely related to a lemur

Lena ('liːnə; *Russian* 'ljɛnə) *n* a river in Russia, rising in S Siberia and flowing generally north through the Sakha Republic to the Laptev Sea by an extensive delta: the longest river in Russia. Length: 4271 km (2653 miles)

lend (lɛnd) *vb* **lends, lending, lent** (lɛnt) **1** (*tr*) to permit the use of (something) with the expectation of return of the same or an equivalent **2** to provide (money) temporarily, often at interest **3** (*intr*) to provide loans, esp as a profession **4** (*tr*) to impart or contribute (something, esp some abstract quality): *her presence lent beauty* **5** (*tr*) to provide, esp in order to assist or support: *he lent his skill to the company* **6** **lend an ear** to listen **7** **lend itself** to possess the right characteristics or qualities for: *the novel lends itself to serialization* **8** **lend oneself** to give support, cooperation, etc [C15 *lende* (originally the past tense), from Old English *lǣnan,* from *lǣn* LOAN[1]; related to Icelandic *lāna,* Old High German *lēhanōn*] > **'lender** *n*

lender of last resort *n* the central bank of a country with authority for controlling its banking system

lending library *n* **1** Also called (esp US): **circulating library** the department of a public library providing books for use outside the building **2** a small commercial library

lend-lease *n* (during World War II) the system organized by the US in 1941 by which equipment and services were provided for countries fighting Germany

length (lɛŋkθ, lɛŋθ) *n* **1** the linear extent or measurement of something from end to end, usually being the longest dimension or, for something fixed, the longest horizontal dimension **2** the extent of something from beginning to end, measured in some more or less regular units or intervals: *the book was 600 pages in length* **3** a specified distance, esp between two positions or locations: *the length of a race* **4** a period of time, as between specified limits or moments **5** something of a specified, average, or known size or extent measured in one dimension, often used as a unit of measurement: *a length of cloth* **6** a piece or section of something narrow and long: *a length of tubing* **7** the quality, state, or fact of being long rather than short **8** (*usually plural*) the amount of trouble taken in pursuing or achieving something (esp in the phrase **to great lengths**) **9** (*often plural*) the extreme or limit of action (in phrases such as **to any length(s)**, **to what length(s) would someone go**, etc) **10** *prosody, phonetics* the metrical quantity or temporal duration of a vowel or syllable **11** the distance from one end of a rectangular swimming bath to the other. Compare **width** (sense 4) **12** *prosody* the quality of a vowel, whether stressed or unstressed, that distinguishes it from another vowel of similar articulatory characteristics. Thus (iː) in English *beat* is of greater length than (ɪ) in English *bit* **13** *cricket* the distance from the batsman at which the ball pitches **14** *bridge* a holding of four or more cards in a suit **15** *NZ informal* the general idea; the main purpose **16** **at length a** in depth; fully **b** eventually **c** for a long time; interminably [Old English *lengthu;* related to Middle Dutch *lengede,* Old Norse *lengd*]

lengthen ('lɛŋkθən, 'lɛŋθən) *vb* to make or become longer > **'lengthener** *n*

lengthman ('lɛŋkθmən, 'lɛŋθ-) *n, pl* **-men** a person whose job it is to maintain a particular length of road or railway line

lengthways ('lɛŋkθ,weɪz, 'lɛŋθ-) *or* **lengthwise** *adv, adj* in, according to, or along the direction of length

lengthy ('lɛŋkθɪ, 'lɛŋθɪ) *adj* **lengthier, lengthiest** of relatively great or tiresome extent or duration > **'lengthily** *adv* > **'lengthiness** *n*

lenient ('liːnɪənt) *adj* **1** showing or characterized by mercy or tolerance **2** *archaic* caressing or soothing [C17 from Latin *lēnīre* to soothe, from *lēnis* soft] > **'leniency** *or* **'lenience** *n* > **'leniently** *adv*

Leninabad (*Russian* lɪninaˈbat) *n* the former name (1937–91) of **Khojent**

Leninakan (*Russian* lɪninaˈkan) *n* the former name (1925–91) of **Kumayri**

Leningrad ('lɛnɪn,græd; *Russian* lɪnin'grat) *n* the former name (1937–91) of **Saint Petersburg**

Leninism ('lɛnɪ,nɪzəm) *n* **1** the political and economic theories of Vladimir Ilyich Lenin (original surname *Ulyanov;* 1870–1924) the Russian statesman and Marxist theoretician **2** another name for **Marxism-Leninism.** > **'Leninist** *or* **'Leninite** *n, adj*

Lenin Peak *n* a mountain in Tajikistan; the highest peak in the Trans Alai Range. Height: 7134 m (23 406 ft)

lenis ('liːnɪs) *phonetics* ▷ *adj* **1** (of a consonant) articulated with weak muscular tension ▷ *n, pl* **lenes** ('liːniːz) **2** a consonant, such as English *b* or *v,* pronounced with weak muscular force ▷ Compare **fortis** [C19 from Latin: gentle]

lenitive ('lɛnɪtɪv) *adj* **1** soothing or alleviating pain or distress ▷ *n* **2** *obsolete* a lenitive drug [C16 from Medieval Latin *lēnītīvus,* from Latin *lēnīre* to soothe]

lenity ('lɛnɪtɪ) *n, pl* **-ties** the state or quality of being lenient [C16 from Latin *lēnitās* gentleness, from *lēnis* soft]

leno ('liːnəʊ) *n, pl* **-nos 1** (in textiles) a weave in which the warp yarns are twisted together in pairs between the weft or filling yarns **2** a fabric of this weave [C19 probably from French *linon* lawn, from *lin* flax, from Latin *līnum.* See LINEN]

lens (lɛnz) *n* **1** a piece of glass or other transparent material, used to converge or diverge transmitted light and form optical images **2** Also called: **compound lens** a combination of such lenses for forming images or concentrating a beam of light **3** a device that diverges or converges a beam of electromagnetic radiation, sound, or particles. See **electron lens 4** *anatomy* See **crystalline lens** ▷ Related adjective: **lenticular** [C17 from Latin *lēns* lentil, referring to the similarity of a lens to the shape of a lentil]

Lens (lɛnz; *French* lɑ̃) *n* an industrial town in N France, in the Pas de Calais department; badly damaged in both World Wars. Pop: 36 206 (1999)

lens hood *n photog* an extension piece fixed to a camera lens to shield it from a direct light source

lent (lɛnt) *vb* the past tense and past participle of **lend**

Lent (lɛnt) *n* **1** *Christianity* the period of forty weekdays lasting from Ash Wednesday to Holy Saturday, observed as a time of penance and fasting commemorating Jesus' fasting in the wilderness **2** (*modifier*) falling within or associated with the season before Easter: *Lent observance* **3** (*plural*) (at Cambridge University) Lent term boat races [Old English *lencten, lengten* spring, literally: lengthening (of hours of daylight)]

lentamente (,lɛntə'mɛntɪ) *adv music* to be played slowly [C18 Italian, from LENTO]

lenten ('lɛntən) *adj* **1** (*often capital*) of or relating to Lent **2** *archaic or literary* spare, plain, or meagre: *lenten fare* **3** *archaic* cold, austere, or sombre

lentic ('lɛntɪk) *adj ecology* of, relating to, or inhabiting still water: *a lentic fauna.* Compare **lotic** [C20 from Latin *lentus* slow]

lenticel ('lɛntɪ,sɛl) *n* any of numerous pores in the stem of a woody plant allowing exchange of gases between the stem and the exterior [C19 from New Latin *lenticella,* from Latin *lenticula* diminutive of *lēns* LENTIL] > **lenticellate** (,lɛntɪ'sɛlɪt) *adj*

lenticle ('lɛntɪkəl) *n geology* a lens-shaped layer of mineral or rock embedded in a matrix of different constitution

lenticular (lɛnˈtɪkjʊlə) or **lentiform** (ˈlɛntɪˌfɔːm) adj **1** Also: **lentoid** (ˈlɛntɔɪd) shaped like a biconvex lens **2** of or concerned with a lens or lenses **3** shaped like a lentil seed **4** of or relating to a galaxy with a large central bulge, small disc, but no spiral arms, intermediate in shape between spiral and elliptical galaxies [c17 from Latin *lenticulāris* like a LENTIL]

lentigo (lɛnˈtaɪɡəʊ) n, pl lentigines (lɛnˈtɪdʒɪˌniːz) a technical name for a **freckle** [c14 from Latin, from *lēns* LENTIL] > **len'tiginous** or **len'tiginose** adj

lentil (ˈlɛntɪl) n **1** a small annual leguminous plant, *Lens culinaris*, of the Mediterranean region and W Asia, having edible brownish convex seeds **2** any of the seeds of this plant, which are cooked and eaten as a vegetable, in soups, etc [c13 from Old French *lentille*, from Latin *lenticula*, diminutive of *lēns* lentil]

lentissimo (lɛnˈtɪsɪˌməʊ) adj, adv music to be played very slowly [Italian, superlative of *lento* slow]

lentivirus (ˈlɛntɪˌvaɪrəs) n any of a group of slowly acting viruses that includes the human immunodeficiency virus (HIV), which causes AIDS [c20 from Latin *lentus* slow + VIRUS]

lent lily n another name for the **daffodil**

lento (ˈlɛntəʊ) music ▷ adj, adv **1** to be performed slowly ▷ n, pl **-tos 2** a movement or passage performed in this way [c18 Italian, from Latin *lentus* slow]

Lent term n the spring term at Cambridge University and some other educational establishments

Lenz's law (ˈlɛntsɪz) n physics the principle that the direction of the current induced in a circuit by a changing magnetic field is such that the magnetic field produced by this current will oppose the original field [c19 named after H. F. E. Lenz (1804–65), German physicist]

Leo¹ (ˈliːəʊ) n a name for a lion, used in children's tales, fables, etc [from Latin: lion]

Leo² (ˈliːəʊ) n, Latin genitive Leonis (liːˈəʊnɪs) **1** astronomy a zodiacal constellation in the N hemisphere, lying between Cancer and Virgo on the ecliptic, that contains the star Regulus and the radiant of the Leonid meteor shower **2** astrology **a** Also called: **the Lion** the fifth sign of the zodiac, symbol ♌, having a fixed fire classification and ruled by the sun. The sun is in this sign between about July 23 and Aug 22 **b** a person born during a period when the sun is in this sign ▷ adj **3** astrology born under or characteristic of Leo ▷ Also (for senses 2b, 3): **Leonian** (liːˈəʊnɪən)

LEO abbreviation for low earth orbit

Leoben (German leˈoːbən) n a city in E central Austria, in Styria on the Mur River: lignite mining. Pop: 25 804 (2001)

Leo Minor n a small faint constellation in the N hemisphere lying near Leo and Ursa Major

León (Spanish leˈɔn) n **1** a region and former kingdom of NW Spain, which united with Castile in 1230 **2** a city of NW Spain: capital of the kingdom of León (10th century). Pop: 135 634 (2003 est) **3** a city in central Mexico, in W Guanajuato state: commercial centre of a rich agricultural region. Pop: 1 438 000 (2005 est). Official name: **León de los Aldamas** (de los ˈaldamas) **4** a city in W Nicaragua: one of the oldest towns of Central America, founded in 1524; capital of Nicaragua until 1855; university (1812). Pop: 168 000 (2005 est)

Leonardesque (ˌliːənɑːˈdɛsk) adj of, relating to, or in the style of Leonardo da Vinci, the Italian painter, sculptor, architect, and engineer (1452–1519)

leone (liːˈəʊnɪ) n the standard monetary unit of Sierra Leone, divided into 100 cents [c20 from SIERRA LEONE]

Leonid (ˈliːənɪd) n, pl Leonids or Leonides (lɪˈɒnɪˌdiːz) any member of a meteor shower that is usually insignificant, but more spectacular every 33 years, and occurs annually in mid-November,

appearing to radiate from a point in the constellation Leo [c19 from New Latin *Leōnidēs*, from *leō* lion]

leonine (ˈliːəˌnaɪn) adj of, characteristic of, or resembling a lion [c14 from Latin *leōnīnus*, from *leō* lion]

Leonine (ˈliːəˌnaɪn) adj **1** connected with one of the popes called Leo **2 Leonine City** a district of Rome on the right bank of the Tiber fortified by Pope Leo IV **3** of or relating to certain prayers in the Mass prescribed by Pope Leo XIII (1810–1903; pope 1878–1903) ▷ n **4** Also called: **Leonine verse a** a type of medieval hexameter or elegiac verse having internal rhyme **b** a type of English verse with internal rhyme

leontopodium (lɪˌɒntəˈpəʊdɪəm) n any plant of the Eurasian alpine genus *Leontopodium*, esp *L. alpinum*. See **edelweiss** [New Latin, from Greek *leōn* lion + *podion*, diminutive of *pous* foot (from the shape of the flowers)]

leopard (ˈlɛpəd) n **1** Also called: **panther** a large feline mammal, *Panthera pardus*, of forests of Africa and Asia, usually having a tawny yellow coat with black rosette-like spots **2** any of several similar felines, such as the snow leopard and cheetah **3** **clouded leopard** a feline, *Neofelis nebulosa*, of SE Asia and Indonesia with a yellowish-brown coat marked with darker spots and blotches **4** heraldry a stylized leopard, painted as a lion with the face turned towards the front **5** the pelt of a leopard [c13 from Old French *lepart*, from Late Latin *leōpardus*, from Late Greek *leópardos*, from *leōn* lion + *pardos* PARD² (the leopard was thought at one time to be the result of cross-breeding)] > **'leopardess** fem n

leopard lily n a North American lily plant, *Lilium pardalinum*, cultivated for its large orange-red flowers, with brown-spotted petals and long stamens

leopard moth n a nocturnal European moth, *Zeuzera pyrina*, having white wings and body, both marked with black spots: family *Cossidae*

leopard's-bane n any of several Eurasian perennial plants of the genus *Doronicum*, esp *D. plantagineum*, having clusters of yellow flowers: family *Asteraceae* (composites)

Léopoldville (ˈliːəpəʊldˌvɪl; French leɔpɔlvil) n the former name (until 1966) of **Kinshasa**

leotard (ˈliːəˌtɑːd) n **1** a tight-fitting garment covering the body from the shoulders down to the thighs and worn by acrobats, ballet dancers, etc **2** (plural) US and Canadian another name for **tights** (sense 1b) [c19 named after Jules *Léotard*, French acrobat]

Lepanto n **1** (lɪˈpæntəʊ) a port in W Greece, between the Gulfs of Corinth and Patras: scene of a naval battle (1571) in which the Turkish fleet was defeated by the fleets of the Holy League. Pop: 8170 (latest est). Greek name: **Návpaktos 2 Gulf of Lepanto** another name for the (Gulf of) **Corinth**

Lepaya (lɪˈpɑːjə) n a variant spelling of **Liepāja**

Lepcha (ˈlɛptʃə) n **1** (pl **-cha** or **-chas**) a member of a Mongoloid people of Sikkim **2** the language of this people, belonging to the Tibeto-Burman branch of the Sino-Tibetan family ▷ adj **3** of or relating to this people or their language

leper (ˈlɛpə) n **1** a person who has leprosy **2** a person who is ignored or despised [c14 via Late Latin from Greek *lepra*, noun use of *lepros* scaly, from *lepein* to peel]

lepido- or before a vowel **lepid-** combining form scale or scaly: *lepidopterous* [from Greek *lepis* scale; see LEPER]

lepidolite (lɪˈpɪdəˌlaɪt, ˈlɛpɪdəˌlaɪt) n a lilac, pink, or greyish mica consisting of a hydrous silicate of lithium, potassium, aluminium, and fluorine, containing rubidium as an impurity: a source of lithium and rubidium. Formula: $K_2Li_3Al_4Si_7O_{21}(OH,F)_3$

lepidopteran (ˌlɛpɪˈdɒptərən) n, pl **-terans** or **-tera** (-tərə) also **lepidopteron 1** any of numerous insects of the order *Lepidoptera*, typically having

two pairs of wings covered with fragile scales, mouthparts specialized as a suctorial proboscis, and caterpillars as larvae: comprises the butterflies and moths ▷ adj also **lepidopterous 2** of, relating to, or belonging to the order *Lepidoptera* [c19 from New Latin *lepidoptera*, from LEPIDO- + Greek *pteron* wing]

lepidopterist (ˌlɛpɪˈdɒptərɪst) n a person who studies or collects moths and butterflies

lepidosiren (ˌlɛpɪdəʊˈsaɪərən) n a South American lungfish, *Lepidosiren paradoxa*, having an eel-shaped body and whiplike paired fins

lepidote (ˈlɛpɪˌdəʊt) adj biology covered with scales, scaly leaves, or spots [c19 via New Latin *lepidōtus*, from Greek, from *lepis* scale]

Lepontine Alps (lɪˈpɒntaɪn) pl n a range of the S central Alps, in S Switzerland and N Italy. Highest peak: Monte Leone, 3553 m (11 657 ft)

leporid (ˈlɛpərɪd) adj **1** of, relating to, or belonging to the *Leporidae*, a family of lagomorph mammals having long ears and limbs and a short tail: includes rabbits and hares ▷ n **2** any animal belonging to the family *Leporidae* [c19 from Latin *lepus* hare]

leporine (ˈlɛpəˌraɪn) adj of, relating to, or resembling a hare [c17 from Latin *leporīnus*, from *lepus* hare]

LEPRA (ˈlɛprə) n acronym for Leprosy Relief Association

leprechaun (ˈlɛprəˌkɔːn) n (in Irish folklore) a mischievous elf, often believed to have a treasure hoard [c17 from Irish Gaelic *leipreachán*, from Middle Irish *lūchorpān*, from *lū* small + *corp* body, from Latin *corpus* body]

leprosarium (ˌlɛprəˈsɛərɪəm) n, pl **-ia** (-ɪə) a hospital or other centre for the treatment or care of lepers [c20 from Medieval Latin: see LEPER]

leprose (ˈlɛprəʊs, -rəʊz) adj biology having or denoting a whitish scurfy surface

leprosy (ˈlɛprəsɪ) n pathol a chronic infectious disease occurring mainly in tropical and subtropical regions, characterized by the formation of painful inflamed nodules beneath the skin and disfigurement and wasting of affected parts, caused by the bacillus *Mycobacterium leprae*. Also called: **Hansen's disease** [c16 from LEPROUS + -Y³]

leprous (ˈlɛprəs) adj **1** having leprosy **2** relating to or resembling leprosy **3** biology a less common word for **leprose** [c13 from Old French, from Late Latin *leprosus*, from *lepra* LEPER] > **'leprously** adv > **'leprousness** n

-lepsy or sometimes **-lepsia** n combining form indicating a seizure or attack: *catalepsy* [from New Latin *-lepsia*, from Greek, from *lēpsis* a seizure, from *lambanein* to seize] > **-leptic** adj combining form

leptin (ˈlɛptɪn) n a protein, produced by fat cells in the body, that acts on the brain to regulate the amount of additional fat laid down in the body [c20 from LEPTO- + -IN]

lepto- or before a vowel **lept-** combining form fine, slender, or slight: *leptosome* [from Greek *leptos* thin, literally: peeled, from *lepein* to peel]

leptocephalic (ˌlɛptəʊsɪˈfælɪk) or **leptocephalous** (ˌlɛptəʊˈsɛfələs) adj having a narrow skull

leptocephalus (ˌlɛptəʊˈsɛfələs) n, pl **-li** (-ˌlaɪ) the slender transparent oceanic larva of eels of the genus *Anguilla* that migrates from its hatching ground in the Caribbean to European freshwater habitats

leptocercal (ˌlɛptəʊˈsɜːkəl) adj zoology having a long thin tail [from LEPTO- + Greek *kerkos* tail]

leptodactylous (ˌlɛptəʊˈdæktɪləs) adj zoology having slender digits

leptokurtic (ˌlɛptəʊˈkɜːtɪk) adj statistics (of a distribution) having kurtosis B_2 greater than 3, more heavily concentrated about the mean than a normal distribution. Compare **platykurtic**, **mesokurtic** [c20 from LEPTO- + Greek *kurtos* arched, bulging + -IC]

lepton¹ (ˈlɛptɒn) n, pl **-ta** (-tə) **1** a former Greek monetary unit worth one hundredth of a drachma **2** a small coin of ancient Greece [from Greek *lepton (nomisma)* small (coin)]

lepton² (ˈlɛptɒn) *n physics* any of a group of elementary particles and their antiparticles, such as an electron, muon, or neutrino, that participate in electromagnetic and weak interactions and have a half-integral spin [C20 from LEPTO- + -ON] > **lepˈtonic** *adj*

lepton number *n physics* a quantum number describing the behaviour of elementary particles, equal to the number of leptons present minus the number of antileptons. It is thought to be conserved in all processes. Symbol: **l**

leptophyllous (ˌlɛptəʊˈfɪləs) *adj* (of plants) having long slender leaves

leptorrhine (ˈlɛptərɪn) *adj* another word for **catarrhine** (sense 2)

leptosome (ˈlɛptəˌsəʊm) *n* a person with a small bodily frame and a slender physique > ˌ**leptoˈsomic** *or* **leptosomatic** (ˌlɛptəʊsəˈmætɪk) *adj*

leptospirosis (ˌlɛptəʊspaɪˈrəʊsɪs) *n* any of several infectious diseases caused by spirochaete bacteria of the genus *Leptospira*, transmitted to man by animals and characterized by jaundice, meningitis, and kidney failure. Also called: **Weil's disease** [C20 from New Latin *Leptospira* (LEPTO- + Greek *speira* coil + -OSIS)]

leptosporangiate (ˌlɛptəʊspəˈrændʒɪɪt) *adj* (of ferns) having each sporangium developing from a single cell, rather than from a group, and normally with specialized explosive spore dispersal ▷ Compare **eusporangiate**

leptotene (ˈlɛptəʊˌtiːn) *n* the first stage of the prophase of meiosis during which the nuclear material becomes resolved into slender single-stranded chromosomes [C20 from LEPTO- + *-tene*, from Greek *tainia* band, filament]

Lepus (ˈlɛpəs, ˈliː-) *n, Latin genitive* **Leporis** (ˈlɛpərɪs) a small constellation in the S hemisphere lying between Orion and Columba [New Latin, from Latin: hare]

lequear (ləˈkwɪə) *n* another name for **lacunar** (sense 1)

Lérida (*Spanish* ˈleriða) *n* a city in NE Spain, in Catalonia: commercial centre of an agricultural region. Pop: 118 035 (2003 est). Catalan name: **Lleida**

Lerwick (ˈlɜːwɪk) *n* a town in Shetland, administrative centre of the island authority of Shetland, on the island of Mainland: the most northerly town in the British Isles; knitwear, oil refining. Pop: 6830 (2001)

lesbian (ˈlɛzbɪən) *n* **1** a female homosexual ▷ *adj* **2** of or characteristic of lesbians [C19 from the homosexuality attributed to Sappho (6th century BC), poetess of Lesbos] > ˈ**lesbianism** *n*

Lesbian (ˈlɛzbɪən) *n* **1** a native or inhabitant of Lesbos **2** the Aeolic dialect of Ancient Greek spoken in Lesbos ▷ *adj* **3** of or relating to Lesbos **4** of or relating to the poetry of Lesbos, esp that of Sappho

Lesbos (ˈlɛzbɒs) *n* an island in the E Aegean, off the NW coast of Turkey: a centre of lyric poetry, led by Alcaeus and Sappho (6th century BC); annexed to Greece in 1913. Chief town: Mytilene. Pop: 90 642 (2001). Area: 1630 sq km (630 sq miles). Modern Greek name: **Lésvos** Former name: **Mytilene**

Les Cayes (leɪ ˈkeɪ; *French* le kaj) *n* a port in SW Haiti, on the S Tiburon Peninsula. Pop: 45 904 (1992). Also called: **Cayes** Former name: **Aux Cayes**

lese-majesty (ˈliːzˈmædʒɪstɪ) *n* **1** any of various offences committed against the sovereign power in a state; treason **2** an attack on authority or position [C16 from French *lèse majesté*, from Latin *laesa mājestās* wounded majesty]

lesion (ˈliːʒən) *n* **1** any structural change in a bodily part resulting from injury or disease **2** an injury or wound [C15 via Old French from Late Latin *laesiō* injury, from Latin *laedere* to hurt]

Lesotho (lɪˈsuːtʊ, ləˈsəʊtəʊ) *n* a kingdom in southern Africa, forming an enclave in the Republic of South Africa: annexed to British Cape Colony in 1871; made a protectorate in 1884; gained independence in 1966; a member of the Commonwealth. It is generally mountainous, with temperate grasslands throughout. Languages: Sesotho and English. Religion: Christian majority. Currency: loti and South African rand. Capital: Maseru. Pop: 1 800 000 (2004 est). Area: 30 344 sq km (11 716 sq miles). Former name (1884–1966): **Basutoland**

less (lɛs) *determiner* **1 a** the comparative of **little** (sense 1) *less sugar; less spirit than before* **b** (*as pronoun; functioning as sing or plural*): *she has less than she needs; the less you eat, the less you want* **2** (usually preceded by *no*) lower in rank or importance: *no less a man than the president; St James the Less* **3 no less** *informal* used to indicate surprise or admiration, often sarcastic, at the preceding statement: *she says she's been to Italy, no less* **4 less of** to a smaller extent or degree: *we see less of John these days; less of a success than I'd hoped* ▷ *adv* **5** the comparative of **little** (sense 1): *she walks less than she should; less quickly; less beautiful* **6 much** *or* **still less** used to reinforce a negative: *we don't like it, still less enjoy it* **7 think less of** to have a lower opinion of ▷ *prep* **8** subtracting; minus: *three weeks less a day* [Old English *lǣssa* (adj), *lǣs* (adv, n)]

> USAGE *Less* should not be confused with *fewer*. *Less* refers strictly only to quantity and not to number: *there is less water than before*. *Fewer* means smaller in number: *there are fewer people than before*

-less *suffix forming adjectives* **1** without; lacking: *speechless* **2** not able to (do something) or not able to be (done, performed, etc): *countless* [Old English *-lās*, from *lēas* lacking]

lessee (lɛˈsiː) *n* a person to whom a lease is granted; a tenant under a lease [C15 via Anglo-French from Old French *lessé*, from *lesser* to LEASE¹] > **lesˈseeship** *n*

lessen (ˈlɛsᵊn) *vb* **1** to make or become less **2** (*tr*) to make little of

lesser (ˈlɛsə) *adj* not as great in quantity, size, or worth

Lesser Antilles *pl n* **the** a group of islands in the Caribbean, including the Leeward Islands, the Windward Islands, Barbados, and the Netherlands Antilles. Formerly called: **Caribbees**

lesser celandine *n* a Eurasian ranunculaceous plant, *Ranunculus ficaria*, having yellow flowers and heart-shaped leaves. Also called: **pilewort** Compare **greater celandine**

lesser panda *n* See **panda** (sense 2)

Lesser Sunda Islands *pl n* the English name of **Nusa Tenggara**

lesson (ˈlɛsᵊn) *n* **1 a** a unit, or single period of instruction in a subject; class: *an hour-long music lesson* **b** the content of such a unit **2** material assigned for individual study **3** something from which useful knowledge or principles can be learned; example **4** the principles, knowledge, etc, gained **5** a reprimand or punishment intended to correct **6** a portion of Scripture appointed to be read at divine service ▷ *vb* **7** (*tr*) *rare* to censure or punish [C13 from Old French *leçon*, from Latin *lēctiō*, from *legere* to read]

lessor (ˈlɛsɔː, lɛˈsɔː) *n* a person who grants a lease of property

lest (lɛst) *conj* (*subordinating;* takes *should* or a subjunctive verb) **1** so as to prevent any possibility that: *he fled the country lest he be captured and imprisoned* **2** (*after verbs or phrases expressing fear, worry, anxiety, etc*) for fear that; in case: *he was alarmed lest she should find out* [Old English *thē lǣste*, earlier *thȳ lǣs the*, literally: whereby less that]

Lésvos (ˈlɛzvɔs) *n* transliteration of the Modern Greek name for **Lesbos**

let¹ (lɛt) *vb* **lets, letting, let** (*tr;* usually takes an infinitive without *to* or an implied infinitive) **1** to permit; allow: *she lets him roam around* **2** (*imperative or dependent imperative*) **a** used as an auxiliary to express a request, proposal, or command, or to convey a warning or threat: *let's get on; just let me catch you here again!* **b** (in mathematical or philosophical discourse) used as an auxiliary to express an assumption or hypothesis: *let "a" equal "b"* **c** used as an auxiliary to express resigned acceptance of the inevitable: *let the worst happen* **3 a** to allow the occupation of (accommodation) in return for rent **b** to assign (a contract for work) **4** to allow or cause the movement of (something) in a specified direction: *to let air out of a tyre* **5** *Irish informal* to utter: *to let a cry* **6 let alone** (*conjunction*) much less; not to mention: *I can't afford wine, let alone champagne* **7 let** *or* **leave alone** *or* **be** to refrain from annoying or interfering with: *let the poor cat alone* **8 let go** See **go¹** (sense 59) **9 let loose a** to set free **b** *informal* to make (a sound or remark) suddenly: *he let loose a hollow laugh* **c** *informal* to discharge (rounds) from a gun or guns: *they let loose a couple of rounds of ammunition* ▷ *n* **10** *Brit* the act of letting property or accommodation: *the majority of new lets are covered by the rent regulations* ▷ See also **let down, let in, let into, let off, let on, let out, let through, let up** [Old English *lǣtan* to permit; related to Gothic *lētan*, German *lassen*]

let² (lɛt) *n* **1** an impediment or obstruction (esp in the phrase **without let or hindrance**) **2** *tennis, squash* **a** a minor infringement or obstruction of the ball, requiring a point to be replayed **b** the point so replayed ▷ *vb* **lets, letting, letted** *or* **let 3** (*tr*) *archaic* to hinder; impede [Old English *lettan* to hinder, from *lǣt* LATE; related to Old Norse *letja*]

-let *suffix forming nouns* **1** small or lesser: *booklet; starlet* **2** an article of attire or ornament worn on a specified part of the body: *anklet* [from Old French *-elet*, from Latin *-āle*, neuter of adj suffix *-ālis* or from Latin *-ellus*, diminutive suffix]

letch (lɛtʃ) *vb, n* a variant spelling of **lech** [C18 perhaps back formation from LECHER]

Letchworth (ˈlɛtʃwəθ, -ˌwɜːθ) *n* a town in SE England, in N Hertfordshire: the first garden city in Great Britain (founded in 1903). Pop: 32 932 (2001)

let down *vb* (*tr, mainly adverb*) **1** (*also preposition*) to lower **2** to fail to fulfil the expectations of (a person); disappoint **3** to undo, shorten, and resew (the hem) so as to lengthen (a dress, skirt, etc) **4** to untie (long hair that is bound up) and allow to fall loose **5** to deflate: *to let down a tyre* ▷ *n* **letdown 6** a disappointment **7** the gliding descent of an aircraft in preparation for landing **8** the release of milk from the mammary glands following stimulation by the hormone oxytocin

lethal (ˈliːθəl) *adj* **1** able to cause or causing death **2** of or suggestive of death [C16 from Latin *lēthālis*, from *lētum* death] > **lethality** (liːˈθælɪtɪ) *n* > ˈ**lethally** *adv*

lethal dose *n* the amount of a drug or other agent that if administered to an animal or human will prove fatal. Abbreviation: **LD** See also **median lethal dose**

lethargy (ˈlɛθədʒɪ) *n, pl* **-gies 1** sluggishness, slowness, or dullness **2** an abnormal lack of energy, esp as the result of a disease [C14 from Late Latin *lēthargīa*, from Greek *lēthargos* drowsy, from *lēthē* forgetfulness] > **lethargic** (lɪˈθɑːdʒɪk) *or* **leˈthargical** *adj* > **leˈthargically** *adv*

Lethbridge (ˈlɛθbrɪdʒ) *n* a city in Canada, in S Alberta: coal-mining. Pop: 67 374 (2001)

Lethe (ˈliːθɪ) *n* **1** *Greek myth* a river in Hades that caused forgetfulness in those who drank its waters **2** forgetfulness [C16 via Latin from Greek, from *lēthē* oblivion] > **Lethean** (lɪˈθiːən) *adj*

let in *vb* (*tr, adverb*) **1** to allow to enter **2 let in for** to involve (oneself or another) in (something more than is expected): *he let himself in for a lot of extra work* **3 let in on** to allow (someone) to know about or participate in

let into *vb* (*tr, preposition*) **1** to allow to enter **2** to put into the surface of: *to let a pipe into the wall* **3** to allow (someone) to share (a secret)

Leto ('li:təʊ) *n* the mother by Zeus of Apollo and Artemis. Roman name: **Latona**

let off *vb* (*tr, mainly adverb*) **1** (*also preposition*) to allow to disembark or leave **2** to explode or fire (a bomb, gun, etc) **3** (*also preposition*) to excuse from (work or other responsibilities): *I'll let you off for a week* **4** to allow to get away without the expected punishment, work, etc **5** to let (accommodation) in portions **6** to release (liquid, air, etc) **7** **let off steam** See **steam** (sense 6) **8** **let (someone) off with** to give (a light punishment) to (someone)

let on *vb* (*adverb; when tr, takes a clause as object*) *informal* **1** to allow (something, such as a secret) to be known; reveal: *he never let on that he was married* **2** (*tr*) to cause or encourage to be believed; pretend

let out *vb* (*adverb, mainly tr*) **1** to give vent to; emit: *to let out a howl* **2** to allow to go or run free; release **3** (*may take a clause as object*) to reveal (a secret) **4** to make available to tenants, hirers, or contractors **5** to permit to flow out: *to let air out of the tyres* **6** to make (a garment) larger, as by unpicking (the seams) and sewing nearer the outer edge ▷ *n* **let-out 7** a chance to escape

LETS (lɛts) *n acronym for* Local Exchange and Trading System: an economic system in which members of a community exchange goods and services using a cashless local currency

let's (lɛts) *contraction of* let us: used to express a suggestion, command, etc, by the speaker to himself and his hearers

Lett (lɛt) *n* another name for a **Latvian**

letter ('lɛtə) *n* **1** any of a set of conventional symbols used in writing or printing a language, each symbol being associated with a group of phonetic values in the language; character of the alphabet **2** a written or printed communication addressed to a person, company, etc, usually sent by post in an envelope. Related adj: **epistolary 3** (often preceded by *the*) the strict legalistic or pedantic interpretation of the meaning of an agreement, document, etc; exact wording as distinct from actual intention (esp in the phrase **the letter of the law**). Compare **spirit¹** (sense 10) **4** *printing archaic* a style of typeface: *a fancy letter* **5** **to the letter a** following the literal interpretation or wording exactly **b** attending to every detail ▷ *vb* **6** to write or mark letters on (a sign, etc), esp by hand **7** (*tr*) to set down or print using letters ▷ See also **letters** [c13 from Old French *lettre*, from Latin *littera* letter of the alphabet] > **letterer** *n*

letter bomb *n* a thin explosive device inside an envelope, detonated when the envelope is opened

letter box *n chiefly Brit* **1 a** a slot, usually covered with a hinged flap, through which letters, etc are delivered to a building **b** a private box into which letters, etc, are delivered **2** Also called: **postbox** a public box into which letters, etc, are put for collection and delivery

letterboxing ('lɛtə,bɒksɪŋ) *n* **1** a method of formatting film that enables all of a wide-screen film to be transmitted on a television screen, resulting in a blank strip of screen above and below the picture **2** a type of treasure hunt in which a box, known as a **letterbox**, is hidden in a remote rural location and clues are provided as to its whereabouts

letter card *n* **1** a card, usually one on which the postage is prepaid, that is sealed by being folded in half so that its gummed edges come into contact with each other **2** a long card consisting of a number of postcard views, with space for writing a letter on the backs, that is folded like a concertina for posting

lettered ('lɛtəd) *adj* **1** well educated in literature, the arts, etc **2** literate **3** of or characterized by learning or culture **4** printed or marked with letters

letterhead ('lɛtə,hɛd) *n* a sheet of paper printed with one's address, name, etc, for writing a letter on

letter-high *adj* another term for **type-high**

lettering ('lɛtərɪŋ) *n* **1** the act, art, or technique of

inscribing letters on to something **2** the letters so inscribed

letter of advice *n* a commercial letter giving a specific notification, such as the consignment of goods

letter of attorney *n* a less common term for **power of attorney**

letter of credit *n* **1** a letter issued by a bank entitling the bearer to draw funds up to a specified maximum from that bank or its agencies **2** a letter addressed by a bank instructing the addressee to allow the person named to draw a specified sum on the credit of the addressor bank

letter of intent *n* a letter indicating that the writer has the serious intention of doing something, such as signing a contract in the circumstances specified. It does not constitute either a promise or a contract

letter of introduction *n* a letter given by one person to another, as an introduction to a third party

letter of marque *or* **letters of marque** *n* **1** a licence granted by a state to a private citizen to arm a ship and seize merchant vessels of another nation **2** a similar licence issued by a nation allowing a private citizen to seize goods or citizens of another nation ▷ Also called: **letter of marque and reprisal**

letter-perfect *adj* another term (esp in the US) for **word-perfect**

letterpress ('lɛtə,prɛs) *n* **1 a** a method of printing in which ink is transferred from raised surfaces to paper by pressure; relief printing **b** matter so printed **2** text matter as distinct from illustrations

letter-quality printing *n computing* high-quality output in printed form from a printer linked to a word processor. Compare **draft-quality printing**

letters ('lɛtəz) *n* (*functioning as plural or singular*) **1** literary knowledge, ability, or learning: *a man of letters* **2** literary culture in general **3** an official title, degree, etc, indicated by an abbreviation: *letters after one's name*

letterset ('lɛtə,sɛt) *n* a method of rotary printing in which ink is transferred from raised surfaces to paper via a rubber-covered cylinder [c20 from LETTER(PRESS) + (OFF)SET]

letters of administration *pl n law* a formal document nominating a specified person to take over, administer, and dispose of an estate when there is no executor to carry out the testator's will

letters of credence *or* **letters credential** *pl n* a formal document accrediting a diplomatic officer to a foreign court or government

letters patent *pl n* See **patent** (sense 1)

let through *vb* (*tr*) to allow to pass (through): *the invalid was let through to the front of the queue*

Lettish ('lɛtɪʃ) *n, adj* another word for **Latvian**

lettre de cachet French (lɛtrə də kaʃɛ) *n, pl lettres de cachet* (lɛtrə də kaʃɛ) *French history* a letter under the sovereign's seal, often authorizing imprisonment without trial [literally: letter with a seal]

lettuce ('lɛtɪs) *n* **1** any of various plants of the genus *Lactuca*, esp *L. sativa*, which is cultivated in many varieties for its large edible leaves: family *Asteraceae* (composites) **2** the leaves of any of these varieties, which are eaten in salads **3** any of various plants that resemble true lettuce, such as lamb's lettuce and sea lettuce [c13 probably from Old French *laitues*, pl of *laitue*, from Latin *lactūca*, from *lac-* milk, because of its milky juice]

let up *vb* (*intr, adverb*) **1** to diminish, slacken, or stop **2** (foll by *on*) *informal* to be less harsh (towards someone) ▷ *n* **let-up 3** *informal* a lessening or abatement

leu ('leɪu) *n, pl* **lei** (leɪ) the standard monetary unit of Romania and Moldova, divided into 100 bani [from Romanian: lion]

Leucas ('lu:kəs) *n* a variant spelling of **Leukas**

leucine ('lu:si:n) *or* **leucin** ('lu:sɪn) *n* an essential

amino acid found in many proteins

leucite ('lu:saɪt) *n* a grey or white mineral consisting of potassium aluminium silicate: a source of potash for fertilizers and of aluminium. Formula: $KAlSi_2O_6$ > **leucitic** (lu:'sɪtɪk) *adj*

leuco-, leuko- *or before a vowel* **leuc-, leuk-** *combining form* white or lacking colour: *leucocyte; leucorrhoea; leukaemia* [from Greek *leukos* white]

leuco base ('lu:kəʊ) *n* a colourless compound formed by reducing a dye so that the original dye can be regenerated by oxidation

leucoblast *or esp US* **leukoblast** ('lu:kəʊ,blɑ:st) *n* an immature leucocyte

leucocratic (,lu:kə'krætɪk) *adj* (of igneous rocks) light-coloured because of a low content of ferromagnesian minerals [c20 from German *leukokrat*, from LEUCO- + Greek *kratein* to rule]

leucocyte *or esp US* **leukocyte** ('lu:kə,saɪt) *n* any of the various large unpigmented cells in the blood of vertebrates. Also called: **white blood cell, white (blood) corpuscle** See also **lymphocyte, granulocyte, monocyte.** > **leucocytic** *or esp US* **leukocytic** (,lu:kə'sɪtɪk) *adj*

leucocytosis *or esp US* **leukocytosis** (,lu:kəʊsaɪ'təʊsɪs) *n* a gross increase in the number of white blood cells in the blood, usually as a response to an infection > **leucocytotic** *or esp US* **leukocytotic** (,lu:kəʊsaɪ'tɒtɪk) *adj*

leucodepleted ('lu:kəʊdɪ,pli:tɪd) *adj* of or denoting blood from which the white cells have been removed

leucoderma *or esp US* **leukoderma** (,lu:kəʊ'dɜ:mə) *n* any area of skin that is white from congenital **albinism** (see **albino**) or acquired absence or loss of melanin pigmentation. Also called: **vitiligo** > ,**leuco'dermal**, ,**leuco'dermic** *or esp US* ,**leuko'dermal**, ,**leuko'dermic** *adj*

leucoma (lu:'kəʊmə) *n pathol* a white opaque scar of the cornea

leucomaine ('lu:kə,meɪn) *n biochem* any of a group of toxic amines produced during animal metabolism [c20 from LEUCO- + -*maine*, as in *ptomaine*]

leucopenia *or esp US* **leukopenia** (,lu:kəʊ'pi:nɪə) *n pathol* an abnormal reduction in the number of white blood cells in the blood, characteristic of certain diseases [c19 from LEUCO- + Greek *penia* poverty] > ,**leuco'penic** *or esp US* ,**leuko'penic** *adj*

leucoplast ('lu:kə,plæst) *or* **leucoplastid** *n* any of the small colourless bodies occurring in the cytoplasm of plant cells and used for storing food material, esp starch

leucopoiesis *or esp US* **leukopoiesis** (,lu:kəʊpɔɪ'i:sɪs) *n physiol* formation of leucocytes in the body. Also called: **leucocytopoiesis** > **leucopoietic** *or esp US* **leukopoietic** (,lu:kəʊpɔɪ'ɛtɪk) *adj*

leucorrhoea *or esp US* **leukorrhea** (,lu:kə'ri:ə) *n pathol* a white or yellowish discharge of mucous material from the vagina, often an indication of infection > ,**leucor'rhoeal** *or esp US or* ,**leukor'rheal** *adj*

leucotomy (lu:'kɒtəmɪ) *n* the surgical operation of cutting some of the nerve fibres in the frontal lobes of the brain for treating intractable mental disorders. See also **lobotomy** [c20 from LEUCO- (with reference to the white brain tissue) + -TOMY]

Leuctra ('lu:ktrə) *n* an ancient town in Greece southwest of Thebes in Boeotia: site of a victory of Thebes over Sparta (371BC), which marked the end of Spartan military supremacy in Greece

leukaemia *or esp US* **leukemia** (lu:'ki:mɪə) *n* an acute or chronic disease characterized by a gross proliferation of leucocytes, which crowd into the bone marrow, spleen, lymph nodes, etc, and suppress the blood-forming apparatus [c19 from LEUCO- + Greek *haima* blood]

Leukas *or* **Leucas** ('lu:kəs) *n* another name for **Levkás**

leuko- *combining form* a variant of **leuco-**

leukotriene (,lu:kəʊ'traɪi:n) *n* one of a class of products of metabolic conversion of arachidonic acid; the active constituents of slow-reacting substance, responsible for bronchial constriction, contraction of smooth muscle, and inflammatory processes [c20 from *leukocyte*, in which they were discovered + *triene* from the conjugated triene unit that they contain]

Leuven ('lø:və) *n* the Flemish name for **Louvain**

lev (lɛf) *n, pl* **leva** ('lɛvə) the standard monetary unit of Bulgaria, divided into 100 stotinki [from Bulgarian: lion]

Lev. *Bible abbreviation for* Leviticus

Levalloisian (ˌlɛvə'lɔɪzɪən) *or* **Levallois** (lə'vælwɑ:) *adj* of or relating to a Lower Palaeolithic culture in W Europe, characterized by a method of flaking flint tools so that one side of the core is flat and the other domed

levant[1] (lɪ'vænt) *n* a type of leather made from the skins of goats, sheep, or seals, having a pattern of irregular creases [c19 shortened from *Levant morocco* (type of leather)]

levant[2] (lɪ'vænt) *vb* (*intr*) *Brit* to bolt or abscond, esp to avoid paying debts [c18 perhaps from Spanish *levantar (el campo)* to break (camp)]

Levant (lɪ'vænt) *n* **the** a former name for the area of the E Mediterranean now occupied by Lebanon, Syria, and Israel [c15 from Old French, from the present participle of *lever* to raise (referring to the rising of the sun in the east), from Latin *levāre*]

levanter[1] (lɪ'væntə) *n* (*sometimes capital*) **1** an easterly wind in the W Mediterranean area, esp in the late summer **2** an inhabitant of the Levant

levanter[2] (lɪ'væntə) *n Brit* a person who bolts or absconds

levantine ('lɛvənˌtaɪn) *n* a cloth of twilled silk

Levantine ('lɛvənˌtaɪn) *adj* **1** of or relating to the Levant ▷ *n* **2** (esp formerly) an inhabitant of the Levant

levator (lɪ'veɪtə, -tɔ:) *n* **1** *anatomy* any of various muscles that raise a part of the body **2** *surgery* an instrument for elevating a part or structure [c17 New Latin, from Latin *levāre* to raise]

levee[1] ('lɛvɪ) *n US* **1** an embankment alongside a river, produced naturally by sedimentation or constructed by man to prevent flooding **2** an embankment that surrounds a field that is to be irrigated **3** a landing place on a river; quay [c18 from French, from Medieval Latin *levāta*, from Latin *levāre* to raise]

levee[2] ('lɛvɪ, 'lɛveɪ) *n* **1** a formal reception held by a sovereign just after rising from bed **2** (in Britain) a public court reception for men, held in the early afternoon [c17 from French, variant of *lever* a rising, from Latin *levāre* to raise]

level ('lɛvᵊl) *adj* **1** on a horizontal plane **2** having a surface of completely equal height **3** being of the same height as something else **4** (of quantities to be measured, as in recipes) even with the top of the cup, spoon, etc **5** equal to or even with (something or someone else) **6** not having or showing inconsistency or irregularities **7** Also: **level-headed** even-tempered; steady ▷ *vb* **-els, -elling, -elled** *or US* **-els, -eling, -eled 8** (*tr*; sometimes foll by *off*) to make (a surface) horizontal, level, or even **9** to make (two or more people or things) equal, as in position or status **10** (*tr*) to raze to the ground **11** (*tr*) to knock (a person) down by or as if by a blow **12** (*tr*) to direct (a gaze, criticism, etc) emphatically at someone **13** (*intr*; often foll by *with*) *informal* to be straightforward and frank **14** (*intr*; foll by *off* or *out*) to manoeuvre an aircraft into a horizontal flight path after a dive, climb, or glide **15** (often foll by *at*) to aim (a weapon) horizontally **16** *surveying* to determine the elevation of a section of (land), sighting through a levelling instrument to a staff at successive pairs or points ▷ *n* **17** a horizontal datum line or plane **18** a device, such as a spirit level, for determining whether a surface is horizontal **19** a surveying instrument consisting basically of a telescope with a spirit level attached, used for measuring relative heights of land. See **Abney level, dumpy level 20** a reading of the difference in elevation of two points taken with such an instrument **21** position or status in a scale of values **22** amount or degree of progress; stage **23** a specified vertical position; altitude **24** a horizontal line or plane with respect to which measurement of elevation is based: *sea level* **25** a flat even surface or area of land **26** a horizontal passage or drift in a mine **27** any of the successive layers of material that have been deposited with the passage of time to build up and raise the height of the land surface **28** *physics* the ratio of the magnitude of a physical quantity to an arbitrary magnitude: *sound-pressure level* **29 do one's level best** to make every possible effort; try one's utmost **30 find one's level** to find one's most suitable place socially, professionally, etc **31 on a level** on the same horizontal plane as another **32 on the level** *informal* sincere, honest, or genuine [c14 from Old French *livel*, from Vulgar Latin *lībellum* (unattested), from Latin *lībella*, diminutive of *lībra* scales] > **'levelly** *adv* > **'levelness** *n*

level crossing *n Brit* a point at which a railway and a road cross, esp one with barriers that close the road when a train is scheduled to pass. US and Canadian name: **grade crossing**

level descriptor (dɪ'skrɪptə) *n Brit education* one of a set of criteria used to assess the performance of a pupil in a particular subject

level-headed *adj* even-tempered, balanced, and reliable; steady > **ˌlevel-'headedly** *adv* > **ˌlevel-'headedness** *n*

leveller *or US* **leveler** ('lɛvələ) *n* **1** a person or thing that levels **2** a person who works for the abolition of inequalities

Levellers ('lɛvələz) *n* **the** *English history* a radical group on the Parliamentarian side during the Civil War that advocated republicanism, freedom of worship, etc

levelling screw *n* a screw, often one of three, for adjusting the level of an apparatus

level of attainment *n Brit education* one of ten groupings, each with its own attainment criteria based on pupil age and ability, within which a pupil is assessed

level pegging *Brit informal* ▷ *n* **1** equality between two contestants ▷ *adj* **2** (of two contestants) equal

level playing field *n* a situation in which none of the competing parties has an advantage at the outset of a competitive activity

Leven ('li:vᵊn) *n* **Loch 1** a lake in E central Scotland: one of the shallowest of Scottish lochs, with seven islands, on one of which Mary, Queen of Scots was imprisoned (1567–8). Length: 6 km (3.7 miles). Width: 4 km (2.5 miles) **2** a sea loch in W Scotland, extending for about 14 km (9 miles) east from Loch Linnhe

lever ('li:və) *n* **1** a rigid bar pivoted about a fulcrum, used to transfer a force to a load and usually to provide a mechanical advantage **2** any of a number of mechanical devices employing this principle **3** a means of exerting pressure in order to accomplish something; strategic aid ▷ *vb* **4** to prise or move (an object) with a lever [c13 from Old French *leveour*, from *lever* to raise, from Latin *levāre*, from *levis* light] > **'lever-ˌlike** *adj*

leverage ('li:vərɪdʒ, -vrɪdʒ) *n* **1** the action of a lever **2** the mechanical advantage gained by employing a lever **3** power to accomplish something; strategic advantage **4** the enhanced power available to a large company: *the supermarket chains have greater leverage than single-outlet enterprises* **5** US word for **gearing** (sense 3) **6** the use made by a company of its limited assets to guarantee the substantial loans required to finance its business

leveraged buyout ('li:vərɪdʒd) *n* a takeover bid in which a small company makes use of its limited assets, and those of the usually larger target company, to raise the loans required to finance the takeover. Abbreviation: **LBO**

leveret ('lɛvərɪt, -vrɪt) *n* a young hare, esp one less than one year old [c15 from Norman French *levrete*, diminutive of *levre*, from Latin *lepus* hare]

Leverkusen (*German* 'le:vərˌku:zən) *n* a town in NW Germany, in North Rhine-Westphalia on the Rhine: chemical industries. Pop: 161 543 (2003 est)

Levi[1] ('li:vaɪ) *n* **1** *Old Testament* **a** the third son of Jacob and Leah and the ancestor of the tribe of Levi (Genesis 29:34) **b** the priestly tribe descended from this patriarch (Numbers 18:21–24) **2** *New Testament* another name for **Matthew** (the apostle)

Levi[2] ('li:vaɪ; *Hebrew* 'levi) *or* **Levite** ('li:vaɪt) *n Judaism* a descendant of the tribe of Levi who has certain privileges in the synagogue service

leviable ('lɛvɪəbᵊl) *adj* **1** (of taxes, tariffs, etc) liable to be levied **2** (of goods, etc) liable to bear a levy; taxable

leviathan (lɪ'vaɪəθən) *n* **1** *Bible* a monstrous beast, esp a sea monster **2** any huge or powerful thing [c14 from Late Latin, ultimately from Hebrew *liwyāthān*, of obscure origin]

levigate ('lɛvɪˌgeɪt) *vb chem* **1** (*tr*) to grind into a fine powder or a smooth paste **2** to form or cause to form a homogeneous mixture, as in the production of gels **3** (*tr*) to suspend (fine particles) by grinding in a liquid, esp as a method of separating fine from coarse particles ▷ *adj* **4** *botany* having a smooth polished surface; glabrous [c17 from Latin *lēvigāre*, from *lēvis* smooth] > **ˌlevi'gation** *n* > **'leviˌgator** *n*

levin ('lɛvɪn) *n* an archaic word for **lightning** [c13 probably from Scandinavian; compare Danish *lygnild*]

levirate ('lɛvɪrɪt) *n* the practice, required by Old Testament law, of marrying the widow of one's brother [c18 from Latin *lēvir* a husband's brother] > **leviratic** (ˌlɛvɪ'rætɪk) *or* **ˌlevi'ratical** *adj*

Levi's ('li:vaɪz) *pl n trademark* jeans, usually blue and made of denim

levitate ('lɛvɪˌteɪt) *vb* **1** to rise or cause to rise and float in the air, without visible agency, attributed, esp formerly, to supernatural causes **2** (*tr*) *med* to support (a patient) on a cushion of air in the treatment of severe burns [c17 from Latin *levis* light + *-tate*, as in *gravitate*] > **ˌlevi'tation** *n* > **'leviˌtator** *n*

Levite ('li:vaɪt) *n* **1** *Old Testament* a member of the priestly tribe of Levi **2** *Judaism* another word for **Levi**[2]

Levitical (lɪ'vɪtɪkᵊl) *or* **Levitic** *adj* **1** of or relating to the Levites **2** of or relating to the book of Leviticus containing moral precepts and many of the laws concerning the Temple ritual and construction > **Le'vitically** *adv*

Leviticus (lɪ'vɪtɪkəs) *n Old Testament* the third book of the Old Testament, containing Levitical law and ritual precepts

levity ('lɛvɪtɪ) *n, pl* **-ties 1** inappropriate lack of seriousness **2** fickleness or instability **3** *archaic* lightness in weight [c16 from Latin *levitās* lightness, from *levis* light]

Levkás (lɛf'kæs), **Leukas** *or* **Leucas** *n* a Greek island in the Ionian Sea, in the Ionian Islands. Pop: 20 751 (2001). Area: 295 sq km (114 sq miles). Italian name: **Santa Maura**

Levkosia (lɛf'kəʊsɪə) *or* **Leukosia** *n* the Greek name for **Nicosia**

levo- *combining form* a US variant of **laevo-** [from Latin *laevus* left, on the left]

levodopa (ˌli:vəʊ'dəʊpə) *n* another name for **L-dopa**

levy ('lɛvɪ) *vb* **levies, levying, levied** (*tr*) **1** to impose and collect (a tax, tariff, fine, etc) **2** to conscript troops for service **3** to seize or attach (property) in accordance with the judgment of a court ▷ *n, pl* **levies 4 a** the act of imposing and collecting a tax, tariff, etc **b** the money so raised **5 a** the conscription of troops for service **b** a person conscripted in this way [c15 from Old French *levée* a raising, from *lever*, from Latin *levāre* to raise] > **'levier** *n*

levy en masse ('lɛvɪ ɒn 'mæs) *n* the conscription of the civilian population in large numbers in the face of impending invasion. Also called: **levée en masse** (*French* ləve ā mas)

lewd (luːd) *adj* **1** characterized by or intended to excite crude sexual desire; obscene **2** *obsolete* **a** wicked **b** ignorant [c14 from Old English *lǣwde* lay, ignorant; see LAY³] > **'lewdly** *adv* > **'lewdness** *n*

Lewes ('luːɪs) *n* a market town in S England, administrative centre of East Sussex, on the River Ouse: site of a battle (1264) in which Henry III was defeated by Simon de Montfort. Pop: 15 988 (2001)

lewis ('luːɪs) or **lewisson** *n* a lifting device for heavy stone or concrete blocks consisting of a number of curved pieces of metal or wedges fitting into a dovetailed recess cut into the block [c18 perhaps from the name of the inventor]

Lewis ('luːɪs) *n* the N part of the island of Lewis with Harris, in the Outer Hebrides. Area: 1634 sq km (631 sq miles)

Lewis acid *n* a substance capable of accepting a pair of electrons from a base to form a covalent bond. Compare **Lewis base** [c20 named after G. N. *Lewis* (1875–1946), US chemist]

Lewis base *n* a substance capable of donating a pair of electrons to an acid to form a covalent bond. Compare **Lewis acid** [c20 named after G. N. *Lewis* (1875–1946), US chemist]

Lewis gun *n* a light air-cooled drum-fed gas-operated machine gun used chiefly in World War I [c20 named after I. N. *Lewis* (1858–1931), US soldier]

Lewisham ('luːɪʃəm) *n* a borough of S Greater London, on the River Thames. Pop: 248 300 (2003 est). Area: 35 sq km (13 sq miles)

lewisite ('luːɪˌsaɪt) *n* a colourless oily poisonous liquid with an odour resembling that of geraniums, having a powerful vesicant action and used as a war gas; 1-chloro-2-dichloroarsinoethene. Formula: ClCH:CHAsCl₂ [c20 named after W. L. *Lewis* (1878–1943), US chemist]

Lewis with Harris or **Lewis and Harris** *n* an island in the Outer Hebrides, separated from the NW coast of Scotland by the Minch: consists of Lewis in the north and Harris in the south; many lakes and peat moors; economy based chiefly on the Harris tweed industry, with some fishing. Chief town: Stornoway. Pop: 19 918 (2001). Area: 2134 sq km (824 sq miles)

Lewy bodies ('luːɪ) *pl n* abnormal proteins that occur in the nerve cells of the cerebral cortex and the basal ganglia, causing Parkinson's disease and dementia [c20 named after F. H. *Lewy* (1885–1950), German neurologist]

lex (lɛks) *n*, *pl* **leges** ('liːdʒiːz) **1** a system or body of laws **2** a particular specified law [Latin]

lexeme ('lɛksiːm) *n linguistics* a minimal meaningful unit of language, the meaning of which cannot be understood from that of its component morphemes. *Take off* (in the senses to mimic, to become airborne, etc) is a lexeme, as well as the independent morphemes *take* and *off* [c20 from LEX(ICON) + -EME]

lexical ('lɛksɪkᵊl) *adj* **1** of or relating to items of vocabulary in a language **2** of or relating to a lexicon > **lexicality** (ˌlɛksɪ'kælɪtɪ) *n* > **'lexically** *adv*

lexical decision task *n psychol* an experimental task in which subjects have to decide as fast as possible whether a given letter string is a word

lexical insertion *n generative grammar* the process in which actual morphemes of a language are substituted either for semantic material or for place-fillers in the course of a derivation of a sentence

lexicalize or **lexicalise** ('lɛksɪkəˌlaɪz) *vb linguistics* to form (a word or lexeme) or (of a word or lexeme) to be formed from constituent morphemes, words, or lexemes, as to form *cannot* from *can* and *not* > ˌlexicali'zation or ˌlexicali'sation *n*

lexical meaning *n* the meaning of a word in relation to the physical world or to abstract concepts, without reference to any sentence in which the word may occur. Compare **grammatical meaning, content word**

lexical order *n* the arrangement of a set of items in accordance with a recursive algorithm, such as the entries in a dictionary whose order depends on their first letter unless these are the same in which case it is the second which decides, and so on

lexicog. *abbreviation for* **1** lexicographical **2** lexicography

lexicography (ˌlɛksɪ'kɒgrəfɪ) *n* the process or profession of writing or compiling dictionaries > ˌlexi'cographer *n* > lexicographic (ˌlɛksɪkə'græfɪk) or ˌlexico'graphical *adj* > ˌlexico'graphically *adv*

lexicology (ˌlɛksɪ'kɒlədʒɪ) *n* the study of the overall structure and history of the vocabulary of a language > lexicological (ˌlɛksɪkə'lɒdʒɪkᵊl) *adj* > ˌlexico'logically *adv* > ˌlexi'cologist *n*

lexicon ('lɛksɪkən) *n* **1** a dictionary, esp one of an ancient language such as Greek or Hebrew **2** a list of terms relating to a particular subject **3** the vocabulary of a language or of an individual **4** *linguistics* the set of all the morphemes of a language [c17 New Latin, from Greek *lexikon*, n use of *lexikos* relating to words, from Greek *lexis* word, from *legein* to speak]

lexicostatistics (ˌlɛksɪkəʊstə'tɪstɪks) *n* (*functioning as singular*) the statistical study of the vocabulary of a language, with special attention to the historical links with other languages. See also **glottochronology**

lexigram ('lɛksɪˌgræm) *n* a figure or symbol that represents a word [c20 from Greek *lexis* word + -GRAM]

lexigraphy (lɛk'sɪgrəfɪ) *n* a system of writing in which each word is represented by a sign [c19 from Greek *lexis* word + -GRAPHY]

Lexington ('lɛksɪŋtən) *n* **1** a city in NE central Kentucky, in the bluegrass region: major centre for horse-breeding. Pop (including Fayette): 266 798 (2003 est) **2** a city in Massachusetts, northwest of Boston: site of the first action (1775) of the War of American Independence. Pop: 30 631 (2003 est)

lexis ('lɛksɪs) *n* the totality of vocabulary items in a language, including all forms having lexical meaning or grammatical function [c20 from Greek *lexis* word]

lex loci ('ləʊsaɪ, -kiː) *n* the law of the place [from Latin]

lex non scripta (nɒn 'skrɪptə) *n* the unwritten law; common law [from Latin]

lex scripta ('skrɪptə) *n* the written law; statute law [from Latin]

lex talionis (ˌtælɪ'əʊnɪs) *n* the law of revenge or retaliation [c16 New Latin]

ley (leɪ, liː) *n* **1** arable land put down to grass; grassland or pastureland **2** Also called: **ley line** a line joining two prominent points in the landscape, thought to be the line of a prehistoric track [c14 variant of LEA¹]

Leyden ('laɪdᵊn; *Dutch* 'lɛɪdə) *n* a variant spelling of **Leiden**

Leyden jar *n physics* an early type of capacitor consisting of a glass jar with the lower part of the inside and outside coated with tin foil [c18 first made in Leiden]

ley farming *n* the alternation at intervals of several years of crop growing and grassland pasture

Leyland cypress ('leɪlənd) *n* a fast-growing cypress, *Cupressocyparis leylandii*, that is a hybrid produced by crossing the macrocarpa with the Nootka cypress (*Chamaecyparis nootkatensis*): widely grown for hedging. Also called: **Leylandii, Leylandi** [c19 named after C. J. *Leyland* (1849–1926), British horticulturalist]

leylandii (leɪ'lændɪaɪ) or **leylandi** (-'lændɪ) *n* other names for **Leyland cypress**

Leyte ('leɪteɪ) *n* an island in the central Philippines, in the Visayan Islands. Chief town: Tacloban. Pop: 1 362 050 (1990). Area: 7215 sq km (2786 sq miles)

Leyte Gulf *n* an inlet of the Pacific in the E Philippines, east of Leyte and south of Samar: scene of a battle (Oct 23–26, 1944) during World War II, in which the Americans defeated almost the entire Japanese navy, thereby ensuring ultimate Allied victory

lezzie ('lɛzɪ) or **lezza** ('lɛzə) *n slang* a lesbian

LF *radio abbreviation for* **low frequency**

LG *abbreviation for* **Low German**

lg. or **lge** *abbreviation for* **large**

LGBT *abbreviation for* **1** lesbian, gay, bisexual, and transgender ▷ *n* (ɛldʒiːbiːtiː) *pl* LGBT's or LGBTs **2** a lesbian, gay, bisexual, or transgender person

lgth *abbreviation for* **length**

LGV (in Britain) *abbreviation for* large goods vehicle

lh or **LH** *abbreviation for* **left hand**

LH *abbreviation for* **luteinizing hormone**

Lhasa or **Lassa** ('lɑːsə) *n* a city in SW China, capital of Tibet AR, at an altitude of 3606 m (11 830 ft): for centuries the sacred city of Lamaism and residence of the Dalai Lamas from the 17th century until 1950; known as the Forbidden City because it was closed to Westerners until the beginning of the 20th century; annexed by China in 1951. The Dalai Lama fled after an unsuccessful revolt against Chinese rule in 1959. Pop: 131 000 (2005 est)

Lhasa apso ('lɑːsə 'æpsəʊ) *n*, *pl* Lhasa apsos a small dog of a Tibetan breed having a long straight dense coat, often gold or greyish, and a well-feathered tail carried curled over its back [Tibetan]

lhd *abbreviation for* left-hand drive

LH-RH *abbreviation for* **luteinizing hormone-releasing hormone**

li¹ (liː) *n* a Chinese unit of length, approximately equal to 590 yards [from Chinese]

li² *the internet domain name for* Liechtenstein

Li *the chemical symbol for* lithium

LI *abbreviation for* **1** Long Island **2** Light Infantry

liabilities (ˌlaɪə'bɪlɪtɪz) *pl n accounting* business obligations incurred but not discharged and entered as claims on the assets shown on the balance sheet. Compare **assets** (sense 1)

liability (ˌlaɪə'bɪlɪtɪ) *n*, *pl* **-ties** **1** the state of being liable **2** a financial obligation **3** a hindrance or disadvantage **4** likelihood or probability

liability engineering *n* the practice by a company of taking steps to avoid liability for any fraudulent dealings with it, such as making a credit card owner responsible for any abuses of the card by a third party

liable ('laɪəbᵊl) *adj* (*postpositive*) **1** legally obliged or responsible; answerable **2** susceptible or exposed; subject **3** probable, likely, or capable: *it's liable to happen soon* [c15 perhaps via Anglo-French, from Old French *lier* to bind, from Latin *ligāre*] > 'liableness *n*

USAGE The use of *liable to* to mean *likely to* was formerly considered incorrect, but is now acceptable

liaise (lɪ'eɪz) *vb* (*intr*; usually foll by *with*) to communicate and maintain contact (with) [c20 back formation from LIAISON]

liaison (lɪ'eɪzɒn) *n* **1** communication and contact between groups or units **2** (*modifier*) of or relating to liaison between groups or units: *a liaison officer* **3** a secretive or adulterous sexual relationship **4** one who acts as an agent between parties; an intermediary **5** the relationship between military units necessary to ensure unity of purpose **6** (in the phonology of several languages, esp French) the pronunciation of a normally silent consonant at the end of a word immediately before another word commencing with a vowel, in such a way that the consonant is taken over as the initial sound of the following word. Liaison is seen between French *ils* (il) and *ont* (ɔ̃), to give *ils ont* (il zɔ̃) **7** any thickening for soups, sauces, etc, such as egg yolks or cream [c17 via French from Old French, from *lier* to bind, from Latin *ligāre*]

liaison officer *n* **1** a person who liaises between groups or units **2** NZ a university official who oversees the operation of the accrediting system in schools

Liákoura ('ljakura) *n* transliteration of the Modern Greek name for (Mount) **Parnassus**

liana (lɪ'ɑːnə) *or* **liane** (lɪ'ɑːn) *n* any of various woody climbing plants mainly of tropical forests [c19 changed from earlier *liane* (through influence of French *lier* to bind), from French, of obscure origin] > li'anoid *adj*

Lianyungang ('ljænˌjʊŋ'gæn), **Sinhailien** *or* **Hsin-hai-lien** *n* a city in E China, near the coast of Jiangsu. Pop: 645 000 (2005 est)

Liao (ljau) *n* a river in NE China, rising in SE Inner Mongolia and flowing northeast then southwest to the Gulf of Liaodong. Length: about 1100 km (700 miles)

Liaodong Peninsula ('ljaʊ'dʊŋ) *or* **Liaotung Peninsula** ('ljaʊ'tʊŋ) *n* **1** a peninsula of NE China, in S Manchuria extending south into the Yellow Sea: forms the S part of Liaoning province **2 Gulf of** the N part of the Gulf of Chihli, west of the Liaodong Peninsula

Liaoning ('ljaʊ'nɪŋ) *n* a province of NE China, in S Manchuria. Capital: Shenyang. Pop: 42 100 000 (2003 est). Area: 150 000 sq km (58 500 sq miles)

Liaoyang ('ljaʊ'jæŋ) *n* a city in NE China, in S Manchuria, in Liaoning province: a regional capital in the early dynasties. Pop: 752 000 (2005 est)

liar ('laɪə) *n* a person who has lied or lies repeatedly

liard (lɪ'ɑːd) *n* a former small coin of various European countries [c16 after G. *Liard*, French minter]

Liard (li'ɑːd, liː'ɑːd, -'ɑː) *n* a river in W Canada, rising in the SE Yukon and flowing east and then northwest to the Mackenzie River. Length: 885 km (550 miles)

liar paradox *n logic* the paradox that *this statement is false* is true only if it is false and false only if it is true: attributed to Epimenides the Cretan in the form *all Cretans are liars*

Lias ('laɪəs) *n* the lowest series of rocks of the Jurassic system [c15 (referring to a kind of limestone), c19 (geological sense) from Old French *liois*, perhaps from *lie* lees, dregs, so called from its appearance] > Liassic (laɪ'æsɪk) *adj*

liatris (laɪ'ætrɪs) *n* See **blazing star** (sense 2) [c18 New Latin, of uncertain origin]

lib (lɪb) *n informal, sometimes derogatory* short for **liberation** (sense 2)

lib. *abbreviation for* **1** librarian **2** library

Lib. *abbreviation for* Liberal

libation (laɪ'beɪʃən) *n* **1 a** the pouring out of wine, etc, in honour of a deity **b** the liquid so poured out **2** *usually facetious* an alcoholic drink [c14 from Latin *lībātiō*, from *lībāre* to pour an offering of drink] > li'bational *or* li'bationary *adj*

Libau ('liːbau) *n* the German name for **Liepāja**

Libava (lɪ'bavə) *n* transliteration of the Russian name for **Liepāja**

Lib Dem *abbreviation for* **Liberal Democrat**

libeccio (lɪ'bɛtʃɪəʊ) *or* **libecchio** (lɪ'bɛkɪəʊ) *n* a strong westerly or southwesterly wind blowing onto the W coast of Corsica [Italian, via Latin, from Greek *libs*]

libel ('laɪbəl) *n* **1** *law* **a** the publication of defamatory matter in permanent form, as by a written or printed statement, picture, etc **b** the act of publishing such matter **2** any defamatory or unflattering representation or statement **3** *ecclesiastical law* a claimant's written statement of claim **4** *Scots law* the formal statement of a charge ▷ *vb* -bels, -belling, -belled *or US* -bels, -beling, -beled (*tr*) **5** *law* to make or publish a defamatory statement or representation about (a person) **6** to misrepresent injuriously **7** *ecclesiastical law* to bring an action against (a person) in the ecclesiastical courts [c13 (in the sense: written statement), hence c14 legal sense:

a plaintiff's statement, via Old French from Latin *libellus* a little book, from *liber* a book] > 'libeller *or* 'libelist *n* > 'libellous *or* 'libelous *adj*

libellant *or US* **libelant** ('laɪbələnt) *n* **1** a party who brings an action in the ecclesiastical courts by presenting a libel **2** a person who publishes a libel

libellee *or US* **libelee** (ˌlaɪbə'liː) *n* a person against whom a libel has been filed in an ecclesiastical court

liber ('laɪbə) *n* a rare name for **phloem** [c18 from Latin, in original sense: tree bark]

liberal ('lɪbərəl, 'lɪbrəl) *adj* **1** relating to or having social and political views that favour progress and reform **2** relating to or having policies or views advocating individual freedom **3** giving and generous in temperament or behaviour **4** tolerant of other people **5** abundant; lavish: *a liberal helping of cream* **6** not strict; free: *a liberal translation* **7** of or relating to an education that aims to develop general cultural interests and intellectual ability ▷ *n* **8** a person who has liberal ideas or opinions [c14 from Latin *līberālis* of freedom, from *līber* free] > 'liberally *adv* > 'liberalness *n*

Liberal ('lɪbərəl, 'lɪbrəl) *n* **1** a member or supporter of a Liberal Party or Liberal Democrat party ▷ *adj* **2** of or relating to a Liberal Party

liberal arts *pl n* the fine arts, humanities, sociology, languages, and literature. Often shortened to: **arts**

Liberal Democrat *n* a member or supporter of the Liberal Democrats

Liberal Democrats *pl n* (in Britain) a political party with centrist policies; established in 1988 as the Social and Liberal Democrats when the Liberal Party merged with the Social Democratic Party; renamed Liberal Democrats in 1989

liberal elite *n often derogatory* the group of people in a society who are considered as having a high level of education and liberal ideas

liberalism ('lɪbərəˌlɪzəm, 'lɪbrə-) *n* **1** liberal opinions, practices, or politics **2** a movement in modern Protestantism that rejects biblical authority > 'liberalist *n, adj* > ˌliberal'istic *adj*

liberality (ˌlɪbə'rælɪtɪ) *n, pl* -ties **1** generosity; bounty **2** the quality or condition of being liberal

liberalize *or* **liberalise** ('lɪbərəˌlaɪz, 'lɪbrə-) *vb* to make or become liberal > ˌliberali'zation *or* ˌliberali'sation *n* > 'liberalˌizer *or* 'liberalˌiser *n*

Liberal Party *n* **1** one of the former major political parties in Britain; in 1988 merged with the Social Democratic Party to form the Social and Liberal Democrats; renamed the Liberal Democrats in 1989 **2** one of the major political parties in Australia, a conservative party, generally opposed to the Labor Party **3** one of the major political parties in Canada, generally representing viewpoints between those of the Progressive Conservative Party and the New Democratic Party **4** any other party supporting liberal policies

liberal studies *n* (*functioning as singular*) *Brit* a supplementary arts course for those specializing in scientific, technical, or professional studies

Liberal Unionist *n* a Liberal who opposed Gladstone's policy of Irish Home Rule in 1886 and after > Liberal Unionism *n*

liberate ('lɪbəˌreɪt) *vb* (*tr*) **1** to give liberty to; make free **2** to release (something, esp a gas) from chemical combination during a chemical reaction **3** to release from occupation or subjugation by a foreign power **4** to free from social prejudices or injustices **5** *euphemistic or facetious* to steal > 'liberˌator *n*

liberated ('lɪbəˌreɪtɪd) *adj* **1** given liberty; freed; released **2** released from occupation or subjugation by a foreign power **3** (esp in feminist theory) not bound by traditional sexual and social roles

liberation (ˌlɪbə'reɪʃən) *n* **1** a liberating or being liberated **2** the seeking of equal status or just

treatment for or on behalf of any group believed to be discriminated against: *women's liberation; animal liberation* > ˌliber'ationist *n, adj*

liberation theology *n* the belief that Christianity involves not only faith in the teachings of the Church but also a commitment to change social and political conditions from within in societies in which it is considered exploitation and oppression exist

Liberec (*Czech* 'lɪbɛrɛts) *n* a city in the N Czech Republic, on the Neisse River: a centre of the German Sudeten movement in 1938. Pop: 97 000 (2005 est). German name: Reichenberg

Liber Extra ('laɪbər 'ɛkstrə) *n* See **Decretals** [Latin: book of additional (decretals)]

Liberia (laɪ'bɪərɪə) *n* a republic in W Africa, on the Atlantic: originated in 1822 as a home for freed Afro-American slaves, with land purchased by the American Colonization Society; republic declared in 1847; exports are predominantly rubber and iron ore. Official language: English. Religion: Christian majority, also animist. Currency: dollar. Capital: Monrovia. Pop: 3 487 000 (2004 est). Area: 111 400 sq km (43 000 sq miles)

Liberian (laɪ'bɪərɪən) *adj* **1** of or relating to Liberia or its inhabitants ▷ *n* **2** a native or inhabitant of Liberia

libero ('liːbero) *n* another name for **sweeper** (sense 3)

libertarian (ˌlɪbə'tɛərɪən) *n* **1** a believer in freedom of thought, expression, etc **2** *philosophy* a believer in the doctrine of free will. Compare **determinism** ▷ *adj* **3** of, relating to, or characteristic of a libertarian [c18 from LIBERTY] > ˌliber'tarianism *n*

liberticide (lɪ'bɜːtɪˌsaɪd) *n* **1** a destroyer of freedom **2** the destruction of freedom > liˌberti'cidal *adj*

libertine ('lɪbəˌtiːn, -ˌtaɪn) *n* **1** a morally dissolute person ▷ *adj* **2** morally dissolute [c14 (in the sense: freedman, dissolute person): from Latin *lībertīnus* freedman, from *lībertus* freed, from *līber* free] > 'liberˌtinage *or* 'libertinˌism *n*

liberty ('lɪbətɪ) *n, pl* -ties **1** the power of choosing, thinking, and acting for oneself; freedom from control or restriction **2** the right or privilege of access to a particular place; freedom **3** (*often plural*) a social action regarded as being familiar, forward, or improper **4** (*often plural*) an action that is unauthorized or unwarranted in the circumstances: *he took liberties with the translation* **5 a** authorized leave granted to a sailor **b** (*as modifier*): *liberty man; liberty boat* **6** at liberty free, unoccupied, or unrestricted **7** take liberties (with) to be overfamiliar or overpresumptuous **8** take the liberty (of *or* to) to venture or presume (to do something) [c14 from Old French *liberté*, from Latin *lībertās*, from *līber* free]

Liberty bodice *n trademark* a sleeveless vest-like undergarment made from thick cotton and covering the upper part of the body, formerly worn esp by young children

liberty cap *n* **1** a cap of soft felt worn as a symbol of liberty, esp during the French Revolution, from the practice in ancient Rome of giving a freed slave such a cap **2** a poisonous hallucinogenic basidiomycetous fungus, *Psilocybe semilanceata*, yellowish-brown with a distinctive pointed cap, found in groups in grassland

liberty hall *n* (*sometimes capitals*) *informal* a place or condition of complete liberty

liberty horse *n* (in a circus) a riderless horse that performs movements to verbal commands

Liberty Island *n* a small island in upper New York Bay: site of the Statue of Liberty. Area: 5 hectares (12 acres). Former name (until 1956): Bedloe's Island

liberty ship *n* a supply ship of World War II

Libia ('liːbja) *n* the Italian name for **Libya**

libidinous (lɪ'bɪdɪnəs) *adj* **1** characterized by excessive sexual desire **2** of or relating to the libido > li'bidinously *adv* > li'bidinousness *n*

libido (lɪˈbiːdəʊ) *n, pl* **-dos** **1** *psychoanal* psychic energy emanating from the id **2** sexual urge or desire [C20 (in psychoanalysis): from Latin: desire] > **libidinal** (lɪˈbɪdɪnᵊl) *adj* > **liˈbidinally** *adv*
libra (ˈlaɪbrə) *n, pl* **-brae** (-briː) an ancient Roman unit of weight corresponding to 1 pound, but equal to about 12 ounces [C14 from Latin, literally: scales]
Libra (ˈliːbrə) *n, Latin genitive* **Librae** (ˈliːbriː) **1** *astronomy* a small faint zodiacal constellation in the S hemisphere, lying between Virgo and Scorpius on the ecliptic **2** *astrology* **a** Also called: **the Scales, the Balance** the seventh sign of the zodiac, symbol ♎, having a cardinal air classification and ruled by the planet Venus. The sun is in this sign between about Sept 23 and Oct 22 **b** a person born under this sign ▷ *adj* **3** *astrology* born under or characteristic of Libra ▷ Also (for senses 2b, 3): **Libran** (ˈlɪbrən)
librarian (laɪˈbrɛərɪən) *n* a person in charge of or assisting in a library
librarianship (lɪˈbrɛərɪənʃɪp, laɪ-) *n* the professional administration of library resources and services. Also called: **library science**
library (ˈlaɪbrərɪ) *n, pl* **-braries** **1** a room or set of rooms where books and other literary materials are kept **2** a collection of literary materials, films, CDs, children's toys, etc, kept for borrowing or reference **3** the building or institution that houses such a collection: *a public library* **4** a set of books published as a series, often in a similar format **5** *computing* a collection of standard programs and subroutines for immediate use, usually stored on disk or some other storage device **6** a collection of specific items for reference or checking against: *a library of genetic material* [C14 from Old French *librairie*, from Medieval Latin *librāris*, n use of Latin *librārius* relating to books, from *liber* book]
library edition *n* an edition of a book having a superior quality of paper, binding, etc
librate (ˈlaɪbreɪt) *vb (intr)* **1** to oscillate or waver **2** to hover or be balanced [C17 from Latin *librātus*, from *librāre* to balance] > **libratory** (ˈlaɪbrətərɪ, -trɪ) *adj*
libration (laɪˈbreɪʃən) *n* **1** the act or an instance of oscillating **2** a real or apparent oscillation of the moon enabling approximately 59 per cent of the surface to be visible from the earth over a period of time > **liˈbrational** *adj*
librettist (lɪˈbrɛtɪst) *n* the author of a libretto
libretto (lɪˈbrɛtəʊ) *n, pl* **-tos** *or* **-ti** (-tiː) a text written for and set to music in an opera, etc [C18 from Italian, diminutive of *libro* book]
Libreville (*French* librəvil) *n* the capital of Gabon, in the west on the estuary of the Gabon River: founded as a French trading post in 1843 and expanded with the settlement of freed slaves in 1848. Pop: 649 000 (2005 est)
libriform (ˈlaɪbrɪˌfɔːm) *adj* (of a fibre of woody tissue) elongated and having a pitted thickened cell wall
Librium (ˈlɪbrɪəm) *n trademark* a brand of the drug chlordiazepoxide. See also **benzodiazepine**
Libya (ˈlɪbɪə) *n* a republic in N Africa, on the Mediterranean: became an Italian colony in 1912; divided after World War II into Tripolitania and Cyrenaica (under British administration) and Fezzan (under French); gained independence in 1951; monarchy overthrown by a military junta in 1969. It consists almost wholly of desert and is a major exporter of oil. Official language: Arabic. Official religion: (Sunni) Muslim. Currency: Libyan dinar. Capital: Tripoli. Pop: 5 659 000 (2004 est). Area: 1 760 000 sq km (680 000 sq miles). Official name: **Al-Jumhuria al-Arabia al-Libya ash-Shabiya al-Ishtirakiya al-Uzma**
Libyan (ˈlɪbɪən) *adj* **1** of or relating to Libya, its people, or its language ▷ *n* **2** a native or inhabitant of Libya **3** the extinct Hamitic language of ancient Libya
Libyan Desert *n* a desert in N Africa, in E Libya, W Egypt, and the NW Sudan: the NE part of the Sahara
lice (laɪs) *n* the plural of **louse**
licence *or US* **license** (ˈlaɪsəns) *n* **1** a certificate, tag, document, etc, giving official permission to do something **2** formal permission or exemption **3** liberty of action or thought; freedom **4** intentional disregard of or deviation from conventional rules to achieve a certain effect: *poetic licence* **5** excessive freedom **6** licentiousness [C14 via Old French and Medieval Latin *licentia* permission, from Latin: freedom, from *licet* it is allowed]
license (ˈlaɪsəns) *vb (tr)* **1** to grant or give a licence for (something, such as the sale of alcohol) **2** to give permission to or for > **ˈlicensable** *adj* > **ˈlicenser** *or* **ˈlicensor** *n*
licensed aircraft engineer *n* the official name for **ground engineer**
licensee (ˌlaɪsənˈsiː) *n* a person who holds a licence, esp one to sell alcoholic drink
license plate *or Canadian* **licence plate** *n US and Canadian* a plate mounted on the front and back of a motor vehicle bearing the registration number. Also called (in Britain and certain other countries): **numberplate**
licentiate (laɪˈsɛnʃɪɪt) *n* **1** a person who has received a formal attestation of professional competence to practise a certain profession or teach a certain skill or subject **2** a degree between that of bachelor and doctor awarded now only by certain chiefly European universities **3** a person who holds this degree **4** *chiefly Presbyterian Church* a person holding a licence to preach [C15 from Medieval Latin *licentiātus*, from *licentiāre* to permit] > **liˈcentiateˌship** *n* > **liˌcentiˈation** *n*
licentious (laɪˈsɛnʃəs) *adj* **1** sexually unrestrained or promiscuous **2** *now rare* showing disregard for convention [C16 from Latin *licentiōsus* capricious, from *licentia* LICENCE] > **liˈcentiously** *adv* > **liˈcentiousness** *n*
lichee (ˌlaɪˈtʃiː) *n* a variant spelling of **litchi**
lichen (ˈlaɪkən, ˈlɪtʃən) *n* **1** an organism that is formed by the symbiotic association of a fungus and an alga or cyanobacterium and occurs as crusty patches or bushy growths on tree trunks, bare ground, etc Lichens are now classified as a phylum of fungi (*Mycophycophyta*) **2** *pathol* any of various eruptive disorders of the skin [C17 via Latin from Greek *leikhēn*, from *leikhein* to lick] > **ˈlichened** *adj* > **ˈlichen-ˌlike** *adj* > **ˈlichenˌoid** *adj* > **ˈlichenous** *or* **ˈlichenˌose** *adj*
lichenin (ˈlaɪkənɪn) *n* a complex polysaccharide occurring in certain species of mosses
lichenology (ˌlaɪkəˈnɒlədʒɪ, ˌlɪ-) *n* the study of the structure, physiology, and ecology of lichens
Lichfield (ˈlɪtʃˌfiːld) *n* a city in central England, in SE Staffordshire: cathedral with three spires (13th-14th century); birthplace of Samuel Johnson, during whose lifetime the **Lichfield Group** (a literary circle) flourished. Pop: 28 435 (2001)
lich gate (lɪtʃ) *n* a variant spelling of **lych gate**
lichi (ˌlaɪˈtʃiː) *n* a variant spelling of **litchi**
licht (lɪxt) *n, adj, vb* a Scot word for **light**¹ and **light**²
licit (ˈlɪsɪt) *adj* a less common word for **lawful** [C15 from Latin *licitus* permitted, from *licēre* to be permitted] > **ˈlicitly** *adv* > **ˈlicitness** *n*
lick (lɪk) *vb* **1** *(tr)* to pass the tongue over, esp in order to taste or consume **2** to flicker or move lightly over or round (something): *the flames licked around the door* **3** *(tr) informal* **a** to defeat or vanquish **b** to flog or thrash **c** to be or do much better than **4** **lick into shape** to put into a satisfactory condition: from the former belief that bear cubs were born formless and had to be licked into shape by their mother **5** **lick one's lips** to anticipate or recall something with glee or relish **6** **lick one's wounds** to retire after a defeat or setback in order to husband one's resources **7** **lick the boots of** See **boot**¹ (sense 14) ▷ *n* **8** an instance of passing the tongue over something **9** a small amount: *a lick of paint* **10** Also called: **salt lick** a block of compressed salt or chemical matter provided for domestic animals to lick for medicinal and nutritional purposes **11** a place to which animals go to lick exposed natural deposits of salt **12** *informal* a hit; blow **13** *slang* a short musical phrase, usually on one instrument **14** *informal* speed; rate of movement: *he was going at quite a lick when he hit it* **15** **a lick and a promise** something hastily done, esp a hurried wash [Old English *liccian*; related to Old High German *leckon*, Latin *lingere*, Greek *leikhein*] > **ˈlicker** *n*
lick-alike *adj Irish informal* very similar: *he and his father are lick-alike*
lickerish *or* **liquorish** (ˈlɪkərɪʃ) *adj archaic* **1** lecherous or lustful **2** greedy; gluttonous **3** appetizing or tempting [C16 changed from C13 *lickerous*, via Norman French from Old French *lechereus* lecherous; see LECHER] > **ˈlickerishly** *or* **ˈliquorishly** *adv* > **ˈlickerishness** *or* **ˈliquorishness** *n*
lickety-split (ˈlɪkɪtɪˈsplɪt) *adv US and Canadian informal* very quickly; speedily [C19 from LICK + SPLIT]
licking (ˈlɪkɪŋ) *n informal* **1** a beating **2** a defeat
lickspittle (ˈlɪkˌspɪtᵊl) *n* a flattering or servile person
licorice (ˈlɪkərɪs) *n* the usual US and Canadian spelling of **liquorice**
lictor (ˈlɪktə) *n* one of a group of ancient Roman officials, usually bearing fasces, who attended magistrates, etc [C16 *lictor*, C14 *littour*, from Latin *ligāre* to bind]
lid (lɪd) *n* **1** a cover, usually removable or hinged, for a receptacle: *a saucepan lid; a desk lid* **2** short for **eyelid** **3** *botany* another name for **operculum** (sense 2) **4** *slang* short for **skidlid** **5** *US dated slang* a quantity of marijuana, usually an ounce **6** **dip one's lid** *Austral informal* to raise one's hat as a greeting, etc **7** **flip one's lid** *slang* to become crazy or angry **8** **put the lid on** *informal* **a** *Brit* to be the final blow to **b** to curb, prevent, or discourage **9** **take the lid off** *informal* to make startling or spectacular revelations about [Old English *hlid*; related to Old Friesian *hlid*, Old High German *hlit* cover] > **ˈlidded** *adj*
Lidice (*Czech* ˈlidjtsɛ) *n* a mining village in the Czech Republic: destroyed by the Germans in 1942 in reprisal for the assassination of Reinhard Heydrich; rebuilt as a national memorial
lidless (ˈlɪdlɪs) *adj* **1** having no lid or top **2** (of animals) having no eyelids **3** *archaic* vigilant and watchful
lido (ˈliːdəʊ) *n, pl* **-dos** *Brit* a public place of recreation, including a pool for swimming or water sports [C20 after the *Lido*, island bathing beach near Venice, from Latin *litus* shore]
lidocaine (ˈlaɪdəˌkeɪn) *n* a powerful local anaesthetic administered by injection, or topically to mucous membranes. Formula: $C_{14}H_{22}N_2O.HCl.H_2O$. Also called: **lignocaine** [C20 from (ACETANI)LID(D) + *-caine* on the model of *cocaine*]
lie¹ (laɪ) *vb* **lies, lying, lied** **1** *(intr)* to speak untruthfully with intent to mislead or deceive **2** *(intr)* to convey a false impression or practise deception: *the camera does not lie* ▷ *n* **3** an untrue or deceptive statement deliberately used to mislead **4** something that is deliberately intended to deceive **5** **give the lie to** **a** to disprove **b** to accuse of lying ▷ Related adjective: **mendacious** [Old English *lyge* (n), *lēogan* (vb); related to Old High German *liogan*, Gothic *liugan*]
lie² (laɪ) *vb* **lies, lying, lay** (leɪ) **lain** (leɪn) *(intr)* **1** (often foll by *down*) to place oneself or be in a prostrate position, horizontal to the ground **2** to be situated, esp on a horizontal surface: *the pencil is lying on the desk; India lies to the south of Russia* **3** to be buried: *here lies Jane Brown* **4** *(copula)* to be and remain (in a particular state or condition): *to lie dormant* **5** to stretch or extend: *the city lies before us* **6** (usually foll by *on* or *upon*) to rest or weigh: *my sins lie heavily on my mind* **7** (usually foll by *in*) to exist or consist inherently: *strength lies in unity* **8**

(foll by *with*) **a** to be or rest (with): *the ultimate decision lies with you* **b** *archaic* to have sexual intercourse (with) **9** (of an action, claim, appeal, etc) to subsist; be maintainable or admissible **10** *archaic* to stay temporarily **11 lie in state** See **state** (sense 13) **12 lie low a** to keep or be concealed or quiet **b** to wait for a favourable opportunity ▷ *n* **13** the manner, place, or style in which something is situated **14** the hiding place or lair of an animal **15** *golf* **a** the position of the ball after a shot: *a bad lie* **b** the angle made by the shaft of the club before the upswing **16 lie of the land a** the topography of the land **b** the way in which a situation is developing or people are behaving ▷ See also **lie down, lie in, lie to, lie up** [Old English *licgan* akin to Old High German *ligen* to lie, Latin *lectus* bed]

USAGE See at **lay**[1]

Liebfraumilch ('li:bfraʊˌmɪlk; *German* 'li:pfraumɪlç) *or* **Liebfrauenmilch** (*German* li:p'frauənmɪlç) *n* a white table wine from the Rhine vineyards [German: from *Liebfrau* the Virgin Mary + *Milch* milk; after *Liebfrauenstift* convent in Worms where the wine was originally made]

Liebig condenser (*German* 'li:bɪç) *n chem* a laboratory condenser consisting of a glass tube surrounded by a glass envelope through which cooling water flows [named after Justus, Baron von *Liebig* (1803–73), German chemist]

Liechtenstein ('lɪktənˌstaɪn; *German* 'lɪçtənʃtain) *n* a small mountainous principality in central Europe on the Rhine: formed in 1719 by the uniting of the lordships of Schellenburg and Vaduz, which had been purchased by the Austrian family of Liechtenstein; customs union formed with Switzerland in 1924. Official language: German. Religion: Roman Catholic majority. Currency: Swiss franc. Capital: Vaduz. Pop: 34 000 (2003 est). Area: 160 sq km (62 sq miles)

Liechtensteiner ('lɪktənˌstaɪnə) *n* **1** a native or inhabitant of Liechtenstein ▷ *adj* **2** of or relating to Liechtenstein or its inhabitants

lied (li:d; *German* li:t) *n, pl* **lieder** ('li:də; *German* 'li:dər) *music* any of various musical settings for solo voice and piano of a romantic or lyrical poem, for which composers such as Schubert, Schumann, and Wolf are famous [from German: song]

lie detector *n* a polygraph used esp by a police interrogator to detect false or devious answers to questions, a sudden change in one or more involuntary physiological responses being considered a manifestation of guilt, fear, etc. See **polygraph** (sense 1), **galvanic skin response**

lie down *vb* (*intr, adverb*) **1** to place oneself or be in a prostrate position in order to rest or sleep **2** to accept without protest or opposition (esp in the phrases **lie down under, take something lying down**) ▷ *n* **lie-down 3** a rest

lief (li:f) *adv* **1** *now rare* gladly; willingly: *I'd as lief go today as tomorrow* ▷ *adj* **2** *archaic* **a** ready; glad **b** dear; beloved [Old English *leof;* related to *lufu* love]

liege (li:dʒ) *adj* **1** (of a lord) owed feudal allegiance (esp in the phrase **liege lord**) **2** (of a vassal or servant) owing feudal allegiance: *a liege subject* **3** of or relating to the relationship or bond between liege lord and liegeman: *liege homage* **4** faithful; loyal ▷ *n* **5** a liege lord **6** a liegeman or true subject [c13 from Old French *lige,* from Medieval Latin *līticus,* from *lītus, laetus* serf, of Germanic origin]

Liège (lɪ'eɪʒ; *French* ljɛʒ) *n* **1** a province of E Belgium: formerly a principality of the Holy Roman Empire, much larger than the present-day province. Pop: 1 029 605 (2004 est). Area: 3877 sq km (1497 sq miles) **2** a city in E Belgium, capital of Liège province: the largest French-speaking city in Belgium; river port and industrial centre. Pop: 185 488 (2004 est) ▷ Flemish name: **Luik**

liegeman ('li:dʒˌmæn) *n, pl* **-men 1** (formerly) the subject of a sovereign or feudal lord; vassal **2** a loyal follower

Liegnitz ('li:gnɪts) *n* the German name for **Legnica**

lie in *vb* (*intr, adverb*) **1** to remain in bed late in the morning **2** to be confined in childbirth ▷ *n* **lie-in 3** a long stay in bed in the morning

lien ('li:ən, li:n) *n law* a right to retain possession of another's property pending discharge of a debt [c16 via Old French from Latin *ligāmen* bond, from *ligāre* to bind]

lienal ('laɪənᵊl) *adj* of or relating to the spleen [c19 from Latin *lien* SPLEEN]

lientery ('laɪəntərɪ, -trɪ) *n pathol* the passage of undigested food in the faeces [c16 from French, from Medieval Latin, from Greek *leienteria,* from *leios* smooth + *enteron* intestine] > ˌ**lien'teric** *adj*

Liepāja *or* **Lepaya** (lɪ'pɑ:jə) *n* a port in W Latvia on the Baltic Sea; founded by the Teutonic Knights in 1263: a naval and industrial centre, with a fishing fleet. Pop: 86 985 (2002 est). Russian name: **Libava** German name: **Libau**

lierne (lɪ'ɜ:n) *n architect* a short secondary rib that connects the intersections of the primary ribs, esp as used in Gothic vaulting [c19 from French, perhaps related to *lier* to bind]

Liestal (*German* 'li:sta:l) *n* a city in NW Switzerland, capital of Basel-Land demicanton. Pop: 12 930 (2000)

lie to *vb* (*intr, adverb*) *nautical* (of a vessel) to be hove to with little or no swinging

Lietuva (lɪə'tu:və) *n* the Lithuanian name for **Lithuania**

lieu (lju:, lu:) *n* stead; place (esp in the phrases **in lieu, in lieu of**) [c13 from Old French, ultimately from Latin *locus* place]

lie up *vb* (*intr, adverb*) **1** to go into or stay in one's room or bed, as through illness **2** to be out of commission or use: *my car has been lying up for months*

Lieut *abbreviation for* lieutenant. Also: **Lt**

lieutenant (lɛf'tɛnənt; *US* lu:'tɛnənt) *n* **1** a military officer holding commissioned rank immediately junior to a captain **2** a naval officer holding commissioned rank immediately junior to a lieutenant commander **3** *US* an officer in a police or fire department ranking immediately junior to a captain **4** a person who holds an office in subordination to or in place of a superior [c14 from Old French, literally: place-holding] > **lieu'tenancy** *n*

lieutenant colonel *n* an officer holding commissioned rank immediately junior to a colonel in certain armies, air forces, and marine corps

lieutenant commander *n* an officer holding commissioned rank in certain navies immediately junior to a commander

lieutenant general *n* an officer holding commissioned rank in certain armies, air forces, and marine corps immediately junior to a general

lieutenant governor *n* **1** a deputy governor **2** (in the US) an elected official who acts as deputy to a state governor and succeeds him if he dies **3 lieutenant-governor** (in Canada) the representative of the Crown in a province: appointed by the federal government acting for the Crown

life (laɪf) *n, pl* **lives** (laɪvz) **1** the state or quality that distinguishes living beings or organisms from dead ones and from inorganic matter, characterized chiefly by metabolism, growth, and the ability to reproduce and respond to stimuli. Related adjs: **animate, vital 2** the period between birth and death **3** a living person or being: *to save a life* **4** the time between birth and the present time **5 a** the remainder or extent of one's life **b** (*as modifier*): *a life sentence; life membership; life subscription; life work* **6** short for **life imprisonment 7** the amount of time that something is active or functioning: *the life of a battery* **8** a present condition, state, or mode of existence: *my life is very dull here* **9 a** a biography **b** (*as modifier*): *a life story* **10 a** a characteristic state or mode of existence: *town life* **b** (*as modifier*): *life style* **11** the sum or course of human events and activities **12** liveliness or high spirits: *full of life* **13** a source of strength, animation, or vitality: *he was the life of the show* **14** all living things, taken as a whole: *there is no life on Mars; plant life* **15** sparkle, as of wines **16** strong or high flavour, as of fresh food **17** (*modifier*) *arts* drawn or taken from a living model: *life drawing; a life mask* **18** *physics* another name for **lifetime 19** (in certain games) one of a number of opportunities of participation **20 as large as life** *informal* real and living **21 larger than life** in an exaggerated form **22 come to life a** to become animate or conscious **b** to be realistically portrayed or represented **23 for dear life** urgently or with extreme vigour or desperation **24 for the life of me (him, her, etc)** though trying desperately **25 go for your life** *Austral and NZ informal* an expression of encouragement **26 a matter of life and death** a matter of extreme urgency **27 not on your life** *informal* certainly not **28 the life and soul** *informal* a person regarded as the main source of merriment and liveliness: *the life and soul of the party* **29 the life of Riley** *informal* an easy life **30 to the life** (of a copy or image) resembling the original exactly **31 to save (one's) life** *informal* in spite of all considerations or attempts: *he couldn't play football to save his life* **32 the time of one's life** a memorably enjoyable time **33 true to life** faithful to reality [Old English *līf;* related to Old High German *lib,* Old Norse *līf* life, body]

life assurance *n* a form of insurance providing for the payment of a specified sum to a named beneficiary on the death of the policyholder. Also called: **life insurance**

life belt *n* a ring filled with buoyant material or air, used to keep a person afloat when in danger of drowning

lifeblood ('laɪfˌblʌd) *n* **1** the blood, considered as vital to sustain life **2** the essential or animating force

lifeboat ('laɪfˌbəʊt) *n* **1** a boat, propelled by oars or a motor, used for rescuing people at sea, escaping from a sinking ship, etc **2** *informal* a fund set up by the dealers in a market to rescue any member who may become insolvent as a result of a collapse in market prices

life buoy *n* any of various kinds of buoyant device for keeping people afloat in an emergency

life coach *n* a person whose job is to improve the quality of his or her client's life, by offering advice on professional and personal matters, such as career, health, personal relationships, etc

life cycle *n* the series of changes occurring in an animal or plant between one development stage and the identical stage in the next generation

life estate *n* property that may be held only for the extent of the holder's lifetime

life expectancy *n* the statistically determined average number of years of life remaining after a specified age for a given group of individuals. Also called: **expectation of life**

life form *n* **1** *biology* the characteristic overall form and structure of a mature organism on the basis of which it can be classified **2** any living creature **3** (in science fiction) an alien

lifeguard ('laɪfˌgɑ:d) *n* a person present at a beach or pool to guard people against the risk of drowning. Also called: **life-saver**

Life Guards *pl n* (in Britain) a cavalry regiment forming part of the Household Brigade, who wear scarlet jackets and white plumes in their helmets

life history *n* **1** the series of changes undergone by an organism between fertilization of the egg and death **2** the series of events that make up a person's life

life imprisonment *n* (in Britain) an indeterminate sentence always given for murder and as a maximum sentence in several other crimes. There is no remission, although the Home Secretary may order the prisoner's release on licence

life instinct *n psychoanal* the instinct for reproduction and self-preservation

life insurance *n* another name for **life assurance**

life interest *n* interest (esp from property) that is payable to a person during his life but ceases with his death

life jacket *n* an inflatable sleeveless jacket worn to keep a person afloat when in danger of drowning

lifeless (ˈlaɪflɪs) *adj* **1** without life; inanimate; dead **2** not sustaining living organisms **3** having no vitality or animation **4** unconscious > ˈ**lifelessly** *adv* > ˈ**lifelessness** *n*

life lesson *n* something from which useful knowledge or principles can be learned

lifelike (ˈlaɪfˌlaɪk) *adj* closely resembling or representing life > ˈ**lifeˌlikeness** *n*

lifeline (ˈlaɪfˌlaɪn) *n* **1** a line thrown or fired aboard a vessel for hauling in a hawser for a breeches buoy **2** any rope or line attached to a vessel or trailed from it for the safety of passengers, crew, swimmers, etc **3** a line by which a deep-sea diver is raised or lowered **4** a vital line of access or communication

lifelong (ˈlaɪfˌlɒŋ) *adj* lasting for or as if for a lifetime

lifelong learning *n* the provision or use of both formal and informal learning opportunities throughout people's lives in order to foster the continuous development and improvement of the knowledge and skills needed for employment and personal fulfilment

life mask *n* a cast taken from the face of a living person, usually using plaster of Paris

life partner *n* either member of a couple in a long-term relationship

life peer *n Brit* a peer whose title lapses at his death

life preserver *n* **1** *Brit* a club or bludgeon, esp one kept for self-defence **2** *US and Canadian* a life belt or life jacket

lifer (ˈlaɪfə) *n informal* a prisoner sentenced to life imprisonment

life raft *n* a raft for emergency use at sea

life-saver *n* **1** the saver of a person's life **2** another name for **lifeguard** **3** *informal* a person or thing that gives help in time of need

life-saving *adj* **1** acting to save a person's life **2** *informal* giving help in time of need ▷ *n* **3** the practice or techniques of saving people's lives

life science *n* any one of the branches of science concerned with the structure and behaviour of living organisms, such as biology, botany, zoology, physiology, or biochemistry. Compare **physical science** See also **social science**

life-size *or* **life-sized** *adj* representing actual size

life space *n psychol* a spatial representation of all the forces that control a person's behaviour

life span *n* the period of time during which a human being, animal, machine, etc, may be expected to live or function under normal conditions

lifestyle (ˈlaɪfˌstaɪl) *n* **1** a set of attitudes, habits, or possessions associated with a particular person or group **2** such attitudes, etc, regarded as fashionable or desirable **3** *NZ* **a** a luxurious semirural manner of living **b** (*as modifier*): *a lifestyle property* ▷ *adj* **4** suggestive of a fashionable or desirable lifestyle: *a lifestyle café* **5** (of a drug) designed to treat problems, such as impotence or excess weight, which affect a person's quality of life rather than their health

lifestyle block *n NZ* a semi-rural property comprising a house and land for small-scale farming

lifestyle business *n* a small business in which the owners are more anxious to pursue interests that reflect their lifestyle than to make more than a comfortable living

lifestyle guru *n* a person hired to give someone advice on various aspects of his or her life, work, and relationships

lifestyler (ˈlaɪfˌstaɪlə) *n informal* a person who adopts a particular lifestyle: *new lifestyler; vampire lifestyler*

life-support *adj* of or providing the equipment required to sustain human life in an unnatural environment, such as in space, or in severe illness or disability

life table *n* another name for **mortality table**

lifetime (ˈlaɪfˌtaɪm) *n* **1** **a** the length of time a person or animal is alive **b** (*as modifier*): *a lifetime supply* **2** the length of time that something functions, is useful, etc **3** *physics* the average time of existence of an unstable or reactive entity, such as a nucleus, excited state, elementary particle, etc; mean life

Liffey (ˈlɪfɪ) *n* a river in E Republic of Ireland, rising in the Wicklow Mountains and flowing west, then northeast through Dublin into Dublin Bay. Length: 80 km (50 miles)

Lifford (ˈlɪfərd) *n* the county town of Donegal, Republic of Ireland; market town. Pop: 1395 (2002)

LIFO (ˈlaɪfəʊ) *acronym for* last in, first out (as an accounting principle in sorting stock). Compare **FIFO**

lift[1] (lɪft) *vb* **1** to rise or cause to rise upwards from the ground or another support to a higher place: *to lift a sack* **2** to move or cause to move upwards: *to lift one's eyes* **3** (*tr*) to take hold of in order to carry or remove: *to lift something down from a shelf* **4** (*tr*) to raise in status, spirituality, estimation, etc: *his position lifted him from the common crowd* **5** (*tr*) to revoke or rescind: *to lift tax restrictions* **6** to make or become audible or louder: *to lift one's voice in song* **7** (*tr*) to take (plants or underground crops) out of the ground for transplanting or harvesting **8** (*intr*) to disappear by lifting or as if by lifting: *the fog lifted* **9** to transport in a vehicle **10** (*tr*) *informal* to take unlawfully or dishonourably; steal **11** (*tr*) *informal* to make dishonest use of (another person's idea, writing, etc); plagiarize **12** (*tr*) *slang* to arrest **13** (*tr*) to perform a face-lift on **14** (*tr*) *US and Canadian* to pay off (a mortgage, etc) ▷ *n* **15** the act or an instance of lifting **16** the power or force available or used for lifting **17** **a** *Brit* a platform, compartment, or cage raised or lowered in a vertical shaft to transport persons or goods in a building. US and Canadian word: **elevator** **b** See **chairlift, ski lift** **18** the distance or degree to which something is lifted **19** a usually free ride as a passenger in a car or other vehicle **20** a rise in the height of the ground **21** a rise in morale or feeling of cheerfulness usually caused by some specific thing or event **22** the force required to lift an object **23** a layer of the heel of a shoe, etc, or a detachable pad inside the shoe to give the wearer added height **24** aid; help **25** *mining* **a** the thickness of ore extracted in one operation **b** a set of pumps used in a mine **26** **a** the component of the aerodynamic forces acting on a wing, etc, at right angles to the airflow **b** the upward force exerted by the gas in a balloon, airship, etc **27** See **airlift** (sense 1) [C13 from Scandinavian; related to Old Norse *lypta*, Old English *lyft* sky; compare LOFT] > ˈ**liftable** *adj* > ˈ**lifter** *n*

lift[2] (lɪft) *n Scot* the sky [Old English *lyft*]

liftboy (ˈlɪftˌbɔɪ) *or* **liftman** *n, pl* **-boys** *or* **-men** a person who operates a lift, esp in large public or commercial buildings and hotels

lifting body *n* a wingless aircraft or spacecraft that derives its aerodynamic lift from the shape of its body

liftoff (ˈlɪftˌɒf) *n* **1** the initial movement or ascent of a rocket from its launch pad **2** the instant at which this occurs ▷ *vb* **lift off** **3** (*intr, adverb*) (of a rocket) to leave its launch pad

lift pump *n* a pump that raises a fluid to a higher level. It usually consists of a piston and vertical cylinder with flap or ball valves in both piston and cylinder base. Compare **force pump**

lig (lɪg) *Brit slang* ▷ *n* **1** (esp in the entertainment industry and the media) a function at which free entertainment and refreshments are available ▷ *vb* **ligs, ligging, ligged** **2** (*intr*) to attend such a function in order to take advantage of free entertainment and refreshments; freeload [C20 origin uncertain] > ˈ**ligger** *n* > ˈ**ligging** *n*

ligament (ˈlɪɡəmənt) *n* **1** *anatomy* any one of the bands or sheets of tough fibrous connective tissue that restrict movement in joints, connect various bones or cartilages, support muscles, etc **2** any physical or abstract connection or bond [C14 from Medieval Latin *ligāmentum*, from Latin (in the sense: bandage), from *ligāre* to bind]

ligamentous (ˌlɪɡəˈmɛntəs), **ligamental** *or* **ligamentary** *adj* relating to or shaped like a ligament

ligan (ˈlaɪɡən) *n* a variant of **lagan**

ligand (ˈlɪɡənd, ˈlaɪ-) *n chem* an atom, molecule, radical, or ion forming a complex with a central atom [C20 from Latin *ligandum*, gerund of *ligāre* to bind]

ligase (ˈlaɪˌɡeɪz) *n* any of a class of enzymes that catalyse the formation of covalent bonds and are important in the synthesis and repair of biological molecules, such as DNA

ligate (ˈlaɪɡeɪt) *vb* (*tr*) to tie up or constrict (something) with a ligature [C16 from Latin *ligātus*, from *ligāre* to bind] > **liˈgation** *n* > **ligative** (ˈlɪɡətɪv) *adj*

ligature (ˈlɪɡətʃə, -ˌtʃʊə) *n* **1** the act of binding or tying up **2** something used to bind **3** a link, bond, or tie **4** *surgery* a thread or wire for tying around a vessel, duct, etc, as for constricting the flow of blood to a part **5** *printing* a character of two or more joined letters, such as, ﬁ, ﬂ, ﬃ, ﬄ **6** *music* **a** a slur or the group of notes connected by it **b** (in plainsong notation) a symbol indicating two or more notes grouped together ▷ *vb* **7** (*tr*) to bind with a ligature; ligate [C14 from Late Latin *ligātūra*, ultimately from Latin *ligāre* to bind]

liger (ˈlaɪɡə) *n* the hybrid offspring of a female tiger and a male lion

light[1] (laɪt) *n* **1** the medium of illumination that makes sight possible **2** Also called: **visible radiation** electromagnetic radiation that is capable of causing a visual sensation and has wavelengths from about 380 to about 780 nanometres **3** (*not in technical usage*) electromagnetic radiation that has a wavelength outside this range, esp ultraviolet radiation: *ultraviolet light* **4** the sensation experienced when electromagnetic radiation within the visible spectrum falls on the retina of the eye. Related prefix: **photo-** **5** anything that illuminates, such as a lamp or candle **6** See **traffic light** **7** a particular quality or type of light: *a good light for reading* **8** **a** illumination from the sun during the day; daylight **b** the time this appears; daybreak; dawn **9** anything that allows the entrance of light, such as a window or compartment of a window **10** the condition of being visible or known (esp in the phrases **bring** *or* **come to light**) **11** an aspect or view: *he saw it in a different light* **12** mental understanding or spiritual insight **13** a person considered to be an authority or leader **14** brightness of countenance, esp a sparkle in the eyes **15** **a** the act of igniting or kindling something, such as a cigarette **b** something that ignites or kindles, esp in a specified manner, such as a spark or flame **c** something used for igniting or kindling, such as a match **16** See **lighthouse** **17** **a** the effect of illumination on objects or scenes, as created in a picture **b** an area of brightness in a picture, as opposed to shade **18** a poetic or archaic word for **eyesight** **19** the answer to a clue in a crossword **20** **in (the) light of** in view of; taking into account; considering **21** **light at the end of the tunnel** hope for the ending of a difficult or unpleasant situation **22** **out like a light** quickly asleep or unconscious **23** **see the light** **a** to gain sudden insight into or understanding of something **b** to experience a religious conversion **24** **see the light (of day)** **a** to come into being **b** to come to public notice **25**

shed (*or* throw) light on to clarify or supply additional information on **26 stand in a person's light** to stand so as to obscure a person's vision **27 strike a light a** (*verb*) to ignite something, esp a match, by friction **b** (*interjection*) *Brit* an exclamation of surprise ▷ *adj* **28** full of light; well-lighted **29** (of a colour) reflecting or transmitting a large amount of light: *light yellow.* Compare **medium** (sense 2), **dark** (sense 2) **30** *phonetics* relating to or denoting an (l) pronounced with front vowel resonance; clear: *the French "l" is much lighter than that of English.* Compare **dark** (sense 9) ▷ *vb* **lights, lighting, lighted** *or* **lit** (lɪt) **31** to ignite or cause to ignite **32** (often foll by *up*) to illuminate or cause to illuminate **33** to make or become cheerful or animated **34** (*tr*) to guide or lead by light ▷ See also **lights¹, light up** [Old English *lēoht*; related to Old High German *lioht*, Gothic *liuhath*, Latin *lux*] > 'lightish *adj* > 'lightless *adj*

light² (laɪt) *adj* **1** not heavy; weighing relatively little **2** having relatively low density: *magnesium is a light metal* **3** lacking sufficient weight; not agreeing with standard or official weights **4** not great in degree, intensity, or number: *light rain; a light eater* **5** without burdens, difficulties, or problems; easily borne or done: *a light heart; light work* **6** graceful, agile, or deft: *light fingers* **7** not bulky or clumsy **8** not serious or profound; entertaining: *light verse* **9** without importance or consequence; insignificant: *no light matter* **10** frivolous or capricious **11** loose in morals **12** dizzy or unclear: *a light head* **13** (of bread, cake, etc) spongy or well leavened **14** easily digested: *a light meal* **15** relatively low in alcoholic content: *a light wine* **16** (of a soil) having a crumbly texture **17** (of a vessel, lorry, etc) **a** designed to carry light loads **b** not loaded **18** carrying light arms or equipment: *light infantry* **19** (of an industry) engaged in the production of small consumer goods using light machinery. Compare **heavy** (sense 10) **20** *aeronautics* (of an aircraft) having a maximum take-off weight less than 5670 kilograms (12 500 pounds) **21** *chem* (of an oil fraction obtained from coal tar) having a boiling range between about 100° and 210°C **22** (of a railway) having a narrow gauge, or in some cases a standard gauge with speed or load restrictions not applied to a main line **23** *bridge* **a** (of a bid) made on insufficient values **b** (of a player) having failed to take sufficient tricks to make his contract **24** *phonetics, prosody* (of a syllable, vowel, etc) unaccented or weakly stressed; short. Compare **heavy** (sense 13) See also **light¹** (sense 30) **25** *phonetics* the least of three levels of stress in an utterance, in such languages as English **26 light on** *informal* lacking a sufficient quantity of (something) **27 make light of** to treat as insignificant or trifling ▷ *adv* **28** a less common word for **lightly 29** with little equipment, baggage, etc: *to travel light* ▷ *vb* **lights, lighting, lighted** *or* **lit** (lɪt) (*intr*) **30** (esp of birds) to settle or land after flight **31** to get down from a horse, vehicle, etc **32** (foll by *on* or *upon*) to come upon unexpectedly **33** to strike or fall on: *the choice lighted on me* ▷ See also **light into, light out, lights²** [Old English *lēoht*; related to Dutch *licht*, Gothic *leihts*] > 'lightish *adj* > 'lightly *adv* > 'lightness *n*

Light (laɪt) *n* **1** God regarded as a source of illuminating grace and strength **2** *Quakerism* short for **Inner Light**

light air *n* very light air movement of force one on the Beaufort scale

light box *n* a light source contained in a box and covered with a diffuser, used for viewing photographic transparencies, negatives, etc

light breeze *n* a very light wind of force two on the Beaufort scale

light bulb *n* a glass bulb containing a gas, such as argon or nitrogen, at low pressure and enclosing a thin metal filament that emits light when an electric current is passed through it. Sometimes shortened to: **bulb**

light bulb moment *n informal* a moment of sudden inspiration, revelation, or recognition [c20 from the cartoon image of a light bulb lighting up above a character's head when he or she has an idea]

light cannon *n* a particularly powerful torch, spotlight, or searchlight

light-emitting diode *n* a diode of semiconductor material, such as gallium arsenide, that emits light when a forward bias is applied, the colour depending on the semiconductor material: used as off/on indicators. Abbreviation: **LED**

lighten¹ (ˈlaɪt³n) *vb* **1** to become or make light **2** (*intr*) to shine; glow **3** (*intr*) (of lightning) to flash **4** (*tr*) an archaic word for **enlighten**

lighten² (ˈlaɪt³n) *vb* **1** to make or become less heavy **2** to make or become less burdensome or oppressive; mitigate **3** to make or become more cheerful or lively

light engine *n* a railway locomotive in motion without drawing any carriages or wagons. US equivalent: **wildcat**

lightening (ˈlaɪt³nɪŋ) *n obstetrics* the sensation, experienced by many women late in pregnancy when the head of the fetus enters the pelvis, of a reduction in pressure on the diaphragm, making it easier to breathe

lighter¹ (ˈlaɪtə) *n* **1** a small portable device for providing a naked flame or red-hot filament to light cigarettes, etc **2** a person or thing that ignites something

lighter² (ˈlaɪtə) *n* a flat-bottomed barge used for transporting cargo, esp in loading or unloading a ship [c15 probably from Middle Dutch; compare C16 Dutch *lichter*]

lighterage (ˈlaɪtərɪdʒ) *n* **1** the conveyance or loading and unloading of cargo by means of a lighter **2** the charge for this service

lighter than air *adj* (**lighter-than-air** *when prenominal*) **1** having a lower density than that of air **2** of or relating to an aircraft, such as a balloon or airship, that depends on buoyancy for support in the air

light face *n* **1** *printing* a weight of type characterized by light thin lines. Compare **bold face** ▷ *adj also* **light-faced 2** (of type) having this weight

light-fast *adj* (of a dye or dyed article) unaffected by light

light-fingered *adj* having nimble or agile fingers, esp for thieving or picking pockets > ˌlight-ˈfingeredness *n*

light flyweight *n* **a** an amateur boxer weighing not more than 48 kg (106 pounds) **b** (*as modifier*): a *light-flyweight fight*

light-footed *adj* having a light or nimble tread > ˌlight-ˈfootedly *adv* > ˌlight-ˈfootedness *n*

light-headed *adj* **1** frivolous in disposition or behaviour **2** giddy; feeling faint or slightly delirious > ˌlight-ˈheadedly *adv* > ˌlight-ˈheadedness *n*

light-hearted *adj* cheerful or carefree in mood or disposition > ˌlight-ˈheartedly *adv* > ˌlight-ˈheartedness *n*

light heavyweight *n* **1** Also called (in Britain): cruiserweight **a** a professional boxer weighing 160–175 pounds (72.5–79.5 kg) **b** an amateur boxer weighing 75–81 kg (165–179 pounds) **c** (*as modifier*): a *light-heavyweight bout* **2** a wrestler in a similar weight category (usually 192–214 pounds (87–97 kg))

light horse *n* lightly armed and highly mobile cavalry > ˌlight-ˈhorseman *n*

lighthouse (ˈlaɪtˌhaʊs) *n* a fixed structure in the form of a tower equipped with a light visible to mariners for warning them of obstructions, for marking harbour entrances, etc

lighting (ˈlaɪtɪŋ) *n* **1** the act or quality of illumination or ignition **2** the apparatus for supplying artificial light effects to a stage, film, or television set **3** the distribution of light on an object or figure, as in painting, photography, etc

lighting cameraman *n films* the person who designs and supervises the lighting of scenes to be filmed

lighting-up time *n* the time when vehicles are required by law to have their lights switched on

light into *vb* (*intr, preposition*) *informal* to assail physically or verbally

light meter *n* another name for **exposure meter**

light middleweight *n* **a** an amateur boxer weighing 67–71 kg (148–157 pounds) **b** (*as modifier*): a *light-middleweight bout.* Compare **junior middleweight**

light music *n* music for popular entertainment

lightness (ˈlaɪtnɪs) *n* the attribute of an object or colour that enables an observer to judge the extent to which the object or colour reflects or transmits incident light. See also **colour**

lightning (ˈlaɪtnɪŋ) *n* **1** a flash of light in the sky, occurring during a thunderstorm and caused by a discharge of electricity, either between clouds or between a cloud and the earth. Related adjs: **fulgurous, fulminous 2** (*modifier*) fast and sudden: *a lightning raid* [c14 variant of *lightening*]

lightning arrester *n* a device that protects electrical equipment, such as an aerial, from an excessive voltage resulting from a lightning discharge or other accidental electric surge, by discharging it to earth

lightning bug *n US and Canadian* another name for the **firefly**

lightning chess *n* rapid chess in which either each move has a fixed time allowed (usually 10 seconds) or each player is allotted a fixed time (often 5 minutes) for all his moves. US name: **rapid transit chess**

lightning conductor *or* **rod** *n* a metal strip terminating in a series of sharp points, attached to the highest part of a building, etc, to discharge the electric field before it can reach a dangerous level and cause a lightning strike

lightning stroke *n* **1** a discharge of lightning between a cloud and the earth, esp one that causes damage **2** *vet science* sudden death due to being struck by lightning, esp of cattle, horses or sheep

light opera *n* another term for **operetta**

light out *vb* (*intr, adverb*) *informal* to depart quickly, as if being chased

light pen *n computing* **a** a rodlike device which, when applied to the screen of a cathode-ray tube, can detect the time of passage of the illuminated spot across that point thus enabling a computer to determine the position on the screen being pointed at **b** a penlike device, used to read bar codes, that emits light and determines the intensity of that light as reflected from a small area of an adjacent surface

light pollution *n* the glow from street and domestic lighting that obscures the night sky and hinders the observation of faint stars

light rail *n* a transport system using small trains or trams, often serving parts of a large metropolitan area

light reaction *n botany* the stage of photosynthesis during which light energy is absorbed by chlorophyll and transformed into chemical energy stored in ATP. Compare **dark reaction**

lights¹ (laɪts) *pl n* a person's ideas, knowledge, or understanding: *he did it according to his lights*

lights² (laɪts) *pl n* the lungs, esp of sheep, bullocks, and pigs, used for feeding pets and occasionally in human food [c13 plural noun use of LIGHT², referring to the light weight of the lungs]

light-sensitive *adj physics* (of a surface) having a photoelectric property, such as the ability to generate a current, change its electrical resistance, etc, when exposed to light

lightship (ˈlaɪtˌʃɪp) *n* a ship equipped as a lighthouse and moored where a fixed structure would prove impracticable

light show *n* a kaleidoscopic display of moving lights, etc, projected onto a screen, esp during pop concerts

lightsome¹ ('laɪtsəm) *adj archaic or poetic* **1** lighthearted **2** airy or buoyant **3** not serious; frivolous > '**lightsomely** *adv* > '**lightsomeness** *n*

lightsome² ('laɪtsəm) *adj archaic or poetic* **1** producing or reflecting light **2** full of or flooded with light

lights out *n* **1** the time when those resident at an institution, such as soldiers in barracks or children at a boarding school, are expected to retire to bed **2** a fanfare or other signal indicating or signifying this

light table *n printing* a translucent surface of ground glass or a similar substance, illuminated from below and used for the examination of positive or negative film, and for the make-up of photocomposed pages

light trap *n* any mechanical arrangement that allows some form of movement to take place while excluding light, such as a light-proof door or the lips of a film cassette

light up *vb (adverb)* **1** to light a cigarette, pipe, etc **2** to illuminate or cause to illuminate **3** to make or become cheerful or animated

light water *n* a name for water (H_2O), as distinct from heavy water

lightweight ('laɪt,weɪt) *adj* **1** of a relatively light weight **2** not serious; trivial ▷ *n* **3** a person or animal of a relatively light weight **4 a** a professional boxer weighing 130–135 pounds (59–61 kg) **b** an amateur boxer weighing 57–60 kg (126–132 pounds) **c** (*as modifier*): *the lightweight contender* **5** a wrestler in a similar weight category (usually 115–126 pounds (52–57 kg)) **6** *informal* a person of little importance or influence

light welterweight *n* **a** an amateur boxer weighing 60–63.5 kg (132–140 pounds) **b** (*as modifier*): *the light welterweight champion*. Compare **junior welterweight**

light year *n* a unit of distance used in astronomy, equal to the distance travelled by light in one year, i.e. 9.4607×10^{12} kilometres or 0.3066 parsecs

lignaloes (laɪ'næləʊz, lɪg-) *n* (*functioning as singular*) another name for **eaglewood** (sense 2) [C14 *ligne aloes*, from Medieval Latin *lignum aloēs* wood of the aloe]

ligneous ('lɪgnɪəs) *adj* of or resembling wood [C17 from Latin *ligneus*, from *lignum* wood]

ligni-, ligno- *or before a vowel* **lign-** *combining form* indicating wood: *lignocellulose* [from Latin *lignum* wood]

lignicolous (lɪg'nɪkələs) *or* **lignicole** ('lɪgnɪ,kəʊl) *adj* growing or living on or in wood [C19 LIGNI- + -COLOUS]

ligniform ('lɪgnɪ,fɔːm) *adj* having the appearance of wood

lignify ('lɪgnɪ,faɪ) *vb* -**fies, -fying, -fied** *botany* to make or become woody as a result of the deposition of lignin in the cell walls > ,lignifi'cation *n*

lignin ('lɪgnɪn) *n* a complex polymer occurring in certain plant cell walls making the plant rigid

lignite ('lɪgnaɪt) *n* a brown carbonaceous sedimentary rock with woody texture that consists of accumulated layers of partially decomposed vegetation: used as a fuel. Fixed carbon content: 46–60 per cent; calorific value: 1.28×10^7 to 1.93×10^7 J/kg (5500 to 8300 Btu/lb). Also called: **brown coal** > **lignitic** (lɪg'nɪtɪk) *adj*

lignivorous (lɪg'nɪvərəs) *adj* (of animals) feeding on wood

lignocaine ('lɪgnə,keɪn) *n* another name for **lidocaine** [C20 from LIGNO- + *caine*, on the model of *cocaine*]

lignocellulose (,lɪgnəʊ'sɛljʊ,ləʊs, -,ləʊz) *n* a compound of lignin and cellulose that occurs in the walls of xylem cells in woody tissue

lignum ('lɪgnəm) *n Austral* another name for **polygonum**

lignum vitae ('vaɪtɪ) *n* **1** either of two zygophyllaceous tropical American trees, *Guaiacum officinale* or *G. sanctum*, having blue or purple flowers **2** the heavy resinous wood of either of these trees, which is used in machine bearings, casters, etc: formerly thought to have medicinal properties ▷ See also **guaiacum** [New Latin, from Late Latin, literally: wood of life]

ligroin ('lɪgrəʊɪn) *n* a volatile fraction of petroleum containing aliphatic hydrocarbons of the paraffin series. It has an approximate boiling point range of 70°–130°C and is used as a solvent [origin unknown]

ligula ('lɪgjʊlə) *n, pl* -**lae** (-,liː) *or* -**las 1** *entomol* the terminal part of the labium of an insect consisting of paired lobes **2** a variant spelling of **ligule** [C18 New Latin; see LIGULE] > '**ligular** *adj* > '**ligu,loid** *adj*

ligulate ('lɪgjʊlɪt, -,leɪt) *adj* **1** having the shape of a strap **2** *biology* of, relating to, or having a ligule or ligula

ligule ('lɪgjuːl) *or* **ligula** *n* **1** a membranous outgrowth at the junction between the leaf blade and sheath in many grasses and sedges **2** a strap-shaped corolla, such as that of a ray floret in the daisy [C19 via French, from Latin *ligula* strap, variant of *lingula*, from *lingua* tongue]

ligure ('lɪgjʊə) *n Old Testament* any of the 12 precious stones used in the breastplates of high priests [C14 from Late Latin *ligūrius*, from Late Greek *ligurion*]

Liguria (lɪ'gjʊərɪə) *n* a region of NW Italy, on the **Ligurian Sea** (an arm of the Mediterranean): the third smallest of the regions of Italy. Pop: 1 572 197 (2003 est). Area: 5410 sq km (2089 sq miles)

Ligurian (lɪ'gjʊərɪən) *adj* **1** of or relating to Liguria, a region of NW Italy, or its inhabitants ▷ *n* **2** a native or inhabitant of Liguria

likable *or* **likeable** ('laɪkəbᵊl) *adj* easy to like; pleasing > '**likableness** *or* '**likeableness** *n*

Likasi (lɪ'kaːsɪ) *n* a city in the S Democratic Republic of Congo (formerly Zaïre): a centre of copper and cobalt production. Pop: 345 000 (2005 est). Former name: **Jadotville**

like¹ (laɪk) *adj* **1** (*prenominal*) similar; resembling ▷ *prep* **2** similar to; similarly to; in the manner of: *acting like a maniac; he's so like his father* **3** used correlatively to express similarity in certain proverbs: *like mother, like daughter* **4** such as: *there are lots of ways you might amuse yourself — like taking a long walk, for instance* ▷ *adv* **5** a dialect word for **likely 6** *not standard* as it were: often used as a parenthetic filler: *there was this policeman just staring at us, like* ▷ *conj* **7** *not standard* as though; as if: *you look like you've just seen a ghost* **8** in the same way as; in the same way that: *she doesn't dance like you do* ▷ *n* **9** the equal or counterpart of a person or thing, esp one respected or prized: *compare like with like; her like will never be seen again* **10** the like similar things: *dogs, foxes, and the like* **11** the likes (*or* like) of people or things similar to (someone or something specified): *we don't want the likes of you around here* [shortened from Old English *gelīc*; compare Old Norse *glīkr* and *līkr* like]

▌ USAGE The use of *like* to mean *such as* was formerly thought to be undesirable in formal writing, but has now become acceptable. It was also thought that *as* rather than *like* should be used to mean in the same way that, but now both *as* and *like* are acceptable: *they hunt and catch fish as/like their ancestors used to*. The use of *look like* and *seem like* before a clause, although very common, is thought by many people to be incorrect or non-standard: *it looks as though he won't come* (not *it looks like he won't come*)

like² (laɪk) *vb* **1** (*tr*) to find (something) enjoyable or agreeable or find it enjoyable or agreeable (to do something): *he likes boxing; he likes to hear music* **2** (*tr*) to be fond of **3** (*tr*) to prefer or wish (to do

something): *we would like you to go* **4** (*tr*) to feel towards; consider; regard: *how did she like it?* **5** (*intr*) to feel disposed or inclined; choose; wish **6** (*tr*) *archaic* to please; agree with: *it likes me not to go* ▷ *n* **7** (*usually plural*) a favourable feeling, desire, preference, etc (esp in the phrase **likes and dislikes**) [Old English *līcian*; related to Old Norse *līka*, Dutch *lijken*]

-like *suffix forming adjectives* **1** resembling or similar to: *lifelike; springlike* **2** having the characteristics of: *childlike; ladylike* [from LIKE¹ (prep)]

likelihood ('laɪklɪ,hʊd) *or* **likeliness** *n* **1** the condition of being likely or probable; probability **2** something that is probable **3** *statistics* the probability of a given sample being randomly drawn regarded as a function of the parameters of the population. The likelihood ratio is the ratio of this to the maximized likelihood. See also **maximum likelihood**

likely ('laɪklɪ) *adj* **1** (usually foll by an infinitive) tending or inclined; apt: *likely to rain* **2** probable: *a likely result* **3** believable or feasible; plausible **4** appropriate for a purpose or activity **5** having good possibilities of success: *a likely candidate* **6** *dialect, chiefly US* attractive, agreeable, or enjoyable: *her likely ways won her many friends* ▷ *adv* **7** probably or presumably **8** as likely as not very probably [C14 from Old Norse *līkligr*]

▌ USAGE *Likely* as an adverb is preceded by another, intensifying adverb, as in *it will very likely rain* or *it will most likely rain*. Its use without an intensifier, as in *it will likely rain* is regarded as unacceptable by most users of British English, though it is common in colloquial US English

like-minded *adj* agreeing in opinions, goals, etc > ,like-'mindedly *adv* > ,like-'mindedness *n*

liken ('laɪkən) *vb* (*tr*) to see or represent as the same or similar; compare [C14 from LIKE¹ (adj)]

likeness ('laɪknɪs) *n* **1** the condition of being alike; similarity **2** a painted, carved, moulded, or graphic image of a person or thing **3** an imitative appearance; semblance

likewise ('laɪk,waɪz) *adv* **1** in addition; moreover; also **2** in like manner; similarly

liking ('laɪkɪŋ) *n* **1** the feeling of a person who likes; fondness **2** a preference, inclination, or pleasure

likuta (liː'kuːtaː) *n, pl* **makuta** (maː'kuːtaː) (formerly) a coin used in Zaïre [C20 from Congolese]

lilac ('laɪlək) *n* **1** Also called: **syringa** any of various Eurasian oleaceous shrubs or small trees of the genus *Syringa*, esp *S. vulgaris* (**common lilac**) which has large sprays of purple or white fragrant flowers **2** French lilac another name for **goat's-rue** (sense 1) **3 a** a light or moderate purple colour, sometimes with a bluish or reddish tinge **b** (*as adjective*): *a lilac carpet* [C17 via French from Spanish, from Arabic *līlak*, changed from Persian *nīlak* bluish, from *nīl* blue]

lilangeni ('lɪlə,ŋgeɪnɪ) *n, pl* **emalangeni** ('ɛmaːlaː,ŋgeɪnɪ) the standard monetary unit of Swaziland, divided into 100 cents

liliaceous (,lɪlɪ'eɪʃəs) *adj* of, relating to, or belonging to the *Liliaceae*, a family of plants having showy flowers and a bulb or bulblike organ: includes the lily, tulip, and bluebell [C18 from Late Latin *līliāceus*, from *līlium* lily]

Lilith ('lɪlɪθ) *n* **1** (in the Old Testament and in Jewish folklore) a female demon, who attacks children **2** (in Talmudic literature) Adam's first wife **3** a witch notorious in medieval demonology

Lille (*French* lil) *n* an industrial city in N France: the medieval capital of Flanders; forms with Roubaix and Tourcoing one of the largest conurbations in France. Pop: 184 657 (1999)

Lille Bælt ('lilə 'bɛld) *n* the Danish name for the **Little Belt**

Lilliputian (,lɪlɪ'pjuːʃɪən) *n* **1** a tiny person or

being ▷ *adj* **2** tiny; very small **3** petty or trivial [c18 from *Lilliput*, an imaginary country of tiny inhabitants in Swift's *Gulliver's Travels* (1726)]

lilly-pilly ('lɪlɪ,pɪlɪ) *n Austral* a tall myrtaceous tree, *Acmena smithii*, having dark green leaves, spikes of feathery flowers, and white to purplish edible berries [c19 of uncertain origin]

Lilo ('laɪləʊ) *n, pl* **-los** *trademark* a type of inflatable plastic or rubber mattress

Lilongwe (lɪ'lɒŋwɪ) *n* the capital of Malawi, in the central part west of Lake Malawi. Pop: 655 000 (2005 est)

lilt (lɪlt) *n* **1** (in music) a jaunty rhythm **2** a buoyant motion ▷ *vb* (*intr*) **3** (of a melody) to have a lilt **4** to move in a buoyant manner [C14 *lulten*, origin obscure] > **'lilting** *adj*

lily ('lɪlɪ) *n, pl* **lilies 1** any liliaceous perennial plant of the N temperate genus *Lilium*, such as the Turk's-cap lily and tiger lily, having scaly bulbs and showy typically pendulous flowers **2** the bulb or flower of any of these plants **3** any of various similar or related plants, such as the water lily, plantain lily, and day lily [Old English, from Latin *līlium*; related to Greek *leirion* lily] > **'lily-,like** *adj*

lily iron *n* a harpoon, the head of which is detachable [c19 from the shape of its shaft, which resembles lily leaves]

lily-livered *adj* cowardly; timid

lily of the valley *n, pl* **lilies of the valley** a small liliaceous plant, *Convallaria majalis*, of Eurasia and North America cultivated as a garden plant, having two long oval leaves and spikes of white bell-shaped flowers

lily pad *n* any of the floating leaves of a water lily

lily-trotter *n* another name for **jaçana**

lily-white *adj* **1** of a pure white: *lily-white skin* **2** *informal* pure; irreproachable **3** *US informal* **a** discriminating against Blacks: *a lily-white club* **b** racially segregated

Lima ('liːmə) *n* **1** the capital of Peru, near the Pacific coast on the Rímac River: the centre of Spanish colonization in South America; university founded in 1551 (the oldest in South America); an industrial centre with a port at nearby Callao. Pop: 8 180 000 (2005 est) **2** *communications* a code word for the letter L

lima bean ('laɪmə, 'liː-) *n* **1** any of several varieties of the bean plant, *Phaseolus lunatus* (or *P. limensis*), native to tropical America but cultivated in the US for its flat pods containing pale green edible beans **2** the seed of such a plant ▷ See also **butter bean** [c19 named after LIMA]

limacine ('lɪmə,saɪn, -sɪn, 'laɪ-) *adj* **1** of, or relating to slugs, esp those of the genus *Limax* **2** Also: **limaciform** (lɪ'mæsɪ,fɔːm) resembling a slug [c19 from New Latin, from Latin *līmax*, from *līmus* mud]

limaçon ('lɪmə,sɒn) *n* a heart-shaped curve generated by a point lying on a line at a fixed distance from the intersection of the line with a fixed circle, the line rotating about a point on the circumference of the circle [French, literally: snail (so named by Pascal)]

Limassol ('lɪmə,sɒl) *n* a port in S Cyprus: trading centre. Pop: 163 000 (2005 est). Ancient name: Lemessus (lə'mɛsəs)

Limavady (,lɪmə'vædɪ) *n* a district of N Northern Ireland, in Co Londonderry. Pop: 33 571 (2003 est). Area: 586 sq km (226 sq miles)

limb¹ (lɪm) *n* **1** an arm or leg, or the analogous part on an animal, such as a wing **2** any of the main branches of a tree **3** a branching or projecting section or member; extension **4** a person or thing considered to be a member, part, or agent of a larger group or thing **5** *chiefly Brit* a mischievous child (esp in *limb of Satan* or *limb of the devil*) **6** **out on a limb a** in a precarious or questionable position **b** *Brit* isolated, esp because of unpopular opinions ▷ *vb* **7** (*tr*) a rare word for **dismember** [Old English *lim*; related to Old Norse *limr*] > **limbed** *adj* > **'limbless** *adj*

limb² (lɪm) *n* **1** the edge of the apparent disc of

the sun, a moon, or a planet **2** a graduated arc attached to instruments, such as the sextant, used for measuring angles **3** *botany* **a** the expanded upper part of a bell-shaped corolla **b** the expanded part of a leaf, petal, or sepal **4** either of the two halves of a bow **5** Also called: **fold limb** either of the sides of a geological fold [c15 from Latin *limbus* edge]

limbate ('lɪmbeɪt) *adj biology* having an edge or border of a different colour from the rest: *limbate flowers* [c19 from Late Latin *limbātus* bordered, from LIMBUS]

limbed (lɪmd) *adj* **a** having limbs **b** (in combination): *short-limbed; strong-limbed*

limber¹ ('lɪmbə) *adj* **1** capable of being easily bent or flexed; pliant **2** able to move or bend freely; agile [c16 origin uncertain] > **'limberly** *adv* > **'limberness** *n*

limber² ('lɪmbə) *n* **1** part of a gun carriage, often containing ammunition, consisting of an axle, pole, and two wheels, that is attached to the rear of an item of equipment, esp field artillery ▷ *vb* **2** (usually foll by *up*) to attach the limber (to a gun, etc) [C15 *lymour* shaft of a gun carriage, origin uncertain]

limber³ ('lɪmbə) *n* (*often plural*) *nautical* (in the bilge of a vessel) a fore-and-aft channel through a series of holes in the frames (**limber holes**) where water collects and can be pumped out [c17 probably changed from French *lumière* hole (literally: light)]

limber up *vb* (*adverb*) **1** (*intr*) (esp in sports) to exercise in order to be limber and agile **2** (*tr*) to make flexible

limbic system ('lɪmbɪk) *n* the part of the brain bordering on the corpus callosum: concerned with basic emotion, hunger, and sex [C19 *limbic*, from French *limbique*, from *limbe* limbus, from New Latin *limbus*, from Latin: border]

limbo¹ ('lɪmbəʊ) *n, pl* **-bos 1** (*often capital*) *Christianity* the supposed abode of infants dying without baptism and the just who died before Christ **2** an imaginary place for lost, forgotten, or unwanted persons or things **3** an unknown intermediate place or condition between two extremes: *in limbo* **4** a prison or confinement [c14 from Medieval Latin *in limbo* on the border (of hell)]

limbo² ('lɪmbəʊ) *n, pl* **-bos** a Caribbean dance in which dancers pass, while leaning backwards, under a bar [c20 origin uncertain]

Limbourg (lɛbur) *n* the French name for **Limburg** (sense 3)

Limburg ('lɪmbɜːɡ; *Dutch* 'lɪmbyrx) *n* **1** a medieval duchy of W Europe: divided between the Netherlands and Belgium in 1839 **2** a province of the SE Netherlands: contains a coalfield and industrial centres. Capital: Maastricht. Pop: 1 142 000 (2003 est). Area: 2253 sq km (809 sq miles) **3** a province of NE Belgium: contains the industrial regions of the Kempen coalfield. Capital: Hasselt. Pop: 805 786 (2004 est). Area: 2422 sq km (935 sq miles). French name: Limbourg

Limburger ('lɪmbɜːɡə) *n* a semihard white cheese of very strong smell and flavour. Also called: **Limburg cheese**

limbus ('lɪmbəs) *n, pl* **-bi** (-baɪ) *anatomy* the edge or border of any of various structures or parts [c15 from Latin: edge] > **'limbic** *adj*

lime¹ (laɪm) *n* **1** short for **quicklime, birdlime, slaked lime 2** *agriculture* any of certain calcium compounds, esp calcium hydroxide, spread as a dressing on lime-deficient land ▷ *vb* (*tr*) **3** to spread (twigs, etc) with birdlime **4** to spread a calcium compound upon (land) to improve plant growth **5** to catch (animals, esp birds) with or as if with birdlime **6** to whitewash or cover (a wall, ceiling, etc) with a mixture of lime and water (**limewash**) [Old English *līm*; related to Icelandic *līm* glue, Latin *līmus* slime]

lime² (laɪm) *n* **1** a small Asian citrus tree, *Citrus aurantifolia*, with stiff sharp spines and small

round or oval greenish fruits **2 a** the fruit of this tree, having acid fleshy pulp rich in vitamin C **b** (*as modifier*): *lime juice* ▷ *adj* **3** having the flavour of lime fruit [c17 from French, from Provençal, from Arabic *līmah*]

lime³ (laɪm) *n* any linden tree, such as *Tilia europaea*, planted in many varieties for ornament [c17 changed from obsolete *line*, from Old English *lind* LINDEN]

lime⁴ (laɪm) *vb* (*intr*) *Caribbean slang* (of young people) to sit or stand around on the pavement [of unknown origin]

limeade (,laɪm'eɪd) *n* a drink made from sweetened lime juice and plain or carbonated water

lime burner *n* a person whose job it is to burn limestone to make lime

lime green *n* **a** a moderate greenish-yellow colour **b** (*as adjective*): *a lime-green dress*

limekiln ('laɪm,kɪln) *n* a kiln in which calcium carbonate is calcined to produce quicklime

limelight ('laɪm,laɪt) *n* **1 the** a position of public attention or notice (esp in the phrase **in the limelight**) **2 a** a type of lamp, formerly used in stage lighting, in which light is produced by heating lime to white heat **b** Also called: **calcium light** brilliant white light produced in this way > **'lime,lighter** *n*

limen ('laɪmɛn) *n, pl* **limens** or **limina** ('lɪmɪnə) *psychol* another term for **threshold** (sense 4) See also **liminal** [c19 from Latin]

lime pit *n* (in tanning) a pit containing lime in which hides are placed to remove the hair

limerick ('lɪmərɪk) *n* a form of comic verse consisting of five anapaestic lines of which the first, second, and fifth have three metrical feet and rhyme together and the third and fourth have two metrical feet and rhyme together [c19 allegedly from *will you come up to Limerick?*, a refrain sung between nonsense verses at a party]

Limerick ('lɪmərɪk) *n* **1** a county of SW Republic of Ireland, in N Munster province: consists chiefly of an undulating plain with rich pasture and mountains in the south. County town: Limerick. Pop: 175 304 (2002). Area: 2686 sq km (1037 sq miles) **2** a port in SW Republic of Ireland, county town of Limerick, at the head of the Shannon estuary. Pop: 86 998 (2002)

limes ('laɪmiːz) *n, pl* **limites** ('lɪmɪ,tiːz) the fortified boundary of the Roman Empire [from Latin]

limescale ('laɪmskeɪl) *n* a flaky deposit left in containers such as kettles by the action of heat on water containing calcium salts. Often shortened to: **scale** [from LIME¹ (sense 1) + SCALE¹ (sense 3)]

limestone ('laɪm,stəʊn) *n* a sedimentary rock consisting mainly of calcium carbonate, deposited as the calcareous remains of marine animals or chemically precipitated from the sea: used as a building stone and in the manufacture of cement, lime, etc

limestone pavement *n geology* a horizontal surface of exposed limestone in which the joints have been enlarged, cutting the surface into roughly rectangular blocks. See also **clint, grike**

limewater ('laɪm,wɔːtə) *n* **1** a clear colourless solution of calcium hydroxide in water, formerly used in medicine as an antacid **2** water that contains dissolved lime or calcium salts, esp calcium carbonate or calcium sulphate

limey ('laɪmɪ) *US and Canadian slang* ▷ *n* **1** a British person **2** a British sailor or ship ▷ *adj* **3** British [abbreviated from C19 *lime-juicer*, because British sailors were required to drink lime juice as a protection against scurvy]

limicoline (laɪ'mɪkə,laɪn, -lɪn) *adj* of, relating to, or belonging to the *Charadrii*, a suborder of birds containing the plovers, sandpipers, snipes, oystercatchers, avocets, etc [c19 from New Latin *Limicolae* former name of order, from Latin *līmus* mud + *colere* to inhabit]

limicolous (laɪ'mɪkələs) *adj* (of certain animals) living in mud or muddy regions

943

liminal (ˈlɪmɪnᵊl) *adj psychol* relating to the point (or threshold) beyond which a sensation becomes too faint to be experienced [c19 from Latin *līmen* threshold]

limit (ˈlɪmɪt) *n* **1** (*sometimes plural*) the ultimate extent, degree, or amount of something: *the limit of endurance* **2** (*often plural*) the boundary or edge of a specific area: *the city limits* **3** (*often plural*) the area of premises within specific boundaries **4** the largest quantity or amount allowed **5** *maths* **a** a value to which a function f(x) approaches as closely as desired as the independent variable approaches a specified value (x = a) or approaches infinity **b** a value to which a sequence a_n approaches arbitrarily close as n approaches infinity **c** the limit of a sequence of partial sums of a convergent infinite series: *the limit of* $1 + \frac{1}{2} + \frac{1}{4} + \frac{1}{8} + ...$ *is* 2 **6** *maths* one of the two specified values between which a definite integral is evaluated **7** the limit *informal* a person or thing that is intolerably exasperating **8** off limits **a** out of bounds **b** forbidden to do or use: *smoking was off limits everywhere* **9** within limits to a certain or limited extent: *I approve of it within limits* ▷ *vb* (*tr*) **-its, -iting, -ited 10** to restrict or confine, as to area, extent, time, etc **11** *law* to agree, fix, or assign specifically [c14 from Latin *līmes* boundary] > ˈlimitable *adj* > ˈlimitableness *n* > ˈlimitless *adj* > ˈlimitlessly *adv* > ˈlimitlessness *n*

limitarian (ˌlɪmɪˈtɛərɪən) *n Christianity* a person who regards salvation as limited to only a part of mankind

limitary (ˈlɪmɪtərɪ, -trɪ) *adj* **1** of, involving, or serving as a limit **2** restricted or limited

limitation (ˌlɪmɪˈteɪʃən) *n* **1** something that limits a quality or achievement **2** the act of limiting or the condition of being limited **3** *law* a certain period of time, legally defined, within which an action, claim, etc, must be commenced **4** *property law* a restriction upon the duration or extent of an estate

limited (ˈlɪmɪtɪd) *adj* **1** having a limit; restricted; confined **2** without fullness or scope; narrow **3** (of governing powers, sovereignty, etc) restricted or checked, by or as if by a constitution, laws, or an assembly: *limited government* **4** *US and Canadian* (of a train) stopping only at certain stations and having only a set number of cars for passengers **5** *chiefly Brit* (of a business enterprise) owned by shareholders whose liability for the enterprise's debts is restricted ▷ *n* **6** *US and Canadian* a limited train, bus, etc > ˈlimitedly *adv* > ˈlimitedness *n*

limited company *n Brit* a company whose owners enjoy limited liability for the company's debts and losses

limited edition *n* an edition of something such as a book, plate, etc, that is limited to a specified number

limited liability *n Brit* liability restricted to the unpaid portion (if any) of the par value of the shares of a limited company. It is a feature of share ownership

limited monarchy *n* another term for **constitutional monarchy**

limited partner *n* a business partner who has no management authority and no personal liability

limited war *n* a war in which the belligerents do not seek the total destruction of the enemy, esp one in which nuclear weapons are deliberately not used

limiter (ˈlɪmɪtə) *n* an electronic circuit that produces an output signal whose positive or negative amplitude, or both, is limited to some predetermined value above which the peaks become flattened. Also called: **clipper**

limit man *n* (in a handicap sport or game) the competitor with the maximum handicap

limit point *n maths* (of a set) a point that is the limit of a sequence of points in the set. Also called: **accumulation point**

limitrophe (ˈlɪmɪˌtrəʊf) *adj* (of a country or region) on or near a frontier [c19 via French from

Late Latin *limitrophus*, from *limit-* LIMIT + Greek *-trophus* supporting; originally referring to borderland that supported frontier troops]

limit-state design *n* a design criterion specifying that with acceptable probabilities a structure will not reach a limit state in which it either is unfit for the use for which it was designed (unavailability limit state) or fails (ultimate limit state)

limivorous (lɪˈmɪvərəs) *adj* (of certain invertebrate animals) feeding on mud [c19 from Latin *līmus* mud + -VOROUS]

limn (lɪm) *vb* (*tr*) **1** to represent in drawing or painting **2** *archaic* to describe in words **3** an obsolete word for **illuminate** [c15 from Old French *enluminer* to illumine (a manuscript) from Latin *inlūmināre* to brighten, from *lūmen* light] > **limner** (ˈlɪmnə) *n*

limnetic (lɪmˈnɛtɪk) *adj* of, relating to, or inhabiting the open water of lakes down to the depth of light penetration: *the limnetic zone* [c20 from Greek *limnē* pool]

limnology (lɪmˈnɒlədʒɪ) *n* the study of bodies of fresh water with reference to their plant and animal life, physical properties, geographical features, etc [c20 from Greek *limnē* lake] > **limnological** (ˌlɪmnəˈlɒdʒɪkᵊl) *or* ˌlimnoˈlogic *adj* > ˌlimnoˈlogically *adv* > limˈnologist *n*

limnophilous (lɪmˈnɒfɪləs) *adj* (of animals) living in lakes or freshwater marshes

Límnos (ˈlɪmnɔs) *n* transliteration of the Modern Greek name for **Lemnos**

limo (ˈlɪməʊ) *n, pl* -**mos** *informal* short for **limousine**

Limoges (lɪˈməʊʒ; *French* limɔʒ) *n* a city in S central France, on the Vienne River: a centre of the porcelain industry since the 18th century. Pop: 133 968 (1999)

limonene (ˈlɪməˌniːn) *n* a liquid optically active terpene with a lemon-like odour, found in lemon, orange, peppermint, and other essential oils and used as a wetting agent and in the manufacture of resins. Formula: $C_{10}H_{16}$ [c19 from New Latin *limonum* lemon]

limonite (ˈlaɪməˌnaɪt) *n* a common brown, black, or yellow amorphous secondary mineral that consists of hydrated ferric oxides and is a source of iron. Formula: $FeO(OH).nH_2O$ [c19 probably from Greek *leimōn*, translation of earlier German name, *Wiesenerz* meadow ore] > **limonitic** (ˌlaɪməˈnɪtɪk) *adj*

Limousin¹ (*French* limuzɛ̃) *n* a region and former province of W central France, in the W part of the Massif Central

Limousin² (ˌlɪmuˌzɛ̃) *n* a breed of fairly large yellowish-to-reddish-gold beef cattle originally from France

limousine (ˈlɪməˌziːn, ˌlɪməˈziːn) *n* **1** any large and luxurious car, esp one that has a glass division between the driver and passengers **2** a former type of car in which the roof covering the rear seats projected over the driver's compartment [c20 from French, literally: cloak (originally one worn by shepherds in *Limousin*), hence later applied to the car]

limousine liberal *n US derogatory* a wealthy left-wing person

limp¹ (lɪmp) *vb* (*intr*) **1** to walk with an uneven step, esp with a weak or injured leg **2** to advance in a labouring or faltering manner ▷ *n* **3** an uneven walk or progress [c16 probably a back formation from obsolete *limphalt* lame, from Old English *lemphealt*; related to Middle High German *limpfen* to limp] > ˈlimper *n* > ˈlimping *adj, n* > ˈlimpingly *adv*

limp² (lɪmp) *adj* **1** not firm or stiff **2** not energetic or vital **3** (of the binding of a book) not stiffened with boards [c18 probably of Scandinavian origin; related to Icelandic *limpa* looseness] > ˈlimply *adv* > ˈlimpness *n*

limpet (ˈlɪmpɪt) *n* **1** any of numerous marine gastropods, such as *Patella vulgata* (**common**

limpet) and *Fissurella* (or *Diodora*) *apertura* (**keyhole limpet**), that have a conical shell and are found clinging to rocks **2** any of various similar freshwater gastropods, such as *Ancylus fluviatilis* (**river limpet**) **3** (*modifier*) relating to or denoting certain weapons that are attached to their targets by magnetic or adhesive properties and resist removal: *limpet mines* **4** a small open caisson shaped to fit against a dock wall, used mainly in repair work [Old English *lempedu*, from Latin *lepas*, from Greek]

limpid (ˈlɪmpɪd) *adj* **1** clear or transparent **2** (esp of writings, style, etc) free from obscurity **3** calm; peaceful [c17 from French *limpide*, from Latin *limpidus* clear] > limˈpidity *or* ˈlimpidness *n* > ˈlimpidly *adv*

limpkin (ˈlɪmpkɪn) *n* a rail-like wading bird, *Aramus guarauna*, of tropical American marshes, having dark brown plumage with white markings and a wailing cry: order *Gruiformes* (cranes, rails, etc). Also called: **courlan** [c19 named from its awkward gait]

Limpopo (lɪmˈpəʊpəʊ) *n* **1** a province of NE South Africa, comprising the N part of the former province of Transvaal: agriculture and service industries. Capital: Polokwane (formerly Pietersburg). Pop: 5 511 962 (2004 est). Area: 123 910 sq km (47 842 sq miles). Former name (1994–2002): **Northern Province 2** a river in SE Africa, rising in E South Africa and flowing northeast, then southeast as the border between South Africa and Zimbabwe and through Mozambique to the Indian Ocean. Length: 1770 km (1100 miles)

limp-wristed *adj* ineffectual; effete

limulus (ˈlɪmjʊləs) *n, pl* -**li** (-ˌlaɪ) any horseshoe crab of the genus *Limulus*, esp *L. polyphemus* [c19 from New Latin (name of genus), from Latin *līmus* sidelong]

limy¹ (ˈlaɪmɪ) *adj* **limier, limiest 1** of, like, or smeared with birdlime **2** containing or characterized by the presence of lime > ˈliminess *n*

limy² (ˈlaɪmɪ) *adj* **limier, limiest** of or tasting of lime (the fruit)

linac (ˈlaɪnæk) *n* short for **linear accelerator**

linage *or* **lineage** (ˈlaɪnɪdʒ) *n* **1** the number of lines in a piece of written or printed matter **2** payment for written material calculated according to the number of lines **3** a less common word for **alignment**

linalool (lɪˈnæləʊˌɒl, ˌlɪnəˌluː) *or* **linalol** (ˈlɪnəˌlɒl) *n* an optically active colourless fragrant liquid found in many essential oils and used in perfumery. Formula: $C_{10}H_{18}O$ [from LIGNALOES + -OL¹]

Linares (*Spanish* liˈnares) *n* a city in S Spain: site of Scipio Africanus' defeat of the Carthaginians (208 BC); lead mines. Pop: 58 257 (2003 est)

linchpin *or* **lynchpin** (ˈlɪntʃˌpɪn) *n* **1** a pin placed transversely through an axle to keep a wheel in position **2** a person or thing regarded as an essential or coordinating element: *the linchpin of the company* [c14 *lynspin*, from Old English *lynis*]

Lincoln (ˈlɪŋkən) *n* **1** a city in E central England, administrative centre of Lincolnshire: an important ecclesiastical and commercial centre in the Middle Ages; Roman ruins, a castle (founded by William the Conqueror) and a famous cathedral (begun in 1086). Pop: 85 963 (2001). Latin name: **Lindum** (ˈlɪndəm) **2** a city in SE Nebraska: state capital; University of Nebraska (1869). Pop: 235 594 (2003 est) **3** short for **Lincolnshire 4** a breed of long-woolled sheep, originally from Lincolnshire

Lincoln Center *n* a centre for the performing arts in New York City, including theatres, a library, and a school. Official name: **Lincoln Center for the Performing Arts**

Lincoln green *n, adj* **1 a** a yellowish-green or brownish-green colour **b** (*as adjective*): *a Lincoln-green suit* **2** a cloth of this colour [c16 so named after a green fabric formerly made at LINCOLN, England]

Lincolnshire (ˈlɪŋkənʃɪə, -ʃə) *n* a county of E England, on the North Sea and the Wash: mostly low-lying and fertile, with fenland around the Wash and hills (the **Lincoln Wolds**) in the east; one of the main agricultural counties of Great Britain: the geographical and ceremonial county includes the unitary authorities of North Lincolnshire and North East Lincolnshire (both part of Humberside county from 1974 to 1996). Administrative centre: Lincoln. Pop (excluding unitary authorities): 665 300 (2003 est). Area (excluding unitary authorities): 5880 sq km (2270 sq miles). Abbreviation: Lincs

Lincoln's Inn *n* one of the four legal societies in London which together form the Inns of Court

lincrusta (lɪnˈkrʌstə) *n* a type of wallpaper having a hard embossed surface [C19 from Latin *linum* flax + *crusta* rind]

Lincs (lɪŋks) *abbreviation for* Lincolnshire

linctus (ˈlɪŋktəs) *n, pl* -**tuses** a syrupy medicinal formulation taken to relieve coughs and sore throats [C17 (in the sense: medicine to be licked with the tongue): from Latin, past participle of *lingere* to lick]

lindane (ˈlɪndeɪn) *n* a white poisonous crystalline powder with a slight musty odour: used as an insecticide, weedkiller, and, in low concentrations, in treating scabies; 1,2,3,4,5,6-hexachlorocyclohexane. Formula: $C_6H_6Cl_6$ [C20 named after T. van der *Linden*, Dutch chemist]

linden (ˈlɪndən) *n* any of various tiliaceous deciduous trees of the N temperate genus *Tilia*, having heart-shaped leaves and small fragrant yellowish flowers: cultivated for timber and as shade trees. See also **lime³, basswood** [C16 n use of obsolete adj *linden*, from Old English *linde* lime tree]

Lindesnes (ˈlɪndɪsˌnɛs) *n* a cape at the S tip of Norway, projecting into the North Sea. Also called: **the Naze**

Lindisfarne (ˈlɪndɪsˌfɑːn) *n* another name for **Holy Island**

Lindsey (ˈlɪndzɪ) *n* **Parts of** an area in E England constituting a former administrative division of Lincolnshire

line¹ (laɪn) *n* **1** a narrow continuous mark, as one made by a pencil, pen, or brush across a surface **2** such a mark cut into or raised from a surface **3** a thin indented mark or wrinkle **4** a straight or curved continuous trace having no breadth that is produced by a moving point **5** *maths* **a** any straight one-dimensional geometrical element whose identity is determined by two points. A **line segment** lies between any two points on a line **b** a set of points (x, y) that satisfies the equation $y = mx + c$, where *m* is the gradient and *c* is the intercept with the *y*-axis **6** a border or boundary: *the county line* **7** *sport* **a** a white or coloured band indicating a boundary or division on a field, track, etc **b** a mark or imaginary mark at which a race begins or ends **8** *American football* **a** See **line of scrimmage b** the players arranged in a row on either side of the line of scrimmage at the start of each play **9** a specified point of change or limit: *the dividing line between sanity and madness* **10** **a** the edge or contour of a shape, as in sculpture or architecture, or a mark on a painting, drawing, etc, defining or suggesting this **b** the sum or type of such contours or marks, characteristic of a style or design: *the line of a draughtsman; the line of a building* **11** anything long, flexible, and thin, such as a wire or string: *a washing line; a fishing line* **12** a telephone connection: *a direct line to New York* **13** **a** a conducting wire, cable, or circuit for making connections between pieces of electrical apparatus, such as a cable for electric-power transmission, telecommunications, etc **b** (*as modifier*): *the line voltage* **14** a system of travel or transportation, esp over agreed routes: *a shipping line* **15** a company operating such a system **16** a route between two points on a railway **17** *chiefly*

Brit **a** a railway track, including the roadbed, sleepers, etc **b** one of the rails of such a track **18** *NZ* a roadway usually in a rural area **19** a course or direction of movement or advance: *the line of flight of a bullet* **20** a course or method of action, behaviour, etc: *take a new line with him* **21** a policy or prescribed course of action or way of thinking (often in the phrases **bring** *or* **come into line**) **22** **a** field of study, interest, occupation, trade, or profession: *this book is in your line* **23** alignment; true (esp in the phrases **in line, out of line**) **24** one kind of product or article: *a nice line in hats* **25** *NZ* a collection of bales of wool all of the one type **26** a row of persons or things: *a line of cakes on the conveyor belt* **27** a chronological or ancestral series, esp of people: *a line of prime ministers* **28** a row of words printed or written across a page or column **29** a unit of verse consisting of the number of feet appropriate to the metre being used and written or printed with the words in a single row **30** a short letter; note: *just a line to say thank you* **31** a piece of useful information or hint about something: *give me a line on his work* **32** one of a number of narrow horizontal bands forming a television picture **33** *physics* a narrow band in an electromagnetic spectrum, resulting from a transition in an atom, ion, or molecule of a gas or plasma **34** *music* **a** any of the five horizontal marks that make up the stave. Compare **space** (sense 10) **b** the musical part or melody notated on one such set **c** a discernible shape formed by sequences of notes or musical sounds: *a meandering melodic line* **d** (in polyphonic music) a set of staves that are held together with a bracket or brace **35** a unit of magnetic flux equal to 1 maxwell **36** a defensive or fortified position, esp one that marks the most forward position in war or a national boundary: *the front line* **37** **line ahead** *or* **line abreast** a formation adopted by a naval unit for manoeuvring **38** a formation adopted by a body or a number of military units when drawn up abreast **39** the combatant forces of certain armies and navies, excluding supporting arms **40** *fencing* one of four divisions of the target on a fencer's body, considered as areas to which specific attacks are made **41** the scent left by a fox **42** **a** the equator (esp in the phrase **crossing the line**) **b** any circle or arc on the terrestrial or celestial sphere **43** the amount of insurance written by an underwriter for a particular risk **44** *US and Canadian* a line of people, vehicles, etc, waiting for something. Also called (in Britain and certain other countries): **queue 45** *slang* a portion of a powdered drug for snorting **46** *slang* something said for effect, esp to solicit for money, sex, etc: *he gave me his usual line* **47** **above the line a** *accounting* denoting entries above a horizontal line on a profit and loss account, separating those that establish the profit or loss from those that show how the profit is distributed **b** denoting revenue transactions rather than capital transactions in a nation's accounts **c** *marketing* expenditure on media advertising through an agency, rather than internally arranged advertising, such as direct mail, free samples, etc **d** *bridge* denoting bonus points, marked above the horizontal line on the score card **48** **below the line a** *accounting* denoting entries below a horizontal line on a profit and loss account, separating those that establish the profit or loss from those that show how the profit is distributed **b** denoting capital transactions rather than revenue transactions in a nation's accounts **c** *marketing* denoting expenditure on advertising by other means than the traditional media, such as the provision of free gifts, special displays, direct mailshots, etc **d** *bridge* denoting points scored towards game and rubber, marked below the horizontal line on the score card **49** **all along the line a** at every stage in a series **b** in every detail **50** **do a line (with)** *Irish and Austral informal* to associate (with a person of the opposite sex) regularly; go out (with): *he is*

doing a line with her **51** **draw the line (at)** to reasonably object (to) or set a limit (on): *her father draws the line at her coming in after midnight* **52** **get a line on** *informal* to obtain information about **53** **hold the line a** to keep a telephone line open **b** *football* to prevent the opponents from taking the ball forward **c** (of soldiers) to keep formation, as when under fire **54** **in line for** in the running for; a candidate for: *he's in line for a directorship* **55** **in line with** conforming to **56** **in the line of duty** as a necessary and usually undesired part of the performance of one's responsibilities **57** **lay** *or* **put on the line a** to pay money **b** to speak frankly and directly **c** to risk (one's career, reputation, etc) on something **58** **shoot a line** *informal* to try to create a false image, as by boasting or exaggerating **59** **step out of line** to fail to conform to expected standards, attitudes, etc **60** **toe the line** to conform to expected standards, attitudes, etc ▷ *vb* **61** (*tr*) to mark with a line or lines **62** (*tr*) to draw or represent with a line or lines **63** (*tr*) to be or put as a border to: *tulips lined the lawns* **64** to place in or form a row, series, or alignment ▷ See also **lines, line-up** [C13 partly from Old French *ligne*, ultimately from Latin *līnea*, n use of *līneus* flaxen, from *līnum* flax; partly from Old English *līn*, ultimately also from Latin *līnum* flax] > 'linable *or* 'lineable *adj* > lined *adj* > 'line,like *adj* > 'liny *or* 'liney *adj*

line² (laɪn) *vb* (*tr*) **1** to attach an inside covering to (a garment, curtain, etc), as for protection, to hide the seaming, or so that it should hang well **2** to cover or fit the inside of: *to line the walls with books* **3** to fill plentifully: *a purse lined with money* **4** to reinforce the back of (a book) with fabric, paper, etc [C14 ultimately from Latin *līnum* flax, since linings were often made of linen]

lineage¹ (ˈlɪnɪɪdʒ) *n* **1** direct descent from an ancestor, esp a line of descendants from one ancestor **2** a less common word for **derivation** [C14 from Old French *lignage*, from Latin *līnea* LINE¹]

lineage² (ˈlaɪnɪdʒ) *n* a variant spelling of **linage**

lineal (ˈlɪnɪəl) *adj* **1** being in a direct line of descent from an ancestor **2** of, involving, or derived from direct descent **3** a less common word for **linear** [C14 via Old French from Late Latin *līneālis*, from Latin *līnea* LINE¹] > 'lineally *adv*

lineament (ˈlɪnɪəmənt) *n* (*often plural*) **1** a facial outline or feature **2** a distinctive characteristic or feature **3** *geology* any long natural feature on the surface of the earth, such as a fault, esp as revealed by aerial photography [C15 from Latin: line, from *līneāre* to draw a line] > lineamental (ˌlɪnɪəˈmɛntəl) *adj*

linear (ˈlɪnɪə) *adj* **1** of, in, along, or relating to a line **2** of or relating to length **3** resembling, represented by, or consisting of a line or lines **4** having one dimension **5** designating a style in the arts, esp painting, that obtains its effects through line rather than colour or light and in which the edges of forms and planes are sharply defined. Compare **painterly 6** *maths* of or relating to the first degree: *a linear equation* **7** narrow and having parallel edges: *a linear leaf* **8** *electronics* **a** (of a circuit, etc) having an output that is directly proportional to input: *linear amplifier* **b** having components arranged in a line [C17 from Latin *līneāris* of or by means of lines] > linearity (ˌlɪnɪˈærɪtɪ) *n* > 'linearly *adv*

Linear A *n* a hitherto undeciphered script, partly syllabic and partly ideographic, found on tablets and pottery in Crete and dating mainly from the 15th century BC

linear accelerator *n* an accelerator in which charged particles are accelerated along a linear path by potential differences applied to a number of electrodes along their path. Sometimes shortened to: **linac**

Linear B *n* an ancient system of writing, apparently a modified form of Linear A, found on clay tablets and jars of the second millennium BC The earliest excavated examples, dating from about 1400, came from Knossos, in Crete, but all the later finds are at Pylos and Mycenae on the Greek mainland, dating from the 14th–12th centuries. The script is generally accepted as being an early representation of Mycenaean Greek

linear collider *n physics* a particle accelerator in which two beams of particles are made to collide

linear equation *n* a polynomial equation of the first degree, such as $x + y = 7$

linear measure *n* a unit or system of units for the measurement of length. Also called: **long measure**

linear motor *n* a form of electric motor in which the stator and the rotor are linear and parallel. It can be used to drive a train, one part of the motor being in the locomotive, the other in the track

linear perspective *n* the branch of perspective in which the apparent size and shape of objects and their position with respect to foreground and background are established by actual or suggested lines converging on the horizon

linear programming *n maths* a technique used in economics, etc, for determining the maximum or minimum of a linear function of non-negative variables subject to constraints expressed as linear equalities or inequalities

linear space *n maths* another name for **vector space**

lineate ('lɪnɪɪt, -ˌeɪt) *or* **lineated** *adj* marked with lines; streaked [C17 from Latin *līneātus* drawn with lines]

lineation (ˌlɪnɪˈeɪʃən) *n* 1 the act of marking with lines 2 an arrangement of or division into lines 3 an outline or contour 4 any linear arrangement involving rocks or minerals, such as a parallel arrangement of elongated mineral grains

linebacker ('laɪnˌbækə) *n* a defensive player in American or Canadian football who is positioned just behind the line of scrimmage

line block *n* a letterpress printing block made by a photoengraving process without the use of a screen

line breeding *n* selective inbreeding that produces individuals possessing one or more of the favourable characteristics of their common ancestor

line call *n tennis* the judgment of the umpire or linesman as to whether the ball has landed in or out of court

linecaster ('laɪnˌkɑːstə) *n* a typesetting machine that casts metal type in lines

line composition *n printing* type produced on a linecaster

line dancing *n* a form of dancing performed by rows of people to country and western music

line drawing *n* a drawing made with lines only, gradations in tone being provided by the spacing and thickness of the lines

line-engraving *n* 1 the art or process of hand-engraving in intaglio and copper plate 2 a plate so engraved 3 a print taken from such a plate ▷ **line-enˌgraver** *n*

line fish *n South African* fish caught by lines rather than nets

Line Islands *pl n* a group of coral islands in the central Pacific, including Tabuaeran, Teraina, and Kiritimati: part of Kiribati, with Palmyra and Jarvis administered by the US

lineman ('laɪnmən) *n, pl* **-men** 1 another name for **platelayer** 2 a person who does the chaining, taping, or marking of points for a surveyor 3 *Austral and NZ* (formerly) the member of a beach life-saving team who controlled the line used to help drowning swimmers and surfers 4 *American football* a member of the row of players who start each down positioned on either side of the line of scrimmage 5 *US and Canadian* another word for **linesman** (sense 2)

line management *n commerce* those managers in an organization who are responsible for the main activity or product of the organization, as distinct from those, such as transport, accounting, or

personnel, who provide services to the line management ▷ **line manager** *n*

linen ('lɪnɪn) *n* 1 **a** a hard-wearing fabric woven from the spun fibres of flax **b** (*as modifier*): *a linen tablecloth* 2 yarn or thread spun from flax fibre 3 clothes, sheets, tablecloths, etc, made from linen cloth or from a substitute such as cotton 4 See **linen paper** [Old English *linnen*, ultimately from Latin *līnum* flax, LINE²]

linen paper *n* paper made from flax fibres or having a similar texture

line of battle *n* a formation adopted by a military or naval force when preparing for action

line of credit *n US and Canadian* another name for **credit line**

line of fire *n* the flight path of a missile discharged or to be discharged from a firearm

line of force *n* an imaginary line representing a field of force, such as an electric or magnetic field, such that the tangent at any point is the direction of the field vector at that point

line of scrimmage *n American football* an imaginary line, parallel to the goal lines, on which the ball is placed at the start of a down and on either side of which the offense and defense line up

line of sight *n* 1 the straight line along which an observer looks or a beam of radiation travels 2 *ophthalmol* another term for **line of vision**

line of vision *n ophthalmol* a straight line extending from the fovea centralis of the eye to an object on which the eye is focused. Also called: **line of sight**

lineolate ('lɪnɪəˌleɪt) *or* **lineolated** *adj biology* marked with very fine parallel lines [C19 from Latin *līneola*, diminutive of *līnea* LINE¹]

line-out *n rugby union* the method of restarting play when the ball goes into touch, the forwards forming two parallel lines at right angles to the touchline and jumping for the ball when it is thrown in

line printer *n* an electromechanical device that prints a line of characters at a time rather than a character at a time, at speeds from about 200 to 3000 lines per minute: used in printing and in computer systems

liner¹ ('laɪnə) *n* 1 a passenger ship or aircraft, esp one that is part of a commercial fleet 2 See **Freightliner** 3 Also called: **eye liner** a cosmetic used to outline the eyes, consisting of a liquid or cake mixed with water and applied by brush or a grease pencil 4 a person or thing that uses lines, esp in drawing or copying

liner² ('laɪnə) *n* 1 a material used as a lining 2 a person who supplies or fits linings 3 *engineering* a sleeve, usually of a metal that will withstand wear or corrosion, fixed inside or outside a structural component or vessel: *cylinder liner*

liner notes *pl n* the US name for **sleeve notes**

lines (laɪnz) *pl n* 1 general appearance or outline: *a car with fine lines* 2 a plan of procedure or construction: *built on traditional lines* 3 **a** the spoken words of a theatrical presentation **b** the words of a particular role: *he forgot his lines* 4 *informal, chiefly Brit* a marriage certificate: *marriage lines* 5 luck, fate, or fortune (esp in the phrase **hard lines**) 6 **a** rows of tents, buildings, temporary stabling, etc, in a military camp: *transport lines* **b** a defensive position, row of trenches, or other fortification: *we broke through the enemy lines* 7 **a** a school punishment of writing the same sentence or phrase out a specified number of times **b** the phrases or sentences so written out: *a hundred lines* 8 **read between the lines** to understand or find an implicit meaning in addition to the obvious one

linesman ('laɪnzmən) *n, pl* **-men** 1 an official who helps the referee or umpire in various sports, esp by indicating when the ball has gone out of play 2 *chiefly Brit* a person who installs, maintains, or repairs telephone or electric-power lines. US and Canadian name: **lineman**

line squall *n* a squall or series of squalls along a cold front

line-up *n* 1 a row or arrangement of people or things assembled for a particular purpose: *the line-up for the football match* 2 the members of such a row or arrangement 3 an identity parade ▷ *vb* **line up** (*adverb*) 4 to form, put into, or organize a line-up 5 (*tr*) to produce, organize, and assemble: *they lined up some questions* 6 (*tr*) to align

ling¹ (lɪŋ) *n, pl* **ling** *or* **lings** 1 any of several gadoid food fishes of the northern coastal genus *Molva*, esp *M. molva*, having an elongated body with long fins 2 another name for **burbot** (a fish) [C13 probably from Low German; related to LONG¹]

ling² (lɪŋ) *n* another name for **heather** (sense 1) [C14 from Old Norse *lyng*] ▷ **'lingy** *adj*

ling. *abbreviation for* linguistics

-ling¹ *suffix forming nouns* 1 *often disparaging* a person or thing belonging to or associated with the group, activity, or quality specified: *nestling; underling* 2 used as a diminutive: *duckling* [Old English *-ling*, of Germanic origin; related to Icelandic *-lingr*, Gothic *-lings*]

-ling² *suffix forming adverbs* in a specified condition, manner, or direction: *darkling; sideling* [Old English *-ling*, adverbial suffix]

Lingala (ˌlɪŋˈgɑːlə) *n* a Bantu language which is spoken in the Democratic Republic of the Congo, Congo-Brazzaville, and Angola

lingam ('lɪŋgəm) *or* **linga** ('lɪŋgə) *n* 1 (in Sanskrit grammar) the masculine gender 2 **a** the Hindu phallic image of the god Siva **b** the penis [C18 from Sanskrit]

Lingayen Gulf ('lɪŋgɑːˈjɛn) *n* a large inlet of the South China Sea in the Philippines, on the NW coast of Luzon: site of the Japanese landing in the 1941 invasion

lingcod ('lɪŋˌkɒd) *n, pl* **-cod** *or* **-cods** any scorpaenoid food fish of the family *Ophiodontidae*, esp *Ophiodon elongatus*, of the N Pacific Ocean

linger ('lɪŋgə) *vb* (*mainly intr*) 1 to delay or prolong departure 2 to go in a slow or leisurely manner; saunter 3 to remain just alive for some time prior to death 4 to persist or continue, esp in the mind 5 to be slow to act; dither; procrastinate [C13 (northern dialect) *lengeren* to dwell, from *lengen* to prolong, from Old English *lengan*; related to Old Norse *lengja*; see LONG¹] ▷ **'lingerer** *n* ▷ **'lingering** *adj* ▷ **'lingeringly** *adv*

lingerie ('lænʒərɪ) *n* 1 women's underwear and nightwear 2 *archaic* linen goods collectively [C19 from French, from *linge*, from Latin *līneus* linen, from *līnum* flax]

lingo ('lɪŋgəʊ) *n, pl* **-goes** *informal* any foreign or unfamiliar language, jargon, etc [C17 perhaps from LINGUA FRANCA; compare Portuguese *lingoa* tongue]

lingua ('lɪŋgwə) *n, pl* **-guae** (-gwiː) *anatomy* 1 the technical name for **tongue** 2 any tongue-like structure [C17 Latin]

lingua franca ('fræŋkə) *n, pl* **lingua francas** *or* **linguae francae** ('frænsiː) 1 a language used for communication among people of different mother tongues 2 a hybrid language containing elements from several different languages used in this way 3 any system of communication providing mutual understanding [C17 Italian, literally: Frankish tongue]

Lingua Franca *n* a particular lingua franca spoken from the time of the Crusades to the 18th century in the ports of the Mediterranean, based on Italian, Spanish, French, Arabic, Greek, and Turkish

lingual ('lɪŋgwəl) *adj* 1 *anatomy* of or relating to the tongue or a part or structure resembling a tongue 2 *rare* of or relating to language or languages **b** (*in combination*): *polylingual* 3 articulated with the tongue ▷ *n* 4 a lingual consonant, such as Scots (r) ▷ **'lingually** *adv*

linguiform ('lɪŋgwɪˌfɔːm) *adj* shaped like a tongue

linguine *or* **linguini** (lɪŋˈgwiːnɪ) *n* a kind of long pasta in the shape of thin flat strands [from

Italian: small tongues]

linguist ('lɪŋgwɪst) *n* **1** a person who has the capacity to learn and speak foreign languages **2** a person who studies linguistics **3** *West African, esp Ghanaian* the spokesman for a chief [c16 from Latin *lingua* tongue]

linguistic (lɪŋ'gwɪstɪk) *adj* **1** of or relating to language **2** of or relating to linguistics > lin'guistically *adv*

linguistic atlas *n* an atlas showing the distribution of distinctive linguistic features of languages or dialects

linguistic borrowing *n* another name for **loan word**

linguistic geography *n* the study of the distribution of dialectal speech elements > linguistic geographer *n*

linguistic philosophy *n* the approach to philosophy common in the mid 20th century that tends to see philosophical problems as arising from inappropriate theoretical use of language and therefore as being resolved by detailed attention to the common use of expressions

linguistics (lɪŋ'gwɪstɪks) *n* (*functioning as singular*) the scientific study of language. See also **historical linguistics, descriptive linguistics**

lingulate ('lɪŋgjʊˌleɪt) *or* **lingulated** *adj* shaped like a tongue: *a lingulate leaf* [c19 from Latin *lingulātus*]

linhay ('lɪnɪ) *n dialect* a farm building with an open front [c17 of unknown origin]

liniment ('lɪnɪmənt) *n* a medicated liquid, usually containing alcohol, camphor, and an oil, applied to the skin to relieve pain, stiffness, etc [c15 from Late Latin *linīmentum*, from *linere* to smear, anoint]

linin ('laɪnɪn) *n* the network of viscous material in the nucleus of a cell that connects the chromatin granules [c19 from Latin *līnum* flax + -IN]

lining ('laɪnɪŋ) *n* **1 a** material used to line a garment, curtain, etc **b** (*as modifier*): *lining satin* **2** a material, such as mull or brown paper, used to strengthen the back of a book **3** *civil engineering* a layer of concrete, brick, or timber, etc, used in canals to prevent them leaking or in tunnels or shafts to prevent them falling in **4** any material used as an interior covering

link¹ (lɪŋk) *n* **1** any of the separate rings, loops, or pieces that connect or make up a chain **2** something that resembles such a ring, loop, or piece **3** a road, rail, air, or sea connection, as between two main routes **4** a connecting part or episode **5** a connecting piece in a mechanism, often having pivoted ends **6** Also called: **radio link** a system of transmitters and receivers that connect two locations by means of radio and television signals **7** a unit of length equal to one hundredth of a chain. 1 link of a Gunter's chain is equal to 7.92 inches, and of an engineer's chain to 1 foot **8** *computing* short for **hyperlink 9 weak link** an unreliable person or thing within an organization or system ▷ *vb* **10** (often foll by *up*) to connect or be connected with or as if with links **11** (*tr*) to connect by association, etc [c14 from Scandinavian; compare Old Norse *hlekkr* link] > 'linkable *adj*

link² (lɪŋk) *n* (formerly) a torch used to light dark streets [c16 perhaps from Latin *lychnus*, from Greek *lukhnos* lamp]

linkage ('lɪŋkɪdʒ) *n* **1** the act of linking or the state of being linked **2** a system of interconnected levers or rods for transmitting or regulating the motion of a mechanism **3** *electronics* the product of the total number of lines of magnetic flux and the number of turns in a coil or circuit through which they pass **4** *genetics* the occurrence of two genes close together on the same chromosome so that they are unlikely to be separated during crossing over and tend to be inherited as a single unit **5** the fact of linking separate but related issues in the course of political negotiations

linkboy ('lɪŋkˌbɔɪ) *or* **linkman** *n, pl* **-boys** *or* **-men**

(formerly) a boy who carried a torch for pedestrians in dark streets

linked list *n computing* a list in which each item contains both data and a pointer to one or both neighbouring items, thus eliminating the need for the data items to be ordered in memory

linker ('lɪŋkə) *n* **1** *computing* a program that adjusts two or more machine-language program segments so that they may be simultaneously loaded and executed as a unit **2** (in systemic grammar) a word that links one word, phrase, sentence, or clause to another; a co-ordinating conjunction or a sentence connector. Compare **binder** (sense 11)

linkman ('lɪŋkmən) *n, pl* **-men 1** a presenter of a television or radio programme, esp a sports transmission, consisting of a number of outside broadcasts from different locations **2** another word for **linkboy**

link motion *n* a mechanism controlling the valves of a steam engine, consisting of a slotted link terminating in a pair of eccentrics

Linköping (*Swedish* 'lintɕøːpiŋ) *n* a city in S Sweden: a political and ecclesiastical centre in the Middle Ages; engineering industry. Pop: 137 004 (2004 est)

links (lɪŋks) *pl n* **1 a** short for **golf links b** (*as modifier*): *a links course* **2** *chiefly Scot* undulating sandy ground near the shore [Old English *hlincas* plural of *hlinc* ridge]

Link trainer *n trademark* a ground-training device for training pilots and aircrew in the use of flight instruments. Compare **flight simulator** [named after E. A. *Link* (1904–81), its US inventor]

linkup ('lɪŋkˌʌp) *n* **1** the establishing of a connection or union between objects, groups, organizations, etc **2** the connection or union established

linkwork ('lɪŋkˌwɜːk) *n* **1** something made up of links **2** a mechanism consisting of a series of links to impart or control motion; linkage

Linlithgow (lɪn'lɪθgəʊ) *n* **1** a town in SE Scotland, in West Lothian: ruined palace, residence of Scottish kings and birthplace of Mary, Queen of Scots. Pop: 13 370 (2001) **2** the former name of **West Lothian**

linn (lɪn) *n chiefly Scot* **1** a waterfall or a pool at the foot of it **2** a ravine or precipice [c16 probably from a confusion of two words, Scottish Gaelic *linne* pool and Old English *hlynn* torrent]

Linnean *or* **Linnaean** (lɪ'niːən, -'neɪ-) *adj* **1** of or relating to Carolus Linnaeus (original name *Carl von Linné*; 1707–78), the Swedish botanist who established the binomial system of biological nomenclature **2** relating to the system of classification of plants and animals using binomial nomenclature

linnet ('lɪnɪt) *n* **1** a brownish Old World finch, *Acanthis cannabina*: the male has a red breast and forehead **2** Also called: **house finch** a similar and related North American bird, *Carpodacus mexicanus* [c16 from Old French *linotte*, ultimately from Latin *līnum* flax (because the bird feeds on flaxseeds)]

linney ('lɪnɪ) *n Southwest English dialect* a lean-to shed

Linnhe ('lɪnɪ) *n* **Loch** a sea loch of W Scotland, at the SW end of the Great Glen. Length: about 32 km (20 miles)

lino ('laɪnəʊ) *n* short for **linoleum**

linocut ('laɪnəʊˌkʌt) *n* **1** a design cut in relief on linoleum mounted on a wooden block **2** a print made from such a design

linoleate (lɪ'nəʊlɪˌeɪt) *n* an ester or salt of linoleic acid

linoleic acid (ˌlɪnəʊ'liːɪk) *n* a colourless oily essential fatty acid found in many natural oils, such as linseed, used in the manufacture of soaps, emulsifiers, and driers. Formula: $C_{18}H_{32}O_2$ [c19 from Latin *līnum* flax + OLEIC ACID; so named because it is found in linseed oil]

linolenic acid (ˌlɪnəʊ'lɛnɪk, -'liː-) *n* a colourless unsaturated essential fatty acid found in drying

oils, such as linseed oil, and used in making paints and synthetic resins; 9,12,15-octadecatrienoic acid. Formula: $C_{18}H_{30}O_2$. Also called: alpha-linolenic acid

linoleum (lɪ'nəʊlɪəm) *n* a sheet material made of hessian, jute, etc, coated under pressure and heat with a mixture of powdered cork, linseed oil, rosin, and pigment, used as a floor covering. Often shortened to: **lino** [c19 from Latin *līnum* flax + *oleum* oil]

lino tile *n* a tile made of linoleum or a similar substance, used as a floor covering

Linotype ('laɪnəʊˌtaɪp) *n* **1** *trademark* a typesetting machine, operated by a keyboard, that casts an entire line on one solid slug of metal **2** type produced by such a machine

linsang ('lɪnsæŋ) *n* any of several forest-dwelling viverrine mammals, *Poiana richardsoni* of W Africa or either of the two species of *Prionodon* of S Asia: closely related to the genets, having a very long tail and a spotted or banded coat of thick fur [c19 Malay]

linseed ('lɪnˌsiːd) *n* another name for **flaxseed** [Old English *līnsǣd*, from *līn* flax + *sǣd* seed]

linseed oil *n* a yellow oil extracted from seeds of the flax plant. It has great drying qualities and is used in making oil paints, printer's ink, linoleum, etc

linsey-woolsey ('lɪnzɪ'wʊlzɪ) *n* **1** a thin rough fabric of linen warp and coarse wool or cotton filling **2** a strange nonsensical mixture or confusion [c15 probably from *Lindsey*, Suffolk village where the fabric was first made + WOOL (with rhyming suffix -*sey*)]

linstock ('lɪnˌstɒk) *n* a long staff holding a lighted match, formerly used to fire a cannon [c16 from Dutch *lontstok*, from *lont* match + *stok* stick]

lint (lɪnt) *n* **1** an absorbent cotton or linen fabric with the nap raised on one side, used to dress wounds, etc **2** shreds of fibre, yarn, etc **3** *chiefly US* staple fibre for making cotton yarn [c14 probably from Latin *linteus* made of linen, from *līnum* flax] > 'linty *adj*

lintel ('lɪntªl) *n* a horizontal beam, as over a door or window [c14 via Old French probably from Late Latin *līmitāris* (unattested) of the boundary, influenced in meaning by *līminaris* of the threshold]

linter ('lɪntə) *n* **1** a machine for stripping the short fibres of ginned cotton seeds **2** (*plural*) the fibres so removed

lintie ('lɪntɪ) *n* a Scot word for **linnet** (sense 1)

lintwhite ('lɪntˌwaɪt) *n archaic or poetic, chiefly Scot* the linnet [Old English *līnetwige*, probably from *līn* flax + -*twige*, perhaps related to Old High German *zwigon* to pluck]

linum ('laɪnəm) *n* any plant of the annual or perennial genus *Linum*, of temperate regions, esp *L. grandiflorum*, from N Africa, cultivated for its showy red or blue flowers: family *Linaceae*. See also **flax** [Latin, from Greek *linon* flax]

linux ('laɪnʌks) *n* a nonproprietary computer operating system suitable for use on personal computers

Linz¹ (lɪnts) *n* a port in N Austria, capital of Upper Austria, on the River Danube: cultural centre; steelworks. Pop: 183 504 (2001). Latin name: **Lentia** ('lɛntɪə, 'lɛnsɪə)

Linz² (lɪnz) *n acronym for* Land Information New Zealand; the official body responsible for land registration, mapping, and surveying in New Zealand

lion ('laɪən) *n* **1** a large gregarious predatory feline mammal, *Panthera leo*, of open country in parts of Africa and India, having a tawny yellow coat and, in the male, a shaggy mane. Related adj: **leonine 2** a conventionalized lion, the principal beast used as an emblem in heraldry. It has become the national emblem of Great Britain **3** a courageous, strong, or bellicose person **4** a celebrity or idol who attracts much publicity and a large following **5 beard the lion in his den** to approach a feared or influential person, esp in order to ask a favour **6 the lion's share** the largest portion [Old English *līo, lēo* (Middle English *lioun,* from Anglo-French *liun*), both from Latin *leo,* Greek *leōn*]

Lion ('laɪən) *n* **the** the constellation Leo, the fifth sign of the zodiac

lioness ('laɪənɪs) *n* a female lion

lionfish ('laɪən,fɪʃ) *n, pl* **-fish** or **-fishes** any of various scorpion fishes of the tropical Pacific genus *Pterois,* having a striped body and elongated spiny fins

lion-hearted *adj* very brave; courageous > '**lion-,heartedly** *adv* > '**lion,heartedness** *n*

lionize or **lionise** ('laɪə,naɪz) *vb* (*tr*) to treat as or make into a celebrity > ,**lioni'zation** or ,**lioni'sation** *n* > '**lion,izer** or '**lion,iser** *n*

Lions ('laɪənz) *n* **Gulf of** a wide bay of the Mediterranean off the S coast of France, between the Spanish border and Toulon. French name: **Golfe du Lion** (gɔlf dy ljɔ̃)

Lions Club *n* any of the local clubs that form the International Association of Lions Clubs, formed in the US in 1917 to foster local and international good relations and service to the community

lip (lɪp) *n* **1** *anatomy* **a** either of the two fleshy folds surrounding the mouth, playing an important role in the production of speech sounds, retaining food in the mouth, etc. Related adj: **labial b** (*as modifier*): *lip salve* **2** the corresponding part in animals, esp mammals **3** any structure resembling a lip, such as the rim of a crater, the margin of a gastropod shell, etc **4** a nontechnical word for **labium** and **labellum** (sense 1) **5** *slang* impudent talk or backchat **6** the embouchure and control in the lips needed to blow wind and brass instruments **7 bite one's lip a** to stifle one's feelings **b** to be annoyed or irritated **8 button (up) one's lip** *slang* to stop talking: often imperative **9 keep a stiff upper lip** to maintain one's courage or composure during a time of trouble without giving way to or revealing one's emotions **10 lick** or **smack one's lips** to anticipate or recall something with glee or relish ▷ *vb* **lips, lipping, lipped 11** (*tr*) to touch with the lip or lips **12** (*tr*) to form or be a lip or lips for **13** (*tr*) *rare* to murmur or whisper **14** (*intr*) to use the lips in playing a wind instrument ▷ See also **lip out** [Old English *lippa;* related to Old High German *leffur,* Norwegian *lepe,* Latin *labium*] > '**lipless** *adj* > '**lip,like** *adj*

lip- *combining form* a variant of **lipo-** before a vowel

lipa ('liːpə) *n, pl* **lipa** a monetary unit of Croatia worth one hundredth of a kuna

lipaemia or US **lipemia** (lɪ'piːmɪə) *n pathol* an abnormally large amount of fat in the blood [from Greek *lipos* fat + -AEMIA]

Lipari Islands ('lɪpərɪ) *pl n* a group of volcanic islands under Italian administration off the N coast of Sicily: remains that form a continuous record from Neolithic times. Chief town: Lipari. Pop: 10 300 (latest est). Area: 114 sq km (44 sq miles). Also called: **Aeolian Islands** Italian name: **Isole Eolie** ('iːzɔle e'ɔːlje)

lipase ('laɪpeɪs, 'lɪpeɪs) *n* any of a group of fat-digesting enzymes found in the stomach, pancreas, and liver and also occurring widely in the seeds of plants [c19 from Greek *lipos* fat + -ASE]

Lipetsk (*Russian* 'lipitsk) *n* a city in central Russia, on the Voronezh River: steelworks. Pop: 518 000 (2005 est)

lip gloss *n* a cosmetic preparation applied to the lips to give a sheen

lipid or **lipide** ('laɪpɪd, 'lɪpɪd) *n biochem* any of a large group of organic compounds that are esters of fatty acids (**simple lipids,** such as fats and waxes) or closely related substances (**compound lipids,** such as phospholipids): usually insoluble in water but soluble in alcohol and other organic solvents. They are important structural materials in living organisms. Former name: **lipoid** [c20 from French *lipide,* from Greek *lipos* fat]

Lipizzaner (,lɪpɪt'saːnə) *n* a breed of riding and

carriage horse used by the Spanish Riding School in Vienna and nearly always grey in colour [German, after *Lipizza,* near Trieste, where these horses were bred]

lip microphone *n* a microphone designed and shaped to be held close to the mouth, for use in noisy environments

lipo ('laɪpəʊ, 'laɪpəʊ) *n informal* short for **liposuction**

lipo- or *before a vowel* **lip-** *combining form* fat or fatty: *lipoprotein* [from Greek *lipos* fat]

lipodystrophy (,lɪpəʊ'dɪstrəfɪ) *n* any condition resulting in bodily loss or redistribution of fat tissue

lipogenesis (,lɪpəʊ'dʒɛnɪsɪs) *adj biochem* the synthesis of fatty acids in the body from glucose and other substrates

lipogram ('lɪpəʊ,græm) *n* a piece of writing from which all words containing a particular letter have been deliberately omitted

lipography (lɪ'pɒgrəfɪ) *n* the accidental omission of words or letters in writing [c19 from Greek *lip-,* stem of *leipein* to omit + -GRAPHY]

lipoic acid *n biochem* a sulphur-containing fatty acid, regarded as an element of the vitamin B complex, minute amounts of which are required for carbohydrate metabolism

lipoid ('lɪpɔɪd, 'laɪ-) *adj also* **lipoidal 1** resembling fat; fatty ▷ *n* **2** a fatlike substance, such as wax **3** *biochem* a former name for **lipid**

lipolysis (lɪ'pɒlɪsɪs) *n chem* the hydrolysis of fats resulting in the production of carboxylic acids and glycerol > **lipolytic** (,lɪpəʊ'lɪtɪk) *adj*

lipoma (lɪ'pəʊmə) *n, pl* **-mas** or **-mata** (-mətə) *pathol* a benign tumour composed of fatty tissue [c19 New Latin] > **lipomatous** (lɪ'pɒmətəs) *adj*

lipophilic (,lɪpəʊ'fɪlɪk) or **lipotropic** (,lɪpəʊ'trɒpɪk, ,laɪ-) *adj chem* having an affinity for lipids

lipoplast ('lɪpəʊ,plaːst) or **lipidoplast** ('lɪpɪdəʊ,plaːst) *n botany* a small particle in plant cytoplasm, esp that of seeds, in which fat is stored

lipopolysaccharide (,lɪpəʊ,pɒlɪ'sækə,raɪd) *n* a molecule, consisting of lipid and polysaccharide components, that is the main constituent of the cell walls of Gram-negative bacteria

lipoprotein (,lɪpəʊ'prəʊtiːn, ,laɪ-) *n* any of a group of proteins to which a lipid molecule is attached, important in the transport of lipids in the bloodstream. They exist in two main forms: high-density lipoproteins and low-density lipoproteins. See also **low-density lipoprotein**

liposculpture ('lɪpəʊ,skʌlptʃə) *n* a cosmetic surgical operation in which the shape of the body is altered by the removal by suction of excess body fat

liposome ('lɪpəʊ,səʊm) *n* a particle formed by lipids, consisting of a double layer similar to a natural biological membrane, enclosing an aqueous compartment

liposuck ('lɪpəʊ,sʌk, 'laɪpəʊ,sʌk) *vb* (*tr*) *informal* to subject to liposuction: *she's already had her thighs liposucked*

liposuction ('lɪpəʊ,sʌkʃən, 'laɪpəʊ,sʌkʃən) *n* a cosmetic surgical operation in which subcutaneous fat is removed from the body by suction

lipotropic (,lɪpəʊ'trɒpɪk) *adj biochem* (of a substance) increasing the utilization of fat by the tissues

lip out *vb* (*intr, adverb*) *golf* (of a ball) to reach the edge of the hole without dropping in

Lippe ('lɪpə) *n* **1** a former state of NW Germany, now part of the German state of North Rhine-Westphalia **2** a river in NW Germany, flowing west to the Rhine. Length: about 240 km (150 miles)

-lipped *adj* having a lip or lips as specified: *tight-lipped*

Lippizaner (,lɪpɪt'zaːnə) *n* a variant spelling of **Lipizzaner**

lippy¹ ('lɪpɪ) *adj informal* **-pier, -piest** insolent or cheeky

lippy² ('lɪpɪ) *n informal* lipstick

lip-read ('lɪp,riːd) *vb* **-reads, -reading, -read** (-'rɛd) to interpret (words) by lip-reading

lip-reading *n* a method used by deaf people to comprehend spoken words by interpreting movements of the speaker's lips. Also called: **speech-reading** > '**lip-,reader** *n*

lip service *n* insincere support or respect expressed but not put into practice

lipstick ('lɪp,stɪk) *n* a cosmetic for colouring the lips, usually in the form of a stick

lip-synch or **lip-sync** ('lɪp,sɪŋk) *vb* to mouth (prerecorded words) on television or film

lipuria (lɪ'pjʊərɪə) *n pathol* the presence of fat in the urine

liq. *abbreviation for* liquid

liquate ('laɪkweɪt) *vb* (*tr;* often foll by *out*) to separate one component of (an alloy, impure metal, or ore) by heating so that the more fusible part melts [c17 from Latin *liquāre* to dissolve] > **li'quation** *n*

liquefacient (,lɪkwɪ'feɪʃənt) *n* **1** a substance that liquefies or causes liquefaction ▷ *adj* **2** becoming or causing to become liquid [c19 from Latin *liquefacere* to make LIQUID]

liquefied natural gas *n* a mixture of various gases, esp methane, liquefied under pressure for transportation and used as an engine fuel. Abbreviation: LNG

liquefied petroleum gas *n* a mixture of various petroleum gases, esp propane and butane, stored as a liquid under pressure and used as an engine fuel. See also **bottled gas** Abbreviation: LPG or LP gas

liquefy ('lɪkwɪ,faɪ) *vb* **-fies, -fying, -fied** (esp of a gas) to become or cause to become liquid [c15 via Old French from Latin *liquefacere* to make liquid] > **liquefaction** (,lɪkwɪ'fækʃən) *n* > ,**lique'factive** *adj* > '**lique,fiable** *adj* > '**lique,fier** *n*

liquesce (lɪ'kwɛs) *vb* (*intr*) to become liquid

liquescent (lɪ'kwɛsᵊnt) *adj* (of a solid or gas) becoming or tending to become liquid [c18 from Latin *liquescere*] > **li'quescence** or **li'quescency** *n*

liqueur (lɪ'kjʊə; *French* likœr) *n* **1 a** any of several highly flavoured sweetened spirits such as kirsch or cointreau, intended to be drunk after a meal **b** (*as modifier*): *liqueur glass* **2** a small hollow chocolate sweet containing liqueur [c18 from French; see LIQUOR]

liquid ('lɪkwɪd) *n* **1** a substance in a physical state in which it does not resist change of shape but does resist change of size. Compare **gas** (sense 1), **solid** (sense 1) **2** a substance that is a liquid at room temperature and atmospheric pressure **3** *phonetics* a frictionless continuant, esp (l) or (r) ▷ *adj* **4** of, concerned with, or being a liquid or having the characteristic state of liquids: *liquid wax* **5** shining, transparent, or brilliant **6** flowing, fluent, or smooth **7** (of assets) in the form of money or easily convertible into money [c14 via Old French from Latin *liquidus,* from *liquēre* to be fluid] > '**liquidly** *adv* > '**liquidness** *n*

liquid air *n* air that has been liquefied by cooling. It is a pale blue and consists mainly of liquid oxygen (boiling pt.: −182.9°C) and liquid nitrogen (boiling pt.: −195.7°C): used in the production of pure oxygen, nitrogen, and the inert gases, and as a refrigerant

liquidambar (,lɪkwɪd'æmbə) *n* **1** any deciduous tree of the hamamelidaceous genus *Liquidambar,* of Asia and North and Central America, with star-shaped leaves, and exuding a yellow aromatic balsam. See also **sweet gum 2** the balsam of this tree, used in medicine. See also **storax** (sense 3) [c16 New Latin, from Latin *liquidus* liquid + Medieval Latin *ambar* AMBER]

liquidate ('lɪkwɪ,deɪt) *vb* **1 a** to settle or pay off (a debt, claim, etc) **b** to determine by litigation or agreement the amount of (damages, indebtedness, etc) **2 a** to terminate the operations of (a commercial firm, bankrupt estate, etc) by assessment of liabilities and appropriation of assets for their settlement **b** (of a commercial firm, etc) to terminate operations in this manner **3** (*tr*) to convert (assets) into cash **4** (*tr*) to eliminate or kill

liquidation (ˌlɪkwɪ'deɪʃən) *n* **1 a** the process of terminating the affairs of a business firm, etc, by realizing its assets to discharge its liabilities **b** the state of a business firm, etc, having its affairs so terminated (esp in the phrase **to go into liquidation**) **2** destruction; elimination

liquidator (ˈlɪkwɪˌdeɪtə) *n* a person assigned to supervise the liquidation of a business concern and whose legal authorization, rights, and duties differ according to whether the liquidation is compulsory or voluntary

liquid crystal *n* a liquid that has some crystalline characteristics, such as the presence of different optical properties in different directions; a substance in a mesomorphic state. See also **smectic, nematic**

liquid-crystal display *n* a flat-screen display in which an array of liquid-crystal elements can be selectively activated to generate an image, an electric field applied to each element altering its optical properties; it is used, for example, in portable computers, digital watches, and calculators. Abbreviation: **LCD**

liquid ecstasy *n* another name for **gamma hydroxybutyrate**

liquid fire *n* inflammable petroleum or other liquid used as a weapon of war in flamethrowers, etc

liquid glass *n* another name for **water glass**

liquidity (lɪ'kwɪdɪtɪ) *n* **1** the possession of sufficient liquid assets to discharge current liabilities **2** the state or quality of being liquid

liquidity event *n* the ending of an investor's involvement in a business venture with a view to realizing a gain or loss from the investment

liquidity preference *n economics* the desire to hold money rather than other assets, in Keynsian theory based on motives of transactions, precaution, and speculation

liquidity ratio *n* **1** the ratio of those assets that can easily be exchanged for money to the total assets of a bank or other financial institution. Also called: **liquid assets ratio 2** the ratio of a company's liquid assets to its current liabilities, used as a measure of its solvency **3** another name for **cash ratio**

liquidize *or* **liquidise** (ˈlɪkwɪˌdaɪz) *vb* **1** to make or become liquid; liquefy **2** (*tr*) to pulverize (food) in a liquidizer so as to produce a fluid

liquidizer *or* **liquidiser** (ˈlɪkwɪˌdaɪzə) *n* a kitchen appliance with blades for cutting and puréeing vegetables, blending liquids, etc. Also called: **blender**

liquid measure *n* a unit or system of units for measuring volumes of liquids or their containers

liquid oxygen *n* the clear pale blue liquid state of oxygen produced by liquefying air and allowing the nitrogen to evaporate: used in rocket fuels. Also called: **lox**

liquid paraffin *n* a colourless almost tasteless oily liquid obtained by petroleum distillation and used as a laxative. Also called (esp US and Canadian): **mineral oil**

liquid x *n* another name for **gamma-hydroxybutyrate**

liquor (ˈlɪkə) *n* **1** any alcoholic drink, esp spirits, or such drinks collectively **2** any liquid substance, esp that in which food has been cooked **3** *pharmacol* a solution of a pure substance in water **4** *brewing* warm water added to malt to form wort **5 in liquor** drunk; intoxicated ▷ *vb* **6** *brewing* to steep (malt) in warm water to form wort; mash [c13 via Old French from Latin, from *liquēre* to be liquid]

liquorice *or US and Canadian* **licorice** (ˈlɪkərɪs, -ərɪʃ) *n* **1** a perennial Mediterranean leguminous shrub, *Glycyrrhiza glabra*, having spikes of pale blue flowers and flat red-brown pods **2** the dried root of this plant, used as a laxative and in

confectionery **3** a sweet having a liquorice flavour [c13 via Anglo-Norman and Old French from Late Latin *liquirītia*, from Latin *glycyrrhīza*, from Greek *glukurrhiza*, from *glukus* sweet + *rhiza* root]

liquorish (ˈlɪkərɪʃ) *adj* **1** a variant spelling of **lickerish 2** *Brit* a variant of **liquorice**. > ˈ**liquorishly** *adv* > ˈ**liquorishness** *n*

liquor store *n US and Canadian* See **package store**

liquor up *vb* (*adverb*) *US and Canadian slang* to become or cause to become drunk

lira (ˈlɪərə; *Italian* 'li:ra) *n, pl* **lire** (ˈlɪərɪ; *Italian* 'li:re) *or* **liras 1** the former standard monetary unit of Italy, San Marino, and the Vatican City, divided into 100 centesimi; replaced by the euro in 2002 **2** Also called: **pound** the standard monetary unit of Turkey, divided into 100 kuruş **3** the standard monetary unit of Malta, divided into 100 cents or 1000 mils [Italian, from Latin *lībra* pound]

liriodendron (ˌlɪrɪəʊ'dendrən) *n, pl* **-drons** *or* **-dra** (-drə) either of the two deciduous trees of the magnoliaceous genus *Liriodendron*, the tulip trees of North America or China [c18 New Latin, from Greek *leiron* lily + *dendron* tree]

liripipe (ˈlɪrɪˌpaɪp) *or* **liripoop** (ˈlɪrɪˌpuːp) *n* the tip of a graduate's hood [c14 Medieval Latin *liripipium*, origin obscure]

Lisbon (ˈlɪzbən) *n* the capital and chief port of Portugal, in the southwest on the Tagus estuary: became capital in 1256; subject to earthquakes and severely damaged in 1755; university (1911). Pop: 1 892 891 (2001). Portuguese name: Lisboa (liʒ'boə)

Lisburn (ˈlɪzbɜːn) *n* **1** a city in Northern Ireland in Lisburn district, Co Antrim, noted for its linen industry: headquarters of the British Army in Northern Ireland. Pop: 71 465 (2001) **2** a district of S Northern Ireland, in Co. Antrim and Co. Down. Pop: 109 565 (2003 est). Area: 446 sq km (172 sq miles)

Lisieux (*French* lizjø) *n* a town in NW France: Roman Catholic pilgrimage centre, for its shrine of St Thérèse, who lived there. Pop: 23 166 (1999)

lisle (laɪl) *n* **a** a strong fine cotton thread or fabric **b** (*as modifier*): lisle stockings [c19 named after *Lisle* (now Lille), town in France where this type of thread was originally manufactured]

lisp (lɪsp) *n* **1** the articulation of *s* and *z* like or nearly like the *th* sounds in English *thin* and *then* respectively **2** the habit or speech defect of pronouncing *s* and *z* in this manner **3** the sound of a lisp in pronunciation ▷ *vb* **4** to use a lisp in the pronunciation of (speech) **5** to speak or pronounce imperfectly or haltingly [Old English *āwlispian*, from *wlisp* lisping (adj), of imitative origin; related to Old High German *lispen*] > ˈ**lisper** *n* > ˈ**lisping** *adj, n* > ˈ**lispingly** *adv*

LISP (lɪsp) *n* a high-level computer-programming language suitable for work in artificial intelligence [c20 from *lis*(t) *p*(*rocessing*)]

lis pendens (lɪs 'pɛndɛnz) *n* **1** a suit pending in a court that concerns the title to land **2** a notice filed to warn interested persons of such a suit [Latin: pending lawsuit]

Lissajous figure (ˈliːsəˌʒuː, ˌliːsə'ʒuː) *n* a curve traced out by a point that undergoes two simple harmonic motions in mutually perpendicular directions. The shape of these curves is characteristic of the relative phases and frequencies of the motion; they are used to determine the frequencies and phases of alternating voltages [c19 named after Jules A. *Lissajous* (1822–80), French physicist]

lissom *or* **lissome** (ˈlɪsəm) *adj* **1** supple in the limbs or body; lithe; flexible **2** agile; nimble [c19 variant of LITHESOME] > ˈ**lissomly** *or* ˈ**lissomely** *adv* > ˈ**lissomness** *or* ˈ**lissomeness** *n*

list¹ (lɪst) *n* **1** an item by item record of names or things, usually written or printed one under the other **2** *computing* a linearly ordered data structure **3 be on the danger list** to be in a critical medical or physical condition ▷ *vb* **4** (*tr*) to make a list of **5** (*tr*) to include in a list **6** (*tr*) *Brit*

to declare to be a listed building **7** (*tr*) *stock exchange* to obtain an official quotation for (a security) so that it may be traded on the recognized market **8** an archaic word for **enlist** [c17 from French, ultimately related to LIST²; compare Italian *lista* list of names (earlier: border, strip, as of paper), Old High German *līsta* border] > ˈ**listable** *adj*

list² (lɪst) *n* **1** a border or edging strip, esp of cloth **2** a less common word for **selvage 3** a strip of bark, sapwood, etc, trimmed from a board or plank **4** another word for **fillet** (sense 8) **5** a strip, band, ridge or furrow **6** *agriculture* a ridge in ploughed land formed by throwing two furrows together ▷ *vb* (*tr*) **7** to border with or as if with a list or lists **8** *agriculture* to plough (land) so as to form lists **9** to cut a list from (a board, plank, etc) ▷ See also **lists** [Old English *līst*; related to Old High German *līsta*]

list³ (lɪst) *vb* **1** (esp of ships) to lean over or cause to lean over to one side ▷ *n* **2** the act or an instance of leaning to one side [c17 origin unknown]

list⁴ (lɪst) *archaic* ▷ *vb* **1** to be pleasing to (a person) **2** (*tr*) to desire or choose ▷ *n* **3** a liking or desire [Old English *lystan*; related to Old High German *lusten* and Gothic *lūston* to desire]

list⁵ (lɪst) *vb* an archaic or poetic word for **listen** [Old English *hlystan*; related to Old Norse *hlusta*]

listed building *n* (in Britain) a building officially recognized as having special historical or architectural interest and therefore protected from demolition or alteration

listed company *n stock exchange* a company whose shares are quoted on the main market of the London Stock Exchange

listed security *n stock exchange* a security that is quoted on the main market of the London Stock Exchange and appears in its *Official List of Securities*. Compare **Third Market, unlisted securities market**

listel (ˈlɪst°l) *n* another name for **fillet** (sense 8) [c16 via French from Italian *listello*, diminutive of *lista* band, LIST²]

listen (ˈlɪs°n) *vb* (*intr*) **1** to concentrate on hearing something **2** to take heed; pay attention: *I told you many times but you wouldn't listen* [Old English *hlysnan*; related to Old High German *lūstrēn*] > ˈ**listener** *n*

listenable (ˈlɪs°nəb°l) *adj* easy or pleasant to listen to > ˌ**listena'bility** *n*

listenership (ˈlɪsnəʃɪp) *n* all the listeners collectively of a particular radio programme, station, or broadcaster

listen in *vb* (*intr, adverb*; often foll by *to*) **1** to listen to the radio **2** to intercept radio communications **3** to listen but not contribute (to a discussion), esp surreptitiously

listening post *n* **1** *military* a forward position set up to obtain early warning of enemy movement. Abbreviation: LP **2** any strategic position or place for obtaining information about another country or area

lister (ˈlɪstə) *n US and Canadian agriculture* a plough with a double mouldboard designed to throw soil to either side of a central furrow. Also called: **lister plough, middlebreaker, middle buster** [c19 from LIST²]

listeria (lɪs'tɪərɪə) *n* any rodlike Gram-positive bacterium of the genus *Listeria*, esp *L. monocytogenes*, the cause of listeriosis [c20 named after Joseph, 1st Baron *Lister* (1827–1912), British surgeon] > lis'**terial** *adj*

listeriosis (lɪˌstɪərɪ'əʊsɪs) *n* a serious form of food poisoning, caused by bacteria of the genus *Listeria*. Its symptoms can include meningitis and in pregnant women it may cause damage to the fetus

Listerism (ˈlɪstəˌrɪzəm) *n surgery* the use of or theory of using antiseptic techniques

listing (ˈlɪstɪŋ) *n* **1** a list or an entry in a list **2** *computing* a printed copy of a program or file in a form that can be read by humans **3** a place on the Official List of Securities of the London Stock

Exchange obtained by a company that has fulfilled the listing requirements and whose shares are quoted on the main market **4** (*plural*) lists of concerts, films, and other events printed in newspapers or magazines, showing details, such as times and venues

listless ('lɪstlɪs) *adj* disinclined for any effort or exertion; lacking vigour, enthusiasm, or energy [c15 from *list* desire + -LESS] > **'listlessly** *adv* > **'listlessness** *n*

list price *n* the selling price of merchandise as quoted in a catalogue or advertisement

list renting *n* the practice of renting a list of potential customers to a direct-mail seller of goods or to the fundraisers of a charity

lists (lɪsts) *pl n* **1** *history* **a** the enclosed field of combat at a tournament **b** the barriers enclosing the field at a tournament **2** any arena or scene of conflict, controversy, etc **3** **enter the lists** to engage in a conflict, controversy, etc [c14 plural of LIST² (border, boundary)]

listserv (,lɪst'sɜ:v) *n* a service on the internet that provides an electronic mailing to subscribers with similar interests

lit (lɪt) *vb* **1** a past tense and past participle of **light¹** **2** an alternative past tense and past participle of **light²**

lit. *abbreviation for* **1** literal(ly) **2** literary **3** literature

litany ('lɪtənɪ) *n*, *pl* **-nies** **1** *Christianity* **a** a form of prayer consisting of a series of invocations, each followed by an unvarying response **b** the Litany the general supplication in this form included in the Book of Common Prayer **2** any long or tedious speech or recital [c13 via Old French from Medieval Latin *litanīa* from Late Greek *litaneia* prayer, ultimately from Greek *litē* entreaty]

litas ('li:tɑ:s) *n*, *pl* **litai** ('li:teɪ) the standard monetary unit of Lithuania, divided into 100 centai

litchi, lichee, lichi or **lychee** (,laɪ'tʃi:) *n* **1** a Chinese sapindaceous tree, *Litchi chinensis*, cultivated for its round edible fruits **2** the fruit of this tree, which has a whitish juicy edible aril [c16 from Cantonese *lai chi*]

lite (laɪt) *adj* **1** (of food and drink) containing few calories or little alcohol or fat **2** denoting a more restrained or less extreme version of a person or thing: *reggae lite* [c20 variant spelling of LIGHT²]

-lite *n combining form* (in names of minerals) stone: *chrysolite*. Compare **-lith** [from French *-lite* or *-lithe*, from Greek *lithos* stone]

liter ('li:tə) *n* the US spelling of **litre**

literacy ('lɪtərəsɪ) *n* **1** the ability to read and write **2** the ability to use language proficiently

literacy hour *n* (in England and Wales) a daily reading and writing lesson that was introduced into the national primary school curriculum in 1998 to raise standards of literacy

literae humaniores ('lɪtə,riː hjuː,mænɪ'ɔːriːz) *n* (at Oxford University) the faculty concerned with Greek and Latin literature, ancient history, and philosophy; classics [Latin, literally: the more humane letters]

literal ('lɪtərəl) *adj* **1** in exact accordance with or limited to the primary or explicit meaning of a word or text **2** word for word **3** dull, factual, or prosaic **4** consisting of, concerning, or indicated by letters **5** true; actual **6** *maths* containing or using coefficients and constants represented by letters: $ax^2 + b$ is a literal expression. Compare **numerical** (sense 3a) ⊳ *n* **7** Also called: **literal error** a misprint or misspelling in a text [c14 from Late Latin *litterālis* concerning letters, from Latin *littera* LETTER] > **'literalness** or **literality** (,lɪtə'rælɪtɪ) *n*

literalism ('lɪtərə,lɪzəm) *n* **1** the disposition to take words and statements in their literal sense **2** literal or realistic portrayal in art or literature > **'literalist** *n* > ,literal'istic *adj* > ,literal'istically *adv*

literally ('lɪtərəlɪ) *adv* **1** in a literal manner **2** (intensifier): *there were literally thousands of people*

▬▬ **USAGE** The use of *literally* as an

intensifier is common, esp in informal contexts. In some cases, it provides emphasis without adding to the meaning: *the house was literally only five minutes walk away*. Often, however, its use results in absurdity: *the news was literally an eye-opener to me*. It is therefore best avoided in formal contexts

literary ('lɪtərərɪ, 'lɪtrərɪ) *adj* **1** of, relating to, concerned with, or characteristic of literature or scholarly writing: *a literary discussion; a literary style* **2** versed in or knowledgeable about literature: *a literary man* **3** (of a word) formal; not colloquial [c17 from Latin *litterārius* concerning reading and writing. See LETTER] > **'literarily** *adv* > **'literariness** *n*

literary agent *n* a person who manages the business affairs of an author > **literary agency** *n*

literate ('lɪtərɪt) *adj* **1** able to read and write **2** educated; learned **3** used to words rather than numbers as a means of expression. Compare **numerate** ⊳ *n* **4** a literate person [c15 from Latin *litterātus* learned. See LETTER] > **'literately** *adv*

literati (,lɪtə'rɑːtiː) *pl n* literary or scholarly people [c17 from Latin]

literatim (,lɪtə'rɑːtɪm) *adv* letter for letter [c17 from Medieval Latin, from Latin *littera* LETTER]

literation (,lɪtə'reɪʃən) *n* the use of letters to represent sounds or words

literator ('lɪtə,reɪtə) *n* another word for **littérateur** [c18 from Latin, from Latin *littera* letter]

literature ('lɪtərɪtʃə, 'lɪtrɪ-) *n* **1** written material such as poetry, novels, essays, etc, esp works of imagination characterized by excellence of style and expression and by themes of general or enduring interest **2** the body of written work of a particular culture or people: *Scandinavian literature* **3** written or printed matter of a particular type or on a particular subject: *scientific literature; the literature of the violin* **4** printed material giving a particular type of information: *sales literature* **5** the art or profession of a writer **6** *obsolete* learning [c14 from Latin *litterātūra* writing; see LETTER]

Lith. *abbreviation for* Lithuania(n)

-lith *n combining form* indicating stone or rock: *megalith*. Compare **-lite** [from Greek *lithos* stone]

litharge ('lɪθɑːdʒ) *n* another name for **lead monoxide** [c14 via Old French from Latin *lithargyrus*, from Greek, from *lithos* stone + *arguros* silver]

lithe (laɪð) *adj* flexible or supple [Old English (in the sense: gentle; c15 supple); related to Old High German *lindi* soft, Latin *lentus* slow] > **'lithely** *adv* > **'litheness** *n*

lithesome ('laɪðsəm) *adj* a less common word for **lissom** [c18 from LITHE + -SOME¹]

lithia ('lɪθɪə) *n* **1** another name for **lithium oxide** **2** lithium present in mineral waters as lithium salts [c19 New Latin, ultimately from Greek *lithos* stone]

lithiasis (lɪ'θaɪəsɪs) *n* *pathol* the formation of a calculus [c17 New Latin; see LITHO-, -IASIS]

lithia water *n* a natural or artificial mineral water that contains lithium salts

lithic ('lɪθɪk) *adj* **1** of, relating to, or composed of stone **2** containing abundant fragments of previously formed rock: *a lithic sandstone* **3** *pathol* of or relating to a calculus or calculi, esp one in the urinary bladder **4** of or containing lithium [c18 from Greek *lithikos* stony]

-lithic *adj combining form* (in anthropology) relating to the use of stone implements in a specified cultural period: *Neolithic* [from Greek *lithikos*, from *lithos* stone]

lithification (,lɪθɪfɪ'keɪʃən) *n* the consolidation of a loosely deposited sediment into a hard sedimentary rock

lithium ('lɪθɪəm) *n* a soft silvery element of the alkali metal series: the lightest known metal, used as an alloy hardener, as a reducing agent, and in batteries. Symbol: Li; atomic no.: 3; atomic

wt.: 6.941; valency: 1; relative density: 0.534; melting pt.: 180.6°C; boiling pt.: 1342°C [c19 New Latin, from LITHO- + -IUM]

lithium carbonate *n* a white crystalline solid used in the treatment of manic-depressive illness and mania. Formula: Li_2CO_3. Lithium citrate is also sometimes used for this purpose

lithium citrate *n* a white crystalline solid sometimes used in the treatment of manic-depressive illness and mania. Formula: $Li_3C_6H_5O_7$

lithium oxide *n* a white crystalline compound. It absorbs carbon dioxide and water vapour

litho ('laɪθəʊ) *n*, *pl* **-thos**, *adj*, *adv* short for **lithography, lithograph, lithographic** or **lithographically**

litho- or before a vowel **lith-** *combining form* stone: *lithograph* [from Latin, from Greek, from *lithos* stone]

lithogenous (lɪ'θɒdʒɪnəs) *adj* (of animals, esp certain corals) rock-building

lithograph ('lɪθə,grɑːf, -,græf) *n* **1** a print made by lithography ⊳ *vb* **2** (*tr*) to reproduce (pictures, text, etc) by lithography > **lithographic** (,lɪθə'græfɪk) or ,litho'graphical *adj* > ,litho'graphically *adv*

lithography (lɪ'θɒgrəfɪ) *n* a method of printing from a metal or stone surface on which the printing areas are not raised but made ink-receptive while the non-image areas are made ink-repellent [c18 from New Latin *lithographia*, from LITHO- + -GRAPHY] > li'thographer *n*

lithoid ('lɪθɔɪd) or **lithoidal** (lɪ'θɔɪdəl) *adj* resembling stone or rock [c19 from Greek *lithoeidēs*, from *lithos* stone]

lithology (lɪ'θɒlədʒɪ) *n* **1** the physical characteristics of a rock, including colour, composition, and texture **2** the study of rocks > **lithologic** (,lɪθə'lɒdʒɪk) or ,litho'logical *adj* > ,litho'logically *adv* > li'thologist *n*

lithomarge ('lɪθə,mɑːdʒ) *n* a smooth compact type of kaolin: white or reddish and often mottled [c18 from New Latin *lithomarga* from LITHO- + Latin *marga* marl]

lithometeor (,lɪθə'miːtɪə) *n* a mass of solid particles, such as dust, sand, etc, falling through the atmosphere

lithophyte ('lɪθə,faɪt) *n* **1** a plant that grows on rocky or stony ground **2** an organism, such as a coral, that is partly composed of stony material > **lithophytic** (,lɪθə'fɪtɪk) *adj*

lithopone ('lɪθə,pəʊn) *n* a white pigment consisting of a mixture of zinc sulphide, zinc oxide, and barium sulphate [c20 from LITHO- + Greek *ponos* work]

lithosol ('lɪθə,sɒl) *n* chiefly US a type of azonal soil consisting chiefly of unweathered or partly weathered rock fragments, usually found on steep slopes [c20 from LITHO- + Latin *solum* soil]

lithosphere ('lɪθə,sfɪə) *n* the rigid outer layer of the earth, having an average thickness of about 75 km and comprising the earth's crust and the solid part of the mantle above the asthenosphere

lithostatic (,lɪθəʊ'stætɪk) another name for **geostatic¹**

lithotomy (lɪ'θɒtəmɪ) *n*, *pl* **-mies** the surgical removal of a calculus, esp one in the urinary bladder [c18 via Late Latin from Greek, from LITHO- + -TOMY] > **lithotomic** (,lɪθə'tɒmɪk) or ,litho'tomical *adj* > li'thotomist *n*

lithotripsy ('lɪθəʊ,trɪpsɪ) *n* the use of ultrasound, often generated by a lithotripter, to pulverize kidney stones and gallstones *in situ* [c20 from LITHO- + Greek *thruptein* to crush]

lithotripter ('lɪθə,trɪptə) *n* a machine that pulverizes kidney stones by ultrasound as an alternative to their surgical removal

lithotrity (lɪ'θɒtrɪtɪ) *n*, *pl* **-ties** *surgery* the crushing of a calculus in the bladder by means of an instrument (**lithotrite**) so that it can be expelled by urinating [c19 from LITHO- + Latin *trītus*, from *terere* to crush]

Lithuania (,lɪθjʊ'eɪnɪə) *n* a republic in NE Europe,

on the Baltic Sea: a grand duchy in medieval times; united with Poland in 1569; occupied by Russia in 1795 and by Germany during World War I; independent Lithuania formed in 1918, but occupied by Soviet troops in 1919 and then by Poland; became a Soviet republic in 1940; unilaterally declared independence from the Soviet Union in 1990; recognized as independent in 1991; joined the EU in 2004. Official language: Lithuanian. Religion: Roman Catholic majority. Currency: litas. Capital: Vilnius. Pop: 3 422 000 (2004 est). Area: 65 200 sq km (25 174 sq miles). Also called: **Lithuanian Republic** Lithuanian name: **Lietuva**

Lithuanian (ˌlɪθjʊˈeɪnɪən) adj **1** of, relating to, or characteristic of Lithuania, its people, or their language ▷ n **2** the official language of Lithuania: belonging to the Baltic branch of the Indo-European family **3** a native or inhabitant of Lithuania

litigable (ˈlɪtɪɡəbəl) adj law that may be the subject of litigation

litigant (ˈlɪtɪɡənt) n **1** a party to a lawsuit ▷ adj **2** engaged in litigation

litigate (ˈlɪtɪˌɡeɪt) vb **1** to bring or contest (a claim, action, etc) in a lawsuit **2** (intr) to engage in legal proceedings [c17 from Latin lītigāre, from līt-, stem of līs lawsuit + agere to carry on] > ˈlitiˌgator n

litigation (ˌlɪtɪˈɡeɪʃən) n **1** the act or process of bringing or contesting a legal action in court **2** a judicial proceeding or contest

litigation friend n law a person acting on behalf of an infant or other person under legal disability. Former name: **next friend**

litigious (lɪˈtɪdʒəs) adj **1** excessively ready to go to law **2** of or relating to litigation **3** inclined to dispute or disagree [c14 from Latin lītigiōsus quarrelsome, from lītigium strife] > liˈtigiously adv > liˈtigiousness n

litmus (ˈlɪtməs) n a soluble powder obtained from certain lichens. It turns red under acid conditions and blue under basic conditions and is used as an indicator [c16 perhaps from Scandinavian; compare Old Norse litmosi, from litr dye + mosi moss]

litmus test n **1** a test to establish the acidity or alkalinity of a mixture **2** a critical indication of future success or failure

litotes (ˈlaɪtəʊˌtiːz) n, pl -tes understatement for rhetorical effect, esp when achieved by using negation with a term in place of using an antonym of that term, as in "She was not a little upset" for "She was extremely upset." [c17 from Greek, from litos small]

litre or US **liter** (ˈliːtə) n **1** one cubic decimetre **2** (formerly) the volume occupied by 1 kilogram of pure water at 4°C and 760 millimetres of mercury. This is equivalent to 1.000 028 cubic decimetres or about 1.76 pints [c19 from French, from Medieval Latin litra, from Greek: a unit of weight]

LittB or **LitB** abbreviation for Bachelor of Letters or Bachelor of Literature [Latin: Litterarum Baccalaureus]

LittD or **LitD** abbreviation for Doctor of Letters or Doctor of Literature [Latin: Litterarum Doctor]

litter (ˈlɪtə) n **1 a** small refuse or waste materials carelessly dropped, esp in public places **b** (as modifier): litter bin **2** a disordered or untidy condition or a collection of objects in this condition **3** a group of offspring produced at one birth by a mammal such as a sow **4** a layer of partly decomposed leaves, twigs, etc, on the ground in a wood or forest **5** straw, hay, or similar material used as bedding, protection, etc, by animals or plants **6** See **cat litter 7** a means of conveying people, esp sick or wounded people, consisting of a light bed or seat held between parallel sticks ▷ vb **8** to make (a place) untidy by strewing (refuse) **9** to scatter (objects, etc) about or (of objects) to lie around or upon (anything) in an untidy fashion **10** (of pigs, cats, etc) to give birth to (offspring) **11** (tr) to provide (an animal or

plant) with straw or hay for bedding, protection, etc [c13 (in the sense: bed): via Anglo-French, ultimately from Latin lectus bed]

littérateur (ˌlɪtərəˈtɜː; French literatœr) n an author, esp a professional writer [c19 from French from Latin litterātor a grammarian]

litter lout or US and Canadian **litterbug** (ˈlɪtəˌbʌɡ) n slang a person who tends to drop refuse in public places

little (ˈlɪtəl) determiner **1** (often preceded by a) **a** a small quantity, extent, or duration of: the little hope there is left; very little milk **b** (as pronoun): save a little for me **2** not much: little damage was done **3** make little of See **make of** (sense 3) **4** not a little a very **b** a lot **5** quite a little a considerable amount **6** think little of to have a low opinion of ▷ adj **7** of small or less than average size **8** young: a little boy; our little ones **9** endearingly familiar; dear: my husband's little ways **10** contemptible, mean, or disagreeable: your filthy little mind **11** (of a region or district) resembling another country or town in miniature: little Venice **12** little game a person's secret intention or business: so that's his little game! **13** no little considerable ▷ adv **14** (usually preceded by a) in a small amount; to a small extent or degree; not a lot: to laugh a little **15** (used preceding a verb) not at all, or hardly: he little realized his fate **16** not much or often: we go there very little now **17** little by little by small degrees ▷ See also **less, lesser, least, littler, littlest** [Old English lȳtel; related to lȳr few, Old High German luzzil]

Little America n originally the chief US base in the Antarctic, on the Ross Ice Shelf: first established by Admiral Richard E. Byrd (1928); used for polar exploration. It closed in the 1960s

Little Bear n **the** the English name for **Ursa Minor**

Little Belt n a strait in Denmark, between Jutland and Funen Island, linking the Kattegat with the Baltic. Length: about 48 km (30 miles). Width: up to 29 km (18 miles). Danish name: **Lille Bælt**

Little Bighorn n a river in the W central US, rising in N Wyoming and flowing north to the Bighorn River. Its banks were the scene of the defeat (1876) and killing of General Custer and his command by Indians

Little Corporal n **the** a nickname of Napoleon Bonaparte

Little Diomede n **the** the smaller of the two Diomede Islands in the Bering Strait: administered by the US Area: about 10 sq km (4 sq miles)

Little Dipper n US and Canadian **the** a small faint constellation, the brightest star of which is the Pole Star, lying 1° from the true celestial pole. Also called: **Ursa Minor, the Bear, the Little Bear**

Little Dog n **the** the English name for **Canis Minor**

little end n Brit **1** Also called (in vertical engines): **top end** the smaller end of a connecting rod in an internal-combustion engine or reciprocating pump. Compare **big end 2** the bearing surface between the smaller end of a connecting rod and the gudgeon pin

Little Englander (ˈɪŋɡləndə) n **1** (esp in the 19th century) a person opposed to the extension of the British Empire **2** Brit informal a person who perceives most foreign influences on Britain's culture and institutions as damaging or insidious

little grebe n a small brownish European diving bird, Podiceps ruficollis, frequenting lakes, family Podicipitidae (grebes)

little hours pl n RC Church the canonical hours of prime, terce, sext, and nones in the divine office

Little John n one of Robin Hood's companions, noted for his great size and strength

little lion dog n another name for **Lowchen**

little magazine n a literary magazine that features experimental or other writing of interest to a limited number of readers

little man n **1** a man of no importance or significance **2** Brit a tradesman or artisan operating on a small scale

little office n RC Church a series of psalms and prayers similar to the divine office but shorter

little owl n a small Old World owl, Athene noctua, having a speckled brown plumage and flattish head

little people or **folk** pl n folklore small supernatural beings, such as elves, pixies, or leprechauns

littler (ˈlɪtlə) determiner not standard the comparative of **little**

Little Rock n a city in central Arkansas, on the Arkansas River: state capital. Pop: 184 053 (2003 est)

Little Russia n a region of the former SW Soviet Union, consisting chiefly of Ukraine

Little Russian n, adj a former word for **Ukrainian**

little slam n bridge the winning of all tricks except one by one side, or the contract to do so. Also called: **small slam**

littlest (ˈlɪtlɪst) determiner not standard the superlative of **little**

Little St Bernard Pass n a pass over the Savoy Alps, between Bourg-Saint-Maurice, France, and La Thuile, Italy: 11th-century hospice. Height: 2187 m (7177 ft)

little theatre n theatre, chiefly US and Canadian experimental or avant-garde drama, usually amateur, originating from a theatrical movement of the 1920s

little woman n **the** Brit old-fashioned a facetious term for **wife**

littlie (ˈlɪtlɪ) n Austral informal a young child

littoral (ˈlɪtərəl) adj **1** of or relating to the shore of a sea, lake, or ocean **2** biology inhabiting the shore of a sea or lake or the shallow waters near the shore: littoral fauna ▷ n **3** a coastal or shore region [c17 from Late Latin littorālis, from lītorālis, from lītus shore]

Littoria (Italian litˈtɔːrja) n the former name (until 1947) of **Latina**

lit up adj slang **1** drunk **2** drugged, esp on heroin

liturgical (lɪˈtɜːdʒɪkəl) or **liturgic** adj **1** of or relating to public worship **2** of or relating to the liturgy > liˈturgically adv

liturgics (lɪˈtɜːdʒɪks) n (functioning as singular) the study of liturgies. Also called: **liturgiology**

liturgist (ˈlɪtədʒɪst) n a student or composer of liturgical forms > ˈliturgism n > ˌliturˈgistic adj

liturgy (ˈlɪtədʒɪ) n, pl -gies **1** the forms of public services officially prescribed by a Church **2** (often capital) Also called: **Divine Liturgy** chiefly Eastern Churches the Eucharistic celebration **3** a particular order or form of public service laid down by a Church [c16 via Medieval Latin, from Greek leitourgia, from leitourgos minister, from leit- people + ergon work]

livable or **liveable** (ˈlɪvəbəl) adj **1** (of a room, house, etc) suitable for living in **2** worth living; tolerable **3** (foll by with) pleasant to live (with) > ˈlivableness, ˈliveableness, ˌlivaˈbility or ˌliveaˈbility n

live¹ (lɪv) vb (mainly intr) **1** to show the characteristics of life; be alive **2** to remain alive or in existence **3** to exist in a specified way: to live poorly **4** (usually foll by in or at) to reside or dwell: to live in London **5** (often foll by on) to continue or last: the pain still lives in her memory **6** (usually foll by by) to order one's life (according to a certain philosophy, religion, etc) **7** (foll by on, upon, or by) to support one's style of life; subsist: to live by writing **8** (foll by with) to endure the effects (of a crime, mistake, etc) **9** (foll by through) to experience and survive: he lived through the war **10** (tr) to pass or spend (one's life, etc) **11** to enjoy life to the full: he knows how to live **12** (tr) to put into practice in one's daily life, express: he lives religion every day **13** live and let live to refrain from interfering in others' lives; to be tolerant **14** where one lives US informal in one's sensitive or defenceless position ▷ See also **live down, live in, live out, live together, live up, live with** [Old

English *libban, lifian;* related to Old High German *libēn,* Old Norse *lifa*]

live² (laɪv) *adj* **1** *(prenominal)* showing the characteristics of life **2** *(usually prenominal)* of, relating to, or abounding in life: *the live weight of an animal* **3** *(usually prenominal)* of current interest; controversial: *a live issue* **4** actual: *a real live cowboy* **5** *informal* full of life and energy **6** (of a coal, ember, etc) glowing or burning **7** (esp of a volcano) not extinct **8** loaded or capable of exploding: *a live bomb* **9** *radio, television* transmitted or present at the time of performance, rather than being a recording: *a live show* **10** (of a record) **a** recorded in concert **b** recorded in one studio take, without overdubs or splicing **11** connected to a source of electric power: *a live circuit* **12** (esp of a colour or tone) brilliant or splendid **13** acoustically reverberant: *a live studio* **14** *sport* (of a ball) in play **15** (of rocks, ores, etc) not quarried or mined; native **16** being in a state of motion or transmitting power; positively connected to a driving member **17** *printing* **a** (of copy) not yet having been set into type **b** (of type that has been set) still in use ▷ *adv* **18** during, at, or in the form of a live performance: *the show went out live* [C16 from *on live* ALIVE]

live axle *n* an axle which rotates with the wheel; driving axle

live-bearer *n* a fish, esp a cyprinodont, that gives birth to living young

live birth *n* the birth of a living child. Compare **stillbirth**

live centre (laɪv) *n* a conically pointed rod mounted in the headstock of a lathe that locates and turns with the workpiece. Compare **dead centre** (sense 2)

-lived (-lɪvd) *adj* having or having had a life as specified: *short-lived*

live data *n* *computing* data that is still relevant

lived-in *adj* having a comfortable, natural, or homely appearance, as if subject to regular use or habitation

livedo (lɪˈviːdəʊ) *n, pl* **livedos** *med* a reddish discoloured patch on the skin [from Latin]

live down (lɪv) *vb* (*tr, adverb*) to withstand the effects of (a crime, mistake, etc) by waiting until others forget or forgive it

live in (lɪv) *vb* (*intr, adverb*) **1** (of an employee, as in a hospital or hotel) to dwell at one's place of employment ▷ *adj* **live-in 2** living in the place at which one works: *a live-in maid* **3** living with someone else in that person's home: *a live-in lover*

livelihood (ˈlaɪvlɪˌhʊd) *n* occupation or employment

live load (laɪv) *n* a variable weight on a structure, such as moving traffic on a bridge. Also called: **superload** Compare **dead load**

livelong (ˈlɪvˌlɒŋ) *adj chiefly poetic* **1** (of time) long or seemingly long, esp in a tedious way (esp in the phrase **all the livelong day**) **2** whole; entire ▷ *n* **3** *Brit* another name for **orpine**

lively (ˈlaɪvlɪ) *adj* **-lier, -liest 1** full of life or vigour **2** vivacious or animated, esp when in company **3** busy; eventful **4** characterized by mental or emotional intensity; vivid **5** having a striking effect on the mind or senses **6** refreshing: *a lively breeze* **7** springy or bouncy or encouraging springiness: *a lively ball* **8** (of a boat or ship) readily responsive to the helm ▷ *adv also* **livelily 9** in a brisk manner: *step lively* **10** look lively (*interjection*) make haste > **liveliness** *n*

liven (ˈlaɪvən) *vb* (usually foll by *up*) to make or become lively; enliven > **livener** *n*

live oak (laɪv) *n* a hard-wooded evergreen oak, *Quercus virginianus,* of S North America: used for shipbuilding

live out (lɪv) *vb* (*intr, adverb*) (of an employee, as in a hospital or hotel) to dwell away from one's place of employment

liver¹ (ˈlɪvə) *n* **1** a multilobed highly vascular reddish-brown glandular organ occupying most of the upper right part of the human abdominal

cavity immediately below the diaphragm. It secretes bile, stores glycogen, detoxifies certain poisons, and plays an important part in the metabolism of carbohydrates, proteins, and fat, helping to maintain a correct balance of nutrients. Related adj: **hepatic 2** the corresponding organ in animals **3** the liver of certain animals used as food **4** a reddish-brown colour, sometimes with a greyish tinge [Old English *lifer;* related to Old High German *lebrav,* Old Norse *lefr,* Greek *liparos* fat] > **liverless** *adj*

liver² (ˈlɪvə) *n* a person who lives in a specified way: *a fast liver*

liver extract *n* an extract of raw mammalian liver containing vitamin B₁₂: sometimes used to treat pernicious anaemia

liver fluke *n* any of various parasitic flatworms, esp *Fasciola hepatica,* that inhabit the bile ducts of sheep, cattle, etc, and have a complex life cycle: class *Digenea.* See also **trematode**

liveried (ˈlɪvərɪd) *adj* (esp of servants or footmen) wearing livery

liverish (ˈlɪvərɪʃ) *adj* **1** *informal* having a disorder of the liver **2** disagreeable; peevish: *I was liverish and nettled* > **liverishness** *n*

liver of sulphur *n* a mixture of potassium sulphides used as a fungicide and insecticide and in the treatment of skin diseases

liver opal *n* a form of opal having a reddish-brown coloration. Also called: **menilite**

Liverpolitan (ˌlɪvəˈpɒlɪtᵊn) *n* **1** a native or inhabitant of Liverpool ▷ *adj* **2** of or relating to Liverpool [C20 a supposedly status-enhancing adaptation of LIVERPUDLIAN from Liverpool + Greek *politēs* citizen]

Liverpool (ˈlɪvəˌpuːl) *n* **1** a city in NW England, in Liverpool unitary authority, Merseyside, on the Mersey estuary: second largest seaport in Great Britain; developed chiefly in the 17th century with the industrialization of S Lancashire; Liverpool University (1881) and John Moores University (1992). Pop: 469 017 (2001) **2** a unitary authority in NW England, in Merseyside. Pop: 441 800 (2003 est). Area: 113 sq km (44 sq miles)

Liverpudlian (ˌlɪvəˈpʌdlɪən) *n* **1** a native or inhabitant of Liverpool ▷ *adj* **2** of or relating to Liverpool [C19 from LIVERPOOL, with humorous alteration of *pool* to *puddle*]

liver salts *pl n* a preparation of mineral salts used to treat indigestion

liver sausage *or esp US* **liverwurst** (ˈlɪvəˌwɜːst) *n* a sausage made of or containing liver

liverwort (ˈlɪvəˌwɜːt) *n* any bryophyte plant of the phylum *Hepatophyta,* growing in wet places and resembling green seaweeds or leafy mosses. See also **scale moss** [late Old English *liferwyrt*]

livery¹ (ˈlɪvərɪ) *n, pl* **-eries 1** the identifying uniform, badge, etc, of a member of a guild or one of the servants of a feudal lord **2** a uniform worn by some menservants and chauffeurs **3** an individual or group that wears such a uniform **4** distinctive dress or outward appearance **5 a** the stabling, keeping, or hiring out of horses for money **b** (*as modifier*): *a livery horse* **6** at livery being kept in a livery stable **7** *legal history* an ancient method of conveying freehold land [C14 via Anglo-French from Old French *livrée* allocation, from *livrer* to hand over, from Latin *līberāre* to set free]

livery² (ˈlɪvərɪ) *adj* **1** of or resembling liver **2** another word for **liverish**

livery company *n Brit* one of the chartered companies of the City of London originating from the craft guilds

liveryman (ˈlɪvərɪmən) *n, pl* **-men 1** *Brit* a member of a livery company **2** a worker in a livery stable

livery stable *n* a stable where horses are accommodated and from which they may be hired out

lives (laɪvz) *n* the plural of **life**

live steam (laɪv) *n* steam supplied directly from a

boiler at full pressure, before it has performed any work

livestock (ˈlaɪvˌstɒk) *n* (*functioning as singular or plural*) cattle, horses, poultry, and similar animals kept for domestic use but not as pets, esp on a farm or ranch

live together (lɪv) *vb* (*intr, adverb*) (esp of an unmarried couple) to dwell in the same house or flat; cohabit

live trap (laɪv) *n* **1** a box constructed to trap an animal without injuring it ▷ *vb* **livetrap -traps, -trapping, -trapped 2** (*tr*) to catch (an animal) in such a box

live up (lɪv) *vb* **1** (*intr, adverb;* foll by *to*) to fulfil (an expectation, obligation, principle, etc) **2** live it up *informal* to enjoy oneself, esp flamboyantly

liveware (ˈlaɪvˌwɛə) *n* the programmers, systems analysts, operating staff, and other personnel working in a computer system. Compare **hardware** (sense 2), **software**

live wire (laɪv) *n* **1** *informal* an energetic or enterprising person **2** a wire carrying an electric current

live with (lɪv) *vb* (*tr, preposition*) to dwell with (a person to whom one is not married)

liveyer *or* **liveyere** (ˈlɪvjə) *n Canadian* (in Newfoundland) a full-time resident [altered from LIVER, a dweller]

livid (ˈlɪvɪd) *adj* **1** (of the skin) discoloured, as from a bruise or contusion **2** of a greyish tinge or colour: *livid pink* **3** *informal* angry or furious [C17 via French from Latin *līvidus,* from *līvēre* to be black and blue] > **lividly** *adv* > **lividness** *or* **liˈvidity** *n*

living (ˈlɪvɪŋ) *adj* **1 a** possessing life; not dead **b** (*as collective noun* preceded by *the*): *the living* **2** having the characteristics of life (used esp to distinguish organisms from nonliving matter) **3** currently in use or valid **4** seeming to be real **5** (of animals or plants) existing in the present age; extant. Compare **extinct** (sense 1) **6** *geology* another word for **live²** (sense 15) **7** presented by actors before a live audience **8** *(prenominal)* (*intensifier*): *the living daylights* ▷ *n* **9** the condition of being alive **10** the manner in which one conducts one's life **11** the means, esp the financial means, whereby one lives **12** *Church of England* another term for **benefice 13** (*modifier*) of, involving, or characteristic of everyday life: *living area* **14** (*modifier*) of or involving those now alive (esp in the phrase **living memory**)

living bandage *n* a method of treating severe burns or other skin injuries in which cultured cells grown from a sample of the patient's own skin are applied to the wound in order to stimulate new cell growth and avoid problems of graft rejection

living death *n* a life or lengthy experience of constant misery

living fossil *n* an animal or plant, such as the coelacanth and ginkgo, belonging to a group most of whose members are extinct

living history *n* any of various activities involving the re-enactment of historical events or the recreation of living conditions of the past

living picture *n* another term for **tableau vivant**

living room *n* a room in a private house or flat used for relaxation and entertainment of guests

Livingston (ˈlɪvɪŋstən) *n* a town in SE Scotland, the administrative centre of West Lothian: founded as a new town in 1962. Pop: 50 826 (2001)

Livingstone daisy *n* a gardener's name for various species of *Mesembryanthemum,* especially *M. criniflorum,* grown as garden annuals (though several are perennial) for their brightly coloured showy flowers: family *Aizoaceae* [C20 of unknown origin]

living wage *n* a wage adequate to permit a wage earner to live and support a family in reasonable comfort

living will *n* a document stating that if its author becomes terminally ill, his or her life should not be prolonged by artificial means, such as a life-support machine

Livonia (lɪˈvəʊnɪə) *n* **1** a former Russian province on the Baltic, north of Lithuania: became Russian in 1721; divided between Estonia and Latvia in 1918 **2** a city in SE Michigan, west of Detroit. Pop: 99 487 (2003 est)

Livonian (lɪˈvəʊnɪən) *adj* **1** of or relating to Livonia, a former Russian Baltic province, or its inhabitants ▷ *n* **2** a native or inhabitant of Livonia

Livorno (*Italian* liˈvorno) *n* a port in W central Italy, in Tuscany on the Ligurian Sea: shipyards; oil-refining. Pop: 156 274 (2001). English name: **Leghorn**

livraison *French* (livrɛzõ) *n rare* one of the numbers of a book published in parts [literally: delivery (of goods)]

livre (ˈliːvrə; *French* livrə) *n* a former French unit of money of account, equal to 1 pound of silver [c16 via Old French from Latin *lībra* the Roman pound]

lixiviate (lɪkˈsɪvɪˌeɪt) *vb* (*tr*) *chem* a less common word for **leach¹** (senses 1, 2) [c17 from LIXIVIUM] > **lixˈivial** *adj* > **lixˌiviˈation** *n*

lixivium (lɪkˈsɪvɪəm) *n, pl* **- iums** *or* **-ia** (-ɪə) **1** the alkaline solution obtained by leaching wood ash with water; lye **2** any solution obtained by leaching [c17 from Late Latin, from *lix* lye]

lizard (ˈlɪzəd) *n* **1** any reptile of the suborder *Lacertilia* (or *Sauria*), esp those of the family *Lacertidae* (Old World lizards), typically having an elongated body, four limbs, and a long tail: includes the geckos, iguanas, chameleons, monitors, and slow worms. Related adjs: **lacertilian, saurian 2 a** leather made from the skin of such an animal **b** (*as modifier*): *a lizard handbag* [c14 via Old French from Latin *lacerta*]

Lizard (ˈlɪzəd) *n* **the** a promontory in SW England, in SW Cornwall: the southernmost point in Great Britain. Also called: **Lizard Head, Lizard Peninsula**

lizard fish *n* any small teleost fish of the family *Synodontidae*, having a slender body and a lizard-like head and living at the bottom of warm seas

lizard orchid *n* a European orchid, *Himantoglossum hircinum*, rare in Britain, having a spike of grey-green flowers smelling of goats

LJ *Brit* ▷ *abbreviation for* Lord Justice

Ljubljana (luˈbljɑːnə) *n* the capital of Slovenia: capital of Illyria (1816–49); part of Yugoslavia (1918–91); university (1595). Pop: 265 881 (2002). German name: **Laibach**

lk *the internet domain name for* Sri Lanka

LL *abbreviation for* **1** Late Latin **2** Low Latin **3** Lord Lieutenant

ll. *abbreviation for* lines (of written matter)

llama (ˈlɑːmə) *n* **1** a domesticated South American cud-chewing mammal, *Lama glama* (or *L. peruana*), that is used as a beast of burden and is valued for its hair, flesh, and hide: family *Camelidae* (camels) **2** the cloth made from the wool of this animal **3** any other animal of the genus *Lama*. See **alpaca¹**, **guanaco** [c17 via Spanish from Quechua]

Llandaff (ˈlændəf, -dæf) *or* **Llandaf** (*Welsh* hlanˈdav) *n* a town in SE Wales, now a suburb of Cardiff; the oldest bishopric in Wales (6th century)

Llandudno (θlænˈdɪdnəʊ, lænˈdɪdnəʊ; *Welsh* hlanˈdɪdnɔ) *n* a town and resort in NW Wales, in Conwy county borough on the Irish Sea. Pop: 14 872 (2001)

Llanelli *or* **Llanelly** (θlæˈnɛθlɪ; *Welsh* hlaˈnɛhliː) *n* an industrial town in S Wales, in SE Carmarthenshire on an inlet of Carmarthen Bay. Pop: 46 357 (2001)

Llanfairpwllgwyngyll (*Welsh* hlanˌvaɪrpʊhlˈgwɪŋɪhl), **Llanfairpwll** *or* **Llanfair P. G.** *n* a village in NW Wales, in SE Anglesey: reputed to be the longest place name in Great Britain when unabbreviated; means: St Mary's Church in the hollow of the white hazel near the rapid whirlpool of Llandysilio of the red cave. Full name: **Llanfairpwllgwyngyllgogerychwyrndrobwllllantysiliogogogoch** (*Welsh* hlanˌvaɪrpʊhlˈgwɪŋɪhlgɔˈgɛrəxwɪrnˈdrɔbʊhlˈhlantəˈsɪljɔˈgɔgɔˈgɔx)

Llangollen (*Welsh* hlanˈgɔhlɛn) *n* a town in NE Wales, in Denbighshire on the River Dee: International Musical Eisteddfod held annually since 1946. Pop: 2930 (2001)

llano (ˈlɑːnəʊ; *Spanish* ˈʎano) *n, pl* **-nos** (-nəʊz; *Spanish* -nos) an extensive grassy treeless plain, esp in South America [c17 Spanish, from Latin *plānum* level ground]

Llano Estacado (ˈlɑːnəʊ ˌɛstəˈkɑːdəʊ) *n* the S part of the Great Plains of the US, extending over W Texas and E New Mexico: oil and natural gas resources. Chief towns: Lubbock and Amarillo. Area: 83 700 sq km (30 000 sq miles). Also called: **Staked Plain**

LLB *abbreviation for* Bachelor of Laws [Latin: *Legum Baccalaureus*]

LLD *abbreviation for* Doctor of Laws [Latin: *Legum Doctor*]

Lleida (ˈʎeiðə) *n* the Catalan name for **Lérida**

Lleyn Peninsula (*Welsh* hliːn) *n* a peninsula in NW Wales between Cardigan Bay and Caernarvon Bay

LLM *abbreviation for* Master of Laws [Latin: *Legum Magister*]

Lloyd's (lɔɪdz) *n* an association of London underwriters, set up in the late 17th century. Originally concerned exclusively with marine insurance and a shipping information service, it now subscribes a variety of insurance policies and publishes a daily list (**Lloyd's List**) of shipping data and news [c17 named after Edward Lloyd (died ?1726) at whose coffee house in London the underwriters originally carried on their business]

Lloyd's Register *n* **1** a society formed in 1760 by a group of merchants operating at Lloyd's coffee house to draw up rules concerning the construction of merchant ships **2** an annual publication giving details of all ships that have been built according to the various classifications established by this society ▷ In full: **Lloyd's Register of Shipping**

lm *symbol for* lumen

LMS (in Britain) *abbreviation for* local management of schools: the system of making each school responsible for controlling its total budget, after the budget has been calculated by the Local Education Authority

LMVD (in New Zealand) *abbreviation for* Licensed Motor Vehicle Dealer

ln *abbreviation for* (natural) logarithm

LNG *abbreviation for* **liquefied natural gas**

lo (ləʊ) *interj* look! see! (now often in the phrase **lo and behold**) [Old English *lā*]

LO *text messaging abbreviation for* hello

loach (ləʊtʃ) *n* any carplike freshwater cyprinoid fish of the family *Cobitidae*, of Eurasia and Africa, having a long narrow body with barbels around the mouth [c14 from Old French *loche*, of obscure origin]

load (ləʊd) *n* **1** something to be borne or conveyed; weight **2 a** the usual amount borne or conveyed **b** (*in combination*): *a carload* **3** something that weighs down, oppresses, or burdens: *that's a load off my mind* **4** a single charge of a firearm **5** the weight that is carried by a structure. See also **dead load, live load 6** *electrical engineering, electronics* **a** a device that receives or dissipates the power from an amplifier, oscillator, generator, or some other source of signals **b** the power delivered by a machine, generator, circuit, etc **7** the force acting on a component in a mechanism or structure **8** the resistance overcome by an engine or motor when it is driving a machine, etc **9** an external force applied to a component or mechanism **10** a load of *informal* a quantity of: *a load of nonsense* **11 get a load of** *informal* pay attention to **12 have a load on** *US and Canadian slang* to be intoxicated **13 shoot one's load** *slang* (of a man) to ejaculate at orgasm ▷ *vb* (*mainly tr*) **14** (*also intr*) to place or receive (cargo, goods, etc)

upon (a ship, lorry, etc) **15** to burden or oppress **16** to supply or beset (someone) with in abundance or overwhelmingly: *they loaded her with gifts* **17** to cause to be biased: *to load a question* **18** (*also intr*) to put an ammunition charge into (a firearm) **19** *photog* to position (a film, cartridge, or plate) in (a camera) **20** to weight or bias (a roulette wheel, dice, etc) **21** *insurance* to increase (a premium) to cover expenses, etc **22** to draw power from (an electrical device, such as a generator) **23** to add material of high atomic number to (concrete) to increase its effectiveness as a radiation shield **24** to increase the power output of (an electric circuit) **25** to increase the work required from (an engine or motor) **26** to apply force to (a mechanism or component) **27** *computing* to transfer (a program) to a memory **28 load the dice a** to add weights to dice in order to bias them **b** to arrange to have a favourable or unfavourable position ▷ See also **loads** [Old English *lād* course; in meaning, influenced by LADE¹; related to LEAD¹]

load displacement *n nautical* the total weight of a cargo vessel loaded so that its waterline reaches the summer load line

loaded (ˈləʊdɪd) *adj* **1** carrying a load **2** (of dice, a roulette wheel, etc) weighted or otherwise biased **3** (of a question or statement) containing a hidden trap or implication **4** charged with ammunition **5** (of concrete) containing heavy metals, esp iron or lead, for use in making radiation shields **6** *slang* wealthy **7** (*postpositive*) *slang, chiefly US and Canadian* **a** drunk **b** drugged; influenced by drugs

loader (ˈləʊdə) *n* **1** a person who loads a gun or other firearm **2** (*in combination*) designating a firearm or machine loaded in a particular way: *breech-loader; top-loader* **3** *computing* a system program that takes a program in a form close to machine code and places it into a memory for execution

load factor *n* **1** the ratio of the average electric load to the peak load over a period of time **2** *aeronautics* **a** the ratio of a given external load to the weight of an aircraft **b** the actual payload carried by an aircraft as a percentage of its maximum payload

loading (ˈləʊdɪŋ) *n* **1** a load or burden; weight **2** the addition of an inductance to electrical equipment, such as a transmission line or aerial, to improve its performance. See **loading coil 3** an addition to an insurance premium to cover expenses, provide a safer profit margin, etc **4** the ratio of the gross weight of an aircraft to its engine power (**power loading**), wing area (**wing loading**), or some other parameter, or of the gross weight of a helicopter to its rotor disc area (**disc loading**) **5** *psychol* the correlation of a factor, such as a personality trait, with a performance score derived from a psychological test **6** material, such as china clay or size, added to paper, textiles, or similar materials to produce a smooth surface, increase weight, etc **7** *Austral and NZ* a payment made in addition to a basic wage or salary to reward special skills, compensate for unfavourable conditions, etc

loading coil *n* an inductance coil inserted at regular intervals and in series with the conductors of a transmission line in order to improve its characteristics

load line *n nautical* a pattern of lines painted on the hull of a ship, approximately midway between the bow and the stern, indicating the various levels that the waterline should reach if the ship is properly loaded under given circumstances

load-lugger *n* a motor vehicle that is capable of carrying a load rather than, or as well as, passengers

loads (ləʊdz) *informal* ▷ *pl n* **1** (*often foll by of*) a lot: *loads to eat* ▷ *adv* **2** (*intensifier*): *loads better; thanks loads*

load shedding *n* the act or practice of temporarily reducing the supply of electricity to an area to avoid overloading the generators

loadspace ('ləʊd,speɪs) *n* the area in a motor vehicle where a load can be carried

loadstar ('ləʊd,stɑː) *n* a variant spelling of lodestar

loadstone ('ləʊd,stəʊn) *n* a variant spelling of lodestone

loaf¹ (ləʊf) *n, pl* **loaves** (ləʊvz) **1** a shaped mass of baked bread **2** any shaped or moulded mass of food, such as cooked meat **3** *slang* the head; *sense: use your loaf!* [Old English *hlāf*; related to Old High German *hleib* bread, Old Norse *hleifr*, Latin *libum* cake]

loaf² (ləʊf) *vb* **1** (*intr*) to loiter or lounge around in an idle way **2** (*tr; foll by away*) to spend (time) idly: *he loafed away his life* [C19 perhaps back formation from LOAFER]

loafer ('ləʊfə) *n* **1** a person who avoids work; idler **2** a moccasin-like shoe for casual wear [C19 perhaps from German *Landläufer* vagabond]

loaf sugar *n* (esp formerly) **1** a large conical mass of hard refined sugar; sugar loaf **2** small cube-shaped lumps of this, the form in which it was often sold

loam (ləʊm) *n* **1** rich soil consisting of a mixture of sand, clay, and decaying organic material **2** a paste of clay and sand used for making moulds in a foundry, plastering walls, etc ▷ *vb* **3** (*tr*) to cover, treat, or fill with loam [Old English *lām*; related to Old Swedish *lēmo* clay, Old High German *leimo*] > 'loamy *adj* > 'loaminess *n*

loan¹ (ləʊn) *n* **1** the act of lending: *the loan of a car* **2 a** property lent, esp money lent at interest for a period of time **b** (*as modifier*): *loan holder* **3** the adoption by speakers of one language of a form current in another language **4** short for **loan word 5 on loan a** lent out; borrowed **b** (esp of personnel) transferred from a regular post to a temporary one elsewhere ▷ *vb* **6** to lend (something, esp money) [C13 *loon, lan*, from Old Norse *lān*; related to Old English *læn* loan; compare German *Lehen* fief, *Lohn* wages] > 'loanable *adj* > 'loaner *n*

loan² (ləʊn), **loaning** ('ləʊnɪŋ) *n Scot and northern English dialect* **1** a lane **2** a place where cows are milked [Old English *lone*, variant of LANE¹]

loanback ('ləʊn,bæk) *n* **1** a facility offered by some life-assurance companies in which an individual can borrow from his pension fund ▷ *vb* **loan back 2** to make use of this facility

loan collection *n* a number of works of art lent by their owners for a temporary public exhibition

Loan Council *n* (in Australia) a statutory body that controls borrowing by the states

Loanda (ləʊ'ændə) *n* a variant spelling of **Luanda**

loan shark *n informal* a person who lends funds at illegal or exorbitant rates of interest

loan translation *n* the adoption by one language of a phrase or compound word whose components are literal translations of the components of a corresponding phrase or compound in a foreign language: *English "superman" is a loan translation from German "Übermensch".* Also called: **calque**

loan word *n* a word adopted, often with some modification of its form, from one language into another

loath *or* **loth** (ləʊθ) *adj* **1** (usually foll by *to*) reluctant or unwilling **2 nothing loath** willing [Old English *lāth* (in the sense: hostile); related to Old Norse *leithr*] > 'loathness *or* 'lothness *n*

loathe (ləʊð) *vb* (*tr*) to feel strong hatred or disgust for [Old English *lāthian*, from LOATH] > 'loather *n*

loathing ('ləʊðɪŋ) *n* abhorrence; disgust > 'loathingly *adv*

loathly¹ ('ləʊðlɪ) *adv* with reluctance; unwillingly

loathly² ('ləʊðlɪ) *adj* an archaic word for **loathsome**

loathsome ('ləʊðsəm) *adj* causing loathing; abhorrent > 'loathsomely *adv* > 'loathsomeness *n*

loaves (ləʊvz) *n* the plural of **loaf¹**

lob¹ (lɒb) *sport* ▷ *n* **1** a ball struck in a high arc **2** *cricket* a ball bowled in a slow high arc ▷ *vb* **lobs, lobbing, lobbed 3** to hit or kick (a ball) in a high arc **4** *informal* to throw, esp in a high arc [C14 probably of Low German origin, originally in the sense: something dangling; compare Middle Low German *lobbe* hanging lower lip, Old English *loppe* spider]

lob² (lɒb) *n* short for **lobworm** [C17 (in the sense: pendulous object): related to LOB¹]

lobar ('ləʊbə) *adj* of, relating to, or affecting a lobe

lobate ('ləʊbeɪt) *or* **lobated** *adj* **1** having or resembling lobes **2** (of birds) having separate toes that are each fringed with a weblike lobe > 'lobately *adv*

lobby ('lɒbɪ) *n, pl* **-bies 1** a room or corridor used as an entrance hall, vestibule, etc **2** *chiefly Brit* a hall in a legislative building used for meetings between the legislators and members of the public **3** Also called: **division lobby** *chiefly Brit* one of two corridors in a legislative building in which members vote **4** a group of persons who attempt to influence legislators on behalf of a particular interest ▷ *vb* **-bies, -bying, -bied 5** to attempt to influence (legislators, etc) in the formulation of policy **6** (*intr*) to act in the manner of a lobbyist **7** (*tr*) to apply pressure or influence for the passage of (a bill, etc) [C16 from Medieval Latin *lobia* portico, from Old High German *lauba* arbor, from *laub* leaf] > 'lobbyer *n*

lobbyist ('lɒbɪɪst) *n* a person employed by a particular interest to lobby > 'lobby,ism *n*

lobe (ləʊb) *n* **1** any rounded projection forming part of a larger structure **2** any of the subdivisions of a bodily organ or part, delineated by shape or connective tissue **3** short for **ear lobe 4** any of the loops that form part of the graphic representation in cylindrical coordinates of the radiation pattern of a transmitting aerial. Compare **radiation pattern 5** any of the parts, not entirely separate from each other, into which a flattened plant part, such as a leaf, is divided [C16 from Late Latin *lobus*, from Greek *lobos* lobe of the ear or of the liver]

lobectomy (ləʊ'bɛktəmɪ) *n, pl* **-mies** surgical removal of a lobe from any organ or gland in the body, esp removal of tissue from the frontal lobe of the brain in an attempt to alleviate mental disorder

lobelia (ləʊ'biːlɪə) *n* any plant of the campanulaceous genus *Lobelia*, having red, blue, white, or yellow five-lobed flowers with the three lower lobes forming a lip [C18 from New Latin, named after Matthias de *Lobel* (1538–1616), Flemish botanist]

lobeline ('ləʊbə,liːn) *n* a crystalline alkaloid extracted from the seeds of the Indian tobacco plant, used as a smoking deterrent and respiratory stimulant [C19 from LOBELIA]

Lobito (*Portuguese* lu'βitu) *n* the chief port in Angola, in the west on **Lobito Bay**: terminus of the railway through Benguela to Mozambique. Pop: 70 000 (latest est)

loblolly ('lɒb,lɒlɪ) *n, pl* **-lies 1** a southern US pine tree, *Pinus taeda*, with bright red-brown bark, green needle-like leaves, and reddish-brown cones **2** *nautical* a thick gruel **3** *US dialect* a mire; mudhole [C16 perhaps from dialect *lob* to boil + obsolete dialect *lolly* thick soup]

loblolly boy *or* **man** *n Brit naval* (formerly) a boy or man acting as a medical orderly on board ship [C18 from LOBLOLLY sense 2, applied to a ship's doctor's medicines]

lobo ('ləʊbəʊ) *n, pl* **-bos** *Western US* another name for **timber wolf** [Spanish, from Latin *lupus* wolf]

lobola *or* **lobolo** (lɔː'bɔːlə, lə'bəʊ-) *n* (in southern Africa) an African custom by which a bridegroom's family makes a payment in cattle or cash to the bride's family shortly before the marriage [from Nguni *ukulobola* to give the bride price]

lobotomized *or* **lobotomised** (ləʊ'bɒtəmaɪzd) *adj informal* apathetic, sluggish, and zombie-like [C20 from *lobotomize* (chiefly US) to perform a lobotomy on]

lobotomy (ləʊ'bɒtəmɪ) *n, pl* **-mies 1** surgical incision into a lobe of any organ **2** Also called: **prefrontal leucotomy** surgical interruption of one or more nerve tracts in the frontal lobe of the brain: used in the treatment of intractable mental disorders [C20 from LOBE + -TOMY]

lobscouse ('lɒb,skaʊs) *n* a sailor's stew of meat, vegetables, and hardtack [C18 perhaps from dialect *lob* to boil + *scouse*, broth; compare LOBLOLLY]

lobster ('lɒbstə) *n, pl* **-sters** *or* **-ster 1** any of several large marine decapod crustaceans of the genus *Homarus*, esp *H. vulgaris*, occurring on rocky shores and having the first pair of limbs modified as large pincers **2** any of several similar crustaceans, esp the spiny lobster **3** the flesh of any of these crustaceans, eaten as a delicacy [Old English *loppestre*, from *loppe* spider]

lobster moth *n* a large sombre-hued prominent moth, *Stauropus fagi*, that when at rest resembles dead leaves. The modified thoracic legs of the larva, carried curled over its body, look like a lobster's claw

lobster Newburg ('njuː'bɜːg) *n* lobster cooked in a rich cream sauce flavoured with sherry

lobster pot *or* **trap** *n* a round basket or trap made of open slats used to catch lobsters

lobster thermidor ('θɜːmɪ,dɔː) *n* a dish of cooked lobster, replaced in its shell with a creamy cheese sauce

lobule ('lɒbjuːl) *n* a small lobe or a subdivision of a lobe [C17 from New Latin *lobulus*, from Late Latin *lobus* LOBE] > lobular ('lɒbjʊlə), lobulate ('lɒbjʊlɪt), 'lobu,lated *or* 'lobulose *adj* > ,lobu'lation *n*

lobworm ('lɒb,wɜːm) *n* **1** another name for **lugworm** Sometimes shortened to: **lob 2** a large earthworm used as bait in fishing [C17 from obsolete *lob* lump + WORM]

local ('ləʊkəl) *adj* **1** characteristic of or associated with a particular locality or area **2** of, concerned with, or relating to a particular place or point in space **3** *med* of, affecting, or confined to a limited area or part. Compare **general** (sense 10), **systemic** (sense 2) **4** (of a train, bus, etc) stopping at all stations or stops ▷ *n* **5** a train, bus, etc, that stops at all stations or stops **6** an inhabitant of a specified locality **7** *Brit informal* a pub close to one's home or place of work **8** *med* short for **local anaesthetic 9** *US and Canadian* an item of local interest in a newspaper **10** *US and Canadian* a local or regional branch of an association **11** *Canadian* a telephone extension [C15 via Old French from Late Latin *locālis*, from Latin *locus* place, LOCUS] > 'localness *n*

local anaesthetic *n med* a drug that produces local anaesthesia. Often shortened to: **local** See **anaesthesia** (sense 2)

local area network *n computing* the linking of a number of different devices by cable within a system. Abbreviation: **LAN**

local authority *n Brit and NZ* the governing body of a county, district, etc. US equivalent: **local government**

local colour *n* the characteristic features or atmosphere of a place or time

locale (ləʊ'kɑːl) *n* a place or area, esp with reference to events connected with it [C18 from French *local* (n use of adj); see LOCAL]

local examinations *pl n* any of various examinations, such as the GCE, set by university boards and conducted in local centres, schools, etc

local government *n* **1** government of the affairs of counties, towns, etc, by locally elected political bodies **2** the US equivalent of **local authority**

Local Group *n astronomy* the cluster of galaxies to which our galaxy and the Andromeda Galaxy belong

localism ('ləʊkə,lɪzəm) *n* **1** a pronunciation,

phrase, etc, peculiar to a particular locality **2** another word for **provincialism**. > 'localist *n* > ,local'istic *adj*

locality (ləʊˈkælɪtɪ) *n, pl* -ties **1** a neighbourhood or area **2** the site or scene of an event **3** the fact or condition of having a location or position in space

localize *or* **localise** ('ləʊkə,laɪz) *vb* **1** to make or become local in attitude, behaviour, etc **2** (*tr*) to restrict or confine (something) to a particular area or part **3** (*tr*) to assign or ascribe to a particular region > 'local,izable *or* 'local,isable *adj* > ,locali'zation *or* ,locali'sation *n* > 'local,izer *or* 'local,iser *n*

local loan *n* (in Britain) a loan issued by a local government authority

locally ('ləʊkəlɪ) *adv* within a particular area or place

local option *n* (esp in Scotland, New Zealand, and the US) the privilege of a municipality, county, etc, to determine by referendum whether a particular activity, esp the sale of liquor, shall be permitted there

local oscillator *n electronics* the oscillator in a superheterodyne receiver whose output frequency is mixed with the incoming modulated radio-frequency carrier signal to produce the required intermediate frequency

local sign *n physiol* the information from a receptor in the eye or the skin signifying respectively a direction in space or a given point on the body

local time *n* the time in a particular region or area expressed with reference to the meridian passing through it

Locarno (*Italian* loˈkarno) *n* a town in S Switzerland, in Ticino canton at the N end of Lake Maggiore: tourist resort. Pop: 14 561 (2000)

Locarno Pact (ləʊˈkɑːnəʊ) *n* a series of treaties, concluded in Locarno, Switzerland in 1925, between Germany, France, Belgium, the United Kingdom, Italy, Poland, and Czechoslovakia. The principal treaty, between Germany, France, and Belgium, concerned the maintenance of their existing frontiers, settlement of disputes by arbitration without resort to force, and the demilitarization of the Rhineland. This treaty was guaranteed by the United Kingdom and Italy but was violated when Germany occupied the Rhineland in 1936. Also called: **Treaties of Locarno**

locate (ləʊˈkeɪt) *vb* **1** (*tr*) to discover the position, situation, or whereabouts of; find **2** (*tr; often passive*) to situate or place: *located on the edge of the city* **3** (*intr*) to become established or settled > lo'catable *adj* > lo'cater *n*

location (ləʊˈkeɪʃən) *n* **1** a site or position; situation **2** the act or process of locating or the state of being located **3** a place outside a studio where filming is done: *shot on location* **4** (in South Africa) **a** a Black African or Coloured township, usually located near a small town. See also **township** (sense 4) **b** (formerly) an African tribal reserve **5** *computing* a position in a memory capable of holding a unit of information, such as a word, and identified by its address **6** *Roman and Scots law* the letting out on hire of a chattel or of personal services [c16 from Latin *locātiō*, from *locāre* to place]

locative ('lɒkətɪv) *grammar* ▷ *adj* **1** (of a word or phrase) indicating place or direction **2** denoting a case of nouns, etc, that refers to the place at which the action described by the verb occurs ▷ *n* **3 a** the locative case **b** a word or speech element in this case [c19 LOCATE + -IVE, on the model of *vocative*]

loc. cit. (in textual annotation) *abbreviation for* loco citato

loch (lɒx, lɒk) *n* **1** a Scot word for **lake**¹ **2** Also called: **sea loch** a long narrow bay or arm of the sea in Scotland [c14 from Gaelic]

lochan ('lɒxən, 'lɒkᵊn) *n Scot* a small inland loch [c18 Gaelic, diminutive of LOCH]

lochia ('lɒkɪə) *n* a vaginal discharge of cellular debris, mucus, and blood following childbirth [c17 New Latin from Greek *lokhia*, from *lokhios*, from *lokhos* childbirth] > 'lochial *adj*

loci ('ləʊsaɪ) *n* the plural of **locus**

lock¹ (lɒk) *n* **1** a device fitted to a gate, door, drawer, lid, etc, to keep it firmly closed and often to prevent access by unauthorized persons **2** a similar device attached to a machine, vehicle, etc, to prevent use by unauthorized persons: *a steering lock* **3 a** a section of a canal or river that may be closed off by gates to control the water level and the raising and lowering of vessels that pass through it **b** (*as modifier*): *a lock gate* **4** the jamming, fastening, or locking together of parts **5** *Brit* the extent to which a vehicle's front wheels will turn to the right or left: *this car has a good lock* **6** a mechanism that detonates the charge of a gun **7** *US and Canadian informal* a person or thing that is certain to win or to succeed: *she is a lock for the Academy Award* **8** *lock, stock, and barrel* completely; entirely **9** any wrestling hold in which a wrestler seizes a part of his opponent's body and twists it or otherwise exerts pressure upon it **10** Also called: **lock forward** *rugby* either of two players who make up the second line of the scrum and apply weight to the forwards in the front line **11** a gas bubble in a hydraulic system or a liquid bubble in a pneumatic system that stops or interferes with the fluid flow in a pipe, capillary, etc: *an air lock* ▷ *vb* **12** to fasten (a door, gate, etc) or (of a door, etc) to become fastened with a lock, bolt, etc, so as to prevent entry or exit **13** (*tr*) to secure (a building) by locking all doors, windows, etc **14** to fix or become fixed together securely or inextricably **15** to become or cause to become rigid or immovable: *the front wheels of the car locked* **16** (when *tr, often passive*) to clasp or entangle (someone or each other) in a struggle or embrace **17** (*tr*) to furnish (a canal) with locks **18** (*tr*) to move (a vessel) through a system of locks **20** *lock horns* (esp of two equally matched opponents) to become engaged in argument or battle **21** *lock the stable door after the horse has bolted or been stolen* to take precautions after harm has been done ▷ See also **lock on to, lock out, lock up** [Old English *loc*; related to Old Norse *lok*] > 'lockable *adj*

lock² (lɒk) *n* **1** a strand, curl, or cluster of hair **2** a tuft or wisp of wool, cotton, etc **3** (*plural*) *chiefly literary* hair, esp when curly or fine [Old English *loc*; related to Old Frisian *lok*, Old Norse *lokkr* lock of wool]

lockage ('lɒkɪdʒ) *n* **1** a system of locks in a canal **2** passage through a lock or the fee charged for such passage

lockdown ('lɒk,daʊn) *n US* a security measure in which those inside a building such as a prison, school, or hospital are required to remain confined in it for a time: *many schools remained under lockdown yesterday*

locked-in syndrome *n* a condition in which a person is conscious but unable to move any part of the body except the eyes: results from damage to the brainstem

locker ('lɒkə) *n* **1 a** a small compartment or drawer that may be locked, as one of several in a gymnasium, etc, for clothes and valuables **b** (*as modifier*): *a locker room* **2** a person or thing that locks **3** *US and Canadian* a refrigerated compartment for keeping frozen foods, esp one rented in an establishment

Lockerbie ('lɒkəbɪ) *n* a town in SW Scotland, in Dumfries and Galloway: scene (1988) of the UK's worst air disaster when a jumbo jet was brought down by a terrorist bomb, killing 270 people, including eleven residents of the town

locket ('lɒkɪt) *n* a small ornamental case, usually on a necklace or chain, that holds a picture, keepsake, etc [c17 from French *loquet* latch, diminutive of *loc* LOCK¹]

lockfast ('lɒk,fɑːst) *adj Scot* securely fastened

with a lock

lock-in *n* an illegal session of selling alcohol in a bar after the time when it should, by law, be closed

lockjaw ('lɒk,dʒɔː) *n pathol* a nontechnical name for **trismus** and (often) **tetanus**

locknut ('lɒk,nʌt) *n* **1** a supplementary nut screwed down upon a primary nut to prevent it from shaking loose **2** a threaded nut having a feature, such as a nylon insert, to prevent it from shaking loose

lock on to *vb* (*intr, adverb + preposition*) (of a radar beam) to automatically follow (a target)

lock out *vb* (*tr, adverb*) **1** to prevent from entering by locking a door **2** to prevent (employees) from working during an industrial dispute, as by closing a factory ▷ *n* **lockout 3** the closing of a place of employment by an employer, in order to bring pressure on employees to agree to terms

locksmith ('lɒk,smɪθ) *n* a person who makes or repairs locks > 'lock,smithery *or* 'lock,smithing *n*

lockstep ('lɒk,stɛp) *n* **1** a method of marching in step such that the men follow one another as closely as possible **2** *chiefly US and Canadian* a standard procedure that is closely, often mindlessly, followed **3** *in lockstep with* progressing at exactly the same speed and in the same direction as other people or things, esp as a matter of course rather than by choice

lock stitch *n* a sewing-machine stitch in which the top thread interlocks with the bobbin thread

lock up *vb* (*adverb*) **1** (*tr*) Also: **lock in, lock away** to imprison or confine **2** to lock or secure the doors, windows, etc, of (a building) **3** (*tr*) to keep or store securely: *secrets locked up in history* **4** (*tr*) to invest (funds) so that conversion into cash is difficult **5** *printing* to secure (type, etc) in a chase or in the bed of the printing machine by tightening the quoins ▷ *n* **lockup 6** the action or time of locking up **7** a jail or block of cells **8** *Brit* a small shop with no attached quarters for the owner or shopkeeper **9** *Brit* a garage or storage place separate from the main premises **10** *stock exchange* an investment that is intended to be held for a relatively long period **11** *printing* the pages of type held in a chase by the positioning of quoins ▷ *adj* **12** *lock-up Brit and NZ* (of premises) without living accommodation: *a lock-up shop*

Lockwood home ('lɒk,wʊd) *n trademark NZ* a house built of timber planks that lock together without the use of nails

loco¹ ('ləʊkəʊ) *n informal* short for **locomotive**

loco² ('ləʊkəʊ) *adj* **1** *slang, chiefly US* insane **2** (of an animal) affected with loco disease ▷ *n, pl* -cos **3** short for **locoweed** ▷ *vb* (*tr*) **4** to poison with locoweed **5** *US slang* to make insane [c19 via Mexican Spanish from Spanish: crazy]

loco³ ('ləʊkəʊ) *adj* denoting a price for goods, esp goods to be exported, that are in a place specified or known, the buyer being responsible for all transport charges from that place: *loco Bristol; a loco price* [c20 from Latin *locō* from a place]

loco citato ('lɒkəʊ sɪ'tɑːtəʊ) (in the place or passage quoted. Abbreviations: **loc. cit, lc** [Latin: in the place cited]

loco disease *or* **poisoning** *n* a disease of cattle, sheep, and horses characterized by paralysis and faulty vision, caused by ingestion of locoweed

locoism ('ləʊkəʊ,ɪzəm) *n* another word for **loco disease**

locoman ('ləʊkəʊmən) *n, pl* -men *Brit informal* a railwayman, esp an engine-driver

locomotion (,ləʊkə'məʊʃən) *n* the act, fact, ability, or power of moving [c17 from Latin *locō* from a place, ablative of *locus* place + MOTION]

locomotive (,ləʊkə'məʊtɪv) *n* **1 a** Also called: **locomotive engine** a self-propelled engine driven by steam, electricity, or diesel power and used for drawing trains along railway tracks **b** (*as modifier*): *a locomotive shed; a locomotive works* ▷ *adj* **2** of or relating to locomotion **3** moving or able to move, as by self-propulsion > ,loco'motively *adv*

> ˌloco'motiveness *n*

locomotor (ˌləʊkə'məʊtə) *adj* of or relating to locomotion [c19 from Latin *locō* from a place, ablative of *locus* place + MOTOR (mover)]

locomotor ataxia *n pathol* another name for **tabes dorsalis**

locoweed ('ləʊkəʊˌwiːd) *n* any of several perennial leguminous plants of the genera *Oxytropis* and *Astragalus* of W North America that cause loco disease in horses, cattle, and sheep

Locrian or **Lokrian** ('ləʊkrɪən, 'lɒk-) *adj* **1** of or relating to Locris, an ancient region of central Greece, or its inhabitants ▷ *n* **2** a native or inhabitant of Locris

Locris or **Lokris** ('ləʊkrɪs, 'lɒk-) *n* an ancient region of central Greece

locular ('lɒkjʊlə) or **loculate** ('lɒkjʊˌleɪt, -lɪt) *adj biology* divided into compartments by septa: *the locular ovary of a plant* [c19 from New Latin *loculāris* kept in boxes] > ˌlocu'lation *n*

locule ('lɒkjuːl) or **loculus** ('lɒkjʊləs) *n, pl* **locules** or **loculi** ('lɒkjʊˌlaɪ) **1** *botany* any of the chambers of an ovary or anther **2** *biology* any small cavity or chamber [c19 New Latin, from Latin: compartment, from *locus* place]

locum tenens ('ləʊkəm 'tiːnɛnz) *n, pl* **locum tenentes** (tə'nɛntiːz) *chiefly Brit* a person who stands in temporarily for another member of the same profession, esp for a physician, chemist, or clergyman. Often shortened to: **locum** [c17 Medieval Latin: (someone) holding the place (of another)]

locus ('ləʊkəs) *n, pl* **loci** ('ləʊsaɪ) **1** (in many legal phrases) a place or area, esp the place where something occurred **2** *maths* a set of points whose location satisfies or is determined by one or more specified conditions: *the locus of points equidistant from a given point is a circle* **3** *genetics* the position of a particular gene on a chromosome [c18 Latin]

locus classicus ('klæsɪkəs) *n, pl* **loci classici** ('klæsɪˌsaɪ) an authoritative and often quoted passage from a standard work [Latin: classical place]

locus sigilli (sɪ'dʒɪlaɪ) *n, pl* **loci sigilli** the place to which the seal is affixed on legal documents, etc [Latin]

locus standi ('stændaɪ) *n law* the right of a party to appear and be heard before a court [from Latin: a place for standing]

locust ('ləʊkəst) *n* **1** any of numerous orthopterous insects of the genera *Locusta*, *Melanoplus*, etc, such as *L. migratoria*, of warm and tropical regions of the Old World, which travel in vast swarms, stripping large areas of vegetation. See also **grasshopper** (sense 1) Compare **seventeen-year locust 2** Also called: **locust tree**, **false acacia** a North American leguminous tree, *Robinia pseudoacacia*, having prickly branches, hanging clusters of white fragrant flowers, and reddish-brown seed pods **3** the yellowish durable wood of this tree **4** any of several similar trees, such as the honey locust and carob [c13 (the insect): from Latin *locusta* locust; applied to the tree (c17) because the pods resemble locusts] > 'locust-ˌlike *adj*

locust bird *n* any of various pratincoles, esp *Glareola nordmanni* (**black-winged pratincole**), that feed on locusts

locution (ləʊ'kjuːʃən) *n* **1** a word, phrase, or expression **2** manner or style of speech or expression [c15 from Latin *locūtiō* an utterance, from *loquī* to speak] > lo'cutionary *adj*

locutionary act *n* the act of uttering a sentence considered only as such. Compare **illocution**, **perlocution**

Lod (lɒd) *n* a town in central Israel, southeast of Tel Aviv: Israel's chief airport. Pop: 66 800 (2003 est). Also called: **Lydda**

lode (ləʊd) *n* **1** a deposit of valuable ore occurring between definite limits in the surrounding rock; vein **2** a deposit of metallic ore filling a fissure in the surrounding rock [Old English *lād* course. Compare LOAD]

loden ('ləʊdᵊn) *n* **1** a thick heavy waterproof woollen cloth with a short pile, used to make garments, esp coats **2** a dark bluish-green colour, in which the cloth is often made [German, from Old High German *lodo* thick cloth, perhaps related to Old English *lotha* cloak]

lodestar or **loadstar** ('ləʊdˌstɑː) *n* **1** a star, esp the North Star, used in navigation or astronomy as a point of reference **2** something that serves as a guide or model [c14 literally, guiding star. See LODE]

lodestone or **loadstone** ('ləʊdˌstəʊn) *n* **1 a** a rock that consists of pure or nearly pure magnetite and thus is naturally magnetic **b** a piece of such rock, which can be used as a magnet and which was formerly used as a primitive compass **2** a person or thing regarded as a focus of attraction [c16 literally: guiding stone]

lodge (lɒdʒ) *n* **1** *chiefly Brit* a small house at the entrance to the grounds of a country mansion, usually occupied by a gatekeeper or gardener **2** a house or cabin used occasionally, as for some seasonal activity **3** *US and Canadian* a central building in a resort, camp, or park **4** (*capital when part of a name*) a large house or hotel **5** a room for the use of porters in a university, college, etc **6** a local branch or chapter of certain societies **7** the building used as the meeting place of such a society **8** the dwelling place of certain animals, esp the dome-shaped den constructed by beavers **9** a hut or tent of certain North American Indian peoples **10** (at Cambridge University) the residence of the head of a college ▷ *vb* **11** to provide or be provided with accommodation or shelter, esp rented accommodation **12** to live temporarily, esp in rented accommodation **13** to implant, embed, or fix or be implanted, embedded, or fixed **14** (*tr*) to deposit or leave for safety, storage, etc **15** (*tr*) to bring (a charge or accusation) against someone **16** (*tr; often foll by in* or *with*) to place (authority, power, etc) in the control (of someone) **17** (*intr; often foll by in*) *archaic* to exist or be present (in) **18** (*tr*) (of wind, rain, etc) to beat down (crops) [c15 from Old French *loge*, perhaps from Old High German *louba* porch] > 'lodgeable *adj*

Lodge¹ (lɒdʒ) *n* (*preceded by the*) the official Canberra residence of the Australian Prime Minister

Lodge (lɒdʒ) *n* **the** the official Canberra residence of the Australian Prime Minister

lodger ('lɒdʒə) *n* a person who pays rent in return for accommodation in someone else's house

lodging ('lɒdʒɪŋ) *n* **1** a temporary residence **2** (*sometimes plural*) sleeping accommodation **3** (*sometimes plural*) (at Oxford University) the residence of the head of a college ▷ See also **lodgings**

lodging house *n* a private home providing accommodation and meals for lodgers

lodgings ('lɒdʒɪŋz) *pl n* a rented room or rooms in which to live, esp in another person's house

lodging turn *n* a period of work or duty, esp among railway workers, which involves sleeping away from home

lodgment or **lodgement** ('lɒdʒmənt) *n* **1** the act of lodging or the state of being lodged **2** a blockage or accumulation **3** a small area gained and held in enemy territory

Lodi (*Italian* 'lɔːdi) *n* a town in N Italy, in Lombardy: scene of Napoleon's defeat of the Austrians in 1796. Pop: 40 805 (2001)

lodicule ('lɒdɪˌkjuːl) *n* any of two or three minute scales at the base of the ovary in grass flowers that represent the corolla [c19 from Latin *lōdīcula*, diminutive of *lōdix* blanket]

Łódź (*Polish* wudʒ) *n* a city in central Poland: the country's second largest city; major centre of the textile industry; university (1945). Pop: 943 000 (2005 est)

loerie ('laʊrɪ) *n* a variant of **lourie**

loess ('ləʊɪs; *German* lœs) *n* a light-coloured fine-grained accumulation of clay and silt particles that have been deposited by the wind [c19 from German *Löss*, from Swiss German dialect *lösch* loose] > **loessial** (ləʊ'ɛsɪəl) or **lo'essal** *adj*

lo-fi ('ləʊˌfaɪ) or **low-fi** *adj informal* (of sound reproduction) of or giving an impression of poor quality [c20 modelled on HI-FI]

Lofoten and Vesterålen (*Norwegian* 'luːfutən, 'vɛstərɔːlən) *pl n* a group of islands off the NW coast of Norway, within the Arctic Circle. Largest island: Hinnoy. Pop: 54 589 (2004 est). Area: about 5130 sq km (1980 sq miles)

loft (lɒft) *n* **1** the space inside a roof **2** a gallery, esp one for the choir in a church **3** a room over a stable used to store hay **4** an upper storey of a warehouse or factory, esp when converted into living space **5** a raised house or coop in which pigeons are kept **6** *sport* **a** (in golf) the angle from the vertical made by the club face to give elevation to a ball **b** elevation imparted to a ball **c** a lofting stroke or shot ▷ *vb* (*tr*) **7** *sport* to strike or kick (a ball) high in the air **8** to store or place in a loft **9** to lay out a full-scale working drawing of (the lines of a vessel's hull) [Late Old English, from Old Norse *lopt* air, ceiling; compare Old Danish and Old High German *loft* (German *Luft* air)]

loftsman ('lɒftsmən) *n, pl* **-men** a person who reproduces in actual size a draughtsman's design for a ship or an aircraft, working on the floor of a building (**mould loft**) with a large floor area

lofty ('lɒftɪ) *adj* **loftier, loftiest 1** of majestic or imposing height **2** exalted or noble in character or nature **3** haughty or supercilious **4** elevated, eminent, or superior > 'loftily *adv* > 'loftiness *n*

log¹ (lɒg) *n* **1 a** a section of the trunk or a main branch of a tree, when stripped of branches **b** (*modifier*) constructed out of logs: *a log cabin* **2 a** a detailed record of a voyage of a ship or aircraft **b** a record of the hours flown by pilots and aircrews **c** a book in which these records are made; logbook **3** a written record of information about transmissions kept by radio stations, amateur radio operators, etc **4 a** a device consisting of a float with an attached line, formerly used to measure the speed of a ship. See also **chip log b heave the log** to determine a ship's speed with such a device **5** *Austral* a claim for better pay and conditions presented by a trade union to an employer **6 like a log** without stirring or being disturbed (in the phrase **sleep like a log**) ▷ *vb* **logs, logging, logged 7** (*tr*) to fell the trees of (a forest, area, etc) for timber **8** (*tr*) to saw logs from (trees) **9** (*intr*) to work at the felling of timber **10** (*tr*) to enter (a distance, event, etc) in a logbook or log **11** (*tr*) to record the punishment received by (a sailor) in a logbook **12** (*tr*) to travel (a specified distance or time) or move at (a specified speed) [c14 origin obscure]

log² (lɒg) *n* short for **logarithm**

-log *combining form* a US variant of **-logue**

logagraphia (ˌlɒgə'græfɪə) *n med* inability to express ideas in writing

logan¹ ('ləʊgən) or **logan-stone** *n* other names for **rocking stone** [c18 from *logging-stone*, from dialect *log* to rock]

logan² ('ləʊgən) *n Canadian* another name for **bogan** (a backwater)

Logan ('ləʊgən) *n* **Mount** a mountain in NW Canada, in SW Yukon in the St Elias Range: the highest peak in Canada and the second highest in North America. Height (after a re-survey in 1993): 5959 m (19 550 ft)

loganberry ('ləʊgənbərɪ, -brɪ) *n, pl* **-ries 1 a** trailing prickly hybrid rosaceous plant, *Rubus loganobaccus*, cultivated for its edible fruit: probably a hybrid between an American blackberry and a raspberry **2 a** the purplish-red acid fruit of this plant **b** (*as modifier*): *loganberry pie* [c19 named after James H. Logan (1841–1928),

American judge and horticulturist who first grew it (1881)]

loganiaceous (ləʊˌgeɪnɪ'eɪʃəs) *adj* of, relating to, or belonging to the *Loganiaceae,* a tropical and subtropical family of plants that includes nux vomica, pinkroot, and gelsemium [C19 from New Latin *Logania,* named after James *Logan* (1674–1751) Irish-American botanist]

logaoedic (ˌlɒgə'iːdɪk) (in classical prosody) *adj* **1** of or relating to verse in which mixed metres are combined within a single line to give the effect of prose ▷ *n* **2** a line or verse of this kind [C19 via Late Latin from Greek *logaoidikos,* from *logos* speech + *aoidē* poetry]

logarithm ('lɒgəˌrɪðəm) *n* the exponent indicating the power to which a fixed number, the base, must be raised to obtain a given number or variable. It is used esp to simplify multiplication and division: if $a^x = M$, then the logarithm of *M* to the base *a* (written $\log_a M$) is *x*. Often shortened to: **log** See also **common logarithm, natural logarithm** [C17 from New Latin *logarithmus,* coined 1614 by John Napier (1550–1617), Scottish mathematician who invented them, from Greek, *logos* ratio, reckoning + *arithmos* number]

logarithmic (ˌlɒgə'rɪðmɪk) *or* **logarithmical** *adj* **1** of, relating to, using, or containing logarithms of a number or variable **2** consisting of, relating to, or using points or lines whose distances from a fixed point or line are proportional to the logarithms of numbers ▷ Abbreviation: **log** > ˌloga'rithmically *adv*

logarithmic function *n* **a** the mathematical function $y = \log x$ **b** a function that can be expressed in terms of this function

logbook ('lɒgˌbʊk) *n* **1** a book containing the official record of trips made by a ship or aircraft; **log 2** *Brit* (formerly) a document listing the registration, manufacture, ownership and previous owners, etc, of a motor vehicle. Compare **registration document**

log chip *n nautical* the chip of a chip log

loge (ləʊʒ) *n* **1** a small enclosure or box in a theatre or opera house **2** the upper section in a theatre or cinema [C18 French; see LODGE]

logger ('lɒgə) *n* **1** another word for **lumberjack 2** a tractor or crane for handling logs

loggerhead ('lɒgəˌhed) *n* **1** Also called: **loggerhead turtle** a large-headed turtle, *Caretta caretta,* occurring in most seas: family *Chelonidae* **2 loggerhead shrike** a North American shrike, *Lanius ludovicianus,* having a grey head and body, black-and-white wings and tail, and black facial stripe **3** a tool consisting of a large metal sphere attached to a long handle, used for warming liquids, melting tar, etc **4** a strong round upright post in a whaleboat for belaying the line of a harpoon **5** *archaic or dialect* a blockhead; dunce **6 at loggerheads** engaged in dispute or confrontation [C16 probably from dialect *logger* wooden block + HEAD] > 'loggerˌheaded *adj*

loggia ('lɒdʒə, 'lɒdʒɪə) *n, pl* **-gias** *or* **-gie** (-dʒɛ) **1** a covered area on the side of a building, esp one that serves as a porch **2** an open balcony in a theatre [C17 Italian, from French *loge.* See LODGE]

logging ('lɒgɪŋ) *n* the work of felling, trimming, and transporting timber

logia ('lɒgɪə) *n* **1** a supposed collection of the sayings of Christ held to have been drawn upon by the writers of the gospels **2** the plural of **logion**

logic ('lɒdʒɪk) *n* **1** the branch of philosophy concerned with analysing the patterns of reasoning by which a conclusion is properly drawn from a set of premises, without reference to meaning or content. See also **formal logic, deduction** (sense 4), **induction** (sense 4) **2** any particular formal system in which are defined axioms and rules of inference. Compare **formal system, formal language 3** the system and principles of reasoning used in a specific field of

study **4** a particular method of argument or reasoning **5** force or effectiveness in argument or dispute **6** reasoned thought or argument, as distinguished from irrationality **7** the relationship and interdependence of a series of events, facts, etc **8 chop logic** to use excessively subtle or involved logic or argument **9** *electronics, computing* **a** the principles underlying the units in a computer system that perform arithmetical and logical operations. See also **logic circuit b** (*as modifier*): *a logic element* [C14 from Old French *logique* from Medieval Latin *logica* (neuter plural, treated in Medieval Latin as feminine singular), from Greek *logikos* concerning speech or reasoning]

logical ('lɒdʒɪk³l) *adj* **1** relating to, used in, or characteristic of logic **2** using, according to, or deduced from the principles of logic: *a logical conclusion* **3** capable of or characterized by clear or valid reasoning **4** reasonable or necessary because of facts, events, etc: *the logical candidate* **5** *computing* of, performed by, used in, or relating to the logic circuits in a computer > ˌlogi'cality *or* 'logicalness *n* > 'logically *adv*

logical atomism *n* the philosophical theory of Bertrand Russell, the British philosopher (1872–1970), and the early Ludwig Wittgenstein, the Austrian-born British philosopher (1889–1951), which held that all meaningful expressions must be analysable into atomic elements which refer directly to atomic elements of the real world

logical consequence *n* the relation that obtains between the conclusion and the premises of a formally valid argument

logical constant *n* one of the connectives of a given system of formal logic, esp those of the sentential calculus, *not, and, or,* and *if … then …*

logical form *n* the syntactic structure that may be shared by different expressions as abstracted from their content and articulated by the logical constants of a particular logical system, esp the structure of an argument by virtue of which it can be shown to be formally valid. Thus *John is tall and thin, so John is tall* has the same logical form as *London is large and dirty, so London is large,* namely *P & Q, so P*

logically possible *adj* capable of being described without self-contradiction

logical operation *n computing* an operation involving the use of logical functions, such as *and* or *or,* that are applied to the input signals of a particular logic circuit

logical positivism *n* a philosophical theory that holds to be meaningful only those propositions that can be analysed by the tools of logic into elementary propositions that are either tautological or are empirically verifiable. It therefore rejects metaphysics, theology, and sometimes ethics as meaningless

logical sum *n* another name for **disjunction** (sense 3)

logical truth *n* **1** another term for **tautology** (sense 2) **2** the property of being logically tautologous

logic array *n computing* an integrated circuit consisting of interconnected logic gates

logic bomb *n computing* an unauthorized program that is inserted into a computer system; when activated it interferes with the operation of the computer

logic cell *n* a logic circuit forming part of a chip

logic circuit *n* an electronic circuit used in computers to perform a logical operation on its two or more input signals. There are six basic circuits, the AND, NOT, NAND, OR, NOR, and exclusive OR circuits, which can be combined into more complex circuits

logician (lɒ'dʒɪʃən) *n* a person who specializes in or is skilled at logic

logicism ('lɒdʒɪˌsɪzəm) *n* the philosophical theory that all of mathematics can be deduced from logic. Compare **intuitionism, formalism**

logic level *n* the voltage level representing one or

zero in an electronic logic circuit

logic programming *n* the study or implementation of computer programs capable of discovering or checking proofs of formal expressions or segments

Logie ('ləʊgɪ) *n* (in Australia) one of the awards made annually for outstanding television performances [C20 after (John) *Logie* Baird (1888–1946), the Scottish inventor of the television]

log in *computing* ▷ *vb* **1** Also: **log on** to enter (an identification number, password, etc) from a remote terminal to gain access to a multiaccess system ▷ *n* **2** Also: **login** the process by which a computer user logs in

logion ('lɒgɪˌɒn) *n, pl* **logia** ('lɒgɪə) a saying of Christ regarded as authentic. See also **logia** [C16 from Greek: a saying, oracle, from *logos* word]

logistic¹ (lɒ'dʒɪstɪk) *n* **1** an uninterpreted calculus or system of symbolic logic. Compare **formal language** ▷ *adj* **2** *maths* (of a curve) having an equation of the form $y = k/(1 + e^{a+bx})$, where *b* is less than zero **3** *rare* of, relating to, or skilled in arithmetical calculations [C17 via French, from Late Latin *logisticus* of calculation, from Greek *logistikos* rational, from *logos* word, reason]

logistic² (lɒ'dʒɪstɪk) *or* **logistical** *adj* of or relating to logistics > lo'gistically *adv*

logistics (lɒ'dʒɪstɪks) *n* (*functioning as singular or plural*) **1** the science of the movement, supplying, and maintenance of military forces in the field **2** the management of materials flow through an organization, from raw materials through to finished goods **3** the detailed planning and organization of any large complex operation [C19 from French *logistique,* from *loger* to LODGE] > lo'gistically *adv* > logistician (ˌlɒdʒɪ'stɪʃən) *n*

log jam *n chiefly US and Canadian* **1** blockage caused by the crowding together of a number of logs floating in a river **2** a deadlock; standstill

loglog ('lɒglɒg) *n* the logarithm of a logarithm (in equations, etc)

logo ('ləʊgəʊ, 'lɒg-) *n, pl* **-os** short for **logotype** (sense 2)

logo- *combining form* indicating word or speech: *logogram* [from Greek; see LOGOS]

log of wood *n* NZ **the** an informal name for **Ranfurly Shield**

logogram ('lɒgəˌgræm) *or* **logograph** ('lɒgəˌgrɑːf, -ˌgræf) *n* a single symbol representing an entire morpheme, word, or phrase, as for example the symbol (%) meaning *per cent* > logogrammatic (ˌlɒgəgrə'mætɪk), logographic (ˌlɒgə'græfɪk) *or* ˌlogo'graphical *adj* > ˌlogogram'matically *or* ˌlogo'graphically *adv*

logography (lɒ'gɒgrəfɪ) *n* (formerly) a method of longhand reporting > lo'gographer *n*

logogriph ('lɒgəʊˌgrɪf) *n* a word puzzle, esp one based on recombination of the letters of a word [C16 via French from LOGO- + Greek *griphos* puzzle] > ˌlogo'griphic *adj*

logomachy (lɒ'gɒməkɪ) *n, pl* **-chies** argument about words or the meaning of words [C16 from Greek *logomakhia,* from *logos* word + *makhē* battle] > lo'gomachist *n*

logopaedics *or US* **logopedics** (ˌlɒgə'piːdɪks) *n* (*functioning as singular*) another name for **speech therapy.** > ˌlogo'paedic *or US* ˌlogo'pedic *adj*

logorrhoea *or esp US* **logorrhea** (ˌlɒgə'rɪə) *n* excessive, uncontrollable, or incoherent talkativeness

logos ('lɒgɒs) *n philosophy* reason or the rational principle expressed in words and things, argument, or justification; esp personified as the source of order in the universe [C16 from Greek: word, reason, discourse, from *legein* to speak]

Logos ('lɒgɒs) *n christian theol* the divine Word; the second person of the Trinity incarnate in the person of Jesus

logotype ('lɒgəʊˌtaɪp) *n* **1** *printing* a piece of type with several uncombined characters cast on it **2** Also called: **logo** a trademark, company emblem, or similar device > 'logo,typy n

log out *computing* ▷ *vb* **1** Also: **log off** to disconnect a remote terminal from a multiaccess system by entering (an identification number, password, etc) ▷ *n* **2** Also: **logout** the process by which a computer user logs out

logroll ('lɒg,rəʊl) *vb chiefly US* to use logrolling in order to procure the passage of (legislation) > 'log,roller *n*

logrolling ('lɒg,rəʊlɪŋ) *n* **1** *US* the practice of undemocratic agreements between politicians involving mutual favours, the trading of votes, etc **2** another name for **birling** See **birl¹**

Logroño (*Spanish* lo'ɣroɲo) *n* a walled city in N Spain, on the Ebro River: trading centre of an agricultural region noted for its wine. Pop: 139 615 (2003 est)

-logue *or US* **-log** *n combining form* indicating speech or discourse of a particular kind: *travelogue; monologue* [from French, from Greek *-logos*]

logway ('lɒg,weɪ) *n* another name for **gangway** (sense 4)

logwood ('lɒg,wʊd) *n* **1** a leguminous tree, *Haematoxylon campechianum,* of the Caribbean and Central America **2** the heavy reddish-brown wood of this tree, yielding the dye haematoxylin. See also **haematoxylon**

logy ('ləʊgɪ) *adj* **logier, logiest** *chiefly US* dull or listless [c19 perhaps from Dutch *log* heavy] > 'loginess *n*

-logy *n combining form* **1** indicating the science or study of: *musicology* **2** indicating writing, discourse, or body of writings: *trilogy; phraseology; martyrology* [from Latin *-logia,* from Greek, from *logos* word; see LOGOS] > -logical *or* -logic *adj combining form* > -logist *n combining form*

lohan ('ləʊ'hɑːn) *n* (*sometimes capital*) another word for **arhat**

Lohengrin ('ləʊɪngrɪn) *n* (in German legend) a son of Parzival and knight of the Holy Grail

loin (lɔɪn) *n* **1** Also called: **lumbus** *anatomy* the part of the lower back and sides between the pelvis and the ribs. Related adj: **lumbar 2** a cut of meat from this part of an animal ▷ See also **loins** [c14 from Old French *loigne,* perhaps from Vulgar Latin *lumbra* (unattested), from Latin *lumbus* loin]

loincloth ('lɔɪn,klɒθ) *n* a piece of cloth worn round the loins. Also called: **breechcloth**

loins (lɔɪnz) *pl n* **1** the hips and the inner surface of the legs where they join the trunk of the body; crotch **2 a** *euphemistic* the reproductive organs **b** *chiefly literary* the womb

Loire (*French* lwar) *n* **1** a department of E central France, in Rhône-Alpes region. Capital: St Étienne. Pop: 726 613 (2003 est). Area: 4799 sq km (1872 sq miles) **2** a river in France, rising in the Massif Central and flowing north and west in a wide curve to the Bay of Biscay: the longest river in France. Its valley is famous for its wines and châteaux. Length: 1020 km (634 miles). Ancient name: Liger

Loire-Atlantique (*French* lwaratlɑ̃tik) *n* a department of W France, in Pays de la Loire region. Capital: Nantes. Pop: 1 174 120 (2003 est). Area: 6980 sq km (2722 sq miles)

Loiret (*French* lwarɛ) *n* a department of central France, in Centre region. Capital: Orléans. Pop: 629 377 (2003 est). Area: 6812 sq km (2657 sq miles)

Loir-et-Cher (*French* lwarʃɛr) *n* a department of N central France, in Centre region. Capital: Blois. Pop: 318 853 (2003 est). Area: 6422 sq km (2505 sq miles)

loiter ('lɔɪtə) *vb* (*intr*) to stand or act aimlessly or idly [c14 perhaps from Middle Dutch *lōteren* to wobble: perhaps related to Old English *lūtian* to lurk] > 'loiterer *n* > 'loitering *n, adj*

Loki ('ləʊkɪ) *n Norse myth* the god of mischief and destruction

Lok Sabha ('ləʊk 'sʌbə) *n* the lower chamber of India's Parliament. Compare **Rajya Sabha** [Hindi, from *lok* people + *sabha* assembly]

LOL *text messaging abbreviation for* laughing out loud

Lolita (ˌlɒ'liːtə) *n* a sexually precocious young girl [c20 after the character in Nabokov's novel *Lolita* (1955)]

loll (lɒl) *vb* **1** (*intr*) to lie, lean, or lounge in a lazy or relaxed manner **2** to hang or allow to hang loosely ▷ *n* **3** an act or instance of lolling [c14 perhaps imitative; perhaps related to Middle Dutch *lollen* to doze] > 'loller *n* > 'lolling *adj*

Lolland *or* **Laaland** (*Danish* 'lɔlan) *n* an island of Denmark in the Baltic Sea, south of Sjælland. Pop: 69 796 (2003 est). Area: 1240 sq km (480 sq miles)

lollapalooza (ˌlɒləpə'luːzə) *or* **lalapalooza** *n US slang* something excellent [c20 origin unknown]

Lollard ('lɒləd) *n English history* a follower of John Wycliffe during the 14th, 15th, and 16th centuries [c14 from Middle Dutch; mutterer, from *lollen* to mumble (prayers)] > 'Lollardy, 'Lollardry *or* 'Lollardism *n*

lollipop ('lɒlɪ,pɒp) *n* **1** a boiled sweet or toffee stuck on a small wooden stick **2** *Brit* another word for **ice lolly** [c18 perhaps from Northern English dialect *lolly* the tongue (compare LOLL) + POP¹]

lollipop man *or* **lady** *n* (in Britain) a person wearing a white coat and carrying a pole bearing a circular warning sign who stops traffic to allow children travelling to or from school to cross a road safely. Official name: **school crossing patrol**

lollop ('lɒləp) *vb* (*intr*) *chiefly Brit* **1** to walk or run with a clumsy or relaxed bouncing movement **2** a less common word for **lounge** [c18 probably from LOLL + *-op* as in GALLOP, to emphasize the contrast in meaning]

lollo rosso ('lɒləʊ 'rɒsəʊ) *n* a variety of lettuce originating in Italy, having curly red-tipped leaves and a slightly bitter taste

lolly ('lɒlɪ) *n, pl* **-lies 1** an informal word for **lollipop 2** *Brit* short for **ice lolly 3** *Brit, Austral, and NZ* a slang word for **money 4** *Austral and NZ informal* a sweet, esp a boiled one **5** **do the** (or one's) **lolly** *Austral informal* to lose one's temper [shortened from LOLLIPOP]

lollygag ('lɒlɪ,gæg) *vb* **-gags, -gagging, -gagged** (*intr*) a variant of **lallygag**

lolly water *n Austral and NZ informal* any of various coloured soft drinks

Lombard ('lɒmbəd, -bɑːd, 'lʌm-) *n* **1** a native or inhabitant of Lombardy **2** Also called: **Langobard** a member of an ancient Germanic people who settled in N Italy after 568 A.D ▷ *adj* **also** **Lombardic 3** of or relating to Lombardy or the Lombards

Lombard Street *n* the British financial and banking world [c16 from a street in London once occupied by Lombard bankers]

Lombardy ('lɒmbədɪ, 'lʌm-) *n* a region of N central Italy, bordering on the Alps: dominated by prosperous lordships and city-states during the Middle Ages; later ruled by Spain and then by Austria before becoming part of Italy in 1859; intensively cultivated and in parts highly industrialized. Pop: 9 108 645 (2003 est). Area: 23 804 sq km (9284 sq miles). Italian name: Lombardia (ˌlombar'diːa)

Lombardy poplar *n* an Italian poplar tree, *Populus nigra italica,* with upwardly pointing branches giving it a columnar shape

Lombok ('lɒmbɒk) *n* an island of Indonesia, in the Nusa Tenggara Islands east of Java: came under Dutch rule in 1894; important biologically as being transitional between Asian and Australian in flora and fauna, the line of demarcation beginning at **Lombok Strait** (a channel between Lombok and Bali, connecting the Flores Sea with the Indian Ocean). Chief town: Mataram. Pop: 2 500 000 (1991). Area: 4730 sq km (1826 sq miles)

Lombrosian (lɒm'brəʊzɪən) *adj* of or relating to the doctrine propounded by the Italian criminologist Cesare Lombroso (1836–1909) that criminals are a product of hereditary and atavistic factors and can be classified as a definite

abnormal type

Lomé (*French* lɔme) *n* the capital and chief port of Togo, on the Bight of Benin. Pop: 865 000 (2005 est)

loment ('ləʊmɛnt) *or* **lomentum** (ləʊ'mɛntəm) *n, pl* **-ments** *or* **-menta** (-'mɛntə) the pod of certain leguminous plants, constricted between each seed and breaking into one-seeded portions when ripe [c19 from Latin *lomentum* bean meal] > **lomentaceous** (ˌləʊmən'teɪʃəs) *adj*

Lomond ('ləʊmənd) *n* **1 Loch** a lake in W Scotland, north of Glasgow: the largest Scottish lake; designated a national park in 2002. Length: about 38 km (24 miles). Width: up to 8 km (5 miles) **2** See **Ben Lomond**

London ('lʌndən) *n* **1** the capital of the United Kingdom, a port in S England on the River Thames near its estuary on the North Sea: consists of the **City** (the financial quarter), the **West End** (the entertainment and major shopping centre), the **East End** (the industrial and former dock area), and extensive suburbs. Latin name: Londinium See also **City 2 Greater** the administrative area of London, consisting of the City of London and 32 boroughs (13 Inner London boroughs and 19 Outer London boroughs): formed in 1965 from the City, parts of Surrey, Kent, Essex, and Hertfordshire, and almost all of Middlesex, and abolished for administrative purposes in 1996: a Mayor of London and a new London Assembly took office in 2000. Pop: 7 387 900 (2003 est). Area: 1579 sq km (610 sq miles) **3** a city in SE Canada, in SE Ontario on the Thames River: University of Western Ontario (1878). Pop: 337 318 (2001)

Londonderry ('lʌndənˌdɛrɪ) *or* **Derry** *n* **1** a historical county of NW Northern Ireland, on the Atlantic: in 1973 replaced for administrative purposes by the districts of Coleraine, Derry, Limavady, and Magherafelt. Area: 2108 sq km (814 sq miles) **2** a port in N Northern Ireland, second city of Northern Ireland: given to the City of London in 1613 to be colonized by Londoners; besieged by James II's forces (1688–89). Pop: 83 699 (2001) ▷ See also **Derry**

Londoner ('lʌndənə) *n* a native or inhabitant of London

London pride *n* a saxifragaceous plant, a hybrid between *Saxifraga spathularis* and *S. umbrosa,* having a basal rosette of leaves and pinkish-white flowers

Londrina (*Portuguese* lon'drina) *n* a city in S Brazil, in Paraná: centre of a coffee-growing area. Pop: 679 000 (2005 est)

lone (ləʊn) *adj* (*prenominal*) **1** unaccompanied; solitary **2** single or isolated: *a lone house* **3** a literary word for **lonely 4** unmarried or widowed [c14 from the mistaken division of ALONE into *a lone*] > 'loneness *n*

lone hand *n* **1** (in card games such as euchre) an independent player or hand played without a partner **2 play a lone hand** to operate without assistance

lonely ('ləʊnlɪ) *adj* **-lier, -liest 1** unhappy as a result of being without the companionship of others: *a lonely man* **2** causing or resulting from the state of being alone: *a lonely existence* **3** isolated, unfrequented, or desolate **4** without companions; solitary > 'loneliness *n*

lonely hearts *adj* (*often capitals*) of or for people who wish to meet a congenial companion or marriage partner: *a lonely hearts advertisement*

lone pair *n chem* a pair of valency electrons of opposite spin that are not shared between the atoms in a molecule and are responsible for the formation of coordinate bonds

loner ('ləʊnə) *n informal* a person or animal who avoids the company of others or prefers to be alone

lonesome ('ləʊnsəm) *adj* **1** *chiefly US and Canadian* another word for **lonely** ▷ *n* **2 on** *or* (*US*) **by one's lonesome** *informal* on one's own > 'lonesomely *adv*

> ˈlonesomeness *n*

lone wolf *n* a person who prefers to be alone

long¹ (lɒŋ) *adj* **1** having relatively great extent in space on a horizontal plane **2** having relatively great duration in time **3 a** (*postpositive*) of a specified number of units in extent or duration: *three hours long* **b** (*in combination*): *a two-foot-long line* **4** having or consisting of a relatively large number of items or parts: *a long list* **5** having greater than the average or expected range: *a long memory* **6** being the longer or longest of alternatives: *the long way to the bank* **7** having more than the average or usual quantity, extent, or duration: *a long match* **8** seeming to occupy a greater time than is really so: *she spent a long afternoon waiting in the departure lounge* **9** intense or thorough (esp in the phrase **a long look**) **10** (of drinks) containing a large quantity of nonalcoholic beverage **11** (of a garment) reaching to the wearer's ankles **12** *informal* (foll by *on*) plentifully supplied or endowed (with): *long on good ideas* **13** *phonetics* (of a speech sound, esp a vowel) **a** of relatively considerable duration **b** classified as long, as distinguished from the quality of other vowels **c** (in popular usage) denoting the qualities of the five English vowels in such words as *mate, mete, mite, moat, moot,* and *mute* **14** from end to end; lengthwise **15** unlikely to win, happen, succeed, etc: *a long chance* **16** *prosody* **a** denoting a vowel of relatively great duration or (esp in classical verse) followed by more than one consonant **b** denoting a syllable containing such a vowel **c** (in verse that is not quantitative) carrying the emphasis or ictus **17** *finance* having or characterized by large holdings of securities or commodities in anticipation of rising prices: *a long position* **18** *cricket* (of a fielding position) near the boundary: *long leg* **19** *informal* (of people) tall and slender **20** in the long run See **run** (sense 82) **21** long in the tooth *informal* old or ageing ▷ *adv* **22** for a certain time or period: *how long will it last?* **23** for or during an extensive period of time: *long into the next year* **24** at a distant time; quite a bit of time: *long before I met you; long ago* **25** *finance* into a position with more security or commodity holdings than are required by sale contracts and therefore dependent on rising prices for profit: *to go long* **26** as (or so) long as **a** for or during just the length of time that **b** inasmuch as; since **c** provided that; if **27** no longer not any more; formerly but not now ▷ *n* **28** a long time (esp in the phrase **for long**) **29** a relatively long thing, such as a signal in Morse code **30** a clothing size for tall people, esp in trousers **31** *phonetics* a long vowel or syllable **32** *finance* a person with large holdings of a security or commodity in expectation of a rise in its price; bull **33** *music* a note common in medieval music but now obsolete, having the time value of two breves **34** before long soon **35** the long and the short of it the essential points or facts ▷ See also **longs** [Old English *lang*; related to Old High German *lang*, Old Norse *langr*, Latin *longus*]

long² (lɒŋ) *vb* (*intr*; foll by *for* or an infinitive) to have a strong desire [Old English *langian*; related to LONG¹]

long³ (lɒŋ) *vb* (*intr*) *archaic* to belong, appertain, or be appropriate [Old English *langian* to belong, from *gelang* at hand, belonging to; compare ALONG]

long. *abbreviation for* longitude

long- *adv* (*in combination*) for or lasting a long time: *long-awaited; long-established; long-lasting*

long-acting *adj* (of a drug) slowly effective after initial dosage, but maintaining its effects over a long period of time, being slowly absorbed and persisting in the tissues before being excreted. Compare **intermediate-acting, short-acting**

longan (ˈlɒŋɡən) *or* **lungan** (ˈlʌŋɡən) *n* **1** a sapindaceous tree, *Euphoria longan,* of tropical and subtropical Asia, with small yellowish-white flowers and small edible fruits **2** the fruit of this tree, which is similar to but smaller than the litchi, having white juicy pulp and a single seed [c18 from Chinese *lung yen* dragon's eye]

long-and-short work *n architect* the alternation in masonry of vertical and horizontal blocks of stone

longanimity (ˌlɒŋɡəˈnɪmɪtɪ) *n now rare* patience or forbearance [c15 from Late Latin *longanimitās,* from *longanimis* forbearing, from *longus* long + *animus* mind, soul] > **longanimous** (lɒŋˈɡænɪməs) *adj*

long arm *n informal* **1** power, esp far-reaching power: *the long arm of the law* **2** make a long arm to reach out for something, as from a sitting position

Long Beach *n* a city in SW California, on San Pedro Bay: resort and naval base; oil-refining. Pop: 475 460 (2003 est)

Longbenton (ˌlɒŋˈbɛntən) *n* a town in N England, in North Tyneside unitary authority, Tyne and Wear. Pop: 34 878 (2001)

longboard (ˈlɒŋˌbɔːd) *n* **1** a type of surfboard **2** a type of skateboard

longboat (ˈlɒŋˌbəʊt) *n* **1** the largest boat carried aboard a commercial sailing vessel **2** another term for **longship**

longbow (ˈlɒŋˌbəʊ) *n* a large powerful hand-drawn bow, esp as used in medieval England

longcase clock (ˈlɒŋˌkeɪs) *n* another name for **grandfather clock**

long-chain *adj chem* having a relatively long chain of atoms in the molecule

longcloth (ˈlɒŋˌklɒθ) *n* **1** a fine plain-weave cotton cloth made in long strips **2** *US* a light soft muslin

long-coats *pl n* dress-like garments formerly worn by a baby. Archaic name: **long clothes**

long-dated *adj* (of a gilt-edged security) having more than 15 years to run before redemption. Compare **medium-dated, short-dated**

long-day *adj* (of certain plants) able to mature and flower only if exposed to long periods of daylight (more than 12 hours), each followed by a shorter period of darkness. Compare **short-day**

long-distance *n* **1** (*modifier*) covering relatively long distances: *a long-distance driver* **2** (*modifier*) (of telephone calls, lines, etc) connecting points a relatively long way apart **3** *chiefly US and Canadian* a long-distance telephone call **4** a long-distance telephone system or its operator ▷ *adv* **5** by a long-distance telephone line: *he phoned long-distance*

long-drawn-out *adj* over-prolonged or extended

longe (lʌndʒ, lɒndʒ) *n* an older variant of **lunge²** [c17 via Old French from Latin *longus* LONG¹]

long-eared owl *n* a slender European owl, *Asio otus,* with long ear tufts: most common in coniferous forests

Long Eaton (ˈiːtᵊn) *n* a town in N central England, in SE Derbyshire. Pop: 46 490 (2001)

longeron (ˈlɒndʒərən) *n* a main longitudinal structural member of an aircraft [c20 from French: side support, ultimately from Latin *longus* LONG¹]

longevity (lɒnˈdʒɛvɪtɪ) *n* **1** long life **2** relatively long duration of employment, service, etc [c17 from Late Latin *longaevitās,* from Latin *longaevus* long-lived, from *longus* LONG¹ + *aevum* age] > **longevous** (lɒnˈdʒiːvəs) *adj*

long face *n* a disappointed, solemn, or miserable facial expression > **long-ˈfaced** *adj*

long finger *n* put (something) on the long finger *Irish* to postpone (something) for a long time

Longford (ˈlɒŋfəd) *n* **1** a county of N Republic of Ireland, in Leinster province. County town: Longford. Pop: 31 068 (2002). Area: 1043 sq km (403 sq miles) **2** a town in N Republic of Ireland, county town of Co Longford. Pop: 7557 (2002)

longhand (ˈlɒŋˌhænd) *n* ordinary handwriting, in which letters, words, etc, are set down in full, as opposed to shorthand or to typing

long haul *n* **1** a journey over a long distance, esp one involving the transport of goods **2** a lengthy job

long-headed *adj* astute; shrewd; sagacious

> ˌlong-ˈheadedly *adv* > ˌlong-ˈheadedness *n*

long hop *n cricket* a short-pitched ball, which can easily be hit

longhorn (ˈlɒŋˌhɔːn) *n* **1** Also called: Texas longhorn a long-horned breed of beef cattle, usually red or variegated, formerly common in SW US **2** a now rare British breed of beef cattle with long curved horns

long-horned beetle *n* another name for **longicorn beetle** (see **longicorn** (sense 1))

long house *n* **1** a long communal dwelling of the Iroquois and other North American Indian peoples. It often served as a council house as well **2** a long dwelling found in other parts of the world, such as Borneo

long hundredweight *n* the full name for **hundredweight** (sense 1)

longicorn (ˈlɒndʒɪˌkɔːn) *n* **1** Also called: longicorn beetle, long-horned beetle any beetle of the family *Cerambycidae,* having a long narrow body, long legs, and long antennae ▷ *adj* **2** *zoology* having or designating long antennae [c19 from New Latin *longicornis* long-horned]

longing (ˈlɒŋɪŋ) *n* **1** a prolonged unfulfilled desire or need ▷ *adj* **2** having or showing desire or need: *a longing look* > ˈlongingly *adv*

longipennate (ˌlɒndʒɪˈpɛneɪt) *adj* (of birds) having long slender wings or feathers

longirostral (ˌlɒndʒɪˈrɒstrəl) *adj* (of birds) having a long beak

longish (ˈlɒŋɪʃ) *adj* rather long

Long Island *n* an island in SE New York State, separated from the S shore of Connecticut by **Long Island Sound** (an arm of the Atlantic): contains the New York City boroughs of Brooklyn and Queens in the west, many resorts (notably Coney Island), and two large airports (La Guardia and John F. Kennedy). Area: 4462 sq km (1723 sq miles)

longitude (ˈlɒndʒɪˌtjuːd, ˈlɒŋɡ-) *n* **1** distance in degrees east or west of the prime meridian at 0° measured by the angle between the plane of the prime meridian and that of the meridian through the point in question, or by the corresponding time difference. See **latitude** (sense 1) **2** *astronomy* short for **celestial longitude** [c14 from Latin *longitūdō* length, from *longus* LONG¹]

longitudinal (ˌlɒndʒɪˈtjuːdᵊnᵊl, ˌlɒŋɡ-) *adj* **1** of or relating to longitude or length **2** placed or extended lengthways. Compare **transverse** (sense 1) **3** *psychol* (of a study of behaviour) carried on over a protracted period of time > ˌlongiˈtudinally *adv*

longitudinal wave *n* a wave that is propagated in the same direction as the displacement of the transmitting medium. Compare **transverse wave**

long jenny *n billiards* an in-off up the cushion into a far pocket. Compare **short jenny** [from *Jenny,* pet form of *Janet*]

long johns *pl n informal* underpants with long legs

long jump *n* an athletic contest in which competitors try to cover the farthest distance possible with a running jump from a fixed board or mark. US and Canadian equivalent: broad jump > **long jumping** *n*

longleaf pine (ˈlɒŋˌliːf) *n* a North American pine tree, *Pinus palustris,* with long needle-like leaves and orange-brown bark: the most important timber tree of the southeastern US

long lease *n* (in England and Wales) a lease, originally for a period of over 21 years, on a whole house of low rent and ratable value, which is the occupants' only or main residence. The leaseholder is entitled to buy the freehold, claim an extension of 50 years, or become a statutory tenant

Longleat House (ˈlɒŋˌliːt) *n* an Elizabethan mansion near Warminster in Wiltshire, built (from 1568) by Robert Smythson for Sir John Thynne; the grounds, landscaped by Capability Brown, now contain a famous safari park

long leg *n cricket* **a** a fielding position on the leg side near the boundary almost directly behind the batsman's wicket **b** a fielder in this position

long-legged ('lɒŋˌlɛgd, -ˌlɛgɪd) *adj* **1** having long legs **2** *informal* (of a person or animal) able to run fast

long list *chiefly Brit* ▷ *n* **1** a list of suitable applicants for a job, post, etc, from which a short list will be selected ▷ *vb* **long-list 2** (*tr*) to put (someone) on a long list

long-lived *adj* having long life, existence, or currency > ˌlong-'livedness *n*

Long March *n* **the** a journey of about 10 000 km (6000 miles) undertaken (1934–35) by some 100 000 Chinese Communists when they were forced out of their base in Kiangsi in SE China. They made their way to Shensi in NW China; only about 8000 survived the rigours of the journey

long mark *n* another name for **macron**

long measure *n* another name for **linear measure**

long metre *n* a stanzaic form consisting of four octosyllabic lines, used esp for hymns

long moss *n* another name for **Spanish moss**

longneck ('lɒŋˌnɛk) *n US, Canadian, and Austral* **a** a 330-ml beer bottle with a long narrow neck **b** (*as modifier*): *a longneck bottle*

Longobard ('lɒŋgəˌbɑːd) *n, pl* **-bards** or **-bardi** (-ˌbɑːdɪ) a rare name for an ancient **Lombard** > ˌLongo'bardian or ˌLongo'bardic *adj*

long-off *n cricket* **a** a fielding position on the off side near the boundary almost directly behind the bowler **b** a fielder in this position

long-on *n cricket* **a** a fielding position on the leg side near the boundary almost directly behind the bowler **b** a fielder in this position

Long Parliament *n English history* **1** the Parliament summoned by Charles I that assembled on Nov 3, 1640, was expelled by Cromwell in 1653, and was finally dissolved in 1660. See also **Rump Parliament 2** the Cavalier Parliament of 1661–79 **3** the Parliament called in Henry IV's reign that met from March 1 to Dec 22, 1406

long pig *n obsolete* human flesh eaten by cannibals [translation of a Māori and Polynesian term]

long-playing *adj* of or relating to an LP (long-playing record)

long primer *n* (formerly) a size of printer's type, approximately equal to 10 point

long purse *n informal* wealth; riches

long-range *adj* **1** of or extending into the future: *a long-range weather forecast* **2** (of vehicles, aircraft, etc) capable of covering great distances without refuelling **3** (of weapons) made to be fired at a distant target

longs (lɒŋz) *pl n* **1** full-length trousers **2** long-dated gilt-edged securities **3** *finance* unsold securities or commodities held in anticipation of rising prices

long s *n* a lower-case *s*, printed ſ, formerly used in handwriting and printing. Also called: **long ess**

longship ('lɒŋˌʃɪp) *n* a narrow open vessel with oars and a square sail, used esp by the Vikings during medieval times

longshore ('lɒŋˌʃɔː) *adj* situated on, relating to, or along the shore [c19 shortened form of *alongshore*]

longshore drift *n* the process whereby beach material is gradually shifted laterally as a result of waves meeting the shore at an oblique angle

longshoreman ('lɒŋˌʃɔːmən) *n, pl* **-men** *US and Canadian* a man employed in the loading or unloading of ships. Also called (in Britain and certain other countries): **docker**

long shot *n* **1** a competitor, as in a race, considered to be unlikely to win **2** a bet against heavy odds **3** an undertaking, guess, or possibility with little chance of success **4** *films, television* a shot where the camera is or appears to be distant from the object to be photographed **5 by a long shot** by any means: *he still hasn't finished by a long shot*

long-sighted *adj* **1** related to or suffering from

hyperopia **2** able to see distant objects in focus **3** having foresight > ˌlong-'sightedly *adv* > ˌlong-'sightedness *n*

Longs Peak *n* a mountain in N Colorado, in the Front Range of the Rockies: the highest peak in the Rocky Mountain National Park. Height: 4345 m (14 255 ft)

longspur ('lɒŋˌspɜː) *n* any of various Arctic and North American buntings of the genera *Calcarius* and *Rhyncophanes*, all of which have a long claw on the hind toe

long-standing *adj* existing or in effect for a long time

long-suffering *adj* **1** enduring pain, unhappiness, etc, without complaint ▷ *n* also **long-sufferance 2** long and patient endurance > ˌlong-'sufferingly *adv*

long suit *n* **1 a** the longest suit in a hand of cards **b** a holding of four or more cards of a suit **2** *informal* an outstanding advantage, personal quality, or talent

long-tailed cuckoo *n* another name for **koekoea**

long-tailed tit *n* a small European songbird, *Aegithalos caudatus*, with a black, white, and pink plumage and a very long tail: family *Paridae* (tits)

long-term *adj* **1** lasting, staying, or extending over a long time: *long-term prospects* **2** *finance* maturing after a long period of time: *a long-term bond*

long-termism *n* the tendency to focus attention on long-term gains

long-term memory *n psychol* that section of the memory storage system in which experiences are stored on a semipermanent basis. Compare **short-term memory**

longtime ('lɒŋˌtaɪm) *adj* of long standing

long tin *n Brit* a tall long loaf of bread

long tom *n* **1** a long swivel cannon formerly used in naval warfare **2** a long-range land gun **3** an army slang name for **cannon** (sense 1)

long ton *n* the full name for **ton¹** (sense 1)

Longueuil (lɒŋˈgeɪl; *French* lɔ̃gœj) *n* a city in SE Canada, in S Quebec: a suburb of Montreal. Pop: 128 016 (2001)

longueur (*French* lɔ̃gœr) *n* a period of boredom or dullness [literally: length]

long vacation *n* the long period of holiday in the summer during which universities, law courts, etc, are closed

long view *n* the consideration of events or circumstances likely to occur in the future

long wave *n* **a** a radio wave with a wavelength greater than 1000 metres **b** (*as modifier*): *a long-wave broadcast*

longways ('lɒŋˌweɪz) or *US and Canadian* **longwise** ('lɒŋˌwaɪz) *adv* another word for **lengthways**

long weekend *n* a weekend holiday extended by a day or days on either side

long white lop-eared *n* a former name for **British lop**

long-winded *adj* **1** tiresomely long **2** capable of energetic activity without becoming short of breath > ˌlong-'windedly *adv* > ˌlong-'windedness *n*

long-wire aerial *n* a travelling-wave aerial consisting of one or more conductors, the length of which usually exceeds several wavelengths

Longyearbyen ('lɒŋjɪəˌbjɛn) *n* a village on Spitsbergen island, administrative centre of the Svalbard archipelago: coal-mining

lonicera (lɒˈnɪsərə) *n* See **honeysuckle**

Lonk (lɒŋk) *n* a breed of large mountain sheep having horns in both male and female, a trim even fleece, and black face and legs, found only in Lancashire and Derbyshire, England [possibly from a local Lancashire pronunciation of *Lancs*]

Lonsdale Belt ('lɒnzˌdeɪl) *n* (in Britain) a belt conferred as a trophy on professional boxing champions, in various weight categories: if a champion wins it three times it becomes his personal property [named after Hugh Cecil Lowther, 5th Earl of *Lonsdale* (1857–1944), who presented the first one]

Lons-le-Saunier (*French* lɔ̃ləsonje) *n* a town in E France: saline springs; manufactures sparkling wines. Pop: 25 867 (1999)

loo¹ (luː) *n, pl* **loos** *Brit* an informal word for **lavatory** (sense 1) [c20 perhaps from French *lieux d'aisance* water closet]

loo² (luː) *n, pl* **loos 1** a gambling card game **2** a stake used in this game [c17 shortened form of *lanterloo*, via Dutch from French *lanterelu*, originally a meaningless word from the refrain of a popular song]

loo³ (luː) *vb* a variant spelling of **lou**

looby ('luːbɪ) *n, pl* **-bies** a foolish or stupid person [c14 of unknown origin]

loofah ('luːfə) *n* **1** the fibrous interior of the fruit of the dishcloth gourd, which is dried, bleached, and used as a bath sponge or for scrubbing **2** another name for **dishcloth gourd** ▷ Also called (esp US): **loofa, luffa** [c19 from New Latin *luffa*, from Arabic *lūf*]

look (lʊk) *vb* (*mainly intr*) **1** (*often foll by at*) to direct the eyes (towards): *to look at the sea* **2** (*often foll by at*) to direct one's attention (towards): *let's look at the circumstances* **3** (*often foll by to*) to turn one's interests or expectations (towards): *to look to the future* **4** (*copula*) to give the impression of being by appearance to the eye or mind; seem: *that looks interesting* **5** to face in a particular direction: *the house looks north* **6** to expect, hope, or plan (to do something): *I look to hear from you soon; he's looking to get rich* **7** (foll by *for*) **a** to search or seek: *I looked for you everywhere* **b** to cherish the expectation (of); hope (for): *I look for success* **8** (foll by *to*) **a** to be mindful (of): *to look to the promise one has made* **b** to have recourse (to): *look to your swords, men!* **9** to be a pointer or sign: *these early inventions looked towards the development of industry* **10** (foll by *into*) to carry out an investigation: *to look into a mystery* **11** (*tr*) to direct a look at (someone) in a specified way: *she looked her rival up and down* **12** (*tr*) to accord in appearance with (something): *to look one's age* **13 look alive** or **lively** hurry up; get busy **14 look daggers** See **dagger** (sense 4) **15 look here** an expression used to attract someone's attention, add emphasis to a statement, etc **16 look sharp** or **smart** (*imperative*) to hurry up; make haste **17 not look at** to refuse to consider: *they won't even look at my offer of £5000* **18 not much to look at** unattractive; plain ▷ *n* **19** the act or an instance of looking: *a look of despair* **20** a view or sight (of something): *let's have a look* **21** (*often plural*) appearance to the eye or mind; aspect: *the look of innocence; I don't like the looks of this place* **22** style; fashion: *the new look for summer* ▷ *sentence connector* **23** an expression demanding attention or showing annoyance, determination, etc: *look, I've had enough of this* ▷ See also **look after, look back, look down, look forward to, look-in, look on, lookout, look over, look through, look up** [Old English *lōcian*; related to Middle Dutch *lǣken*, Old High German *luogen* to look out]

■ USAGE See at **like**

look after *vb* (*intr, preposition*) **1** to take care of; be responsible for: *she looked after the child while I was out* **2** to follow with the eyes: *he looked after the girl thoughtfully*

lookalike ('lʊkəˌlaɪk) *n* **a** a person, esp a celebrity, or thing that is the double of another **b** (*as modifier*): *a lookalike Minister; a lookalike newspaper*

look back *vb* (*intr, adverb*) **1** to cast one's mind to the past **2 to never look back** to become increasingly successful: *after his book was published, he never looked back* **3** *chiefly Brit* to pay another visit later

look down *vb* **1** (*intr, adverb*; foll by *on* or *upon*) to express or show contempt or disdain (for) **2 look down one's nose at** *informal* to be contemptuous or disdainful of

looker ('lʊkə) *n informal* **1** a person who looks **2** a very attractive person, esp a woman or girl

look forward to *vb* (*intr, adverb + preposition*) to wait or hope for, esp with pleasure

lookie-likie *n informal* a lookalike

look-in *informal* ▷ *n* **1** a chance to be chosen, participate, etc **2** a short visit ▷ *vb* **look in 3** (*intr, adverb*; often foll by *on*) to pay a short visit

looking glass *n* **1** a mirror, esp a ladies' dressing mirror ▷ *modifier* **looking-glass 2** with normal or familiar circumstances reversed; topsy-turvy: *a looking-glass world* [sense 2 in allusion to Lewis Carroll's *Through the Looking-Glass*]

lookism ('lʊkɪzəm) *n* discrimination against a person on the grounds of physical appearance > **'lookist** *adj*

look on *vb* (*intr*) **1** (*adverb*) to be a spectator at an event or incident **2** (*preposition*) Also: **look upon** to consider or regard: *she looked on the whole affair as a joke; he looks on his mother-in-law with disapproval* > **,looker-'on** *n*

lookout ('lʊk,aʊt) *n* **1** the act of keeping watch against danger, etc **2** a person or persons instructed or employed to keep such a watch, esp on a ship **3** a strategic point from which a watch is kept **4** *informal* worry or concern: *that's his lookout* **5** *chiefly Brit* outlook, chances, or view ▷ *vb* **look out** (*adverb, mainly intr*) **6** to heed one's behaviour; be careful: *look out for the children's health* **7** to be on the watch: *look out for my mother at the station* **8** (*tr*) to search for and find: *I'll look out some curtains for your new house* **9** (foll by *on* or *over*) to face in a particular direction: *the house looks out over the moor*

look over *vb* **1** (*intr, preposition*) to inspect by making a tour of (a factory, house, etc): *we looked over the country house* **2** (*tr, adverb*) to examine (a document, letter, etc): *please look the papers over quickly* ▷ *n* **lookover 3** an inspection: often, specifically, a brief or cursory one

look-see *n informal* a brief inspection or look

look through *vb* **1** (*intr, preposition or tr, adverb*) to examine, esp cursorily: *he looked through his notes before the lecture* **2** (*intr, preposition*) to ignore (a person) deliberately: *whenever he meets his ex-girlfriend, she looks straight through him*

look up *vb* (*adverb*) **1** (*tr*) to discover (something required to be known) by resorting to a work of reference, such as a dictionary **2** (*intr*) to increase, as in quality or value: *things are looking up* **3** (*intr; foll by to*) to have respect (for): *I've always wanted a girlfriend I could look up to* **4** (*tr*) to visit or make contact with (a person): *I'll look you up when I'm in town*

loom¹ (luːm) *n* **1** an apparatus, worked by hand or mechanically (**power loom**), for weaving yarn into a textile **2** the middle portion of an oar, which acts as a fulcrum swivelling in the rowlock [C13 (meaning any kind of tool): variant of Old English *gelōma* tool; compare HEIRLOOM]

loom² (luːm) *vb* (*intr*) **1** to come into view indistinctly with an enlarged and often threatening aspect **2** (of an event) to seem ominously close **3** (often foll by *over*) (of large objects) to dominate or overhang ▷ *n* **4** a rising appearance, as of something far away [c16 perhaps from East Frisian *lomen* to move slowly]

loom³ (luːm) *n archaic or dialect* **1** another name for **diver** (the bird) **2** any of various other birds, esp the guillemot [c17 from Old Norse *lomr*]

loo mask *n* a half-mask worn during the 18th century for masquerades, etc. Also called: **loup** [C17 *loo*, from French *loup*, literally: wolf, from Latin *lupus*]

loom-state *adj* (of a woven cotton fabric) not yet dyed

loon¹ (luːn) *n* the US and Canadian name for **diver** (the bird) [c17 of Scandinavian origin; related to Old Norse *lōmr*]

loon² (luːn) *n* **1** *informal* a simple-minded or stupid person **2** *Northeast Scot dialect* a lad **3** *archaic* a person of low rank or occupation (esp in the phrase **lord and loon**) [c15 origin obscure]

loonie ('luːnɪ) *n Canadian slang* **a** a Canadian dollar coin with a loon bird on one of its faces **b** the Canadian currency

loony, looney *or* **luny** ('luːnɪ) *slang* ▷ *adj* **loonier, looniest** *or* **lunier, luniest 1** lunatic; insane **2** foolish or ridiculous ▷ *n, pl* **loonies, looneys** *or* **lunies 3** a foolish or insane person > **'looniness** *or* **'luniness** *n*

loony bin *n slang* a mental hospital or asylum

loop¹ (luːp) *n* **1** the round or oval shape formed by a line, string, etc, that curves around to cross itself **2** any round or oval-shaped thing that is closed or nearly closed **3** a piece of material, such as string, curved round and fastened to form a ring or handle for carrying by **4** an intrauterine contraceptive device in the shape of a loop **5** *electronics* **a** a closed electric or magnetic circuit through which a signal can circulate **b** short for **loop aerial 6** a flight manoeuvre in which an aircraft flies one complete circle in the vertical plane **7** Also called: **loop line** *chiefly Brit* a railway branch line which leaves the main line and rejoins it after a short distance **8** *maths, physics* a closed curve on a graph: *hysteresis loop* **9** another name for **antinode 10** *anatomy* **a** the most common basic pattern of the human fingerprint, formed by several sharply rising U-shaped ridges. Compare **arch¹** (sense 4b), **whorl** (sense 3) **b** a bend in a tubular structure, such as the U-shaped curve in a kidney tubule (**Henle's loop** or **loop of Henle**) **11** *computing* a series of instructions in a program, performed repeatedly until some specified condition is satisfied **12** *skating* a jump in which the skater takes off from a back outside edge, makes one, two, or three turns in the air, and lands on the same back outside edge **13** a group of people to whom information is circulated (esp in the phrases in *or* **out of the loop**) ▷ *vb* **14** (*tr*) to make a loop in or of (a line, string, etc) **15** (*tr*) to fasten or encircle with a loop or something like a loop **16** Also: **loop the loop** to cause (an aircraft) to perform a loop or (of an aircraft) to perform a loop **17** (*intr*) to move in loops or in a path like a loop [c14 *loupe*, origin unknown]

loop² (luːp) *n* an archaic word for **loophole** [c14 perhaps related to Middle Dutch *lupen* to watch, peer]

loop aerial *n* an aerial that consists of one or more coils of wire wound on a frame. Maximum radiation or reception is in the plane of the loop, the minimum occurring at right angles to it. Sometimes shortened to: **loop** Also called: **frame aerial**

loop diuretic *n med* any of a group of diuretics, including frusemide, that act by inhibiting resorption of salts from Henle's loop of the kidney tubule

looper ('luːpə) *n* **1** a person or thing that loops or makes loops **2** another name for a **measuring worm**

loophole ('luːp,həʊl) *n* **1** an ambiguity, omission, etc, as in a law, by which one can avoid a penalty or responsibility **2** a small gap or hole in a wall, esp one in a fortified wall ▷ *vb* **3** (*tr*) to provide with loopholes [c16 from LOOP² + HOLE]

loop knot *n* a knot that leaves a loop extending from it

loopy ('luːpɪ) *adj* **loopier, loopiest 1** full of loops; curly or twisted **2** *informal* slightly mad, crazy, or stupid

loose (luːs) *adj* **1** free or released from confinement or restraint **2** not close, compact, or tight in structure or arrangement **3** not fitted or fitting closely: *loose clothing is cooler* **4** not bundled, packaged, fastened, or put in a container: *loose nails* **5** inexact; imprecise: *a loose translation* **6** (of funds, cash, etc) not allocated or locked away; readily available **7 a** (esp of women) promiscuous or easy **b** (of attitudes, ways of life, etc) immoral or dissolute **8** lacking a sense of responsibility or propriety: *loose talk* **9 a** (of the bowels) emptying easily, esp excessively; lax **b** (of a cough) accompanied by phlegm, mucus, etc **10** (of a dye or dyed article) fading as a result of washing; not

fast **11** *informal, chiefly US and Canadian* very relaxed; easy ▷ *n* **12** the loose *rugby* the part of play when the forwards close round the ball in a ruck or loose scrum. See **scrum 13** on the loose **a** free from confinement or restraint **b** *informal* on a spree ▷ *adv* **14 a** in a loose manner; loosely **b** (*in combination*): *loose-fitting* **15** hang loose *informal, chiefly US* to behave in a relaxed, easy fashion ▷ *vb* **16** (*tr*) to set free or release, as from confinement, restraint, or obligation **17** (*tr*) to unfasten or untie **18** to make or become less strict, tight, firmly attached, compact, etc **19** (when *intr*, often foll by *off*) to let fly (a bullet, arrow, or other missile) [C13 (in the sense: not bound): from Old Norse *lauss* free; related to Old English *lēas* free from, -LESS] > **'loosely** *adv* > **'looseness** *n*

loosebox ('luːs,bɒks) *n* an enclosed and covered stall with a door in which an animal can be confined

loose cannon *n* a person or thing that appears to be beyond control and is potentially a source of unintentional damage

loose change *n* money in the form of coins suitable for small expenditures

loose cover *n* a fitted but easily removable cloth cover for a chair, sofa, etc. US and Canadian name: slipcover

loose end *n* **1** a detail that is left unsettled, unexplained, or incomplete **2** at a loose end without purpose or occupation

loose forward *n rugby* one of a number of forwards who play at the back or sides of the scrum and who are not bound wholly into it. Compare **tight forward**

loose head *n rugby* the prop on the hooker's left in the front row of a scrum. Compare **tight head**

loose-jointed *adj* **1** supple and easy in movement **2** loosely built; with ill-fitting joints > **,loose-'jointedness** *n*

loose-leaf *adj* **1** (of a binder, album, etc) capable of being opened to allow removal and addition of pages ▷ *n* **2** a serial publication published in loose leaves and kept in such a binder

loose-limbed *adj* (of a person) having supple limbs

loose metal *n* NZ shingle on a road

loosen ('luːsˀn) *vb* **1** to make or become less tight, fixed, etc **2** (often foll by *up*) to make or become less firm, compact, or rigid **3** (*tr*) to untie **4** (*tr*) to let loose; set free **5** (often foll by *up*) to make or become less strict, severe, etc **6** (*tr*) to rid or relieve (the bowels) of constipation [c14 from LOOSE] > **'loosener** *n*

loose order *n military* a formation in which soldiers, units, etc, are widely separated from each other

loose smut *n* a disease of cereal grasses caused by smut fungi of the genus *Ustilago*, in which powdery spore masses replace the host tissue

loosestrife ('luːs,straɪf) *n* **1** any of various primulaceous plants of the genus *Lysimachia*, esp the yellow-flowered *L. vulgaris* (**yellow loosestrife**). See also **moneywort 2** purple loosestrife a purple-flowered lythraceous marsh plant, *Lythrum salicaria* **3** any of several similar or related plants, such as the primulaceous plant *Naumburgia thyrsiflora* (**tufted loosestrife**) [c16 LOOSE + STRIFE, an erroneous translation of Latin *lysimachia*, as if from Greek *lusimakhos* ending strife, instead of from the name of the supposed discoverer, *Lusimakhos*]

loose-tongued *adj* careless or irresponsible in talking

loosie ('luːsɪ) *n chiefly Austral and NZ informal* short for **loose forward**

loosies ('luːsɪz) *pl n Northern English informal* cigarettes sold individually

loosing *or* **lowsening** ('luːsɪŋ, -zɪŋ, 'lɔɪ-) *n Yorkshire dialect* a celebration of one's 21st birthday

loot (luːt) *n* **1** goods stolen during pillaging, as in wartime, during riots, etc **2** goods, money, etc, obtained illegally **3** *informal* money or wealth **4**

the act of looting or plundering ▷ *vb* **5** to pillage (a city, settlement, etc) during war or riots **6** to steal (money or goods), esp during pillaging [C19 from Hindi *lūt*] > **'looter** *n*

lop¹ (lɒp) *vb* **lops, lopping, lopped** (*tr*; usually foll by *off*) **1** to sever (parts) from a tree, body, etc, esp with swift strokes **2** to cut out or eliminate from as excessive ▷ *n* **3** a part or parts lopped off, as from a tree [C15 *loppe* branches cut off; compare LOB¹] > **'lopper** *n*

lop² (lɒp) *vb* **lops, lopping, lopped 1** to hang or allow to hang loosely **2** (*intr*) to slouch about or move awkwardly **3** (*intr*) a less common word for **lope** [C16 perhaps related to LOP¹; compare LOB¹]

lop³ (lɒp) *n* *Northern English dialect* a flea [probably from Old Norse *hloppa* (unattested) flea, from *hlaupa* to LEAP]

lope (ləʊp) *vb* **1** (*intr*) (of a person) to move or run with a long swinging stride **2** (*intr*) (of four-legged animals) to run with a regular bounding movement **3** to cause (a horse) to canter with a long easy stride or (of a horse) to canter in this manner ▷ *n* **4** a long steady gait or stride [C15 from Old Norse *hlaupa* to LEAP; compare Middle Dutch *lopen* to run] > **'loper** *n*

lop-eared *adj* (of animals) having ears that droop

lopho- *combining form* indicating a crested or tufted part: *lophophore* [from Greek *lophos* crest]

lophobranch ('ləʊfə,bræŋk) *n* **1** any teleost fish of the suborder *Lophobranchii*, having the gills arranged in rounded tufts: includes the pipefishes and sea horses ▷ *adj* **2** of, relating to, or belonging to the *Lophobranchii* > **lophobranchiate** (,ləʊfə'bræŋkɪɪt, -,eɪt) *adj*

lophophore ('ləʊfə,fɔː) *n* a circle or horseshoe of ciliated tentacles surrounding the mouth and used for the capture of food in minute sessile animals of the phyla *Brachiopoda, Phoronida,* and *Ectoprocta* > **'lopho'phorate** *adj*

lopolith ('lɒpəlɪθ) *n* a saucer- or lens-shaped body of intrusive igneous rock, formed by the penetration of magma between the beds or layers of existing rock and subsequent subsidence beneath the intrusion. Compare **laccolith** [C20 from Greek *lopas* dish + -LITH]

loppy ('lɒpɪ) *n*, *pl* **-pies**, *Austral informal* a man employed to do maintenance tasks on a ranch

lopsided (,lɒp'saɪdɪd) *adj* **1** leaning or inclined to one side **2** greater in weight, height, or size on one side > **,lop'sidedly** *adv* > **,lop'sidedness** *n*

loq. *abbreviation for* loquitur

loquacious (lɒ'kweɪʃəs) *adj* characterized by or showing a tendency to talk a great deal [C17 from Latin *loquāx* from *loquī* to speak] > **lo'quaciously** *adv* > **loquacity** (lɒ'kwæsɪtɪ) *n* > **lo'quaciousness** *n*

loquat ('ləʊkwɒt, -kwət) *n* **1** an ornamental evergreen rosaceous tree, *Eriobotrya japonica*, of China and Japan, having reddish woolly branches, white flowers, and small yellow edible plumlike fruits **2** the fruit of this tree ▷ Also called: **Japan plum** [C19 from Chinese (Cantonese) *lō kwat*, literally: rush orange]

loquitur *Latin* ('lɒkwɪtə) he (or she) speaks: used, esp formerly, as a stage direction. Usually abbreviated to: **loq**

lor (lɔː) *interj* *not standard* an exclamation of surprise or dismay [from LORD (interj)]

loran ('lɔːrən) *n* a radio navigation system operating over long distances. Synchronized pulses are transmitted from widely spaced radio stations to aircraft or shipping, the time of arrival of the pulses being used to determine position [C20 *lo(ng-)ra(nge) n(avigation)*]

Lorca (*Spanish* 'lɔrka) *n* a town in SE Spain, on the Guadalentín River. Pop: 82 511 (2003 est)

lord (lɔːd) *n* **1** a person who has power or authority over others, such as a monarch or master **2** a male member of the nobility, esp in Britain **3** (in medieval Europe) a feudal superior, esp the master of a manor. Compare **lady** (sense 5) **4** a husband considered as head of the household (archaic except in the facetious phrase **lord and**

master) **5** *astrology* a planet having a dominating influence **6 my lord** a respectful form of address used to a judge, bishop, or nobleman ▷ *vb* **7** (*tr*) *now rare* to make a lord of (a person) **8** to act in a superior manner towards (esp in the phrase **lord it over**) [Old English *hlāford* bread keeper; see LOAF¹, WARD] > **'lordless** *adj* > **'lord,like** *adj*

Lord (lɔːd) *n* **1** a title given to God or Jesus Christ **2** *Brit* **a** a title given to men of high birth, specifically to an earl, marquess, baron, or viscount **b** a courtesy title given to the younger sons of a duke or marquess **c** the ceremonial title of certain high officials or of a bishop or archbishop: *Lord Mayor; Lord of Appeal; Law Lord; Lord Bishop of Durham* ▷ *interj* **3** (*sometimes not capital*) an exclamation of dismay, surprise, etc: *Good Lord!; Lord only knows!*

Lord Advocate *n* (in Scotland) the chief law officer of the Crown: he acts as public prosecutor and is in charge of the administration of criminal justice

Lord Chamberlain *n* (in Britain) the chief official of the royal household

Lord Chancellor *n* *Brit government* the cabinet minister who is head of the judiciary in England and Wales and Speaker of the House of Lords

Lord Chief Justice *n* the judge who is second only to the Lord Chancellor in the English legal hierarchy; president of one division of the High Court of Justice

Lord High Chancellor *n* another name for the **Lord Chancellor**

Lord Howe Island (haʊ) *n* an island in the Tasman Sea, southeast of Australia: part of New South Wales. Area: 17 sq km (6 sq miles). Pop: 401 (2001)

lording ('lɔːdɪŋ) *n* **1** *archaic* a gentleman; lord: used in the plural as a form of address **2** an obsolete word for **lordling** [Old English *hlāfording*, from *hlāford* LORD + -ING³, suffix indicating descent]

Lord Justice of Appeal *n* an ordinary judge of the Court of Appeal

Lord Lieutenant *n* **1** (in Britain) the representative of the Crown in a county **2** (formerly) the British viceroy in Ireland

lordling ('lɔːdlɪŋ) *n* *now rare* a young lord

lordly ('lɔːdlɪ) *adj* **-lier, -liest 1** haughty; arrogant; proud **2** of or befitting a lord ▷ *adv* **3** *archaic* in the manner of a lord > **'lordliness** *n*

Lord Mayor *n* the mayor in the City of London and in certain other important boroughs and large cities

Lord Muck *n* *informal* an ordinary man behaving or being treated as if he were aristocratic. See also **Lady Muck**

Lord of Appeal *n* *Brit* one of several judges appointed to assist the House of Lords in hearing appeals

Lord of Hosts *n* Jehovah or God when regarded as having the angelic forces at his command

Lord of Misrule *n* (formerly, in England) a person appointed master of revels at a Christmas celebration

Lord of the Flies *n* a name for **Beelzebub** [translation of Hebrew: see BEELZEBUB]

lordosis (lɔː'dəʊsɪs) *n* **1** *pathology* forward curvature of the lumbar spine: congenital or caused by trauma or disease. Nontechnical name: **hollow-back** Compare **kyphosis, scoliosis 2** *zoology* concave arching of the back occurring in many female animals during sexual stimulation [C18 New Latin from Greek *lordōsis*, from *lordos* bent backwards] > **lordotic** (lɔː'dɒtɪk) *adj*

Lord President of the Council *n* (in Britain) the cabinet minister who presides at meetings of the Privy Council

Lord Privy Seal *n* (in Britain) the senior cabinet minister without official duties

Lord Protector *n* See **Protector**

Lord Provost *n* the provost of one of the five major Scottish cities (Edinburgh, Glasgow,

Aberdeen, Dundee, and Perth)

Lords (lɔːdz) *n* **the** short for **House of Lords**

Lord's (lɔːdz) *n* a cricket ground in N London; headquarters of the MCC

lords-and-ladies *n* (*functioning as singular*) another name for **cuckoopint**

Lord's Day *n* **the** the Christian Sabbath; Sunday

lordship ('lɔːdʃɪp) *n* the position or authority of a lord

Lordship ('lɔːdʃɪp) *n* (preceded by *Your* or *His*) *Brit* a title used to address or refer to a bishop, a judge of the high court, or any peer except a duke

Lordship of the Isles *n* an overlordship of the Western Isles of Scotland and adjacent lands instituted in 1266 when Magnus of Norway ceded the Hebrides, the Isle of Man, and Kintyre to the King of Scotland, and claimed by the chiefs of Clan Dougall and later by those of Clan Donald. The title was forfeited to James IV in 1493 and is now held by the eldest son of the sovereign > **Lord of the Isles** *n*

Lord's Prayer *n* **the** the prayer taught by Jesus Christ to his disciples, as in Matthew 6:9–13, Luke 11:2–4. Also called: **Our Father,** (esp Latin version) **Paternoster**

Lords Spiritual *pl n* **the** the two Anglican archbishops and 24 most senior bishops of England and Wales who sit as members of the House of Lords

Lord's Supper *n* **the** another term for **Holy Communion** (I Corinthians 11:20)

Lord's table *n* **the** *chiefly Protestantism* **1** Holy Communion **2** another name for **altar**

Lords Temporal *pl n* **the** (in Britain) peers other than bishops in their capacity as members of the House of Lords

lordy ('lɔːdɪ) *interj* *chiefly US and Canadian* an exclamation of surprise or dismay

lore¹ (lɔː) *n* **1** collective knowledge or wisdom on a particular subject, esp of a traditional nature **2** knowledge or learning **3** *archaic* teaching, or something that is taught [Old English *lār*; related to *leornian* to LEARN]

lore² (lɔː) *n* **1** the surface of the head of a bird between the eyes and the base of the bill **2** the corresponding area in a snake or fish [C19 from New Latin *lōrum*, from Latin: strap]

Lorelei ('lɒrə,laɪ) *n* (in German legend) a siren, said to dwell on a rock at the edge of the Rhine south of Koblenz, who lures boatmen to destruction [C19 from German *Lurlei* name of the rock; from a poem by Clemens Brentano (1778–1842)]

Lorentz-Fitzgerald contraction *n* the supposed contraction of a body in the direction of its motion through the ether, postulated to explain the result of the Michelson-Morley experiment. The special theory of relativity denies that any such real change can occur in a body as a result of uniform motion but shows that an observer moving with respect to the body will determine an apparent change given by a formula similar to that of Lorentz and Fitzgerald [C20 named after Hendrik Antoon *Lorentz* (1853–1928), Dutch physicist, and G. F. *Fitzgerald* (1851–1901), Irish physicist]

Lorentz transformation *n* a set of equations relating the coordinates of space and time used by two hypothetical observers in uniform relative motion. According to the special theory of relativity the laws of physics are invariant under this transformation [C20 named after Hendrik Antoon *Lorentz* (1853–1928), Dutch physicist]

lorgnette (lɔː'njɛt) *n* a pair of spectacles or opera glasses mounted on a handle [C19 from French, from *lorgner* to squint, from Old French *lorgne* squinting]

lorgnon (*French* lɔrɲɔ̃) *n* **1** a monocle or pair of spectacles **2** another word for **lorgnette** [C19 from French, from *lorgner*; see LORGNETTE]

lorica (lɒ'raɪkə) *n*, *pl* **-cae** (-siː, -kiː) **1** the hard outer covering of rotifers, ciliate protozoans, and similar organisms **2** an ancient Roman cuirass of leather or metal [C18 from New Latin, from Latin: leather cuirass; related to *lōrum* thong] > **loricate** ('lɒrɪˌkeɪt) *or* '**loriˌcated** *adj*

Lorient (*French* lɔrjɑ̃) *n* a port in W France, on the Bay of Biscay. Pop: 59 189 (1999)

lorikeet ('lɒrɪˌkiːt, ˌlɒrɪ'kiːt) *n* any of various small lories, such as *Glossopsitta versicolor* (**varied lorikeet**) or *Trichoglossus moluccanus* (**rainbow lorikeet**) [C18 from LORY + *-keet*, as in PARAKEET]

lorimer ('lɒrɪmə) *or* **loriner** ('lɒrɪnə) *n Brit* (formerly) a person who made bits, spurs, and other small metal objects [C15 from Old French, from *lorain* harness strap, ultimately from Latin *lōrum* strap]

loris ('lɔːrɪs) *n, pl* **-ris** any of several omnivorous nocturnal slow-moving prosimian primates of the family *Lorisidae*, of S and SE Asia, esp *Loris tardigradus* (**slow loris**) and *Nycticebus coucang* (**slender loris**), having vestigial digits and no tails [C18 from French; of uncertain origin]

lorn (lɔːn) *adj poetic* forsaken or wretched [Old English *loren*, past participle of *-lēosan* to lose] > '**lornness** *n*

Lorraine (lɒ'reɪn; *French* lɔrɛn) *n* **1** a region and former province of E France; ceded to Germany in 1871 after the Franco-Prussian war and regained by France in 1919; rich iron-ore deposits. German name: **Lothringen** **2** **Kingdom of** an early medieval kingdom on the Meuse, Moselle, and Rhine rivers: later a duchy **3** a former duchy in E France, once the S half of this kingdom

Lorraine cross *n* See **cross of Lorraine**

lorry ('lɒrɪ) *n, pl* **-ries** **1** a large motor vehicle designed to carry heavy loads, esp one with a flat platform. US and Canadian name: **truck** See also **articulated vehicle** **2** **off the back of a lorry** *Brit informal* a phrase used humorously to imply that something has been dishonestly acquired: *it fell off the back of a lorry* **3** any of various vehicles with a flat load-carrying surface, esp one designed to run on rails [C19 perhaps related to northern English dialect *lurry* to pull, tug]

lory ('lɔːrɪ) *n, pl* **-ries** any of various small brightly coloured parrots of Australia and Indonesia, having a brush-tipped tongue with which to feed on nectar and pollen [C17 via Dutch from Malay *lūrī*, variant of *nūrī*]

Los Alamos (lɒs 'æləmɒs) *n* a town in the US, in New Mexico: the first atomic bomb was developed here. Pop: 18 343 (2000 est)

Los Angeles (lɒs 'ændʒɪˌliːz) *n* a city in SW California, on the Pacific: the second largest city in the US, having absorbed many adjacent townships; industrial centre and port, with several universities. Pop: 3 819 951 (2003 est). Abbreviation: **LA**

lose (luːz) *vb* **loses, losing, lost** (*mainly tr*) **1** to part with or come to be without, as through theft, accident, negligence, etc **2** to fail to keep or maintain: *to lose one's balance* **3** to suffer the loss or deprivation of: *to lose a parent* **4** to cease to have or possess **5** to fail to get or make use of: *to lose a chance* **6** (*also intr*) to fail to gain or win (a contest, game, etc): *to lose the match* **7** to fail to see, hear, perceive, or understand: *I lost the gist of his speech* **8** to waste: *to lose money gambling* **9** to wander from so as to be unable to find: *to lose one's way* **10** to cause the loss of: *his delay lost him the battle* **11** to allow to go astray or out of sight: *we lost him in the crowd* **12** (*usually passive*) to absorb or engross: *he was lost in contemplation* **13** (*usually passive*) to cause the death or destruction of: *two men were lost in the attack* **14** to outdistance or elude: *he soon lost his pursuers* **15** (*intr*) to decrease or depreciate in value or effectiveness: *poetry always loses in translation* **16** (*also intr*) (of a timepiece) to run slow (by a specified amount): *the clock loses ten minutes every day* **17** (of a physician) to fail to sustain the life of (a patient) **18** (of a woman) to fail to give birth to (a viable baby), esp as the result of a miscarriage **19** *motor racing slang* to lose control of (the car), as on a bend: *he lost it going into Woodcote* **20** **lose it** *slang* to lose control of oneself or one's temper [Old English *losian* to perish; related to Old English *-lēosan* as in *forlēosan* to forfeit. Compare LOOSE] > '**losable** *adj* > '**losableness** *n*

losel ('ləʊzəl) *archaic or dialect* ▷ *n* **1** a worthless person ▷ *adj* **2** (of a person) worthless, useless, or wasteful [C14 from *losen*, from the past participle of LOSE]

lose out *vb informal* **1** (*intr, adverb*) to be defeated or unsuccessful **2** **lose out on** to fail to secure or make use of: *we lost out on the sale*

loser ('luːzə) *n* **1** a person or thing that loses **2** a person or thing that seems destined to be taken advantage of, fail, etc: *a born loser* **3** *bridge* a card that will not take a trick

losing ('luːzɪŋ) *adj* unprofitable; failing: *the business was a losing concern*

losings ('luːzɪŋz) *pl n* losses, esp money lost in gambling

loslyf ('lɔːsˌlɛf) *n South African slang* a promiscuous female [Afrikaans]

loss (lɒs) *n* **1** the act or an instance of losing **2** the disadvantage or deprivation resulting from losing: *a loss of reputation* **3** the person, thing, or amount lost: *a large loss* **4** (*plural*) military personnel lost by death or capture **5** (*sometimes plural*) the amount by which the costs of a business transaction or operation exceed its revenue **6** a measure of the power lost in an electrical system expressed as the ratio of or difference between the input power and the output power **7** *insurance* **a** an occurrence of something that has been insured against, thus giving rise to a claim by a policyholder **b** the amount of the resulting claim **8** **at a loss** **a** uncertain what to do; bewildered **b** rendered helpless (for lack of something): *at a loss for words* **c** at less than the cost of buying, producing, or maintaining (something): *the business ran at a loss for several years* [C14 noun probably formed from *lost*, past participle of *losen* to perish, from Old English *lōsian* to be destroyed, from *los* destruction]

loss adjuster *n insurance* a person qualified to adjust losses incurred through fire, explosion, accident, theft, natural disaster, etc, to agree the loss and the compensation to be paid

loss leader *n* an article offered below cost in the hope that customers attracted by it will buy other goods

lossmaker ('lɒsˌmeɪkə) *n Brit* an organization, industry, or enterprise that consistently fails to make a profit

lossmaking ('lɒsˌmeɪkɪŋ) *adj Brit* unprofitable; losing money

loss ratio *n* the ratio of the annual losses sustained to the premiums received by an insurance company

lossy ('lɒsɪ) *adj* (of a dielectric material, transmission line, etc) designed to have a high attenuation; dissipating energy: *lossy line* [C20 from LOSS]

lost (lɒst) *adj* **1** unable to be found or recovered **2** unable to find one's way or ascertain one's whereabouts **3** confused, bewildered, or helpless: *he is lost in discussions of theory* **4** (sometimes foll by *on*) not utilized, noticed, or taken advantage of (by): *rational arguments are lost on her* **5** no longer possessed or existing because of defeat, misfortune, or the passage of time: *a lost art* **6** destroyed physically: *the lost platoon* **7** (foll by *to*) no longer available or open (to) **8** (foll by *to*) insensible or impervious (to a sense of shame, justice, etc) **9** (foll by *in*) engrossed (in): *he was lost in his book* **10** morally fallen: *a lost woman* **11** damned: *a lost soul* **12** **get lost** (*usually imperative*) *informal* go away and stay away

lost cause *n* a cause with no chance of success

Lost Generation *n* (*sometimes not capitals*) **1** the large number of talented young men killed in World War I **2** the generation of writers, esp American authors such as Scott Fitzgerald and Hemingway, active after World War I

lost tribes *pl n* **the** *Old Testament* the ten tribes deported from the N kingdom of Israel in 721 BC and believed never to have returned to Palestine

lot (lɒt) *pron* **1** (*functioning as singular or plural; preceded by* a) a great number or quantity: *a lot to do; a lot of people; a lot of trouble* ▷ *n* **2** a collection of objects, items, or people: *a nice lot of youngsters* **3** portion in life; destiny; fortune: *it falls to my lot to be poor* **4** any object, such as a straw or slip of paper, drawn from others at random to make a selection or choice (esp in the phrase **draw** *or* **cast lots**) **5** the use of lots in making a selection or choice (esp in the phrase **by lot**) **6** an assigned or apportioned share **7** an item or set of items for sale in an auction **8** *chiefly US and Canadian* an area of land: *a parking lot* **9** *US and Canadian* a piece of land with fixed boundaries **10** *chiefly US and Canadian* a film studio and the site on which it is located **11** **a bad lot** an unpleasant or disreputable person **12** **cast** *or* **throw in one's lot with** to join with voluntarily and share the fortunes of **13** **the lot** the entire amount or number ▷ *adv* (preceded by *a*) *informal* **14** to a considerable extent, degree, or amount; very much: *to delay a lot* **15** a great deal of the time or often: *to sing madrigals a lot* ▷ *vb* **lots, lotting, lotted** **16** to draw lots for (something) **17** (*tr*) to divide (land, etc) into lots **18** (*tr*) another word for **allot** ▷ See also **lots** [Old English *hlot*; related to Old High German *lug* portion of land, Old Norse *hlutr* lot, share]

Lot[1] (lɒt) *n* **1** a department of S central France, in Midi-Pyrénées region. Capital: Cahors. Pop: 164 413 (2003 est). Area: 5226 sq km (2038 sq miles) **2** a river in S France, rising in the Cévennes and flowing west into the Garonne River. Length: about 483 km (300 miles)

Lot[2] (lɒt) *n Old Testament* Abraham's nephew: he escaped the destruction of Sodom, but his wife was changed into a pillar of salt for looking back as they fled (Genesis 19)

lota *or* **lotah** ('ləʊtə) *n* a globular water container, usually of brass, used in India, Myanmar, etc [C19 from Hindi *lotā*]

lo tech *n, adj* a variant spelling of **low tech**

Lot-et-Garonne (*French* lɔtegarɔn) *n* a department of SW France, in Aquitaine. Capital: Agen. Pop: 309 993 (2003 est). Area: 5385 sq km (2100 sq miles)

loth (ləʊθ) *adj* a variant spelling of **loath** > '**lothness** *n*

Lothario (ləʊ'θɑːrɪˌəʊ) *n, pl* **-os** (*sometimes not capital*) a rake, libertine, or seducer [C18 after a seducer in Nicholas Rowe's tragedy *The Fair Penitent* (1703)]

Lothian Region ('ləʊðɪən) *n* a former local government region in SE central Scotland, formed in 1975 from East Lothian, most of Midlothian, and West Lothian; replaced in 1996 by the council areas of East Lothian, Midlothian, West Lothian, and Edinburgh

Lothians ('ləʊðɪənz) *pl n* **the** three historic counties of SE central Scotland (now council areas): East Lothian, West Lothian, and Midlothian (including Edinburgh)

Lothringen ('loːtrɪŋən) *n* the German name for **Lorraine**

loti ('ləʊtɪ, 'luːtɪ) *n, pl* **maloti** (mə'ləʊtɪ, -'luːtɪ) the standard monetary unit of Lesotho, divided into 100 lisente

lotic ('ləʊtɪk) *adj ecology* of, relating to, or designating natural communities living in rapidly flowing water. Compare **lentic** [C20 from Latin *lotus*, a past participle of *lavāre* to wash]

lotion ('ləʊʃən) *n* a liquid preparation having a soothing, cleansing, or antiseptic action, applied to the skin, eyes, etc [C14 via Old French from Latin *lōtiō* a washing, from *lōtus* past participle of *lavāre* to wash]

lots (lɒts) *informal* ▷ *pl n* **1** (often foll by *of*) great numbers or quantities: *lots of people; to eat lots* ▷ *adv*

2 a great deal **3** (intensifier): *the journey is lots quicker by train*

lottery (ˈlɒtərɪ) *n, pl* -teries **1** a method of raising money by selling numbered tickets and giving a proportion of the money raised to holders of numbers drawn at random **2** a similar method of raising money in which players select a small group of numbers out of a larger group printed on a ticket. If a player's selection matches some or all of the numbers drawn at random the player wins a proportion of the prize fund **3** an activity or endeavour the success of which is regarded as a matter of fate or luck [C16 from Old French *loterie*, from Middle Dutch *loterije*. See LOT]

lotto (ˈlɒtəʊ) *n* **1** Also called: **housey-housey** a children's game in which numbered discs, counters, etc, are drawn at random and called out, while the players cover the corresponding numbers on cards, the winner being the first to cover all the numbers, a particular row, etc. Compare **bingo 2** a lottery [C18 from Italian, from Old French *lot*, from Germanic. See LOT]

lotus (ˈləʊtəs) *n* **1** (in Greek mythology) a fruit that induces forgetfulness and a dreamy languor in those who eat it **2** the plant bearing this fruit, thought to be the jujube, the date, or any of various other plants **3** any of several water lilies of tropical Africa and Asia, esp the **white lotus** (*Nymphaea lotus*), which was regarded as sacred in ancient Egypt **4** a similar plant, *Nelumbo nucifera,* which is the sacred lotus of India, China, and Tibet and also sacred in Egypt: family *Nelumbonaceae* **5** a representation of such a plant, common in Hindu, Buddhist, and ancient Egyptian carving and decorative art **6** any leguminous plant of the genus *Lotus,* of the Old World and North America, having yellow, pink, or white pealike flowers ▷ Also called (rare): **lotos** [C16 via Latin from Greek *lōtos,* from Semitic; related to Hebrew *lōt* myrrh]

lotus-eater *n Greek myth* one of a people encountered by Odysseus in North Africa who lived in indolent forgetfulness, drugged by the fruit of the legendary lotus

lotus position *n* a seated cross-legged position used in yoga, meditation, etc

Lotus Sutra *n* a central scripture of Mahayana Buddhism, emphasizing that anyone can attain enlightenment

lou *or* **loo** (luː) *vb* a Scot word for **love**

louche (luːʃ) *adj* shifty or disreputable [C19 from French, literally: squinting]

loud (laʊd) *adj* **1** (of sound) relatively great in volume: *a loud shout* **2** making or able to make sounds of relatively great volume: *a loud voice* **3** clamorous, insistent, and emphatic: *loud protests* **4** (of colours, designs, etc) offensive or obtrusive to look at **5** characterized by noisy, vulgar, and offensive behaviour ▷ *adv* **6** in a loud manner **7** out loud audibly, as distinct from silently [Old English *hlud;* related to Old Swedish *hlūd,* German *laut*] > **loudly** *adv* > **loudness** *n*

louden (ˈlaʊdᵊn) *vb* to make or become louder

loud-hailer *n* a portable loudspeaker having a built-in amplifier and microphone. Also called (US and Canadian): **bullhorn**

loudish (ˈlaʊdɪʃ) *adj* fairly loud; somewhat loud

loudmouth (ˈlaʊdˌmaʊθ) *n* **1** a person who brags or talks too loudly **2** a person who is gossipy or tactless > **loudmouthed** (ˈlaʊdˌmaʊðd, -ˌmaʊθt) *adj*

loudspeaker (ˌlaʊdˈspiːkə) *n* a device for converting audio-frequency signals into the equivalent sound waves by means of a vibrating conical diaphragm. Sometimes shortened to: **speaker** Also called: **reproducer**

loudspeaker van *n* a motor vehicle carrying a public address system. US and Canadian name: **sound truck**

Lou Gehrig's disease (luː ˈgɛrɪg) *n* another name for **amyotrophic lateral sclerosis** [C20 named after *Lou Gehrig* (1903–41), US baseball player who suffered from it]

lough (lɒx, lɒk) *n* **1** an Irish word for **lake¹ 2** a long narrow bay or arm of the sea in Ireland ▷ Compare **loch** [C14 from Irish *loch* lake]

Loughborough (ˈlʌfbərə, -brə) *n* a town in central England, in N Leicestershire: university (1966). Pop: 55 258 (2001)

louis (ˈluːɪ; *French* lwi) *n, pl* **louis** (ˈluːɪz; *French* lwi) short for **louis d'or**

Louisbourg (ˈluːɪsˌbɜːg) *n* a fortress in Canada, in Nova Scotia on SE Cape Breton Island: founded in 1713 by the French and strongly fortified (1720–40); captured by the British (1758) and demolished; reconstructed as a historic site

louis d'or (ˌluːɪ ˈdɔː; *French* lwi dɔr) *n, pl* **louis d'or** (ˌluːɪ ˈdɔː; *French* lwi dɔr) **1** a former French gold coin worth 20 francs **2** an old French coin minted in the reign of Louis XIII ▷ Often shortened to: **louis** [C17 from French: golden louis, named after Louis XIII]

Louisiana (luːˌiːzɪˈænə) *n* a state of the southern US, on the Gulf of Mexico: originally a French colony; bought by the US in 1803 as part of the Louisiana Purchase; chiefly low-lying. Capital: Baton Rouge. Pop: 4 496 334 (2003 est). Area: 116 368 sq km (44 930 sq miles). Abbreviations: **La,** (with zip code) **LA**

Louisiana Purchase *n* the large region of North America sold by Napoleon I to the US in 1803 for 15 million dollars: consists of the W part of the Mississippi basin. Area: about 2 292 150 sq km (885 000 sq miles)

Louis Quatorze (kəˈtɔːz) *adj* of or relating to the baroque style of furniture, decoration, and architecture of the time of Louis XIV of France (1638–1715; king 1643–1715) and characterized by massive forms and heavy ornamentation

Louis Quinze (kænz) *adj* of or relating to the rococo style of the furniture, decoration, and architecture of the time of Louis XV of France (1710–74; king 1715–74)

Louis Seize (sɛz) *adj* of or relating to the style of furniture, decoration, and architecture of the time of Louis XVI of France (1754–93; king 1774–92), belonging to the late French rococo and early neoclassicism

Louis Treize (trɛz) *adj* of or relating to the style of furniture, decoration, and architecture of the time of Louis XIII of France (1601–43; king 1610–43), with rich decorative features based on classical models

Louisville (ˈluːɪˌvɪl) *n* a port in N Kentucky, on the Ohio River: site of the annual Kentucky Derby; university (1837). Pop: 248 762 (2003 est)

lounge (laʊndʒ) *vb* **1** (intr; often foll by *about* or *around*) to sit, lie, walk, or stand in a relaxed manner **2** to pass (time) lazily or idly ▷ *n* **3** a **a** communal room in a hotel, ship, theatre, etc, used for waiting or relaxing in **b** (*as modifier*): *lounge chair* **4** *chiefly Brit* a living room in a private house **5** Also called: **lounge bar, saloon bar** *Brit* a more expensive bar in a pub or hotel **6** *chiefly US and Canadian* an expensive bar, esp in a hotel **b** short for **cocktail lounge 7** a sofa or couch, esp one with a headrest and no back **8** the act or an instance of lounging [C16 origin unknown]

lounge lizard *n informal* an idle frequenter of places where rich or prominent people gather

lounger (ˈlaʊndʒə) *n* **1** a comfortable sometimes adjustable couch or extending chair designed for someone to relax on **2** a loose comfortable leisure garment **3** a person who lounges

lounge suit *n* the customary suit of matching jacket and trousers worn by men for the normal business day

loup¹ (luː) *n* another name for **loo mask** [C19 from French, from Latin *lupus* wolf]

loup² *or* **lowp** (laʊp) *vb,* a Scot word for **leap**

loupe (luːp) *n* a magnifying glass used by jewellers, horologists, etc [C20 from French (formerly an imperfect precious stone), from Old French, of obscure origin]

louping ill (ˈlaʊpɪŋ, ˈləʊ-) *n* a viral disease of sheep causing muscular twitching and partial paralysis: transmitted by the bite of an infected tick (*Ixodes ricinus*) [C18 *louping,* from LOUP²]

lour *or* **lower** (laʊə) *vb* (*intr*) **1** (esp of the sky, weather, etc) to be overcast, dark, and menacing **2** to scowl or frown ▷ *n* **3** a menacing scowl or appearance [C13 *louren* to scowl; compare German *lauern* to lurk] > **louring** *or* **lowering** *adj* > **louringly** *or* **loweringly** *adv*

Lourdes (*French* lurd) *n* a town in SW France: a leading place of pilgrimage for Roman Catholics after a peasant girl, Bernadette Soubirous, had visions of the Virgin Mary in 1858. Pop: 15 203 (1999)

Lourenço Marques (ləˈrɛnsəʊ ˈmɑːk, ˈmɑːks; *Portuguese* loˈrẽsu ˈmarkiʃ) *n* the former name (until 1975) of **Maputo**

lourie *or* **loerie** (ˈlaʊrɪ) *n South African* any of several species of touraco: louries are divided into two groups, the arboreal species having a mainly green plumage and crimson wings and the species which inhabits the more open savanna areas having a plain grey plumage [from Malay *luri*]

Lourie (ˈlaʊrɪ) *South African* any of several awards for excellence in advertising and marketing, given by the Marketing Federation of South Africa

louse (laʊs) *n, pl* **lice** (laɪs) **1** any wingless bloodsucking insect of the order *Anoplura:* includes *Pediculus capitis* (**head louse**), *Pediculus corporis* (**body louse**), and the crab louse, all of which infest man. Related adj: **pedicular 2** biting *or* bird louse any wingless insect of the order *Mallophaga,* such as the chicken louse: external parasites of birds and mammals with biting mouthparts **3** any of various similar but unrelated insects, such as the plant louse and book louse **4** *pl* **louses** *slang* an unpleasant or mean person ▷ *vb* (*tr*) **5** to remove lice from **6** (foll by *up*) *slang* to ruin or spoil [Old English *lūs;* related to Old High German, Old Norse *lūs*]

louser (ˈlaʊzə) *n Irish slang* a mean nasty person [C20 from *louse* (up) + -ER¹]

lousewort (ˈlaʊsˌwɜːt) *n* any of various N temperate scrophulariaceous plants of the genus *Pedicularis,* having spikes of white, yellow, or mauve flowers. See also **betony** (sense 3)

lousy (ˈlaʊzɪ) *adj* **lousier, lousiest 1** *slang* very mean or unpleasant: *a lousy thing to do* **2** *slang* inferior or bad: *this is a lousy film* **3** infested with lice **4** (foll by *with*) *slang* **a** provided with an excessive amount (of): *he's lousy with money* **b** full of or teeming with > **lousily** *adv* > **lousiness** *n*

lout¹ (laʊt) *n* a crude or oafish person; boor [C16 perhaps from LOUT²]

lout² (laʊt) *vb* (*intr*) *archaic* to bow or stoop [Old English *lūtan;* related to Old Norse *lūta*]

Louth (laʊð) *n* a county of NE Republic of Ireland, in Leinster province on the Irish Sea: the smallest of the counties. County town: Dundalk. Pop: 101 821 (2002). Area: 821 sq km (317 sq miles)

loutish (ˈlaʊtɪʃ) *adj* characteristic of a lout; unpleasant and uncouth > **loutishly** *adv* > **loutishness** *n*

Louvain (*French* luvɛ̃) *n* a town in central Belgium, in Flemish Brabant province: capital of the duchy of Brabant (11th–15th centuries) and centre of the cloth trade; university (1426). Pop: 89 777 (2004 est). Flemish name: **Leuven**

louvar (ˈluːvɑː) *n* a large silvery whalelike scombroid fish, *Luvarus imperialis,* that occurs in most tropical and temperate seas and feeds on plankton: family *Luvaridae* [from Italian (Calabrian and Sicilian dialect) *lùvaru,* perhaps from Latin *ruber* red]

louvre *or US* **louver** (ˈluːvə) *n* **1 a** any of a set of horizontal parallel slats in a door or window, sloping outwards to throw off rain and admit air **b** Also called: **louvre boards** the slats together with the frame supporting them **2** *architect* a lantern or turret that allows smoke to escape [C14 from Old French *lovier*, of obscure origin]

Louvre (*French* luvrə) *n* the national museum and art gallery of France, in Paris: formerly a royal palace, begun in 1546; used for its present purpose since 1793

louvred *or US* **louvered** (ˈluːvəd) *adj* (of a window, door, etc) having louvres

lovable *or* **loveable** (ˈlʌvəb°l) *adj* attracting or deserving affection > ˌlovaˈbility, ˌloveaˈbility, ˈlovableness *or* ˈloveableness *n* > ˈlovably *or* ˈloveably *adv*

lovage (ˈlʌvɪdʒ) *n* **1** a European umbelliferous plant, *Levisticum officinale*, with greenish-white flowers and aromatic fruits, which are used for flavouring food **2** **Scotch lovage** a similar and related plant, *Ligusticum scoticum*, of N Europe [C14 *loveache*, from Old French *luvesche*, from Late Latin *levisticum*, from Latin *ligusticum*, literally: Ligurian (plant)]

lovat (ˈlʌvət) *n* a yellowish-green or bluish-green mixture, esp in tweeds or woollens [named after *Lovat*, Inverness-shire]

love (lʌv) *vb* **1** (*tr*) to have a great attachment to and affection for **2** (*tr*) to have passionate desire, longing, and feelings for **3** (*tr*) to like or desire (to do something) very much **4** (*tr*) to make love to **5** (*intr*) to be in love ▷ *n* **6 a** an intense emotion of affection, warmth, fondness, and regard towards a person or thing **b** (*as modifier*): *love song; love story* **7** a deep feeling of sexual attraction and desire **8** wholehearted liking for or pleasure in something **9** *Christianity* **a** God's benevolent attitude towards man **b** man's attitude of reverent devotion towards God **10** Also: **my love** a beloved person: used esp as an endearment **11** *Brit informal* a term of address, esp but not necessarily for a person regarded as likable **12** (in tennis, squash, etc) a score of zero **13** **fall in love** to become in love **14** **for love** without payment **15** **for love or money** (*used with a negative*) in any circumstances: *I wouldn't eat a snail for love or money* **16** **for the love of** for the sake of **17** **in love** in a state of strong emotional attachment and usually sexual attraction **18** **make love (to) a** to have sexual intercourse (with) **b** *now archaic* to engage in courtship (with) ▷ Related adjective: **amatory** [Old English *lufu*; related to Old High German *luba*; compare also Latin *libēre* (originally *lubēre*) to please]

love affair *n* **1** a romantic or sexual relationship, esp a temporary one, between two people **2** a great enthusiasm or liking for something: *a love affair with ballet*

love apple *n* an archaic name for **tomato**

lovebird (ˈlʌvˌbɜːd) *n* **1** any of several small African parrots of the genus *Agapornis*, often kept as cage birds **2** another name for **budgerigar 3** *informal* a lover: *the lovebirds are in the garden*

lovebite (ˈlʌvˌbaɪt) *n* a temporary red mark left on a person's skin by a partner's biting or sucking it during lovemaking

love child *n* *euphemistic* an illegitimate child; bastard

Lovecraftian (ˈlʌvˌkrɑːftɪən) *adj* referring to or reminiscent of the work of the American fantasy and horror fiction author H.P. Lovecraft (1870–1937)

loved-up *adj* *slang* experiencing feelings of love, through or as if through taking a drug, esp the drug ecstasy

love feast *n* **1** Also called: **agape** (among the early Christians) a religious meal eaten with others as a sign of mutual love and fellowship **2** a ritual meal modelled upon this

love game *n* *tennis* a game in which the loser has a score of zero

love handles *pl n* *informal* folds of excess fat on either side of the waist

love-in *n* a gathering at which people express feelings of love, friendship, or physical attraction towards each other

love-in-a-mist *n* an erect S European ranunculaceous plant, *Nigella damascena*, cultivated

as a garden plant, having finely cut leaves and white or pale blue flowers. See also **fennelflower**

love-in-idleness *n* another name for the **wild pansy**

love knot *n* a stylized bow, usually of ribbon, symbolizing the bond between two lovers. Also called: **lover's knot**

loveless (ˈlʌvlɪs) *adj* **1** without love: *a loveless marriage* **2** receiving or giving no love > ˈlovelessly *adv* > ˈlovelessness *n*

love letter *n* **1** a letter or note written by someone to his or her sweetheart or lover **2** (in Malaysia) a type of biscuit, made from eggs and rice flour and rolled into a cylinder

love-lies-bleeding *n* any of several amaranthaceous plants of the genus *Amaranthus*, esp *A. caudatus*, having drooping spikes of small red flowers

love life *n* the part of a person's life consisting of his or her sexual relationships

lovelock (ˈlʌvˌlɒk) *n* a long lock of hair worn on the forehead

lovelorn (ˈlʌvˌlɔːn) *adj* miserable because of unrequited love or unhappiness in love > ˈloveˌlornness *n*

lovely (ˈlʌvlɪ) *adj* **-lier, -liest 1** very attractive or beautiful **2** highly pleasing or enjoyable: *a lovely time* **3** loving and attentive **4** inspiring love; lovable ▷ *n, pl* **-lies 5** *slang* a lovely woman > ˈloveliness *n*

lovemaking (ˈlʌvˌmeɪkɪŋ) *n* **1** sexual play and activity between lovers, esp including sexual intercourse **2** an archaic word for **courtship**

love match *n* a betrothal or marriage based on mutual love rather than any other considerations

love nest *n* a place suitable for or used for making love

love potion *n* any drink supposed to arouse sexual love in the one who drinks it

lover (ˈlʌvə) *n* **1** a person, esp a man, who has an extramarital or premarital sexual relationship with another person **2** (*often plural*) either of the two people involved in a love affair **3 a** someone who loves a specified person or thing: *a lover of music* **b** (*in combination*): *a music-lover; a cat-lover*

love seat *n* a small upholstered sofa for two people

love set *n* *tennis* a set in which the loser has a score of zero

lovesick (ˈlʌvˌsɪk) *adj* pining or languishing because of love > ˈloveˌsickness *n*

lovey (ˈlʌvɪ) *n* *Brit informal* another word for **love** (sense 11)

lovey-dovey *adj* making an excessive or ostentatious display of affection

loving (ˈlʌvɪŋ) *adj* feeling, showing, or indicating love and affection > ˈlovingly *adv* > ˈlovingness *n*

loving cup *n* **1** a large vessel, usually two-handled, out of which people drink in turn at a banquet **2** a similar cup awarded to the winner of a competition

low¹ (ləʊ) *adj* **1** having a relatively small distance from base to top; not tall or high: *a low hill; a low building* **2 a** situated at a relatively short distance above the ground, sea level, the horizon, or other reference position: *low cloud* **b** (*in combination*): *low-lying* **3** involving or containing a relatively small amount of something: *a low supply* **b** (*in combination*): *low-pressure* **4 a** having little value or quality **b** (*in combination*): *low-grade* **5** of less than the usual or expected height, depth, or degree: *low temperature* **6 a** (of numbers) small **b** (of measurements) expressed in small numbers **7** unfavourable: *a low opinion* **8** not advanced in evolution: *a low form of plant life* **9** deep: *a low obeisance* **10** coarse or vulgar: *a low conversation* **11 a** inferior in culture or status **b** (*in combination*): *low-class* **12** in a physically or mentally depressed or weakened state **13** designed so as to reveal the wearer's neck and part of the bosom: *a low neckline* **14** with a hushed tone; quiet or soft: *a low whisper*

15 of relatively small price or monetary value: *low cost* **16** *music* relating to or characterized by a relatively low pitch **17** (of latitudes) situated not far north or south of the equator **18** having little or no money **19** abject or servile **20** *phonetics* of, relating to, or denoting a vowel whose articulation is produced by moving the back of the tongue away from the soft palate or the blade away from the hard palate, such as for the *a* in English *father*. Compare **high** (sense 22) **21** (of a gear) providing a relatively low forward speed for a given engine speed **22** (*usually capital*) of or relating to the Low Church ▷ *adv* **23** in a low position, level, degree, intensity, etc: *to bring someone low* **24** at a low pitch; deep: *to sing low* **25** at a low price; cheaply: *to buy low* **26** **lay low a** to cause to fall by a blow **b** to overcome, defeat or destroy **27** **lie low a** to keep or be concealed or quiet **b** to wait for a favourable opportunity ▷ *n* **28** a low position, level, or degree: *an all-time low* **29** an area of relatively low atmospheric pressure, esp a depression **30** *electronics* the voltage level in a logic circuit corresponding to logical zero. Compare **high** (sense 40) [C12 *lāh*, from Old Norse *lāgr*; related to Old Frisian *lēch* low, Dutch *laag*] > ˈlowness *n*

low² (ləʊ) *n* also **lowing 1** the sound uttered by cattle; moo ▷ *vb* **2** to make or express by a low or moo [Old English *hlōwan*; related to Dutch *loeien*, Old Saxon *hlōian*]

low-alcohol *adj* (of beer or wine) containing only a small amount of alcohol. Compare **alcohol-free**

lowan (ˈləʊən) *n* *Austral* another name for **mallee fowl**

Low Archipelago *n* another name for the **Tuamotu Archipelago**

lowball (ˈləʊˌbɔːl) *n* **1** a game of poker in which the player with the lowest hand wins **2 a** a very low estimate or offer **b** (*as modifier*): *a lowball bid* ▷ *vb* (*tr*) **3** to make a very low estimate or offer for (a service, product, company, etc)

lowborn (ˌləʊˈbɔːn) *or* **lowbred** (ˌləʊˈbrɛd) *adj* *now rare* of ignoble or common parentage; not royal or noble

lowboy (ˈləʊˌbɔɪ) *n* *US and Canadian* a table fitted with drawers

lowbrow (ˈləʊˌbraʊ) *disparaging* ▷ *n* **1** a person who has uncultivated or nonintellectual tastes ▷ *adj* *also* **lowbrowed 2** of or characteristic of such a person > ˈlowˌbrowism *n*

low camp *n* an unsophisticated form of **camp** (the style)

low-carbon steel *n* *engineering* steel containing between 0.04 and 0.25 per cent carbon

Lowchen (ˌləʊˈtʃɛn) *n* a small dog of a breed with a long wavy coat, often having the hindquarters and tail clipped to resemble a lion. Also called: little lion dog [from German *Löwchen* little lion]

Low Church *n* **1** the school of thought in the Church of England stressing evangelical beliefs and practices. Compare **Broad Church, High Church** ▷ *adj* **Low-Church 2** of or relating to this school > ˌLow-ˈChurchman *n*

low comedy *n* comedy characterized by slapstick and physical action > **low comedian** *n*

low-context *adj* tending to communicate by electronic methods such as e-mail, rather than in person. Compare **high-context**

Low Countries *pl n* the lowland region of W Europe, on the North Sea: consists of Belgium, Luxembourg, and the Netherlands

low-density lipoprotein *n* a lipoprotein that is the form in which cholesterol is transported in the bloodstream to the cells and tissues of the body. High levels of low-density lipoprotein in the blood are associated with atheroma. Abbreviation: LDL

low-down *informal* ▷ *adj* **1** mean, underhand, or despicable ▷ *n* **lowdown 2** information, esp secret or true information

lower¹ (ˈləʊə) *adj* **1** being below one or more other things: *the lower shelf; the lower animals* **2** reduced in amount or value: *a lower price* **3** *maths* (of a limit or bound) less than or equal to one or more numbers or variables **4** (*sometimes capital*) *geology* denoting the early part or division of a period, system, formation, etc: *Lower Silurian* ▷ *vb* **5** (*tr*) to cause to become low or on a lower level; bring, put, or cause to move down **6** (*tr*) to reduce or bring down in estimation, dignity, value, etc: *to lower oneself* **7** to reduce or be reduced: *to lower one's confidence* **8** (*tr*) to make quieter: *to lower the radio* **9** (*tr*) to reduce the pitch of **10** (*tr*) *phonetics* to modify the articulation of (a vowel) by bringing the tongue further away from the roof of the mouth **11** (*intr*) to diminish or become less [C12 (comparative of LOW¹); C17 (vb)] > 'lowerable *adj*

lower² ('laʊə) *vb* a variant spelling of **lour**

Lower Austria *n* a state of NE Austria: the largest Austrian province, containing most of the Vienna basin. Capital: Sankt Pölten. Pop: 1 552 848 (2003 est). Area: 19 170 sq km (7476 sq miles). German name: **Niederösterreich**

Lower California *n* a mountainous peninsula of NW Mexico, between the Pacific and the Gulf of California: administratively divided into the states of Baja California (or Baja California Norte) and Baja California Sur. Spanish name: **Baja California**

Lower Canada *n* (from 1791 to 1841) the official name of the S region of the present-day province of Quebec. Compare **Upper Canada**

lower case *n* **1** a compositor's type case, in which the small letters are kept ▷ *adj* **lower-case 2** of or relating to small letters ▷ *vb* **lower-case 3** (*tr*) to print with lower-case letters

lower chamber *n* another name for a **lower house**

lower class *n* **1** the social stratum having the lowest position in the social hierarchy. Compare **middle class, upper class, working class** ▷ *adj* **lower-class 2** of or relating to the lower class **3** inferior or vulgar

lowerclassman (ˌlaʊəˈklɑːsmən) *n*, *pl* **-men** *US* a freshman or sophomore. Also called: **underclassman**

lower criticism *n* textual criticism, esp the study of the extant manuscripts of the Scriptures in order to establish the original text. Compare **higher criticism**

lower deck *n* **1** the deck of a ship situated immediately above the hold **2** *informal* the petty officers and seamen of a ship collectively

Lower Egypt *n* one of the two main administrative districts of Egypt: consists of the Nile Delta

lower house *n* one of the two houses of a bicameral legislature: usually the larger and more representative house. Also called: **lower chamber** Compare **upper house**

Lower Hutt (hʌt) *n* an industrial town in New Zealand on the S coast of North Island. Pop: 100 300 (2004 est)

Lower Lakes *pl n chiefly Canadian* Lakes Erie and Ontario

lower mordent *n* another term for **mordent**

lowermost ('laʊəˌməʊst) *adj* lowest

Lower Palaeolithic *n* **1** the earliest of the three sections of the Palaeolithic, beginning about 3 million years ago and ending about 70 000 BC with the emergence of Neanderthal man ▷ *adj* **2** of or relating to this period

lower regions *pl n* (usually preceded by *the*) hell

Lower Saxony *n* a state of N Germany, on the North Sea and including the E Frisian Islands; formerly in West Germany: a leading European producer of petroleum. Capital: Hanover. Pop: 7 993 000 (2003 est). Area: 47 408 sq km (18 489 sq miles). German name: **Niedersachsen**

lower school *n* the younger pupils in a secondary school, usually those in the first three or four year groups

lower world *n* **1** the earth as opposed to heaven or the spiritual world **2** another name for **hell**

lowest common denominator *n* the smallest integer or polynomial that is exactly divisible by each denominator of a set of fractions. Abbreviations: **LCD, lcd** Also called: **least common denominator**

lowest common multiple *n* the smallest number or quantity that is exactly divisible by each member of a set of numbers or quantities. Abbreviations: **LCM, lcm** Also called: **least common multiple**

Lowestoft ('laʊstɒft) *n* a fishing port and resort in E England, in NE Suffolk on the North Sea. Pop: 68 340 (2001)

low explosive *n* an explosive of relatively low power, as used in firearms

low-fi ('laʊˈfaɪ) *adj informal* a variant spelling of **lo-fi**

low frequency *n* a radio-frequency band or a frequency lying between 300 and 30 kilohertz. Abbreviation: **LF**

Low German *n* a language of N Germany, spoken esp in rural areas: more closely related to Dutch than to standard High German. Also called: **Plattdeutsch** Abbreviation: **LG** See also **German, High German**

low-hanging fruit *n* **1** the fruit that grows low on a tree and is therefore easy to reach **2** a course of action that can be undertaken quickly and easily as part of a wider range of changes or solutions to a problem **3** a suitable company to buy as a straightforward investment opportunity

low-impact *adj* **1** designed to cause minimal damage to the environment **2** designed to provide exercise without being over-strenuous

low-key *or* **low-keyed** *adj* **1** having a low intensity or tone **2** restrained, subdued, or understated **3** (of a photograph, painting, etc) having a predominance of dark grey tones or dark colours with few highlights. Compare **high-key**

lowland ('laʊlənd) *n* **1** relatively low ground **2** (*often plural*) a low generally flat region ▷ *adj* **3** of or relating to a lowland or lowlands > 'lowlander *n*

Lowland ('laʊlənd) *adj* of or relating to the Lowlands of Scotland or the dialect of English spoken there

Lowlands ('laʊləndz) *pl n* **the** a low generally flat region of central Scotland, around the Forth and Clyde valleys, separating the Southern Uplands from the Highlands > 'Lowlander *n*

Low Latin *n* any form or dialect of Latin other than the classical, such as Vulgar or Medieval Latin

low-level language *n* a computer programming language that is closer to machine language than to human language. Compare **high-level language**

low-level waste *n* waste material contaminated by traces of radioactivity that can be disposed of in steel drums in concrete-lined trenches but not (since 1983) in the sea. Compare **high-level waste, intermediate-level waste**

lowlife ('laʊˌlaɪf) *n*, *pl* **-lifes** *slang* **a** a member or members of the underworld **b** (*as modifier*): *his lowlife friends*

lowlight ('laʊˌlaɪt) *n* **1** an unenjoyable or unpleasant part of an event **2** (*usually plural*) a streak of darker colour artificially applied to the hair

low-loader *n* a road or rail vehicle for heavy loads with a low platform for ease of access

lowly ('laʊlɪ) *now rare* ▷ *adj* **-lier, -liest 1** humble or low in position, rank, status, etc **2** full of humility; meek **3** simple, unpretentious, or plain ▷ *adv* **4** in a low or lowly manner > 'lowliness *n*

Low Mass *n* a Mass that has a simplified ceremonial form and is spoken rather than sung. Compare **High Mass**

low-minded *adj* having a vulgar or crude mind and character > ˌlow-'mindedly *adv* > ˌlow-'mindedness *n*

low-necked *adj* (of a woman's garment) having a low neckline

lowp (laʊp) *vb, n Scot* a variant spelling of **loup²**

low-pass filter *n electronics* a filter that transmits all frequencies below a specified value, substantially attenuating frequencies above this value. Compare **high-pass filter, band-pass filter**

low-pitched *adj* **1** pitched low in tone **2** (of a roof) having sides with a shallow slope

low-pressure *adj* **1** having, using, or involving a pressure below normal **2** relaxed or calm

low profile *n* **1 a** a position or attitude characterized by a deliberate avoidance of prominence or publicity **b** (*as modifier*): *a low-profile approach* ▷ *adj* **low-profile 2** (of a tyre) wide in relation to its height ▷ Compare **high profile**

low relief *n* another term for **bas-relief**

low-rent *adj informal* cheap and inferior

low-rise *adj* **1** of or relating to a building having only a few storeys. Compare **high-rise** ▷ *n* **2** such a building

lowry *or* **lowrie** ('laʊrɪ) *n* another name for **lory**

lowse (laʊz, laʊs) *Scot* ▷ *adj* **1** loose ▷ *vb* **2** (*tr*) to release; loose **3** (*intr*) to finish work **4** lowsing time the time at which work or school finishes; knocking-off time [a Scot variant of LOOSE]

low-spirited *adj* depressed, dejected, or miserable > ˌlow-'spiritedly *adv* > ˌlow-'spiritedness *n*

Low Sunday *n* the Sunday after Easter [probably so named because of its relative unimportance in contrast with Easter Sunday]

low tech *n* **1** short for **low technology 2** a style of interior design using items associated with low technology ▷ *adj* **low-tech 3** of or using low technology **4** of or in the interior design style ▷ Compare **hi tech**

low technology *n* simple unsophisticated technology, often that used for centuries, that is limited to the production of basic necessities

low-tension *adj* subjected to, carrying, or capable of operating at a low voltage. Abbreviation: **LT**

low tide *n* **1** the tide when it is at its lowest level or the time at which it reaches this **2** a lowest point

lowveld ('laʊˌfɛlt, -ˌvɛlt) *n* **the** another name for **bushveld**

low-velocity zone *n* a layer or zone in the earth in which the velocity of seismic waves is slightly lower than in the layers above and below. The asthenosphere is thought to be such a zone. See **asthenosphere**

low water *n* **1** another name for **low tide** (sense 1) **2** the state of any stretch of water at its lowest level **3** a situation of difficulty or point of least success, excellence, etc

low-water mark *n* **1** the level reached by seawater at low tide or by other stretches of water at their lowest level **2** the lowest point or level

lox¹ (lɒks) *n* a kind of smoked salmon [C19 from Yiddish *laks*, from Middle High German *lahs* salmon]

lox² (lɒks) *n* short for **liquid oxygen,** esp when used as an oxidizer for rocket fuels

loxodromic (ˌlɒksəˈdrɒmɪk) *or* **loxodromical** *adj* of or relating to rhumb lines or to map projections on which rhumb lines appear straight, as on a Mercator projection [C17 from Greek *loxos* oblique + *dromikos* relating to a course] > ˌloxo'dromically *adv*

loxodromics (ˌlɒksəˈdrɒmɪks) *or* **loxodromy** (lɒkˈsɒdrəmɪ) *n* (*functioning as singular*) the technique of navigating using rhumb lines

loy (lɔɪ) *n Irish* a narrow spade with a single footrest [C18 from Irish Gaelic *láí*]

loya jirga (ˌlɔɪə ˈdʒɜːɡə) *n* (*often with capitals*) an assembly of regional leaders and tribal chiefs in Afghanistan [from Pashto, literally: grand assembly]

loyal ('lɔɪəl) *adj* **1** having or showing continuing allegiance **2** faithful to one's country, government, etc **3** of or expressing loyalty [C16 from Old French *loial, leial,* from Latin *lēgālis* LEGAL] > 'loyally *adv* > 'loyalness *n*

loyalist ('lɔɪəlɪst) *n* a patriotic supporter of his sovereign or government > 'loyalism *n*

Loyalist ('lɔɪəlɪst) *n* **1** (in Northern Ireland) any of the Protestants wishing to retain Ulster's link with Britain **2** (in North America) an American colonist who supported Britain during the War of American Independence **3** (during the Spanish Civil War) a supporter of the republican government

loyalty ('lɔɪəltɪ) *n, pl* -ties **1** the state or quality of being loyal **2** (*often plural*) a feeling of allegiance

loyalty card *n* a swipe card issued by a supermarket or chain store to a customer, used to record credit points awarded for money spent in the store

Loyang ('ləʊ'jæŋ) *n* a variant transliteration of the Chinese name for **Luoyang**

lozenge ('lɒzɪndʒ) *n* **1** Also called: **pastille, troche** *med* a medicated tablet held in the mouth until it has dissolved **2** *geometry* another name for **rhombus 3** *heraldry* a diamond-shaped charge [C14 from Old French *losange*, of Gaulish origin; compare Vulgar Latin *lausa* flat stone]

lozenged ('lɒzɪndʒd) *adj* decorated with lozenges

lozengy ('lɒzɪndʒɪ) *adj* (*usually postpositive*) *heraldry* divided by diagonal lines to form a lattice

Lozère (*French* lɔzɛr) *n* a department of S central France, in Languedoc-Roussillon region. Capital: Mende. Pop: 74 234 (2003 est). Area: 5180 sq km (2020 sq miles)

Lozi ('ləʊzɪ) *n* the language of the Barotse people of Zambia, belonging to the Bantu group of the Niger-Congo family

LP[1] *n* **1 a** a long-playing gramophone record: usually one 12 inches (30 cm) or 10 inches (25 cm) in diameter, designed to rotate at 33⅓ revolutions per minute. Compare **EP b** (*as modifier*): *an LP sleeve* **2** long play: a slow-recording facility on a VCR which allows twice the length of material to be recorded on a tape from that of standard play

LP[2] *abbreviation for* **1** (in Britain) **Lord Provost 2** Also: **lp** low pressure

L/P *printing abbreviation for* letterpress

LPG *abbreviation for* **liquefied petroleum gas**

L-plate *n Brit* a white rectangle with an "L" sign fixed to the back and front of a motor vehicle; a red "L" sign is used to show that a driver using it is a learner who has not passed the driving test; a green "L" sign may be displayed by new drivers for up to a year after passing the driving test

LPO *abbreviation for* London Philharmonic Orchestra

L'pool *abbreviation for* Liverpool

LPS (in Britain) *abbreviation for* **Lord Privy Seal**

lr *the internet domain name for* Liberia

Lr *the chemical symbol for* lawrencium

LRSC *abbreviation for* Licentiate of the Royal Society of Chemistry

LRT (in the US and Canada) *abbreviation for* **1** light-rail transit **2** light-rapid transit

ls[1] *abbreviation for* (on a document) the place of the seal [from Latin *locus sigilli*]

ls[2] *the internet domain name for* Lesotho

LS *international car registration for* Lesotho

LSD *n* lysergic acid diethylamide; a crystalline compound prepared from lysergic acid, used in experimental medicine and taken illegally as a hallucinogenic drug. Informal name (as an illegal hallucinogen): acid

L.S.D., £.s.d. *or* **l.s.d.** (in Britain, esp formerly) *abbreviation for* librae, solidi, denarii [Latin: pounds, shillings, pence]

LSE *abbreviation for* London School of Economics

LSI *electronics abbreviation for* large scale integration

LSO *abbreviation for* London Symphony Orchestra

LSZ (in New Zealand) *abbreviation for* limited speed zone

lt[1] *abbreviation for* **1** long ton **2** (esp in the US) local time

lt[2] *the internet domain name for* Lithuania

Lt *abbreviation for* Lieutenant

LT 1 *abbreviation for* low-tension **2** ▷ *international car registration for* Lithuania

LTA *abbreviation for* Lawn Tennis Association

Lt Cdr *abbreviation for* lieutenant commander

Lt Col *abbreviation for* lieutenant colonel

Ltd *or* **ltd** (esp after the names of British business organizations) *abbreviation for* limited (liability). US equivalent: **Inc**

Lt Gen *abbreviation for* lieutenant general

Lt Gov *abbreviation for* lieutenant governor

LTNS *text messaging abbreviation for* long time no see

LTR *abbreviation for* long-term relationship: used in lonely hearts columns and personal advertisements

LTSA (in New Zealand) *abbreviation for* Land Transport Safety Authority

lu *the internet domain name for* Luxembourg

Lu *the chemical symbol for* lutetium

LU *physics abbreviation for* loudness unit

luach ('lʊɑx) *n Judaism* a calendar that shows the dates of festivals and, usually, the times of start and finish of the Sabbath

Lualaba (ˌluːə'lɑːbə) *n* a river in the SE Democratic Republic of Congo (formerly Zaïre), rising in Katanga province and flowing north as the W headstream of the River Congo. Length: about 1800 km (1100 miles)

Luanda *or* **Loanda** (lʊ'ændə) *n* the capital of Angola, a port in the west, on the Atlantic: founded in 1576, it became a centre of the slave trade to Brazil in the 17th and 18th centuries; oil refining. Pop: 2 839 000 (2005 est). Official name: São Paulo de Loanda

Luang Prabang (luːˈæŋ prɑːˈbæŋ) *n* a market town in N Laos, on the Mekong River: residence of the monarch of Laos (1946–75). Pop: 26 400 (2003 est)

luau (luːˈaʊ, ˈluːaʊ) *n* **1** a feast of Hawaiian food **2** a dish of taro leaves usually prepared with coconut cream and octopus or chicken [from Hawaiian *lu'au*]

Luba ('luːbə) *n* **1** (*pl* Luba) a member of a Negroid people of Africa living chiefly in the S Democratic Republic of Congo (formerly Zaïre) **2** Also called: **Tshiluba** the language of this people, belonging to the Bantu group of the Niger-Congo family

lubber ('lʌbə) *n* **1** a big, awkward, or stupid person **2** short for **landlubber** [C14 *lobre*, probably from Scandinavian. See LOB[1]] > **'lubberly** *adj, adv* > **'lubberliness** *n*

lubber line *n* a mark on a ship's compass that designates the fore-and-aft axis of the vessel. Also called: **lubber's line**

lubber's hole *n nautical* a hole in a top or platform on a mast through which a sailor can climb

Lubbock ('lʌbək) *n* a city in NW Texas: cotton market. Pop: 206 481 (2003 est)

Lübeck (*German* 'lyːbɛk) *n* a port in N Germany, in Schleswig-Holstein on the Baltic: the leading member of the Hanseatic League, and a major European commercial centre until the 15th century. Pop: 212 754 (2003 est)

Lublin (*Polish* 'lublin) *n* an industrial city in E Poland: provisional seat of the government in 1918 and 1944. Pop: 397 000 (2005 est). Russian name: Lyublin

lubra ('luːbrə) *n Austral* an Aboriginal woman [C19 from a native Australian language]

lubricant ('luːbrɪkənt) *n* **1** a lubricating substance, such as oil ▷ *adj* **2** serving to lubricate [C19 from Latin *lūbricāns*, present participle of *lūbricāre*. See LUBRICATE]

lubricate ('luːbrɪˌkeɪt) *vb* **1** (*tr*) to cover or treat with an oily or greasy substance so as to lessen friction **2** (*tr*) to make greasy, slippery, or smooth **3** (*intr*) to act as a lubricant [C17 from Latin *lūbricāre*, from *lūbricus* slippery] > ˌlubri'cation *n* > ˌlubri'cational *adj* > 'lubriˌcative *adj*

lubricator ('luːbrɪˌkeɪtə) *n* **1** a person or thing that lubricates **2** a device for applying lubricant

lubricious (luːˈbrɪʃəs) *or* **lubricous** ('luːbrɪkəs) *adj* **1** *formal or literary* lewd, lascivious **2** *rare* oily or slippery [C16 from Latin *lūbricus*] > lu'briciously *or* 'lubricously *adv*

lubricity (luːˈbrɪsɪtɪ) *n* **1** *formal or literary* lewdness

or salaciousness **2** *rare* smoothness or slipperiness **3** capacity to lubricate [C15 (lewdness), C17 (slipperiness): from Old French *lubricité*, from Medieval Latin *lubricitās*, from Latin, from *lūbricus* slippery]

lubritorium (ˌluːbrɪˈtɔːrɪəm) *n, pl* -ria (-rɪə) *chiefly US* a place, as in a service station, for the lubrication of motor vehicles [C20 from LUBRICATE + -*orium*, as in *sanatorium*]

Lubumbashi (ˌluːbʊmˈbæʃɪ) *n* a city in the S Democratic Republic of Congo (formerly Zaïre): founded in 1910 as a copper-mining centre; university (1955). Pop: 1 102 000 (2005 est). Former name (until 1966): Elisabethville

Lucan ('luːkən) *adj* of or relating to St Luke, a fellow worker of Paul and a physician (Colossians 4:14), or St. Luke's gospel

Lucania (luːˈkeɪnɪə) *n* the Latin name for **Basilicata**

lucarne (luːˈkɑːn) *n* a type of dormer window [C16 from French, from Provençal *lucana*, of obscure origin]

Lucca (*Italian* 'lukka) *n* a city in NW Italy, in Tuscany: centre of a rich agricultural region, noted for the production of olive oil. Pop: 81 862 (2001). Ancient name: Luca ('luːkə)

luce (luːs) *n* another name for the **pike** (the fish) [C14 from Old French *lus*, from Late Latin *lūcius* pike]

lucent ('luːs³nt) *adj* brilliant, shining, or translucent [C16 from Latin *lūcēns*, present participle of *lūcēre* to shine] > 'lucently *adv*

lucerne (luːˈsɜːn) *n Brit* another name for **alfalfa**

Lucerne (luːˈsɜːn; *French* lysɛrn) *n* **1** a canton in central Switzerland, northwest of Lake Lucerne: joined the Swiss Confederacy in 1332. Pop: 352 300 (2002 est). Area: 1494 sq km (577 sq miles) **2** a city in central Switzerland, capital of Lucerne canton, on Lake Lucerne: tourist centre. Pop: 59 496 (2000) **3 Lake** a lake in central Switzerland: fed and drained chiefly by the River Reuss. Area: 115 sq km (44 sq miles). German name: Vierwaldstättersee ▷ German name (for senses 1 and 2): Luzern

lucid ('luːsɪd) *adj* **1** readily understood; clear **2** shining or glowing **3** *psychiatry* of or relating to a period of normality between periods of insane or irresponsible behaviour [C16 from Latin *lūcidus* full of light, from *lūx* light] > lu'cidity *or* 'lucidness *n* > 'lucidly *adv*

lucifer ('luːsɪfə) *n* a friction match: originally a trade name for a match manufactured in England in the 19th century

Lucifer ('luːsɪfə) *n* **1** the leader of the rebellion of the angels: usually identified with Satan **2** the planet Venus when it rises as the morning star [Old English, from Latin *Lūcifer*, light-bearer, from *lūx* light + *ferre* to bear]

luciferin (luːˈsɪfərɪn) *n biochem* a substance occurring in bioluminescent organisms, such as glow-worms and fireflies. It undergoes an enzyme-catalysed oxidation and emits light on decaying to its ground state [C20 from Latin *lucifer* (literally: light-bearer) + -IN]

luciferous (luːˈsɪfərəs) *adj rare* bringing or giving light

lucifugous (luːˈsɪfjʊgəs) *adj* avoiding light [C17 from Latin *lucifugus*, from *lux* (genitive *lūcis*) light + *fugere* to flee + -OUS]

Lucina (luːˈsaɪnə) *n Roman myth* a title or name given to Juno as goddess of childbirth [C14 from Latin *lūcīnus* bringing to the light, from *lūx* light]

luck (lʌk) *n* **1** events that are beyond control and seem subject to chance; fortune **2** success or good fortune **3** something considered to bring good luck **4 down on one's luck** having little or no good luck to the point of suffering hardships **5 no such luck** *informal* unfortunately not **6 try one's luck** to attempt something that is uncertain ▷ See also **luck out** [C15 from Middle Dutch *luc*; related to Middle High German *gelücke*, late Old Norse *lukka, lykka*]

luckless ('lʌklɪs) *adj* having no luck; unlucky

> **'lucklessly** *adv* > **'lucklessness** *n*

Lucknow ('lʌknaʊ) *n* a city in N India, capital of Uttar Pradesh: capital of Oudh (1775–1856); the British residency was besieged (1857) during the Indian Mutiny. Pop: 2 207 340 (2001)

luck out *vb* (*intr, adverb*) to have good fortune; be lucky: *the US economy lucked out for most of the decade*

luckpenny ('lʌk,pɛnɪ) *n, pl* **-nies** *Brit* **1** a coin kept for luck **2** a small amount of money returned for luck by a seller to a customer

lucky ('lʌkɪ) *adj* **luckier, luckiest 1** having or bringing good fortune **2** happening by chance, esp as desired > **'luckily** *adv* > **'luckiness** *n*

Lucky Country *n Austral slang* a jocular name for **Australia**

lucky dip *n Brit* **1** a barrel or box filled with sawdust and small prizes for which children search **2** *informal* an undertaking of uncertain outcome

lucrative ('lu:krətɪv) *adj* producing a profit; profitable; remunerative [c15 from Old French *lucratif*; see LUCRE] > **'lucratively** *adv* > **'lucrativeness** *n*

lucre ('lu:kə) *n usually facetious* money or wealth (esp in the phrase **filthy lucre**) [c14 from Latin *lucrum* gain; related to Old English *lēan* reward, German *Lohn* wages]

Lucretia (lu:'kri:ʃɪə) *n* (in Roman legend) a Roman woman who killed herself after being raped by a son of Tarquin the Proud

lucubrate ('lu:kjʊ,breɪt) *vb* (*intr*) to write or study, esp at night [c17 from Latin *lūcubrāre* to work by lamplight] > **'lucu,brator** *n*

lucubration (,lu:kjʊ'breɪʃən) *n* **1** laborious study, esp at night **2** (*often plural*) a solemn literary work

luculent ('lu:kjʊlənt) *adj rare* **1** easily understood; lucid **2** bright or shining [c15 from Latin *lūculentus* full of light, from *lūx* light] > **'luculently** *adv*

Lucullan (lu:'kʌlən) *or* **Lucullean, Lucullian** (,lu:kʌ'lɪən) *adj* luxurious or sumptuous [named after Lucius Licinius *Lucullus*, the Roman general and consul (?110–56 BC), famous for his luxurious banquets]

lud (lʌd) *Brit* ▷ *n* **1** lord (in the phrase **my lud, m'lud**): used when addressing a judge in court ▷ *interj* **2** *archaic* an exclamation of dismay or surprise

Lüda ('lu:'dɑ:) *or* **Lü-ta** *n* a port in NE China, in S Liaoning province, comprising the two cities of Lüshun and Dalian at the S end of the Liaodong peninsula: the chief northern port. Pop: 2 400 000 (1991 est)

Luddite ('lʌdaɪt) *n English history* **1** any of the textile workers opposed to mechanization who rioted and organized machine-breaking between 1811 and 1816 **2** any opponent of industrial change or innovation ▷ *adj* **3** of or relating to the Luddites [c19 alleged to be named after Ned *Ludd*, an 18th-century Leicestershire workman, who destroyed industrial machinery] > **'Luddism** *n*

Lüdenscheid (*German* 'ly:dənʃaɪt) *n* a city in W Germany, in North Rhine-Westphalia. Pop: 79 829 (2003 est)

luderick ('lu:dərɪk) *n* an estuarine and rock fish, *Girella tricuspidata*, of Australia, usually black or dark brown in colour: a kind of blackfish. Also called: **black bream** [c19 from a native Australian language]

Lüderitz (*German* 'ly:dərɪts) *n* a port in Namibia: diamond-mining centre. Pop: 6000 (1990)

Ludhiana (,lʊdɪ'ɑ:nə) *n* a city in N India, in the central Punjab: Punjab Agricultural University (1962). Pop: 1 395 053 (2001)

ludic ('lu:dɪk) *adj literary* playful [c20 from French *ludique*, from Latin *lūdus* game]

ludicrous ('lu:dɪkrəs) *adj* absurd or incongruous to the point of provoking ridicule or laughter [c17 from Latin *lūdicrus* done in sport, from *lūdus* game; related to *lūdere* to play] > **'ludicrously** *adv* > **'ludicrousness** *n*

Ludlow¹ ('lʌdləʊ) *n trademark* a machine for casting type from matrices set by hand, used esp for headlines

Ludlow² ('lʌdləʊ) *n* a market town in W central England, in Shropshire: castle (11th–16th century). Pop: 9548 (2001)

ludo ('lu:dəʊ) *n Brit* a simple board game in which players advance counters by throwing dice [c19 from Latin: I play]

Ludwigsburg (*German* 'lu:tvɪçsbʊrk) *n* a city in SW Germany, in Baden-Württemberg north of Stuttgart: expanded in the 18th century around the palace of the dukes of Württemberg. Pop: 87 581 (2003 est)

Ludwigshafen (*German* 'lu:tvɪçsha:fən) *n* a city in SW Germany, in the Rhineland-Palatinate, on the Rhine: chemical industry. Pop: 162 836 (2003 est)

lues ('lu:i:z) *n, pl* **lues** *rare* **1** any venereal disease **2** a pestilence [c17 from New Latin, from Latin: calamity] > **luetic** (lu:'ɛtɪk) *adj* > **lu'etically** *adv*

luff (lʌf) *n* **1** *nautical* the leading edge of a fore-and-aft sail ▷ *n* **2** tackle consisting of a single and a double, block for use with rope having a large diameter ▷ *vb* **3** *nautical* to head (a sailing vessel) into the wind so that her sails flap **4** (*intr*) *nautical* (of a sail) to flap when the wind is blowing equally on both sides **5** to move the jib of (a crane) or raise or lower the boom of (a derrick) in order to shift a load [c13 (in the sense: steering gear): from Old French *lof*, perhaps from Middle Dutch *loef* peg of a tiller; compare Old High German *laffa* palm of hand, oar blade, Russian *lapa* paw]

luffa ('lʌfə) *n* **1** any tropical climbing plant of the cucurbitaceous genus *Luffa*, esp the dishcloth gourd **2** *US* another name for **loofah**

Luftwaffe *German* ('lʊftvafə) *n* the German Air Force [c20 German, literally: air weapon]

lug¹ (lʌg) *vb* **lugs, lugging, lugged 1** to carry or drag (something heavy) with great effort **2** (*tr*) to introduce (an irrelevant topic) into a conversation or discussion **3** (*tr*) (of a sailing vessel) to carry too much (sail) for the amount of wind blowing ▷ *n* **4** the act or an instance of lugging [c14 probably from Scandinavian; apparently related to Norwegian *lugge* to pull by the hair]

lug² (lʌg) *n* **1** a projecting piece by which something is connected, supported, or lifted **2** Also called: **tug** a leather loop used in harness for various purposes **3** a box or basket for vegetables or fruit with a capacity of 28 to 40 pounds **4** *Scot and northern English dialect* another word for **ear¹ 5** *slang* a man, esp a stupid or awkward one [c15 (Scots dialect) *lugge* ear, perhaps related to LUG¹ (in the sense: to pull by the ear)]

lug³ (lʌg) *n nautical* short for **lugsail**

lug⁴ (lʌg) *n* short for **lugworm** [c16 origin uncertain]

Luganda (lu:'gændə, -'gɑ:ndə) *n* the language of the Buganda, spoken chiefly in Uganda, belonging to the Bantu group of the Niger-Congo family

Lugano (lʊ'gɑ:nəʊ) *n* a town in S Switzerland, on Lake Lugano: a financial centre and tourist resort. Pop: 26 560 (2000)

Lugansk (*Russian* lu'gansk) *n* an industrial city in E Ukraine, in the Donbass mining region: established in 1795 as an iron-founding centre. Pop: 454 000 (2005 est). Former name (1935–91): Voroshilovgrad

luge (lu:ʒ) *n* **1** a racing toboggan on which riders lie on their backs, descending feet first ▷ *vb* **2** (*intr*) to ride on a luge [c20 from French]

Luger ('lu:gə) *n trademark* a German 9 mm calibre automatic pistol [c20 named after George *Luger* (1849–1923), German gun designer]

luggage ('lʌgɪdʒ) *n* suitcases, trunks, etc, containing personal belongings for a journey; baggage [c16 perhaps from LUG¹, influenced in form by BAGGAGE]

luggage van *n Brit* a railway carriage used to transport passengers' luggage, bicycles, etc. US and Canadian name: **baggage car**

lugger ('lʌgə) *n nautical* a small working boat

rigged with a lugsail [c18 from LUGSAIL]

Lughnasadh ('lu:nasa) *n* an ancient Celtic festival held on Aug 1. It is also celebrated by modern pagans. Also called: **Lammas** [from Old Irish]

lughole ('lʌg,həʊl) *n Brit* an informal word for **ear¹** See also **lug²** (sense 4)

Lugo (*Spanish* 'luɣo) *n* a city in NW Spain: Roman walls; Romanesque cathedral. Pop: 91 158 (2003 est). Latin name: **Lucus Augusti** ('lu:kəs aʊ'gu:sti:, ɔ:'gʌsti:)

lugsail ('lʌgseɪl) *or* **lug** (lʌg) *n nautical* a four-sided sail bent and hoisted on a yard [c17 perhaps from Middle English *lugge* pole, or from *lugge* ear]

lug screw *n* a small screw without a head

lugubrious (lʊ'gu:brɪəs) *adj* excessively mournful; doleful [c17 from Latin *lūgubris* mournful, from *lūgēre* to grieve] > **lu'gubriously** *adv* > **lu'gubriousness** *n*

lugworm ('lʌg,wɜ:m) *n* any polychaete worm of the genus *Arenicola*, living in burrows on sandy shores and having tufted gills: much used as bait by fishermen. Sometimes shortened to: **lug** Also called: **lobworm** [c17 of uncertain origin]

lug wrench *n* a spanner with a lug or lugs projecting from its jaws to engage the component to be rotated

Luichow Peninsula ('lu:'tʃaʊ) *n* a variant transliteration of the Chinese name for **Leizhou Peninsula**

Luik (lœik) *n* the Flemish name for **Liège**

Luke (lu:k) *n New Testament* **1 Saint** a fellow worker of Paul and a physician (Colossians 4:14). Feast day: Oct 18 **2** the third Gospel, traditionally ascribed to Luke. Related adj: **Lucan**

lukewarm (,lu:k'wɔ:m) *adj* **1** moderately warm; tepid **2** having or expressing little enthusiasm or conviction [c14 *luke* probably from Old English *hlēow* warm; compare German *lauwarm*] > **,luke'warmly** *adv* > **,luke'warmness** *n*

Luleå (*Swedish* 'lu:leɔ:) *n* a port in N Sweden, on the Gulf of Bothnia: industrial and shipbuilding centre; icebound in winter. Pop: 72 608 (2004 est)

lull (lʌl) *vb* **1** to soothe (a person or animal) by soft sounds or motions (esp in the phrase **lull to sleep**) **2** to calm (someone or someone's fears, suspicions, etc), esp by deception ▷ *n* **3** a short period of calm or diminished activity [c14 possibly imitative of crooning sounds; related to Middle Low German *lollen* to soothe, Middle Dutch *lollen* to talk drowsily, mumble] > **'lulling** *adj*

lullaby ('lʌlə,baɪ) *n, pl* **-bies 1** a quiet song to lull a child to sleep **2** the music for such a song ▷ *vb* **-bies, -bying, -bied 3** (*tr*) to quiet or soothe with or as if with a lullaby [c16 perhaps a blend of LULL + GOODBYE]

lulu ('lu:lu:) *n slang* a person or thing considered to be outstanding in size, appearance, etc [c19 probably from the nickname for *Louise*]

Luluabourg (lu:'lu:ə,bʊə) *n* the former name (until 1966) of **Kananga**

lum (lʌm) *n Scot* a chimney [c17 of obscure origin]

luma (lu:mə) *n* a monetary unit of Armenia worth one hundredth of a dram

lumbago (lʌm'beɪgəʊ) *n* pain in the lower back; backache affecting the lumbar region [c17 from Late Latin *lumbāgo*, from Latin *lumbus* loin]

lumbar ('lʌmbə) *adj* of, near, or relating to the part of the body between the lowest ribs and the hipbones [c17 from New Latin *lumbāris*, from Latin *lumbus* loin]

lumbar puncture *n med* insertion of a hollow needle into the lower region of the spinal cord to withdraw cerebrospinal fluid, introduce drugs, etc

lumber¹ ('lʌmbə) *n* **1** *chiefly US and Canadian* **a** logs; sawn timber **b** cut timber, esp when sawn and dressed ready for use in joinery, carpentry, etc **c** (*as modifier*): *the lumber trade* **2** *Brit* **a** useless household articles that are stored away **b** (*as modifier*): *lumber room* ▷ *vb* **3** (*tr*) to pile together in a disorderly manner **4** (*tr*) to fill up or encumber with useless household articles **5** *chiefly US and Canadian* to convert (the trees) of (a forest) into marketable timber **6** (*tr*) *Brit informal* to burden with something unpleasant, tedious, etc **7** (*tr*) *Austral* to arrest; imprison [C17 perhaps from a noun use of LUMBER²] > **'lumberer** *n*

lumber² ('lʌmbə) *vb* (*intr*) **1** to move awkwardly **2** an obsolete word for **rumble** [C14 *lomeren*; perhaps related to *lome* LAME¹, Swedish dialect *loma* to move ponderously]

lumbering¹ ('lʌmbərɪŋ) *n chiefly US and Canadian* the business or trade of cutting, transporting, preparing, or selling timber

lumbering² ('lʌmbərɪŋ) *adj* **1** awkward in movement **2** moving with a rumbling sound > **'lumberingly** *adv* > **'lumberingness** *n*

lumberjack ('lʌmbə,dʒæk) *n* (esp in North America) a person whose work involves felling trees, transporting the timber, etc [C19 from LUMBER¹ + JACK¹ (man)]

lumberjacket ('lʌmbə,dʒækɪt) *n* a boldly coloured, usually checked jacket in warm cloth, as worn by lumberjacks. US name: **lumberjack**

lumberyard ('lʌmbə,jɑːd) *n US and Canadian* an establishment where timber and sometimes other building materials are stored or sold. Also called (in Britain and certain other countries): **timberyard**

lumbricalis (,lʌmbrɪ'keɪlɪs) *n anatomy* any of the four wormlike muscles in the hand or foot [C18 New Latin, from Latin *lumbrīcus* worm] > **lumbrical** ('lʌmbrɪkᵊl) *adj*

lumbricoid ('lʌmbrɪ,kɔɪd) *adj* **1** *anatomy* designating any part or structure resembling a worm **2** of, relating to, or resembling an earthworm [C19 from New Latin *lumbricoides,* from Latin *lumbrīcus* worm]

lumen ('luːmɪn) *n, pl* **-mens** *or* **-mina** (-mɪnə) **1** the derived SI unit of luminous flux; the flux emitted in a solid angle of 1 steradian by a point source having a uniform intensity of 1 candela. Symbol: lm **2** *anatomy* a passage, duct, or cavity in a tubular organ **3** a cavity within a plant cell enclosed by the cell walls [C19 New Latin, from Latin: light, aperture] > **'lumenal** *or* **'luminal** *adj*

lum-hat (,lʌm'hæt) *n Scot* a top hat [C19 from LUM]

luminance ('luːmɪnəns) *n* **1** a state or quality of radiating or reflecting light **2** a measure (in candelas per square metre) of the brightness of a point on a surface that is radiating or reflecting light. It is the luminous intensity in a given direction of a small element of surface area divided by the orthogonal projection of this area onto a plane at right angles to the direction. Symbol: *L* [C19 from Latin *lūmen* light]

luminary ('luːmɪnərɪ) *n, pl* **-naries 1** a person who enlightens or influences others **2** a famous person **3** *literary* something, such as the sun or moon, that gives off light ▷ *adj* **4** of, involving, or characterized by light or enlightenment [C15 via Old French, from Latin *lūmināre* lamp, from *lūmen* light]

luminesce (,luːmɪ'nɛs) *vb* (*intr*) to exhibit luminescence [back formation from LUMINESCENT]

luminescence (,luːmɪ'nɛsəns) *n physics* **a** the emission of light at low temperatures by any process other than incandescence, such as phosphorescence or chemiluminescence **b** the light emitted by such a process [C19 from Latin *lūmen* light] > **,lumi'nescent** *adj*

luminosity (,luːmɪ'nɒsɪtɪ) *n, pl* **-ties 1** the condition of being luminous **2** something that is luminous **3** *astronomy* a measure of the radiant power emitted by a star **4** *physics* the attribute of an object or colour enabling the extent to which an object emits light to be observed. Former name: **brightness** See also **colour**

luminous ('luːmɪnəs) *adj* **1** radiating or reflecting light; shining; glowing: *luminous colours* **2** (*not in technical use*) exhibiting luminescence: *luminous*

paint **3** full of light; well-lit **4** (of a physical quantity in photometry) evaluated according to the visual sensation produced in an observer rather than by absolute energy measurements: *luminous flux; luminous intensity.* Compare **radiant 5** easily understood; lucid; clear **6** enlightening or wise [C15 from Latin *lūminōsus* full of light, from *lūmen* light] > **'luminously** *adv* > **'luminousness** *n*

luminous efficacy *n* **1** the quotient of the luminous flux of a radiation and its corresponding radiant flux. Symbol: *K* **2** the quotient of the luminous flux emitted by a source of radiation and the power it consumes. It is measured in lumens per watt. Symbol: η_v, Φ_v

luminous efficiency *n* the efficiency of polychromatic radiation in producing a visual sensation. It is the radiant flux weighed according to the spectral luminous efficiencies of its constituent wavelengths divided by the corresponding radiant flux. Symbol: *V*

luminous energy *n* energy emitted or propagated in the form of light; the product of a luminous flux and its duration, measured in lumen seconds. Symbol: Q_v

luminous exitance *n* the ability of a surface to emit light expressed as the luminous flux per unit area at a specified point on the surface. Symbol: M_v

luminous flux *n* a measure of the rate of flow of luminous energy, evaluated according to its ability to produce a visual sensation. For a monochromatic light it is the radiant flux multiplied by the spectral luminous efficiency of the light. It is measured in lumens. Symbol: Φ_v

luminous intensity *n* a measure of the amount of light that a point source radiates in a given direction. It is expressed by the luminous flux leaving the source in that direction per unit of solid angle. Symbol: I_v

lumisterol (luː'mɪstə,rɒl) *n biochem* a steroid compound produced when ergosterol is exposed to ultraviolet radiation. Formula: $C_{28}H_{44}O$ [C20 from Latin *lumin-, lūmen* light + STEROL]

lumme *or* **lummy** ('lʌmɪ) *interj Brit* an exclamation of surprise or dismay [C19 alteration of *Lord love me*]

lummox ('lʌməks) *n informal* a clumsy or stupid person [C19 origin unknown]

lump¹ (lʌmp) *n* **1** a small solid mass without definite shape **2** *pathol* any small swelling or tumour **3** a collection of things; aggregate **4** *informal* an awkward, heavy, or stupid person **5** (*plural*) *US informal* punishment, defeat, or reverses: *he took his lumps* **6 the lump** *Brit* **a** self-employed workers in the building trade considered collectively, esp with reference to tax and national insurance evasion **b** (*as modifier*): *lump labour* **7** (*modifier*) in the form of a lump or lumps: *lump sugar* **8** a lump in one's throat a tight dry feeling in one's throat, usually caused by great emotion ▷ *vb* **9** (*tr*; often foll by *together*) to collect into a mass or group **10** (*intr*) to grow into lumps or become lumpy **11** (*tr*) to consider as a single group, often without justification **12** (*tr*) to make or cause lumps in or on **13** (*intr*; often foll by *along*) to move or proceed in a heavy manner [C13 probably related to early Dutch *lompe* piece, Scandinavian dialect *lump* block, Middle High German *lumpe* rag]

lump² (lʌmp) *vb* (*tr*) *informal* to tolerate or put up with; endure (in the phrase **lump it**) [C16 origin uncertain]

lumpectomy (lʌm'pɛktəmɪ) *n, pl* **-mies** the surgical removal of a tumour in a breast [C20 from LUMP¹ + -ECTOMY]

lumpen ('lʌmpᵊn) *adj informal* stupid or unthinking [from German *Lump* vagabond, influenced in meaning by *Lumpen* rag, as in LUMPENPROLETARIAT]

lumpenproletariat (,lʌmpən,prəʊlɪ'tɛərɪət) *n* (esp in Marxist theory) the amorphous urban social group below the proletariat, consisting of

criminals, tramps, etc [German, literally: ragged proletariat]

lumper ('lʌmpə) *n US* a stevedore; docker

lumpfish ('lʌmp,fɪʃ) *n, pl* **-fish** *or* **-fishes 1** a North Atlantic scorpaenoid fish, *Cyclopterus lumpus,* having a globular body covered with tubercles, pelvic fins fused into a sucker, and an edible roe: family *Cyclopteridae* **2** any other fish of the family *Cyclopteridae* ▷ Also called: **lumpsucker** [C16 *lump* (now obsolete) *lumpfish,* from Middle Dutch *lumpe,* perhaps related to LUMP¹]

lump hammer *n* a heavy hammer used for driving stakes or breaking stone

lumpish ('lʌmpɪʃ) *adj* **1** resembling a lump **2** stupid, clumsy, or heavy > **'lumpishly** *adv* > **'lumpishness** *n*

lumpsucker ('lʌmp,sʌkə) *n* See **lumpfish**

lump sum *n* a relatively large sum of money, paid at one time, esp in cash

lumpy ('lʌmpɪ) *adj* **lumpier, lumpiest 1** full of or having lumps **2** (esp of the sea) rough **3** (of a person) heavy or bulky > **'lumpily** *adv* > **'lumpiness** *n*

lumpy jaw *n vet science* a nontechnical name for **actinomycosis**

Luna¹ ('luːnə) *n* **1** the alchemical name for **silver 2** the Roman goddess of the moon. Greek counterpart: **Selene** [from Latin: moon]

Luna² ('luːnə), **Lunik** ('luːnɪk) *n* any of a series of Soviet lunar space-probes, one of which, **Luna 9,** made the first soft landing on the moon (1966)

lunacy ('luːnəsɪ) *n, pl* **-cies 1** (formerly) any severe mental illness **2** foolishness or a foolish act

luna moth *n* a large American saturniid moth, *Tropaea* (*or Actias*) *luna,* having light green wings with a yellow crescent-shaped marking on each forewing [C19 so named from the markings on its wings]

lunar ('luːnə) *adj* **1** of or relating to the moon **2** occurring on, used on, or designed to land on the surface of the moon: *lunar module* **3** relating to, caused by, or measured by the position or orbital motion of the moon **4** of or containing silver [C17 from Latin *lūnāris,* from *lūna* the moon]

lunar caustic *n* silver nitrate fused into sticks, which were formerly used in cauterizing

lunar eclipse *n* See **eclipse** (sense 1)

lunarian (luː'nɛərɪən) *n* **1** an archaic word for **selenographer 2** *myth* an inhabitant of the moon

lunar module *n* the module used to carry two of the three astronauts on an Apollo spacecraft to the surface of the moon and back to the spacecraft

lunar month *n* another name for **synodic month** See **month** (sense 6)

lunar year *n* See **year** (sense 6)

lunate ('luːneɪt) *adj* **also lunated 1** *anatomy, botany* shaped like a crescent ▷ *n* **2** a crescent-shaped bone forming part of the wrist [C18 from Latin *lūnātus* crescent-shaped, from *lūnāre,* from *lūna* moon]

lunatic ('luːnətɪk) *adj* **also** *or rarely* **lunatical** (luː'nætɪkᵊl) **1** an archaic word for **insane 2** foolish; eccentric; crazy ▷ *n* **3** a person who is insane [C13 (adj) via Old French from Late Latin *lūnāticus* crazy, moonstruck, from Latin *lūna* moon] > **lu'natically** *adv*

lunatic asylum *n* another name, usually regarded as offensive, for **mental home**

lunatic fringe *n* the members of a society or group who adopt or support views regarded as extreme or fanatical

lunation (luː'neɪʃən) *n* another name for **synodic month** See **month** (sense 6)

lunch (lʌntʃ) *n* **1** a meal eaten during the middle of the day **2** *Caribbean* (among older people) mid-afternoon tea ▷ *vb* **3** (*intr*) to eat lunch **4** (*tr*) to provide or buy lunch for [C16 probably short form of LUNCHEON] > **'luncher** *n*

lunchbox ('lʌntʃ,bɒks) *n* **1** a container for carrying a packed lunch **2** *Brit and Austral humorous* a man's genitals

luncheon ('lʌntʃən) *n* a lunch, esp a formal one [c16 probably variant of *nuncheon*, from Middle English *noneschench*, from *none* NOON + *schench* drink]

luncheon club *n* **1** *social welfare* (in Britain) an arrangement or organization for serving hot midday meals for a small charge to old people in clubs or daycentres **2** a society or group of people who meet regularly for an organized lunch

luncheonette (,lʌntʃə'nɛt) *n* US and Canadian a café or small informal restaurant where light meals and snacks are served

luncheon meat *n* a ground mixture of meat (often pork) and cereal, usually tinned

luncheon voucher *n* a voucher worth a specified amount issued to employees and redeemable at a restaurant for food. Abbreviation: LV US equivalent: **meal ticket**

lunch hour *n* **1** Also called: **lunch break** a break in the middle of the working day, during which lunch may be eaten **2** Also called: **lunch time** the time at which lunch is usually eaten

lunchroom ('lʌntʃ,ruːm, -,rʊm) *n* US and Canadian a room where lunch is served or where students, employees, etc, may eat lunches they bring

Lund (lʊnd) *n* a city in SE Sweden, northeast of Malmö: founded in about 1020 by the Danish King Canute; the archbishopric for all Scandinavia in the Middle Ages; university (1668). Pop: 101 427 (2004 est)

Lundy ('lʌndɪ) *n* an island in SW England, in Devon, in the Bristol Channel: now a bird sanctuary. Pop: 50 (latest est)

Lundy's Lane ('lʌndɪz) *n* the site, near Niagara Falls, of a major battle (1814) in the War of 1812, in which British and Canadian forces defeated the Americans

lune¹ (luːn) *n* **1 a** a section of the surface of a sphere enclosed between two semicircles that intersect at opposite points on the sphere **b** a crescent-shaped figure formed on a plane surface by the intersection of the arcs of two circles **2** something shaped like a crescent **3** *RC Church* another word for **lunette** (sense 6) [c18 from Latin *lūna* moon]

lune² (luːn) *n* falconry a leash for hawks or falcons [c14 *loigne*, from Old French, from Medieval Latin *longia, longea*, from Latin *longus* LONG¹]

Lüneburg (*German* 'lyːnəbʊrk) *n* a city in N Germany, in Lower Saxony: capital of the duchy of Brunswick-Lüneburg from 1235 to 1369; prominent Hanse town; saline springs. Pop: 70 614 (2003 est)

lunette (luː'nɛt) *n* **1** anything that is shaped like a crescent **2** an oval or circular opening to admit light in a dome **3** a semicircular panel containing a window, mural, or sculpture **4** a ring attached to a vehicle, into which a hook is inserted so that it can be towed **5** a type of fortification like a detached bastion **6** Also called: **lune** *RC Church* a case fitted with a bracket to hold the consecrated host [c16 from French: crescent, from *lune* moon, from Latin *lūna*]

Lunéville (*French* lynevil) *n* a city in NE France: scene of the signing of the **Peace of Lunéville** between France and Austria (1801). Pop: 20 200 (1999)

lung (lʌŋ) *n* **1** either one of a pair of spongy saclike respiratory organs within the thorax of higher vertebrates, which oxygenate the blood and remove its carbon dioxide **2** any similar or analogous organ in other vertebrates or in invertebrates **3 at the top of one's lungs** in one's loudest voice; yelling ▷ Related adjectives: **pneumonic, pulmonary, pulmonic** [Old English *lungen*; related to Old High German *lungun* lung. Compare LIGHTS²]

lungan ('lʌŋgən) *n* another name for **longan**

lunge¹ (lʌndʒ) *n* **1** a sudden forward motion **2** *fencing* a thrust made by advancing the front foot and straightening the back leg, extending the sword arm forwards ▷ *vb* **3** to move or cause to move with a lunge **4** (*intr*) *fencing* to make a lunge

[c18 shortened form of obsolete c17 *allonge*, from French *allonger* to stretch out (one's arm), from Late Latin *ēlongāre* to lengthen. Compare ELONGATE] ▷ '**lunger** *n*

lunge² (lʌndʒ) *n* **1** a rope used in training or exercising a horse ▷ *vb* **2** to exercise or train (a horse) on a lunge [c17 from Old French *longe*, shortened from *allonge*, ultimately from Latin *longus* LONG¹; related to LUNGE¹]

lungfish ('lʌŋ,fɪʃ) *n, pl* **-fish** or **-fishes** any freshwater bony fish of the subclass *Dipnoi*, having an air-breathing lung, fleshy paired fins, and an elongated body. The only living species are those of the genera *Lepidosiren* of South America, *Protopterus* of Africa, and *Neoceratodus* of Australia

lungi or **lungee** ('lʊŋgiː) *n* a long piece of cotton cloth worn as a loincloth, sash, or turban by Indian men or as a skirt [c17 Hindi, from Persian]

Lungki or **Lung-chi** ('lʊŋ'kiː) *n* the former name of **Zhangzhou**

lungworm ('lʌŋ,wɜːm) *n* **1** any parasitic nematode worm of the family *Metastrongylidae*, occurring in the lungs of mammals, esp *Metastrongylus apri* which infects pigs **2** any of certain other nematodes that are parasitic in the lungs

lungwort ('lʌŋ,wɜːt) *n* **1** any of several Eurasian plants of the boraginaceous genus *Pulmonaria*, esp *P. officinalis*, which has spotted leaves and clusters of blue or purple flowers: formerly used to treat lung diseases **2** any of various boraginaceous plants of the N temperate genus *Mertensia*, such as *Mertensia maritima* (sea lungwort), having drooping clusters of tubular usually blue flowers

Lunik ('luːnɪk) *n* another name for **Luna²**

lunisolar (,luːnɪ'səʊlə) *adj* resulting from, relating to, or based on the combined gravitational attraction of the sun and moon [c17 from Latin *lūna* moon + SOLAR]

lunitidal (,luːnɪ'taɪdəl) *adj* of or relating to tidal phenomena as produced by the moon [c19 from Latin *lūna* moon + TIDAL]

lunitidal interval *n* the difference in time between the moon crossing a meridian and the following high tide at that meridian

lunk (lʌŋk) *n* an awkward, heavy, or stupid person

lunula ('luːnjʊlə) or **lunule** ('luːnjuːl) *n, pl* **-nulae** (-njʊ,liː) or **-nules** the white crescent-shaped area at the base of the human fingernail. Nontechnical name: **half-moon** [c16 from Latin: small moon, from *lūna*]

lunulate ('luːnjʊ,leɪt) or **lunulated** *adj* **1** having markings shaped like crescents: *lunulate patterns on an insect* **2** Also: **lunular** shaped like a crescent

Luo (lə'wəʊ, 'luːəʊ) *n* (*pl* **Luo** or **Luos**) a member of a cattle-herding Nilotic people living chiefly east of Lake Victoria in Kenya **2** the language of this people, belonging to the Nilotic group of the Nilo-Saharan family

Luoyang or **Loyang** ('ləʊ'jæn) *n* a city in E China, in N Henan province on the Luo River near its confluence with the Yellow River; an important Buddhist centre in the 5th and 6th centuries. Pop: 1 594 000 (2005 est)

Lupercalia (,luːpɜː'keɪlɪə) *n, pl* **-lia** or **-lias** an ancient Roman festival of fertility, celebrated annually on Feb 15. See also **Saint Valentine's Day** [Latin, from *Lupercālis* belonging to *Lupercus*, a Roman god of the flocks] ,**Luper'calian** *adj*

lupin or US **lupine** ('luːpɪn) *n* any leguminous plant of the genus *Lupinus*, of North America, Europe, and Africa, with large spikes of brightly coloured flowers and flattened pods [c14 from Latin *lupīnus* wolfish (see LUPINE); from the belief that the plant ravenously exhausted the soil]

lupine ('luːpaɪn) *adj* of, relating to, or resembling a wolf [c17 from Latin *lupīnus*, from *lupus* wolf]

lupulin ('luːpjʊlɪn) *n* a resinous powder extracted from the female flowers of the hop plant and used as a sedative [c19 from New Latin *lupulus*, diminutive of *lupus* the hop plant]

lupus ('luːpəs) *n* any of various ulcerative skin

diseases [c16 via Medieval Latin from Latin: wolf; said to be so called because it rapidly eats away the affected part]

> **USAGE** In current usage the word *lupus* alone is generally understood to signify lupus vulgaris, lupus erythematosus being normally referred to in full or by the abbreviation LE

Lupus ('luːpəs) *n, Latin genitive* **Lupi** ('luːpaɪ) a constellation in the S hemisphere lying between Centaurus and Ara

lupus erythematosus (,ɛrɪ,θiːmə'təʊsəs) *n* either of two inflammatory diseases of the connective tissue. **Discoid lupus erythematosus** is characterized by a scaly rash over the cheeks and bridge of the nose; **disseminated** and **systemic lupus erythematosus** affects the joints, lungs, kidneys, or skin. Abbreviation: LE

lupus vulgaris (vʌl'gɛərɪs) *n* tuberculosis of the skin, esp of the face, with the formation of raised translucent nodules. Sometimes shortened to: **lupus**

lur or **lure** (lʊə) *n, pl* **lures** ('lʊərɪz) a large bronze musical horn found in Danish peat bogs and probably dating to the Bronze Age [from Danish (and Swedish and Norwegian) *lur*, from Old Norse *lūthr* trumpet]

lurch¹ (lɜːtʃ) *vb* (*intr*) **1** to lean or pitch suddenly to one side **2** to stagger or sway ▷ *n* **3** the act or an instance of lurching [c19 origin unknown] > '**lurching** *adj*

lurch² (lɜːtʃ) *n* **1** leave (someone) in the lurch to desert (someone) in trouble **2** *cribbage* the state of a losing player with less than 30 points at the end of a game (esp in the phrase **in the lurch**) [c16 from French *lourche* a game similar to backgammon, apparently from *lourche* (adj) deceived, probably of Germanic origin]

lurch³ (lɜːtʃ) *vb* (*intr*) archaic or dialect to prowl or steal about suspiciously [c15 perhaps a variant of LURK]

lurcher ('lɜːtʃə) *n* **1** a crossbred hunting dog, usually a greyhound cross with a collie, esp one trained to hunt silently **2** archaic a person who prowls or lurks [c16 from LURCH³]

lurdan ('lɜːdən) archaic ▷ *n* **1** a stupid or dull person ▷ *adj* **2** dull or stupid [c14 from Old French *lourdin*, Old French *lourd* heavy, from Latin *lūridus* LURID]

lure (lʊə) *vb* (*tr*) **1** (sometimes foll by *away* or *into*) to tempt or attract by the promise of some type of reward **2** *falconry* to entice (a hawk or falcon) from the air to the falconer by a lure ▷ *n* **3** a person or thing that lures **4** *angling* any of various types of brightly-coloured artificial spinning baits, usually consisting of a plastic or metal body mounted with hooks and trimmed with feathers, etc. See **jig, plug, spoon** **5** *falconry* a feathered decoy to which small pieces of meat can be attached and which is equipped with a long thong [c14 from Old French *loirre* falconer's lure, from Germanic; related to Old English *lathian* to invite] > '**lurer** *n*

Lurex ('lʊərɛks) *n trademark* **1** a thin metallic thread coated with plastic **2** fabric containing such thread, which gives it a glittering appearance

lurgy ('lɜːgɪ) *n, pl* **-gies** *facetious* any undetermined illness

lurid ('lʊərɪd) *adj* **1** vivid in shocking detail; sensational **2** horrible in savagery or violence **3** pallid in colour; wan **4** glowing with an unnatural glare [c17 from Latin *lūridus* pale yellow; probably related to *lūtum* a yellow vegetable dye] > '**luridly** *adv* > '**luridness** *n*

lurk (lɜːk) *vb* (*intr*) **1** to move stealthily or be concealed, esp for evil purposes **2** to be present in an unobtrusive way; go unnoticed ▷ *n* **3** to read messages posted on an electronic network without contributing messages oneself **4** *Austral and NZ slang* a scheme or stratagem for success [c13 probably frequentative of LOUR; compare Middle Dutch *loeren* to lie in wait] > 'lurker *n*

lurking ('lɜːkɪŋ) *adj* **1** lingering and persistent, though unsuspected or unacknowledged: *a lurking suspicion* **2** dimly perceived

Lusaka (luːˈzɑːkə, -ˈsɑːkə) *n* the capital of Zambia, in the southeast at an altitude of 1280 m (4200 ft): became capital of Northern Rhodesia in 1932 and of Zambia in 1964; University of Zambia (1966). Pop: 1 450 000 (2005 est)

Lusatia (luːˈseɪʃɪə) *n* a region of central Europe, lying between the upper reaches of the Elbe and Oder Rivers: now mostly in E Germany, extending into SW Poland; inhabited chiefly by Sorbs

Lusatian (luːˈseɪʃɪən) *adj* **1** of or relating to Lusatia, its people, or their language ▷ *n* **2** a native or inhabitant of Lusatia; a Sorb **3** the Sorbian language

luscious ('lʌʃəs) *adj* **1** extremely pleasurable, esp to the taste or smell **2** very attractive **3** *archaic* cloying [C15 *lucius, licius,* perhaps a shortened form of DELICIOUS] > 'lusciously *adv* > 'lusciousness *n*

luser ('luːzə) *n facetious* a user of a computer system, as considered by a systems administrator or other member of a technical support team [C20 a blend of LOSER + USER]

lush[1] (lʌʃ) *adj* **1** (of vegetation) abounding in lavish growth **2** (esp of fruits) succulent and fleshy **3** luxurious, elaborate, or opulent [C15 probably from Old French *lasche* lax, lazy, from Latin *laxus* loose; perhaps related to Old English *lǣc,* Old Norse *lakr* weak, German *lasch* loose] > 'lushly *adv* > 'lushness *n*

lush[2] (lʌʃ) *slang* ▷ *n* **1** a heavy drinker, esp an alcoholic **2** alcoholic drink ▷ *vb* **3** *US and Canadian* to drink (alcohol) to excess [C19 origin unknown]

Lüshun ('luːʃʊn) *n* a port in NE China, in S Liaoning province, at the S end of the Liaodong peninsula; together with the city of Dalian it comprises the port complex of Lüda: jointly held by China and the Soviet Union (1945–55). Former name: Port Arthur

Lusitania (ˌluːsɪˈteɪnɪə) *n* an ancient region of the W Iberian Peninsula: a Roman province from 27 BC to the late 4th century AD; corresponds to most of present-day Portugal and the Spanish provinces of Salamanca and Cáceres

Lusitanian (ˌluːsɪˈteɪnɪən) *adj* **1** *chiefly poetic* of or relating to Lusitania or Portugal **2** *biology* denoting flora or fauna characteristically found only in the warm, moist, west-facing coastal regions of Portugal, Spain, France, and the west and southwest coasts of Great Britain and Ireland

Luso- *combining form* indicating Portugal or Portuguese [from Portuguese *lusitano,* from Latin, from LUSITANIA]

lust (lʌst) *n* **1** a strong desire for sexual gratification **2** a strong desire or drive ▷ *vb* **3** (*intr; often foll by after or for*) to have a lust (for) [Old English; related to Old High German *lust* desire, Old Norse *losti* sexual desire, Latin *lascīvus* playful, wanton, lustful. Compare LISTLESS]

lustful ('lʌstfʊl) *adj* **1** archaic vigorous or lusty > 'lustfully *adv* > 'lustfulness *n*

lustral ('lʌstrəl) *adj* **1** of or relating to a ceremony of purification **2** taking place at intervals of five years; quinquennial [C16 from Latin *lūstrālis* adj from LUSTRUM]

lustrate ('lʌstreɪt) *vb* (*tr*) to purify by means of religious rituals or ceremonies [C17 from Latin *lūstrāre* to brighten] > lus'tration *n* > lustrative ('lʌstrətɪv) *adj*

lustre *or US* **luster** ('lʌstə) *n* **1** reflected light; sheen; gloss **2** radiance or brilliance of light **3** great splendour of accomplishment, beauty, etc **4** a substance used to polish or put a gloss on a surface **5** a vase or chandelier from which hang cut-glass drops **6** a drop-shaped piece of cut glass or crystal used as a decoration on a chandelier, vase, etc **7 a** a shiny metallic surface on some pottery and porcelain **b** (*as modifier*): *lustre decoration* **8** *mineralogy* the way in which light is

reflected from the surface of a mineral. It is one of the properties by which minerals are defined ▷ *vb* **9** to make, be, or become lustrous [C16 from Old French, from Old Italian *lustro,* from Latin *lustrāre* to make bright; related to LUSTRUM] > 'lustreless *or US* 'lusterless *adj* > 'lustrous *adj*

lustreware *or US* **lusterware** ('lʌstəˌwɛə) *n* pottery or porcelain ware with lustre decoration

lustring ('lʌstrɪŋ) *or* **lutestring** ('luːtˌstrɪŋ) *n* a glossy silk cloth, formerly used for clothing, upholstery, etc [C17 from Italian *lustrino,* from *lustro* LUSTRE]

lustrum ('lʌstrəm) *or* **lustre** *n, pl* -**trums** *or* -**tra** (-trə) a period of five years [C16 from Latin: ceremony of purification, from *lustrāre* to brighten, purify]

lusty ('lʌstɪ) *adj* **lustier, lustiest 1** having or characterized by robust health **2** strong or invigorating: *a lusty brew* **3** lustful > 'lustily *adv* > 'lustiness *n*

lusus naturae ('luːsʊs næˈtʊərɪ:) *n* a freak, mutant, or monster [C17 Latin: whim of nature]

Lü-ta ('luːˈtɑː) *n* a variant transliteration of the Chinese name for **Lüda**

lutanist ('luːtənɪst) *n* a variant spelling of **lutenist**

lute[1] (luːt) *n* an ancient plucked stringed instrument, consisting of a long fingerboard with frets and gut strings, and a body shaped like a sliced pear [C14 from Old French *lut,* via Old Provençal from Arabic *al 'ūd,* literally: the wood]

lute[2] (luːt) *n* **1** *Also called:* **luting** a mixture of cement and clay used to seal the joints between pipes, etc **2** *dentistry* a thin layer of cement used to fix a crown or inlay in place on a tooth ▷ *vb* **3** (*tr*) to seal (a joint or surface) with lute [C14 via Old French ultimately from Latin *lutum* clay]

luteal ('luːtɪəl) *adj* relating to or characterized by the development of the corpus luteum: *the luteal phase of the oestrous cycle* [C20 from Latin *lūteus* yellow, relating to *lūtum* a yellow weed]

lutein ('luːtɪɪn) *n* a xanthophyll pigment, occurring in plants, that has a light-absorbing function in photosynthesis [C20 from Latin *lūteus* yellow + -IN]

luteinizing hormone ('luːtɪɪˌnaɪzɪŋ) *n* a gonadotrophic hormone secreted by the anterior lobe of the pituitary gland. In female vertebrates it stimulates ovulation, and in mammals it also induces the conversion of the ruptured follicle into the corpus luteum. In male vertebrates it promotes maturation of the interstitial cells of the testes and stimulates androgen secretion. Abbreviation: LH *Also called:* **interstitial cell-stimulating hormone** *See also* **follicle-stimulating hormone, prolactin** [C19 from Latin *lūteum* egg yolk, from *lūteus* yellow]

luteinizing hormone-releasing hormone *n* a hypothalamic peptide that stimulates the pituitary gland to release luteinizing hormone. Abbreviation: LH-RH

lutenist ('luːtənɪst), **lutanist** *or US and Canadian* (*sometimes*) **lutist** ('luːtɪst) *n* a person who plays the lute [C17 from Medieval Latin *lūtānista,* from *lūtāna,* apparently from Old French *lut* LUTE[1]]

luteolin ('luːtɪəlɪn) *n* a yellow crystalline compound found, in the form of its glycoside, in many plants. Formula: $C_{15}H_{10}O_6$ [C19 via French from New Latin *reseda lūteola,* dyer's rocket, from which this substance is obtained; *lūteola* from Latin *lūteus* yellow]

luteotrophin (ˌluːtɪəʊˈtrəʊfɪn), **luteotrophic hormone,** *esp US* **luteotropin, luteotropic hormone** *n* other names for **prolactin**

luteous ('luːtɪəs) *adj* of a light to moderate greenish-yellow colour [C17 from Latin *lūteus* yellow]

lutestring ('luːtˌstrɪŋ) *n textiles* a variant of **lustring**

Lutetia *or* **Lutetia Parisiorum** (luːˈtiːʃə pəˌrɪzɪˈɔːrəm) *n* an ancient name for **Paris** (the French city)

lutetium *or* **lutecium** (lʊˈtiːʃɪəm) *n* a silvery-white metallic element of the lanthanide series, occurring in monazite and used as a catalyst in cracking, alkylation, and polymerization. Symbol: Lu; atomic no.: 71; atomic wt.: 174.967; valency: 3; relative density: 9.841; melting pt.: 1663°C; boiling pt.: 3402°C [C19 New Latin, from Latin *Lūtētia* ancient name of Paris, home of G. Urbain (1872–1938), French chemist, who discovered it]

Luth. *abbreviation for* Lutheran

Lutheran ('luːθərən) *n* **1** a follower of Martin Luther (1483–1546), the German leader of the Protestant Reformation, or a member of a Lutheran Church ▷ *adj* **2** of or relating to Luther or his doctrines, the most important being justification by faith alone, consubstantiation, and the authority of the Bible **3** of or denoting any Protestant Church that follows Luther's doctrines > 'Lutheranism *n*

Lutherism ('luːθərɪzəm) *n* the religious doctrines of Martin Luther, the German leader of the Protestant Reformation (1483–1546)

luthern ('luːθən) *n* another name for **dormer** [C17 probably from LUCARNE, perhaps influenced by LUTHERAN]

Lutine bell ('luːtiːn, luːˈtiːn) *n* a bell, taken from the ship *Lutine,* kept at Lloyd's in London and rung before important announcements, esp the loss of a vessel

luting ('luːtɪŋ) *n* **1** another name for **lute**[2] (sense 1) **2** *Also called:* **luting paste** a strip of pastry placed around the dish to seal the lid of a pie

lutist ('luːtɪst) *n* **1** *US and Canadian* another word for **lutenist** **2** a person who makes lutes

lutite ('luːtaɪt) *n* another name for **pelite** [C20 from Latin *lutum* mud + -ITE[1]]

Luton ('luːt³n) *n* **1** a town in SE central England, in Luton unitary authority, S Bedfordshire: airport; motor-vehicle industries; university (1993). Pop: 185 543 (2001) **2** a unitary authority in SE central England, in Bedfordshire. Pop: 185 200 (2003 est). Area: 43 sq km (17 sq miles)

Luton Hoo (huː) *n* a mansion near Luton in Bedfordshire: built (1766–67) for the 3rd Earl of Bute by Robert Adam; rebuilt in the 19th century: houses the Wernher Collection of tapestries, porcelain, and paintings

lutz (luːts) *n skating* a jump in which the skater takes off from the back outside edge of one skate, makes one, two, or three turns in the air, and lands on the back outside edge of the other skate [C20 of uncertain origin]

Lützen (*German* 'lytsən) *n* a town near Leipzig in E Germany, in Saxony; site of a battle (1632) in the Thirty Years' War in which the army of the Holy Roman Empire under Wallenstein was defeated by the Swedes under Gustavus Adolphus, who died in the battle

Lützow-Holm Bay ('lʊtsəʊˈhəʊm) *n* an inlet of the Indian Ocean on the coast of Antarctica, between Enderby Land and Queen Maud Land

LUV *text messaging abbreviation for* love

luvvie *or* **luvvy** ('lʌvɪ) *n, pl* -**vies** *facetious* a person who is involved in the acting profession or the theatre, esp one with a tendency to affectation [C20 from LOVEY]

lux (lʌks) *n, pl* **lux** the derived SI unit of illumination equal to a luminous flux of 1 lumen per square metre. 1 lux is equivalent to 0.0929 foot-candle. Symbol: lx [C19 from Latin: light]

Lux. *abbreviation for* Luxembourg

luxate ('lʌkseɪt) *vb* (*tr*) *pathol* to put (a shoulder, knee, etc) out of joint; dislocate [C17 from Latin *luxāre* to displace, from *luxus* dislocated; related to Greek *loxos* oblique] > lux'ation *n*

luxe (lʌks, lʊks; *French* lyks) *n See* de luxe [C16 from French from Latin *luxus* extravagance, LUXURY]

Luxembourg ('lʌksəmˌbɜːɡ; *French* lyksɑ̃buːr) *n* **1** a grand duchy in W Europe: it formed the Benelux customs union with the Belgium and the Netherlands in 1948 and was a founder member of the Common Market, now the European Union . Languages: French, German, and Luxemburgish. Religion: Roman Catholic majority. Currency: euro. Capital: Luxembourg. Pop: 459 000 (2004 est). Area: 2586 sq km (999 sq miles) **2** the capital of Luxembourg, on the Alzette River: an industrial centre. Pop: 77 300 (2003 est) **3** a province in SE Belgium, in the Ardennes. Capital: Arlon. Pop: 254 120 (2004 est). Area: 4416 sq km (1705 sq miles)

Luxembourger ('lʌksəm,bɜːɡə) *n* a native or inhabitant of Luxembourg

Luxor ('lʌksɔː) *n* a town in S Egypt, on the River Nile: the southern part of the site of ancient Thebes; many ruins and tombs, notably the temple built by Amenhotep III (about 1411–1375 BC). Pop: 183 000 (2005 est)

luxulianite *or* **luxullianite** (lʌk'suːljə,naɪt) *n* a rare variety of granite containing tourmaline embedded in quartz and feldspar [C19 named after *Luxulyan*, a village in Cornwall near which it was first found]

luxuriant (lʌɡ'zjʊərɪənt) *adj* **1** rich and abundant; lush **2** very elaborate or ornate **3** extremely productive or fertile [C16 from Latin *luxuriāns*, present participle of *luxuriāre* to abound to excess] > lux'uriance *n* > lux'uriantly *adv*

▪ USAGE See at **luxurious**

luxuriate (lʌɡ'zjʊərɪ,eɪt) *vb* (*intr*) **1** (foll by *in*) to take voluptuous pleasure; revel **2** to flourish extensively or profusely **3** to live in a sumptuous way [C17 from Latin *luxuriāre*] > lux,uri'ation *n*

luxurious (lʌɡ'zjʊərɪəs) *adj* **1** characterized by luxury **2** enjoying or devoted to luxury **3** an archaic word for **lecherous** [C14 via Old French from Latin *luxuriōsus* excessive] > lux'uriously *adv* > lux'uriousness *n*

▪ USAGE *Luxurious* is sometimes wrongly used where *luxuriant* is meant: *he had a luxuriant* (not *luxurious*) *moustache; the walls were covered with a luxuriant growth of wisteria*

luxury ('lʌkʃərɪ) *n*, *pl* **-ries 1** indulgence in and enjoyment of rich, comfortable, and sumptuous living **2** (*sometimes plural*) something that is considered an indulgence rather than a necessity **3** something pleasant and satisfying: *the luxury of independence* **4** (*modifier*) relating to, indicating, or supplying luxury: *a luxury liner* [C14 (in the sense: lechery): via Old French from Latin *luxuria* excess, from *luxus* extravagance]

Luzern (lu'tsɛrn) *n* the German name for **Lucerne**

Luzon (luː'zɒn) *n* the main and largest island of the Philippines, in the N part of the archipelago, separated from the other islands by the Sibuyan Sea: important agriculturally, with large forests and rich mineral resources; industrial centres at Manila and Batangas. Capital: Quezon City. Pop: 32 558 000 (1995 est). Area: 108 378 sq km (41 845 sq miles)

lv *the internet domain name for* Latvia

Lv *currency abbreviation for* lev(a)

LV 1 (in Britain) *abbreviation for* luncheon voucher **2** ▷ *international car registration for* Latvia

LVAD *abbreviation for* left ventricular assist device; an implanted device that boosts the output of the heart on a short-term basis; for example in people awaiting heart transplants

Lviv (lvif) *n* an industrial city in W Ukraine: it has belonged to Poland (1340–1772; 1919–39), Austria (1772–1918), Germany (1939–45), and the Soviet Union (1945–91); Ukrainian cultural centre, with a university (1661). Pop: 719 000 (2005 est). Russian name: **Lvov** Polish name: **Lwów** German name: **Lemberg**

Lvov (*Russian* ljvɔf) *n* the Russian name for **Lviv**

LVP *abbreviation for* least valuable player

Lw *the former chemical symbol for* lawrencium (now superseded by **Lr**)

LW *abbreviation for* **1** radio long wave **2** low water

lwl *or* **LWL** *abbreviation for* length waterline; the length of a vessel at the waterline, taken at the centre axis

LWM *or* **lwm** *abbreviation for* low water mark

Lwów (lvuf) *n* the Polish name for **Lviv**

lx *physics symbol for* lux

LXX *symbol for* Septuagint

ly *the internet domain name for* Libyan Arab Jamahiriya

-ly¹ *suffix forming adjectives* **1** having the nature or qualities of: *brotherly; godly* **2** occurring at certain intervals; every: *daily; yearly* [Old English *-lic*]

-ly² *suffix forming adverbs* in a certain manner; to a certain degree: *quickly; recently; chiefly* [Old English *-lice*, from *-lic* -LY¹]

Lyallpur (,laɪəl'pʊə) *n* the former name (until 1979) of **Faisalabad**

lyase ('laɪeɪz) *n* any enzyme that catalyses the separation of two parts of a molecule by the formation of a double bond between them [C20 from Greek *lusis* a loosening + -ASE]

lycanthrope ('laɪkən,θrəʊp, laɪ'kænθrəʊp) *n* **1** a werewolf **2** *psychiatry* a person who believes that he is a wolf [C17 via New Latin, from Greek *lukanthrōpos*, from *lukos* wolf + *anthrōpos* man]

lycanthropy (laɪ'kænθrəpɪ) *n* **1** the supposed magical transformation of a person into a wolf **2** *psychiatry* a delusion in which a person believes that he is a wolf [C16 from Greek *lukánthropía*, from *lukos* wolf + *anthrōpos* man] > lycanthropic (,laɪkən'θrɒpɪk) *adj*

Lycaon (laɪ'keɪɒn) *n Greek myth* a king of Arcadia said to have offered Zeus a plate of human flesh to learn whether the god was omniscient

Lycaonia (,laɪkə'əʊnɪə) *n* an ancient region of S Asia Minor, north of the Taurus Mountains; corresponds to present-day S central Turkey

lycée French (lise; *English* 'liːseɪ) *n*, *pl lycées* (lise; *English* 'liːseɪz) a secondary school [C19 French, from Latin: LYCEUM]

lyceum (laɪ'sɪəm) *n* (now chiefly in the names of buildings) **1** a public building for concerts, lectures, etc **2** *US* a cultural organization responsible for presenting concerts, lectures, etc **3** another word for **lycée**

Lyceum (laɪ'sɪəm) *n* **the 1** a school and sports ground of ancient Athens: site of Aristotle's discussions with his pupils **2** the Aristotelian school of philosophy [from Greek *Lukeion*, named after a temple nearby dedicated to *Apollo Lukeios*, an epithet of unknown origin]

lychee (,laɪ'tʃiː) *n* a variant spelling of **litchi**

lych gate *or* **lich gate** (lɪtʃ) *n* a roofed gate to a churchyard, formerly used during funerals as a temporary shelter for the bier [C15 *lich*, from Old English *līc* corpse]

lychnis ('lɪknɪs) *n* any caryophyllaceous plant of the genus *Lychnis*, having red, pink, or white five-petalled flowers. See also **ragged robin** [C17 New Latin, via Latin, from Greek *lukhnis* a red flower; related to *lukhnos* lamp]

Lycia ('lɪsɪə) *n* an ancient region on the coast of SW Asia Minor: a Persian, Rhodian, and Roman province

Lycian ('lɪsɪən) *adj* **1** of or relating to ancient Lycia, its inhabitants, or their language ▷ *n* **2** an inhabitant of Lycia **3** the extinct language of the Lycians, belonging to the Anatolian group or family

lycopene ('laɪkə,piːn) *n* **1** an acyclic carotenoid occuring in tomatoes and some other ripe fruit as a red pigment. As an antioxidant its consumption can reduce the risk of some cancers

lycopod ('laɪkə,pɒd) *n* another name for a **club moss**, esp one of the genus *Lycopodium*

lycopodium (,laɪkə'pəʊdɪəm) *n* any club moss of the genus *Lycopodium*, resembling moss but having vascular tissue and spore-bearing cones: family *Lycopodiaceae*. See also **ground pine** (sense 2) [C18 New Latin, from Greek, from *lukos* wolf + *pous* foot]

Lycra ('laɪkrə) *n trademark* a type of synthetic elastic fabric and fibre used for tight-fitting garments, such as swimming costumes

Lydda ('lɪdə) *n* another name for **Lod**

lyddite ('lɪdaɪt) *n* **1** an explosive consisting chiefly of fused picric acid **2** a dense black variety of chert, formerly used as a touchstone [C19 (sense 1) named after *Lydd*, a town in Kent near which the first tests were made]

Lydia ('lɪdɪə) *n* an ancient region on the coast of W Asia Minor: a powerful kingdom in the century and a half before the Persian conquest (546 BC). Chief town: Sardis

Lydian ('lɪdɪən) *adj* **1** of or relating to ancient Lydia, its inhabitants, or their language **2** *music* of or relating to an authentic mode represented by the ascending natural diatonic scale from F to F. See also **Hypo-** Compare **Hypolydian** ▷ *n* **3** an inhabitant of Lydia **4** the extinct language of the Lydians, thought to belong to the Anatolian group or family

lye (laɪ) *n* **1** any solution obtained by leaching, such as the caustic solution obtained by leaching wood ash **2** a concentrated solution of sodium hydroxide or potassium hydroxide [Old English *lēag*; related to Middle Dutch *lōghe*, Old Norse *laug* bath, Latin *lavāre* to wash]

lying¹ ('laɪɪŋ) *vb* the present participle and gerund of **lie¹**

lying² ('laɪɪŋ) *vb* the present participle and gerund of **lie²**

lying-in *n*, *pl* lyings-in **a** confinement in childbirth **b** (*as modifier*): *a lying-in hospital*

lyke-wake ('laɪk,weɪk) *n Brit* a watch held over a dead person, often with festivities [C16 perhaps from Old Norse; see LYCH GATE, WAKE¹]

Lyme disease (laɪm) *n* a disease of domestic animals and humans, caused by the spirochaete *Borrelia burghdorferi* and transmitted by ticks, and variously affecting the joints, heart, and brain [C20 named after *Lyme*, Connecticut, the town where it was first identified in humans]

lyme grass (laɪm) *n* a N temperate perennial dune grass, *Elymus arenarius*, with a creeping stem and rough bluish leaves [C18 probably a respelling (influenced by its genus name, *Elymus*) of LIME¹, referring to its stabilizing effect (like lime in mortar)]

Lyme Regis (laɪm 'riːdʒɪs) *n* a resort in S England, in Dorset, on the English Channel: noted for finds of prehistoric fossils. Pop: 4406 (2001)

Lymington ('lɪmɪŋtən) *n* a market town in S England, in SW Hampshire, on the Solent. Pop: 14 227 (2001)

lymph (lɪmf) *n* the almost colourless fluid, containing chiefly white blood cells, that is collected from the tissues of the body and transported in the lymphatic system [C17 from Latin *lympha* water, from earlier *limpa* influenced in form by Greek *numphē* nymph]

lymphadenitis (lɪm,fædɪ'naɪtɪs, ,lɪmfæd-) *n* inflammation of a lymph node [C19 New Latin. See LYMPH, ADENITIS]

lymphadenopathy (lɪm,fædɪ'nɒpəθɪ, ,lɪmfæd-) *n* a swelling of the lymph nodes, usually caused by inflammation associated with a viral infection such as rubella

lymphangial (lɪm'fændʒɪəl) *adj* of or relating to a lymphatic vessel

lymphangitis (,lɪmfæn'dʒaɪtɪs) *n*, *pl* -gitides (-'dʒɪtɪ,diːz) inflammation of one or more of the lymphatic vessels [C19 see LYMPH, ANGIO-, -ITIS] > lymphangitic (,lɪmfæn'dʒɪtɪk) *adj*

lymphatic (lɪm'fætɪk) *adj* **1** of, relating to, or containing lymph: *the lymphatic vessels* **2** of or relating to the lymphatic system **3** sluggish or lacking vigour ▷ *n* **4** a lymphatic vessel [C17 (meaning: mad): from Latin *lymphāticus*. Original meaning perhaps arose from a confusion between *nymph* and LYMPH; compare Greek *numphaleptos* frenzied] > lym'phatically *adv*

lymphatic system *n* an extensive network of capillary vessels that transports the interstitial fluid of the body as lymph to the venous blood circulation

lymphatic tissue *n* tissue, such as the lymph nodes, tonsils, spleen, and thymus, that produces lymphocytes. Also called: lymphoid tissue

lymph cell *n* another name for **lymphocyte**

lymph gland *n* a former name for **lymph node**

lymph node *n* any of numerous bean-shaped masses of tissue, situated along the course of lymphatic vessels, that help to protect against infection by killing bacteria and neutralizing toxins and are the source of lymphocytes

lympho- *or before a vowel* **lymph-** *combining form* indicating lymph or the lymphatic system: *lymphogranuloma*

lymphoblast ('lɪmfəʊˌblɑːst) *n* an abnormal cell consisting of a large nucleus and small cytoplasm that was once thought to be an immature lymphocyte and is now associated with a type of leukaemia (**lymphoblastic leukaemia**) > lymphoblastic (ˌlɪmfəʊˈblæstɪk) *adj*

lymphocyte ('lɪmfəʊˌsaɪt) *n* a type of white blood cell formed in lymphoid tissue. See also **B-lymphocyte, T-lymphocyte.** > lymphocytic (ˌlɪmfəʊˈsɪtɪk) *adj*

lymphocytopenia (ˌlɪmfəʊˌsaɪtəʊˈpiːnɪə) *n pathol* an abnormally low level of lymphocytes in the blood. Also called: lymphopenia

lymphocytosis (ˌlɪmfəʊsaɪˈtəʊsɪs) *n* an abnormally large number of lymphocytes in the blood: often found in diseases such as glandular fever and smallpox > lymphocytotic (ˌlɪmfəʊsaɪˈtɒtɪk) *adj*

lymphoid ('lɪmfɔɪd) *adj* of or resembling lymph, or relating to the lymphatic system

lymphoid tissue *n* another name for **lymphatic tissue**

lymphokine ('lɪmfəʊˌkaɪn) *n immunol* a protein, released by lymphocytes, that affects other cells involved in the immune response

lymphoma (lɪmˈfəʊmə) *n, pl* **-mata** (-mətə) *or* **-mas** any form of cancer of the lymph nodes. Also called: lymphosarcoma (ˌlɪmfəʊsɑːˈkəʊmə) > lym'phomatous *or* lym'phoma,toid *adj*

lymphopoiesis (ˌlɪmfəʊpɔɪˈiːsɪs) *n, pl* **-ses** (-siːz) the formation of lymphatic tissue or lymphocytes > lymphopoietic (ˌlɪmfəʊpɔɪˈɛtɪk) *adj*

lyncean (lɪnˈsiːən) *adj* **1** of or resembling a lynx **2** *rare* having keen sight [c17 probably via Latin, from Greek *Lunkeios* concerning *Lunkeos*, an Argonaut renowned for his sharpsightedness, from *lunx* lynx]

lynch (lɪntʃ) *vb* (*tr*) (of a mob) to punish (a person) for some supposed offence by hanging without a trial [probably after Charles *Lynch* (1736–96), Virginia justice of the peace, who presided over extralegal trials of Tories during the American War of Independence] > 'lyncher *n* > 'lynching *n*

lynchet ('lɪntʃɪt) *n* a terrace or ridge formed in prehistoric or medieval times by ploughing a hillside [Old English *hlinc* ridge]

lynch law *n* the practice of condemning and punishing a person by mob action without a proper trial

Lynn (lɪn) *n* another name for **King's Lynn** Also called: Lynn Regis ('riːdʒɪs)

lynx (lɪŋks) *n, pl* **lynxes** *or* **lynx 1** a feline mammal, *Felis lynx* (or *canadensis*), of Europe and North America, with grey-brown mottled fur, tufted ears, and a short tail. Related adj: **lyncean 2** the fur of this animal **3** **bay lynx** another name for **bobcat 4** **desert lynx** another name for **caracal 5** Also called: **Polish lynx** a large fancy pigeon from Poland, with spangled or laced markings [c14 via Latin from Greek *lunx*; related to Old English *lox*, German *Luchs*] > 'lynx,like *adj*

Lynx (lɪŋks) *n, Latin genitive* Lyncis ('lɪnsɪs) a faint constellation in the N hemisphere lying between Ursa Major and Cancer

lynx-eyed *adj* having keen sight

lyo- *combining form* indicating dispersion or dissolution: *lyophilic; lyophilize; lyophobic* [from Greek *luein* to loose]

lyolysis (laɪˈɒlɪsɪs) *n chem* the formation of an acid and a base from the interaction of a salt with a solvent

Lyon (*French* ljɔ̃) *n* a city in SE central France, capital of Rhône department, at the confluence of the Rivers Rhône and Saône: the third largest city in France; a major industrial centre and river port. Pop: 445 452 (1999). English name: Lyons ('laɪənz) Ancient name: Lugdunum (lʊɡˈduːnəm)

Lyon King of Arms ('laɪən) *n* the chief herald of Scotland. Also called: Lord Lyon [c14 archaic spelling of LION, referring to the figure on the royal shield]

Lyonnais (*French* ljɔnɛ) *n* a former province of E central France, on the Rivers Rhône and Saône: occupied by the present-day departments of Rhône and Loire. Chief town: Lyon

lyonnaise (ˌlaɪəˈneɪz; *French* ljɔnɛz) *adj* (of food) cooked or garnished with onions, usually fried

Lyonnesse (ˌlaɪəˈnɛs) *n* (in Arthurian legend) the mythical birthplace of Sir Tristram, situated in SW England and believed to have been submerged by the sea

lyophilic (ˌlaɪəʊˈfɪlɪk) *adj chem* (of a colloid) having a dispersed phase with a high affinity for the continuous phase: *a lyophilic sol*. Compare **lyophobic**

lyophilize *or* **lyophilise** (laɪˈɒfɪˌlaɪz) *vb* (*tr*) to dry (blood, serum, tissue, etc) by freezing in a high vacuum; freeze dry

lyophobic (ˌlaɪəʊˈfəʊbɪk) *adj chem* (of a colloid) having a dispersed phase with little or no affinity for the continuous phase. Compare **lyophilic**

lyosorption (ˌlaɪəʊˈsɔːpʃən) *n chem* the adsorption of a liquid on a solid surface, esp of a solvent on suspended particles

Lyra ('laɪərə) *n, Latin genitive* Lyrae ('laɪriː) a small constellation in the N hemisphere lying near Cygnus and Draco and containing the star Vega, an eclipsing binary (**Beta Lyrae**), a planetary nebula (the **Ring Nebula**), and a variable star, **RR Lyrae**

lyrate ('laɪərɪt) *or* **lyrated** *adj* **1** shaped like a lyre **2** (of leaves) having a large terminal lobe and smaller lateral lobes [c18 from New Latin *lyrātus*, Latin from *lyra* LYRE] > 'lyrately *adv*

lyra viol ('laɪərə) *n* a lutelike musical instrument popular in the 16th and 17th centuries: the forerunner of the mandolin

lyre (laɪə) *n* **1** an ancient Greek stringed instrument consisting of a resonating tortoise shell to which a crossbar was attached by two projecting arms. It was plucked with a plectrum and used for accompanying songs **2** any ancient instrument of similar design **3** a medieval bowed instrument of the violin family [c13 via Old French from Latin *lyra*, from Greek *lura*]

lyrebird ('laɪəˌbɜːd) *n* either of two pheasant-like Australian birds, *Menura superba* and *M. alberti*, constituting the family *Menuridae*: during courtship displays, the male spreads its tail into the shape of a lyre

lyric ('lɪrɪk) *adj* **1** (of poetry) **a** expressing the writer's personal feelings and thoughts **b** having the form and manner of a song **2** of or relating to such poetry **3** (of a singing voice) having a light quality and tone **4** intended for singing, esp (in classical Greece) to the accompaniment of the lyre ▷ *n* **5** a short poem of songlike quality **6** (*plural*) the words of a popular song ▷ Also (for senses 1–3): lyrical [c16 from Latin *lyricus*, from Greek *lurikos*, from *lura* LYRE] > 'lyrically *adv* > 'lyricalness *n*

lyrical ('lɪrɪkəl) *adj* **1** another word for **lyric** (senses 1–3) **2** enthusiastic; effusive (esp in the phrase **to wax lyrical**)

lyricism ('lɪrɪˌsɪzəm) *n* **1** the quality or style of lyric poetry **2** emotional or enthusiastic outpouring

lyricist ('lɪrɪsɪst) *n* **1** a person who writes the words for a song, opera, or musical play **2** Also called: lyrist a lyric poet

lyrism ('lɪrɪzəm) *n* **1** the art or technique of playing the lyre **2** a less common word for **lyricism**

lyrist *n* **1** ('laɪərɪst) a person who plays the lyre **2**

('lɪrɪst) another word for **lyricist** (sense 2)

lys- *combining form* a variant of **lyso-** before a vowel

lyse (laɪs, laɪz) *vb* to undergo or cause to undergo lysis

Lysenkoism (lɪˈsɛŋkəʊˌɪzəm) *n* a form of Neo-Lamarckism advocated by Trofim Denisovich Lysenko, the Russian biologist and geneticist (1898–1976), emphasizing the importance of the inheritance of acquired characteristics

lysergic acid (lɪˈsɜːdʒɪk, laɪ-) *n* a crystalline compound with a polycyclic molecular structure: used in medical research. Formula $C_{16}H_{16}N_2O_2$ [c20 from (HYDRO)LYS(IS) + ERG(OT) + -IC]

lysergic acid diethylamide (daɪˌɛθɪlˈeɪmaɪd, -ˌiːˈθaɪl-) *n* See LSD

lysimeter (laɪˈsɪmɪtə) *n* an instrument for determining solubility, esp the amount of water-soluble matter in soil [c20 from *lysi-* (variant of LYSO-) + -METER]

lysin ('laɪsɪn) *n* any of a group of antibodies or other agents that cause dissolution of cells against which they are directed

lysine ('laɪsiːn, -sɪn) *n* an essential amino acid that occurs in proteins

lysis ('laɪsɪs) *n, pl* **-ses** (-siːz) **1** the destruction or dissolution of cells by the action of a particular lysin **2** *med* the gradual reduction in severity of the symptoms of a disease [c19 New Latin, from Greek, from *luein* to release]

-lysis *n combining form* indicating a loosening, decomposition, or breaking down: *electrolysis* [from Greek, from *lusis* a loosening; see LYSIS]

Lysithea (laɪˈsɪθɪə) *n astronomy* a small satellite of Jupiter in an intermediate orbit

lyso- *or before a vowel* **lys-** *combining form* indicating a dissolving or loosening: *lysozyme* [from Greek *lusis* a loosening]

lysogeny (laɪˈsɒdʒənɪ) *n* the biological process in which a bacterium is infected by a bacteriophage that integrates its DNA into that of the host such that the host is not destroyed > lysogenic (ˌlaɪsəʊˈdʒɛnɪk) *adj*

Lysol ('laɪsɒl) *n trademark* a solution containing a mixture of cresols in water, used as an antiseptic and disinfectant

lysosome ('laɪsəˌsəʊm) *n* any of numerous small particles, containing digestive enzymes, that are present in the cytoplasm of most cells > ˌlyso'somal *adj*

lysozyme ('laɪsəˌzaɪm) *n* an enzyme occurring in tears, certain body tissues, and egg white: destroys bacteria by hydrolysing polysaccharides in their cell walls [c20 from LYSO- + (EN)ZYME]

lyssa ('lɪsə) *n pathol* a less common word for **rabies**

-lyte *n combining form* indicating a substance that can be decomposed or broken down: *electrolyte* [from Greek *lutos* soluble, from *luein* to loose]

Lytham Saint Anne's ('lɪðəm sənt 'ænz) *n, usually abbreviated to* Lytham St Anne's a resort in NW England, in Lancashire on the Irish Sea. Pop: 41 327 (2001)

lythraceous (lɪˈθreɪʃəs, laɪˈθreɪ-) *adj* of, relating to, or belonging to the *Lythraceae*, a mostly tropical American family of herbaceous plants, shrubs, and trees that includes purple loosestrife and crape myrtle [c19 from New Latin *Lythrum* type genus, from Greek *luthron* blood, from the red flowers]

lytic ('lɪtɪk) *adj* **1** relating to, causing, or resulting from lysis **2** of or relating to a lysin [c19 Greek *lutikos* capable of loosing]

-lytic *adj combining form* indicating a loosening or dissolving: *paralytic* [from Greek, from *lusis*; see -LYSIS]

lytta ('lɪtə) *n, pl* **-tas** *or* **-tae** (-tiː) a rodlike mass of cartilage beneath the tongue in the dog and other carnivores [c17 New Latin, from Greek *lussa* madness; in dogs, it was believed to be a cause of rabies]

Lyublin ('ljublɪn) *n* transliteration of the Russian name for **Lublin**

M m

m *or* **M** (ɛm) *n, pl* **m's, M's** *or* **Ms 1** the 13th letter and tenth consonant of the modern English alphabet **2** a speech sound represented by this letter, usually a bilabial nasal, as in *mat*

m *symbol for* **1** metre(s) **2** mile(s) **3** milli- **4** minute(s)

M *symbol for* **1** mach **2** medium (size) **3** mega- **4** *currency* mark(s) **5** million **6** *astronomy* Messier catalogue; a catalogue published in 1784, in which 103 nebulae and clusters are listed using a numerical system: *M13 is the globular cluster in Hercules* **7** Middle **8** *physics* modulus **9** (in Britain) motorway: *the M1 runs from London to Leeds* **10** (in Australia) **a** mature audience (used to describe a category of film certified as suitable for viewing by anyone over the age of 15) **b** (*as modifier*): *an M film* **11** *logic* the middle term of a syllogism **12** *physics* mutual inductance **13** *chem* molar **14** ▷ *the Roman numeral for* 1000. See **Roman numerals 15** ▷ *international car registration for* Malta

m *abbreviation for* **1** *cricket* maiden (over) **2** male **3** mare **4** married **5** masculine

M. *abbreviation for* **1** Majesty **2** (in titles) Member **3** million **4** *pl* MM *or* MM **5** *French* Monsieur [French equivalent of *Mr*] **5** mountain

m- *prefix* short for **meta-** (sense 4)

M'- *prefix* a variant of **Mac-**

'm *contraction of* **1** (*verb*) am **2** (*noun*) madam: *yes'm*

M0 *symbol for* the amount of money in circulation in notes and coin, plus the banks' till money and the banks' balances at the Bank of England. Informal name: **narrow money**

M1 *symbol for* the amount of money in circulation in notes, coin, current accounts, and deposit accounts transferable by cheque

M2 *symbol for* the amount of money in circulation in notes and coin plus non-interest-bearing bank deposits, building-society deposits, and National Savings accounts

M3 *symbol for* the amount of money in circulation given by M1 plus all private-sector bank deposits and certificates of deposit. Former symbol: £M3 (sterling M3)

M3c *symbol for* the amount of money in circulation given by M3 plus foreign currency bank deposits. Former symbol: M3 Informal name: **broad money**

M4 *symbol for* the amount of money in circulation given by M1 plus most private-sector bank deposits and holdings of money-market instruments. Also called: **PSL1**

M5 *symbol for* the amount of money in circulation given by M4 plus building-society deposits. Also called: **PSL2**

M8 *text messaging abbreviation for* mate

ma¹ (mɑː) *n* an informal word for **mother¹**

ma² *the internet domain name for* Morocco

MA *abbreviation for* **1** Massachusetts **2** Master of Arts **3** *psychol* **mental age 4** Military Academy **5** ▷ *international car registration for* Morocco [from French *Maroc*]

ma'am (mæm, mɑːm; *unstressed* məm) *n* short for **madam**: used as a title of respect, esp for female royalty

maar (mɑː) *n, pl* **maars** *or* **maare** ('mɑːrə) (*sometimes capital*) a coneless volcanic crater that has been formed by a single explosion [c19 from German]

Maarianhamina (ˌmɑːriənhɑminə) *n* the Finnish name for **Mariehamn**

Ma'ariv *Hebrew* (mɑɑˈriv; *Yiddish* 'mɑɪriv) *n Judaism* the evening service

maas (mɑːs) *n South African* thick soured milk [from Nguni *amasi* milk]

Maas (mɑːs) *n* the Dutch name for the **Meuse**

Maastricht *or* **Maestricht** ('mɑːstrɪxt; *Dutch* mɑːˈstrɪxt) *n* a city in the SE Netherlands near the Belgian and German borders: capital of Limburg province, on the River Maas (Meuse); a European Community treaty (**Maastricht Treaty**) was signed here in 1992, setting out the terms for the creation of the European Union. Pop: 122 000 (2003 est)

Mab (mæb) *n* (in English and Irish folklore) a fairy queen said to create and control men's dreams

mabela (mɑːˈbɛlə) *n South African* ground kaffir corn used for making porridge [from Zulu *amabele* kaffir corn]

Mabinogion (ˌmæbɪˈnɒɡɪən) *n* **the** a collection of Welsh tales based on old Celtic legends and mythology in which magic and the supernatural play a large part [from Welsh *mabinogi* instruction for young bards]

mac *or* **mack** (mæk) *n Brit informal* short for **mackintosh** (senses 1, 3)

Mac (mæk) *n chiefly US and Canadian* an informal term of address to a man [c20 abstracted from MAC-, prefix of Scottish surnames]

MAC *abbreviation for* multiplexed analogue component: a transmission coding system for colour television using satellite broadcasting

Mac. *abbreviation for* Maccabees (books of the Apocrypha)

Mac-, Mc- *or* **M'-** *prefix* (in surnames of Scottish or Irish Gaelic origin) son of: *MacDonald; MacNeice* [from Goidelic *mac* son of; compare Welsh *mab*, Cornish *mab*]

macabre (məˈkɑːbə, -brə) *adj* **1** gruesome; ghastly; grim **2** resembling or associated with the danse macabre [c15 from Old French *danse macabre* dance of death, probably from *macabé* relating to the Maccabees, who were associated with death because of the doctrines and prayers for the dead in II Macc. (12:43–46)] > ma'**cabrely** *adv*

macaco (məˈkɑːkəʊ, -ˈkeɪ-) *n, pl* **-cos** any of various lemurs, esp *Lemur macaco*, the males of which are usually black and the females brown [c18 from French *macoco*, of unknown origin]

macadam (məˈkædəm) *n* a road surface made of compressed layers of small broken stones, esp one that is bound together with tar or asphalt [c19 named after John *McAdam* (1756–1836), Scottish engineer, the inventor]

macadamia (ˌmækəˈdeɪmɪə) *n* **1** any tree of the Australian proteaceous genus *Macadamia*, esp *M. ternifolia*, having clusters of small white flowers and edible nutlike seeds **2** **macadamia nut** the seed of this tree [c19 New Latin, named after John *Macadam* (1827–1865), Australian chemist]

macadamize *or* **macadamise** (məˈkædəˌmaɪz) *vb* (*tr*) to construct or surface (a road) with macadam > mac,adami'**zation** *or* mac,adami'**sation** *n* > mac'**adam,izer** *or* mac'**adam,iser** *n*

Macao (məˈkaʊ) *n* a special administrative region of S China, across the estuary of the Zhu Jiang from Hong Kong: chief centre of European trade with China in the 18th century; attained partial autonomy in 1976; formerly (until 1999) a Portuguese overseas province under a long-term lease from China, as with Hong Kong (a UK territory until 1997); transit trade with rest of China; tourism and financial services. It retains its own currency, the pataca. Pop: 448 500 (2003 est). Area: 16 sq km (6 sq miles). Portuguese name: **Macáu**

Macapá (*Portuguese* makaˈpa) *n* a town in NE Brazil, capital of the federal territory of Amapá, on the Canal do Norte of the Amazon delta. Pop: 377 000 (2005 est)

macaque (məˈkɑːk) *n* any of various Old World monkeys of the genus *Macaca*, inhabiting wooded or rocky regions of Asia and Africa. Typically the tail is short or absent and cheek pouches are present [c17 from French, from Portuguese *macaco*, from Fiot (a W African language) *makaku*, from *kaku* monkey]

macaroni *or* **maccaroni** (ˌmækəˈrəʊnɪ) *n, pl* **-nis** *or* **-nies 1** pasta tubes made from wheat flour **2** (in 18th-century Britain) a dandy who affected foreign manners and style [c16 from Italian (Neapolitan dialect) *maccarone*, probably from Greek *makaria* food made from barley]

macaronic (ˌmækəˈrɒnɪk) *adj* **1** (of verse) characterized by a mixture of vernacular words jumbled together with Latin words or Latinized words or with words from one or more other foreign languages ▷ *n* **2** (*often plural*) macaronic verse [c17 from New Latin *macarōnicus*, literally: resembling macaroni (in lack of sophistication); see MACARONI] > ˌmaca'**ronically** *adv*

macaroni cheese *n* a dish of macaroni with a cheese sauce

macaroon (ˌmækəˈruːn) *n* a kind of sweet biscuit made of ground almonds, sugar, and egg whites [c17 via French *macaron* from Italian *maccarone* MACARONI]

Macassar (məˈkæsə) *n* a variant spelling of **Makasar**

Macassar oil *n* an oily preparation formerly put on the hair to make it smooth and shiny [c19 so called because its ingredients were originally claimed to have come from MAKASAR]

Macáu (məˈkau) *n* the Portuguese name for **Macao**

macaw (məˈkɔː) *n* any large tropical American

parrot of the genera *Ara* and *Anodorhynchus,* having a long tail and brilliant plumage [c17 from Portuguese *macau,* of unknown origin]

Macc. *abbreviation for* Maccabees (books of the Apocrypha)

Maccabean (ˌmækəˈbiːən) *adj* of or relating to the Maccabees or to Judas Maccabaeus, the Jewish leader of a revolt (166–161 BC) against Seleucid oppression

Maccabees (ˈmækəˌbiːz) *n* any of four books of Jewish history, including the last two of the Apocrypha [from the *Maccabees,* a Jewish family of patriots who freed Judaea from Seleucid oppression (168–142 BC)]

maccaboy, maccoboy (ˈmækəˌbɔɪ) *or* **maccabaw** (ˈmækəˌbɔː) *n* a dark rose-scented snuff [c18 from French *macouba,* from the name of the district of Martinique where it is made]

maccaroni (ˌmækəˈrəʊnɪ) *n, pl* -nis *or* -nies a variant spelling of **macaroni**

McCarthyism (məˈkɑːθɪˌɪzəm) *n chiefly US* **1** the practice of making unsubstantiated accusations of disloyalty or Communist leanings **2** the use of unsupported accusations for any purpose [c20 after Joseph Raymond *McCarthy* (1908–57), US Republican senator, who led (1950–54) the notorious investigations of alleged Communist infiltration into the US government] > Mc'Carthyite *n, adj*

maccheroncini (ˌmækərənˈtʃiːnɪ) *n* thin pasta tubes made from wheat flour [Italian]

macchiato (ˌmækɪˈɑːtəʊ) *n, pl* -tos espresso coffee served with a dash of hot or cold milk [Italian, literally: stained]

Macclesfield (ˈmækᵊlzˌfiːld) *n* a market town in NW England, in Cheshire: former centre of the silk industry; pharmaceuticals, services. Pop: 50 688 (2001)

McCoy (məˈkɔɪ) *n slang* the genuine person or thing (esp in the phrase **the real McCoy**) [c20 perhaps after Kid *McCoy,* professional name of Norman Selby (1873–1940), American boxer, who was called "the real McCoy" to distinguish him from another boxer of that name]

Macdonnell Ranges (məkˈdɒnəl) *pl n* a mountain system of central Australia, in S central Northern Territory, extending about 160 km (100 miles) east and west of Alice Springs. Highest peak: Mount Zeil, 1531 m (5024 ft)

mace[1] (meɪs) *n* **1** a club, usually having a spiked metal head, used esp in the Middle Ages **2** a ceremonial staff of office carried by certain officials **3** See **macebearer 4** an early form of billiard cue [c13 from Old French, probably from Vulgar Latin *mattea* (unattested); apparently related to Latin *mateola* mallet]

mace[2] (meɪs) *n* a spice made from the dried aril round the nutmeg seed [c14 formed as a singular from Old French *macis* (wrongly assumed to be plural), from Latin *macir* an oriental spice]

Mace (meɪs) *US* ▷ *n* **1** *trademark* a liquid causing tears and nausea, used as a spray for riot control, etc ▷ *vb* **2** (*tr; sometimes not capital*) to use Mace on

macebearer (ˈmeɪsˌbɛərə) *n* a person who carries a mace in processions or ceremonies

Maced. *abbreviation for* Macedonia(n)

macedoine (ˌmæsɪˈdwɑːn) *n* **1** a hot or cold mixture of diced vegetables **2** a mixture of fruit served in a syrup or in jelly **3** any mixture; medley [c19 from French, literally: Macedonian, alluding to the mixture of nationalities in Macedonia]

Macedon (ˈmæsɪˌdɒn) *or* **Macedonia** *n* a region of the S Balkans, now divided among Greece, Bulgaria, and Macedonia (Former Yugoslav Republic of Macedonia). As a kingdom in the ancient world it achieved prominence under Philip II (359–336 BC) and his son Alexander the Great

Macedonia (ˌmæsɪˈdəʊnɪə) *n* **1** a country in SE Europe, comprising the NW half of ancient Macedon: it became part of the kingdom of Serbs,

Croats, and Slovenes (subsequently Yugoslavia) in 1913; it declared independence in 1992, but Greece objected to the use of the historical name Macedonia; in 1993 it was recognized by the UN under its current official name. Official language: Macedonian. Religion: Christian majority, Muslim, nonreligious, and Jewish minorities. Currency: denar. Capital: Skopje. Pop: 2 066 000 (2004 est). Area: 25 713 sq km (10 028 sq miles). Serbian name: Makedonija Official name: Former Yugoslav Republic of Macedonia (FYROM) **2** an area of N Greece, comprising the regions of Macedonia Central, Macedonia West, and part of Macedonia East and Thrace. Modern Greek name: Makedhonia **3** a district of SW Bulgaria, now occupied by Blagoevgrad province. Area: 6465 sq km (2496 sq miles)

Macedonian (ˌmæsɪˈdəʊnɪən) *adj* **1** of or relating to Macedonia, its inhabitants, or any of their languages or dialects ▷ *n* **2** a native or inhabitant of Macedonia **3** the language of the Former Yugoslav Republic of Macedonia, belonging to the south Slavonic branch of the Indo-European family **4** an extinct language spoken in ancient Macedonia

Maceió (maseˈjɔ) *n* a port in NE Brazil, capital of Alagôas state, on the Atlantic. Pop: 1 137 000 (2005 est)

macer (ˈmeɪsə) *n* a macebearer, esp (in Scotland) an official who acts as usher in a court of law [c14 from Old French *massier,* from *masse* MACE[1]]

maceral (ˈmæsərəl) *n geology* any of the organic units that constitute coal: equivalent to any of the mineral constituents of a rock [c20 from Latin *mācerāre* to MACERATE]

macerate (ˈmæsəˌreɪt) *vb* **1** to soften or separate or be softened or separated as a result of soaking **2** to break up or cause to break up by soaking: *macerated peaches* **3** to become or cause to become thin [c16 from Latin *mācerāre* to soften] > 'macerˌater *or* 'macerˌator *n* > 'macerative *adj* > ˌmacer'ation *n*

Macgillicuddy's Reeks (məˌgɪlɪˈkʌdɪz ˈriːks) *pl n* a range of mountains in SW Republic of Ireland in Kerry: includes Ireland's highest mountain (Carrantuohill)

McGuffin *or* **MacGuffin** (məˈgʌfɪn) *n* an object or event in a book or a film that serves as the impetus for the plot [c20 coined (c. 1935) by Sir Alfred Joseph Hitchcock (1899–1980), English film director]

Mach (mæk) *n* short for **Mach number**

machair (ˈmæxər) *n Scot* (in the western Highlands of Scotland) a strip of sandy, grassy, often lime-rich land just above the high-water mark at a sandy shore: used as grazing or arable land [c17 from Scottish Gaelic]

machan (məˈtʃɑːn) *n* (in India) a raised platform used in tiger hunting [c19 from Hindi]

macher Yiddish (ˈmɑxər) *n* an important or influential person: often used ironically [Yiddish, from German, literally: doer]

machete (məˈʃɛtɪ, -ˈtʃeɪ-) *or* **matchet** *n* a broad heavy knife used for cutting or as a weapon, esp in parts of Central and South America [C16 *macheto,* from Spanish *machete,* from *macho* club, perhaps from Vulgar Latin *mattea* (unattested) club]

machi chips (ˈmʌtʃiː) *pl n Hinglish* fish and chips [Hindi]

Machiavellian *or* **Machiavelian** (ˌmækɪəˈvɛlɪən) *adj* (*sometimes not capital*) **1** of or relating to the alleged political principles of Niccolò Machiavelli (1469–1527), Florentine statesman and political philosopher; cunning, amoral, and opportunist ▷ *n* **2** a cunning, amoral, and opportunist person, esp a politician > ˌMachia'vellianism *or* ˌMachia'vellism *n* > ˌMachia'vellist *adj, n*

machicolate (məˈtʃɪkəˌleɪt) *vb* (*tr*) to construct machicolations at the top of (a wall) [c18 from Old French *machicoller,* ultimately from Provençal *machacol,* from *macar* to crush + *col* neck]

machicolation (məˌtʃɪkəʊˈleɪʃən) *n* **1** (esp in medieval castles) a projecting gallery or parapet supported on corbels having openings through which missiles could be dropped **2** any such opening

machinate (ˈmækɪˌneɪt, ˈmæʃ-) *vb* (*usually tr*) to contrive, plan, or devise (schemes, plots, etc) [c17 from Latin *māchinārī* to plan, from *māchina* MACHINE] > 'machiˌnator *n*

machination (ˌmækɪˈneɪʃən, ˌmæʃ-) *n* **1** an intrigue, plot, or scheme **2** the act of devising plots or schemes

machine (məˈʃiːn) *n* **1** an assembly of interconnected components arranged to transmit or modify force in order to perform useful work **2** Also called: **simple machine** a device for altering the magnitude or direction of a force, esp a lever, screw, wedge, or pulley **3** a mechanically operated device or means of transport, such as a car, aircraft, etc **4** any mechanical or electrical device that automatically performs tasks or assists in performing tasks **5 a** (*modifier*) denoting a firearm that is fully automatic as distinguished from semiautomatic **b** (*in combination*): *machine pistol; machine gun* **6** any intricate structure or agency: *the war machine* **7** a mechanically efficient, rigid, or obedient person **8** an organized body of people that controls activities, policies, etc **9** (esp in the classical theatre) a device such as a pulley to provide spectacular entrances and exits for supernatural characters **10** an event, etc, introduced into a literary work for special effect ▷ *vb* **11** (*tr*) to shape, cut, or remove (excess material) from (a workpiece) using a machine tool **12** to use a machine to carry out a process on (something) [c16 via French from Latin *māchina* machine, engine, from Doric Greek *makhana* pulley; related to *makhos* device, contrivance] > ma'chinable *or* ma'chineable *adj* > maˌchina'bility *n* > ma'chineless *adj* > ma'chine-ˌlike *adj*

machine bolt *n* a fastening bolt with a machine-cut thread

machine code *or* **language** *n* instructions for the processing of data in a binary, octal, or hexadecimal code that can be understood and executed by a computer

machine gun *n* **1 a** a rapid-firing automatic gun, usually mounted, from which small-arms ammunition is discharged **b** (*as modifier*): *machine-gun fire* ▷ *vb* **machine-gun -guns, -gunning, -gunned 2** (*tr*) to shoot or fire at with a machine gun > **machine gunner** *n*

machine head *n* a metal peg-and-gear mechanism for tuning a string on an instrument such as a guitar

machine intelligence *n Brit now rare* another term for **artificial intelligence**

machine learning *n* a branch of artificial intelligence in which a computer generates rules underlying or based on raw data that has been fed into it

machine moulding *n engineering* the process of making moulds and cores for castings by mechanical means, usually by compacting the moulding sand by vibration instead of by ramming down

machine readable *adj* (of data) in a form in which it can be fed into a computer

machinery (məˈʃiːnərɪ) *n, pl* -eries **1** machines, machine parts, or machine systems collectively **2** a particular machine system or set of machines **3** a system similar to a machine **4** literary devices used for effect in epic poetry

machine screw *n* a fastening screw with a machine-cut thread throughout the length of its shank

machine shop *n* a workshop in which machine tools are operated

machine tool *n* a power-driven machine, such as a lathe, miller, or grinder, that is used for cutting, shaping, and finishing metals or other materials > ma'chine-ˌtooled *adj*

m

machine translation *n* the production of text in one natural language from that in another by means of computer procedures

machinist (məˈʃiːnɪst) *n* **1** a person who operates machines to cut or process materials **2** a maker or repairer of machines

machismo (mæˈkɪzməʊ, -ˈtʃɪz-) *n* exaggerated masculine pride [Mexican Spanish, from Spanish *macho* male, from Latin *masculus* MASCULINE]

Machmeter (ˈmækˌmiːtə) *n* an instrument for measuring the Mach number of an aircraft in flight

Mach number *n* (*often not capital*) the ratio of the speed of a body in a particular medium to the speed of sound in that medium. Mach number 1 corresponds to the speed of sound. Often shortened to: **Mach** [c19 named after Ernst *Mach* (1838–1916), Austrian physicist and philosopher]

macho (ˈmætʃəʊ) *adj* **1** denoting or exhibiting pride in characteristics believed to be typically masculine, such as physical strength, sexual appetite, etc ▷ *n, pl* **machos 2** a man who displays such characteristics [c20 from Spanish: male; see MACHISMO]

machree (məˈkriː) *adj* (*postpositive*) *Irish* my dear: *mother machree* [from Irish *mo croidhe*]

machtpolitik (ˈmɑːxtˌpɒliˌtiːk) *n* power politics [from German]

Machu Picchu (ˈmɑːtʃuː ˈpiːktʃuː) *n* a ruined Incan city in S Peru

machzor or **mahzor** *Hebrew* (maxˈzɔr; *English* mɑːkˈzɔː) *n, pl* **-zorim** (-zɔˈriːm; *English* -zəˈriːm) a Jewish prayer book containing prescribed holiday rituals [literally: cycle]

Macías Nguema (məˈsiːəs əŋˈɡweɪmə) *n* the former name (until 1979) of **Bioko**

macintosh (ˈmækɪnˌtɒʃ) *n* a variant spelling of **mackintosh**

McIntosh (ˈmækɪnˌtɒʃ) or **McIntosh red** *n* a Canadian variety of red-skinned eating apple [c19 named after John *McIntosh* (1777–c. 1845), US-born Canadian farmer on whose property the variety was first found growing wild]

mack[1] (mæk) *n Brit informal* a variant spelling of **mac** short for **mackintosh** (senses 1, 3)

mack[2] (mæk) *n slang* a pimp [c19 shortened from obsolete *mackerel,* from Old French, of uncertain origin]

Mackay (məˈkaɪ) *n* a port in E Australia, in Queensland: artificial harbour. Pop: 57 649 (2001)

Mackem (ˈmækəm) *Brit* ▷ *n* **1** a person who comes from or lives in the Sunderland and Wearside area **2** the dialect spoken by these people ▷ *adj* **3** of or relating to these people or their dialect

Mackenzie (məˈkɛnzɪ) *n* a river in NW Canada, in the Northwest Territories and Nunavut, flowing northwest from Great Slave Lake to the Beaufort Sea: the longest river in Canada; navigable in summer. Length: 1770 km (1100 miles)

mackerel (ˈmækrəl) *n, pl* **-rel** or **-rels 1** a spiny-finned food fish, *Scomber scombrus,* occurring in northern coastal regions of the Atlantic and in the Mediterranean: family *Scombridae.* It has a deeply forked tail and a greenish-blue body marked with wavy dark bands on the back. Compare **Spanish mackerel** (sense 1) **2** any of various other fishes of the family *Scombridae,* such as *Scomber colias* (**Spanish mackerel**) and *S. japonicus* (**Pacific mackerel**) ▷ Compare **horse mackerel** [c13 from Anglo-French, from Old French *maquerel,* of unknown origin]

mackerel breeze *n* a strong breeze [c18 so named because the ruffling of the water by the wind aids mackerel fishing]

mackerel shark *n* another name for **porbeagle**

mackerel sky *n* a sky patterned with cirrocumulus or small altocumulus clouds [from the similarity in the pattern to a mackerel's back]

Mackinac (ˈmækɪˌnɔː, -ˌnæk) *n* a wooded island in N Michigan, in the **Straits of Mackinac** (a channel between the lower and upper peninsulas of Michigan): an ancient Indian burial ground; state park. Length: 5 km (3 miles)

Mackinaw coat (ˈmækɪˌnɔː) *n chiefly US and Canadian* a thick short double-breasted plaid coat. Also called: **mackinaw** [c19 named after *Mackinaw,* variant of MACKINAC]

McKinley (məˈkɪnlɪ) *n* **Mount** a mountain in S central Alaska, in the Alaska Range: the highest peak in North America. Height: 6194 m (20 320 ft)

mackintosh or **macintosh** (ˈmækɪnˌtɒʃ) *n* **1** a waterproof raincoat made of rubberized cloth **2** such cloth **3** any raincoat [c19 named after Charles *Macintosh* (1760–1843), who invented it]

mackle[1] (ˈmækᵊl), **macule** (ˈmækjuːl) *n printing* a double or blurred impression caused by shifting paper or type [c16 via French from Latin *macula* spot, stain]

mackle[2] (ˈmækᵊl) *vb* **mackles, mackled, mackling** (*tr*) *Midland English dialect* to mend hurriedly or in a makeshift way

Maclaurin's series (məˈklɔːrɪnz) *n maths* an infinite sum giving the value of a function f(x) in terms of the derivatives of the function evaluated at zero: f(x) = f(0) + (f′(0)x)/1! + (f″(0)x²)/2! + ... Also called: **Maclaurin series** [c18 named after Colin *Maclaurin* (1698–1746), British mathematician who formulated it]

macle (ˈmækᵊl) *n* another name for **chiastolite** and **twin** (sense 3) [c19 via French from Latin *macula* spot, stain]

McMurdo Sound (məkˈmɜːdəʊ) *n* an inlet of the Ross Sea in Antarctica, north of Victoria Land

McNaughten Rules or **McNaghten Rules** (məkˈnɔːtᵊn) *pl n* (in English law) a set of rules established by the case of Regina v. McNaughten (1843) by which legal proof of insanity in the commission of a crime depends upon whether or not the accused can show either that he did not know what he was doing or that he is incapable of realizing that what he was doing was wrong

Macon (ˈmeɪkən) *n* a city in the US, in central Georgia, on the Ocmulgee River. Pop: 95 267 (2003 est)

Mâcon (*French* mɑkɔ̃) *n* **1** a city in E central France, in the Saône valley: a centre of the wine-producing region of lower Burgundy. Pop: 34 469 (1999) **2** a red or white wine from the Mâcon area, heavier than the other burgundies

Macquarie (məˈkwɒrɪ) *n* **1** an Australian island in the Pacific, SE of Tasmania: noted for its species of albatross and penguin. Area: about 168 sq km (65 sq miles) **2** a river in SE Australia, in E central New South Wales, rising in the Blue Mountains and flowing NW to the Darling. Length: about 1200 km (750 miles)

macramé (məˈkrɑːmɪ) *n* a type of ornamental work made by knotting and weaving coarse thread into a pattern [c19 via French and Italian from Turkish *makrama* towel, from Arabic *migramah* striped cloth]

macrencephaly (ˌmækrənˈsɛfəlɪ) or less commonly **macrencephalia** (ˌmækrənsɪˈfeɪlɪə) *n* the condition of having an abnormally large brain

macro (ˈmækrəʊ) *n, pl* **macros 1** a macro lens **2** Also: **macro instruction** a single computer instruction that initiates a set of instructions to perform a specific task

macro- or before a vowel **macr-** *combining form* **1** large, long, or great in size or duration: *macroscopic* **2** (in pathology) indicating abnormal enlargement or overdevelopment: *macrocyte.* Compare **micro-** (sense 5) **3** producing larger than life images: *macrophotography* [from Greek *makros* large; compare Latin *macer* MEAGRE]

macrobiotic (ˌmækrəʊbaɪˈɒtɪk) *adj* **1** of or relating to macrobiotics **2** of a diet comprising only food conforming to the principles of macrobiotics

macrobiotics (ˌmækrəʊbaɪˈɒtɪks) *n* (*functioning as singular*) a dietary system in which foods are classified according to the principles of Yin and Yang. It advocates diets of whole grains and vegetables grown without chemical additives [c20 from MACRO- + Greek *biotos* life + -ICS]

macrocarpa (ˌmækrəʊˈkɑːpə) *n* a large coniferous tree of New Zealand, *Cupressus macrocarpa,* used for shelter belts on farms and for rough timber. Also called: **Monterey cypress** [c19 from New Latin, from Greek MACRO- + *karpos* fruit]

macrocephaly (ˌmækrəʊˈsɛfəlɪ) or less commonly **macrocephalia** (ˌmækrəʊsɪˈfeɪlɪə) *n* the condition of having an abnormally large head or skull > **macrocephalic** (ˌmækrəʊsɪˈfælɪk) or ˌmacro'cephalous *adj*

macroclimate (ˈmækrəʊˌklaɪmɪt) *n* the prevailing climate of a large area > **macroclimatic** (ˌmækrəʊklaɪˈmætɪk) *adj* > ˌmacroclimatically *adv*

macrocosm (ˈmækrəˌkɒzəm) *n* **1** a complex structure, such as the universe or society, regarded as an entirety, as opposed to microcosms, which have a similar structure and are contained within it **2** any complex entity regarded as a complete system in itself ▷ Compare **microcosm** [c16 via French and Latin from Greek *makros kosmos* great world] > ˌmacro'cosmic *adj* > ˌmacro'cosmically *adv*

macrocyst (ˈmækrəʊˌsɪst) *n* **1** an unusually large cyst **2** (in slime moulds) an encysted resting protoplasmic mass. See **plasmodium** (sense 1)

macrocyte (ˈmækrəʊˌsaɪt) *n pathol* an abnormally large red blood cell, over 10 μm in diameter > **macrocytic** (ˌmækrəʊˈsɪtɪk) *adj*

macrocytosis (ˌmækrəʊsaɪˈtəʊsɪs) *n pathol* the presence in the blood of macrocytes

macroeconomics (ˌmækrəʊˌiːkəˈnɒmɪks, -ˌɛk-) *n* (*functioning as singular*) the branch of economics concerned with aggregates, such as national income, consumption, and investment. Compare **microeconomics**. > ˌmacro,eco'nomic *adj*

macroevolution (ˌmækrəʊˌiːvəˈluːʃən) *n biology* the evolution of large taxonomic groups such as genera and families > ˌmacro,evo'lutionary *adj*

macrogamete (ˌmækrəʊˈgæmiːt) or **megagamete** (ˌmɛgəˈgæmiːt) *n* the larger and apparently female of two gametes in conjugating protozoans. Compare **microgamete**

macroglia (ˌmækrəʊˈgliːə) *n* one of the two types of non-nervous tissue (glia) found in the central nervous system: includes astrocytes. Compare **microglia**

macroglobulin (ˌmækrəʊˈglɒbjʊlɪn) *n immunol* **1** an immunoglobulin of unusually high relative molecular mass, observed in the blood in some diseases **2** Also called: **immunoglobulin M** the normal form of this immunoglobulin

macrograph (ˈmækrəʊˌgrɑːf, -ˌgræf) *n* a photograph, drawing, etc, in which an object appears as large as or several times larger than the original > **macrographic** (ˌmækrəʊˈgræfɪk) *adj*

macro lens *n* a camera lens used for close-up photography (2–10 cm)

macrolepidoptera (ˌmækrəʊˌlɛpɪˈdɒptərə) *pl n* a collector's name for that part of the lepidoptera that comprises the butterflies and the larger moths (noctuids, geometrids, bombycids, springtails, etc): a term without taxonomic significance. Compare **microlepidoptera**

macromere (ˈmækrəʊˌmɪə) *n embryol* any of the large yolk-filled cells formed by unequal cleavage of a fertilized ovum

macromolecule (ˌmækrəʊˈmɒlɪˌkjuːl) *n* any very large molecule, such as a protein or synthetic polymer > **macromolecular** (ˌmækrəʊməˈlɛkjʊlə) *adj*

macron (ˈmækrɒn) *n* a diacritical mark (ˉ) placed over a letter, used in prosody, in the orthography of some languages, and in several types of phonetic respelling systems, to represent a long vowel [c19 from Greek *makron* something long, from *makros* long]

macronucleus (ˌmækrəʊˈnjuːkliəs) *n, pl* **-clei** (-klɪˌaɪ) the larger of the two nuclei in ciliated protozoans. Compare **micronucleus**

macronutrient (ˌmækrəʊˈnjuːtrɪənt) *n* any substance, such as carbon, hydrogen, or oxygen, that is required in large amounts for healthy growth and development

macrophage ('mækrəʊˌfeɪdʒ) *n* any large phagocytic cell occurring in the blood, lymph, and connective tissue of vertebrates. See also **histiocyte**. > macrophagic (ˌmækrəʊˈfædʒɪk) *adj*

macrophagous (məˈkrɒfəgəs) *adj zoology* (of an animal) feeding on relatively large particles of food

macrophotography (ˌmækrəʊfəˈtɒgrəfɪ) *n* extremely close-up photography in which the image on the film is as large as, or larger than, the object

macrophysics (ˌmækrəʊˈfɪzɪks) *n* (*functioning as singular*) the branch of physics concerned with macroscopic systems and objects

macropsia (məˈkrɒpsɪə) *n* the condition of seeing everything in the field of view as larger than it really is, which can occur in diseases of the retina or in some brain disorders

macropterous (məˈkrɒptərəs) *adj* (of certain animals, esp some types of ant) having large wings

macroscopic (ˌmækrəʊˈskɒpɪk) *adj* **1** large enough to be visible to the naked eye. Compare **microscopic 2** comprehensive; concerned with large units **3** *physics* capable of being described by the statistical properties of a large number of parts ▷ Also: **megascopic** [C19 see MACRO-, -SCOPIC] > ˌmacroˈscopically *adv*

macrosociology (ˌmækrəʊˌsəʊsɪˈɒlədʒɪ) *n* the branch of sociology concerned with the study of human societies on a wide scale > ˌmacroˌsocioˈlogical *adj*

macrosporangium (ˌmækrəʊspɔːˈrændʒɪəm) *n*, *pl* **-gia** (-dʒɪə) another name for **megasporangium**

macrospore ('mækrəʊˌspɔː) *n* another name for **megaspore** (sense 1)

macrotous (məˈkrəʊtəs) *adj zoology* having large ears [from MACRO- + Greek *ous* ear]

macruran (məˈkrʊərən) *n* **1** any decapod crustacean of the group (formerly suborder) *Macrura*, which includes the lobsters, prawns, and crayfish ▷ *adj also* **macrurous macrural** or **macruroid 2** of, relating to, or belonging to the *Macrura* [C19 via New Latin, from Greek *makros* long + *oura* tail]

macula ('mækjʊlə) or **macule** ('mækjuːl) *n*, *pl* **-ulae** (-jʊˌliː) or **-ules** *anatomy* **1** a small spot or area of distinct colour, esp the macula lutea **2** any small discoloured spot or blemish on the skin, such as a freckle [C14 from Latin] > ˈmacular *adj*

macula lutea ('luːtɪə) *n*, *pl* **maculae luteae** ('luːtɪˌiː) a small yellowish oval-shaped spot, rich in cones, near the centre of the retina of the eye, where vision is especially sharp. See also **fovea centralis** [New Latin, literally: yellow spot]

macular degeneration *n* pathological changes in the macula lutea, resulting in loss of central vision: a common cause of blindness in the elderly

maculate *archaic or literary* ▷ *vb* ('mækjʊˌleɪt) **1** (*tr*) to spot, stain, or pollute ▷ *adj* ('mækjʊlɪt) **2** spotted or polluted [C15 from Latin *maculāre* to stain]

maculation (ˌmækjʊˈleɪʃən) *n* **1** a pattern of spots, as on certain animals and plants **2** *archaic* the act of maculating or the state of being maculated

macule ('mækjuːl) *n* **1** *anatomy* another name for **macula 2** *printing* another name for **mackle** [C15 from Latin *macula* spot]

Macumba (*Portuguese* maˈkumba) *n* a religious cult in Brazil that combines Christian and voodoo elements

mad (mæd) *adj* **madder, maddest 1** mentally deranged; insane **2** senseless; foolish **3** (*often foll by of*) *informal* angry; resentful **4** (*foll by about, on,* or *over*; often postpositive) wildly enthusiastic (about) or fond (of): *mad about football* **5** extremely excited or confused; frantic **6** temporarily overpowered by violent reactions, emotions, etc:

mad with grief **7** (of animals) **a** unusually ferocious: *a mad buffalo* **b** afflicted with rabies **8** like mad *informal* with great energy, enthusiasm, or haste; wildly **9** mad as a hatter crazily eccentric ▷ *vb* **mads, madding, madded 10** *archaic* to make or become mad; act or cause to act as if mad [Old English *gemǣded,* past participle of *gemǣdan* to render insane; related to *gemād* insane, and to Old High German *gimeit* silly, crazy, Old Norse *meitha* to hurt, damage] > ˈmaddish *adj*

MAD (mæd) *n US* ▷ *acronym for* mutual assured destruction: a theory of nuclear deterrence whereby each side in a conflict has the capacity to destroy the other in retaliation for a nuclear attack

madafu (maˈdafuː) *n E African* coconut milk [C19 from Swahili]

Madag. *abbreviation for* Madagascar

Madagascan (ˌmædəˈgæskən) *adj* **1** of or relating to Madagascar or its inhabitants ▷ *n* **2** a native or inhabitant of Madagascar

Madagascar (ˌmædəˈgæskə) *n* an island republic in the Indian Ocean, off the E coast of Africa: made a French protectorate in 1895; became autonomous in 1958 and fully independent in 1960; contains unique flora and fauna. Languages: Malagasy and French. Religions: animist and Christian. Currency: franc. Capital: Antananarivo. Pop: 17 901 000 (2004 est). Area: 587 041 sq km (266 657 sq miles). Official name (since 1975): Democratic Republic of Madagascar Former name (1958–75): Malagasy Republic > ˌMadaˈgascan *n, adj*

Madagascar aquamarine *n* a form of blue beryl from Madagascar, used as a gemstone

madam ('mædəm) *n, pl* **madams** or *for sense 1* **mesdames** ('meɪˌdæm) **1** a polite term of address for a woman, esp one considered to be of relatively high social status **2** a woman who runs a brothel **3** *Brit informal* a precocious or pompous little girl **4** *South African informal* the lady of the house [C13 from Old French *ma dame* my lady]

madame ('mædəm; *French* madam) *n, pl* **mesdames** ('meɪˌdæm; *French* medam) a married Frenchwoman: usually used as a title equivalent to *Mrs,* and sometimes extended to older unmarried women to show respect and to women of other nationalities [C17 from French. See MADAM]

madcap ('mædˌkæp) *adj* **1** impulsive, reckless, or lively ▷ *n* **2** an impulsive, reckless, or lively person [C16 from MAD + *cap* (in the figurative sense: head)]

mad cow disease *n* an informal name for **BSE**

madden ('mædⁿn) *vb* to make or become mad or angry

maddening ('mædⁿnɪŋ) *adj* **1** serving to send mad **2** extremely annoying; exasperating > ˈmaddeningly *adv* > ˈmaddeningness *n*

madder[1] ('mædə) *n* **1** any of several rubiaceous plants of the genus *Rubia,* esp the Eurasian *R. tinctoria,* which has small yellow flowers and a red fleshy root **2** the root of this plant **3** a dark reddish-purple dye formerly obtained by fermentation of this root; identical to the synthetic dye, alizarin **4** a red lake obtained from alizarin and an inorganic base; used as a pigment in inks and paints [Old English *mædere;* related to Middle Dutch *mēde,* Old Norse *mathra*]

madder[2] ('mædə) *adj* the comparative of **mad**

madding ('mædɪŋ) *adj archaic* **1** acting or behaving as if mad: *the madding crowd* **2** making mad; maddening > ˈmaddingly *adv*

made (meɪd) *vb* **1** the past tense and past participle of **make**[1] ▷ *adj* **2** artificially produced **3** (*in combination*) produced or shaped as specified: *handmade* **4** *get or have it made informal* to be assured of success **5** *made of money* very rich

made dish *n cookery* a dish consisting of a number of different ingredients cooked together

Madeira (məˈdɪərə; *Portuguese* məˈðeirə) *n* **1** a group of volcanic islands in the N Atlantic, west

of Morocco: since 1976 an autonomous region of Portugal; consists of the chief island, Madeira, Porto Santo, and the uninhabited Deserta and Selvagen Islands. Capital: Funchal. Pop: 245 012 (2001). Area: 797 sq km (311 sq miles) **2** a river in W Brazil, flowing northeast to the Amazon below Manaus. Length: 3241 km (2013 miles) **3** a rich strong fortified white wine made on Madeira

Madeira cake *n* a kind of rich sponge cake

madeleine ('mædəlɪn, -ˌleɪn) *n* a small fancy sponge cake [C19 perhaps after *Madeleine* Paulmier, French pastry cook]

mademoiselle (ˌmædmwɑːˈzɛl; *French* madmwazɛl) *n, pl* **mesdemoiselles** (ˌmeɪdmwɑːˈzɛl; *French* medmwazɛl) **1** a young unmarried French girl or woman: usually used as a title equivalent to *Miss* **2** a French teacher or governess [C15 French, from *ma my* + *demoiselle* DAMSEL]

made-up *adj* **1** invented; fictional **2** wearing make-up **3** put together; assembled **4** (of a road) surfaced with asphalt, concrete, etc

madhouse ('mædˌhaʊs) *n informal* **1** a mental hospital or asylum **2** a state of uproar or confusion

Madhya Bharat ('mʌdjə 'bɑːrət) *n* a former state of central India: part of Madhya Pradesh since 1956

Madhya Pradesh ('mʌdjə prɑːˈdɛʃ) *n* a state of central India, situated on the Deccan Plateau: rich in mineral resources, with several industrial cities; formerly the largest Indian state, it lost much of the SE to the new state of Chhattisgarh in 2000. Capital: Bhopal. Pop: 60 385 118 (2001). Area: 308 332 sq km (119 016 sq miles)

Madiba (məˈdiːbə) *n South African* a title of respect for Nelson Mandela, deriving from his Xhosa clan name

madison ('mædɪsⁿn) *n* a type of cycle relay race [C20 from *Madison Square Gardens* in New York City, early venue for such races]

Madison ('mædɪsⁿn) *n* a city in the US, in S central Wisconsin, on an isthmus between Lakes Mendota and Monona: the state capital. Pop: 218 432 (2003 est)

Madison Avenue *n* a street in New York City: a centre of American advertising and public-relations firms and a symbol of their attitudes and methods

madly ('mædlɪ) *adv* **1** in an insane or foolish manner **2** with great speed and energy **3** *informal* extremely or excessively: *I love you madly*

madman ('mædmən) *n, pl* **-men** a man who is insane, esp one who behaves violently; lunatic

madness ('mædnɪs) *n* **1** insanity; lunacy **2** extreme anger, excitement, or foolishness **3** a nontechnical word for **rabies**

Madonna (məˈdɒnə) *n* **1** *chiefly RC Church* a designation of the Virgin Mary **2** (*sometimes not capital*) a picture or statue of the Virgin Mary [C16 Italian, from *ma my* + *donna* lady]

Madonna lily *n* a perennial widely cultivated Mediterranean lily plant, *Lilium candidum,* with white trumpet-shaped flowers. Also called: Annunciation lily

madras ('mædrəs, məˈdræs, -ˈdrɑːs) *n* **1 a** a strong fine cotton or silk fabric, usually with a woven stripe **b** (*as modifier*): *madras cotton* **2** something made of this, esp a scarf **3** a medium-hot curry: *chicken madras* [C19 so named because the material originated in the MADRAS area]

Madras (məˈdrɑːs, -ˈdræs) *n* **1** a port in SE India, capital of Tamil Nadu, on the Bay of Bengal: founded in 1639 by the English East India Company as **Fort St George;** traditional burial place of St Thomas; university (1857). Pop: 4 216 268 (2001). Official name: Chennai **2** the former name (until 1968) for the state of **Tamil Nadu**

madrasah, madrasa (məˈdræsə, 'mɑːdræsə) or **medrese** (məˈdresɛɪ) *n Islam* an educational institution, particularly for Islamic religious instruction [from Arabic, literally: place of learning]

m

977

Madre de Dios (*Spanish* ˈmaðre ðe ˈðiɔs) *n* a river in NE South America, rising in SE Peru and flowing northeast to the Beni River in N Bolivia. Length: about 965 km (600 miles)

madrepore (ˌmædrɪˈpɔː) *n* any coral of the genus *Madrepora,* many of which occur in tropical seas and form large coral reefs: order *Zoantharia* [c18 via French from Italian *madrepora* mother-stone, from *madre* mother + *-pora,* from Latin *porus* or Greek *poros* calcareous stone, stalactite] > ˌmadreˈporal, madreporic (ˌmædrɪˈpɒrɪk) *or* madreporitic (ˌmædrɪpəˈrɪtɪk) *or* ˌmadreˈporian *adj*

Madrid (məˈdrɪd) *n* the capital of Spain, situated centrally in New Castile: the highest European capital, at an altitude of about 700 m (2300 ft); a Moorish fortress in the 10th century, captured by Castile in 1083 and made capital of Spain in 1561; university (1836). Pop: 3 092 759 (2003 est)

madrigal (ˈmædrɪgʰl) *n* **1** *music* a type of 16th- or 17th-century part song for unaccompanied voices with an amatory or pastoral text. Compare **glee** (sense 2) **2** a 14th-century Italian song, related to a pastoral stanzaic verse form [c16 from Italian, from Medieval Latin *mātricāle* primitive, apparently from Latin *mātrīcālis* of the womb, from *matrix* womb] > ˈmadrigalˌesque *or* > madrigalian (ˌmædrɪˈgeɪlɪən, -ˈgeɪ-) *adj* > ˈmadrigalist *n*

madrilène (ˈmædrɪˌlen, -ˌleɪn; *French* madrilɛn) *n* a cold consommé flavoured with tomato juice [shortened from French (*consommé*) *madrilène* from Spanish *madrileño* of Madrid]

madroña (məˈdrəʊnjə), **madroño** (məˈdrəʊnjəʊ) *or* **madrone** (məˈdrəʊn) *n, pl* **-ñas, -ños** *or* **-nes** an ericaceous North American evergreen tree or shrub, *Arbutus menziesii,* with white flowers and red berry-like fruits. See also **strawberry tree** [c19 from Spanish]

Madura (məˈdʊərə) *n* an island in Indonesia, off the NE coast of Java: extensive forests and saline springs. Capital: Pamekasan. Area: 5472 sq km (2113 sq miles)

Madurai (ˈmædjʊˌraɪ) *n* a city in S India, in S Tamil Nadu: centre of Dravidian culture for over 2000 years; cotton industry. Pop: 922 913 (2001). Former name: **Madura**

Madurese (ˌmædjʊəˈriːz) *adj* **1** of or relating to the Indonesian island of Madura or its inhabitants ▷ *n, pl* **-ese** **2** a native or inhabitant of Madura

maduro (məˈdʊərəʊ) *adj* **1** (of cigars) dark and strong ▷ *n, pl* **-ros** **2** a cigar of this type [Spanish, literally: ripe, from Latin *mātūrus* ripe, MATURE]

madwoman (ˈmædˌwʊmən) *n, pl* **-women** a woman who is insane, esp one who behaves violently; lunatic

madwort (ˈmædˌwɜːt) *n* **1** a low-growing Eurasian boraginaceous plant, *Asperugo procumbens,* with small blue flowers **2** any of certain other plants, such as alyssum [c16 once alleged to be a cure for madness]

madzoon (maˈdzuːn) *n* a variant of **matzoon**

Maeander (miːˈændə) *n* ancient name of the river **Menderes** (sense 1) Also spelt: **Meander**

Maebashi (maˈbaːʃiː) *n* a city in central Japan, on central Honshu: centre of sericulture and silk-spinning; university (1949). Pop: 283 005 (2002 est)

Maecenas (miːˈsiːnæs) *n* a wealthy patron of the arts [from Gaius *Maecenas* (?70–8 BC) Roman statesman and patron of Horace and Virgil]

maelstrom (ˈmeɪlstrəʊm) *n* **1** a large powerful whirlpool **2** any turbulent confusion [c17 from obsolete Dutch *maelstroom,* from *malen* to grind, whirl round + *stroom* STREAM]

Maelstrom (ˈmeɪlstrəʊm) *n* a strong tidal current in a restricted channel in the Lofoten Islands off the NW coast of Norway

maenad *or* **menad** (ˈmiːnæd) *n* **1** *classical myth* a woman participant in the orgiastic rites of Dionysus; bacchante **2** a frenzied woman [c16 from Latin *Maenas,* from Greek *mainas* madwoman] > **maeˈnadic** *adj* > **maeˈnadically** *adv* > ˈmaenadism *n*

maestoso (maɪˈstəʊsəʊ) *music* ▷ *adj, adv* **1** to be performed majestically ▷ *n, pl* **-tos** **2** a piece or passage directed to be played in this way [c18 Italian: majestic, from Latin *māiestās* MAJESTY]

Maestricht (ˈmaːstrɪxt; *Dutch* maːˈstrɪxt) *n* an obsolete spelling of **Maastricht**

maestro (ˈmaɪstrəʊ) *n, pl* **-tri** (-trɪ) *or* **-tros** **1** a distinguished music teacher, conductor, or musician **2** any man regarded as the master of an art: often used as a term of address **3** See **maestro di cappella** [c18 Italian: master]

maestro di cappella (dɪ kəˈpɛlə) *n* a person in charge of an orchestra, esp a private one attached to the palace of a prince in Italy during the baroque period. See **capellmeister** [Italian: master of the chapel]

mae west (meɪ) *n* *slang* an inflatable life jacket, esp as issued to the US armed forces for emergency use [c20 after *Mae West,* 1892–1980, American actress, renowned for her generous bust]

Maewo (maːˈeɪwəʊ) *n* an almost uninhabited island in Vanuatu. Also called: **Aurora**

MAF (mæf) *n* (in New Zealand) ▷ *acronym for* Ministry of Agriculture and Forestry

Mafeking (ˈmæfɪˌkɪŋ) *n* the former name (until 1980) of **Mafikeng**

MAFF (mæf) *n* (formerly, in Britain) ▷ *acronym for* Ministry of Agriculture, Fisheries, and Food

maffick (ˈmæfɪk) *vb* (*intr*) *Brit archaic* to celebrate extravagantly and publicly [c20 back formation from *Mafeking* (now Mafikeng), from the rejoicings at the relief of the siege there in 1900] > ˈmafficker *n*

Mafia *or* **Maffia** (ˈmæfɪə) *n* **1** **the** an international secret organization founded in Sicily, probably in opposition to tyranny. It developed into a criminal organization and in the late 19th century was carried to the US by Italian immigrants **2** any group considered to resemble the Mafia. See also **Black Hand, Camorra, Cosa Nostra** [c19 from Sicilian dialect of Italian, literally hostility to the law, boldness, perhaps from Arabic *mahyah* bragging]

Mafikeng (ˈmæfɪˌkɛŋ) *n* a town in N South Africa: besieged by the Boers for 217 days (1899–1900) during the second Boer War: administrative headquarters of the British protectorate of Bechuanaland until 1965, although outside its borders. Pop: 23 650 (2001). Former name (until 1980): **Mafeking**

mafioso (ˌmæfɪˈəʊsəʊ; *Italian* mafiˈoso) *n, pl* **-sos** *or* **-si** (*Italian* -si) a person belonging to the Mafia

mafted (ˈmæftɪd) *adj* *Northern English dialect* suffering under oppressive heat

maftir (ˈmaftɪr) *n* *Judaism* **1** the final section of the weekly Torah reading **2** the person to whom it is read, who also reads the Haftarah

mag¹ (mæg) *n* *informal* See **magazine**

mag² (mæg) *informal,* (*intr*) *Now chiefly Austral* ▷ *vb* **mags, magging, magged** **1** to talk; chatter ▷ *n* **2** talk; chatter [c18 from *Mag,* see MAGPIE]

mag. *abbreviation for* **1** magazine **2** magnitude

magainin (məˈgeɪnɪn) *n* any of a series of related substances with antibacterial properties, derived from the skins of frogs [c20 from Hebrew *magain* a shield]

Magallanes (*Spanish* maɣaˈʎanes) *n* the former name of **Punta Arenas**

magalogue *or US* **magalog** (ˈmagəˌlɒg) *n* a combination of a magazine and a catalogue [c20 from MAG(AZINE) + (CAT)ALOGUE]

magazine (ˌmægəˈziːn) *n* **1** a periodical paperback publication containing articles, fiction, photographs, etc **2** a metal box or drum holding several cartridges used in some kinds of automatic firearms; it is removed and replaced when empty **3** a building or compartment for storing weapons, explosives, military provisions, etc **4** a stock of ammunition **5** a device for continuously recharging a handling system, stove, or boiler with solid fuel **6** *photog* another name for **cartridge** (sense 5) **7** a rack for automatically feeding a number of slides through a projector **8** a TV or radio programme made up of a series of short nonfiction items [c16 via French *magasin* from Italian *magazzino,* from Arabic *makhāzin,* plural of *makhzan* storehouse, from *khazana* to store away]

magdalen (ˈmægdəlɪn) *or* **magdalene** (ˈmægdəˌlɪn, ˌmægdəˈliːn) *n* **1** *literary* a reformed prostitute **2** *rare* a reformatory for prostitutes [from MARY MAGDALENE]

Magdalena (ˌmægdəˈleɪnə, -ˈliː-; *Spanish* maɣðaˈlena) *n* a river in SW Colombia, rising on the E slopes of the Andes and flowing north to the Caribbean near Barranquilla. Length: 1540 km (956 miles)

Magdalena Bay *n* an inlet of the Pacific on the coast of NW Mexico, in Lower California

Magdalene (ˈmægdəˌliːn, ˌmægdəˈliːnɪ) *n* See **Mary Magdalene**

Magdalenian (ˌmægdəˈliːnɪən) *adj* **1** of or relating to the latest Palaeolithic culture in Europe, which ended about 10 000 years ago ▷ *n* **2** the Magdalenian culture [c19 from French *magdalénien,* after *La Madeleine,* village in Dordogne, France, near which artefacts of the culture were found]

Magdeburg (ˈmægdəˌbɜːg; *German* ˈmakdəbʊrk) *n* an industrial city and port in central Germany, on the River Elbe, capital of Saxony-Anhalt: a leading member of the Hanseatic League, whose local laws, the **Magdeburg Laws** were adopted by many European cities. Pop: 227 535 (2003 est)

mage (meɪdʒ) *n* an archaic word for **magician** [c14 from MAGUS]

Magellan (məˈgɛlən) *n* **Strait of** a strait between the mainland of S South America and Tierra del Fuego, linking the S Pacific with the S Atlantic. Length: 600 km (370 miles). Width: up to 32 km (20 miles)

Magellanic Cloud (ˌmægɪˈlænɪk) *n* either of two small irregular galaxies, the **Large Magellanic Cloud** (Nubecula Major) and the **Small Magellanic Cloud** (Nubecula Minor), lying near the S celestial pole; they are probably satellites of the Galaxy. Distances: 163 000 light years (Large), 196 000 light years (Small)

Magen David *or* **Mogen David** (ˈmɔːgən ˈdeɪvɪd) *n* *Judaism* another name for the **Star of David** [c20 from Hebrew *māghēn Dāwīdh* shield of David; David (about 1000–962 BC) was the second king of the Hebrews, and was responsible for uniting Israel as a kingdom]

magenta (məˈdʒɛntə) *n* **1 a** a deep purplish red that is the complementary colour of green and, with yellow and cyan, forms a set of primary colours **b** (*as adjective*): *a magenta filter* **2** another name for **fuchsin** [c19 named after *Magenta,* Italy, alluding to the blood shed in a battle there (1859)]

maggie (ˈmægɪ) *n* *slang* a magpie

Maggiore (ˌmædʒɪˈɔːrɪ; *Italian* madˈdʒore) *n* **Lake** a lake in N Italy and S Switzerland, in the S Lepontine Alps

maggot (ˈmægət) *n* **1** the soft limbless larva of dipterous insects, esp the housefly and blowfly, occurring in decaying organic matter **2** *rare* a fancy or whim [c14 from earlier *mathek;* related to Old Norse *mathkr* worm, Old English *matha,* Old High German *mado* grub]

maggoty (ˈmægətɪ) *adj* **1** relating to, resembling, or ridden with maggots **2** *slang* very drunk **3** *Austral slang* annoyed, angry

Magherafelt (ˈmæhərəˌfɛlt) *n* a district of N Northern Ireland, in Co Londonderry. Pop: 40 837 (2003 est). Area: 572 sq km (221 sq miles)

Maghreb *or* **Maghrib** (ˈmʌgrəb) *n* NW Africa, including Morocco, Algeria, Tunisia, and sometimes Libya [from Arabic, literally: the West]

Maghrebi *or* **maghribi** (ˈmʌgrəbɪ) *adj* **1** of or relating to the Maghreb region of NW Africa or its inhabitants ▷ *n* **2** a native or inhabitant of the Maghreb

magi (ˈmeɪdʒaɪ) *pl n, sing* **magus** (ˈmeɪgəs) **1** the Zoroastrian priests of the ancient Medes and

Persians **2 the three magi** the wise men from the East who came to do homage to the infant Jesus (Matthew 2:1–12) and traditionally called Caspar, Melchior, and Balthazar > **magian** ('meɪdʒɪən) *adj*

magic ('mædʒɪk) *n* **1** the art that, by use of spells, supposedly invokes supernatural powers to influence events; sorcery **2** the practice of this art **3** the practice of illusory tricks to entertain other people; conjuring **4** any mysterious or extraordinary quality or power: *the magic of springtime* **5 like magic** very quickly ▷ *adj also* **magical 6** of or relating to magic: *a magic spell* **7** possessing or considered to possess mysterious powers: *a magic wand* **8** unaccountably enchanting: *magic beauty* **9** *informal* wonderful; marvellous; exciting ▷ *vb* **-ics, -icking, -icked** (*tr*) **10** to transform or produce by or as if by magic **11** (foll by *away*) to cause to disappear by or as if by magic [c14 via Old French *magique,* from Greek *magikē* witchcraft, from *magos* MAGUS] > '**magical** *adj* > '**magically** *adv*

magic bullet *n informal* any therapeutic agent, esp one in the early stages of development, reputed to be very effective in treating a condition, such as a malignant tumour, by specifically targeting the diseased tissue

magic carpet *n* (in fairy stories) a carpet capable of transporting people through the air

Magic Circle *n* **1** the British association of magicians, traditionally forbidden to reveal any of the secrets of their art **2** (*not capitals*) a group of influential people involved in a conspiracy

magic eye *n* a miniature cathode-ray tube in some radio receivers, on the screen of which a pattern is displayed in order to assist tuning

magician (mə'dʒɪʃən) *n* **1** another term for **conjuror 2** a person who practises magic **3** a person who has extraordinary skill, influence, or qualities

magic lantern *n* an early type of slide projector. Sometimes shortened to: **lantern**

magic mushroom *n informal* any of various types of fungi that contain a hallucinogenic substance, esp *Psilocybe mexicana,* which contains psilocybin

magic number *n* **1** *physics* any of the numbers 2, 8, 20, 28, 50, 82, and 126. Nuclides with these numbers of nucleons appear to have greater stability than other nuclides **2** *chem* a number of atoms that is particularly stable in certain types of compound that have clusters of the same type of atom

magic realism *or* **magical realism** *n* a style of painting or writing that depicts images or scenes of surreal fantasy in a representational or realistic way > **magic realist** *or* **magical realist** *n*

magic square *n* a square array of rows of integers arranged so that the sum of the integers is the same when taken vertically, horizontally, or diagonally

magic wand *n* **1** a thin rod brandished by a conjuror in peforming magic tricks **2** any seemingly magical solution to a difficult problem: *there is no magic wand for us to fix it*

magilp (mə'gɪlp) *n arts* a variant spelling of **megilp**

Maginot line ('mæʒɪˌnəʊ; *French* maʒino) *n* **1** a line of fortifications built by France to defend its border with Germany prior to World War II; it proved ineffective against the German invasion **2** any line of defence in which blind confidence is placed [named after André *Maginot* (1877–1932), French minister of war when the fortifications were begun in 1929]

magisterial (ˌmædʒɪ'stɪərɪəl) *adj* **1** commanding; authoritative **2** domineering; dictatorial **3** of or relating to a teacher or person of similar status **4** of or relating to a magistrate [c17 from Late Latin *magisteriālis,* from *magister* master] > ˌmagis'terially *adv* > ˌmagis'terialness *n*

magisterium (ˌmædʒɪ'stɪərɪəm) *n* the teaching authority or function of the Roman Catholic Church [c19 see MAGISTERY]

magistery ('mædʒɪstərɪ, -trɪ) *n, pl* **-teries** *alchemy* **1** an agency or substance, such as the philosopher's stone, believed to transmute other substances **2** any substance capable of healing [c16 from Medieval Latin *magisterium,* from Latin: mastery, from *magister* master]

magistracy ('mædʒɪstrəsɪ) *or* **magistrature** ('mædʒɪstrəˌtjʊə) *n, pl* **-cies** *or* **-tures 1** the office or function of a magistrate **2** magistrates collectively **3** the district under the jurisdiction of a magistrate

magistral (mə'dʒɪstrəl) *adj* **1** of, relating to, or characteristic of a master **2** *pharmacol obsolete* made up according to a special prescription. Compare **officinal 3** *fortifications* determining the location of other fortifications: *the magistral line* ▷ *n* **4** a fortification in a determining position [c16 from Latin *magistrālis* concerning a master, from *magister* master] > **magistrality** (ˌmædʒɪ'strælɪtɪ) *n* > **magistratically** (ˌmædʒɪ'strætɪkəlɪ) *adv*

magistrate ('mædʒɪˌstreɪt, -strɪt) *n* **1** a public officer concerned with the administration of law. Related adj: **magisterial 2** another name for **justice of the peace 3** NZ the former name for **district court judge** [c17 from Latin *magistrātus,* from *magister* master] > '**magisˌtrateship** *n*

magistrates' court *n* (in England) a court of summary jurisdiction held before two or more justices of the peace or a stipendiary magistrate to deal with minor crimes, certain civil actions, and preliminary hearings

Maglemosian *or* **Maglemosean** (ˌmæglə'məʊzɪən) *n* **1** the first Mesolithic culture of N Europe, dating from 8000 BC to about 5000 BC: important for the rare wooden objects that have been preserved, such as dugout canoes ▷ *adj* **2** designating or relating to this culture [c20 named after the site at *Maglemose,* Denmark, where the culture was first classified]

maglev ('mæɡˌlɛv) *n* a type of high-speed train that runs on magnets supported by a magnetic field generated around the track [c20 from *mag(netic) lev(itation)*]

magma ('mæɡmə) *n, pl* **-mas** *or* **-mata** (-mətə) **1** a paste or suspension consisting of a finely divided solid dispersed in a liquid **2** hot molten rock, usually formed in the earth's upper mantle, some of which finds its way into the crust and onto the earth's surface, where it solidifies to form igneous rock [c15, from Latin: dregs (of an ointment), from Greek: salve made by kneading, from *massein* to knead] > **magmatic** (mæɡ'mætɪk) *adj* > '**magmatism** *n*

magma chamber *n* a reservoir of magma in the earth's crust where the magma may reside temporarily on its way from the upper mantle to the earth's surface

Magna Carta *or* **Magna Charta** ('mæɡnə 'kɑːtə) *n English history* the charter granted by King John at Runnymede in 1215, recognizing the rights and privileges of the barons, church, and freemen [Medieval Latin: great charter]

magna cum laude ('mæɡnə kʊm 'laʊdeɪ) *chiefly US* with great praise: the second of three designations for above-average achievement in examinations. Compare **cum laude, summa cum laude** [Latin]

Magna Graecia ('mæɡnə 'griːʃɪə) *n* (in the ancient world) S Italy, where numerous colonies were founded by Greek cities [Latin: Great Greece]

magnanimity (ˌmæɡnə'nɪmɪtɪ) *n, pl* **-ties** generosity [c14 via Old French from Latin *magnanimitās,* from *magnus* great + *animus* soul]

magnanimous (mæɡ'nænɪməs) *adj* generous and noble [c16 from Latin *magnanimus* great-souled] > mag'**nanimously** *adv* > mag'**nanimousness** *n*

magnate ('mæɡneɪt, -nɪt) *n* **1** a person of power and rank in any sphere, esp in industry **2** *history* a great nobleman **3** (formerly) a member of the upper chamber in certain European parliaments, as in Hungary [c15 back formation from earlier

magnates from Late Latin: great men, plural of *magnās,* from Latin *magnus* great] > '**magnateˌship** *n*

magnesia (mæɡ'niːʃə) *n* another name for **magnesium oxide** [c14 via Medieval Latin from Greek *Magnēsia,* of *Magnēs* ancient mineral-rich region] > mag'**nesian, magnesic** (mæɡ'niːsɪk) *or* mag'**nesial** *adj*

magnesite ('mæɡnɪˌsaɪt) *n* a white, colourless, or lightly tinted mineral consisting of naturally occurring magnesium carbonate in hexagonal crystalline form: a source of magnesium and also used in the manufacture of refractory bricks. Formula: $MgCO_3$ [c19 from MAGNESIUM + -ITE[1]]

magnesium (mæɡ'niːzɪəm) *n* a light silvery-white metallic element of the alkaline earth series that burns with an intense white flame, occurring principally in magnesite, dolomite, and carnallite: used in light structural alloys, flashbulbs, flares, and fireworks. Symbol: Mg; atomic no.: 12; atomic wt.: 24.3050; valency: 2; relative density: 1.738; melting pt.: 650°C; boiling pt.: 1090°C [c19 New Latin, from MAGNESIA]

magnesium oxide *n* a white tasteless substance occurring naturally as periclase: used as an antacid and laxative and in refractory materials, such as crucibles and fire bricks. Formula: MgO. Also called: **magnesia**

magnet ('mæɡnɪt) *n* **1** a body that can attract certain substances, such as iron or steel, as a result of a magnetic field; a piece of ferromagnetic substance. See also **electromagnet 2** a person or thing that exerts a great attraction [c15 via Latin from Greek *magnēs,* shortened from *ho Magnēs lithos* the Magnesian stone. See MAGNESIA]

magnetar ('mæɡnɪtɑː) *n* a type of neutron star that has a very intense magnetic field, over 1000 times greater than that of a pulsar [c20 from MAGNET(IC) (ST)AR, on the model of QUASAR]

magnetic (mæɡ'nɛtɪk) *adj* **1** of, producing, or operated by means of magnetism **2** of or concerned with a magnet **3** of or concerned with the magnetism of the earth: *the magnetic equator* **4** capable of being magnetized **5** exerting a powerful attraction: *a magnetic personality* > mag'**netically** *adv*

magnetic bottle *n* a configuration of magnetic fields for containing plasma

magnetic bubble *n physics* a small round magnetic domain induced by a magnetic field in a thin film of magnetic material, used in certain types of computer memories

magnetic character reader *n* a device that automatically scans and interprets characters printed with magnetic ink. It operates by the process of **magnetic character recognition**

magnetic compass *n* a compass containing a magnetic needle pivoted in a horizontal plane, that indicates the direction of magnetic north at points on the earth's surface

magnetic confinement *n* another name for **containment** (sense 3)

magnetic constant *n* the permeability of free space, which has the value $4\pi \times 10^{-7}$ henry per metre. Symbol: M_0 Also called: **absolute permeability**

magnetic course *n* an aircraft's course in relation to the magnetic north. Also called: **magnetic heading**

magnetic declination *n* the angle that a compass needle makes with the direction of the geographical north pole at any given point on the earth's surface. Also called: **declination, magnetic variation**

magnetic dip *or* **inclination** *n* another name for **dip** (sense 28)

magnetic dipole moment *n* a measure of the magnetic strength of a magnet or current-carrying coil, expressed as the torque per unit magnetic-flux density produced when the magnet or coil is set with its axis perpendicular to the magnetic field. Symbol: *m, j* Also called:

m

magnetic moment Compare **electromagnetic moment**

magnetic disk *n computing* another name for **disk** (sense 2)

magnetic epoch *n geology* a geologically long period of time during which the magnetic field of the earth retains the same polarity. The magnetic field may reverse during such a period for a geologically short period of time (a **magnetic event**)

magnetic equator *n* an imaginary line on the earth's surface, near the equator, at all points on which there is no magnetic dip. Also called: aclinic line

magnetic field *n* a field of force surrounding a permanent magnet or a moving charged particle, in which another permanent magnet or moving charge experiences a force. Compare **electric field**

magnetic flux *n* a measure of the strength of a magnetic field over a given area perpendicular to it, equal to the product of the area and the magnetic flux density through it. Symbol: φ

magnetic flux density *n* a measure of the strength of a magnetic field at a given point, expressed by the force per unit length on a conductor carrying unit current at that point. Symbol: *B* Also called: magnetic induction

magnetic induction *n* another name for **magnetic flux density**

magnetic ink *n* ink containing particles of a magnetic material used for printing characters for magnetic character recognition

magnetic ink character recognition *n* the process of reading characters printed in magnetic ink. Abbreviation: MICR

magnetic lens *n* a set of magnets, esp electromagnets, used to focus or defocus a beam of charged particles in an electron microscope, particle accelerator, or similar device

magnetic meridian *n* a continuous imaginary line around the surface of the earth passing through both magnetic poles

magnetic mine *n* a mine designed to activate when a magnetic field such as that generated by the metal of a ship's hull is detected

magnetic mirror *n physics* a configuration of magnetic fields used to confine charged particles, as in a magnetic bottle

magnetic moment *n* short for **magnetic dipole moment** *or* **electromagnetic moment**

magnetic monopole *n* another name for **monopole** (sense 2)

magnetic needle *n* a slender magnetized rod used in certain instruments, such as the magnetic compass, for indicating the direction of a magnetic field

magnetic north *n* the direction in which a compass needle points, at an angle (the declination) from the direction of true (geographic) north

magnetic particle inspection *n engineering* a method of testing for cracks and other defects in a magnetic material, such as steel, by covering it with a magnetic powder and magnetizing it: any variation in the concentration of the powder indicates a flaw in the material

magnetic pick-up *n* a type of record player pick-up in which the stylus moves an iron core in a coil, causing a changing magnetic field that produces the current

magnetic pole *n* **1** either of two regions in a magnet where the magnetic induction is concentrated **2** either of two variable points on the earth's surface towards which a magnetic needle points, where the lines of force of the earth's magnetic field are vertical

magnetic resonance *n* the response by atoms, molecules, or nuclei subjected to a magnetic field to radio waves or other forms of energy: used in medicine for scanning. See **magnetic resonance imaging**, **magnetic resonance angiography**

magnetic resonance angiography *n* a form of magnetic resonance imaging in which either the injection of a magnetic resonance contrast agent or the movement of the blood provides information of value in diagnosis. Abbreviation: MRA

magnetic resonance imaging *n* a noninvasive medical diagnostic technique in which the absorption and transmission of high-frequency radio waves are analysed as they irradiate the hydrogen atoms in water molecules and other tissue components placed in a strong magnetic field. This computerized analysis provides a powerful aid to the diagnosis and treatment planning of many diseases, including cancer. Abbreviation: MRI

magnetics (mæɡ'nɛtɪks) *n* (*functioning as singular*) the branch of physics concerned with magnetism

magnetic storm *n* a sudden severe disturbance of the earth's magnetic field, caused by emission of charged particles from the sun

magnetic stripe *n* (across the back of various types of cheque card, credit card, etc) a dark stripe of magnetic material consisting of several tracks onto which information may be coded and which may be read or written to electronically

magnetic tape *n* a long narrow plastic or metal strip coated or impregnated with a ferromagnetic material such as iron oxide, used to record sound or video signals or to store information in computers. Sometimes (*informal*) shortened to: **mag tape**

magnetic tape unit *or* **drive** *n* a computer device that moves reels of magnetic tape past read-write heads so that data can be transferred to or from the computer

magnetic variation *n* another name for **magnetic declination**

magnetic wood *n* wood containing fine particles of nickel-zinc ferrite which absorb microwave radio signals, used to line rooms where mobile phone use is undesirable

magnetism ('mæɡnɪˌtɪzəm) *n* **1** the property of attraction displayed by magnets **2** any of a class of phenomena in which a field of force is caused by a moving electric charge. See also **electromagnetism**, **ferromagnetism**, **diamagnetism**, **paramagnetism** **3** the branch of physics concerned with magnetic phenomena **4** powerful attraction > '**magnetist** *n*

magnetite ('mæɡnɪˌtaɪt) *n* a black magnetic mineral, found in igneous and metamorphic rocks and as a separate deposit. It is a source of iron. Composition: iron oxide. Formula: Fe_3O_4. Crystal structure: cubic > **magnetitic** (ˌmæɡnɪ'tɪtɪk) *adj*

magnetize *or* **magnetise** ('mæɡnɪˌtaɪz) *vb* (*tr*) **1** to make (a substance or object) magnetic **2** to attract strongly **3** an obsolete word for **mesmerize** > ˌmagnet'izable *or* ˌmagnet'isable *adj* > ˌmagneti'zation *or* ˌmagneti'sation *n* > 'magnetˌizer *or* 'magnetˌiser *n*

magneto (mæɡ'niːtəʊ) *n, pl* **-tos** a small electric generator in which the magnetic field is produced by a permanent magnet, esp one for providing the spark in an internal-combustion engine [c19 short for *magnetoelectric generator*]

magneto- *combining form* indicating magnetism or magnetic properties: *magnetosphere*

magnetochemistry (mæɡˌniːtəʊ'kɛmɪstrɪ) *n* the branch of chemistry concerned with the relationship between magnetic and chemical properties > magˌneto'chemical *adj*

magnetoelectricity (mæɡˌniːtəʊɪlɛk'trɪsɪtɪ) *n* electricity produced by the action of magnetic fields > magˌnetoe'lectric *or* magˌnetoe'lectrical *adj*

magnetograph (mæɡ'niːtəʊˌɡrɑːf, -ˌɡræf) *n* a recording magnetometer, usually used for studying variations in the earth's magnetic field

magnetohydrodynamics (mæɡˌniːtəʊˌhaɪdrəʊdaɪ'næmɪks) *n* (*functioning as singular*) **1** the study of the behaviour of conducting fluids, such as liquid metals or plasmas, in magnetic fields **2** the generation of electricity by subjecting a plasma to a magnetic field and collecting the deflected free electrons ▷ Abbreviation: MHD > magˌneto,hydrody'namic *adj*

magnetometer (ˌmæɡnɪ'tɒmɪtə) *n* any instrument for measuring the intensity or direction of a magnetic field, esp the earth's field > magnetometric (ˌmæɡnɪtəʊ'mɛtrɪk) *adj* > ˌmagne'tometry *n*

magnetomotive (mæɡˌniːtəʊ'məʊtɪv) *adj* causing a magnetic flux

magnetomotive force *n* the agency producing a magnetic flux, considered analogous to the electromotive force in an electric circuit; equal to the circular integral of the magnetic field strength. Symbol: *F*

magneton ('mæɡnɪˌtɒn, mæɡ'niːtɒn) *n* **1** Also called: Bohr magneton a unit of magnetic moment equal to $eh/4\pi m$ where *e* and *m* are the charge and mass of an electron and *h* is the Planck constant. It has the value $9.274\,096 \times 10^{-24}$ joule per tesla. Symbol: β *or* m_B **2** Also called: nuclear magneton a similar unit equal to $\beta m/M$ where *M* is the mass of the proton [c20 from MAGNET + (ELECTR)ON]

magnetosphere (mæɡ'niːtəʊˌsfɪə) *n* the region surrounding a planet, such as the earth, in which the behaviour of charged particles is controlled by the planet's magnetic field > magnetospheric (mæɡˌniːtəʊ'sfɛrɪk) *adj*

magnetostatics (mæɡˌniːtəʊ'stætɪks) *n* (*functioning as singular*) *physics* the study of steady-state magnetic fields

magnetostriction (mæɡˌniːtəʊ'strɪkʃən) *n* a change in dimensions of a ferromagnetic material that is subjected to a magnetic field [c19 from MAGNETO- + CONSTRICTION] > magˌneto'strictive *adj*

magnetron ('mæɡnɪˌtrɒn) *n* an electronic valve with two coaxial electrodes used with an applied magnetic field to generate high-power microwave oscillations, esp for use in radar [c20 from MAGNET + ELECTRON]

magnet school *n* a school that provides a focus on one subject area throughout its curriculum in order to attract, often from an early age, pupils who wish to specialize in this subject

magnet steel *n engineering* steel used for the manufacture of permanent magnets, often having a high cobalt content and smaller amounts of nickel, aluminium, or copper

magnific (mæɡ'nɪfɪk) *or* **magnifical** *adj archaic* magnificent, grandiose, or pompous [c15 via Old French from Latin *magnificus* great in deeds, from *magnus* great + *facere* to do] > mag'nifically *adv*

Magnificat (mæɡ'nɪfɪˌkæt) *n Christianity* the hymn of the Virgin Mary (Luke 1:46-55), used as a canticle [from the opening phrase in the Latin version, *Magnificat anima mea Dominum* (my soul doth magnify the Lord)]

magnification (ˌmæɡnɪfɪ'keɪʃən) *n* **1** the act of magnifying or the state of being magnified **2** the degree to which something is magnified **3** a copy, photograph, drawing, etc, of something magnified **4** a measure of the ability of a lens or other optical instrument to magnify, expressed as the ratio of the size of the image to that of the object

magnificence (mæɡ'nɪfɪsəns) *n* the quality of being magnificent [c14 via French from Latin *magnificentia*]

magnificent (mæɡ'nɪfɪsənt) *adj* **1** splendid or impressive in appearance **2** superb or very fine **3** (esp of ideas) noble or elevated **4** *archaic* great or exalted in rank or action [c16 from Latin *magnificentio* more splendid; irregular comparative of *magnificus* great in deeds; see MAGNIFIC] > mag'nificently *adv* > mag'nificentness *n*

magnifico (mæɡ'nɪfɪˌkəʊ) *n, pl* **-coes** a magnate; grandee [c16 Italian from Latin *magnificus*; see MAGNIFIC]

magnify ('mægnɪ,faɪ) vb -fies, -fying, -fied **1** to increase, cause to increase, or be increased in apparent size, as through the action of a lens, microscope, etc **2** to exaggerate or become exaggerated in importance: *don't magnify your troubles* **3** (*tr*) *rare* to increase in actual size **4** (*tr*) *archaic* to glorify [c14 via Old French from Latin *magnificāre* to praise; see MAGNIFIC] > 'magni,fiable *adj*

magnifying glass *or* **magnifier** *n* a convex lens used to produce an enlarged image of an object

magniloquent (mæg'nɪləkwənt) *adj* (of speech) lofty in style; grandiloquent [c17 from Latin *magnus* great + *loquī* to speak] > mag'niloquence *n* > mag'niloquently *adv*

Magnitogorsk (*Russian* məgnita'gɔrsk) *n* a city in central Russia, on the Ural River: founded in 1930 to exploit local magnetite ores; site of one of the world's largest, metallurgical plants. Pop: 415 000 (2005 est)

magnitude ('mægnɪ,tjuːd) *n* **1** relative importance or significance: *a problem of the first magnitude* **2** relative size or extent: *the magnitude of the explosion* **3** *maths* a number assigned to a quantity, such as weight, and used as a basis of comparison for the measurement of similar quantities **4** Also called: **apparent magnitude** *astronomy* the apparent brightness of a celestial body expressed on a numerical scale on which bright stars have a low value. Values are measured by eye (**visual magnitude**) or more accurately by photometric or photographic methods, and range from –26.7 (the sun), through 1.5 (Sirius), down to about +30. Each integral value represents a brightness 2.512 times greater than the next highest integral value. See also **absolute magnitude 5** Also called: **earthquake magnitude** *geology* a measure of the size of an earthquake based on the quantity of energy released: specified on the Richter scale. See **Richter scale** [c14 from Latin *magnitūdō* size, from *magnus* great] > ,magni'tudinous *adj*

magnolia (mæg'nəʊlɪə) *n* **1** any tree or shrub of the magnoliaceous genus *Magnolia* of Asia and North America: cultivated for their white, pink, purple, or yellow showy flowers **2** the flower of any of these plants **3** a very pale pinkish-white or purplish-white colour [c18 New Latin, named after Pierre *Magnol* (1638–1715), French botanist]

magnoliaceous (mæg,nəʊlɪ'eɪʃəs) *adj* of, relating to, or belonging to the *Magnoliaceae*, a family of trees and shrubs, including magnolias and the tulip tree, having large showy flowers

magnolia metal *n* *engineering* an alloy used for bearings, consisting largely of lead (up to 80 per cent) and antimony, with the addition of smaller quantities of iron and tin

magnox ('mægnɒks) *n* an alloy consisting mostly of magnesium with small amounts of aluminium and other metals, used in fuel elements of nuclear reactors [c20 from *mag(nesium) n(o) ox(idation)*]

magnox reactor *n* a nuclear reactor using carbon dioxide as the coolant, graphite as the moderator, and uranium cased in magnox as the fuel

magnum ('mægnəm) *n, pl* -nums a wine bottle holding the equivalent of two normal bottles (approximately 52 fluid ounces) [c18 from Latin: a big thing, from *magnus* large]

magnum opus *n* a great work of art or literature, esp the greatest single work of an artist [Latin]

magnus hitch ('mægnəs) *n* a knot similar to a clove hitch but having one more turn [C19 *magnus*, of unknown origin]

Magog ('meɪgɒg) *n* See **Gog and Magog**

magot (mɑː'gəʊ, 'mægət) *n* **1** a Chinese or Japanese figurine in a crouching position, usually grotesque **2** a less common name for **Barbary ape** [c17 from French: grotesque figure, after the Biblical giant MAGOG]

magpie ('mægpaɪ) *n* **1** any of various passerine birds of the genus *Pica*, esp *P. pica*, having a black-and-white plumage, long tail, and a chattering call: family *Corvidae* (crows, etc) **2** any of various similar birds of the Australian family *Cracticidae*. See also **butcherbird** (sense 2) **3** any of various other similar or related birds **4** (*often capital*) a variety of domestic fancy pigeon typically having black-and-white markings **5** *Brit* a person who hoards small objects **6** a person who chatters **7 a** the outmost ring but one on a target **b** a shot that hits this ring [c17 from *Mag* diminutive of *Margaret*, used to signify a chatterbox + PIE²]

magpie goose *n* a large black-and-white goose, *Anseranas semipalmata*, of N Australia and adjacent islands

magpie lark *n* a common black-and-white bird of Australia, *Grallina cyanoleuca*, that builds a mud nest. Also called: **peewee**

magpie moth *n* **1** a geometrid moth, *Abraxas grossulariata*, showing variable patterning in black on white or yellow, whose looper larvae attack currant and gooseberry bushes. The paler **clouded magpie** is *A. sylvata* **2** small magpie an unrelated micro, *Eurrhypara hortulata*

MAgr *abbreviation for* Master of Agriculture

magsman ('mægz,mæn) *n, pl* -men *Austral slang* **1** a raconteur **2** a confidence trickster

mag tape *n* *informal* short for **magnetic tape**

maguey ('mægweɪ) *n* **1** any of various tropical American agave plants of the genera *Agave* or *Furcraea*, esp one that yields a fibre or is used in making an alcoholic beverage **2** the fibre from any of these plants, used esp for rope [c16 Spanish, from Taino]

magus ('meɪgəs) *n, pl* magi ('meɪdʒaɪ) **1** a Zoroastrian priest **2** an astrologer, sorcerer, or magician of ancient times [c14 from Latin, from Greek *magos*, from Old Persian *magus* magician]

Magus ('meɪgəs) *n* Simon *New Testament* a sorcerer who tried to buy spiritual powers from the apostles (Acts 8:9-24)

Magyar ('mægjɑː) *n* **1** (*pl* -yars) a member of the predominant ethnic group of Hungary, also found in NW Siberia **2** the Hungarian language ▷ *adj* **3** of or relating to the Magyars or their language **4** *sewing* of or relating to a style of sleeve cut in one piece with the bodice

Magyarország ('mɒdjɔrorsaːg) *n* the Hungarian name for **Hungary**

Mahabharata (mə,hɑː'bɑːrətə) *or* **Mahabharatam, Mahabharatum** (mə,hɑː'bɑːrətəm) *n* an epic Sanskrit poem of India, dealing chiefly with the struggle between two rival families. It contains many separate episodes, the most notable of which is the *Bhagavad-Gita* [Sanskrit, from *mahā* great + *bhārata* story]

Mahajanga (,mæhə'dʒæŋgə) *n* a port in NW Madagascar, on Bombetoka Bay. Pop: 147 000 (2005 est). Former name: Majunga

Mahalla el Kubra (mə'hælə ɛl 'kuːbrə) *n* a city in N Egypt, on the Nile delta: one of the largest diversified textile centres in Egypt. Pop: 433 000 (2005 est)

Mahanadi (mə'hɑːnədɪ) *n* a river in E India, rising in Chhattisgarh and flowing north, then south and east to the Bay of Bengal. Length: 885 km (550 miles)

maharajah *or* **maharaja** (,mɑːhə'rɑːdʒə) *n* any of various Indian princes, esp any of the rulers of the former native states [c17 Hindi, from *mahā* great + RAJAH]

maharani *or* **maharanee** (,mɑːhə'rɑːniː) *n* **1** the wife of a maharajah **2** a woman holding the rank of maharajah [c19 from Hindi, from *mahā* great + RANI]

Maharashtra (,mɑːhə'ræʃtrə) *n* a state of W central India, formed in 1960 from the Marathi-speaking S and E parts of former Bombay state: lies mainly on the Deccan plateau; mainly agricultural. Capital: Bombay. Pop: 96 752 247 (2001). Area: 307 690 sq km (118 800 sq miles)

maharishi (,mɑːhɑː'riːʃɪ, mə'hɑː,riːʃɪ) *n* *Hinduism* a Hindu teacher of religious and mystical knowledge [from Hindi, from *mahā* great + *rishi* sage, saint]

mahatma (mə'hɑːtmə, -'hæt-) *n* (*sometimes capital*) **1** *Hinduism* a Brahman sage **2** *theosophy* an adept or sage [c19 from Sanskrit *mahātman*, from *mahā* great + *ātman* soul] > ma'hatmaism *n*

Mahayana (,mɑːhə'jɑːnə) *n* **a** a liberal Buddhist school of Tibet, China, and Japan, whose adherents aim to disseminate Buddhist doctrines, seeking enlightenment not for themselves alone, but for all sentient beings **b** (*as modifier*): *Mahayana Buddhism* [from Sanskrit, from *mahā* great + *yāna* vehicle] > ,Maha'yanist *n*

Mahdi ('mɑːdɪ) *n* *Islam* any of a number of Muslim messiahs expected to forcibly convert all mankind to Islam [Arabic *mahdīy* one who is guided, from *madā* to guide aright]

Mahdist ('mɑːdɪst) *adj* **1** of or relating to the Mahdi, the title assumed by Mohammed Ahmed, the Sudanese military leader (?1843–85), or his followers ▷ *n* **2** a follower or admirer of the Madhi > 'Mahdism *n*

Mahé (mɑː'heɪ) *n* an island in the Indian Ocean, the chief island of the Seychelles. Capital: Victoria. Pop: 71 900 (2002 est). Area: 147 sq km (57 sq miles)

mahewu (mɑ'hewʊ, -'xe-) *n* (in South Africa) fermented liquid mealie-meal porridge, used as a stimulant, esp by Black Africans [from Xhosa *amarewu*]

Mahican (mə'hiːkən) *n, pl* -cans *or* -can a variant of **Mohican**

mahi-mahi ('mɑːhɪ,mɑːhɪ) *n* another name for **dolphin** (sense 3) [c20 from Hawaiian, literally: strong-strong]

mah jong *or* **mah-jongg** (,mɑː'dʒɒŋ) *n* a game of Chinese origin, usually played by four people, in which tiles bearing various designs are drawn and discarded until one player has an entire hand of winning combinations [from Chinese, literally: sparrows]

mahlstick ('mɔːl,stɪk) *n* a variant spelling of **maulstick**

mahoe (mɑ'həʊ) *n, pl* mahoe a small New Zealand tree, *Melicytus ramiflorus*, with white flowers and bark. Also called: hinahina, whitewood *or* whiteywood [Māori]

mahogany (mə'hɒgənɪ) *n, pl* -nies **1** any of various tropical American trees of the meliaceous genus *Swietenia*, esp *S. mahogani* and *S. macrophylla*, valued for their hard reddish-brown wood **2** any of several trees with similar wood, such as African mahogany (genus *Khaya*) and Philippine mahogany (genus *Shorea*) **3 a** the wood of any of these trees. See also **acajou** (sense 1) **b** (*as modifier*): *a mahogany table* **4** a reddish-brown colour [c17 origin obscure]

Mahometan (mə'hɒmɪtᵊn) *n, adj* a former word for **Muslim**. > Ma'hometanism *n*

mahonia (mə'həʊnɪə) *n* any evergreen berberidaceous shrub of the Asian and American genus *Mahonia*, esp *M. aquifolium*: cultivated for their ornamental spiny divided leaves and clusters of small yellow flowers [c19 New Latin, named after Bernard *McMahon* (died 1816), American botanist]

mahout (mə'haʊt) *n* (in India and the East Indies) an elephant driver or keeper [c17 Hindi *mahāut*, from Sanskrit *mahāmātra* of great measure, originally a title]

Mahratta (mə'rɑːtə) *n* a variant spelling of **Maratha**. > Mah'ratti *n, adj*

Mähren ('meːrən) *n* the German name for **Moravia**

mahseer ('mɑːsɪə) *n* any of various large freshwater Indian cyprinid fishes, such as *Barbus tor* [from Hindi]

mahzor *Hebrew* (max'zɔr; *English* mɑːk'zɔː) *n, pl* -zorim (-'zɔːriːm; *English* -zə'riːm) a variant spelling of **machzor**

m

Maia ('maɪə) n *Greek myth* the eldest of the seven Pleiades, mother by Zeus of Hermes

maid (meɪd) n **1** *archaic or literary* a young unmarried girl; maiden **2 a** a female servant **b** (*in combination*): *a housemaid* **3** a spinster [c12 shortened form of MAIDEN] > 'maidish *adj* > 'maidishness n

maidan (mæˈdɑːn) n (in Pakistan, India, etc) an open space used for meetings, sports, etc [Urdu, from Arabic]

maiden ('meɪdᵊn) n **1** *archaic or literary* **a** a young unmarried girl, esp when a virgin **b** (*as modifier*): *a maiden blush* **2** *horse racing* **a** a horse that has never won a race **b** (*as modifier*): *a maiden race* **3** *cricket* See **maiden over** **4** Also called: **clothes maiden** *Northern English dialect* a frame on which clothes are hung to dry; clothes horse **5** (*modifier*) of or relating to an older unmarried woman: *a maiden aunt* **6** (*modifier*) of or involving an initial experience or attempt: *a maiden voyage; maiden speech* **7** (*modifier*) (of a person or thing) untried; unused **8** (*modifier*) (of a place) never trodden, penetrated, or captured [Old English mægden; related to Old High German magad, Old Norse mogr young man, Old Irish mug slave] > 'maidenish *adj* > 'maiden-ˌlike *adj*

maidenhair fern or **maidenhair** ('meɪdᵊn,hɛə) n any fern of the cosmopolitan genus *Adiantum*, esp *A. capillis-veneris*, having delicate fan-shaped fronds with small pale-green leaflets: family *Adiantaceae* [c15 so called from the hairlike appearance of its fine fronds]

maidenhair tree n another name for **ginkgo**

maidenhead ('meɪdᵊn,hɛd) n **1** a nontechnical word for the **hymen 2** virginity; maidenhood [c13 from *maiden* + -*hood*, variant of -HOOD]

Maidenhead ('meɪdᵊn,hɛd) n a town in S England, in Windsor and Maidenhead unitary authority, Berkshire, on the River Thames. Pop: 58 848 (2001)

maidenhood ('meɪdᵊn,hʊd) n **1** the time during which a woman is a maiden or a virgin **2** the condition of being a maiden or virgin

maidenly ('meɪdᵊnlɪ) *adj* of or befitting a maiden > 'maidenliness n

maiden name n a woman's surname before marriage

maiden over n *cricket* an over in which no runs are scored

maiden voyage n *nautical* the first voyage of a vessel

Maid Marian n **1** a character in morris dancing, played by a man dressed as a woman **2** *legend* the sweetheart of Robin Hood

maid of all work n **1** a maid who does all types of housework **2** a general factotum

maid of honour n **1** *US and Canadian* the principal unmarried attendant of a bride. Compare **bridesmaid, matron of honour 2** *Brit* a small tart with an almond-flavoured filling **3** an unmarried lady attending a queen or princess

maidservant ('meɪd,sɜːvᵊnt) n a female servant

Maidstone ('meɪdstən, -ˌstəʊn) n a town in SE England, administrative centre of Kent, on the River Medway. Pop: 89 684 (2001)

Maiduguri (ˌmaɪdʊˈgʊːrɪ) n a city in NE Nigeria, capital of Bornu State; agricultural trade centre. Pop: 828 000 (2005 est). Also called: Yerwa-Maiduguri

maieutic (meɪˈjuːtɪk) or **maieutical** *adj* *philosophy* of or relating to the Socratic method of eliciting knowledge by a series of questions and answers [c17 from Greek *maieutikos* relating to midwifery (used figuratively by Socrates), from *maia* midwife]

maigre ('meɪgə) *adj* RC Church **1** not containing flesh, and so permissible as food on days of religious abstinence: *maigre food* **2** of or designating such a day [c17 from French: thin; see MEAGRE]

maihem ('meɪhɛm) n a variant spelling of **mayhem**

maik (mek) n *Scot* an old halfpenny. Also called: **meck** [of obscure origin]

maiko ('maɪkəʊ) n, pl -ko or -kos an apprentice geisha [from Japanese, literally: dancer]

Maikop (Russian majˈkɔp) n a city in SW Russia, capital of the Adygei Republic: extensive oilfields to the southwest; mineral springs. Pop: 165 000 (2005 est)

mail¹ (meɪl) n **1** Also called (esp Brit): **post** letters, packages, etc, that are transported and delivered by the post office **2** the postal system **3** a single collection or delivery of mail **4** a train, ship, or aircraft that carries mail **5** short for **electronic mail 6** (*modifier*) of, involving, or used to convey mail: *a mail train* ⊳ vb (tr) **7** *chiefly US and Canadian* to send by mail. Usual Brit word: **post 8** to contact (a person) by electronic mail **9** to send (a message, document, etc) by electronic mail [c13 from Old French *male* bag, probably from Old High German *malha* wallet] > 'mailable *adj* > ˌmaila'bility n

mail² (meɪl) n **1** a type of flexible armour consisting of riveted metal rings or links **2** the hard protective shell of such animals as the turtle and lobster ⊳ vb **3** (tr) to clothe or arm with mail [c14 from Old French *maille* mesh, from Latin *macula* spot] > 'mail-less *adj*

mail³ (meɪl) n *archaic, chiefly Scot* a monetary payment, esp of rent or taxes [Old English māl terms, from Old Norse māl agreement]

mail⁴ (meɪl) n *Austral informal* a rumour or report, esp a racing tip

mailbag ('meɪl,bæg), **mailsack** or sometimes US **mailpouch** n a large bag used for transporting or delivering mail

mailbox ('meɪl,bɒks) n **1** *chiefly US and Canadian* **a** a slot, usually covered with a hinged flap, through which letters, etc are delivered to a building **b** a private box into which letters, etc, are delivered. Also called (in Britain and certain other countries): **letter box 2** *chiefly US and Canadian* a public box into which letters, etc, are put for collection and delivery. Also called (in Britain and certain other countries): **postbox 3** (on a computer) the directory in which e-mail messages are stored; also used of the icon that can be clicked to provide access to e-mails

mailcoach ('meɪl,kəʊtʃ) or US and Canadian **mailcar** n a railway coach specially constructed for the transportation of mail

mail drop n *chiefly US and Canadian* a receptacle or chute for mail

mailer ('meɪlə) n **1** a person who addresses or mails letters, etc **2** *US and Canadian* a machine used for stamping and addressing mail **3** *US and Canadian* a container for mailing things

mailing list n a register of names and addresses to which advertising matter, etc, is sent by post or electronic mail

maillot (mæˈjəʊ) n **1** tights worn for ballet, gymnastics, etc **2** a woman's swimsuit **3** a jersey [from French]

mailman ('meɪl,mæn) n, pl -men *chiefly US and Canadian* another name for **postman**

mail merging n *computing* a software facility that can produce a large number of personalized letters by combining a file containing a list of names and addresses with one containing a single standard document

mail order n **1** an order for merchandise sent by post **2 a** a system of buying and selling merchandise through the post **b** (*as modifier*): *a mail-order firm*

mailsack ('meɪl,sæk) n another name for a **mailbag**

mailshot ('meɪl,ʃɒt) n a circular, leaflet, or other advertising material sent by post, or the posting of such material to a large group of people at one time

maim (meɪm) vb (tr) **1** to mutilate, cripple, or disable a part of the body of (a person or animal) **2** to make defective ⊳ n **3** *obsolete* an injury or defect [c14 from Old French *mahaignier* to wound, probably of Germanic origin] > **maimedness** ('meɪmdnɪs) n > 'maimer n

mai mai ('maɪ maɪ) n NZ a duck-shooter's shelter; hide [probably from Australian aboriginal *mia-mia* shelter]

main¹ (meɪn) *adj* (*prenominal*) **1** chief or principal in rank, importance, size, etc **2** sheer or utmost (esp in the phrase **by main force**) **3** *nautical* of, relating to, or denoting any gear, such as a stay or sail, belonging to the mainmast **4** *obsolete* significant or important ⊳ n **5** a principal pipe, conduit, duct, or line in a system used to distribute water, electricity, etc **6** (*plural*) **a** the main distribution network for water, gas, or electricity **b** (*as modifier*): *mains voltage* **7** the chief or most important part or consideration **8** great strength or force (now chiefly in the phrase (**with**) **might and main**) **9** *literary* the open ocean **10** *archaic* short for **Spanish Main 11** *archaic* short for **mainland 12** in (or for) **the main** on the whole; for the most part [c13 from Old English *mægen* strength]

main² (meɪn) n **1** a throw of the dice in dice games **2** a cockfighting contest **3** a match in archery, boxing, etc [c16 of unknown origin]

Main (meɪn; German main) n a river in central and W Germany, flowing west through Würzburg and Frankfurt to the Rhine. Length: about 515 km (320 miles)

mainbrace ('meɪn,breɪs) n *nautical* a brace attached to the main yard

main clause n *grammar* a clause that can stand alone as a sentence. Compare **subordinate clause**

main course n **1** the principal dish of a meal **2** *nautical* a square mainsail

main deck n the uppermost sheltered deck that runs the entire length of a vessel

Maine (meɪn) n a state of the northeastern US, on the Atlantic: chiefly hilly, with many lakes, rivers, and forests. Capital: Augusta. Pop: 1 305 728 (2003 est). Area: 86 156 sq km (33 265 sq miles). Abbreviation: **Me**, (with zip code) **ME**

Maine Coon n a breed of large powerfully-built long-haired indigenous American cat [c20 so-called because it was first recognized as a specific breed in MAINE, USA, and because it somewhat resembles a raccoon in appearance]

Maine-et-Loire (French mɛnelwar) n a department of W France, in Pays de la Loire region. Capital: Angers. Pop: 745 486 (2003 est). Area: 7218 sq km (2815 sq miles)

mainframe ('meɪn,freɪm) n **1 a** a high-speed general-purpose computer, usually with a large store capacity **b** (*as modifier*): *mainframe systems* **2** the central processing unit of a computer

mainland ('meɪnlənd) n **1** the main part of a land mass as opposed to an island or peninsula **2** the mainland a particular landmass as viewed from a nearby island with which it has close links, such as Great Britain as viewed from Northern Ireland or continental Australia as viewed from Tasmania > 'mainlander n

Mainland ('meɪnlənd) n **1** an island off N Scotland: the largest of the Shetland Islands. Chief town: Lerwick. Pop: 17 550 (2001). Area: about 583 sq km (225 sq miles) **2** Also called: Pomona an island off N Scotland: the largest of the Orkney Islands. Chief town: Kirkwall. Pop: 15 315 (2001). Area: 492 sq km (190 sq miles) **3** the Mainland NZ a South Islanders' name for **South Island**

main line n **1** *railways* **a** the trunk route between two points, usually fed by branch lines **b** (*as modifier*): *a main-line station* **2** *US* a main road ⊳ vb **mainline 3** (*intr*) *slang* to inject a drug into a vein ⊳ *adj* **mainline 4** having an important position, esp having responsibility for the main areas of activity > 'main,liner n

mainly ('meɪnlɪ) *adv* **1** for the most part; to the greatest extent; principally **2** *obsolete* strongly; very much

main man *n slang, chiefly US* **1** one's best friend **2** a boss or leader

main market *n* the market for trading in the listed securities of companies on the London Stock Exchange. Compare **Third Market, unlisted securities market**

mainmast ('meɪn,mɑːst) *n nautical* the chief mast of a sailing vessel with two or more masts, being the foremast of a yawl, ketch, or dandy and the second mast from the bow of most others

main memory *n* the central memory-storage facility in a computer

main plane *n* **a** one of the principal supporting surfaces of an aircraft, esp either of the wings **b** both wings considered together

mainsail ('meɪn,seɪl; *Nautical* 'meɪnsᵊl) *n nautical* the largest and lowermost sail on the mainmast

main sequence *n astronomy* **a** a diagonal band on the Hertzsprung Russell diagram containing about 90% of all known stars; stars evolve onto and then off the band during their lifetime **b** (*as modifier*): *a main-sequence star*

mainsheet ('meɪn,ʃiːt) *n nautical* the line used to control the angle of the mainsail to the wind

mainspring ('meɪn,sprɪŋ) *n* **1** the principal power spring of a mechanism, esp in a watch or clock **2** the chief cause or motive of something

mainstay ('meɪn,steɪ) *n* **1** *nautical* the forestay that braces the mainmast **2** a chief support

main store *n computing* another name for **memory** (sense 7)

mainstream ('meɪn,striːm) *n* **1 a** the main current (of a river, cultural trend, etc): *in the mainstream of modern literature* **b** (*as modifier*): *mainstream politics* ▷ *adj* **2** of or relating to the style of jazz that lies between the traditional and the modern

mainstream corporation tax *n* (in Britain) the balance of the corporation tax formerly paid by a company for an accounting period after the advance corporation tax had been deducted

mainstreeting ('meɪn,striːtɪŋ) *n Canadian* the practice of a politician walking about the streets of a town or city to gain votes and greet supporters

maintain (meɪn'teɪn) *vb* (*tr*) **1** to continue or retain; keep in existence **2** to keep in proper or good condition: *to maintain a building* **3** to support a style of living: *the money maintained us for a month* **4** (*takes a clause as object*) to state or assert: *he maintained that Talbot was wrong* **5** to defend against contradiction; uphold: *she maintained her innocence* **6** to defend against physical attack [c13 from Old French *maintenir*, ultimately from Latin *manū tenēre* to hold in the hand] > **main'tainable** *adj* > **main'tainer** *n*

maintained school *n* a school financially supported by the state

maintenance ('meɪntɪnəns) *n* **1** the act of maintaining or the state of being maintained **2** a means of support; livelihood **3** (*modifier*) of or relating to the maintaining of buildings, machinery, etc: *maintenance man* **4** *law* (formerly unlawful) the interference in a legal action by a person having no interest in it, as by providing funds to continue the action. See also **champerty 5** *law* a provision ordered to be made by way of periodical payments or a lump sum, as after a divorce for a spouse **6** *computing* **a** the correction or prevention of faults in hardware by a programme of inspection and the replacement of parts **b** the removal of existing faults and the modification of software in response to changes in specification or environment [c14 from Old French; see MAINTAIN]

maintop ('meɪn,tɒp) *n* a top or platform at the head of the mainmast

main-topmast *n nautical* the mast immediately above the mainmast

maintopsail (,meɪn'tɒpseɪl; *Nautical* ,meɪn'tɒpsᵊl) *n nautical* a topsail set on the mainmast

main yard *n nautical* a yard for a square mainsail

Mainz (*German* maints) *n* a port in W Germany, capital of the Rhineland-Palatinate, at the confluence of the Main and Rhine: an archbishopric from about 780 until 1801; important in the 15th century for the development of printing (by Johann Gutenberg). Pop: 185 532 (2003 est). French name: **Mayence**

maiolica (maˈjɒlɪkə) *n* a variant of **majolica**

maire (mɑːˈiːrə) *n, pl* **maire** a tall native New Zealand tree, *olea cunninghami*, with dark brown wood [Māori]

mairehau (mɑːˈiːrəhɑːuː) *n* a small aromatic shrub *Phebalium nudum*, of New Zealand's North Island [Māori]

maisonette *or* **maisonnette** (,meɪzəˈnɛt) *n* self-contained living accommodation often occupying two floors of a larger house and having its own outside entrance [c19 from French, diminutive of *maison* house]

maist (mest) *determiner* a Scot word for **most**

Maitland ('meɪtlənd) *n* a town in SE Australia, in E New South Wales: industrial centre of an agricultural region. Pop: 53 470 (2001)

maître d'hôtel (,mɛtrə dəʊ'tɛl; *French* mɛtrə dɔtɛl) *n, pl* **maîtres d'hôtel 1** a head waiter or steward **2** the manager or owner of a hotel [c16 from French: master of (the) hotel]

maître d'hôtel butter *n* melted butter mixed with parsley and lemon juice

Maitreya (miˈtreɪjə) *n* the future Buddha [Sanskrit]

maize (meɪz) *n* **1** Also called: **Indian corn a** a tall annual grass, *Zea mays*, cultivated for its yellow edible grains, which develop on a spike **b** the grain of this plant, used for food, fodder, and as a source of oil. Usual US and Canadian name: **corn** See also **sweet corn 2** a yellow colour [c16 from Spanish *maiz*, from Taino *mahiz*]

Maj. *abbreviation for* Major

majestic (məˈdʒɛstɪk) *or less commonly* **majestical** *adj* having or displaying majesty or great dignity; grand; lofty > **maˈjestically** *adv*

majesty ('mædʒɪstɪ) *n* **1** great dignity of bearing; loftiness; grandeur **2** supreme power or authority **3** an archaic word for **royalty** [c13 from Old French, from Latin *mājestās*; related to Latin *major*, comparative of *magnus* great]

Majesty ('mædʒɪstɪ) *n, pl* **-ties** (preceded by *Your, His, Her,* or *Their*) a title used to address or refer to a sovereign or the wife or widow of a sovereign

Maj. Gen. *abbreviation for* Major General

Majlis ('mædʒlɪs) *n* **1** the parliament of Iran **2** (in various N African and Middle Eastern countries) an assembly; council [from Persian: assembly]

majolica (məˈdʒɒlɪkə, məˈjɒl-) *or* **maiolica** *n* a type of porous pottery glazed with bright metallic oxides that was originally imported into Italy via Majorca and was extensively made in Italy during the Renaissance [c16 from Italian, from Late Latin *Mājorica* Majorca]

major ('meɪdʒə) *n* **1** *military* an officer immediately junior to a lieutenant colonel **2** a person who is superior in a group or class **3** a large or important company: *the oil majors* **4** (often preceded by *the*) *music* a major key, chord, mode, or scale **5** *US, Canadian, Austral, and NZ* **a** the principal field of study of a student at a university, etc: *his major is sociology* **b** a student who is studying a particular subject as his principal field: *a sociology major* **6** a person who has reached the age of legal majority **7** *logic* a major term or premise **8** (*plural*) **the** *US and Canadian* the major leagues ▷ *adj* **9** larger in extent, number, etc: *the major part* **10** of greater importance or priority **11** very serious or significant: *a major disaster* **12** main, chief, or principal **13** of, involving, or making up a majority **14** *music* **a** (of a scale or mode) having notes separated by the interval of a whole tone, except for the third and fourth degrees, and seventh and eighth degrees, which are separated by a semitone **b** relating to or employing notes from the major scale: *a major key*

c (*postpositive*) denoting a specified key or scale as being major: *C major* **d** denoting a chord or triad having a major third above the root **e** (in jazz) denoting a major chord with a major seventh added above the root **15** *logic* constituting the major term or major premise of a syllogism **16** *chiefly US, Canadian, Austral, and NZ* of or relating to a student's principal field of study at a university, etc **17** *Brit* the elder: used after a schoolboy's surname if he has one or more younger brothers in the same school: *Price major* **18** of full legal age **19** (*postpositive*) *bell-ringing* of, relating to, or denoting a method rung on eight bells ▷ *vb* **20** (*intr; usually foll by in*) *US, Canadian, Austral, and NZ* to do one's principal study (in a particular subject): *to major in English literature* [c15 (adj): from Latin, comparative of *magnus* great; c17 (n, in military sense): from French, short for SERGEANT MAJOR] > **'majorship** *n*

major axis *n* the longer or longest axis of an ellipse or ellipsoid

Majorca (məˈjɔːkə, -ˈdʒɔː-) *n* an island in the W Mediterranean: the largest of the Balearic Islands; tourism. Capital: Palma. Pop: 730 778 (2002 est). Area: 3639 sq km (1465 sq miles). Spanish name: **Mallorca**

major-domo (,meɪdʒəˈdəʊməʊ) *n, pl* **-mos 1** the chief steward or butler of a great household **2** *facetious* a steward or butler [c16 from Spanish *mayordomo*, from Medieval Latin *mājor domūs* head of the household]

majorette (,meɪdʒəˈrɛt) *n* See **drum majorette**

major general *n military* an officer immediately junior to a lieutenant general > **'major-'generalship** *or* **'major-'generalcy** *n*

major histocompatibility complex *n* the full name for **MHC**

majority (məˈdʒɒrɪtɪ) *n, pl* **-ties 1** the greater number or part of something: *the majority of the constituents* **2** (in an election) the number of votes or seats by which the strongest party or candidate beats the combined opposition or the runner-up. See **relative majority, absolute majority 3** the largest party or group that votes together in a legislative or deliberative assembly **4** the time of reaching or state of having reached full legal age, when a person is held competent to manage his own affairs, exercise civil rights and duties, etc **5** the rank, office, or commission of major **6** *euphemistic* the dead (esp in the phrases **join the majority, go** *or* **pass over to the majority**) **7** *obsolete* the quality or state of being greater; superiority **8** (*modifier*) of, involving, or being a majority: *a majority decision; a majority verdict* **9** in the majority forming or part of the greater number of something [c16 from Medieval Latin *mājorītās*, from MAJOR (adj)]

m

> USAGE *The majority of* can only refer to a number of things or people. When talking about an amount, *most of* should be used: *most of* (not *the majority of*) *the harvest was saved*

majority carrier *n* the entity responsible for carrying the greater part of the current in a semiconductor. In n-type semiconductors the majority carriers are electrons; in p-type semiconductors they are positively charged holes. Compare **minority carrier**

major league *n US and Canadian* a league of highest classification in baseball, football, hockey, etc

majorly ('meɪdʒəlɪ) *adv slang, chiefly US and Canadian* very; really; extremely: *it was majorly important for us to do that*

Major Mitchell *n* an Australian cockatoo, *Kakatoe leadbeateri*, with a white-and-pink plumage. Also called: **Leadbeater's cockatoo** [c19 named after *Major* (later Sir) Thomas Mitchell (1792–1855), Scots-born Australian explorer]

major orders *pl n RC Church* the three higher degrees of holy orders: bishop, priest, and deacon

major planet *n* a planet of the solar system, as

opposed to an asteroid (minor planet)

major premise *n logic* the premise of a syllogism containing the predicate of its conclusion

major seventh chord *n* a chord much used in modern music, esp jazz and pop, consisting of a major triad with an added major seventh above the root. Compare **minor seventh chord** Often shortened to: **major seventh**

major suit *n bridge* hearts or spades. Compare **minor suit**

major term *n logic* the predicate of the conclusion of a syllogism, also occurring as the subject or predicate in the major premise

Majunga (*French* maʒœ̃ga) *n* the former name of **Mahajanga**

majuscule (ˈmædʒəˌskjuːl) *n* **1** a large letter, either capital or uncial, used in printing or writing ▷ *adj* **2** relating to, printed, or written in such letters. Compare **minuscule** [C18 via French from Latin *mājusculus*, diminutive of *mājor* bigger, MAJOR] > **majuscular** (məˈdʒʌskjʊlə) *adj*

mak (mæk) *vb* a Scot word for **make[1]**

Makalu (ˈmʌkəˌluː) *n* a massif in NE Nepal, on the border with Tibet in the Himalayas

makar (ˈmækər) *n Scot* a creative artist, esp a poet [a Scot variant of *maker*]

Makasar, Makassar *or* **Macassar** (məˈkæsə, -ˈkɑː-) *n* another name for **Ujung Pandang**

make[1] (meɪk) *vb* **makes, making, made** (*mainly tr*) **1** to bring into being by shaping, changing, or combining materials, ideas, etc; form or fashion; create: *to make a chair from bits of wood; make a poem* **2** to draw up, establish, or form: *to make a decision; make one's will* **3** to cause to exist, bring about, or produce: *don't make a noise* **4** to cause, compel, or induce: *please make him go away* **5** to appoint or assign, as to a rank or position: *they made him chairman* **6** to constitute: *one swallow doesn't make a summer* **7** (*also intr*) to come or cause to come into a specified state or condition: *to make merry; make someone happy* **8** (*copula*) to be or become through development: *he will make a good teacher* **9** to cause or ensure the success of: *your news has made my day* **10** to amount to: *twelve inches make a foot* **11** to be part of or a member of: *did she make one of the party?* **12** to serve as or be suitable for: *that piece of cloth will make a coat* **13** to prepare or put into a fit condition for use: *to make a bed* **14** to be the essential element in or part of: *charm makes a good salesman* **15** to carry out, effect, or do: *to make a gesture* **16** (*intr*; foll by *to, as if to*, or *as though to*) to act with the intention or with a show of doing something: *they made to go out; he made as if to hit her* **17** to use for a specified purpose: *I will make this town my base* **18** to deliver or pronounce: *to make a speech* **19** to judge, reckon, or give one's own opinion or information as to: *what time do you make it?* **20** to cause to seem or represent as being: *that furniture makes the room look dark* **21** to earn, acquire, or win for oneself: *to make friends; make a fortune* **22** to engage in: *make love not war* **23** to traverse or cover (distance) by travelling: *we can make a hundred miles by nightfall* **24** to arrive in time for: *he didn't make the first act of the play* **25** *cards* **a** to win a trick with (a specified card) **b** to shuffle (the cards) **c** *bridge* to fulfil (a contract) by winning the necessary number of tricks **26** *cricket* to score (runs) **27** *electronics* to close (a circuit) permitting a flow of current. Compare **break** (sense 44) **28** (*intr*) to increase in depth: *the water in the hold was making a foot a minute* **29** (*intr*) (of hay) to dry and mature **30** *informal* to gain a place or position on or in: *to make the headlines; make the first team* **31** *informal* to achieve the rank of **32** *slang* to seduce **33** **make a book** to take bets on a race or other contest **34** **make a day, night, etc, of it** to cause an activity to last a day, night, etc **35** **make do** See **do[1]** (sense 37) **36** **make eyes at** to flirt with or ogle **37** **make good** See **good** (sense 44) **38** **make heavy weather (of)** **a** *nautical* to roll and pitch in heavy seas **b** *informal* to carry out with great difficulty or unnecessarily great effort **39** **make it** **a** *informal* to be successful in doing something **b** (foll by *with*) *slang* to have sexual intercourse **c** *slang* to inject a narcotic drug **40** **make like** *slang, chiefly US and Canadian* to imitate **41** **make love (to)** **a** to have sexual intercourse (with) **b** *now archaic* to engage in courtship (with) **42** **make or break** to bring success or ruin **43** **make time** See **time** (sense 45) **44** **make water** **a** another term for **urinate** **b** (of a boat, hull, etc) to let in water ▷ *n* **45** brand, type, or style: *what make of car is that?* **46** the manner or way in which something is made **47** disposition or character; make-up **48** the act or process of making **49** the amount or number made **50** *bridge* the contract to be played **51** *cards* a player's turn to shuffle **52** **on the make** **a** *informal* out for profit or conquest **b** *slang* in search of a sexual partner ▷ See also **make after, make away, make for, make of, make off, make out, make over, make-up, make with** [Old English *macian*; related to Old Frisian *makia* to construct, Dutch *maken*, German *machen* to make] > ˈ**makable** *adj*

make[2] (meɪk) *n archaic* **1** a peer or consort **2** a mate or spouse [Old English *gemaca* mate; related to MATCH[1]] > ˈ**makeless** *adj*

make after *vb* (*intr, preposition*) *archaic* to set off in pursuit of; chase

make away *vb* (*intr, adverb*) **1** to depart in haste **2** **make away with** **a** to steal or abduct **b** to kill, destroy, or get rid of

make believe *vb* **1** to pretend or enact a fantasy: *the children made believe they were doctors* ▷ *n* **make-believe** **2** **a** a fantasy, pretence, or unreality **b** (*as modifier*): *a make-believe world* **3** a person who pretends

Makedhonia (ˌmakɛðoˈnia) *n* transliteration of the Modern Greek name for **Macedonia** (sense 2)

makefast (ˈmeɪkˌfɑːst) *n* a strong support to which a vessel is secured

make for *vb* (*intr, preposition*) **1** to head towards, esp in haste **2** to prepare to attack **3** to help to bring about: *your cooperation will make for the success of our project*

make of *vb* (*tr, preposition*) **1** to interpret as the meaning of: *what do you make of this news?* **2** to produce or construct from: *houses made of brick* **3** **make little, nothing, etc, of** **a** not to understand **b** to attribute little, no, etc, importance to **c** to gain little or no benefit from **4** **make much, a lot, etc, of** **a** (*used with a negative*) to make sense of: *he couldn't make much of her babble* **b** to give importance to **c** to gain benefit from **d** to pay flattering attention to: *the reporters made much of the film star*

make off *vb* **1** (*intr, adverb*) to go or run away in haste **2** **make off with** to steal or abduct

make out *vb* (*adverb*) **1** (*tr*) to discern or perceive: *can you make out that house in the distance?* **2** (*tr*) to understand or comprehend: *I can't make out this letter* **3** (*tr*) to write out: *he made out a cheque* **4** (*tr*) to attempt to establish or prove: *he made me out to be a liar* **5** (*intr*) to pretend: *he made out that he could cook* **6** (*intr*) to manage or fare: *how did you make out in the contest?* **7** (*intr*; often foll by *with*) *informal, chiefly US and Canadian* to engage in necking or petting: *Alan is making out with Jane*

make over *vb* (*tr, adverb*) **1** to transfer the title or possession of (property, etc) **2** to renovate or remodel: *she made over the dress to fit her sister* ▷ *n* **makeover** (ˈmeɪkˌəʊvə) **3** a complete remodelling **4** a series of alterations, including beauty treatments and new clothes, intended to make a noticeable improvement in a person's appearance

maker (ˈmeɪkə) *n* **1** a person who makes (something); fabricator; constructor **2** a person who executes a legal document, esp one who signs a promissory note **3** *archaic, Scot* Also called (esp Scot): **makar** a poet

Maker (ˈmeɪkə) *n* **1** a title given to **God** (as Creator) **2** **(go to) meet one's Maker** to die

make-ready *n printing* the process of preparing the forme and the cylinder or platen packing to achieve the correct impression all over the forme

makeshift (ˈmeɪkˌʃɪft) *adj* **1** serving as a temporary or expedient means, esp during an emergency ▷ *n* **2** something serving in this capacity

make-up *n* **1** cosmetics, such as powder, lipstick, etc, applied to the face to improve its appearance **2** **a** the cosmetics, false hair, etc, used by an actor to highlight his features or adapt his appearance **b** the art or result of applying such cosmetics **3** the manner of arrangement of the parts or qualities of someone or something **4** the arrangement of type matter and illustrations on a page or in a book **5** mental or physical constitution ▷ *vb* **make up** (*adverb*) **6** (*tr*) to form or constitute: *these arguments make up the case for the defence* **7** (*tr*) to devise, construct, or compose, sometimes with the intent to deceive: *to make up a song; to make up an excuse* **8** (*tr*) to supply what is lacking or deficient in; complete: *these extra people will make up our total* **9** (*tr*) to put in order, arrange, or prepare: *to make up a bed* **10** (*intr*; foll by *for*) to compensate or atone (for): *his kindness now makes up for his rudeness yesterday* **11** to settle (differences) amicably (often in the phrase **make it up**) **12** to apply cosmetics to (the face) to enhance one's appearance or so as to alter the appearance for a theatrical role **13** to assemble (type and illustrations) into (columns or pages) **14** (*tr*) to surface (a road) with asphalt, concrete, etc **15** (*tr*) **a** to set in order and balance (accounts) **b** to draw up (accounting statements) **16** **make up one's mind** to decide (about something or to do something): *he made up his mind to take vengeance* **17** **make up to** *informal* **a** to make friendly overtures to **b** to flirt with

makeweight (ˈmeɪkˌweɪt) *n* **1** something put on a scale to make up a required weight **2** an unimportant person or thing added to make up a lack

make with *vb* (*intr, preposition*) *slang, chiefly US* to proceed with the doing, showing, etc, of: *make with the music*

Makeyevka (*Russian* maˈkjejɪfkə) *n* a city in SE Ukraine: coal-mining centre. Pop: 380 000 (2005 est)

Makhachkala (*Russian* məxətʃkaˈla) *n* a port in SW Russia, capital of the Dagestan Republic, on the Caspian Sea: fishing fleet; oil refining. Pop: 503 000 (2005 est). Former name (until 1921): **Petrovsk**

maki (ˈmækɪ) *n* (in Japanese cuisine) a small segment cut from a long roll of cold rice and various other ingredients wrapped in a sheet of seaweed [from Japanese, literally: roll]

making (ˈmeɪkɪŋ) *n* **1** **a** the act of a person or thing that makes or the process of being made **b** (*in combination*): *watchmaking* **2** **be the making of** to cause the success of **3** **in the making** in the process of becoming or being made: *a politician in the making* **4** something made or the quantity of something made at one time **5** make-up; composition

makings (ˈmeɪkɪŋz) *pl n* **1** potentials, qualities, or materials: *he had the makings of a leader* **2** Also called: **rollings** *slang* the tobacco and cigarette paper used for rolling a cigarette **3** profits; earnings

Makkah *or* **Makah** (ˈmækə, -kɑː) *n* transliteration of the Arabic name for **Mecca**

mako[1] (ˈmɑːkəʊ) *n, pl* **-kos** **1** any shark of the genus *Isurus*, esp *I. glaucus* of Indo-Pacific and Australian seas: family *Isuridae* **2** *NZ* the teeth of the mako worn as a decoration by early Māoris [from Māori]

mako[2] (ˈmɑːkəʊ), **mako-mako** (ˈmɑːkəʊˌmɑːkəʊ) *n, pl* **-kos** **1** Also called: **wineberry** a small evergreen New Zealand tree, *Aristotelia serrata*: family *Elaeocarpaceae* **2** *NZ* another name for the **bellbird**, *Anthornis melanura* [from Māori]

Makurdi (məˈkɜːdɪ) *n* a port in E central Nigeria, capital of Benue State on the Benue River: agricultural trade centre. Pop: 259 000 (2005 est)

makuta (mɑːˈkuːtɑː) *n* the plural of **likuta**

makutu (ˈmɑːkuːtuː) *n NZ* **1** witchcraft or magic ▷ *vb* (*tr*) **2** to cast a spell on (a person) [Māori]

MAL *international car registration for* Malaysia

Mal. *abbreviation for* **1** *Bible* Malachi **2** Malay(an)

mal- *combining form* bad or badly; wrong or wrongly; imperfect or defective: *maladjusted; malfunction* [Old French, from Latin *malus* bad, *male* badly]

mala (ˈmɑːlaː) *n Hinduism* a string of beads or knots, used in praying and meditating

Malabar Coast *or* **Malabar** (ˈmælə,bɑː) *n* a region along the SW coast of India, extending from Goa to Cape Comorin: includes most of Kerala state

Malabo (məˈlɑːbəʊ) *n* the capital and chief port of Equatorial Guinea, on the island of Bioko in the Gulf of Guinea. Pop: 105 000 (2005 est). Former name (until 1973): Santa Isabel

malabsorption (,mæləbˈsɔːpʃən) *n* a failure of absorption, esp by the small intestine in coeliac disease, cystic fibrosis, etc

malacca *or* **malacca cane** (məˈlækə) *n* **1** the stem of the rattan palm **2** a walking stick made from this stem

Malacca (məˈlækə) *n* a state of SW Peninsular Malaysia: rubber plantations. Capital: Malacca. Pop: 635 791 (2000). Area: 1650 sq km (637 sq miles)

Malachi (ˈmæləˌkaɪ) *n Old Testament* **1** a Hebrew prophet of the 5th century BC **2** the book containing his oracles. Douay spelling: Malachias (,mæləˈkaɪəs)

malachite (ˈmæləˌkaɪt) *n* a bright green mineral, found in veins and in association with copper deposits. It is a source of copper and is used as an ornamental stone. Composition: hydrated copper carbonate. Formula: $Cu_2CO_3(OH)_2$. Crystal structure: monoclinic [c16 via Old French from Latin *molochītes*, from Greek *molokhitis* mallow-green stone, from *molokhē* mallow]

malacia (məˈleɪʃɪə) *n* the pathological softening of an organ or tissue, such as bone

malaco- *or before a vowel* **malac-** *combining form* denoting softness: *malacology; malacostracan* [from Greek *malakos*]

malacology (,mæləˈkɒlədʒɪ) *n* the branch of zoology concerned with the study of molluscs > **malacological** (,mæləkəˈlɒdʒɪk²l) *adj* > ,mala'cologist *n*

malacophily (,mæləˈkɒfɪlɪ) *n botany* pollination of plants by snails > ,mala'cophilous *adj*

malacophyllous (,mæləˈkɒfɪləs) *adj* (of plants living in dry regions) having fleshy leaves in which water is stored

malacopterygian (,mæləˌkɒptəˈrɪdʒɪən) *adj* **1** of, relating to, or belonging to the *Malacopterygii,* a group of teleost fishes, including herrings and salmon, having soft fin rays ▷ *n* **2** any malacopterygian fish; a soft-finned fish ▷ Compare **acanthopterygian** [c19 from New Latin *Malacopterygii,* from MALACO- + Greek *pterux* wing, fin]

malacostracan (,mæləˈkɒstrək²n) *n* **1** any crustacean of the subclass or group *Malacostraca,* including lobsters, crabs, woodlice, sand hoppers, and opossum shrimps ▷ *adj also* **malacostracous** **2** of, relating to, or belonging to the *Malacostraca* [c19 from New Latin, from Greek *malakōstrakos,* from MALACO- + *ostrakon* shell]

maladaptive (,mæləˈdæptɪv) *adj* **1** unsuitably adapted or adapting poorly to (a situation, purpose, etc) **2** not encouraging adaptation > ,mala'dapted *adj* > ,mala'daptively *adv*

maladdress (,mæləˈdrɛs) *n* awkwardness; tactlessness

maladjusted (,mæləˈdʒʌstɪd) *adj psychol* suffering from maladjustment **2** badly adjusted

maladjustment (,mæləˈdʒʌstmənt) *n* **1** *psychol* a failure to meet the demands of society, such as coping with problems and social relationships: usually reflected in emotional instability **2** faulty or bad adjustment

maladminister (,mælədˈmɪnɪstə) *vb* (*tr*) to administer badly, inefficiently, or dishonestly > ,malad'minis,trator *n*

maladministration (,mæləd,mɪnɪˈstreɪʃən) *n* bad, inefficient, or dishonest management of the affairs of an organization, such as a business or institution

maladroit (,mæləˈdrɔɪt) *adj* **1** showing or characterized by clumsiness; not dexterous **2** tactless and insensitive in behaviour or speech [c17 from French, from *mal* badly + ADROIT] > ,mala'droitly *adv* > ,mala'droitness *n*

malady (ˈmælədɪ) *n, pl* **-dies** **1** any disease or illness **2** any unhealthy, morbid, or desperate condition: *a malady of the spirit* [c13 from Old French, from Vulgar Latin *male habitus* (unattested) in poor condition, from Latin *male* badly + *habitus,* from *habēre* to have]

mala fide (ˈmælə ˈfaɪdɪ) *adj* undertaken in bad faith [from Latin]

Málaga (ˈmæləgə; *Spanish* ˈmalaɣa) *n* **1** a port and resort in S Spain, in Andalusia on the Mediterranean. Pop: 547 105 (2003 est) **2** a sweet fortified dessert wine from Málaga

Malagasy (,mæləˈgæzɪ) *n* **1** (*pl* **-gasy** *or* **-gasies**) a native or inhabitant of Madagascar **2** the official language of Madagascar belonging to the Malayo-Polynesian family ▷ *adj* **3** of or relating to Madagascar, its people, or their language

Malagasy Republic *n* the former name (1958–75) of **Madagascar**

malagueña (,mæləˈgeɪnjə) *n* a Spanish dance similar to the fandango [Spanish: of MÁLAGA]

malaise (mæˈleɪz) *n* **1** a feeling of unease or depression **2** a mild sickness, not symptomatic of any disease or ailment **3** a complex of problems affecting a country, economy, etc: *Bulgaria's economic malaise* [c18 from Old French, from *mal* bad + *aise* EASE]

malam (ˈmæləm, -əm) *n* a variant spelling of **mallam**

malamute *or* **malemute** (ˈmæləˌmuːt) *n* an Alaskan sled dog of the spitz type, having a dense usually greyish coat [from the name of an Inuit tribe]

malanders, mallanders *or* **mallenders** (ˈmæləndəz) *pl n* (*functioning as singular*) a disease of horses characterized by an eczematous inflammation behind the knee [c15 via Old French from Latin *malandria* sore on the neck of a horse]

Malang (ˈmælæŋ) *n* a city in S Indonesia, on E Java: commercial centre. Pop: 756 982 (2000)

malapert (ˈmæləˌpɜːt) *archaic or literary* **1** saucy or impudent ▷ *n* **2** a saucy or impudent person [c15 from Old French: unskilful (see MAL-, EXPERT); meaning in English influenced by *apert* frank, from Latin *apertus* open] > 'mala,pertly *adv* > 'mala,pertness *n*

malapropism (ˈmæləprɒp,ɪzəm) *n* **1** the unintentional misuse of a word by confusion with one of similar sound, esp when creating a ridiculous effect, as in *I am not under the affluence of alcohol* **2** the habit of misusing words in this manner [c18 after Mrs *Malaprop* in Sheridan's play *The Rivals* (1775), a character who misused words, from MALAPROPOS] > 'malaprop *or* ,mala'propian *adj*

malapropos (,mæləprəˈpəʊ) *adj* **1** of an inappropriate or misapplied nature or kind ▷ *adv* **2** in an inappropriate way or manner ▷ *n* **3** something inopportune or inappropriate [c17 from French *mal à propos* not to the purpose]

malar (ˈmeɪlə) *adj* **1** of or relating to the cheek or cheekbone ▷ *n* **2** Also called: **malar bone** another name for **zygomatic bone** [c18 from New Latin *mālāris,* from Latin *māla* jaw]

Mälar (ˈmeɪlə) *n* Lake a lake in S Sweden, extending 121 km (75 miles) west from Stockholm, where it joins with an inlet of the Baltic Sea (the **Saltsjön**). Area: 1140 sq km (440 sq miles). Swedish name: Mälaren (ˈmelaren)

malaria (məˈlɛərɪə) *n* an infectious disease characterized by recurring attacks of chills and fever, caused by the bite of an anopheles mosquito infected with any of four protozoans of the genus *Plasmodium* (*P. vivax, P. falciparum, P. malariae,* or *P. ovale*) [c18 from Italian *mala aria* bad air, from the belief that the disease was caused by the unwholesome air in swampy districts] > ma'larial, ma'larian *or* ma'larious *adj*

malariology (mə,lɛərɪˈɒlədʒɪ) *n* the study of malaria > ma,lari'ologist *n*

malarkey *or* **malarky** (məˈlɑːkɪ) *n slang* nonsense; rubbish [c20 of unknown origin]

malassimilation (,mæləˌsɪmɪˈleɪʃən) *n pathol* defective assimilation of nutrients

malate (ˈmæleɪt, ˈmeɪ-) *n* any salt or ester of malic acid [c18 from MALIC ACID]

Malathion (,mæləˈθaɪɒn) *n trademark* a yellow organophosphorus insecticide used as a dust or mist for the control of house flies and garden pests. Formula: $C_{10}H_{19}O_6PS_2$ [c20 from (*diethyl*) MAL(EATE) + THIO- + -ON]

Malatya (,mɑːlɑːˈtjɑː) *n* a city in E central Turkey: nearby is the ruined Roman and medieval city of Melitene (Old Malatya). Pop: 448 000 (2005 est)

Malawi (məˈlɑːwɪ) *n* **1** a republic in E central Africa: established as a British protectorate in 1891; became independent in 1964 as a republic, within the Commonwealth, in 1966; lies along the Great Rift Valley, with Lake Nyasa (Malawi) along the E border, the Nyika Plateau in the northwest, and the Shire (or Shiré) Highlands in the southeast. Official language: Chichewa; English and various other Bantu languages are also widely spoken. Religion: Christian majority, Muslim, and animist minorities. Currency: kwacha. Capital: Lilongwe. Pop: 12 337 000 (2004 est). Area: 118 484 sq km (45 747 sq miles). Former name: Nyasaland **2** Lake the Malawi name for (Lake) Nyasa

Malawian (məˈlɑːwɪən) *adj* **1** of or relating to Malawi or its inhabitants ▷ *n* **2** a native or inhabitant of Malawi

Malay (məˈleɪ) *n* **1** a member of a people living chiefly in Malaysia and Indonesia who are descendants of Mongoloid immigrants **2** the language of this people, belonging to the Malayo-Polynesian family ▷ *adj* **3** of or relating to the Malays or their language

Malaya (məˈleɪə) *n* **1** States of the Federation of part of Malaysia, in the S Malay Peninsula, constituting Peninsular Malaysia: consists of the former Federated Malay States, the former Unfederated Malay States, and the former Straits Settlements. Capital: Kuala Lumpur. Pop: 17 144 322 (2000). Area: 131 587 sq km (50 806 sq miles) **2** Federation of a federation of the nine Malay States of the Malay Peninsula and two of the Straits Settlements (Malacca and Penang): formed in 1948: became part of the British Commonwealth in 1957 and joined Malaysia in 1963

Malayalam *or* **Malayalaam** (,mælɪˈɑːləm) *n* a language of SW India, belonging to the Dravidian family and closely related to Tamil: the state language of Kerala

Malayali *or* **Malayalee** (,mælɪˈɑːlɪ) *n* a speaker of the Malayalam language

Malayan (məˈleɪən) *adj* **1** of or relating to Malaya or its inhabitants ▷ *n* **2** a native or inhabitant of Malaya

Malay Archipelago *n* a group of islands in the Indian and Pacific Oceans, between SE Asia and Australia: the largest group of islands in the world; includes over 3000 Indonesian islands, about 7000 islands of the Philippines, and, sometimes, New Guinea

Malayo-Polynesian *n* **1** Also called: Austronesian a family of languages extending from Madagascar to the central Pacific, including Malagasy, Malay, Indonesian, Tagalog, and Polynesian. See also **Austro-Asiatic** ▷ *adj* **2** of or relating to this family of languages

m

Malay Peninsula *n* a peninsula of SE Asia, extending south from the Isthmus of Kra in Thailand to Cape Tanjong Piai in Malaysia: consists of SW Thailand and the states of Malaya (Peninsular Malaysia). Ancient name: Chersonesus Aurea (ˌkɜːsəˈniːsəs ˈɔːrɪə)

Malaysia (məˈleɪzɪə) *n* a federation in SE Asia (within the Commonwealth), consisting of **Peninsular Malaysia** on the Malay Peninsula, and **East Malaysia** (Sabah and Sarawak), occupying the N part of the island of Borneo: formed in 1963 as a federation of Malaya, Sarawak, Sabah, and Singapore (the latter seceded in 1965); densely forested and mostly mountainous. Official language: Malay; English and various Chinese and Indian minority languages are also spoken. Official religion: Muslim. Currency: ringgit. Capital: Putrajaya (the transfer of government from Kuala Lumpur is taking place in stages over several years starting 1999). Pop: 24 876 000 (2004 est). Area: 333 403 sq km (128 727 sq miles)

Malaysian (məˈleɪzɪən) *adj* **1** of or relating to Malaysia or its inhabitants ▷ *n* **2** a native or inhabitant of Malaysia

Malay States *pl n* the former states of the Malay Peninsula that, together with Penang and Malacca, formed the Union of Malaya (1946) and the Federation of Malaya (1948). Perak, Selangor, Negri Sembilan, and Pahang were established as the **Federated Malay States** by the British in 1895 and Perlis, Kedah, Kelantan, and Trengannu as the **Unfederated Malay States** in 1909 (joined by Johore in 1914)

Malbec (mælˈbɛk) *n* **1** a black grape originally grown in the Bordeaux region of France and now in Argentina and Chile, used for making wine **2** a rustic mid-bodied red wine made from this grape

malcontent (ˈmælkənˌtɛnt) *adj* **1** disgusted or discontented ▷ *n* **2** a person who is malcontent [C16 from Old French]

mal de mer *French* (mal də mɛr) *n* seasickness

maldistribution (ˌmældɪstrɪˈbjuːʃən) *n* faulty, unequal, or unfair distribution (as of wealth, business, etc)

Maldives (ˈmɔːldiːvz) *pl n* **Republic of** a republic occupying an archipelago of 1087 coral islands in the Indian Ocean, southwest of Sri Lanka: came under British protection in 1887; became independent in 1965 and a republic in 1968; a member of the Commonwealth. The economy and infrastructure were severely damaged in the Indian Ocean tsunami of December 2004. Official language: Divehi. Official religion: (Sunni) Muslim. Currency: rufiyaa. Capital: Malé. Pop: 328 000 (2004 est). Area: 298 sq km (115 sq miles). Also called: **Maldive Islands**

Maldivian (mɔːlˈdɪvɪən) *or* **Maldivan** (ˈmɔːldaɪvʲən, -dɪ-) *adj* **1** of or relating to the Maldives or their inhabitants ▷ *n* **2** a native or inhabitant of the Maldives

Maldon (ˈmɔːldən) *n* a market town in SE England, in Essex; scene of a battle (991) between the East Saxons and the victorious Danes, celebrated in *The Battle of Maldon*, an Old English poem; notable for Maldon salt, used in cookery. Pop: 20 731 (2001)

male (meɪl) *adj* **1** of, relating to, or designating the sex producing gametes (spermatozoa) that can fertilize female gametes (ova) **2** of, relating to, or characteristic of a man; masculine **3** for or composed of men or boys: *a male choir* **4** (of gametes) capable of fertilizing an egg cell in sexual reproduction **5** (of reproductive organs, such as a testis or stamen) capable of producing male gametes **6** (of flowers) bearing stamens but lacking a functional pistil **7** *electronics, mechanical engineering* having a projecting part or parts that fit into a female counterpart: *a male plug* ▷ *n* **8** a male person, animal, or plant [C14 via Old French from Latin *masculus* MASCULINE] > **maleness** *n*

Malé (ˈmɑːleɪ) *n* the capital of the Republic of Maldives, on Malé Island in the centre of the island group. Pop: 90 000 (2005 est)

maleate (ˈmælɪˌeɪt) *n* any salt or ester of maleic acid [C19 from MALE(IC ACID) + -ATE¹]

male chauvinism *n* the belief, held or alleged to be held by certain men, that men are inherently superior to women > **male chauvinist** *n, adj*

male chauvinist pig *n informal, derogatory* a man who exhibits male chauvinism. Abbreviation: MCP

maledict (ˈmælɪdɪkt) *vb* **1** (*tr*) *literary* to utter a curse against ▷ *adj* **2** *archaic* cursed or detestable

malediction (ˌmælɪˈdɪkʃən) *n* **1** the utterance of a curse against someone or something **2** slanderous accusation or comment [C15 from Latin *maledictiō* a reviling, from *male* ill + *dīcere* to speak] > ˌmale'dictive *or* ˌmale'dictory *adj*

malefactor (ˈmælɪˌfæktə) *n* a criminal; wrongdoer [C15 via Old French from Latin, from *malefacere* to do evil] > ˈmaleˌfaction *n* > ˈmaleˌfactress *fem n*

male fern *n* a fern, *Dryopteris filix-mas*, having scaly stalks and pinnate fronds with kidney-shaped spore-producing bodies on the underside: family *Polypodiaceae* [C16 so called because it was formerly believed to be the male of the lady fern]

maleficent (məˈlɛfɪsənt) *adj* causing or capable of producing evil or mischief; harmful or baleful [C17 from Latin *maleficent-*, from *maleficus* wicked, prone to evil, from *malum* evil] > **ma'lefic** *adj* > **ma'leficence** *n*

maleic acid (məˈleɪɪk) *n* a colourless soluble crystalline substance used to synthesize other compounds. Formula: HOOCCH:CHCOOH. Systematic name: **cis-butanedioic acid** [C19 from French *maléique*, altered form of *malique*; see MALIC ACID]

male menopause *n* a period in a man's later middle age in which he may experience an identity crisis as he feels age overtake his sexual powers

malemute (ˈmæləˌmjuːt) *n* a variant spelling of **malamute**

malevolent (məˈlɛvələnt) *adj* **1** wishing or appearing to wish evil to others; malicious **2** *astrology* having an evil influence [C16 from Latin *malevolens*, from *male* ill + *volens*, present participle of *velle* to wish] > **ma'levolence** *n* > **ma'levolently** *adv*

malfeasance (mælˈfiːzəns) *n law* the doing of a wrongful or illegal act, esp by a public official. Compare **misfeasance**, **nonfeasance** [C17 from Old French *mal faisant*, from *mal* evil + *faisant* doing, from *faire* to do, from Latin *facere*] > **mal'feasant** *n, adj*

malformation (ˌmælfɔːˈmeɪʃən) *n* **1** the condition of being faulty or abnormal in form or shape **2** *pathol* a deformity in the shape or structure of a part, esp when congenital > **mal'formed** *adj*

malfunction (mælˈfʌŋkʃən) *n* **1** (*intr*) to function imperfectly or irregularly or fail to function ▷ *n* **2** failure to function or defective functioning

malgré lui *French* (malgre lyi) *adv* in spite of himself

Mali (ˈmɑːlɪ) *n* a landlocked republic in West Africa: conquered by the French by 1898 and incorporated (as French Sudan) into French West Africa; became independent in 1960; settled chiefly in the basins of the Rivers Senegal and Niger in the south. Official language: French. Religion: Muslim majority, also animist. Currency: franc. Capital: Bamako. Pop: 13 408 000 (2004 est). Area: 1 248 574 sq km (482 077 sq miles). Former name (1898–1959): **French Sudan**.

malibu board (ˈmælɪbuː) *n* a lightweight surfboard, usually having a fin [C20 named after *Malibu beach*, California]

malic acid (ˈmælɪk, ˈmeɪ-) *n* a colourless crystalline compound occurring in apples and other fruits. Formula: HOOCCH₂CH(OH)COOH [C18 *malic*, via French *malique* from Latin *mālum* apple]

malice (ˈmælɪs) *n* **1** the desire to do harm or mischief **2** evil intent **3** *law* the state of mind with which an act is committed and from which the intent to do wrong may be inferred. See also **malice aforethought** [C13 via Old French from Latin *malitia*, from *malus* evil]

malice aforethought *n criminal law* **1** the predetermination to do an unlawful act, esp to kill or seriously injure **2** the intent with which an unlawful killing is effected, which must be proved for the crime to constitute murder. See also **murder**, **manslaughter**

malicious (məˈlɪʃəs) *adj* **1** characterized by malice **2** motivated by wrongful, vicious, or mischievous purposes > **ma'liciously** *adv* > **ma'liciousness** *n*

malign (məˈlaɪn) *adj* **1** evil in influence, intention, or effect ▷ *vb* **2** (*tr*) to slander or defame [C14 via Old French from Latin *malīgnus* spiteful, from *malus* evil] > **ma'ligner** *n* > **ma'lignly** *adv*

malignancy (məˈlɪgnənsɪ) *n, pl* -cies **1** the state or quality of being malignant **2** *pathol* a cancerous growth

malignant (məˈlɪgnənt) *adj* **1** having or showing desire to harm others **2** tending to cause great harm; injurious **3** *pathol* (of a tumour) uncontrollable or resistant to therapy; rapidly spreading ▷ *n* **4** *history* (in the English Civil War) a Parliamentarian term for a **royalist** [C16 from Late Latin *malīgnāre* to behave spitefully, from Latin *malīgnus* MALIGN] > **ma'lignantly** *adv*

malignity (məˈlɪgnɪtɪ) *n, pl* -ties **1** the condition or quality of being malign, malevolent, or deadly **2** (*often plural*) a malign or malicious act or feeling

malihini (ˌmɑːlɪˈhiːnɪ) *n, pl* -nis (in Hawaii) a foreigner or stranger [from Hawaiian]

malimprinted (ˌmælɪmˈprɪntɪd) *adj* (of an animal or person) suffering from a defect in the behavioural process of imprinting, resulting in attraction to members of other species, fetishism, etc > ˌmalim'printing *n*

malines (məˈliːn) *n* **1** a type of silk net used in dressmaking **2** another name for **Mechlin lace** [C19 from French *Malines* (Mechelen), where this lace was traditionally made]

Malines (malin) *n* the French name for **Mechelen**

malinger (məˈlɪŋgə) *vb* (*intr*) to pretend or exaggerate illness, esp to avoid work [C19 from French *malingre* sickly, perhaps from *mal* badly + Old French *haingre* feeble] > **ma'lingerer** *n*

Malinke (məˈlɪŋkɪ) *or* **Maninke** *n* **1** (*pl* -ke *or* -kes) a member of a Negroid people of W Africa, living chiefly in Guinea and Mali, noted for their use of cowry shells as currency **2** the language of this people, belonging to the Mande branch of the Niger-Congo family

Maliseet (ˈmælɪˌsiːt) *n* a member of a Native Canadian people of New Brunswick and E Quebec **2** the Algonquian language of this people [from Micmac *malisiit* one speaking an incomprehensible language]

malison (ˈmælɪzən, -sən) *n* an archaic or poetic word for **curse** [C13 via Old French from Latin *maledictiō* MALEDICTION]

malkin (ˈmɔːkɪn, ˈmɔːl-, ˈmæl-) *n* **1** an archaic or dialect name for a **cat¹**. Compare **grimalkin** **2** a variant of **mawkin** [C13 diminutive of *Maud*]

mall (mæl, mɔːl) *n* **1** a shaded avenue, esp one that is open to the public **2** *US, Canadian, Austral, and NZ* short for **shopping mall** [C17 after *The Mall*, in St James's Park, London. See PALL-MALL]

mallam *or* **malam** (ˈmæləm, -əm) *n W African* **1** (in Islamic W Africa) a man learned in Koranic studies **2** (in N Nigeria) a title and form of address for a learned or educated man [C20 from Hausa]

mallanders (ˈmæləndəz) *n* a variant spelling of **malanders**

mallard (ˈmælɑːd) *n, pl* -lard *or* -lards a duck, *Anas platyrhynchos*, common over most of the N hemisphere, the male of which has a dark green head and reddish-brown breast: the ancestor of all domestic breeds of duck [C14 from Old French *mallart,* perhaps from *maslart* (unattested); see MALE, -ARD]

malleable ('mælɪəb³l) *adj* **1** (esp of metal) able to be worked, hammered, or shaped under pressure or blows without breaking **2** able to be influenced; pliable or tractable [C14 via Old French from Medieval Latin *malleābilis,* from Latin *malleus* hammer] > ˌmallea'bility *or less commonly* 'malleableness *n* > 'malleably *adv*

malleable iron *n* **1** Also called: malleable cast iron cast iron that has been toughened by gradual heating or slow cooling **2** a less common name for **wrought iron**

mallee ('mælɪː) *n* **1** any of several low shrubby eucalyptus trees that flourish in desert regions of Australia **2** (usually preceded by *the*) *Austral informal* another name for the **bush** (sense 4) **3** See **mallee root** [C19 native Australian name]

mallee fowl *n* an Australian megapode, *Leipoa ocellata,* that allows its eggs to incubate naturally in a sandy mound

mallee root *n Austral* the rootstock (rhizome) of a mallee tree, often used as fuel

mallemuck ('mælɪˌmʌk) *n* any of various sea birds, such as the albatross, fulmar, or shearwater [C17 from Dutch *mallemok* from *mal* silly + *mok* gull]

mallenders ('mæləndəz) *n* a less common spelling of **malanders**

malleolus (mə'liːələs) *n, pl* -li (-ˌlaɪ) either of two rounded bony projections of the tibia and fibula on the sides of each ankle joint [C17 diminutive of Latin *malleus* hammer] > mal'leolar *adj*

mallet ('mælɪt) *n* **1** a tool resembling a hammer but having a large head of wood, copper, lead, leather, etc, used for driving chisels, beating sheet metal, etc **2** a long stick with a head like a hammer used to strike the ball in croquet or polo **3** *chiefly US* a very large powerful steam locomotive with a conventional boiler but with two separate articulated engine units [C15 from Old French *maillet* wooden hammer, diminutive of *mail* MAUL (n)]

malleus ('mælɪəs) *n, pl* -lei (-lɪˌaɪ) the outermost and largest of the three small bones in the middle ear of mammals. Nontechnical name: hammer See also **incus, stapes** [C17 from Latin: hammer]

Mallorca (ma'ʎɔrka) *n* the Spanish name for **Majorca**

mallow ('mæləʊ) *n* **1** any plant of the malvaceous genus *Malva,* esp *M. sylvestris* of Europe, having purple, pink, or white flowers. See also **dwarf mallow, musk mallow 2** any of various related plants, such as the marsh mallow, rose mallow, Indian mallow, and tree mallow [Old English *mealuwe,* from Latin *malva;* probably related to Greek *malakhē* mallow]

mallowpuff ('mæləʊˌpʌf) *n NZ* a white marshmallow on a biscuit base and covered with chocolate

mallowpuff Māori *n NZ informal, derogatory* a Māori who is considered to behave like a white person

mall rat (mɔːl) *n slang, chiefly US* a youngster who spends much of his or her time in shopping malls

malm (mɑːm) *n* **1** a soft greyish limestone that crumbles easily **2** a chalky soil formed from this limestone **3** an artificial mixture of clay and chalk used to make bricks [Old English *mealm-* (in compound words); related to Old Norse *malmr* ore, Gothic *malma* sand]

Malmédy (*French* malmedi) *n* See **Eupen and Malmédy**

Malmö ('mælməʊ; *Swedish* 'malmøː) *n* a port in S Sweden, on the Sound: part of Denmark until 1658; industrial centre. Pop: 268 971 (2004 est)

malmsey ('mɑːmzɪ) *n* a sweet Madeira wine [C15 from Medieval Latin *Malmasia,* corruption of Greek *Monembasia,* Greek port from which the wine was shipped]

malnourished (mæl'nʌrɪʃt) *adj* undernourished

malnutrition (ˌmælnjuː'trɪʃən) *n* lack of adequate nutrition resulting from insufficient food,

unbalanced diet, or defective assimilation

malocclusion (ˌmælə'kluːʒən) *n dentistry* a defect in the normal position of the upper and lower teeth when the mouth is closed, as from abnormal development of the jaw > ˌmaloc'cluded *adj*

malodorous (mæl'əʊdərəs) *adj* having a bad smell > mal'odorously *adv* > mal'odorousness *n*

malonic acid (mə'lɒnɪk, -'lɒn-) *n* another name for **propanedioic acid** [C19 from French *malonique,* altered form of *malique;* see MALIC ACID]

malonylurea (ˌmælənɪljʊ'rɪə, -'jʊərɪə, -niː-l-) *n* another name for **barbituric acid**

maloti (mə'ləʊtɪ, -'luːtɪ) *n* the plural of **loti**

malpighiaceous (mælˌpɪɡɪ'eɪʃəs) *adj* of, relating to, or belonging to the *Malpighiaceae,* a family of tropical plants many of which are lianas [C19 from New Latin *Malpighia,* after Marcello *Malpighi* (1628–94), Italian physiologist]

Malpighian (mæl'pɪɡɪən) *adj* of or relating to Marcello Malpighi (1628–94), the Italian physiologist

Malpighian corpuscle *or* **body** (mæl'pɪɡɪən) *n anatomy* an encapsulated cluster of capillaries at the end of each urine-secreting tubule of the kidney

Malpighian layer *n anatomy* the innermost layer of the epidermis

Malpighian tubules *or* **tubes** *pl n* organs of excretion in insects and many other arthropods: narrow tubules opening into the anterior part of the hindgut

malposition (ˌmælpə'zɪʃən) *n* abnormal position of a bodily part > malposed (mæl'pəʊzd) *adj*

malpractice (mæl'præktɪs) *n* **1** immoral, illegal, or unethical professional conduct or neglect of professional duty **2** any instance of improper professional conduct > malpractitioner (ˌmælpræk'tɪʃənə) *n*

malt (mɔːlt) *n* **1** cereal grain, such as barley, that is kiln-dried after it has germinated by soaking in water **2** See **malt liquor 3** short for **malt whisky** ▷ *vb* **4** to make into or become malt **5** to make (something, esp liquor) with malt [Old English *mealt;* related to Dutch *mout,* Old Norse *malt;* see also MELT]

Malta ('mɔːltə) *n* a republic occupying the islands of Malta, Gozo, and Comino, in the Mediterranean south of Sicily: governed by the Knights Hospitallers from 1530 until Napoleon's conquest in 1798; French driven out, with British help, 1800; became British dependency 1814; suffered severely in World War II; became independent in 1964 and a republic in 1974; joined the EU in 2004; a member of the Commonwealth. Official languages: Maltese and English. Official religion: Roman Catholic. Currency: Maltese lira. Capital: Valletta. Pop: 396 000 (2004 est). Area: 316 sq km (122 sq miles)

Malta fever *n* another name for **brucellosis**

maltase ('mɔːlteɪz) *n* an enzyme that hydrolyses maltose and similar glucosides (α-glucosides) to glucose. Also called: α-glucosidase [C19 from MALT + -ASE]

malted milk *n* **1** a soluble powder made from dehydrated milk and malted cereals **2** a drink made from this powder

Maltese (mɔːl'tiːz) *adj* **1** of or relating to Malta, its inhabitants, or their language ▷ *n* **2** (*pl* -tese) a native or inhabitant of Malta **3** the official language of Malta, a form of Arabic with borrowings from Italian, etc **4** a breed of toy dog having a very long straight silky white coat **5** a domestic fancy pigeon having long legs and a long neck

Maltese cross *n* **1** a cross with triangular arms that taper towards the centre, sometimes having indented outer sides; formerly worn by the Knights of Malta **2** (in a film projector) a cam mechanism of this shape that produces intermittent motion

malt extract *n* a sticky substance obtained from

an infusion of malt

maltha ('mælθə) *n* **1** another name for **mineral tar 2** any of various naturally occurring mixtures of hydrocarbons, such as ozocerite [C15 via Latin from Greek: a mixture of wax and pitch]

Malthusian (mæl'θjuːzɪən) *adj* **1** of or relating to the theory of the English economist Thomas Robert Malthus (1766–1834) stating that increases in population tend to exceed increases in the means of subsistence and that therefore sexual restraint should be exercised ▷ *n* **2** a supporter of this theory > Mal'thusianism *n*

malting ('mɔːltɪŋ) *n* a building in which malt is made or stored. Also called: malt house

malt liquor *n* any alcoholic drink brewed from malt

maltose ('mɔːltəʊz) *n* a disaccharide of glucose formed by the enzymic hydrolysis of starch: used in bacteriological culture media and as a nutrient in infant feeding. Formula: $C_{12}H_{22}O_{11}$ [C19 from MALT + -OSE²]

maltreat (mæl'triːt) *vb* (*tr*) to treat badly, cruelly, or inconsiderately [C18 from French *maltraiter*] > mal'treater *n* > mal'treatment *n*

maltster ('mɔːltstə) *n* a person who makes or deals in malt

malt whisky *n* whisky made from malted barley

malty ('mɔːltɪ) *adj* maltier, maltiest of, like, or containing malt > 'maltiness *n*

Maluku (mɑː'luːkuː) *n* the Indonesian name for the **Moluccas**

malvaceous (mæl'veɪʃəs) *adj* of, relating to, or belonging to the *Malvaceae,* a family of plants that includes mallow, cotton, okra, althaea, and abutilon [C17 from Latin *malvāceus,* from *malva* MALLOW]

Malvasia (ˌmælvə'sɪə) *n* **1** another word for **malmsey 2** the type of grape used to make malmsey [C19 from Italian, from Greek *Monembasia;* see MALMSEY] > ˌMalva'sian *adj*

Malvern ('mɔːlvən) *n* a town and resort in W England, in S Worcestershire on the E slopes of the **Malvern Hills**: annual dramatic festival; mineral springs. Pop: 35 588 (2001)

malversation (ˌmælvɜː'seɪʃən) *n rare* professional or public misconduct [C16 from French, from *malverser* to behave badly, from Latin *male versārī*]

Malvinas (*Spanish* mal'βinas) *pl n* **Islas** ('izlas) the Argentine name for the **Falkland Islands**

malvoisie ('mælvɔɪzɪ, -və-) *n* an amber dessert wine made in France, similar to malmsey [C14 via Old French from Italian *Malvasia,* from Greek *Monembasia;* see MALMSEY]

malwa ('malwə) *n* a Ugandan drink brewed from millet [from Rutooro, a language of W Uganda]

malware ('mælwɛə) *n* a computer program designed specifically to damage or disrupt a system, such as a virus [C20 from MAL(ICIOUS) + (SOFT)WARE]

mam (mæm) *n informal or dialect* another word for **mother¹**

mama (mə'mɑː) *n old-fashioned* an informal word for **mother¹**

mamaguy ('mɑːməˌɡaɪ) *Caribbean* ▷ *vb* **1** (*tr*) to deceive or tease, either in jest or by deceitful flattery ▷ *n* **2** an instance of such deception or flattery [from Spanish *mamar el gallo,* literally: to feed the cock]

mamaku, mamakau *or* **mamako** ('mɑːmɑːkuː) *n, pl* mamaku a tall edible New Zealand tree fern, *Cyathea medullaris,* with a black trunk. Also called: black tree fern [Māori]

mamba ('mæmbə) *n* any aggressive partly arboreal tropical African venomous elapid snake of the genus *Dendroaspis,* esp *D. angusticeps* (**green** and **black mambas**) [from Zulu *im-amba*]

mambo ('mæmbəʊ) *n, pl* -bos **1** a modern Latin American dance, resembling the rumba, derived from the ritual dance of voodoo **2** a voodoo priestess ▷ *vb* -bos, -boing, -boed **3** (*intr*) to perform this dance [American Spanish, probably from Haitian Creole: voodoo priestess]

m

mamelon ('mæmələⁿn) *n* a small rounded hillock [C19 from French: nipple]

Mameluke, Mamaluke ('mæmə,lu:k) *or* **Mamluk** ('mæmlu:k) *n* **1** a member of a military class, originally of Turkish slaves, ruling in Egypt from about 1250 to 1517 and remaining powerful until crushed in 1811 **2** (in Muslim countries) a slave [C16 via French, ultimately from Arabic *mamlūk* slave, from *malaka* to possess]

mamey, mammee *or* **mammee apple** (mæ'mi:) *n* **1** a tropical American tree, *Mammea americana*, cultivated for its large edible fruits: family *Clusiaceae* **2** the fruit of this tree, having yellow pulp and a red skin **3** another name for the **marmalade tree** [C16 from Spanish *mamey*, from Haitian]

mamilla *or US* **mammilla** (mæ'mɪlə) *n, pl* -**lae** (-li:) **1** a nipple or teat **2** any nipple-shaped part or prominence [C17 from Latin, diminutive of *mamma* breast] > **'mamillary** *or US* **'mammillary** *adj*

mamillate ('mæmɪ,leɪt), **mamillated,** *US* **mammillate, mammillated** *adj* having nipples or nipple-like protuberances

mamma¹ *n chiefly US* **1** ('mɑ:mə, mə'mɑ:) *Also:* **momma** another word for **mother¹ 2** ('mɑ:mə) *informal* a buxom and voluptuous woman [C16 reduplication of childish syllable *ma;* compare Welsh *mam,* French *maman,* Russian *mama*]

mamma² ('mæmə) *n, pl* -**mae** (-mi:) **1** the milk-secreting organ of female mammals: the breast in women, the udder in cows, sheep, etc **2** (*functioning as plural*) breast-shaped protuberances, esp from the base of cumulonimbus clouds [C17 from Latin: breast]

mammal ('mæml) *n* any animal of the *Mammalia,* a large class of warm-blooded vertebrates having mammary glands in the female, a thoracic diaphragm, and a four-chambered heart. The class includes the whales, carnivores, rodents, bats, primates, etc [C19 via New Latin from Latin *mamma* breast] > **mammalian** (mæ'meɪlɪən) *adj, n* > **'mammal-,like** *adj*

mammalogy (mæ'mælədʒɪ) *n* the branch of zoology concerned with the study of mammals > **mammalogical** (,mæmə'lɒdʒɪk^əl) *adj* > **mam'malogist** *n*

mammary ('mæmərɪ) *adj* of, relating to, or like a mamma or breast

mammary gland *n* any of the milk-producing glands in mammals. In higher mammals each gland consists of a network of tubes and cavities connected to the exterior by a nipple

mammee (mæ'mi:) *n* a variant spelling of **mamey**

mammet ('mæmɪt) *n* another word for **maumet**

mammiferous (mæ'mɪfərəs) *adj* having breasts or mammae

mammilla (mæ'mɪlə) *n, pl* -**lae** (-li:) the US spelling of **mamilla.** > **'mammillary** *adj*

mammillate ('mæmɪ,leɪt) *or* **mammillated** *adj* the US spellings of **mamillate, mamillated**

mammock ('mæmək) *dialect* ⊳ *n* **1** a fragment ⊳ *vb* **2** (*tr*) to tear or shred [C16 of unknown origin]

mammography (mæ'mɒɡrəfɪ) *n* the technique of using X-rays to examine the breast in the early detection of cancer > **'mammo,graph** *or* **'mammo,gram** *n*

mammon ('mæmən) *n* **1** riches or wealth regarded as a source of evil and corruption **2** avarice or greed [C14 via Late Latin from New Testament Greek *mammōnas,* from Aramaic *māmōnā* wealth] > **'mammonish** *adj* > **'mammonism** *n* > **'mammonist** *or* **'mammonite** *n* > **,mammon'istic** *adj*

Mammon ('mæmən) *n New Testament* the personification of riches and greed in the form of a false god

mammoth ('mæməθ) *n* **1** any large extinct elephant of the Pleistocene genus *Mammuthus* (or *Elephas*), such as *M. primigenius* (**woolly mammoth**), having a hairy coat and long curved tusks ⊳ *adj* **2** of gigantic size or importance [C18 from Russian *mamot,* from Tatar *mamont,* perhaps from *mamma* earth, because of a belief that the animal made burrows]

Mammoth Cave National Park *n* a national park in W central Kentucky: established in 1941 to protect a system of limestone caverns

mammy *or* **mammie** ('mæmɪ) *n, pl* -**mies 1** a child's word for **mother¹ 2** *chiefly Southern US* a Black woman employed as a nurse or servant to a White family

mammy wagon *n* a W African vehicle built on a lorry chassis, capable of carrying both passengers and goods

Mamoré (*Spanish* mamo're) *n* a river in central Bolivia, flowing north to the Beni River to form the Madeira River. Length: about 1500 km (930 miles)

mampara (mam'pɑ:rə) *n South African informal* **1** a foolish person, idiot **2** *obsolete* an incompetent worker [of unknown origin]

mampoer (məm'puə) *n South African* a home-distilled brandy made from peaches, prickly pears, etc [Afrikaans, possibly from Sotho *mampuru,* strong man]

mamzer ('mamzə) *n* **1** a Yiddish slang word for **bastard 2** *Judaism* a child of an incestuous or adulterous union [from Hebrew]

man (mæn) *n, pl* **men** (mɛn) **1** an adult male human being, as distinguished from a woman **2** (*modifier*) male; masculine: *a man child* **3** a human being regardless of sex or age, considered as a representative of mankind; a person **4** (*sometimes capital*) human beings collectively; mankind: *the development of man* **5** *Also called:* **modern man a** a member of any of the living races of *Homo sapiens,* characterized by erect bipedal posture, a highly developed brain, and powers of articulate speech, abstract reasoning, and imagination **b** any extinct member of the species *Homo sapiens,* such as Cro-Magnon man **6** a member of any of the extinct species of the genus *Homo,* such as Java man, Heidelberg man, and Solo man **7** an adult male human being with qualities associated with the male, such as courage or virility: *be a man* **8** manly qualities or virtues: *the man in him was outraged* **9 a** a subordinate, servant, or employee contrasted with an employer or manager **b** (*in combination*): *the number of man-days required to complete a job* **10** (*usually plural*) a member of the armed forces who does not hold commissioned, warrant, or noncommissioned rank (as in the phrase **officers and men**) **11** a member of a group, team, etc **12** a husband, boyfriend, etc: *man and wife* **13** an expression used parenthetically to indicate an informal relationship between speaker and hearer **14** a movable piece in various games, such as draughts **15** *South African slang* any person: used as a term of address **16** a vassal of a feudal lord **17 as one man** with unanimous action or response **18 be one's own man** to be independent or free **19 he's your man** he's the person needed (for a particular task, role, job, etc) **20 man and boy** from childhood **21 sort out** *or* **separate the men from the boys** to separate the experienced from the inexperienced **22 to a man a** unanimously **b** without exception: *they were slaughtered to a man* ⊳ *interj* **23** *informal* an exclamation or expletive, often indicating surprise or pleasure ⊳ *vb* **mans, manning, manned** (*tr*) **24** to provide with sufficient men for operation, defence, etc: *to man a ship* **25** to take one's place at or near in readiness for action **26** *falconry* to induce (a hawk or falcon) to endure the presence of and handling by man, esp strangers [Old English *mann;* related to Old Frisian *man,* Old High German *man,* Dutch *man,* Icelandic *mathr*] > **'manless** *adj*

Man¹ (mæn) *n* **the** (*sometimes not capital*) *US* **1** *Black slang* a White man or White men collectively, esp when in authority, in the police, or held in contempt **2** *slang* a drug peddler

Man² (mæn) *n* **Isle of** an island in the British Isles, in the Irish Sea between Cumbria and Northern Ireland: a UK Crown Dependency (but not part of the United Kingdom), with its own ancient parliament, the Court of Tynwald; a dependency of Norway until 1266, when for a time it came under Scottish rule; its own language, Manx, became extinct in the 19th century but has been revived to some extent. Capital: Douglas. Pop: 75 000 (2003 est). Area: 588 sq km (227 sq miles)

-man *n combining form* indicating a person who has a role, works in a place, or operates equipment as specified: *salesman; barman; cameraman*

⸰ **USAGE** The use of words ending in *-man* is avoided as implying a male in job advertisements, where sexual discrimination is illegal, and in many other contexts where a term that is not gender-specific is available, such as *salesperson, barperson, camera operator*

mana ('mɑ:nə) *n anthropol* **1** (in Polynesia, Melanesia, etc) a concept of a life force, believed to be seated in the head, and associated with high social status and ritual power **2** any power achieved by ritual means; prestige; authority [from Polynesian]

man about town *n* a fashionable sophisticate, esp one in a big city

manacle ('mænək^əl) *n* **1** (*usually plural*) a shackle, handcuff, or fetter, used to secure the hands of a prisoner, convict, etc ⊳ *vb* (*tr*) **2** to put manacles on **3** to confine or constrain [C14 via Old French from Latin *manicula,* diminutive of *manus* hand]

Manado (mə'nɑ:dəʊ) *n* a variant of **Menado**

manage ('mænɪdʒ) *vb* (*mainly tr*) **1** (*also intr*) to be in charge (of); administer: *to manage one's affairs; to manage a shop* **2** to succeed in being able (to do something) despite obstacles; contrive: *did you manage to go to sleep?* **3** to have room, time, etc, for: *can you manage dinner tomorrow?* **4** to exercise control or domination over, often in a tactful or guileful manner **5** (*intr*) to contrive to carry on despite difficulties, esp financial ones: *he managed quite well on very little money* **6** to wield or handle (a weapon) **7** *rare* to be frugal in the use of ⊳ *n* **8** an archaic word for **manège** [C16 from Italian *maneggiare* to control, train (esp horses), ultimately from Latin *manus* hand]

manageable ('mænɪdʒəb^əl) *adj* able to be managed or controlled > **,managea'bility** *or less commonly* **'manageableness** > **'manageably** *adv*

managed bonds *pl n* investment in a combination of fixed interest securities, equities, gilts, and property, in which an investment manager, acting on a client's behalf, varies the amount invested in each according to the returns expected

managed currency *n* a currency that is subject to governmental control with respect to the amount in circulation and the rate of exchange with other currencies

managed forest *n* a sustainable forest in which usually at least one tree is planted for every tree felled

management ('mænɪdʒmənt) *n* **1** the members of the executive or administration of an organization or business. See also **line management, middle management, top management 2** managers or employers collectively **3** the technique, practice, or science of managing, controlling or dealing with: *anger management* **4** the skilful or resourceful use of materials, time, etc **5** the specific treatment of a disease, disorder, etc

management accounting *n* another name for **cost accounting**

management buyout *n* the purchase of a company by its managers, usually with outside backing from a bank or other institution. Abbreviation: **MBO**

management company *n* a company that

manages a unit trust

management information system *n* an arrangement of equipment and procedures, often computerized, that is designed to provide managers with information

management union *n* a union that represents managers in negotiations with their employers concerning terms and conditions of employment

manager ('mænɪdʒə) *n* **1** a person who directs or manages an organization, industry, shop, etc **2** a person who controls the business affairs of an actor, entertainer, etc **3** a person who controls the training of a sportsman or team **4** a person who has a talent for managing efficiently **5** *law* a person appointed by a court to carry on a business during receivership **6** (in Britain) a member of either House of Parliament appointed to arrange a matter in which both Houses are concerned **7** a computer program that organizes a resource, such as a set of files or a database > 'manager,ship *n*

manageress (,mænɪdʒə'rɛs, 'mænɪdʒə,rɛs) *n* a woman who is in charge of a shop, department, canteen, etc

managerial (,mænɪ'dʒɪərɪəl) *adj* of or relating to a manager or to the functions, responsibilities, or position of management > ,mana'gerially *adv*

managerialism (,mænɪ'dʒɪərɪə,lɪzəm) *n* the application of managerial techniques of businesses to the running of other organizations, such as the civil service or local authorities > ,mana'gerialist *n*

manage up *vb* (*intr, adverb*) *informal* to build a successful working relationship with a superior, manager, or employer

managing ('mænɪdʒɪŋ) *adj* having administrative control or authority: *a managing director*

Managua (mə'nægwə; *Spanish* ma'naɣwa) *n* **1** the capital of Nicaragua, on the S shore of Lake Managua: chosen as capital in 1857. Pop: 1 159 000 (2005 est) **2 Lake** a lake in W Nicaragua: drains into Lake Nicaragua by the Tipitapa River. Length: 61 km (38 miles). Width: about 26 km (16 miles)

manaia (mɑ:nɑ:i:ə) *n, pl* **manaia** a common figure in Māori carving consisting of a human body and a bird-like head [Māori]

manakin ('mænəkɪn) *n* **1** any small South American passerine bird of the family *Pipridae*, having a colourful plumage, short bill, and elaborate courtship behaviour **2** a variant of **manikin**

Manama (mə'nɑ:mə) *n* the capital of Bahrain, at the N end of Bahrain Island: transit port. Pop: 142 000 (2005 est)

mañana *Spanish* (ma'ɲana; *English* mə'njɑ:nə) *n, adv* **a** tomorrow **b** some other and later time

Manáos (*Portuguese* mə'naus) *n* a variant spelling of **Manaus**

Manassas (mə'næsəs) *n* a town in NE Virginia, west of Alexandria: site of the victory of Confederate forces in the Battles of Bull Run, or First and Second Manassas (1861; 1862), during the American Civil War. Pop: 37 166 (2003 est)

Manasseh (mə'næsɪ) *n Old Testament* **1** the elder son of Joseph (Genesis 41:51) **2** the Israelite tribe descended from him **3** the territory of this tribe, in the upper Jordan valley. Douay spelling: **Manases** (mə'næsi:z)

manat (mæ'næt) *n* **1** the standard monetary unit of Azerbaijan, divided into 100 gopik **2** the standard monetary unit of Turkmenistan, divided into 100 tenesi

man-at-arms *n, pl* **men-at-arms** a soldier, esp a heavily armed mounted soldier in medieval times

manatee ('mænə,ti:, ,mænə'ti:) *n* any sirenian mammal of the genus *Trichechus*, occurring in tropical coastal waters of America, the Caribbean, and Africa: family *Trichechidae*. They resemble whales and have a prehensile upper lip and a broad flattened tail [c16 via Spanish from Carib *Manattouí*] > 'mana,toid *adj*

manatu ('mɑ:nɑ:tu:) *n, pl* **manatu** a large flowering deciduous New Zealand tree, *Plagianthus regius* [Māori]

Manaus *or* **Manáos** (*Portuguese* mə'naus) *n* a port in N Brazil, capital of Amazonas state, on the Rio Negro 19 km (12 miles) above its confluence with the Amazon: chief commercial centre of the Amazon basin. Pop: 1 673 000 (2005 est)

manawa ('mɑ:nɑ:wɑ;) *n NZ* another word for **mangrove** [Māori]

man boobs *pl n Brit informal derogatory* overdeveloped breasts on a man, casued by excess weight or lack of exercise

Man Booker Prize *n* an annual prize for a work of Commonwealth or Irish fiction of £50,000, awarded as the **Booker Prize** from 1969–2002

Manc (mæŋk) *n, adj Brit informal* short for **Mancunian**

Manche (*French* mɑ̃ʃ) *n* **1** a department of NW France, in Basse-Normandie region. Capital: St-Lô. Pop: 484 967 (2003 est). Area: 6412 sq km (2501 sq miles) **2 La** the French name for the **English Channel**

manchester ('mæntʃɪstə) *n Austral and NZ* **1** household linen or cotton goods, such as sheets and towels **2** Also called: **manchester department** a section of a store where such goods are sold [from MANCHESTER, England]

Manchester ('mæntʃɪstə) *n* **1** a city in NW England, in Manchester unitary authority, Greater Manchester: linked to the Mersey estuary by the **Manchester Ship Canal**: commercial, industrial, and cultural centre; formerly the centre of the cotton and textile trades; two universities. Pop: 394 269 (2001). Latin name: **Man'cunium 2** a unitary authority in NW England, in Greater Manchester. Pop: 432 500 (2003 est). Area: 116 sq km (45 sq miles)

Manchester terrier *n* a small breed of terrier with a glossy black-and-tan coat. Also called (less commonly): **black-and-tan terrier**

manchineel (,mæntʃɪ'ni:l) *n* a tropical American euphorbiaceous tree, *Hippomane mancinella*, having fruit and milky highly caustic poisonous sap, which causes skin blisters [c17 via French from Spanish MANZANILLA]

Manchu (mæn'tʃu:) *n* **1** (*pl* **-chus** *or* **-chu**) a member of a Mongoloid people of Manchuria who conquered China in the 17th century, establishing an imperial dynasty that lasted until 1912 **2** the language of this people, belonging to the Tungusic branch of the Altaic family ▷ *adj* **3** Also: **Ching** of or relating to the dynasty of the Manchus [from Manchu, literally: pure]

Manchukuo *or* **Manchoukuo** ('mæn'tʃu:'kwəu) *n* a former state of E Asia (1932–45), consisting of the three provinces of old Manchuria and Jehol

Manchuria (mæn'tʃʊərɪə) *n* a region of NE China, historically the home of the Manchus, rulers of China from 1644 to 1912: includes part of the Inner Mongolian AR and the provinces of Heilongjiang, Jilin, and Liaoning. Area: about 1 300 000 sq km (502 000 sq miles)

Manchurian (mæn'tʃʊərɪən) *adj* **1** of or relating to Manchuria, a region of NE China, or its inhabitants ▷ *n* **2** a native or inhabitant of Manchuria

manciple ('mænsɪpəl) *n* a steward who buys provisions, esp in a college, Inn of Court, or monastery [c13 via Old French from Latin *mancipium* purchase, from *manceps* purchaser, from *manus* hand + *capere* to take]

Mancunian (mæn'kju:nɪən) *n* **1** a native or inhabitant of Manchester ▷ *adj* **2** of or relating to Manchester [from Medieval Latin *Mancunium* Manchester]

-mancy *n combining form* indicating divination of a particular kind: *chiromancy* [from Old French *-mancie*, from Latin *-mantia*, from Greek *manteia* soothsaying] > **-mantic** *adj combining form*

Mandaean *or* **Mandean** (mæn'dɪən) *n* **1** a member of a Gnostic sect of Iraq **2** the form of

Aramaic used by this sect ▷ *adj* **3** of or relating to this sect [c19 from Aramaic *mandaya* Gnostics, from *mandā* knowledge] > **Man'daeanism** *or* **Man'deanism** *n*

mandala ('mændələ, mæn'dɑ:lə) *n* **1** *Hindu and Buddhist art* any of various designs symbolizing the universe, usually circular **2** *psychol* such a symbol expressing a person's striving for unity of the self [Sanskrit: circle]

Mandalay (,mændə'leɪ) *n* a city in central Myanmar, on the Irrawaddy River: the second largest city in the country and former capital of Burma and of Upper Burma; Buddhist religious centre. Pop: 927 000 (2005 est)

mandamus (mæn'deɪməs) *n, pl* **-muses** *law* formerly a writ from, now an order of, a superior court commanding an inferior tribunal, public official, corporation, etc, to carry out a public duty [c16 Latin, literally: we command, from *mandāre* to command]

mandarin ('mændərɪn) *n* **1** (in the Chinese Empire) a member of any of the nine senior grades of the bureaucracy, entered by examinations **2** a high-ranking official whose powers are extensive and thought to be outside political control **3** a person of standing and influence, as in literary or intellectual circles **4 a** a small citrus tree, *Citrus nobilis*, cultivated for its edible fruit **b** the fruit of this tree, resembling the tangerine [c16 from Portuguese *mandarim*, via Malay *menteri* from Sanskrit *mantrin* counsellor, from *mantra* counsel] > 'mandarinate *n*

Mandarin Chinese *or* **Mandarin** *n* the official language of China since 1917; the form of Chinese spoken by about two thirds of the population and taught in schools throughout China. See also **Chinese, Pekingese**

Mandarin collar *n* a high stiff round collar

mandarin duck *n* an Asian duck, *Aix galericulata*, the male of which has a brightly coloured and patterned plumage and crest

mandate *n* ('mændeɪt, -dɪt) **1** an official or authoritative instruction or command **2** *politics* the support or commission given to a government and its policies or an elected representative and his policies through an electoral victory **3** (*often capital*) Also called: **mandated territory** (formerly) any of the territories under the trusteeship of the League of Nations administered by one of its member states **4 a** *Roman law* a contract by which one person commissions another to act for him gratuitously and the other accepts the commission **b** *contract law* a contract of bailment under which the party entrusted with goods undertakes to perform gratuitously some service in respect of such goods **c** *Scots law* a contract by which a person is engaged to act in the management of the affairs of another ▷ *vb* ('mændeɪt) (*tr*) **5** *international law* to assign (territory) to a nation under a mandate **6** to delegate authority to **7** *obsolete* to give a command to [c16 from Latin *mandātum* something commanded, from *mandāre* to command, perhaps from *manus* hand + *dāre* to give] > 'man,dator *n*

mandatory ('mændətərɪ, -trɪ) *adj* **1** having the nature or powers of a mandate **2** obligatory; compulsory **3** (of a state) having received a mandate over some territory ▷ *n, pl* **-ries 4** Also called: **mandatary** a person or state holding a mandate > 'mandatorily *adv*

Mande ('mɑ:ndeɪ) *n, pl* **-de** *or* **-des 1** a group of African languages, a branch of the Niger-Congo family, spoken chiefly in Mali, Guinea, and Sierra Leone ▷ *adj* **2** of or relating to this group of languages

Mandelbrot set ('mændəl,brɒt) *n maths* a set of points in the complex plane that is self-replicating according to some predetermined rule such that the boundary of the set has fractal dimensions, used in the study of fractal geometry and in producing patterns in computer graphics [c20 after Benoît *Mandelbrot* (born 1924), French

m

mathematician, born in Poland]

mandi ('mʌndɪ) *n* (in India) a big market [Hindi]

mandible ('mændɪbᵊl) *n* **1** the lower jawbone in vertebrates. See **jaw** (sense 1) **2** either of a pair of mouthparts in insects and other arthropods that are usually used for biting and crushing food **3** *ornithol* either the upper or the lower part of the bill, esp the lower part [c16 via Old French from Late Latin *mandibula* jaw, from *mandere* to chew] > **mandibular** (mæn'dɪbjʊlə) *adj* > **mandibulate** (mæn'dɪbjʊlɪt, -ˌleɪt) *n, adj*

mandibular disease *n vet science* another name for **shovel beak**

Mandingo (mæn'dɪŋɡəʊ) *n, pl* **-gos** *or* **-goes** a former name for **Mande** *or* **Malinke**

mandir ('mʌndɪə) *n* a Hindu or Jain temple [Hindi, from Sanskrit *mandira*]

mandola ('mændələ) *n* an early type of mandolin [from Italian]

mandolin *or* **mandoline** (ˌmændə'lɪn) *n* **1** a plucked stringed instrument related to the lute, having four pairs of strings tuned in ascending fifths stretched over a small light body with a fretted fingerboard. It is usually played with a plectrum, long notes being sustained by the tremolo **2** a vegetable slicer consisting of a flat stainless-steel frame with adjustable cutting blades [c18 via French from Italian *mandolino*, diminutive of *mandora* lute, ultimately from Greek *pandoura* musical instrument with three strings] > ˌmando'linist *n*

mandorla (mæn'dɔːlə) *n* (in painting, sculpture, etc) an almond-shaped area of light, usually surrounding the resurrected Christ or the Virgin at the Assumption. Also called: **vesica** [from Italian, literally: almond, from Late Latin *amandula*; see ALMOND]

mandrake ('mændreɪk) *or* **mandragora** (mæn'dræɡərə) *n* **1** a Eurasian solanaceous plant, *Mandragora officinarum*, with purplish flowers and a forked root. It was formerly thought to have magic powers and a narcotic was prepared from its root **2** another name for the **May apple** [c14 probably via Middle Dutch from Latin *mandragoras* (whence Old English *mandragora*), from Greek. The form *mandrake* was probably adopted through folk etymology, because of the allegedly human appearance of the root and because *drake* (dragon) suggested magical powers]

mandrel *or* **mandril** ('mændrəl) *n* **1** a spindle on which a workpiece is supported during machining operations **2** a shaft or arbor on which a machining tool is mounted **3** the driving spindle in the headstock of a lathe **4** *Brit* a miner's pick [c16 perhaps related to French *mandrin* lathe]

mandrill ('mændrɪl) *n* an Old World monkey, *Mandrillus sphinx*, of W Africa. It has a short tail and brown hair, and the ridged muzzle, nose, and hindquarters are red and blue [c18 from MAN + DRILL⁴]

manducate ('mændjʊˌkeɪt) *vb* (tr) *literary* to eat or chew [c17 from Latin *mandūcāre* to chew] > ˌmandu'cation *n* > ˌmandu'catory *adj*

mane (meɪn) *n* **1** the long coarse hair that grows from the crest of the neck in such mammals as the lion and horse **2** long thick human hair [Old English *manu*; related to Old High German *mana*, Old Norse *mön*, and perhaps to Old English *mene* and Old High German *menni* necklace] > **maned** *adj* > 'maneless *adj*

man-eater *n* **1** an animal, such as a tiger, that has become accustomed to eating human flesh **2** any of various sharks that feed on human flesh, esp the great white shark (*Carcharodon carcharias*) **3** a human cannibal **4** *informal* a woman with many lovers

man-eating *adj* **1** eating human flesh **2** *informal* (of a woman) having many lovers

manège *or* **manege** (mæ'neɪʒ) *n* **1** the art of training horses and riders. Compare **dressage 2** a riding school [c17 via French from Italian *maneggio*,

from *maneggiare* to MANAGE]

manes ('mɑːneɪz; *Latin* 'mɑːnɛs) *pl n* (*sometimes capital*) (in Roman legend) **1** the spirits of the dead, often revered as minor deities **2** (*functioning as singular*) the shade of a dead person [c14 from Latin, probably: the good ones, from Old Latin *mānus* good]

maneuver (mə'nuːvə) *n, vb* the usual US spelling of **manoeuvre**. > ma'neuverable *adj* > maˌneuvera'bility *n* > ma'neuverer *n* > ma'neuvering *n*

man Friday *n* a loyal male servant or assistant [after the native in Daniel Defoe's novel *Robinson Crusoe* (1719)]

manful ('mænfʊl) *adj* a less common word for **manly**. > 'manfully *adv* > 'manfulness *n*

manga ('mæŋɡə) *n, pl* **manga a** a type of Japanese comic book with an adult theme **b** (*as modifier*): *manga videos*

mangabey ('mæŋɡəˌbeɪ) *n* any of several large agile arboreal Old World monkeys of the genus *Cercocebus*, of central Africa, having long limbs and tail and white upper eyelids [c18 after the name of a region in Madagascar]

Mangalore (ˌmæŋɡə'lɔː) *n* a port in S India, in Karnataka on the Malabar Coast. Pop: 398 745 (2001)

manganate ('mæŋɡəˌneɪt) *n* a salt of manganic acid

manganese ('mæŋɡəˌniːz) *n* a brittle greyish-white metallic element that exists in four allotropic forms, occurring principally in pyrolusite and rhodonite: used in making steel and ferromagnetic alloys. Symbol: Mn; atomic no.: 25; atomic wt.: 54.93805; valency: 1, 2 ,3, 4, 6, or 7; relative density: 7.21–7.44; melting pt.: 1246±3°C; boiling pt.: 2062°C [c17 via French from Italian *manganese*, probably altered form of Medieval Latin MAGNESIA]

manganese bronze *n* any of various alloys containing copper (55–60 per cent), zinc (35–42 per cent), and manganese (about 3.5 per cent)

manganese nodule *n geology* a small irregular concretion found on deep ocean floors having high concentrations of certain metals, esp manganese

manganese steel *n* any very hard steel containing manganese (11–14 per cent), used in dredger buckets, rock-crushers, railway points, etc

manganic (mæn'ɡænɪk) *adj* of or containing manganese in the trivalent state

manganic acid *n* a hypothetical dibasic acid known only in solution and in the form of manganate salts. Formula: H_2MnO_4

Manganin ('mæŋɡənɪn) *n trademark* an alloy of copper containing manganese (13–18 per cent) and nickel (1–4 per cent): it has a high electrical resistance that does not vary greatly with temperature and is used in resistors

manganite ('mæŋɡəˌnaɪt) *n* a blackish mineral consisting of basic manganese oxide in monoclinic crystalline form: a source of manganese. Formula: MnO(OH)

manganous ('mæŋɡənəs, mæn'ɡænəs) *adj* of or containing manganese in the divalent state

mange (meɪndʒ) *n* an infectious disorder mainly affecting domestic animals, characterized by itching, formation of papules and vesicles, and loss of hair: caused by parasitic mites [c14 from Old French *mangeue* itch, literally: eating, from *mangier* to eat]

mangeao ('mɑːˀŋɑːˈəʊ) *n, pl* **mangeao** a small tree with glossy leaves, *Litsea calicaris*, of New Zealand's North Island [Māori]

mangelwurzel ('mæŋɡᵊlˌwɜːzᵊl) *or* **mangoldwurzel** ('mæŋɡəʊldˌwɜːzᵊl) *n* a Eurasian variety of the beet plant, *Beta vulgaris*, cultivated as a cattle food, having a large yellowish root. Often shortened to: **mangel** *or* **mangold** [c18 from German *Mangoldwurzel*, from *Mangold* beet + *Wurzel* root]

mangemange (mɑːˀŋəmɑːˀŋə) *n, pl*

mangemange a climbing fern, *Lygodium articulatum*, of New Zealand's North Island [Māori]

manger ('meɪndʒə) *n* **1** a trough or box in a stable, barn, etc, from which horses or cattle feed **2** *nautical* a basin-like construction in the bows of a vessel for catching water draining from an anchor rode or coming in through the hawseholes [c14 from Old French *maingeure* food trough, from *mangier* to eat, ultimately from Latin *mandūcāre* to chew]

mangetout ('mɑːʒˈtuː) *n* a variety of garden pea in which the pod is also edible. Also called: **sugar pea** [c20 from French: eat all]

mangey ('meɪndʒɪ) *adj* **-gier, -giest** a variant spelling of **mangy**

mangle¹ ('mæŋɡᵊl) *vb* (tr) **1** to mutilate, disfigure, or destroy by cutting, crushing, or tearing **2** to ruin, spoil, or mar [c14 from Norman French *mangler*, probably from Old French *mahaignier* to maim] > 'mangler *n* > 'mangled *adj*

mangle² ('mæŋɡᵊl) *n* **1** Also called: **wringer** a machine for pressing or drying wet textiles, clothes, etc, consisting of two heavy rollers between which the cloth is passed ▷ *vb* (tr) **2** to press or dry in a mangle [c18 from Dutch *mangel*, ultimately from Late Latin *manganum*. See MANGONEL]

mango ('mæŋɡəʊ) *n, pl* **-goes** *or* **-gos 1** a tropical Asian anacardiaceous evergreen tree, *Mangifera indica*, cultivated in the tropics for its fruit **2** the ovoid edible fruit of this tree, having a smooth rind and sweet juicy orange-yellow flesh [c16 via Portuguese from Malay *mangā*, from Tamil *mānkāy* from *mān* mango tree + *kāy* fruit]

mango madness *n Austral informal* the irrational behaviour of a person suffering from the effects of living in tropical heat

mangonel ('mæŋɡəˌnɛl) *n history* a war engine for hurling stones [c13 via Old French from Medieval Latin *manganellus*, ultimately from Greek *manganon*]

mangosteen ('mæŋɡəʊˌstiːn) *n* **1** an East Indian tree, *Garcinia mangostana*, with thick leathery leaves and edible fruit: family *Clusiaceae* **2** the fruit of this tree, having a sweet juicy pulp and a hard skin [c16 from Malay *mangustan*]

mangrove ('mæŋɡrəʊv, 'mæn-) *n* **1 a** any tropical evergreen tree or shrub of the genus *Rhizophora*, having stiltlike intertwining aerial roots and growing below the highest tide levels in estuaries and along coasts, forming dense thickets: family *Rhizophoraceae* **b** (*as modifier*): *mangrove swamp* **2** any of various similar trees or shrubs of the genus *Avicennia*: family *Avicenniaceae* [c17 *mangrow* (changed through influence of *grove*), from Portuguese *mangue*, ultimately from Taino]

mangrove fish *n* another name for **parore**

mangrove Jack *n* a predatory food and game fish, *Lutjanus argentimaculatus*, of Australian rivers and tidal creeks dominated by mangroves

mangulate ('mæŋɡjʊˌleɪt) *vb* (tr) *Austral slang* to bend or twist out of shape; mangle

mangy *or* **mangey** ('meɪndʒɪ) *adj* **-gier, -giest 1** having or caused by mange: *a mangy dog* **2** scruffy or shabby: *a mangy carpet* **3** *Irish informal* stingy or miserly: *a mangy reward* > 'mangily *adv* > 'manginess *n*

manhandle ('mænˌhændᵊl, ˌmæn'hændᵊl) *vb* (tr) **1** to handle or push (someone) about roughly **2** to move or do by manpower rather than by machinery [c19 from MAN + HANDLE; sense 1 perhaps also influenced by Devon dialect *manangle* to mangle]

Manhattan (mæn'hætᵊn, mən-) *n* **1** an island at the N end of New York Bay, between the Hudson, East, and Harlem Rivers: administratively (with adjacent islets) a borough of New York City; a major financial, commercial, and cultural centre. Pop: 1 537 195 (2000). Area: 47 sq km (22 sq miles) **2** a mixed drink consisting of four parts whisky, one part vermouth, and a dash of bitters

Manhattan District *n* (during World War II) the code name for a unit of US army engineers established in 1942 to construct secret sites for the development of the atomic bomb. Also called: Manhattan Project

Manhattan Project *n* (during World War II) the code name for the secret US project set up in 1942 to develop an atomic bomb

manhole ('mæn,həʊl) *n* **1** Also called: inspection chamber a shaft with a removable cover that leads down to a sewer or drain **2** a hole, usually with a detachable cover, through which a man can enter a boiler, tank, etc

manhood ('mænhʊd) *n* **1** the state or quality of being a man or being manly **2** men collectively **3** the state of being human

manhood suffrage *n* the right of adult male citizens to vote

man-hour *n* a unit for measuring work in industry, equal to the work done by one man in one hour

manhunt ('mæn,hʌnt) *n* an organized search, usually by police, for a wanted man or fugitive > 'man,hunter *n*

mania ('meɪnɪə) *n* **1** a mental disorder characterized by great excitement and occasionally violent behaviour. See also **manic-depressive 2** an obsessional enthusiasm or partiality: *a mania for mushrooms* [c14 via Late Latin from Greek: madness]

-mania *n combining form* indicating extreme desire or pleasure of a specified kind or an abnormal excitement aroused by something: *kleptomania; nymphomania; pyromania* [from MANIA] > -maniac *n and adj combining form*

maniac ('meɪnɪ,æk) *n* **1** a wild disorderly person **2** a person who has a great craving or enthusiasm for something: *a football maniac* **3** *psychiatry obsolete* a person afflicted with mania [c17 from Late Latin *maniacus* belonging to madness, from Greek]

maniacal (mə'naɪək³l) *or* **maniac** ('meɪnɪæk) *adj* **1** affected with or characteristic of mania **2** characteristic of or befitting a maniac: *maniacal laughter* > ma'niacally *adv*

manic ('mænɪk) *adj* **1** characterizing, denoting, or affected by mania ▷ *n* **2** a person afflicted with mania [c19 from Greek, from MANIA]

manic-depressive *psychiatry* ▷ *adj* **1** denoting a mental disorder characterized either by an alternation between extreme euphoria and deep depression (bipolar manic-depressive disorder or syndrome) or by depression on its own or (rarely) by elation on its own (unipolar disorder) ▷ *n* **2** a person afflicted with this disorder. Compare **cyclothymia**

Manichaean *or* **Manichean** (,mænɪ'kiːən) *adj* **1** of or relating to Manichaeism **2** *chiefly RC Church* involving a radical dualism ▷ *n* **3** an adherent of Manichaeism

Manichaeism *or* **Manicheism** ('mænɪki:,ɪzəm) *n* **1** the system of religious doctrines, including elements of Gnosticism, Zoroastrianism, Christianity, Buddhism, etc, taught by the Persian prophet Mani (??216–?276 AD), based on a supposed primordial conflict between light and darkness or goodness and evil **2** *chiefly RC Church* any similar heretical philosophy involving a radical dualism [c14 from Late Latin *Manichaeus*, from Late Greek *Manikhaios* of Mani] > 'Manichee *n*

manicotti (,mænɪ'kɒtɪ) *pl n* large tubular noodles, usually stuffed with ricotta cheese and baked in a tomato sauce [Italian: sleeves, plural of *manicotto*, diminutive of *manica* sleeve]

manicure ('mænɪ,kjʊə) *n* **1** care of the hands and fingernails, involving shaping the nails, removing cuticles, etc **2** another word for **manicurist** ▷ *vb* **3** to care for (the hands and fingernails) in this way **4** (*tr*) to trim neatly [c19 from French, from Latin *manus* hand + *cūra* care]

manicurist ('mænɪ,kjʊərɪst) *n* a person who gives manicures, esp as a profession

manifest ('mænɪ,fɛst) *adj* **1** easily noticed or perceived; obvious; plain **2** *psychoanal* of or relating to the ostensible elements of a dream:

manifest content. Compare **latent** (sense 5) ▷ *vb* **3** (*tr*) to show plainly; reveal or display: *to manifest great emotion* **4** (*tr*) to prove beyond doubt **5** (*intr*) (of a disembodied spirit) to appear in visible form **6** (*tr*) to list in a ship's manifest ▷ *n* **7** a customs document containing particulars of a ship, its cargo, and its destination **8 a** a list of cargo, passengers, etc, on an aeroplane **b** a list of railway trucks or their cargo **c** *chiefly US and Canadian* a fast freight train carrying perishables [c14 from Latin *manifestus* plain, literally: struck with the hand, from *manū* with the hand + *-festus* struck] > 'mani,festable *adj* > 'mani,festly *adv* > 'mani,festness *n*

manifestation (,mænɪfɛ'steɪʃən) *n* **1** the act of demonstrating; display: *a manifestation of solidarity* **2** the state of being manifested **3** an indication or sign **4** a public demonstration of feeling **5** the materialization of a disembodied spirit > ,manifes'tational *adj* > ,mani'festative *adj*

Manifest Destiny *n* (esp in the 19th-century US) the belief that the US was a chosen land that had been allotted the entire North American continent by God

manifesto (,mænɪ'fɛstəʊ) *n, pl* -tos *or* -toes a public declaration of intent, policy, aims, etc, as issued by a political party, government, or movement [c17 from Italian, from *manifestare* to MANIFEST]

manifold ('mænɪ,fəʊld) *adj formal* **1** of several different kinds; multiple: *manifold reasons* **2** having many different forms, features, or elements: *manifold breeds of dog* ▷ *n* **3** something having many varied parts, forms, or features **4** a copy of a page, book, etc **5** a chamber or pipe with a number of inlets or outlets used to collect or distribute a fluid. In an internal-combustion engine the **inlet manifold** carries the vaporized fuel from the carburettor to the inlet ports and the **exhaust manifold** carries the exhaust gases away **6** *maths* **a** a collection of objects or a set **b** a topological space having specific properties **7** (in the philosophy of Kant) the totality of the separate elements of sensation which are then organized by the active mind and conceptualized as a perception of an external object ▷ *vb* **8** (*tr*) to duplicate (a page, book, etc) **9** to make manifold; multiply [Old English *manigfeald.* See MANY, -FOLD] > 'mani,folder *n* > 'mani,foldly *adv* > 'mani,foldness *n*

manikin, mannikin ('mænɪkɪn) *or formerly* **manakin** *n* **1** a little man; dwarf or child **2 a** an anatomical model of the body or a part of the body, esp for use in medical or art instruction **b** Also called: phantom an anatomical model of a fully developed fetus, for use in teaching midwifery or obstetrics **3** variant spellings of **mannequin** [c17 from Dutch *manneken*, diminutive of MAN]

Manila (mə'nɪlə) *n* **1** the chief port of the Philippines, on S Luzon on Manila Bay: capital of the republic until 1948 and from 1976; seat of the Far Eastern University and the University of Santo Tomas (1611). Pop: 10 677 000 (2005 est) **2** a type of cigar made in this city **3** (*often not capital*) short for **Manila hemp, Manila paper**

Manila Bay *n* an almost landlocked inlet of the South China Sea in the Philippines, in W Luzon: mostly forms Manila harbour. Area: 1994 sq km (770 sq miles)

Manila hemp *or* **Manilla hemp** *n* a fibre obtained from the plant abaca, used for rope, paper, etc

Manila paper *or* **Manilla paper** *n* a strong usually brown paper made from Manila hemp or similar fibres

Manila rope *or* **Manilla rope** *n* rope of Manila hemp

manilla (mə'nɪlə) *n* an early form of currency in W Africa in the pattern of a small bracelet [from Spanish: bracelet, diminutive of *mano* hand, from Latin *manus*]

manille (mæ'nɪl) *n* (in ombre and quadrille) the second best trump [c17 from French, from Spanish *malilla*, diminutive of *mala* bad]

Maninke (mə'nɪŋkə) *n, pl* -ke *or* -kes a variant of **Malinke**

man in the moon *n* **1** the moon when considered to resemble the face of a man **2** (in folklore and nursery rhyme) a character dwelling in the moon

man in the street *n* the typical or ordinary person, esp as a hypothetical unit in statistics

manioc ('mænɪ,ɒk) *or* **manioca** (,mænɪ'əʊkə) *n* another name for **cassava** (sense 1) [c16 from Tupi *mandioca*; earlier form *manihot* from French, from Guarani *mandio*]

maniple ('mænɪp³l) *n* **1** (in ancient Rome) a unit of 120 to 200 foot soldiers **2** *Christianity* an ornamental band formerly worn on the left arm by the celebrant at the Eucharist [c16 from Medieval Latin *manipulus* (the Eucharistic vestment), from Latin, literally: a handful, from *manus* hand]

manipular (mə'nɪpjʊlə) *adj* **1** of or relating to an ancient Roman maniple **2** of or relating to manipulation

manipulate (mə'nɪpjʊ,leɪt) *vb* **1** (*tr*) to handle or use, esp with some skill, in a process or action: *to manipulate a pair of scissors* **2** to negotiate, control, or influence (something or someone) cleverly, skilfully, or deviously **3** to falsify (a bill, accounts, etc) for one's own advantage **4** (in physiotherapy) to examine or treat manually, as in loosening a joint [c19 back formation from *manipulation*, from Latin *manipulus* handful] > manipulability (mə,nɪpjʊlə'bɪlɪtɪ) *n* > ma'nipu,latable *or* ma'nipulable *adj* > ma,nipu'lation *n* > ma'nipulative *adj* > ma'nipulatively *adv* > ma'nipu,lator *n* > ma'nipulatory *adj*

Manipur (,mʌnɪ'pʊə) *n* a state in NE India: largely densely forested mountains. Capital: Imphal. Pop: 2 388 634 (2001). Area: 22 327 sq km (8621 sq miles)

Manisa ('mɑːnɪ,sɑː) *n* a city in W Turkey: the Byzantine seat of government (1204–1313). Pop: 237 000 (2005 est)

Manitoba (,mænɪ'təʊbə) *n* **1** a province of W Canada: consists of prairie in the southwest, with extensive forests in the north and tundra near Hudson Bay in the northeast. Capital: Winnipeg. Pop: 1 170 268 (2004 est). Area: 650 090 sq km (251 000 sq miles). Abbreviation: MB **2 Lake** a lake in W Canada, in S Manitoba: fed by the outflow from Lake Winnipegosis; drains into Lake Winnipeg. Area: 4706 sq km (1817 sq miles)

Manitoba maple *n* a Canadian fast-growing variety of maple

Manitoban (,mænɪ'təʊbən) *n* **1** a native or inhabitant of Manitoba ▷ *adj* **2** of or relating to Manitoba or its inhabitants

manitou, manitu ('mænɪ,tuː) *or* **manito** ('mænɪ,təʊ) *n, pl* -tous, -tus, -tos *or* -tou, -tu, -to (among the Algonquian Indians) a deified spirit or force [c17 from Algonquian; related to Ojibwa *manito* spirit]

Manitoulin Island (,mænɪ'tuːlɪn) *n* an island in N Lake Huron in Ontario: the largest freshwater island in the world. Length: 129 km (80 miles). Width: up to 48 km (30 miles)

Manizales (,mænɪ'zɑːles; *Spanish* mani'θales) *n* a city in W Colombia, in the Cordillera Central of the Andes at an altitude of 2100 m (7000 ft): commercial centre of a rich coffee-growing area. Pop: 401 000 (2005 est)

man jack *n informal* a single individual (in the phrases **every man jack, no man jack**)

mankind (,mæn'kaɪnd) *n* **1** human beings collectively; humanity **2** men collectively, as opposed to womankind

■ USAGE Some people object to the use of *mankind* to refer to all human beings and prefer the term *humankind*

manky ('mæŋkɪ) *adj* mankier, mankiest *slang* **1** worthless, rotten, or in bad taste **2** dirty, filthy, or bad [via Polari from Italian *mancare* to be lacking]

m

manlike ('mæn,laɪk) *adj* resembling or befitting a man

man lock *n civil engineering* an airlock that allows workmen to pass in and out of spaces with differing air pressures, esp one providing access to and from a tunnel, shaft, or caisson in which the air is compressed

manly ('mænlɪ) *adj* -lier, -liest **1** possessing qualities, such as vigour or courage, generally regarded as appropriate to or typical of a man; masculine **2** characteristic of or befitting a man: *a manly sport* > **'manliness** *n*

man-made *adj* made or produced by man; artificial

man-mark *vb sport, Brit* (*tr*) to stay close to (a specific opponent) to hamper his or her play

man-mountain *n informal* a man who is very tall and heavily built

manna ('mænə) *n* **1** *Old Testament* the miraculous food which sustained the Israelites in the wilderness (Exodus 16:14–36) **2** any spiritual or divine nourishment **3** a windfall; an unexpected gift (esp in the phrase **manna from heaven**) **4** a sweet substance obtained from various plants, esp from an ash tree, *Fraxinus ornus* (**manna** or **flowering ash**) of S Europe, used as a mild laxative [Old English via Late Latin from Greek, from Hebrew *mān*]

Mannar (mə'nɑ:) *n* **Gulf of** the part of the Indian Ocean between SE India and the island of Sri Lanka: pearl fishing

manned (mænd) *adj* **1** supplied or equipped with men, esp soldiers **2** (of spacecraft, aircraft, etc) having a human crew

mannequin ('mænɪkɪn) *n* **1** a woman who wears the clothes displayed at a fashion show; model **2** a life-size dummy of the human body used to fit or display clothes **3** *arts* another name for **lay figure** [c18 via French from Dutch *manneken* MANIKIN]

manner ('mænə) *n* **1** a way of doing or being **2** a person's bearing and behaviour: *she had a cool manner* **3** the style or customary way of doing or accomplishing something: *sculpture in the Greek manner* **4** type or kind: *what manner of man is this?* **5** mannered style, as in art; mannerism **6** **by all manner of means** certainly; of course **7** **by no manner of means** definitely not: *he was by no manner of means a cruel man* **8** **in a manner of speaking** in a way; so to speak **9** **to the manner born** naturally fitted to a specified role or activity ▷ See also **manners** [c12 via Norman French from Old French *maniere*, from Vulgar Latin *manuāria* (unattested) a way of handling something, noun use of Latin *manuārius* belonging to the hand, from *manus* hand]

mannered ('mænəd) *adj* **1** having idiosyncrasies or mannerisms; affected: *mannered gestures* **2** of or having mannerisms of style, as in art or literature **3** (*in combination*) having manners as specified: *ill-mannered*

mannerism ('mænə,rɪzəm) *n* **1** a distinctive and individual gesture or trait; idiosyncrasy **2** (*often capital*) a principally Italian movement in art and architecture between the High Renaissance and Baroque periods (1520–1600) that sought to represent an ideal of beauty rather than natural images of it, using characteristic distortion and exaggeration of human proportions, perspective, etc **3** adherence to a distinctive or affected manner, esp in art or literature > **'mannerist** *n* > ,manner'istic *or* ,manner'istical *adj* > ,manner'istically *adv*

mannerless ('mænəlɪs) *adj* having bad manners; boorish > **'mannerlessness** *n*

mannerly ('mænəlɪ) *adj* **1** well-mannered; polite; courteous ▷ *adv* **2** *now rare* with good manners; politely; courteously > **'mannerliness** *n*

manners ('mænəz) *pl n* **1** social conduct: *he has the manners of a pig* **2** a socially acceptable way of behaving

Mannheim ('mænhaɪm; *German* 'manhaɪm) *n* a

city in SW Germany, in Baden-Württemberg at the confluence of the Rhine and Neckar: one of Europe's largest inland harbours; a cultural and musical centre. Pop: 308 353 (2003 est)

Mannheim School ('mænhaɪm) *n music* a group of musicians and composers connected with the court orchestra at Mannheim during the mid-18th century, who evolved the controlled orchestral crescendo as well as a largely homophonic musical style

mannikin ('mænɪkɪn) *n* a variant spelling of **manikin**

mannish ('mænɪʃ) *adj* **1** (of a woman) having or displaying qualities regarded as typical of a man **2** of or resembling a man > **'mannishly** *adv* > **'mannishness** *n*

mannitol ('mænɪ,tɒl) *or* **mannite** ('mænaɪt) *n* a white crystalline water-soluble sweet-tasting alcohol, found in plants and used in diet sweets and as a dietary supplement (**E421**). Formula: $C_6H_{14}O_6$ [from MANNOSE + -ITE² + -OL¹] > **mannitic** (mə'nɪtɪk) *adj*

mannose ('mænəʊs, -nəʊz) *n* a hexose sugar found in mannitol and many polysaccharides. Formula: $C_6H_{12}O_6$ [c20 from MANNA + -OSE²]

Mann-Whitney test ('mæn'wɪtnɪ) *n* a statistical test of the difference between the distributions of data collected in two experimental conditions applied to unmatched groups of subjects but comparing the distributions of the ranks of the scores. Also called: Wilcoxon Mann-Whitney test

manoao (mɑ:'nəʊɑ:əʊ) *n, pl* **manoao** a coniferous forest tree, *Manoao colensoi*, found in New Zealand's North Island [Māori]

manoeuvre *or US* **maneuver** (mə'nu:və) *n* **1** a contrived, complicated, and possibly deceptive plan or action: *political manoeuvres* **2** a movement or action requiring dexterity and skill **3** **a** a tactic or movement of one or a number of military or naval units **b** (*plural*) tactical exercises, usually on a large scale **4** a planned movement of an aircraft in flight **5** any change from the straight steady course of a ship ▷ *vb* **6** (*tr*) to contrive or accomplish with skill or cunning **7** (*intr*) to manipulate situations, etc, in order to gain some end: *to manoeuvre for the leadership* **8** (*intr*) to perform a manoeuvre or manoeuvres **9** to move or deploy or be moved or deployed, as military units, etc [c15 from French, from Medieval Latin *manuopera* manual work, from Latin *manū operāre* to work with the hand] > **ma'noeuvrable** *or US* **ma'neuverable** *adj* > **ma,noeuvra'bility** *or US* **ma,neuvera'bility** *n* > **ma'noeuvrer** *or US* **ma'neuverer** *n* > **ma'noeuvring** *or US* **ma'neuvering** *n*

man of God *n* **1** a saint or prophet **2** a clergyman

man of straw *n* **1** a person of little substance **2** Also called: **straw man** *chiefly US* a person used as a cover for some dubious plan or enterprise; front man

man-of-war *or* **man o' war** *n, pl* **men-of-war, men o' war 1** a warship **2** See **Portuguese man-of-war**

man-of-war bird *or* **man-o'-war bird** *n* another name for **frigate bird**

manometer (mə'nɒmɪtə) *n* an instrument for comparing pressures; typically a glass U-tube containing mercury, in which pressure is indicated by the difference in levels in the two arms of the tube [c18 from French *manomètre*, from Greek *manos* sparse + *metron* measure] > **manometric** (,mænəʊ'mɛtrɪk) *or* ,mano'metrical *adj* > ,mano'metrically *adv* > **ma'nometry** *n*

manor ('mænə) *n* **1** (in medieval Europe) the manor house of a lord and the lands attached to it **2** (before 1776 in some North American colonies) a tract of land granted with rights of inheritance by royal charter **3** a manor house **4** a landed estate **5** *Brit slang* a geographical area of operation, esp of a local police force [c13 from Old French *manoir* dwelling, from *maneir* to dwell, from Latin *manēre* to remain] > **manorial** (mə'nɔ:rɪəl) *adj*

man orchid *n* an orchid, *Aceras anthropophorum*, having greenish or reddish flowers in a loose spike, with a deeply lobed dark brown lip thought to resemble the silhouette of a man

manor house *n* (esp formerly) the house of the lord of a manor

manoscopy (mə'nɒskəpɪ) *n chem* the measurement of the densities of gases

manpower ('mæn,paʊə) *n* **1** power supplied by men **2** a unit of power based on the rate at which a man can work; approximately 75 watts **3** available or suitable power: *the manpower of a battalion*

manpower planning *n* a procedure used in organizations to balance future requirements for all levels of employee with the availability of such employees

Manpower Services Commission *n Brit* the former name of the **Training Agency**

manqué *French* (māke; *English* 'mɒŋkeɪ) *adj* (*postpositive*) unfulfilled; potential; would-be: *the manager is an actor manqué* [c19 literally: having missed]

Manresa (*Spanish* man'rɛsa) *n* a city in NE Spain: contains a cave used as the spiritual retreat of St Ignatius Loyola. Pop: 67 269 (2003 est)

manrope ('mæn,rəʊp) *n nautical* a rope railing

mansard ('mænsɑ:d, -səd) *n* **1** Also called: **mansard roof** a roof having two slopes on both sides and both ends, the lower slopes being steeper than the upper. Compare **gambrel roof 2** an attic having such a roof [c18 from French *mansarde*, after François *Mansart* (1598–1666), French architect]

manse (mæns) *n* (in certain religious denominations) the house provided for a minister [c15 from Medieval Latin *mansus* dwelling, from the past participle of Latin *manēre* to stay]

manservant ('mæn,sɜ:vənt) *n, pl* **menservants** a male servant, esp a valet

Mansfield ('mæns,fi:ld) *n* a town in central England, in W Nottinghamshire: former coal-mining and cotton-textiles industries. Pop: 69 987 (2001)

mansion ('mænʃən) *n* **1** Also called: **mansion house** a large and imposing house **2** a less common word for **manor house 3** *archaic* any residence **4** *Brit* (*plural*) a block of flats **5** *astrology* any of 28 divisions of the zodiac each occupied on successive days by the moon [c14 via Old French from Latin *mansio* a remaining, from *mansus*; see MANSE]

Mansion House *n* the **1** the residence of the Lord Mayor of London **2** the residence of the Lord Mayor of Dublin

man-sized *adj* **1** of a size appropriate for or convenient for a man **2** *informal* big; large

manslaughter ('mæn,slɔ:tə) *n* **1** *law* the unlawful killing of one human being by another without malice aforethought. Compare **murder** See also **homicide, malice aforethought 2** (loosely) the killing of a human being

mansuetude ('mænswɪ,tju:d) *n archaic* gentleness or mildness [c14 from Latin *mansuētūdō*, from *mansuētus*, past participle of *mansuēscere* to make tame by handling, from *manus* hand + *suescere* to train]

Mansûra (mæn'sʊərə) *n* See **El Mansûra**

manta ('mæntə; *Spanish* 'manta) *n* **1** Also called: **manta ray, devilfish, devil ray** any large ray (fish) of the family *Mobulidae*, having very wide winglike pectoral fins and feeding on plankton **2** a rough cotton cloth made in Spain and Spanish America **3** a piece of this used as a blanket or shawl **4** another word for **mantelet** (sense 2) [Spanish: cloak, from Vulgar Latin; see MANTLE. The manta ray is so called because it is caught in a trap resembling a blanket]

manteau ('mæntəʊ; *French* māto) *n, pl* **-teaus** (-təʊz) *or* **-teaux** (*French* -to) a cloak or mantle [c17 via French from Latin *mantellum* MANTLE]

mantel *or less commonly* **mantle** ('mæntᵊl) *n* **1** a wooden or stone frame around the opening of a fireplace, together with its decorative facing **2** Also called: mantel shelf a shelf above this frame [c15 from French, variant of MANTLE]

mantelet ('mænt³ˌlɛt) or **mantlet** n **1** a woman's short mantle, often lace-trimmed, worn in the mid-19th century **2** a portable bulletproof screen or shelter [c14 from Old French, diminutive of *mantel* MANTLE]

mantelletta (ˌmæntɪˈlɛtə) n *RC Church* a sleeveless knee-length vestment, worn by cardinals, bishops, etc [Italian, from Old French *mantelet* or Medieval Latin *mantelletum*, diminutive of Latin *mantellum* MANTLE]

mantelpiece ('mænt³lˌpiːs) n **1** Also called: mantel shelf, chimneypiece a shelf above a fireplace often forming part of the mantel **2** another word for **mantel** (sense 1)

manteltree or **mantletree** ('mænt³lˌtriː) n a beam of stone or wood that forms the lintel over a fireplace

mantic ('mæntɪk) adj **1** of or relating to divination and prophecy **2** having divining or prophetic powers [c19 from Greek *mantikos* prophetic, from *mantis* seer] > 'mantically adv

-mantic adj combining form forming adjectives corresponding to nouns ending in **-mancy**: *necromantic*

manticore ('mæntɪˌkɔː) n a monster with a lion's body, a scorpion's tail, and a man's head with three rows of teeth. It roamed the jungles of India and, like the Sphinx, would ask travellers a riddle and kill them when they failed to answer it [c21 from Latin *manticora*, from Greek *mantichōras*, corruption of *martichorās*, from Persian *mardkhora* man-eater]

mantilla (mænˈtɪlə) n **1** a woman's lace or silk scarf covering the shoulders and head, often worn over a comb in the hair, esp in Spain **2** a similar covering for the shoulders only [c18 Spanish, diminutive of *manta* cloak]

Mantinea or **Mantineia** (ˌmæntɪˈneɪə) n (in ancient Greece) a city in E Arcadia; site of several battles

mantis ('mæntɪs) n, pl **-tises** or **-tes** (-tiːz) any carnivorous typically green insect of the family *Mantidae*, of warm and tropical regions, having a long body and large eyes and resting with the first pair of legs raised as if in prayer: order *Dictyoptera*. Also called: **praying mantis** See also **cockroach** [c17 New Latin, from Greek: prophet, alluding to its praying posture]

mantissa (mænˈtɪsə) n the fractional part of a common logarithm representing the digits of the associated number but not its magnitude: *the mantissa of 2.4771 is .4771*. Compare **characteristic** (sense 2a) [c17 from Latin: something added, of Etruscan origin]

mantis shrimp or **crab** n any of various burrowing marine shrimplike crustaceans of the order *Stomatopoda* that have a pair of large grasping appendages: subclass *Malacostraca*. See also **squilla**

mantle ('mænt³l) n **1** *archaic* a loose wrap or cloak **2** such a garment regarded as a symbol of someone's power or authority: *he assumed his father's mantle* **3** anything that covers completely or envelops: *a mantle of snow* **4** a small dome-shaped or cylindrical mesh impregnated with cerium or thorium nitrates, used to increase illumination in a gas or oil lamp **5** Also called: pallium *zoology* **a** a protective layer of epidermis in molluscs that secretes a substance forming the shell **b** a similar structure in brachiopods **6** *ornithol* the feathers of the folded wings and back, esp when these are of a different colour from the remaining feathers **7** *geology* the part of the earth between the crust and the core, accounting for more than 82% of the earth's volume (but only 68% of its mass) and thought to be composed largely of peridotite. See also **asthenosphere** **8** a less common spelling of **mantel** **9** *anatomy*

another word for **pallium** (sense 3) **10** a clay mould formed around a wax model which is subsequently melted out ▷ vb **11** (tr) to envelop or supply with a mantle **12** to spread over or become spread over: *the trees were mantled with snow* **13** (tr) (of the face, cheeks) to become suffused with blood; flush **14** (intr) *falconry* (of a hawk or falcon) to spread the wings and tail over food [c13 via Old French from Latin *mantellum*, diminutive of *mantum* cloak]

mantle plume n another name for **plume** (sense 6)

mantling ('mæntlɪŋ) n *heraldry* the drapery or scrollwork around a shield [c16 from MANTLE]

man-to-man adj characterized by directness or candour: *a man-to-man discussion*

Mantoux test (mænˈtuː; *French* mɑ̃tu) n *med* a test for determining the presence of a tubercular infection by injecting tuberculin into the skin [c19 named after C. *Mantoux*, French physician (1877–1956)]

Mantova ('mantova) n the Italian name for **Mantua**

mantra ('mæntrə, 'mʌn-) n **1** *Hinduism* any of those parts of the Vedic literature which consist of the metrical psalms of praise **2** *Hinduism, Buddhism* any sacred word or syllable used as an object of concentration and embodying some aspect of spiritual power [c19 from Sanskrit, literally: speech, instrument of thought, from *man* to think]

Man fern n another name for **soft tree fern**

mantrap ('mænˌtræp) n a snare for catching people, esp trespassers

mantua ('mæntjʊə) n a loose gown of the 17th and 18th centuries, worn open in front to show the underskirt [c17 changed from MANTEAU, through the influence of MANTUA]

Mantua ('mæntjʊə) n a city in N Italy, in E Lombardy, surrounded by lakes: birthplace of Virgil. Pop: 47790 (2001). Italian name: Mantova

manual ('mænjʊəl) adj **1** of or relating to a hand or hands **2** operated or done by hand: *manual controls* **3** physical, as opposed to mental or mechanical: *manual labour* **4** by human labour rather than automatic or computer-aided means **5** of, relating to, or resembling a manual ▷ n **6** a book, esp of instructions or information: *a car manual* **7** *music* one of the keyboards played by hand on an organ **8** *military* the prescribed drill with small arms [c15 via Old French from Latin *manuālis*, from *manus* hand] > 'manually adv

manubrium (məˈnjuːbrɪəm) n, pl **-bria** (-brɪə) or **-briums 1** *anatomy* any handle-shaped part, esp the upper part of the sternum **2** *zoology* the tubular mouth that hangs down from the centre of a coelenterate medusa such as a jellyfish [c17 from New Latin, from Latin: handle, from *manus* hand] > ma'nubrial adj

manuf. or **manufac.** abbreviation for **1** manufacture **2** manufactured

manufactory (ˌmænjʊˈfæktərɪ, -trɪ) n, pl **-ries** an obsolete word for **factory** [c17 from obsolete *manufact*; see MANUFACTURE]

manufacture (ˌmænjʊˈfæktʃə) vb **1** to process or make (a product) from a raw material, esp as a large-scale operation using machinery **2** (tr) to invent or concoct: *to manufacture an excuse* ▷ n **3** the production of goods, esp by industrial processes **4** a manufactured product **5** the creation or production of anything [c16 from obsolete *manufact* hand-made, from Late Latin *manūfactus*, from Latin *manus* hand + *facere* to make] > ,manu'facturable adj > ,manu'facturing n, adj

manufacturer (ˌmænjʊˈfæktʃərə) n a person or business concern that manufactures goods or owns a factory

manuhiri (ˌmɑːnuːˈhiːriː) n *NZ* a visitor to a Māori marae **2** a Māori term for a non-Māori person, seen as a guest in the country [Māori]

manuka ('mɑːnuːkə) n a New Zealand myrtaceous tree, *Leptospermum scoparium*, with strong elastic wood and aromatic leaves. Also

called: red tea tree, kahikatoa

Manukau ('mɑːnuˌkaʊ) n a city in New Zealand, on **Manukau Harbour** (an inlet of the Tasman Sea) near Auckland on NW North Island. Pop: 326 200 (2004 est)

manumission (ˌmænjʊˈmɪʃən) n the act of freeing or the state of being freed from slavery, servitude, etc

manumit (ˌmænjʊˈmɪt) vb **-mits**, **-mitting**, **-mitted** (tr) to free from slavery, servitude, etc; emancipate [c15 from Latin *manūmittere* to release, from *manū* from one's hand + *ēmittere* to send away] > ,manu'mitter n

manure (məˈnjʊə) n **1** animal excreta, usually with straw, used to fertilize land **2** *chiefly Brit* any material, esp chemical fertilizer, used to fertilize land ▷ vb **3** (tr) to spread manure upon (fields or soil) [c14 from Medieval Latin *manuopera*; manual work; see MANOEUVRE] > ma'nurer n

manus ('meɪnəs) n, pl **-nus 1** *anatomy* the wrist and hand **2** the corresponding part in other vertebrates **3** *Roman law* the authority of a husband over his wife **4** *English law* (formerly) an oath or the person taking an oath [c19 Latin: hand]

Manu Samoa ('mænʊ) n the international Rugby Union football team of Western Samoa

manuscript ('mænjʊˌskrɪpt) n **1** a book or other document written by hand **2** the original handwritten or typed version of a book, article, etc, as submitted by an author for publication **3 a** handwriting, as opposed to printing **b** (as modifier): *a manuscript document* [c16 from Medieval Latin *manūscriptus*, from Latin *manus* hand + *scribere* to write]

Manx (mæŋks) adj **1** of, relating to, or characteristic of the Isle of Man, its inhabitants, their language, or their dialect of English ▷ n **2** a language of the Isle of Man, belonging to the N Celtic branch of the Indo-European family and closely related to Scottish Gaelic **3** (functioning as plural) the people of the Isle of Man [c16 earlier *Maniske*, from Scandinavian, from *Mana* Isle of Man + *-iske* -ISH]

Manx cat n a short-haired tailless variety of cat, believed to originate on the Isle of Man

Manxman ('mæŋksmən) or feminine **Manxwoman** ('mæŋkswʊmən) n, pl **-men** or **-women** a native or inhabitant of the Isle of Man

Manx shearwater n a European oceanic bird, *Puffinus puffinus*, with long slender wings and black-and-white plumage: family *Procellariidae* (shearwaters)

many ('mɛnɪ) determiner **1** (sometimes preceded by a great or a good) **a** a large number of: *many coaches; many times* **b** (as pronoun; functioning as plural): *many are seated already* **2** (foll by a, an, or another, and a singular noun) each of a considerable number of: *many a man* **3** (preceded by as, too, that, etc) **a** a great number of: *as many apples as you like; too many clouds to see* **b** (as pronoun; functioning as plural): *I have as many as you* ▷ n **4** the many the majority of mankind, esp the common people. Compare **few** (sense 7) ▷ See also **more, most** [Old English *manig*; related to Old Frisian *manich*, Middle Dutch *menech*, Old High German *manag*]

many-one adj maths, logic (of a function) associating a single element of a range with more than one member of the domain

manyplies ('mɛnɪˌplaɪz) n (functioning as singular) another name for **psalterium** [c18 from the large number of plies or folds of its membrane]

many-sided adj having many sides, aspects, etc: *a many-sided personality* > ,many-'sidedness n

many-valued logic n **a** the study of logical systems in which the truth-values that a proposition may have are not restricted to two, representing only truth and falsity **b** such a logical system

manzanilla (ˌmænzəˈnɪlə) n a very dry pale sherry [c19 from Spanish: camomile (referring to its bouquet)]

m

MAO *abbreviation for* **monoamine oxidase**

MAOI *abbreviation for* **monoamine oxidase inhibitor**

Maoism ('maʊɪzəm) *n* **1** Marxism-Leninism as interpreted by Mao Tse-tung (1893–1976), the Chinese Marxist theoretician and statesman: distinguished by its theory of guerrilla warfare and its emphasis on the revolutionary potential of the peasantry **2** adherence to or reverence for Mao Tse-tung and his teachings > **'Maoist** *n, adj*

maomao ('mɑːˌɒmɑːˌɒ) *n, pl* maomao either of two small New Zealand edible fish, the pink maomao *caprodon langimanus* and the blue maomao *scorpis acquipinnus* [Māori]

Māori ('maʊrɪ) *n* **1** (*pl* -ri *or* -ris) a member of the people living in New Zealand and the Cook Islands since before the arrival of European settlers. They are descended from Polynesian voyagers who migrated in successive waves from the ninth century onwards **2** the language of this people, belonging to the Malayo-Polynesian family ▷ *adj* **3** of or relating to this people or their language

Māori Battalion *n* the Māori unit of the 2nd New Zealand Expeditionary Force in World War II

Māori bread *n* NZ bread made with fermented potato yeast

Māori bug *n* a large shining black wingless cockroach of New Zealand, *Platyzosteria novae-zelandiae*. Also called: **black beetle, kekerengu**

Māori bunk *n* NZ a raised sleeping platform

Māori hen *n* NZ another name for **weka**

Māoriland ('maʊrɪˌlænd) *n* an obsolete name for **New Zealand**

Māorilander ('maʊrɪˌlændə) *n* an obsolete name for a **New Zealander**

Māori mint *n* another name for **hioi**

Māori oven *n* another name for **hangi** (sense 1)

Māori rat *n* a small brown rat, *Rattus exulans*, native to New Zealand. Also called: **kiore**

Māoritanga ('maʊrɪˌtʌŋə) *n* NZ the Māori culture; Māori way of life [Māori]

Māori warden *n* a person appointed to exercise advisory and minor disciplinary powers in Māori communities

Mao suit (maʊ) *n* a simple style of clothing, traditionally made of cotton and commonly worn in Communist China, consisting of loose trousers and a straight jacket with a close-fitting stand-up collar [c20 named after *Mao* Tse-tung (1893–1976), Chinese Marxist theoretician and statesman, who popularized the style]

map (mæp) *n* **1** a diagrammatic representation of the earth's surface or part of it, showing the geographical distributions, positions, etc, of natural or artificial features such as roads, towns, relief, rainfall, etc **2** a diagrammatic representation of the distribution of stars or of the surface of a celestial body: *a lunar map* **3** a maplike drawing of anything **4** *maths* another name for **function** (sense 4) **5** a slang word for **face** (sense 1) **6 off the map** no longer important or in existence (esp in the phrase **wipe off the map**) **7 put on the map** to make (a town, company, etc) well-known ▷ *vb* **maps, mapping, mapped** (*tr*) **8** to make a map of **9** *maths* to represent or transform (a function, figure, set, etc): *the results were mapped onto a graph*. See also **map out** **10** (*intr*) **map onto** to fit in with or correspond to [c16 from Medieval Latin *mappa* (*mundi*) map (of the world), from Latin *mappa* cloth] > **'mappable** *adj* > **'mapless** *adj* > **'mapper** *n*

mapau ('mɑːpɑːuː) *n, pl* mapau a small New Zealand tree, *Myrsine australis*, with reddish bark, aromatic leaves, and dark berries. Also called: **red matipo** [Māori]

maple ('meɪpəl) *n* **1** any tree or shrub of the N temperate genus *Acer*, having winged seeds borne in pairs and lobed leaves: family *Aceraceae* **2** the hard close-grained wood of any of these trees, used for furniture and flooring **3** the flavour of the sap of the sugar maple ▷ See also **sugar maple, silver maple, Norway maple, sycamore** [c14 from Old English *mapel-*, as in *mapeltrēow* maple tree]

Maple Leaf *n* **the** the national flag of Canada, consisting of a representation of a maple leaf in red on a white central panel with a vertical red bar on either side

maple sugar *n* US and Canadian sugar made from the sap of the sugar maple

maple syrup *n* a very sweet syrup made from the sap of the sugar maple

map out *vb* (*tr, adverb*) to plan or design: *to map out a route*

mapping ('mæpɪŋ) *n* maths another name for **function** (sense 4)

map projection *n* a means of representing or a representation of the globe or celestial sphere or part of it on a flat map, using a grid of lines of latitude and longitude

Maputo (məˈpuːtəʊ) *n* the capital and chief port of Mozambique, in the south on Delagoa Bay: became capital in 1907; the nearest port to the Rand gold-mining and industrial region of South Africa. Pop: 1 316 000 (2005 est). Former name (until 1975): **Lourenço Marques**

maquette (mæˈkɛt) *n* a sculptor's small preliminary model or sketch [c20 from French, from Italian *macchietta* a little sketch, from *macchia*, from *macchiare*, from Latin *maculāre* to stain, from *macula* spot, blemish]

maquillage French (makijaʒ) *n* **1** make-up; cosmetics **2** the application of make-up [from *maquiller* to make up]

maquis (mɑːˈkiː) *n, pl* -quis (-ˈkiː) **1** shrubby mostly evergreen vegetation found in coastal regions of the Mediterranean: includes myrtles, heaths, arbutus, cork oak, and ilex **2** (*often capital*) **a** the French underground movement that fought against the German occupying forces in World War II **b** a member of this movement [c20 from French, from Italian *macchia* thicket, from Latin *macula* spot]

mar (mɑː) *vb* **mars, marring, marred 1** (*tr*) to cause harm to; spoil or impair ▷ *n* **2** a disfiguring mark; blemish [Old English *merran*; compare Old Saxon *merrian* to hinder, Old Norse *merja* to bruise] > **'marrer** *n*

Mar *abbreviation for* March

mara (məˈrɑː) *n* a harelike South American rodent, *Dolichotis patagonum*, inhabiting the pampas of Argentina: family *Caviidae* (cavies) [from American Spanish *mará*, perhaps of Araucanian origin]

marabi (ˌmaˈrɑːbɪ) *n* South African a kind of music popular in townships in the 1930s [of uncertain origin, possibly from Sotho]

marabou ('mærəˌbuː) *n* **1** a large black-and-white African carrion-eating stork, *Leptoptilos crumeniferus*, with a very short naked neck and a straight heavy bill. See also **adjutant bird 2 a** a down feather of this bird, used to trim garments **3 a** a fine white raw silk **b** fabric made of this [c19 from French, from Arabic *murābit* MARABOUT, so called because the stork is considered a holy bird in Islam]

marabout ('mærəˌbuː) *n* **1** a Muslim holy man or hermit of North Africa **2** a shrine of the grave of a marabout [c17 via French and Portuguese *marabuto*, from Arabic *murābit*]

marabunta ('mærəˌbʌntə) *n* Caribbean **1** any of several social wasps **2** slang an ill-tempered woman [c19 perhaps of W African origin]

maraca (məˈrækə) *n* a percussion instrument, usually one of a pair, consisting of a gourd or plastic shell filled with dried seeds, pebbles, etc It is used chiefly in Latin American music [c20 Brazilian Portuguese, from Tupi]

Maracaibo (ˌmærəˈkaɪbəʊ; Spanish maraˈkaiβo) *n* **1** a port in NW Venezuela, on the channel from Lake Maracaibo to the Gulf of Venezuela: the second largest city in the country; University of Zulia (1891); major oil centre. Pop: 2 182 000 (2005 est) **2 Lake** a lake in NW Venezuela, linked with the Gulf of Venezuela by a dredged channel: centre of the Venezuelan and South American oil industry. Area: about 13 000 sq km (500 sq miles)

Maracanda (ˌmærəˈkændə) *n* the ancient name for **Samarkand**

Maracay (Spanish maraˈkai) *n* a city in N central Venezuela: developed greatly as the headquarters of Juan Vicente Gómez (1857–1935) during his dictatorship; textile industries. Pop: 1 138 000 (2005 est)

marae (məˈraɪ) *n* **1** NZ a traditional Māori tribal meeting place, originally one in the open air, now frequently a purpose-built building **2** (in Polynesia) an open-air place of worship [Māori]

maraging steel ('mɑːˌreɪdʒɪŋ) *n* a strong low-carbon steel containing nickel and small amounts of titanium, aluminium, and niobium, produced by transforming to a martensitic structure and heating at 500°C [c20 *maraging*, from MAR(TENSITE) + *aging*]

Marajó (Portuguese maraˈʒɔ) *n* an island in N Brazil, at the mouth of the Amazon. Area: 38 610 sq km (15 444 sq miles)

Maranhão (Portuguese maraˈɲ̃ɐu) *n* a state of NE Brazil, on the Atlantic: forested and humid in the northwest, with high plateaus in the east and south. Capital: São Luís. Pop: 5 803 224 (2002). Area: 328 666 sq km (128 179 sq miles)

Marañón (Spanish maraˈɲɔn) *n* a river in NE Peru, rising in the Andes and flowing northwest into the Ucayali River, forming the Amazon. Length: about 1450 km (900 miles)

maranta (məˈræntə) *n* any plant of the tropical American rhizomatous genus *Maranta*, some species of which are grown as pot plants for their showy leaves in variegated shades of green: family *Marantaceae* [named after Bartolomea *Maranti*, died 1571, Venetian botanist]

marari ('mɑːrɑːriː) *n* NZ a Māori name for **butterfish** (sense 2)

Maraş (mæˈræʃ) *n* a town in S Turkey: noted formerly for the manufacture of weapons but now for carpets and embroidery. Pop: 366 000 (2005 est)

marasca (məˈræskə) *n* a European cherry tree, *Prunus cerasus marasca*, with red acid-tasting fruit from which maraschino is made [c19 from Italian, variant of *amarasca* from *amaro*, from Latin *amārus* bitter]

maraschino (ˌmærəˈskiːnəʊ, -ˈʃiːnəʊ) *n* a liqueur made from marasca cherries and flavoured with the kernels, having a taste like bitter almonds [c18 from Italian; see MARASCA]

maraschino cherry *n* a cherry preserved in maraschino or an imitation of this liqueur, used as a garnish

marasmus (məˈræzməs) *n* pathol general emaciation and wasting, esp of infants, thought to be associated with severe malnutrition or impaired utilization of nutrients [c17 from New Latin, from Greek *marasmos*, from *marainein* to waste] > **ma'rasmic** *adj*

Maratha *or* **Mahratta** (məˈrɑːtə) *n* a member of a people of India living chiefly in Maharashtra

Marathi *or* **Mahratti** (məˈrɑːtɪ) *adj* **1** of or relating to Maharashtra state in India, its people, or their language ▷ *n* **2** the state language of Maharashtra, belonging to the Indic branch of the Indo-European family

marathon ('mærəθən) *n* **1** a race on foot of 26 miles 385 yards (42.195 kilometres): an event in the modern Olympics **2 a** any long or arduous task, assignment, etc **b** (*as modifier*): *a marathon effort* [referring to the feat of the messenger who ran more than 20 miles from Marathon to Athens to bring the news of victory in 490 BC]

Marathon ('mærəθən) *n* a plain in Attica northeast of Athens: site of a victory of the Athenians and Plataeans over the Persians (490 BC)

marathoner ('mærəθənə) *n* a person who runs in a marathon

marathon group *n* (in psychotherapy) an encounter group that lasts for many hours or days

maraud (məˈrɔːd) *vb* **1** to wander or raid in search

of plunder ▷ *n* **2** an archaic word for **foray** [c18 from French *marauder* to prowl, from *maraud* vagabond] > ma'rauder *n*

marauding (məˈrɔːdɪŋ) *adj* wandering or raiding in search of plunder or victims

maravedi (ˌmærəˈveɪdɪ) *n, pl* -dis any of various Spanish coins of copper or gold [c15 from Spanish, from Arabic *Murābitīn* (plural of *murābit* MARABOUT), the Moorish dynasty in Córdoba, 1087–1147]

Marbella (maːˈbeɪjə) *n* a coastal resort in S Spain, on the Costa del Sol. Pop: 100 000 (2004 est)

marble (ˈmaːbᵊl) *n* **1 a** a hard crystalline metamorphic rock resulting from the recrystallization of a limestone: takes a high polish and is used for building and sculpture **b** (*as modifier*): *a marble bust.* Related adj: **marmoreal 2** a block or work of art of marble **3** a small round glass or stone ball used in playing marbles **4** **make one's marble good** *Austral and NZ informal* to succeed or do the right thing **5 pass in one's marble** *Austral informal* to die ▷ *vb* **6** (*tr*) to mottle with variegated streaks in imitation of marble ▷ *adj* **7** cold, hard, or unresponsive **8** white like some kinds of marble ▷ See also **marbles** [c12 via Old French from Latin *marmor*, from Greek *marmaros*, related to Greek *marmairein* to gleam] > 'marbled *adj* > 'marbler *n* > 'marbly *adj*

marble cake *n* a cake with a marbled appearance obtained by incompletely mixing dark and light mixtures

marbled white *n* any butterfly of the satyrid genus *Melanargia*, with panelled black-and-white wings, but technically a brown butterfly; found in grassland

marbles (ˈmaːbᵊlz) *n* **1** (*functioning as singular*) a game in which marbles are rolled at one another, similar to bowls **2** (*functioning as plural*) *informal* wits: *to lose one's marbles*

marblewood (ˈmaːbᵊlˌwʊd) *n* **1** a Malaysian tree, *Diospyros marmorata*: family *Ebenaceae* **2** the distinctively marked wood of this tree, having black bands on a lighter background

marbling (ˈmaːblɪŋ) *n* **1** a mottled effect or pattern resembling marble **2** such an effect obtained by transferring floating colours from a bath of gum solution **3** the streaks of fat in lean meat

Marburg (ˈmaːˌbɜːg; *German* ˈmaːrbʊrk) *n* **1** a city in W central Germany, in Hesse: famous for the religious debate between Luther and Zwingli in 1529; Europe's first Protestant university (1527). Pop: 78 511 (2003 est) **2** the German name for **Maribor**

Marburg disease *n* a severe, sometimes fatal, viral disease of the green monkey, which may be transmitted to humans. Symptoms include fever, vomiting, and internal bleeding. Also called: **green monkey disease**

marc (maːk; *French* mar) *n* **1** the remains of grapes or other fruit that have been pressed for wine-making **2** a brandy distilled from these [c17 from French, from Old French *marchier* to trample (grapes), MARCH¹]

marcasite (ˈmaːkəˌsaɪt) *n* **1** a metallic pale yellow mineral consisting of iron sulphide in orthorhombic crystalline form used in jewellery. Formula: FeS₂ **2** a cut and polished form of steel or any white metal used for making jewellery [c15 from Medieval Latin *marcasita*, from Arabic *marqashītā*, perhaps from Persian] > marcasitical (ˌmaːkəˈsɪtɪkᵊl) *adj*

marcato (maːˈkaːtəʊ) *music* ▷ *adj* **1** (of notes) heavily accented ▷ *adv* **2** with each note heavily accented [c19 from Italian: marked]

marcel (maːˈsɛl) *n* **1** Also called: **marcel wave** a hairstyle characterized by repeated regular waves, popular in the 1920s ▷ *vb* -cels, -celling, -celled **2** (*tr*) to make such waves in (the hair) with special hot irons [c20 after *Marcel* Grateau (1852–1936), French hairdresser] > mar'celler *n*

marcescent (maːˈsɛsᵊnt) *adj* (of the parts of certain plants) remaining attached to the plant when withered [c18 from Latin *marcescere* to grow weak, from *marcēre* to wither] > mar'cescence *n*

march¹ (maːtʃ) *vb* **1** (*intr*) to walk or proceed with stately or regular steps, usually in a procession or military formation **2** (*tr*) to make (a person or group) proceed: *he marched his army to the town* **3** (*tr*) to traverse or cover by marching ▷ *n* **4** the act or an instance of marching **5** a regular stride **6** a long or exhausting walk **7** advance; progression (of time, etc) **8** a distance or route covered by marching **9** a piece of music, usually in four beats to the bar, having a strongly accented rhythm **10 steal a march on** to gain an advantage over, esp by a secret or underhand enterprise [c16 from Old French *marchier* to tread, probably of Germanic origin; compare Old English *mearcian* to MARK¹] > 'marcher *n*

march² (maːtʃ) *n* **1** Also called: **marchland** a frontier, border, or boundary or the land lying along it, often of disputed ownership ▷ *vb* **2** (*intr*; often foll by *upon* or *with*) to share a common border (with) [c13 from Old French *marche*, from Germanic; related to MARK¹]

March¹ (maːtʃ) *n* the third month of the year, consisting of 31 days [from Old French, from Latin *Martius* (month) of Mars]

March² (març) *n* the German name for the **Morava** (sense 1)

MArch *abbreviation for* Master of Architecture

March. *abbreviation for* Marchioness

march brown *n* an angler's name for the dun and spinner of various mayflies or an artificial fly imitating one of these

Marche (*French* marʃ) *n* a former province of central France

marcher (ˈmaːtʃə) *n* **1** an inhabitant of any of the Marches **2** (*formerly*) **a** a lord governing and defending such a borderland **b** (*as modifier*): *the marcher lords*

Marches (ˈmaːtʃɪz) *n* **the 1** the border area between England and Wales or Scotland, both characterized by continual feuding (13th–16th centuries) **2** a region of central Italy. Capital: Ancona. Pop: 1 484 601 (2003 est). Area: 9692 sq km (3780 sq miles). Italian name: Le Marche (le 'marke) **3** any of various other border regions

marchesa *Italian* (marˈkeːza) *n, pl* -se (-ze) (in Italy) the wife or widow of a marchese; marchioness

marchese *Italian* (marˈkeːze) *n, pl* -si (-zi) (in Italy) a nobleman ranking below a prince and above a count; marquis

Marcheshvan *Hebrew* (marxɛʃˈvan) *n* another word for **Cheshvan** [from Hebrew *mar* bitter (because it contains no festivals) + CHESHVAN]

March hare *n* a hare during its breeding season in March, noted for its wild and excitable behaviour (esp in the phrase **mad as a March hare**)

marching girl *n* (*often plural*) *Austral and NZ* one of a team of girls dressed in fancy uniform who perform marching formations

marching orders *pl n* **1** military orders, esp to infantry, giving instructions about a march, its destination, etc **2** *informal* notice of dismissal, esp from employment **3** *informal* the instruction to proceed with a task

marchioness (ˈmaːʃənɪs, ˌmaːʃəˈnɛs) *n* **1** the wife or widow of a marquis **2** a woman who holds the rank of marquis [c16 from Medieval Latin *marchionissa*, feminine of *marchiō* MARQUIS]

marchland (ˈmaːtʃˌlænd, -lənd) *n* a less common word for **borderland** or **march²**

marchpane (ˈmaːtʃˌpeɪn) *n* an archaic word for **marzipan** (sense 1) [c15 from French]

march past *n* the marching of troops on parade past a person who is reviewing them

Marcionism (ˈmaːʃəˌnɪzəm) *n* a Gnostic movement of the 2nd and 3rd centuries A.D [c16 after *Marcion* of Sinope, 2nd-century Gnostic]

Marconi rig (maːˈkəʊnɪ) *n* *nautical* a fore-and-aft sailing boat rig with triangular sails [c20 from Gugliemo *Marconi* (1874–1937), the Italian physicist who developed radiotelegraphy, from its resemblance to some types of radio aerial] > Mar'coni-ˌrigged *adj*

Mar del Plata (*Spanish* 'mar ðɛl 'plata) *n* a city and resort in E Argentina, on the Atlantic: fishing port. Pop: 552 000 (2005 est)

Mardi Gras (ˈmaːdɪ ˈgraː) *n* the festival of Shrove Tuesday, celebrated in some cities with great revelry [French: fat Tuesday]

Marduk (ˈmaːdʊk) *n* the chief god of the Babylonian pantheon

mardy (ˈmaːdɪ) *adj dialect* **1** (of a child) spoilt **2** irritable [from *marred*, past participle of MAR]

mare¹ (mɛə) *n* the adult female of a horse or zebra [c12 from Old English, of Germanic origin; related to Old High German *mariha*, Old Norse *merr* mare]

mare² (ˈmaːreɪ, -rɪ) *n, pl* maria (ˈmaːrɪə) **1** (*capital when part of a name*) any of a large number of huge dry plains on the surface of the moon, visible as dark markings and once thought to be seas: *Mare Imbrium (Sea of Showers)* **2** a similar area on the surface of Mars, such as *Mare Sirenum* [from Latin: sea]

mare clausum (ˈmaːreɪ ˈklaʊsʊm) *n law* a sea coming under the jurisdiction of one nation and closed to all others. Compare **mare liberum** [Latin: closed sea]

mare liberum (ˈmaːreɪ ˈliːbərʊm) *n law* a sea open to navigation by shipping of all nations. Compare **mare clausum** [Latin: free sea]

maremma (məˈrɛmə) *n, pl* -me (-miː) a marshy unhealthy region near the shore, esp in Italy [c19 from Italian, from Latin *maritima* MARITIME]

maremma sheepdog *n* a large strongly-built sheepdog of a breed with a long, slightly wavy, white coat

Marengo¹ (məˈrɛŋgəʊ) *adj* (*postpositive*) browned in oil and cooked with tomatoes, mushrooms, garlic, wine, etc: *chicken Marengo* [c19 after a dish prepared for Napoleon after the battle of Marengo]

Marengo² (məˈrɛŋgəʊ; *Italian* maˈrɛngo) *n* a village in NW Italy: site of a major battle in which Napoleon decisively defeated the Austrians (1800)

mare nostrum *Latin* (ˈmaːreɪ ˈnɒstrʊm) *n* the Latin name for the **Mediterranean** [literally: our sea]

mare's-nest *n* **1** a discovery imagined to be important but proving worthless **2** a disordered situation

mare's-tail *n* **1** a wisp of trailing cirrus cloud, often indicating high winds in the upper troposphere **2** an erect cosmopolitan pond plant, *Hippuris vulgaris*, with minute flowers and crowded whorls of narrow leaves: family *Hippuridaceae*

Mareva injunction (məˈriːvə) *n law* the former name for **freezing injunction** [c20 named after *Mareva Compañia Naviera SA*, the plaintiff in an early case (1975) in which such an order was made]

marg (maːdʒ) *n Brit informal* short for **margarine**

margaric (maːˈgærɪk) *or* **margaritic** *adj* of or resembling pearl [c19 from Greek *margaron* pearl]

margaric acid *n* another name for **heptadecanoic acid**

margarine (ˌmaːdʒəˈriːn, ˌmaːgə-) *n* a substitute for butter, prepared from vegetable and animal fats by emulsifying them with water and adding small amounts of milk, salt, vitamins, colouring matter, etc [c19 from MARGARIC]

margarita (ˌmaːgəˈriːtə) *n* a mixed drink consisting of tequila and lemon juice [c20 from the woman's name]

Margarita (ˌmaːgəˈriːtə) *n* an island in the Caribbean, off the NE coast of Venezuela: pearl fishing. Capital: La Asunción

margarite (ˈmaːgəˌraɪt) *n* **1** a pink pearly micaceous mineral consisting of hydrated calcium aluminium silicate. Formula: CaAl₄Si₂O₁₀(OH)₂ **2** an aggregate of minute beadlike masses occurring in some glassy igneous rocks [c19 via German from Greek *margaron* pearl]

Margate (ˈmaːgeɪt) *n* a town and resort in SE England, in E Kent on the Isle of Thanet. Pop: 58 465 (2001)

m

Margaux (*French* margo) *n* a red wine produced in the region around the village of Margaux near Bordeaux

margay ('mɑːˌgeɪ) *n* a feline mammal, *Felis wiedi,* of Central and South America, having a dark-striped coat [c18 from French, from Tupi *mbaracaiá*]

marge[1] (mɑːdʒ) *n Brit informal* short for **margarine**

marge[2] (mɑːdʒ) *n archaic* a margin [c16 from French]

margin ('mɑːdʒɪn) *n* **1** an edge or rim, and the area immediately adjacent to it; border **2** the blank space surrounding the text on a page **3** a vertical line on a page, esp one on the left-hand side, delineating this space **4** an additional amount or one beyond the minimum necessary: *a margin of error* **5** *chiefly Austral* a payment made in addition to a basic wage, esp for special skill or responsibility **6** a bound or limit **7** the amount by which one thing differs from another: *a large margin separated the parties* **8** *commerce* the profit on a transaction **9** *economics* the minimum return below which an enterprise becomes unprofitable **10** *finance* **a** collateral deposited by a client with a broker as security **b** the excess of the value of a loan's collateral over the value of the loan ▷ Also (*archaic*): **margent** ('mɑːdʒənt) ▷ *vb* (*tr*) **11** to provide with a margin; border **12** *finance* to deposit a margin upon [c14 from Latin *margō* border; related to MARCH[2], MARK[1]]

marginal ('mɑːdʒɪnᵊl) *adj* **1** of, in, on, or constituting a margin **2** close to a limit, esp a lower limit: *marginal legal ability* **3** not considered central or important; insignificant, minor, small **4** *economics* relating to goods or services produced and sold at the margin of profitability: *marginal cost* **5** *politics, chiefly Brit and NZ* of or designating a constituency in which elections tend to be won by small margins: *a marginal seat* **6** designating agricultural land on the margin of cultivated zones **7** *economics* relating to a small change in something, such as total cost, revenue, or consumer satisfaction > **marginality** (ˌmɑːdʒɪˈnælɪtɪ) *n* > **'marginally** *adv*

marginal costing *n* a method of cost accounting and decision making used for internal reporting in which only marginal costs are charged to cost units and fixed costs are treated as a lump sum. Compare **absorption costing**

marginalia (ˌmɑːdʒɪˈneɪlɪə) *pl n* notes in the margin of a book, manuscript, or letter [c19 New Latin, noun (neuter plural) from *marginālis* marginal]

marginalize or **marginalise** ('mɑːdʒɪnᵊˌlaɪz) *vb* (*tr*) to relegate to the fringes, out of the mainstream; make seem unimportant: *various economic assumptions marginalize women* > ˌmarginaliˈzation or ˌmarginaliˈsation *n*

marginal probability *n statistics* (in a multivariate distribution) the probability of one variable taking a specific value irrespective of the values of the others

marginate ('mɑːdʒɪˌneɪt) *vb* **1** (*tr*) to provide with a margin or margins ▷ *adj* **2** *biology* having a margin of a distinct colour or form: *marginate leaves* [c18 from Latin *margināre*] > ˌmarginˈation *n*

margravate ('mɑːgrəvɪt) or **margraviate** (mɑːˈgreɪvɪɪt) *n* the domain of a margrave

margrave ('mɑːgreɪv) *n* a German nobleman ranking above a count. Margraves were originally counts appointed to govern frontier provinces, but all had become princes of the Holy Roman Empire by the 12th century [c16 from Middle Dutch *markgrave*, literally: count of the MARCH[2]]

margravine ('mɑːgrəˌviːn) *n* **1** the wife or widow of a margrave **2** a woman who holds the rank of margrave [c17 from Middle Dutch, feminine of MARGRAVE]

marguerite (ˌmɑːgəˈriːt) *n* **1** a cultivated garden plant, *Chrysanthemum frutescens,* whose flower heads have white or pale yellow rays around a yellow disc: family *Asteraceae* (composites) **2** any of

various related plants with daisy-like flowers, esp *C. leucanthemum* [c19 from French: daisy, pearl, from Latin *margarīta,* from Greek *margaritēs,* from *margaron*]

Marheshvan or **Marcheshvan** *Hebrew* (marxɛʃˈvan) *n* another word for **Cheshvan**

Mari ('mɑːrɪ) *n, pl* **Mari** or **Maris** another name for **Cheremiss**

maria ('mɑːrɪə) *n* the plural of **mare[2]**

mariachi (ˌmɑːrɪˈɑːtʃɪ) *n* a small ensemble of street musicians in Mexico [c20 from Mexican Spanish]

mariage blanc *French* (marjaʒ blɑ̃) *n, pl* **mariages blancs** (marjaʒ blɑ̃) unconsummated marriage [c20 literally: white marriage]

mariage de convenance *French* (marjaʒ də kɔ̃vənɑ̃s) *n, pl* **mariages de convenance** another term for **marriage of convenience**

Marian ('mɛərɪən) *adj* **1** of or relating to the Virgin Mary, the mother of Jesus **2** of or relating to some other Mary, such as Mary Queen of Scots (1542–87; queen 1542–67) or Mary I of England (1516–58; queen 1553–58) ▷ *n* **3** a person who has a special devotion to the Virgin Mary **4** a supporter of some other Mary

Mariana Islands (ˌmærɪˈɑːnə) *pl n* a chain of volcanic and coral islands in the W Pacific, east of the Philippines and north of New Guinea: divided politically into Guam (a US unincorporated territory) and the islands north of Guam constituting the Commonwealth of the Northern Mariana Islands (a US commonwealth territory). Pop: (Guam) 165 000 (2004 est); (Northern Marianas) 79 000 (2003 est). Area: 958 sq km (370 sq miles). Former name (1521–1668): **Ladrone Islands**

Marianao (*Spanish* marjaˈnao) *n* a city in NW Cuba, adjacent to W Havana city: the chief Cuban military base. Pop: 133 015 (latest est)

Marianne (*French* marjan) *n* a female figure personifying the French republic after the Revolution (1789)

Mariánské Lázně (*Czech* 'marjanskɛ: 'la:znjɛ) *n* a town in the W Czech Republic: a fashionable spa in the 18th and 19th centuries. Pop: 15 380 (1991). German name: **Marienbad**

Maribor ('mærɪbɔː) *n* an industrial city in N Slovenia on the Drava River: a flourishing Hapsburg trading centre in the 13th century; resort. Pop: 110 668 (2002). German name: **Marburg**

mariculture ('mærɪˌkʌltʃə) *n* the cultivation of marine plants and animals in their natural environment [c20 from Latin *mari-, mare* sea + CULTURE]

Marie Byrd Land ('mɑːrɪ 'bɜːd) *n* the former name of **Byrd Land**

Marie Galante (*French* mari galɑ̃t) *n* an island in the E Caribbean southeast of Guadeloupe, of which it is a dependency. Chief town: Grand Bourg. Pop: 13 463 (1990). Area: 155 sq km (60 sq miles)

Mariehamn (mariəˈhamn) *n* a city in SW Finland, chief port of the Åland Islands. Pop: 10 693 (2004 est). Finnish name: **Maarianhamina**

Mari El Republic ('mɑːrɪ) *n* a constituent republic of W central Russia, in the middle Volga basin. Capital: Yoshkar-Ola. Pop: 728 000 (2002). Area: 23 200 sq km (8955 sq miles)

Marienbad ('mærɪənˌbæd; *German* ma'ri:ənba:t) *n* the German name for **Mariánské Lázně**

marigold ('mærɪˌgəʊld) *n* **1** any of various tropical American plants of the genus *Tagetes,* esp *T. erecta* (**African marigold**) and *T. patula* (**French marigold**), cultivated for their yellow or orange flower heads and strongly scented foliage: family *Asteraceae* (composites) **2** any of various similar or related plants, such as the marsh marigold, pot marigold, bur marigold, and fig marigold [c14 from *Mary* (the Virgin) + GOLD]

marigram ('mærɪˌgræm) *n* a graphic record of the tide levels at a particular coastal station [from

Latin *mare* sea + -GRAM]

marigraph ('mærɪˌgræf, -ˌgrɑːf) *n* a gauge for recording the levels of the tides [from Latin *mare* sea + -GRAPH]

marijuana or **marihuana** (ˌmærɪˈhwɑːnə) *n* **1** the dried leaves and flowers of the hemp plant, used for its euphoric effects, esp in the form of cigarettes. See also **cannabis 2** another name for **hemp** (the plant) [c19 from Mexican Spanish]

marimba (məˈrɪmbə) *n* a Latin American percussion instrument consisting of a set of hardwood plates placed over tuned metal resonators, played with two soft-headed sticks in each hand [c18 of West African origin]

marina (məˈriːnə) *n* an elaborate docking facility for pleasure boats [c19 via Italian and Spanish from Latin: MARINE]

marinade *n* (ˌmærɪˈneɪd) **1** a spiced liquid mixture of oil, wine, vinegar, herbs, etc, in which meat or fish is soaked before cooking **2** meat or fish soaked in this liquid ▷ *vb* ('mærɪˌneɪd) **3** a variant of **marinate** [c17 from French, from Spanish *marinada,* from *marinar* to pickle in brine, MARINATE]

marinate ('mærɪˌneɪt) *vb* to soak in marinade [c17 probably from Italian *marinato,* from *marinare* to pickle, ultimately from Latin *marīnus* MARINE] > ˌmariˈnation *n*

Marinduque (ˌmɑːrɪnˈduːkeɪ) *n* an island of the central Philippines, east of Mindoro: forms, with offshore islets, a province of the Philippines. Capital: Boac. Pop (Marinduque province): 217 392 (2000). Area: 960 sq km (370 sq miles)

marine (məˈriːn) *adj* (*usually prenominal*) **1** of, found in, or relating to the sea **2** of or relating to shipping, navigation, etc **3** of or relating to a body of seagoing troops: *marine corps* **4** of or relating to a government department concerned with maritime affairs **5** used or adapted for use at sea: *a marine camera* ▷ *n* **6** shipping and navigation in general: *the merchant marine* **7** (*capital when part of a name*) a member of a marine corps or similar body **8** a picture of a ship, seascape, etc **9** **tell it to the marines** *informal* an expression of disbelief [c15 from Old French *marin,* from Latin *marīnus,* from *mare* sea]

marine borer *n* any mollusc or crustacean that lives usually in warm seas and destroys wood by boring into and eating it. The gribble and shipworm are the best known since they penetrate any wood in favourable water. See also **piddock**

marine engineer *n* an engineer responsible for all heavy machinery on a ship or an offshore structure

marine insurance *n* insurance covering damage to or loss of ship, passengers, or cargo caused by the sea

mariner ('mærɪnə) *n* a formal or literary word for **seaman** [c13 from Anglo-French, ultimately from Latin *marīnus* MARINE]

Mariner ('mærɪnə) *n* any of a series of US space probes launched between 1962 and 1971 that sent back photographs and information concerning the surface of Mars and Venus and also studied interplanetary matter

marine railway *n* another term for **slipway** (sense 2)

marine snow *n* small particles of organic biogenic marine sediment, including the remains of organisms, faecal matter, and the shells of planktonic oganisms, that slowly drift down to the sea floor

Mariolatry or **Maryolatry** (ˌmɛərɪˈɒlətrɪ) *n derogatory* exaggerated veneration of the Virgin Mary > ˌMariˈolater or ˌMaryˈolater *n* > ˌMariˈolatrous or ˌMaryˈolatrous *adj*

Mariology or **Maryology** (ˌmɛərɪˈɒlədʒɪ) *n RC Church* the study of the traditions and doctrines concerning the Virgin Mary > ˌMariˈologist or ˌMaryˈologist *n*

marionette (ˌmærɪəˈnɛt) *n* an articulated puppet

or doll whose jointed limbs are moved by strings [c17 from French, from *Marion,* diminutive of *Marie* Mary + -ETTE]

mariposa (ˌmærɪˈpəʊzə, -sə) *n* any of several liliaceous plants of the genus *Calochortus,* of the southwestern US and Mexico, having brightly coloured tulip-like flowers. Also called: **mariposa lily** *or* **tulip** [c19 from Spanish: butterfly; from the likeness of the blooms to butterflies]

marish (ˈmærɪʃ) *adj obsolete* marshy, swampy [c14 from Old French *marais* MARSH]

Marist (ˈmɛərɪst) *RC Church* ▷ *n* **1** a member of the Society of Mary, a religious congregation founded in 1824 **2** *NZ* a teacher or pupil in a school belonging to the Marist Order ▷ *adj* **3** of a Marist [c19 from French *Mariste,* from *Marie* Mary (the virgin)]

maritage (ˈmærɪtɪdʒ) *n feudal history* **1** the right of a lord to choose the spouses of his wards **2** a sum paid to a lord in lieu of his exercising this right [c16 from Medieval Latin *marītāgium,* a Latinized form of French *mariage* marriage]

marital (ˈmærɪtᵊl) *adj* **1** of or relating to marriage: *marital status* **2** of or relating to a husband [c17 from Latin *marītālis,* from *marītus* married (adj), husband (n); related to *mās* male] > ˈmaritally *adv*

maritime (ˈmærɪˌtaɪm) *adj* **1** of or relating to navigation, shipping, etc; seafaring **2** of, relating to, near, or living near the sea **3** (of a climate) having small temperature differences between summer and winter; equable [c16 from Latin *maritimus* from *mare* sea]

Maritime Alps *pl n* a range of the W Alps in SE France and NW Italy. Highest peak: Argentera, 3297 m (10 817 ft)

Maritime Command *n Canadian* the naval branch of the Canadian armed forces

Maritime Provinces *or* **Maritimes** *pl n* **the** another name for the **Atlantic Provinces,** but often excluding Newfoundland and Labrador

Maritimer (ˈmærɪˌtaɪmə) *n* a native or inhabitant of the Maritime Provinces of Canada

Maritsa (*Bulgarian* maˈritsa) *n* a river in S Europe, rising in S Bulgaria and flowing east into Turkey, then south from Edirne as part of the border between Turkey and Greece to the Aegean. Length: 483 km (300 miles). Turkish name: **Meriç** Greek name: **Évros**

Mariupol (*Russian* məriˈupəlj) *n* a port in SE Ukraine, on an estuary leading to the Sea of Azov. Pop: 485 000 (2005 est). Former name (1948–91): Zhdanov

marjoram (ˈmɑːdʒərəm) *n* **1** Also called: **sweet marjoram** an aromatic Mediterranean plant, *Origanum* (or *Marjorana*) *hortensis,* with small pale purple flowers and sweet-scented leaves, used for seasoning food and in salads: family *Lamiaceae* (labiates) **2** Also called: **wild marjoram, pot marjoram, origan** a similar and related European plant, *Origanum vulgare* See also **oregano, origanum** [c14 via Old French *majorane,* from Medieval Latin *marjorana*]

mark¹ (mɑːk) *n* **1** a visible impression, stain, etc, on a surface, such as a spot or scratch **2** a sign, symbol, or other indication that distinguishes something: *an owner's mark* **3** a cross or other symbol made instead of a signature **4** a written or printed sign or symbol, as for punctuation: *a question mark* **5** a letter, number, or percentage used to grade academic work **6** a thing that indicates position or directs; marker **7** a desired or recognized standard: *he is not up to the mark* **8** an indication of some quality, feature, or prowess: *he has the mark of an athlete* **9** quality or importance; note: *a person of little mark* **10** a target or goal **11** impression or influence: *he left his mark on German literature* **12** one of the temperature settings on a gas oven: *gas mark 5* **13** (*often capital*) (in trade names) **a** model, brand, or type: *the car is a Mark 4* **b** a variation on a particular model: *a Mark 3 Cortina* **14** *slang* a suitable victim, esp for swindling **15** *nautical* one of the intervals

distinctively marked on a sounding lead. Compare **deep** (sense 21) **16** *bowls* another name for the **jack 17** *rugby union* an action in which a player standing inside his own 22m line catches a forward kick by an opponent and shouts "mark", entitling himself to a free kick **18** *Australian rules football* a catch of the ball from a kick of at least 10 yards, after which a free kick is taken **19** the **mark** *boxing* the middle of the stomach at or above the line made by the boxer's trunks **20** (in medieval England and Germany) a piece of land held in common by the free men of a community **21** an obsolete word for **frontier 22** *statistics* See **class mark 23** make one's mark to succeed or achieve recognition **24** on your mark *or* marks a command given to runners in a race to prepare themselves at the starting line ▷ *vb* **25** to make or receive (a visible impression, trace, or stain) on (a surface) **26** (*tr*) to characterize or distinguish: *his face was marked by anger* **27** (often foll by *off* or *out*) to set boundaries or limits (on): *to mark out an area for negotiation* **28** (*tr*) to select, designate, or doom by or as if by a mark: *to mark someone as a criminal* **29** (*tr*) to put identifying or designating labels, stamps, etc, on, esp to indicate price: *to mark the book at one pound* **30** (*tr*) to pay heed or attention to: *mark my words* **31** to observe; notice **32** to grade or evaluate (scholastic work): *she marks fairly* **33** *Brit sport* to stay close to (an opponent) to hamper his or her play **34** to keep (score) in some games **35** mark time **a** to move the feet alternately as in marching but without advancing **b** to act in a mechanical and routine way **c** to halt progress temporarily, while awaiting developments ▷ *interj* **36** *rugby union* the shout given by a player when calling for a mark ▷ See also **markdown, mark-up** [Old English *mearc* mark; related to Old Norse *mörk* boundary land, Old High German *marha* boundary, Latin *margō* MARGIN]

mark² (mɑːk) *n* **1** See **Deutschmark, markka, Reichsmark, Ostmark 2** a former monetary unit and coin in England and Scotland worth two thirds of a pound sterling **3** a silver coin of Germany until 1924 [Old English *marc* unit of weight of precious metal, perhaps from the marks on metal bars; apparently of Germanic origin and related to MARK¹]

Mark (mɑːk) *n New Testament* **1** one of the four Evangelists. Feast day: April 25 **2** the second Gospel, traditionally ascribed to him

marka (ˈmɑːkə) *n* a unit of currency introduced as an interim currency in Bosnia-Herzegovina; replaced by the euro in 2002

markdown (ˈmɑːkˌdaʊn) *n* **1** a price reduction ▷ *vb* mark down **2** (*tr, adverb*) to reduce in price

marked (mɑːkt) *adj* **1** obvious, evident, or noticeable **2** singled out, esp for punishment, killing, etc: *a marked man* **3** *linguistics* distinguished by a specific feature, as in phonology. For example, of the two phonemes /t/ and /d/, the /d/ is marked because it exhibits the feature of voice > **markedly** (ˈmɑːkɪdlɪ) *adv* > ˈmarkedness *n*

marker (ˈmɑːkə) *n* **1 a** something used for distinguishing or marking **b** (*as modifier*): *a marker buoy* **2** a person or thing that marks **3** a person or object that keeps or shows scores in a game **4** a trait, condition, gene, or substance that indicates the presence of, or a probable increased predisposition to, a medical or psychological disorder. Compare **biological marker, genetic marker, medical marker**

market (ˈmɑːkɪt) *n* **1 a** an event or occasion, usually held at regular intervals, at which people meet for the purpose of buying and selling merchandise **b** (*as modifier*): *market day* **2** a place, such as an open space in a town, at which a market is held **3** a shop that sells a particular merchandise: *an antique market* **4** the market business or trade in a commodity as specified: *the sugar market* **5** the trading or selling opportunities provided by a particular group of people: *the foreign*

market **6** demand for a particular product or commodity: *there is no market for furs here* **7** See **stock market 8** See **market price, market value 9** at market at the current price **10** be in the market for to wish to buy or acquire **11** on the market available for purchase **12** play the market **a** to speculate on a stock exchange **b** to act aggressively or unscrupulously in one's own commercial interests **13** seller's (*or* buyer's) market a market characterized by excess demand (or supply) and thus favourable to sellers (or buyers) ▷ *vb* -kets, -keting, -keted **14** (*tr*) to offer or produce for sale **15** (*intr*) to buy or deal in a market [c12 from Latin *mercātus;* from *mercārī* to trade, from *merx* merchandise] > ˈmarketer *n*

marketable (ˈmɑːkɪtəbᵊl) *adj* **1** (of commodities, assets, etc) **a** being in good demand; saleable **b** suitable for sale **2** of or relating to buying or selling on a market > ˌmarketaˈbility *or* ˈmarketableness *n* > ˈmarketably *adv*

market abuse *n* (in Britain) a statutory offence which covers insider trading and stockmarket manipulation

marketeer (ˌmɑːkɪˈtɪə) *n* **1** *Brit* a supporter of the European Union and of Britain's membership of it **2** a marketer

marketeer (ˌmɑːkəˈtɪə) *n* a person employed in marketing

market forces *pl n* the effect of supply and demand on trading within a free market

market garden *n chiefly Brit* an establishment where fruit and vegetables are grown for sale > market gardener *n*

market gardening *n chiefly Brit* the business of growing fruit and vegetables on a commercial scale. Also called (in the US and Canada): **truck farming, trucking**

marketing (ˈmɑːkɪtɪŋ) *n* the provision of goods or services to meet customer or consumer needs

marketing mix *n* the variables, such as price, promotion, and service, managed by an organization to influence demand for a product or service

marketing research *or* **market research** *n* the study of influences upon customer and consumer behaviour and the analysis of market characteristics and trends

market maker *n* a dealer in securities on the London Stock Exchange who buys and sells as a principal and since 1986 can also deal with the public as a broker

market order *n* an instruction to a broker to sell or buy at the best price currently obtainable on the market

marketplace (ˈmɑːkɪtˌpleɪs) *n* **1** a place where a public market is held **2** any centre where ideas, opinions, etc, are exchanged **3** the commercial world of buying and selling

market price *n* the prevailing price, as determined by supply and demand, at which goods, services, etc, may be bought or sold

market rent *n* (in Britain) the rent chargeable for accommodation, allowing for the scarcity of that kind of property and the willingness of tenants to pay

market research *n* the study of influences upon customer and consumer behaviour and the analysis of market characteristics and trends

market segment *n* a part of a market identifiable as having particular customers with specific buying characteristics

market segmentation *n* the division of a market into identifiable groups, esp to improve the effectiveness of a marketing strategy

market share *n* the percentage of a total market, in terms of either value or volume, accounted for by the sales of a specific brand

market-test *vb* (*tr*) to put (a section of a public-sector enterprise) out to tender, often as a prelude to full-scale privatization

market town *n chiefly Brit* a town that holds a market, esp an agricultural centre in a rural area

m

market value *n* the amount obtainable on the open market for the sale of property, financial assets, or goods and services. Compare **par value, book value**

Markham ('mɑːkəm) *n* **Mount** a mountain in Antarctica, in Victoria Land. Height: 4350 m (14 272 ft)

markhor ('mɑːkɔː) *or* **markhoor** ('mɑːkʊə) *n, pl* -khors, -khor *or* -khoors, -khoor a large wild Himalayan goat, *Capra falconeri,* with a reddish-brown coat and large spiralled horns [C19 from Persian, literally: snake-eater, from *mār* snake + -*khōr* eating]

marking ('mɑːkɪŋ) *n* **1** a mark or series of marks **2** the arrangement of colours on an animal, plant, etc **3** assessment and correction of school children's or students' written work by teaching staff

marking ink *n* indelible ink used for marking linen, clothes, etc

markka ('mɑːkɑː, -kə) *n, pl* -kaa (-kɑː) the former standard monetary unit of Finland, divided into 100 penniä; replaced by the euro in 2002 [Finnish. See MARK²]

Markov chain ('mɑːkɒf) *n statistics* a sequence of events the probability for each of which is dependent only on the event immediately preceding it [C20 named after Andrei *Markov* (1856–1922), Russian mathematician]

marksman ('mɑːksmən) *n, pl* -men **1** a person skilled in shooting **2** a serviceman selected for his skill in shooting, esp for a minor engagement **3** a qualification awarded in certain armed services for skill in shooting > '**marksman,ship** *n* > '**marks,woman** *feminine noun*

mark-up *n* **1** a percentage or amount added to the cost of a commodity to provide the seller with a profit and to cover overheads, costs, etc **2 a** an increase in the price of a commodity **b** the amount of this increase > *vb* **mark up** (*tr, adverb*) **3** to add a percentage for profit, overheads, etc, to the cost of (a commodity) **4** to increase the price of

marl¹ (mɑːl) *n* **1** a fine-grained sedimentary rock consisting of clay minerals, calcite or aragonite, and silt: used as a fertilizer > *vb* **2** (*tr*) to fertilize (land) with marl [C14 via Old French, from Late Latin *margila,* diminutive of Latin *marga*] > **marlacious** (mɑːˈleɪʃəs) *or* '**marly** *adj*

marl² (mɑːl) *vb nautical* to seize (a rope) with marline, using a hitch at each turn [C15 *marlyn* to bind; related to Dutch *marlen* to tie, Old English *mǣrels* cable]

Marlborough ('mɑːlbərə, -brə, 'mɔːl-) *n* a town in S England, in Wiltshire: besieged and captured by Royalists in the Civil War (1642); site of Marlborough College, a public school founded in 1843. Pop: 7713 (2001)

marlin ('mɑːlɪn) *n, pl* -lin *or* -lins any of several large scombroid fish and game fishes of the genera *Makaira, Istiompax,* and *Tetrapturus,* of warm and tropical seas, having a very long upper jaw: family *Istiophoridae.* Also called: **spearfish** [C20 from MARLINESPIKE; with allusion to the shape of the beak]

marline, marlin ('mɑːlɪn) *or less commonly* **marling** ('mɑːlɪŋ) *n nautical* a light rope, usually tarred, made of two strands laid left-handed [C15 from Dutch *marlijn,* from *marren* to tie + *lijn* line]

marlinespike, marlinspike ('mɑːlɪn,spaɪk) *or less commonly* **marlingspike** ('mɑːlɪŋ,spaɪk) *n nautical* a pointed metal tool used as a fid, spike, and for various other purposes

marlite ('mɑːlaɪt) *or* **marlstone** ('mɑːl,stəʊn) *n* a type of marl that contains clay and calcium carbonate and is resistant to the decomposing action of air

marmalade ('mɑːmə,leɪd) *n* **1** a preserve made by boiling the pulp and rind of citrus fruits, esp oranges, with sugar > *adj* **2** (of cats) streaked orange or yellow and brown [C16 via French from Portuguese *marmelada,* from *marmelo* quince, from

Latin, from Greek *melimēlon,* from *meli* honey + *mēlon* apple]

marmalade tree *n* a tropical American sapotaceous tree, *Calocarpum sapota,* with durable wood: its fruit is used to make preserves. Also called: mamey

marmalise *or* **marmalize** ('mɑːmə,laɪz) *vb* (*tr*) *slang* to beat soundly or defeat utterly; thrash [C20 a humorous coinage]

Marmara *or* **Marmora** ('mɑːmərə) *n* **Sea of** a deep inland sea in NW Turkey, linked with the Black Sea by the Bosporus and with the Aegean by the Dardanelles: separates Turkey in Europe from Turkey in Asia. Area: 11 471 sq km (4429 sq miles). Ancient name: Propontis

marmite ('mɑːmaɪt) *n* **1** a large cooking pot **2** soup cooked in such a pot **3** an individual covered casserole for serving soup **4** *US military* a container used to bring food to troops in the field [from French: pot]

Marmite ('mɑːmaɪt) *n trademark Brit* a yeast and vegetable extract used as a spread, flavouring, etc

Marmolada (*Italian* marmoˈlaːda) *n* a mountain in NE Italy: highest peak in the Dolomites. Height: 3342 m (10 965 ft)

marmoreal (mɑːˈmɔːrɪəl) *or less commonly* **marmorean** *adj* of, relating to, or resembling marble: *a marmoreal complexion* [C18 from Latin *marmoreus,* from *marmor* marble] > marˈmoreally *adv*

marmoset ('mɑːmə,zɛt) *n* **1** any small South American monkey of the genus *Callithrix* and related genera, having long hairy tails, clawed digits, and tufts of hair around the head and ears: family *Callithricidae* **2 pygmy marmoset** a related form, *Cebuella pygmaea*: the smallest monkey, inhabiting tropical forests of the Amazon [C14 from Old French *marmouset* grotesque figure, of obscure origin]

marmot ('mɑːmət) *n* **1** any burrowing sciurine rodent of the genus *Marmota,* of Europe, Asia, and North America. They are heavily built, having short legs, a short furry tail, and coarse fur **2 prairie marmot** another name for **prairie dog** [C17 from French *marmotte,* perhaps ultimately from Latin *mūr-* (stem of *mūs*) mouse + *montis* of the mountain]

Marne (*French* marn) *n* **1** a department of NE France, in Champagne-Ardenne region. Capital: Châlons-sur-Marne. Pop: 563 027 (2003 est). Area: 8205 sq km (3200 sq miles) **2** a river in NE France, rising on the plateau of Langres and flowing north, then west to the River Seine, north of Paris: linked by canal with the Rivers Saône, Rhine, and Aisne; scene of two unsuccessful German offensives (1914, 1918) during World War I. Length: 525 km (326 miles)

Maroc (marɔk) *n* the French name for **Morocco**

marocain ('mærə,keɪn) *n* **1** a fabric of ribbed crepe **2** a garment made from this fabric [C20 from French *maroquin* Moroccan]

Maronite ('mærə,naɪt) *n Christianity* a member of a body of Uniats of Syrian origin, now living chiefly in Lebanon [C16 from Late Latin *Marōnīta,* after *Maro,* 5th-century Syrian monk]

maroon¹ (məˈruːn) *vb* (*tr*) **1** to leave ashore and abandon, esp on an island **2** to isolate without resources > *n* **3** a descendant of a group of runaway slaves living in the remoter areas of the Caribbean or Guyana **4** *US and Canadian informal* a person who has been marooned, esp on an island [C17 (applied to fugitive slaves): from American Spanish *cimarrón* wild, literally: dwelling on peaks, from Spanish *cima* summit]

maroon² (məˈruːn) *n* **1 a** a dark red to purplish-red colour **b** (*as adjective*): *a maroon carpet* **2** an exploding firework, esp one used as a warning signal [C18 from French, literally: chestnut, MARRON¹]

maroquin (,mærəˈkiːn, 'mærəkɪn, -kwɪn) *n tanning* morocco leather [C16 from French: Moroccan]

Maros ('mɒrɒʃ) *n* the Hungarian name for the **Mureș**

Marq. *abbreviation for* Marquis

marque (mɑːk) *n* **1** a brand of product, esp of a car **2** an emblem or nameplate used to identify a product, esp a car **3** See **letter of marque** [from French, from *marquer* to MARK¹]

marquee (mɑːˈkiː) *n* **1** a large tent used for entertainment, exhibition, etc **2** Also called: marquise *chiefly US and Canadian* a canopy over the entrance to a theatre, hotel, etc **3** (*modifier*) *chiefly US and Canadian* celebrated or pre-eminent: *a marquee player* [C17 (originally an officer's tent): invented singular form of MARQUISE, erroneously taken to be plural]

Marquesan (mɑːˈkeɪzᵊn, -sᵊn) *adj* **1** of or relating to the Marquesas Islands or their inhabitants > *n* **2** a native or inhabitant of the Marquesas Islands

Marquesas Islands (mɑːˈkeɪsəs) *pl n* a group of volcanic islands in the S Pacific, in French Polynesia. Pop: 8712 (2002). Area: 1287 sq km (497 sq miles). French name: Îles Marquises (il markiz)

marquess ('mɑːkwɪs) *n* **1** (in the British Isles) a nobleman ranking between a duke and an earl **2** See **marquis**

marquessate ('mɑːkwɪzɪt) *n* (in the British Isles) the dignity, rank, or position of a marquess; marquisate

marquetry *or* **marqueterie** ('mɑːkɪtrɪ) *n, pl* -quetries *or* -queteries a pattern of inlaid veneers of wood, brass, ivory, etc, fitted together to form a picture or design, used chiefly as ornamentation in furniture. Compare **parquetry** [C16 from Old French, from *marqueter* to inlay, from *marque* MARK¹]

marquis ('mɑːkwɪs, mɑːˈkiː; *French* marki) *n, pl* -quises *or* -quis (in various countries) a nobleman ranking above a count, corresponding to a British marquess. The title of marquis is often used in place of that of marquess [C14 from Old French *marchis,* literally: count of the march, from *marche* MARCH²]

marquisate ('mɑːkwɪzɪt) *n* **1** the rank or dignity of a marquis **2** the domain of a marquis

marquise (mɑːˈkiːz; *French* markiz) *n* **1** (in various countries) another word for **marchioness 2 a** a gemstone, esp a diamond, cut in a pointed oval shape and usually faceted **b** a piece of jewellery, esp a ring, set with such a stone or with an oval cluster of stones **3** another name for **marquee** (sense 2) [C18 from French, feminine of MARQUIS]

marquisette (,mɑːkɪˈzɛt, -kwɪ-) *n* a leno-weave fabric of cotton, silk, etc [C20 from French, diminutive of MARQUISE]

Marrakech *or* **Marrakesh** (məˈrækɛʃ, ,mærəˈkɛʃ) *n* a city in W central Morocco: several times capital of Morocco; tourist centre. Pop: 672 000 (2003)

marram grass ('mærəm) *n* any of several grasses of the genus *Ammophila,* esp *A. arenaria,* that grow on sandy shores and can withstand drying: often planted to stabilize sand dunes [C17 *marram,* from Old Norse *marálmr,* from *marr* sea + *hálmr* HAULM]

Marrano (məˈrɑːnəʊ) *n, pl* -nos a Spanish or Portuguese Jew of the late Middle Ages who was converted to Christianity, esp one forcibly converted but secretly adhering to Judaism [from Spanish, literally: pig, with reference to the Jewish prohibition against eating pig meat]

marri ('mærɪ) *n, pl* -ris a species of eucalyptus, *Eucalyptus calophylla,* of Western Australia, widely cultivated for its coloured flowers [C19 from a native Australian language]

marriage ('mærɪdʒ) *n* **1** the state or relationship of being husband and wife **2 a** the legal union or contract made by a man and woman to live as husband and wife **b** (*as modifier*): *marriage licence; marriage certificate* **3** the religious or legal ceremony formalizing this union; wedding **4** a close or intimate union, relationship, etc: *a marriage of ideas* **5** (in certain card games, such as bezique, pinochle) the king and queen of the same suit > Related adjectives: **conjugal, marital, nuptial** [C13 from Old French; see MARRY¹, -AGE]

marriageable ('mærɪdʒəbᵊl) *adj* (esp of women)

suitable for marriage, usually with reference to age > ˌmarriageaˈbility *or* ˈmarriageableness *n*

marriage bureau *n* an agency that provides introductions to single people seeking a marriage partner

marriage guidance *n* **a** advice given to couples who have problems in their married life **b** (*as modifier*): *a marriage guidance counsellor*

marriage of convenience *n* a marriage based on expediency rather than on love

married ('mærɪd) *adj* **1** having a husband or wife **2** joined in marriage **3** of or involving marriage or married persons **4** closely or intimately united ▷ *n* **5** (*usually plural*) a married person (esp in the phrase *young marrieds*)

marron¹ ('mærən; *French* marɔ̃) *n* a large edible sweet chestnut [from French, of obscure origin]

marron² ('mærən) *n* a large freshwater crayfish of Western Australia, *Cherax tenuimanus* [from a native Australian language]

marrons glacés *French* (marɔ̃ glase) *pl n* chestnuts cooked in syrup and glazed

marrow¹ ('mærəʊ) *n* **1** the fatty network of connective tissue that fills the cavities of bones **2** the vital part; essence **3** vitality **4** rich food **5** *Brit* short for **vegetable marrow** [Old English *mærg*; related to Old Frisian *merg*, Old Norse *mergr*] > ˈmarrowy *adj*

marrow² ('mærəʊ, -rə) *n* *Northeastern English dialect, chiefly Durham* a companion, esp a workmate [C15 *marwe* fellow worker, perhaps of Scandinavian origin; compare Icelandic *margr* friendly]

marrowbone ('mærəʊˌbəʊn) *n* **a** a bone containing edible marrow **b** (*as modifier*): *marrowbone jelly*

marrowbones ('mærəʊˌbəʊnz) *pl n* **1** *facetious* the knees **2** a rare word for **crossbones**. See **skull and crossbones**

marrow fat ('mærəʊˌfæt) *or* **marrow pea** *n* **1** any of several varieties of pea plant that have large seeds **2** the seed of such a plant

marrow squash *n* *US and Canadian* any of several oblong squashes that have a hard smooth rind, esp the vegetable marrow

marry¹ ('mærɪ) *vb* -ries, -rying, -ried **1** to take (someone as one's husband or wife) in marriage **2** (*tr*) to join or give in marriage **3** (*tr*) to acquire (something) by marriage: *marry money* **4** to unite closely or intimately **5** (*tr; sometimes foll by up*) to fit together or align (two things); join **6** (*tr*) *nautical* **a** to match up (the strands) of unlaid ropes before splicing **b** to seize (two ropes) together at intervals along their lengths ▷ See also **marry up** [C13 from Old French *marier*, from Latin *marītāre*, from *marītus* married (man), perhaps from *mās* male] > ˈmarrier *n*

marry² ('mærɪ) *interj archaic* an exclamation of surprise, anger, etc [C14 euphemistic for the Virgin *Mary*]

marry into *vb* (*intr, preposition*) to become a member of (a family) by marriage

marry off *vb* (*tr, adverb*) to find a husband or wife for (a person, esp one's son or daughter)

marry up *vb* (*adverb*) **1** (*tr*) to join **2** (*intr*) to tally or correspond **3** (*intr*) to marry someone of a higher social class than oneself

Mars¹ (mɑːz) *n* the Roman god of war, the father of Romulus and Remus. Greek counterpart: **Ares**

Mars² (mɑːz) *n* **1** Also called: **the Red Planet** the fourth planet from the sun, having a reddish-orange surface with numerous dark patches and two white polar caps. It has a thin atmosphere, mainly carbon dioxide, and low surface temperatures. Spacecraft encounters have revealed a history of volcanic activity and running surface water. The planet has two tiny satellites, Phobos and Deimos. Mean distance from sun: 228 million km; period of revolution around sun: 686.98 days; period of axial rotation: 24.6225 hours; diameter and mass: 53.2 and 10.7 per cent that of earth respectively **2** the alchemical name for **iron**

Marsala (mɑːˈsɑːlə) *n* **1** a port in W Sicily: landing place of Garibaldi at the start of his Sicilian campaign (1860). Pop: 77 784 (2001) **2** (*sometimes not capital*) a dark sweet dessert wine made in Sicily

Marsanne (mɑːˈsæn) *n* **1** a white grape grown in the N Rhône region of France and in California and Australia, used for making wine **2** a full-bodied white wine made from this grape

Marseillaise (ˌmɑːseɪˈleɪz; *French* marsɛjɛz) *n* **the** the French national anthem. Words and music were composed in 1792 by C. J. Rouget de Lisle as a war song for the Rhine army of revolutionary France [C18 from French (*chanson*) *Marseillaise* song of Marseille (it was first sung in Paris by the battalion of Marseille)]

marseille (mɑːˈseɪl) *or* **marseilles** (mɑːˈseɪlz) *n* a strong cotton fabric with a raised pattern, used for bedspreads, etc [C18 from *Marseille* quilting, made in Marseille]

Marseille (*French* marsɛj) *n* a port in SE France, on the Gulf of Lions: second largest city in the country and a major port; founded in about 600 BC by Greeks from Phocaea; oil refining. Pop: 798 430 (1999). Ancient name: **Massilia** English name: **Marseilles** (mɑːˈseɪ, -ˈseɪlz)

marsh (mɑːʃ) *n* low poorly drained land that is sometimes flooded and often lies at the edge of lakes, streams, etc. Related adj: **paludal** Compare **swamp** (sense 1) [Old English *merisc*; related to German *Marsch*, Dutch *marsk*; related to MERE²] > ˈmarshˌlike *adj*

marshal ('mɑːʃəl) *n* **1** (in some armies and air forces) an officer of the highest rank **2** (in England) an officer, usually a junior barrister, who accompanies a judge on circuit and performs miscellaneous secretarial duties **3** (in the US) **a** a Federal court officer assigned to a judicial district whose functions are similar to those of a sheriff **b** (in some states) the chief police or fire officer **4** an officer who organizes or conducts ceremonies, parades, etc **5** Also called: **knight marshal** (formerly in England) an officer of the royal family or court, esp one in charge of protocol **6** an obsolete word for **ostler** ▷ *vb* -shals, -shalling, -shalled *or US* -shals, -shaling, -shaled (*tr*) **7** to arrange in order: *to marshal the facts* **8** to assemble and organize (troops, vehicles, etc) prior to onward movement **9** to arrange (assets, mortgages, etc) in order of priority **10** to guide or lead, esp in a ceremonious way **11** to combine (two or more coats of arms) on one shield [C13 from Old French *mareschal*; related to Old High German *marahscalc* groom, from *marah* horse + *scalc* servant] > ˈmarshalcy *or* ˈmarshalˌship *n* > ˈmarshaller *or US* ˈmarshalar *n*

marshalling yard *n* *railways* a place or depot where railway wagons are shunted and made up into trains and where engines, carriages, etc, are kept when not in use

Marshall Islands (ˈmɑːʃəl) *pl n* a republic, consisting of a group of 34 coral islands in the W central Pacific: administratively part of the Trust Territory of the Pacific Islands (1947–87); status of free association with the US from 1986; consists of two parallel chains, Ralik and Ratak. Official languages: Marshallese and English. Religion: Roman Catholic majority. Currency: US dollar. Capital: Majuro. Pop: 53 000 (2003 est). Area: (land) 181 sq km (70 sq miles); (lagoon) 11 655 sq km (4500 sq miles)

Marshall Plan *n* a programme of US economic aid for the reconstruction of post-World War II Europe (1948–52). Official name: **European Recovery Programme**

Marshal of the Royal Air Force *n* a rank in the Royal Air Force comparable to that of Field Marshal in the British army

Marshalsea (ˈmɑːʃəlˌsiː) *n* **1** (formerly in England) a court held before the knight marshal: abolished 1849 **2** a prison for debtors and others, situated in Southwark, London: abolished in 1842 [C14 see MARSHAL, -CY]

marsh andromeda *n* a low-growing pink-flowered ericaceous evergreen shrub, *Andromeda polifolia*, that grows in peaty bogs of northern regions. Also called: **moorwort, bog rosemary**

marshbuck ('mɑːʃˌbʌk) *n* an antelope of the central African swamplands, *Strepsiceros spekei*, with spreading hoofs adapted to boggy ground; an important vector of the tsetse fly. Also called: **sitatunga**

marsh elder *n* any of several North American shrubs of the genus *Iva*, growing in salt marshes: family *Asteraceae* (composites). Compare **elder²**

marsh fern *n* a fern of marshy woodlands, *Thelypteris palustris*, having pale green pinnate leaves and an underground rootstock

marsh fever *n* another name for **malaria**

marsh gas *n* a hydrocarbon gas largely composed of methane formed when organic material decays in the absence of air

marsh harrier *n* **1** a European harrier, *Circus aeruginosus*, that frequents marshy regions **2** Also: **marsh hawk** *US and Canadian* a common harrier, *Circus cyaneus*, that flies over fields and marshes and nests in marshes and open land. Also called (in Britain and certain other countries): **hen harrier**

marsh hawk *n* another name for **marsh harrier** (sense 2)

marsh hen *n* any bird that frequents marshes and swamps, esp a rail, coot, or gallinule

marshland ('mɑːʃlənd) *n* land consisting of marshes

marshmallow (ˌmɑːʃˈmæləʊ) *n* **1** a sweet of a spongy texture containing gum arabic or gelatine, sugar, etc **2** a sweetened paste or confection made from the root of the marsh mallow > ˌmarshˈmallowy *adj*

marsh mallow *n* **1** a malvaceous plant, *Althaea officinalis*, that grows in salt marshes and has pale pink flowers. The roots yield a mucilage formerly used to make marshmallows **2** *US and Canadian* another name for **rose mallow** (sense 1)

marsh marigold *n* a yellow-flowered ranunculaceous plant, *Caltha palustris*, that grows in swampy places. Also called: **kingcup, May blobs**, and (*US*) **cowslip**

marsh orchid *n* any of various orchids of the genus *Dactylorhiza*, growing in damp places and having mostly purplish flowers

marsh tit *n* a small European songbird, *Parus palustris*, with a black head and greyish-brown body: family *Paridae* (tits)

marshwort ('mɑːʃˌwɜːt) *n* a prostrate creeping aquatic perennial umbelliferous plant of the genus *Apium*, esp *A. inundatum*, having small white flowers: related to wild celery

marshy ('mɑːʃɪ) *adj* marshier, marshiest of, involving, or like a marsh > ˈmarshiness *n*

marsipobranch ('mɑːsɪpəʊˌbræŋk) *n, adj* another word for **cyclostome** [C19 from New Latin *Marsipobranchia*, from Greek *marsipos* pouch + *branchia* gills]

Marston Moor *n* a flat low-lying area in NE England, west of York: scene of a battle (1644) in which the Parliamentarians defeated the Royalists

marsupial (mɑːˈsjuːpɪəl, -ˈsuː-) *n* **1** any mammal of the order *Marsupialia*, in which the young are born in an immature state and continue development in the marsupium. The order occurs mainly in Australia and South and Central America and includes the opossums, bandicoots, koala, wombats, and kangaroos ▷ *adj* **2** of, relating to, or belonging to the *Marsupialia* **3** of or relating to a marsupium [C17 see MARSUPIUM] > marsupialian (mɑːˌsjuːpɪˈeɪlɪən, -ˌsuː-) *or* marˈsupian *n, adj*

marsupial mole *n* any molelike marsupial of the family *Notoryctidae*

marsupial mouse *n* any mouselike insectivorous marsupial of the subfamily *Phascogalinae*: family *Dasyuridae*

m

marsupium (maːˈsjuːpɪəm, -ˈsuː-) *n, pl* **-pia** (-pɪə) an external pouch in most female marsupials within which the newly born offspring are suckled and complete their development [c17 New Latin, from Latin: purse, from Greek *marsupion*, diminutive of *marsipos*]

mart (maːt) *n* a market or trading centre [c15 from Middle Dutch *mart* MARKET]

Martaban (ˌmaːtaːˈbaːn) *n* **Gulf of** an inlet of the Bay of Bengal in Myanmar

martagon or **martagon lily** (ˈmaːtəgən) *n* a Eurasian lily plant, *Lilium martagon*, cultivated for its mottled purplish-red flowers with reflexed petals. Also called: **Turk's-cap lily** [c15 from French, from Turkish *martagān* a type of turban]

martellato (ˌmaːtəˈlaːtəʊ) or **martellando** *n* (in string playing) the practice of bowing the string with a succession of short sharp blows [Italian: hammered]

Martello tower or **Martello** (maːˈtɛləʊ) *n* a small circular tower for coastal defence, formerly much used in Europe [c18 after Cape *Mortella* in Corsica, where the British navy captured a tower of this type in 1794]

marten (ˈmaːtɪn) *n, pl* **-tens** or **-ten** **1** any of several agile arboreal musteline mammals of the genus *Martes*, of Europe, Asia, and North America, having bushy tails and golden brown to blackish fur. See also **pine marten** **2** the highly valued fur of these animals, esp that of *M. americana* ▷ See also **sable** (sense 1) [c15 from Middle Dutch *martren*, from Old French (*peau*) *martrine* skin of a marten, from *martre*, probably of Germanic origin]

martensite (ˈmaːtɪnˌzaɪt) *n* a constituent formed in steels by rapid quenching, consisting of a supersaturated solid solution of carbon in iron. It is formed by the breakdown of austenite when the rate of cooling is large enough to prevent pearlite forming [c20 named after Adolf *Martens* (died 1914), German metallurgist] > **martensitic** (ˌmaːtɪnˈzɪtɪk) *adj*

martial (ˈmaːʃəl) *adj* of, relating to, or characteristic of war, soldiers, or the military life [c14 from Latin *martiālis* of MARS¹] > **'martialism** *n* > **'martialist** *n* > **'martially** *adv* > **'martialness** *n*

Martial (ˈmaːʃəl) *adj* of or relating to Mars

martial art *n* any of various philosophies of self-defence and techniques of single combat, such as judo or karate, originating in the Far East

martial law *n* the rule of law established and maintained by the military in the absence of civil law

Martian (ˈmaːʃən) *adj* **1** of, occurring on, or relating to the planet Mars ▷ *n* **2** an inhabitant of Mars, esp in science fiction

martin (ˈmaːtɪn) *n* any of various swallows of the genera *Progne, Delichon, Riparia*, etc, having a square or slightly forked tail. See also **house martin** [c15 perhaps from St *Martin* (??316–??397 AD), bishop of Tours, because the birds were believed to migrate at the time of Martinmas]

martinet (ˌmaːtɪˈnɛt) *n* a person who maintains strict discipline, esp in a military force [c17 from French, from the name of General *Martinet*, drillmaster under Louis XIV] > ˌmarti'netish *adj* > ˌmarti'netism *n*

martingale (ˈmaːtɪnˌgeɪl) *n* **1** a strap from the reins to the girth of a horse preventing it from carrying its head too high **2** any gambling system in which the stakes are raised, usually doubled, after each loss **3** Also called: **martingale boom** *nautical* **a** a chain or cable running from a jib boom to the dolphin striker, serving to counteract strain **b** another term for **dolphin striker** [c16 from French, of uncertain origin]

Martini (maːˈtiːnɪ) *n, pl* **-nis** **1** *trademark* an Italian vermouth **2** a cocktail of gin and vermouth [C19 (sense 2): perhaps from the name of the inventor]

Martinican (ˌmaːtɪˈniːkən) *adj* **1** of or relating to the Caribbean island of Martinique or its inhabitants ▷ *n* **2** a native or inhabitant of Martinique

Martinique (ˌmaːtɪˈniːk) *n* an island in the E Caribbean, in the Windward Islands of the Lesser Antilles: administratively an overseas region of France. Capital: Fort-de-France. Pop: 395 000 (2004 est). Area: 1090 sq km (420 sq miles)

Martinmas (ˈmaːtɪnməs) *n* the feast of St Martin on Nov 11; one of the four quarter days in Scotland

martlet (ˈmaːtlɪt) *n* **1** an archaic name for a **martin 2** *heraldry* a footless bird often found in coats of arms, standing for either a martin or a swallow [c16 from French *martelet*, variant of *martinet*, diminutive of MARTIN]

martyr (ˈmaːtə) *n* **1** a person who suffers death rather than renounce his religious beliefs **2** a person who suffers greatly or dies for a cause, belief, etc **3** a person who suffers from poor health, misfortune, etc: *he's a martyr to rheumatism* **4** *facetious or derogatory* a person who feigns suffering to gain sympathy, help, etc ▷ *vb also* **'martyr'ize** or **'martyr'ise** (*tr*) **5** to kill as a martyr **6** to make a martyr of [Old English *martir*, from Church Latin *martyr*, from Late Greek *martur-, martus* witness] > ˌmartyri'zation or ˌmartyri'sation *n*

martyrdom (ˈmaːtədəm) *n* **1** the sufferings or death of a martyr **2** great suffering or torment

martyrology (ˌmaːtəˈrɒlədʒɪ) *n, pl* **-gies 1** an official list of martyrs **2** *Christianity* the study of the lives of the martyrs **3** a historical account of the lives of martyrs > **martyrological** (ˌmaːtərəˈlɒdʒɪkəl) or ˌmartyro'logic *adj* > ˌmarty'rologist *n*

martyry (ˈmaːtərɪ) *n, pl* **-tyries** a shrine or chapel erected in honour of a martyr

MARV (maːv) *n acronym for* manoeuvrable re-entry vehicle: a missile that has one or more warheads that may be controlled so as to avoid enemy defences

marvel (ˈmaːvəl) *vb* **-vels, -velling, -velled** or *US* **-vels, -veling, -veled** **1** (when *intr*, often foll by *at* or *about*; when *tr, takes a clause as object*) to be filled with surprise or wonder ▷ *n* **2** something that causes wonder **3** *archaic* astonishment [c13 from Old French *merveille*, from Late Latin *mīrābilia*, from Latin *mīrābilis*, from *mīrārī* to wonder at]

marvellous or *US* **marvelous** (ˈmaːvələs) *adj* **1** causing great wonder, surprise, etc; extraordinary **2** improbable or incredible **3** excellent; splendid > **'marvellously** or *US* **'marvelously** *adv* > **'marvellousness** or *US* **'marvelousness** *n*

marvel-of-Peru *n, pl* **marvels-of-Peru** another name for **four-o'clock** (the plant) [c16 first found in Peru]

Marxian (ˈmaːksɪən) *adj* of or relating to Karl Marx (1818–83), the German founder of modern Communism, and his theories > **'Marxianism** *n*

Marxism (ˈmaːksɪzəm) *n* the economic and political theory and practice originated by the German political philosophers Karl Marx (1818–83) and Friedrich Engels (1820–95), that holds that actions and human institutions are economically determined, that the class struggle is the basic agency of historical change, and that capitalism will ultimately be superseded by communism

Marxism-Leninism *n* the modification of Marxism by the Russian statesman and Marxist theoretician V. I. Lenin (1870–1924) stressing that imperialism is the highest form of capitalism > **'Marxist-'Leninist** *n, adj*

Marxist (ˈmaːksɪst) *n* **1** a follower of Marxism ▷ *adj* **2** (of an economic or political theory) analogous to or derived from the doctrines of Karl Marx (1818–83), the German founder of modern Communism **3** of or relating to Marx, Marxism, or Marxists and their theories

Mary (ˈmɛərɪ) *n* **1** *New Testament* **a** **Saint** Also called: the **Virgin Mary**. the mother of Jesus, believed to have conceived and borne him while still a virgin; she was married to Joseph (Matthew 1:18–25). Major feast days: Feb 2, Mar 25, May 31, Aug 15, Sept 8 **b** the sister of Martha and Lazarus (Luke 10:38–42; John 11:1–2) **2** *pl* **Maries** *Austral*

obsolete derogatory slang an Aboriginal woman or girl

mary jane *n US and Canadian* a slang term for **marijuana**

Maryland (ˈmɛərɪˌlænd, ˈmɛrɪlənd) *n* a state of the eastern US, on the Atlantic: divided into two unequal parts by Chesapeake Bay: mostly low-lying, with the Alleghenies in the northwest. Capital: Annapolis. Pop: 5 508 909 (2003 est). Area: 31 864 sq km (12 303 sq miles). Abbreviations: Md, (with zip code) MD

Mary Magdalene *n New Testament* **Saint** a woman of **Magdala** (ˈmægdələ) in Galilee whom Jesus cured of evil spirits (Luke 8:2) and who is often identified with the sinful woman of Luke 7:36–50. In Christian tradition she is usually taken to have been a prostitute. See **magdalen**. Feast day: July 22

Maryolatry (ˌmɛərɪˈɒlətrɪ) *n* a variant spelling of **Mariolatry**

Maryology (ˌmɛərɪˈɒlədʒɪ) *n* a variant spelling of **Mariology**

marzipan (ˈmaːzɪˌpæn) *n* **1** a paste made from ground almonds, sugar, and egg whites, used to coat fruit cakes or moulded into sweets. Also called (esp formerly): **marchpane** ▷ *modifier* **2** *informal* of or relating to the stratum of middle managers in a financial institution or other business: *marzipan layer job losses* [c19 via German from Italian *marzapane*. See MARCHPANE]

mas (maːs) *n* **1** *Caribbean* a carnival **2** music played for a carnival, or a band playing this [c20 from MASQUERADE]

-mas *n combining form* indicating a Christian festival: *Christmas; Michaelmas* [from MASS]

Masada (məˈsaːdə) *n* an ancient mountaintop fortress in Israel, 400 m (1300 ft) above the W shore of the Dead Sea: the last Jewish stronghold during a revolt in Judaea (66–73 AD). Besieged by the Romans for a year, almost all of the inhabitants killed themselves rather than surrender. The site is an Israeli national monument

Masai (ˈmaːsaɪ, maːˈsaɪ, ˈmæsaɪ) *n* **1** (*pl* **-sais** or **-sai**) a member of a Nilotic people, formerly noted as warriors, living chiefly in Kenya and Tanzania **2** the language of this people, belonging to the Nilotic group of the Nilo-Saharan family

Masakhane (ˌmasaˈkanɪ) *sentence substitute South African* a political slogan of solidarity [c20 Nguni, literally: let us build together]

masala (maːˈsaːlə) *n* **1** a mixture of spices ground into a paste, used in Indian cookery ▷ *adj* **2** *Hinglish* spicy; dramatic: *it was a typical masala film* [from Urdu *masalah*, from Arabic *masalih* ingredients]

Masan (ˈmaːˌsaːn) *n* a port in SE South Korea, on an inlet of the Korea Strait: first opened to foreign trade in 1899. Pop: 428 000 (2005 est)

Masbate (mæsˈbaːtɪ) *n* **1** an island in the central Philippines, between Negros and SE Luzon: agricultural, with resources of gold, copper, and manganese. Pop (Masbate province): 707 668 (2000). Area: 4045 sq km (1562 sq miles) **2** the capital of this island, a port in the northeast. Pop: 71 441 (2000)

masc. *abbreviation for* masculine

mascara (mæˈskaːrə) *n* a cosmetic substance for darkening, colouring, and thickening the eyelashes, applied with a brush or rod [c20 from Spanish: mask]

Mascarene Islands (ˌmæskəˈriːn) *pl n* a group of volcanic islands in the W Indian Ocean, east of Madagascar: consists of the islands of Réunion, Mauritius, and Rodrigues. French name: Îles Mascareignes

mascarpone (ˌmæskəˈpəʊnɪ) *n* a soft Italian cream cheese [from Italian, from dialect (Lombardy) *mascherpa* ricotta]

mascle (ˈmaːskəl) *n heraldry* a charge consisting of a lozenge with a lozenge-shaped hole in the middle. Also called: **voided lozenge** [c14 from Old

French *macle*, perhaps from Latin *macula* spot]

mascon ('mæskɒn) *n* any of several lunar regions of high gravity [c20 from MAS(S) + CON(CENTRATION)]

mascot ('mæskət) *n* a person, animal, or thing considered to bring good luck [c19 from French *mascotte*, from Provençal *mascotto* charm, from *masco* witch]

masculine ('mæskjʊlɪn) *adj* 1 possessing qualities or characteristics considered typical of or appropriate to a man; manly 2 unwomanly 3 *grammar* **a** denoting a gender of nouns, occurring in many inflected languages, that includes all kinds of referents as well as some male animate referents **b** (*as noun*): German "*Weg*" is a masculine [c14 via French from Latin *masculīnus*, from *masculus* male, from *mās* a male] > 'masculinely *adv* > ,mascu'linity *or less commonly* 'masculineness *n*

masculine ending *n prosody* a stressed syllable at the end of a line of verse. Compare **feminine ending**

masculine rhyme *n prosody* a rhyme between stressed monosyllables or between the final stressed syllables of polysyllabic words: *book, cook; collect, direct*. Compare **feminine rhyme**

masculinist ('mæskjʊlɪnɪst) *or* **masculist** ('mæskjʊlɪst) *n* 1 an advocate of the rights of men ▷ *adj* 2 of, characterized by, or relating to men's rights

masculinize *or* **masculinise** ('mæskjʊlɪn,aɪz) *vb* to make or become masculine, esp to cause (a woman) to show male secondary sexual characteristics as a result of taking steroids > ,masculini'zation *or* ,masculini'sation *n*

maser ('meɪzə) *n* a device for amplifying microwaves, working on the same principle as a laser [c20 m(icrowave) a(mplification by) s(timulated) e(mission of) r(adiation)]

Maseru (mə'sɛəruː) *n* the capital of Lesotho, in the northwest near the W border with South Africa; established as capital of Basutoland in 1869. Pop: 175 000 (2005 est)

mash (mæʃ) *n* 1 a soft pulpy mass or consistency 2 *agriculture* a feed of bran, meal, or malt mixed with water and fed to horses, cattle, or poultry 3 (esp in brewing) a mixture of mashed malt grains and hot water, from which malt is extracted 4 *Brit informal* mashed potatoes 5 *Northern English dialect* a brew of tea ▷ *vb* (*tr*) 6 to beat or crush into a mash 7 to steep (malt grains) in hot water in order to extract malt, esp for making malt liquors 8 *Northern English dialect* to brew (tea) 9 *archaic* to flirt with [Old English *māsc-* (in compound words); related to Middle Low German *mēsch*] > mashed *adj* > 'masher *n*

MASH (mæʃ) *n* (in the US) ▷ *acronym for* Mobile Army Surgical Hospital

Masham ('mæsəm) *n* a crossbreed of large sheep having a black and white face and a long curly fleece: kept for lamb production [c20 named after *Masham*, town in N Yorkshire]

mashed (mæʃt) *adj slang* intoxicated; drunk

Masherbrum *or* **Masharbrum** ('mʌʃə,brʊm) *n* a mountain in N India, in N Kashmir in the Karakoram Range of the Himalayas. Height: 7822 m (25 660 ft)

Mashhad (mæʃ'hæd) *or* **Meshed** *n* a city in NE Iran: an important holy city of Shi'ite Muslims; carpet manufacturing. Pop: 2 147 000 (2005 est)

mashiach (mə'ʃiɑx) *n Judaism* the messiah [Hebrew, literally: anointed; compare MESSIAH]

mashie *or* **mashy** ('mæʃɪ) *n, pl* **mashies** *golf* (formerly) a club, corresponding to the modern No. 5 or No. 6 iron, used for approach shots [c19 perhaps from French *massue* club, ultimately from Latin *mateola* mallet]

Mashona (mə'ʃəʊnə) *n, pl* **-na** *or* **-nas** another name for the **Shona** (sense 1)

mashup ('mæʃʌp) *n* a piece of recorded or live music in which a producer or DJ blends together two or more tracks, often of contrasting genres [c20 from MASH blend + UP]

masjid *or* **musjid** ('mʌsdʒɪd) *n* a mosque in an Arab country [Arabic; see MOSQUE]

mask (mɑːsk) *n* 1 any covering for the whole or a part of the face worn for amusement, protection, disguise, etc 2 a fact, action, etc, that conceals something: *his talk was a mask for his ignorance* 3 another name for **masquerade** 4 a likeness of a face or head, either sculpted or moulded, such as a death mask 5 an image of a face worn by an actor, esp in ancient Greek and Roman drama, in order to symbolize the character being portrayed 6 a variant spelling of **masque** 7 *surgery* a sterile gauze covering for the nose and mouth worn esp during operations to minimize the spread of germs 8 *sport* a protective covering for the face worn for fencing, ice hockey, etc 9 a carving in the form of a face or head, used as an ornament 10 a natural land feature or artificial object which conceals troops, etc, from view 11 a device placed over the nose and mouth to facilitate or prevent inhalation of a gas 12 *photog* a shield of paper, paint, etc, placed over an area of unexposed photographic surface to stop light falling on it 13 *electronics* a thin sheet of material from which a pattern has been cut, placed over a semiconductor chip so that an integrated circuit can be formed on the exposed areas 14 *computing* a bit pattern which, by convolution with a second pattern in a logical operation, can be used to isolate a specific subset of the second pattern for examination 15 *entomol* a large prehensile mouthpart (labium) of the dragonfly larva 16 the face or head of an animal, such as a fox, or the dark coloration of the face of some animals, such as Siamese cats and certain dogs 17 another word for **face pack** 18 *now rare* a person wearing a mask ▷ *vb* 19 to cover with or put on a mask 20 (*tr*) to conceal; disguise: *to mask an odour* 21 (*tr*) *photog* to shield a particular area of (an unexposed photographic surface) in order to prevent or reduce the action of light there 22 (*tr*) to shield a particular area of (a surface to be painted) with masking tape 23 (*tr*) to cover (cooked food, esp meat) with a savoury sauce or glaze 24 a Scot variant of **mash** (sense 8) [c16 from Italian *maschera*, ultimately from Arabic *maskharah* clown, from *sakhira* mockery] > 'mask,like *adj*

maskanonge ('mæskə,nɒndʒ), **maskinonge** ('mæskɪ,nɒndʒ) *or* **maskalonge** ('mæskə,lɒndʒ) *n, pl* **-nonges, -nonge** *or* **-longes, -longe** variants of **muskellunge**

masked (mɑːskt) *adj* 1 disguised or covered by or as if by a mask 2 *botany* another word for **personate²**

masked ball *n* a ball at which masks are worn

masker *or* **masquer** ('mɑːskə) *n* a person who wears a mask or takes part in a masque

masking ('mɑːskɪŋ) *n* 1 the act or practice of masking 2 *psychol* the process by which a stimulus (usually visual or auditory) is obscured by the presence of another almost simultaneous stimulus

masking tape *n* an adhesive tape used to mask and protect surfaces surrounding an area to be painted

masochism ('mæsə,kɪzəm) *n* 1 *psychiatry* an abnormal condition in which pleasure, esp sexual pleasure, is derived from pain or from humiliation, domination, etc, by another person 2 *psychoanal* the directing towards oneself of any destructive tendencies 3 a tendency to take pleasure from one's own suffering. Compare **sadism** [c19 named after Leopold von Sacher *Masoch* (1836–95), Austrian novelist, who described it] > 'masochist *n, adj* > ,maso'chistic *adj* > ,maso'chistically *adv*

mason ('meɪsˀn) *n* 1 a person skilled in building with stone 2 a person who dresses stone ▷ *vb* 3 (*tr*) to construct or strengthen with masonry [c13 from Old French *masson*, of Frankish origin; perhaps related to Old English *macian* to make]

Mason ('meɪsˀn) *n* short for **Freemason**

mason bee *n* any bee of the family *Megachilidae*

that builds a hard domelike nest of sand, clay, etc, held together with saliva

Mason-Dixon Line *or* **Mason and Dixon Line** ('meɪsˀn 'dɪksən) *n* the state boundary between Maryland and Pennsylvania: surveyed between 1763 and 1767 by Charles Mason and Jeremiah Dixon; popularly regarded as the dividing line between North and South, esp between the free and the slave states before the American Civil War

masonic (mə'sɒnɪk) *adj* 1 (*often capital*) of, characteristic of, or relating to Freemasons or Freemasonry 2 of or relating to masons or masonry > ma'sonically *adv*

Masonite ('meɪsə,naɪt) *n Austral and NZ trademark* a kind of dark brown hardboard used for partitions, lining, etc

mason jar *n US* an airtight glass jar for preserving food [c20 named after its US inventor, John L. *Mason* (1832–1902)]

masonry ('meɪsənrɪ) *n, pl* **-ries** 1 the craft of a mason 2 work that is built by a mason; stonework or brickwork 3 (*often capital*) short for **Freemasonry**

mason wasp *n* a solitary wasp of the genus *Odynerus* that excavates its nest in sand or the mortar of old walls

Masora, Masorah, Massora *or* **Massorah** (mə'sɔːrə) *n* 1 the text of the Hebrew Bible as officially revised by the Masoretes from the 6th to the 10th centuries AD, with critical notes and commentary 2 the collection of these notes, commentaries, etc [c17 from Hebrew: tradition]

Masorete, Massorete ('mæsə,riːt) *or* **Masorite** ('mæsə,raɪt) *n* 1 a member of the school of rabbis that produced the Masora 2 a Hebrew scholar who is expert in the Masora [c16 from Hebrew *māsōreth* MASORA]

Masoretic, Massoretic (,mæsə'rɛtɪk) *or* **Masoretical, Massoretical** *adj* of or relating to the Masora, the Masoretes, or the system of textual criticism and explanation evolved by them

Masqat ('mʌskət, -kæt) *n* a transliteration of the Arabic name for **Muscat**

masque *or* **mask** (mɑːsk) *n* 1 a dramatic entertainment of the 16th to 17th centuries in England, consisting of pantomime, dancing, dialogue, and song, often performed at court 2 the words and music written for a masque 3 short for **masquerade** [c16 variant of MASK]

masquer ('mɑːskə) *n* a variant spelling of **masker**

masquerade (,mæskə'reɪd) *n* 1 a party or other gathering to which the guests wear masks and costumes 2 the disguise worn at such a function 3 a pretence or disguise ▷ *vb* (*intr*) 4 to participate in a masquerade; disguise oneself 5 to dissemble [c16 from Spanish *mascarada*, from *mascara* MASK] > ,masquer'ader *n*

mass (mæs) *n* 1 a large coherent body of matter without a definite shape 2 a collection of the component parts of something 3 a large amount or number, such as a great body of people 4 the main part or majority: *the mass of the people voted against the government's policy* 5 **in the mass** in the main; collectively 6 the size of a body; bulk 7 *physics* a physical quantity expressing the amount of matter in a body. It is a measure of a body's resistance to changes in velocity (**inertial mass**) and also of the force experienced in a gravitational field (**gravitational mass**): according to the theory of relativity, inertial and gravitational masses are equal 8 (in painting, drawing, etc) an area of unified colour, shade, or intensity, usually denoting a solid form or plane 9 *pharmacol* a pastelike composition of drugs from which pills are made 10 *mining* an irregular deposit of ore not occurring in veins 11 ▷ *modifier* done or occurring on a large scale: *mass hysteria, mass radiography* 12 consisting of a mass or large number, esp of people: *a mass meeting* ▷ *vb* 13 to form (people or things) or (of people or things) to join together into a mass: *the crowd massed outside the embassy* ▷ See also **masses, mass in** [c14 from

Old French *masse,* from Latin *massa* that which forms a lump, from Greek *maza* barley cake; perhaps related to Greek *massein* to knead]
> **massed** *adj* > **massedly** ('mæsɪdlɪ, 'mæstlɪ) *adv*

Mass (mæs, mɑ:s) *n* **1** (in the Roman Catholic Church and certain Protestant Churches) the celebration of the Eucharist. See also **High Mass, Low Mass 2** a musical setting of those parts of the Eucharistic service sung by choir or congregation [Old English *mæsse,* from Church Latin *missa,* ultimately from Latin *mittere* to send away; perhaps derived from the concluding dismissal in the Roman Mass, *Ite, missa est,* Go, it is the dismissal]

Mass. *abbreviation for* Massachusetts

Massa (*Italian* 'massa) *n* a town in W Italy, in NW Tuscany. Pop: 66 769 (2001)

Massachuset (ˌmæsə'tʃu:sɪt) *or* **Massachusetts** *n* **1** (*pl* -sets, -set *or* -setts) a member of a North American Indian people formerly living around Massachusetts Bay **2** the language of this people, belonging to the Algonquian family [probably from Algonquian, literally: at the big hill]

Massachusetts (ˌmæsə'tʃu:sɪts) *n* a state of the northeastern US, on the Atlantic: a centre of resistance to English colonial policy during the War of American Independence; consists of a coastal plain rising to mountains in the west. Capital: Boston. Pop: 6 433 422 (2003 est). Area: 20 269 sq km (7826 sq miles). Abbreviations: Mass, (with zip code) MA

Massachusetts Bay *n* an inlet of the Atlantic on the E coast of Massachusetts

massacre ('mæsəkə) *n* **1** the wanton or savage killing of large numbers of people, as in battle **2** *informal* an overwhelming defeat, as in a game ▷ *vb* (*tr*) **3** to kill indiscriminately or in large numbers **4** *informal* to defeat overwhelmingly [c16 from Old French, of unknown origin] > **massacrer** ('mæsəkrə) *n*

Massacre of the Innocents *n* the slaughter of all the young male children of Bethlehem at Herod's command in an attempt to destroy Jesus (Matthew 2:16–18)

mass affluent *pl n* the large number of individuals with liquid assets of around £250,000

massage ('mæsɑ:ʒ, -sɑ:dʒ) *n* **1** the act of kneading, rubbing, etc, parts of the body to promote circulation, suppleness, or relaxation ▷ *vb* (*tr*) **2** to give a massage to **3** to treat (stiffness, aches, etc) by a massage **4** to manipulate (statistics, data, etc) so that they appear to support a particular interpretation or to be better than they are; doctor **5** **massage (someone's) ego** to boost (someone's) sense of self-esteem by flattery [c19 from French, from *masser* to rub; see MASS] > **massager** *or* **massagist** *n*

massage parlour *n* **1** a business providing massage services **2** *euphemistic* a brothel

massasauga (ˌmæsə'sɔːgə) *n* a North American venomous snake, *Sistrurus catenatus,* that has a horny rattle at the end of the tail: family *Crotalidae* (pit vipers) [c19 named after the *Missisauga* River, Ontario, Canada, where it was first found]

Massawa *or* **Massaua** (mə'sɑːwə) *n* a port in E central Eritrea, on the Red Sea: capital of Eritrea during Italian occupation, from 1885 until 1900. Pop: 40 000 (1992)

mass defect *n physics* the amount by which the mass of a particular nucleus is less than the total mass of its constituent particles. See also **binding energy**

massé *or* **massé shot** ('mæsɪ) *n billiards* a stroke made by hitting the cue ball off centre with the cue held nearly vertically, esp so as to make the ball move in a curve around another ball before hitting the object ball [c19 from French, from *masser* to hit from above with a hammer, from *masse* sledgehammer, from Old French *mace* MACE¹]

massed practice *n psychol* learning with no intervals or short intervals between successive bouts of learning. Compare **distributed practice**

mass-energy *n* mass and energy considered as equivalent and interconvertible, according to the theory of relativity

masses ('mæsɪz) *pl n* **1** (preceded by *the*) the body of common people **2** (often foll by *of*) *informal, chiefly Brit* great numbers or quantities: *masses of food*

masseter (mæ'si:tə) *n anatomy* a muscle of the cheek used in moving the jaw, esp in chewing [c17 from New Latin from Greek *masētēr* one who chews, from *masāsthai* to chew] > **masseteric** (ˌmæsɪ'tɛrɪk) *adj*

masseur (mæ'sɜ:) *n* a man who gives massages, esp as a profession [c19 from French *masser* to MASSAGE]

masseuse (mæ'sɜ:z) *n* a woman who gives massages, esp as a profession

massicot ('mæsɪˌkɒt) *n* a yellow earthy secondary mineral consisting of lead oxide. Formula: PbO [c15 via French from Italian *marzacotto* ointment, perhaps from Arabic *shabb qubti* Egyptian alum]

massif ('mæsi:f; *French* masif) *n* **1** a geologically distinct mass of rock or a series of connected masses forming the peaks of a mountain range **2** a topographically high part of the earth's crust that is bounded by faults and may be shifted by tectonic movements [c19 from French, noun use of *massif* MASSIVE]

Massif Central (*French* masif sɑ̃tral) *n* a mountainous plateau region of S central France, occupying about one sixth of the country: contains several extinct volcanic cones, notably Puy de Dôme, 1465 m (4806 ft). Highest point: Puy de Sancy, 1886 m (6188 ft). Area: about 85 000 sq km (33 000 sq miles)

mass in *vb* (*adverb*) to fill or block in (the areas of unified colour, shade, etc) in a painting or drawing

massive ('mæsɪv) *adj* **1** (of objects) large in mass; bulky, heavy, and usually solid **2** impressive or imposing in quality, degree, or scope: *massive grief* **3** relatively intensive or large; considerable: *a massive dose* **4** *pathol* affecting a large area of the body: *a massive cancer* **5** *geology* **a** (of igneous rocks) having no stratification, cleavage, etc; homogeneous **b** (of sedimentary rocks) arranged in thick poorly defined strata **6** *mineralogy* without obvious crystalline structure ▷ *n* **7** *slang* a group of friends or associates; gang: *the Staines massive* [c15 from French *massif,* from *masse* MASS] > **massively** *adv* > **massiveness** *n*

mass leave *n* (in India) leave taken by a large number of employees at the same time, as a form of protest

mass-market *adj* of, for, or appealing to a large number of people; popular: *mass-market paperbacks*

mass media *pl n* the means of communication that reach large numbers of people in a short time, such as television, newspapers, magazines, and radio

mass noun *n* a noun that refers to an extended substance rather than to each of a set of isolable objects, as, for example, *water* as opposed to *lake*. In English when used indefinitely they are characteristically preceded by *some* rather than *a* or *an;* they do not have normal plural forms. Compare **count noun**

mass number *n* the total number of neutrons and protons in the nucleus of a particular atom. Symbol: *A* Also called: **nucleon number**

mass observation *n chiefly Brit* (*sometimes capitals*) the study of the social habits of people through observation, interviews, etc

Massorete ('mæsəˌriːt) *n* a variant spelling of **Masorete**

massotherapy (ˌmæsəʊ'θɛrəpɪ) *n* medical treatment by massage [c20 from MASS(AGE) + THERAPY] > **massotherapeutic** (ˌmæsəʊˌθɛrə'pju:tɪk) *adj* > **masso'therapist** *n*

mass-produce *vb* (*tr*) to manufacture (goods) to a standardized pattern on a large scale by means of extensive mechanization and division of labour

> ˌmass-pro'duced *adj* > ˌmass-pro'ducer *n* > mass production *n*

mass ratio *n* the ratio of the mass of a fully-fuelled rocket at liftoff to the mass of the rocket without fuel

mass spectrograph *n* a mass spectrometer that produces a photographic record of the mass spectrum

mass spectrometer *or* **spectroscope** *n* an analytical instrument in which ions, produced from a sample, are separated by electric or magnetic fields according to their ratios of charge to mass. A record is produced (**mass spectrum**) of the types of ion present and their relative amounts

massy ('mæsɪ) *adj* massier, massiest a literary word for **massive**. > 'massiness *n*

mast¹ (mɑ:st) *n* **1** *nautical* any vertical spar for supporting sails, rigging, flags, etc, above the deck of a vessel or any components of such a composite spar **2** any sturdy upright pole used as a support **3** Also called: **captain's mast** *nautical* a hearing conducted by the captain of a vessel into minor offences of the crew **4** **before the mast** *nautical* as an apprentice seaman ▷ *vb* **5** (*tr*) *nautical* to equip with a mast or masts [Old English *mæst;* related to Middle Dutch *mast* and Latin *mālus* pole] > 'mastless *adj* > 'mast‚like *adj*

mast² (mɑ:st) *n* the fruit of forest trees, such as beech, oak, etc, used as food for pigs [Old English *mæst;* related to Old High German *mast* food, and perhaps to MEAT]

mast- *combining form* a variant of **masto-** before a vowel

mastaba *or* **mastabah** ('mæstəbə) *n* a mudbrick superstructure above tombs in ancient Egypt from which the pyramid developed [from Arabic: bench]

mast cell *n* a type of granular basophil cell in connective tissue that releases heparin, histamine, and serotonin during inflammation and allergic reactions [c19 from MAST², on the model of German *Mastzelle*]

mastectomy (mæ'stɛktəmɪ) *n, pl* -mies the surgical removal of a breast

-masted *adj* (*in combination*) *nautical* having a mast or masts of a specified kind or number: *three-masted; tall-masted*

master ('mɑ:stə) *n* **1** the man in authority, such as the head of a household, the employer of servants, or the owner of slaves or animals. Related adj: **magistral 2 a** a person with exceptional skill at a certain thing: *a master of the violin* **b** (*as modifier*): *a master thief* **3** (*often capital*) a great artist, esp an anonymous but influential artist **4 a** a person who has complete control of a situation **b** an abstract thing regarded as having power or influence: *they regarded fate as the master of their lives* **5 a** a workman or craftsman fully qualified to practise his trade and to train others in it **b** (*as modifier*): *master carpenter* **6 a** an original copy, stencil, tape, etc, from which duplicates are made **b** (*as modifier*): *master copy* **7** a player of a game, esp chess or bridge, who has won a specified number of tournament games **8** the principal of some colleges **9** a highly regarded teacher or leader whose religion or philosophy is accepted by followers **10** a graduate holding a master's degree **11** the chief executive officer aboard a merchant ship **12** a person presiding over a function, organization, or institution **13** *chiefly Brit* a male teacher **14** an officer of the Supreme Court of Judicature subordinate to a judge **15** the superior person or side in a contest **16** a machine or device that operates to control a similar one **17** (*often capital*) the heir apparent of a Scottish viscount or baron **18** ▷ *modifier* overall or controlling: *master plan* **19** ▷ *modifier* designating a device or mechanism that controls others: *master switch* **20** ▷ *modifier* main; principal: *master bedroom* **21** *South African informal* **the** the man of the house ▷ *vb* (*tr*) **22** to become thoroughly proficient in: *to* master the art of driving **23** to overcome; defeat: *to master your emotions* **24** to rule or control as master [Old English *magister* teacher, from Latin; related to Latin *magis* more, to a greater extent] > ˈmasterdom *n* > ˈmaster,hood *n* > ˈmasterless *adj* > ˈmastership *n*

Master (ˈmɑːstə) *n* **1** a title of address placed before the first name or surname of a boy **2** a respectful term of address, esp as used by disciples when addressing or referring to a religious teacher **3** an archaic equivalent of **Mr**

master aircrew *n* a warrant rank in the Royal Air Force, equal to but before a warrant officer

master-at-arms *n, pl* masters-at-arms the senior rating, of Chief Petty Officer rank, in a naval unit responsible for discipline, administration, and police duties

master builder *n* **1** a person skilled in the design and construction of buildings, esp before the foundation of the profession of architecture **2** a self-employed builder who employs labour

masterclass (ˈmɑːstəˌklɑːs) *n* a session of tuition by an expert, esp a musician, for exceptional students, usually given in public or on television

master corporal *n* a noncommissioned officer in the Canadian forces senior to a corporal and junior to a sergeant

master cylinder *n* a large cylinder in a hydraulic system in which the working fluid is compressed by a piston enabling it to drive one or more slave cylinders. See also **slave cylinder**

masterful (ˈmɑːstəfʊl) *adj* **1** having or showing mastery **2** fond of playing the master; imperious **3** masterly > ˈmasterfully *adv* > ˈmasterfulness *n*

USAGE The use of *masterful* to mean masterly as in *a masterful performance*, although common, is considered incorrect by many people

master key *n* a key that opens all the locks of a set, the individual keys of which are not interchangeable. Also called: **pass key**

masterly (ˈmɑːstəlɪ) *adj* of the skill befitting a master: *a masterly performance* > ˈmasterliness *n*

mastermind (ˈmɑːstəˌmaɪnd) *vb* **1** (tr) to plan and direct (a complex undertaking): *he masterminded the robbery* ▷ *n* **2** a person of great intelligence or executive talent, esp one who directs an undertaking

Master of Arts *n* a degree, usually postgraduate and in a nonscientific subject, or the holder of this degree. Abbreviation: **MA**

master of ceremonies *n* a person who presides over a public ceremony, formal dinner, or entertainment, introducing the events, performers, etc. Abbreviation: **MC**

master of foxhounds *n* a person responsible for the maintenance of a pack of foxhounds and the associated staff, equipment, hunting arrangements, etc. Abbreviation: **MFH**

Master of Science *n* a postgraduate degree, usually in science, or the holder of this degree. Abbreviation: **MSc**

Master of the Horse *n* (in England) the third official of the royal household

Master of the Queen's Music *n* (in Britain when the sovereign is female) a court post dating from the reign of Charles I. It is an honorary title and normally held by an established English composer. Also called (when the sovereign is male): **Master of the King's Music**

Master of the Rolls *n* (in England) a judge of the court of appeal: the senior civil judge in the country and the Keeper of the Records at the Public Record Office

masterpiece (ˈmɑːstəˌpiːs) *or less commonly* **masterwork** (ˈmɑːstəˌwɜːk) *n* **1** an outstanding work, achievement, or performance **2** the most outstanding piece of work of a creative artist, etc [C17 compare Dutch *meesterstuk*, German *Meisterstück*, a sample of work submitted to a guild by a craftsman in order to qualify for the rank of master]

master plan *n* a comprehensive long-term strategy

master race *n* a race, nation, or group, such as the Germans or Nazis as viewed by Hitler, believed to be superior to other races. German name: Herrenvolk

master sergeant *n* a senior noncommissioned officer in the US Army, Air Force, and Marine Corps and certain other military forces, ranking immediately below the most senior noncommissioned rank

mastersinger (ˈmɑːstəˌsɪŋə) *n* an English spelling of **Meistersinger**

masterstroke (ˈmɑːstəˌstrəʊk) *n* an outstanding piece of strategy, skill, talent, etc: *your idea is a masterstroke*

master warrant officer *n* a noncommissioned officer in the Canadian forces junior to a chief warrant officer

mastery (ˈmɑːstərɪ) *n, pl* -teries **1** full command or understanding of a subject **2** outstanding skill; expertise **3** the power of command; control **4** victory or superiority

masthead (ˈmɑːstˌhɛd) *n* **1** *nautical* **a** the head of a mast **b** (*as modifier*): *masthead sail* **2** Also called: **flag** the name of a newspaper or periodical, its proprietors, staff, etc, printed in large type at the top of the front page ▷ *vb* (tr) **3** to send (a sailor) to the masthead as a punishment **4** to raise (a sail) to the masthead

mastic (ˈmæstɪk) *n* **1** an aromatic resin obtained from the mastic tree and used as an astringent and to make varnishes and lacquers **2** mastic tree **a** a small Mediterranean anacardiaceous evergreen tree, *Pistacia lentiscus*, that yields the resin mastic **b** any of various similar trees, such as the pepper tree **3** any of several sticky putty-like substances used as a filler, adhesive, or seal in wood, plaster, or masonry **4** a liquor flavoured with mastic gum [C14 via Old French from Late Latin *mastichum*, from Latin, from Greek *mastikhē* resin used as chewing gum; from *mastikhan* to grind the teeth]

masticate (ˈmæstɪˌkeɪt) *vb* **1** to chew (food) **2** to reduce (materials such as rubber) to a pulp by crushing, grinding, or kneading [C17 from Late Latin *masticāre*, from Greek *mastikhan* to grind the teeth] > ˈmasticable *adj* > ˌmastiˈcation *n* > ˈmastiˌcator *n*

masticatory (ˈmæstɪkətərɪ, -trɪ) *adj* **1** of, relating to, or adapted to chewing ▷ *n, pl* -tories **2** *obsolete* a medicinal substance chewed to increase the secretion of saliva

mastiff (ˈmæstɪf) *n* an old breed of large powerful short-haired dog, usually fawn or brindle with a dark mask [C14 from Old French, ultimately from Latin *mansuētus* tame; see MANSUETUDE]

mastigophoran (ˌmæstɪˈɡɒfərən) *n* also **mastigophore** (ˈmæstɪɡəˌfɔː) **1** any protozoan having one or more flagella ▷ *adj* also **mastigophorous 2** of or relating to flagellated protozoans. Also: **flagellate** [C19 *mastigophore* whip-bearer, from Greek *mastigophoros*, from *mastix* whip + *-phoros* -PHORE]

mastitis (mæˈstaɪtɪs) *n* inflammation of a breast or an udder

masto- *or before a vowel* **mast-** *combining form* indicating the breast, mammary glands, or something resembling a breast or nipple: *mastodon; mastoid* [from Greek *mastos* breast]

mastodon (ˈmæstəˌdɒn) *n* any extinct elephant-like proboscidean mammal of the genus *Mammut* (or *Mastodon*), common in Pliocene times [C19 from New Latin, literally: breast-tooth, referring to the nipple-shaped projections on the teeth] > ˌmastoˈdontic *adj*

mastoid (ˈmæstɔɪd) *adj* **1** shaped like a nipple or breast **2** designating or relating to a nipple-like process of the temporal bone behind the ear ▷ *n* **3** the mastoid process **4** *informal* mastoiditis

mastoidectomy (ˌmæstɔɪˈdɛktəmɪ) *n, pl* -mies surgical removal of the mastoid process

mastoiditis (ˌmæstɔɪˈdaɪtɪs) *n* inflammation of the mastoid process

masturbate (ˈmæstəˌbeɪt) *vb* to stimulate the genital organs of (oneself or another) to achieve sexual pleasure [C19 from Latin *masturbārī*, of unknown origin; formerly thought to be derived from *manus* hand + *stuprāre* to defile] > ˌmasturˈbation *n* > ˈmasturˌbator *n*

masturbatory (ˈmæstəˌbeɪtərɪ) *adj* involving, conducive to, or suggestive of masturbation

Masuria (məˈsjʊərɪə) *n* a region of NE Poland: until 1945 part of East Prussia: includes the **Masurian Lakes,** scene of Russian defeats by the Germans (1914, 1915) during World War I

Masurian (məˈsjʊərɪən) *adj* **1** of or relating to Masuria, a region of NE Poland, or its inhabitants ▷ *n* **2** a native or inhabitant of Masuria

masurium (məˈsʊərɪəm) *n* the former name for **technetium** [C20 New Latin, after MASURIA, where it was discovered]

mat¹ (mæt) *n* **1** a thick flat piece of fabric used as a floor covering, a place to wipe one's shoes, etc **2** a smaller pad of material used to protect a surface from the heat, scratches, etc, of an object placed upon it **3** a large piece of thick padded material put on the floor as a surface for wrestling, judo, or gymnastic sports **4** NZ a Māori cloak **5** go back to the mat NZ to abandon urban civilization **6** any surface or mass that is densely interwoven or tangled: *a mat of grass and weeds* **7** the solid part of a lace design **8 a** a heavy net of cable or rope laid over a blasting site to prevent the scatter of debris **b** a heavy mesh of reinforcement in a concrete slab **c** (esp US) a steel or concrete raft serving as a footing to support a post **9** *civil engineering* short for **mattress** (sense 3) ▷ *vb* mats, matting, matted **10** to tangle or weave or become tangled or woven into a dense mass **11** (tr) to cover with a mat or mats [Old English *matte*; related to Old High German *matta*] > ˈmatless *adj*

mat² (mæt) *n* **1** a border of cardboard, cloth, etc, placed around a picture to act as a frame or as a contrast between picture and frame **2** a surface, as on metal or paint ▷ *adj* **3** having a dull, lustreless, or roughened surface ▷ *vb* mats, matting, matted (tr) **4** to furnish (a picture) with a mat **5** to give (a surface) a mat finish ▷ Also (for senses 2, 3, 5): **matt** [C17 from French, literally: dead; see CHECKMATE]

mat³ (mæt) *n printing informal* short for **matrix** (sense 5)

mat. *abbreviation for* matinée

Matabele (ˌmætəˈbiːlɪ, -ˈbɛlɪ) *n* (*pl* **-les** *or* **-le**) a member of a formerly warlike people of southern Africa, now living in Zimbabwe: driven out of the Transvaal by the Boers in 1837. Now known as: **Ndebele 2** the language of this people, belonging to the Bantu group of the Niger-Congo family

Matabeleland (ˌmætəˈbiːlɪˌlænd, -ˈbɛlɪ-) *n* a region of W Zimbabwe, between the Rivers Limpopo and Zambezi, comprises three provinces, Matabeleland North, Matabeleland South, and Bulawayo: rich gold deposits. Chief town: Bulawayo. Area: 181 605 sq km (70 118 sq miles)

Matadi (məˈtɑːdɪ) *n* the chief port of the Democratic Republic of Congo (formerly Zaïre), in the west at the mouth of the River Congo. Pop: 256 000 (2005 est)

matador (ˈmætəˌdɔː) *n* **1** the principal bullfighter who is appointed to kill the bull **2** (in some card games such as skat) one of the highest ranking cards **3** a game played with dominoes in which the dots on adjacent halves must total seven [C17 from Spanish, from *matar* to kill]

matagouri (ˌmætəˈɡuːrɪ) *n, pl* -ris a thorny bush of New Zealand, *Discaria toumatou*, that forms thickets in open country. Also called: **wild Irishman, tumatakuru** [from Māori *tumatakuru*]

matai (ˈmɑːtaɪ) *n, pl* -tais a coniferous evergreen tree of New Zealand, *Podocarpus spicatus*, having a bluish bark and small linear leaves arranged in two rows: timber used for flooring and

m

weatherboards. Also called: black pine [Māori]

mata-mata ('mata'mata) *n* (in Malaysia) a former name for **police** [from Malay, reduplicated plural of *mata* eye]

Matamoros (,mætə'mɔːrəs; *Spanish* mata'moros) *n* a port in NE Mexico, on the Río Grande: scene of bitter fighting during the US-Mexican War; centre of a cotton-growing area. Pop: 481 000 (2005 est)

Matanzas (mə'tænzəs; *Spanish* ma'tanθas) *n* a port in W central Cuba: founded in 1693 and developed into the second city of Cuba in the mid-19th century; exports chiefly sugar. Pop: 130 000 (2005 est)

Matapan ('mætə,pæn, ,mætə'pæn) *n* **Cape** a cape in S Greece, at the S central tip of the Peloponnese: the southern point of the mainland of Greece. Modern Greek name: **Taínaron**

matata (mɑː'tɑːtɑː) *n, pl* matata NZ another name for **fernbird** [Māori]

match¹ (mætʃ) *n* **1** a formal game or sports event in which people, teams, etc, compete to win **2** a person or thing able to provide competition for another: *she's met her match in talking ability* **3** a person or thing that resembles, harmonizes with, or is equivalent to another in a specified respect: *that coat is a good match for your hat* **4** a person or thing that is an exact copy or equal of another **5 a** a partnership between a man and a woman, as in marriage **b** an arrangement for such a partnership **6** a person regarded as a possible partner, as in marriage ▷ *vb* **7** (*mainly tr*) to fit (parts) together: *to match the tongue and groove of boards* **8** (*also intr*; sometimes foll by *up*) to resemble, harmonize with, correspond to, or equal (one another or something else): *the skirt matches your shoes well* **9** (sometimes foll by *with* or *against*) to compare in order to determine which is the superior: *they matched wits* **10** (often foll by *to* or *with*) to adapt so as to correspond with: *to match hope with reality* **11** (often foll by *with* or *against*) to arrange a competition between **12** to find a match for **13** *electronics* to connect (two circuits) so that their impedances are equal or are equalized by a coupling device, to produce a maximum transfer of energy [Old English *gemæcca* spouse; related to Old High German *gimahha* wife, Old Norse *maki* mate] ▷ **'matchable** *adj* ▷ **'matcher** *n* ▷ **'matching** *adj*

match² (mætʃ) *n* **1** a thin strip of wood or cardboard tipped with a chemical that ignites by friction when rubbed on a rough surface or a surface coated with a suitable chemical (see **safety match**) **2** a length of cord or wick impregnated with a chemical so that it burns slowly. It is used to fire cannons, explosives, etc [c14 from Old French *meiche*, perhaps from Latin *myxa* wick, from Greek *muxa* lamp nozzle]

matchboard ('mætʃ,bɔːd) *n* a long thin board with a tongue along one edge and a corresponding groove along the other, used with similar boards to line walls, ceilings, etc

matchbox ('mætʃ,bɒks) *n* a small box for holding matches

matched-pairs design *n* (*modifier*) *statistics* (of an experiment) concerned with measuring the values of the dependent variables for pairs of subjects that have been matched to eliminate individual differences and that are respectively subjected to the control and the experimental condition. Compare **between-subjects design, within-subjects design**

matched sample *n* *statistics* a sample in which the individuals selected for analysis share all properties except that under investigation

matchet ('mætʃət) *n* an earlier name for **machete**

match-fit *adj* in good physical condition for competing in a match

match-funding *n* the stipulation set by a grant-providing body that the recipients of a grant raise a certain percentage of the money they require, generally a sum more or less equal to that of the

sum of money being granted

matchless ('mætʃlɪs) *adj* unequalled; incomparable; peerless ▷ **'matchlessly** *adv* ▷ **'matchlessness** *n*

matchlock ('mætʃ,lɒk) *n* **1** an obsolete type of gunlock igniting the powder by means of a slow match **2** a gun having such a lock

matchmaker¹ ('mætʃ,meɪkə) *n* **1** a person who brings together suitable partners for marriage **2** a person who arranges competitive matches ▷ **'match,making** *n, adj*

matchmaker² ('mætʃ,meɪkə) *n* a person who makes matches (for igniting) ▷ **'match,making** *n, adj*

matchmark ('mætʃ,mɑːk) *n* **1** a mark made on mating components of an engine, machine, etc, to ensure that the components are assembled in the correct relative positions ▷ *vb* **2** (*tr*) to stamp (an object) with matchmarks

match play *n* *golf* **a** scoring according to the number of holes won and lost **b** (*as modifier*): *a matchplay tournament* ▷ Compare **Stableford, stroke play.** ▷ match player *n*

match point *n* **1** *sport* the final point needed to win a match **2** *bridge* the unit used for scoring in tournaments

matchstick ('mætʃ,stɪk) *n* **1** the wooden part of a match ▷ *adj* **2** made with or as if with matchsticks: *a matchstick model* **3** (esp of figures drawn with single strokes) thin and straight: *matchstick men*

matchup ('mætʃʌp) *n* *US and Canadian* a sports match

matchwood ('mætʃ,wʊd) *n* **1** wood suitable for making matches **2** splinters or fragments: *the bomb blew the house to matchwood*

mate¹ (meɪt) *n* **1** the sexual partner of an animal **2** a marriage partner **3 a** *informal, chiefly Brit, Austral, and NZ* a friend, usually of the same sex: often used between males in direct address **b** (*in combination*) an associate, colleague, fellow sharer, etc: *a classmate; a flatmate* **4** one of a pair of matching items **5** *nautical* **a** short for **first mate b** any officer below the master on a commercial ship **c** a warrant officer's assistant on a ship **6** (in some trades) an assistant: *a plumber's mate* **7** *archaic* a suitable associate **8** mate rates *Austral slang* the reduced rate charged for work done for a friend ▷ *vb* **9** to pair (a male and female animal) or (of animals) to pair for reproduction **10** to marry or join in marriage **11** (*tr*) to join as a pair; match [c14 from Middle Low German; related to Old English *gemetta* table-guest, from *mete* MEAT] ▷ **'mateless** *adj*

mate² (meɪt) *n, vb chess* See **checkmate**

maté *or* **mate** ('mɑːteɪ, 'mæteɪ) *n* **1** an evergreen tree, *Ilex paraguariensis*, cultivated in South America for its leaves, which contain caffeine: family *Aquifoliaceae* **2** a stimulating milky beverage made from the dried leaves of this tree ▷ Also called: Paraguay tea, yerba, yerba maté [c18 from American Spanish (originally referring to the vessel in which the drink was brewed), from Quechua *máti* gourd]

matelassé (mæt'læseɪ) *adj* (in textiles) having a raised design, as quilting; embossed [c19 from French *matelasser* to quilt, from *matelas* MATTRESS]

matelot, matlo *or* **matlow** ('mætləʊ) *n* *slang, chiefly Brit* a sailor [c20 from French]

matelote *or* **matelotte** ('mætəˌləʊt; *French* matlɔt) *n* fish served with a sauce of wine, onions, seasonings, and fish stock [c18 from French, feminine of *matelot* sailor]

mater ('meɪtə) *n* *Brit public school slang* a word for **mother¹**: often used facetiously [c16 from Latin]

mater dolorosa (,dɒlə'rəʊsə) *n* the Virgin Mary sorrowing for the dead Christ, esp as depicted in art [Latin: sorrowful mother]

materfamilias (,meɪtəfə'mɪliˌæs) *n, pl* matresfamilias (,meɪtreɪzfə'mɪliˌæs) the mother of a family or the female head of a family [c18 from Latin]

material (mə'tɪəriəl) *n* **1** the substance of which a thing is made or composed; component or constituent matter: *raw material* **2** facts, notes, etc, that a finished work may be based on or derived from: *enough material for a book* **3** cloth or fabric **4** a person who has qualities suitable for a given occupation, training, etc: *that boy is not university material* ▷ *adj* **5** of, relating to, or composed of physical substance; corporeal **6** *philosophy* composed of or relating to physical as opposed to mental or spiritual substance: *the material world* **7** of, relating to, or affecting economic or physical wellbeing: *material ease* **8** of or concerned with physical rather than spiritual interests **9** of great import or consequence: *of material benefit to the workers* **10** (often foll by *to*) relevant **11** *philosophy* of or relating to matter as opposed to form **12** *law* relevant to the issue before court: applied esp to facts or testimony of much significance: *a material witness* ▷ See also **materials** [c14 via French from Late Latin *māteriālis*, from Latin *māteria* MATTER] ▷ **ma'terialness** *n*

material implication *n* *logic* **1** the truth-functional connective that forms a compound sentence from two given sentences and assigns the value false to it only when its antecedent is true and its consequent false, without consideration of relevance; loosely corresponds to the English *if … then* **2** a compound sentence formed with this connective

materialism (mə'tɪəriəˌlɪzəm) *n* **1** interest in and desire for money, possessions, etc, rather than spiritual or ethical values **2** *philosophy* the monist doctrine that matter is the only reality and that the mind, the emotions, etc, are merely functions of it. Compare **idealism** (sense 3), **dualism** (sense 2) See also **identity theory** **3** *ethics* the rejection of any religious or supernatural account of things ▷ **ma'terialist** *n, adj* ▷ **ma,terial'istic** *adj* ▷ **ma,terial'istically** *adv*

materiality (mə,tɪəri'ælɪtɪ) *n* **1** the state or quality of being physical or material **2** substance; matter

materialize *or* **materialise** (mə'tɪəriəˌlaɪz) *vb* **1** (*intr*) to become fact; actually happen: *our hopes never materialized* **2** to invest or become invested with a physical shape or form **3** to cause (a spirit, as of a dead person) to appear in material form or (of a spirit) to appear in such form **4** (*intr*) to take shape; become tangible: *after hours of discussion, the project finally began to materialize* **5** *physics* to form (material particles) from energy, as in pair production ▷ **ma,teriali'zation** *or* **ma,teriali'sation** *n* ▷ **ma'terial,izer** *or* **ma'terial,iser** *n*

materially (mə'tɪəriəlɪ) *adv* **1** to a significant extent; considerably: *his death alters the situation materially* **2** with respect to material objects **3** *philosophy* with respect to substance as distinct from form

material mode *n* *philosophy* the normal use of language that refers to extra-linguistic subjects without explicit mention of the words themselves. *Fido is a dog* is in the material mode, while *"Fido" is a dog's name* is in the formal mode. See also **use** (sense 18)

materials (mə'tɪəriəlz) *pl n* the equipment necessary for a particular activity

materia medica (mə'tɪəriə 'mɛdɪkə) *n* **1** the branch of medical science concerned with the study of drugs used in the treatment of disease: includes pharmacology, clinical pharmacology, and the history and physical and chemical properties of drugs **2** the drugs used in the treatment of disease [c17 from Medieval Latin: medical matter]

materiel *or* **matériel** (mə,tɪəri'ɛl) *n* the materials and equipment of an organization, esp of a military force. Compare **personnel** [c19 from French: MATERIAL]

maternal (mə'tɜːnʳl) *adj* **1** of, relating to, derived from, or characteristic of a mother **2** related through the mother's side of the family: *his*

maternal uncle [c15 from Medieval Latin *māternālis*, from Latin *māternus*, from *māter* mother]
> ma'**ternalism** *n* > ma,**ternal'istic** *adj*
> ma'**ternally** *adv*

maternity (mə'tɜːnɪtɪ) *n* **1** motherhood **2** the characteristics associated with motherhood; motherliness **3** (*modifier*) relating to pregnant women or women at the time of childbirth: *a maternity ward*

maternity benefit *n* (in the British National Insurance scheme) a payment (**maternity allowance**) made to a pregnant woman who usually works but does not qualify for statutory maternity pay, normally from 11 weeks before confinement for a period of 18 weeks; there is also a flat-rate benefit (**maternity grant**) for those on low incomes

maternity leave *n* a period of paid absence from work, in Britain currently six months, to which a woman is legally entitled during the months immediately before and after childbirth

mateship ('meɪtʃɪp) *n Austral* the comradeship of friends, usually male, viewed as an institution

mate's rates *pl n NZ informal* preferential rates of payment offered to a friend

matey *or* **maty** ('meɪtɪ) *Brit informal* ▷ *adj* **1** friendly or intimate; on good terms ▷ *n* **2** friend or fellow: usually used in direct address
> '**mateyness** *or* '**matiness** *n*

mat grass *n* a widespread perennial European grass, *Nardus stricta*, with dense tufts of bristly leaves, characteristic of peaty moors

math (mæθ) *n US and Canadian informal* short for **mathematics** *Brit equivalent:* maths

math. *US and Canadian* ▷ *abbreviation for* mathematics

mathematical (,mæθə'mætɪkªl, ,mæθ'mæt-) *or less commonly* **mathematic** *adj* **1** of, used in, or relating to mathematics **2** characterized by or using the precision of mathematics; exact **3** using, determined by, or in accordance with the principles of mathematics > ,mathe'**matically** *adv*

mathematical expectation *n statistics* another name for **expected value**

mathematical logic *n* symbolic logic, esp that branch concerned with the foundations of mathematics

mathematical probability *n statistics* **1** the probability of an event consisting of *n* out of *m* possible equally likely occurrences, defined to be *n/m*. See also **principle of indifference 2** the study of such probabilities ▷ *Also called:* classical probability

mathematician (,mæθəmə'tɪʃən, ,mæθmə-) *n* an expert or specialist in mathematics

mathematics (,mæθə'mætɪks, ,mæθ'mæt-) *n* **1** (*functioning as singular*) a group of related sciences, including algebra, geometry, and calculus, concerned with the study of number, quantity, shape, and space and their interrelationships by using a specialized notation **2** (*functioning as singular or plural*) mathematical operations and processes involved in the solution of a problem or study of some scientific field [c14 *mathematik* (n), via Latin from Greek (adj), from *mathēma* a science, *mathēmatikos* (adj); related to *manthanein* to learn]

maths (mæθs) *n* (*functioning as singular*) *Brit informal* short for **mathematics** *US and Canadian equivalent:* math

maths. *Brit* ▷ *abbreviation for* mathematics

Mathura ('mʌtʊərə, mʌ'θʊərə) *n* a city in N India, in W Uttar Pradesh on the Jumna River: a place of Hindu pilgrimage, revered as the birthplace of Krishna. Pop: 298 827 (2001). Former name: Muttra

Matie ('mɑːtɪ) *n South African informal* a student at the University of Stellenbosch, esp one representing the University in a sport [perhaps from Afrikaans *tamatie* tomato, from the red colour of the rugby jersey]

Matilda (mə'tɪldə) *n Austral informal* **1** a bushman's swag **2** walk *or* waltz Matilda to travel the road carrying one's swag [c20 from the Christian name]

matin, mattin ('mætɪn) *or* **matinal** *adj* of or relating to matins [c14 see MATINS]

matinée ('mætɪ,neɪ) *n* a daytime, esp afternoon, performance of a play, concert, etc [c19 from French; see MATINS]

matinée coat *or* **jacket** *n* a short coat for a baby

matinée idol *n* (esp in the 1930s and 1940s) an actor popular as a romantic figure among women

matins *or* **mattins** ('mætɪnz) *n* (*functioning as singular or plural*) **1 a** *chiefly RC Church* the first of the seven canonical hours of prayer, originally observed at night but now often recited with lauds at daybreak **b** the service of morning prayer in the Church of England **2** *literary* a morning song, esp of birds [c13 from Old French, ultimately from Latin *mātūtīnus* of the morning, from *Mātūta* goddess of dawn]

matlo *or* **matlow** ('mætləʊ) *n* variant spellings of **matelot**

Matlock ('mæt,lɒk) *n* a town in England, on the River Derwent, administrative centre of Derbyshire: mineral springs. Pop: 11 265 (2001)

Mato Grosso *or* **Matto Grosso** ('mætəʊ 'grɒsəʊ; *Portuguese* 'matu 'grosu) *n* **1** a high plateau in SW Brazil: forms the watershed separating the Amazon and Plata river systems **2** a state of W central Brazil: mostly on the Mato Grosso Plateau, with the Amazon basin to the north; valuable mineral resources. Capital: Cuiabá. Pop: 2 604 742 (2002). Area: 881 001 sq km (340 083 sq miles)

Mato Grosso do Sul ('duː sul) *n* a state of W central Brazil: formed in 1979 from part of Mato Grosso state. Capital: Campo Grande. Pop: 2 140 624 (2002). Area: 350 548 sq km (135 318 sq miles)

matoke (ma'tɔkɛ) *n* (in Uganda) the flesh of bananas, boiled and mashed as a food [c20 from Luganda]

Matopo Hills (mə'təʊpə) *or* **Matopos** *pl n* the granite hills south of Bulawayo, Zimbabwe, where Cecil Rhodes chose to be buried

Matosinhos *or* **Matozinhos** (*Portuguese* mətu'ʒiɲuʃ) *n* a port in N Portugal, on the estuary of the Leça River north of Oporto: fishing industry. Pop: 167 026 (2001)

matrass *or* **mattrass** ('mætrəs) *n chem obsolete* a long-necked glass flask, used for distilling, dissolving substances, etc [c17 from French, perhaps related to Latin *mētiri* to measure]

matri- *combining form* mother or motherhood: *matriarchy* [from Latin *māter* mother]

matriarch ('meɪtrɪ,ɑːk) *n* **1** a woman who dominates an organization, community, etc **2** the female head of a tribe or family, esp in a matriarchy **3** a very old or venerable woman [c17 from MATRI- + -ARCH, by false analogy with PATRIARCH] > 'matri,**archal** *or less commonly* 'matri,**archic** *adj* > ,matri'**archalism** *n*

matriarchate ('meɪtrɪ,ɑːkɪt, -keɪt) *n rare* a family or people under female domination or government

matriarchy ('meɪtrɪ,ɑːkɪ) *n, pl* -chies **1** a form of social organization in which a female is head of the family or society, and descent and kinship are traced through the female line **2** any society dominated by women

matric (mə'trɪk) *n Brit and South African* short for **matriculation** (sense 2)

matrices ('meɪtrɪ,siːz, 'mæ-) *n* a plural of **matrix**

matricide ('mætrɪ,saɪd, 'meɪ-) *n* **1** the act of killing one's own mother **2** a person who kills his mother [c16 from Latin *mātrīcīdium* (the act), *mātrīcīda* (the agent). See MATRI-, -CIDE]
> ,matri'**cidal** *adj*

matriclinous (,mætrə'klaɪnəs), **matroclinous** *or* **matroclinal** *adj* (of an animal or plant) showing the characters of the female parent. Compare **patriclinous** [c20 from MATRI- + Greek *klīnein* to lean]

matriculate *vb* (mə'trɪkjʊ,leɪt) **1** to enrol or be enrolled in an institution, esp a college or university **2** (*intr*) to attain the academic standard required for a course at such an institution ▷ *n* (mə'trɪkjʊlɪt) **3** *Also called:* **matriculant** a person who has matriculated [c16 from Medieval Latin *mātrīculāre* to register, from *mātrīcula*, diminutive of *matrix* list, MATRIX] > ma'**tricu,lator** *n*

matriculation (mə,trɪkjʊ'leɪʃən) *n* **1** the process of matriculating **2** (in Britain, except Scotland) a former school examination, which was replaced by the General Certificate of Education (Ordinary Level), now superseded by the General Certificate of Secondary Education

matrilineal (,mætrɪ'lɪnɪəl, ,meɪ-) *adj* relating to descent or kinship through the female line > ,matri'**lineally** *adv*

matrilocal ('mætrɪ,ləʊkªl, ,meɪ-) *adj* denoting, having, or relating to a marriage pattern in which the couple live with the wife's family
> matrilocality (,mætrɪləʊ'kælɪtɪ, ,meɪ-) *n*
> ,matri'**locally** *adv*

matrimonial (,mætrɪ'məʊnɪəl) *adj* relating to marriage: *matrimonial troubles* > ,matri'**monially** *adv*

matrimony ('mætrɪmənɪ) *n, pl* -nies **1** the state or condition of being married **2** the ceremony or sacrament of marriage **3 a** a card game in which the king and queen together are a winning combination **b** such a combination [c14 via Norman French from Latin *mātrimōnium* wedlock, from *māter* mother]

matrimony vine *n* any of various shrubs of the solanaceous genus *Lycium*, cultivated for their purple flowers and colourful berries. *Also called:* boxthorn

matrix ('meɪtrɪks, 'mæ-) *n, pl* matrices ('meɪtrɪ,siːz, 'mæ-) *or* matrixes **1** a substance, situation, or environment in which something has its origin, takes form, or is enclosed **2** *anatomy* the thick tissue at the base of a nail from which a fingernail or toenail develops **3** the intercellular substance of bone, cartilage, connective tissue, etc **4 a** the rock material in which fossils, pebbles, etc, are embedded **b** the material in which a mineral is embedded; gangue **5** *printing* **a** a metal mould for casting type **b** a papier-mâché or plastic mould impressed from the forme and used for stereotyping. Sometimes shortened to: mat **6** (formerly) a mould used in the production of gramophone records. It is obtained by electrodeposition onto the master **7** a bed of perforated material placed beneath a workpiece in a press or stamping machine against which the punch operates **8** *metallurgy* **a** the shaped cathode used in electroforming **b** the metal constituting the major part of an alloy **c** the soft metal in a plain bearing in which the hard particles of surface metal are embedded **9** the main component of a composite material, such as the plastic in a fibre-reinforced plastic **10** *maths* a rectangular array of elements set out in rows and columns, used to facilitate the solution of problems, such as the transformation of coordinates. Usually indicated by parentheses: $\begin{pmatrix} a & b & c \\ d & e & f \end{pmatrix}$. Compare **determinant** (sense 3) **11** *linguistics* the main clause of a complex sentence **12** *computing* a rectangular array of circuit elements usually used to generate one set of signals from another **13** *obsolete* the womb [c16 from Latin: womb, female animal used for breeding, from *māter* mother]

matrix printer *n computing* another name for **dot-matrix printer**

matroclinous (,mætrə'klaɪnəs) *adj* a variant of **matriclinous**

matron ('meɪtrən) *n* **1** a married woman regarded as staid or dignified, esp a middle-aged woman with children **2** a woman in charge of the domestic or medical arrangements in an institution, such as a boarding school **3** *US* a wardress in a prison **4** *Official name:* **nursing officer** *Brit* the former name for the administrative head of the nursing staff in a

m

hospital [C14 via Old French from Latin *mātrōna*, from *māter* mother] > 'matron,al *adj* > 'matron,hood *or* 'matron,ship *n* > 'matron-,like *adj*

matronage ('meɪtrənɪdʒ) *n* **1** the state of being a matron **2** supervision or care by a matron **3** matrons collectively

matronly ('meɪtrənlɪ) *adj* of, characteristic of, or suitable for a matron; staid and dignified in a manner associated with a middle-aged, usually plump, woman > 'matronliness *n*

matron of honour *n*, *pl* matrons of honour **1** a married woman serving as chief attendant to a bride. Compare **bridesmaid**, **maid of honour 2** a married woman, usually a member of the nobility, who attends a queen or princess

matronymic (,mætrə'nɪmɪk) *adj*, *n* a less common word for **metronymic**

matryoshka, **matryoshka doll** *or* **matrioshka** (,mætrɪ'ɒʃkə) *n* another word for **Russian doll** [C20 from Russian *matreshka* mother, highly respected lady]

Matsu *or* **Mazu** (mæt'su:) *n* an island group in Formosa Strait, off the SE coast of mainland China: belongs to Taiwan. Pop: 3145 (1990 est). Area: 44 sq km (17 sq miles)

Matsuyama (,mætsʊ'jɑːmə) *n* a port in SW Japan, on NW Shikoku: textile and chemical industries; Ehime University (1949). Pop: 473 039 (2002 est)

matt *or* **matte** (mæt) *adj*, *n*, *vb* variant spellings of **mat²** (senses 2, 3, 5)

Matt. *Bible abbreviation for* **Matthew**

mattamore ('mætə,mɔ:) *n* a subterranean storehouse or dwelling [C17 from French, from Arabic *matmūrā*, from *tamara* to store, bury]

matte¹ (mæt) *n* an impure fused material consisting of metal sulphides produced during the smelting of a sulphide ore [C19 from French]

matte² (mæt) *n* films, television a mask used to blank out part of an image so that another image can be superimposed

matted ('mætɪd) *adj* **1** tangled into a thick mass: *matted hair* **2** covered with or formed of matting

matter ('mætə) *n* **1** that which makes up something, esp a physical object; material **2** substance that occupies space and has mass, as distinguished from substance that is mental, spiritual, etc **3** substance of a specified type: *vegetable matter; reading matter* **4** (sometimes foll by *of* or *for*) thing; affair; concern; question: *a matter of taste; several matters to attend to; no laughing matter* **5** a quantity or amount: *a matter of a few pence* **6** the content of written or verbal material as distinct from its style or form **7** (usually with a negative) importance; consequence **8** philosophy (in the writings of Aristotle and the Scholastics) that which is itself formless but can receive form and become substance **9** philosophy (in the Cartesian tradition) one of two basic modes of existence, the other being **mind**: matter being extended in space as well as time **10** printing **a** type set up, either standing or for use **b** copy to be set in type **11** a secretion or discharge, such as pus **12** law **a** something to be proved **b** statements or allegations to be considered by a court **13** for that matter as regards that **14** See **grey matter 15** no matter **a** regardless of; irrespective of: *no matter what the excuse, you must not be late* **b** (sentence substitute) it is unimportant **16** the matter wrong; the trouble: *there's nothing the matter* ▷ *vb* (*intr*) **17** to be of consequence or importance **18** to form and discharge pus [C13 (n), C16 (vb): from Latin *māteria* cause, substance, esp wood, or a substance that produces something else; related to *māter* mother]

Matterhorn ('mætə,hɔ:n) *n* a mountain on the border between Italy and Switzerland, in the Pennine Alps. Height: 4477 m (14 688 ft). French name: Mont Cervin Italian name: Monte Cervino ('monte tʃer'vi:no)

matter of course *n* **1** an event or result that is natural or inevitable ▷ *adj* **matter-of-course 2** (*usually postpositive*) occurring as a matter of course

3 accepting things as inevitable or natural: *a matter-of-course attitude*

matter of fact *n* **1** a fact that is undeniably true **2** law a statement of facts the truth of which the court must determine on the basis of the evidence before it: contrasted with **matter of law 3** philosophy a proposition that is amenable to empirical testing, as contrasted with the truths of logic or mathematics **4** as a matter of fact actually; in fact ▷ *adj* **matter-of-fact 5** unimaginative or emotionless: *he gave a matter-of-fact account of the murder*

matter of law *n* law an issue requiring the court's interpretation of the law or relevant principles of the law: contrasted with **matter of fact**

matter of opinion *n* a point open to question; a debatable statement

matter waves *pl n* See **de Broglie waves**

mattery ('mætərɪ) *adj* discharging pus

Matthew ('mæθju:) *n* New Testament **1** Saint Also called: Levi a tax collector of Capernaum called by Christ to be one of the 12 apostles (Matthew 9:9–13; 10:3). Feast day: Sept 21 or Nov 16 **2** the first Gospel, traditionally ascribed to him

Matthew Walker ('wɔ:kə) *n* a knot made at the end of a rope by unlaying the strands and passing them up through the loops formed in the next two strands [C19 probably named after the man who introduced it]

mattify ('mætɪ,faɪ) *vb* **-fies**, **-fying**, **-fied** (*tr*) to make (the skin of the face) less oily or shiny using cosmetics [C20 from MAT²]

matting¹ ('mætɪŋ) *n* **1** a coarsely woven fabric, usually made of a natural fibre such as straw or hemp and used as a floor covering, packing material, etc **2** the act or process of making mats **3** material for mats

matting² ('mætɪŋ) *n* **1** another word for **mat²** (sense 1) **2** the process of producing a mat finish

mattins ('mætɪnz) *n* a variant spelling of **matins**

mattock ('mætək) *n* a type of large pick that has one end of its blade shaped like an adze, used for loosening soil, cutting roots, etc [Old English *mattuc*, of unknown origin; related to Latin *mateola* club, mallet]

Matto Grosso ('mætəʊ 'grɒsəʊ) *n* a variant spelling of **Mato Grosso**

mattoid ('mætɔɪd) *n* rare a person displaying eccentric behaviour and mental characteristics that approach the psychotic [C19 from Italian, from *matto* insane]

mattrass ('mætrəs) *n* a variant spelling of **matrass**

mattress ('mætrɪs) *n* **1** a large flat pad with a strong cover, filled with straw, foam rubber, etc, and often incorporating coiled springs, used as a bed or as part of a bed **2** Also called: Dutch mattress a woven mat of brushwood, poles, etc, used to protect an embankment, dyke, etc, from scour **3** a concrete or steel raft or slab used as a foundation or footing. Sometimes shortened to: mat **4** a network of reinforcing rods or expanded metal sheeting, used in reinforced concrete **5** civil engineering another name for **blinding** (sense 3) [C13 via Old French from Italian *materasso*, from Arabic *almatrah* place where something is thrown]

maturate ('mætjʊ,reɪt, 'mætʃʊ-) *vb* **1** to mature or bring to maturity **2** a less common word for **suppurate**. > maturative (mə'tjʊərətɪv, mə'tʃʊ-) *adj*

maturation (,mætjʊ'reɪʃən, ,mætʃʊ-) *n* **1** the process of maturing or ripening **2** zoology the development of ova and spermatozoa from precursor cells in the ovary and testis, involving meiosis **3** a less common word for **suppuration** > ,matu'rational *adj*

mature (mə'tjʊə, -'tʃʊə) *adj* **1** relatively advanced physically, mentally, emotionally, etc; grown-up **2** (of plans, theories, etc) fully considered; perfected **3** due or payable: *a mature debenture* **4** biology **a** fully developed or differentiated: *a mature cell* **b** fully grown; adult: *a mature animal* **5** (of fruit,

wine, cheese, etc) ripe or fully aged **6** (of a river valley or land surface) in the middle stage of the cycle of erosion, characterized by meanders, maximum relief, etc. See also **youthful** (sense 4), **old** (sense 18) ▷ *vb* **7** to make or become mature **8** (*intr*) (of notes, bonds, etc) to become due for payment or repayment [C15 from Latin *mātūrus* early, developed] > ma'turely *adv* > ma'tureness *n*

mature student *n* a student at a college or university who has passed the usual age for formal education

maturity (mə'tjʊərɪtɪ, -'tʃʊə-) *n* **1** the state or quality of being mature; full development **2** finance **a** the date upon which a bill of exchange, bond, note, etc, becomes due for repayment **b** the state of a bill, note, etc, when due

matutinal (,mætjʊ'taɪnºl) *adj* of, occurring in, or during the morning [C17 from Late Latin *mātūtinālis*, from Latin *mātūtinus*, from *Mātūta* goddess of the dawn] > ,matu'tinally *adv*

maty ('meɪtɪ) *n*, *pl* maties, *adj* matier, matiest a variant of **matey**

matzo, matzoh ('mætsəʊ) *or* **matza, matzah** ('mætsə) *n*, *pl* matzos, matzohs, matzas, matzahs *or* matzoth (Hebrew ma'tsɔt) a brittle very thin biscuit of unleavened bread, traditionally eaten during Passover [from Hebrew *matsāh*]

matzoon (mɑ:'tsu:n) *or* **madzoon** (mɑ:d'zu:n) *n* a fermented milk product similar to yogurt [from Armenian *madzun*]

Maubeuge (French mobøʒ) *n* an industrial town in N France, near the border with Belgium. Pop: 33 546 (1999)

mauby ('mɑ:bɪ, 'mɔ:-) *n*, *pl* -bies (in the E Caribbean) a bittersweet drink made from the bark of a rhamnaceous tree [C20 of uncertain origin]

maud (mɔ:d) *n* a shawl or rug of grey wool plaid formerly worn in Scotland [C18 of unknown origin]

maudlin ('mɔ:dlɪn) *adj* foolishly tearful or sentimental, as when drunk [C17 from Middle English *Maudelen* Mary Magdalene, typically portrayed as a tearful penitent] > 'maudlinism *n* > 'maudlinly *adv* > 'maudlinness *n*

maugre *or* **mauger** ('mɔ:gə) *prep* obsolete in spite of [C13 (meaning: ill will): from Old French *maugre*, literally: bad pleasure]

Maui ('maʊɪ) *n* a volcanic island in S central Hawaii: the second largest of the Hawaiian Islands. Pop: 117 644 (2000). Area: 1885 sq km (728 sq miles)

maul (mɔ:l) *vb* (*tr*) **1** to handle clumsily; paw **2** to batter or lacerate ▷ *n* **3** a heavy two-handed hammer suitable for driving piles, wedges, etc **4** rugby a loose scrum that forms around a player who is holding the ball and on his feet [C13 from Old French *mail*, from Latin *malleus* hammer. See MALLET] > 'mauler *n*

Maulana (mɔ:'lɑ:nɑ:) *n* (in Pakistan, India, etc) a title used for a scholar of Persian and Arabic [Urdu, from Arabic *mawlānā*]

maulers ('mɔ:ləz) *pl n* Brit slang the hands

Maulmain (maʊl'meɪn) *n* a variant spelling of **Moulmein**

maulstick *or* **mahlstick** ('mɔ:l,stɪk) *n* a long stick used by artists to steady the hand holding the brush [C17 partial translation of Dutch *maalstok*, from obsolete *malen* to paint + *stok* STICK¹]

Mau Mau ('maʊ ,maʊ) *n*, *pl* Mau Maus *or* Mau Mau **1** a secret political society consisting chiefly of Kikuyu tribesmen that was founded in 1952 to drive European settlers from Kenya by acts of terrorism **2** E African slang a Ugandan motorcycle policeman who directs traffic

maumet ('mɔ:mɪt) *or* **mammet** ('mæmɪt) *n* **1** obsolete a false god; idol **2** English dialect a figure dressed up, such as a guy or scarecrow [C13 from Old French *mahomet* idol, literally: the prophet *Mohammed*, from the belief that his image was worshipped] > 'maumetry *n*

maun, man (mɑ:n, mɔ:n) *or* **mun** (mʌn) *vb* a

dialect word for **must¹** [c14 from Old Norse *man* must, will]

Mauna Kea ('maʊnə 'keɪɑ:) *n* an extinct volcano in Hawaii, on N central Hawaii Island: the highest island mountain in the world. Height: 4206 m (13 799 ft)

Mauna Loa ('maʊnə 'ləʊɑ:) *n* an active volcano in Hawaii, on S central Hawaii Island. Height: 4171 m (13 684 ft)

maund (mɔːnd) *n* a unit of weight used in Asia, esp India, having different values in different localities. A common value in India is 82 pounds or 37 kilograms [c17 from Hindi *man*, from Sanskrit *manā*]

maunder ('mɔːndə) *vb* (*intr*) to move, talk, or act aimlessly or idly [c17 perhaps from obsolete *maunder* to beg, from Latin *mendicāre*; see MENDICANT] ▷ '**maunderer** *n* ▷ '**maundering** *adj*

maundy ('mɔːndɪ) *n, pl* **maundies** *Christianity* the ceremonial washing of the feet of poor persons in commemoration of Jesus' washing of his disciples' feet (John 13:4–34) re-enacted in some churches on Maundy Thursday [c13 from Old French *mandé* something commanded, from Latin *mandatum* commandment, from the words of Christ: *Mandātum novum dō vōbīs* A new commandment give I unto you]

Maundy money *n* specially minted coins distributed by the British sovereign on Maundy Thursday

Maundy Thursday *n Christianity* the Thursday before Easter observed as a commemoration of the Last Supper

maungy ('mɔːndʒɪ) *adj* **-gier, -giest** *West Yorkshire dialect* (esp of a child) sulky, bad-tempered, or peevish [variant of MANGY, in extended sense: restless, dissatisfied]

Mauretania (ˌmɒrɪ'teɪnɪə) *n* an ancient region of N Africa, corresponding approximately to the N parts of modern Algeria and Morocco

Mauretanian (ˌmɒrɪ'teɪnɪən) *adj* **1** of or relating to Mauretania, an ancient region of N Africa, or its inhabitants ▷ *n* **2** a native or inhabitant of Mauretania

mauri ('maːuːriː) *n NZ* the life force or essence of the emotions [Māori]

Maurist ('mɔːrɪst) *n* a member of a congregation of French Benedictine monks founded in 1621 and noted for its scholarly work [c19 named after *St Maurus*, 6th-century disciple of St Benedict]

Mauritania (ˌmɒrɪ'teɪnɪə) *n* a republic in NW Africa, on the Atlantic: established as a French protectorate in 1903 and a colony in 1920; gained independence in 1960; lies in the Sahara; contains rich resources of iron ore. Official language: Arabic; Fulani, Soninke, Wolof, and French are also spoken. Official religion: Muslim. Currency: ouguiya. Capital: Nouakchott. Pop: 2 980 000 (2004 est). Area: 1 030 700 sq km (398 000 sq miles). Official name: **Islamic Republic of Mauritania**

Mauritanian (ˌmɒrɪ'teɪnɪən) *adj* **1** of or relating to Mauritania, a republic in NW Africa, or its inhabitants ▷ *n* **2** a native or inhabitant of Mauritania

Mauritian (mə'rɪʃən) *adj* **1** of or relating to the Indian Ocean island of Mauritius or its inhabitants ▷ *n* **2** a native or inhabitant of Mauritius

Mauritius (mə'rɪʃəs) *n* an island and state in the Indian Ocean, east of Madagascar: originally uninhabited, it was settled by the Dutch (1638–1710) then abandoned; taken by the French in 1715 and the British in 1810; became an independent member of the Commonwealth in 1968. It is economically dependent on sugar. Official language: English; a French creole is widely spoken. Religion: Hindu majority, large Christian minority. Currency: rupee. Capital: Port Louis. Pop: 1 233 000 (2004 est). Area: 1865 sq km (720 sq miles). Former name (1715–1810): Île-de-France

Maurya ('maʊrjə) *n* a dynasty (?321–?185 BC) that united most of the Indian subcontinent and presided over a great flowering of Indian civilization

Mauser ('maʊzə) *n trademark* **1** a high-velocity magazine rifle **2** a type of automatic pistol [c19 named after P. P. von *Mauser* (1838–1914), German firearms inventor]

mausoleum (ˌmɔːsə'lɪəm) *n, pl* **-leums** *or* **-lea** (-'lɪə) a large stately tomb [c16 via Latin from Greek *mausōleion*, the tomb of *Mausolus*, king of Caria; built at Halicarnassus in the 4th century BC] ▷ ˌmauso'lean *adj*

mauvaise foi French (movɛ fwa) *n* (in the philosophy of Sartre) the expression usually rendered as *bad faith*: see **bad faith** (sense 2)

mauvais pas ('məʊvɛ 'pɑ:) *n, pl* **mauvais pas** (-'pɑ:, -'pɑ:z) *mountaineering* a place that presents a particular difficulty on a climb or walk [c19 from French: bad step]

mauvais quart d'heure French (movɛ kar dœr) *n Brit* a brief unpleasant experience [literally: (a) bad quarter of an hour]

mauve (məʊv) *n* **1 a** any of various pale to moderate pinkish-purple or bluish-purple colours **b** (*as adjective*): *a mauve flower* **2** Also called: **Perkin's mauve, mauveine** ('məʊviːn, -vɪn) a reddish-purple aniline dye [c19 from French, from Latin *malva* MALLOW]

maven *or* **mavin** ('meɪvən) *n US* an expert or connoisseur [c20 from Yiddish, from Hebrew *mevin* understanding]

maverick ('mævərɪk) *n* **1** (in US and Canadian cattle-raising regions) an unbranded animal, esp a stray calf **2 a** a person of independent or unorthodox views **b** (*as modifier*): *a maverick politician* [c19 after Samuel A. *Maverick* (1803–70), Texas rancher, who did not brand his cattle]

mavis ('meɪvɪs) *n* a popular name for the **song thrush** [c14 from Old French *mauvis* thrush; origin obscure]

mavourneen *or* **mavournin** (mə'vʊəniːn) *n Irish* my darling [c18 from Irish, from *mo* my + *muirnīn* love]

maw (mɔː) *n* **1** the mouth, throat, crop, or stomach of an animal, esp of a voracious animal **2** *informal* the mouth or stomach of a greedy person [Old English *maga*; related to Middle Dutch *maghe*, Old Norse *magi*]

mawger ('mɔːgə) *adj Caribbean* (of persons or animals) thin or lean [from Dutch *mager* thin, MEAGRE]

mawkin ('mɔːkɪn) *n* **1** a variant of **malkin 2** *Brit dialect* **a** a slovenly woman **b** a scarecrow

mawkish ('mɔːkɪʃ) *adj* **1** falsely sentimental, esp in a weak or maudlin way **2** nauseating or insipid in flavour, smell, etc [c17 from obsolete *mawk* MAGGOT + -ISH] ▷ '**mawkishly** *adv* ▷ '**mawkishness** *n*

max (mæks) *n informal* **1** the most significant, highest, furthest, or greatest thing **2** to the max to the ultimate extent ▷ See also **max out**

max. *abbreviation for* maximum

maxi ('mæksɪ) *adj* **1 a** (of a garment) reaching the ankle **b** (*as noun*): *she wore a maxi* **c** (in combination): *a maxidress* ▷ *n* **2** a type of large racing yacht [c20 shortened from MAXIMUM]

maxilla (mæk'sɪlə) *n, pl* **-lae** (-liː) **1** the upper jawbone in vertebrates. See **jaw** (sense 1) **2** any member of one or two pairs of mouthparts in insects and other arthropods used as accessory jaws [c17 New Latin, from Latin: jaw] ▷ **maxillar** (mæk'sɪlə) *or* **maxil**lary *adj*

maxilliped (mæk'sɪlɪˌpɛd) *n* any member of three pairs of appendages in crustaceans, behind the maxillae: specialized for feeding [c19 *maxilli-*, from MAXILLA + -PED] ▷ max,illi'pedary *adj*

maxillofacial (mækˌsɪləʊ'feɪʃəl, ˌmæksɪləʊ-) *adj* of, relating to, or affecting the upper jawbone and face: *maxillofacial surgery* [c20 from MAXILLA + -O- + FACIAL]

maxim ('mæksɪm) *n* a brief expression of a general truth, principle, or rule of conduct [c15 via French from Medieval Latin, from *maxima*, in the phrase *maxima prōpositiō* basic axiom (literally: greatest proposition); see MAXIMUM]

maxima ('mæksɪmə) *n* a plural of **maximum**

maximal ('mæksɪməl) *adj* **1** of, relating to, or achieving a maximum; being the greatest or best possible **2** *maths* (of a member of an ordered set) being preceded, in order, by all other members of the set ▷ '**maximally** *adv*

maximalist ('mæksɪməlɪst) *n* a person who favours direct action to achieve all his goals and rejects compromise

Maximalist ('mæksɪməlɪst) *n* (in early 20th-century Russia) **1** a member of the radical faction of Social Revolutionaries that supported terrorism against the tsarist regime and advocated a short period of postrevolutionary working-class dictatorship **2** a less common name for a **Bolshevik** ▷ Compare **Minimalist** [c20 from French, a translation of Russian; see BOLSHEVIK]

Maxim gun ('mæksɪm) *n* an obsolete water-cooled machine gun having a single barrel and utilizing the recoil force of each shot to maintain automatic fire [c19 named after Sir Hiram Stevens *Maxim* (1840–1916), its US-born British inventor]

maximin ('mæksɪˌmɪn) *n* **1** *maths* the highest of a set of minimum values **2** (in game theory, etc) the procedure of choosing the strategy that most benefits the least advantaged member of a group. Compare **minimax** [c20 from MAXI(MUM) + MIN(IMUM)]

maximize *or* **maximise** ('mæksɪˌmaɪz) *vb* **1** (*tr*) to make as high or great as possible; increase to a maximum **2** *maths* to find the maximum of (a function) ▷ ˌmaximi'zation, ˌmaximi'sation *or* ˌmaxi'mation *n* ▷ 'maxiˌmizer *or* 'maxiˌmiser *n*

maximum ('mæksɪməm) *n, pl* **-mums** *or* **-ma** (-mə) **1** the greatest possible amount, degree, etc **2** the highest value of a variable quantity **3** *maths* **a** a value of a function that is greater than any neighbouring value **b** a stationary point on a curve at which the tangent changes from a positive value on the left of this point to a negative value on the right. Compare **minimum** (sense 4) **c** the largest number in a set **4** *astronomy* **a** the time at which the brightness of a variable star has its greatest value **b** the magnitude of the star at that time ▷ *adj* **5** of, being, or showing a maximum or maximums Abbreviation: **max** [c18 from Latin: greatest (the neuter form used as noun), from *magnus* great]

maximum likelihood *n statistics* **1** the probability of randomly drawing a given sample from a population maximized over the possible values of the population parameters **2** the non-Bayesian rule that, given an experimental observation, one should utilize as point estimates of parameters of a distribution those values which give the highest conditional probability to that observation, irrespective of the prior probability assigned to the parameters

maximum-minimum thermometer *n* a thermometer that records the highest and lowest temperatures since it was last set

maximus ('mæksɪməs) *n bell-ringing* a method rung on twelve bells [from Latin: superlative of *magnus* great]

maxixe (mə'fiːʃ, mæk'siːks, mə'fiːʃeɪ) *n* a Brazilian dance in duple time, a precursor of the tango [from Brazilian Portuguese]

max out *vb* (*adverb*) *informal* to reach or cause to reach the full extent or allowance: *the goal was to max out the customer's credit card*

maxwell ('mækswəl) *n* the cgs unit of magnetic flux equal to the flux through one square centimetre normal to a field of one gauss. It is equivalent to 10^{-8} weber. Symbol: Mx [c20 named after James Clerk *Maxwell* (1831–79), Scottish physicist]

Maxwell equations ('mækswəl) *pl n* equations developed by James Clerk Maxwell (1831–79) upon

m

which classical electromagnetic theory is based

may¹ (meɪ) *vb, past* **might** (takes an infinitive without *to* or an implied infinitive *used as an auxiliary*) **1** to indicate that permission is requested by or granted to someone: *he may go to the park tomorrow if he behaves himself* **2** (often foll by *well*) to indicate possibility: *the rope may break; he may well be a spy* **3** to indicate ability or capacity, esp in questions: *may I help you?* **4** to express a strong wish: *long may she reign* **5** to indicate result or purpose: used only in clauses introduced by *that* or *so that: he writes so that the average reader may understand* **6** another word for **might¹** **7** to express courtesy in a question: *whose child may this little girl be?* **8** **be that as it may** in spite of that: a sentence connector conceding the possible truth of a previous statement and introducing an adversative clause: *be that as it may, I still think he should come* **9** **come what may** whatever happens **10** **that's as may be** (foll by a clause introduced by *but*) that may be so [Old English *mæg*, from *magan*: compare Old High German *mag*, Old Norse *mā*]

> **USAGE** It was formerly considered correct to use *may* rather than *can* when referring to permission as in: *you may use the laboratory for your experiments*, but this use of *may* is now almost entirely restricted to polite questions such as: *may I open the window?* The use of *may* with *if* in constructions such as: *your analysis may have been more credible if ... is* generally regarded as incorrect, *might* being preferred: *your analysis might have been more credible if ...*

may² (meɪ) *n* an archaic word for **maiden** [Old English *mæg*; related to Old High German *māg* kinsman, Old Norse *māgr* a relative by marriage]

may³ (meɪ) *n* **1** Also: **may tree** a Brit name for **hawthorn** **2** short for **may blossom** [c16 from the month of MAY, when it flowers]

May (meɪ) *n* the fifth month of the year, consisting of 31 days [from Old French, from Latin *Maius*, probably from *Maia*, Roman goddess, identified with the Greek goddess MAIA]

maya (ˈmɑːɪə, ˈmɑːjə, ˈmɑːjɑː) *n* Hinduism illusion, esp the material world of the senses regarded as illusory [c19 from Sanskrit] > ˈ**mayan** *adj*

Maya¹ (ˈmɑːɪə, ˈmɑːjə, ˈmɑːjɑː) *n* the Hindu goddess of illusion, the personification of the idea that the material world is illusory > ˈ**Mayan** *adj*

Maya² (ˈmaɪə) *n* **1** *pl* **-ya** or **-yas** Also called: **Mayan** a member of an American Indian people of Yucatan, Belize, and N Guatemala, having an ancient culture once characterized by outstanding achievements in architecture, astronomy, chronology, painting, and pottery **2** the language of this people. See also **Mayan**

Mayagüez (*Spanish* majaˈɣweθ) *n* a port in W Puerto Rico; needlework industry. Pop: 97 627 (2003 est)

Mayan (ˈmaɪən) *adj* **1** of, relating to, or characteristic of the Maya or any of their languages ▷ *n* **2** a family of Central American Indian languages, including Maya, possibly a member of the Penutian phylum **3** another name for a **Maya²**

May apple *n* **1** an American berberidaceous plant, *Podophyllum peltatum*, with edible yellowish egg-shaped fruit **2** the fruit of this plant

maybe (ˈmeɪˌbiː) *adv* **1 a** perhaps **b** (*as sentence modifier*): *maybe I'll come tomorrow* ▷ *sentence substitute* **2** possibly; neither yes nor no

May beetle or **bug** *n* another name for **cockchafer** and **June bug**

May blobs *n* (*functioning as singular*) another name for **marsh marigold**

may blossom or **may** *n* the blossom of the may tree or hawthorn

Mayday (ˈmeɪˌdeɪ) *n* the international radiotelephone distress signal [c20 phonetic spelling of French *m'aidez* help me]

May Day *n* **a** the first day of May, traditionally a celebration of the coming of spring: in some countries now observed as a holiday in honour of workers **b** (*as modifier*): *May-Day celebrations*

Mayence (majɑ̃s) *n* the French name for **Mainz**

Mayenne (*French* majɛn) *n* a department of NW France, in Pays de la Loire region. Capital: Laval. Pop: 290 780 (2003 est). Area: 5212 sq km (2033 sq miles)

mayest (ˈmeɪɪst) *vb* a variant of **mayst**

Mayfair (ˈmeɪˌfɛə) *n* a fashionable district of west central London

mayflower (ˈmeɪˌflaʊə) *n* **1** any of various plants that bloom in May **2** *US and Canadian* another name for **trailing arbutus** **3** *Brit* another name for **hawthorn, cowslip** or **marsh marigold**

Mayflower (ˈmeɪˌflaʊə) *n* **the** the ship in which the Pilgrim Fathers sailed from Plymouth to Massachusetts in 1620

mayfly (ˈmeɪˌflaɪ) *n, pl* **-flies 1** Also called: **dayfly** any insect of the order *Ephemeroptera* (or *Ephemerida*). The short-lived adults, found near water, have long tail appendages and large transparent wings; the larvae are aquatic **2** *angling* an artificial fly resembling this

mayhap (ˈmeɪˌhæp) *adv* an archaic word for **perhaps** [c16 shortened from *it may hap*]

mayhem or **maihem** (ˈmeɪhɛm) *n* **1** *law* the wilful and unlawful infliction of injury upon a person, esp (formerly) the injuring or removing of a limb rendering him less capable of defending himself against attack **2** any violent destruction or confusion [c15 from Anglo-French *mahem* injury, from Germanic; related to Icelandic *meitha* to hurt. See MAIM]

Maying (ˈmeɪɪŋ) *n* the traditional celebration of May Day

mayn't (ˈmeɪənt, meɪnt) *vb contraction of* may not

Mayo (ˈmeɪəʊ) *n* a county of NW Republic of Ireland, in NW Connacht province, on the Atlantic: has many offshore islands and several large lakes. County town: Castlebar. Pop: 117 446 (2002). Area: 5397 sq km (2084 sq miles)

Mayon (mɑːˈjɔːn) *n* a volcano in the Philippines, on SE Luzon: Height: 2421 m (7943 ft)

mayonnaise (ˌmeɪəˈneɪz) *n* a thick creamy sauce made from egg yolks, oil, and vinegar or lemon juice, eaten with salads, eggs, etc [c19 from French, perhaps from *Mahonnais* of *Mahón*, a port in Minorca]

mayor (mɛə) *n* the chairman and civic head of a municipal corporation in many countries. Scottish equivalent: **provost** [c13 from Old French *maire*, from Latin *maior* greater. See MAJOR] > ˈ**mayoral** *adj* > ˈ**mayorship** *n*

mayoralty (ˈmɛərəltɪ) *n, pl* **-ties** the office or term of office of a mayor [c14 from Old French *mairalté*]

mayoress (ˈmɛərɪs) *n* **1** *chiefly Brit* the wife of a mayor **2** a female mayor

Mayotte (*French* majɔt) *n* an island in the Indian Ocean, northwest of Madagascar; administered by France. Pop (including Pamanzi): 186 026 (2004 est). Area: 374 sq km (146 sq miles)

maypole (ˈmeɪˌpəʊl) *n* a tall pole fixed upright in an open space during May-Day celebrations, around which people dance holding streamers attached at its head

May queen *n* a girl chosen, esp for her beauty, to preside over May-Day celebrations

mayst (meɪst) or **mayest** (ˈmeɪɪst) *vb archaic or dialect* (used with the pronoun *thou* or its relative equivalent) a singular form of the present tense of **may**

may tree *n* a Brit name for **hawthorn**

May Two-Four *n* *Canadian* an informal name for **Victoria Day**

mayweed (ˈmeɪˌwiːd) *n* **1** Also called: **dog fennel, stinking mayweed** a widespread Eurasian weedy plant, *Anthemis cotula*, having evil-smelling leaves and daisy-like flower heads: family *Asteraceae* (composites) **2** **scentless mayweed** a similar and related plant, *Matricaria maritima*, with scentless leaves [c16 changed from Old English *mægtha*

mayweed + WEED¹]

mazard or **mazzard** (ˈmæzəd) *n* **1** an obsolete word for the **head** or **skull 2** another word for **mazer** [c17 altered from MAZER]

Mazar-e-Sharif or **Mazar-i-Sharif** (ˈmæzaː iː ʒəˈriːf) *n* a city in N Afghanistan, reputed burial place of the caliph Ali; trading, agricultural, and military centre. Pop: 254 000 (2005 est)

Mazatlán (*Spanish* maθaˈtlan) *n* a port in W Mexico, in S Sinaloa on the Pacific: situated opposite the tip of the peninsula of Lower California, for which it is the chief link with the mainland. Pop: 406 000 (2005 est)

Mazdaism or **Mazdeism** (ˈmæzdəˌɪzəm) *n* another word for **Zoroastrianism**

maze (meɪz) *n* **1** a complex network of paths or passages, esp one with high hedges in a garden, designed to puzzle those walking through it. Compare **labyrinth** (sense 1) **2** a similar system represented diagrammatically as a pattern of lines **3** any confusing network of streets, pathways, etc: *a maze of paths* **4** a state of confusion ▷ *vb* **5** an archaic or dialect word for **amaze** [c13 see AMAZE] > ˈ**maze**ˌ**like** *adj* > ˈ**mazement** *n*

mazer (ˈmeɪzə) or **mazard, mazzard** (ˈmæzəd) *n obsolete* a large hardwood drinking bowl [c12 from Old French *masere*, of Germanic origin; compare Old Norse *mösurr* maple]

mazey (ˈmeɪzɪ) *adj* mazier, maziest *Northern English dialect* dizzy

Mazu (maˈzuː) *n* the Pinyin transliteration of the Chinese name for **Matsu**

mazuma (məˈzuːmə) *n slang, chiefly US* money [c20 from Yiddish]

mazurka or **mazourka** (məˈzɜːkə) *n* **1** a Polish national dance in triple time **2** a piece of music composed for this dance [c19 from Polish: (dance) of *Mazur* (Mazovia) province in Poland]

mazy (ˈmeɪzɪ) *adj* mazier, maziest of or like a maze; perplexing or confused > ˈ**mazily** *adv* > ˈ**maziness** *n*

mazzard or **mazard** (ˈmæzəd) *n* a wild sweet cherry tree, *Prunus avium*, often used as a grafting stock for cultivated cherries [c16 perhaps related to MAZER]

mb *symbol for* millibar

Mb *computing abbreviation for* megabyte

MB *abbreviation for* **1** Bachelor of Medicine **2** maternity benefit **3** (esp in postal addresses) Manitoba **4** (in Canada) Medal of Bravery

MBA *abbreviation for* Master of Business Administration

Mbabane (ˌəmbɑːˈbɑːnɪ) *n* the capital of Swaziland, in the northwest: administrative and financial centre, with a large iron mine nearby. Pop: 71 000 (2005 est)

m-banking *n* the practice of making financial transactions or managing bank accounts using mobile phone technology [c20 M(OBILE) + BANKING]

mbaqanga (ˌəmbɑːˈkæŋɡə) *n* a style of Black popular music of urban South Africa [c20 perhaps from Zulu *umbaqanga* mixture]

MBE *abbreviation for* Member of the Order of the British Empire (a Brit title)

mbira (ˌəmˈbiːrə) *n* an African musical instrument consisting of tuned metal strips attached to a resonating box, which are plucked with the thumbs. Also called: **thumb piano** [Shona]

MBO *abbreviation for* management buyout

Mbujimayi (ˌəmˈbuːdʒɪˌmaɪɪ) *n* a city in S Democratic Republic of Congo (formerly Zaïre): diamond mining. Pop: 821 000 (2005 est)

mbyte *computing abbreviation for* megabyte

mc *the internet domain name for* Monaco

MC *abbreviation for* **1** Master of Ceremonies **2** *astrology* Medium Coeli [Latin: Midheaven.] **3** (in the US) Member of Congress **4** (in Britain) Military Cross **5** ▷ *international car registration for* Monaco

Mc- *prefix* a variant of **Mac-**. For names beginning

with this prefix, see under **Mac-**

MCB *abbreviation for* miniature circuit breaker; a small trip switch operated by an overload and used to protect an electric circuit, esp a domestic circuit as an alternative to a fuse

MCC (in Britain) *abbreviation for* Marylebone Cricket Club

MCG (in Australia) *abbreviation for* Melbourne Cricket Ground

MCh *abbreviation for* Master of Surgery [Latin *Magister Chirurgiae*]

McJob (mək'dʒɒb) *n informal* a job that is poorly paid and menial [c20 a humorous corruption of *McDonald's*, a major American fast-food enterprise]

MCom *abbreviation for* Master of Commerce

m-commerce ('ɛm,kɒmɜːs) *n* business transactions conducted on the internet using a mobile phone [c20 from M(OBILE) + COMMERCE]

MCP *informal* ▷ *abbreviation for* male chauvinist pig

MCPS *abbreviation for* Mechanical Copyright Protection Society

M.C.S. (in the US and Canada) *abbreviation for* Master of Computer Science

md *the internet domain name for* Moldova

Md *the chemical symbol for* mendelevium

MD *abbreviation for* **1** Doctor of Medicine [from Latin *Medicinae Doctor*] **2** Maryland **3** Medical Department **4** mentally deficient **5** Managing Director **6** ▷ *international car registration for* Moldova

Md. *abbreviation for* Maryland

MDF *abbreviation for* medium-density fibreboard: a wood-substitute material used in interior decoration

MDMA *abbreviation for* 3,4-methylenedioxymethamphetamine. Also called (informal): **ecstasy**

MDNA *abbreviation for* mitochondrial DNA

MDR *abbreviation for* multi-drug resistant: *MDR tuberculosis*

MDS *abbreviation for* Master of Dental Surgery

me¹ (miː; *unstressed* mɪ) *pron* (*objective*) **1** refers to the speaker or writer: *that shocks me; he gave me the glass* **2** *chiefly US* a dialect word for **myself** when used as an indirect object: *I want to get me a car* ▷ *n* **3** *informal* the personality of the speaker or writer or something that expresses it: *the real me comes out when I'm happy* [Old English *mē* (dative); compare Dutch, German *mir*, Latin *mē* (accusative), *mihi* (dative)]

me² (miː) *n* a variant spelling of **mi**

Me *the chemical symbol for* the methyl group

ME *abbreviation for* **1** Maine **2** Marine Engineer **3** Mechanical Engineer **4** Methodist Episcopal **5** Mining Engineer **6** Middle English **7** (in titles) Most Excellent **8** **myalgic encephalopathy**

Me. *abbreviation for* Maine

mea culpa *Latin* ('meɪə 'kʊlpɑː) an acknowledgment of guilt [literally: my fault]

mead¹ (miːd) *n* an alcoholic drink made by fermenting a solution of honey, often with spices added [Old English *meodu*; related to Old High German *metu*, Greek *methu*, Welsh *medd*]

mead² (miːd) *n* an archaic or poetic word for **meadow** [Old English *mǣd*]

Mead (miːd) *n* **Lake** a reservoir in NW Arizona and SE Nevada, formed by the Hoover Dam across the Colorado River: one of the largest man-made lakes in the world. Area: 588 sq km (227 sq miles)

meadow ('mɛdəʊ) *n* **1** an area of grassland, often used for hay or for grazing of animals **2** a low-lying piece of grassland, often boggy and near a river [Old English *mǣdwe*, from *mǣd* MEAD²; related to *māwan* to MOW¹] ▷ **'meadowy** *adj*

meadow fescue *n* an erect Eurasian perennial grass, *Festuca pratensis*, with lustrous leaves and stem bases surrounded by dark brown sheaths

meadow grass *n* a perennial grass, *Poa pratensis*, that has erect hairless leaves and grows in meadows and similar places in N temperate regions

meadowlark ('mɛdəʊ,lɑːk) *n* either of two North American yellow-breasted songbirds, *Sturnella*

magna (**eastern meadowlark**) or *S. neglecta* (**western meadowlark**): family *Icteridae* (American orioles)

meadow lily *n* another name for **Canada lily**

meadow mouse *n US* another name for **vole¹**

meadow mushroom *n* a saprotrophic agaricaceous edible fungus, *Agaricus campestris*, having a white cap with pink or brown gills on the underside

meadow pipit *n* a common European songbird, *Anthus pratensis*, with a pale brown speckled plumage: family *Motacillidae* (pipits and wagtails)

meadow rue *n* any ranunculaceous plant of the N temperate genus *Thalictrum*, esp *T. flavum*, having clusters of small yellowish-green, white, or purple flowers

meadow saffron *n* another name for **autumn crocus**

meadowsweet ('mɛdəʊ,swiːt) *n* **1** a Eurasian rosaceous plant, *Filipendula ulmaria*, with dense heads of small fragrant cream-coloured flowers. See also **dropwort** (sense 1) **2** any of several North American rosaceous plants of the genus *Spiraea*, having pyramid-shaped sprays of small flowers

meagre *or US* **meager** ('miːɡə) *adj* **1** deficient in amount, quality, or extent **2** thin or emaciated **3** lacking in richness or strength [c14 from Old French *maigre*, from Latin *macer* lean, poor] ▷ **'meagrely** *or US* **'meagerly** *adv* ▷ **'meagreness** *or US* **'meagerness** *n*

meal¹ (miːl) *n* **1 a** any of the regular occasions, such as breakfast, lunch, dinner, etc, when food is served and eaten **b** (in combination): *mealtime*. Related adj: **prandial 2** the food served and eaten **3** **make a meal of** *informal* to perform (a task) with unnecessarily great effort [Old English *mǣl* measure, set time, meal; related to Old High German *māl* mealtime]

meal² (miːl) *n* **1** the edible part of a grain or pulse (excluding wheat) ground to a coarse powder, used chiefly as animal food **2** *Scot* oatmeal **3** *chiefly US* maize flour [Old English *melu*; compare Dutch *meel*, Old High German *melo*, Old Norse *mjöl*] ▷ **'meal-less** *adj*

mealie *or* **mielie** ('miːlɪ) *n South African* an ear of maize. See also **mealies** [c19 from Afrikaans *milie*, from Portuguese *milho*, from Latin *milium* millet]

mealie meal *or* **mielie meal** *n South African* finely ground maize

mealie pap *or* **mielie pap** *n South African* mealie porridge [Afrikaans]

mealies *or* **mielies** ('miːlɪz) *n* (*functioning as singular*) a South African word for **maize**

meal moth *n* a small pyralid moth, *Pyralis farinalis*, whose larvae are an important pest of stored cereals. The **Indian meal moth** (*Plodia interpunctella*) and the **Mediterranean flour moth** (*Ephestia kuehniella*) are other pyralids with similar habits

meals on wheels *or* **meals-on-wheels** *n* (*functioning as singular*) social welfare, *Brit* a service, usually subsidized, and run by a social services department or voluntary body, which delivers hot meals to elderly or housebound people who might otherwise be unable to have them

meal ticket *n slang* a person, situation, etc, providing a source of livelihood or income [from original US sense of ticket entitling holder to a meal]

mealworm ('miːl,wɜːm) *n* the larva of various beetles of the genus *Tenebrio*, esp *T. molitor*, feeding on meal, flour, and similar stored foods: family *Tenebrionidae*

mealy ('miːlɪ) *adj* mealier, mealiest **1** resembling meal; powdery **2** containing or consisting of meal or grain **3** sprinkled or covered with meal or similar granules **4** (esp of horses) spotted; mottled **5** pale in complexion **6** short for **mealy-mouthed**. ▷ **'mealiness** *n*

mealy bug *n* any plant-eating homopterous insect of the genus *Pseudococcus* and related genera, coated with a powdery waxy secretion: some species are pests of citrus fruits and greenhouse plants: family *Pseudococcidae*

mealy-mouthed *adj* hesitant or afraid to speak plainly; not outspoken [c16 from MEALY (in the sense: soft, soft-spoken)] ▷ **,mealy-'mouthedness** *n*

mean¹ (miːn) *vb* means, meaning, meant (*mainly tr*) **1** (*may take a clause as object or an infinitive*) to intend to convey or express **2** (*may take a clause as object or an infinitive*) intend: *she didn't mean to hurt it* **3** (*may take a clause as object*) to say or do in all seriousness: *the boss means what he says about strikes* **4** (*often passive; often foll by* for) to destine or design (for a certain person or purpose): *she was meant for greater things* **5** (*may take a clause as object*) to denote or connote; signify; represent: *examples help show exactly what a word means* **6** (*may take a clause as object*) to produce; cause: *the weather will mean long traffic delays* **7** (*may take a clause as object*) to foretell; portend: *those dark clouds mean rain* **8** to have the importance of: *money means nothing to him* **9** (*intr*) to have the intention of behaving or acting (esp in the phrases **mean well** or **mean ill**) **10** **mean business** to be in earnest [Old English *mǣnan*; compare Old Saxon *mēnian* to intend, Dutch *meenen*]

> USAGE In standard English, *mean* should not be followed by *for* when expressing intention: *I didn't mean this to happen* (not *I didn't mean for this to happen*)

mean² (miːn) *adj* **1** *chiefly Brit* miserly, ungenerous, or petty **2** humble, obscure, or lowly: *he rose from mean origins to high office* **3** despicable, ignoble, or callous: *a mean action* **4** poor or shabby: *mean clothing; a mean abode* **5** *informal, chiefly US and Canadian* bad-tempered; vicious **6** *informal* ashamed: *he felt mean about not letting the children go to the zoo* **7** *informal, chiefly US* unwell; in low spirits **8** *slang* excellent; skilful: *he plays a mean trombone* **9** **no mean a** of high quality: *no mean performer* **b** difficult: *no mean feat* [c12 from Old English *gemǣne* common; related to Old High German *gimeini*, Latin *communis* common, at first with no pejorative sense] ▷ **'meanly** *adv* ▷ **'meanness** *n*

mean³ (miːn) *n* **1** the middle point, state, or course between limits or extremes **2** moderation **3** *maths* **a** the second and third terms of a proportion, as *b* and *c* in *a/b = c/d* **b** another name for **average** (sense 2) See also **geometric mean 4** *statistics* a statistic obtained by multiplying each possible value of a variable by its probability and then taking the sum or integral over the range of the variable ▷ *adj* **5** intermediate or medium in size, quantity, etc **6** occurring halfway between extremes or limits; average ▷ See also **means** [c14 via Anglo-Norman from Old French *moien*, from Late Latin *mediānus* MEDIAN]

meander (mɪ'ændə) *vb* (*intr*) **1** to follow a winding course **2** to wander without definite aim or direction ▷ *n* **3** (*often plural*) a curve or bend, as in a river **4** (*often plural*) a winding course or movement **5** an ornamental pattern, esp as used in ancient Greek architecture [c16 from Latin *maeander*, from Greek *Maiandros* the River Maeander; see MENDERES (sense 1)] ▷ **me'anderer** *n* ▷ **me'andering** *adj* ▷ **me'anderingly** *adv* ▷ **me'androus** *adj*

Meander (miː'ændə) *n* a variant spelling of **Maeander**

mean deviation *n statistics* **1** the difference between an observed value of a variable and its mean **2** Also called: **mean deviation from the mean** (or **median**), **average deviation** a measure of dispersion derived by computing the mean of the absolute values of the differences between observed values of a variable and the variable's mean

mean distance *n* the average of the greatest and least distances of a celestial body from its primary

mean free path *n* the average distance travelled by a particle, atom, etc, between collisions

meanie *or* **meany** ('miːnɪ) *n, pl* meanies *informal* **1** *chiefly Brit* a miserly or stingy person **2** *chiefly US* a nasty ill-tempered person

meaning ('miːnɪŋ) *n* **1** the sense or significance of a word, sentence, symbol, etc; import; semantic or lexical content **2** the purpose underlying or intended by speech, action, etc **3** the inner, symbolic, or true interpretation, value, or message: *the meaning of a dream* **4** valid content; efficacy: *a law with little or no meaning* **5** *philosophy* **a** the sense of an expression; its connotation **b** the reference of an expression; its denotation. In recent philosophical writings meaning can be used in both the above senses. See also **sense** (sense 13) ▷ *adj* **6** expressive of some sense, intention, criticism, etc: *a meaning look* ▷ See also **well-meaning**

meaningful ('miːnɪŋfʊl) *adj* **1** having great meaning or validity **2** eloquent, expressive: *a meaningful silence* > 'meaningfully *adv* > 'meaningfulness *n*

meaningless ('miːnɪŋlɪs) *adj* futile or empty of meaning > 'meaninglessly *adv* > 'meaninglessness *n*

mean lethal dose *n* another term for **median lethal dose**

mean life *n physics* the average time of existence of an unstable or reactive entity, such as a nucleus, elementary particle, charge carrier, etc; lifetime. It is equal to the half-life divided by 0.693 15. Symbol: τ

means (miːnz) *n* **1** (*functioning as singular or plural*) the medium, method, or instrument used to obtain a result or achieve an end: *a means of communication* **2** (*functioning as plural*) resources or income **3** (*functioning as plural*) considerable wealth or income: *a man of means* **4** by all means without hesitation or doubt; certainly: *come with us by all means* **5** by means of with the use or help of **6** by no manner of means definitely not: *he was by no manner of means a cruel man* **7** by no (*or* not by any) means on no account; in no way: *by no means come!*

mean sea level *n* (in the UK) the sea level used by the Ordnance Survey as a datum level, determined at Newlyn in Cornwall. See **sea level**

means of production *pl n* (in Marxist theory) the raw materials and means of labour (tools, machines, etc) employed in the production process

mean solar day *n* the time between two successive passages of the mean sun across the meridian at noon. It is equal to 24 hours 3 minutes and 56.555 seconds of mean sidereal time

means test *n* a test involving the checking of a person's income to determine whether he qualifies for financial or social aid from a government. Compare **needs test**. > 'means-tested *adj*

mean sun *n* an imaginary sun moving along the celestial equator at a constant rate and completing its annual course in the same time as the sun takes to move round the ecliptic at a varying rate. It is used in the measurement of mean solar time

meant (mɛnt) *vb* the past tense and past participle of **mean¹**

mean time *or* **mean solar time** *n* the time, at a particular place, measured in terms of the passage of the mean sun; the timescale is not precisely constant. See **mean solar day**

meantime ('miːnˌtaɪm) *n* **1** the intervening time or period, as between events (esp in the phrase **in the meantime**) ▷ *adv* **2** another word for meanwhile

mean-tone tuning *n* See **temperament** (sense 4)

meanwhile ('miːnˌwaɪl) *adv* **1** during the intervening time or period **2** at the same time, esp in another place ▷ *n* **3** another word for meantime

meany ('miːnɪ) *n informal* a variant spelling of meanie

Mearns (mɛənz) *n* the another name for Kincardineshire

measled ('miːzəld) *adj* (of cattle, sheep, or pigs)

infested with tapeworm larvae; measly

measles ('miːzəlz) *n* (*functioning as singular or plural*) **1** a highly contagious viral disease common in children, characterized by fever, profuse nasal discharge of mucus, conjunctivitis, and a rash of small red spots spreading from the forehead down to the limbs. Technical names: **morbilli**, **rubeola** See also **German measles** **2** a disease of cattle, sheep, and pigs, caused by infestation with tapeworm larvae [c14 from Middle Low German *masele* spot on the skin; influenced by Middle English *mesel* leper, from Latin *misellus*, diminutive of *miser* wretched]

measly ('miːzlɪ) *adj* **-slier, -sliest** **1** *informal* meagre in quality or quantity **2** (of meat) measled **3** having or relating to measles [c17 see MEASLES]

measurable ('mɛʒərəbᵊl, 'mɛʒrə-) *adj* able to be measured; perceptible or significant > ˌmeasura'bility *or* 'measurableness *n* > 'measurably *adv*

measure ('mɛʒə) *n* **1** the extent, quantity, amount, or degree of something, as determined by measurement or calculation **2** a device for measuring distance, volume, etc, such as a graduated scale or container **3** a system of measurement: *give the size in metric measure* **4** a standard used in a system of measurements: *the international prototype kilogram is the measure of mass in SI units* **5** a specific or standard amount of something: *a measure of grain; short measure; full measure* **6** a basis or standard for comparison: *his work was the measure of all subsequent attempts* **7** reasonable or permissible limit or bounds: *we must keep it within measure* **8** degree or extent (often in phrases such as **in some measure, in a measure**, etc): *they gave him a measure of freedom* **9** (*often plural*) a particular action intended to achieve an effect: *they took measures to prevent his leaving* **10** a legislative bill, act, or resolution: *to bring in a measure* **11** *music* another word for **bar¹** (sense 15a) **12** *prosody* poetic rhythm or cadence; metre **13** a metrical foot **14** *poetic* a melody or tune **15** the act of measuring; measurement **16** *archaic* a dance **17** *printing* the width of a page or column of type **18** **for good measure** as an extra precaution or beyond requirements **19** **get the measure of** *or* **get someone's measure** to assess the nature, character, quality, etc, of someone or something **20** **made to measure** (of clothes) made to fit an individual purchaser ▷ *vb* **21** (*tr; often foll by up*) to determine the size, amount, etc, of by measurement **22** (*intr*) to make a measurement or measurements **23** (*tr*) to estimate or determine: *I measured his strength to be greater than mine* **24** (*tr*) to function as a measurement of: *the ohm measures electrical resistance* **25** (*tr*) to bring into competition or conflict: *he measured his strength against that of his opponent* **26** (*intr*) to be as specified in extent, amount, etc: *the room measures six feet* **27** (*tr*) to travel or move over as if measuring **28** (*tr*) to adjust or choose: *he measured his approach to suit the character of his client* **29** (*intr*) to allow or yield to measurement ▷ See also **measure off, measure out, measures, measure up** [c13 from Old French, from Latin *mēnsūra* measure, from *mēnsus*, past participle of *mētīrī* to measure] > 'measurer *n*

measured ('mɛʒəd) *adj* **1** determined by measurement **2** slow, stately, or leisurely **3** carefully considered; deliberate > 'measuredly *adv* > 'measuredness *n*

measured daywork ('deɪˌwɜːk) *n* a system of wage payment, usually determined by work-study techniques, whereby the wage of an employee is fixed on the understanding that a specific level of work performance will be maintained

measureless ('mɛʒəlɪs) *adj* limitless, vast, or infinite > 'measurelessly *adv* > 'measurelessness *n*

measurement ('mɛʒəmənt) *n* **1** the act or process of measuring **2** an amount, extent, or size determined by measuring **3** a system of measures based on a particular standard

measurement ton *n* the full name for **ton¹** (sense 5)

measure off *or* **out** *vb* (*tr, adverb*) to determine the limits of; mark out: *to measure off an area*

measure out *vb* (*tr, adverb*) **1** to pour or dole out: *they measure out a pint of fluid* **2** to administer; mete out: *they measured out harsh punishments*

measures ('mɛʒəz) *pl n* rock strata that are characterized by a particular type of sediment or deposit: *coal measures*

measure up *vb* **1** (*adverb*) to determine the size of (something) by measurement **2** **measure up to** to fulfil (expectations, standards, etc)

measuring jug *n* a graduated jug used in cooking to measure ingredients

measuring worm *n* the larva of a geometrid moth: it has legs on its front and rear segments only and moves in a series of loops. Also called: **looper, inchworm**

meat (miːt) *n* **1** the flesh of mammals used as food, as distinguished from that of birds and fish **2** anything edible, esp flesh with the texture of meat: *crab meat* **3** food, as opposed to drink **4** the essence or gist **5** an archaic word for **meal¹** **6** **meat and drink** a source of pleasure **7** **have one's meat and one's manners** *Irish informal* to lose nothing because one's offer is not accepted [Old English *mete*; related to Old High German *maz* food, Old Saxon *meti*, Gothic *mats*] > 'meatless *adj*

meataxe ('miːtˌæks) *n* **1** a cleaver **2** **mad as a meataxe** *Austral and NZ informal* raving

meatball ('miːtˌbɔːl) *n* **1** minced beef, shaped into a ball before cooking **2** *US and Canadian slang* a stupid or boring person

Meath (miːð, miːθ) *n* a county of E Republic of Ireland, in Leinster province on the Irish Sea: formerly a kingdom much larger than the present county; livestock farming. County town: Trim. Pop: 134 005 (2002). Area: 2338 sq km (903 sq miles)

meatspace ('miːtˌspeɪs) *n slang* the real physical world, as contrasted with the world of cyberspace

meatus (mɪˈeɪtəs) *n, pl* **-tuses** *or* **-tus** *anatomy* a natural opening or channel, such as the canal leading from the outer ear to the eardrum [c17 from Latin: passage, from *meāre* to pass]

meaty ('miːtɪ) *adj* **meatier, meatiest** **1** of, relating to, or full of meat: *a meaty stew* **2** heavily built; fleshy or brawny **3** full of import or interest: *a meaty discussion* **4** *Judaism* another word for **fleishik** > 'meatily *adv* > 'meatiness *n*

mebi- ('mɛbɪ) *prefix computing* denoting 2²⁰: *mebibyte*. Symbol: **Mi** [c20 from ME(GA-) + BI(NARY)]

MEC (in South Africa) *abbreviation for* Member of the Executive Council

mecamylamine (ˌmɛkəˈmɪləˌmiːn) *n* a ganglion-blocking drug administered orally to lower high blood pressure. Formula: $C_{11}H_{21}N$ [c20 from ME(THYL) + cam(phane) (a former name of bornane) + -YL + AMINE]

Mecca *or* **Mekka** ('mɛkə) *n* **1** a city in W Saudi Arabia, joint capital (with Riyadh) of Saudi Arabia: birthplace of Mohammed; the holiest city of Islam, containing the Kaaba. Pop: 1 529 000 (2005 est). Arabic name: **Makkah** **2** (*sometimes not capital*) a place that attracts many visitors: *Athens is a Mecca for tourists*

Meccano (mɪˈkɑːnəʊ) *n trademark* a construction set consisting of miniature metal or plastic parts from which mechanical models can be made

mechanic (mɪˈkænɪk) *n* **1** a person skilled in maintaining or operating machinery, motors, etc **2** *archaic* a common labourer [c14 from Latin *mēchanicus*, from Greek *mēkhanikos*, from *mēkhanē* MACHINE]

mechanical (mɪˈkænɪkᵊl) *adj* **1** made, performed, or operated by or as if by a machine or machinery: *a mechanical process* **2** concerned with machines or machinery **3** relating to or controlled or operated by physical forces **4** of or concerned with mechanics **5** (of a gesture, etc) automatic; lacking thought, feeling, etc **6** *philosophy* accounting for phenomena by physically determining forces **7** (of paper, such as newsprint) made from pulp that has been mechanically ground and contains impurities ▷ *n* **8** *printing* another name for **camera-ready copy** **9** *archaic* another word for **mechanic** (sense 2) > me'chanicalism *n* > me'chanically *adv* > me'chanicalness *n*

mechanical advantage *n* the ratio of the working force exerted by a mechanism to the applied effort

mechanical drawing *n* a drawing to scale of a machine, machine component, architectural plan, etc, from which dimensions can be taken for manufacture

mechanical engineering *n* the branch of engineering concerned with the design, construction, and operation of machines and machinery > **mechanical engineer** *n*

mechanical equivalent of heat *n physics* a factor for converting units of energy into heat units. It has the value 4.1868 joules per calorie. Symbol: *J*

mechanical instrument *n* a musical instrument, such as a barrel organ or music box, that plays a preselected piece of music by mechanical means

mechanically recovered meat *n* an amalgamation of the gristle, cartilage, and fat removed from animal carcasses, sometimes used in the manufacture of meat products such as sausages and hamburgers. Also called: MRM

mechanician (ˌmɛkəˈnɪʃən) *or* **mechanist** *n* a person skilled in making machinery and tools; technician

mechanics (mɪˈkænɪks) *n* **1** (*functioning as singular*) the branch of science, divided into statics, dynamics, and kinematics, concerned with the equilibrium or motion of bodies in a particular frame of reference. See also **quantum mechanics, wave mechanics, statistical mechanics 2** (*functioning as singular*) the science of designing, constructing, and operating machines **3** the working parts of a machine **4** the technical aspects of something: *the mechanics of poetic style*

mechanism (ˈmɛkəˌnɪzəm) *n* **1** a system or structure of moving parts that performs some function, esp in a machine **2** something resembling a machine in the arrangement and working of its parts: *the mechanism of the ear* **3** any form of mechanical device or any part of such a device **4** a process or technique, esp of execution: *the mechanism of novel writing* **5** *philosophy* **a** the doctrine that human action can be explained in purely physical terms, whether mechanical or biological **b** the explanation of phenomena in causal rather than teleological or essentialist terms **c** the view that the task of science is to seek such explanations **d** strict determinism ▷ Compare **dynamism, vitalism 6** *psychoanal* **a** the ways in which psychological forces interact and operate **b** a structure having an influence on the behaviour of a person, such as a defence mechanism

mechanist (ˈmɛkənɪst) *n* **1** a person who accepts a mechanistic philosophy **2** another name for a **mechanician**

mechanistic (ˌmɛkəˈnɪstɪk) *adj* **1** *philosophy* of or relating to the theory of mechanism **2** *maths* of or relating to mechanics > ˌmechaˈnistically *adv*

mechanize *or* **mechanise** (ˈmɛkəˌnaɪz) *vb* (*tr*) **1** to equip (a factory, industry, etc) with machinery **2** to make mechanical, automatic, or monotonous **3** to equip (an army, etc) with motorized or armoured vehicles > ˌmechaniˈzation *or* ˌmechaniˈsation *n* > ˈmechaˌnizer *or* ˈmechaˌniser *n*

mechanoreceptor (ˌmɛkənəʊrɪˈsɛptə) *n physiol* a sensory receptor, as in the skin, that is sensitive to a mechanical stimulus, such as pressure

mechanotherapy (ˌmɛkənəʊˈθɛrəpɪ) *n* the treatment of disorders or injuries by means of mechanical devices, esp devices that provide exercise for bodily parts

mechatronics (ˌmɛkəˈtrɒnɪks) *n* (*functioning as singular*) the combination of mechanical engineering, computing, and electronics, as used in the design and development of new manufacturing techniques [c20 from MECHA(NICS) + (ELEC)TRONICS]

Mechelen (ˈmɛxələn) *n* a city in N Belgium, in Antwerp province: capital of the Netherlands from 1507 to 1530; formerly famous for lace-making, now has an important vegetable market. Pop: 76 981 (2004 est). French name: Malines English name: Mechlin

Mechlin (ˈmɛklɪn) *n* the English name for **Mechelen**

Mechlin lace *n* bobbin lace made at Mechlin, characterized by patterns outlined by a heavier flat thread. Also called: **malines**

meck (mɛk) *n Northeastern Scot dialect* a variant of **maik**

Mecklenburg (ˈmɛklənˌbɜːg; *German* ˈmeːklənbʊrk) *n* a historic region and former state of NE Germany, along the Baltic coast; now part of Mecklenburg-West Pomerania

Mecklenburg-West Pomerania (ˌpɒməˈreɪnɪə) *n* a state of NE Germany, along the Baltic coast: consists of the former state of Mecklenburg and those parts of W Pomerania not incorporated into Poland after World War II: part of East Germany until 1990. Pop: 1 732 000 (2003 est)

MEcon *abbreviation for* Master of Economics

meconium (mɪˈkəʊnɪəm) *n* **1** the dark green mucoid material that forms the first faeces of a newborn infant **2** opium or the juice from the opium poppy [c17 from New Latin, from Latin: poppy juice (used also of infant's excrement because of similarity in colour), from Greek *mēkōneion*, from *mēkōn* poppy]

meconopsis (ˌmɛkəˈnɒpsɪs) *n* any plant of the mostly Asiatic papaveraceous genus *Meconopsis*, esp *M. betonicifolia* (the Tibetan or blue poppy), grown for its showy sky-blue flowers. *M. cambrica* is the Welsh poppy [New Latin, from Greek *mēkōn* poppy + -OPSIS]

Med (mɛd) *n* **the** *informal* the Mediterranean region

MEd *abbreviation for* Master of Education

med. *abbreviation for* **1** medical **2** medicine **3** medium

médaillons (medaɪˈjɔ̃) *pl n cookery* small round thin pieces of meat, fish, vegetables, etc. Also called: **medallions** [c20 French: medallions]

medal (ˈmɛdᵊl) *n* **1** a small flat piece of metal bearing an inscription or image, given as an award or commemoration of some outstanding action, event, etc ▷ *vb* **-als, -alling, -alled** *or US* **-als, -aling, -aled 2** (*tr*) to honour with a medal [c16 from French *médaille*, probably from Italian *medaglia*, ultimately from Latin *metallum* METAL] > **medallic** (mɪˈdælɪk) *adj*

medallion (mɪˈdæljən) *n* **1** a large medal **2** an oval or circular decorative device resembling a medal, usually bearing a portrait or relief moulding, used in architecture and textile design [c17 from French, from Italian *medaglione*, from *medaglia* MEDAL]

medallist *or US* **medalist** (ˈmɛdᵊlɪst) *n* **1** a designer, maker, or collector of medals **2** *chiefly sport* a winner or recipient of a medal or medals

Medal of Bravery *n* a Canadian award for courage. Abbreviation: MB

Medal of Honor *n* the highest US military decoration, awarded by Congress for conspicuous bravery in action: instituted in 1861 (Navy), 1862 (Army)

medal play *n golf* another name for **stroke play**

Medan (ˈmɛdɑːn) *n* a city in Indonesia, in NE Sumatra; seat of the University of North Sumatra (1952) and the Indonesian Islam University (1952). Pop: 1 904 273 (2000)

meddle (ˈmɛdᵊl) *vb* (*intr*) **1** (usually foll by *with*) to interfere officiously or annoyingly **2** (usually foll by *in*) to involve oneself unwarrantably: *to meddle in someone's private affairs* [c14 from Old French *medler*, ultimately from Latin *miscēre* to mix] > **meddler** *n* > **meddling** *adj* > **meddlingly** *adv*

meddlesome (ˈmɛdᵊlsəm) *adj* intrusive or meddling > **meddlesomely** *adv* > **meddlesomeness** *n*

Mede (miːd) *n* a member of an Indo-European people of West Iranian speech who established an empire in SW Asia in the 7th and 6th centuries BC > **Median** *n, adj*

Medea (mɪˈdɪə) *n Greek myth* a princess of Colchis, who assisted Jason in obtaining the Golden Fleece from her father

Medellín (*Spanish* meðeˈʎin) *n* a city in W Colombia, at an altitude of 1554 m (5100 ft): the second largest city in the country, with three universities; important coffee centre, with large textile mills; dominated by drug cartels in recent years. Pop: 3 236 000 (2005 est)

medevac (ˈmɛdɪˌvæk) *n* **1** *military* the evacuation of casualties from forward areas to the nearest hospital or base **2** a helicopter used for transporting wounded or sick people to hospital ▷ *vb* **-vacs, -vacking, -vacked 3** (*tr*) to transport (a wounded or sick person) to hospital by medevac [c20 from med(ical) evac(uation)]

medfly (ˈmɛdˌflaɪ) *n, pl* **-fly** *or* **-flies** another name for **Mediterranean fruit fly**

media¹ (ˈmiːdɪə) *n* **1** a plural of **medium 2** the means of communication that reach large numbers of people, such as television, newspapers, and radio ▷ *adj* **3** of or relating to the mass media: *media hype*

USAGE When *media* refers to the mass media, it is sometimes treated as a singular form, as in: *the media has shown great interest in these events*. Many people think this use is incorrect and that *media* should always be treated as a plural form: *the media have shown great interest in these events*

media² (ˈmiːdɪə) *n, pl* **-diae** (-dɪˌiː) **1** the middle layer of the wall of a blood or lymph vessel **2** one of the main veins in the wing of an insect **3** *phonetics* **a** a consonant whose articulation lies midway between that of a voiced and breathed speech sound **b** a consonant pronounced with weak voice, as *c* in French *second* [c19 from Latin *medius* middle]

Media (ˈmiːdɪə) *n* an ancient country of SW Asia, south of the Caspian Sea: inhabited by the Medes; overthrew the Assyrian Empire in 612 BC in alliance with Babylonia; conquered by Cyrus the Great in 550 BC; corresponds to present-day NW Iran

mediacy (ˈmiːdɪəsɪ) *n* **1** the quality or state of being mediate **2** a less common word for **mediation**

mediad (ˈmiːdɪæd) *adj anatomy, zoology* situated near the median line or plane of an organism

mediaeval (ˌmɛdɪˈiːvᵊl) *adj* a variant spelling of **medieval**

media event *n* an event that is staged for or exploited by the mass media, whose attention lends it an apparent importance

mediagenic (ˌmiːdɪəˈdʒɛnɪk) *adj* presenting an attractive or positive image when portrayed in the media

medial (ˈmiːdɪəl) *adj* **1** of or situated in the middle **2** ordinary or average in size **3** *maths* relating to an average **4** another word for **median** (senses 1, 2, 3) **5** *zoology* of or relating to a media ▷ *n* **6** *phonetics* a speech sound between being fortis and lenis; media [c16 from Late Latin *mediālis*, from *medius* middle] > **medially** *adv*

median (ˈmiːdɪən) *adj* **1** of, relating to, situated in, or directed towards the middle **2** *biology* of or relating to the plane that divides an organism or organ into symmetrical parts **3** *statistics* of or relating to the median ▷ *n* **4** a middle point, plane, or part **5** *geometry* **a** a straight line joining one vertex of a triangle to the midpoint of the

m

opposite side. See also **centroid b** a straight line joining the midpoints of the nonparallel sides of a trapezium **6** *statistics* the middle value in a frequency distribution, below and above which lie values with equal total frequencies **7** *statistics* the middle number or average of the two middle numbers in an ordered sequence of numbers: *7 is the median of both 1, 7, 31 and 2, 5, 9, 16* **8** *Canadian* the strip, often covered with grass, that separates the two sides of a highway. Also called (chiefly Brit): **central reserve** [c16 from Latin *mediānus*, from *medius* middle] > **'medianly** *adv*

median lethal dose *or* **mean lethal dose** *n* **1** the amount of a drug or other substance that, when administered to a group of experimental animals, will kill 50 per cent of the group in a specified time **2** the amount of ionizing radiation that will kill 50 per cent of a population in a specified time ▷ Abbreviation: LD$_{50}$

median strip *n* the US term for **central reserve**

mediant ('miːdɪənt) *n music* **a** the third degree of a major or minor scale **b** *(as modifier)*: *a mediant chord* [c18 from Italian *mediante*, from Late Latin *mediāre* to be in the middle]

mediastinum (ˌmiːdɪəˈstaɪnəm) *n, pl* **-na** (-nə) *anatomy* **1** a membrane between two parts of an organ or cavity such as the pleural tissue between the two lungs **2** the part of the thoracic cavity that lies between the lungs, containing the heart, trachea, etc [c16 from medical Latin, neuter of Medieval Latin *mediastīnus* median, from Latin: low grade of servant, from *medius* mean] > ˌmedias'tinal *adj*

mediate *vb* ('miːdɪˌeɪt) **1** *(intr; usually foll by between or in)* to intervene (between parties or in a dispute) in order to bring about agreement **2** to bring about (an agreement) **3** to bring about (an agreement) between parties in a dispute **4** to resolve (differences) by mediation **5** *(intr)* to be in a middle or intermediate position **6** *(tr)* to serve as a medium for causing (a result) or transferring (objects, information, etc) ▷ *adj* ('miːdɪɪt) **7** occurring as a result of or dependent upon mediation **8** a rare word for **intermediate 9** *logic* (of an inference) having more than one premise, esp being syllogistic in form [c16 from Late Latin *mediāre* to be in the middle] > **'mediately** *adv* > **'mediateness** *n* > **'mediative, 'mediatory** *or* ˌmedia'torial *adj* > 'medi,ator *n* > ˌmedia'torially *adv*

mediation (ˌmiːdɪˈeɪʃən) *n* **1** the act of mediating; intercession **2** *international law* an attempt to reconcile disputed matters arising between states, esp by the friendly intervention of a neutral power **3** a method of resolving an industrial dispute whereby a third party consults with those involved and recommends a solution which is not, however, binding on the parties

mediatize *or* **mediatise** ('miːdɪəˌtaɪz) *vb* *(tr)* to annex (a state) to another state, allowing the former ruler to retain his title and some authority [c19 from French *médiatiser*; see MEDIATE, -IZE] > ˌmediati'zation *or* ˌmediati'sation *n*

medic[1] ('mɛdɪk) *n informal* a doctor, medical orderly, or medical student [c17 from MEDICAL]

medic[2] ('mɛdɪk) *n* the usual US spelling of **medick**

medicable ('mɛdɪkəbºl) *adj* potentially able to be treated or cured medically > **'medicably** *adv*

Medicaid ('mɛdɪˌkeɪd) *n US* a health assistance programme financed by federal, state, and local taxes to help pay hospital and medical costs for persons of low income [c20 MEDIC(AL) + AID]

medical ('mɛdɪkºl) *adj* **1** of or relating to the science of medicine or to the treatment of patients by drugs, etc, as opposed to surgery **2** a less common word for **medicinal** ▷ *n* **3** *informal* a medical examination [c17 from Medieval Latin *medicālis*, from Latin *medicus* physician, surgeon, from *medērī* to heal] > **'medically** *adv*

medical audit *n* a review of the professional standards of doctors, usually within a hospital, conducted by a medical committee

medical certificate *n* **1** a document stating the

result of a satisfactory medical examination **2** a doctor's certificate giving evidence of a person's unfitness for work

medical examination *n* an examination carried out to determine the physical fitness of an applicant for a job, life insurance, etc

medical examiner *n* **1** *chiefly US* a medical expert, usually a physician, employed by a state or local government to determine the cause of sudden death in cases of suspected violence, suicide, etc. Compare **coroner 2** a physician who carries out medical examinations

medical jurisprudence *n* another name for **forensic medicine**

medical marker *n* **1** a trait, condition, etc that indicates the presence of, or a probable increased predisposition towards, a medical or psychological disorder **2** a pen or an inklike substance used in medicine, for example to mark on a surgical patient the places where incisions are to be made

medicament (mɪˈdɪkəmənt, ˈmɛdɪ-) *n* a medicine or remedy in a specified formulation [c16 via French from Latin *medicāmentum*, from *medicāre* to cure] > **medicamental** (ˌmɛdɪkəˈmɛntºl) *or* ˌmedica'mentary *adj*

Medicare ('mɛdɪˌkɛə) *n* **1** (in the US) a federally sponsored health insurance programme for persons of 65 or older **2** *(often not capital)* (in Canada) a similar programme covering all citizens **3** (in Australia) a government-controlled general health-insurance scheme [c20 MEDI(CAL) + CARE]

medicate ('mɛdɪˌkeɪt) *vb (tr)* **1** to cover or impregnate (a wound, etc) with an ointment, cream, etc **2** to treat (a patient) with a medicine **3** to add a medication to (a bandage, shampoo, etc) [c17 from Latin *medicāre* to heal] > **'medicative** *adj*

medicated *adj* **1** (of a patient) having been treated with a medicine or drug **2** (of a bandage, shampoo, etc) containing medication

medication (ˌmɛdɪˈkeɪʃən) *n* **1** treatment with drugs or remedies **2** a drug or remedy

Medicean (ˌmɛdɪˈsiːən, -ˈtʃiː-) *adj* of or relating to the Medici, the Italian family of bankers, merchants, and rulers of Florence and Tuscany, prominent in Italian political and cultural history in the 15th, 16th, and 17th centuries

medicinal (mɛˈdɪsɪnºl) *adj* **1** relating to or having therapeutic properties ▷ *n* **2** a medicinal substance > me'dicinally *adv*

medicinal leech *n* a large European freshwater leech, *Hirudo medicinalis*, formerly used in medical bloodletting

medicine ('mɛdɪsɪn, 'mɛdsɪn) *n* **1** any drug or remedy for use in treating, preventing, or alleviating the symptoms of disease **2** the science of preventing, diagnosing, alleviating, or curing disease **3** any nonsurgical branch of medical science **4** the practice or profession of medicine: *he's in medicine*. Related adjs: **Aesculapian, iatric 5** something regarded by primitive people as having magical or remedial properties **6** **take one's medicine** to accept a deserved punishment **7** **a taste (or dose) of one's own medicine** an unpleasant experience in retaliation for and by similar methods to an unkind or aggressive act [c13 via Old French from Latin *medicīna (ars)* (art of) healing, from *medicus* doctor, from *medērī* to heal]

medicine ball *n* a heavy ball used for physical training

medicine chest *n* a small chest or cupboard for storing medicines, bandages, etc

medicine lodge *n* a wooden structure used for magical and religious ceremonies among certain North American Indian peoples

medicine man *n* (among certain peoples, esp North American Indians) a person believed to have supernatural powers of healing; a magician or sorcerer

medicine shop *n* (in Malaysia) a Chinese

chemist's shop where traditional herbs are sold as well as modern drugs. It is not, however, a dispensary for prescribed medicines

medicine wheel *n* a Native American ceremonial tool representing a sacred circle

medick *or US* **medic** ('mɛdɪk) *n* any small leguminous plant of the genus *Medicago*, such as black medick or sickle medick, having yellow or purple flowers and trifoliate leaves [c15 from Latin *mēdica*, from Greek *mēdikē (poa)* Median (grass), a type of clover]

medico ('mɛdɪˌkəʊ) *n, pl* **-cos** a doctor or medical student [c17 via Italian from Latin *medicus*]

medico- *combining form* medical: *medicolegal*

medieval *or* **mediaeval** (ˌmɛdɪˈiːvºl) *adj* **1** of, relating to, or in the style of the Middle Ages **2** *informal* old-fashioned; primitive [c19 from New Latin *medium aevum* the middle age. See MEDIUM, AGE] > ˌmedi'evally *or* ˌmedi'aevally *adv*

Medieval Greek *n* the Greek language from the 7th century AD to shortly after the sacking of Constantinople in 1204. Also called: **Middle Greek, Byzantine Greek** Compare **Koine, Late Greek, Ancient Greek**

medievalism *or* **mediaevalism** (ˌmɛdɪˈiːvəˌlɪzəm) *n* **1** the beliefs, life, or style of the Middle Ages or devotion to those **2** a belief, custom, or point of style copied or surviving from the Middle Ages

medievalist *or* **mediaevalist** (ˌmɛdɪˈiːvəlɪst) *n* a student or devotee of the Middle Ages > ˌmedi'eval'istic *or* ˌmedi,aeval'istic *adj*

Medieval Latin *n* the Latin language as used throughout Europe in the Middle Ages. It had many local forms incorporating Latinized words from other languages

medina (mɛˈdiːnə) *n (sometimes capital)* the ancient quarter of any of various North African cities. Compare **kasbah** [c20 Arabic, literally: town]

Medina (mɛˈdiːnə) *n* a city in W Saudi Arabia: the second most holy city of Islam (after Mecca), with the tomb of Mohammed; university (1960). Pop: 1 044 000 (2005 est). Arabic name: **Al Madinah** Ancient Arabic name: **Yathrib**

mediocre (ˌmiːdɪˈəʊkə, ˈmiːdɪˌəʊkə) *adj often derogatory* average or ordinary in quality: *a mediocre book* [c16 via French from Latin *mediocris* moderate, literally: halfway up the mountain, from *medius* middle + *ocris* stony mountain]

mediocrity (ˌmiːdɪˈɒkrɪtɪ, ˌmɛd-) *n, pl* **-ties 1** the state or quality of being mediocre **2** a mediocre person or thing

meditate ('mɛdɪˌteɪt) *vb* **1** *(intr; foll by on or upon)* to think about something deeply **2** *(intr)* to reflect deeply on spiritual matters, esp as a religious act: *I make space to meditate every day* **3** *(tr)* to plan, consider, or think of doing (something) [c16 from Latin *meditārī* to reflect upon] > **'meditative** *adj* > **'meditatively** *adv* > **'meditativeness** *n* > 'medi,tator *n*

meditation (ˌmɛdɪˈteɪʃən) *n* **1** the act of meditating; contemplation; reflection **2** contemplation of spiritual matters, esp as a religious practice

Mediterranean (ˌmɛdɪtəˈreɪnɪən) *n* **1** short for the **Mediterranean Sea 2** a native or inhabitant of a Mediterranean country ▷ *adj* **3** of, relating to, situated or dwelling on or near the Mediterranean Sea **4** denoting a postulated subdivision of the Caucasoid race, characterized by slender build and dark complexion **5** *meteorol* (of a climate) characterized by hot summers and relatively warm winters when most of the annual rainfall occurs **6** *(often not capital)* *obsolete* situated in the middle of a landmass; inland [c16 from Latin *mediterrāneus*, from *medius* middle + *-terrāneus*, from *terra* land, earth]

Mediterranean fever *n* another name for **brucellosis**

Mediterranean fruit fly *n* a species of dipterous fly, *Ceratitis capitata*, having marbled wings, whose maggots tunnel into fruits such as citrus, peach, and vine in the Mediterranean area, South Africa, and elsewhere: family *Trypetidae*. Also called: **medfly**

Mediterranean Sea *n* a large inland sea between S Europe, N Africa, and SW Asia: linked with the Atlantic by the Strait of Gibraltar, with the Red Sea by the Suez Canal, and with the Black Sea by the Dardanelles, Sea of Marmara, and Bosporus; many ancient civilizations developed around its shores. Greatest depth: 4770 m (15 900 ft). Length: (west to east) over 3700 km (2300 miles). Greatest width: about 1368 km (850 miles). Area: (excluding the Black Sea) 2 512 300 sq km (970 000 sq miles). Ancient name: Mare Internum

medium ('mi:dɪəm) *adj* **1** midway between extremes; average: *a medium size* **2** (of a colour) reflecting or transmitting a moderate amount of light: *a medium red*. Compare **light**¹ (sense 29), **dark** (sense 2) ▷ *n, pl* **-dia** (-dɪə) *or* **-diums 3** an intermediate or middle state, degree, or condition; mean: *the happy medium* **4** an intervening substance or agency for transmitting or producing an effect; vehicle: *air is a medium for sound* **5** a means or agency for communicating and diffusing information, news, etc, to the public: *television is a powerful medium* **6** a person supposedly used as a spiritual intermediary between the dead and the living **7** the substance in which specimens of animals and plants are preserved or displayed **8** *biology* short for **culture medium 9** the substance or surroundings in which an organism naturally lives or grows **10** *art* **a** the category of a work of art, as determined by its materials and methods of production: *the medium of wood engraving* **b** the materials used in a work of art **11** any solvent in which pigments are mixed and thinned **12** any one of various sizes of writing or printing paper, esp 18½ by 23½ inches or 17½ by 22 inches (**small medium**) ▷ See also **mediums** [c16 from Latin: neuter singular of *medius* middle]

▪ USAGE See at **media**

medium-dated *adj* (of a gilt-edged security) having between five and fifteen years to run before redemption. Compare **long-dated, short-dated**

medium frequency *n* a radio-frequency band or radio frequency lying between 3000 and 300 kilohertz. Abbreviation: MF

mediumistic (ˌmi:dɪə'mɪstɪk) *adj* of or relating to a spiritual medium

medium of exchange *n* anything acceptable as a measure of value and a standard of exchange for goods and services in a particular country, region, etc

medium-range ballistic missile *n* a missile that can carry a nuclear weapon with a range of 800 to 2400 km. Abbreviation: MRBM

mediums ('mi:dɪəmz) *pl n* medium-dated gilt-edged securities

medium wave *n* **a** a radio wave with a wavelength between 100 and 1000 metres **b** (*as modifier*): *a medium-wave broadcast*

medivac ('mɛdɪˌvæk) *n* ▷ *vb* **-vacs, -vacking, -vacked** a variant spelling of **medevac**

medlar ('mɛdlə) *n* **1** a small Eurasian rosaceous tree, *Mespilus germanica* **2** the fruit of this tree, which resembles the crab apple and is not edible until it has begun to decay **3** any of several other rosaceous trees or their fruits [c14 from Old French *medlier,* from Latin *mespilum* medlar fruit, from Greek *mespilon*]

medley ('mɛdlɪ) *n* **1** a mixture of various types or elements **2** a musical composition consisting of various tunes arranged as a continuous whole **3** Also called: **medley relay a** *swimming* a race in which a different stroke is used for each length **b** *athletics* a relay race in which each leg has a different distance **4** an archaic word for **melee** ▷ *adj* **5** of, being, or relating to a mixture or variety [c14 from Old French *medlee,* from *medler* to mix, quarrel]

Médoc (meɪ'dɒk, 'mɛdɒk; *French* medɔk) *n* **1** a district of SW France, on the left bank of the Gironde estuary: famous vineyards **2** a fine red wine from this district

medrese (mə'dreseɪ) *n* a variant of **madrasah**

medulla (mɪ'dʌlə) *n, pl* **-las** *or* **-lae** (-li:) **1** *anatomy* **a** the innermost part of an organ or structure **b** short for **medulla oblongata 2** *botany* another name for **pith** (sense 4) [c17 from Latin: marrow, pith, probably from *medius* middle] > **me'dullary** *or* **me'dullar** *adj*

medulla oblongata (ˌɒblɒŋ'gɑːtə) *n, pl* **medulla oblongatas** *or* **medullae oblongatae** (mɪ'dʌli: ˌɒblɒŋ'gɑːti:) the lower stalklike section of the brain, continuous with the spinal cord, containing control centres for the heart and lungs [c17 New Latin: oblong-shaped medulla]

medullary ray *n* any of the sheets of conducting tissue that run radially through the vascular tissue of some higher plants

medullary sheath *n* **1** *anatomy* a myelin layer surrounding and insulating certain nerve fibres **2** a layer of thick-walled cells surrounding the pith of the stems of some higher plants

medullated ('mɛdəˌleɪtɪd, mɪ'dʌl-) *adj* **1** *anatomy* encased in a myelin sheath **2** having a medulla

medulloblastoma (mɪˌdʌləʊblæs'təʊmə) *n* a rapidly growing brain tumour that develops in children and is responsive to radiotherapy

medusa (mɪ'dju:zə) *n, pl* **-sas** *or* **-sae** (-zi:) **1** another name for **jellyfish** (senses 1, 2) **2** one of the two forms in which a coelenterate exists. It has a jelly-like umbrella-shaped body, is free swimming, and produces gametes. Also called: **medusoid, medusan** Compare **polyp** [c18 from the likeness of its tentacles to the snaky locks of Medusa] > **me'dusan** *adj*

Medusa (mɪ'dju:zə) *n Greek myth* a mortal woman who was transformed by Athena into one of the three Gorgons. Her appearance was so hideous that those who looked directly at her were turned to stone. Perseus eventually slew her. See also **Pegasus**¹ ▷ Me'dusan *adj*

medusoid (mɪ'dju:zɔɪd) *adj* **1** of, relating to, or resembling a medusa ▷ *n* **2** another name for **medusa** (sense 2)

Medway ('mɛdˌweɪ) *n* **1** a river in SE England, flowing through Kent and the **Medway towns** (Rochester, Chatham, and Gillingham) to the Thames estuary. Length: 110 km (70 miles) **2** a unitary authority in SE England, in Kent. Pop: 251 100 (2003 est). Area: 204 sq km (79 sq miles)

mee (mi:) *n* (in Malaysia) noodles or a dish containing noodles [from Chinese (Cantonese) *mien* noodles]

Meech Lake Accord (mi:tʃ) *n* the agreement reached in 1987 at Meech Lake, Quebec, at a Canadian federal-provincial conference that accepted Quebec's conditions for signing the Constitution Act of 1982. The Accord lapsed when the legislatures of two provinces, Newfoundland and Quebec, failed to ratify it by the deadline of June 23, 1990

meed (mi:d) *n archaic* a recompense; reward [Old English: wages; compare Old High German *mēta* pay]

meek (mi:k) *adj* **1** patient, long-suffering, or submissive in disposition or nature; humble **2** spineless or spiritless; compliant **3** an obsolete word for **gentle** [c12 related to Old Norse *mjūkr* amenable; compare Welsh *mwytho* to soften] > **'meekly** *adv* > **'meekness** *n*

meerkat ('mɪəˌkæt) *n* any of several South African mongooses, esp *Suricata suricatta* (**slender-tailed meerkat** or **suricate**), which has a lemur-like face and four-toed feet [c19 from Dutch: sea-cat]

meerschaum ('mɪəʃəm) *n* **1** Also called: **sepiolite** a white, yellowish, or pink compact earthy mineral consisting of hydrated magnesium silicate: used to make tobacco pipes and as a building stone. Formula: $Mg_2Si_3O_6(OH)_4$ **2** a tobacco pipe having a bowl made of this mineral [c18 German, literally: sea foam]

Meerut ('mɪərət) *n* an industrial city in N India, in W Uttar Pradesh: founded as a military base by the British in 1806 and scene of the first uprising (1857) of the Indian Mutiny. Pop: 1 074 229 (2001)

meet¹ (mi:t) *vb* **meets, meeting, met 1** (sometimes foll by *up* or (*US*) *with*) to come together (with), either by design or by accident; encounter: *I met him unexpectedly; we met at the station* **2** to come into or be in conjunction or contact with (something or each other): *the roads meet in the town; the sea meets the sky* **3** (*tr*) to come to or be at the place of arrival of: *to meet a train* **4** to make the acquaintance of or be introduced to (someone or each other): *have you two met?* **5** to gather in the company of (someone or each other): *the board of directors meets on Tuesday* **6** to come into the presence of (someone or each other) as opponents: *Joe meets Fred in the boxing match* **7** (*tr*) to cope with effectively; satisfy: *to meet someone's demands* **8** (*tr*) to be apparent to (esp in the phrase **meet the eye**) **9** (*tr*) to return or counter: *to meet a blow with another* **10** to agree with (someone or each other): *we met him on the price he suggested* **11** (*tr;* sometimes foll by *with*) to experience; suffer: *he met his death in a road accident* **12** to occur together: *courage and kindliness met in him* **13** (*tr*) *Caribbean* to find (a person, situation, etc) in a specified condition: *I met the door open* **14 meet and greet** (of a celebrity, politician, etc) to have a session of being introduced to and questioned by members of the public or journalists ▷ *n* **15** the assembly of hounds, huntsmen, etc, prior to a hunt **16** a meeting, esp a sports meeting **17** *US* the place where the paths of two railway trains meet or cross **18 meet-and-greet** a session where a celebrity, etc, is introduced to or questioned by members of the public or journalists [Old English *mētan;* related to Old Norse *mæta*, Old Saxon *mōtian*] > **'meeter** *n*

meet² (mi:t) *adj archaic* proper, fitting, or correct [c13 from variant of Old English *gemǣte;* related to Old High German *māza* suitability, Old Norse *mætr* valuable] > **'meetly** *adv*

meeting ('mi:tɪŋ) *n* **1** an act of coming together; encounter **2** an assembly or gathering **3** a conjunction or union **4** a sporting competition, as of athletes, or of horse racing

meeting house *n* **1** the place in which certain religious groups, esp Quakers, hold their meetings for worship **2** Also called: **wharepuni** NZ a large Māori tribal hall

meff (mɛf) *n dialect* **1** *Northern English* a tramp **2** a stupid or worthless person

mefloquine ('mɛfləʊˌkwi:n) *n* a synthetic drug administered orally to prevent or treat malaria [c20]

meg (mɛg) *n informal* short for **megabyte**

mega ('mɛgə) *adj slang* extremely good, great, or successful [c20 probably independent use of MEGA-]

mega- *combining form* **1** denoting 10⁶: *megawatt*. Symbol: M **2** (in computer technology) denoting 2²⁰ (1 048 576): *megabyte* **3** large or great: *megalith* **4** *informal* great in importance or amount: *megastar* [from Greek *megas* huge, powerful]

megabit ('mɛgəˌbɪt) *n computing* **1** one million bits **2** 2²⁰ bits

megabuck ('mɛgəˌbʌk) *n US and Canadian slang* **a** a million dollars **b** (*as modifier*): *a megabuck movie*

megabyte ('mɛgəˌbaɪt) *n computing* 2²⁰ or 1 048 576 bytes. Abbreviations: MB, mbyte See also **mega-** (sense 2)

megacephaly (ˌmɛgə'sɛfəlɪ) *or* **megalocephaly** *n* the condition of having an unusually large head or cranial capacity. It can be of congenital origin or result from an abnormal overgrowth of the facial bones. Compare **microcephaly** > **megacephalic** (ˌmɛgəsɪ'fælɪk), ˌmega'cephalous, ˌmegaloce'phalic *or* ˌmegalo'cephalous *adj*

megacity ('mɛgəˌsɪtɪ) *n, pl* **-cities** a city with over 10 million inhabitants

m

megadeath ('mɛgə,dɛθ) *n* the death of a million people, esp in a nuclear war or attack

megadose ('mɛgə,dəʊs) *n* a very large dose, as of a medicine, vitamin, etc

Megaera (mɪ'dʒɪərə) *n Greek myth* one of the three Furies; the others are Alecto and Tisiphone

megafauna ('mɛgə,fɔ:nə) *n* the component of the fauna of a region or period that comprises the larger terrestrial animals

megaflop ('mɛgə,flɒp) *n computing* a measure of processing speed, consisting of a million floating-point operations a second [c20 from MEGA- + *flo(ating) p(oint)*]

megagamete (,mɛgə'gæmi:t) *n* another name for **macrogamete**

megahertz ('mɛgə,hɜ:ts) *n, pl* **-hertz** one million hertz; one million cycles per second. Symbol: MHz Former name: **megacycle**

megalith ('mɛgəlɪθ) *n* a stone of great size, esp one forming part of a prehistoric monument. See also **alignment** (sense 6), **circle** (sense 11) > ,mega'lithic *adj*

megalithic tomb *n* a burial chamber constructed of large stones, either underground or covered by a mound and usually consisting of long transepted corridors (**gallery graves**) or of a distinct chamber and passage (**passage graves**). The tombs may date from the 4th millennium BC

megalitre ('mɛgə,li:tə) *n* one million litres

megalo- *or before a vowel* **megal-** *combining form* indicating greatness, or abnormal size: *megalopolis; megaloblast* [from Greek *megas* great]

megaloblast ('mɛgələʊ,blɑ:st) *n* an abnormally large red blood cell precursor, present in certain types of anaemia > megaloblastic (,mɛgələʊ'blæstɪk) *adj*

megaloblastic anaemia *n* any anaemia, esp pernicious anaemia, characterized by the presence of megaloblasts in the blood or bone marrow

megalocardia (,mɛgələʊ'kɑ:dɪə) *n pathol* abnormal increase in the size of the heart. Also called: **cardiomegaly**

megalocephaly (,mɛgələʊ'sɛfəlɪ) *n* another word for **megacephaly**

megalomania (,mɛgələʊ'meɪnɪə) *n* 1 a mental illness characterized by delusions of grandeur, power, wealth, etc 2 *informal* a lust or craving for power > ,megalo'maniac *adj, n* > megalomaniacal (,mɛgələʊmə'naɪək³l) *adj*

megalopolis (,mɛgə'lɒpəlɪs) *n* an urban complex, usually comprising several large towns [c20 MEGALO- + Greek *polis* city] > megalopolitan (,mɛgələ'pɒlɪt³n) *adj, n*

megalosaur ('mɛgələʊ,sɔ:) *n* any very large Jurassic or Cretaceous bipedal carnivorous dinosaur of the genus *Megalosaurus*, common in Europe: suborder *Theropoda* (theropods) [c19 from New Latin *megalosaurus*, from MEGALO- + Greek *sauros* lizard] > ,megalo'saurian *adj, n*

megaphanerophyte (,mɛgə'fænərəʊ,faɪt) *n botany* any tree with a height over 30 metres

megaphone ('mɛgə,fəʊn) *n* a funnel-shaped instrument used to amplify the voice. See also **loud-hailer**. > megaphonic (,mɛgə'fɒnɪk) *adj* > ,mega'phonically *adv*

megaphyll ('mɛgəfɪl) *n botany* the relatively large type of leaf produced by ferns and seed plants. Compare **microphyll**

megapixel ('mɛgə,pɪks³l) *n computing* one million pixels: a term used to describe the degree of resolution supplied by digital cameras, scanners, etc

megaplex ('mɛgə,plɛks) *n* **a** a cinema complex containing a large number of separate screens, and usually a restaurant or bar **b** (*as modifier*): *a megaplex cinema*

megapode ('mɛgə,pəʊd) *n* any ground-living gallinaceous bird of the family *Megapodiidae*, of Australia, New Guinea, and adjacent islands. Their eggs incubate in mounds of sand, rotting vegetation, etc, by natural heat. Also called:

mound-builder See also **brush turkey, mallee fowl**

megaproject ('mɛgə,prɒdʒɛkt) *n* a very large, expensive, or ambitious business project

Megara ('mɛgərə) *n* a town in E central Greece: an ancient trading city, founding many colonies in the 7th and 8th centuries BC. Pop: 26 562 (1991 est)

megaron ('mɛgə,rɒn) *n, pl* **-ra** (-rə) a tripartite rectangular room containing a central hearth surrounded by four pillars, found in Bronze Age Greece and Asia Minor [from Greek, literally: hall, from *megas* large]

megascopic (,mɛgə'skɒpɪk) *adj* another word for **macroscopic**

megasporangium (,mɛgəspɔ:'rændʒɪəm) *n, pl* **-gia** (-dʒɪə) the structure in certain spore-bearing plants in which the megaspores are formed: corresponds to the ovule in seed plants. Compare **microsporangium**

megaspore ('mɛgə,spɔ:) *n* 1 Also called: macrospore the larger of the two types of spore produced by some spore-bearing plants, which develops into the female gametophyte. Compare **microspore** (sense 1) 2 the cell in flowering plants that gives rise to the embryo sac > ,mega'sporic *adj*

megasporophyll (,mɛgə'spɔ:rəfɪl) *n* a leaf on which the megaspores are formed: corresponds to the carpel of a flowering plant. Compare **microsporophyll** [c20 from MEGA- + SPOROPHYLL]

megass *or* **megasse** (mə'gæs) *n* another name for **bagasse** (sense 2) [c19 of obscure origin]

megastar ('mɛgə,stɑ:) *n* a very well-known personality in the entertainment business

megathere ('mɛgə,θɪə) *n* any of various gigantic extinct American sloths of the genus *Megatherium* and related genera, common in late Cenozoic times [c19 from New Latin *megathērium*, from MEGA- + -*there*, from Greek *thērion* wild beast] > ,mega'therian *adj*

megaton ('mɛgə,tʌn) *n* 1 one million tons 2 an explosive power, esp of a nuclear weapon, equal to the power of one million tons of TNT. Abbreviation: mt > megatonic (,mɛgə'tɒnɪk) *adj*

megavolt ('mɛgə,vɒlt) *n* one million volts. Symbol: MV

megawatt ('mɛgə,wɒt) *n* one million watts. Symbol: MW

Me generation *n* the generation, originally in the 1970s, characterized by self-absorption; in the 1980s, characterized by material greed

Megger ('mɛgə) *n trademark* an instrument that generates a high voltage in order to test the resistance of insulation, etc

Meghalaya (,meɪgə'leɪə) *n* a state of NE India, created in 1969 from part of Assam. Capital: Shillong. Pop: 2 306 069 (2001). Area: 22 429 sq km (7800 sq miles)

Megiddo (mə'gɪdəʊ) *n* an ancient town in N Palestine, strategically located on a route linking Egypt to Mesopotamia: site of many battles, including an important Egyptian victory over rebel chieftains in 1469 or 1468 BC. See also **Armageddon**

megillah (mə'gɪlə; *Hebrew* migi'la) *n, pl* **-lahs** *or* **-loth** (*Hebrew* -'lɔt) *Judaism* 1 a scroll of the Book of Esther, read on the festival of Purim 2 a scroll of the Book of Ruth, Song of Songs, Lamentations, or Ecclesiastes 3 *slang* anything, such as a story or letter, that is too long or unduly drawn out [Hebrew: scroll, from *galal* to roll]

megilp *or* **magilp** (mə'gɪlp) *n* an oil-painting medium of linseed oil mixed with mastic varnish or turpentine [c18 of unknown origin]

megohm ('mɛg,əʊm) *n* one million ohms. Symbol: MΩ

megrim[1] ('mi:grɪm) *n archaic* 1 (*often plural*) a caprice 2 a migraine [c14 from MIGRAINE]

megrim[2] ('mi:grɪm) *n* a flatfish, *Lepidorhombus whiffiagonis*, of the turbot family, having a yellowish translucent body up to 50 cm (20 in.) in length, found in European waters, and caught for food [c19 of uncertain origin]

megrims ('mi:grɪmz) *n (functioning as singular)* 1 *archaic* a fit of depression 2 *archaic* a disease of horses and cattle; staggers

mehndi ('mendi:) *n (esp in India)* the practice of painting designs on the hands, feet, etc using henna [c20 from Hindi]

meibomian cyst (maɪ'bəʊmɪən) *n* another name for **chalazion** [c19 named after H. *Meibom* (1638–1700), German anatomist]

meibomian gland *n* any of the small sebaceous glands in the eyelid, beneath the conjunctiva

Meiji ('meɪdʒi:) *n Japanese history* the reign of Emperor Mutsuhito (1867–1912), during which Japan began a rapid process of Westernization, industrialization, and expansion in foreign affairs [Japanese, from Chinese *ming* enlightened + *dji* government]

meiny *or* **meinie** ('meɪnɪ) *n, pl* **meinies** *obsolete* 1 a retinue or household 2 *Scot* a crowd [c13 from Old French *mesnie*, from Vulgar Latin *mansiōnāta* (unattested), from Latin *mansiō* a lodging; see MANSION]

meiocyte ('maɪəʊ,saɪt) *n botany* a cell that divides by meiosis to produce four haploid spores (meiospores)

meiofauna ('maɪəʊ,fɔ:nə) *n* the component of the fauna of a sea or lake bed comprising small (but not microscopic) animals, such as tiny worms and crustaceans [c20 from Greek *meiōn* less + FAUNA] > ,meio'faunal *adj*

meiosis (maɪ'əʊsɪs) *n, pl* **-ses** (-,si:z) 1 a type of cell division in which a nucleus divides into four daughter nuclei, each containing half the chromosome number of the parent nucleus: occurs in all sexually reproducing organisms in which haploid gametes or spores are produced. Compare **mitosis** See also **prophase** (sense 2) 2 *rhetoric* another word for **litotes** [c16 via New Latin from Greek: a lessening, from *meioun* to diminish, from *meiōn* less] > meiotic (maɪ'ɒtɪk) *adj* > mei'otically *adv*

Meissen (*German* 'maɪsən) *n* a town in E Germany, in Saxony, in Dresden district on the River Elbe: famous for its porcelain (Dresden china), first made here in 1710. Pop: 28 640 (2003 est)

Meissner effect ('maɪsnə) *n physics* the phenomenon in which magnetic flux is excluded from a substance when it is in a superconducting state, except for a thin layer at the surface [c20 named after Fritz Walther *Meissner* (1882–1974), German physicist]

-meister ('maɪstə) *n combining form* a person who excels at a particular activity: *spinmeister; horror-meister* [c20 from German *Meister* master]

Meistersinger ('maɪstə,sɪŋə) *n, pl* **-singer** *or* **-singers** a member of one of the various German guilds of workers or craftsmen organized to compose and perform poetry and music. These flourished in the 15th and 16th centuries [c19 German: master singer]

meitnerium ('maɪtnɪərɪəm) *n* a synthetic element produced in small quantities by high-energy ion bombardment. Symbol: Mt; atomic no.: 109 [c20 named after Lise *Meitner* (1878–1968), Austrian nuclear physicist]

Méjico ('mexiko) *n* the Spanish name for **Mexico**

Mekka ('mɛkə) *n* a variant spelling of **Mecca**

Meknès (mɛk'nɛs) *n* a city in N central Morocco, in the Middle Atlas Mountains: noted for the making of carpets. Pop: 234 000 (2003)

Mekong (,mi:'kɒŋ) *n* a river in SE Asia, rising in SW China in Qinghai province: flows southeast forming the border between Laos and Myanmar, and part of the border between Laos and Thailand, then continues south across Cambodia and Vietnam to the South China Sea by an extensive delta, one of the greatest rice-growing areas in Asia. Length: about 4025 km (2500 miles)

mel (mel) *n pharmacol* a pure form of honey formerly used in pharmaceutical products [from Latin]

mela ('mi:lə, 'mɛlə) *n* an Asian cultural or

religious fair or festival [C19 Hindi, from Sanskrit *mēlā* an assembly, from *mil* to meet]

melaleuca (ˌmɛləˈluːkə) *n* any shrub or tree of the mostly Australian myrtaceous genus *Melaleuca*, found in sandy or swampy regions [C19 New Latin, from Greek *melas* black + *leukos* white, from its black trunk and white branches]

melamine (ˈmɛləˌmiːn) *n* **1** a colourless crystalline compound used in making synthetic resins; 2,4,6-triamino-1,3,5 triazine. Formula: $C_3H_6N_6$ **2** melamine resin or a material made from this resin [C19 from German *Melamin*, from *Melam* distillate of ammonium thiocyanate, with *-am* representing *ammonia*]

melamine resin *n* a thermosetting amino resin, stable to heat and light, produced from melamine and used for moulded products, adhesives, and surface coatings

melancholia (ˌmɛlənˈkəʊliə) *n* a former name for **depression**. > ˌmelanˈcholiˌac *adj, n*

melancholic (ˌmɛlənˈkɒlɪk) *adj* **1** relating to or suffering from melancholy or melancholia ▷ *n* **2** a person who suffers from melancholia > ˌmelanˈcholically *adv*

melancholy (ˈmɛlənkəlɪ) *n, pl* -cholies **1** a constitutional tendency to gloominess or depression **2** a sad thoughtful state of mind; pensiveness **3** *archaic* **a** a gloomy character, thought to be caused by too much black bile **b** one of the four bodily humours; black bile. See **humour** (sense 8) ▷ *adj* **4** characterized by, causing, or expressing sadness, dejection, etc [C14 via Old French from Late Latin *melancholia*, from Greek *melankholia*, from *melas* black + *kholē* bile] > melancholily (ˈmɛlənˌkɒlɪlɪ) *adv* > ˈmelanˌcholiness *n*

Melanesia (ˌmɛləˈniːzɪə) *n* one of the three divisions of islands in the Pacific (the others being Micronesia and Polynesia); the SW division of Oceania: includes Fiji, New Caledonia, Vanuatu, the Bismarck Archipelago, the Louisiade, Solomon, Santa Cruz, and Loyalty Islands, which all lie northeast of Australia [C19 from Greek *melas* black + *nēsos* island; with reference to the dark skins of the inhabitants; on the model of *Polynesia*]

Melanesian (ˌmɛləˈniːzɪən) *adj* **1** of or relating to Melanesia, its people, or their languages ▷ *n* **2** a native or inhabitant of Melanesia: generally Negroid with frizzy hair and small stature **3** a group or branch of languages spoken in Melanesia, belonging to the Malayo-Polynesian family **4** See also **Neo-Melanesian**

melange *or* **mélange** (meɪˈlɑːnʒ) *n* **1** a mixture; confusion **2** *geology* a totally disordered mixture of rocks of different shapes, sizes, ages, and origins [C17 from French *mêler* to mix. See MEDLEY]

melanic (məˈlænɪk) *adj* relating to melanism or melanosis

melanin (ˈmɛlənɪn) *n* any of a group of black or dark brown pigments present in the hair, skin, and eyes of man and animals: produced in excess in certain skin diseases and in melanomas

melanism (ˈmɛləˌnɪzəm) *n* **1** the condition in man and animals of having dark-coloured or black skin, feathers, etc. **Industrial melanism** is the occurrence of dark varieties of animals, esp moths, in smoke-blackened industrial regions, in which they are well camouflaged **2** another name for **melanosis**. > ˌmelaˈnistic *adj*

melanite (ˈmɛləˌnaɪt) *n* a black variety of andradite garnet

melano- *or before a vowel* **melan-** *combining form* black or dark: *melanin; melanism; melanocyte; melanoma* [from Greek *melas* black]

Melanochroi (ˌmɛləˈnɒkrəʊˌaɪ) *pl n* a postulated subdivision of the Caucasoid race, characterized by dark hair and pale complexion [C19 New Latin (coined by T. H. Huxley), from Greek, from *melas* dark + *ōchros* pale] > Melanochroid (ˌmɛləˈnɒkrɔɪd) *adj*

melanocyte (ˈmɛlənəʊˌsaɪt) *n anatomy, zoology* a

cell, usually in the epidermis, that contains melanin

melanoid (ˈmɛləˌnɔɪd) *adj* **1** resembling melanin; dark coloured **2** characterized by or resembling melanosis

melanoma (ˌmɛləˈnəʊmə) *n, pl* -mas *or* -mata (-mətə) *pathol* a malignant tumour composed of melanocytes, occurring esp in the skin, often as a result of excessive exposure to sunlight

melanosis (ˌmɛləˈnəʊsɪs) *or* **melanism** (ˈmɛləˌnɪzəm) *n pathol* a skin condition characterized by excessive deposits of melanin > melanotic (ˌmɛləˈnɒtɪk) *adj*

melanous (ˈmɛlənəs) *adj* having a dark complexion and black hair > melanosity (ˌmɛləˈnɒsɪtɪ) *n*

melaphyre (ˈmɛləˌfaɪə) *n geology obsolete* a type of weathered amygdaloidal basalt or andesite [C19 via French from Greek *melas* black + (*por*)*phura* purple]

melatonin (ˌmɛləˈtəʊnɪn) *n* the hormone-like secretion of the pineal gland, causing skin colour changes in some animals and thought to be involved in reproductive function [C20 probably from MELA(NOCYTE) + (SERO)TONIN]

Melba (ˈmɛlbə) *n* **do a Melba** *Austral slang* to make repeated farewell appearances [from Dame Nellie *Melba*, stage name of Helen Porter Mitchell (1861–1931), Australian operatic soprano]

Melba sauce *n* a sweet sauce made from fresh raspberries and served with peach melba, fruit sundaes, etc [C20 named after Dame Nellie *Melba*, stage name of Helen Porter Mitchell (1861–1931), Australian operatic soprano]

Melba toast *n* very thin crisp toast [C20 named after Dame Nellie *Melba*, stage name of Helen Porter Mitchell (1861–1931), Australian operatic soprano]

Melbourne (ˈmɛlbən) *n* a port in SE Australia, capital of Victoria, on Port Phillip Bay: the second largest city in the country; settled in 1835 and developed rapidly with the discovery of rich goldfields in 1851; three universities. Pop: 3 160 171 (2001)

Melbourne Cup *n* an annual horse race run in Melbourne, since 1861

Melburnian (mɛlˈbɜːnɪən) *n* **1** a native or inhabitant of Melbourne ▷ *adj* **2** of or relating to Melbourne or its inhabitants

Melchior (ˈmɛlkɪˌɔː) *n* (in Christian tradition) one of the Magi, the others being Balthazar and Caspar

Melchite (ˈmɛlkaɪt) *Eastern Churches* ▷ *adj* **1** of or relating to the Uniat Greek Catholic Church in Syria, Egypt, and Israel ▷ *n* **2** a member of this Church [C17 from Church Latin *Melchīta*, from Medieval Greek *Melkhītēs*, literally: royalist, from Syriac *malkā* king]

Melchizedek (mɛlˈkɪzəˌdɛk) *n Old Testament* the priest-king of Salem who blessed Abraham (Genesis 14:18-19) and was taken as a prototype of Christ's priesthood (Hebrews 7). Douay spelling: Melchisedech

meld¹ (mɛld) *vb* **1** (in some card games) to declare or lay down (cards), which then score points ▷ *n* **2** the act of melding **3** a set of cards for melding [C19 from German *melden* to announce; related to Old English *meldian*]

meld² (mɛld) *vb* to blend or become blended; combine [C20 blend of MELT + WELD¹]

Meldrew (ˈmɛldruː) *n informal* a person, esp a middle-aged or elderly man, who is habitually peevish, pessimistic, and cynical; curmudgeon [C20 named after Victor *Meldrew*, curmudgeonly hero of the 1990s BBC television situation comedy *One Foot in the Grave*, written by David Renwick] > ˈMeldrewish *adj*

Meleager (ˌmɛlɪˈeɪgə) *n Greek myth* one of the Argonauts, slayer of the Calydonian boar

melee *or* **mêlée** (ˈmɛleɪ) *n* a noisy riotous fight or brawl [C17 from French *mêlée*. See MEDLEY]

meliaceous (ˌmiːlɪˈeɪʃəs) *adj* of, relating to, or

belonging to the *Meliaceae*, a family of tropical and subtropical trees, including mahogany, some of which yield valuable timber [C19 from New Latin *Melia* type genus, from Greek: ash]

melic (ˈmɛlɪk) *adj* (of poetry, esp ancient Greek lyric poems) intended to be sung [C17 via Latin from Greek *melikos*, from *melos* song]

melick (ˈmɛlɪk) *n* either of two pale green perennial grasses of the genus *Melica*, related to fescue, esp **wood melick** (*M. uniflora*) having branching flower heads, that are common in woodlands [New Latin *melica*, of unknown origin]

Melilla (*Spanish* meliʎa) *n* the chief town of a Spanish enclave in Morocco, on the Mediterranean coast: founded by the Phoenicians; exports iron ore. Pop: 68 463 (2003 est)

melilot (ˈmɛlɪˌlɒt) *n* any leguminous plant of the Old World genus *Melilotus*, having narrow clusters of small white or yellow fragrant flowers. Also called: **sweet clover** [C15 via Old French from Latin *melilotos*, from Greek: sweet clover, from *meli* honey + *lōtos* LOTUS]

melinite (ˈmɛlɪˌnaɪt) *n* a high explosive made from picric acid [C19 via French from Greek *mēlinos* (colour) of a quince, from *mēlon* fruit, quince]

meliorate (ˈmiːlɪəˌreɪt) *vb* a variant of **ameliorate** > ˈmelioˌrable *adj* > meliorative (ˈmiːlɪərətɪv) *adj, n* > ˈmelioˌrator *n*

melioration (ˌmiːlɪəˈreɪʃən) *n* the act or an instance of improving or the state of being improved

meliorism (ˈmiːlɪəˌrɪzəm) *n* the notion that the world can be improved by human effort [C19 from Latin *melior* better] > ˈmeliorist *adj, n* > ˌmelioˈristic *adj*

melisma (mɪˈlɪzmə) *n, pl* -mata (-mətə) *or* -mas *music* an expressive vocal phrase or passage consisting of several notes sung to one syllable [C19 from Greek: melody] > melismatic (ˌmɛlɪzˈmætɪk) *adj*

Melitopol (*Russian* mɪliˈtɔpəlj) *n* a city in SE Ukraine. Pop: 157 000 (2005 est)

Melk (mɛlk) *n* a town in N Austria, on the River Danube: noted for its baroque Benedictine abbey. Pop: 5222 (2001)

melliferous (mɪˈlɪfərəs) *or* **mellific** (mɪˈlɪfɪk) *adj* forming or producing honey [C17 from Latin *mellifer*, from *mel* honey + *ferre* to bear]

mellifluous (mɪˈlɪflʊəs) *or* **mellifluent** *adj* (of sounds or utterances) smooth or honeyed; sweet [C15 from Late Latin *mellifluus* flowing with honey, from Latin *mel* honey + *fluere* to flow] > melˈlifluously *or* melˈlifluently *adv* > melˈlifluousness *or* melˈlifluence *n*

melliphagous (mɪˈlɪfəgəs) *or* **mellivorous** (mɪˈlɪvərəs) *adj zoology* (of an animal) feeding on honey [C19 from Latin *mel* honey + Greek *-phagos*, from *phagein* to consume]

mellophone (ˈmɛləˌfəʊn) *n music* a brass band instrument similar in tone to a French horn [C20 from MELLOW + -PHONE]

mellow (ˈmɛləʊ) *adj* **1** (esp of fruits) full-flavoured; sweet; ripe **2** (esp of wines) well-matured **3** (esp of colours or sounds) soft or rich **4** kind-hearted, esp through maturity or old age **5** genial, as through the effects of alcohol **6** (of soil) soft and loamy ▷ *vb* **7** to make or become mellow; soften; mature **8** (foll by *out*) to become calm and relaxed or (esp of a drug) to have a calming or relaxing effect on (someone) [C15 perhaps from Old English *meru* soft (as through ripeness)] > ˈmellowly *adv* > ˈmellowness *n*

melodeon *or* **melodion** (mɪˈləʊdɪən) *n music* **1** a type of small accordion **2** a type of keyboard instrument similar to the harmonium [C19 from German *Melodie* melody]

melodic (mɪˈlɒdɪk) *adj* **1** of or relating to melody **2** of or relating to a part in a piece of music **3** tuneful or melodious > meˈlodically *adv*

melodic minor scale *n music* a minor scale modified from the natural by the sharpening of the sixth and seventh when taken in ascending order and the restoration of their original pitches when taken in descending order. See **minor** (sense 4a) Compare **harmonic minor scale**

melodious (mɪ'ləʊdɪəs) adj **1** having a tune that is pleasant to the ear **2** of or relating to melody; melodic > me'lodiously adv > me'lodiousness n

melodist ('mɛlədɪst) n **1** a composer of melodies **2** a singer

melodize or **melodise** ('mɛlə,daɪz) vb **1** (tr) to provide with a melody **2** (tr) to make melodious **3** (intr) to sing or play melodies > 'melo,dizer or 'melo,diser n

melodrama ('mɛlə,drɑːmə) n **1** a play, film, etc, characterized by extravagant action and emotion **2** (formerly) a romantic drama characterized by sensational incident, music, and song **3** overdramatic emotion or behaviour **4** a poem or part of a play or opera spoken to a musical accompaniment [c19 from French mélodrame, from Greek melos song + drame DRAMA] > melodramatist (,mɛlə'dræmətɪst) n > melodramatic (,mɛlədrə'mætɪk) adj > ,melodra'matically adv

melodramatize or **melodramatise** (,mɛləʊ'dræmə,taɪz) vb (tr) to make melodramatic

melody ('mɛlədɪ) n, pl **-dies 1** music **a** a succession of notes forming a distinctive sequence; tune **b** the horizontally represented aspect of the structure of a piece of music. Compare **harmony** (sense 4b) **2** sounds that are pleasant because of tone or arrangement, esp words of poetry [c13 from Old French, from Late Latin melōdia, from Greek melōidia singing, from melos song + -ōidia, from aoidein to sing]

meloid ('mɛlɔɪd) n **1** any long-legged beetle of the family Meloidae, which includes the blister beetles and oil beetles ▷ adj **2** of, relating to, or belonging to the Meloidae [c19 from New Latin Meloē name of genus]

melon ('mɛlən) n **1** any of several varieties of two cucurbitaceous vines (see **muskmelon**, **watermelon**), cultivated for their edible fruit **2** the fruit of any of these plants, which has a hard rind and juicy flesh **3** **cut a melon** US and Canadian slang to declare an abnormally high dividend to shareholders [c14 via Old French from Late Latin mēlo, shortened form of mēlopepō, from Greek mēlopepōn, from mēlon apple + pepōn gourd]

Melos ('miːlɒs) n an island in the SW Aegean Sea, in the Cyclades: of volcanic origin, with hot springs; centre of early Aegean civilization, where the Venus de Milo was found. Pop: 4771 (2001). Area: 132 sq km (51 sq miles). Modern Greek name: **Mílos**

Melpomene (mɛl'pɒmɪnɪ) n Greek myth the Muse of tragedy

Melrose Abbey ('mɛlrəʊz) n a ruined Cistercian abbey in Melrose in Scottish Borders: founded in 1136 and sacked by the English in 1385 and 1547: repaired in 1822 by Sir Walter Scott

melt (mɛlt) vb **melts, melting, melted; melted** or **molten** ('məʊltən) **1** to liquefy (a solid) or (of a solid) to become liquefied, as a result of the action of heat **2** to become or make liquid; dissolve: cakes that melt in the mouth **3** (often foll by away) to disappear; fade **4** (foll by down) to melt (metal scrap) for reuse **5** (often foll by into) to blend or cause to blend gradually **6** to make or become emotional or sentimental; soften ▷ n **7** the act or process of melting **8** something melted or an amount melted [Old English meltan to digest; related to Old Norse melta to malt (beer), digest, Greek meldein to melt] > 'meltable adj > ,melta'bility n > 'melter n > 'meltingly adv > 'meltingness n

meltage ('mɛltɪdʒ) n the process or result of melting or the amount melted: rapid meltage of ice

meltdown ('mɛlt,daʊn) n **1** (in a nuclear reactor) the melting of the fuel rods as a result of a defect in the cooling system, with the possible escape of radiation into the environment **2** informal a sudden disastrous failure with potential for widespread harm, as a stock-exchange crash **3**

informal the process or state of irreversible breakdown or decline: the community is slowly going into meltdown

meltemi (mɛl'tɛmɪ) n a northerly wind in the northeast Mediterranean; etesian wind [c20 from Modern Greek, from Turkish meltem]

melting point n the temperature at which a solid turns into a liquid. It is equal to the freezing point

melting pot n **1** a pot in which metals or other substances are melted, esp in order to mix them **2** an area in which many races, ideas, etc, are mixed

melton ('mɛltən) n a heavy smooth woollen fabric with a short nap, used esp for overcoats. Also called: **melton cloth** [c19 from MELTON MOWBRAY, Leicestershire, a former centre for making this cloth]

Melton Mowbray ('mɛltən 'məʊbrɪ) n a town in central England, in Leicestershire: pork pies and Stilton cheese. Pop: 25 554 (2001)

meltwater ('mɛlt,wɔːtə) n melted snow or ice

melungeon (mə'lʌndʒən) n any of a dark-skinned group of people of the Appalachians in E Tennessee, of mixed Indian, White, and Black ancestry [c20 of unknown origin]

Melville Island ('mɛlvɪl) n **1** a Canadian island in the Arctic Ocean, north of Victoria Island: in the Northwest Territories and Nunavut. Area: 41 865 sq km (16 164 sq miles) **2** an island in the Arafura Sea, off the N central coast of Australia, separated from the mainland by Clarence Strait. Area: 6216 sq km (2400 sq miles)

Melville Peninsula n a peninsula of N Canada, in Nunavut, between the Gulf of Boothia and Foxe Basin

mem (mɛm) n the 13th letter in the Hebrew alphabet (מ or, at the end of a word, ם), transliterated as m [Hebrew, literally: water]

member ('mɛmbə) n **1** a person who belongs to a club, political party, etc **2** any individual plant or animal in a taxonomic group: a member of the species **3** any part of an animal body, such as a limb **4** another word for **penis 5** any part of a plant, such as a petal, root, etc **6** maths any individual object belonging to a set or logical class **7** a distinct part of a whole, such as a proposition in a syllogism **8** a component part of a building or construction [c13 from Latin membrum limb, part] > 'memberless adj

Member ('mɛmbə) n (sometimes not capital) **1** short for **Member of Parliament 2** short for **Member of Congress 3** a member of some other legislative body

Member of Congress n a member of the US Congress, esp of the House of Representatives

Member of Parliament n a member of the House of Commons or similar legislative body, as in many Commonwealth countries. Abbreviation: **MP**

membership ('mɛmbəʃɪp) n **1** the members of an organization collectively **2** the state of being a member

membrane ('mɛmbreɪn) n **1** any thin pliable sheet of material **2** a pliable sheetlike usually fibrous tissue that covers, lines, or connects plant and animal organs or cells **3** biology a double layer of lipid, containing some proteins, that surrounds biological cells and some of their internal structures **4** physics a two-dimensional entity postulated as a fundamental constituent of matter in superstring theories of particle physics **5** a skin of parchment forming part of a roll [c16 from Latin membrāna skin covering a part of the body, from membrum MEMBER]

membrane bone n any bone that develops within membranous tissue, such as the clavicle and bones of the skull, without cartilage formation. Compare **cartilage bone**

membrane transport n the process by which physiologically important substances, such as calcium ions, sugars, etc, are conveyed across a biological membrane

membranous ('mɛmbrənəs, mɛm'breɪnəs),

membraneous (mɛm'breɪnɪəs) or **membranaceous** (,mɛmbrə'neɪʃəs) adj of or relating to a membrane > 'membranously adv

meme (miːm) n an idea or element of social behaviour passed on through generations in a culture, esp by imitation [c20 possibly from MIMIC, on the model of GENE]

Memel ('meɪməl) n **1** the German name for **Klaipeda 2** the lower course of the Neman River

memento (mɪ'mɛntəʊ) n, pl **-tos** or **-toes 1** something that reminds one of past events; souvenir **2** RC Church either of two prayers occurring during the Mass [c15 from Latin, imperative of meminisse to remember]

memento mori ('mɔːriː) n an object, such as a skull, intended to remind people of the inevitability of death [c16 Latin: remember you must die]

Memnon ('mɛmnɒn) n **1** Greek myth a king of Ethiopia, son of Eos: slain by Achilles in the Trojan War **2** a colossal statue of Amenhotep III at Thebes in ancient Egypt, which emitted a sound thought by the Greeks to be the voice of Memnon > Memnonian (mɛm'nəʊnɪən) adj

memo ('mɛmaʊ, 'miːməʊ) n, pl **memos** short for **memorandum**

memoir ('mɛmwɑː) n **1** a biography or historical account, esp one based on personal knowledge **2** an essay or monograph, as on a specialized topic **3** obsolete a memorandum [c16 from French, from Latin memoria MEMORY] > 'memoirist n

memoirs ('mɛmwɑːz) pl n **1** a collection of reminiscences about a period, series of events, etc, written from personal experience or special sources **2** an autobiographical record **3** a collection or record, as of transactions of a society, etc

memorabilia (,mɛmərə'bɪlɪə) pl n, sing **-rabile** (-'ræbɪlɪ) **1** memorable events or things **2** objects connected with famous people or events [c17 from Latin, from memorābilis MEMORABLE]

memorable ('mɛmərəb(ə)l, 'mɛmrə-) adj worth remembering or easily remembered; noteworthy [c15 from Latin memorābilis, from memorāre to recall, from memor mindful] > ,memora'bility or 'memorableness n > 'memorably adv

memorandum (,mɛmə'rændəm) n, pl **-dums** or **-da** (-də) **1** a written statement, record, or communication such as within an office **2** a note of things to be remembered **3** an informal diplomatic communication, often unsigned: often summarizing the point of view of a government **4** law a short written summary of the terms of a transaction ▷ Often (esp for senses 1, 2) shortened to: **memo** [c15 from Latin: (something) to be remembered]

memorial (mɪ'mɔːrɪəl) adj **1** serving to preserve the memory of the dead or a past event **2** of or involving memory ▷ n **3** something serving as a remembrance **4** a written statement of facts submitted to a government, authority, etc, in conjunction with a petition **5** an informal diplomatic paper [c14 from Late Latin memoriāle a reminder, neuter of memoriālis belonging to remembrance] > me'morially adv

Memorial Day n a holiday in the United States, May 30th in most states, commemorating the servicemen killed in all American wars

memorialist (mɪ'mɔːrɪəlɪst) n **1** a person who writes or presents a memorial **2** a writer of a memoir or memoirs

memorialize or **memorialise** (mɪ'mɔːrɪə,laɪz) vb (tr) **1** to honour or commemorate **2** to present or address a memorial to > me,moriali'zation or me,moriali'sation n > me'morial,izer or me'morial,iser n

memoria technica (mɪ'mɔːrɪə 'tɛknɪkə) n a method or device for assisting the memory [c18 New Latin: artificial memory]

memorize or **memorise** ('mɛmə,raɪz) vb (tr) to commit to memory; learn so as to remember > 'memo,rizable or 'memo,risable adj

> ˌmemoriˈzation *or* ˌmemoriˈsation *n* > ˈmemoˌrizer *or* ˈmemoˌriser *n*

memory (ˈmɛməri) *n, pl* -ries **1 a** the ability of the mind to store and recall past sensations, thoughts, knowledge, etc: *he can do it from memory* **b** the part of the brain that appears to have this function **2** the sum of everything retained by the mind **3** a particular recollection of an event, person, etc **4** the time over which recollection extends: *within his memory* **5** commemoration or remembrance: *in memory of our leader* **6** the state of being remembered, as after death **7** Also called: **RAM, main store, store** a part of a computer in which information is stored for immediate use by the central processing unit. See also **backing store, virtual storage 8** the tendency for a material, system, etc, to show effects that depend on its past treatment or history **9** the ability of a material, etc, to return to a former state after a constraint has been removed [c14 from Old French *memorie,* from Latin *memoria,* from *memor* mindful]

memory mapping *n* a technique whereby computer peripherals may be addressed as though they formed part of the main memory of the computer

memory span *n psychol* the capacity of short-term memory, usually between 5 and 10 items

memory trace *n psychol* the hypothetical structural alteration in brain cells following learning. See also **engram**

Memphian (ˈmɛmfiən) *adj* **1** of or relating to ancient Memphis or its inhabitants ▷ *n* **2** an inhabitant or native of ancient Memphis

Memphis (ˈmɛmfɪs) *n* **1** a port in SW Tennessee, on the Mississippi River: the largest city in the state; a major cotton and timber market; Memphis State University (1909). Pop: 645 978 (2003 est) **2** a ruined city in N Egypt, the ancient centre of Lower Egypt, on the Nile: administrative and artistic centre, sacred to the worship of Ptah

Memphremagog (ˌmɛmfriˈmeɪɡɒɡ) *n* **Lake a** lake on the border between the US and Canada, in N Vermont and S Quebec. Length: about 43 km (27 miles). Width: up to 6 km (4 miles)

memsahib (ˈmɛmˌsaːɪb, -hɪb) *n* (formerly in India) a term of respect used of a European married woman [c19 from MA'AM + SAHIB]

men (mɛn) *n* the plural of **man**

menace (ˈmɛnɪs) *vb* **1** to threaten with violence, danger, etc ▷ *n* **2** *literary* a threat or the act of threatening **3** something menacing; a source of danger **4** *informal* a nuisance [c13 ultimately related to Latin *minax* threatening, from *mināri* to threaten] > ˈmenacer *n* > ˈmenacing *adj* > ˈmenacingly *adv*

menad (ˈmiːnæd) *n* a variant spelling of **maenad**

menadione (ˌmɛnəˈdaɪəʊn) *n* a yellow crystalline compound used in fungicides and as an additive to animal feeds. Formula: $C_{11}H_8O_2$. Also called: **vitamin K₃** [c20 from ME(THYL) + NA(PHTHA) + DI-¹ + -ONE]

Menado (mɛˈnaːdəʊ) *or* **Manado** *n* a port in NE Indonesia, on NE Sulawesi: founded by the Dutch in 1657. Pop: 372 887 (2000)

ménage (meɪˈnaːʒ; *French* menaʒ) *n* the persons of a household [c17 from French, from Vulgar Latin *mansiōnāticum* (unattested) household; see MANSION]

ménage à trois French (menaʒ a trwa) *n, pl ménages à trois* (menaʒ a trwa) a sexual arrangement involving a married couple and the lover of one of them [literally: household of three]

menagerie (mɪˈnædʒəri) *n* **1** a collection of wild animals kept for exhibition **2** the place where such animals are housed [c18 from French: household management, which formerly included care of domestic animals. See MÉNAGE]

Menai Strait (ˈmɛnaɪ) *n* a channel of the Irish Sea between the island of Anglesey and the mainland of NW Wales: famous suspension bridge (1819–26) designed by Thomas Telford and tubular bridge (1846–50) by Robert Stephenson.

Length: 24 km (15 miles). Width: up to 3 km (2 miles)

Menam (miˈnæm) *n* another name for the **Chao Phraya**

menaquinone (ˌmɛnəkwɪˈnəʊn) *n* a form of vitamin K synthesized by bacteria in the intestine or in putrefying organic matter. Also called: **vitamin K₂** [c20 from *me(thyl)-na(phtho)quinone*]

menarche (mɛˈnaːkɪ) *n* the first occurrence of menstruation in a woman's life [c20 New Latin, from Greek *mēn* month + *arkhē* beginning] > menˈarcheal *or* menˈarchial *adj*

mend (mɛnd) *vb* **1** (*tr*) to repair (something broken or unserviceable) **2** to improve or undergo improvement; reform (often in the phrase **mend one's ways**) **3** (*intr*) to heal or recover **4** (*intr*) (of conditions) to improve; become better **5** (*tr*) *Northern English* to feed or stir (a fire) ▷ *n* **6** the act of repairing **7** a mended area, esp on a garment **8** **on the mend** becoming better, esp in health [c12 shortened from AMEND] > ˈmendable *adj* > ˈmender *n*

mendacity (mɛnˈdæsɪtɪ) *n, pl* -ties **1** the tendency to be untruthful **2** a falsehood [c17 from Late Latin *mendācitās,* from Latin *mendāx* untruthful] > mendacious (mɛnˈdeɪʃəs) *adj* > menˈdaciously *adv* > menˈdaciousness *n*

mendelevium (ˌmɛndɪˈliːvɪəm) *n* a transuranic element artificially produced by bombardment of einsteinium. Symbol: Md; atomic no.: 101; half-life of most stable isotope, ²⁵⁸Md: 60 days (approx.); valency: 2 or 3 [c20 named after Dmitri Ivanovich *Mendeleyev* (1834–1907), Russian chemist]

Mendelian (mɛnˈdiːliən) *adj* of or relating to Mendel's laws

Mendelism (ˈmɛndəˌlɪzəm) *or* **Mendelianism** (mɛnˈdiːliəˌnɪzəm) *n* the science of heredity based on Mendel's laws with some modifications in the light of more recent knowledge

Mendel's laws (ˈmɛnd²lz) *pl n* the principles of heredity proposed by Gregor Mendel (1822–84), the Austrian monk and botanist. The **Law of Segregation** states that each hereditary character is determined by a pair of units in the reproductive cells: the pairs separate during meiosis so that each gamete carries only one unit of each pair. The **Law of Independent Assortment** states that the separation of the units of each pair is not influenced by that of any other pair

Menderes (ˌmɛndeˈrɛs) *n* **1** a river in SW Turkey flowing southwest, then west to the Aegean. Length: about 386 km (240 miles). Ancient name: Maeander **2** a river in NW Turkey flowing west and northwest to the Dardanelles. Length: 104 km (65 miles). Ancient name: Scamander

mendicant (ˈmɛndɪkənt) *adj* **1** begging **2** (of a member of a religious order) dependent on alms for sustenance: *mendicant friars* **3** characteristic of a beggar ▷ *n* **4** a mendicant friar **5** a less common word for **beggar** [c16 from Latin *mendīcāre* to beg, from *mendīcus* beggar, from *mendus* flaw] > ˈmendicancy *or* mendicity (mɛnˈdɪsɪtɪ) *n*

mending (ˈmɛndɪŋ) *n* something to be mended, esp clothes

Mendips (ˈmɛndɪps) *pl n* a range of limestone hills in SW England, in N Somerset: includes the Cheddar Gorge and numerous caves. Highest point: 325 m (1068 ft). Also called: Mendip Hills

Mendoza (mɛnˈdəʊzə; *Spanish* menˈdoθa) *n* a city in W central Argentina, in the foothills of the Sierra de los Paramillos: largely destroyed by an earthquake in 1861; commercial centre of an intensively cultivated irrigated region; University of Cuyo (1939). Pop: 1 072 000 (2005 est)

meneer (məˈnɪə) *n* a South African title of address equivalent to *sir* when used alone or *Mr* when placed before a name [Afrikaans]

Menelaus (ˌmɛnɪˈleɪəs) *n Greek myth* a king of Sparta and the brother of Agamemnon. He was the husband of Helen, whose abduction led to the Trojan War

mene, mene, tekel, upharsin (ˈmiːni ˈmiːni ˈtɛkəl

juːˈfaːsɪn) *n Old Testament* the words that appeared on the wall during Belshazzar's Feast (Daniel 5:25), interpreted by Daniel to mean that God had doomed the kingdom of Belshazzar [Aramaic: numbered, numbered, weighed, divided]

menfolk (ˈmɛnˌfəʊk) *or US sometimes* **menfolks** *pl n* men collectively, esp the men of a particular family

menhaden (mɛnˈheɪd²n) *n, pl* -den a marine North American fish, *Brevoortia tyrannus:* source of fishmeal, fertilizer, and oil: family *Clupeidae* (herrings, etc) [c18 from Algonquian; probably related to Narragansett *munnawhatteaúg* fertilizer, menhaden]

menhir (ˈmɛnhɪə) *n* a single standing stone, often carved, dating from the middle Bronze Age in the British Isles and from the late Neolithic Age in W Europe [c19 from Breton *men* stone + *hir* long]

menial (ˈmiːnɪəl) *adj* **1** consisting of or occupied with work requiring little skill, esp domestic duties such as cleaning **2** of, involving, or befitting servants **3** servile ▷ *n* **4** a domestic servant **5** a servile person [c14 from Anglo-Norman *meignial,* from Old French *meinie* household. See MEINY] > ˈmenially *adv*

Ménière's syndrome *or* **disease** (meɪnˈjɛəz) *n* a disorder of the inner ear characterized by a ringing or buzzing in the ear, dizziness, and impaired hearing [c19 named after Prosper *Ménière* (1799–1862), French physician]

menilite (ˈmɛnɪˌlaɪt) *n* another name for **liver opal,** esp a brown or grey variety

meninges (mɪˈnɪndʒiːz) *pl n, sing* meninx (ˈmiːnɪŋks) the three membranes (**dura mater, arachnoid, pia mater**) that envelop the brain and spinal cord [c17 from Greek, pl of *meninx* membrane] > meningeal (mɪˈnɪndʒɪəl) *adj*

meningitis (ˌmɛnɪnˈdʒaɪtɪs) *n* inflammation of the membranes that surround the brain or spinal cord, caused by infection > meningitic (ˌmɛnɪnˈdʒɪtɪk) *adj*

meningocele (mɛˈnɪŋɡəʊˌsiːl) *n pathol* protrusion of the meninges through the skull or backbone [c19 from *meningo-* (see MENINGES) + -CELE]

meningococcal (mɛˌnɪŋɡəʊˈkɒkəl) *adj* of or relating to the meningococcus bacterium

meningococcus (mɛˌnɪŋɡəʊˈkɒkəs) *n, pl* -cocci (-ˈkɒkaɪ) the bacterium that causes cerebrospinal meningitis

meniscus (mɪˈnɪskəs) *n, pl* -nisci (-ˈnɪsaɪ) *or* -niscuses **1** the curved upper surface of a liquid standing in a tube, produced by the surface tension **2** a crescent or half-moon-shaped body or design **3** a crescent-shaped fibrous cartilage between the bones at certain joints, esp at the knee **4** a crescent-shaped lens; a concavo-convex or convexo-concave lens [c17 from New Latin, from Greek *mēniskos* crescent, diminutive of *mēnē* moon] > meˈniscoid *adj*

menispermaceous (ˌmɛnɪspɜːˈmeɪʃəs) *adj* of, relating to, or belonging to the *Menispermaceae,* a family of mainly tropical and subtropical plants, most of which are woody climbers with small flowers [c19 from New Latin *Mēnispermum* name of genus, from Greek *mēnē* moon + *sperma* seed]

Mennonite (ˈmɛnəˌnaɪt) *n* a member of a Protestant sect that rejects infant baptism, Church organization, and the doctrine of transubstantiation and in most cases refuses military service, public office, and the taking of oaths [c16 from German *Mennonit,* after *Menno* Simons (1496–1561), Frisian religious leader] > ˈMennoˌnitism *n*

meno (ˈmɛnəʊ) *adv music* **1** (esp preceding a dynamic or tempo marking) to be played less quickly, less softly, etc **2** short for **meno mosso** [from Italian, from Latin *minus* less]

meno- *combining form* menstruation: *menorrhagia* [from Greek *mēn* month]

menology (mɪˈnɒlədʒɪ) *n, pl* -gies **1** an ecclesiastical calendar of the months **2** *Eastern Churches* a liturgical book containing the lives of

m

the saints arranged by months [c17 from New Latin *mēnologium*, from Late Greek *mēnologion*, from Greek *mēn* month + *logos* word, account]

Menomini *or* **Menominee** (məˈnɒmənɪ) *n* **1** (*pl* -ni, -nis *or* -nee, -nees) a member of a North American Indian people formerly living between Lake Michigan and Lake Superior **2** the language of this people, belonging to the Algonquian family

meno mosso (ˈmɛnəʊ ˈmɒsəʊ) *adv music* to be played at reduced speed. Often shortened to: **meno** [Italian: less rapid]

menopause (ˈmɛnəʊˌpɔːz) *n* the period during which a woman's menstrual cycle ceases, normally occurring at an age of 45 to 50. Nontechnical name: change of life [c19 from French, from Greek *mēn* month + *pausis* halt] > ˌmenoˈpausal *or rarely* ˌmenoˈpausic *adj*

menopolis (mɛˈnɒpəlɪs) *n informal* an area or city with a high proportion of single men [c21 from MEN + (METR)OPOLIS]

menorah (mɪˈnɔːrə; *Hebrew* məˈnaʊrɔ) *n Judaism* **1** a seven-branched candelabrum used in the Temple and now an emblem of Judaism and the badge of the state of Israel **2** a candelabrum having eight branches and a shammes that is lit during the festival of Hanukkah [from Hebrew: candlestick]

Menorca (meˈnɔrka) *n* the Spanish name for **Minorca** (sense 1)

menorrhagia (ˌmɛnɔːˈreɪdʒɪə) *n* excessive bleeding during menstruation > **menorrhagic** (ˌmɛnəˈrædʒɪk) *adj*

menorrhoea (ˌmɛnəˈrɪə) *n* normal bleeding in menstruation

Mensa[1] (ˈmɛnsə) *n, Latin genitive* Mensae (ˈmɛnsiː) a faint constellation in the S hemisphere lying between Hydrus and Volans and containing part of the Large Magellanic Cloud [Latin, literally: the table]

Mensa[2] (ˈmɛnsə) *n* an international society, membership of which is restricted to people whose intelligence test scores exceed those expected of 98 per cent of the population

mensal[1] (ˈmɛnsəl) *adj rare* monthly [c15 from Latin *mensis* month]

mensal[2] (ˈmɛnsəl) *adj rare* relating to or used at the table [c15 from Latin *mensalis*, from *mensa* table]

menses (ˈmɛnsiːz) *n, pl* menses **1** another name for **menstruation 2** the period of time, usually from three to five days, during which menstruation occurs **3** the matter discharged during menstruation [c16 from Latin, pl of *mensis* month]

Menshevik (ˈmɛnʃɪvɪk) *or* **Menshevist** *n* a member of the moderate wing of the Russian Social Democratic Party, advocating gradual reform to achieve socialism. Compare **Bolshevik** [c20 from Russian, literally: minority, from *menshe* less, from *malo* few] > ˈMenshevism *n*

mens rea (ˈmɛnz ˈreɪə) *n law* a criminal intention or knowledge that an act is wrong. It is assumed to be an ingredient of all criminal offences although some minor statutory offences are punishable irrespective of it. Compare **actus reus** [Latin, literally: guilty mind]

men's room *n chiefly US and Canadian* a public lavatory for men

menstrual (ˈmɛnstrʊəl) *adj* of or relating to menstruation or the menses

menstruate (ˈmɛnstrʊˌeɪt) *vb* (*intr*) to undergo menstruation [c17 from Latin *menstruāre*, from *mensis* month]

menstruation (ˌmɛnstrʊˈeɪʃən) *n* the approximately monthly discharge of blood and cellular debris from the uterus by nonpregnant women from puberty to the menopause. Also called: **menses** Nontechnical name: **period** > **menstruous** (ˈmɛnstrʊəs) *adj*

menstruum (ˈmɛnstrʊəm) *n, pl* -struums *or* -strua (-strʊə) *obsolete* **1** a solvent, esp one used in the preparation of a drug **2** a solid formulation of a

drug [c17 (meaning: solvent), c14 (menstrual discharge): from Medieval Latin, from Latin *mēnstruus* monthly, from *mēnsis* month; from an alchemical comparison between a base metal being transmuted into gold and the supposed action of the menses]

mensurable (ˈmɛnsjʊrəbᵊl, -ʃə-) *adj* a less common word for **measurable** [c17 from Late Latin *mēnsūrābilis*, from *mēnsūra* MEASURE] > ˌmensuraˈbility *n*

mensural (ˈmɛnʃərəl) *adj* **1** of or involving measure **2** *music* of or relating to music in which notes have fixed values in relation to each other [c17 from Late Latin *mēnsūrālis*, from *mēnsūra* MEASURE]

mensuration (ˌmɛnʃəˈreɪʃən) *n* **1** the study of the measurement of geometric magnitudes such as length **2** the act or process of measuring; measurement > ˌmensuˈrational *adj* > **mensurative** (ˈmɛnʃərətɪv) *adj*

menswear (ˈmɛnzˌwɛə) *n* clothing for men

-ment *suffix forming nouns, esp from verbs* **1** indicating state, condition, or quality: *enjoyment* **2** indicating the result or product of an action: *embankment* **3** indicating process or action: *management* [from French, from Latin *-mentum*]

mental[1] (ˈmɛntᵊl) *adj* **1** of or involving the mind or an intellectual process **2** occurring only in the mind: *mental calculations* **3** affected by mental illness: *a mental patient* **4** concerned with care for persons with mental illness: *a mental hospital* **5** *slang* insane [c15 from Late Latin *mentālis*, from Latin *mēns* mind] > ˈmentally *adv*

mental[2] (ˈmɛntᵊl) *adj anatomy* of or relating to the chin. Also: **genial** [c18 from Latin *mentum* chin]

mental age *n psychol* the mental ability of a child, expressed in years and based on a comparison of his test performance with the performance of children with a range of chronological ages. See also **intelligence quotient**

mental block *n* See **block** (sense 21)

mental cruelty *n* behaviour that causes distress to another person but that does not involve physical assault

mental deficiency *n psychiatry* a less common term for **mental retardation**

mental disorder *n law* (in England, according to the Mental Health Act 1983) mental illness, arrested or incomplete development of mind, psychopathic disorder, or any other disorder or disability of the mind > **mentally disordered** *adj*

mental handicap *n* a general or specific intellectual disability, resulting directly or indirectly from injury to the brain or from abnormal neurological development > **mentally handicapped** *adj*

mental healing *n* the healing of a disorder by mental concentration or suggestion > **mental healer** *n*

mental home, hospital *or* **institution** *n* a home, hospital, or institution for people who are mentally ill

mental illness *n* any of various disorders in which a person's thoughts, emotions, or behaviour are so abnormal as to cause suffering to himself, herself, or other people

mental impairment *n law* (in England, according to the Mental Health Act 1983) a state of arrested or incomplete development of mind, which includes significant impairment of intelligence and social functioning and is associated with abnormally aggressive or seriously irresponsible conduct > **mentally impaired** *adj*

mentalism (ˈmɛntᵊˌlɪzəm) *n philosophy* the doctrine that mind is the fundamental reality and that objects of knowledge exist only as aspects of the subject's consciousness. Compare **physicalism, idealism** (sense 3) See also **monism** (sense 1), **materialism** (sense 2) > ˈmentalist *n* > ˌmentalˈistic *adj* > ˌmentalˈistically *adv*

mentality (mɛnˈtælɪtɪ) *n, pl* -ties **1** the state or

quality of mental or intellectual ability **2** a way of thinking; mental inclination or character

mental lexicon *n* the store of words in a person's mind

mental reservation *n* a tacit withholding of full assent or an unexpressed qualification made when one is taking an oath, making a statement, etc

mental retardation *n psychiatry* the condition of having a low intelligence quotient (below 70)

mentation (mɛnˈteɪʃən) *n* the process or result of mental activity

menthaceous (mɛnˈθeɪʃɪəs) *adj* of, relating to, or belonging to the labiate plant genus *Mentha* (mints, etc) the members of which have scented leaves [from New Latin, from Latin *mentha* MINT[1]]

menthol (ˈmɛnθɒl) *n* an optically active organic compound found in peppermint oil and used as an antiseptic, in inhalants, and as an analgesic. Formula: $C_{10}H_{20}O$ [c19 from German, from Latin *mentha* MINT[1]]

mentholated (ˈmɛnθəˌleɪtɪd) *adj* containing, treated, or impregnated with menthol

mention (ˈmɛnʃən) *vb* (*tr*) **1** to refer to or speak about briefly or incidentally **2** to acknowledge or honour **3** not to mention (something) to say nothing of (something too obvious to mention) ⊳ *n* **4** a recognition or acknowledgment **5** a slight reference or allusion: *he only got a mention in the article; the author makes no mention of that* **6** the act of mentioning **7** *philosophy, logic, linguistics* the occurrence (of an expression) in such a context that it is itself referred to rather than performing its own linguistic function. In "*Fido*" names Fido, the word *Fido* is first mentioned and then used to refer to the dog. Compare **use** (sense 18) See also **formal mode** [c14 via Old French from Latin *mentiō* a calling to mind, naming, from *mēns* mind] > ˈmentionable *adj* > ˈmentioner *n*

Mentmore (ˈmɛntˌmɔː) *n* a mansion in Mentmore in Buckinghamshire: built by Sir Joseph Paxton in the 19th century for the Rothschild family; now owned by the Maharishi University of Natural Law

Menton (mɛnˈtəʊn; *French* mãtɔ̄) *n* a town and resort in SE France, on the Mediterranean: belonged to Monaco from the 14th century until 1848, then an independent republic until purchased by France in 1860. Pop: 28 812 (1999)

mentor (ˈmɛntɔː) *n* **1** a wise or trusted adviser or guide ⊳ *vb* **2** to act as a mentor to (someone); train [c18 from MENTOR] > menˈtorial *adj*

Mentor (ˈmɛntɔː) *n* the friend whom Odysseus put in charge of his household when he left for Troy. He was the adviser of the young Telemachus

mentoring (ˈmɛntərɪŋ) *n* (in business) the practice of assigning a junior member of staff to the care of a more experienced person who assists him in his career

menu (ˈmɛnjuː) *n* **1** a list of dishes served at a meal or that can be ordered in a restaurant **2** a list of options displayed on a visual display unit from which the operator selects an action to be carried out by positioning the cursor or by depressing the appropriate key [c19 from French *menu* small, detailed (list), from Latin *minūtus* MINUTE[2]]

menu-driven *adj* (of a computer system) operated through menus

meow, miaou, miaow (mɪˈaʊ, mjaʊ) *or* **miaul** (mɪˈaʊl, mjaʊl) *vb* **1** (*intr*) (of a cat) to make a characteristic crying sound ⊳ *interj* **2** an imitation of this sound

MEP (in Britain) *abbreviation for* Member of the European Parliament

mepacrine (ˈmɛpəkrɪn) *n Brit* a drug, mepacrine dihydrochloride, one of the first synthetic substitutes for quinine, formerly widely used to treat malaria but now largely replaced by chloroquine. Formula: $C_{23}H_{30}ClN_3O.2HCl.2H_2O$. US name: **quinacrine** [c20 from ME(THYL) + PA(LUDISM + A)CR(ID)INE]

Mephistopheles (ˌmɛfɪˈstɒfɪˌliːz) or **Mephisto** (məˈfɪstəʊ) n a devil in medieval mythology and the one to whom Faust sold his soul in the Faust legend > Mephistophelean or Mephistophelian (ˌmɛfɪstəˈfiːlɪən) adj

mephitic (mɪˈfɪtɪk) or **mephitical** adj 1 poisonous; foul 2 foul-smelling; putrid [c17 from Late Latin *mephīticus* pestilential] > meˈphitically adv

meprobamate (məˈprəʊbəˌmeɪt, ˌmɛprəʊˈbæmeɪt) n a white bitter powder used as a hypnotic. Formula: $C_9H_{18}N_2O_4$ [ME(THYL) + PRO(PYL + CAR)BAMATE]

mer. abbreviation for meridian

-mer suffix forming nouns chem denoting a substance of a particular class: *monomer; polymer* [from Greek *meros* part]

Merano (məˈrɑːnəʊ; Italian me'rɑːno) n a town and resort in NE Italy, in the foothills of the central Alps: capital of the Tyrol (12th–15th century); under Austrian rule until 1919. Pop: 33 656 (2001). German name: Meran (me'rɑːn)

meranti (mɪˈræntɪ) n wood from any of several Malaysian trees of the dipterocarpaceous genus *Shorea* [c18 from Malay]

merbromin (məˈbrəʊmɪn) n a green iridescent crystalline compound that forms a red solution in water: used in medicine as an antiseptic. Formula: $C_{20}H_8Br_2HgNa_2O_6$. See also **Mercurochrome** [c20 blend of MERCURIC + *dibromofluorescein*]

Merca (ˈmɛəkə) n a port in S Somalia on the Indian Ocean. Pop: 189 000 (2005 est)

Mercalli scale (mɜːˈkælɪ) n a 12-point scale for expressing the intensity of an earthquake, ranging from 1 (not felt, except by few under favourable circumstances) to 12 (total destruction). Compare **Richter scale** See also **intensity** (sense 4) [c20 named after Giuseppe *Mercalli* (1850–1914), Italian volcanologist and seismologist]

mercantile (ˈmɜːkənˌtaɪl) adj 1 of, relating to, or characteristic of trade or traders; commercial 2 of or relating to mercantilism [c17 from French, from Italian, from *mercante* MERCHANT]

mercantile agency n an enterprise that collects and supplies information about the financial credit standing of individuals and enterprises

mercantile paper n another name for **commercial paper**

mercantilism (ˈmɜːkəntɪˌlɪzəm) n 1 Also called: **mercantile system** *economics* a theory prevalent in Europe during the 17th and 18th centuries asserting that the wealth of a nation depends on its possession of precious metals and therefore that the government of a nation must maximize the foreign trade surplus, and foster national commercial interests, a merchant marine, the establishment of colonies, etc 2 a rare word for **commercialism** (sense 1) > ˈmercanˌtilist n, adj

mercaptan (mɜːˈkæptæn) n another name (not in technical usage) for **thiol** [c19 from German, from Medieval Latin *mercurium captans*, literally: seizing quicksilver]

mercaptide (məˈkæptaɪd, mɜː-) n a salt of a mercaptan, containing the ion RS⁻, where R is an alkyl or aryl group

mercapto- (mɜːˈkæptəʊ) combining form (in chemical compounds) indicating the presence of an HS- group

mercaptopurine (məˌkæptəʊˈpjʊəriːn) n a drug used in the treatment of leukaemia. Formula: $C_5H_4N_4S$

mercat (ˈmɛrkət) n a Scot word for **market**

Mercator projection (mɜːˈkeɪtə) n an orthomorphic map projection on which parallels and meridians form a rectangular grid, scale being exaggerated with increasing distance from the equator. Also called: **Mercator's projection** [c17 named after Gerardus *Mercator*, Latinized name of Gerhard Kremer (1512–94), Flemish cartographer and mathematician]

mercenary (ˈmɜːsɪnərɪ, -sɪnrɪ) adj 1 influenced by greed or desire for gain 2 of or relating to a mercenary or mercenaries ▷ n, pl -naries 3 a man hired to fight for a foreign army, etc 4 rare any person who works solely for pay [c16 from Latin *mercēnārius*, from *mercēs* wages] > ˈmercenarily adv > ˈmercenariness n

mercer (ˈmɜːsə) n Brit a dealer in textile fabrics and fine cloth [c13 from Old French *mercier* dealer, from Vulgar Latin *merciārius* (unattested), from Latin *merx* goods, wares] > ˈmercery n

mercerize or **mercerise** (ˈmɜːsəˌraɪz) vb (tr) to treat (cotton yarn) with an alkali to increase its strength and reception to dye and impart a lustrous silky appearance [c19 named after John *Mercer* (1791–1866), English maker of textiles] > ˌmerceriˈzation or ˌmerceriˈsation n

merchandise n (ˈmɜːtʃənˌdaɪs, -ˌdaɪz) 1 commercial goods; commodities ▷ vb (ˈmɜːtʃənˌdaɪz) 2 to engage in the commercial purchase and sale of (goods or services); trade [c13 from Old French. See MERCHANT] > ˈmerchanˌdiser n

merchandising (ˈmɜːtʃənˌdaɪzɪŋ) n 1 the selection and display of goods in a retail outlet 2 commercial goods, esp ones issued to exploit the popularity of a pop group, sporting event, etc

merchant (ˈmɜːtʃənt) n 1 a person engaged in the purchase and sale of commodities for profit, esp on international markets; trader 2 chiefly US and Canadian a person engaged in retail trade 3 (esp in historical contexts) any trader 4 derogatory a person dealing or involved in something undesirable: *a gossip merchant* 5 (modifier) **a** of the merchant navy: *a merchant sailor* **b** of or concerned with trade: *a merchant ship* ▷ vb 6 (tr) to conduct trade in; deal in [c13 from Old French, probably from Vulgar Latin *mercātāre* (unattested), from Latin *mercārī* to trade, from *merx* goods, wares] > ˈmerchant-ˌlike adj

merchantable (ˈmɜːtʃəntəbəl) adj suitable for trading

merchant bank n (in Britain) a financial institution engaged primarily in accepting foreign bills, advising companies on flotations and takeovers, underwriting new issues, hire-purchase finance, making long-term loans to companies, and managing investment portfolios, funds, and trusts > merchant banker n

merchantman (ˈmɜːtʃəntmən) n, pl -men a merchant ship

merchant navy or **marine** n the ships or crew engaged in a nation's commercial shipping

merchant prince n a very wealthy merchant

merchet (ˈmɜːtʃɪt) n (in feudal England) a fine paid by a tenant, esp a villein, to his lord for allowing the marriage of his daughter [c13 from Anglo-French, literally: MARKET]

Mercia (ˈmɜːʃɪə) n a kingdom and earldom of central and S England during the Anglo-Saxon period that reached its height under King Offa (757–96)

Mercian (ˈmɜːʃɪən) adj 1 of or relating to Mercia or the dialect spoken there ▷ n 2 the dialect of Old and Middle English spoken in the Midlands of England south of the River Humber. See also **Anglian, Northumbrian**

merciful (ˈmɜːsɪfʊl) adj showing or giving mercy; compassionate > ˈmercifulness n

mercifully (ˈmɜːsɪfʊlɪ) adv 1 in a way that shows mercy; compassionately: *mercifully put down* 2 (sentence modifier) fortunately; one is relieved to say that: *mercifully, all went well*

merciless (ˈmɜːsɪlɪs) adj without mercy; pitiless, cruel, or heartless > ˈmercilessly adv > ˈmercilessness n

Mercosur (ˈmɜːkəˌsə) n a trading block composed of Argentina, Bolivia, Brazil, Chile, Paraguay, and Uruguay [c20 from Spanish *Mercado Común del Cono Sur* common market of the southern cone]

mercurate (ˈmɜːkjʊˌreɪt) vb 1 (tr) to treat or mix with mercury 2 to undergo or cause to undergo a chemical reaction in which a mercury atom is added to a compound > ˌmercuˈration n

mercurial (mɜːˈkjʊərɪəl) adj 1 of, like, containing, or relating to mercury 2 volatile; lively: *a mercurial temperament* 3 (sometimes capital) of, like, or relating to the god or the planet Mercury ▷ n 4 med any salt of mercury for use as a medicine [c14 from Latin *mercuriālis*] > merˈcurially adv > merˈcurialness or merˌcuriˈality n

mercurialism (mɜːˈkjʊərɪəˌlɪzəm) n poisoning caused by chronic ingestion of mercury

mercurialize or **mercurialise** (mɜːˈkjʊərɪəˌlaɪz) vb (tr) 1 to make mercurial 2 to treat with mercury or a mercury compound > merˌcurialiˈzation or merˌcurialiˈsation n

mercuric (mɜːˈkjʊərɪk) adj of or containing mercury in the divalent state; denoting a mercury(II) compound

mercuric chloride n a white poisonous soluble crystalline substance used as a pesticide, antiseptic, and preservative for wood. Formula: $HgCl_2$. Systematic name: mercury(II) chloride Also called: bichloride of mercury, corrosive sublimate

mercuric oxide n a soluble poisonous substance existing in red and yellow powdered forms: used as pigments. Formula: HgO. Systematic name: mercury(II) oxide

mercuric sulphide n a compound of mercury, usually existing as a black solid (**metacinnabarite**) or a red solid (**cinnabar** or **vermilion**), which is used as a pigment. Formula: HgS. Systematic name: mercury(II) sulphide

Mercurochrome (məˈkjʊərəˌkrəʊm) n trademark a solution of merbromin, used as topical antibacterial agent

mercurous (ˈmɜːkjʊrəs) adj of or containing mercury in the monovalent state; denoting a mercury(I) compound. Mercurous salts contain the divalent ion Hg_2^{2+}

mercurous chloride n a white tasteless insoluble powder used as a fungicide and formerly as a medical antiseptic, cathartic, and diuretic. Formula: Hg_2Cl_2. Systematic name: mercury(I) chloride Also called: calomel

mercury (ˈmɜːkjʊrɪ) n, pl -ries 1 Also called: quicksilver, hydrargyrum a heavy silvery-white toxic liquid metallic element occurring principally in cinnabar: used in thermometers, barometers, mercury-vapour lamps, and dental amalgams. Symbol: Hg; atomic no.: 80; atomic wt.: 200.59; valency: 1 or 2; relative density: 13.546; melting pt.: –38.842°C; boiling pt.: 357°C 2 any plant of the euphorbiaceous genus *Mercurialis*. See **dog's mercury** 3 archaic a messenger or courier [c14 from Latin *Mercurius* messenger of Jupiter, god of commerce; related to *merx* merchandise]

Mercury[1] (ˈmɜːkjʊrɪ) n Roman myth the messenger of the gods. Greek counterpart: Hermes

Mercury[2] (ˈmɜːkjʊrɪ) n the second smallest planet and the nearest to the sun. Mean distance from sun: 57.9 million km; period of revolution around sun: 88 days; period of axial rotation: 59 days; diameter and mass: 38 and 5.4 per cent that of earth respectively

mercury arc n **a** an electric discharge through ionized mercury vapour, producing a brilliant bluish-green light containing ultraviolet radiation **b** (as modifier): *a mercury-arc rectifier*. See also **ignitron**

mercury chloride n See **mercurous chloride, mercuric chloride**

mercury switch n electrical engineering a switch in which a circuit is completed between two terminals by liquid mercury when the switch is tilted

mercury-vapour lamp n a lamp in which an electric discharge through a low pressure of mercury vapour is used to produce a greenish-blue light. It is used for street lighting and is also a source of ultraviolet radiation

mercy (ˈmɜːsɪ) n, pl -cies 1 compassionate treatment of or attitude towards an offender,

m

adversary, etc, who is in one's power or care; clemency; pity **2** the power to show mercy: *to throw oneself on someone's mercy* **3** a relieving or welcome occurrence or state of affairs: *his death was a mercy after weeks of pain* **4 at the mercy of** in the power of [c12 from Old French, from Latin *mercēs* wages, recompense, price, from *merx* goods]

mercy flight *n* an aircraft flight to bring a seriously ill or injured person to hospital from an isolated community

mercy killing *n* another term for **euthanasia**

mercy seat *n* **1** *Old Testament* the gold platform covering the Ark of the Covenant and regarded as the throne of God where he accepted sacrifices and gave commandments (Exodus 25:17, 22) **2** *Christianity* the throne of God

mere[1] (mɪə) *adj, superlative* **merest** being nothing more than something specified: *she is a mere child* [c15 from Latin *merus* pure, unmixed]

mere[2] (mɪə) *n* **1** *dialect or archaic* a lake or marsh **2** *obsolete* the sea or an inlet of it [Old English *mere* sea, lake; related to Old Saxon *meri* sea, Old Norse *marr*, Old High German *mari*; compare Latin *mare*]

mere[3] (mɪə) *n archaic* a boundary or boundary marker [Old English *gemære*]

mere[4] ('mɛrɪ) *n* NZ a short flat striking weapon [Māori]

-mere *n combining form* indicating a part or division: *blastomere* [from Greek *meros* part, portion] > **-meric** *adj combining form*

merely ('mɪəlɪ) *adv* only; nothing more than

merengue (mə'rɛŋɡeɪ) *n* **1** a type of lively dance music originating in the Dominican Republic, which combines African and Spanish elements **2** a Caribbean dance in duple time with syncopated rhythm performed to such music [from American Spanish and Haitian Creole]

mereology (ˌmiːrɪ'ɒlədʒɪ) *n* the formal study of the logical properties of the relation of part and whole [c20 via French from Greek *meros* part + -LOGY] > **mereo'logical** *adj*

meretricious (ˌmɛrɪ'trɪʃəs) *adj* **1** superficially or garishly attractive **2** insincere: *meretricious praise* **3** *archaic* of, like, or relating to a prostitute [c17 from Latin *merētrīcius*, from *merētrix* prostitute, from *merēre* to earn money] > ˌmere'triciously *adv* > ˌmere'triciousness *n*

merganser (mɜː'ɡænsə) *n, pl* **-sers** or **-ser** any of several typically crested large marine diving ducks of the genus *Mergus*, having a long slender hooked bill with serrated edges. Also called: **sawbill** See also **goosander** [c18 from New Latin, from Latin *mergus* waterfowl, from *mergere* to plunge + *anser* goose]

merge (mɜːdʒ) *vb* **1** to meet and join or cause to meet and join **2** to blend or cause to blend; fuse [c17 from Latin *mergere* to plunge] > 'mergence *n*

merger ('mɜːdʒə) *n* **1** *commerce* the combination of two or more companies, either by the creation of a new organization or by absorption by one of the others. Often called (Brit): **amalgamation 2** *law* the extinguishment of an estate, interest, contract, right, offence, etc, by its absorption into a greater one **3** the act of merging or the state of being merged

Mergui Archipelago (mɜː'ɡwiː) *n* a group of over 200 islands in the Andaman Sea, off the Tenasserim coast of S Myanmar: mountainous and forested

Meriç (mə'riːtʃ) *n* the Turkish name for the Maritsa

Mérida (*Spanish* 'meriða) *n* **1** a city in SE Mexico, capital of Yucatán state: founded in 1542 on the site of the ancient Mayan city of T'ho; centre of the henequen industry; university. Pop: 919 000 (2005 est) **2** a city in W Venezuela: founded in 1558 by Spanish conquistadores; University of Los Andes (1785). Pop: 319 000 (2005 est) **3** a market town in W Spain, in Extremadura, on the Guadiana River: founded in 25 BC; became the capital of Lusitania and one of the chief cities of Iberia. Pop: 52 110 (2003 est). Latin name: **Augusta Emerita**

meridian (mə'rɪdɪən) *n* **1 a** one of the imaginary lines joining the north and south poles at right angles to the equator, designated by degrees of longitude from 0° at Greenwich to 180° **b** the great circle running through both poles. See **prime meridian 2** *astronomy* **a** the great circle on the celestial sphere passing through the north and south celestial poles and the zenith and nadir of the observer **b** (*as modifier*): *a meridian instrument* **3** Also called: **meridian section** *maths* a section of a surface of revolution, such as a paraboloid, that contains the axis of revolution **4** the peak; zenith: *the meridian of his achievements* **5** (in acupuncture, etc) any of the channels through which vital energy is believed to circulate round the body **6** *obsolete* noon ▷ *adj* **7** along or relating to a meridian **8** of or happening at noon **9** relating to the peak of something [c14 from Latin *merīdiānus* of midday, from *merīdiēs* midday, from *medius* MID[1] + *diēs* day]

meridian circle *n* an instrument used in astronomy for determining the declination and right ascension of stars. It consists of a telescope attached to a graduated circle

meridional (mə'rɪdɪən°l) *adj* **1** along, relating to, or resembling a meridian **2** characteristic of or located in the south, esp of Europe ▷ *n* **3** an inhabitant of the south, esp of France [c14 from Late Latin *merīdiōnālis* southern; see MERIDIAN; for form, compare *septentriōnālis* SEPTENTRIONAL] > me'ridionally *adv*

mering ('mɪərɪŋ) *n chiefly Irish* **a** another word for **mere**[3] **b** (*as modifier*): *the mering wall* [c16 from MERE[3]]

meringue (mə'ræŋ) *n* **1** stiffly beaten egg whites mixed with sugar and baked, often as a topping for pies, cakes, etc **2** a small cake or shell of this mixture, often filled with cream [c18 from French, origin obscure]

merino (mə'riːnəʊ) *n, pl* **-nos 1** a breed of sheep, originating in Spain, bred for their fleece **2** the long fine wool of this sheep **3** the yarn made from this wool, often mixed with cotton **4** *pure merino Austral informal* **a** *history* a free settler rather than a convict **b** an affluent and socially prominent person **c** (*as modifier*): *a pure merino cricketer* ▷ *adj* **5** made from merino wool [c18 from Spanish, origin uncertain]

Merionethshire (ˌmɛrɪ'ɒnɪθˌʃɪə, -ʃə) *n* (until 1974) a county of N Wales, now part of Gwynedd

meristem ('mɛrɪˌstɛm) *n* a plant tissue responsible for growth, whose cells divide and differentiate to form the tissues and organs of the plant. Meristems occur within the stem (see **cambium**) and leaves and at the tips of stems and roots [c19 from Greek *meristos* divided, from *merizein* to divide, from *meris* portion] > **meristematic** (ˌmɛrɪstɪ'mætɪk) *adj*

meristic (mə'rɪstɪk) *adj biology* **1** of or relating to the number of organs or parts in an animal or plant body: *meristic variation* **2** segmented: *meristic worms*

merit ('mɛrɪt) *n* **1** worth or superior quality; excellence: *work of great merit* **2** (*often plural*) a deserving or commendable quality or act: *judge him on his merits* **3** *Christianity* spiritual credit granted or received for good works **4** the fact or state of deserving; desert **5** an obsolete word for **reward** ▷ *vb* **-its, -iting, -ited 6** (*tr*) to be worthy of; deserve: *he merits promotion* ▷ See also **merits** [c13 via Old French from Latin *meritum* reward, desert, from *merēre* to deserve] > 'merited *adj* > 'meritless *adj*

meritocracy (ˌmɛrɪ'tɒkrəsɪ) *n, pl* **-cies 1** rule by persons chosen not because of birth or wealth, but for their superior talents or intellect **2** the persons constituting such a group **3** a social system formed on such a basis > 'merito,crat *n* > meritocratic (ˌmɛrɪtə'krætɪk) *adj*

meritorious (ˌmɛrɪ'tɔːrɪəs) *adj* praiseworthy; showing merit [c15 from Latin *meritōrius* earning money] > ˌmeri'toriously *adv* > ˌmeri'toriousness *n*

merits ('mɛrɪts) *pl n* **1** the actual and intrinsic rights and wrongs of an issue, esp in a law case, as distinct from extraneous matters and technicalities **2 on its (his, her, etc) merits** on the intrinsic qualities or virtues

merit system *n* US the system of employing and promoting civil servants solely on the basis of ability rather than patronage. Compare **spoils system**

merkin ('mɜːkɪn) *n* **1** an artificial hairpiece for the pudendum; a pubic wig **2** *obsolete* the pudendum itself [c16 of unknown origin]

merle[1] or **merl** (mɜːl; *Scot* mɛrl) *n Scot* another name for the (European) **blackbird** [c15 via Old French from Latin *merula*]

merle[2] (mɜːl) *adj* (of a dog, esp a collie) having a bluish-grey coat with speckles or streaks of black. Often called: **blue merle** [c20 from dialect *mirlet, mirly* speckled]

merlin ('mɜːlɪn) *n* a small falcon, *Falco columbarius*, that has a dark plumage with a black-barred tail: used in falconry. See also **pigeon hawk** [c14 from Old French *esmerillon*, from *esmeril*, of Germanic origin]

Merlin ('mɜːlɪn) *n* (in Arthurian legend) a wizard and counsellor to King Arthur eternally imprisoned in a tree by a woman to whom he revealed his secret craft

merlon ('mɜːlən) *n fortifications* the solid upright section in a crenellated battlement [c18 from French, from Italian *merlone*, from *merlo* battlement]

Merlot ('mɜːləʊ) *n* (*sometimes not capital*) **1** a black grape grown in France and now throughout the wine-producing world, used, often in a blend, for making wine **2** any of various wines made from this grape [from French *merlot*, literally: young blackbird, diminutive of *merle* MERLE[1], probably alluding to the colour of the grape]

mermaid ('mɜːˌmeɪd) *n* an imaginary sea creature fabled to have a woman's head and upper body and a fish's tail [c14 from *mere* lake, inlet + MAID]

mermaid's purse *n* another name for **sea purse**

merman ('mɜːˌmæn) *n, pl* **-men** a male counterpart of the mermaid [c17 see MERMAID]

mero- *combining form* part or partial: *merocrine* [from Greek *meros* part, share]

meroblastic (ˌmɛrəʊ'blæstɪk) *adj embryol* of or showing cleavage of only the non-yolky part of the zygote, as in birds' eggs. Compare **holoblastic** > ˌmero'blastically *adv*

merocrine ('mɛrəˌkraɪn, -krɪn) *adj* (of the secretion of glands) characterized by formation of the product without undergoing disintegration. Compare **holocrine, apocrine** [c20 from MERO- + Greek *krinein* to separate]

Meroë ('mɛrəʊˌiː) *n* an ancient city in N Sudan, on the Nile; capital of a kingdom that flourished from about 700 BC to about 350 A.D

meronym ('mɛrəʊˌnɪm) *n* a part of something used to refer to the whole, such as *faces* meaning *people*, as in *they've seen a lot of faces come and go* [from Greek *meros* part + *onuma* name]

meroplankton (ˌmɛrəʊ'plæŋktən) *n* plankton consisting of organisms at a certain stage of their life cycles, esp larvae, the other stages not being spent as part of the plankton community. Compare **holoplankton**

-merous *adj combining form* (in biology) having a certain number or kind of parts: *dimerous* [from Greek *meros* part, division]

Merovingian (ˌmɛrəʊ'vɪndʒɪən) *adj* **1** of or relating to a Frankish dynasty founded by Clovis I, which ruled Gaul and W Germany from about 500 to 751 A.D ▷ *n* **2** a member or supporter of this dynasty [c17 from French, from Medieval Latin *Merovingi* offspring of *Merovaeus*, Latin form of *Merowig*, traditional founder of the line]

merozoite (ˌmɛrəʊ'zəʊaɪt) *n* any of the cells formed by fission of a schizont during the life cycle of sporozoan protozoans, such as the malaria parasite. Compare **trophozoite** [C20 from MERO- + ZO(O) + -ITE¹]

merriment ('mɛrɪmənt) n gaiety, fun, or mirth

merry ('mɛrɪ) adj -rier, -riest **1** cheerful; jolly **2** very funny; hilarious **3** Brit informal slightly drunk **4** archaic delightful **5 make merry** to revel; be festive **6 play merry hell with** informal to disturb greatly; disrupt [Old English merige agreeable] > 'merrily adv > 'merriness n

merry-andrew n a joker, clown, or buffoon [C17 original reference of Andrew unexplained]

merry dancers pl n Scot the aurora borealis

merry-go-round n **1** another name for **roundabout** (sense 1) **2** a whirl of activity or events: the merry-go-round of the fashion world

merrymaking ('mɛrɪ,meɪkɪŋ) n fun, revelry, or festivity > 'merry,maker n

merry men pl n facetious a person's assistants or followers [C19 originally, the companions of a knight, outlaw, etc]

merrythought ('mɛrɪ,θɔ:t) n Brit a less common word for **wishbone**

merse (mɜːs; Scot mɛrs) n Scot **1** low level ground by a river or shore, often alluvial and fertile **2** a marsh [Old English merse marsh]

Merse (mɜːs; Scot mɛrs) n **the** a fertile lowland area of SE Scotland, in Scottish Borders, north of the Tweed

Merseburg (German 'mɛrzəburk) n a city in E Germany, on the Saale River, in Saxony-Anhalt: residence of the dukes of Saxe-Merseburg (1656–1738); chemical industry. Pop: 35 358 (2003 est)

Mersey ('mɜːzɪ) n a river in W England, rising in N Derbyshire and flowing northwest and west to the Irish Sea through a large estuary on which is situated the port of Liverpool. Length: about 112 km (70 miles)

Mersey beat n **a** the characteristic pop music of the Beatles and other groups from Liverpool in the 1960s **b** (as modifier): the Merseybeat years

Merseyside ('mɜːzɪ,saɪd) n a metropolitan county of NW England, administered since 1986 by the unitary authorities of Sefton, Liverpool, St Helens, Knowsley, and Wirral. Area: 652 sq km (252 sq miles)

Mersin (mɛə'siːn) n a port in S Turkey, on the Mediterranean: oil refinery. Pop: 603 000 (2005 est). Also called: **İçel**

Merthyr Tydfil ('mɜːθə 'tɪdvɪl) n **1** a town in SE Wales, in Merthyr Tydfil county borough: formerly an important centre for the mining industry. Pop: 30 483 (2001) **2** a county borough in SE Wales, created from part of N Mid Glamorgan in 1996. Pop: 55 400 (2003 est). Area: 111 sq km (43 sq miles)

Merton ('mɜːtᵊn) n a borough in SW Greater London. Pop: 191 400 (2003 est). Area: 38 sq km (15 sq miles)

mes- combining form a variant of **meso-** before a vowel: mesarch; mesencephalon; mesenteron

mesa ('meɪsə) n a flat tableland with steep edges, common in the southwestern US [from Spanish: table]

mésalliance (mɛ'zælɪəns; French mezaljɑ̃s) n marriage with a person of lower social status [C18 from French: MISALLIANCE]

mesarch ('mɛsɑːk) adj botany (of a xylem strand) having the first-formed xylem surrounded by that formed later, as in fern stems. Compare **exarch²**, **endarch** [C19 from MES(O)- + Greek arkhē beginning]

Mesa Verde ('meɪsə 'vɜːd) n a high plateau in SW Colorado: remains of numerous prehistoric cliff dwellings, inhabited by the Pueblo Indians

mescal (mɛ'skæl) n **1** Also called: **peyote** a spineless globe-shaped cactus, Lophophora williamsii, of Mexico and the southwestern US. Its button-like tubercles (**mescal buttons**) contain mescaline and are chewed by certain Indian tribes for their hallucinogenic effects **2** a colourless alcoholic spirit distilled from the fermented juice of certain

agave plants [C19 from American Spanish, from Nahuatl mexcalli the liquor, from metl MAGUEY + ixcalli stew]

mescaline or **mescalin** ('mɛskə,liːn, -lɪn) n a hallucinogenic drug derived from mescal buttons. Formula: $C_{11}H_{17}NO_3$

mesdames ('meɪ,dæm; French medam) n the plural of **madame** and **madam** (sense 1)

mesdemoiselles (,meɪdmwɑ'zɛl; French medmwazɛl) n the plural of **mademoiselle**

meseems (mɪ'siːmz) vb, past **meseemed** (tr; takes a clause as object) archaic it seems to me

mesembryanthemum (mɪz,ɛmbrɪ'ænθɪməm) n any plant of a South African genus (Mesembryanthemum) of succulent-leaved prostrate or erect plants widely grown in gardens and greenhouses: family Aizoaceae. See **fig marigold**, **ice plant**, **Livingstone daisy** [C18 New Latin, from Greek mesēmbria noon + anthemon flower]

mesencephalon (,mɛsɛn'sɛfə,lɒn) n the part of the brain that develops from the middle portion of the embryonic neural tube. Nontechnical name: midbrain. Related adj: **prosencephalon, rhombencephalon** Nontechnical name: midbrain > mesencephalic (,mɛsɛnsɪ'fælɪk) adj

mesenchyme ('mɛsɛŋ,kaɪm) n embryol the part of the mesoderm that develops into connective tissue, cartilage, lymph, blood, etc [C19 New Latin, from MESO- + -ENCHYMA] > mesenchymal (mɛs'ɛŋkɪməl) or mesenchymatous (,mɛsɛŋ'kɪmətəs) adj

mesenteritis (mɛs,ɛntə'raɪtɪs) n inflammation of the mesentery

mesenteron (mɛs'ɛntə,rɒn) n, pl **-tera** (-tərə) a former name for **midgut** (sense 1) > mes,enter'onic adj

mesentery ('mɛsəntərɪ, 'mɛz-) n, pl **-teries** the double layer of peritoneum that is attached to the back wall of the abdominal cavity and supports most of the small intestine [C16 from New Latin mesenterium; see MESO- + ENTERON] > ,mesen'teric adj

mesh (mɛʃ) n **1** a network; net **2** an open space between the strands of a network **3** (often plural) the strands surrounding these spaces **4** anything that ensnares, or holds like a net: the mesh of the secret police **5** the engagement of teeth on interacting gearwheels: the gears are in mesh **6** a measure of spacing of the strands of a mesh or grid, expressed as the distance between strands for coarse meshes or a number of strands per unit length for fine meshes ▷ vb **7** to entangle or become entangled **8** (of gear teeth) to engage or cause to engage **9** (intr; often foll by with) to coordinate (with): to mesh with a policy **10** to work or cause to work in harmony [C16 probably from Dutch maesche; related to Old English masc, Old High German masca] > 'meshy adj

Meshach ('miːʃæk) n Old Testament one of Daniel's three companions who, together with Shadrach and Abednego, was miraculously saved from destruction in Nebuchadnezzar's fiery furnace (Daniel 3:12-30)

mesh connection n electrical engineering (in a polyphase system) an arrangement in which the end of each phase is connected to the beginning of the next, forming a ring, each junction being connected to a terminal. See also **delta connection, star connection**

Meshed (mɛ'ʃɛd) n a variant of **Mashhad**

meshuga Yiddish (mɪ'ʃʊgə) adj crazy [from Hebrew]

meshugas Yiddish (mɪ'ʃʊgəs) n craziness [from Hebrew]

mesiad ('miːzɪæd) adj anatomy, zoology relating to or situated at the middle or centre

mesial ('miːzɪəl) adj anatomy another word for **medial** (sense 1) [C19 from MESO- + -IAL] > 'mesially adv

mesic ('miːzɪk) adj **1** of, relating to, or growing in conditions of medium water supply: mesic plants **2** of or relating to a meson > 'mesically adv

mesitylene (mɪ'sɪtɪ,liːn, 'mɛsɪtɪ,liːn) n a

colourless liquid that occurs in crude petroleum; 1,3,5-trimethylbenzene. Formula: $C_6H_3(CH_3)_3$ [C19 from mesityl, from mesite, from New Latin mesita, from Greek mesitēs mediator + -ENE]

mesmeric (mɛz'mɛrɪk) adj **1** holding (someone) as if spellbound **2** of or relating to mesmerism > mes'merically adv

mesmerism ('mɛzmə,rɪzəm) n psychol **1** a hypnotic state induced by the operator's imposition of his will on that of the patient **2** an early doctrine concerning this [C19 named after F. A. Mesmer (1734–1815), Austrian physician] > 'mesmerist n

mesmerize or **mesmerise** ('mɛzmə,raɪz) vb (tr) **1** a former word for **hypnotize 2** to hold (someone) as if spellbound > ,mesmeri'zation or ,mesmeri'sation n > 'mesmer,izer or 'mesmer,iser n

mesnalty ('miːnəltɪ) n, pl **-ties** history the lands of a mesne lord [C16 from legal French, from MESNE]

mesne (miːn) adj law **1** intermediate or intervening: used esp of any assignment of property before the last: a mesne assignment **2 mesne profits** rents or profits accruing during the rightful owner's exclusion from his land [C15 from legal French meien in the middle, MEAN³]

mesne lord n (in feudal society) a lord who held land from a superior lord and kept his own tenants on it

meso- or before a vowel **mes-** combining form middle or intermediate: mesomorph [from Greek misos middle]

Mesoamerica or **Meso-America** (,mɛsəʊə'mɛrɪkə) n another name for **Central America**. > ,Mesoa'merican or ,Meso-A'merican adj, n

mesobenthos (,mɛzə'bɛnθəs, ,mɛsə-) n flora and fauna living at the bottom of seas 182 to 914 metres deep [from MESO- + Greek benthos depth of the sea]

mesoblast ('mɛsəʊ,blæst) n another name for **mesoderm**. > ,meso'blastic adj

mesocarp ('mɛsəʊ,kɑːp) n the middle layer of the pericarp of a fruit, such as the flesh of a peach

mesocephalic (,mɛsəʊsɪ'fælɪk) anatomy ▷ adj **1** having a medium-sized head, esp one with a cephalic index between 75 and 80 ▷ n **2** an individual with such a head ▷ Compare **brachycephalic, dolichocephalic**. > mesocephaly (,mɛsəʊ'sɛfəlɪ) n

mesocratic (,mɛsə'krætɪk) adj (of igneous rocks) containing 30–60 per cent of ferromagnesian minerals [C20 from MESO- + -CRAT, with allusion to the moderately dark colour of the rock. Compare LEUCOCRATIC]

mesoderm ('mɛsəʊ,dɜːm) n the middle germ layer of an animal embryo, giving rise to muscle, blood, bone, connective tissue, etc. See also **ectoderm, endoderm**. > ,meso'dermal or ,meso'dermic adj

mesogastrium (,mɛsəʊ'gæstrɪəm) n the mesentery supporting the embryonic stomach > ,meso'gastric adj

mesoglea or **mesogloea** (,mɛsəʊ'gliːə) n the gelatinous material between the outer and inner cellular layers of jellyfish and other coelenterates [C19 New Latin, from MESO- + Greek gloia glue]

mesognathous (mɪ'sɒgnəθəs) adj anthropol having slightly projecting jaws > me'sognathism or me'sognathy n

mesokurtic (,mɛsəʊ'kɜːtɪk) adj statistics (of a distribution) having kurtosis B_2 = 3, concentrated around its mean like a normal distribution. Compare **leptokurtic, platykurtic** [C20 from MESO- + Greek kurtos arched, bulging + -IC]

Mesolithic (,mɛsəʊ'lɪθɪk) n **1** the period between the Palaeolithic and the Neolithic, in Europe from about 12 000 to 3000 BC, characterized by the appearance of microliths ▷ adj **2** of or relating to the Mesolithic

Mesolonghi (,mɛsə'lɔ:ŋgɪ) n a variant of **Missolonghi**

Mesolóngion (,mɛsə'lɒŋgɪ,ɒn) n transliteration

m

of the Modern Greek name for **Missolonghi**

mesomorph ('mɛsəʊˌmɔːf) *n* a person with a muscular body build: said to be correlated with somatotonia. Compare **ectomorph, endomorph** (sense 1)

mesomorphic (ˌmɛsəʊˈmɔːfɪk) *adj* also **mesomorphous 1** *chem* existing in or concerned with an intermediate state of matter between a true liquid and a true solid. See also **liquid crystal, smectic, nematic 2** relating to or being a mesomorph > ˌmeso'morphism *n* > 'mesoˌmorphy *n*

meson ('miːzɒn) *n* any of a group of elementary particles, such as a pion or kaon, that usually has a rest mass between those of an electron and a proton, and an integral spin. They are responsible for the force between nucleons in the atomic nucleus. Former name: **mesotron** See also **muon** [c20 from MESO- + -ON] > me'sonic *or* 'mesic *adj*

mesonephros (ˌmɛsəʊˈnɛfrɒs) *n* the middle part of the embryonic kidney in vertebrates, becoming the adult kidney in fishes and amphibians and the epididymis in reptiles, birds, and mammals. See also **pronephros, metanephros** [c19 New Latin, from MESO- + Greek *nephros* kidney] > ˌmeso'nephric *adj*

mesopause ('mɛsəʊˌpɔːz) *n meteorol* the zone of minimum temperature between the mesosphere and the thermosphere

mesopelagic (ˌmɛsəʊpəˈlædʒɪk) *adj* of, relating to, or inhabiting the intermediate depths of the ocean between approximately 100 and 1000 metres

mesophilic (ˌmɛsəʊˈfɪlɪk) *adj biology* (esp of bacteria) having an ideal growth temperature of 20–45°C > **mesophile** ('mɛsəʊˌfaɪl) *n*

mesophyll ('mɛsəʊˌfɪl) *n* the soft chlorophyll-containing tissue of a leaf between the upper and lower layers of epidermis: involved in photosynthesis > ˌmeso'phyllic *or* ˌmeso'phyllous *adj*

mesophyte ('mɛsəʊˌfaɪt) *n* any plant that grows in surroundings receiving an average supply of water > **mesophytic** (ˌmɛsəʊˈfɪtɪk) *adj*

Mesopotamia (ˌmɛsəpəˈteɪmɪə) *n* a region of SW Asia between the lower and middle reaches of the Tigris and Euphrates rivers: site of several ancient civilizations [Latin from Greek *mesopotamia* (khora) (the land) between rivers]

Mesopotamian (ˌmɛsəpəˈteɪmɪən) *adj* **1** of or relating to Mesopotamia, a region of SW Asia, or its inhabitants ▷ *n* **2** a native or inhabitant of Mesopotamia

mesosphere ('mɛsəʊˌsfɪə) *n* **1** the atmospheric layer lying between the stratosphere and the thermosphere, characterized by a rapid decrease in temperature with height **2** the solid part of the earth's mantle lying between the asthenosphere and the core > **mesospheric** (ˌmɛsəʊˈsfɛrɪk) *adj*

mesothelioma (ˌmɛzəʊˌθiːlɪˈəʊmə) *n, pl* **-mata** (-mətə) *or* **-mas** a tumour of the epithelium lining the lungs, abdomen, or heart: often associated with exposure to asbestos dust [c20 from MESOTHELI(UM) + -OMA]

mesothelium (ˌmɛsəʊˈθiːlɪəm) *n, pl* **-liums** *or* **-lia** (-lɪə) epithelium, derived from embryonic mesoderm lining body cavities [from New Latin, from MESO- + (EPI)THELIUM] > ˌmeso'thelial *adj*

mesothorax (ˌmɛsəʊˈθɔːræks) *n, pl* **-raxes** *or* **-races** (-rəˌsiːz) the middle segment of the thorax of an insect, bearing the second pair of walking legs and the first pair of wings. See also **prothorax, metathorax.** > **mesothoracic** (ˌmɛsəʊθɔːˈræsɪk) *adj*

mesothorium (ˌmɛsəʊˈθɔːrɪəm) *n physics obsolete* either of the two radioactive elements which are decay products of thorium. **Mesothorium I** is now called radium-228. **Mesothorium II** is now called actinium-228

mesotron ('mɛsəˌtrɒn) *n* a former name for **meson**

Mesozoic (ˌmɛsəʊˈzəʊɪk) *adj* **1** of, denoting, or relating to an era of geological time that began 250 000 000 years ago with the Triassic period and lasted about 185 000 000 years until the end of the Cretaceous period ▷ *n* **2** the the Mesozoic era

mesquite *or* **mesquit** (mɛˈskiːt, ˈmɛskiːt) *n* any small leguminous tree of the genus *Prosopis*, esp the tropical American *P. juliflora*, whose sugary pods (**mesquite beans**) are used as animal fodder. Also called: algarroba, honey locust, honey mesquite [c19 from Mexican Spanish, from Nahuatl *mizquitl*]

mess (mɛs) *n* **1** a state of confusion or untidiness, esp if dirty or unpleasant: *the house was in a mess* **2** a chaotic or troublesome state of affairs; muddle: *his life was a mess* **3** *informal* a dirty or untidy person or thing **4** *archaic* a portion of food, esp soft or semiliquid food **5** a place where service personnel eat or take recreation: *an officers' mess* **6** a group of people, usually servicemen, who eat together **7** the meal so taken **8** mess of pottage a material gain involving the sacrifice of a higher value ▷ *vb* **9** (*tr; often foll by up*) to muddle or dirty **10** (*intr*) to make a mess **11** (*intr; often foll by with*) to interfere; meddle **12** (*intr; often foll by with or together*) *military* to group together, esp for eating [c13 from Old French *mes* dish of food, from Late Latin *missus* course (at table), from Latin *mittere* to send forth, set out]

mess about *or* **around** *vb* (*adverb*) **1** (*intr*) to occupy oneself trivially; potter **2** (when *intr*, often foll by *with*) to interfere or meddle (with) **3** (*intr; sometimes foll by with*) *chiefly US* to engage in adultery

message ('mɛsɪdʒ) *n* **1** a communication, usually brief, from one person or group to another **2** an implicit meaning or moral, as in a work of art **3** a formal communiqué **4** an inspired communication of a prophet or religious leader **5** a mission; errand **6** (*plural*) *Scot* shopping: *going for the messages* **7** get the message *informal* to understand what is meant ▷ *vb* **8** (*tr*) to send as a message, esp to signal (a plan, etc) [c13 from Old French, from Vulgar Latin *missāticum* (unattested) something sent, from Latin *missus*, past participle of *mittere* to send]

message stick *n* a stick bearing carved symbols, carried by a native Australian as identification

message switching *n computing* the maintenance of a telecommunication link between two devices for the duration of a message

messaging ('mɛsɪdʒɪŋ) *n* the practice of sending and receiving written communications by computer or mobile phone

messaline (ˌmɛsəˈliːn, ˌmɛsəˈliːn) *n* a light lustrous twilled-silk fabric [c20 from French, origin obscure]

Messapian (məˈseɪpɪən) *or* **Messapic** (məˈseɪpɪk, -ˈsæpɪk) *n* a scantily recorded language of an ancient people of Calabria (the **Messapii**), thought by some to be related to ancient Illyrian

Messeigneurs *French* (mesɛɲœr) *n* the plural of **Monseigneur**

Messene (mɛˈsiːnɪ) *n* an ancient Greek city in the SW Peloponnese: founded in 369 BC as the capital of Messenia

messenger ('mɛsɪndʒə) *n* **1** a person who takes messages from one person or group to another or others **2** a person who runs errands or is employed to run errands **3** a carrier of official dispatches; courier **4** *nautical* **a** a light line used to haul in a heavy rope **b** an endless belt of chain, rope, or cable, used on a powered winch to take off power **5** *archaic* a herald [c13 from Old French *messagier*, from MESSAGE]

messenger RNA *n biochem* a form of RNA, transcribed from a single strand of DNA, that carries genetic information required for protein synthesis from DNA to the ribosomes. Sometimes shortened to: **mRNA** See also **transfer RNA, genetic code**

Messenia (məˈsiːnɪə) *n* the southwestern area of the Peloponnese in S Greece

mess hall *n* a military dining room, usually large

Messiah (mɪˈsaɪə) *n* **1** *Judaism* the awaited redeemer of the Jews, to be sent by God to free them **2** Jesus Christ, when regarded in this role **3** an exceptional or hoped for liberator of a country or people [c14 from Old French *Messie*, ultimately from Hebrew *māshīach* anointed] > **Mes'siah**ˌship *n*

messianic (ˌmɛsɪˈænɪk) *adj* **1** (*sometimes capital*) *Bible* **a** of or relating to the Messiah, his awaited deliverance of the Jews, or the new age of peace expected to follow this **b** of or relating to Jesus Christ or the salvation believed to have been brought by him **2 a** of or relating to any popular leader promising deliverance or an ideal era of peace and prosperity **b** of or relating to promises of this kind or to an ideal era of this kind > ˌmessi'anically *adv* > messianism (mɛˈsaɪənɪzəm) *n*

Messidor *French* (mesidɔr) *n* the month of harvest: the tenth month of the French revolutionary calendar, extending from June 20 to July 19 [c19 from French, from Latin *messis* harvest + Greek *dōron* gift]

Messier catalogue ('mɛsɪeɪ) *n astronomy* a catalogue of 103 nonstellar objects, such as nebulae and galaxies, prepared in 1781–86. An object is referred to by its number in this catalogue, for example the Andromeda Galaxy is referred to as *M*31 [c18 named after Charles *Messier* (1730–1817), French astronomer]

messieurs ('mɛsəz; *French* mesjø) *n* the plural of **monsieur**

Messina (mɛˈsiːnə) *n* a port in NE Sicily, on the **Strait of Messina**: colonized by Greeks around 730 BC; under Spanish rule (1282–1676 and 1678–1713); university (1549). Pop: 252 026 (2001)

mess jacket *n* a waist-length jacket tapering to a point at the back, worn by officers in the mess for formal dinners

mess kit *n military* **1** *Brit* formal evening wear for officers **2** Also called: **mess gear** eating utensils used esp in the field

messmate ('mɛsˌmeɪt) *n* **1** a person with whom one shares meals in a mess, esp in the army **2** *Austral* any of various eucalyptus trees that grow amongst other species

Messrs ('mɛsəz) *n* the plural of **Mr** [c18 abbreviation from French *messieurs*]

messuage ('mɛswɪdʒ) *n property law* a dwelling house together with its outbuildings, curtilage, and the adjacent land appropriated to its use [c14 from Norman French: household, perhaps through misspelling of Old French *mesnage* MÉNAGE]

messy ('mɛsɪ) *adj* **messier, messiest** dirty, confused, or untidy > 'messily *adv* > 'messiness *n*

mestee (mɛˈstiː) *n* a variant of **mustee**

mester ('mɛstə) *n South Yorkshire dialect* **1** master: used as a term of address for a man who is the head of a house **2** bad mester a term for the devil, used when speaking to children

mestizo (mɛˈstiːzəʊ, mɪ-) *n, pl* **-zos** *or* **-zoes** a person of mixed parentage, esp the offspring of a Spanish American and an American Indian [c16 from Spanish, ultimately from Latin *miscēre* to mix] > **mestiza** (mɛˈstiːzə) *fem n*

mestome ('mɛstəʊm) *or* **mestom** *n botany* **a** conducting tissue associated with parenchyma **b** (*as modifier*): *a mestome sheath* [c19 from Greek *mestōma* filling up]

mestranol ('mɛstrəˌnɒl, -ˌnəʊl) *n* a synthetic oestrogen used in combination with progestogens as an oral contraceptive. Formula: $C_{21}H_{26}O_2$ [c20 from M(ETHYL) + (O)ESTR(OGEN) + (pregn)an(e) $(C_{21}H_{36})$ + -OL]

met (mɛt) *vb* the past tense and past participle of **meet**

met. abbreviation for **1** meteorological: *the met. office weather report* **2** meteorology

Meta ('meɪtə; *Spanish* 'meta) *n* a river in Colombia, rising in the Andes and flowing northeast and east, forming part of the border between

Colombia and Venezuela, to join the Orinoco River. Length: about 1000 km (620 miles)

meta- *or sometimes before a vowel* **met-** *prefix* **1** indicating change, alteration, or alternation: *metabolism; metamorphosis* **2** (of an academic discipline, esp philosophy) concerned with the concepts and results of the named discipline: *metamathematics; meta-ethics.* See also **metatheory** **3** occurring or situated behind or after: *metaphase* **4** (*often in italics*) denoting that an organic compound contains a benzene ring with substituents in the 1,3-positions: *metadinitrobenzene; meta-cresol.* Abbreviation: *m-* Compare **ortho-** (sense 4), **para-**¹ (sense 6) **5** denoting an isomer, polymer, or compound related to a specified compound (often differing from similar compounds that are prefixed by *para-*): *metaldehyde* **6** denoting an oxyacid that is a lower hydrated form of the anhydride or a salt of such an acid: *metaphosphoric acid.* Compare **ortho-** (sense 5) [Greek, from *meta* with, after, between, among. Compare Old English *mid, mith* with, Old Norse *meth* with, between]

metabolic pathway *n* any of the sequences of biochemical reactions, catalysed by enzymes, that occur in all living cells: concerned mainly with the exchange of energy and chemicals. See also Krebs cycle

metabolic syndrome *n* a condition associated with obesity including symptoms such as glucose intolerance, insulin resistance, and raised blood pressure, which increases the risk of cardiovascular disease and diabetes

metabolism (mɪˈtæbəˌlɪzəm) *n* **1** the sum total of the chemical processes that occur in living organisms, resulting in growth, production of energy, elimination of waste material, etc. See **anabolism, basal metabolism, catabolism 2** the sum total of the chemical processes affecting a particular substance in the body: *carbohydrate metabolism; iodine metabolism* [C19 from Greek *metabolē* change, from *metaballein* to change, from META- + *ballein* to throw] > metabolic (ˌmɛtəˈbɒlɪk) *adj* > ˌmetaˈbolically *adv*

metabolite (mɪˈtæbəˌlaɪt) *n* a substance produced during or taking part in metabolism [C19 METABOL(ISM) + -ITE¹]

metabolize *or* **metabolise** (mɪˈtæbəˌlaɪz) *vb* to bring about or subject to metabolism > meˈtaboˌlizable *or* meˈtaboˌlisable *adj*

metabolome (mɪˈtæbəˌləʊm) *n* the full complement of metabolites present in a cell, tissue, or organism in a particular physiological or developmental state [C20 from METABOLITE + -OME]

metabolomics (mɪˌtæˌbəˈlɒmɪks) *n* (*functioning as singular*) the study of all the metabolites present in cells, tissues, and organs

metaboly (mɪˈtæbəlɪ) *n* biology the ability of some cells, esp protozoans, to alter their shape

metabotropic receptor (mɪˌtæbəˈtrɒpɪk) *n* physiology an indirect receptor which initiates an intracellular biochemical cascade after it is triggered by an agonistic ligand. Compare ionotropic receptor

metacarpal (ˌmɛtəˈkɑːpˀl) anatomy ▷ adj **1** of or relating to the metacarpus ▷ n **2** a metacarpal bone

metacarpus (ˌmɛtəˈkɑːpəs) *n, pl* -pi (-paɪ) **1** the skeleton of the hand between the wrist and the fingers, consisting of five long bones **2** the corresponding bones in other vertebrates

metacentre *or US* **metacenter** (ˈmɛtəˌsɛntə) *n* the intersection of a vertical line through the centre of buoyancy of a floating body at equilibrium with the formerly vertical line through the centre of gravity of the body when the body is tilted > ˌmetaˈcentric *adj*

metachromatic (ˌmɛtəkrəʊˈmætɪk) *adj* **1** (of tissues and cells stained for microscopical examination) taking a colour different from that of the dye solution **2** (of dyes) capable of staining

tissues or cells a colour different from that of the dye solution **3** of or relating to metachromatism

metachromatism (ˌmɛtəˈkrəʊməˌtɪzəm) *n* a change in colour, esp when caused by a change in temperature [C19 from META- + CHROMATO- + -ISM]

metachrosis (ˌmɛtəˈkrəʊsɪs) *n* zoology the ability of some animals, such as chameleons, to change their colour [C19 from META- + Greek *khrōs* colour]

metacinnabarite (ˌmɛtəsɪˈnæbəˌraɪt) *n* the black solid form of mercuric sulphide

metacognition (ˌmɛtəkɒgˈnɪʃən) *n* psychol thinking about one's own mental processes

metacomputer (ˌmɛtəkəmˈpjuːtə) *n* an interconnected and balanced set of computers that operate as a single unit > ˌmetacomˈputing *n*

meta-data *pl n* computing information that is held as a description of stored data

meta-ethics *n* (*functioning as singular*) the philosophical study of questions about the nature of ethical judgment as distinct from questions of normative ethics, for example, whether ethical judgments state facts or express attitudes, whether there are objective standards of morality, and how moral judgments can be justified > ˌmeta-ˈethical *adj*

metafemale (ˌmɛtəˈfiːmeɪl) *n* genetics a sterile female organism, esp a fruit fly (*Drosophila*) that has three X chromosomes. Former name: superfemale

metagalaxy (ˌmɛtəˈgæləksɪ) *n, pl* -axies the total system of galaxies and intergalactic space making up the universe > metagalactic (ˌmɛtəgəˈlæktɪk) *adj*

metage (ˈmiːtɪdʒ) *n* **1** the official measuring of weight or contents **2** a charge for this [C16 from METE¹]

metagenesis (ˌmɛtəˈdʒɛnɪsɪs) *n* another name for alternation of generations. > metagenetic (ˌmɛtədʒɪˈnɛtɪk) *or* ˌmetaˈgenic *adj* > ˌmetageˈnetically *adv*

metagnathous (mɪˈtægnəθəs) *adj* (of the beaks of birds such as the crossbill) having crossed tips [C19 from META- + -GNATHOUS] > meˈtagnaˌthism *n*

metal (ˈmɛtˀl) *n* **1 a** any of a number of chemical elements, such as iron or copper, that are often lustrous ductile solids, have basic oxides, form positive ions, and are good conductors of heat and electricity **b** an alloy, such as brass or steel, containing one or more of these elements **2** printing type made of metal **3** the substance of glass in a molten state or as the finished product **4** short for road metal **5** informal short for heavy metal (sense 1) **6** navy **a** the total weight of projectiles that can be shot by a ship's guns at any one time **b** the total weight or number of a ship's guns **7** astronomy any element heavier than helium. Also called: heavy element **8** heraldry gold or silver **9** (*plural*) the rails of a railway ▷ adj **10** made of metal ▷ vb -als, -alling, -alled *or US* -als, -aling, -aled (*tr*) **11** to fit or cover with metal **12** to make or mend (a road) with road metal [C13 from Latin *metallum* mine, product of a mine, from Greek *metallon*] > ˈmetalled *adj* > ˈmetal-ˌlike *adj*

metal. *or* **metall.** *abbreviation for* **1** metallurgical **2** metallurgy

metalanguage (ˈmɛtəˌlæŋgwɪdʒ) *n* a language or system of symbols used to discuss another language or system. See also formal language, natural language Compare object language

metal detector *n* a device that gives an audible or visual signal when its search head comes close to a metallic object embedded in food, buried in the ground, etc

metalled (ˈmɛtˀld) *adj* **1** made or mended with road metal **2** fitted or covered with metal

metallic (mɪˈtælɪk) *adj* **1** of, concerned with, or consisting of metal or a metal **2** suggestive of a metal: *a metallic click; metallic lustre* **3** chem (of a metal element) existing in the free state rather than in combination: *metallic copper* > meˈtallically *adv*

metallic bond *n* chem the covalent bonding

between atoms in metals, in which the valence electrons are free to move through the crystal

metallic lens *n* an arrangement of louvres used to direct and focus electromagnetic or sound waves

metallic soap *n* any one of a number of colloidal stearates, palmitates, or oleates of various metals, including aluminium, calcium, magnesium, iron, and zinc. They are used as bases for ointments, fungicides, fireproofing and waterproofing agents, and dryers for paints and varnishes

metalliferous (ˌmɛtˀlˈɪfərəs) *adj* containing a high concentration of metallic elements: *a metalliferous ore* [C17 from Latin *metallifer* yielding metal, from *metallum* metal + *ferre* to bear]

metalline (ˈmɛtəˌlaɪn) *adj* **1** of, resembling, or relating to metals **2** containing metals or metal ions

metallist *or US* **metalist** (ˈmɛtˀlɪst) *n* **1** a person who works with metals **2** a person who advocates a system of currency based on a metal, such as gold or silver

metallize, metallise *or US* **metalize** (ˈmɛtəˌlaɪz) *vb* (*tr*) to make metallic or to coat or treat with metal > ˌmetalliˈzation, ˌmetalliˈsation *or US* ˌmetaliˈzation *n*

metallo- *combining form* denoting metal: *metallography; metalloid; metallurgy* [from Greek *metallon*]

metallocene (mɪˈtæləʊˌsiːn) *n* chem any one of a class of organometallic sandwich compounds of the general formula $M(C_5H_5)_2$, where M is a metal atom. See ferrocene [C20 from METALLO- + -cene, as in FERROCENE]

metallography (ˌmɛtəˈlɒgrəfɪ) *n* **1** the branch of metallurgy concerned with the composition and structure of metals and alloys **2** a lithographic process using metal plates instead of stone; metal lithography > ˌmetalˈlographer *or* ˌmetalˈlographist *n* > metallographic (mɪˌtæləˈgræfɪk) *adj* > meˌtalloˈgraphically *adv*

metalloid (ˈmɛtəˌlɔɪd) *n* **1** a nonmetallic element, such as arsenic or silicon, that has some of the properties of a metal ▷ adj also **metalloidal** (ˌmɛtəˈlɔɪdˀl) **2** of or being a metalloid **3** resembling a metal

metallophone (mɪˈtæləˌfəʊn) *n* any of various musical instruments consisting of tuned metal bars struck with a hammer, such as the glockenspiel

metallurgy (mɪˈtælədʒɪ; US ˈmɛtˀlˌɜːdʒɪ) *n* the scientific study of the extraction, refining, alloying, and fabrication of metals and of their structure and properties > ˌmetalˈlurgic *or* ˌmetalˈlurgical *adj* > ˌmetalˈlurgically *adv* > metallurgist (mɪˈtælədʒɪst, ˈmɛtˀlˌɜːdʒɪst) *n*

metal spraying *n* a process in which a layer of one metal is sprayed onto another in the molten state

metal tape *n* a magnetic recording tape coated with pure iron rather than iron oxide or chromedioxide: it gives enhanced recording quality

metalwork (ˈmɛtˀlˌwɜːk) *n* **1** the craft of working in metal **2** work in metal or articles made from metal

metalworking (ˈmɛtˀlˌwɜːkɪŋ) *n* the processing of metal to change its shape, size, etc, as by rolling, forging, etc, or by making metal articles > ˈmetalˌworker *n*

metamale (ˈmɛtəˌmeɪl) *n* genetics a sterile male organism, esp a fruit fly (*Drosophila*) that has one X chromosome and three sets of autosomes. Former name: supermale

metamathematics (ˌmɛtəˌmæθɪˈmætɪks) *n* (*functioning as singular*) the logical analysis of the reasoning, principles, and rules that control the use and combination of mathematical symbols, numbers, etc > ˌmetaˌmatheˈmatical *adj* > ˌmetaˌmathemaˈtician *n*

metamer (ˈmɛtəmə) *n* any of two or more

m

isomeric compounds exhibiting metamerism

metamere ('mɛtə,mɪə) *n* one of the similar body segments into which earthworms, crayfish, and similar animals are divided longitudinally. Also called: **somite** [C19 from META- + -MERE] > **metameral** (mɪˈtæmərəl) *adj*

metameric (,mɛtəˈmɛrɪk) *adj* **1** divided into or consisting of metameres. See also **metamerism** (sense 1) **2** of or concerned with metamerism > ,meta'merically *adv*

metamerism (mɪˈtæmə,rɪzəm) *n* **1** Also called: **(metameric) segmentation** the division of an animal into similar segments (metameres). In many vertebrates it is confined to the embryonic nervous and muscular systems **2** *chem* a type of isomerism in which molecular structures differ by the attachment of different groups to the same atom, as in $CH_3OC_3H_7$ and $C_2H_5OC_2H_5$

metamict ('mɛtə,mɪkt) *adj* of or denoting the amorphous state of a substance that has lost its crystalline structure as a result of the radioactivity of uranium or thorium within it: *metamict minerals* [C19 from Danish *metamikt*, from META- + Greek *miktos* mixed] > ,metamicti'zation *or* ,metamicti'sation *n*

metamorphic (,mɛtəˈmɔːfɪk) *or* **metamorphous** *adj* **1** relating to or resulting from metamorphosis or metamorphism **2** (of rocks) altered considerably from their original structure and mineralogy by pressure and heat. Compare **igneous, sedimentary**

metamorphism (,mɛtəˈmɔːfɪzəm) *n* **1** the process by which metamorphic rocks are formed **2** a variant of **metamorphosis**

metamorphose (,mɛtəˈmɔːfəʊz) *vb* to undergo or cause to undergo metamorphosis or metamorphism

metamorphosis (,mɛtəˈmɔːfəsɪs) *n, pl* **-ses** (-,siːz) **1** a complete change of physical form or substance **2** a complete change of character, appearance, etc **3** a person or thing that has undergone metamorphosis **4** *zoology* the rapid transformation of a larva into an adult that occurs in certain animals, for example the stage between tadpole and frog or between chrysalis and butterfly [C16 via Latin from Greek: transformation, from META- + *morphē* form]

metanephros (,mɛtəˈnɛfrɒs) *n, pl* **-roi** (-,rɔɪ) the last-formed posterior part of the embryonic kidney in reptiles, birds, and mammals, which remains functional in the adult. See also **pronephros, mesonephros** [C19 New Latin, from META- + Greek *nephros* kidney]

metaphase ('mɛtə,feɪz) *n* **1** *biology* the second stage of mitosis during which the condensed chromosomes attach to the centre of the spindle. See also **prophase** (sense 1), **anaphase** (sense 1), **telophase** (sense 1) **2** the corresponding stage of the first division of meiosis

metaphor ('mɛtəfə, -,fɔː) *n* a figure of speech in which a word or phrase is applied to an object or action that it does not literally denote in order to imply a resemblance, for example *he is a lion in battle*. Compare **simile** [C16 from Latin from Greek *metaphora*, from *metapherein* to transfer, from META- + *pherein* to bear] > **metaphoric** (,mɛtəˈfɒrɪk) *or* ,meta'phorical *adj* > ,meta'phorically *adv* > ,meta'phoricalness *n*

metaphosphate (,mɛtəˈfɒsfeɪt) *n* any salt of metaphosphoric acid

metaphosphoric acid (,mɛtəfɒsˈfɒrɪk) *n* a glassy deliquescent highly polymeric solid, used as a dehydrating agent. Formula: $(HPO_3)_n$. See also **polyphosphoric acid**

metaphrase ('mɛtə,freɪz) *n* **1** a literal translation. Compare **paraphrase** ▷ *vb* (*tr*) **2** to alter or manipulate the wording of **3** to translate literally [C17 from Greek *metaphrazein* to translate]

metaphrast ('mɛtə,fræst) *n* a person who metaphrases, esp one who changes the form of a text, as by rendering verse into prose [C17 from Medieval Greek *metaphrastēs* translator]

> ,meta'phrastic *or* ,meta'phrastical *adj*
> ,meta'phrastically *adv*

metaphysic (,mɛtəˈfɪzɪk) *n* **1** the system of first principles and assumptions underlying an enquiry or philosophical theory **2** an obsolete word for **metaphysician** ▷ *adj* **3** *rare* another word for **metaphysical**

metaphysical (,mɛtəˈfɪzɪkəl) *adj* **1** relating to or concerned with metaphysics **2** (of a statement or theory) having the form of an empirical hypothesis, but in fact immune from empirical testing and therefore (in the view of the logical positivists) literally meaningless **3** (popularly) abstract, abstruse, or unduly theoretical **4** incorporeal; supernatural > ,meta'physically *adv*

Metaphysical (,mɛtəˈfɪzɪkəl) *adj* **1** denoting or relating to certain 17th-century poets who combined intense feeling with ingenious thought and often used elaborate imagery and conceits. Notable among them were Donne, Herbert, and Marvell ▷ *n* **2** a poet of this group

metaphysicize *or* **metaphysicise** (,mɛtəˈfɪzɪ,saɪz) *vb* **1** (*intr*) to think, write, etc, metaphysically **2** (*tr*) to treat (a subject) metaphysically

metaphysics (,mɛtəˈfɪzɪks) *n* (*functioning as singular*) **1** the branch of philosophy that deals with first principles, esp of being and knowing **2** the philosophical study of the nature of reality, concerned with such questions as the existence of God, the external world, etc **3** See **descriptive metaphysics 4** (popularly) abstract or subtle discussion or reasoning [C16 from Medieval Latin, from Greek *ta meta ta phusika* the things after the physics, from the arrangement of the subjects treated in the works of Aristotle] > **metaphysician** (,mɛtəfɪˈzɪʃən) *or* **metaphysicist** (,mɛtəˈfɪzɪsɪst) *n*

metaplasia (,mɛtəˈpleɪzɪə) *n* the transformation of one kind of tissue into a different kind

metaplasm ('mɛtə,plæzəm) *n* the nonliving constituents, such as starch and pigment granules, of the cytoplasm of a cell > ,meta'plasmic *adj*

metapolitics (,mɛtəˈpɒlɪtɪks) *n* (*functioning as singular*) political theory (often used derogatorily) > **metapolitical** (,mɛtəpəˈlɪtɪkəl) *adj*

metapsychology (,mɛtəsaɪˈkɒlədʒɪ) *n psychol* **1** the study of philosophical questions, such as the relation between mind and body, that go beyond the laws of experimental psychology **2** any attempt to state the general laws of psychology **3** another word for **parapsychology** > **metapsychological** (,mɛtə,saɪkəˈlɒdʒɪkəl) *adj*

metarchon (mɪˈtɑːkɒn) *n* a nontoxic substance, such as a chemical to mask pheromones, that reduces the persistence of a pest

metasoma (,mɛtəˈsəʊmə) *n zoology* the posterior part of an arachnid's abdomen (opisthosoma) that never carries appendages

metasomatism (,mɛtəˈsəʊmə,tɪzəm) *or* **metasomatosis** (,mɛtə,səʊməˈtəʊsɪs) *n* change in the composition of a rock or mineral by the addition or replacement of chemicals [C19 from New Latin; see META-, SOMATO-]

metastable (,mɛtəˈsteɪbəl) *physics* ▷ *adj* **1** (of a body or system) having a state of apparent equilibrium although capable of changing to a more stable state **2** (of an atom, molecule, ion, or atomic nucleus) existing in an excited state with a relatively long lifetime ▷ *n* **3** a metastable atom, ion, molecule, or nucleus > ,metasta'bility *n*

metastasis (mɪˈtæstəsɪs) *n, pl* **-ses** (-,siːz) **1** *pathol* the spreading of a disease, esp cancer cells, from one part of the body to another **2** a transformation or change, as in rhetoric, from one point to another **3** a rare word for **metabolism** [C16 via Latin from Greek: transition] > **metastatic** (,mɛtəˈstætɪk) *adj* > ,meta'statically *adv*

metastasize *or* **metastasise** (mɪˈtæstə,saɪz) *vb* (*intr*) *pathol* (esp of cancer cells) to spread to a new site in the body via blood or lymph vessels

meta tag *or* **metatag** ('mɛtə,tæg) *n* an element of HTML that describes the contents of a Web page, and is placed near the beginning of the page's source code, and used by search engines to index pages by subject

metatarsal (,mɛtəˈtɑːsəl) *anatomy* ▷ *adj* **1** of or relating to the metatarsus ▷ *n* **2** any bone of the metatarsus

metatarsus (,mɛtəˈtɑːsəs) *n, pl* **-si** (-,saɪ) **1** the skeleton of the human foot between the toes and the tarsus, consisting of five long bones **2** the corresponding skeletal part in other vertebrates

metatheory ('mɛtə,θɪərɪ) *n* **1** philosophical discussion of the foundations, structure, or results of some theory, such as metamathematics **2** a formal system that describes the structure of some other system. See also **metalanguage** > **metatheoretical** (,mɛtəθɪəˈrɛtɪkəl) *adj*

metatherian (,mɛtəˈθɪərɪən) *adj* **1** of, relating to, or belonging to the *Metatheria*, a subclass of mammals comprising the marsupials ▷ *n* **2** any metatherian mammal; a marsupial ▷ Compare **eutherian, prototherian** [C19 from New Latin, from META- + Greek *thērion* animal]

metathesis (mɪˈtæθəsɪs) *n, pl* **-ses** (-,siːz) **1** the transposition of two sounds or letters in a word **2** *chem* another name for **double decomposition** [C16 from Late Latin, from Greek, from *metatithenai* to transpose] > **metathetic** (,mɛtəˈθɛtɪk) *or* ,meta'thetical *adj*

metathesize *or* **metathesise** (mɪˈtæθɪ,saɪz) *vb* to change or cause to change by metathesis

metathorax (,mɛtəˈθɔːræks) *n, pl* **-raxes** *or* **-races** (-rə,siːz) the third and last segment of an insect's thorax, which bears the third pair of walking legs and the second pair of wings. See also **prothorax, mesothorax.** > **metathoracic** (,mɛtəθɔːˈræsɪk) *adj*

metaxylem (,mɛtəˈzaɪlɛm) *n* xylem tissue that consists of rigid thick-walled cells and occurs in parts of the plant that have finished growing. Compare **protoxylem**

metazoan (,mɛtəˈzəʊən) *n* **1** any multicellular animal of the group *Metazoa*: includes all animals except sponges ▷ *adj* also **metazoic 2** of, relating to, or belonging to the *Metazoa* [C19 from New Latin *Metazoa*; see META-, -ZOA]

mete[1] (miːt) *vb* (*tr*) **1** (usually foll by *out*) *formal* to distribute or allot (something, often unpleasant) ▷ *vb* ▷ *n* **2** *poetic, dialect* (to) measure [Old English *metan*; compare Old Saxon *metan*, Old Norse *meta*, German *messen* to measure]

mete[2] (miːt) *n rare* a mark, limit, or boundary (esp in the phrase **metes and bounds**) [C15 from Old French, from Latin *mēta* goal, turning post (in race)]

metecdysis (,mɛtɛkˈdaɪsɪs) *n, pl* **-ses** (-,siːz) the period following the moult (ecdysis) of an arthropod, when the new cuticle is forming

metempirical (,mɛtɛmˈpɪrɪkəl) *or* **metempiric** *adj* **1** beyond the realm of experience **2** of or relating to metempirics > ,metem'pirically *adv*

metempirics (,mɛtɛmˈpɪrɪks) *n* (*functioning as singular*) the branch of philosophy that deals with things existing beyond the realm of experience > ,metem'piricist *n*

metempsychosis (,mɛtəmsaɪˈkəʊsɪs) *n, pl* **-ses** (-,siːz) **1** the migration of a soul from one body to another **2** the entering of a soul after death upon a new cycle of existence in a new body either of human or animal form [C16 via Late Latin from Greek, from *metempsukhousthai*, from META- + *-em-* in + *psukhē* soul] > ,metempsy'chosist *n*

metencephalon (,mɛtɛnˈsɛfə,lɒn) *n, pl* **-lons** *or* **-la** (-lə) the part of the embryonic hindbrain that develops into the cerebellum and pons Varolii > **metencephalic** (,mɛtɛnsɪˈfælɪk) *adj*

meteor ('miːtɪə) *n* **1** a very small meteoroid that has entered the earth's atmosphere. Such objects have speeds approaching 70 kilometres per second **2** Also called: **shooting star, falling star** the bright streak of light appearing in the sky due to the incandescence of such a body heated by friction at its surface [C15 from Medieval Latin *meteōrum*, from Greek *meteōron* something aloft, from *meteōros* lofty, from *meta-* (intensifier) + *aeirein* to raise]

meteoric (ˌmiːtɪˈɒrɪk) *adj* **1** of, formed by, or relating to meteors **2** like a meteor in brilliance, speed, or transience **3** *rare* of or relating to the weather; meteorological > **mete'orically** *adv*

meteoric water *n geology* ground water that has recently originated from the atmosphere

meteorism (ˈmiːtɪəˌrɪzəm) *n med* another name for **tympanites**

meteorite (ˈmiːtɪəˌraɪt) *n* a rocklike object consisting of the remains of a meteoroid that has fallen on earth. It may be stony (see **chondrite**), iron, or stony iron (see **pallasite**) > **meteoritic** (ˌmiːtɪəˈrɪtɪk) *adj*

meteoritics (ˌmiːtɪəˈrɪtɪks) *n* (*functioning as singular*) the branch of science concerned with meteors and meteorites > **meteor'iticist** *n*

meteorograph (ˈmiːtɪərəˌgrɑːf, -ˌgræf) *n obsolete* an instrument that records various meteorological conditions > **meteoro'graphic** *or* **meteoro'graphical** *adj*

meteoroid (ˈmiːtɪəˌrɔɪd) *n* any of the small celestial bodies that are thought to orbit the sun, possibly as the remains of comets. When they enter the earth's atmosphere, they become visible as meteors > **meteor'oidal** *adj*

meteorol. *or* **meteor.** *abbreviation for* **1** meteorological **2** meteorology

meteorology (ˌmiːtɪəˈrɒlədʒɪ) *n* the study of the earth's atmosphere, esp of weather-forming processes and weather forecasting [C17 from Greek *meteōrologia*, from *meteōron* something aloft + *-logia* -LOGY. See METEOR] > **meteorological** (ˌmiːtɪərəˈlɒdʒɪkᵊl) *or* **meteoro'logic** *adj* > **meteoro'logically** *adv* > **meteor'ologist** *n*

meteor shower *n* a transient rain of meteors, such as the Perseids, occurring at regular intervals and coming from a particular region in the sky. It is caused by the earth passing through a large number of meteoroids (a **meteor swarm**)

meter¹ (ˈmiːtə) *n* the US spelling of **metre¹**

meter² (ˈmiːtə) *n* the US spelling of **metre²**

meter³ (ˈmiːtə) *n* **1** any device that measures and records the quantity of a substance, such as gas, that has passed through it during a specified period **2** any device that measures and sometimes records an electrical or magnetic quantity, such as current, voltage, etc **3** See **parking meter** ▷ *vb* (*tr*) **4** to measure (a rate of flow) with a meter **5** to print with stamps by means of a postage meter [C19 see METE¹]

-meter *n combining form* **1** indicating an instrument for measuring: *barometer* **2** *prosody* indicating a verse having a specified number of feet: *pentameter* [from Greek *metron* measure]

metered mail *n* mail franked privately, under licence, with a machine bearing special markings (**meter marks**)

meter maid *n informal* a female traffic warden

metestrus (mɛtˈɛstrəs, -ˈiːstrəs) *n* the US spelling of **metoestrus**. > **met'estrous** *adj*

Meth. *abbreviation for* Methodist

meth- *combining form* indicating a chemical compound derived from methane or containing methyl groups: *methacrylate resin*

methacrylate (mɛˈθækrɪˌleɪt) *n* **1** any ester of methacrylic acid **2** See **methacrylate resin**

methacrylate resin *n* any acrylic resin derived from methacrylic acid

methacrylic acid (ˌmɛθəˈkrɪlɪk) *n* a colourless crystalline water-soluble substance used in the manufacture of acrylic resins; 2-methylpropenoic acid. Formula: $CH_2:C(CH_3)COOH$

methadone (ˈmɛθəˌdəʊn) *or* **methadon** (ˈmɛθəˌdɒn) *n* a narcotic analgesic drug similar to morphine, used to treat opiate addiction. Formula: $C_{21}H_{27}NO$ [C20 from (di)*meth*(yl) + A(MINO) + D(IPHENYL) + -ONE]

methaemoglobin (ˌmɛtˌhiːməˈgləʊbɪn, mɛˌθiːmə-) *n* a brown compound of oxygen and haemoglobin

formed in the blood by the action of certain drugs

methamphetamine (ˌmɛθæmˈfɛtəmɪn) *n* a variety of amphetamine used for its stimulant action [C20 from METH- + AMPHETAMINE]

methanal (ˈmɛθəˌnæl) *n* the systematic name for **formaldehyde**

methane (ˈmiːθeɪn) *n* a colourless odourless flammable gas, the simplest alkane and the main constituent of natural gas: used as a fuel. Formula: CH_4. See also **marsh gas, firedamp** [C19 from METH(YL) + -ANE]

methane series *n* another name for the **alkane series** See **alkane**

methanoic acid (ˌmɛθəˈnəʊɪk) *n* the systematic name for **formic acid**

methanol (ˈmɛθəˌnɒl) *n* a colourless volatile poisonous liquid compound used as a solvent and fuel. Formula: CH_3OH. Also called: **methyl alcohol, wood alcohol** [C20 from METHANE + -OL¹]

metheglin (məˈθɛglɪn) *n* (esp formerly) spiced or medicated mead [C16 from Welsh *meddyglyn*, from *meddyg* healer (from Latin *medicus* MEDICAL) + *llyn* liquor]

methenamine (mɛˈθiːnəˌmiːn, -ˌmaɪn) *n* another name for **hexamethylenetetramine** [C20 METH- + -ENE + AMINE]

methicillin (ˌmɛθɪˈsɪlɪn) *n* a semisynthetic penicillin used to treat various infections

methinks (mɪˈθɪŋks) *vb*, *past* methought (*tr*; *takes a clause as object*) *archaic* it seems to me

methionine (mɛˈθaɪəˌniːn, -ˌnaɪn) *n* an essential amino acid containing sulphur, which occurs in many proteins: important in methylating reactions [C20 METH- + THIONINE]

metho (ˈmɛθəʊ) *n Austral* an informal name for **methylated spirits**

method (ˈmɛθəd) *n* **1** a way of proceeding or doing something, esp a systematic or regular one **2** orderliness of thought, action, etc **3** (*often plural*) the techniques or arrangement of work for a particular field or subject **4** *bell-ringing* any of several traditional sets of changes. See **major** (sense 19), **minor** (sense 8) [C16 via French from Latin *methodus*, from Greek *methodos*, literally: a going after, from *meta-* after + *hodos* way]

Method (ˈmɛθəd) *n* (*sometimes not capital*) **a** a technique of acting based on the theories of Stanislavsky, in which the actor bases his role on the inner motivation of the character he plays **b** (*as modifier*): *a Method actor*

methodical (mɪˈθɒdɪkᵊl) *or less commonly* **methodic** *adj* characterized by method or orderliness; systematic > **me'thodically** *adv* > **me'thodicalness** *n*

Methodism (ˈmɛθəˌdɪzəm) *n* the system and practices of the Methodist Church, developed by the English preacher John Wesley (1703–91) and his followers

Methodist (ˈmɛθədɪst) *n* **1** a member of any of the Nonconformist denominations that derive from the system of faith and practice initiated by the English preacher John Wesley (1703–91) and his followers ▷ *adj also* Methodistic *or* Methodistical **2** of or relating to Methodism or the Church embodying it (the **Methodist Church**) > **Method'istically** *adv*

methodize *or* **methodise** (ˈmɛθəˌdaɪz) *vb* (*tr*) to organize according to a method; systematize > **methodi'zation** *or* **methodi'sation** *n* > **'method,izer** *or* **'method,iser** *n*

methodology (ˌmɛθəˈdɒlədʒɪ) *n*, *pl* -gies **1** the system of methods and principles used in a particular discipline **2** the branch of philosophy concerned with the science of method and procedure > **methodological** (ˌmɛθədəˈlɒdʒɪkᵊl) *adj* > **methodo'logically** *adv* > **method'ologist** *n*

methotrexate (ˌmɛθəʊˈtrɛkseɪt, ˌmiːθəʊ-) *n* an antimetabolite drug used in the treatment of certain cancers. Formula: $C_{20}H_{22}N_8O_5$

methought (mɪˈθɔːt) *vb archaic* the past tense of **methinks**

methoxide (mɛˈθɒksaɪd) *n* a saltlike compound

in which the hydrogen atom in the hydroxyl group of methanol has been replaced by a metal atom, usually an alkali metal atom as in sodium methoxide, $NaOCH_3$. Also called: **methylate**

meths (mɛθs) *n chiefly Brit, Austral, and NZ* an informal name for **methylated spirits**

Methuselah¹ (məˈθjuːzələ) *n* a wine bottle holding the equivalent of eight normal bottles

Methuselah² (mɪˈθjuːzələ) *n Old Testament* a patriarch supposed to have lived 969 years (Genesis 5:21–27) who has come to be regarded as epitomizing longevity. Douay spelling: Mathusala

methyl (ˈmiːθaɪl, ˈmɛθɪl) *n* **1** (*modifier*) of, consisting of, or containing the monovalent group of atoms CH_3 **2** an organometallic compound in which methyl groups are bound directly to a metal atom [C19 from French *méthyle*, back formation from METHYLENE] > **methylic** (məˈθɪlɪk) *adj*

methyl acetate *n* a colourless volatile flammable liquid ester with a fragrant odour, used as a solvent, esp in paint removers. Formula: CH_3COOCH_3

methylal (ˈmɛθɪˌlæl) *n* a colourless volatile flammable liquid with an odour resembling that of chloroform, used as a solvent and in the manufacture of perfumes and adhesives. Formula: $(CH_3O)_2CH_2$. Also called: **formal**

methyl alcohol *n* another name for **methanol**

methylamine (ˌmiːθaɪlˈæˌmiːn) *n* a colourless flammable water-soluble gas, used in the manufacture of herbicides, dyes, and drugs. Formula: CH_3NH_2

methylate (ˈmɛθɪˌleɪt) *vb* **1** (*tr*) to mix with methanol **2** to undergo or cause to undergo a chemical reaction in which a methyl group is introduced into a molecule ▷ *n* **3** another name for **methoxide**. > **methyl'ation** *n* > **'methyl,ator** *n*

methylated spirits *or* **spirit** *n* (*functioning as singular or plural*) alcohol that has been denatured by the addition of methanol and pyridine and a violet dye. Also called: **metho, meths**

methyl bromide *n* a colourless poisonous gas or volatile liquid with an odour resembling that of chloroform, used as a solvent, and extinguishant. Formula: CH_3Br

methyl chloride *n* a colourless gas with an ether-like odour, used as a refrigerant and anaesthetic. Formula: CH_3Cl. Systematic name: chloromethane

methyl chloroform *n* the traditional name for **trichloroethane**

methyldopa (ˌmiːθaɪlˈdəʊpə) *n* a drug used to treat hypertension. Formula: $C_{10}H_{13}NO_4$ [C20 from *methyl* + d(*ihydr*)o(*xy*)p(*henyl*)a(*lanine*)]

methylene (ˈmɛθɪˌliːn) *n* (*modifier*) of, consisting of, or containing the divalent group of atoms $=CH_2$: *a methylene group or radical* [C19 from French *méthylène*, from Greek *methu* wine + *hulē* wood + -ENE: originally referring to a substance distilled from wood]

methylene blue *n* a dark-green crystalline compound forming a blue aqueous solution, used as a mild antiseptic and biological stain. Formula: $C_{16}H_{18}N_3SCl.3H_2O$. Also called: **methylthionine chloride**

methylene chloride *n* another name for **dichloromethane**

methyl ethyl ketone *n* another name for **butanone**

methyl isobutyl ketone (ˌaɪsəʊˈbjuːtaɪl, -tɪl) *n* a colourless insoluble liquid ketone used as a solvent for organic compounds, esp nitrocellulose; 4-methylpentan-2-one. Formula: $(CH_3)_2CHCH_2COCH_3$. Also called: **hexone**

methyl methacrylate *n* a colourless liquid compound, used in the manufacture of certain methacrylate resins. Formula: $CH_2C(CH_3)COOCH_3$

methylnaphthalene (ˌmiːθaɪlˈnæfθəˌliːn) *n* either of two isomeric derivatives of naphthalene: a liquid (1-methylnaphthalene), used in standardizing diesel fuels, or a solid (2-methylnaphthalene), an insecticide

m

methylthionine chloride (ˌmiːθaɪlˈθaɪəˌniːn) *n* another name for **methylene blue**

metic ('mɛtɪk) *n* (in ancient Greece) an alien having some rights of citizenship in the city in which he lives [C19 from Greek *metoikos*, from META- (indicating change) + *-oikos* dwelling]

meticulous (mɪˈtɪkjʊləs) *adj* very precise about details, even trivial ones; painstaking [C16 (meaning: timid): from Latin *meticulōsus* fearful, from *metus* fear] > me'**ticulously** *adv* > me'**ticulousness** *n*

métier ('mɛtɪeɪ) *n* **1** a profession or trade, esp that to which one is well suited **2** a person's strong point or speciality [C18 from French, ultimately from Latin *ministerium* service]

me-time *n* the time a person has to himself or herself, in which to do something for his or her own enjoyment

Métis (meˈtiːs) *n*, *pl* **-tis** (-'tiːs, -'tiːz) **1** a person of mixed parentage **2** *Canadian* **a** the offspring or a descendant of a French Canadian and a North American Indian **b** a member or descendant of a group of such people, who established themselves in Manitoba and Saskatchewan as a distinct political and cultural force during the nineteenth century **3** *US* a person having one eighth Black ancestry; octoroon [C19 from French, from Vulgar Latin *mixtícius* (unattested) of mixed race; compare MESTIZO] > **Métisse** (meˈtiːs) *fem n*

metoestrus (mɛtˈiːstrəs, -ˈɛstrəs) *or US* **metestrus** *n* *zoology* the period in the oestrous cycle following oestrus, characterized by lack of sexual activity > met'**oestrous** *or US* met'**estrous** *adj*

metol ('miːtɒl) *n* a colourless soluble organic substance used, in the form of its sulphate, as a photographic developer; *p*-methylaminophenol. See also **aminophenol** [C20 from German, an arbitrary coinage]

Metonic cycle (mɪˈtɒnɪk) *n* a cycle of nearly 235 synodic months after which the phases of the moon recur on the same days of the year. See also **golden number** [C17 named after *Meton*, 5th-century BC Athenian astronomer]

metonym ('mɛtənɪm) *n* a word used in a metonymy. For example *the bottle* is a metonym for *alcoholic drink*

metonymy (mɪˈtɒnɪmɪ) *n*, *pl* **-mies** the substitution of a word referring to an attribute for the thing that is meant, as for example the use of *the crown* to refer to a monarch. Compare **synecdoche** [C16 from Late Latin from Greek: a changing of name, from *meta-* (indicating change) + *onoma* name] > **metonymical** (ˌmɛtəˈnɪmɪkəl) *or* ˌmeto'**nymic** *adj* > ˌmeto'**nymically** *adv*

me-too *n* *slang* a person who does something merely because someone else has done it

me-tooism (ˌmiːˈtuːɪzəm) *n* the practice of imitating other people's work or ideas

metope ('mɛtəʊp, 'mɛtəpɪ) *n architect* a square space between two triglyphs in a Doric frieze [C16 via Latin from Greek *metopē*, from *meta* between + *opē* one of the holes for the beam-ends]

metopic (mɪˈtɒpɪk) *adj* of or relating to the forehead

metralgia (mɪˈtrældʒɪə) *n* pain in the uterus [C20 from METRO-¹ + -ALGIA]

metre¹ *or US* **meter** ('miːtə) *n* **1** a metric unit of length equal to approximately 1.094 yards **2** the basic SI unit of length; the length of the path travelled by light in free space during a time interval of 1/299 792 458 of a second. In 1983 this definition replaced the previous one based on krypton-86, which in turn had replaced the definition based on the platinum-iridium metre bar kept in Paris Symbol: m [C18 from French; see METRE²]

metre² *or US* **meter** ('miːtə) *n* **1** *prosody* the rhythmic arrangement of syllables in verse, usually according to the number and kind of feet in a line **2** *music* another word (esp US) for **time** (sense 22) [C14 from Latin *metrum*, from Greek *metron* measure]

metre-kilogram-second *n* See **mks units**

metric ('mɛtrɪk) *adj* **1** of or relating to the metre or metric system **2** *maths* denoting or relating to a set containing pairs of points for each of which a non-negative real number $\rho(x, y)$ (the distance) can be defined, satisfying specific conditions ▷ *n* **3** *maths* the function $\rho(x, y)$ satisfying the conditions of membership of such a set (a **metric space**)

metrical ('mɛtrɪkəl) *or* **metric** ('mɛtrɪk) *adj* **1** of or relating to measurement **2** of or in poetic metre > '**metrically** *adv*

metrical psalm *n* a translation of one of the psalms into rhyming strict-metre verse usually sung as a hymn

metricate ('mɛtrɪˌkeɪt) *vb* to convert (a measuring system, instrument, etc) from nonmetric to metric units > ˌmetri'**cation** *n*

metric hundredweight *n* See **hundredweight** (sense 3)

metric madness *n informal* excessive devotion to metrication

metric martyr *n Brit* a shopkeeper or trader willing to be prosecuted for continuing to use only imperial measures as a protest against the perceived imposition of metric measures by the European Union

metrics ('mɛtrɪks) *n* (*functioning as singular*) *prosody* the art of using poetic metre

metric system *n* any decimal system of units based on the metre. For scientific purposes the Système International d'Unités (SI units) is used

metric ton *n* another name (not in technical use) for **tonne**

metrify ('mɛtrɪˌfaɪ) *vb* **-fies, -fying, -fied** (*tr*) *prosody* to render into poetic metre > '**metri**ˌ**fier** *n*

metrist ('mɛtrɪst) *n prosody* a person skilled in the use of poetic metre

metritis (mɪˈtraɪtɪs) *n* inflammation of the uterus

metro ('mɛtrəʊ) *or* **métro** (*French* metro) *n*, *pl* **-ros** an underground, or largely underground, railway system in certain cities, esp in Europe, such as that in Paris [C20 from French, short for *chemin de fer métropolitain* metropolitan railway]

metro-¹ *or before a vowel* **metr-** *combining form* indicating the uterus: *metrorrhagia* [from Greek *mētra* womb]

metro-² *combining form* indicating a measure: *metronome* [from Greek *metron* measure]

metrology (mɪˈtrɒlədʒɪ) *n*, *pl* **-gies 1** the science of weights and measures; the study of units of measurement **2** a particular system of units [C19 from Greek *metron* measure] > **metrological** (ˌmɛtrəˈlɒdʒɪkəl) *adj* > ˌmetro'**logically** *adv* > me'**trologist** *n*

metronidazole (ˌmɛtrəˈnaɪdəˌzəʊl) *n* a pale yellow crystalline compound used to treat vaginal trichomoniasis. Formula: $C_6H_9N_3O_3$ [C20 from ME(THYL) + (NI)TRO- + -n- + (IM)ID(E) + AZOLE]

metronome ('mɛtrəˌnəʊm) *n* a mechanical device which indicates the exact tempo of a piece of music by producing a clicking sound from a pendulum with an adjustable period of swing [C19 from Greek *metron* measure + *nomos* rule, law] > **metronomic** (ˌmɛtrəˈnɒmɪk) *adj*

metronymic (ˌmɛtrəˈnɪmɪk) *or less commonly* **matronymic** *adj* **1** (of a name) derived from the name of its bearer's mother or another female ancestor ▷ *n* **2** a metronymic name [C19 from Greek *mētronumikos*, from *mētēr* mother + *onoma* name]

metropolis (mɪˈtrɒpəlɪs) *n*, *pl* **-lises 1** the main city, esp of a country or region; capital **2** a centre of activity **3** the chief see in an ecclesiastical province [C16 from Late Latin from Greek: mother city or state, from *mētēr* mother + *polis* city]

metropolitan (ˌmɛtrəˈpɒlɪtən) *adj* **1** of or characteristic of a metropolis **2** constituting a city and its suburbs: *the metropolitan area* **3** of, relating to, or designating an ecclesiastical metropolis **4** of or belonging to the home territories of a country, as opposed to overseas territories: *metropolitan France* ▷ *n* **5 a** *Eastern Churches* the head of an ecclesiastical province, ranking between archbishop and patriarch **b** *Church of England* an archbishop **c** *RC Church* an archbishop or bishop having authority in certain matters over the dioceses in his province > ˌmetro'**politanism** *n*

metropolitan county *n* (in England) any of the six conurbations established as administrative units in the new local government system in 1974; the metropolitan county councils were abolished in 1986

metropolitan district *n* any of the districts making up the metropolitan counties of England: since 1986 they have functioned as unitary authorities, forming the sole principal tier of local government. Each metropolitan district has an elected council responsible for education, social services, etc. See also **district** (sense 4)

Metropolitan Museum of Art *n* the principal museum in New York City: founded in 1870 and housed in its present premises in Central Park since 1880

metrorrhagia (ˌmiːtrɔːˈreɪdʒɪə, ˌmɛt-) *n* abnormal bleeding from the uterus

metrosexual (ˌmɛtrəʊˈsɛksjʊəl) *adj informal* of or relating to a heterosexual man who spends a lot of time and money on his appearance and likes to shop

-metry *n combining form* indicating the process or science of measuring: *anthropometry; geometry* [from Old French *-metrie*, from Latin *-metria*, from Greek, from *metron* measure] > **-metric** *adj combining form*

mettle ('mɛtəl) *n* **1** courage; spirit **2** inherent character **3 on one's mettle** roused to putting forth one's best efforts [C16 originally variant spelling of METAL]

mettled ('mɛtəld) *or* **mettlesome** ('mɛtəlsəm) *adj* spirited, courageous, or valiant

Metz (mɛts; *French* mɛs) *n* a city in NE France on the River Moselle: a free imperial city in the 13th century; annexed by France in 1552; part of Germany (1871–1918); centre of the Lorraine iron-mining region. Pop: 123 776 (1999)

meu (mjuː) *n* another name for **spignel** [C16 from Latin *mēum*, from Greek *mēon*]

meum et tuum *Latin* ('meɪʊm ɛt 'tuːʊm) mine and thine: used to express rights to property [C16 neuter of *mēus* mine and *tuus* yours]

meunière (mənˈjɛə; *French* mønjɛr) *adj* (of fish) dredged with flour, fried in butter, and served with butter, lemon juice, and parsley [French, literally: miller's wife]

Meurthe-et-Moselle (*French* mœrtemozɛl) *n* a department of NE France, in Lorraine region. Capital: Nancy. Pop: 718 250 (2003 est). Area: 5280 sq km (2059 sq miles)

Meuse (mɜːz; *French* møz) *n* **1** a department of N France, in Lorraine region: heavy fighting occurred here in World War I. Capital: Bar-le-Duc. Pop: 191 728 (2003 est). Area: 6241 sq km (2434 sq miles) **2** a river in W Europe, rising in NE France and flowing north across E Belgium and the S Netherlands to join the Waal River before entering the North Sea. Length: 926 km (575 miles). Dutch name: **Maas**

MeV *symbol for* million electronvolts (10^6 electronvolts)

mevrou (məˈfrəʊ) *n* a South African title of address equivalent to *Mrs* when placed before a surname or *madam* when used alone [Afrikaans]

mew¹ (mjuː) *vb* **1** (*intr*) (esp of a cat) to make a characteristic high-pitched cry ▷ *n* **2** such a sound [C14 imitative]

mew² (mjuː) *n* any seagull, esp the common gull, *Larus canus*. Also called: **mew gull, sea mew** [Old English *mǣw*; compare Old Saxon *mēu*, Middle Dutch *mēwe*]

mew³ (mjuː) *n* **1** a room or cage for hawks, esp while moulting ▷ *vb* **2** (*tr*; often foll by *up*) to confine (hawks or falcons) in a shelter, cage, etc, usually by tethering them to a perch **3** to confine, conceal [c14 from Old French *mue,* from *muer* to moult, from Latin *mūtāre* to change]

mew⁴ (mjuː) *vb* **1** (*intr*) (of hawks or falcons) to moult **2** (*tr*) *obsolete* to shed (one's covering, clothes, etc) [c14 from Old French *muer* to moult, from Latin *mūtāre* to change]

Mewar (mɛˈwɑː) *n* another name for **Udaipur** (sense 1)

mewl (mjuːl) *vb* **1** (*intr*) (esp of a baby) to cry weakly; whimper (often in the phrase **mewl and puke**) ▷ *n* **2** such a cry [c17 imitative] > ˈmewler *n*

mews (mjuːz) *n* (*functioning as singular or plural*) *chiefly Brit* **1** a yard or street lined by buildings originally used as stables but now often converted into dwellings **2** the buildings around a mews **3** *informal* an individual residence in a mews [c14 pl of MEW³, originally referring to royal stables built on the site of hawks' mews at Charing Cross in London]

MEX *international car registration for* Mexico

Mex. *abbreviation for* **1** Mexican **2** Mexico

Mexicali (ˌmɛksɪˈkɑːlɪ; *Spanish* mexiˈkali) *n* a city in NW Mexico, capital of Baja California (Norte) state, on the border with the US adjoining Calexico, California: centre of a rich irrigated agricultural region. Pop: 840 000 (2005 est)

Mexican (ˈmɛksɪkən) *adj* **1** of or relating to Mexico or its inhabitants ▷ *n* **2** a native or inhabitant of Mexico

Mexican hairless *n* a breed of small hairless dog with mottled skin, originating from Mexico

Mexican War *n* the war fought between the US and Mexico (1846–48), through which the US acquired the present-day Southwest

Mexican wave *n* the rippling effect produced when the spectators in successive sections of a sports stadium stand up while raising their arms and then sit down [c20 so called because it was first demonstrated at the World Cup in Mexico in 1986]

Mexico (ˈmɛksɪˌkəʊ) *n* **1** a republic in North America, on the Gulf of Mexico and the Pacific: early Mexican history includes the Maya, Toltec, and Aztec civilizations; conquered by the Spanish between 1519 and 1525 and achieved independence in 1821; lost Texas to the US in 1836 and California and New Mexico in 1848. It is generally mountainous with three ranges of the Sierra Madre (east, west, and south) and a large central plateau. Official language: Spanish. Religion: Roman Catholic majority. Currency: peso. Capital: Mexico City. Pop: 104 931 000 (2004 est). Area: 1 967 183 sq km (761 530 sq miles). Official name: **United Mexican States** *Spanish name:* **Méjico 2** a state of Mexico, on the central plateau surrounding Mexico City, which is not administratively part of the state. Capital: Toluca. Pop: 13 096 686 (2000). Area: 21 461 sq km (8287 sq miles) **3 Gulf of** an arm of the Atlantic, bordered by the US, Cuba, and Mexico: linked with the Atlantic by the Straits of Florida and with the Caribbean by the Yucatán Channel. Area: about 1 600 000 sq km (618 000 sq miles)

Mexico City *n* the capital of Mexico, on the central plateau at an altitude of 2240 m (7350 ft): founded as the Aztec capital (Tenochtitlán) in about 1300; conquered and rebuilt by the Spanish in 1521; forms, with its suburbs, the federal district of Mexico; the largest industrial complex in the country. Pop: 19 013 000 (2005 est)

MEZ *abbreviation for* Central European Time [from German *Mitteleuropäische Zeit*]

mezcal (mɛˈskæl) *n* a variant spelling of **mescal**

mezcaline (ˈmɛskəˌliːn) *n* a variant spelling of **mescaline**

meze (ˈmɛzɛ) *n* a type of hors d'oeuvre eaten esp with an apéritif or other drink in Greece and the Near East [c20 from Turkish *meze* snack, appetizer]

mezereon (mɛˈzɪərɪən) *n* **1** a Eurasian thymelaeaceous shrub, *Daphne mezereum,* with fragrant early-blooming purplish-pink flowers and small scarlet fruits **2** another name for

mezereum [c15 via Medieval Latin from Arabic *māzaryūn*]

mezereum (mɪˈzɪərɪəm) or **mezereon** *n* the dried bark of certain shrubs of the genus *Daphne,* esp mezereon, formerly used as a vesicant and to treat arthritis

Mézières (*French* mezjɛr) *n* a town in NE France, on the River Meuse opposite Charleville. See **Charleville-Mézières**

mezuzah (məˈzʊzə, -ˈzuː-; *Hebrew* məzuˈza; *Yiddish* məˈzʊzə) *n, pl* **-zuzahs** or **-zuzoth** (*Hebrew* -zuˈzɔt) *Judaism* **1** a piece of parchment inscribed with biblical passages and fixed to the doorpost of the rooms of a Jewish house **2** a metal case for such a parchment, sometimes worn as an ornament [from Hebrew, literally: doorpost]

mezzanine (ˈmɛzəˌniːn, ˈmɛtsəˌniːn) *n* **1** Also called: **mezzanine floor, entresol** an intermediate storey, esp a low one between the ground and first floor of a building **2** *theatre, US and Canadian* the first balcony **3** *theatre, Brit* a room or floor beneath the stage ▷ *adj* **4** Often shortened to: **mezz** of or relating to an intermediate stage in a financial process: *mezzanine funding* [c18 from French, from Italian, diminutive of *mezzano* middle, from Latin *mediānus* MEDIAN]

mezza voce (ˈmɛtsə ˈvəʊtʃɪ; *Italian* ˈmɛddza ˈvotʃe) *adv music* (in singing) softly; quietly [Italian, literally: half voice]

mezzo (ˈmɛtsəʊ) *music* ▷ *adv* **1** moderately; quite: *mezzo forte; mezzo piano* ▷ *n, pl* **-zos 2** See **mezzo-soprano** (sense 1) [c19 from Italian, literally: half, from Latin *medius* middle]

mezzo-relievo or **mezzo-rilievo** (ˌmɛtsəʊrɪˈliːvəʊ) *n* carving in which the depth of the relief is halfway between that of high relief and low relief [from Italian: half relief]

mezzo-soprano *n, pl* **-nos 1** a female voice intermediate between a soprano and contralto and having a range from the A below middle C to the F an eleventh above it. Sometimes shortened to: **mezzo 2** a singer with such a voice

mezzotint (ˈmɛtsəʊˌtɪnt) *n* **1** a method of engraving a copper plate by scraping and burnishing the roughened surface **2** a print made from a plate so treated ▷ *vb* **3** (*tr*) to engrave (a copper plate) in this fashion [c18 from Italian *mezzotinto* half tint] > ˈmezzoˌtinter *n*

mf *music abbreviation for* mezzo forte [Italian: moderately loud]

MF *abbreviation for* **1** *radio* **medium frequency 2** Middle French

M.F.A. (in the US and Canada) *abbreviation for* Master of Fine Arts

MFAT (ˈɛmfæt) *n* (in New Zealand) ▷ *acronym for* Ministry of Foreign Affairs and Trade

mfd *abbreviation for* manufactured

mfg *abbreviation for* manufacturing

MFH *hunting abbreviation for* Master of Foxhounds

mfr *abbreviation for* **1** manufacture **2** manufacturer

mg¹ *symbol for* milligram

mg² *the internet domain name for* Madagascar

Mg *the chemical symbol for* magnesium

MG *abbreviation for* machine gun

MGB *abbreviation for* Ministry of State Security; the Soviet secret police from 1946 to 1954 [from Russian *Ministerstvo gosudarstvennoi bezopasnosti*]

MGL *international car registration for* Mongolia

Mgr *abbreviation for* **1** manager **2** Monseigneur **3** Monsignor

mh *the internet domain name for* Marshall Islands

MHA (in Australia and Newfoundland, Canada) *abbreviation for* Member of the House of Assembly

MHC *abbreviation for* major histocompatibility complex; a series of genes located on chromosome 6 that code for antigens. They are important in determining histocompatibility

MHD *abbreviation for* magnetohydrodynamics

MHG *abbreviation for* Middle High German

mho (məʊ) *n, pl* **mhos** the former name for **siemens** [c19 formed by reversing the letters of OHM (first used by Lord Kelvin)]

MHR (in the US and Australia) *abbreviation for* Member of the House of Representatives

MHz *symbol for* megahertz

mi or **me** (miː) *n music* (in tonic sol-fa) the third degree of any major scale; mediant [c16 see GAMUT]

MI *abbreviation for* **1** Michigan **2** Military Intelligence

mi. *abbreviation for* mile

MI5 *abbreviation for* Military Intelligence, section five; a former official and present-day popular name for the counterintelligence agency of the British Government

MI6 *abbreviation for* Military Intelligence, section six; a former official and present-day popular name for the intelligence and espionage agency of the British Government

MIA *abbreviation for* **1** *military, chiefly US* missing in action: officially unaccounted for following combat **2** (in Australia) Murrumbidgee Irrigation Area

Miami (maɪˈæmɪ) *n* a city and resort in SE Florida, on Biscayne Bay: developed chiefly after 1896, esp with the Florida land boom of the 1920s; centre of an extensive tourist area. Pop: 376 815 (2003 est)

mia mia (ˈmiːə ˈmiːə) *n* a native Australian's hut [from a native Australian language]

Miami Beach *n* a resort in SE Florida, on an island separated from Miami by Biscayne Bay. Pop: 89 312 (2003 est)

miaou or **miaow** (mɪˈaʊ, mjaʊ) *vb, interj* variant spellings of **meow**

miasma (mɪˈæzmə) *n, pl* **-mata** (-mətə) or **-mas 1** an unwholesome or foreboding atmosphere **2** pollution in the atmosphere, esp noxious vapours from decomposing organic matter [c17 New Latin, from Greek: defilement, from *miainein* to defile] > miˈasmal, miasmatic (ˌmiːəzˈmætɪk) or ˌmiasˈmatical, miˈasmic *adj*

miaul (mɪˈaʊl) *vb* (*intr*) another word for **meow**

mic (maɪk) *n informal* short for **microphone**

Mic. *Bible abbreviation for* Micah

mica (ˈmaɪkə) *n* any of a group of lustrous rock-forming minerals consisting of hydrous silicates of aluminium, potassium, etc, in monoclinic crystalline form, occurring in igneous and metamorphic rock. Because of their resistance to electricity and heat they are used as dielectrics, in heating elements, etc [c18 from Latin: grain, morsel] > micaceous (maɪˈkeɪʃəs) *adj*

Micah (ˈmaɪkə) *n Old Testament* **1** a Hebrew prophet of the late 8th century BC **2** the book containing his prophecies. Douay spelling: **Micheas** (maɪˈkiːəs)

Micawber (mɪˈkɔːbə) *n* a person who idles and trusts to fortune [c19 after a character in *David Copperfield*, a novel (1850) by English novelist Charles Dickens (1812–70)] > Miˈcawberish *adj* > Miˈcawberism *n*

mice (maɪs) *n* the plural of **mouse**

micelle, micell (mɪˈsɛl) or **micella** (mɪˈsɛlə) *n chem* **a** a charged aggregate of molecules of colloidal size in a solution **b** any molecular aggregate of colloidal size, such as a particle found in coal [c19 from New Latin *micella,* diminutive of Latin *mīca* crumb] > miˈcellar *adj*

mich (mɪtʃ) *vb* (*intr*) a variant spelling of **mitch**

Mich. *abbreviation for* Michigan

Michaelmas (ˈmɪkəlməs) *n* Sept 29, the feast of St Michael the archangel; in England, Ireland, and Wales, one of the four quarter days

Michaelmas daisy *n Brit* any of various plants of the genus *Aster* that have small autumn-blooming purple, pink, or white flowers: family *Asteraceae* (composites)

Michaelmas term *n* the autumn term at Oxford and Cambridge Universities, the Inns of Court, and some other educational establishments

Michelson-Morley experiment (ˌmaɪkəlsᵊnˈmɔːlɪ) *n* an experiment first performed in 1887 by A. A. Michelson and E. W. Morley, in which an interferometer was used to

m

attempt to detect a difference in the velocities of light in directions parallel and perpendicular to the earth's motion. The negative result was explained by the special theory of relativity

michigan ('mɪʃɪgən) *n* the US name for **newmarket** (sense 2)

Michigan ('mɪʃɪgən) *n* **1** a state of the N central US, occupying two peninsulas between Lakes Superior, Huron, Michigan, and Erie: generally low-lying. Capital: Lansing. Pop: 10 079 985 (2003 est). Area: 147 156 sq km (56 817 sq miles). Abbreviations: **Mich,** (with zip code) **MI 2 Lake** a lake in the N central US between Wisconsin and Michigan: the third largest of the five Great Lakes and the only one wholly in the US; linked with Lake Huron by the Straits of Mackinac. Area: 58 000 sq km (22 400 sq miles)

Michigander (ˌmɪʃɪ'gændə) *n* a native or inhabitant of Michigan

Michiganite ('mɪʃɪgənˌaɪt) *n* **1** a native or inhabitant of Michigan ▷ *adj* **2** of or relating to Michigan or its inhabitants

Michoacán (*Spanish* mitʃoa'kan) *n* a state of SW Mexico, on the Pacific: rich mineral resources. Capital: Morelia. Pop: 3 979 177 (2000). Area: 59 864 sq km (23 114 sq miles)

micht (mɪxt) *vb, n* a Scot word for **might¹** and **might²**

Mick (mɪk) or **Mickey** ('mɪkɪ) *n* (*sometimes not capital*) *derogatory* a slang name for an Irishman or a Roman Catholic [C19 from the nickname for *Michael*]

mickey¹ or **micky** ('mɪkɪ) *n* **take the mickey (out of)** *informal* to tease [C20 of unknown origin]

mickey² or **micky** ('mɪkɪ) *n Austral informal* a young bull, esp one that is wild and unbranded

mickey³ ('mɪkɪ) *n Canadian* a liquor bottle of 0.375 litre capacity, flat on one side and curved on the other to fit into a pocket [C20 of unknown origin]

Mickey Finn *n slang* **a** a drink containing a drug to make the drinker unconscious, usually formed by the combination of chloral hydrate and alcohol. It can be poisonous **b** the drug itself ▷ Often shortened to: **Mickey** [C20 of unknown origin]

Mickey Mouse *adj* (*sometimes not capitals*) *slang* **1** ineffective; trivial; insignificant: *he settled for a Mickey Mouse job instead of something challenging* **2** *chiefly US and Canadian* (of music, esp that of dance bands) mechanical or spiritless [C20 from the name of a cartoon character known for his simple-minded attitudes, created by Walt Disney (1901–66), the US film producer]

mickle ('mɪkəl) or **muckle** ('mʌkəl) *Scot and Northern English dialect* ▷ *adj* **1** great or abundant ▷ *adv* **2** much; greatly ▷ *n* **3** a great amount, esp in the proverb, *mony a little makes a mickle* **4** *Scot* a small amount, esp in the proverb, *many a mickle maks a muckle* [C13 *mikel,* from Old Norse *mikell,* replacing Old English *micel* MUCH]

Micmac ('mɪkmæk) *n* **1** (*pl* **-macs** or **-mac**) a member of a North American Indian people formerly living in the Maritime Provinces of Canada **2** the language of this people, belonging to the Algonquian family

MICR *abbreviation for* **magnetic ink character recognition**

micra ('maɪkrə) *n* a plural of **micron**

micro ('maɪkrəʊ) *adj* **1** very small ▷ *n, pl* **-cros 2** short for **microcomputer, microlepidoptera, microprocessor, microwave oven**

micro- or **micr-** *combining form* **1** small or minute: *microspore* **2** involving the use of a microscope: *micrography* **3** indicating a method or instrument for dealing with small quantities: *micrometer* **4** (in pathology) indicating abnormal smallness or underdevelopment: *microcephaly; microcyte.* Compare **macro-** (sense 2) **5** denoting 10⁻⁶: *microsecond.* Symbol: μ [from Greek *mikros* small]

microaerophile (ˌmaɪkrəʊ'ɛərəʊˌfaɪl) *n* an organism, esp a bacterium, that thrives in an environment low in oxygen ▷ **microaerophilic**

(ˌmaɪkrəʊˌɛərəʊ'fɪlɪk) *adj*

microanalysis (ˌmaɪkrəʊə'nælɪsɪs) *n, pl* **-ses** (-ˌsiːz) the qualitative or quantitative chemical analysis of very small amounts of substances ▷ **microanalyst** (ˌmaɪkrəʊ'ænəlɪst) *n* ▷ **microanalytic** (ˌmaɪkrəʊˌænə'lɪtɪk) *or* ˌmicroˌana'lytical *adj*

microarray (ˌmaɪkrəʊə'reɪ) *n* another name for **biochip**

microbalance ('maɪkrəʊˌbæləns) *n* a precision balance designed to weigh quantities between 10⁻⁶ and 10⁻⁹ kilogram

microbarograph (ˌmaɪkrəʊ'bærəˌgrɑːf, -ˌgræf) *n* a barograph that records minute changes in atmospheric pressure

microbe ('maɪkrəʊb) *n* any microscopic organism, esp a disease-causing bacterium [C19 from French, from MICRO- + Greek *bios* life] ▷ **mi'crobial, mi'crobic** *or less commonly* **mi'crobian** *adj*

microbiology (ˌmaɪkrəʊbaɪ'ɒlədʒɪ) *n* the branch of biology involving the study of microorganisms ▷ **microbiological** (ˌmaɪkrəʊˌbaɪə'lɒdʒɪkəl) *or* ˌmicroˌbio'logic *adj* ▷ ˌmicroˌbio'logically *adv* ▷ ˌmicrobi'ologist *n*

microbrewery ('maɪkrəʊˌbrʊərɪ) *n, pl* **-ries** a small, usually independent brewery that produces limited quantities of specialized beers, often sold for consumption on the premises

microbubbles ('maɪkrəʊˌbʌbᵊlz) *pl n medicine* a contrast medium used with ultrasound, consisting of tiny bubbles of gas introduced into the vascular system or Fallopian tubes to enhance the images obtained

microburst ('maɪkrəʊˌbɜːst) *n* another name for **downburst**

microcelebrity (ˌmaɪkrəʊsɪ'lɛbrɪtɪ) *n, pl* **-ties** a celebrity whose fame is relatively narrow in scope and likely to be transient

microcephaly (ˌmaɪkrəʊ'sɛfəlɪ) *n* the condition of having an abnormally small head or cranial capacity. Compare **megacephaly.** ▷ **microcephalic** (ˌmaɪkrəʊsɪ'fælɪk) *adj, n* ▷ ˌmicro'cephalous *adj*

microchemistry (ˌmaɪkrəʊ'kɛmɪstrɪ) *n* chemical experimentation with minute quantities of material ▷ ˌmicro'chemical *adj*

microchip ('maɪkrəʊˌtʃɪp) *n* **1** a small piece of semiconductor material carrying many integrated circuits ▷ *vb* **-chips, -chipping, -chipped 2** (*tr*) to implant (an animal) with a microchip tag linked to a national computer network for purposes of identification

microcircuit ('maɪkrəʊˌsɜːkɪt) *n* a miniature electronic circuit, esp one in which a number of permanently connected components are contained in one small chip of semiconducting material. See **integrated circuit.** ▷ ˌmicro'circuitry *n*

microclimate ('maɪkrəʊˌklaɪmɪt) *n ecology* **1** the atmospheric conditions affecting an individual or a small group of organisms, esp when they differ from the climate of the rest of the community **2** the entire environment of an individual or small group of organisms ▷ **microclimatic** (ˌmaɪkrəʊklaɪ'mætɪk) *adj* ▷ ˌmicrocli'matically *adv*

microclimatology (ˌmaɪkrəʊˌklaɪmə'tɒlədʒɪ) *n* the study of climate on a small scale, as of a city ▷ **microclimatologic** (ˌmaɪkrəʊˌklaɪmətə'lɒdʒɪk) *or* ˌmicroˌclimato'logical *adj* ▷ ˌmicroˌclima'tologist *n*

microcline ('maɪkrəʊˌklaɪn) *n* a white, creamy yellow, red, or green mineral of the feldspar group, found in igneous, sedimentary, and metamorphic rocks: used in the manufacture of glass and ceramics. Composition: potassium aluminium silicate. Formula: $KAlSi_3O_8$. Crystal structure: triclinic [C19 from German *Mikroklin,* from *mikro* MICRO- + Greek *klinein* to lean; so called because its cleavage plane is slightly different from 90°]

micrococcus (ˌmaɪkrəʊ'kɒkəs) *n, pl* **-cocci** (-'kɒksaɪ) any spherical Gram-positive bacterium of the genus *Micrococcus*: family *Micrococcaceae*

microcomputer ('maɪkrəʊkəm'pjuːtə) *n* a small

computer in which the central processing unit is contained in one or more silicon chips. Sometimes shortened to: **micro**

microcopy ('maɪkrəʊˌkɒpɪ) *n, pl* **-copies** a greatly reduced photographic copy of a printed page, drawing, etc, on microfilm or microfiche. Sometimes called: **microphotograph**

microcosm ('maɪkrəʊˌkɒzəm) *or* **microcosmos** (ˌmaɪkrəʊ'kɒzmɒs) *n* **1** a miniature representation of something, esp a unit, group, or place regarded as a copy of a larger one **2** man regarded as epitomizing the universe ▷ Compare **macrocosm** [C15 via Medieval Latin from Greek *mikros kosmos* little world] ▷ ˌmicro'cosmic *or* ˌmicro'cosmical *adj*

microcosmic salt *n* a white soluble solid obtained from human urine; ammonium sodium hydrogen phosphate. It is used as a flux in bead tests on metal oxides

micro-credit ('maɪkrəʊˌkrɛdɪt) *n* the practice of lending small amounts of money on minimal security, esp to help small businesses and communities in the developing world

microcrystalline (ˌmaɪkrəʊ'krɪstᵊˌlaɪn) *adj* (of a solid) composed of microscopic crystals

microcyte ('maɪkrəʊˌsaɪt) *n* an unusually small red blood cell ▷ **microcytic** (ˌmaɪkrəʊ'sɪtɪk) *adj*

microdetector (ˌmaɪkrəʊdɪ'tɛktə) *n* any instrument for measuring small quantities or detecting small effects, esp a sensitive galvanometer

microdont ('maɪkrəʊˌdɒnt) *or* **microdontous** (ˌmaɪkrəʊ'dɒntəs) *adj* having unusually small teeth

microdot ('maɪkrəʊˌdɒt) *n* **1** a microcopy about the size of a pinhead, used esp in espionage **2** a tiny tablet containing LSD

microdrive ('maɪkrəʊˌdraɪv) *n* a type of memory card that has moving parts and can store large amounts of data

microeconomics (ˌmaɪkrəʊˌiːkə'nɒmɪks, -ˌɛkə-) *n* (*functioning as singular*) the branch of economics concerned with particular commodities, firms, or individuals and the economic relationships between them. Compare **macroeconomics** ▷ ˌmicroˌeco'nomic *adj*

microelectronics (ˌmaɪkrəʊɪlɛk'trɒnɪks) *n* (*functioning as singular*) the branch of electronics concerned with microcircuits ▷ ˌmicroelec'tronic *adj*

microenvironment ('maɪkrəʊɪnˌvaɪrənmənt) *n ecology* the environment of a small area, such as that around a leaf or plant

microfarad (ˌmaɪkrəʊˌfærəd) *n* one millionth of a farad; 10⁻⁶ farad. Symbol: μF

microfibre *or US* **microfiber** ('maɪkrəʊˌfaɪbə) *n* a very fine synthetic fibre used for textiles

microfiche ('maɪkrəʊˌfiːʃ) *n* a sheet of film, usually the size of a filing card, on which books, newspapers, documents, etc, can be recorded in miniaturized form. Sometimes shortened to: **fiche** See also **ultrafiche** [C20 from French, from MICRO- + *fiche* small card, from Old French *fichier* to fix]

microfilament (ˌmaɪkrəʊ'fɪləmənt) *n* thin filament, composed of the protein actin and associated proteins, that occurs abundantly in muscle and in the cytoplasm of other cells

microfilaria (ˌmaɪkrəʊfɪ'lɛərɪə) *n, pl* **-iae** (-ˌiːiː) *zoology* the early larval stage of certain parasitic nematodes (filariae), found in the blood of infected individuals

microfilm ('maɪkrəʊˌfɪlm) *n* **1** a strip of film of standard width on which books, newspapers, documents, etc, can be recorded in miniaturized form ▷ *vb* **2** to photograph (a page, document, etc) on microfilm ▷ See also **microfiche**

microfilm plotter *n computing* a type of incremental plotter that has a film rather than a paper output

microfilter ('maɪkrəʊˌfɪltə) *n* a device plugged into a phone socket to separate the phone line from the broadband line

microflora (ˈmaɪkrəʊˌflɔːrə) *n* the community of microorganisms, including algae, fungi, and bacteria that live in or on another living organism or in a particular habitat

microform (ˈmaɪkrəʊˌfɔːm) *n computing* a method of storing symbolic information by using photographic reduction techniques, such as microfilm, microfiche, etc

microfossil (ˈmaɪkrəʊˌfɒsəl) *n* a fossil generally less than 0.5 millimetre in size, such as a protozoan, bacterium, or pollen grain

microgamete (ˌmaɪkrəʊˈgæmiːt) *n* the smaller and apparently male of two gametes in conjugating protozoans. Compare **macrogamete**

microglia (ˌmaɪkrəʊˈgliːə) *n* one of the two types of non-nervous tissue (glia) found in the central nervous system, having macrophage activity. Compare **macroglia**

micrograph (ˈmaɪkrəʊˌɡrɑːf, -ˌgræf) *n* **1** a photograph or drawing of an object as viewed through a microscope **2** an instrument or machine for producing very small writing or engraving

micrography (maɪˈkrɒɡrəfɪ) *n* **1** the description, study, drawing, or photography of microscopic objects **2** the technique of using a microscope **3** the art or practice of writing in minute characters > mi'crographer *n* > micrographic (ˌmaɪkrəʊˈɡræfɪk) *adj* > ˌmicro'graphically *adv*

microgravity (ˈmaɪkrəʊˌɡrævɪtɪ) *n* the very low apparent gravity experienced in a spacecraft in earth orbit

microgroove (ˈmaɪkrəʊˌɡruːv) *n* **a** the narrow groove in a long-playing gramophone record **b** (*as modifier*): *a microgroove record*

microhabitat (ˌmaɪkrəʊˈhæbɪtæt) *n ecology* the smallest part of the environment that supports a distinct flora and fauna, such as a fallen log in a forest

microinstruction (ˈmaɪkrəʊɪnˌstrʌkʃən) *n computing* an instruction produced within an arithmetic and logic unit in accordance with a microprogram, that activates a particular circuit to perform part of the operation specified by a machine instruction

microjet (ˈmaɪkrəʊˌdʒɛt) *n* a light jet-propelled aircraft

microlepidoptera (ˌmaɪkrəʊˌlɛpɪˈdɒptərə) *pl n* a collector's name for the smaller moths: a term without taxonomic significance. Compare **macrolepidoptera**

microlight *or* **microlite** (ˈmaɪkrəʊˌlaɪt) *n* a small private aircraft carrying no more than two people, with an empty weight of not more than 150 kg and a wing area not less than 10 square metres: used in pleasure flying and racing

microlith (ˈmaɪkrəʊˌlɪθ) *n archaeol* a small Mesolithic flint tool which was made from a blade and formed part of hafted tools > ˌmicro'lithic *adj*

micromanage (ˈmaɪkrəʊˌmænɪdʒ) *vb* (*tr*) to control (a business or project) with excessive attention to minor details

micromarketing (ˈmaɪkrəʊˌmɑːkɪtɪŋ) *n* the marketing of products or services designed to meet the needs of a very small section of the market

micromere (ˈmaɪkrəʊˌmɪə) *n embryol* any of the small cells formed by unequal cleavage of a fertilized ovum

micrometeorite (ˌmaɪkrəʊˈmiːtɪəˌraɪt) *n* a tiny meteorite having a diameter of 10–40 micrometres, found esp in rainwater and seawater, having entered the atmosphere as a **micrometeoroid** (extremely small meteoroid)

micrometeorology (ˌmaɪkrəʊˌmiːtɪəˈrɒlədʒɪ) *n* the study of the layer of air immediately above the earth and of small-scale meteorological processes

micrometer (maɪˈkrɒmɪtə) *n* **1** any of various instruments or devices for the accurate measurement of distances or angles **2** Also

called: **micrometer gauge**, **micrometer calliper** a type of gauge for the accurate measurement of small distances, thicknesses, diameters, etc. The gap between its measuring faces is adjusted by a fine screw, the rotation of the screw giving a sensitive measure of the distance moved by the face > mi'crometry *n* > micrometric (ˌmaɪkrəʊˈmɛtrɪk) *or* ˌmicro'metrical *adj*

micrometer screw *n* a screw with a fine thread of definite pitch, such as that of a micrometer gauge

micrometre (ˈmaɪkrəʊˌmiːtə) *n* a unit of length equal to 10⁻⁶ metre. Symbol: μm Former name: micron

microminiaturization *or* **microminiaturisation** (ˌmaɪkrəʊˌmɪnɪtʃəraɪˈzeɪʃən) *n* the production and application of very small semiconductor components and the circuits and equipment in which they are used

micron (ˈmaɪkrɒn) *n, pl* **-crons** *or* **-cra** (-krə) a unit of length equal to 10⁻⁶ metre. It is being replaced by the micrometre, the equivalent SI unit [C19 New Latin, from Greek *mikros* small]

Micronesia (ˌmaɪkrəʊˈniːzɪə) *n* **1** one of the three divisions of islands in the Pacific (the others being Melanesia and Polynesia); the NW division of Oceania: includes the Mariana, Caroline, Marshall, and Kiribati island groups, and Nauru Island **2 Federated States of** an island group in the W Pacific, formerly within the United States Trust Territory of the Pacific Islands: comprises the islands of Truk, Yap, Ponape, and Kosrae: formed in 1979 when the islands became self-governing: status of free association with the US from 1982. Languages: English and Micronesian languages. Religion: Christian majority. Currency: US dollar. Capital: Palikir. Pop: 111 000 (2004 est) [C19 from MICRO- + Greek *nēsos* island; so called from the small size of many of the islands; on the model of *Polynesia*]

Micronesian (ˌmaɪkrəʊˈniːzɪən) *adj* **1** of or relating to Micronesia, its inhabitants, or their languages ▷ *n* **2** a native or inhabitant of Micronesia, more akin to the Polynesians than the Melanesians, but having Mongoloid traces **3** a group of languages spoken in Micronesia, belonging to the Malayo-Polynesian family

micronize *or* **micronise** (ˈmaɪkrəʊˌnaɪz) *vb* (*tr*) to reduce (a material) to a very fine powder, esp to particles only a few microns in diameter > ˌmicroni'zation *or* ˌmicroni'sation *n*

micronucleus (ˌmaɪkrəʊˈnjuːklɪəs) *n, pl* **-clei** (-klɪˌaɪ) *or* **-cleuses** the smaller of two nuclei in ciliated protozoans, involved in reproduction. Compare **macronucleus**

micronutrient (ˌmaɪkrəʊˈnjuːtrɪənt) *n* any substance, such as a vitamin or trace element, essential for healthy growth and development but required only in minute amounts

microorganism (ˌmaɪkrəʊˈɔːɡəˌnɪzəm) *n* any organism, such as a bacterium, protozoan, or virus, of microscopic size

micropalaeontology (ˌmaɪkrəʊˌpælɪɒnˈtɒlədʒɪ) *n* the branch of palaeontology concerned with the study of microscopic fossils > micropalaeontological (ˌmaɪkrəʊˌpælɪɒntəˈlɒdʒɪkᵊl) *or* ˌmicro,palaeonto'logic *adj* > ˌmicro,palaeon'tologist *n*

microparasite (ˌmaɪkrəʊˈpærəˌsaɪt) *n* any parasitic microorganism > microparasitic (ˌmaɪkrəʊˌpærəˈsɪtɪk) *adj*

micropayment (ˈmaɪkrəʊˌpeɪmənt) *n* a system whereby a user pays a small fee to access a specific area of a website

microphagous (maɪˈkrɒfəgəs) *adj zoology* (of an animal) feeding on small particles of food

microphanerophyte (ˌmaɪkrəʊˈfænərəʊˌfaɪt) *n botany* any shrub or tree having a height of 2 to 8 metres

microphone (ˈmaɪkrəˌfəʊn) *n* a device used in

sound-reproduction systems for converting sound into electrical energy, usually by means of a ribbon or diaphragm set into motion by the sound waves. The vibrations are converted into the equivalent audio-frequency electric currents. Informal name: mike See also **carbon microphone** Compare **loudspeaker**

microphonic (ˌmaɪkrəˈfɒnɪk) *adj* **1** of or relating to microphones **2** (of valves or other electronic components) unusually sensitive to incident sound or mechanical shock

microphotograph (ˌmaɪkrəʊˈfəʊtəˌɡrɑːf, -ˌgræf) *n* **1** a photograph in which the image is greatly reduced and therefore requires optical enlargement for viewing purposes **2** a less common name for **microcopy** or **photomicrograph** (sense 1) > ˌmicro,photo'graphic *adj* > microphotography (ˌmaɪkrəʊfəˈtɒɡrəfɪ) *n*

microphyll (ˈmaɪkrəʊˌfɪl) *n botany* the relatively small type of leaf produced by club mosses and horsetails. Compare **megaphyll**

microphysics (ˌmaɪkrəʊˈfɪzɪks) *n* (*functioning as singular*) the branch of physics concerned with small objects and systems, such as atoms, molecules, nuclei, and elementary particles > ˌmicro'physical *adj*

microphyte (ˈmaɪkrəʊˌfaɪt) *n* an obsolete name for a **bacterium**. > microphytic (ˌmaɪkrəʊˈfɪtɪk) *adj*

micropower (ˈmaɪkrəʊˌpaʊə) *n* power distributed on a small scale using local generators

microprint (ˈmaɪkrəʊˌprɪnt) *n* a microphotograph reproduced on paper and read by a magnifying device. It is used in order to reduce the size of large books, etc

microprism (ˈmaɪkrəʊˌprɪzəm) *n photog* a small prism incorporated in the focusing screen of many single-lens reflex cameras. The prism stops shimmering when the subject is in focus

microprocessor (ˌmaɪkrəʊˈprəʊsɛsə) *n computing* a single integrated circuit performing the basic functions of the central processing unit in a small computer

microprogram (ˈmaɪkrəʊˌprəʊɡræm) *n computing* a sequence of microinstructions that controls the operation of an arithmetic and logic unit so that machine code instructions are executed

micropropagation (ˌmaɪkrəʊˌprɒpəˈɡeɪʃən) *n botany* the production of a large number of individual plants from a small piece of plant tissue cultured in a nutrient medium

micropsia (maɪˈkrɒpsɪə) *n* a defect of vision in which objects appear to be smaller than they appear to a person with normal vision

micropterous (maɪˈkrɒptərəs) *adj* (of certain animals, esp some types of ant) having small reduced wings

micropyle (ˈmaɪkrəʊˌpaɪl) *n* **1** a small opening in the integuments of a plant ovule through which the male gametes pass **2** a small pore in the shell of an insect's eggs through which the sperm passes [C19 from MICRO- + Greek *pulē* gate] > ˌmicro'pylar *adj*

micropyrometer (ˌmaɪkrəʊpaɪˈrɒmɪtə) *n* a pyrometer for measuring the temperature of very small objects

microreader (ˈmaɪkrəʊˌriːdə) *n* an apparatus that produces an enlarged image of a microphotograph

microsatellite (ˌmaɪkrəʊˈsætᵊˌlaɪt) *n genetics* a section of DNA consisting of very short nucleotide sequences repeated many times, the number of repeats varying between members of the species: used as a marker in determining genetic diversity, identifying important genetic traits, and in forensics, population studies, and paternity studies

micro scooter *n* a foldable lightweight aluminium foot-propelled scooter, used by both adults and children

microscope (ˈmaɪkrəˌskəʊp) *n* **1** an optical instrument that uses a lens or combination of lenses to produce a magnified image of a small,

m

close object. Modern optical microscopes have magnifications of about 1500 to 2000. See also **simple microscope, compound microscope, ultramicroscope 2** any instrument, such as the electron microscope, for producing a magnified visual image of a small object

microscopic (ˌmaɪkrəˈskɒpɪk) *or less commonly* **microscopical** *adj* **1** not large enough to be seen with the naked eye but visible under a microscope. Compare **macroscopic 2** very small; minute **3** of, concerned with, or using a microscope **4** characterized by or done with great attention to detail > ˌmicroˈscopically *adv*

Microscopium (ˌmaɪkrəˈskəʊpɪəm) *n, Latin genitive* Microscopii (ˌmaɪkrəˈskəʊpɪˌaɪ) a faint constellation in the S hemisphere lying near Sagittarius and Capricornus

microscopy (maɪˈkrɒskəpɪ) *n* **1** the study, design, and manufacture of microscopes **2** investigation by use of a microscope > **microscopist** (maɪˈkrɒskəpɪst) *n*

microsecond (ˈmaɪkrəʊˌsɛkənd) *n* one millionth of a second. Symbol: μs

microseism (ˈmaɪkrəʊˌsaɪzəm) *n* a very slight tremor of the earth's surface, thought not to be caused by an earthquake > **microseismic** (ˌmaɪkrəʊˈsaɪzmɪk) *or* ˌmicroˈseismical *adj*

microsite (ˈmaɪkrəʊˌsaɪt) *n* a website that is intended for a specific limited purpose and is often temporary

microsleep (ˈmaɪkrəʊˌsliːp) *n* a period of sleep which is so momentary as to be imperceptible

microsmatic (ˌmaɪkrɒzˈmætɪk) *adj* (of humans and certain animals) having a poor sense of smell [from MICRO- + Greek *osmē* smell]

microsome (ˈmaɪkrəʊˌsəʊm) *n* any of the small particles consisting of ribosomes and fragments of attached endoplasmic reticulum that can be isolated from cells by centrifugal action > ˌmicroˈsomal *adj*

microspecies (ˈmaɪkrəʊˌspiːʃiːz) *n, pl* -cies another name for **biotype**

microsporangium (ˌmaɪkrəʊspɔːˈrændʒɪəm) *n, pl* -gia (-dʒɪə) the structure in certain spore-bearing plants in which the microspores are formed: corresponds to the pollen sac in seed plants. Compare **megasporangium**

microspore (ˈmaɪkrəʊˌspɔː) *n* **1** the smaller of two types of spore produced by some spore-bearing plants, which develops into the male gametophyte. Compare **megaspore** (sense 1) **2** the pollen grain of seed plants > ˌmicroˈsporic *or* ˌmicroˈsporous *adj*

microsporophyll (ˌmaɪkrəʊˈspɔːrəfɪl) *n* a leaf on which the microspores are formed: corresponds to the stamen of a flowering plant. Compare **megasporophyll** [C19 from MICRO- + SPOROPHYLL]

microstate (ˈmaɪkrəʊˌsteɪt) *n* a very small nation that is internationally-recognized sovereign state. Also called: **mini-state**

microstomatous (ˌmaɪkrəʊˈstɒmətəs) *or* **microstomous** (maɪˈkrɒstəməs) *adj anatomy* having an unusually small mouth

microstructure (ˈmaɪkrəʊˌstrʌktʃə) *n* structure on a microscopic scale, esp the structure of an alloy as observed by etching, polishing, and observation under a microscope

microsurgery (ˌmaɪkrəʊˈsɜːdʒərɪ) *n* intricate surgery performed on cells, tissues, etc, using a specially designed operating microscope and miniature precision instruments > ˌmicroˈsurgical *adj*

microswitch (ˈmaɪkrəʊˌswɪtʃ) *n electrical engineering* a switch that operates at small movements of a lever

microtechnology (ˌmaɪkrəʊtɛkˈnɒlədʒɪ) *n* technology that uses microelectronics

micro-time *n* **1** the most accurate expression of a time that a computer is able to produce **2** the time taken (1/30 000 second) by the human eye to register consciously an image before it

microtome (ˈmaɪkrəʊˌtəʊm) *n* an instrument

used for cutting thin sections, esp of biological material, for microscopical examination

microtomy (maɪˈkrɒtəmɪ) *n, pl* -mies the cutting of sections with a microtome > **microtomic** (ˌmaɪkrəʊˈtɒmɪk) *or* ˌmicroˈtomical *adj* > miˈcrotomist *n*

microtone (ˈmaɪkrəʊˌtəʊn) *n* any musical interval smaller than a semitone > ˌmicroˈtonal *adj* > ˌmicroˈtonality *n* > ˌmicroˈtonally *adv*

microtubule (ˌmaɪkrəʊˈtjuːbjuːl) *n biology* a tubular aggregate of protein subunits that forms structures, such as the mitotic spindle or the cilia of animal cells or of protozoans, in which the protein interacts with other proteins to generate various cellular movements

microvillus (ˌmaɪkrəʊˈvɪləs) *n, pl* -li (-laɪ) *physiol* a thin protuberance present in great abundance at the surface of some epithelial cells, notably in the gut, thus increasing the surface area available for absorption

microwave (ˈmaɪkrəʊˌweɪv) *n* **1 a** electromagnetic radiation in the wavelength range 0.3 to 0.001 metres: used in radar, cooking, etc **b** (*as modifier*): *microwave generator* **2** short for **microwave oven** ▷ *vb* (*tr*) **3** to cook in a microwave oven

microwave background *n* a background of microwave electromagnetic radiation with a black-body spectrum discovered in 1965, understood to be the thermal remnant of the big bang with which the universe began

microwave detector *n* a device for recording the speed of a motorist

microwave oven *n* an oven in which food is cooked by microwaves. Often shortened to: **micro, microwave**

microwave spectroscopy *n* a type of spectroscopy in which information is obtained on the structure and chemical bonding of molecules and crystals by measurements of the wavelengths of microwaves emitted or absorbed by the sample > **microwave spectroscope** *n*

microwriter (ˈmaɪkrəʊˌraɪtə) *n* a small device with six keys for creating text that can be printed or displayed on a visual display unit

micrurgy (ˈmaɪkrɜːdʒɪ) *n* **1** *biology* the manipulation and examination of single cells under a microscope **2** dissection under a microscope [C20 from MICRO- + Greek -*ourgia* work]

micturate (ˈmɪktjʊˌreɪt) *vb* (*intr*) a less common word for **urinate** [C19 from Latin *micturīre* to desire to urinate, from *mingere* to urinate] > **micturition** (ˌmɪktjʊˈrɪʃən) *n*

mid¹ (mɪd) *adj* **1** *phonetics* of, relating to, or denoting a vowel whose articulation lies approximately halfway between high and low, such as *e* in English *bet* ▷ *n* **2** an archaic word for **middle** [C12 *midre* (inflected form of *midd*, unattested); related to Old Norse *mithr*, Gothic *midjis*]

mid² *or* **'mid** (mɪd) *prep* a poetic word for **amid**

mid. *abbreviation for* middle

Mid. *abbreviation for* Midshipman

mid- *combining form* indicating a middle part, point, time, or position: *midday; mid-April; mid-Victorian* [Old English; see MIDDLE, MID¹]

midair (ˌmɪdˈɛə) *n* **a** some point above ground level, in the air **b** (*as modifier*): *a midair collision of aircraft*

Midas (ˈmaɪdəs) *n* **1** *Greek legend* a king of Phrygia given the power by Dionysus of turning everything he touched to gold **2** the Midas touch ability to make money

MIDAS (ˈmaɪdəs) *n acronym for* Missile Defence Alarm System

mid-Atlantic *adj* characterized by a blend of British and American styles, elements, etc: *a disc jockey's mid-Atlantic accent*

midbrain (ˈmɪdˌbreɪn) *n* the nontechnical name for **mesencephalon**

midday (ˈmɪdˌdeɪ) *n* **a** the middle of the day; noon **b** (*as modifier*): *a midday meal*

Middelburg (ˈmɪdəlˌbɜːg; *Dutch* ˈmɪdəlbyrx) *n* a city in the SW Netherlands, capital of Zeeland province, on Walcheren Island: an important trading centre in the Middle Ages and member of the Hanseatic League; 12th-century abbey; market town. Pop: 46 000 (2003 est)

middelmannetjie (ˌmɪdəlˈmænɪkɪ) *n* a continuous hump between wheel ruts on a dirt road [from Afrikaans, literally: little man in the middle]

midden (ˈmɪdən) *n* **1 a** *archaic or dialect* a dunghill or pile of refuse **b** *dialect* a dustbin **c** *Northern English dialect* an earth closet **2** See **kitchen midden** [C14 from Scandinavian; compare Danish *mödding* from *mög* MUCK + *dynge* pile]

middie (ˈmɪdɪ) *n Austral* a glass or bottle containing 285ml of beer

middle (ˈmɪdəl) *adj* **1** equally distant from the ends or periphery of something; central **2** intermediate in status, situation, etc **3** located between the early and late parts of a series, time sequence, etc **4** not extreme, esp in size; medium **5** (esp in Greek and Sanskrit grammar) denoting a voice of verbs expressing reciprocal or reflexive action. Compare **active** (sense 5), **passive** (sense 5) **6** (*usually capital*) (of a language) intermediate between the earliest and the modern forms: *Middle English* ▷ *n* **7** an area or point equal in distance from the ends or periphery or in time between the early and late parts **8** an intermediate part or section, such as the waist **9** *grammar* the middle voice **10** *logic* See **middle term 11** the ground between rows of growing plants **12** a discursive article in a journal, placed between the leading articles and the book reviews ▷ *vb* (*tr*) **13** to place in the middle **14** *nautical* to fold in two **15** *football* to return (the ball) from the wing to midfield **16** *cricket* to hit (the ball) with the middle of the bat [Old English *middel*; compare Old Frisian *middel*, Dutch *middel*, German *mittel*]

middle age *n* the period of life between youth and old age, usually (in man) considered to occur approximately between the ages of 40 and 60

middle-aged *adj* of, relating to, or being in the time in a person's life between youth and old age

Middle Ages *n the European history* **1** (broadly) the period from the end of classical antiquity (or the deposition of the last W Roman emperor in 476 AD) to the Italian Renaissance (or the fall of Constantinople in 1453) **2** (narrowly) the period from about 1000 AD to the 15th century. Compare **Dark Ages**

middle-age spread *or* **middle-aged spread** *n* the fat that appears round many people's waist during middle age

Middle America *n* **1** the territories between the US and South America: Mexico, Central America, Panama, and the Greater and Lesser Antilles **2** the US middle class, esp those groups that are politically conservative

Middle American *adj* **1** of or relating to the territories between the US and South America or their inhabitants **2** of or relating to the US middle class, esp those groups that are politically conservative ▷ *n* **3** a native or inhabitant of Middle America **4** a member of the US middle class

Middle Atlantic States *or* **Middle States** *pl n* the states of New York, Pennsylvania, and New Jersey

middlebreaker (ˈmɪdəlˌbreɪkə) *or* **middlebuster** *n* a type of plough that cuts a furrow with the soil heaped on each side, often used for sowing. Also called: **lister**

middlebrow (ˈmɪdəlˌbraʊ) *disparaging* ▷ *n* **1** a person with conventional tastes and limited cultural appreciation ▷ *adj* *also* **middlebrowed 2** of or appealing to middlebrows: *middlebrow culture* > ˈmiddleˌbrowism *n*

middle C *n music* the note graphically represented on the first ledger line below the treble staff or the first ledger line above the bass staff and corresponding in pitch to an internationally standardized fundamental frequency of 261.63 hertz

middle class *n* **1** Also called: **bourgeoisie** a social stratum that is not clearly defined but is positioned between the lower and upper classes. It consists of businessmen, professional people, etc, along with their families, and is marked by bourgeois values. Compare **lower class, upper class, working class** ▷ *adj* **middle-class 2** of, relating to, or characteristic of the middle class

middle common room *n* (in certain universities and colleges) a common room for the use of postgraduate students. Compare **junior common room, senior common room**

Middle Congo *n* one of the four territories of former French Equatorial Africa, in W central Africa: became an autonomous member of the French Community, as the Republic of the Congo, in 1958

middle-distance *adj* **1** *athletics* relating to or denoting races of a length between the sprints and the distance events, esp the 800 metres and the 1500 metres ▷ *n* **middle distance 2** Also called: **middle ground** part of a painting, esp a landscape between the foreground and far distance

Middle Dutch *n* the Dutch language from about 1100 to about 1500. Abbreviation: **MD**

middle ear *n* the sound-conducting part of the ear, containing the malleus, incus, and stapes

Middle East *n* **1** (loosely) the area around the E Mediterranean, esp Israel and the Arab countries from Turkey to North Africa and eastwards to Iran **2** (formerly) the area extending from the Tigris and Euphrates to Myanmar

Middle Eastern *adj* of or relating to the Middle East or its inhabitants

middle eight *n* the third contrasting eight-bar section of a 32-bar pop song

Middle England *n* a characterization of a predominantly middle-class, middle-income section of British society living mainly in suburban and rural England

Middle English *n* the English language from about 1100 to about 1450: main dialects are Kentish, Southwestern (West Saxon), East Midland (which replaced West Saxon as the chief literary form and developed into Modern English), West Midland, and Northern (from which the Scots of Lowland Scotland and other modern dialects developed). Compare **Old English, Modern English** Abbreviation: **ME**

middle game *n* *chess* the central phase between the opening and the endgame

Middle Greek *n* another name for **Medieval Greek**

middle ground *n* **1** another term for **middle distance 2** a position of compromise between two opposing views, parties, etc

Middle High German *n* High German from about 1200 to about 1500. Abbreviation: **MHG**

Middle Irish *n* Irish Gaelic from about 1100 to about 1500

Middle Kingdom *n* **1** a period of Egyptian history extending from the late 11th to the 13th dynasty (?2040–?1670 BC) **2 a** the former Chinese empire (from the belief that it lay at the centre of the earth) **b** the original 18 provinces of China; China proper

Middle Low German *n* Low German from about 1200 to about 1500. Abbreviation: **MLG**

middleman ('mɪdəlˌmæn) *n*, *pl* -men **1** an independent trader engaged in the distribution of goods from producer to consumer **2** an intermediary **3** *theatre* the interlocutor in minstrel shows

middle management *n* a level of management in an organization or business consisting of executives or senior supervisory staff in charge of the detailed running of an organization or business and reporting to top management. Compare **top management.** ▷ **middle manager** *n*

middlemost ('mɪdəlˌməʊst) *adj* another word for **midmost**

middle name *n* **1** a name between a person's first name and surname **2** a characteristic quality for which a person is known: *caution is my middle name*

middle-of-the-road *adj* **1** not extreme, esp in political views; moderate **2** of, denoting, or relating to popular music having a wide general appeal ▷ 'middle-of-the-'roader *n*

Middle Palaeolithic *n* **1** the period between the Lower and the Upper Palaeolithic, usually taken as equivalent to the Mousterian ▷ *adj* **2** of or relating to this period

middle passage *n* the *history* the journey across the Atlantic Ocean from the W coast of Africa to the Caribbean: the longest part of the journey of the slave ships sailing to the Caribbean or the Americas

Middle Persian *n* the classical form of modern Persian, spoken from about 300 AD to about 900. See also **Pahlavi²**

Middlesbrough ('mɪdəlzbrə) *n* **1** an industrial town in NE England, in Middlesbrough unitary authority, North Yorkshire: on the Tees estuary; university (1992). Pop: 142 691 (2001) **2** a unitary authority in NE England, in North Yorkshire: formerly (1974–96) part of Cleveland county. Pop: 139 000 (2003 est). Area: 54 sq km (21 sq miles)

middle school *n* (in England and Wales) a school for children aged between 8 or 9 and 12 or 13. Compare **first school**

Middlesex ('mɪdəlˌsɛks) *n* a former county of SE England: became mostly part of N and W Greater London in 1965. Abbreviation: **Middx**

Middle States *pl n* another name for the **Middle Atlantic States**

Middle Temple *n* (in England) one of the four legal societies in London which together form the Inns of Court

middle term *n* *logic* the term that appears in both the major and minor premises of a syllogism, but not in the conclusion. Also called: **mean, middle**

Middleton ('mɪdəltən) *n* a town in NW England, in Rochdale Unitary Authority, Greater Manchester. Pop: 45 314 (2001)

middle watch *n* *nautical* the watch between midnight and 4 a.m

middleweight ('mɪdəlˌweɪt) *n* **1 a** a professional boxer weighing 154–160 pounds (70–72.5 kg) **b** an amateur boxer weighing 71–75 kg (157–165 pounds) **c** (*as modifier*): *a middleweight contest* **2** a wrestler in a similar weight category (usually 172–192 pounds (78–87 kg))

Middle West *n* another name for the **Midwest**

Middle Western *adj* another name for **Midwestern**

Middle Westerner *n* another name for **Midwesterner**

middle white *n* (*often capitals*) a breed of medium-sized white pig commonly kept for pork and bacon, and for fattening

middle youth *n* the period of life between about 30 and 50

middling ('mɪdlɪŋ) *adj* **1** mediocre in quality, size, etc; neither good nor bad, esp in health (often in the phrase **fair to middling**) ▷ *adv* **2** *informal* moderately: *middling well* [C15 (northern English and Scottish): from MID¹ + -LING²] ▷ 'middlingly *adv*

middlings ('mɪdlɪŋz) *pl n* **1** the poorer or coarser part of flour or other products **2** commodities of intermediate grade, quality, size, or price **3** *chiefly US* the part of a pig between the ham and shoulder

Middx *abbreviation for* Middlesex

middy ('mɪdɪ) *n*, *pl* -dies **1** *informal* See **midshipman** (sense 1) **2** See **middy blouse 3** *Austral* a middle-sized glass of beer

middy blouse *n* a blouse with a sailor collar, worn by women and children, esp formerly

Mideast (ˌmɪd'iːst) *n* *chiefly US* another name for **Middle East**

midfield (ˌmɪd'fiːld) *n* *soccer* **a** the general area between the two opposing defences **b** (*as modifier*): *a midfield player*

mid-flight *adj*, *adv* **1** during a flight; whilst airborne: *a mid-flight celebration; doors opening mid-flight* ▷ *n* **2** in mid-flight during a flight; whilst airborne

Midgard ('mɪdgɑːd), **Midgarth** ('mɪdgɑːθ) *or* **Mithgarthr** ('mɪðgɑːθə) *n* *Norse myth* the dwelling place of mankind, formed from the body of the giant Ymir and linked by the bridge Bifrost to Asgard, home of the gods [C19 from Old Norse *mithgarthr*; see MID¹, YARD²]

midge (mɪdʒ) *n* **1** any fragile mosquito-like dipterous insect of the family *Chironomidae*, occurring in dancing swarms, esp near water **2** any similar or related insect, such as the biting midge and gall midge **3** a small or diminutive person or animal [Old English *mycge*; compare Old High German *mucca*, Danish *myg*] ▷ 'midgy *adj*

midget ('mɪdʒɪt) *n* **1** a dwarf whose skeleton and features are of normal proportions **2 a** something small of its kind **b** (*as modifier*): *a midget car* [C19 from MIDGE + -ET]

midgie ('mɪdʒɪ) *n* *Scot, Austral, and NZ informal* a small winged biting insect such as the midge or sandfly

Mid Glamorgan *n* a former county of S Wales, formed in 1974 from parts of Breconshire, Glamorgan, and Monmouthshire: replaced in 1996 by the county boroughs of Bridgend, Rhondda Cynon Taff, Merthyr Tydfil, and part of Caerphilly

midgut ('mɪdˌgʌt) *n* **1** the middle part of the digestive tract of vertebrates, including the small intestine **2** the middle part of the digestive tract of arthropods ▷ See also **foregut, hindgut**

Midheaven ('mɪdˌhɛvən) *n* *astrology* **1** the point on the ecliptic, measured in degrees, that crosses the meridian of a particular place at a particular time. On a person's birth chart it relates to the time of birth. Abbreviation: **MC 2** the sign of the zodiac containing this point [C16 initials MC represent Latin *medium caeli* middle of the sky]

midi ('mɪdɪ) *adj* **a** (of a skirt, coat, etc) reaching to below the knee or midcalf **b** (*as noun*): *she wore her new midi* [C20 from MID-; on the model of MAXI and MINI]

Midi (French midi) *n* **1** the south of France **2 Canal du** a canal in S France, extending from the River Garonne at Toulouse to the Mediterranean at Sète and providing a link between the Mediterranean and Atlantic coasts: built between 1666 and 1681. Length: 181 km (150 miles)

MIDI ('mɪdɪ) *n* (*modifier*) a generally accepted specification for the external control of electronic musical instruments: *a MIDI synthesizer; a MIDI system* [C20 from m(usical) i(nstrument) d(igital) i(nterface)]

Midian ('mɪdɪən) *n* *Old Testament* **1** a son of Abraham (Genesis 25:1–2) **2** a nomadic nation claiming descent from him ▷ 'Midian,ite *n*, *adj* ▷ 'Midian,itish *adj*

midinette (ˌmɪdɪ'nɛt; *French* midinɛt) *n*, *pl* -nettes (-'nɛts; *French* -nɛt) a Parisian seamstress or salesgirl in a clothes shop [C20 from French, from *midi* noon + *dinette* light meal, since the girls had time for no more than a snack at midday]

Midi-Pyrénées (*French* midipirene) *n* a region of SW France: consists of N slopes of the Pyrenees in the south, a fertile lowland area in the west crossed by the River Garonne, and the edge of the Massif Central in the north and east

midiron ('mɪdˌaɪən) *n* *golf* a club, usually a No. 5, 6, or 7 iron, used for medium-length approach shots

midi system *n* a complete set of hi-fi sound equipment designed as a single unit that is more compact than the standard equipment

midland ('mɪdlənd) *n* **a** the central or inland part of a country **b** (*as modifier*): *a midland region*

Midlander ('mɪdləndə) *n* a native or inhabitant of the Midlands of England

m

Midlands ('mɪdləndz) *n* (*functioning as plural or singular*) **the**. the central counties of England, including Warwickshire, Northamptonshire, Leicestershire, Nottinghamshire, Derbyshire, Staffordshire, the former West Midlands metropolitan county, and Worcestershire: characterized by manufacturing industries

midlife crisis ('mɪd,laɪf) *n* a crisis that may be experienced in middle age involving frustration, panic, and feelings of pointlessness, sometimes resulting in radical and often ill-advised changes of lifestyle

mid-list *n* **a** a section of a publisher's list containing those books that are not bestsellers **b** (*as modifier*): *a mid-list writer*. See also **backlist**, **front list**

Midlothian (mɪd'ləʊðɪən) *n* a council area of SE central Scotland: the historical county of Midlothian (including Edinburgh) became part of Lothian region in 1975; separate unitary authorities were created for Midlothian and City of Edinburgh in 1996; mainly agricultural. Administrative centre: Dalkeith. Pop: 79 710 (2003 est). Area: 356 sq km (137 sq miles)

midmost ('mɪd,məʊst) *adj, adv* in the middle or midst

midnight ('mɪd,naɪt) *n* **1 a** the middle of the night; 12 o'clock at night **b** (*as modifier*): *the midnight hour* **2 burn the midnight oil** to work or study late into the night > '**mid**,**nightly** *adj, adv*

midnight blue *n* **a** a very dark blue colour; bluish black **b** (*as adjective*): *a midnight-blue suit*

midnight sun *n* the sun visible at midnight during local summer inside the Arctic and Antarctic circles

mid-off *n* *cricket* **1** the fielding position on the off side closest to the bowler **2** a fielder in this position

mid-on *n* *cricket* **1** the fielding position on the on side closest to the bowler **2** a fielder in this position

midpoint ('mɪd,pɔɪnt) *n* **1** the point on a line that is at an equal distance from either end **2** a point in time halfway between the beginning and end of an event

midrash ('mɪdræʃ; *Hebrew* mi'draʃ) *n, pl* **midrashim** (mɪ'drɔʃɪm; *Hebrew* midra'ʃim) *Judaism* **1** a homily on a scriptural passage derived by traditional Jewish exegetical methods and consisting usually of embellishment of the scriptural narrative **2** one of a number of collections of such homilies composed between 400 and 1200 AD [C17 from Hebrew: commentary, from *darash* to search] > **midrashic** (mɪd'ræʃɪk) *adj*

midrib ('mɪd,rɪb) *n* the main vein of a leaf, running down the centre of the blade

midriff ('mɪdrɪf) *n* **1 a** the middle part of the human body, esp between waist and bust **b** (*as modifier*): *midriff bulge* (sense 1) **2** *anatomy* another name for the **diaphragm** (sense 1) **3** the part of a woman's garment covering the midriff **4** *US* a woman's garment which exposes the midriff [Old English *midhrif*, from MID[1] + *hrif* belly]

midsection ('mɪd,sɛkʃən) *n* **1** the middle of something **2** the middle region of the human body; midriff

midship ('mɪdʃɪp) *nautical* ▷ *adj* **1** in, of, or relating to the middle of a vessel ▷ *n* **2** the middle of a vessel

midshipman ('mɪdʃɪpmən) *n, pl* -**men** **1** a probationary rank held by young naval officers under training, or an officer holding such a rank **2** any of several American toadfishes of the genus *Porichthys*, having small light-producing organs on the undersurface of their bodies

midships ('mɪdʃɪps) *adv, adj* *nautical* See **amidships**

midsole (,mɪd'səʊl) *n* a layer between the inner and the outer sole of a shoe, contoured for absorbing shock

midst[1] (mɪdst) *n* **1 in the midst of** surrounded or enveloped by; at a point during, esp a climactic one **2 in our midst** among us **3** *archaic* the centre

[C14 back formation from *amiddes* AMID]

midst[2] (mɪdst) *prep poetic* See **amid**

midstream ('mɪd,striːm) *n* **1** the middle of a stream or river **2** the middle of a process or action: *they tried to change the rules in midstream* ▷ *adv, adj* **3** in or towards the middle of a stream or river: *moored midstream*

midsummer ('mɪd'sʌmə) *n* **1 a** the middle or height of the summer **b** (*as modifier*): *a midsummer carnival* **2** another name for **summer solstice**

midsummer madness *n* foolish or extravagant behaviour, supposed to occur during the summer

midsummer-men *n* (*functioning as singular or plural*) another name for **rose-root**

Midsummer's Day or **Midsummer Day** *n* June 24, the feast of St John the Baptist; in England, Ireland, and Wales, one of the four quarter days. See also **summer solstice**

midterm ('mɪd'tɜːm) *n* **1 a** the middle of a term in a school, university, etc **b** (*as modifier*): *midterm exam* **2** *US politics* **a** the middle of a term of office, esp of a presidential term, when congressional and local elections are held **b** (*as modifier*): *midterm elections* **3 a** the middle of the gestation period **b** (*as modifier*): *midterm checkup*. See **term** (sense 6)

midtown ('mɪd,taʊn) *n* *US and Eastern Canadian* the centre of a town. See also **downtown**, **uptown**

mid-Victorian *adj* **1** *Brit history* of or relating to the middle period of the reign of Queen Victoria (1837–1901) ▷ *n* **2** a person of the mid-Victorian era

midway ('mɪd,weɪ) *adj, adv* **1** in or at the middle of the distance; halfway ▷ *n* **2** *US and Canadian* a place in a fair, carnival, etc, where sideshows are located **3** *obsolete* a middle place, way, etc

Midway Islands *pl n* an atoll in the central Pacific, about 2100 km (1300 miles) northwest of Honolulu: annexed by the US in 1867: scene of a decisive battle (June, 1942), in which the US combined fleets destroyed Japan's carrier fleet. Pop: 30 (2004 est). Area: 5 sq km (2 sq miles)

midweek ('mɪd'wiːk) *n* **a** the middle of the week **b** (*as modifier*): *a midweek holiday* > ,**mid'weekly** *adj*

Midwest ('mɪd'wɛst) or **Middle West** *n* the N central part of the US; the region consisting of the states from Ohio westwards that border on the Great Lakes, often extended to include the upper Mississippi and Missouri valleys

Midwestern ('mɪd'wɛstən) or **Middle Western** *adj* of or relating to the Midwest of the US or its inhabitants

Midwesterner ('mɪd'wɛstənə) or **Middle Westerner** *n* a native or inhabitant of the Midwest of the US

mid-wicket *n* *cricket* **1** the fielding position on the on side, approximately midway between square leg and mid-on **2** a fielder in this position

midwife ('mɪd,waɪf) *n, pl* -**wives** (-,waɪvz) a person qualified to deliver babies and to care for women before, during, and after childbirth [C14 from Old English *mid* with + *wif* woman]

midwifery ('mɪd,wɪfərɪ) *n* the art or practice of a midwife; obstetrics

midwife toad *n* a European toad, *Alytes obstetricans*, the male of which carries the fertilized eggs on its hind legs until they hatch: family *Discoglossidae*

midwinter ('mɪd'wɪntə) *n* **1 a** the middle or depth of the winter **b** (*as modifier*): *a midwinter festival* **2** another name for **winter solstice**

midyear ('mɪd'jɪə) *n* **a** the middle of the year **b** (*as modifier*): *a midyear examination*

mielie ('miːlɪ) *n* a variant of **mealie**

mien (miːn) *n* *literary* a person's manner, bearing, or appearance, expressing personality or mood: *a noble mien* [C16 probably variant of obsolete *demean* appearance; related to French *mine* aspect]

Mieres (*Spanish* 'mjeres) *n* a city in N Spain, south of Oviedo: steel and chemical industries; iron and coal mines. Pop: 47 618 (2003 est)

mifepristone (mɪ'fɛprɪ,stəʊn) *n* an antiprogestogenic steroid, used in the medical termination of pregnancy. Formula: $C_{29}H_{35}NO_2$ [C20 from *amino*phenol + *propyne* + *oestradiol* + -ONE]

miff (mɪf) *informal* ▷ *vb* **1** to take offence or offend ▷ *n* **2** a petulant mood **3** a petty quarrel [C17 perhaps an imitative expression of bad temper]

miffy ('mɪfɪ) *adj* -**fier**, -**fiest** *informal* easily upset; oversensitive > '**miffily** *adv* > '**miffiness** *n*

MiG (mɪg) *n* any of various types of Russian and former Soviet fighter aircraft [from *Mi(koyan)* and *G(urevich)*, names of designers]

might[1] (maɪt) *vb* (takes an implied infinitive or an infinitive without *to*) used as an auxiliary **1** making the past tense or subjunctive mood of **may**[1] *he might have come last night* **2** (often foll by *well*) expressing theoretical possibility: *he might well come*. In this sense *might* looks to the future and functions as a weak form of *may*. See **may**[1] (sense 2)

■ USAGE See at **may**[1]

might[2] (maɪt) *n* **1** power, force, or vigour, esp of a great or supreme kind **2** physical strength **3** (**with**) **might and main** See **main**[1] (sense 8) [Old English *miht*; compare Old High German *maht*, Dutch *macht*]

mightily ('maɪtɪlɪ) *adv* **1** to a great extent, amount, or degree **2** with might; powerfully or vigorously

mighty ('maɪtɪ) *adj* **mightier**, **mightiest** **1 a** having or indicating might; powerful or strong **b** (*as collective noun*; preceded by *the*): *the mighty* **2** very large; vast **3** very great in extent, importance, etc ▷ *adv* **4** *informal, chiefly US and Canadian* (intensifier): *he was mighty tired* > '**mightiness** *n*

migmatite ('mɪgmə,taɪt) *n* a composite rock body containing two types of rock (esp igneous and metamorphic rock) that have interacted with each other but are nevertheless still distinguishable [C20 alteration of Swedish *migmatit*, from Greek *migma* mixture + -ITE[1]]

mignon ('mɪnjɒn; *French* miɲɔ̃) *adj* small and pretty; dainty [C16 from French, from Old French *mignot* dainty] > **mignonne** ('mɪnjɒn; *French* miɲɔn) *fem n*

mignonette (,mɪnjə'nɛt) *n* **1** any of various mainly Mediterranean plants of the resedaceous genus *Reseda*, such as *R. odorata* (**garden mignonette**), that have spikes of small greenish-white flowers with prominent anthers **2** a type of fine pillow lace ▷ *adj* **3** of a greyish-green colour; reseda [C18 from French, diminutive of MIGNON]

migraine ('miːgreɪn, 'maɪ-) *n* a throbbing headache usually affecting only one side of the head and commonly accompanied by nausea and visual disturbances [C18 (earlier form, C14 *mygrame* MEGRIM[1]): from French, from Late Latin *hēmicrānia* pain in half of the head, from Greek *hēmikrania*, from HEMI- + *kranion* CRANIUM] > '**migrainous** *adj*

migrant ('maɪgrənt) *n* **1** a person or animal that moves from one region, place, or country to another **2** an itinerant agricultural worker who travels from one district to another **3** *chiefly Austral* **a** an immigrant, esp a recent one **b** (*as modifier*): *a migrant hostel* ▷ *adj* **4** moving from one region, place, or country to another; migratory [C17 from Latin *migrāre* to change one's abode]

migrate (maɪ'greɪt) *vb* (*intr*) **1** to go from one region, country, or place of abode to settle in another, esp in a foreign country **2** (of birds, fishes, etc) to journey between different areas at specific times of the year [C17 from Latin *migrāre* to change one's abode] > mi'**grator** *n*

migration (maɪ'greɪʃən) *n* **1** the act or an instance of migrating **2** a group of people, birds, etc, migrating in a body **3** *chem* a movement of atoms, ions, or molecules, such as the motion of ions in solution under the influence of electric fields > mi'**grational** *adj*

migratory ('maɪgrətərɪ, -trɪ) *adj* **1** of, relating to, or characterized by migration **2** nomadic; itinerant

MIG welding (mɪg) *n* metal inert gas welding: a method of welding in which the filler metal wire supplies the electric current to maintain the arc, which is shielded from the access of air by an inert gas, usually argon. Compare **TIG welding**

miha ('miːhɑː) *n, pl* **miha** NZ a young fern frond which has not yet opened [Māori]

mihi ('miːhɪ) NZ ▷ *n* **1** a Māori ceremonial greeting ▷ *vb* **2** (*tr*) to greet [Māori]

MIHL *abbreviation for* music-induced hearing loss; a condition that can afflict both rock and classical musicians in which loss of sensitivity to high notes can be followed by headaches and tinnitus

mihrab ('miːræb, -rəb) *n Islam* the niche in a mosque showing the direction of Mecca [from Arabic]

mikado (mɪ'kɑːdəʊ) *n, pl* **-dos** (*often capital*) *archaic* the Japanese emperor. Compare **tenno** [c18 from Japanese, from *mi-* honourable + *kado* gate]

mike (maɪk) *n informal* short for **microphone** ▷ See also **mike up**

Mike (maɪk) *n communications* a code word for the letter *m*

mike up *vb* (*tr, adv*) to supply with a microphone

Míkonos (*Greek* 'mikonos) *n* transliteration of the Modern Greek name for **Mykonos**

mikvah *or* **mikveh** (mik'vɑ, 'mikvə) *n Judaism* a pool used esp by women for ritual purification after their monthly period [from Hebrew]

mil (mɪl) *n* **1** a unit of length equal to one thousandth of an inch **2** an obsolete pharmaceutical unit of volume equal to one millilitre **3** a unit of angular measure, used in gunnery, equal to one sixty-four-hundredth of a circumference [c18 short for Latin *millēsimus* thousandth]

mil *an internet domain name for* a US military department

mil. *abbreviation for* **1** military **2** militia

milady *or* **miladi** (mɪ'leɪdɪ) *n, pl* **-dies** (formerly) a continental title used for an English gentlewoman

milage ('maɪlɪdʒ) *n* a variant spelling of **mileage**

Milan (mɪ'læn) *n* a city in N Italy, in central Lombardy: Italy's second largest city and chief financial and industrial centre; a centre of the Renaissance under the Visconti and Sforza families. Pop: 1 256 211 (2001). Italian name: **Milano** (mi'laːno)

Milanese (ˌmɪlə'niːz) *adj* **1** of or relating to Milan, its people, culture, etc **2** of a fine lightweight knitted fabric of silk, rayon, etc ▷ *n* **3** the Italian dialect spoken in Milan **4** (*pl* **-ese**) a native or inhabitant of Milan

Milazzo (*Italian* mi'lattso) *n* a port in NE Sicily: founded in the 8th century BC; scene of a battle (1860), in which Garibaldi defeated the Bourbon forces. Pop: 32 108 (2001). Ancient name: **Mylae** ('maɪliː)

milch (mɪltʃ) *n* **1** (*modifier*) (esp of cattle) yielding milk **2 milch cow** *informal* a source of easy income, esp a person [c13 from Old English *-milce* (in compounds); related to Old English *melcan* to milk]

milchik *or* **milchig** ('mɪlxɪk) *adj Judaism* containing or used in the preparation of milk products and so not to be used with meat products. Also called: **milky** Compare **fleishik** See also **kashruth** [Yiddish, from *milch* milk, ultimately from Old High German; compare MILCH; see also MILK]

mild (maɪld) *adj* **1** (of a taste, sensation, etc) not powerful or strong; bland: *a mild curry* **2** gentle or temperate in character, climate, behaviour, etc **3** not extreme; moderate: *a mild rebuke* **4** feeble; unassertive ▷ *n* **5** *Brit* draught beer, of darker colour than bitter and flavoured with fewer hops [Old English *milde*; compare Old Saxon *mildi*, Old Norse *mildr*] > **'mildly** *adv* > **'mildness** *n*

milden ('maɪldən) *vb* to make or become mild or milder

mildew ('mɪlˌdjuː) *n* **1** any of various diseases of plants that affect mainly the leaves and are caused by parasitic fungi. See also **downy mildew, powdery mildew 2** any fungus causing this kind of disease **3** another name for **mould**² ▷ *vb* **4** to affect or become affected with mildew [Old English *mildēaw*, from *mil-* honey (compare Latin *mel*, Greek *mēli*) + *dēaw* DEW] > **'mil,dewy** *adj*

mild steel *n* any of a class of strong tough steels that contain a low quantity of carbon (0.1–0.25 per cent)

mile (maɪl) *n* **1** Also called: **statute mile** a unit of length used in the UK, the US, and certain other countries, equal to 1760 yards. 1 mile is equivalent to 1.609 34 kilometres **2** See **nautical mile 3** See **Swedish mile 4** any of various units of length used at different times and places, esp the Roman mile, equivalent to 1620 yards **5** (*often plural*) *informal* a great distance: *he missed by a mile* **6** a race extending over a mile ▷ *adv* **7 miles** (*intensifier*): *he likes his new job miles better* [Old English *mīl*, from Latin *mīlia (passuum)* a thousand (paces)]

mileage *or* **milage** ('maɪlɪdʒ) *n* **1** a distance expressed in miles **2** the total number of miles that a motor vehicle has travelled **3** allowance for travelling expenses, esp as a fixed rate per mile **4** the number of miles a motor vehicle will travel on one gallon of fuel **5** *informal* use, benefit, or service provided by something: *this scheme has a lot of mileage left* **6** *informal* grounds, substance, or weight: *some mileage in the objectors' arguments*

mileometer *or* **milometer** (maɪ'lɒmɪtə) *n* a device that records the number of miles that a bicycle or motor vehicle has travelled. Usual US and Canadian name: **odometer**

milepost ('maɪlˌpəʊst) *n* **1** *horse racing* a marking post on a racecourse a mile before the finishing line **2** Also called (esp Brit): **milestone** *chiefly US and Canadian* a signpost that shows the distance in miles to or from a place

miler ('maɪlə) *n* an athlete, horse, etc, that runs or specializes in races of one mile

miles gloriosus Latin ('miːleɪs ˌglɔːrɪ'əʊsʊs) *n, pl milites gloriosi* ('miːlɪˌteɪs ˌglɔːrɪ'əʊsaɪ) a braggart soldier, esp as a stock figure in comedy [from the title of a comedy by Plautus]

Milesian¹ (maɪ'liːzɪən) *adj* **1** of or relating to Miletus ▷ *n* **2** an inhabitant of Miletus [via Latin from Greek *Milēsios*]

Milesian² (maɪ'liːzɪən) *facetious* ▷ *adj* **1** Irish ▷ *n* **2** an Irishman [c16 from *Milesius*, a fictitious king of Spain whose sons were supposed to have conquered Ireland]

milestone ('maɪlˌstəʊn) *n* **1** a stone pillar that shows the distance in miles to or from a place **2** a significant event in life, history, etc

Miletus (mɪ'liːtəs) *n* an ancient city on the W coast of Asia Minor: a major Ionian centre of trade and learning in the ancient world

milfoil ('mɪlˌfɔɪl) *n* **1** another name for **yarrow 2** See **water milfoil** [c13 from Old French, from Latin *milifolium*, from *mille* thousand + *folium* leaf]

Milford Haven ('mɪlfəd) *n* a port in SW Wales, in Pembrokeshire on **Milford Haven** (a large inlet of St George's Channel): major oil port. Pop: 12 830 (2001)

miliaria (ˌmɪlɪ'ɛərɪə) *n* an acute itching eruption of the skin, caused by blockage of the sweat glands. Nontechnical names: **heat rash, prickly heat** [c19 from New Latin, from Latin *miliārius* MILIARY]

miliary ('mɪljərɪ) *adj* **1** resembling or relating to millet seeds **2** (of a disease or skin eruption) characterized by small lesions resembling millet seeds: *miliary tuberculosis* [c17 from Latin *miliārius*, from *milium* MILLET]

miliary fever *n* an acute infectious fever characterized by profuse sweating and the formation on the skin of minute fluid-filled vesicles. Nontechnical name: **sweating sickness**

milieu ('miːljɜː; *French* miljø) *n, pl* **-lieux** (-ljɜː; -ljɜːz; *French* -ljø) *or* **-lieus** surroundings, location, or setting [c19 from French, from *mi-* MID¹ + *lieu* place]

militant ('mɪlɪtənt) *adj* **1** aggressive or vigorous, esp in the support of a cause: *a militant protest* **2** warring; engaged in warfare ▷ *n* **3** a militant person [c15 from Latin *mīlitāre* to be a soldier, from *mīles* soldier] > **'militancy** *or less commonly* **'militantness** *n* > **'militantly** *adv*

Militant ('mɪlɪtənt) *n* **1** short for **Militant Tendency 2** a member of Militant Tendency

Militant Tendency *n* a Trotskyist group formerly operating within the Labour Party

militaria (ˌmɪlɪ'tɛərɪə) *pl n* items of military interest, such as weapons, uniforms, medals, etc, esp from the past

militarism ('mɪlɪtəˌrɪzəm) *n* **1** military spirit; pursuit of military ideals **2** domination by the military in the formulation of policies, ideals, etc, esp on a political level **3** a policy of maintaining a strong military organization in aggressive preparedness for war

militarist ('mɪlɪtərɪst) *n* **1** a supporter of or believer in militarism **2** a devotee of military history, strategy, etc > **,milita'ristic** *adj* > **,milita'ristically** *adv*

militarize *or* **militarise** ('mɪlɪtəˌraɪz) *vb* (*tr*) **1** to convert to military use **2** to imbue with militarism > **,militari'zation** *or* **,militari'sation** *n*

military ('mɪlɪtərɪ, -trɪ) *adj* **1** of or relating to the armed forces (esp the army), warlike matters, etc **2** of, characteristic of, or about soldiers ▷ *n, pl* **-taries** *or* **-tary 3** (preceded by *the*) the armed services (esp the army) [c16 via French from Latin *mīlitāris*, from *mīles* soldier] > **'militarily** *adv*

military academy *n* a training establishment for young officer cadets entering the army

military engineering *n* the design, construction, etc, of military fortifications and communications

military honours *pl n* ceremonies performed by troops in honour of royalty, at the burial of an officer, etc

military-industrial complex *n* (in the US) the combined interests of the military establishment and industries involved in producing military material considered as exerting influence on US foreign and economic policy

military law *n* articles or regulations that apply to those belonging to the armed services. Compare **martial law**

military orchid *n* another name for **soldier orchid**

military pace *n* the pace of a single step in marching, taken to be 30 inches for quick time (120 paces to the minute) in both the British and US armies

military police *n* a corps within an army that performs police and disciplinary duties > **military policeman** *n*

militate ('mɪlɪˌteɪt) *vb* (*intr*; usually foll by *against* or *for*) (of facts, actions, etc) to have influence or effect: *the evidence militated against his release* [c17 from Latin *mīlitātus*, from *mīlitāre* to be a soldier] > **,mili'tation** *n*

USAGE See at **mitigate**

militia (mɪ'lɪʃə) *n* **1** a body of citizen (as opposed to professional) soldiers **2** an organization containing men enlisted for service in emergency only [c16 from Latin: soldiery, from *mīles* soldier]

militiaman (mɪ'lɪʃəmən) *n, pl* **-men** a man serving with the militia

milium ('mɪlɪəm) *n, pl* **-ia** (-ɪə) *pathol* a small whitish nodule on the skin, usually resulting from a clogged sebaceous gland [c19 from Latin: millet]

milk (mɪlk) *n* **1 a** a whitish nutritious fluid produced and secreted by the mammary glands of mature female mammals and used for feeding their young until weaned **b** the milk of cows, goats, or other animals used by man as a food or in the production of butter, cheese, etc. Related adjs: **lacteal, lactic 2** any similar fluid in plants,

m

such as the juice of a coconut **3** any of various milklike pharmaceutical preparations, such as milk of magnesia **4** *cry over spilt milk* to lament something that cannot be altered ▷ *vb* **5** to draw milk from the udder of (a cow, goat, or other animal) **6** (*intr*) (of cows, goats, or other animals) to yield milk **7** (*tr*) to draw off or tap in small quantities: *to milk the petty cash* **8** (*tr*) to extract as much money, help, etc, as possible from: *to milk a situation of its news value* **9** (*tr*) to extract venom, sap, etc, from [Old English *milc*; compare Old Saxon *miluk*, Old High German *miluh*, Old Norse *mjolk*]

milk-and-water *adj* (**milk and water** *when postpositive*) weak, feeble, or insipid

milk bar *n* **1** a snack bar at which milk drinks and light refreshments are served **2** (in Australia) a shop selling, in addition to milk, basic provisions and other items

milk cap *n* any of a large genus (*Lactarius*) of basidiomycetous fungi that are brittle to touch and exude a milky liquid when crushed. Some are funnel-shaped and some parasol-shaped, and most, except for *L. deliciosus*, are inedible

milk chocolate *n* chocolate that has been made with milk, having a creamy taste. Compare **plain chocolate**

milker ('mɪlkə) *n* **1** a cow, goat, etc, that yields milk, esp of a specified quality or amount: *a poor milker* **2** a person who milks **3** another name for **milking machine**

milk fever *n* **1** a fever that sometimes occurs shortly after childbirth, once thought to result from engorgement of the breasts with milk but now thought to be caused by infection **2** Also called: **parturient fever, eclampsia** *vet science* a disease of cows, goats, etc, occurring shortly after parturition, characterized by low blood calcium levels, paralysis, and loss of consciousness

milkfish ('mɪlk,fɪʃ) *n, pl* **-fish** *or* **-fishes** a large silvery tropical clupeoid food and game fish, *Chanos chanos*: family *Chanidae*

milk float *n Brit* a small motor vehicle used to deliver milk to houses

milk glass *n* opaque white glass, originally produced in imitation of Chinese porcelain

milking machine *n* an apparatus for milking cows

milking shed *n* a building in which a herd of cows is milked. Compare **milking parlour** (see **parlour** (sense 6))

milking stool *n* a low three-legged stool

milk lameness *n vet science* a disease of cattle that produce a high milk yield, characterized by hip lameness associated with a low concentration of phosphorus in the blood

milk leg *n* inflammation and thrombosis of the femoral vein following childbirth, characterized by painful swelling of the leg. Also called: **white leg** Technical name: **phlegmasia alba dolens**

milkmaid ('mɪlk,meɪd) *n* a girl or woman who milks cows

milkman ('mɪlkmən) *n, pl* **-men 1** a man who delivers or sells milk **2** a man who milks cows; dairyman

milko ('mɪlkəʊ) *n, pl* **milkos** *Austral* an informal name for **milkman** (sense 1)

milk of magnesia *n* a suspension of magnesium hydroxide in water, used as an antacid and laxative

milk pudding *n chiefly Brit* a hot or cold pudding made by boiling or baking milk with a grain, esp rice

milk punch *n* a spiced drink made of milk and spirits

milk round *n Brit* **1** a route along which a milkman regularly delivers milk **2 a** a regular series of visits, esp as made by recruitment officers from industry to universities **b** (*as modifier*): *milk-round recruitment*

milk run *n aeronautics informal* a routine and uneventful flight, esp on a dangerous mission [c20 referring to the regular and safe routine of a milkman's round]

milk shake *n* a cold frothy drink made of milk, flavouring, and sometimes ice cream, whisked or beaten together

milk sickness *n* **1** an acute disease characterized by weakness, vomiting, and constipation, caused by ingestion of the flesh or dairy products of cattle affected with trembles **2** *vet science* another name for **trembles** (sense 1)

milk snake *n* a nonvenomous brown-and-grey North American colubrid snake *Lampropeltis doliata*, related to the king snakes

milksop ('mɪlk,sɒp) *n* **1** a feeble or ineffectual man or youth **2** *Brit* a dish of bread soaked in warm milk, given esp to infants and invalids > 'milk,soppy *or* 'milk,sopping *adj* > 'milk,sopism *n*

milk stout *n Brit* a rich mellow stout lacking a bitter aftertaste [c20 so called because its ingredients include LACTOSE]

milk sugar *n* another name for **lactose**

milk thistle *n* another name for **sow thistle**

milktoast ('mɪlk,təʊst) *n* a variant spelling of **milquetoast**

milk tooth *n* any of the first teeth to erupt; a deciduous tooth. Also called: **baby tooth** See also **dentition**

milk vetch *n* any of various leguminous plants of the genus *Astragalus*, esp *A. glycyphyllos*, with clusters of purple, white, or yellowish flowers: formerly reputed to increase milk production in goats

milkweed ('mɪlk,wiːd) *n* **1** Also called: **silkweed** any plant of the mostly North American genus *Asclepias*, having milky sap and pointed pods that split open to release tufted seeds: family *Asclepiadaceae*. See also **asclepias 2** any of various other plants having milky sap **3** orange milkweed another name for **butterfly weed 4** another name for **monarch** (the butterfly)

milkwort ('mɪlk,wɜːt) *n* any of several plants of the genus *Polygala*, having small blue, pink, or white flowers with two petal-like sepals: family *Polygalaceae*. They were formerly believed to increase milk production in cows. See also **senega**

milky ('mɪlkɪ) *adj* **milkier, milkiest 1** resembling milk, esp in colour or cloudiness **2** of or containing milk **3** spiritless or spineless **4** *Judaism* another word for **milchik**. > 'milkily *adv* > 'milkiness *n*

Milky Way *n the* **1** the diffuse band of light stretching across the night sky that consists of millions of faint stars, nebulae, etc, within our Galaxy **2** another name for the **Galaxy** [c14 translation of Latin *via lactea*]

mill¹ (mɪl) *n* **1** a building in which grain is crushed and ground to make flour **2** a factory, esp one which processes raw materials: *a steel mill* **3** any of various processing or manufacturing machines, esp one that grinds, presses, or rolls **4** any of various small hand mills used for grinding pepper, salt, or coffee for domestic purposes. See also **coffee mill, pepper mill 5** a hard roller for impressing a design, esp in a textile-printing machine or in a machine for printing banknotes **6** a system, institution, etc, that influences people or things in the manner of a factory: *going through the educational mill* **7** an unpleasant experience; ordeal (esp in the phrases **go** *or* **be put through the mill**) **8** a fist fight **9** *run of the mill* ordinary or routine ▷ *vb* **10** (*tr*) to grind, press, or pulverize in or as if in a mill **11** (*tr*) to process or produce in or with a mill **12** to cut or roll (metal) with or as if with a milling machine **13** (*tr*) to groove or flute the edge of (a coin) **14** (*intr*; often foll by *about* or *around*) to move about in a confused manner **15** (*usually tr*) *now rare* to beat (chocolate, etc) **16** *archaic slang* to fight, esp with the fists [Old English *mylen* from Late Latin *molīna* a mill, from Latin *mola* mill, millstone, from *molere* to grind] > 'millable *adj*

mill² (mɪl) *n* a US and Canadian monetary unit used in calculations, esp for property taxes, equal to one thousandth of a dollar [c18 short for Latin *mīllēsimum* a thousandth (part)]

Millau Bridge (miyo) *n* a road bridge, the highest in the world, crossing the River Tarn in the Massif Central in SW France; designed by Sir Norman Foster and opened in 2004

millboard ('mɪl,bɔːd) *n* strong pasteboard, used esp in book covers [c18 changed from *milled board*]

milldam ('mɪl,dæm) *n* a dam built in a stream to raise the water level sufficiently for it to turn a millwheel

milled (mɪld) *adj* **1** (of coins, etc) having a grooved or fluted edge **2** made or treated in a mill

millefeuille *French* (milfœj) *n Brit* a small iced cake made of puff pastry filled with jam and cream. US name: **napoleon** [literally: thousand leaves]

millefiori (,mɪlɪˈfjɔːrɪ) *n* **a** decorative glassware in which coloured glass rods are fused and cut to create flower patterns: an ancient technique revived in Venice in the sixteenth century and in France and England in the nineteenth century **b** (*as modifier*): *a millefiori paperweight* [c19 from Italian: thousand flowers]

millefleurs (ˈmiːlˌflɜː) *n* a design of stylized floral patterns, used in textiles, tapestries, etc [French: thousand flowers]

millenarian (,mɪlɪˈnɛərɪən) *or* **millenary** *adj* **1** of or relating to a thousand or to a thousand years **2** of or relating to the millennium or millenarianism ▷ *n* **3** an adherent of millenarianism

millenarianism (,mɪlɪˈnɛərɪəˌnɪzəm) *n* **1** *Christianity* the belief in a future millennium following the Second Coming of Christ during which he will reign on earth in peace: based on Revelation 20:1–5 **2** any belief in a future period of ideal peace and happiness

millenary (mɪˈlɛnərɪ) *n, pl* **-naries 1** a sum or aggregate of one thousand, esp one thousand years **2** another word for a **millennium** ▷ *adj* ▷ *n* **3** another word for **millenarian** [c16 from Late Latin *millēnārius* containing a thousand, from Latin *mille* thousand]

millennium (mɪˈlɛnɪəm) *n, pl* **-nia** (-nɪə) *or* **-niums 1** *the Christianity* the period of a thousand years of Christ's awaited reign upon earth **2** a period or cycle of one thousand years **3** a time of peace and happiness, esp in the distant future **4** a thousandth anniversary [c17 from New Latin, from Latin *mille* thousand + *annus* year; for form, compare QUADRENNIUM] > mil'lennial *adj* > mil'lenniaist *n* > mil'lennially *adv*

Millennium Bridge *n* a pedestrian-crossing steel bridge over the River Thames linking the City of London at St Paul's Cathedral with the Tate Modern Gallery at Bankside: it has a span of 325 m (1056 ft)

millennium bug *n computing* any software problem arising from the change in date at the start of the 21st century

millepede ('mɪlɪ,piːd) *or* **milleped** ('mɪlɪ,pɛd) *n* variants of **millipede**

millepore ('mɪlɪ,pɔː) *n* any tropical colonial coral-like medusoid hydrozoan of the order *Milleporina*, esp of the genus *Millepora*, having a calcareous skeleton [c18 from New Latin, from Latin *mille* thousand + *porus* hole]

miller ('mɪlə) *n* **1** a person who keeps, operates, or works in a mill, esp a corn mill **2** another name for **milling machine 3** a person who operates a milling machine **4** any of various pale coloured or white moths, especially the medium-sized noctuid *Apatele leporina* **5** an edible basidiomycetous fungus, *Clitopilus prunulus*, with a white funnel-shaped cap and pinkish spores, often forming rings in grass

millerite ('mɪlə,raɪt) *n* a yellow mineral consisting of nickel sulphide in hexagonal crystalline form: a minor ore of nickel. Formula: NiS [c19 named after W. H. *Miller* (1801–80), English mineralogist]

miller's disease *n vet science* osteofibrosis of

horses due to low concentration of phosphorus in the blood caused by eating bran exclusively

miller's thumb *n* any of several small freshwater European fishes of the genus *Cottus*, esp *C. gobio*, having a flattened body: family *Cottidae* (bullheads, etc) [c15 from the alleged likeness of the fish's head to a thumb]

millesimal (mɪ'lɛsɪməl) *adj* **1 a** denoting a thousandth **b** (*as noun*): *a millesimal* **2** of, consisting of, or relating to a thousandth [c18 from Latin *millēsimus*]

millet ('mɪlɪt) *n* **1** a cereal grass, *Setaria italica*, cultivated for grain and animal fodder **2 a** an East Indian annual grass, *Panicum miliaceum*, cultivated for grain and forage, having pale round shiny seeds **b** the seed of this plant **3** any of various similar or related grasses, such as pearl millet and Indian millet. Related adj: **miliary** [c14 via Old French from Latin *milium*; related to Greek *melinē* millet]

milli- *prefix* denoting 10⁻³: *millimetre*. Symbol: m [from French, from Latin *mille* thousand, this meaning being maintained in words borrowed from Latin (*millipede*)]

milliard ('mɪlɪˌɑːd, 'mɪljɑːd) *n Brit* (no longer in technical use) a thousand million. US and Canadian equivalent: billion [c19 from French]

milliary ('mɪljərɪ) *adj* relating to or marking a distance equal to an ancient Roman mile of a thousand paces [c17 from Latin *milliārius* containing a thousand, from *mille* thousand]

millibar ('mɪlɪˌbɑː) *n* a cgs unit of atmospheric pressure equal to 10⁻³ bar, 100 newtons per square metre or 0.7500617 millimetre of mercury

millie ('mɪlɪ) *n Northern Irish informal derogatory* a young working-class woman who dresses in casual sports clothes [perhaps from *mill worker*]

millieme (miː'ljɛm) *n* a Tunisian monetary unit worth one thousandth of a dinar. Also called: **millime** [from French *millième* thousandth]

millième (miː'ljɛm) *n* an Egyptian monetary unit worth one thousandth of a lira

milligram or **milligramme** ('mɪlɪˌɡræm) *n* one thousandth of a gram. Symbol: mg [c19 from French]

millilitre or US **milliliter** ('mɪlɪˌliːtə) *n* one thousandth of a litre. Symbol: ml

millimetre or US **millimeter** ('mɪlɪˌmiːtə) *n* one thousandth of a metre. Symbol: mm

millimicron ('mɪlɪˌmaɪkrɒn) *n* an obsolete name for a nanometre; one millionth of a millimetre

milliner ('mɪlɪnə) *n* a person who makes or sells women's hats [c16 originally *Milaner*, a native of *Milan*, at that time famous for its fancy goods]

millinery ('mɪlɪnərɪ, -ɪnrɪ) *n* **1** hats, trimmings, etc, sold by a milliner **2** the business or shop of a milliner

milling ('mɪlɪŋ) *n* **1** the act or process of grinding, cutting, pressing, or crushing in a mill **2** the vertical grooves or fluting on the edge of a coin, etc **3** (in W North America) a method of halting a stampede of cattle by turning the leaders in a wide arc until the herd turns in upon itself in a tightening spiral

milling machine *n* a machine tool in which a horizontal arbor or vertical spindle rotates a cutting tool above a horizontal table, which is used to move a workpiece

million ('mɪljən) *n, pl* **-lions** or **-lion** **1** the cardinal number that is the product of 1000 multiplied by 1000. See also **number** (sense 1) **2** a numeral, 1 000 000, 10⁶, M, etc, representing this number **3** (*often plural*) *informal* an extremely large but unspecified number, quantity, or amount: *I have millions of things to do* ▷ *determiner* **4** (preceded by *a* or by a numeral) **a** amounting to a million: *a million light years away* **b** (*as pronoun*): *I can see a million under the microscope* **5** **gone a million** *Austral informal* done for; sunk ▷ Related prefix: **mega-** [c17 via Old French from early Italian *millione*, from *mille* thousand, from Latin]

millionaire or **millionnaire** (ˌmɪljə'nɛə) *n* a

person whose assets are worth at least a million of the standard monetary units of his country ▷ ˌmillion'airess or ˌmillion'nairess *fem n*

millionth ('mɪljənθ) *adj* **1 a** one of 1 000 000 approximately equal parts of something **b** (*as modifier*): *a millionth part* **2** one of 1 000 000 equal divisions of a particular scientific quantity. Related prefix: **micro-** **3** the fraction equal to one divided by 1 000 000 ▷ *adj* **4** (*usually prenominal*) **a** being the ordinal number of 1 000 000 in numbering or counting order, etc **b** (*as noun*): *the millionth to be manufactured*

millipede, millepede ('mɪlɪˌpiːd) or **milliped** *n* any terrestrial herbivorous arthropod of the class *Diplopoda*, having a cylindrical body made up of many segments, each of which bears two pairs of walking legs. See also **myriapod** [c17 from Latin, from *mille* thousand + *pēs* foot]

millisecond ('mɪlɪˌsɛkənd) *n* one thousandth of a second. Symbol: ms

millpond ('mɪlˌpɒnd) *n* **1** a pool formed by damming a stream to provide water to turn a millwheel **2** any expanse of calm water: *the sea was a millpond*

millrace ('mɪlˌreɪs) or **millrun** *n* **1** the current of water that turns a millwheel **2** the channel for this water

mill-rind *n* an iron support fitted across an upper millstone

millrun ('mɪlˌrʌn) *n* **1** another name for **millrace 2** *mining* **a** the process of milling an ore or rock in order to determine the content or quality of the mineral **b** the mineral so examined ▷ *adj* **millrun 3** *chiefly US* (of commodities) taken straight from the production line; unsorted as to quality

Mills bomb (mɪlz) *n* a type of high-explosive hand grenade [c20 named after Sir William *Mills* (1856–1932), English inventor]

millstone ('mɪlˌstəʊn) *n* **1** one of a pair of heavy flat disc-shaped stones that are rotated one against the other to grind grain **2** a heavy burden, such as a responsibility or obligation: *his debts were a millstone round his neck*

millstream ('mɪlˌstriːm) *n* a stream of water used to turn a millwheel

millwheel ('mɪlˌwiːl) *n* a wheel, esp a waterwheel, that drives a mill

millwork ('mɪlˌwɜːk) *n* work done in a mill

millwright ('mɪlˌraɪt) *n* a person who designs, builds, or repairs grain mills or mill machinery

milo ('maɪləʊ) *n, pl* **-los** any of various early-growing cultivated varieties of sorghum with heads of yellow or pinkish seeds resembling millet [c19 from Sotho *maili*]

milometer (maɪ'lɒmɪtə) *n* a variant spelling of **mileometer**

milord (mɪ'lɔːd) *n* (formerly) a continental title used for an English gentleman [c19 via French from English *my lord*]

Mílos ('miːlɒs) *n* transliteration of the Modern Greek name for **Melos**

milquetoast ('mɪlkˌtəʊst) *n US and Canadian* a meek, submissive, or timid person [c20 from Caspar *Milquetoast*, a cartoon character invented by H. T. Webster (1885–1952)]

milreis ('mɪlˌreɪs; *Portuguese* mil'rɛiʃ) *n, pl* **-reis** a former monetary unit of Portugal and Brazil, divided into 1000 reis [c16 from Portuguese, from *mil* thousand + *réis*, pl of *real* royal]

milt (mɪlt) *n* **1** the testis of a fish **2** the spermatozoa and seminal fluid produced by a fish **3** *rare* the spleen of certain animals, esp fowls and pigs ▷ *vb* **4** to fertilize (the roe of a female fish) with milt, esp artificially [Old English *milte* spleen; in the sense: fish sperm, probably from Middle Dutch *milte*]

milter ('mɪltə) *n* a male fish that is mature and ready to breed

Miltonic (mɪl'tɒnɪk) or **Miltonian** (mɪl'təʊnɪən) *adj* characteristic of or resembling the literary style of the English poet John Milton (1608–74), esp in being sublime and majestic

Milton Keynes ('mɪltən 'kiːnz) *n* **1** a new town in central England, in Milton Keynes unitary authority, N Buckinghamshire: founded in 1967: electronics, clothing, machinery; seat of the Open University. Pop: 215 700 (2003 est) **2** a unitary authority in central England, in Buckinghamshire. Pop: 184 506 (2001). Area: 310 sq km (119 sq miles)

Milton Work count *n bridge* a system of hand valuation in which aces count 4, kings 3, queens 2, and jacks 1 [c20 named after *Milton Work*, authority on auction bridge]

Milwaukee (mɪl'wɔːkiː) *n* a port in SE Wisconsin, on Lake Michigan: the largest city in the state; established as a trading post in the 18th century; an important industrial centre. Pop: 586 941 (2003 est)

Milwaukeean (mɪl'wɔːkɪən) *adj* **1** of or relating to Milwaukee or its inhabitants ▷ *n* **2** a native or inhabitant of Milwaukee

mim (mɪm) *adj dialect* prim, modest, or demure [c17 perhaps imitative of lip-pursing]

Mimas ('maɪməs, -mæs) *n* a satellite of the planet Saturn

mime (maɪm) *n* **1** the theatrical technique of expressing an idea or mood or portraying a character entirely by gesture and bodily movement without the use of words **2** Also called: **mime artist** a performer specializing in such a technique, esp a comic actor **3** a dramatic presentation using such a technique **4** (in the classical theatre) **a** a comic performance depending for effect largely on exaggerated gesture and physical action **b** an actor in such a performance ▷ *vb* **5** to express (an idea) in actions or gestures without speech **6** (of singers or musicians) to perform as if singing (a song) or playing (a piece of music) that is actually prerecorded [Old English *mīma*, from Latin *mīmus* mimic actor, from Greek *mimos* imitator] ▷ 'mimer *n*

MIME *computing abbreviation for* multipurpose internet mail extensions

Mimeograph ('mɪmɪəˌɡrɑːf, -ˌɡræf) *n* **1** *trademark* an office machine for printing multiple copies of text or line drawings from an inked drum to which a cut stencil is fixed **2** a copy produced by this machine ▷ *vb* **3** to print copies from (a prepared stencil) using this machine

mimesis (mɪ'miːsɪs) *n* **1** *art, literature* the imitative representation of nature or human behaviour **2 a** any disease that shows symptoms of another disease **b** a condition in a hysterical patient that mimics an organic disease **3** *biology* another name for **mimicry** (sense 2) **4** *rhetoric* representation of another person's alleged words in a speech [c16 from Greek, from *mimeisthai* to imitate]

mimetic (mɪ'mɛtɪk) *adj* **1** of, resembling, or relating to mimesis or imitation, as in art, etc **2** *biology* of or exhibiting mimicry ▷ mi'metically *adv*

mimetite ('mɪmɪˌtaɪt, 'maɪmɪ-) *n* a rare secondary mineral consisting of a chloride and arsenate of lead in the form of white or yellowish needle-like hexagonal crystals. Formula: Pb₅Cl(AsO₄)₃ [c19 from German, from Greek *mimētēs* imitator (of pyromorphite)]

mimic ('mɪmɪk) *vb* **-ics, -icking, -icked** (*tr*) **1** to imitate (a person, a manner, etc), esp for satirical effect; ape: *known mainly for its ability to mimic other singers* **2** to take on the appearance of; resemble closely: *certain flies mimic wasps* **3** to copy closely or in a servile manner ▷ *n* **4** a person or an animal, such as a parrot, that is clever at mimicking **5** an animal that displays mimicry ▷ *adj* **6** of, relating to, or using mimicry; imitative **7** simulated, make-believe, or mock [c16 from Latin *mīmicus*, from Greek *mimikos*, from *mimos* MIME] ▷ 'mimicker *n*

mimic panel *n* a panel simulating the geographical layout of a television studio, railway points system, traffic interchange, etc, in which small indicator lamps display the selected state of the lighting circuits, signalling, traffic lights, etc

mimicry ('mɪmɪkrɪ) *n, pl* **-ries** **1** the act or art of copying or imitating closely; mimicking **2** the resemblance shown by one animal species, esp an insect, to another, which protects it from predators

MIMinE *abbreviation for* Member of the Institute of Mining Engineers

miminy-piminy (,mɪmɪnɪ'pɪmɪnɪ) *adj* a variant of **niminy-piminy**

Mimir ('miːmɪə) *n Norse myth* a giant who guarded the well of wisdom near the roots of Yggdrasil

mimosa (mɪ'məʊsə, -zə) *n* **1** any tropical shrub or tree of the leguminous genus *Mimosa,* having ball-like clusters of yellow or pink flowers and compound leaves that are often sensitive to touch or light. See also **sensitive plant** **2** any similar or related tree [c18 from New Latin, probably from Latin *mīmus* MIME, because the plant's sensitivity to touch imitates the similar reaction of animals]

mimsy ('mɪmzɪ) *adj* **-sier, -siest** prim, underwhelming, and ineffectual [c19 a blend of MISERABLE and FLIMSY, coined by the English writer Lewis Carroll (1832–98), real name *Charles Lutwidge Dodgson*]

mimulus ('mɪmjʊləs) *n* See **monkey flower** [New Latin, from Greek *mimō* ape (from the shape of the corolla)]

MIMunE *abbreviation for* Member of the Institution of Municipal Engineers

min *symbol for* minim (liquid measure)

Min (mɪn) *n* any of the dialects or forms of Chinese spoken in Fukien province. Also called: **Fukien**

min. *abbreviation for* **1** minimum **2** minute(s)

Min. *abbreviation for* **1** Minister **2** Ministry

mina ('maɪnə) *n, pl* **-nae** (-niː) *or* **-nas** an ancient unit of weight and money, used in Asia Minor, equal to one sixtieth of a talent [c16 via Latin from Greek *mnā,* of Semitic origin; related to Hebrew *māneh* mina]

minacious (mɪ'neɪʃəs) *adj* threatening [c17 from Latin *minax,* from *minārī* to threaten] > **mi'naciously** *adv* > **minacity** (mɪ'næsɪtɪ) *n*

Mina Hassan Tani ('miːnə haː'saːn 'taːnɪ) *n* another name for **Kénitra**

minaret (,mɪnə'rɛt, 'mɪnə,rɛt) *n* **1** a slender tower of a mosque having one or more balconies from which the muezzin calls the faithful to prayer **2** any structure resembling this [c17 from French, from Turkish, from Arabic *manārat* lamp, from *nār* fire] > **,mina'reted** *adj*

Minas Basin ('maɪnəs) *n* a bay in E Canada, in central Nova Scotia: the NE arm of the Bay of Fundy, with which it is linked by **Minas Channel**

Minas Gerais (*Portuguese* 'minaʒ ʒə'raɪʒ) *n* an inland state of E Brazil: situated on the high plateau of the Brazilian Highlands; large reserves of iron ore and manganese. Capital: Belo Horizonte. Pop: 18 343 517 (2002). Area: 587 172 sq km (226 707 sq miles)

minatory ('mɪnətərɪ, -trɪ) *or* **minatorial** *adj* threatening or menacing [c16 from Late Latin *minātōrius,* from Latin *minārī* to threaten] > **'minatorily** *or* **,mina'torially** *adv*

mince (mɪns) *vb* **1** (*tr*) to chop, grind, or cut into very small pieces **2** (*tr*) to soften or moderate, esp for the sake of convention or politeness: *I didn't mince my words* **3** (*intr*) to walk or speak in an affected dainty manner ▷ *n* **4** *chiefly Brit* minced meat **5** *informal* nonsensical rubbish [c14 from Old French *mincier,* from Vulgar Latin *minūtiāre* (unattested), from Late Latin *minūtia* smallness; see MINUTIAE]

mincemeat ('mɪns,miːt) *n* **1** a mixture of dried fruit, spices, etc, used esp for filling pies **2** minced meat **3** **make mincemeat of** *informal* to defeat completely

mince pie *n* **1** a small round pastry tart filled with mincemeat **2** (*usually plural*) Cockney rhyming slang an eye

mincer (mɪnsə) *n* an appliance used to mince meat

Minch (mɪntʃ) *n* **the** a channel of the Atlantic divided into the **North Minch** between the mainland of Scotland and the Isle of Lewis, and the **Little Minch** between the Isle of Skye and Harris and North Uist

Mincha *Hebrew* (min'xɑː; *Yiddish* 'minxa) *n Judaism* the afternoon service

mincing ('mɪnsɪŋ) *adj* (of a person) affectedly elegant in gait, manner, or speech > **'mincingly** *adv*

mind (maɪnd) *n* **1** the human faculty to which are ascribed thought, feeling, etc; often regarded as an immaterial part of a person **2** intelligence or the intellect, esp as opposed to feelings or wishes **3** recollection or remembrance; memory: *it comes to mind* **4** the faculty of original or creative thought; imagination: *it's all in the mind* **5** a person considered as an intellectual being: *the great minds of the past* **6** opinion or sentiment: *we are of the same mind; to change one's mind; to have a mind of one's own; to know one's mind; to speak one's mind* **7** condition, state, or manner of feeling or thought: *no peace of mind; his state of mind* **8** an inclination, desire, or purpose: *I have a mind to go* **9** attention or thoughts: *keep your mind on your work* **10** a sound mental state; sanity (esp in the phrase **out of one's mind**) **11** intelligence, as opposed to material things: *the mind of the universe* **12** (in Cartesian philosophy) one of two basic modes of existence, the other being matter **13** **blow someone's mind** *slang* **a** to cause someone to have a psychedelic experience **b** to astound or surprise someone **14** **give (someone) a piece of one's mind** to criticize or censure (someone) frankly or vehemently **15** **in** *or* **of two minds** undecided; wavering: *he was in two minds about marriage* **16** **make up one's mind** to decide (something or to do something): *he made up his mind to go* **17** **on one's mind** in one's thoughts **18** **put (one) in mind of** to remind (one) of ▷ *vb* **19** (when *tr,* may take a clause as object) to take offence at: *do you mind if I smoke? I don't mind* **20** to pay attention to (something); heed; notice: *to mind one's own business* **21** (*tr;* takes a clause as object) to make certain; ensure: *mind you tell her* **22** to take care of; have charge of: *to mind the shop* **23** (when *tr,* may take a clause as object) to be cautious or careful about (something): *mind how you go; mind your step* **24** (*tr*) to obey (someone or something); heed: *mind your father!* **25** to be concerned (about); be troubled (about): *never mind your hat; never mind about your hat; never mind* **26** (*tr; passive;* takes an infinitive) to be intending or inclined (to do something): *clearly he was not minded to finish the story* **27** (*tr*) *Scot and English dialect* to remember: *do ye mind his name?* **28** (*tr*) *Scot* to remind: *that minds me of another story* **29** **mind you** an expression qualifying a previous statement: *Dogs are nice. Mind you, I don't like all dogs* ▷ Related adjectives: **mental, noetic, phrenic** ▷ See also **mind out** [Old English *gemynd* mind; related to Old High German *gimunt* memory]

Mindanao (,mɪndə'naʊ) *n* the second largest island of the Philippines, in the S part of the archipelago: mountainous and volcanic. Chief towns: Davao, Zamboanga. Pop: 13 626 338 (2000). Area: (including offshore islands) 94 631 sq km (36 537 sq miles)

mind-bending *adj informal* **1** very difficult to understand; complex **2** altering one's state of consciousness: *mind-bending drugs* **3** reaching the limit of credibility: *they offered a mind-bending salary* ▷ *n* **4** the process of brainwashing

mind-blowing *adj informal* producing euphoria; psychedelic

mind-body problem *n* the traditional philosophical problem concerning the nature of mind, body, and the relationship between them. See **dualism** (sense 2), **interactionism, parallelism** (sense 3), **monism** (sense 1), **idealism** (sense 3), **materialism** (sense 2), **identity theory, behaviourism** (sense 2)

mind-boggling *adj informal* astonishing; bewildering

minded ('maɪndɪd) *adj* **1** having a mind, inclination, intention, etc, as specified: *politically minded* **2** (in combination): *money-minded*

Mindel ('mɪndᵊl) *n* the second major Pleistocene glaciation of Alpine Europe. See also **Günz, Riss, Würm** [c20 named after the River *Mindel,* in Bavaria, Germany]

minder ('maɪndə) *n* **1** someone who looks after someone or something **2** short for **child minder** **3** *slang* an aide to someone in public life, esp a politician or political candidate, who keeps control of press and public relations **4** *slang* someone acting as a bodyguard, guard, or assistant, esp in the criminal underworld

mind-expanding *adj* (of a drug such as LSD) causing a sensation of heightened consciousness; psychedelic

mindfuck ('maɪnd,fʌk) *n taboo slang* the deliberate infliction of psychological damage

mindful ('maɪndfʊl) *adj* (usually *postpositive* and foll by *of*) keeping aware; heedful: *mindful of your duties* > **'mindfully** *adv* > **'mindfulness** *n*

mind games *pl n* actions or statements intended to undermine or mislead someone else, often to gain advantage for oneself: *she started playing mind games with me*

mindless ('maɪndlɪs) *adj* **1** stupid or careless **2** requiring little or no intellectual effort: *a mindless task* > **'mindlessly** *adv* > **'mindlessness** *n*

mind-numbing *adj* extremely boring and uninspiring > **'mind-,numbingly** *adv*

Mindoro (mɪn'dɔːrəʊ) *n* a mountainous island in the central Philippines, south of Luzon. Pop: 912 000 (1995 est). Area: 9736 sq km (3759 sq miles)

mind out *vb* (*intr, adverb*) *Brit* to be careful or pay attention

mind-reader *n* a person seemingly able to discern the thoughts of another > **'mind-,reading** *n*

mind-set *n* the ideas and attitudes with which a person approaches a situation, esp when these are seen as being difficult to alter

mind's eye *n* the visual memory or the imagination

mindshare ('maɪnd,ʃɛə) *n* the level of awareness in the minds of consumers that a particular product commands

mind-your-own-business *n* a Mediterranean urticaceous plant, *Helxine soleirolii,* with small dense leaves: used for cover

mine¹ (maɪn) *pron* **1** something or someone belonging to or associated with me: *mine is best* **2** **of mine** belonging to or associated with me ▷ *determiner* **3** (*preceding a vowel*) an archaic word for **my**: *mine eyes; mine host* [Old English *mīn;* compare Old High German, Old Norse *mīn,* Dutch *mijn*]

mine² (maɪn) *n* **1** a system of excavations made for the extraction of minerals, esp coal, ores, or precious stones **2** any deposit of ore or minerals **3** a lucrative source or abundant supply: *she was a mine of information* **4** a device containing an explosive designed to destroy ships, vehicles, or personnel, usually laid beneath the ground or in water **5** a tunnel or sap dug to undermine a fortification **6** a groove or tunnel made by certain insects, esp in a leaf ▷ *vb* **7** to dig into (the earth) for (minerals) **8** to make (a hole, tunnel, etc) by digging or boring **9** to place explosive mines in position below the surface of (the sea or land) **10** to undermine (a fortification) by digging mines or saps **11** another word for **undermine** [c13 from Old French *mine,* probably of Celtic origin; compare Irish *mein,* Welsh *mwyn* ore, mine] > **'minable** *or* **'mineable** *adj*

mine detector *n* an instrument designed to detect explosive mines > **mine detection** *n*

mine dump *n South African* a large mound of residue, esp from gold-mining operations

minefield ('maɪn,fiːld) *n* **1** an area of ground or water containing explosive mines **2** a subject, situation, etc, beset with hidden problems

minehunter ('maɪnˌhʌntə) *n* a naval vessel that searches for mines by electronic means

minelayer ('maɪnˌleɪə) *n* a warship or aircraft designed for the carrying and laying of mines

miner ('maɪnə) *n* **1** a person who works in a mine **2** Also called: **continuous miner** a large machine for the automatic extraction of minerals, esp coal, from a mine **3** any of various insects or insect larvae that bore into and feed on plant tissues. See also **leaf miner** **4** *Austral* any of several honey-eaters of the genus *Manorina*, esp *M. melanocephala* (**noisy miner**), of scrub regions

mineral ('mɪnərəl, 'mɪnrəl) *n* **1** any of a class of naturally occurring solid inorganic substances with a characteristic crystalline form and a homogeneous chemical composition **2** any inorganic matter **3** any substance obtained by mining, esp a metal ore **4** (*often plural*) *Brit* short for **mineral water** **5** *Brit* a soft drink containing carbonated water and flavourings. Usual US word: **soda** ▷ *adj* **6** of, relating to, containing, or resembling minerals [c15 from Medieval Latin *minerāle* (n), from *minerālis* (adj); related to *minera* mine, ore, of uncertain origin]

mineral. *abbreviation for* mineralogy *or* mineralogical

mineralize *or* **mineralise** ('mɪnərəˌlaɪz, 'mɪnrə-) *vb* (*tr*) **1 a** to impregnate (organic matter, water, etc) with a mineral substance **b** to convert (such matter) into a mineral; petrify **2** (of gases, vapours, etc, in magma) to transform (a metal) into an ore ▷ ˌminerali'zation *or* ˌminerali'sation *n*

mineralizer *or* **mineraliser** ('mɪnərəˌlaɪzə) *n* **1** any of various gases dissolved in magma that affect the crystallization of igneous rocks and the formation of minerals when the magma cools **2** an element, such as oxygen, that combines with a metal to form an ore

mineral jelly *n* another name for **petrolatum**

mineral kingdom *n* all nonliving material, esp rocks and minerals. Compare **animal kingdom, plant kingdom**

mineralocorticoid (ˌmɪnərələʊˈkɔːtɪˌkɔɪd) *n* any corticosteroid that controls electrolyte and water balance, esp by promoting retention of sodium by the kidney tubules

mineralogy (ˌmɪnəˈrælədʒɪ) *n* the branch of geology concerned with the study of minerals ▷ **mineralogical** (ˌmɪnərəˈlɒdʒɪkəl) *or* ˌmineral'ogic *adj* ▷ ˌmineral'ogically *adv* ▷ ˌmineral'ogist *n*

mineral oil *n* **1** *Brit* any oil of mineral origin, esp petroleum **2** *US and Canadian* a colourless almost tasteless oily liquid obtained by petroleum distillation and used as a laxative. Also called (in Britain and certain other countries): **liquid paraffin**

mineral pitch *n* another name for **asphalt**

mineral spring *n* a spring of water that contains a high proportion of dissolved mineral salts

mineral tar *n* a natural black viscous tar intermediate in properties between petroleum and asphalt. Also called: **maltha**

mineral water *n* water containing dissolved mineral salts or gases, usually having medicinal properties

mineral wax *n* another name for **ozocerite**

mineral wool *n* a fibrous material made by blowing steam or air through molten slag and used for packing and insulation. Also called: **rock wool**

miner's right *n* *Austral and NZ history* a licence to prospect for minerals, esp gold [c19]

Minerva (mɪˈnɜːvə) *n* the Roman goddess of wisdom. Greek counterpart: **Athena**

minestrone (ˌmɪnɪˈstrəʊnɪ) *n* a soup made from a variety of vegetables and pasta [from Italian, from *minestrare* to serve]

minesweeper ('maɪnˌswiːpə) *n* a naval vessel equipped to detect and clear mines ▷ 'mineˌsweeping *n*

Ming (mɪŋ) *n* **1** the imperial dynasty of China from 1368 to 1644 ▷ *adj* **2** of or relating to Chinese porcelain produced during the Ming dynasty, characterized by the use of brilliant colours and a fine-quality body

minge (mɪndʒ) *n* *Brit taboo slang* **1** the female genitals **2** women collectively considered as sexual objects [c20 from Romany; of obscure origin]

minger ('mɪŋə) *n* *Brit informal* an unattractive or malodorous person

mingimingi ('miːⁱŋiːmiːⁱŋiː) *n* an evergreen New Zealand, *Cyathodes juniperina*, with grey bark, narrow leaves, and blue berries [Māori]

minging ('mɪŋɪŋ) *adj Brit informal* **1** ugly, disgusting, or malodorous **2** extremely poor in quality [c20 originally Scottish, of obscure origin]

mingle ('mɪŋgəl) *vb* **1** to mix or cause to mix **2** (*intr*; *often foll by with*) to come into close association [c15 from Old English *mengan* to mix; related to Middle Dutch *mengen*, Old Frisian *mengja*] ▷ 'mingler *n*

Mingrelian (mɪŋˈgriːlɪən) *or* **Mingrel** ('mɪŋgrəl) *n* **1** a member of a people of Georgia living in the mountains northeast of the Black Sea **2** the language of this people, belonging to the South Caucasian family and closely related to Georgian ▷ *adj* **3** of or relating to the Mingrelians or their language

ming tree *n* an artificial plant resembling a bonsai plant [perhaps from MING]

mingy ('mɪndʒɪ) *adj* **-gier, -giest** *Brit informal* miserly, stingy, or niggardly [c20 probably a blend of MEAN² + STINGY¹]

Minho ('miːnjʊ) *n* the Portuguese name for the **Miño**

mini ('mɪnɪ) *adj* **1** (of a woman's dress, skirt, etc) very short; thigh-length **2** (*prenominal*) small; miniature ▷ *n, pl* **minis** **3** something very small of its kind, esp a small car or a miniskirt

mini- *combining form* smaller or shorter than the standard size: *minibus; miniskirt* [c20 from MINIATURE and MINIMUM]

miniature ('mɪnɪtʃə) *n* **1** a model, copy, or similar representation on a very small scale **2** anything that is very small of its kind **3** a very small painting, esp a portrait, showing fine detail on ivory or vellum **4** a very small bottle of whisky or other spirits, which can hold 50 millilitres **5** an illuminated letter or other decoration in a manuscript **6 in miniature** on a small scale: *games are real life in miniature* ▷ *adj* **7** greatly reduced in size **8** on a small scale; minute [c16 from Italian, from Medieval Latin *miniātūra*, from *miniāre* to paint red, (in illuminating manuscripts); from MINIUM]

miniature camera *n* a small camera using 35 millimetre film

miniaturist ('mɪnɪtʃərɪst) *n* a person who paints miniature portraits

miniaturize *or* **miniaturise** ('mɪnɪtʃəˌraɪz) *vb* (*tr*) to make or construct (something, esp electronic equipment) on a very small scale; reduce in size ▷ ˌminiaturi'zation *or* ˌminiaturi'sation *n*

minibar ('mɪnɪˌbɑː) *n* a selection of drinks and confectionery provided in a hotel bedroom and charged to the guest's bill if used

minibus ('mɪnɪˌbʌs) *n* a small bus able to carry approximately ten passengers

minicab ('mɪnɪˌkæb) *n* *Brit* a small saloon car used as a taxi

minicom ('mɪnɪˌkɒm) *n* a device used by deaf and hard-of-hearing people, allowing typed telephone messages to be sent and received

minicomputer (ˌmɪnɪkəmˈpjuːtə) *n* a small comparatively cheap digital computer

minidisc ('mɪnɪˌdɪsk) *n* a small recordable compact disc

minidish ('mɪnɪˌdɪʃ) *n* a small parabolic aerial for reception or transmission to a communications satellite

minidress ('mɪnɪˌdrɛs) *n* a very short dress, at least four inches above the knee. Often shortened to: **mini**

Minié ball ('mɪnɪˌeɪ; French miɲe) *n* a conical rifle bullet, used in the 19th century, manufactured with a hollow base designed to expand when fired to fit the rifling [c19 named after Capt. C. E. *Minié* (1814–1879), French army officer who invented it]

minify ('mɪnɪˌfaɪ) *vb* **-fies, -fying, -fied** (*tr*) *rare* to minimize or lessen the size or importance of (something) [c17 from Latin *minus* less; for form, compare MAGNIFY] ▷ **minification** (ˌmɪnɪfɪˈkeɪʃən) *n*

minikin ('mɪnɪkɪn) *obsolete* ▷ *n* **1** a small, dainty, or affected person or thing ▷ *adj* **2** dainty, prim, or affected [c16 from Dutch *minneken*, diminutive of *minne* love]

minim ('mɪnɪm) *n* **1** a unit of fluid measure equal to one sixtieth of a drachm. It is approximately equal to one drop. Symbol: M, ♍ **2** *music* a note having the time value of half a semibreve. Usual US and Canadian name: **half-note** **3** a small or insignificant person or thing **4** a downward stroke in calligraphy ▷ *adj* **5** *rare* very small; tiny [c15 (in its musical meaning): from Latin *minimus* smallest]

minima ('mɪnɪmə) *n* a plural of **minimum**

minimal ('mɪnɪməl) *adj* of the least possible; minimum or smallest ▷ 'minimally *adv*

minimal art *n* abstract painting or sculpture in which expressiveness and illusion are minimized by the use of simple geometric shapes, flat colour, and arrangements of ordinary objects ▷ **minimal artist** *n*

minimalism ('mɪnɪməˌlɪzəm) *n* **1** another name for **minimal art 2** a type of music based on simple elements and avoiding elaboration or embellishment **3** design or style in which the simplest and fewest elements are used to create the maximum effect

minimalist ('mɪnɪməlɪst) *n* **1** a person advocating a minimal policy, style, technique, action, etc **2** a minimal artist ▷ *adj* **3** of or relating to minimal art or artists

Minimalist ('mɪnɪməlɪst) *n* (in early 20th-century Russia) **1** a member of the faction of the Social Revolutionaries that advocated immediate postrevolutionary democracy **2** a less common name for a **Menshevik** ▷ Compare **Maximalist**

minimally *or* **minimal invasive** *adj* (of surgery) involving as little incision into the body as possible, through the use of techniques such as keyhole surgery and laser treatment

minimal pair *n* *linguistics* a pair of speech elements in a given language differing in only one respect and thus serving to identify minimum units such as phonemes, morphemes, etc. For example, *tin* and *din* constitute a minimal pair in English

minimax ('mɪnɪˌmæks) *n* **1** *maths* the lowest of a set of maximum values **2** (in game theory, etc) the procedure of choosing the strategy that least benefits the most advantaged member of a group. Compare **maximin** [c20 from MINI(MUM) + MAX(IMUM)]

Mini-Me ('mɪnɪˌmiː) *n informal* **1** a person who resmbles a smaller or younger version of another person **2** a person who adopts the opinions or mannerisms of a more powerful or senior person in order to win favour, achieve promotion, etc [c20 after a character in the 1999 film *Austin Powers: The Spy who Shagged Me*]

minimize *or* **minimise** ('mɪnɪˌmaɪz) *vb* (*tr*) **1** to reduce to or estimate at the least possible degree or amount: *to minimize a risk* **2** to rank or treat at less than the true worth; belittle: *to minimize someone's achievements* ▷ ˌminimi'zation *or* ˌminimi'sation *n* ▷ 'miniˌmizer *or* 'miniˌmiser *n*

minimoto ('mɪnɪˌməʊtəʊ) *n* a reduced-size replica racing motorcycle powered by a two-stroke petrol engine and used for racing. Also called: **pocketbike**

minimum ('mɪnɪməm) *n, pl* **-mums** *or* **-ma** (-mə) **1** the least possible amount, degree, or quantity **2** the least amount recorded, allowed, or reached: *the minimum in our temperature record this month was 50°*

m

3 (*modifier*) being the least possible, recorded, allowed, etc: *minimum age* **4** *maths* a value of a function that is less than any neighbouring value ▷ *adj* **5** of or relating to a minimum or minimums [C17 from Latin: smallest thing, from *minimus* least]

minimum lending rate *n* (in Britain) the minimum rate at which the Bank of England would lend to discount houses between 1971 and 1981, after which it was replaced by the less formal base rate. Abbreviation: **MLR**

minimum wage *n* the lowest wage that an employer is permitted to pay by law or union contract

minimus ('mɪnɪməs) *adj* (*immediately postpositive*) *Brit* the youngest: sometimes used after the surname of a schoolboy having elder brothers at the same school: *Hunt minimus*

mining ('maɪnɪŋ) *n* **1** the act, process, or industry of extracting coal, ores, etc, from the earth **2** *military* the process of laying mines

mining bee *n* a solitary bee of the genera *Andrena* and *Halictus*, which sometimes resemble honey bees [named from their burrowing habits]

minion ('mɪnjən) *n* **1** a favourite or dependant, esp a servile or fawning one **2** a servile agent: *the minister's minions* **3** a size of printer's type, approximately equal to 7 point ▷ *adj* **4** dainty, pretty, or elegant [C16 from French *mignon*, from Old French *mignot*, of Gaulish origin]

minipill ('mɪnɪˌpɪl) *n* a low-dose oral contraceptive containing a progestogen only

miniseries ('mɪnɪˌsɪərɪːz) *n* a television programme in several parts that is shown on consecutive days or weeks for a short period

miniskirt ('mɪnɪˌskɜːt) *n* a very short skirt, originally in the 1960s one at least four inches above the knee. Often shortened to: **mini** ▷ '**mini**ˌskirted *adj*

mini-state *n* same as **microstate**

minister ('mɪnɪstə) *n* **1** (esp in Presbyterian and some Nonconformist Churches) a member of the clergy **2** a person appointed to head a government department **3** any diplomatic agent accredited to a foreign government or head of state **4** short for **minister plenipotentiary** or **envoy extraordinary and minister plenipotentiary** See **envoy¹** (sense 1) **5** Also called (in full): **minister resident** a diplomat ranking after an envoy extraordinary and minister plenipotentiary **6** a person who attends to the needs of others, esp in religious matters **7** a person who acts as the agent or servant of a person or thing ▷ *vb* **8** (*intr*; often foll by *to*) to attend to the needs (of); take care (of) **9** (*tr*) *archaic* to provide; supply [C13 via Old French from Latin: servant; related to *minus* less] ▷ '**minister**ˌship *n*

ministerial (ˌmɪnɪˈstɪərɪəl) *adj* **1** of or relating to a minister of religion or his office **2** of or relating to a government minister or ministry: *a ministerial act* **3** (*often capital*) of or supporting the ministry or government against the opposition **4** *law* relating to or possessing delegated executive authority **5** *law* (of an office, duty, etc) requiring the following of instructions, without power to exercise any personal discretion in doing so **6** acting as an agent or cause; instrumental ▷ ˌ**minis**ˈterially *adv*

ministerialist (ˌmɪnɪˈstɪərɪəlɪst) *n Brit* a supporter of the governing ministry

ministerium (ˌmɪnɪˈstɪərɪəm) *n, pl* -ria (-rɪə) the body of the Lutheran ministers in a district [C19 Latin: MINISTRY]

minister of state *n* **1** (in the British Parliament) a minister, usually below cabinet rank, appointed to assist a senior minister with heavy responsibilities **2** any government minister

Minister of the Crown *n Brit* any Government minister of cabinet rank

minister plenipotentiary *n, pl* ministers plenipotentiary See **envoy¹** (sense 1)

ministrant ('mɪnɪstrənt) *adj* **1** ministering or

serving as a minister ▷ *n* **2** a person who ministers [C17 from Latin *ministrans,* from *ministrāre* to wait upon]

ministration (ˌmɪnɪˈstreɪʃən) *n* **1** the act or an instance of serving or giving aid **2** the act or an instance of ministering religiously [C14 from Latin *ministrātiō,* from *ministrāre* to wait upon] ▷ **ministrative** ('mɪnɪstrətɪv) *adj*

ministroke (ˌmɪnɪˈstrəʊk) *n* an informal name for **TIA**

ministry ('mɪnɪstrɪ) *n, pl* -tries **1 a** the profession or duties of a minister of religion **b** the performance of these duties **2** ministers of religion or government ministers considered collectively **3** the tenure of a minister **4 a** a government department headed by a minister **b** the buildings of such a department [C14 from Latin *ministerium* service, from *minister* servant; see MINISTER]

Minitrack ('mɪnɪˌtræk) *n trademark obsolete* a system for tracking the course of rockets or satellites by radio signals received at ground stations

minium ('mɪnɪəm) *n* another name for **red lead** [C14 (meaning: vermilion): from Latin]

minivan ('mɪnɪˌvæn) *n* a small van, esp one with seats in the back for carrying passengers

miniver ('mɪnɪvə) *n* white fur, used in ceremonial costumes [C13 from Old French *menu vair,* from *menu* small + *vair* variegated fur, VAIR]

minivet ('mɪnɪvɛt) *n* any brightly coloured tropical Asian cuckoo shrike of the genus *Pericrocotus* [C19 of unknown origin]

mink (mɪŋk) *n, pl* mink *or* minks **1** any of several semiaquatic musteline mammals of the genus *Mustela,* of Europe, Asia, and North America, having slightly webbed feet **2** the highly valued fur of these animals, esp that of the American mink (*M. vison*) **3** a garment made of this, esp a woman's coat or stole [C15 from Scandinavian; compare Danish *mink,* Swedish *mänk*]

minke whale ('mɪŋkə) *n* a type of small whalebone whale or rorqual, *Balaenoptera acutorostrata,* up to 10 metres long. Also called: **minke** [C20 probably from Norwegian *minkehval,* from *minke* lesser + *hval* whale]

Minkowski space-time (mɪŋˈkɒfskɪ) *n* a four-dimensional space in which three coordinates specify the position of a point in space and the fourth represents the time at which an event occurred at that point [C20 named after Hermann Minkowski (1864–1909), Russian-born German mathematician]

min min (mɪn mɪn) *n Austral* will-o'-the-wisp [from a native Australian language]

Minn. abbreviation for Minnesota

Minna ('mɪnə) *n* a city in W central Nigeria, capital of Niger state. Pop: 278 000 (2005 est)

Minneapolis (ˌmɪnɪˈæpəlɪs) *n* a city in SE Minnesota, on the Mississippi River adjacent to St Paul: the largest city in the state; important centre for the grain trade. Pop: 373 188 (2003 est)

minneola (ˌmɪnɪˈəʊlə) *n* a juicy citrus fruit that is a cross between a tangerine and a grapefruit [C20 perhaps from *Mineola, Texas*]

minnesinger ('mɪnɪˌsɪŋə) *n* one of the German lyric poets and musicians of the 12th to 14th centuries [C19 from German: love-singer]

Minnesota (ˌmɪnɪˈsəʊtə) *n* **1** a state of the N central US: chief US producer of iron ore. Capital: St Paul. Pop: 5 059 375 (2003 est). Area: 218 600 sq km (84 402 sq miles). Abbreviations: **Minn,** (with zip code) **MN 2** a river in S Minnesota, flowing southeast and northeast to the Mississippi River near St Paul. Length: 534 km (332 miles)

Minnesotan (ˌmɪnɪˈsəʊtən) *n* **1** a native or inhabitant of Minnesota ▷ *adj* **2** of or relating to Minnesota or its inhabitants

minnow ('mɪnəʊ) *n, pl* -nows *or* -now **1** a small slender European freshwater cyprinid fish, *Phoxinus phoxinus* **2** any other small cyprinid **3** *angling* a spinning lure imitating a minnow **4** a

small or insignificant person [C15 related to Old English *myne* minnow; compare Old High German *muniwa* fish]

Miño (Spanish 'mino) *n* a river in SW Europe, rising in NW Spain and flowing southwest (as part of the border between Spain and Portugal) to the Atlantic. Length: 338 km (210 miles). Portuguese name: Minho

Minoan (mɪˈnəʊən) *adj* **1** denoting the Bronze Age culture of Crete from about 3000 BC to about 1100 BC. Compare **Mycenaean 2** of or relating to the linear writing systems used in Crete and later in mainland Greece. See **Linear A, Linear B** ▷ *n* **3** a Cretan belonging to the Minoan culture [C19 named after MINOS, from the excavations at his supposed palace at Knossos]

minor ('maɪnə) *adj* **1** lesser or secondary in amount, extent, importance, or degree: *a minor poet; minor burns* **2** of or relating to the minority **3** below the age of legal majority **4** *music* **a** (of a scale) having a semitone between the second and third and fifth and sixth degrees (**natural minor**). See also **harmonic minor scale, melodic minor scale b** (of a key) based on the minor scale **c** (*postpositive*) denoting a specified key based on the minor scale: *C minor* **d** (of an interval) reduced by a semitone from the major **e** (of a chord, esp a triad) having a minor third above the root **f** (esp in jazz) of or relating to a chord built upon a minor triad and containing a minor seventh: *a minor ninth.* See also **minor key, minor mode 5** *logic* (of a term or premise) having less generality or scope than another term or proposition **6** *US education* of or relating to an additional secondary subject taken by a student **7** (*immediately postpositive*) *Brit* the younger or junior: sometimes used after the surname of a schoolboy if he has an older brother in the same school: *Hunt minor* **8** (*postpositive*) *bell-ringing* of, relating to, or denoting a set of changes rung on six bells: *grandsire minor* ▷ *n* **9** a person or thing that is lesser or secondary in amount **10** a person below the age of legal majority **11** *US and Canadian education* a subsidiary subject in which a college or university student needs fewer credits than in his or her major **12** *music* a minor key, chord, mode, or scale **13** *logic* a minor term or premise **14** *maths* **a** a determinant associated with a particular element of a given determinant and formed by removing the row and column containing that element **b** Also called: **cofactor, signed minor** the number equal to this reduced determinant **15** (*capital*) another name for **Minorite** ▷ *vb* **16** (*intr*; usually foll by *in*) *US education* to take a minor ▷ Compare **major** [C13 from Latin: less, smaller; related to Old High German *minniro* smaller, Gothic *minniza* least, Latin *minuere* to diminish, Greek *meiōn* less]

minor axis *n* the shorter or shortest axis of an ellipse or ellipsoid

Minorca (mɪˈnɔːkə) *n* **1** an island in the W Mediterranean, northeast of Majorca: the second largest of the Balearic Islands. Chief town: Mahón. Pop: 78 796 (2002 est). Area: 702 sq km (271 sq miles). Spanish name: Menorca **2** a breed of light domestic fowl with glossy white, black, or blue plumage

Minorcan (mɪˈnɔːkən) *adj* **1** of or relating to Minorca or its inhabitants ▷ *n* **2** a native or inhabitant of Minorca

minor canon *n Church of England* a clergyman who is attached to a cathedral to assist at daily services but who is not a member of the chapter

Minorite ('maɪnəˌraɪt) *n* a member of the Franciscan Friars Minor. Also called: **Minor** [C16 from Medieval Latin *frātrēs minōrēs* lesser brethren, name adopted by St Francis as a token of humility]

minority (maɪˈnɒrɪtɪ, mɪ-) *n, pl* -ties **1** the smaller in number of two parts, factions, or groups **2** a group that is different racially, politically, etc, from a larger group of which it is a part **3 a** the state of being a minor **b** the period during which a person is below legal age ▷ Compare **majority 4** (modifier) relating to or being a minority: *a minority interest; a minority opinion* [c16 from Medieval Latin *minōritās*, from Latin MINOR]

minority carrier *n* the entity responsible for carrying the lesser part of the current in a semiconductor. Compare **majority carrier**

minor key *n music* a key based on notes taken from a corresponding minor scale

minor league *n* **1** *US and Canadian* any professional league in baseball other than a major league. Compare **major league 2** (modifier) of relatively little importance: *that firm is very minor league*

minor mode *n music* any arrangement of notes present in or characteristic of a minor scale or key

minor orders *pl n RC Church* the four lower degrees of holy orders, namely porter, exorcist, lector, and acolyte. Compare **major orders**

minor planet *n* another name for **asteroid** (sense 1)

minor premise *n logic* the premise of a syllogism containing the subject of its conclusion

minor seventh chord *n* a chord consisting of a minor triad with an added minor seventh above the root. Compare **major seventh chord** Often shortened to: **minor seventh**

minor suit *n bridge* diamonds or clubs. Compare **major suit**

minor term *n logic* the subject of the conclusion of a syllogism, also occurring as the subject or predicate in the minor premise

Minos ('maɪnɒs) *n Greek myth* a king of Crete for whom Daedalus built the Labyrinth to contain the Minotaur

Minotaur ('maɪnətɔː) *n Greek myth* a monster with the head of a bull and the body of a man. It was kept in the Labyrinth in Crete, feeding on human flesh, until destroyed by Theseus [c14 via Latin from Greek *Minōtauros*, from MINOS + *tauros* bull]

Minsk (mɪnsk) *n* the capital of Belarus: an industrial city and educational and cultural centre, with a university (1921). Pop: 1 709 000 (2005 est)

minster ('mɪnstə) *n Brit* any of certain cathedrals and large churches, usually originally connected to a monastery [Old English *mynster*, probably from Vulgar Latin *monisterium* (unattested), variant of Church Latin *monastērium* MONASTERY]

minstrel ('mɪnstrəl) *n* **1** a medieval wandering musician who performed songs or recited poetry with instrumental accompaniment **2** a performer in a minstrel show **3** *archaic or poetic* any poet, musician, or singer [c13 from Old French *menestral*, from Late Latin *ministeriālis* an official, from Latin MINISTER]

minstrel show *n* a theatrical entertainment consisting of songs, dances, comic turns, etc, performed by a troupe of actors wearing black face make-up

minstrelsy ('mɪnstrəlsɪ) *n, pl* -sies **1** the art of a minstrel **2** the poems, music, or songs of a minstrel **3** a troupe of minstrels

mint¹ (mɪnt) *n* **1** any N temperate plant of the genus *Mentha*, having aromatic leaves and spikes of small typically mauve flowers: family *Lamiaceae* (labiates). The leaves of some species are used for seasoning and flavouring. See also **peppermint, spearmint, horsemint, water mint 2** stone mint another name for **dittany** (sense 2) **3** a sweet flavoured with mint [Old English *minte*, from Latin *mentha*, from Greek *minthē*; compare Old High German *minza*] > 'minty *adj*

mint² (mɪnt) *n* **1** a place where money is coined by governmental authority **2** a very large amount of money: *he made a mint in business* ▷ *adj* **3** (of coins, postage stamps, etc) in perfect condition as issued **4** *Brit informal* excellent; impressive **5** in mint condition in perfect condition; as if new ▷ *vb* **6** to make (coins) by stamping metal **7** (tr) to invent (esp phrases or words) [Old English *mynet* coin, from Latin *monēta* money, mint, from the

temple of Juno *Monēta*, used as a mint in ancient Rome] > 'minter *n*

mintage ('mɪntɪdʒ) *n* **1** the process of minting **2** money minted **3** a fee paid for minting a coin **4** an official impression stamped on a coin

mint bush *n* an aromatic shrub of the genus *Prostanthera* with a mintlike odour: family *Lamiaceae* (labiates): native to Australia

minted ('mɪntɪd) *adj Brit slang* wealthy

mint julep *n chiefly US* a long drink consisting of bourbon whiskey, crushed ice, sugar, and sprigs of mint

Minton ('mɪntən) *n* a fine-quality porcelain ware produced in Stoke-on-Trent since 1798 **b** (as modifier): *Minton plate* [c19 named after Thomas Minton (1765–1836), English potter]

mint sauce *n* a sauce made from mint leaves, sugar, and vinegar, usually served with lamb

minuend ('mɪnjʊˌend) *n* the number from which another number, the **subtrahend** is to be subtracted [c18 from Latin *minuendus* (numerus) (the number) to be diminished]

minuet (ˌmɪnjʊˈet) *n* **1** a stately court dance of the 17th and 18th centuries in triple time **2** a piece of music composed for or in the rhythm of this dance, sometimes as a movement in a suite, sonata, or symphony. See also **scherzo** [c17 from French *menuet* dainty (referring to the dance steps), from *menu* small]

minus ('maɪnəs) *prep* **1** reduced by the subtraction of: *four minus two* (written 4 – 2) **2** *informal* deprived of; lacking: *minus the trimmings, that hat would be ordinary* ▷ *adj* **3 a** indicating or involving subtraction: *a minus sign* **b** Also: **negative** having a value or designating a quantity less than zero: *a minus number* **4** on the negative part of a scale or coordinate axis: *a value of minus 40°C* **5** involving a disadvantage, harm, etc: *a minus factor* **6** (postpositive) *education* slightly below the standard of a particular grade: *he received a B minus for his essay* **7** *botany* designating the strain of a fungus that can only undergo sexual reproduction with a plus strain **8** denoting a negative electric charge ▷ *n* **9** short for **minus sign 10** a negative quantity **11** a disadvantage, loss, or deficit **12** *informal* something detrimental or bad ▷ Mathematical symbol: – [c15 from Latin, neuter of MINOR]

minuscule ('mɪnəˌskjuːl) *n* **1** a lower-case letter **2** writing using such letters **3** a small cursive 7th-century style of lettering derived from the uncial ▷ *adj* **4** relating to, printed in, or written in small letters. Compare **majuscule 5** very small **6** (of letters) lower-case [c18 from French, from Latin (*littera*) *minuscula* very small (letter), diminutive of MINOR] > **minuscular** (mɪˈnʌskjʊlə) *adj*

minus sign *n* the symbol –, indicating subtraction or a negative quantity

minute¹ ('mɪnɪt) *n* **1** a period of time equal to 60 seconds; one sixtieth of an hour **2** a unit of angular measure equal to one sixtieth of a degree. Symbol: ′ Also called: **minute of arc 3** any very short period of time; moment **4** a short note or memorandum **5** the distance that can be travelled in a minute: *it's only two minutes away* **6** up to the minute (**up-to-the-minute** when prenominal) very latest or newest ▷ *vb* **7** to record in minutes: *to minute a meeting* **8** to time in terms of minutes ▷ See also **minutes** [c14 from Old French from Medieval Latin *minūta*, n. use of Latin *minūtus* MINUTE²]

minute² (maɪˈnjuːt) *adj* **1** very small; diminutive; tiny **2** unimportant; petty **3** precise or detailed: *a minute examination* [c15 from Latin *minūtus*, past participle of *minuere* to diminish] > mi'nuteness *n*

minute gun ('mɪnɪt) *n* a gun fired at one-minute intervals as a sign of distress or mourning

minute hand ('mɪnɪt) *n* the pointer on a timepiece that indicates minutes, typically the longer hand of two. Compare **hour hand, second hand**

minutely¹ (maɪˈnjuːtlɪ) *adv* in great detail

minutely² ('mɪnɪtlɪ) *adj* **1** occurring every minute ▷ *adv* **2** every minute

Minuteman ('mɪnɪtˌmæn) *n, pl* -men **1** (sometimes not capital) (in the War of American Independence) a colonial militiaman who promised to be ready to fight at one minute's notice **2** a US three-stage intercontinental ballistic missile

minute mark ('mɪnɪt) *n* the symbol ′ used for minutes of arc and linear feet

minutes ('mɪnɪts) *pl n* an official record of the proceedings of a meeting, conference, convention, etc

minute steak ('mɪnɪt) *n* a small thinly-cut piece of steak that can be cooked quickly

minutiae (mɪˈnjuːʃɪˌiː) *pl n, sing* -tia (-ʃɪə) small, precise, or trifling details [c18 pl of Late Latin *minūtia* smallness, from Latin *minūtus* MINUTE²]

minx (mɪŋks) *n* a bold, flirtatious, or scheming woman [c16 of unknown origin] > 'minxish *adj*

Minya ('mɪnjə) *n* See **El Minya**

minyan *Hebrew* (min'jan; *English* 'mɪnjən) *n, pl* **minyanim** (minja'nim) **minyans** the number of persons required by Jewish law to be present at a religious service, namely, at least ten males over thirteen years of age [literally: number]

Miocene ('maɪəˌsiːn) *adj* **1** of, denoting, or formed in the fourth epoch of the Tertiary period, between the Oligocene and Pliocene epochs, which lasted for 19 million years ▷ *n* **2** the this epoch or rock series [c19 from Greek *meiōn* less + -CENE]

miombo (mɪˈɒmbo) *n* (in E Africa) a dry wooded area with sparse deciduous growth [c19 probably from a Niger-Congo language]

miosis or **myosis** (maɪˈəʊsɪs) *n, pl* -ses (-siːz) **1** excessive contraction of the pupil of the eye, as in response to drugs **2** a variant spelling of **meiosis** (sense 1) [c20 from Greek *muein* to shut the eyes + -OSIS] > **miotic** or **myotic** (maɪˈɒtɪk) *adj, n*

MIP *abbreviation for* **1** monthly investment plan **2** maximum investment plan: an endowment assurance policy designed to produce maximum profits

MIPS (mɪps) *n computing* ▷ *acronym for* million instructions per second

Miquelon ('miːkəˌlɒn; *French* miklɔ̃) *n* a group of islands in the French territory of **Saint Pierre and Miquelon**

mir *Russian* (mir) *n, pl* **miri** ('miri) a peasant commune in prerevolutionary Russia [literally: world]

Mir (mɪə) *n* the Russian (formerly Soviet) manned space station launched in February 1986 and scuttled in 2001 [c20 Russian: peace]

mirabelle ('mɪrəˌbel) *n* **1** a small sweet yellow-orange fruit that is a variety of greengage **2** a liqueur distilled from this [c18 from French]

mirabile dictu *Latin* (mɪˈræbɪleɪ ˈdɪktuː) wonderful to relate; amazing to say

Mira Ceti ('maɪrə 'siːtaɪ) *n* a binary star one component of which, a red supergiant, is a long-period variable with an average period of 332 days

miracidium (ˌmaɪrəˈsɪdɪəm) *n, pl* -ia (-ɪə) the flat ciliated larva of flukes that hatches from the egg and gives rise asexually to other larval forms [c20 New Latin, via Late Latin *miracidion*, from Greek *meirax* boy, girl] > ˌmira'cidial *adj*

miracle ('mɪrəkᵊl) *n* **1** an event that is contrary to the established laws of nature and attributed to a supernatural cause **2** any amazing or wonderful event **3** a person or thing that is a marvellous example of something: *the bridge was a miracle of engineering* **4** short for **miracle play 5** (modifier) being or seeming a miracle: *a miracle cure* [c12 from Latin *mīrāculum*, from *mīrārī* to wonder at]

miracle play *n* a medieval play based on a biblical story or the life of a saint. Compare **mystery play**

miraculous (mɪˈrækjʊləs) *adj* **1** of, like, or caused by a miracle; marvellous **2** surprising **3** having the power to work miracles > mi'raculously *adv* > mi'raculousness *n*

mirador (ˌmɪrəˈdɔː) *n* a window, balcony, or turret

m

[c17 from Spanish, from *mirar* to look]

Miraflores (ˌmɪrəˈflɔːrəs; *Spanish* miraˈflores) *n* **Lake** an artificial lake in Panama, in the S Canal Zone of the Panama Canal

mirage (mɪˈrɑːʒ) *n* **1** an image of a distant object or sheet of water, often inverted or distorted, caused by atmospheric refraction by hot air **2** something illusory [c19 from French, from (*se*) *mirer* to be reflected]

Miranda (mɪˈrændə) *n* one of the larger satellites of the planet Uranus

MIRAS (ˈmaɪˌræs) *n* (formerly in Britain) *acronym for* mortgage interest relief at source

mirchi (miːrˈtʃiː) *adj Hinglish* hot [c21 Hindi]

mire (maɪə) *n* **1** a boggy or marshy area **2** mud, muck, or dirt ▷ *vb* **3** to sink or cause to sink in a mire **4** (*tr*) to make dirty or muddy **5** (*tr*) to involve, esp in difficulties [c14 from Old Norse *mȳrr*; related to MOSS] > ˈmiry *adj*

Mirena (maɪˈriːnə) *n trademark* a type of intrauterine system. See IUS

mirepoix (mɪəˈpwɑː) *n* a mixture of sautéed root vegetables used as a base for braising meat or for various sauces [French, probably named in honour of C. P. G. F. de Lévis, Duke of *Mirepoix*, 18th-century French general]

Miriam (ˈmɪrɪəm) *n Old Testament* the sister of Moses and Aaron. (Numbers 12:1–15). Douay name: Mary

mirk (mɜːk) *n* a variant spelling of **murk**. > ˈmirky *adj* > ˈmirkily *adv* > ˈmirkiness *n*

mirliton (ˈmɜːlɪtɒn) *n* another name (chiefly US) for **chayote** [c19 French, literally: reed pipe, of imitative origin]

miro (ˈmiːrɒ) *n, pl* miro a tall New Zealand coniferous timber tree, *Podocarpus ferrugineus, with large red fruit* [Māori]

miromiro (miːˈrɒmiːrɒ) *n, pl* miromiro a small white-breasted New Zealand tit, *Petroica Macrocephala* [Māori]

mirror (ˈmɪrə) *n* **1** a surface, such as polished metal or glass coated with a metal film, that reflects light without diffusion and produces an image of an object placed in front of it **2** such a reflecting surface mounted in a frame **3** any reflecting surface **4** a thing that reflects or depicts something else: *the press is a mirror of public opinion* ▷ *vb* **5** (*tr*) to reflect, represent, or depict faithfully: *he mirrors his teacher's ideals* [c13 from Old French from *mirer* to look at, from Latin *mīrārī* to wonder at] > ˈmirror-ˌlike *adj*

mirror ball *n* a large revolving ball covered with small pieces of mirror glass so that it reflects light in changing patterns: used in discos and ballrooms

mirror canon *n music* **1** a canon in which the parts are written as though seen in a mirror placed between them: one part or set of parts is the upside-down image of the other **2** sometimes, less accurately, a piece that can be played backwards

mirror carp *n* a variety of the common carp (*Cyprinus carpio*) with reduced scales, giving a smooth shiny body surface

mirror finish *n* a smooth highly polished surface produced on metal by mechanical or electrolytic polishing or lapping

mirror image *n* **1** an image as observed in a mirror **2** an object that corresponds to another object in the same way as it would correspond to its image in a mirror

mirror lens *n photog* a lens of long focal length in which some of the lens elements are replaced by mirrors in order to shorten its overall length and reduce its weight

mirror symmetry *n* symmetry about a plane (**mirror plane**) that divides the object or system into two mutual mirror images

mirror writing *n* backward writing that forms a mirror image of normal writing

mirth (mɜːθ) *n* laughter, gaiety, or merriment [Old English *myrgth*; compare MERRY] > ˈmirthful

adj > ˈmirthfully *adv* > ˈmirthfulness *n* > ˈmirthless *adj* > ˈmirthlessly *adv* > ˈmirthlessness *n*

MIRV (mɜːv) *n acronym for* multiple independently targeted re-entry vehicle **a** a missile that has several warheads, each one being directed to different enemy targets **b** any of the warheads

mirza (ˈmɜːzə, mɪəˈzɑː) *n* (in Iran) **1** a title of respect placed before the surname of an official, scholar, or other distinguished man **2** a royal prince: used as a title after a name [c17 from Persian: son of a lord]

mis-¹ *prefix* **1** wrong, bad, or erroneous; wrongly, badly, or erroneously: *misunderstanding; misfortune; misspelling; mistreat; mislead* **2** lack of; not: *mistrust* [Old English *mis*(*se*)-; related to Middle English *mes-*, from Old French *mes-*; compare Old High German *missa-*, Old Norse *mis-*]

mis-² *prefix* a variant of **miso-** before a vowel

misadventure (ˌmɪsədˈventʃə) *n* **1** an unlucky event; misfortune **2** *law* accidental death not due to crime or negligence

misaligned (ˌmɪsəˈlaɪnd) *adj* placed or positioned wrongly or badly > ˌmisaˈlignment *n*

misalliance (ˌmɪsəˈlaɪəns) *n* an unsuitable alliance or marriage

misandry (ˈmɪsəndrɪ) *n* hatred of men [c20 from Greek, from MISO- + -*andria*, from *anēr* man] > misˈandrist *n, adj* > misˈandrous *adj*

misanthrope (ˈmɪzənˌθrəʊp) *or* **misanthropist** (mɪˈzænθrəpɪst) *n* a person who dislikes or distrusts other people or mankind in general [c17 from Greek *mīsanthrōpos, from misos* hatred + *anthrōpos* man] > misanthropic (ˌmɪzənˈθrɒpɪk) *or* ˌmisanˈthropical *adj* > ˌmisanˈthropically *adv* > misanthropy (mɪˈzænθrəpɪ) *n*

misapply (ˌmɪsəˈplaɪ) *vb* -plies, -plying, -plied (*tr*) **1** to apply wrongly or badly **2** another word for **misappropriate**. > misapplication (ˌmɪsæplɪˈkeɪʃən) *n*

misapprehend (ˌmɪsæprɪˈhend) *vb* (*tr*) to misunderstand > ˌmisappreˈhensive *adj* > ˌmisappreˈhensively *adv* > ˌmisappreˈhensiveness *n*

misapprehension (ˌmɪsæprɪˈhenʃən) *n* a failure to understand fully; misconception: *the misapprehension that acting was easy*

misappropriate (ˌmɪsəˈprəʊprɪˌeɪt) *vb* (*tr*) to appropriate for a wrong or dishonest use; embezzle or steal > ˌmisapˈpropriˈation *n*

misbecome (ˌmɪsbɪˈkʌm) *vb* -comes, -coming, -came (*tr*) to be unbecoming to or unsuitable for

misbegotten (ˌmɪsbɪˈɡɒtᵊn) *adj* **1** unlawfully obtained: *misbegotten gains* **2** badly conceived, planned, or designed: *a misbegotten scheme* **3** Also: misbegot (ˌmɪsbɪˈɡɒt) *literary and dialect* illegitimate; bastard

misbehave (ˌmɪsbɪˈheɪv) *vb* to behave (oneself) badly > ˌmisbeˈhaver *n* > misbehaviour (ˌmɪsbɪˈheɪvjə) *n*

misbelief (ˌmɪsbɪˈliːf) *n* a false or unorthodox belief

misc. *abbreviation for* miscellaneous

miscalculate (ˌmɪsˈkælkjʊˌleɪt) *vb* (*tr*) to calculate wrongly > ˌmiscalcuˈlation *n* > ˌmisˈcalcuˌlator *n*

miscall (ˌmɪsˈkɔːl) *vb* (*tr*) **1** to call by the wrong name **2** *dialect* to abuse or malign > ˌmisˈcaller *n*

miscanthus (mɪsˈkænθəs) *n* any tall perennial bamboo-like grass of the genus *Miscanthus*, native from southern Africa to SE Asia and cultivated for ornament in temperate regions

miscarriage (mɪsˈkærɪdʒ) *n* **1** (*also* ˈmɪskær-) spontaneous expulsion of a fetus from the womb, esp prior to the 20th week of pregnancy **2** an act of mismanagement or failure: *a miscarriage of justice* **3** *Brit* the failure of freight to reach its destination

miscarry (mɪsˈkærɪ) *vb* -ries, -rying, -ried (*intr*) **1** to expel a fetus prematurely from the womb; abort **2** to fail: *all her plans miscarried* **3** *Brit* (of freight, mail, etc) to fail to reach a destination

miscast (ˌmɪsˈkɑːst) *vb* -casts, -casting, -cast (*tr*) **1** to cast badly **2** (*often passive*) **a** to cast (a role or

the roles) in (a play, film, etc) inappropriately: *Falstaff was certainly miscast* **b** to assign an inappropriate role to: *he was miscast as Othello*

miscegenation (ˌmɪsɪdʒɪˈneɪʃən) *n* interbreeding of races, esp where differences of pigmentation are involved [c19 from Latin *miscēre* to mingle + *genus* race] > miscegenetic (ˌmɪsɪdʒɪˈnetɪk) *adj*

miscellanea (ˌmɪsəˈleɪnɪə) *pl n* a collection of miscellaneous items, esp literary works [c16 from Latin: neuter pl of *miscellāneus* MISCELLANEOUS]

miscellaneous (ˌmɪsəˈleɪnɪəs) *adj* **1** composed of or containing a variety of things; mixed; varied **2** having varied capabilities, sides, etc [c17 from Latin *miscellāneus*, from *miscellus* mixed, from *miscēre* to mix] > ˌmiscelˈlaneously *adv* > ˌmiscelˈlaneousness *n*

miscellanist (mɪˈselənɪst) *n* a writer of miscellanies

miscellany (mɪˈselənɪ; *US* ˈmɪsəˌleɪnɪ) *n, pl* -nies **1** a mixed assortment of items **2** (*sometimes plural*) a miscellaneous collection of essays, poems, etc, by different authors in one volume [c16 from French *miscellanées* (pl) MISCELLANEA]

mischance (mɪsˈtʃɑːns) *n* **1** bad luck **2** a stroke of bad luck

mischief (ˈmɪstʃɪf) *n* **1** wayward but not malicious behaviour, usually of children, that causes trouble, irritation, etc **2** a playful inclination to behave in this way or to tease or disturb **3** injury or harm caused by a person or thing **4** a person, esp a child, who is mischievous **5** a source of trouble, difficulty, etc: *floods are a great mischief to the farmer* [c13 from Old French *meschief* disaster, from *meschever* to meet with calamity; from *mes-* MIS-¹ + *chever* to reach an end, from *chef* end, CHIEF]

mischievous (ˈmɪstʃɪvəs) *adj* **1** inclined to acts of mischief **2** teasing; slightly malicious: *a mischievous grin* **3** causing or intended to cause harm: *a mischievous plot* > ˈmischievously *adv* > ˈmischievousness *n*

misch metal (mɪʃ) *n* an alloy of cerium and other rare earth metals, used esp as a flint in cigarette lighters [c20 from German *Mischmetall*, from *mischen* to mix]

miscible (ˈmɪsɪbᵊl) *adj* capable of mixing: *alcohol is miscible with water* [c16 from Medieval Latin *miscibilis*, from Latin *miscēre* to mix] > ˌmisciˈbility *n*

misconceive (ˌmɪskənˈsiːv) *vb* to have the wrong idea; fail to understand > ˌmisconˈceiver *n*

misconceived (ˌmɪskənˈsiːvd) *adj* faultily or wrongly planned or based

misconception (ˌmɪskənˈsepʃən) *n* a false or mistaken view, opinion, or attitude

misconduct *n* (mɪsˈkɒndʌkt) **1** behaviour, such as adultery or professional negligence, that is regarded as immoral or unethical ▷ *vb* (ˌmɪskənˈdʌkt) (*tr*) **2** to conduct (oneself) in such a way **3** to manage (something) badly

misconstruction (ˌmɪskənˈstrʌkʃən) *n* **1** a false interpretation of evidence, facts, etc **2** a faulty construction, esp in grammar

misconstrue (ˌmɪskənˈstruː) *vb* -strues, -struing, -strued (*tr*) to interpret mistakenly

miscount (ˌmɪsˈkaʊnt) *vb* **1** to count or calculate incorrectly ▷ *n* **2** a false count or calculation

miscreance (ˈmɪskrɪəns) *or* **miscreancy** *n archaic* lack of religious belief or faith

miscreant (ˈmɪskrɪənt) *n* **1** a wrongdoer or villain **2** *archaic* an unbeliever or heretic ▷ *adj* **3** evil or villainous **4** *archaic* unbelieving or heretical [c14 from Old French *mescreant* unbelieving, from *mes-* MIS-¹ + *creant*, ultimately from Latin *credere* to believe]

miscreate *vb* (ˌmɪskrɪˈeɪt) **1** to create (something) badly or incorrectly ▷ *adj* (ˈmɪskriːt, -eɪt) **2** *archaic* badly or unnaturally formed or made > ˌmiscreˈation *n*

miscue (ˌmɪsˈkjuː) *n* **1** *billiards* a faulty stroke in which the cue tip slips off the cue ball or misses it altogether **2** *informal* a blunder or mistake ▷ *vb* -cues, -cuing, -cued **3** (*intr*) *billiards* to make a

miscue 4 (*intr*) *theatre* to fail to answer one's own cue or answer the cue of another **5** *radio* to start (a record or tape) at the wrong point **6** (*intr*) *informal* to blunder

miscue analysis *n Brit education* analysis of the errors a pupil makes while reading

misdate (ˌmɪsˈdeɪt) *vb* (*tr*) to date (a letter, event, etc) wrongly

misdeal (ˌmɪsˈdiːl) *vb* **-deals, -dealing, -dealt 1** (*intr*) to deal out cards incorrectly ▷ *n* **2** a faulty deal > **ˈmisˈdealer** *n*

misdeed (ˌmɪsˈdiːd) *n* an evil or illegal action

misdemean (ˌmɪsdɪˈmiːn) *vb* a rare word for misbehave

misdemeanant (ˌmɪsdɪˈmiːnənt) *n criminal law* (formerly) a person who has committed or been convicted of a misdemeanour. Compare **felon¹**

misdemeanour or US **misdemeanor** (ˌmɪsdɪˈmiːnə) *n* **1** *criminal law* (formerly) an offence generally less heinous than a felony and which until 1967 involved a different form of trial. Compare **felony 2** any minor offence or transgression

misdiagnose (ˌmɪsˈdaɪəgˌnəʊz) *vb* (*tr*) to diagnose (an illness or problem) wrongly or mistakenly

misdiagnosis (ˌmɪsdaɪəgˈnəʊsɪs) *n, pl* **-ses** (-siːz) the act or an instance of misdiagnosing or being misdiagnosed

misdirect (ˌmɪsdɪˈrɛkt) *vb* (*tr*) **1** to give (a person) wrong directions or instructions **2** to address (a letter, parcel, etc) wrongly > **ˈmisdiˈrection** *n*

misdoubt (mɪsˈdaʊt) *vb* an archaic word for **doubt** or **suspect**

mise (miːz, maɪz) *n law* **1** the issue in the obsolete writ of right **2** an agreed settlement [c15 from Old French: action of putting, from *mettre* to put]

mise en place *French* (miz ɑ̃ plas) *n* (in a restaurant kitchen) the preparation of equipment and food before service begins

mise en scène *French* (miz ɑ̃ sɛn) *n* **1 a** the arrangement of properties, scenery, etc, in a play **b** the objects so arranged; stage setting **2** the environment of an event

Miseno (*Italian* miˈzɛːno) *n* a cape in SW Italy, on the N shore of the Bay of Naples: remains of the town of **Misenum**, a naval base constructed by Agrippa in 31 BC

miser¹ (ˈmaɪzə) *n* **1** a person who hoards money or possessions, often living miserably **2** selfish person [c16 from Latin: wretched]

miser² (ˈmaɪzə) *n civil engineering* a large hand-operated auger used for loose soils [c19 origin unknown]

miserabilism (ˈmɪzərəbɪlˌɪzəm, ˈmɪzrə-) or **miserablism** (ˈmɪzərəblɪzəm, ˈmɪzrə-) *n* the quality of seeming to enjoy being depressed, or the type of gloomy music, art, etc, that evokes this

miserabilist (ˈmɪzərəbɪlɪst, ˈmɪzrə-) or **miserablist** (ˈmɪzərəblɪst, ˈmɪzrə-) *n* **1** a person who appears to enjoy being depressed, esp a performer of or listener to gloomy music ▷ *adj* **2** of, resembling, or likely to be enjoyed by a miserabilist or miserabilists

miserable (ˈmɪzərəbᵊl, ˈmɪzrə-) *adj* **1** unhappy or depressed; wretched **2** causing misery, discomfort, etc: *a miserable life* **3** contemptible: *a miserable villain* **4** sordid or squalid: *miserable living conditions* **5** *Scot, Austral, and NZ* mean; stingy **6** (pejorative intensifier): *you miserable wretch* [c16 from Old French, from Latin *miserābilis* worthy of pity, from *miserārī* to pity, from *miser* wretched] > **ˈmiserableness** *n* > **ˈmiserably** *adv*

misère (mɪˈzɛə) *n* **1** a call in solo whist and other card games declaring a hand that will win no tricks **2** a hand that will win no tricks [c19 from French: misery]

miserere (ˌmɪzəˈrɛərɪ, -ˈrɪərɪ) *n* another word for **misericord** (sense 1)

Miserere (ˌmɪzəˈrɛərɪ, -ˈrɪərɪ) *n* the 51st psalm, the Latin version of which begins "Miserere mei, Deus" ("Have mercy on me, O God")

misericord or **misericorde** (mɪˈzɛrɪˌkɔːd) *n* **1** a ledge projecting from the underside of the hinged seat of a choir stall in a church, on which the occupant can support himself while standing **2** *Christianity* **a** a relaxation of certain monastic rules for infirm or aged monks or nuns **b** a monastery where such relaxations can be enjoyed **3** a small medieval dagger used to give the death stroke to a wounded foe [c14 from Old French, from Latin *misericordia* compassion, from *miserēre* to pity + *cor* heart]

miserly (ˈmaɪzəlɪ) *adj* of or resembling a miser; avaricious > **ˈmiserliness** *n*

misery (ˈmɪzərɪ) *n, pl* **-eries 1** intense unhappiness, discomfort, or suffering; wretchedness **2** a cause of such unhappiness, discomfort, etc **3** squalid or poverty-stricken conditions **4** *Brit informal* a person who is habitually depressed: *he is such a misery* **5** *dialect* a pain or ailment [c14 via Anglo-Norman from Latin *miseria*, from *miser* wretched]

misfeasance (mɪsˈfiːzəns) *n law* the improper performance of an act that is lawful in itself. Compare **malfeasance, nonfeasance** [c16 from Old French *mesfaisance*, from *mesfaire* to perform misdeeds] > **misˈfeasor** *n*

misfile (ˌmɪsˈfaɪl) *vb* to file (papers, records, etc) wrongly

misfire (ˌmɪsˈfaɪə) *vb* (*intr*) **1** (of a firearm or its projectile) to fail to fire, explode, or ignite as or when expected **2** (of a motor engine or vehicle, etc) to fail to fire at the appropriate time, often causing a backfire **3** to fail to operate or occur as intended ▷ *n* **4** the act or an instance of misfiring

misfit *n* (ˈmɪsˌfɪt) **1** a person not suited in behaviour or attitude to a particular social environment **2** something that does not fit or fits badly ▷ *vb* (ˌmɪsˈfɪt) **-fits, -fitting, -fitted** (*intr*) **3** to fail to fit or be fitted

misfortune (mɪsˈfɔːtʃən) *n* **1** evil fortune; bad luck **2** an unfortunate or disastrous event; calamity

misgive (mɪsˈgɪv) *vb* **-gives, -giving, -gave, -given** to make or be apprehensive or suspicious

misgiving (mɪsˈgɪvɪŋ) *n* (*often plural*) a feeling of uncertainty, apprehension, or doubt

misgovern (ˌmɪsˈgʌvən) *vb* to govern badly > **ˌmisˈgovernment** *n* > **ˌmisˈgovernor** *n*

misguide (ˌmɪsˈgaɪd) *vb* (*tr*) to guide or direct wrongly or badly > **ˌmisˈguidance** *n* > **ˌmisˈguider** *n*

misguided (ˌmɪsˈgaɪdɪd) *adj* foolish or unreasonable, esp in action or behaviour > **ˌmisˈguidedly** *adv*

mishandle (mɪsˈhændᵊl) *vb* (*tr*) to handle or treat badly or inefficiently

mishap (ˈmɪshæp) *n* **1** an unfortunate accident **2** bad luck

mishear (ˌmɪsˈhɪə) *vb* **-hears, -hearing, -heard** to fail to hear correctly

mishit *sport* ▷ *n* (ˈmɪsˌhɪt) **1** a faulty shot or stroke ▷ *vb* (ˌmɪsˈhɪt) **-hits, -hitting, -hit 2** to hit (a ball) with a faulty stroke

mishmash (ˈmɪʃˌmæʃ) *n* a confused collection or mixture; hotchpotch [c15 reduplication of MASH]

Mishmi (ˈmɪʃmɪ) *n* **1** (*pl* **-mi** or **-mis**) a member of a Mongoloid hill people of the Brahmaputra area of NE India **2** the language of this people, belonging to the Tibeto-Burman branch of the Sino-Tibetan family ▷ *adj* **3** of or relating to this people or their language

Mishna (ˈmɪʃnə; *Hebrew* miʃˈna) *n, pl* **Mishnayoth** (mɪˈʃnɑːjəʊt; *Hebrew* miʃnaˈjɔt) *Judaism* a compilation of precepts passed down as an oral tradition and collected by Judah ha-Nasi in the late second century AD. It forms the earlier part of the Talmud. See also **Gemara** [c17 from Hebrew: instruction by repetition, from *shānāh* to repeat] > **Mishnaic** (mɪʃˈneɪɪk), **Mishnic** or **Mishnical** *adj*

misinform (ˌmɪsɪnˈfɔːm) *vb* (*tr*) to give incorrect information to > **ˌmisinˈformant** or **ˌmisinˈformer** *n* > **misinformation** (ˌmɪsɪnfəˈmeɪʃən) *n*

misinterpret (ˌmɪsɪnˈtɜːprɪt) *vb* (*tr*) to interpret badly, misleadingly, or incorrectly > **ˌmisinˌterpreˈtation** *n* > **ˌmisinˈterpreter** *n*

misjoinder (mɪsˈdʒɔɪndə) *n law* the improper joining of parties as coplaintiffs or codefendants or of different causes of action in one suit. Compare **nonjoinder**

misjudge (ˌmɪsˈdʒʌdʒ) *vb* to judge (a person or persons) wrongly or unfairly > **ˌmisˈjudger** *n* > **ˈmisˈjudgment** or **ˈmisˈjudgement** *n*

Miskolc (*Hungarian* ˈmɪʃkolts) *n* a city in NE Hungary: the second most important industrial centre in Hungary; iron and steel industries. Pop: 180 282 (2003 est)

mislay (mɪsˈleɪ) *vb* **-lays, -laying, -laid** (*tr*) **1** to lose (something) temporarily, esp by forgetting where it is **2** to lay (something) badly > **misˈlayer** *n*

mislead (mɪsˈliːd) *vb* **-leads, -leading, -led** (*tr*) **1** to give false or misleading information to **2** to lead or guide in the wrong direction > **misˈleader** *n*

misleading (mɪsˈliːdɪŋ) *adj* tending to confuse or mislead; deceptive > **misˈleadingly** *adv*

mislike (mɪsˈlaɪk) *archaic* ▷ *vb* (*tr*) **1** to dislike ▷ *n also* **misliking 2** dislike or aversion > **misˈliker** *n*

mismanage (ˌmɪsˈmænɪdʒ) *vb* (*tr*) to manage badly or wrongly > **ˌmisˈmanagement** *n* > **ˌmisˈmanager** *n*

mismatch (ˌmɪsˈmætʃ) *vb* **1** to match badly, esp in marriage ▷ *n* **2** a bad or inappropriate match

misnomer (ˌmɪsˈnəʊmə) *n* **1** an incorrect or unsuitable name or term for a person or thing **2** the act of referring to a person by the wrong name [c15 via Anglo-Norman from Old French *mesnommer* to misname, from Latin *nōmināre* to call by name]

miso (ˈmiːsəʊ) *n* a thick brown salty paste made from soya beans, used to flavour savoury dishes, esp soups [from Japanese]

miso- or before a vowel **mis-** *combining form* indicating hatred: *misogyny* [from Greek *misos* hatred]

misogamy (mɪˈsɒgəmɪ, maɪ-) *n* hatred of marriage > **miˈsogamist** *n*

misogyny (mɪˈsɒdʒɪnɪ, maɪ-) *n* hatred of women [c17 from Greek, from MISO- + *gunē* woman] > **miˈsogynist** *n, adj* > **miˌsogyˈnistic** or **miˈsogynous** *adj*

misology (mɪˈsɒlədʒɪ, maɪ-) *n* hatred of reasoning or reasoned argument [c19 from Greek *misologia*, from *misos* hatred + *logos* word, reasoning. See LOGOS] > **miˈsologist** *n*

misoneism (ˌmɪsəʊˈniːˌɪzəm, ˌmaɪ-) *n* hatred of anything new [c19 from Italian *misoneismo*; see MISO-, NEO-, -ISM] > **ˌmisoˈneist** *n* > **ˌmisoneˈistic** *adj*

mispickel (ˈmɪsˌpɪkᵊl) *n* another name for **arsenopyrite** [c17 from German]

misplace (ˌmɪsˈpleɪs) *vb* (*tr*) **1** to put (something) in the wrong place, esp to lose (something) temporarily by forgetting where it was placed; mislay **2** (*often passive*) to bestow (trust, confidence, affection, etc) unadvisedly > **ˌmisˈplacement** *n*

misplaced modifier *n grammar* a participle intended to modify a noun but having the wrong grammatical relationship to it as for example *having left* in the sentence *Having left Europe for good, Peter's future seemed bleak indeed.* Usual US and Canadian name: dangling participle

misplay (ˌmɪsˈpleɪ) *vb* **1** (*tr*) to play badly or wrongly in games or sports: *the batsman misplayed the ball* ▷ *n* **2** a wrong or unskilful play

misplead (mɪsˈpliːd) *vb* **-pleads, -pleading, -pleaded, -plead** (-ˈplɛd) or **-pled** (*tr*) to plead incorrectly

mispleading (mɪsˈpliːdɪŋ) *n law* an error or omission in pleading

misprint *n* (ˈmɪsˌprɪnt) **1** an error in printing, made through damaged type, careless reading, etc ▷ *vb* (ˌmɪsˈprɪnt) **2** (*tr*) to print (a letter) incorrectly

misprision¹ (mɪsˈprɪʒən) *n* **a** a failure to inform the proper authorities of the commission of an act of treason **b** the deliberate concealment of

m

the commission of a felony [C15 via Anglo-French from Old French *mesprision* error, from *mesprendre* to mistake, from *mes-* MIS-¹ + *prendre* to take]

misprision² (mɪsˈprɪʒən) *n archaic* **1** contempt **2** failure to appreciate the value of something [C16 from MISPRIZE]

misprize or **misprise** (mɪsˈpraɪz) *vb* to fail to appreciate the value of; undervalue or disparage [C15 from Old French *mesprisier*, from *mes-* MIS-¹ + *prisier* to PRIZE²]

mispronounce (ˌmɪsprəˈnaʊns) *vb* to pronounce (a word) wrongly > mispronunciation (ˌmɪsprəˌnʌnsɪˈeɪʃən) *n*

misquote (ˌmɪsˈkwəʊt) *vb* to quote (a text, speech, etc) inaccurately > ˌmisquoˈtation *n*

misread (ˌmɪsˈriːd) *vb* -reads, -reading, -read (-ˈrɛd) (*tr*) **1** to read incorrectly **2** to misinterpret

misreport (ˌmɪsrɪˈpɔːt) *vb* **1** (*tr*) to report falsely or inaccurately ▷ *n* **2** an inaccurate or false report > ˌmisreˈporter *n*

misrepresent (ˌmɪsrɛprɪˈzɛnt) *vb* (*tr*) to represent wrongly or inaccurately > ˌmisrepresenˈtation *n* > ˌmisrepreˈsentative *adj* > ˌmisrepreˈsenter *n*

misrule (ˌmɪsˈruːl) *vb* (*tr*) to govern inefficiently or without humanity or justice ▷ *n* **2** inefficient or inhumane government **3** disorder

miss¹ (mɪs) *vb* **1** to fail to reach, hit, meet, find, or attain (some specified or implied aim, goal, target, etc) **2** (*tr*) to fail to attend or be present for: *to miss a train; to miss an appointment* **3** (*tr*) to fail to see, hear, understand, or perceive: *to miss a point* **4** (*tr*) to lose, overlook, or fail to take advantage of: *to miss an opportunity* **5** (*tr*) to leave out; omit: *to miss an entry in a list* **6** (*tr*) to discover or regret the loss or absence of: *he missed his watch; she missed him* **7** (*tr*) to escape or avoid (something, esp a danger), usually narrowly: *he missed death by inches* **8** miss the boat or bus to lose an opportunity ▷ *n* **9** a failure to reach, hit, meet, find, etc **10** give (something) a miss *informal* to avoid (something): *give the lecture a miss; give the pudding a miss* ▷ See also **miss out** [Old English *missan* (meaning: to fail to hit); related to Old High German *missan*, Old Norse *missa*] > ˈmissable *adj*

miss² (mɪs) *n informal* an unmarried woman or girl, esp a schoolgirl [C17 shortened form of MISTRESS]

Miss (mɪs) *n* a title of an unmarried woman or girl, usually used before the surname or sometimes alone in direct address [C17 shortened from MISTRESS]

Miss. *abbreviation for* Mississippi

missal (ˈmɪsəl) *n RC Church* a book containing the prayers, rites, etc, of the Masses for a complete year [C14 from Church Latin *missale* (n), from *missālis* concerning the MASS]

mis-sell *vb, pl* -sells, -selling -sold to sell a financial product that is inappropriate for the needs of the customer

missel thrush (ˈmɪsəl) *n* a variant spelling of mistle thrush

misshape *vb* (ˌmɪsˈʃeɪp) -shapes, -shaping, -shaped; -shaped or -shapen (*tr*) **1** to shape badly; deform ▷ *n* (ˈmɪsˌʃeɪp) **2** something that is badly shaped

misshapen (ˌmɪsˈʃeɪpən) *adj* badly shaped; deformed > ˌmisˈshapenly *adv* > ˌmisˈshapenness *n*

missile (ˈmɪsaɪl) *n* **1** any object or weapon that is thrown at a target or shot from an engine, gun, etc **2 a** a rocket-propelled weapon that flies either in a fixed trajectory (**ballistic missile**) or in a trajectory that can be controlled during flight (**guided missile**) **b** (*as modifier*): *a missile carrier* [C17 from Latin: *missilis*, from *mittere* to send]

missileer (ˌmɪsaɪˈlɪə) *n* a serviceman or servicewoman who is responsible for firing missiles

missilery or **missilry** (ˈmɪsaɪlrɪ) *n* **1** missiles collectively **2** the design, operation, or study of missiles

missing (ˈmɪsɪŋ) *adj* **1** not present; absent or lost **2** not able to be traced and not known to be dead:

nine men were missing after the attack **3** go missing to become lost or disappear

missing fundamental *n* a tone, not present in the sound received by the ear, whose pitch is that of the difference between the two tones that are sounded

missing link *n* **1** (*sometimes capitals; usually preceded by the*) a hypothetical extinct animal or animal group, formerly thought to be intermediate between the anthropoid apes and man **2** any missing section or part in an otherwise complete series

missiology (ˌmɪsɪˈɒlədʒɪ) *n christian theol* the study of the missionary function of the Christian Church

mission (ˈmɪʃən) *n* **1** a specific task or duty assigned to a person or group of people: *their mission was to irrigate the desert* **2** a person's vocation (often in the phrase **mission in life**) **3** a group of persons representing or working for a particular country, business, etc, in a foreign country **4 a** a special embassy sent to a foreign country for a specific purpose **b** US a permanent legation **5 a** a group of people sent by a religious body, esp a Christian church, to a foreign country to do religious and social work **b** the campaign undertaken by such a group **6 a** the work or calling of a missionary **b** a building or group of buildings in which missionary work is performed **c** the area assigned to a particular missionary **7** the dispatch of aircraft or spacecraft to achieve a particular task **8** a church or chapel that has no incumbent of its own **9** a charitable centre that offers shelter, aid, or advice to the destitute or underprivileged **10** (*modifier*) of or relating to an ecclesiastical mission: *a mission station* **11** *South African* a long and difficult process **12** (*modifier*) US (of furniture) in the style of the early Spanish missions of the southwestern US ▷ *vb* **13** (*tr*) to direct a mission to or establish a mission in (a given region) [C16 from Latin *missiō*, from *mittere* to send]

missionary (ˈmɪʃənərɪ) *n, pl* -aries **1** a member of a religious mission ▷ *adj* **2** of or relating to missionaries: *missionary work* **3** resulting from a desire to convert people to one's own beliefs: *missionary zeal*

missionary position *n informal* a position for sexual intercourse in which the man lies on top of the woman and they are face to face [C20 from the belief that missionaries advocated this as the proper position to primitive peoples among whom it was unknown]

Missionary Ridge *n* a ridge in NW Georgia and SE Tennessee: site of a battle (1863) during the Civil War: Northern victory leading to the campaign in Georgia

mission creep *n* the tendency for a task, esp a military operation, to become unintentionally wider in scope than its initial objectives

missioner (ˈmɪʃənə) *n* **1** a less common name for **missionary 2** a person heading a parochial mission in a Christian country

mission statement *n* an official statement of the aims and objectives of a business or other organization

missis (ˈmɪsɪz, -ɪs) *n* a variant spelling of **missus**

Mississauga (ˌmɪsəˈsɔːgə) *n* a town in SE Ontario: a SW suburb of Toronto. Pop: 612 925 (2001)

Mississippi (ˌmɪsɪˈsɪpɪ) *n* **1** a state of the southeastern US, on the Gulf of Mexico: consists of a largely forested undulating plain, with swampy regions in the northwest and on the coast, the Mississippi River forming the W border; cotton, rice, and oil. Capital: Jackson. Pop: 2 881 281 (2003 est). Area: 122 496 sq km (47 296 sq miles). Abbreviations: Miss, (with zip code) MS **2** a river in the central US, rising in NW Minnesota and flowing generally south to the Gulf of Mexico through several mouths, known as the Passes: the second longest river in North America (after its tributary, the Missouri), with the third largest

drainage basin in the world (after the Amazon and the Congo). Length: 3780 km (2348 miles)

Mississippian (ˌmɪsɪˈsɪpɪən) *adj* **1** of or relating to the state of Mississippi or the Mississippi River **2** (in North America) of, denoting, or formed in the lower of two subdivisions of the Carboniferous period (see also **Pennsylvanian** (sense 2)), which lasted for 30 million years ▷ *n* **3** an inhabitant or native of the state of Mississippi **4** the Mississippian period or rock system equivalent to the lower Carboniferous of Europe

missive (ˈmɪsɪv) *n* **1** a formal or official letter **2** a formal word for **letter** ▷ *adj* **3** *rare* sent or intended to be sent [C15 from Medieval Latin *missivus*, from *mittere* to send]

Missolonghi (ˌmɪsəˈlɒŋgɪ) or **Mesolonghi** *n* a town in W Greece, near the Gulf of Patras: famous for its defence against the Turks in 1822–23 and 1825–26 and for its association with Lord Byron, who died here in 1824. Pop: 11 275 (latest est). Modern Greek name: **Mesolóngion**

Missouri (mɪˈzʊərɪ) *n* **1** a state of the central US: consists of rolling prairies in the north, the Ozark Mountains in the south, and part of the Mississippi flood plain in the southeast, with the Mississippi forming the E border; chief US producer of lead and barytes. Capital: Jefferson City. Pop: 5 704 484 (2003 est). Area: 178 699 sq km (68 995 sq miles). Abbreviations: Mo, (with zip code) MO **2** a river in the W and central US, rising in SW Montana: flows north, east, and southeast to join the Mississippi above St Louis; the longest river in North America; chief tributary of the Mississippi. Length: 3970 km (2466 miles)

Missourian (mɪˈzʊərɪən) *n* **1** a native or inhabitant of Missouri ▷ *adj* **2** of or relating to Missouri or its inhabitants

miss out *vb* **1** (*tr, adverb*) to leave out; overlook **2** (*intr, adverb; often foll by on*) to fail to experience: *by leaving early you missed out on the celebrations*

misspell (ˌmɪsˈspɛl) *vb* -spells, -spelling, -spelt or -spelled to spell (a word or words) wrongly

misspelling (ˌmɪsˈspɛlɪŋ) *n* a wrong spelling

misspend (ˌmɪsˈspɛnd) *vb* -spends, -spending, -spent to spend thoughtlessly or wastefully > ˌmisˈspender *n*

misstate (ˌmɪsˈsteɪt) *vb* (*tr*) to state incorrectly > ˌmisˈstatement *n*

misstep (ˌmɪsˈstɛp) *n* **1** a false step **2** an error

missus or **missis** (ˈmɪsɪz, -ɪs) *n* **1** (*usually preceded by the*) *informal* one's wife or the wife of the person addressed or referred to **2** an informal term of address for a woman [C19 spoken version of MISTRESS]

missy (ˈmɪsɪ) *n, pl* missies *informal* an affectionate or sometimes disparaging form of address to a young girl

mist (mɪst) *n* **1** a thin fog resulting from condensation in the air near the earth's surface **2** *meteorol* such an atmospheric condition with a horizontal visibility of 1–2 kilometres **3** a fine spray of any liquid, such as that produced by an aerosol container **4** *chem* a colloidal suspension of a liquid in a gas **5** condensed water vapour on a surface that blurs the surface **6** something that causes haziness or lack of clarity, such as a film of tears ▷ *vb* **7** to cover or be covered with or as if with mist [Old English; related to Middle Dutch, Swedish *mist*, Greek *omikhlē* fog]

mistakable or **mistakeable** (mɪˈsteɪkəbəl) *adj* liable to be mistaken > misˈtakably or misˈtakeably *adv*

mistake (mɪˈsteɪk) *n* **1** an error or blunder in action, opinion, or judgment **2** a misconception or misunderstanding ▷ *vb* -takes, -taking, -took, -taken **3** (*tr*) to misunderstand; misinterpret: *she mistook his meaning* **4** (*tr; foll by for*) to take (for), interpret (as), or confuse (with): *she mistook his direct manner for honesty* **5** (*tr*) to choose badly or incorrectly: *he mistook his path* **6** (*intr*) to make a mistake in action, opinion, judgment, etc [C13 (meaning: to do wrong, err): from Old Norse *mistaka* to take erroneously] > mis'taker *n*

mistaken (mɪˈsteɪkən) *adj* **1** (*usually predicative*) wrong in opinion, judgment, etc: *she is mistaken* **2** arising from error in judgment, opinion, etc: *a mistaken viewpoint* > mis'takenly *adv* > mis'takenness *n*

mistal (ˈmɪstəl) *n dialect* a cow shed; byre [c17 of uncertain origin]

Mistassini (ˌmɪstəˈsiːnɪ) *n* **Lake** a lake in E Canada, in N Quebec: the largest lake in the province; drains through the Rupert River into James Bay. Area: 2175 sq km (840 sq miles). Length: about 160 km (100 miles)

mister (ˈmɪstə) (*sometimes capital*) *n* **1** an informal form of address for a man **2** *naval* **a** the official form of address for subordinate or senior warrant officers **b** the official form of address for all officers in a merchant ship, other than the captain **c** *US navy* the official form of address used by the commanding officer to his officers, esp the more junior **3** *Brit* the form of address for a surgeon **4** the form of address for officials holding certain positions: *mister chairman* ▷ *vb* **5** (*tr*) *informal* to call (someone) mister [c16 variant of MASTER]

Mister (ˈmɪstə) *n* the full form of **Mr**

Misti (*Spanish* ˈmisti) *n* See **El Misti**

mistigris (ˈmɪstɪɡriː) *n* **1** the joker or a blank card used as a wild card in a variety of draw poker **2** the variety of draw poker using this card [c19 from French *mistigris* jack of clubs, game in which this card was wild]

mistime (ˌmɪsˈtaɪm) *vb* (*tr*) to time (an action, utterance, etc) wrongly

misting (ˈmɪstɪŋ) *n* the act or an instance of having an artificial suntan applied to the skin by a fine spray of liquid

mistle thrush *or* **missel thrush** (ˈmɪsˀl) *n* a large European thrush, *Turdus viscivorus*, with a brown back and spotted breast, noted for feeding on mistletoe berries [c18 from Old English *mistel* MISTLETOE]

mistletoe (ˈmɪsˀlˌtəʊ) *n* **1** a Eurasian evergreen shrub, *Viscum album*, with leathery leaves, yellowish flowers, and waxy white berries: grows as a partial parasite on various trees: used as a Christmas decoration: family *Viscaceae* **2** any of several similar and related American plants in the families *Loranthaceae* or *Viscaceae*, esp *Phoradendron flavescens* **3** **mistletoe cactus** an epiphytic cactus, *Rhipsalis cassytha*, that grows in tropical America [Old English *misteltān*, from *mistel* mistletoe + *tān* twig; related to Old Norse *mistilteinn*]

mistletoe bird *n* a small Australian flowerpecker, *Dicaeum hirundinaceum*, that feeds on mistletoe berries

mistook (mɪˈstʊk) *vb* the past tense of **mistake**

mistral (ˈmɪstrəl, mɪˈstrɑːl) *n* **1** a strong cold dry wind that blows through the Rhône valley and S France to the Mediterranean coast, mainly in the winter **2** the class of board used in international windsurfing competitions, weighing 15kg and measuring 372cm × 64cm [c17 via French from Provençal, from Latin *magistrālis* MAGISTRAL, as in *magistrālis ventus* master wind]

mistreat (ˌmɪsˈtriːt) *vb* (*tr*) to treat badly > ˌmisˈtreatment *n*

mistress (ˈmɪstrɪs) *n* **1** a woman who has a continuing extramarital sexual relationship with a man **2** a woman in a position of authority, ownership, or control, such as the head of a household **3** a woman or female personification having control over something specified: *she was mistress of her own destiny* **4** *chiefly Brit* short for **schoolmistress 5** an archaic or dialect word for **sweetheart** [c14 from Old French; see MASTER, -ESS]

Mistress (ˈmɪstrɪs) *n* an archaic or dialect title equivalent to **Mrs**

Mistress of the Robes *n* (in Britain) a lady of high rank in charge of the Queen's wardrobe

mistrial (mɪsˈtraɪəl) *n* **1** a trial made void because of some error, such as a defect in procedure **2** (in the US) an inconclusive trial, as when a jury cannot agree on a verdict

mistrust (ˌmɪsˈtrʌst) *vb* **1** to have doubts or suspicions about (someone or something) ▷ *n* **2** distrust > ˌmisˈtruster *n* > ˌmisˈtrustful *adj* > ˌmisˈtrustfully *adv* > ˌmisˈtrustfulness *n*

misty (ˈmɪstɪ) *adj* mistier, mistiest **1** consisting of or resembling mist **2** obscured by or as if by mist **3** indistinct; blurred: *the misty past* > ˈmistily *adv* > ˈmistiness *n*

misunderstand (ˌmɪsʌndəˈstænd) *vb* -stands, -standing, -stood to fail to understand properly

misunderstanding (ˌmɪsʌndəˈstændɪŋ) *n* **1** a failure to understand properly **2** a disagreement

misunderstood (ˌmɪsʌndəˈstʊd) *adj* not properly or sympathetically understood: *a misunderstood work of art; a misunderstood adolescent*

misuse *n* (ˌmɪsˈjuːs) *also* **misusage 1** erroneous, improper, or unorthodox use: *misuse of words* **2** cruel or inhumane treatment ▷ *vb* (ˌmɪsˈjuːz) (*tr*) **3** to use wrongly **4** to treat badly or harshly **5** to use (something, esp alcohol, drugs, etc) improperly

misuser (ˌmɪsˈjuːzə) *n* **1** *law* an abuse of some right, privilege, office, etc, such as one that may lead to its forfeiture **2** (*often in combination*) a person who regularly abuses alcohol, drugs, etc: *heroin misusers* [c17 from Old French *mesuser* (infinitive used as noun)]

MIT *abbreviation for* Massachusetts Institute of Technology

mitch *or* **mich** (mɪtʃ) *vb* (*intr*) *dialect* to play truant from school [c13 probably from Old French *muchier*, *mucier* to hide, lurk]

mite¹ (maɪt) *n* any of numerous small free-living or parasitic arachnids of the order *Acarina* (or *Acari*) that can occur in terrestrial or aquatic habitats. See also **gall mite, harvest mite, itch mite, spider mite** Related *adj*: **acaroid** Compare **tick²** [Old English *mīte*; compare Old High German *mīza* gnat, Dutch *mijt*]

mite² (maɪt) *n* **1** a very small particle, creature, or object **2** a very small contribution or sum of money. See also **widow's mite 3** a former Flemish coin of small value **4 a mite** *informal* somewhat: *he's a mite foolish* [c14 from Middle Low German, Middle Dutch *mite*; compare MITE¹]

miter (ˈmaɪtə) *n, vb* the usual US spelling of **mitre**

miterwort (ˈmaɪtəˌwɜːt) *n* the US spelling of **mitrewort**

mither¹ (ˈmɪðə) *n* a Scot word for **mother¹**

mither² (ˈmaɪðə) *vb* (*intr*) *Northern English dialect* to fuss over or moan about something [c17 of unknown origin]

Mithgarthr (ˈmɪðˌɡɑːðə) *n* a variant of **Midgard**

Mithraism (ˈmɪθreɪˌɪzəm) *or* **Mithraicism** (mɪθˈreɪɪˌsɪzəm) *n* the ancient Persian religion of Mithras. It spread to the Roman Empire during the first three centuries AD > **Mithraic** (mɪθˈreɪɪk) *or* ˌMithraˈistic *adj* > ˈMithraist *n, adj*

Mithras (ˈmɪθræs) *or* **Mithra** (ˈmɪθrə) *n persian myth* the god of light, identified with the sun, who slew a primordial bull and fertilized the world with its blood

mithridate (ˈmɪθrɪˌdeɪt) *n obsolete* a substance believed to be an antidote to every poison and a cure for every disease [c16 from Late Latin *mithradatium*, after *Mithridates* VI (?132–63 BC), king of Pontus, alluding to his legendary immunity to poisons]

mithridatism (ˈmɪθrɪdeɪˌtɪzəm) *n* immunity to large doses of poison by prior ingestion of gradually increased doses > **mithridatic** (ˌmɪθrɪˈdætɪk, -ˈdeɪ-) *adj*

miticide (ˈmɪtɪˌsaɪd) *n* any drug or agent that destroys mites > ˌmitiˈcidal *adj*

mitigate (ˈmɪtɪˌɡeɪt) *vb* to make or become less severe or harsh; moderate [c15 from Latin *mītigāre*, from *mītis* mild + *agere* to make] > **mitigable** (ˈmɪtɪɡəbˀl) *adj* > ˌmitiˈgation *n* > ˈmitiˌgative *or* ˈmitiˌgatory *adj* > ˈmitiˌgator *n*

USAGE *Mitigate* is sometimes wrongly used where *militate* is meant: *his behaviour militates* (not *mitigates*) *against his chances of promotion*

mitigating circumstances *pl n* circumstances that may be considered to lessen the culpability of an offender

Mitilíni (mitiˈlini) *n* transliteration of the Modern Greek name for **Mytilene** (sense 1)

mitis (ˈmaɪtɪs, ˈmiː-) *or* **mitis metal** *n* a malleable iron, fluid enough for casting, made by adding a small amount of aluminium to wrought iron [c19 from Latin: soft]

Mitnaged (ˌmitnaˈɡed) *or* **Misnaged** (misˈnaɡed) *n, pl* **Mitnagdim** (ˌmitnaˈɡdim) *or* **Misnagdim** (misˈnaɡdim) *Judaism* an orthodox opponent of Chassidism. See **Chassid** [from Hebrew, literally: opponent]

mitochondrial DNA *n* DNA found in mitochondria, which contains some structural genes and is generally inherited only through the female line. Abbreviation: mtDNA

mitochondrion (ˌmaɪtəʊˈkɒndriən) *n, pl* -dria (-drɪə) a small spherical or rodlike body, bounded by a double membrane, in the cytoplasm of most cells: contains enzymes responsible for energy production. Also called: **chondriosome** [c19 New Latin, from Greek *mitos* thread + *khondrion* small grain] > ˌmitoˈchondrial *adj*

mitogen (ˈmaɪtədʒən) *n* any agent that induces mitosis > **mitogenic** (ˌmaɪtəʊˈdʒɛnɪk) *adj*

mitosis (maɪˈtəʊsɪs, mɪ-) *n* a method of cell division, in which the nucleus divides into daughter nuclei, each containing the same number of chromosomes as the parent nucleus. See **prophase, metaphase, anaphase, telophase** Compare **meiosis** (sense 1) [c19 from New Latin, from Greek *mitos* thread] > **mitotic** (maɪˈtɒtɪk, mɪ-) *adj* > miˈtotically *adv*

mitrailleuse (ˌmiːtraɪˈɜːz) *n* **1** an early form of breech-loading machine gun having several parallel barrels **2** any French machine gun [c19 from French, from *mitraille* small shot, from Old French *mistraille* pieces of money, from MITE²]

mitral (ˈmaɪtrəl) *adj* **1** of or like a mitre **2** *anatomy* of or relating to the mitral valve

mitral valve *n* the valve between the left atrium and the left ventricle of the heart, consisting of two membranous flaps, that prevents regurgitation of blood into the atrium. Also called: **bicuspid valve**

mitre *or US* **miter** (ˈmaɪtə) *n* **1** *Christianity* the liturgical headdress of a bishop or abbot, in most western churches consisting of a tall pointed cleft cap with two bands hanging down at the back **2** short for **mitre joint 3** a bevelled surface of a mitre joint **4** (in sewing) a diagonal join where the hems along two sides meet at a corner of the fabric ▷ *vb* (*tr*) **5** to make a mitre joint between (two pieces of material, esp wood) **6** to make a mitre in (a fabric) **7** to confer a mitre upon: *a mitred abbot* [c14 from Old French, from Latin *mitra*, from Greek *mitra* turban]

mitre block *n* a block of wood with slots for cutting mitre joints with a saw

mitre box *n* an open-ended box with sides having narrow slots to guide a saw in cutting mitre joints

mitre gear *n* one of a pair of similar bevel gears or shafts at right angles to each other having a pitch cone angle of 45°

mitre joint *n* a corner joint formed between two pieces of material, esp wood, by cutting bevels of equal angles at the ends of each piece. Sometimes shortened to: **mitre**

mitre square *n* a tool with two blades that are at a fixed angle to one another, used to bevel a mitre joint

mitrewort *or US* **miterwort** (ˈmaɪtəˌwɜːt) *n* any of several Asian and North American saxifragaceous plants of the genus *Mitella*, having clusters of small white flowers and capsules resembling a bishop's mitre. Also called:

m

bishop's-cap

mitt (mɪt) *n* **1** any of various glovelike hand coverings, such as one that does not cover the fingers **2** short for **mitten** (sense 1) **3** *baseball* a large round thickly padded leather mitten worn by the catcher. See also **glove** (sense 2) **4** (*often plural*) a slang word for **hand 5** *slang* a boxing glove [C18 shortened from MITTEN]

Mittelland Canal (*German* 'mɪtəllant) *n* a canal in Germany, linking the Rivers Rhine and Elbe. Length: 325 km (202 miles)

mitten ('mɪtªn) *n* **1** a glove having one section for the thumb and a single section for the other fingers. Sometimes shortened to: **mitt 2** *slang* a boxing glove [C14 from Old French *mitaine*, of uncertain origin]

mittimus ('mɪtɪməs) *n, pl* **-muses** *law* a warrant of commitment to prison or a command to a jailer directing him to hold someone in prison [C15 from Latin: we send, the first word of such a command]

Mitty ('mɪtɪ) *n* Walter **a** a fictional character given to grand and elaborate fantasies; daydreamer **b** (*as modifier*): *a Walter Mitty character; a Mitty act* [C20 from a short story *The Secret Life of Walter Mitty* (1939), by James Thurber (1894–1961), the US humorist and illustrator] > ˌMitty'esque *or* 'Mitty-ˌlike *adj*

mitumba (mɪ'tʊmbə) *n* **a** used clothes imported for sale in African countries from more developed western countries **b** (*as modifier*): *the mitumba economy* [C20 Swahili, literally: bale]

mitzvah ('mɪtsvə; *Hebrew* mits'va) *n, pl* **-vahs** *or* **-voth** (*Hebrew* -'vɔt) *Judaism* **1** a commandment or precept, esp one found in the Bible **2** a good deed [from Hebrew: commandment]

mix (mɪks) *vb* **1** (*tr*) to combine or blend (ingredients, liquids, objects, etc) together into one mass **2** (*intr*) to become or have the capacity to become combined, joined, etc: *some chemicals do not mix* **3** (*tr*) to form (something) by combining two or more constituents: *to mix cement* **4** (*tr*; often foll by *in* or *into*) to add as an additional part or element (to a mass or compound): *to mix flour into a batter* **5** (*tr*) to do at the same time; combine: *to mix study and pleasure* **6** (*tr*) to consume (drinks or foods) in close succession **7** to come or cause to come into association socially: *Pauline has never mixed well* **8** (*tr*; often foll by *with*) to go together; complement **9** (*tr*) to crossbreed (differing strains of plants or breeds of livestock), esp more or less at random **10** (*tr*) *electronics* to combine (two or more signals) **11** *music* **a** (in sound recording) to balance and adjust (the recorded tracks) on a multitrack tape machine **b** (in live performance) to balance and adjust (the output levels from microphones and pick-ups) **12** (*tr*) to merge (two lengths of film) so that the effect is imperceptible **13** mix it *informal* **a** to cause mischief or trouble, often for a person named: *she tried to mix it for John* **b** to fight ▷ *n* **14** the act or an instance of mixing **15** the result of mixing; mixture **16** a mixture of ingredients, esp one commercially prepared for making a cake, bread, etc **17** *music* the sound obtained by mixing **18** *building trades, civil engineering* the proportions of cement, sand, and aggregate in mortar, plaster, or concrete **19** *informal* a state of confusion, bewilderment ▷ See also **mix-up** [C15 back formation from *mixt* mixed, via Old French from Latin *mixtus*, from *miscēre* to mix] > 'mixable *adj* > ˌmixa'bility *n*

mixdown ('mɪks,daʊn) *n* (in sound recording) the transfer of a multitrack master mix to two-track stereo tape

mixed (mɪkst) *adj* **1** formed or blended together by mixing **2** composed of different elements, races, sexes, etc: *a mixed school* **3** consisting of conflicting elements, thoughts, attitudes, etc: *mixed feelings; mixed motives* **4** (of a legal action) **a** having the nature of both a real and a personal action, such as a demand for the return of wrongfully withheld property as well as for damages to compensate for the loss **b** having

aspects or issues determinable by different persons or bodies: *a mixed question of law and fact* **5** (of an inflorescence) containing cymose and racemose branches **6** (of a nerve) containing both motor and sensory nerve fibres **7** *maths* **a** (of a number) consisting of the sum of an integer and a fraction, as 5½ **b** (of a decimal) consisting of the sum of an integer and a decimal fraction, as 17.43 **c** (of an algebraic expression) consisting of the sum of a polynomial and a rational fraction, such as $2x + 4x^2 + 2/3x$ > mixedly ('mɪksɪdlɪ) *adv* > mixedness ('mɪksɪdnɪs) *n*

mixed bag *n informal* something composed of diverse elements, characteristics, people, etc

mixed blessing *n* an event, situation, etc, having both advantages and disadvantages

mixed bud *n* a bud containing both rudimentary flowers and foliage leaves

mixed crystal *n chem* a crystal consisting of a solid solution of two or more distinct compounds

mixed doubles *pl n tennis* a doubles game with a man and a woman as partners on each side

mixed economy *n* an economy in which some industries are privately owned and others are publicly owned or nationalized

mixed farming *n* combined arable and livestock farming (on **mixed farms**)

mixed-flow turbine *n* a water turbine in which water flows radially and axially through the rotating vanes

mixed grill *n* a dish made of several kinds of grilled meats, often served with grilled tomatoes and mushrooms

mixed language *n* any language containing items of vocabulary or other linguistic characteristics borrowed from two or more existing languages. See also **pidgin, creole** (sense 1), **lingua franca**

mixed marriage *n* a marriage between persons of different races or religions

mixed media *n* **a** the integrated use of different forms of media, esp within the arts **b** (*as modifier*): *mixed-media musical presentations*

mixed metaphor *n* a combination of incongruous metaphors, as *when the Nazi jackboots sing their swan song*

mixed-up *adj* in a state of mental confusion; perplexed

mixer ('mɪksə) *n* **1** a person or thing that mixes **2** *informal* **a** a person considered in relation to his ability to mix socially **b** a person who creates trouble for others **3** a kitchen appliance, usually electrical, used for mixing foods, etc **4** a drink such as ginger ale, fruit juice, etc, used in preparing cocktails **5** *electronics* a device in which two or more input signals are combined to give a single output signal **6** short for **sound mixer, vision mixer**

mixer tap *n* a tap in which hot and cold water supplies have a joint outlet but are controlled separately

Mixe-Zoque ('mɪks'zɒk) *n* **1** a member of an American Indian people of Mexico **2** any of the languages of this people

mixmaster ('mɪks,mɑːstə) *n informal* a disc jockey

mixologist (ˌmɪk'sɒlədʒɪst) *n* **1** *humorous* a person who serves drinks, esp cocktails, at a bar **2** *music* a person skilled at mixing sounds in recording or live performance

mixolydian (ˌmɪksəʊ'lɪdɪən) *adj music* of, relating to, or denoting an authentic mode represented by the ascending natural diatonic scale from G to G. See **Hypo-** [C16 from Greek *mixoludios* half-Lydian]

mixte ('mɪkstɪ) *adj* of or denoting a type of bicycle frame, usually for women, in which angled twin lateral tubes run back to the rear axle [C20 from French]

Mixtec ('miːstɛk) *n* (*pl* **-tecs** *or* **-tec**) a member of an American Indian people of Mexico **2** the language of this people > Mix'tecan *adj, n*

mixter-maxter ('mɪkstər'mækstər) *Scot* ▷ *adj* **1** chaotic or confused ▷ *n* **2** a chaotic or confused

mixture; jumble [C19 reduplicated form based on MIX]

mixture ('mɪkstʃə) *n* **1** the act of mixing or state of being mixed **2** something mixed; a result of mixing **3** *chem* a substance consisting of two or more substances mixed together without any chemical bonding between them **4** *pharmacol* a liquid medicine in which an insoluble compound is suspended in the liquid **5** *music* an organ stop that controls several ranks of pipes sounding the upper notes in a harmonic series **6** the mixture of petrol vapour and air in an internal-combustion engine [C16 from Latin *mixtūra*, from *mixtus*, past participle of *miscēre* to mix]

mix-up *n* **1** a confused condition or situation **2** *informal* a fight ▷ *vb* mix up (*tr, adverb*) **3** to make into a mixture: *to mix up ingredients* **4** to confuse or confound: *Tom mixes John up with Bill* **5** (*often passive*) to put (someone) into a state of confusion: *I'm all mixed up* **6** (foll by *in* or *with*; usually passive) to involve (in an activity or group, esp one that is illegal): *why did you get mixed up in that drugs racket?* **7** mix it up *US and Canadian informal* to fight

Mizar ('maɪzɑː) *n* a multiple star having four components that lies in the Plough in the constellation Ursa Major and forms a visible binary with the star Alcor. Visual magnitude: 2.1; spectral type: A2V [from Arabic *mi'zar* cloak]

Mizoram (mɪ'zɔːrəm) *n* a state (since 1986) in NE India, created in 1972 from the former Mizo Hills District of Assam. Capital: Aijal. Pop: 891 058 (2001). Area: about 21 081 sq km (8140 sq miles)

mizuna (mɪ'zuːnə) *n* a Japanese variety of lettuce having crisp green leaves [Japanese]

mizzen *or* **mizen** ('mɪzªn) *nautical* ▷ *n* **1** a sail set on a mizzenmast **2** short for **mizzenmast** ▷ *adj* **3** of or relating to any kind of gear used with a mizzenmast: *a mizzen staysail* [C15 from French *misaine*, from Italian *mezzana, mezzano* middle]

mizzenmast *or* **mizenmast** ('mɪzªn,mɑːst; *Nautical* 'mɪzªnməst) *n nautical* **1** (on a yawl, ketch, or dandy) the after mast **2** (on a vessel with three or more masts) the third mast from the bow

mizzle[1] ('mɪzªl) *vb, n* a dialect word for **drizzle** [C15 perhaps from Low German *miseln* to drizzle; compare Dutch dialect *miezelen* to drizzle] > 'mizzly *adj*

mizzle[2] ('mɪzªl) *vb* (*intr*) *Brit slang* to decamp [C18 of unknown origin]

mizzy maze ('mɪzɪ) *n Southwestern English dialect* a state of confusion

mk[1] *currency symbol for* **1** mark **2** markka

mk[2] *the internet domain name for* Macedonia

Mk *abbreviation for* mark (type of car)

MK *international car registration for* (Federal Republic of) Macedonia [from Macedonian *Makedonija*]

MKSA system *n* another name for **Giorgi system**

mks units *pl n* a metric system of units based on the metre, kilogram, and second as the units of length, mass, and time; it forms the basis of the SI units

mkt *abbreviation for* market

ml[1] *symbol for* **1** millilitre **2** mile

ml[2] *the internet domain name for* Mali

ML *abbreviation for* Medieval Latin

MLA *abbreviation for* **1** Member of the Legislative Assembly (of Northern Ireland) **2** Modern Language Association (of America)

MLC (in India and Australia) *abbreviation for* Member of the Legislative Council

MLD *abbreviation for* minimum lethal dose (the smallest amount of a drug or toxic agent that will kill a laboratory animal)

MLF *abbreviation for* multilateral (nuclear) force

MLG *abbreviation for* Middle Low German

MLitt *abbreviation for* Master of Letters [Latin *Magister Litterarum*]

Mlle *n, pl* Mlles the French equivalent of **Miss** [from French *Mademoiselle*]

MLR *abbreviation for* minimum lending rate

mm[1] **1** *symbol for* millimetre **2** ▷ *abbreviation for* mutatis mutandis

mm² *the internet domain name for* Myanmar

MM 1 *abbreviation for* Military Medal **2** the French equivalent of **Messrs** [from French *Messieurs*]

Mmabatho (ˌmæbˈæθəʊ) *n* the capital of the former homeland of Bophuthatswana

MMC (formerly, in Britain) *abbreviation for* Monopolies and Mergers Commission

MMDS *abbreviation for* multipoint microwave distribution system: a radio alternative to cable television. Sometimes shortened to: MDS

Mme *n*, *pl* **Mmes** the French equivalent of **Mrs** [from French *Madame*, *Mesdames*]

mmf *abbreviation for* magnetomotive force

mmHg *abbreviation for* millimetre(s) of mercury (a unit of pressure equal to the pressure that can support a column of mercury 1 millimetre high)

MMM (in Canada) *abbreviation for* Member of the Order of Military Merit

mmorpg *abbreviation for* massive(ly) multiplayer online role-playing game: an internet-based computer game set in a virtual world, which can be played by many people at the same time, each of whom can interact with the others

MMP *abbreviation for* mixed member proportional: a system of proportional representation, used in Germany and New Zealand

MMR *n* a combined vaccine against measles, mumps, and rubella, given to young children

MMS *abbreviation for* multimedia messaging service: a method of transmitting graphics, video or sound files and short text messages over wireless networks, esp on mobile phones

MMus. *abbreviation for* Master of Music

MMV (in Canada) *abbreviation for* Medal of Military Valour

mn *the internet domain name for* Mongolia

Mn *the chemical symbol for* manganese

MN *abbreviation for* **1** (in Britain) Merchant Navy **2** Minnesota

MNA (in Canada) *abbreviation for* Member of the National Assembly (of Quebec)

mnemonic (nɪˈmɒnɪk) *adj* **1** aiding or meant to aid one's memory **2** of or relating to memory or mnemonics ▷ *n* **3** something, such as a verse, to assist memory [c18 from Greek *mnēmonikos*, from *mnēmōn* mindful, from *mnasthai* to remember] > **mneˈmonically** *adv*

mnemonics (nɪˈmɒnɪks) *n* (*usually functioning as singular*) **1** the art or practice of improving or of aiding the memory **2** a system of rules to aid the memory

Mnemosyne (niːˈmɒzɪˌniː, -ˈmɒs-) *n Greek myth* the goddess of memory and mother by Zeus of the Muses

mo¹ (məʊ) *n informal* **1** *chiefly Brit* short for **moment** (sense 1) (esp in the phrase **half a mo**) **2** *chiefly Austral* short for **moustache** (sense 1)

mo² *the internet domain name for* Macau

Mo *the chemical symbol for* molybdenum

MO *abbreviation for* **1** Missouri **2** Medical Officer **3** modus operandi

Mo. *abbreviation for* Missouri

mo. or **MO** *abbreviation for* **1** mail order **2** money order

-mo *suffix forming nouns* (in bookbinding) indicating book size by specifying the number of leaves formed by folding one sheet of paper: *12mo*, *twelvemo*, or *duodecimo*; *16mo* or *sixteenmo* [abstracted from DUODECIMO]

moa (ˈməʊə) *n* any large flightless bird of the recently extinct order *Dinornithiformes* of New Zealand (see **ratite**) [c19 from Māori]

Moab (ˈməʊæb) *n Old Testament* an ancient kingdom east of the Dead Sea, in what is now the SW part of Jordan: flourished mainly from the 9th to the 6th centuries BC > **Moabite** (ˈməʊəˌbaɪt) *adj*, *n*

Moabite (ˈməʊəˌbaɪt) *Old Testament* ▷ *adj* **1** of or relating to Moab, an ancient kingdom east of the Dead Sea, or its inhabitants ▷ *n* **2** a native or inhabitant of Moab

moa hunter *n* the name given by anthropologists to the early Māori inhabitants of New Zealand

moai (ˈməʊaɪ) *n*, *pl* **moai** any of the gigantic carved stone figures found on Easter Island (Rapa Nui) [from Rapanui (the Polynesian language of Easter Island), literally: statue, figurine]

moan (məʊn) *n* **1** a low prolonged mournful sound expressive of suffering or pleading **2** any similar mournful sound, esp that made by the wind **3** a grumble or complaint ▷ *vb* **4** to utter (words) in a low mournful manner **5** (*intr*) to make a sound like a moan **6** (*usually intr*) to grumble or complain (esp in the phrase **moan and groan**) [c13 related to Old English *mǣnan* to grieve over] > **ˈmoaner** *n* > **ˈmoanful** *adj* > **ˈmoaning** *n*, *adj* > **ˈmoaningly** *adv*

moat (məʊt) *n* **1** a wide water-filled ditch surrounding a fortified place, such as a castle ▷ *vb* **2** (*tr*) to surround with or as if with a moat: *a moated grange* [c14 from Old French *motte* mound]

mob (mɒb) *n* **1 a** a riotous or disorderly crowd of people; rabble **b** (*as modifier*): *mob law*; *mob violence* **2** *often derogatory* a group or class of people, animals, or things **3** *Austral and NZ* a flock (of sheep) or a herd (of cattle, esp when droving) **4** *often derogatory* the masses **5** *slang* a gang of criminals ▷ *vb* **mobs**, **mobbing**, **mobbed** (*tr*) **6** to attack in a group resembling a mob **7** to surround, esp in order to acclaim: *they mobbed the film star* **8** to crowd into (a building, plaza, etc) **9** (of a group of animals of a prey species) to harass (a predator) ▷ See also **mobs** [c17 shortened from Latin *mōbile vulgus* the fickle populace; see MOBILE] **ˈmobber** *n* > **ˈmobbish** *adj*

MOB *abbreviation for* mobile phone

mobcap (ˈmɒbˌkæp) *n* a woman's large cotton cap with a pouched crown and usually a frill, worn esp during the 18th century. Often shortened to: mob [c18 from obsolete *mob* woman, esp a loose-living woman, + CAP]

mobe (məʊb) *n informal* a mobile phone

mob-handed *adj*, *adv informal* in or with a large group of people: *the police turned up mob-handed*

mobie (ˈməʊbi) *n informal* a mobile phone

mobile (ˈməʊbaɪl) *adj* **1** having freedom of movement; movable **2** changing quickly in expression: *a mobile face* **3** *sociol* (of individuals or social groups) moving within and between classes, occupations, and localities: *upwardly mobile* **4** (of military forces) able to move freely and quickly to any given area **5** (*postpositive*) *informal* having transport available: *are you mobile tonight?* ▷ *n* **6 a** a sculpture suspended in midair with delicately balanced parts that are set in motion by air currents **b** (*as modifier*): *mobile sculpture*. Compare **stabile** **7** short for **mobile phone** [c15 via Old French from Latin *mōbilis*, from *movēre* to move]

Mobile (ˈməʊbiːl, məʊˈbiːl) *n* a port in SW Alabama, on **Mobile Bay** (an inlet of the Gulf of Mexico): the state's only port and its first permanent settlement, made by French colonists in 1711. Pop: 193 464 (2003 est)

-mobile (məʊˌbiːl) *suffix forming nouns* indicating a vehicle designed for a particular person or purpose: *Popemobile*

Mobile Command *n Canadian* the Canadian army and other land forces

mobile home *n* living quarters mounted on wheels and capable of being towed by a motor vehicle

mobile library *n* a vehicle providing lending library facilities. US and Canadian equivalent: bookmobile

mobile phone *n* a portable telephone that works by means of a cellular radio system

mobility (məʊˈbɪlɪtɪ) *n* **1** the ability to move physically: *a knee operation has restricted his mobility*; *mobility is part of physical education* **2** *sociol* (of individuals or social groups) movement within or between classes and occupations. See also **vertical mobility**, **horizontal mobility** **3** time that a resident of a secure unit is allowed to spend

outside the unit, as preparation for an eventual return to society

mobility housing *n social welfare* houses designed or adapted for people who have difficulty in walking but are not necessarily chairbound. See also **wheelchair housing**

mobilize or **mobilise** (ˈməʊbɪˌlaɪz) *vb* **1** to prepare for war or other emergency by organizing (national resources, the armed services, etc) **2** (*tr*) to organize for a purpose; marshal **3** (*tr*) to put into motion, circulation, or use > **ˈmobiˌlizable** or **ˈmobiˌlisable** *adj* > **ˌmobiliˈzation** or **ˌmobiliˈsation** *n*

Möbius strip (ˈmɜːbɪəs; *German* ˈmøːbiʊs) *n maths* a one-sided continuous surface, formed by twisting a long narrow rectangular strip of material through 180° and joining the ends [c19 named after August *Möbius* (1790–1868), German mathematician who invented it]

moblog (ˈmɒbˌlɒg) *n* a chronicle, which may be shared with others, of someone's thoughts and experiences recorded in the form of mobile phone calls, text messages, and photographs [c21 MOB(ILE) + LOG¹] > **ˈmobˌlogger** *n*

MOBO (ˈməʊbəʊ) (in Britain) *n acronymn for* Music of Black Origin: any of several awards given annually to musicians and performers of a variety of musical genres originating in Black culture

mobocracy (mɒˈbɒkrəsɪ) *n*, *pl* **-cies 1** rule or domination by a mob **2** the mob that rules > **mobocrat** (ˈmɒbəˌkræt) *n* > **ˌmoboˈcratic** or **ˌmoboˈcratical** *adj*

mobs (mɒbz) *informal* ▷ *pl n* **1** (usually foll by *of*) great numbers or quantities; lots: *mobs of people* ▷ *adv* **2** *Austral and NZ* a great deal: *mobs better*

mobster (ˈmɒbstə) *n* a US slang word for **gangster**

Mobutu (məˈbuːtuː) *n* the former name (until 1997) of **Lake Albert**. See **Albert**

moby (ˈməʊbɪ) *n*, *pl* **-bies** *informal* a mobile phone

MoC *abbreviation for* mother of the chapel

MOC *international car registration for* Mozambique [from Portuguese *Moçambique*]

Moçambique (musəmˈbikə) *n* the Portuguese name for **Mozambique**

moccasin (ˈmɒkəsɪn) *n* **1** a shoe of soft leather, esp deerskin, worn by North American Indians **2** any soft shoe resembling this **3** *NZ* a sheepshearer's footgear, usually made of sacking **4** short for **water moccasin** [c17 from Algonquian; compare Narraganset *mocussin* shoe]

moccasin flower *n* any of several North American orchids of the genus *Cypripedium* with a pink solitary flower. See also **lady's-slipper**, **cypripedium** (sense 1)

moccasin telegraph *n Canadian informal* the transmission of rumour or secret information; the grapevine

moccies (ˈmɒkɪz) *pl n Austral informal* moccasin shoes or slippers

mocha (ˈmɒkə) *n* **1** a strongly flavoured dark brown coffee originally imported from Arabia **2** a flavouring made from coffee and chocolate **3** a soft glove leather with a suede finish, made from goatskin or sheepskin **4 a** a dark brown colour **b** (*as adjective*): *mocha shoes*

Mocha or **Mokha** (ˈmɒkə) *n* a port in Yemen, on the Red Sea; in the former North Yemen until 1990: formerly important for the export of Arabian coffee. Pop: about 2000 (1990 est)

mocha stone *n* another name for **moss agate**

mock (mɒk) *vb* **1** (when *intr*, often foll by *at*) to behave with scorn or contempt (towards); show ridicule (for) **2** (*tr*) to imitate, esp in fun; mimic **3** (*tr*) to deceive, disappoint, or delude **4** (*tr*) to defy or frustrate: *the team mocked the visitors' attempt to score* ▷ *n* **5** the act of mocking **6** a person or thing mocked **7** a counterfeit; imitation **8** (*often plural*) *informal* (in England and Wales) the school examinations taken as practice before public examinations ▷ *adj* (*prenominal*) **9** sham or counterfeit **10** serving as an imitation or substitute, esp for practice purposes: *a mock battle*;

m

mock finals ▷ See also **mock-up** [c15 from Old French *mocquer*] > 'mockable *adj* > 'mocker *n* > 'mocking *n*, *adj* > 'mockingly *adv*

mocker ('mɒkə) *Austral slang, old-fashioned* ▷ *verb* **1** clothing ▷ *n* (*tr*) **2** all mockered up dressed up [of unknown origin]

mockernut ('mɒkə,nʌt) *n* **1** Also called: black hickory a species of smooth-barked hickory, *Carya tomentosa*, with fragrant foliage that turns bright yellow in autumn **2** the nut of this tree [so called because the nut is difficult to extract]

mockers ('mɒkəz) *pl n* put the mockers on *informal* to ruin the chances of success of. Also (Austral): put the mock (*or* mocks) on [c20 perhaps from MOCK]

mockery ('mɒkərɪ) *n*, *pl* -eries **1** ridicule, contempt, or derision **2** a derisive action or comment **3** an imitation or pretence, esp a derisive one **4** a person or thing that is mocked **5** a person, thing, or action that is inadequate or disappointing

mock-heroic *adj* **1** (of a literary work, esp a poem) imitating the style of heroic poetry in order to satirize an unheroic subject, as in Pope's *The Rape of the Lock* ▷ *n* **2** burlesque imitation of the heroic style or of a single work in this style

mockingbird ('mɒkɪŋ,bɜːd) *n* **1** any American songbird of the family *Mimidae*, having a long tail and grey plumage: noted for their ability to mimic the song of other birds *Austral* **2** a small scrb bird, *Atrichornis rufescens*, noted for its mimicry

mock moon *n* another name for **paraselene**

mockney ('mɒknɪ) *n* **1** (*often capital*) a person who affects a cockney accent **2** an affected cockney accent ▷ *adj* **3** denoting an affected cockney accent or a person who has one [c20 MOCK + COCKNEY]

mock orange *n* **1** Also called: syringa any shrub of the genus *Philadelphus*, esp *P. coronarius*, with white fragrant flowers that resemble those of the orange: family *Philadelphaceae* **2** any other shrub or tree that resembles the orange tree

mock sun *n* another name for **parhelion**

mock turtle soup *n* an imitation turtle soup made from a calf's head

mockumentary (,mɒkjʊ'mɛntərɪ, -trɪ) *n*, *pl* -ries a satirical television or radio programme in the form of a parody of a documentary [c20 from MOCK + (DOC)UMENTARY]

mock-up *n* **1** a working full-scale model of a machine, apparatus, etc, for testing, research, etc **2** a layout of printed matter ▷ *vb* mock up **3** (*tr, adverb*) to build or make a mock-up of

mod[1] (mɒd) *n Brit* **a** a member of a group of teenagers in the mid-1960s, noted for their clothes-consciousness and opposition to the rockers **b** a member of a revived group of this type in the late 1970s and early 1980s, noted for their clothes-consciousness and opposition to the skinheads **c** (*as modifier*): *a mod haircut* [c20 from MODERNIST]

mod[2] (mɒd) *n* an annual Highland Gaelic meeting with musical and literary competitions [c19 from Gaelic *mòd* assembly, from Old Norse; related to MOOT]

mod[3] (mɒd) *maths* abbreviation for **modulus**

MOD (in Britain) abbreviation for Ministry of Defence

mod. abbreviation for **1** moderate **2** moderato **3** modern

modal ('məʊdᵊl) *adj* **1** of, relating to, or characteristic of mode or manner **2** *grammar* (of a verb form or auxiliary verb) expressing a distinction of mood, such as that between possibility and actuality. The modal auxiliaries in English include *can, could, may, must, need, ought, shall, should, will,* and *would* **3** *philosophy, logic* **a** qualifying or expressing a qualification of the truth of some statement, for example, as necessary or contingent **b** relating to analogous qualifications such as that of rules as obligatory or permissive **4** *metaphysics* of or relating to the

form of a thing as opposed to its attributes, substance, etc **5** *music* of or relating to a mode **6** of or relating to a statistical mode > 'modally *adv*

modality (məʊ'dælɪtɪ) *n*, *pl* -ties **1** the condition of being modal **2** a quality, attribute, or circumstance that denotes mode, mood, or manner **3** *logic* the property of a statement of being classified under one of the concepts studied by modal logic, esp necessity or possibility **4** any physical or electrical therapeutic method or agency **5** any of the five senses

modal logic *n* **1** the logical study of such philosophical concepts as necessity, possibility, contingency, etc **2** the logical study of concepts whose formal properties resemble certain moral, epistemological, and psychological concepts. See also **alethic, deontic, epistemic, doxastic 3** any formal system capable of being interpreted as a model for the behaviour of such concepts

mod cons *pl n informal* modern conveniences; the usual installations of a modern house, such as hot water, heating, etc

mode (məʊd) *n* **1** a manner or way of doing, acting, or existing **2** the current fashion or style **3** *music* **a** any of the various scales of notes within one octave, esp any of the twelve natural diatonic scales taken in ascending order used in plainsong, folk song, and art music until 1600 **b** (in the music of classical Greece) any of the descending diatonic scales from which the liturgical modes evolved **c** either of the two main scale systems in music since 1600: *major mode; minor mode* **4** *logic, linguistics* another name for **modality** (sense 3), **mood**[2] (sense 2) **5** *philosophy* a complex combination of ideas the realization of which is not determined by the component ideas **6** that one of a range of values that has the highest frequency as determined statistically. Compare **mean**[3] (sense 4), **median** (sense 6) **7** the quantitative mineral composition of an igneous rock **8** *physics* one of the possible configurations of a travelling or stationary wave **9** *physics* one of the fundamental vibrations [c14 from Latin *modus* measure, manner]

model ('mɒdᵊl) *n* **1 a** a representation, usually on a smaller scale, of a device, structure, etc **b** (*as modifier*): *a model train* **2** a standard to be imitated: *she was my model for good scholarship* **b** (*as modifier*): *a model wife* **3** a representative form, style, or pattern **4** a person who poses for a sculptor, painter, or photographer **5** a person who wears clothes to display them to prospective buyers; mannequin **6** a preparatory sculpture in clay, wax, etc, from which the finished work is copied **7** a design or style, esp one of a series of designs of a particular product: *last year's model* **8** *Brit* **a** an original unique article of clothing **b** (*as modifier*): *a model coat* **9** a simplified representation or description of a system or complex entity, esp one designed to facilitate calculations and predictions **10** *logic* **a** an interpretation of a formal system under which the theorems derivable in that system are mapped onto truths **b** a theory in which a given sentence is true ▷ *vb* -els, -elling, -elled *or US* -els, -eling, -eled **11** to make a model of (something or someone) **12** to form in clay, wax, etc; mould **13** to display (clothing and accessories) as a mannequin **14** to plan or create according to a model or models **15** to arrange studio lighting so that highlights and shadows emphasize the desired features of a human form or an inanimate object [c16 from Old French *modelle*, from Italian *modello*, from Latin *modulus*, diminutive of *modus* MODE] > 'modeller *or US* 'modeler *n*

modelling *or US* **modeling** ('mɒdᵊlɪŋ) *n* **1** the act or an instance of making a model **2** the practice or occupation of a person who models clothes **3** a technique in psychotherapy in which the therapist encourages the patient to model his behaviour on his own

model theory *n* the branch of logic that deals

with the properties of models; the semantic study of formal systems > 'model-,theo'retic *adj*

modem ('məʊdɛm) *n computing* a device for connecting two computers by a telephone line, consisting of a modulator that converts computer signals into audio signals and a corresponding demodulator [c20 from *mo(dulator) dem(odulator)*]

Modena (Italian 'mɔːdena) *n* **1** a city in N Italy, in Emilia-Romagna: ruled by the Este family (18th–19th century); university (1678). Pop: 175 502 (2001. Ancient name: Mutina **2** (*sometimes not capital*) a popular variety of domestic fancy pigeon originating in Modena

moderate *adj* ('mɒdərɪt, 'mɒdrɪt) **1** not extreme or excessive; within due or reasonable limits: *moderate demands* **2** not violent; mild or temperate **3** of average quality or extent: *moderate success* ▷ *n* ('mɒdərɪt, 'mɒdrɪt) **4** a person who holds moderate views, esp in politics ▷ *vb* ('mɒdə,reɪt) **5** to become or cause to become less extreme or violent **6** (when *intr*, often foll by *over*) to preside over a meeting, discussion, etc **7** *Brit and NZ* to act as an external moderator of the overall standards and marks for (some types of educational assessment) **8** *physics* to slow down (neutrons), esp by using a moderator **9** (*tr*) to monitor the conversations in an on-line chatroom for bad language, inappropriate content, etc [c14 from Latin *moderātus* observing moderation, from *moderārī* to restrain] > 'moderately *adv* > 'moderateness *n* > 'moderatism *n*

moderate breeze *n* a wind of force four on the Beaufort scale

moderate gale *n* a gale of force seven on the Beaufort scale, capable of swaying trees

moderation (,mɒdə'reɪʃən) *n* **1** the state or an instance of being moderate; mildness; balance **2** the act of moderating **3** in moderation within moderate or reasonable limits

Moderations (,mɒdə'reɪʃənz) *pl n* short for **Honour Moderations**

moderato (,mɒdə'rɑːtəʊ) *adv music* **1** at a moderate tempo **2** (preceded by a tempo marking) a direction indicating that the tempo specified is to be used with restraint: *allegro moderato* [c18 from Italian, from Latin *moderātus*; see MODERATE]

moderator ('mɒdə,reɪtə) *n* **1** a person or thing that moderates **2** *Presbyterian Church* a minister appointed to preside over a Church court, synod, or general assembly **3** a presiding officer at a public or legislative assembly **4** a material, such as heavy water or graphite, used for slowing down neutrons in the cores of nuclear reactors so that they have more chance of inducing nuclear fission **5** an examiner at Oxford or Cambridge Universities in first public examinations **6** (in Britain and New Zealand) one who is responsible for consistency of standards in the grading of some educational assessments **7** a person who moniters the conversations in an on-line chatroom for bad language, inappropriate content, etc > 'mode,ratorship *n*

modern ('mɒdən) *adj* **1** of, involving, or befitting the present or a recent time; contemporary **2** of, relating to, or characteristic of contemporary styles or schools of art, literature, music, etc, esp those of an experimental kind **3** belonging or relating to the period in history from the end of the Middle Ages to the present ▷ *n* **4** a contemporary person **5** *printing* a type style that originated around the beginning of the 19th century, characterized chiefly by marked contrast between thick and thin strokes. Compare **old face** [c16 from Old French, from Late Latin *modernus*, from *modō* (adv) just recently, from *modus* MODE] > 'modernly *adv* > 'modernness *n*

modern apprenticeship *n* an arrangement that allows a school leaver to gain vocational qualifications while being trained in a job

modern dance *n* a style of free and expressive theatrical dancing not bound by the classical rules of ballet

moderne (məˈdɛən) *adj chiefly US* of or relating to the style of architecture and design, prevalent in Europe and the US in the late 1920s and 1930s, typified by the use of straight lines, tubular chromed steel frames, contrasting inlaid woods, etc. Compare **Art Deco**

Modern English *n* the English language since about 1450, esp any of the standard forms developed from the S East Midland dialect of Middle English. See also **English, Middle English, Old English**

modern greats *pl n* (at Oxford University) the Honour School of Philosophy, Politics, and Economics

Modern Greek *n* the Greek language since about 1453 AD (the fall of Byzantium). Compare **Demotic, Katharevusa**

Modern Hebrew *n* the official language of the state of Israel; a revived form of ancient Hebrew

modernism (ˈmɒdəˌnɪzəm) *n* **1** modern tendencies, characteristics, thoughts, etc, or the support of these **2** something typical of contemporary life or thought **3** a 20th-century divergence in the arts from previous traditions, esp in architecture. See **International Style 4** (*capital*) RC Church the movement at the end of the 19th and beginning of the 20th centuries that sought to adapt doctrine to the supposed requirements of modern thought > ˈmodernist *n, adj* > ˌmodernˈistic *adj* > ˌmodernˈistically *adv*

modernity (mɒˈdɜːnɪtɪ) *n, pl* **-ties 1** the quality or state of being modern **2** something modern

modernize *or* **modernise** (ˈmɒdəˌnaɪz) *vb* **1** (*tr*) to make modern in appearance or style: *to modernize a room* **2** (*intr*) to adopt modern ways, ideas, etc > ˌmoderniˈzation *or* moderniˈsation *n* > ˈmodernˌizer *or* ˈmodernˌiser *n*

modern jazz *n* any of the styles of jazz that evolved between the early 1940s and the later emergence of avant-garde jazz, characterized by a greater harmonic and rhythmic complexity than hitherto

modern language *n* any of the languages spoken in present-day Europe, with the exception of English

modern pentathlon *n* an athletic contest consisting of five different events: horse riding with jumps, fencing with electric épée, freestyle swimming, pistol shooting, and cross-country running

modern sequence dancing *n* a form of dancing in which ballroom dance steps are used as the basis of a wide variety of different dances typically performed in a sequence

modest (ˈmɒdɪst) *adj* **1** having or expressing a humble opinion of oneself or one's accomplishments or abilities **2** reserved or shy: *modest behaviour* **3** not ostentatious or pretentious **4** not extreme or excessive; moderate **5** decorous or decent [C16 via Old French from Latin *modestus* moderate, from *modus* MODE] > ˈmodestly *adv*

modesty (ˈmɒdɪstɪ) *n, pl* **-ties 1** the quality or condition of being modest **2** (*modifier*) designed to prevent inadvertent exposure of part of the body: *a modesty flap*

modge (mɒdʒ) *vb* (*tr*) *Midland English dialect* to do shoddily; make a mess of [C20 perhaps a variant of *mudge* to crush (hops)]

modicum (ˈmɒdɪkəm) *n* a small amount or portion [C15 from Latin: a little way, from *modicus* moderate]

modification (ˌmɒdɪfɪˈkeɪʃən) *n* **1** the act of modifying or the condition of being modified **2** something modified; the result of a modification **3** a small change or adjustment **4** *grammar* the relation between a modifier and the word or phrase that it modifies > ˈmodifiˌcatory *or* ˈmodifiˌcative *adj*

modified-release *adj* denoting a formulation of a medicinal drug taken orally that releases the active ingredients over several hours, in order to maintain a relatively constant plasma concentration of the drug. Also called: sustained-release, continuous-release

modifier (ˈmɒdɪˌfaɪə) *n* **1** Also called: qualifier *grammar* a word or phrase that qualifies the sense of another word; for example, the noun *alarm* is a modifier of *clock* in *alarm clock* and the phrase *every day* is an adverbial modifier of *walks* in *he walks every day* **2** a person or thing that modifies

modify (ˈmɒdɪˌfaɪ) *vb* **-fies, -fying, -fied** (*mainly tr*) **1** to change the structure, character, intent, etc, of **2** to make less extreme or uncompromising: *to modify a demand* **3** *grammar* (of a word or group of words) to bear the relation of modifier to (another word or group of words) **4** *linguistics* to change (a vowel) by umlaut **5** (*intr*) to be or become modified [C14 from Old French *modifier*, from Latin *modificāre* to limit, control, from *modus* measure + *facere* to make] > ˈmodiˌfiable *adj* > ˌmodiˌfiaˈbility *or* ˈmodiˌfiableness *n*

modillion (məˈdɪljən) *n architect* one of a set of ornamental brackets under a cornice, esp as used in the Corinthian order. Compare **mutule** [C16 via French from Italian *modiglione*, probably from Vulgar Latin *mutiliō* (unattested), from Latin *mūtulus* MUTULE]

modiolus (məʊˈdaɪəʊləs, mə-) *n, pl* **-li** (-ˌlaɪ) the central bony pillar of the cochlea [C19 New Latin, from Latin: hub of a wheel, from *modus* a measure]

modish (ˈməʊdɪʃ) *adj* in the current fashion or style; contemporary > ˈmodishly *adv* > ˈmodishness *n*

modiste (məʊˈdiːst) *n* a fashionable dressmaker or milliner [C19 from French, from *mode* fashion]

Modred (ˈməʊdrɪd) *or* **Mordred** (ˈmɔːdrɛd) *n* (in Arthurian legend) a knight of the Round Table who rebelled against and killed his uncle King Arthur

Mods (mɒdz) *plural noun* (at Oxford University) short for **Honour Moderations**

modular (ˈmɒdjʊlə) *adj* of, consisting of, or resembling a module or modulus > **modularity** (ˌmɒdjʊˈlærɪtɪ) *n*

modulate (ˈmɒdjʊˌleɪt) *vb* **1** (*tr*) to change the tone, pitch, or volume of **2** (*tr*) to adjust or regulate the degree of **3** *music* **a** to subject to or undergo modulation in music **b** (*often foll by to*) to make or become in tune (with a pitch, key, etc) **4** (*tr*) *physics, electronics* to cause to vary by a process of modulation [C16 from Latin *modulātus* in due measure, melodious, from *modulārī* to regulate, from *modus* measure] > **modulability** (ˌmɒdjʊləˈbɪlɪtɪ) *n* > ˈmodulative *or* ˈmodulatory *adj* > ˈmoduˌlator *n*

modulation (ˌmɒdjʊˈleɪʃən) *n* **1** the act of modulating or the condition of being modulated **2** *music* the transition from one key to another **3** *grammar* **a** another word for **intonation** (sense 1) **b** the grammatical expression of modality **4** *electrical engineering* **a** the act or process of superimposing the amplitude, frequency, phase, etc, of a wave or signal onto another wave (the carrier wave) or signal or onto an electron beam. See also **amplitude modulation, frequency modulation, phase modulation, velocity modulation b** the variation of the modulated signal

module (ˈmɒdjuːl) *n* **1** a self-contained unit or item, such as an assembly of electronic components and associated wiring or a segment of computer software, which itself performs a defined task and can be linked with other such units to form a larger system **2** a standard unit of measure, esp one used to coordinate the dimensions of buildings and components; in classical architecture, half the diameter of a column at the base of the shaft **3** a standardized unit designed to be added to or used as part of an arrangement of similar units, as in furniture **4** *astronautics* any of several self-contained separable units making up a spacecraft or launch vehicle, each of which has one or more specified tasks: *command module; service module* **5** *education* a short course of study, esp of a vocational or technical subject, that together with other such completed courses can count towards a particular qualification [C16 from Latin *modulus*, diminutive of *modus* MODE]

modulus (ˈmɒdjʊləs) *n, pl* **-li** (-ˌlaɪ) **1** *physics* a coefficient expressing a specified property of a specified substance. See **bulk modulus, modulus of rigidity, Young's modulus 2** *maths* another name for the **absolute value** (sense 2) of a complex number **3** *maths* the number by which a logarithm to one base is multiplied to give the corresponding logarithm to another base **4** *maths* an integer that can be divided exactly into the difference between two other integers: *7 is a modulus of 25 and 11.* See also **congruence** (sense 2) [C16 from Latin, diminutive of *modus* measure]

modulus of elasticity *n* the ratio of the stress applied to a body or substance to the resulting strain within the elastic limit. Also called: elastic modulus See also **Young's modulus, bulk modulus, modulus of rigidity**

modulus of rigidity *n* a modulus of elasticity equal to the ratio of the tangential force per unit area to the resulting angular deformation. Symbol: G

modus operandi (ˈməʊdəs ˌɒpəˈrændiː, -ˈrændaɪ) *n, pl* **modi operandi** (ˈməʊdiː ˌɒpəˈrændiː, ˈməʊdaɪ ˌɒpəˈrændaɪ) procedure; method of operating [C17 from Latin]

modus ponens Latin (ˈməʊdəs ˈpəʊˌnɛnz) *n logic* the principle that whenever a conditional statement and its antecedent are given to be true its consequent may be validly inferred, as in *if it's Tuesday this must be Belgium* and *it's Tuesday so this must be Belgium* [literally: mood that affirms]

modus tollens Latin (ˈməʊdəs ˈtɒlˌɛnz) *n logic* the principle that whenever a conditional statement and the negation of its consequent are given to be true, the negation of its antecedent may be validly inferred, as in *if it's Tuesday this must be Belgium and this isn't Belgium so it's not Tuesday* [literally: mood that denies]

modus vivendi (ˈməʊdəs vɪˈvɛndiː, -ˈvɛndaɪ) *n, pl* **modi vivendi** (ˈməʊdiː vɪˈvɛndiː, ˈməʊdaɪ vɪˈvɛndaɪ) a working arrangement between conflicting interests; practical compromise [C19 from Latin: way of living]

moer (muːr) *South African taboo slang* ⊳ *n* **1** the womb **2** a despicable person **3 the moer in** furious; enraged ⊳ *vb* **4** (*tr*) to attack (someone or something) violently [from Afrikaans, literally: mother]

Moers (*German* møːrs) *n* a city in W Germany, in North Rhine-Westphalia: coalmining centre. Pop: 107 903 (2003 est)

mofette (məʊˈfɛt) *n* an opening in a region of nearly extinct volcanic activity, through which carbon dioxide, nitrogen, and other gases pass [C19 from French, from Neapolitan Italian *mofeta*; compare dialect German *muffezen* to smell fetid]

moffie (ˈmɒfɪ) *South African slang* ⊳ *n* **1** a homosexual ⊳ *adj* **2** homosexual [C18 from *mophrodite*, a variant of HERMAPHRODITE]

mofo (ˈməʊfəʊ) *n, pl* **mofos** *slang, chiefly US* short for **motherfucker**

Mogadishu (ˌmɒgəˈdɪʃuː) *or* **Mogadiscio** (ˌmɒgəˈdɪʃɪˌəʊ, -ˈdɪʃəʊ) *n* the capital and chief port of Somalia, on the Indian Ocean: founded by Arabs around the 10th century; taken by the Sultan of Zanzibar in 1871 and sold to Italy in 1905. Pop: 1 257 000 (2005 est)

Mogadon (ˈmɒgəˌdɒn) *n trademark* a drug of the benzodiazepine group, a brand of nitrazepam, used to treat insomnia

Mogador (ˌmɒgəˈdɔː; *French* mɔgadɔr) *n* the former name (until 1956) of **Essaouira**

Mogen David (ˈməʊgən ˈdeɪvɪd) *n* another name for the **Star of David**

moggy (ˈmɒgɪ) *n, pl* **moggies** *Brit* a slang name for **cat¹** (sense 1) Sometimes shortened to: **mog**

m

[C20 of dialect origin, originally a pet name for a cow]

Mogilev (*Russian* məgi'ljɔf) *or* **Mohilev** *n* an industrial city in E Belarus on the Dnieper River: passed to Russia in 1772 after Polish rule. Pop: 353 000 (2005 est)

mogul[1] ('məʊgʌl, məʊ'gʌl) *n* **1** an important or powerful person **2** a type of steam locomotive with a wheel arrangement of two leading wheels, six driving wheels, and no trailing wheels [C18 from MOGUL]

mogul[2] ('məʊgᵊl) *n* a mound of hard snow on a ski slope [C20 perhaps from South German dialect *Mugl*]

Mogul ('məʊgʌl, məʊ'gʌl) *n* **1** a member of the Muslim dynasty of Indian emperors established by Baber in 1526. See **Great Mogul 2** a Muslim Indian, Mongol, or Mongolian ▷ *adj* **3** of or relating to the Moguls or their empire [C16 from Persian *mughul* Mongol]

mogul skiing *n* a skiing event in which skiers descend a slope which is covered in mounds of snow, making two jumps during the descent

MOH (formerly in Britain) *abbreviation for* Medical Officer of Health

mohair ('məʊˌhɛə) *n* **1** Also called: angora the long soft silky hair that makes up the outer coat of the Angora goat **2 a** a fabric made from the yarn of this hair and cotton or wool **b** (*as modifier*): *a mohair suit* [C16 variant (influenced by *hair*) of earlier *mocayare*, ultimately from Arabic *mukhayyar*, literally: choice, from *khayyara* to choose]

Moham. *abbreviation for* Mohammedan

Mohammedan (məʊ'hæmɪdᵊn) *n, adj* another word, formerly common in Western usage but never used among Muslims, for **Muslim**

Mohammedanism (məʊ'hæmɪdᵊˌnɪzəm) *n* a name, formerly common in Western usage but never used among Muslims, for the Muslim religion; Islam. See **Islam**

Mohammedanize *or* **Mohammedanise** (məʊ'hæmɪdᵊˌnaɪz) *vb* (*tr*) another word, formerly common in Western usage but never used among Muslims, for **Islamize**

Moharram (məʊ'hærəm) *n* a variant of **Muharram**

Mohave *or* **Mojave** (məʊ'hɑːvɪ) *n* **1** (*pl* -ves *or* -ve) a member of a North American Indian people formerly living along the Colorado River **2** the language of this people, belonging to the Yuman family

Mohave Desert *n* another name for **Mojave Desert**

mohawk ('məʊhɔːk) *n* **1** *skating* a half turn from either edge of either skate to the corresponding edge of the other skate **2** *US and Canadian* a punk hairstyle in which the head is shaved at the sides and the remaining strip of hair is worn stiffly erect and sometimes brightly coloured. Also called (in Britain and certain other countries): mohican [C19 after MOHAWK[1]]

Mohawk[1] ('məʊhɔːk) *n* (*pl* -hawks *or* -hawk) a member of a North American Indian people formerly living along the Mohawk River; one of the Iroquois peoples **2** the language of this people, belonging to the Iroquoian family

Mohawk[2] ('məʊhɔːk) *n* a river in E central New York State, flowing south and east to the Hudson River at Cohoes: the largest tributary of the Hudson. Length: 238 km (148 miles)

mohel ('mɔɛl, mɔɪl) *n* *Judaism* a man qualified to conduct circumcisions [from Hebrew]

Mohenjo-Daro (məˈhɛndʒəʊˈdɑːrəʊ) *n* an excavated city in SE Pakistan, southwest of Sukkur near the River Indus: flourished during the third millennium BC

mohican (məʊ'hiːkən) *n* **1** a punk hairstyle in which the head is shaved at the sides and the remaining strip of hair is worn stiffly erect and sometimes brightly coloured **2** a person wearing such a hairstyle

Mohican ('məʊɪkən, məʊ'hiːkən) *or* **Mahican**

(məˈhiːkən) *n* **1** (*pl* -cans *or* -can) a member of a North American Indian people formerly living along the Hudson river and east of it **2** the language of this people, belonging to the Algonquian family

Moho ('məʊhəʊ) *n* short for **Mohorovičić discontinuity**

Mohock ('məʊhɒk) *n* (in 18th-century London) one of a group of aristocratic ruffians, who attacked people in the streets at night [C18 variant of MOHAWK[1]]

Mohole ('məʊˌhəʊl) *n* an abandoned research project to drill through the earth's crust down to the Mohorovičić discontinuity to obtain samples of mantle rocks [C20 from *Moho(rovičić)* + HOLE. See MOHOROVIČIĆ DISCONTINUITY]

Mohorovičić discontinuity (ˌməʊhəˈrəʊvɪtʃɪtʃ) *n* the boundary between the earth's crust and mantle, across which there is a sudden change in the velocity of seismic waves. Often shortened to: Moho [C20 named after Andrija *Mohorovičić* (1857–1936), Croatian geologist]

Mohr's circle (mɔːz) *n* a graphical construction enabling the stresses in the cross-section of a body to be determined if the principal stresses are known [C20 named after Otto *Mohr* (1773–1839), German scientist]

Mohs scale (məʊz) *n* a scale for expressing the hardness of solids by comparing them with ten standards ranging from talc, with a value of 1, to diamond, with a value of 10 [C19 named after Friedrich *Mohs* (1773–1839), German mineralogist]

mohua (mɒhuːɑ:) *n, pl* mohua NZ another name for **yellowhead** [Māori]

mohur ('məʊhə) *n* a former Indian gold coin worth 15 rupees [C17 from Hindi]

MOI *abbreviation for* Ministry of Information (now superseded by **COI**)

moidore ('mɔɪdɔ:) *n* a former Portuguese gold coin [C18 from Portuguese *moeda de ouro*: money of gold]

moiety ('mɔɪɪtɪ) *n, pl* -ties *archaic* **1** a half **2** one of two parts or divisions of something [C15 from Old French *moitié*, from Latin *medietās* middle, from *medius*]

moil (mɔɪl) *archaic or dialect* ▷ *vb* **1** to moisten or soil or become moist, soiled, etc **2** (*intr*) to toil or drudge (esp in the phrase **toil and moil**) ▷ *n* **3** toil; drudgery **4** confusion; turmoil [C14 (to moisten; later: to work hard in unpleasantly wet conditions) from Old French *moillier*, ultimately from Latin *mollis* soft] > 'moiler *n*

Moirai ('mɔɪriː) *pl n, sing* Moira ('mɔɪrə) **the** the Greek goddesses of fate. Roman counterparts: the Parcae See **Fates**

moire (mwɑ:) *n* a fabric, usually silk, having a watered effect [C17 from French, earlier *mouaire*, from MOHAIR]

moiré ('mwɑːreɪ) *adj* **1** having a watered or wavelike pattern ▷ *n* **2** such a pattern, impressed on fabrics by means of engraved rollers **3** any fabric having such a pattern; moire **4** Also: moiré pattern a pattern seen when two geometrical patterns, such as grids, are visually superimposed [C17 from French, from *moire* MOHAIR]

Moism ('məʊɪzəm) *n* the religious and ethical teaching of Mo-Zi, the Chinese philosopher (?470–?391 BC), and his followers, emphasizing universal love, ascetic self-discipline, and obedience to the will of Heaven

moist (mɔɪst) *adj* **1** slightly damp or wet **2** saturated with or suggestive of moisture [C14 from Old French, ultimately related to Latin *mūcidus* musty, from *mūcus* MUCUS] > 'moistly *adv* > 'moistness *n*

moisten ('mɔɪsᵊn) *vb* to make or become moist > 'moistener *n*

moisture ('mɔɪstʃə) *n* water or other liquid diffused as vapour or condensed on or in objects > 'moistureless *adj*

moisturize *or* **moisturise** ('mɔɪstʃəˌraɪz) *vb* (*tr*) to add or restore moisture to (the air, the skin, etc)

moisturizer *or* **moisturiser** ('mɔɪstʃəˌraɪzə) *n* a cosmetic cream, lotion, etc applied to the skin to add or restore moisture to it

moither ('mɔɪðə) *or* **moider** ('mɔɪdə) *vb* dialect **1** (*tr; usually passive*) to bother or bewilder **2** (*intr*) to talk in a rambling or confused manner [C17 of obscure origin]

Mojave (məʊ'hɑːvɪ) *n* a variant spelling of **Mohave**

Mojave Desert *or* **Mohave Desert** *n* a desert in S California, south of the Sierra Nevada: part of the Great Basin. Area: 38 850 sq km (15 000 sq miles)

mojo ('məʊdʒəʊ) *n, pl* mojos *or* mojoes *US slang* **1 a** an amulet, charm, or magic spell **b** (*as modifier*): *ancient mojo spells* **2** the art of casting magic spells [C20 of W African origin]

moke (məʊk) *n* **1** *Brit* a slang name for **donkey** (sense 1) **2** *Austral slang* an inferior type of horse [C19 origin obscure]

Mokha ('məʊkə, 'mɒk-) *n* a variant of **Mocha**

moki ('məʊkɪ) *n, pl* mokis *or* moki either of two edible sea fish of New Zealand, the blue cod (*Percis colias*) or the bastard trumpeter (*Latridopsis ciliaris*) [Māori]

mokihi ('məʊkiːhi:) *n, pl* mokihi NZ a type of raft, usually made out of flax stems [Māori]

moko ('məʊkəʊ) *n, pl* mokos NZ a Māori tattoo or tattoo pattern. Also called: nanua [Māori]

mokomoko (mɒkɒmɒkɒ) *n, pl* mokomoko a New Zealand skink, *Leiolopisma zelandica* [Māori]

mokopuna (ˌməʊkəʊˈpuːnə) *n* NZ a grandchild or young person [Māori]

mokoro (mo'koro) *n, pl* -ro *or* -ros (in Botswana) the traditional dugout canoe of the people of the Okavango Delta [from a Bantu language of Botswana]

Mokpo (ˌməʊkˈpəʊ) *n* a port in SW South Korea, on the Yellow Sea. Pop: 253 000 (2005 est)

moksha ('mɒkʃə) *n* *Hinduism* freedom from the endless cycle of transmigration into a state of bliss [from Sanskrit *mokṣa* liberation]

mol the chemical symbol for **mole**[3]

mol. *abbreviation for* **1** molecular **2** molecule

mola ('məʊlə) *n, pl* -la *or* -las another name for **sunfish** (sense 1) [C17 from Latin, literally: millstone]

molal ('məʊlᵊl) *adj* *chem* of or consisting of a solution containing one mole of solute per thousand grams of solvent [C20 from MOLE[3] + -AL[1]]

molality (mɒ'lælɪtɪ) *n, pl* -ties (not in technical usage) a measure of concentration equal to the number of moles of solute in a thousand grams of solvent

molar[1] ('məʊlə) *n* **1** any of the 12 broad-faced grinding teeth in man **2** a corresponding tooth in other mammals ▷ *adj* **3** of, relating to, or designating any of these teeth **4** used for or capable of grinding [C16 from Latin *molāris* for grinding, from *mola* millstone]

molar[2] ('məʊlə) *adj* **1** (of a physical quantity) per unit amount of substance: *molar volume* **2** (not recommended in technical usage) (of a solution) containing one mole of solute per litre of solution [C19 from Latin *mōlēs* a mass]

molarity (mɒ'lærɪtɪ) *n* another name (not in technical usage) for **concentration** (sense 4)

molasse (mə'læs) *n* a soft sediment produced by the erosion of mountain ranges after the final phase of mountain building [C18 from French, perhaps alteration of *mollasse*, from Latin *mollis* soft]

molasses (mə'læsɪz) *n* (*functioning as singular*) **1** the thick brown uncrystallized bitter syrup obtained from sugar during refining **2** *US and Canadian* a dark viscous syrup obtained during the refining of sugar. Also called (in Britain and certain other countries): treacle [C16 from Portuguese *melaço*, from Late Latin *mellāceum* must, from Latin *mel* honey]

mold (məʊld) *n, vb* the US spelling of **mould**

Moldau ('mɔldaʊ) *n* **1** the German name for

Moldavia 2 the German name for the **Vltava**

Moldavia (mɒlˈdeɪvɪə) *n* **1** another name for **Moldova 2** a former principality of E Europe, consisting of the basins of the Rivers Prut and Dniester: the E part (Bessarabia) became Moldova; the W part remains a province of Romania. Romanian name: **Moldova** (mɒlˈdova) German name: **Moldau**

Moldavian (mɒlˈdeɪvɪən) *adj, n* **1** another name for **Moldovan** ▷ *adj* **2** of or relating to the former E European principality of Moldavia or its inhabitants ▷ *n* **3** a native or inhabitant of Moldavia

moldavite (ˈmɒldəˌvaɪt) *n* a green tektite found in the Czech Republic, thought to be the product of an ancient meteorite impact in Germany [C19 named after MOLDAVIA]

moldboard (ˈməʊldˌbɔːd) *n* the US spelling of **mouldboard**

molder (ˈməʊldə) *vb, n* the US spelling of **moulder**

molding (ˈməʊldɪŋ) *n* the US spelling of **moulding**

Moldova (mɒlˈdəʊvə) *n* a republic in SE Europe: comprising the E part of the former principality of Moldavia, the E part of which (Bessarabia) was ceded to the Soviet Union in 1940 and formed the Moldavian Soviet Socialist Republic until it gained independence in 1991; an agricultural region with many vineyards. Official language: Romanian. Religion: nonreligious and Christian. Currency: leu. Capital: Kishinev. Pop: 4 263 000 (2004 est). Area: 33 670 sq km (13 000 sq miles). Also called: **Moldavia** (mɒlˈdeɪvɪə)

Moldovan (mɒlˈdəʊvən) *or* **Moldavian** *adj* **1** of or relating to Moldova or its inhabitants ▷ *n* **2** a native or inhabitant of Moldova

moldy (ˈməʊldɪ) *adj* **moldier, moldiest** the US spelling of **mouldy**. > **ˈmoldiness** *n*

mole¹ (məʊl) *n pathol* a nontechnical name for **naevus** [Old English *māl*; related to Old High German *meil* spot]

mole² (məʊl) *n* **1** any small burrowing mammal, of the family *Talpidae*, of Europe, Asia, and North and Central America: order *Insectivora* (insectivores). They have velvety, typically dark fur and forearms specialized for digging **2 golden mole** any small African burrowing molelike mammal of the family *Chrysochloridae*, having copper-coloured fur: order *Insectivora* (insectivores) **3** *informal* a spy who has infiltrated an organization and, often over a long period, become a trusted member of it [C14 from Middle Dutch *mol*, of Germanic origin; compare Middle Low German *mol*]

mole³ (məʊl) *n* the basic SI unit of amount of substance; the amount that contains as many elementary entities as there are atoms in 0.012 kilogram of carbon-12. The entity must be specified and may be an atom, a molecule, an ion, a radical, an electron, a photon, etc. Symbol: mol [C20 from German *Mol*, short for *Molekül* MOLECULE]

mole⁴ (məʊl) *n* **1** a breakwater **2** a harbour protected by a breakwater **3** a large tunnel excavator for use in soft rock [C16 from French *môle*, from Latin *mōlēs* mass]

mole⁵ (məʊl) *n pathol* a fleshy growth in the uterus formed by the degeneration of fetal tissues [C17 medical use of Latin *mola* millstone]

mole⁶ (ˈməʊleɪ) *n* a spicy Mexican sauce made from chili and chocolate [C20 from Mexican Spanish from Nahuatl *molli* sauce]

Molech (ˈməʊlɛk) *n Old Testament* a variant of **Moloch**

mole cricket *n* any subterranean orthopterous insect of the family *Gryllotalpidae*, of Europe and North America, similar and related to crickets but having the first pair of legs specialized for digging

molecular (məʊˈlɛkjʊlə, mə-) *adj* **1** of or relating to molecules: *molecular hydrogen* **2** *logic* (of a sentence, formula, etc) capable of analysis into atomic formulae of the appropriate kind > **molecularity** (məʊˌlɛkjʊˈlærɪtɪ) *n*

> mo'lecularly *adv*

molecular beam *or* **ray** *n physics* a parallel beam of molecules that are at low pressure and suffer no interatomic or intermolecular collisions

molecular biology *n* the study of biological phenomena at the molecular level

molecular cloud *n* a cool dense interstellar region composed of a wide variety of molecules, mainly hydrogen, plus some dust, in which stars are forming

molecular distillation *n* distillation in which a substance is heated under vacuum, the pressure being so low that no intermolecular collisions can occur before condensation

molecular film *n* another name for **monolayer**

molecular formula *n* a chemical formula indicating the numbers and types of atoms in a molecule: H_2SO_4 *is the molecular formula of sulphuric acid*. Compare **empirical formula, structural formula**

molecular genetics *n* (*functioning as singular*) the study of the molecular constitution of genes and chromosomes

molecular sieve *n chem* a material that can absorb large amounts of certain compounds while not absorbing others and is thus suitable for use in separating mixtures

molecular volume *n* the volume occupied by one mole of a substance. Also called: **molar volume**

molecular weight *n* the former name for **relative molecular mass**

molecule (ˈmɒlɪˌkjuːl) *n* **1** the simplest unit of a chemical compound that can exist, consisting of two or more atoms held together by chemical bonds **2** a very small particle [C18 via French from New Latin *mōlēcula*, diminutive of Latin *mōlēs* mass, MOLE⁴]

mole drain *n* an underground cylindrical drainage channel cut by a special plough to drain heavy agricultural soil

molehill (ˈməʊlˌhɪl) *n* **1** the small mound of earth thrown up by a burrowing mole **2** **make a mountain out of a molehill** to exaggerate an unimportant matter out of all proportion

mole mapping *n* the procedure of using a digital camera to record the positions and appearances of moles on a person's body so that regular checks will detect any changes that might lead to skin cancer

mole rat *n* **1** any burrowing molelike African rodent of the family *Bathyergidae* **2** any similar rodent, esp any member of the genus *Spalax*, of Asia and North Africa: family *Spalacidae* **3** another name for **bandicoot rat** (see **bandicoot** (sense 2))

mole run *n* (*usually plural*) *informal* any part of a system of underground tunnels, rooms, etc, prepared for use in the event of nuclear war

moleskin (ˈməʊlˌskɪn) *n* **1** the dark grey dense velvety pelt of a mole, used as a fur **2** a hard-wearing cotton fabric of twill weave used for work clothes, etc **3** (*modifier*) made from moleskin: *a moleskin waistcoat*

moleskins (ˈməʊlˌskɪnz) *pl n* clothing of moleskin

molest (məˈlɛst) *vb* (*tr*) **1** to disturb or annoy by malevolent interference **2** to accost or attack, esp with the intention of assaulting sexually [C14 from Latin *molestāre* to annoy, from *molestus* troublesome, from *mōlēs* mass] > **molestation** (ˌməʊlɛˈsteɪʃən) *n* > mo'lester *n*

moline (məˈlaɪn) *adj heraldry* (of a cross) having arms of equal length, forked and curved back at the ends [C16 probably from Anglo-French *moliné*, from *molin* MILL¹, referring to the arms curved back like the ends of a mill-rind]

Molinism (ˈmɒlɪnɪzəm) *n RC Church* a doctrine of grace that attempts to reconcile the efficacy of divine grace with human free will in responding to it [C17 named after *Luis de Molina* (1535–1600), Spanish Jesuit who taught such a doctrine]

Molise (Italian moˈliːze) *n* a region of S central Italy, the second smallest of the regions: separated from **Abruzzi e Molise** in 1965. Capital:

Campobasso. Pop: 321 047 (2003 est). Area: 4438 sq km (1731 sq miles)

moll (mɒl) *n slang* **1** the female accomplice of a gangster **2** a prostitute [C17 from *Moll*, familiar form of *Mary*]

mollah (ˈmɒːlə) *n* an older spelling of **mullah**

mollify (ˈmɒlɪˌfaɪ) *vb* **-fies, -fying, -fied** (*tr*) **1** to pacify; soothe **2** to lessen the harshness or severity of [C15 from Old French *mollifier*, via Late Latin, from Latin *mollis* soft + *facere* to make] > **ˈmolliˌfiable** *adj* > **ˌmollifiˈcation** *n* > **ˈmolliˌfier** *n*

mollusc *or US* **mollusk** (ˈmɒləsk) *n* any invertebrate of the phylum *Mollusca*, having a soft unsegmented body and often a shell, secreted by a fold of skin (the mantle). The group includes the gastropods (snails, slugs, etc), bivalves (clams, mussels, etc), and cephalopods (cuttlefish, octopuses, etc) [C18 via New Latin from Latin *molluscus*, from *mollis* soft] > **molluscan** *or US* **molluskan** (mɒˈlʌskən) *adj, n* > **ˈmolluscˌlike** *or US* **ˈmolluskˌlike** *adj*

molluscoid (mɒˈlʌskɔɪd) *or* **molluscoidal** (ˌmɒlʌsˈkɔɪdᵊl) *adj* of, relating to, or belonging to the *Molluscoidea*, a former phylum including the brachiopods and bryozoans now classified separately [C19 via New Latin from Latin *molluscus* soft]

Mollweide projection (ˈmɒlˌvaɪdə) *n* an equal-area map projection with the parallels and the central meridian being straight lines and the other meridians curved. It is often used to show world distributions of various phenomena [C19 named after Karl B. *Mollweide* (1774–1825), German mathematician and astronomer]

molly¹ (ˈmɒlɪ) *n, pl* **-lies** any brightly coloured tropical or subtropical American freshwater cyprinodont fish of the genus *Mollienisia* [C19 from New Latin *Molliensia*, from Comte F. N. *Mollien* (1758–1850), French statesman]

molly² (ˈmɒlɪ) *n, pl* **-lies** *Irish informal* an effeminate, weak, or cowardly boy or man [C18 perhaps from *Molly*, pet name for *Mary*]

mollycoddle (ˈmɒlɪˌkɒdᵊl) *vb* **1** (*tr*) to treat with indulgent care; pamper ▷ *n* **2** a pampered person [C19 from MOLLY² + CODDLE] > **ˈmollyˌcoddler** *n*

mollyhawk (ˈmɒlɪˌhɔːk) *n NZ* the juvenile of the southern black-backed gull (*Larus dominicanus*)

Molly Maguire (ˈmɒlɪ məˈgwaɪə) *n* **1** *Irish history* a member of a secret society that terrorized law officers during the 1840s to prevent evictions **2** (in Pennsylvania from about 1865 to 1877) a member of a society of miners that terrorized mine owners and their agents in an effort to obtain better pay [C19 the name refers to the female disguise adopted by members of these societies]

mollymawk (ˈmɒlɪˌmɔːk) *n NZ* an informal name for **mallemuck**

moloch (ˈməʊlɒk) *n* a spiny Australian desert-living lizard, *Moloch horridus*, that feeds on ants: family *Agamidae* (agamas). Also called: **mountain devil, spiny lizard**

Moloch (ˈməʊlɒk) *or* **Molech** (ˈməʊlɛk) *n Old Testament* a Semitic deity to whom parents sacrificed their children

Molokai (ˌməʊləʊˈkaːɪ) *n* an island in central Hawaii. Pop: 7404 (2000). Area: 676 sq km (261 sq miles)

Molopo (məˈləʊpəʊ) *n* a seasonal river rising in N South Africa and flowing west and southwest to the Orange river. Length: about 1000 km (600 miles)

Molossian (məˈlɒsɪən), **Molossian dog** *or* **Molossian hound** *n* a breed of dog native to Epirus in NW Greece, used in classical antiquity as a hunting dog and guard dog [from *Molossia*, a district of Epirus]

Molotov (ˈmɒləˌtɒf; *Russian* ˈmɔlətəf) *n* the former name (1940–62) for **Perm**

Molotov cocktail (ˈmɒləˌtɒf) *n* an elementary incendiary weapon, usually a bottle of petrol with a short-delay fuse or wick; petrol bomb [C20

m

named after Vyacheslav Mikhailovich *Molotov* (1890–1986), Soviet statesman]

molt ('məʊlt) *vb, n* the usual US spelling of **moult**

molten ('məʊltən) *adj* **1** liquefied; melted: *molten lead* **2** made by having been melted: *molten casts* ▷ *vb* **3** the past participle of **melt**

molto ('mɒltəʊ) *adv music* (preceded or followed by a musical direction, esp a tempo marking) very: *allegro molto; molto adagio* [from Italian, from Latin *multum* (adv) much]

Moluccas (məʊ'lʌkəz, mə-) *or* **Molucca Islands** *pl n* a group of islands in the Malay Archipelago, between Sulawesi (Celebes) and New Guinea. Capital: Amboina. Pop: 2 223 000 (1999 est). Area: about 74 505 sq km (28 766 sq miles). Indonesian name: Maluku. Former name: Spice Islands

mol. wt. *abbreviation for* molecular weight

moly ('məʊlɪ) *n, pl* **-lies 1** *Greek myth* a magic herb given by Hermes to Odysseus to nullify the spells of Circe **2** a liliaceous plant, *Allium moly*, that is native to S Europe and has yellow flowers in a dense cluster [C16 from Latin *mōly*, from Greek *mōlu*]

molybdate (mɒ'lɪbdeɪt) *n* a salt or ester of a molybdic acid

molybdenite (mɒ'lɪbdɪˌnaɪt) *n* a soft grey mineral consisting of molybdenum sulphide in hexagonal crystalline form with rhenium as an impurity: the main source of molybdenum and rhenium. Formula: MoS_2

molybdenous (mɒ'lɪbdɪnəs) *adj* of or containing molybdenum in the divalent state

molybdenum (mɒ'lɪbdɪnəm) *n* a very hard ductile silvery-white metallic element occurring principally in molybdenite: used mainly in alloys, esp to harden and strengthen steels. Symbol: Mo; atomic no.: 42; atomic wt.: 95.94; valency: 2–6; relative density: 10.22; melting pt.: 2623°C; boiling pt.: 4639°C [C19 from New Latin, from Latin *molybdaena* galena, from Greek *molubdaina*, from *molubdos* lead]

molybdic (mɒ'lɪbdɪk) *adj* of or containing molybdenum in the trivalent or hexavalent state

molybdous (mɒ'lɪbdəs) *adj* of or containing molybdenum, esp in a low valence state

mom (mɒm) *n chiefly US and Canadian* an informal word for **mother¹**

Mombasa (mɒm'bæsə) *n* a port in S Kenya, on a coral island in a bay of the Indian Ocean: the chief port for Kenya, Uganda, and NE Tanzania; became British in 1887, capital of the East African Protectorate until 1907. Pop: 828 000 (2005 est)

moment ('məʊmənt) *n* **1** a short indefinite period of time: *he'll be here in a moment* **2** a specific instant or point in time: *at that moment the doorbell rang* **3** the moment the present point of time: *at the moment it's fine* **4** import, significance, or value: *a man of moment* **5** *physics* **a** a tendency to produce motion, esp rotation about a point or axis **b** the product of a physical quantity, such as force or mass, and its distance from a fixed reference point. See also **moment of inertia 6** *statistics* the mean of a specified power of the deviations of all the values of a variable in its frequency distribution. The power of the deviations indicates the order of the moment and the deviations may be from the origin (giving a **moment about the origin**) or from the mean (giving a **moment about the mean**) [C14 from Old French, from Latin *mōmentum*, from *movēre* to move]

momentarily ('məʊməntərəlɪ, -trɪlɪ) *adv* **1** for an instant; temporarily **2** from moment to moment; every instant **3** *US and Canadian* very soon ▷ Also (for senses 1, 2): momently ('məʊməntlɪ)

momentary ('məʊməntərɪ, -trɪ) *adj* lasting for only a moment; temporary > 'momentariness *n*

moment of inertia *n* > the tendency of a body to resist angular acceleration, expressed as the sum of the products of the mass of each particle in the body and the square of its perpendicular distance from the axis of rotation. Symbol: *I*

moment of truth *n* **1** a moment when a person or thing is put to the test **2** the point in a bullfight when the matador is about to kill the bull

momentous (məʊ'mɛntəs) *adj* of great significance > mo'mentously *adv* > mo'mentousness *n*

momentum (məʊ'mɛntəm) *n, pl* -ta (-tə) *or* -tums **1** *physics* the product of a body's mass and its velocity. Symbol: *p* See also **angular momentum 2** the impetus of a body resulting from its motion **3** driving power or strength [C17 from Latin: movement; see MOMENT]

momism ('mɒmɪzəm) *n US informal* the excessive domination of a child by his or her mother

momma ('mɒmə) *n US and Canada* another word for **mother**

mommy track ('mɒmɪ) *n US* a path in life in which a woman devotes most of her time to her children and home rather than to her career

mom test *n US informal* a test of the user-friendliness of a computer device or software based on the extent to which a user's mother is able to use it

Momus ('məʊməs) *n, pl* -muses *or* -mi (-maɪ) **1** *Greek myth* the god of blame and mockery **2** a cavilling critic

Mon (məʊn) *n* **1** (*pl* Mon *or* Mons) a member of a people of Myanmar and Thailand related to the Khmer of Cambodia **2** the language of this people, belonging to the Mon-Khmer family ▷ Also called: Talaing

Mon. *abbreviation for* Monday

mon- *combining form* a variant of **mono-** before a vowel

mona ('məʊnə) *n* a W African guenon monkey, *Cercopithecus mona*, with dark fur on the back and white or yellow underparts [C18 from Spanish or Portuguese: monkey]

Monacan ('mɒnəkən, mə'nɑː-) *adj* **1** of or relating to Monaco or its inhabitants ▷ *n* **2** a native or inhabitant of Monaco

monachal ('mɒnək⁰l) *adj* a less common word for **monastic** [C16 from Old French, from Church Latin *monachālis*, from *monachus* MONK] > 'monachism *n* > 'monachist *adj, n*

monacid (mɒn'æsɪd) *or* **monacidic** (ˌmɒnə'sɪdɪk) *adj* variants of **monoacid**

Monaco ('mɒnəˌkəʊ, mə'nɑːkəʊ; *French* mɒnako) *n* a principality in SW Europe, on the Mediterranean and forming an enclave in SE France: the second smallest sovereign state in the world (after the Vatican); consists of **Monaco-Ville** (the capital) on a rocky headland, **La Condamine** (a business area and port), **Monte Carlo** (the resort centre), and **Fontvieille**, a light industrial area. Language: French. Religion: Roman Catholic. Currency: euro. Pop: 34 000 (2003 est). Area: 189 hectares (476 acres). Related adj: **Monegasque**

monad ('mɒnæd, 'məʊ-) *n* **1** *pl* -ads *or* -ades (-əˌdiːz) *philosophy* **a** any fundamental singular metaphysical entity, esp if autonomous **b** (in the metaphysics of Leibnitz) a simple indestructible nonspatial element regarded as the unit of which reality consists **c** (in the pantheistic philosophy of Giordano Bruno) a fundamental metaphysical unit that is spatially extended and psychically aware **2** a single-celled organism, esp a flagellate protozoan **3** an atom, ion, or radical with a valency of one ▷ Also called (for senses 1, 2): monas [C17 from Late Latin *monas*, from Greek: unit, from *monos* alone] > mo'nadical *adj* > mo'nadically *adv*

monadelphous (ˌmɒnə'dɛlfəs) *adj* **1** (of stamens) having united filaments forming a tube around the style **2** (of flowers) having monadelphous stamens [C19 from MONO- + Greek *adelphos* brother, twin + -OUS]

monadic (mɒ'nædɪk) *adj* **1** being or relating to a monad **2** *logic, maths* (of an operator, predicate, etc) having only a single argument place

monadism ('mɒnəˌdɪzm, 'məʊ-) *or* **monadology**

(ˌmɒnə'dɒlədʒɪ, ˌməʊ-) *n* (esp in the writings of Gottfried Leibnitz, the German rationalist philosopher and mathematician (1646–1716)) the philosophical doctrine that monads are the ultimate units of reality > ˌmonad'istic *adj*

monadnock (mə'nædnɒk) *n* a residual hill that consists of hard rock in an otherwise eroded area [C19 named after Mount *Monadnock*, in New Hampshire]

Monaghan ('mɒnəhən) *n* **1** a county of NE Republic of Ireland, in Ulster province: many small lakes. County town: Monaghan. Pop: 52 593 (2002). Area: 1292 sq km (499 sq miles) **2** a town in NE Republic of Ireland, county town of Co Monaghan. Pop: 5717 (2002)

monal *or* **monaul** ('mɒnɔːl) *n* any of several S Asian pheasants of the genus *Lophophorus*, the males of which have a brilliantly coloured plumage [C18 from Hindi]

Mona Lisa ('məʊnə 'liːzə) *n* a portrait of a young woman painted by Leonardo da Vinci, admired for her enigmatic smile. Also called: La Gioconda

monandrous (mɒ'nændrəs) *adj* **1** having or preferring only one male sexual partner over a period of time **2** (of plants) having flowers with only one stamen **3** (of flowers) having only one stamen [C19 from MONO- + -ANDROUS] > mo'nandry *n*

monanthous (mɒ'nænθəs) *adj* (of certain plants) having or producing only one flower [C19 from MONO- + Greek *anthos* flower]

Mona Passage ('məʊnə) *n* a strait between Puerto Rico and the Dominican Republic, linking the Atlantic with the Caribbean

monarch ('mɒnək) *n* **1** a sovereign head of state, esp a king, queen, or emperor, who rules usually by hereditary right **2** a supremely powerful or pre-eminent person or thing **3** Also called: milkweed a large migratory butterfly, *Danaus plexippus*, that has orange-and-black wings and feeds on the milkweed plant: family *Danaidae* [C15 from Late Latin *monarcha*, from Greek; see MONO-, -ARCH] > monarchal (mɒ'nɑːk⁰l) *or* monarchial (mɒ'nɑːkɪəl) *adj* > mo'narchally *adv* > mo'narchical *or* mo'narchic *adj* > mo'narchically *adv* > 'monarchism *n* > 'monarchist *n, adj* > ˌmonar'chistic *adj*

monarchy ('mɒnəkɪ) *n, pl* -chies **1** a form of government in which supreme authority is vested in a single and usually hereditary figure, such as a king, and whose powers can vary from those of an absolute despot to those of a figurehead **2** a country reigned over by a king, prince, or other monarch

monarda (mɒ'nɑːdə) *n* any mintlike North American plant of the genus *Monarda*: family *Lamiaceae* (labiates). See also **horsemint** (sense 2), **bergamot** (sense 4) [C19 from New Latin, named after N. *Monardés* (1493–1588), Spanish botanist]

monas ('mɒnæs, 'məʊ-) *n, pl* monades ('mɒnəˌdiːz) another word for **monad** (senses 1, 2)

monastery ('mɒnəstərɪ, -strɪ) *n, pl* -teries the residence of a religious community, esp of monks, living in seclusion from secular society and bound by religious vows [C15 from Church Latin *monastērium*, from Late Greek *monastērion*, from Greek *monázein* to live alone, from *monos* alone] > monasterial (ˌmɒnə'stɪərɪəl) *adj*

monastic (mə'næstɪk) *adj* also less commonly monastical **1** of or relating to monasteries or monks, nuns, etc **2** resembling this sort of life; reclusive ▷ *n* **3** a person who is committed to this way of life, esp a monk > mo'nastically *adv*

monasticism (mə'næstɪˌsɪzəm) *n* the monastic system, movement, or way of life

Monastral (mə'næstrəl) *adj trademark* denoting certain fast pigments used in paints and inks, derived from phthalocyanine

monatomic (ˌmɒnə'tɒmɪk) *or* **monoatomic** (ˌmɒnəʊə'tɒmɪk) *adj chem* **1** (of an element) having or consisting of single atoms: *argon is a monatomic gas* **2** (of a compound or molecule) having only one atom or group that can be replaced in a chemical reaction **3** a less common word for **monovalent**

monaul ('mɒnɔːl) *n* a variant spelling of **monal**

monaural (mɒˈnɔːrəl) *adj* **1** relating to, having, or hearing with only one ear **2** another word for **monophonic**. > mon'aurally *adv*

monaxial (mɒˈnæksɪəl) *adj* another word for **uniaxial**

monazite ('mɒnəˌzaɪt) *n* a yellow to reddish-brown mineral consisting of a phosphate of thorium, cerium, and lanthanum in monoclinic crystalline form [C19 from German, from Greek *monazein* to live alone, so called because of its rarity]

Mönchengladbach (German mœnçən'glatbax) *n* a city in W Germany, in W North Rhine-Westphalia: headquarters of NATO forces in N central Europe; textile industry. Pop: 262 391 (2003 est). Former name: München-Gladbach

Moncton ('mɒŋktən) *n* a city in E Canada, in SE New Brunswick. Pop: 90 359 (2001)

mondain (*French* mɔ̃dɛ̃) *n* **1** a man who moves in fashionable society ▷ *adj* **2** characteristic of fashionable society; worldly [C19 from French; see MUNDANE]

mondaine (*French* mɔ̃dɛn) *n* **1** a woman who moves in fashionable society ▷ *adj* **2** characteristic of fashionable society; worldly [C19 from French; see MUNDANE]

Monday ('mʌndɪ) *n* the second day of the week; first day of the working week [Old English *mōnandæg* moon's day, translation of Late Latin *lūnae diēs*]

Monday Club *n* (in Britain) a club made up of right-wing Conservatives who originally met together for lunch on Monday: founded in 1961

Mondayize *or* **Mondayise** ('mʌndɪˌaɪz) *vb* (*tr*) NZ to move (a statutory holiday, such as the Queen's birthday) to the nearest Monday in order to secure a long weekend > ˌMondayi'zation *or* ˌMondayi'sation *n*

Monday morning quarterback *n* *chiefly US and Canadian informal* a person who criticizes or suggests alternative courses of action from a position of hindsight after the event in question

mondegreen ('mɒndɪˌgriːn) *n* a word or phrase that is misinterpreted as another word or phrase, usually with an amusing result [C20 from the Scottish ballad 'The Bonny Earl of Murray', in which the line *laid him on the green* can be misheard as *Lady Mondegreen*]

Mondeo Man (mɒnˈdeɪəʊ) *n* Brit informal a middle-class man, seen as typically driving a Ford Mondeo and preferring to do this rather than use public transport

mondial ('mɒndɪəl) *adj* of or involving the whole world [C20 from French, ultimately from Latin *mundus*]

Mond process (mɒnd; *German* mɔnt) *n* a process for obtaining nickel by heating the ore in carbon monoxide to produce nickel carbonyl vapour, which is then decomposed at a higher temperature to yield the metal [C19 named after Ludwig *Mond* (1839–1909), German chemist and industrialist]

monecious (mɒˈniːʃəs) *adj* a variant spelling of **monoecious**. > mo'neciously *adv*

Monegasque (ˌmɒnəˈgæsk) *n* **1** a native or inhabitant of Monaco ▷ *adj* **2** of or relating to Monaco or its inhabitants [from French, from Provençal *mounegasc,* from *Mouneque* Monaco]

Monel metal *or* **Monell metal** (mɒˈnɛl) *n trademark* any of various silvery corrosion-resistant alloys containing copper (28 per cent), nickel (67 per cent), and smaller quantities of such metals as iron, manganese, and aluminium [C20 named after A. *Monell* (died 1921), president of the International Nickel Co, New York, which introduced the alloys]

moneme ('mɒuniːm) *n linguistics* a less common word for **morpheme** [C20 from MONO- + -EME]

monetarism (ˈmʌnɪtəˌrɪzəm) *n* **1** the theory that inflation is caused by an excess quantity of money in an economy **2** an economic policy based on this theory and on a belief in the efficiency of free market forces, that gives priority to achieving price stability by monetary control, balanced budgets, etc, and maintains that unemployment results from excessive real wage rates and cannot be controlled by Keynesian demand management > 'monetarist *n, adj*

monetary ('mʌnɪtərɪ, -trɪ) *adj* **1** of or relating to money or currency **2** of or relating to monetarism: *a monetary policy* [C19 from Late Latin *monētārius,* from Latin *monēta* MONEY] > 'monetarily *adv*

monetary unit *n* a unit of value and money of a country, esp the major or standard unit

monetize *or* **monetise** ('mʌnɪˌtaɪz) *vb* (*tr*) **1** to establish as the legal tender of a country **2** to give a legal value to (a coin) > ˌmoneti'zation *or* ˌmoneti'sation *n*

money ('mʌnɪ) *n* **1** a medium of exchange that functions as legal tender **2** the official currency, in the form of banknotes, coins, etc, issued by a government or other authority **3** a particular denomination or form of currency: *silver money* **4** property or assets with reference to their realizable value **5** *formal pl* **moneys** *or* **monies** a pecuniary sum or income **6** an unspecified amount of paper currency or coins: *money to lend* **7** *for one's money* in one's opinion **8** *in the money informal* well-off; rich **9** *money for old rope informal* profit obtained by little or no effort **10** *money to burn* more money than one needs **11** *one's money's worth* full value for the money one has paid for something **12** *put money into* to invest money in **13** *put money on* to place a bet on **14** *put one's money where one's mouth is* See **mouth** (sense 19) Related adj: **pecuniary** [C13 from Old French *moneie,* from Latin *monēta* coinage; see MINT²]

moneybags ('mʌnɪˌbægz) *n* (*functioning as singular*) *informal* a very rich person

moneychanger ('mʌnɪˌtʃeɪndʒə) *n* **1** a person engaged in the business of exchanging currencies or money **2** *chiefly US* a machine for dispensing coins

money cowry *n* **1** a tropical marine gastropod, *Cypraea moneta* **2** the shell of this mollusc, used as money in some parts of Africa and S Asia

moneyed *or* **monied** ('mʌnɪd) *adj* **1** having a great deal of money; rich **2** arising from or characterized by money

moneyer ('mʌnɪə) *n* **1** *archaic* a person who coins money **2** an obsolete word for **banker¹**

money-grubbing *adj informal* seeking greedily to obtain money at every opportunity > 'money-ˌgrubber *n*

moneylender ('mʌnɪˌlɛndə) *n* a person who lends money at interest as a living > 'money,lending *adj, n*

moneymaker ('mʌnɪˌmeɪkə) *n* **1** a person who is intent on accumulating money **2** a person or thing that is or might be profitable > 'money,making *adj, n*

money market *n finance* the financial institutions dealing with short-term loans and capital and with foreign exchange. Compare **capital market**

money of account *n* another name (esp US and Canadian) for **unit of account**

money order *n US and Canadian* a written order for the payment of a sum of money, to a named payee, obtainable and payable at a post office. Also called (in Britain and certain other countries): **postal order**

money-purchase *n* **1** (*modifier*) relating to a pension scheme in which both employer and employee make contributions to a fund that is used to buy an annuity on retirement. The amount paid as a pension depends on the size of the fund

money shot *n slang* a shot in a pornographic film in which a male performer is seen to ejaculate [C20 from the idea that the performer is only paid if he does this]

money spider *n* any of certain small shiny brownish spiders of the family *Linyphiidae*

money-spinner *n informal* an enterprise, idea, person, or thing that is a source of wealth

moneyspinning ('mʌnɪˌspɪnɪŋ) *adj informal* earning money or making a profit

money supply *n* the total amount of money in a country's economy at a given time. See also **M0, M1, M2, M3, M3c, M4, M5**

money wages *pl n economics* wages evaluated with reference to the money paid rather than the equivalent purchasing power. Also called: nominal wages Compare **real wages**

moneywort ('mʌnɪˌwɜːt) *n* a European and North American creeping primulaceous plant, *Lysimachia nummularia,* with round leaves and yellow flowers. Also called: **creeping Jennie**

mong¹ (mʌŋ) *n Austral informal* short for **mongrel**

mong² (mɒŋ) *n Brit slang* a stupid or foolish person [C20 a shortening of MONGOL]

monged (mɒŋd) *adj slang* under the influence of drugs [C20 from a shortening of MONGOL]

monger ('mʌŋgə) *n* **1** (*in combination except in archaic use*) a trader or dealer: *ironmonger* **2** (*in combination*) a promoter of something unpleasant: *warmonger* [Old English *mangere,* ultimately from Latin *mangō* dealer; compare Old High German *mangari*] > 'mongering *n, adj*

mongo *or* **mongoe** ('mɒŋgəʊ) *n* a variant of **mungo**

möngö *or* **mongoe** ('mɒŋgəʊ) *n, pl* **-gos** *or* **-goes** a Mongolian monetary unit worth one hundredth of a tugrik

mongol ('mɒŋgəl) *n offensive* a person affected by Down's syndrome

Mongol ('mɒŋgɒl, -gəl) *n* **1** a native or inhabitant of Mongolia, esp a nomad **2** the Mongolian language

Mongolia (mɒŋˈgəʊlɪə) *n* **1** a republic in E central Asia: made a Chinese province in 1691; became autonomous in 1911 and a republic in 1924; multiparty democracy introduced in 1990. It consists chiefly of a high plateau, with the Gobi Desert in the south, a large lake district in the northwest, and the Altai and Khangai Mountains in the west. Official language: Khalkha. Religion: nonreligious majority. Currency: tugrik. Capital: Ulan Bator. Pop: 2 630 000 (2004 est). Area: 1 565 000 sq km (604 095 sq miles). Former names: Outer Mongolia (until 1924), Mongolian People's Republic (1924–92) **2** a vast region of central Asia, inhabited chiefly by Mongols: now divided into the republic of Mongolia, the Inner Mongolian Autonomous Region of China, and the Tuva Republic of S Russia; at its height during the 13th century under Genghis Khan

mongolian (mɒŋˈgəʊlɪən) *adj* (not in technical use) of, relating to, or affected by Down's syndrome

Mongolian (mɒŋˈgəʊlɪən) *adj* **1** of or relating to Mongolia, its people, or their language ▷ *n* **2** a native of Mongolia **3** the language of Mongolia: see **Khalkha**

Mongolian People's Republic *n* the former name of **Mongolia** (sense 1)

Mongolic (mɒŋˈgɒlɪk) *n* **1** a branch or subfamily of the Altaic family of languages, including Mongolian, Kalmuck, and Buryat **2** another word for **Mongoloid**

mongolism ('mɒŋgəˌlɪzəm) *n pathol* a former name (not in technical use) for **Down's syndrome** [C20 so named because Down's syndrome produces facial features similar to those of the Mongoloid peoples]

mongoloid ('mɒŋgəˌlɔɪd) (not in technical use) *adj* **1** relating to or characterized by Down's syndrome ▷ *n* **2** a person affected by Down's syndrome

Mongoloid ('mɒŋgəˌlɔɪd) *adj* **1** denoting, relating

m

to, or belonging to one of the major racial groups of mankind, characterized by yellowish complexion, straight black hair, slanting eyes, short nose, and scanty facial hair, including most of the peoples of Asia, the Inuit, and the North American Indians ▷ *n* **2** a member of this group

mongoose ('mɒŋ,guːs) *n*, *pl* **-gooses** any small predatory viverrine mammal of the genus *Herpestes* and related genera, occurring in Africa and from S Europe to SE Asia, typically having a long tail and brindled coat [C17 from Marathi *maṅgūs*, of Dravidian origin]

mongrel ('mʌŋgrəl) *n* **1** a plant or animal, esp a dog, of mixed or unknown breeding; a crossbreed or hybrid **2** *derogatory* a person of mixed race **3** *Austral and NZ sport* toughness and physical aggression: *a tall southpaw with plenty of mongrel* ▷ *adj* **4** of mixed origin, breeding, character, etc [C15 from obsolete *mong* mixture; compare Old English *gemong* a mingling] > 'mongrelism *n* > 'mongrelly *adj*

mongrelize or **mongrelise** ('mʌŋgrə,laɪz) *vb* (*tr*) to make mixed or mongrel in breed, race, character, kind, etc >,mongreli'zation or ,mongreli'sation *n* > 'mongrel,izer or 'mongrel,iser *n*

'mongst (mʌŋst) *prep poetic* short for **amongst**

monied ('mʌnɪd) *adj* a less common spelling of **moneyed**

monies ('mʌnɪz) *n formal* a plural of **money**

moniker or **monicker** ('mɒnɪkə) *n slang* a person's name or nickname [C19 from Shelta *munnik*, altered from Irish *ainm* name]

monilial (mə'nɪlɪəl) *adj pathol* denoting a thrush infection, caused by the fungus *Candida* (formerly *Monilia*) *albicans* [C20 from New Latin *monilia*, from Latin *monīle* necklace (referring to the beadlike form of the fungus)]

moniliform (mɒ'nɪlɪ,fɔːm) *adj biology* shaped like a string of beads: *moniliform fungi* [C19 from New Latin *monīliformis*, from Latin *monīle* necklace + *forma* shape]

monism ('mɒnɪzəm) *n* **1** *philosophy* the doctrine that the person consists of only a single substance, or that there is no crucial difference between mental and physical events or properties. Compare **dualism** (sense 2) See also **materialism** (sense 2), **idealism** (sense 3) **2** *philosophy* the doctrine that reality consists of an unchanging whole in which change is mere illusion. Compare **pluralism** (sense 5) **3** the epistemological theory that the object and datum of consciousness are identical **4** the attempt to explain anything in terms of one principle only [C19 from Greek *monos* single + -ISM] > 'monist *n*, *adj* > mo'nistic *adj* > mo'nistically *adv*

monition (məʊ'nɪʃən) *n* **1** a warning or caution; admonition **2** *Christianity* a formal notice from a bishop or ecclesiastical court requiring a person to refrain from committing a specific offence [C14 via Old French from Latin *monitiō*, from *monēre* to warn]

monitor ('mɒnɪtə) *n* **1** a person or piece of equipment that warns, checks, controls, or keeps a continuous record of something **2** *education* **a** a senior pupil with various supervisory duties **b** a pupil assisting a teacher in classroom organization, etc **3** a television screen used to display certain kinds of information in a television studio, airport, etc **4** the unit in a desk computer that contains the screen **5 a** a loudspeaker used in a recording studio control room to determine quality or balance **b** a loudspeaker used on stage to enable musicians to hear themselves **6** a device for controlling the direction of a water jet in fire fighting **7** any large predatory lizard of the genus *Varanus* and family *Varanidae*, inhabiting warm regions of Africa, Asia, and Australia. See also **Komodo dragon 8** Also called: giant *mining* a nozzle for directing a high-pressure jet of water at the material to be excavated **9** (formerly) a small heavily armoured shallow-draught warship used

for coastal assault ▷ *vb* (*tr*) **10** to act as a monitor of **11** to observe or record (the activity or performance) of (an engine or other device) **12** to check (the technical quality of) (a radio or television broadcast) [C16 from Latin, from *monēre* to advise] > **monitorial** (,mɒnɪ'tɔːrɪəl) *adj* >,moni'torially *adv* > 'monitor,ship *n* > 'monitress *fem n*

monitory ('mɒnɪtərɪ, -trɪ) *adj also* monitorial **1** warning or admonishing: *a monitory look* ▷ *n*, *pl* **-ries 2** *rare* a letter containing a monition

monk (mʌŋk) *n* **1** a male member of a religious community bound by vows of poverty, chastity, and obedience. Related adj: **monastic 2** (*sometimes capital*) a fancy pigeon having a bald pate and often large feathered feet [Old English *munuc*, from Late Latin *monachus*, from Late Greek: solitary (man), from Greek *monos* alone]

monkery ('mʌŋkərɪ) *n*, *pl* **-eries** *derogatory* **1** monastic life or practices **2** a monastery or monks collectively

monkey ('mʌŋkɪ) *n* **1** any of numerous long-tailed primates excluding the prosimians (lemurs, tarsiers, etc): comprise the families *Cercopithecidae* (see **Old World monkey**), *Cebidae* (see **New World monkey**), and *Callithricidae* (marmosets). Related adj: **simian 2** any primate except man **3** a naughty or mischievous person, esp a child **4** the head of a pile-driver (**monkey engine**) or of some similar mechanical device **5** (*modifier*) *nautical* denoting a small light structure or piece of equipment contrived to suit an immediate purpose: *a monkey foresail; a monkey bridge* **6** *US and Canadian slang* an addict's dependence on a drug (esp in the phrase **have a monkey on one's back**) **7** *slang* a butt of derision; someone made to look a fool (esp in the phrase **make a monkey of**) **8** *slang* (esp in bookmaking) £500 **9** *US and Canadian slang* $500 **10** *Austral slang, archaic* a sheep **11** **give a monkey's** *Brit slang* to care about or regard as important: *who gives a monkey's what he thinks?* ▷ *vb* **12** (*intr; usually foll by* around, with, *etc*) to meddle, fool, or tinker **13** (*tr*) *rare* to imitate; ape [C16 perhaps from Low German; compare Middle Low German *Moneke* name of the ape's son in the tale of Reynard the Fox]

monkey bread *n* **1** the gourdlike fruit of the baobab tree **2** **monkey bread tree** another name for **baobab**

monkey business *n informal* mischievous, suspect, dishonest, or meddlesome behaviour or acts

monkey climb *n* a wrestling throw in which a contestant seizes his opponent's arms or neck, places his feet on his opponent's stomach, and falls backwards, straightening his legs and throwing the opponent over his head

monkey flower *n* any of various scrophulariaceous plants of the genus *Mimulus*, cultivated for their yellow or red flowers. See also **musk** (sense 3)

monkeygland sauce ('mʌŋkɪ,glænd) *n South African* a piquant sauce, made from tomatoes, ketchup, fruit chutney, garlic, spices, etc

monkey jacket *n* a short close-fitting jacket, esp a waist-length jacket similar to a mess jacket

monkey nut *n Brit* another name for a **peanut**

monkey orchid *n* a European orchid, *Orchis simia*, rare in Britain, having a short dense flower spike that opens from the top downwards. The flowers are white streaked with pink or violet and have five spurs thought to resemble a monkey's arms, legs, and tail

monkeypot ('mʌŋkɪ,pɒt) *n* **1** any of various tropical trees of the genus *Lecythis*: family *Lecythidaceae* **2** the large urn-shaped pod of any of these trees, formerly used to catch monkeys by baiting it with sugar **3** a melting pot used in making flint glass

monkey puzzle *n* a South American coniferous tree, *Araucaria araucana*, having branches shaped like a candelabrum and stiff sharp leaves: family

Araucariaceae. Also called: Chile pine [so called because monkeys allegedly have difficulty climbing them]

monkey suit *n US slang* a man's evening dress

monkey's wedding *n South African informal* a combination of sunshine and light rain

monkey tricks or *US* **monkey shines** *pl n informal* mischievous behaviour or acts, such as practical jokes

monkey wrench *n* a wrench with adjustable jaws

monkfish ('mʌŋk,fɪʃ) *n*, *pl* **-fish** or **-fishes 1** Also called (US): goosefish any of various anglers of the genus *Lophius* **2** another name for the **angel shark**

Mon-Khmer *n* **1** a family of languages spoken chiefly in Cambodia, Myanmar, and Assam; probably a member of the Austro-Asiatic phylum ▷ *adj* **2** of or belonging to this family of languages

monkhood ('mʌŋkhʊd) *n* **1** the condition of being a monk **2** monks collectively

monkish ('mʌŋkɪʃ) *adj* of, relating to, or resembling a monk or monks > 'monkishly *adv* > 'monkishness *n*

monk's cloth *n* a heavy cotton fabric of basket weave, used mainly for bedspreads [C19 so called because a similar material was used for making monks' habits]

monkshood ('mʌŋkshʊd) *n* any of several poisonous N temperate plants of the ranunculaceous genus *Aconitum*, esp *A. napellus*, that have hooded blue-purple flowers

Monmouth ('mɒnməθ) *n* a market town in E Wales, in Monmouthshire: Norman castle, where Henry V was born in 1387. Pop: 8547 (2001)

Monmouthshire ('mɒnməθ,ʃɪə, -ʃə) *n* a county of E Wales: administratively part of England for three centuries (until 1830); mainly absorbed into the county of Gwent in 1974; reinstated with reduced boundaries in 1996: chiefly agricultural, with the Black Mountains in the N. Administrative centre: Cwmbran. Pop: 86 200 (2003 est). Area: 851 sq km (329 sq miles)

mono ('mɒnəʊ) *adj* **1** short for **monophonic** ▷ *n* **2** monophonic sound; monophony

mono- or *before a vowel* **mon-** *combining form* **1** one; single: *monochrome; monorail* **2** indicating that a chemical compound contains a single specified atom or group: *monoxide* [from Greek *monos*]

monoacid (,mɒnəʊ'æsɪd), **monacid**, **monoacidic** (,mɒnəʊə'sɪdɪk) or **monacidic** *adj chem* (of a base) capable of reacting with only one molecule of a monobasic acid; having only one hydroxide ion per molecule

monoamine (,mɒnəʊ'eɪmiːn) *n* a substance, such as adrenaline, noradrenaline, or serotonin, that contains a single amine group

monoamine oxidase *n biochem* an enzyme present in nerve tissue that is responsible for the inactivation of neurotransmitters. Abbreviation: MAO

monoamine oxidase inhibitor *n biochem* an agent that inhibits the action of monoamine oxidase. Such inhibitors are used in the treatment of depression. Abbreviation: MAOI

monoao (mɒnɒɑːɒ) *n*, *pl* monoao a New Zealand plant, *Dracophyllum subulatum*, with rigid leaves, found esp in volcanic soil [Māori]

monoatomic (,mɒnəʊə'tɒmɪk) *adj* a variant of **monatomic**

monobasic (,mɒnəʊ'beɪsɪk) *adj chem* (of an acid, such as hydrogen chloride) having only one replaceable hydrogen atom per molecule

monobrow ('mɒnəʊ,braʊ) *n informal* the appearance of a single eyebrow as a result of the eyebrows joining above a person's nose

monocarp ('mɒnəʊ,kɑːp) *n* a plant that is monocarpic

monocarpellary (,mɒnəʊ'kɑːpɪlərɪ) or **monocarpous** (,mɒnəʊ'kɑːpəs) *adj* **1** (of flowers) having only one carpel **2** (of a plant gynoecium) consisting of one carpel

monocarpic (ˌmɒnəʊˈkɑːpɪk) or **monocarpous** adj botany another name for **semelparous** Also: hapaxanthic

Monoceros (məˈnɒsərəs) n, Latin genitive Monocerotis (məˌnɒsəˈrəʊtɪs) a faint constellation on the celestial equator crossed by the Milky Way and lying close to Orion and Canis Major [c14 via Old French from Latin: unicorn, from Greek monokeros with a single horn, from MONO- + keras horn]

monochasium (ˌmɒnəʊˈkeɪzɪəm) n, pl -sia (-zɪə) botany a cymose inflorescence in which each branch gives rise to one other branch only, as in the forget-me-not and buttercup. Compare **dichasium** [c19 MONO- + -chasium as in DICHASIUM] > ˌmono'chasial adj

monochlamydeous (ˌmɒnəʊkləˈmɪdɪəs) adj (of a flower) having a perianth of one whorl of members; not having a separate calyx and corolla [c19 from Greek, from MONO- + khlamus a cloak + -EOUS]

monochloride (ˌmɒnəˈklɔːraɪd) n a chloride containing one atom of chlorine per molecule

monochord (ˈmɒnəʊˌkɔːd) n an instrument employed in acoustic analysis or investigation, consisting usually of one string stretched over a resonator of wood. Also called: sonometer (səˈnɒmɪtə) [c15 from Old French, from Late Latin, from Greek monokhordon, from MONO- + khordē string]

monochromat (ˌmɒnəʊˈkrəʊmæt) or **monochromate** (ˌmɒnəʊˈkrəʊmeɪt) n a person who perceives all colours as a single hue

monochromatic (ˌmɒnəʊkrəʊˈmætɪk) or **monochroic** (ˌmɒnəʊˈkrəʊɪk) adj 1 Also: homochromatic (of light or other electromagnetic radiation) having only one wavelength 2 physics (of moving particles) having only one kinetic energy 3 of or relating to monochromatism ▷ n 4 a person who is totally colour-blind > ˌmonochro'matically adv

monochromatism (ˌmɒnəʊˈkrəʊməˌtɪzəm) n a visual defect in which all colours appear as variations of a single hue

monochromator (ˌmɒnəʊˈkrəʊmeɪtə) n physics a device that isolates a single wavelength of radiation

monochrome (ˈmɒnəˌkrəʊm) n 1 a black-and-white photograph or transparency 2 photog black and white 3 a a painting, drawing, etc, done in a range of tones of a single colour b the technique or art of this 4 (modifier) executed in or resembling monochrome: a monochrome print ▷ adj 5 devoid of any distinctive or stimulating characteristics ▷ Also called (for senses 3, 4): monotint [c17 via Medieval Latin from Greek monokhrōmos of one colour] > ˌmono'chromic or ˌmono'chromical adj > ˌmono'chromist n

monocle (ˈmɒnəkəl) n a lens for correcting defective vision of one eye, held in position by the facial muscles [c19 from French, from Late Latin monoculus one-eyed, from MONO- + oculus eye] > 'monocled adj

monocline (ˈmɒnəʊˌklaɪn) n a local steepening in stratified rocks with an otherwise gentle dip [c19 from MONO- + Greek klīnein to lean] > ˌmono'clinal adj, n > ˌmono'clinally adv

monoclinic (ˌmɒnəʊˈklɪnɪk) adj crystallog relating to or belonging to the crystal system characterized by three unequal axes, one pair of which are not at right angles to each other [c19 from MONO- + Greek klīnein to lean + -IC]

monoclinous (ˌmɒnəʊˈklaɪnəs, ˈmɒnəʊˌklaɪnəs) adj (of flowering plants) having the male and female reproductive organs on the same flower. Compare **diclinous** [c19 from MONO- + Greek klīnē bed + -OUS] > 'monoˌclinism n

monoclonal antibody (ˌmɒnəʊˈkləʊnəl) n an antibody, produced by a single clone of cells grown in culture, that is both pure and specific and is capable of proliferating indefinitely to produce unlimited quantities of identical antibodies: used in diagnosis, therapy, and biotechnology

monocoque (ˈmɒnəˌkɒk) n 1 a type of aircraft fuselage, car body, etc, in which all or most of the loads are taken by the skin 2 a type of racing-car, racing-cycle, or powerboat design with no separate chassis and body ▷ adj 3 of or relating to the design characteristic of a monocoque [c20 from French, from MONO- + coque shell]

monocotyledon (ˌmɒnəʊˌkɒtɪˈliːdən) n any flowering plant of the class Monocotyledonae, having a single embryonic seed leaf, leaves with parallel veins, and flowers with parts in threes: includes grasses, lilies, palms, and orchids. Often shortened to: monocot Compare **dicotyledon** > ˌmono'coty'ledonous adj

monocracy (mɒˈnɒkrəsɪ) n, pl -cies government by one person > monocrat ('mɒnəˌkræt) n > ˌmono'cratic adj

monocular (mɒˈnɒkjʊlə) adj 1 having to do with or using only one eye ▷ n 2 a device for use with one eye, such as a field glass [c17 from Late Latin monoculus one-eyed] > mo'nocularly adv

monoculture (ˈmɒnəʊˌkʌltʃə) n the continuous growing of one type of crop

monocycle (ˈmɒnəˌsaɪkəl) n another name for **unicycle**

monocyclic (ˌmɒnəʊˈsaɪklɪk) adj 1 Also: mononuclear (of a chemical compound) containing only one ring of atoms 2 (of sepals, petals, or stamens) arranged in a single whorl 3 (of a plant) having a life cycle that is completed in one year

monocyte (ˈmɒnəˌsaɪt) n a large phagocytic leucocyte with a spherical nucleus and clear cytoplasm > monocytic (ˌmɒnəˈsɪtɪk) adj > ˌmono'cytoid adj

monodactylous (ˌmɒnəʊˈdæktɪləs) adj (of certain animals) having a single functional digit

monodisperse (ˌmɒnəʊdɪsˈpɜːs) adj chem (of a colloidal system) having particles of similar size

monodont (ˈmɒnəʊˌdɒnt) adj (of certain animals, esp the male narwhal) having a single tooth throughout life

monodrama (ˈmɒnəʊˌdrɑːmə) n a play or other dramatic piece for a single performer > ˌmonodra'matic adj

monody (ˈmɒnədɪ) n, pl -dies 1 (in Greek tragedy) an ode sung by a single actor 2 any poem of lament for someone's death 3 music a style of composition consisting of a single vocal part, usually with accompaniment [c17 via Late Latin from Greek monōidia, from MONO- + aeidein to sing] > monodic (mɒˈnɒdɪk) or mo'nodical adj > mo'nodically adv > 'monodist n

monoecious, monecious (mɒˈniːʃəs) or **monoicous** (mɒˈnɔɪkəs) adj 1 (of some flowering plants) having the male and female reproductive organs in separate flowers on the same plant 2 (of some animals and lower plants) hermaphrodite ▷ Compare **dioecious** [c18 from New Latin monoecia, from MONO- + Greek oikos house] > mo'noeciously or mo'neciously adv

monofilament (ˌmɒnəˈfɪləmənt) or **monofil** (ˈmɒnəfɪl) n 1 synthetic thread or yarn composed of a single strand rather than twisted fibres 2 a fishing line made of monofilaments

monogamist (mɒˈnɒɡəmɪst) n a person who advocates or practises monogamy > moˌnoga'mistic adj

monogamy (mɒˈnɒɡəmɪ) n 1 the state or practice of having only one husband or wife over a period of time. Compare **bigamy, polygamy** (sense 1), **digamy** 2 zoology the practice of having only one mate [c17 via French from Late Latin monogamia, from Greek; see MONO- + -GAMY] > mo'nogamous adj > mo'nogamously adv > mo'nogamousness n

monogenesis (ˌmɒnəʊˈdʒɛnɪsɪs) or **monogeny** (mɒˈnɒdʒɪnɪ) n 1 the hypothetical descent of all organisms from a single cell or organism 2 asexual reproduction in animals 3 the direct development of an ovum into an organism resembling the adult 4 the hypothetical descent of all human beings from a single pair of ancestors ▷ Compare **polygenesis**

monogenetic (ˌmɒnəʊdʒɪˈnɛtɪk) or **monogenous** (mɒˈnɒdʒɪnəs) adj 1 of, relating to, or showing monogenesis 2 of or relating to parasitic animals, such as some flukes, that complete their life cycle on only one host 3 (of rocks and rock formations) formed from one source or by one process

monogenic (ˌmɒnəʊˈdʒɛnɪk) adj 1 genetics of or relating to an inherited character difference that is controlled by a single gene 2 (of animals) producing offspring of one sex

monogram (ˈmɒnəˌɡræm) n 1 a design of one or more letters, esp initials, embroidered on clothing, printed on stationery, etc ▷ vb monograms, monogramming, monogrammed 2 (tr; usually passive) to decorate (clothing, stationery, etc) with a monogram [c17 from Late Latin monogramma, from Greek; see MONO-, -GRAM] > monogrammatic (ˌmɒnəɡrəˈmætɪk) adj

monograph (ˈmɒnəˌɡrɑːf, -ˌɡræf) n 1 a paper, book, or other work concerned with a single subject or aspect of a subject ▷ vb 2 (tr) to write a monograph on > monographer (mɒˈnɒɡrəfə) or mo'nographist n > ˌmono'graphic adj > ˌmono'graphically adv

monogyny (mɒˈnɒdʒɪnɪ) n the custom of having only one female sexual partner over a period of time > mo'nogynist n > mo'nogynous adj

monohull (ˈmɒnəʊˌhʌl) n a sailing vessel with a single hull. Compare **multihull**

monohybrid (ˌmɒnəʊˈhaɪbrɪd) n genetics the offspring of two individuals that differ in respect of a single gene

monohydrate (ˌmɒnəʊˈhaɪdreɪt) n a hydrate, such as ferrous sulphate monohydrate, $FeSO_4.H_2O$, containing one molecule of water per molecule of the compound > mono'hydrated adj

monohydric (ˌmɒnəʊˈhaɪdrɪk) adj another word for **monohydroxy**, esp when applied to alcohols

monohydroxy (ˌmɒnəʊhaɪˈdrɒksɪ) adj (of a chemical compound) containing one hydroxyl group per molecule. Also: monohydric

monoicous (mɒˈnɔɪkəs) adj a variant of **monoecious**. > mo'noicously adv

Monola (mɒˈnəʊlə) n trademark Austral a form of canola, modified through selective breeding, which yields a cooking oil low in saturated fat [from Monsanto the company that developed the oil + CANOLA]

monolatry (mɒˈnɒlətrɪ) n the exclusive worship of one god without excluding the existence of others > monolater (mɒˈnɒlətə) or mo'nolatrist n > mo'nolatrous adj

monolayer (ˈmɒnəʊˌleɪə) n a single layer of atoms or molecules adsorbed on a surface. Also called: molecular film

monolingual (ˌmɒnəʊˈlɪŋɡwəl) adj 1 knowing or expressed in only one language ▷ n 2 a monolingual person ▷ Compare **bilingual, multilingual**

monolith (ˈmɒnəlɪθ) n 1 a large block of stone or anything that resembles one in appearance, intractability, etc 2 a statue, obelisk, column, etc, cut from one block of stone 3 a large hollow foundation piece sunk as a caisson and having a number of compartments that are filled with concrete when it has reached its correct position [c19 via French from Greek monolithos made from a single stone]

monolithic (ˌmɒnəˈlɪθɪk) adj 1 of, relating to, or like a monolith 2 characterized by hugeness, impenetrability, or intractability: a monolithic government 3 electronics (of an integrated circuit) having all components manufactured into or on top of a single chip of silicon. Compare **hybrid** (sense 6) > ˌmono'lithically adv

monologue (ˈmɒnəˌlɒɡ) n 1 a long speech made by one actor in a play, film, etc, esp when alone 2 a dramatic piece for a single performer 3 any long

m

speech by one person, esp when interfering with conversation [c17 via French from Greek *monologos* speaking alone] > monologic (ˌmɒnəˈlɒdʒɪk) or ˌmonoˈlogical *adj* > monologist (ˈmɒnəˌlɒgɪst, məˈnɒləgɪst) *n* > monology (mɒˈnɒlədʒɪ) *n*

▓ USAGE See at **soliloquy**

monomania (ˌmɒnəʊˈmeɪnɪə) *n* an excessive mental preoccupation with one thing, idea, etc > ˌmonoˈmaniˌac *n, adj* > monomaniacal (ˌmɒnəʊməˈnaɪəkᵊl) *adj*

monomark (ˈmɒnəmɑːk) *n Brit* a series of letters or figures to identify goods, personal articles, etc

monomer (ˈmɒnəmə) *n chem* a compound whose molecules can join together to form a polymer > monomeric (ˌmɒnəˈmɛrɪk) *adj*

monomerous (mɒˈnɒmərəs) *adj* (of flowers) having whorls consisting of only one member [c19 from Greek *monomerēs* of one part; see MONO-, -MERE]

monometallic (ˌmɒnəʊmɪˈtælɪk) *adj* 1 (esp of coins) consisting of one metal only 2 relating to monometallism

monometallism (ˌmɒnəʊˈmɛtᵊˌlɪzəm) *n* 1 the use of one metal, esp gold or silver, as the sole standard of value and currency 2 the economic policies supporting a monometallic standard > ˌmonoˈmetallist *n*

monometer (mɒˈnɒmɪtə) *n prosody* a line of verse consisting of one metrical foot > monometrical (ˌmɒnəʊˈmɛtrɪkᵊl) or ˌmonoˈmetric *adj*

monomial (mɒˈnəʊmɪəl) *n* 1 *maths* an expression consisting of a single term, such as 5*ax* ▷ *adj* 2 consisting of a single algebraic term 3 *biology* of, relating to, or denoting a taxonomic name that consists of a single term [c18 MONO- + (BIN)OMIAL]

monomode (ˈmɒnəʊˌməʊd) *adj* denoting or relating to a type of optical fibre with a core less than 10 micrometres in diameter

monomolecular (ˌmɒnəʊməˈlɛkjʊlə) *adj* of, concerned with, or involving single molecules: *a monomolecular layer*

monomorphic (ˌmɒnəʊˈmɔːfɪk) or **monomorphous** *adj* 1 (of an individual organism) showing little or no change in structure during the entire life history 2 (of a species) existing or having parts that exist in only one form 3 (of a chemical compound) having only one crystalline form > ˌmonoˈmorphism *n*

Monongahela (məˌnɒŋɡəˈhiːlə) *n* a river in the northeastern US, flowing generally north to the Allegheny River at Pittsburgh, Pennsylvania, forming the Ohio River. Length: 206 km (128 miles)

mononuclear (ˌmɒnəʊˈnjuːklɪə) *adj* 1 (of a cell) having only one nucleus 2 another word for **monocyclic** (sense 1)

mononucleosis (ˌmɒnəʊˌnjuːklɪˈəʊsɪs) *n* 1 *pathol* the presence of a large number of monocytes in the blood 2 See **infectious mononucleosis**

mononym (ˈmɒnəʊˌnɪm) *n* a person who is famous enough to be known only by one name, usually the first name [c20 from MONO- + (EPO)NYM]

monopetalous (ˌmɒnəʊˈpɛtᵊləs) *adj* (of flowers) having only one petal

monophagous (məˈnɒfəɡəs) *adj* feeding on only one type of food > moˈnophagy *n*

monophobia (ˌmɒnəʊˈfəʊbɪə) *n* a strong fear of being alone > ˌmonoˈphobic *adj*

monophonic (ˌmɒnəʊˈfɒnɪk) *adj* 1 Also: monaural (of a system of broadcasting, recording, or reproducing sound) using only one channel between source and loudspeaker. Sometimes shortened to: mono Compare **stereophonic** 2 *music* of or relating to a style of musical composition consisting of a single melodic line. See also **monody** (sense 3) > monophony (mɒˈnɒfənɪ) *n*

monophthong (ˈmɒnəfˌθɒŋ) *n* a simple or pure vowel [c17 from Greek *monophthongos,* from MONO- + *thongos* sound] > monophthongal (ˌmɒnəfˈθɒŋɡᵊl) *adj*

monophyletic (ˌmɒnəʊfaɪˈlɛtɪk) *adj* 1 relating to or characterized by descent from a single ancestral group of animals or plants 2 (of animals or plants) of or belonging to a single stock

monophyllous (ˌmɒnəʊˈfɪləs) *adj botany* having or consisting of only one leaf or leaflike part

Monophysite (mɒˈnɒfɪˌsaɪt) *Christianity* ▷ *n* 1 a person who holds that there is only one nature in the person of Christ, which is primarily divine with human attributes ▷ *adj* 2 of or relating to this belief [c17 via Church Latin from Late Greek, from MONO- + *phusis* nature] > Monophysitic (ˌmɒnəʊfɪˈsɪtɪk) *adj* > Moˈnophyˌsitism *n*

monoplane (ˈmɒnəʊˌpleɪn) *n* an aeroplane with only one pair of wings. Compare **biplane**

monoplegia (ˌmɒnəʊˈpliːdʒɪə) *n pathol* paralysis limited to one limb or a single group of muscles > monoplegic (ˌmɒnəʊˈpliːdʒɪk) *adj*

monoploid (ˈmɒnəˌplɔɪd) *adj, n* a less common word for **haploid**

monopode (ˈmɒnəˌpəʊd) *n* 1 a member of a legendary one-legged race of Africa 2 another word for **monopodium** [c19 from Late Latin *monopodius*]

monopodium (ˌmɒnəˈpəʊdɪəm) *n, pl* -dia (-dɪə) the main axis of growth in the pine tree and similar plants: the main stem, which elongates from the tip and gives rise to lateral branches. Compare **sympodium** [c19 New Latin, from Greek *monopous,* from MONO- + *pous* foot] > ˌmonoˈpodial *adj* > ˌmonoˈpodially *adv*

monopole (ˈmɒnəˌpəʊl) *n physics* 1 a magnetic pole considered in isolation 2 Also called: magnetic monopole a hypothetical elementary particle postulated in certain theories of particle physics to exist as an isolated north or south magnetic pole

monopolistic competition *n economics* the form of imperfect competition that exists when there are many producers or sellers of similar but differentiated goods or services

monopolize or **monopolise** (məˈnɒpəˌlaɪz) *vb* (*tr*) 1 to have, control, or make use of fully, excluding others 2 to obtain, maintain, or exploit a monopoly of (a market, commodity, etc) > moˌnopoliˈzation or moˌnopoliˈsation *n* > moˈnopoˌlizer or moˈnopoˌliser *n*

monopoly (məˈnɒpəlɪ) *n, pl* -lies 1 exclusive control of the market supply of a product or service 2 a an enterprise exercising this control b the product or service so controlled 3 *law* the exclusive right or privilege granted to a person, company, etc, by the state to purchase, manufacture, use, or sell some commodity or to carry on trade in a specified country or area 4 exclusive control, possession, or use of something [c16 from Late Latin, from Greek *monopōlion,* from MONO- + *pōlein* to sell] > moˈnopolism *n* > moˈnopolist *n* > moˌnopoˈlistic *adj* > moˌnopoˈlistically *adv*

Monopoly (məˈnɒpəlɪ) *n trademark* a board game for two to six players who throw dice to advance their tokens around a board, the object being to acquire the property on which their tokens land

monopropellant (ˌmɒnəʊprəˈpɛlənt) *n* a solid or liquid rocket propellant containing both the fuel and the oxidizer

monopsony (məˈnɒpsənɪ) *n, pl* -nies a situation in which the entire market demand for a product or service consists of only one buyer [c20 MONO- + Greek *opsōnia* purchase, from *opsōnein* to buy] > moˌnopsoˈnistic *adj*

monopteros (mɒnˈɒptəˌrɒs) or **monopteron** *n, pl* -teroi (-təˌrɔɪ) or -tera (-tərə) a circular classical building, esp a temple, that has a single ring of columns surrounding it [c18 Late Latin from Greek, from MONO- + *pteron* a wing] > monˈopteral *adj*

monorail (ˈmɒnəʊˌreɪl) *n* a single-rail railway, often elevated and with suspended cars

monorchid (mɒnˈɔːkɪd) *adj* 1 having only one

testicle ▷ *n* 2 an animal or person with only one testicle

monosaccharide (ˌmɒnəʊˈsækəˌraɪd, -rɪd) *n* a simple sugar, such as glucose or fructose, that does not hydrolyse to yield other sugars

monosaturated (ˌmɒnəʊˈsætʃəˌreɪtɪd) *adj* of or relating to fats that are liquid at room temperature and derive mostly from foods such as olives, avocados, and nuts

monosemy (ˈmɒnəʊˌsiːmɪ) *n* the fact of having only a single meaning; absence of ambiguity in a word. Compare **polysemy** [c20 from MONO- + (POLY)SEMY]

monosepalous (ˌmɒnəʊˈsɛpələs) *adj* (of flowers) having only one sepal

monoski (ˈmɒnəʊˌskiː) *n* a wide ski on which the skier stands with both feet > ˈmonoˌskier *n* > ˈmonoˌskiing *n*

monosodium glutamate (ˌmɒnəʊˈsəʊdɪəm) *n* a white crystalline substance, the sodium salt of glutamic acid, that has little flavour itself but enhances the flavour of proteins either by increasing the amount of saliva produced in the mouth or by stimulating the taste buds: used as a food additive, esp in Chinese foods. Formula: $NaC_5H_8O_4$. Also called: sodium glutamate Abbreviation: MSG

monosome (ˈmɒnəˌsəʊm) *n* an unpaired chromosome, esp an X-chromosome in an otherwise diploid cell > monosomic (ˌmɒnəˈsəʊmɪk) *adj*

monospaced type (ˈmɒnəʊˌspeɪst) *n computing* a typeface in which the width of all letters, including the space around them, is the same

monospermous (ˌmɒnəʊˈspɜːməs) or **monospermal** *adj* (of certain plants) producing only one seed

monostable (ˌmɒnəʊˈsteɪbᵊl) *adj physics* (of an electronic circuit) having only one stable state but able to pass into a second state in response to an input pulse

monostich (ˈmɒnəˌstɪk) *n* a poem of a single line [c16 via Late Latin from Greek; see MONO-, STICH] > ˌmonoˈstichic *adj*

monostichous (ˌmɒnəʊˈstaɪkəs) *adj botany* (of parts) forming one row

monostome (ˈmɒnəˌstəʊm) or **monostomous** (mɒˈnɒstəməs) *adj zoology, botany* having only one mouth, pore, or similar opening

monostrophe (mɒˈnɒstrəfɪ, ˈmɒnəˌstrəʊf) *n* a poem in which all the stanzas or strophes are written in the same metre > monostrophic (ˌmɒnəˈstrɒfɪk) *adj*

monostylous (ˌmɒnəʊˈstaɪləs) *adj botany* having only one style

monosyllabic (ˌmɒnəsɪˈlæbɪk) *adj* 1 (of a word) containing only one syllable 2 characterized by monosyllables; curt: *a monosyllabic answer* > ˌmonosylˈlabically *adv*

monosyllable (ˈmɒnəˌsɪləbᵊl) *n* a word of one syllable, esp one used as a sentence > ˌmonoˈsyllaˌbism *n*

monosymmetric (ˌmɒnəsɪˈmɛtrɪk) or **monosymmetrical** *adj* 1 *crystallog* variants of **monoclinic** 2 *botany* variants of **zygomorphic** > ˌmonosymˈmetrically *adv* > monosymmetry (ˌmɒnəˈsɪmɪtrɪ) *n*

monoterpene (ˌmɒnəˈtɜːpiːn) *n chem* an isoprene unit, C_5H_8, forming a terpene

monotheism (ˈmɒnəʊθɪˌɪzəm) *n* the belief or doctrine that there is only one God > ˈmonoˌtheist *n, adj* > ˌmonotheˈistic *adj* > ˌmonotheˈistically *adv*

monotint (ˈmɒnəˌtɪnt) *n* another word for **monochrome** (senses 3, 4)

monotocous (məˈnɒtəkəs) *adj* (of certain animals) producing a single offspring at a birth [from MONO- + Greek *tokos* birth]

monotone (ˈmɒnəˌtəʊn) *n* 1 a single unvaried pitch level in speech, sound, etc 2 utterance, etc, without change of pitch 3 lack of variety in style, expression, etc ▷ *adj* 4 unvarying or monotonous 5 Also: monotonic (ˌmɒnəˈtɒnɪk) *maths* (of a sequence or function) consistently increasing or decreasing in value

monotonize or **monotonise** (məˈnɒtəˌnaɪz) vb (tr) to make monotonous

monotonous (məˈnɒtənəs) adj **1** dull and tedious, esp because of repetition **2** unvarying in pitch or cadence > moˈnotonously adv > moˈnotonousness n

monotony (məˈnɒtənɪ) n, pl -nies **1** wearisome routine; dullness **2** lack of variety in pitch or cadence

monotreme (ˈmɒnəˌtriːm) n any mammal of the primitive order Monotremata, of Australia and New Guinea: egg-laying toothless animals with a single opening (cloaca) for the passage of eggs or sperm, faeces, and urine. The group contains only the echidnas and the platypus [c19 via New Latin from MONO- + Greek trēma hole] > monotrematous (ˌmɒnəˈtriːmətəs) adj

monotrichous (mɒˈnɒtrɪkəs) or **monotrichic** (ˌmɒnəˈtrɪkɪk) adj (of bacteria) having a single flagellum

monotype (ˈmɒnəˌtaɪp) n **1** a single print made from a metal or glass plate on which a picture has been painted **2** biology a monotypic genus or species

Monotype (ˈmɒnəˌtaɪp) n **1** trademark any of various typesetting systems, esp originally one in which each character was cast individually from hot metal **2** type produced by such a system

monotypic (ˌmɒnəˈtɪpɪk) adj **1** (of a genus or species) consisting of only one type of animal or plant **2** of or relating to a monotype

monounsaturated (ˌmɒnəʊʌnˈsætʃəˌreɪtɪd) adj of or relating to a class of vegetable oils, such as olive oil, the molecules of which have long chains of carbon atoms containing only one double bond. See also **polyunsaturated**

monovalent (ˌmɒnəʊˈveɪlənt) adj chem **a** having a valency of one **b** having only one valency ▷ Also: univalent > ˌmonoˈvalence or ˌmonoˈvalency n

monoxide (mɒˈnɒksaɪd) n an oxide that contains one oxygen atom per molecule: carbon monoxide, CO

monozygotic (ˌmɒnəʊzaɪˈɡɒtɪk) or **monzygous** (ˌmɒnəʊˈzaɪɡəs) adj (of twins) derived from a single fertilized ovum, and so identical [c20]

Monroe doctrine n a principle of US foreign policy that opposes the influence or interference of outside powers in the Americas

Monrovia (mɒnˈrəʊvɪə) n the capital and chief port of Liberia, on the Atlantic: founded in 1822 as a home for freed American slaves; University of Liberia (1862). Pop: 614 000 (2005 est)

Mons (French mɔ̃s) n a town in SW Belgium, capital of Hainaut province: scene of the first battle (1914) of the British Expeditionary Force during World War I. Pop: 91 185 (2004 est). Flemish name: Bergen

Monseigneur French (mɔ̃sɛɲœr) n, pl Messeigneurs (mesɛɲœr) a title given to French bishops, prelates, and princes. Abbreviation: Mgr [literally: my lord]

monsieur (French məsjø; English məsˈjɜː) n, pl messieurs (French mesjø; English ˈmɛsəz) a French title of address equivalent to sir when used alone or Mr when placed before a name [literally: my lord]

Monsignor (mɒnˈsiːnjə; Italian monsiɲˈɲor) n, pl Monsignors or Monsignori (Italian monsiɲˈɲoːri) RC Church an ecclesiastical title attached to certain offices or distinctions usually bestowed by the Pope. Abbreviations: Mgr, Msgr [c17 from Italian, from French MONSEIGNEUR]

monsoon (mɒnˈsuːn) n **1** a seasonal wind of S Asia that blows from the southwest in summer, bringing heavy rains, and from the northeast in winter **2** the rainy season when the SW monsoon blows, from about April to October **3** any wind that changes direction with the seasons [c16 from obsolete Dutch monssoen, from Portuguese monção, from Arabic mawsim season] > monˈsoonal adj

mons pubis (ˈmɒnz ˈpjuːbɪs) n, pl montes pubis (ˈmɒntiːz) the fatty cushion of flesh in human males situated over the junction of the pubic bones. Compare **mons veneris** [c17 New Latin: hill of the pubes]

monster (ˈmɒnstə) n **1** an imaginary beast, such as a centaur, usually made up of various animal or human parts **2** a person, animal, or plant with a marked structural deformity **3** a cruel, wicked, or inhuman person **4 a** a very large person, animal, or thing **b** (as modifier): a monster cake ▷ vb (tr) **5** Austral and NZ informal to criticize (a person or group) severely **6** Austral and NZ sport to use intimidating tactics against (an opponent) [c13 from Old French monstre, from Latin monstrum portent, from monēre to warn]

monstera (mɒnˈstɪərə) n any plant of the tropical climbing genus Monstera, some species of which are grown as greenhouse or pot plants for their unusual leathery perforated leaves: family Araceae. M. deliciosa is the Swiss cheese plant [New Latin, perhaps because the leaves were regarded as an aberration]

monstering (ˈmɒnstərɪŋ) n informal a severe reprimand or scolding; highly critical verbal attack

monster truck n a pick-up truck with extremely large tyres, often used for racing over rough terrain

monstrance (ˈmɒnstrəns) n RC Church a receptacle, usually of gold or silver, with a transparent container in which the consecrated Host is exposed for adoration [c16 from Medieval Latin mōnstrantia, from Latin mōnstrāre to show]

monstrosity (mɒnˈstrɒsɪtɪ) n, pl -ties **1** an outrageous or ugly person or thing; monster **2** the state or quality of being monstrous

monstrous (ˈmɒnstrəs) adj **1** abnormal, hideous, or unnatural in size, character, etc **2** (of plants and animals) abnormal in structure **3** outrageous, atrocious, or shocking: it is monstrous how badly he is treated **4** huge: a monstrous fire **5** of, relating to, or resembling a monster > ˈmonstrously adv > ˈmonstrousness n

mons veneris (ˈmɒnz ˈvɛnərɪs) n, pl montes veneris (ˈmɒntiːz) the fatty cushion of flesh in human females situated over the junction of the pubic bones. Compare **mons pubis** [c17 New Latin: hill of Venus]

Mont. abbreviation for Montana

montage (mɒnˈtɑːʒ; French mɔ̃taʒ) n **1** the art or process of composing pictures by the superimposition or juxtaposition of miscellaneous elements, such as other pictures or photographs **2** such a composition **3** a method of film editing involving the juxtaposition or partial superimposition of several shots to form a single image **4** a rapidly cut film sequence of this kind [c20 from French, from monter to MOUNT¹]

Montagnais (ˌmɒntənˈjeɪ) n, pl -gnais (jeɪ, jeɪz) or -gnaises (jeɪz) **1** a member of an Innu people living in Labrador and eastern Quebec **2** the Algonquian language of this people [c18 from French: of the mountain, from montagne MOUNTAIN]

Montagnard (ˌmɒntənˈjɑːd, -ˈjɑː) n, pl -gnards or -gnard **1** a member of a hill people living on the border between Vietnam, Laos, and NE Cambodia **2** a member of a North American Indian people living in the N Rocky Mountains [c19 from French: mountaineer, from montagne MOUNTAIN]

Montague grammar (ˈmɒntəˌɡjuː) n logic, linguistics a model-theoretic semantic theory for natural language that seeks to encompass indexical expressions and opaque contexts within an extensional theory by constructing set-theoretic representations of the intension of an expression in terms of functions of possible worlds [named after Richard Merett Montague (1930–71), US logician]

Montagu's harrier (ˈmɒntəˌɡjuːz) n a brownish European bird of prey, Circus pygargus, with long

narrow wings and a long tail: family Accipitridae (hawks, harriers, etc) [c19 named after Col George Montagu (1751–1815), British naturalist]

Montana (mɒnˈtænə) n a state of the western US: consists of the Great Plains in the east and the Rocky Mountains in the west. Capital: Helena. Pop: 917 621 (2003 est). Area: 377 070 sq km (145 587 sq miles). Abbreviations: Mont, (with zip code) MT

Montanan (mɒnˈtænən) n **1** a native or inhabitant of Montana ▷ adj **2** of or relating to Montana or its inhabitants

montane (ˈmɒntein) adj of or inhabiting mountainous regions: a montane flora [c19 from Latin montānus, from mons MOUNTAIN]

montan wax (ˈmɒntæn) n a hard wax obtained from lignite and peat, varying in colour from white to dark brown. It is used in polishes and candles [c20 from Latin montānus of a mountain]

Montauban (French mɔ̃tobɑ̃) n a city in SW France: a stronghold in the 16th and 17th centuries, taken by Richelieu in 1629. Pop: 51 855 (1999)

Montbéliard (French mɔ̃beljar) n an industrial town in E France: former capital of the duchy of Burgundy. Pop: 27 570 (1999)

Mont Blanc (French mɔ̃ blɑ̃) n a massif in SW Europe, mainly between France and Italy: the highest mountain in the Alps; beneath it is **Mont Blanc Tunnel**, 12 km (7.5 miles) long. Highest peak (in France): 4807 m (15 771 ft). Italian name: **Monte Bianco** (ˈmonte ˈbjaŋko)

montbretia (mɒnˈbriːʃə) n a widely cultivated plant of the African iridaceous genus Crocosmia, a cross between C. aurea and C. pottsii, with ornamental orange or yellow flowers, grown mostly as pot plants [c19 New Latin, named after A. F. E. Coquebert de Montbret (1780–1801), French botanist]

Mont Cenis (French mɔ̃səni) n See (Mont) **Cenis**

Mont Cervin (mɔ̃ sɛrvɛ̃) n the French name for the **Matterhorn**

mont-de-piété French (mɔ̃dpjete) n, pl monts-de-piété (mɔ̃dpjete) (formerly) a public pawnshop [from Italian monte di pietà bank of pity]

monte (ˈmɒntɪ) n **1** a gambling card game of Spanish origin **2** Austral informal a certainty [c19 from Spanish: mountain, hence pile of cards]

Monte Carlo (ˈmɒntɪ ˈkɑːləʊ; French mɔ̃te karlo) n a town and resort forming part of the principality of Monaco, on the Riviera: famous casino and the destination of an annual car rally (the **Monte Carlo Rally**). Pop: 15 507 (2000)

Monte Carlo method n a heuristic mathematical technique for evaluation or estimation of intractable problems by probabilistic simulation and sampling [c20 named after the casino at Monte Carlo, where systems for winning at roulette, etc, are often tried]

Monte Cassino (ˈmɒntɪ kəˈsiːnəʊ; Italian ˈmonte kasˈsiːno) n a hill above Cassino in central Italy: site of intense battle during World War II: site of Benedictine monastery (530 AD), destroyed by Allied bombing in 1944, later restored

Monte Corno (Italian ˈmonte ˈkorno) n See (Monte) **Corno**

Montego Bay (mɒnˈtiːɡəʊ) n a port and resort in NW Jamaica: the second largest town on the island Pop: 83 446 (1991)

monteith (mɒnˈtiːθ) n a large ornamental bowl, usually of silver, for cooling wineglasses, which are suspended from the notched rim [c17 said to be from the name of a Scot who wore a cloak with a scalloped edge]

Montenegrin (ˌmɒntɪˈniːɡrɪn) adj **1** of or relating to Montenegro or its inhabitants ▷ n **2** a native or inhabitant of Montenegro

Montenegro (ˌmɒntɪˈniːɡrəʊ) n a constituent republic of the Union of Serbia and Montenegro, bordering on the Adriatic: declared a kingdom in 1910 and united with Serbia, Croatia, and other territories in 1918 to form Yugoslavia; remained

m

united with Serbia as the Federal Republic of Yugoslavia when the other Yugoslav constituent republics became independent in 1991–92; Union of Serbia and Montenegro formed in 2002. Capital: Podgorica. Pop: 658 000 (2001 est). Area: 13 812 sq km (5387 sq miles)

Monterey (ˌmɒntəˈreɪ) *n* a city in W California: capital of Spain's Pacific empire from 1774 to 1825; taken by the US (1846). Pop: 29 960 (2003 est)

Monterey cypress *n* another name for **macrocarpa**

montero (mɒnˈtɛərəʊ; *Spanish* monˈtero) *n, pl* -ros (-rəʊz; *Spanish* -ros) a round cap with a flap at the back worn by hunters, esp in Spain in the 17th and 18th centuries [C17 from Spanish, literally: mountaineer]

Monterrey (ˌmɒntəˈreɪ; *Spanish* mɒnteˈrrei) *n* a city in NE Mexico, capital of Nuevo Léon state: the third largest city in Mexico; a major industrial centre, esp for metals. Pop: 1 353 000 (2005 est)

Montessori method *n* a method of nursery education in which children are provided with generous facilities for practical play and allowed to develop at their own pace

Montevideo (ˌmɒntɪvɪˈdeɪəʊ; *Spanish* mɒnteβiˈðeo) *n* the capital and chief port of Uruguay, in the south on the Río de la Plata estuary: the largest city in the country: University of the Republic (1849); resort. Pop: 1 378 707 (1996)

Montezuma's revenge (ˌmɒntɪˈzuːmə) *n informal* an acute attack of infectious diarrhoea, esp when experienced in Mexico by tourists [C20 after *Montezuma* II (1466–1520), the Aztec emperor of Mexico overthrown and killed by the Spanish conquistador Hernando Cortés (1485–1527)]

montgolfier (mɒntˈɡɒlfɪə; *French* mɔ̃ɡɔlfje) *n obsolete* a hot-air balloon [C18 after Jacques Etienne *Montgolfier* (1745–99) and his brother Joseph Michel *Montgolfier* (1740–1810), the French inventors who built (1782) and ascended in (1783) the first practical hot-air balloon]

Montgomery (məntˈɡʌmərɪ) *n* a city in central Alabama, on the Alabama River: state capital; capital of the Confederacy (1861). Pop: 200 123 (2003 est)

Montgomeryshire (məntˈɡʌmərɪˌʃɪə, -ʃə) *n* (until 1974) a county of central Wales, now part of Powys

month (mʌnθ) *n* **1** one of the twelve divisions (**calendar months**) of the calendar year **2** a period of time extending from one date to a corresponding date in the next calendar month **3** a period of four weeks or of 30 days **4** the period of time (**tropical month**) taken by the moon to return to the same longitude after one complete revolution around the earth; 27.321 58 days (approximately 27 days, 7 hours, 43 minutes, 4.5 seconds) **5** the period of time (**sidereal month**) taken by the moon to make one complete revolution around the earth, measured between two successive conjunctions with a distant star; 27.321 66 days (approximately 27 days, 7 hours, 43 minutes, 11 seconds) **6** Also called: **lunation** the period of time (**lunar** or **synodic month**) taken by the moon to make one complete revolution around the earth, measured between two successive new moons; 29.530 59 days (approximately 29 days, 12 hours, 44 minutes, 3 seconds) **7** a month of Sundays *informal* a long unspecified period ▷ Related adjective: **mensal** [Old English *mōnath*; related to Old High German *mānōd*, Old Norse *mānathr*; compare Gothic *mena* moon]

monthly (ˈmʌnθlɪ) *adj* **1** occurring, done, appearing, payable, etc, once every month **2** lasting or valid for a month: *a monthly subscription* ▷ *adv* **3** once a month ▷ *n, pl* -lies **4** a book, periodical, magazine, etc, published once a month **5** *informal* a menstrual period

month's mind *n* RC Church a Mass celebrated in remembrance of a person one month after his death

monticule (ˈmɒntɪˌkjuːl) *n* a small hill or mound,

such as a secondary volcanic cone [C18 via French from Late Latin *monticulus*, diminutive of Latin *mons* mountain]

Montluçon (*French* mɔ̃lysɔ̃) *n* an industrial city in central France, on the Cher River. Pop: 41 362 (1999)

Montmartre (*French* mɔ̃martrə) *n* a district of N Paris, on a hill above the Seine: the highest point in the city; famous for its associations with many artists

montmorillonite (ˌmɒntməˈrɪləˌnaɪt) *n* a clay mineral consisting of hydrated aluminium silicate: an important component of bentonite [C19 named after *Montmorillon*, French town where it was first found, + -ITE[1]]

Montparnasse (*French* mɔ̃parnas) *n* a district of S Paris, on the left bank of the Seine: noted for its cafés, frequented by artists, writers, and students

Montpelier (mɒntˈpiːljə) *n* a city in N central Vermont, on the Winooski River: the state capital. Pop: 7945 (2003 est)

Montpellier (*French* mɔ̃pelje) *n* a city in S France, the chief town of Languedoc: its university was founded by Pope Nicholas IV in 1289; wine trade. Pop: 225 392 (1999)

Montreal (ˌmɒntrɪˈɔːl) *n* a city and major port in central Canada, in S Quebec on **Montreal Island** at the junction of the Ottawa and St Lawrence Rivers. Pop: 1 039 534 (2001). French name: **Montréal** (mɔ̃real)

Montreuil (*French* mɔ̃trœj) *n* an E suburb of Paris: formerly famous for peaches, but now increasingly industrialized. Pop: 90 674 (1999)

Montreux (*French* mɔ̃trø) *n* a town and resort in W Switzerland, in Vaud canton on Lake Geneva annual television festival. Pop: 22 454 (2000)

Mont-Saint-Michel (*French* mɔ̃sɛ̃miʃɛl) *n* a rocky islet off the coast of NW France, accessible at low tide by a causeway, in the **Bay of St Michel** (an inlet of the Gulf of St Malo): Benedictine abbey (966), used as a prison from the Revolution until 1863; reoccupied by Benedictine monks since 1966. Area: 1 hectare (3 acres)

Montserrat *n* **1** (ˌmɒntsəˈræt) a volcanic island in the Caribbean, in the Leeward Islands: a UK Overseas Territory: much of the island rendered uninhabitable by volcanic eruptions in 1997. Capital: Plymouth (effectively destroyed by the eruption). Pop: 4000 (2003 est). Area: 103 sq km (40 sq miles) **2** (*Spanish* mɔnseˈrrat) a mountain in NE Spain, northwest of Barcelona: famous Benedictine monastery. Height: 1235 m (4054 ft). Ancient name: Mons Serratus (mɒnz səˈrætəs)

monument (ˈmɒnjʊmənt) *n* **1** an obelisk, statue, building, etc, erected in commemoration of a person or event or in celebration of something **2** a notable building or site, esp one preserved as public property **3** a tomb or tombstone **4** a literary or artistic work regarded as commemorative of its creator or a particular period **5** *US* a boundary marker **6** an exceptional example: *his lecture was a monument of tedium* **7** an obsolete word for **statue** [C13 from Latin *monumentum*, from *monēre* to remind, advise]

Monument (ˈmɒnjʊmənt) *n* **the** a tall columnar building designed (1671) by Sir Christopher Wren to commemorate the Fire of London (1666), which destroyed a large part of the medieval city

monumental (ˌmɒnjʊˈmentᵊl) *adj* **1** like a monument, esp in large size, endurance, or importance: *a monumental work of art* **2** of, relating to, or being a monument **3** *informal* (intensifier): *monumental stupidity* ▷ ˌmonumenˈtality *n* ▷ ˌmonuˈmentally *adv*

mony (ˈmɒnɪ) *determiner* a Scot word for **many**

Monza (*Italian* ˈmontsa) *n* a city in N Italy, northeast of Milan: the ancient capital of Lombardy; scene of the assassination of King Umberto I in 1900; motor-racing circuit. Pop: 120 204 (2001)

monzonite (ˈmɒnzəˌnaɪt) *n* a coarse-grained plutonic igneous rock consisting of equal

amounts of plagioclase and orthoclase feldspar, with ferromagnesian minerals [C19 from German, named after *Monzoni*, Tyrolean mountain where it was found] ▷ monzonitic (ˌmɒnzəˈnɪtɪk) *adj*

moo (muː) *vb* **1** (*intr*) (of a cow, bull, etc) to make a characteristic deep long sound; low ▷ *interj* **2** an instance or imitation of this sound

mooch (muːtʃ) *vb slang* **1** (*intr*; often foll by *around*) to loiter or walk aimlessly **2** (*intr*) to behave in an apathetic way **3** (*intr*) to sneak or lurk; skulk **4** (*tr*) to cadge **5** (*tr*) *chiefly US and Canadian* to steal [C17 perhaps from Old French *muchier* to skulk] ▷ ˈmoocher *n*

mood[1] (muːd) *n* **1** a temporary state of mind or temper: *a cheerful mood* **2** a sullen or gloomy state of mind, esp when temporary: *she's in a mood* **3** a prevailing atmosphere or feeling **4** in the mood in a favourable state of mind (for something or to do something) [Old English *mōd* mind, feeling; compare Old Norse *mōthr* grief, wrath]

mood[2] (muːd) *n* **1** *grammar* a category of the verb or verbal inflections that expresses semantic and grammatical differences, including such forms as the indicative, subjunctive, and imperative **2** *logic* one of the possible arrangements of the syllogism, classified solely by whether the component propositions are universal or particular and affirmative or negative. Compare **figure** (sense 18) ▷ Also called: **mode** [C16 from MOOD[1], influenced in meaning by MODE]

mood music *n* **1** recorded music played in the background in a place to establish a mood of relaxation, calm, etc **2** a prevailing atmosphere or feeling

moody (ˈmuːdɪ) *adj* moodier, moodiest **1** sullen, sulky, or gloomy **2** temperamental or changeable ▷ ˈmoodily *adv* ▷ ˈmoodiness *n*

Moog (muːɡ, məʊɡ) *n trademark music* a type of synthesizer [C20 named after Robert *Moog* (born 1934), US engineer]

mooi (mɔɪ) *adj South African slang* pleasing; nice [Afrikaans]

mook (muːk) *n US slang* a person regarded with contempt, esp a stupid person [of uncertain origin]

moolah (ˈmuːlɑː) *n* a slang word for **money**

mooli (ˈmuːlɪ) *n* a type of large white radish [E African native name]

mooloo (ˈmuːluː) *n NZ* a person from the Waikato [originally the name of the cow mascot of the Waikato rugby team]

moolvie or **moolvi** (ˈmuːlvɪː) *n* (esp in India) a Muslim doctor of the law, teacher, or learned man also used as a title of respect [C17 from Urdu, from Arabic *mawlawīy*; compare MULLAH]

Moomba (ˈmuːmbə) *n Austral* **1** a festival held annually in Melbourne since 1954, named in the belief that *moomba* was an Aboriginal word meaning "Let's get together and have fun" **2** a natural gas field in South Australia [from a native Australian language *moom* buttocks, anus]

moon (muːn) *n* **1** (*sometimes capital*) the natural satellite of the earth. Diameter: 3476 km; mass: 7.35×10^{22} kg; mean distance from earth: 384 400 km; periods of rotation and revolution: 27.32 days. Related adj: **lunar** **2** the face of the moon as it is seen during its revolution around the earth, esp at one of its phases: *new moon; full moon* **3** any natural satellite of a planet **4** moonlight; moonshine **5** something resembling a moon **6** a month, esp a lunar one **7** once in a blue moon very seldom **8** over the moon *informal* extremely happy; ecstatic **9** reach for the moon to desire or attempt something unattainable or difficult to obtain ▷ *vb* **10** (when *tr*, often foll by *away*; when *intr*, often foll by *around*) to be idle in a listless way, as if in love, or to idle (time) away **11** (*intr*) *slang* to expose one's buttocks to passers-by [Old English *mōna*; compare Old Frisian *mōna*, Old High German *māno*] ▷ ˈmoonless *adj*

Moon (muːn) *n* a system of embossed alphabetical signs for blind readers, the fourteen basic characters of which can, by rotation, mimic most of the letters of the Roman alphabet, thereby making learning easier for those who learned to read before going blind. Compare **Braille¹**

moon bag *n South African* a small bag worn on a belt, round the waist. Brit equivalent: **bum bag**

moonbeam ('muːnˌbiːm) *n* a ray of moonlight

moon blindness *n* 1 *ophthalmol* a nontechnical name for **nyctalopia** 2 *Also called:* **mooneye** *vet science* a disorder affecting horses, which causes inflammation of the eyes and sometimes blindness > **'moon-ˌblind** *adj*

mooncalf ('muːnˌkɑːf) *n, pl* -calves (-ˌkɑːvz) 1 a born fool; dolt 2 a person who idles time away 3 *obsolete* a freak or monster

Moon Child *n* a euphemistic name for **Cancer** (sense 2b)

mooned (muːnd) *adj* decorated with a moon

mooneye ('muːnˌaɪ) *n* 1 any of several North American large-eyed freshwater clupeoid fishes of the family *Hiodontidae,* esp *Hiodon tergisus.* See also **goldeye** 2 *vet science* another name for **moon blindness** (sense 2)

moon-eyed *adj* 1 having the eyes open wide, as in awe 2 *vet science* affected with moon blindness

moon-faced *adj* having a round face; full-faced

moonfish ('muːnˌfɪʃ) *n, pl* -fishes *or* -fish 1 any of several deep-bodied silvery carangid fishes, occurring in warm and tropical American coastal waters 2 any of various other round silvery fishes, such as the Indo-Pacific *Monodactylus argenteus* 3 another name for **opah**

moonflower ('muːnˌflaʊə) *n* 1 any of several night-blooming convolvulaceous plants, esp the white-flowered *Calonyction* (or *Ipomoea*) *aculeatum* 2 *Also called:* **angels' tears** a Mexican solanaceous plant, *Datura suaveolens,* planted in the tropics for its white night-blooming flowers

Moonie ('muːnɪ) *n informal* 1 a member of the Unification Church 2 (*plural;* preceded by *the*) the Unification Church [c20 named after the founder Sun Myung *Moon* (born 1920), S Korean industrialist]

moonlight ('muːnˌlaɪt) *n* 1 *Also called:* **moonshine** light from the sun received on earth after reflection by the moon 2 (*modifier*) illuminated by the moon: *a moonlight walk* 3 short for **moonlight flit** ▷ *vb* -lights, -lighting, -lighted 4 (*intr*) *informal* to work at a secondary job, esp at night, and often illegitimately > **'moonˌlighter** *n*

moonlight flit *n Brit informal* a hurried departure at night, esp from rented accommodation to avoid payment of rent owed. Often shortened to: **moonlight**

moonlighting ('muːnˌlaɪtɪŋ) *n* 1 working at a secondary job 2 (in 19th-century Ireland) the carrying out of cattle-maiming, murders, etc, during the night in protest against the land-tenure system

moonlit ('muːnˌlɪt) *adj* illuminated by the moon

moon pool *n* (in the oil industry) an open shaft in the centre of the hull of a ship engaged in deep-sea drilling through which drilling takes place

moonquake ('muːnˌkweɪk) *n* a light tremor of the moon, detected on the moon's surface

moonraker ('muːnˌreɪkə) *n nautical* a small square sail set above a skysail

moon rat *n* a ratlike SE Asian nocturnal mammal, *Echinosorex gymnurus,* with greyish fur and an elongated snout: family *Erinaceidae* (hedgehogs): the largest living insectivore

moonrise ('muːnˌraɪz) *n* the moment when the moon appears above the horizon

moonscape ('muːnˌskeɪp) *n* the general surface of the moon or a representation of it

moonseed ('muːnˌsiːd) *n* any menispermaceous climbing plant of the genus *Menispermum* and related genera, having red or black fruits with crescent-shaped or ring-shaped seeds

moonset ('muːnˌsɛt) *n* the moment when the

moon disappears below the horizon

moonshine ('muːnˌʃaɪn) *n* 1 another word for **moonlight** (sense 1) 2 *US and Canadian* illegally distilled or smuggled whisky or other spirit 3 foolish talk or thought

moonshiner ('muːnˌʃaɪnə) *n US and Canadian* a person who illegally makes or smuggles distilled spirits

moonshot ('muːnˌʃɒt) *n* the launching of a spacecraft, rocket, etc, to the moon

moonstone ('muːnˌstəʊn) *n* a gem variety of orthoclase or albite that is white and translucent with bluish reflections

moonstruck ('muːnˌstrʌk) *or* **moonstricken** ('muːnˌstrɪkən) *adj* deranged or mad

moonwort ('muːnˌwɜːt) *n* 1 *Also called* (US): **grape fern** any of various ferns of the genus *Botrychium,* esp *B. lunaria,* which has crescent-shaped leaflets 2 another name for **honesty** (sense 4)

moony ('muːnɪ) *adj* moonier, mooniest 1 *informal* dreamy or listless 2 of or like the moon 3 *Brit slang* crazy or foolish > **'moonily** *adv* > **'mooniness** *n*

moor¹ (mʊə, mɔː) *n* a tract of unenclosed ground, usually having peaty soil covered with heather, coarse grass, bracken, and moss [Old English *mōr;* related to Old Saxon *mōr,* Old High German *muor* swamp] > **'moory** *adj*

moor² (mʊə, mɔː) *vb* 1 to secure (a ship, boat, etc) with cables or ropes 2 (of a ship, boat, etc) to be secured in this way 3 (not in technical usage) a less common word for **anchor** (sense 11) [c15 of Germanic origin; related to Old English *mǣrelsrāp* rope for mooring]

Moor (mʊə, mɔː) *n* a member of a Muslim people of North Africa, of mixed Arab and Berber descent. In the 8th century they were converted to Islam and established power in North Africa and Spain, where they established a civilization (756–1492) [c14 via Old French from Latin *Maurus,* from Greek *Mauros,* possibly from Berber]

moorage ('mʊərɪdʒ, 'mɔːrɪdʒ) *n* 1 a place for mooring a vessel 2 a charge for mooring 3 the act of mooring

moorburn *or* **muirburn** ('mʊərˌbʌrn, 'mʊəˌbɜːn) *n Scot* the practice of burning off old growth on a heather moor to encourage new growth for grazing

moorcock ('mʊəˌkɒk, 'mɔː-) *n* the male of the red grouse

Moore ('mʊərə) *n* another name for **Mossi**

moorfowl ('mʊəˌfaʊl, 'mɔː-) *n* (in British game laws) an archaic name for **red grouse** Compare **heathfowl**

moor grass *n* a grass characteristic of moors, especially **purple moor grass** (*Molinia caerulea*) of heath and fenland and **blue moor grass** (*Sesleria caerulea*) of limestone uplands

moorhen ('mʊəˌhɛn, 'mɔː-) *n* 1 a bird, *Gallinula chloropus,* inhabiting ponds, lakes, etc, having a black plumage, red bill, and a red shield above the bill: family *Rallidae* (rails) 2 the female of the red grouse

mooring ('mʊərɪŋ, 'mɔː-) *n* 1 a place for mooring a vessel 2 a permanent anchor, dropped in the water and equipped with a floating buoy, to which vessels can moor ▷ See also **moorings**

mooring mast *n* a mast or tower to which a balloon or airship may be moored. Also called: **mooring tower**

moorings ('mʊərɪŋz, 'mɔː-) *pl n* 1 *nautical* the ropes, anchors, etc, used in mooring a vessel 2 (*sometimes singular*) something that provides security or stability

Moorish ('mʊərɪʃ, 'mɔː-) *adj* 1 of or relating to the Moors 2 denoting the style of architecture used in Spain from the 13th to 16th century, characterized by the horseshoe arch. Also: **Morisco** *or* **Moresco**

Moorish idol *n* a tropical marine spiny-finned fish, *Zanclus canescens,* that is common around

coral reefs: family *Zanclidae.* It has a deeply compressed body with yellow and black stripes, a beaklike snout, and an elongated dorsal fin

moorland ('mʊələnd, 'mɔː-) *n Brit* an area of moor

moorwort ('mʊəˌwɜːt, 'mɔː-) *n* another name for **marsh andromeda**

moose (muːs) *n, pl* moose a large North American deer, *Alces alces,* having large flattened palmate antlers: also occurs in Europe and Asia where it is called an elk [c17 from Algonquian; related to Narraganset *moos,* from *moosu* he strips, alluding to the moose's habit of stripping trees]

Moose Jaw *n* a city in W Canada, in S Saskatchewan. Pop: 32 631 (2001)

moose milk *n Canadian* a mixed alcoholic drink made with ingredients such as milk and eggs and usually rum

moose pasture *n Canadian informal* land considered to be worthless, esp when lacking in extractable mineral deposits

moot (muːt) *adj* 1 subject or open to debate: *a moot point* ▷ *vb* 2 (*tr*) to suggest or bring up for debate 3 (*intr*) to plead or argue theoretical or hypothetical cases, as an academic exercise or as vocational training for law students ▷ *n* 4 a discussion or debate of a hypothetical case or point, held as an academic activity 5 (in Anglo-Saxon England) an assembly, mainly in a shire or hundred, dealing with local legal and administrative affairs [Old English *gemōt;* compare Old Saxon *mōt,* Middle High German *muoze* meeting] > **'mooter** *n*

moot court *n* a mock court trying hypothetical legal cases

mop¹ (mɒp) *n* 1 an implement with a wooden handle and a head made of twists of cotton or a piece of synthetic sponge, used for polishing or washing floors, or washing dishes 2 something resembling this, such as a tangle of hair ▷ *vb* mops, mopping, mopped 3 (*tr;* often foll by *up*) to clean or soak up with or as if with a mop ▷ See also **mop up** [c15 *mappe,* from earlier *mappel,* from Medieval Latin *mappula* cloth, from Latin *mappa* napkin]

mop² (mɒp) *rare* ▷ *vb* mops, mopping, mopped 1 (*intr*) to make a grimace or sad expression (esp in the phrase **mop and mow**) ▷ *n* 2 such a face or expression [c16 perhaps from Dutch *moppen* to pour; compare Dutch *mop* pug dog]

mop³ (mɒp) *n* (in various parts of England) an annual fair at which formerly servants were hired [c17 from the practice of servants carrying a mop, broom, or flail, etc, to signify the job sought]

mopani *or* **mopane** (mɒˈpɑːnɪ) *n* a leguminous tree, *Colophospermum* (or *Copaifera*) *mopane,* native to southern Africa, that is highly resistant to drought and produces very hard wood. Also called: **ironwood** [c19 from Setswana (a Bantu language) *mo-pane*]

mopani worm *n* an edible caterpillar that feeds on mopani leaves

mopboard ('mɒpˌbɔːd) *n* a US word for **skirting board**

mope (məʊp) *vb* (*intr*) 1 to be gloomy or apathetic: *there's no time to mope* 2 to move or act in an aimless way: *he moped around the flat* ▷ *n* 3 a gloomy person ▷ See also **mopes** [c16 perhaps from obsolete *mope* fool and related to MOP²] > **'moper** *n* > **'mopy** *adj*

moped ('məʊpɛd) *n Brit* a light motorcycle, not over 50cc [c20 from MOTOR + PEDAL¹, originally equipped with auxiliary pedals]

mopes (məʊps) *pl n* **the** low spirits

mopoke ('məʊˌpəʊk) *n* 1 *Also called* (NZ): **ruru** a small spotted owl, *Ninox novaeseelandiae,* of Australia and New Zealand. In Australia the tawny frogmouth, *Podargus strigoides,* is very often wrongly identified as the mopoke 2 *Austral and NZ slang* a slow or lugubrious person ▷ *Also called:* **morepork** [c19 imitative of the bird's cry]

moppet ('mɒpɪt) *n* a less common word for

m

poppet (sense 1) [C17 from obsolete *mop* rag doll; of obscure origin]

mop up *vb* (*tr, adverb*) **1** to clean with a mop **2** *informal* to complete (a task, etc) **3** *military* to clear (remaining enemy forces) after a battle, as by killing, taking prisoner, etc ▷ *n* mop-up **4** the act or an instance of mopping up

moquette (mɒˈkɛt) *n* a thick velvety fabric used for carpets, upholstery, etc [C18 from French; of uncertain origin]

mor (mɔː) *n* a layer of acidic humus formed in cool moist areas where decomposition is slow. Compare **mull⁴** [Danish]

MOR *abbreviation for* middle-of-the-road: used esp in radio programming

Mor. *abbreviation for* Morocco

mora (ˈmɔːrə) *n, pl* -rae (-riː) *or* -ras *prosody* the quantity of a short syllable in verse represented by the breve (˘) [C16 from Latin: pause]

moraceous (mɔːˈreɪʃəs) *adj* of, relating to, or belonging to the *Moraceae*, a mostly tropical and subtropical family of trees and shrubs, including fig, mulberry, breadfruit, and hop, many of which have latex in the stems and heads enclosed in a fleshy receptacle [C20 via New Latin from Latin *morus* mulberry tree]

Moradabad (ˌmɔːrədəˈbæd) *n* a city in N India, in N Uttar Pradesh. Pop: 641 240 (2001)

moraine (mɒˈreɪn) *n* a mass of debris, carried by glaciers and forming ridges and mounds when deposited [C18 from French, from Savoy dialect *morena*, of obscure origin] > moˈrainal *or* moˈrainic *adj*

moral (ˈmɒrəl) *adj* **1** concerned with or relating to human behaviour, esp the distinction between good and bad or right and wrong behaviour: *moral sense* **2** adhering to conventionally accepted standards of conduct **3** based on a sense of right and wrong according to conscience: *moral courage; moral law* **4** having psychological rather than tangible effects: *moral support* **5** having the effects but not the appearance of (victory or defeat): *a moral victory; a moral defeat* **6** having a strong probability: *a moral certainty* **7** *law* (of evidence, etc) based on a knowledge of the tendencies of human nature ▷ *n* **8** the lesson to be obtained from a fable or event: *point the moral* **9** a concise truth; maxim **10** (*plural*) principles of behaviour in accordance with standards of right and wrong [C14 from Latin *mōrālis* relating to morals or customs, from *mōs* custom] > ˈmorally *adv*

morale (mɒˈrɑːl) *n* the degree of mental or moral confidence of a person or group; spirit of optimism [C18 morals, from French, n. use of MORAL (adj)]

moral hazard *n insurance* a risk incurred by an insurance company with respect to the possible lack of honesty or prudence among policyholders

moralism (ˈmɒrəˌlɪzəm) *n* **1** the habit or practice of moralizing **2** a moral saying **3** the practice of moral principles without reference to religion

moralist (ˈmɒrəlɪst) *n* **1** a person who seeks to regulate the morals of others or to imbue others with a sense of morality **2** a person who lives in accordance with moral principles **3** a philosopher who is concerned with casuistic discussions of right action, or who seeks a general characterization of right action, often contrasted with a moral philosopher whose concern is with general philosophical questions about ethics > ˌmoralˈistic *adj* > ˌmoralˈistically *adv*

morality (məˈrælɪtɪ) *n, pl* -ties **1** the quality of being moral **2** conformity, or degree of conformity, to conventional standards of moral conduct **3** a system of moral principles **4** an instruction or lesson in morals **5** short for **morality play**

morality play *n* a type of drama written between the 14th and 16th centuries concerned with the conflict between personified virtues and vices

moralize *or* **moralise** (ˈmɒrəˌlaɪz) *vb* **1** (*intr*) to make moral pronouncements **2** (*tr*) to interpret or

explain in a moral sense **3** (*tr*) to improve the morals of > ˌmoraliˈzation *or* ˌmoraliˈsation *n* > ˈmoralˌizer *or* ˈmoralˌiser *n*

moral majority *n* a presumed majority of people believed to be in favour of a stricter code of public morals [C20 after *Moral Majority*, a right-wing US religious organization, based on SILENT MAJORITY]

moral philosophy *n* the branch of philosophy dealing with both argument about the content of morality and meta-ethical discussion of the nature of moral judgment, language, argument, and value

Moral Rearmament *n* a worldwide movement for moral and spiritual renewal founded by Frank Buchman in 1938. Also called: Buchmanism Former name: Oxford Group

moral theology *n* the branch of theology dealing with ethics

Morar (ˈmɔːrə) *n* **Loch** a lake in W Scotland, in the SW Highlands: the deepest in Scotland Length: 18 km (11 miles). Depth: 296 m (987 ft)

morass (məˈræs) *n* **1** a tract of swampy low-lying land **2** a disordered or muddled situation or circumstance, esp one that impedes progress [C17 from Dutch *moeras*, ultimately from Old French *marais* MARSH]

moratorium (ˌmɒrəˈtɔːrɪəm) *n, pl* -ria (-rɪə) *or* -riums **1** a legally authorized postponement of the fulfilment of an obligation **2** an agreed suspension of activity [C19 New Latin, from Late Latin *morātōrius* dilatory, from *mora* delay] > moratory (ˈmɒrətərɪ, -trɪ) *adj*

Morava (məˈrɑːvə) *n* **1** a river in central Europe, rising in the Sudeten Mountains, in the Czech Republic, and flowing south through Slovakia to the Danube: forms part of the border between the Czech Republic, Slovakia, and Austria. Length: 370 km (230 miles). German name: March **2** a river in E Serbia and Montenegro, formed by the confluence of the Southern Morava and the Western Morava near Stalac: flows north to the Danube. Length: 209 km (130 miles) **3** (ˈmɒrəvə) the Czech name for **Moravia**

Moravia (məˈreɪvɪə, mɒ-) *n* a region of the Czech Republic around the Morava River, bounded by the Bohemian-Moravian Highlands, the Sudeten Mountains, and the W Carpathians: became a separate Austrian crownland in 1848; part of Czechoslovakia 1918–92; valuable mineral resources. Czech name: Morava German name: Mähren

Moravian (məˈreɪvɪən, mɒ-) *adj* **1** of or relating to Moravia, its people, or their dialect of Czech **2** of or relating to the Moravian Church ▷ *n* **3** the Moravian dialect **4** a native or inhabitant of Moravia **5** a member of the Moravian Church > Moˈravianism *n*

Moravian Church *n* a Protestant Church originating in Moravia in 1722 as a revival of the sect of Bohemian Brethren. It has close links with the Lutheran Church

Moravian Gate *n* a low mountain pass linking S Poland and Moravia (the Czech Republic), between the SE Sudeten Mountains and the W Carpathian Mountains

moray (mɒˈreɪ) *n, pl* -rays any voracious marine coastal eel of the family Muraenidae, esp *Muraena helena*, marked with brilliant patterns and colours [C17 from Portuguese *moréia*, from Latin *mūrēna*, from Greek *muraina*]

Moray (ˈmʌrɪ) *n* a council area and historical county of NE Scotland: part of Grampian region from 1975 to 1996: mainly hilly, with the Cairngorm mountains in the S. Administrative centre: Elgin. Pop: 87 460 (2003 est). Area: 2238 sq km (874 sq miles). Former name: Elgin

Moray Firth *n* an inlet of the North Sea on the NE coast of Scotland. Length: about 56 km (35 miles)

morbid (ˈmɔːbɪd) *adj* **1** having an unusual interest in death or unpleasant events **2** gruesome **3** relating to or characterized by disease; pathologic:

a morbid growth [C17 from Latin *morbidus* sickly, from *morbus* illness] > ˈmorbidly *adv* > ˈmorbidness *n*

morbid anatomy *n* the branch of medical science concerned with the study of the structure of diseased organs and tissues

morbidity (mɔːˈbɪdɪtɪ) *n* **1** the state of being morbid **2** Also called: morbidity rate the relative incidence of a particular disease in a specific locality

morbific (mɔːˈbɪfɪk) *adj* causing disease; pathogenic > morˈbifically *adv*

Morbihan (French mɔrbiɑ̃) *n* a department of NW France, in S Brittany. Capital: Vannes. Pop: 665 540 (2003 est). Area: 7092 sq km (2766 sq miles)

morbilli (mɔːˈbɪlaɪ) *n* a technical name for **measles** [C17 from Medieval Latin *morbillus* pustule, diminutive of Latin *morbus* illness]

morceau *French* (mɔrso) *n, pl* -ceaux (-so) **1** a fragment or morsel **2** a short composition, esp a musical one [C18 from Old French: MORSEL]

morcha (ˈmɔːtʃɑː) *n* (in India) a hostile demonstration against the government [Hindi: entrenchment]

mordacious (mɔːˈdeɪʃəs) *adj* sarcastic, caustic, or biting [C17 from Latin *mordax*, from *mordēre* to bite] > morˈdaciously *adv* > mordacity (mɔːˈdæsɪtɪ) *or* morˈdaciousness *n*

mordant (ˈmɔːdənt) *adj* **1** sarcastic or caustic **2** having the properties of a mordant **3** pungent ▷ *n* **4** a substance used before the application of a dye, possessing the ability to fix colours in textiles, leather, etc. See also **lake²** (sense 1) **5** an acid or other corrosive fluid used to etch lines on a printing plate ▷ *vb* **6** (*tr*) to treat (a fabric, yarn, etc) with a mordant [C15 from Old French: biting, from *mordre* to bite, from Latin *mordēre*] > ˈmordancy *n* > ˈmordantly *adv*

Mordecai (ˌmɔːdɪˈkaɪ, ˈmɔːdəˌkaɪ) *n* Old Testament the cousin of Esther who averted a massacre of the Jews (Esther 2–9)

mordent (ˈmɔːdənt) *n music* a melodic ornament consisting of the rapid alternation of a note with a note one degree lower than it. Also called: lower mordent [C19 from German, from Italian *mordente*, from *mordere* to bite]

Mordred (ˈmɔːdrɛd) *n* a variant of **Modred**

Mordvin (ˈmɔːdvɪn) *n* **1** (*pl* -vin *or* -vins) a member of a Finnish people of the middle Volga region, living chiefly in the Mordvinian Republic **2** the language of this people, belonging to the Finno-Ugric family

Mordvinian Republic (mɔːˈdvɪnɪən) *n* a constituent republic of W central Russia, in the middle Volga basin. Capital: Saransk. Pop: 888 700 (2002). Area: 26 200 sq km (10 110 sq miles). Also called: Mordovian Republic (mɔːˈdəʊvɪən), Mordovia

more (mɔː) *determiner* **1 a** the comparative of **much** or **many** *more joy than you know; more pork sausages* **b** (*as pronoun; functioning as sing or plural*): *he has more than she has; even more are dying every day* **2 a** additional; further: *no more bananas* **b** (*as pronoun; functioning as sing or plural*): *I can't take any more; more than expected* **3** more of to a greater extent or degree: *we see more of Sue these days; more of a nuisance than it should be* ▷ *adv* **4** used to form the comparative of some adjectives and adverbs: *a more believable story; more quickly* **5** the comparative of **much** *people listen to the radio more now* **6** additionally; again: *I'll look at it once more* **7** more or less **a** as an estimate; approximately **b** to an unspecified extent or degree: *the party was ruined, more or less* **8** more so to a greater extent or degree **9** neither more nor less than simply **10** think more of to have a higher opinion of **11** what is more moreover [Old English *māra*; compare Old Saxon, Old High German *mēro*, Gothic *maiza*. See also MOST]

■ USAGE See at **most**

Morea (mɔːˈrɪə) *n* the medieval name for the **Peloponnese**

Morecambe (ˈmɔːkəm) *n* a port and resort in NW

England, in NW Lancashire on **Morecambe Bay** (an inlet of the Irish Sea). Pop (with Heysham): 49 569 (2001)

moreen (mʊˈriːn) *n* a heavy, usually watered, fabric of wool or wool and cotton, used esp in furnishing [c17 perhaps from MOIRE, influenced by VELVETEEN]

moreish *or* **morish** (ˈmɔːrɪʃ) *adj informal* (of food) causing a desire for more: *these cakes are very moreish*

morel (mʊˈrɛl) *n* any edible saprotrophic ascomycetous fungus of the genus *Morchella*, in which the mushroom has a pitted cap: order *Pezizales* [c17 from French *morille*, probably of Germanic origin; compare Old High German *morhila*, diminutive of *morha* carrot]

Morelia (*Spanish* moˈrelja) *n* a city in central Mexico, capital of Michoacán state: a cultural centre during colonial times; two universities. Pop: 668 000 (2005 est). Former name (until 1828): Valladolid

morello (məˈrɛləʊ) *n, pl* **-los** a variety of small very dark sour cherry, *Prunus cerasus austera* [c17 perhaps from Medieval Latin *amārellum* diminutive of Latin *amārus* bitter, but also influenced by Italian *morello* blackish]

Morelos (*Spanish* moˈrelɔs) *n* an inland state of S central Mexico, on the S slope of the great plateau. Capital: Cuernavaca. Pop: 1 552 878 (2000 est). Area: 4988 sq km (1926 sq miles)

moreover (mɔːˈrəʊvə) *sentence connector* in addition to what has already been said; furthermore

morepork (ˈmɔːˌpɔːk) *n* NZ **1** a small spotted owl, *Ninox novaeseelandiae*, of Australia and New Zealand. Also called (NZ): ruru, (Austral) mopoke **2** *slang* a slow or lugubrious person. Also called (Austral): mopoke

mores (ˈmɔːreɪz) *pl n sociol* the customs and conventions embodying the fundamental values of a group or society [c20 from Latin, plural of *mōs* custom]

Moresco (məˈrɛskəʊ) *n, adj* a variant of **Morisco**

Moresque (mɔːˈrɛsk) *adj* **1** (esp of decoration and architecture) of Moorish style ▷ *n* **2 a** Moorish design or decoration **b** a specimen of this [c17 from French, from Italian *moresco*, from *Moro* MOOR]

Moreton Bay bug (ˈmɔːt³n) *n* a flattish edible shellfish, *Thenus orientalis*, of Northern Australian waters [named after *Moreton Bay*, Queensland, Australia]

Moreton Bay fig *n* a large Australian fig tree, *Ficus macrophylla*, having glossy leaves and smooth bark [named after *Moreton Bay*, Queensland, Australia]

Morgan (ˈmɔːgən) *n* an American breed of small compact saddle horse [c19 named after Justin Morgan (1747–98), American owner of the original sire]

morganatic (ˌmɔːgəˈnætɪk) *adj* of or designating a marriage between a person of high rank and a person of low rank, by which the latter is not elevated to the higher rank and any issue have no rights to the succession of the higher party's titles, property, etc [c18 from the Medieval Latin phrase *mātrimōnium ad morganāticum* marriage based on the morning-gift (a token present after consummation representing the husband's only liability); *morganātica*, ultimately from Old High German *morgan* morning; compare Old English *morgengiefu* morning-gift] > ˌmorga'natically *adv*

morganite (ˈmɔːgəˌnaɪt) *n* a pink variety of beryl, used as a gemstone [c20 named after John Pierpoint *Morgan* (1837–1913), US financier, philanthropist, and art collector]

Morgan le Fay (ˈmɔːgən lə ˈfeɪ) *or* **Morgain le Fay** (ˈmɔːgaɪn, -gən) *n* a wicked sorceress of Arthurian legend, the half-sister of King Arthur

morgen (ˈmɔːgən) *n* **1** a South African unit of area, equal to about two acres or 0.8 hectare **2** a unit of area, formerly used in Prussia and Scandinavia, equal to about two thirds of an acre

[c17 from Dutch: morning, a morning's ploughing]

morgue¹ (mɔːg) *n* **1** another word for **mortuary** (sense 1) **2** *informal* a room or file containing clippings, files, etc, used for reference in a newspaper [c19 from French *la Morgue*, a Paris mortuary]

morgue² *French* (mɔrg) *n* superiority; haughtiness

MORI (ˈmɔːrɪ) *n acronym for* Market and Opinion Research Institute: *a MORI poll*

moribund (ˈmɒrɪˌbʌnd) *adj* **1** near death **2** stagnant; without force or vitality [c18 from Latin, from *morī* to die] > ˌmoriˈbundity *n* > ˈmoriˌbundly *adv*

morion¹ (ˈmɔːrɪən) *n* a 16th-century helmet with a brim and wide comb [c16 via Old French from Spanish *morrión*, perhaps from *morra* crown of the head]

morion² (ˈmɔːrɪən) *n* a smoky brown, grey, or blackish variety of quartz, used as a gemstone [c16 via French from Latin *mōrion*, a misreading of *mormorion*]

Moriori (ˌmɒrɪˈɔːrɪ) *n* **1** a Polynesian people of New Zealand, esp of the Chatham Islands, closely related to the mainland Māori, now racially intermixed **2** (*pl* **-ri** *or* **-ris**) a member of this people **3** the language of the Moriori, belonging to the Malayo-Polynesian family ▷ *adj* **4** of or relating to the Moriori or their language

Morisco (məˈrɪskəʊ) *or* **Moresco** (məˈrɛskəʊ) *n, pl* **-cos** *or* **-coes 1** a Spanish Moor **2** a morris dance ▷ *adj* **3** another word for **Moorish** [c16 from Spanish, from *Moro* MOOR]

morish (ˈmɔːrɪʃ) *adj* a variant spelling of **moreish**

Morley (ˈmɔːlɪ) *n* an industrial town in N England, in Leeds unitary authority, West Yorkshire. Pop: 54 051 (2001)

Mormon (ˈmɔːmən) *n* **1** a member of the Church of Jesus Christ of Latter-day Saints, founded in 1830 at La Fayette, New York, by Joseph Smith (1805–44) **2** a prophet whose supposed revelations were recorded by Joseph Smith in the Book of Mormon ▷ *adj* **3** of or relating to the Mormons, their Church, or their beliefs > ˈMormonism *n*

morn (mɔːn) *n* **1** a poetic word for **morning 2** the morn *Scot* tomorrow **3** the morn's nicht *Scot* tomorrow night [Old English *morgen*; compare Old High German *morgan*, Old Norse *morginn*]

mornay (ˈmɔːneɪ) *adj* (*often immediately postpositive*) denoting a cheese sauce used in several dishes: *eggs mornay* [perhaps named after Philippe de Mornay, Seigneur du Plessis-Marly (1549–1623), French Huguenot leader]

morning (ˈmɔːnɪŋ) *n* **1** the first part of the day, ending at or around noon **2** sunrise; daybreak; dawn **3** the beginning or early period: *the morning of the world* **4** the morning after *informal* the aftereffects of excess, esp a hangover **5** (*modifier*) of, used, or occurring in the morning: *morning coffee* ▷ See also **mornings** [c13 *morwening*, from MORN, formed on the model of EVENING]

morning-after pill *n* an oral contraceptive that is effective if taken some hours after intercourse

morning coat *n* a cutaway frock coat, part of morning dress. Also called: tail coat, swallow-tailed coat

morning dress *n* formal day dress for men, comprising a morning coat, usually with grey trousers and top hat

morning-glory *n, pl* **-ries** any of various mainly tropical convolvulaceous plants of the genus *Ipomoea* and related genera, with trumpet-shaped blue, pink, or white flowers, which close in late afternoon

mornings (ˈmɔːnɪŋz) *adv informal* in the morning, esp regularly, or during every morning

morning sickness *n* nausea occurring shortly after rising: an early symptom of pregnancy

morning star *n* a planet, usually Venus, seen just before sunrise during the time that the planet is west of the sun. Also called: daystar Compare **evening star**

morning tea *n Austral and NZ* a mid-morning snack with a cup of tea. Brit equivalent: elevenses

morning watch *n nautical* the watch between 4 and 8 am

Moro (ˈmɔːrəʊ) *n* **1** (*pl* **-ros** *or* **-ro**) a member of a group of predominantly Muslim peoples of the S Philippines: noted for their manufacture of weapons **2** the language of these peoples, belonging to the Malayo-Polynesian family [c19 via Spanish from Latin *Maurus* MOOR]

Moroccan (məˈrɒkən) *adj* **1** of or relating to Morocco or its inhabitants ▷ *n* **2** a native or inhabitant of Morocco

morocco (məˈrɒkəʊ) *n* **a** a fine soft leather made from goatskins, used for bookbinding, shoes, etc **b** (*as modifier*): *morocco leather* [c17 after MOROCCO, where it was originally made]

Morocco (məˈrɒkəʊ) *n* a kingdom in NW Africa, on the Mediterranean and the Atlantic: conquered by the Arabs in about 683, who introduced Islam; at its height under Berber dynasties (11th–13th centuries); became a French protectorate in 1912 and gained independence in 1956. It is mostly mountainous, with the Atlas Mountains in the centre and the Rif range along the Mediterranean coast, with the Sahara in the south and southeast; an important exporter of phosphates. Official language: Arabic; Berber and French are also widely spoken. Official religion: (Sunni) Muslim. Currency: dirham. Capital: Rabat. Pop: 31 064 000 (2004 est). Area: 458 730 sq km (177 117 sq miles). French name: Maroc

moron (ˈmɔːrɒn) *n* **1** a foolish or stupid person **2** a person having an intelligence quotient of between 50 and 70, able to work under supervision [c20 from Greek *mōros* foolish] > moronic (mɒˈrɒnɪk) *adj* > moˈronically *adv* > ˈmoronism *or* moˈronity *n*

Moroni (məˈrəʊnɪ; *French* mɔrɔni) *n* the capital of the Comoros, on the island of Njazidja (Grande Comore). Pop: 59 000 (2005 est)

morose (məˈrəʊs) *adj* ill-tempered or gloomy [c16 from Latin *mōrōsus* peevish, capricious, from *mōs* custom, will, caprice] > mo'rosely *adv* > mo'roseness *n*

Morpeth (ˈmɔːpəθ) *n* a town in NE England, the administrative centre of Northumberland. Pop: 13 555 (2001)

morph¹ (mɔːf) *n linguistics* the phonological representation of a morpheme [c20 shortened form of MORPHEME]

morph² (mɔːf) *n biology* any of the different forms of individual found in a polymorphic species [c20 from Greek *morphē* shape]

morph³ (mɔːf) *vb* **1** to undergo or cause to undergo morphing **2** to transform or be transformed completely in appearance or character: *he morphed from nerd into pop icon* ▷ *n* **3** a morphed image

morph. *or* **morphol.** *abbreviation for* **1** morphological **2** morphology

-morph *n combining form* indicating shape, form, or structure of a specified kind: *ectomorph* [from Greek *-morphos*, from *morphē* shape] > **-morphic** *or* **-morphous** *adj combining form* > **-morphy** *n combining form*

morphallaxis (ˌmɔːfəˈlæksɪs) *n, pl* **-laxes** (-ˈlæksiːz) *zoology* the transformation of one part into another that sometimes occurs during regeneration of organs in certain animals [c20 New Latin, from MORPHO- + Greek *allaxis* exchange, from *allassein* to exchange, from *allos* other]

morpheme (ˈmɔːfiːm) *n linguistics* a speech element having a meaning or grammatical function that cannot be subdivided into further such elements [c20 from French, from Greek *morphē* form, coined on the model of PHONEME; see -EME] > mor'phemic *adj* > mor'phemically *adv*

Morpheus (ˈmɔːfɪəs, -fjuːs) *n Greek myth* the god of sleep and dreams > ˈMorphean *adj*

morphic resonance (ˈmɔːfɪk) *n* the idea that,

through a telepathic effect or sympathetic vibration, an event or act can lead to similar events or acts in the future or an idea conceived in one mind can then arise in another

morphine ('mɔːfiːn) or **morphia** ('mɔːfɪə) n an alkaloid extracted from opium: used in medicine as an analgesic and sedative, although repeated use causes addiction. Formula: $C_{17}H_{19}NO_3$ [C19 from French, from MORPHEUS]

morphing ('mɔːfɪŋ) n a computer technique used for graphics and in films, in which one image is gradually transformed into another image without individual changes being noticeable in the process [C20 from METAMORPHOSIS]

morphinism ('mɔːfɪˌnɪzəm) n morphine addiction

morpho- or before a vowel **morph-** combining form **1** indicating form or structure: morphology **2** morpheme: morphophonemics [from Greek morphē form, shape]

morphogenesis (ˌmɔːfəʊˈdʒɛnɪsɪs) n **1** the development of form and structure in an organism during its growth from embryo to adult **2** the evolutionary development of form in an organism or part of an organism > morphogenetic (ˌmɔːfəʊdʒɪˈnɛtɪk) or ˌmorphoˈgenic adj

morphology (mɔːˈfɒlədʒɪ) n **1** the branch of biology concerned with the form and structure of organisms **2** the form and structure of words in a language, esp the consistent patterns of inflection, combination, derivation and change, etc, that may be observed and classified **3** the form and structure of anything > morphologic (ˌmɔːfəˈlɒdʒɪk) or ˌmorphoˈlogical adj > ˌmorphoˈlogically adv > morˈphologist n

morphometrics (ˌmɔːfəʊˈmɛtrɪks) zoology ⊳ n a technique of taxonomic analysis using measurements of the form of organisms > ˌmorphoˈmetric adj **2** the evolutionary development of form in an organism or part of an organism > morphogenetic (ˌmɔːfəʊdʒɪˈnɛtɪk) or ˌmorphoˈgenic adj

morphophoneme (ˌmɔːfəʊˈfəʊniːm) n linguistics the set of phonemes or sequences of phonemes that constitute the various allomorphs of a morpheme [C20 from MORPHEME + PHONEME]

morphophonemics (ˌmɔːfəʊfəʊˈniːmɪks) n (functioning as singular) linguistics the study of the phonemic realization of the allomorphs of the morphemes of a language > ˌmorphophoˈnemic adj

morphosis (mɔːˈfəʊsɪs) n, pl -ses (-siːz) biology development in an organism or its parts characterized by structural change [C17 via New Latin from Greek, from morphoun to form, from morphē form] > morphotic (mɔːˈfɒtɪk) adj

morrell (məˈrɛl) n a tall eucalyptus, Eucalyptus longicornis, of SW Australia, having pointed buds [from a native Australian language]

Morris chair ('mɒrɪs) n an armchair with an adjustable back and large cushions [C19 named after William Morris (1834–96), English poet, designer, craftsman, and socialist writer]

morris dance ('mɒrɪs) n any of various old English folk dances usually performed by men (**morris men**) to the accompaniment of violin, concertina, etc The dancers are adorned with bells and often represent characters from folk tales. Often shortened to: morris [C15 moreys daunce Moorish dance. See MOOR] > morris dancing n

morro ('mɒrəʊ; Spanish 'morro) n, pl -ros (-rəʊz; Spanish -ros) a rounded hill or promontory [from Spanish]

morrow ('mɒrəʊ) n (usually preceded by the) archaic or poetic **1** the next day **2** the period following a specified event **3** the morning [C13 morwe, from Old English morgen morning; see MORN]

Mors (mɔːz) n the Roman god of death. Greek counterpart: Thanatos

morse (mɔːs) n a clasp or fastening on a cope [C15 from Old French mors, from Latin morsus clasp, bite, from mordēre to bite]

Morse code (mɔːs) n a telegraph code formerly used internationally for transmitting messages; it was superseded by satellite technology (the Global Marine Distress and Safety System) in 1999. Letters, numbers, etc, are represented by groups of shorter dots and longer dashes, or by groups of the corresponding sounds, dits and dahs, the groups being separated by spaces. Also called: international Morse code [C19 named after Samuel Finley Breese Morse (1791–1872), US inventor of the first electric telegraph]

morsel ('mɔːsəl) n **1** a small slice or mouthful of food **2** a small piece; bit **3** Irish informal a term of endearment for a child [C13 from Old French, from mors a bite, from Latin morsus, from mordēre to bite]

Morse taper n trademark engineering a taper that is one of a standard series used in the shank of tools to fit a matching taper in the mandrel of a machine tool [probably named after the Morse Twist Drill Co, Massachusetts, US]

mort[1] (mɔːt) n a call blown on a hunting horn to signify the death of the animal hunted [C16 via Old French from Latin mors death]

mort[2] (mɔːt) n a great deal; a great many [possibly a shortened form of MORTAL used as an intensifier]

mortal ('mɔːtəl) adj **1** (of living beings, esp human beings) subject to death **2** of or involving life or the world **3** ending in or causing death; fatal: a mortal blow **4** deadly or unrelenting: a mortal enemy **5** of or like the fear of death; dire: mortal terror **6** great or very intense: mortal pain **7** possible: there was no mortal reason to go **8** slang long and tedious: for three mortal hours ⊳ n **9** a mortal being **10** informal a person: a mean mortal [C14 from Latin mortālis, from mors death] > 'mortally adv

mortality (mɔːˈtælɪtɪ) n, pl -ties **1** the condition of being mortal **2** great loss of life, as in war or disaster **3** the number of deaths in a given period **4** mankind; humanity **5** an obsolete word for **death**

mortality rate n another term for **death rate**

mortality table n insurance an actuarial table indicating life expectancy and death frequency for a given age, occupation, etc

mortal sin n Christianity a sin regarded as involving total loss of grace. Compare **venial sin**

mortar ('mɔːtə) n **1** a mixture of cement or lime or both with sand and water, used as a bond between bricks or stones or as a covering on a wall **2** a muzzle-loading cannon having a short barrel and relatively wide bore that fires low-velocity shells in high trajectories over a short range **3** a similar device for firing lifelines, fireworks, etc **4** a vessel, usually bowl-shaped, in which substances are pulverized with a pestle **5** mining a cast-iron receptacle in which ore is crushed ⊳ vb (tr) **6** to join (bricks or stones) or cover (a wall) with mortar **7** to fire on with mortars **8** Midland English dialect to trample (on) [C13 from Latin mortārium basin in which mortar is mixed; in some senses, via Old French mortier substance mixed inside such a vessel]

mortarboard ('mɔːtəˌbɔːd) n **1** a black tasselled academic cap with a flat square top covered with cloth **2** Also called: hawk a small square board with a handle on the underside for carrying mortar

mortgage ('mɔːgɪdʒ) n **1** an agreement under which a person borrows money to buy property, esp a house, and the lender may take possession of the property if the borrower fails to repay the money **2** the deed effecting such an agreement **3** the loan obtained under such an agreement: a mortgage of £48 000 **4** a regular payment of money borrowed under such an agreement: a mortgage of £247 per month ⊳ vb (tr) **5** to pledge (a house or other property) as security for the repayment of a loan ⊳ adj **6** of or relating to a mortgage: a mortgage payment [C14 from Old French, literally: dead pledge, from mort dead + gage security, GAGE[1]] > 'mortgageable adj

mortgagee (ˌmɔːgɪˈdʒiː) n law **1** the party to a mortgage who makes the loan **2** a person who holds mortgaged property as security for repayment of a loan

mortgage rate n the level of interest charged by building societies and banks on house-purchase loans

mortgagor ('mɔːgɪdʒə, ˌmɔːgɪˈdʒɔː) or **mortgager** n property law a person who borrows money by mortgaging his property to the lender as security

mortician (mɔːˈtɪʃən) n chiefly US another word for **undertaker** [C19 from MORTUARY + -ician, as in physician]

mortification (ˌmɔːtɪfɪˈkeɪʃən) n **1** a feeling of loss of prestige or self-respect; humiliation **2** something causing this **3** Christianity the practice of mortifying the senses **4** another word for **gangrene**

mortify ('mɔːtɪˌfaɪ) vb -fies, -fying, -fied **1** (tr) to humiliate or cause to feel shame **2** (tr) Christianity to subdue and bring under control by self-denial, disciplinary exercises, etc **3** (intr) to undergo tissue death or become gangrenous [C14 via Old French from Church Latin mortificāre to put to death, from Latin mors death + facere to do] > 'mortiˌfier n > 'mortiˌfying adj > 'mortiˌfyingly adv

mortise or **mortice** ('mɔːtɪs) n **1** a slot or recess, usually rectangular, cut into a piece of wood, stone, etc, to receive a matching projection (tenon) of another piece, or a mortise lock **2** printing a cavity cut into a letterpress printing plate into which type or another plate is inserted ⊳ vb (tr) **3** to cut a slot or recess in (a piece of wood, stone, etc) **4** to join (two pieces of wood, stone, etc) by means of a mortise and tenon **5** to cut a cavity in (a letterpress printing plate) for the insertion of type, etc [C14 from Old French mortoise, perhaps from Arabic murtazza fastened in position] > 'mortiser n

mortise lock n a lock set into a mortise in a door so that the mechanism of the lock is enclosed by the door

mortmain ('mɔːtˌmeɪn) n law the state or condition of lands, buildings, etc, held inalienably, as by an ecclesiastical or other corporation [C15 from Old French mortemain, from Medieval Latin mortua manus dead hand, inalienable ownership]

mortsafe ('mɔːtˌseɪf) n a heavy iron cage or grille placed over the grave of a newly deceased person during the 19th century in order to deter body snatchers [C19 from mort dead body (via Old French from Latin mors death) + SAFE]

mortuary ('mɔːtʃʊərɪ) n, pl -aries Also called: morgue a building where dead bodies are kept before cremation or burial ⊳ adj **2** of or relating to death or burial [C14 (as n, a funeral gift to a parish priest): via Medieval Latin mortuārium (n) from Latin mortuārius of the dead]

morula ('mɒrjʊlə) n, pl -las or -lae (-ˌliː) embryol a solid ball of cells resulting from cleavage of a fertilized ovum [C19 via New Latin, diminutive of Latin morum mulberry, from Greek moron] > 'morular adj

morwong ('mɔːˌwɒŋ) n a food fish of Australasian coastal waters belonging to the Cheilodactylidae family [from a native Australian language]

moryah (mɒrˈjæ) interj Irish an exclamation of annoyance, disbelief, etc [from Irish Gaelic Mar dhea forsooth]

MOS electronics abbreviation for metal oxide silicon

mosaic (məˈzeɪɪk) n **1** a design or decoration made up of small pieces of coloured glass, stone, etc **2** the process of making a mosaic **3 a** a mottled yellowing that occurs in the leaves of plants affected with any of various virus diseases **b** Also called: mosaic disease any of the diseases, such as **tobacco mosaic**, that produce this discoloration **4** genetics another name for **chimera** (sense 4) **5** an assembly of aerial photographs forming a composite picture of a large area on the ground **6** a light-sensitive surface on a television camera tube, consisting of a large number of granules of photoemissive material deposited on an insulating medium [C16 via French and Italian from Medieval Latin *mōsaicus,* from Late Greek *mouseion* mosaic work, from Greek *mouseios* of the Muses, from *mousa* MUSE] > **mosaicist** (mə'zeɪɪsɪst) *n*

Mosaic (məʊ'zeɪɪk) *or* **Mosaical** *adj* of or relating to Moses or the laws and traditions ascribed to him

mosaic disease (mə'zeɪɪk) *n* a serious viral disease of plants, esp tobacco, maize, and sugar cane, in which the leaves become mottled by discoloration

mosaic gold (mə'zeɪɪk) *n* stannic sulphide, esp when suspended in lacquer for use in gilding surfaces

Mosaic law (məʊ'zeɪɪk) *n Old Testament* the laws of the Hebrews ascribed to Moses and contained in the Pentateuch

mosasaur ('məʊsəˌsɔː) *or* **mosasaurus** (ˌməʊsə'sɔːrəs) *n, pl* -**saurs** *or* -**sauri** (-'sɔːraɪ) any of various extinct Cretaceous giant marine lizards of the genus *Mosasaurus* and related genera, typically having paddle-like limbs [C18 from Latin *Mosa* the river MEUSE (near which remains were first found) + -SAUR]

moschatel (ˌmɒskə'tɛl) *n* a small N temperate plant, *Adoxa moschatellina,* with greenish-white musk-scented flowers on top of the stem, arranged as four pointing sideways at right angles to each other and one facing upwards: family *Adoxaceae*. Also called: **townhall clock, five-faced bishop** [C18 via French from Italian *moscatella,* diminutive of *moscato* MUSK]

Moscow ('mɒskəʊ) *n* the capital of Russia and of the Moscow Autonomous Region, on the Moskva River: dates from the 11th century; capital of the grand duchy of Russia from 1547 to 1712; capital of the Soviet Union 1918–91; centres on the medieval Kremlin; chief political, cultural, and industrial centre of Russia, with two universities. Pop: 10 672 000 (2005 est). Russian name: **Moskva** Related noun: **Muscovite**

Moselle (məʊ'zɛl) *n* **1** a department of NE France, in Lorraine region. Capital: Metz. Pop: 1 027 854 (2003 est). Area: 6253 sq km (2439 sq miles) **2** a river in W Europe, rising in NE France and flowing northwest, forming part of the border between Luxembourg and Germany, then northeast to the Rhine: many vineyards along its lower course. Length: 547 km (340 miles). German name: **Mosel** ('moːz°l) **3** (*sometimes not capital*) a German white wine from the Moselle valley

Moses ('məʊzɪz) *n Old Testament* the Hebrew prophet who led the Israelites out of Egypt to the Promised Land and gave them divinely revealed laws

Moses basket ('məʊzɪz) *n* a portable cradle for a baby, often made of straw or wicker [C20 from Moses being left in a cradle of bulrushes (Exodus 2:3)]

mosey ('məʊzɪ) *vb* (*intr*) *informal* (often foll by *along* or *on*) to walk in a leisurely manner; amble [C19 origin unknown]

MOSFET ('mɒsfɛt) *n electronics* metal-oxide-silicon field-effect transistor; a type of IGFET

mosh (mɒʃ) *n* **1** a type of dance, performed to loud rock music, in which people throw themselves about in a frantic and violent manner ▷ *vb* **2** (*intr*) to dance in this manner [C20 of uncertain origin]

moshav (*Hebrew* mɔː'ʃav) *n, pl* -**shavim** (-ʃa'vim) a cooperative settlement in Israel, consisting of a number of small farms [C20 from Hebrew *mōshābh* a dwelling]

mosher ('mɒʃə) *n* **1** someone who moshes **2** (in Britain) a young person who typically enjoys rock music and skateboarding

mosh pit *n informal* an area at a rock-music concert, usually in front of the stage, where members of the audience dance in a frantic and

violent manner

Moskva (*Russian* mas'kva) *n* **1** transliteration of the Russian name for **Moscow 2** a river in W central Russia, rising in the Smolensk-Moscow upland, and flowing southeast through Moscow to the Oka River: linked with the River Volga by the Moscow Canal. Length: about 500 km (310 miles)

Moslem ('mɒzləm) *n, pl* -**lems** *or* -**lem,** *adj* a variant of **Muslim.** > **Moslemic** (mɒz'lɛmɪk) *adj* > '**Moslemism** *n*

Mosotho (mʊ'suːtʊ) *n, pl* -**tho** *or* -**thos** a member of the Basotho people. Former name: **Basuto**

mosque (mɒsk) *n* a Muslim place of worship, usually having one or more minarets and often decorated with elaborate tracery and texts from the Koran. Also called: **masjid, musjid** [C14 earlier *mosquee,* from Old French via Italian *moschea,* ultimately from Arabic *masjid* temple, place of prostration]

mosquito (mə'skiːtəʊ) *n, pl* -**toes** *or* -**tos** any dipterous insect of the family *Culicidae*: the females have a long proboscis adapted for piercing the skin of man and animals to suck their blood. See also **aedes, anopheles, culex** [C16 from Spanish, diminutive of *mosca* fly, from Latin *musca*]

mosquito boat *n* another name for **MTB**

mosquito hawk *n* another name for **nighthawk** (sense 1)

mosquito net *or* **netting** *n* a fine curtain or net put in windows, around beds, etc, to keep mosquitoes out

moss (mɒs) *n* **1** any bryophyte of the phylum *Bryophyta,* typically growing in dense mats on trees, rocks, moist ground, etc. See also **peat moss 2** a clump or growth of any of these plants **3** any of various similar but unrelated plants, such as club moss, Spanish moss, Ceylon moss, rose moss, and reindeer moss **4** *Scot and Northern English* a peat bog or marsh [Old English *mos* swamp; compare Middle Dutch, Old High German *mos* bog, Old Norse *mosi*; compare also Old Norse *mȳrr* MIRE] > '**moss,like** *adj* > '**mossy** *adj* > '**mossiness** *n*

Mossad ('mɒsæd) *n* the secret intelligence service of Israel [C20 Hebrew *Mosad LeModi'in U-LeTafkidim Miyuhadim* establishment for information and special tasks]

moss agate *n* a variety of chalcedony with dark greenish mossy markings, used as a gemstone

mossback ('mɒsˌbæk) *n US and Canadian* **1** an old turtle, shellfish, etc, that has a growth of algae on its back **2** *informal* a provincial or conservative person > '**moss,backed** *adj*

Mössbauer effect ('mɒsˌbaʊə; *German* 'mœsbaʊər) *n physics* the phenomenon in which an atomic nucleus in a crystal of certain substances emits a gamma ray without any recoil to the atom. The study of the emitted gamma rays (**Mössbauer spectroscopy**) is used to determine the energy levels in a nucleus, the structure of molecules, etc [C20 named after Rudolf Ludwig *Mössbauer* (born 1929), German physicist]

mossbunker ('mɒsˌbʌŋkə) *n US* another name for **menhaden** [C18 from Dutch *marsbanker* scad, horse-mackerel]

moss-grown *adj* covered with moss

Mossi ('mɒsɪ) *n* **1** (*pl* -**sis** *or* -**si**) a member of a Negroid people of W Africa, living chiefly in Burkina-Faso: noted for their use of cowry shells as currency and for their trading skill **2** the language of this people, belonging to the Gur branch of the Niger-Congo family ▷ Also called: **Moore**

mossie[1] *or* **mozzie** ('mɒzɪ) *n Austral and NZ* an informal name for **mosquito**

mossie[2] ('mɒsɪ) *n* another name for the **Cape sparrow** [Afrikaans]

moss layer *n* See **layer** (sense 2)

mosso ('mɒsəʊ) *adv music* to be performed with rapidity. See also **meno mosso** [Italian, past participle of *muovere* to MOVE]

moss pink *n* a North American plant, *Phlox subulata,* forming dense mosslike mats: cultivated for its pink, white, or lavender flowers: family *Polemoniaceae*. Also called: **ground pink**

moss rose *n* a variety of rose, *Rosa centifolia muscosa,* that has a mossy stem and calyx and fragrant pink flowers

moss stitch *n* a knitting stitch made up of alternate plain and purl stitches

mosstrooper ('mɒsˌtruːpə) *n* a raider in the border country of England and Scotland in the mid-17th century [C17 *moss,* in northern English dialect sense: bog]

most (məʊst) *determiner* **1 a** a great majority of; nearly all: *most people like eggs* **b** (*as pronoun; functioning as sing or plural*): *most of them don't know; most of it is finished* **2** the **a** the superlative of **many** and **much**: *you have the most money; the most apples* **b** (*as pronoun*): *the most he can afford is two pounds* **3 at (the) most** at the maximum: *that girl is four at the most* **4** for the most part generally **5 make the most of** to use to the best advantage: *she makes the most of her accent* **6 than most** than most others: *the leaves are greener than most* **7** the most *slang, chiefly US* wonderful: *that chick's the most* ▷ *adv* **8** the most used to form the superlative of some adjectives and adverbs: *the most beautiful daughter of all* **9** the superlative of **much** *people welcome a drink most after work* **10** (*intensifier*): *a most absurd story* **11** *US and Canadian informal or dialect* almost: *most every town in this state* [Old English *māst* or *mǣst,* whence Middle English *moste, mēst*; compare Old Frisian *maest,* Old High German *meist,* Old Norse *mestr*]

⬛ USAGE *More* and *most* should be distinguished when used in comparisons. *More* applies to cases involving two persons, objects, etc, *most* to cases involving three or more: *John is the more intelligent of the two; he is the most intelligent of the students*

-most *suffix* forming the superlative degree of some adjectives and adverbs: *hindmost; uppermost* [Old English *-māst, -mest,* originally a superlative suffix, later mistakenly taken as derived from *mǣst* (adv) most]

Mostaganem (məˌstægə'nɛm) *n* a port in NW Algeria, on the Mediterranean Sea: exports wine, fruit, and vegetables. Pop: 133 000 (2005 est)

Most Honourable *n* a courtesy title applied to marquesses and members of the Privy Council and the Order of the Bath

mostly ('məʊstlɪ) *adv* **1** almost entirely; chiefly **2** on many or most occasions; usually

Most Reverend *n* (in Britain) a courtesy title applied to Anglican and Roman Catholic archbishops

Mosul ('məʊs°l) *n* a city in N Iraq, on the River Tigris opposite the ruins of Nineveh: an important commercial centre with nearby Ayn Zalah oilfield; university. Pop: 1 236 000 (2005 est)

mot[1] (məʊ) *n* short for **bon mot** [C16 via French from Vulgar Latin *mottum* (unattested) utterance, from Latin *muttum* a mutter, from *muttīre* to mutter]

mot[2] (mɒt) *n Dublin slang* a girl or young woman, esp one's girlfriend [perhaps a variant of *mort,* obsolete slang for girl or woman, of unknown origin]

MOT *abbreviation for* **1** (in New Zealand and formerly in Britain) Ministry of Transport (in Britain now part of the **DTLR**) **2** (in Britain) MOT test: a compulsory annual test for all road vehicles over a certain age, which require a valid **MOT** certificate

mote[1] (məʊt) *n* a tiny speck [Old English *mot;* compare Middle Dutch *mot* grit, Norwegian *mutt* speck]

mote[2] (məʊt) *vb, past* moste (məʊst) (takes an infinitive without *to*) *archaic* may or might [Old English *mōt,* first person singular present tense of *mōtan* to be allowed]

m

motel (məʊˈtɛl) *n* a roadside hotel for motorists, usually having direct access from each room or chalet to a parking space or garage [c20 from *motor* + *hotel*]

motet (məʊˈtɛt) *n* a polyphonic choral composition used as an anthem in the Roman Catholic service [c14 from Old French, diminutive of *mot* word; see MOT¹]

moth (mɒθ) *n* any of numerous insects of the order *Lepidoptera* that typically have stout bodies with antennae of various shapes (but not clubbed), including such brightly coloured species, such as hawk moths, and small inconspicuous types, such as the clothes moths. Compare **butterfly** (sense 1) [Old English *moththe*; compare Middle Dutch *motte*, Old Norse *motti*]

mothball (ˈmɒθˌbɔːl) *n* 1 Also called: camphor ball a small ball of camphor or naphthalene used to repel clothes moths in stored clothing, blankets, etc 2 put in mothballs to postpone work on (a project, activity, etc) ▷ *vb* (*tr*) 3 to prepare (a ship, aircraft, etc) for a long period of storage by sealing all openings with plastic to prevent corrosion 4 to take (a factory, plant, etc) out of operation but maintain it so that it can be used in the future 5 to postpone work on (a project, activity, etc)

moth-eaten *adj* 1 decayed, decrepit, or outdated 2 eaten away by or as if by moths

mother¹ (ˈmʌðə) *n* 1 a a female who has given birth to offspring (*as modifier*): *a mother bird* 2 (*often capital, esp as a term of address*) a person's own mother 3 a female substituting in the function of a mother 4 (*often capital*) *chiefly archaic* a term of address for an old woman 5 a motherly qualities, such as maternal affection: *it appealed to the mother in her* b (*as modifier*): *mother love* c (*in combination*): *mothercraft* 6 a a female or thing that creates, nurtures, protects, etc, something b (*as modifier*): *mother church; mother earth* 7 a title given to certain members of female religious orders: *mother superior* 8 *Christian Science* God as the eternal Principle 9 (*modifier*) native or innate: *mother wit* 10 *offensive taboo slang, chiefly US* short for **motherfucker** 11 be mother to pour the tea: *I'll be mother* 12 the mother of all ... *informal* the greatest example of its kind: *the mother of all parties* ▷ *vb* (*tr*) 13 to give birth to or produce 14 to nurture, protect, etc as a mother ▷ Related adjective: **maternal** [Old English *mōdor*; compare Old Saxon *mōdar*, Old High German *muotar*, Latin *māter*, Greek *mētēr*] > 'mothering *n*

mother² (ˈmʌðə) *n* a stringy slime containing various bacteria that forms on the surface of liquids undergoing acetous fermentation. It can be added to wine, cider, etc to promote vinegar formation. Also called: mother of vinegar [c16 perhaps from MOTHER¹, but compare Spanish *madre* scum, Dutch *modder* dregs, Middle Low German *modder* decaying object, *mudde* sludge] > 'mothery *adj*

motherboard (ˈmʌðəˌbɔːd) *n* (in an electronic system) a printed circuit board through which signals between all other boards are routed

Mother Carey's chicken (ˈkɛərɪz) *n* another name for **storm petrel** [origin unknown]

mother country *n* 1 the original country of colonists or settlers 2 another term for **fatherland**

motherese (ˌmʌðəˈriːz) *n* the simplified and repetitive type of speech, with exaggerated intonation and rhythm, often used by adults when speaking to babies

motherfucker (ˈmʌðəˌfʌkə) *n offensive taboo slang, chiefly US* a person or thing, esp an exasperating or unpleasant one. Often shortened to: mother

Mother Goose *n* the imaginary author of the collection of nursery rhymes published in 1781 in London as *Mother Goose's Melody* [c18 translated from French *Contes de ma mère l'Oye* (1697), title of a collection of tales by Charles Perrault (1628–1703), French author]

motherhood (ˈmʌðəˌhʊd) *n* 1 the state of being a mother 2 the qualities characteristic of a mother

Mother Hubbard (ˈhʌbəd) *n* (*sometimes not capitals*)

a woman's full-length unbelted dress [c19 after *Mother Hubbard*, a character in a nursery rhyme]

Mothering Sunday (ˈmʌðərɪŋ) *n* See **Mother's Day**

mother-in-law *n*, *pl* mothers-in-law the mother of one's wife or husband

mother-in-law's tongue *n* See **sansevieria**

motherland (ˈmʌðəˌlænd) *n* another word for **fatherland**

motherless (ˈmʌðələs) *adj* 1 not having a mother ▷ *adv* 2 (*intensifier*) *Austral informal* motherless broke

mother lode *n mining* the principal lode in a system

motherly (ˈmʌðəlɪ) *adj* of or resembling a mother, esp in warmth, or protectiveness > 'motherliness *n*

Mother of God *n* a title given to the Virgin Mary: used in Orthodox and Roman Catholic churches to emphasize the belief that Jesus was God

Mother of Parliaments *n* the the British Parliament: the model and creator of many other Parliaments [c19 first used of England in 1865 by John Bright (1811–89), British Liberal statesman]

mother-of-pearl *n* a hard iridescent substance, mostly calcium carbonate, that forms the inner layer of the shells of certain molluscs, such as the oyster. It is used to make buttons, inlay furniture, etc. Also called: nacre Related adj: **nacreous**

mother-of-pearl moth *n* a pyralid moth, *Pleuroptya ruralis*, having a pale sheen, that is often seen around nettles, on which its green larvae feed

mother of the chapel *n* (in British trade unions in the publishing and printing industries) a woman shop steward. Abbreviation: MoC

mother-of-thousands *n* 1 a S European perennial creeping plant, *Linaria cymbalaria*, having small pale blue or lilac flowers 2 a saxifragaceous plant, *Saxifraga sarmentosa* or *S. stolonifera*, having white flowers and creeping red runners

mother-out-law *n informal* the mother of one's ex-husband or ex-wife

Mother's Day *n* 1 US, Canadian, Austral & NZ the second Sunday in May, observed as a day in honour of mothers 2 Brit & S African the fourth Sunday in Lent, when mothers traditionally receive presents from their children. Also called: Mothering Sunday

mother ship *n* a ship providing facilities and supplies for a number of small vessels

Mother Shipton (ˈʃɪptən) *n* a day-flying noctuid moth, *Callistege mi*, mottled brown in colour and named from a fancied resemblance between its darker marking and a haggish profile [named after *Mother Shipton*, a legendary prophetess in 15th-century Yorkshire]

mother superior *n*, *pl* mother superiors *or* mothers superior the head of a community of nuns

mother tongue *n* 1 the language first learned by a child 2 a language from which another has evolved

Motherwell (ˈmʌðəwəl) *n* a town in S central Scotland, the administrative centre of North Lanarkshire on the River Clyde: industrial centre. Pop: 30 311 (2001)

mother wit *n* native practical intelligence; common sense

motherwort (ˈmʌðəˌwɜːt) *n* any of several plants of the Eurasian genus *Leonurus*, esp *L cardiaca*, having divided leaves and clusters of small purple or pink flowers: family *Lamiaceae* (labiates) [c14 so named because it was thought to be beneficial in uterine disorders]

mothproof (ˈmɒθˌpruːf) *adj* 1 (esp of clothes) chemically treated so as to repel clothes moths ▷ *vb* 2 (*tr*) to make (clothes, etc) mothproof

mothy (ˈmɒθɪ) *adj* mothier, mothiest 1 ragged; moth-eaten 2 containing moths; full of moths

moti (məʊˈtiː) *n Hinglish derogatory* a fat woman or girl [c21 Hindi]

motif (məʊˈtiːf) *n* 1 a distinctive idea, esp a theme elaborated on in a piece of music,

literature, etc 2 Also: motive a recurring form or shape in a design or pattern 3 a single added piece of decoration, such as a symbol or name on a jumper, sweatshirt, etc [c19 from French. See MOTIVE]

motile (ˈməʊtaɪl) *adj* 1 capable of moving spontaneously and independently ▷ *n* 2 *psychol* a person whose mental imagery strongly reflects movement, esp his own [c19 from Latin *mōtus* moved, from *movēre* to move] > motility (məʊˈtɪlɪtɪ) *n*

motion (ˈməʊʃən) *n* 1 the process of continual change in the physical position of an object; movement: *linear motion* ▷ Related adjective: **kinetic** 2 a movement or action, esp of part of the human body; a gesture 3 a the capacity for movement b a manner of movement, esp walking; gait 4 a mental impulse 5 a formal proposal to be discussed and voted on in a debate, meeting, etc 6 *law* an application made to a judge or court for an order or ruling necessary to the conduct of legal proceedings 7 Brit a the evacuation of the bowels b excrement 8 a part of a moving mechanism b the action of such a part 9 *music* the upward or downward course followed by a part or melody. Parts whose progressions are in the same direction exhibit **similar motion**, while two parts whose progressions are in opposite directions exhibit **contrary motion**. See also **parallel** (sense 3) 10 go through the motions a to act or perform the task (of doing something) mechanically or without sincerity b to mimic the action (of something) by gesture 11 in motion operational or functioning (often in the phrases **set in motion, set the wheels in motion**) ▷ *vb* 12 (when *tr*, may take a clause as object or an infinitive) to signal or direct (a person) by a movement or gesture [c15 from Latin *mōtiō* a moving, from *movēre* to move] > 'motional *adj*

motion capture *n* a process by which a device can be used to capture patterns of live movement; the data is then transmitted to a computer, where simulation software displays it applied to a virtual actor

motionless (ˈməʊʃənlɪs) *adj* not moving; absolutely still > 'motionlessly *adv* > 'motionlessness *n*

motion picture *n US and Canadian* a a sequence of images of moving objects photographed by a camera and providing the optical illusion of continuous movement when projected onto a screen b a form of entertainment, information, etc, composed of such a sequence of images and shown in a cinema, etc. Also called: film

motion sickness *n* the state or condition of being dizzy or nauseous from riding in a moving vehicle

motion study *n* short for **time and motion study**

motivate (ˈməʊtɪˌveɪt) *vb* (*tr*) to give incentive to

motivation (ˌməʊtɪˈveɪʃən) *n* 1 the act or an instance of motivating 2 desire to do; interest or drive 3 incentive or inducement 4 *psychol* the process that arouses, sustains and regulates human and animal behaviour > ˌmoti'vational *adj* > 'moti,vative *adj*

motivational research *n* the application of psychology to the study of consumer behaviour, esp the planning of advertising and sales campaigns. Also called: motivation research

motive (ˈməʊtɪv) *n* 1 the reason for a certain course of action, whether conscious or unconscious 2 a variant of **motif** (sense 2) ▷ *adj* 3 of or causing motion or action: *a motive force* 4 of or acting as a motive; motivating ▷ *vb* (*tr*) 5 to motivate [c14 from Old French *motif*, from Late Latin *mōtīvus* (adj) moving, from Latin *mōtus*, past participle of *movēre* to move] > 'motiveless *adj* > 'motivelessly *adv* > 'motivelessness *n*

motive power *n* 1 any source of energy used to produce motion 2 the means of supplying power to an engine, vehicle, etc 3 any driving force

motivity (məʊˈtɪvɪtɪ) *n* the power of moving or of

initiating motion

mot juste French (mo ʒyst) *n*, *pl* **mots justes** (mo ʒyst) the appropriate word or expression

motley ('mɒtlɪ) *adj* **1** made up of elements of varying type, quality, etc **2** multicoloured ▷ *n* **3** a motley collection or mixture **4** the particoloured attire of a jester **5** *obsolete* a jester [c14 perhaps from *mot* speck, MOTE¹]

motmot ('mɒtmɒt) *n* any tropical American bird of the family *Momotidae*, having a long tail and blue and brownish-green plumage: order *Coraciiformes* (kingfishers, etc) [c19 from American Spanish, imitative of the bird's call]

motocross ('məʊtəˌkrɒs) *n* **1** a motorcycle race across very rough ground **2** another name for **rallycross** See also **autocross** [c20 from MOTO(R) + CROSS(-COUNTRY)]

motoneuron (ˌməʊtəʊ'njʊərɒn) *n anatomy* an efferent nerve cell; motor neuron

moto perpetuo ('məʊtəʊ pə'pɛtjʊəʊ) *n music* a fast instrumental passage made up of notes of equal length [Italian, literally: perpetual motion]

motor ('məʊtə) *n* **1 a** the engine, esp an internal-combustion engine, of a vehicle **b** (*as modifier*): *a motor scooter* **2** Also called: **electric motor** a machine that converts electrical energy into mechanical energy by means of the forces exerted on a current-carrying coil placed in a magnetic field **3** any device that converts another form of energy into mechanical energy to produce motion **4** an indispensable part or player that moves a process or system along **5 a** *chiefly Brit* a car or other motor vehicle **b** *as modifier: motor spares* ▷ *adj* **6** producing or causing motion **7** *physiol* **a** of or relating to nerves or neurons that carry impulses that cause muscles to contract **b** of or relating to movement or to muscles that induce movement ▷ *vb* **8** (*intr*) to travel by car **9** (*tr*) *Brit* to transport by car **10** (*intr*) *informal* to move fast; make good progress **11** (*tr*) to motivate [c16 from Latin *mōtor* a mover, from *movēre* to move]

motorable ('məʊtərəb³l) *adj* (of a road) suitable for use by motor vehicles

motorbicycle ('məʊtəˌbaɪsɪk³l) *n* **1** a motorcycle **2** a moped

motorbike ('məʊtəˌbaɪk) *n* a less formal name for **motorcycle**

motorboat ('məʊtəˌbəʊt) *n* any boat powered by a motor

motorbus ('məʊtəˌbʌs) *n* a bus driven by an internal-combustion engine

motorcade ('məʊtəˌkeɪd) *n* a parade of cars or other motor vehicles [c20 from MOTOR + CAVALCADE]

motor camp *n NZ* a camp for motorists, tents, and caravans

motorcar ('məʊtəˌkɑː) *n* **1** a more formal word for **car** (sense 1) **2** a self-propelled electric railway car

motor caravan *n Brit* a former name for **motorhome**

motorcoach ('məʊtəˌkəʊtʃ) *n* a coach driven by an internal-combustion engine

motorcycle ('məʊtəˌsaɪk³l) *n* **1** Also called: **motorbike** a two-wheeled vehicle, having a stronger frame than a bicycle, that is driven by a petrol engine, usually with a capacity of between 125 cc and 1000 cc ▷ *vb* (*intr*) **2** to ride on a motorcycle > 'motor,cyclist *n*

motor drive *n photog* a battery-operated motorized system to give fast film advance between exposures. Compare **autowinder**

-motored *adj* (*in combination*) having a specified type of motor or number of motors

motor generator *n* a generator driven by an electric motor, by means of which the voltage, frequency, or phases of an electrical power supply can be changed

motorhome ('məʊtəˌhəʊm) *n* a large motor vehicle with living quarters behind the driver's compartment. Former name: **motor caravan**

motorist ('məʊtərɪst) *n* a driver of a car, esp when considered as a car-owner

---

motorize *or* **motorise** ('məʊtəˌraɪz) *vb* (*tr*) **1** to equip with a motor **2** to provide (military units) with motor vehicles > ˌmotori'zation *or* ˌmotori'sation *n*

motorman ('məʊtəmən) *n, pl* -men **1** the driver of an electric train **2** the operator of a motor

motor neurone disease *n* a progressively degenerative disease of the motor system causing muscle weakness and wasting

motor park *n* a W African name for **car park**

motor scooter *n* a light motorcycle with small wheels and an enclosed engine. Often shortened to: **scooter**

motor vehicle *n* a road vehicle driven by a motor or engine, esp an internal-combustion engine

motor vessel *or* **ship** *n* a ship whose main propulsion system is a diesel or other internal-combustion engine

motorway ('məʊtəˌweɪ) *n Brit* a main road for fast-moving traffic, having limited access, separate carriageways for vehicles travelling in opposite directions, and usually a total of four or six lanes. US names: **superhighway**, (also Canadian) **expressway**

Motown ('məʊˌtaʊn) *n trademark* music combining rhythm and blues and pop, or gospel rhythms and modern ballad harmony [c20 from *Motown Records* of Detroit; from *Mo(tor)Town*, a nickname for Detroit, Michigan, centre of the US car industry]

motser *or* **motza** ('mɒtsə) *n Austral informal* a large sum of money, esp a gambling win [of uncertain origin; possibly Yiddish]

motte (mɒt) *n history* a natural or man-made mound on which a castle was erected [c14 see MOAT]

MOT test *n* (in Britain) See **MOT** (sense 2)

mottle ('mɒt³l) *vb* **1** (*tr*) to colour with streaks or blotches of different shades ▷ *n* **2** a mottled appearance, as of the surface of marble **3** one streak or blotch of colour in a mottled surface [c17 back formation from MOTTLEY]

mottled ('mɒt³ld) *adj* coloured with streaks or blotches of different shades

motto ('mɒtəʊ) *n, pl* -toes *or* -tos **1** a short saying expressing the guiding maxim or ideal of a family, organization, etc, esp when part of a coat of arms **2** a short explanatory phrase inscribed on or attached to something **3** a verse or maxim contained in a paper cracker **4** a quotation prefacing a book or chapter of a book **5** a recurring musical phrase [c16 via Italian from Latin *muttum* utterance]

motty ('mɒtɪ) *n Irish* the target at which coins are aimed in pitch-and-toss

motu (məʊ'tuː) *n Hinglish derogatory* a fat man or boy [c21 Hindi]

Motu ('məʊtuː) *n* **1** (*pl* -tu *or* -tus) a member of an aboriginal people of S Papua **2** the language of this people, belonging to the Malayo-Polynesian family **3** Also called: **Hiri Motu**, (esp formerly) **Police Motu** a pidgin version of this language, widely used in Papua-New Guinea. Compare **Neo-Melanesian**

motu proprio ('məʊtuː 'prəʊprɪˌəʊ) *n* an administrative papal bull [Latin: of his own accord]

moue French (mu) *n* a disdainful or pouting look

mouflon *or* **moufflon** ('muːflɒn) *n* a wild short-fleeced mountain sheep, *Ovis musimon*, of Corsica and Sardinia [c18 via French from Corsican *mufrone*, from Late Latin *mufrō*]

mouillé ('mwiːeɪ) *adj phonetics* palatalized, as in the sounds represented by Spanish *ll* or *ñ*, Italian *gl* or *gn* (pronounced as (ʎ) and (ɲ) respectively), or French *ll* (representing a (j) sound) [c19 from French, past participle of *mouiller* to moisten, from Latin *mollis* soft]

moujik ('muːʒɪk) *n* a variant spelling of **muzhik**

mould¹ *or US* **mold** (məʊld) *n* **1** a shaped cavity used to give a definite form to fluid or plastic material **2** a frame on which something may be

---

constructed **3** something shaped in or made on a mould **4** shape, form, design, or pattern **5** specific nature, character, or type ▷ *vb* (*tr*) **6** to make in a mould **7** to shape or form, as by using a mould **8** to influence or direct **9** to cling to **10** *metallurgy* to make (a material such as sand) into a mould that is used in casting [c13 (n): changed from Old French *modle*, from Latin *modulus* a small measure, MODULE] > 'mouldable *or US* 'moldable *adj* > ˌmoulda'bility *or US* ˌmolda'bility *n*

mould² *or US* **mold** (məʊld) *n* **1** a coating or discolouration caused by various saprotrophic fungi that develop in a damp atmosphere on the surface of stored food, fabrics, wallpaper, etc **2** any of the fungi that causes this growth ▷ *vb* **3** to become or cause to become covered with this growth. Also called: **mildew** [c15 dialect (Northern English) *mowlde* mouldy, from the past participle of *moulen* to become mouldy, probably of Scandinavian origin; compare Old Norse *mugla* mould]

mould³ *or US* **mold** (məʊld) *n* **1** loose soil, esp when rich in organic matter **2** *poetic* the earth [Old English *molde*; related to Old High German *molta* soil, Gothic *mulde*]

mouldboard *or US* **moldboard** ('məʊldˌbɔːd) *n* the curved blade of a plough, which turns over the furrow

moulder¹ *or US* **molder** ('məʊldə) *vb* (often foll by *away*) to crumble or cause to crumble, as through decay [c16 verbal use of MOULD³]

moulder² *or US* **molder** ('məʊldə) *n* **1** a person who moulds or makes moulds **2** *printing* one of the set of electrotypes used for making duplicates

moulding *or US* **molding** ('məʊldɪŋ) *n* **1** *architect* **a** a shaped outline, esp one used on cornices, etc **b** a shaped strip made of wood, stone, etc **2** something moulded

moulding board *n* a board on which dough is kneaded

mouldwarp ('məʊldˌwɔːp) *or* **mouldywarp** ('məʊldɪˌwɔːp) *n* an archaic or dialect name for a **mole²** (sense 1) [c14 *moldewarpe*; ultimately from Germanic *moldeworpon* (unattested) earth-thrower, from *moldā* MOULD³ + *wurp, werp* to throw (both unattested)]

mouldy *or US* **moldy** ('məʊldɪ) *adj* **mouldier, mouldiest** *or US* **moldier, moldiest** **1** covered with mould **2** stale or musty, esp from age or lack of use **3** *slang* boring; dull > 'mouldiness *or US* 'moldiness *n*

mouldy fig *n dated slang* a rigid adherent to older jazz forms

moulin ('muːlɪn) *n* a vertical shaft in a glacier, maintained by a constant descending stream of water and debris [c19 from French: a mill]

Moulins (French mulɛ̃) *n* a market town in central France, on the Allier River. Pop: 21 892 (1999)

Moulmein *or* **Maulmain** (maʊl'meɪn) *n* a port in S Myanmar, near the mouth of the Salween River: exports teak and rice. Pop: 390 000 (2005 est)

moult *or US* **molt** (məʊlt) *vb* **1** (of birds, mammals, reptiles, and arthropods) to shed (feathers, hair, skin, or cuticle) ▷ *n* **2** the periodic process of moulting. See also **ecdysis** [c14 *mouten*, from Old English *mūtian*, as in *bimūtian* to exchange for, from Latin *mūtāre* to change] > 'moulter *or US* 'molter *n*

mound¹ (maʊnd) *n* **1** a raised mass of earth, debris, etc **2** any heap or pile: *a mound of washing* **3** a small natural hill **4** *archaeol* another word for **barrow²** **5** an artificial ridge of earth, stone, etc, as used for defence ▷ *vb* **6** (often foll by *up*) to gather into a mound; heap **7** (*tr*) to cover or surround with a mound: *to mound a grave* ▷ Related adjective: **tumular** [c16 earthwork, perhaps from Old English *mund* hand, hence defence: compare Middle Dutch *mond* protection]

mound² (maʊnd) *n heraldry* a rare word for **orb** (sense 1) [c13 (meaning: world, c16 orb): from French *monde*, from Latin *mundus* world]

Mound Builder *n* a member of a group of

prehistoric inhabitants of the Mississippi region who built altar-mounds, tumuli, etc

mound-builder *n* another name for **megapode**

mount¹ (maʊnt) *vb* **1** to go up (a hill, stairs, etc); climb **2** to get up on (a horse, a platform, etc) **3** (*intr; often foll by up*) io increase; accumulate: *excitement mounted* **4** (*tr*) to fix onto a backing, setting, or support: *to mount a photograph; to mount a slide* **5** (*tr*) to provide with a horse for riding, or to place on a horse **6** (of male animals) to climb onto (a female animal) for copulation **7** (*tr*) to prepare (a play, musical comedy, etc) for production **8** (*tr*) to plan and organize (a compaign, an exhibition, etc) **9** (*tr*) *military* to prepare or launch (an operation): *the Allies mounted an offensive* **10** (*tr*) to prepare (a skeleton, dead animal, etc) for exhibition as a specimen **11** (*tr*) to place or carry (weapons) in such a position that they can be fired **12** mount guard See **guard** (sense 26) ▷ *n* **13** a backing, setting, or support onto which something is fixed **14** the act or manner of mounting **15** a horse for riding **16** a slide used in microscopy **17** *philately* **a** a small transparent pocket in an album for a postage stamp **b** another word for **hinge** (sense 5) [C16 from Old French *munter*, from Vulgar Latin *montāre* (unattested) from Latin *mons* MOUNT²] ▷ '**mountable** *adj* ▷ '**mounter** *n*

mount² (maʊnt) *n* **1** a mountain or hill: used in literature and (when cap.) in proper names: *Mount Everest* **2** (in palmistry) any of the seven cushions of flesh on the palm of the hand [Old English *munt,* from Latin *mons* mountain, but influenced in Middle English by Old French *mont*]

mountain ('maʊntɪn) *n* **1** a natural upward projection of the earth's surface, higher and steeper than a hill and often having a rocky summit **b** (*as modifier*): *mountain people; mountain scenery* **c** (*in combination*): *a mountaintop* **2** a huge heap or mass: *a mountain of papers* **3** anything of great quantity or size **4** a surplus of a commodity, esp in the European Union: *the butter mountain* **5** a mountain to climb *Brit informal* a serious or considerable difficulty or obstruction to overcome **6** make a mountain out of a molehill See **molehill** (sense 2) [C13 from Old French *montaigne,* from Vulgar Latin *montānea* (unattested) mountainous, from Latin *montānus,* from *mons* mountain]

Mountain ('maʊntɪn) *n* **the** an extremist faction during the French Revolution led by Danton and Robespierre [C18 so called because its members sat in the highest row of seats at the National Convention Hall in 1793]

mountain ash *n* **1** any of various trees of the rosaceous genus *Sorbus,* such as *S aucuparia* (**European mountain ash** or **rowan**), having clusters of small white flowers and bright red berries **2** any of several Australian eucalyptus trees, such as *Eucalyptus regnans*

mountain avens *n* See **avens** (sense 2)

mountain bike *n* a type of sturdy bicycle with at least 16 and up to 21 gears, straight handlebars, and heavy-duty tyres

mountainboard ('maʊntɪnˌbɔːd) *n* a type of skateboard specially designed for rough terrain and steep slopes, having four large wheels linked by a suspension system ▷ 'mountainˌboarding *n* ▷ 'mountainˌboarder *n*

mountain cat *n* any of various wild feline mammals, such as the bobcat, lynx, or puma

mountain chain *n* a series of ranges of mountains

mountain devil *n* another name for **moloch**

mountaineer (ˌmaʊntɪ'nɪə) *n* **1** a person who climbs mountains **2** a person living in a mountainous area ▷ *vb* **3** (*intr*) to climb mountains ▷ ˌmountain'eering *n*

mountain everlasting *n* another name for **cat's-foot**

mountain goat *n* **1** short for **Rocky Mountain goat** **2** any wild goat inhabiting mountainous regions

mountain laurel *n* any of various ericaceous shrubs or trees of the genus *Kalmia,* esp *K. latifolia* of E North America, which has leathery poisonous leaves and clusters of pink or white flowers. Also called: calico bush

mountain lion *n* another name for **puma**

mountainous ('maʊntɪnəs) *adj* **1** of or relating to mountains: *a mountainous region* **2** like a mountain, esp in size or impressiveness ▷ 'mountainously *adv* ▷ 'mountainousness *n*

mountain range *n* a series of adjoining mountains or of lines of mountains of similar origin

mountain sheep *n* **1** another name for **bighorn 2** any wild sheep inhabiting mountainous regions

mountain sickness *n* **1** Also called: altitude sickness nausea, headache, and shortness of breath caused by climbing to high altitudes (usually above 12 000 ft) **2** *vet science* a disease of cattle kept at high altitude in S and N America, characterized by congestive heart failure

Mountain Standard Time *n* one of the standard times used in North America, seven hours behind Greenwich Mean Time. Abbreviation: MST

Mount Cook lily *n* a large white buttercup, *Ranunculus lyallii,* of the South Island alpine country of New Zealand. Also called: great mountain buttercup

Mount Desert Island *n* an island off the coast of Maine: lakes and granite peaks. Area: 279 sq km (108 sq miles)

mountebank ('maʊntɪˌbæŋk) *n* **1** (formerly) a person who sold quack medicines in public places **2** a charlatan; fake ▷ *vb* **3** (*intr*) to play the mountebank [C16 from Italian *montambanco* a climber on a bench, from *montare* to MOUNT² + *banco* BENCH (see also BANK¹)] ▷ ˌmounte'bankery *n*

mounted ('maʊntɪd) *adj* **1** equipped with or riding horses: *mounted police* **2** provided with a support, backing, etc

Mountie *or* **Mounty** ('maʊntɪ) *n, pl* Mounties *informal* a member of the Royal Canadian Mounted Police [nickname evolved from MOUNTED]

mounting ('maʊntɪŋ) *n* another word for **mount¹** (sense 13)

mounting-block *n* a block of stone formerly used to aid a person when mounting a horse

Mount Isa ('aɪzə) *n* a city in NE Australia in NW Queensland: mining of copper and other minerals. Pop: 20 525 (2001)

Mount McKinley National Park (mə'kɪnlɪ) *n* a national park in S central Alaska: contains part of the Alaska Range Area: 7847 sq km (3030 sq miles)

Mount Rainier National Park ('raɪnɪə, reɪ'nɪə, rə-) *n* a national park in W Washington, in the Cascade Range. Area: 976 sq km (377 sq miles)

mourn (mɔːn) *vb* **1** to feel or express sadness for the death or loss of (someone or something) **2** (*intr*) to observe the customs of mourning, as by wearing black **3** (*tr*) to grieve over (loss or misfortune) [Old English *murnan;* compare Old High German *mornēn* to be troubled, Gothic *maurnan* to grieve, Greek *mermeros* worried]

Mourne Mountains (mɔːn) *pl n* a mountain range in SE Northern Ireland. Highest peak: Slieve Donard, 853 m (2798 ft)

mourner ('mɔːnə) *n* **1** a person who mourns, esp at a funeral **2** (at US revivalist meetings) a person who repents publicly

mournful ('mɔːnfʊl) *adj* **1** evoking grief; sorrowful **2** gloomy; sad ▷ 'mournfully *adv* ▷ 'mournfulness *n*

mourning ('mɔːnɪŋ) *n* **1** the act or feelings of one who mourns; grief **2** the conventional symbols of grief, such as the wearing of black **3** the period of time during which a death is officially mourned **4** in mourning observing the conventions of mourning ▷ *adj* **5** of or relating to mourning ▷ 'mourningly *adv*

mourning band *n* a piece of black material, esp an armband, worn to indicate that the wearer is

in mourning

mourning cloak *n* the US name for **Camberwell beauty**

mourning dove *n* a brown North American dove, *Zenaidura macroura,* with a plaintive song

mouse (maʊs) *n, pl* mice (maɪs) **1** any of numerous small long-tailed rodents of the families *Muridae* and *Cricetidae* that are similar to but smaller than rats. See also **fieldmouse, harvest mouse, house mouse** Related adj: **murine 2** any of various related rodents, such as the jumping mouse **3** a quiet, timid, or cowardly person **4** *computing* a hand-held device used to control the cursor movement and select computing functions without keying **5** *slang* a black eye **6** *nautical* another word for **mousing** ▷ *vb* (maʊz) **7** to stalk and catch (mice) **8** (*intr*) to go about stealthily **9** (*tr*) *nautical* to secure (a hook) with mousing [Old English *mūs;* compare Old Saxon *mūs,* German *Maus,* Old Norse *mūs,* Latin *mūs,* Greek *mūs*] ▷ 'mouseˌlike *adj*

mousebird ('maʊsˌbɜːd) *n* another name for **coly**

mouse deer *n* another name for **chevrotain**

mouse-ear *n* short for **mouse-ear chickweed** (see **chickweed** (sense 2))

mousemat ('maʊsˌmæt) *n* a piece of material on which a computer mouse is moved

mouseover ('maʊsˌəʊvə) *n* *computing* (on the page of a website) an item, esp a graphic, that changes or pops up when the pointer of a mouse moves over it

mouser ('maʊzə, 'maʊsə) *n* a cat or other animal that is used to catch mice: usually qualified: *a good mouser*

mousetail ('maʊsˌteɪl) *n* any of various N temperate ranunculaceous plants of the genus *Myosurus,* esp *M. minimus,* with tail-like flower spikes

mousetrap ('maʊsˌtræp) *n* **1** any trap for catching mice, esp one with a spring-loaded metal bar that is released by the taking of the bait **2** *Brit informal* cheese of indifferent quality

mousey ('maʊsɪ) *adj* mousier, mousiest a variant spelling of **mousy.** ▷ 'mousily *adv* ▷ 'mousiness *n*

mousing ('maʊzɪŋ) *n* *nautical* a lashing, shackle, etc, for closing off a hook to prevent a load from slipping off

moussaka *or* **mousaka** (mʊ'sɑːkə) *n* a dish originating in the Balkan States, consisting of meat, aubergines, and tomatoes, topped with cheese sauce [C20 from Modern Greek]

mousse (muːs) *n* **1** a light creamy dessert made with eggs, cream, fruit, etc, set with gelatine **2** a similar dish made from fish or meat **3** the layer of small bubbles on the top of a glass of champagne or other sparkling wine **4** short for **styling mousse** [C19 from French: froth]

mousseline (French muslin) *n* **1** a fine fabric made of rayon or silk **2** a type of fine glass **3** short for **mousseline sauce** [C17 French: MUSLIN]

mousseline de laine French (muslin də lɛn) *n* a light woollen fabric [literally: muslin of wool]

mousseline de soie French (muslin də swa) *n* a thin gauzelike fabric of silk or rayon [literally: muslin of silk]

mousseline sauce *n* a light sauce, made by adding whipped cream or egg whites to hollandaise sauce [from French *mousseline,* literally: muslin]

moustache *or US* **mustache** (mə'stɑːʃ) *n* **1** the unshaved growth of hair on the upper lip, and sometimes down the sides of the mouth **2** a similar growth of hair or bristles (in animals) or feathers (in birds) **3** a mark like a moustache [C16 via French from Italian *mostaccio,* ultimately from Doric Greek *mustax* upper lip] ▷ mous'tached *or US* mus'tached *adj*

moustache cup *n* a cup with a partial cover to protect a drinker's moustache

Mousterian (muː'stɪərɪən) *n* **1** a culture characterized by flint flake tools and associated with Neanderthal man, found throughout

Europe, North Africa, and the Near East, dating from before 70 000–32 000 BC ▷ *adj* **2** of or relating to this culture [c20 from French *Moustérien* from archaeological finds of the same period in the cave of *Le Moustier,* Dordogne, France]

mousy *or* **mousey** ('maʊsɪ) *adj* **mousier, mousiest 1** resembling a mouse, esp in having a light brown or greyish hair colour **2** shy or ineffectual: *a mousy little woman* **3** infested with mice > 'mousily *adv* > 'mousiness *n*

mouth *n* (maʊθ) *pl* mouths (maʊðz) **1** the opening through which many animals take in food and issue vocal sounds **2** the system of organs surrounding this opening, including the lips, tongue, teeth, etc **3** the visible part of the lips on the face. Related adjs: **oral, oscular 4** a person regarded as a consumer of food: *four mouths to feed* **5** verbal expression (esp in the phrase **give mouth to**) **6** a particular manner of speaking: *a foul mouth* **7** *informal* boastful, rude, or excessive talk: *he is all mouth* **8** the point where a river issues into a sea or lake **9** the opening of a container, such as a jar **10** the opening of or place leading into a cave, tunnel, volcano, etc **11** that part of the inner lip of a horse on which the bit acts, esp when specified as to sensitivity: *a hard mouth* **12** *music* the narrow slit in an organ pipe **13** the opening between the jaws of a vice or other gripping device **14** a pout; grimace **15** by word of mouth orally rather than by written means **16** down in *or* at the mouth in low spirits **17** have a big mouth *or* open one's big mouth *informal* to speak indiscreetly, loudly, or excessively **18** keep one's mouth shut to keep a secret **19** put one's money where one's mouth is to take appropriate action to support what one has said **20** put words into someone's mouth **a** to represent, often inaccurately, what someone has said **b** to tell someone what to say **21** run off at the mouth *informal* to talk incessantly, esp about unimportant matters ▷ *vb* (maʊð) **22** to speak or say (something) insincerely, esp in public **23** (*tr*) to form (words) with movements of the lips but without speaking **24** (*tr*) to accustom (a horse) to wearing a bit **25** (*tr*) to take (something) into the mouth or to move (something) around inside the mouth **26** (*intr*; usually foll by *at*) to make a grimace [Old English *mūth*; compare Old Norse *muthr,* Gothic *munths,* Dutch *mond*] > mouther ('maʊðə) *n*

mouthbrooder ('maʊθˌbruːdə) *or* **mouthbreeder** ('maʊθˌbriːdə) *n* any of various African cichlid fishes of the genera *Tilapia Haplochromis* that carry their eggs and young around in the mouth

mouthfeel ('maʊθˌfiːl) *n* the texture of a substance as it is perceived in the mouth: *the wine has a good mouthfeel*

mouthful ('maʊθˌfʊl) *n, pl* -fuls **1** as much as is held in the mouth at one time **2** a small quantity, as of food **3** a long word or phrase that is difficult to say **4** *Brit informal* an abusive response **5** *informal, chiefly US and Canadian* an impressive remark (esp in the phrase **say a mouthful**)

mouth off *vb* (*intr, adv*) *Brit informal* to give an opinion or speak emotionally, often without much care or consideration

mouth organ *n* another name for **harmonica** (sense 1)

mouthpart ('maʊθˌpaːt) *n* any of the paired appendages in arthropods that surround the mouth and are specialized for feeding

mouthpiece ('maʊθˌpiːs) *n* **1** the part of a wind instrument into which the player blows **2** the part of a telephone receiver into which a person speaks **3** the part of a container forming its mouth **4** a person who acts as a spokesman, as for an organization **5** a publication, esp a periodical, expressing the official views of an organization **6** *boxing* another name for **gumshield**

mouth-to-mouth *adj* designating a method of artificial respiration involving blowing air

rhythmically into the mouth of a person who has stopped breathing, to stimulate return of spontaneous breathing

mouthwash ('maʊθˌwɒʃ) *n* a medicated aqueous solution, used for gargling and for cleansing the mouth

mouthwatering ('maʊθˌwɔːtərɪŋ) *adj* whetting the appetite, as from smell, appearance, or description

mouthy ('maʊðɪ) *adj* mouthier, mouthiest bombastic; excessively talkative

mouton ('muːtɒn) *n* sheepskin processed to resemble the fur of another animal, esp beaver or seal [from French: sheep. See MUTTON]

movable *or* **moveable** ('muːvəbᵊl) *adj* **1** able to be moved or rearranged; not fixed **2** (esp of religious festivals such as Easter) varying in date from year to year **3** (usually spelt **moveable**) *law* denoting or relating to personal property as opposed to realty **4** *printing* (of type) cast singly so that each character is on a separate piece of type suitable for composition by hand, as founder's type ▷ *n* **5** (*often plural*) a movable article, esp a piece of furniture > ˌmovaˈbility *or* ˈmovableness *n* > ˈmovably *adv*

move (muːv) *vb* **1** to go or take from one place to another; change in location or position **2** (*usually intr*) to change (one's dwelling, place of business, etc) **3** to be or cause to be in motion; stir **4** (*intr*) (of machines, etc) to work or operate **5** (*tr*) to cause (to do something); prompt **6** (*intr*) to begin to act: *move soon or we'll lose the order* **7** (*intr*) to associate oneself with a specified social circle: *to move in exalted spheres* **8** (*intr*) to make progress **9** (*tr*) to arouse affection, pity, or compassion in; touch **10** (in board games) to change the position of (a piece) or (of a piece) to change position **11** (*intr*) (of merchandise) to be disposed of by being bought **12** (when *tr, often takes a clause as object; when intr, often foll by for*) to suggest (a proposal) formally, as in debating or parliamentary procedure **13** (*intr; usually foll by on or along*) to go away or to another place; leave **14** to cause (the bowels) to evacuate or (of the bowels) to be evacuated **15** (*intr*) *informal* to be exciting or active: *the party started moving at twelve* **16** move heaven and earth to take every step possible (to achieve something) ▷ *n* **17** the act of moving; movement **18** one of a sequence of actions, usually part of a plan; manoeuvre **19** the act of moving one's residence, place of business, etc **20** (in board games) **a** a player's turn to move his piece or take other permitted action **b** a permitted manoeuvre of a piece **21** get a move on *informal* **a** to get started **b** to hurry up **22** make a move (*usually used with a negative*) *informal* to take even the slightest action **23** make one's move to commit oneself to a position or course of action **24** on the move **a** travelling from place to place **b** advancing; succeeding **c** very active; busy ▷ See also **move in, move on, move out** [c13 from Anglo-French *mover,* from Latin *movēre*]

move in *vb* (*mainly adverb*) **1** (*also preposition*) Also (when preposition): move into to occupy or take possession of (a new residence, place of business, etc) or help (someone) to do this **2** (*intr; often foll by on*) *informal* to creep close (to), as in preparing to capture **3** (*intr; often foll by on*) *informal* to try to gain power or influence (over) or interfere (with)

movement ('muːvmənt) *n* **1 a** the act, process, or result of moving **b** an instance of moving **2** the manner of moving **3 a** a group of people with a common ideology, esp a political or religious one **b** the organized action of such a group **4** a trend or tendency in a particular sphere **5** the driving and regulating mechanism of a watch or clock **6** (*often plural*) a person's location and activities during a specific time **7 a** the evacuation of the bowels **b** the matter evacuated **8** *music* a principal self-contained section of a symphony, sonata, etc, usually having its own structure **9** tempo or pace, as in music or literature **10** *fine arts*

the appearance of motion in painting, sculpture, etc **11** *prosody* the rhythmic structure of verse **12** a positional change by one or a number of military units **13** a change in the market price of a security or commodity

move on *vb* (*intr, adv*) to put a difficult experience behind one and progress mentally or emotionally

move out *vb* (*adverb*) to vacate a residence, place of business, etc, or help (someone) to do this

mover ('muːvə) *n* **1** *informal* a person, business, idea, etc, that is advancing or progressing **2** a person who moves a proposal, as in a debate **3** *US and Canadian* a removal firm or a person who works for one

movers and shakers *pl n informal* the people with power and influence in a particular field of activity [c20 perhaps from the line "We are the movers and shakers of the world for ever" in 'Ode' by Arthur O'Shaughnessy (1844–81), British poet]

movie ('muːvɪ) *n* **1 a** an informal word for **film** (sense 1) **b** (*as modifier*): movie ticket [c20 from MOV(ING PICTURE) + -IE]

movie camera *n US and Canadian* a camera in which a strip of film moves past the lens, usually to give 16 or 24 exposures per second, thus enabling moving pictures to be taken. Also called (Brit): cine camera

movie film *n US and Canadian* photographic film, wound on a spool, usually 8, 16, or 35 millimetres wide, up to several hundred metres long, and having one or two lines of sprocket holes along its length enabling it to be used in a movie camera. Also called (Brit): cine film

movieoke (ˌmuːvɪˈəʊkɪ) *n* an entertainment in which people take it in turns, with the help of subtitles and the audience, to act out well-known scenes from movies while they are silently shown in the background [c20 from MOVIE + KARAOKE]

Movietone ('muːvɪˌtəʊn) *n trademark US* the earliest technique of including a soundtrack on film

moving ('muːvɪŋ) *adj* **1** arousing or touching the emotions **2** changing or capable of changing position **3** causing motion > 'movingly *adv*

moving average *n statistics* (of a sequence of values) a derived sequence of the averages of successive subsequences of a given number of members, often used in time series to even out short-term fluctuations and make a trend clearer: *the 3-term moving average of 4, 6, 8, 7, 9, 8 is 6, 7, 8*

moving coil *adj* denoting an electromechanical device in which a suspended coil is free to move in a magnetic field. A current passing through the coil causes it to move, as in loudspeakers and electrical measuring instruments, or movement of the coil gives rise to induced currents, as in microphones and some record-player pick-ups

moving picture *n* another name for **motion picture**

moving staircase *or* **stairway** *n* less common terms for **escalator** (sense 1)

Moviola (ˌmuːvɪˈəʊlə) *n trademark* a viewing machine used in cutting and editing film

mow¹ (maʊ) *vb* mows, mowing, mowed, mowed *or* mown **1** to cut down (grass, crops, etc) with a hand implement or machine **2** (*tr*) to cut the growing vegetation of (a field, lawn, etc) [Old English *māwan*; related to Old High German *māen,* Middle Dutch *maeyen* to mow, Latin *metere* to reap, Welsh *medi*] > 'mower *n*

mow² (maʊ) *n* **1** the part of a barn where hay, straw, etc, is stored **2** the hay, straw, etc, stored [Old English *mūwa*; compare Old Norse *mūgr* heap, Greek *mukōn*]

mow³ (maʊ) *n, vb* an archaic word for **grimace** [c14 from Old French *moe* a pout, or Middle Dutch *mouwe*]

mowburnt ('məʊˌbɜːnt) *adj* (of hay, straw, etc) damaged by overheating in a mow

mowdie ('maʊdɪ) *or* **mowdiewart** ('maʊdɪˌwært) *n* Scot words for **mole²** [c18 a Scot variant of MOULDWARP]

m

mow down *vb* (*tr, adverb*) to kill in large numbers, esp by gunfire

mown (məʊn) *vb* a past participle of **mow¹**

MOX (mɒks) *n* a blend of plutonium and uranium oxides, used as a nuclear fuel in breeder reactors [C20 from *m*(*ixed*) *ox*(*ides*)]

moxa ('mɒksə) *n* **1** a downy material obtained from various plants and used in Oriental medicine by being burned on the skin as a cauterizing agent or counterirritant for the skin **2** any of various plants yielding this material, such as the wormwood *Artemisia chinensis* [C17 anglicized version of Japanese *mogusa*, contraction of *moe gusa* burning herb]

moxibustion (,mɒksɪ'bʌstʃən) *n* a method of treatment, originally in Chinese medicine, in which a moxa is burned on the skin [C20 from MOXA + (COM)BUSTION]

moxie ('mɒksɪ) *n US and Canadian slang* courage, nerve, or vigour [from the trademark *Moxie*, a soft drink]

Moyle (mɔɪl) *n* a district of NE Northern Ireland, in Co Antrim. Pop: 16 302 (2003 est). Area: 494 sq km (191 sq miles)

moz *or* **mozz** (mɒz) *n Austral slang, obsolete* **1** a hoodoo; hex **2** **put the moz on** to jinx [short for *mozzle*, from Hebrew *mazzal* luck]

Mozambican *or* **Mozambiquan** (,məʊzəm'bi:kən) *adj* **1** of or relating to Mozambique or its inhabitants ▷ *n* **2** a native or inhabitant of Mozambique

Mozambiquan *adj, n* **2** a variant of **Mozambican**

Mozambique (,məʊzəm'bi:k) *n* a republic in SE Africa: colonized by the Portuguese from 1505 onwards and a slave-trade centre until 1878; made an overseas province of Portugal in 1951; became an independent republic in 1975; became a member of the Commonwealth in 1995. Official language: Portuguese. Religion: animist majority. Currency: metical. Capital: Maputo. Pop: 19 183 000 (2004 est). Area: 812 379 sq km (313 661 sq miles). Portuguese name: Moçambique Also called (until 1975): Portuguese East Africa

Mozambique Channel *n* a strait between Mozambique and Madagascar. Length: about 1600 km (1000 miles). Width: 400 km (250 miles)

Mozarab (məʊ'zærəb) *n* (formerly) a Christian of Moorish Spain [C18 via Spanish from Arabic *musta'rib* a would-be Arab] ▷ Moz'arabic *adj*

Mozartian *or* **Mozartean** (məʊ'tsɑːtɪən) *adj* **1** of, relating to, or reminiscent of Wolfgang Amadeus Mozart, the Austrian composer (1756–91) ▷ *n* **2** a follower or admirer of Mozart

mozzarella (,mɒtsə'rɛlə) *n* a moist white Italian curd cheese made originally from buffalo milk [from Italian, diminutive of *mozza* a type of cheese, from *mozzare* to cut off]

mozzetta (məʊ'zɛtə; *Italian* mot'tsetta) *or* **mozetta** *n RC Church* a short hooded cape worn by the pope, cardinals, etc [C18 from Italian, shortened from *almozzetta*, from Medieval Latin *almutia* ALMUCE]

mozzie ('mɒzɪ) *n* a variant spelling of **mossie¹**

mp¹ *abbreviation for* **1** melting point **2** *music* mezzo piano [Italian: moderately soft]

mp² *the internet domain name for* Northern Mariana Islands

MP *abbreviation for* **1** (in Britain and Canada) Member of Parliament **2** (in Britain) Metropolitan Police **3** Military Police **4** Mounted Police

MP3 *abbreviation for* **1** MPEG-1 Audio Layer-3: tradename for software created by the Motion Picture Experts Group that enables files to be compressed quickly to 10% or less of their original size for storage on disk or hard drive or esp for transfer across the internet **2** an audio or video file created in this way

MPAA *abbreviation for* Motion Picture Association of America

m-payment *n* a point-of-sale payment made through a wireless device such as a mobile phone or PDA [C20 M(OBILE) + PAYMENT]

MPC (in Britain) *abbreviation for* **1** Medical Practices Committee **2** Monetary Policy Committee (of the Bank of England)

MPEG ('ɛm,pɛg) *n computing* a standard file format for compressing video images and audio sounds [C20 technique devised by the *M*(*otion*) *P*(*icture*) *E*(*xperts*) *G*(*roup*)]

mpg *abbreviation for* miles per gallon

MPG (in Britain) *abbreviation for* main professional grade: the basic salary scale for classroom teachers

mph *abbreviation for* miles per hour

MPhil *or* **MPh** *abbreviation for* Master of Philosophy

MPLA *abbreviation for* Movimento Popular de Libertacão de Angola [Portuguese: Popular Movement for the Liberation of Angola]

MP/M *n computing* a multiuser operating system that resembles a CP/M

MPP (in Canada) *abbreviation for* Member of the Provincial Parliament (of Ontario)

MPS *abbreviation for* **1** Member of the Pharmaceutical Society **2** Member of the Philological Society

Mpumalanga (m'pʌmɑːlaːŋgə) *n* a province of E South Africa; formed in 1994 from part of the former province of Transvaal: agriculture and service industries. Capital: Nelspruit. Pop: 3 244 306 (2004 est). Area: 78 370 sq km (30 259 sq miles)

MPV *abbreviation for* **multipurpose vehicle**

mq *the internet domain name for* Martinique

Mr ('mɪstə) *n, pl* Messrs ('mɛsəz) **1** a title used before a man's name or names or before some office that he holds; *Mr Jones; Mr President* **2** (in military contexts) a title used in addressing a warrant officer, officer cadet, or junior naval officer **3** a title placed before the surname of a surgeon [C17 abbreviation of MISTER]

MR *abbreviation for* **1** (in Britain) **Master of the Rolls 2** motivation(al) research

MRA *abbreviation for* **1** magnetic resonance **2** **Moral Rearmament**

Mr Big *n slang, chiefly US* the head of an organization, esp of a criminal organization

MRBM *abbreviation for* **medium-range ballistic missile**

MRC (in Britain) *abbreviation for* Medical Research Council

MRCA *abbreviation for* multirole combat aircraft

MRE *abbreviation for* meal ready to eat, a US military precooked ration pack

MRI *abbreviation for* magnetic resonance imaging

MRIA *abbreviation for* Member of the Royal Irish Academy

mridang (mrɪ'dʌŋg) *n* a drum used in Indian music [Hindi]

M-1 rifle *n* a semiautomatic .30 calibre rifle: the basic infantry weapon of the US Army in World War II and the Korean War. Also called: Garand rifle

MRM *abbreviation for* mechanically recovered meat: a reconstituted meat product created from offal and other meat waste, often used in hamburgers, sausages, pies etc

mRNA *abbreviation for* messenger RNA

MRP *abbreviation for* manufacturers' recommended price

Mr Right *n informal* the man considered by a woman to be her perfect marriage partner

Mrs ('mɪsɪz) *n, pl* Mrs *or* Mesdames a title used before the name or names of a married woman [C17 originally an abbreviation of MISTRESS]

MRSA *abbreviation for* methicillin-resistant *Staphylococcus aureus*: a bacterium that enters the skin through open wounds to cause septicaemia and is extremely resistant to most antibiotics. It has been responsible for outbreaks of untreatable infections among patients in hospitals

MRSC *abbreviation for* Member of the Royal Society of Chemistry

Mrs Mop *n informal* a cleaning lady

ms *the internet domain name for* Montserrat

Ms (mɪz, məs) *n* a title substituted for **Mrs** or **Miss** before a woman's name to avoid making a distinction between married and unmarried women

MS *abbreviation for* **1** Master of Surgery **2** (on gravestones) memoriae sacrum [Latin: sacred to the memory of] **3** Mississippi **4** motor ship **5** **multiple sclerosis** **6** ▷ *international car registration for* Mauritius

MS. *or* **ms.** *pl* MSS. *or* mss. *abbreviation for* manuscript

msb *computing abbreviation for* most significant bit; the bit of binary number with the greatest numerical value or the bit in some other binary pattern which occupies this position

MSc *abbreviation for* Master of Science

MSC (in Canada) *abbreviation for* Meritorious Service Cross

MSD (in New Zealand) *abbreviation for* Ministry of Social Development

MS-DOS (ɛm'ɛs'dɒs) *n trademark computing* a type of disk operating system [C20 from *M*(*icro*)*s*(*oft*), the company that developed it, + DOS]

MSF (formerly, in Britain) *abbreviation for* Manufacturing, Science, Finance (a trade union)

MSG *abbreviation for* **monosodium glutamate**

Msgr *abbreviation for* Monsignor

MSI *electronics abbreviation for* medium-scale integration

msl *or* **MSL** *abbreviation for* mean sea level

MSM (in Canada) *abbreviation for* Meritorious Service Medal

MSP *abbreviation for* Member of the Scottish Parliament

MSS *or* **mss** *abbreviation for* manuscripts

MST *abbreviation for* **Mountain Standard Time**

Ms-Th *physics symbol for* mesothorium

mt *the internet domain name for* Malta

Mt *or* **mt** *abbreviation for* **1** mount: *Mt Everest* **2** Also: mtn mountain

MT *abbreviation for* Montana

MTB *n Brit* a motor torpedo boat

MTBE *abbreviation for* methyl tertiary-butyl ether: a lead-free antiknock petrol additive

MTBF *abbreviation for* mean time between failures

mtDNA *abbreviation for* mitochondrial deoxyribonucleic acid. See **mitochondrial DNA**

MTech *abbreviation for* Master of Technology

mtg *abbreviation for* meeting

MTNG *text messaging abbreviation for* meeting

Mt Rev. *abbreviation for* Most Reverend

MTV *abbreviation for* music television: a US music channel that operates 24 hours a day

mu¹ (mju:) *n* the 12th letter in the Greek alphabet (M, μ), a consonant, transliterated as *m*

mu² *the internet domain name for* Mauritius

MU *abbreviation for* Musicians' Union

Muay Thai ('mu:eɪ 'taɪ) *n* a martial art developed in Thailand in which blows may be struck with the fists, elbows, knees, and shins

muc- *combining form* a variant of **muco-** before a vowel

much (mʌtʃ) *determiner* **1 a** (usually used with a negative) a great quantity or degree of: *there isn't much honey left* **b** (as pronoun): *much has been learned from this* **2** a bit much *informal* rather excessive **3** as much exactly that: *I suspected as much when I heard* **4** make much of See **make of** (sense 4) **5** not much of not to any appreciable degree or extent: *he's not much of an actor really* **6** not up to much *informal* of a low standard: *this beer is not up to much* **7** think much of (used with a negative) to have a high opinion of: *I don't think much of his behaviour* ▷ *adv* **8** considerably: *they're much better now* **9** practically; nearly (esp in the phrase **much the same**) **10** (usually used with a negative) often, a great deal: *it doesn't happen much in this country* **11** (as) much as even though; although: *much as I'd like to, I can't come* ▷ *adj* **12** (predicative; usually used with a negative) impressive or important: *this car isn't much* ▷ See also **more, most** [Old English *mycel*; related to Old English *micel* great, Old Saxon *mikil*, Gothic *mikils*; compare also Latin *magnus*, Greek *megas*]

muchness ('mʌtʃnɪs) *n* **1** *archaic or informal* magnitude **2** much of a muchness *Brit* very similar

mucic acid ('mju:sɪk) *n* a colourless crystalline solid carboxylic acid found in milk sugar and used in the manufacture of pyrrole. Formula: $C_4H_4(OH)_4(COOH)_2$ [C19 *mucic,* from French *mucique;* see MUCUS, -IC]

mucid ('mju:sɪd) *adj rare* mouldy, musty, or slimy [C17 from Latin *mūcidus,* from *mucēre* to be mouldy] > mu'cidity *or* 'mucidness *n*

mucigen ('mju:sɪdʒən) *n* a substance present in mucous cells that is converted into mucin

mucilage ('mju:sɪlɪdʒ) *n* **1** a sticky preparation, such as gum or glue, used as an adhesive **2** a complex glutinous carbohydrate secreted by certain plants [C14 via Old French from Late Latin *mūcilāgo* mouldy juice; see MUCID] > mucilaginous (,mju:sɪ'lædʒɪnəs) *adj* > ,muci'laginously *adv* > ,muci'laginousness *n*

mucin ('mju:sɪn) *n biochem* any of a group of nitrogenous mucoproteins occurring in saliva, skin, tendon, etc, that produce a very viscous solution in water [C19 via French from Latin MUCUS] > 'mucinous *adj*

muck (mʌk) *n* **1** farmyard dung or decaying vegetable matter **2** Also called: muck soil an organic soil rich in humus and used as a fertilizer **3** dirt or filth **4** earth, rock material, etc, removed during mining excavations **5** *slang, chiefly Brit* rubbish **6** See **Lord Muck, Lady Muck 7** make a muck of *slang, chiefly Brit* to ruin or spoil > *vb* (*tr*) **8** to spread manure upon (fields, gardens, etc) **9** to soil or pollute **10** (often foll by *out*) to clear muck from > See also **muck about, muck in, muck up** [C13 probably of Scandinavian origin; compare Old Norse *myki* dung, Norwegian *myk*]

muck about *vb Brit slang* **1** (*intr*) to waste time; misbehave **2** (when *intr,* foll by *with*) to interfere with, annoy, or waste the time of

muckamuck ('mʌkə,mʌk) *Canadian W coast* > *n* **1** food > *vb* **2** (*intr*) to consume food; eat [Chinook Jargon]

mucker ('mʌkə) *n* **1** *mining* a person who shifts broken rock or waste **2** *Brit slang* **a** a friend; mate **b** a coarse person > 'muckerish *adj*

muck in *vb* (*intr, adverb*) *Brit slang* to share something, such as duties, work, etc (with other people)

muckle ('mʌkəl) *Scot* > *adj* **1** large; much > *adv* **2** much; greatly [dialect variant of MICKLE]

muckrake ('mʌk,reɪk) *n* **1** an agricultural rake for spreading manure > *vb* **2** (*intr*) to seek out and expose scandal, esp concerning public figures > 'muck,raker *n* > 'muck,raking *n*

mucksweat ('mʌk,swɛt) *n Brit informal* profuse sweat or a state of profuse sweating

muck up *vb* (*adverb*) *informal* **1** (*tr*) *Brit and Austral* to ruin or spoil; make a mess of **2** (*intr*) *Austral* to misbehave

muck-up day *n Austral slang* the last day of school before the annual examinations, marked by practical jokes and other student pranks

muckworm ('mʌk,wɜ:m) *n* **1** any larva or worm that lives in mud **2** *informal* a miser

mucky ('mʌki) *adj* muckier, muckiest **1** dirty **2** of or like muck > 'muckily *adv* > 'muckiness *n*

muco- *or before a vowel* **muc-** *combining form* mucus or mucous: *mucoprotein; mucin*

mucoid ('mju:kɔɪd) *or* **mucoidal** *adj* of the nature of or resembling mucin

mucopolysaccharide (,mju:kəʊ,pɒlɪ'sækəraɪd) *n biochem* any of a group of complex polysaccharides composed of repeating units of two sugars, one of which contains an amino group

mucoprotein (,mju:kəʊ'prəʊti:n) *n* any of a group of conjugated proteins containing small quantities of mucopolysaccharides; glycoprotein

mucopurulent (,mju:kəʊ'pjʊərələnt) *adj pathol* composed of or containing both mucus and pus

mucor ('mju:kɔ:) *n* any fungus belonging to the genus *Mucor,* which comprises many common moulds [C20 New Latin, from Latin: mould]

mucosa (mju:'kəʊsə) *n, pl* -sae (-si:) another word for **mucous membrane** [C19 New Latin, from Latin *mūcōsus* slimy] > mu'cosal *adj*

mucous ('mju:kəs) *or* **mucose** ('mju:kəʊs, -kəʊz) *adj* of, resembling, or secreting mucus [C17 from Latin *mūcōsus* slimy, from MUCUS] > mucosity (mju:'kɒsɪtɪ) *n*

▪ **USAGE** The noun *mucus* is often misspelled *mucous. Mucous* can only be correctly used as an adjective

mucous membrane *n* a mucus-secreting membrane that lines body cavities or passages that are open to the external environment. Also called: mucosa > mucomembranous (,mju:kəʊ'mɛmbrənəs) *adj*

mucro ('mju:krəʊ) *n, pl* mucrones (mju:'krəʊni:z) *biology* a short pointed projection from certain parts or organs, as from the tip of a leaf [C17 from Latin *mūcrō* point]

mucronate ('mju:krəʊnɪt, -,neɪt) *or* **mucronated** *adj* terminating in a sharp point [C18 from Latin *mūcrōnātus* pointed, from MUCRO] > ,mucro'nation *n*

mucus ('mju:kəs) *n* the slimy protective secretion of the mucous membranes, consisting mainly of mucin [C17 from Latin: nasal secretions; compare *mungere* to blow the nose; related to Greek *muxa* mucus, *muktēr* nose]

▪ **USAGE** See at **mucous**

mud (mʌd) *n* **1** a fine-grained soft wet deposit that occurs on the ground after rain, at the bottom of ponds, lakes, etc **2** *informal* slander or defamation **3** clear as mud not at all clear **4** drag (someone's) name in the mud to disgrace or defame (someone) **5** here's mud in your eye *informal* a humorous drinking toast **6** (someone's) name is mud *informal* (someone) is disgraced **7** throw (*or* sling) mud at *informal* to slander; vilify > *vb* muds, mudding, mudded **8** (*tr*) to soil or cover with mud [C14 probably from Middle Low German *mudde;* compare Middle High German *mot* swamp, mud, Swedish *modd* slush]

mud bath *n* **1** a medicinal bath in heated mud **2** a dirty or muddy occasion, state, etc

mudcat ('mʌd,kæt) *n* any of several large North American catfish living in muddy rivers, esp in the Mississippi valley

mud crab *n* a large edible crab, *Scylla serrata,* of Australian mangrove regions

mud dauber *n* any of various wasps of the family *Sphecidae,* that construct cells of mud or clay in which they lay their eggs and store live insects as food for the developing larvae. See also **digger wasp**

muddle ('mʌdəl) *vb* (*tr*) **1** (often foll by *up*) to mix up (objects, items, etc); jumble **2** to confuse **3** to make (water) muddy or turbulent **4** *US* to mix or stir (alcoholic drinks, etc) > *n* **5** a state of physical or mental confusion [C16 perhaps from Middle Dutch *moddelen* to make muddy] > 'muddled *adj* > 'muddledness *or* 'muddlement *n* > 'muddling *adj, n* > 'muddlingly *adv* > 'muddly *adj*

muddle along *or* **on** *vb* (*intr, adverb*) to proceed in a disorganized way

muddleheaded (,mʌdəl'hɛdɪd) *adj* mentally confused or vague > ,muddle'headedness *n*

muddler ('mʌdlə) *n* **1** a person who muddles or muddles through **2** *US* an instrument for mixing drinks thoroughly

muddle through *vb* (*intr, adverb*) *chiefly Brit* to succeed in some undertaking in spite of lack of organization

muddy ('mʌdɪ) *adj* -dier, -diest **1** covered or filled with mud **2** not clear or bright: *muddy colours* **3** cloudy: *a muddy liquid* **4** (esp of thoughts) confused or vague > *vb* -dies, -dying, -died **5** to become or cause to become muddy > 'muddily *adv* > 'muddiness *n*

Mudéjar Spanish (mu'ðexar) *n, pl -jares* (-xares) **1** *medieval history* a Spanish Moor, esp one permitted

to stay in Spain after the Christian reconquest > *adj* **2** of or relating to a style of architecture orginated by Mudéjares [from Arabic *mudajjan* one permitted to remain]

mudeye ('mʌdaɪ) *n Austral* the larva of the dragonfly, commonly used as a fishing bait

mud fever *n* another name for **scratches**

mudfish ('mʌd,fɪʃ) *n, pl -fish or -fishes* any of various fishes, such as the bowfin and cichlids, that live at or frequent the muddy bottoms of rivers, lakes, etc

mud flat *n* a tract of low muddy land, esp near an estuary, that is covered at high tide and exposed at low tide

mudflow ('mʌd,fləʊ) *n geology* a flow of soil or fine-grained sediment mixed with water down a steep unstable slope

mud gecko *n Austral* another name for **crocodile**

mudguard ('mʌd,gɑ:d) *n* a curved part of a motorcycle, bicycle, etc, attached above the wheels to reduce the amount of water or mud thrown up by them. US and Canadian name: fender

mud hen *n* any of various birds that frequent marshes or similar places, esp the coots, rails, etc

mudir (mu:'dɪə) *n* a local governor [C19 via Turkish, from Arabic, from *adāra* to administrate]

mudlark ('mʌd,lɑ:k) *n* **1** *slang, now rare* a street urchin **2** (formerly) one who made a living by picking up odds and ends in the mud of tidal rivers **3** *Austral slang* a racehorse that runs well on a wet or muddy course

mud map *n Austral informal* a map drawn on the ground with a stick, or any other roughly drawn map

mudpack ('mʌd,pæk) *n* a cosmetic astringent paste containing fuller's earth, used to improve the complexion

mud pie *n* a mass of mud moulded into a pie-like shape by a child

mud puppy *n* any aquatic North American salamander of the genus *Necturus,* esp *N. maculosus,* having red feathery external gills and other persistent larval features: family *Proteidae.* See also **neoteny**

mudra (mə'drɑ:) *n* any of various ritual hand movements in Hindu religious dancing [Sanskrit, literally: sign, token]

mudskipper ('mʌd,skɪpə) *n* any of various gobies of the genus *Periophthalmus* and related genera that occur in tropical coastal regions of Africa and Asia and can move on land by means of their strong pectoral fins

mudslinging ('mʌd,slɪŋɪŋ) *n* casting malicious slurs on an opponent, esp in politics > 'mud,slinger *n*

mudstone ('mʌd,stəʊn) *n* a dark grey clay rock similar to shale but with the lamination less well developed

mud turtle *n* any of various small turtles of the genus *Kinosternon* and related genera that inhabit muddy rivers in North and Central America: family *Kinosternidae*

mud volcano *n* a cone-shaped mound formed from fine mud ejected, with gases and water, from hot springs, geysers, etc, in volcanic regions

muenster ('mʌnstə) *n* a whitish-yellow semihard whole milk cheese, often flavoured with caraway or aniseed [after *Muenster,* Haut-Rhin, France]

muesli ('mju:zlɪ) *n* a mixture of rolled oats, nuts, fruit, etc, eaten with milk [Swiss German, from German *Mus* mush, purée + -*li,* diminutive suffix]

muesli bar *n* a snack made of compressed muesli ingredients

muezzin (mu:'ɛzɪn) *n Islam* the official of a mosque who calls the faithful to prayer five times a day from the minaret [C16 changed from Arabic *mu'adhdhin*]

muff[1] (mʌf) *n* **1** an open-ended cylinder of fur or cloth into which the hands are placed for warmth **2** the tuft on either side of the head of certain

m

fowls [c16 probably from Dutch *mof*, ultimately from French *mouffle* MUFFLE¹]

muff² (mʌf) *vb* **1** to perform (an action) awkwardly **2** (*tr*) to bungle (a shot, catch, etc) in a game ▷ *n* **3** any unskilful play in a game, esp a dropped catch **4** any clumsy or bungled action **5** a bungler [c19 of uncertain origin]

muffin (ˈmʌfɪn) *n* **1** *Brit* a thick round baked yeast roll, usually toasted and served with butter **2** *US and Canadian* a small cup-shaped sweet bread roll, usually eaten hot with butter [c18 perhaps from Low German *muffen*, cakes]

muffin man *n Brit* (formerly) an itinerant seller of muffins

muffle¹ (ˈmʌfəl) *vb* (*tr*) **1** (often foll by *up*) to wrap up (the head) in a scarf, cloak, etc, esp for warmth **2** to deaden (a sound or noise), esp by wrapping **3** to prevent (the expression of something) by (someone) ▷ *n* **4** something that muffles **5** a kiln with an inner chamber for firing porcelain, enamel, etc, at a low temperature [c15 probably from Old French; compare Old French *moufle* mitten, *emmouflé* wrapped up]

muffle² (ˈmʌfəl) *n* the fleshy hairless part of the upper lip and nose in ruminants and some rodents [c17 from French *mufle*, of unknown origin]

muffler (ˈmʌflə) *n* **1** a thick scarf, collar, etc **2** *US and Canadian* any device designed to reduce noise, esp the tubular device containing baffle plates in the exhaust system of a motor vehicle. Also called (in Britain and certain other countries): **silencer 3** something that muffles

mufti¹ (ˈmʌftɪ) *n, pl* **-tis 1** a Muslim legal expert and adviser on the law of the Koran **2** (in the former Ottoman empire) the leader of the religious community [c16 from Arabic *muftī*, from *aftā* to give a (legal) decision]

mufti² (ˈmʌftɪ) *n, pl* **-tis** civilian dress, esp as worn by a person who normally wears a military uniform [c19 perhaps from MUFTI¹]

Mufulira (ˌmuːfuːˈlɪərə) *n* a mining town in the Copper Belt of Zambia. Pop: 220 000 (2005 est)

mug¹ (mʌg) *n* **1** a drinking vessel with a handle, usually cylindrical and made of earthenware **2** Also called: **mugful** the quantity held by a mug or its contents [c16 probably from Scandinavian; compare Swedish *mugg*]

mug² (mʌg) *n* **1** *slang* a person's face or mouth: *get your ugly mug out of here!* **2** *slang* a grimace **3** *Brit slang* a gullible person, esp one who is swindled easily **4 a mug's game** a worthless activity ▷ *vb* **mugs, mugging, mugged 5** (*tr*) *informal* to attack or rob (someone) violently **6** (*intr*) *Brit slang* to pull faces or overact, esp in front of a camera ▷ See also **mug up** [c18 perhaps from MUG¹, since drinking vessels were sometimes modelled into the likeness of a face]

mugga (ˈmʌgə) *n* an Australian eucalyptus tree with dark bark and pink flowers, *Eucalyptus sideroxylon* [from a native Australian language]

mugger¹ (ˈmʌgə) *n informal* a person who commits robbery with violence, esp in the street **2** *chiefly US and Canadian* a person who overacts

mugger², muggar or **muggur** (ˈmʌgə) *n* a large freshwater crocodile, *Crocodylus niloticus*, inhabiting marshes and pools of India and Ceylon. Also called: **marsh crocodile** [c19 from Hindi *magar*]

muggins (ˈmʌgɪnz) *n* **1** *Brit slang* **a** a simpleton; silly person **b** a title used humorously to refer to oneself **2** a variation on the game of dominoes **3** a card game [c19 probably from the surname *Muggins*]

muggy (ˈmʌgɪ) *adj* **-gier, -giest** (of weather, air, etc) unpleasantly warm and humid [c18 dialect *mug* drizzle, probably from Scandinavian; compare Old Norse *mugga* mist] ▷ **ˈmuggily** *adv* ▷ **ˈmugginess** *n*

Mughal (ˈmuːgaːl) *n* a variant spelling of **Mogul**

mug punter *n Brit slang* a customer or client who is gullible and easily swindled

mug up *vb* (*adverb*) *Brit slang* to study (a subject)

hard, esp for an exam [c19 of unknown origin]

mugwort (ˈmʌgˌwɜːt) *n* **1** a N temperate perennial herbaceous plant, *Artemisia vulgaris*, with aromatic leaves and clusters of small greenish-white flowers: family *Asteraceae* (composites) **2** another name for **crosswort** [Old English *mucgwyrt*, perhaps from Old English *mycg* MIDGE]

mugwump (ˈmʌgˌwʌmp) *n US* a neutral or independent person, esp in politics [c19 from Algonquian: great chief, from *mogki* great + *-omp* man] ▷ **ˈmugˌwumpery** or **ˈmugˌwumpism** *n* ▷ **ˈmugˌwumpish** *adj*

Muhammadan or **Muhammedan** (muˈhæmədᵊn) *n, adj* another word (not in Muslim use) for **Muslim**

Muharram (muˈhærəm) or **Moharram** *n* the first month of the Islamic year [from Arabic: sacred]

Mühlhausen (myːlˈhauzən) *n* the German name for **Mulhouse**

muir (muːr, mjuːr, myr) *n* **a** a Scot word for **moor¹ b** (in place names): *Sheriffmuir*

muirburn (ˈmuːrˌbʌrn, ˈmjuːr-, ˈmyr-) *n Scot* a variant of **moorburn**

Muir Glacier (mjʊə) *n* a glacier in SE Alaska, in the St Elias Mountains, flowing southeast from Mount Fairweather. Area: about 900 sq km (350 sq miles)

mujaheddin, mujahedeen or **mujahideen** (ˌmuːdʒæhəˈdiːn) *pl n* (preceded by *the; sometimes capital*) (in Afghanistan and Iran) fundamentalist Muslim guerrillas; in Afghanistan in 1992 the mujaheddin overthrew the government but were unable to agree on a constitution due to factional conflict and in 1996 Taliban forces seized power [c20 from Arabic *mujāhidīn* fighters, ultimately from JIHAD]

mujik (ˈmuːʒɪk) *n* a variant spelling of **muzhik**

Mukden (ˈmʊkdən) *n* a former name of **Shenyang**

mukluk (ˈmʌklʌk) *n* a soft boot, usually of sealskin, worn by the Inuit [from Inuktitut *muklok* large seal]

muktuk (ˈmʌktʌk) *n Canadian* the thin outer skin of the beluga, used as food [from Inuktitut]

mulatto (mjuːˈlætəʊ) *n, pl* **-tos** or **-toes 1** a person having one Black and one White parent ▷ *adj* **2** of a light brown colour [c16 from Spanish *mulato* young mule, variant of *mulo* MULE¹]

mulberry (ˈmʌlbərɪ, -brɪ) *n, pl* **-ries 1** any moraceous tree of the temperate genus *Morus*, having edible blackberry-like fruit, such as *M. alba* (**white mulberry**), the leaves of which are used to feed silkworms **2** the fruit of any of these trees **3** any of several similar or related trees, such as the paper mulberry and Indian mulberry **4 a** a dark purple colour **b** (*as adjective*): *a mulberry dress* [c14 from Latin *mōrum*, from Greek *moron*; related to Old English *mōrberie*; compare Dutch *moerbezie*, Old High German *mūrberi*]

Mulberry Harbour *n* either of two prefabricated floating harbours towed across the English Channel to the French coast for the Allied invasion of Normandy in 1944 [from the code name Operation *Mulberry*]

mulch (mʌltʃ) *n* **1** half-rotten vegetable matter, peat, etc, used to prevent soil erosion or enrich the soil ▷ *vb* **2** (*tr*) to cover (the surface of land) with mulch [c17 from obsolete *mulch* soft; related to Old English *mylisc* mellow; compare dialect German *molsch* soft, Latin *mollis* soft]

Mulciber (ˈmʌlsɪbə) *n* another name for **Vulcan¹**

mulct (mʌlkt) *vb* (*tr*) **1** to cheat or defraud **2** to fine (a person) ▷ *n* **3** a fine or penalty [c15 via French from Latin *multa* a fine]

mule¹ (mjuːl) *n* **1** the sterile offspring of a male donkey and a female horse, used as a beast of burden. Compare **hinny¹ 2** any hybrid animal: *a mule canary* **3** Also called: **spinning mule** a machine invented by Samuel Crompton that spins cotton into yarn and winds the yarn on spindles **4** *informal* an obstinate or stubborn person **5** *slang* a person who is paid to transport

illegal drugs for a dealer [c13 from Old French *mul*, from Latin *mūlus* ass, mule]

mule² (mjuːl) *n* a backless shoe or slipper [c16 from Old French from Latin *mulleus* a magistrate's shoe]

mule deer *n* a W North American deer, *Odocoileus hemionus*, with long ears and a black-tipped tail

mules (mjuːlz) *vb* (*tr*) *Austral* to perform the Mules operation on (a sheep)

mule skinner *n US and Canadian* an informal term for **muleteer**

Mules operation (mjuːlz) *n Austral* the surgical removal of folds of skin in the breech of a sheep to reduce blowfly strike [named after J. H. W. *Mules* (died 1946), Australian grazier who first suggested it]

muleta (mjuːˈlɛtə) *n* the small cape attached to a stick used by the matador during the final stages of a bullfight [Spanish: small mule, crutch, from *mula* MULE¹]

muleteer (ˌmjuːlɪˈtɪə) *n* a person who drives mules

muley (ˈmjuːlɪ) or **mulley** (ˈmʌlɪ) *adj* **1** (of cattle) having no horns ▷ *n* **2** any hornless cow [c16 variant of dialect *moiley*, from Gaelic *maol*, Welsh *moel* bald]

mulga (ˈmʌlgə) *n Austral* **1** any of various Australian acacia shrubs, esp *Acacia aneura*, which grows in the central desert regions and has leaflike leafstalks **2** scrub comprised of a dense growth of acacia **3** the outback; bush [from a native Australian language]

Mulhacén (*Spanish* mulaˈθen) *n* a mountain in S Spain, in the Sierra Nevada: the highest peak in Spain Height: 3478 m (11 410 ft)

Mülheim an der Ruhr (*German* ˈmyːlhaɪm an der ˈ'ruːr) or **Mülheim** *n* an industrial city in W Germany, in North Rhine-Westphalia on the River Ruhr: river port. Pop: 170 745 (2003 est)

Mulhouse (*French* myluz) *n* a city in E France, on the Rhône-Rhine canal: under German rule (1871–1918); textiles. Pop: 110 359 (1999). German name: **Mühlhausen**

muliebrity (ˌmjuːlɪˈɛbrɪtɪ) *n* **1** the condition of being a woman **2** femininity [c16 via Late Latin from Latin *muliēbris* womanly, from *mulier* woman]

mulish (ˈmjuːlɪʃ) *adj* stubborn; obstinate; headstrong ▷ **ˈmulishly** *adv* ▷ **ˈmulishness** *n*

Mulki (ˈmʊlkɪ) *n* a native or inhabitant of the former Hyderabad State in India [Urdu, from *mulk* country]

mull¹ (mʌl) *vb* (*tr*; often foll by *over*) to study or ponder [c19 probably from MUDDLE]

mull² (mʌl) *vb* (*tr*) to heat (wine, ale, etc) with sugar and spices to make a hot drink [c17 of unknown origin]

mull³ (mʌl) *n* a light muslin fabric of soft texture [c18 earlier *mulmull*, from Hindi *malmal*]

mull⁴ (mʌl) *n* a layer of nonacidic humus formed in well drained and aerated soils. Compare **mor** [c20 from Danish *muld*; see MOULD³]

mull⁵ (mʌl) *n Scot* a promontory [c14 related to Gaelic *maol*, Icelandic *múli*]

Mull (mʌl) *n* a mountainous island off the west coast of Scotland, in the Inner Hebrides, separated from the mainland by the **Sound of Mull**. Chief town: Tobermory. Pop: 2667 (2001). Area: 909 sq km (351 sq miles)

mullah, mulla (ˈmʌlə, ˈmʊlə) or **mollah** (ˈmɒlə) *n* (formerly) a Muslim scholar, teacher, or religious leader: also used as a title of respect [c17 from Turkish *molla*, Persian and Hindi *mulla*, from Arabic *mawlā* master]

mullein or **mullen** (ˈmʌlɪn) *n* any of various European herbaceous plants of the scrophulariaceous genus *Verbascum*, such as *V. thapsus* (**common mullein** or **Aaron's rod**), typically having tall spikes of yellow flowers and broad hairy leaves [c15 from Old French *moleine*, probably from Old French *mol* soft, from Latin *mollis*]

muller (ˈmʌlə) *n* a flat heavy implement of stone or iron used to grind material against a slab of stone [c15 probably from *mullen* to grind to powder; compare Old English *myl* dust]

mullered ('mʌləd) *adj slang* **1** drunk **2** heavily defeated; trounced [c20 of unknown origin]

Müllerian mimicry (muːˈliəriən) *n zoology* mimicry in which two or more harmful or inedible species resemble each other, so that predators tend to avoid them [c19 named after J.F.T. *Müller* (1821–97), German zoologist who first described it]

Müller-Lyer illusion ('muːləˈlaɪə) *n* an optical illusion in which a line with inward pointing arrowheads is seen as longer than an equal line with outward pointing arrowheads [c19 named after Franz *Müller-Lyer* (1857–1916), German sociologist and psychiatrist]

mullet[1] ('mʌlɪt) *n* **1** any of various teleost food fishes belonging to the families *Mugilidae* (see **grey mullet**) or *Mullidae* (see **red mullet**) **2** the US name for **grey mullet** [c15 via Old French from Latin *mullus*, from Greek *mullos*]

mullet[2] ('mʌlɪt) *n* a hairstyle in which the hair is short at the top and long at the back [c20 origin unknown]

mulley ('mʌlɪ) *adj, n* a variant of **muley**

mulligan ('mʌlɪɡən) *n US and Canadian* a stew made from odds and ends of food [c20 perhaps from the surname]

mulligatawny (ˌmʌlɪɡəˈtɔːnɪ) *n* a curry-flavoured soup of Anglo-Indian origin, made with meat stock [c18 from Tamil *milakutanni*, from *milaku* pepper + *tanni* water]

Mullingar (ˌmʌlɪnˈɡɑː) *n* a town in N central Republic of Ireland, the county town of Co Westmeath; site of cathedral; cattle raised. Pop: 15 621 (2002)

mullion ('mʌlɪən) *n* **1** a vertical member between the casements or panes of a window or the panels of a screen **2** one of the ribs on a rock face ▷ *vb* **3** (*tr*) to furnish (a window, screen, etc) with mullions [c16 variant of Middle English *munial*, from Old French *moinel*, of unknown origin]

mullite ('mʌlaɪt) *n* a colourless mineral consisting of aluminium silicate in orthorhombic crystalline form: used as a refractory. Formula: $Al_6Si_2O_{13}$ [from island of MULL]

mullock ('mʌlək) *n* **1** *Austral* waste material from a mine **2** *dialect* a mess or muddle **3** *poke mullock at Austral informal* to ridicule [c14 related to Old English *myl* dust, Old Norse *mylja* to crush; see MULLER] > 'mullocky *adj*

mulloway ('mʌləˌweɪ) *n* a large Australian marine sciaenid fish, *Sciaena antarctica*, valued for sport and food [c19 of unknown origin]

Multan (ˌmʊlˈtɑːn) *n* a city in central Pakistan, near the Chenab River. Pop: 1 459 000 (2005 est)

multangular (mʌlˈtæŋɡjʊlə) or **multiangular** *adj* having many angles

multeity (mʌlˈtiːɪtɪ) *n* manifoldness [c19 from Latin *multus* many, perhaps formed by analogy with HAECCEITY]

multi- *combining form* **1** many or much: *multiflorous; multimillion* **2** more than one: *multiparous; multistorey* [from Latin *multus* much, many]

multiaccess (ˌmʌltɪˈæksɛs) *n computing* a system in which several users are permitted to have apparently simultaneous access to a computer

multicast (ˌmʌltɪˈkɑːst) *n* a broadcast from one source simultaneously to several receivers on a network

multichannel analyser (ˌmʌltɪˈtʃænᵊl) *n* an electronic instrument, such as a pulse height analyser, that splits an input waveform into a large number of channels in accordance with a particular parameter of the input

multicide (ˈmʌltɪˌsaɪd) *n* mass murder

multicollinearity (ˌmʌltɪkəʊˌlɪnɪˈærɪtɪ) *n statistics* the condition occurring when two or more of the independent variables in a regression equation are correlated

multicoloured (ˈmʌltɪˌkʌləd) *adj* having many colours

multicultural (ˌmʌltɪˈkʌltʃərəl) *adj* consisting of, relating to, or designed for the cultures of several different races

multiculturalism (ˌmʌltɪˈkʌltʃərəˌlɪzəm) *n* **1** the state or condition of being multicultural **2** the policy of maintaining a diversity of ethnic cultures within a community > ˌmultiˈculturaˌlist *adj, n*

multidisciplinary (ˌmʌltɪˈdɪsɪˌplɪnərɪ) *adj* of or relating to the study of one topic, involving several subject disciplines

multiethnic (ˌmʌltɪˈɛθnɪk) *adj* consisting of, relating to, or designed for various different races

multifaceted (ˌmʌltɪˈfæsɪtɪd) *adj* **1** (of a gem) having many facets **2** having many aspects, abilities, etc

multifactorial (ˌmʌltɪfækˈtɔːrɪəl) *adj* **1** *genetics* of or designating inheritance that depends on more than one gene **2** involving or including a number of elements or factors

multifarious (ˌmʌltɪˈfɛərɪəs) *adj* having many parts of great variety [c16 from Late Latin *multifārius* manifold, from Latin *multifāriam* on many sides] > ˌmultiˈfariously *adv* > ˌmultiˈfariousness *n*

multifid ('mʌltɪfɪd) or **multifidous** (mʌlˈtɪfɪdəs) *adj* having or divided into many lobes or similar segments: *a multifid leaf* [c18 from Latin *multifidus*, from *multus* many + *findere* to split] > 'multifidly *adv*

multiflora rose (ˌmʌltɪˈflɔːrə) *n* an Asian climbing shrubby rose, *Rosa multiflora*, having clusters of small fragrant flowers: the source of many cultivated roses

multifoil ('mʌltɪˌfɔɪl) *n* an ornamental design having a large number of foils. See also **trefoil** (sense 4), **quatrefoil** (sense 2), **cinquefoil** (sense 2)

multifold ('mʌltɪˌfəʊld) *adj* many times doubled; manifold

multifoliate (ˌmʌltɪˈfəʊlɪɪt, -ˌeɪt) *adj botany* having many leaves or leaflets: *a multifoliate compound leaf*

multiform ('mʌltɪˌfɔːm) *adj* having many forms or kinds > multiformity (ˌmʌltɪˈfɔːmɪtɪ) *n*

multifunctional (ˌmʌltɪˈfʌŋkʃənᵊl) or **multifunction** ('mʌltɪˌfʌŋkʃən) *adj* having or able to perform many functions

multigravida (ˌmʌltɪˈɡrævɪdə) *n* a woman who is pregnant for at least the third time. Compare **multipara** [c20 New Latin; see MULTI-, GRAVID]

multigym ('mʌltɪˌdʒɪm) *n* an exercise apparatus incorporating a variety of weights, used for toning the muscles

multihull ('mʌltɪˌhʌl) *n* a sailing vessel with two or more hulls. Compare **monohull**

multilateral (ˌmʌltɪˈlætərəl, -ˈlætrəl) *adj* **1** of or involving more than two nations or parties: *a multilateral pact* **2** having many sides > ˌmultiˈlaterally *adv*

multilingual (ˌmʌltɪˈlɪŋɡwəl) *adj* **1** able to speak more than two languages **2** written or expressed in more than two languages. Compare **bilingual**, **monolingual**

multimedia (ˌmʌltɪˈmiːdɪə) *pl n* **1** the combined use of media such as television, slides, etc, esp in education ▷ *adj* **2** of or relating to the use of a combination of media: *multimedia teaching aids* **3** *computing* of or relating to any of various systems which can manipulate data in a variety of forms, such as sound, graphics, or text

multimeter ('mʌltɪˌmiːtə) *n* an electrical test instrument offering measurement of several values, usually voltage, current, and resistance

multimillionaire (ˌmʌltɪˌmɪljəˈnɛə) *n* a person with a fortune of several million pounds, dollars, etc

multinational (ˌmʌltɪˈnæʃənᵊl) *adj* **1** (of a large business company) operating in several countries ▷ *n* **2** such a company

multinomial (ˌmʌltɪˈnəʊmɪəl) *n* another name for **polynomial** (sense 2b) [c17 from MULTI- + -*nomial* as in BINOMIAL]

multinuclear (ˌmʌltɪˈnjuːklɪə) or **multinucleate** (ˌmʌltɪˈnjuːklɪɪt, -ˌeɪt) *adj* (of a cell, microorganism, etc) having two or more nuclei

multipack ('mʌltɪˌpæk) *n* a form of packaging of foodstuffs, etc, that contains several units and is offered at a price below that of the equivalent number of units

multipara (mʌlˈtɪpərə) *n, pl* -**rae** (-ˌriː) a woman who has given birth to more than one viable fetus or living child. Compare **multigravida** [c19 New Latin, feminine of *multiparus* MULTIPAROUS]

multiparous (mʌlˈtɪpərəs) *adj* **1** (of certain species of mammal) producing many offspring at one birth **2** of, relating to, or designating a multipara [c17 from New Latin *multiparus*] > multiparity (ˌmʌltɪˈpærɪtɪ) *n*

multipartite (ˌmʌltɪˈpɑːtaɪt) *adj* **1** divided into many parts or sections **2** *government* a less common word for **multilateral**

multi-part stationery *n computing* continuous stationery comprising two or more sheets, either carbonless or with carbon paper between the sheets

multiparty (ˌmʌltɪˈpɑːtɪ) *adj* of or relating to a state, political system, etc, in which more than one political party is permitted: *multiparty democracy*

multipath (ˌmʌltɪˌpɑːθ) *adj* relating to television or radio signals that travel by more than one route from a transmitter and arrive at slightly different times, causing ghost images or audio distortion

multiped ('mʌltɪˌpɛd) or **multipede** ('mʌltɪˌpiːd) *rare* ▷ *adj* **1** having many feet ▷ *n* **2** an insect or animal having many feet [c17 from Latin *multipēs*]

multiphase ('mʌltɪˌfeɪz) *adj* another word for **polyphase** (sense 1)

multiplane ('mʌltɪˌpleɪn) *n* an aircraft that has more than one pair of wings. Compare **monoplane**

multiplayer ('mʌltɪˌpleɪə) *n* a mode of play involving more than one player at one time in a computer or video game

multiple ('mʌltɪpᵊl) *adj* **1** having or involving more than one part, individual, etc: *he had multiple injuries* **2** *electronics, US and Canadian* (of a circuit) having a number of conductors in parallel ▷ *n* **3** the product of a given number or polynomial and any other one: *6 is a multiple of 2* **4** *telephony* an electrical circuit accessible at a number of points to any one of which a connection can be made **5** short for **multiple store** [c17 via French from Late Latin *multiplus*, from Latin MULTIPLEX] > 'multiply *adv*

multiple alleles *pl n* three or more alternative forms of a particular gene existing in a population > multiple allelism *n*

multiple birth *n* a birth at which two or more children are born at the same time

multiple-choice *adj* having a number of possible given answers out of which the correct one must be chosen

multiple factors *pl n genetics* two or more genes that act as a unit, producing cumulative effects in the phenotype

multiple fission *n zoology* asexual reproduction in unicellular organisms, esp sporozoans, in which the nucleus divides a number of times, followed by division of the cytoplasm, to form daughter cells

multiple fruit *n* a fruit, such as a pineapple, formed from the ovaries of individual flowers in an inflorescence

multiple personality *n psychiatry* a mental disorder in which an individual's personality appears to have become separated into two or more distinct personalities, each with its own complex organization. Nontechnical name: **split personality**

multiplepoinding (ˌmʌltɪpᵊlˈpɪndɪŋ) *n Scots law* an action to determine the division of a property or fund between several claimants, brought by or on behalf of the present holder

multiple sclerosis *n* a chronic progressive

m

disease of the central nervous system characterized by loss of some of the myelin sheath surrounding certain nerve fibres and resulting in speech and visual disorders, tremor, muscular incoordination, partial paralysis, etc. Also called: disseminated sclerosis

multiple star *n* a system of three or more stars associated by gravitation. See also **binary star**

multiple store *n* one of several retail enterprises under the same ownership and management. Also called: **multiple shop**

multiplet ('mʌltɪˌplɛt, -plɪt) *n* *physics* **1** a set of closely spaced lines in a spectrum, resulting from small differences between the energy levels of atoms or molecules **2** a group of related elementary particles that differ only in electric charge [from MULTIPLE; on the model of DOUBLET]

multiple voting *n* the practice of voting in more than one constituency in the same election

multiplex ('mʌltɪˌplɛks) *n* **1** *telecomm* **a** the use of a common communications channel for sending two or more messages or signals. In **frequency-division multiplex** the frequency band transmitted by the common channel is split into narrower bands each of which constitutes a distinct channel. In **time-division multiplex** different channels are established by intermittent connections to the common channel **b** (*as modifier*): *a multiplex transmitter* **2 a** a purpose-built complex containing a number of cinemas and usually a restaurant or bar **b** (*as modifier*): *a multiplex cinema* ▷ *adj* **3** designating a method of map-making using three cameras to produce a stereoscopic effect **4** a less common word for **multiple** ▷ *vb* **5** to send (messages or signals) or (of messages or signals) be sent by multiplex [c16 from Latin: having many folds, from MULTI- + *plicāre* to fold] > 'multi,plexer *n*

multiplexer *or* **multiplexor** ('mʌltɪˌplɛksə) *n* *computing* a device that enables the simultaneous transmission of several messages or signals over one communications channel

multiplicand (ˌmʌltɪplɪ'kænd) *n* a number to be multiplied by another number, the **multiplier** [c16 from Latin *multiplicandus*, gerund of *multiplicāre* to MULTIPLY]

multiplicate ('mʌltɪplɪˌkeɪt) *adj* *rare* manifold

multiplication (ˌmʌltɪplɪ'keɪʃən) *n* **1** an arithmetical operation, defined initially in terms of repeated addition, usually written $a × b$, $a.b$, or ab, by which the product of two quantities is calculated: to multiply a by a positive integral b is to add a to itself b times. Multiplication by fractions can then be defined in the light of the associative and commutative properties; multiplication by $1/n$ is equivalent to multiplication by 1 followed by division by n: for example $0.3 × 0.7 = 0.3 × 7/10 = (0.3 × 7)/10 = 2.1/10 = 0.21$ **2** the act of multiplying or state of being multiplied **3** the act or process in animals, plants, or people of reproducing or breeding > ˌmultipli'cational *adj*

multiplication sign *n* the symbol ×, placed between numbers to be multiplied, as in $3 × 4 × 5 = 60$

multiplication table *n* one of a group of tables giving the results of multiplying two numbers together

multiplicative ('mʌltɪplɪˌkeɪtɪv, ˌmʌltɪ'plɪkətɪv) *adj* **1** tending or able to multiply **2** *maths* involving multiplication > 'multipli,catively *adv*

multiplicity (ˌmʌltɪ'plɪsɪtɪ) *n*, *pl* -ties **1** a large number or great variety **2** the state of being multiple **3** *physics* **a** the number of levels into which the energy of an atom, molecule, or nucleus splits as a result of coupling between orbital angular momentum and spin angular momentum **b** the number of elementary particles in a multiplet

multiplier ('mʌltɪˌplaɪə) *n* **1** a person or thing that multiplies **2** the number by which another number, the **multiplicand** is multiplied **3** *physics* any device or instrument, such as a

photomultiplier, for increasing an effect **4** *economics* **a** the ratio of the total change in income (resulting from successive rounds of spending) to an initial autonomous change in expenditure **b** (*as modifier*): *multiplier effects*

multiply ('mʌltɪˌplaɪ) *vb* -plies, -plying, -plied **1** to increase or cause to increase in number, quantity, or degree **2** (*tr*) to combine (two numbers or quantities) by multiplication **3** (*intr*) to increase in number by reproduction [c13 from Old French *multiplier*, from Latin *multiplicāre* to multiply, from *multus* much, many + *plicāre* to fold] > 'multi,pliable *or* 'multi,plicable *adj*

multiprocessor (ˌmʌltɪ'prəʊsɛsə) *n* *computing* a number of central processing units linked together to enable parallel processing to take place

multiprogramming (ˌmʌltɪ'prəʊɡræmɪŋ) *n* a time-sharing technique by which several computer programs are each run for a short period in rotation

multipurpose (ˌmʌltɪ'pɜːpəs) *adj* able to be used for many purposes: *a multipurpose gadget*

multipurpose vehicle *n* a large car, similar to a van, designed to carry up to eight passengers. Abbreviation: MPV

multiracial (ˌmʌltɪ'reɪʃəl) *adj* comprising people of many races > ˌmulti'racialism *n*

multirole ('mʌltɪˌrəʊl) *adj* having a number of roles, functions, etc

multiseriate (ˌmʌltɪ'sɪərɪeɪt) *adj* *botany* arranged in rows or composed of more than one cell layer

multi-skilled *adj* possessing or trained in more than one skill or area of expertise

multi-skilling *n* the practice of training employees to do a number of different tasks

multistage ('mʌltɪˌsteɪdʒ) *adj* **1** (of a rocket or missile) having several stages, each of which can be jettisoned after it has burnt out **2** (of a turbine, compressor, or supercharger) having more than one rotor **3** (of any process or device) having more than one stage

multistorey (ˌmʌltɪ'stɔːrɪ) *adj* **1** (of a building) having many storeys ▷ *n* **2** a multistorey car park

multitask ('mʌltɪˌtɑːsk) *vb* (*intr*) to work at several different tasks simultaneously

multitasking ('mʌltɪˌtɑːskɪŋ) *n* **1** *computing* the execution of various diverse tasks simultaneously **2** the carrying out of two or more tasks at the same time by one person

multitrack ('mʌltɪˌtræk) *adj* (in sound recording) using tape containing two or more tracks, usually four to twenty-four

multitude ('mʌltɪˌtjuːd) *n* **1** a large gathering of people **2** **the** the common people **3** a large number **4** the state or quality of being numerous [c14 via Old French from Latin *multitūdō*]

multitudinous (ˌmʌltɪ'tjuːdɪnəs) *adj* **1** very numerous **2** *rare* great in extent, variety, etc **3** *poetic* crowded > ˌmulti'tudinously *adv* > ˌmulti'tudinousness *n*

multi-user *adj* (of a computer) capable of being used by several people at once

multi-utility *n*, *pl* -ties a public utility that provides more than one essential service, such as supplying both gas and electricity

multivalent (ˌmʌltɪ'veɪlənt) *adj* another word for **polyvalent**. > ˌmulti'valency *n*

multivariate (ˌmʌltɪ'vɛərɪɪt) *adj* *statistics* (of a distribution) involving a number of distinct, though not usually independent, random variables

multiverse ('mʌltɪˌvɜːs) *n* *astronomy* the aggregate of all existing matter, of which the universe is but a tiny fragment

multiversity (ˌmʌltɪ'vɜːsɪtɪ) *n* *chiefly US and Canadian* a university with many constituent and affiliated institutions [c20 MULTI- + UNIVERSITY]

multivibrator (ˌmʌltɪvaɪ'breɪtə) *n* an electronic oscillator consisting of two transistors or other electronic devices, coupled so that the input of each is derived from the output of the other

multivocal (ˌmʌltɪ'vəʊkᵊl) *adj* having many meanings [c19 from Latin *multus* many + *vocare* to call; on the model of EQUIVOCAL]

multiwindow (ˌmʌltɪ'wɪndəʊ) *n* a visual display unit screen that can be divided to show a number of different documents simultaneously

multum in parvo ('mʊltʊm ɪn 'pɑːvəʊ) much in a small space [Latin]

multure ('mʌltʃə) *n* *Scot* **1** a fee formerly paid to a miller for grinding grain **2** the right to receive such a fee [c13 from Old French *moulture*, from Medieval Latin *molitūra* a grinding, from Latin *molere*]

mum¹ (mʌm) *n* *chiefly Brit* an informal word for **mother¹** [c19 a child's word]

mum² (mʌm) *adj* **1** keeping information to oneself; silent ▷ *n* **2** **mum's the word** silence or secrecy is to be observed [c14 suggestive of closed lips]

mum³ *or* **mumm** (mʌm) *vb* mums, mumming, mummed (*intr*) to act in a mummer's play [c16 verbal use of MUM²]

mum⁴ (mʌm) *n* *Brit* *obsolete* a type of beer made from cereals, beans, etc [c17 from German *Mumme*, perhaps from the name of its original brewer]

Mumbai ('mʊmˌbaɪ) *n* the official and Hindi name for **Bombay**

mumble ('mʌmbᵊl) *vb* **1** to utter indistinctly, as with the mouth partly closed; mutter **2** *rare* to chew (food) ineffectually or with difficulty ▷ *n* **3** an indistinct or low utterance or sound [c14 *momelen*, from MUM²] > 'mumbler *n* > 'mumbling *adj* > 'mumblingly *adv*

mumbletypeg ('mʌmbᵊltɪˌpɛɡ) *n* *US* a game in which players throw a knife in various prescribed ways, the aim being to make the blade stick in the ground [c17 from *mumble the peg*, a loser in the game being required to pull the knife out of the ground using the teeth]

mumbo jumbo ('mʌmbəʊ) *n*, *pl* mumbo jumbos **1** foolish religious reverence, ritual, or incantation **2** meaningless or unnecessarily complicated language **3** an object of superstitious awe or reverence [c18 probably from Mandingo *mama dyumbo*, name of a tribal god]

mumchance ('mʌmˌtʃɑːns) *adj* silent; struck dumb [c16 (masquerade, dumb show): from Middle Low German *mummenschanze* masked serenade; from *mummen* (see MUMMER) + *schanze* CHANCE]

mu meson (mjuː) *n* a former name for **muon**

mummer ('mʌmə) *n* **1** one of a group of masked performers in folk play or mime **2** a mime artist **3** *humorous or derogatory* an actor [c15 from Old French *momeur*, from *momer* to mime; related to *momon* mask]

Mummerset ('mʌmˌəsɪt, -ˌsɛt) *n* an imitation West Country accent used in drama [c20 from MUMMER + (SOMER)SET]

mummery ('mʌmərɪ) *n*, *pl* -meries **1** a performance by mummers **2** hypocritical or ostentatious ceremony

mummify ('mʌmɪˌfaɪ) *vb* -fies, -fying, -fied **1** (*tr*) to preserve the body of (a human or animal) as a mummy **2** (*intr*) to dry up; shrivel **3** (*tr*) to preserve (an outdated idea, institution, etc) while making lifeless > ˌmummifi'cation *n*

mummy¹ ('mʌmɪ) *n*, *pl* -mies **1** an embalmed or preserved body, esp as prepared for burial in ancient Egypt **2** *obsolete* the substance of such a body used medicinally **3** a mass of pulp **4** a dark brown pigment [c14 from Old French *momie*, from Medieval Latin *mumia*, from Arabic *mūmiyah*, from Persian *mūm* wax]

mummy² ('mʌmɪ) *n*, *pl* -mies *chiefly Brit* a child's word for **mother** [c19 variant of MUM¹]

mummy bag *n* a sleeping bag with a hood [c20 so called because the wearer resembles a mummified body]

mump¹ (mʌmp) *vb* (*intr*) *archaic* to be silent [c16 (to grimace, sulk, be silent): of imitative origin, alluding to the shape of the mouth when mumbling or chewing]

mump² (mʌmp) *vb* (*intr*) *archaic* to beg [C17 perhaps from Dutch *mompen* to cheat]

mumps (mʌmps) *n* (*functioning as singular or plural*) an acute contagious viral disease of the parotid salivary glands, characterized by swelling of the affected parts, fever, and pain beneath the ear: usually affects children. Also called: epidemic parotitis [C16 from MUMP¹ (to grimace)] > 'mumpish *adj*

mumsy ('mʌmzɪ) *adj* -sier, -siest out of fashion; homely or drab

munch (mʌntʃ) *vb* to chew (food) steadily, esp with a crunching noise [C14 *monche*, of imitative origin; compare CRUNCH] > 'muncher *n*

Munchausen (*German* 'mʏnçhauzən) *n* 1 an exaggerated story 2 a person who tells such a story [C19 after Baron *Münchhausen*, subject of a series of exaggerated adventure tales written in English by R. E. Raspe (1737–94)]

Munchausen's syndrome *n* a mental disorder in which a patient feigns illness to obtain hospital treatment

Munchausen's syndrome by proxy *or* **Munchausen by proxy** *n* a mental disorder in which an individual derives emotional satisfaction from inflicting injury on others and then subjecting them to medical treatment

München ('mʏnçən) *n* the German name for Munich

München-Gladbach (mʏnçən'glatbax) *n* the former name of **Mönchengladbach**

munchies ('mʌntʃɪz) *pl n slang* 1 the a craving for food, induced by alcohol or drugs 2 snacks or food collectively

munchkin ('mʌntʃkɪn) *n* 1 *informal, chiefly US* an undersized person or a child, esp an appealing one 2 a breed of medium-sized cat with short legs [C20 from the *Munchkins*, a dwarfish race of people in L. Frank Baum's *The Wonderful Wizard of Oz* (1900)]

Munda ('mʊndə) *n* 1 a family of languages spoken by scattered peoples throughout central India 2 (*pl* -das) a member of any of these peoples

mundane (mʌndeɪn, mʌn'deɪn) *adj* 1 everyday, ordinary, or banal 2 relating to the world or worldly matters [C15 from French *mondain*, via Late Latin, from Latin *mundus* world] > 'mundanely *adv* > mun'danity *or* 'mundaneness *n*

mung (mʌŋ) *vb* (*tr*) *computing jargon* to process (computer data) [C20 *m*(ash) *u*(ntil) *n*(o) *g*(ood)]

munga ('mʌŋgə) *n NZ informal* an army canteen [C20 perhaps from French *manger* to eat or from Māori *manga* food remains]

mung bean (mʌŋ) *n* 1 an E Asian bean plant, *Phaseolus aureus,* grown for forage and as the source of bean sprouts used in oriental cookery 2 the seed of this plant [C20 *mung,* changed from *mungo,* from Tamil *mūngu,* ultimately from Sanskrit *mudga*]

mungo ('mʌŋgəʊ), **mongo** *or* **mongoe** *n, pl* -gos *or* -goes a cheap felted fabric made from waste wool [C19 of unknown origin]

Munich ('mju:nɪk) *n* a city in S Germany, capital of the state of Bavaria, on the Isar River: became capital of Bavaria in 1508; headquarters of the Nazi movement in the 1920s; a major financial, commercial, and manufacturing centre. Pop: 1 247 873 (2003 est). German name: München

Munich Pact *or* **Agreement** *n* the pact signed by Germany, the United Kingdom, France, and Italy on Sept 29, 1938, to settle the crisis over Czechoslovakia, by which the Sudetenland was ceded to Germany

municipal (mju:'nɪsɪpºl) *adj* of or relating to a town, city, or borough or its local government [C16 from Latin *mūnicipium* a free town, from *mūniceps* citizen from *mūnia* responsibilities + *capere* to take] > mu'nicipalism *n* > mu'nicipalist *n* > mu'nicipally *adv*

municipality (mju:ˌnɪsɪ'pælɪtɪ) *n, pl* -ties 1 a city, town, or district enjoying some degree of local

self-government 2 the governing body of such a unit

municipalize *or* **municipalise** (mju:'nɪsɪpəˌlaɪz) *vb* (*tr*) 1 to bring under municipal ownership or control 2 to make a municipality of > muˌnicipali'zation *or* muˌnicipali'sation *n*

munificent (mju:'nɪfɪsənt) *adj* 1 (of a person) very generous 2 (of a gift) generous [C16 back formation from Latin *mūnificentia* liberality, from *munificus,* from *munus* gift + *facere* to make] > mu'nificence *or* mu'nificentness *n* > mu'nificently *adv*

muniment ('mju:nɪmənt) *n rare* a means of defence [C15 via Old French, from Latin *munīre* to defend]

muniments ('mju:nɪmənts) *pl n* 1 *law* the title deeds and other documentary evidence relating to the title to land 2 *archaic* furnishings or supplies

munition (mju:'nɪʃən) *vb* (*tr*) to supply with munitions [C16 via French from Latin *mūnītiō* fortification, from *mūnīre* to fortify. See AMMUNITION] > mu'nitioner *n*

munitions (mju:'nɪʃənz) *pl n* (*sometimes singular*) military equipment and stores, esp ammunition

munnion ('mʌnjən) *n* an archaic word for **mullion** [C16 from *monial* mullion]

Munro (mʌn'rəʊ) *n, pl* Munros *mountaineering* any separate mountain peak over 3000 feet high: originally used of Scotland only but now sometimes extended to other parts of the British Isles [C20 named after Hugh Thomas *Munro* (1856–1919), who published a list of these in 1891]

Munsell scale ('mʌnsºl) *n* a standard chromaticity scale used in specifying colour. It gives approximately equal changes in visual hue [C20 named after A. H. *Munsell* (1858–1918), US inventor]

münster ('mʏnstə) *n* a variant of **muenster**

Munster ('mʌnstə) *n* a province of SW Republic of Ireland: the largest of the four provinces and historically a kingdom; consists of the counties of Clare, Cork, Kerry, Limerick, Tipperary, and Waterford. Capital: Cork. Pop: 1 100 614 (2002). Area: 24 125 sq km (9315 sq miles)

Münster (*German* 'mʏnstər) *n* a city in NW Germany, in North Rhine-Westphalia on the Dortmund-Ems Canal: one of the treaties comprising the Peace of Westphalia (1648) was signed here; became capital of Prussian Westphalia in 1815. Pop: 269 579 (2003 est)

munt (mʊnt) *n South African and Zimbabwean slang, derogatory* a Black African [from Zulu *umuntu* person]

munter ('mʌntə) *n slang* an unattractive person [C20 of unknown origin]

muntin ('mʌntɪn) *n* another name (esp US) for **glazing-bar** [C17 variant of C15 *mountant,* from Old French *montant,* present participle of *monter* to MOUNT]

muntjac *or* **muntjak** ('mʌntˌdʒæk) *n* any small Asian deer of the genus *Muntiacus,* typically having a chestnut-brown coat, small antlers, and a barklike cry. Also called: barking deer [C18 probably changed from Javanese *mindjangan* deer]

muntrie ('mʌntrɪ) *n* a SE Australian myrtaceous shrub, *Kunzea pomifera,* that has green-red edible berries [from a native Australian language]

Muntz metal (mʌnts) *n* a type of brass consisting of three parts copper and two parts zinc, used in casting and extrusion [C19 named after G. F. *Muntz* (1794–1857), English metallurgist]

muon ('mju:ɒn) *n* a positive or negative elementary particle with a mass 207 times that of an electron and spin ½. It was originally called the **mu meson** but is now classified as a lepton [C20 short for MU MESON] > muonic (mju:'ɒnɪk) *adj*

muon-catalysed fusion *n physics* an experimental form of nuclear fusion in which hydrogen and deuterium muonic atoms are formed. Because the mass of the muon is much larger than that of the electron, the atoms are smaller, and the nuclei are close enough for

fusion to occur

muonic atom *n physics* an atom in which an orbiting electron has been replaced by a muon

muppet ('mʌpɪt) *n slang* a stupid person [C20 from the name for the puppets used in the television programme *The Muppet Show*]

murage ('mjʊərɪdʒ) *n Brit archaic* a tax levied for the construction or maintenance of town walls [C13 from Old French, ultimately from Latin *mūrus* wall]

mural ('mjʊərəl) *n* 1 a large painting or picture on a wall ▷ *adj* 2 of or relating to a wall [C15 from Latin *mūrālis,* from *mūrus* wall] > 'muralist *n*

Murcia (*Spanish* 'mur θja) *n* 1 a region and ancient kingdom of SE Spain, on the Mediterranean: taken by the Moors in the 8th century; an independent Muslim kingdom in the 11th and 12th centuries 2 a city in SE Spain, capital of Murcia province: trading centre for a rich agricultural region; silk industry; university (1915). Pop: 391 146 (2003 est)

murdabad ('mʊədaːˌbaːd) *vb* (*tr*) *Indian* down with; death to: used as part of a slogan in India, Pakistan, etc. Compare **zindabad** [from Urdu, from Persian *murda* dead]

murder ('mɜːdə) *n* 1 the unlawful premeditated killing of one human being by another. Compare **manslaughter, homicide** 2 *informal* something dangerous, difficult, or unpleasant 3 cry blue murder *informal* to make an outcry 4 get away with murder *informal* to escape censure; do as one pleases ▷ *vb* (*mainly tr*) 5 (*also intr*) to kill (someone) unlawfully with premeditation or during the commission of a crime 6 to kill brutally 7 *informal* to destroy: *he murdered her chances of happiness* 8 *informal* to defeat completely; beat decisively: *the home team murdered their opponents* ▷ Also (archaic or dialect): murther [Old English *morthor;* related to Old English *morth,* Old Norse *morth,* Latin *mors* death; compare French *meurtre*] > 'murderer *n* > 'murderess *fem n*

m

murderous ('mɜːdərəs) *adj* 1 intending, capable of, or guilty of murder 2 *informal* very dangerous, difficult, or unpleasant: *a murderous road* > 'murderously *adv* > 'murderousness *n*

mure (mjʊə) *vb* (*tr*) an archaic or literary word for **immure** [C14 from Old French *murer,* from Latin *mūrus* wall]

Mureş ('mʊəreʃ) *n* a river in SE central Europe, rising in central Romania in the Carpathian Mountains and flowing west to the Tisza River at Szeged, Hungary. Length: 885 km (550 miles). Hungarian name: Maros

murex ('mjʊəreks) *n, pl* murices ('mjʊərɪˌsiːz) any of various spiny-shelled marine gastropods of the genus *Murex* and related genera: formerly used as a source of the dye Tyrian purple [C16 from Latin *mūrex* purple fish; related to Greek *muax* sea mussel]

muriate ('mjʊərɪɪt, -ˌeɪt) *n* an obsolete name for a **chloride** [C18 back formation from *muriatic;* see MURIATIC ACID]

muriatic acid (ˌmjʊərɪ'ætɪk) *n* a former name for **hydrochloric acid** [C17 from Latin *muriāticus* pickled, from *muria* brine]

muricate ('mjʊərɪˌkeɪt) *or* **muricated** *adj biology* having a surface roughened by numerous short points: *muricate stems* [C17 from Latin *mūricātus* pointed like a MUREX]

murine ('mjʊəraɪn, -rɪn) *adj* 1 of, relating to, or belonging to the *Muridae,* an Old World family of rodents, typically having long hairless tails: includes rats and mice 2 resembling a mouse or rat ▷ *n* 3 any animal belonging to the *Muridae* [C17 from Latin *mūrīnus* of mice, from *mūs* MOUSE]

murk *or* **mirk** (mɜːk) *n* 1 gloomy darkness ▷ *adj* 2 an archaic variant of **murky** [C13 probably from Old Norse *myrkr* darkness; compare Old English *mirce* dark]

murky *or* **mirky** ('mɜːkɪ) *adj* murkier, murkiest *or* mirkier, mirkiest 1 gloomy or dark 2 cloudy or impenetrable as with smoke or fog > 'murkily *or* 'mirkily *adv* > 'murkiness *or* 'mirkiness *n*

Murman Coast ('moəmən) *or* **Murmansk Coast** *n* a coastal region of NW Russia, in the north of the Kola Peninsula within the Arctic Circle, but ice-free

Murmansk (*Russian* 'murmənsk) *n* a port in NW Russia, on the Kola Inlet of the Barents Sea: founded in 1915; the world's largest town north of the Arctic Circle, with a large fishing fleet. Pop: 316 000 (2005 est)

murmur ('mɜːmə) *n* **1** a continuous low indistinct sound, as of distant voices **2** an indistinct utterance: *a murmur of satisfaction* **3** a complaint; grumble: *he made no murmur at my suggestion* **4** *med* any abnormal soft blowing sound heard within the body, usually over the chest. See also **heart murmur** ▷ *vb* -murs, -muring, -mured **5** to utter (something) in a murmur **6** (*intr*) to complain in a murmur [c14 as n, from Latin *murmur*; vb via Old French *murmurer* from Latin *murmurāre* to rumble] > 'murmurer *n* > 'murmuring *n, adj* > 'murmuringly *adv* > 'murmurous *adj*

murphy ('mɜːfɪ) *n, pl* -phies a dialect or informal word for **potato** [c19 from the common Irish surname *Murphy*]

Murphy bed *n US and Canadian* a bed designed to be folded or swung into a cabinet when not in use [c20 named after William *Murphy*, US inventor]

Murphy's Law *n informal* another term for **Sod's law** [c20 of uncertain origin]

murra ('mʌrə) *n* See **murrhine** (sense 2)

murragh ('mʌrə) *n* an angler's name for the **great red sedge**, a large caddis fly, *Phryganea grandis*, of still and running water, esteemed by trout [perhaps from MURREY]

murrain ('mʌrɪn) *n archaic* **1** any plaguelike disease in cattle **2** a plague [c14 from Old French *morine*, from *morir* to die, from Latin *morī*]

Murray ('mʌrɪ) *n* a river in SE Australia, rising in New South Wales and flowing northwest into SE South Australia, then south into the sea at Encounter Bay: the main river of Australia, important for irrigation and power. Length: 2590 km (1609 miles)

Murray cod *n* a large Australian freshwater fish, *Maccullochella peeli*, chiefly of the Murray and Darling rivers

murre (mɜː) *n US and Canadian* any guillemot of the genus *Uria* [c17 origin unknown]

murree *or* **murri** ('mʌrɪ) *n, pl* -rees *or* -ris a native Australian [c19 from a native Australian language]

murrelet ('mɜːlɪt) *n* any of several small diving birds of the genus *Brachyramphus* and related genera, similar and related to the auks: family *Alcidae*, order *Charadriiformes* [c19 from MURRE + -LET]

murrey ('mʌrɪ) *adj Brit archaic* mulberry-coloured [c14 from Old French *moré*, ultimately from Latin *mōrum* mulberry]

murrhine *or* **murrine** ('mʌraɪn, -ɪn) *adj* **1** of or relating to an unknown substance used in ancient Rome to make vases, cups, etc ▷ *n* **2** Also called: **murra** the substance so used [c16 from Latin *murr(h)inus* belonging to *murra*]

murrhine glass *n* a type of Eastern glassware made from fluorspar and decorated with pieces of coloured metal

Murrumbidgee (,mʌrəm'bɪdʒɪ) *n* a river in SE Australia, rising in S New South Wales and flowing north and west to the Murray River: important for irrigation. Length: 1690 km (1050 miles)

murther ('mɜːðə) *n, vb* an archaic word for **murder**. > 'murtherer *n*

murti ('muːrtɪ) *n Hinduism* an image of a deity, which itself is considered divine once consecrated [from Sanskrit, literally: embodiment]

mus. *abbreviation for* **1** museum **2** music

musaceous (mju:'zeɪʃəs) *adj* of, relating to, or belonging to the *Musaceae*, a family of tropical flowering plants having large leaves and clusters of elongated berry fruits: includes the banana, edible plantain, and Manila hemp [c19 from New Latin *Mūsāceae*, from *Mūsa* genus name, from Arabic *mawzah* banana]

Musaf *Hebrew* (mʊ'saf; *Yiddish* 'mʊsəf) *n Judaism* the additional prayers added to the morning service on Sabbaths, festivals, and Rosh Chodesh [literally: addition]

musar *Hebrew* (mʊ'sa:; *Yiddish* 'mʊsə) *n Judaism* **1** rabbinic literature concerned with ethics, right conduct, etc **2** any moralizing speech, esp one which is critical [literally: instruction]

MusB *or* **MusBac** *abbreviation for* Bachelor of Music

Musca ('mʌskə) *n, Latin genitive* Muscae ('mʌski:) a small constellation in the S hemisphere lying between the Southern Cross and Chamaeleon [Latin: a fly]

muscadel *or* **muscadelle** (,mʌskə'dɛl) *n* another name for **muscatel**

Muscadet ('mʌskə,deɪ; *French* myskadɛ) *n* (*sometimes not capital*) **1** a white grape, grown esp in the Loire valley, used for making wine **2** any of various dry white wines made from this grape [c20 from the region of Brittany where the grape was first grown]

muscadine ('mʌskədɪn, -,daɪn) *n* **1** a woody climbing vitaceous plant, *Vitis rotundifolia*, of the southeastern US **2** Also called: **scuppernong, bullace grape** the thick-skinned musk-scented purple grape produced by this plant: used to make wine [c16 from MUSCADEL]

muscae volitantes ('mʌsiː vɒlɪ'tænti:z) *pl n pathol* moving black specks or threads seen before the eyes, caused by opaque fragments floating in the vitreous humour or a defect in the lens [c18 New Latin: flying flies]

muscarine ('mʌskərɪn, -,ri:n) *n* a poisonous alkaloid occurring in certain mushrooms. Formula: $C_9H_{21}NO_3$ [c19 from Latin *muscārius* of flies, from *musca* fly]

muscat ('mʌskət, -kæt) *n* **1** any of various grapevines that produce sweet white grapes used for making wine or raisins **2** another name for **muscatel** (sense 1) [c16 via Old French from Provençal *muscat*, from *musc* MUSK]

Muscat ('mʌskət, -kæt) *n* the capital of the Sultanate of Oman, a port on the Gulf of Oman: a Portuguese port from the early 16th century; controlled by Persia (1650–1741). Pop: 689 000 (2005 est). Arabic name: **Masqat**

Muscat and Oman *n* the former name (until 1970) of (the Sultanate of) **Oman**

muscatel (,mʌskə'tɛl), **muscadel** *or* **muscadelle** *n* **1** Also called: **muscat** a rich sweet wine made from muscat grapes **2** the grape or raisin from a muscat vine [c14 from Old French *muscadel*, from Old Provençal, from *moscadel*, from *muscat* musky. See MUSK]

muscid ('mʌsɪd) *n* **1** any fly of the dipterous family *Muscidae*, including the housefly and tsetse fly ▷ *adj* **2** of, relating to, or belonging to the *Muscidae* [c19 via New Latin from Latin *musca* fly]

muscle ('mʌsəl) *n* **1** a tissue composed of bundles of elongated cells capable of contraction and relaxation to produce movement in an organ or part **2** an organ composed of muscle tissue **3** strength or force ▷ *vb* (*intr; often foll by in, on, etc*) *informal* to force one's way (in) [c16 from medical Latin *musculus* little mouse, from the imagined resemblance of some muscles to mice, from Latin *mūs* mouse] > 'muscly *adj*

muscle-bound *adj* **1** having overdeveloped and inelastic muscles **2** lacking flexibility

muscle fibre *n* any of the numerous elongated contractile cells that make up striated muscle

muscleman ('mʌsəl,mæn) *n, pl* -men **1** a man with highly developed muscles **2** a henchman employed by a gangster to intimidate or use violence upon victims

muscle mary *n, pl* maries *informal* a homosexual man who practises bodybuilding

muscle sense *n* another name for **kinaesthesia**

muscovado *or* **muscavado** (,mʌskə'vɑ:dəʊ) *n* raw sugar obtained from the juice of sugar cane by evaporating the molasses [c17 from Portuguese *açúcar mascavado* separated sugar; *mascavado* from *mascavar* to separate, probably from Latin]

muscovite ('mʌskə,vaɪt) *n* a pale brown, or green, or colourless mineral of the mica group, found in plutonic rocks such as granite and in sedimentary rocks. It is used in the manufacture of lubricants, insulators, paints, and Christmas "snow". Composition: potassium aluminium silicate. Formula: $KAl_2(AlSi_3)O_{10}(OH)_2$. Crystal structure: monoclinic. See also **mica** [c19 from the phrase *Muscovy glass*, an early name for mica]

Muscovite ('mʌskə,vaɪt) *n* **1** a native or inhabitant of Moscow ▷ *adj* **2** an archaic word for **Russian**

Muscovy ('mʌskəvɪ) *n* **1** a Russian principality (13th to 16th centuries), of which Moscow was the capital **2** an archaic name for **Russia** and **Moscow**

Muscovy duck *or* **musk duck** *n* a large crested widely domesticated South American duck, *Cairina moschata*, having a greenish-black plumage with white markings and a large red caruncle on the bill [c17 originally *musk duck*, a name later mistakenly associated with MUSCOVY]

muscular ('mʌskjʊlə) *adj* **1** having well-developed muscles; brawny **2** of, relating to, or consisting of muscle [c17 from New Latin *muscularis*, from *musculus* MUSCLE] > **muscularity** (,mʌskjʊ'lærɪtɪ) *n* > 'muscularly *adv*

muscular dystrophy *n* a genetic disease characterized by progressive deterioration and wasting of muscle fibres, causing difficulty in walking

musculature ('mʌskjʊlətʃə) *n* **1** the arrangement of muscles in an organ or part **2** the total muscular system of an organism

musculocutaneous (,mʌskjʊləʊkju:'teɪnɪəs) *adj* of, relating to, or supplying the muscles and skin: *musculocutaneous nerve*

musculoskeletal (,mʌskjʊləʊ'skɛlɪt²l) *adj* of or relating to the skeleton and musculature taken together

MusD *or* **MusDoc** *abbreviation for* Doctor of Music

muse¹ (mju:z) *vb* **1** (*when intr, often foll by on or about*) to reflect (about) or ponder (on), usually in silence **2** (*intr*) to gaze thoughtfully ▷ *n* **3** *archaic* a state of abstraction [c14 from Old French *muser*, perhaps from *mus* snout, from Medieval Latin *mūsus*] > 'muser *n* > 'museful *adj* > 'musefully *adv*

muse² (mju:z) *n* a goddess that inspires a creative artist, esp a poet [c14 from Old French, from Latin *Mūsa*, from Greek *Mousa* a Muse]

Muse (mju:z) *n Greek myth* any of nine sister goddesses, each of whom was regarded as the protectress of a different art or science. Daughters of Zeus and Mnemosyne, the nine are Calliope, Clio, Erato, Euterpe, Melpomene, Polyhymnia, Terpsichore, Thalia, and Urania

museology (,mju:zɪ'ɒlədʒɪ) *n* the science of museum organization > ,museo'logical *adj* > ,muse'ologist *n*

musette (mju:'zɛt; *French* myzɛt) *n* **1** a type of bagpipe with a bellows popular in France during the 17th and 18th centuries **2** a dance, with a drone bass originally played by a musette [c14 from Old French, diminutive of *muse* bagpipe]

musette bag *n US* an army officer's haversack

museum (mju:'zɪəm) *n* a place or building where objects of historical, artistic, or scientific interest are exhibited, preserved, or studied [c17 via Latin from Greek *Mouseion* home of the Muses, from *Mousa* MUSE]

museum beetle *n* See **dermestid**

museum piece *n* **1** an object of sufficient age or interest to be kept in a museum **2** *informal* a person or thing regarded as antiquated or decrepit

mush¹ (mʌʃ) *n* **1** a soft pulpy mass or consistency **2** *US* a thick porridge made from corn meal **3** *informal* cloying sentimentality **4** *radio* interference in reception, esp a hissing noise ▷ *vb*

5 (*tr*) to reduce (a substance) to a soft pulpy mass [C17 from obsolete *moose* porridge; probably related to MASH; compare Old English *mōs* food]

mush² (mʌʃ) *Canadian* ▷ *interj* **1** an order to dogs in a sled team to start up or go faster ▷ *vb* **2** to travel by or drive a dog sled **3** (*intr*) to travel on foot, esp with snowshoes ▷ *n* **4** a journey with a dogsled [C19 perhaps from French *marchez* or *marchons*, imperatives of *marcher* to advance] > 'musher *n*

mush³ (muʃ) *n Brit* a slang word for **face** (sense 1) [C19 from MUSH¹, alluding to the softness of the face]

mush⁴ (muʃ) *n Brit slang* a familiar or contemptuous term of address [C19 probably from Gypsy *moosh* a man]

mush area *n* a region where signals from two or more radio transmitters overlap, causing fading and distortion

mushroom ('mʌʃruːm, -rʊm) *n* **1 a** the fleshy spore-producing body of any of various basidiomycetous fungi, typically consisting of a cap (see **pileus**) at the end of a stem arising from an underground mycelium. Some species, such as the field mushroom, are edible. Compare **toadstool b** (*as modifier*): *mushroom soup* **2** the fungus producing any of these structures **3 a** something resembling a mushroom in shape or rapid growth **b** (*as modifier*): *mushroom expansion* ▷ *vb* (*intr*) **4** to grow rapidly: *demand mushroomed overnight* **5** to assume a mushroom-like shape **6** to gather mushrooms [C15 from Old French *mousseron*, from Late Latin *mussiriō*, of obscure origin]

mushroom cloud *n* the large mushroom-shaped cloud of dust, debris, etc produced by a nuclear explosion

mushy ('mʌʃɪ) *adj* mushier, mushiest **1** soft and pulpy **2** *informal* excessively sentimental or emotional > 'mushily *adv* > 'mushiness *n*

music ('mjuːzɪk) *n* **1** an art form consisting of sequences of sounds in time, esp tones of definite pitch organized melodically, harmonically, rhythmically and according to tone colour **2** such an art form characteristic of a particular people, culture, or tradition: *Indian music; rock music; baroque music* **3** the sounds so produced, esp by singing or musical instruments **4** written or printed music, such as a score or set of parts **5** any sequence of sounds perceived as pleasing or harmonious **6** *rare* a group of musicians: *the Queen's music* **7 face the music** *informal* to confront the consequences of one's actions **8 music to one's ears** something that is very pleasant to hear: *his news is music to my ears* [C13 via Old French from Latin *mūsica*, from Greek *mousikē (tekhnē)* (art) belonging to the Muses, from *Mousa* MUSE]

musical ('mjuːzɪkᵊl) *adj* **1** of, relating to, or used in music: *a musical instrument* **2** harmonious; melodious: *musical laughter* **3** talented in or fond of music **4** involving or set to music: *a musical evening* ▷ *n* **5** short for **musical comedy**. > 'musically *adv* > 'musicalness or ,musi'cality *n*

musical chairs *n* (*functioning as singular*) **1** a party game in which players walk around chairs while music is played, there being one fewer chair than players. Whenever the music stops, the player who fails to find a chair is eliminated **2** any situation involving a number of people in a series of interrelated changes

musical comedy *n* **1** a play or film, usually having a light romantic story, that consists of dialogue interspersed with singing and dancing **2** such plays and films collectively

musicale (,mjuːzɪ'kɑːl) *n US and Canadian* a party or social evening with a musical programme [C19 shortened from French *soirée musicale* musical evening]

musical glasses *pl n* another term for **glass harmonica**

music box *or* **musical box** *n* a mechanical instrument that plays tunes by means of pins on a revolving cylinder striking the tuned teeth of a comblike metal plate, contained in a box

music centre *n* a single hi-fi unit containing eg a turntable, amplifier, radio, cassette player, and compact disc player

music drama *n* **1** an opera in which the musical and dramatic elements are of equal importance and strongly interfused **2** the genre of such operas [C19 translation of German *Musikdrama*, coined by Wagner to describe his later operas]

music hall *n chiefly Brit* **1 a** a variety entertainment consisting of songs, comic turns, etc. US and Canadian name: vaudeville **b** (*as modifier*): *a music-hall song* **2** a theatre at which such entertainments are staged

musician (mjuː'zɪʃən) *n* a person who plays or composes music, esp as a profession > mu'sicianly *adj*

musicianship (mjuː'zɪʃənʃɪp) *n* skill or artistry in performing music

music of the spheres *n* the celestial music supposed by Pythagoras to be produced by the regular movements of the stars and planets

musicology (,mjuːzɪ'kɒlədʒɪ) *n* the scholarly study of music > musicological (,mjuːzɪkə'lɒdʒɪkᵊl) *adj* > ,musico'logically *adv* > ,musi'cologist *n*

music paper *n* paper ruled or printed with a stave for writing music

music roll *n* a roll of perforated paper for use in a mechanical instrument such as a player piano

music stand *n* a frame, usually of wood or metal, upon which a musical score or orchestral part is supported

music theatre *n* a modern musical-dramatic work that is performed on a smaller scale than, and without the conventions of, traditional opera

musique concrète *French* (myzik kɔ̃krɛt) *n* another term for **concrete music**

musjid ('mʌsdʒɪd) *n* a variant spelling of **masjid**

musk (mʌsk) *n* **1** a strong-smelling glandular secretion of the male musk deer, used in perfumery **2** a similar substance produced by certain other animals, such as the civet and otter, or manufactured synthetically **3** any of several scrophulariaceous plants of the genus *Mimulus*, esp the North American *M. moschatus*, which has yellow flowers and was formerly cultivated for its musky scent. See also **monkey flower 4** the smell of musk or a similar heady smell **5** (*modifier*) containing or resembling musk: *musk oil; a musk flavour* [C14 from Late Latin *muscus*, from Greek *moskhos*, from Persian *mushk*, probably from Sanskrit *mushká* scrotum (from the appearance of the musk deer's musk bag), diminutive of *mūsh* MOUSE]

musk deer *n* a small central Asian mountain deer, *Moschus moschiferus*. The male has long tusklike canine teeth and secretes musk

musk duck *n* **1** another name for **Muscovy duck 2** a duck, *Biziura lobata*, inhabiting swamps, lakes, and streams in Australia. The male has a leathery pouch beneath the bill and emits a musky odour

muskeg ('mʌs,kɛg) *n chiefly Canadian* **1** undrained boggy land characterized by sphagnum moss vegetation: *vast areas of muskeg* **2** a bog or swamp of this nature [C19 from Algonquian: grassy swamp]

muskellunge ('mʌskə,lʌndʒ), **maskalonge** ('mæskə,lɒndʒ) *or* **maskanonge** ('mæskə,nɒndʒ) *n, pl* -lunges, -longes, -nonges *or* -lunge, -longe, -nonge a large North American freshwater game fish, *Esox masquinongy*: family *Esocidae* (pikes, etc). Often (informal) shortened to: musky *or* muskie [C18 *maskinunga*, of Algonquian origin; compare Ojibwa *mashkinonge* big pike]

musket ('mʌskɪt) *n* a long-barrelled muzzle-loading shoulder gun used between the 16th and 18th centuries by infantry soldiers [C16 from French *mousquet*, from Italian *moschetto* arrow, earlier: sparrow hawk, from *moscha* a fly, from Latin *musca*]

musketeer (,mʌskɪ'tɪə) *n* (formerly) a soldier armed with a musket

musketry ('mʌskɪtrɪ) *n* **1** muskets or musketeers

collectively **2** the technique of using small arms

muskie ('mʌskɪ) *n Canadian* an informal name for the **muskellunge**

musk mallow *n* **1** a malvaceous plant, *Malva moschata*, of Europe and N Africa, with purple-spotted stems, pink flowers, and a faint scent of musk **2** another name for **abelmosk**

muskmelon ('mʌsk,mɛlən) *n* **1** any of several varieties of the melon *Cucumis melo*, such as the cantaloupe and honeydew **2** the fruit of any of these melons, having ribbed or warty rind and sweet yellow, white, or green flesh with a musky aroma

Muskogean *or* **Muskhogean** (mʌs'kəʊɡiən) *n* a family of North American Indian languages, probably distantly related to the Algonquian family

musk orchid *n* a small Eurasian orchid, *Herminium monorchis*, with dense spikes of musk-scented greenish-yellow flowers

musk ox *n* a large bovid mammal, *Ovibos moschatus*, which has a dark shaggy coat, short legs, and widely spaced downward-curving horns and emits a musky smell: now confined to the tundras of Canada and Greenland

muskrat ('mʌsk,ræt) *n, pl* -rats *or* -rat **1** a North American beaver-like amphibious rodent, *Ondatra zibethica*, closely related to but larger than the voles: family *Cricetidae* **2** the brown fur of this animal **3** either of two closely related rodents, *Ondatra obscurus* or *Neofiber alleni* (**round-tailed muskrat**) ▷ Also called: musquash [C17 by folk etymology, from the same source as MUSQUASH]

musk rose *n* a prickly shrubby Mediterranean rose, *Rosa moschata*, cultivated for its white musk-scented flowers

musk turtle *n* any of several small turtles of the genus *Sternotherus*, esp *S. odoratus* (**common musk turtle** or **stinkpot**), that emit a strong unpleasant odour: family *Kinosternidae*

musky¹ ('mʌskɪ) *adj* muskier, muskiest resembling the smell of musk; having a heady or pungent sweet aroma > 'muskiness *n*

musky² ('mʌskɪ) *n, pl* muskies an informal name for the **muskellunge**

Muslim ('mʊzlɪm, 'mʌz-) *or* **Moslem** *n, pl* -lims *or* -lim **1** a follower of the religion of Islam ▷ *adj* **2** of or relating to Islam, its doctrines, culture, etc ▷ Also (but not in Muslim use): Muhammadan, Muhammedan, Mohammedan [C17 from Arabic, literally: one who surrenders] > 'Muslimism *or* 'Moslemism *n*

muslin ('mʌzlɪn) *n* a fine plain-weave cotton fabric [C17 from French *mousseline*, from Italian *mussolina*, from Arabic *mawṣiliy* of Mosul, from *Mawṣil* Mosul, Iraq, where it was first produced]

MusM *abbreviation for* Master of Music

muso ('mjuːzəʊ) *n, pl* musos *slang* **1** *Brit derogatory* a musician, esp a pop musician, regarded as being overconcerned with technique rather than musical content or expression **2** *Austral* any musician, esp a professional one

musquash ('mʌskwɒʃ) *n* another name for **muskrat**, esp the fur [C17 from Algonquian: compare Natick *musquash*, Abnaki *muskwessu*]

muss (mʌs) *US and Canadian informal* ▷ *vb* **1** (*tr*; often foll by *up*) to make untidy; rumple ▷ *n* **2** a state of disorder; muddle [C19 probably a blend of MESS + FUSS]

mussel ('mʌsᵊl) *n* **1** any of various marine bivalves of the genus *Mytilus* and related genera, esp *M. edulis* (**edible mussel**), having a dark slightly elongated shell and living attached to rocks, etc, **2** any of various freshwater bivalves of the genera *Anodonta*, *Unio*, etc, attached to rocks, sand, etc having a flattened oval shell (a source of mother-of-pearl). The **zebra mussel**, *Dreissena polymorpha*, can be a serious nuisance in water mains [Old English *muscle*, from Vulgar Latin *muscula* (unattested), from Latin *musculus*, diminutive of *mūs* mouse]

musselcracker ('mʌsᵊl,krækə) *n South African* a

large variety of sea bream, *Sparodon durbanensis*, that feeds on shellfish and is a popular food and game fish

Mussulman *or* **Mussalman** ('mʌsᵊlmən) *n, pl* -mans an archaic word for **Muslim** [c16 from Persian *Musulmān* (pl) from Arabic *Muslimūn*, pl of MUSLIM]

mussy ('mʌsɪ) *adj* mussier, mussiest untidy or disordered > 'mussily *adv* > 'mussiness *n*

must[1] (mʌst; *unstressed* məst, məs) *vb* (takes an infinitive without *to* or an implied infinitive) **1** used as an auxiliary to express obligation or compulsion: *you must pay your dues*. In this sense, *must* does not form a negative. If used with a negative infinitive it indicates obligatory prohibition **2** used as an auxiliary to indicate necessity: *I must go to the bank tomorrow* **3** used as an auxiliary to indicate the probable correctness of a statement: *he must be there by now* **4** used as an auxiliary to indicate inevitability: *all good things must come to an end* **5** used as an auxiliary to express resolution **a** on the part of the speaker when used with *I* or *we*: *I must finish this* **b** on the part of another or others as imputed to them by the speaker, when used with *you, he, she, they*, etc: *let him get drunk if he must* **6** (used emphatically) used as an auxiliary to express conviction or certainty on the part of the speaker: *he must have reached the town by now, surely; you must be joking* **7** (foll by *away*) used with an implied verb of motion to express compelling haste: *I must away* ▷ *n* **8** an essential or necessary thing: *strong shoes are a must for hill walking* [Old English *mōste* past tense of *mōtan* to be allowed, be obliged to; related to Old Saxon *mōtan*, Old High German *muozan*, German *müssen*]

must[2] (mʌst) *n* the newly pressed juice of grapes or other fruit ready for fermentation [Old English, from Latin *mustum* new wine, must, from *mustus* (adj) newborn]

must[3] (mʌst) *n* mustiness or mould [c17 back formation from MUSTY]

must[4] (mʌst) *n* a variant spelling of **musth**

must- *combining form* indicating that something is highly recommended or desirable: *a must-see film; this season's must-haves*

mustache (mə'stɑ:ʃ) *n* the US spelling of **moustache**. > mus'tached *adj*

mustachio (mə'stɑ:ʃɪ,əʊ) *n, pl* -chios (*often plural when considered as two halves*) *often humorous* a moustache, esp when bushy or elaborately shaped [c16 from Spanish *mostacho* and Italian *mostaccio*]

mustachioed (mə'stɑ:ʃɪ,əʊd) *adj often humorous* having a moustache, esp when bushy or elaborately shaped

mustang ('mʌstæŋ) *n* a small breed of horse, often wild or half wild, found in the southwestern US [c19 from Mexican Spanish *mestengo*, from *mesta* a group of stray animals]

mustard ('mʌstəd) *n* **1** any of several Eurasian plants of the genus *Brassica*, esp black mustard and white mustard, having yellow or white flowers and slender pods and cultivated for their pungent seeds: family *Brassicaceae* (crucifers). See also **charlock 2** a paste made from the powdered seeds of any of these plants and used as a condiment **3 a** a brownish-yellow colour **b** (*as adjective*): *a mustard carpet* **4** *slang, chiefly US* zest or enthusiasm **5** cut the mustard *slang* to come up to expectations [c13 from Old French *moustarde*, from Latin *mustum* MUST², since the original condiment was made by adding must]

mustard and cress *n* seedlings of white mustard and garden cress, used in salads

mustard gas *n* an oily liquid vesicant compound used in chemical warfare. Its vapour causes blindness and burns. Formula: (ClCH₂CH₂)₂S

mustard oil *n* an oil that is obtained from mustard seeds and used in making soap

mustard plaster *n med* a mixture of powdered black mustard seeds and an adhesive agent applied to the skin for its relaxing, stimulating, or counterirritant effects

mustee (mʌ'sti:, 'mʌsti:) *or* **mestee** (mɛ'sti:) *n* **1** the offspring of a White and a quadroon **2** any person of mixed ancestry [c17 shortened from MESTIZO]

musteline ('mʌstɪ,laɪn, -lɪn) *adj* **1** of, relating to, or belonging to the *Mustelidae*, a family of typically predatory mammals including weasels, ferrets, minks, polecats, badgers, skunks, and otters: order *Carnivora* (carnivores) ▷ *n* **2** any musteline animal [c17 from Latin *mustēlīnus*, from *mustēla* weasel, from *mūs* mouse + *-tēla*, of unknown origin]

muster ('mʌstə) *vb* **1** to call together (numbers of men) for duty, inspection, etc, or (of men) to assemble in this way **2** muster in *or* out *US* to enlist into or discharge from military service **3** (*tr*) *Austral and NZ* to round up (livestock) **4** (*tr*; sometimes foll by *up*) to summon or gather: *to muster one's arguments; to muster up courage* ▷ *n* **5** an assembly of military personnel for duty, inspection, etc **6** a collection, assembly, or gathering **7** *Austral and NZ* the rounding up of livestock **8** a flock of peacocks **9** pass muster to be acceptable [c14 from old French *moustrer*, from Latin *monstrāre* to show, from *monstrum* portent, omen]

muster roll *n* a list of the officers and men in a regiment, ship's company, etc

musth *or* **must** (mʌst) *n* (often preceded by *in*) a state of frenzied sexual excitement in the males of certain large mammals, esp elephants, associated with discharge from a gland between the ear and eye [c19 from Urdu *mast*, from Persian: drunk]

must-have *n* **1** an essential possession: *the mobile phone is now a must-have for children* ▷ *adj* **2** essential: *a must-have fashion accessory*

musty ('mʌstɪ) *adj* -tier, -tiest **1** smelling or tasting old, stale, or mouldy **2** old-fashioned, dull, or hackneyed: *musty ideas* [c16 perhaps a variant of obsolete *moisty*, influenced by MUST³] > 'mustily *adv* > 'mustiness *n*

mut (mʌt) *n printing* another word for **em** (sense 1) [c20 shortened from MUTTON]

mutable ('mju:təbᵊl) *adj* **1** able to or tending to change **2** *astrology* of or relating to four of the signs of the zodiac, Gemini, Virgo, Sagittarius, and Pisces, which are associated with the quality of adaptability. Compare **cardinal** (sense 9), **fixed** (sense 10) [c14 from Latin *mūtābilis* fickle, from *mūtāre* to change] > muta'bility *or less commonly* 'mutableness *n* > 'mutably *adv*

mutagen ('mju:tədʒən) *n* a substance or agent that can induce genetic mutation [c20 from MUTATION + -GEN] > mutagenic (ˌmju:tə'dʒɛnɪk) *adj* > ˌmutagen'icity *n*

mutagenesis (ˌmju:tə'dʒɛnɪsɪs) *n genetics* the generation, usually intentional, of mutations [c20 from MUTATION + -GENESIS]

mutagenize *or* **mutagenise** ('mju:tədʒə,naɪz) *vb* (*tr*) to subject (cells, DNA, etc) to mutagens to induce mutations

mutant ('mju:tᵊnt) *n* **1** Also called: mutation an animal, organism, or gene that has undergone mutation ▷ *adj* **2** of, relating to, undergoing, or resulting from change or mutation [c20 from Latin *mutāre* to change]

Mutare (mu:'tɑ:rɪ) *n* a city in E Zimbabwe, near the Mozambique border: rail and trade centre in a mining and tobacco-growing region. Pop: 160 000 (2005 est). Former name (until 1982): **Umtali**

mutate (mju:'teɪt) *vb* to undergo or cause to undergo mutation [c19 from Latin *mūtātus* changed, from *mūtāre* to change] > **mutative** ('mju:tətɪv, mju:'teɪtɪv) *adj*

mutation (mju:'teɪʃən) *n* **1** the act or process of mutating; change; alteration **2** a change or alteration **3** a change in the chromosomes or genes of a cell. When this change occurs in the gametes the structure and development of the resultant offspring may be affected. See also **inversion** (sense 11) **4** another word for **mutant**

(sense 1) **5** a physical characteristic of an individual resulting from this type of chromosomal change **6** *phonetics* **a** (in Germanic languages) another name for **umlaut b** (in Celtic languages) a phonetic change in certain initial consonants caused by a preceding word > mu'tational *adj* > mu'tationally *adv*

mutation stop *n* an organ pipe sounding the harmonic of the note normally produced

mutatis mutandis *Latin* (mu:'tɑ:tɪs mu:'tændɪs) the necessary changes having been made

Mutazilite (mu:'tɑ:zɪ,laɪt) *n* a member of an 8th-century liberal Muslim sect, later merged into the Shiahs [from Arabic *mu'tazilah* body of seceders + -ITE¹]

mutch[1] (mʌtʃ) *n* a close-fitting linen cap formerly worn by women and children in Scotland [c15 from Middle Dutch *mutse* cap, from Medieval Latin *almucia* ALMUCE]

mutch[2] (mʌtʃ) *vb dialect* **1** (*tr*) to cadge; beg **2** (*intr*) another word for **mitch**

mutchkin ('mʌtʃkɪn) *n* a Scottish unit of liquid measure equal to slightly less than one pint [c15 from Middle Dutch *mudseken*, from Latin *modius* measure for grain]

mute[1] (mju:t) *adj* **1** not giving out sound or speech; silent **2** unable to speak; dumb **3** unspoken or unexpressed: *mute dislike* **4** *law* (of a person arraigned on indictment) refusing to answer a charge **5** *phonetics* another word for **plosive 6** (of a letter in a word) silent ▷ *n* **7** a person who is unable to speak **8** *law* a person who refuses to plead when arraigned on indictment for an offence **9** any of various devices used to soften the tone of stringed or brass instruments **10** *phonetics* a plosive consonant; stop **11** a silent letter **12** an actor in a dumb show **13** a hired mourner at a funeral ▷ *vb* (*tr*) **14** to reduce the volume of (a musical instrument) by means of a mute, soft pedal, etc **15** to subdue the strength of (a colour, tone, lighting, etc) [c14 *muwet* from Old French *mu*, from Latin *mūtus* silent] > 'mutely *adv* > 'muteness *n*

mute[2] (mju:t) *archaic* ▷ *vb* **1** (of birds) to discharge (faeces) ▷ *n* **2** birds' faeces [c15 from Old French *meutir*, variant of *esmeltir*, of Germanic origin; probably related to SMELT¹ and MELT]

muted ('mju:tɪd) *adj* **1** (of a sound or colour) softened: *a muted pink shirt* **2** (of an emotion or action) subdued or restrained: *his response was muted* **3** (of a musical instrument) being played while fitted with a mute: *muted trumpet*

mute swan *n* a Eurasian swan, *Cygnus olor*, with a pure white plumage, an orange-red bill with a black base, and a curved neck. Compare **whistling swan**

mutha ('mʌðə) *n offensive taboo slang, chiefly US* short for **motherfucker** [c20 from a pronunciation of *mother*]

muti ('mu:tɪ) *n South African informal* medicine, esp herbal medicine [from Zulu *umuthi* tree, medicine]

muticous ('mju:tɪkəs) *adj botany* lacking an awn, spine, or point. Also: **muticate** [c19 from Latin *muticus* awnless, curtailed]

mutilate ('mju:tɪ,leɪt) *vb* (*tr*) **1** to deprive of a limb, essential part, etc; maim; dismember **2** to mar, expurgate, or damage (a text, book, etc) [c16 from Latin *mutilāre* to cut off; related to *mutilus* maimed] > ˌmuti'lation *n* > 'muti,lative *adj* > 'muti,lator *n*

mutineer (ˌmju:tɪ'nɪə) *n* a person who mutinies

mutinous ('mju:tɪnəs) *adj* **1** openly rebellious or disobedient: *a mutinous child* **2** characteristic or indicative of mutiny > 'mutinously *adv* > 'mutinousness *n*

mutiny ('mju:tɪnɪ) *n, pl* -nies **1** open rebellion against constituted authority, esp by seamen or soldiers against their officers ▷ *vb* -nies, -nying, -nied **2** (*intr*) to engage in mutiny [c16 from obsolete *mutine*, from Old French *mutin* rebellious, from *meute* mutiny, ultimately from Latin *movēre* to move]

mutism ('mju:tɪzəm) *n* **1** the state of being mute **2** *psychiatry* **a** a refusal to speak although the mechanism of speech is not damaged **b** the lack of development of speech, due usually to early deafness

mutt (mʌt) *n slang* **1** an inept, ignorant, or stupid person **2** a mongrel dog; cur [C20 shortened from MUTTONHEAD]

mutter ('mʌtə) *vb* **1** to utter (something) in a low and indistinct tone **2** (*intr*) to grumble or complain **3** (*intr*) to make a low continuous murmuring sound ▷ *n* **4** a muttered sound or complaint [C14 *moteren;* related to Norwegian (dialect) *mutra,* Old High German *mutilôn;* compare Old English *mōtian* to speak] > 'mutterer *n* > 'muttering *n, adj* > 'mutteringly *adv*

mutton ('mʌt³n) *n* **1** the flesh of sheep, esp of mature sheep, used as food **2** mutton dressed as lamb an older woman dressed up to look young **3** *printing* another word for **em** (sense 1) Compare **nut** (sense 12) [C13 *moton* sheep, from Old French, from Medieval Latin *multō,* of Celtic origin; the term was adopted in printing to distinguish the pronunciation of *em quad* from *en quad*] > 'muttony *adj*

mutton bird *n* **1** any of several shearwaters, having a dark plumage with greyish underparts, esp the sooty shearwater (*Puffinus griseus*) of New Zealand, which is collected for food by Māoris. It inhabits the Pacific Ocean and in summer nests in Australia and New Zealand *Austral* **2** any of various petrels esp the short tailed shearwater, *Puffinus tenuirostris,* which inhabits the Pacific Ocean and in summer nests in S Australia [C19 so named because their cooked flesh is claimed to taste like mutton]

mutton-birder *n* NZ a person who hunts mutton birds

mutton chop *n* a piece of mutton from the loin

muttonchops ('mʌt³n,tʃɒps) *pl n* side whiskers trimmed in the shape of chops, widening out from the temples

muttonhead ('mʌt³n,hɛd) *n slang* a stupid or ignorant person; fool > 'mutton,headed *adj*

Muttra ('mʌtrə) *n* the former name of **Mathura**

mutual ('mju:tʃʊəl) *adj* **1** experienced or expressed by each of two or more people or groups about the other; reciprocal: *mutual distrust* **2** common to or shared by both or all of two or more parties: *a mutual friend; mutual interests* **3** denoting an insurance company, etc, in which the policyholders share the profits and expenses and there are no shareholders [C16 from Old French *mutuel,* from Latin *mūtuus* reciprocal (originally: borrowed); related to *mūtāre* to change] > mutuality (,mju:tjʊ'ælɪtɪ) *or* 'mutualness *n* > 'mutually *adv*

> USAGE The use of *mutual* to mean *common to or shared by two or more parties* was formerly considered incorrect, but is now acceptable. Tautologous use of *mutual* should be avoided: *cooperation* (not *mutual cooperation*) *between the two countries*

mutual fund *n US and Canadian* an investment trust that issues units for public sale, the holders of which are creditors and not shareholders with their interests represented by a trust company independent of the issuing agency. British equivalent: unit trust

mutual inductance *n* a measure of the mutual induction between two magnetically linked circuits, given as the ratio of the induced electromotive force to the rate of change of current producing it. It is usually measured in henries. Symbol: *M or* L_{12} Also called: coefficient of mutual induction

mutual induction *n* the production of an electromotive force in a circuit by a current change in a second circuit magnetically linked to the first. See also **mutual inductance** Compare **self-induction**

mutual insurance *n* a system of insurance by which all policyholders become company members under contract to pay premiums into a common fund out of which claims are paid. See also **mutual** (sense 3)

mutualism ('mju:tʃʊə,lɪzəm) *n* another name for **symbiosis**. > 'mutualist *n, adj* > ,mutual'istic *adj*

mutualize *or* **mutualise** ('mju:tʃʊə,laɪz) *vb* **1** to make or become mutual **2** (*tr*) *US* to organize or convert (a business enterprise) so that customers or employees own a majority of shares > ,mutuali'zation *or* ,mutuali'sation *n*

mutual savings bank *n chiefly US* a savings bank having no subscribed capital stock and distributing all available net profit to depositors who, however, remain creditors without voting power

mutuel ('mju:tjʊəl) *n* short for **pari-mutuel**

mutule ('mju:tju:l) *n architect* one of a set of flat blocks below the corona of a Doric cornice. Compare **modillion** [C16 via French from Latin *mūtulus* modillion]

muu-muu ('mu:,mu:) *n* a loose brightly-coloured dress worn by women in Hawaii [from Hawaiian]

Muzak ('mju:zæk) *n trademark* recorded light music played in shops, restaurants, factories, etc, to entertain, increase sales or production, etc

muzhik, moujik *or* **mujik** ('mu:ʒɪk) *n* a Russian peasant, esp under the tsars [C16 from Russian: peasant]

muzz (mʌz) *vb* (*tr*) *Brit informal* to make (something) muzzy

muzzle ('mʌz³l) *n* **1** the projecting part of the face, usually the jaws and nose, of animals such as the dog and horse **2** a guard or strap fitted over an animal's nose and jaws to prevent it biting or eating **3** the front end of a gun barrel ▷ *vb* (*tr*) **4** to prevent from being heard or noticed: *to muzzle the press* **5** to put a muzzle on (an animal) **6** to take in (a sail) [C15 *mosel,* from Old French *musel,* diminutive of *muse* snout, from Medieval Latin *mūsus,* of unknown origin] > 'muzzler *n*

muzzle-loader *n* a firearm receiving its ammunition through the muzzle > 'muzzle-,loading *adj*

muzzle velocity *n* the velocity of a projectile as it leaves a firearm's muzzle

muzzy ('mʌzɪ) *adj* -zier, -ziest **1** blurred, indistinct, or hazy **2** confused, muddled, or befuddled [C18 origin obscure] > 'muzzily *adv* > 'muzziness *n*

mv¹ *music abbreviation for* mezzo voce

mv² *the internet domain name for* Maldives

MV *abbreviation for* **1** motor vessel **2** muzzle velocity **3** ▷ *symbol for* megavolt

MVD *abbreviation for* Ministry of Internal Affairs; the police organization in the former Soviet Union, formed in 1946 [from Russian *Ministerstvo vnutrennikh del*]

MVDI (in New Zealand) *abbreviation for* Motor Vehicle Dealers Institute

MVO (in Britain) *abbreviation for* Member of the Royal Victorian Order

MVP (in the US and Australia) *abbreviation for* most valuable player: the man or woman judged to be the outstanding player in a sport during a particular season or championship

MVS *abbreviation for* Master of Veterinary Surgery

MVSc *abbreviation for* Master of Veterinary Science

mw *the internet domain name for* Malawi

MW **1** *symbol for* megawatt **2** *radio abbreviation for* medium wave **3** Master of Wine **4** *international car registration for* Malawi

mwalimu (mwa:'li:mu:) *n E African* a teacher [Swahili]

Mweru ('mwɛəru:) *n* a lake in central Africa, on the border between Zambia and the Democratic Republic of Congo (formerly Zaïre). Area: 4196 sq km (1620 sq miles)

mx *the internet domain name for* Mexico

Mx *physics symbol for* maxwell

MX *US abbreviation for* missile-experimental: an intercontinental ballistic missile with up to ten nuclear warheads

my (maɪ) *determiner* **1** of, belonging to, or associated with the speaker or writer (me): *my own ideas; do you mind my smoking?* **2** used in various forms of address: *my lord; my dear boy* **3** used in various exclamations: *my goodness! ▷ interj* **4** an exclamation of surprise, awe, etc: *my, how you've grown!* [C12 *mī,* variant of Old English *mīn* when preceding a word beginning with a consonant]

> USAGE See at me

my *the internet domain name for* Malaysia

MY *abbreviation for* motor yacht

my- *combining form* a variant of **myo-** before a vowel

myalgia (maɪ'ældʒɪə) *n* pain in a muscle or a group of muscles [C19 from MYO- + -ALGIA] > my'algic *adj*

myalgic encephalopathy (maɪ'ældʒɪk ɛn,sɛfə'lɒpfɪ) *n* a condition characterized by painful muscles, extreme fatigue, and general debility, sometimes occurring as a sequel to viral illness. Also called **chronic fatigue syndrome** Formerly called: myalgic encephalomyelitis Abbreviation: ME

myalism ('maɪə,lɪzəm) *n* a kind of witchcraft, similar to obi, practised esp in the Caribbean [C19 from *myal,* probably of West African origin] > 'myalist *n*

myall ('maɪəl) *n* **1** any of several Australian acacias, esp *Acacia pendula,* having hard scented wood used for fences **2** a native Australian living independently of society [C19 from a native Australian name]

Myanmar *or* **Myanma** ('maɪænma:, 'mjænma:) *n* a republic in SE Asia, on the Bay of Bengal and the Andaman Sea: unified from small states in 1752; annexed by Britain (1823–85) and made a province of India in 1886; became independent in 1948. It is generally mountainous, with the basins of the Chindwin and Irrawaddy Rivers in the central part and the Irrawaddy delta in the south. Official language: Burmese. Religion: Buddhist majority. Currency: kyat. Capital: Yangon. Pop: 50 101 000 (2004 est). Area: 676 577 sq km (261 228 sq miles). Official name: Union of Myanmar Former name (until 1989): Burma

myasthenia (,maɪəs'θi:nɪə) *n* **1** any muscular weakness **2** short for **myasthenia gravis** [C19 from MYO- + ASTHENIA] > myasthenic (,maɪəs'θɛnɪk) *adj*

myasthenia gravis ('gra:vɪs) *n* a chronic progressive disease in which the muscles, esp those of the head and face, become weak and easily fatigued

myc- *combining form* a variant of **myco-** before a vowel

mycelium (maɪ'si:lɪəm) *n, pl* -lia (-lɪə) the vegetative body of fungi: a mass of branching filaments (hyphae) that spread throughout the nutrient substratum [C19 (literally: nail of fungus): from MYCO- + Greek *hēlos* nail] > my'celial *adj* > myceloid ('maɪsɪ,lɔɪd) *adj*

mycella (maɪ'sɛlə) *n* a blue-veined Danish cream cheese, less strongly flavoured than Danish blue [C20 New Latin, from Greek *mukēs* fungus]

Mycenae (maɪ'si:ni:) *n* an ancient Greek city in the NE Peloponnesus on the plain of Argos

Mycenaean (,maɪsɪ'ni:ən) *adj* **1** of or relating to ancient Mycenae or its inhabitants **2** of or relating to the Aegean civilization of Mycenae (1400 to 1100BC)

-mycete *n combining form* indicating a fungus: *ascomycete* [from New Latin *-mycetes,* from Greek *mukētes,* plural of *mukēs* fungus]

myceto- *or before a vowel* **mycet-** *combining form* fungus: *mycetophagous* [from Greek *mukēs* fungus]

mycetoma (,maɪsɪ'təʊmə) *n, pl* -mas *or* -mata (-mətə) a chronic fungal infection, esp of the foot, characterized by swelling, usually resulting from a wound

mycetophagous (,maɪsɪ'tɒfəgəs) *adj zoology* feeding on fungi

mycetozoan (maɪ,si:təʊ'zəʊən) *n* a former name

m

for a **slime mould**

-mycin *n combining form* indicating an antibiotic compound derived from a fungus: *streptomycin* [from Greek *mukēs* fungus + -IN]

myco- or before a vowel **myc-** *combining form* indicating fungus: *mycology* [from Greek *mukēs* fungus]

mycobacterium (ˌmaɪkəʊbækˈtɪərɪəm) *n, pl* -ria (-rɪə) any of the rod-shaped Gram-positive bacteria of the genus *Mycobacterium*, some of which cause human diseases, such as tuberculosis and leprosy

mycobiont (ˌmaɪkəʊˈbaɪɒnt) *n botany* the fungal constituent of a lichen. Compare **phycobiont**

mycol. *abbreviation for* **1** mycological **2** mycology

mycology (maɪˈkɒlədʒɪ) *n* **1** the branch of biology concerned with the study of fungi **2** the fungi of a particular region ▷ **mycological** (ˌmaɪkəˈlɒdʒɪkəl) or ˌmyco'logic *adj* ▷ my'cologist *n*

mycoplasma (ˌmaɪkəʊˈplæzmə) *n* any prokaryotic microorganism of the genus *Mycoplasma*, some species of which cause disease (**mycoplasmosis**) in animals and humans

mycorrhiza or **mycorhiza** (ˌmaɪkəˈraɪzə) *n, pl* -zae (-ziː) or -zas an association of a fungus and a plant in which the fungus lives within or on the outside of the plant's roots forming a symbiotic or parasitic relationship. See **ectotrophic mycorrhiza, endotrophic mycorrhiza** [C19 from MYCO- + Greek *rhiza* root] ▷ ˌmycor'rhizal or ˌmyco'rhizal *adj*

mycosis (maɪˈkəʊsɪs) *n* any infection or disease caused by fungus ▷ **mycotic** (maɪˈkɒtɪk) *adj*

Mycostatin (ˌmaɪkəʊˈstætɪn) *n trademark* (in the US and Australia) a form of **nystatin**

mycotoxin (ˌmaɪkəˈtɒksɪn) *n* any of various toxic substances produced by fungi some of which may affect food and others of which are alleged to have been used in warfare. See also **aflatoxin, yellow rain.** ▷ ˌmyco'toxin'ology *n*

mycotrophic (ˌmaɪkəʊˈtrɒfɪk) *adj botany* (of a plant) symbiotic with a fungus, esp a mycorrhizal fungus

mydriasis (mɪˈdraɪəsɪs, maɪ-) *n* abnormal dilation of the pupil of the eye, produced by drugs, coma, etc [C17 via Late Latin from Greek; origin obscure]

mydriatic (ˌmɪdrɪˈætɪk) *adj* **1** relating to or causing mydriasis ▷ *n* **2** a mydriatic drug

myel- or before a consonant **myelo-** *combining form* the spinal cord or bone marrow: *myeloid* [from Greek *muelos* marrow, spinal cord, from *mus* muscle]

myelencephalon (ˌmaɪɪlɛnˈsɛfəˌlɒn) *n, pl* -lons or -la (-lə) the part of the embryonic hindbrain that develops into the medulla oblongata. Nontechnical name: **afterbrain** ▷ **myelencephalic** (ˌmaɪɪlɛnsəˈfælɪk) *adj*

myelin (ˈmaɪɪlɪn) or **myeline** (ˈmaɪɪˌliːn) *n* a white tissue forming an insulating sheath (**myelin sheath**) around certain nerve fibres. Damage to the myelin sheath causes neurological disease, as in multiple sclerosis ▷ ˌmye'linic *adj*

myelinated (ˈmaɪɪlɪˌneɪtɪd) *adj* (of a nerve fibre) having a myelin sheath

myelitis (ˌmaɪɪˈlaɪtɪs) *n* inflammation of the spinal cord or of the bone marrow

myeloblast (ˈmaɪɪləʊˌblɑːst) *n* a cell that gives rise to a granulocyte, normally occurring in the bone marrow but detected in the blood in certain diseases, esp leukaemia ▷ **myeloblastic** (ˌmaɪɪləʊˈblæstɪk) *adj*

myelocyte (ˈmaɪɪləʊˌsaɪt) *n* an immature granulocyte, normally occurring in the bone marrow but detected in the blood in certain diseases ▷ **myelocytic** (ˌmaɪɪləʊˈsɪtɪk) *adj*

myelogram (ˈmaɪɪlə,græm) *n* an X-ray of the spinal cord, after injection with a radio-opaque medium ▷ ˌmye'lography *n*

myeloid (ˈmaɪɪˌlɔɪd) *adj* of or relating to the spinal cord or the bone marrow

myeloma (ˌmaɪɪˈləʊmə) *n, pl* -mas or -mata

(-mətə) a usually malignant tumour of the bone marrow or composed of cells normally found in bone marrow ▷ ˌmye'loma,toid *adj*

myiasis (ˈmaɪəsɪs) *n, pl* -ses (-ˌsiːz) **1** infestation of the body by the larvae of flies **2** any disease resulting from such infestation [C19 New Latin, from Greek *muia* a fly]

Mykonos (ˈmɪkɒnɒs, -əʊs, ˈmiːkə-) *n* a Greek island in the S Aegean Sea, one of the Cyclades: a popular tourist resort with many churches. Pop: 9306 (2001). Greek name: Míkonos

My Lai (ˈmaɪ ˈlaɪ, ˈmiː) *n* a village in S Vietnam where in 1968 US troops massacred over 400 civilians

mylonite (ˈmaɪlə,naɪt, ˈmɪlə-) *n* a fine-grained metamorphic rock, often showing banding and micaceous fracture, formed by the crushing, grinding, or rolling of the original structure [C19 from Greek *mulōn* mill]

mynah or **myna** (ˈmaɪnə) *n* any of various tropical Asian starlings of the genera *Acridotheres, Gracula*, etc, esp *G. religiosa* (see **hill mynah**), some of which can mimic human speech [C18 from Hindi *mainā*, from Sanskrit *madana*]

Mynheer (məˈnɪə) *n* a Dutch title of address equivalent to *Sir* when used alone or to *Mr* when placed before a name [C17 from Dutch *mijnheer*, my lord]

myo- or before a vowel **my-** *combining form* muscle: *myocardium* [from Greek *mus* MUSCLE]

myocardial (ˌmaɪəʊˈkɑːdɪəl) *adj* of or relating to the muscular tissue of the heart

myocardial infarction *n* destruction of an area of heart muscle as the result of occlusion of a coronary artery. Compare **coronary thrombosis**

myocardiograph (ˌmaɪəʊˈkɑːdɪəˌɡrɑːf, -ˌɡræf) *n* an instrument for recording the movements of heart muscle

myocarditis (ˌmaɪəʊkɑːˈdaɪtɪs) *n* inflammation of the heart muscle

myocardium (ˌmaɪəʊˈkɑːdɪəm) *n, pl* -dia (-dɪə) the muscular tissue of the heart [C19 myo- + cardium, from Greek *kardia* heart]

myoelectric (ˌmaɪəʊɪˈlɛktrɪk) *adj* denoting a type of powered artificial hand or limb that detects electrical changes in the muscles of the stump and converts these into movements

myogenic (ˌmaɪəʊˈdʒɛnɪk) *adj* originating in or forming muscle tissue

myoglobin (ˌmaɪəʊˈɡləʊbɪn) *n* a protein that is the main oxygen-carrier of muscle

myograph (ˈmaɪəˌɡrɑːf, -ˌɡræf) *n* an instrument for recording tracings (**myograms**) of muscular contractions ▷ ˌmyo'graphic *adj* ▷ ˌmyo'graphically *adv* ▷ **myography** (maɪˈɒɡrəfɪ) *n*

myology (maɪˈɒlədʒɪ) *n* the branch of medical science concerned with the structure and diseases of muscles ▷ **myologic** (ˌmaɪəˈlɒdʒɪk) or ˌmyo'logical *adj* ▷ my'ologist *n*

myoma (maɪˈəʊmə) *n, pl* -mas or -mata (-mətə) a benign tumour composed of muscle tissue ▷ my'omatous *adj*

myomectomy (ˌmaɪəˈmɛktəmɪ) *n, pl* -mies surgical removal of a myoma, especially in the uterus

myopathy (maɪˈɒpəθɪ) *n, pl* -thies any disease affecting muscles or muscle tissue

myope (ˈmaɪəʊp) *n* any person afflicted with myopia [C18 via French from Greek *muōps*; see MYOPIA]

myophily or **myiophily** (maɪˈɒfɪlɪ) *n* pollination of plants by flies [from Greek *muia* fly + *philos* loving] ▷ my'ophilous or myi'ophilous *adj*

myopia (maɪˈəʊpɪə) *n* inability to see distant objects clearly because the images are focused in front of the retina; short-sightedness [C18 via New Latin from Greek *muōps* short-sighted, from *muein* to close (the eyes), blink + *ōps* eye] ▷ **myopic** (maɪˈɒpɪk) *adj* ▷ my'opically *adv*

myosin (ˈmaɪəsɪn) *n* the chief protein of muscle that interacts with actin to form actomyosin during muscle contraction; it is also present in

many other cell types [C19 from MYO- + -OSE² + -IN]

myosis (maɪˈəʊsɪs) *n, pl* -ses (-siːz) a variant spelling of **miosis**

myosotis (ˌmaɪəˈsəʊtɪs) or **myosote** (ˈmaɪəˌsəʊt) *n* any plant of the boraginaceous genus *Myosotis*. See **forget-me-not** [C18 New Latin from Greek *muosōtis* mouse-ear (referring to its furry leaves), from *muos*, genitive of *mus* mouse + -ōt-, stem of *ous* ear]

myotome (ˈmaɪəˌtəʊm) *n* **1** any segment of embryonic mesoderm that develops into skeletal muscle in the adult **2** any of the segmentally arranged blocks of muscle in lower vertebrates such as fishes

myotonia (ˌmaɪəˈtəʊnɪə) *n* lack of muscle tone, frequently including muscle spasm or rigidity. Also called: **amyotonia** ▷ **myotonic** (ˌmaɪəˈtɒnɪk) *adj*

myria- *combining form* indicating a very great number: *myriapod* [from Greek *murios* countless]

myriad (ˈmɪrɪəd) *adj* **1** innumerable ▷ *n* **2** (also used in plural) a large indefinite number **3** archaic ten thousand [C16 via Late Latin from Greek *murias* ten thousand]

myriapod (ˈmɪrɪəˌpɒd) *n* **1** any terrestrial arthropod of the group *Myriapoda*, having a long segmented body and many walking limbs: includes the centipedes and millipedes ▷ *adj* **2** of, relating to, or belonging to the *Myriapoda* [C19 from New Latin *Myriapoda*. See MYRIAD, -POD] ▷ **myriapodan** (ˌmɪrɪˈæpədən) *adj* ▷ ˌmyri'apodous *adj*

myrica (mɪˈraɪkə) *n* the dried root bark of the wax myrtle, used as a tonic and to treat diarrhoea [C18 via Latin from Greek *murikē* the tamarisk]

myrmeco- *combining form* ant: *myrmecology; myrmecophile* [from Greek *murmēx*]

myrmecochory (ˌmɜːmɪkəʊˈkɔːrɪ) *n* the dispersal of fruits and seeds by ants

myrmecology (ˌmɜːmɪˈkɒlədʒɪ) *n* the branch of zoology concerned with the study of ants ▷ **myrmecological** (ˌmɜːmɪkəˈlɒdʒɪkəl) *adj* ▷ ˌmyrme'cologist *n*

myrmecophagous (ˌmɜːmɪˈkɒfəɡəs) *adj* **1** (of jaws) specialized for feeding on ants **2** feeding on ants

myrmecophile (ˈmɜːmɪkəʊˌfaɪl) *n* an animal that lives in a colony of ants ▷ **myrmecophilous** (ˌmɜːmɪˈkɒfɪləs) *adj*

myrmecophily (ˌmɜːmɪˈkɒfɪlɪ) *n biology* **1** symbiosis with ants **2** pollination of plants by ants

Myrmidon (ˈmɜːmɪ,dɒn, -dən) *n, pl* Myrmidons or Myrmidones (mɜːˈmɪdəˌniːz) **1** *Greek myth* one of a race of people whom Zeus made from a nest of ants. They settled in Thessaly and were led against Troy by Achilles **2** (*often not capital*) a follower or henchman

myrobalan (maɪˈrɒbələn, mɪ-) *n* **1** the dried plumlike fruit of various tropical trees of the genus *Terminalia*, used in dyeing, tanning, ink, and medicine **2** a dye extracted from this fruit **3** another name for **cherry plum** [C16 via Latin from Greek *murobalanos*, from *muron* ointment + *balanos* acorn]

myrrh (mɜː) *n* **1** any of several burseraceous trees and shrubs of the African and S Asian genus *Commiphora*, esp *C. myrrha*, that exude an aromatic resin. Compare **balm of Gilead** (sense 1) **2** the resin obtained from such a plant, used in perfume, incense, and medicine **3** another name for **sweet cicely** (sense 1) [Old English *myrre*, via Latin from Greek *murrha*, ultimately from Akkadian *murrū*; compare Hebrew *mōr*, Arabic *murr*]

myrtaceous (mɜːˈteɪʃəs) *adj* of, relating to, or belonging to the *Myrtaceae*, a family of mostly tropical and subtropical trees and shrubs having oil glands in the leaves: includes eucalyptus, clove, myrtle, and guava [C19 via New Latin from Latin *myrtus* myrtle, from Greek *murtos*]

myrtle (ˈmɜːtəl) *n* **1** any evergreen shrub or tree of the myrtaceous genus *Myrtus*, esp *M. communis*, a S

European shrub with pink or white flowers and aromatic blue-black berries **2** short for **crape myrtle 3** bog myrtle. another name for **sweet gale 4** creeping *or* trailing myrtle *US and Canadian* another name for **periwinkle** (the plant) [c16 from Medieval Latin *myrtilla*, from Latin *myrtus*, from Greek *murtos*]

mySAP ('maɪˌsæp) *n trademark* a Web-integrated software application used by businesses to plan and control product distribution, human resources, budgets, etc

myself (maɪ'sɛlf) *pron* **1 a** the reflexive form of *I* or *me* **b** (intensifier): *I myself know of no answer* **2** (*preceded by a copula*) my usual self: *I'm not myself today* **3** *not standard* used instead of *I* or *me* in compound noun phrases: *John and myself are voting together*

Mysia ('mɪsɪə) *n* an ancient region in the NW corner of Asia Minor

Mysian ('mɪsɪən) *adj* **1** of or relating to Mysia, an ancient region in Asia Minor, or its inhabitants ▷ *n* **2** a native or inhabitant of Mysia

Mysore (maɪ'sɔː) *n* **1** a city in S India, in S Karnataka state: former capital of the state of Mysore; manufacturing and trading centre; university (1916). Pop: 742 261 (2001) **2** the former name (until 1973) of **Karnataka**

mystagogue ('mɪstəˌɡɒɡ) *n* (in Mediterranean mystery religions) a person who instructs those who are preparing for initiation into the mysteries [c16 via Latin from Greek *mustagōgos*, from *mustēs* candidate for initiation + *agein* to lead. See MYSTIC] > **mystagogic** (ˌmɪstə'ɡɒdʒɪk) *or* ˌmysta'gogical *adj* > ˌmysta'gogically *adv* > **mystagogy** ('mɪstəˌɡɒdʒɪ) *n*

mysterious (mɪ'stɪərɪəs) *adj* **1** characterized by or indicative of mystery **2** puzzling, curious, or enigmatic > mys'teriously *adv* > mys'teriousness *n*

mystery¹ ('mɪstərɪ, -trɪ) *n, pl* -teries **1** an unexplained or inexplicable event, phenomenon, etc **2** a person or thing that arouses curiosity or suspense because of an unknown, obscure, or enigmatic quality **3** the state or quality of being obscure, inexplicable, or enigmatic **4** a story, film, etc, which arouses suspense and curiosity because of facts concealed **5** *Christianity* any truth that is divinely revealed but otherwise unknowable **6** *Christianity* a sacramental rite, such as the Eucharist, or (*when plural*) the consecrated elements of the Eucharist **7** (*often plural*) any of various rites of certain ancient Mediterranean religions **8** short for **mystery play** [c14 via Latin from Greek *mustērion* secret rites. See MYSTIC]

mystery² ('mɪstərɪ) *n, pl* -teries *archaic* **1** a trade, occupation, or craft **2** a guild of craftsmen [c14 from Medieval Latin *mistērium*, from Latin *ministerium* occupation, from *minister* official]

mystery bag *n Austral slang* **1** a sausage **2** a meat pie

mystery play *n* (in the Middle Ages) a type of drama based on the life of Christ. Compare

miracle play

mystery tour *n* an excursion to an unspecified destination

mystic ('mɪstɪk) *n* **1** a person who achieves mystical experience or an apprehension of divine mysteries ▷ *adj* **2** another word for **mystical** [c14 via Latin from Greek *mustikos*, from *mustēs* mystery initiate; related to *muein* to initiate into sacred rites]

mystical ('mɪstɪkəl) *adj* **1** relating to or characteristic of mysticism **2** *Christianity* having a divine or sacred significance that surpasses natural human apprehension **3** having occult or metaphysical significance, nature, or force **4** a less common word for **mysterious**. > 'mystically *adv* > 'mysticalness *n*

mysticism ('mɪstɪˌsɪzəm) *n* **1** belief in or experience of a reality surpassing normal human understanding or experience, esp a reality perceived as essential to the nature of life **2** a system of contemplative prayer and spirituality aimed at achieving direct intuitive experience of the divine **3** obscure or confused belief or thought

mystify ('mɪstɪˌfaɪ) *vb* -fies, -fying, -fied (*tr*) **1** to confuse, bewilder, or puzzle **2** to make mysterious or obscure [c19 from French *mystifier*, from *mystère* MYSTERY¹ *or* *mystique* MYSTIC] > ˌmystifi'cation *n* > 'mysti,fier *n* > 'mysti,fying *adj* > 'mysti,fyingly *adv*

mystique (mɪ'stiːk) *n* an aura of mystery, power, and awe that surrounds a person or thing: *the mystique of the theatre; the mystique of computer programming* [c20 from French (adj): MYSTIC]

myth (mɪθ) *n* **1 a** a story about superhuman beings of an earlier age taken by preliterate society to be a true account, usually of how natural phenomena, social customs, etc, came into existence **b** another word for **mythology** (senses 1, 3) **2** a person or thing whose existence is fictional or unproven **3** (in modern literature) a theme or character type embodying an idea: *Hemingway's myth of the male hero* **4** *philosophy* (esp in the writings of Plato) an allegory or parable [c19 via Late Latin from Greek *muthos* fable, word]

myth. *abbreviation for* **1** mythological **2** mythology

mythical ('mɪθɪkəl) *or* **mythic** ('mɪθɪk) *adj* **1** of or relating to myth **2** imaginary or fictitious > 'mythically *adv*

mythicize *or* **mythicise** ('mɪθɪˌsaɪz) *vb* (*tr*) to make into or treat as a myth > ˌmythici'zation *or* ˌmythici'sation *n* > 'mythicist, 'mythi,cizer *or* 'mythi,ciser *n*

mytho- *combining form* myth: *mythogenesis; mythography*

mythological (ˌmɪθə'lɒdʒɪkəl) *adj* **1** of or relating to mythology **2** mythical > ˌmytho'logically *adv*

mythologist (mɪ'θɒlədʒɪst) *n* **1** an expert in or student of mythology **2** a writer or editor of myths

mythologize *or* **mythologise** (mɪ'θɒləˌdʒaɪz) *vb* **1** to tell, study, or explain (myths) **2** (*intr*) to create

or make up myths **3** (*tr*) to convert into a myth > myˌthologi'zation *or* myˌthologi'sation *n* > my'thologer, my'tholo,gizer *or* my'tholo,giser *n*

mythology (mɪ'θɒlədʒɪ) *n, pl* -gies **1** a body of myths, esp one associated with a particular culture, institution, person, etc **2** a body of stories about a person, institution, etc: *the mythology of Hollywood* **3** myths collectively **4** the study or collecting of myths

mythomania (ˌmɪθəʊ'meɪnɪə) *n psychiatry* the tendency to lie, exaggerate, or relate incredible imaginary adventures as if they had really happened, occurring in some mental disorders > mythomaniac (ˌmɪθəʊ'meɪnɪˌæk) *n, adj*

mythopoeia (ˌmɪθəʊ'piːə) *or* **mythopoesis** (ˌmɪθəpəʊ'iːsɪs) *n* the composition or making of myths [c19 from Greek, from *muthopoiein*, from *muthos* myth + *poiein* to make]

mythopoeic (ˌmɪθəʊ'piːɪk) *adj* of or relating to the composition of myths; productive of myths > ˌmytho'poeism *n* > ˌmytho'poeist *n*

mythos ('maɪθɒs, 'mɪθɒs) *n, pl* -thoi (-θɔɪ) **1** the complex of beliefs, values, attitudes, etc, characteristic of a specific group or society **2** another word for **myth** *or* **mythology**

Mytilene (ˌmɪtɪ'liːnɪ) *n* **1** a port on the Greek island of Lesbos: Roman remains; Byzantine fortress Pop: 25 000 (latest est). Modern Greek name: Mitilíni **2** a former name for **Lesbos**

myxo ('mɪksəʊ) *n Austral slang* short for **myxomatosis**

myxo- *or before a vowel* **myx-** *combining form* mucus or slime: *myxomycete* [from Greek *muxa* slime, mucus]

myxoedema *or US* **myxedema** (ˌmɪksɪ'diːmə) *n* a disease resulting from underactivity of the thyroid gland characterized by puffy eyes, face, and hands and mental sluggishness. See also **cretinism**. > myxoedemic (ˌmɪksɪ'dɛmɪk), myxoedematous (ˌmɪksɪ'dɛmətəs, -'diː-) *or US* ˌmyxe'demic *or* ˌmyxe'dematous *adj*

myxoma (mɪk'səʊmə) *n, pl* -mas *or* -mata (-mətə) a tumour composed of mucous connective tissue, usually situated in subcutaneous tissue > myxomatous (mɪk'sɒmətəs) *adj*

myxomatosis (ˌmɪksəmə'təʊsɪs) *n* an infectious and usually fatal viral disease of rabbits characterized by swelling of the mucous membranes and formation of skin tumours; transmitted by flea bites

myxomycete (ˌmɪksəʊmaɪ'siːt) *n* a slime mould, esp a slime mould of the phylum *Myxomycota* (division *Myxomycetes* in traditional classifications) > ˌmyxomy'cetous *adj*

myxovirus (ˌmɪksəʊ,vaɪərəs) *n* any of a group of viruses that cause influenza, mumps, and certain other diseases

mz *the internet domain name for* Mozambique

mzee (ə'mˈzeɪ) *E African* ▷ *n* **1** an old person ▷ *adj* **2** advanced in years [c19 from Swahili]

mzungu (ə'mˈzʊŋɡuː) *n E African* a White person [c20 from Swahili]

m

N n

n or **N** (ɛn) *n, pl* **n's**, **N's** or **Ns 1** the 14th letter and 11th consonant of the modern English alphabet **2** a speech sound represented by this letter, usually an alveolar nasal, as in *nail*

n¹ *symbol for* **1** neutron **2** *optics* index of refraction **3** nano-

n² (ɛn) *determiner* an indefinite number (of): *there are n objects in a box*

N *symbol for* **1** Also: **kt** *chess* knight **2** neper **3** neutral **4** newton(s) **5** *chem* nitrogen **6** North **7** Avogadro's number **8** noun **9** *international car registration for* Norway

n. *abbreviation for* **1** natus **2** neuter **3** new **4** nominative **5** noun [(for sense 1) Latin: born]

n- *prefix chem* short for **normal** (sense 6)

na¹ (nɑː) *n, determiner* a variant of **nae**

na² *the internet domain name for* Namibia

Na *the chemical symbol for* sodium [Latin *natrium*]

NA 1 *abbreviation for* North America **2** *international car registration for* Netherlands Antilles

n/a *abbreviation for* not applicable

NAACP (in the US) *abbreviation for* National Association for the Advancement of Colored People

NAAFI or **Naafi** ('næfɪ) *n* **1** *acronym for* Navy, Army, and Air Force Institutes: an organization providing canteens, shops, etc, for British military personnel at home or overseas **2** a canteen, shop, etc, run by this organization

naan (nɑːn) *n* another name for **nan bread**

naartjie ('nɑːtʃɪ) *n South African* a tangerine [Afrikaans]

nab (næb) *vb* **nabs**, **nabbing**, **nabbed** (*tr*) *informal* **1** to arrest **2** to catch (someone) in wrongdoing **3** to seize suddenly; snatch [c17 perhaps of Scandinavian origin; compare Danish *nappe*, Swedish *nappa* to snatch. See KIDNAP]

Nabataean or **Nabatean** (ˌnæbə'tiːən) *n* **1** a member of an Arab trading people who flourished southeast of Palestine, around Petra, in the Hellenistic and Roman periods **2** the extinct form of Aramaic spoken by this people

Nabis (*French* nabi) *pl n, sing* -**bi** (-bi) a group of French artists much influenced by Gauguin, including Bonnard and Vuillard, who reacted against the naturalism of the impressionists. See also **synthetism** [c19 French, from Hebrew *nābhi* prophet]

nabla ('næblə) *n maths* another name for **del** [c19 from Greek *nabla* stringed instrument, because it is shaped like a harp]

Nablus ('nɑːbləs) *n* a town in the West Bank: near the site of ancient Shechem. Pop: 136 000 (2005 est)

nabob ('neɪbɒb) *n* **1** *informal* a rich, powerful, or important man **2** (formerly) a European who made a fortune in the Orient, esp in India **3** another name for a **nawab** [c17 from Portuguese *nababo*, from Hindi *nawwāb*; see NAWAB] > **nabobery** ('neɪbɒbərɪ, neɪ'bɒbərɪ) or '**nabobism** *n* > '**nabobish** *adj*

Nabokovian (ˌnæbə'kəʊvɪən) *adj* of, relating to, or reminiscent of Vladimir Vladimirovich Nabokov, the Russian-born US novelist (1899–1977)

Nabonidus (ˌnæbə'naɪdəs) *n Old Testament* the father of Belshazzar last king of Babylon before it was captured by Cyrus in 539 BC

Naboth ('neɪbɒθ) *n Old Testament* an inhabitant of Jezreel, murdered by King Ahab at the instigation of his wife Jezebel for refusing to sell his vineyard (I Kings 21)

nacelle (nə'sɛl) *n* a streamlined enclosure on an aircraft, not part of the fuselage, to accommodate an engine, passengers, crew, etc [c20 from French: small boat, from Late Latin *nāvicella*, a diminutive of Latin *nāvis* ship]

nacho ('nɑːtʃəʊ) *n, pl* **nachos** *Mexican cookery* a snack consisting of a piece of tortilla topped with cheese, hot peppers, etc, and grilled

NACODS ('neɪkɒdz) *n acronym for* National Association of Colliery Overmen, Deputies, and Shotfirers

nacre ('neɪkə) *n* the technical name for **mother-of-pearl** [c16 via French from Old Italian *naccara*, from Arabic *naqqārah* shell, drum] > '**nacred** *adj*

nacreous ('neɪkrɪəs) *adj* **1** relating to or consisting of mother-of-pearl **2** having the lustre of mother-of-pearl: *nacreous minerals*

NACRO or **Nacro** ('nækrəʊ) *n acronym for* National Association for the Care and Resettlement of Offenders

NAD *n biochem* nicotinamide adenine dinucleotide; a coenzyme that is a hydrogen carrier in metabolic reactions, esp in tissue respiration. Former name: DPN

nada ('nɑːdə) *n chiefly US informal* nothing [c20 Spanish]

Na-Dene or **Na-Déné** (nɑː'deɪnɪ, nə'diːn) *n* a phylum of North American Indian languages including Athapascan, Tlingit, and Haida [from Haida *na* to dwell + Athapascan *dene* people; coined by Edward Sapir (1884–1939), American anthropologist]

NADH *n biochem* the chemically reduced form of NAD

nadir ('neɪdɪə, 'næ-) *n* **1** the point on the celestial sphere directly below an observer and diametrically opposite the zenith **2** the lowest or deepest point; depths: *the nadir of despair* [c14 from Old French, from Arabic *nazīr as-samt*, literally: opposite the zenith]

nadors ('nɑːdɔːz) *n South African* a thirst brought on by excessive consumption of alcohol [from Afrikaans *na* after + *dors* thirst]

NADP *n biochem* nicotinamide adenine dinucleotide phosphate; a coenzyme with functions similar to those of NAD. Former name: TPN

NADPH *n biochem* the chemically reduced form of NADP

nads (nædz) *pl n slang* another word for **testicles** [c20 (GO)NAD]

nae (neɪ) or **na** (nɑː) *n, determiner* a Scot word for **no** or **not**

naevus or US **nevus** ('niːvəs) *n, pl* -**vi** (-vaɪ) any congenital growth or pigmented blemish on the skin; birthmark or mole [c19 from Latin; related to (*g*)*natus* born, produced by nature] > '**naevoid** or US '**nevoid** *adj*

naff (næf) *adj Brit slang* inferior; in poor taste [c19 perhaps back slang for *fan*, short for FANNY] > '**naffness** *n*

naff off *sentence substitute Brit slang* a forceful expression of dismissal or contempt

NAFTA ('næftə) *n acronym for* North American Free Trade Agreement

nag¹ (næg) *vb* **nags**, **nagging**, **nagged 1** to scold or annoy constantly **2** (when *intr*, often foll by *at*) to be a constant source of discomfort or worry (to): *toothache nagged him all day* ▷ *n* **3** a person, esp a woman, who nags [c19 of Scandinavian origin; compare Swedish *nagga* to GNAW, irritate, German *nagen*] > '**nagger** *n* > '**naggingly** *adv*

nag² (næg) *n* **1** *often derogatory* a horse **2** a small riding horse [c14 of Germanic origin; related to NEIGH]

Naga ('nɑːgə) *n* **1** (*pl* **Nagas** or **Naga**) a member of a people of NE India and W Myanmar: until the early 20th century they practised head-hunting **2** the language of this people, belonging to the Sino-Tibetan family of languages and having many dialects

Nagaland ('nɑːgəˌlænd) *n* a state of NE India: formed in 1962 from parts of Assam and the North-East Frontier Agency; inhabited chiefly by Naga tribes; consists of almost inaccessible forested hills and mountains (the **Naga Hills**); shifting cultivation predominates. Capital: Kohima. Pop: 1 988 636 (2001). Area: 16 579 sq km (6401 sq miles)

nagana (nə'gɑːnə) *n* a disease of all domesticated animals of central and southern Africa, caused by parasitic protozoa of the genus *Trypanosoma* transmitted by tsetse flies [from Zulu *u-nakane*]

Nagano (nə'gɑːnəʊ) *n* a city in central Japan, on central Honshu: Buddhist shrine; two universities. Pop: 359 045 (2002 est)

Nagari ('nɑːgərɪ) *n* **1** a set of scripts, including Devanagari, used as the writing systems for several languages of India **2** another word for **Devanagari**

Nagasaki (ˌnɑːgə'sɑːkɪ) *n* a port in SW Japan, on W Kyushu: almost completely destroyed in 1945 by the second atomic bomb dropped on Japan by the US; shipbuilding industry. Pop: 419 901 (2002 est)

nagor ('neɪgɔː) *n* another name for **reedbuck** [c18 from French, arbitrarily named by Buffon, from earlier *nanguer*]

Nagorno-Karabakh Autonomous Region (nə'gɔː:nəʊkərʌ'bɑːk) *n* an administrative division in S Azerbaijan. In 1990–94 Armenian claims to the region led to violent unrest and fighting between national forces. Capital: Stepanakert. Pop: 143 000 (2000 est). Area: 4400 sq km (1700 sq miles)

Nagoya ('nɑːɡəʊjə) *n* a city in central Japan, on S Honshu on Ise Bay: a major industrial centre. Pop: 2 109 681 (2002 est)

Nagpur (næɡˈpʊə) *n* a city in central India, in NE Maharashtra state: became capital of the kingdom of Nagpur (1743); capital of the Central Provinces (later Madhya Pradesh) from 1861 to 1956. Pop: 2 051 320 (2001)

Nagyszeben ('nɔdjseˌben) *n* the Hungarian name for **Sibiu**

Nagyvárad ('nɔdjvaːrɔd) *n* the Hungarian name for **Oradea**

Nah. *Bible abbreviation for* Nahum

Naha ('nɑːhə) *n* a port in S Japan, on the SW coast of Okinawa Island: chief city of the Ryukyu Islands. Pop: 303 146 (2002 est)

Nahal (nə'hɑːl) *n* 1 (in Israel) a military youth organization 2 (*not capital*) an agricultural settlement, esp in a border area, set up or manned by Nahal members [c20 from Hebrew acronym for *No'ar Halutzi Lohem* Pioneer and Military Youth]

NAHT (in Britain) *abbreviation for* National Association of Head Teachers

Nahuatl ('nɑːwɑːtʰəl, nɑːˈwɑːtʰəl) *n* 1 (*pl* -tl *or* -tls) a member of one of a group of Central American and Mexican Indian peoples including the Aztecs 2 the language of these peoples, belonging to the Uto-Aztecan family ▷ Also: Nahuatlan

Nahum ('neɪhəm) *n Old Testament* 1 a Hebrew prophet of the 7th century BC 2 the book containing his oracles

NAI (in Britain) *abbreviation for* **nonaccidental injury**

naiad ('naɪæd) *n*, *pl* -ads *or* -ades (-əˌdiːz) 1 *Greek myth* a nymph dwelling in a lake, river, spring, or fountain 2 the aquatic larva of the dragonfly, mayfly, and related insects 3 Also called: **water nymph** any monocotyledonous submerged aquatic plant of the genus *Naias* (or *Najas*), having narrow leaves and small flowers: family *Naiadaceae* (or *Najadaceae*) 4 any of certain freshwater mussels of the genus *Unio*. See **mussel** (sense 2) [c17 via Latin from Greek *naias* water nymph; related to *náein* to flow]

NAIC *abbreviation for* National Astronomy and Ionosphere Center (headquarters Cornell University, New York State)

naïf (nɑːˈiːf) *adj*, *n* a less common word for **naive**

nail (neɪl) *n* 1 a fastening device usually made from round or oval wire, having a point at one end and a head at the other 2 anything resembling such a fastening device, esp in function or shape 3 the horny plate covering part of the dorsal surface of the fingers or toes. See **fingernail, toenail** Related adjs: **ungual, ungular** 4 the claw of a mammal, bird, or reptile 5 *slang* a hypodermic needle, used for injecting drugs 6 a unit of length, formerly used for measuring cloth, equal to two and a quarter inches 7 a nail in one's coffin an experience or event that tends to shorten life or hasten the end of something 8 bite one's nails **a** to chew off the ends of one's fingernails **b** to be worried or apprehensive 9 hard as nails **a** in tough physical condition **b** without sentiment or feelings 10 hit the nail on the head to do or say something correct or telling 11 on the nail (of payments) at once (esp in the phrase **pay on the nail**) ▷ *vb* (*tr*) 12 to attach with or as if with nails 13 *informal* to arrest or seize 14 *informal* to hit or bring down, as with a shot: *I nailed the sniper* 15 *informal* to expose or detect (a lie or liar) 16 to fix or focus (one's eyes, attention, etc) on an object 17 to stud with nails ▷ See also **nail down, nail up** [Old English *nægl*, related to Old High German *nagal* nail, Latin *unguis* fingernail, claw, Greek *onux*] ▷ 'nailer *n* ▷ 'nail-less *adj*

nail bar *n* a type of beauty salon specializing in manicure and the decoration of, esp women's, fingernails

nailbiter ('neɪlˌbaɪtə) *n* 1 a person who bites his or her nails 2 a person who is anxious or tense 3 something that causes anxiety or tension

nail-biting *n* 1 the act or habit of biting one's fingernails 2 **a** anxiety or tension **b** (*as modifier*): *nail-biting suspense*

nail bomb *n* an explosive device containing nails, used by terrorists to cause serious injuries in crowded situations

nailbrush ('neɪlˌbrʌʃ) *n* a small stiff-bristled brush for cleaning the fingernails

nail down *vb* (*tr, adverb*) 1 to fasten down with or as if with nails 2 *informal* to extort a definite promise or consent from: *I nailed him down on the deadline* 3 *informal* to settle in a definite way: *they nailed down the agreement*

nailed-on *adj slang* certain, definite; guaranteed to be successful

nailfile ('neɪlˌfaɪl) *n* a small file, chiefly either of metal or of board coated with emery, used to trim the nails

nailhead ('neɪlˌhɛd) *n* a decorative device, as on tooled leather, resembling the round head of a nail

nail polish, varnish *or US* **enamel** *n* a quick-drying lacquer applied to colour the nails or make them shiny or esp both

nail set *or* **punch** *n* a punch for driving the head of a nail below or flush with the surrounding surface

nail technician *n* a person whose job is to take care of and decorate people's fingernails

nail up *vb* (*tr, adverb*) to shut in or fasten tightly with or as if with nails

nainsook ('neɪnsʊk, 'næn-) *n* a light soft plain-weave cotton fabric, used esp for babies' wear [c19 from Hindi *nainsukh*, literally: delight to the eye, from *nain* eye + *sukh* delight, from Sanskrit *sukha*]

naira ('naɪrə) *n* the standard monetary unit of Nigeria, divided into 100 kobo [c20 altered from NIGERIA]

NAI register *n social welfare* (in Britain) a list of children deemed to be at risk of abuse or injury from their parents or guardians, compiled and held by a local authority, area health authority, or NSPCC Special Unit. Also called: **child abuse register**

Nairnshire ('nɛənˌʃɪə, -ʃə) *n* (until 1975) a county of NE Scotland, now part of Highland

Nairobi (naɪˈrəʊbɪ) *n* the capital of Kenya, in the southwest at an altitude of 1650 m (5500 ft): founded in 1899; became capital in 1905; commercial and industrial centre; the **Nairobi National Park** (a game reserve) is nearby. Pop: 2 818 000 (2005 est)

NAIRU ('naɪruː) *n economics acronym for* non-accelerating inflation rate of unemployment: the rate of unemployment at which inflation is neither accelerating nor decelerating. Also called: **natural rate of unemployment**

Naismith's rule ('neɪsmɪθs) *n mountaineering* a rule of thumb for calculating the time needed for a climbing expedition, allowing 1 hour for every 3 miles of distance plus 1 hour for every 2000 feet of height [c19 named after W W *Naismith* (1856–1935), Scottish climber, who formulated it]

naissant ('neɪsᵊnt) *adj heraldry* (of a beast) having only the forepart shown above a horizontal division of a shield [c16 from Old French, literally: being born. See NASCENT]

naive, naïve (nɑːˈiːv, naɪˈiːv) *or* **naïf** *adj* 1 **a** having or expressing innocence and credulity; ingenuous **b** (*as collective noun; preceded by the*): *only the naive believed him* 2 artless or unsophisticated 3 lacking developed powers of analysis, reasoning, or criticism: *a naive argument* 4 another word for **primitive** (sense 5) ▷ *n* 5 *rare* a person who is naive, esp in artistic style. See **primitive** (sense 10) [c17 from French, feminine of *naïf*, from Old French *naif* native, spontaneous, from Latin *nātīvus* NATIVE, from *nasci* to be born] ▷ na'ively, na'ïvely *or* na'ïfly *adv* ▷ na'iveness,

na'iveness *or* na'ïfness *n*

naive realism *n philosophy* the doctrine that in perception of physical objects what is before the mind is the object itself and not a representation of it. Compare **representationalism** (sense 1)

naivety (naɪˈiːvtɪ) *or* **naiveté, naïveté** (ˌnɑːiːvˈteɪ) *n*, *pl* -ties *or* -tés 1 the state or quality of being naive; ingenuousness; simplicity 2 a naive act or statement

Najaf ('nædʒæf) *n* a holy city in central Iraq, near the River Euphrates; burial place of the Caliph Ali and a centre of the Shiite faith. Pop: 639 000 (2005 est)

naked ('neɪkɪd) *adj* 1 having the body completely unclothed; undressed. Compare **bare¹** 2 having no covering; bare; exposed: *a naked flame* 3 with no qualification or concealment; stark; plain: *the naked facts* 4 unaided by any optical instrument, such as a telescope or microscope (esp in the phrase **the naked eye**) 5 with no defence, protection, or shield 6 (usually foll by *of*) stripped or destitute: *naked of weapons* 7 (of the seeds of gymnosperms) not enclosed in a pericarp 8 (of flowers) lacking a perianth 9 (of stems) lacking leaves and other appendages 10 (of animals) lacking hair, feathers, scales, etc 11 *law* **a** unsupported by authority or financial or other consideration: *a naked contract* **b** lacking some essential condition to render valid; incomplete [Old English *nacod*; related to Old High German *nackot* (German *nackt*), Old Norse *noktr*, Latin *nudus*] ▷ 'nakedly *adv* ▷ 'nakedness *n*

naked ladies *n* (*functioning as singular*) another name for **autumn crocus**

naked lady *n* a leafless pink orchid found in Australia and New Zealand

naked singularity *n astronomy* an infinitely dense point mass without a surrounding black hole. See also **black hole**

naker ('neɪkə, 'næk-) *n* one of a pair of small kettledrums used in medieval music [c14 from Old French *nacre*, via Medieval Greek *anakara*, from Arabic *naqāra*]

nakfa ('nækfə) *n* the standard currency unit of Eritrea

Nakhichevan (*Russian* nəxitʃɪˈvanj) *n* a city in W Azerbaijan, capital of the Nakhichevan Autonomous Republic: an ancient trading town; ceded to Russia in 1828. Pop: 66 800 (1994). Ancient name: Naxuana (ˌnækˈswɑːnə)

Nakhichevan Autonomous Republic (nəˌkɪtʃᵊˈvɑːn) *n* a region belonging to Azerbaijan, from which it is separated by part of Armenia; annexed by Russia in 1828; unilaterally declared secession from the Soviet Union in 1990. Capital: Nakhichevan. Pop: 363 000 (2000 est). Area: 5500 sq km (2120 sq miles)

Nakuru (nəˈkuːruː) *n* a town in W Kenya, on Lake Nakuru: commercial centre of an agricultural region. Pop: 264 000 (2005 est)

nalbuphine hydrochloride ('nælbuːˌfiːn) *n* an opiate drug used as a painkiller. See also **Nubain**

Nalchik (*Russian* 'naljtʃik) *n* a city in SW Russia, capital of the Kabardino-Balkar Republic, in a valley of the Greater Caucasus: health resort. Pop: 283 000 (2005 est)

NALGO ('nælɡəʊ) *n* (formerly, in Britain) *acronym for* National and Local Government Officers' Association

naloxone (nəˈlɒksəʊn) *n* a chemical substance that counteracts the effects of opiates by binding to opiate receptors on cells [c20 from N-al(lylnor)ox(ymorph)one, the chemical name]

naltrexone (nælˈtrɛksəʊn) *n* a narcotic antagonist, similar to morphine, used chiefly in the treatment of heroin addiction [c20 from N-al(lylnor)ox(ymorph)one, 1 the arbitrary insertion of -trex-]

Nam *or* **'Nam** (næm) *n chiefly US informal* Vietnam

NAM *international car registration for* Namibia

Nama ('nɑːmə) *or* **Namaqua** (nəˈmɑːkwə) *n* 1 (*pl*

n

-ma, -mas *or* **-qua, -quas** a member of a Khoikhoi people living chiefly in Namaqualand **2** the Khoikhoi language spoken by this people, belonging to the Khoisan family. See also **Damara** ⊳ 'Naman *or* Na'maquan *n, adj*

Namangan (*Russian* nəman'gan) *n* a city in E Uzbekistan. Pop: 471 000 (2005 est)

Namaqualand (nə'mɑ:kwə,lænd) *n* a semiarid coastal region of SW Africa, extending from near Windhoek, Namibia, into W South Africa: divided by the Orange River into **Little Namaqualand** in South Africa, and **Great Namaqualand** in Namibia; rich mineral resources. Area: 47 961 sq km (18 518 sq miles). Also called: Namaland ('nɑ:mə,lænd)

namas kar (nə'mʌs kɑ:) *n* a salutation used in India [Sanskrit, from *namas* salutation, bow + *kara* doing]

namaste (,nʌməs'teɪ) *interj* a salutation used in India [c21 via Hindi from Sanskrit, from *namas* salutation, bow + *te* to you]

namby-pamby (,næmbɪ'pæmbɪ) *adj* **1** sentimental or prim in a weak insipid way: *namby-pamby manners* **2** clinging, feeble, or spineless: *a namby-pamby child* ⊳ *n, pl* **-bies 3** a person who is namby-pamby [c18 a nickname of Ambrose Phillips (died 1749), whose pastoral verse was ridiculed for being insipid]

Nam Co ('nɑ:m 'kɔ:) *or* **Nam Tso** *n* a salt lake in SW China, in SE Tibet at an altitude of 4629 m (15 186 ft). Area: about 1800 sq km (700 sq miles). Also called: Tengri Nor

name (neɪm) *n* **1** a word or term by which a person or thing is commonly and distinctively known. Related adj: **nominal 2** mere outward appearance or form as opposed to fact (esp in the phrase **in name**): *he was a ruler in name only* **3** a word, title, or phrase descriptive of character, usually abusive or derogatory: *to call a person names* **4** reputation, esp, if unspecified, good reputation: *he's made quite a name for himself* **5 a** a famous person or thing: *a name in the advertising world* **b** *chiefly US and Canadian* (*as modifier*): *a name product* **6** a member of Lloyd's who provides part of the capital of a syndicate and shares in its profits or losses but does not arrange its business **7 in** *or* **under the name of** using as a name **8 in the name of a** for the sake of **b** by the sanction or authority of **9 know by name** to have heard of without having met **10 name of the game a** anything that is essential, significant, or important **b** expected or normal conditions, circumstances, etc: *in gambling, losing money's the name of the game* to one: *I haven't a penny to my name* ⊳ *vb* (*tr*) **12** to give a name to; call by a name: *she named the child Edward* **13** to refer to by name; cite: *he named three French poets* **14** to determine, fix, or specify: *they have named a date for the meeting* **15** to appoint to or cite for a particular title, honour, or duty; nominate: *he was named Journalist of the Year* **16** to ban (an MP) from the House of Commons by mentioning him formally by name as being guilty of disorderly conduct **17 name and shame** to reveal the identity of a person or organization guilty of illegal or unacceptable behaviour in order to embarrass them into not repeating the offence **18 name names** to cite people, esp in order to blame or accuse them **19 name the day** to choose the day for one's wedding **20 you name it** whatever you need, mention, etc [Old English *nama*, related to Latin *nomen*, Greek *noma*, Old High German *namo*, German *Namen*] ⊳ 'namable *or* 'nameable *adj*

name-calling *n* verbal abuse, esp as a crude form of argument

namecheck ('neɪm,tʃek) *vb* (*tr*) **1** to mention (someone) specifically by name ⊳ *n* **2** a specific mention of someone's name, for example on a radio programme

name day *n* **1** *RC Church* the feast day of a saint whose name one bears **2** another name for **ticket day**

name-dropping *n informal* the practice of referring frequently to famous or fashionable people, esp as though they were intimate friends, in order to impress others ⊳ 'name-,dropper *n*

nameless ('neɪmlɪs) *adj* **1** without a name; anonymous **2** incapable of being named; indescribable: *a nameless horror seized him* **3** too unpleasant or disturbing to be mentioned: *nameless atrocities* **4** having no legal name; illegitimate: *a nameless child* ⊳ 'namelessly *adv* ⊳ 'namelessness *n*

namely ('neɪmlɪ) *adv* that is to say: *it was another colour, namely green*

Namen ('nɑ:mə) *n* the Flemish name for **Namur**

name part *n* another name for **title role**

nameplate ('neɪm,pleɪt) *n* a small panel on or next to the door of a room or building, bearing the occupant's name and profession

namesake ('neɪm,seɪk) *n* **1** a person or thing named after another **2** a person or thing with the same name as another [c17 probably a shortening of the phrase describing people connected *for the name's sake*]

nametape ('neɪm,teɪp) *n* a narrow cloth tape bearing the owner's name and attached to an article

Namhoi ('nɑ:m'hɔɪ) *n* another name for **Foshan**

Namibe (næ'mi:b) *n* a port in SW Angola: fishing industry. Pop: 77 000 (latest est)

Namibia (nɑ:'mɪbɪə, nə-) *n* a country in southern Africa bordering on South Africa: annexed by Germany in 1884 and mandated by the League of Nations to South Africa in 1920. The mandate was terminated by the UN in 1966 but this was ignored by South Africa, as was the 1971 ruling by the International Court of Justice that the territory be surrendered. Independence was achieved in 1990 and Namibia became a member of the Commonwealth; Walvis Bay remained a South African enclave until 1994 when it was returned to Namibia. Official language: English; Afrikaans and German also spoken. Religion: mostly animist, with some Christians. Currency: dollar. Capital: Windhoek. Pop: 2 011 000 (2004 est). Area: 823 328 sq km (317 887 sq miles). Also called: South West Africa Former name (1885–1919): German Southwest Africa

Namibian (nɑ:'mɪbɪən, nə-) *adj* **1** of or relating to Namibia or its inhabitants ⊳ *n* **2** a native or inhabitant of Namibia

namma hole ('næmə) *n Austral* a natural well in a rock [c19 from a native Australian language]

nam pla (,næm 'plɑ:) *n* a fermented fish sauce with a strong aroma and a salty taste, often used in Thai cookery [Thai]

Nam Tso ('nɑ:m 'tsɔ:) *n* a variant transliteration of the Chinese name for **Nam Co**

namu ('nɑ:mu:) *n, pl* **namu** a black New Zealand sandfly, *Austrosimulium australense* [Māori]

Namur (næ'mʊə; *French* namyr) *n* **1** a province of S Belgium. Capital: Namur. Pop: 452 856 (2004 est). Area: 3660 sq km (1413 sq miles) **2** a town in S Belgium, capital of Namur province: strategically situated on a promontory between the Sambre and Meuse Rivers, besieged and captured many times. Pop: 106 213 (2004 est). Flemish name: Namen

nan (næn) *or* **nana, nanna** ('nænə) *n* a child's words for **grandmother** [see NANNY; compare Greek *nanna* aunt, Medieval Latin *nonna* old woman]

nana ('nɑ:nə) *n* **1** *slang* a fool **2** *Austral slang* the head **3** **do one's nana** *Austral slang* to become very angry **4** **off one's nana** *Austral slang* mad; insane [c19 probably from BANANA]

Nanaimo bar (nə'naɪmoʊ) *n Canadian* a chocolate-coated sweet with a filling made from butter and icing sugar [c20 named after *Nanaimo*, a city on Vancouver Island]

nan bread *or* **naan** (nɑ:n) *n* (in Indian cookery) a slightly leavened bread in a large flat leaf shape [from Hindi]

Nanchang *or* **Nan-ch'ang** ('næn'tʃæŋ) *n* a walled city in SE China, capital of Jiangxi province, on the Kan River: largest city in the Poyang basin. Pop: 1 742 000 (2005 est)

Nan-ching ('næn'tʃɪŋ) *n* a variant spelling of **Nanjing**

nancy ('nænsɪ) *n, pl* **-cies a** an effeminate or homosexual boy or man **b** (*as modifier*): *his nancy ways* ⊳ Also called: nancy boy [c20 from the girl's name *Nancy*]

Nancy ('nænsɪ; *French* nɑ̃si) *n* a city in NE France: became the capital of the dukes of Lorraine in the 12th century, becoming French in 1766; administrative and financial centre. Pop: 103 605 (1999)

Nanda Devi ('nʌndə 'di:vɪ) *n* a mountain in N India, in Uttaranchal in the Himalayas. Height: 7817 m (25 645 ft)

NAND circuit *or* **gate** (nænd) *n electronics* a computer logic circuit having two or more input wires and one output wire that has an output signal if one or more of the input signals are at a low voltage. Compare **OR circuit** [c20 from *not* + AND; see NOT CIRCUIT, AND CIRCUIT]

nandrolone ('nændrə,ləʊn) *n* an anabolic steroid present in the body in small amounts but also produced by metabolism of other steroids, sometimes taken as performance-enhancing drugs by athletes and bodybuilders

nane (nen) *pron* a Scot word for **none**[1]

Nanga Parbat ('nʌŋgə 'pɑ:bʌt) *n* a mountain in N India, in NW Kashmir in the W Himalayas. Height: 8126 m (26 660 ft)

Nanhai ('nɑ:n'haɪ) *n* the Chinese name for the **South China Sea**

Nanjing ('næn'dʒɪŋ), **Nanking** ('næn'kɪŋ) *or* **Nan-ching** *n* a port in E central China, capital of Jiangsu province, on the Yangtze River: capital of the Chinese empire and a literary centre from the 14th to 17th centuries; capital of Nationalist China (1928–37); site of a massacre of about 300 000 civilians by the invading Japanese army in 1937; university (1928). Pop: 2 806 000 (2005 est)

nankeen (næŋ'ki:n) *or* **nankin** ('nænkɪn) *n* **1** a hard-wearing buff-coloured cotton fabric **2 a** a pale greyish-yellow colour **b** (*as adjective*): *a nankeen carpet* [c18 named after *Nanking*, China, where it originated]

Nanning *or* **Nan-ning** ('næn'nɪŋ) *n* a port in S China, capital of Guanxi Zhuang AR, on the Xiang River: rail links with Vietnam. Pop: 1 395 000 (2005 est)

nanny ('nænɪ) *n, pl* **-nies 1** a nurse or nursemaid for children **2 a** any person or thing regarded as treating people like children, esp by being patronizing or overprotective **b** (*as modifier*): *the nanny state* **3** a child's word for **grandmother** ⊳ *vb* **nannies, nannying, nannied 4** (*intr*) to nurse or look after someone else's children **5** (*tr*) to be overprotective towards [c19 child's name for a nurse]

nanny cam *n* a camera that transmits images to a computer, used to monitor children in another location

nannygai ('nænɪ,gaɪ) *n, pl* **-gais** an edible sea fish, *Centroberyx affinis*, of Australia which is red in colour and has large prominent eyes. Also called: red fish [c19 from a native Australian language]

nanny goat *n* a female goat. Compare **billy goat**

nanny state *n* a government that makes decisions for people that they might otherwise make for themselves, esp those relating to private and personal behaviour

nano- *combining form* **1** denoting 10⁻⁹: *nanosecond*. Symbol: n **2** indicating extreme smallness: *nanoplankton* [from Latin *nanus* dwarf, from Greek *nanos*]

nanobe ('nænəʊb) *n* a microbe that measures between 50 and 100 nanometres across and is smaller than the smallest known bacterium

nanodot ('nænəʊ,dɒt) *n* a microscopic cluster of several hundred nickel atoms that can be used to store extremely large amounts of data in a computer chip

nanogram or **nanogramme** ('nænəʊˌgræm) n one billionth (10⁻⁹) of a gram. Symbol: ng

nanomaterial ('nænəʊməˌtɪərɪəl) n any material that has an average particle size of between 1 and 100 nanometres

nanometre or US **nanometer** ('nænəʊˌmiːtə) n one thousand-millionth of a metre. Symbol: nm

nanook ('nænuːk) n N Canadian the polar bear [from Inuktitut nanug]

nanoparticle ('nænəʊˌpɑːtɪkəl) n a particle with dimensions less than 100 nanometres

nanophysics ('nænəʊˌfɪzɪks) n the physics of structures and artefacts with dimensions in the nanometre range or of phenomena occurring in nanaseconds

nanoplankton or **nannoplankton** ('nænəʊˌplæŋktən) n microscopic organisms in plankton

nanosecond ('nænəʊˌsɛkənd) n one thousand-millionth of a second. Symbol: ns

nanotechnology (ˌnænəʊtɛkˈnɒlədʒɪ) n a branch of technology dealing with the manufacture of objects with dimensions of less than 100 nanometres and the manipulation of individual molecules and atoms

nanoworld ('nænəʊˌwɜːld) n the world at a microscopic level, as dealt with by nanotechnology

Nansei-shoto ('nænˈseɪˌʃəʊˌtɒ) n the official Japanese name for **Ryukyu Islands**

Nansen bottle ('nænsən) n an instrument used by oceanographers for obtaining samples of sea water from a desired depth [c19 named after Fridtjof Nansen (1861–1930), Norwegian arctic explorer, statesman, and scientist]

Nansen passport n a passport issued to stateless persons by the League of Nations after World War I [c20 named after Fridtjof Nansen (1861–1930), Norwegian arctic explorer, statesman, and scientist]

Nan Shan ('næn 'ʃæn) pl n a mountain range in N central China, mainly in Qinghai province, with peaks over 6000 m (20 000 ft)

Nanterre (French nɑ̃tɛr) n a town in N France, on the Seine: an industrial suburb of Paris. Pop: 84 281 (1999)

Nantes (French nɑ̃t) n 1 a port in W France, at the head of the Loire estuary: scene of the signing of the Edict of Nantes and of the Noyades (drownings) during the French Revolution; extensive shipyards, and large metallurgical and food processing industries. Pop: 270 251 (1999) 2 history See **Edict of Nantes**

Nantong or **Nantung** ('næn'tʌŋ) n a city in E China, in Jiangsu province on the Yangtze estuary. Pop: 898 000 (2005 est)

Nantucket (næn'tʌkɪt) n an island off SE Massachusetts: formerly a centre of the whaling industry; now a resort. Length: nearly 24 km (15 miles). Width: 5 km (3 miles). Pop (county and town): 10 724 (2003 est)

nanua ('nɑːnuːˌɑː) n, pl nanua NZ another name for **moki** [Māori]

Naoise ('niːʃə) n Irish myth the husband of Deirdre, killed by his uncle Conchobar. See also **Deirdre**

Naomi ('neɪəmɪ) n Old Testament the mother-in-law of Ruth (Ruth 1:2). Douay spelling: Noemi

naos ('neɪɒs) n, pl naoi ('neɪɔɪ) 1 rare an ancient classical temple 2 architect another name for **cella** [c18 from Greek: inner part of temple]

nap¹ (næp) vb naps, napping, napped (intr) 1 to sleep for a short while; doze 2 to be unaware or inattentive; be off guard (esp in the phrase **catch someone napping**) ▷ n 3 a short light sleep; doze [Old English hnappian; related to Middle High German napfen]

nap² (næp) n 1 a the raised fibres of velvet or similar cloth b the direction in which these fibres lie when smoothed down 2 any similar downy coating 3 Austral informal blankets,

bedding ▷ vb naps, napping, napped 4 (tr) to raise the nap of (cloth, esp velvet) by brushing or similar treatment [c15 probably from Middle Dutch noppe; related to Old English hnoppian to pluck]

nap³ (næp) n 1 Also called: napoleon a card game similar to whist, usually played for stakes 2 a call in this card game, undertaking to win all five tricks 3 horse racing a tipster's choice for an almost certain winner 4 go nap a to undertake to win all five tricks at nap b to risk everything on one chance 5 not to go nap on Austral slang to hold in disfavour 6 nap hand a position in which there is a very good chance of success if a risk is taken ▷ vb naps, napping, napped 7 (tr) horse racing to name (a horse) as likely to win a race [c19 short for NAPOLEON, the original name of the card game]

napalm ('neɪpɑːm, 'næ-) n 1 a thick and highly incendiary liquid, usually consisting of petrol gelled with aluminium soaps, used in firebombs, flame-throwers, etc ▷ vb 2 (tr) to attack with napalm [c20 from NA(PHTHENE) + PALM(ITATE)]

nape¹ (neɪp) n the back of the neck. Related adj: **nuchal** [c13 of unknown origin]

nape² (neɪp) vb (tr) US military slang to attack with napalm

napery ('neɪpərɪ) n rare household linen, esp table linen [c14 from Old French naperie, from nape tablecloth, from Latin mappa. See NAPKIN]

Naphtali ('næftəˌlaɪ) n Old Testament 1 Jacob's sixth son, whose mother was Rachel's handmaid (Genesis 30:7–8) 2 the tribe descended from him 3 the territory of this tribe, between the Sea of Galilee and the mountains of central Galilee. Douay spelling: Nephtali

naphtha ('næfθə, 'næp-) n 1 a distillation product from coal tar boiling in the approximate range 80–170°C and containing aromatic hydrocarbons 2 a distillation product from petroleum boiling in the approximate range 100–200°C and containing aliphatic hydrocarbons: used as a solvent and in petrol 3 an obsolete name for **petroleum** [c16 via Latin from Greek, of Iranian origin; related to Persian neft naphtha]

naphthalene, naphthaline ('næfθəˌliːn, 'næp-) or **naphthalin** ('næfθəlɪn, 'næp-) n a white crystalline volatile solid with a characteristic penetrating odour: an aromatic hydrocarbon used in mothballs and in the manufacture of dyes, explosives, etc Formula: $C_{10}H_8$ [c19 from NAPHTHA + ALCOHOL + -ENE] > naphthalic (næf'θælɪk, næp-) adj

naphthene ('næfθiːn, 'næp-) n any of a class of cycloalkanes, mainly derivatives of cyclopentane, found in petroleum [c20 from NAPHTHA + -ENE]

naphthol ('næfθɒl, 'næp-) n a white crystalline solid having two isomeric forms, **alpha-naphthol**, used in dyes, and **beta-naphthol**, used in dyes and as an antioxidant. Formula: $C_{10}H_7OH$ [c19 from NAPHTHA + -OL¹]

naphthyl ('næfθaɪl, -θɪl, 'næp-) n (modifier) of, consisting of, or containing either of two forms of the monovalent group $C_{10}H_7-$ [c19 from NAPHTHA + -YL]

Napier ('neɪpɪə) n a port in New Zealand, on E North Island on Hawke Bay: wool trade centre. Pop: 56 100 (2004 est)

Napierian logarithm (nə'pɪərɪən, neɪ-) n another name for **natural logarithm**

Napier's bones ('neɪpɪəz) pl n a set of graduated rods formerly used for multiplication and division [c17 based on a method invented by John Napier (1550–1617), Scottish mathematician]

napiform ('neɪpɪˌfɔːm) adj botany shaped like a turnip [c19 from Latin nāpus turnip]

napkin ('næpkɪn) n 1 Also called: table napkin a usually square piece of cloth or paper used while eating to protect the clothes, wipe the mouth, etc; serviette 2 rare a similar piece of cloth used for example as a handkerchief or headscarf 3 a more formal name for **nappy¹** 4 a less common term

for **sanitary towel** [c15 from Old French, from nape tablecloth, from Latin mappa small cloth, towel; see MAP]

Naples ('neɪpəlz) n 1 a port in SW Italy, capital of Campania region, on the Bay of Naples: the third largest city in the country; founded by Greeks in the 6th century BC; incorporated into the Kingdom of the Two Sicilies in 1140 and its capital (1282–1503); university (1224). Pop: 1 004 500 (2001). Ancient name: Neapolis Italian name: Napoli Related adj: **Neapolitan** 2 **Bay of** an inlet of the Tyrrhenian Sea in the SW coast of Italy

Naples yellow n 1 a yellow pigment, used by artists; lead antimonate 2 a similar pigment consisting of a mixture of zinc oxide with yellow colouring matter 3 the colour of either of these pigments

napoleon (nə'pəʊlɪən) n 1 a former French gold coin worth 20 francs bearing a portrait of either Napoleon I (1769–1821), Emperor of the French (1804–15), or Napoleon III (1808–73), Emperor of the French (1852–70) 2 cards the full name for **nap³** (sense 1) 3 the US name for **millefeuille** [c19 from French napoléon, after Napoleon I]

Napoleonic (nəˌpəʊlɪ'ɒnɪk) adj relating to or characteristic of Napoleon I (1769–1821), Emperor of the French (1804–15), or his era

Napoleonic Code n the English name for the Code Napoléon

Napoleonic Wars pl n the series of wars fought between France, under Napoleon Bonaparte, and (principally) Great Britain, Prussia, Russia, and Austria either alone or in alliances (1799–1815)

Napoli ('nɑːpoli) n the Italian name for **Naples**

nappa ('næpə) n a soft leather, used in gloves and clothes, made from sheepskin, lambskin, or kid [c19 named after Napa, California, where it was originally made]

nappe (næp) n 1 a large sheet or mass of rock, commonly a recumbent fold, that has been thrust from its original position by earth movements 2 the sheet of water that flows over a dam or weir 3 geometry either of the two parts into which a **cone** (sense 2) is divided by the vertex [c20 from French: tablecloth]

napper¹ ('næpə) n a person or thing that raises the nap on cloth

napper² ('næpə) n Brit a slang or dialect word for **head** (sense 1) [c18 from NAP¹]

nappy¹ ('næpɪ) n, pl -pies Brit a piece of soft material, esp towelling or a disposable material, wrapped around a baby in order to absorb its excrement. Also called: napkin US and Canadian name: diaper [c20 changed from NAPKIN]

nappy² ('næpɪ) adj -pier, -piest 1 having a nap; downy; fuzzy 2 (of alcoholic drink, esp beer) a having a head; frothy b strong or heady 3 dialect, chiefly Brit slightly intoxicated; tipsy 4 (of a horse) jumpy or irritable; nervy ▷ n 5 any strong alcoholic drink, esp heady beer > 'nappiness n

nappy rash n Brit (in babies) any irritation to the skin around the genitals, anus, or buttocks, usually caused by contact with urine or excrement. Formal name: napkin rash US and Canadian name: diaper rash

Nara ('nɑːrə) n a city in central Japan, on S Honshu: the first permanent capital of Japan (710–784). Pop: 364 411 (2002 est)

Narayanganj (nə'rɑːjənˌgʌndʒ) n a city in central Bangladesh, on the Ganges delta just southeast of Dhaka. Pop: 276 549 (1991)

Narbada (nə'bʌdə) n another name for the **Narmada**

Narbonne (French narbɔn) n a city in S France: capital of the Roman province of **Gallia Narbonensis**; harbour silted up in the 14th century. Pop: 46 510 (1999)

narc (nɑːk) n US slang a narcotics agent

narceine or **narceen** ('nɑːsiːn) n a narcotic alkaloid that occurs in opium. Formula: $C_{23}H_{27}O_8N$ [c19 via French from Greek narkē numbness]

narcissism ('nɑːsɪˌsɪzəm) or **narcism** ('nɑːˌsɪzəm)

n

n **1** an exceptional interest in or admiration for oneself, esp one's physical appearance **2** sexual satisfaction derived from contemplation of one's own physical or mental endowments [C19 from NARCISSUS] > **narcissist** *n* > **narcis'sistic** *adj*

narcissus (naːˈsɪsəs) *n, pl* **-cissuses** or **-cissi** (-ˈsɪsaɪ, -ˈsɪsiː) any amaryllidaceous plant of the Eurasian genus *Narcissus*, esp *N. poeticus*, whose yellow, orange, or white flowers have a crown surrounded by spreading segments [C16 via Latin from Greek *nárkissos*, perhaps from *narkē* numbness, because of narcotic properties attributed to species of the plant]

Narcissus (naːˈsɪsəs) *n Greek myth* a beautiful youth who fell in love with his reflection in a pool and pined away, becoming the flower that bears his name

narco- or sometimes before a vowel **narc-** *combining form* **1** indicating numbness or torpor: *narcolepsy* **2** connected with or derived from illicit drug production: *narcoeconomies* [from Greek *narkē* numbness]

narcoanalysis (ˌnaːkəʊəˈnælɪsɪs) *n* psychoanalysis of a patient in a trance induced by a narcotic drug

narcolepsy (ˈnaːkəˌlɛpsɪ) *n pathol* a rare condition characterized by sudden and uncontrollable episodes of deep sleep > **narco'leptic** *adj*

narcosis (naːˈkəʊsɪs) *n* unconsciousness induced by narcotics or general anaesthetics

narcoterrorism (ˌnaːkəʊˈtɛrəˌrɪzəm) *n* terrorism funded by the sale of illegal drugs [C20 from NARCO- + TERRORISM] > **narco'terrorist** *n, adj*

narcotic (naːˈkɒtɪk) *n* **1** any of a group of drugs, such as heroin, morphine, and pethidine, that produce numbness and stupor. They are used medicinally to relieve pain but are sometimes also taken for their pleasant effects; prolonged use may cause addiction **2** anything that relieves pain or induces sleep, mental numbness, etc **3** any illegal drug ▷ *adj* **4** of, relating to, or designating narcotics **5** of or relating to narcotics addicts or users **6** of or relating to narcosis [C14 via Medieval Latin from Greek *narkōtikós*, from *narkoūn* to render numb, from *narkē* numbness] > **nar'cotically** *adv*

narcotism (ˈnaːkəˌtɪzəm) *n* stupor or addiction induced by narcotic drugs

narcotize or **narcotise** (ˈnaːkəˌtaɪz) *vb* (*tr*) to place under the influence of a narcotic drug > ˌnarcoti'zation or ˌnarcoti'sation *n*

nard (naːd) *n* **1** another name for **spikenard** (senses 1, 2) **2** any of several plants, such as certain valerians, whose aromatic roots were formerly used in medicine [C14 via Latin from Greek *nárdos*, perhaps ultimately from Sanskrit *nalada* Indian spikenard, perhaps via Semitic (Hebrew *nēr'd*, Arabic *nārdīn*)]

nardoo (naːˈduː) *n* **1** any of certain cloverlike ferns of the genus *Marsilea*, which grow in swampy areas **2** the spores of such a plant, used as food in Australia [C19 from a native Australian language]

nares (ˈnɛəriːz) *pl n, sing* **naris** (ˈnɛərɪs) *anatomy* the nostrils [C17 from Latin; related to Old English *nasu*, Latin *nāsus* nose]

narghile, nargile or **nargileh** (ˈnaːgɪlɪ, -ˌleɪ) *n* another name for **hookah** [C19 from French *narguilé*, from Persian *nārgīleh* a pipe having a bowl made of coconut shell, from *nārgīl* coconut]

narial (ˈnɛərɪəl) or **narine** (ˈnɛərɪn, -raɪn) *adj anatomy* of or relating to the nares [C19 from Latin *nāris* nostril]

nark (naːk) *slang* ▷ *n* **1** *Brit, Austral, and NZ* an informer or spy, esp one working for the police (**copper's nark**) **2** *Brit* a person who complains irritatingly: *an old nark* **3** *Austral and NZ* a spoilsport ▷ *vb* **4** *Brit, Austral, and NZ* to annoy, upset, or irritate: *he was narked by her indifference* **5** (*intr*) *Brit, Austral, and NZ* to inform or spy, esp for the police **6** (*intr*) *Brit* to complain irritatingly **7** **nark at (someone)** *NZ* to nag (someone) **8** **nark it**

Brit stop it! [C19 probably from Romany *nāk* nose]

narky (ˈnaːkɪ) *adj* **narkier, narkiest** *slang* irritable, complaining, or sarcastic

Narmada (nəˈmʌdə) or **Narbada** *n* a river in central India, rising in Madhya Pradesh and flowing generally west to the Gulf of Cambay in a wide estuary: the second most sacred river in India. Length: 1290 km (801 miles)

Narraganset or **Narragansett** (ˌnærəˈgænsɪt) *n* **1** (*pl* **-set, -sets** or **-sett, -setts**) a member of a North American Indian people formerly living in Rhode Island **2** the language of this people, belonging to the Algonquian family

Narragansett Bay *n* an inlet of the Atlantic in SE Rhode Island: contains several islands, including Rhode Island, Prudence Island, and Conanicut Island

narrate (nəˈreɪt) *vb* **1** to tell (a story); relate **2** to speak in accompaniment of (a film, television programme, etc) [C17 from Latin *narrāre* to recount, from *gnārus* knowing] > **nar'ratable** *adj*

narration (nəˈreɪʃən) *n* **1** the act or process of narrating **2** a narrated account or story; narrative **3** (in traditional rhetoric) the third step in making a speech, the putting forward of the question

narrative (ˈnærətɪv) *n* **1** an account, report, or story, as of events, experiences, etc **2** (sometimes preceded by *the*) the part of a literary work that relates events **3** the process or technique of narrating ▷ *adj* **4** telling a story: *a narrative poem* **5** of or relating to narration: *narrative art* > **'narratively** *adv*

narrator (nəˈreɪtə) *n* **1** a person who tells a story or gives an account of something **2** a person who speaks in accompaniment of a film, television programme, etc

narrow (ˈnærəʊ) *adj* **1** small in breadth, esp in comparison to length **2** limited in range or extent **3** limited in outlook; lacking breadth of vision **4** limited in means or resources; meagre: *narrow resources* **5** barely adequate or successful (esp in the phrase **a narrow escape**) **6** painstakingly thorough; minute: *a narrow scrutiny* **7** *finance* denoting an assessment of liquidity as including notes and coin in circulation with the public, banks' till money, and banks' balances: *narrow money*. Compare **broad** (sense 14) **8** *dialect* overcareful with money; parsimonious **9** *phonetics* **a** another word for **tense¹** (sense 4) **b** relating to or denoting a transcription used to represent phonetic rather than phonemic distinctions **c** another word for **close¹** (sense 21) **10** (of agricultural feeds) especially rich in protein **11** **narrow squeak** *informal* an escape only just managed ▷ *vb* **12** to make or become narrow; limit; restrict ▷ *n* **13** a narrow place, esp a pass or strait ▷ See also **narrows** [Old English *nearu*; related to Old Saxon *naru*] > **'narrowly** *adv* > **'narrowness** *n*

narrowband (ˈnærəʊˌbænd) *n* a limited-capacity transmission channel such as that used for transmitting telephone calls and faxes. Compare **broadband**

narrow boat *n* a long narrow bargelike boat with a beam of 2.1 m (7 ft) or less, used on canals

narrowcast (ˈnærəʊˌkaːst) *vb* **-casts, -casting, -cast** or **-casted** **1** (*tr*) to supply (television programmes) to a small area by cable television **2** (*intr*) (of programmers or advertisers) to target a specialized audience on radio or television ▷ Compare **broadcast**. > **'narrow,casting** *n*

narrow gauge *n* **1** a railway track with a smaller distance between the lines than the standard gauge of 56½ in ▷ *adj* **narrow-gauge** or **narrow-gauged** **2** of, relating to, or denoting a railway with a narrow gauge

narrow-minded *adj* having a biased or illiberal viewpoint; bigoted, intolerant, or prejudiced > ˌnarrow-'mindedly *adv* > ˌnarrow-'mindedness *n*

narrows (ˈnærəʊz) *pl n* a narrow part of a strait, river, current, etc

narrow seas *pl n archaic* the channels between Great Britain and the Continent and Great Britain and Ireland

narthex (ˈnaːθɛks) *n* **1** a portico at the west end of a basilica or church, esp one that is at right angles to the nave **2** a rectangular entrance hall between the porch and nave of a church [C17 via Latin from Medieval Greek: enclosed porch, enclosure (earlier: box), from Greek *narthēx* giant fennel, the stems of which were used to make boxes]

Narva (*Russian* ˈnarvə) *n* a port in Estonia on the Narva River near the Gulf of Finland: developed around a Danish fortress in the 13th century; textile centre. Pop: 77770 (1995)

Narvik (ˈnaːvɪk; *Norwegian* ˈnarvik) *n* a port in N Norway: scene of two naval battles in 1940; exports iron ore from Kiruna and Gällivare (Sweden). Pop: 18542 (2004 est)

narwhal, narwal (ˈnaːwəl) or **narwhale** (ˈnaːˌweɪl) *n* an arctic toothed whale, *Monodon monoceros*, having a black-spotted whitish skin and, in the male, a long spiral tusk: family *Monodontidae* [C17 of Scandinavian origin; compare Danish, Norwegian *narhval*, from Old Norse *nāhvalr*, from *nār* corpse + *hvalr* whale, from its white colour, supposed to resemble a human corpse]

nary (ˈnɛərɪ) *adv dialect* not; never: *nary a man was left* [C19 variant of *ne'er a* never a]

NASA (ˈnæsə) *n* (in the US) *acronym for* National Aeronautics and Space Administration

nasal (ˈneɪzᵊl) *adj* **1** of or relating to the nose **2** *phonetics* pronounced with the soft palate lowered allowing air to escape via the nasal cavity instead of or as well as through the mouth ▷ *n* **3** a nasal speech sound, such as English *m, n,* or *ng* **4** another word for **nosepiece** (sense 1) [C17 from French from Late Latin *nāsālis*, from Latin *nāsus* nose] > **nasality** (neɪˈzælɪtɪ) *n* > **'nasally** *adv*

nasal index *n* the ratio of the widest part of the nose to its length multiplied by 100

nasalize or **nasalise** (ˈneɪzᵊˌlaɪz) *vb* (*tr*) to pronounce nasally > ˌnasali'zation or ˌnasali'sation *n*

NASCAR dad (ˈnæsˌkaː) *n US* a stereotypical representation of a white working-class American male with a family [C21 from *NASCAR* (National Association Stock Car Racing), a form of motor racing supposedly popular with this type of man]

nascent (ˈnæsᵊnt, ˈneɪ-) *adj* **1** starting to grow or develop; being born **2** *chem* (of an element or simple compound, esp hydrogen) created within the reaction medium in the atomic form and having a high activity [C17 from Latin *nāscēns* present participle of *nāscī* to be born] > **'nascence** or **'nascency** *n*

NASDAQ (ˈnæzdæk) *n* (in the US) *acronym for* National Association of Securities Dealers Automated Quotations System

naseberry (ˈneɪzˌbɛrɪ) *n, pl* **-berries** another name for **sapodilla** [C17 from Spanish *néspera* medlar + BERRY]

Naseby (ˈneɪzbɪ) *n* a village in Northamptonshire: site of a major Parliamentarian victory (1645) in the Civil War, when Cromwell routed Prince Rupert's force

nashi (ˈnæʃɪ) *n, pl* **nashi** or **nashis** another name for **Asian pear** [Japanese: pear]

Nasho (ˈnæʃəʊ) *n obsolete, Austral slang* **1** compulsory military training; conscription **2** (*pl* **Nashos**) a conscript [C20 shortening and alteration of *national service*]

Nashville (ˈnæʃvɪl) *n* a city in central Tennessee, the state capital, on the Cumberland River: an industrial and commercial centre, noted for its recording industry. Pop (including Davidson): 544765 (2003 est)

nasi goreng (ˈnaːsɪ gəˈrɛŋ) *n* a dish, originating in Malaysia, consisting of rice fried with a selection of other ingredients [C20 from Malay *nasi* (cooked) rice + *goreng* fry]

Nasik (ˈnaːsɪk) *n* a city in W India, in

Maharashtra: a centre for Hindu pilgrims. Pop: 1 076 967 (2001)

nasion ('neɪzɪən) *n* a craniometric point where the top of the nose meets the ridge of the forehead [c20 New Latin, from Latin *nāsus* nose] > 'nasial *adj*

Nasiriyah (ˌnæzɪ'riːə) *n* a city in S Iraq, on the River Euphrates; agricultural and trading centre. Pop. 425 000 (2005 est)

Naskapi (nə'skæpɪ) *n* a member of an Innu people living in Quebec [from Cree]

naso- *combining form* nose: nasopharynx [from Latin *nāsus* nose]

nasofrontal (ˌneɪzəʊ'frʌntəl) *adj anatomy* of or relating to the nasal and frontal bones

nasogastric (ˌneɪzəʊ'gæstrɪk) *adj anatomy* of or relating to the nose and stomach: *a nasogastric tube*

nasopharynx (ˌneɪzəʊ'færɪŋks) *n, pl* -pharynges (-fə'rɪndʒiːz) *or* -pharynxes the part of the pharynx situated above and behind the soft palate > nasopharyngeal (ˌneɪzəʊfə'rɪndʒɪəl, -ˌfærɪn'dʒɪəl) *adj*

Nassau *n* **1** (*German* 'nasaʊ) a region of W central Germany: formerly a duchy (1816–66), from which a branch of the House of Orange arose (represented by the present rulers of the Netherlands and Luxembourg); annexed to the Prussian province of Hesse-Nassau in 1866; corresponds to present-day W Hesse and NE Rhineland-Palatinate states **2** ('næsɔː) the capital and chief port of the Bahamas, on the NE coast of New Providence Island: resort. Pop: 229 000 (2005 est)

nassella tussock (nə'sɛlə) *n* a type of tussock grass, originally of South America, now regarded as a noxious weed in New Zealand

Nassella Tussock Board *n NZ* one of many local statutory organizations set up in different regions of New Zealand to eradicate the invasive nassella tussock weed

nastic movement ('næstɪk) *n* a response of plant parts that is independent of the direction of the external stimulus, such as the opening of buds caused by an alteration in light intensity [c19 *nastic,* from Greek *nastos* close-packed, from *nassein* to press down]

nasturtium (nə'stɜːʃəm) *n* any of various plants of the genus *Tropaeolum,* esp *T. major,* having round leaves and yellow, red, or orange trumpet-shaped spurred flowers: family *Tropaeolaceae* [c17 from Latin: kind of cress, from *nāsus* nose + *tortus* twisted, from *torquēre* to twist, distort; so called because the pungent smell causes one to wrinkle one's nose]

nasty ('nɑːstɪ) *adj* -tier, -tiest **1** unpleasant, offensive, or repugnant **2** (of an experience, condition, etc) unpleasant, dangerous, or painful: *a nasty wound* **3** spiteful, abusive, or ill-natured **4** obscene or indecent **5** *nasty piece of work Brit informal* a cruel or mean person ▷ *n, pl* -ties **6** an offensive or unpleasant person or thing: *a video nasty* [c14 origin obscure; probably related to Swedish dialect *nasket* and Dutch *nestig* dirty] > 'nastily *adv* > 'nastiness *n*

-nasty *n combining form* indicating a nastic movement to a certain stimulus: *nyctinasty* [from Greek *nastos* pressed down, close-pressed] > -nastic *adj combining form*

NAS/UWT (in Britain) *abbreviation for* National Association of Schoolmasters/Union of Women Teachers

Nat (næt) *n informal* **1** a member or supporter of the Scottish National Party **2** *NZ* a member of the National Party **3** *NZ* a Member of Parliament for the National Party

nat. *abbreviation for* **1** national **2** natural

natal¹ ('neɪtəl) *adj* **1** of or relating to birth **2** a rare word for **native**: *natal instincts* [c14 from Latin *nātālis* of one's birth, from *nātus,* from *nascī* to be born]

natal² ('neɪtəl) *adj anatomy* of or relating to the buttocks [from New Latin *nates* buttocks]

Natal *n* **1** (nə'tæl) a former province of E South Africa, between the Drakensberg and the Indian Ocean: set up as a republic by the Boers in 1838; became a British colony in 1843; joined South Africa in 1910; replaced by KwaZulu/Natal in 1994. Capital: Pietermaritzburg **2** (*Portuguese* na'tal) a port in NE Brazil, capital of Rio Grande do Norte state, near the mouth of the Potengi River. Pop: 1 049 000 (2005 est)

natality (neɪ'tælɪtɪ) *n, pl* -ties another name (esp US) for **birth rate**

natant ('neɪtənt) *adj* **1** (of aquatic plants) floating on the water **2** *rare* floating or swimming [c18 from Latin *natāns,* present participle of *natāre* to swim]

natation (nə'teɪʃən) *n* a formal or literary word for **swimming** [c16 from Latin *natātiō* a swimming, from *natāre* to swim] > na'tational *adj*

natatorium (ˌneɪtə'tɔːrɪəm) *n, pl* -riums *or* -ria (-rɪə) *rare* a swimming pool, esp an indoor pool [c20 from Late Latin: swimming place, pool]

natatory (nə'teɪtərɪ) *or* **natatorial** (ˌnætə'tɔːrɪəl, ˌneɪtə'tɔːrɪəl) *adj* of or relating to swimming [c18 from Late Latin *natātōrius,* from *natāre* to swim]

natch (nætʃ) *sentence substitute informal* short for **naturally** (sense 3)

nates ('neɪtiːz) *pl n, sing* -tis (-tɪs) a technical word for the **buttocks** [c17 from Latin; compare Greek *nōton* back, *nosthi* buttocks]

NATFHE *abbreviation for* National Association of Teachers in Further and Higher Education

Nathan ('neɪθən) *n Old Testament* a prophet at David's court (II Samuel 7:1–17; 12:1–15)

Nathanael (nə'θænjəl) *n New Testament* a Galilean who is perhaps to be identified with Bartholomew among the apostles (John 1:45–51; 21:1)

natheless ('neɪθlɪs) *or* **nathless** ('næθlɪs) *archaic* ▷ *sentence connector* **1** another word for **nonetheless** ▷ *prep* **2** notwithstanding; despite [Old English *nāthylēs,* from *nā* never + *thȳ* for that + *lēs* less]

nation ('neɪʃən) *n* **1** an aggregation of people or peoples of one or more cultures, races, etc, organized into a single state: *the Australian nation* **2** a community of persons not constituting a state but bound by common descent, language, history, etc: *the French-Canadian nation* **3 a** a federation of tribes, esp American Indians **b** the territory occupied by such a federation [c13 via Old French from Latin *nātiō* birth, tribe, from *nascī* to be born] > 'nationˌhood *n* > 'nationless *adj*

national ('næʃənəl) *adj* **1** of, involving, or relating to a nation as a whole **2** of, relating to, or characteristic of a particular nation: *the national dress of Poland* **3** *rare* nationalistic or patriotic ▷ *n* **4** a citizen or subject **5** a national newspaper > 'nationally *adv*

National ('næʃənəl) *n* **the** short for the **Grand National**

national accounting *n* another name for **social accounting**

national agreement *n* written formal agreements covering rates of pay and other terms and conditions of employment that are the result of collective bargaining at national level between one or more trade unions and employers in a sector of the economy

national anthem *n* a patriotic hymn or other song adopted by a nation for use on public or state occasions

National Assembly *n French history* the body constituted by the French third estate in June 1789 after the calling of the Estates General. It was dissolved in Sept 1791 to be replaced by the new Legislative Assembly

national assistance *n* (in Britain) formerly a weekly allowance paid to certain people by the state to bring their incomes up to minimum levels established by law. Now replaced by **income support**

national bank *n* **1** (in the US) a commercial bank incorporated under a Federal charter and legally required to be a member of the Federal Reserve System. Compare **state bank 2** a bank owned and operated by a government

National Bureau of Standards *n* (in the US) an organization, founded in 1901, whose function is to establish and maintain standards for units of measurements. Compare **British Standards Institution**

national code *n* another term for **Australian Rules**

National Convention *n* **1** a convention held every four years by each major US political party to choose its presidential candidate **2** *French history* the longest-lasting of the revolutionary assemblies, lasting from Sept 1792 to Oct 1795, when it was replaced by the Directory

National Country Party *n* (in Australia) a former name for **National Party.** Abbreviation: NCP

National Covenant *n* See **Covenant**

National Curriculum *n* (in England and Wales) the curriculum of subjects taught in state schools progressively from 1989. There are ten foundation subjects: English, maths, and science (the core subjects); art, design and technology, geography, history, music, physical education, and a foreign language. Pupils are assessed according to specified attainment targets throughout each of four key stages. Schools must also provide religious education and from 1999 lessons in citizenship

national debt *n* the total outstanding borrowings of a nation's central government. Also called (esp US): public debt

National Economic Development Council *n* an advisory body on general economic policy in Britain, composed of representatives of government, management, and trade unions: established in 1962; abolished in 1992 Abbreviations: NEDC, (informal) Neddy

National Enterprise Board *n* a public corporation established in 1975 to help the economy of the UK. In 1981 it merged with the National Research and Development Council to form the British Technology Group. Abbreviation: NEB

National Front *n* (in Britain) a small political party of the right with racist and other extremist policies. Abbreviation: NF

National Gallery *n* a major art gallery in London, in Trafalgar Square. Founded in 1824, it contains the largest collection of paintings in Britain

national grid *n* **1** *Brit* a network of high-voltage power lines connecting major power stations **2** a grid of metric coordinates used by the Ordnance Survey in Britain and Ireland and in New Zealand by the New Zealand Lands and Survey Department and printed on their maps

National Guard *n* **1** (*sometimes not capitals*) the armed force, first commanded by Lafayette, that was established in France in 1789 and existed intermittently until 1871 **2** (in the US) a state military force that can be called into federal service by the president

National Health Service *n* (in Britain) the system of national medical services since 1948, financed mainly by taxation

national hunt *n Brit* (*often capital*) **a** the racing of horses on racecourses with jumps **b** (*as modifier*): *a National Hunt jockey*

national income *n economics* the total of all incomes accruing over a specified period to residents of a country and consisting of wages, salaries, profits, rent, and interest

national insurance *n* (in Britain) state insurance based on weekly contributions from employees and employers and providing payments to the unemployed, the sick, the retired, etc, as well as medical services. See also **social security**

nationalism ('næʃənəˌlɪzəm, 'næʃnə-) *n* **1** a sentiment based on common cultural

n

characteristics that binds a population and often produces a policy of national independence or separatism **2** loyalty or devotion to one's country; patriotism **3** exaggerated, passionate, or fanatical devotion to a national community. See also **chauvinism**. > ˈnationalist *n, adj* > ˌnationalˈistic *adj*

Nationalist China *n* an unofficial name for (the Republic of) **China**

nationality (ˌnæʃəˈnælɪtɪ) *n, pl* **-ties 1** the state or fact of being a citizen of a particular nation **2** a body of people sharing common descent, history, language, etc; a nation **3** a national group: *30 different nationalities are found in this city* **4** national character or quality **5** the state or fact of being a nation; national status

nationalize *or* **nationalise** (ˈnæʃənəˌlaɪz, ˈnæʃnə-) *vb (tr)* **1** to put (an industry, resources, etc) under state control or ownership **2** to make national in scope, character, or status **3** a less common word for **naturalize**. > ˌnationaliˈzation *or* ˌnationaliˈsation *n*

National Liberation Front *n* **1** (*sometimes not capitals*) a revolutionary movement that seeks the national independence of a country, usually by guerrilla warfare **2** Also called: **National Liberation Front of South Vietnam** a political organization formed in South Vietnam in 1960 by the Vietcong

national park *n* an area of countryside for public use designated by a national government as being of notable scenic, environmental, or historical importance

National Park *n* a mountainous volcanic region in New Zealand, in the central North Island: ski resort

National Party *n* **1** (in New Zealand) the more conservative of the two main political parties **2** (in Australia) a political party drawing its main support from rural areas. Former name: **National Country Party 3** (in South Africa) a political party composed mainly of centre-to-right-wing Afrikaners, which ruled from 1948 until the country's first multiracial elections in 1994: renamed the **New National Party** (NNP) in 1999. See also **Progressive Federal Party, United Party**

National Physical Laboratory *n* a UK establishment founded in 1900 at Teddington to carry out research in physics and monitor standards of measurement. Abbreviation: NPL

National Portrait Gallery *n* an art gallery in London, established in 1856, displaying portraits and photographs of eminent figures in British history

National Savings Bank *n* (in Britain) a government savings bank, run through the post office, esp for small savers

National School *n* **1** (in Ireland) a state primary school **2** (in England in the 19th century) a school run by the Church of England for the children of the poor

national service *n* compulsory military service

National Socialism *n German history* the doctrines and practices of the Nazis, involving the supremacy of the Austrian-born German dictator Adolf Hitler (1889–1945) as Führer (1934–45), anti-Semitism, state control of the economy, and national expansion. Also called: **Nazism, Naziism** > **National Socialist** *n, adj*

national superannuation *n NZ* a means-related pension paid to elderly people

National Tests *pl n* (*sometimes not capitals*) *Brit education* externally devised assessments in the core subjects of English, mathematics and science that school students in England and Wales sit at the end of Key Stages 1 to 3. Often referred to as: SATs

National Theatre *n* the former name of the **Royal National Theatre**

National Trust *n* **1** (in Britain) an organization concerned with the preservation of historic buildings and monuments and areas of the countryside of great beauty in England, Wales,

and Northern Ireland. It was founded in 1895 and incorporated by act of parliament in 1907. The **National Trust for Scotland** was founded in 1931 **2** (in Australia) a similar organization in each of the states

nation-building *n South African* the advocacy of national solidarity in South Africa in the post-apartheid era

Nation of Islam *n* the official name for the **Black Muslims**. Abbreviation: NOI

nation-state *n* an independent state inhabited by all the people of one nation and one nation only

nationwide (ˈneɪʃənˌwaɪd) *adj* covering or available to the whole of a nation; national: *a nationwide survey*

native (ˈneɪtɪv) *adj* **1** relating or belonging to a person or thing by virtue of conditions existing at the time of birth: *my native city* **2** inherent, natural, or innate: *a native strength* **3** born in a specified place: *a native Indian* **4** (when *postpositive*, foll by *to*) originating in a specific place or area: *kangaroos are native to Australia* **5** characteristic of or relating to the indigenous inhabitants of a country or area: *the native art of the New Guinea Highlands* **6** (of chemical elements, esp metals) found naturally in the elemental form **7** unadulterated by civilization, artifice, or adornment; natural **8** *archaic* related by birth or race **9** **go native** (of a settler) to adopt the lifestyle of the local population, esp when it appears less civilized ▷ *n* **10** (usually foll by *of*) a person born in a particular place: *a native of Geneva* **11** (usually foll by *of*) a species originating in a particular place or area: *the kangaroo is a native of Australia* **12** a member of an indigenous people of a country or area, esp a non-White people, as opposed to colonial settlers and immigrants **13** *derogatory, rare* any non-White [c14 from Latin *nātīvus* innate, natural, from *nascī* to be born] > ˈnatively *adv* > ˈnativeness *n*

Native American *n* another name for an **American Indian**

native bear *n* an Austral name for **koala**

native-born *adj* born in the country or area indicated

native bush *n NZ* indigenous forest

native cat *n Austral* any of various Australian catlike carnivorous marsupials of the genus *Dasyurus*

native companion *n Austral* another name for the **brolga** [c19 so called because the birds were observed in pairs]

native dog *n Austral* a dingo

native oak *n Austral* another name for **casuarina**

native speaker *n* a person having a specified native language: *a native speaker of Cree*

Native States *pl n* the former 562 semi-independent states of India, ruled by Indians but subject to varying degrees of British authority: merged with provinces by 1948; largest states were Hyderabad, Gwalior, Baroda, Mysore, Cochin, Jammu and Kashmir, Travancore, Sikkim, and Indore. Also called: **Indian States and Agencies**

nativism (ˈneɪtɪˌvɪzəm) *n* **1** *chiefly US* the policy of favouring the natives of a country over the immigrants **2** *anthropol* the policy of protecting and reaffirming native tribal cultures in reaction to acculturation **3** the doctrine that the mind and its capacities are innately structured and that much knowledge is innate > ˈnativist *n, adj* > ˌnativˈistic *adj*

nativity (nəˈtɪvɪtɪ) *n, pl* **-ties** birth or origin, esp in relation to the circumstances surrounding it [c14 via Old French from Late Latin *nātīvitas* birth: see **NATIVE**]

Nativity (nəˈtɪvɪtɪ) *n* **1** the birth of Jesus Christ **2** the feast of Christmas as a commemoration of this **3 a** an artistic representation of the circumstances of the birth of Christ **b** (*as modifier*): *a Nativity play*

natl *abbreviation for* national

NATO *or* **Nato** (ˈneɪtəʊ) *n acronym for* North Atlantic Treaty Organization, an international organization composed of the US, Canada, Britain, and a number of European countries: established by the **North Atlantic Treaty** (1949) for purposes of collective security. In 1994 it launched the partnerships for peace initiative, in order to forge alliances with former Warsaw Pact countries; in 1997 a treaty of cooperation with Russia was signed and in 1999 Hungary, Poland, and the Czech Republic became full NATO members

natrium (ˈneɪtrɪəm) *n* an obsolete name for **sodium** [c19 New Latin; see **NATRON**]

natrolite (ˈnætrəˌlaɪt, ˈneɪ-) *n* a colourless, white, or yellow zeolite mineral consisting of sodium aluminium silicate in the form of needle-like orthorhombic crystals. Formula: $Na_2Al_2Si_3O_{10}.2H_2O$ [c19 from **NATRON** + **-LITE**]

natron (ˈneɪtrən) *n* a whitish or yellow mineral that consists of hydrated sodium carbonate and occurs in saline deposits and salt lakes. Formula: $Na_2CO_3.10H_2O$ [c17 via French and Spanish from Arabic *natrūn*, from Greek *nitron*]

NATSOPA (nætˈsəʊpə) *n* (formerly, in Britain) *acronym for* National Society of Operative Printers, Graphical and Media Personnel

natter (ˈnætə) *chiefly Brit* ▷ *vb* **1** (*intr*) to talk idly and at length; chatter or gossip ▷ *n* **2** prolonged idle chatter or gossip [c19 changed from *gnatter* to grumble, of imitative origin; compare Low German *gnatteren*] > ˈnatterer *n*

natterjack (ˈnætəˌdʒæk) *n* a European toad, *Bufo calamita*, of sandy regions, having a greyish-brown body marked with reddish warty processes: family *Bufonidae* [c18 of unknown origin]

natty (ˈnætɪ) *adj* **-tier, -tiest** *informal* smart in appearance or dress; spruce; dapper: *a natty outfit* [c18 perhaps from obsolete *netty*, from *net* **NEAT**[1]; compare Old French *net* trim] > ˈnattily *adv* > ˈnattiness *n*

natural (ˈnætʃrəl, -tʃərəl) *adj* **1** of, existing in, or produced by nature: *natural science; natural cliffs* **2** in accordance with human nature: *it is only natural to want to be liked* **3** as is normal or to be expected; ordinary or logical: *the natural course of events* **4** not acquired; innate: *a natural gift for sport* **5** being so through innate qualities: *a natural leader* **6** not supernatural or strange: *natural phenomena* **7** not constrained or affected; genuine or spontaneous **8** not artificially dyed or coloured: *a natural blonde* **9** following or resembling nature or life; lifelike: *she looked more natural without her make-up* **10** not affected by man or civilization; uncultivated; wild: *in the natural state this animal is not ferocious* **11** illegitimate; born out of wedlock **12** not adopted but rather related by blood: *her natural parents* **13** *music* **a** not sharp or flat **b** (*postpositive*) denoting a note that is neither sharp nor flat: *B natural* **c** (of a key or scale) containing no sharps or flats. Compare **flat**[1] (sense 23), **sharp** (sense 12) **14** *music* of or relating to a trumpet, horn, etc, without valves or keys, on which only notes of the harmonic series of the keynote can be obtained **15** determined by inborn conviction: *natural justice; natural rights* **16** *cards* **a** (of a card) not a joker or wild card **b** (of a canasta or sequence) containing no wild cards **c** (of a bid in bridge) describing genuine values; not conventional **17** based on the principles and findings of human reason and what is to be learned of God from nature rather than on revelation: *natural religion* ▷ *n* **18** *informal* a person or thing regarded as certain to qualify for success, selection, etc: *the horse was a natural for first place* **19** *music* **a** Also called (US): **cancel** an accidental cancelling a previous sharp or flat. Usual symbol: ♮ **b** a note affected by this accidental. Compare **flat**[1] (sense 35), **sharp** (sense 19) **20** *pontoon* the combination of an ace with a ten or court card when dealt to a player as his or her first two cards **21** *obsolete* an imbecile; idiot

> ꞌnaturally *adv* > ꞌnaturalness *n*

natural-born *adj* being as specified through one's birth: *a natural-born Irishman*

natural childbirth *n* a method of childbirth characterized by the absence of anaesthetics, in which the expectant mother is given special breathing and relaxing exercises

natural classification *n biology* classification of organisms according to relationships based on descent from a common ancestor

natural deduction *n* a system of formal logic that has no axioms but permits the assumption of premises of an argument. Such a system uses sequents to record which assumptions are operative at any stage. Compare **axiomatic** (sense 3)

natural frequency *n physics* the frequency at which a system vibrates when set in free vibration. Compare **forcing frequency**

natural gas *n* a gaseous mixture consisting mainly of methane trapped below ground; used extensively as a fuel

natural gender *n* grammatical gender that reflects, as in English, the sex or animacy of the referent of a noun rather than the form or any other feature of the word

natural history *n* **1** the study of animals and plants in the wild state **2** the study of all natural phenomena **3** the sum of these phenomena in a given place or at a given time: *the natural history of Iran* > natural historian *n*

natural immunity *n* immunity with which an individual is born, which has a genetic basis

naturalism (ꞌnætʃrəˌlɪzəm, -tʃərə-) *n* **1 a** a movement, esp in art and literature, advocating detailed realistic and factual description, esp that in 19th-century France in the writings of the novelists Emile Zola (1840–1902), Gustave Flaubert (1821–80), etc **b** the characteristics or effects of this movement **2** a school of painting or sculpture characterized by the faithful imitation of appearances for their own sake **3** the belief that all religious truth is based not on revelation but rather on the study of natural causes and processes **4** *philosophy* **a** a scientific account of the world in terms of causes and natural forces that rejects all spiritual, supernatural, or teleological explanations **b** the meta-ethical thesis that moral properties are reducible to natural ones, or that ethical judgments are derivable from nonethical ones. See **naturalistic fallacy** Compare **descriptivism 5** action or thought caused by natural desires and instincts **6** devotion to that which is natural

naturalist (ꞌnætʃrəlɪst, -tʃərəl-) *n* **1** a person who is expert or interested in botany or zoology, esp in the field **2** a person who advocates or practises naturalism, esp in art or literature

naturalistic (ˌnætʃrəꞌlɪstɪk, -tʃərə-) *adj* **1** of, imitating, or reproducing nature in effect or characteristics **2** of or characteristic of naturalism, esp in art or literature **3** of or relating to naturalists **4** (of an ethical theory) permitting the inference of ethical judgments from statements of nonethical fact. See **Hume's law.** > ˌnaturalꞌistically *adv*

naturalistic fallacy *n* the supposed fallacy of inferring evaluative conclusions from purely factual premises. See **Hume's law** Compare **non-naturalism**

naturalize *or* **naturalise** (ꞌnætʃrəˌlaɪz, -tʃərə-) *vb* **1** (*tr*) to give citizenship to (a person of foreign birth) **2** to be or cause to be adopted in another place, as a word, custom, etc **3** (*tr*) to introduce (a plant or animal from another region) and cause it to adapt to local conditions **4** (*intr*) (of a plant or animal) to adapt successfully to a foreign environment and spread there **5** (*tr*) to explain (something unusual) with reference to nature, excluding the supernatural **6** (*tr*) to make natural or more lifelike > ˌnaturaliꞌzation *or* ˌnaturaliꞌsation *n*

natural justice *n* the principles and procedures that govern the adjudication of disputes between persons or organizations, chief among which are that the adjudication should be unbiased and given in good faith, and that each party should have equal access to the tribunal and should be aware of arguments and documents adduced by the other

natural language *n* **1** a language that has evolved naturally as a means of communication among people. Compare **artificial language, formal language 2** languages of this kind considered collectively

natural law *n* **1** an ethical belief or system of beliefs supposed to be inherent in human nature and discoverable by reason rather than revelation **2** a nonlogically necessary truth; law of nature. See also **nomological** (sense 2) **3** the philosophical doctrine that the authority of the legal system or of certain laws derives from their justifiability by reason, and indeed that a legal system which cannot be so justified has no authority

natural logarithm *n* a logarithm to the base e (see **e** (sense 1)). Usually written log$_e$ or ln. Also called: **Napierian logarithm** Compare **common logarithm**

naturally (ꞌnætʃrəlɪ, -tʃərə-) *adv* **1** in a natural or normal way **2** through nature; inherently; instinctively ▷ *adv, sentence substitute* **3** of course; surely

natural number *n* any of the numbers 0,1,2,3,4,... that can be used to count the members of a set; the nonnegative integers

natural philosophy *n* (now only used in Scottish universities) physical science, esp physics > natural philosopher *n*

natural rate of unemployment *n* another name for NAIRU

natural resources *pl n* naturally occurring materials such as coal, fertile land, etc, that can be used by man

natural science *n* **1** the sciences collectively that are involved in the study of the physical world and its phenomena, including biology, physics, chemistry, and geology, but excluding social sciences, abstract or theoretical sciences, such as mathematics, and applied sciences **2** any one of these sciences > natural scientist *n*

natural selection *n* a process resulting in the survival of those individuals from a population of animals or plants that are best adapted to the prevailing environmental conditions. The survivors tend to produce more offspring than those less well adapted, so that the characteristics of the population change over time, thus accounting for the process of evolution

natural slope *n civil engineering* the maximum angle at which soil will lie in a bank without slipping

natural theology *n* the attempt to derive theological truth, and esp the existence of God, from empirical facts by reasoned argument. Compare **revealed religion, fideism, revelation** (sense 3) > natural theologian *n*

natural virtues *pl n* (esp among the scholastics) those virtues of which man is capable without direct help from God, specifically justice, temperance, prudence, and fortitude. Compare **theological virtues**

natural wastage *n* another term for **attrition** (sense 3)

nature (ꞌneɪtʃə) *n* **1** the fundamental qualities of a person or thing; identity or essential character **2** (*often capital, esp when personified*) the whole system of the existence, arrangement, forces, and events of all physical life that are not controlled by man **3** all natural phenomena and plant and animal life, as distinct from man and his creations **4** a wild primitive state untouched by man or civilization **5** natural unspoilt scenery or countryside **6** disposition or temperament **7** tendencies, desires, or instincts governing

behaviour **8** the normal biological needs or urges of the body **9** sort; kind; character **10** the real appearance of a person or thing: *a painting very true to nature* **11** accepted standards of basic morality or behaviour **12** *biology* the complement of genetic material that partly determines the structure of an organism; genotype. Compare **nurture** (sense 3) **13** *Irish* sympathy and fondness for one's own people or native place: *she is full of nature* **14** against nature unnatural or immoral **15** by nature essentially or innately **16** call of nature *informal, euphemistic or humorous* the need to urinate or defecate **17** from nature using natural models in drawing, painting, etc **18** in (*or* of) the nature of essentially the same as; by way of [c13 via Old French from Latin *nātūra,* from *nātus,* past participle of *nascī* to be born]

Nature Conservancy Council *n* (in Britain) a body set up by act of parliament in 1973 to establish and manage nature reserves, identify SSSIs, and provide information and advice about nature conservation. In 1991–92 it was replaced by English Nature, Scottish Natural Heritage, and the Countryside Council for Wales. Abbreviation: NCC

nature reserve *n* an area of land that is protected and managed in order to preserve a particular type of habitat and its flora and fauna which are often rare or endangered

nature strip *n Austral informal* a grass strip in front of a house between a fence or footpath and a roadway

nature study *n* the study of the natural world, esp animals and plants, by direct observation at an elementary level

nature trail *n* a path through countryside designed and usually signposted to draw attention to natural features of interest

naturism (ꞌneɪtʃəˌrɪzəm) *n* another name for **nudism.** > ꞌnaturist *n, adj*

naturopathy (ˌneɪtʃəꞌrɒpəθɪ) *n* a method of treating disorders, involving the use of herbs and other naturally grown foods, sunlight, fresh air, etc. Also called: **nature cure** > naturopath (ꞌneɪtʃərəˌpæθ) *n* > naturopathic (ˌneɪtʃərəꞌpæθɪk) *adj*

NAU *international car registration for* Nauru

nauch (nɔːtʃ) *n* a variant spelling of **nautch**

Naucratis (ꞌnɔːkrətɪs) *n* an ancient Greek city in N Egypt, in the Nile delta: founded in the 7th century BC

naught (nɔːt) *n* **1** *archaic or literary* nothing or nothingness; ruin or failure **2** a variant spelling (esp US) of **nought 3** set at naught to have disregard or scorn for; disdain ▷ *adv* **4** *archaic or literary* not at all: *it matters naught* ▷ *adj* **5** *obsolete* worthless, ruined, or wicked [Old English *nāwiht,* from *nā* NO¹ + *wiht* thing, person; see WIGHT¹, WHIT]

naughty (ꞌnɔːtɪ) *adj* -tier, -tiest **1** (esp of children or their behaviour) mischievous or disobedient; bad **2** mildly indecent; titillating ▷ *n, pl* -ties **3** *Austral and NZ slang* an act of sexual intercourse [C14 (originally: needy, of poor quality): from NAUGHT] > ꞌnaughtily *adv* > ꞌnaughtiness *n*

naughty nineties *pl n* the (in Britain) the 1890s, considered to be a period of fun-loving and laxity, esp in sexual morals

naumachia (nɔːꞌmeɪkɪə) *or* **naumachy** (ꞌnɔːməkɪ) *n, pl* -chiae (-kɪˌiː) -chias *or* -chies (in ancient Rome) **1** a mock sea fight performed as an entertainment **2** an artificial lake used in such a spectacle [c16 via Latin from Greek *naumakhia,* from *naus* ship + *makhē* battle]

nauplius (ꞌnɔːplɪəs) *n, pl* -plii (-plɪˌaɪ) the larva of many crustaceans, having a rounded unsegmented body with three pairs of limbs [c19 from Latin: type of shellfish, from Greek *Nauplios,* one of the sons of Poseidon]

Nauru (nɑːꞌuːruː) *n* an island republic in the SW Pacific, west of Kiribati: administered jointly by Australia, New Zealand, and Britain as a UN trust

n

territory before becoming independent in 1968; a member of the Commonwealth (formerly a special member not represented at all meetings, until 1999). The economy is based on export of phosphates. Languages: Nauruan (a Malayo-Polynesian language) and English. Religion: Christian. Currency: Australian dollar. Pop: 13 000 (2003 est). Area: 2130 hectares (5263 acres). Former name: Pleasant Island

Nauruan (nɑːˈuːruːən) *adj* **1** of or relating to Nauru, its inhabitants, or their language ▷ *n* **2** a native or inhabitant of Nauru **3** the Malayo-Polynesian language of Nauru

nausea ('nɔːzɪə, -sɪə) *n* **1** the sensation that precedes vomiting **2** a feeling of disgust or revulsion [C16 via Latin from Greek: seasickness, from *naus* ship]

nauseate ('nɔːzɪˌeɪt, -sɪ-) *vb* **1** (*tr*) to arouse feelings of disgust or revulsion in **2** to feel or cause to feel sick > 'nause,ating *adj* > ,nause'ation *n*

nauseous ('nɔːzɪəs, -sɪəs) *adj* **1** feeling sick **2** causing nausea **3** distasteful to the mind or senses; repulsive > 'nauseously *adv* > 'nauseousness *n*

Nausicaä (nɔːˈsɪkɪə) *n Greek myth* a daughter of Alcinous, king of the Phaeacians, who assisted the shipwrecked Odysseus after discovering him on a beach

-naut *n combining form* indicating a person engaged in the navigation of a vehicle, esp one used for scientific investigation: *astronaut*

nautch *or* **nauch** (nɔːtʃ) *n* **a** an intricate traditional Indian dance performed by professional dancing girls **b** (*as modifier*): *a nautch girl* [C18 from Hindi *nāc*, from Sanskrit *nrtya*, from *nrtyati* he acts or dances]

nautical ('nɔːtɪkəl) *adj* of, relating to, or involving ships, navigation, or sailors [C16 from Latin *nauticus*, from Greek *nautikos*, from *naus* ship] > 'nautically *adv*

nautical mile *n* **1** Also called: **international nautical mile, air mile** a unit of length, used esp in navigation, equivalent to the average length of a minute of latitude, and corresponding to a latitude of 45°, i.e. 1852 m (6076.12 ft) **2** a former British unit of length equal to 1853.18 m (6080 ft), which was replaced by the international nautical mile in 1970. Former name: **geographical mile** Compare **sea mile**

nautiloid ('nɔːtɪˌlɔɪd) *n* **1** any mollusc of the *Nautiloidea*, a group of cephalopods that includes the pearly nautilus and many extinct forms ▷ *adj* **2** of, relating to, or belonging to the *Nautiloidea*

nautilus ('nɔːtɪləs) *n, pl* **-luses** *or* **-li** (-ˌlaɪ) **1** any cephalopod mollusc of the genus *Nautilus*, esp the pearly nautilus **2** short for **paper nautilus** [C17 via Latin from Greek *nautilos* sailor, from *naus* ship]

NAV *abbreviation for* **net asset value**

Navaho *or* **Navajo** ('nævəˌhəʊ, 'nɑː-) *n* **1** (*pl* **-ho, -hos, -hoes** *or* **-jo, -jos, -joes**) **1** a member of a North American Indian people of Arizona, New Mexico, and Utah **2** the language of this people, belonging to the Athapascan group of the Na-Dene phylum [C18 from Spanish *Navajó* pueblo, from Tena *Navahu* large planted field]

naval ('neɪvəl) *adj* **1** of, relating to, characteristic of, or having a navy **2** of or relating to ships; nautical [C16 from Latin *nāvālis*, from *nāvis* ship; related to Greek *naus*, Old Norse *nōr* ship, Sanskrit *nau*]

naval architecture *n* the designing of ships > **naval architect** *n*

navar ('nævɑː) *n* a system of air navigation in which a ground radar station relays signals to each aircraft indicating the relative positions of neighbouring aircraft [C20 from *nav*(*igational and traffic control rad*)*ar*]

Navaratri (nævəˈrɑːtrɪ) *n* an annual Hindu festival celebrated over nine days in September-October. Observed throughout India, it commemorates the slaying of demons by Rama and the goddess Durga; in some places it is

dedicated to all female deities. Also called: **Durga Puja** [from Sanskrit *navaratri* nine nights]

navarin ('nævərɪn; *French* navarɛ̃) *n* a stew of mutton or lamb with root vegetables [from French]

Navarino (nava'riːno) *n* **1** the Italian name for **Pylos 2** a sea battle (Oct 20, 1827) in which the defeat of the Turkish-Egyptian fleet by a combined British, French, and Russian fleet decided Greek independence

Navarre (nəˈvɑː) *n* a former kingdom of SW Europe: established in the 9th century by the Basques; the parts south of the Pyrenees joined Spain in 1515 and the N parts passed to France in 1589. Capital: Pamplona. Spanish name: **Navarra** (naˈβarra)

nave[1] (neɪv) *n* the central space in a church, extending from the narthex to the chancel and often flanked by aisles [C17 via Medieval Latin from Latin *nāvis* ship, from the similarity of shape]

nave[2] (neɪv) *n* the central block or hub of a wheel [Old English *nafu, nafa*; related to Old High German *naba*]

navel ('neɪvəl) *n* **1** the scar in the centre of the abdomen, usually forming a slight depression, where the umbilical cord was attached. Technical name: **umbilicus** Related adj: **umbilical 2** a central part, location, or point; middle **3** short for **navel orange** [Old English *nafela*; related to Old Frisian *navla*, Old High German *nabulo* (German *Nabel*), Latin *umbilīcus*]

navel-gazing *n informal* self-absorbed behaviour

navel orange *n* a sweet orange that is usually seedless and has at its apex a navel-like depression enclosing an underdeveloped secondary fruit

navelwort ('neɪvəlˌwɜːt) *n* another name for **pennywort** (sense 1)

navew ('neɪvjuː) *n* another name for **turnip** (senses 1, 2) [C16 from Old French *navel*, from Latin *nāpus*]

navicert ('nævɪˌsɜːt) *n* a certificate specifying the contents of a neutral ship's cargo, issued esp in time of war by a blockading power [C20 from Latin *nāvi*(*s*) ship + CERT(IFICATE)]

navicular (nəˈvɪkjʊlə) *anatomy* ▷ *adj* **1** shaped like a boat ▷ *n also* **naviculare** (nəˌvɪkjʊ'lɑːrɪ) **2** a small boat-shaped bone of the wrist or foot [C16 from Late Latin *nāviculāris*, from Latin *nāvicula*, diminutive of *nāvis* ship]

navig. *abbreviation for* navigation

navigable ('nævɪgəbəl) *adj* **1** wide, deep, or safe enough to be sailed on or through: *a navigable channel* **2** capable of being steered or controlled: *a navigable raft* > ,naviga'bility *or* 'navigableness *n* > 'navigably *adv*

navigate ('nævɪˌgeɪt) *vb* **1** to plan, direct, or plot the path or position of (a ship, an aircraft, etc) **2** (*tr*) to travel over, through, or on (water, air, or land) in a boat, aircraft, etc **3** *informal* to direct (oneself, one's way, etc) carefully or safely: *he navigated his way to the bar* **4** (*intr*) (of a passenger in a motor vehicle) to give directions to the driver; point out the route **5** (*intr*) *rare* to voyage in a ship; sail [C16 from Latin *nāvigāre* to sail, from *nāvis* ship + *agere* to drive]

navigation (ˌnævɪˈgeɪʃən) *n* **1** the skill or process of plotting a route and directing a ship, aircraft, etc, along it **2** the act or practice of navigating: *dredging made navigation of the river possible* **3** *US rare* ship traffic; shipping **4** *Midland English dialect* an inland waterway; canal > ,navi'gational *adj*

Navigation Acts *pl n* a series of acts of Parliament, the first of which was passed in 1381, that attempted to restrict to English ships the right to carry goods to and from England and its colonies. The attempt to enforce the acts helped cause the War of American Independence

navigator ('nævɪˌgeɪtə) *n* **1** a person who is skilled in or performs navigation, esp on a ship or aircraft **2** (esp formerly) a person who explores by

ship **3** an instrument or device for assisting a pilot to navigate an aircraft

Návpaktos (*Greek* 'nafpaktos) *n* the Greek name for **Lepanto**

navvy ('nævɪ) *n, pl* **-vies** *Brit informal* a labourer on a building site, excavations, etc [C19 shortened from *navigator*, builder of a NAVIGATION (sense 4)]

navy ('neɪvɪ) *n, pl* **-vies 1** the warships and auxiliary vessels of a nation or ruler **2** (*often capital*; usually preceded by *the*) the branch of a country's armed services comprising such ships, their crews, and all their supporting services and equipment **3** short for **navy blue 4** *archaic or literary* a fleet of ships **5** (*as modifier*): *a navy custom* [C14 via Old French from Vulgar Latin *nāvia* (unattested) ship, from Latin *nāvis* ship]

navy blue *n* a dark greyish-blue colour **b** (*as adjective*): *a navy-blue suit* ▷ Sometimes shortened to: **navy** [C19 from the colour of the British naval uniform]

navy cut *n* tobacco finely cut from a block

Navy List *n* (in Britain) an official list of all serving commissioned officers of the Royal Navy and reserve officers liable for recall

navy yard *n* a naval shipyard, esp in the US

nawab (nəˈwɑːb) *n* (formerly) a Muslim ruling prince or powerful landowner in India. Also called: **nabob** [C18 from Hindi *nawwāb*, from Arabic *nuwwāb*, plural of *na'ib* viceroy, governor]

Naxalite ('nʌksəˌlaɪt) *n* a member of an extreme Maoist group in India that originated in 1967 in West Bengal and which employs tactics of agrarian terrorism and direct action [C20 named after *Naxalbari*, a town in West Bengal where the movement started]

Naxos ('næksɒs) *n* a Greek island in the S Aegean, the largest of the Cyclades: ancient centre of the worship of Dionysius. Pop: 18 188 (2001). Area: 438 sq km (169 sq miles)

nay (neɪ) *sentence substitute* **1** a word for **no**[1]: archaic or dialectal except in voting by voice ▷ *n* **2 a** a person who votes in the negative **b** a negative vote ▷ *adv* **3** (*sentence modifier*) *archaic* an emphatic form of **no**[1] ▷ Compare **aye**[1] [C12 from Old Norse *nei*, from *ne* not + *ei* ever, AY[1]]

Nayarit (*Spanish* naja'rit) *n* a state of W Mexico, on the Pacific: includes the offshore Tres Marías Islands. Capital: Tepic. Pop: 919 739 (2000). Area: 27 621 sq km (10 772 sq miles)

Nazarene (ˌnæzəˈriːn, 'næz-) *n also* Nazarite **1** an early name for a **Christian** (Acts 24:5) or (when preceded by *the*) for Jesus Christ (?4 BC–?29 AD), the founder of Christianity **2** a member of one of several groups of Jewish-Christians found principally in Syria **3** a member of an association of German artists called the Nazarenes or Brotherhood of St Luke, including Friedrich Overbeck (1789–1869) and Peter von Cornelius (1783–1867), founded (1809) in Vienna to revive German religious art after the examples of the Middle Ages and early Renaissance ▷ *adj* **4** of or relating to Nazareth or the Nazarenes

Nazareth ('næzərɪθ) *n* a town in N Israel, in Lower Galilee: the home of Jesus in his youth. Pop: 62 700 (2003 est)

Nazarite[1] ('næzəˌraɪt) *n* another word for **Nazarene** (senses 1, 2)

Nazarite[2] *or* **Nazirite** ('næzəˌraɪt) *n* a religious ascetic of ancient Israel [C16 from Latin *Nazaraeus*, from Hebrew *nāzīr*, from *nāzar* to consecrate + -ITE[1]]

Naze (neɪz) *n* **the 1** a flat marshy headland in SE England, in Essex on the North Sea coast **2** another name for **Lindesnes**

Nazi ('nɑːtsɪ) *n, pl* **Nazis 1** a member of the fascist National Socialist German Workers' Party, which was founded in 1919 and seized political control in Germany in 1933 under the Austrian-born German dictator Adolf Hitler (1889–1945) **2** *derogatory* anyone who thinks or acts like a Nazi, esp showing racism, brutality, etc ▷ *adj* **3** of, characteristic of, or relating to the Nazis [C20 from German, phonetic spelling of the first two

syllables of *Nationalsozialist* National Socialist]
> Nazism (ˈnɑːtˌsɪzəm) *or* Naziism (ˈnɑːtsɪˌɪzəm) *n*

Nazify (ˈnɑːtsɪˌfaɪ) *vb* -fies, -fying, -fied (*tr*) to make Nazi in character > ˌNaziˈfication *n*

nb *cricket abbreviation for* no ball

Nb *the chemical symbol for* niobium

NB[1] *abbreviation for* New Brunswick

NB[2]**, N.B., nb** *or* **n.b.** *abbreviation for* nota bene [Latin: note well]

NBA *abbreviation for* **1** (in the US) National Basketball Association **2** (the former) **Net Book Agreement**

NBC *abbreviation for* **1** (in the US) National Broadcasting Company **2** (of weapons or warfare) nuclear, biological, and chemical

NBG *informal abbreviation for* no bloody good. Also: **nbg**

nc *the internet domain name for* New Caledonia

NC *or* **N.C.** *abbreviation for* **1** North Carolina **2** *Brit education* **National Curriculum**

NCC (in Britain) *abbreviation for* (the former) **Nature Conservancy Council**

NCCL *abbreviation for* National Council for Civil Liberties

NCEA (in New Zealand) *abbreviation for* National Certificate of Educational Attainment

NCIS (in Britain) *abbreviation for* National Criminal Intelligence Service

NCM (in the Canadian armed forces) *abbreviation for* noncommissioned member

NCO *abbreviation for* noncommissioned officer

NCP (in Australia) *abbreviation for* **National Country Party**

NCVO (in Britain) *abbreviation for* National Council for Voluntary Organizations

nd *abbreviation for* no date

Nd *the chemical symbol for* neodymium

ND, N.D. *or* **N. Dak.** *abbreviation for* North Dakota

NDE *abbreviation for* **near-death experience**

Ndebele (ənˈdɛbɛle) *n* **1** (*pl* **Ndebele**) a member of a Negroid people of Zimbabwe. See also **Matabele 2** the language of this people, belonging to the Bantu grouping of the Niger-Congo family

Ndjamena *or* **N'djamena** (əndʒɑːˈmeɪnə) *n* the capital of Chad, in the southwest, at the confluence of the Shari and Logone Rivers: trading centre for livestock. Pop: 866 000 (2005 est). Former name (until 1973): **Fort Lamy**

Ndola (ənˈdəʊlə) *n* a city in N Zambia: copper, cobalt, and sugar refineries. Pop: 478 000 (2005 est)

NDP *abbreviation for* **1 net domestic product 2** (in Canada) **New Democratic Party**

NDT *abbreviation for* **nondestructive testing**

ne *the internet domain name for* Niger

Ne *the chemical symbol for* neon

NE[1] **1** *symbol for* northeast(ern) **2** *abbreviation for* Nebraska

NE[2] *or* **N.E.** *abbreviation for* New England

ne- *combining form* a variant of **neo-**, esp before a vowel *Nearctic*

NE1 *text messaging abbreviation for* anyone

Neagh (neɪ) *n* **Lough** a lake in Northern Ireland, in SW Co Antrim: the largest lake in the British Isles. Area: 388 sq km (150 sq miles)

Neanderthal (nɪˈændəˌtɑːl) (*sometimes not capital*) *adj* **1** relating to or characteristic of Neanderthal man **2** primitive; uncivilized **3** *informal* ultraconservative; reactionary ⊳ *n* **4** a person showing any such characteristics

Neanderthal man (nɪˈændəˌtɑːl) *n* a type of primitive man, *Homo neanderthalensis*, or *H. sapiens neanderthalensis*, occurring throughout much of Europe in late Palaeolithic times: it is thought that they did not interbreed with other early humans and are not the ancestors of modern humans [c19 from the anthropological findings (1857) in the Neandertal, a valley near Düsseldorf, Germany]

neanic (nɪˈænɪk) *adj zoology* of or relating to the early stages in the life cycle of an organism, esp the pupal stage of an insect [c19 from Greek

neanikus youthful]

neap (niːp) *adj* **1** of, relating to, or constituting a neap tide ⊳ *n* **2** short for **neap tide** [Old English, as in *nēpflōd* neap tide, of uncertain origin]

Neapolitan (ˌnɪəˈpɒlɪtən) *n* **1** a native or inhabitant of Naples ⊳ *adj* **2** of or relating to Naples [c15 from Latin *Neāpolītānus*, ultimately from Greek *Neapolis* new town]

Neapolitan ice cream *n* ice cream, usually in brick form, with several layers of different colours and flavours

Neapolitan sixth *n* (in musical harmony) a chord composed of the subdominant of the key, plus a minor third and a minor sixth. Harmonically it is equivalent to the first inversion of a major chord built upon the flattened supertonic

neap tide *n* either of the two tides that occur at the first or last quarter of the moon when the tide-generating forces of the sun and moon oppose each other and produce the smallest rise and fall in tidal level. Compare **spring tide** (sense 1)

near (nɪə) *prep* **1** at or to a place or time not far away from; close to ⊳ *adv* **2** at or to a place or time not far away; close by **3** *near to* not far from; near **4** short for **nearly** (esp in phrases such as **damn near**): *I was damn near killed* ⊳ *adj* **5** at or in a place not far away **6** (*postpositive*) not far away in time; imminent **7** (*prenominal*) only just successful or only just failing: *a near escape* **8** (*postpositive*) *informal* miserly, mean **9** (*prenominal*) closely connected or intimate: *a near relation* ⊳ *vb* **10** to come or draw close (to) ⊳ *n* **11** Also called: **nearside a** the left side of a horse, team of animals, vehicle, etc **b** (*as modifier*): *the near foreleg* [Old English *nēar* (adv), comparative of *nēah* close, NIGH; related to Old Frisian *niar*, Old Norse *nǣr*, Old High German *nāhōr*] > ˈnearness *n*

near- *combining form* nearly; almost: *a near-perfect landing*

nearby *adj* (ˈnɪəˌbaɪ), *adv* (ˌnɪəˈbaɪ) not far away; close at hand

Nearctic (nɪˈɑːktɪk) *adj* of or denoting a zoogeographical region consisting of North America, north of the tropic of Cancer, and Greenland

near-death experience *n* an experience, instances of which have been widely reported, in which a person near death is apparently outside his body and aware of it and the attendant circumstances as separate from him. Abbreviation: **NDE**

Near East *n* **1** another term for the **Middle East 2** (formerly) the Balkan States and the area of the Ottoman Empire

near gale *n meteorol* a wind of force seven on the Beaufort scale or from 32–38 mph

nearly (ˈnɪəlɪ) *adv* **1** not quite; almost; practically **2** not nearly nowhere near; not at all: *not nearly enough money* **3** closely: *the person most nearly concerned*

near-market research *n* scientific research that, while not linked to the development of a specific product, is likely to be commercially exploitable

near miss *n* **1** a bomb, shell, etc, that does not exactly hit the target **2** any attempt or shot that just fails to be successful **3** an incident in which two vehicles narrowly avoid collision

near money *n* liquid assets that can be converted to cash very quickly, such as a bank deposit or bill of exchange

near point *n optics* the nearest point to the eye at which an object remains in focus

near rhyme *n prosody* another term for **half-rhyme**

nearside (ˈnɪəˌsaɪd) *n* **1** (usually preceded by *the*) *chiefly Brit* **a** the side of a vehicle normally nearer the kerb (in Britain, the left side) **b** (*as modifier*): *the nearside door* ⊳ Compare **offside 2 a** the left side of an animal, team of horses, etc **b** (*as modifier*): *the nearside flank*

near-sighted (ˌnɪəˈsaɪtɪd) *adj* relating to or suffering from myopia > ˌnear-ˈsightedly *adv* > ˌnear-ˈsightedness *n*

near thing *n informal* an event or action whose outcome is nearly a failure, success, disaster, etc

nearthrosis (ˌniːɑːˈθrəʊsɪs) *n, pl* -ses (-siːz) another name for **pseudoarthrosis**

neat[1] (niːt) *adj* **1** clean, tidy, and orderly **2** liking or insisting on order and cleanliness; fastidious **3** smoothly or competently done; efficient: *a neat job* **4** pat or slick: *his excuse was suspiciously neat* **5** (of alcoholic drinks) without added water, lemonade, etc; undiluted **6** a less common word for **net**[2]: *neat profits* **7** *slang, chiefly US and Canadian* good; pleasing; admirable [c16 from Old French *net*, from Latin *nitidus* clean, shining, from *nitēre* to shine; related to Middle Irish *niam* beauty, brightness, Old Persian *naiba-* beautiful] > ˈneatly *adv* > ˈneatness *n*

neat[2] (niːt) *n, pl* neat *archaic or dialect* a domestic bovine animal [Old English *neat*]

neaten (ˈniːtⁿn) *vb* (*tr*) to make neat; tidy

neath *or* **'neath** (niːθ) *prep archaic* short for **beneath**

Neath Port Talbot (ˈniːθ ˈpɔːt ˈtɔːlbət, ˈtæl-) *n* a county borough in S Wales, created from part of West Glamorgan in 1996. Administrative centre: Port Talbot. Pop: 135 300 (2003 est). Area: 439 sq km (169 sq miles)

neat's-foot oil *n* a yellow fixed oil obtained by boiling the feet and shinbones of cattle and used esp to dress leather

neb (neb) *n archaic or dialect* **1** *chiefly Scot and northern English* the peak of a cap **2** the beak of a bird or the nose or snout of an animal **3** a person's mouth or nose **4** the projecting part or end of anything **5 a** a peak, esp in N England **b** a prominent gritstone overhang [Old English *nebb*; related to Old Norse *nef*, Old High German *snabul* (German *Schnabel*)]

NEB *abbreviation for* **1** New English Bible **2** (the former) National Enterprise Board

Nebelung (ˈneɪbəˌlʊŋ) *n* a breed of cat with a long body, long silky bluish hair, and a plumelike tail

Nebo (ˈniːbəʊ) *n* **Mount** a mountain in Jordan, northeast of the Dead Sea: the highest point of a ridge known as Pisgah, from which Moses viewed the Promised Land just before his death (Deuteronomy 34:1). Height: 802 m (2631 ft)

Nebr. *abbreviation for* Nebraska

Nebraska (nɪˈbræskə) *n* a state of the western US: consists of an undulating plain. Capital: Lincoln. Pop: 1 739 291 (2003 est). Area: 197 974 sq km (76 483 sq miles). Abbreviations: **Nebr**, (with zip code) **NE**

Nebraskan (nɪˈbræskən) *adj* **1** of or relating to Nebraska or its inhabitants ⊳ *n* **2** a native or inhabitant of Nebraska

Nebuchadnezzar[1] (ˌnɛbjʊkədˈnɛzə) *n* a wine bottle, used esp for display, holding the equivalent of twenty normal bottles (approximately 520 ounces) [c20 named after NEBUCHADNEZZAR[2], from the custom of naming large wine bottles after Old Testament figures; compare JEROBOAM]

Nebuchadnezzar[2] (ˌnɛbjʊkədˈnɛzə) *or* **Nebuchadrezzar** *n Old Testament* a king of Babylon, 605–562 BC, who conquered and destroyed Jerusalem and exiled the Jews to Babylon (II Kings 24–25)

nebula (ˈnɛbjʊlə) *n, pl* -lae (-ˌliː) *or* -las **1** *astronomy* a diffuse cloud of particles and gases (mainly hydrogen) that is visible either as a hazy patch of light (either an **emission** or a **reflection nebula**) or an irregular dark region against a brighter background (**dark nebula**). Compare **planetary nebula 2** *pathol* **a** opacity of the cornea **b** cloudiness of the urine **3** any substance for use in an atomizer spray [c17 from Latin: mist, cloud, related to Greek *nephélē* cloud, Old High German *nebul* cloud, Old Norse *njól* night] > ˈnebular *adj*

nebular hypothesis *n* the theory that the solar system evolved from the gravitational collapse of nebular matter

n

nebulize *or* **nebulise** (ˈnɛbjʊˌlaɪz) *vb* (*tr*) to convert (a liquid) into a mist or fine spray; atomize > ˌnebuliˈzation *or* ˌnebuliˈsation *n*

nebulizer *or* **nebuliser** (ˈnɛbjʊˌlaɪzə) *n* a device for converting a drug in liquid form into a mist or fine spray which is inhaled through a mask to provide medication for the respiratory system. Also called: **inhalator**

nebulosity (ˌnɛbjʊˈlɒsɪtɪ) *n, pl* **-ties 1** the state or quality of being nebulous **2** *astronomy* a nebula

nebulous (ˈnɛbjʊləs) *adj* **1** lacking definite form, shape, or content; vague or amorphous: *nebulous reasons* **2** of, characteristic of, or resembling a nebula **3** *rare* misty or hazy > ˈ**nebulously** *adv* > ˈ**nebulousness** *n*

NEC *abbreviation for* National Executive Committee

necessaries (ˈnɛsɪsərɪz) *pl n* **1** (*sometimes singular*) what is needed; essential items: *the necessaries of life* **2** *law* food, clothing, etc, essential for the maintenance of a dependant in the condition of life to which he or she is accustomed

necessarily (ˈnɛsɪsərɪlɪ, ˌnɛsɪˈsɛrɪlɪ) *adv* **1** as an inevitable or natural consequence: *girls do not necessarily like dolls* **2** as a certainty: *he won't necessarily come*

necessary (ˈnɛsɪsərɪ) *adj* **1** needed to achieve a certain desired effect or result; required **2** resulting from necessity; inevitable: *the necessary consequences of your action* **3** *logic* **a** (of a statement, formula, etc) true under all interpretations or in all possible circumstances **b** (of a proposition) determined to be true by its meaning, so that its denial would be self-contradictory **c** (of a property) essential, so that without it its subject would not be the entity it is **d** (of an inference) always yielding a true conclusion when its premises are true; valid **e** (of a condition) entailed by the truth of some statement or the obtaining of some state of affairs ▷ Compare **sufficient** (sense 2) **4** *philosophy* (in a nonlogical sense) expressing a law of nature, so that if it is in this sense necessary that all As are B, even although it is not contradictory to conceive of an A which is not B, we are licensed to infer that if something were an A it would have to be B **5** *rare* compelled, as by necessity or law; not free ▷ *n* **6** *informal* (preceded by *the*) the money required for a particular purpose **7 do the necessary** *informal* to do something that is necessary in a particular situation ▷ See also **necessaries** [C14 from Latin *necessārius* indispensable, from *necesse* unavoidable]

necessitarianism (nɪˌsɛsɪˈtɛərɪəˌnɪzəm) *or* **necessarianism** (ˌnɛsɪˈsɛərɪəˌnɪzəm) *n philosophy* another word for **determinism** Compare **libertarian.** > **neˌcessiˈtarian** *or* **ˌnecesˈsarian** *n, adj*

necessitate (nɪˈsɛsɪˌteɪt) *vb* (*tr*) **1** to cause as an unavoidable and necessary result **2** (*usually passive*) to compel or require (someone to do something) > **neˌcessiˈtation** *n* > **neˈcessitative** *adj*

necessitous (nɪˈsɛsɪtəs) *adj* very needy; destitute; poverty-stricken > **neˈcessitously** *adv*

necessity (nɪˈsɛsɪtɪ) *n, pl* **-ties 1** (*sometimes plural*) something needed for a desired result; prerequisite: *necessities of life* **2** a condition or set of circumstances, such as physical laws or social rules, that inevitably requires a certain result: *it is a matter of necessity to wear formal clothes when meeting the Queen* **3** the state or quality of being obligatory or unavoidable **4** urgent requirement, as in an emergency or misfortune: *in time of necessity we must all work together* **5** poverty or want **6** *rare* compulsion through laws of nature; fate **7** *philosophy* **a** a condition, principle, or conclusion that cannot be otherwise **b** the constraining force of physical determinants on all aspects of life. Compare **freedom** (sense 8) **8** *logic* **a** the property of being necessary **b** a statement asserting that some property is essential or statement is necessarily true **c** the operator that indicates that the expression it modifies is true in all possible worlds. Usual symbol: □ *or* L **9 of necessity** inevitably; necessarily

neck (nɛk) *n* **1** the part of an organism connecting the head with the rest of the body. Related adjs: **cervical, jugular 2** the part of a garment around or nearest the neck **3** something resembling a neck in shape or position: *the neck of a bottle* **4** *anatomy* a constricted portion of an organ or part, such as the cervix of the uterus **5** a narrow or elongated projecting strip of land; a peninsula or isthmus **6** a strait or channel **7** the part of a violin, cello, etc, that extends from the body to the tuning pegs and supports the fingerboard **8** a solid block of lava from the opening of an extinct volcano, exposed after erosion of the surrounding rock **9** *botany* the upper, usually tubular, part of the archegonium of mosses, ferns, etc **10** the length of a horse's head and neck taken as an approximate distance by which one horse beats another in a race: *to win by a neck* **11** *informal* a short distance, amount, or margin: *he is always a neck ahead in new techniques* **12** *informal* impudence; audacity: *he had the neck to ask for a rise* **13** *architect* the narrow band at the top of the shaft of a column between the necking and the capital, esp as used in the Tuscan order **14** another name for **beard** (sense 7), on printer's type **15 break one's neck** *informal* to exert oneself greatly, esp by hurrying, in order to do something **16 by the neck** *Irish and Scot slang* (of a bottle of beer) served unpoured: *give me two bottles of stout by the neck* **17 get it in the neck** *informal* to be reprimanded or punished severely **18 neck and neck** absolutely level or even in a race or competition **19 neck of the woods** *informal* an area or locality: *a quiet neck of the woods* **20 risk one's neck** to take a great risk **21 save one's** *or* **someone's neck** *informal* to escape from or help someone else to escape from a difficult or dangerous situation **22 stick one's neck out** *informal* to risk criticism, ridicule, failure, etc, by speaking one's mind **23 up to one's neck (in)** deeply involved (in): *he's up to his neck in dodgy dealings* ▷ *vb* **24** (*intr*) *informal* to kiss, embrace, or fondle someone or one another passionately **25** (*tr*) *Brit informal* to swallow (something, esp a drink): *he's been necking pints all night* [Old English *hnecca*; related to Old High German *hnack*, Old Irish *cnocc* hill] > ˈ**necker** *n*

Neckar (ˈnɛkɑː) *n* a river in SW Germany, rising in the Black Forest and flowing generally north into the Rhine at Mannheim. Length: 394 km (245 miles)

neckband (ˈnɛkˌbænd) *n* a band around the neck of a garment as finishing, decoration, or a base for a collar

neckcloth (ˈnɛkˌklɒθ) *n* a large ornamental usually white cravat worn formerly by men

neckerchief (ˈnɛkətʃɪf, -ˌtʃiːf) *n* a piece of ornamental cloth, often square, worn around the neck [C14 from NECK + KERCHIEF]

Necker cube (ˈnɛkə) *n* a line drawing showing the 12 edges of a transparent cube, so that it can be seen alternately facing in two different directions: an example of an ambiguous figure [C19 named after Louis Albert *Necker* (1786–1861), Swiss mineralogist]

necking (ˈnɛkɪŋ) *n* **1** *informal* the activity of kissing and embracing passionately **2** Also called: **gorgerin** *architect* one or more mouldings at the top of a column between the shaft and the capital

necklace (ˈnɛklɪs) *n* **1** a chain, band, or cord, often bearing beads, pearls, jewels, etc, worn around the neck as an ornament, esp by women **2** (in South Africa) a tyre soaked in petrol, placed round a person's neck, and set on fire in order to burn the person to death ▷ *vb* **3** (*tr*) *South African* to kill (someone) by placing a burning tyre round his or her neck

necklace bomb *n* a bomb consisting of linked charges hung around a victim's neck, used by terrorists or in hostage situations

necklet (ˈnɛklɪt) *n* an ornament worn round the neck

neckline (ˈnɛkˌlaɪn) *n* the shape or position of the upper edge of a dress, blouse, etc: *a plunging neckline*

neckpiece (ˈnɛkˌpiːs) *n* a piece of fur, cloth, etc, worn around the neck or neckline

necktie (ˈnɛkˌtaɪ) *n* the US name for **tie** (sense 11)

neckwear (ˈnɛkˌwɛə) *n* articles of clothing, such as ties, scarves, etc, worn around the neck

necro- *or before a vowel* **necr-** *combining form* indicating death, a dead body, or dead tissue: *necrology; necrophagous; necrosis* [from Greek *nekros* corpse]

necrobiosis (ˌnɛkrəʊbaɪˈəʊsɪs) *n physiol* the normal degeneration and death of cells. Compare **necrosis.** > **necrobiotic** (ˌnɛkrəʊbaɪˈɒtɪk) *adj*

necrolatry (nɛˈkrɒlətrɪ) *n* the worship of the dead

necrology (nɛˈkrɒlədʒɪ) *n, pl* **-gies 1** a list of people recently dead **2** a less common word for **obituary.** > **necrological** (ˌnɛkrəˈlɒdʒɪkᵊl) *adj* > **neˈcrologist** *n*

necromancy (ˈnɛkrəʊˌmænsɪ) *n* **1** the art or practice of supposedly conjuring up the dead, esp in order to obtain from them knowledge of the future **2** black magic; sorcery [C13 (as in sense 1) ultimately from Greek *nekromanteia*, from *nekros* corpse; (as in sense 2) from Medieval Latin *nigromantia*, from Latin *niger* black, which replaced *necro-* through folk etymology] > ˈ**necroˌmancer** *n* > ˌ**necroˈmantic** *adj*

necromania (ˌnɛkrəʊˈmeɪnɪə) *n* another word for **necrophilia.** > ˌ**necroˈmaniˌac** *n*

necrophagous (nəˈkrɒfəgəs) *adj* (of an animal, bird, etc) feeding on carrion

necrophilia (ˌnɛkrəʊˈfɪlɪə) *n* sexual attraction for or sexual intercourse with dead bodies. Also called: **necromania, necrophilism** > ˌ**necroˈphiliˌac** *or* **necrophile** (ˈnɛkrəʊˌfaɪl) *n* > ˌ**necroˈphilic** *adj*

necrophilism (nɛˈkrɒfɪˌlɪzəm) *n* **1** another word for **necrophilia 2** a strong desire to be dead

necrophobia (ˌnɛkrəʊˈfəʊbɪə) *n* an abnormal fear of death or dead bodies > ˈ**necroˌphobe** *n* > ˌ**necroˈphobic** *adj*

necrophorous (nɪˈkrɒfərəs) *adj* denoting animals, such as certain beetles, that carry away the bodies of dead animals

necropolis (nɛˈkrɒpəlɪs) *n, pl* **-lises** *or* **-leis** (-ˌleɪs) a burial site or cemetery [C19 Greek, from *nekros* dead + *polis* city]

necropsy (ˈnɛkrɒpsɪ) *or* **necroscopy** (nɛˈkrɒskəpɪ) *n, pl* **-sies** *or* **-pies** another name for **autopsy** [C19 from Greek *nekros* dead body + *opsis* sight]

necrose (nɛˈkrəʊs, ˈnɛkrəʊs) *vb* (*intr*) to cause or undergo necrosis [C19 back formation from NECROSIS]

necrosis (nɛˈkrəʊsɪs) *n* **1** the death of one or more cells in the body, usually within a localized area, as from an interruption of the blood supply to that part **2** death of plant tissue due to disease, frost, etc [C17 New Latin from Greek *nekrōsis*, from *nekroun* to kill, from *nekros* corpse] > **necrotic** (nɛˈkrɒtɪk) *adj*

necrotic enteritis *n vet science* an infectious disease of calves, lambs, foals, and piglets, characterized by acute diarrhoea and death, caused by the toxin of the organism *Clostridium perfringens type C*

necrotomy (nɛˈkrɒtəmɪ) *n, pl* **-mies 1** dissection of a dead body **2** surgical excision of dead tissue from a living organism

necrotroph (ˈnɛkrəʊˌtrəʊf) *n* a parasitic organism that kills the living cells of its host and then feeds on the dead matter > **necrotrophic** (ˌnɛkrəʊˈtrɒfɪk) *adj*

nectar (ˈnɛktə) *n* **1** a sugary fluid produced in the nectaries of plants and collected by bees and other animals **2** *classical myth* the drink of the gods. Compare **ambrosia** (sense 1) **3** any delicious drink, esp a sweet one **4** something very pleasant or welcome: *your words are nectar to me* **5** *chiefly US* **a** the undiluted juice of a fruit **b** a mixture of fruit juices [C16 via Latin from Greek *néktar*, perhaps *nek-* death (related to *nekros* corpse) + *-tar*, related to Sanskrit *tarati* he overcomes; compare Latin *nex* death and *trans* across] > **nectareous** (nɛkˈtɛərɪəs) *or* ˈ**nectarous** *adj*

nectarine (ˈnɛktərɪn) *n* **1** a variety of peach tree, *Prunus persica nectarina* **2** the fruit of this tree, which has a smooth skin [c17 apparently from NECTAR]

nectarivorous (ˌnɛktəˈrɪvərəs) *adj zoology* feeding on nectar

nectary (ˈnɛktərɪ) *n, pl* -ries **1** any of various glandular structures secreting nectar that occur in the flowers, leaves, stipules, etc, of a plant **2** any of the abdominal tubes in aphids through which honeydew is secreted [c18 from New Latin *nectarium*, from NECTAR] > **nectarial** (nɛkˈtɛərɪəl) *adj*

ned (nɛd) *n Scot slang derogatory* a young working-class male who dresses in casual sports clothes [c20 a shortened form of *Edward*] > ˈ**neddy** *or* ˈ**neddish** *adj*

NEDC *abbreviation for* (the former) National Economic Development Council. Also (informal): **Neddy** (ˈnɛdɪ)

neddy (ˈnɛdɪ) *n, pl* -dies **1** a child's word for a **donkey 2** *informal* a silly person; fool **3** *Austral informal* a horse, esp a racehorse: *he lost his money on the neddies* [c18 from *Ned*, pet form of *Edward*]

Nederland (ˈneːdərlant) *n* the Dutch name for the **Netherlands**

nedette (nɛdˈɛt) *n Scot derogatory* a young working-class female who dresses in casual sports clothes [c20 from NED + -ETTE (sense 2)]

née *or* **nee** (neɪ) *adj* indicating the maiden name of a married woman: *Mrs Bloggs née Blandish* [c19 from French: past participle (fem) of *naître* to be born, from Latin *nascī*]

need (niːd) *vb* **1** (*tr*) to be in want of: *to need money* **2** (*tr*) to require or be required of necessity (to be or do something); be obliged: *to need to do more work* **3** (takes an infinitive without *to*) used as an auxiliary in negative and interrogative sentences to express necessity or obligation and does not add -*s* when used with *he, she, it,* and singular nouns: *need he go?* **4** (*intr*) *archaic* to be essential or necessary to: *there needs no reason for this* ▷ *n* **5** the fact or an instance of feeling the lack of something: *he has need of a new coat* **6** a requirement: *the need for vengeance* **7** necessity or obligation resulting from some situation: *no need to be frightened* **8** distress or extremity: *a friend in need* **9** extreme poverty or destitution; penury ▷ See also **needs** [Old English *nēad, nied*; related to Old Frisian *nēd*, Old Saxon *nōd*, Old High German *nōt*]

needful (ˈniːdfʊl) *adj* **1** necessary; needed; required **2** *archaic* needy; poverty-stricken ▷ *n* **3** *informal* money or funds: *do you have the needful?* **4 do the needful** to perform a necessary task > ˈ**needfully** *adv* > ˈ**needfulness** *n*

neediness (ˈniːdɪnɪs) *n* the state of being needy; poverty

needle (ˈniːdəl) *n* **1** a pointed slender piece of metal, usually steel, with a hole or eye in it through which thread is passed for sewing **2** a somewhat larger rod with a point at one or each end, used in knitting **3** a similar instrument with a hook at one end for crocheting **4 a** another name for **stylus** (sense 3) **b** a small thin pointed device, esp one made of stainless steel, used to transmit the vibrations from a gramophone record to the pick-up **5** *med* **a** the long hollow pointed part of a hypodermic syringe, which is inserted into the body **b** an informal name for **hypodermic syringe 6** *surgery* a pointed steel instrument, often curved, for suturing, puncturing, or ligating **7** a long narrow stiff leaf, esp of a conifer, in which water loss is greatly reduced: *pine needles* **8** any slender sharp spine, such as the spine of a sea urchin **9** any slender pointer for indicating the reading on the scale of a measuring instrument **10** short for **magnetic needle 11** a crystal resembling a needle in shape **12** a sharp pointed metal instrument used in engraving and etching **13** anything long and pointed, such as an obelisk: *a needle of light* **14** a short horizontal beam passed through a wall and supported on vertical posts to take the load of the upper part of the wall **15** *informal* **a** anger or intense rivalry, esp in a sporting encounter **b** (*as modifier*): *a needle match* **16 have** *or* **get the needle** (**to**) *Brit informal* to feel dislike, distaste, nervousness, or annoyance (for): *she got the needle after he had refused her invitation* ▷ *vb* **17** (*tr*) *informal* to goad or provoke, as by constant criticism **18** (*tr*) to sew, embroider, or prick (fabric) with a needle **19** (*tr*) *US* to increase the alcoholic strength of (beer or other beverages) **20** (*intr*) (of a substance) to form needle-shaped crystals [Old English *nǣdl*; related to Gothic *nēthla*, German *Nadel*]

needle bearing *n engineering* an antifriction roller bearing in which long rollers of very small diameter fill the race without a cage to provide spacers between them

needlecord (ˈniːdəlˌkɔːd) *n* a corduroy fabric with narrow ribs

needlecraft (ˈniːdəlˌkrɑːft) *n* the art or practice of needlework

needle exchange *n* a centre where drug users can exchange used hypodermic syringes for new ones

needlefish (ˈniːdəlˌfɪʃ) *n, pl* -fish *or* -fishes **1** any ferocious teleost fish of the family *Belonidae* of warm and tropical regions, having an elongated body and long toothed jaws **2** another name for **pipefish**

needle fly *n* a small stonefly of the genus *Leuctra*, whose rolled-up wings at rest give it a slender pointed appearance

needleful (ˈniːdəlfʊl) *n* a length of thread cut for use in a needle

needlepoint (ˈniːdəlˌpɔɪnt) *n* **1** embroidery done on canvas with the same stitch throughout so as to resemble tapestry **2** another name for **point lace**

needless (ˈniːdlɪs) *adj* not required or desired; unnecessary > ˈ**needlessly** *adv* > ˈ**needlessness** *n*

needlestick (ˈniːdəlˌstɪk) *adj* (of an injury) caused by accidentally pricking the skin with a hypodermic needle

needle time *n* the limited time allocated by a radio channel to the broadcasting of music from records

needle valve *n* a valve containing a tapered rod that can be moved in or out to control the flow of a fluid

needlewoman (ˈniːdəlˌwʊmən) *n, pl* -women a woman who does needlework; seamstress

needlework (ˈniːdəlˌwɜːk) *n* **1** work done with a needle, esp sewing and embroidery **2** the result of such work

needs (niːdz) *adv* **1** (preceded or foll by *must*) of necessity: *we must needs go; we will go, if needs must* ▷ *pl n* **2** what is required; necessities: *the needs of the third world; his needs are modest*

needs test *n social welfare* an examination of a person's physical or social, rather than financial, circumstances, to determine whether he is eligible for a particular welfare benefit or service. Compare **means test**

needy (ˈniːdɪ) *adj* needier, neediest **a** in need of practical or emotional support; distressed **b** (*as collective noun; preceded by the*): *the needy*

Néel point *or* **temperature** (neɪˈɛl) *n* the temperature above which an antiferromagnetic substance loses its antiferromagnetism and becomes paramagnetic

neem (niːm) *n* a large tree of India, *Azadirachta indica*, all parts of which are useful to man: the leaves act as a natural pesticide, the fruit and seeds yield a medicinal oil, the bark is used to make a tonic, and the trunk exudes a gum [c19 from Hindi *nīm*, from Sanskrit *nimba*]

neep (niːp) *n Brit* a dialect name for a **turnip** [Old English *nǣp*, from Latin *nāpus* turnip]

ne'er (nɛə) *adv* a poetic contraction of **never**

Ne'erday (ˈnɛːdeɪ) *n Scot* New Year's Day

ne'er-do-well *n* **1** an improvident, irresponsible, or lazy person ▷ *adj* **2** useless; worthless: *your ne'er-do-well schemes*

nefarious (nɪˈfɛərɪəs) *adj* evil; wicked; sinful [c17 from Latin *nefārius*, from *nefās* unlawful deed, from *nē* not + *fās* divine law] > **neˈfariously** *adv* > **neˈfariousness** *n*

NEG (in transformational grammar) *abbreviation for* negative

neg. *abbreviation for* negative(ly)

negate (nɪˈgeɪt) *vb* (*tr*) **1** to make ineffective or void; nullify; invalidate **2** to deny or contradict [c17 from Latin *negāre*, from *neg-*, variant of *nec* not + *aio* I say] > **neˈgator** *or* **neˈgater** *n*

negation (nɪˈgeɪʃən) *n* **1** the opposite or absence of something **2** a negative thing or condition **3** the act or an instance of negating **4** *logic* **a** the operator that forms one sentence from another and corresponds to the English *not* **b** a sentence so formed. It is usually written –*p*, -*p*, *p̄* or →*p*, where *p* is the given sentence, and is false when the given sentence is true, and true when it is false

negative (ˈnɛgətɪv) *adj* **1** expressing or meaning a refusal or denial: *a negative answer* **2** lacking positive or affirmative qualities, such as enthusiasm, interest, or optimism **3** showing or tending towards opposition or resistance **4 a** measured in a direction opposite to that regarded as positive **b** having the same magnitude but opposite sense to an equivalent positive quantity **5** *biology* indicating movement or growth away from a particular stimulus: *negative geotropism* **6** *med* (of the results of a diagnostic test) indicating absence of the disease or condition for which the test was made **7** another word for **minus** (senses 3b, 5) **8** *physics* **a** (of an electric charge) having the same polarity as the charge of an electron **b** (of a body, system, ion, etc) having a negative electric charge; having an excess of electrons **c** (of a point in an electric circuit) having a lower electrical potential than some other point with an assigned zero potential **9** short for **electronegative 10** of or relating to a photographic negative **11** *logic* (of a categorial proposition) denying the satisfaction by the subject of the predicate, as in *some men are irrational; no pigs have wings* **12** *astrology* of, relating to, or governed by the signs of the zodiac of the earth and water classifications, which are thought to be associated with a receptive passive nature **13** short for **Rh negative** ▷ *n* **14** a statement or act of denial, refusal, or negation **15** a negative person or thing **16** *photog* a piece of photographic film or a plate, previously exposed and developed, showing an image that, in black-and-white photography, has a reversal of tones. In colour photography the image is in complementary colours to the subject so that blue sky appears yellow, green grass appears purple, etc **17** *physics* a negative object, such as a terminal or a plate in a voltaic cell **18** a sentence or other linguistic element with a negative meaning, as the English word *not* **19** a quantity less than zero or a quantity to be subtracted **20** *logic* a negative proposition **21** *archaic* the right of veto **22 in the negative** indicating denial or refusal ▷ *sentence substitute* **23** (esp in military communications) a signal code word for **no¹** ▷ *vb* (*tr*) **24** to deny or nullify; negate **25** to show to be false; disprove **26** to refuse consent to or approval of: *the proposal was negatived* ▷ Compare **positive, affirmative**. > ˈ**negatively** *adv* > ˈ**negativeness** *or* ˌ**negaˈtivity** *n*

negative equity *n* the state of holding a property the value of which is less than the amount of mortgage still unpaid

negative feedback *n* See **feedback**

negative hallucination *n psychol* an apparent abnormal inability to perceive an object

negative polarity *n grammar* the grammatical character of a word or phrase, such as *ever* or *any*, that may normally only be used in a semantically

n

or syntactically negative or interrogative context

negative profit *n* a financial loss

negative-raising *n transformational grammar* a rule that moves a negative element out of the complement clause of certain verbs, such as *think*, into the main clause, as in the derivation of *He doesn't think that he'll finish*

negative reinforcement *n psychol* the reinforcing of a response by giving an aversive stimulus when the response is not made and omitting the aversive stimulus when the response is made

negative resistance *n* a characteristic of certain electronic components in which an increase in the applied voltage increases the resistance, producing a proportional decrease in current

negative sign *n* the symbol (–) used to indicate a negative quantity or a subtraction; minus sign

negative tax *n* a payment by the State to a person with a low income, the magnitude of the payment increasing as the income decreases. It is regarded as a form of social welfare. Also called: **negative income tax**

negativism ('nɛgətɪv,ɪzəm) *n* **1** a tendency to be or a state of being unconstructively critical **2** any sceptical or derisive system of thought **3** *psychiatry* refusal to do what is expected or suggested or the tendency to do the opposite > 'negativist *n, adj* > ,negativ'istic *adj*

negator (nɪ'geɪtə) *n electronics* another name for **NOT circuit**

negatron ('nɛgə,trɒn) *n* an obsolete word for **electron** [C20 from NEGA(TIVE + ELEC)TRON]

Negev ('nɛgɛv) *or* **Negeb** ('nɛgɛb) *n* the S part of Israel, on the Gulf of Aqaba: a triangular-shaped semidesert region, with large areas under irrigation; scene of fighting between Israeli and Egyptian forces in 1948. Chief town: Beersheba. Area: 12 820 sq km (4950 sq miles)

neglect (nɪ'glɛkt) *vb (tr)* **1** to fail to give due care, attention, or time to: *to neglect a child* **2** to fail (to do something) through thoughtlessness or carelessness: *he neglected to tell her* **3** to ignore or disregard: *she neglected his frantic signals* ▷ *n* **4** lack of due care or attention; negligence: *the child starved through neglect* **5** the act or an instance of neglecting or the state of being neglected [C16 from Latin *neglegere* to neglect, from *nec* not + *legere* to select] > ne'glecter *or* ne'glector *n*

neglectful (nɪ'glɛktfʊl) *adj* (when *postpositive,* foll by *of*) not giving due care and attention (to); careless; heedless > ne'glectfully *adv* > ne'glectfulness *n*

negligee *or* **negligée** ('nɛglɪ,ʒeɪ) *n* **1** a woman's light dressing gown, esp one that is lace-trimmed **2** any informal attire [C18 from French *négligée*, past participle (fem) of *négliger* to NEGLECT]

negligence ('nɛglɪdʒəns) *n* **1** the state or quality of being negligent **2** a negligent act **3** *law* a civil wrong whereby a person or party is in breach of a legal duty of care to another which results in loss or injury to the claimant

negligent ('nɛglɪdʒənt) *adj* **1** habitually neglecting duties, responsibilities, etc; lacking attention, care, or concern; neglectful **2** careless or nonchalant > 'negligently *adv*

negligible ('nɛglɪdʒəb³l) *adj* so small, unimportant, etc, as to be not worth considering; insignificant > ,negligi'bility *or* 'negligibleness *n* > 'negligibly *adv*

negotiable (nɪ'gəʊʃəb³l) *adj* **1** able to be negotiated **2** (of a bill of exchange, promissory note, etc) legally transferable in title from one party to another > ne,gotia'bility *n*

negotiable instrument *n* a legal document, such as a cheque or bill of exchange, that is freely negotiable

negotiant (nɪ'gəʊʃɪənt) *n* a person, nation, organization, etc, involved in a negotiation

negotiate (nɪ'gəʊʃɪ,eɪt) *vb* **1** to work or talk (with others) to achieve (a transaction, an agreement, etc) **2** *(tr)* to succeed in passing through, around,

or over: *to negotiate a mountain pass* **3** *(tr) finance* **a** to transfer (a negotiable commercial paper) by endorsement to another in return for value received **b** to sell (financial assets) **c** to arrange for (a loan) [C16 from Latin *negōtiārī* to do business, from *negōtium* business, from *nec* not + *ōtium* leisure] > ne'goti,ator *n*

negotiation (nɪ,gəʊʃɪ'eɪʃən) *n* **1** a discussion set up or intended to produce a settlement or agreement **2** the act or process of negotiating

Negress ('niːgrɪs) *n* a female Black person

Negrillo (nɪ'grɪləʊ) *n, pl* **-los** *or* **-loes** a member of a dwarfish Negroid race of central and southern Africa [C19 from Spanish, diminutive of *negro* black]

Negri Sembilan ('nɛgrɪ sɛm'biːlən) *n* a state of S Peninsular Malaysia: mostly mountainous, with large areas under paddy and rubber. Capital: Seremban. Pop: 859 924 (2000). Area: 6643 sq km (2565 sq miles)

Negritic (nɪ'grɪtɪk) *adj* relating to the Negroes or the Negritos

Negrito (nɪ'griːtəʊ) *n, pl* **-tos** *or* **-toes** a member of any of various dwarfish Negroid peoples of SE Asia and Melanesia [C19 from Spanish, diminutive of *negro* black]

negritude ('niːgrɪ,tjuːd, 'nɛg-) *n* **1** the fact of being a Negro **2** awareness and cultivation of the Negro heritage, values, and culture [C20 from French, from *nègre* NEGRO[1]]

Negro[1] ('niːgrəʊ) *old-fashioned offensive* ▷ *n, pl* **-groes** **1** a member of any of the dark-skinned indigenous peoples of Africa and their descendants elsewhere ▷ *adj* **2** relating to or characteristic of Negroes [C16 from Spanish or Portuguese: black, from Latin *niger* black] > 'Negro,ism *n*

Negro[2] ('neɪgrəʊ, 'nɛg-) *n* Río **1** a river in NW South America, rising in E Colombia (as the Guainía) and flowing east, then south as part of the border between Colombia and Venezuela, entering Brazil and continuing southeast to join the Amazon at Manáus. Length: about 2250 km (1400 miles) **2** a river in S central Argentina, formed by the confluence of the Neuquén and Limay Rivers and flowing east and southeast to the Atlantic. Length: about 1014 km (630 miles) **3** a river in central Uruguay, rising in S Brazil and flowing southwest into the Uruguay River. Length: about 467 km (290 miles)

Negroid ('niːgrɔɪd) *adj* **1** denoting, relating to, or belonging to one of the major racial groups of mankind, characterized by brown-black skin, tightly-curled hair, a short nose, and full lips. This group includes the indigenous peoples of Africa south of the Sahara, their descendants elsewhere, and some Melanesian peoples ▷ *n* **2** a member of this racial group

Negrophil ('niːgrəʊfɪl) *or* **Negrophile** ('niːgrəʊ,faɪl) *n* a person who admires Negroes and their culture > **Negrophilism** (niː'grɒfɪ,lɪzəm) *n*

Negrophobe ('niːgrəʊ,fəʊb) *n* a person who dislikes or fears Negroes > ,Negro'phobia *n* > ,Negro'phobic *adj*

Negropont ('nɛgrəʊ,pɒnt) *n* **1** the former English name for **Euboea** **2** the medieval English name for **Chalcis**

Negros ('neɪgrəʊs; *Spanish* 'neɣrɔs) *n* an island of the central Philippines, one of the Visayan Islands. Capital: Bacolod. Pop: 3 168 000 (1990 est). Area: 12 704 sq km (4904 sq miles)

Negro spiritual ('niːgrəʊ) *n* a type of religious song originating among Black slaves in the American South

negus ('niːgəs) *n, pl* **-guses** a hot drink of port and lemon juice, usually spiced and sweetened [C18 named after Col Francis *Negus* (died 1732), its English inventor]

Negus ('niːgəs) *n, pl* **-guses** a title of the emperor of Ethiopia [from Amharic: king]

Neh. *Bible abbreviation for* Nehemiah

Nehemiah (,niːɪ'maɪə) *n Old Testament* **1** a Jewish

official at the court of Artaxerxes, king of Persia, who in 444 BC became a leader in the rebuilding of Jerusalem after the Babylonian captivity **2** the book recounting the acts of Nehemiah

neigh (neɪ) *n* **1** the high-pitched cry of a horse; whinny ▷ *vb* **2** *(intr)* to make a neigh or a similar noise **3** *(tr)* to utter with a sound like a neigh [Old English *hnǣgan*; related to Old Saxon *hnēgian*]

neighbour *or US* **neighbor** ('neɪbə) *n* **1** a person who lives near or next to another **2 a** a person or thing near or next to another **b** *(as modifier)*: *neighbour states* ▷ *vb* **3** (when *intr*, often foll by *on*) to be or live close (to a person or thing) [Old English *nēahbūr*, from *nēah* NIGH + *būr*, *gebūr* dweller; see BOOR] > 'neighbouring *or US* 'neighboring *adj* > 'neighbourless *or US* 'neighborless *adj*

neighbourhood *or US* **neighborhood** ('neɪbə,hʊd) *n* **1** the immediate environment; surroundings; vicinity. Related adj: **vicinal 2** a district where people live **3** the people in a particular area; neighbours **4** neighbourly feeling **5** *maths* the set of all points whose distance from a given point is less than a specified value **6** *(modifier)* of or for a neighbourhood: *a neighbourhood community worker* **7** **in the neighbourhood of** approximately (a given number)

neighbourhood warden *n Brit* a person employed by a local authority to patrol residential areas and deal with anti-social behaviour

neighbourhood watch *n* a scheme under which members of a community agree together to take responsibility for keeping an eye on each other's property, as a way of preventing crime

neighbourly *or US* **neighborly** ('neɪbəlɪ) *adj* kind, friendly, or sociable, as befits a neighbour > 'neighbourliness *or US* 'neighborliness *n*

neinei (,neɪ'neɪ:) *n* a New Zealand shrub, *Dracophyllum latifolium*, with clusters of long narrow leaves. Also called: **spiderwood** [Māori]

Neisse ('naɪsə) *n* **1** Also called: **Glatzer Neisse** ('glɑːtsə) Polish name: **Nysa** a river in SW Poland, rising on the northern Czech border, and flowing northeast to join the Oder near Brzeg. Length: about 193 km (120 miles) **2** Also called: **Lusatian Neisse** a river in E Europe, rising near Liberec in the Czech Republic and flowing north to join the Oder: forms part of the German-Polish border. Length: 225 km (140 miles)

neither ('naɪðə, 'niːðə) *determiner* **1 a** not one nor the other (of two); not either: *neither foot is swollen* **b** *(as pronoun)*: *neither can win* ▷ *conj* **2** *(coordinating)* **a** (used preceding alternatives joined by *nor*) not: *neither John nor Mary nor Joe went* **b** another word for **nor** (sense 2) ▷ *adv* **3** *(sentence modifier) not standard* another word for **either** (sense 4) [C13 (literally, *ne either* not either): changed from Old English *nāwther*, from *nāhwæther*, from *nā* not + *hwæther* which of two; see WHETHER]

> USAGE A verb following a compound subject that uses *neither...* should be in the singular if both subjects are in the singular: *neither Jack nor John has done the work*

Nejd (nɛʒd, neɪd) *n* a region of central Saudi Arabia: formerly an independent sultanate of Arabia; united with Hejaz to form the kingdom of Saudi Arabia (1932)

nek (nɛk) *n (capital when part of name) South African* a mountain pass: *Lundeans Nek*

nekton ('nɛktɒn) *n* the population of free-swimming animals that inhabits the middle depths of a sea or lake. Compare **plankton** [C19 via German from Greek *nēkton* a swimming thing, from *nēkhein* to swim] > **nek'tonic** *adj*

nelly ('nɛlɪ) *n* **not on your nelly** *(sentence substitute) Brit slang* not under any circumstances; certainly not

nelson ('nɛlsən) *n* any wrestling hold in which a wrestler places his arm or arms under his opponent's arm or arms from behind and exerts pressure with his palms on the back of his opponent's neck. See **full nelson, half-nelson** [C19 from a proper name]

Nelson ('nɛlsən) *n* **1** a town in NW England, in E Lancashire: textile industry. Pop: 28 998 (2001) **2** a port in New Zealand, on N South Island on Tasman Bay. Pop: 45 300 (2004 est) **3 River** a river in central Canada, in N central Manitoba, flowing from Lake Winnipeg northeast to Hudson Bay. Length: about 650 km (400 miles)

Nelspruit ('nɛlsˌprɔɪt) *n* a city in NE South Africa, the capital of Mpumalanga province on the Crocodile River: trading and agricultural centre, esp for fruit, with a growing tourist trade. Pop: 21 541 (2001)

nelumbo (nɪ'lʌmbəʊ) *n, pl* -bos either of the two aquatic plants of the genus *Nelumbo*: family *Nelumbonaceae.* See **lotus** (sense 4), **water chinquapin** [C19 New Latin, from Sinhalese *nelumbu* lotus]

Neman or **Nyeman** (*Russian* 'njɛmən) *n* a river in NE Europe, rising in Belarus and flowing northwest through Lithuania to the Baltic. Length: 937 km (582 miles). Polish name: Niemen

nemathelminth (ˌnɛmə'θɛlmɪnθ) *n* any unsegmented worm of the group *Nemathelminthes,* including the nematodes, nematomorphs, and acanthocephalans

nematic (nɪ'mætɪk) *adj chem* (of a substance) existing in or having a mesomorphic state in which a linear orientation of the molecules causes anisotropic properties. Compare **smectic** See also **liquid crystal** [C20 NEMAT(O)- (referring to the threadlike chains of molecules in liquid) + -IC]

nemato- or before a vowel **nemat-** combining form indicating a threadlike form: *nematocyst* [from Greek *nēma* thread]

nematocyst ('nɛmətəˌsɪst, nɪ'mætə-) *n* a structure in coelenterates, such as jellyfish, consisting of a capsule containing a hollow coiled thread that can be everted to sting or paralyse prey and enemies > *nemato'cystic adj*

nematode ('nɛməˌtəʊd) *n* any unsegmented worm of the phylum (or class) *Nematoda,* having a tough outer cuticle. The group includes free-living forms and disease-causing parasites, such as the hookworm and filaria. Also called: nematode worm, roundworm

Nembutal ('nɛmbjʊˌtɑːl) *n* a trademark for **pentobarbital sodium**

nem. con. abbreviation for nemine contradicente [Latin: no-one contradicting; unanimously]

Nemea (nɪ'miːə) *n* (in ancient Greece) a valley in N Argolis in the NE Peloponnese; site of the **Nemean Games,** a Panhellenic festival and athletic competition held every other year

Nemean (nɪ'miːən) *adj* of or relating to the valley of Nemea in ancient Greece or its inhabitants

Nemean lion *n Greek myth* an enormous lion that was strangled by Hercules as his first labour

nemertean (nɪ'mɜːtɪən) or **nemertine** ('nɛməˌtaɪn) *n* **1** Also called: ribbon worm any soft flattened ribbon-like marine worm of the phylum (or class) *Nemertea* (or *Nemertina*), having an eversible threadlike proboscis ▷ *adj* **2** of, relating to, or belonging to the *Nemertea* [C19 via New Latin from Greek *Nēmertēs* a NEREID[1]]

nemesia (nɪ'miːzə) *n* any plant of the southern African scrophulariaceous genus *Nemesia*: cultivated for their brightly coloured (often reddish) flowers [C19 New Latin, from Greek *nemesion,* name of a plant resembling this]

Nemesis ('nɛmɪsɪs) *n, pl* -ses (-ˌsiːz) **1** Greek myth the goddess of retribution and vengeance **2** (sometimes not capital) any agency of retribution and vengeance [C16 via Latin from Greek: righteous wrath, from *némein* to distribute what is due]

nemophila (nɪ'mɒfɪlə) *n* any of a genus, *Nemophila,* of low-growing hairy annual plants, esp *N. menziesii,* grown for its blue or white flowers: family *Hydrophyllaceae* [New Latin, from Greek *nemos* a grove + *philein* to love]

nene ('neɪˌneɪ) *n* a rare black-and-grey short-winged Hawaiian goose, *Branta sandvicensis,* having partly webbed feet [from Hawaiian]

neo- or sometimes before a vowel **ne-** combining form **1** (sometimes capital) new, recent, or a new or modern form or development: *neoclassicism; neocolonialism* **2** (usually capital) the most recent subdivision of a geological period: *Neogene* [from Greek *neos* new]

neoanthropic (ˌniːəʊæn'θrɒpɪk) *adj anthropol* of, relating to, or resembling modern man

neoarsphenamine (ˌniːəʊɑːs'fɛnəˌmiːn, -fɪ'næmɪn) *n* a derivative of arsenic formerly used in treating syphilis

Neocene ('niːəˌsiːn) *adj, n* a former word for **Neogene**

neoclassical (ˌniːəʊ'klæsɪkˀl) or **neoclassic** *adj* **1** of, relating to , or in the style of neoclassicism in art, architecture, etc **2** of, relating to , or in the style of neoclassicism in music

neoclassicism (ˌniːəʊ'klæsɪˌsɪzəm) *n* **1** a late 18th- and early 19th-century style in architecture, decorative art, and fine art, based on the imitation of surviving classical models and types **2** music a movement of the 1920s, involving Hindemith, Stravinsky, etc, that sought to avoid the emotionalism of late romantic music by reviving the use of counterpoint, forms such as the classical suite, and small instrumental ensembles > *neo'classicist n*

neocolonialism (ˌniːəʊkə'ləʊnɪəˌlɪzəm) *n* (in the modern world) political control by an outside power of a country that is in theory sovereign and independent, esp through the domination of its economy > *neoco'lonial adj* > *neoco'lonialist n*

neo-con (ˌniːəʊ'kɒn) *n US informal* **a** a neo-conservative **b** (as modifier): a neo-con think tank

neo-conservatism *n* (in the US) a right-wing tendency that originated amongst supporters of the political left and has become characterized by its support of hawkish foreign policies > *neo-con'servative adj, n*

Neo-Darwinism (ˌniːəʊ'dɑːwɪnˌɪzəm) *n* the modern version of the Darwinian theory of evolution, which incorporates the principles of genetics to explain how inheritable variations can arise by mutation > *Neo-Dar'winian adj, n*

neodymium (ˌniːəʊ'dɪmɪəm) *n* a toxic silvery-white metallic element of the lanthanide series, occurring principally in monazite: used in colouring glass. Symbol: Nd; atomic no.: 60; atomic wt.: 144.24; valency: 3; relative density: 6.80 and 7.00 (depending on allotrope); melting pt.: 1024°C; boiling pt.: 3127°C [C19 New Latin; see NEO- + DIDYMIUM]

Neogaea (ˌniːəʊ'dʒiːə) *n* a zoogeographical area comprising the Neotropical region. Compare **Arctogaea, Notogaea** [C19 New Latin, from NEO- + GAEA, from Greek *gaia* earth]

Neogaean (ˌniːəʊ'dʒiːən) *adj* of or relating to Neogaea, a zoogeographical area comprising the Neotropical region

Neogene ('niːəˌdʒiːn) *adj* **1** of, denoting, or formed during the Miocene and Pliocene epochs ▷ *n* **2** the the Neogene period or system

neogothic (ˌniːəʊ'gɒθɪk) *n* another name for **Gothic Revival**

neoimpressionism (ˌniːəʊɪm'prɛʃəˌnɪzəm) *n* a movement in French painting initiated mainly by Georges Seurat (1859–91) in the 1880s and combining his vivid colour technique with strictly formal composition. See also **pointillism** > *neoim'pressionist n, adj*

Neo-Lamarckism (ˌniːəʊlə'mɑːkɪzəm) *n* a theory of evolution based on Lamarckism, proposing that environmental factors could lead to adaptive genetic changes > *Neo-La'marckian adj, n*

Neo-Latin (ˌniːəʊ'lætɪn) *n* **1** another term for **New Latin** ▷ *adj* **2** denoting or relating to New Latin **3** denoting or relating to language that developed from Latin; Romance

neoliberalism (ˌniːəʊ'lɪbərəˌlɪzəm, -'lɪbrəˌlɪzəm) *n* a modern politico-economic theory favouring free trade, privatization, minimal government

intervention in business, reduced public expenditure on social services, etc > *neo'liberal adj, n*

neolith ('niːəʊlɪθ) *n* a Neolithic stone implement

Neolithic (ˌniːəʊ'lɪθɪk) *n* **1** the cultural period that lasted in SW Asia from about 9000 to 6000 BC and in Europe from about 4000 to 2400 BC and was characterized by primitive crop growing and stock rearing and the use of polished stone and flint tools and weapons ▷ *adj* **2** relating to this period ▷ See also **Mesolithic, Palaeolithic**

neologism (nɪ'ɒləˌdʒɪzəm) or **neology** *n, pl* -gisms or -gies **1** a newly coined word, or a phrase or familiar word used in a new sense **2** the practice of using or introducing neologisms **3** rare a tendency towards adopting new views, esp rationalist views, in matters of religion [C18 via French from NEO- + -logism, from Greek *logos* word, saying] > *ne'ologist n* > *ne,olo'gistic, ne,olo'gistical* or *neological* (ˌniːə'lɒdʒɪkˀl) *adj* > *ne,olo'gistically* or *neo'logically adv*

neologize or **neologise** (nɪ'ɒləˌdʒaɪz) *vb* (*intr*) to invent or use neologisms

Neo-Melanesian *n* an English-based creole language widely spoken in the SW Pacific, with borrowings from other languages, esp Motu. Also called: **Beach-la-Mar**

neomycin (ˌniːəʊ'maɪsɪn) *n* an antibiotic obtained from the bacterium *Streptomyces fradiae,* administered locally in the treatment of skin and eye infections or orally for bowel infections. Formula: $C_{12}H_{26}N_4O_6$ [C20 from NEO- + Greek *mukēs* fungus + -IN]

neon ('niːɒn) *n* **1** a colourless odourless rare gaseous element, an inert gas occurring in trace amounts in the atmosphere: used in illuminated signs and lights. Symbol: Ne; atomic no.: 10; atomic wt.: 20.1797; valency: 0; density: 0.899 90 kg/m³; melting pt.: –248.59°C; boiling pt.: –246.08°C **2** (modifier) of or illuminated by neon or neon lamps: *neon sign* [C19 via New Latin from Greek *neon* new]

neonatal (ˌniːəʊ'neɪtˀl) *adj* of or relating to newborn children, esp in the first week of life and up to four weeks old > *neo'natally adv*

neonate ('niːəʊˌneɪt) *n* a newborn child, esp in the first week of life and up to four weeks old

neonaticide (ˌniːəʊ'neɪtɪˌsaɪd) *n* the act of killing a baby in the first 24 hours of its life

neonatology (ˌniːəʊnə'tɒlədʒɪ) *n* the branch of medicine concerned with the development and disorders of newborn babies > *neona'tologist n*

neon lamp *n* a glass bulb or tube containing neon at low pressure that gives a pink or red glow when a voltage is applied

neo-noir (ˌniːəʊ'nwɑː) *adj* (of a film) set in contemporary modern times, but showing characteristics of a film noir, in plot or style

neo-orthodoxy (ˌniːəʊ'ɔːθəˌdɒksɪ) *n* a movement in 20th-century Protestantism, reasserting certain older traditional Christian doctrines > *neo-'orthodox adj*

neophilia (ˌniːəʊ'fɪlɪə) *n* a tendency to like anything new; love of novelty > *neo,philiac n*

neophobia (ˌniːəʊ'fəʊbɪə) *n* a tendency to dislike anything new; fear of novelty > *neo,phobe n* > *neo'phobic adj*

neophyte ('niːəʊˌfaɪt) *n* **1** a person newly converted to a religious faith **2** RC Church a novice in a religious order **3** a novice or beginner [C16 via Church Latin from New Testament Greek *neophutos* recently planted, from *neos* new + *phuton* a plant] > *neophytic* (ˌniːəʊ'fɪtɪk) *adj*

neoplasm ('niːəʊˌplæzəm) *n pathol* any abnormal new growth of tissue; tumour > *neoplastic* (ˌniːəʊ'plæstɪk) *adj*

neoplasticism (ˌniːəʊ'plæstɪˌsɪzəm) *n* the style of abstract painting evolved by the Dutch painter Piet Mondrian (1872–1944) and the Dutch de Stijl movement, characterized by the use of horizontal and vertical lines and planes and by black, white, grey, and primary colours

n

neoplasty ('niːəʊ,plæstɪ) *n* the surgical formation of new tissue structures or repair of damaged structures

Neo-Platonism or **Neoplatonism** (,niːəʊ'pleɪtə,nɪzəm) *n* a philosophical system which was first developed in the 3rd century AD as a synthesis of Platonic, Pythagorean, and Aristotelian elements, and which, although originally opposed to Christianity, later incorporated it. It dominated European thought until the 13th century and re-emerged during the Renaissance > Neo-Platonic (,niːəʊplə'tɒnɪk) *adj* > ,Neo-'Platonist *n, adj*

neoprene ('niːəʊ,priːn) *n* a synthetic rubber obtained by the polymerization of chloroprene. It is resistant to oil and ageing and is used in waterproof products, such as diving suits, paints, and adhesives [C20 from NEO- + PR(OPYL) + -ENE]

Neoptolemus (,niːɒp'tɒləməs) *n Greek myth* a son of Achilles and slayer of King Priam of Troy. Also called: Pyrrhus

neorealism (,niːəʊ'riːəlɪzəm) *n films* a movement to depict directly the poor in society: originating in postwar Italy > ,neo'realist *n, adj*

neoteny (nɪ'ɒtənɪ) *n* the persistence of larval or fetal features in the adult form of an animal. For example, the adult axolotl, a salamander, retains larval external gills. See also **paedogenesis** [C19 from New Latin *neotenia*, from Greek NEO- + *teinein* to stretch] > neotenic (,niːəʊ'tɛnɪk) or ne'otenous *adj*

neoteric (,niːəʊ'tɛrɪk) *rare* ▷ *adj* 1 belonging to a new fashion or trend; modern: *a neoteric genre* ▷ *n* 2 a new writer or philosopher [C16 via Late Latin from Greek *neōterikos* young, fresh, from *neoteros* younger, more recent, from *neos* new, recent] > ,neo'terically *adv*

Neotropical (,niːəʊ'trɒpɪkᵊl) *adj* of or denoting a zoogeographical region consisting of South America and North America south of the tropic of Cancer

neotype ('niːəʊ,taɪp) *n biology* a specimen selected to replace a type specimen that has been lost or destroyed

Neozoic (,niːəʊ'zəʊɪk) *adj obsolete* of or formed at any time after the end of the Mesozoic era

NEP 1 *abbreviation for* **New Economic Policy** 2 *international car registration for* Nepal

NEPAD ('niːpæd) *n acronym for* New Partnership for African Development

Nepal (nɪ'pɔːl) *n* a kingdom in S Asia: the world's only Hindu kingdom; united in 1768 by the Gurkhas; consists of swampy jungle in the south and great massifs, valleys, and gorges of the Himalayas over the rest of the country, with many peaks over 8000 m (26 000 ft) (notably Everest and Kangchenjunga). A multiparty democracy was instituted in 1990. Official language: Nepali. Official religion: Hinduism; Mahayana Buddhist minority. Currency: rupee. Capital: Katmandu. Pop: 25 724 000 (2004 est). Area: 147 181 sq km (56 815 sq miles)

Nepalese (,nɛpə'liːz) *adj* 1 of or relating to Nepal or its inhabitants ▷ *n, pl* -ese 2 a native or inhabitant of Nepal

Nepali (nɪ'pɔːlɪ) *n* 1 the official language of Nepal, also spoken in Sikkim and parts of India. It forms the E group of Pahari and belongs to the Indic branch of Indo-European 2 (*pl* -pali or -palis) a native or inhabitant of Nepal; a Nepalese ▷ *adj* 3 of or relating to Nepal, its inhabitants, or their language; Nepalese

nepenthe (nɪ'pɛnθɪ) *n* 1 a drug, or the plant providing it, that ancient writers referred to as a means of forgetting grief or trouble 2 anything that produces sleep, forgetfulness, or pleasurable dreaminess [C16 via Latin from Greek *nēpenthes* sedative made from a herb, from *nē*- not + *penthos* grief] > ne'penthean *adj*

neper ('neɪpə, 'niː-) *n* a unit expressing the ratio of two quantities, esp amplitudes in telecommunications, equal to the natural

logarithm of the ratio of the two quantities. Symbol: Np, N [C20 named after John *Napier* (1550–1617), Scottish mathematician; the name was approved in 1928]

nepeta ('nɛpətə) *n* See **catmint** [Latin: catmint]

nepheline ('nɛfɪlɪn, -,liːn) or **nephelite** ('nɛfɪ,laɪt) *n* a whitish mineral consisting of sodium potassium aluminium silicate in hexagonal crystalline form: used in the manufacture of glass and ceramics. Formula: (Na,K)(AlSi)$_2$O$_4$ [C19 from French *néphéline*, from Greek *nephelē* cloud, so called because pieces of it become cloudy if dipped in nitric acid]

nephelinite ('nɛfɪlɪ,naɪt) *n* a fine-grained basic laval rock consisting of pyroxene and nepheline

nephelometer (,nɛfɪ'lɒmɪtə) *n chem* an instrument for measuring the size or density of particles suspended in a fluid [C19 (in the sense: an instrument for measuring the cloudiness of the sky): from Greek *nephelē* cloud + -O- + -METER] > nephelometric (,nɛfɪləʊ'mɛtrɪk) *adj* > ,nephe'lometry *n*

nephew ('nɛvjuː, 'nɛf-) *n* a son of one's sister or brother [C13 from Old French *neveu*, from Latin *nepōs*; related to Old English *nefa*, Old High German *nevo* relative]

nepho- *combining form* concerning cloud or clouds [from Greek *nephos* cloud]

nephogram ('nɛfə,græm) *n meteorol* a photograph of a cloud

nephograph ('nɛfə,grɑːf, -,græf) *n* an instrument for photographing clouds

nephology (nɪ'fɒlədʒɪ) *n* the study of clouds > nephological (,nɛfə'lɒdʒɪkᵊl) *adj* > ne'phologist *n*

nephoscope ('nɛfə,skəʊp) *n* an instrument for measuring the altitude, velocity, and direction of movement of clouds

nephralgia (nɪ'frældʒɪə) *n* pain in a kidney > ne'phralgic *adj*

nephrectomy (nɪ'frɛktəmɪ) *n, pl* -mies surgical removal of a kidney

nephridium (nɪ'frɪdɪəm) *n, pl* -ia (-ɪə) a simple excretory organ of many invertebrates, consisting of a tube through which waste products pass to the exterior [C19 New Latin: little kidney] > ne'phridial *adj*

nephrite ('nɛfraɪt) *n* a tough fibrous amphibole mineral: a variety of jade consisting of calcium magnesium silicate in monoclinic crystalline form. Formula: Ca$_2$Mg$_5$Si$_8$O$_{22}$(OH)$_2$. Also called: kidney stone [C18 via German *Nephrit* from Greek *nephrós* kidney, so called because it was thought to be beneficial in kidney disorders]

nephritic (nɪ'frɪtɪk) *adj* 1 of or relating to the kidneys 2 relating to or affected with nephritis

nephritis (nɪ'fraɪtɪs) *n* inflammation of a kidney

nephro- or before a vowel **nephr-** *combining form* kidney or kidneys: *nephrotomy* [from Greek *nephros*]

nephroblastoma (,nɛfrəʊblæs'təʊmə) *n, pl* -mata or -mas a malignant tumour arising from the embryonic kidney that occurs in young children, esp in the age range 3–8 years

nephrolepis (,nɛfrə'liːpɪs) *n* any fern of the tropical genus *Nephrolepis*, some species of which are grown as ornamental greenhouse or house plants for their handsome deeply-cut drooping fronds: family *Polypodiaceae*. Also called: ladder fern, Boston fern [New Latin, from Greek *nephros* kidney + *lepis* scale (from the shape of the indusium)]

nephrology (nɪ'frɒlədʒɪ) *n* the branch of medicine concerned with diseases of the kidney > ne'phrologist *n*

nephron ('nɛfrɒn) *n* any of the minute urine-secreting tubules that form the functional unit of the kidneys

nephroscope ('nɛfrə,skəʊp) *n* a tubular medical instrument inserted through an incision in the skin to enable examination of a kidney > nephroscopy (nɪ'frɒskəpɪ) *n*

nephrosis (nɪ'frəʊsɪs) *n* any noninflammatory degenerative kidney disease > ne'phrotic *adj*

nephrotomy (nɪ'frɒtəmɪ) *n, pl* -mies surgical incision into a kidney

nepionic (,nɛpɪ'ɒnɪk) *adj zoology* of or relating to the juvenile period in the life cycle of an organism

nepit ('niːpɪt) *n* another word for **nit**⁴

ne plus ultra *Latin* ('neɪ 'plʊs 'ʊltrɑː) *n* the extreme or perfect point or state [literally: not more beyond (that is, go no further), allegedly a warning to sailors inscribed on the Pillars of Hercules at Gibraltar]

nepotism ('nɛpə,tɪzəm) *n* favouritism shown to relatives or close friends by those with power or influence [C17 from Italian *nepotismo*, from *nepote* NEPHEW, from the former papal practice of granting special favours to nephews or other relatives] > nepotic (nɪ'pɒtɪk) or ,nepo'tistic *adj* > 'nepotist *n*

Neptune¹ ('nɛptjuːn) *n* the Roman god of the sea. Greek counterpart: Poseidon

Neptune² ('nɛptjuːn) *n* the eighth planet from the sun, having eight satellites, the largest being Triton and Nereid, and a faint planar system of rings or ring fragments. Mean distance from sun: 4497 million km; period of revolution around sun: 164.8 years; period of rotation: 14 to 16 hours; diameter and mass: 4.0 and 17.2 times that of earth respectively

Neptunian (nɛp'tjuːnɪən) *adj* 1 of or relating to the Roman god Neptune or the sea 2 of, occurring on, or relating to the planet Neptune 3 *geology* (of sedimentary rock formations such as dykes) formed under water

neptunium (nɛp'tjuːnɪəm) *n* a silvery metallic transuranic element synthesized in the production of plutonium and occurring in trace amounts in uranium ores. Symbol: Np; atomic no.: 93; half-life of most stable isotope, ^{237}Np: 2.14 × 10⁶ years; valency: 3, 4, 5, or 6; relative density: 20.25; melting pt.: 639±1°C; boiling pt.: 3902°C (est) [C20 from NEPTUNE², the planet beyond Uranus, because neptunium is the element beyond uranium in the periodic table]

neptunium series *n* a radioactive series that starts with plutonium-241 and ends with bismuth-209. Neptunium-237 is the longest-lived member of the series. The series does not occur in nature

neral ('nɪəræl) *n chem* the *trans*- isomer of citral [C20 from *nerol* (an alcohol from NEROLI OIL) + -AL³]

NERC *abbreviation for* Natural Environment Research Council

nerd or **nurd** (nɜːd) *n slang* 1 a boring or unpopular person, esp one obsessed with something specified: *a computer nerd* 2 a stupid and feeble person > 'nerdish or 'nurdish *adj* > 'nerdy or 'nurdy *adj*

Nereid¹ ('nɪərɪɪd) *n, pl* Nereides (nə'riːə,diːz) *Greek myth* any of the 50 sea nymphs who were the daughters of the sea god Nereus [C17 via Latin from Greek *Nērēid*, from NEREUS; compare Latin *nāre* to swim]

Nereid² ('nɪərɪɪd) *n* a satellite of the planet Neptune, in a large and highly eccentric orbit

nereis ('nɪərɪɪs) *n* any polychaete worm of the genus *Nereis*. See **ragworm** [C18 from Latin; see NEREID¹]

Nereus ('nɪərɪ,uːs) *n Greek myth* a sea god who lived in the depths of the sea with his wife Doris and their daughters the Nereides

nerine (nə'riːnɪ) *n* any plant of the bulbous S. African genus *Nerine*, related to the amaryllis; several species are grown as garden or pot plants for their beautiful pink, orange, red, or white flowers. *N. sarniensis* is the pink-flowered Guernsey lily: family *Amaryllidaceae* [Latin, from Greek *nērēis* a sea nymph]

neritic (nɛ'rɪtɪk) *adj* of or formed in the region of shallow seas near a coastline [C20 perhaps from Latin *nērīta* sea mussel, from Greek *nērítēs*, from NEREUS]

Nernst heat theorem (nɛənst) *n* the principle that reactions in crystalline solids involve changes in entropy that tend to zero as the temperature approaches absolute zero. See **law of thermodynamics** (sense 1)

neroli oil or **neroli** (ˈnɪərəlɪ) n a brown oil distilled from the flowers of various orange trees, esp the Seville orange: used in perfumery [C17 named after Anne Marie de la Tremoïlle of *Neroli*, French-born Italian princess believed to have discovered it]

nervate (ˈnɜːveɪt) adj (of leaves) having veins

nervation (nɜːˈveɪʃən) or **nervature** (ˈnɜːvətʃə) n a less common word for **venation**

nerve (nɜːv) n 1 any of the cordlike bundles of fibres that conduct sensory or motor impulses between the brain or spinal cord and another part of the body. Related adj: **neural** 2 courage, bravery, or steadfastness 3 **lose one's nerve** to become timid, esp failing to perform some audacious act 4 *informal* boldness or effrontery; impudence: *he had the nerve to swear at me* 5 muscle or sinew (often in the phrase **strain every nerve**) 6 a large vein in a leaf 7 any of the veins of an insect's wing 8 **touch, hit,** or **strike a (raw) nerve** to mention or bring to mind a sensitive issue or subject ▷ vb (tr) 9 to give courage to (oneself); steel (oneself) 10 to provide with nerve or nerves ▷ See also **nerves** [C16 from Latin *nervus*; related to Greek *neuron*; compare Sanskrit *snāvan* sinew]

nerve block n induction of anaesthesia in a specific part of the body by injecting a local anaesthetic close to the sensory nerves that supply it

nerve cell n another name for **neurone**

nerve centre n 1 a group of nerve cells associated with a specific function 2 a principal source of control over any complex activity

nerve fibre n a threadlike extension of a nerve cell; axon

nerve gas n (esp in chemical warfare) any of various poisonous gases that have a paralysing effect on the central nervous system that can be fatal

nerve growth factor n 1 a polypeptide produced by neurones and their supporting tissues as well as some other tissues that stimulate the growth of neurones 2 any of various related polypeptides that promote the growth of neurones. Abbreviation: NGF

nerve impulse n the electrical wave transmitted along a nerve fibre, usually following stimulation of the nerve-cell body. See also **action potential**

nerveless (ˈnɜːvlɪs) adj 1 calm and collected 2 listless or feeble > ˈnervelessly adv > ˈnervelessness n

nerve-racking or **nerve-wracking** adj very distressing, exhausting, or harrowing

nerves (nɜːvz) pl n *informal* 1 the imagined source of emotional control: *my nerves won't stand it* 2 anxiety, tension, or imbalance: *she's all nerves* 3 **bundle of nerves** a very nervous person 4 **get on one's nerves** to irritate, annoy, or upset one

nervine (ˈnɜːviːn) adj 1 having a soothing or calming effect upon the nerves ▷ n 2 *obsolete* a nervine drug or agent [C17 from New Latin *nervīnus*, from Latin *nervus* NERVE]

nerving (ˈnɜːvɪŋ) n *vet science* surgical removal of part of a nerve trunk, or the use of chemicals to block the nerve supply, to relieve pain; usually because of chronic and disabling inflammation

nervous (ˈnɜːvəs) adj 1 very excitable or sensitive; highly strung 2 (often foll by *of*) apprehensive or worried: *I'm nervous of traffic* 3 of, relating to, or containing nerves; neural: *nervous tissue* 4 affecting the nerves or nervous tissue: *a nervous disease* 5 *archaic* active, vigorous, or forceful > ˈnervously adv > ˈnervousness n

nervous breakdown n any mental illness not primarily of organic origin, in which the patient ceases to function properly, often accompanied by severely impaired concentration, anxiety, insomnia, and lack of self-esteem; used esp of episodes of depression

nervous system n the sensory and control apparatus of all multicellular animals above the level of sponges, consisting of a network of nerve cells (see **neurone**). See also **central nervous system**

nervure (ˈnɜːvjʊə) n 1 *entomol* any of the stiff chitinous rods that form the supporting framework of an insect's wing; vein 2 *botany* any of the veins or ribs of a leaf [C19 from French; see NERVE, -URE]

nervy (ˈnɜːvɪ) adj nervier, nerviest 1 *Brit informal* tense or apprehensive 2 having or needing bravery or endurance 3 *US and Canadian informal* brash or cheeky 4 *archaic* muscular; sinewy > ˈnervily adv > ˈnerviness n

nescience (ˈnɛsɪəns) n a formal or literary word for **ignorance** [C17 from Late Latin *nescientia*, from Latin *nescīre* to be ignorant of, from *ne* not + *scīre* to know; compare SCIENCE] > ˈnescient adj

nesh (nɛʃ) adj *dialect* 1 sensitive to the cold 2 timid or cowardly [from Old English *hnesce*; related to Gothic *hnasqus* tender, soft; of obscure origin]

ness (nɛs) n **a** *archaic* a promontory or headland **b** (*capital as part of a name*): *Orford Ness* [Old English *næs* headland; related to Old Norse *nes*, Old English *nasu* NOSE]

Ness (nɛs) n **Loch** a lake in NW Scotland, in the Great Glen: said to be inhabited by an aquatic monster. Length: 36 km (22.5 miles). Depth: 229 m (754 ft)

-ness suffix forming nouns chiefly from adjectives and participles indicating state, condition, or quality, or an instance of one of these: *greatness; selfishness; meaninglessness; a kindness* [Old English *-nes*, of Germanic origin; related to Gothic *-nassus*]

nesselrode (ˈnɛsəlˌrəʊd) n a rich frozen pudding, made of chestnuts, eggs, cream, etc [C19 named after Count Karl Robert *Nesselrode* (1780–1862), Russian diplomat, whose chef invented the dish]

Nessus (ˈnɛsəs) n *Greek myth* a centaur that killed Hercules. A garment dipped in its blood fatally poisoned Hercules, who had been given it by Deianira who thought it was a love charm

nest (nɛst) n 1 a place or structure in which birds, fishes, insects, reptiles, mice, etc, lay eggs or give birth to young 2 a number of animals of the same species and their young occupying a common habitat: *an ants' nest* 3 a place fostering something undesirable: *a nest of thievery* 4 the people in such a place: *a nest of thieves* 5 a cosy or secluded place 6 a set of things, usually of graduated sizes, designed to fit together: *a nest of tables* 7 *military* a weapon emplacement: *a machine-gun nest* ▷ vb 8 (intr) to make or inhabit a nest 9 (intr) to hunt for birds' nests 10 (tr) to place in a nest [Old English; related to Latin *nīdus* (nest) and to BENEATH, SIT] > ˈnester n > ˈnestˌlike adj

NESTA (ˈnɛstə) n (in Britain) acronym for National Endowment for Science, Technology and the Arts

nest box or **nesting box** n 1 a box in a henhouse in which domestic chickens lay eggs 2 a box designed as a nesting place for wild birds and positioned in a garden, park, or reserve to encourage them to breed there

nest egg n 1 a fund of money kept in reserve; savings 2 a natural or artificial egg left in a nest to induce hens to lay their eggs in it

nesting (ˈnɛstɪŋ) n the tendency to arrange one's immediate surroundings, such as a work station, to create a place where one feels secure, comfortable, or in control

nestle (ˈnɛsəl) vb 1 (intr; often foll by *up* or *down*) to snuggle, settle, or cuddle closely 2 (intr) to be in a sheltered or protected position; lie snugly 3 (tr) to shelter or place snugly or partly concealed, as in a nest [Old English *nestlian*. See NEST] > ˈnestler n

nestling (ˈnɛstlɪŋ, ˈnɛslɪŋ) n 1 **a** a young bird not yet fledged **b** (*as modifier*): *a nestling thrush* 2 any young person or animal [C14 from NEST + -LING¹]

Nestor (ˈnɛstɔː) n 1 *Greek myth* the oldest and wisest of the Greeks in the Trojan War 2

(*sometimes not capital*) a wise old man; sage

Nestorianism (nɛˈstɔːrɪəˌnɪzəm) n the doctrine that Christ was two distinct persons, divine and human, implying a denial that the Virgin Mary was the mother of God. It is attributed to Nestorius (died ?451 AD), the Syrian patriarch of Constantinople, and survives in the Iraqi Church > Nesˈtorian n, adj

net¹ (nɛt) n 1 an openwork fabric of string, rope, wire, etc; mesh. Related adj: **retiary** 2 a device made of net, used to protect or enclose things or to trap animals 3 **a** a thin light mesh fabric of cotton, nylon, or other fibre, used for curtains, dresses, etc **b** (*as modifier*): *net curtains* 4 a plan, strategy, etc, intended to trap or ensnare: *the murderer slipped through the police net* 5 *sport* **a** a strip of net that divides the playing area into two equal parts **b** a shot that hits the net, whether or not it goes over 6 the goal in soccer, hockey, etc 7 (*often plural*) *cricket* **a** a pitch surrounded by netting, used for practice **b** a practice session in a net 8 *informal* short for **internet** 9 another word for **network** (sense 2) ▷ vb nets, netting, netted 10 (tr) to catch with or as if with a net; ensnare 11 (tr) to shelter or surround with a net 12 (intr) *sport* to score a goal: *Rangers netted three times in seven minutes* 13 to make a net out of (rope, string, etc) [Old English *net*; related to Gothic *nati*, Dutch *net*]

net² or **nett** (nɛt) adj 1 remaining after all deductions, as for taxes, expenses, losses, etc: *net profit*. Compare **gross** (sense 2) 2 (of weight) after deducting tare 3 ultimate; final; conclusive (esp in the phrase **net result**) ▷ n 4 net income, profits, weight, etc ▷ vb nets, netting, netted 5 (tr) to yield or earn as clear profit [C14 clean, neat, from French *net* NEAT¹; related to Dutch *net*, German *nett*]

net³ an internet domain name for a company or organization

net asset value n the total value of the assets of an organization less its liabilities and capital charges. Abbreviation: NAV

netball (ˈnɛtˌbɔːl) n a team game similar to basketball, played mainly by women > ˈnetˌballer n

Net Book Agreement n a former agreement between UK publishers and booksellers that until 1995 prohibited booksellers from undercutting the price of books sold in bookshops. Abbreviation: NBA

net domestic product n *economics* the gross domestic product minus an allowance for the depreciation of capital goods. Abbreviation: NDP

Neth. *abbreviation for* Netherlands

nethead (ˈnɛtˌhɛd) n *informal* a person who is enthusiastic about or an expert on the internet [C20 from (INTER)NET + HEAD, meaning enthusiast, expert]

nether (ˈnɛðə) adj placed or situated below, beneath, or underground: *nether regions; a nether lip* [Old English *niothera, nithera*, literally: further down, from *nither* down. Related to Old Irish *nitaram*, German *nieder*]

Netherlander (ˈnɛðəˌlændə) n a native or inhabitant of the Netherlands

Netherlands (ˈnɛðələndz) n (*functioning as singular or plural*) **the** 1 Also called: Holland a kingdom in NW Europe, on the North Sea: declared independence from Spain in 1581 as the United Provinces; became a major maritime and commercial power in the 17th century, gaining many overseas possessions; it formed the Benelux customs union with the Belgium and Luxembourg in 1948 and was a founder member of the Common Market, now the European Union. It is mostly flat and low-lying, with about 40 per cent of the land being below sea level, much of it on polders protected by dykes. Official language: Dutch. Religion: Christian majority, Protestant and Roman Catholic, large nonreligious minority. Currency: euro. Capital: Amsterdam, with the seat of government at The Hague. Pop: 16 227 000 (2004 est). Area: 41 526 sq km (16 033 sq miles). Dutch

n

name: Nederland **2** the kingdom of the Netherlands together with the Flemish-speaking part of Belgium, esp as ruled by Spain and Austria before 1581; the Low Countries

Netherlands Antilles *pl n* **the** two groups of islands in the Caribbean, in the Lesser Antilles: overseas division of the Netherlands, consisting of the S group of Curaçao, Aruba, and Bonaire, and the N group of Saint Eustatius, Saba, and the S part of Saint Martin; economy based on refining oil from Venezuela. Capital: Willemstad (on Curaçao). Pop: 222 000 (2004 est). Area: 996 sq km (390 sq miles). Former names: Curaçao (until 1949), Dutch West Indies, Netherlands West Indies

Netherlands East Indies *pl n* **the** a former name (1798–1945) for **Indonesia**

Netherlands Guiana *n* a former name for **Surinam**

Netherlands West Indies *pl n* **the** a former name for the **Netherlands Antilles**

nethermost ('nɛðə,məʊst) *adj* farthest down; lowest

nether world *n* **1** the world after death; the underworld **2** hell **3** a criminal underworld ▷ Also called (for sense 1, 2): nether regions

netiquette ('nɛtɪ,kɛt) *n* the informal code of behaviour on the internet [c20 from NET(WORK) + (ET)IQUETTE]

netizen ('nɛtɪz³n) *n* informal a person who regularly uses the internet [c20 from (INTER)NET + (CIT)IZEN]

net national product *n* gross national product minus an allowance for the depreciation of capital goods. Abbreviation: NNP

net present value *n* accounting an assessment of the long-term profitability of a project made by adding together all the revenue it can be expected to achieve over its whole life and deducting all the costs involved, discounting both future costs and revenue at an appropriate rate. Abbreviation: NPV

net profit *n* gross profit minus all operating costs not included in the calculation of gross profit, esp wages, overheads, and depreciation

net realizable value *n* the net value of an asset if it were to be sold, taking into account the cost of making the sale and of bringing the asset into a saleable state. Abbreviation: NRV

netspeak ('nɛt,spiːk) *n* informal the jargon, abbreviations, and emoticons typically used by frequent internet users [c20 from (INTER)NET + -SPEAK]

netsuke ('nɛtsʊkɪ) *n* (in Japan) a carved toggle, esp of wood or ivory, originally used to tether a medicine box, purse, etc, worn dangling from the waist [c19 from Japanese]

nett (nɛt) *adj, n, vb* a variant spelling of **net²**

nettie ('nɛtɪ) *n* informal a habitual and enthusiastic user of the internet [c20 from (INTER)NET]

netting ('nɛtɪŋ) *n* any netted fabric or structure

nettle ('nɛt³l) *n* **1** any weedy plant of the temperate urticaceous genus *Urtica*, such as *U. dioica* (**stinging nettle**), having serrated leaves with stinging hairs and greenish flowers **2** any of various other urticaceous plants with stinging hairs or spines **3** any of various plants that resemble urticaceous nettles, such as the dead-nettle, hemp nettle, and horse nettle **4** grasp the nettle to attempt or approach something with boldness and courage ▷ *vb* (*tr*) **5** to bother; irritate **6** to sting as a nettle does [Old English *netele*; related to Old High German *nazza* (German *Nessel*)] > 'nettle-,like *adj* > 'nettly *adj*

nettle rash *n* a nontechnical name for **urticaria**

nettlesome ('nɛt³lsəm) *adj* causing or susceptible to irritation

net ton *n* the full name for **ton¹** (sense 2)

netty ('nɛtɪ) *n, pl* -ties *Northeast English dialect* a lavatory, originally an earth closet [of obscure origin]

Neturei Karta (nə'tʊrɛɪ 'kɑːtə) *n* a small ultra-orthodox Jewish group living mainly in Jerusalem

and New York who oppose the establishment of a Jewish state by temporal means [Aramaic: guardians of the walls]

network ('nɛt,wɜːk) *n* **1** an interconnected group or system: *a network of shops* **2** Also: net a system of intersecting lines, roads, veins, etc **3** another name for **net¹** (sense 1) or **netting** **4** *radio, television* a group of broadcasting stations that all transmit the same programme simultaneously **5** *electronics* a system of interconnected components or circuits **6** *computing* a system of interconnected computer systems, terminals, and other equipment allowing information to be exchanged ▷ *vb* **7** (*tr*) *radio, television* to broadcast on stations throughout the country **8** *computing* (of computers, terminals, etc) to connect or be connected **9** (*intr*) to form business contacts through informal social meetings

networker ('nɛt,wɜːkə) *n* a person who forms business contacts through informal social meetings

networking ('nɛt,wɜːkɪŋ) *n* **1** *computing* the interconnection of two or more networks in different places, as in working at home with a link to a central computer in an office **2** forming business connections and contacts through informal social meetings ▷ *adj* **3** of or for networking: *networking systems*

Neubrandenburg (*German* nɔʏ'brandənbʊrk) *n* a city in NE Germany, in Mecklenburg-West Pomerania: 14th-century city walls. Pop: 69 157 (2003 est)

Neuchâtel (*French* nøʃatɛl) *n* **1** a canton in the Jura Mountains of W Switzerland. Capital: Neuchâtel. Pop: 167 000 (2002 est). Area: 798 sq km (308 sq miles) **2** a town in W Switzerland, capital of Neuchâtel canton, on Lake Neuchâtel: until 1848 the seat of the last hereditary rulers in Switzerland. Pop: 32 914 (2000) **3** Lake a lake in W Switzerland: the largest lake wholly in Switzerland. Area: 216 sq km (83 sq miles) ▷ German name (for senses 1, 2): Neuenburg ('nɔʏənbʊrk)

Neufchâtel (*French* nøʃatɛl) *n* a soft creamy whole-milk cheese, similar to cream cheese [named after *Neufchâtel*, town in N France where it is made]

Neuilly-sur-Seine (*French* nœjisyrsɛn) *n* a town in N France, on the Seine: a suburb of NW Paris. Pop: 59 848 (1999)

neuk (njuːk) *n* a Scot word for **nook**

neume *or* **neum** (njuːm) *n* *music* one of a series of notational symbols used before the 14th century [c15 from Medieval Latin *neuma* group of notes sung on one breath, from Greek *pneuma* breath] > 'neumic *adj*

Neumünster (*German* nɔʏ'mʏnstər) *n* a town in N Germany, in Schleswig-Holstein: manufacturing of textiles and machinery. Pop: 78 951 (2003 est)

neural ('njʊərəl) *adj* of or relating to a nerve or the nervous system > 'neurally *adv*

neural chip *n* another name for **neurochip**

neural computer *n* another name for **neurocomputer**

neuralgia (njʊ'rældʒɪə) *n* severe spasmodic pain caused by damage to or malfunctioning of a nerve and often following the course of the nerve > neu'ralgic *adj*

neural network *n* **1** an interconnected system of neurons, as in the brain or other parts of the nervous system **2** Also called: neural net an analogous network of electronic components, esp one in a computer designed to mimic the operation of the human brain

neural tube *n* the structure in mammalian embryos that develops into the brain and spinal cord. Incomplete development results in **neural-tube defects**, such as spina bifida, in a newborn baby

neuraminidase (,njʊərə'mɪnɪdeɪz) *n* any of various enzymes, found esp in viruses, that catalyse the breakdown of glucosides containing

neuraminic acid, an amino sugar [c20 from *neuramin(ic acid)* (from NEURO- + AMINE + -IC) + -IDE + -ASE]

neurasthenia (,njʊərəs'θiːnɪə) *n* an obsolete technical term for a neurosis characterized by extreme lassitude and inability to cope with any but the most trivial tasks > neurasthenic (,njʊərəs'θɛnɪk) *adj* > ,neuras'thenically *adv*

neurectomy (njʊ'rɛktəmɪ) *n, pl* -mies the surgical removal of a nerve segment

neurilemma (,njʊərɪ'lɛmə) *n* a variant of **neurolemma** [c19 from French *névrilème*, from Greek *neuron* nerve + *eilēma* covering, but influenced also by Greek *lemma* husk]

neuritis (njʊ'raɪtɪs) *n* inflammation of a nerve or nerves, often accompanied by pain and loss of function in the affected part > neuritic (njʊ'rɪtɪk) *adj*

neuro- *or before a vowel* **neur-** *combining form* indicating a nerve or the nervous system: *neuroblast; neurology* [from Greek *neuron* nerve; related to Latin *nervus*]

neuroanatomy (,njʊərəʊə'nætəmɪ) *n* the study of the structure of the nervous system > ,neuroa'natomist *n*

neurobiology (,njʊərəʊbaɪ'ɒlədʒɪ) *n* the study of the anatomy, physiology, and biochemistry of the nervous system > ,neurobi'ologist *n*

neuroblast ('njʊərəʊ,blæst) *n* an embryonic nerve cell

neuroblastoma (,njʊərəʊblæs'təʊmə) *n, pl* -mata *or* -mas *pathol* a malignant tumour that derives from neuroblasts, occurring mainly in the adrenal gland

neurochip ('njʊərəʊ,tʃɪp) *n* *computing* a semiconductor chip designed for use in an electronic neural network. Also called: neural chip

neurocoele ('njʊərə,siːl) *n* *embryol* a cavity in the embryonic brain and spinal cord that develops into the ventricles and central canal respectively [c19 from NEURO- + Greek *koilos* hollow]

neurocognitive (,njʊərə'kɒgnɪtɪv) *adj* of or relating to cognitive functions associated with particular areas of the brain

neurocomputer ('njʊərəʊkəm,pjuːtə) *n* a type of computer designed to mimic the action of the human brain by use of an electronic neural network. Also called: neural computer

neuroendocrine (,njʊərəʊ'ɛndəʊ,kraɪn) *adj* of, relating to, or denoting the dual control of certain body functions by both nervous and hormonal stimulation: *neuroendocrine system*

neuroendocrinology (,njʊərəʊ,ɛndəʊkrɪ'nɒlədʒɪ) *n* the study of neuroendocrine systems and neurohormones

neurofeedback (,njʊərəʊ'fiːdbæk) *n* *physiol, psychol* a technique, for dealing with brain-based functional disorders without the use of medication or invasive procedures, in which brain activity is recorded using electrodes and presented visually or audibly so that the patient can know the state of the function he or she is trying to control. Compare **biofeedback**

neurofibril (,njʊərəʊ'faɪbrɪl) *n* any of the delicate threads within the body of a nerve cell that extend into the axon and dendrites > ,neuro'fibrilar, ,neurofi'brillar *or* ,neurofi'brillary *adj*

neurofibromatosis (,njʊərəʊ,faɪbrəmə'təʊsɪs) *n* a condition characterized by the formation of benign tumours on the fibrous coverings of the peripheral nerves and the development of areas of *café-au-lait* spots

neurogenic (,njʊərəʊ'dʒɛnɪk) *adj* originating in or stimulated by the nervous system or nerve impulses

neuroglia (njʊ'rɒglɪə) *n* another name for **glia**

neurohormone ('njʊərəʊ,hɔːməʊn) *n* a hormone, such as noradrenaline, oxytocin, or vasopressin, that is produced by specialized nervous tissue rather than by endocrine glands

neurohypophysis (,njʊərəʊhaɪ'pɒfɪsɪs) *n, pl* -ses

(-ˌsiːz) the posterior lobe of the pituitary gland. Compare **adenohypophysis**

neurol. *abbreviation for* neurology

neurolemma (ˌnjʊərəʊˈlɛmə) *n* the thin membrane that forms a sheath around nerve fibres. Also: **neurilemma** [C19 New Latin, from NEURO- + Greek *eilēma* covering]

neuroleptic (ˌnjʊərəʊˈlɛptɪk) *adj* **1** capable of affecting the brain, esp by reducing the intensity of nerve function; tranquillizing ▷ *n* **2** a neuroleptic drug; major tranquillizer: used in the treatment of psychoses

neurolinguistics (ˌnjʊərəʊlɪŋˈɡwɪstɪks) *n* (*functioning as singular*) the branch of linguistics that deals with the encoding of the language faculty in the brain

neurological (ˌnjʊərəˈlɒdʒɪkəl) *adj* of or relating to the nervous system or neurology

neurology (njʊˈrɒlədʒɪ) *n* the study of the anatomy, physiology, and diseases of the nervous system > **neuˈrologist** *n*

neuroma (njʊˈrəʊmə) *n, pl* -mata (-mətə) *or* -mas any tumour composed of nerve tissue > **neuromatous** (njʊˈrɒmətəs) *adj*

neuromarketing (ˈnjʊərəʊˌmɑːkɪtɪŋ) *n* the process of researching the brain patterns of consumers to reveal their responses to particular advertisements and products before developing new advertising campaigns and branding techniques

neuromuscular (ˌnjʊərəʊˈmʌskjʊlə) *adj* of, relating to, or affecting nerves and muscles

neurone (ˈnjʊərəʊn) *or* **neuron** (ˈnjʊərɒn) *n* a cell specialized to conduct nerve impulses: consists of a cell body, axon, and dendrites. Also called: **nerve cell** > **neuˈronal** *adj* > **neuronic** (njʊˈrɒnɪk) *adj*

neuropath (ˈnjʊərəʊˌpæθ) *n* a person suffering from or predisposed to a disorder of the nervous system

neuropathology (ˌnjʊərəʊpəˈθɒlədʒɪ) *n* the study of diseases of the nervous system > neuropathological (ˌnjʊərəʊˌpæθəˈlɒdʒɪkəl) *adj* > ˌneuropaˈthologist *n*

neuropathy (njʊˈrɒpəθɪ) *n* disease of the nervous system > neuropathic (ˌnjʊərəʊˈpæθɪk) *adj* > ˌneuroˈpathically *adv*

neuropeptide (ˌnjʊərəʊˈpɛptaɪd) *n* a peptide produced by neural tissue, esp one with hormonal activity

neurophysiology (ˌnjʊərəʊˌfɪzɪˈɒlədʒɪ) *n* the study of the functions of the nervous system > neurophysiological (ˌnjʊərəʊˌfɪzɪəˈlɒdʒɪkəl) *adj* > ˌneuroˌphysioˈlogically *adv* > ˌneuroˌphysiˈologist *n*

neuropil (ˈnjʊərəʊpɪl) *n* a dense network of neurons and glia in the central nervous system [from NEURO- + Greek *pilos* hair]

neuropsychiatry (ˌnjʊərəʊsaɪˈkaɪətrɪ) *n* the branch of psychiatry that investigates the links between mental illness and organic disease of the brain > neuropsychiatric (ˌnjʊərəʊˌsaɪkɪˈætrɪk) *adj* > ˌneuropsyˈchiatrist *n*

neuropsychology (ˌnjʊərəʊsaɪˈkɒlədʒɪ) *n* the study of the effects of brain damage on behaviour and the mind > ˌneuropsyˈchologist *n*

neuropteran *or* **neuropteron** (njʊˈrɒptərən) *n, pl* -terans *or* -tera (-tərə) any neuropterous insect

neuropterous (njʊˈrɒptərəs) *or* **neuropteran** *adj* of, relating to, or belonging to the *Neuroptera*, an order of insects having two pairs of large muchveined wings and biting mouthparts: includes the lacewings and antlions [C18 from New Latin *Neuroptera*; see NEURO-, -PTEROUS]

neuroscience (ˈnjʊərəʊˌsaɪəns) *n* the study of the anatomy, physiology, biochemistry, and pharmacology of the nervous system > ˈneuroˌscientist *n*

neurosis (njʊˈrəʊsɪs) *n, pl* -ses (-siːz) a relatively mild mental disorder, characterized by symptoms such as hysteria, anxiety, depression, or obsessive behaviour. Also called: **psychoneurosis**

neurosurgery (ˌnjʊərəʊˈsɜːdʒərɪ) *n* the branch of surgery concerned with the nervous system > ˈneuroˌsurgeon *n* > ˌneuroˈsurgical *adj* > ˌneuroˈsurgically *adv*

neurotic (njʊˈrɒtɪk) *adj* **1** of, relating to, or afflicted by neurosis ▷ *n* **2** a person who is afflicted with a neurosis or who tends to be emotionally unstable or unusually anxious > neuˈrotically *adv*

neuroticism (njʊˈrɒtɪˌsɪzəm) *n* a personality trait characterized by instability, anxiety, aggression, etc

neurotomy (njʊˈrɒtəmɪ) *n, pl* -mies the surgical cutting of a nerve, esp to relieve intractable pain > neuˈrotomist *n*

neurotoxin (ˌnjʊərəʊˈtɒksɪn) *n* any of several natural substances that interfere with the electrical activities of nerves, thus preventing them from functioning > ˌneuroˈtoxic *adj*

neurotransmitter (ˌnjʊərəʊtrænzˈmɪtə) *n* a chemical by which a nerve cell communicates with another nerve cell or with a muscle

neurovascular (ˌnʊərəʊˈvæskjʊlə) *adj* of, relating to, or affecting both the nerves and the blood vessels

Neusatz (ˈnɔyzats) *n* the German name for **Novi Sad**

Neuss (*German* nɔys) *n* an industrial city in W Germany, in North Rhine-Westphalia west of Düsseldorf: founded as a Roman fortress in the 1st century AD. Pop: 152 050 (2003 est). Latin name: Novaesium

neuston (ˈnjuːstən) *n* **1** organisms, similar to plankton, that float on the surface film of open water **2** the ecosystem of the surface film of open water in which such organisms as copepods graze on tiny flagellates, bacteria, etc [C20 via German from Greek *neustos* swimming, from *nein* to swim] > neusˈtonic *adj*

Neustria (ˈnjuːstrɪə) *n* the western part of the kingdom of the Merovingian Franks formed in 561 AD in what is now N France

Neustrian (ˈnjuːstrɪən) *adj* of or relating to Neustria, the western part of the kingdom of the Merovingian Franks, or its inhabitants

neut. *abbreviation for* neuter

neuter (ˈnjuːtə) *adj* **1** *grammar* **a** denoting or belonging to a gender of nouns which for the most part have inanimate referents or do not specify the sex of their referents **b** (*as noun*): *German "Mädchen" (meaning "girl") is a neuter* **2** (of animals and plants) having nonfunctional, underdeveloped, or absent reproductive organs **3** sexless or giving no indication of sex: *a neuter sort of name* ▷ *n* **4** a sexually underdeveloped female insect, such as a worker bee **5** a castrated animal, esp a domestic animal **6** a flower in which the stamens and pistil are absent or nonfunctional ▷ *vb* **7** (*tr*) to castrate or spay (an animal) [C14 from Latin, from *ne* not + *uter* either (of two)]

neutral (ˈnjuːtrəl) *adj* **1** not siding with any party to a war or dispute **2** of, belonging to, or appropriate to a neutral party, country, etc: *neutral land* **3** of no distinctive quality, characteristics, or type; indifferent **4** (of a colour such as white or black) having no hue; achromatic **5** (of a colour) dull, but harmonizing with most other colours **6** a less common term for **neuter** (sense 2) **7** *chem* neither acidic nor alkaline **8** *physics* having zero charge or potential **9** *rare* having no magnetism **10** *phonetics* (of a vowel) articulated with the tongue relaxed in mid-central position and the lips midway between spread and rounded: *the word "about" begins with a neutral vowel* ▷ *n* **11** a neutral person, nation, etc **12** a citizen of a neutral state **13** the position of the controls of a gearbox that leaves the transmission disengaged [C16 from Latin *neutrālis*; see NEUTER] > ˈneutrally *adv*

neutral axis *n* engineering the line or plane through the section of a beam or plate which does not suffer extension or compression when the beam or plate bends

neutral density *n* **a** black, white, or a shade of grey; a colourless tone **b** (*as modifier*): *a neutraldensity filter*

neutralism (ˈnjuːtrəˌlɪzəm) *n* (in international affairs) the policy, practice, or attitude of neutrality, noninvolvement, or nonalignment with power blocs > ˈneutralist *n, adj*

neutrality (njuːˈtrælɪtɪ) *n* **1** the state or character of being neutral, esp in a dispute, contest, etc **2** the condition of being chemically or electrically neutral

neutralize *or* **neutralise** (ˈnjuːtrəˌlaɪz) *vb* (*mainly tr*) **1** (*also intr*) to render or become ineffective or neutral by counteracting, mixing, etc; nullify **2** (*also intr*) to make or become electrically or chemically neutral **3** to exclude (a country) from the sphere of warfare or alliances by international agreement **4** to render (an army) incapable of further military action > ˌneutraliˈzation *or* ˌneutraliˈsation *n* > ˈneutralˌizer *or* ˈneutralˌiser *n*

neutral monism *n* the philosophical doctrine that mind and body are both constructs of the same elements which cannot themselves be classified either as mental or physical. See also **monism** (sense 1)

neutral spirits *n* (*functioning as singular or plural*) US ethanol of more than 190° proof

neutretto (njuːˈtrɛtəʊ) *n, pl* -tos *physics* **1** the neutrino associated with the muon **2** (formerly) any of various hypothetical neutral particles [C20 from NEUTR(INO) + diminutive suffix *-etto*]

neutrino (njuːˈtriːnəʊ) *n, pl* -nos *physics* a stable leptonic neutral elementary particle with very small or possibly zero rest mass and spin $\frac{1}{2}$ that travels at the speed of light. Three types exist, associated with the electron, the muon, and the tau particle [C20 from Italian, diminutive of *neutrone* NEUTRON]

neutrino astronomy *n* the detection of neutrinos emitted by the sun or by supernovae from which information about the solar interior can be obtained

neutron (ˈnjuːtrɒn) *n physics* a neutral elementary particle with a rest mass of $1.674\ 92716 \times 10^{-27}$ kilogram and spin $\frac{1}{2}$; classified as a baryon. In the nucleus of an atom it is stable but when free it decays [C20 from NEUTRAL, on the model of ELECTRON]

neutron bomb *n* a type of nuclear weapon designed to provide a high yield of neutrons but to cause little blast or long-lived radioactive contamination. The neutrons destroy all life in the target area, which theoretically can be entered relatively soon after the attack. Technical name: **enhanced radiation weapon**

neutron gun *n physics* a device used for producing a beam of fast neutrons

neutron number *n* the number of neutrons in the nucleus of an atom. Symbol: *N*

neutron poison *n physics* a nonfissionable material used to absorb neutrons and thus to control nuclear reactions

neutron star *n* a star that has collapsed under its own gravity to a diameter of about 10 to 15 km. It is composed mostly of neutrons, has a mass of between 1.4 and about 3 times that of the sun, and a density in excess of 10^{17} kilograms per cubic metre

neutropenia (ˌnjuːtrəˈpiːnɪə) *n* an abnormal reduction in the number of neutrophils in the blood, as seen in certain anaemias and leukaemias

neutrophil (ˈnjuːtrəˌfɪl) *or* **neutrophile** (ˈnjuːtrəˌfaɪl) *n* **1** a leucocyte having a lobed nucleus and a fine granular cytoplasm, which stains with neutral dyes ▷ *adj* **2** (of cells and tissues) readily stainable by neutral dyes

Nev. *abbreviation for* Nevada

Neva (ˈniːvə; *Russian* nɪˈva) *n* a river in NW Russia, flowing west to the Gulf of Finland by the delta on which Saint Petersburg stands. Length: 74 km (46 miles)

Nevada (nɪˈvɑːdə) *n* a state of the western US: lies

n

almost wholly within the Great Basin, a vast desert plateau; noted for production of gold and copper. Capital: Carson City. Pop: 2 241 154 (2003 est). Area: 284 612 sq km (109 889 sq miles). Abbreviations: **Nev.** (with zip code) **NV**

névé ('nɛveɪ) *n* **1** Also called: **firn** a mass of porous ice, formed from snow, that has not yet become frozen into glacier ice **2** a snowfield at the head of a glacier that becomes transformed to ice [C19 from Swiss French *névé* glacier, from Late Latin *nivātus* snow-cooled, from *nix* snow]

never ('nɛvə) *adv, sentence substitute* **1** at no time; not ever **2** certainly not; by no means; in no case ▷ *interj* **3** Also: **well I never! surely not!** [Old English *nǣfre*, from *ne* not + *ǣfre* EVER]

> USAGE In informal speech and writing, *never* can be used instead of *not* with the simple past tenses of certain verbs for emphasis (*I never said that; I never realized how clever he was*), but this usage should be avoided in serious writing

never-ending *adj* having or seeming to have no end; interminable

nevermore (,nɛvə'mɔ:) *adv literary* never again

never-never *informal* ▷ *n* **1** the hire-purchase system of buying **2** *Austral* remote desert country, as that of W Queensland and central Australia ▷ *adj* **3** imaginary; idyllic (esp in the phrase **never-never land**)

Nevers (*French* nəvɛr) *n* a city in central France: capital of the former duchy of Nivernais; engineering industry. Pop: 40 932 (1999)

nevertheless (,nɛvəðə'lɛs) *sentence connector* in spite of that; however; yet

Nevis *n* **1** ('ni:vɪs, 'nɛvɪs) an island in the Caribbean, part of St Kitts-Nevis; the volcanic cone of **Nevis Peak,** which rises to 1002 m (3287 ft), lies in the centre of the island. Capital: Charlestown. Pop: 11 181 (2001. Area: 129 sq km (50 sq miles) **2** ('nɛvɪs) See **Ben Nevis**

nevus ('ni:vəs) *n, pl* **-vi** (-vaɪ) the usual US spelling of **naevus**

new (nju:) *adj* **1 a** recently made or brought into being: *a new dress; our new baby* **b** (*as collective noun; preceded by the*): *the new* **2** of a kind never before existing; novel: *a new concept in marketing* **3** having existed before but only recently discovered: *a new comet* **4** markedly different from what was before: *the new liberalism* **5** fresh and unused; not second-hand: *a new car* **6** (*prenominal*) having just or recently become: *a new bride* **7** (often foll by *to* or *at*) recently introduced (to); inexperienced (in) or unaccustomed (to): *new to this neighbourhood* **8** (*capital in names or titles*) more or most recent of two or more things with the same name: *the New Testament* **9** (*prenominal*) fresh; additional: *I'll send some new troops* **10** (often foll by *to*) unknown; novel: *this is new to me* **11** (*prenominal*) beginning or occurring again: *a new year* **12** (*prenominal*) (of crops) harvested early: *new carrots* **13** changed, esp for the better: *she returned a new woman from her holiday* **14** up-to-date; fashionable **15** (*capital when part of a name; prenominal*) being the most recent, usually living, form of a language: *New High German* **16** (**be**) **the new** (to be) set to become the new vogue: *comedy is the new rock'n'roll* **17** **turn over a new leaf** to reform; make a fresh start ▷ *adv* (*usually in combination*) **18** recently, freshly: *new-laid eggs* **19** anew; again ▷ See also **news** ▷ Related prefix: **neo-** [Old English *nīowe*; related to Gothic *niujis*, Old Norse *naujas*, Latin *novus*] > **'newness** *n*

New Age *n* **1 a** a philosophy, originating in the late 1980s, characterized by a belief in alternative medicine, astrology, spiritualism, etc **b** (*as modifier*): *New Age therapies* **2** short for **New Age music**

New Age music or **New Age** *n* a type of gentle melodic popular music originating in the US in the late 1980s, which takes in elements of jazz, folk, and classical music and is played largely on synthesizers and acoustic instruments

New Amsterdam *n* the Dutch settlement established on Manhattan (1624–26); capital of New Netherlands; captured by the English and renamed New York in 1664

Newark ('nju:ək) *n* **1** a town in N central England, in Nottinghamshire. Pop: 35 454 (2001). Official name: **Newark-on-Trent 2** a port in NE New Jersey, just west of New York City, on Newark Bay and the Passaic River: the largest city in the state; founded in 1666 by Puritans from Connecticut; industrial and commercial centre. Pop: 277 911 (2003 est)

New Australia *n* the colony on socialist principles founded by William Lane in Paraguay in 1893

New Australian *n* an immigrant to Australia, esp one whose native tongue is not English

New Bedford *n* a port and resort in SE Massachusetts, near Buzzards Bay: settled by Plymouth colonists in 1652; a leading whaling port (18th–19th centuries). Pop: 94 112 (2003 est)

newbie ('nju:bɪ) *n slang* a newcomer, esp in computing or on the internet [C20 origin unknown; possibly from *new boy*]

newborn ('nju:,bɔ:n) *adj* **1 a** recently or just born **b** (*as collective noun; preceded by the*): *the newborn* **2** (of hope, faith, etc) reborn

New Britain *n* an island in the S Pacific, northeast of New Guinea: the largest island of the Bismarck Archipelago; part of Papua New Guinea; mountainous, with several active volcanoes. Capital: Rabaul. Pop: 435 307 (1999 est). Area: 36 519 sq km (14 100 sq miles)

new broom *n* a newly appointed person eager to make changes

New Brunswick *n* a province of SE Canada on the Gulf of St Lawrence and the Bay of Fundy: extensively forested. Capital: Fredericton. Pop: 751 384 (2004 est). Area: 72 092 sq km (27 835 sq miles). Abbreviation: **NB**

New Brunswicker ('brʌnzwɪkə) *n* a native or inhabitant of New Brunswick

new brutalism *n* another name for **brutalism**

Newburg ('nju:bɜ:g) *adj* (*immediately postpositive*) (of shellfish, esp lobster) cooked in a rich sauce of butter, cream, sherry, and egg yolks [of unknown origin]

Newbury ('nju:bərɪ) *n* a market town in West Berkshire unitary authority, S England: scene of a Parliamentarian victory (1643) and a Royalist victory (1644) during the Civil War; telecommunications, racecourse. Pop: 32 675 (2001)

Newby Hall ('nju:bɪ) *n* a mansion near Ripon in Yorkshire: built in 1705 and altered (1770–76) by Robert Adam

New Caledonia *n* an island in the SW Pacific, east of Australia: forms, with its dependencies, a French Overseas Country; discovered by Captain Cook in 1774; rich mineral resources. Capital: Nouméa. Pop: 232 000 (2004 est). Area: 19 103 sq km (7374 miles). French name: **Nouvelle-Calédonie**

New Castile *n* a region and former province of central Spain. Chief town: Toledo

Newcastle ('nju:,kɑ:sᵊl) *n* a port in SE Australia, in E New South Wales near the mouth of the Hunter River: important industrial centre, with extensive steel, metalworking, engineering, shipbuilding, and chemical industries. It suffered Australia's first fatal earthquake in 1989. Pop: 279 975 (2001)

Newcastle disease *n* an acute viral disease of birds, esp poultry, characterized by pneumonia and inflammation of the central nervous system [C20 named after NEWCASTLE UPON TYNE, where it was recorded in 1926]

Newcastle-under-Lyme *n* a town in W central England, in Staffordshire. Pop: 74 427 (2001). Often shortened to: **Newcastle**

Newcastle upon Tyne *n* **1** a port in NE England in Newcastle upon Tyne unitary authority, Tyne and Wear, near the mouth of the River Tyne

opposite Gateshead: Roman remains; engineering industries, including ship repairs; two universities (1937, 1992). Pop: 189 863 (2001). Often shortened to: **Newcastle 2** a unitary authority in NE England, in Tyne and Wear. Pop: 266 600 (2003 est). Area: 112 sq km (43 sq miles)

new chum *n* **1** *Austral and NZ archaic informal* a recent British immigrant **2** *Austral* a novice in any activity **3** *Austral* (in the 19th century) a new arrival in a hulk

New Church *n* another name for the **New Jerusalem Church**

newcomer ('nju:,kʌmə) *n* a person who has recently arrived or started to participate in something

New Country *n* a style of country music that emerged in the late 1980s characterized by a more contemporary sound and down-to-earth rather than sentimental lyrics

new criticism *n* an approach to literary criticism through close analysis of the text > **new critic** *n* > **new critical** *adj*

New Deal *n* **1** the domestic policies of Franklin D Roosevelt for economic and social reform **2** the period of the implementation of these policies (1933–40) > **New Dealer** *n*

New Delhi *n* See **Delhi**

New Democratic Party *n* the Canadian social democratic party formed in 1961. Abbreviation: **NDP**

New Economic Policy *n* an economic programme in the former Soviet Union from 1921 to 1928, that permitted private ownership of industries, etc. Abbreviation: **NEP**

new economy *n* the postindustrial world economy based on internet trading and advanced technology

newel ('nju:əl) *n* **1** the central pillar of a winding staircase, esp one that is made of stone **2** See **newel post** [C14 from Old French *nouel* knob, from Medieval Latin *nōdellus,* diminutive of *nōdus* NODE]

newel post *n* the post at the top or bottom of a flight of stairs that supports the handrail. Sometimes shortened to: **newel**

New England *n* **1** the NE part of the US, consisting of the states of Maine, New Hampshire, Vermont, Massachusetts, Rhode Island, and Connecticut: settled originally chiefly by Puritans in the mid-17th century **2** a region in SE Australia, in the northern tablelands of New South Wales

New Englander *n* a native or inhabitant of New England

New England Range *n* a mountain range in SE Australia, in NE New South Wales: part of the Great Dividing Range. Highest peak: Ben Lomond, 1520 m (4986 ft)

New English Bible *n* a new Modern English version of the Bible and Apocrypha, published in full in 1970

newfangled ('nju:'fæŋɡᵊld) *adj* **1** newly come into existence or fashion, esp excessively modern **2** *rare* excessively fond of new ideas, fashions, etc [C14 *newefangel* liking new things, from *new* + *-fangel,* from Old English *fōn* to take] > **'new'fangledness** *n*

new-fashioned *adj* of or following a recent design, trend, etc

Newfie ('nju:fɪ) *n informal* **1** a native or inhabitant of Newfoundland **2** the province or island of Newfoundland

New Forest *n* a region of woodland and heath in S England, in SW Hampshire: a hunting ground of the West Saxon kings; tourist area, noted for its ponies. Area: 336 sq km (130 sq miles)

New Forest disease *n* vet science an infectious eye disease causing acute eye pain in cattle

New Forest fly *n* vet science a blood-sucking fly, *Hippobosca equinus,* that attacks horses and cattle

new-found *adj* newly or recently discovered: *new-found confidence*

Newfoundland ('nju:fəndlənd, -fənlənd, -,lænd,

nju:'faʊndlənd) *n* **1** an island of E Canada, separated from the mainland by the Strait of Belle Isle: with the Coast of Labrador forms the province of Newfoundland and Labrador; consists of a rugged plateau with the Long Range Mountains in the west. Area: 110 681 sq km (42 734 sq miles) **2** the former name for **Newfoundland and Labrador 3** a very large heavy breed of dog similar to a Saint Bernard with a flat coarse usually black coat

Newfoundland and Labrador *n* a province of E Canada, consisting of the island of Newfoundland and the Coast of Labrador: usually known as Newfoundland until its official long form was adopted as the main name in 2001. Capital: St John's. Pop: 517 027 (2004 est). Area: 404 519 sq km (156 185 sq miles). Abbreviations: **Nfld** or **NF**

Newfoundlander (nju:'faʊndləndə) *n* a native or inhabitant of Newfoundland

Newfoundland Standard Time *n* one of the standard times used in Canada, three and a half hours behind Greenwich Mean Time

New France *n* the former French colonies and possessions in North America, most of which were lost to England and Spain by 1763: often restricted to the French possessions in Canada

Newgate ('nju:gɪt, -ˌgeɪt) *n* a famous London prison, in use from the Middle Ages: demolished in 1902

New Georgia *n* **1** a group of islands in the SW Pacific, in the Solomon Islands **2** the largest island in this group. Area: about 1300 sq km (500 sq miles)

New Granada *n* **1** a former Spanish presidency and later viceroyalty in South America. At its greatest extent it consisted of present-day Panama, Colombia, Venezuela, and Ecuador **2** the name of Colombia when it formed, with Panama, part of Great Colombia (1819–30)

New Guinea *n* **1** an island in the W Pacific, north of Australia: divided politically into Papua (formerly Irian Jaya, a province of Indonesia) in the west and Papua New Guinea in the east. There is a central chain of mountains and a lowland area of swamps in the south and along the Sepik River in the north. Area: 775 213 sq km (299 310 sq miles) **2 Trust Territory of** (until 1975) an administrative division of the former Territory of Papua and New Guinea, consisting of the NE part of the island of New Guinea together with the Bismarck Archipelago; now part of Papua New Guinea

New Guinea macrophylum (ˌmækrəʊ'faɪləm) *n* the older term for **Trans-New Guinea phylum**

New Guinea Pidgin *n* the variety of Neo-Melanesian spoken in Papua New Guinea and neighbouring islands

Newham ('nju:əm) *n* a borough of E Greater London, on the River Thames: established in 1965. Pop: 250 600 (2003 est). Area: 36 sq km (14 sq miles)

New Hampshire *n* a state of the northeastern US: generally hilly. Capital: Concord. Pop: 1 287 687 (2003 est). Area: 23 379 sq km (9027 sq miles). Abbreviations: **N.H.**, (with zip code) **NH**

New Harmony *n* a village in SW Indiana, on the Wabash River: scene of two experimental cooperative communities, the first founded in 1815 by George Rapp, a German religious leader, and the second by Robert Owen in 1825

Newhaven ('nju:ˌheɪvᵊn) *n* a ferry port and resort on the S coast of England, in East Sussex. Pop: 12 276 (2001)

New Haven *n* an industrial city and port in S Connecticut, on Long Island Sound: settled in 1638 by English Puritans, who established it as a colony in 1643; seat of Yale University (1701). Pop: 124 512 (2003 est)

New Hebrides *pl n* the former name (until 1980) of **Vanuatu**

New Ireland *n* an island in the S Pacific, in the Bismarck Archipelago, separated from New Britain by St George's Channel: part of Papua New

Guinea. Chief town and port: Kavieng. Pop: 87 194 (1990.). Area (including adjacent islands): 9850 sq km (3800 sq miles)

newish ('nju:ɪʃ) *adj* fairly new > **'newishly** *adv* > **'newishness** *n*

new issue *n stock exchange* an issue of shares being offered to the public for the first time

New Jersey *n* a state of the eastern US, on the Atlantic and Delaware Bay: mostly low-lying, with a heavy industrial area in the northeast and many coastal resorts. Capital: Trenton. Pop: 8 638 396 (2003 est). Area: 19 479 sq km (7521 sq miles). Abbreviations: **N.J.**, (with zip code) **NJ**

New Jerusalem *n Christianity* heaven regarded as the prototype of the earthly Jerusalem; the heavenly city

New Jerusalem Church *n* a sect founded in 1787, based on Swedenborgianism. Often shortened to: **New Church**

New Journalism *n* a style of journalism originating in the US in the 1960s, which uses techniques borrowed from fiction to portray a situation or event as vividly as possible

New Kingdom *n* a period of Egyptian history, extending from the 18th to the 20th dynasty (?1570–?1080 BC)

New Latin *n* the form of Latin used since the Renaissance, esp for scientific nomenclature. Also called: **Neo-Latin**

New Learning *n* the classical and Biblical studies of Renaissance Europe in the 15th and 16th centuries

New Left *n* a loose grouping of left-wing radicals, esp among students, that arose in many countries after 1960

New Look *n* **the** a fashion in women's clothes introduced in 1947, characterized by long full skirts

newly ('nju:lɪ) *adv* **1** recently; lately or just: *a newly built shelf* **2** again; afresh; anew: *newly raised hopes* **3** in a new manner; differently: *a newly arranged room*

Newlyn datum ('nju:lɪn) *n* another name for **ordnance datum** [named after *Newlyn*, Cornwall, where the observations were taken]

newlywed ('nju:lɪˌwɛd) *n* (*often plural*) a recently married person

New Man *n* **the** a type of modern man who allows the caring side of his nature to show by being supportive and by sharing child care and housework

newmarket ('nju:ˌmɑ:kɪt) *n* **1** a double-breasted waisted coat with a full skirt worn, esp for riding, in the 19th century **2** a simple gambling card game

Newmarket ('nju:ˌmɑ:kɪt) *n* a town in SE England, in W Suffolk: a famous horse-racing centre since the reign of James I. Pop: 16 947 (2001)

new maths *n* (*functioning as singular*) *Brit* an approach to mathematics in which the basic principles of set theory are introduced at an elementary level

new media *n* **a** the internet and other postindustrial forms of telecommunication **b** (*as modifier*): *the new-media industry* ▷ Compare **old media**

New Mexican *adj* **1** of or relating to New Mexico or its inhabitants ▷ *n* **2** a native or inhabitant of New Mexico

New Mexico *n* a state of the southwestern US: has high semiarid plateaus and mountains, crossed by the Rio Grande and the Pecos River; large Spanish-American and Indian populations; contains over two-thirds of US uranium reserves. Capital: Santa Fé. Pop: 1 874 614 (2003 est). Area: 314 451 sq km (121 412 sq miles). Abbreviations: **N. Mex.**, (with zip code) **NM**

New Model Army *n* the army established (1645) during the Civil War by the English parliamentarians, which exercised considerable political power under Cromwell

new moon *n* **1** the moon when it appears as a narrow waxing crescent **2** the time at which this

occurs **3** *astronomy* one of the four principal phases of the moon, occurring when it lies between the earth and the sun

New National Party *n* see **National Party** (sense 3)

New Netherland ('nɛðələnd) *n* a Dutch North American colony of the early 17th century, centred on the Hudson valley. Captured by the English in 1664, it was divided into New York and New Jersey

New Orleans ('ɔ:li:ənz, -lənz, ɔ:'li:nz) *n* a port in SE Louisiana, on the Mississippi River about 172 km (107 miles) from the sea: the largest city in the state and the second most important port in the US; founded by the French in 1718; belonged to Spain (1763–1803). It is largely below sea level, built around the Vieux Carré (French quarter); famous for its annual Mardi Gras festival and for its part in the history of jazz; a major commercial, industrial, and transportation centre. Pop: 469 032 (2003 est)

New Orleans jazz *n* the jazz originating in New Orleans from about 1914; traditional jazz

new penny *n* another name for **penny** (sense 1)

new planets *pl n* the outer planets Uranus, Neptune, and Pluto, only discovered comparatively recently

New Plymouth *n* a port in New Zealand, on W North Island: founded in 1841. Pop: 69 200 (2004 est)

Newport ('nju:pɔ:t) *n* **1** a city and port in SE Wales, in Newport county borough on the River Usk: electronics. Pop: 116 143 (2001) **2** a county borough in SE Wales, created from part of Gwent in 1996. Pop: 139 300 (2003 est). Area: 190 sq km (73 sq miles) **3** a port in SE Rhode Island: founded in 1639, it became one of the richest towns of colonial America; centre of a large number of US naval establishments. Pop: 26 136 (2003 est) **4** a town in S England, administrative centre of the Isle of Wight. Pop: 22 957 (2001)

Newport News *n* (*functioning as singular*) a port in SE Virginia, at the mouth of the James River: an industrial centre, with one of the world's largest shipyards. Pop: 181 647 (2003 est)

New Providence *n* an island in the Atlantic, in the Bahamas. Chief town: Nassau. Pop: 210 832 (2000). Area: 150 sq km (58 sq miles)

New Quebec *n* a region of E Canada, formerly the Ungava district of Northwest Territories (1895–1912), extending from the line of the Eastmain and Hamilton Rivers north between Hudson Bay and Labrador: absorbed by Quebec in 1912: contains extensive iron deposits. Area: about 777 000 sq km (300 000 sq miles)

New Right *n* a range of radical right-wing groups and ideologies which advocate laissez-faire economic policies, anti-welfarism, and the belief in the rights of the individual over the common good

New Romney *n* a market town in SE England, in Kent on Romney Marsh: of early importance as one of the Cinque Ports, but is now over 1.6 km (1 mile) inland. Pop: 9406 (2001). Former name (until 1563): **Romney**

Newry ('njʊərɪ) *n* a city and port in Northern Ireland, in Newry and Mourne district, Co Down: close to the border with the Republic of Ireland, it has been the scene of sectarian violence in recent years. Pop: 27 433 (2001)

Newry and Mourne ('mɔ:n) *n* a district of SE Northern Ireland, in Co Down. Pop: 89 644 (2003 est). Area: 909 sq km (351 sq miles)

news (nju:z) *n* (*functioning as singular*) **1** current events; important or interesting recent happenings **2** information about such events, as in the mass media **3 a** **the** a presentation, such as a radio broadcast, of information of this type: *the news is at six* **b** (*in combination*): *a newscaster* **4** interesting or important information not previously known or realized: *it's news to me* **5** a person, fashion, etc, widely reported in the mass media: *she is no longer news in the film world* [c15 from

n

Middle English *newes*, plural of *newe* new (*adj*) on model of Old French *noveles* or Medieval Latin *nova* new things] > **'newsless** *adj*

newsagency ('nju:z,eɪdʒənsɪ) *n Austral* a newsagent's shop

news agency *n* an organization that collects news reports for newspapers, periodicals, etc. Also called: **press agency**

newsagent ('nju:z,eɪdʒənt) *or US* **newsdealer** ('nju:z,di:lə) *n* a shopkeeper who sells newspapers, stationery, etc

newsboy ('nju:z,bɔɪ) *n* a boy who sells or delivers newspapers

newscast ('nju:z,kɑ:st) *n* a radio or television broadcast of the news [C20 from NEWS + (BROAD)CAST] > **'news,caster** *n*

news conference *n* another name for **press conference**

newsflash ('nju:z,flæʃ) *n* a brief item of important news, often interrupting a radio or television programme

newsgirl ('nju:z,gɜ:l) *n* **1** *informal* a female newsreader or reporter **2** a girl who sells or delivers newspapers

newsgroup ('nju:z,gru:p) *n computing* a forum where subscribers exchange information about a specific subject by electronic mail

newshawk ('nju:z,hɔ:k) *n US and Canadian informal* a newspaper reporter. Also called: **newshound** ('nju:z,haʊnd)

New Siberian Islands *pl n* an archipelago in the Arctic Ocean, off the N mainland of Russia, in the Sakha Republic. Area: about 37 555 sq km (14 500 sq miles)

newsletter ('nju:z,lɛtə) *n* **1** Also called: **news-sheet** a printed periodical bulletin circulated to members of a group **2** *history* a written or printed account of the news

newsman ('nju:z,mæn) *n, pl* -men *informal* a male newsreader or reporter

newsmonger ('nju:z,mʌŋgə) *n old-fashioned* a gossip

new sol (sɒl) *n* the standard monetary unit of Peru, divided into 100 céntimos. Spanish name: **nuevo sol**

New South *n Austral informal* See **New South Wales**

New South Wales *n* a state of SE Australia: originally contained over half the continent, but was reduced by the formation of other states (1825–1911); consists of a narrow coastal plain, separated from extensive inland plains by the Great Dividing Range; the most populous state; mineral resources. Capital: Sydney. Pop: 6 716 277 (2003 est). Area: 801 428 sq km (309 433 sq miles)

New Spain *n* a Spanish viceroyalty of the 16th to 19th centuries, composed of Mexico, Central America north of Panama, the Spanish West Indies, the southwestern US, and the Philippines

newspaper ('nju:z,peɪpə) *n* **1 a** a weekly or daily publication consisting of folded sheets and containing articles on the news, features, reviews, and advertisements. Often shortened to: **paper b** (*as modifier*): *a newspaper article* **2** a less common name for **newsprint**

newspaperman ('nju:z,peɪpə,mæn) *n, pl* -men **1** a man who works for a newspaper as a reporter or editor **2** the male owner of a newspaper

newspaperwoman ('nju:z,peɪpə,wʊmən) *n, pl* -women **1** a woman who works for a newspaper as a reporter or editor **2** the female owner of a newspaper

newspeak ('nju:,spi:k) *n* the language of bureaucrats and politicians, regarded as deliberately ambiguous and misleading [C20 from *1984*, a novel by George Orwell]

newsprint ('nju:z,prɪnt) *n* an inexpensive wood-pulp paper used for newspapers

newsreader ('nju:z,ri:də) *n* a news announcer on radio or television

newsreel ('nju:z,ri:l) *n* a short film with a commentary presenting current events

newsroom ('nju:z,ru:m, -,rʊm) *n* a room in a newspaper office or television or radio station, where news is received and prepared for publication or broadcasting

newsstand ('nju:z,stænd) *n* a portable stand in the street, from which newspapers are sold

new start *n* an employee who has just joined a company or organization

New Stone Age *n* (not now in technical use) another term for **Neolithic**

New Style *n* the present method of reckoning dates using the Gregorian calendar

news vendor *n* a person who sells newspapers

newswoman ('nju:z,wʊmən) *n, pl* -women *informal* a female newsreader or reporter

newsworthy ('nju:z,wɜ:ðɪ) *adj* sufficiently interesting to be reported in a news bulletin > **'news,worthiness** *n*

newsy ('nju:zɪ) *adj* newsier, newsiest full of news, esp gossipy or personal news: *a newsy letter* > **'newsiness** *n*

newt (nju:t) *n* **1** any of various small semiaquatic urodele amphibians, such as *Triturus vulgaris* (**common newt**) of Europe, having a long slender body and tail and short feeble legs **2** *chiefly Brit* any other urodele amphibian, including the salamanders [C15 from *a newt*, a mistaken division of *an ewt*; ewt, from Old English *eveta* EFT[1]]

New Test. *abbreviation for* New Testament

New Testament *n* the collection of writings consisting of the Gospels, Acts of the Apostles, Pauline and other Epistles, and the book of Revelation, composed soon after Christ's death and added to the Jewish writings of the Old Testament to make up the Christian Bible

New Thought *n* a movement interested in spiritual healing and the power of constructive thinking

newton ('nju:t'n) *n* the derived SI unit of force that imparts an acceleration of 1 metre per second per second to a mass of 1 kilogram; equivalent to 10^5 dynes or 7.233 poundals. Symbol: N [C20 named after Sir Isaac *Newton* (1642–1727), English mathematician, physicist, astronomer, and philosopher]

Newton ('nju:t'n) *n* one of the deepest craters on the moon, over 7300 m deep and about 112 km in diameter, situated in the SE quadrant

Newtonian (nju:'təʊnɪən) *adj* of, relating to, or based on the theories of Sir Isaac Newton, the English mathematician, physicist, astronomer, and philosopher (1642–1727)

Newtonian mechanics *n* (*functioning as singular*) a system of mechanics based on Newton's laws of motion

Newtonian telescope *n* a type of astronomical reflecting telescope in which light is reflected from a large concave mirror, onto a plane mirror, and through a hole in the side of the body of the telescope to form an image

Newton's cradle *n* an ornamental puzzle consisting of a frame in which five metal balls are suspended in such a way that when one is moved it sets all the others in motion in turn

Newton's law of gravitation *n* the principle that two particles attract each other with forces directly proportional to the product of their masses divided by the square of the distance between them

Newton's laws of motion *pl n* three laws of mechanics describing the motion of a body. **The first law** states that a body remains at rest or in uniform motion in a straight line unless acted upon by a force. **The second law** states that a body's rate of change of momentum is proportional to the force causing it. **The third law** states that when a force acts on a body due to another body then an equal and opposite force acts simultaneously on that body

Newtown ('nju:taʊn) *n* a new town in central Wales, in Powys. Pop: 10 358 (2001)

new town *n* (in Britain) a town that has been planned as a complete unit and built with government sponsorship, esp to accommodate overspill population

Newtownabbey (,nju:t'n'æbɪ) *n* **1** a town in Northern Ireland, in Newtownabbey district, Co Antrim on Belfast Lough: the third largest town in Northern Ireland, formed in 1958 by the amalgamation of seven villages; light industrial centre, esp for textiles. Pop: 62 056 (2001) **2** a district of E Northern Ireland, in Co Antrim. Pop: 80 285 (2003 est). Area: 151 sq km (58 sq miles)

Newtown St Boswells ('nju:taʊn sənt 'bɒzwəlz) *n* a village in SE Scotland, administrative centre of Scottish Borders: agricultural centre. Pop: 1199 (2001)

New Urbanism *n* an international movement concerned with tackling the problems associated with urban sprawl and car dependency > **New Urbanist** *n*

new-variant Creutzfeldt-Jakob disease *or* **variant Creutzfeldt-Jakob disease** *n* a form of Creutzfeldt-Jakob disease thought to be transmitted by eating beef or beef products infected with BSE. Often shortened to: **new-variant CJD, variant CJD** Abbreviations: **nvCJD, vCJD**

new wave *n* a movement in art, film-making, politics, etc, that consciously breaks with traditional ideas

New Wave[1] *n* **the** a movement in the French cinema of the 1960s, led by such directors as Godard, Truffaut, and Resnais, and characterized by a fluid use of the camera and an abandonment of traditional editing techniques. Also called: **Nouvelle Vague**

New Wave[2] *n* rock music of the late 1970s, related to punk but more complex: sometimes used to include punk

New Windsor *n* the official name of **Windsor**[1] (sense 1)

new wool *n* wool that is being processed or woven for the first time. Usual US term: **virgin wool**

New World *n* **the** the Americas; the western hemisphere

New World monkey *n* any monkey of the family *Cebidae*, of Central and South America, having widely separated nostrils: many are arboreal and have a prehensile tail. Compare **Old World monkey**

New Year *n* the first day or days of the year in various calendars, usually celebrated as a holiday

New Year's Day *n* Jan 1, celebrated as a holiday in many countries. Often (US and Canadian informal) shortened to: **New Year's**

New Year's Eve *n* the evening of Dec 31, often celebrated with parties. See also **Hogmanay**

New York *n* **1** Also called: **New York City** a city in SE New York State, at the mouth of the Hudson River: the largest city and chief port of the US; settled by the Dutch as New Amsterdam in 1624 and captured by the British in 1664, when it was named New York; consists of five boroughs (Manhattan, the Bronx, Queens, Brooklyn, and Richmond) and many islands, with its commercial and financial centre in Manhattan; the country's leading commercial and industrial city. Pop: 8 085 742 (2003 est). Abbreviations: N.Y.C., NYC **2** a state of the northeastern US: consists chiefly of a plateau with the Finger Lakes in the centre, the Adirondack Mountains in the northeast, the Catskill Mountains in the southeast, and Niagara Falls in the west. Capital: Albany. Pop: 19 190 115 (2003 est). Area: 123 882 sq km (47 831 sq miles). Abbreviations: N.Y., (with zip code) NY

New York Bay *n* an inlet of the Atlantic at the mouth of the Hudson River: forms the harbour of the port of New York

New Yorker *n* a native or inhabitant of New York

New York minute *n chiefly US and Canadian informal* a very short period of time; instant [C20

from the supposedly fast pace of life in New York]

New York State Barge Canal *n* a system of inland waterways in New York State, connecting the Hudson River with Lakes Erie and Ontario and, via Lake Champlain, with the St Lawrence. Length: 845 km (525 miles)

New Zealand ('zi:lənd) *n* an independent dominion within the Commonwealth, occupying two main islands (the North Island and the South Island), Stewart Island, the Chatham Islands, and a number of minor islands in the SE Pacific: original Māori inhabitants ceded sovereignty to the British government in 1840; became a dominion in 1907; a major world exporter of dairy products, wool, and meat. Official languages: English and Māori. Religion: Christian majority, nonreligious and Māori minorities. Currency: New Zealand dollar. Capital: Wellington. Pop: 3 905 000 (2004 est). Area: 270 534 sq km (104 454 sq miles)

New Zealand ash *n* another name for **titoki**

New Zealander ('zi:ləndə) *n* a native or inhabitant of New Zealand

New Zealand fur seal *n* an Australasian seal, *Arctocephalus forsteri*. Also called: kekeno, southern fur seal

New Zealand greenstone *n* a variety of nephrite from New Zealand, used as a gemstone

New Zealand on Air *n* the operational name for the New Zealand Broadcasting Commission

New Zealand pepper tree *n* another name for **horopito**

New Zealand pigeon *n* a large fruit-eating native pigeon, *Hemiphagia novaeseelandiae*, of forest areas. Also called: kereru, kuku

next (nɛkst) *adj* **1** immediately following: *the next patient to be examined; do it next week* **2** immediately adjoining: *the next room* **3** closest to in degree: *the tallest boy next to James* **4** the next (Sunday) but one the (Sunday) after the next ▷ *adv* **5** at a time or on an occasion immediately to follow: *next, he started to unscrew the telephone receiver* **6** next to **a** adjacent to; at or on one side of: *the house next to ours* **b** following in degree: *next to your mother, who do you love most?* **c** almost: *next to impossible* ▷ *prep* **7** *archaic* next to [Old English *nēhst*, superlative of *nēah* NIGH; compare NEAR, NEIGHBOUR]

next door *adj* (**next-door** when prenominal), *adv* at, in, or to the adjacent house, flat, building, etc: *we live next door to the dentist; the next-door house*

next friend *n law* (formerly) a person acting on behalf of an infant or other person under legal disability. Official name: **litigation friend**

next of kin *n* a person's closest relative or relatives

nexus ('nɛksəs) *n, pl* **nexus 1** a means of connection between members of a group or things in a series; link; bond **2** a connected group or series [C17 from Latin: a binding together, from *nectere* to bind]

Nez Percé ('nɛz 'pɜːs; *French* ne pɛrse) *n* **1** (*pl* **Nez Percés** ('pɜːsɪz; *French* pɛrse) or **Nez Percé**) a member of a North American Indian people of the Pacific coast, a tribe of the Sahaptin **2** the Sahaptin language of this people [French, literally: pierced nose]

nf *the internet domain name for* Norfolk Island

NF *abbreviation for* **1** Norman French (language) **2** (in Britain) **National Front 3** (esp in postal addresses) Newfoundland

N/F *or* **NF** *banking abbreviation for* no funds

NFA *abbreviation for* **1** (in the US) National Futures Association **2** (in Britain) no fixed abode

NFB (in Canada) *abbreviation for* National Film Board

NFL (in the US) *abbreviation for* National Football League

NFS (in Britain) *abbreviation for* National Fire Service

NFT *abbreviation for* National Film Theatre

NFU (in Britain) *abbreviation for* National Farmers' Union

NFWI (in Britain) *abbreviation for* National Federation of Women's Institutes

ng *the internet domain name for* Nigeria

NG *abbreviation for* **1** (in the US) National Guard **2** New Guinea **3** *Also:* **ng** no good

NGA (formerly, in Britain) *abbreviation for* National Graphical Association

ngai (ˈᵊŋˈgɑːi) *prefix* NZ clan or tribe: used before the names of certain Māori tribes: *Ngai Tahu* [Māori]

ngaio ('naɪəʊ) *n, pl* **ngaios** a small New Zealand tree, *Myoporum laetum*, yielding useful timber: family *Myoporaceae* [from Māori]

Ngaliema Mountain (ᵊŋgɑːˈljeɪmə) *n* the Congolese name for (Mount) **Stanley**

ngarara (ˌᵊŋgɑːˈrɑːrɑː) *n, pl* **ngarara** NZ **1** a lizard **2** (in Māori mythology) a lizard-like monster [Māori]

ngati ('nɑːti:) *n* NZ (occurring as part of the name of a tribe) tribe or clan [Māori]

NGC *abbreviation for* New General Catalogue of Nebulae and Clusters of Stars; a catalogue in which over 8000 nebulae, galaxies, and clusters are listed numerically

NGF *abbreviation for* **nerve growth factor**

NGk *abbreviation for* New Greek

NGL *abbreviation for* natural gas liquids: liquid hydrocarbons derived from natural gas

NGO *abbreviation for* **1** Non-Governmental Organization **2** (in India) nongazetted officer

ngoma (ᵊŋˈgəʊmə, ᵊŋˈgɒm-) *n E African* a type of drum [Swahili]

ngultrum (ᵊŋˈguːltrəm) *n* the standard monetary unit of Bhutan, divided into 100 chetrum

Nguni (ᵊŋˈguːni) *n* a group of Bantu languages of southern Africa, consisting chiefly of Zulu, Xhosa, and Swazi

ngwee (ᵊŋˈgweɪ) *n* a Zambian monetary unit worth one hundredth of a kwacha

NH *or* **N.H.** *abbreviation for* New Hampshire

Nha Trang ('njɑː ˈtræŋ) *n* a port in SE Vietnam, on the South China Sea: nearby temples of the Cham civilization; fishing industry. Pop: 382 000 (2005 est)

NHI (in Britain) *abbreviation for* National Health Insurance

NHL (in Canada) *abbreviation for* National Hockey League

NHS (in Britain) *abbreviation for* **National Health Service**

ni *the internet domain name for* Nicaragua

Ni *the chemical symbol for* nickel

NI *abbreviation for* **1** (in Britain) **national insurance 2** Northern Ireland **3** NZ North Island

niacin ('naɪəsɪn) *n* another name for **nicotinic acid** [C20 from NI(COTINIC) AC(ID) + -IN]

Niagara (naɪˈægrə, -ˈægərə) *n* **1** a river in NE North America, on the border between W New York State and Ontario, Canada, flowing from Lake Erie to Lake Ontario. Length: 45 km (28 miles) **2** a torrent

Niagara Falls *n* **1** (*functioning as plural*) the falls of the Niagara River, on the border between the US and Canada: divided by Goat Island into the American Falls, 50 m (167 ft) high, and the Horseshoe or Canadian Falls, 47 m (158 ft) high **2** (*functioning as singular*) a city in W New York State, situated at the falls of the Niagara River. Pop: 78 815 (2001) **3** (*functioning as singular*) a city in S Canada, in SE Ontario on the Niagara River just below the falls: linked to the city of Niagara Falls in the US by three bridges. Pop: 78 815 (2001)

Niamey (njɑːˈmeɪ) *n* the capital of Niger, in the southwest on the River Niger: became capital in 1926; airport and land route centre. Pop: 997 000 (2005 est)

nib (nɪb) *n* **1** the writing point of a pen, esp an insertable tapered metal part with a split tip **2** a point, tip, or beak **3** (*plural*) crushed cocoa beans ▷ *vb* **nibs, nibbing, nibbed** (*tr*) **4** to provide with a nib **5** to prepare or sharpen the nib of [C16 (in the sense: beak): origin obscure; compare Northern

German *nibbe* tip. See NEB, NIBBLE] ▷ 'nib,like *adj*

nibble ('nɪbᵊl) *vb* (when *intr*, often foll by *at*) **1** (esp of animals, such as mice) to take small repeated bites (of) **2** to take dainty or tentative bites: *to nibble at a cake* **3** to bite (at) gently or caressingly **4** (*intr*) to make petty criticisms **5** (*intr*) to consider tentatively or cautiously: *to nibble at an idea* ▷ *n* **6** a small mouthful **7** an instance or the act of nibbling **8** (*plural*) *informal* small items of food, esp savouries, usually served with drinks [C15 related to Low German *nibbelen*. Compare NIB, NEB]

nibbler ('nɪblə) *n* **1** a person, animal, or thing that nibbles **2** *engineering* a tool that cuts sheet material by a series of small rapidly reciprocating cuts

Nibelung ('niːbəˌlʊŋ) *n, pl* -lungs *or* -lungen (-ˌlʊŋən) *German myth* **1** any of the race of dwarfs who possessed a treasure hoard stolen by Siegfried **2** one of Siegfried's companions or followers **3** (in the *Nibelungenlied*) a member of the family of Gunther, king of Burgundy

Nibelungenlied *German* ('niːbəlʊŋənliːt) *n* a medieval High German heroic epic of unknown authorship based on German history and legend and written about 1200 [literally: song of the Nibelungs]

niblick ('nɪblɪk) *n golf* (formerly) a club, a No. 9 iron, giving a great deal of lift [C19 of unknown origin]

nibs (nɪbz) *n* his nibs (*functioning as singular*) *slang* a mock title used of someone in authority [C19 of unknown origin]

NIC 1 *abbreviation for* newly industrialized country ▷ *international car registration for* Nicaragua

nicad ('naɪˌkæd) *n* a rechargeable dry-cell battery with a nickel anode and a cadmium cathode [C20 NI(CKEL) + CAD(MIUM)]

Nicaea (naɪˈsiːə) *n* an ancient city in NW Asia Minor, in Bithynia: site of the **first council of Nicaea** (325 AD), which composed the Nicene Creed. Modern Turkish name: Iznik

Nicaean (naɪˈsiːən) *adj* a variant of **Nicene**

NICAM ('naɪkæm) *n acronym for* near-instantaneous companding system: a technique for coding audio signals into digital form

Nicaragua (ˌnɪkəˈrægjuə, -gwə; *Spanish* nikaˈraɣwa) *n* **1** a republic in Central America, on the Caribbean and the Pacific: colonized by the Spanish from the 1520s; gained independence in 1821 and was annexed by Mexico, becoming a republic in 1838. Official language: Spanish. Religion: Roman Catholic majority. Currency: córdoba. Capital: Managua. Pop: 5 596 000 (2004 est). Area: 131 812 sq km (50 893 sq miles) **2 Lake** a lake in SW Nicaragua, separated from the Pacific by an isthmus 19 km (12 miles) wide: the largest lake in Central America. Area: 8264 sq km (3191 sq miles)

Nicaraguan (ˌnɪkəˈrægjuən, -gwən) *adj* **1** of or relating to Nicaragua or its inhabitants ▷ *n* **2** a native or inhabitant of Nicaragua

niccolite ('nɪkəˌlaɪt) *n* a copper-coloured mineral consisting of nickel arsenide in hexagonal crystalline form, occurring associated with copper and silver ores: a source of nickel. Formula: NiAs. Also called: nickeline [C19 from New Latin *niccolum* NICKEL + -ITE¹]

nice (naɪs) *adj* **1** pleasant or commendable: *a nice day* **2** kind or friendly: *a nice gesture of help* **3** good or satisfactory: *they made a nice job of it* **4** subtle, delicate, or discriminating: *a nice point in the argument* **5** precise; skilful: *a nice fit* **6** *now rare* fastidious; respectable: *he was not too nice about his methods* **7** *obsolete* **a** foolish or ignorant **b** delicate **c** shy; modest **d** wanton **8** nice and pleasingly: *it's nice and cool* [C13 (originally: foolish): from Old French *nice* simple, silly, from Latin *nescius* ignorant, from *nescīre* to be ignorant; see NESCIENCE] ▷ 'nicely *adv* ▷ 'niceness *n* ▷ 'nicish *adj*

Nice (*French* nis) *n* a city in SE France, on the Mediterranean: a leading resort of the French Riviera; founded by Phocaeans from Marseille in about the 3rd century BC Pop: 342 738 (1999)

NICE (naɪs) *n* (in Britain) *acronym for* National Institute for Clinical Excellence: a body established in 1999 to provide authoritative guidance on current best practice in medicine and to promote high-quality cost-effective medical treatment in the NHS

nice-looking *adj informal* attractive in appearance; pretty or handsome

Nicene ('naɪsi:n) or **Nicaean** (naɪ'si:ən) *adj* of or relating to Nicaea, an ancient city in NW Asia Minor, or its inhabitants

Nicene Council *n* 1 the first council of Nicaea, the first general council of the Church, held in 325 AD to settle the Arian controversy 2 the second council of Nicaea, the seventh general council of the Church, held in 787 AD to settle the question of images

Nicene Creed *n* 1 the formal summary of Christian beliefs promulgated at the first council of Nicaea in 325 AD 2 a longer formulation of Christian beliefs authorized at the council of Constantinople in 381, and now used in most Christian liturgies

nicety ('naɪsɪtɪ) *n, pl* -ties 1 a subtle point of delicacy or distinction: *a nicety of etiquette* 2 (*usually plural*) a refinement or delicacy: *the niceties of first-class travel* 3 subtlety, delicacy, or precision 4 excessive refinement; fastidiousness 5 **to a nicety** with precision

nicey-nicey (,naɪsɪ'naɪsɪ) *adj, adv informal* trying to be pleasant, but in a way that suggests artifice or exaggeration; ingratiating(ly)

niche (nɪtʃ, ni:ʃ) *n* 1 a recess in a wall, esp one that contains a statue 2 any similar recess, such as one in a rock face 3 a position particularly suitable for the person occupying it: *he found his niche in politics* 4 (*modifier*) relating to or aimed at a small specialized group or market 5 *ecology* the role of a plant or animal within its community and habitat, which determines its activities, relationships with other organisms, etc ▷ *vb* 6 (*tr*) to place (a statue) in a niche; ensconce (oneself) [c17 from French, from Old French *nichier* to nest, from Vulgar Latin *nīdicāre* (unattested) to build a nest, from Latin *nīdus* NEST]

niche market *n* a demand for a very specialized product or commodity

Nichiren ('ni:tʃi:,ren) *n* a Buddhist sect of Japan based on the teachings of the Buddhist priest Nichiren (1222–82), who claimed that the Lotus Sutra contained the only way to salvation

Nichrome ('naɪkrəʊm) *n trademark* any of various alloys containing nickel, iron, and chromium, with smaller amounts of other components. It is used in electrical heating elements, furnaces, etc

nicht (nɪxt) *n* a Scot word for **night**

nick¹ (nɪk) *n* 1 a small notch or indentation on an edge or surface 2 a groove on the shank of a printing type, used to orientate type and often to distinguish the fount 3 *Brit* a slang word for **prison** or **police station** 4 **in good nick** *informal* in good condition 5 **in the nick of time** at the last possible moment; at the critical moment ▷ *vb* 6 (*tr*) to chip or cut 7 (*tr*) *slang, chiefly Brit* **a** to steal **b** to take into legal custody; arrest 8 (*intr; often foll by off*) *informal* to move or depart rapidly 9 to divide and reset (certain of the tail muscles of a horse) to give the tail a high carriage 10 (*tr*) to guess, catch, etc, exactly 11 (*intr*) (of breeding stock) to mate satisfactorily 12 **nick (someone)** for *US and Canadian slang* to defraud (someone) to the extent of [c15 perhaps changed from C14 *nocke* NOCK]

nick² (nɪk) *n computing* an alias adopted by a member of a chatroom or forum; nickname [short for NICKNAME]

nickel ('nɪkᵊl) *n* 1 a malleable ductile silvery-white metallic element that is strong and corrosion-resistant, occurring principally in pentlandite and niccolite: used in alloys, esp in toughening steel, in electroplating, and as a

catalyst in organic synthesis. Symbol: Ni; atomic no.: 28; atomic wt.: 58.6934; valency: 0, 1, 2, or 3; relative density: 8.902; melting pt.: 1455°C; boiling pt.: 2914°C 2 a US and Canadian coin and monetary unit worth five cents ▷ *vb* -els, -elling, -elled or US -els, -eling, -eled 3 (*tr*) to plate with nickel [c18 shortened form of German *Kupfernickel* NICCOLITE, literally: copper demon, so called by miners because it was mistakenly thought to contain copper]

nickel bloom *n* another name for **annabergite**

nickelic (nɪ'kɛlɪk) *adj* 1 of or containing metallic nickel 2 of or containing nickel in the trivalent state

nickeliferous (,nɪkə'lɪfərəs) *adj* containing nickel

nickeline ('nɪkə,li:n) *n* another name for **niccolite**

nickelodeon (,nɪkə'ləʊdɪən) *n US* 1 an early form of jukebox 2 (*formerly*) a cinema charging five cents for admission 3 (*formerly*) a Pianola, esp one operated by inserting a five-cent piece [c20 from NICKEL + (MEL)ODEON]

nickelous ('nɪkələs) *adj* of or containing nickel, esp in the divalent state

nickel plate *n* a thin layer of nickel deposited on a surface, usually by electrolysis

nickel silver *n* any of various white alloys containing copper (46–63 per cent), zinc (18–36 per cent), and nickel (6–30 per cent): used in making tableware, etc. Also called: German silver, pakthong

nickel steel *n engineering* steel containing between 0.5 and 6.0 per cent nickel to increase its strength

nicker¹ ('nɪkə) *vb* (*intr*) 1 (of a horse) to neigh softly 2 to laugh quietly; snigger [c18 perhaps from NEIGH]

nicker² ('nɪkə) *n, pl* -er *Brit slang* a pound sterling [c20 of unknown origin]

nick-nack ('nɪk,næk) *n* a variant spelling of **knick-knack**

nickname ('nɪk,neɪm) *n* 1 a familiar, pet, or derisory name given to a person, animal, or place: *his nickname was Lefty because he was left-handed* 2 a shortened or familiar form of a person's name: *Joe is a nickname for Joseph* ▷ *vb* 3 (*tr*) to call by a nickname; give a nickname to [c15 *a nekename*, mistaken division of *an ekename* an additional name, from *eke* addition + NAME]

nickpoint ('nɪk,pɔɪnt) *n* a variant spelling (esp US) of **knickpoint**

nicky nicky nine doors ('nɪkɪ) *n Canadian informal* the practice of knocking on a door or ringing a doorbell and running away before it is answered

nicky-tam ('nɪkɪ'tæm) *n Scot* a strap or string secured round a trouser leg below the knee, formerly worn esp by farm workers to keep the trouser bottoms clear of dirt [c20 from *knicker* + *tam, taum* a fishing line or string]

Nicobar Islands ('nɪkə,bɑ:) *pl n* a group of 19 islands in the Indian Ocean, south of the Andaman Islands, with which they form a territory of India. Area: 1645 sq km (635 sq miles)

Nicodemus (,nɪkə'di:məs) *n New Testament* a Pharisee and a member of the Sanhedrin, who supported Jesus against the other Pharisees (John 8:50–52)

Nicol prism ('nɪkᵊl) *n* a device composed of two prisms of Iceland spar or calcite cut at specified angles and cemented together with Canada balsam. It is used for producing plane-polarized light [c19 named after William *Nicol* (?1768–1851), Scottish physicist, its inventor]

Nicosia (,nɪkə'si:ə, -'sɪə) *n* the capital of Cyprus, in the central part on the Pedieos River: capital since the 10th century. Pop (Greek and Turkish): Pop: 211 000 (2005 est). Greek name: Levkosia or Leukosia Turkish name: Lefkoşa

nicotiana (nɪ,kəʊʃɪ'ɑ:nə, -'eɪnə) *n* any solanaceous plant of the American and Australian genus *Nicotiana*, such as tobacco, having white, yellow, or purple fragrant flowers [c16 see NICOTINE]

nicotinamide (,nɪkə'tɪnə,maɪd, -'ti:n-) *n* the

amide of nicotinic acid: a component of the vitamin B complex and essential in the diet for the prevention of pellagra. Formula: $C_6H_6ON_2$

nicotine ('nɪkə,ti:n) *n* a colourless oily acrid toxic liquid that turns yellowish-brown in air and light: the principal alkaloid in tobacco, used as an agricultural insecticide. Formula: $C_{10}H_{14}N_2$ [c19 from French, from New Latin *herba nicotiana* Nicot's plant, named after J *Nicot* (1530–1600), French diplomat who introduced tobacco into France] > 'nico,tined *adj* > nicotinic (,nɪkə'tɪnɪk) *adj*

nicotinic acid *n* a vitamin of the B complex that occurs in milk, liver, yeast, etc. Lack of it in the diet leads to the disease pellagra. Formula: $(C_5H_4N)COOH$. Also called: niacin

nicotinism ('nɪkəti:,nɪzəm) *n pathol* a toxic condition of the body or a bodily organ or part caused by nicotine

Nictheroy (*Portuguese* nite'rɔɪ) *n* another name for **Niterói**

nictitate ('nɪktɪ,teɪt) or **nictate** ('nɪkteɪt) *vb* technical words for **blink** (sense 1) [c19 from Medieval Latin *nictitāre* to wink repeatedly, from Latin *nictāre* to wink, from *nicere* to beckon] > ,nicti'tation or nic'tation *n*

nictitating membrane ('nɪktɪ,teɪtɪŋ) *n* (in reptiles, birds, and some mammals) a thin fold of skin beneath the eyelid that can be drawn across the eye. Also called: third eyelid, haw

NICU *abbreviation for* neonatal intensive care unit

Nidaros (*Norwegian* 'ni:daro:s) *n* the former name (1930–31) of **Trondheim**

nidation (naɪ'deɪʃən) *n physiol* another name for **implantation** (sense 2) [from Latin *nīdus* nest]

niddering or **nidering** ('nɪdərɪŋ) *archaic* ▷ *n* 1 a coward ▷ *adj* 2 cowardly [c16 a mistaken reading of Old English *nithing* coward; related to *nīth* malice]

niddick ('nɪdɪk) *n Southwest English dialect* the nape of the neck

niddle-noddle ('nɪdᵊl,nɒdᵊl) *adj* 1 nodding ▷ *vb* 2 to nod rapidly or unsteadily [c18 reduplication of NOD]

NIDDM *abbreviation for* noninsulin-dependent diabetes mellitus; a form of diabetes in which insulin production is inadequate or the body becomes resistant to insulin

nide (naɪd) *n* another word for **nye** [c17 from Latin *nīdus* nest]

nidicolous (nɪ'dɪkələs) *adj* (of young birds) remaining in the nest for some time after hatching [c19 from Latin *nīdus* nest + *colere* to inhabit]

nidifugous (nɪ'dɪfjʊgəs) *adj* (of young birds) leaving the nest very soon after hatching [c19 from Latin *nīdus* nest + *fugere* to flee]

nidify ('nɪdɪ,faɪ) or **nidificate** ('nɪdɪfɪ,keɪt) *vb* -fies, -fying, -fied or -cates, -cating, -cated (*intr*) (of a bird) to make or build a nest [c17 from Latin *nīdificāre*, from *nīdus* a nest + *facere* to make] > ,nidifi'cation *n*

nid-nod ('nɪd,nɒd) *vb* to nod repeatedly [c18 reduplication of NOD]

nidus ('naɪdəs) *n, pl* -di (-daɪ) 1 the nest in which insects or spiders deposit their eggs 2 *pathol* a focus of infection 3 a cavity in which plant spores develop [c18 from Latin: NEST] > 'nidal *adj*

niece (ni:s) *n* a daughter of one's sister or brother [c13 from Old French: niece, granddaughter, ultimately from Latin *neptis* granddaughter]

Niederösterreich ('ni:dərø:stəraɪç) *n* the German name for **Lower Austria**

Niedersachsen ('ni:dərzaksən) *n* the German name for **Lower Saxony**

niello (nɪ'eləʊ) *n, pl* -li (-lɪ) or -los 1 a black compound of sulphur and silver, lead, or copper used to incise a design on a metal surface 2 the process of decorating surfaces with niello 3 a surface or object decorated with niello ▷ *vb* -los, -loing, -loed 4 (*tr*) to decorate or treat with niello [c19 from Italian from Latin *nigellus* blackish, from *niger* black] > ni'ellist *n*

Niemen ('njɛmɛn) *n* the Polish name for the **Neman**

Niersteiner (*German* 'niːrʃtainər) *n* a white wine from the region around Nierstein, Germany

Nietzschean ('niːtʃiən) *adj* **1** of or relating to Friedrich Wilhelm Nietzsche, the German philosopher, poet, and critic (1844–1900) ▷ *n* **2** a follower or admirer of Nietzsche > 'Nietzsche,ism *or* 'Nietzschean,ism *n*

nieve (niːv) *n Scot and northern English dialect* the closed hand; fist [c14 from Old Norse *hnefi*]

Nièvre (*French* njɛvrə) *n* a department of central France, in Burgundy region. Capital: Nevers. Pop: 222 298 (2003 est). Area: 6888 sq km (2686 sq miles)

nife (naɪf, 'naɪfɪ) *n* the earth's core, thought to be composed of nickel and iron [c20 from the chemical symbols Ni (nickel) and Fe (iron)]

nifedipine (naɪˈfɛdɪpiːn) *n med* a calcium-channel blocker used in the treatment of hypertension, angina pectoris, and heart failure

niff (nɪf) *Brit slang* ▷ *n* **1** a bad smell ▷ *vb* (*intr*) **2** to smell badly [c20 perhaps from SNIFF] > 'niffy *adj*

Niflheim ('nɪvªl,heɪm) *n Norse myth* the abode of the dead [Old Norse, literally: mist home]

nifty ('nɪftɪ) *adj* -tier, -tiest *informal* **1** pleasing, apt, or stylish **2** quick, agile: *he's nifty on his feet* [c19 of uncertain origin] > 'niftily *adv* > 'niftiness *n*

nigella (naɪˈdʒɛlə) *n* any plant of the ranunculaceous genus *Nigella,* from the Mediterranean and W Asia, esp *N damascena:* see **love-in-a-mist** [New Latin, diminutive of Latin *niger* black, from the colour of the seeds]

Niger *n* **1** (niːˈʒɛə, ˈnaɪdʒə) a landlocked republic in West Africa: important since earliest times for its trans-Saharan trade routes; made a French colony in 1922 and became fully independent in 1960; exports peanuts and livestock. Official language: French. Religion: Muslim majority. Currency: franc. Capital: Niamey. Pop: 12 415 000 (2004 est). Area: 1 267 000 sq km (489 000 sq miles) **2** ('naɪdʒə) a river in West Africa, rising in S Guinea and flowing in a great northward curve through Mali, then southwest through Niger and Nigeria to the Gulf of Guinea: the third longest river in Africa, with the largest delta, covering an area of 36 260 sq km (14 000 sq miles). Length: 4184 km (2600 miles) **3** ('naɪdʒə) a state of W central Nigeria, formed in 1976 from part of North-Western State. Capital: Minna. Pop: 2 775 526 (1995 est). Area: 76 363 sq km (29 476 sq miles)

Niger-Congo *n* **1** a family of languages of Africa consisting of the Bantu languages together with most of the languages of the coastal regions of West Africa. The chief branches are Benue-Congo (including Bantu), Kwa, Mande, and West Atlantic ▷ *adj* **2** relating to or belonging to this family of languages

Nigeria (naɪˈdʒɪərɪə) *n* a republic in West Africa, on the Gulf of Guinea: Lagos annexed by the British in 1861; protectorates of Northern and Southern Nigeria formed in 1900 and united as a colony in 1914; gained independence as a member of the Commonwealth in 1960 (membership suspended from 1995 to 1999 following human rights violations); Eastern Region seceded as the Republic of Biafra for the duration of the severe civil war (1967–70); ruled by military governments from 1966. It consists of a belt of tropical rain forest in the south, with semidesert in the extreme north and highlands in the east; the main export is petroleum. Official language: English; Hausa, Ibo, and Yoruba are the chief regional languages. Religion: animist, Muslim, and Christian. Currency: naira. Capital: Abuja. Pop: 127 117 000 (2004 est). Area: 923 773 sq km (356 669 sq miles)

Nigerian (naɪˈdʒɪərɪən) *adj* **1** of or relating to Nigeria or its inhabitants ▷ *n* **2** a native or inhabitant of Nigeria

Nigerien (niːˈʒɛərɪən) *adj* **1** of or relating to Niger or its inhabitants ▷ *n* **2** a native or inhabitant of Niger

Niger seed *n* another name for **ramtil** (sense 2)

niggard ('nɪgəd) *n* **1** a stingy person ▷ *adj* **2** *archaic* miserly [c14 perhaps of Scandinavian origin; related to Swedish dialect *nygg* and Old English *hnēaw* stingy]

niggardly ('nɪgədlɪ) *adj* **1** stingy or ungenerous **2** meagre: *a niggardly salary* ▷ *adv* **3** stingily; grudgingly > 'niggardliness *n*

nigger ('nɪgə) *n taboo* **1 a** a derogatory name for a Black person **b** (*as modifier*): *nigger minstrels* **2** *derogatory* a member of any dark-skinned race **3** nigger in the woodpile *old-fashioned offensive* a hidden snag or hindrance [c18 from c16 dialect *neeger,* from French *nègre,* from Spanish NEGRO[1]]

niggle ('nɪgªl) *vb* **1** (*intr*) to find fault continually **2** (*intr*) to be preoccupied with details; fuss **3** (*tr*) to irritate; worry ▷ *n* **4** a slight or trivial objection or complaint **5** a slight feeling as of misgiving, uncertainty, etc [c16 from Scandinavian; related to Norwegian *nigla*. Compare NIGGARD] > 'niggler *n* > 'niggly *adj*

niggling ('nɪglɪŋ) *adj* **1** petty **2** fussy **3** irritating **4** requiring painstaking work ▷ *n* **5** an act or instance of niggling > 'nigglingly *adv*

nigh (naɪ) *adj, adv, prep* an archaic, poetic, or dialect word for **near** [Old English *nēah, nēh;* related to German *nah,* Old Frisian *nei.* Compare NEAR, NEXT]

night (naɪt) *n* **1** the period of darkness each 24 hours between sunset and sunrise, as distinct from day **2** (*modifier*) of, occurring, working, etc, at night: *a night nurse* **3** the occurrence of this period considered as a unit: *four nights later they left* **4** the period between sunset and retiring to bed; evening **5** the time between bedtime and morning: *she spent the night alone* **6** the weather conditions of the night: *a clear night* **7** the activity or experience of a person during a night **8** (*sometimes capital*) any evening designated for a special observance or function **9** nightfall or dusk **10** a state or period of gloom, ignorance, etc **11** make a night of it to go out and celebrate for most of the night **12** night and day continually: *that baby cries night and day* ▷ Related adjective: **nocturnal** [Old English *niht;* compare Dutch *nacht,* Latin *nox,* Greek *nux*] > 'nightless *adj* > 'night,like *adj*

night blindness *n pathol* a nontechnical term for **nyctalopia.** > 'night,blind *adj*

night-blooming cereus *n* any of several cacti of the genera *Hylocereus, Selenicereus,* etc, having large fragrant flowers that open at night

nightcap ('naɪt,kæp) *n* **1** a bedtime drink, esp an alcoholic or hot one **2** a soft cap formerly worn in bed

nightclothes ('naɪt,kləʊðz) *pl n* clothes worn in bed

nightclub ('naɪt,klʌb) *n* a place of entertainment open until late at night, usually offering food, drink, a floor show, dancing, etc > 'night,clubber *n*

night dancer *n* (in Uganda) a person believed to employ the help of the dead in destroying other people

nightdress ('naɪt,drɛs) *n Brit* a loose dress worn in bed by women. Also called: nightgown, nightie

nightfall ('naɪt,fɔːl) *n* the approach of darkness; dusk

night fighter *n* an interceptor aircraft used for operations at night

nightgown ('naɪt,gaʊn) *n* **1** another name for **nightdress 2** a man's nightshirt

nighthawk ('naɪt,hɔːk) *n* **1** Also called: bullbat, mosquito hawk any American nightjar of the genus *Chordeiles* and related genera, having a dark plumage and, in the male, white patches on the wings and tail **2** *informal* another name for **night owl**

night heron *n* any nocturnal heron of the genus *Nycticorax* and related genera, having short legs and neck, a heavy body, and a short heavy bill

nightie *or* **nighty** ('naɪtɪ) *n, pl* nighties *informal* short for **nightdress**

nightingale ('naɪtɪŋ,geɪl) *n* **1** a brownish European songbird, *Luscinia megarhynchos,* with a broad reddish-brown tail: well known for its musical song, usually heard at night **2** any of various similar or related birds, such as *Luscinia luscinia* (**thrush nightingale**) [Old English *nihtegale,* literally: night-singer, from NIGHT + *galan* to sing]

Nightingale ward *n* a long hospital ward with beds on either side and the nurses' station in the middle [c20 after Florence *Nightingale* (1820–1910), English nurse famous for her work during the Crimean War]

nightjar ('naɪt,dʒɑː) *n* any nocturnal bird of the family *Caprimulgidae,* esp *Caprimulgus europaeus* (**European nightjar**): order *Caprimulgiformes.* They have a cryptic plumage and large eyes and feed on insects [c17 NIGHT + JAR[2], so called from its discordant cry]

night latch *n* a door lock that is operated by means of a knob on the inside and a key on the outside

night letter *n* (formerly, in the US and Canada) a telegram sent for delivery the next day at a cheaper rate than a regular telegram

nightlife ('naɪt,laɪf) *n* social life or entertainment taking place in the late evening or night, as in nightclubs

night-light *n* a dim light burning at night, esp for children

nightlong ('naɪt,lɒŋ) *adj, adv* throughout the night

nightly ('naɪtlɪ) *adj* **1** happening or relating to each night **2** happening at night ▷ *adv* **3** at night or each night

nightmare ('naɪt,mɛə) *n* **1** a terrifying or deeply distressing dream **2 a** an event or condition resembling a terrifying dream: *the nightmare of shipwreck* **b** (*as modifier*): *a nightmare drive* **3** a thing that is feared **4** (*formerly*) an evil spirit supposed to harass or suffocate sleeping people [c13 (meaning: incubus; c16 bad dream): from NIGHT + Old English *mare, mære* evil spirit, from Germanic; compare Old Norse *mara* incubus, Polish *zmora,* French *cauchemar* nightmare] > 'night,marish *adj* > 'night,marishly *adv* > 'night,marishness *n*

night-night *sentence substitute* an informal word for **good night**

night nurse *n* a nurse whose duty is to look after a patient or patients during the night

night owl *or* **hawk** *n informal* a person who is or prefers to be up and about late at night

night raven *n poetic* any bird, esp the night heron, that is most active at night

nightrider ('naɪt,raɪdə) *n* a member of a band of mounted and usually masked Whites in the southern US who carried out acts of revenge and intimidation at night after the Civil War > 'night,riding *n*

night robe *n US and Canadian* a loose dress worn in bed by women. Also called (in Britain and certain other countries): nightdress

nights (naɪts) *adv informal* at night, esp regularly: *he works nights*

night safe *n* a safe built into the outside wall of a bank, in which customers can deposit money at times when the bank is closed

night school *n* an educational institution that holds classes in the evening for those who are not free during the day

nightshade ('naɪt,ʃeɪd) *n* **1** any of various solanaceous plants, such as deadly nightshade, woody nightshade, and black nightshade **2** See **enchanter's nightshade** [Old English *nihtscada,* apparently NIGHT + SHADE, referring to the poisonous or soporific qualities of these plants]

night shift *n* **1** a group of workers who work a shift during the night in an industry or occupation where a day shift or a back shift are also worked **2** the period worked ▷ See also **back shift**

nightshirt ('naɪt,ʃɜːt) *n* a loose knee-length or longer shirtlike garment worn in bed by men

night soil *n* human excrement collected at night

n

from cesspools, privies, etc, and sometimes used as a fertilizer

nightspot ('naɪtˌspɒt) *n* an informal word for **nightclub**

night stick *n* *US and Canadian* a heavy baton or club carried by a policeman. British equivalent: **truncheon**

night terrors *pl n* a condition in which a person, usually a child, suddenly starts from sleep in a state of extreme fear but cannot later remember the incident

night-time *n* **a** the time from sunset to sunrise; night as distinct from day **b** (*as modifier*): *a night-time prowler*

night watch *n* **1** a watch or guard kept at night, esp for security **2** the period of time the watch is kept **3** a person who keeps such a watch; night watchman

night watchman *n* **1** *Also called:* night watch a person who keeps guard at night on a factory, public building, etc **2** *cricket* a batsman sent in to bat to play out time when a wicket has fallen near the end of a day's play

nightwear ('naɪtˌwɛə) *n* apparel worn in bed or before retiring to bed; pyjamas, nightdress, dressing gown, etc

nigiri (niˈɡiːriː) *n* (in Japanese cuisine) a small oval block of cold rice topped with wasabi and a thin slice of fish, prawn, etc, and sometimes held together by a thin band of seaweed [Japanese, literally: grasp, as the rice is shaped by hand]

nigrescent (naɪˈɡrɛsᵊnt) *adj* blackish; dark [c18 from Latin *nigrescere* to grow black, from *niger* black; see NEGRO¹] > niˈgrescence *n*

nigritude ('nɪɡrɪˌtjuːd) *n rare* blackness; darkness [c17 from Latin *nigritūdō,* from *niger* black]

nigrosine ('nɪɡrəˌsiːn, -sɪn) or **nigrosin** ('nɪɡrəsɪn) *n* any of a class of black pigments and dyes obtained from aniline: used in inks and shoe polishes and for dyeing textiles [c19 from Latin *niger* black + -OSE¹ + -INE¹]

NIHE (in Ireland) *abbreviation for* National Institute for Higher Education

nihil *Latin* ('naɪhɪl, 'niːhɪl) *n* nil; nothing

nihilism ('naɪɪˌlɪzəm) *n* **1** a complete denial of all established authority and institutions **2** *philosophy* an extreme form of scepticism that systematically rejects all values, belief in existence, the possibility of communication, etc **3** a revolutionary doctrine of destruction for its own sake **4** the practice or promulgation of terrorism [c19 from Latin *nihil* nothing + -ISM, on the model of German *Nihilismus*] > 'nihilist *n, adj* > ˌnihil'istic *adj*

Nihilism ('naɪɪˌlɪzəm) *n* (in tsarist Russia) any of several revolutionary doctrines that upheld terrorism

nihility (naɪˈhɪlɪtɪ) *n* the state or condition of being nothing; nothingness; nullity

nihil obstat ('ɒbstæt) the phrase used by a Roman Catholic censor to declare publication inoffensive to faith or morals [Latin, literally: nothing hinders]

Nihon ('niːˈhɒn) *n* transliteration of a Japanese name for **Japan**

NII (in Britain) *abbreviation for* nuclear installations inspectorate

Niigata ('niːˌɡɑːtə) *n* a port in central Japan, on NW Honshu at the mouth of the Shinano River: the chief port on the Sea of Japan. Pop: 514 678 (2002 est)

Nijmegen ('naɪˌmeɪɡən; *Dutch* 'nɛimeːxə) *n* an industrial town in the E Netherlands, in Gelderland province on the Waal River: the oldest town in the country; scene of the signing (1678) of the peace treaty between Louis XIV, the Netherlands, Spain, and the Holy Roman Empire. Pop: 156 000 (2003 est). Latin name: **Noviomagus** German name: **Nimwegen**

-nik *suffix forming nouns* denoting a person associated with a specified state, belief, or quality: *beatnik; refusenik* [c20 from Russian *-nik,* as in

SPUTNIK, and influenced by Yiddish *-nik* (agent suffix)]

Nikaria (nɪˈkɛərɪə, naɪ-) *n* another name for **Icaria**

nikau or **nikau palm** ('niːkaʊ) *n* a palm tree of the genus *Rhopalostylis,* esp *R. sapida,* native to New Zealand. The leaves were used by the Māoris to build their whares and the top of the stem is sometimes eaten [Māori]

Nike ('naɪkiː) *n Greek myth* the winged goddess of victory. Roman counterpart: Victoria [from Greek: victory]

Nikkei Stock Average ('nɪkeɪ) *n* an index of prices on the Tokyo Stock Exchange [c20 from *Nik(on) Kei(zai Shimbun),* a Japanese newspaper group]

Nikko ('niːkəʊ) *n* a town in central Japan, on NE Honshu: a major pilgrimage centre, with a 4th-century Shinto shrine, a Buddhist temple (767), and the shrines and mausoleums of the Tokugawa shoguns. Pop: 17 527 (2002 est)

Nikolainkaupunki (*Finnish* ˌnikəlaɪnˈkaʊpʊŋki) *n* the former name of **Vaasa**

Nikolayev (*Russian* nikaˈlajɪf) *n* a city in S Ukraine on the Southern Bug about 64 km (40 miles) from the Black Sea: founded as a naval base in 1788; one of the leading Black Sea ports. Pop: 518 000 (2005 est). Former name: **Vernoleninsk**

nil (nɪl) *n* another word for nothing: used esp in the scoring of certain games [c19 from Latin]

nil desperandum ('nɪl ˌdɛspəˈrændəm) *sentence substitute* never despair [from Latin, literally: nothing to be despaired of]

Nile (naɪl) *n* a river in Africa, rising in S central Burundi in its remotest headstream, the **Luvironza:** flows into Lake Victoria and leaves the lake as the **Victoria Nile,** flowing to Lake Albert, which is drained by the **Albert Nile,** becoming the White Nile on the border between Uganda and the Sudan; joined by its chief tributary, the **Blue Nile** (which rises near Lake Tana, Ethiopia) at Khartoum, and flows north to its delta on the Mediterranean; the longest river in the world. Length: (from the source of the Luvironza to the Mediterranean) 6741 km (4187 miles)

Nile blue *n* a pale greenish-blue colour **b** (*as adjective*): *a Nile-blue carpet*

Nile green *n* a pale bluish-green colour **b** (*as adjective*): *a Nile-green dress*

nilgai ('nɪlɡaɪ) or **nilghau, nylghau** ('nɪlɡɔː) *n, pl* **-gai, -gais** or **-ghau, -ghaus** a large Indian antelope, *Boselaphus tragocamelus.* The male is blue-grey with white markings and has small horns; the female is brownish and has no horns [c19 from Hindi *nīlgāw* blue bull, from Sanskrit *nīla* dark blue + *go* bull]

Nilgiri Hills ('nɪlɡɪrɪ) or **Nilgiris** *pl n* a plateau in S India, in Tamil Nadu. Average height: 2000 m (6500 ft), reaching 2635 m (8647 ft) in Doda Betta

Nilometer (naɪˈlɒmɪtə) *n archaic* a graduated pillar by which the rise and fall of the Nile can be measured

Nilo-Saharan (ˌnaɪləʊsəˈhɑːrən) *n* **1** a family of languages of Africa, spoken chiefly by Nilotic peoples in a region extending from the Sahara to Kenya and Tanzania, including the Chari-Nile, Saharan, Songhai, and other branches. Classification is complicated by the fact that many languages spoken in this region belong to the unrelated Afro-Asiatic, Kordofanian, and Niger-Congo families ▷ *adj* **2** relating to or belonging to this family of languages

Nilotic (naɪˈlɒtɪk) *adj* **1** of or relating to the Nile **2** of, relating to, or belonging to a tall Negroid pastoral people inhabiting the S Sudan, parts of Kenya and Uganda, and neighbouring countries **3** relating to or belonging to the group of languages spoken by the Nilotic peoples ▷ *n* **4** a group of languages of E Africa, including Luo, Dinka, and Masai, now generally regarded as belonging to the Chari-Nile branch of the Nilo-Saharan family [c17 via Latin from Greek *Neilotikós,* from *Neilos* the NILE]

nil return *n* a reply of zero to a request for a quantified reply

nim (nɪm) *n* a game in which two players alternately remove one or more small items, such as matchsticks, from one of several rows or piles, the object being to take (or avoid taking) the last item remaining on the table [c20 perhaps from archaic *nim* to take, from Old English *niman*]

nimble ('nɪmbᵊl) *adj* **1** agile, quick, and neat in movement: *nimble fingers* **2** alert; acute: *a nimble intellect* [Old English *nǣmel* quick to grasp, and *numol* quick at seizing, both from *niman* to take] > 'nimbleness *n* > 'nimbly *adv*

nimblewit ('nɪmbəlˌwɪt) *n chiefly US and Canadian* an alert, bright, and clever person > 'nimbleˌwitted *adj*

nimbostratus (ˌnɪmbəʊˈstreɪtəs, -ˈstrɑːtəs) *n, pl* -ti (-taɪ) a dark-coloured rain-bearing stratus cloud

nimbus ('nɪmbəs) *n, pl* -bi (-baɪ) or -buses **1 a** a dark grey rain-bearing cloud **b** (*in combination*): *cumulonimbus clouds* **2 a** an emanation of light surrounding a saint or deity **b** a representation of this emanation **3** a surrounding aura or atmosphere [c17 from Latin: cloud, radiance] > 'nimbused *adj*

NIMBY ('nɪmbɪ) *n acronym for* not in my back yard: a person who objects to the occurrence of something if it will affect him or her or take place in his or her locality

nimbyism ('nɪmbɪˌɪzəm) *n* the practice of objecting to something that will affect one or take place in one's locality

Nîmes (*French* nim) *n* a city in S France: Roman remains including an amphitheatre and the Pont du Gard aqueduct. Pop: 133 424 (1999)

nimiety (nɪˈmaɪɪtɪ) *n, pl* -ties a rare word for **excess** [c16 from Late Latin *nimietās,* from Latin *nimis* too much]

niminy-piminy ('nɪmɪnɪ'pɪmɪnɪ) *adj* excessively refined; prim [c19 imitative of a prim affected enunciation]

nimonic alloy (nɪˈmɒnɪk) *n* any of various nickel-based alloys used at high temperatures, as in gas turbine blades [c20 from NI(CKEL) + MO(LYBDENUM) + -IC]

n'importe *French* (nɛ̃pɔrt) no matter

nimps (nɪmps) *adj Northern English dialect* easy

Nimrod ('nɪmrɒd) *n* **1** *Old Testament* a hunter, who was famous for his prowess (Genesis 10:8–9) **2** a person who is dedicated to or skilled in hunting. Douay spelling: Nemrod > Nim'rodian or Nim'rodic *adj*

Nimrud (nɪmˈruːd) *n* an ancient city in Assyria, near the present-day city of Mosul (Iraq): founded in about 1250 BC and destroyed by the Medes in 612 BC; excavated by Sir Austen Henry Layard

Nimwegen ('nɪmveːɡən) *n* the German name for **Nijmegen**

Niña ('niːnə; *Spanish* 'niɲa) *n* **the** one of the three ships commanded by Columbus in 1492

nincompoop ('nɪnkəmˌpuːp, 'nɪŋ-) *n* a stupid person; fool; idiot [c17 of unknown origin]

nine (naɪn) *n* **1** the cardinal number that is the sum of one and eight. See also **number** (sense 1) **2** a numeral, 9, IX, etc, representing this number **3** something representing, represented by, or consisting of nine units, such as a playing card with nine symbols on it **4** *Also:* nine o'clock nine hours after noon or midnight: *the play starts at nine* **5** dressed (up) to the nines *informal* elaborately dressed **6** 999 (in Britain) the telephone number of the emergency services **7** nine to five normal office hours: *he works nine to five; a nine-to-five job* ▷ *determiner* **8 a** amounting to nine: *nine days* **b** (*as pronoun*): *nine of the ten are ready* ▷ Related prefix: **nona-** [Old English *nigon;* related to Gothic *niun,* Latin *novem*]

nine-days wonder *n* something that arouses great interest, but only for a short period

nine-eleven, 9-11 or **9/11** *n* the 11th of September 2001, the day on which the twin towers of the World Trade Center in New York were flown into and destroyed by aeroplanes hijacked by Islamic fundamentalists. Also called: September eleven [C21 from the US custom of expressing dates in figures, the day of the month following the number of the month]

ninefold ('naɪnˌfəʊld) *adj* **1** equal to or having nine times as many or as much **2** composed of nine parts ▷ *adv* **3** by or up to nine times as many or as much

ninepins ('naɪnˌpɪnz) *n* **1** (*functioning as singular*) another name for **skittles 2** (*singular*) one of the pins used in this game

nineteen (ˌnaɪn'tiːn) *n* **1** the cardinal number that is the sum of ten and nine and is a prime number. See also **number** (sense 1) **2** a numeral, 19, XIX, etc, representing this number **3** something represented by, representing, or consisting of 19 units **4** talk nineteen to the dozen to talk incessantly ▷ *determiner* **5 a** amounting to nineteen: *nineteen pictures* **b** (*as pronoun*): *only nineteen voted* [Old English *nigontĩne*]

nineteenth (ˌnaɪn'tiːnθ) *adj* **1** (*usually prenominal*) **a** coming after the eighteenth in numbering or counting order, position, time, etc, being the ordinal number of *nineteen*. Often written: 19th **b** (*as noun*): *the nineteenth was rainy* ▷ *n* **2 a** one of 19 approximately equal parts of something **b** (*as modifier*): *a nineteenth part* **3** the fraction that is equal to one divided by 19 (1/19)

nineteenth hole *n golf slang* the bar in a golf clubhouse [C20 from its being the next objective after a standard 18-hole round]

nineteenth man *n* **1** *Australian rules football* the first reserve in a team **2** any person acting as a reserve or substitute

ninetieth ('naɪntɪɪθ) *adj* **1** (*usually prenominal*) **a** being the ordinal number of *ninety* in numbering or counting order, position, time, etc Often written: 90th **b** (*as noun*): *the ninetieth in succession* ▷ *n* **2 a** one of 90 approximately equal parts of something **b** (*as modifier*): *a ninetieth part* **3** the fraction equal to one divided by 90 (1/90)

ninety ('naɪntɪ) *n, pl* -ties **1** the cardinal number that is the product of ten and nine. See also **number** (sense 1) **2** a numeral, 90, XC, etc, representing this number **3** something represented by, representing, or consisting of 90 units ▷ *determiner* **4 a** amounting to ninety: *ninety times out of a hundred* **b** (*as pronoun*): *at least ninety are thought to be missing* [Old English *nigontig*]

Nineveh ('nɪnɪvə) *n* the ancient capital of Assyria, on the River Tigris opposite the present-day city of Mosul (N Iraq): at its height in the 8th and 7th centuries BC; destroyed in 612 BC by the Medes and Babylonians

Ninevite ('nɪnɪˌvaɪt) *n* a native or inhabitant of Nineveh, the ancient capital of Assyria

Ningbo *or* **Ningpo** ('nɪŋ'pəʊ) *n* a port in E China, in NE Zhejiang, on the Yung River, about 20 km (12 miles) from its mouth at Hangzhou Bay: one of the first sites of European settlement in China. Pop: 1 188 000 (2005 est)

Ningsia *or* **Ninghsia** ('nɪŋ'ʃjaː) *n* **1** a former province of NW China: mostly included in the Inner Mongolian AR in 1956, with the smaller part constituted as the Ningxia Hui AR in 1958 **2** the former name of **Yinchuan**

Ningxia Hui Autonomous Region ('nɪŋ'ʃjaː 'huːɪ) *n* an administrative division of NW China, south of the Inner Mongolian AR. Capital: Yinchuan. Pop: 5 800 000 (2003 est). Area: 66 400 sq km (25 896 sq miles)

ninhydrin (nɪn'haɪdrɪn) *n* a chemical reagent used for the detection and analysis of primary amines, esp amino acids, with which it forms a derivative with an intense purple colour [C20 from the chemical name *triketo hydrindene*]

ninja ('nɪndʒə) *n, pl* -ja *or* -jas (*sometimes capital*) a person skilled in **ninjutsu**, a Japanese martial art characterized by stealthy movement and camouflage [Japanese]

ninny ('nɪnɪ) *n, pl* -nies a dull-witted person [C16

perhaps from *an innocent simpleton*] > 'ninnyish *adj*

ninnyhammer ('nɪnɪˌhæmə) *n US and Canadian* a ninny [origin unknown]

ninon ('niːnɒn, 'naɪnɒn; *French* ninɔ̃) *n* a fine strong silky fabric [C20 from French]

ninth (naɪnθ) *adj* **1** (*usually prenominal*) **a** coming after the eighth in counting order, position, time, etc; being the ordinal number of *nine*. Often written: 9th **b** (*as noun*): *he came on the ninth; ninth in line* ▷ *n* **2 a** one of nine equal or nearly equal parts of an object, quantity, measurement, etc **b** (*as modifier*): *a ninth part* **3** the fraction equal to one divided by nine (1/9) **4** *music* **a** an interval of one octave plus a second **b** one of two notes constituting such an interval **c** See **ninth chord** ▷ *adv* **5** Also: ninthly after the eighth person, position, event, etc ▷ *sentence connector* **6** Also: ninthly as the ninth point: linking what follows to the previous statement [Old English *nigotha*; related to Old High German *niunto*, Old Norse *nīundi*]

ninth chord *n* a chord much used in jazz and pop, consisting of a major or minor triad with the seventh and ninth added above the root. Often shortened to: ninth

Niobe ('naɪəbɪ) *n Greek myth* a daughter of Tantalus, whose children were slain after she boasted of them: although turned into stone, she continued to weep > Niobean (naɪ'əʊbɪən) *adj*

niobic (naɪ'əʊbɪk, -'ɒbɪk) *adj* of or containing niobium in the pentavalent state. Also: columbic

niobite ('naɪəˌbaɪt) *n* another name for **columbite** [C19 NIOBIUM + -ITE[1]]

niobium (naɪ'əʊbɪəm) *n* a ductile white superconductive metallic element that occurs principally in columbite and tantalite: used in steel alloys. Symbol: Nb; atomic no.: 41; atomic wt.: 92.90638; valency: 2, 3, or 5; relative density: 8.57; melting pt.: 2469±10°C; boiling pt.: 4744°C. Former name: columbium [C19 from New Latin, from NIOBE (daughter of Tantalus), so named because it occurred in TANTALITE]

niobous (naɪ'əʊbəs) *adj* of or containing niobium in the trivalent state. Also: columbous

Niort (*French* njɔr) *n* a market town in W France. Pop: 56 663 (1999)

nip[1] (nɪp) *vb* nips, nipping, nipped (*mainly tr*) **1** to catch or tightly compress, as between a finger and the thumb; pinch **2** (*often foll by off*) to remove by clipping, biting, etc **3** (*when intr, often foll by at*) to give a small sharp bite (to): *the dog nipped at his heels* **4** (*esp of the cold*) to affect with a stinging sensation **5** to harm through cold: *the frost nipped the young plants* **6** to check or destroy the growth of (esp in the phrase **nip in the bud**) **7** *slang* to steal **8** (*intr; foll by along, up, out, etc*) *Brit informal* to hurry; dart **9** *slang, chiefly US and Canadian* to snatch ▷ *n* **10** the act of nipping; a pinch, snip, etc **11 a** a frosty or chilly quality **b** severe frost or cold: *the first nip of winter* **12** a small piece or quantity: *he went out for a nip of fresh air* **13** a sharp flavour or tang **14** *archaic* a taunting remark **15** nip and tuck **a** *chiefly US and Canadian* neck and neck **b** *informal* plastic surgery performed for cosmetic reasons **16** put the nips in *Austral and NZ slang* to exert pressure on someone, esp in order to extort money [C14 of Scandinavian origin; compare Old Norse *hnippa* to prod]

nip[2] (nɪp) *n* **1** a small drink of spirits; dram **2** *chiefly Brit* a measure of spirits usually equal to one sixth of a gill ▷ *vb* nips, nipping, nipped **3** to drink (spirits), esp habitually in small amounts [C18 shortened from *nipperkin* a vessel holding a half-pint or less, of uncertain origin; compare Dutch *nippen* to sip]

Nip (nɪp) *n slang* a derogatory word for a **Japanese** [C20 short for *Nipponese*]

nipa ('niːpə, 'naɪ-) *n* **1** a palm tree, *Nipa fruticans*, of S and SE Asia, having feathery leaves, used for thatching, and edible fruit **2** the fruit or thatch obtained from this tree **3** the sap of this tree, used to make a liquor [C16 from Malay *nipah*]

nip curn (kɜːn) *n Northern English dialect* a tightfisted woman [from NIP[1] (to bite) and *curn* currant; the allusion being that the currant is divided in two to make it go further]

Nipigon ('nɪpəgɒn) *n* **Lake** a lake in central Canada, in NW Ontario, draining into Lake Superior via the **Nipigon River**. Area: 4843 sq km (1870 sq miles)

Nipissing ('nɪpɪsɪŋ) *n* **Lake** a lake in central Canada, in E Ontario between the Ottawa River and Georgian Bay. Area: 855 sq km (330 sq miles)

nipper ('nɪpə) *n* **1** a person or thing that nips **2** the large pincer-like claw of a lobster, crab, or similar crustacean **3** *informal* a small child **4** *Austral* a type of small prawn used as bait

nippers ('nɪpəz) *pl n* an instrument or tool, such as a pair of pliers, for snipping, pinching, or squeezing

nipping ('nɪpɪŋ) *adj* **1** sharp and biting: *a nipping wind* **2** sarcastic; bitter > 'nippingly *adv*

nipple ('nɪpəl) *n* **1** Also called: mamilla, papilla, teat the small conical projection in the centre of the areola of each breast, which in women contains the outlet of the milk ducts. Related adj: **mamillary 2** something resembling a nipple in shape or function **3** Also called: grease nipple a small drilled bush, usually screwed into a bearing, through which grease is introduced **4** *US and Canadian* an informal word for **dummy** (sense 11) [C16 from earlier *neble, nible*, perhaps from NEB, NIB]

nipplewort ('nɪpəlˌwɜːt) *n* an annual Eurasian plant, *Lapsana communis*, with pointed oval leaves and small yellow flower heads: family *Asteraceae* (composites)

Nippon ('nɪpɒn) *n* transliteration of a Japanese name for **Japan**

Nipponese (ˌnɪpə'niːz) *adj, n, pl* -nese another word for **Japanese**

Nippur (nɪ'pʊə) *n* an ancient Sumerian and Babylonian city, the excavated site of which is in SE Iraq: an important religious centre, abandoned in the 12th or 13th century

nippy ('nɪpɪ) *adj* -pier, -piest **1** (of weather) chilly, keen, or frosty **2** *Brit informal* **a** quick; nimble; active **b** (of a motor vehicle) small and relatively powerful **3** (of the taste of food) biting, sharp, or pungent **4** (of a dog) inclined to bite > 'nippily *adv* > 'nippiness *n*

niqab (nɪ'kɑːb) *n Islam* a type of veil worn by some Muslim women that is made of lightweight opaque fabric and leaves only the eyes uncovered [C20 from Arabic]

NIREX ('naɪrɛks) *n acronym for* Nuclear Industry Radioactive Waste Executive

nirvana (nɪə'vɑːnə, nɜː-) *n Buddhism, Hinduism* final release from the cycle of reincarnation attained by extinction of all desires and individual existence, culminating (in Buddhism) in absolute blessedness, or (in Hinduism) in absorption into Brahman [C19 from Sanskrit: extinction, literally: a blowing out, from *nir-* out + *vāti* it blows] > nir'vanic *adj*

Niš *or* **Nish** (niːʃ) *n* an industrial town in E Serbia and Montenegro, in SE Serbia: situated on routes between central Europe and the Aegean. Pop: 203 670 (2002)

Nisan (ni:'san) *n* (in the Jewish calendar) the first month of the year according to biblical reckoning and the seventh month of the civil year, usually falling within March and April [from Hebrew]

Nisei ('niːseɪ) *n* a native-born citizen of the United States or Canada whose parents were Japanese immigrants [Japanese, literally: second generation]

nisgul ('nɪsɡʌl) *n Midland English dialect* the smallest and weakest bird in a brood of chickens

nish (nɪʃ) *n Northern English dialect* nothing

Nishapur (ˌniːʃɑː'pʊə) *n* a town in NE Iran, at an altitude of 1195 m (3920 ft): birthplace and burial place of Omar Khayyám. Pop: 208 000 (2005 est)

Nishinomiya (ˌniːʃɪ'nɒmɪjə) *n* an industrial city

in central Japan, on S Honshu, northwest of Osaka. Pop: 436 877 (2002 est)

nisi ('naɪsaɪ) *adj* (*postpositive*) *law* (of a court order) coming into effect on a specified date unless cause is shown within a certain period why it should not: *a decree nisi* [C19 from Latin: unless, if not]

nisi prius ('praɪəs) *n* **1** *English legal history* **a** a direction that a case be brought up to Westminster for trial before a single judge and a jury **b** the writ giving this direction **c** trial before the justices taking the assizes **2** (in the US) a court where civil actions are tried by a single judge sitting with a jury as distinguished from an appellate court [C15 from Latin: unless previously]

Nissen hut ('nɪsᵊn) *n* a military shelter of semicircular cross section, made of corrugated steel sheet. US and Canadian equivalent: **Quonset hut** [C20 named after Lt Col. Peter *Nissen* (1871–1930), British mining engineer, its inventor]

nisus ('naɪsəs) *n, pl* -**sus** an impulse towards or striving after a goal [C17 from Latin: effort, from *nītī* to strive]

nit¹ (nɪt) *n* **1** the egg of a louse, usually adhering to human hair **2** the larva of a louse or similar insect [Old English *hnitu*; related to Dutch *neet*, Old High German *hniz*]

nit² (nɪt) *n* a unit of luminance equal to 1 candela per square metre [C20 from Latin *nitor* brightness]

nit³ (nɪt) *n informal, chiefly Brit* short for **nitwit**

nit⁴ (nɪt) *n* a unit of information equal to 1.44 bits. Also called: **nepit** [C20 from N(*apierian dig*)*it*]

nit⁵ (nɪt) *n* **keep nit** *Austral informal* to keep watch, esp during illegal activity [C19 from NIX¹]

niter ('naɪtə) *n* the usual US spelling of **nitre**

niterie ('naɪtərɪ, -trɪ) *n slang* a nightclub

Niterói (Portuguese niteˈrɔi) *n* a port in SE Brazil, on Guanabara Bay opposite Rio de Janeiro: contains Brazil's chief shipyards. Pop: 458 465 (2000). Also called: **Nictheroy**

nither ('naɪðə) *vb* (*intr*) *Northern English dialect* to shiver

nitid ('nɪtɪd) *adj poetic* bright; glistening [C17 from Latin *nitidus*, from *nitēre* to shine]

niton ('naɪtɒn) *n* a less common name for **radon** [C20 from Latin *nitēre* to shine]

nit-pick *vb* (*intr*) *informal* to raise petty objections or concern oneself with insignificant details

nit-picking *informal* ▷ *n* **1** a concern with insignificant details, esp with the intention of finding fault ▷ *adj* **2** showing such a concern; fussy [C20 from NIT¹ + PICK¹] ▷ **'nit-picker** *n*

nit-picky *adj informal* tending to raise petty objections; pernickety

nitramine ('naɪtrəˌmiːn) *n* another name for **tetryl**

nitrate ('naɪtreɪt) *n* **1** any salt or ester of nitric acid, such as sodium nitrate, NaNO₃ **2** a fertilizer consisting of or containing nitrate salts ▷ *vb* **3** (*tr*) to treat with nitric acid or a nitrate **4** to convert or be converted into a nitrate **5** to undergo or cause to undergo the chemical process in which a nitro group is introduced into a molecule ▷ **niˈtration** *n*

nitrazepam (naɪˈtreɪzɪˌpæm, naɪˈtræz-) *n* a synthetic chemical compound belonging to the benzodiazepine group of drugs; a minor tranquillizer used mainly in sleeping tablets, such as Mogadon. Formula: C₁₅H₁₁N₃O₃ [C20 from NITRO- + -*azepam*; see DIAZEPAM]

nitre *or US* **niter** ('naɪtə) *n* another name for **potassium nitrate** *or* **sodium nitrate** [C14 via Old French from Latin *nitrum*, from Greek *nitron* NATRON]

nitric ('naɪtrɪk) *adj* of or containing nitrogen, esp in the pentavalent state

nitric acid *n* a colourless or yellowish fuming corrosive liquid usually used in aqueous solution. It is an oxidizing agent and a strong monobasic acid: important in the manufacture of fertilizers, explosives, and many other chemicals. Formula: HNO₃. Former name: **aqua fortis**

nitric bacteria *pl n* bacteria that convert nitrites to nitrates in the soil. See also **nitrobacteria**

nitric oxide *n* a colourless slightly soluble gas forming red fumes of nitrogen dioxide in air. Formula: NO. Systematic name: **nitrogen monoxide**

nitride ('naɪtraɪd) *n* a compound of nitrogen with a more electropositive element, for example magnesium nitride, Mg₃N₂

nitriding ('naɪtraɪdɪŋ) *n* a type of case-hardening in which steel is heated for long periods in ammonia vapour so that nitrogen produced by dissociation on the surface enters the steel

nitrification (ˌnaɪtrɪfɪˈkeɪʃən) *n* **1** the oxidation of the ammonium compounds in dead organic material into nitrites and nitrates by soil nitrobacteria, making nitrogen available to plants. See also **nitrogen cycle 2 a** the addition of a nitro group to an organic compound **b** the substitution of a nitro group for another group in an organic compound

nitrify ('naɪtrɪˌfaɪ) *vb* -**fies**, -**fying**, -**fied** (*tr*) **1** to treat or cause to react with nitrogen or a nitrogen compound **2** to treat (soil) with nitrates **3** (of nitrobacteria) to convert (ammonium compounds) into nitrates by oxidation ▷ **'nitriˌfiable** *adj*

nitrile ('naɪtrɪl, -traɪl) *n* any one of a class of organic compounds containing the monovalent group, -CN. Also called (not in technical usage): **cyanide**

nitrite ('naɪtraɪt) *n* any salt or ester of nitrous acid

nitro ('naɪtrəʊ) *n slang* short for **nitroglycerine**

nitro- *or before a vowel* **nitr-** *combining form* **1** indicating that a chemical compound contains a nitro group, -NO₂: *nitrobenzene* **2** indicating that a chemical compound is a nitrate ester: *nitrocellulose* [from Greek *nitron* NATRON]

nitrobacteria (ˌnaɪtrəʊbækˈtɪərɪə) *pl n, sing* -**terium** (-ˈtɪərɪəm) soil bacteria of the order *Pseudomonadales* that are involved in nitrification, including species of *Nitrosomonas* and *Nitrobacter*

nitrobenzene (ˌnaɪtrəʊˈbɛnziːn) *n* a yellow oily toxic water-insoluble liquid compound, used as a solvent and in the manufacture of aniline. Formula: C₆H₅NO₂

nitrocellulose (ˌnaɪtrəʊˈsɛljʊˌləʊs) *n* another name (not in chemical usage) for **cellulose nitrate**

Nitro-chalk *n trademark* a chemical fertilizer containing calcium carbonate and ammonium nitrate

nitrochloroform (ˌnaɪtrəʊˈklɔːrəˌfɔːm) *n* another name for **chloropicrin**

nitro compound (ˈnaɪtrəʊ) *n* any one of a class of usually organic compounds that contain the monovalent group, -NO₂ (**nitro group** or **radical**), linked to a carbon atom. The commonest example is nitrobenzene, C₆H₅NO₂

nitrogen ('naɪtrədʒən) *n* **a** a colourless odourless relatively unreactive gaseous element that forms 78 per cent (by volume) of the air, occurs in many compounds, and is an essential constituent of proteins and nucleic acids: used in the manufacture of ammonia and other chemicals and as a refrigerant. Symbol: N; atomic no: 7; atomic wt: 14.00674; valency: 3 or 5; density: 1/2506 kg/m³; melting pt: –210.00°C; boiling pt: –195.80°C **b** (*as modifier*): *nitrogen cycle*

nitrogen cycle *n* the natural circulation of nitrogen by living organisms. Nitrates in the soil, derived from dead organic matter by bacterial action (see **nitrification**, **nitrogen fixation**), are absorbed and synthesized into complex organic compounds by plants and reduced to nitrates again when the plants and the animals feeding on them die and decay

nitrogen dioxide *n* a red-brown poisonous irritating gas that, at ordinary temperatures, exists in equilibrium with dinitrogen tetroxide. It is an intermediate in the manufacture of nitric acid, a nitrating agent, and also an oxidizer for

rocket fuels. Formula: NO₂

nitrogen fixation *n* **1** the conversion of atmospheric nitrogen into nitrogen compounds by certain bacteria, such as *Rhizobium* in the root nodules of legumes **2** a process, such as the Haber process, in which atmospheric nitrogen is converted into a nitrogen compound, used esp for the manufacture of fertilizer ▷ **'nitrogen-ˌfixing** *adj*

nitrogenize *or* **nitrogenise** (naɪˈtrɒdʒɪˌnaɪz) *vb* to combine or treat with nitrogen or a nitrogen compound ▷ **niˌtrogeniˈzation** *or* **niˌtrogeniˈsation** *n*

nitrogen monoxide *n* the systematic name for **nitric oxide**

nitrogen mustard *n* any of a class of organic compounds resembling mustard gas in their molecular structure. General formula: RN(CH₂CH₂Cl)₂, where R is an organic group: important in the treatment of cancer

nitrogenous (naɪˈtrɒdʒɪnəs) *adj* containing nitrogen or a nitrogen compound: *a nitrogenous fertilizer*

nitrogen peroxide *n* **1** an obsolete name for **nitrogen dioxide 2** the equilibrium mixture of nitrogen dioxide and dinitrogen tetroxide

nitrogen tetroxide *n* **1** another name for **dinitrogen tetroxide 2** a brown liquefied mixture of nitrogen dioxide and dinitrogen tetroxide, used as a nitrating, bleaching, and oxidizing agent

nitroglycerine (ˌnaɪtrəʊˈglɪsəˌriːn) *or* **nitroglycerin** (ˌnaɪtrəʊˈglɪsərɪn) *n* a pale yellow viscous explosive liquid substance made from glycerol and nitric and sulphuric acids and used in explosives and in medicine as a vasodilator. Formula: CH₂NO₃CHNO₃CH₂NO₃. Also called: **trinitroglycerine**

nitrohydrochloric acid (ˌnaɪtrəʊˌhaɪdrəʊˈklɒrɪk) *n* another name for **aqua regia**

nitrometer (naɪˈtrɒmɪtə) *n* an instrument for measuring the amount of nitrogen in a substance ▷ **nitrometric** (ˌnaɪtrəʊˈmɛtrɪk) *adj*

nitromethane (ˌnaɪtrəʊˈmiːθeɪn) *n* an oily colourless liquid obtained from methane and used as a solvent and rocket fuel and in the manufacture of synthetic resins. Formula: CH₃NO₂

nitroparaffin (ˌnaɪtrəʊˈpærəfɪn) *n* any of a class of colourless toxic compounds with the general formula CₙH₂ₙ₊₁NO₂

nitrophilous (naɪˈtrɒfɪləs) *adj* (of plants) growing in soil well supplied with nitrogen

nitrosamine (ˌnaɪtrəʊsəˈmiːn, ˌnaɪtrəʊsˈæmiːn) *n* any one of a class of neutral, usually yellow oily compounds containing the divalent group =NNO

nitroso (naɪˈtrəʊsəʊ) *n* (*modifier*) of, consisting of, or containing the monovalent group O:N-: *a nitroso compound* [C19 from Latin *nitrōsus* full of natron; see NITRE]

nitrosyl ('naɪtrəsɪl, -ˌsaɪl) *n* (*modifier*) another word for **nitroso**, esp when applied to inorganic compounds *nitrosyl chloride* [C19 see NITROSO]

nitrous ('naɪtrəs) *adj* of, derived from, or containing nitrogen, esp in a low valency state [C17 from Latin *nitrōsus* full of natron]

nitrous acid *n* a weak monobasic acid known only in solution and in the form of nitrite salts. Formula: HNO₂. Systematic name: **dioxonitric(III) acid**

nitrous bacteria *pl n* bacteria that convert ammonia to nitrites in the soil. See also **nitrobacteria**

nitrous oxide *n* a colourless nonflammable slightly soluble gas with a sweet smell: used as an anaesthetic in dentistry and surgery. Formula: N₂O. Systematic name: **dinitrogen oxide** Also called: **laughing gas**

nitty¹ ('nɪtɪ) *adj* -**tier**, -**tiest** infested with nits

nitty² ('nɪtɪ) *adj* -**tier**, -**tiest** *informal* foolish; stupid [C20 from NITWIT]

nitty-gritty ('nɪtɪˈgrɪtɪ) *n* the *informal* the basic facts of a matter, situation, etc; the core [C20 perhaps rhyming compound formed from GRIT]

nitwit ('nɪtˌwɪt) *n informal* a foolish person [C20

perhaps from NIT¹ + WIT¹]

Niue ('nju:eɪ) *n* an island in the S Pacific, between Tonga and the Cook Islands: annexed by New Zealand (1901); achieved full internal self-government in 1974. Chief town and port: Alofi. Pop: 2000 (2003 est). Area: 260 sq km (100 sq miles). Also called: **Savage Island**

Niuean (nju:'ɪən) *adj* **1** of or relating to the S Pacific island of Niue or its inhabitants ▷ *n* **2** a native or inhabitant of Niue

Niu Tireni or **Niu Tirani** ('ni:u 'ti:rɛni:, 'nu:-'ti:,rɛni:) *n* a Māori name for **New Zealand** [Māori: from a corruption of European names for New Zealand]

nival ('naɪvᵊl) *adj* of or growing in or under snow [c17 from Latin *nivālis*, from *nix* snow]

nivation (naɪ'veɪʃən) *n* the weathering of rock around a patch of snow by alternate freezing and thawing [c19 from Latin *nix*, stem *niv-* snow]

niveous ('nɪvɪəs) *adj* resembling snow, esp in colour [c17 from Latin *niveus*, from *nix* snow]

Nivernais (*French* niverne) *n* a former province of central France, around Nevers

Nivôse *French* (nivoz) *n* the fourth month of the French revolutionary calendar, extending from Dec 22 to Jan 20 [c18 via French from Latin *nivōsus* snowy, from *nix* snow]

nix¹ (nɪks) *US and Canadian informal* ▷ *sentence substitute* **1** another word for **no¹** (sense 1) **2** be careful! watch out! ▷ *n* **3** a rejection or refusal **4** nothing at all ▷ *vb* **5** (*tr*) to veto, deny, reject, or forbid (plans, suggestions, etc) [c18 from German, colloquial form of *nichts* nothing]

nix² (nɪks) *n German myth* a male water sprite, usually unfriendly to humans [c19 from German *Nixe* nymph or water spirit, from Old High German *nihhus*; related to Old English *nicor* sea monster]

nixer ('nɪksə) *n Dublin dialect* a spare-time job [from NIX¹, in the sense no (tax or insurance) + -ER¹]

nixie ('nɪksɪ) *n German myth* a female water sprite, usually unfriendly to humans [c19 see NIX]

Nixie tube ('nɪksɪ) *n electronics* another name for **digitron**

nizam (naɪ'zæm) *n* (formerly) a Turkish regular soldier [c18 ultimately from Arabic *nizām* order, arrangement]

Nizam (nɪ'zɑːm) *n* the title of the ruler of Hyderabad, India, from 1724 to 1948

Nizhni Novgorod (*Russian* 'niʒnij 'nɔvgərət) *n* a city and port in central Russia, at the confluence of the Volga and Oka Rivers: situated on the Volga route from the Baltic to central Asia; birthplace of Maxim Gorki. Pop: 1 288 000 (2005 est). Former name (1932–91): Gorki

Nizhni Tagil (*Russian* 'niʒnij ta'gil) *n* a city in central Russia, on the E slopes of the Ural Mountains: a major metallurgical centre. Pop: 382 000 (2005 est

NJ or **N.J.** *abbreviation for* New Jersey

Njord (njɔːd) or **Njorth** (njɔːθ) *n Norse myth* the god of the sea, fishing, and prosperity

NKGB *abbreviation for* (formerly) People's Commissariat of State Security: the Soviet secret police from 1943 to 46 [from Russian *Narodny komissariat gosudarstvennoi bezopasnosti*]

nkosi (ᵊŋ'kɔːsɪ) *n South African* a term of address to a superior; master; chief [Nguni *inkosi* chief, lord]

Nkosi Sikelel' iAfrica (ŋ'kɔsɪ ,sɪke'lɛlɪ ,afrɪ'ka) *n* the unofficial anthem of the Black people of South Africa, officially recognized as a national anthem (along with parts of 'Die Stem' and an English verse) in 1991 [from Xhosa, Lord Bless Africa]

NKVD *abbreviation for* (formerly) People's Commissariat of Internal Affairs: the Soviet police and secret police from 1934 to 1943: the police from 1943–46 [from Russian *Narodny komissariat vnutrennikh del* People's Commissariat of Internal Affairs]

nl¹ *abbreviation for* **1** non licet **2** non liquet [Latin:

(for sense 1) it is not permitted: (for sense 2) it is not clear]

nl² *the internet domain name for* the Netherlands

NL *abbreviation for* **1** New Latin **2** *international car registration for* the Netherlands

NLC *abbreviation for* National Liberal Club

NLF *abbreviation for* National Liberation Front

NLLST *abbreviation for* National Lending Library for Science and Technology

NLS *abbreviation for* National Library of Scotland

NLW *abbreviation for* National Library of Wales

nm *abbreviation for* **1** nautical mile **2** nanometre

NM or **N. Mex.** *abbreviation for* New Mexico

NMR *abbreviation for* nuclear magnetic resonance

NNE *symbol for* north-northeast

NNP *abbreviation for* **1** net national product **2** (in South Africa) New National Party

NNW *symbol for* north-northwest

no¹ (nəʊ) *sentence substitute* **1** used to express denial, disagreement, refusal, disapproval, disbelief, or acknowledgment of negative statements **2** used with question intonation to query a previous negative statement, as in disbelief: *Alfred isn't dead yet. No?* ▷ *n*, *pl* **noes** or **nos** **3** an answer or vote of *no* **4** (*often plural*) a person who votes in the negative **5** **the noes have it** there is a majority of votes in the negative **6** **not take no for an answer** to continue in a course of action despite refusals ▷ Compare **yes**, (for senses 3–5) **aye¹** [Old English *nā*, from *ne* not, no + *ā* ever; see AY¹]

no² (nəʊ) *determiner* **1** not any, not a, or not one: *there's no money left; no card in the file* **2** not by a long way; not at all: *she's no youngster* **3** (foll by comparative adjectives and adverbs) not: *no less than forty men; no more quickly than before* **4** **no go** See **go** (sense 74) [Old English *nā*, changed from *nān* NONE¹]

no³ *the internet domain name for* Norway

No¹ or **Noh** (nəʊ) *n*, *pl* **No** or **Noh** the stylized classic drama of Japan, developed in the 15th century or earlier, using music, dancing, chanting, elaborate costumes, and themes from religious stories or myths [from Japanese *nō* talent, from Chinese *neng*]

No² (nəʊ) *n Lake* a lake in the S central Sudan, where the Bahr el Jebel (White Nile) is joined by the Bahr el Ghazal. Area: about 103 sq km (40 sq miles)

No³ *the chemical symbol for* nobelium

No. *abbreviation for* **1** north(ern) **2** *pl* **Nos** or **nos** Also: **no.** number [from French *numéro*]

n.o. *cricket abbreviation for* not out

no' (no, nəʊ) *adv Scot* not

NO1 *text messaging abbreviation for* no-one

no-account *adj* **1** worthless; good-for-nothing ▷ *n* **2** a worthless person

Noachian (nəʊ'eɪkɪən) or **Noachic** (nəʊ'ækɪk, -'eɪkɪk) *adj Old Testament* of or relating to the patriarch Noah

noah ('nəʊə) *n Austral* a shark [from Australian rhyming slang *Noah's Ark*]

Noah ('nəʊə) *n Old Testament* a Hebrew patriarch, who saved himself, his family, and specimens of each species of animal and bird from the Flood by building a ship (**Noah's Ark**) in which they all survived (Genesis 6–8)

Noahide Laws ('nəʊə,haɪd) *pl n Judaism* the seven laws given to Noah after the Flood, which decree the establishment of a fair system of justice in society, and prohibit idolatry, blasphemy, murder, adultery and incest, robbery, and the eating of flesh taken from a living animal

nob¹ (nɒb) *n cribbage* **1** the jack of the suit turned up **2** **one for his nob** the call made with this jack, scoring one point [c19 of uncertain origin]

nob² (nɒb) *n slang, chiefly Brit* a person of social distinction [c19 of uncertain origin] ▷ '**nobby** *adj* ▷ '**nobbily** *adv*

nob³ (nɒb) *n slang* the head [c17 perhaps a variant of KNOB]

nob⁴ (nɒb) *n* a variant spelling of **knob** (sense 4)

no-ball *n* **1** *cricket* an illegal ball, as for overstepping the crease, throwing, etc, for which the batting side scores a run, and from which the batsman can be out only by being run out **2** *rounders* an illegal ball, esp one bowled too high or too low ▷ *sentence substitute* **3** *cricket, rounders* a call by the umpire indicating a no-ball ▷ *vb* **4** (*tr*) *cricket* (of an umpire) **a** to declare (a bowler) to have bowled a no-ball **b** to declare (a delivery) to be a no-ball

nobble ('nɒbᵊl) *vb* (*tr*) *Brit slang* **1** to disable (a racehorse), esp with drugs **2** to win over or outwit (a person) by underhand means **3** to suborn (a person, esp a juror) by threats, bribery, etc **4** to steal; filch **5** to get hold of; grab **6** to kidnap [c19 back formation from *nobbler*, from false division of *an hobbler* (one who hobbles horses) as *a nobbler*] ▷ '**nobbler** *n*

nobbut ('nɒbət) *adv dialect* nothing but; only [c14 from NO² + BUT¹]

nobelium (nəʊ'bi:lɪəm) *n* a transuranic element produced artificially from curium. Symbol: No; atomic no: 102; half-life of most stable isotope, ²⁵⁵No: 180 seconds (approx); valency: 2 or 3 [c20 New Latin, named after *Nobel* Institute, Stockholm, where it was discovered]

Nobel prize (nəʊ'bel) *n* a prize for outstanding contributions to chemistry, physics, physiology or medicine, literature, economics, and peace that may be awarded annually. It was established in 1901; the prize for economics being added in 1969. The recipients are chosen by an international committee centred in Sweden, except for the peace prize which is awarded in Oslo by a committee of the Norwegian parliament

nobiliary (nə'bɪlɪərɪ) *adj* of or relating to the nobility [c18 from French *nobiliaire*; see NOBLE, -ARY]

nobiliary particle *n* a preposition, such as French *de* or German *von*, occurring as part of a title or surname: *Marquis de Sade*

nobility (nəʊ'bɪlɪtɪ) *n*, *pl* -ties **1** a socially or politically privileged class whose titles are conferred by descent or by royal decree **2** the state or quality of being morally or spiritually good; dignity: *the nobility of his mind* **3** (in the British Isles) the class of people holding the title of dukes, marquesses, earls, viscounts, or barons and their feminine equivalents collectively; peerage

noble ('nəʊbᵊl) *adj* **1** of or relating to a hereditary class with special social or political status, often derived from a feudal period **2** of or characterized by high moral qualities; magnanimous: *a noble deed* **3** having dignity or eminence; illustrious **4** grand or imposing; magnificent: *a noble avenue of trees* **5** of superior quality or kind; excellent: *a noble strain of horses* **6** *chem* **a** (of certain elements) chemically unreactive **b** (of certain metals, esp copper, silver, and gold) resisting oxidation **7** *falconry* **a** designating long-winged falcons that capture their quarry by stooping on it from above. Compare **ignoble b** designating the type of quarry appropriate to a particular species of falcon ▷ *n* **8** a person belonging to a privileged social or political class whose status is usually indicated by a title conferred by sovereign authority or descent **9** (in the British Isles) a person holding the title of duke, marquess, earl, viscount, or baron, or a feminine equivalent **10** a former Brit gold coin having the value of one third of a pound [c13 via Old French from Latin *nōbilis*, originally, capable of being known, hence well-known, noble, from *noscere* to know] ▷ '**nobleness** *n* ▷ '**nobly** *adv*

noble art or **science** *n* the boxing

noble gas *n* another name for **inert gas** (sense 1)

nobleman ('nəʊbᵊlmən) *n*, *pl* -men a man of noble rank, title, or status; peer; aristocrat

noble rot *n* *winemaking* a condition in which grapes are deliberately affected by *Botrytis cinerea*, resulting in the shrivelling of the ripened grapes, which in turn leads to an increased sugar content

n

[C20 translation of French *pourriture noble*]

noble savage *n* (in romanticism) an idealized view of primitive man

noblesse (nəʊˈblɛs) *n literary* **1** noble birth or condition **2** the noble class [C13 from Old French; see NOBLE]

noblesse oblige (nəʊˈblɛs əʊˈbliːʒ; *French* nɔblɛs ɔbliʒ) *n often ironic* the supposed obligation of nobility to be honourable and generous [French, literally: nobility obliges]

noblewoman (ˈnəʊbəlˌwʊmən) *n, pl* -women a woman of noble rank, title, or status; peer; aristocrat

nobody (ˈnəʊbədɪ) *pron* **1** no person; no-one ▷ *n, pl* -bodies **2** an insignificant person

USAGE See at **everyone**

no-brainer (ˌnəʊˈbreɪnə) *n slang* something which requires little or no mental effort

nociceptive (ˌnəʊsɪˈsɛptɪv) *adj* causing or reacting to pain [C20 from Latin *nocēre* to injure + RECEPTIVE]

nocireceptor (ˈnəʊsɪrɪˌsɛptə) or **nociceptor** (ˈnəʊsɪˌsɛptə) *n physiol* a receptor sensitive to pain

nock (nɒk) *n* **1** a notch on an arrow that fits on the bowstring **2** either of the grooves at each end of a bow that hold the bowstring ▷ *vb* (*tr*) **3** to fit (an arrow) on a bowstring **4** to put a groove or notch in (a bow or arrow) [C14 related to Swedish *nock* tip]

nocking point *n* a marked part of the bowstring where the arrow is placed

no-claims bonus *n* a reduction on an insurance premium, esp one covering a motor vehicle, if no claims have been made within a specified period. Also called: **no-claim bonus**

noctambulism (nɒkˈtæmbjʊˌlɪzəm) or **noctambulation** (nɒkˌtæmbjʊˈleɪʃən) *n* another word for **somnambulism** [C19 from Latin *nox* night + *ambulāre* to walk] > nocˈtambulist *n*

nocti- or before a vowel **noct-** *combining form* night: *noctilucent* [from Latin *nox, noct-*]

noctiluca (ˌnɒktɪˈluːkə) *n, pl* -cae (-siː) any bioluminescent marine dinoflagellate of the genus *Noctiluca* [C17 from Latin, from *nox* night + *lūcēre* to shine]

noctilucent (ˌnɒktɪˈluːsənt) *adj* shining at night, usu. of very thin high altitude clouds observable in the summer twilight sky > ˌnoctiˈlucence *n*

noctuid (ˈnɒktjʊɪd) *n* **1** any nocturnal moth of the family *Noctuidae*: includes the underwings and antler moth. See also **cutworm, army worm** ▷ *adj* **2** of, relating to, or belonging to the *Noctuidae* [C19 via New Latin from Latin *noctua* night owl, from *nox* night]

noctule (ˈnɒktjuːl) *n* any of several large Old World insectivorous bats of the genus *Nyctalus*, esp *N. noctula*: family Vespertilionidae [C18 probably from Late Latin *noctula* small owl, from Latin *noctua* night owl]

nocturia (nɒkˈtjʊərɪə) *n* abnormally excessive urination during the night

nocturn (ˈnɒktɜːn) *n RC Church* any of the main sections of the office of matins [C13 from Medieval Latin *nocturna* (n), from Latin *nocturnus* nocturnal, from *nox* night]

nocturnal (nɒkˈtɜːnəl) *adj* **1** of, used during, occurring in, or relating to the night **2** (of animals) active at night **3** (of plants) having flowers that open at night and close by day ▷ Compare **diurnal** [C15 from Late Latin *nocturnālis*, from Latin *nox* night] > nocˈturnality *n* > nocˈturnally *adv*

nocturne (ˈnɒktɜːn) *n* **1** a short, lyrical piece of music, esp one for the piano **2** a painting or tone poem of a night scene

nocuous (ˈnɒkjʊəs) *adj rare* harmful; noxious [C17 from Latin *nocuus*, from *nocēre* to hurt] > ˈnocuously *adv* > ˈnocuousness *n*

nod (nɒd) *vb* nods, nodding, nodded **1** to lower and raise (the head) briefly, as to indicate agreement, invitation, etc **2** (*tr*) to express or indicate by nodding: *she nodded approval* **3** (*tr*) to

bring or direct by nodding: *she nodded me towards the manager's office* **4** (*intr*) (of flowers, trees, etc) to sway or bend forwards and back **5** (*intr*) to let the head fall forward through drowsiness; be almost asleep: *the old lady sat nodding by the fire* **6** (*intr*) to be momentarily inattentive or careless: *even Homer sometimes nods* **7** nodding acquaintance a slight, casual, or superficial knowledge (of a subject or a person) ▷ *n* **8** a quick down-and-up movement of the head, as in assent, command, etc: *she greeted him with a nod* **9** a short sleep; nap. See also **land of Nod** **10** a swaying motion, as of flowers, etc, in the wind **11** on the nod *informal* **a** agreed, as in a committee meeting, without any formal procedure **b** (formerly) on credit **12** the nod *boxing informal* the award of a contest to a competitor on the basis of points scored ▷ See also **nod off, nod out** [C14 *nodde*, of obscure origin] > ˈnodding *adj, n*

nodal (ˈnəʊdəl) *adj* of or like a node > noˈdality *n* > ˈnodally *adv*

nodding dog *n* a small model of a dog carried as a mascot in a motor vehicle, with a head so mounted that it moves up and down with the motion of the vehicle

nodding donkey *n informal* (in the oil industry) a type of reciprocating pump used to extract oil from an inland well [C20 so called from its shape and movement]

noddle[1] (ˈnɒdəl) *n informal, chiefly Brit* the head or brains: *use your noddle!* [C15 origin obscure]

noddle[2] (ˈnɒdəl) *vb informal, chiefly Brit* to nod (the head), as through drowsiness [C18 from NOD]

noddy[1] (ˈnɒdɪ) *n, pl* -dies **1** any of several tropical terns of the genus *Anous*, esp *A. stolidus* (**common noddy**), typically having a dark plumage **2** a fool or dunce [C16 perhaps noun use of obsolete *noddy* foolish, drowsy, perhaps from NOD (vb); the bird is so called because it allows itself to be caught by hand]

noddy[2] (ˈnɒdɪ) *n, pl* -dies (*usually plural*) television film footage of an interviewer's reactions to comments made by an interviewee, used in editing the interview after it has been recorded [C20 from NOD]

noddy[3] (ˈnɒdɪ) *adj informal* very easy to use or understand; simplistic [C20 origin unknown]

node (nəʊd) *n* **1** a knot, swelling, or knob **2** the point on a plant stem from which the leaves or lateral branches grow **3** *physics* a point at which the amplitude of one of the two kinds of displacement in a standing wave has zero or minimum value. Generally the other kind of displacement has its maximum value at this point. See also **standing wave** Compare **antinode** **4** Also called: crunode *maths* a point at which two branches of a curve intersect, each branch having a distinct tangent **5** *maths, linguistics* one of the objects of which a graph or a tree consists; vertex **6** *astronomy* either of the two points at which the orbit of a body intersects the plane of the ecliptic. When the body moves from the south to the north side of the ecliptic it passes the **ascending node** and from the north to the south side it passes the **descending node** **7** *anatomy* **a** any natural bulge or swelling of a structure or part, such as those that occur along the course of a lymphatic vessel (**lymph node**) **b** a finger joint or knuckle **8** *computing* an interconnection point on a computer network ▷ See also **nod off, nod out** [C16 from Latin *nōdus* knot]

node house *n* a prefabricated shelter used by welders during the construction of an oil rig

node of Ranvier (ˈrɑːnvɪˌeɪ) *n* any of the gaps that occur at regular intervals along the length of the sheath of a myelinated nerve fibre, at which the axon is exposed [C19 named after Louis-Antoine *Ranvier* (1835–1922), French histologist]

nodical (ˈnəʊdɪkəl, ˈnɒdɪ-) *adj* of or relating to the nodes of a celestial body, esp of the moon

nodical month *n* another name for **draconic month**

nod off *vb* (*intr, adverb*) *informal* to fall asleep

nodose (ˈnəʊdəʊs, nəʊˈdəʊs) or **nodous** (ˈnəʊdəs) *adj* having nodes or knotlike swellings: *nodose stems* [C18 from Latin *nōdōsus* knotty] > nodosity (nəʊˈdɒsɪtɪ)

nod out *vb* (*intr, adverb*) *slang* to lapse into stupor, esp on heroin

nodule (ˈnɒdjuːl) *n* **1** a small knot, lump, or node **2** Also called: root nodule any of the knoblike outgrowths on the roots of clover and many other legumes: contain bacteria involved in nitrogen fixation **3** *anatomy* any small node or knoblike protuberance **4** a small rounded lump of rock or mineral substance, esp in a matrix of different rock material [C17 from Latin *nōdulus*, from *nōdus* knot] > ˈnodular, ˈnodulose or ˈnodulous *adj*

nodus (ˈnəʊdəs) *n, pl* -di (-daɪ) **1** a problematic idea, situation, etc **2** another word for **node** [C14 from Latin: knot]

Noel or **Noël** (nəʊˈɛl) *n* **1** (esp in carols) another word for **Christmas** **2** (*often not capital*) *rare* a Christmas carol [C19 from French, from Latin *nātālis* a birthday; see NATAL]

noesis (nəʊˈiːsɪs) *n* **1** *philosophy* the exercise of reason, esp in the apprehension of universal forms. Compare **dianoia** **2** *psychol* the mental process used in thinking and perceiving; the functioning of the intellect. See also **cognition** [C19 from Greek *noēsis* thought, from *noein* to think]

noetic (nəʊˈɛtɪk) *adj* of or relating to the mind, esp to its rational and intellectual faculties [C17 from Greek *noētikos*, from *noein* to think, from *nous* the mind]

no-fly zone *n* **1** an area in which aeroplanes may not fly, esp during wartime **2** a taboo subject

nog[1] or **nogg** (nɒg) *n* **1** Also called: flip a drink, esp an alcoholic one, containing beaten egg **2** *East Anglian dialect* strong local beer [C17 (originally: a strong beer): of obscure origin]

nog[2] (nɒg) *n* **1** a wooden peg or block built into a masonry or brick wall to provide a fixing for nails **2** short for **nogging** (sense 1) [C17 origin unknown]

noggin (ˈnɒgɪn) *n* **1** a small quantity of spirits, usually 1 gill **2** a small mug or cup **3** an informal word for **head** (sense 1) [C17 of obscure origin]

nogging (ˈnɒgɪŋ) *n* **1** Also called: nog, (Scot and NZ) dwang a short horizontal timber member used between the studs of a framed partition **2** masonry or brickwork between the timber members of a framed construction **3** a number of wooden pieces fitted between the timbers of a half-timbered wall

no-go area *n* **1** a district in a town that is barricaded off, usually by a paramilitary organization, within which the police, army, etc, can only enter by force **2** an area that is barred to certain individuals, groups, etc

Noh (nəʊ) *n* a variant spelling of No[1]

no-hoper *n informal* a useless person; failure

nohow (ˈnəʊˌhaʊ) *adv not standard* (in negative constructions) **a** under any conditions **b** in any manner

NOI *abbreviation for* **Nation of Islam**

noil (nɔɪl) *n textiles* the short or knotted fibres that are separated from the long fibres, or staple, by combing [C17 of unknown origin]

nointer (ˈnɔɪntə) *n Austral slang* a mischievous child; rascal

noir (nwɑː) *adj* (of a film) showing characteristics of a *film noir*, in plot or style

noise (nɔɪz) *n* **1** a sound, esp one that is loud or disturbing **2** loud shouting; clamour; din **3** any undesired electrical disturbance in a circuit, degrading the useful information in a signal. See also **signal-to-noise ratio** **4** undesired or irrelevant elements in a visual image: *removing noise from pictures* **5** talk or interest: *noise about strikes* **6** (*plural*) conventional comments or sounds conveying a reaction, attitude, feeling, etc: *she made sympathetic noises* **7** make a noise to talk a great deal or complain **8** make noises about *informal* to give indications of one's intentions: *the government is making noises about new social security arrangements* **9 noises off** *theatre* sounds made offstage intended for the ears of the audience: used as a stage direction ▷ *vb* **10** (*tr*; usually foll by *abroad* or *about*) to spread (news, gossip, etc) **11** (*intr*) *rare* to talk loudly or at length **12** (*intr*) *rare* to make a din or outcry; be noisy [c13 from Old French, from Latin: NAUSEA]

noise generator *n* **1** a device used in synthesizers to produce high-frequency sound effects **2** a generator of electronic noise used to test equipment

noiseless ('nɔɪzlɪs) *adj* making little or no sound; silent > 'noiselessly *adv* > 'noiselessness *n*

noisemaker ('nɔɪz,meɪkə) *n US and Canadian* something, such as a clapper or bell, used to make a loud noise at football matches, celebrations, etc > 'noise,making *n, adj*

noisenik ('nɔɪznɪk) *n* a rock musician who performs loud harsh music

noise pollution *n* annoying or harmful noise in an environment

noisette (nwɑː'zɛt) *adj* **1** flavoured or made with hazelnuts ▷ *n* **2** a small round boneless slice of lamb from the fillet or leg **3** a chocolate made with hazelnuts [from French: hazelnut]

noisome ('nɔɪsəm) *adj* **1** (esp of smells) offensive **2** harmful or noxious [c14 from obsolete *noy*, variant of ANNOY + -SOME¹] > 'noisomely *adv* > 'noisomeness *n*

noisy ('nɔɪzɪ) *adj* noisier, noisiest **1** making a loud or constant noise **2** full of or characterized by noise > 'noisily *adv* > 'noisiness *n*

noisy miner *n* a honey-eater, *Manorina melanocephala*, of eastern Australia, having a grey-white plumage and brown wings and noted for its raucous cries

nolens volens Latin ('nəʊlɛnz 'vəʊlɛnz) *adv* whether willing or unwilling

noli-me-tangere ('nəʊlɪˌmeɪ'tæŋgərɪ) *n* **1** a warning against interfering or against touching a person or thing **2** a work of art depicting Christ appearing to Mary Magdalene after His Resurrection **3** another name for **touch-me-not 4** a cancerous ulcer affecting soft tissue and bone [from Latin: do not touch me, the words spoken by Christ to Mary Magdalene (Vulgate, John 20:17)]

nolle prosequi ('nɒlɪ 'prɒsɪˌkwaɪ) *n law* an entry made on the court record when the plaintiff in a civil suit or prosecutor in a criminal prosecution undertakes not to continue the action or prosecution. Compare **non prosequitur** [Latin: do not pursue (prosecute)]

nolo contendere ('nəʊləʊ kɒn'tɛndərɪ) *n law, chiefly US* a plea made by a defendant to a criminal charge having the same effect in those proceedings as a plea of guilty but not precluding him from denying the charge in a subsequent action [Latin: I do not wish to contend]

nol. pros. *or* **nolle pros.** *abbreviation for* nolle prosequi

nom. *abbreviation for* **1** nominal **2** nominative

noma ('nəʊmə) *n* a gangrenous inflammation of the mouth, esp one affecting malnourished children [c19 New Latin, from Latin *nomē* ulcer, from Greek *nomē* feeding; related to Greek *nemein* to feed]

nomad ('nəʊmæd) *n* **1** a member of a people or tribe who move from place to place to find pasture and food **2** a person who continually moves from place to place; wanderer [c16 via French from Latin *nomas* wandering shepherd, from Greek; related to *nemein* to feed, pasture] > 'nomadism *n*

nomadic (nəʊ'mædɪk) *adj* relating to or characteristic of nomads or their way of life > no'madically *adv*

nomadize *or* **nomadise** ('nəʊmæd,aɪz) *vb* **1** (*intr*) to live as nomads **2** (*tr*) to make into nomads **3** (*tr*) to people (a place) with nomads

no-man's-land *n* **1** land between boundaries, esp

an unoccupied zone between opposing forces **2** an unowned or unclaimed piece of land **3** an ambiguous area of activity or thought

nomarch ('nɒmɑːk) *n* **1** the head of an ancient Egyptian nome **2** the senior administrator in a Greek nomarchy [c17 from Greek *nomarkhēs*]

nomarchy ('nɒmɑːkɪ, -əkɪ) *n, pl* -chies any of the provinces of modern Greece; nome [c19 from Greek; see NOME, -ARCHY]

no-mates *adj slang* (*used postpositively after a name*) designating a person with no friends: *Norman No-Mates*

nombles ('nʌmbᵊlz) *pl n* a variant spelling of numbles

nombril ('nɒmbrɪl) *n heraldry* a point on a shield between the fesse point and the lowest point [c16 from French, literally: navel]

nom de guerre ('nɒm də 'gɛə) *n, pl* noms de guerre ('nɒm də 'gɛə) an assumed name; pseudonym [French, literally: war name]

nom de plume ('nɒm də 'pluːm) *n, pl* noms de plume ('nɒm də 'pluːm) another term for **pen name**

nome (nəʊm) *n* **1** any of the former provinces of modern Greece; nomarchy **2** an administrative division of ancient Egypt [c18 from Greek *nomos* pasture, region]

nomen ('nəʊmɛn) *n, pl* nomina ('nɒmɪnə) an ancient Roman's second name, designating his gens or clan. See also **agnomen, cognomen, praenomen** [Latin: a name]

nomenclator ('nəʊmen,kleɪtə) *n* a person who invents or assigns names, as in scientific classification [c16 from Latin, from *nōmen* name + *calāre* to call]

nomenclature (nəʊ'mɛnklətʃə; US 'nəʊmən,kleɪtʃər) *n* the terminology used in a particular science, art, activity, etc [c17 from Latin *nōmenclātūra* list of names; see NOMENCLATOR]

nomenklatura (,nəʊmɛnklə'tʃʊːrə) *n* (formerly, in the USSR and E Europe) a list of individuals drawn up by the Communist Party from which were selected candidates for vacant senior positions in the state, party, and other important organizations [c20 Russian, from Latin *nōmenclātūra* list of names]

nominal ('nɒmɪnᵊl) *adj* **1** in name only; theoretical: *the nominal leader* **2** minimal in comparison with real worth or what is expected; token: *a nominal fee* **3** of, relating to, constituting, bearing, or giving a name **4** *grammar* of or relating to a noun or noun phrase ▷ *n* **5** *grammar* a nominal element; a noun, noun phrase, or syntactically similar structure **6** *bell-ringing* the harmonic an octave above the strike tone of a bell [c15 from Latin *nōminālis* of a name, from *nōmen* name] > 'nominally *adv*

nominal aphasia *n* aphasia in which the primary symptom is an inability to recall or recognize the names of objects

nominalism ('nɒmɪnᵊ,lɪzəm) *n* the philosophical theory that the variety of objects to which a single general word, such as *dog*, applies have nothing in common but the name. Compare **conceptualism, realism.** > 'nominalist *n, adj* > ,nominal'istic *adj*

nominal scale *n statistics* a discrete classification of data, in which data are neither measured nor ordered but subjects are merely allocated to distinct categories: for example, a record of students' course choices constitutes nominal data which could be correlated with school results. Compare **ordinal scale, interval scale, ratio scale**

nominal value *n* another name for **par value**

nominal wages *pl n* another name for **money wages**

nominate *vb* ('nɒmɪ,neɪt) (*mainly tr*) **1** to propose as a candidate, esp for an elective office **2** to appoint to an office or position **3** to name (someone) to act on one's behalf, esp to conceal one's identity **4** (*intr*) *Austral* to stand as a candidate in an election **5** *archaic* to name, entitle, or designate ▷ *adj* ('nɒmɪnɪt) **6** *rare*

having a particular name [c16 from Latin *nōmināre* to call by name, from *nōmen* name] > 'nomi,nator *n*

nomination (,nɒmɪ'neɪʃən) *n* the act of nominating or state of being nominated, esp as an election candidate

nominative ('nɒmɪnətɪv, 'nɒmnə-) *adj* **1** *grammar* denoting a case of nouns and pronouns in inflected languages that is used esp to identify the subject of a finite verb. See also **subjective** (sense 6) **2** appointed rather than elected to a position, office, etc **3** bearing the name of a person ▷ *n* **4** *grammar* **a** the nominative case **b** a word or speech element in the nominative case [c14 from Latin *nōminātīvus* belonging to naming, from *nōmen* name] > nominatival (,nɒmɪnə'taɪvᵊl, ,nɒmnə-) *adj* > 'nominatively *adv*

nominee (,nɒmɪ'niː) *n* **1** a person who is nominated to an office or as a candidate **2 a** a person or organization named to act on behalf of someone else, esp to conceal the identity of the nominator **b** (*as modifier*): *nominee shareholder* [c17 from NOMINATE + -EE]

nomism ('nəʊmɪzəm) *n* adherence to a law or laws as a primary exercise of religion [c20 from Greek *nomos* law, custom] > no'mistic *adj*

nomo- *combining form* indicating law or custom: *nomology* [from Greek *nomos* law, custom]

nomocracy (nɒ'mɒkrəsɪ, nəʊ-) *n, pl* -cies government based on the rule of law rather than arbitrary will, terror, etc [c19 from Greek, from *nomos* law + -CRACY]

nomogram ('nɒmə,græm, 'nəʊmə-) *or* **nomograph** *n* **1** an arrangement of two linear or logarithmic scales such that an intersecting straight line enables intermediate values or values on a third scale to be read off **2** any graphic representation of numerical relationships [c20 from Greek *nomos* law + -GRAM, on the model of French *nomogramme*]

nomography (nɒ'mɒgrəfɪ) *n, pl* -phies the science of constructing nomographs. See **nomogram.** > no'mographer *n* > nomographic (,nɒmə'græfɪk) *or* ,nomo'graphical *adj* > ,nomo'graphically *adv*

nomological (,nɒmə'lɒdʒɪkᵊl) *adj* **1** of or relating to nomology **2** stating or relating to a nonlogical necessity or law of nature. The difference between a nomological and a merely universal statement is that from the universal *all As are Bs* one cannot, but from the nomological *all As must be Bs* one can, infer the counterfactual *if this were an A it would (have to) be a B* > ,nomo'logically *adv*

nomology (nɒm'ɒlədʒɪ) *n* **1** the science of law and law-making **2** the branch of science concerned with the formulation of laws explaining natural phenomena > no'mologist *n*

nomothetic (,nɒmə'θɛtɪk) *or* **nomothetical** *adj* **1** giving or enacting laws; legislative **2** *psychol* of or relating to the search for general laws or traits, esp in personality theory. Compare **idiographic** [c17 from Greek *nomothetikos*, from *nomothetēs* lawgiver]

-nomy *n combining form* indicating a science or the laws governing a certain field of knowledge: *agronomy; economy* [from Greek *-nomia* law; related to *nemein* to distribute, control] > -nomic *adj combining form*

non- *prefix* **1** indicating negation: *nonexistent* **2** indicating refusal or failure: *noncooperation* **3** indicating exclusion from a specified class of persons or things: *nonfiction* **4** indicating lack or absence, esp of a quality associated with what is specified: *nonobjective; nonevent* [from Latin *nōn* not]

nona- *or before a vowel* **non-** *combining form* nine: *nonagon* [from Latin *nōnus*]

nonacademic (,nɒnækə'dɛmɪk) *adj* not related to, involved in, or trained in academic disciplines

nonacceptance (,nɒnək'sɛptəns) *n* the act or an instance of not accepting or being accepted

nonaccidental injury (,nɒnæksɪ'dɛntᵊl) *n social welfare* damage, such as a bruise, burn, or fracture, deliberately inflicted on a child or an old person. Abbreviation: NAI See also **child abuse**

n

nonaddictive (ˌnɒnəˈdɪktɪv) *adj* not of, relating to, or causing addiction

nonage (ˈnəʊnɪdʒ) *n* **1** *law* the state of being under any of various ages at which a person may legally enter into certain transactions, such as the making of binding contracts, marrying, etc **2** any period of immaturity

nonagenarian (ˌnəʊnədʒɪˈnɛərɪən) *n* **1** a person who is from 90 to 99 years old ▷ *adj* **2** of, relating to, or denoting a nonagenarian [c19 from Latin *nōnāgēnārius,* from *nōnāginta* ninety]

nonaggression (ˌnɒnəˈɡrɛʃən) *n* **a** restraint of aggression, esp between states **b** (*as modifier*): *a nonaggression pact*

nonagon (ˈnɒnəˌɡɒn) *n* a polygon having nine sides. Also called: enneagon > **nonagonal** (nɒnˈæɡən°l) *adj*

nonagricultural (ˌnɒnəɡrɪˈkʌltʃərəl) *adj* not of or relating to agriculture

nonalcoholic (ˌnɒnælkəˈhɒlɪk) *adj* not containing alcohol: *nonalcoholic drinks*

nonaligned (ˌnɒnəˈlaɪnd) *adj* (of states) not part of a major alliance or power bloc, esp not allied to the US, China, or formerly the Soviet Union > ˌnonaˈlignment *n*

nonanoic acid (ˌnɒnəˈnəʊɪk) *n* a colourless oily fatty acid with a rancid odour: used in making pharmaceuticals, lacquers, and plastics. Formula: $CH_3(CH_2)_7COOH$. Also called: pelargonic acid [c19 from *nonane* a paraffin, ninth in the methane series, from Latin *nōnus* ninth + -ANE]

non-A, non-B hepatitis *n* a form of viral hepatitis, not caused by the agents responsible for hepatitis A and hepatitis B, that is commonly transmitted by infected blood transfusions. The causative virus has been isolated. Also called: hepatitis C

nonappearance (ˌnɒnəˈpɪərəns) *n* failure to appear or attend, esp as a defendant or witness in court

nonattendance (ˌnɒnəˈtɛndəns) *n* the act or an instance of not attending an event, meeting, etc

nonbeing (nɒnˈbiːɪŋ) *n* the philosophical problem arising from the fact that the ability to refer appears to presuppose the existence of whatever is referred to, and yet we can talk intelligibly about nonexistent objects. See also **subsistence** (sense 5)

nonbeliever (ˌnɒnbɪˈliːvə) *n* a person who does not believe, esp in God and religion

nonbiological (ˌnɒnbaɪəˈlɒdʒɪkəl) *adj* **1** not related by birth: *nonbiological mother* **2** (of a detergent) not containing enzymes said to be capable of removing stains of organic origin from items to be washed **3** not of or relating to biology

non-Catholic *adj* **1** not of or relating to the Roman Catholic Church ▷ *n* **2** a person who does not practise Roman Catholicism

nonce¹ (nɒns) *n* the present time or occasion (now only in the phrase **for the nonce**) [c12 from the phrase *for the nonce,* a mistaken division of *for then anes,* literally: for the once, from *then* dative singular of *the* + *anes* ONCE]

nonce² (nɒns) *n prison slang* a rapist or child molester; a sexual offender [c20 of unknown origin]

nonce word *n* a word coined for a single occasion

nonchalant (ˈnɒnʃələnt) *adj* casually unconcerned or indifferent; uninvolved [c18 from French, from *nonchaloir* to lack warmth, from NON- + *chaloir,* from Latin *calēre* to be warm] > ˈnonchalance *n* > ˈnonchalantly *adv*

non-Christian *adj* **1** (of a person, country, etc) not adhering to the Christian faith ▷ *n* **2** a person who does not adhere to the Christian faith

noncognitivism (nɒnˈkɒɡnɪˌtɪˌvɪzəm) *n philosophy* the semantic meta-ethical thesis that moral judgments do not express facts and so do not have a truth value thus excluding both naturalism and non-naturalism. See **emotivism, prescriptivism**

non-com (ˈnɒnˌkɒm) *n US* short for **noncommissioned officer**

noncombatant (nɒnˈkɒmbətənt) *n* **1** a civilian in time of war **2** a member of the armed forces whose duties do not include fighting, such as a chaplain or surgeon

noncommercial (ˌnɒnkəˈmɜːʃəl) *adj* not of, connected with, or involved in commerce: *noncommercial organizations*

noncommissioned officer (ˌnɒnkəˈmɪʃənd) *n* (in the armed forces) a person, such as a sergeant or corporal, who is appointed from the ranks as a subordinate officer

noncommittal (ˌnɒnkəˈmɪt°l) *adj* **1** not involving or revealing commitment to any particular opinion or course of action: *a noncommittal reply* **2** *rare* having no outstanding quality, meaning, etc

noncommunist (nɒnˈkɒmjʊnɪst) *adj* **1** relating to a government or state that does not practise communism ▷ *n* **2** a person who does not practise communism: *re-enter politics as a noncommunist*

noncompetitive (ˌnɒnkəmˈpɛtɪtɪv) *adj* not involving or determined by rivalry or competition

noncompliance (ˌnɒnkəmˈplaɪəns) *n* the act or state of not complying

non compos mentis *Latin* (ˈnɒn ˈkɒmpəs ˈmɛntɪs) *adj* mentally incapable of managing one's own affairs; of unsound mind [Latin: not in control of one's mind]

nonconductor (ˌnɒnkənˈdʌktə) *n* a substance that is a poor conductor of heat, electricity, or sound

nonconformist (ˌnɒnkənˈfɔːmɪst) *n* **1** a person who does not conform to generally accepted patterns of behaviour or thought ▷ *adj* **2** of or characterized by behaviour that does not conform to generally accepted patterns > ˌnonconˈformism *n*

Nonconformist (ˌnɒnkənˈfɔːmɪst) *n* **1** a member of a Protestant denomination that dissents from an Established Church, esp the Church of England ▷ *adj* **2** of, relating to, or denoting Nonconformists > ˌNonconˈformity *or* ˌNonconˈformism *n*

nonconformity (ˌnɒnkənˈfɔːmɪtɪ) *n* **1** failure or refusal to conform **2** absence of agreement or harmony

noncontributory (ˌnɒnkənˈtrɪbjʊtərɪ, -trɪ) *adj* **1 a** denoting an insurance or pension scheme for employees, the premiums of which are paid entirely by the employer **b** (of a state benefit) not dependent on national insurance contributions **2** not providing contribution; noncontributing

noncontroversial (ˌnɒnkɒntrəˈvɜːʃəl) *adj* not causing dispute, argument, debate, etc

nonconventional (ˌnɒnkənˈvɛnʃən°l) *adj* **1** not established by accepted usage or general agreement; non-traditional: *a nonconventional lifestyle* **2** (of weapons, warfare, etc) nuclear or chemical

noncooperation (ˌnɒnkəʊˌɒpəˈreɪʃən) *n* **1** failure or refusal to cooperate **2** refusal to pay taxes, obey government decrees, etc, as a protest > **noncooperative** (ˌnɒnkəʊˈɒpərətɪv) *adj* > ˌnoncoˈoperator *n*

noncritical (nɒnˈkrɪtɪk°l) *adj* not containing or making severe or negative judgments

nondemocratic (ˌnɒndɛməˈkrætɪk) *adj* not adhering to the principles or practice of democracy

nondenominational (ˌnɒndɪˌnɒmɪˈneɪʃən°l) *adj* not of or related to any religious denomination

nondescript (ˈnɒndɪˌskrɪpt) *adj* **1** lacking distinct or individual characteristics; having no outstanding features ▷ *n* **2** a nondescript person or thing [c17 from NON- + Latin *dēscriptus,* past participle of *dēscribere* to copy, DESCRIBE]

nondestructive testing (ˌnɒndɪˈstrʌktɪv) *n* any of several methods of detecting flaws in metals without causing damage. The most common techniques involve the use of X-rays, gamma rays, and ultrasonic vibrations. Abbreviation: NDT

nondirective therapy (ˌnɒndɪˈrɛktɪv, ˌnɒndaɪ) *n*

psychiatry another name for **client-centred therapy**

nondisjunction (ˌnɒndɪsˈdʒʌŋkʃən) *n* the failure of paired homologous chromosomes to move to opposite poles of the cell during meiosis

nondomiciled (nɒnˈdɒmɪsaɪld) *adj* of, relating to, or denoting a person who is not domiciled in his country of origin

nondrinker (nɒnˈdrɪŋkə) *n* someone who does not drink alcohol

nondrip (nɒnˈdrɪp) *adj* (of paint) specially formulated to minimize dripping during application

none¹ (nʌn) *pron* **1** not any of a particular class: *none of my letters has arrived* **2** no-one; nobody: *there was none to tell the tale* **3** no part (of a whole); not any (of): *none of it looks edible* **4** none other no other person: *none other than the Queen herself* **5** none (foll by a comparative adjective) in no degree: *she was none the worse for her ordeal* **6** none too not very: *he was none too pleased with his car* [Old English *nān,* literally: not one]

> **USAGE** None is a singular pronoun and should be used with a singular form of a verb: *none of the students has* (not *have*) *a car*

none² (nəʊn) *n* another word for **nones**

noneconomic (ˌnɒniːkəˈnɒmɪk, -ɛkəˈnɒmɪk) *adj* not of or relating to economic factors: *noneconomic benefits*

noneffective (ˌnɒnɪˈfɛktɪv) *chiefly US* ▷ *adj* **1** not effective **2** unfit for or incapable of active military service ▷ *n* **3** *military* a noneffective person

nonego (nɒnˈiːɡəʊ, -ˈɛɡəʊ) *n philosophy* everything that is outside one's conscious self, such as one's environment

nonentity (nɒnˈɛntɪtɪ) *n, pl* -ties **1** an insignificant person or thing **2** a nonexistent thing **3** the state of not existing; nonexistence

nonequivalence (ˌnɒnɪˈkwɪvələns) *n* **1** the relationship of being unequal or incomparable **2** *logic* **a** the relation between two statements only one of which can be true in any circumstances **b** a function of two statements that takes the value true only when one but not both of its arguments is true **c** a compound statement asserting that just one of its components is true ▷ Also called: exclusive or

nones (nəʊnz) *n (functioning as singular or plural)* **1** (in the Roman calendar) the ninth day before the ides of each month: the seventh day of March, May, July, and October, and the fifth of each other month. See also **calends 2** *chiefly RC Church* the fifth of the seven canonical hours of the divine office, originally fixed at the ninth hour of the day, about 3 p.m [Old English *nōn,* from Latin *nōna hora* ninth hour, from *nōnus* ninth]

nonessential (ˌnɒnɪˈsɛnʃəl) *adj* **1** not essential; not necessary **2** *biochem* (of an amino acid in a particular organism) able to be synthesized from other substances ▷ *n* **3** a nonessential person or thing

nonesuch *or* **nonsuch** (ˈnʌnˌsʌtʃ) *n* **1** *archaic* a matchless person or thing; nonpareil **2** another name for **black medick**

nonet (nɒˈnɛt) *n* **1** a piece of music composed for a group of nine instruments **2** an instrumental group of nine players [c19 from Italian *nonetto,* from *nono* ninth, from Latin *nōnus*]

nonetheless (ˌnʌnðəˈlɛs) *sentence connector* despite that; however; nevertheless

non-Euclidean geometry *n* the branch of modern geometry in which certain axioms of Euclidean geometry are restated. It introduces fundamental changes into the concept of space

nonevent (ˌnɒnɪˈvɛnt) *n* a disappointing or insignificant occurrence, esp one predicted to be important

nonexclusive (ˌnɒnɪksˈkluːsɪv) *adj* not belonging to a particular individual or group: *a nonexclusive deal*

nonexecutive (ˌnɒnɪɡˈzɛkjʊtɪv) *adj* not having

the function or purpose of carrying plans, orders, laws, etc, into practical effect: *a nonexecutive role*

nonexecutive director *n* a director of a commercial company who is not a full-time member of the company but is brought in to advise the other directors

nonexistent (ˌnɒnɪɡˈzɪstənt) *adj* **1** not having being or existence **2** not present under specified conditions or in a specified place > ˌnonexˈistence *n*

nonfatal (nɒnˈfeɪtəl) *adj* not resulting in or capable of causing death

nonfattening (nɒnˈfætənɪŋ) *adj* not causing weight gain: *a nonfattening alternative*

nonfeasance (nɒnˈfiːzəns) *n law* a failure to act when under an obligation to do so. Compare **malfeasance, misfeasance** [c16 from NON- + *feasance* (obsolete) performing or doing, from French *faisance*, from *faire* to do, from Latin *facere*]

nonferrous (nɒnˈfɛrəs) *adj* **1** denoting any metal other than iron **2** not containing iron: *a nonferrous alloy*

nonfiction (nɒnˈfɪkʃən) *n* **1** writing dealing with facts and events rather than imaginative narration **2** (*modifier*) relating to or denoting nonfiction > nonˈfictional *adj* > nonˈfictionally *adv*

nonflammable (nɒnˈflæməbəl) *adj* incapable of burning or not easily set on fire; not flammable

nong (nɒŋ) *n Austral slang* a stupid or incompetent person [c19 perhaps alteration of obsolete English dialect *nigmenog* silly fellow, of unknown origin]

nongovernmental (ˌnɒnɡʌvənˈmɛntəl) *adj* not related to government affairs or procedures

nonharmonic (ˌnɒnhɑːˈmɒnɪk) *adj music* not relating to the harmony formed by a chord or chords

non-Hodgkin's lymphoma (-ˈhɒdʒkɪnz) *n* any form of lymphoma other than Hodgkin's disease

noni (ˈnəʊnɪ) *n* a tree, *Morinda citrifolia*, native to SE Asia and the Pacific islands, juice from the fruit of which is marketed as a health supplement [Hawaiian]

nonillion (nəʊˈnɪljən) *n* **1** (in Britain, France, and Germany) the number represented as one followed by 54 zeros (10⁵⁴) **2** (in the US and Canada) the number represented as one followed by 30 zeros (10³⁰). Brit word: **quintillion** [c17 from French, from Latin *nōnus* ninth, on the model of MILLION] > noˈnillionth *adj, n*

non-impact printer *n computing* any printing device in which the images are created without being struck onto the paper, such as a laser printer or ink-jet printer

nonindustrial (ˌnɒnɪnˈdʌstrɪəl) *adj* not of or relating to an industrial society, place, or age

nonintellectual (ˌnɒnɪntɪˈlɛktʃʊəl) *adj* not appealing to or characteristic of people with a developed intellect

nonintervention (ˌnɒnɪntəˈvɛnʃən) *n* refusal to intervene, esp the abstention by a state from intervening in the affairs of other states or in its own internal disputes > ˌnoninterˈventional *adj* > ˌnoninterˈventionist *n, adj*

noninvasive (ˌnɒnɪnˈveɪsɪv) *adj* (of medical treatment) not involving the making of a relatively large incision in the body or the insertion of instruments, etc, into the patient

noniron (nɒnˈaɪən) *adj* (of a fabric) composed of any of various man-made fibres that are crease-resistant and do not require ironing

nonjoinder (nɒnˈdʒɔɪndə) *n law* the failure to join as party to a suit a person who should have been included either as a plaintiff or as a defendant. Compare **misjoinder**

nonjudgmental *or* **nonjudgemental** (ˌnɒndʒʌdʒˈmɛntəl) *adj* of, relating to, or denoting an attitude, approach, etc, that is open and not incorporating a judgment one way or the other

nonjuror (nɒnˈdʒʊərə) *n* a person who refuses to take an oath, as of allegiance

Nonjuror (nɒnˈdʒʊərə) *n* any of a group of clergy

in England and Scotland who declined to take the oath of allegiance to William and Mary in 1689

nonlethal (nɒnˈliːθəl) *adj* not resulting in or capable of causing death

non licet (ˈnɒn ˈlaɪsɪt) *adj* not permitted; unlawful [c17 Latin, literally: it is not allowed]

nonlinear (nɒnˈlɪnɪə) *adj* **1** not of, in, along, or relating to a line **2** denoting digital editing in which edits are saved on computer, rather than videotape, thus enabling further edits to be made

non liquet (ˈnɒn ˈlaɪkwɪt) *adj Roman law* (of a cause, evidence, etc) not clear [c17 Latin, literally: it is not clear]

nonliterary (nɒnˈlɪtərərɪ, -ˈlɪtrərɪ) *adj* not of, relating to, concerned with, or characteristic of literature or scholarly writing

nonlocal (nɒnˈləʊkəl) *adj* not of, affecting, or confined to a limited area or part: *the nonlocal aspect of the psyche*

non-malignant (ˌnɒnməˈlɪɡnənt) *adj* (of a tumour) not uncontrollable or resistant to therapy

nonmedical (nɒnˈmɛdɪkəl) *adj* not of, relating to, or using medical theory or practice

nonmember (nɒnˈmɛmbə) *n* a person who is not a member of a club, etc

nonmetal (nɒnˈmɛtəl) *n* any of a number of chemical elements that form negative ions, have acidic oxides, and are generally poor conductors of heat and electricity

nonmetallic (ˌnɒnmɪˈtælɪk) *adj* **1** not of metal **2** of, concerned with, or being a nonmetal

nonmonetary advantages (nɒnˈmʌnɪtərɪ) *pl n* the beneficial aspects of an employment, such as the stimulation of the work, attractiveness of the workplace, or its nearness to one's home, that do not reflect its financial remuneration

nonmoral (nɒnˈmɒrəl) *adj* not involving or related to morality or ethics; neither moral nor immoral

non-native *n* a person who is not a native of a particular place or country

non-naturalism *n* the meta-ethical doctrine that moral properties exist but are not reducible to "natural", empirical, or supernatural ones, and that moral judgments therefore state a special kind of fact. Compare **naturalistic fallacy** See also **descriptivism**

non-negotiable *adj* not open to negotiation or discussion: *the policy is non-negotiable*

Nonne's syndrome (nɒnz) *n* another name for **cerebellar syndrome**

non-nuclear *adj* **1** not of, concerned with, or operated by energy from fission or fusion of atomic nuclei: *non-nuclear weapons* **2** not involving, concerned with, or possessing nuclear weapons: *non-nuclear states*

nonobjective (ˌnɒnəbˈdʒɛktɪv) *adj* of or designating an art movement in which things are depicted in an abstract or purely formalized way, not as they appear in reality

nonofficial (ˌnɒnəˈfɪʃəl) *adj* not official or formal

no-nonsense (ˌnəʊˈnɒnsəns) *adj* sensible, practical, straightforward; without nonsense of any kind: *a businesslike no-nonsense approach; a severe no-nonsense look*

nonoperational (ˌnɒnɒpəˈreɪʃənəl) *adj* not in working order or ready to use

nonorthodox (nɒnˈɔːθəˌdɒks) *adj* not conforming with established or accepted standards, as in religion, behaviour, or attitudes

nonparametric statistics (ˌnɒnpærəˈmɛtrɪk) *n* (*functioning as singular*) the branch of statistics that studies data measurable on an ordinal or nominal scale, to which arithmetic operations cannot be applied

nonpareil (ˈnɒnpərəl, ˌnɒnpəˈreɪl) *n* **1** a person or thing that is unsurpassed or unmatched; peerless example **2** (formerly) a size of printers' type equal to 6 point **3** US a small bead of coloured sugar used to decorate cakes, biscuits, etc **4** chiefly US a flat round piece of chocolate covered with this

sugar ▷ *adj* **5** having no match or equal; peerless [c15 from French, from NON- + *pareil* similar]

nonparous (nɒnˈpærəs) *adj* never having given birth

nonparticipating (ˌnɒnpɑːˈtɪsɪˌpeɪtɪŋ) *adj* **1** not participating **2** (of an assurance policy, share, etc) not carrying the right to share in a company's profit

nonpartisan *or* **nonpartizan** (ˌnɒnpɑːˈtɪˈzæn) *adj* not partisan or aligned, esp not affiliated to, influenced by, or supporting any one political party > ˌnonpartiˈsanˌship *or* ˌnonpartiˈzanˌship *n*

nonparty (nɒnˈpɑːtɪ) *adj* not connected with any one political party

nonpaying (nɒnˈpeɪɪŋ) *adj* (of guests, customers, etc) not expected or requested to pay

nonpayment (nɒnˈpeɪmənt) *n* the act or state of not paying

nonpermanent (nɒnˈpɜːmənənt) *adj* not existing or intended to exist for an indefinite time

nonpersistent (ˌnɒnpəˈsɪstənt) *adj* (of pesticides) breaking down rapidly after application; not persisting in the environment

non-person *n* a person regarded as nonexistent or unimportant; a nonentity

nonphysical (nɒnˈfɪzɪkəl) *adj* **1** not of or relating to the body or nature **2** not sexual; platonic: *intimate nonphysical friendships*

nonplaying (nɒnˈpleɪɪŋ) *adj* belonging to a team, group, etc, but not participating in their pursuit: *appointed nonplaying captain*

nonplus (nɒnˈplʌs) *vb* -plusses, -plussing, -plussed *or US* -pluses, -plusing, -plused **1** (*tr*) to put at a loss; confound: *he was nonplussed by the sudden announcement* ▷ *n, pl* -pluses **2** a state of utter perplexity prohibiting action or speech [c16 from Latin *nōn plūs* no further (that is, nothing further can be said or done)]

nonpoisonous (nɒnˈpɔɪzənəs) *adj* not having the effects or qualities of a poison

nonpolitical (ˌnɒnpəˈlɪtɪkəl) *adj* not of, dealing with, or relating to politics: *a nonpolitical organization*

nonpolluting (ˌnɒnpəˈluːtɪŋ) *adj* (of a fuel, vehicle, technology, etc) not resulting in or causing pollution

nonporous (nɒnˈpɔːrəs) *adj* not permeable to water, air, or other fluids

nonpractising (nɒnˈpræktɪsɪŋ) *adj* of or relating to a person who no longer observes or pursues his or her religious faith

nonproductive (ˌnɒnprəˈdʌktɪv) *adj* **1** (of workers) not directly responsible for producing goods **2** having disappointing results; unproductive > ˌnonproˈductiveness *n* > nonproductivity (ˌnɒnprɒdʌkˈtɪvɪtɪ) *n*

nonprofessional (ˌnɒnprəˈfɛʃənəl) *adj* **1** not of, relating to, suitable for, or engaged in a profession **2** not undertaken or performed for gain or by people who are paid

nonprofit (nɒnˈprɒfɪt) *US* ▷ *adj* **1** another word for **non-profit-making** ▷ *n* **2** an organization that is not intended to make a profit

non-profit-making *adj* not yielding a profit, esp because organized or established for some other reason: *a non-profit-making organization*

nonproliferation (ˌnɒnprəˌlɪfərˈeɪʃən) *n* **1 a** limitation of the production or spread of something, esp nuclear or chemical weapons **b** (*as modifier*): *a nonproliferation treaty* **2** failure or refusal to proliferate

non pros. *law abbreviation for* non prosequitur

non-pros (ˌnɒnˈprɒs) *n* **1** short for **non prosequitur** ▷ *vb* -prosses, -prossing, -prossed **2** (*tr*) to enter a judgment of non prosequitur against (a plaintiff)

non prosequitur (ˈnɒn prɒˈsɛkwɪtə) *n law* (formerly) a judgment in favour of a defendant when the plaintiff failed to take the necessary steps in an action within the time allowed. Compare **nolle prosequi** [Latin, literally: he does not prosecute]

n

nonracial (nɒnˈreɪʃəl) *adj* not related to racial factors or discrimination

nonrational (nɒnˈræʃənəl) *adj* not in accordance with the principles of logic or reason

nonrecognition (ˌnɒnrɛkəgˈnɪʃən) *n* the act or an instance of refusing to acknowledge formally a government or the independence of a country

nonreflexive (ˌnɒnrɪˈflɛksɪv) *adj logic* (of a relation) neither reflexive nor irreflexive; holding between some members of its domain and themselves, and failing to hold between others

nonreligious (ˌnɒnrɪˈlɪdʒəs) *adj* not of or relating to religious beliefs and practices

nonrenewable (ˌnɒnrɪˈnjuːəbəl) *adj* not able to be restored, replaced, recommenced, etc: *nonrenewable resources*

nonrepresentational (ˌnɒnˌrɛprɪzɛnˈteɪʃənəl) *adj art* another word for **abstract** (sense 4)

nonresident (nɒnˈrɛzɪdənt) *n* **1** a person who is not residing in the place implied or specified: *the hotel restaurant is open to nonresidents* **2** a British person employed abroad on a contract for a minimum of one year, who is exempt from UK income tax provided that he does not spend more than 90 days in the UK during that tax year ▷ *adj* **3** not residing in the place specified > non'residence *or* non'residency *n*

nonresidential (ˌnɒnrɛzɪˈdɛnʃəl) *adj* **1** not suitable or allocated for residence: *nonresidential areas* **2** not having residence: *nonresidential customers*

nonresistant (ˌnɒnrɪˈzɪstənt) *adj* **1** incapable of resisting something, such as a disease; susceptible **2** *history* (esp in 17th-century England) practising passive obedience to royal authority even when its commands were unjust > ˌnonre'sistance *n*

nonrestrictive (ˌnɒnrɪˈstrɪktɪv) *adj* **1** not restrictive or limiting **2** *grammar* denoting a relative clause that is not restrictive. Compare **restrictive** (sense 2)

nonreturn (ˌnɒnrɪˈtɜːn) *adj* denoting a mechanism that permits flow in a pipe, tunnel, etc, in one direction only: *a nonreturn valve*

nonreturnable (ˌnɒnrɪˈtɜːnəbəl) *adj* denoting a container, esp a bottle, on which no returnable deposit is paid on purchase of the contents

nonreturn valve *n* another name for **check valve**

nonrhotic (nɒnˈrəʊtɪk) *adj phonetics* denoting or speaking a dialect of English in which preconsonantal *r*s are not pronounced > ˌnonrho'ticity *n*

nonrigid (nɒnˈrɪdʒɪd) *adj* **1** not rigid; flexible **2** (of the gas envelope of an airship) flexible and held in shape only by the internal gas pressure

nonscheduled (nɒnˈʃɛdjuːld; *also, esp US* nɒnˈskɛdʒʊəld) *adj* **1** not according to a schedule or plan; unscheduled **2** (of an airline) operating without published flight schedules

nonscientific (ˌnɒnsaɪənˈtɪfɪk) *adj* not of, relating to, derived from, or used in science

nonsectarian (ˌnɒnsɛkˈtɛərɪən) *adj* not narrow-minded, esp as a result of rigid adherence to a particular sect; broad-minded

non-secure *adj computing* of or relating to a channel of communication, esp on the internet, that is not restricted to authorized users and is not therefore guaranteed to be private and confidential

nonselective (ˌnɒnsɪˈlɛktɪv) *adj* (of a school, education system, etc) admitting all pupils regardless of ability; inclusive

nonsense (ˈnɒnsəns) *n* **1** something that has or makes no sense; unintelligible language; drivel **2** conduct or action that is absurd **3** foolish or evasive behaviour or manners: *she'll stand no nonsense* **4** See **no nonsense** **5** things of little or no value or importance; trash ▷ *interj* **6** an exclamation of disagreement > nonsensical (nɒnˈsɛnsɪkəl) *adj* > non'sensically *adv* > non'sensicalness *or* non,sensi'cality *n*

nonsense correlation *n statistics* a correlation supported by data but having no basis in reality,

as between incidence of the common cold and ownership of televisions

nonsense syllable *n psychol* a syllable, like *bik*, having no meaning. Lists of such syllables have been used to investigate memory and learning

nonsense verse *n* verse in which the sense is nonexistent or absurd, such as that of Edward Lear

non seq. *abbreviation for* non sequitur

non sequitur (ˈnɒn ˈsɛkwɪtə) *n* **1** a statement having little or no relevance to what preceded it **2** *logic* a conclusion that does not follow from the premises. Abbreviation: non seq [Latin, literally: it does not follow]

nonsexist (nɒnˈsɛksɪst) *adj* not discriminating on the basis of sex, esp not against women

nonsexual (nɒnˈsɛksjʊəl) *adj* not of, relating to, or characterized by sex or sexuality

nonslip (nɒnˈslɪp) *adj* designed to reduce or prevent slipping

nonsmoker (nɒnˈsməʊkə) *n* **1** a person who does not smoke **2** a train compartment in which smoking is forbidden > non'smoking *adj*

nonspeaking (nɒnˈspiːkɪŋ) *adj* (of a part in a play) not having any lines to speak

nonspecialist (nɒnˈspɛʃəlɪst) *n* **1** someone who does not specialize in a particular area, activity, field of research, etc ▷ *adj* **2** not specializing in a particular area, activity, field of research, etc

nonspecific (ˌnɒnspɪˈsɪfɪk) *adj* not explicit, particular, or definite

nonspecific urethritis *n* inflammation of the urethra as a result of a venereal infection that cannot be traced to a specific cause. Abbreviation: NSU

nonspecular reflection (nɒnˈspɛkjʊlə) *n physics* the diffuse reflection of sound or light waves

nonsporting (nɒnˈspɔːtɪŋ) *adj* **1** not of or related to sport **2** having no aptitude for sport

nonstandard (nɒnˈstændəd) *adj* **1** denoting or characterized by idiom, vocabulary, etc, that is not regarded as correct and acceptable by educated native speakers of a language; not standard **2** deviating from a given standard

nonstarter (nɒnˈstɑːtə) *n* **1** a horse that fails to run in a race for which it has been entered **2** a person or thing that is useless, has little chance of success, etc

nonstative (nɒnˈsteɪtɪv) *grammar* ▷ *adj* **1** denoting a verb describing an action rather than a state, as for example *throw* or *thank* as opposed to *know* or *hate*. Compare **stative** ▷ *n* **2** a nonstative verb ▷ Also: **active**

nonstick (ˈnɒnˈstɪk) *adj* (of saucepans, frying pans, etc) coated with a substance such as polytetrafluoroethylene (PTFE) that prevents food sticking to them

nonstoichiometric (nɒnˌstɔɪkɪəˈmɛtrɪk) *adj chem* (of a solid compound) having a composition in which the ratio of the atoms present is not a simple integer

nonstop (ˈnɒnˈstɒp) *adj, adv* done without pause or interruption: *a nonstop flight*

nonstrategic (ˌnɒnstrəˈtiːdʒɪk) *adj* not of, relating to, or characteristic of strategy

nonstriated (nɒnˈstraɪeɪtɪd) *adj* (esp of certain muscle fibres) having no striations

non-striker *n cricket* the batsman who is not facing the bowling

nonsuch (ˈnʌnˌsʌtʃ) *n* a variant spelling of **nonesuch**

Nonsuch Palace (ˈnʌnˌsʌtʃ) *n* a former royal palace in Cuddington in London: built in 1538 for Henry VIII; later visited by Elizabeth I, James I, Charles I, and Charles II; demolished (1682–1702)

nonsuit (nɒnˈsuːt, -ˈsjuːt) *law* ▷ *n* **1** an order of a judge dismissing a suit when the plaintiff fails to show he has a good cause of action or fails to produce any evidence ▷ *vb* **2** (*tr*) to order the dismissal of the suit of (a person)

nonsurgical (nɒnˈsɜːdʒɪkəl) *adj* not of, relating to, involving, or used in surgery

nonswimmer (nɒnˈswɪmə) *n* a person who cannot swim

nonsymmetric (ˌnɒnsɪˈmɛtrɪk) *adj logic, maths* (of a relation) not symmetric, asymmetric, or antisymmetric; holding between some pairs of arguments *x* and *y* and failing to hold for some other pairs when it holds between *y* and *x*

nontaxable (nɒnˈtæksəbəl) *adj* not subject to tax

nonteaching (nɒnˈtiːtʃɪŋ) *adj* of or relating to a post within an academic or vocational environment that does not entail teaching

nontechnical (nɒnˈtɛknɪkəl) *adj* not relating to, characteristic of, or skilled in a particular field of activity and its terminology

nontoxic (nɒnˈtɒksɪk) *adj* not of, relating to, or caused by a toxin or poison: *safe, nontoxic paint*

nontraditional (ˌnɒntrəˈdɪʃənəl) *adj* not traditional; unconventional: *nontraditional lifestyles*

nontransitive (nɒnˈtrænsɪtɪv) *adj logic* (of a relation) neither transitive nor intransitive

non troppo (ˈnɒn ˈtrɒpəʊ) *adv music* (preceded by a musical direction, esp a tempo marking) not to be observed too strictly (esp in the phrases **allegro ma non troppo, adagio ma non troppo**)

non-U (nɒnˈjuː) *adj Brit informal* (esp of language) not characteristic of or used by the upper class. Compare **U¹**

nonunion (nɒnˈjuːnjən) *adj* **1** not belonging or related to a trade union: *nonunion workers* **2** not favouring or employing union labour **3** not produced by union labour ▷ *n* **4** *pathol* failure of broken bones or bone fragments to heal

nonunionism (nɒnˈjuːnjəˌnɪzəm) *n chiefly US* opposition to trade unionism > non'unionist *n, adj*

nonvenomous (nɒnˈvɛnəməs) *adj* (of a snake, spider, etc) not venomous

nonverbal (nɒnˈvɜːbəl) *adj* not spoken: *the nonverbal signals of body movement*

nonverbal communication *n psychol* those aspects of communication, such as gestures and facial expressions, that do not involve verbal communication but which may include nonverbal aspects of speech itself (accent, tone of voice, speed of speaking, etc)

nonvintage (nɒnˈvɪntɪdʒ) *adj* **1** (of wine) not of an outstandingly good year **2** not representative of the best: *two nonvintage teams*

nonviolence (nɒnˈvaɪələns) *n* abstention from the use of physical force to achieve goals > non'violent *adj*

nonvoter (nɒnˈvəʊtə) *n* **1** a person who does not vote **2** a person not eligible to vote

nonvoting (nɒnˈvəʊtɪŋ) *adj* **1** of or relating to a nonvoter **2** *finance* (of shares) not entitling the holder to vote at company meetings

non-White *n* a person not of the Caucasoid or White race

nonworking (nɒnˈwɜːkɪŋ) *adj* **1** not engaged in payed employment: *nonworking mothers* **2** (of machinery, technology, etc) not operating properly or effectively: *nonworking telephones*

noodle¹ (ˈnuːdəl) *n* (*often plural*) a ribbon-like strip of pasta: noodles are often served in soup or with a sauce [C18 from German *Nudel*, origin obscure]

noodle² (ˈnuːdəl) *n* **1** *US and Canadian* a slang word for **head** (sense 1) **2** a simpleton [C18 perhaps a blend of NODDLE¹ and NOODLE¹]

noodle³ (ˈnuːdəl) *vb* (*intr*) *slang* to improvise aimlessly on a musical instrument

noodling (ˈnuːdlɪŋ) *n slang* aimless musical improvisation

Noogoora burr (nəˈguːrə) *n Austral* a European cocklebur, *Xanthium pungens*, that is poisonous to stock [from *Noogoora* a sheep station in Queensland]

nooit (nɔɪt) *interj South African* an exclamation expressive of surprise, admiration, disgust, etc [from Afrikaans, literally: never]

nook (nʊk) *n* **1** a corner or narrow recess, as in a room **2** a secluded or sheltered place; retreat [C13 origin obscure; perhaps related to Norwegian dialect *nok* hook]

nooky or **nookie** ('nʊkɪ) n slang sexual intercourse [c20 of uncertain origin; perhaps from NOOK]

noon (nuːn) n 1 a the middle of the day; 12 o'clock in the daytime or the time or point at which the sun crosses the local meridian b (as modifier): the noon sun 2 poetic the highest, brightest, or most important part; culmination [Old English nōn, from Latin nōna (hōra) ninth hour (originally 3 pm, the ninth hour from sunrise)]

noonday ('nuːnˌdeɪ) n a the middle of the day; noon b (as modifier): the noonday sun

no-one or **no one** pron no person; nobody

▪ USAGE See at everyone

nooning ('nuːnɪŋ) n dialect, chiefly US 1 a midday break for rest or food 2 midday; noon

noontime ('nuːnˌtaɪm) or **noontide** n a the middle of the day; noon b (as modifier): a noontime drink

Noordbrabant (noːrd'braːbɑnt) n the Dutch name for North Brabant

Noordholland (noːrt'hɔlɑnt) n the Dutch name for North Holland

noose (nuːs) n 1 a loop in the end of a rope or cord, such as a lasso, snare, or hangman's halter, usually tied with a slipknot 2 something that restrains, binds, or traps 3 put one's head in a noose to bring about one's own downfall ▷ vb (tr) 4 to secure or catch in or as if in a noose 5 to make a noose of or in [c15 perhaps from Provençal nous, from Latin nōdus NODE]

noosphere ('nəʊˌsfɪə) n philosophy the part of the biosphere that is affected by human thought, culture, and knowledge [c20 from French noösphere, based on Greek noos mind]

Nootka ('nʊtkə, 'nuːt-) n 1 (pl -ka or -kas) a member of a North American Indian people living in British Columbia and Vancouver Island 2 the language of this people, belonging to the Wakashan family

nopal ('nəʊpªl) n 1 any of various cactuses of the genus Nopalea, esp the red-flowered N. cochinellifera, which is a host plant of the cochineal insect 2 a cactus, Opuntia lindheimeri, having yellow flowers and purple fruits. See also prickly pear [c18 from Spanish, from Nahuatl nopälli cactus]

no-par adj (of securities) without a par value

nope (nəʊp) sentence substitute an informal word for no¹ [c19 originally US, a variant of NO¹]

Nopo ('nəʊˌpəʊ) n acronym for no person operation; driverless trains suggested as a means of increasing the efficiency of some railway systems

nor (nɔː; unstressed nə) conj (coordinating) ▷ prep 1 (used to join alternatives, the first of which is preceded by neither) and not: neither measles nor mumps 2 (foll by an auxiliary verb or have, do, or be used as main verbs) (and) not...either: they weren't talented — nor were they particularly funny 3 dialect than: better nor me 4 poetic neither: nor wind nor rain [c13 contraction of Old English nōther, from nāhwæther NEITHER]

nor- combining form 1 indicating that a chemical compound is derived from a specified compound by removal of a group or groups: noradrenaline 2 indicating that a chemical compound is a normal isomer of a specified compound [by shortening from NORMAL]

noradrenaline (ˌnɔːrə'drɛnəlɪn, -liːn) or **noradrenalin** n a hormone secreted by the adrenal medulla, increasing blood pressure and heart rate, and by the endings of sympathetic nerves, when it acts as a neurotransmitter both centrally and peripherally. Formula: $C_8H_{11}NO_3$. US name: norepinephrine

Noraid ('nɔːˌreɪd) n an American organization that supports the Republicans in Northern Ireland

NOR circuit or **gate** (nɔː) n computing a logic circuit having two or more input wires and one output wire that has a high-voltage output signal only if all input signals are at a low voltage. Compare AND circuit [c20 from NOR, so named

because the action performed is similar to the operation of the conjunction nor in logic]

Nord (French nɔr) n a department of N France, in Nord-Pas-de-Calais region. Capital: Lille. Pop: 2 561 800 (2003 est). Area: 5774 sq km (2252 sq miles)

Nordenskjöld Sea (Swedish 'nuːrdənʃœld) n the former name of the Laptev Sea [named after Nils Adolf Erik Nordenskjöld (1832–1901), Swedish Arctic explorer and geologist]

nordic ('nɔːdɪk) adj skiing of or relating to competitions in cross-country racing and ski-jumping. Compare alpine (sense 4)

Nordic ('nɔːdɪk) adj of, relating to, or belonging to a subdivision of the Caucasoid race typified by the tall blond blue-eyed long-headed inhabitants of N Britain, Scandinavia, N Germany, and the Netherlands [c19 from French nordique, from nord NORTH]

Nordkyn Cape (Norwegian 'nuːrçyːn) n a cape in N Norway: the northernmost point of the European mainland

Nord-Pas-de-Calais (French nɔrpɑdəkalɛ) n a region of N France, on the Straits of Dover (the Pas de Calais): coal-mining, textile, and metallurgical industries

Nordrhein-Westfalen ('nɔrtrainvɛst'faːlən) n the German name for North Rhine-Westphalia

norepinephrine (ˌnɔːrɛpɪ'nɛfrɪn, -riːn) n the US name for noradrenaline

Norfolk ('nɔːfək) n 1 a county of E England, on the North Sea and the Wash: low-lying, with large areas of fens in the west and the Broads in the east; rich agriculturally. Administrative centre: Norwich. Pop: 810 700 (2003 est). Area: 5368 sq km (2072 sq miles) 2 a port in SE Virginia, on the Elizabeth River and Hampton Roads: headquarters of the US Atlantic fleet; shipbuilding. Pop: 241 727 (2003 est)

Norfolk Island n an island in the S Pacific, between New Caledonia and N New Zealand: an Australian external territory; discovered by Captain Cook in 1774; a penal settlement in early years. Pop: 2601 (2001). Area: 36 sq km (14 sq miles)

Norfolk Island pine n a tall coniferous tree, Araucaria heterophylla, native to Norfolk Island and widely cultivated

Norfolk jacket n a man's single-breasted belted jacket with one or two chest pockets and a box pleat down the back [c19 worn in NORFOLK for duck shooting]

Norfolk terrier n a small wiry-coated breed of terrier having a short tail and pendent ears

Norge ('nɔrgə) n the Norwegian name for Norway

nori ('nɔːrɪ) n an edible seaweed often used in Japanese cookery, esp for wrapping sushi or rice balls [Japanese]

noria ('nɔːrɪə) n a water wheel with buckets attached to its rim for raising water from a stream into irrigation canals: common in Spain and the Orient [c18 via Spanish from Arabic nā'ūra, from na'ara to creak]

Noricum ('nɒrɪkəm) n an Alpine kingdom of the Celts, south of the Danube: comprises present-day central Austria and parts of Bavaria; a Roman province from about 16 BC

norite ('nɔːraɪt) n a variety of gabbro composed mainly of hypersthene and labradorite feldspar [c19 from Norwegian norit, from NORGE Norway + -it -ITE¹]

nork (nɔːk) n (usually plural) Austral slang a female breast [c20 of unknown origin]

norland ('nɔːlənd) n archaic the north part of a country or the earth [c17 contraction of NORTH + LAND]

norm (nɔːm) n 1 an average level of achievement or performance, as of a group or person 2 a standard of achievement or behaviour that is required, desired, or designated as normal 3 sociol an established standard of behaviour shared by members of a social group to which each member is expected to conform 4 maths a the length of a vector expressed as the square root of the sum of

the square of its components b another name for mode (sense 6) 5 geology the theoretical standard mineral composition of an igneous rock [c19 from Latin norma carpenter's rule, square]

Norm (nɔːm) n a stereotype of the unathletic Australian male [from a cartoon figure in the government-sponsored Life, Be In It campaign]

norm. abbreviation for normal

Norm. abbreviation for Norman

Norma ('nɔːmə) n, Latin genitive Normae ('nɔːmiː) a constellation in the S hemisphere crossed by the Milky Way lying near Scorpius and Ara

normal ('nɔːmªl) adj 1 usual; regular; common; typical: the normal way of doing it; the normal level 2 constituting a standard: if we take this as normal 3 psychol a being within certain limits of intelligence, educational success or ability, etc b conforming to the conventions of one's group 4 biology, med (of laboratory animals) maintained in a natural state for purposes of comparison with animals treated with drugs, etc 5 chem (of a solution) containing a number of grams equal to the equivalent weight of the solute in each litre of solvent. Symbol: N 6 chem denoting a straight-chain hydrocarbon: a normal alkane. Prefix: n-, eg n-octane 7 geometry another word for perpendicular (sense 1) ▷ n 8 the usual, average, or typical state, degree, form, etc 9 anything that is normal 10 geometry a line or plane perpendicular to another line or plane or to the tangent of a curved line or plane at the point of contact [c16 from Latin normālis conforming to the carpenter's square, from norma NORM] > normality (nɔː'mælɪtɪ) or esp US 'normalcy n

normal curve n statistics a symmetrical bell-shaped curve representing the probability density function of a normal distribution. The area of a vertical section of the curve represents the probability that the random variable lies between the values which delimit the section

normal distribution n statistics a continuous distribution of a random variable with its mean, median, and mode equal, the probability density function of which is given by (exp-[$(x-\mu)^2/2\sigma^2]/\sigma\sqrt{(2\pi)}$) where μ is the mean and σ² the variance. Also called: Gaussian distribution

normalization or **normalisation** (ˌnɔːməlaɪ'zeɪʃən) n 1 the act or process of normalizing 2 social welfare the policy of offering mentally or physically handicapped people patterns, conditions, and experiences of everyday life as close as possible to those of nonhandicapped people, by not segregating them physically, socially, and administratively from the rest of society

normalize or **normalise** ('nɔːməˌlaɪz) vb (tr) 1 to bring or make into the normal state 2 to bring into conformity with a standard 3 to heat (steel) above a critical temperature and allow it to cool in air to relieve internal stresses; anneal

normally ('nɔːməlɪ) adv 1 as a rule; usually; ordinarily 2 in a normal manner

normal matrix n a square matrix A for which AA* = A*A, where A* is the Hermitian conjugate of A

normal school n (in France, and formerly England, the US, and Canada) a school or institution for training teachers [c19 from French école normale: the first French school so named was intended as a model for similar institutions]

normal time n sport the standard length of time allowed for a match before any extra time, such as injury time, is added

Norman ('nɔːmən) n 1 (in the Middle Ages) a member of the people of Normandy descended from the 10th-century Scandinavian conquerors of the country and the native French 2 a native or inhabitant of Normandy 3 another name for Norman French ▷ adj 4 of, relating to, or characteristic of the Normans, esp the Norman kings of England, the Norman people living in England, or their dialect of French 5 of, relating to, or characteristic of Normandy or its

n

inhabitants **6** denoting, relating to, or having the style of Romanesque architecture used in Britain from the Norman Conquest until the 12th century. It is characterized by the rounded arch, the groin vault, massive masonry walls, etc

Norman arch *n chiefly Brit* a semicircular arch, esp one in the Romanesque style of architecture developed by the Normans in England. Also called: **Roman arch**

Norman Conquest *n* the invasion and settlement of England by the Normans, following the Battle of Hastings (1066)

Normandy ('nɔːməndɪ) *n* a former province of N France, on the English Channel: settled by Vikings under Rollo in the 10th century; scene of the Allied landings in 1944. Chief town: Rouen. French name: **Normandie** (nɔrmãdi)

Norman English *n* the dialect of English used by the Norman conquerors of England

Norman French *n* the medieval Norman and English dialect of Old French. See also **Anglo-French** (sense 3)

Normanize *or* **Normanise** ('nɔːmə,naɪz) *vb* to make or become Norman in character, style, customs, etc > ,Normani'zation *or* ,Normani'sation *n*

normative ('nɔːmətɪv) *adj* **1** implying, creating, or prescribing a norm or standard, as in language: *normative grammar* **2** expressing value judgments or prescriptions as contrasted with stating facts: *normative economics* **3** of, relating to, or based on norms > 'normatively *adv* > 'normativeness *n*

normotensive (,nɔːməʊ'tɛnsɪv) *adj* having or denoting normal blood pressure

Norn[1] (nɔːn) *n Norse myth* any of the three virgin goddesses of fate, who predestine the lives of the gods and men [C18 Old Norse]

Norn[2] (nɔːn) *n* the medieval Norse language of the Orkneys, Shetlands, and parts of N Scotland. It was extinct by 1750 [C17 from Old Norse *norréna* Norwegian, from *northr* north]

Norrköping (*Swedish* 'nɔrtɕø·piŋ) *n* a port in SE Sweden, near the Baltic. Pop: 124 378 (2004 est)

Norroy ('nɒrɔɪ) *n* the third King-of-Arms in England: since 1943, called **Norroy and Ulster** [C15 Old French *nor* north + *roy* king]

Norse (nɔːs) *adj* **1** of, relating to, or characteristic of ancient and medieval Scandinavia or its inhabitants **2** of, relating to, or characteristic of Norway > *n* **3 a** the N group of Germanic languages, spoken in Scandinavia; Scandinavian **b** any one of these languages, esp in their ancient or medieval forms. See also **Proto-Norse, Old Norse 4** the **Norse** (*functioning as plural*) **a** the Norwegians **b** the Vikings

Norseman ('nɔːsmən) *n, pl* -men another name for a **Viking**

north (nɔːθ) *n* **1** one of the four cardinal points of the compass, at 0° or 360°, that is 90° from east and west and 180° from south **2** the direction along a meridian towards the North Pole **3** the direction in which a compass needle points; magnetic north **4** the North (*often capital*) any area lying in or towards the north. Related adjs: **arctic, boreal 5** *cards* (*usually capital*) the player or position at the table corresponding to north on the compass > *adj* **6** situated in, moving towards, or facing the north **7** (esp of the wind) from the north > *adv* **8** in, to, or towards the north **9** *archaic* (of the wind) from the north > Symbol: N [Old English; related to Old Norse *northr*, Dutch *noord*, Old High German *nord*]

North (nɔːθ) *n* the **1** the northern area of England, generally regarded as reaching approximately the southern boundaries of Yorkshire and Lancashire **2** (in the US) the area approximately north of Maryland and the Ohio River, esp those states north of the Mason-Dixon Line that were known as the Free States during the Civil War **3** the northern part of North America, esp the area consisting of Alaska, the Yukon, the Northwest Territories, and Nunavut;

the North Country **4** the countries of the world that are economically and technically advanced **5** *poetic* the north wind > *adj* **6 a** of or denoting the northern part of a specified country, area, etc **b** (*as part of a name*): *North Africa*

North Africa *n* the part of Africa between the Mediterranean and the Sahara: consists chiefly of Morocco, Algeria, Tunisia, Libya, and N Egypt

North African *adj* **1** of or relating to North Africa or its inhabitants > *n* **2** a native or inhabitant of North Africa

Northallerton (nɔː'ælətⁿn) *n* a market town in N England, administrative centre of North Yorkshire. Pop: 15 517 (2001)

North America *n* the third largest continent, linked with South America by the Isthmus of Panama and bordering on the Arctic Ocean, the N Pacific, the N Atlantic, the Gulf of Mexico, and the Caribbean. It consists generally of a great mountain system (the Western Cordillera) extending along the entire W coast, actively volcanic in the extreme north and south, with the Great Plains to the east and the Appalachians still further east, separated from the Canadian Shield by an arc of large lakes (Great Bear, Great Slave, Winnipeg, Superior, Michigan, Huron, Erie, Ontario); reaches its greatest height of 6194 m (20 320 ft) in Mount McKinley, Alaska, and its lowest point of 85 m (280 ft) below sea level in Death Valley, California, and ranges from snowfields, tundra, and taiga in the north to deserts in the southwest and tropical forests in the extreme south. Pop: 332 156 000 (2005 est). Area: over 24 000 000 sq km (9 500 000 sq miles)

North American *adj* **1** of or relating to North America or its inhabitants > *n* **2** a native or inhabitant of North America

North American Free Trade Agreement *n* an international trade agreement between the United States, Canada, and Mexico. Abbreviation: NAFTA

Northampton (nɔː'θæmptən, nɔː'θ'hæmp-) *n* **1** a town in central England, administrative centre of Northamptonshire, on the River Nene: footwear and engineering industries. Pop: 189 474 (2001) **2** short for **Northamptonshire**

Northamptonshire (nɔː'θæmptən,ʃɪə, -ʃə, nɔː'θ'hæmp-) *n* a county of central England: agriculture, food processing, engineering, and footwear industries. Administrative centre: Northampton. Pop: 642 700 (2003 est). Area: 2367 sq km (914 sq miles). Abbreviation: **Northants**

Northants (nɔː'θænts) *abbreviation for* Northamptonshire

North Atlantic Drift *or* **Current** *n* the warm ocean current flowing northeast, under the influence of prevailing winds, from the Gulf of Mexico towards NW Europe and warming its climate. Also called: **Gulf Stream**

North Atlantic Treaty Organization *n* the full name of NATO

North Ayrshire ('ɛəʃɪə, -ʃə) *n* a council area of W central Scotland, on the Firth of Clyde: comprises the N part of the historical county of Ayrshire, including the Isle of Arran; formerly part of Strathclyde Region (1975–96): chiefly agricultural, with fishing and tourism. Administrative centre: Irvine. Pop: 136 030 (2003 est). Area: 884 sq km (341 sq miles)

North Borneo *n* the former name (until 1963) of **Sabah**

northbound ('nɔːθ,baʊnd) *adj* going or leading towards the north

North Brabant *n* a province of the S Netherlands: formed part of the medieval duchy of Brabant. Capital: 's Hertogenbosch. Pop: 2 400 000 (2003 est). Area: 4965 sq km (1917 sq miles). Dutch name: **Noordbrabant**

north by east *n* **1** one point on the compass east of north, 11° 15′ clockwise from north > *adj, adv* **2** in, from, or towards this direction

north by west *n* **1** one point on the compass

west of north, 348° 45′ clockwise from north > *adj, adv* **2** in, from, or towards this direction

North Cape *n* **1** a cape on N Magerøy Island, in the Arctic Ocean off the N coast of Norway **2** a cape on N North Island, New Zealand

North Carolina *n* a state of the southeastern US, on the Atlantic: consists of a coastal plain rising to the Piedmont Plateau and the Appalachian Mountains in the west. Capital: Raleigh. Pop: 8 407 248 (2003 est). Area: 126 387 sq km (48 798 sq miles). Abbreviations: N.C., (with zip code) NC

North Carolinian (,kærə'lɪnɪən) *adj* **1** of or relating to North Carolina or its inhabitants > *n* **2** a native or inhabitant of North Carolina

North Channel *n* a strait between NE Ireland and SW Scotland, linking the North Atlantic with the Irish Sea

North Country *n* (usually preceded by *the*) **1** another name for **North**[1] (sense 1) **2** the geographic region formed by Alaska, the Yukon, the Northwest Territories, and Nunavut

northcountryman (,nɔː'kʌntrɪmən) *n, pl* -men a native or inhabitant of the North of England

Northd *abbreviation for* Northumberland

North Dakota *n* a state of the western US: mostly undulating prairies and plains, rising from the Red River valley in the east to the Missouri plateau in the west, with the infertile Bad Lands in the extreme west. Capital: Bismarck. Pop: 633 837 (2003 est). Area: 183 019 sq km (70 664 sq miles). Abbreviations: N.Dak., N.D., (with zip code) ND

North Dakotan *adj* **1** of or relating to North Dakota or its inhabitants > *n* **2** a native or inhabitant of North Dakota

North Down *n* a district of E Northern Ireland, in Co Down. Pop: 77 110 (2003 est). Area: 82 sq km (32 sq miles)

northeast (,nɔː'θi:st; *Nautical* ,nɔː'ri:st) *n* **1** the point of the compass or direction midway between north and east, 45° clockwise from north **2** (*often capital;* usually preceded by *the*) any area lying in or towards this direction > *adj also* **northeastern 3** (*sometimes capital*) of or denoting the northeastern part of a specified country, area, etc: *northeast Lincolnshire* **4** situated in, proceeding towards, or facing the northeast **5** (esp of the wind) from the northeast > *adv* **6** in, to, towards, or (esp of the wind) from the northeast > Symbol: NE > ,north'easternmost *adj*

Northeast (,nɔː'θi:st) *n* (usually preceded by *the*) the northeastern part of England, esp Northumberland, Durham, and the Tyneside area

northeast by east *n* **1** one point on the compass east of northeast, 56° 15′ clockwise from north > *adj, adv* **2** in, from, or towards this direction

northeast by north *n* **1** one point on the compass north of northeast, 33° 45′ clockwise from north > *adj, adv* **2** in, from, or towards this direction

northeaster (,nɔː'θi:stə; *Nautical* ,nɔː'ri:stə) *n* a strong wind or storm from the northeast

northeasterly (,nɔː'θi:stəlɪ; *Nautical* ,nɔː'ri:stəlɪ) *adj, adv* **1** in, towards, or (esp of a wind) from the northeast > *n, pl* -lies **2** a wind or storm from the northeast

North East Frontier Agency *n* the former name (until 1972) of Arunachal Pradesh

North East Lincolnshire ('lɪŋkənʃɪə, -ʃə) *n* a unitary authority in E England, in Lincolnshire: formerly (1974–96) part of the county of Humberside. Pop: 157 400 (2003 est). Area: 192 sq km (74 sq miles)

Northeast Passage *n* a shipping route along the Arctic coasts of Europe and Asia, between the Atlantic and Pacific: first navigated by Nordenskjöld (1878–79)

northeastward (,nɔː'θi:stwəd; *Nautical* ,nɔː'ri:stwəd) *adj* **1** towards or (esp of a wind) from the northeast > *n* **2** a direction towards or area in the northeast > ,north'eastwardly *adj, adv*

northeastwards (,nɔː'θi:stwədz; *Nautical*

,nɔːˈriːstwədz) *or* **northeastward** *adv* to the northeast

norther ('nɔːðə) *n chiefly Southern US* a wind or storm from the north

northerly ('nɔːðəlɪ) *adj* **1** of, relating to, or situated in the north ▷ *adv, adj* **2** towards or in the direction of the north **3** from the north: *a northerly wind* ▷ *n, pl* -**lies 4** a wind from the north > '**northerliness** *n*

northern ('nɔːðən) *adj* **1** situated in or towards the north: *northern towns* **2** directed or proceeding towards the north: *a northern flow of traffic* **3** (esp of winds) proceeding from the north **4** (*sometimes capital*) of, relating to, or characteristic of the north or North **5** (*sometimes capital*) *astronomy* north of the celestial equator

Northern Cape *n* the largest but least populated province in South Africa, in the NW part of the country; created in 1994 from part of Cape Province: agriculture, mining (esp diamonds). Capital: Kimberley. Pop: 899 349 (2004 est). Area: 139 703 sq km (361 830 sq miles)

Northern Cross *n* a group of the five brightest stars that form a large cross in the constellation Cygnus

Northern Dvina *n* See **Dvina** (sense 1)

Northerner ('nɔːðənə) *n* (*sometimes not capital*) a native or inhabitant of the north of any specified region, esp England or the US

northern hemisphere *n* (*often capitals*) **1** that half of the globe lying north of the equator **2** *astronomy* that half of the celestial sphere north of the celestial equator ▷ Abbreviation: **N hemisphere**

Northern Ireland *n* that part of the United Kingdom occupying the NE part of Ireland: separated from the rest of Ireland, which became independent in law in 1920; it remained part of the United Kingdom, with a separate Parliament (Stormont), inaugurated in 1921, and limited self-government: scene of severe conflict between Catholics and Protestants, including terrorist bombing from 1969: direct administration from Westminster from 1972: assembly and powersharing executive established in 1998–99 following the Good Friday Agreement of 1998 and suspended indefinitely in 2002. Capital: Belfast. Pop: 1 702 628 (2003 est). Area: 14 121 sq km (5452 sq miles)

Northern Isles *pl n* Orkney and Shetland

northern lights *pl n* another name for **aurora borealis**

northernmost ('nɔːðən,məʊst) *adj* situated or occurring farthest north

Northern Province *n* the former name for **Limpopo** (sense 1)

Northern Rhodesia *n* the former name (until 1964) of **Zambia**

Northern Sotho *n* another name for **Pedi** (the language)

Northern Territories *pl n* a former British protectorate in W Africa, established in 1897; attached to the Gold Coast in 1901; constitutes the Northern Region of Ghana (since 1957)

Northern Territory *n* an administrative division of N central Australia, on the Timor and Arafura Seas: includes Ashmore and Cartier Islands; the Arunta Desert lies in the east, the Macdonnell Ranges in the south, and Arnhem Land in the north (containing Australia's largest Aboriginal reservation). Capital: Darwin. Pop: 198 700 (2003 est). Area: 1 347 525 sq km (520 280 sq miles)

North Germanic *n* a subbranch of the Germanic languages that consists of Danish, Norwegian, Swedish, Icelandic, and their associated dialects. See also **Old Norse**

North Holland *n* a province of the NW Netherlands, on the peninsula between the North Sea and IJsselmeer: includes the West Frisian Island of Texel. Capital: Haarlem. Pop: 2 573 000 (2003 est). Area: 2663 sq km (1029 sq miles). Dutch name: Noordholland

northing ('nɔːθɪŋ, -ðɪŋ) *n* **1** *navigation* movement or distance covered in a northerly direction, esp as expressed in the resulting difference in latitude **2** *astronomy* a north or positive declination **3** *cartography* **a** the distance northwards of a point from a given parallel indicated by the second half of a map grid reference **b** a latitudinal grid line. Compare **easting** (sense 2)

North Island *n* the northernmost of the two main islands of New Zealand. Pop: 3 087 200 (2004 est). Area: 114 729 sq km (44 297 sq miles)

North Island muttonbird *n* NZ another name for **grey-faced petrel**

North Korea *n* a republic in NE Asia, on the Sea of Japan and the Yellow Sea: established in 1948 as a people's republic; mostly rugged and mountainous, with fertile lowlands in the west. Language: Korean. Currency: won. Capital: Pyongyang. Pop: 22 776 000 (2004 est). Area: 122 313 sq km (47 225 sq miles). Official name: Democratic People's Republic of Korea Korean name: Chosŏn

North Korean *adj* **1** of or relating to North Korea or its inhabitants ▷ *n* **2** a native or inhabitant of North Korea

North Lanarkshire ('lænəkʃɪə, -ʃə) *n* a council area of central Scotland: consists of the NE part of the historical county of Lanarkshire; formerly (1974–96) part of Strathclyde Region: engineering and metalworking industries. Administrative centre: Motherwell. Pop: 321 820 (2003 est). Area: 1771 sq km (684 sq miles)

Northland ('nɔːðlənd) *n* **1** the peninsula containing Norway and Sweden **2** (in Canada) the far north

Northlander ('nɔːðləndə) *n* **1** a native or inhabitant of the peninsula containing Norway and Sweden **2** (in Canada) a native or inhabitant of the far north

North Lincolnshire ('lɪŋkənʃɪə, -ʃə) *n* a unitary authority of NE England, in Lincolnshire: formerly (1975–96) part of the county of Humberside. Pop: 155 000 (2003 est). Area: 1497 sq km (578 sq miles)

Northman ('nɔːθmən) *n, pl* -**men** another name for a **Viking**

north-northeast *n* **1** the point on the compass or the direction midway between north and northeast, 22° 30′ clockwise from north ▷ *adj, adv* **2** in, from, or towards this direction ▷ Symbol: NNE

north-northwest *n* **1** the point on the compass or the direction midway between northwest and north, 337° 30′ clockwise from north ▷ *adj, adv* **2** in, from, or towards this direction ▷ Symbol: NNW

North Ossetian Republic (əˈsiːʃən) *n* a constituent republic of S Russia, on the N slopes of the central Caucasus Mountains. Capital: Vladikavkaz. Pop: 709 900 (2002). Area: about 8000 sq km (3088 sq miles). Also called: North Ossetia, Alania

North Pole *n* **1** the northernmost point on the earth's axis, at a latitude of 90°N **2** Also called: north celestial pole *astronomy* the point of intersection of the earth's extended axis and the northern half of the celestial sphere, lying about 1° from Polaris **3** (*usually not capitals*) the pole of a freely suspended magnet, which is attracted to the earth's magnetic North Pole

North Rhine-Westphalia *n* a state of W Germany: formed in 1946 by the amalgamation of the Prussian province of Westphalia with the N part of the Prussian Rhine province and later with the state of Lippe; part of West Germany until 1990: highly industrialized. Capital: Düsseldorf. Pop: 18 080 000 (2003 est). Area: 34 039 sq km (13 142 sq miles). German name: Nordrhein-Westfalen

North Riding *n* (until 1974) an administrative division of Yorkshire, now constituting most of North Yorkshire

North Saskatchewan *n* a river in W Canada,

rising in W Alberta and flowing northeast, east, and southeast to join the South Saskatchewan River and form the Saskatchewan River. Length: 1223 km (760 miles)

North Sea *n* an arm of the Atlantic between Great Britain and the N European mainland. Area: about 569 800 sq km (220 000 sq miles). Former name: German Ocean

North-Sea gas *n* (in Britain) natural gas obtained from deposits below the North Sea

North Somerset ('sʌməsɛt) *n* a unitary authority of SW England, in Somerset: formerly (1974–96) part of the county of Avon. Pop: 191 400 (2003 est). Area: 375 sq km (145 sq miles)

North Star *n* the another name for **Polaris** (sense 1)

North Tyneside ('taɪnsaɪd) *n* a unitary authority of NE England, in Tyne and Wear. Pop: 190 800 (2003 est). Area: 84 sq km (32 sq miles)

Northumberland (nɔːˈθʌmbələnd) *n* the northernmost county of England, on the North Sea: hilly in the north (the Cheviots) and west (the Pennines), with many Roman remains, notably Hadrian's Wall. Administrative centre: Morpeth. Pop: 309 200 (2003 est). Area: 5032 sq km (1943 sq miles). Abbreviation: Northd

Northumbria (nɔːˈθʌmbrɪə) *n* **1** (in Anglo-Saxon Britain) a region that stretched from the Humber to the Firth of Forth: formed in the 7th century AD, it became an important intellectual centre; a separate kingdom until 876 AD **2** an area of NE England roughly corresponding to the Anglo-Saxon region of Northumbria

Northumbrian (nɔːˈθʌmbrɪən) *adj* **1** of or relating to the English county of Northumberland, its inhabitants, or their dialect of English **2** of or relating to ancient Northumbria, its inhabitants, or their dialect ▷ *n* **3 a** the dialect of Old and Middle English spoken north of the River Humber. See also **Anglian, Mercian b** the dialect of Modern English spoken in Northumberland

North Vietnam *n* a region of N Vietnam, on the Gulf of Tonkin: an independent Communist state from 1954 until 1976. Area: 164 061 sq km (63 344 sq miles)

northward ('nɔːθwəd; *Nautical* 'nɔːðəd) *adj* **1** moving, facing, or situated towards the north ▷ *n* **2** the northward part, direction, etc; the north ▷ *adv* **3** a variant of **northwards.** > 'northwardly *adj, adv*

northwards ('nɔːθwədz) *or* **northward** *adv* towards the north

northwest (,nɔːθˈwɛst; *Nautical* ,nɔːˈwɛst) *n* **1** the point of the compass or direction midway between north and west, clockwise 315° from north **2** (*often capital;* usually preceded by *the*) any area lying in or towards this direction ▷ *adj* *also* northwestern **3** (*sometimes capital*) of or denoting the northwestern part of a specified country, area, etc: *northwest Greenland* ▷ *adj, adv* **4** in, to, towards, or (esp of the wind) from the northwest ▷ Symbol: NW > ,north'westernmost *adj*

Northwest (,nɔːθˈwɛst) *n* (usually preceded by *the*) **1** the northwestern part of England, esp Lancashire and the Lake District **2** the northwestern part of the US, consisting of the states of Washington, Oregon, and sometimes Idaho **3** (in Canada) the region north and west of the Great Lakes

North West *n* a province in N South Africa, created in 1994 from the NE part of Cape Province and part of Transvaal: agriculture and service industries. Capital: Mafikeng. Pop: 3 807 469 (2004 est). Area: 116 320 sq km (44 911 sq miles)

northwest by north *n* **1** one point on the compass north of northwest, 326° 15′ clockwise from north ▷ *adj, adv* **2** in, from, or towards this direction

northwest by west *n* **1** one point on the compass south of northwest, 303° 45′ clockwise from north ▷ *adj, adv* **2** in, from, or towards this direction

n

northwester (ˌnɔːθ'wɛstə; *Nautical* ˌnɔː'wɛstə) *n* a strong wind or storm from the northwest

northwesterly (ˌnɔːθ'wɛstəlɪ; *Nautical* ˌnɔː'wɛstəlɪ) *adj, adv* **1** in, towards, or (esp of a wind) from the northwest ▷ *n, pl* **-lies 2** a wind or storm from the northwest

North-West Frontier Province *n* a province in N Pakistan between Afghanistan and Jammu and Kashmir: part of British India from 1901 until 1947; of strategic importance, esp for the Khyber Pass. Capital: Peshawar. Pop: 20 170 000 (2003 est). Area: 74 522 sq km (28 773 sq miles)

Northwest Passage *n* the passage by sea from the Atlantic to the Pacific along the N coast of America: attempted for over 300 years by Europeans seeking a short route to the Far East, before being successfully navigated by Amundsen (1903–06)

Northwest Territories *pl n* a territory of NW Canada including part of Victoria Island and several other islands of the Arctic; comprised over a third of Canada's total area until Nunavut became a separate territory in 1999: rich mineral resources. Pop: 42 810 (2004 est). Area: 2 082 910 sq km (804 003 sq miles). Abbreviation: **NWT**

Northwest Territory *n* See **Old Northwest**

northwestward (ˌnɔːθ'wɛstwəd; *Nautical* ˌnɔː'wɛstwəd) *adj* **1** towards or (esp of a wind) from the northwest ▷ *n* **2** a direction towards or area in the northwest > ˌnorth'westwardly *adj, adv*

northwestwards (ˌnɔːθ'wɛstwədz; *Nautical* ˌnɔː'wɛstwədz) *or* **northwestward** *adv* towards or (esp of a wind) from the northwest

Northwich (ˈnɔːθwɪtʃ) *n* a town in NW England, in Cheshire: salt and chemical industries. Pop: 39 568 (2001)

North Yemen *n* a former republic in SW Arabia, on the Red Sea; now part of Yemen: declared a republic in 1962: united with South Yemen in 1990. Official name: **Yemen Arab Republic** See also **Yemen, South Yemen**

North Yorkshire *n* a county in N England, formed in 1974 from most of the North Riding of Yorkshire and parts of the East and West Ridings: the geographical and ceremonial county includes the unitary authorities of Middlesbrough, Redcar and Cleveland, and part of Stockton on Tees (all within Cleveland until 1996), and York (created in 1997). Administrative centre: Northallerton. Pop (excluding unitary authorities): 576 100 (2003 est). Area (excluding unitary authorities): 8037 sq km (3102 sq miles)

Norw. *abbreviation for* **1** Norway **2** Norwegian

Norway (ˈnɔːˌweɪ) *n* a kingdom in NW Europe, occupying the W part of the Scandinavian peninsula: first united in the Viking age (800–1050); under the rule of Denmark (1523–1814) and Sweden (1814–1905); became an independent monarchy in 1905. Its coastline is deeply indented with fjords and fringed with islands, rising inland to plateaus and mountains. Norway has a large fishing fleet and its merchant navy is among the world's largest. Official language: Norwegian. Official religion: Evangelical Lutheran. Currency: krone. Capital: Oslo. Pop: 4 552 000 (2004 est). Area: 323 878 sq km (125 050 sq miles). Norwegian name: **Norge**

Norway lobster *n* a European lobster, *Nephrops norvegicus,* fished for food

Norway maple *n* a large Eurasian maple tree, *Acer platanoides,* with broad five-lobed pale green leaves

Norway rat *n* another name for **brown rat**

Norway spruce *n* a European spruce tree, *Picea abies,* having drooping branches and dark green needle-like leaves

Norwegian (nɔː'wiːdʒən) *adj* **1** of, relating to, or characteristic of Norway, its language, or its people ▷ *n* **2** any of the various North Germanic languages of Norway. See also **Nynorsk, Bokmål** Compare **Norse 3** a native, citizen, or inhabitant of Norway

Norwegian buhund ('buːˌhʊnd) *n* a slightly-built medium-sized dog of a breed with erect pointed ears and a short thick tail carried curled over its back [from Norwegian *bu* homestead, livestock + *hund* dog]

Norwegian forest cat *n* a breed of long-haired cat with a long bushy tail and a long mane

Norwegian Sea *n* part of the Arctic Ocean between Greenland and Norway

nor'wester (ˌnɔː'wɛstə) *n* **1** a less common name for **sou'wester 2** a drink of strong liquor **3** a strong northwest wind **4** *NZ* a hot dry wind from the Southern Alps [C18 (in the sense: storm from the northwest): a contraction of NORTHWESTER]

Norwich (ˈnɒrɪdʒ) *n* a city in E England, administrative centre of Norfolk: cathedral (founded 1096); University of East Anglia (1963); traditionally a centre of the footwear industry, now has engineering, financial services. Pop: 174 047 (2001)

Norwich terrier *n* a small wiry-coated breed of terrier having either erect or pendent ears

Nos. *or* **nos.** *abbreviation for* numbers

nose (nəʊz) *n* **1** the organ of smell and entrance to the respiratory tract, consisting of a prominent structure divided into two hair-lined air passages by a median septum. Related adjs: **nasal, rhinal 2** the sense of smell itself: in hounds and other animals, the ability to follow trails by scent (esp in the phrases **a good nose, a bad nose**) **3** another word for **bouquet** (sense 2) **4** instinctive skill or facility, esp in discovering things (sometimes in the phrase **follow one's nose**): *he had a nose for good news stories* **5** any part regarded as resembling a nose in form or function, such as a nozzle or spout **6** the forward part of a vehicle, aircraft, etc, esp the front end of an aircraft **7** narrow margin of victory (in the phrase (**win**) **by a nose**) **8** cut off one's nose to spite one's face to carry out a vengeful action that hurts oneself more than another **9** get up (someone's) nose *informal* to annoy or irritate (someone) **10** keep one's nose clean to stay out of trouble; behave properly **11** keep one's nose to the grindstone to work hard and continuously **12** lead (someone) by the nose to make (someone) do unquestioningly all one wishes; dominate (someone) **13** look down one's nose at *informal* to be contemptuous or disdainful of **14** nose to tail (of vehicles) moving or standing very close behind one another **15** on the nose *slang* **a** (in horse-race betting) to win only: *I bet twenty pounds on the nose on that horse* **b** *chiefly US and Canadian* precisely; exactly **c** *Austral* bad or bad-smelling **16** pay through the nose *informal* to pay an exorbitant price **17** poke, stick, etc, one's nose into *informal* to pry into or interfere in **18** put someone's nose out of joint *informal* to thwart or offend someone, esp by supplanting him or gaining something he regards as his **19** rub someone's nose in it *informal* to remind someone unkindly of his failing or error **20** see no further than (the end of) one's nose *informal* **a** to be short-sighted; suffer from myopia **b** to lack insight or foresight **21** turn up one's nose (at) *informal* to behave disdainfully (towards) **22** under one's nose **a** directly in front of one **b** without one noticing **23** with one's nose in the air haughtily ▷ *vb* **24** (*tr*) (esp of horses, dogs, etc) to rub, touch, or sniff with the nose; nuzzle **25** to smell or sniff (wine, etc) **26** (*intr*; usually foll by *after* or *for*) to search (for) by or as if by scent **27** to move or cause to move forwards slowly and carefully: *the car nosed along the cliff top; we nosed the car into the garage* **28** (*intr*; foll by *into, around, about,* etc) to pry or snoop (into) or meddle (in) ▷ See also **nose out** [Old English *nosu;* related to Old Frisian *nose,* Norwegian *nosa* to smell and *nus* smell] > 'noseless *adj* > 'nose,like *adj*

nosebag ('nəʊz,bæg) *n* a bag, fastened around the head of a horse and covering the nose, in which feed is placed

noseband ('nəʊz,bænd) *n* the detachable part of a horse's bridle that goes around the nose. Also called: nosepiece > 'nose,banded *adj*

nosebleed ('nəʊz,bliːd) *n* bleeding from the nose, as the result of injury, etc. Technical name: epistaxis

nose cone *n* the conical forward section of a missile, spacecraft, etc, designed to withstand high temperatures, esp during re-entry into the earth's atmosphere

nose dive *n* **1** a sudden plunge with the nose or front pointing downwards, esp of an aircraft **2** *informal* a sudden drop or sharp decline: *prices took a nose dive* ▷ *vb* **nose-dive 3** to perform or cause to perform a nose dive **4** (*intr*) *informal* to drop suddenly

nose flute *n* (esp in the South Sea Islands) a type of flute blown through the nose

nosegay ('nəʊz,geɪ) *n* a small bunch of flowers; posy [C15 from NOSE + archaic *gay* a toy]

nose job *n* *slang* a surgical remodelling of the nose for cosmetic reasons

nose out *vb* (*tr, adverb*) **1** to discover by smelling **2** to discover by cunning or persistence: *the reporter managed to nose out a few facts* **3** *informal* to beat by a narrow margin: *he was nosed out of first place*

nosepiece ('nəʊz,piːs) *n* **1** Also called: nasal a piece of armour, esp part of a helmet, that serves to protect the nose **2** the connecting part of a pair of spectacles that rests on the nose; bridge **3** the part of a microscope to which one or more objective lenses are attached **4** a less common word for **noseband**

nose rag *n* *slang* a handkerchief

nose ring *n* a ring fixed through the nose, as for leading a bull

nose wheel *n* a wheel fitted to the forward end of a vehicle, esp the landing wheel under the nose of an aircraft

nosey ('nəʊzɪ) *adj* a variant spelling of **nosy**

nosh (nɒʃ) *slang* ▷ *n* **1** food or a meal ▷ *vb* **2** to eat [C20 from Yiddish; compare German *naschen* to nibble] > 'nosher *n*

noshery *or* **nosherie** ('nɒʃərɪ) *n, pl* -eries *informal* a restaurant or other place where food is served

no-show *n* a person who fails to take up a reserved seat, place, etc, without having cancelled it

nosh-up *n* *Brit slang* a large and satisfying meal

no-side *n* *rugby* the end of a match, signalled by the referee's whistle

nosing ('nəʊzɪŋ) *n* **1** the edge of a step or stair tread that projects beyond the riser **2** a projecting edge of a moulding, esp one that is half-round [C18 from NOSE + -ING¹]

noso- *or before a vowel* **nos-** *combining form* disease: *nosology* [from Greek *nosos*]

nosocomial (ˌnɒsə'kəʊmɪəl) *adj med* originating in hospital: *nosocomial disease* [C19 New Latin *nosocomialis,* via Late Latin from Greek, from *nosokomos* one that tends the sick, from *nosos* (see NOSO-) + *komein* to tend]

nosography (nɒ'sɒgrəfɪ) *n* a written classification and description of various diseases > no'sographer *n* > nosographic (ˌnɒsə'græfɪk) *adj*

nosology (nɒ'sɒlədʒɪ) *n* the branch of medicine concerned with the classification of diseases > nosological (ˌnɒsə'lɒdʒɪkᵊl) *adj* > ˌnoso'logically *adv* > no'sologist *n*

nosophobia (ˌnɒsə'fəʊbɪə) *n* the morbid dread of contracting disease

nostalgia (nɒ'stældʒə, -dʒɪə) *n* **1** a yearning for the return of past circumstances, events, etc **2** the evocation of this emotion, as in a book, film, etc **3** longing for home or family; homesickness [C18 New Latin (translation of German *Heimweh* homesickness), from Greek *nostos* a return home + -ALGIA]

nostalgic (nɒ'stældʒɪk) *adj* **1** of or characterized by nostalgia ▷ *n* **2** a person who indulges in nostalgia

nostalgist (nɒ'stældʒɪst) *n* a person who indulges in nostalgia

nostoc ('nɒstɒk) *n* any cyanobacterium of the genus *Nostoc,* occurring in moist places as rounded colonies consisting of coiled filaments in a gelatinous substance [c17 New Latin, coined by Paracelsus]

nostology (nɒ'stɒlədʒɪ) *n med* another word for **gerontology** [c20 from Greek *nostos* a return home (with reference to ageing or second childhood) + -LOGY] > **nostologic** (ˌnɒstə'lɒdʒɪk) *adj*

nostril ('nɒstrɪl) *n* either of the two external openings of the nose. Related adjs: **narial, narine** [Old English *nosthyrl,* from *nosu* NOSE + *thyrel* hole]

nostro account ('nɒstrəʊ) *n* a bank account conducted by a British bank with a foreign bank, usually in the foreign currency. Compare **vostro account**

nostrum ('nɒstrəm) *n* **1** a patent or quack medicine **2** a favourite remedy, as for political or social problems [c17 from Latin: our own (make), from *noster* our]

nosy *or* **nosey** ('nəʊzɪ) *adj* nosier, nosiest *informal* prying or inquisitive > **'nosily** *adv* > **'nosiness** *n*

nosy parker *n informal* a prying person [c20 apparently arbitrary use of surname *Parker*]

not (nɒt) *adv* **1 a** used to negate the sentence, phrase, or word that it modifies: *I will not stand for it* **b** (in combination): *they cannot go* **2** not that (*conjunction*) Also (archaic): not but what which is not to say or suppose that: *I expect to lose the game — not that I mind* ▷ *sentence substitute* **3** used to indicate denial, negation, or refusal: *certainly not* [c14 *not,* variant of *nought* nothing, from Old English *nāwiht,* from *nā* no + *wiht* creature, thing. See NAUGHT, NOUGHT]

not- *combining form* a variant of **noto-** before a vowel

nota ('nəʊtə) *n* the plural of **notum**

nota bene Latin ('nəʊtə 'biːnɪ) note well; take note. Abbreviations: NB, N.B., nb, n.b.

notability (ˌnəʊtə'bɪlɪtɪ) *n, pl* -ties **1** the state or quality of being notable **2** a distinguished person; notable

notable ('nəʊtəb²l) *adj* **1** worthy of being noted or remembered; remarkable; distinguished ▷ *n* **2** a notable person [c14 via Old French from Latin *notābilis,* from *notāre* to NOTE] > **'notableness** *n*

notably ('nəʊtəblɪ) *adv* particularly or especially; in a way worthy of being noted

notarize *or* **notarise** ('nəʊtəˌraɪz) *vb* (*tr*) to attest to or authenticate (a document, contract, etc), as a notary

notary ('nəʊtərɪ) *n, pl* -ries **1** a notary public **2** (formerly) a clerk licensed to prepare legal documents **3** *archaic* a clerk or secretary [c14 from Latin *notārius* clerk, from *nota* a mark, note] > **notarial** (nəʊ'tɛərɪəl) *adj* > **no'tarially** *adv* > **'notaryship** *n*

notary public *n, pl* notaries public a public official, usually a solicitor, who is legally authorized to administer oaths, attest and certify certain documents, etc

notate (nəʊ'teɪt) *vb* to write (esp music) in notation [c20 back formation from NOTATION]

notation (nəʊ'teɪʃən) *n* **1** any series of signs or symbols used to represent quantities or elements in a specialized system, such as music or mathematics **2** the act or process of notating **3 a** the act of noting down **b** a note or record [c16 from Latin *notātiō* a marking, from *notāre* to NOTE] > **no'tational** *adj*

notch (nɒtʃ) *n* **1** a V-shaped cut or indentation; nick **2** a cut or nick made in a tally stick or similar object **3** *US and Canadian* a narrow pass or gorge **4** *informal* a step or level (esp in the phrase **a notch above**) ▷ *vb* (*tr*) **5** to cut or make a notch in **6** to record with or as if with a notch **7** (usually foll by *up*) *informal* to score or achieve: *the team notched up its fourth win* [c16 from incorrect division of *an otch* (as *a notch*), from Old French *oche* notch, from Latin *obsecāre* to cut off, from *secāre* to cut]

notch effect *n metallurgy, building trades* the increase in stress in an area of a component near a crack, depression, etc, or a change in section, such as a sharp angle: can be enough to cause failure of the component although the calculated average stress may be quite safe

notchy ('nɒtʃɪ) *adj* (of a motor vehicle gear mechanism) requiring careful gear-changing, as if having to fit the lever into narrow notches

NOT circuit *or* **gate** (nɒt) *n computing* a logic circuit that has a high-voltage output signal if the input signal is low, and vice versa: used extensively in computers. Also called: inverter, negator [c20 so named because the action performed on electrical signals is similar to the operation of *not* in logical constructions]

note (nəʊt) *n* **1** a brief summary or record in writing, esp a jotting for future reference **2** a brief letter, usually of an informal nature **3** a formal written communication, esp from one government to another **4** a short written statement giving any kind of information **5** a critical comment, explanatory statement, or reference in the text of a book, often preceded by a number **6** short for **banknote 7** a characteristic element or atmosphere: *a note of sarcasm* **8** a distinctive vocal sound, as of a species of bird or animal: *the note of the nightingale* **9** any of a series of graphic signs representing a musical sound whose pitch is indicated by position on the stave and whose duration is indicated by the sign's shape **10** Also called (esp US and Canadian): tone a musical sound of definite fundamental frequency or pitch **11** a key on a piano, organ, etc **12** a sound, as from a musical instrument, used as a signal or warning: *the note to retreat was sounded* **13** short for **promissory note 14** *archaic or poetic* a tune or melody **15** of note **a** distinguished or famous: *an athlete of note* **b** worth noticing or paying attention to; important: *nothing of note* **16** strike the right (*or* a false) note to behave appropriately (or inappropriately) **17** take note (often foll by *of*) to observe carefully; pay close attention (to) ▷ *vb* (*tr; may take a clause as object*) **18** to notice; perceive: *he noted that there was a man in the shadows* **19** to pay close attention to; observe: *they noted every movement* **20** to make a written note or memorandum of: *she noted the date in her diary* **21** to make particular mention of; remark upon: *I note that you do not wear shoes* **22** to write down (music, a melody, etc) in notes **23** to take (an unpaid or dishonoured bill of exchange) to a notary public to re-present the bill and if it is still unaccepted or unpaid to note the circumstances in a register. See **protest** (sense 12) **24** a brief letter [c13 via Old French from Latin *nota* sign, indication] > **'noteless** *adj*

notebook ('nəʊtˌbʊk) *n* **1** a book for recording notes or memoranda **2** a book for registering promissory notes

notebook computer *n* a portable computer smaller than a laptop model, often approximately the size of a sheet of A4 paper

notecase ('nəʊtˌkeɪs) *n* a less common word for **wallet** (sense 1)

noted ('nəʊtɪd) *adj* **1** distinguished; celebrated; famous **2** of special note or significance; noticeable: *a noted increase in the crime rate* > **'notedly** *adv*

notelet ('nəʊtlɪt) *n* a folded card with a printed design on the front, for writing a short informal letter

note of hand *n* another name for **promissory note**

notepaper ('nəʊtˌpeɪpə) *n* paper for writing letters; writing paper

note-perfect *adj* **1** (of a singer or musician) able to sing or play without making any errors **2** (of a piece of music) sung or performed without any errors

note row (rəʊ) *n music* another name for **tone row**

notes (nəʊts) *pl n* **1** short descriptive or summarized jottings taken down for future reference **2** a record of impressions, reflections, etc, esp as a literary form

notes inégales French (nɔts inegal) *pl n* **1** (esp in French baroque music) notes written down evenly but executed as if they were divided into pairs of long and short notes **2** the style of playing in this manner [literally: unequal notes]

note value *n* another term for **time value**

noteworthy ('nəʊtˌwɜːðɪ) *adj* worthy of notice; notable > **'note,worthily** *adv* > **'note,worthiness** *n*

not-for-profit organization *or esp US* **nonprofit organization** *n* an organization that is not intended to make a profit, esp one set up to provide a public service

nothing ('nʌθɪŋ) *pron* **1** (*indefinite*) no thing; not anything, as of an implied or specified class of things: *I can give you nothing* **2** no part or share: *to have nothing to do with this crime* **3** a matter of no importance or significance: *it doesn't matter, it's nothing* **4** indicating the absence of anything perceptible; nothingness **5** indicating the absence of meaning, value, worth, etc: *to amount to nothing* **6** zero quantity; nought **7** be nothing to **a** not to concern or be significant to (someone) **b** to be not nearly as good as **8** have *or* be nothing to do with **a** to have no connection with **9** have (got) nothing on **a** to have no engagements to keep **b** to be undressed or naked **c** *informal* to compare unfavourably with **10** in nothing flat *informal* in almost no time; very quickly or soon **11** nothing but not something other than; only **12** nothing doing *informal* an expression of dismissal, disapproval, lack of compliance with a request, etc **13** nothing if not at the very least; certainly **14** nothing less than *or* nothing short of downright; truly **15** (there's) nothing for it (there's) no choice; (there's) no other course **16** there's nothing like a general expression of praise: *there's nothing like a good cup of tea* **17** there's nothing to it it is very simple, easy, etc **18** think nothing of **a** to regard as routine, easy, or natural **b** to have no compunction or hesitation about **c** to have a very low opinion of **19** to say nothing of as well as; even disregarding: *he was warmly dressed in a shirt and heavy jumper, to say nothing of his thick overcoat* **20** stop at nothing to be prepared to do anything; be unscrupulous or ruthless ▷ *adv* **21** in no way; not at all: *he looked nothing like his brother* ▷ *n* **22** *informal* a person or thing of no importance or significance **23** sweet nothings words of endearment or affection [Old English *nāthing, nān thing,* from *nān* NONE[1] + THING[1]]

> **USAGE** *Nothing* normally takes a singular verb, but when *nothing but* is followed by a plural form of a noun, a plural verb is usually used: *it was a large room where nothing but souvenirs were sold*

nothingness ('nʌθɪŋnɪs) *n* **1** the state or condition of being nothing; nonexistence **2** absence of consciousness or life **3** complete insignificance or worthlessness **4** something that is worthless or insignificant

notice ('nəʊtɪs) *n* **1** the act of perceiving; observation; attention: *to escape notice* **2** take notice to pay attention; attend **3** take no notice of to ignore or disregard **4** information about a future event; warning; announcement **5** a displayed placard or announcement giving information **6** advance notification of intention to end an arrangement, contract, etc, as of renting or employment (esp in the phrase **give notice**) **7** at short, two hours', etc, notice with notification only a little, two hours, etc, in advance **8** *chiefly Brit* dismissal from employment **9** favourable, interested, or polite attention: *she was beneath his notice* **10** a theatrical or literary review: *the play received very good notices* ▷ *vb* (*tr*) **11** to become conscious or aware of; perceive; note **12** to point out or remark upon **13** to pay polite or interested attention to **14** to recognize or acknowledge (an acquaintance) [c15 via Old French from Latin *notitia* fame, from *nōtus* known, celebrated]

noticeable ('nəʊtɪsəbəl) *adj* easily seen or detected; perceptible: *the stain wasn't noticeable* > ˌnoticea'bility *n* > 'noticeably *adv*

notice board *n Brit* a board on which notices, advertisements, bulletins, etc, are displayed. US and Canadian name: **bulletin board**

notifiable ('nəʊtɪˌfaɪəbəl) *adj* **1** denoting certain infectious diseases of humans, such as smallpox and tuberculosis, outbreaks of which must be reported to the public health authorities **2** denoting certain infectious diseases of animals, such as BSE, foot-and-mouth disease, and rabies, outbreaks of which must be reported to the appropriate veterinary authority

notification (ˌnəʊtɪfɪ'keɪʃən) *n* **1** the act of notifying **2** a formal announcement **3** something that notifies; a notice

notify ('nəʊtɪˌfaɪ) *vb* **-fies, -fying, -fied** (*tr*) **1** to inform; tell **2** *chiefly Brit* to draw attention to; make known; announce [c14 from Old French *notifier*, from Latin *notificāre* to make known, from *nōtus* known + *facere* to make] > 'notiˌfier *n*

no-tillage *n* a system of farming in which planting is done in a narrow trench, without tillage, and weeds are controlled with herbicide

notion ('nəʊʃən) *n* **1** a vague idea; impression **2** an idea, concept, or opinion **3** an inclination or whim ▷ See also **notions** [c16 from Latin *nōtiō* a becoming acquainted (with), examination (of), from *noscere* to know]

notional ('nəʊʃənəl) *adj* **1** relating to, expressing, or consisting of notions or ideas **2** not evident in reality; hypothetical or imaginary: *a notional tax credit* **3** characteristic of a notion or concept, esp in being speculative or imaginary; abstract **4** *grammar* **a** (of a word) having lexical meaning **b** another word for **semantic**. > 'notionally *adv*

notions ('nəʊʃənz) *pl n chiefly US and Canadian* pins, cotton, ribbon, and similar wares used for sewing; haberdashery

notitia (nəʊ'tɪʃɪə) *n* a register or list, esp of ecclesiastical districts [c18 Latin, literally: knowledge, from *notus* known]

noto- *or before a vowel* **not-** *combining form* the back: *notochord* [from Greek *nōton* the back]

notochord ('nəʊtəˌkɔːd) *n* a fibrous longitudinal rod in all embryo and some adult chordate animals, immediately above the gut, that supports the body. It is replaced in adult vertebrates by the vertebral column > ˌnoto'chordal *adj*

Notogaea (ˌnəʊtə'dʒiːə) *n* a zoogeographical area comprising the Australasian region. Compare **Arctogaea, Neogaea** [c19 from Greek *notos* south wind + *gaia* land]

Notogaean (ˌnəʊtə'dʒiːən) *n* **1** a native or inhabitant of Notogaea, a zoogeographical area comprising the Australasian region ▷ *adj* **2** of or relating to Notogaea or its inhabitants

notorious (nəʊ'tɔːrɪəs) *adj* **1** well-known for some bad or unfavourable quality, deed, etc; infamous **2** *rare* generally known or widely acknowledged [c16 from Medieval Latin *notōrius* well-known, from *nōtus* known, from *noscere* to know] > notoriety (ˌnəʊtə'raɪɪtɪ) *or* no'toriousness *n* > no'toriously *adv*

notornis (nəʊ'tɔːnɪs) *n* a rare flightless rail of the genus *Notornis*, of New Zealand. See **takahe** [c19 New Latin, from Greek *notos* south + *ornis* bird]

nototherium (ˌnəʊtəʊ'θɪərɪəm) *n* an extinct Pleistocene rhinoceros-sized marsupial of the genus *Notothrium*, related to the wombats [c19 New Latin, from Greek *notos* south (referring to their discovery in the S hemisphere) + *thērion* beast]

notour ('nəʊtə) *adj* (in Scots Law) short for **notorious**. A **notour bankrupt** is one who has failed to discharge his debts within the days of grace allowed by the court

not proven ('prəʊvən) *adj* (*postpositive*) a third

verdict available to Scottish courts, returned when there is evidence against the defendant but insufficient to convict

Notre Dame ('nəʊtrə 'dɑːm, 'nɒtrə; *French* nɔtrə dam) *n* the early Gothic cathedral of Paris, on the Île de la Cité: built between 1163 and 1257

no-trump *bridge* ▷ *n* also **no-trumps 1** a bid or contract to play without trumps ▷ *adj* also **no-trumper 2** (of a hand) of balanced distribution suitable for playing without trumps

Nottingham ('nɒtɪŋəm) *n* **1** a city in N central England, administrative centre of Nottinghamshire, on the River Trent: scene of the outbreak of the Civil War (1642); famous for its associations with the Robin Hood legend; two universities. Pop: 249 584 (2001) **2** a unitary authority in N central England, in Nottinghamshire. Pop: 273 900 (2003 est). Area: 78 sq km (30 sq miles)

Nottinghamshire ('nɒtɪŋəmˌʃɪə, -ʃə) *n* an inland county of central England: generally low-lying, with part of the S Pennines and the remnant of Sherwood Forest in the east. Nottingham became an independent unitary authority in 1998. Administrative centre: Nottingham. Pop (excluding Nottingham): 755 400 (2003 est). Area (excluding Nottingham): 2086 sq km (805 sq miles). Abbreviation: **Notts**

Nottm *abbreviation for* Nottingham

Notts (nɒts) *abbreviation for* Nottinghamshire

notum ('nəʊtəm) *n, pl* **-ta** (-tə) a cuticular plate covering the dorsal surface of a thoracic segment of an insect [c19 New Latin, from Greek *nōton* back] > 'notal *adj*

Notus ('nəʊtəs) *n classical myth* a personification of the south or southwest wind

notwithstanding (ˌnɒtwɪθ'stændɪŋ, -wɪð-) *prep* **1** (*often immediately postpositive*) in spite of; despite ▷ *conj* **2** (*subordinating*) despite the fact that; although ▷ *sentence connector* **3** in spite of that; nevertheless [c14 NOT + *withstanding*, from Old English *withstandan*, on the model of Medieval Latin *non obstante*, Old French *non obstant*]

Nouakchott (*French* nwakʃɔt) *n* the capital of Mauritania, near the Atlantic coast: replaced St Louis as capital in 1957; situated on important caravan routes. Pop: 559 000 (2002 est)

nougat ('nuːɡɑː, 'nʌɡət) *n* a hard chewy pink or white sweet containing chopped nuts, cherries, etc [c19 via French from Provençal *nogat*, from *noga* nut, from Latin *nux* nut]

nought (nɔːt) *n also* **naught, ought, aught 1** another name for **zero**: used esp in counting or numbering ▷ *n, adj, adv* **2** a variant spelling of **naught** [Old English *nōwiht*, from *ne* not, no + *ōwiht* something; see WHIT]

noughties ('nɔːtɪz) *pl n informal* the years from 2000 to 2009

noughts and crosses *n* (*functioning as singular*) a game in which two players, one using a nought, "O", the other a cross, "X", alternately mark one square out of nine formed by two pairs of crossed lines, the winner being the first to get three of his symbols in a row. US and Canadian term: **tick-tack-toe, (US) crisscross**

Nouméa (ˌnuː'meɪə; *French* numea) *n* the capital and chief port of the French Overseas Territory of New Caledonia. Pop: 146 000 (2005 est)

noumenon ('nuːmɪnən, 'nəʊ-) *n, pl* **-na** (-nə) **1** (in the philosophy of Kant) a thing as it is in itself, not perceived or interpreted, incapable of being known, but only inferred from the nature of experience. Compare **phenomenon** (sense 3) See also **thing-in-itself 2** the object of a purely intellectual intuition [c18 via German from Greek: thing being thought of, from *noein* to think, perceive; related to *nous* mind] > 'noumenal *adj* > 'noumenalism *n* > 'noumenalist *n, adj* > ˌnoume'nality *n* > 'noumenally *adv*

noun (naʊn) *n* **a** a word or group of words that refers to a person, place, or thing or any syntactically similar word **b** (*as modifier*): *a noun*

phrase. Abbreviations: **N, n** Related *adj:* **nominal** [c14 via Anglo-French from Latin *nōmen* NAME] > 'nounal *adj* > 'nounally *adv* > 'nounless *adj*

noun phrase *n grammar* a constituent of a sentence that consists of a noun and any modifiers it may have, a noun clause, or a word, such as a pronoun, that takes the place of a noun. Abbreviation: **NP**

nourish ('nʌrɪʃ) *vb* (*tr*) **1** to provide with the materials necessary for life and growth **2** to support or encourage (an idea, feeling, etc); foster: *to nourish resentment* [c14 from Old French *norir*, from Latin *nūtrīre* to feed, care for] > 'nourisher *n* > 'nourishing *adj* > 'nourishingly *adv*

nourishment ('nʌrɪʃmənt) *n* **1** the act or state of nourishing **2** a substance that nourishes; food; nutriment

nous (naʊs) *n* **1** *metaphysics* mind or reason, esp when regarded as the principle governing all things **2** *Brit slang* common sense; intelligence [c17 from Greek, literally: mind]

nouveau *or before a plural noun* **nouveaux** ('nuːvəʊ) *adj* (*prenominal*) facetious *or derogatory* having recently become the thing specified: *a nouveau hippy* [c20 French, literally: new; on the model of NOUVEAU RICHE]

nouveau riche (ˌnuːvəʊ 'riːʃ; *French* nuvo riʃ) *n, pl* **nouveaux riches** (ˌnuːvəʊ 'riːʃ; *French* nuvo riʃ) **1** (*often plural and preceded by the*) a person who has acquired wealth recently and is regarded as vulgarly ostentatious or lacking in social graces ▷ *adj* **2** of or characteristic of the nouveaux riches [French, literally: new rich]

nouveau roman *French* (nuvo rɔmɑ̃) *n, pl* **nouveaux romans** (nuvo rɔmɑ̃) another term for *anti-roman*. See **antinovel** [literally: new novel]

Nouvelle-Calédonie (nuvɛlkaledɔni) *n* the French name for **New Caledonia**

nouvelle cuisine ('nuːvɛl kwiː'ziːn) *n* a style of preparing and presenting food, often raw or only lightly cooked, with light sauces, and unusual combinations of flavours and garnishes [c20 French, literally: new cookery]

Nouvelle Vague *French* (nuvɛl vaɡ) *n films* another term for **New Wave¹**

Nov. *abbreviation for* November

nova ('nəʊvə) *n, pl* **-vae** (-viː) *or* **-vas** a variable star that undergoes a cataclysmic eruption, observed as a sudden large increase in brightness with a subsequent decline over months or years; it is a close binary system with one component a white dwarf. Compare **supernova** [c19 New Latin *nova* (*stella*) new (star), from Latin *novus* new]

novaculite (nəʊ'vækjʊˌlaɪt) *n* a fine-grained dense hard rock containing quartz and feldspar: used as a whetstone [c18 from Latin *novācula* sharp knife, razor, from *novāre* to renew]

Nova Lisboa (*Portuguese* 'nɔvə liʒ'βɔə) *n* the former name (1928–73) of **Huambo**

Novara (*Italian* no'vaːra) *n* a city in NW Italy, in NE Piedmont: scene of the Austrian defeat of the Piedmontese in 1849. Pop: 100 910 (2001)

Nova Scotia ('nəʊvə 'skəʊʃə) *n* **1** a peninsula in E Canada, between the Gulf of St Lawrence and the Bay of Fundy **2** a province of E Canada, consisting of the Nova Scotia peninsula and Cape Breton Island: first settled by the French as Acadia. Capital: Halifax. Pop: 936 960 (2004 est). Area: 52 841 sq km (20 402 sq miles). Abbreviation: **NS**

Nova Scotia duck tolling retriever *n* a Canadian variety of retriever

Nova Scotian ('nəʊvə 'skəʊʃən) *n* **1** a native or inhabitant of Nova Scotia ▷ *adj* **2** of or relating to Nova Scotia or its inhabitants

novated lease (nəʊ'veɪtɪd) *n Austral* a system for purchasing a car in which an employer makes lease payments on behalf of an employee who eventually owns the car

novation (nəʊ'veɪʃən) *n* **1** *law* the substitution of a new obligation for an old one by mutual agreement between the parties, esp of one debtor or creditor for another **2** an obsolete word for

innovation [c16 from Late Latin *novātio* a renewing, from Latin *novāre* to renew]

Novaya Zemlya (*Russian* 'nɔvəjə zɪm'lja) *n* an archipelago in the Arctic Ocean, off the NE coast of Russia: consists of two large islands and many islets. Area: about 81 279 sq km (31 382 sq miles)

novel¹ ('nɒvəl) *n* **1** an extended work in prose, either fictitious or partly so, dealing with character, action, thought, etc, esp in the form of a story **2** **the** the literary genre represented by novels **3** (*usually plural*) *obsolete* a short story or novella, as one of those in the *Decameron* of Boccaccio [c15 from Old French *novelle,* from Latin *novella* (*narrātiō*) new (story); see NOVEL²]

novel² ('nɒvəl) *adj* of a kind not seen before; fresh; new; original: *a novel suggestion* [c15 from Latin *novellus* new, diminutive of *novus* new]

novel³ ('nɒvəl) *n* *Roman law* a new decree or an amendment to an existing statute. See also **Novels**

novelese (ˌnɒvə'liːz) *n* *derogatory* a style of writing characteristic of poor novels

novelette (ˌnɒvə'lɛt) *n* **1** an extended prose narrative story or short novel **2** a novel that is regarded as being slight, trivial, or sentimental **3** a short piece of lyrical music, esp one for the piano

novelettish (ˌnɒvə'lɛtɪʃ) *adj* characteristic of a novelette; trite or sentimental

novelist ('nɒvəlɪst) *n* a writer of novels

novelistic (ˌnɒvə'lɪstɪk) *adj* of or characteristic of novels, esp in style or method of treatment: *his novelistic account annoyed other historians*

novelize or **novelise** (ˌnɒvə,laɪz) *vb* to convert (a true story, film, etc) into a novel ▷ ˌnoveli'zation or ˌnoveli'sation *n*

novella (nəʊ'vɛlə) *n, pl* **-las** or **-le** (-leɪ) **1** (formerly) a short narrative tale, esp a popular story having a moral or satirical point, such as those in Boccaccio's *Decameron* **2** a short novel; novelette [c20 from Italian; see NOVEL¹]

Novels ('nɒvəlz) *pl n Roman law* the new statutes of Justinian and succeeding emperors supplementing the Institutes, Digest, and Code: now forming part of the Corpus Juris Civilis [Latin *Novellae* (*constitūtiōnēs*) new (laws)]

novelty ('nɒvəltɪ) *n, pl* **-ties 1 a** the quality of being new and fresh and interesting **b** (*as modifier*): *novelty value* **2** a new or unusual experience or occurrence **3** (*often plural*) a small usually cheap new toy, ornament, or trinket [c14 from Old French *noveltë*; see NOVEL²]

November (nəʊ'vɛmbə) *n* **1** the eleventh month of the year, consisting of 30 days **2** *communications* a code word for the letter *n* [c13 via Old French from Latin: ninth month, from *novem* nine]

novena (nəʊ'viːnə) *n, pl* **-nas** or **-nae** (-niː) *RC Church* a devotion consisting of prayers or services on nine consecutive days [c19 from Medieval Latin, from Latin *novem* nine]

novercal (nəʊ'vɜːkᵊl) *adj rare* stepmotherly [c17 from Latin *novercālis,* from *noverca* stepmother]

Novgorod (*Russian* 'nɔvgərət) *n* a city in NW Russia, on the Volkhov River; became a principality in 862 under Rurik, an event regarded as the founding of the Russian state; a major trading centre in the Middle Ages; destroyed by Ivan the Terrible in 1570. Pop: 215 000 (2005 est)

novice ('nɒvɪs) *n* **1 a** a person who is new to or inexperienced in a certain task, situation, etc; beginner; tyro **b** (*as modifier*): *novice driver* **2** a probationer in a religious order **3** a sportsman, esp an oarsman, who has not won a recognized prize, performed to an established level, etc **4** a racehorse, esp a steeplechaser or hurdler, that has not won a specified number of races [c14 via Old French from Latin *novīcius,* from *novus* new]

Novi Sad (*Serbo-Croat* 'nɔviː 'sɑːd) *n* a port in NE Serbia and Montenegro, in Serbia, on the River Danube: founded in 1690 as the seat of the Serbian patriarch; university (1960). Pop: 234 151 (2002). German name: Neusatz

novitiate or **noviciate** (nəʊ'vɪʃɪɪt, -,eɪt) *n* **1** the state of being a novice, esp in a religious order, or the period for which this lasts **2** the part of a religious house where the novices live **3** a less common word for **novice** [c17 from French *noviciat,* from Latin *novīcius* NOVICE]

Novocaine ('nəʊvə,keɪn) *n* a trademark for procaine hydrochloride. See **procaine**

Novokuznetsk (*Russian* nɔvəkuz'njetsk) *n* a city in S central Russia: iron and steel works. Pop: 542 000 (2005 est). Former name (1932–61): Stalinsk

Novosibirsk (*Russian* nəvəsi'birsk) *n* a city in W central Russia, on the River Ob: the largest town in Siberia; developed with the coming of the Trans-Siberian railway in 1893; important industrial centre. Pop: 1 425 000 (2005 est)

now (naʊ) *adv* **1** at or for the present time or moment **2** at this exact moment; immediately **3** in these times; nowadays **4** given the present circumstances: *now we'll have to stay to the end* **5** (*preceded by just*) very recently: *he left just now* **6** (*often preceded by just*) very soon: *he is leaving just now* **7** (*every*) *now and again* or *then* occasionally; on and off **8** *for now* for the time being **9** *now now!* (*interjection*) an exclamation used to rebuke or pacify someone **10** *now then* **a** (*sentence connector*) used to preface an important remark, the next step in an argument, etc **b** (*interjection*) an expression of mild reproof: *now then, don't tease!* ▷ *conj* **11** (*subordinating; often foll by that*) seeing that; since it has become the case that: *now you're in charge, things will be better* ▷ *sentence connector* **12 a** used as a transitional particle or hesitation word: *now, I can't really say* **b** used for emphasis: *now listen to this* **c** used at the end of a command, esp in dismissal: *run along, now* ▷ *n* **13** the present moment or time: *now is the time to go* ▷ *adj* **14** *informal* of the moment; fashionable: *the now look is street fashion* [Old English *nū;* compare Old Saxon *nū,* German *nun,* Latin *nunc,* Greek *nu*]

nowadays ('naʊə,deɪz) *adv* in these times [c14 from NOW + *adays* from Old English *a* on + *dæges* genitive of DAY]

noway ('nəʊ,weɪ) *adv* **1** Also in the US (not standard): **noways** in no manner; not at all; nowise ▷ *sentence substitute* **no way 2** used to make an emphatic refusal, denial etc

Nowel or **Nowell** (nəʊ'ɛl) *n* archaic spellings of **Noel**

nowhence ('nəʊ,wɛns) *adv archaic* from no place; from nowhere

nowhere ('nəʊ,wɛə) *adv* **1** in, at, or to no place; not anywhere **2** *get nowhere* (*fast*) *informal* to fail completely to make any progress **3** *nowhere near* far from; not nearly ▷ *n* **4** a nonexistent or insignificant place **5** *middle of nowhere* a completely isolated, featureless, or insignificant place

nowhither ('nəʊ,wɪðə) *adv archaic* to no place; to nowhere [Old English *nāhwider.* See NEITHER]

no-win *adj* offering no possibility of a favourable outcome (esp in the phrase **a no-win situation**)

nowise ('nəʊ,waɪz) *adv* another word for **noway**

now-now *adv South African informal* right away; immediately: *I'll do it now-now!*

nowt¹ (naʊt) *n Northern English* a dialect word for **nothing** [from NAUGHT]

nowt² (naʊt) *n Scot and Northern English* a dialect word for **bullock** and **cattle** [c13 from Old Norse *naut;* see NEAT²]

nowty ('naʊtɪ) *adj* nowtier, nowtiest *Northern English dialect* bad-tempered

Nox (nɒks) *n* the Roman goddess of the night. Greek counterpart: **Nyx**

noxious ('nɒkʃəs) *adj* **1** poisonous or harmful **2** harmful to the mind or morals; corrupting [c17 from Latin *noxius* harmful, from *noxa* injury] ▷ 'noxiously *adv* ▷ 'noxiousness *n*

noyade (nwa:'ja:d; *French* nwajad) *n French history* execution by drowning, esp as practised during the Reign of Terror at Nantes from 1793 to 1794 [c19 from French, from *noyer* to drown, from Late Latin

necāre to drown, from Latin: to put to death]

noyau ('nwaɪəʊ) *n* a liqueur made from brandy flavoured with nut kernels [c18 from French: kernel, from Latin *nux* nut]

Noyon (*French* nwajɔ̃) *n* a town in N France: scene of the coronations of Charlemagne (768) and Hugh Capet (987); birthplace of John Calvin. Pop: 14 471 (1999)

nozzle ('nɒzᵊl) *n* **1** a projecting pipe or spout from which fluid is discharged **2** Also called: propelling nozzle a pipe or duct, esp in a jet engine or rocket, that directs the effluent and accelerates or diffuses the flow to generate thrust **3** a socket, such as the part of a candlestick that holds the candle [c17 *nosle, nosel,* diminutive of NOSE]

np¹ *abbreviation for* **1** *printing* new paragraph **2** *law* nisi prius **3** no place of publication

np² *the internet domain name for* Nepal

Np 1 *symbol for* neper **2** *the chemical symbol for* neptunium

NP *abbreviation for* **1** neuropsychiatric **2** neuropsychiatry **3** Also: np. Notary Public **4** noun phrase

NPA *abbreviation for* Newspaper Publishers' Association

NPC (*in New Zealand*) *abbreviation for* National Provincial Championship, an interprovincial rugby competition

NPD *commerce abbreviation for* new product development

NPL *abbreviation for* National Physical Laboratory

NPV *abbreviation for* **1** net present value **2** no par value

NQA (*in New Zealand*) *abbreviation for* National Qualifications Authority

nr¹ *abbreviation for* near

nr² *the internet domain name for* Nauru

NRA (*in Britain*) *abbreviation for* **1** National Rifle Association **2** National Rivers Authority

NRC (*in Canada*) *abbreviation for* National Research Council

NRI (*in India*) *abbreviation for* Non-Resident Indian: an Indian citizen or person of Indian origin living abroad

NRL (*in Australia*) *abbreviation for* National Rugby League

NRMA (*in Australia*) *abbreviation for* National Roads and Motorists Association

NRN *text messaging abbreviation for* no reply necessary

NRT *abbreviation for* nicotine replacement therapy: a type of treatment designed to help people give up smoking in which gradually decreasing doses of nicotine are administered through patches on the skin etc to avoid the effects of sudden withdrawal from the drug

NRV *abbreviation for* **net realizable value**

ns *abbreviation for* **1** new series **2** not specified

NS *abbreviation for* **1** New Style (method of reckoning dates) **2** not sufficient or not satisfactory **3** (*esp in postal addresses*) Nova Scotia **4** nuclear ship

N/S *abbreviation for* non-smoker: used in lonely hearts columns and personal advertisements

NSAID *abbreviation for* nonsteroidal anti-inflammatory drug: any of a class of drugs, including aspirin and ibuprofen, used for reducing inflammation and pain in rheumatic diseases. Possible adverse effects include gastric ulceration

NSB *abbreviation for* **National Savings Bank**

NSF or **N/S/F** *banking abbreviation for* not sufficient funds

NSG *Brit education abbreviation for* nonstatutory guidelines: practical nonmandatory advice and information on the implementation of the National Curriculum

NSPCC *abbreviation for* National Society for the Prevention of Cruelty to Children

NSU *abbreviation for* **nonspecific urethritis**

NSW *abbreviation for* New South Wales

n

NT *abbreviation for* **1** National Trust **2** New Testament **3** Northern Territory (of Australia) **4** (esp in postal addresses) Northwest Territories (of Australia) **5** (esp in postal addresses) Nunavut **6** no-trump **7** (in Ireland) National Teacher (teacher in a National School)

-n't *contraction of* not: used as an enclitic after *be* and *have* when they function as main verbs and after auxiliary verbs or verbs operating syntactically as auxiliaries: *can't; don't; shouldn't; needn't; daren't; isn't*

nth (εnθ) *adj* **1** *maths* of or representing an unspecified ordinal number, usually the greatest in a series of values: *the nth power* **2** *informal* being the last, most recent, or most extreme of a long series: *for the nth time, eat your lunch!* **3** to the nth degree *informal* to the utmost extreme; as much as possible

Nth *abbreviation for* North

NTO (in Britain) *abbreviation for* National Training Organization

NTP *abbreviation for* normal temperature and pressure: standard conditions of 0°C temperature and 101.325 kPa (760 mmHg) pressure. Also: STP

NTS *abbreviation for* National Trust for Scotland

n-tuple *n logic, maths* an ordered set of *n* elements

nt. wt. *or* **nt wt** *abbreviation for* net weight

n-type *adj* **1** (of a semiconductor) having more conduction electrons than mobile holes **2** associated with or resulting from the movement of electrons in a semiconductor: *n-type conductivity* ▷ Compare **p-type**

nu¹ (njuː) *n* the 13th letter in the Greek alphabet (N, ν), a consonant, transliterated as *n* [from Greek, of Semitic origin; compare NUN²]

nu² *the internet domain name for* Niue

nu- *prefix informal* indicating an updated or modern version of something: *nu-metal music* [c20 from NEW]

nuance (njuːˈɑːns, ˈnjuːɑːns) *n* **1** a subtle difference in colour, meaning, tone, etc; a shade or graduation ▷ *vb* (tr; passive) **2** to give subtle differences to: *carefully nuanced words* [c18 from French, from *nuer* to show light and shade, ultimately from Latin *nūbēs* a cloud]

nub (nʌb) *n* **1** a small lump or protuberance **2** a small piece or chunk **3** the point or gist: *the nub of a story* **4** a small fibrous knot in yarn [c16 variant of *knub*, from Middle Low German *knubbe* KNOB] ▷ 'nubbly *adj*

Nuba ('njuːbə) *n* **1** (*pl* -bas *or* -ba) a member of a formerly warlike Nilotic people living chiefly in the hills of S central Sudan **2** the language or group of related dialects spoken by this people, belonging to the Chari-Nile branch of the Nilo-Saharan family

Nubain ('njuːbeɪn) *n trademark* an opiate drug, nalbuphine hydrochloride, used as a painkiller and, illegally, by bodybuilders and others to increase their pain threshold and as a recreational drug, being a cheap alternative to heroin

nubbin ('nʌbɪn) *n chiefly US and Canadian* something small or undeveloped, esp a fruit or ear of corn [c19 diminutive of NUB]

nubble ('nʌbᵊl) *n* a small lump [c19 diminutive of NUB] ▷ 'nubbly *adj*

nubby ('nʌbɪ) *adj* having small lumps or protuberances; knobbly

nubecula (njuːˈbɛkjʊlə) *n, pl* -lae (-liː) See **Magellanic Cloud** [c19 from Latin, diminutive of *nubes* cloud]

Nubia ('njuːbɪə) *n* an ancient region in NE Africa, on the Nile, extending from Aswan to Khartoum

Nubian ('njuːbɪən) *n* **1** a native or inhabitant of Nubia, an ancient region of NE Africa **2** the language spoken by the people of Nubia ▷ *adj* **3** of or relating to Nubia or its inhabitants **4** *informal* of or relating to Black culture

Nubian Desert *n* a desert in the NE Sudan, between the Nile valley and the Red Sea: mainly a sandstone plateau

---

nubile ('njuːbaɪl) *adj* (of a girl or woman) **1** ready or suitable for marriage by virtue of age or maturity **2** sexually attractive [c17 from Latin *nūbilis*, from *nūbere* to marry] > **nubility** (njuːˈbɪlɪtɪ) *n*

Nubuck ('njuːˌbʌk) *n* (*sometimes not capital*) leather that has been rubbed on the flesh side of the skin to give it a fine velvet-like finish

nucellus (njuːˈsɛləs) *n, pl* -li (-laɪ) the central part of a plant ovule containing the embryo sac [c19 New Latin, from Latin *nucella*, from *nux* nut] > nu'cellar *adj*

nucha ('njuːkə) *n, pl* -chae (-kiː) *zoology, anatomy* the back or nape of the neck [c14 from Medieval Latin, from Arabic *nukhā'* spinal marrow] > 'nuchal *adj*

nucivorous (njuːˈsɪvərəs) *adj* (of animals) feeding on nuts [from Latin *nux* nut + -VOROUS]

nuclear ('njuːklɪə) *adj* **1** of, concerned with, or involving the nucleus of an atom: *nuclear fission* **2** *biology* of, relating to, or contained within the nucleus of a cell: *a nuclear membrane* **3** of, relating to, forming, or resembling any other kind of nucleus **4** of, concerned with, or operated by energy from fission or fusion of atomic nuclei: *a nuclear weapon* **5** involving, concerned with, or possessing nuclear weapons: *nuclear war*

nuclear bomb *n* a bomb whose force is due to uncontrolled nuclear fusion or nuclear fission

nuclear chemistry *n* the branch of chemistry concerned with nuclear reactions

nuclear energy *n* energy released during a nuclear reaction as a result of fission or fusion. Also called: atomic energy

nuclear family *n sociol, anthropol* a primary social unit consisting of parents and their offspring. Compare **extended family**

nuclear fission *n* the splitting of an atomic nucleus into approximately equal parts, either spontaneously or as a result of the impact of a particle usually with an associated release of energy. Sometimes shortened to: fission Compare **nuclear fusion**

nuclear-free zone *n* an area barred, esp by local authorities, to the storage or deployment of nuclear weapons

nuclear fuel *n* a fuel that provides nuclear energy, used in nuclear power stations, nuclear submarines, etc

nuclear fusion *n* a reaction in which two nuclei combine to form a nucleus with the release of energy. Sometimes shortened to: fusion Compare **nuclear fission** See also **thermonuclear reaction**

nuclear isomer *n* the more formal name for **isomer** (sense 2) > nuclear isomerism *n*

nuclear magnetic resonance *n* a technique for determining the magnetic moments of nuclei by subjecting a substance to high-frequency radiation and a large magnetic field. The technique is used as a method of determining structure. Abbreviation: NMR See also **electron spin resonance**

nuclear magnetic resonance scanner *n* a machine for the medical technique in which changes in the constituent atoms of the body under the influence of a powerful electromagnet are used to generate computed images of the internal organs

nuclear medicine *n* the branch of medicine concerned with the use of radionuclides in the diagnosis and treatment of disease

nuclear option *n* **1** the use of or power to use nuclear weapons **2** the use of or power to use a measure considered to be particularly drastic

nuclear physics *n* (*functioning as singular*) the branch of physics concerned with the structure and behaviour of the nucleus and the particles of which it consists > nuclear physicist *n*

nuclear power *n* power, esp electrical or motive, produced by a nuclear reactor. Also called: atomic power

nuclear reaction *n* a process in which the structure and energy content of an atomic

---

nucleus is changed by interaction with another nucleus or particle

nuclear reactor *n* a device in which a nuclear reaction is maintained and controlled for the production of nuclear energy. Sometimes shortened to: reactor Former name: atomic pile See also **fission reactor, fusion reactor**

nuclear threshold *n* the point in war at which a combatant brings nuclear weapons into use

nuclear transfer *n* the procedure used to produce the first cloned mammals, in which the nucleus of a somatic cell is transferred into an egg cell whose own nucleus has been removed: this cell is then stimulated by an electric shock to divide and form an embryo

nuclear waste *n* another name for **radioactive waste**

nuclear winter *n* a period of extremely low temperatures and little light that has been suggested would occur as a result of a nuclear war

nuclease ('njuːklɪˌeɪz) *n* any of a group of enzymes that hydrolyse nucleic acids to simple nucleotides

nucleate *adj* ('njuːklɪɪt, -ˌeɪt) **1** having a nucleus ▷ *vb* ('njuːklɪˌeɪt) (*intr*) **2** to form a nucleus > ,nucle'ation *n* > 'nucle,ator *n*

nucleating agent *n meteorol* a substance used to seed clouds to control rainfall and fog formation

nuclei ('njuːklɪˌaɪ) *n* a plural of **nucleus**

nucleic acid (njuːˈkliːɪk, -ˈkleɪ-) *n biochem* any of a group of complex compounds with a high molecular weight that are vital constituents of all living cells. See also **RNA, DNA**

nuclein ('njuːklɪɪn) *n* any of a group of proteins, containing phosphorus, that occur in the nuclei of living cells

nucleo- *or before a vowel* **nucle-** *combining form* **1** nucleus or nuclear: *nucleoplasm* **2** nucleic acid: *nucleoprotein*

nucleolus (ˌnjuːklɪˈəʊləs) *n, pl* -li (-laɪ) a small rounded body within a resting nucleus that contains RNA and proteins and is involved in the production of ribosomes. Also called: 'nucle"ole [c19 from Latin, diminutive of NUCLEUS] > ,nucle'olar, 'nucleo,late *or* ,nucleo'lated *adj*

nucleon ('njuːklɪˌɒn) *n* a proton or neutron, esp one present in an atomic nucleus [c20 from NUCLE(US) + -ON]

nucleonics (ˌnjuːklɪˈɒnɪks) *n* (*functioning as singular*) the branch of physics concerned with the applications of nuclear energy > ,nucle'onic *adj* > ,nucle'onically *adv*

nucleon number *n* another name for **mass number**

nucleophilic (ˌnjuːklɪəʊˈfɪlɪk) *adj chem* having or involving an affinity for positive charge. Nucleophilic reagents (**nucleophiles**) are molecules, atoms, and ions that behave as electron donors. Compare **electrophilic**

nucleoplasm ('njuːklɪəˌplæzəm) *n* the protoplasm in the nucleus of a plant or animal cell that surrounds the chromosomes and nucleolus. Also called: karyoplasm > ,nucleo'plasmic *or* ,nucleoplas'matic *adj*

nucleoprotein (ˌnjuːklɪəʊˈprəʊtiːn) *n* a compound within a cell nucleus that consists of a protein bound to a nucleic acid

nucleoside ('njuːklɪəˌsaɪd) *n biochem* a compound containing a purine or pyrimidine base linked to a sugar (usually ribose or deoxyribose) [c20 from NUCLEO- + -OSE² + -IDE]

nucleosome ('njuːklɪəˌsəʊm) *n* a repeating structural unit of chromatin that contains DNA and histones

nucleosynthesis (ˌnjuːklɪəʊˈsɪnθɪsɪs) *n astronomy* the formation of heavier elements from lighter elements by nuclear fusion in stars

nucleotide ('njuːklɪəˌtaɪd) *n biochem* a compound consisting of a nucleoside linked to phosphoric acid. Nucleic acids are made up of long chains (polynucleotides) of such compounds [c20 from NUCLEO- + *t* + -IDE]

nucleus ('nju:klɪəs) *n, pl* **-clei** (-klɪ,aɪ) *or* **-cleuses 1** a central or fundamental part or thing around which others are grouped; core **2** a centre of growth or development; basis; kernel: *the nucleus of an idea* **3** *biology* (in the cells of eukaryotes) a large compartment, bounded by a double membrane, that contains the chromosomes and associated molecules and controls the characteristics and growth of the cell **4** *anatomy* any of various groups of nerve cells in the central nervous system **5** *astronomy* the central portion in the head of a comet, consisting of small solid particles of ice and frozen gases, which vaporize on approaching the sun to form the coma and tail **6** *physics* the positively charged dense region at the centre of an atom, composed of protons and neutrons, about which electrons orbit **7** *chem* a fundamental group of atoms in a molecule serving as the base structure for related compounds and remaining unchanged during most chemical reactions: *the benzene nucleus* **8** *botany* **a** the central point of a starch granule **b** a rare name for **nucellus 9** *phonetics* the most sonorous part of a syllable, usually consisting of a vowel or frictionless continuant **10** *logic* the largest individual that is a mereological part of every member of a given class [c18 from Latin: kernel, from *nux* nut]

nuclide ('nju:klaɪd) *n* a species of atom characterized by its atomic number and its mass number. See also **isotope** [c20 from NUCLEO- + *-ide*, from Greek *eidos* shape]

nuddy ('nʌdɪ) *n* in the nuddy *informal, chiefly Brit and Austral* in the nude; naked [c20 originally Australian, a variant of NUDE]

nude (nju:d) *adj* **1** completely unclothed; undressed **2** having no covering; bare; exposed **3** *law* **a** lacking some essential legal requirement, esp supporting evidence **b** (of a contract, agreement, etc) made without consideration and void unless under seal ▷ *n* **4** the state of being naked (esp in the phrase **in the nude**) **5** a naked figure, esp in painting, sculpture, etc [c16 from Latin *nūdus*] > **'nudely** *adv* > **'nudeness** *n*

nudge (nʌdʒ) *vb* (*tr*) **1** to push or poke (someone) gently, esp with the elbow, to get attention; jog **2** to push slowly or lightly: *as I drove out, I just nudged the gatepost* **3** to give (someone) a gentle reminder or encouragement ▷ *n* **4** a gentle poke or push **5** a gentle reminder [c17 perhaps from Scandinavian; compare Icelandic *nugga* to push] > **'nudger** *n*

nudi- *combining form* naked or bare: *nudibranch* [from Latin *nūdus*]

nudibranch ('nju:dɪ,bræŋk) *n* any marine gastropod of the order *Nudibranchia*, characterized by a shell-less, often beautifully coloured, body bearing external gills and other appendages. Also called: **sea slug** [c19 from NUDI- + *branche*, from Latin *branchia* gills]

nudicaudate (,nju:dɪ'kɔ:deɪt) *adj* (of such animals as rats) having a hairless tail

nudicaul ('nju:dɪ,kɔ:l) *or* **nudicaulous** (,nju:dɪ'kɔ:ləs) *adj* (of plants) having stems without leaves [c20 from NUDI- + *caul*, from Latin *caulis* stem]

nudism ('nju:dɪzəm) *n* the practice of nudity, esp for reasons of health, religion, etc > **'nudist** *n, adj*

nudity ('nju:dɪtɪ) *n, pl* **-ties 1** the state or fact of being nude; nakedness **2** *rare* a nude figure, esp in art

nudnik ('nʌdnɪk) *n US informal* an annoying or boring person [c20 from Yiddish *nudyen* to bore + -NIK]

nudum pactum ('nju:dʊm 'pæktʊm) *n law* an agreement made without consideration and void unless made under seal [Latin: nude (sense 3b) agreement]

nuée ardente ('nʊeɪ ɑː'dɑ̃t) *n* a rapidly moving turbulent incandescent cloud of gas, ash, and rock fragments flowing close to the ground after violent ejection from a volcano. See also

ignimbrite [c20 from French, literally: burning cloud]

Nuevo Laredo (*Spanish* 'nweβo la'reðo) *n* a city and port of entry in NE Mexico, in Tamaulipas state on the Rio Grande opposite Laredo, Texas: oil industries. Pop: 353 000 (2005 est)

Nuevo León ('nweɪvəʊ leɪ'əʊn, nu:'eɪ-; *Spanish* 'nweβo le'ɔn) *n* a state of NE Mexico: the first centre of heavy industry in Latin America. Capital: Monterrey. Pop: 3 826 240 (2000). Area: 64 555 sq km (24 925 sq miles)

nuevo sol ('nweɪvəʊ 'sɒl) *n* the Spanish name for **new sol**

Nuffield teaching project ('nʌfi:ld) *n* (in Britain) a complete school programme in mathematics, science, languages, etc, with suggested complementary theory and practical work

nugatory ('nju:gətərɪ, -trɪ) *adj* **1** of little value; trifling **2** not valid: *a nugatory law* [c17 from Latin *nūgātōrius*, from *nūgārī* to jest, from *nūgae* trifles]

nuggar ('nʌgə) *n* a sailing boat used to carry cargo on the Nile [from Arabic]

nugget ('nʌgɪt) *n* **1** a small piece or lump, esp of gold in its natural state **2** something small but valuable or excellent [c19 origin unknown]

Nugget ('nʌgɪt) NZ ▷ *n* **1** *trademark* shoe polish ▷ *vb* **2** (*tr; sometimes not capital*) *informal* to shine (shoes)

nuggety ('nʌgɪtɪ) *adj* **1** of or resembling a nugget **2** *Austral and NZ informal* (of a person) thickset; stocky

nuisance ('nju:səns) *n* **1** **a** a person or thing that causes annoyance or bother **b** (*as modifier*): *nuisance calls* **2** *law* something unauthorized that is obnoxious or injurious to the community at large (**public nuisance**) or to an individual, esp in relation to his ownership or occupation of property (**private nuisance**) **3** **nuisance value** the usefulness of a person's or thing's capacity to cause difficulties or irritation [c15 via Old French from *nuire* to injure, from Latin *nocēre*]

Nuits-Saint-Georges (*French* nɥisɛ̃ʒɔrʒ) *n* a fine red wine produced near the town of Nuits-Saint-Georges in Burgundy

NUJ (in Britain) *abbreviation for* National Union of Journalists

Nu Jiang ('nu: 'dʒjæŋ) *n* the Chinese name for the **Salween**

nuke (nju:k) *slang* ▷ *vb* **1** (*tr*) to attack or destroy with nuclear weapons ▷ *n* **2** a nuclear bomb **3** a military strike with nuclear weapons **4** nuclear power **5** *chiefly US* a nuclear power plant

Nuku'alofa (,nu:ku:ə'lɔ:fə) *n* the capital of Tonga, a port on the N coast of Tongatapu Island. Pop: 36 000 (2005 est)

Nukus (*Russian* nu'kus) *n* a city in Uzbekistan, capital of the Kara-Kalpak Autonomous Republic, on the Amu Darya River. Pop: 325 000 (2005 est)

null (nʌl) *adj* **1** without legal force; invalid; (esp in the phrase **null and void**) **2** without value or consequence; useless **3** lacking distinction; characterless: *a null expression* **4** nonexistent **5** *maths* **a** quantitatively zero **b** relating to zero **c** (of a set) having no members **d** (of a sequence) having zero as a limit **6** *physics* involving measurement in which an instrument has a zero reading, as with a Wheatstone bridge [c16 from Latin *nullus* none, from *ne* not + *ullus* any]

nullah ('nʌlə) *n* a stream or drain [c18 from Hindi *nālā*]

nulla-nulla (,nʌlə'nʌlə) *n Austral* a wooden club used by native Australians [from a native Australian language]

Nullarbor Plain ('nʌlə,bɔ:) *n* a vast low plateau of S Australia: extends north from the Great Australian Bight to the Great Victoria Desert; has no surface water or trees. Area: 260 000 sq km (100 000 sq miles)

null hypothesis *n statistics* the residual hypothesis if the alternative hypothesis tested against it fails to achieve a predetermined

significance level. See **hypothesis testing** Compare **alternative hypothesis**

nullifidian (,nʌlɪ'fɪdɪən) *n* **1** a person who has no faith or belief; sceptic; disbeliever ▷ *adj* **2** having no faith or belief [c16 from Latin, from *nullus* no + *fidēs* faith]

nullify ('nʌlɪ,faɪ) *vb* **-fies, -fying, -fied** (*tr*) **1** to render legally void or of no effect **2** to render ineffective or useless; cancel out [c16 from Late Latin *nullificāre* to despise, from Latin *nullus* of no account + *facere* to make] > ,nulli'fication *n* > 'nulli,fier *n*

nullipara (nʌ'lɪpərə) *n, pl* **-rae** (-,ri:) a woman who has never borne a child [c19 New Latin, from *nullus* no, not any + *-para,* from *parere* to bring forth; see -PAROUS] > nul'liparous *adj*

nullipore ('nʌlɪ,pɔ:) *n* any of several red seaweeds that secrete and become encrusted with calcium carbonate: family *Rhodophyceae* [c19 from Latin, from *nullus* no + PORE²]

nulli secundus *Latin* ('nʊli: sə'kʊndʊs) *adj* second to none

nullity ('nʌlɪtɪ) *n, pl* **-ties 1** the state of being null **2** a null or legally invalid act or instrument **3** something null, ineffective, characterless, etc [c16 from Medieval Latin *nullitās*, from Latin *nullus* no, not any]

NUM (in Britain and South Africa) *abbreviation for* National Union of Mineworkers

Num. *Bible abbreviation for* Numbers

Numantia (nju:'mæntɪə) *n* an ancient city in N Spain: a centre of Celtic resistance to Rome in N Spain: captured by Scipio the Younger in 133 BC

Numantian (nju:'mæntɪən) *adj* **1** of or relating to Numantia or its inhabitants ▷ *n* **2** a native or inhabitant of Numantia

numb (nʌm) *adj* **1** deprived of feeling through cold, shock, etc **2** unable to move; paralysed **3** characteristic of or resembling numbness: *a numb sensation* ▷ *vb* **4** (*tr*) to make numb; deaden, shock, or paralyse [c15 *nomen,* literally: taken (with paralysis), from Old English *niman* to take; related to Old Norse *nema,* Old High German *niman*] > 'numbly *adv* > 'numbness *n*

numbat ('nʌm,bæt) *n* a small Australian marsupial, *Myrmecobius fasciatus,* having a long snout and tongue and strong claws for hunting and feeding on termites: family *Dasyuridae.* Also called: banded anteater [c20 from a native Australian language]

number ('nʌmbə) *n* **1** a concept of quantity that is or can be derived from a single unit, the sum of a collection of units, or zero. Every number occupies a unique position in a sequence, enabling it to be used in counting. It can be assigned to one or more sets that can be arranged in a hierarchical classification: every number is a **complex number**; a complex number is either an **imaginary number** or a **real number**, and the latter can be a **rational number** or an **irrational number**; a rational number is either an **integer** or a **fraction**, while an irrational number can be a **transcendental number** or an **algebraic number**. See also **cardinal number, ordinal number 2** the symbol used to represent a number; numeral **3** a numeral or string of numerals used to identify a person or thing, esp in numerical order: *a telephone number* **4** the person or thing so identified or designated **5** the sum or quantity of equal or similar units or things **6** one of a series, as of a magazine or periodical; issue **7 a** a self-contained piece of pop or jazz music **b** a self-contained part of an opera or other musical score, esp one for the stage **8** a group or band of people, esp an exclusive group **9** *slang* a person, esp a woman: *who's that nice little number?* **10** *informal* an admired article, esp an item of clothing for a woman **11** *slang* a cannabis cigarette: *roll another number* **12** a grammatical category for the variation in form of nouns, pronouns, and any words agreeing with them, depending on how many persons or things are referred to, esp as singular or plural in number

n

and in some languages dual or trial **13** any number of several or many **14** by numbers *military* (of a drill procedure, etc) performed step by step, each move being made on the call of a number **15** do a number on (someone) *US slang* to manipulate or trick (someone) **16** get *or* have someone's number *informal* to discover someone's true character or intentions **17** in numbers in large numbers; numerously **18** one's number is up *Brit informal* one is finished; one is ruined or about to die **19** without *or* beyond number of too great a quantity to be counted; innumerable ▷ *vb* (*mainly tr*) **20** to assign a number to **21** to add up to; total **22** (*also intr*) to list (items) one by one; enumerate **23** (*also intr*) to put or be put into a group, category, etc **24** to limit the number of [c13 from Old French *nombre*, from Latin *numerus*]

number crunching *n computing* the large-scale processing of numerical data > **number cruncher** *n*

numbered account *n banking* an account identified only by a number, esp one in a Swiss bank that could contain funds illegally obtained

number eight wire *n NZ* **1** a standard gauge of fencing wire **2** this wire or something similar used for emergency repairs

numberless ('nʌmbəlɪs) *adj* **1** too many to be counted; countless **2** not containing or consisting of numbers > '**numberlessly** *adv* > '**numberlessness** *n*

number line *n* an infinite line on which points represent the real numbers

number off *vb* (*adverb*) to call out or cause to call out one's number or place in a sequence, esp in a rank of soldiers: *the sergeant numbered his men off from the right*

number one *n* **1** the first in a series or sequence **2** an informal phrase for **oneself, myself**, etc **3** *informal* the most important person; leader, chief **4** *informal* the bestselling pop record in any one week **5** *euphemistic* the act or an instance of urination **6** a haircut in which the hair is cut very close to the head with an electric shaver ▷ *adj* **7** first in importance, urgency, quality, etc: *number one priority* **8** *informal* (of a pop record) having reached the top of the charts

numberplate ('nʌmbə,pleɪt) *n* a plate mounted on the front and back of a motor vehicle bearing the registration number. Usual US term: **license plate**, (*Canadian*) **licence plate**

Numbers ('nʌmbəz) *n* (*functioning as singular*) the fourth book of the Old Testament, recording the numbers of the Israelites who followed Moses out of Egypt

numbers game *or* **racket** *n US* an illegal lottery in which money is wagered on a certain combination of digits appearing at the beginning of a series of numbers published in a newspaper, as in share prices or sports results. Often shortened to: **numbers**

Number Ten *n* 10 Downing Street, the British prime minister's official London residence

number theory *n* the study of integers, their properties, and the relationship between integers

number two *n* **1** *euphemistic* the act or an instance of defecation **2** a haircut in which the hair is cut close to the head with an electric shaver

number work *n* simple arithmetic and similar mathematical procedures as used and studied at primary level. Also called (esp formerly): **sums**

numbfish ('nʌm,fɪʃ) *n, pl* **-fish** *or* **-fishes** any of several electric rays, such as *Narcine tasmaniensis* (**Australian numbfish**) [c18 so called because it numbs its victims]

numbles ('nʌmbᵊlz) *pl n archaic* the heart, lungs, liver, etc, of an animal, cooked for food [c14 from Old French *nombles*, plural of *nomble* thigh muscle of a deer, changed from Latin *lumbulus* a little loin, from *lumbus* loin; see HUMBLE PIE]

numbskull *or* **numskull** ('nʌm,skʌl) *n* a stupid person; dolt; blockhead [c18 from NUMB + SKULL]

numdah ('nʌmdɑː) *n* **1** a coarse felt made esp in India **2** a saddle pad made from this **3** an

embroidered rug made from this ▷ Also called (for senses 1, 2): **numnah** [c19 from Urdu *namdā*]

numen ('njuːmɛn) *n, pl* **-mina** (-mɪnə) **1** (esp in ancient Roman religion) a deity or spirit presiding over a thing or place **2** a guiding principle, force, or spirit [c17 from Latin: a nod (indicating a command), divine power; compare *nuere* to nod]

numerable ('njuːmərəbᵊl) *adj* able to be numbered or counted > '**numerably** *adv*

numeracy ('njuːmərəsɪ) *n* the ability to use numbers, esp in arithmetical operations

numeral ('njuːmərəl) *n* **1** a symbol or group of symbols used to express a number: for example, *6* (*Arabic*), *VI* (*Roman*), *110* (*binary*) ▷ *adj* **2** of, consisting of, or denoting a number [c16 from Late Latin *numerālis* belonging to number, from Latin *numerus* number]

numerary ('njuːmərərɪ) *adj* of or relating to numbers

numerate *adj* ('njuːmərɪt) **1** able to use numbers, esp in arithmetical operations. Compare **literate** ▷ *vb* ('njuːmə,reɪt) (*tr*) **2** to read (a numerical expression) **3** a less common word for **enumerate** [c18 (*vb*): from Latin *numerus* number + -ATE¹, by analogy with *literate*]

numeration (,njuːmə'reɪʃən) *n* **1** the act or process of writing, reading, or naming numbers **2** a system of numbering or counting > '**numerative** *adj*

numerator ('njuːmə,reɪtə) *n* **1** *maths* the dividend of a fraction: *the numerator of ⅞ is 7.* Compare **denominator 2** a person or thing that numbers; enumerator

numerical (njuː'mɛrɪkᵊl) *or* **numeric** *adj* **1** of, relating to, or denoting a number or numbers **2** measured or expressed in numbers: *numerical value* **3** *maths* **a** containing or using constants, coefficients, terms, or elements represented by numbers: $3x^2 + 4y = 2$ *is a numerical equation*. Compare **literal** (sense 6) **b** another word for **absolute** (sense 11a) > nu'**merically** *adv*

numerical analysis *n* a branch of mathematics concerned with methods, usually iterative, for obtaining solutions to problems by means of a computer

numerical control *n engineering* a form of computer control applied to machine tools, by which an operation is directed from numerical data stored on tape or punched on cards

numerical identity *n logic* the relation that holds between two relata when they are the selfsame entity, that is, when the terms designating them have the same reference. Compare **qualitative identity** See also **Leibnitz's law**

numerology (,njuːmə'rɒlədʒɪ) *n* the study of numbers, such as the figures in a birth date, and of their supposed influence on human affairs > **numerological** (,njuːmərə'lɒdʒɪkᵊl) *adj* > ,**numer'ologist** *n*

numerous ('njuːmərəs) *adj* **1** being many **2** consisting of many units or parts: *a numerous collection* > '**numerously** *adv* > '**numerousness** *n*

nu-metal (,njuː'mɛtᵊl) *n* **a** a type of rock music popular from the late 1990s, featuring much of the sound typical of heavy metal but also influenced by rap and hip-hop **b** (*as modifier*): *a nu-metal band* [c20 from NU-, a form of NEW + (HEAVY) METAL]

Numidia (njuː'mɪdɪə) *n* an ancient country of N Africa, corresponding roughly to present-day Algeria: flourished until its invasion by Vandals in 429; chief towns were Cirta and Hippo Regius

Numidian (njuː'mɪdɪən) *adj* **1** of or relating to Numidia or its inhabitants ▷ *n* **2** a native or inhabitant of Numidia

Numidian crane *n* another name for **demoiselle crane** (see **demoiselle** (sense 1))

numina ('njuːmɪnə) *n* the plural of **numen**

numinous ('njuːmɪnəs) *adj* **1** denoting, being, or relating to a numen; divine **2** arousing spiritual or religious emotions **3** mysterious or awe-

inspiring [c17 from Latin *numin-*, NUMEN + -OUS]

numismatics (,njuːmɪz'mætɪks) *n* (*functioning as singular*) the study or collection of coins, medals, etc. Also called: **numismatology** [c18 from French *numismatique*, from Latin *nomisma*, from Greek: piece of currency, from *nomizein* to have in use, from *nōmos* use] > ,**numis'matic** *adj* > ,**numis'matically** *adv*

numismatist (njuː'mɪzmətɪst) *or* **numismatologist** (njuː,mɪzmə'tɒlədʒɪst) *n* a person who studies or collects coins, medals, etc

nummary ('nʌmərɪ) *adj* of or relating to coins [c17 from Latin *nummārius*, from *nummus* coin]

nummular ('nʌmjʊlə) *adj* shaped like a coin; disc-shaped; circular [c19 from Latin *nummulus* a small coin]

nummulite ('nʌmjʊ,laɪt) *n* any of various large fossil protozoans of the family *Nummulitidae*, common in Tertiary times: phylum *Foraminifera* (foraminifers) [c19 from New Latin *Nummulites* genus name, from Latin *nummulus*, from *nummus* coin] > **nummulitic** (,nʌmjʊ'lɪtɪk) *adj*

numnah ('nʌmnɑː) *n* another word for **numdah** (senses 1, 2)

numpty ('nʌmptɪ) *n, pl* **-ties** *Scot informal* a stupid person [c20 of unknown origin]

numskull ('nʌm,skʌl) *n* a variant spelling of **numbskull**

nun¹ (nʌn) *n* **1** a female member of a religious order **2** (*sometimes capital*) a variety of domestic fancy pigeon usually having a black-and-white plumage with a ridged peak or cowl of short white feathers [Old English *nunne*, from Church Latin *nonna*, from Late Latin: form of address used for an elderly woman] > '**nunlike** *adj*

nun² (nʊn) *n* the 14th letter in the Hebrew alphabet (נ or, at the end of a word, ן), transliterated as *n*

nunatak ('nʌnə,tæk) *n* an isolated mountain peak projecting through the surface of surrounding glacial ice and supporting a distinct fauna and flora after recession of the ice [c19 via Danish from Inuktitut]

Nunavut ('nuːnəvuːt) *n* a territory of NW Canada, formed in 1999 from part of the Northwest Territories as a semiautonomous region for the Inuit; includes Baffin Island and Ellesmere Island. Capital: Iqaluit. Pop: 29 644 (2004 est). Area: 2 093 190 sq km (808 185 sq miles)

nun buoy (nʌn) *n nautical* a buoy, conical at the top, marking the right side of a channel leading into a harbour: green in British waters but red in US waters. Compare **can buoy** [c18 from obsolete *nun* a child's spinning top + BUOY]

Nunc Dimittis ('nʌŋk dɪ'mɪtɪs, 'nʊŋk) *n* **1** the Latin name for the Canticle of Simeon (Luke 2:29–32) **2** a musical setting of this [from the opening words (Vulgate): now let depart]

nunciature ('nʌnsɪətʃə) *n* the office or term of office of a nuncio [c17 from Italian *nunziatura*; see NUNCIO]

nuncio ('nʌnʃɪ,əʊ, -sɪ-) *n, pl* **-cios** *RC Church* a diplomatic representative of the Holy See, ranking above an internuncio and esp having ambassadorial status [c16 via Italian from Latin *nuntius* messenger]

nuncle ('nʌŋkᵊl) *n* an archaic or dialect word for **uncle** [c17 from division of *mine uncle* as *my nuncle*]

nuncupative ('nʌŋkjʊ,peɪtɪv, nʌŋ'kjuːpətɪv) *adj* (of a will) declared orally by the testator and later written down [c16 from Late Latin *nuncupātīvus* nominal, from Latin *nuncupāre* to name]

Nuneaton (nʌn'iːtᵊn) *n* a town in central England, in Warwickshire. Pop: 70 721 (2001)

nunhood ('nʌnhʊd) *n* **1** the condition, practice, or character of a nun **2** nuns collectively

nunnery ('nʌnərɪ) *n, pl* **-neries** the convent or religious house of a community of nuns

nunny bag ('nʌnɪ) *n Canadian* a small sealskin haversack, used chiefly in Newfoundland [c19 *nunny*, probably from Scottish dialect *noony* luncheon, from NOON]

nun's cloth *or* **veiling** (nʌnz) *n* a thin soft plain-weave silk or worsted fabric used for veils, dresses, etc

Nupe ('nuːpeɪ) *n* **1** (*pl* **-pe** *or* **-pes**) a member of a Negroid people of Nigeria, noted as fishermen, who live near the confluence of the Niger and Benue Rivers **2** the language of this people, belonging to the Kwa branch of the Niger-Congo family

NUPE ('njuːpɪ) *n* (formerly, in Britain) *acronym for* National Union of Public Employees

nuptial ('nʌpʃəl, -tʃəl) *adj* **1** relating to marriage; conjugal: *nuptial vows* **2** *zoology* of or relating to mating [c15 from Latin *nuptiālis,* from *nuptiae* marriage, from *nubere* to marry] > 'nuptially *adv*

nuptials ('nʌpʃəlz, -tʃəlz) *pl n* (*sometimes singular*) a marriage ceremony; wedding

NUR (in Britain, formerly) *abbreviation for* National Union of Railwaymen

nurd (nɜːd) *n* a variant spelling of **nerd**

Nuremberg ('njuərəm,bɜːg) *n* a city in S Germany, in N Bavaria: scene of annual Nazi rallies (1933–38), the anti-Semitic Nuremberg decrees (1935), and the trials of Nazi leaders for their war crimes (1945–46); important metalworking and electrical industries. Pop: 493 553 (2003 est). German name: **Nürnberg**

Nuri ('nʊərɪ) *n* **1** (*pl* **-ris** *or* **-ri**) Also called: **Kafir** a member of an Indo-European people of Nuristan and neighbouring parts of Pakistan **2** Also called: **Kafiri** the Indo-Iranian language of this people

Nuristan (,nʊərɪ'staːn) *n* a region of E Afghanistan: consists mainly of high mountains (including part of the Hindu Kush), steep narrow valleys, and forests. Area: about 13 000 sq km (5000 sq miles). Former name: **Kafiristan**

Nürnberg ('nyrnberk) *n* the German name for **Nuremberg**

nurse (nɜːs) *n* **1** a person who tends the sick, injured, or infirm **2** short for **nursemaid 3** a woman employed to breast-feed another woman's child; wet nurse **4** a worker in a colony of social insects that takes care of the larvae ▷ *vb* (*mainly tr*) **5** (*also intr*) to tend (the sick) **6** (*also intr*) to feed (a baby) at the breast; suckle **7** to try to cure (an ailment) **8** to clasp carefully or fondly: *she nursed the crying child* **9** (*also intr*) (of a baby) to suckle at the breast (of) **10** to look after (a child) as one's employment **11** to attend to carefully; foster, cherish **12** to harbour; preserve: *to nurse a grudge* **13** *billiards* to keep (the balls) together for a series of cannons [c16 from earlier *norice,* Old French *nourice,* from Late Latin *nūtrīcia* nurse, from Latin *nūtrīcius* nourishing, from *nūtrīre* to nourish]

nursehound ('nɜːs,haʊnd) *n* a species of European dogfish, *Scyliorhinus caniculus* [c20 NURSE (SHARK) + HOUND[1]]

nursemaid ('nɜːs,meɪd) *or* **nurserymaid** ('nɜːsrɪ,meɪd) *n* a woman or girl employed to look after someone else's children. Often shortened to: **nurse**

nurse practitioner *n* a nurse who has specialized advanced skills in diagnosis, psychosocial assessment, and patient management and is permitted to prescribe certain drugs

nursery ('nɜːsrɪ) *n, pl* **-ries 1 a** a room in a house set apart for use by children **b** (*as modifier*): *nursery wallpaper* **2** a place where plants, young trees, etc, are grown commercially **3** an establishment providing residential or day care for babies and very young children; crèche **4** short for **nursery school 5** anywhere serving to foster or nourish new ideas, etc **6** Also called: **nursery cannon** *billiards* **a** a series of cannons with the three balls adjacent to a cushion, esp near a corner pocket **b** a cannon in such a series

nurseryman ('nɜːsrɪmən) *n, pl* **-men** a person who owns or works in a nursery in which plants are grown

nursery rhyme *n* a short traditional verse or song for children, such as *Little Jack Horner*

nursery school *n* a school for young children, usually from three to five years old

nursery slopes *pl n* gentle slopes used by beginners in skiing

nursery stakes *pl n* a race for two-year-old horses

nurse shark *n* any of various sharks of the family *Orectolobidae,* such as *Ginglymostoma cirratum* of the Atlantic Ocean, having an external groove on each side of the mouth between the mouth and nostril [c15 *nusse fisshe* (later influenced in spelling by NURSE), perhaps from division of obsolete *an huss* shark, dogfish (of uncertain origin) as *a nuss*]

nursing ('nɜːsɪŋ) *n* **a** the practice or profession of caring for the sick and injured **b** (*as modifier*): *a nursing home*

nursing bottle *n* another term (esp US) for **feeding bottle**

nursing father *n* a biblical name for **foster father**

nursing home *n* **1** a private hospital or residence staffed and equipped to care for aged or infirm persons **2** *Brit* a private maternity home

nursing mother *n* **1** a mother who is breast-feeding her baby **2** a biblical name for **foster mother**

nursing officer *n* (in Britain) the official name for **matron** (sense 4)

nursling *or* **nurseling** ('nɜːslɪŋ) *n* a child or young animal that is being suckled, nursed, or fostered

nurture ('nɜːtʃə) *n* **1** the act or process of promoting the development, etc, of a child **2** something that nourishes **3** *biology* the environmental factors that partly determine the structure of an organism. See also **nature** (sense 12) ▷ *vb* (*tr*) **4** to feed or support **5** to educate or train [c14 from Old French *norriture,* from Latin *nutrīre* to nourish] > 'nurturable *adj* > 'nurturer *n*

NUS (in Britain) *abbreviation for* National Union of Students

Nusa Tenggara ('nuːsə tɛŋ'gɑːrə) *n* an island chain east of Java, mostly in Indonesia: the main islands are Bali, Lombok, Sumbawa, Sumba, Flores, Alor, and Timor. Pop: 7 237 600 (1995 est). Area: 73 144 sq km (28 241 sq miles). English name: **Lesser Sunda Islands**

nut (nʌt) *n* **1** a dry one-seeded indehiscent fruit that usually possesses a woody wall **2** (*not in technical use*) any similar fruit, such as the walnut, having a hard shell and an edible kernel **3** the edible kernel of such a fruit **4** *slang* **a** an eccentric person **b** a person who is mentally disturbed **5** a slang word for **head** (sense 1) **6** **do one's nut** *Brit slang* to be extremely angry; go into a rage **7** **off one's nut** *slang* mad, crazy, or foolish **8** a person or thing that presents difficulties (esp in the phrase **a tough** *or* **hard nut to crack**) **9** a small square or hexagonal block, usu metal, with a threaded hole through the middle for screwing on the end of a bolt **10** *mountaineering* a variously shaped small metal block, usually a wedge or hexagonal prism (originally an ordinary engineer's nut) with a wire or rope loop attached, for jamming into a crack to provide security. Also called: **chock 11** Also called (US and Canadian): **frog** *music* **a** the ledge or ridge at the upper end of the fingerboard of a violin, cello, etc, over which the strings pass to the tuning pegs **b** the end of a violin bow that is held by the player **12** *printing* another word for **en 13** a small usually gingery biscuit **14** *Brit* a small piece of coal ▷ *vb* **nuts, nutting, nutted 15** (*intr*) to gather nuts **16** (*tr*) *slang* to butt (someone) with the head ▷ See also **nuts** [Old English *hnutu;* related to Old Norse *hnot,* Old High German *hnuz* (German *Nuss*)] > 'nut,like *adj*

NUT (in Britain) *abbreviation for* National Union of Teachers

nutant ('njuːt'nt) *adj botany* having the apex hanging down: *nutant flowers* [c18 from Latin *nūtāre* to nod]

nutation (njuː'teɪʃən) *n* **1** *astronomy* a periodic variation in the precession of the earth's axis causing the earth's poles to oscillate about their mean position **2** *physics* a periodic variation in the uniform precession of the axis of any spinning body, such as a gyroscope, about the horizontal **3** Also called: circumnutation the spiral growth of a shoot, tendril, or similar plant organ, caused by variation in the growth rate in different parts **4** the act or an instance of nodding the head [c17 from Latin *nutātiō,* from *nūtāre* to nod] > nu'tational *adj*

nutbrown ('nʌt'braʊn) *adj* of a brownish colour, esp a reddish-brown: *nutbrown hair*

nutcase ('nʌt,keɪs) *n slang* an insane or very foolish person

nutcracker ('nʌt,krækə) *n* **1** (*often plural*) a device for cracking the shells of nuts **2** either of two birds, *Nucifraga caryocatactes* of the Old World or *N. columbianus* (**Clark's nutcracker**) of North America, having speckled plumage and feeding on nuts, seeds, etc: family *Corvidae* (crows)

nutgall ('nʌt,gɔːl) *n* a nut-shaped gall caused by gall wasps on the oak and other trees

nuthatch ('nʌt,hætʃ) *n* a songbird of the family *Sittidae,* esp *Sitta europaea,* having strong feet and bill, and feeding on insects, seeds, and nuts [c14 *notehache,* from *note* nut + *hache* hatchet, from the bird's habit of splitting nuts; see NUT, HACK[1]]

nuthouse ('nʌt,haʊs) *n slang* a mental hospital or asylum

nut key *n mountaineering* a tool for extracting a nut, chock, etc, from a crack after use

nutlet ('nʌtlɪt) *n* **1** any of the one-seeded portions of a fruit, such as a labiate fruit, that fragments when mature **2** the stone of a drupe, such as a plum **3** a small nut

nutmeg ('nʌtmeg) *n* **1** an East Indian evergreen tree, *Myristica fragrans,* cultivated in the tropics for its hard aromatic seed: family *Myristicaceae.* See also **mace[2] 2** the seed of this tree, used as a spice **3** any of several similar trees or their fruit **4** a greyish-brown colour ▷ *vb* **-megs, -megging, -megged** (*tr*) **5** *Brit sport informal* to kick or hit the ball between the legs of (an opposing player) [c13 from Old French *nois muguede,* from Old Provençal *noz muscada* musk-scented nut, from Latin *nux* NUT + *muscus* MUSK]

nut oil *n* oil obtained from walnuts, hazelnuts, etc, used in paints and varnishes and in cooking

nut pine *n* either of two varieties of the pine tree *Pinus cembroides,* of Mexico, Arizona, and California, having edible nuts

nutraceutical (,njuːtrə'sjuːtɪkəl) *n* another name for **functional food**

nutria ('njuːtrɪə) *n* **1** another name for **coypu,** esp the fur **2** a brown colour with a grey tinge [c19 from Spanish: otter, variant of *lutria,* ultimately from Latin *lūtra* otter]

nutrient ('njuːtrɪənt) *n* **1** any of the mineral substances that are absorbed by the roots of plants for nourishment **2** any substance that nourishes an organism ▷ *adj* **3** providing or contributing to nourishment: *a nutrient solution* [c17 from Latin *nūtrīre* to nourish]

nutriment ('njuːtrɪmənt) *n* any material providing nourishment [c16 from Latin *nūtrīmentum,* from *nūtrīre* to nourish] > nutrimental (,njuːtrɪ'mɛnt'l) *adj*

nutrition (njuː'trɪʃən) *n* **1** a process in animals and plants involving the intake of nutrient materials and their subsequent assimilation into the tissues. Related adjs: **alimentary, trophic 2** the act or process of nourishing **3** the study of nutrition, esp in humans [c16 from Late Latin *nūtrītiō,* from *nūtrīre* to nourish] > nu'tritional *or less commonly* nu'tritionary *adj* > nu'tritionally *adv*

nutritionist (njuː'trɪʃənɪst) *n* a person who specializes in nutrition and the nutritive value of various foods

nutritious (njuː'trɪʃəs) *adj* nourishing, sometimes to a high degree [c17 from Latin *nūtrīcius* nourishing, from *nūtrix* a NURSE] > nu'tritiously *adv* > nu'tritiousness *n*

n

nutritive ('njuːtrɪtɪv) *adj* **1** providing nourishment **2** of, concerning, or promoting nutrition ▷ *n* **3** a nutritious food > 'nutritively *adv*

nuts (nʌts) *adj* **1** a slang word for **insane 2** (foll by *about* or *on*) *slang* extremely fond (of) or enthusiastic (about) ▷ *interj* **3** *slang* an expression of disappointment, contempt, refusal, or defiance ▷ *pl n* **4** a slang word for **testicles**

nuts and bolts *pl n informal* the essential or practical details

nutshell ('nʌt,ʃɛl) *n* **1** the shell around the kernel of a nut **2 in a nutshell** in essence; briefly

nutso ('nʌtsəʊ) *adj informal, chiefly US* insane

nutter ('nʌtə) *n Brit slang* a mad or eccentric person

nutting ('nʌtɪŋ) *n* the act or pastime of gathering nuts

nutty ('nʌtɪ) *adj* **-tier, -tiest 1** containing or abounding in nuts **2** resembling nuts, esp in taste **3** a slang word for **insane 4** (foll by *over* or *about*) *informal* extremely fond (of) or enthusiastic (about) > 'nuttily *adv* > 'nuttiness *n*

nutwood ('nʌt,wʊd) *n* **1** any of various nut-bearing trees, such as walnut **2** the wood of any of these trees

Nuuk (nuːk) *n* the capital of Greenland, in the southwest: the oldest Danish settlement in Greenland, founded in 1721. Pop: 14 350 (2004 est). Danish name (official name until 1979): **Godthaab**

Nuxalk (nuːˈxɒlk) *n* a member of a Salishan Native Canadian people of British Columbia. Formerly called: **Bella Coola** [from Salish]

nux vomica ('nʌks 'vɒmɪkə) *n* **1** an Indian spiny loganiaceous tree, *Strychnos nux-vomica*, with orange-red berries containing poisonous seeds **2** any of the seeds of this tree, which contain strychnine and other poisonous alkaloids **3** a medicine manufactured from the seeds of this tree, formerly used as a heart stimulant [C16 from Medieval Latin: vomiting nut]

nuzzle ('nʌzᵊl) *vb* **1** to push or rub gently against the nose or snout **2** (*intr*) to nestle **3** (*tr*) to dig out with the snout [C15 *nosele*, from NOSE (n)]

NV *abbreviation for* Nevada

NVQ (in Britain) *abbreviation for* national vocational qualification: a qualification that rewards competence in a specified type of employment

NW *symbol for* northwest(ern)

n-word *n* (*sometimes capital; preceded by the*) a euphemistic way of referring to the word **nigger**

NWT *abbreviation for* Northwest Territories (of Canada)

NY or **N.Y.** *abbreviation for* New York (city or state)

nyaff (njæf) *n Scot* a small or contemptible person [C19 perhaps imitative of the bark of a small dog]

nyala ('njɑːlə) *n, pl* **-la** or **-las 1** a spiral-horned southern African antelope, *Tragelaphus angasi*, with a fringe of white hairs along the length of the back and neck **2 mountain nyala** a similar and related Ethiopian animal, *T. buxtoni*, lacking the white crest [from Zulu]

Nyanja ('njændʒə) *n* **1** (*pl* **-ja** or **-jas**) a member of a Negroid people of central Africa, living chiefly in Malawi **2** the language of this people, belonging to the Bantu group of the Niger-Congo family. Nyanja forms the basis of a pidgin used as a lingua franca in central Africa

nyanza ('njænzə, nɪˈænzə) *n* (*capital when part of a name*) (in E Africa) a lake [from Bantu]

Nyasa or **Nyassa** (nɪˈæsə, naɪˈæsə) *n* **Lake** a lake in central Africa at the S end of the Great Rift Valley: the third largest lake in Africa, drained by the Shire River into the Zambezi. Area: about 28 500 sq km (11 000 sq miles). Malawi name: **Lake Malawi**

Nyasaland (nɪˈæsə,lænd, naɪˈæsə-) *n* the former name (until 1964) of **Malawi**

NYC *abbreviation for* New York City

nyctaginaceous (,nɪktədʒɪˈneɪʃəs) *adj* of, relating

to, or belonging to the *Nyctaginaceae*, a family of mostly tropical plants, including bougainvillea, having large coloured bracts surrounding each flower [from New Latin, from *Nyctago* type genus, from Greek *nukt-, nux* night]

nyctalopia (,nɪktəˈləʊpɪə) *n* inability to see normally in dim light. Nontechnical name: night blindness Compare **hemeralopia** [C17 via Late Latin from Greek *nuktálōps*, from *nux* night + *alaos* blind + *ōps* eye]

nyctanthous (nɪkˈtænθəs) *adj* (of plants) flowering at night

nyctinasty ('nɪktɪ,næstɪ) *n botany* a nastic movement, such as the closing of petals, that occurs in response to the alternation of day and night [C20 from Greek *nukt-, nux* night + -NASTY] > ,nycti'nastic *adj*

nyctitropism (nɪkˈtɪtrə,pɪzəm) *n* a tendency of some plant parts to assume positions at night that are different from their daytime positions [C19 *nyct-*, from Greek *nukt-, nux* night + -TROPISM] > nyctitropic (,nɪktɪˈtrɒpɪk) *adj*

nyctophobia (,nɪktəʊˈfəʊbɪə) *n psychiatry* an abnormal dread of night or darkness [*nyct-*, from Greek *nukt-, nux* night + -PHOBIA] > ,nycto'phobic *adj*

nye (naɪ) *n* a flock of pheasants. Also called: **nide, eye** [C15 from Old French *ni*, from Latin *nīdus* nest]

Nyeman (*Russian* 'njɛmən) *n* a variant spelling of **Neman**

Nyíregyháza (*Hungarian* 'njiːrɛtjhaːzɔ) *n* a market town in NE Hungary. Pop: 116 899 (2003 est)

Nykøbing (*Danish* 'nykøːbeŋ) *n* a port in Denmark, on the W coast of Falster Island. Pop: 16 784 (2004 est)

nylghau ('nɪlgɔː) *n, pl* **-ghau** or **-ghaus** another name for **nilgai**

nylon ('naɪlɒn) *n* **1** a class of synthetic polyamide materials made by copolymerizing dicarboxylic acids with diamines. They can be moulded into a variety of articles, such as combs and machine parts. Nylon monofilaments are used for bristles, etc, and nylon fibres can be spun into yarn **2 a** yarn or cloth made of nylon, used for clothing, stockings, etc **b** (*as modifier*): *a nylon dress.* See also **nylons** [C20 originally a trademark]

NYLON ('naɪlɒn) *n informal* a high-earning business executive who enjoys a transatlantic lifestyle, living part of the year in New York City and part in London [C20 from N(*ew*) Y(*ork*) + Lon(*don*)]

nylons ('naɪlɒnz) *pl n* stockings made of nylon or other man-made material

nymph (nɪmf) *n* **1** *myth* a spirit of nature envisaged as a beautiful maiden **2** *chiefly poetic* a beautiful young woman **3** the larva of insects such as the dragonfly and mayfly. It resembles the adult, apart from having underdeveloped wings and reproductive organs, and develops into the adult without a pupal stage [C14 via Old French from Latin, from Greek *numphē* nymph; related to Latin *nūbere* to marry] > 'nymphal or nymphean ('nɪmfɪən) *adj* > 'nymphlike *adj*

nympha ('nɪmfə) *n, pl* **-phae** (-fiː) *anatomy* either one of the labia minora. Also called: **labium minus pudendi** [C17 from Latin: bride, NYMPH]

nymphaeaceous (,nɪmfɪˈeɪʃəs) *adj* of, relating to, or belonging to the *Nymphaeaceae*, a family of plants, including the water lilies, that grow in water or marshes and have typically floating leaves and showy flowers [from New Latin, from Latin *nymphaea* water lily, ultimately from Greek *numphaios* sacred to nymphs]

nymphalid ('nɪmfəlɪd) *n* **1** any butterfly of the family *Nymphalidae*, typically having brightly coloured wings: includes the fritillaries, tortoiseshells, red admirals, and peacock ▷ *adj* **2** of, relating to, or belonging to the *Nymphalidae* [C19 from New Latin, from *Nymphalis* genus name, from Latin; see NYMPH]

nymphet ('nɪmfɪt) *n* a young girl who is sexually

precocious and desirable [C17 (meaning: a young nymph): diminutive of NYMPH]

nympho ('nɪmfəʊ) *n, pl* **-phos** *informal* a nymphomaniac

nympholepsy ('nɪmfə,lɛpsɪ) *n, pl* **-sies** a state of violent emotion, esp when associated with a desire for something one cannot have [C18 from NYMPHOLEPT, on the model of *epilepsy*] > ,nympho'leptic *adj*

nympholept ('nɪmfə,lɛpt) *n* a person afflicted by nympholepsy [C19 from Greek *numpholēptos* caught by nymphs, from *numphē* nymph + *lambanein* to seize]

nymphomania (,nɪmfəˈmeɪnɪə) *n* a neurotic condition in women in which the symptoms are a compulsion to have sexual intercourse with as many men as possible and an inability to have lasting relationships with them. Compare **satyriasis** [C18 New Latin, from Greek *numphē* nymph + -MANIA] > ,nympho'maniac *n, adj* > nymphomaniacal (,nɪmfəʊməˈnaɪəkᵊl) *adj*

Nynorsk (*Norwegian* 'nyːnɔːsk; *English* 'niːnɔːsk) *n* one of two mutually intelligible official forms of written Norwegian: it also exists in spoken form and is derived from the dialect of W and N Norway. Also called: **Landsmål** Compare **Bokmål** [Norwegian: new Norse]

Nyoro ('njɔːrəʊ) *n* **1** (*pl* **-ro** or **-ros**) a member of a Negroid people of W Uganda **2** the language of this people, belonging to the Bantu group of the Niger-Congo family

Nysa ('nɪsə) *n* the Polish name for the **Neisse** (sense 1)

NYSE *abbreviation for* New York Stock Exchange

nystagmus (nɪˈstægməs) *n* involuntary movement of the eye comprising a smooth drift followed by a flick back, occurring in several situations, for example after the body has been rotated or in disorders of the cerebellum

nystatin ('nɪstətɪn) *n* an antibiotic obtained from the bacterium *Streptomyces noursei*: used in the treatment of infections caused by certain fungi, esp *Candida albicans* [C20 from *New York State*, where it was originated + -IN]

Nyx (nɪks) *n Greek myth* the goddess of the night, daughter of Chaos. Roman counterpart: **Nox**

nz *the internet domain name for* New Zealand

NZ¹ *international car registration for* New Zealand

NZ² or **N. Zeal.** *abbreviation for* New Zealand

NZC *abbreviation for* New Zealand Cricket

NZCER *abbreviation for* New Zealand Council for Educational Research

NZE *abbreviation for* New Zealand English

NZEF *abbreviation for* New Zealand Expeditionary Force, the New Zealand army that served throughout World War I. **2NZEF** is used to refer to the Second New Zealand Expeditionary Force, in World War II

NZEFIP *abbreviation for* New Zealand Expeditionary Force in the Pacific, the 3rd division of the New Zealand Expeditionary Force serving in the Pacific campaign in World War II

NZEI *abbreviation for* New Zealand Educational Institute

NZLR *abbreviation for* New Zealand Law Reports

NZMA *abbreviation for* New Zealand Medical Association

NZOM *abbreviation for* New Zealand Order of Merit

NZPA *abbreviation for* New Zealand Press Association

NZR *abbreviation for* (the former) New Zealand Railways

NZRFU *abbreviation for* New Zealand Rugby Football Union

NZRN *abbreviation for* New Zealand Registered Nurse

NZSE *abbreviation for* New Zealand Stock Exchange

NZSO *abbreviation for* New Zealand Symphony Orchestra

O o

o or **O** (əʊ) n, pl **o's**, **O's** or **Os** 1 the 15th letter and fourth vowel of the modern English alphabet 2 any of several speech sounds represented by this letter, in English as in *code, pot, cow, move,* or *form* 3 another name for **nought**

O¹ symbol for 1 chem oxygen 2 a human blood type of the ABO group. See **universal donor** 3 logic a particular negative categorial proposition, such as *some men are not married*: often symbolized as **SoP.** Compare **A, E, I² ▷** abbreviation for 4 Austral slang offence [(for sense 3) from Latin (*neg)o* I deny]

O² (əʊ) interj 1 a variant spelling of **oh** 2 an exclamation introducing an invocation, entreaty, wish, etc: *O God!; O for the wings of a dove!*

o- prefix short for **ortho-** (sense 4)

o' (ə) prep informal or archaic shortened form of **of:** *a cup o' tea*

O'- prefix (in surnames of Irish Gaelic origin) descendant of: *O'Corrigan* [from Irish Gaelic *ó, ua* descendant]

-o suffix forming informal and slang variants and abbreviations, esp of nouns: *wino; lie doggo; Jacko* [probably special use of OH]

-o- connective vowel used to connect elements in a compound word: *chromosome; filmography.* Compare **-i-** [from Greek, stem vowel of many nouns and adjectives in combination]

oaf (əʊf) n a stupid or loutish person [C17 variant of Old English *ælf* ELF] **> 'oafish** adj **> 'oafishly** adv **> 'oafishness** n

Oahu (əʊ'ɑːhuː) n an island in central Hawaii: the third largest of the Hawaiian Islands. Chief town: Honolulu. Pop: 876 151 (2000). Area: 1574 sq km (608 sq miles)

oak (əʊk) n 1 any deciduous or evergreen tree or shrub of the fagaceous genus *Quercus,* having acorns as fruits and lobed leaves. See also **holm oak, cork oak, red oak, Turkey oak, durmast** Related adj: **quercine** 2 **a** the wood of any of these trees, used esp as building timber and for making furniture **b** (as modifier): *an oak table* 3 any of various trees that resemble the oak, such as the poison oak, silky oak, and Jerusalem oak 4 **a** anything made of oak, esp a heavy outer door to a set of rooms in an Oxford or Cambridge college **b** sport one's oak to shut this door as a sign one does not want visitors 5 the leaves of an oak tree, worn as a garland 6 the dark brownish colour of oak wood 7 Austral any of various species of casuarina, such as desert oak, swamp oak, or she-oak [Old English *āc;* related to Old Norse *eik,* Old High German *eih,* Latin *aesculus*]

oak apple or **gall** n any of various brownish round galls on oak trees, containing the larva of certain wasps

Oak-apple Day n (in Britain) May 29, the anniversary of the Restoration (1660), formerly commemorated by the wearing of oak apples or oak leaves, recalling the **Boscobel oak** in which Charles II hid after the battle of Worcester

oaked (əʊkt) adj relating to wine that is stored for a time in oak barrels prior to bottling

oaken ('əʊkən) adj made of the wood of the oak

oak fern n a graceful light green polypody fern, *Thelypteris dryopteris,* having a creeping rhizome, found in acid woodlands and on rocks in the northern hemisphere

Oakham ('əʊkəm) n a market town in E central England, the administrative centre of Rutland. Pop: 9620 (2001)

Oakland ('əʊklənd) n a port and industrial centre in W California, on San Francisco Bay; damaged by earthquake in 1989. Pop: 398 844 (2003 est)

oak-leaf cluster n US an insignia consisting of oak leaves and acorns awarded to holders of certain military decorations to indicate a further award of the same decoration

Oaks (əʊks) n (functioning as singular) the 1 a horse race for fillies held annually at Epsom since 1779: one of the classics of English flat racing 2 any of various similar races [named after an estate near Epsom]

oakum ('əʊkəm) n loose fibre obtained by unravelling old rope, used esp for caulking seams in wooden ships [Old English *ācuma,* variant of *ācumba,* literally: off-combings, from *ā-* off + *-cumba,* from *cemban* to COMB]

Oakville ('əʊkvɪl) n a city in SE Canada, in SE Ontario on Lake Ontario southwest of Toronto: motor-vehicle industry. Pop: 144 738 (2001)

oaky¹ ('əʊkɪ) adj oakier, oakiest 1 hard like the wood of an oak 2 (of a wine) having a pleasant flavour imparted by the oak barrel in which it was stored

oaky² ('əʊkɪ) n, pl oakies Midland English dialect an ice cream

Oamaru stone ('ɒmərʊː) n a kind of limestone, of building quality, found at Oamaru on South Island, New Zealand

O & M abbreviation for organization and method (in studies of working methods)

oanshagh ('oːnʃəx) n Irish a foolish girl or woman [from Irish Gaelic *óinseach*]

OAP (in Britain) abbreviation for **old age pension** or **pensioner**

OAPEC (əʊ'eɪpɛk) n acronym for Organization of Arab Petroleum Exporting Countries

oar (ɔː) n 1 a long shaft of wood for propelling a boat by rowing, having a broad blade that is dipped into and pulled against the water. Oars were also used for steering certain kinds of ancient sailing boats 2 short for **oarsman** 3 put one's oar in to interfere or interrupt **▷** vb 4 to row or propel with or as if with oars: *the two men were oaring their way across the lake* [Old English *ār,* of Germanic origin; related to Old Norse *ār*] **> 'oarless** adj **> 'oar,like** adj

oared (ɔːd) adj 1 equipped with oars 2 (in combination) having oars as specified: *two-oared*

oarfish ('ɔːˌfɪʃ) n, pl -fish or -fishes a very long ribbonfish, *Regalecus glesne,* with long slender ventral fins. Also called: king of the herrings [C19 referring to the flattened oarlike body]

oarlock ('ɔːˌlɒk) n US and Canadian a swivelling device attached to the gunwale of a boat that holds an oar in place and acts as a fulcrum during rowing. Also called: rowlock

oarsman ('ɔːzmən) n, pl -men a man who rows, esp one who rows in a racing boat **> 'oarsman,ship** n

oarweed ('ɔːˌwiːd) n any of various brown seaweeds, especially a kelp of the genus *Laminaria,* with long broad fronds, common below the low-water mark [from earlier *oreweed,* from *wore,* from Old English *wār* seaweed + WEED¹]

OAS abbreviation for 1 **Organization of American States** 2 Organisation de l'armée secrète; an organization of European settlers in Algeria who opposed Algerian independence by acts of terrorism (1961–63)

oasis (əʊ'eɪsɪs) n, pl -ses (-siːz) 1 a fertile patch in a desert occurring where the water table approaches or reaches the ground surface 2 a place of peace, safety, or happiness in the midst of trouble or difficulty [C17 via Latin from Greek, probably of Egyptian origin]

Oasis (əʊ'eɪsɪs) n trademark a block of light porous material, used as a base for flower arrangements

oast (əʊst) n chiefly Brit 1 a kiln for drying hops 2 Also called: oast house a building containing such kilns, usually having a conical or pyramidal roof [Old English *āst;* related to Old Norse *eisa* fire]

oat (əʊt) n 1 an erect annual grass, *Avena sativa,* grown in temperate regions for its edible seed 2 (usually plural) the seeds or fruits of this grass 3 any of various other grasses of the genus *Avena,* such as the wild oat 4 poetic a flute made from an oat straw 5 feel one's oats US and Canadian informal **a** to feel exuberant **b** to feel self-important 6 get one's oats slang to have sexual intercourse 7 sow one's (wild) oats to indulge in adventure or promiscuity during youth [Old English *āte,* of obscure origin]

oatcake ('əʊtˌkeɪk) n a brittle unleavened oatmeal biscuit

oaten ('əʊtⁿn) adj made of oats or oat straw

oat grass n any of various oatlike grasses, esp of the genera *Arrhenatherum* and *Danthonia,* of Eurasia and N Africa

oath (əʊθ) n, pl oaths (əʊðz) 1 a solemn pronouncement to affirm the truth of a statement or to pledge a person to some course of action, often involving a sacred being or object as witness. Related adj: **juratory** 2 the form of such a pronouncement 3 an irreverent or blasphemous expression, esp one involving the name of a deity; curse 4 on, upon, or under oath **a** under the obligation of an oath **b** law having sworn to tell the truth, usually with one's hand on the Bible 5 take an oath to declare formally with an oath or pledge, esp before giving evidence [Old English *āth;* related to Old Saxon, Old Frisian *ēth,* Old High German *eid*]

oatmeal (ˈəʊtˌmiːl) *n* **1** meal ground from oats, used for making porridge, oatcakes, etc **2 a** a greyish-yellow colour **b** (*as adjective*): *an oatmeal coat*

OAU *abbreviation for* the former Organization of African Unity, now the **African Union**

Oaxaca (wəˈhɑːkə; *Spanish* oaˈxaka) *n* **1** a state of S Mexico, on the Pacific: includes most of the Isthmus of Tehuantepec; inhabited chiefly by Indians. Capital: Oaxaca de Juárez. Pop: 3 432 180 (2000). Area: 95 363 sq km (36 820 sq miles) **2** a city in S Mexico, capital of Oaxaca state: founded in 1486 by the Aztecs and conquered by Spain in 1521. Pop: 483 000 (2005 est). Official name: Oaxaca de Juárez (de ˈxwaɾɛθ)

Ob (*Russian* ɔpj) *n* a river in N central Russia, formed at Bisk by the confluence of the Biya and Katun Rivers and flowing generally north to the **Gulf of Ob** (an inlet of the Arctic Ocean): one of the largest rivers in the world, with a drainage basin of about 2 930 000 sq km (1 131 000 sq miles). Length: 3682 km (2287 miles)

OB *Brit abbreviation for* **1** Old Boy **2** outside broadcast

ob. *abbreviation for* **1** (on tombstones) obiit **2** obiter **3** oboe [(for sense 1) Latin: he (or she) died; (for sense 2) Latin: incidentally; in passing]

ob- *prefix* inverse or inversely: *obovate* [from Old French, from Latin *ob*. In compound words of Latin origin, *ob-* (and *oc-*, *of-*, *op-*) indicates: to, towards (*object*); against (*oppose*); away from (*obsolete*); before (*obstetric*); down, over (*obtect*); for the sake of (*obsecrate*); and is used as an intensifier (*oblong*)]

oba (ˈɔːbɑː, -bə) *n* (in W Africa) a Yoruba chief or ruler

Obad. *Bible abbreviation for* Obadiah

Obadiah (ˌəʊbəˈdaɪə) *n Old Testament* **1** a Hebrew prophet **2** the book containing his oracles, chiefly directed against Edom. Douay spelling: Abdias (ˈæbˈdaɪəs)

Oban (ˈəʊbᵊn) *n* a small port and resort in W Scotland, in Argyll and Bute on the Firth of Lorne. Pop: 8120 (2001)

obb. *abbreviation for* obbligato

obbligato *or* **obligato** (ˌɒblɪˈɡɑːtəʊ) *music* ⊳ *adj* **1** not to be omitted in performance ⊳ *n, pl* **-tos** *or* **-ti** (-tiː) **2** an essential part in a score: *with oboe obbligato* ⊳ See also **ad-lib** [c18 from Italian, from *obbligare* to OBLIGE]

obconic (ɒbˈkɒnɪk) *or* **obconical** *adj botany* (of a fruit or similar part) shaped like a cone and attached at the pointed end

obcordate (ɒbˈkɔːdeɪt) *adj botany* heart-shaped and attached at the pointed end: *obcordate leaves*

obdt *abbreviation for* obedient

obdurate (ˈɒbdjʊrɪt) *adj* **1** not easily moved by feelings or supplication; hardhearted **2** impervious to persuasion, esp to moral persuasion [c15 from Latin *obdūrāre* to make hard, from *ob-* (intensive) + *dūrus* hard; compare ENDURE] > ˈobduracy *or* ˈobdurateness *n* > ˈobdurately *adv*

OBE *abbreviation for* **1** Officer of the Order of the British Empire (a Brit title) **2** out-of-body experience

obeah (ˈəʊbɪə) *n* another word for **obi²**

obedience (əˈbiːdɪəns) *n* **1** the condition or quality of being obedient **2** the act or an instance of obeying; dutiful or submissive behaviour **3** the authority vested in a Church or similar body **4** the collective group of persons submitting to this authority. See also **passive obedience**

obedient (əˈbiːdɪənt) *adj* obeying or willing to obey [c13 from Old French, from Latin *oboediens*, present participle of *oboedīre* to OBEY] > oˈbediently *adv*

obedientiary (əʊˌbiːdɪˈɛnʃərɪ) *n, pl* **-ries** *Christianity* the holder of any monastic office under the superior [c18 from Medieval Latin *obedientiarius*; see OBEDIENT, -ARY]

obeisance (əʊˈbeɪsəns, əʊˈbiː-) *n* **1** an attitude of deference or homage **2** a gesture expressing obeisance [c14 from Old French *obéissant*, present participle of *obéir* to OBEY] > oˈbeisant *adj* > oˈbeisantly *adv*

obelisk (ˈɒbɪlɪsk) *n* **1** a stone pillar having a square or rectangular cross section and sides that taper towards a pyramidal top, often used as a monument in ancient Egypt **2** *printing* another name for **dagger** (sense 2) [c16 via Latin from Greek *obeliskos* a little spit, from *obelos* spit] > ˌobeˈliscal *adj* > ˌobeˈliskoid *adj*

obelize *or* **obelise** (ˈɒbɪˌlaɪz) *vb* (*tr*) to mark (a word or passage) with an obelus [c17 from Greek *obelizein*]

obelus (ˈɒbɪləs) *n, pl* **-li** (-ˌlaɪ) **1** a mark (— or ÷) used in editions of ancient documents to indicate spurious words or passages **2** another name for **dagger** (sense 2) [c14 via Late Latin from Greek *obelos* spit]

Oberammergau (German oːbərˈamərɡaʊ) *n* a village in S Germany, in Bavaria in the foothills of the Alps: famous for its Passion Play, performed by the villagers every ten years (except during the World Wars) since 1634, in thanksgiving for the end of the Black Death. Pop: 5363 (2003 est)

Oberhausen (German ˈoːbərhauzən) *n* an industrial city in W Germany, in North Rhine-Westphalia on the Rhine-Herne Canal: site of the first ironworks in the Ruhr. Pop: 220 033 (2003 est)

Oberland (ˈəʊbəˌlænd) *n* the lower parts of the Bernese Alps in central Switzerland, mostly in S Bern canton

Oberon¹ (ˈəʊbəˌrɒn) *n* (in medieval folklore) the king of the fairies, husband of Titania

Oberon² (ˈəʊbəˌrɒn) *n* the outermost of the satellites of Uranus

Oberösterreich (ˈoːbərˌøːstəraiç) *n* the German name for **Upper Austria**

obese (əʊˈbiːs) *adj* excessively fat or fleshy; corpulent [c17 from Latin *obēsus*, from *ob-* (intensive) + *edere* to eat] > oˈbesity *or* oˈbeseness *n*

obey (əˈbeɪ) *vb* **1** to carry out (instructions or orders); comply with (demands) **2** to behave or act in accordance with (one's feelings, whims, etc) [c13 from Old French *obéir*, from Latin *oboedīre*, from *ob-* to, towards + *audīre* to hear] > oˈbeyer *n*

obfuscate (ˈɒbfʌsˌkeɪt) *vb* (*tr*) **1** to obscure or darken **2** to perplex or bewilder [c16 from Latin *ob-* (intensive) + *fuscāre* to blacken, from *fuscus* dark] > ˌobfusˈcatory *adj*

obfuscation (ˌɒbfʌsˈkeɪʃən) *n* the act or an instance of making something obscure, dark, or difficult to understand

obi¹ (ˈəʊbɪ) *n, pl* obis *or* obi **1** a broad sash tied in a large flat bow at the back, worn by Japanese women and children as part of the national costume **2** a narrow sash worn by Japanese men [c19 from Japanese]

obi² (ˈəʊbɪ) *or* **obeah** *n, pl* obis *or* obeahs **1** a kind of witchcraft originating in Africa and practised by some West Indians **2** a charm or amulet used in this [of West African origin; compare Edo *obi* poison] > ˈobiism *n*

obit (ˈɒbɪt, ˈəʊbɪt) *n informal* **1** short for **obituary 2** a memorial service

obiter dictum (ˈɒbɪtə ˈdɪktəm, ˈəʊ-) *n, pl* obiter dicta (ˈdɪktə) **1** *law* an observation by a judge on some point of law not directly in issue in the case before him and thus neither requiring his decision nor serving as a precedent, but nevertheless of persuasive authority **2** any comment, remark, or observation made in passing [Latin: something said in passing]

obituary (əˈbɪtjʊərɪ) *n, pl* **-aries** a published announcement of a death, often accompanied by a short biography of the dead person [c18 from Medieval Latin *obituārius*, from Latin *obīre* to fall, from *ob-* down + *īre* to go] > oˈbituarist *n*

obj. *abbreviation for* **1** *grammar* object(ive) **2** objection

object¹ (ˈɒbdʒɪkt) *n* **1** a tangible and visible thing **2** a person or thing seen as a focus or target for feelings, thought, etc: *an object of affection* **3** an aim, purpose, or objective **4** *informal* a ridiculous or pitiable person, spectacle, etc **5** *philosophy* that towards which cognition is directed, as contrasted with the thinking subject; anything regarded as external to the mind, esp in the external world **6** *grammar* a noun, pronoun, or noun phrase whose referent is the recipient of the action of a verb. See also **direct object, indirect object 7** *grammar* a noun, pronoun, or noun phrase that is governed by a preposition **8 no object** not a hindrance or obstacle: *money is no object* **9** *computing* a self-contained identifiable component of a software system or design: *object-oriented programming* [c14 from Late Latin *objectus* something thrown before (the mind), from Latin *obicere*; see OBJECT²]

object² (əbˈdʒɛkt) *vb* **1** (*tr; takes a clause as object*) to state as an objection: *he objected that his motives had been good* **2** (*intr; often foll by to*) to raise or state an objection (to); present an argument (against) [c15 from Latin *obicere*, from *ob-* against + *jacere* to throw]

object ball *n billiards, snooker* any ball except the cue ball, esp one which the striker aims to hit with the cue ball

object glass *n optics* another name for **objective** (sense 11)

objectify (əbˈdʒɛktɪˌfaɪ) *vb* **-fies, -fying, -fied** (*tr*) to represent concretely; present as an object > ˌobjectifiˈcation *n*

objection (əbˈdʒɛkʃən) *n* **1** an expression, statement, or feeling of opposition or dislike **2** a cause for such an expression, statement, or feeling **3** the act of objecting

objectionable (əbˈdʒɛkʃənəbᵊl) *adj* unpleasant, offensive, or repugnant > obˌjectionaˈbility *or* obˈjectionableness *n* > obˈjectionably *adv*

objective (əbˈdʒɛktɪv) *adj* **1** existing independently of perception or an individual's conceptions: *are there objective moral values?* **2** undistorted by emotion or personal bias **3** of or relating to actual and external phenomena as opposed to thoughts, feelings, etc **4** *med* (of disease symptoms) perceptible to persons other than the individual affected **5** *grammar* denoting a case of nouns and pronouns, esp in languages having only two cases, that is used to identify the direct object of a finite verb or preposition and for various other purposes. In English the objective case of pronouns is also used in many elliptical constructions (as in *Poor me! Who, him?*), as the subject of a gerund (as in *It was me helping him*), informally as a predicate complement (as in *It's me*), and in nonstandard use as part of a compound subject (as in *John, Larry, and me went fishing*). See also **accusative 6** of or relating to a goal or aim ⊳ *n* **7** the object of one's endeavours; goal; aim **8** Also called: objective point *military* a place or position towards which forces are directed **9** an actual phenomenon; reality **10** *grammar* **a** the objective case **b** a word or speech element in the objective case **11** Also called: object glass *optics* **a** the lens or combination of lenses nearest to the object in an optical instrument **b** the lens or combination of lenses forming the image in a camera or projector ⊳ Abbreviation: obj. Compare **subjective** > objectival (ˌɒbdʒɛkˈtaɪvəl) *adj* > obˈjectively *adv* > obˈjecˈtivity *or less commonly* obˈjectiveness *n*

objective danger *n mountaineering* a danger, such as a stone fall or avalanche, to which climbing skill is irrelevant

objective genitive *n grammar* a use of the genitive case to express an objective relationship, as in Latin *timor mortis* (fear of death)

objective point *n military* another term for **objective** (sense 8)

objective test *n* a test, such as one using multiple-choice questions, in which the feelings or opinions of the person marking it cannot affect the marks given

objectivism (əbˈdʒɛktɪˌvɪzəm) *n* **1** the tendency to

stress what is objective **2** *philosophy* **a** the meta-ethical doctrine that there are certain moral truths that are independent of the attitudes of any individuals **b** the philosophical doctrine that reality is objective, and that sense data correspond with it > ob'jectivist *n, adj* > objectiv'istic *adj* > objectiv'istically *adv*

object language *n* a language described by or being investigated by another language. Compare **metalanguage**

object lesson *n* **1** a convincing demonstration of some principle or ideal **2** (esp formerly) a lesson in which a material object forms the basis of the teaching and is available to be inspected

object linking and embedding *n* See OLE

object program *n* a computer program translated from the equivalent source program into machine language by the compiler or assembler

object relations theory *n* a form of psychoanalytic theory postulating that people relate to others in order to develop themselves

objet d'art *French* (ɔbʒe dar) *n, pl* objets d'art (ɔbʒe dar) a small object considered to be of artistic worth [literally: object of art]

objet de vertu (ɔbʒei də vɜ:ˈtu:) *n, pl* objets de vertu (ɔbʒei də vɜ:ˈtu:) another name for **object of virtu**: see **virtu** [French, coined by the British as a translation of *object of virtu* but literally meaning only "object of virtue"]

objet trouvé *French* (ɔbʒe truve) *n, pl* objets trouvés (ɔbʒe truve) any ordinary object considered from an aesthetic viewpoint [c20 literally: found object]

objure (ɒbˈdʒʊə) *vb rare* **1** (*tr*) to put on oath **2** (*intr*) to swear [c17 from Latin *objūrāre* to bind by oath] > ,obju'ration *n*

objurgate (ˈɒbdʒə,geit) *vb* (*tr*) to scold or reprimand [c17 from Latin *objurgāre*, from *ob-* against + *jurgāre* to scold] > ,objur'gation *n* > 'objur,gator *n* > objurgatory (ɒbˈdʒɜː,gətəri, -tri) *or* ob'jurgative *adj*

oblanceolate (ɒbˈlɑːnsiəlit, -,leit) *adj botany* (esp of leaves) having a rounded apex and a tapering base

oblast (ˈɒblɑːst) *n* **1** an administrative division of the constituent republics of Russia **2** an administrative and territorial division in some republics of the former Soviet Union [from Russian, from Old Slavonic, *vlast* government]

oblate¹ (ˈɒbleit) *adj* having an equatorial diameter of greater length than the polar diameter: *the earth is an oblate sphere* Compare **prolate** [c18 from New Latin *oblātus* lengthened, from Latin *ob-* towards + *lātus*, past participle of *ferre* to bring] > 'oblately *adv*

oblate² (ˈɒbleit) *n* a person dedicated to a monastic or religious life [c19 from French *oblat*, from Medieval Latin *oblātus*, from Latin *offerre* to OFFER]

oblation (ɒˈbleiʃən) *n Christianity* **1** the offering of the bread and wine of the Eucharist to God **2** any offering made for religious or charitable purposes [c15 from Church Latin *oblātiō*; see OBLATE²] > oblatory (ˈɒblətəri, -tri) *or* ob'lational *adj*

obligate (ˈɒbli,geit) *vb* **1** to compel, constrain, or oblige morally or legally **2** (in the US) to bind (property, funds, etc) as security ▷ *adj* **3** compelled, bound, or restricted **4** *biology* able to exist under only one set of environmental conditions: *an obligate parasite cannot live independently of its host.* Compare **facultative** (sense 4) [c16 from Latin *obligāre* to OBLIGE] > 'obligable *adj* > 'obligative *adj* > 'obli,gator *n*

obligation (,ɒbliˈgeiʃən) *n* **1** a moral or legal requirement; duty **2** the act of obligating or the state of being obligated **3** *law* a legally enforceable agreement to perform some act, esp to pay money, for the benefit of another party **4** *law* a written contract containing a penalty **b** an instrument acknowledging indebtedness to secure the repayment of money borrowed **5** a person or thing to which one is bound morally or legally **6** something owed in return for a service

or favour **7** a service or favour for which one is indebted > ,obli'gational *adj*

obligato (,ɒbliˈgɑːtəʊ) *adj, n music* a variant spelling of **obbligato**

obligatory (ɒˈbligətəri, -tri) *adj* **1** required to be done, obtained, possessed, etc **2** of the nature of or constituting an obligation > ob'ligatorily *adv*

oblige (əˈblaidʒ) *vb* **1** (*tr; often passive*) to bind or constrain (someone to do something) by legal, moral, or physical means **2** (*tr; usually passive*) to make indebted or grateful (to someone) by doing a favour or service: *we are obliged to you for dinner* **3** to do a service or favour to (someone): *she obliged the guest with a song* [c13 from Old French *obliger*, from Latin *obligāre*, from *ob-* to, towards + *ligāre* to bind] > o'bliger *n*

obligee (,ɒbliˈdʒiː) *n* **1** a person in whose favour an obligation, contract, or bond is created; creditor **2** a person who receives a bond

obligement (əˈblaidʒmənt) *n Now chiefly Scot* a kind helpful action; favour

obliging (əˈblaidʒiŋ) *adj* ready to do favours; agreeable; kindly > o'bligingly *adv* > o'bligingness *n*

obligor (,ɒbliˈgɔː) *n* **1** a person who binds himself by contract to perform some obligation; debtor **2** a person who gives a bond

oblique (əˈbliːk) *adj* **1** at an angle; slanting; sloping **2** *geometry* **a** (of lines, planes, etc) neither perpendicular nor parallel to one another or to another line, plane, etc **b** not related to or containing a right angle **3** indirect or evasive **4** *grammar* denoting any case of nouns, pronouns, etc, other than the nominative and vocative **5** *biology* having asymmetrical sides or planes: *an oblique leaf* **6** (of a map projection) constituting a type of zenithal projection in which the plane of projection is tangential to the earth's surface at some point between the equator and the poles ▷ *n* **7** something oblique, esp a line **8** another name for **solidus** (sense 1) **9** *navigation* the act of changing course by less than 90° **10** an aerial photograph taken at an oblique angle ▷ *vb* (*intr*) **11** to take or have an oblique direction **12** (of a military formation) to move forward at an angle [c15 from Old French, from Latin *oblīquus*, of obscure origin] > o'bliquely *adv* > o'bliqueness *n*

oblique angle *n* an angle that is not a right angle or any multiple of a right angle

oblique fault *n* a fault that runs obliquely to, rather than parallel to or perpendicular to, the strike of the affected rocks

oblique sailing *n* a ship's movement on a course that is not due north, south, east, or west

oblique-slip fault *n* a fault on which the movement is along both the strike and the dip of the fault

obliquity (əˈblikwiti) *n, pl* -ties **1** the state or condition of being oblique **2** a deviation from the perpendicular or horizontal **3** a moral or mental deviation **4** Also called: **obliquity of the ecliptic** *astronomy* the angle between the plane of the earth's orbit and that of the celestial equator, equal to approximately 23° 27′ at present > o'bliquitous *adj*

obliterate (əˈblitə,reit) *vb* (*tr*) to destroy every trace of; wipe out completely [c16 from Latin *oblitterāre* to erase, from *ob-* out + *littera* letter] > o,blite'ration *n* > o'bliterative *adj* > o'bliter,ator *n*

oblivion (əˈbliviən) *n* **1** the condition of being forgotten or disregarded **2** the state of being mentally withdrawn or blank **3** *law* an intentional overlooking, esp of political offences; amnesty; pardon [c14 via Old French from Latin *oblīviō* forgetfulness, from *oblīviscī* to forget]

oblivious (əˈbliviəs) *adj* (foll by *to* or *of*) unaware or forgetful > ob'liviously *adv* > ob'liviousness *n*

> **USAGE** It was formerly considered incorrect to use *oblivious* to mean *unaware*, but this use is now acceptable

oblong (ˈɒb,lɒŋ) *adj* **1** having an elongated, esp

rectangular, shape ▷ *n* **2** a figure or object having this shape [c15 from Latin *oblongus*, from *ob-* (intensive) + *longus* LONG¹]

obloquy (ˈɒbləkwi) *n, pl* -quies **1** defamatory or censorious statements, esp when directed against one person **2** disgrace brought about by public abuse [c15 from Latin *obloquium* contradiction, from *ob-* against + *loquī* to speak]

obmutescence (,ɒbmjuːˈtɛsəns) *n archaic* persistent silence [c17 from Latin *obmūtescere* to become mute] > ,obmu'tescent *adj*

obnoxious (əbˈnɒkʃəs) *adj* **1** extremely unpleasant **2** *obsolete* exposed to harm, injury, etc [c16 from Latin *obnoxius*, from *ob-* to + *noxa* injury, from *nocēre* to harm] > ob'noxiously *adv* > ob'noxiousness *n*

obnubilate (ɒbˈnjuːbi,leit) *vb* (*tr*) *literary* to darken or obscure [c16 ultimately from Latin *obnūbilāre* to cover with clouds, from *nubes* cloud]

oboe (ˈəʊbəʊ) *n* **1** a woodwind instrument of the family that includes the bassoon and cor anglais, consisting of a conical tube fitted with a mouthpiece having a double reed. It has a penetrating nasal tone. Range: about two octaves plus a sixth upwards from B flat below middle C **2** a person who plays this instrument in an orchestra: *second oboe* ▷ *Archaic form:* **hautboy** [c18 via Italian *oboe*, phonetic approximation to French *haut bois*, literally: high wood (referring to its pitch)] > 'oboist *n*

oboe da caccia (də ˈkætʃə) *n* a member of the oboe family; the predecessor of the cor anglais [Italian: hunting oboe]

oboe d'amore (dɑːˈmɔːrei) *n* a type of oboe pitched a minor third lower than the oboe itself. It is used chiefly in the performance of baroque music [Italian: oboe of love]

obolus (ˈɒbələs) *or* **obol** (ˈɒbɒl) *n, pl* -li (-,lai) *or* -ols **1** a modern Greek unit of weight equal to one tenth of a gram **2** a silver coin of ancient Greece worth one sixth of a drachma [c16 via Latin from Greek *obolos* small coin, nail; related to *obelos* spit, variant of OBELUS]

obovate (ɒbˈəʊveit) *adj* (of a leaf or similar flat part) shaped like the longitudinal section of an egg with the narrower end at the base; inversely ovate

obovoid (ɒbˈəʊvɔid) *adj* (of a fruit or similar solid part) egg-shaped with the narrower end at the base. Compare **ovoid** (sense 2)

obreption (ɒˈbrɛpʃən) *n now rare* the obtaining of something, such as a gift, in Scots Law esp a grant from the Crown, by giving false information. Compare **subreption** (sense 1) [c17 from Latin *obreptio*, from *obrepere* to creep up to]

obs. *abbreviation for* obsolete

obscene (əbˈsiːn) *adj* **1** offensive or outrageous to accepted standards of decency or modesty **2** *law* (of publications) having a tendency to deprave or corrupt **3** disgusting; repellent: *an obscene massacre* [c16 from Latin *obscēnus* inauspicious, perhaps related to *caenum* filth] > ob'scenely *adv*

obscenity (əbˈsɛniti) *n, pl* -ties **1** the state or quality of being obscene **2** an obscene act, statement, word, etc

obscurant (əbˈskjʊərənt) *n* **1** an opposer of reform and enlightenment ▷ *adj* **2** of or relating to an obscurant **3** causing obscurity > ,obscu'rantism *n* > ,obscu'rantist *n, adj*

obscure (əbˈskjʊə) *adj* **1** unclear or abstruse **2** indistinct, vague, or indefinite **3** inconspicuous or unimportant **4** hidden, secret, or remote **5** (of a vowel) reduced to or transformed into a neutral vowel (ə) **6** gloomy, dark, clouded, or dim ▷ *vb* (*tr*) **7** to make unclear, vague, or hidden **8** to cover or cloud over **9** *phonetics* to pronounce (a vowel) with articulation that causes it to become a neutral sound represented by (ə) ▷ *n* **10** a rare word for **obscurity** [c14 via Old French from Latin *obscūrus* dark] > obscuration (,ɒbskjʊˈreiʃən) *n* > ob'scurely *adv* > ob'scureness *n*

obscurity (əbˈskjʊəriti) *n, pl* -ties **1** the state or

O

quality of being obscure **2** an obscure person or thing

obscurum per obscurius (əbˈskjʊərəm pɜːr əbˈskjʊərɪəs) *n* another term for **ignotum per ignotius** [Latin: the obscure by the more obscure]

obsecrate (ˈɒbsɪˌkreɪt) *vb* (*tr*) a rare word for **beseech** [C16 from Latin *obsecrāre* to entreat (in the name of the gods), from *ob-* for the sake of + *sacrāre* to hold in reverence; see SACRED] > ˌ**obseˈcration** *n*

obsequent (ˈɒbsɪkwənt) *adj* (of a river) flowing into a subsequent stream in the opposite direction to the original slope of the land [C16 (in the obsolete sense: yielding): from Latin *obsequī*, from *sequī* to follow]

obsequies (ˈɒbsɪkwɪz) *pl n, sing* **-quy** funeral rites [C14 via Anglo-Norman from Medieval Latin *obsequiae* (influenced by Latin *exsequiae*), from *obsequium* compliance] > **obsequial** (ɒbˈsiːkwɪəl) *adj*

obsequious (əbˈsiːkwɪəs) *adj* **1** obedient or attentive in an ingratiating or servile manner **2** *now rare* submissive or compliant [C15 from Latin *obsequiōsus* compliant, from *obsequium* compliance, from *obsequi* to follow, from *ob-* to + *sequi* to follow] > **obˈsequiously** *adv* > **obˈsequiousness** *n*

observance (əbˈzɜːvəns) *n* **1** recognition of or compliance with a law, custom, practice, etc **2** the act of such recognition **3** a ritual, ceremony, or practice, esp of a religion **4** observation or attention **5** the degree of strictness of a religious order or community in following its rule **6** *archaic* respectful or deferential attention

observant (əbˈzɜːvənt) *adj* **1** paying close attention to detail; watchful or heedful **2** adhering strictly to rituals, ceremonies, laws, etc > **obˈservantly** *adv*

observation (ˌɒbzəˈveɪʃən) *n* **1** the act of observing or the state of being observed **2** a comment or remark **3** detailed examination of phenomena prior to analysis, diagnosis, or interpretation: *the patient was under observation* **4** the facts learned from observing **5** an obsolete word for **observance** **6** *navigation* **a** a sight taken with an instrument to determine the position of an observer relative to that of a given heavenly body **b** the data so taken > ˌ**obserˈvational** *adj* > ˌ**obserˈvationally** *adv*

observation car *n* a railway carriage fitted with large expanses of glass to provide a good view of the scenery

observation post *n* *military* a position from which observations can be made or from which fire can be directed. Abbreviation: **OP**

observatory (əbˈzɜːvətərɪ, -trɪ) *n, pl* **-ries** **1** an institution or building specially designed and equipped for observing meteorological and astronomical phenomena **2** any building or structure providing an extensive view of its surroundings

observe (əbˈzɜːv) *vb* **1** (*tr; may take a clause as object*) to see; perceive; notice: *we have observed that you steal* **2** (*when tr, may take a clause as object*) to watch (something) carefully; pay attention to (something) **3** to make observations of (something), esp scientific ones **4** (*when intr, usually foll by* on *or* upon; *when tr, may take a clause as object*) to make a comment or remark: *the speaker observed that times had changed* **5** (*tr*) to abide by, keep, or follow (a custom, tradition, law, holiday, etc) [C14 via Old French from Latin *observāre*, from *ob-* to + *servāre* to watch] > **obˈservable** *adj* > **obˈservableness** *or* **obˌservaˈbility** *n* > **obˈservably** *adv*

observer (əbˈzɜːvə) *n* **1** a person or thing that observes **2** a person who attends a conference solely to note the proceedings **3** a person trained to identify aircraft, esp, formerly, a member of an aircrew

obsess (əbˈsɛs) *vb* **1** (*tr; when passive, foll by* with *or* by) to preoccupy completely; haunt **2** (*intr; usually foll by* on *or* over) to worry neurotically or obsessively; brood [C16 from Latin *obsessus* besieged, past participle of *obsidēre*, from *ob-* in front of + *sedēre* to sit]

obsession (əbˈsɛʃən) *n* **1** *psychiatry* a persistent idea or impulse that continually forces its way into consciousness, often associated with anxiety and mental illness **2** a persistent preoccupation, idea, or feeling **3** the act of obsessing or the state of being obsessed > **obˈsessional** *adj* > **obˈsessionally** *adv*

obsessive (əbˈsɛsɪv) *adj* **1** *psychiatry* motivated by a persistent overriding idea or impulse, often associated with anxiety and mental illness **2** continually preoccupied with a particular activity, person, or thing ▷ *n* **3** *psychiatry* a person subject to obsession **4** a person who is continually preoccupied with a particular activity, person, or thing > **obˈsessively** *adv* > **obˈsessiveness** *n*

obsessive-compulsive disorder *n* *psychiatry* an anxiety disorder in which patients are driven to repeat the same act, such as washing their hands, over and over again, usually for many hours. Abbreviation: **OCD**

obsidian (ɒbˈsɪdɪən) *n* a dark volcanic glass formed by very rapid solidification of lava. Also called: **Iceland agate** [C17 from Latin *obsidiānus*, erroneous transcription of *obsiānus* (*lapis*) (stone of) *Obsius*, the name (in Pliny) of the discoverer of a stone resembling obsidian]

obsolesce (ˌɒbsəˈlɛs) *vb* (*intr*) to become obsolete

obsolescent (ˌɒbsəˈlɛsᵊnt) *adj* becoming obsolete or out of date [C18 from Latin *obsolescere*; see OBSOLETE] > ˌ**obsoˈlescence** *n* > ˌ**obsoˈlescently** *adv*

obsolete (ˈɒbsəˌliːt, ˌɒbsəˈliːt) *adj* **1** out of use or practice; not current **2** out of date; unfashionable or outmoded **3** *biology* (of parts, organs, etc) vestigial; rudimentary [C16 from Latin *obsolētus* worn out, past participle of *obsolēre* (unattested), from *ob-* opposite to + *solēre* to be used] > ˈ**obsoˌletely** *adv* > ˈ**obsoˌleteness** *n*

USAGE The word *obsoleteness* is hardly ever used, *obsolescence* standing as the noun form for both *obsolete* and *obsolescent*

obstacle (ˈɒbstəkᵊl) *n* **1** a person or thing that opposes or hinders something **2** *Brit* a fence or hedge used in showjumping [C14 via Old French from Latin *obstāculum*, from *obstāre*, from *ob-* against + *stāre* to stand]

obstacle race *n* a race in which competitors have to negotiate various obstacles

obstet. *abbreviation for* obstetric(s)

obstetric (ɒbˈstɛtrɪk) *or* **obstetrical** *adj* of or relating to childbirth or obstetrics [C18 via New Latin from Latin *obstetrīcius*, from *obstetrix* a midwife, literally: woman who stands opposite, from *obstāre* to stand in front of; see OBSTACLE] > **obˈstetrically** *adv*

obstetrician (ˌɒbstɪˈtrɪʃən) *n* a physician who specializes in obstetrics

obstetrics (ɒbˈstɛtrɪks) *n* (*functioning as singular*) the branch of medicine concerned with childbirth and the treatment of women before and after childbirth

obstinacy (ˈɒbstɪnəsɪ) *n, pl* **-cies** **1** the state or quality of being obstinate **2** an obstinate act, attitude, etc

obstinate (ˈɒbstɪnɪt) *adj* **1** adhering fixedly to a particular opinion, attitude, course of action, etc **2** self-willed or headstrong **3** difficult to subdue or alleviate; persistent: *an obstinate fever* [C14 from Latin *obstinātus*, past participle of *obstināre* to persist in, from *ob-* (intensive) + *stin-*, variant of *stare* to stand] > ˈ**obstinately** *adv*

obstipation (ˌɒbstɪˈpeɪʃən) *n* *pathol* a severe form of constipation, usually resulting from obstruction of the intestinal tract [C16 from Latin *obstīpātiō*, from *ob-* (intensive) + *stīpāre* to press together]

obstreperous (əbˈstrɛpərəs) *adj* noisy or rough, esp in resisting restraint or control [C16 from Latin, from *obstrepere*, from *ob-* against + *strepere* to roar] > **obˈstreperously** *adv* > **obˈstreperousness** *n*

obstruct (əbˈstrʌkt) *vb* (*tr*) **1** to block (a road, passageway, etc) with an obstacle **2** to make (progress or activity) difficult **3** to impede or block a clear view of [C17 Latin *obstructus* built against, past participle of *obstruere*, from *ob-* against + *struere* to build] > **obˈstructor** *n* > **obˈstructive** *adj, n* > **obˈstructively** *adv* > **obˈstructiveness** *n*

obstruction (əbˈstrʌkʃən) *n* **1** a person or thing that obstructs **2** the act or an instance of obstructing **3** delay of business, esp in a legislature by means of procedural devices **4** *sport* the act of unfairly impeding an opposing player **5** the state or condition of being obstructed > **obˈstructional** *adj* > **obˈstructionally** *adv*

obstructionist (əbˈstrʌkʃənɪst) *n* **a** a person who deliberately obstructs business, esp in a legislature **b** (*as modifier*): *obstructionist tactics* > **obˈstructionism** *n*

obstruent (ˈɒbstrʊənt) *med* ▷ *adj* **1** causing obstruction, esp of the intestinal tract ▷ *n* **2** anything that causes obstruction [C17 from Latin *obstruere* to OBSTRUCT]

obtain (əbˈteɪn) *vb* **1** (*tr*) to gain possession of; acquire; get **2** (*intr*) to be customary, valid, or accepted: *a new law obtains in this case* **3** (*tr*) *archaic* to arrive at **4** (*intr*) *archaic* to win a victory; succeed [C15 via Old French from Latin *obtinēre* to take hold of, from *ob-* (intensive) + *tenēre* to hold] > **obˈtainable** *adj* > **obˌtainaˈbility** *n* > **obˈtainer** *n* > **obˈtainment** *n*

obtaining by deception *n* *law* the offence of dishonestly obtaining the property of another by some deception or misrepresentation of facts

obtect (ɒbˈtɛkt) *adj* (of a pupa) encased in a hardened secretion so that the wings, legs, etc, are held immovably to the body, as in butterflies. Also: **obtected** [C19 from Latin *obtectus* covered, past participle of *obtegere*, from *ob-* (intensive) + *tegere* to cover]

obtemper (ɒbˈtɛmpə) *vb* *Scots law* to comply (with) [C15 from Latin *obtemperāre* to obey, from *ob-* towards + *temperāre* to temper]

obtest (ɒbˈtɛst) *vb* *rare* **1** (*tr; may take a clause as object or an infinitive*) to beg (someone) earnestly **2** (*when tr, takes a clause as object; when intr, may be foll by* with *or* against) to object; protest **3** (*tr*) to call (a supernatural power) to witness [C16 from Latin *obtestārī* to protest, from *ob-* to + *testārī* to bear or call as witness] > ˌ**obtesˈtation** *n*

obtrude (əbˈtruːd) *vb* **1** to push (oneself, one's opinions, etc) on others in an unwelcome way **2** (*tr*) to push out or forward [C16 from Latin *obtrūdere*, from *ob-* against + *trūdere* to push forward] > **obˈtruder** *n* > **obtrusion** (əbˈtruːʒən) *n*

obtrusive (əbˈtruːsɪv) *adj* **1** obtruding or tending to obtrude **2** sticking out; protruding; noticeable > **obˈtrusively** *adv* > **obˈtrusiveness** *n*

obtund (ɒbˈtʌnd) *vb* (*tr*) *rare* to deaden or dull [C14 from Latin *obtundere* to beat against, from *ob-* against + *tundere* to belabour] > **obˈtundent** *adj, n*

obturate (ˈɒbtjʊəˌreɪt) *vb* (*tr*) to stop up (an opening, esp the breech of a gun) [C17 from Latin *obtūrāre* to block up, of obscure origin] > ˌ**obtuˈration** *n* > ˈ**obtuˌrator** *n*

obtuse (əbˈtjuːs) *adj* **1** mentally slow or emotionally insensitive **2** *maths* **a** (of an angle) lying between 90° and 180° **b** (of a triangle) having one interior angle greater than 90° **3** not sharp or pointed **4** indistinctly felt, heard, etc; dull: *obtuse pain* **5** (of a leaf or similar flat part) having a rounded or blunt tip [C16 from Latin *obtūsus* dulled, past participle of *obtundere* to beat down; see OBTUND] > **obˈtusely** *adv* > **obˈtuseness** *n*

obverse (ˈɒbvɜːs) *adj* **1** facing or turned towards the observer **2** forming or serving as a counterpart **3** (of certain plant leaves) narrower at the base than at the top ▷ *n* **4** a counterpart or complement **5** the side of a coin that bears the main design or device. Compare **reverse** (sense 15) **6** *logic* a categorial proposition derived from another by replacing the original predicate by its negation and changing the proposition from affirmative to negative or vice versa, as *no sum is correct* from *every sum is incorrect* [C17 from Latin *obversus* turned towards, past participle of *obvertere*, from *ob-* to + *vertere* to turn] > ob'versely *adv*

obvert (ɒb'vɜːt) *vb* (*tr*) **1** *logic* to deduce the obverse of (a proposition) **2** *rare* to turn so as to show the main or other side [C17 from Latin *obvertere* to turn towards; see OBVERSE]
> ob'version *n*

obviate ('ɒbvɪˌeɪt) *vb* (*tr*) to do away with or counter [C16 from Late Latin *obviātus* prevented, past participle of *obviāre*; see OBVIOUS]
> ˌobvi'ation *n*

> **USAGE** Only things that have not yet occurred can be *obviated*. For example, one can *obviate* a possible future difficulty, but not one that already exists

obvious ('ɒbvɪəs) *adj* **1** easy to see or understand; evident **2** exhibiting motives, feelings, intentions, etc, clearly or without subtlety **3** naive or unsubtle: *the play was rather obvious* **4** *obsolete* being or standing in the way [C16 from Latin *obvius*, from *obviam* in the way, from *ob-* against + *via* way] > 'obviousness *n*

obviously ('ɒbvɪəslɪ) *adv* **1** in a way that is easy to see or understand; evidently **2** without subtlety **3** (*sentence modifier*) it is obvious that; clearly: *obviously not everyone wants a bank account*

obvolute ('ɒbvəˌluːt) *adj* **1** (of leaves or petals in the bud) folded so that the margins overlap each other **2** turned in or rolled [C16 from Latin *obvolūtus* past participle of *obvolvere*, from *ob-* to, over + *volvere* to roll] > ˌobvo'lution *n*
> 'obvoˌlutive *adj*

OC *abbreviation for* **1** Officer Commanding **2** Officer of the Order of Canada

o/c *abbreviation for* overcharge

oca ('əʊkə) *n* any of various South American herbaceous plants of the genus *Oxalis*, cultivated for their edible tubers: family *Oxalidaceae* [C20 via Spanish from Quechua *okka*]

OCAM *abbreviation for Organisation commune africaine et malgache*: an association of the 14 principal Francophone states of Africa, established in 1965 to further political cooperation and economic and social development

O Canada *n* the Canadian national anthem

ocarina (ˌɒkəˈriːnə) *n* an egg-shaped wind instrument with a protruding mouthpiece and six to eight finger holes, producing an almost pure tone. Also called (*US informal*): sweet potato [C19 from Italian: little goose, from *oca* goose, ultimately from Latin *avis* bird]

Occam's razor *n* a variant spelling of **Ockham's razor**

occasion (əˈkeɪʒən) *n* **1** (sometimes foll by *of*) the time of a particular happening or event **2** (sometimes foll by *for*) a reason or cause (to do or be something); grounds: *there was no occasion to complain* **3** an opportunity (to do something); chance **4** a special event, time, or celebration: *the party was quite an occasion* **5** on occasion every so often **6** rise to the occasion to have the courage, wit, etc, to meet the special demands of a situation **7** take occasion to avail oneself of an opportunity (to do something) > *vb* **8** (*tr*) to bring about, esp incidentally or by chance > See also **occasions** [C14 from Latin *occāsiō* a falling down, from *occidere*, from *ob-* down + *cadere* to fall]

occasional (əˈkeɪʒənᵊl) *adj* **1** taking place from time to time; not frequent or regular **2** of, for, or happening on special occasions **3** serving as an occasion (for something)

occasionalism (əˈkeɪʒənəˌlɪzəm) *n* the post-Cartesian theory that the seeming interconnection of mind and matter is effected by God

occasional licence *n Brit* a licence granted to sell alcohol only at specified times

occasionally (əˈkeɪʒənəlɪ) *adv* from time to time

occasional table *n* a small table with no regular use

occasions (əˈkeɪʒənz) *pl n archaic* **1** (*sometimes singular*) needs; necessities **2** personal or business affairs

occident ('ɒksɪdənt) *n* a literary or formal word for **west**. Compare **orient** [C14 via Old French from Latin *occidere* to fall, go down (with reference to the setting sun); see OCCASION]

Occident ('ɒksɪdənt) *n* (usually preceded by *the*) **1** the countries of Europe and America **2** the western hemisphere

occidental (ˌɒksɪˈdentᵊl) *adj* a literary or formal word for **western**. Compare **oriental**

Occidental (ˌɒksɪˈdentᵊl) (*sometimes not capital*) *adj* **1** of or relating to the Occident ▷ *n* **2** an inhabitant, esp a native, of the Occident
> ˌOcciˈdentalism *n* > ˌOcciˈdentalist *n, adj*
> ˌOcciˈdentally *adv*

Occidentalize *or* **Occidentalise** (ˌɒksɪˈdentəˌlaɪz) *vb* to make or become Occidental
> ˌOcciˌdentaliˈzation *or* ˌOcciˌdentaliˈsation *n*

occipital (ɒkˈsɪpɪtᵊl) *adj* **1** of or relating to the back of the head or skull ▷ *n* **2** short for **occipital bone**

occipital bone *n* the saucer-shaped bone that forms the back part of the skull and part of its base

occipital lobe *n* the posterior portion of each cerebral hemisphere, concerned with the interpretation of visual sensory impulses

occiput ('ɒksɪˌpʌt, -pət) *n, pl* **occiputs** *or* **occipita** (ɒkˈsɪpɪtə) the back part of the head or skull [C14 from Latin, from *ob-* at the back of + *caput* head]

occlude (əˈkluːd) *vb* **1** (*tr*) to block or stop up (a passage or opening); obstruct **2** (*tr*) to prevent the passage of **3** (*tr*) *chem* (of a solid) to incorporate (a substance) by absorption or adsorption **4** *meteorol* to form or cause to form an occluded front **5** *dentistry* to produce or cause to produce occlusion, as in chewing [C16 from Latin *occlūdere*, from *ob-* (intensive) + *claudere* to close] > oc'cludent *adj*

occluded front *n meteorol* the line or plane occurring where the cold front of a depression has overtaken the warm front, raising the warm sector from ground level. Also called: **occlusion**

occlusion (əˈkluːʒən) *n* **1** the act or process of occluding or the state of being occluded **2** *meteorol* another term for **occluded front** **3** *dentistry* the normal position of the teeth when the jaws are closed **4** *phonetics* the complete closure of the vocal tract at some point, as in the closure prior to the articulation of a plosive > **occlusal** (əˈkluːsəl) *adj*

occlusive (əˈkluːsɪv) *adj* **1** of or relating to the act of occlusion ▷ *n* **2** *phonetics* an occlusive speech sound > oc'clusiveness *n*

occult *adj* (ɒˈkʌlt, ˈɒkʌlt) **1 a** of or characteristic of magical, mystical, or supernatural arts, phenomena, or influences **b** (*as noun*): *the occult* **2** beyond ordinary human understanding **3** secret or esoteric ▷ *vb* (ɒˈkʌlt) **4** *astronomy* (of a celestial body) to hide (another celestial body) from view by occultation or (of a celestial body) to become hidden by occultation **5** to hide or become hidden or shut off from view **6** (*intr*) (of lights, esp in lighthouses) to shut off at regular intervals [C16 from Latin *occultus*, past participle of *occulere*, from *ob-* over, up + *culere*, related to *cēlāre* to conceal] > oc'cultly *adv* > oc'cultness *n*

occultation (ˌɒkʌlˈteɪʃən) *n* **1** the temporary disappearance of one celestial body as it moves out of sight behind another body **2** the act of occulting or the state of being occulted

occultism ('ɒkʌlˌtɪzəm) *n* belief in and the study and practice of magic, astrology, etc > 'occultist *n, adj*

occupancy ('ɒkjʊpənsɪ) *n, pl* **-cies** **1** the act of occupying; possession of a property **2** *law* the possession and use of property by or without agreement and without any claim to ownership **3** *law* the act of taking possession of unowned property, esp land, with the intent of thus

acquiring ownership **4** the condition or fact of being an occupant, esp a tenant **5** the period of time during which one is an occupant, esp of property

occupant ('ɒkjʊpənt) *n* **1** a person, thing, etc, holding a position or place **2** *law* a person who has possession of something, esp an estate, house, etc; tenant **3** *law* a person who acquires by occupancy the title to something previously without an owner

occupation (ˌɒkjʊˈpeɪʃən) *n* **1** a person's regular work or profession; job or principal activity **2** any activity on which time is spent by a person **3** the act of occupying or the state of being occupied **4** the control of a country by a foreign military power **5** the period of time that a nation, place, or position is occupied **6** (*modifier*) for the use of the occupier of a particular property: *occupation road; occupation bridge*

occupational (ˌɒkjʊˈpeɪʃənᵊl) *adj* of, relating to, or caused by an occupation: *an occupational pension scheme; an occupational disease* > ˌoccuˈpationally *adv*

occupational pension *n* **1** a pension scheme provided for the members of a particular occupation or by a specific employer or group of employers **2** a pension derived from such a scheme

occupational psychology *n psychol* the study of human behaviour at work, including ergonomics, selection procedures, and the effects of stress

occupational therapy *n med* treatment of people with physical, emotional, or social problems, using purposeful activity to help them overcome or learn to deal with their problems
> occupational therapist *n*

occupation franchise *n Brit* the right of a tenant to vote in national and local elections

occupation groupings *pl n* a system of classifying people according to occupation, based originally on information obtained by government census and subsequently developed by market research. The classifications are used by the advertising industry to identify potential markets. The groups are **A, B, C1, C2, D,** and **E**

occupier ('ɒkjʊˌpaɪə) *n* **1** *Brit* a person who is in possession or occupation of a house or land **2** a person or thing that occupies

occupy ('ɒkjʊˌpaɪ) *vb* **-pies, -pying, -pied** (*tr*) **1** to live or be established in (a house, flat, office, etc) **2** (*often passive*) to keep (a person) busy or engrossed; engage the attention of **3** (*often passive*) to take up (a certain amount of time or space) **4** to take and hold possession of, esp as a demonstration: *students occupied the college buildings* **5** to fill or hold (a position or rank) [C14 from Old French *occuper*, from Latin *occupāre* to seize hold of, from *ob-* (intensive) + *capere* to take]

occur (əˈkɜː) *vb* **-curs, -curring, -curred** (*intr*) **1** to happen; take place; come about **2** to be found or be present; exist **3** (foll by *to*) to be realized or thought of (by); suggest itself (to) [C16 from Latin *occurrere* to run up to, from *ob-* to + *currere* to run]

> **USAGE** It is usually regarded as incorrect to talk of pre-arranged events *occurring* or *happening*: *the wedding took place* (not *occurred* or *happened*) *in the afternoon*

occurrence (əˈkʌrəns) *n* **1** something that occurs; a happening; event **2** the act or an instance of occurring: *a crime of frequent occurrence*

occurrent (əˈkʌrənt) *adj philosophy* (of a property) relating to some observable feature of its bearer. Compare **disposition** (sense 4)

occy ('ɒkɪ) *n* all over the occy *Midland English dialect* in every direction

OCD *abbreviation for* **obsessive-compulsive disorder**

ocean ('əʊʃən) *n* **1** a very large stretch of sea, esp one of the five oceans of the world, the Atlantic, Pacific, Indian, Arctic, and Antarctic **2** the body of salt water covering approximately 70 per cent of the earth's surface **3** a huge quantity or expanse: *an ocean of replies* **4** *literary* the sea [C13 via

O

Old French from Latin *ōceanus*, from Greek *ōkeanos* OCEANUS]

oceanarium (ˌəʊʃəˈnɛərɪəm) *n, pl* **-iums** *or* **-ia** (-ɪə) a large saltwater aquarium for marine life

ocean floor spreading *n* another term for **seafloor spreading**

ocean-going *adj* (of a ship, boat, etc) suited for travel on the open ocean

ocean greyhound *n* a fast ship, esp a liner

Oceania (ˌəʊʃɪˈɑːnɪə) *n* the islands of the central and S Pacific, including Melanesia, Micronesia, and Polynesia: sometimes also including Australasia and the Malay Archipelago

Oceanian (ˌəʊʃɪˈɑːnɪən) *adj* **1** of or relating to Oceania or its inhabitants ▷ *n* **2** a native or inhabitant of Oceania

oceanic (ˌəʊʃɪˈænɪk) *adj* **1** of or relating to the ocean **2** living in the depths of the ocean beyond the continental shelf at a depth exceeding 200 metres: *oceanic fauna* **3** huge or overwhelming **4** (of geological formations) of volcanic origin, arising from the ocean: *oceanic islands*

Oceanic (ˌəʊʃɪˈænɪk) *n* **1** a branch, group, or subfamily of the Malayo-Polynesian family of languages, comprising Polynesian and Melanesian ▷ *adj* **2** of, relating to, or belonging to this group of languages **3** of or relating to Oceania

oceanic ridge *n* any section of the narrow, largely continuous range of submarine mountains that extends into all the major oceans and at which new oceanic lithosphere is created by the rise of magma from the earth's interior. See also **seafloor spreading**

oceanic trench *n* a long narrow steep-sided depression in the earth's oceanic crust, usually lying above a subduction zone

Oceanid (əʊˈsɪənɪd) *n, pl* **Oceanids** *or* **Oceanides** (ˌəʊsɪˈænɪˌdiːz) *Greek myth* any of the ocean nymphs born of Oceanus and Tethys

Ocean of Storms *n* the largest of the dark plains (maria) on the surface of the moon, situated in the second and third quadrant. Also called: **Oceanus Procellarum** (ˌəʊʃɪˈænəs ˌprəʊsɪˈlɛərəm)

oceanog. *abbreviation for* oceanography

oceanography (ˌəʊʃəˈnɒɡrəfɪ, ˌəʊʃɪə-) *n* the branch of science dealing with the physical, chemical, geological, and biological features of the oceans and ocean basins > ˌocean'ographer *n* > oceanographic (ˌəʊʃənəˈɡræfɪk, ˌəʊʃɪ-) *or* ˌoceano'graphical *adj* > ˌoceano'graphically *adv*

oceanology (ˌəʊʃəˈnɒlədʒɪ, ˌəʊʃɪə-) *n* the study of the sea, esp of its economic geography

Oceanus (əʊˈsɪənəs) *n Greek myth* a Titan, divinity of the stream believed to flow around the earth

ocellus (ɒˈsɛləs) *n, pl* **-li** (-laɪ) **1** the simple eye of insects and some other invertebrates, consisting basically of light-sensitive cells **2** any eyelike marking in animals, such as the eyespot on the tail feather of a peacock **3** *botany* an enlarged discoloured cell in a leaf **b** a swelling on the sporangium of certain fungi [C19 via New Latin from Latin: small eye, from *oculus* eye] > o'cellar *adj* > ocellate (ˈɒsɪˌleɪt) *or* ocellated (ˈɒsɪˌleɪtɪd) *adj* > ˌocel'lation *n*

ocelot (ˈɒsɪˌlɒt, ˈəʊ-) *n* a feline mammal, *Felis pardalis*, inhabiting the forests of Central and South America and having a dark-spotted buff-brown coat [C18 via French from Nahuatl *ocelotl* jaguar]

och (ɒx) *Scot and Irish* ▷ *interj* **1** an expression of surprise, contempt, annoyance, impatience, or disagreement ▷ *sentence connector* **2** an expression used to preface a remark, gain time, etc: *och, I suppose so* ▷ Also: **ach**

oche (ˈɒkɪ) *n darts* the mark or ridge on the floor behind which a player must stand to throw [of unknown origin; perhaps connected with obsolete *oche* to chop off, from Old French *ocher* to cut a notch in]

ocher (ˈəʊkə) *n, adj, vb* the US spelling of **ochre** > 'ocherous *or* 'ochery *adj* > ochroid (ˈəʊkrɔɪd) *adj*

ochlocracy (ɒkˈlɒkrəsɪ) *n, pl* **-cies** rule by the mob; mobocracy [C16 via French, from Greek *okhlokratia*, from *okhlos* mob + *kratos* power] > **ochlocrat** (ˈɒkləˌkræt) *n* > **ochlocratic** (ˌɒkləˈkrætɪk) *adj*

ochlophobia (ˌɒkləˈfəʊbɪə) *n psychol* the fear of crowds [C19 from New Latin, from Greek *okhlos* mob + -PHOBIA]

ochone (ɒˈxəʊn) *interj Scot and Irish* an expression of sorrow or regret [from Gaelic *ochóin*]

ochre *or US* **ocher** (ˈəʊkə) *n* **1** any of various natural earths containing ferric oxide, silica, and alumina: used as yellow or red pigments **2 a** a moderate yellow-orange to orange colour **b** (*as adjective*): *an ochre dress* ▷ *vb* **3** (*tr*) to colour with ochre [C15 from Old French *ocre*, from Latin *ōchra*, from Greek *ōkhra*, from *ōkhros* pale yellow] > **ochreous** (ˈəʊkrɪəs, ˈəʊkərəs), **ochrous** (ˈəʊkrəs), **ochry** (ˈəʊkərɪ, ˈəʊkrɪ) *or US* **ocherous**, **ochery** *adj* > **ochroid** (ˈəʊkrɔɪd) *adj*

ochrea *or* **ocrea** (ˈɒkrɪə) *n, pl* **-reae** (-rɪˌiː) a cup-shaped structure that sheathes the stems of certain plants, formed from united stipules or leaf bases [C19 from Latin *ocrea* greave, legging, of obscure origin]

ocicat (ˈɒsɪˌkæt) *n* a breed of large short-haired cat with a spotted coat [C20 from OC(ELOT) + -i- + CAT]

-ock *suffix forming nouns* indicating smallness: *hillock* [Old English *-oc, -uc*]

ocker (ˈɒkə) *Austral slang* ▷ *n* **1** (*often capital*) an uncultivated or boorish Australian ▷ *adj, adv* **2** typical of such a person [C20 of uncertain origin]

Ockham's razor *or* **Occam's razor** (ˈɒkəmz) *n* a maxim, attributed to the English nominalist philosopher William of Ockham (died ?1349), stating that in explaining something assumptions must not be needlessly multiplied. Also called: **the principle of economy**

ockodols (ˈɒkədɒlz) *pl n Northern English dialect* one's feet when wearing boots

o'clock (əˈklɒk) *adv* **1** used after a number from one to twelve to indicate the hour of the day or night **2** used after a number to indicate direction or position relative to the observer, twelve o'clock being directly ahead or overhead and other positions being obtained by comparisons with a clock face [C18 abbreviation for *of the clock*]

ocotillo (ˌəʊkəˈtiːljəʊ) *n, pl* **-los** a cactus-like tree, *Fouquieria splendens*, of Mexico and the southwestern US, with scarlet tubular flowers: used for hedges and candlewood: family *Fouquieriaceae* [Mexican Spanish: diminutive of *ocote* pine, from Nahuatl *ocotl* torch]

OCR *abbreviation for* optical character reader or recognition

ocrea (ˈɒkrɪə) *n, pl* **-reae** (-rɪˌiː) a variant spelling of **ochrea**

ocreate (ˈɒkrɪɪt, -ˌeɪt) *adj* **1** *botany* possessing an ocrea; sheathed **2** *ornithol* another word for **booted** (sense 2)

OCS *abbreviation for* Officer Candidate School

Oct *abbreviation for* October

oct- *combining form* a variant of **octo-** before a vowel

octa (ˈɒktə) *n* a variant spelling of **okta**

octa- *combining form* a variant of **octo-**

octachord (ˈɒktəˌkɔːd) *n* **1** an eight-stringed musical instrument **2** a series of eight notes, esp a scale

octad (ˈɒktæd) *n* **1** a group or series of eight **2** *chem* an element or group with a valency of eight [C19 from Greek *oktás*, from *oktō* eight] > **oc'tadic** *adj*

octagon (ˈɒktəgən) *or less commonly* **octangle** *n* a polygon having eight sides [C17 via Latin from Greek *oktagōnos*, having eight angles]

octagonal (ɒkˈtægənˌl) *adj* **1** having eight sides and eight angles **2** of or relating to an octagon > **oc'tagonally** *adv*

octahedral (ˌɒktəˈhiːdrəl) *adj* **1** having eight plane surfaces **2** shaped like an octahedron

octahedrite (ˌɒktəˈhiːdraɪt) *n* another name for **anatase**

octahedron (ˌɒktəˈhiːdrən) *n, pl* **-drons** *or* **-dra** (-drə) a solid figure having eight plane faces

octal notation *or* **octal** (ˈɒktəl) *n* a number system having a base 8: often used in computing, one octal digit being equivalent to a group of three bits

octamerous (ɒkˈtæmərəs) *adj* consisting of eight parts, esp (of flowers) having the parts arranged in groups of eight

octameter (ɒkˈtæmɪtə) *n prosody* a verse line consisting of eight metrical feet

octane (ˈɒkteɪn) *n* a liquid alkane hydrocarbon found in petroleum and existing in 18 isomeric forms, esp the isomer *n*-octane. Formula: C_8H_{18}. See also **isooctane**

octanedioic acid (ˌɒkteɪndaɪˈəʊɪk) *n* a colourless crystalline dicarboxylic acid found in suberin and castor oil and used in the manufacture of synthetic resins. Formula: $HOOC(CH_2)_6COOH$. Also called: **suberic acid** [C20 from OCTANE + DIOL]

octane number *or* **rating** *n* a measure of the quality of a petrol expressed as the percentage of isooctane in a mixture of isooctane and *n*-heptane that gives a fuel with the same antiknock qualities as the given petrol

octangle (ˈɒktæŋgˌl) *n* a less common name for **octagon**

octangular (ɒkˈtæŋgjʊlə) *adj* having eight angles

Octans (ˈɒktænz) *n, Latin genitive* **Octantis** (ɒkˈtæntɪs) a faint constellation in the S hemisphere in which the S celestial pole is situated

octant (ˈɒktənt) *n* **1** *maths* **a** any of the eight parts into which the three planes containing the Cartesian coordinate axes divide space **b** an eighth part of a circle **2** *astronomy* the position of a celestial body when it is at an angular distance of 45° from another body **3** an instrument used for measuring angles, similar to a sextant but having a graduated arc of 45° [C17 from Latin *octans* half quadrant, from *octo* eight]

octarchy (ˈɒktɑːkɪ) *n, pl* **-chies 1** government by eight rulers **2** a confederacy of eight kingdoms, tribes, etc

octaroon (ˌɒktəˈruːn) *n* a variant spelling of **octoroon**

octavalent (ˌɒktəˈveɪlənt) *adj chem* having a valency of eight

octave (ˈɒktɪv) *n* **1 a** the interval between two musical notes one of which has twice the pitch of the other and lies eight notes away from it counting inclusively along the diatonic scale **b** one of these two notes, esp the one of higher pitch **c** (*as modifier*): *an octave leap* ▷ See also **perfect** (sense 9), **diminished** (sense 2), **interval** (sense 5) **2** *prosody* a rhythmic group of eight lines of verse **3** (ˈɒkteɪv) **a** a feast day and the seven days following **b** the final day of this period **4** the eighth of eight basic positions in fencing **5** any set or series of eight ▷ *adj* **6** consisting of eight parts [C14 (originally: eighth day) via Old French from Medieval Latin *octāva diēs* eighth day (after a festival), from Latin *octo* eight]

octave coupler *n* a mechanism on an organ and on some harpsichords that enables keys or pedals an octave apart to be played simultaneously

octavo (ɒkˈteɪvəʊ) *n, pl* **-vos 1** Also called: **eightvo** a book size resulting from folding a sheet of paper of a specified size to form eight leaves: *demi-octavo*. Often written: **8vo, 8° 2** a book of this size **3** (formerly) a size of cut paper 8 inches by 5 inches (20.3 cm by 12.7 cm) [C16 from New Latin phrase *in octavo* in an eighth (of a whole sheet)]

octennial (ɒkˈtɛnɪəl) *adj* **1** occurring every eight years **2** lasting for eight years [C17 from Latin *octennium* eight years, from *octo* eight + *annus* year] > **oc'tennially** *adv*

octet (ɒkˈtɛt) *n* **1** any group of eight, esp eight singers or musicians **2** a piece of music composed for such a group **3** *prosody* another word for **octave** (sense 2) **4** *chem* a group of eight electrons forming a stable shell in an atom ▷ Also (for senses 1, 2, 3): octette [C19 from Latin *octo* eight, on the model of DUET]

octillion (ɒkˈtɪljən) *n* **1** (in Britain and Germany) the number represented as one followed by 48 zeros (10^{48}) **2** (in the US, Canada, and France) the number represented as one followed by 27 zeros (10^{27}) [C17 from French, on the model of MILLION] ▷ ocˈtillionth *adj*

octo-. **octa-** *or before a vowel* **oct-** *combining form* eight: *octosyllabic*; *octagon* [from Latin *octo*, Greek *okto*]

October (ɒkˈtəʊbə) *n* the tenth month of the year, consisting of 31 days [Old English, from Latin, from *octo* eight, since it was the eighth month in Roman reckoning]

October Revolution *n* another name for the **Russian Revolution** (sense 2)

Octobrist (ɒkˈtəʊbrɪst) *n* a member of a Russian political party favouring the constitutional reforms granted in a manifesto issued by Nicholas II in Oct 1905

octocentenary (ˌɒktəʊsɛnˈtiːnərɪ) *n*, *pl* -naries an eight-hundredth anniversary

octodecimo (ˌɒktəʊˈdɛsɪməʊ) *n*, *pl* -mos *bookbinding* another word for **eighteenmo** [C18 from New Latin phrase *in octodecimo* in an eighteenth (of a whole sheet)]

octogenarian (ˌɒktəʊdʒɪˈnɛərɪən) *or less commonly* **octogenary** (ɒkˈtɒdʒɪnərɪ) *n*, *pl* -narians *or* -naries **1** a person who is from 80 to 89 years old ▷ *adj* **2** of or relating to an octogenarian [C19 from Latin *octōgēnārius* containing eighty, from *octōgēnī* eighty each]

octonary (ˈɒktənərɪ) *rare* ▷ *adj* **1** relating to or based on the number eight ▷ *n*, *pl* -naries **2** *prosody* a stanza of eight lines **3** a group of eight [C16 from Latin *octōnārius*, from *octōnī* eight at a time]

octopod (ˈɒktəˌpɒd) *n* **1** any cephalopod mollusc of the order *Octopoda*, including octopuses and the paper nautilus, having eight tentacles, and lacking an internal shell ▷ *adj* **2** of, relating to, or belonging to the *Octopoda*

octopus (ˈɒktəpəs) *n*, *pl* -puses **1** any cephalopod mollusc of the genera *Octopus, Eledone*, etc, having a soft oval body with eight long suckered tentacles and occurring at the sea bottom: order *Octopoda* (octopods) **2** a powerful influential organization with far-reaching effects, esp harmful ones **3** another name for **spider** (sense 8) [C18 via New Latin from Greek *oktōpous* having eight feet]

octoroon *or* **octaroon** (ˌɒktəˈruːn) *n* a person having one quadroon and one White parent and therefore having one-eighth Black blood. Compare **quadroon** [C19 OCTO- + -*roon* as in QUADROON]

octosyllable (ˈɒktəˌsɪləbˀl) *n* **1** a line of verse composed of eight syllables **2** a word of eight syllables > **octosyllabic** (ˌɒktəsɪˈlæbɪk) *adj*

octroi (ˈɒktrwɑː) *n* **1** (in some European countries, esp France) a duty on various goods brought into certain towns or cities **2** the place where such a duty is collected **3** the officers responsible for its collection [C17 from French *octroyer* to concede, from Medieval Latin *auctorizāre* to AUTHORIZE]

octuple (ˈɒktjʊpˀl) *n* **1** a quantity or number eight times as great as another ▷ *adj* **2** eight times as much or as many **3** consisting of eight parts ▷ *vb* **4** (*tr*) to multiply by eight [C17 from Latin *octuplus*, from *octo* eight + -*plus* as in *duplus* double]

ocular (ˈɒkjʊlə) *adj* **1** of or relating to the eye ▷ *n* **2** another name for **eyepiece** [C16 from Latin *oculāris* from *oculus* eye] > ˈocularly *adv*

ocularist (ˈɒkjʊlərɪst) *n* a person who makes artificial eyes

oculate (ˈɒkjʊˌleɪt) *adj zoology* **1** possessing eyes **2** relating to or resembling eyes: *oculate markings*

oculist (ˈɒkjʊlɪst) *n med* a former term for **ophthalmologist** [C17 via French from Latin *oculus* eye]

oculo- *or sometimes before a vowel* **ocul-** *combining form* indicating the eye: *oculomotor* [from Latin *oculus* eye]

oculoauriculovertebral displasia (ˈɒkjʊˌəʊʊˈrɪkjʊˌləʊˈvɜːtɪˌbrəl dɪsˈpleɪʒə) *n* the technical name for **Goldenhar's Syndrome**

oculomotor (ˌɒkjʊləʊˈməʊtə) *adj* relating to or causing eye movements [C19 from OCULO- + MOTOR]

oculomotor nerve *n* the third cranial nerve, which supplies most of the eye muscles

od (ɒd, əʊd) *or* **odyl, odyle** (ˈɒdɪl) *n archaic* a hypothetical force formerly thought to be responsible for many natural phenomena, such as magnetism, light, and hypnotism [C19 coined arbitrarily by Baron Karl von Reichenbach (1788–1869), German scientist] > ˈodic *adj*

Od, 'Od *or* **Odd** (ɒd) *euphemistic* (used in mild oaths) an archaic word for **God**

OD[1] (ˌəʊˈdiː) *informal* ▷ *n* **1** an overdose of a drug ▷ *vb* OD's, OD'ing, OD'd **2** (*intr*) to take an overdose of a drug [C20 from O(*ver*)D(*ose*)]

OD[2] *abbreviation for* **1** Officer of the Day **2** Old Dutch **3** ordnance datum **4** outside diameter **5** Also: o.d. *military* olive drab **6** Also: O/D *banking* **a** on demand **b** overdraft **c** overdrawn

ODA (in Britain, formerly) *abbreviation for* Overseas Development Administration, now superseded by the Department for International Development (DFID)

odalisque *or* **odalisk** (ˈəʊdəlɪsk) *n* a female slave or concubine [C17 via French, changed from Turkish *ōdalik*, from *ōdah* room + -*lik* n suffix]

odd (ɒd) *adj* **1** unusual or peculiar in appearance, character, etc **2** occasional, incidental, or random: *odd jobs* **3** leftover or additional: *odd bits of wool* **4 a** not divisible by two **b** represented or indicated by a number that is not divisible by two: *graphs are on odd pages*. Compare **even**[1] (sense 7) **5** being part of a matched pair or set when the other or others are missing: *an odd sock; odd volumes* **6** (*in combination*) used to designate an indefinite quantity more than the quantity specified in round numbers: *fifty-odd pounds* **7** out-of-the-way or secluded: *odd corners* **8** *maths* (of a function) changing sign but not absolute value when the sign of the independent variable is changed, as in *y=x³*. Compare **even**[1] (sense 13) **9 odd man out** a person or thing excluded from others forming a group, unit, etc ▷ *n* **10** *golf* **a** one stroke more than the score of one's opponent **b** an advantage or handicap of one stroke added to or taken away from a player's score **11** a thing or person that is odd in sequence or number ▷ See also **odds** [C14 *odde*: from Old Norse *oddi* point, angle, triangle, third or odd number. Compare Old Norse *oddr* point, spot, place; Old English *ord* point, beginning] > ˈoddly *adv* > ˈoddness *n*

oddball (ˈɒdˌbɔːl) *informal* ▷ *n* **1** Also called: **odd bod, odd fish** a strange or eccentric person ▷ *adj* **2** strange or peculiar

Oddfellow (ˈɒdˌfɛləʊ) *n* a member of the **Independent Order of Oddfellows,** a secret benevolent and fraternal association founded in England in the 18th century

oddity (ˈɒdɪtɪ) *n*, *pl* -ties **1** an odd person or thing **2** an odd quality or characteristic **3** the condition of being odd

odd-jobman *or* **odd-jobber** *n*, *pl* -men *or* -bers a person who does casual work, esp domestic repairs

odd lot *n* **1** a batch of merchandise that contains less than or more than the usual number of units **2** *stock exchange* a number of securities less than the standard trading unit of 100

odd-man rush *n ice hockey* an attacking move when the defence is outnumbered by the opposing team

oddment (ˈɒdmənt) *n* **1** (*often plural*) an odd piece or thing; leftover **2** (*plural*) NZ pieces of wool, such as belly wool or neck wool, removed from a fleece and sold separately

odd-pinnate *adj* (of a plant leaf) pinnate with a single leaflet at the apex

odds (ɒdz) *pl n* **1** (foll by *on or against*) the probability, expressed as a ratio, that a certain event will take place: *the odds against the outsider are a hundred to one* **2** the amount, expressed as a ratio, by which the wager of one better is greater than that of another: *he was offering odds of five to one* **3** the likelihood that a certain state of affairs will be found to be so: *the odds are that he is drunk* **4** the chances or likelihood of success in a certain undertaking: *their odds were very poor after it rained* **5** an equalizing allowance, esp one given to a weaker side in a contest **6** the advantage that one contender is judged to have over another: *the odds are on my team* **7** *Brit* a significant difference (esp in the phrase **it makes no odds**) **8 at odds a** on bad terms **b** appearing not to correspond or match: *the silvery hair was at odds with her youthful shape* **9 give** *or* **lay odds** to offer a bet with favourable odds **10 take odds** to accept such a bet **11 over the odds** a more than is expected, necessary, etc: *he got two pounds over the odds for this job* **b** unfair or excessive **12 what's the odds?** *Brit informal* what difference does it make?

odds and ends *pl n* miscellaneous items

odds and sods *pl n Brit informal* miscellaneous people or things

odds-on *adj* **1** (of a chance, horse, etc) rated at even money or less to win **2** regarded as more or most likely to win, succeed, happen, etc

ode (əʊd) *n* **1** a lyric poem, typically addressed to a particular subject, with lines of varying lengths and complex rhythms. See also **Horatian ode, Pindaric ode 2** (formerly) a poem meant to be sung [C16 via French from Late Latin *ōda*, from Greek *ōidē*, from *aeidein* to sing]

-ode[1] *n combining form* denoting resemblance: *nematode* [from Greek -*ōdēs*, from *eidos* shape, form]

-ode[2] *n combining form* denoting a path or way: *electrode* [from Greek -*odos*, from *hodos* a way]

odea (ˈəʊdɪə) *n* the plural of **odeum**

Odelsting *or* **Odelsthing** (ˈəʊdˀlsˌtɪŋ) *n* the lower chamber of the Norwegian parliament. See also **Lagting, Storting**

Odense (*Danish* ˈoːðənsə) *n* a port in S Denmark, on Funen Island: cathedral founded by King Canute in the 11th century. Pop: 145 554 (2004 est)

Oder (ˈəʊdə) *n* a river in central Europe, rising in the NE Czech Republic and flowing north and west, forming part of the border between Germany and Poland, to the Baltic. Length: 913 km (567 miles). Czech and Polish name: **Odra**

Oder-Neisse Line (ˈəʊdəˈnaɪsə) *n* the present-day boundary between Germany and Poland along the Rivers Oder and Neisse. Established in 1945, it originally separated the Soviet Zone of Germany from the regions under Polish administration

Odessa (əʊˈdɛsə; *Russian* aˈdjɛsa) *n* a port in S Ukraine on the Black Sea: the chief Russian grain port in the 19th century; university (1865); industrial centre and important naval base. Pop: 1 010 000 (2005 est)

odeum (ˈəʊdɪəm) *n*, *pl* odea (ˈəʊdɪə) (esp in ancient Greece and Rome) a building for musical performances. Also called: odeon [C17 from Latin, from Greek *ōideion*, from *ōidē* ODE]

ODI *cricket abbreviation for* one-day international

Odin (ˈəʊdɪn) *or* **Othin** (ˈəʊðɪn) *n Norse myth* the supreme creator god; the divinity of wisdom, culture, war, and the dead. Germanic counterpart: Wotan, Woden

odious (ˈəʊdɪəs) *adj* offensive; repugnant [C17 from Latin; see ODIUM] > ˈodiously *adv* > ˈodiousness *n*

odium (ˈəʊdɪəm) *n* **1** the dislike accorded to a hated person or thing **2** hatred; repugnance [C17 from Latin; related to *ōdī* I hate, Greek *odussasthai* to be angry]

odometer (ɒˈdɒmɪtə, əʊ-) *n US and Canadian* a device that records the number of miles that a bicycle or motor vehicle has travelled. Also called:

O

mileometer [C18 *hodometer*, from Greek *hodos* way + -METER] > o'dometry *n*

-odont *adj and n combining form* having teeth of a certain type; -toothed: *acrodont* [from Greek *odōn* tooth]

odontalgia (ˌɒdɒnˈtældʒɪə) *n* a technical name for **toothache**. > odonˈtalgic *adj*

odonto- *or before a vowel* **odont-** *combining form* indicating a tooth or teeth: *odontology* [from Greek *odōn* tooth]

odontoblast (ɒˈdɒntəˌblæst) *n* any of a layer of cells lining the pulp cavity of a tooth and giving rise to the dentine > oˌdontoˈblastic *adj*

odontoglossum (ˌɒdɒntəˈɡlɒsəm) *n* any epiphytic orchid of the tropical American genus *Odontoglossum*, having clusters of brightly coloured flowers

odontoid (ɒˈdɒntɔɪd) *adj* **1** toothlike **2** of or relating to the odontoid process

odontoid process *n anatomy* the toothlike upward projection at the back of the second vertebra of the neck

odontolite (ɒˈdɒntəˌlaɪt) *n* another name for **bone turquoise**

odontology (ˌɒdɒnˈtɒlədʒɪ) *n* the branch of science concerned with the anatomy, development, and diseases of teeth and related structures > odontological (ɒˌdɒntəˈlɒdʒɪkəl) *adj* > ˌodonˈtologist *n*

odontophore (ɒˈdɒntəˌfɔː) *n* an oral muscular protrusible structure in molluscs that supports the radula > odontophoral (ˌɒdɒnˈtɒfərəl) *or* ˌodonˈtophorous *adj*

odontorhynchous (ɒˌdɒntəˈrɪŋkəs) *adj* (of birds) having toothlike ridges inside the beak [C19 from ODONTO- + Greek *rhunkhos* snout + -OUS]

odor (ˈəʊdə) *n* the US spelling of **odour** > 'odorless *adj*

odoriferous (ˌəʊdəˈrɪfərəs) *adj* having or emitting an odour, esp a fragrant one > ˌodorˈiferously *adv* > ˌodorˈiferousness *n*

odorimetry (ˌəʊdəˈrɪmɪtrɪ) *n chem* the measurement of the strength and permanence of odours. Also called: **olfactometry**

odoriphore (əʊˈdɒrɪˌfɔː) *n chem* the group of atoms in an odorous molecule responsible for its odour

odorous (ˈəʊdərəs) *adj* having or emitting a characteristic smell or odour > 'odorously *adv* > 'odorousness *n*

odour *or US* **odor** (ˈəʊdə) *n* **1** the property of a substance that gives it a characteristic scent or smell **2** a pervasive quality about something: *an odour of dishonesty* **3** repute or regard (in the phrases **in good odour**, **in bad odour**) [C13 from Old French *odur*, from Latin *odor*; related to Latin *olēre* to smell, Greek *ōzein*] > 'odourless *or US* 'odorless *adj*

odour of sanctity *n derogatory* sanctimoniousness [C18 originally, the sweet smell said to be exhaled by the bodies of dead saints]

Odra (ˈɔdra) *n* the Czech and Polish name for the **Oder**

odyl *or* **odyle** (ˈɒdɪl) *n* other words for **od**

Odysseus (əˈdiːsɪəs) *n Greek myth* one of the foremost of the Greek heroes at the siege of Troy, noted for his courage and ingenuity. His return to his kingdom of Ithaca was fraught with adventures in which he lost all his companions and he was acknowledged by his wife Penelope only after killing her suitors. Roman name: Ulysses

Odyssey (ˈɒdɪsɪ) *n* **1** a Greek epic poem, attributed to Homer (c. 800 BC), describing the ten-year homeward wanderings of Odysseus after the fall of Troy **2** (*often not capital*) any long eventful journey > **Odyssean** (ˌɒdɪˈsiːən) *adj*

Oe *symbol for* oersted

OE *abbreviation for* Old English (language)

o.e. *commerce abbreviation for* omissions excepted

OECD *abbreviation for* Organization for Economic

Cooperation and Development; an association of 21 nations to promote growth and trade, set up in 1961 to supersede the OEEC

oecology (iːˈkɒlədʒɪ) *n* a less common spelling of **ecology**. > oecological (ˌɛkəˈlɒdʒɪkəl, ˌiː-) *adj* > ˌoecoˈlogically *adv* > oeˈcologist *n*

oecumenical (ˌiːkjʊˈmɛnɪkəl) *adj* a less common spelling of **ecumenical**

OED *abbreviation for* Oxford English Dictionary

oedema *or* **edema** (ɪˈdiːmə) *n, pl* **-mata** (-mətə) **1** *pathol* an excessive accumulation of serous fluid in the intercellular spaces of tissue **2** *plant pathol* an abnormal swelling in a plant caused by a large mass of parenchyma or an accumulation of water in the tissues [C16 via New Latin from Greek *oidēma*, from *oidein* to swell] > **oedematous, edematous** (ɪˈdɛmətəs) *or* oeˈdemaˌtose, eˈdemaˌtose *adj*

Oedipus (ˈiːdɪpəs) *n Greek myth* the son of Laius and Jocasta, the king and queen of Thebes, who killed his father, being unaware of his identity, and unwittingly married his mother, by whom he had four children. When the truth was revealed, he put out his eyes and Jocasta killed herself

Oedipus complex *n psychoanal* a group of emotions, usually unconscious, involving the desire of a child, esp a male child, to possess sexually the parent of the opposite sex while excluding the parent of the same sex. Compare **Electra complex**. > 'oedipal *or* ˌoediˈpean *adj*

oedometer (iːˈdɒmɪtə) *n civil engineering* an instrument for measuring the rate and amount of consolidation of a soil specimen under pressure [C20 from Greek *oidēma* (see OEDEMA) + -METER]

OEEC *abbreviation for* Organization for European Economic Cooperation; an organization of European nations set up in 1948 to allocate postwar US aid and to stimulate trade and cooperation. It was superseded by the OECD in 1961

oeil-de-boeuf *French* (œjdəbœf) *n, pl* **oeils-de-boeuf** (œjdəbœf) a circular window, esp in 17th- and 18th-century French architecture [literally: bull's eye]

oeillade (ɜːˈjɑːd; *French* œjad) *n literary* an amorous or suggestive glance; ogle [C16 from French, from *oeil* eye, from Latin *oculus* + *-ade* as in FUSILLADE]

OEM *abbreviation for* original equipment manufacturer: a computer company whose products are made by customizing basic parts supplied by others

oenology *or* **enology** (iːˈnɒlədʒɪ) *n* the study of wine [C19 from Greek *oinos* wine + -LOGY] > **oenological** *or* **enological** (ˌiːnəˈlɒdʒɪkəl) *adj* > oeˈnologist *or* eˈnologist *n*

oenomel (ˈiːnəˌmɛl) *n* **1** a drink made of wine and honey **2** *literary* a source of strength and sweetness [C16 via Latin from Greek *oinos* wine + *meli* honey]

Oenone (iːˈnəʊnɪ) *n Greek myth* a nymph of Mount Ida, whose lover Paris left her for Helen

oenophile (ˈiːnəˌfaɪl) *n* a lover or connoisseur of wines [C20 from Greek *oinos* wine + -PHILE]

oenothera (ˌiːnəˈθɪərə) *n* any plant of the large taxonomically complicated American genus *Oenothera*, typically having yellow flowers that open in the evening: family Onagraceae. See **evening primrose**

o'er (ɔː, əʊə) *prep, adv* a poetic contraction of **over**

oersted (ˈɜːstɛd) *n* the cgs unit of magnetic field strength; the field strength that would cause a unit magnetic pole to experience a force of 1 dyne in a free space. It is equivalent to 79.58 amperes per metre. Symbol: Oe [C20 named after H C Oersted (1777–1851), Danish physicist, who discovered electromagnetism]

oesophagoscope *or US* **esophagoscope** (iːˈsɒfəɡəʊˌskəʊp) *n med* an instrument for examining the oesophagus > **oesophagoscopy** (iːˌsɒfəˈɡɒskəpɪ) *n*

oesophagus *or US* **esophagus** (iːˈsɒfəɡəs) *n, pl* **-gi** (-ˌɡaɪ) the part of the alimentary canal

between the pharynx and the stomach; gullet [C16 via New Latin from Greek *oisophagos*, from *oisein*, future infinitive of *pherein* to carry + *-phagos*, from *phagein* to eat] > **oesophageal** *or US* **esophageal** (iːˌsɒfəˈdʒiːəl) *adj*

oestradiol (ˌiːstrəˈdaɪɒl, ˌɛstrə-) *or US* **estradiol** *n* the most potent oestrogenic hormone secreted by the mammalian ovary: synthesized and used to treat oestrogen deficiency and cancer of the breast. Formula: $C_{18}H_{24}O_2$ [C20 from New Latin, from OESTRIN + DI-[1] + -OL[1]]

oestrin (ˈiːstrɪn, ˈɛstrɪn) *or US* **estrin** *n* an obsolete term for **oestrogen** [C20 from OESTR(US) + -IN]

oestriol (ˈiːstrɪˌɒl, ˈɛstrɪ-) *or US* **estriol** *n* a weak oestrogenic hormone secreted by the mammalian ovary: a synthetic form is used to treat oestrogen deficiency. Formula: $C_{18}H_{24}O_3$ [C20 from OESTRIN + TRI- + -OL[1]]

oestrogen (ˈiːstrədʒən, ˈɛstrə-) *or US* **estrogen** *n* any of several steroid hormones, that are secreted chiefly by the ovaries and placenta, that induce oestrus, stimulate changes in the female reproductive organs during the oestrous cycle, and promote development of female secondary sexual characteristics [C20 from OESTRUS + -GEN] > **oestrogenic** (ˌiːstrəˈdʒɛnɪk, ˌɛstrə-) *or US* **estrogenic** (ˌɛstrəˈdʒɛnɪk, ˌiːstrə-) *adj* > ˌoestroˈgenically *or US* ˌestroˈgenically *adv*

oestrone (ˈiːstrəʊn, ˈɛstrəʊn) *or US* **estrone** *n* a weak oestrogenic hormone secreted by the mammalian ovary and having the same medical uses as oestradiol. Formula: $C_{18}H_{22}O_2$ [C20 from OESTR(US) + -ONE]

oestrous cycle *n* a hormonally controlled cycle of activity of the reproductive organs in many female mammals. The follicular stage (growth of the Graafian follicles, thickening of the lining of the uterus, secretion of oestrogen, and ovulation (see **oestrus**)), is succeeded by the luteal phase (formation of the corpus luteum and secretion of progesterone), followed by regression and a return to the first stage

oestrus (ˈiːstrəs, ˈɛstrəs) *or US* **estrus, estrum** (ˈiːstrəm, ˈɛstrəm) *n* a regularly occurring period of sexual receptivity in most female mammals, except humans, during which ovulation occurs and copulation can take place; heat [C17 from Latin *oestrus* gadfly, hence frenzy, from Greek *oistros*] > 'oestrous, 'oestral *or US* 'estrous, 'estral *adj*

oeuvre *French* (œvrə) *n* **1** a work of art, literature, music, etc **2** the total output of a writer, painter, etc [ultimately from Latin *opera*, plural of *opus* work]

of (ɒv; *unstressed* əv) *prep* **1** used with a verbal noun or gerund to link it with a following noun that is either the subject or the object of the verb embedded in the gerund: *the breathing of a fine swimmer* (subject); *the breathing of clean air* (object) **2** used to indicate possession, origin, or association: *the house of my sister; to die of hunger* **3** used after words or phrases expressing quantities: *a pint of milk* **4** constituted by, containing, or characterized by: *a family of idiots; a rod of iron; a man of some depth* **5** used to indicate separation, as in time or space: *within a mile of the town; within ten minutes of the beginning of the concert* **6** used to mark apposition: *the city of Naples; a speech on the subject of archaeology* **7** about; concerning: *speak to me of love* **8** used in passive constructions to indicate the agent: *he was beloved of all* **9** *informal* used to indicate a day or part of a period of time when some activity habitually occurs: *I go to the pub of an evening* **10** *US* before the hour of: *a quarter of nine* [Old English (as prep and adv); related to Old Norse *af*, Old High German *aba*, Latin *ab*, Greek *apo*]

◼ USAGE See at **off**

OF *abbreviation for* Old French (language)

ofay (ˈəʊfeɪ) *n US slang* a derogatory term for a White person [C20 origin unknown]

Ofcom (ˈɒfkɒm) *n* (in Britain) *acronym for* Office of Communications: a government body regulating the telecommunications industries; a super-regulator merging the Radio Authority, Independent Television Commission, and Oftel

off (ɒf) *prep* **1** used to indicate actions in which contact is absent or rendered absent, as between an object and a surface: *to lift a cup off the table* **2** used to indicate the removal of something that is or has been appended to or in association with something else: *to take the tax off potatoes* **3** out of alignment with: *we are off course* **4** situated near to or leading away from: *just off the High Street* **5** not inclined towards: *I'm off work; I've gone off you* ▷ *adv* **6** (*particle*) so as to be deactivated or disengaged: *turn off the radio* **7** (*particle*) **a** so as to get rid of: *sleep off a hangover* **b** so as to be removed from, esp as a reduction: *he took ten per cent off* **8** spent away from work or other duties: *take the afternoon off* **9 a** on a trip, journey, or race: *I saw her off at the station* **b** (*particle*) so as to be completely absent, used up, or exhausted: *this stuff kills off all vermin* **10** out from the shore or land: *the ship stood off* **11 a** out of contact; at a distance: *the ship was 10 miles off* **b** out of the present location: *the girl ran off* **12** away in the future: *August is less than a week off* **13** (*particle*) so as to be no longer taking place: *the match has been rained off* **14** (*particle*) removed from contact with something, as clothing from the body: *the girl took all her clothes off* **15** offstage: *noises off* **16** *commerce* (used with a preceding number) indicating the number of items required or produced: *please supply 100 off* **17 off and on** *or* **on and off** occasionally; intermittently: *he comes here off and on* **18 off with** (*interjection*) a command, often peremptory, or an exhortation to remove or cut off (something specified): *off with his head; off with that coat, my dear* ▷ *adj* **19** not on; no longer operative: *the off position on the dial* **20** (*postpositive*) not or no longer taking place; cancelled or postponed: *the meeting is off* **21** in a specified condition regarding money, provisions, etc: *well off; how are you off for bread?* **22** unsatisfactory or disappointing: *his performance was rather off; an off year for good tennis* **23** (*postpositive*) in a condition as specified: *I'd be better off without this job* **24** (*postpositive*) no longer on the menu; not being served at the moment: *sorry, love, haddock is off* **25** (*postpositive*) (of food or drink) having gone bad, sour, etc: *this milk is off* ▷ *n* **26** *cricket* **a** the part of the field on that side of the pitch to which the batsman presents his bat when taking strike: thus for a right-hander, off is on the right-hand side. Compare **leg** (sense 13) **b** (*in combination*) a fielding position in this part of the field: *mid-off* **c** (*as modifier*): *the off stump* ▷ *vb* **27** (*tr*) to kill (someone) [originally variant of OF; fully distinguished from it in the 17th century]

> USAGE In standard English, *off* is not followed by *of*: *he stepped off* (not *off of*) *the platform*

OFFA (ˈɒfə) *n acronym for* Orthopaedic Foundation for Animals

off-air *adj, adv* **1** obtained by reception of a radiated broadcasting signal rather than by line feed: *an off-air recording* **2** connected with a radio or television programme but not broadcast: *an off-air phone-in*

offal (ˈɒfᵊl) *n* **1** the edible internal parts of an animal, such as the heart, liver, and tongue **2** dead or decomposing organic matter **3** refuse; rubbish [C14 from OFF + FALL, referring to parts fallen or cut off; compare German *Abfall* rubbish]

Offaly (ˈɒfəlɪ) *n* an inland county of E central Republic of Ireland, in Leinster province: formerly an ancient kingdom, which also included parts of Tipperary, Leix, and Kildare. County town: Tullamore. Pop: 63 663 (2002). Area: 2000 sq km (770 sq miles)

off-balance sheet reserve *n accounting* a sum of money or an asset that should appear on a company's balance but does not; hidden reserve

offbeat (ˈɒfˌbiːt) *n* **1** *music* any of the normally unaccented beats in a bar, such as the second and fourth beats in a bar of four-four time. They are stressed in most rock and some jazz and dance music, such as the bossa nova ▷ *adj* **2 a** unusual, unconventional, or eccentric **b** (*as noun*): *he liked the offbeat in fashion*

off break *n cricket* a bowled ball that spins from off to leg on pitching

off-Broadway *adj* **1** designating the kind of experimental, low-budget, or noncommercial productions associated with theatre outside the Broadway area in New York **2** (of theatres) not located on Broadway ▷ Compare **off-off-Broadway**

off-centre *adj* **1** displaced from a centre point or axis **2** slightly eccentric or unconventional; not completely sound or balanced

off chance *n* **1** a slight possibility **2 on the off chance** with the hope: *on the off chance of getting the job*

off colour *adj* (**off-colour** *when prenominal*) **1** *chiefly Brit* slightly ill; unwell **2** indecent or indelicate; risqué

offcut (ˈɒfˌkʌt) *n* a piece of paper, plywood, fabric, etc, remaining after the main pieces have been cut; remnant

Offenbach (*German* ˈɔfənbax) *n* a city in central Germany, on the River Main in Hesse opposite Frankfurt am Main: leather-goods industry. Pop: 119 208 (2003 est)

offence *or US* **offense** (əˈfɛns) *n* **1** a violation or breach of a law, custom, rule, etc **2 a** any public wrong or crime **b** a nonindictable crime punishable on summary conviction **3** annoyance, displeasure, or resentment **4 give offence** (to) to cause annoyance or displeasure (to) **5 take offence** to feel injured, humiliated, or offended **6** a source of annoyance, displeasure, or anger **7** attack; assault **8** *archaic* injury or harm **9** (ˈɒfɛns) *American football* (usually preceded by *the*) **a** the team that has possession of the ball **b** the members of a team that play in such circumstances > **ofˈfenceless** *or US* **ofˈfenseless** *adj*

offend (əˈfɛnd) *vb* **1** to hurt the feelings, sense of dignity, etc, of (a person) **2** (*tr*) to be disagreeable to; disgust: *the smell offended him* **3** (*intr except in archaic uses*) to break (a law or laws in general) [C14 via Old French *offendre* to strike against, from Latin *offendere*, from *ob-* against + *fendere* to strike] > **ofˈfender** *n* > **ofˈfending** *adj*

offensive (əˈfɛnsɪv) *adj* **1** unpleasant or disgusting, as to the senses **2** causing anger or annoyance; insulting **3** for the purpose of attack rather than defence ▷ *n* **4** (usually preceded by *the*) an attitude or position of aggression **5** an assault, attack, or military initiative, esp a strategic one > **ofˈfensively** *adv* > **ofˈfensiveness** *n*

offer (ˈɒfə) *vb* **1** to present or proffer (something, someone, oneself, etc) for acceptance or rejection **2** (*tr*) to present as part of a requirement: *she offered English as a second subject* **3** (*tr*) to provide or make accessible: *this stream offers the best fishing* **4** (*intr*) to present itself: *if an opportunity should offer* **5** (*tr*) to show or express willingness or the intention (to do something) **6** (*tr*) to put forward (a proposal, opinion, etc) for consideration **7** (*tr*) to present for sale **8** (*tr*) to propose as payment; bid or tender **9** (when *tr*, often foll by *up*) to present (a prayer, sacrifice, etc) as or during an act of worship **10** (*tr*) to show readiness for: *to offer battle* **11** (*intr*) *archaic* to make a proposal of marriage **12** (*tr*; sometimes foll by *up* or *to*) *engineering* to bring (a mechanical piece) near to or in contact with another, and often to proceed to fit the pieces together ▷ *n* **13** something, such as a proposal or bid, that is offered **14** the act of offering or the condition of being offered **15** *contract law* a proposal made by one person that will create a binding contract if accepted unconditionally by the person to whom it is made. See also **acceptance** **16** a proposal of marriage **17** short for **offer price** **18 on offer** for sale at a reduced price [Old English, from Latin *offerre* to present, from *ob-* to + *ferre* to bring] > **ˈofferer** *or* **ˈofferor** *n*

Offer (ˈɒfə) *n* (formerly, in Britain) *acronym for* Office of Electricity Regulation: merged with Ofgas in 1999 to form Ofgem

offer document *n* a document sent by a person or firm making a takeover bid to the shareholders of the target company, giving details of the offer that has been made and, usually, reasons for accepting it

offering (ˈɒfərɪŋ) *n* **1** something that is offered **2** a contribution to the funds of a religious organization **3** a sacrifice, as of an animal, to a deity

offer price *n stock exchange* the price at which a market maker is prepared to sell a specific security. Often shortened to: **offer** Compare **bid price**

offertory (ˈɒfətərɪ) *n, pl* **-tories** **1** the oblation of the bread and wine at the Eucharist **2** the offerings of the worshippers at this service **3** the prayers said or sung while the worshippers' offerings are being received [C14 from Church Latin *offertōrium* place appointed for offerings, from Latin *offerre* to OFFER]

off-glide *n phonetics* a glide caused by the movement of the articulators away from their position in articulating the previous speech sound. Compare **on-glide**

offhand (ˌɒfˈhænd) *adj also* **offhanded**, *adv* **1** without care, thought, or consideration; sometimes, brusque or ungracious: *an offhand manner* **2** without preparation or warning; impromptu > ˌ**offˈhandedly** *adv* > ˌ**offˈhandedness** *n*

office (ˈɒfɪs) *n* **1 a** a room or set of rooms in which business, professional duties, clerical work, etc, are carried out **b** (*as modifier*): *office furniture; an office boy* **2** (*often plural*) the building or buildings in which the work of an organization, such as a business or government department, is carried out **3** a commercial or professional business: *the architect's office approved the plans* **4** the group of persons working in an office: *it was a happy office until she came* **5** (*capital when part of a name*) (in Britain) a department of the national government: *the Home Office* **6** (*capital when part of a name*) (in the US) **a** a governmental agency, esp of the Federal government **b** a subdivision of such an agency or of a department: *Office of Science and Technology* **7 a** a position of trust, responsibility, or duty, esp in a government or organization: *the office of president; to seek office* **b** (*in combination*): *an office-holder* **8** duty or function: *the office of an administrator* **9** (*often plural*) a minor task or service: *domestic offices* **10** (*often plural*) an action performed for another, usually a beneficial action: *through his good offices* **11** a place where tickets, information, etc, can be obtained: *a ticket office* **12** *Christianity* **a** (*often plural*) a ceremony or service, prescribed by ecclesiastical authorities, esp one for the dead **b** the order or form of these **c** *RC Church* the official daily service **d** short for **divine office** **13** (*plural*) the parts of a house or estate where work is done, goods are stored, etc **14** (*usually plural*) *Brit euphemistic* a lavatory (esp in the phrase **usual offices**) **15 in** (*or* **out of**) **office** (of a government) in (or out of) power **16 the office** *slang* a hint or signal [C13 via Old French from Latin *officium* service, duty, from *opus* work, service + *facere* to do]

office bearer *n* a person who holds an office, as in a society, company, club, etc; official

office block *n* a large building designed to provide office accommodation

office boy *n* a former name for **office junior**

office hours *pl n* **1** the hours during which an office is open for business **2** the number of hours worked in an office

office junior *n* a young person, esp a school-leaver, employed in an office for running errands and doing other minor jobs

officer (ˈɒfɪsə) *n* **1** a person in the armed services who holds a position of responsibility, authority, and duty, esp one who holds a commission **2** See **police officer** **3** (on a non-naval ship) any person including the captain and mate, who holds a position of authority and responsibility: *radio* *officer; engineer officer* **4** a person appointed or elected to a position of responsibility or authority in a government, society, etc **5** a government official: *a customs officer* **6** (in the Order of the British Empire) a member of the grade below commander ▷ *vb* (*tr*) **7** to furnish with officers **8** to act as an officer over (some section, group, organization, etc)

officer of arms *n heraldry* a pursuivant or herald

officer of the day *n* a military officer whose duty is to take charge of the security of the unit or camp for a day. Also called: **orderly officer**

officer of the guard *n* a junior officer whose duty is to command a ceremonial guard. Abbreviation: **OG**

official (ə'fɪʃəl) *adj* **1** of or relating to an office, its administration, or its duration **2** sanctioned by, recognized by, or derived from authority: *an official statement* **3** appointed by authority, esp for some special duty **4** having a formal ceremonial character: *an official dinner* ▷ *n* **5** a person who holds a position in an organization, government department, etc, esp a subordinate position

Official (ə'fɪʃəl) *adj* **1** of or relating to one of the two factions of the IRA and Sinn Féin, created by a split in 1969. The Official movement subsequently renounced terrorism and entered constitutional politics in the Irish Republic as the Workers' Party (now the Democratic Left) ▷ *n* **2** a member of the Official IRA and Sinn Féin. ▷ Compare **Provisional**

officialdom (ə'fɪʃəldəm) *n* **1** the outlook or behaviour of officials, esp those rigidly adhering to regulations; bureaucracy **2** officials or bureaucrats collectively

officialese (ə,fɪʃə'li:z) *n* language characteristic of official documents, esp when verbose or pedantic

officially (ə'fɪʃəlɪ) *adv* **1** in a formal or authoritative manner: *the Queen officially opened the dome* **2** in a way that is formally acknowledged but is not necessarily the case: *officially on the dole but actually holding a job*

Official Receiver *n* an officer appointed by the Department of Trade and Industry to receive the income and manage the estate of a bankrupt pending the appointment of a trustee in bankruptcy. See also **receiver** (sense 2)

Official Referee *n law* (in England) a circuit judge attached to the High Court who is empowered to try certain cases, esp where a detailed examination of accounts or other documents is involved

Official Solicitor *n* an officer of the Supreme Court of Judicature with special responsibilities for protecting the interests of persons under disability

official strike *n* a collective stoppage of work by part or all of the workforce of an organization with the approval of the trade union concerned. The stoppage may be accompanied by the payment of strike pay by the trade union concerned

officiant (ə'fɪʃɪənt) *n* a person who presides and officiates at a religious ceremony

officiary (ə'fɪʃɪərɪ) *n, pl* -aries **1** a body of officials ▷ *adj* **2** of, relating to, or derived from office

officiate (ə'fɪʃɪ,eɪt) *vb* (*intr*) **1** to hold the position, responsibility, or function of an official **2** to conduct a religious or other ceremony [c17 from Medieval Latin *officiāre*, from Latin *officium*; see OFFICE] > of,fici'ation *n* > of'fici,ator *n*

officinal (ɒ'fɪsɪnᵊl, ,ɒfɪ'saɪnᵊl) *pharmacol obsolete* ▷ *adj* **1** (of pharmaceutical products) available without prescription **2** (of a plant) having pharmacological properties ▷ *n* **3** an officinal preparation or plant [c17 from Medieval Latin *officīnālis*, from Latin *officīna* workshop; see OFFICE] > of'ficinally *adv*

officious (ə'fɪʃəs) *adj* **1** unnecessarily or obtrusively ready to offer advice or services **2** marked by such readiness **3** *diplomacy* informal or unofficial **4** *obsolete* attentive or obliging [c16 from Latin *officiōsus* kindly, from *officium* service;

see OFFICE] > of'ficiously *adv* > of'ficiousness *n*

offing ('ɒfɪŋ) *n* **1** the part of the sea that can be seen from the shore **2 in the offing** likely to occur soon

offish ('ɒfɪʃ) *adj informal* aloof or distant in manner > 'offishly *adv* > 'offishness *n*

off key *adj* (**off-key** *when prenominal*) *adv* **1** *music* **a** not in the correct key **b** out of tune **2** out of keeping; discordant

off label *adj* (**off-label** *when prenominal*) *adv* (of a prescription drug) relating to use, or being used, in ways for which it has not been approved

off-licence *n Brit* **1** a shop, or a counter in a pub or hotel, where alcoholic drinks are sold for consumption elsewhere. US equivalents: **package store**, **liquor store 2** a licence permitting such sales

off limits *adj* (**off-limits** *when prenominal*) **1** not to be entered; out of bounds ▷ *adv* **2** in or into an area forbidden by regulations

off line *adj* (**off-line** *when prenominal*) **1** of, relating to, or concerned with a part of a computer system not connected to the central processing unit but controlled by a computer storage device. Compare **on line 2** disconnected from a computer; switched off **3** extra to or not involving a continuous sequence of operations, such as a production line **4** *radio, television* (of processes, such as editing) not carried out on the actual transmission medium

off-load *vb* (*tr*) to get rid of (something unpleasant or burdensome), as by delegation to another

off message *adj* (**off-message** *when prenominal*) not adhering to or reflecting the official line of a political party, government, or other organization

off-off-Broadway *adj* of or relating to highly experimental informal small-scale theatrical productions in New York, usually taking place in cafés, small halls, etc. Compare **off-Broadway**

off-peak *adj* of or relating to services as used outside periods of intensive use or electricity supplied at cheaper rates during the night

off-piste *adj* of or relating to skiing on virgin snow off the regular runs

off plan *adj* (**off-plan** *when prenominal*) (of a new building) considered with reference to its plans, before it has been built

offprint ('ɒf,prɪnt) *n* **1** Also called (US): **separate** a separate reprint of an article that originally appeared in a larger publication ▷ *vb* **2** (*tr*) to reprint (an article taken from a larger publication) separately

off-putting *adj Brit informal* disconcerting or disturbing

off-ramp *n* a short steep one-way road by which traffic can leave a motorway or highway

off-road *adj* (of a motor vehicle) designed or built for use away from public roads, esp on rough terrain

off-roader *n* **1** a motor vehicle designed for use away from public roads, esp on rough terrain **2** an owner or driver of an off-road vehicle

off-roading *n* the sport or activity of driving vehicles over rough terrain

off-sales *pl n Brit* sales of alcoholic drink for consumption off the premises by a pub or an off-licence attached to a pub

offscourings ('ɒf,skaʊərɪŋz) *pl n* scum; dregs

off season *adj* (**off-season** *when prenominal*) **1** denoting or occurring during a period of little activity in a trade or business ▷ *n* **2** such a period ▷ *adv* **3** in an off-season period

offset *n* ('ɒf,sɛt) **1** something that counterbalances or compensates for something else **2** an allowance made to counteract some effect **3 a** a printing method in which the impression is made onto an intermediate surface, such as a rubber blanket, which transfers it to the paper **b** (*modifier*) relating to, involving, or printed by offset: *offset letterpress; offset lithography* **4** another name for **set-off 5** *botany* **a** a short

runner in certain plants, such as the houseleek, that produces roots and shoots at the tip **b** a plant produced from such a runner **6** a ridge projecting from a range of hills or mountains **7** the horizontal component of displacement on a fault **8** a narrow horizontal or sloping surface formed where a wall is reduced in thickness towards the top **9** a person or group descended collaterally from a particular group or family; offshoot **10** *surveying* a measurement of distance to a point at right angles to a survey line ▷ *vb* (,ɒf'sɛt) -sets, -setting, -set **11** (*tr*) to counterbalance or compensate for **12** (*tr*) to print (pictures, text, etc) using the offset process **13** (*tr*) to construct an offset in (a wall) **14** (*intr*) to project or develop as an offset

offshoot ('ɒf,ʃu:t) *n* **1** a shoot or branch growing from the main stem of a plant **2** something that develops or derives from a principal source or origin

offshore (,ɒf'ʃɔ:) *adj, adv* **1** from, away from, or at some distance from the shore **2** NZ overseas; abroad ▷ *adj* **3** sited or conducted at sea as opposed to on land: *offshore industries* **4** based or operating abroad in places where the tax system is more advantageous than that of the home country: *offshore banking; offshore fund*

offshoring ('ɒf,ʃɔ:rɪŋ) *n* the practice of moving a company's operating base to a foreign country where labour costs are cheaper

offside ('ɒf'saɪd) *adj, adv* **1** *sport* (in football, hockey, etc) in a position illegally ahead of the ball or puck when it is played, usually when within one's opponents' half or the attacking zone ▷ *n* **2** (usually preceded by *the*) *chiefly Brit* **a** the side of a vehicle nearest the centre of the road (in Britain, the right side) **b** (*as modifier*): *the offside passenger door* ▷ Compare **nearside**

offsider (,ɒf'saɪdə) *n Austral and NZ* a partner or assistant

off-site *adj, adv* away from the principle area of activity

offspring ('ɒf,sprɪŋ) *n* **1** the immediate descendant or descendants of a person, animal, etc; progeny **2** a product, outcome, or result

offstage ('ɒf'steɪdʒ) *adj, adv* out of the view of the audience; off the stage

off-street *adj* located away from a street: *off-street parking*

off the record *adj* (**off-the-record** *when prenominal*) **1** not intended for publication or disclosure; confidential ▷ *adv* **2** with such an intention; unofficially

off the shelf *adv* **1** from stock and readily available: *you can have this model off the shelf* ▷ *adj* (**off-the-shelf** *when prenominal*) **2** of or relating to a product that is readily available: *an off-the-shelf model* **3** of or denoting a company that has been registered with the Registrar of Companies for the sole purpose of being sold

off-the-wall *adj* (**off the wall** *when postpositive*) *slang* new or unexpected in an unconventional or eccentric way: *an off-the-wall approach to humour* [c20 possibly from the use of the phrase in handball and squash to describe a shot that is unexpected]

off-white *n* **1** a colour, such as cream or bone, consisting of white mixed with a tinge of grey or with a pale hue ▷ *adj* **2** of such a colour: *an off-white coat*

off-year election *n* (in the US) an election held in a year when a presidential election does not take place

Ofgas ('ɒf,gæs) *n* (formerly, in Britain) *acronym for* Office of Gas Supply: merged with Offer in 1999 to form Ofgem

Ofgem ('ɒf,dʒɛm) *n* (in Britain) *acronym for* Office of Gas and Electricity Markets: a government body formed in 1999 by the merger of the separate regulatory bodies for gas and electricity; its functions are to promote competition and protect consumers' interests

oflag ('ɒf,lɑ:g) *n* a German prisoner-of-war camp

for officers in World War II [German, short for *Offizierslager* officers' camp]

Oflot (ˈɒf‚lɒt) *n* (in Britain, formerly) *acronym for* Office of the National Lottery, now superseded by the National Lottery Commission

OFM *abbreviation for* Ordo Fratrum Minorum (the Franciscans) [Latin: Order of Minor Friars]

OFris *abbreviation for* Old Frisian

OFS *abbreviation for* (Orange) Free State

Ofsted (ˈɒf‚stɛd) *n* (in Britain) *acronym for* Office for Standards in Education: a government body set up in 1993 to inspect and assess the educational standards of schools and colleges in England and Wales

oft (ɒft) *adv* short for **often** (archaic or poetic except in combinations such as **oft-repeated** and **oft-recurring**) [Old English *oft*; related to Old High German *ofto*]

OFT (in Britain) *abbreviation for* Office of Fair Trading

Oftel (ˈɒf‚tɛl) *n* (in Britain) *acronym for* Office of Telecommunications: a government body set up in 1984 to supervise telecommunications activities in the UK, and to protect the interests of the consumers

often (ˈɒfⁿn, ˈɒftⁿn) *adv* **1** frequently or repeatedly; much of the time. Archaic equivalents: oftentimes, ofttimes **2** as often as not quite frequently **3** every so often at intervals **4** more often than not in more than half the instances ▷ *adj* **5** *archaic* repeated; frequent [c14 variant of OFT before vowels and h]

Ofwat (ˈɒf‚wɒt) *n* (in Britain) *acronym for* Office of Water Services: a government body set up in 1989 to regulate the activities of the water companies in England and Wales, and to protect the interests of their consumers

OG *abbreviation for* **1** officer of the guard **2** Also: o.g *philately* original gum

o.g. *abbreviation for* own goal

Ogaden (‚ɒgəˈdɛn) *n* the a region of SE Ethiopia, bordering on Somalia: consists of a desert plateau, inhabited by Somali nomads; a secessionist movement, supported by Somalia, has existed within the region since the early 1960s and led to bitter fighting between Ethiopia and Somalia (1977–78)

Ogasawara Gunto (‚ɒgəsəˈwɑːrə ˈgʌntəʊ) *n* transliteration of the Japanese name for the **Bonin Islands**

Ogbomosho (‚ɒgbəˈməʊʃəʊ) *n* a city in SW Nigeria: the third largest town in Nigeria; trading centre for an agricultural region. Pop: 959 000 (2005 est)

ogdoad (ˈɒgdəʊ‚æd) *n* a group of eight [c17 via Late Latin from Greek *ogdoos* eighth, from *oktō* eight]

ogee (ˈəʊdʒiː) *n architect* **1** Also called: **talon** a moulding having a cross section in the form of a letter S **2** short for **ogee arch** [c15 probably variant of OGIVE]

ogee arch *n architect* a pointed arch having an S-shaped curve on both sides. Sometimes shortened to: ogee Also called: **keel arch**

Ogen melon (ˈəʊgɛn) *n* a variety of small melon having a green skin and sweet pale green flesh [c20 named after a kibbutz in Israel where it was first developed]

ogham or **ogam** (ˈɒgəm, ˈɔːm) *n* an ancient alphabetical writing system used by the Celts in Britain and Ireland, consisting of straight lines drawn or carved perpendicular to or at an angle to another long straight line [c17 from Old Irish *ogom*, of uncertain origin but associated with the name *Ogma*, legendary inventor of this alphabet]

ogive (ˈəʊdʒaɪv, əʊˈdʒaɪv) *n* **1** a diagonal rib or groin of a Gothic vault **2** another name for **lancet arch 3** *statistics* a graph the ordinates of which represent cumulative frequencies of the values indicated by the corresponding abscissas **4** the conical head of a missile or rocket that protects the payload during its passage through the

atmosphere [c17 from Old French, of uncertain origin] > o'gival *adj*

ogle (ˈəʊg³l) *vb* **1** to look at (someone) amorously or lustfully **2** (*tr*) to stare or gape at ▷ *n* **3** a flirtatious or lewd look [c17 probably from Low German *oegeln*, from *oegen* to look at] > 'ogler *n*

Ogooué or **Ogowe** (ɒˈgəʊweɪ) *n* a river in W central Africa, rising in SW Congo-Brazzaville and flowing generally northwest and north through Gabon to the Atlantic. Length: about 970 km (683 miles)

Ogopogo (‚əʊgəʊˈpəʊgəʊ) *n* an aquatic monster said to live in Okanagan Lake in British Columbia, Canada [apparently an arbitrary coinage]

Ogpu (ˈɒgpuː) *n* the Soviet police and secret police from 1923 to 1934 [c20 from Russian O(byedinyonnoye) g(osudarstvennoye) p(oliticheskoye) u(pravleniye) United State Political Administration]

O grade *n* (formerly, in Scotland) **1 a** the basic level of the Scottish Certificate of Education, now replaced by **Standard Grade b** (*as modifier*): *O grade history* **2** a pass in a particular subject at O grade: *she has ten O grades* ▷ Formal name: **Ordinary grade**

ogre (ˈəʊgə) *n* **1** (in folklore) a giant, usually given to eating human flesh **2** any monstrous or cruel person [c18 from French, perhaps from Latin *Orcus* god of the infernal regions] > 'ogreish *adj* > 'ogress *fem n*

Ogun (əʊˈgʊn) *n* a state of SW Nigeria, formed in 1976 from part of Western State. Capital: Abeokuta. Pop: 2 614 747 (1995 est). Area: 16 762 sq km (6472 sq miles)

Ogygian (əʊˈdʒɪdʒɪən) *adj* of very great age; prehistoric [c19 from Greek *ōgugios* relating to *Ogyges*, the most ancient king of Greece, mythical ruler of Boeotia or Attica]

oh (əʊ) *interj* **1** an exclamation expressive of surprise, pain, pleasure, etc ▷ *sentence connector* **2** an expression used to preface a remark, gain time, etc: *oh, I suppose so*

OH *abbreviation for* Ohio

OHAC *abbreviation for* own house and car: used in lonely hearts columns and personal advertisements

OHG *abbreviation for* Old High German

Ohio (əʊˈhaɪəʊ) *n* **1** a state of the central US, in the Midwest on Lake Erie: consists of prairies in the W and the Allegheny plateau in the E, the Ohio River forming the S and most of the E borders. Capital: Columbus. Pop: 11 435 798 (2003 est). Area: 107 044 sq km (41 330 sq miles). Abbreviation and zip code: OH **2** a river in the eastern US, formed by the confluence of the Allegheny and Monongahela Rivers at Pittsburgh: flows generally W and SW to join the Mississippi at Cairo, Illinois, as its chief E tributary. Length: 1570 km (975 miles)

ohm (əʊm) *n* the derived SI unit of electrical resistance; the resistance between two points on a conductor when a constant potential difference of 1 volt between them produces a current of 1 ampere. Symbol: Ω [c19 named after Georg Simon *Ohm* (1787–1854), German physicist]

ohmage (ˈəʊmɪdʒ) *n* electrical resistance in ohms

ohmic (ˈəʊmɪk) *adj* of or relating to a circuit element, the electrical resistance of which obeys Ohm's law

ohmmeter (ˈəʊm‚miːtə) *n* an instrument for measuring electrical resistance

OHMS (in Britain and the dominions of the Commonwealth) *abbreviation for* On Her (*or* His) Majesty's Service

Ohm's law (əʊmz) *n* the principle that the electric current passing through a conductor is directly proportional to the potential difference across it, provided that the temperature remains constant. The constant of proportionality is the resistance of the conductor [c19 named after Georg Simon *Ohm* (1787–1854), German physicist]

oho (əʊˈhəʊ) *interj* an exclamation expressing surprise, exultation, or derision

ohv *abbreviation for* overhead valve

oi¹ (ɔɪ) *interj* **1** *Brit* a cry used to attract attention, esp in an aggressive way ▷ *adj* **2** of or relating to a form of punk rock popular esp among skinheads in the late 1970s and 1980s

oi² (ˈɒɪ) *n, pl* oi NZ another name for **grey-faced petrel** [Māori]

OIC *text messaging abbreviation for* oh I see

-oid *suffix forming adjectives and associated nouns* indicating likeness, resemblance, or similarity: *anthropoid* [from Greek *-oeidēs* resembling, form of, from *eidos* form]

-oidea *suffix forming plural proper nouns* forming the names of zoological classes or superfamilies: *Crinoidea; Canoidea* [from New Latin, from Latin *-ōidēs -OID*]

oidium (əʊˈɪdɪəm) *n, pl* -ia (-ɪə) *botany* any of various fungal spores produced in the form of a chain by the development of septa in a hypha [New Latin: from oo- + -idium diminutive suffix]

oik (ɔɪk) *n Brit derogatory, slang* a person regarded as inferior because ignorant, ill-educated, or lower-class

oil (ɔɪl) *n* **1** any of a number of viscous liquids with a smooth sticky feel. They are usually flammable, insoluble in water, soluble in organic solvents, and are obtained from plants and animals, from mineral deposits, and by synthesis. They are used as lubricants, fuels, perfumes, foodstuffs, and raw materials for chemicals. See also **essential oil, fixed oil 2** another name for **petroleum** (*as modifier*): *an oil engine; an oil rig* **3 a** Also called: **lubricating oil** any of a number of substances usually derived from petroleum and used for lubrication **b** (*in combination*): *an oilcan; an oilstone* **c** (*as modifier*): *an oil pump* **4** Also called: **fuel oil** a petroleum product used as a fuel in domestic heating, industrial furnaces, marine engines, etc **5** *Brit* **a** paraffin, esp when used as a domestic fuel **b** (*as modifier*): *an oil lamp; an oil stove* **6** any substance of a consistency resembling that of oil: *oil of vitriol* **7** the solvent, usually linseed oil, with which pigments are mixed to make artists' paints **8 a** (*often plural*) oil colour or paint **b** (*as modifier*): *an oil painting* **9** an oil painting **10** the good (dinkum) oil *Austral and NZ slang* facts or news **11** strike oil **a** to discover petroleum while drilling for it **b** *informal* to become very rich or successful ▷ *vb* (*tr*) **12** to lubricate, smear, polish, etc, with oil or an oily substance **13** *informal* to bribe (esp in the phrase oil someone's palm) **14** oil the wheels to make things run smoothly **15** See well-oiled [c12 from Old French *oile*, from Latin *oleum* (olive) oil, from *olea* olive tree, from Greek *elaia* OLIVE] > 'oil-‚like *adj*

oil beetle *n* any of various beetles of the family *Meloidae* that exude an oily evil-smelling blood from their joints, which deters enemies

oilbird (ˈɔɪl‚bɜːd) *n* a nocturnal gregarious cave-dwelling bird, *Steatornis caripensis*, of N South America and Trinidad, having a hooked bill and dark plumage: family *Steatornithidae*, order *Caprimulgiformes*. Also called: **guacharo**

oil cake *n* stock feed consisting of compressed cubes made from the residue of the crushed seeds of oil-bearing crops such as linseed

oilcan (ˈɔɪl‚kæn) *n* a container with a long nozzle for applying lubricating oil to machinery

oilcloth (ˈɔɪl‚klɒθ) *n* **1** waterproof material made by treating one side of a cotton fabric with a drying oil, or a synthetic resin **2** another name for **linoleum**

oil-cooled *adj engineering* (of an engine, apparatus, etc) having its heat removed by the circulation of oil > oil cooler *n*

oilcup (ˈɔɪl‚kʌp) *n* a cup-shaped oil reservoir in a machine providing continuous lubrication for a bearing

oil drum *n* a metal drum used to contain or transport oil

oiled silk (ɔɪld) *n* silk treated with oil to make it waterproof

O

oiler ('ɔɪlə) n **1** a person, device, etc, that lubricates or supplies oil **2** an oil tanker **3** an oil well

oilfield ('ɔɪl,fiːld) n an area containing reserves of petroleum, esp one that is already being exploited

oilfired ('ɔɪl,faɪəd) adj (of central heating) using oil as fuel

oilgas ('ɔɪl,gæs) n a gaseous mixture of hydrocarbons used as a fuel, obtained by the destructive distillation of mineral oils

oil hardening n a process of hardening high-carbon or alloy steels by heating and cooling in oil. Compare **air hardening**

oilman ('ɔɪlmən) n, pl -men **1** a person who owns or operates oil wells **2** a person who makes or sells oil

oil of turpentine n another name for **turpentine** (sense 3)

oil of vitriol n another name for **sulphuric acid**

oil paint or **colour** n paint made of pigment ground in oil, usually linseed oil, used for oil painting

oil painting n **1** a picture painted with oil paints **2** the art or process of painting with oil paints **3** he's or she's no oil painting informal he or she is not good-looking

oil palm n a tropical African palm tree, Elaeis guineensis, the fruits of which yield palm oil

oil rig n See **rig** (sense 6)

Oil Rivers pl n the delta of the Niger River in S Nigeria

oil sand n a sandstone impregnated with hydrocarbons, esp such deposits in Alberta, Canada

oil-seed rape n another name for **rape²**

oil shale n a fine-grained shale containing oil, which can be extracted by heating

oilskin ('ɔɪl,skɪn) n **1 a** a cotton fabric treated with oil and pigment to make it waterproof **b** (as modifier): an oilskin hat **2** (often plural) a protective outer garment of this fabric

oil slick n a mass of floating oil covering an area of water, esp oil that has leaked or been discharged from a ship

oilstone ('ɔɪl,stəʊn) n a stone with a fine grain lubricated with oil and used for sharpening cutting tools. See also **whetstone**

oil varnish n another name for **varnish** (sense 1)

oil well n a boring into the earth or sea bed for the extraction of petroleum

oily ('ɔɪlɪ) adj oilier, oiliest **1** soaked in or smeared with oil or grease **2** consisting of, containing, or resembling oil **3** flatteringly servile or obsequious ▷ 'oilily adv ▷ 'oiliness n

oink (ɔɪŋk) interj an imitation or representation of the grunt of a pig

ointment ('ɔɪntmənt) n **1** a fatty or oily medicated formulation applied to the skin to heal or protect **2** a similar substance used as a cosmetic [c14 from Old French oignement, from Latin unguentum UNGUENT]

Oireachtas ('ɛrəkθəs; Gaelic 'ɛrəxtəs) n the parliament of the Republic of Ireland, consisting of the president, the Dáil Éireann, and the Seanad Éireann. See also **Dáil Éireann, Seanad Éireann** [Irish: assembly, from Old Irish airech nobleman]

Oise (French waz) n **1** a department of N France, in Picardy region. Capital: Beauvais. Pop: 776 999 (2003 est). Area: 5887 sq km (2296 sq miles) **2** a river in N France, rising in Belgium, in the Ardennes, and flowing southwest to join the Seine at Conflans. Length: 302 km (188 miles)

Oita ('ɔɪtə) n an industrial city in SW Japan, on NE Kyushu: dominated most of Kyushu in the 16th century. Pop: 437 699 (2002 est)

OJ abbreviation for Order of Jamaica

Ojibwa (əʊ'dʒɪbwə) n **1** (pl -was or -wa) a member of a North American Indian people living in a region west of Lake Superior **2** the language of this people, belonging to the Algonquian family ▷ Also called: **Chippewa**

OK abbreviation for Oklahoma

O.K. (,əʊ'keɪ) informal ▷ sentence substitute **1** an expression of approval, agreement, etc ▷ adj (usually postpositive) ▷ adv **2** in good or satisfactory condition **3** permissable: is it O.K. if I go home now? **4** acceptable but not outstanding: the party was O.K. ▷ vb O.K.s, O.K.ing (,əʊ'keɪɪŋ), O.K.ed (,əʊ'keɪd) **5** (tr) to approve or endorse ▷ n, pl O.K.s **6** approval or agreement ▷ Also: OK, o.k., okay [c19 perhaps from o(ll) k(orrect), jocular alteration of all correct]

oka ('əʊkə) or **oke** (əʊk) n **1** a unit of weight used in Turkey, equal to about 2.75 pounds or 1.24 kilograms **2** a unit of liquid measure used in Turkey, equal to about 1.3 pints or 0.75 litres [c17 from Turkish ōqah, from Arabic ūqiyah, probably from Greek ounkia; perhaps related to Latin uncia one twelfth; see OUNCE¹]

Oka ('əʊkə) n a brine-cured Canadian cheese [named after Oka, Quebec, where it is made at a monastery]

Okanagan (,əʊkə'nɑːgən) n **1** Also (US): Okanogan a river in North America that flows south from Okanagan Lake in Canada into the Columbia River in NE Washington, US Length: about 483 km (300 miles) **2** Also: Okanogan, Okinagan a member of a North American Indian people living in the Okanagan River valley in British Columbia and Washington **3** Also: Okanogan, Okinagan the language of this people, belonging to the Salish family

Okanagan Lake n a lake in SW Canada, in S British Columbia: drained by the Okanagan River into the Columbia River. Length: about 111 km (69 miles). Width: from 3.2–6.4 km (2–4 miles)

okapi (əʊ'kɑːpɪ) n, pl -pis or -pi a ruminant mammal, Okapia johnstoni, of the forests of central Africa, having a reddish-brown coat with horizontal white stripes on the legs and small horns: family Giraffidae [c20 from a Central African word]

Okavango or **Okovango** (,əʊkə'vɑːŋɡəʊ) n a river in SW central Africa, rising in central Angola and flowing southeast, then east as part of the border between Angola and Namibia, then southeast across the Caprivi Strip into Botswana to form a great marsh known as the **Okavango Basin, Delta or Swamp**. Length: about 1600 km (1000 miles)

okay (,əʊ'keɪ) sentence substitute, adj, vb, n a variant of **O.K.**

Okayama (,ɒkə'jɑːmə) n a city in SW Japan, on W Honshu on the Inland Sea. Pop: 621 809 (2002 est)

oke¹ (əʊk) n another name for **oka**

oke² (əʊk) adj, adv informal another term for **O.K.**

oke³ (əʊk) n South African an informal word for **man** [from Afrikaans]

Okeechobee (,əʊkɪ'tʃəʊbɪ) n **Lake** a lake in S Florida, in the Everglades: second largest freshwater lake wholly within the US Area: 1813 sq km (700 sq miles)

Okefenokee Swamp (,əʊkɪfɪ'nəʊkɪ) n a swamp in the US, in SE Georgia and N Florida: protected flora and fauna. Area: 1554 sq km (600 sq miles)

okey-doke ('əʊkɪ'dəʊk) or **okey-dokey** ('əʊkɪ'dəʊkɪ) sentence substitute, adj, adv informal another term for **O.K.**

Okhotsk ('əʊkɒtsk; Russian a'ɔxtsk) n **Sea of** part of the NW Pacific, surrounded by the Kamchatka Peninsula, the Kurile Islands, Sakhalin Island, and the E coast of Siberia. Area: 1 589 840 sq km (613 838 sq miles)

Okie ('əʊkɪ) n US slang, sometimes considered offensive **1** an inhabitant of Oklahoma **2** an impoverished migrant farm worker, esp one who left Oklahoma during the Depression of the 1930s to work elsewhere in the US

Okinawa (,əʊkɪ'nɑːwə) n a coral island of SW Japan, the largest of the Ryukyu Islands in the N Pacific: scene of heavy fighting in World War II; administered by the US (1945–72); agricultural. Chief town: Naha City. Pop: 1 273 508 (1995). Area: 1176 sq km (454 sq miles)

Okla. abbreviation for Oklahoma

Oklahoma (,əʊklə'həʊmə) n a state in the S central US: consists of plains in the west, rising to mountains in the southwest and east; important for oil. Capital: Oklahoma City. Pop: 3 511 532 (2003 est). Area: 181 185 sq km (69 956 sq miles). Abbreviations: Okla., (with zip code) OK

Oklahoma City n a city in central Oklahoma: the state capital and a major agricultural and industrial centre. Pop: 523 303 (2003 est)

Oklahoman (,əʊklə'həʊmən) n **1** a native or inhabitant of Oklahoma ▷ adj **2** of or relating to Oklahoma or its inhabitants

Okovango (,əʊkə'vɑːŋɡəʊ) n a variant spelling of **Okovango**

okra ('əʊkrə) n **1** Also called: ladies' fingers an annual malvaceous plant, Hibiscus esculentus, of the Old World tropics, with yellow-and-red flowers and edible oblong sticky green pods **2** the pod of this plant, eaten in soups, stews, etc. See also **gumbo** (sense 1) [c18 of W African origin]

okta or **octa** ('ɒktə) n a unit used in meteorology to measure cloud cover, equivalent to a cloud cover of one eighth of the sky [c20 from Greek okta-, oktō eight]

-ol¹ suffix forming nouns denoting an organic chemical compound containing a hydroxyl group, esp alcohols and phenols: ethanol; quinol [from ALCOHOL]

-ol² n combining form (not used systematically) a variant of **-ole¹**

Öland (Swedish 'øːland) n an island in the Baltic Sea, separated from the mainland of SE Sweden by Kalmar Sound: the second largest Swedish island. Chief town: Borgholm. Pop: 24 628 (2004 est). Area: 1347 sq km (520 sq miles)

old (əʊld) adj **1** having lived or existed for a relatively long time: an old man; an old tradition; old wine; an old house; an old country **2 a** of or relating to advanced years or a long life: old age **b** (as collective noun; preceded by the): the old **c** old and young people of all ages **3** decrepit or senile **4** worn with age or use: old clothes; an old car **5 a** (postpositive) having lived or existed for a specified period: a child who is six years old **b** (in combination): a six-year-old child **c** (as noun in combination): a six-year-old **6** (capital when part of a name or title) earlier or earliest of two or more things with the same name: the old edition; the Old Testament; old Norwich **7** (capital when part of a name) designating the form of a language in which the earliest known records are written: Old English **8** (prenominal) familiar through long acquaintance or repetition: an old friend; an old excuse **9** practised; hardened: old in cunning **10** (prenominal; often preceded by good) cherished; dear: used as a term of affection or familiarity: good old George **11** informal (with any of several nouns) used as a familiar form of address to a person: old thing; old bean; old stick; old fellow **12** skilled through long experience (esp in the phrase **an old hand**) **13** out-of-date; unfashionable **14** remote or distant in origin or time of origin: an old culture **15** (prenominal) former; previous: my old house was small **16 a** (prenominal) established for a relatively long time: an old member **b** (in combination): old-established **17** sensible, wise, or mature: old beyond one's years **18** (of a river, valley, or land surface) in the final stage of the cycle of erosion, characterized by flat extensive flood plains and minimum relief. See also **youthful** (sense 4), **mature** (sense 6) **19** (intensifier) (esp in phrases such as **a good old time, any old thing, any old how**, etc) **20** (of crops) harvested late **21** good old days an earlier period of time regarded as better than the present **22** little old informal indicating affection, esp humorous affection: my little old wife **23** the old one (or gentleman) informal a jocular name for **Satan** ▷ n **24** an earlier or past time (esp in the phrase **of old**): in days of old [Old English eald; related to Old Saxon ald, Old High German, German alt, Latin altus high] ▷ 'oldish adj ▷ 'oldness n

old age pension n a former name for the state

retirement pension. ▷ **old age pensioner** *n*

Old Bailey *n* the chief court exercising criminal jurisdiction in London; the Central Criminal Court of England

Old Bill *n* *Brit slang* **1** a policeman **2** (*functioning as plural*; *preceded by the*) policemen collectively or in general [C20 of uncertain origin: perhaps derived from the World War I cartoon of a soldier with a drooping moustache]

old bird *n* *jocular* a wary and astute person

old boy *n* **1** (*sometimes capitals*) *Brit* a male ex-pupil of a school **2** *informal, chiefly Brit* **a** a familiar name used to refer to a man **b** an old man

old boy network *n* *Brit informal* the appointment to power of former pupils of the same small group of public schools or universities

Old Bulgarian *n* another name for **Old Church Slavonic**

Old Castile *n* a region of N Spain, on the Bay of Biscay: formerly a province. Spanish name: Castilla la Vieja

Old Catholic *adj* **1** of or relating to several small national Churches which have broken away from the Roman Catholic Church on matters of doctrine ▷ *n* **2** a member of one of these Churches

old chum *n* *Austral informal* (*formerly*) **1** a person who is experienced, esp in life in colonial Australia **2** an experienced convict

Old Church Slavonic *or* **Slavic** *n* the oldest recorded Slavonic language: the form of Old Slavonic into which the Bible was translated in the ninth century, preserved as a liturgical language of various Orthodox Churches: belonging to the South Slavonic subbranch of languages

old clothes man *n* a person who deals in second-hand clothes

Old Contemptibles *pl n* the British expeditionary force to France in 1914 [so named from the Kaiser's alleged reference to them as a "contemptible little army"]

old country *n* the country of origin of an immigrant or an immigrant's ancestors

Old Dart *n* the *Austral slang* England [C19 of unknown origin]

Old Delhi *n* See **Delhi**

Old Dutch *n* the Dutch language up to about 1100, derived from the Low Franconian dialect of Old Low German. See also **Franconian** Abbreviation: **OD**

olden (ˈəʊldᵊn) *adj* an archaic or poetic word for **old** (often in phrases such as **in olden days** and **in olden times**)

Oldenburg (ˈəʊldᵊnˌbɜːɡ; *German* ˈɔldənburk) *n* **1** a city in NW Germany, in Lower Saxony: former capital of Oldenburg state. Pop: 158 340 (2003 est) **2** a former state of NW Germany: became part of Lower Saxony in 1946

Old English *n* **1** Also called: **Anglo-Saxon** the English language from the time of the earliest settlements in the fifth century AD to about 1100. The main dialects were West Saxon (the chief literary form), Kentish, and Anglian. Compare **Middle English, Modern English** Abbreviation: **OE 2** *printing* a Gothic typeface commonly used in England up until the 18th century

Old English sheepdog *n* a breed of large bobtailed sheepdog with a profuse shaggy coat

older (ˈəʊldə) *adj* **1** the comparative of **old 2** Also (of people, esp members of the same family): **elder** having lived or existed longer; of greater age

old-established *adj* established for a long time

olde-worlde (ˈəʊldɪˈwɜːldɪ) *adj* sometimes facetious old-world or quaint

old face *n* *printing* a type style that originated in the 18th century, characterized by little contrast between thick and thin strokes. Compare **modern** (sense 5)

oldfangled (ˈəʊldˈfæŋɡᵊld) *adj* derogatory out-of-date; old-fashioned [C20 formed on analogy with NEWFANGLED]

old-fashioned *adj* **1** belonging to, characteristic of, or favoured by former times; outdated: *old-fashioned ideas* **2** favouring or adopting the dress, manners, fashions, etc, of a former time **3** quizzically doubtful or disapproving: *she did not reply, but gave him an old-fashioned look* **4** *Scot and northern English dialect* old for one's age: *an old-fashioned child* ▷ *n* **5** a cocktail containing spirit, bitters, fruit, etc ▷ ˌold-ˈfashionedly *adv*

Old French *n* the French language in its earliest forms, from about the 9th century up to about 1400. Abbreviation: **OF**

Old Frisian *n* the Frisian language up to about 1400. Abbreviation: **OFris**

old girl *n* **1** (*sometimes capitals*) *Brit* a female ex-pupil of a school **2** *informal, chiefly Brit* **a** a familiar name used to refer to a woman **b** an old woman

Old Glory *n* a nickname for the flag of the United States of America

old gold *n* **a** a dark yellow colour, sometimes with a brownish tinge **b** (*as adjective*): *an old-gold carpet*

old guard *n* **1** a group that works for a long-established or old-fashioned cause or principle **2** the conservative element in a political party or other group [C19 from OLD GUARD]

Old Guard *n* the French imperial guard created by Napoleon in 1804

Oldham (ˈəʊldəm) *n* **1** a town in NW England, in Oldham unitary authority, Greater Manchester. Pop: 103 544 (2001) **2** a unitary authority in NW England, in Greater Manchester. Pop: 218 100 (2003 est). Area: 141 sq km (54 sq miles)

old hand *n* **1** a person who is skilled at something through long experience **2** *Austral informal* (*in the 19th century*) an ex-convict **3** *Austral informal* a person who is long established in a place

Old Harry *n* *informal* a jocular name for **Satan**

old hat *adj* (*postpositive*) old-fashioned or trite

Old High German *n* a group of West Germanic dialects that eventually developed into modern German; High German up to about 1200: spoken in the Middle Ages on the upper Rhine, in Bavaria, Alsace, and elsewhere, including Alemannic, Bavarian, Langobardic, and Upper Franconian. Abbreviation: **OHG**

Old Icelandic *n* the dialect of Old Norse spoken and written in Iceland; the Icelandic language up to about 1600

old identity *n* *NZ* a person known for a long time in the one locality

oldie (ˈəʊldɪ) *n* **1** *informal* an old person or thing **2** *Austral informal* a parent: *children and their oldies*

Old Irish *n* the Celtic language of Ireland up to about 900 AD, introduced to Scotland by Irish settlers about 500 AD

Old Kingdom *n* a period of Egyptian history: usually considered to extend from the third to the sixth dynasty (?2700–?2150 BC)

old lady *n* **1** an informal term for **mother**[1] *or* **wife** (sense 1) **2** a large noctuid moth, *Mormo maura*, that has drab patterned wings originally thought to resemble an elderly Victorian lady's shawl

Old Latin *n* the Latin language before the classical period, up to about 100 BC

old-line *adj* **1** *US and Canadian* conservative; old-fashioned **2** well-established; traditional ▷ ˌold-ˈliner *n*

Old Low German *n* the Saxon and Low Franconian dialects of German up to about 1200; the old form of modern Low German and Dutch. Abbreviation: **OLG**

old maid *n* **1** a woman regarded as unlikely ever to marry; spinster **2** *informal* a prim, fastidious, or excessively cautious person **3** a card game using a pack from which one card has been removed, in which players try to avoid holding the unpaired card at the end of the game ▷ ˌold-ˈmaidish *adj*

old man *n* **1** an informal term for **father** *or* **husband** (sense 1) **2** (*sometimes capitals*) *informal* a man in command, such as an employer, foreman,

or captain of a ship **3** *sometimes facetious* an affectionate term used in addressing a man **4** another name for **southernwood 5** *Austral informal* **a** an adult male kangaroo **b** (*as modifier*) very large **6** *Christianity* the unregenerate aspect of human nature

old man's beard *n* any of various plants having a white feathery appearance, esp traveller's joy and Spanish moss

old master *n* **1** one of the great European painters of the period 1500 to 1800 **2** a painting by one of these

old media *n* **a** the media in existence before the arrival of the internet, such as newspapers, books, television, and cinema **b** (*as modifier*): *Warner's vast old-media holdings.* Compare **new media**

old moon *n* **1** a phase of the moon lying between last quarter and new moon, when it appears as a waning crescent **2** the moon when it appears as a waning crescent **3** the time at which this occurs

Old Nick *n* *informal* a jocular name for **Satan**

Old Norse *n* the language or group of dialects of medieval Scandinavia and Iceland from about 700 to about 1350, forming the North Germanic branch of the Indo-European family of languages. See also **Proto-Norse, Old Icelandic** Abbreviation: **ON**

Old North French *n* any of the dialects of Old French spoken in N France, such as Norman French

Old Northwest *n* (in the early US) the land between the Great Lakes, the Mississippi, and the Ohio River. Awarded to the US in 1783, it was organized into the **Northwest Territory** in 1787 and now forms the states of Ohio, Indiana, Illinois, Wisconsin, Michigan, and part of Minnesota

Old Persian *n* an ancient language belonging to the West Iranian branch of the Indo-European family, recorded in cuneiform inscriptions of the 6th to the 4th centuries BC. See also **Middle Persian**

Old Prussian *n* the former language of the non-German Prussians, belonging to the Baltic branch of the Indo-European family: extinct by 1700

Old Red Sandstone *n* **1** a thick sequence of sedimentary rock (generally, but not always, red) deposited in Britain and NW Europe during the Devonian period **2** (in Britain) another term for **Devonian** ▷ Abbreviation: **ORS**

old rose *n* **a** a greyish-pink colour **b** (*as adjective*): *old-rose gloves*

Old Saxon *n* the Saxon dialect of Low German up to about 1200, from which modern Low German is derived. Abbreviation: **OS**

old school *n* **1** *chiefly Brit* a school formerly attended by a person **2** a group of people favouring traditional ideas or conservative practices

old school tie *n* **1** *Brit* a distinctive tie that indicates which school the wearer attended **2** the attitudes, loyalties, values, etc, associated with British public schools

old skool (skuːl) *n* **a** the hip-hop music of the 1980s or modern music imitating this style **b** (*as modifier*): *old-skool hip-hop* [C20 *skool* is a phonetic rendering of SCHOOL]

Old Slavonic *or* **Slavic** *n* the South Slavonic language up to about 1400: the language of the Macedonian Slavs that developed into Serbo-Croat and Bulgarian. See also **Old Church Slavonic**

old sod *n* *informal* one's native country: *back to the old sod*

old soldier *n* **1** a former soldier or veteran **2** an experienced or practised person

Old South *n* the American South before the Civil War

old squaw *n* *US and Canadian* a long-tailed northern sea duck, *Clangula hyemalis*, having dark wings and a white-and-brown head and body. Also called: **oldwife**

old stager *n* a person with experience; old hand

O

oldster ('əuldstə) *n* **1** *informal* an older person **2** *Brit navy* a person who has been a midshipman for four years

Old Stone Age *n* (*not now in technical usage*) another term for **Palaeolithic**

old style *n printing* a type style reviving the characteristics of old face

Old Style *n* the former method of reckoning dates using the Julian calendar. Compare **New Style**

old sweat *n Brit informal* **1** an old soldier; veteran **2** a person who has a great deal of experience in some activity

old talk *Caribbean* ▷ *n* **1** superficial chatting ▷ *vb* **old-talk 2** (*intr*) to indulge in such chatting

Old Test. *abbreviation for* Old Testament

Old Testament *n* the collection of books comprising the sacred Scriptures of the Hebrews and essentially recording the history of the Hebrew people as the chosen people of God; the first part of the Christian Bible

old-time *adj* (*prenominal*) of or relating to a former time; old-fashioned: *old-time dancing*

old-time dance *n Brit* a formal or formation dance, such as the lancers > **old-time dancing** *n*

old-timer *n* **1** a person who has been in a certain place, occupation, etc, for a long time **2** *US* an old man

Olduvai Gorge ('ɒldu,vaɪ) *n* a gorge in N Tanzania, north of the Ngorongoro Crater: fossil evidence of early man and other closely related species, together with artefacts

oldwife ('əuld,waɪf) *n, pl* **-wives 1** another name for **old squaw 2** any of various fishes, esp the menhaden or the alewife

old wives' tale *n* a belief, usually superstitious or erroneous, passed on by word of mouth as a piece of traditional wisdom

old woman *n* **1** an informal term for **mother¹** or **wife** (sense 1) **2** a timid, fussy, or cautious person > **,old-'womanish** *adj*

Old World *n* that part of the world that was known before the discovery of the Americas, comprising Europe, Asia, and Africa; the eastern hemisphere

old-world *adj* of or characteristic of former times, esp, in Europe, quaint or traditional > **,old-'worldly** *adv*

Old World monkey *n* any monkey of the family *Cercopithecidae*, including macaques, baboons, and mandrills. They are more closely related to anthropoid apes than are the New World monkeys, having nostrils that are close together and nonprehensile tails. Compare **New World monkey**

olé (əʊ'leɪ) *interj* **1** an exclamation of approval or encouragement customary at bullfights, flamenco dancing, and other Spanish or Latin American events ▷ *n* **2** a cry of olé [Spanish, from Arabic *wa-llāh*, from *wa* and + *allāh* God]

OLE *computing abbreviation for* object linking and embedding: a system for linking and embedding data, images, and programs from different sources

-ole¹ *or* **-ol** *n combining form* **1** denoting an organic unsaturated compound containing a 5-membered ring: *thiazole* **2** denoting an aromatic organic ether: *anisole* [from Latin *oleum* oil, from Greek *elaion*, from *elaia* olive]

-ole² *suffix of nouns* indicating something small: *arteriole* [from Latin *-olus*, diminutive suffix]

olea ('əʊliə) *n* a plural of **oleum**

oleaceous (,əʊlɪ'eɪʃəs) *adj* of, relating to, or belonging to the *Oleaceae*, a family of trees and shrubs, including the ash, jasmine, privet, lilac, and olive [C19 via New Latin from Latin *olea* OLIVE; see also OIL]

oleaginous (,əʊlɪ'ædʒɪnəs) *adj* **1** resembling or having the properties of oil **2** containing or producing oil [C17 from Latin *oleāginus*, from *olea* OLIVE; see also OIL]

oleander (,əʊlɪ'ændə) *n* a poisonous evergreen Mediterranean apocynaceous shrub or tree, *Nerium oleander*, with fragrant white, pink, or purple flowers. Also called: **rosebay** [C16 from Medieval Latin, variant of *arodandrum*, perhaps from Latin RHODODENDRON]

olearia (,ɒlɪ'ɛərɪə) *n Austral* another word for **daisy bush**

oleaster (,əʊlɪ'æstə) *n* **1** any of several shrubs of the genus *Elaeagnus*, esp E. *angustifolia*, of S Europe, Asia, and North America, having silver-white twigs, yellow flowers, and an olive-like fruit: family *Elaeagnaceae* **2** Also called: **wild olive** a wild specimen of the cultivated olive [Latin: from *olea*; see OLIVE, OIL]

oleate ('əʊlɪ,eɪt) *n* any salt or ester of oleic acid, containing the ion $C_{17}H_{33}COO^-$ or the group $C_{17}H_{33}COO-$: common components of natural fats

olecranon (əʊ'lekrə,nɒn, ,əʊlɪ'kreɪnən) *n anatomy* the bony projection of the ulna behind the elbow joint [C18 from Greek, shortened from *ōlenokrānon*, from *ōlenē* elbow + *krānion* head] > **olecranal** (əʊ'lekrən°l, ,əʊlɪ'kreɪn°l) *adj*

OLED *abbreviation for* organic light-emitting diode

olefine *or* **olefin** ('əʊlɪ,fiːn, -fɪn, 'ɒl-) *n* other names for **alkene** [C19 from French *oléfiant*, ultimately from Latin *oleum* oil + *facere* to make] > **,ole'finic** *adj*

oleic acid (əʊ'liːɪk) *n* a colourless oily liquid unsaturated acid occurring, as the glyceride, in almost all natural fats used in making soaps, ointments, cosmetics, and lubricating oils. Formula: $CH_3(CH_2)_7CH:CH(CH_2)_7COOH$. Systematic name: *cis*-9-octadecenoic acid [C19 *oleic*, from Latin *oleum* oil + -IC]

olein ('əʊlɪɪn) *n* another name for **triolein** [C19 from French *oléine*, from Latin *oleum* oil + -IN]

oleo- *combining form* oil: *oleomargarine* [from Latin *oleum* OIL]

oleograph ('əʊlɪə,grɑːf, -,græf) *n* **1** a chromolithograph printed in oil colours to imitate the appearance of an oil painting **2** the pattern formed by a drop of oil spreading on water > **oleographic** (,əʊlɪə'græfɪk) *adj* > **oleography** (,əʊlɪ'ɒgrəfɪ) *n*

oleomargarine (,əʊlɪəʊ,mɑː'dʒəriːn) *or* **oleomargarin** (,əʊlɪəʊ'mɑːdʒərɪn) *n* other names (esp US) for **margarine**

oleo oil ('əʊlɪəʊ) *n* an oil extracted from beef fat, consisting mainly of a mixture of olein and palmitin. It is used in the manufacture of margarine

oleoresin (,əʊlɪəʊ'rɛzɪn) *n* **1** a semisolid mixture of a resin and essential oil, obtained from certain plants **2** *pharmacol* a liquid preparation of resins and oils, obtained by extraction from plants > **,oleo'resinous** *adj*

oleum ('əʊlɪəm) *n, pl* **olea** ('əʊlɪə) *or* **oleums** another name for **fuming sulphuric acid** [from Latin: oil, referring to its oily consistency]

O level *n* (formerly, in Britain) **1 a** the basic level of the General Certificate of Education, now replaced by **GCSE b** (*as modifier*): *O level maths* **2** a pass in a particular subject at O level: *he has eight O levels* ▷ Formal name: **Ordinary level**

olfaction (ɒl'fækʃən) *n* **1** the sense of smell **2** the act or function of smelling

olfactometry (,ɒlfæk'tɒmɪtrɪ) *n chem* another name for **odorimetry**

olfactory (ɒl'fæktərɪ, -trɪ) *adj* **1** of or relating to the sense of smell ▷ *n, pl* **-ries 2** (*usually plural*) an organ or nerve concerned with the sense of smell [C17 from Latin *olfactus*, past participle of *olfacere*, from *olere* to smell + *facere* to make]

olfactory bulb *n* the anterior and slightly enlarged end of the olfactory tract, from which the cranial nerves concerned with the sense of smell originate

olfactory nerve *n* either one of the first pair of cranial nerves, supplying the mucous membrane of the nose

olfactory tract *n* a long narrow triangular band of white tissue originating in the olfactory bulb and extending back to the point at which its fibres enter the base of the cerebrum

OLG *abbreviation for* Old Low German

olibanum (ɒ'lɪbənəm) *n* another name for **frankincense** [C14 from Medieval Latin, from Greek *libanos*]

olid ('ɒlɪd) *adj* foul-smelling [C17 from Latin *olidus*, from *olēre* to smell]

oligaemia *or US* **oligemia** (,ɒlɪ'giːmɪə) *n med* a reduction in the volume of the blood, as occurs after haemorrhage > **,oli'gaemic** *or US* **,oli'gemic** *adj*

oligarch ('ɒlɪ,gɑːk) *n* a member of an oligarchy

oligarchy ('ɒlɪ,gɑːkɪ) *n, pl* **-chies 1** government by a small group of people **2** a state or organization so governed **3** a small body of individuals ruling such a state **4** *chiefly US* a small clique of private citizens who exert a strong influence on government [C16 via Medieval Latin from Greek *oligarkhia*, from *olígos* few + -ARCHY] > **,oli'garchic** *or* **,oli'garchical** *adj* > **,oli'garchically** *adv*

oligo- *or before a vowel* **olig-** *combining form* indicating a few or little: *oligopoly* [from Greek *olígos* little, few]

Oligocene ('ɒlɪgəʊ,siːn, ɒ'lɪg-) *adj* **1** of, denoting, or formed in the third epoch of the Tertiary period, which lasted for 10 000 000 years ▷ *n* **2** **the** the Oligocene epoch or rock series [C19 OLIGO- + -CENE]

oligochaete ('ɒlɪgəʊ,kiːt) *n* **1** any freshwater or terrestrial annelid worm of the class *Oligochaeta*, having bristles (chaetae) borne singly along the length of the body: includes the earthworms ▷ *adj* **2** of, relating to, or belonging to the class *Oligochaeta* [C19 from New Latin; see OLIGO-, CHAETA]

oligoclase ('ɒlɪgəʊ,kleɪs) *n* a white, bluish, or reddish-yellow feldspar mineral of the plagioclase series, consisting of aluminium silicates of sodium and calcium. Formula: $NaAlSi_3O_8.CaAl_2Si_2O_8$ [C19 from OLIGO- + -CLASE]

oligodendrocyte (,ɒlɪgəʊ'dɛndrəʊsaɪt) *n anatomy* a glial cell involved in the formation of the myelin sheaths of nerve cell axons

oligomer (ɒ'lɪgəmə) *n* a compound of relatively low molecular weight containing up to five monomer units. Compare **polymer, copolymer** [C20 from OLIGO- + -mer, as in *polymer*]

oligomerous (,ɒlɪ'gɒmərəs) *adj biology* having a small number of component parts

oligonucleotide (,ɒlɪgəʊ'njuːklɪə,taɪd) *n* a polymer consisting of a small number of nucleotides

oligopeptide (,ɒlɪgəʊ'pɛptaɪd) *n biochem* a peptide comprising a small number of amino acids

oligopoly (,ɒlɪ'gɒpəlɪ) *n, pl* **-lies** *economics* a market situation in which control over the supply of a commodity is held by a small number of producers each of whom is able to influence prices and thus directly affect the position of competitors [C20 from OLIGO- + Greek *pōlein* to sell, on the model of MONOPOLY] > **,oli,gopo'listic** *adj*

oligopsony (,ɒlɪ'gɒpsənɪ) *n, pl* **-nies** a market situation in which the demand for a commodity is represented by a small number of purchasers [C20 from OLIGO- + -opsony, from Greek *opsōnia* purchase of food] > **,oli,gopso'nistic** *adj*

oligosaccharide (,ɒlɪgəʊ'sækə,raɪd, -rɪd) *n* any one of a class of carbohydrates consisting of a few monosaccharide units linked together. Compare **polysaccharide**

oligospermia (,ɒlɪgəʊ'spɜːmɪə) *n* the condition of having less than the normal number of spermatozoa in the semen: a cause of infertility in men

oligotrophic (,ɒlɪgəʊ'trɒfɪk) *adj* (of lakes and similar habitats) poor in nutrients and plant life and rich in oxygen. Compare **eutrophic** [C20 from OLIGO- + Greek *trophein* to nourish + -IC] > **oligotrophy** (,ɒlɪ'gɒtrəfɪ) *n*

oliguria (,ɒlɪ'gjʊərɪə) *or* **oliguresis** (,ɒlɪgjʊ'riːsɪs) *n* excretion of an abnormally small volume of urine, often as the result of a kidney disorder. Compare **anuria** [C19 from OLIGO- + -URIA] > **oliguretic**

(ˌɒlɪɡjʊˈrɛtɪk) *adj*

Ōlimbos (ˈɒlɪmbɒs) *n* transliteration of the Modern Greek name for (Mount) **Olympus** (sense 1)

olio (ˈəʊlɪˌəʊ) *n, pl* **olios 1** a dish of many different ingredients **2** a miscellany or potpourri [C17 from Spanish *olla* stew, from Latin: jar]

olivaceous (ˌɒlɪˈveɪʃəs) *adj* of an olive colour

olivary (ˈɒlɪvərɪ) *adj* **1** shaped like an olive **2** *anatomy* of or relating to either of two masses of tissue (**olivary bodies**) on the forward portion of the medulla oblongata [C16 from Latin *olivārius*, from *oliva* OLIVE]

olive (ˈɒlɪv) *n* **1** an evergreen oleaceous tree, *Olea europaea*, of the Mediterranean region but cultivated elsewhere, having white fragrant flowers, and edible shiny black fruits **2** the fruit of this plant, eaten as a relish and used as a source of olive oil **3** the wood of the olive tree, used for ornamental work **4** any of various trees or shrubs resembling the olive **5 a** a yellow-green colour **b** (*as adjective*): *an olive coat* **6** an angler's name for the dun of various mayflies or an artificial fly in imitation of this ▷ *adj* **7** of, relating to, or made of the olive tree, its wood, or its fruit [C13 via Old French from Latin *oliva*, related to Greek *elaia* olive tree; compare Greek *elaion* oil]

olive branch *n* **1** a branch of an olive tree used to symbolize peace **2** any offering of peace or conciliation

olive brown *n* **a** a dull yellowish-brown to yellowish-green colour **b** (*as adjective*): *an olive-brown coat*

olive crown *n* (esp in ancient Greece and Rome) a garland of olive leaves awarded as a token of victory

olive drab *n US* **1 a** a dull but fairly strong greyish-olive colour **b** (*as adjective*): *an olive-drab jacket* **2** cloth or clothes in this colour, esp the uniform of the US Army. Abbreviation: **OD**

olive green *n* **a** a colour that is greener, stronger, and brighter than olive; deep yellowish-green **b** (*as adjective*): *an olive-green coat*

olivenite (ɒˈlɪvɪˌnaɪt) *n* a green to black rare secondary mineral consisting of hydrated basic copper arsenate in orthorhombic crystalline form. Formula: $Cu_2(AsO_4)(OH)$ [C19 from German *Oliven(erz)* olive (ore) + -ITE[1]]

olive oil *n* a pale yellow oil pressed from ripe olive fruits and used in cooking, medicines, soaps, etc

Olives (ˈɒlɪvz) *n* **Mount of** a hill to the east of Jerusalem: in New Testament times the village Bethany (Mark 11:11) was on its eastern slope and Gethsemane on its western one

olivine (ˈɒlɪˌviːn, ˌɒlɪˈviːn) *n* **1** an olive-green mineral of the olivine group, found in igneous and metamorphic rocks. The clear-green variety (peridot) is used as a gemstone. Composition: magnesium iron silicate. Formula: $(MgFe)_2SiO_4$. Crystal structure: orthorhombic. Also called: **chrysolite 2** any mineral in the group having the general formula $(Mg,Fe,Mn,Ca)_2SiO_4$ [C18 from German, named after its colour]

olla (ˈɒlə; *Spanish* ˈoʎa) *n* **1** a cooking pot **2** short for **olla podrida** [Spanish, from Latin *olla*, variant of *aulla* pot]

olla podrida (pɒˈdriːdə; *Spanish* poˈðriða) *n* **1** a Spanish dish, consisting of a stew with beans, sausages, etc **2** an assortment; miscellany [literally: rotten pot]

oller (ˈɒlə) *n Northern English dialect* waste ground

ollie (ˈɒlɪ) *n, pl* **-lies** (in skateboarding and snowboarding) a jump into the air executed by stamping on the tail of the board [C20 of uncertain origin]

olm (əʊlm, ɒlm) *n* a pale blind eel-like salamander, *Proteus anguinus*, of underground streams in SE Europe, that retains its larval form throughout its life: family *Proteidae*. See also **mud puppy** [C20 from German]

Olmec (ˈɒlmɛk) *n, pl* **-mecs** or **-mec 1** a member of an ancient Central American Indian people who inhabited the southern Gulf Coast of Mexico and flourished between about 1200 and 400 BC ▷ *adj* **2** of or relating to these people or their civilization or culture

Olmütz (ˈɒlmyts) *n* the German name for **Olomouc**

ologoan (ˌʌləˈɡoːn) *vb* (*intr*) *Irish* to complain loudly without reason; *she's always ologoaning about something* [from Irish Gaelic *olagón* lament]

ology (ˈɒlədʒɪ) *n, pl* **-gies** *informal* a science or other branch of knowledge [C19 abstracted from words with this ending, such as *theology, biology*, etc; see -LOGY]

Olomouc (*Czech* ˈɒlɒmɒuts) *n* a city in the Czech Republic, in North Moravia on the Morava River: capital of Moravia until 1640; university (1576). Pop: 102 000 (2005 est). German name: **Olmütz**

oloroso (ˌɒləˈrəʊsəʊ) *n* a full-bodied golden-coloured sweet sherry [from Spanish: fragrant]

Olsztyn (*Polish* ˈɔlʃtin) *n* a town in NE Poland: founded in 1334 by the Teutonic Knights; communications centre. Pop: 176 000 (2005 est)

Olympia (əˈlɪmpɪə) *n* **1** a plain in Greece, in the NW Peloponnese: in ancient times a major sanctuary of Zeus and site of the original Olympic Games **2** a port in W Washington, the state capital, on Puget Sound. Pop: 43 963 (2003 est)

Olympiad (əˈlɪmpɪˌæd) *n* **1** a staging of the modern Olympic Games **2** the four-year period between consecutive celebrations of the Olympic Games; a unit of ancient Greek chronology dating back to 776 BC **3** an international contest in chess, bridge, etc

Olympian (əˈlɪmpɪən) *adj* **1** of or relating to Mount Olympus or to the classical Greek gods **2** majestic or godlike in manner or bearing **3** superior to mundane considerations, esp when impractical **4** of or relating to ancient Olympia or its inhabitants ▷ *n* **5** a god of Olympus **6** an inhabitant or native of ancient Olympia **7** *chiefly US* a competitor in the Olympic Games

Olympic (əˈlɪmpɪk) *adj* **1** of or relating to the Olympic Games **2** of or relating to ancient Olympia

Olympic Games *n* (*functioning as singular or plural*) **1** the greatest Panhellenic festival, held every fourth year in honour of Zeus at ancient Olympia. From 472 BC, it consisted of five days of games, sacrifices, and festivities **2** Also called: **the Olympics** the modern revival of these games, consisting of international athletic and sporting contests held every four years in a selected country since their inception in Athens in 1896. See also **Winter Olympic Games**

Olympic Mountains *pl n* a mountain range in NW Washington: part of the Coast Range. Highest peak: Mount Olympus, 2427 m (7965 ft)

Olympic Peninsula *n* a large peninsula of W Washington

Olympus (əʊˈlɪmpəs) *n* **1** **Mount** a mountain in NE Greece: the highest mountain in Greece, believed in Greek mythology to be the dwelling place of the greater gods. Height: 2911 m (9550 ft). Modern Greek name: **Ōlimbos 2** **Mount** a mountain in NW Washington: highest peak of the Olympic Mountains. Height: 2427 m (7965 ft) **3** a poetic word for **heaven**

Olympus Mons *n* the highest of the giant shield volcanoes on Mars, lying 18°N of the equator. Height: 26 km; base diameter: over 600 km

Olynthus (əʊˈlɪnθəs) *n* an ancient city in N Greece: the centre of Chalcidice

om *the internet domain name for* Oman

Om (əʊm) *n Hinduism* a sacred syllable typifying the three gods Brahma, Vishnu, and Siva, who are concerned in the threefold operation of integration, maintenance, and disintegration [from Sanskrit]

OM 1 *abbreviation for* Order of Merit (a Brit title) **2** *currency symbol for* (the former) Ostmark

-oma *n combining form* indicating a tumour: *carcinoma* [from Greek *-ōma*]

omadhaun (ˈɒmədɔːn) *n Irish* a foolish man or boy [C19 from Irish Gaelic *amadán*]

Omagh (əʊˈmɑː, ˈəʊmə) *n* **1** a market town in Northern Ireland. Pop: 19 910 (2001) **2** a district of W Northern Ireland, in Co Tyrone. Pop: 49 560 (2003 est). Area: 1130 sq km (436 sq miles)

Omaha (ˈəʊməˌhɑː) *n* a city in E Nebraska, on the Missouri River opposite Council Bluffs, Iowa: the largest city in the state; the country's largest livestock market and meat-packing centre. Pop: 404 267 (2003 est)

Oman (əʊˈmɑːn) *n* a sultanate in SE Arabia, on the **Gulf of Oman** and the Arabian Sea: the most powerful state in Arabia in the 19th century, ruling Zanzibar, much of the Persian coast, and part of Pakistan. Official language: Arabic. Official religion: Muslim. Currency: rial. Capital: Muscat. Pop: 2 935 000 (2004 est). Area: about 306 000 sq km (118 150 sq miles). Former name (until 1970): **Muscat and Oman**

OMAN *international car registration for* Oman

Omani (əʊˈmɑːnɪ) *n* **1** a native or inhabitant of Oman ▷ *adj* **2** of or relating to Oman or its inhabitants

omasum (əʊˈmeɪsəm) *n, pl* **-sa** (-sə) another name for **psalterium** [C18 from Latin: bullock's tripe]

ombre *or US* **omber** (ˈɒmbə) *n* an 18th-century card game [C17 from Spanish *hombre* man, referring to the player who attempts to win the stakes]

ombro- *combining form* indicating rain: *ombrogenous; ombrophilous* [from Greek *ombros* shower of rain]

ombrogenous (ɒmˈbrɒdʒɪnəs) *adj* (of plants) able to flourish in wet conditions

ombrophilous (ɒmˈbrɒfɪləs) *adj* (of plants) tolerant of wet conditions

ombrophobous (ɒmˈbrɒfəbəs) *adj* (of plants) not able to tolerate wet conditions

ombudsman (ˈɒmbʊdzmən) *n, pl* **-men 1** a commissioner who acts as independent referee between individual citizens and their government or its administration **2** (in Britain) an official, without power of sanction or mechanism of appeal, who investigates complaints of maladministration by members of the public against national or local government or its servants. Formal names: **Commissioner for Local Administration, Health Service Commissioner, Parliamentary Commissioner** See also **Financial Ombudsman** [C20 from Swedish: commissioner]

Omdurman (ˌɒmdɜːˈmɑːn) *n* a city in the central Sudan, on the White Nile, opposite Khartoum: the largest town in the Sudan; scene of the **Battle of Omdurman** (1898), in which the Mahdi's successor was defeated by Lord Kitchener's forces. Pop: 1 267 077 (1993)

-ome *n combining form* denoting a mass or part of a specified kind: *rhizome* [variant of -OMA]

omega (ˈəʊmɪɡə) *n* **1** the 24th and last letter of the Greek alphabet (Ω, ω), a long vowel, transliterated as *o* or *ō* **2** the ending or last of a series [C16 from Greek *ō mega* big o; see MEGA-, OMICRON]

omega-3 fatty acid *n* an unsaturated fatty acid that occurs naturally in fish oil and is valuable in reducing blood-cholesterol levels

omega minus *n* an unstable negatively charged elementary particle, classified as a baryon, that has a mass 3273 times that of the electron

omelette *or esp US* **omelet** (ˈɒmlɪt) *n* a savoury or sweet dish of beaten eggs cooked in fat [C17 from French *omelette*, changed from *alumette*, from *alumelle* sword blade, changed by mistaken division from *la lemelle*, from Latin (see LAMELLA); apparently from the flat shape of the omelette]

omen (ˈəʊmən) *n* **1** a phenomenon or occurrence regarded as a sign of future happiness or disaster **2** prophetic significance ▷ *vb* **3** (*tr*) to portend [C16 from Latin]

omentum (əʊˈmɛntəm) *n, pl* **-ta** (-tə) *anatomy* a

double fold of peritoneum connecting the stomach with other abdominal organs [C16 from Latin: membrane, esp a caul, of obscure origin]

omer ('əʊmə) *n* an ancient Hebrew unit of dry measure equal to one tenth of an ephah [C17 from Hebrew *'ōmer* a measure]

Omer ('əʊmə) *n Judaism* a period of seven weeks extending from the second day of Passover to the first day of Shavuoth, and observed as a period of semimourning [named because sacrifices of an OMER of grain were made]

omertà Italian (omer'ta) *n* a conspiracy of silence

omicron (əʊ'maɪkrɒn, 'ɒmɪkrɒn) *n* the 15th letter in the Greek alphabet (O, o), a short vowel, transliterated as *o* [from Greek *ō mikron* small o; see MICRO-, OMEGA]

omigod (,əʊmaɪ'gɒd) *interj* an exclamation of surprise, pleasure, dismay, etc [C20 from *Oh, my God*]

ominous ('ɒmɪnəs) *adj* 1 foreboding evil 2 serving as or having significance as an omen [C16 from Latin *ōminōsus*, from OMEN] > **'ominously** *adv* > **'ominousness** *n*

omission (əʊ'mɪʃən) *n* 1 something that has been omitted or neglected 2 the act of omitting or the state of having been omitted [C14 from Latin *omissiō*, from *omittere* to OMIT] > **o'missive** *adj*

omit (əʊ'mɪt) *vb* omits, omitting, omitted (*tr*) 1 to neglect to do or include 2 to fail (to do something) [C15 from Latin *omittere*, from *ob-* away + *mittere* to send] > **o'missible** (əʊ'mɪsɪbᵊl) *adj* > **o'mitter** *n*

OMM (in Canada) *abbreviation for* Officer of the Order of Military Merit

ommatidium (,ɒmə'tɪdɪəm) *n*, *pl* -tidia (-'tɪdɪə) any of the numerous cone-shaped units that make up the compound eyes of some arthropods [C19 via New Latin from Greek *ommatidion*, from *omma* eye] > **,omma'tidial** *adj*

ommatophore (ɒ'mætə,fɔː) *n zoology* a movable stalk or tentacle bearing an eye, occurring in lower animals such as crabs and snails [C19 from Greek *omma* eye + -PHORE] > **ommatophorous** (,ɒmə'tɒfərəs) *adj*

omni- *combining form* all or everywhere: *omnipresent* [from Latin *omnis* all]

omnia vincit amor Latin ('ɒmnɪə 'vɪnsɪt 'æmɒː) love conquers all things [from Virgil's *Eclogues* 10:69]

omnibus ('ɒmnɪˌbʌs, -bəs) *n*, *pl* -buses 1 a less common word for **bus** (sense 1) Also called: **omnibus volume** a collection of works by one author or several works on a similar topic, reprinted in one volume 3 Also called: **omnibus edition** a television or radio programme consisting of two or more programmes broadcast earlier in the week ▷ *adj* 4 (*prenominal*) of, dealing with, or providing for many different things or cases [C19 from Latin, literally: for all, from *omnis* all]

omnicompetent (,ɒmnɪ'kɒmpɪtənt) *adj* able to judge or deal with all matters > **,omni'competence** *n*

omnidirectional (,ɒmnɪdɪ'rɛkʃənᵊl, -daɪ-) *adj* 1 (of an antenna) capable of transmitting and receiving radio signals equally in any direction in the horizontal plane 2 (of a microphone or antenna) equally sensitive in all directions

omnifarious (,ɒmnɪ'fɛərɪəs) *adj* of many or all varieties or forms [C17 from Late Latin *omnifārius*, from Latin *omnis* all + *-farius* doing, related to *facere* to do] > **,omni'fariously** *adv* > **,omni'fariousness** *n*

omnific (ɒm'nɪfɪk) or **omnificent** (ɒm'nɪfɪsᵊnt) *adj rare* creating all things [C17 via Medieval Latin from Latin *omni-* + *-ficus*, from *facere* to do] > **om'nificence** *n*

omnipotent (ɒm'nɪpətənt) *adj* 1 having very great or unlimited power ▷ *n* 2 **the Omnipotent** an epithet for God [C14 via Old French from Latin *omnipotens* all-powerful, from OMNI- + *potens*, from *posse* to be able] > **om'nipotence** *n*
> **om'nipotently** *adv*

omnipresent (,ɒmnɪ'prɛzᵊnt) *adj* (esp of a deity) present in all places at the same time
> **,omni'presence** *n*

omnirange (,ɒmnɪ,reɪndʒ) *n* a very-high-frequency ground radio navigational system to assist a pilot in plotting his exact position

omniscient (ɒm'nɪsɪənt) *adj* 1 having infinite knowledge or understanding 2 having very great or seemingly unlimited knowledge [C17 from Medieval Latin *omnisciens*, from Latin OMNI- + *scīre* to know] > **om'niscience** *n* > **om'nisciently** *adv*

omnium-gatherum ('ɒmnɪəm'gæðərəm) *n often facetious* a miscellaneous collection; assortment [C16 from Latin *omnium* of all, from *omnis* all + Latinized form of English *gather*]

omnivore ('ɒmnɪ,vɔː) *n* an omnivorous person or animal

omnivorous (ɒm'nɪvərəs) *adj* 1 eating food of both animal and vegetable origin, or any type of food indiscriminately 2 taking in or assimilating everything, esp with the mind [C17 from Latin *omnivorus* all-devouring, from OMNI- + *vorāre* to eat greedily] > **om'nivorously** *adv* > **om'nivorousness** *n*

omophagia (,əʊmə'feɪdʒɪə) or **omophagy** (əʊ'mɒfədʒɪ) *n* the eating of raw food, esp meat [C18 via New Latin from Greek *ōmophagia*, from *ōmos* raw + *-phagia*; see PHAGY] > **omophagic** (,əʊmə'fædʒɪk) or **omophagous** (əʊ'mɒfəgəs) *adj*

OMOV or **omov** ('əʊmɒv) *n acronym for* one member one vote: a voting system in which each voter has one vote to cast. Compare **block vote**

Omphale ('ɒmfə,liː) *n Greek myth* a queen of Lydia, whom Hercules was required to serve as a slave to atone for the murder of Iphitus

omphalos ('ɒmfə,lɒs) *n* 1 (in the ancient world) a sacred conical object, esp a stone. The most famous omphalos at Delphi was assumed to mark the centre of the earth 2 the central point 3 *literary* another word for **navel** [Greek: navel]

OMS *abbreviation for* Organisation Mondiale de la Santé [French: World Health Organization]

Omsk (ɒmsk) *n* a city in W central Russia, at the confluence of the Irtysh and Om Rivers: a major industrial centre, with pipelines from the second Baku oilfield. Pop: 1 132 000 (2005 est)

Omuta ('əʊmuː,tɑː) *n* a city in SW Japan, on W Kyushu on Ariake Bay: former coal-mining centre; chemical industries and manufacturing. Pop: 139 345 (2002 est)

on (ɒn) *prep* 1 in contact or connection with the surface of; at the upper surface of: *an apple on the ground; a mark on the table cloth* 2 attached to: *a puppet on a string* 3 carried with: *I've no money on me* 4 in the immediate vicinity of; close to or along the side of: *a house on the sea; this verges on the ridiculous!* 5 within the time limits of a day or date: *he arrived on Thursday* 6 being performed upon or relayed through the medium of: *what's on the television?* 7 at the occasion of: *on his retirement* 8 used to indicate support, subsistence, contingency, etc: *he lives on bread; it depends on what you want* 9 a regularly taking (a drug): *she's on the pill* b addicted to: *he's on heroin* 10 by means of (something considered as a mode of transport) (esp in such phrases as **on foot, on wheels, on horseback,** etc) 11 in the process or course of: *on a journey; on strike* 12 concerned with or relating to: *a tax on potatoes; a programme on archaeology* 13 used to indicate the basis, grounds, or cause, as of a statement or action: *I have it on good authority* 14 against: used to indicate opposition: *they marched on the city at dawn* 15 used to indicate a meeting or encounter: *he crept up on her* 16 (used with an adjective preceded by *the*) indicating the manner or way in which an action is carried out: *on the sly; on the cheap* 17 *informal* a staked or wagered as a bet: *ten pounds on that horse* b charged to: *the drinks are on me* 18 **on it** *Austral informal* drinking alcoholic liquor 19 *informal or dialect* to the loss or disadvantage of: *the old car gave out on us* ▷ *adv* (often used as a particle) 20 in the position or state required for the commencement or sustained

continuation, as of a mechanical operation: *the radio's been on all night* 21 a attached to, surrounding, or placed in contact with something: *the girl had nothing on* b taking place: *what's on tonight?* 22 in a manner indicating continuity, persistence, concentration, etc: *don't keep on about it; the play went on all afternoon* 23 in a direction towards something, esp forwards; so as to make progress: *we drove on towards London; march on!* 24 **on and off** or **off and on** intermittently; from time to time 25 **on and on** without ceasing; continually ▷ *adj* 26 functioning; operating: *turn the switch to the on position* 27 (*postpositive*) *informal* a performing, as on stage: *I'm on in five minutes* b definitely taking place: *the match is on for Friday; their marriage is still on* c tolerable, practicable, acceptable, etc: *your plan just isn't on* d (of a person) willing to do something: *she was always on at her husband* 29 *cricket* (of a bowler) bowling ▷ *n* 30 *cricket* a (*modifier*) relating to or denoting the leg side of a cricket field or pitch: *the on side; an on drive* b (in combination) used to designate certain fielding positions on the leg side: *long-on; mid-on* [Old English *an, on;* related to Old Saxon *an*, Old High German, Gothic *ana*]

On (ɒn) *n* the ancient Egyptian and biblical name for Heliopolis

ON *abbreviation for* 1 Old Norse 2 (esp in postal addresses) Ontario

-on *suffix forming nouns* 1 indicating a chemical substance: *interferon; parathion* 2 (in physics) indicating an elementary particle or quantum: *electron; photon* 3 (in chemistry) indicating an inert gas: *neon; radon* 4 (in biochemistry) a molecular unit: *codon; operon* [from ION]

onager ('ɒnədʒə) *n, pl* -gri (-,graɪ) or -gers 1 a Persian variety of the wild ass, *Equus hemionus*. Compare **kiang** 2 an ancient war engine for hurling stones [C14 from Late Latin: military engine for stone throwing, from Latin: wild ass, from Greek *onagros*, from *onos* ass + *agros* field]

onagraceous (,ɒnə'greɪʃəs) *adj* of, relating to, or belonging to the *Onagraceae*, a family of flowering plants including fuchsia and willowherb [C19 via New Latin *Onagrāceae*, from Latin *onager*; see ONAGER]

onanism ('əʊnə,nɪzəm) *n* another name for **masturbation** or **coitus interruptus** [C18 after *Onan*, son of Judah; see Genesis 38:9] > **'onanist** *n, adj*
> **,onan'istic** *adj*

onbeat ('ɒn,biːt) *n music* the first and third beats in a bar of four-four time

ONC (in Britain, formerly) *abbreviation for* Ordinary National Certificate

once (wʌns) *adv* 1 one time; on one occasion or in one case 2 at some past time; formerly: *I could speak French once* 3 by one step or degree (of relationship): *a cousin once removed* 4 (in conditional clauses, negatives, etc) ever; at all: *if you once forget it* 5 multiplied by one 6 **once and away** a conclusively b occasionally 7 **once and for all** conclusively; for the last time 8 **once in a while** occasionally; now and then 9 **once or twice** or **once and again** a few times 10 **once upon a time** used to begin fairy tales and children's stories ▷ *conj* 11 (*subordinating*) as soon as; if ever or whenever: *once you begin, you'll enjoy it* ▷ *n* 12 one occasion or case: *you may do it, this once* 13 **all at once** a suddenly or without warning b simultaneously 14 **at once** a immediately b simultaneously 15 **for once** this time, if (or but) at no other time [C12 *ones, ānes,* adverbial genitive of *on, ān* ONE]

once-over *n informal* 1 a quick examination or appraisal 2 a quick but comprehensive piece of work 3 a violent beating or thrashing (esp in the phrase **give** (**a person** or **thing**) **the** (or **a**) **once-over**)

oncer ('wʌnsə) *n slang* 1 Brit (formerly) a one-pound note 2 Austral a person elected to Parliament who can only expect to serve one term

3 *NZ* something that happens on only one occasion [C20 from ONCE]

onchocerciasis (ˌɒŋkəʊsəˈkaɪəsɪs) *n, pl* -ses (-siːz) a disease found in parts of Africa and tropical America that is caused by a parasitic worm, *Onchocerca volvulus*, and transmitted to humans by various species of black fly. It results in inflammation of the skin and in some cases blindness. Also called: river blindness [C20 from *Onchocerca*, the genus of worms + -IASIS]

onco- *combining form* denoting a tumour: *oncology* [from Greek *onkos*]

oncogene (ˈɒŋkəʊˌdʒiːn) *n* any of several genes, first identified in viruses but present in all cells, that when abnormally activated can cause cancer

oncogenic (ˌɒŋkəʊˈdʒɛnɪk) *or* **oncogenous** (ɒŋˈkɒdʒənəs) *adj* causing the formation of a tumour: *an oncogenic virus* > ˌonco'genesis *n*

oncology (ɒŋˈkɒlədʒɪ) *n* the branch of medicine concerned with the study, classification, and treatment of tumours > oncological (ˌɒŋkəˈlɒdʒɪkᵊl) *adj* > on'cologist *n*

oncoming (ˈɒnˌkʌmɪŋ) *adj* **1** coming nearer in space or time; approaching ▷ *n* **2** the approach or onset: *the oncoming of winter*

oncost (ˈɒnˌkɒst) *n Brit* **1** another word for **overhead** (sense 7) **2** (*sometimes plural*) another word for **overheads**

OND (in Britain, formerly) *abbreviation for* Ordinary National Diploma

ondes Martenot (ɔ̃d mɑːtəˈnəʊ) *n music* an electronic keyboard instrument in which the frequency of an oscillator is varied to produce separate musical notes [C20 French, literally: Martenot waves, invented by Maurice *Martenot* (1898–1980)]

on dit *French* (ɔ̃ di) *n, pl on dits* (ɔ̃ di) a rumour; piece of gossip [literally: it is said, they say]

Ondo (ˈɒndəʊ) *n* a state of SW Nigeria, on the Bight of Benin: formed in 1976 from part of Western State. Capital: Akure. Pop: 4 343 230 (1995 est). Area: 20 959 sq km (8092 sq miles)

ondograph (ˈɒndəʊˌɡrɑːf, -ˌɡræf) *n* an instrument for producing a graphical recording of an alternating current by measuring the charge imparted to a capacitor at different points in the cycle [C20 from French, from *onde* wave + -GRAPH]

one (wʌn) *determiner* **1 a** single; lone; not two or more: *one car* **b** (*as pronoun*): *one is enough for now; one at a time* **c** (*in combination*): *one-eyed; one-legged* **2 a** distinct from all others; only; unique: *one girl in a million* **b** (*as pronoun*): *one of a kind* **3 a** a specified (person, item, etc) as distinct from another or others of its kind: *raise one hand and then the other* **b** (*as pronoun*): *which one is correct?* **4** a certain, indefinite, or unspecified (time); some: *one day you'll be sorry* **5** *informal* an emphatic word for **a¹** or **an¹**: *it was one hell of a fight* **6** a certain (person): *one Miss Jones was named* **7** (**all**) **in one** combined; united **8** all one **a** all the same **b** of no consequence: *it's all one to me* **9** at one (often foll by *with*) in a state of agreement or harmony **10** be made one (of a man and a woman) to become married **11** many a one indefinite; many people **12** neither one thing nor the other indefinite, undecided, or mixed **13** never a one none **14** one and all everyone, without exception **15** one by one one at a time; individually **16** one or two a few **17** one way and another indefinite; taking all in all **18** off on one *informal* exhibiting bad temper; ranting **19** one with another on average ▷ *pron* **20** an indefinite person regarded as typical of every person: *one can't say any more than that* **21** any indefinite person: used as the subject of a sentence to form an alternative grammatical construction to that of the passive voice: *one can catch fine trout in this stream* **22** *archaic* an unspecified person: *one came to him* ▷ *n* **23** the smallest whole number and the first cardinal number; unity. See also **number** (sense 1) **24** a numeral (1, I, i, etc) representing this number **25** *music* the numeral 1 used as the lower figure in a time signature to indicate that the beat is measured in semibreves **26** something representing, represented by, or consisting of one unit **27** Also called: one o'clock one hour after noon or midnight **28** a blow or setback (esp in the phrase **one in the eye for**) **29** the one (in Neo-Platonic philosophy) the ultimate being **30** the Holy One *or* the One above God **31** the Evil One Satan; the devil ▷ Related prefixes: **mono-, uni-** Related adj: **single** [Old English *ān*, related to Old French *ān*, *ēn*, Old High German *ein*, Old Norse *einn*, Latin *unus*, Greek *oinē* ace]

-one *suffix forming nouns* indicating that a chemical compound is a ketone: *acetone* [arbitrarily from Greek *-ōnē*, feminine patronymic suffix, but perhaps influenced by *-one* in OZONE]

one another *pron* the reflexive form of plural pronouns when the action, attribution, etc, is reciprocal: *they kissed one another; knowing one another.* Also: **each other**

one-armed bandit *n* a fruit machine operated by pulling down a lever at one side

one-down *adj informal* having conceded an advantage or lead to someone or something

Onega (*Russian* aˈnjɛɡa) *n* a lake in NW Russia, mostly in the Karelian Republic: the second largest lake in Europe. Area: 9891 sq km (3819 sq miles)

one-horse *adj* **1** drawn by or using one horse **2** (*prenominal*) *informal* small or obscure: *a one-horse town*

Oneida (əʊˈnaɪdə) *n, pl* -das *or* -da **1 Lake** a lake in central New York State: part of the New York State Barge Canal system. Length: about 35 km (22 miles). Greatest width: 9 km (6 miles) **2** (*preceded by the; functioning as plural*) a North American Indian people formerly living east of Lake Ontario; one of the Iroquois peoples **3** a member of this people **4** the language of this people, belonging to the Iroquoian family [from Iroquois *onēyóte'*, literally: standing stone]

oneiric (əʊˈnaɪərɪk) *adj* of or relating to dreams

oneiro- *combining form* indicating a dream: *oneirocritic* [from Greek *oneiros* dream]

oneirocritic (əʊˌnaɪərəʊˈkrɪtɪk) *n* a person who interprets dreams [C17 from Greek *oneirokritikos*] > oˌneiro'critical *adj* > oˌneiro'critically *adv*

oneiromancy (əʊˈnaɪərəʊˌmænsɪ) *n rare* divination by the interpretation of dreams [C17 from Greek *oneiros* dream + -MANCY] > o'neiroˌmancer *n*

one-liner *n informal* a short joke or witty remark or riposte

one-man *adj* consisting of or done by or for one man: *a one-man band; a one-man show*

one-many *adj maths, logic* (of a relation) holding between more than one ordered pair of elements with the same first member

oneness (ˈwʌnnɪs) *n* **1** the state or quality of being one; singleness **2** the state of being united; agreement **3** uniqueness **4** sameness

one-night stand *n* **1** a performance given only once at any one place **2** *informal* **a** a sexual encounter lasting only one evening or night **b** a person regarded as being only suitable for such an encounter

one-off *n Brit* **a** something that is carried out or made only once **b** (*as modifier*): *a one-off job.* Also: **one-shot** [See OFF (sense 15)]

one-on-one *adj* denoting a relationship or encounter in which someone is involved with only one other person: *a one-on-one meeting*

one-parent family *n* a household consisting of at least one dependent child and the mother or father, the other parent being dead or permanently absent

one-piece *adj* **1** (of a garment, esp a bathing costume) made in one piece ▷ *n* **2** a garment, esp a bathing costume, made in one piece

oner (ˈwʌnə) *n Brit informal* **1** a single continuous action (esp in the phrase **down it in a oner**) **2** an outstanding person or thing **3** a heavy blow [C20 from ONE]

onerous (ˈɒnərəs, ˈəʊ-) *adj* **1** laborious or oppressive **2** *law* (of a contract, lease, etc) having or involving burdens or obligations that counterbalance or outweigh the advantages [C14 from Latin *onerōsus* burdensome, from *onus* load] > 'onerously *adv* > 'onerousness *n*

oneself (wʌnˈsɛlf) *pron* **1 a** the reflexive form of **one** (senses 20, 21) **b** (intensifier): *one doesn't do that oneself* **2** (*preceded by a copula*) one's normal or usual self: *one doesn't feel oneself after such an experience*

one-sided *adj* **1** considering or favouring only one side of a matter, problem, etc **2** having all the advantage on one side **3** larger or more developed on one side **4** having, existing on, or occurring on one side only **5** another term for **unilateral 6** denoting a surface on which any two points can be joined without crossing an edge. See **Möbius strip.** > ˌone-'sidedly *adv* > ˌone-'sidedness *n*

one-size-fits-all *adj* relating to policies or approaches that are standard and not tailored to individual needs

one-step *n* **1** an early 20th-century ballroom dance with long quick steps, the precursor of the foxtrot **2** a piece of music composed for or in the rhythm of this dance

one-stop *adj* having or providing a range of related services or goods in one place: *a one-stop shop*

one-tailed *adj statistics* (of a significance test) concerned with the hypothesis that an observed value of a sampling statistic either significantly exceeds or falls significantly below a given value, where the error is relevant only in one direction: for instance, in testing whether scales are fair a customer does not regard overweight goods as a relevant error. Compare **two-tailed**

One Thousand Guineas *n* See **Thousand Guineas**

one-time *adj* **1** (*prenominal*) at some time in the past; former ▷ *adv* **2** *Caribbean informal* at once

one-to-one *adj* **1** (of two or more things) corresponding exactly **2** denoting a relationship or encounter in which someone is involved with only one other person: *one-to-one tuition* **3** *maths* characterized by or involving the pairing of each member of one set with only one member of another set, without remainder ▷ *n* **4** a conversation, encounter, or relationship between two people

one-track *adj* **1** *informal* obsessed with one idea, subject, etc **2** having or consisting of a single track

one-trick pony *n informal, chiefly US* a person or thing considered as being limited to only one single talent, capability, quality, etc

one-two *n* **1** *boxing* a jab with the leading hand followed by a cross with the other hand **2** *soccer* another term for **wall pass**

one-up *adj informal* having or having scored an advantage or lead over someone or something

one-upmanship (wʌnˈʌpmənʃɪp) *n informal* the art or practice of achieving or maintaining an advantage over others, often by slightly unscrupulous means

one-way *adj* **1** moving or allowing travel in one direction only: *one-way traffic* **2** entailing no reciprocal obligation, action, etc: *a one-way agreement*

one-way ticket *n* a ticket entitling a passenger to travel only to his destination, without returning. Also called (chiefly *Brit*): **single ticket**

ongaonga (ˌɒŋɡɑːˈɒŋɡɑː) *n* a New Zealand nettle, *Urtica ferox*, with a painful or even fatal sting [Māori]

on-glide *n phonetics* a glide immediately preceding a speech sound, for which the articulators are taking position. Compare **off-glide**

ongoing (ˈɒnɡəʊɪŋ) *adj* **1** actually in progress: *ongoing projects* **2** continually moving forward; developing **3** remaining in existence; continuing

ongoings (ˈɒnɡəʊɪŋz) *pl n* a Scot word for **goings-on**

onie (ˈəʊnɪ) *determiner Scot* a variant of **ony**

O

onion ('ʌnjən) *n* **1** an alliaceous plant, *Allium cepa*, having greenish-white flowers: cultivated for its rounded edible bulb **2** the bulb of this plant, consisting of concentric layers of white succulent leaf bases with a pungent odour and taste **3** any of several related plants similar to *A. cepa*, such as *A. fistulosum* (Welsh onion) **4** know one's onions *Brit slang* to be fully acquainted with a subject [c14 via Anglo-Norman from Old French *oignon*, from Latin *unio* onion, related to UNION] > 'oniony *adj*

onion dome *n* a bulb-shaped dome characteristic of Byzantine and Russian church architecture

onion fly *n* a small grey dipterous insect, *Delia antiqua*, that is a serious pest of onions. The larvae destroy the bulbs

onionskin ('ʌnjən,skɪn) *n* a glazed translucent paper

onion weed *n* a plant of Australia and New Zealand, *Nuthoscordum inodorum*, having a strong onion-like smell and reproducing from bulbs and seeds

Onitsha (ə'nɪtʃə) *n* a port in S Nigeria, in Anambra State on the Niger River: industrial centre. Pop: 565 000 (2005 est)

onium compound *or* **salt** ('əʊnɪəm) *n chem* any salt in which the positive ion (**onium ion**) is formed by the attachment of a proton to a neutral compound, as in ammonium, oxonium, and sulphonium compounds [c20 from (AMM)ONIUM]

on key *adj* (**on-key** *when prenominal*), *adv* **1** in the right key **2** in tune

on line *or* **online** ('ɒn,laɪn) *adj* (**on-line** *or* **online** *when prenominal*) **1** of, relating to, or concerned with a peripheral device that is directly connected to and controlled by the central processing unit of a computer **2** of or relating to the internet: *online shopping* **3** occurring as part of, or involving, a continuous sequence of operations, such as a production line ▷ Compare **off line**

onliner (ɒn'laɪnə) *n* a person who uses the internet regularly

onlooker ('ɒn,lʊkə) *n* a person who observes without taking part > 'on,looking *adj*

only ('əʊnlɪ) *adj* (*prenominal*) **1 the** being single or very few in number: *the only men left in town were too old to bear arms* **2** (of a child) having no siblings **3** unique by virtue of being superior to anything else; peerless **4 one and only a** (*adjective*) incomparable; unique **b** (*as noun*) the object of all one's love: *you are my one and only* ▷ *adv* **5** without anyone or anything else being included; alone: *you have one choice only; only a genius can do that* **6** merely or just: *it's only Henry* **7** no more or no greater than: *we met only an hour ago* **8** (intensifier): *she was only marvellous; it was only dreadful* **9** used in conditional clauses introduced by *if* to emphasize the impossibility of the condition ever being fulfilled: *if I had only known, this would never have happened* **10** not earlier than; not...until: *I only found out yesterday* **11** if only *or* if...only an expression used to introduce a wish, esp one felt to be unrealizable **12** only if never...except when **13** only too **a** (intensifier): *he was only too pleased to help* **b** most regrettably (esp in the phrase **only too true**) ▷ *sentence connector* **14** but; however: used to introduce an exception or condition: *play outside: only don't go into the street* [Old English *ānlīc*, from *ān* ONE + -*līc* -LY²]

USAGE In informal English, *only* is often used as a sentence connector: *I would have phoned you, only I didn't know your number*. This use should be avoided in formal writing: *I would have phoned you if I'd known your number*. In formal speech and writing, *only* is placed directly before the word or words that it modifies: *she could interview only three applicants in the morning*. In all but the most formal contexts, however, it is generally regarded as acceptable to put *only* before the verb: *she could only*

interview three applicants in the morning. Care must be taken not to create ambiguity, esp in written English, in which intonation will not, as it does in speech, help to show to which item in the sentence *only* applies. A sentence such as *she only drinks tea in the afternoon* is capable of two interpretations and is therefore better rephrased either as *she drinks only tea in the afternoon* (ie no other drink) or *she drinks tea only in the afternoon* (ie at no other time)

only-begotten *adj archaic* (of a child) being the only offspring of its father

on message *adj* (**on-message** *when prenominal*) adhering to or reflecting the official line of a political party, government, or other organization

o.n.o. (in advertisements in Britain, Australia, and New Zealand) *abbreviation for* or near(est) offer: £50 o.n.o.

on-off *adj* **1** (of an electrical switch, button, etc) having an 'on' position and an 'off' position **2** existing at times and not at others; discontinuous: *an on-off relationship*

onomasiology (,ɒnəʊ,meɪsɪ'ɒlədʒɪ) *n* **1** another name for **onomastics** (sense 1) **2** the branch of semantics concerned with the meanings of and meaning relations between individual words

onomastic (,ɒnə'mæstɪk) *adj* **1** of or relating to proper names **2** *law* denoting a signature in a different handwriting from that of the document to which it is attached [c17 from Greek *onomastikos*, from *onomazein* to name, from *onoma* NAME]

onomastics (,ɒnə'mæstɪks) *n* **1** (*functioning as singular*) the study of proper names, esp of their origins **2** (*functioning as singular or plural*) a systematization of the facts about how proper names are formed in a given language

onomatopoeia (,ɒnə,mætə'piːə) *n* **1** the formation of words whose sound is imitative of the sound of the noise or action designated, such as *hiss*, *buzz*, and *bang* **2** the use of such words for poetic or rhetorical effect [c16 via Late Latin from Greek *onoma* name + *poiein* to make] > ,ono,mato'poeic *or* onomatopoetic (,ɒnə,mætəpəʊ'ɛtɪk) *adj* > ,ono,mato'poeically *or* ,ono,matopo'etically *adv*

Onondaga (,ɒnən'dɑːgə) *n* **1 Lake** a salt lake in central New York State. Area: about 13 sq km (5 sq miles) **2** (*pl* -gas *or* -ga) a member of a North American Indian Iroquois people formerly living between Lake Champlain and the St Lawrence River **3** the language of this people, belonging to the Iroquoian family [from Iroquois *onōtáge'*, literally: on the top of the hill (the name of their principal village)]

Onondagan (,ɒnən'dɑːgən) *adj* of or relating to the Onondaga people or their language

on-ramp *n* **1** a ramp that provides access to the specified part of a road system: *an interstate highway on-ramp* **2** a method of accessing a service or facility: *an important on-ramp to the on-line world*

onrush ('ɒn,rʌʃ) *n* a forceful forward rush or flow

ONS (in Britain) *abbreviation for* Office for National Statistics

onset ('ɒn,sɛt) *n* **1** an attack; assault **2** a start; beginning

onshore ('ɒn'ʃɔː) *adj*, *adv* **1** towards the land: *an onshore gale* **2** on land; not at sea

onshoring ('ɒn,ʃɔːrɪŋ) *n* the practice of employing white-collar workers from abroad

onside (,ɒn'saɪd) *adj*, *adv* **1** *sport* (of a player) in a legal position, as when behind the ball or with a required number of opponents between oneself and the opposing team's goal line ▷ *adj* **2** taking one's part or side; working towards the same goal (esp in the phrase **get someone onside**). Compare **offside**

onslaught ('ɒn,slɔːt) *n* a violent attack [c17 from Middle Dutch *aenslag*, from *aan* ON + *slag* a blow, related to SLAY]

Ont. *abbreviation for* Ontario

Ontarian (ɒn'tɛərɪən) *or* **Ontarioan** (ɒn'tɛərɪ,əʊən) *n* **1** a native or inhabitant of Ontario ▷ *adj* **2** of or relating to Ontario or its inhabitants

Ontario (ɒn'tɛərɪəʊ) *n* **1** a province of central Canada: lies mostly on the Canadian Shield and contains the fertile plain of the lower Great Lakes and the St Lawrence River, one of the world's leading industrial areas; the second largest and the most populous province. Capital: Toronto. Pop: 12 392 721 (2004 est). Area: 891 198 sq km (344 092 sq miles). Abbreviations: **Ont.** *or* **ON 2 Lake** a lake between the US and Canada, bordering on New York State and Ontario province: the smallest of the Great Lakes; linked with Lake Erie by the Niagara River and Welland Canal; drained by the St Lawrence. Area: 19 684 sq km (7600 sq miles)

onto *or* **on to** ('ɒntʊ; *unstressed* 'ɒntə) *prep* **1** to a position that is on: *step onto the train as it passes* **2** having become aware of (something illicit or secret): *the police are onto us* **3** into contact with: *get onto the factory*

USAGE *Onto* is now generally accepted as a word in its own right. *On to* is still used, however, where *on* is considered to be part of the verb: *he moved on to a different town* as contrasted with *he jumped onto the stage*

onto- *combining form* existence or being: *ontogeny; ontology* [from Late Greek, from *ōn* (stem *ont-*) being, present participle of *einai* to be]

ontogeny (ɒn'tɒdʒənɪ) *or* **ontogenesis** (,ɒntə'dʒɛnɪsɪs) *n* the entire sequence of events involved in the development of an individual organism. Compare **phylogeny.** > ontogenic (,ɒntə'dʒɛnɪk) *or* ontogenetic (,ɒntədʒɪ'nɛtɪk) *adj* > ,onto'genically *or* ,ontoge'netically *adv*

ontological argument *n philosophy* **1** the traditional a priori argument for the existence of God on the grounds that the concept itself necessitates existence. Compare **cosmological argument, teleological argument 2** any analogous argument from the nature of some concept to the existence of whatever instantiates it

ontology (ɒn'tɒlədʒɪ) *n* **1** *philosophy* the branch of metaphysics that deals with the nature of being **2** *logic* the set of entities presupposed by a theory > ,onto'logical *adj* > ,onto'logically *adv*

onus ('əʊnəs) *n*, *pl* **onuses** a responsibility, task, or burden [c17 from Latin: burden]

onus probandi ('əʊnəs prəʊ'bændɪ) *n law* the Latin phrase for **burden of proof**

onward ('ɒnwəd) *adj* **1** directed or moving forwards, onwards, etc ▷ *adv* **2** a variant of **onwards**

onwards ('ɒnwədz) *or* **onward** ('ɒnwəd) *adv* at or towards a point or position ahead, in advance, etc

ony ('əʊnɪ) *determiner* a Scot word for **any**

onychia (,ɒnɪ'kɪə) *n vet science* inflammation of the nails or claws of animals

onychophoran (,ɒnɪ'kɒfərən) *n* any wormlike terrestrial invertebrate of the phylum *Onychophora*, having a segmented body, short unjointed limbs, and breathing by means of tracheae: intermediate in structure and evolutionary development between annelids and arthropods [from New Latin *Onychophora*, from Greek *onukh-* nail, claw + -PHORE]

-onym *n combining form* indicating a name or word: *acronym; pseudonym* [from Greek *-onumon*, from *onuma*, Doric variant of *onoma* name]

onymous ('ɒnɪməs) *adj* (of a book) bearing its author's name [c18 back formation from ANONYMOUS]

onyx ('ɒnɪks) *n* **1** a variety of chalcedony with alternating black and white parallel bands, used as a gemstone. Formula: SiO_2 **2** a compact variety of calcite used as an ornamental stone; onyx marble. Formula: $CaCO_3$ [c13 from Latin from

Greek: fingernail (so called from its veined appearance)]

ONZ *abbreviation for* Order of New Zealand (a NZ title)

oo- *or* **oö-** *combining form* egg or ovum: *oosperm* [from Greek *ōion* EGG¹]

oocyst ('əʊəˌsɪst) *n* an encysted zygote of sporozoan protozoans that undergoes sporogony to produce infective sporozoites

oocyte ('əʊəˌsaɪt) *n* an immature female germ cell that gives rise to an ovum after two meiotic divisions

oodles ('uːdᵊlz) *pl n informal* great quantities: *oodles of money* [c20 of uncertain origin]

oof (uːf) *n slang* money [c19 from Yiddish *ooftisch,* from German *auf dem Tische* on the table (referring to gambling stakes)] > **'oofy** *adj*

oogamy (əʊˈɒgəmɪ) *n* sexual reproduction involving a small motile male gamete and a large much less motile female gamete: occurs in all higher animals and some plants > **o'ogamous** *adj*

oogenesis (ˌəʊəˈdʒɛnɪsɪs) *n* the formation and maturation of ova from undifferentiated cells in the ovary. See also **oocyte.** > **oogenetic** (ˌəʊədʒɪˈnɛtɪk) *adj*

oogonium (ˌəʊəˈgəʊnɪəm) *n, pl* **-nia** (-nɪə) *or* **-niums 1** an immature female germ cell forming oocytes by repeated divisions **2** a female sex organ of some algae and fungi producing female gametes (oospheres) > **oo'gonial** *adj*

ooh (uː) *interj* an exclamation of surprise, pleasure, pain, etc

Ookpik ('uːkpɪk) *n trademark Canadian* a sealskin doll resembling an owl, first made in 1963 by an Inuit and used abroad as a symbol of Canadian handicrafts [from Inuktitut *ukpik* a snowy owl]

oolite ('əʊəˌlaɪt) *n* any sedimentary rock, esp limestone, consisting of tiny spherical concentric grains within a fine matrix [c18 from French from New Latin *oolitēs,* literally: egg stone; probably a translation of German *Rogenstein* roe stone] > **oolitic** (ˌəʊəˈlɪtɪk) *adj*

oolith ('əʊəˌlɪθ) *n* any of the tiny spherical grains of sedimentary rock of which oolite is composed

oology (əʊˈɒlədʒɪ) *n* the branch of ornithology concerned with the study of birds' eggs > **oological** (ˌəʊəˈlɒdʒɪkᵊl) *adj* > **o'ologist** *n*

oolong ('uːˌlɒŋ) *n* a kind of dark tea, grown in China, that is partly fermented before being dried [c19 from Chinese *wu lung,* from *wu* black + *lung* dragon]

oom ('uːəm) *n South African* a title of respect used to address an elderly man [Afrikaans: literally, uncle]

oomiak *or* **oomiac** ('uːmɪˌæk) *n* other words for **umiak**

oompah ('uːmˌpɑː) *n* a representation of the sound made by a deep brass instrument, esp in military band music

oomph (ʊmf) *n informal* **1** enthusiasm, vigour, or energy **2** sex appeal [c20 perhaps imitative of the bellow of a mating bull]

oomycete (ˌəʊəˈmaɪsiːt) *n* any organism of the phylum *Oomycota* (or *Oomycetes*), formerly classified as fungi but now usually included in the kingdom *Protoctista* or *Protista:* includes the water moulds and downy mildews

oont (ʊnt) *n Anglo-Indian dialect* a camel [c19 from Hindi *unt*]

oophorectomy (ˌəʊəfəˈrɛktəmɪ) *n, pl* **-mies** surgical removal of an ovary or ovarian tumour. Also called: **ovariectomy** Compare **ovariotomy** [c19 from New Latin *ōophoron* ovary, from Greek *ōion* egg + *phoros* bearing, + -ECTOMY]

oophoritis (ˌəʊəfəˈraɪtɪs) *n* inflammation of an ovary; ovaritis > **oophoritic** (ˌəʊəfəˈrɪtɪk) *adj*

oophyte ('əʊəˌfaɪt) *n* the gametophyte in mosses, liverworts, and ferns > **oophytic** (ˌəʊəˈfɪtɪk) *adj*

oops (ʊps, uːps) *interj* an exclamation of surprise or of apology as when someone drops something or makes a mistake

Oort cloud (ɔːt) *n* a mass of comets orbiting the sun far beyond the orbit of Pluto, whose existence was first proposed by Jan Hendrick Oort (1900–92) in 1950

oose (uːs) *n Scot dialect* dust; fluff [of unknown origin] > **'oosy** *adj*

oosperm ('əʊəˌspɜːm) *n* a fertilized ovum; zygote

oosphere ('əʊəˌsfɪə) *n* a large female gamete produced in the oogonia of algae and fungi

oospore ('əʊəˌspɔː) *n* a thick-walled sexual spore that develops from a fertilized oosphere in some algae and fungi > **oo'sporic** *or* **oo'sporous** *adj*

Oostende (oːstˈɛndə) *n* the Flemish name for **Ostend**

ootheca (ˌəʊəˈθiːkə) *n, pl* **-cae** (-siː) a capsule containing eggs that is produced by some insects and molluscs [c19 New Latin, from OO- + *thēkē* case] > **oo'thecal** *adj*

ootid ('əʊətɪd) *n zoology* an immature female gamete that develops into an ovum [c20 from OO- + (SPERMA)TID]

ooze¹ (uːz) *vb* **1** (*intr*) to flow or leak out slowly, as through pores or very small holes **2** to exude or emit (moisture, gas, etc) **3** (*tr*) to overflow with: *to ooze charm* **4** (*intr;* often foll by *away*) to disappear or escape gradually ▷ *n* **5** a slow flowing or leaking **6** an infusion of vegetable matter, such as sumach or oak bark, used in tanning [Old English *wōs* juice]

ooze² (uːz) *n* **1** a soft thin mud found at the bottom of lakes and rivers **2** a fine-grained calcareous or siliceous marine deposit consisting of the hard parts of planktonic organisms **3** muddy ground, esp of bogs [Old English *wāse* mud; related to Old French *wāse,* Old Norse *veisa*]

ooze leather *n* a very soft leather with a suedelike finish [c19 from OOZE¹ (sense 6)]

oozy¹ ('uːzɪ) *adj* **oozier, ooziest** moist or dripping

oozy² ('uːzɪ) *adj* **oozier, ooziest** of, resembling, or containing mud; slimy > **'oozily** *adv* > **'ooziness** *n*

OP *abbreviation for* **1** *military* observation post **2** Ordo Praedicatorum (the Dominicans) **3** organophosphate [(for sense 2) Latin: Order of Preachers]

op. *abbreviation for* **1** operation **2** opus **3** operator **4** operational

o.p. *or* **O.P.** *abbreviation for* out of print

opacity (əʊˈpæsɪtɪ) *n, pl* **-ties 1** the state or quality of being opaque **2** the degree to which something is opaque **3** an opaque object or substance **4** obscurity of meaning; unintelligibility **5** *physics, photog* the ratio of the intensity of light incident on a medium, such as a photographic film, to that transmitted through the medium **6** *logic, philosophy* the property of being an opaque context

opah ('əʊpə) *n* a large soft-finned deep-sea teleost fish, *Lampris regius* (or *luna*), of the Atlantic and Pacific Oceans and the Mediterranean Sea, having a deep, brilliantly coloured body: family *Lampridae.* Also called: **moonfish, kingfish** [c18 of West African origin]

opal ('əʊpᵊl) *n* an amorphous, usually iridescent, mineral that can be of almost any colour, found in igneous rocks and around hot springs. It is used as a gemstone. Composition: hydrated silica. Formula: $SiO_2.nH_2O$ [c16 from Latin *opalus,* from Greek *opallios,* from Sanskrit *upala* precious stone] > **'opal-ˌlike** *adj*

opalesce (ˌəʊpəˈlɛs) *vb* (*intr*) to exhibit a milky iridescence

opalescent (ˌəʊpəˈlɛsᵊnt) *adj* having or emitting an iridescence like that of an opal > **ˌopal'escence** *n*

opal glass *n* glass that is opalescent or white, made by the addition of fluorides

opaline ('əʊpəˌlaɪn) *adj* **1** opalescent ▷ *n* **2** an opaque or semiopaque whitish glass

opaque (əʊˈpeɪk) *adj* **1** not transmitting light; not transparent or translucent **2** not reflecting light; lacking lustre or shine; dull **3** not transmitting radiant energy, such as electromagnetic or corpuscular radiation, or sound **4** hard to understand; unintelligible **5** unintelligent; dense ▷ *n* **6** *photog* an opaque pigment used to block out particular areas on a negative ▷ *vb* **opaques, opaquing, opaqued** (*tr*) **7** to make opaque **8** *photog* to block out particular areas, such as blemishes, on (a negative), using an opaque [c15 from Latin *opācus* shady] > **o'paquely** *adv* > **o'paqueness** *n*

opaque context *n philosophy, logic* an expression in which the replacement of a term by another with the same reference may change the truth-value of the whole. *John believes that Cicero was a Roman* is opaque, since even though Cicero and Tully are the same person John may know that the given statement is true but not that Tully was a Roman. Compare **transparent context** See also **intensional, Electra paradox**

opaque projector *n US and Canadian* an optical device that projects an enlarged image of an opaque object, such as a printed page or photographic print, onto a screen by means of reflected light. Also called (in Britain and some other countries): **episcope**

op art (ɒp) *n* a style of abstract art chiefly concerned with the exploitation of optical effects such as the illusion of movement [c20 *op,* short for *optical*]

OPC *or* **opc** *abbreviation for* ordinary Portland cement

op. cit. (in textual annotations) *abbreviation for* opere citato [Latin: in the work cited]

ope (əʊp) *vb, adj* an archaic or poetic word for **open**

OPEC ('əʊˌpɛk) *n acronym for* Organization of Petroleum-Exporting Countries: an organization formed in 1961 to administer a common policy for the sale of petroleum. Its members are Algeria, Indonesia, Iran, Iraq, Kuwait, Libya, Nigeria, Qatar, Saudi Arabia, the United Arab Emirates, and Venezuela. Ecuador and Gabon were members but withdrew in 1992 and 1995 respectively

op-ed ('ɒpˌɛd) *n* **a** a page of a newspaper where varying opinions are expressed by columnists, commentators, etc **b** (*as modifier*): *an op-ed column in the New York Times* [c20 from *op(posite) ed(itorial page)*]

open ('əʊpᵊn) *adj* **1** not closed or barred: *the door is open* **2** affording free passage, access, view, etc; not blocked or obstructed: *the road is open for traffic* **3** not sealed, fastened, or wrapped: *an open package* **4** having the interior part accessible: *an open drawer* **5** extended, expanded, or unfolded: *an open newspaper; an open flower* **6** ready for business: *the shops are open* **7** able to be obtained; available: *the position advertised last week is no longer open* **8** unobstructed by buildings, trees, etc: *open countryside* **9** free to all to join, enter, use, visit, etc: *an open competition* **10** unengaged or unoccupied: *the doctor has an hour open for you to call* **11** See **open season 12** not decided or finalized: *an open question* **13** ready to entertain new ideas; not biased or prejudiced: *an open mind* **14** unreserved or candid: *she was very open in her description* **15** liberal or generous: *an open hand* **16** extended or eager to receive (esp in the phrase **with open arms**) **17** exposed to view; blatant: *open disregard of the law* **18** liable or susceptible: *you will leave yourself open to attack if you speak* **19** (of climate or seasons) free from frost; mild **20** free from navigational hazards, such as ice, sunken ships, etc: *open water* **21** *US* without legal restrictions or enforceable regulations, esp in relation to gambling, vice, etc: *an open town* **22** without barriers to prevent absconding: *an open prison* **23** having large or numerous spacing or apertures: *open ranks* **24** full of small openings or gaps; porous: *an open texture* **25** *printing* (of type matter) generously leaded or widely spaced **26** *music* **a** (of a violin or guitar string) not stopped with the finger **b** (of a pipe, such as an organ pipe) not closed at either end **c** (of a note) played on such a string or pipe **27** *commerce* **a** in operation; active: *an open account* **b** unrestricted; unlimited: *open credit; open insurance* *cover* **28** See **open cheque** **29** (of a return ticket) not specifying a date for travel **30** *sport* **a** (of a goal, court, etc) unguarded or relatively unprotected: *the forward missed an open goal* **b** (of a stance, esp in golf) characterized by the front of the body being turned forward **31** (of a wound) exposed to the air **32** (esp of the large intestine) free from obstruction **33** undefended and of no military significance: *an open city* **34** *phonetics* **a** denoting a vowel pronounced with the lips relatively wide apart **b** denoting a syllable that does not end in a consonant, as in *pa* **35** *chess* (of a file) having no pawns on it **36** *maths* (of a set) containing points whose neighbourhood consists of other points of the same set: *points inside a circle are an open set* **37** *computing* (of software or a computer system) designed to an internationally agreed standard in order to allow communication between computers, irrespective of size, maufacturer, etc ▷ *vb* **38** to move or cause to move from a closed or fastened position: *to open a window* **39** (when *intr*, foll by *on* or *onto*) to render, be, or become accessible or unobstructed: *to open a road; to open a parcel; the door opens into the hall* **40** (*intr*) to come into or appear in view: *the lake opened before us* **41** (*tr*) to puncture (a boil) so as to permit drainage **42** to extend or unfold or cause to extend or unfold: *to open a newspaper* **43** to disclose or uncover or be disclosed or uncovered: *to open one's heart* **44** to cause (the mind) to become receptive or (of the mind) to become receptive **45** to operate or cause to operate: *to open a shop* **46** (when *intr*, sometimes folly by *out*) to make or become less compact or dense in structure: *to open ranks* **47** to set or be set in action; start: *to open a discussion; to open the batting* **48** (*tr*) to arrange for (a bank account, savings account, etc) usually by making an initial deposit **49** to turn to a specified point in (a book, magazine, etc): *open at page one* **50** *law* to make the opening statement in (a case before a court of law) **51** (*intr*) *cards* to bet, bid, or lead first on a hand ▷ *n* **52** (often preceded by *the*) any wide or unobstructed space or expanse, esp of land or water **53** See **open air** **54** *sport* a competition which anyone may enter **55** bring (*or* come) into the open to make (or become) evident or public ▷ See also **open up** [Old English; related to Old French *open, epen*, Old Saxon *opan*, Old High German *offan*] > ˈopenable *adj* > ˈopenly *adv* > ˈopenness *n*

open air *n* **a** the place or space where the air is unenclosed; the outdoors **b** (*as modifier*): *an open-air concert*

open-and-shut *adj* easily decided or solved; obvious: *an open-and-shut case*

open book *n* a person or thing without secrecy or concealment that can be easily known or interpreted

Open Brethren *n* one of the two main divisions of the Plymouth Brethren that, in contrast to the Exclusive Brethren, permits contacts with members outside the sect

opencast mining (ˈəʊpˌnˌkɑːst) *n* Brit mining by excavating from the surface. Also called (esp US): **strip mining**, (Austral and NZ) **open-cut mining** [c18 from OPEN + archaic *cast* ditch or cutting]

open chain *n* a chain of atoms in a molecule that is not joined at its ends into the form of a ring

open cheque *n* an uncrossed cheque that can be cashed at the drawee bank

open circuit *n* an incomplete electrical circuit in which no current flows. Compare **closed circuit**

Open College *n* **the** (in Britain) a college of art founded in 1987 for mature students studying foundation courses in arts and crafts by television programmes, written materials, and tutorials

open court *n* a court or trial to which members of the public are freely admitted

open cut *n* *civil engineering* an excavation made in the open rather than in a tunnel. See **cut-and-cover**

open-cut mining *n* Austral and NZ mining by

excavating from the surface. Also called (esp Brit): **opencast mining**, (US and Canadian) **strip mining**

open day *n* an occasion on which an institution, such as a school, is open for inspection by the public. Also called: **at-home** US and Canadian name: **open house**

open door *n* **1** a policy or practice by which a nation grants opportunities for trade to all other nations equally **2** free and unrestricted admission ▷ *adj* **open-door** **3** open to all; accessible **4** (in industrial relations) designating a policy of management being prepared to talk to workers in the office at any time

open-ended *adj* **1** without definite limits, as of duration or amount: *an open-ended contract* **2** denoting a question, esp one on a questionnaire, that cannot be answered "yes", "no", or "don't know"

opener (ˈəʊpənə) *n* **1** an instrument used to open sealed containers such as tins or bottles: *a bottle opener* **2** a person who opens, esp the player who makes the first bid or play **3** the first or opening section or episode in a series **4** US the first song, act, etc, in a variety show **5** (*plural*) a start; beginning (esp in the phrase **for openers**)

open-eyed *adj* **1** with the eyes wide open, as in amazement **2** watchful; alert

open-faced *adj* **1** having an ingenuous expression **2** (of a watch) having no lid or cover other than the glass

open-field *adj* (*prenominal*) *medieval history* of or denoting the system in which an arable area was divided into unenclosed strips, esp cultivated by different tenants

open game *n* *chess* a relatively simple game involving open ranks and files, permitting tactical play, and usually following symmetrical development. Compare **closed game**

open-handed *adj* generous; liberal > ˌopenˈhandedly *adv* > ˌopenˈhandedness *n*

open-hearted *adj* **1** kindly and warm **2** disclosing intentions and thoughts clearly; candid > ˌopenˈheartedly *adv* > ˌopenˈheartedness *n*

open-hearth furnace *n* (esp formerly) a steel-making reverbatory furnace in which pig iron and scrap are contained in a shallow hearth and heated by producer gas

open-hearth process *n* a process for making steel using an open-hearth furnace

open-heart surgery *n* surgical repair of the heart during which the blood circulation is often maintained mechanically

open house *n* **1** US and Canadian an occasion on which an institution, such as a school, is open for inspection by the public. Also called (in Britain and certain other countries): **open day, at-home 2 keep open house** to be always ready to provide hospitality **3** US and NZ a house available for inspection by prospective buyers

opening (ˈəʊpənɪŋ) *n* **1** the act of making or becoming open **2** a vacant or unobstructed space, esp one that will serve as a passageway; gap **3** *chiefly US* a tract in a forest in which trees are scattered or absent **4** the first part or stage of something **5 a** the first performance of something, esp a theatrical production **b** (*as modifier*): *the opening night* **6** a specific or formal sequence of moves at the start of any of certain games, esp chess or draughts **7** an opportunity or chance, esp for employment or promotion in a business concern **8** *law* the preliminary statement made by counsel to the court or jury before adducing evidence in support of his case

opening time *n* Brit the time at which public houses can legally start selling alcoholic drinks

open-jaw *n* (*modifier*) relating to a ticket that allows a traveller to arrive in one place and depart from another

open learning *n* a system of further education on a flexible part-time basis

open letter *n* a letter, esp one of protest,

addressed to a person but also made public, as through the press

open market *n* **a** a market in which prices are determined by supply and demand, there are no barriers to entry, and trading is not restricted to a specific area **b** (*as modifier*): *open-market value*

open-market operations *pl n finance* the purchase and sale on the open market of government securities by the Bank of England for the purpose of regulating the supply of money and credit to the economy

open marriage *n* a marriage in which the partners are free to pursue their own social and sexual lives

open mike *n* **a** a session in a pub or club where members of the public are invited to perform comedy or to sing **b** (*as modifier*): *an open-mike slot for young hopefuls*

open-minded *adj* having a mind receptive to new ideas, arguments, etc; unprejudiced > ˌopenˈmindedly *adv* > ˌopenˈmindedness *n*

open-mouthed *adj* **1** having an open mouth, esp in surprise **2** greedy or ravenous **3** clamorous or vociferous

open order *n military* a formation that allows additional space between the ranks of a guard or inspected unit to allow the inspecting officer to pass

open-plan *adj* having no or few dividing walls between areas: *an open-plan office floor*

open policy *n* an insurance policy in which the amount payable in the event of a claim is settled after the loss or damage has occurred. Compare **valued policy**

open position *n commerce* a situation in which a dealer in commodities, securities, or currencies has either unsold stock or uncovered sales

open primary *n* US government a primary in which any registered voter may participate. Compare **closed primary**

open prison *n* a penal establishment in which the prisoners are trusted to serve their sentences and so do not need to be locked up, thus extending the range of work and occupation they can safely undertake

open punctuation *n* punctuation characterized by sparing use of stops, esp of the comma. Compare **close punctuation**

open question *n* **1** a matter which is undecided **2** a question that cannot be answered with a yes or no but requires a developed answer

open-reel *adj* another term for **reel-to-reel**

open sandwich *n* a slice of bread covered with a spread or filling but without a top

open season *n* **1** a specified period of time in the year when it is legal to hunt or kill game or fish protected at other times by law **2** (often foll by *on*) a time when criticism or mistreatment is common: *open season on women employees*

open secret *n* something that is supposed to be secret but is widely known

open sentence *n logic* an expression containing a free variable that can be replaced by a name to yield a sentence, as *x is wise*. Also called: **propositional function, sentential function**

open sesame *n* a very successful means of achieving a result [from the magical words used by Ali Baba in *The Arabian Nights' Entertainments* to open the door of the robbers' den]

open set *n maths* **1** a set which is not a closed set **2** an interval on the real line excluding its end points, as [0, 1], the set of reals between, but excluding, 0 and 1

open shop *n* an establishment in which persons are hired and employed irrespective of their membership or nonmembership of a trade union. Compare **closed shop, union shop**

open side *n rugby* **1 a** the side of the scrum on which the majority of the backs are ranged **b** (*as modifier*): *an open-side flanker* **2 openside** a flanker who plays on the open side of the scrum

open slather *n* See **slather** (sense 2)

open source *n* **a** intellectual property, esp computer source code, that is made freely available to the general public by its creators **b** (*as modifier*): *open source software*. Compare **closed source**

open system *n* *computing* an operating system that is not specific to a particular supplier, but conforms to more widely compatible standards

open texture *n* *philosophy* the failure of natural languages to determine future usage, particularly the ability of predicates to permit the construction of borderline cases

Open University *n* **the** (in Britain) a university founded in 1969 for mature students studying by television and radio lectures, correspondence courses, local counselling, and summer schools

open up *vb* (*adverb*) **1** (*intr*) to start firing a gun or guns **2** (*intr*) to speak freely or without restraint **3** (*intr*) *informal* (of a motor vehicle) to accelerate **4** (*tr*) to render accessible: *the motorway opened up the remoter areas* **5** to make or become more exciting or lively: *the game opened up after half-time*

open verdict *n* a finding by a coroner's jury of death without stating the cause

openwork (ˈəʊpᵊnˌwɜːk) *n* ornamental work, as of metal or embroidery, having a pattern of openings or holes

opera¹ (ˈɒpərə, ˈɒprə) *n* **1** an extended dramatic work in which music constitutes a dominating feature, either consisting of separate recitatives, arias, and choruses, or having a continuous musical structure **2** the branch of music or drama represented by such works **3** the score, libretto, etc, of an opera **4** a theatre where opera is performed [C17 via Italian from Latin: work, a work, plural of *opus* work]

opera² (ˈɒpərə) *n* a plural of **opus**

operable (ˈɒpərəbᵊl, ˈɒprə-) *adj* **1** capable of being treated by a surgical operation **2** capable of being operated **3** capable of being put into practice > ˌoperaˈbility *n* > ˈoperably *adv*

opéra bouffe (ˈɒpərə ˈbuːf; *French* ɔpera buf) *n, pl* **opéras bouffes** (*French* ɔpera buf) a type of light or satirical opera common in France during the 19th century [from French: comic opera]

opera buffa (ˈbuːfə; *Italian* ˈɔpera ˈbuffa) *n, pl* **opera buffas** *or* **opere buffe** (*Italian* ˈɔpere ˈbuffe) comic opera, esp that originating in Italy during the 18th century [from Italian: comic opera]

opera cloak *n* a large cloak worn over evening clothes. Also called: **opera hood**

opéra comique (kɒˈmiːk; *French* ɔpera kɔmik) *n, pl* **opéras comiques** (*French* ɔpera kɔmik) a type of opera, not necessarily comic, current in France during the 19th century and characterized by spoken dialogue. It originated in satirical parodies of grand opera

opera glasses *pl n* small low-powered binoculars used by audiences in theatres and opera houses

opera hat *n* a collapsible top hat operated by a spring. Also called: **gibus**

opera house *n* a theatre designed for opera

operand (ˈɒpəˌrænd) *n* a quantity or function upon which a mathematical or logical operation is performed [C19 from Latin *operandum* (something) to be worked upon, from *operārī* to work]

operant (ˈɒpərənt) *adj* **1** producing effects; operating ▷ *n* **2** a person or thing that operates **3** *psychol* any response by an organism that is not directly caused by a stimulus

operant learning *n* *psychol* another name for **instrumental learning**

opera seria (ˈsɪərɪə; *Italian* ˈɔpera ˈsɛːrja) *n, pl* **opere serie** (*Italian* ˈɔpere ˈsɛːrje) a type of opera current in 18th-century Italy based on a serious plot, esp a mythological tale [from Italian: serious opera]

operate (ˈɒpəˌreɪt) *vb* **1** to function or cause to function **2** (*tr*) to control the functioning of: *operate a machine* **3** to manage, direct, run, or pursue (a business, system, etc) **4** (*intr*) to perform a surgical operation (upon a person or animal) **5** (*intr*) to produce a desired or intended effect **6** (*tr; usually foll by on*) to treat or process in a particular or specific way **7** (*intr*) to conduct military or naval operations **8** (*intr*) to deal in securities on a stock exchange [C17 from Latin *operārī* to work]

operatic (ˌɒpəˈrætɪk) *adj* **1** of or relating to opera **2** histrionic or exaggerated > ˌoperˈatically *adv*

operating budget *n* *accounting* a forecast of the sales revenue, production costs, overheads, cash flow, etc, of an organization, used to monitor its trading activities, usually for one year

operating system *n* the set of software that controls the overall operation of a computer system, typically by performing such tasks as memory allocation, job scheduling, and input/output control

operating table *n* the table on which the patient lies during a surgical operation

operating theatre *n* a room in which surgical operations are performed

operation (ˌɒpəˈreɪʃən) *n* **1** the act, process, or manner of operating **2** the state of being in effect, in action, or operative (esp in the phrases **in** *or* **into operation**) **3** a process, method, or series of acts, esp of a practical or mechanical nature **4** *surgery* any manipulation of the body or one of its organs or parts to repair damage, arrest the progress of a disease, remove foreign matter, etc **5 a** a military or naval action, such as a campaign, manoeuvre, etc **b** (*capital and prenominal when part of a name*) *Operation Crossbow* **6** *maths* **a** any procedure, such as addition, multiplication, involution, or differentiation, in which one or more numbers or quantities are operated upon according to specific rules **b** a function from a set onto itself **7** a commercial or financial transaction

operational (ˌɒpəˈreɪʃənᵊl) *adj* **1** of or relating to an operation or operations **2** in working order and ready for use **3** *military* capable of, needed in, or actually involved in operations > ˌoperˈationally *adv*

operational amplifier *n* a high-gain direct-coupled amplifier, the response of which may be controlled by negative-feedback circuits externally connected

operationalism (ˌɒpəˈreɪʃənəˌlɪzəm) *or* **operationism** (ˌɒpəˈreɪʃəˌnɪzəm) *n* *philosophy* the theory that scientific terms are defined by the experimental operations which determine their applicability > ˌoperˌationalˈistic *adj*

Operation Barbarossa *n* the codename for Hitler's invasion (1941) of Russia

Operation Desert Storm *n* the codename for the US-led UN operation to liberate Kuwait from Iraq (1991)

Operation Overlord *n* the codename for the Allied invasion (June 1944) of northern France

Operation Sealion *n* the codename for Hitler's proposed invasion (1940) of Great Britain

operations research *n* the analysis of problems in business and industry involving the construction of models and the application of linear programming, critical path analysis, and other quantitative techniques. Also: **operational research**

operations room *n* a room from which all the operations of a military, police, or other disciplined activity are controlled

operative (ˈɒpərətɪv) *adj* **1** in force, effect, or operation **2** exerting force or influence **3** producing a desired effect; significant: *the operative word* **4** of or relating to a surgical procedure ▷ *n* **5** a worker, esp one with a special skill **6** *US* a private detective > ˈoperatively *adv* > ˈoperativeness *or* ˌoperaˈtivity *n*

operatize *or* **operatise** (ˈɒpərəˌtaɪz) *vb* (*tr*) to turn (a play, novel, etc) into an opera

operator (ˈɒpəˌreɪtə) *n* **1** a person who operates a machine, instrument, etc, esp, a person who makes connections on a telephone switchboard or at an exchange **2** a person who owns or operates an industrial or commercial establishment **3** a speculator, esp one who operates on currency or stock markets **4** *informal* a person who manipulates affairs and other people **5** *maths* any symbol, term, letter, etc, used to indicate or express a specific operation or process, such as Δ (the differential operator)

operculum (əʊˈpɜːkjʊləm) *n, pl* **-la** (-lə) *or* **-lums** **1** *zoology* **a** the hard bony flap covering the gill slits in fishes **b** the bony plate in certain gastropods covering the opening of the shell when the body is withdrawn **2** *botany* the covering of the spore-bearing capsule of a moss **3** *biology* any other covering or lid in various organisms [C18 via New Latin from Latin: lid, from *operīre* to cover] > oˈpercular *or* operculate (əʊˈpɜːkjʊlɪt, -ˌleɪt) *adj*

operetta (ˌɒpəˈrɛtə) *n* a type of comic or light-hearted opera [C18 from Italian: a small OPERA¹] > ˌoperˈettist *n*

operon (ˈɒpəˌrɒn) *n* *genetics* a group of adjacent genes in bacteria functioning as a unit, consisting of structural genes and an **operator** [C20 from OPERATE]

operose (ˈɒpəˌrəʊs) *adj* *rare* **1** laborious **2** industrious; busy [C17 from Latin *operōsus* painstaking, from *opus* work] > ˈoperˌosely *adv* > ˈoperˌoseness *n*

opgefok (ˈɒpgəˌfɒk) *adj* *South African taboo slang* damaged; bungled [Afrikaans]

ophicleide (ˈɒfɪˌklaɪd) *n* *music* an obsolete keyed wind instrument of bass pitch [C19 from French *ophiclēide*, from Greek *ophis* snake + *kleis* key]

ophidian (əʊˈfɪdɪən) *adj* **1** snakelike **2** of, relating to, or belonging to the *Ophidia*, a suborder of reptiles that comprises the snakes ▷ *n* **3** any reptile of the suborder *Ophidia*; a snake [C19 from New Latin *Ophidia* name of suborder, from Greek *ophidion*, from *ophis* snake]

ophiology (ˌɒfɪˈɒlədʒɪ) *n* the branch of zoology that is concerned with the study of snakes [C19 from Greek *ophis* snake + -LOGY] > **ophiological** (ˌɒfɪəˈlɒdʒɪkᵊl) *adj* > ˌophiˈologist *n*

Ophir (ˈəʊfə) *n* *Bible* a region, probably situated on the SW coast of Arabia on the Red Sea, renowned, esp in King Solomon's reign, for its gold and precious stones (I Kings 9:28; 10:10)

ophite (ˈəʊfaɪt) *n* any of several greenish mottled rocks with ophitic texture, such as dolerite and diabase [C17 from Latin *ophītēs*, from Greek, from *ophis* snake: because the mottled appearance resembles the markings of a snake]

ophitic (əʊˈfɪtɪk) *adj* (of the texture of rocks such as dolerite) having small elongated unorientated feldspar crystals enclosed within pyroxene grains

Ophiuchus (ɒˈfjuːkəs) *n, Latin genitive* **Ophiuchi** (ɒˈfjuːkaɪ) a large constellation lying on the celestial equator between Hercules and Scorpius and containing the dark nebula, **Ophiuchus Nebula** [C17 via Latin from Greek *Ophioukhos*, from *ophis* snake + *ekhein* to hold]

ophthalmia (ɒfˈθælmɪə) *n* inflammation of the eye, often including the conjunctiva [C16 via Late Latin from Greek, from *ophthalmos* eye; see OPTIC]

ophthalmic (ɒfˈθælmɪk) *adj* of or relating to the eye

ophthalmic optician *n* See **optician**

ophthalmitis (ˌɒfθælˈmaɪtɪs) *n* inflammation of the eye

ophthalmo- *or before a vowel* **ophthalm-** *combining form* indicating the eye or the eyeball: *ophthalmoscope* [from Greek *ophthalmos* EYE¹]

ophthalmol. *or* **ophthal.** *abbreviation for* ophthalmology

ophthalmologist (ˌɒfθælˈmɒlədʒɪst) *n* a medical practitioner specializing in the diagnosis and treatment of eye diseases

ophthalmology (ˌɒfθælˈmɒlədʒɪ) *n* the branch of medicine concerned with the eye and its diseases > **ophthalmological** (ɒfˌθælməˈlɒdʒɪkᵊl) *adj*

ophthalmoscope (ɒfˈθælməˌskəʊp) *n* an instrument for examining the interior of the eye

O

> ophthalmoscopic (ˌɒfˌθælməˈskɒpɪk) adj

ophthalmoscopy (ˌɒfθælˈmɒskəpɪ) n examination of the interior of the eye with an ophthalmoscope

-opia n combining form indicating a visual defect or condition: myopia [from Greek, from ōps eye] > **-opic** adj combining form

opiate n (ˈəʊpɪɪt) **1** any of various narcotic drugs, such as morphine and heroin, that act on opioid receptors **2** any other narcotic or sedative drug **3** something that soothes, deadens, or induces sleep ▷ adj (ˈəʊpɪɪt) **4** containing or consisting of opium **5** inducing relaxation; soporific ▷ vb (ˈəʊpɪˌeɪt) rare **6** to treat with an opiate **7** rare to dull or deaden [c16 from Medieval Latin opiātus; from Latin opium poppy juice, OPIUM]

opine (əʊˈpaɪn) vb (when tr, usually takes a clause as object) to hold or express an opinion: he opined that it was all a sad mistake [c16 from Latin opinārī]

opinion (əˈpɪnjən) n **1** judgment or belief not founded on certainty or proof **2** the prevailing or popular feeling or view: public opinion **3** evaluation, impression, or estimation of the value or worth of a person or thing **4** an evaluation or judgment given by an expert: a medical opinion **5** the advice given by a barrister or counsel on a case submitted to him or her for a view on the legal points involved **6 a matter of opinion** a point open to question **7 be of the opinion (that)** to believe (that) [c13 via Old French from Latin opīniō belief, from opīnārī to think; see OPINE]

opinionated (əˈpɪnjəˌneɪtɪd) adj holding obstinately and unreasonably to one's own opinions; dogmatic > oˈpinionˌatedly adv > oˈpinionˌatedness n

opinionative (əˈpɪnjənətɪv) adj rare **1** of or relating to opinion **2** another word for **opinionated**. > oˈpinionatively adv > oˈpinionativeness n

opinion poll n another term for a **poll** (sense 3)

opioid (ˈəʊpɪˌɔɪd) n **a** any of a group of substances that resemble morphine in their physiological or pharmacological effects, esp in their pain-relieving properties **b** (modifier) of or relating to such substances: opioid receptor; opioid analgesic

opisthobranch (əˈpɪsθəˌbræŋk) n any marine gastropod of the class Opisthobranchia (or Opisthobranchiata), in which the shell is reduced or absent: includes the pteropods, sea hares, and nudibranchs [via New Latin from Greek opisthen behind + -BRANCH]

opisthognathous (ˌɒpɪsˈθɒgnəθəs) adj (of a person or animal) having receding jaws [c19 from Greek opisthen behind + -GNATHOUS] > ˌopisˈthognathism n

opisthosoma (ˌɒpɪsθəˈsəʊmə) n zoology the abdomen of a spider or other arachnid [c19 from Greek opisthen behind + SOMA¹]

opium (ˈəʊpɪəm) n **1** the dried juice extracted from the unripe seed capsules of the opium poppy that contains alkaloids such as morphine and codeine: used in medicine as an analgesic **2** something having a tranquillizing or stupefying effect [c14 from Latin: poppy juice, from Greek opion, diminutive of opos juice of a plant]

opium den n a place where opium is sold and used

opiumism (ˈəʊpɪəˌmɪzəm) n pathol addiction to opium or a condition resulting from prolonged use of opium

opium poppy n a poppy, Papaver somniferum, of SW Asia, with greyish-green leaves and typically white or reddish flowers: widely cultivated as a source of opium

Opium Wars pl n two wars (1839–42; 1856–60) between China and Britain resulting from the Chinese refusal to allow the importation of opium from India. China ceded Hong Kong after the British victory in 1842. The British and French victory in the second war established free trade in Chinese ports and the legalization of the opium trade

Oporto (əˈpɔːtəʊ) n a port in NW Portugal, near the mouth of the Douro River: the second largest city in Portugal, famous for port wine (begun in 1678). Pop: 263 131 (2001). Portuguese name: **Porto**

opossum (əˈpɒsəm) n, pl **-sums** or **-sum** **1** any thick-furred marsupial, esp Didelphis marsupialis (**common opossum**), of the family Didelphidae of S North, Central, and South America, having an elongated snout and a hairless prehensile tail. Sometimes (informal) shortened to: **possum 2** Also called (Austral and NZ): **possum** any of various similar animals, esp the phalanger, Trichosurus vulpecula, of the New Zealand bush [c17 from Algonquian aposoum; related to Delaware apässum, literally: white beast]

opossum block n (in New Zealand) a block of bush allocated to a licensed opossum trapper

opossum shrimp n any of various shrimplike crustaceans of the genera Mysis, Praunus, etc, of the order Mysidacea, in which the females carry the eggs and young around in a ventral brood pouch

oppidan (ˈɒpɪdən) rare ▷ adj **1** of a town; urban ▷ n **2** a person living in a town [c16 from Latin oppidānus, from oppidum town]

oppilate (ˈɒpɪˌleɪt) vb (tr) pathol obsolete to block (the pores, bowels, etc) [c16 from Latin oppilāre, from ob- against + pīlāre to pack closely] > ˌoppiˈlation n

opponent (əˈpəʊnənt) n **1** a person who opposes another in a contest, battle, etc **2** anatomy an opponent muscle ▷ adj **3** opposite, as in position **4** anatomy (of a muscle) bringing two parts into opposition **5** opposing; contrary [c16 from Latin oppōnere to oppose, from ob- against + pōnere to place] > opˈponency n

opportune (ˈɒpəˌtjuːn) adj **1** occurring at a time that is suitable or advantageous **2** fit or suitable for a particular purpose or occurrence [c15 via Old French from Latin opportūnus, from ob- to + portus harbour (originally: coming to the harbour, obtaining timely protection)] > ˈopporˌtunely adv > ˈopporˌtuneness n

opportunist (ˌɒpəˈtjuːnɪst) n **1** a person who adapts his actions, responses, etc, to take advantage of opportunities, circumstances, etc ▷ adj **2** taking advantage of opportunities and circumstances in this way > opporˈtunism n

opportunistic (ˌɒpətjʊˈnɪstɪk) adj **1** of or characterized by opportunism **2** med (of an infection) caused by any microorganism that is harmless to a healthy person but debilitates a person whose immune system has been weakened by disease or drug treatment > ˌopportuˈnistically adv

opportunity (ˌɒpəˈtjuːnɪtɪ) n, pl **-ties 1** a favourable, appropriate, or advantageous combination of circumstances **2** a chance or prospect

opportunity cost n economics the benefit that could have been gained from an alternative use of the same resource

opportunity shop n Austral and NZ a shop selling second-hand goods for charitable funds. Also called: **op-shop**

opposable (əˈpəʊzəbəl) adj **1** capable of being opposed **2** Also: **apposable** (of the thumb of primates, esp man) capable of being moved into a position facing the other digits so as to be able to touch the ends of each **3** capable of being placed opposite something else > opˈposaˌbility n

oppose (əˈpəʊz) vb **1** (tr) to fight against, counter, or resist strongly **2** (tr) to be hostile or antagonistic to; be against **3** (tr) to place or set in opposition; contrast or counterbalance **4** (tr) to place opposite or facing **5** (intr) to be or act in opposition [c14 via Old French from Latin oppōnere, from ob- against + pōnere to place] > opˈposer n > opˈposing adj > opˈposingly adv > oppositive (əˈpɒzɪtɪv) adj

opposed-cylinder adj (of an internal-combustion engine) having cylinders on opposite sides of the crankcase in the same plane

opposite (ˈɒpəzɪt, -sɪt) adj **1** situated or being on the other side or at each side of something between: their houses were at opposite ends of the street **2** facing or going in contrary directions: opposite ways **3** diametrically different in character, tendency, belief, etc: opposite views **4** botany **a** (of leaves, flowers, etc) arranged in pairs on either side of the stem **b** (of parts of a flower) arranged opposite the middle of another part **5** maths **a** (of two vertices or sides in an even-sided polygon) separated by the same number of vertices or sides in both a clockwise and anticlockwise direction **b** (of a side in a triangle) facing a specified angle. Abbreviation: **opp** ▷ n **6** a person or thing that is opposite; antithesis **7** maths the side facing a specified angle in a right-angled triangle **8** a rare word for **opponent** ▷ prep **9** Also: **opposite to** facing; corresponding to (something on the other side of a division): the house opposite ours **10** as a co-star with: she played opposite Olivier in "Hamlet" ▷ adv **11** on opposite sides: she lives opposite > ˈoppositely adv > ˈoppositeness n

opposite number n a person holding an equivalent and corresponding position on another side or situation

opposite prompt n theatre another name for **stage right** See **prompt**

opposite sex n the women in relation to men or men in relation to women

opposition (ˌɒpəˈzɪʃən) n **1** the act of opposing or the state of being opposed **2** hostility, unfriendliness, or antagonism **3** a person or group antagonistic or opposite in aims to another **4 a** (usually preceded by the) a political party or group opposed to the ruling party or government **b** (capital as part of a name, esp in Britain and other Commonwealth countries): Her Majesty's Loyal Opposition **c in opposition** (of a political party) opposing the government **5** a position facing or opposite another **6** the act of placing something facing or opposite something else **7** something that acts as an obstacle to some course or progress **8** astronomy **a** the position of an outer planet or the moon when it is in line or nearly in line with the earth as seen from the sun and is approximately at its nearest to the earth **b** the position of two celestial bodies when they appear to be diametrically opposite each other on the celestial sphere. Compare **conjunction** (sense 4) **9** astrology an exact aspect of 180° between two planets, etc, an orb of 8° being allowed. Compare **conjunction** (sense 5), **square** (sense 10), **trine** (sense 1) **10** logic **a** the relation between propositions having the same subject and predicate but differing in quality, quantity, or both, as with all men are wicked; no men are wicked; some men are not wicked **b square of opposition** a diagram representing these relations with the contradictory propositions at diagonally opposite corners **11 the opposition** chess a relative position of the kings in the endgame such that the player who has the move is at a disadvantage: his opponent has the opposition > ˌoppoˈsitional adj > ˌoppoˈsitionist n > ˌoppoˈsitionless adj

oppress (əˈprɛs) vb (tr) **1** to subjugate by cruelty, force, etc **2** to afflict or torment **3** to lie heavy on (the mind, imagination, etc) **4** an obsolete word for **overwhelm** [c14 via Old French from Medieval Latin oppressāre, from Latin opprimere, from ob- against + premere to press] > opˈpressingly adv > opˈpressor n

oppression (əˈprɛʃən) n **1** the act of subjugating by cruelty, force, etc or the state of being subjugated in this way **2** the condition of being afflicted or tormented **3** the condition of having something lying heavily on one's mind, imagination, etc

oppressive (əˈprɛsɪv) adj **1** cruel, harsh, or tyrannical **2** heavy, constricting, or depressing > opˈpressively adv > opˈpressiveness n

opprobrious (əˈprəʊbrɪəs) adj **1** expressing scorn,

disgrace, or contempt **2** shameful or infamous > op'probriously *adv* > op'probriousness *n*

opprobrium (əˈprəʊbrɪəm) *n* **1** the state of being abused or scornfully criticized **2** reproach or censure **3** a cause of disgrace or ignominy [c17 from Latin *ob-* against + *probrum* a shameful act]

oppugn (əˈpjuːn) *vb* (*tr*) to call into question; dispute [c15 from Latin *oppugnāre*, from *ob-* against + *pugnāre* to fight, from *pugnus* clenched fist; see PUGNACIOUS] > op'pugner *n*

oppugnant (əˈpʌgnənt) *adj rare* combative, antagonistic, or contrary > op'pugnancy *n* > op'pugnantly *adv*

OPRA (ˈɒprə) *n* (in Britain) *acronym for* Occupational Pensions Regulatory Authority

Ops (ɒps) *n* the Roman goddess of abundance and fertility, wife of Saturn. Greek counterpart: Rhea

ops. *abbreviation for* operations

op-shop *n Austral and NZ informal* short for **opportunity shop**

opsimath (ˈɒpsɪˌmæθ) *n* a person who learns late in life [c19 from Greek *opsimathēs*, from *opse* late + *math-* learn] > opsimathy (ɒpˈsɪməθɪ) *n*

opsin (ˈɒpsɪn) *n* the protein that together with retinene makes up the purple visual pigment rhodopsin [c20 back formation from RHODOPSIN]

-opsis *n combining form* indicating a specified appearance or resemblance: *coreopsis* [from Greek *opsis* sight]

opsonic index *n* the ratio of the number of bacteria destroyed by phagocytes in the blood of a test patient to the number destroyed in the blood of a normal individual

opsonin (ˈɒpsənɪn) *n* a constituent of blood serum that renders invading bacteria more susceptible to ingestion by phagocytes in the serum [c20 from Greek *opsōnion* victuals] > opsonic (ɒpˈsɒnɪk) *adj*

opsonize, opsonise (ˈɒpsəˌnaɪz) *or* **opsonify** (ɒpˈsɒnɪˌfaɪ) *vb* (*tr*) to subject (bacteria) to the action of opsonins > ˌopsoniˈzation, ˌopsoniˈsation *or* opˌsoniˈfication *n*

opt (ɒpt) *vb* (when *intr*, foll by *for*) to show preference (for) or choose (to do something). See also **opt out** [c19 from French *opter*, from Latin *optāre* to choose]

optative (ˈɒptətɪv) *adj* **1** indicating or expressing choice, preference, or wish **2** *grammar* denoting a mood of verbs in Greek, Sanskrit, etc, expressing a wish ▷ *n* **3** *grammar* **a** the optative mood **b** a verb in this mood [c16 via French *optatif*, from Late Latin *optātīvus*, from Latin *optāre* to desire]

optic (ˈɒptɪk) *adj* **1** of or relating to the eye or vision **2** a less common word for **optical** ▷ *n* **3** an informal word for **eye¹** [c16 from Medieval Latin *opticus*, from Greek *optikos*, from *optos* visible; related to *ōps* eye]

Optic (ˈɒptɪk) *n trademark Brit* a device attached to an inverted bottle for dispensing measured quantities of liquid, such as whisky, gin, etc

optical (ˈɒptɪkəl) *adj* **1** of, relating to, producing, or involving light **2** of or relating to the eye or to the sense of sight; optic **3** (esp of a lens) aiding vision or correcting a visual disorder > 'optically *adv*

optical activity *n* the ability of substances that are optical isomers to rotate the plane of polarization of a transmitted beam of plane-polarized light

optical bench *n* an apparatus fitted for experimentation in optics, typically consisting of a table and an adjustable arrangement of light source, lenses, prisms, etc

optical character reader *n* a computer peripheral device enabling letters, numbers, or other characters usually printed on paper to be optically scanned and input to a storage device, such as magnetic tape. The device uses the process of **optical character recognition**. Abbreviation (for both *reader* and *recognition*): OCR

optical crown *n* an optical glass of low dispersion and relatively low refractive index. It is

used in the construction of lenses

optical density *n physics* the former name for **reflection density** or **transmission density**

optical disc *n computing* an inflexible disc on which information is stored in digital form by laser technology. Also called: **video disc**

optical double star *n* two stars that appear close together when viewed through a telescope but are not physically associated and are often separated by a great distance. Compare **binary star**

optical fibre *n* a communications cable consisting of a thin glass fibre in a protective sheath. Light transmitted along the fibre may be modulated with vision, sound, or data signals. See also **fibre optics**

optical flint *n* an optical glass of high dispersion and high refractive index containing lead oxide. They are used in the manufacture of lenses, artificial gems, and cut glass. Also called: **flint glass**

optical glass *n* any of several types of clear homogeneous glass of known refractive index used in the construction of lenses, etc. See **optical flint, optical crown**

optical illusion *n* **1** an object causing a false visual impression **2** an instance of deception by such an object

optical isomerism *n* isomerism of chemical compounds in which the two isomers differ only in that their molecules are mirror images of each other. See also **dextrorotation, laevorotatory, racemize**. > **optical isomer** *n*

optical mark reading *n* the reading of marks by an optical device whereby the information can be stored in machine-readable form

optical mouse *n computing* a type of computer mouse that uses light-emitting and -sensing devices to detect where it is

optical pyrometer *n* See **pyrometer**

optical rotation *n* the angle through which plane-polarized light is rotated in its passage through a substance exhibiting optical activity

optical scanner *n* a computer peripheral device enabling printed material, including characters and diagrams, to be scanned and converted into a form that can be stored in a computer. See also **optical character reader**

optical sound *n* sound recorded in the form of a photographic image on cinematograph films

optic axis *n* the direction in a uniaxial crystal or one of the two directions in a biaxial crystal along which a ray of unpolarized light may pass without undergoing double refraction

optic disc *n* a small oval-shaped area on the retina marking the site of entrance into the eyeball of the optic nerve. See **blind spot** (sense 1)

optician (ɒpˈtɪʃən) *n* **a** Also called: optometrist a general name used to refer to **ophthalmic optician**, a person qualified to examine the eyes and prescribe and supply spectacles and contact lenses **b** a general name used to refer to **dispensing optician**, a person who supplies and fits spectacle frames but is not qualified to prescribe lenses ▷ Compare **ophthalmologist**

optic nerve *n* the second cranial nerve, which provides a sensory pathway from the retina to the brain

optics (ˈɒptɪks) *n* (*functioning as singular*) the branch of science concerned with vision and the generation, nature, propagation, and behaviour of electromagnetic light

optic thalamus *n anatomy* an older term for **thalamus** (senses 1, 2)

optimal (ˈɒptɪməl) *adj* another word for **optimum** (sense 2) > ˌopti'mality *n* > 'optimally *adv*

optimism (ˈɒptɪˌmɪzəm) *n* **1** the tendency to expect the best and see the best in all things **2** hopefulness; confidence **3** the doctrine of the ultimate triumph of good over evil **4** the philosophical doctrine that this is the best of all possible worlds ▷ Compare **pessimism** [c18 from French *optimisme*, from Latin *optimus* best,

superlative of *bonus* good] > 'optimist *n* > ˌopti'mistic *or* ˌopti'mistical *adj* > ˌopti'mistically *adv*

optimize *or* **optimise** (ˈɒptɪˌmaɪz) *vb* **1** (*tr*) to take the full advantage of **2** (*tr*) to plan or carry out (an economic activity) with maximum efficiency **3** (*intr*) to be optimistic **4** (*tr*) to write or modify (a computer program) to achieve maximum efficiency in storage capacity, time, cost, etc **5** (*tr*) to find the best compromise among several often conflicting requirements, as in engineering design > ˌopti'zation *or* ˌopti'sation *n*

optimum (ˈɒptɪməm) *n*, *pl* -ma (-mə) *or* -mums **1** a condition, degree, amount or compromise that produces the best possible result ▷ *adj* **2** most favourable or advantageous; best: *optimum conditions* [c19 from Latin: the best (thing), from *optimus* best; see OPTIMISM]

optimum population *n economics* a population that is sufficiently large to provide an adequate workforce with minimal unemployment

option (ˈɒpʃən) *n* **1** the act or an instance of choosing or deciding **2** the power or liberty to choose **3** an exclusive opportunity, usually for a limited period, to buy something at a future date: *he has a six-month option on the Canadian rights to this book* **4** *commerce* the right to buy (**call option**) or sell (**put option**) a fixed quantity of a commodity, security, foreign exchange, etc, at a fixed price at a specified date in the future. See also **traded option** **5** something chosen; choice **6** NZ short for **local option** **7** keep (or leave) one's options open not to commit oneself **8** See **soft option** ▷ *vb* **9** (*tr*) to obtain or grant an option on [c17 from Latin *optiō* free choice, from *optāre* to choose]

optional (ˈɒpʃənəl) *adj* possible but not compulsory; left to personal choice > 'optionally *adv*

option money *n commerce* the price paid for buying an option

optoelectronics (ˌɒptəʊɪlɛkˈtrɒnɪks) *n* (*functioning as singular*) the study or use of devices in which an optical input produces an electrical output, or in which electrical stimulation produces visible or infrared output > ˌoptoelec'tronic *adj*

optometer (ɒpˈtɒmɪtə) *n* any of various instruments for measuring the refractive power of the eye

optometrist (ɒpˈtɒmɪtrɪst) *n* a person who is qualified to examine the eyes and prescribe and supply spectacles and contact lenses. Also called (esp Brit): ophthalmic optician Compare **optician, ophthalmologist**

optometry (ɒpˈtɒmɪtrɪ) *n* the science or practice of testing visual acuity and prescribing corrective lenses > optometric (ˌɒptəˈmɛtrɪk) *adj*

optophone (ˈɒptəˌfəʊn) *n* a device for blind people that converts printed words into sounds

opt out *vb* **1** (*intr, adverb*; often foll by *of*) to choose not to be involved (in) or part (of) ▷ *n* **opt-out 2** the act of opting out, esp of local-authority administration: *opt-outs by hospitals and schools*

opulent (ˈɒpjʊlənt) *adj* **1** having or indicating wealth **2** abundant or plentiful [c17 from Latin *opulens*, from *opēs* (pl) wealth] > 'opulence *or less commonly* 'opulency *n* > 'opulently *adv*

opuntia (əˈpʌnʃɪə) *n* any cactus of the genus *Opuntia*, esp prickly pear, having fleshy branched stems and green, red, or yellow flowers [c17 New Latin, from Latin *Opuntia* (*herba*) the Opuntian (plant), from *Opus*, ancient town of Locris, Greece]

opus (ˈəʊpəs, ˈɒp-) *n*, *pl* opuses *or* opera (ˈɒpərə) **1** an artistic composition, esp a musical work **2** (*often capital*) (usually followed by a number) a musical composition by a particular composer, generally catalogued in order of publication: *Beethoven's opus 61 is his violin concerto.* Abbreviation: op [c18 from Latin: a work; compare Sanskrit *apas* work]

opus anglicanum (ˈəʊpəs æŋglɪˈkɑːnəm) *n* fine embroidery, esp of church vestments, produced in England *c.*1200–*c.*1350; characterized by the rich

O

materials used, esp silver gilt thread [Latin: English work]

opuscule (ɒˈpʌskjuːl) n rare a small or insignificant artistic work [c17 via French from Latin *opusculum*, from *opus* work] > o'**puscular** adj

Opus Dei ('əʊpəs 'deɪɪ) n 1 another name for **divine office** 2 an international Roman Catholic organization of lay people and priests founded in Spain in 1928 by Josemaria Escrivá de Balaguer (1902–75), with the aim of spreading Christian principles

or[1] (ɔː; *unstressed* ə) *conj* (*coordinating*) 1 used to join alternatives: *apples or pears; apples or pears or cheese; apples, pears, or cheese* 2 used to join rephrasings of the same thing: *to serve in the army, or rather to fight in the army; twelve, or a dozen* 3 used to join two alternatives when the first is preceded by *either* or *whether*: *whether it rains or not we'll be there; either yes or no* 4 one or two, four or five, etc a few 5 or else See **else** (sense 3) 6 a poetic word for **either** or **whether** as the first element in correlatives, with *or* also preceding the second alternative ▷ See also **exclusive or, inclusive or** [c13 contraction of *other*, used to introduce an alternative, changed (through influence of EITHER) from Old English *oththe*; compare Old High German *odar* (German *oder*)]

or[2] (ɔː) *archaic* ▷ *conj* 1 (*subordinating*; foll by *ever* or *ere*) before; when ▷ *prep* 2 before [Old English *ār* soon; related to Old Norse *ār* early, Old High German *ēr*]

or[3] (ɔː) *adj* (*usually postpositive*) *heraldry* of the metal gold [c16 via French from Latin *aurum* gold]

OR *abbreviation for* 1 **operations research** 2 Oregon 3 *military* **other ranks**

-or[1] *suffix forming nouns from verbs* a person or thing that does what is expressed by the verb: *actor; conductor; generator; sailor* [via Old French *-eur, -eor*, from Latin *-or* or *-ātor*]

-or[2] *suffix forming nouns* 1 indicating state, condition, or activity: *terror; error* 2 the US spelling of **-our**

ora ('ɔːrə) n the plural of **os**[2]

ORAC ('ɔːræk) n *acronym for* Oxygen Radical Absorbance Capacity: a measure of the ability of a substance, esp the blood, to absorb free radicals, used in determining the antioxidant effects of foods

orache *or esp US* **orach** ('ɒrɪtʃ) n any of several herbaceous plants or small shrubs of the chenopodiaceous genus *Atriplex*, esp *A. hortensis* (**garden orache**), which is cultivated as a vegetable. They have typically greyish-green lobed leaves and inconspicuous flowers [c15 from Old French *arache*, from Latin *atriplex*, from Greek *atraphaxus*, of obscure origin]

oracle ('ɒrəkəl) n 1 a prophecy, often obscure or allegorical, revealed through the medium of a priest or priestess at the shrine of a god 2 a shrine at which an oracular god is consulted 3 an agency through which a prophecy is transmitted 4 any person or thing believed to indicate future action with infallible authority 5 a statement believed to be infallible and authoritative 6 *Bible* a a message from God b the holy of holies in the Israelite temple ▷ See also **oracles** [c14 via Old French from Latin *ōrāculum*, from *ōrāre* to request]

oracles ('ɒrəkəlz) *pl n* another term for **Scripture** (sense 1)

oracular (ɒˈrækjʊlə) *adj* 1 of or relating to an oracle: *Apollo had his oracular shrine at Delphi* 2 wise and prophetic: *an oracular political thriller* 3 mysterious or ambiguous > o'**racularly** adv

oracy ('ɔːrəsɪ) n the capacity to express oneself in and understand speech [c20 from Latin *or-, os* mouth, by analogy with *literacy*]

Oradea (*Romanian* ɒˈradea) n an industrial city in NW Romania, in Transylvania: ceded by Hungary (1919). Pop: 182 000 (2005 est). German name: **Grosswardein** Hungarian name: **Nagyvárad**

ora et labora *Latin* ('ɔːra: ɛt 'læbɔːˌra:) pray and work

oral ('ɔːrəl, 'ɒrəl) *adj* 1 spoken or verbal: *an oral*

agreement 2 relating to, affecting, or for use in the mouth: *an oral thermometer* 3 of or relating to the surface of an animal, such as a jellyfish, on which the mouth is situated 4 denoting a drug to be taken by mouth: *an oral contraceptive*. Compare **parenteral** 5 of, relating to, or using spoken words 6 *phonetics* pronounced with the soft palate in a raised position completely closing the nasal cavity and allowing air to pass out only through the mouth 7 *psychoanal* a relating to a stage of psychosexual development during which the child's interest is concentrated on the mouth b denoting personality traits, such as dependence, selfishness, and aggression, resulting from fixation at the oral stage. Compare **anal** (sense 2), **genital** (sense 2), **phallic** (sense 2) ▷ n 8 an examination in which the questions and answers are spoken rather than written [c17 from Late Latin *orālis*, from Latin *ōs* face] > '**orally** adv

oral eroticism n *psychoanal* libidinal pleasure derived from the lips and mouth, for example by kissing

oral history n the memories of living people about events or social conditions which they experienced in their earlier lives taped and preserved as historical evidence

oral hygiene n another name for **dental hygiene**

oral hygienist n another name for **dental hygienist**

orality (ɔːˈrælɪtɪ) n 1 the quality of being oral 2 a tendency to favour the spoken rather than the written form of language

Oral Law n *Judaism* the traditional body of religious law believed to have been revealed to Moses as an interpretation of the Torah and passed on orally until it was codified and recorded, principally in the Mishna and Gemara

oral society n a society that has not developed literacy

Oran (əˈræn, əˈrɑːn; *French* ɔrã) n a port in NW Algeria: the second largest city in the country; scene of the destruction by the British of most of the French fleet in the harbour in 1940 to prevent its capture by the Germans. Pop: 744 000 (2005 est)

orang (ɔːˈræŋ, ˈɔːræŋ) n short for **orang-utan**

orange ('ɒrɪndʒ) n 1 any of several citrus trees, esp *Citrus sinensis* (**sweet orange**) and the Seville orange, cultivated in warm regions for their round edible fruit. See also **tangerine** (sense 1) 2 a the fruit of any of these trees, having a yellowish-red bitter rind and segmented juicy flesh. See also **navel orange** b (*as modifier*): *orange peel* 3 the hard wood of any of these trees 4 any of a group of colours, such as that of the skin of an orange, that lie between red and yellow in the visible spectrum in the approximate wavelength range 620–585 nanometres 5 a dye or pigment producing these colours 6 orange cloth or clothing: *dressed in orange* 7 any of several trees or herbaceous plants that resemble the orange, such as mock orange ▷ *adj* 8 of the colour orange [c14 via Old French from Old Provençal *auranja*, from Arabic *nāranj*, from Persian *nārang*, from Sanskrit *nāranga*, probably of Dravidian origin]

Orange[1] ('ɒrɪndʒ) n (*modifier*) 1 of or relating to the Orangemen 2 of or relating to the royal dynasty of Orange

Orange[2] n 1 ('ɒrɪndʒ) a river in S Africa, rising in NE Lesotho and flowing generally west across the South African plateau to the Atlantic: the longest river in South Africa. Length: 2093 km (1300 miles) 2 (*French* ɔrã) a town in SE France: a small principality in the Middle Ages, the descendants of which formed the House of Orange. Pop: 27 989 (1999). Ancient name: **Arausio** (əˈrɔːsɪəʊ)

orangeade (ˌɒrɪndʒˈeɪd) n an effervescent or still orange-flavoured drink

orange blossom n the flowers of the orange tree, traditionally worn by brides

orange chromide ('krəʊmaɪd) n an Asian cichlid fish, *Etropus maculatus*, with a brownish-orange spotted body

orange flower water n a distilled infusion of orange blossom, used in cakes, confectionery, etc

Orange Free State n a former province of central South Africa, between the Orange and Vaal rivers: settled by Boers in 1836 after the Great Trek; annexed by Britain in 1848; became a province of South Africa in 1910; replaced in 1994 by the new province of Free State; economy based on agriculture and mineral resources (esp gold and uranium). Capital: Bloemfontein

Orangeism ('ɒrɪndʒˌɪzəm) n the practices or principles of Orangemen, esp Protestant supremacy in the Republic of Ireland, Northern Ireland, or Canada

Orangeman ('ɒrɪndʒmən) n, *pl* -men a member of a society founded in Ireland (1795) to uphold the Protestant religion, the Protestant dynasty, and the Protestant constitution. **Orange Lodges** have since spread to many parts of the former British Empire [c18 after William, prince of *Orange* (king of England as William III)]

Orangeman's Day n the 12th of July, celebrated by Protestants in Northern Ireland to commemorate the anniversary of the Battle of the Boyne (1690)

orange peel n 1 the thick pitted rind of an orange 2 anything resembling this in surface texture, such as skin or porcelain

orange-peel fungus n See **elf-cup**

orange pekoe n a superior grade of black tea made from the small leaves at the tips of the plant stems and growing in India and Sri Lanka

orange roughy ('rʌfɪ) n a marine food fish, *Hoplosthenus atlanticus*, of S Pacific waters

orangery ('ɒrɪndʒərɪ, -dʒrɪ) n, *pl* -eries a building, such as a greenhouse, in which orange trees are grown

orange stick n a small stick used to clean the fingernails and cuticles, having one pointed and one rounded end

orange-tip n a European butterfly, *Anthocharis cardamines*, having whitish wings with orange-tipped forewings: family *Pieridae*

orangewood ('ɒrɪndʒˌwʊd) n a the hard fine-grained yellowish wood of the orange tree b (*as modifier*): *an orangewood table*

orang-utan (ɔːˌræŋuːˈtæn, ˌɔːræŋˈuːtæn) *or* **orang-utang** (ɔːˌræŋuːˈtæŋ, ˌɔːræŋˈuːtæŋ) n a large anthropoid ape, *Pongo pygmaeus*, of the forests of Sumatra and Borneo, with shaggy reddish-brown hair and strong arms. Sometimes shortened to: **orang** [c17 from Malay *orang hutan*, from *ōrang* man + *hūtan* forest]

ora pro nobis *Latin* ('ɔːra: prəʊ 'nəʊbɪs) a Latin invocation meaning *pray for us*

orate (ɔːˈreɪt) *vb* (*intr*) 1 to make or give an oration 2 to speak pompously and lengthily

oration (ɔːˈreɪʃən) n 1 a formal public declaration or speech 2 any rhetorical, lengthy, or pompous speech 3 an academic exercise or contest in public speaking [c14 from Latin *ōrātiō* speech, harangue, from *ōrāre* to plead, pray]

orator ('ɒrətə) n 1 a public speaker, esp one versed in rhetoric 2 a person given to lengthy or pompous speeches 3 *obsolete* the claimant in a cause of action in chancery

Oratorian (ˌɒrəˈtɔːrɪən) n a member of the religious congregation of the Oratory

oratorio (ˌɒrəˈtɔːrɪəʊ) n, *pl* -rios a dramatic but unstaged musical composition for soloists, chorus, and orchestra, based on a religious theme [c18 from Italian, literally: ORATORY[2], referring to the Church of the Oratory at Rome where musical services were held]

oratory[1] ('ɒrətərɪ, -trɪ) n 1 the art of public speaking 2 rhetorical skill or style [c16 from Latin (*ars*) *ōrātōria* (the art of) public speaking] > ˌora'**torical** adj > ˌora'**torically** adv

oratory[2] ('ɒrətərɪ, -trɪ) n, *pl* -ries a small room or secluded place, set apart for private prayer [c14 from Anglo-Norman, from Church Latin *ōrātōrium* place of prayer, from *ōrāre* to plead, pray]

Oratory ('ɒrətərɪ, -trɪ) *n RC Church* **1** Also called: **Congregation of the Oratory** the religious society of secular priests (**Oratorians**) living in a community founded by St Philip Neri **2** any church belonging to this society: *the Brompton Oratory*

orb (ɔːb) *n* **1** (in royal regalia) an ornamental sphere surmounted by a cross, representing the power of a sovereign **2** a sphere; globe **3** *poetic* another word for **eye**[1] **4** *obsolete or poetic* **a** a celestial body, esp the earth or sun **b** the orbit of a celestial body **5** an archaic word for **circle** ▷ *vb* **6** to make or become circular or spherical **7** (*tr*) an archaic word for **encircle** [C16 from Latin *orbis* circle, disc]

orbicular (ɔːˈbɪkjʊlə), **orbiculate** *or* **orbiculated** *adj* **1** circular or spherical **2** (of a leaf or similar flat part) circular or nearly circular **3** *rare* rounded or total > **orbicularity** (ɔːˌbɪkjʊˈlærɪtɪ) *n* > **orˈbicularly** *adv*

orbit ('ɔːbɪt) *n* **1** *astronomy* the curved path, usually elliptical, followed by a planet, satellite, comet, etc, in its motion around another celestial body under the influence of gravitation **2** a range or field of action or influence; sphere: *he is out of my orbit* **3** *anatomy* the bony cavity containing the eyeball. Nontechnical name: **eye socket** **4** *zoology* **a** the skin surrounding the eye of a bird **b** the hollow in which lies the eye or eyestalk of an insect or other arthropod **5** *physics* the path of an electron in its motion around the nucleus of an atom ▷ *vb* **6** to move around (a body) in a curved path, usually circular or elliptical **7** (*tr*) to send (a satellite, spacecraft, etc) into orbit **8** (*intr*) to move in or as if in an orbit [C16 from Latin *orbita* course, from *orbis* circle, ORB]

orbital ('ɔːbɪtᵊl) *adj* **1** of or denoting an orbit ▷ *n* **2** a region surrounding an atomic nucleus in which the probability distribution of the electrons is given by a wave function > **ˈorbitally** *adv*

orbital velocity *n* the velocity required by a spacecraft, satellite, etc, to enter and maintain a given orbit

orbiter ('ɔːbɪtə) *n* a spacecraft or satellite designed to orbit a planet or other body without landing on it. Compare **lander**

orc (ɔːk) *n* **1** any of various whales, such as the killer and grampus **2** one of an imaginary race of evil goblins, esp in the fiction of JRR Tolkien [C16 via Latin *orca*, perhaps from Greek *orux* whale]

Orcadian (ɔːˈkeɪdɪən) *n* **1** a native or inhabitant of Orkney ▷ *adj* **2** of or relating to Orkney [from Latin *Orcades* the Orkney Islands]

orcein ('ɔːsɪɪn) *n* a brown crystalline material formed by the action of ammonia on orcinol and present in orchil: used as a dye, biological stain, and antiseptic. Formula: $C_{28}H_{24}O_7N_2$ [C19 see ORCINOL]

orchard ('ɔːtʃəd) *n* **1** an area of land devoted to the cultivation of fruit trees **2** a collection of fruit trees especially cultivated [Old English *orceard*, *ortigeard*, from *ort-*, from Latin *hortus* garden + *geard* YARD[2]]

orchard bush *n W African* open savanna country with occasional trees and scrub, as found north of the W African forest belt

orchardman ('ɔːtʃədmən) *n, pl* **-men** a person who grows and sells orchard fruits

orchestra ('ɔːkɪstrə) *n* **1** a large group of musicians, esp one whose members play a variety of different instruments. See also **symphony orchestra, string orchestra, chamber orchestra** **2** a group of musicians, each playing the same type of instrument: *a balalaika orchestra* **3** Also called: **orchestra pit** the space reserved for musicians in a theatre, immediately in front of or under the stage **4** *chiefly US and Canadian* the stalls in a theatre **5** (in the ancient Greek theatre) the semicircular space in front of the stage [C17 via Latin from Greek: the space in the theatre reserved for the chorus, from *orkheisthai* to dance] > **orchestral** (ɔːˈkɛstrəl) *adj* > **orˈchestrally** *adv*

orchestrate ('ɔːkɪˌstreɪt) *vb* (*tr*) **1** to score or arrange (a piece of music) for orchestra **2** to arrange, organize, or build up for special or maximum effect > **ˌorchesˈtration** *n* > **ˈorchesˌtrator** *n*

orchestrina (ˌɔːkɪsˈtriːnə) *or* **orchestrion** (ɔːˈkɛstrɪən) *n* any of various types of mechanical musical instrument designed to imitate the sound of an orchestra

orchid ('ɔːkɪd) *n* any terrestrial or epiphytic plant of the family *Orchidaceae*, often having flowers of unusual shapes and beautiful colours, specialized for pollination by certain insects. See **bee orchid, burnt-tip orchid, fly orchid, frog orchid, lady orchid, lizard orchid, man orchid, monkey orchid, purple-fringed orchid, pyramidal orchid, scented orchid, spider orchid, spotted orchid** [C19 from New Latin *Orchideae*; see ORCHIS]

orchidaceous (ˌɔːkɪˈdeɪʃəs) *adj* of, relating to, or belonging to the *Orchidaceae*, a family of flowering plants including the orchids

orchidectomy (ˌɔːkɪˈdɛktəmɪ) *n, pl* **-mies** the surgical removal of one or both testes [C19 from Greek *orkhis* testicle + -ECTOMY]

orchil ('ɔːkɪl, -tʃɪl) *or* **archil** *n* **1** any of various lichens, esp any of the genera *Roccella*, *Dendrographa*, and *Lecanora* **2** Also called: **cudbear** a purplish dye obtained by treating these lichens with aqueous ammonia: contains orcinol, orcein, and litmus [C15 from Old French *orcheil*, of uncertain origin]

orchis ('ɔːkɪs) *n* **1** any terrestrial orchid of the N temperate genus *Orchis*, having fleshy tubers and spikes of typically pink flowers **2** any of various temperate or tropical orchids of the genus *Habenaria*, such as the fringed orchis [C16 via Latin from Greek *orkhis* testicle; so called from the shape of its roots]

orchitis (ɔːˈkaɪtɪs) *n* inflammation of one or both testicles [C18 from New Latin, from Greek *orkhis* testicle + -ITIS] > **orchitic** (ɔːˈkɪtɪk) *adj*

orcinol ('ɔːsɪˌnɒl) *or* **orcin** ('ɔːsɪn) *n* a colourless crystalline water-soluble solid that occurs in many lichens and from which the dyes found in litmus are derived. Formula: $CH_3C_6H_3(OH)_2$ [C20 from New Latin *orcina*, from Italian *orcello* ORCHIL]

OR circuit *or* **gate** (ɔː) *n computing* a logic circuit having two or more input wires and one output wire that gives a high-voltage output signal if one or more input signals are at a high voltage: used extensively as a basic circuit in computers. Compare **AND circuit, NAND circuit** [C20 so named from its similarity to the function of *or* in logical constructions]

Orcus ('ɔːkəs) *n* another name for **Dis** (sense 1)

Ord (ɔːd) *n* a river in NE Western Australia, rising on the Kimberley Plateau and flowing generally north to the Timor Sea: subject of a major irrigation scheme. Length: about 500 km (300 miles)

ordain (ɔːˈdeɪn) *vb* (*tr*) **1** to consecrate (someone) as a priest; confer holy orders upon **2** (*may take a clause as object*) to decree, appoint, or predestine irrevocably **3** (*may take a clause as object*) to order, establish, or enact with authority **4** *obsolete* to select for an office [C13 from Anglo-Norman *ordeiner*, from Late Latin *ordināre*, from Latin *ordo* ORDER] > **orˈdainer** *n* > **orˈdainment** *n*

ordeal (ɔːˈdiːl) *n* **1** a severe or trying experience **2** *history* a method of trial in which the guilt or innocence of an accused person was determined by subjecting him to physical danger, esp by fire or water. The outcome was regarded as an indication of divine judgment [Old English *ordāl*, *ordēl*; related to Old Frisian *ordēl*, Old High German *urteili* (German *Urteil*) verdict. See DEAL[1], DOLE[1]]

order ('ɔːdə) *n* **1** a state in which all components or elements are arranged logically, comprehensibly, or naturally **2** an arrangement or disposition of things in succession; sequence: *alphabetical order* **3** an established or customary method or state, esp of society **4** a peaceful or harmonious condition of society: *order reigned in the streets* **5** (*often plural*) a class, rank, or hierarchy: *the lower orders* **6** *biology* any of the taxonomic groups into which a class is divided and which contains one or more families. *Carnivora*, *Primates*, and *Rodentia* are three orders of the class *Mammalia* **7** an instruction that must be obeyed; command **8** a decision or direction of a court or judge entered on the court record but not included in the final judgment **9** **a** a commission or instruction to produce or supply something in return for payment **b** the commodity produced or supplied **c** (*as modifier*): *order form* **10** a procedure followed by an assembly, meeting, etc **11** (*capital when part of a name*) a body of people united in a particular aim or purpose **12** Also called: **religious order** (*usually capital*) a group of persons who bind themselves by vows in order to devote themselves to the pursuit of religious aims **13** *history* a society of knights constituted as a fraternity, such as the Knights Templars **14** **a** a group of people holding a specific honour for service or merit, conferred on them by a sovereign or state **b** the insignia of such a group **15** **a** any of the five major classical styles of architecture classified by the style of columns and entablatures used. See also **Doric, Ionic, Corinthian, Tuscan, Composite** **b** any style of architecture **16** *Christianity* **a** the sacrament by which bishops, priests, etc, have their offices conferred upon them **b** any of the degrees into which the ministry is divided **c** the office of an ordained Christian minister **17** a form of Christian Church service prescribed to be used on specific occasions **18** *Judaism* one of the six sections of the Mishna or the corresponding tractates of the Talmud **19** *maths* **a** the number of times a function must be differentiated to obtain a given derivative **b** the order of the highest derivative in a differential equation **c** the number of rows or columns in a determinant or square matrix **d** the number of members of a finite group **20** short for **order of magnitude** **21** *military* (often preceded by *the*) the dress, equipment, or formation directed for a particular purpose or undertaking: *drill order; battle order* **22** **a tall order** something difficult, demanding, or exacting **23** **in order** **a** in sequence **b** properly arranged **c** appropriate or fitting **24** **in order to** (*preposition; foll by an infinitive*) so that it is possible to: *to eat in order to live* **25** **in order that** (*conjunction*) with the purpose that; so that **26** **keep order** to maintain or enforce order **27** **of** *or* **in the order of** having an approximately specified size or quantity **28** **on order** having been ordered or commissioned but not having been delivered **29** **out of order** **a** not in sequence **b** not working **c** not following the rules or customary procedure **30** **to order** **a** according to a buyer's specifications **b** on request or demand ▷ *vb* **31** (*tr*) to give a command to (a person or animal to do or be something) **32** to request (something) to be supplied or made, esp in return for payment: *he ordered a hamburger* **33** (*tr*) to instruct or command to move, go, etc (to a specified place): *they ordered her into the house* **34** (*tr; may take a clause as object*) to authorize; prescribe: *the doctor ordered a strict diet* **35** (*tr*) to arrange, regulate, or dispose (articles) in their proper places **36** (of fate or the gods) to will; ordain **37** (*tr*) *rare* to ordain ▷ *interj* **38** an exclamation of protest against an infringement of established procedure **39** an exclamation demanding that orderly behaviour be restored ▷ See also **orders** [C13 from Old French *ordre*, from Latin *ordō*] > **ˈorderer** *n* > **ˈorderless** *adj*

order about *or* **around** *vb* (*tr*) to bully or domineer

order arms *interj, n military* the order in drill to hold the rifle close to the right side with the butt resting on the ground

order-driven *adj* denoting an electronic market system, esp for stock exchanges, in which prices are determined by the publication of orders to buy

O

or sell. Compare **quote-driven**

ordered set *n logic, maths* a sequence of elements that is distinguished from the other sequences of the same element by the order of the elements. Thus <a, b> is not identical with <b, a>

order in council *n* (in Britain and various other Commonwealth countries) a decree of the Cabinet, usually made under the authority of a statute: in theory a decree of the sovereign and Privy Council

ordering ('ɔːdərɪŋ) *n logic* any of a number of categories of relations that permit at least some members of their domain to be placed in order. A **linear** or **simple ordering** is reflexive, antisymmetric, transitive, and connected, as *less than or equal to* on the integers. A **partial ordering** is reflexive, antisymmetric, and transitive, as set inclusion. Either of these orderings is called *strict* if it is asymmetric instead of reflexive and antisymmetric. It is a *well-ordering* if every nonempty subset has a least member under the relation

orderly ('ɔːdəlɪ) *adj* **1** in order, properly arranged, or tidy **2** obeying or appreciating method, system, and arrangement **3** harmonious or peaceful **4** *military* of or relating to orders: *an orderly book* ▷ *adv* **5** *now rare* according to custom or rule ▷ *n, pl* **-lies 6** *med* a male hospital attendant **7** *military* a junior rank detailed to carry orders or perform minor tasks for a more senior officer > 'orderliness *n*

orderly officer *n* another name for **officer of the day**

orderly room *n military* a room in the barracks of a battalion or company used for general administrative purposes

Order of Australia *n* an order awarded to Australians for outstanding achievement or for service to Australia or to humanity at large; established in 1975

Order of Canada *n* an order awarded to Canadians for outstanding achievement; established in 1967

order of magnitude *n* the approximate size of something, esp measured in powers of 10: *the order of magnitude of the deficit was as expected; their estimates differ by an order of magnitude*. Also called: **order**

Order of Merit *n Brit* an order conferred on civilians and servicemen for eminence in any field

Order of Military Merit *n* an order awarded to members of the Canadian Forces for conspicuous merit; established in 1972

order of the day *n* **1** the general directive of a commander in chief or the specific instructions of a commanding officer **2** *informal* the prescribed or only thing offered or available: *prunes were the order of the day* **3** (in Parliament and similar legislatures) any item of public business ordered to be considered on a specific day **4** an agenda or programme

Order of the Garter *n* the highest order of British knighthood (but see also **Order of the Thistle**) open to women since 1987. It consists of the sovereign, 24 knight companions, and extra members created by statute. Also called: **the Garter**

Order of the Thistle *n* an ancient Scottish order of knighthood revived by James VII of Scotland in 1687. It consists of the sovereign, 16 knights brethren, and extra members created by statute. It is the equivalent of the Order of the Garter, and is usually conferred on Scots. Also called: **the Thistle**

order paper *n* a list indicating the order in which business is to be conducted, esp in Parliament

orders ('ɔːdəz) *pl n* **1** short for **holy orders 2** **in** (holy) orders ordained **3** **take** (holy) orders to become ordained **4** short for **major orders** *or* **minor orders**

ordinal ('ɔːdɪnᵊl) *adj* **1** denoting a certain position in a sequence of numbers **2** of, relating to, or characteristic of an order in biological

classification ▷ *n* **3** short for **ordinal number 4** a book containing the forms of services for the ordination of ministers **5** *RC Church* a service book [C14 (in the sense: orderly): from Late Latin *ordinalis* denoting order or place in a series, from Latin *ordō* ORDER]

ordinal number *n* **1** a number denoting relative position in a sequence, such as *first, second, third*. Sometimes shortened to: **ordinal 2** *logic, maths* a measure of not only the size of a set but also the order of its elements ▷ Compare **cardinal number**

ordinal scale *n statistics* a scale on which data is shown simply in order of magnitude since there is no standard of measurement of differences: for instance, a squash ladder is an ordinal scale since one can say only that one person is better than another, but not by how much. Compare **interval scale, ratio scale, nominal scale**

ordinance ('ɔːdɪnəns) *n* an authoritative regulation, decree, law, or practice [C14 from Old French *ordenance*, from Latin *ordināre* to set in order]

ordinand ('ɔːdɪ,nænd) *n Christianity* a candidate for ordination

ordinarily ('ɔːdᵊnrɪlɪ, ,ɔːdᵊ'nɛrɪlɪ) *adv* in ordinary, normal, or usual practice; usually; normally

ordinary ('ɔːdᵊnrɪ) *adj* **1** of common or established type or occurrence **2** familiar, everyday, or unexceptional **3** uninteresting or commonplace **4** having regular or ex officio jurisdiction: *an ordinary judge* **5** *maths* (of a differential equation) containing two variables only and derivatives of one of the variables with respect to the other ▷ *n, pl* **-naries 6** a common or average situation, amount, or degree (esp in the phrase **out of the ordinary**) **7** a normal or commonplace person or thing **8** *civil law* a judge who exercises jurisdiction in his own right **9** (*usually capital*) an ecclesiastic, esp a bishop, holding an office to which certain jurisdictional powers are attached **10** *RC Church* **a** the parts of the Mass that do not vary from day to day. Compare **proper** (sense 13) **b** a prescribed form of divine service, esp the Mass **11** the US name for **penny-farthing 12** *heraldry* any of several conventional figures, such as the bend, the fesse, and the cross, commonly charged upon shields **13** *history* a clergyman who visited condemned prisoners before their death **14** *Brit obsolete* **a** a meal provided regularly at a fixed price **b** the inn providing such meals **15** **in ordinary** *Brit* (used esp in titles) in regular service or attendance: *physician in ordinary to the sovereign* [C16 (adj) and C13 (some n senses): ultimately from Latin *ordinārius* orderly, from *ordō* order]

Ordinary grade *n* (in Scotland) the formal name for **O grade**

ordinary lay *n* the form of lay found in a cable-laid rope

Ordinary level *n* (in Britain) the formal name for **O level**

ordinary rating *n* a rank in the Royal Navy comparable to that of a private in the army

ordinary ray *n* the plane-polarized ray of light that obeys the laws of refraction in a doubly-refracting crystal. See **double refraction** Compare **extraordinary ray**

ordinary seaman *n* a seaman of the lowest rank, being insufficiently experienced to be an able-bodied seaman

ordinary shares *pl n Brit* shares representing part of the capital issued by a company and entitling their holders to a dividend that varies according to the prosperity of the company, to vote at all meetings of members, and to a claim on the net assets of the company, after the holders of preference shares have been paid. US equivalent: **common stock** Compare **preference shares** See also **A shares**

ordinate ('ɔːdɪnɪt) *n* the vertical or *y*-coordinate of a point in a two-dimensional system of Cartesian coordinates. Compare **abscissa**. See also **Cartesian coordinates** [C16 from New Latin phrase (*linea*) *ordināte* (*applicāta*) (line applied) in an orderly

manner, from *ordināre* to arrange in order]

ordination (,ɔːdɪ'neɪʃən) *n* **1 a** the act of conferring holy orders **b** the reception of holy orders **2** the condition of being ordained or regulated **3** an arrangement or order

ordnance ('ɔːdnəns) *n* **1** cannon or artillery **2** military supplies; munitions **3** **the** a department of an army or government dealing with military supplies [C14 variant of ORDINANCE]

ordnance datum *n* mean sea level calculated from observation taken at Newlyn, Cornwall, and used as the official basis for height calculation on British maps. Abbreviation: **OD**

Ordnance Survey *n* the official map-making body of the British or Irish government

ordonnance ('ɔːdənəns; *French* ɔrdɔnɑ̃s) *n* **1** the proper disposition of the elements of a building or an artistic or literary composition **2** an ordinance, law, or decree, esp in French law [C17 from Old French *ordenance* arrangement, influenced by *ordonner* to order]

Ordovician (,ɔːdəʊ'vɪʃɪən) *adj* **1** of, denoting, or formed in the second period of the Palaeozoic era, between the Cambrian and Silurian periods, which lasted for 45 000 000 years during which marine invertebrates flourished ▷ *n* **2** **the** the Ordovician period or rock system [C19 from Latin *Ordovices* ancient Celtic tribe in N Wales]

ordure ('ɔːdjʊə) *n* **1** excrement; dung **2** something regarded as being morally offensive [C14 via Old French, from *ord* dirty, from Latin *horridus* shaggy]

Ordzhonikidze *or* **Orjonikidze** (*Russian* ardʒəni'kidzɪ) *n* the former name (1954–1991) of **Vladikavkaz**

ore (ɔː) *n* any naturally occurring mineral or aggregate of minerals from which economically important constituents, esp metals, can be extracted [Old English *ār, ōra*; related to Gothic *aiz*, Latin *aes*, Dutch *oer*]

öre ('ɜːrə) *n, pl* **öre** a Scandinavian monetary unit worth one hundredth of a Swedish krona and (**øre**) one hundredth of a Danish and Norwegian krone

oread ('ɔːrɪ,æd) *n Greek myth* a mountain nymph [C16 via Latin from Greek *Oreias*, from *oros* mountain]

Örebro (*Swedish* œːrə'bruː) *n* a town in S Sweden: one of Sweden's oldest towns; scene of the election of Jean Bernadotte as heir to the throne in 1810. Pop: 126 940 (2004 est)

orecchiette *or* **orecchietti** (,ɒrəkɪ'ɛtɪ) *pl n* small ear-shaped pasta pieces [C21 from Italian, literally: little ears]

orectic (ɒ'rɛktɪk) *adj* of or relating to the desires [C18 from Greek *orektikos* causing desire, from *oregein* to desire]

ore dressing *n* the first stage in the extraction of a metal from an ore in which as much gangue as possible is removed and the ore is prepared for smelting, refining, etc. Also called: **mineral dressing, mineral processing**

Oreg. *abbreviation for* Oregon

oregano (,ɒrɪ'gɑːnəʊ) *n* **1** a Mediterranean variety of wild marjoram (*Origanum vulgare*), with pungent leaves **2** the dried powdered leaves of this plant, used to season food ▷ See also **origanum** [C18 American Spanish, from Spanish, from Latin *orīganum*, from Greek *origanon* an aromatic herb, perhaps marjoram]

Oregon ('ɒrɪgən) *n* a state of the northwestern US, on the Pacific: consists of the Coast and Cascade Ranges in the west and a plateau in the east; important timber production. Capital: Salem. Pop: 3 559 596 (2003 est). Area: 251 418 sq km (97 073 sq miles). Abbreviations: **Oreg.**, (with zip code) **OR**

Oregon fir *or* **pine** *n* other names for **Douglas fir**

Oregon grape *n* **1** an evergreen berberidaceous shrub, *Mahonia aquifolium*, of NW North America, having yellow fragrant flowers and small blue edible berries **2** the berry of this shrub

Oregon trail *n* an early pioneering route across the central US, from Independence, W Missouri, to the Columbia River country of N Oregon: used chiefly between 1804 and 1860. Length: about 3220 km (2000 miles)

Orel *or* **Oryol** (*Russian* a'rjɔl) *n* a city in W Russia; founded in 1564 but damaged during World War II. Pop: 333 000 (2005 est)

Ore Mountains (ɔ:) *pl n* another name for the **Erzgebirge**

Orenburg ('ɒrənˌbɜːg; *Russian* arın'burk) *n* a city in W Russia, on the Ural River. Pop: 550 000 (2005 est). Former name (1938–57): **Chkalov**

Orense (*Spanish* o'rense) *n* a city in NW Spain, in Galicia on the Miño River: warm springs. Pop: 109 475 (2003 est). Galician name: **Ourense**

Orestes (ɒ'rɛstiːz) *n Greek myth* the son of Agamemnon and Clytemnestra, who killed his mother and her lover Aegisthus in revenge for their murder of his father

Øresund (œːrə'sʊnd) *n* the Swedish and Danish name for the **Sound** Swedish name: **Öresund**

orf (ɔ:f) *n vet science* an infectious disease of sheep and sometimes goats and cattle, characterized by scabby pustular lesions on the muzzle and lips; caused by a paramyxovirus. Technical name: **contagious pustular dermatitis** Also called: (*Austral*): **scabby mouth**

orfe (ɔ:f) *n* a small slender European cyprinoid fish, *Idus idus*, occurring in two colour varieties, namely the **silver orfe** and the **golden orfe**, popular aquarium fishes. Compare **goldfish** [c17 from German; related to Latin *orphus*, Greek *orphos* the sea perch]

orfray ('ɔːfri) *n* a less common spelling of **orphrey**

org *an internet domain name for* an organization, usually a nonprofit-making organization

org. *abbreviation for* **1** organic **2** organization

organ ('ɔːgən) *n* **1 a** Also called: **pipe organ** a large complex musical keyboard instrument in which sound is produced by means of a number of pipes arranged in sets or stops, supplied with air from a bellows. The largest instruments possess three or more manuals and one pedal keyboard and have the greatest range of any instrument **b** (*as modifier*): *organ pipe; organ stop; organ loft* **2** any instrument, such as a harmonium, in which sound is produced in this way. See also **reed organ, harmonica 3** short for **electric organ** (sense 1a), **electronic organ 4** a fully differentiated structural and functional unit, such as a kidney or a root, in an animal or plant **5** an agency or medium of communication, esp a periodical issued by a specialist group or party **6** an instrument with which something is done or accomplished **7** a euphemistic word for **penis** [c13 from Old French *organe*, from Latin *organum* implement, from Greek *organon* tool; compare Greek *ergein* to work]

organa ('ɔːgənə) *n* a plural of **organon** and **organum**

organdie *or esp US* **organdy** ('ɔːgəndɪ, ɔː'gæn-) *n, pl* **-dies** a fine and slightly stiff cotton fabric used esp for dresses [c19 from French *organdi*, of unknown origin]

organelle (ˌɔːgə'nɛl) *n* a structural and functional unit, such as a mitochondrion, in a cell or unicellular organism [c20 from New Latin *organella*, from Latin *organum*: see ORGAN]

organ-grinder *n* a street musician playing a hand organ for money

organic (ɔː'gænɪk) *adj* **1** of, relating to, derived from, or characteristic of living plants and animals **2** of or relating to animal or plant constituents or products having a carbon basis **3** of or relating to one or more organs of an animal or plant **4** of, relating to, or belonging to the class of chemical compounds that are formed from carbon: *an organic compound*. Compare **inorganic** (sense 2) **5** constitutional in the structure of something; fundamental; integral **6** of or characterized by the coordination of integral parts; organized **7** developing naturally: *organic change through positive education* **8** of or relating to the essential constitutional laws regulating the government of a state: *organic law* **9** of, relating to, or grown with the use of fertilizers or pesticides deriving from animal or vegetable matter, rather than from chemicals ▷ *n* **10** any substance, such as a fertilizer or pesticide, that is derived from animal or vegetable matter > **or'ganically** *adv*

organic chemistry *n* the branch of chemistry concerned with the compounds of carbon: originally confined to compounds produced by living organisms but now extended to include man-made substances based on carbon, such as plastics. Compare **inorganic chemistry**

organic disease *n* any disease in which there is a physical change in the structure of an organ or part. Compare **functional disease**

organicism (ɔː'gænɪˌsɪzəm) *n* **1** the theory that the functioning of living organisms is determined by the working together of all organs as an integrated system **2** the theory that all symptoms are caused by organic disease **3** the theory that each organ of the body has its own peculiar constitution > **or'ganicist** *n, adj* > **orˌgani'cistic** *adj*

organic light-emitting diode *n* a cell that emits light when voltage is applied: used as a display device replacing LCD technology in hand-held devices such as mobile phones because it is brighter, thinner, faster, and cheaper. Abbreviation: **OLED**

organic psychosis *n* a severe mental illness produced by damage to the brain, as a result of poisoning, alcoholism, disease, etc. Compare **functional** (sense 4b)

organism ('ɔːgəˌnɪzəm) *n* **1** any living biological entity, such as an animal, plant, fungus, or bacterium **2** anything resembling a living creature in structure, behaviour, etc > ˌorgan'ismal *or* ˌorgan'ismic *adj* > ˌorgan'ismally *adv*

organist ('ɔːgənɪst) *n* a person who plays the organ

organization *or* **organisation** (ˌɔːgənaɪ'zeɪʃən) *n* **1** the act of organizing or the state of being organized **2** an organized structure or whole **3** a business or administrative concern united and constructed for a particular end **4** a body of administrative officials, as of a political party, a government department, etc **5** order or system; method > ˌorgani'zational *or* ˌorgani'sational *adj* > ˌorgani'zationally *or* ˌorgani'sationally *adv*

organizational culture *n* the customs, rituals, and values shared by the members of an organization that have to be accepted by new members

organizational psychology *n* the study of the structure of an organization and of the ways in which the people in it interact, usually undertaken in order to improve the organization

organization chart *n* a diagram representing the management structure of a company, showing the responsibilities of each department, the relationships of the departments to each other, and the hierarchy of management

organization man *n* **1** a person who subordinates his personal life to the demands of the organization he works for **2** a person who specializes in or is good at organization

Organization of African Unity *n* the former name for the **African Union**

Organization of American States *n* an association consisting of the US and other republics in the W hemisphere, founded at Bogotá in 1948 to promote military, economic, social, and cultural cooperation among the member states. Abbreviation: **OAS**. See also **Pan American Union**

organize *or* **organise** ('ɔːgəˌnaɪz) *vb* **1** to form (parts or elements of something) into a structured whole; coordinate **2** (*tr*) to arrange methodically or in order **3** (*tr*) to provide with an organic structure **4** (*tr*) to enlist (the workers) of (a factory, concern, or industry) in a trade union **5** (*intr*) to join or form an organization or trade union **6** (*tr*) *informal* to put (oneself) in an alert and responsible frame of mind [c15 from Medieval Latin *organizare*, from Latin *organum* ORGAN]

organized *or* **organised** ('ɔːgəˌnaɪzd) *adj* **1** planned and controlled on a large scale and involving many people: *organized crime* **2** orderly and efficient: *a highly organized campaign* **3** (of the workers in a factory or office) belonging to a trade union: *organized labour*

organizer *or* **organiser** ('ɔːgəˌnaɪzə) *n* **1** a person who organizes or is capable of organizing **2** a container with a number of compartments for storage: *hanging organizers to keep your clothes smart* **3** *embryol* any part of an embryo or any substance produced by it that induces specialization of undifferentiated cells

organo- *combining form* **1** (in biology or medicine) indicating an organ or organs: *organogenesis* **2** (in chemistry) indicating a compound containing an organic group: *organometallic; organosulphur; organophosphate*

organ of Corti ('kɔːtɪ) *n* the sense organ of the cochlea by which sounds are converted into nerve impulses [named after Alfonso *Corti* (died 1876), Italian anatomist]

organogenesis (ˌɔːgənəʊ'dʒɛnɪsɪs) *n* **1** the formation and development of organs in an animal or plant **2** Also called: **organogeny** (ˌɔːgə'nɒdʒənɪ) the study of this process > **organogenetic** (ˌɔːgənəʊdʒɪ'nɛtɪk) *adj* > ˌorganoge'netically *adv*

organography (ˌɔːgə'nɒgrəfɪ) *n* the description of the organs and major structures of animals and plants > **organographic** (ˌɔːgənəʊ'græfɪk) *or* ˌorgano'graphical *adj* > ˌorgan'ographist *n*

organoleptic (ˌɔːgənəʊ'lɛptɪk) *adj physiol* **1** able to stimulate an organ, esp a special sense organ **2** able to perceive a sensory stimulus

organology (ˌɔːgə'nɒlədʒɪ) *n* the study of the structure and function of the organs of animals and plants > **organological** (ˌɔːgənəʊ'lɒdʒɪkəl) *adj* > ˌorgan'ologist *n*

organometallic (ˌɔːgænəʊmɪ'tælɪk) *adj* of, concerned with, or being an organic compound with one or more metal atoms in its molecules: *an organometallic compound*

organon ('ɔːgəˌnɒn) *or* **organum** *n, pl* **organa** ('ɔːgənə), **-nons** *or* **-na, -nums** *Epistemology* **1** a system of logical or scientific rules, esp that of Aristotle **2** *archaic* a sense organ, regarded as an instrument for acquiring knowledge [c16 from Greek: implement; see ORGAN]

organophosphate (ˌɔːgænəʊ'fɒsfeɪt) *n* any of a group of organic compounds containing phosphate groups and used as a pesticide

organotherapy (ˌɔːgənəʊ'θɛrəpɪ) *n* the treatment of disease with extracts of animal endocrine glands > **organotherapeutic** (ˌɔːgənəʊˌθɛrə'pjuːtɪk) *adj*

organotin (ˌɔːgænəʊ'tɪn) *adj* of, concerned with, or being an organic compound with one or more tin atoms in its molecules: used as a pesticide, hitherto considered to decompose safely, now found to be toxic in the food chain

organ screen *n* a wooden or stone screen that supports the organ in a cathedral or church and divides the choir from the nave

organum ('ɔːgənəm) *n, pl* **-na** (-nə) *or* **-nums 1** a form of polyphonic music originating in the ninth century, consisting of a plainsong melody with parts added at the fourth and fifth **2** a variant of **organon** [c17 via Latin from Greek; see ORGAN]

organza (ɔː'gænzə) *n* a thin stiff fabric of silk, cotton, nylon, rayon, etc [c20 perhaps related to ORGANZINE]

organzine ('ɔːgənˌziːn, ɔː'gænziːn) *n* **1** a strong thread made of twisted strands of raw silk **2** fabric made of such threads [c17 from French *organsin*, from Italian *organzino*, probably from

O

Urgench, a town in Uzbekistan where the fabric was originally produced]

orgasm ('ɔːgæzəm) *n* **1** the most intense point during sexual excitement, characterized by extremely pleasurable sensations and in the male accompanied by ejaculation of semen **2** *rare* intense or violent excitement [c17 from New Latin *orgasmus*, from Greek *orgasmos*, from *organ* to mature, swell] > **or'gasmic** *or* **or'gastic** *adj*

orgeat ('ɔːʒɑː; *French* ɔrʒa) *n* a drink made from barley or almonds, and orange flower water [c18 via French, from *orge* barley, from Latin *hordeum*]

orgone ('ɔːgəʊn) *n* a substance postulated by Wilhelm Reich, who thought it was present everywhere and needed to be incorporated in people for sexual activity and mental health [c20 from ORG(ASM) + (HORM)ONE]

orgulous ('ɔːgjʊləs) *adj archaic* proud [c13 from Old French, from *orgueil* pride, from Frankish *urgōli* (unattested)]

orgy ('ɔːdʒɪ) *n, pl* -gies **1** a wild gathering marked by promiscuous sexual activity, excessive drinking, etc **2** an act of immoderate or frenzied indulgence **3** (*often plural*) secret religious rites of Dionysus, Bacchus, etc, marked by drinking, dancing, and songs [c16 from French *orgies*, from Latin *orgia*, from Greek: nocturnal festival] > ,**orgi'astic** *adj*

oribi ('ɒrɪbɪ) *n, pl* -bi *or* -bis a small African antelope, *Ourebia ourebi*, of grasslands and bush south of the Sahara, with fawn-coloured coat and, in the male, ridged spikelike horns [c18 from Afrikaans, probably from Khoikhoi *arab*]

oriel window ('ɔːrɪəl) *n* a bay window, esp one that is supported by one or more brackets or corbels. Sometimes shortened to: **oriel** [c14 from Old French *oriol* gallery, perhaps from Medieval Latin *auleolum* niche]

orient *n* ('ɔːrɪənt) **1** *poetic* another word for **east**. Compare **occident 2** *archaic* the eastern sky or the dawn **3 a** the iridescent lustre of a pearl **b** (*as modifier*): *orient pearls* **4** a pearl of high quality ▷ *adj* ('ɔːrɪənt) **5** *now chiefly poetic* eastern **6** *archaic* (of the sun, stars, etc) rising ▷ *vb* ('ɔːrɪ,ɛnt) **7** to adjust or align (oneself or something else) according to surroundings or circumstances **8** (*tr*) to position, align, or set (a map, surveying instrument, etc) with reference to the points of the compass or other specific directions **9** (*tr*) to set or build (a church) in an easterly direction [c18 via French from Latin *oriēns* rising (sun), from *orīrī* to rise]

Orient ('ɔːrɪənt) *n* (usually preceded by *the*) **1** the countries east of the Mediterranean **2** the eastern hemisphere

oriental (,ɔːrɪ'ɛntªl) *adj* another word for **eastern**. Compare **occidental**

Oriental (,ɔːrɪ'ɛntªl) *adj* **1** (*sometimes not capital*) of or relating to the Orient **2** of or denoting a zoogeographical region consisting of southeastern Asia from India to Borneo, Java, and the Philippines ▷ *n* **3** a breed of slender muscular cat with large ears, long legs, and a long tail **4** (*sometimes not capital*) an inhabitant, esp a native, of the Orient

Oriental almandine *n* a variety of corundum resembling almandine in colour and used as a gemstone

Oriental emerald *n* a green variety of corundum used as a gemstone

Orientalism (,ɔːrɪ'ɛntə,lɪzəm) *n* **1** knowledge of or devotion to the Orient **2** an Oriental quality, style, or trait > **Ori'entalist** *n* > ,**Ori,ental'istic** *adj*

Orientalize *or* **Orientalise** (,ɔːrɪ'ɛntə,laɪz) *vb* to make, become, or treat as Oriental > ,**Ori,entali'zation** *or* ,**Ori,entali'sation** *n*

Oriental topaz *n* a variety of corundum resembling topaz in colour and used as a gemstone

orientate ('ɔːrɪən,teɪt) *vb* a variant of **orient**

orientation (,ɔːrɪən'teɪʃən) *n* **1** the act or process of orienting or the state of being oriented **2**

position or positioning with relation to the points of the compass or other specific directions **3** the adjustment or alignment of oneself or one's ideas to surroundings or circumstances **4** Also called: **orientation course** *chiefly US and Canadian* **a** a course, programme, lecture, etc, introducing a new situation or environment **b** (*as modifier*): *an orientation talk* **5** *psychol* the knowledge of one's own temporal, social, and practical circumstances in life **6** basic beliefs or preferences: *sexual orientation* **7** *biology* the change in position of the whole or part of an organism in response to a stimulus, such as light **8** *chem* the relative dispositions of atoms, ions, or groups in molecules or crystals **9** the siting of a church on an east-west axis, usually with the altar at the E end > **orien'tational** *adj*

-oriented *suffix forming adjectives* designed for, directed towards, motivated by, or concerned with: *computer-oriented courses; managers who are profit-oriented*

orienteer (,ɔːrɪən'tɪə) *vb* (*intr*) **1** to take part in orienteering ▷ *n* **2** a person who takes part in orienteering

orienteering (,ɔːrɪɛn'tɪərɪŋ) *n* a sport in which contestants race on foot over a course consisting of checkpoints found with the aid of a map and a compass [c20 from Swedish *orientering*; compare ORIENT]

orifice ('ɒrɪfɪs) *n chiefly technical* an opening or mouth into a cavity; vent; aperture [c16 via French from Late Latin *ōrificium*, from Latin *ōs* mouth + *facere* to make]

orifice meter *n engineering* a plate having a central hole that is placed across the flow of a liquid, usually between flanges in a pipeline. The pressure difference generated by the flow velocity through the hole enables the flow quantity to be measured

oriflamme ('ɒrɪ,flæm) *n* a scarlet flag, originally of the abbey of St Denis in N France, adopted as the national banner of France in the Middle Ages [c15 via Old French, from Latin *aurum* gold + *flamma* flame]

orig. *abbreviation for* **1** origin **2** original(ly)

origami (,ɒrɪ'gɑːmɪ) *n* the art or process, originally Japanese, of paper folding [from Japanese, from *ori* a folding + *kami* paper]

origan ('ɒrɪgən) *n* another name for **marjoram** (sense 2) [c16 from Latin *orīganum*, from Greek *origanon* an aromatic herb, perhaps marjoram; compare OREGANO]

origanum (ə'rɪgənəm) *n* any plant of the herbaceous aromatic Mediterranean genus *Origanum*: family *Lamiaceae*. See **oregano, marjoram, dittany** (sense 1) [New Latin, from Greek *origanon* wild marjoram]

origin ('ɒrɪdʒɪn) *n* **1** a primary source; derivation **2** the beginning of something; first stage or part **3** (*often plural*) ancestry or parentage; birth; extraction **4** *anatomy* **a** the end of a muscle, opposite its point of insertion **b** the beginning of a nerve or blood vessel or the site where it first starts to branch out **5** *maths* **a** the point of intersection of coordinate axes or planes **b** the point whose coordinates are all zero. See also **pole²** (sense 8) **6** *commerce* the country from which a commodity or product originates: *shipment from origin* [c16 from French *origine*, from Latin *origō* beginning, birth, from *orīrī* to rise, spring from]

original (ə'rɪdʒɪnªl) *adj* **1** of or relating to an origin or beginning **2** fresh and unusual; novel **3** able to think of or carry out new ideas or concepts **4** being that from which a copy, translation, etc, is made ▷ *n* **5** the first and genuine form of something, from which others are derived **6** a person or thing used as a model in art or literature **7** a person whose way of thinking is unusual or creative **8** an unconventional or strange person **9** the first form or occurrence of something **10** an archaic word for **originator**, see **originate**

originality (ə,rɪdʒɪ'nælɪtɪ) *n, pl* -ties **1** the quality or condition of being original **2** the ability to create or innovate **3** something original

originally (ə'rɪdʒɪnəlɪ) *adv* **1** in the first place **2** in an original way **3** with reference to the origin or beginning

original sin *n* a state of sin held to be innate in mankind as the descendants of Adam

originate (ə'rɪdʒɪ,neɪt) *vb* **1** to come or bring into being **2** (*intr*) US and Canadian (of a bus, train, etc) to begin its journey at a specified point > **o,rigi'nation** *n* > **o'rigi,nator** *n*

orihou ('ɔːrɪ,huː) *n, pl* orihou a small New Zealand tree, *Pseudopanax colensoi*, with leaves in five parts [Māori]

orinasal (,ɔːrɪ'neɪzªl) *phonetics* ▷ *adj* **1** pronounced with simultaneous oral and nasal articulation, such as the French nasalized vowels œ (as in *un*), ɔ̃ (as in *bon*), and ɑ̃ (as in *blanc*) ▷ *n* **2** an orinasal speech sound [c19 from Latin *ōr-* (from *ōs* mouth) + NASAL] > ,**ori'nasally** *adv*

O-ring *n* a rubber ring used in machinery as a seal against oil, air, etc

Orinoco (,ɒrɪ'nəʊkəʊ) *n* a river in N South America, rising in S Venezuela and flowing west, then north as part of the border between Colombia and Venezuela, then east to the Atlantic by a great delta: the third largest river system in South America, draining an area of 945 000 sq km (365 000 sq miles); reaches a width of 22 km (14 miles) during the rainy season. Length: about 2575 km (1600 miles)

oriole ('ɔːrɪ,əʊl) *n* **1** any songbird of the mainly tropical Old World family *Oriolidae*, such as *Oriolus oriolus* (**golden oriole**), having a long pointed bill and a mostly yellow-and-black plumage **2** any American songbird of the family *Icteridae*, esp those of the genus *Icterus*, such as the Baltimore oriole, with a typical male plumage of black with either orange or yellow [c18 from Medieval Latin *oryolus*, from Latin *aureolus*, diminutive of *aureus*, from *aurum* gold]

Orion¹ (ə'raɪən) *n Greek myth* a Boeotian giant famed as a great hunter, who figures in several tales

Orion² (ə'raɪən) *n, Latin genitive* Orionis (,ɔːrɪ'əʊnɪs) a conspicuous constellation near Canis Major containing two first magnitude stars (Betelgeuse and Rigel) and a distant bright emission nebula (the **Orion Nebula**) associated with a system of giant molecular clouds and star formation

orisha *or* **orixa** (ə'rɪʃə) *n* any of the minor gods or spirits of traditional Yoruba religion and its S American and Caribbean offshoots such as Santeria and Candomblé [from Yoruba *orisha* and the Portuguese spelling *orixá*]

orison ('ɒrɪzªn) *n literary* another word for **prayer¹** [c12 from Old French *oreison*, from Late Latin *ōrātiō*, from Latin: speech, from *ōrāre* to speak]

Orissa (ɒ'rɪsə) *n* a state of E India, on the Bay of Bengal: part of the province of Bihar and Orissa (1912–36); enlarged by the addition of 25 native states in 1949. Capital: Bhubaneswar. Pop: 36 706 920 (2001). Area: 155 707 sq km (60 119 sq miles)

orixa (ə'rɪʃə) *n* another name for **orisha**

Oriya (ɒ'riːə) *n* **1** (*pl* -ya) a member of a people of India living chiefly in Orissa and neighbouring states **2** the state language of Orissa, belonging to the Indic branch of the Indo-European family

Orizaba (,ɔːrɪ'zɑːbə; *Spanish* ori'θaβa) *n* **1** a city and resort in SE Mexico, in Veracruz state. Pop: 327 000 (2005 est) **2 Pico de** the Spanish name for **Citlaltépetl**

Orjonikidze (*Russian* ardʒəni'kidzɪ) *n* a variant spelling of **Ordzhonikidze**

Orkney ('ɔːknɪ), **Orkneys** ('ɔːknɪz) *or* **Orkney Islands** *pl n* a group of over 70 islands off the N coast of Scotland, separated from the mainland by the Pentland Firth: constitutes an island authority of Scotland; low-lying and treeless; many important prehistoric remains.

Administrative centre: Kirkwall. Pop: 19 310 (2003 est). Area: 974 sq km (376 sq miles). Related word: **Orcadian**

Orkneyman (ˈɔːknɪmən) *n, pl* **-men** a native or inhabitant of Orkney > **ˈOrkneyˌwoman** *n*

Orlando (ɔːˈlændəʊ) *n* a city in the US, in Florida: site of Walt Disney World. Pop: 199 336 (2003 est)

orle (ɔːl) *n heraldry* a border around a shield [C16 from French, from *ourler* to hem]

Orléanais (*French* ɔrleane) *n* a former province of N central France, centred on Orléans

Orleanist (ɔːˈlɪənɪst) *n* an adherent of the Orléans branch of the French Bourbons

Orléans (ɔːˈlɪənz; *French* ɔrleɑ̃) *n* a city in N central France, on the River Loire: famous for its deliverance by Joan of Arc from the long English siege in 1429; university (1305); an important rail and road junction. Pop: 113 126 (1999)

Orlon (ˈɔːlɒn) *n trademark* a crease-resistant acrylic fibre or fabric used for clothing, furnishings, etc

orlop or **orlop deck** (ˈɔːlɒp) *n nautical* (in a vessel with four or more decks) the lowest deck [C15 from Dutch *overloopen* to run over, spill. See OVER, LEAP]

Orly (ˈɔːlɪ; *French* ɔrli) *n* a suburb of SE Paris, France, with an international airport

Ormazd or **Ormuzd** (ˈɔːmæzd) *n Zoroastrianism* the creative deity, embodiment of good and opponent of Ahriman. Also called: **Ahura Mazda** [from Persian, from Avestan *Ahura-Mazda*, from *ahura* spirit + *mazdā* wise]

ormer (ˈɔːmə) *n* **1** Also called: **sea-ear** an edible marine gastropod mollusc, *Haliotis tuberculata*, that has an ear-shaped shell perforated with holes and occurs near the Channel Islands **2** any other abalone [C17 from French (Guernsey dialect), apparently from Latin *auris* ear + *mare* sea]

ormolu (ˈɔːməˌluː) *n* **1 a** a gold-coloured alloy of copper, tin, or zinc used to decorate furniture, mouldings, etc **b** (*as modifier*): *an ormolu clock* **2** gold prepared to be used for gilding [C18 from French *or moulu* ground gold]

Ormuz (ˈɔːmʌz) *n* a variant spelling of **Hormuz**

ornament *n* (ˈɔːnəmənt) **1** anything that enhances the appearance of a person or thing **2** decorations collectively: *she was totally without ornament* **3** a small decorative object **4** something regarded as a source of pride or beauty **5** *music* any of several decorations, such as the trill, mordent, etc, occurring chiefly as improvised embellishments in baroque music ▷ *vb* (ˈɔːnəˌment) (*tr*) **6** to decorate with or as if with ornaments **7** to serve as an ornament to [C14 from Latin *ornāmentum*, from *ornāre* to adorn] > ˌornamenˈtation *n*

ornamental (ˌɔːnəˈmentəl) *adj* **1** of value as an ornament; decorative **2** (of a plant) used to decorate houses, gardens, etc ▷ *n* **3** a plant cultivated for show or decoration > ˌornaˈmentally *adv*

ornate (ɔːˈneɪt) *adj* **1** heavily or elaborately decorated **2** (of style in writing) overembellished; flowery [C15 from Latin *ornāre* to decorate] > orˈnately *adv* > orˈnateness *n*

Orne (*French* ɔrn) *n* a department of NW France, in Basse-Normandie. Capital: Alençon. Pop: 291 274 (2003 est). Area: 6144 sq km (2396 sq miles)

ornery (ˈɔːnərɪ) *adj US and Canadian dialect or informal* **1** stubborn or vile-tempered **2** low; treacherous: *an ornery trick* **3** ordinary [C19 alteration of ORDINARY] > ˈorneriness *n*

ornis (ˈɔːnɪs) *n* a less common word for **avifauna** [C19 from Greek: bird]

ornithic (ɔːˈnɪθɪk) *adj* of or relating to birds or a bird fauna [C19 from Greek *ornithikos*, from *ornis* bird]

ornithine (ˈɔːnɪˌθiːn) *n* an amino acid produced from arginine by hydrolysis: involved in the formation of urea in the liver; diaminopentanoic acid. Formula: $NH_2(CH_2)_3CHNH_2COOH$ [C19 from ORNITHO- + URIC]

ornithischian (ˌɔːnɪˈθɪskɪən) *adj* **1** of, relating to, or belonging to the *Ornithischia*, an order of dinosaurs that included the ornithopods, stegosaurs, ankylosaurs, and triceratops ▷ *n* **2** any dinosaur of the order *Ornithischia*; a bird-hipped dinosaur [C20 from ORNITHO- + Greek *ischion* hip joint]

ornitho- or before a vowel **ornith-** *combining form* bird or birds: *ornithology; ornithomancy; ornithopter; ornithoscopy; ornithosis* [from Greek *ornis, ornith-* bird]

ornithol. or **ornith.** *abbreviation for* **1** ornithological **2** ornithology

ornithology (ˌɔːnɪˈθɒlədʒɪ) *n* the study of birds, including their physiology, classification, ecology, and behaviour > **ornithological** (ˌɔːnɪθəˈlɒdʒɪkəl) *adj* > ˌornithoˈlogically *adv* > ˌorniˈthologist *n*

ornithomancy (ˌɔːnɪˌθəʊˈmænsɪ) *n* divination from the flight and cries of birds

ornithophily (ˌɔːnɪˈθɒfɪlɪ) *n* pollination of flowers by birds > ˌorniˈthophilous *adj*

ornithopod (ˈɔːnɪθəˌpɒd) *n* any herbivorous typically bipedal ornithischian dinosaur of the suborder *Ornithopoda*, including the iguanodon

ornithopter (ˈɔːnɪˌθɒptə) *n* a heavier-than-air craft sustained in and propelled through the air by flapping wings. Also called: **orthopter**

ornithorhynchus (ˌɔːnɪθəʊˈrɪŋkəs) *n* the technical name for **duck-billed platypus** [C19 New Latin, from ORNITHO- + Greek *rhunkhos* bill]

ornithoscopy (ˌɔːnɪˈθɒskəpɪ) *n* divination from the observation of birds

ornithosis (ˌɔːnɪˈθəʊsɪs) *n* a disease identical to psittacosis that occurs in birds other than parrots and can be transmitted to man

oro-¹ *combining form* mountain: *orogeny; orography* [from Greek *oros*]

oro-² *combining form* oral; mouth: *oromaxillary* [from Latin, from *ōs*]

orobanchaceous (ˌɔːrəʊbæŋˈkeɪʃəs) *adj* of, relating to, or belonging to the *Orobanchaceae*, a family of flowering plants all of which are root parasites, including broomrapes [via Latin from Greek *orobankhē* broomrape]

orogeny (ɒˈrɒdʒɪnɪ) or **orogenesis** (ˌɒrəʊˈdʒenɪsɪs) *n* the formation of mountain ranges by intense upward displacement of the earth's crust, usually associated with folding, thrust faulting, and other compressional processes > **orogenic** (ˌɒrəʊˈdʒenɪk) or **orogenetic** (ˌɒrəʊdʒɪˈnetɪk) *adj* > ˌoroˈgenically or ˌorogeˈnetically *adv*

orography (ɒˈrɒɡrəfɪ) or **orology** (ɒˈrɒlədʒɪ) *n* the study or mapping of relief, esp of mountains > oˈrographer or oˈrologist *n* > **orographic** (ˌɒrəʊˈɡræfɪk) or **orological** (ˌɒrəʊˈlɒdʒɪkəl) *adj* > ˌoroˈgraphically or ˌoroˈlogically *adv*

oroide (ˈɔːrəʊˌaɪd) *n* an alloy containing copper, tin, and other metals, used as imitation gold [C19 from French *or* gold + -OID]

orometer (ɒˈrɒmɪtə) *n* an aneroid barometer with an altitude scale [C19 from ORO-¹ (mountain, altitude) + -METER]

oronasal (ˌɔːrəʊˈneɪzəl) *adj anatomy* of or relating to the mouth and nose

Orontes (ɒˈrɒntiːz) *n* a river in SW Asia, rising in Lebanon and flowing north through Syria into Turkey, where it turns west to the Mediterranean. Length: 571 km (355 miles). Arabic name: ʿAsi

orotund (ˈɒrəʊˌtʌnd) *adj* **1** (of the voice) resonant; booming **2** (of speech or writing) bombastic; pompous [C18 from Latin phrase *ore rotundo* with rounded mouth]

orphan (ˈɔːfən) *n* **1 a** a child, one or (more commonly) both of whose parents are dead **b** (*as modifier*): *an orphan child* **2** *printing* the first line of a paragraph separated from the rest of the paragraph by occurring at the foot of a page ▷ *vb* **3** (*tr*) to deprive of one or both parents [C15 from Late Latin *orphanus*, from Greek *orphanos*; compare Latin *orbus* bereaved]

orphanage (ˈɔːfənɪdʒ) *n* **1** an institution for orphans and abandoned children **2** the state of being an orphan

orpharion (ɔːˈfærɪən) *n* a large lute in use during the 16th and 17th centuries [C16 from ORPHEUS + *Arion*, musicians of Greek mythology]

Orphean (ˈɔːfɪən) *adj* **1** of or relating to Orpheus **2** melodious or enchanting

Orpheus (ˈɔːfɪəs, -fjuːs) *n Greek myth* a poet and lyre-player credited with the authorship of the poems forming the basis of Orphism. He married Eurydice and sought her in Hades after her death. He failed to win her back and was killed by a band of bacchantes

Orphic (ˈɔːfɪk) *adj* **1** of or relating to Orpheus or Orphism **2** (*sometimes not capital*) mystical or occult > ˈOrphically *adv*

Orphism (ˈɔːfɪzəm) *n* a mystery religion of ancient Greece, widespread from the 6th century BC onwards, combining pre-Hellenic beliefs, the Thracian cult of (Dionysius) Zagreus, etc > Orˈphistic *adj*

orphrey or less commonly **orfray** (ˈɔːfrɪ) *n* a richly embroidered band or border, esp on an ecclesiastical vestment [C13 *orfreis*, from Old French, from Late Latin *aurifrisium, auriphrygium*, from Latin *aurum* gold + *Phrygius* Phrygian]

orpiment (ˈɔːpɪmənt) *n* a yellow mineral consisting of arsenic trisulphide in monoclinic crystalline form occurring in association with realgar: it is an ore of arsenic. Formula: As_2S_3 [C14 via Old French from Latin *auripigmentum* gold pigment]

orpine (ˈɔːpaɪn) or **orpin** (ˈɔːpɪn) *n* a succulent perennial N temperate crassulaceous plant, *Sedum telephium*, with toothed leaves and heads of small purplish-white flowers. Also called: (Brit) **livelong**, (US) **live-forever** [C14 from Old French, apparently from ORPIMENT (perhaps referring to the yellow flowers of a related species)]

Orpington¹ (ˈɔːpɪŋtən) *n* **1** a heavy breed of domestic fowl of various single colours, laying brown eggs **2** a breed of brown duck with an orange bill

Orpington² (ˈɔːpɪŋtən) *n* a district of SE London, part of the Greater London borough of Bromley from 1965

orra (ˈɒrə) *adj Scot* **1** odd or unmatched; supernumerary **2** occasional or miscellaneous **3 orra man** or **orraman** an odd-jobman [C18 of unknown origin]

orrery (ˈɒrərɪ) *n, pl* **-ries** a mechanical model of the solar system in which the planets can be moved at the correct relative velocities around the sun [C18 originally made for Charles Boyle, Earl of *Orrery*]

orris¹ or **orrice** (ˈɒrɪs) *n* **1** any of various irises, esp *Iris florentina*, that have fragrant rhizomes **2** Also called: ˈorrisroot the rhizome of such a plant, prepared and used as perfume [C16 variant of IRIS]

orris² (ˈɒrɪs) *n* a kind of lace made of gold or silver, used esp in the 18th century [from Old French *orfreis*, from Latin *auriphrygium* Phrygian gold]

Orsk (*Russian* ɔrsk) *n* a city in W Russia, on the Ural River: a major railway and industrial centre, with an oil refinery linked by pipeline with the Emba field (on the Caspian). Pop: 247 000 (2005 est)

ortanique (ˌɔːtəˈniːk) *n* a hybrid between an orange and a tangerine [C20 from OR(ANGE) + TAN(GERINE) + (UN)IQUE]

Ortegal (*Spanish* ɔrteˈɣal) *n* **Cape** a cape in NW Spain, projecting into the Bay of Biscay

Orth. *abbreviation for* Orthodox (religion)

orthicon (ˈɔːθɪˌkɒn) *n* a television camera tube in which an optical image produces a corresponding electrical charge pattern on a mosaic surface that is scanned from behind by an electron beam. The resulting discharge of the mosaic provides the output signal current. See also **image orthicon** [C20 from ORTHO- + ICON(OSCOPE)]

ortho- or before a vowel **orth-** *combining form* **1** straight or upright: *orthotropous* **2** perpendicular or at right angles: *orthoclastic* **3** correct or right: *orthodontics; orthodox; orthography; orthoptics* **4** (*often in*

O

italics) denoting an organic compound containing a benzene ring with substituents attached to adjacent carbon atoms (the 1,2- positions): *orthodinitrobenzene*. Abbreviation: *o-* Compare **para-¹** (sense 6), **meta-** (sense 4) **5** denoting an oxyacid regarded as the highest hydrated form of the anhydride or a salt of such an acid: *orthophosphoric acid*. Compare **meta-** (sense 6) **6** denoting a diatomic substance in which the spins of the two atoms are parallel: *orthohydrogen*. Compare **para-¹** (sense 8) [from Greek *orthos* straight, right, upright]

orthoboric acid (ˌɔːθəʊˈbɔːrɪk) *n* the more formal name for **boric acid** (sense 1)

orthocentre *or US* **orthocenter** (ˈɔːθəʊˌsɛntə) *n* the point of intersection of any two altitudes of a triangle

orthocephalic (ˌɔːθəʊsɪˈfælɪk) *or* **orthocephalous** (ˌɔːθəʊˈsɛfələs) *adj* having a skull whose breadth is between 70 and 75 per cent of its length > ˌortho'cephaly *n*

orthochromatic (ˌɔːθəʊkrəʊˈmætɪk) *adj photog* of or relating to an emulsion giving a rendering of relative light intensities of different colours that corresponds approximately to the colour sensitivity of the eye, esp one that is insensitive to red light Sometimes shortened to: ortho Compare **panchromatic**. > orthochromatism (ˌɔːθəʊˈkrəʊməˌtɪzəm) *n*

orthoclase (ˈɔːθəʊˌkleɪs, -ˌkleɪz) *n* a white to pale yellow, red, or green mineral of the feldspar group, found in igneous, sedimentary, and metamorphic rocks. It is used in the manufacture of glass and ceramics. Composition: potassium aluminium silicate. Formula: $KAlSi_3O_8$. Crystal structure: monoclinic

orthodontics (ˌɔːθəʊˈdɒntɪks) *or* **orthodontia** (ˌɔːθəʊˈdɒntɪə) *n* (*functioning as singular*) the branch of dentistry concerned with preventing or correcting irregularities of the teeth. Also called: **dental orthopaedics** > ˌortho'dontic *adj* > ˌortho'dontist *n*

orthodox (ˈɔːθəˌdɒks) *adj* **1** conforming with established or accepted standards, as in religion, behaviour, or attitudes **2** conforming to the Christian faith as established by the early Church [c16 via Church Latin from Greek *orthodoxos*, from *orthos* correct + *doxa* belief] > 'ortho,doxly *adv*

Orthodox (ˈɔːθəˌdɒks) *adj* **1** of or relating to the Orthodox Church of the East **2** (*sometimes not capital*) **a** of or relating to Orthodox Judaism **b** (of an individual Jew) strict in the observance of Talmudic law and in personal devotions

Orthodox Church *n* **1** Also called: **Byzantine Church, Eastern Orthodox Church, Greek Orthodox Church** the collective body of those Eastern Churches that were separated from the western Church in the 11th century and are in communion with the Greek patriarch of Constantinople **2** any of these Churches

Orthodox Judaism *n* the form of Judaism characterized by allegiance to the traditional interpretation and to strict observance of the Mosaic Law as interpreted in the Talmud, etc, and regarded as divinely revealed. Compare **Conservative Judaism, Reform Judaism**

orthodoxy (ˈɔːθəˌdɒksɪ) *n, pl* -doxies **1** orthodox belief or practice **2** the quality of being orthodox

orthoepy (ˈɔːθəʊˌɛpɪ) *n* the study of correct or standard pronunciation [c17 from Greek *orthoepeia*, from ORTHO- straight + *epos* word] > orthoepic (ˌɔːθəʊˈɛpɪk) *adj* > ˌortho'epically *adv*

orthogenesis (ˌɔːθəʊˈdʒɛnɪsɪs) *n* **1** *biology* **a** evolution of a group of organisms predetermined to occur in a particular direction **b** the theory that proposes such a development **2** the theory that there is a series of stages through which all cultures pass in the same order > **orthogenetic** (ˌɔːθəʊdʒɪˈnɛtɪk) *adj* > ˌorthoge'netically *adv*

orthogenic (ˌɔːθəʊˈdʒɛnɪk) *adj* **1** *med* relating to corrective procedures designed to promote healthy development **2** of or relating to

orthogenesis > ˌortho'genically *adv*

orthognathous (ɔːˈθɒɡnəθəs) *adj anatomy* having normally aligned jaws > or'thogna,thism *or* or'thognathy *n*

orthogonal (ɔːˈθɒɡənᵊl) *adj* **1** relating to, consisting of, or involving right angles; perpendicular **2** *maths* **a** (of a pair of vectors) having a defined scalar product equal to zero **b** (of a pair of functions) having a defined product equal to zero > or'thogonally *adv*

orthogonal matrix *n maths* a matrix that is the inverse of its transpose so that any two rows or any two columns are orthogonal vectors. Compare **symmetric matrix**

orthogonal projection *n engineering* the method used in engineering drawing of projecting views of the object being described, such as plan, elevation, side view, etc, at right angles to each other

orthographic (ˌɔːθəʊˈɡræfɪk) *or* **orthographical** *adj* of or relating to spelling > ˌortho'graphically *adv*

orthographic projection *n* **1** a style of engineering drawing in which true dimensions are represented as if projected from infinity on three planes perpendicular to each other, avoiding the effects of perspective **2** a type of zenithal map projection in which the area is mapped as if projected from infinity, with resulting distortion of scale away from the centre

orthography (ɔːˈθɒɡrəfɪ) *n, pl* -phies **1** a writing system **2 a** spelling considered to be correct **b** the principles underlying spelling **3** the study of spelling **4** orthographic projection > or'thographer *or* or'thographist *n*

orthohydrogen (ˌɔːθəʊˈhaɪdrədʒən) *n chem* the form of molecular hydrogen, constituting about 75 per cent of the total at normal temperatures, in which the nuclei of the atoms spin in the same direction. Compare **parahydrogen**

orthomorphic (ˌɔːθəʊˈmɔːfɪk) *adj geography* another word for **conformal** (sense 2)

orthopaedic *or US* **orthopedic** (ˌɔːθəʊˈpiːdɪk) *adj* **1** of or relating to orthopaedics **2** designed to help correct or ameliorate the discomfort of disorders of the spine and joints: *orthopaedic mattresses*

orthopaedics *or US* **orthopedics** (ˌɔːθəʊˈpiːdɪks) *n* (*functioning as singular*) **1** the branch of surgery concerned with the spine and joints and the repair of deformities of these parts **2** dental orthopaedics another name for orthodontics. > ˌortho'paedist *or US* ˌortho'pedist *n*

orthophosphate (ˌɔːθəʊˈfɒsfeɪt) *n* any salt or ester of orthophosphoric acid

orthophosphoric acid (ˌɔːθəʊfɒsˈfɒrɪk) *n* a colourless soluble solid tribasic acid used in the manufacture of fertilizers and soaps. Formula: H_3PO_4. Also called: **phosphoric acid**

orthophosphorous acid (ˌɔːθəʊˈfɒsfərəs) *n* a white or yellowish hygroscopic crystalline dibasic acid. Formula: H_3PO_3. Also called: **phosphorous acid**

orthopraxy (ˈɔːθəˌpræksɪ) *n theol* the belief that right action is as important as religious faith [from Greek *orthos* correct + *praxis* deed, action]

orthopsychiatry (ˌɔːθəʊsaɪˈkaɪətrɪ) *n* the study and treatment of mental disorders with emphasis on prevention during childhood > orthopsychiatric (ˌɔːθəʊˌsaɪkɪˈætrɪk) *adj* > ˌorthopsy'chiatrist *n*

orthopter (ˈɔːθɒptə) *n* another name for ornithopter

orthopteran (ɔːˈθɒptərən) *n, pl* -terans **1** Also: orthopteron, *pl* -tera (-tərə) any orthopterous insect ▷ *adj* **2** another word for orthopterous

orthopterous (ɔːˈθɒptərəs) *or* **orthopteran** *adj* of, relating to, or belonging to the *Orthoptera*, a large order of insects, including crickets, locusts, and grasshoppers, having leathery forewings and membranous hind wings, hind legs adapted for leaping, and organs of stridulation

orthoptic (ɔːˈθɒptɪk) *adj* relating to normal

binocular vision: *orthoptic exercises*

orthoptics (ɔːˈθɒptɪks) *n* (*functioning as singular*) the science or practice of correcting defective vision, as by exercises to strengthen weak eye muscles

orthoptist (ɔːˈθɒptɪst) *n* a person who is qualified to practise orthoptics

orthopyroxene (ˌɔːθəʊpaɪˈrɒksiːn) *n* a member of the pyroxene group of minerals having an orthorhombic crystal structure, such as enstatite and hypersthene

orthorhombic (ˌɔːθəʊˈrɒmbɪk) *adj crystallog* relating to the crystal system characterized by three mutually perpendicular unequal axes. Also: rhombic, trimetric

orthoscope (ˈɔːθəʊˌskəʊp) *n med obsolete* a 19th-century instrument for viewing the fundus of the eye through a layer of water, which eliminates distortion caused by the cornea

orthoscopic (ˌɔːθəʊˈskɒpɪk) *adj* **1** of, relating to, or produced by normal vision **2** yielding an undistorted image

orthosis (ɔːˈθəʊsɪs) *n, pl* -ses (-siːz) an artificial or mechanical aid, such as a brace, to support or assist movement of a weak or injured part of the body

orthostichy (ɔːˈθɒstɪkɪ) *n, pl* -chies **1** an imaginary vertical line that connects a row of leaves on a stem **2** an arrangement of leaves so connected ▷ Compare **parastichy** [c19 from ORTHO- + Greek *stikhos* line] > or'thostichous *adj*

orthotics (ɔːˈθɒtɪks) *n* (*functioning as singular*) the provision and use of artificial or mechanical aids, such as braces, to prevent or assist movement of weak or injured joints or muscles

orthotist (ɔːˈθɒtɪst) *n* a person who is qualified to practise orthotics

orthotone (ˈɔːθəʊˌtəʊn) *adj* **1** (of a word) having an independent accent ▷ *n* **2** an independently accented word

orthotropic (ˌɔːθəʊˈtrɒpɪk) *adj* **1** *botany* relating to or showing growth that is in direct line with the stimulus **2** (of a material) having different elastic properties in different planes > orthotropism (ɔːˈθɒtrəˌpɪzəm) *n*

orthotropous (ɔːˈθɒtrəpəs) *adj* (of a plant ovule) growing straight during development so that the micropyle is at the apex. Compare **anatropous**

Ortles (Italian ˈɔːtles) *pl n* a range of the Alps in N Italy. Highest peak: 3899 m (12 792 ft). Also called: Ortler (ˈɔːtlə)

ortolan (ˈɔːtələn) *n* **1** Also called: ortolan bunting a brownish Old World bunting, *Emberiza hortulana*, regarded as a delicacy **2** any of various other small birds eaten as delicacies, esp the bobolink [c17 via French from Latin *hortulānus*, from *hortulus*, diminutive of *hortus* garden]

orts (ɔːts) *pl n* (*sometimes singular*) *archaic or dialect* scraps or leavings [c15 of Germanic origin; related to Dutch *oorete*, from *oor-* remaining + *ete* food]

Oruro (Spanish oˈruro) *n* a city in W Bolivia: a former silver-mining centre; university (1892); tin, copper, and tungsten. Pop: 206 000 (2005 est)

Orvieto (Italian orˈvjɛːto) *n* **1** a market town in central Italy, in Umbria: Etruscan remains. Pop: 20 705 (2001). Latin name: Urbs Vetus (ˈvəbz ˈviːtəs) **2** a light white wine from this region

Orwellian (ɔːˈwɛlɪən) *adj* of, relating to, or reminiscent of George Orwell (real name *Eric Arthur Blair*), the English novelist (1903–50), particularly his portrayal of an authoritarian state

-ory¹ *suffix* forming nouns **1** indicating a place for: *observatory* **2** something having a specified use: *directory* [via Old French *-orie*, from Latin *-ōrium, -ōria*]

-ory² *suffix* forming adjectives of or relating to; characterized by; having the effect of: *contributory; promissory* [via Old French *-orie*, from Latin *-ōrius*]

Oryol (Russian aˈrjɔl) *n* a variant spelling of **Orel**

oryx (ˈɒrɪks) *n, pl* -yxes *or* -yx any large African antelope of the genus *Oryx*, typically having long straight nearly upright horns [c14 via Latin from

Greek *orux* stonemason's axe, used also of the pointed horns of an antelope]

os¹ (ɒs) *n, pl* **ossa** ('ɒsə) *anatomy* the technical name for **bone** [c16 from Latin: bone; compare Greek *osteon*]

os² (ɒs) *n, pl* **ora** ('ɔːrə) *anatomy, zoology* a mouth or mouthlike part or opening [c18 from Latin]

os³ (əʊs) *n, pl* **osar** ('əʊsɑː) another name for **esker** [c19 *osar* (pl), from Swedish *ås* (sing) ridge]

Os *the chemical symbol for* osmium

OS *abbreviation for* **1** Old School **2** Old Style (method of reckoning dates) **3** Ordinary Seaman **4** (in Britain) **Ordnance Survey 5** outsize **6** Old Saxon (language)

o.s., OS *or* **O/S** *abbreviation for* **1** out of stock **2** *banking* outstanding

OSA *abbreviation for* Order of Saint Augustine

Osage (əʊ'seɪdʒ, 'əʊseɪdʒ) *n* **1** (*pl* **Osages** *or* **Osage**) a member of a North American Indian people formerly living in an area between the Missouri and Arkansas Rivers **2** the language of this people, belonging to the Siouan family

Osage orange *n* **1** a North American moraceous tree, *Maclura pomifera,* grown for hedges and ornament **2** the warty orange-like fruit of this plant

Osaka (əʊ'sɑːkə) *n* a port in S Japan, on S Honshu on **Osaka Bay** (an inlet of the Pacific): the third largest city in Japan (the chief commercial city during feudal times); university (1931); an industrial and commercial centre. Pop: 2 484 326 (2002 est)

OSB *abbreviation for* Order of Saint Benedict

Osborne House ('ɒz,bɔːn) *n* a house near Cowes on the Isle of Wight: the favourite residence of Queen Victoria, who died there; now a convalescent home

Oscan ('ɒskən) *n* **1** an extinct language of ancient S Italy belonging to the Italic branch of the Indo-European family. See also **Osco-Umbrian 2** a speaker of this language; Samnite ▷ *adj* **3** of or relating to this language

oscar ('ɒskə) *n Austral slang, rare* cash; money [c20 rhyming slang, from *Oscar* Asche (1871–1936), Australian actor]

Oscar ('ɒskə) *n* **1 a** any of several small gold statuettes awarded annually in the United States by the Academy of Motion Picture Arts and Sciences for outstanding achievements in films. Official name: **Academy Award b** (*sometimes not capital*) an award made in recognition of outstanding endeavour in any of various other fields: *the TV Oscars* **2** (*without capital*) any annual award for excellence **3** *communications* a code word for the letter *o* [c20 sense 1 said to have been named after a remark made by an official on first seeing the statuette, that it reminded her of her uncle Oscar]

OSCE *abbreviation for* Organization for Security and Cooperation in Europe

oscillate ('ɒsɪ,leɪt) *vb* **1** (*intr*) to move or swing from side to side regularly **2** (*intr*) to waver between opinions, courses of action, etc **3** *physics* to undergo or produce or cause to undergo or produce oscillation [c18 from Latin *oscillāre* to swing, from *oscillum* a swing]

oscillating universe theory *n* the theory that the universe is oscillating between periods of expansion and collapse

oscillation (,ɒsɪ'leɪʃən) *n* **1** *physics, statistics* **a** regular fluctuation in value, position, or state about a mean value, such as the variation in an alternating current or the regular swinging of a pendulum **b** a single cycle of such a fluctuation **2** the act or process of oscillating ▷ **oscillatory** ('ɒsɪlətərɪ, -trɪ) *adj*

oscillator ('ɒsɪ,leɪtə) *n* **1** a circuit or instrument for producing an alternating current or voltage of a required frequency **2** any instrument for producing oscillations **3** a person or thing that oscillates

oscillogram (ɒ'sɪlə,græm) *n* the recording

obtained from an oscillograph or the trace on an oscilloscope screen

oscillograph (ɒ'sɪlə,grɑːf, -,græf) *n* a device for producing a graphical record of the variation of an oscillating quantity, such as an electric current ▷ **oscillographic** (ɒ,sɪlə'græfɪk) *adj* ▷ **oscillography** (,ɒsɪ'lɒgrəfɪ) *n*

oscilloscope (ɒ'sɪlə,skəʊp) *n* an instrument for producing a representation of a quantity that rapidly changes with time on the screen of a cathode-ray tube. The changes are converted into electric signals, which are applied to plates in the cathode-ray tube. Changes in the magnitude of the potential across the plates deflect the electron beam and thus produce a trace on the screen

oscine ('ɒsaɪn, 'ɒsɪn) *adj* of, relating to, or belonging to the *Oscines,* a suborder of passerine birds that includes most of the songbirds [c17 via New Latin from Latin *oscen* singing bird]

oscitancy ('ɒsɪtənsɪ) *or* **oscitance** *n, pl* **-tancies** *or* **-tances 1** the state of being drowsy, lazy, or inattentive **2** the act of yawning ▷ Also called: **oscitation** [c17 from Latin *oscitāre* to gape, yawn] ▷ **'oscitant** *adj*

Osco-Umbrian (,ɒskəʊ'ʌmbrɪən) *n* **1** a group of extinct languages of ancient Italy, including Oscan, Umbrian, and Sabellian, which were displaced by Latin ▷ *adj* **2** relating to or belonging to this group of languages

osculant ('ɒskjʊlənt) *adj* **1** *biology* (of an organism or group of organisms) possessing some of the characteristics of two different taxonomic groups **2** *zoology* closely joined or adhering [c19 from Latin *ōsculārī* to kiss; see OSCULUM]

oscular ('ɒskjʊlə) *adj* **1** *zoology* of or relating to an osculum **2** of or relating to the mouth or to kissing

osculate ('ɒskjʊ,leɪt) *vb* **1** *usually humorous* to kiss **2** (*intr*) (of an organism or group of organisms) to be intermediate between two taxonomic groups **3** *geometry* to touch in osculation [c17 from Latin *ōsculārī* to kiss; see OSCULUM]

osculation (,ɒskjʊ'leɪʃən) *n* **1** Also called: **tacnode** *maths* a point at which two branches of a curve have a common tangent, each branch extending in both directions of the tangent **2** *rare* the act or an instance of kissing ▷ **osculatory** ('ɒskjʊlətərɪ, -trɪ) *adj*

osculum ('ɒskjʊləm) *n, pl* **-la** (-lə) *zoology* a mouthlike aperture, esp the opening in a sponge out of which water passes [c17 from Latin: a kiss, little mouth, diminutive of *ōs* mouth]

OSD *abbreviation for* Order of Saint Dominic

-ose¹ *suffix forming adjectives* possessing; resembling: *verbose; grandiose* [from Latin *-ōsus;* see -OUS]

-ose² *suffix forming nouns* **1** indicating a carbohydrate, esp a sugar: *lactose* **2** indicating a decomposition product of protein: *albumose* [from GLUCOSE]

OSF *abbreviation for* Order of Saint Francis

Oshawa ('ɒʃəwə) *n* a city in central Canada, in SE Ontario on Lake Ontario: motor-vehicle industry. Pop: 139 051 (2001)

Oshogbo (ə'fɒgbəʊ) *n* a city in SW Nigeria: trade centre. Pop: 629 000 (2005 est)

Oshun (əʊ'ʃʌn) *or* **Osun** *n* a state of SW Nigeria. Capital: Oshogbo. Pop: 2 463 185 (1995 est). Area 9251 sq km (3570 sq miles)

OSI *abbreviation for* open systems interconnection; an international standardization model to facilitate communications among computers with different protocols

osier ('əʊzɪə) *n* **1** any of various willow trees, esp *Salix viminalis,* whose flexible branches or twigs are used for making baskets, etc **2** a twig or branch from such a tree **3** any of several North American dogwoods, esp the red osier [c14 from Old French, probably from Medieval Latin *auseria,* perhaps of Gaulish origin; compare Breton *aoz*]

Osijek (*Serbo-Croat* 'ɔsijɛk) *n* a town in NE Croatia situated on the right bank of the Drava River: under Turkish rule from 1526 to 1687. Pop: 85 000

(2005 est). Ancient name: **Mursa** ('mʊəsə)

Osiris (əʊ'saɪrɪs) *n* an ancient Egyptian god, ruler of the underworld and judge of the dead ▷ **O'sirian** *adj*

-osis *suffix forming nouns* **1** indicating a process or state: *metamorphosis* **2** indicating a diseased condition: *tuberculosis.* Compare **-iasis 3** indicating the formation or development of something: *fibrosis* [from Greek, suffix used to form nouns from verbs with infinitives in *-oein* or *-oun*]

Oslo ('ɒzləʊ; *Norwegian* 'uslu) *n* the capital and chief port of Norway, in the southeast at the head of **Oslo Fjord** (an inlet of the Skagerrak): founded in about 1050; university (1811); a major commercial and industrial centre, producing about a quarter of Norway's total output. Pop: 521 886 (2004 est). Former names: **Christiania** (1624–1877), **Kristiania** (1877–1924)

Osmanli (ɒz'mænlɪ) *adj* **1** of or relating to the Ottoman Empire ▷ *n* **2** (*pl* **-lis**) (formerly) a subject of the Ottoman Empire **3** the Turkish language, esp as written in Arabic letters under the Ottoman Empire [c19 from Turkish, from Osman I (1259–1326), Turkish sultan]

osmic ('ɒzmɪk) *adj* of or containing osmium in a high valence state, esp the tetravalent state

osmious ('ɒzmɪəs) *adj* another word for **osmous**

osmiridium (,ɒzmɪ'rɪdɪəm) *n* a very hard corrosion-resistant white or grey natural alloy of osmium and iridium in variable proportions, often containing smaller amounts of platinum, ruthenium, and rhodium: used esp in pen nibs. Also: **iridosmine** [c19 from OSM(IUM) + IRIDIUM]

osmium ('ɒzmɪəm) *n* a very hard brittle bluish-white metal occurring with platinum and alloyed with iridium in osmiridium: used to produce platinum alloys, mainly for pen tips and instrument pivots, as a catalyst, and in electric-light filaments. Symbol: Os; atomic no.: 76; atomic wt.: 190.2; valency: 0 to 8; relative density: 22.57; melting pt.: 3033±30°C; boiling pt.: 5012±100°C [c19 from Greek *osmē* smell, so called from its penetrating odour]

osmium tetroxide *n* a yellowish poisonous water-soluble crystalline substance with a penetrating odour, used as a reagent and catalyst in organic synthesis. Formula: OsO_4

osmometer (ɒz'mɒmɪtə) *n* an instrument for measuring osmotic pressure [c20 from OSMO(SIS) + -METER] ▷ **osmometric** (,ɒzmə'mɛtrɪk) *adj* ▷ ,osmo'metrically *adv* ▷ os'mometry *n*

osmoregulation (,ɒzməʊ,rɛgjʊ'leɪʃən) *n zoology* the adjustment of the osmotic pressure of a cell or organism in relation to the surrounding fluid

osmose ('ɒzməʊs, -məʊz, -ɒs-) *vb* **1** to undergo or cause to undergo osmosis ▷ *n* **2** a former name for **osmosis** [c19 (n): abstracted from the earlier terms *endosmose* and *exosmose;* related to Greek *ōsmos* push, thrust]

osmosis (ɒz'məʊsɪs, ɒs-) *n* **1** the passage of a solvent through a semipermeable membrane from a less concentrated to a more concentrated solution until both solutions are of the same concentration **2** diffusion through any membrane or porous barrier, as in dialysis **3** gradual or unconscious assimilation or adoption, as of ideas [c19 Latinized form from OSMOSE (n), from Greek *ōsmos* push, thrust] ▷ **osmotic** (ɒz'mɒtɪk, ɒs-) *adj* ▷ os'motically *adv*

osmotic pressure *n* the pressure necessary to prevent osmosis into a given solution when the solution is separated from the pure solvent by a semipermeable membrane

osmous ('ɒzməs) *adj* of or containing osmium in a low valence state, esp the divalent state. Also: osmious

osmunda (ɒz'mʌndə) *or* **osmund** ('ɒzmənd) *n* any fern of the genus *Osmunda,* such as the royal fern, having large spreading fronds: family *Osmundaceae* [c13 from Old French *osmonde,* of unknown origin]

Osnabrück (*German* ɔsna'brʏk) *n* an industrial

O

city in NW Germany, in Lower Saxony: a member of the Hanseatic League in the Middle Ages; one of the treaties comprising the Peace of Westphalia (1648) was signed here. Pop: 165 517 (2003 est)

osnaburg ('ɒznəˌbɜːɡ) *n* a coarse plain-woven cotton used for sacks, furnishings, etc [C16 corruption of OSNABRÜCK, where it was originally made]

osprey ('ɒsprɪ, -preɪ) *n* **1** a large broad-winged fish-eating diurnal bird of prey, *Pandion haliaetus,* with a dark back and whitish head and underparts: family *Pandionidae.* Often called (US and Canadian): **fish hawk 2** any of the feathers of various other birds, used esp as trimming for hats [C15 from Old French *ospres,* apparently from Latin *ossifraga,* literally: bone-breaker, from *os* bone + *frangere* to break]

ossa ('ɒsə) *n* the plural of **os**[1]

Ossa ('ɒsə) *n* a mountain in NE Greece, in E Thessaly: famous in mythology for the attempt of the twin giants, Otus and Ephialtes, to reach heaven by piling Ossa on Olympus and Pelion on Ossa. Height: 1978 m (6489 ft)

ossein ('ɒsɪɪn) *n* a protein that forms the organic matrix of bone, constituting about 40 per cent of its matter [C19 from Latin *osseus* bony, from *os* bone]

osseous ('ɒsɪəs) *adj* consisting of or containing bone, bony [C17 from Latin *osseus,* from *os* bone] > 'osseously *adv*

Osset ('ɒsɪt) *n* a member of an Iranian people living in S Russia and N Georgia, chiefly in Ossetia in the Caucasus

Ossetia (ɒ'siːtjə, ɒ'sɛtjə) *n* a region of central Asia, in the Caucasus: consists administratively of the North Ossetian Republic in Russia and the South Ossetian Autonomous Region in Georgia

Ossetic (ɒ'sɛtɪk) *or* **Ossetian** (ɒ'siːʃən) *adj* **1** of or relating to Ossetia, its people, or their language ▷ *n* **2** the language of the Ossets, belonging to the East Iranian branch of the Indo-European family

Ossi ('ɒsɪ; German 'ɔsɪ) *n informal* a native, inhabitant, or citizen of that part of Germany that was formerly East Germany [C20 from German *ostdeutsch* East German]

Ossianic (ˌɒsɪ'ænɪk) *adj* of, relating to, or reminiscent of Ossian, a legendary Irish hero and bard of the 3rd century A.D

ossicle ('ɒsɪkəl) *n* a small bone, esp one of those in the middle ear [C16 from Latin *ossiculum,* from *os* bone] > **ossicular** (ɒ'sɪkjʊlə) *adj*

Ossie ('ɒzɪ) *adj, n* a variant spelling of **Aussie**

ossiferous (ɒ'sɪfərəs) *adj geology* containing or yielding bones: *ossiferous caves*

ossification (ˌɒsɪfɪ'keɪʃən) *n* **1** the formation or conversion into bone **2** the process of ossifying or the state of being ossified

ossified ('ɒsɪˌfaɪd) *adj* **1** converted into bone **2** having become set and inflexible **3** *Irish slang* intoxicated; drunk

ossifrage ('ɒsɪfrɪdʒ, -ˌfreɪdʒ) *n* an archaic name for the **lammergeier** and **osprey** (sense 1) [C17 from Latin *ossifraga* sea eagle; see OSPREY]

ossify ('ɒsɪˌfaɪ) *vb* **-fies, -fying, -fied 1** to convert or be converted into bone **2** (*intr*) (of habits, attitudes, etc) to become inflexible [C18 from French *ossifier,* from Latin *os* bone + *facere* to make] > 'ossi,fier *n*

osso bucco ('ɒsəʊ 'bʊkəʊ) *n* a stew, originally from Italy, made with knuckle of veal, cooked in tomato sauce [C20 from Italian: marrowbone]

ossuary ('ɒsjʊərɪ) *n, pl* **-aries** any container for the burial of human bones, such as an urn or vault [C17 from Late Latin *ossuārium,* from *os* bone]

OST (in the US) *abbreviation for* Office of Science and Technology

osteal ('ɒstɪəl) *adj* **1** of or relating to bone or to the skeleton **2** composed of bone; osseous [C19 from Greek *osteon* bone]

osteichthyan (ˌɒstɪ'ɪkθɪən) *n zoology* a technical name for **bony fish** [New Latin, from Greek *osteon* bone + *ikhthus* fish]

osteitis (ˌɒstɪ'aɪtɪs) *n* inflammation of a bone > **osteitic** (ˌɒstɪ'ɪtɪk) *adj*

osteitis deformans (dɪ'fɔːmænz) *n* another name for **Paget's disease** (sense 1)

Ostend (ɒs'tɛnd) *n* a port and resort in NW Belgium, in West Flanders on the North Sea. Pop: 68 273 (2004 est). French name: Ostende (ɔstɑ̃d) Flemish name: Oostende

ostensible (ɒ'stɛnsɪbəl) *adj* **1** apparent; seeming **2** pretended [C18 via French from Medieval Latin *ostensibilis,* from Latin *ostendere* to show, from *ob-* before + *tendere* to extend] > os,tensi'bility *n*

ostensibly (ɒ'stɛnsɪblɪ) *adv* (*sentence modifier*) apparently; seemingly

ostensive (ɒ'stɛnsɪv) *adj* **1** obviously or manifestly demonstrative **2** a less common word for **ostensible 3** *philosophy* (of a definition) given by demonstrative means, esp by pointing [C17 from Late Latin *ostentīvus,* from Latin *ostendere* to show; see OSTENSIBLE] > os'tensively *adv*

ostensory (ɒs'tɛnsərɪ) *n, pl* **-sories** *RC Church* another word for **monstrance** [C18 from Medieval Latin *ostensorium;* see OSTENSIBLE]

ostentation (ˌɒstɛn'teɪʃən) *n* pretentious, showy, or vulgar display

ostentatious (ˌɒstɛn'teɪʃəs) *adj* characterized by pretentious, showy, or vulgar display > ˌosten'tatiously *adv*

osteo- *or before a vowel* **oste-** *combining form* indicating bone or bones: *osteopathy* [from Greek *osteon*]

osteoarthritis (ˌɒstɪəʊɑː'θraɪtɪs) *n* chronic inflammation of the joints, esp those that bear weight, with pain and stiffness. Also called: **degenerative joint disease** > **osteoarthritic** (ˌɒstɪəʊɑː'θrɪtɪk) *adj, n*

osteoblast ('ɒstɪəʊˌblæst) *n* a bone-forming cell > ˌosteo'blastic *adj*

osteoclasis (ˌɒstɪ'ɒkləsɪs) *n* **1** surgical fracture of a bone to correct deformity **2** absorption of bone tissue

osteoclast ('ɒstɪəʊˌklæst) *n* **1** a surgical instrument for fracturing bone **2** a large multinuclear cell formed in bone marrow that is associated with the normal absorption of bone > ˌosteo'clastic *adj*

osteofibrosis (ˌɒstɪəʊfaɪ'brəʊsɪs) *n* loss of calcium from the bones, causing them to become fragile

osteogenesis (ˌɒstɪəʊ'dʒɛnɪsɪs) *n* the formation of bone > ˌosteo'genic *adj*

osteogenesis imperfecta (ˌɪmpə'fɛktə) *n* a hereditary disease caused by a collagen abnormality, causing fragility of the skeleton which results in fractures and deformities. Also called: **brittle bone syndrome**

osteoid ('ɒstɪˌɔɪd) *adj* of or resembling bone; bony

osteology (ˌɒstɪ'ɒlədʒɪ) *n* the study of the structure and function of bones > **osteological** (ˌɒstɪə'lɒdʒɪkəl) *adj* > ˌosteo'logically *adv* > ˌoste'ologist *n*

osteoma (ˌɒstɪ'əʊmə) *n, pl* **-mata** (-mətə) *or* **-mas** a benign tumour composed of bone or bonelike tissue

osteomalacia (ˌɒstɪəʊmə'leɪʃɪə) *n* a disease in adults characterized by softening of the bones, resulting from a deficiency of vitamin D and of calcium and phosphorus [C19 from New Latin, from OSTEO- + Greek *malakia* softness] > ˌosteoma'lacial *or* osteomalacic (ˌɒstɪəʊmə'læsɪk) *adj*

osteomyelitis (ˌɒstɪəʊˌmaɪɪ'laɪtɪs) *n* inflammation of bone marrow, caused by infection

osteopath ('ɒstɪəˌpæθ) *or less commonly* **osteopathist** (ˌɒstɪ'ɒpəθɪst) *n* a person who practises osteopathy

osteopathy (ˌɒstɪ'ɒpəθɪ) *n* a system of healing based on the manipulation of bones or other parts of the body > **osteopathic** (ˌɒstɪə'pæθɪk) *adj* > ˌosteo'pathically *adv*

osteophyte ('ɒstɪəˌfaɪt) *n* a small abnormal bony

outgrowth > **osteophytic** (ˌɒstɪə'fɪtɪk) *adj*

osteoplastic (ˌɒstɪə'plæstɪk) *adj* **1** of or relating to osteoplasty **2** of or relating to the formation of bone

osteoplasty ('ɒstɪəˌplæstɪ) *n, pl* **-ties** the branch of surgery concerned with bone repair or bone grafting

osteoporosis (ˌɒstɪəʊpɔː'rəʊsɪs) *n* porosity and brittleness of the bones due to loss of calcium from the bone matrix [C19 from OSTEO- + PORE[2] + -OSIS] > ˌosteopo'rotic *adj*

osteotome ('ɒstɪəˌtəʊm) *n* a surgical instrument for cutting bone, usually a special chisel

osteotomy (ˌɒstɪ'ɒtəmɪ) *n, pl* **-mies** the surgical cutting or dividing of bone, usually to correct a deformity

Österreich ('øːstəraɪç) *n* the German name for Austria

Ostia ('ɒstɪə) *n* an ancient town in W central Italy, originally at the mouth of the Tiber but now about 6 km (4 miles) inland: served as the port of ancient Rome; harbours built by Claudius and Trajan; ruins excavated since 1854

ostiary ('ɒstɪərɪ) *n, pl* **-aries** *RC Church* another word for **porter**[2] (sense 4) [C15 from Latin *ostiārius* doorkeeper, from *ostium* door]

ostinato (ˌɒstɪ'nɑːtəʊ) *n* **a** a continuously reiterated musical phrase **b** (*as modifier*): *an ostinato passage* [Italian: from Latin *obstinātus* OBSTINATE]

ostiole ('ɒstɪˌəʊl) *n biology* **1** the pore in the reproductive bodies of certain algae and fungi through which spores pass **2** any small pore [C19 from Latin *ostiolum,* diminutive of *ostium* door] > **ostiolar** ('ɒstɪələ) *or* 'ostio,late *adj*

ostium ('ɒstɪəm) *n, pl* **-tia** (-tɪə) *biology* **1** any of the pores in sponges through which water enters the body **2** any of the openings in the heart of an arthropod through which blood enters **3** any similar opening [C17 from Latin: door, entrance]

ostler *or* **hostler** ('ɒslə) *n archaic* a stableman, esp one at an inn [C15 variant of *hostler,* from HOSTEL]

Ostmark ('ɒst,mɑːk; German 'ɔstmark) *n* (formerly) the standard monetary unit of East Germany, divided into 100 pfennigs [German, literally: east mark]

ostosis (ɒs'təʊsɪs) *n* the formation of bone; ossification

Ostpreussen ('ɔstprɔysən) *n* the German name for **East Prussia**

ostracize *or* **ostracise** ('ɒstrəˌsaɪz) *vb* (*tr*) **1** to exclude or banish (a person) from a particular group, society, etc **2** (in ancient Greece) to punish by temporary exile [C17 from Greek *ostrakizein* to select someone for banishment by voting on potsherds; see OSTRACON] > 'ostracism *n* > 'ostra,cizable *or* 'ostra,cisable *adj* > 'ostra,cizer *or* 'ostra,ciser *n*

ostracod ('ɒstrəˌkɒd) *n* any minute crustacean of the mainly freshwater subclass *Ostracoda,* in which the body is enclosed in a transparent two-valved carapace [C19 via New Latin from Greek *ostrakōdēs* having a shell, from *ostrakon* shell] > **ostracodan** (ˌɒstrə'kəʊdən) *or* ˌostra'codous *adj*

ostracoderm ('ɒstrəkəˌdɜːm, ɒ'strækə-) *n* any extinct Palaeozoic fishlike jawless vertebrate of the group *Ostracodermi,* characterized by a heavily armoured body [C19 via New Latin from Greek *ostrakon* shell + -DERM]

ostracon ('ɒstrəˌkɒn) *n* (in ancient Greece) a potsherd used for ostracizing [from Greek]

Ostrava (*Czech* 'ɔstrava) *n* an industrial city in the E Czech Republic, on the River Oder: the chief coal-mining area in the Czech Republic, in Upper Silesia. Pop: 316 000 (2005 est)

ostrich ('ɒstrɪtʃ) *n, pl* **-triches** *or* **-trich 1** a fast-running flightless African bird, *Struthio camelus,* that is the largest living bird, with stout two-toed feet and dark feathers, except on the naked head, neck, and legs: order *Struthioniformes* (see **ratite**). Related adj: **struthious 2** American ostrich another name for **rhea 3** a person who refuses to recognize the truth, reality, etc: a reference to the ostrich's supposed habit of burying its head in the sand [C13 from Old French *ostrice*, from Latin *avis* bird + Late Latin *struthio* ostrich, from Greek *strouthion*]

Ostrogoth ('ɒstrə,gɒθ) *n* a member of the eastern group of the Goths, who formed a kingdom in Italy from 493 to 552 [C17 from Late Latin *Ostrogothī*, from *ostro*- east, eastward + GOTH] ▷ ,Ostro'gothic *adj*

Ostyak ('ɒstɪ,æk) *n* 1 (*pl* -aks *or* -ak) a member of an Ugrian people living in NW Siberia E of the Urals 2 the language of this people, belonging to the Finno-Ugric family: related to Hungarian

Osun (ʊ'sʊn) *n* a variant spelling of **Oshun**

Oświęcim (*Polish* ɔʃˈfjɛntʃim) *n* the Polish name for **Auschwitz**

OT *abbreviation for* 1 occupational therapy 2 occupational therapist 3 Old Testament 4 overtime

ot- *combining form* a variant of **oto-** before a vowel: *otalgia*

Otago (ɒˈtɑːgəʊ) *n* a council region of New Zealand, formerly a province, founded by Scottish settlers in the south of South Island. The University of Otago (1869) in Dunedin is the oldest university in New Zealand. Chief town: Dunedin. Pop: 195 000 (2004 est)

otalgia (əʊ'tældʒɪə, -dʒə) *n* the technical name for **earache**

OTC *abbreviation for* 1 (in Britain) Officers' Training Corps 2 **over-the-counter** 3 oxytetracycline

OTE *abbreviation for* on-target earnings: referring to the salary a salesperson should be able to achieve

O tempora! O mores! Latin (əʊ 'tɛmpɔːrɑː əʊ 'mɔːreɪz) *sentence substitute* oh the times! oh the customs!: an exclamation at the evil of them [from Cicero's oration *In Catilinam*]

other ('ʌðə) *determiner* 1 a (when used before a singular noun, usually preceded by *the*) the remaining (one or ones in a group of which one or some have been specified): *I'll read the other sections of the paper later* b **the other** (*as pronoun; functioning as sing*): *one walks while the other rides* 2 (a) different (one or ones from that or those already specified or understood): *he found some other house; no other man but you; other days were happier* 3 additional; further: *there are no other possibilities* 4 (preceded by *every*) alternate; two: *it buzzes every other minute* 5 **other than** a apart from; besides: *a lady other than his wife* b different from: *he couldn't be other than what he is.* Archaic form: **other from** 6 **no other** *archaic* nothing else: *I can do no other* 7 **or other** (preceded by a phrase or word with *some*) used to add vagueness to the preceding pronoun, noun, noun phrase, or adverb: *some dog or other bit him; he's somewhere or other* 8 **other things being equal** conditions being the same or unchanged 9 **the other day, night,** etc a few days, nights, etc, ago 10 **the other thing** an unexpressed alternative ▷ *pron* 11 another: *show me one other* 12 (*plural*) additional or further ones: *the police have found two and are looking for others* 13 (*plural*) other people or things 14 **the others** the remaining ones (of a group): *take these and leave the others* 15 (*plural*) different ones (from those specified or understood): *they'd rather have others, not these.* See also **each other, one another** ▷ *adv* 16 (usually used with a negative and foll by *than*) otherwise; differently: *they couldn't behave other than they do* [Old English *ōther*; related to Old Saxon *āthar, ōthar,* Old High German *andar*]

▮ USAGE See at **otherwise**

other-directed *adj* guided by values derived from external influences. Compare **inner-directed**

otherness ('ʌðənɪs) *n* the quality of being different or distinct in appearance, character, etc

other ranks *pl n* (rarely used in singular) chiefly Brit (in the armed forces) all those who do not hold a commissioned rank

otherwhere ('ʌðə,wɛə) *adv archaic, poetic* elsewhere

otherwise ('ʌðə,waɪz) *sentence connector* 1 or else; if

not, then: *go home — otherwise your mother will worry* ▷ *adv* 2 differently: *I wouldn't have thought otherwise* 3 in other respects: *an otherwise hopeless situation* ▷ *adj* 4 (*predicative*) of an unexpected nature; different: *the facts are otherwise* ▷ *pron* 5 something different in outcome: *success or otherwise* [C14 from Old English *on ōthre wīsan* in other manner]

▮ USAGE The expression *otherwise than* means *in any other way than* and should not be followed by an adjective: *no-one taught by this method can be other than (not otherwise than) successful; you are not allowed to use the building otherwise than as a private dwelling*

other world *n* the spirit world or afterlife

otherworldly (,ʌðə'wɜːldlɪ) *adj* 1 of or relating to the spiritual or imaginative world 2 impractical or unworldly ▷ ,other'worldliness *n*

Othin ('əʊðɪn) *n* a variant of **Odin**

Othman ('ɒθmən, ɒθ'mɑːn) *adj, n* a variant of **Ottoman**

otic ('əʊtɪk, 'ɒtɪk) *adj* of or relating to the ear [C17 from Greek *ōtikos*, from *ous* ear]

-otic *suffix forming adjectives* 1 relating to or affected by: *sclerotic* 2 causing: *narcotic* [from Greek *-ōtikos*]

otiose ('əʊtɪ,əʊs, -,əʊz) *adj* 1 serving no useful purpose: *otiose language* 2 *rare* indolent; lazy [C18 from Latin *otiōsus* leisured, from *ōtium* leisure] ▷ **otiosity** (,əʊtɪ'ɒsɪtɪ) *or* **otioseness** *n*

otitis (əʊ'taɪtɪs) *n* inflammation of the ear, esp the middle ear (**otitis media**), with pain, impaired hearing, etc, or the outer ear (**otitis externa**), with inflammation between the ear drum and the external opening. See also **labyrinthitis**

oto- *or before a vowel* **ot-** *combining form* indicating the ear: *otitis; otolith* [from Greek *ous, ōt-* ear]

otocyst ('əʊtəʊ,sɪst) *n* 1 another name for **statocyst** 2 the embryonic structure in vertebrates that develops into the inner ear in the adult ▷ ,oto'cystic *adj*

otolaryngology (,əʊtəʊ,lærɪŋ'gɒlədʒɪ) *n* the branch of medicine concerned with the ear, nose, and throat and their diseases. Sometimes called: **otorhinolaryngology** ▷ **otolaryngological** (,əʊtəʊlə,rɪŋgə'lɒdʒɪkəl) *adj* ▷ ,oto,laryn'gologist *n*

otolith ('əʊtəʊ,lɪθ) *n* 1 any of the granules of calcium carbonate in the inner ear of vertebrates. Movement of otoliths, caused by a change in position of the animal, stimulates sensory hair cells, which convey the information to the brain 2 another name for **statolith** (sense 1) ▷ ,oto'lithic *adj*

otology (əʊ'tɒlədʒɪ) *n* the branch of medicine concerned with the ear ▷ **otological** (,əʊtə'lɒdʒɪkəl) *adj* ▷ o'tologist *n*

otorrhoea (,əʊtə'rɪə) *n pathol* a discharge from the ears

otoscope ('əʊtəʊ,skəʊp) *n* another name for **auriscope**. ▷ **otoscopic** (,əʊtəʊ'skɒpɪk) *adj*

Otranto (*Italian* 'ɔːtranto) *n* a small port in SE Italy, in Apulia on the **Strait of Otranto:** the most easterly town in Italy; dates back to Greek times and was an important Roman port; its ruined castle was the setting of Horace Walpole's *Castle of Otranto.* Pop: 5282 (2001)

OTT *slang abbreviation for* over the top: see **top¹** (sense 19b)

ottar ('ɒtə) *n* a variant of **attar**

ottava (əʊ'tɑːvə) *n* an interval of an octave. See **all'ottava** [Italian: OCTAVE]

ottava rima ('riːmə) *n prosody* a stanza form consisting of eight iambic pentameter lines, rhyming a b a b a b c c [Italian: eighth rhyme]

Ottawa ('ɒtəwə) *n* 1 the capital of Canada, in E Ontario on the Ottawa River: name changed from Bytown to Ottawa in 1854. Pop: 774 072 (2001) 2 a river in central Canada, rising in W Quebec and flowing west, then southeast to join the St Lawrence River as its chief tributary at Montreal; forms the border between Quebec and Ontario for most of its length. Length: 1120 km (696 miles)

otter ('ɒtə) *n, pl* -ters *or* -ter 1 any freshwater

carnivorous musteline mammal of the subfamily *Lutrinae,* esp *Lutra lutra* (**Eurasian otter**), typically having smooth fur, a streamlined body, and webbed feet 2 the fur of any of these animals 3 Also called: **otter board** a type of fishing tackle consisting of a weighted board to which hooked and baited lines are attached ▷ *vb* 4 to fish using an otter [Old English *otor*; related to Old Norse *otr,* Old High German *ottar,* Greek *hudra,* Sanskrit *udra*]

Otterburn ('ɒtə,bɜːn) *n* a village in NE England, in central Northumberland: scene of a battle (1388) in which the Scots, led by the earl of Douglas, defeated the English, led by Hotspur

otter hound *n* a dog used for otter hunting, esp one of a breed, now rare, that stands about 60 cm (24 in.) high and has a harsh thick coat, often greyish with tan markings

otter shell *n* See **gaper** (sense 2)

otter shrew *n* any small otter-like amphibious mammal, esp *Potamogale velox,* of the family *Potamogalidae* of W and central Africa: order *Insectivora* (insectivores)

otto ('ɒtəʊ) *n* another name for **attar**

Otto cycle *n* an engine cycle used on four-stroke petrol engines (**Otto engines**) in which, ideally, combustion and rejection of heat both take place at constant volume. Compare **diesel cycle** [C19 named after Nikolaus August Otto (1832–91), German engineer]

ottoman ('ɒtəmən) *n, pl* -mans 1 a a low padded seat, usually armless, sometimes in the form of a chest b a cushioned footstool 2 a corded fabric [C17 from French *ottomane,* feminine of OTTOMAN]

Ottoman ('ɒtəmən) *or* **Othman** *adj* 1 *history* of or relating to the Ottomans or the Ottoman Empire 2 denoting or relating to the Turkish language ▷ *n, pl* -mans 3 a member of a Turkish people who invaded the Near East in the late 13th century [C17 from French, via Medieval Latin, from Arabic *Othmāni* Turkish, from Turkish *Othman Osman* I (1259–1326), founder of the Ottoman Empire]

Ottoman Empire *n* the former Turkish empire in Europe, Asia, and Africa, which lasted from the late 13th century until the end of World War I. Also called: **Turkish Empire**

ou (əʊ) *n South African slang* a man, bloke, or chap [Afrikaans]

OU *abbreviation for* 1 the Open University 2 Oxford University

ouabain ('wɑːbɑːɪn) *n* a poisonous white crystalline glycoside extracted from certain trees and used as a heart stimulant and, by some African tribes, on poison darts. Formula: $C_{29}H_{44}O_{12}.8H_2O$ [C19 from French *ouabaïo,* from Somali *waba* yo native name of tree]

Ouachita *or* **Washita** ('wɒʃɪ,tɔː) *n* a river in the S central US, rising in the **Ouachita Mountains** and flowing east, south, and southeast into the Red River in E Louisiana. Length: 974 km (605 miles)

Ouagadougou (,wɑːgə'duːguː) *n* the capital of Burkina-Faso, on the central plateau: terminus of the railway from Abidjan (Côte d'Ivoire). Pop: 870 000 (2005 est)

ouananiche (,wɑːnə'niːʃ) *n* a landlocked variety of the Atlantic salmon, *Salmo salar,* found in lakes in SE Canada [from Canadian French, from Montagnais *wananish,* diminutive of *wanans* salmon]

oubaas ('əʊ,bɑːs) *n South African* a person who is senior in years or rank [Afrikaans]

Oubangui (uː'bɑːngiː, juː'bæŋgɪ) *n* the French name for **Ubangi**

oubliette (,uːblɪ'ɛt) *n* a dungeon the only entrance to which is through the top [C19 from French, from *oublier* to forget]

ouch¹ (aʊtʃ) *interj* an exclamation of sharp sudden pain

ouch² (aʊtʃ) *n archaic* 1 a brooch or clasp set with gems 2 the setting of a gem [C15 *an ouch,* mistaken division of C14 *a nouche,* from Old French *nouche,* of Germanic origin; compare Old High German *nusca* buckle]

O

oud (uːd) *n* an Arabic stringed musical instrument resembling a lute or mandolin [from Arabic *al 'ūd*, literally: the wood. Compare LUTE[1]]

Oudh (aʊd) *n* **1** a region of N India, in central Uttar Pradesh: annexed by Britain in 1856 and a centre of the Indian Mutiny (1857–58); joined with Agra in 1877, becoming the United Provinces of Agra and Oudh in 1902, which were renamed Uttar Pradesh in 1950 **2** another name for **Ayodhya**

Ouessant (wɛsɑ̃) *n* the French name for **Ushant**

ought[1] (ɔːt) *vb* (*foll by to; takes an infinitive or implied infinitive*) used as an auxiliary **1** to indicate duty or obligation: *you ought to pay your dues* **2** to express prudent expediency: *you ought to be more careful with your money* **3** (usually with reference to future time) to express probability or expectation: *you ought to finish this work by Friday* **4** to express a desire or wish on the part of the speaker: *you ought to come next week* [Old English *āhte*, past tense of *āgan* to OWE; related to Gothic *aihta*]

> USAGE In correct English, *ought* is not used with *did* or *had*. *I ought not to do it*, not *I didn't ought to do it*; *I ought not to have done it*, not *I hadn't ought to have done it*

ought[2] (ɔːt) *pron, adv* a variant spelling of **aught**[1]

ought[3] (ɔːt) *n* a less common word for **nought** (zero) [C19 mistaken division of *a nought* as *an ought*; see NOUGHT]

ouguiya (uːˈgiːjə) *n* the standard monetary unit of Mauritania, divided into 5 khoums

Ouija board (ˈwiːdʒə) *n trademark* a board on which are marked the letters of the alphabet. Answers to questions are spelt out by a pointer or glass held by the fingertips of the participants, and are supposedly formed by spiritual forces [C19 from French *oui* yes + German *ja* yes]

Oujda (uːdʒˈdɑː) *n* a city in NE Morocco, near the border with Algeria: frontier post. Pop: 454 000 (2003)

Oulu (ˈɔulu) *n* an industrial city and port in W Finland, on the Gulf of Bothnia: university (1959). Pop: 125 928 (2003 est). Swedish name: **Uleåborg**

ouma (ˈəʊmɑː) *n South African* **1** grandmother, esp in titular use with surname **2** *slang* any elderly woman [Afrikaans]

ounce[1] (aʊns) *n* **1** a unit of weight equal to one sixteenth of a pound (avoirdupois); 1 ounce is equal to 437.5 grains or 28.349 grams. Abbreviation: **oz** **2** a unit of weight equal to one twelfth of a Troy or Apothecaries' pound; 1 ounce is equal to 480 grains or 31.103 grams **3** short for **fluid ounce** **4** a small portion or amount [C14 from Old French *unce*, from Latin *uncia* a twelfth; from *ūnus* one]

ounce[2] (aʊns) *n* another name for **snow leopard** [C18 from Old French *once*, by mistaken division of *lonce* as if *l'once*, from Latin LYNX]

oupa (ˈəʊpɑː) *n South African* **1** grandfather, esp in titular use with surname **2** *slang* any elderly man [Afrikaans]

our (aʊə) *determiner* **1** of, belonging to, or associated in some way with us: *our best vodka; our parents are good to us* **2** belonging to or associated with all people or people in general: *our nearest planet is Venus* **3** a formal word for *my* used by editors or other writers, and monarchs **4** *informal* (often sarcastic) used instead of *your*: *are our feet hurting?* **5** *dialect* belonging to the family of the speaker: *it's our Sandra's birthday tomorrow* [Old English *ūre* (genitive plural), from US; related to Old French, Old Saxon *ūser*, Old High German *unsēr*, Gothic *unsara*]

-our *suffix forming nouns* indicating state, condition, or activity: *behaviour; labour* [in Old French *-eur*, from Latin *-or*, noun suffix]

Our Father *n* another name for the **Lord's Prayer**, taken from its opening words

Our Lady *n* a title given to the **Virgin Mary**

ours (aʊəz) *pron* **1** something or someone belonging to or associated with us: *ours have blue tags* **2** **of ours** belonging to or associated with us

ourself (aʊəˈsɛlf) *pron archaic* a variant of **myself**, formerly used by monarchs or editors in formal contexts

ourselves (aʊəˈsɛlvz) *pron* **1 a** the reflexive form of *we* or *us* **b** (intensifier): *we ourselves will finish it* **2** (*preceded by a copula*) our usual selves: *we are ourselves when we're together* **3** *not standard* used instead of *we* or *us* in compound noun phrases: *other people and ourselves*

-ous *suffix forming adjectives* **1** having, full of, or characterized by: *dangerous; spacious; languorous* **2** (in chemistry) indicating that an element is chemically combined in the lower of two possible valency states: *ferrous; stannous*. Compare **-ic** (sense 2) [from Old French, from Latin *-ōsus* or *-us*, Greek *-os*, adj suffixes]

Ouse (uːz) *n* **1** Also called: **Great Ouse** a river in E England, rising in Northamptonshire and flowing northeast to the Wash near King's Lynn; for the last 56 km (35 miles) follows mainly artificial channels. Length: 257 km (160 miles) **2** a river in NE England, in Yorkshire, formed by the confluence of the Swale and Ure Rivers: flows southeast to the Humber. Length: 92 km (57 miles) **3** a river in S England, rising in Sussex and flowing south to the English Channel. Length: 48 km (30 miles)

ousel (ˈuːzᵊl) *n* a variant spelling of **ouzel**

oust (aʊst) *vb* (*tr*) **1** to force out of a position or place; supplant or expel **2** *property law* to deprive (a person) of the possession of land [C16 from Anglo-Norman *ouster*, from Latin *obstāre* to withstand, from *ob-* against + *stāre* to stand]

ouster (ˈaʊstə) *n property law* the act of dispossessing of freehold property; eviction; ejection

out (aʊt) *adv* **1** (*often used as a particle*) at or to a point beyond the limits of some location; outside: *get out at once* **2** (*particle*) out of consciousness: *she passed out at the sight of blood* **3** (*particle*) used to indicate a burst of activity as indicated by the verb: *fever broke out* **4** (*particle*) used to indicate obliteration of an object: *the graffiti were painted out* **5** (*particle*) used to indicate an approximate drawing or description: *sketch out; chalk out* **6** (*often used as a particle*) away from one's custody or ownership, esp on hire: *to let out a cottage* **7** on sale or on view to the public: *the book is being brought out next May* **8** (of a young woman) in or into polite society: *Lucinda had a fabulous party when she came out* **9** (of a jury) withdrawn to consider a verdict in private **10** (*particle*) used to indicate exhaustion or extinction: *the sugar's run out; put the light out* **11** (*particle*) used to indicate a goal or object achieved at the end of the action specified by the verb: *he worked it out; let's fight it out, then!* **12** (*preceded by a superlative*) existing: *the friendliest dog out* **13** an expression in signalling, radio, etc, to indicate the end of a transmission **14** *Austral and NZ archaic* in or to Australia or New Zealand: *he came out last year* **15** **out of a** at or to a point outside: *out of his reach* **b** away from; not in: *stepping out of line; out of focus* **c** because of, motivated by: *doing it out of jealousy* **d** from (a material or source): *made out of plastic* **e** not or no longer having any of (a substance, material, etc): *we're out of sugar* ▷ *adj* (*postpositive*) **16** not or not any longer worth considering: *that plan is out because of the weather* **17** not allowed: *smoking on duty is out* **18** (*also prenominal*) not in vogue; unfashionable: *that sort of dress is out these days* **19** (of a fire or light) no longer burning or providing illumination: *the fire is out* **20** not working: *the radio's out* **21** unconscious: *he was out for two minutes* **22** **out to it** *Austral and NZ informal* asleep or unconscious, esp because drunk **23** not in; not at home: *call back later, they're out now* **24** desirous of or intent on (something or doing something): *I'm out for as much money as I can get* **25** Also: **out on strike** on strike: *the machine shop is out* **26** (in several games and sports) denoting the state in which a player is caused to discontinue active participation, esp in some specified role **27** used up; exhausted: *our supplies are completely out* **28** worn into holes: *this sweater is out at the elbows* **29** inaccurate, deficient, or discrepant: *out by six pence* **30** not in office or authority: *his party will be out at the election* **31** completed or concluded, as of time: *before the year is out* **32** in flower: *the roses are out now* **33** in arms, esp, in rebellion: *one of his ancestors was out in the Forty-Five* **34** (*also prenominal*) being out: *the out position on the dial* **35** *informal* not concealing one's homosexuality ▷ *prep* **36** out of; out through: *he ran out the door* **37** *archaic or dialect* outside; beyond: *he comes from out our domain* ▷ *interj* **38 a** an exclamation, usually peremptory, of dismissal, reproach, etc **b** (in wireless telegraphy) an expression used to signal that the speaker is signing off **39** **out with it** a command to make something known immediately, without missing any details ▷ *n* **40** *chiefly US* a method of escape from a place, difficult situation, punishment, etc **41** *baseball* an instance of the putting out of a batter; putout **42** *printing* **a** the omission of words from a printed text; lacuna **b** the words so omitted **43** **ins and outs** See **in** (sense 29) ▷ *vb* **44** (*tr*) to put or throw out **45** (*intr*) to be made known or effective despite efforts to the contrary (esp in the phrase **will out**): *the truth will out* **46** (*tr*) *informal* (of homosexuals) to expose (a public figure) as being a fellow homosexual **47** (*tr*) *informal* to expose something secret, embarrassing, or unknown about (a person): *he was eventually outed as a talented goal scorer* [Old English *ūt*; related to Old Saxon, Old Norse *ūt*, Old High German *ūz*, German *aus*]

> USAGE The use of *out* as a preposition, though common in American English, is regarded as incorrect in British English: *he climbed out of* (not *out*) *a window; he went out through the door*

out- *prefix* **1** excelling or surpassing in a particular action: *outlast; outlive* **2** indicating an external location or situation away from the centre: *outpost; outpatient* **3** indicating emergence, an issuing forth, etc: *outcrop; outgrowth* **4** indicating the result of an action: *outcome*

outage (ˈaʊtɪdʒ) *n* **1** a quantity of goods missing or lost after storage or shipment **2** a period of power failure, machine stoppage, etc

out and about *adj* regularly going out of the house to work, take part in social activity, etc, esp after an illness

out and away *adv* by far

out-and-out *adj* (*prenominal*) thoroughgoing; complete

out-and-outer *n slang* **1** a thorough or thoroughgoing person or thing **2** a person or thing that is excellent of its kind **3** an extremist

outasight (ˌaʊtəˈsaɪt) *or* **out-of-sight** *adj, interj slang* another term for **far-out**

outback (ˈaʊtˌbæk) *n* **a** the remote bush country of Australia **b** (*as modifier*): *outback life*

outbalance (ˌaʊtˈbæləns) *vb* another word for **outweigh**

outbid (ˌaʊtˈbɪd) *vb* **-bids, -bidding, -bid, -bidden** *or* **-bid** (*tr*) to bid higher than; outdo in bidding

outboard (ˈaʊtˌbɔːd) *adj* **1** (of a boat's engine) portable, with its own propeller, and designed to be attached externally to the stern. Compare **inboard** (sense 1) **2** in a position away from, or further away from, the centre line of a vessel or aircraft, esp outside the hull or fuselage ▷ *adv* **3** away from the centre line of a vessel or aircraft, esp outside the hull or fuselage ▷ *n* **4** an outboard motor **5** a boat fitted with an outboard motor

outbound (ˈaʊtˌbaʊnd) *adj* going out; outward bound

outbrave (ˌaʊtˈbreɪv) *vb* (*tr*) **1** to surpass in bravery **2** to confront defiantly

outbreak (ˈaʊtˌbreɪk) *n* a sudden, violent, or spontaneous occurrence, esp of disease or strife

outbreed (ˌaʊtˈbriːd) *vb* **-breeds, -breeding, -bred**

1 (*intr*) *anthropol* to produce offspring through sexual relations outside a particular family or tribe **2** to breed (animals that are not closely related) or (of such animals) to be bred ▷ **ˈoutˌbreeding** *n*

outbuilding (ˈaʊtˌbɪldɪŋ) *n* a building subordinate to but separate from a main building; outhouse

outburst (ˈaʊtˌbɜːst) *n* **1** a sudden and violent expression of emotion **2** an explosion or eruption

outcast (ˈaʊtˌkɑːst) *n* **1** a person who is rejected or excluded from a social group **2** a vagabond or wanderer **3** anything thrown out or rejected ▷ *adj* **4** rejected, abandoned, or discarded; cast out

outcaste (ˈaʊtˌkɑːst) *n* **1** a person who has been expelled from a caste **2** a person having no caste ▷ *vb* **3** (*tr*) to cause (someone) to lose his caste

outclass (ˌaʊtˈklɑːs) *vb* (*tr*) **1** to surpass in class, quality, etc **2** to defeat easily

outcome (ˈaʊtˌkʌm) *n* something that follows from an action, dispute, situation, etc; result; consequence

outcrop *n* (ˈaʊtˌkrɒp) **1** part of a rock formation or mineral vein that appears at the surface of the earth **2** an emergence; appearance ▷ *vb* (ˌaʊtˈkrɒp) **-crops, -cropping, -cropped** (*intr*) **3** (of rock strata, mineral veins, etc) to protrude through the surface of the earth **4** another word for **crop out**

outcross *vb* (ˌaʊtˈkrɒs) **1** to breed (animals or plants of the same breed but different strains) ▷ *n* (ˈaʊtˌkrɒs) **2** an animal or plant produced as a result of outcrossing **3** an act of outcrossing

outcry *n*, *pl* **-cries** (ˈaʊtˌkraɪ) **1** a widespread or vehement protest **2** clamour; uproar **3** *commerce* a method of trading in which dealers shout out bids and offers at a prearranged meeting: *sale by open outcry* ▷ *vb* (ˌaʊtˈkraɪ) **-cries, -crying, -cried** **4** (*tr*) to cry louder or make more noise than (someone or something)

outdate (ˌaʊtˈdeɪt) *vb* (*tr*) (of something new) to cause (something else) to become old-fashioned or obsolete

outdated (ˌaʊtˈdeɪtɪd) *adj* old-fashioned or obsolete

outdistance (ˌaʊtˈdɪstəns) *vb* (*tr*) to leave far behind

outdo (ˌaʊtˈduː) *vb* **-does, -doing, -did, -done** (*tr*) to surpass or exceed in performance or execution

outdoor (ˈaʊtˈdɔː) *adj* (*prenominal*) taking place, existing, or intended for use in the open air: *outdoor games; outdoor clothes*. Also: **out-of-door**

outdoor relief *n* another name for **out-relief**

outdoors (ˌaʊtˈdɔːz) *adv* **1** Also: **out-of-doors** in the open air; outside ▷ *n* **2** the world outside or far away from human habitation: *the great outdoors*

outdoorsy (ˌaʊtˈdɔːzɪ) *adj informal* characteristic of, or taking part in activities relating to, the outdoors

outer (ˈaʊtə) *adj* (*prenominal*) **1** being or located on the outside; external **2** further from the middle or central part ▷ *n* **3** *archery* **a** the white outermost ring on a target **b** a shot that hits this ring **4** *Austral* the unsheltered part of the spectator area at a sports ground **5** **on the outer** *Austral and NZ* disadvantaged or neglected

outer bar *n* (in England) a collective name for junior barristers who plead from outside the bar of the court. Compare **Queen's Counsel**

outercourse (ˈaʊtəˌkɔːs) *n* sexual activity between partners that does not include actual penetration

outer garments *pl n* the garments that are worn over a person's other clothes

Outer Hebrides *pl n* See **Hebrides**

Outer Mongolia *n* the former name (until 1924) of the republic of **Mongolia**

outermost (ˈaʊtəˌməʊst) *adj* furthest from the centre or middle; outmost

outer planet *n* any of the planets Jupiter, Saturn, Uranus, Neptune, and Pluto, whose orbit lies outside the asteroid belt

outer space *n* (*not in technical usage*) any region of

space beyond the atmosphere of the earth

outface (ˌaʊtˈfeɪs) *vb* (*tr*) **1** to face or stare down **2** to confront boldly or defiantly

outfall (ˈaʊtˌfɔːl) *n* the end of a river, sewer, drain, etc, from which it discharges

outfield (ˈaʊtˌfiːld) *n* **1** *cricket* the area of the field relatively far from the pitch; the deep. Compare **infield** (sense 1) **2** *baseball* **a** the area of the playing field beyond the lines connecting first, second, and third bases **b** the positions of the left fielder, centre fielder, and right fielder taken collectively. Compare **infield** (sense 2) **3** *agriculture* farmland most distant from the farmstead ▷ **ˈoutˌfielder** *n*

outfighting (ˈaʊtˌfaɪtɪŋ) *n* fighting at a distance and not at close range

outfit (ˈaʊtˌfɪt) *n* **1** a set of articles or equipment for a particular task, occupation, etc **2** a set of clothes, esp a carefully selected one **3** *informal* any group or association regarded as a cohesive unit, such as a military company, business house, etc **4** the act of fitting out **5** *Canadian* (formerly) the annual shipment of trading goods and supplies sent by a fur company to its trading posts ▷ *vb* **-fits, -fitting, -fitted 6** to furnish or be furnished with an outfit, equipment, etc

outfitter (ˈaʊtˌfɪtə) *n chiefly Brit* **1** a shop that sells men's clothes **2** a person who provides outfits

outflank (ˌaʊtˈflæŋk) *vb* (*tr*) **1** to go around the flank of (an opposing army) **2** to get the better of

outflow (ˈaʊtˌfləʊ) *n* **1** anything that flows out, such as liquid, money, ideas, etc **2** the amount that flows out **3** the act or process of flowing out

outfoot (ˌaʊtˈfʊt) *vb* (*tr*) **1** (of a boat) to go faster than (another boat) **2** to surpass in running, dancing, etc

outfox (ˌaʊtˈfɒks) *vb* (*tr*) to surpass in guile or cunning

outgas (ˌaʊtˈɡæs) *vb* **-gases** *or* **-gasses, -gassing, -gassed** to undergo or cause to undergo the removal of adsorbed or absorbed gas from solids, often by heating in free space

outgeneral (ˌaʊtˈdʒɛnərəl) *vb* **-als, -alling, -alled** *or US* **-als, -aling, -aled** (*tr*) to surpass in generalship

outgo *vb* (ˌaʊtˈɡəʊ) **-goes, -going, -went, -gone 1** (*tr*) to exceed or outstrip ▷ *n* (ˈaʊtˌɡəʊ) **2** cost; outgoings; outlay **3** something that goes out; outflow

outgoing (ˈaʊtˌɡəʊɪŋ) *adj* **1** departing; leaving **2** leaving or retiring from office: *the outgoing chairman* **3** friendly and sociable ▷ *n* **4** the act of going out

outgoings (ˈaʊtˌɡəʊɪŋz) *pl n* expenditure

out-group *n sociol* persons excluded from an in-group

outgrow (ˌaʊtˈɡrəʊ) *vb* **-grows, -growing, -grew, -grown** (*tr*) **1** to grow too large for (clothes, shoes, etc) **2** to lose (a habit, idea, reputation, etc) in the course of development or time **3** to grow larger or faster than

outgrowth (ˈaʊtˌɡrəʊθ) *n* **1** a thing growing out of a main body **2** a development, result, or consequence **3** the act of growing out

outgun (ˌaʊtˈɡʌn) *vb* **-guns, -gunning, -gunned** (*tr*) **1** to surpass in fire power **2** to surpass in shooting **3** *informal* to surpass or excel

out-half *n rugby* another term for **stand-off half** Also: **outside half**

outhaul (ˈaʊtˌhɔːl) *n nautical* a line or cable for tightening the foot of a sail by hauling the clew out along the boom or yard. Also: **outhauler**

out-Herod *vb* (*tr*) to surpass in evil, excesses, or cruelty [C17 originally *out-Herod Herod*, from Shakespeare's *Hamlet* (act 3, scene 2); see also HEROD: portrayed in medieval mystery plays as a ranting tyrant]

outhit (ˌaʊtˈhɪt) *vb* **-hits, -hitting, -hit** (*tr*) to hit something further than (someone else)

outhouse (ˈaʊtˌhaʊs) *n* **1** a building near to, but separate from, a main building; outbuilding **2** *US* an outside lavatory

outing (ˈaʊtɪŋ) *n* **1** a short outward and return journey; trip; excursion **2** *informal* the naming by

homosexuals of other prominent homosexuals, often against their will

outjockey (ˌaʊtˈdʒɒkɪ) *vb* (*tr*) to outwit by deception

outland *adj* (ˈaʊtˌlænd, -lənd) **1** outlying or distant **2** *archaic* foreign; alien ▷ *n* (ˈaʊtˌlænd) **3** (*usually plural*) the outlying areas of a country or region

outlander (ˈaʊtˌlændə) *n* a foreigner or stranger

outlandish (aʊtˈlændɪʃ) *adj* **1** grotesquely unconventional in appearance, habits, etc **2** *archaic* foreign ▷ **outˈlandishly** *adv* ▷ **outˈlandishness** *n*

outlaw (ˈaʊtˌlɔː) *n* **1** (formerly) a person excluded from the law and deprived of its protection **2** any fugitive from the law, esp a habitual transgressor **3** a wild or untamed beast ▷ *vb* (*tr*) **4** to put (a person) outside the law and deprive of its protection **5** (in the US) to deprive (a contract) of legal force **6** to ban

outlawry (ˈaʊtˌlɔːrɪ) *n*, *pl* **-ries 1** the act of outlawing or the state of being outlawed **2** disregard for the law

outlay *n* (ˈaʊtˌleɪ) **1** an expenditure of money, effort, etc ▷ *vb* (ˌaʊtˈleɪ) **-lays, -laying, -laid 2** (*tr*) to spend (money)

outlet (ˈaʊtˌlɛt, -lɪt) *n* **1** an opening or vent permitting escape or release **2** a means for release or expression of emotion, creative energy, etc **3 a** a market for a product or service **b** a commercial establishment retailing the goods of a particular producer or wholesaler **4 a** a channel that drains a body of water **b** the mouth of a river **5** a point in a wiring system from which current can be taken to supply electrical devices **6** *anatomy* the beginning or end of a passage, esp the lower opening of the pelvis (**pelvic outlet**)

outlier (ˈaʊtˌlaɪə) *n* **1** an outcrop of rocks that is entirely surrounded by older rocks **2** a person, thing, or part situated away from a main or related body **3** a person who lives away from his place of work, duty, etc **4** *statistics* a point in a sample widely separated from the main cluster of points in the sample. See **scatter diagram**

outline (ˈaʊtˌlaɪn) *n* **1** a preliminary or schematic plan, draft, account, etc **2** (*usually plural*) the important features of an argument, theory, work, etc **3** the line by which an object or figure is or appears to be bounded **4 a** a drawing or manner of drawing consisting only of external lines **b** (*as modifier*): *an outline map* ▷ *vb* (*tr*) **5** to draw or display the outline of **6** to give the main features or general idea of

outline font *n computing* a font format that makes use of fillable geometric outlines of letters and symbols, allowing fonts to be scaled up or down while still retaining their intended shape. Also called: **vector font** Compare **bitmap font**

outlive (ˌaʊtˈlɪv) *vb* (*tr*) **1** to live longer than (someone) **2** to live beyond (a date or period): *he outlived the century* **3** to live through (an experience)

outlook (ˈaʊtˌlʊk) *n* **1** a mental attitude or point of view **2** the probable or expected condition or outcome of something: *the weather outlook* **3** the view from a place **4** view or prospect **5** the act or state of looking out

outlying (ˈaʊtˌlaɪɪŋ) *adj* distant or remote from the main body or centre, as of a town or region

outman (aʊtˈmæn) *vb* **-mans, -manning, -manned** (*tr*) **1** to surpass in manpower **2** to surpass in manliness

outmanoeuvre *or US* **outmaneuver** (ˌaʊtməˈnuːvə) *vb* (*tr*) to secure a strategic advantage over by skilful manoeuvre

outmoded (ˌaʊtˈməʊdɪd) *adj* **1** no longer fashionable or widely accepted **2** no longer practical or usable ▷ **ˌoutˈmodedly** *adv* ▷ **ˌoutˈmodedness** *n*

outmost (ˈaʊtˌməʊst) *adj* another word for **outermost**

O

outness ('aʊtnɪs) *n* **1** the state or quality of being external **2** outward expression

outnumber (,aʊt'nʌmbə) *vb* (*tr*) to exceed in number

out-of-body experience *n* a vivid feeling of being detached from one's body, usually involving observing it and its environment from nearby. Abbreviation: **OBE** *or* **OOBE** Compare **near-death experience**

out of bounds *adj* (*postpositive*), *adv* **1** (often foll by *to*) not to be entered (by); barred (to): *out of bounds to civilians* **2** outside specified or prescribed limits

out of date *adj* (**out-of-date** *when prenominal*), *adv* no longer valid, current, or fashionable; outmoded

out-of-door *adj* (*prenominal*) another term for **outdoor**

out-of-doors *adv, adj* (*postpositive*) in the open air; outside. Also: **outdoors**

out of pocket *adj* (**out-of-pocket** *when prenominal*) **1** (*postpositive*) having lost money, as in a commercial enterprise **2** without money to spend **3** (*prenominal*) (of expenses) unbudgeted and paid for in cash

out-of-the-way *adj* (*prenominal*) **1** distant from more populous areas **2** uncommon or unusual

outpace (aʊt'peɪs) *vb* (*tr*) to run or move faster than (someone or something else)

outpatient ('aʊt,peɪʃənt) *n* a nonresident hospital patient. Compare **inpatient**

outperform (,aʊtpə'fɔːm) *vb* (*tr*) to perform better than (someone or something)

outplacement ('aʊt,pleɪsmənt) *n* a service that offers counselling and careers advice, esp to redundant executives, which is paid for by their previous employer

outplay (aʊt'pleɪ) *vb* (*tr*) to perform better than one's opponent in a sport or game

outpoint (aʊt'pɔɪnt) *vb* (*tr*) **1** to score more points than **2** *nautical* to sail closer to the wind (point higher) than (another sailing vessel)

outport ('aʊt,pɔːt) *n* **1** *chiefly Brit* a subsidiary port built in deeper water than the original port **2** *Canadian* one of the many isolated fishing villages located in the bays and other indentations of the Newfoundland coast

outporter ('aʊt,pɔːtə) *n Canadian* an inhabitant or native of a Newfoundland outport

outpost ('aʊt,pəʊst) *n* **1** *military* **a** a position stationed at a distance from the area occupied by a major formation **b** the troops assigned to such a position **2** an outlying settlement or position **3** a limit or frontier

outpour ('aʊt,pɔː) **1** the act of flowing or pouring out **2** something that pours out ▷ *vb* (,aʊt'pɔː) **3** to pour or cause to pour out freely or rapidly

outpouring ('aʊt,pɔːrɪŋ) *n* **1** a passionate or exaggerated outburst; effusion **2** another word for **outpour** (senses 1, 2)

output ('aʊt,pʊt) *n* **1** the act of production or manufacture **2** Also called: **outturn** the amount produced, as in a given period: *a high weekly output* **3** the material produced, manufactured, yielded, etc **4** *electronics* **a** the power, voltage, or current delivered by a circuit or component **b** the point at which the signal is delivered **5** the power, energy, or work produced by an engine or a system **6** *computing* **a** the information produced by a computer **b** the operations and devices involved in producing this information. See also **input/output 7** (*modifier*) of or relating to electronic, computer, or other output: *output signal; output device; output tax* ▷ *vb* **-puts, -putting, -put** *or* **-putted** (*tr*) **8** *computing* to cause (data) to be emitted as output

outrage ('aʊt,reɪdʒ) *n* **1** a wantonly vicious or cruel act **2** a gross violation of decency, morality, honour, etc **3** profound indignation, anger, or hurt, caused by such an act ▷ *vb* (*tr*) **4** to cause profound indignation, anger, or resentment in **5**

to offend grossly (feelings, decency, human dignity, etc) **6** to commit an act of wanton viciousness, cruelty, or indecency on **7** a euphemistic word for **rape¹** [C13 (meaning: excess): via French from *outré* beyond, from Latin *ultrā*]

outrageous (aʊt'reɪdʒəs) *adj* **1** being or having the nature of an outrage **2** grossly offensive to decency, authority, etc **3** violent or unrestrained in behaviour or temperament **4** extravagant or immoderate > **out'rageously** *adv* > **out'rageousness** *n*

outrank (,aʊt'ræŋk) *vb* (*tr*) **1** to be of higher rank than **2** to take priority over

outré ('uːtreɪ) *adj* deviating from what is usual or proper [C18 from French past participle of *outrer* to pass beyond]

outreach *vb* (,aʊt'riːtʃ) **1** (*tr*) to surpass in reach **2** (*tr*) to go beyond **3** to reach or cause to reach out ▷ *n* ('aʊt,riːtʃ) **4** the act or process of reaching out **5** the length or extent of reach **6** *social welfare* any systematic effort to provide unsolicited and predefined help to groups or individuals deemed to need it **7** (*modifier*) (of welfare work or workers) propagating take-up of a service by seeking out appropriate people and persuading them to accept what is judged good for them. Compare **detached** (sense 3)

out-relief *n English history* money given to poor people not living in a workhouse. Also called: **outdoor relief**

outride *vb* (,aʊt'raɪd) **-rides, -riding, -rode, -ridden** (*tr*) **1** to outdo by riding faster, farther, or better than **2** (of a vessel) to ride out (a storm) ▷ *n* ('aʊt,raɪd) **3** *prosody rare* an extra unstressed syllable within a metrical foot

outrider ('aʊt,raɪdə) *n* **1** a person who goes ahead of a car, group of people, etc, to ensure a clear passage **2** a person who goes in advance to investigate, discover a way, etc; scout **3** a person who rides in front of or beside a carriage, esp as an attendant or guard **4** *US* a mounted herdsman

outrigger ('aʊt,rɪgə) *n* **1** a framework for supporting a pontoon outside and parallel to the hull of a boat to provide stability **2** a boat equipped with such a framework, esp one of the canoes of the South Pacific **3** any projecting framework attached to a boat, aircraft, building, etc, to act as a support **4** *rowing* another name for **rigger** (sense 2) [C18 from OUT- + RIG¹ + -ER¹; perhaps influenced by archaic *outligger* outlier]

outright *adj* ('aʊt,raɪt) (*prenominal*) **1** without qualifications or limitations: *outright ownership* **2** complete; total: *an outright lie* **3** straightforward; direct: *an outright manner* ▷ *adv* (,aʊt'raɪt) **4** without restrictions: *buy outright* **5** without reservation or concealment: *ask outright* **6** instantly: *he was killed outright* **7** *obsolete* straight ahead or out

outro ('aʊtrəʊ) *n, pl* **-tros** *music informal* an instrumental passage that concludes a piece of music [C20 modelled on INTRO]

outrun (,aʊt'rʌn) *vb* **-runs, -running, -ran, -run** (*tr*) **1** to run faster, farther, or better than **2** to escape from by or as if by running **3** to go beyond; exceed

outrunner ('aʊt,rʌnə) *n* **1** an attendant who runs in front of a carriage, etc **2** the leading dog in a sled team

outrush ('aʊt,rʌʃ) *n* a flowing or rushing out

outsell (,aʊt'sɛl) *vb* **-sells, -selling, -sold** (*tr*) to sell or be sold in greater quantities than

outsert ('aʊt,sɜːt) *n* another word for **wraparound** (sense 5) [C20 based on INSERT]

outset ('aʊt,sɛt) *n* a start; beginning (esp in the phrase **from** (*or* **at**) **the outset**)

outshine (,aʊt'ʃaɪn) *vb* **-shines, -shining, -shone 1** (*tr*) to shine more brightly than **2** (*tr*) to surpass in excellence, beauty, wit, etc **3** (*intr*) *rare* to emit light

outshoot *vb* (,aʊt'ʃuːt) **-shoots, -shooting, -shot 1**

(*tr*) to surpass or excel in shooting **2** to go or extend beyond (something) ▷ *n* ('aʊt,ʃuːt) **3** a thing that projects or shoots out **4** the act or state of shooting out or protruding

outside *prep* (,aʊt'saɪd) **1** (sometimes foll by *of*) on or to the exterior of: *outside the house* **2** beyond the limits of: *outside human comprehension* **3** apart from; other than: *no-one knows outside you and me* ▷ *adj* ('aʊt,saɪd) **4** (*prenominal*) situated on the exterior: *an outside lavatory* **5** remote; unlikely: *an outside chance* **6** not a member of **7** the greatest possible or probable (prices, odds, etc) ▷ *adv* (,aʊt'saɪd) **8** outside a specified thing or place; out of doors **9** *slang* not in prison ▷ *n* ('aʊt,saɪd) **10** the external side or surface: *the outside of the garage* **11** the external appearance or aspect **12** the exterior or outer part of something **13** (of a path, pavement, etc) the side nearest the road or away from a wall or building **14** *sport* an outside player, as in football **15** (*plural*) the outer sheets of a ream of paper **16** *Canadian* (in the north) the settled parts of Canada **17 at the outside** *informal* at the most or at the greatest extent: *two days at the outside* **18 outside in** another term for **inside out** See **inside** (sense 5)

USAGE The use of *outside of* and *inside of*, although fairly common, is generally thought to be incorrect or non-standard: *she waits outside* (not *outside of*) *the school*

outside broadcast *n radio, television* a broadcast not made from a studio

outside director *n* a director of a company who is not employed by that company but is often employed by a holding or associated company

outside half *n rugby* another term for **stand-off half**. Also called: **out-half**

outsider (,aʊt'saɪdə) *n* **1** a person or thing excluded from or not a member of a set, group, etc **2** a contestant, esp a horse, thought unlikely to win in a race **3** *Canadian* (in the north) a person who does not live in the Arctic regions

outsider art *n* art produced by untutored artists working by themselves and for themselves > **outsider artist** *n*

outside work *n* work done off the premises of a business

out sister *n* a member of a community of nuns who performs tasks in the outside world on behalf of the community

outsize ('aʊt,saɪz) *adj* **1** Also: **outsized** very large or larger than normal: *outsize tomatoes* ▷ *n* **2** something outsize, such as a garment or person **3** (*modifier*) relating to or dealing in outsize clothes: *an outsize shop*

outskirts ('aʊt,skɜːts) *pl n* (*sometimes singular*) outlying or bordering areas, districts, etc, as of a city

outsmart (,aʊt'smɑːt) *vb* (*tr*) *informal* to get the better of; outwit

outsole ('aʊt,səʊl) *n* the outermost sole of a shoe

outsource (,aʊt'sɔːs) *vb* (*tr*) (of a manufacturer) **1** to subcontract (work) to another company **2** to buy in (components for a product) rather than manufacture them

outspan *South African* ▷ *n* ('aʊt,spæn) **1** an area on a farm kept available for travellers to rest and refresh animals **2** the act of unharnessing or unyoking ▷ *vb* (,aʊt'spæn) **-spans, -spanning, -spanned 3** (*tr*) to unharness or unyoke (animals) **4** (*intr*) to relax [C19 partial translation of Afrikaans *uitspan*, from *uit* out + *spannen* to stretch]

outspoken (,aʊt'spəʊkən) *adj* **1** candid or bold in speech **2** said or expressed with candour or boldness > **out'spokenness** *n*

outspread *vb* (,aʊt'sprɛd) **-spreads, -spreading, -spread 1** to spread out or cause to spread out ▷ *adj* ('aʊt'sprɛd) **2** spread or stretched out **3** scattered or diffused widely ▷ *n* ('aʊt,sprɛd) **4** a spreading out

outsprint (,aʊt'sprɪnt) *vb* (*tr*) to run faster than (someone)

outstand (ˌaʊtˈstænd) *vb* **-stands, -standing, -stood** **1** (*intr*) to be outstanding or excel **2** (*intr*) *nautical* to stand out to sea **3** (*tr*) *archaic* to last beyond

outstanding (ˌaʊtˈstændɪŋ) *adj* **1** superior; excellent; distinguished **2** prominent, remarkable, or striking **3** still in existence; unsettled, unpaid, or unresolved **4** (of shares, bonds, etc) issued and sold **5** projecting or jutting upwards or outwards > ˌ**outˈstandingly** *adv*

outstation (ˈaʊtˌsteɪʃən) *n* **1** a station or post in a remote region **2** in a radio network, any station other than the base station **3** *Austral* a station set up independently of the head station of a large sheep or cattle farm **4** **outstation movement** *Austral* the programme to resettle native Australians on their tribal lands ▷ *adv* **5** (in Malaysia) away from (the speaker's) town or area

outstay (ˌaʊtˈsteɪ) *vb* (*tr*) **1** to stay longer than **2** to stay beyond (a limit) **3** **outstay one's welcome** See **overstay** (sense 4)

outstretch (ˌaʊtˈstrɛtʃ) *vb* (*tr*) **1** to extend or expand; stretch out **2** to stretch or extend beyond

outstrip (ˌaʊtˈstrɪp) *vb* **-strips, -stripping, -stripped** (*tr*) **1** to surpass in a sphere of activity, competition, etc **2** to be or grow greater than **3** to go faster than and leave behind

outswing (ˈaʊtˌswɪŋ) *n* *cricket* the movement of a ball from leg to off through the air. Compare **inswing**

outswinger (ˈaʊtˌswɪŋə) *n* **1** *cricket* a ball bowled so as to move from leg to off through the air **2** *soccer* a ball kicked, esp from a corner, so as to move through the air in a curve away from the goal or the centre

outtake (ˈaʊtˌteɪk) *n* an unreleased take from a recording session, film, or television programme

outtalk (ˌaʊtˈtɔːk) *vb* (*tr*) to talk more, longer, or louder than (someone)

out there *adj* *slang* (**out-there** *when prenominal*) unconventional or eccentric: *he blends sublime pop moments with some real out-there stuff*

outthink (ˌaʊtˈθɪŋk) *vb* **-thinks, -thinking, -thought** (*tr*) **1** to outdo in thinking **2** to outwit

out-tray *n* (in an office) a tray for outgoing correspondence, documents, etc

outturn (ˈaʊtˌtɜːn) *n* **1** another word for **output** (sense 2) **2** outcome; result

outvote (ˌaʊtˈvəʊt) *vb* (*tr*) to defeat by a majority of votes

outward (ˈaʊtwəd) *adj* **1** of or relating to what is apparent or superficial **2** of or relating to the outside of the body **3** belonging or relating to the external, as opposed to the mental, spiritual, or inherent **4** of, relating to, or directed towards the outside or exterior **5** (of a ship, part of a voyage, etc) leaving for a particular destination **6** **the outward man** **a** the body as opposed to the soul **b** *facetious* clothing ▷ *adv* **7** (of a ship) away from port **8** a variant of **outwards** ▷ *n* **9** the outward part; exterior > ˈ**outwardness** *n*

Outward Bound *n* *trademark* (in Britain) a scheme to provide adventure training for young people

outwardly (ˈaʊtwədlɪ) *adv* **1** in outward appearance **2** with reference to the outside or outer surface; externally

outwards (ˈaʊtwədz) *or* **outward** *adv* towards the outside; out

outwash (ˈaʊtˌwɒʃ) *n* a mass of gravel, sand, etc, carried and deposited by the water derived from melting glaciers

outwear (ˌaʊtˈwɛə) *vb* **-wears, -wearing, -wore, -worn** (*tr*) **1** to use up or destroy by wearing **2** to last or wear longer than **3** to outlive, outgrow, or develop beyond **4** to deplete or exhaust in strength, determination, etc

outweigh (ˌaʊtˈweɪ) *vb* (*tr*) **1** to prevail over; overcome: *his desire outweighed his discretion* **2** to be more important or significant than **3** to be heavier than

outwit (ˌaʊtˈwɪt) *vb* **-wits, -witting, -witted** (*tr*) **1** to get the better of by cunning or ingenuity **2** *archaic* to be of greater intelligence than

outwith (ˌaʊtˈwɪθ) *prep* *Scot* outside; beyond

outwork *n* (ˈaʊtˌwɜːk) **1** (*often plural*) defences which lie outside main defensive works **2** work performed away from the factory, office, etc, by which it has been commissioned ▷ *vb* (ˌaʊtˈwɜːk) **-works, -working, -worked** *or* **-wrought** (*tr*) **3** to work better, harder, etc, than **4** to work out to completion > ˈ**outˌworker** *n*

outworn (ˈaʊtwɔːn, ˌaʊtˈwɔːn) *adj* no longer accepted, used, believed, etc; obsolete or outmoded

ouzel *or* **ousel** (ˈuːzᵊl) *n* **1** short for **ring ouzel** or **water ouzel** (see **dipper**) **2** an archaic name for the (European) **blackbird** [Old English *ōsle,* related to Old High German *amsala* (German *Amsel*), Latin *merula* MERLE[1]]

ouzo (ˈuːzəʊ) *n* a strong aniseed-flavoured spirit from Greece [Modern Greek *ouzon,* of obscure origin]

ova (ˈəʊvə) *n* the plural of **ovum**

oval (ˈəʊvᵊl) *adj* **1** having the shape of an ellipse or ellipsoid ▷ *n* **2** anything that is oval in shape, such as a sports ground [c16 from Medieval Latin *ōvālis,* from Latin *ōvum* egg] > ˈ**ovally** *adv* > ˈ**ovalness** *or* **ovality** (əʊˈvælɪtɪ) *n*

Oval (ˈəʊvᵊl) *n* **the** a cricket ground in south London, in the borough of Lambeth

Oval Office *n* **the** **1** the private office of the president of the US, a large oval room in the White House **2** the US presidency

ovals of Cassini (kəˈsiːnɪ) *pl n* *maths* the locus of a point *x*, whose distance from two fixed points, *a* and *b*, is such that |*x–a*| |*x–b*| is a constant [c18 named after J. D. *Cassini* (1625–1712), Italian-French astronomer and mathematician]

Ovambo (əʊˈvæmbəʊ, ɔːˈvambɔː) *n* **1** (*pl* **-bo** *or* **-bos**) a member of a mixed Khoikhoi and Negroid people of southern Africa, living chiefly in N Namibia: noted for their skill in metal work **2** the language of this people, belonging to the Bantu group of the Niger-Congo family

ovariectomy (əʊˌvɛərɪˈɛktəmɪ) *n, pl* **-mies** *surgery* another name for **oophorectomy**

ovariotomy (əʊˌvɛərɪˈɒtəmɪ) *n, pl* **-mies** surgical incision into an ovary. Compare **oophorectomy**

ovaritis (ˌəʊvəˈraɪtɪs) *n* inflammation of an ovary; oophoritis

ovary (ˈəʊvərɪ) *n, pl* **-ries** **1** either of the two female reproductive organs, which produce ova and secrete oestrogen hormones **2** the corresponding organ in vertebrate and invertebrate animals **3** *botany* the hollow basal region of a carpel containing one or more ovules. In some plants the carpels are united to form a single compound ovary [c17 from New Latin *ōvārium,* from Latin *ōvum* egg] > **ovarian** (əʊˈvɛərɪən) *adj*

ovate (ˈəʊveɪt) *adj* **1** shaped like an egg **2** (esp of a leaf) shaped like the longitudinal section of an egg, with the broader end at the base. Compare **obovate** [c18 from Latin *ōvātus* egg-shaped; see OVUM] > ˈ**ovately** *adv*

ovation (əʊˈveɪʃən) *n* **1** an enthusiastic reception, esp one of prolonged applause: *a standing ovation* **2** a victory procession less glorious than a triumph awarded to a Roman general [c16 from Latin *ovātiō* rejoicing, from *ovāre* to exult] > oˈ**vational** *adj*

ovel (ˈɒvəl) *n* *Judaism* a mourner, esp during the first seven days after a death. See also **shivah** [from Hebrew]

oven (ˈʌvᵊn) *n* **1** an enclosed heated compartment or receptacle for baking or roasting food **2** a similar device, usually lined with a refractory material, used for drying substances, firing ceramics, heat-treating, etc ▷ *vb* **3** (*tr*) to cook in an oven [Old English *ofen;* related to Old High German *ofan,* Old Norse *ofn*] > ˈ**oven-ˌlike** *adj*

ovenable (ˈʌvᵊnəbᵊl) *adj* **1** (of food) suitable for cooking in an oven **2** (of a container) suitable for use in an oven

ovenbird (ˈʌvᵊnˌbɜːd) *n* **1** any of numerous small brownish South American passerine birds of the family *Furnariidae* that build oven-shaped clay nests **2** a common North American warbler, *Seiurus aurocapillus,* that has an olive-brown striped plumage with an orange crown and builds a cup-shaped nest on the ground

oven-ready *adj* **1** (of various foods) bought already prepared so that they are ready to be cooked in the oven **2** (of a new employee) ready to start work immediately without further training: *oven-ready graduates*

ovenware (ˈʌvᵊnˌwɛə) *n* heat-resistant dishes in which food can be both cooked and served

over (ˈəʊvə) *prep* **1** directly above; on the top of; via the top or upper surface of: *over one's head* **2** on or to the other side of: *over the river* **3** during; through, or throughout (a period of time) **4** in or throughout all parts of: *to travel over England* **5** throughout the whole extent of: *over the racecourse* **6** above; in preference to: *I like that over everything else* **7** by the agency of (an instrument of telecommunication): *we heard it over the radio* **8** more than: *over a century ago* **9** on the subject of; about: *an argument over nothing* **10** while occupied in: *discussing business over golf* **11** having recovered from the effects of: *she's not over that last love affair yet* **12** **over and above** added to; in addition to: *he earns a large amount over and above his salary* ▷ *adv* **13** in a state, condition, situation, or position that is or has been placed or put over something: *to climb over* **14** (*particle*) so as to cause to fall: *knocking over a policeman* **15** at or to a point across intervening space, water, etc: *come over and see us; over in America* **16** throughout a whole area: *the world over* **17** (*particle*) from beginning to end, usually cursorily: *to read a document over* **18** throughout a period of time: *stay over for this week* **19** (esp in signalling and radio) it is now your turn to speak, act, etc **20** more than is expected or usual: *not over well* **21** **over again** once more **22** **over against** **a** opposite to **b** contrasting with **23** **over and over** (often foll by *again*) repeatedly **24** **over the odds** **a** in addition, esp when not expected **b** unfair or excessive ▷ *adj* **25** (*postpositive*) finished; no longer in progress: *is the concert over yet?* ▷ *adv, adj* **26** remaining; surplus (often in the phrase **left over**) ▷ *n* **27** *cricket* **a** a series of six balls bowled by a bowler from the same end of the pitch **b** the play during this [Old English *ofer;* related to Old High German *ubir, obar,* Old Norse *yfir,* Latin *super,* Greek *huper*]

over- *prefix* **1** excessive or excessively; beyond an agreed or desirable limit: *overcharge; overdue; oversimplify* **2** indicating superior rank: *overseer* **3** indicating location or movement above: *overhang* **4** indicating movement downwards: *overthrow*

overabundance (ˌəʊvərəˈbʌndəns) *n* a supply or amount that is greater than required: *an overabundance of milk*

overachieve (ˌəʊvərəˈtʃiːv) *vb* (*intr*) to perform (for example, in examinations) better than would be expected on the basis of one's age or talents > ˌ**overaˈchiever** *n*

overact (ˌəʊvərˈækt) *vb* to act or behave in an exaggerated manner, as in a theatrical production. Also: **overplay**

overactive (ˌəʊvərˈæktɪv) *adj* **1** inordinately active **2** (of the thyroid or adrenal gland, nervous system, etc) functioning at too high a capacity

overage (ˌəʊvərˈeɪdʒ) *adj* beyond a specified age

overaggressive (ˌəʊvərəˈɡrɛsɪv) *adj* excessively quarrelsome or belligerent

overall *adj* (ˈəʊvərˌɔːl) (*prenominal*) **1** from one end to the other **2** including or covering everything: *the overall cost* ▷ *adv* (ˌəʊvərˈɔːl) **3** in general; on the whole ▷ *n* (ˈəʊvərˌɔːl) **4** *Brit* a protective work garment usually worn over ordinary clothes **5** (*plural*) hard-wearing work trousers with a bib and shoulder straps or jacket attached

overambitious (ˌəʊvəræmˈbɪʃəs) *adj* excessively ambitious

O

overanxious (ˌəʊvərˈæŋkʃəs, -ˈænʃəs) *adj* excessively worried, tense, or uneasy

overarch (ˌəʊvərˈɑːtʃ) *vb* (*tr*) to form an arch over

overarching (ˌəʊvərˈɑːtʃɪŋ) *adj* overall; all-encompassing: *an overarching concept*

overarm (ˈəʊvərˌɑːm) *sport* ▷ *adj* **1** bowled, thrown, or performed with the arm raised above the shoulder ▷ *adv* **2** with the arm raised above the shoulder

overattentive (ˌəʊvərəˈtɛntɪv) *adj* excessively careful to fulfil the needs and wants (of)

overawe (ˌəʊvərˈɔː) *vb* (*tr*) to subdue, restrain, or overcome by affecting with a feeling of awe

overbalance *vb* (ˌəʊvəˈbæləns) **1** to lose or cause to lose balance **2** (*tr*) another word for **outweigh** ▷ *n* (ˈəʊvəˌbæləns) **3** excess of weight, value, etc

overbear (ˌəʊvəˈbɛə) *vb* **-bears, -bearing, -bore, -borne** **1** (*tr*) to dominate or overcome: *to overbear objections* **2** (*tr*) to press or bear down with weight or physical force **3** to produce or bear (fruit, progeny, etc) excessively

overbearing (ˌəʊvəˈbɛərɪŋ) *adj* **1** domineering or dictatorial in manner or action **2** of particular or overriding importance or significance > **over'bearingly** *adv*

overbid *vb* (ˌəʊvəˈbɪd) **-bids, -bidding, -bid, -bidden** *or* **-bid** **1** (*intr*) *bridge* to bid for more tricks than one can expect to win **2** to bid more than the value of (something) ▷ *n* (ˈəʊvəˌbɪd) **3** a bid higher than someone else's bid

overbite (ˈəʊvəˌbaɪt) *n* *dentistry* an extension of the upper front teeth over the lower front teeth when the mouth is closed. Also called: **vertical overlap**

overblouse (ˈəʊvəˌblaʊz) *n* a blouse designed to be worn not tucked into trousers or a skirt but to fit loosely over the waist or hips

overblow (ˌəʊvəˈbləʊ) *vb* **-blows, -blowing, -blew, -blown** **1** *music* to blow into (a wind instrument) with greater force than normal in order to obtain a harmonic or overtone instead of the fundamental tone **2** to blow (a wind instrument) or (of a wind instrument) to be blown too hard **3** to blow over, away, or across

overblown (ˌəʊvəˈbləʊn) *adj* **1** overdone or excessive **2** bombastic; turgid: *overblown prose* **3** (of flowers, such as the rose) past the stage of full bloom

overboard (ˈəʊvəˌbɔːd) *adv* **1** from on board a vessel into the water **2 go overboard** *informal* **a** to be extremely enthusiastic **b** to go to extremes **3 throw overboard** to reject or abandon

overboot (ˈəʊvəˌbuːt) *n* a protective boot worn over an ordinary boot or shoe

overbuild (ˌəʊvəˈbɪld) *vb* **-builds, -building, -built** (*tr*) **1** to build over or on top of **2** to erect too many buildings in (an area) **3** to build too large or elaborately

overburden *vb* (ˌəʊvəˈbɜːdˀn) **1** (*tr*) to load with excessive weight, work, etc ▷ *n* (ˈəʊvəˌbɜːdˀn) **2** an excessive burden or load **3** *geology* the sedimentary rock material that covers coal seams, mineral veins, etc > **over'burdensome** *adj*

overcall *bridge* ▷ *n* (ˈəʊvəˌkɔːl) **1** a bid higher than the preceding one ▷ *vb* (ˌəʊvəˈkɔːl) **2** to bid higher than (an opponent)

overcapacity (ˌəʊvəkəˈpæsɪtɪ) *n* the situation in which an industry or business cannot sell as much as it produces

overcapitalize *or* **overcapitalise** (ˌəʊvəˈkæpɪtəˌlaɪz) *vb* (*tr*) **1** to provide or issue capital for (an enterprise) in excess of profitable investment opportunities **2** to estimate the capital value of (a company) at an unreasonably or unlawfully high level **3** to overestimate the market value of (property) > **over,capitali'zation** *or* **over,capitali'sation** *n*

overcast *adj* (ˈəʊvəˌkɑːst) **1** covered over or obscured, esp by clouds **2** *meteorol* (of the sky) more than 95 per cent cloud-covered **3** gloomy or melancholy **4** sewn over by overcasting ▷ *vb* (ˌəʊvəˈkɑːst) **5** to make or become overclouded or gloomy **6** to sew (an edge, as of a hem) with long stitches passing successively over the edge ▷ *n* (ˈəʊvəˌkɑːst) **7** a covering, as of clouds or mist **8** *meteorol* the state of the sky when more than 95 per cent of it is cloud-covered **9** *mining* a crossing of two passages without an intersection

overcharge *vb* (ˌəʊvəˈtʃɑːdʒ) **1** to charge too much **2** (*tr*) to fill or load beyond capacity **3** *literary* another word for **exaggerate** ▷ *n* (ˈəʊvəˌtʃɑːdʒ) **4** an excessive price or charge **5** an excessive load

overcheck (ˈəʊvəˌtʃɛk) *n* **1** a thin leather strap attached to a horse's bit to keep its head up **2** (in textiles) **a** a checked pattern laid over another checked pattern **b** a fabric patterned in such a way

overcloud (ˌəʊvəˈklaʊd) *vb* **1** to make or become covered with clouds **2** to make or become dark or dim

overcoat (ˈəʊvəˌkəʊt) *n* a warm heavy coat worn over the outer clothes in cold weather

overcome (ˌəʊvəˈkʌm) *vb* **-comes, -coming, -came, -come** **1** (*tr*) to get the better of in a conflict **2** (*tr; often passive*) to render incapable or powerless by laughter, sorrow, exhaustion, etc: *he was overcome by fumes* **3** (*tr*) to surmount (obstacles, objections, etc) **4** (*intr*) to be victorious

overcommit (ˌəʊvəkəˈmɪt) *vb* **-mits, -mitting, -mitted** (*tr*) to promise, undertake, or allocate more than the available resources justify

overcompensate (ˌəʊvəˈkɒmpənˌseɪt) *vb* **1** to compensate (a person or thing) excessively **2** (*intr*) *psychol* to engage in overcompensation > **over'compen,satory** *adj*

overcompensation (ˌəʊvəˌkɒmpənˈseɪʃən) *n* *psychol* an attempt to make up for a character trait by overexaggerating its opposite

overcomplex (ˌəʊvəˈkɒmplɛks) *adj* excessively complicated, intricate, or involved: *an overcomplex pattern*

overconfident (ˌəʊvəˈkɒnfɪdənt) *adj* excessively confident > **over'confidence** *n*

overconsumption (ˌəʊvəkənˈsʌmpʃən) *n* the state or an instance of consuming too much food, drink, fuel, etc

overcook (ˌəʊvəˈkʊk) *vb* (*tr*) to cook (something) until dry, burnt, or inedible

overcrop (ˌəʊvəˈkrɒp) *vb* **-crops, -cropping, -cropped** (*tr*) to exhaust (land) by excessive cultivation

overcrowd (ˌəʊvəˈkraʊd) *vb* (*tr*) to fill (a room, vehicle, city, etc) with more people or things than is desirable

overcrowding (ˌəʊvəˈkraʊdɪŋ) *n* a state of being filled with more people or things than is desirable; congestion

overdependence (ˌəʊvədɪˈpɛndəns) *n* the state or fact of being too dependent, esp for help or support

overdependent (ˌəʊvədɪˈpɛndənt) *adj* excessively dependent on a person or thing for aid, support, etc

overdevelop (ˌəʊvədɪˈvɛləp) *vb* (*tr*) **1** to develop too much or too far **2** *photog* to process (a film, plate, or print) in developer for more than the required time, at too great a concentration, etc > **overde'velopment** *n*

overdeviate (ˌəʊvəˈdiːvɪˌeɪt) *vb* to cause (a frequency-modulated radio transmitter) to exceed its specified frequency excursion from the rest frequency

overdo (ˌəʊvəˈduː) *vb* **-does, -doing, -did, -done** (*tr*) **1** to take or carry too far; do to excess **2** to exaggerate, overelaborate, or overplay **3** to cook or bake too long **4 overdo it** *or* **things** to overtax one's strength, capacity, etc

overdose *n* (ˈəʊvəˌdəʊs) **1** (esp of drugs) an excessive dose ▷ *vb* (ˌəʊvəˈdəʊs) **2** to take an excessive dose or give an excessive dose to > **over'dosage** *n*

overdraft (ˈəʊvəˌdrɑːft) *n* **1** a draft or withdrawal of money in excess of the credit balance on a bank or building-society cheque account **2** the amount of money drawn or withdrawn thus

overdraught (ˈəʊvəˌdrɑːft) *n* a current of air passed above a fire, as in a furnace

overdraw (ˌəʊvəˈdrɔː) *vb* **-draws, -drawing, -drew, -drawn** **1** to draw on (a bank account) in excess of the credit balance **2** (*tr*) to strain or pull (a bow) too far **3** (*tr*) to exaggerate in describing or telling

overdress *vb* (ˌəʊvəˈdrɛs) **1** to dress (oneself or another) too elaborately or finely ▷ *n* (ˈəʊvəˌdrɛs) **2** a dress that may be worn over a jumper, blouse, etc

overdrive *n* (ˈəʊvəˌdraɪv) **1** a very high gear in a motor vehicle used at high speeds to reduce wear and save fuel **2 in** *or* **into overdrive** in *or* into a state of intense activity ▷ *vb* (ˌəʊvəˈdraɪv) **-drives, -driving, -drove, -driven** **3** (*tr*) to drive too hard or too far; overwork or overuse

overdub (in multitrack recording) ▷ *vb* (ˌəʊvəˈdʌb) **-dubs, -dubbing, -dubbed** **1** to add (new sound) on a spare track or tracks ▷ *n* (ˈəʊvəˌdʌb) **2** the addition of new sound to a recording; the blending of various layers of sound in one recording

overdue (ˌəʊvəˈdjuː) *adj* past the time specified, required, or preferred for arrival, occurrence, payment, etc

overdye (ˌəʊvəˈdaɪ) *vb* (*tr*) **1** to dye (a fabric, yarn, etc) excessively **2** to dye for a second or third time with a different colour

overeager (ˌəʊvərˈiːgə) *adj* excessively eager or keen: *overeager supporters*

overeat (ˌəʊvərˈiːt) *vb* **-eats, -eating, -ate, -eaten** (*intr*) to consume too much food

overegg (ˌəʊvərˈɛg) *vb* (*tr*) to exaggerate (a feature of something) to the point of unreasonableness (esp in the phrase **overegg the pudding**)

overelaborate *adj* (ˌəʊvərɪˈlæbərɪt) **1** excessively ornate, detailed, or complex ▷ *vb* (ˌəʊvərɪˈlæbəˌreɪt) **2** (*tr*) to detail or develop (an idea, plan, etc) excessively > **overe,labo'ration** *n*

overemphasize *or* **overemphasise** (ˌəʊvərˈɛmfəˌsaɪz) *vb* (*tr*) to give excessive emphasis or prominence to (something) > **over'emphasis** *n*

overenthusiastic (ˌəʊvərɪnˌθjuːzɪˈæstɪk) *adj* excessively enthusiastic

overestimate *vb* (ˌəʊvərˈɛstɪˌmeɪt) **1** (*tr*) to value or estimate too highly ▷ *n* (ˌəʊvərˈɛstɪmɪt) **2** an estimate that is too high > **over,esti'mation** *n*

overexcited (ˌəʊvərɪkˈsaɪtɪd) *adj* excessively excited

overexpansion (ˌəʊvərɪksˈpænʃən) *n* an excessive increase, enlargement, or development, esp in the activities of a company

overexpose (ˌəʊvərɪksˈpəʊz) *vb* (*tr*) **1** to expose too much or for too long **2** *photog* to expose (a film, plate, or paper) for too long a period or with too bright a light > **overex'posure** *n*

overfall (ˈəʊvəˌfɔːl) *n* **1** a turbulent stretch of water caused by marine currents over an underwater ridge **2** a mechanism that allows excess water to escape from a dam or lock **3** the point at which a sewer or land drainage discharges into the sea or a river

overfamiliar (ˌəʊvəfəˈmɪlɪə) *adj* **1** excessively friendly, informal, or intimate **2** too well-known or easily recognized: *an overfamiliar action movie* > **overfa,mili'arity** *n*

overflight (ˈəʊvəˌflaɪt) *n* the flight of an aircraft over a specific area or territory

overflow *vb* (ˌəʊvəˈfləʊ) **-flows, -flowing, -flowed** *or formerly* **-flown** **1** to flow or run over (a limit, brim, bank, etc) **2** to fill or be filled beyond capacity so as to spill or run over **3** (*intr; usually foll by with*) to be filled with happiness, tears, etc **4** (*tr*) to spread or cover over; flood or inundate ▷ *n* (ˈəʊvəˌfləʊ) **5** overflowing matter, esp liquid **6** any outlet that enables surplus liquid to be discharged or drained off, esp one just below the top of a tank or cistern **7** the amount by which a limit, capacity, etc, is exceeded **8** *computing* a condition that occurs when numeric operations produce results too large to store in the memory space assigned to it

overfly (ˌəʊvəˈflaɪ) *vb* -flies, -flying, -flew, -flown (*tr*) to fly over (a territory) or past (a point)

overfold (ˈəʊvəˌfəʊld) *n geology* a fold in which one or both limbs have been inclined more than 90° from their original orientation

overfond (ˌəʊvəˈfɒnd) *adj* (*postpositive; foll by of*) excessively keen (on)

overfull (ˌəʊvəˈfʊl) *adj* excessively full; overflowing

overfunding (ˈəʊvəˌfʌndɪŋ) *n* (in Britain) a government policy in which it sells more of its securities than would be required to finance public spending, with the object of absorbing surplus funds to curb inflation

overgarment (ˈəʊvəˌɡɑːmənt) *n* any garment worn over other clothes, esp to protect them from wear or dirt

overgear (ˌəʊvəˈɡɪə) *vb* (*tr; usually passive*) to cause (a company) to have too high a proportion of loan stock and preference shares in comparison to its ordinary share capital

overgenerous (ˌəʊvəˈdʒɛnərəs, -ˈdʒɛnrəs) *adj* excessively willing and liberal in giving away one's time, money, etc

overglaze (ˈəʊvəˌɡleɪz) *adj* (of decoration or colours) applied to porcelain or pottery above the glaze

overgraze (ˌəʊvəˈɡreɪz) *vb* (*tr*) to graze (land) beyond its capacity to sustain stock

overground (ˈəʊvəˌɡraʊnd) *adj* 1 on or above the surface of the ground: *an overground railway* 2 having become sufficiently established, known, or accepted so as to no longer be considered avante-garde, experimental, or subversive

overgrow (ˌəʊvəˈɡrəʊ) *vb* -grows, -growing, -grew, -grown 1 (*tr*) to grow over or across (an area, path, lawn, etc) 2 (*tr*) to choke or supplant by a stronger growth 3 (*tr*) to grow too large for 4 (*intr*) to grow beyond normal size ▷ 'over,growth *n*

overhand (ˈəʊvəˌhænd) *adj* 1 thrown or performed with the hand raised above the shoulder 2 sewn with thread passing over two edges in one direction ▷ *adv* 3 with the hand above the shoulder; overarm 4 with shallow stitches passing over two edges ▷ *vb* 5 to sew (two edges) overhand

overhand knot *n* a knot formed by making a loop in a piece of cord and drawing one end through it. Also called: thumb knot

overhang *vb* (ˌəʊvəˈhæŋ) -hangs, -hanging, -hung 1 to project or extend beyond (a surface, building, etc) 2 (*tr*) to hang or be suspended over 3 (*tr*) to menace, threaten, or dominate ▷ *n* (ˈəʊvəˌhæŋ) 4 a formation, object, part of a structure, etc, that extends beyond or hangs over something, such as an outcrop of rock overhanging a mountain face 5 the amount or extent of projection 6 *aeronautics* a half the difference in span of the main supporting surfaces of a biplane or other multiplane b the distance from the outer supporting strut of a wing to the wing tip 7 *finance* the shares, collectively, that the underwriters have to buy when a new issue has not been fully taken up by the market

overhaul *vb* (ˌəʊvəˈhɔːl) (*tr*) 1 to examine carefully for faults, necessary repairs, etc 2 to make repairs or adjustments to (a car, machine, etc) 3 to overtake ▷ *n* (ˈəʊvəˌhɔːl) 4 a thorough examination and repair

overhead *adj* (ˈəʊvəˌhɛd) 1 situated or operating above head height or some other reference level 2 (*prenominal*) inclusive: *the overhead price included meals* ▷ *adv* (ˌəʊvəˈhɛd) 3 over or above head height, esp in the sky ▷ *n* (ˈəʊvəˌhɛd) 4 a a stroke in racket games played from above head height b (*as modifier*): *an overhead smash* 5 *nautical* the interior lining above one's head below decks in a vessel 6 short for **overhead door** 7 (*modifier*) of, concerned with, or resulting from overheads: *overhead costs* ▷ See also **overheads**

overhead camshaft *n* a type of camshaft situated above the cylinder head in an internal-combustion engine. It is usually driven by a chain or a toothed belt from the crankshaft and the cams bear directly onto the valve stems or rocker arms

overhead door *n* a door that rotates on a horizontal axis and is supported horizontally when open. Sometimes shortened to: overhead

overhead projector *n* a projector that throws an enlarged image of a transparency onto a surface above and behind the person using it. Alterations and additions can be made to the material on the transparency while the projector is in use

overheads (ˈəʊvəˌhɛdz) *pl n* business expenses, such as rent, that are not directly attributable to any department or product and can therefore be assigned only arbitrarily. Also called: burden, fixed costs, indirect costs, oncost Compare **prime cost**

overhead-valve engine *n* a type of internal-combustion engine in which the inlet and exhaust valves are in the cylinder head above the pistons. US name: valve-in-head engine Compare **side-valve engine**

overhear (ˌəʊvəˈhɪə) *vb* -hears, -hearing, -heard (*tr*) to hear (a person, remark, etc) without the knowledge of the speaker

overheat (ˌəʊvəˈhiːt) *vb* 1 to make or become excessively hot 2 (*tr; often passive*) to make very agitated, irritated, etc 3 (*intr*) (of an economy) to tend towards inflation, often as a result of excessive growth in demand 4 (*tr*) to cause (an economy) to tend towards inflation ▷ *n* 5 the condition of being overheated

Overijssel (*Dutch* oːvərˈɛisəl) *n* a province of the E Netherlands: generally low-lying. Capital: Zwolle. Pop: 1 101 000 (2003 est). Area: 3929 sq km (1517 sq miles)

overindulge (ˌəʊvərɪnˈdʌldʒ) *vb* 1 to indulge (in something, esp food or drink) immoderately; binge 2 (*tr*) to yield excessively to the wishes of; spoil ▷ ˌoverin'dulgence *n* ▷ ˌoverin'dulgent *adj*

overissue (ˈəʊvərˌɪsjuː, -ˌɪʃuː) *vb* -sues, -suing, -sued (*tr*) 1 to issue (shares, banknotes, etc) in excess of demand or ability to pay ▷ *n* 2 shares, banknotes, etc, thus issued

overjoy (ˌəʊvəˈdʒɔɪ) *vb* (*tr*) to give great delight to

overjoyed (ˌəʊvəˈdʒɔɪd) *adj* delighted; excessively happy

overkill (ˈəʊvəˌkɪl) *n* 1 the capability to deploy more weapons, esp nuclear weapons, than is necessary to ensure military advantage 2 any capacity or treatment that is greater than that required or appropriate

overland (ˈəʊvəˌlænd) *adj* (*prenominal*), *adv* 1 over or across land ▷ *vb* 2 *Austral history* to drive (cattle or sheep) overland ▷ 'over,lander *n*

overlap *vb* (ˌəʊvəˈlæp) -laps, -lapping, -lapped 1 (of two things) to extend or lie partly over (each other) 2 to cover and extend beyond (something) 3 (*intr*) to coincide partly in time, subject, etc ▷ *n* (ˈəʊvəˌlæp) 4 a part that overlaps or is overlapped 5 the amount, length, etc, overlapping 6 the act or fact of overlapping 7 a place of overlapping 8 *geology* the horizontal extension of the upper beds in a series of rock strata beyond the lower beds, usually caused by submergence of the land

overlarge (ˌəʊvəˈlɑːdʒ) *adj* excessively large

overlay *vb* (ˌəʊvəˈleɪ) -lays, -laying, -laid (*tr*) 1 to lay or place something over or upon (something else) 2 (often foll by *with*) to cover, overspread, or conceal (with) 3 (foll by *with*) to cover (a surface) with an applied decoration: *ebony overlaid with silver* 4 to achieve the correct printing pressure all over (a forme or plate) by adding to the appropriate areas of the packing ▷ *n* (ˈəʊvəˌleɪ) 5 something that is laid over something else; covering 6 an applied decoration or layer, as of gold leaf 7 a transparent sheet giving extra details to a map or diagram over which it is designed to be placed 8 *printing* material, such as paper, used to overlay a forme or plate

overleaf (ˌəʊvəˈliːf) *adv* on the other side of the page. Also: overpage

overlie (ˌəʊvəˈlaɪ) *vb* -lies, -lying, -lay, -lain (*tr*) 1 to lie or rest upon. Compare overlay 2 to kill (a baby or newborn animal) by lying upon it

overlive (ˌəʊvəˈlɪv) *vb* 1 to live longer than (another person) 2 to survive or outlive (an event)

overload *vb* (ˌəʊvəˈləʊd) 1 (*tr*) to put too large a load on or in ▷ *n* (ˈəʊvəˌləʊd) 2 an excessive load

overlong (ˌəʊvəˈlɒŋ) *adj, adv* too or excessively long

overlook *vb* (ˌəʊvəˈlʊk) (*tr*) 1 to fail to notice or take into account 2 to disregard deliberately or indulgently 3 to look at or over from above: *the garden is overlooked by the prison* 4 to afford a view of from above: *the house overlooks the bay* 5 to rise above 6 to look after 7 to look at carefully 8 to bewitch or cast the evil eye upon (someone) ▷ *n* (ˈəʊvəˌlʊk) US 9 a high place affording a view 10 an act of overlooking

overlooker (ˈəʊvəˌlʊkə) *n* another word (less common) for overseer (sense 1)

overlord (ˈəʊvəˌlɔːd) *n* a supreme lord or master ▷ 'over,lordship *n*

overly (ˈəʊvəlɪ) *adv* too; excessively

overman *vb* (ˌəʊvəˈmæn) -mans, -manning, -manned 1 (*tr*) to supply with an excessive number of men ▷ *n* (ˈəʊvəˌmæn) *pl* -men 2 a man who oversees others 3 the Nietzschean superman

overmantel (ˈəʊvəˌmæntəl) *n* an ornamental shelf over a mantelpiece, often with a mirror

overmaster (ˌəʊvəˈmɑːstə) *vb* (*tr*) to overpower

overmatch *chiefly US* ▷ *vb* (ˌəʊvəˈmætʃ) (*tr*) 1 to be more than a match for 2 to match with a superior opponent ▷ *n* (ˈəʊvəˌmætʃ) 3 a person superior in ability 4 a match in which one contestant is superior

overmatter (ˈəʊvəˌmætə) *n printing* type that has been set but cannot be used for printing owing to lack of space. Also called: overset

overmuch (ˌəʊvəˈmʌtʃ) *adv, adj* 1 too much; very much ▷ *n* 2 an excessive amount

overnice (ˌəʊvəˈnaɪs) *adj* too fastidious, precise, etc

overnight *adv* (ˌəʊvəˈnaɪt) 1 for the duration of the night: *we stopped overnight* 2 in or as if in the course of one night; suddenly: *the situation changed overnight* ▷ *adj* (ˈəʊvəˌnaɪt) (*usually prenominal*) 3 done in, occurring in, or lasting the night: *an overnight stop* 4 staying for one night: *overnight guests* 5 lasting one night: *an overnight trip; an overnight bank loan* 6 for use during a single night: *overnight clothes* 7 occurring in or as if in the course of one night; sudden: *an overnight victory* ▷ *vb* (*intr*) 8 to stay the night

overoptimism (ˌəʊvərˈɒptɪˌmɪzəm) *n* excessive hopefulness or confidence

overoptimistic (ˌəʊvərˌɒptɪˈmɪstɪk) *adj* excessively optimistic

overpage (ˌəʊvəˈpeɪdʒ) *adv* another word for **overleaf**

overparted (ˌəʊvəˈpɑːtɪd) *adj* (of a performer) having been cast in a role that is beyond his or her abilities

overpass *n* (ˈəʊvəˌpɑːs) 1 another name for **flyover** (sense 1) ▷ *vb* (ˌəʊvəˈpɑːs) -passes, -passing, -passed (*tr*) now rare 2 to pass over, through, or across 3 to exceed 4 to get over 5 to ignore

overpay (ˌəʊvəˈpeɪ) *vb* -pays, -paying, -paid 1 to pay (someone) at too high a rate 2 to pay (someone) more than is due, as by an error

overpersuade (ˌəʊvəpəˈsweɪd) *vb* (*tr*) to persuade (someone) against his inclination or judgment

overpitch (ˌəʊvəˈpɪtʃ) *vb cricket* to bowl (a ball) so that it pitches too close to the stumps

overplay (ˌəʊvəˈpleɪ) *vb* 1 (*tr*) to exaggerate the importance of 2 another word for **overact** 3 **overplay one's hand** to overestimate the worth or strength of one's position

overplus (ˈəʊvəˌplʌs) *n* surplus or excess quantity

overpopulated (ˌəʊvəˈpɒpjʊˌleɪtɪd) *adj* having too

O

many inhabitants for the available space or resources

overpopulation (ˌəʊvəˌpɒpjʊˈleɪʃən) *n* the population of an area in too large numbers

overpower (ˌəʊvəˈpaʊə) *vb (tr)* **1** to conquer or subdue by superior force **2** to have such a strong effect on as to make helpless or ineffective **3** to supply with more power than necessary

overpowering (ˌəʊvəˈpaʊərɪŋ) *adj* **1** so strong or intense as to be unbearable **2** so powerful as to crush or conquer > ˌ**overˈpoweringly** *adv*

overpressure (ˈəʊvəˌprɛʃə) *n* the blast effect of a nuclear weapon expressed as an amount of pressure greater than normal barometric pressure

overpriced (ˌəʊvəˈpraɪst) *adj* charging or charged at too high a price

overprint *vb* (ˌəʊvəˈprɪnt) **1** *(tr)* to print (additional matter or another colour) on a sheet of paper ▷ *n* (ˈəʊvəˌprɪnt) **2** additional matter or another colour printed onto a previously printed sheet **3** additional matter, other than a change in face value, applied to a finished postage stamp by printing, stamping, etc. See also **surcharge** (sense 5), **provisional** (sense 2)

overproduction (ˌəʊvəprəˈdʌkʃən) *n* the production of more of a product or commodity than is required

overprotect (ˌəʊvəprəˈtɛkt) *vb (tr)* to protect more than necessary, esp to shield a child excessively so as to inhibit its development > ˌ**overproˈtective** *adj*

overqualified (ˌəʊvəˈkwɒlɪˌfaɪd) *adj* having more managerial experience or academic qualifications than required for a particular job

overrate (ˌəʊvəˈreɪt) *vb (tr)* to assess too highly

overreach (ˌəʊvəˈriːtʃ) *vb* **1** *(tr)* to defeat or thwart (oneself) by attempting to do or gain too much **2** *(tr)* to aim for but miss by going too far or attempting too much **3** to get the better of (a person) by trickery **4** *(tr)* to reach or extend beyond or over **5** *(intr)* to reach or go too far **6** *(intr)* (of a horse) to strike the back of a forefoot with the edge of the opposite hind foot

overreact (ˌəʊvərɪˈækt) *vb (intr)* to react excessively to something > ˌ**overreˈaction** *n*

overrefine (ˌəʊvərɪˈfaɪn) *vb* **1** to refine (something) to excess **2** *(intr)* to make excessively fine distinctions > ˌ**overreˈfinement** *n*

overreliance (ˌəʊvərɪˈlaɪəns) *n* the state or fact of being too reliant on someone or something

overrich (ˌəʊvəˈrɪtʃ) *adj* **1** (of food) excessively flavoursome or fatty **2** being excessively abundant, strong, etc: *overrich heroin*

override (ˌəʊvəˈraɪd) *vb* **-rides, -riding, -rode, -ridden** *(tr)* **1** to set aside or disregard with superior authority or power **2** to supersede or annul **3** to dominate or vanquish by or as if by trampling down **4** to take manual control of (a system that is usually under automatic control) **5** to extend or pass over, esp to overlap **6** to ride (a horse) too hard **7** to ride over or across ▷ *n* **8** a device or system that can override an automatic control

overrider (ˈəʊvəˌraɪdə) *n* either of two metal or rubber attachments fitted to the bumper of a motor vehicle to prevent the bumpers interlocking with those of another vehicle

overriding (ˌəʊvəˈraɪdɪŋ) *adj* taking precedence

overripe (ˌəʊvəˈraɪp) *adj* **1** (of food, cheese, etc) past the usual stage of being ready to eat or use **2** overused or overly sentimental and emotional: *his love songs are overripe ballads*

overrule (ˌəʊvəˈruːl) *vb (tr)* **1** to disallow the arguments of (a person) by the use of authority **2** to rule or decide against (an argument, decision, etc) **3** to prevail over, dominate, or influence **4** to exercise rule over

overrun *vb* (ˌəʊvəˈrʌn) **-runs, -running, -ran, -run** **1** *(tr)* to attack or invade and defeat conclusively **2** *(tr)* to swarm or spread over rapidly **3** to run over (something); overflow **4** to extend or run beyond a limit **5** *(intr)* (of an engine) to run with a closed throttle at a speed dictated by that of the vehicle it drives, as on a decline **6** *(tr)* **a** to print (a book, journal, etc) in a greater quantity than ordered **b** to print additional copies of (a publication) **7** *(tr) printing* to transfer (set type and other matter) from one column, line, or page, to another **8** *(tr) archaic* to run faster than ▷ *n* (ˈəʊvəˌrʌn) **9** the act or an instance of overrunning **10** the amount or extent of overrunning **11** the number of copies of a publication in excess of the quantity ordered **12** the cleared level area at the end of an airport runway

overrun brake *n* a brake fitted to a trailer or other towed vehicle that prevents the towed vehicle travelling faster than the towing vehicle when slowing down or descending an incline

oversaturated (ˌəʊvəˈsætʃəˌreɪtɪd) *adj* (of igneous rocks) containing excess silica

overscore (ˌəʊvəˈskɔː) *vb (tr)* to cancel or cross out by drawing a line or lines over or through

overseas *adv* (ˌəʊvəˈsiːz) **1** beyond the sea; abroad ▷ *adj* (ˈəʊvəˈsiːz) **2** of, to, in, from, or situated in countries beyond the sea **3** Also: **oversea** (ˌəʊvəˈsiː) of or relating to passage over the sea ▷ *n* (ˌəʊvəˈsiːz) **4** *(functioning as singular) informal* a foreign country or foreign countries collectively

overseas *or* **international telegram** *n Brit* another name for **cable** (sense 5)

oversee (ˌəʊvəˈsiː) *vb* **-sees, -seeing, -saw, -seen** *(tr)* **1** to watch over and direct; supervise **2** to watch secretly or accidentally

overseer (ˈəʊvəˌsiːə) *n* **1** Also called (less commonly): **overlooker** a person who oversees others, esp workmen **2** *Brit history* short for **overseer of the poor;** a minor official of a parish attached to the workhouse or poorhouse

oversell (ˌəʊvəˈsɛl) *vb* **-sells, -selling, -sold** **1** *(tr)* to sell more of (a commodity) than can be supplied **2** to use excessively aggressive methods in selling (commodities) **3** *(tr)* to exaggerate the merits of

oversensitive (ˌəʊvəˈsɛnsɪtɪv) *adj* excessively responsive to or aware of feelings, reactions, etc

overset *vb* (ˌəʊvəˈsɛt) **-sets, -setting, -set** *(tr)* **1** to disturb or upset **2** *printing* to set (type or copy) in excess of the space available ▷ *n* (ˈəʊvəˌsɛt) **3** another name for **overmatter**

oversew (ˈəʊvəˌsəʊ, ˌəʊvəˈsəʊ) *vb* **-sews, -sewing, -sewed, -sewn** to sew (two edges) with close stitches that pass over them both

oversexed (ˌəʊvəˈsɛkst) *adj* having an excessive preoccupation with or need for sexual activity

overshadow (ˌəʊvəˈʃædəʊ) *vb (tr)* **1** to render insignificant or less important in comparison **2** to cast a shadow or gloom over

overshoe (ˈəʊvəˌʃuː) *n* a protective shoe worn over an ordinary shoe

overshoot (ˌəʊvəˈʃuːt) *vb* **-shoots, -shooting, -shot** **1** to shoot or go beyond (a mark or target) **2** to cause (an aircraft) to fly or taxi too far along (a runway) during landing or taking off, or (of an aircraft) to fly or taxi too far along a runway **3** *(tr)* to pass swiftly over or down over, as water over a wheel ▷ *n* **4** an act or instance of overshooting **5** the extent of such overshooting **6** a momentary excessive response of an electrical or mechanical system

overshot (ˈəʊvəˌʃɒt) *adj* **1** having or designating an upper jaw that projects beyond the lower jaw, esp when considered as an abnormality **2** (of a water wheel) driven by a flow of water that passes over the wheel rather than under it. Compare **undershot**

overside (ˈəʊvəˌsaɪd) *adv* over the side (of a ship)

oversight (ˈəʊvəˌsaɪt) *n* **1** an omission or mistake, esp one made through failure to notice something **2** supervision

oversimplify (ˌəʊvəˈsɪmplɪˌfaɪ) *vb* **-fies, -fying, -fied** to simplify (something) to the point of distortion or error > ˌ**overˌsimplifiˈcation** *n*

oversize *adj* (ˌəʊvəˈsaɪz) **1** Also: **oversized** larger than the usual size ▷ *n* (ˈəʊvəˌsaɪz) **2** a size larger than the usual or proper size **3** something that is oversize

overskirt (ˈəʊvəˌskɜːt) *n* an outer skirt, esp one that reveals a decorative underskirt

overslaugh (ˈəʊvəˌslɔː) *n* **1** *military* the passing over of one duty for another that takes precedence ▷ *vb* **2** *(tr) US* to pass over; ignore [C18 from Dutch *overslaan* to pass over]

oversleep (ˌəʊvəˈsliːp) *vb* **-sleeps, -sleeping, -slept** *(intr)* to sleep beyond the intended time for getting up

oversleeve (ˈəʊvəˌsliːv) *n* a protective sleeve covering an ordinary sleeve

overspend *vb* (ˌəʊvəˈspɛnd) **-spends, -spending, -spent** **1** to spend in excess of (one's desires or what one can afford or is allocated) **2** *(tr; usually passive)* to wear out; exhaust ▷ *n* (ˈəʊvəˌspɛnd) **3** the amount by which someone or something is overspent

overspill *n* (ˈəʊvəˌspɪl) **1** **a** something that spills over or is in excess **b** *(as modifier)*: *overspill population* ▷ *vb* (ˌəʊvəˈspɪl) **-spills, -spilling, -spilt** *or* **-spilled** **2** *(intr)* to overflow

overstaff (ˌəʊvəˈstɑːf) *vb (tr)* to provide an excessive number of staff for (a factory, hotel, etc)

overstate (ˌəʊvəˈsteɪt) *vb (tr)* to state too strongly; exaggerate or overemphasize > ˈ**overˌstatement** *n*

overstay (ˌəʊvəˈsteɪ) *vb (tr)* **1** to stay beyond the time, limit, or duration of **2** *finance* to delay a transaction in (a market) until after the point at which the maximum profit would have been made **3** *NZ* to stay in New Zealand beyond (the period sanctioned by the immigration authorities or the period of a visitor's permit) **4** **overstay** *or* **outstay one's welcome** to stay (at a party, on a visit, etc), longer than pleases the host or hostess

overstayer (ˈəʊvəˌsteɪə) *n* a person who illegally remains in a country after the period of the permitted visit has expired

oversteer (ˌəʊvəˈstɪə) *vb (intr)* **1** (of a vehicle) to turn more sharply, for a particular turn of the steering wheel, than is desirable or anticipated ▷ *n* tendency of a vehicle to oversteer

overstep (ˌəʊvəˈstɛp) *vb* **-steps, -stepping, -stepped** *(tr)* to go beyond (a certain or proper limit)

overstock (ˌəʊvəˈstɒk) *vb (tr)* **1** to hold or supply (a commodity) in excess of requirements **2** to run more farm animals on (a piece of land) than it is capable of maintaining

overstretch (ˌəʊvəˈstrɛtʃ) *vb (tr)* **1** to make excessive demands or put excessive pressure on (oneself, finances, etc) **2** to stretch (muscles or limbs) too much or too hard

overstrung (ˌəʊvəˈstrʌŋ) *adj* **1** too highly strung; tense **2** (of a piano) having two sets of strings crossing each other at an oblique angle

overstuff (ˌəʊvəˈstʌf) *vb (tr)* **1** to force too much into **2** to cover (furniture) entirely with upholstery

oversubscribe (ˌəʊvəsəbˈskraɪb) *vb (tr; often passive)* to subscribe or apply for in excess of available supply > ˌ**oversubˈscription** *n*

oversupply (ˈəʊvəˌsəplaɪ) *n* **1** the supply of too much or too many ▷ *vb* (ˌəʊvəˈsəplaɪ) **-plies, -plying, -plied** **2** *(tr)* to supply too much (material, etc) or too many (goods, people, etc)

overt (ˈəʊvɜːt, əʊˈvɜːt) *adj* **1** open to view; observable **2** *law* open; deliberate. Criminal intent may be inferred from an overt act [C14 via Old French, from *ovrir* to open, from Latin *aperīre*] > ˈ**overtly** *adv* > ˈ**overtness** *n*

overtake (ˌəʊvəˈteɪk) *vb* **-takes, -taking, -took, -taken** **1** *chiefly Brit* to move past (another vehicle or person) travelling in the same direction **2** *(tr)* to pass or do better than, after catching up with **3** *(tr)* to come upon suddenly or unexpectedly: *night overtook him* **4** *(tr)* to catch up with; draw level with

overtask (ˌəʊvəˈtɑːsk) *vb (tr)* to impose too heavy a task upon

overtax (ˌəʊvəˈtæks) *vb (tr)* **1** to tax too heavily **2** to impose too great a strain on

over-the-counter *adj* **1** **a** (of securities) not

listed or quoted on a stock exchange **b** (of a security market) dealing in such securities **c** (of security transactions) conducted through a broker's office directly between purchaser and seller and not on a stock exchange **2** (of medicinal drugs) able to be sold without a prescription. Abbreviation: **OTC** Compare **POM**

overthink (ˌəʊvəˈθɪŋk) *vb* **-thinks, -thinking, -thought** to spend more time thinking about something than is necessary or productive

overthrow *vb* (ˌəʊvəˈθrəʊ) **-throws, -throwing, -threw, -thrown 1** (tr) to effect the downfall or destruction of (a ruler, institution, etc), esp by force **2** (tr) to throw or turn over **3** (tr) to throw (something, esp a ball) too far ▷ *n* (ˈəʊvəˌθrəʊ) **4** an act of overthrowing **5** downfall; destruction **6** *cricket* **a** a ball thrown back too far by a fielder **b** a run scored because of this

overthrust (ˈəʊvəˌθrʌst) *n geology* a reverse fault in which the rocks on the upper surface of a fault plane have moved over the rocks on the lower surface. Compare **underthrust**

overtime *n* (ˈəʊvəˌtaɪm) **1 a** work at a regular job done in addition to regular working hours **b** (as *modifier*): *overtime pay* **2** the rate of pay established for such work **3** time in excess of a set period **4** *sport, US and Canadian* extra time ▷ *vb* (ˈəʊvəˌtaɪm) **5** beyond the regular or stipulated time ▷ *vb* (ˌəʊvəˈtaɪm) **6** (tr) to exceed the required time for (a photographic exposure)

overtired (ˌəʊvəˈtaɪəd) *adj* extremely tired; exhausted: *overtired and overworked*

overtone (ˈəʊvəˌtəʊn) *n* **1** (often plural) additional meaning or nuance: *overtones of despair* **2** *music, acoustics* any of the tones, with the exception of the fundamental, that constitute a musical sound and contribute to its quality, each having a frequency that is a multiple of the fundamental frequency. See also **harmonic** (sense 7), **partial** (sense 6)

overtop (ˌəʊvəˈtɒp) *vb* **-tops, -topping, -topped** (tr) **1** to exceed in height **2** to surpass; excel **3** to rise over the top of

overtopping (ˌəʊvəˈtɒpɪŋ) *n* the rising of water over the top of a barrier

overtrade (ˌəʊvəˈtreɪd) *vb* (intr) (of an enterprise) to trade in excess of capacity or working capital

overtrick (ˈəʊvəˌtrɪk) *n bridge* a trick by which a player exceeds his contract

overtrump (ˌəʊvəˈtrʌmp) *vb cards* to play a trump higher than (one previously played to the trick)

overture (ˈəʊvəˌtjʊə) *n* **1** *music* **a** a piece of orchestral music containing contrasting sections that is played at the beginning of an opera or oratorio, often containing the main musical themes of the work **b** a similar piece preceding the performance of a play **c** Also called: **concert overture** a one-movement orchestral piece, usually having a descriptive or evocative title **d** a short piece in three movements (**French overture** or **Italian overture**) common in the 17th and 18th centuries **2** (often plural) a proposal, act, or gesture initiating a relationship, negotiation, etc **3** something that introduces what follows ▷ *vb* (tr) **4** to make or present an overture to **5** to introduce with an overture [C14 via Old French, from Late Latin *apertūra* opening, from Latin *aperīre* to open; see OVERT]

overturn *vb* (ˌəʊvəˈtɜːn) **1** to turn or cause to turn from an upright or normal position **2** (tr) to overthrow or destroy **3** (tr) to invalidate; reverse: *the bill was passed in the Commons but overturned in the Lords* ▷ *n* (ˈəʊvəˌtɜːn) **4** the act of overturning or the state of being overturned

over-under *US* ▷ *adj* **1** (of a two-barrelled firearm) having one barrel on top of the other ▷ *n* **2** an over-under firearm

over-use *vb* (ˌəʊvəˈjuːz) (tr) **1** to use excessively ▷ *n* (ˌəʊvəˈjuːs) **2** excessive use

overview (ˈəʊvəˌvjuː) *n* a general survey

overvoltage (ˈəʊvəˌvəʊltɪdʒ) *n* a voltage above the normal level

overwatch (ˌəʊvəˈwɒtʃ) *vb* (tr) **1** to watch over **2** *archaic* to fatigue with long watching or lack of sleep

overweening (ˌəʊvəˈwiːnɪŋ) *adj* **1** (of a person) excessively arrogant or presumptuous **2** (of opinions, appetites, etc) excessive; immoderate [C14 OVER- + *weening*, from Old English *wēnan*: see WEEN] > ˌover'weeningly *adv* > ˌover'weeningness *n*

overweigh (ˌəʊvəˈweɪ) *vb* (tr) **1** to exceed in weight; overbalance **2** to weigh down; oppress

overweight *adj* (ˌəʊvəˈweɪt) **1** weighing more than is usual, allowed, or healthy ▷ *n* (ˈəʊvəˌweɪt) **2** *finance* **a** having a higher proportion of one's investments in a particular sector of the market than the size of that sector relative to the total market would suggest: *portfolio managers are currently overweight in bonds* **b** (of a fund etc) invested disproportionately in this way **3** extra or excess weight **4** *archaic* greater importance or effect ▷ *vb* (ˌəʊvəˈweɪt) (tr) **5** to give too much emphasis or consideration to **6** to add too much weight to **7** to weigh down

overwhelm (ˌəʊvəˈwɛlm) *vb* (tr) **1** to overpower the thoughts, emotions, or senses of **2** to overcome with irresistible force **3** to overcome, as with a profusion or concentration of something **4** to cover over or bury completely **5** to weigh or rest upon overpoweringly **6** *archaic* to overturn

overwhelming (ˌəʊvəˈwɛlmɪŋ) *adj* overpowering in effect, number, or force > ˌover'whelmingly *adv*

overwind (ˌəʊvəˈwaɪnd) *vb* **-winds, -winding, -wound** (tr) to wind (a watch) beyond the proper limit

overwinter (ˌəʊvəˈwɪntə) *vb* **1** (intr) to spend winter (in or at a particular place) **2** (tr) to keep (animals or plants) alive through the winter **3** (intr) (of an animal or plant) to remain alive throughout the winter

overword (ˈəʊvəˌwɜːd) *n* a repeated word or phrase

overwork *vb* (ˌəʊvəˈwɜːk) (mainly tr) **1** (also intr) to work or cause to work too hard or too long **2** to use too much: *to overwork an excuse* **3** to decorate the surface of **4** to work up ▷ *n* (ˈəʊvəˌwɜːk) **5** excessive or excessively tiring work > ˌover'worked *adj*

overwrite (ˌəʊvəˈraɪt) *vb* **-writes, -writing, -wrote, -written 1** to write (something) in an excessively ornate or prolix style **2** to write too much about (someone or something) **3** to write on top of (other writing) **4** to record on a storage medium, such as a magnetic disk, thus destroying what was originally recorded there

overwrought (ˌəʊvəˈrɔːt) *adj* **1** full of nervous tension; agitated **2** too elaborate; fussy: *an overwrought style* **3** (often postpositive and foll by *with*) with the surface decorated or adorned

overzealous (ˌəʊvəˈzɛləs) *adj* excessively zealous

ovi- or **ovo-** *combining form* egg or ovum: *oviform; ovotestis* [from Latin *ōvum*]

Ovidian (ɒˈvɪdɪən) *adj* of, relating to, or reminiscent of Ovid (Latin name *Publius Ovidius Naso*), the Roman poet (43 BC–?17 AD)

oviduct (ˈɒvɪˌdʌkt, ˈəʊ-) *n* the tube through which ova are conveyed from an ovary. Also called (in mammals): **Fallopian tube** > oviducal (ˌɒvɪˈdjuːkəl, ˌəʊ-) or ˌovi'ductal *adj*

Oviedo (Spanish oˈβjeðo) *n* a city in NW Spain: capital of Asturias from 810 until 1002; centre of a coal- and iron-mining area. Pop: 207 699 (2003 est)

oviferous (əʊˈvɪfərəs) or **ovigerous** (əʊˈvɪdʒərəs) *adj zoology* carrying or producing eggs or ova: *the oviferous legs of certain spiders*

oviform (ˈəʊvɪˌfɔːm) *adj biology* shaped like an egg

ovine (ˈəʊvaɪn) *adj* of, relating to, or resembling a sheep [C19 from Late Latin *ovīnus*, from Latin *ovis* sheep]

oviparous (əʊˈvɪpərəs) *adj* (of fishes, reptiles, birds, etc) producing eggs that hatch outside the body of the mother. Compare **ovoviviparous, viviparous** (sense 1) > oviparity (ˌəʊvɪˈpærɪtɪ) *n* > oˈviparously *adv*

oviposit (ˌəʊvɪˈpɒzɪt) *vb* (intr) (of insects and fishes) to deposit eggs through an ovipositor [C19 OVI- + *positus*, past participle of Latin *pōnere* to place] > oviposition (ˌəʊvɪpəˈzɪʃən) *n*

ovipositor (ˌəʊvɪˈpɒzɪtə) *n* **1** the egg-laying organ of most female insects, consisting of a pair of specialized appendages at the end of the abdomen **2** a similar organ in certain female fishes, formed by an extension of the edges of the genital opening

ovisac (ˈəʊvɪˌsæk) *n* a capsule or sac, such as an ootheca, in which egg cells are produced

ovo- *combining form* a variant of **ovi-**

ovoid (ˈəʊvɔɪd) *adj* **1** egg-shaped **2** *botany* (of a fruit or similar part) egg-shaped with the broader end at the base. Compare **obovoid** ▷ *n* **3** something that is ovoid

ovolo (ˈəʊvəˌləʊ) *n, pl* -li (-ˌlaɪ) *architect* a convex moulding having a cross section in the form of a quarter of a circle or ellipse. Also called: **quarter round, thumb** Compare **congé** (sense 3), **echinus** (sense 1) [C17 from Italian: a little egg, from *ovo* egg, from Latin *ōvum*]

ovotestis (ˌəʊvəˈtɛstɪs) *n, pl* -tes (-tiːz) the reproductive organ of snails, which produces both ova and spermatozoa

ovoviviparous (ˌəʊvəʊvaɪˈvɪpərəs) *adj* (of certain reptiles, fishes, etc) producing eggs that hatch within the body of the mother. Compare **oviparous, viviparous** (sense 1) > ovoviviparity (ˌəʊvəʊˌvaɪvɪˈpærɪtɪ) *n*

ovulate (ˈɒvjʊˌleɪt) *vb* (intr) to produce or discharge eggs from an ovary [C19 from OVULE] > ˌovu'lation *n*

ovulation method *n* another name for **Billings method**

ovule (ˈɒvjuːl) *n* **1** a small body in seed-bearing plants that consists of the integument(s), nucellus, and embryosac (containing the egg cell) and develops into the seed after fertilization **2** *zoology* an immature ovum [C19 via French from Medieval Latin *ōvulum* a little egg, from Latin *ōvum* egg] > 'ovular *adj*

ovum (ˈəʊvəm) *n, pl* ova (ˈəʊvə) an unfertilized female gamete; egg cell [from Latin: egg]

ow (aʊ) *interj* an exclamation of pain

owe (əʊ) *vb* (mainly tr) **1** to be under an obligation to pay (someone) to the amount of **2** (intr) to be in debt: *he still owes for his house* **3** (often foll by to) to have as a result (of): *he owes his success to chance* **4** to feel the need or obligation to do, give, etc: *to owe somebody thanks; to owe it to oneself to rest* **5** to hold or maintain in the mind or heart (esp in the phrase **owe a grudge**) [Old English *āgan* to have (C12 to have to); related to Old Saxon *ēgan*, Old High German *eigan*]

owelty (ˈəʊəltɪ) *n, pl* -ties *law* equality, esp in financial transactions [C16 from Anglo-French *owelté*, ultimately from Latin *aequalitas*, from *aequalis* EQUAL]

Owen gun (ˈəʊən) *n* a type of simple recoil-operated 9 mm sub-machine-gun first used by Australian forces in World War II [named after E E Owen (1915–49), its Australian inventor]

Owen Stanley Range *n* a mountain range in SE New Guinea. Highest peak: Mount Victoria, 4073 m (13 363 ft)

ower or **owre** (ˈaʊər) *prep, adv, adj* a Scot word for **over**

Owerri (əˈwɛrɪ) *n* a market town in S Nigeria, capital of Imo state. Pop: 35 010 (latest est)

owing (ˈəʊɪŋ) *adj* **1** (postpositive) owed; due **2 owing to** (preposition) because of or on account of

owl (aʊl) *n* **1** any nocturnal bird of prey of the order *Strigiformes*, having large front-facing eyes, a small hooked bill, soft feathers, and a short neck **2** any of various breeds of owl-like fancy domestic pigeon (esp the **African owl, Chinese owl,** and **English owl**) **3** a person who looks or behaves like an owl, esp in having a solemn manner [Old English *ūle*; related to Dutch *uil*, Old High German *ūwila*, Old Norse *ugla*] > 'owl-ˌlike *adj*

owlet ('aʊlɪt) *n* a young or nestling owl

owlish ('aʊlɪʃ) *adj* **1** like an owl **2** solemn and wise in appearance > **'owlishly** *adv* > **'owlishness** *n*

own (əʊn) *determiner* (*preceded by a possessive*) **1 a** (*intensifier*): *John's own idea; your own mother* **b** (*as pronoun*): *I'll use my own* **2** on behalf of oneself or in relation to oneself: *he is his own worst enemy* **3** **come into one's own a** to become fulfilled: *she really came into her own when she got divorced* **b** to receive what is due to one **4** **get one's own back** *informal* to have revenge **5** **hold one's own** to maintain one's situation or position, esp in spite of opposition or difficulty **6** **on one's own a** without help **b** by oneself; alone ▷ *vb* **7** (*tr*) to have as one's possession **8** (when *intr*, often foll by *up, to*, or *up to*) to confess or admit; acknowledge **9** (*tr; takes a clause as object*) *now rare* to concede: *I own that you are right* [Old English *āgen*, originally past participle of *āgan* to have; related to Old Saxon *ēgan*, Old Norse *eiginn*. See OWE]

own brand *n* **a** an item packaged and marketed under the brand name of a particular retailer, usually a large supermarket chain, rather than that of the manufacturer **b** (*as modifier*): *own-brand products* ▷ Also: **own label**

owner ('əʊnə) *n* a person who owns; legal possessor

owner-occupier *n Brit* a person who owns or is in the process of buying the house or flat he lives in > ˌowner-'occuˌpied *adj* > 'owner-ˌoccu'pation *n*

ownership ('əʊnəʃɪp) *n* **1** the state or fact of being an owner **2** legal right of possession; proprietorship

ownership flat *n NZ* a flat owned by the occupier

own goal *n* **1** *soccer* a goal scored by a player accidentally playing the ball into his own team's net. Abbreviation: **o.g. 2** *informal* any action that results in disadvantage to the person who took it or to a party, group, etc with which that person is associated

owt (aʊt) *pron Northern English* a dialect word for **anything** [a variant of AUGHT[1]]

ox (ɒks) *n, pl* **oxen** ('ɒksən) **1** an adult castrated male of any domesticated species of cattle, esp *Bos taurus*, used for draught work and meat **2** any bovine mammal, esp any of the domestic cattle [Old English *oxa*; related to Old Saxon, Old High German *ohso*, Old Norse *oxi*]

oxa- *or before a vowel* **ox-** *combining form* indicating that a chemical compound contains oxygen, used esp to denote that a heterocyclic compound is derived from a specified compound by replacement of a carbon atom with an oxygen atom: *oxazine*

oxalate ('ɒksəˌleɪt) *n* a salt or ester of oxalic acid

oxalic acid (ɒkˈsælɪk) *n* a colourless poisonous crystalline dicarboxylic acid found in many plants: used as a bleach and a cleansing agent for metals. Formula: $(COOH)_2$. Systematic name: **ethanedioic acid** [C18 from French *oxalique*, from Latin *oxalis* garden sorrel; see OXALIS]

oxalis ('ɒksəlɪs, ɒkˈsælɪs) *n* any plant of the genus *Oxalis*, having clover-like leaves which contain oxalic acid and white, pink, red, or yellow flowers: family *Oxalidaceae*. See also **wood sorrel** [C18 via Latin from Greek: sorrel, sour wine, from *oxus* acid, sharp]

oxazine ('ɒksəˌziːn) *n* any of 13 heterocyclic compounds with the formula C_4H_5NO [from OXY-[2] + AZINE]

oxblood ('ɒksˌblʌd) *or* **oxblood red** *adj* of a dark reddish-brown colour

oxbow ('ɒksˌbəʊ) *n* **1** a U-shaped piece of wood fitted under and around the neck of a harnessed ox and attached to the yoke **2** Also called: **oxbow lake, cutoff** a small curved lake lying on the flood plain of a river and constituting the remnant of a former meander

Oxbridge ('ɒksˌbrɪdʒ) *n* **a** the British universities of Oxford and Cambridge, esp considered as ancient and prestigious academic institutions, bastions of privilege and superiority, etc **b** (*as modifier*): *Oxbridge graduates*

oxen ('ɒksən) *n* the plural of **ox**

oxeye ('ɒksˌaɪ) *n* **1** any Eurasian plant of the genus *Buphthalmum*, having daisy-like flower heads with yellow rays and dark centres: family *Asteraceae* (composites) **2** any of various North American plants of the related genus *Heliopsis*, having daisy-like flowers **3 oxeye daisy** another name for **daisy** (sense 2)

ox-eyed *adj* having large round eyes, like those of an ox

ox-eye herring *n* a herring-like sea fish, *Megalops cyprinoides*, of northern Australian waters, related to the tarpon

OXFAM *or* **Oxfam** ('ɒksfæm) *n acronym for* Oxford Committee for Famine Relief

Oxford ('ɒksfəd) *n* **1** a city in S England, administrative centre of Oxfordshire, at the confluence of the Rivers Thames and Cherwell: Royalist headquarters during the Civil War; seat of Oxford University, consisting of 40 separate colleges, the oldest being University College (1249), and Oxford Brookes University (1993); motor-vehicle industry. Pop: 143 016 (2001). Related word: **Oxonian 2** Also called: **Oxford Down** a breed of sheep with middle-length wool and a dark brown face and legs **3** a type of stout laced shoe with a low heel **4** a lightweight fabric of plain or twill weave used esp for men's shirts

Oxford accent *n* the accent associated with Oxford English

Oxford bags *pl n* trousers with very wide baggy legs, originally popular in the 1920s. Often shortened to: **bags**

Oxford blue *n* **1 a** a dark blue colour **b** (*as adjective*): *an Oxford-blue scarf* **2** a person who has been awarded a blue from Oxford University

Oxford comma *n* a comma between the final items in a list, often preceding the word 'and' or 'or', such as the final comma in the list *newspapers, magazines, and books* [C20 because it was traditionally a feature of the house style at Oxford University Press]

Oxford English *n* that form of the received pronunciation of English supposed to be typical of Oxford University and regarded by many as affected or pretentious

Oxford frame *n* a type of picture frame in which the sides of the frame cross each other and project outwards

Oxford Group *n* an early name for **Moral Rearmament**

Oxford Movement *n* a movement within the Church of England that began at Oxford in 1833 and was led by Pusey, Newman, and Keble. It affirmed the continuity of the Church with early Christianity and strove to restore the High-Church ideals of the 17th century. Its views were publicized in a series of tracts (**Tracts for the Times**) 1833–41. The teaching and practices of the Movement are maintained in the High-Church tradition within the Church of England. Also called: **Tractarianism**

Oxfordshire ('ɒksfədˌʃɪə, -ʃə) *n* an inland county of S central England: situated mostly in the basin of the Upper Thames, with the Cotswolds in the west and the Chilterns in the southeast. Administrative centre: Oxford. Pop: 615 200 (2003 est). Area: 2608 sq km (1007 sq miles). Abbreviation: **Oxon**

oxhide ('ɒksˌhaɪd) *n* leather made from the hide of an ox

oxidant ('ɒksɪdənt) *n* a substance that acts or is used as an oxidizing agent. Also called (esp in rocketry): **oxidizer**

oxidase ('ɒksɪˌdeɪs, -ˌdeɪz) *n* any of a group of enzymes that bring about biological oxidation

oxidate ('ɒksɪˌdeɪt) *vb* another word for **oxidize**

oxidation (ˌɒksɪˈdeɪʃən) *n* **a** the act or process of oxidizing **b** (*as modifier*): *an oxidation state; an oxidation potential* > ˌoxiˈdational *adj* > 'oxiˌdative *adj*

oxidation-reduction *n* **a** a reversible chemical process usually involving the transfer of electrons, in which one reaction is an oxidation and the reverse reaction is a reduction **b** Also: **redox** (*as modifier*): *an oxidation-reduction reaction*

oxidative phosphorylation *n* the process by which the energy liberated by oxidation of metabolites is used to synthesize the energy-rich molecule ATP

oxide ('ɒksaɪd) *n* **1** any compound of oxygen with another element **2** any organic compound in which an oxygen atom is bound to two alkyl or aryl groups; an ether or epoxide [C18 from French, from *ox(ygène)* + *(ac)ide*; see OXYGEN, ACID]

oxidimetry (ˌɒksɪˈdɪmɪtrɪ) *n chem* a branch of volumetric analysis in which oxidizing agents are used in titrations [C20 from OXID(ATION) + -METRY] > **oxidimetric** (ˌɒksɪdɪˈmɛtrɪk) *adj*

oxidize *or* **oxidise** ('ɒksɪˌdaɪz) *vb* **1** to undergo or cause to undergo a chemical reaction with oxygen, as in formation of an oxide **2** to form or cause to form a layer of metal oxide, as in rusting **3** to lose or cause to lose hydrogen atoms **4** to undergo or cause to undergo a decrease in the number of electrons. Compare **reduce** (sense 12c) > ˌoxidiˈzation *or* ˌoxidiˈsation *n*

oxidizer *or* **oxidiser** ('ɒksɪˌdaɪzə) *n* an oxidant, esp a substance that combines with the fuel in a rocket engine

oxidizing agent *n chem* a substance that oxidizes another substance, being itself reduced in the process. Common oxidizing agents are oxygen, hydrogen peroxide, and ferric salts. Compare **reducing agent**

oxime ('ɒksiːm) *n* any of a class of compounds with the general formula RR′NOH, where R is an organic group and R′ is either an organic group (**ketoxime**) or hydrogen atom (**aldoxime**): used in the chemical analysis of carbonyl compounds [C19 from OX(YGEN) + IM(ID)E]

oxlip ('ɒksˌlɪp) *n* **1** Also called: **paigle** a primulaceous Eurasian woodland plant, *Primula elatior*, with small drooping pale yellow flowers **2** Also called: **false oxlip** a similar and related plant that is a natural hybrid between the cowslip and primrose [Old English *oxanslyppe*, literally: ox's slippery dropping; see SLIP[3], compare COWSLIP]

Oxo ('ɒksəʊ) *n trademark* extract of beef in the shape of small cubes which are mixed with boiling water and used for flavouring, as stock, a drink, etc [C20 from OX + -o]

oxo- *or before a vowel* **ox-** *combining form* indicating that a chemical compound contains oxygen linked to another atom by a double bond, used esp to denote that a compound is derived from a specified compound by replacement of a methylene group with a carbonyl group: *oxobutanoic acid*

oxo acid ('ɒksəʊ) *n* another name for **oxyacid**

Oxon *abbreviation for* Oxfordshire [from Latin *Oxonia*]

Oxon. ('ɒksən) *abbreviation for* (in degree titles) of Oxford [from Latin *Oxoniensis*]

Oxonian (ɒkˈsəʊnɪən) *adj* **1** of or relating to Oxford or Oxford University ▷ *n* **2** a member of Oxford University **3** an inhabitant or native of Oxford

oxonium compound *or* **salt** (ɒkˈsəʊnɪəm) *n chem* any of a class of salts derived from certain organic ethers or alcohols by adding a proton to the oxygen atom and thus producing a positive ion (**oxonium ion**)

oxpecker ('ɒksˌpɛkə) *n* either of two African starlings, *Buphagus africanus* or *B. erythrorhynchus*, having flattened bills with which they obtain food from the hides of cattle. Also called: **tick-bird**

oxtail ('ɒksˌteɪl) *n* the skinned tail of an ox, used esp in soups and stews

oxter ('ɒkstə) *n Scot, Irish, and Northern English dialect* the armpit [C16 from Old English *oxta*; related to Old High German *Ahsala*, Latin *axilla*]

oxtongue ('ɒksˌtʌŋ) *n* **1** any of various Eurasian plants of the genus *Picris*, having oblong bristly leaves and clusters of dandelion-like flowers: family *Asteraceae* (composites) **2** any of various other plants having bristly tongue-shaped leaves, such as alkanet **3** the tongue of an ox, braised or boiled as food

Oxus ('ɒksəs) *n* the ancient name for the **Amu Darya**

oxy-¹ *combining form* denoting something sharp; acute: *oxytone* [from Greek, from *oxus*]

oxy-² *combining form* **1** containing or using oxygen: *oxyacetylene* **2** a former equivalent of **hydroxy-**

oxyacetylene (ˌɒksɪə'sɛtɪˌliːn) *n* **a** a mixture of oxygen and acetylene; used in a blowpipe for cutting or welding metals at high temperatures **b** (*as modifier*): *an oxyacetylene burner*

oxyacid (ˌɒksɪ'æsɪd) *n* any acid that contains oxygen. Also called: **oxo acid**

oxycephaly (ˌɒksɪ'sɛfəlɪ) *n pathol* the condition of having a conical skull [C20 from Greek *oxus* sharp + -CEPHALY] > **oxycephalic** (ˌɒksɪsɪ'fælɪk) *or* ˌoxy'cephalous *adj*

oxycodone hydrochloride (ˌɒksɪ'kəʊdəʊn) *n* an opiate drug used as a painkiller. See also **OxyContin**

OxyContin (ˌɒksɪ'kɒntɪn) *n trademark* an opiate drug, oxycodone hydrochloride, used as a painkiller and, illegally, as an alternative to heroin

oxygen ('ɒksɪdʒən) *n* **a** a colourless odourless highly reactive gaseous element: the most abundant element in the earth's crust (49.2 per cent). It is essential for aerobic respiration and almost all combustion and is widely used in industry. Symbol: O; atomic no.: 8; atomic wt.: 15.9994; valency: 2; density: 1.429 kg/m³; melting pt.: −218.79°C; boiling pt.: −182.97°C **b** (*as modifier*): *an oxygen mask* > **oxygenic** (ˌɒksɪ'dʒɛnɪk) *or* **oxygenous** (ɒk'sɪdʒɪnəs) *adj*

oxygen acid *n* another name for **oxyacid**

oxygenate ('ɒksɪdʒɪˌneɪt), **oxygenize** *or* **oxygenise** *vb* to enrich or be enriched with oxygen: *to oxygenate blood* > ˌoxygen'ation *n* > 'oxygeˌnizer *or* 'oxygeˌniser *n*

oxygenator ('ɒksɪdʒɪˌneɪtə) *n* an apparatus that oxygenates the blood, esp while a patient is undergoing an operation

oxygen bar *n* an establishment where customers pay to inhale pure oxygen in order to combat the effects of air pollution

oxygen effect *n biology* the increased sensitivity to radiation of living organisms, tissues, etc, when they are exposed in the presence of oxygen

oxygen mask *n* a device, worn over the nose and mouth, to which oxygen is supplied from a cylinder or other source: used to aid breathing

oxygen tent *n med* a transparent enclosure covering a bedridden patient, into which oxygen is released to help maintain respiration

oxygen weed *n NZ* another name for **water hyacinth**

oxyhaemoglobin *or US* **oxyhemoglobin** (ˌɒksɪˌhiːməʊ'ɡləʊbɪn, -ˌhɛm-) *n biochem* the bright red product formed when oxygen from the lungs combines with haemoglobin in the blood

oxyhydrogen (ˌɒksɪ'haɪdrədʒən) *n* **a** a mixture of hydrogen and oxygen used to provide an intense flame for welding **b** (*as modifier*): *an oxyhydrogen blowpipe*

oxymoron (ˌɒksɪ'mɔːrɒn) *n, pl* -mora (-'mɔːrə) *rhetoric* an epigrammatic effect, by which contradictory terms are used in conjunction: *living death; fiend angelical* [C17 via New Latin from Greek

oxumōron, from *oxus* sharp + *mōros* stupid]

oxyntic (ɒk'sɪntɪk) *adj physiol* of or denoting stomach cells that secrete acid: *oxyntic cells* [C19 from Greek *oxus* acid, sharp]

oxysalt (ˌɒksɪ'sɔːlt) *n* any salt of an oxyacid

oxysulphide (ˌɒksɪ'sʌlfaɪd) *n chem* a compound containing an element combined with oxygen and sulphur

oxytetracycline (ˌɒksɪˌtɛtrə'saɪklɪn) *n* a broad-spectrum antibiotic, obtained from the bacterium *Streptomyces rimosus*, used in treating various infections. Formula: C₂₂H₂₄N₂O₉. Abbreviation: OTC

oxytocic (ˌɒksɪ'təʊsɪk) *adj* **1** accelerating childbirth by stimulating uterine contractions ▷ *n* **2** an oxytocic drug or agent [C19 from Greek, from OXY-¹ + *tokos* childbirth]

oxytocin (ˌɒksɪ'təʊsɪn) *n* a polypeptide hormone, secreted by the pituitary gland, that stimulates contractions of the uterus or oviduct and ejection of milk in mammals; alphahypophame: used therapeutically for aiding childbirth. Formula: C₄₃H₆₈N₁₂O₁₂S₂. Compare **vasopressin**

oxytone (ˌɒksɪ'təʊn) (in the classical Greek language) *adj* **1** (of a word) having an accent on the final syllable ▷ *n* **2** an oxytone word ▷ Compare **paroxytone, proparoxytone** [C18 from Greek *oxytonos*, from *oxus* sharp + *tonos* tone]

oyer (ɔɪə) *n* **1** *English legal history* (in the 13th century) an assize **2** (formerly) the reading out loud of a document in court **3** See **oyer and terminer**

oyer and terminer ('tɜːmɪnə) *n* **1** *English law* (formerly) a commission issued to judges to try cases on assize. It became obsolete with the abolition of assizes and the setting up of crown courts in 1972 **2** the court in which such a hearing was held **3** (in the US) a court exercising higher criminal jurisdiction [C15 from Anglo-Norman, from *oyer* to hear + *terminer* to judge]

oyez *or* **oyes** (əʊ'jɛs, -'jɛz) *interj* **1** a cry, usually uttered three times, by a public crier or court official for silence and attention before making a proclamation ▷ *n* **2** such a cry [C15 via Anglo-Norman from Old French *oiez*! hear!]

-oyl *suffix of nouns* (in chemistry) indicating an acyl group or radical: *ethanoyl; methanoyl* [C20 from O(XYGEN) + -YL]

Oyo ('əʊjəʊ) *n* a state of SW Nigeria, formed in 1976 from part of Western State. Capital: Ibadan. Pop: 3 900 803 (1995 est). Area: 28 454 sq km (10 986 sq miles)

oyster ('ɔɪstə) *n* **1 a** any edible marine bivalve mollusc of the genus *Ostrea*, having a rough irregularly shaped shell and occurring on the sea bed, mostly in coastal waters **b** (*as modifier*): *oyster farm; oyster knife* **2** any of various similar and related molluscs, such as the pearl oyster and the **saddle oyster** (*Anomia ephippium*) **3** the oyster-shaped piece of dark meat in the hollow of the pelvic bone of a fowl **4** something from which advantage, delight, profit, etc, may be derived: *the world is his oyster* **5** *informal* a very uncommunicative person ▷ *vb* **6** (*intr*) to dredge for, gather, or raise oysters [C14 *oistre*, from Old French *uistre*, from Latin *ostrea*, from Greek *ostreon*; related to Greek *osteon* bone, *ostrakon* shell]

oyster bed *n* a place, esp on the sea bed, where oysters breed and grow naturally or are cultivated for food or pearls. Also called: **oyster bank, oyster park**

oystercatcher ('ɔɪstəˌkætʃə) *n* any shore bird of

the genus *Haematopus* and family *Haematopodidae*, having a black or black-and-white plumage and a long stout laterally compressed red bill

oyster crab *n* any of several small soft-bodied crabs of the genus *Pinnotheres*, esp *P. ostreum*, that live as commensals in the mantles of oysters

oysterman ('ɔɪstəmən) *n, pl* -men *chiefly US* **1** a person who gathers, cultivates, or sells oysters **2** a boat used in gathering oysters

oyster mushroom *n* an edible fungus, *Pleurotus ostreatus*, having an oyster-shaped cap, commonly found growing in clusters on the trunks of broad-leaved trees

oyster pink *n* **a** a delicate pinkish-white colour, sometimes with a greyish tinge **b** (*as adjective*): *oyster-pink shoes*

oyster plant *n* another name for **salsify** (sense 1) and **sea lungwort** (see **lungwort** (sense 2))

oyster white *n* **a** a greyish-white colour **b** (*as adjective*): *oyster-white walls*

oz *or* **oz.** *abbreviation for* **ounce** [from Italian *onza*]

Oz (ɒz) *n Austral slang* Australia

Ozalid ('ɒzəlɪd) *n* **1** *trademark* a method of duplicating typematter, illustrations, etc, when printed on translucent paper. It is used for proofing **2** a reproduction produced by this method [C20 formed by reversing DIAZO and inserting *l*]

Ozark Mountains ('əʊzaːk) *or* **Ozarks** ('əʊzaːks) *pl n* an eroded plateau in S Missouri, N Arkansas, and NE Oklahoma. Area: about 130 000 sq km (50 000 sq miles) Also called: **Ozark Plateau**

ozocerite *or* **ozokerite** (ˌəʊzəʊkəˌraɪt) *n* a brown or greyish wax that occurs associated with petroleum and is used for making candles and wax paper. Also called: **earth wax, mineral wax** [C19 from German *Ozokerit*, from Greek *ozein* to smell + *kēros* beeswax]

ozone ('əʊzəʊn, əʊ'zəʊn) *n* **1** a colourless gas with a chlorine-like odour, formed by an electric discharge in oxygen: a strong oxidizing agent, used in bleaching, sterilizing water, purifying air, etc Formula: O₃; density: 2.14 kg/m³; melting pt.: −192°C; boiling pt.: −110.51°C. Technical name: **trioxygen 2** *informal* clean bracing air, as found at the seaside [C19 from German *Ozon*, from Greek: smell] > **ozonic** (əʊ'zɒnɪk) *or* **ozonous** *adj*

ozone-friendly *adj* not harmful to the ozone layer; using substances that do not produce gases harmful to the ozone layer: *an ozone-friendly refrigerator*

ozone layer *n* the region of the stratosphere with the highest concentration of ozone molecules, which by absorbing high-energy solar ultraviolet radiation protects organisms on earth. Also called: **ozonosphere**

ozonide (əʊ'zəʊnaɪd) *n* any of a class of unstable explosive compounds produced by the addition of ozone to a double bond in an organic compound

ozoniferous (ˌəʊzəʊ'nɪfərəs) *adj* containing ozone

ozonize *or* **ozonise** ('əʊzəʊˌnaɪz) *vb* (*tr*) **1** to convert (oxygen) into ozone **2** to treat (a substance) with ozone > ˌozoni'zation *or* ˌozoni'sation *n* > 'ozoˌnizer *or* 'ozoˌniser *n*

ozonolysis (ˌəʊzəʊ'nɒlɪsɪs) *n chem* the process of treating an organic compound with ozone to form an ozonide: used to locate double bonds in molecules

ozonosphere (əʊ'zəʊnəˌsfɪə, -'zɒnə-) *n* another name for **ozone layer**

ozs *or* **ozs.** *abbreviation for* **ounces**

ozzie ('ɒzɪ) *n Northern English informal* a hospital

O

Pp

p or **P** (pi:) *n, pl* **p's, P's** or **Ps 1** the 16th letter and 12th consonant of the modern English alphabet **2** a speech sound represented by this letter, usually a voiceless bilabial stop, as in *pig* **3 mind one's p's and q's** to be careful to behave correctly and use polite or suitable language

p *symbol for* **1** (in Britain) penny *or* pence **2** *music* piano: an instruction to play quietly **3** pico- **4** *physics* **a** momentum **b** proton **c** pressure

P *symbol for* **1** *chem* phosphorus **2** *physics* **a** pressure **b** power **c** parity **d** poise **3** (on road signs) parking **4** *chess* pawn **5** *currency* **a** (the former) peseta **b** peso **c** pataca **d** pula ▷ *abbreviation for* **6** pharmacy only: used to label medicines that can be obtained without a prescription, but only at a shop at which there is a pharmacist **7** *international car registration for* Portugal

p. *abbreviation for* **1** (*pl* **pp**) page **2** part **3** participle **4** past **5** per **6** post [Latin: after] **7** pro [Latin: in favour of; for]

p- *prefix* short for para-¹ (sense 6)

P45 *n* (in Britain) **1** a severance form issued by the Inland Revenue via an employer to a person leaving employment **2 get one's P45** *informal* to be dismissed from one's employment

pa¹ (pɑ:) *n* an informal word for **father**

pa² or **pah** (pɑ:) *n* NZ **1** a Māori village or settlement **2** *history* a Māori defensive position and settlement on a hilltop **3 go back to the pa** to abandon city life in favour of rural life [Māori]

pa³ *the internet domain name for* Panama

Pa 1 *the chemical symbol for* protactinium **2** ▷ *symbol for* pascal

PA *abbreviation for* **1** Pennsylvania **2** personal appearance **3** personal assistant **4** *military* Post Adjutant **5 power of attorney 6** press agent **7** Press Association **8** *banking* private account **9** public-address system **10** publicity agent **11** Publishers Association **12** purchasing agent **13** *insurance* **particular average 14** (in New Zealand) **probationary assistant 15** ▷ *international car registration for* Panama

Pa. *abbreviation for* Pennsylvania

p.a. *abbreviation for* per annum [Latin: yearly]

paal (pɑ:l) *n Caribbean* a stake driven into the ground [from Dutch: a pile, stake]

pa'anga (pɑːˈɑːŋgə) *n* the standard monetary unit of Tonga, divided into 100 seniti

PABA (ˈpɑːbə) *n acronym for* para-aminobenzoic acid

Pablum (ˈpæbjʊləm) *n trademark* a cereal food for infants, developed in Canada

pabulum (ˈpæbjʊləm) *n rare* **1** food **2** food for thought, esp when bland or dull [c17 from Latin, from *pascere* to feed]

PABX (in Britain) *abbreviation for* **private automatic branch exchange**. See also **PBX**

PAC *abbreviation for* Pan-Africanist Congress

Pac. *abbreviation for* Pacific

paca (ˈpɑːkə, ˈpækə) *n* a large burrowing hystricomorph rodent, *Cuniculus paca*, of Central and South America, having white-spotted brown fur and a large head: family *Dasyproctidae* [c17 from Spanish, from Tupi]

pace¹ (peɪs) *n* **1 a** a single step in walking **b** the distance covered by a step **2** a measure of length equal to the average length of a stride, approximately 3 feet. See also **Roman pace, geometric pace, military pace 3** speed of movement, esp of walking or running **4** rate or style of proceeding at some activity: *to live at a fast pace* **5** manner or action of stepping, walking, etc; gait **6** any of the manners in which a horse or other quadruped walks or runs, the three principal paces being the walk, trot, and canter (or gallop) **7** a manner of moving, natural to the camel and sometimes developed in the horse, in which the two legs on the same side of the body are moved and put down at the same time **8** *architect* a step or small raised platform **9 keep pace with** to proceed at the same speed as **10 put (someone) through his paces** to test the ability of (someone) **11 set the pace** to determine the rate at which a group runs or walks or proceeds at some other activity **12 stand** *or* **stay the pace** to keep up with the speed or rate of others ▷ *vb* **13** (*tr*) to set or determine the pace for, as in a race **14** (often foll by *about, up and down,* etc) to walk with regular slow or fast paces, as in boredom, agitation, etc: *to pace the room* **15** (*tr*; often foll by *out*) to measure by paces: *to pace out the distance* **16** (*intr*) to walk with slow regular strides: *to pace along the street* **17** (*intr*) (of a horse) to move at the pace (the specially developed gait) [c13 via Old French from Latin *passus* step, from *pandere* to spread, unfold, extend (the legs as in walking)]

pace² *Latin* (ˈpeɪsɪ; *English* ˈpɑːkɛ) *prep* with due deference to: used to acknowledge politely someone who disagrees with the speaker or writer [c19 from Latin, from *pāx* peace]

PACE (peɪs) *n* (in England and Wales) ▷ *acronym for* Police and Criminal Evidence Act

pace bowler *n cricket* a bowler who characteristically delivers the ball rapidly

pacemaker (ˈpeɪsˌmeɪkə) *n* **1** a person, horse, vehicle, etc, used in a race or speed trial to set the pace **2** a person, an organization, etc, regarded as being the leader in a particular field of activity **3** Also called: **cardiac pacemaker** a small area of specialized tissue within the wall of the right atrium of the heart whose spontaneous electrical activity initiates and controls the beat of the heart **4** Also called: **artificial pacemaker** an electronic device for use in certain cases of heart disease to assume the functions of the natural cardiac pacemaker

pacer (ˈpeɪsə) *n* **1** a horse trained to move at a special gait, esp for racing **2** another word for **pacemaker** (sense 1)

pacesetter (ˈpeɪsˌsɛtə) *n* another word for **pacemaker** (senses 1, 2)

paceway (ˈpeɪsˌweɪ) *n Austral* a racecourse for trotting and pacing

pacey or **pacy** (ˈpeɪsɪ) *adj* **pacier, paciest** fast-moving, quick, lively: *a pacey story*

pacha (ˈpɑːʃə, ˈpæʃə) *n* a variant spelling of **pasha**

pachalic (ˈpɑːʃəlɪk) *n* a variant spelling of **pashalik**

pachinko (pəˈtʃɪŋkəʊ) *n* a Japanese game similar to pinball [c20 possibly from Japanese *pachin,* imitative of the sound of a ball being fired by a trigger]

pachisi (pəˈtʃiːzɪ, pɑː-) *n* an Indian game somewhat resembling backgammon, played on a cruciform board using six cowries as dice [c18 from Hindi *pacīsī,* from *pacīs* twenty-five (the highest score possible in one throw)]

pachouli (ˈpætʃʊlɪ, pəˈtʃuːlɪ) *n* a variant spelling of **patchouli**

Pachuca (*Spanish* paˈtʃuka) *n* a city in central Mexico, capital of Hidalgo state, in the Sierra Madre Oriental: silver mines; university (1961). Pop: 333 000 (2005 est)

Pachuco (pəˈtʃuːkəʊ) *n, pl* **-cos** *US* a young Mexican living in the US, esp one of low social status who belongs to a street gang [c20 from Mexican Spanish]

pachyderm (ˈpækɪˌdɜːm) *n* any very large thick-skinned mammal, such as an elephant, rhinoceros, or hippopotamus [c19 from French *pachyderme,* from Greek *pakhudermos* thick-skinned, from *pakhus* thick + *derma* skin] ▷ ˌpachy'dermatous *adj*

pachymeningitis (ˌpækɪˌmɛnɪnˈdʒaɪtɪs) *n pathol* inflammation of the dura mater of the brain and spinal cord

pachytene (ˈpækɪˌtiːn) *n* the third stage of the prophase of meiosis during which the chromosomes become shorter and thicker and divide into chromatids [from Greek *pakhus* thick + *tainia* band]

pacific (pəˈsɪfɪk) *adj* **1** tending or conducive to peace; conciliatory **2** not aggressive; opposed to the use of force **3** free from conflict; peaceful [c16 from Old French *pacifique,* from Latin *pācificus,* from *pāx* peace + *facere* to make] ▷ pa'cifically *adv*

Pacific (pəˈsɪfɪk) *n* **1** the short for **Pacific Ocean** ▷ *adj* **2** of or relating to the Pacific Ocean or its islands

pacification (ˌpæsɪfɪˈkeɪʃən) *n* the act, process, or policy of pacifying ▷ 'pacifi,catory *adj*

Pacific Islands *pl n* a former Trust Territory; an island group in the W Pacific Ocean, mandated to Japan after World War I and assigned to the US by the United Nations in 1947: comprised 2141 islands (96 inhabited) of the Caroline, Marshall, and Mariana groups (excluding Guam). In 1978 the Northern Marianas became a commonwealth in union with the US. The three remaining entities consisting of the Marshall Islands, the Republic of Palau (or Belau), and the Federated States of Micronesia became self-governing during the period 1979–80. In 1982 they signed agreements of free association with the US. Land area: about 1800 sq km (700 sq miles), scattered over about 7 500 000 sq km (3 000 000 sq miles) of ocean

Pacific Northwest *n* the region of North America lying north of the Columbia River and west of the Rockies

Pacific Ocean *n* the world's largest and deepest ocean, lying between Asia and Australia and North and South America: almost landlocked in the north, linked with the Arctic Ocean only by the Bering Strait, and extending to Antarctica in the south; has exceptionally deep trenches, and a large number of volcanic and coral islands. Area: about 165 760 000 sq km (64 000 000 sq miles). Average depth: 4215 m (14 050 ft). Greatest depth: Challenger Deep (in the Marianas Trench), 11 033 m (37 073 ft). Greatest width: (between Panama and Mindanao, Philippines) 17 066 km (10 600 miles)

Pacific rim *n* the regions, countries, etc, that lie on the western shores of the Pacific Ocean, esp in the context of their developing manufacturing capacity and consumer markets

Pacific Rose *n* a large variety of eating apple from New Zealand, with sweet flesh

Pacific Standard Time *n* one of the standard times used in North America, based on the local time of the 120° meridian, eight hours behind Greenwich Mean Time. Abbreviation: **PST**

pacifier ('pæsɪˌfaɪə) *n* **1** a person or thing that pacifies **2** *US and Canadian* a baby's dummy or teething ring

pacifism ('pæsɪˌfɪzəm) *n* **1** the belief that violence of any kind is unjustifiable and that one should not participate in war **2** the belief that international disputes can be settled by arbitration rather than war

pacifist ('pæsɪfɪst) *n* **1** a person who supports pacifism **2** a person who refuses military service ▷ *adj* **3** advocating, relating to, or characterized by pacifism

pacify ('pæsɪˌfaɪ) *vb* **-fies, -fying, -fied** (*tr*) **1** to calm the anger or agitation of; mollify **2** to restore to peace or order, esp by the threat or use of force [C15 from Old French *pacifier*; see PACIFIC] > 'paciˌ**fiable** *adj*

pack¹ (pæk) *n* **1 a** a bundle or load, esp one carried on the back **b** (*as modifier*): *a pack animal* **2** a collected amount of anything **3** a complete set of similar things, esp a set of 52 playing cards **4** a group of animals of the same kind, esp hunting animals: *a pack of hounds* **5** any group or band that associates together, esp for criminal purposes **6** *rugby* the forwards of a team or both teams collectively, as in a scrum or in rucking **7** the basic organizational unit of Cub Scouts and Brownie Guides **8 a** a small package, carton, or container, used to retail commodities, esp foodstuffs, cigarettes, etc **b** (*in combination*): *pack-sealed* **9** *US and Canadian* a small or medium-sized container of cardboard, paper, etc, often together with its contents. Also called (in Britain and certain other countries): **packet** **10** short for **pack ice** **11** the quantity of something, such as food, packaged for preservation **12** *med* **a** a sheet or blanket, either damp or dry, for wrapping about the body, esp for its soothing effect **b** a material such as cotton or gauze for temporarily filling a bodily cavity, esp to control bleeding **13** short for **backpack** *or* **rucksack** **14** *mining* a roof support, esp one made of rubble **15** short for **face pack** **16** a parachute folded and ready for use **17** *computing* another name for **deck** (sense 5) **18** **go to the pack** *Austral and NZ informal* to fall into a lower state or condition ▷ *vb* **19** to place or arrange (articles) in (a container), such as clothes in a suitcase **20** (*tr*) to roll up into a bundle **21** (when *passive*, often foll by *out*) to press tightly together; cram: *the audience packed into the foyer; the hall was packed out* **22** (*tr*; foll by *in* or *into*) to fit (many things, experiences, etc) into a limited space or time: *she packed a lot of theatre visits into her holiday* **23** to form (snow, ice, etc) into a hard compact mass or (of snow, ice, etc) to become compacted **24** (*tr*) to press in or cover tightly: *to pack a hole with cement* **25** (*tr*) to load (a horse, donkey, etc) with a burden **26** (often foll by *off* or *away*) to send away or go away, esp hastily **27** (*tr*) to seal (a joint) by inserting a layer of compressible material between the faces **28** (*tr*) to fill (a bearing or gland) with grease to lubricate it **29** (*tr*) to separate (two adjoining components) so that they have a predetermined gap between them, by introducing shims, washers, plates, etc **30** (*tr*) *med* to treat with a pack **31** (*tr*) *slang* to be capable of inflicting (a blow): *he packs a mean punch* **32** (*tr*) *US informal* to carry or wear habitually: *he packs a gun* **33** (*intr*; often foll by *down*) *rugby* to form a scrum **34** (*tr*; often foll by *into, to,* etc) *US, Canadian, and NZ* to carry (goods), esp on the back: *will you pack your camping equipment into the mountains?* **35** **pack one's bags** *informal* to get ready to leave **36** **send packing** *informal* to dismiss peremptorily ▷ See also **pack in, pack up** [C13 related to Middle Low German *pak*, of obscure origin] > '**packable** *adj*

pack² (pæk) *vb* (*tr*) to fill (a legislative body, committee, etc) with one's own supporters: *to pack a jury* [C16 perhaps changed from PACT]

package ('pækɪdʒ) *n* **1** any wrapped or boxed object or group of objects **2 a** a proposition, offer, or thing for sale in which separate items are offered together as a single or inclusive unit **b** (*as modifier*): *a package holiday* **3** a complete unit consisting of a number of component parts sold separately **4** the act or process of packing or packaging **5** *computing* a set of programs designed for a specific type of problem in statistics, production control, etc, making it unnecessary for a separate program to be written for each problem **6** *US and Canadian* another word for **pack** (sense 8) ▷ *vb* (*tr*) **7** to wrap in or put into a package **8** to design and produce a package for (retail goods) **9** to group (separate items) together as a single unit **10** to compile (complete books) for a publisher to market

packager ('pækɪdʒə) *n* an independent firm specializing in design and production, as of illustrated books or television programmes which are sold to publishers or television companies as finished products

package store *n* *US* a store where alcoholic drinks are sold for consumption elsewhere. Canadian name (also sometimes used in the US): **liquor store** Brit equivalent: **off-licence**

packaging ('pækɪdʒɪŋ) *n* **1 a** the box or wrapping in which a product is offered for sale **b** the design of such a box or wrapping, esp with reference to its ability to attract customers **2** the presentation of a person, product, television programme, etc, to the public in a way designed to build up a favourable image **3** the work of a packager

pack animal *n* an animal, such as a donkey, used to transport goods, equipment, etc

pack drill *n* a military punishment by which the offender is made to march about carrying a full pack of equipment

packed (pækt) *adj* **1** completely filled; full: *a packed theatre* **2** (of a picnic type of meal) prepared and put in a container or containers beforehand; prepacked: *a packed lunch*

packer ('pækə) *n* **1** a person or company whose business is to pack goods, esp food: *a meat packer* **2** a person or machine that packs

packet ('pækɪt) *n* **1** a small or medium-sized container of cardboard, paper, etc, often together with its contents: *a packet of biscuits*. Usual US and Canadian word: **package, pack** **2** a small package; parcel **3** Also called: **packet boat** a boat that transports mail, passengers, goods, etc, on a fixed short route **4** *slang* a large sum of money: *to cost a packet* **5** *computing* a unit into which a larger piece of data is broken down for more efficient transmission. See also **packet switching** ▷ *vb* **6** (*tr*) to wrap up in a packet or as a packet [C16 from Old French *pacquet*, from *pacquer* to pack, from Old Dutch *pak* a pack]

packet switching *n* *computing* the concentration of data into units that are allocated an address prior to transmission

packframe ('pækˌfreɪm) *n* *mountaineering* a light metal frame with shoulder straps, used for carrying heavy or awkward loads

packhorse ('pækˌhɔːs) *n* a horse used to transport goods, equipment, etc

pack ice *n* a large area of floating ice, usually occurring in polar seas, consisting of separate pieces that have become massed together. Also called: **ice pack**

pack in *vb* (*tr, adverb*) **1** *Brit and NZ informal* to stop doing (something) (esp in the phrase **pack it in**) **2** to carry (something) to base camp, etc by pack

packing ('pækɪŋ) *n* **1 a** material used to cushion packed goods **b** (*as modifier*): *a packing needle* **2** the packaging of foodstuffs **3** *med* **a** the application of a medical pack **b** gauze or other absorbent material for packing a wound **4** *printing* sheets of material, esp paper, used to cover the platen or impression cylinder of a letterpress machine **5** any substance or material used to make watertight or gastight joints, esp in a stuffing box **6** *engineering* pieces of material of various thicknesses used to adjust the position of a component or machine before it is secured in its correct position or alignment

packing box *n* another name for **stuffing box**

packing density *n* *computing* a measure of the amount of data that can be held by unit length of a storage medium, such as magnetic tape

packing fraction *n* a measure of the stability of a nucleus, equal to the difference between its mass in amu and its mass number, divided by the mass number

pack of lies *n* a completely false story, account, etc

pack rat *n* any rat of the genus *Neotoma*, of W North America, having a long tail that is furry in some species: family *Cricetidae*. Also called: **wood rat**

packsack ('pækˌsæk) *n* *US and Canadian* a bag carried strapped on the back or shoulder. Also called (in Britain and certain other countries): **knapsack**

packsaddle ('pækˌsædᵊl) *n* a saddle hung with packs, equipment, etc, used on a pack animal

pack shot *n* (in television advertising) a close-up of the product being advertised, usually so that the viewer can register its logo and packaging

packthread ('pækˌθrɛd) *n* a strong twine for sewing or tying up packages

pack up *vb* (*adverb*) **1** to put (things) away in a proper or suitable place **2** *informal* to give up (an attempt) or stop doing (something): *if you don't do your work better, you might as well pack up* **3** (*intr*) (of an engine, machine, etc) to fail to operate; break down **4** *engineering* to use packing to adjust the height of a component or machine before it is secured in its correct position or alignment

pact (pækt) *n* an agreement or compact between two or more parties, nations, etc, for mutual advantage [C15 from Old French *pacte*, from Latin *pactum*, from *pacīscī* to agree]

pacy ('peɪsɪ) *adj* a variant spelling of **pacey**

pad¹ (pæd) *n* **1** a thick piece of soft material used to make something comfortable, give it shape, or protect it **2** a guard made of flexible resilient material worn in various sports to protect parts of the body **3** Also called: **stamp pad, ink pad** a block of firm absorbent material soaked with ink for transferring to a rubber stamp **4** Also called: **notepad, writing pad** a number of sheets of paper fastened together along one edge **5** a flat piece of stiff material used to back a piece of blotting paper **6 a** the fleshy cushion-like underpart of the foot of a cat, dog, etc **b** any of the parts constituting such a structure **7** any of various

P

level surfaces or flat-topped structures, such as a launch pad **8** *entomol* a nontechnical name for **pulvillus 9** the large flat floating leaf of the water lily **10** *electronics* a resistive attenuator network inserted in the path of a signal to reduce amplitude or to match one circuit to another **11** *slang* a person's residence **12** *slang* a bed or bedroom ▷ *vb* **pads, padding, padded** (*tr*) **13** to line, stuff, or fill out with soft material, esp in order to protect or give shape to **14** (often foll by *out*) to inflate with irrelevant or false information: *to pad out a story* [c16 origin uncertain; compare Low German *pad* sole of the foot]

pad² (pæd) *vb* **pads, padding, padded 1** (*intr*; often foll by *along, up,* etc) to walk with a soft or muffled tread **2** (when *intr*, often foll by *around*) to travel (a route) on foot, esp at a slow pace; tramp ▷ *n* **3** a dull soft sound, esp of footsteps **4** *archaic* short for **footpad 5** *archaic or dialect* a slow-paced horse; nag **6** *Austral* a path or track [c16 perhaps from Middle Dutch *paden*, from *pad* PATH]

padang ('pædæŋ) *n* (in Malaysia) a playing field [from Malay: plain]

Padang ('pɑːdaːŋ) *n* a port in W Indonesia, in W Sumatra at the foot of the **Padang Highlands** on the Indian Ocean. Pop: 713 242 (2000)

padauk *or* **padouk** (pə'daʊk) *n* **1** any of various tropical African or Asian leguminous trees of the genus *Pterocarpus* that have reddish wood **2** the wood of any of these trees, used in decorative cabinetwork ▷ See also **amboyna** [from a native Burmese word]

padded cell *n* a room, esp one in a mental hospital, with padded surfaces in which violent inmates are placed

padding ('pædɪŋ) *n* **1** any soft material used to pad clothes, furniture, etc **2** superfluous material put into a speech or written work to pad it out; waffle **3** inflated or false entries in a financial account, esp an expense account

paddle¹ ('pædᵊl) *n* **1** a short light oar with a flat blade at one or both ends, used without a rowlock to propel a canoe or small boat **2** Also called: **float** a blade of a water wheel or paddle wheel **3** a period of paddling: *to go for a paddle upstream* **4 a** a paddle wheel used to propel a boat **b** (*as modifier*): *a paddle steamer* **5** the sliding panel in a lock or sluicegate that regulates the level or flow of water **6** any of various instruments shaped like a paddle and used for beating, mixing, etc **7** a table-tennis bat **8** the flattened limb of a seal, turtle, or similar aquatic animal, specialized for swimming ▷ *vb* **9** to propel (a canoe, small boat, etc) with a paddle **10 paddle one's own canoe a** to be self-sufficient **b** to mind one's own business **11** (*tr*) to convey by paddling: *we paddled him to the shore* **12** (*tr*) to stir or mix with or as if with a paddle **13** to row (a boat) steadily, esp (of a racing crew) to row firmly but not at full pressure **14** (*intr*) (of steamships) to be propelled by paddle wheels **15** (*intr*) to swim with short rapid strokes, like a dog **16** (*tr*) *US and Canadian informal* to spank [c15 of unknown origin] > **'paddler** *n*

paddle² ('pædᵊl) *vb* (*mainly intr*) **1** to walk or play barefoot in shallow water, mud, etc **2** to dabble the fingers, hands, or feet in water **3** to walk unsteadily, like a baby **4** (*tr*) *archaic* to fondle with the fingers ▷ *n* **5** the act of paddling in water [c16 of uncertain origin] > **'paddler** *n*

paddleboard ('pædᵊl,bɔːd) *n* a long narrow surfboard

paddlefish ('pædᵊl,fɪʃ) *n, pl* -**fish** *or* -**fishes 1** a primitive bony fish, *Polyodon spathula,* of the Mississippi River, having a long paddle-like projection to the snout: family *Polyodontidae* **2** a similar and related Chinese fish, *Psephurus gladius,* of the Yangtze River

paddle wheel *n* a large wheel fitted with paddles, turned by an engine to propel a vessel on the water

paddle worm *n* any of a family of green-blue faintly iridescent active marine polychaete worms

of the genus *Phyllodoce,* having paddle-shaped swimming lobes, found under stones on the shore

paddock¹ ('pædək) *n* **1** a small enclosed field, often for grazing or training horses, usually near a house or stable **2** (in horse racing) the enclosure in which horses are paraded and mounted before a race, together with the accompanying rooms **3** (in motor racing) an area near the pits where cars are worked on before races **4** *Austral and NZ* any area of fenced land **5** *Austral and NZ* a playing field **6 the long paddock** *Austral informal* a stockroute or roadside area offering feed to sheep and cattle in dry times ▷ *vb* **7** (*tr*) to confine (horses, etc) in a paddock [c17 variant of dialect *parrock,* from Old English *pearruc* enclosure, of Germanic origin. See PARK]

paddock² ('pædək) *n archaic or dialect* a frog or toad. Also called: (*Scot*) **puddock** [c12 from *pad* toad, probably from Old Norse *padda;* see -OCK]

paddock-basher *n Austral slang* a vehicle suited to driving on rough terrain

paddy¹ ('pædɪ) *n, pl* -**dies 1** Also called: **paddy field** a field planted with rice **2** rice as a growing crop or when harvested but not yet milled [from Malay *pādī*]

paddy² ('pædɪ) *n, pl* -**dies** *Brit informal* a fit of temper [c19 from PADDY]

Paddy ('pædɪ) *n, pl* -**dies** (*sometimes not capital*) an informal, often derogatory, name for an Irishman [from *Patrick*]

paddy-last *n Irish* the last person in a race or competition: *she was paddy-last*

paddymelon ('pædɪ,mɛlən) *n Austral* **1** a South African cucurbitaceous vine, *Cucumis myriocarpus,* widely naturalized in Australia **2** *Austral* the melon-like fruit of this plant **3** a variant spelling of **pademelon** [c19 of uncertain origin]

paddy wagon *n US, Austral, and NZ* an informal word for **patrol wagon**

paddywhack *or* **paddywack** ('pædɪ,wæk) *n informal* **1** *Brit* another word for **paddy² 2** a spanking or smack

pademelon *or* **paddymelon** ('pædɪ,mɛlən) *n* a small wallaby of the genus *Thylogale,* of coastal scrubby regions of Australia [c19 from a native Australian name]

Paderborn (*German* pɑːdər'bɔrn) *n* a market town in NW Germany, in North Rhine-Westphalia: scene of the meeting between Charlemagne and Pope Leo III (799 AD) that led to the foundation of the Holy Roman Empire. Pop: 141 800 (2003 est)

Padishah ('pɑːdɪ,ʃɑː) *n* a title of the shah of Iran [from Persian *pādī* lord + SHAH]

padkos ('pad,kɒs) *pl n South African* snacks and provisions for a journey [Afrikaans, literally: road food]

padlock ('pæd,lɒk) *n* **1** a detachable lock having a hinged or sliding shackle, which can be used to secure a door, lid, etc, by passing the shackle through rings or staples ▷ *vb* **2** (*tr*) to fasten with or as if with a padlock [c15 *pad,* of obscure origin]

Padma Shri ('pɑdmə 'ʃriː) *n* (in India) an award for distinguished service in any field [Hindi: lotus decoration]

padouk (pə'daʊk, -'dɔːk) *n* a variant spelling of **padauk**

Padova ('pɑːdova) *n* the Italian name for **Padua**

padre ('pɑːdrɪ) *n informal* (*sometimes capital*) **1** father: used to address or refer to a clergyman, esp a priest **2** a chaplain to the armed forces [via Spanish or Italian from Latin *pater* father]

padrone (pə'drəʊnɪ) *n, pl* -**nes** *or* -**ni** (-niː) **1** the owner or proprietor of an inn, esp in Italy **2** *US* an employer who completely controls his workers, esp a man who exploits Italian immigrants in the US [c17 from Italian; see PATRON¹]

padsaw ('pæd,sɔː) *n* a small narrow saw used for cutting curves [c19 from PAD¹ (in the sense: a handle that can be fitted to various tools) + SAW¹]

Padua ('pædʒʊə, 'pædjʊə) *n* a city in NE Italy, in Veneto: important in Roman and Renaissance times; university (1222); botanical garden (1545).

Pop: 204 870 (2001). Latin name: **Patavium** (pə'teɪvɪəm) Italian name: **Padova**

paduasoy ('pædjʊə,sɔɪ) *n* **1** a rich strong silk fabric used for hangings, vestments, etc **2** a garment made of this [c17 changed (through influence of PADUA) from earlier *poudesoy,* from French *pou-de-soie,* of obscure origin]

Padus ('peɪdəs) *n* the Latin name for the **Po²**

paean *or sometimes US* **pean** ('piːən) *n* **1** a hymn sung in ancient Greece in invocation of or thanksgiving to a deity **2** any song of praise **3** enthusiastic praise: *the film received a paean from the critics* [c16 via Latin from Greek *paiān* hymn to Apollo, from his title *Paiān,* denoting the physician of the gods]

paederast ('pedə,ræst) *n* a less common spelling of **pederast**. > **,paeder'astic** *adj* > **'paeder,asty** *n*

paediatrician *or chiefly US* **pediatrician** (,piːdɪə'trɪʃən) *n* a medical practitioner who specializes in paediatrics

paediatrics *or chiefly US* **pediatrics** (,piːdɪ'ætrɪks) *n* (*functioning as singular*) the branch of medical science concerned with children and their diseases > **,paedi'atric** *or chiefly US* **,pedi'atric** *adj*

paedo-, *before a vowel* **paed-** *or esp US* **pedo-, ped-** *combining form* indicating a child or children: *paedology* [from Greek *pais, paid-* child]

paedogenesis (,piːdəʊ'dʒɛnɪsɪs) *n* sexual reproduction in an animal that retains its larval features. See also **neoteny**. > **paedogenetic** (,piːdəʊdʒə'nɛtɪk) *or* **,paedo'genic** *adj*

paedology *or US* **pedology** (piː'dɒlədʒɪ) *n* the study of the character, growth, and development of children > **paedological** *or US* **pedological** (,piːdᵊ'lɒdʒɪkᵊl) *adj* > **pae'dologist** *or US* **pe'dologist** *n*

paedomorphosis (,piːdə'mɔːfəsɪs) *n* the resemblance of adult animals to the young of their ancestors: seen in the evolution of modern man, who shows resemblances to the young stages of australopithecines

paedophile *or esp US* **pedophile** ('piːdəʊ,faɪl) *n* a person who is sexually attracted to children

paedophilia *or esp US* **pedophilia** (,piːdəʊ'fɪlɪə) *n* the condition of being sexually attracted to children > **,paedo'phili,ac** *or esp US* **,pedo'phili,ac** *n, adj*

paella (paɪ'ɛlə; *Spanish* pa'eʎa) *n, pl* -**las** (-ləz; *Spanish* -ʎas) **1** a Spanish dish made from rice, shellfish, chicken, and vegetables **2** the large flat frying pan in which a paella is cooked [from Catalan, from Old French *paelle,* from Latin *patella* small pan]

paeon ('piːən) *n prosody* a metrical foot of four syllables, with one long one and three short ones in any order [c17 via Latin *paeon* from Greek *paiōn;* variant of PAEAN] > **pae'onic** *adj*

paeony ('piːənɪ) *n, pl* -**nies** a variant spelling of **peony**

Paestum ('pɛstəm) *n* an ancient Greek colony on the coast of Lucania in S Italy

PAGAD *abbreviation for South African* People Against Gangsterism and Drugs, a vigilante organization formed in the Western Cape around 1995 and subsequently associated with Islamic fundamentalism

pagan ('peɪgən) *n* **1** a member of a group professing a polytheistic religion or any religion other than Christianity, Judaism, or Islam **2** a person without any religion; heathen ▷ *adj* **3** of or relating to pagans or their faith or worship **4** heathen; irreligious [c14 from Church Latin *pāgānus* civilian (hence, not a soldier of Christ), from Latin: countryman, villager, from *pāgus* village] > **'pagandom** *n* > **'paganish** *adj* > **'paganism** *n* > **'paganist** *adj, n* > **,pagan'istic** *adj* > **,pagan'istically** *adv*

paganize *or* **paganise** ('peɪgə,naɪz) *vb* to become pagan, render pagan, or convert to paganism > **,pagani'zation** *or* **,pagani'sation** *n* > **'pagan,izer** *or* **'pagan,iser** *n*

page¹ (peɪdʒ) *n* **1** one side of one of the leaves of a book, newspaper, letter, etc or the written or printed matter it bears. Abbreviation: **P** *pl* **PP 2** such a leaf considered as a unit: *insert a new page* **3** a screenful of information from a website, teletext service, etc, displayed on a television monitor or visual display unit **4** an episode, phase, or period: *a glorious page in the revolution* **5** *printing* the type as set up for printing a page ▷ *vb* **6** another word for **paginate 7** (*intr; foll by through*) to look through (a book, report, etc); leaf through [c15 via Old French from Latin *pāgina*]

page² (peɪdʒ) *n* **1** a boy employed to run errands, carry messages, etc, for the guests in a hotel, club, etc **2** a youth in attendance at official functions or ceremonies, esp weddings **3** *medieval history* **a** a boy in training for knighthood in personal attendance on a knight **b** a youth in the personal service of a person of rank, esp in a royal household: *page of the chamber* **4** (in the US) an attendant at Congress or other legislative body **5** *Canadian* a person employed in the debating chamber of the House of Commons, the Senate, or a legislative assembly to carry messages for members ▷ *vb* (*tr*) **6** to call out the name of (a person), esp by a loudspeaker system, so as to give him a message **7** to call (a person) by an electronic device, such as a pager **8** to act as a page to or attend as a page [c13 via Old French from Italian *paggio*, probably from Greek *paidion* boy, from *pais* child]

pageant ('pædʒənt) *n* **1** an elaborate colourful parade or display portraying scenes from history, esp one involving rich costume **2** any magnificent or showy display, procession, etc [c14 from Medieval Latin *pāgina* scene of a play, from Latin: PAGE¹]

pageantry ('pædʒəntrɪ) *n, pl* -**ries 1** spectacular display or ceremony **2** *archaic* pageants collectively

pageboy ('peɪdʒ,bɔɪ) *n* **1** a smooth medium-length hairstyle with the ends of the hair curled under and a long fringe falling onto the forehead from the crown **2** a less common word for **page²** (sense 1) **3** another word for **page²** (sense 2)

pager ('peɪdʒə) *n* a small electronic device, capable of receiving short messages; usually carried by people who need to be contacted urgently (eg doctors)

Paget's disease ('pædʒɪts) *n* **1** Also called: **osteitis deformans** a chronic disease of the bones characterized by inflammation and deformation **2** Also called: **Paget's cancer** cancer of the nipple and surrounding tissue [c19 named after Sir James *Paget* (1814–99), British surgeon and pathologist, who described these diseases]

page-turner *n* an exciting novel, such as a thriller, with a fast-moving story

pageview ('peɪdʒ,vjuː) *n* *computing* an electronic page of information displayed in response to a user's request, such as one page of a website

paginal ('pædʒɪn²l) *adj* **1** page-for-page: *paginal facsimile* **2** of, like, or consisting of pages [c17 from Late Latin *pāgīnālis*, from Latin *pāgina* page]

paginate ('pædʒɪ,neɪt) *vb* (*tr*) to number the pages of (a book, manuscript, etc) in sequence. Compare **foliate**. > ,pagi'nation *n*

pagoda (pə'gəʊdə) *n* an Indian or Far Eastern temple, esp a tower, usually pyramidal and having many storeys [c17 from Portuguese *pagode*, ultimately from Sanskrit *bhagavatī* divine]

pagoda tree *n* a Chinese leguminous tree, *Sophora japonica*, with ornamental white flowers and dark green foliage

Pago Pago ('pɑːŋəʊ 'pɑːŋəʊ) *n* a port in American Samoa, on SE Tutuila Island. Pop: 4278 (2000). Former name: **Pango Pango**

pagurian (pə'gjʊərɪən) *or* **pagurid** (pə'gjʊərɪd, 'pægjʊrɪd) *n* **1** any decapod crustacean of the family *Paguridae*, which includes the hermit crabs ▷ *adj* **2** of, relating to, or belonging to the *Paguridae* [c19 from Latin *pagurus*, from Greek *pagouros* kind of crab]

pah (pɑː) *interj* an exclamation of disgust, disbelief, etc

Pahang (pə'hʌŋ) *n* a state of Peninsular Malaysia, on the South China Sea: the largest Malayan state; mountainous and heavily forested. Capital: Kuantan. Pop: 1 288 376 (2000). Area: 35 964 sq km (13 886 sq miles)

Pahari (pə'hɑːrɪ) *n* a group of Indo-European languages spoken in the Himalayas, divided into **Eastern Pahari** (Nepali) and **Western Pahari** (consisting of many dialects)

pahautea (pɑːhɑːuːtiːə) *n, pl* **pahautea** another name for **kaikawaka** [Māori]

Pahlavi ('pɑːləvɪ) *or* **Pehlevi** *n* the Middle Persian language, esp as used in classical Zoroastrian and Manichean literature [c18 from Persian *pahlavī*, from Old Persian *Parthava* PARTHIA]

Pahsien ('pɑː'ʃjɛn) *n* another name for **Chongqing**

paid (peɪd) *vb* **1** the past tense and past participle of **pay¹ 2 put paid to** *chiefly Brit and NZ* to end or destroy: *breaking his leg put paid to his hopes of running in the Olympics*

paid-up *adj* **1** having paid the due, full, or required fee to be a member of an organization, club, political party, etc **2** denoting a security in which all the instalments have been paid; fully paid: *a paid-up share* **3** denoting all the money that a company has received from its shareholders: *the paid-up capital* **4** denoting an endowment assurance policy on which the payment of premiums has stopped and the surrender value has been used to purchase a new single-premium policy

paigle ('peɪg²l) *n* another name for the **cowslip** and **oxlip** [c16 of uncertain origin]

Paignton ('peɪntən) *n* a town and resort in SW England, in Devon: administratively part of Torbay since 1968

pail (peɪl) *n* **1** a bucket, esp one made of wood or metal **2** Also called: **pailful** the quantity that fills a pail [Old English *pægel*; compare Catalan *paella* frying pan, PAELLA]

paillasse ('pælɪ,æs, ,pælɪ'æs) *n* a variant spelling (esp US) of **palliasse**

paillette (pæl'jɛt; *French* pajɛt) *n* **1** a sequin or spangle sewn onto a costume **2** a small piece of metal or foil, used in enamelling for decoration [c19 from French, diminutive of *paille* straw, from Latin *palea*]

pain (peɪn) *n* **1** the sensation of acute physical hurt or discomfort caused by injury, illness, etc **2** emotional suffering or mental distress **3 on pain of** subject to the penalty of **4** Also called: **pain in the neck**, (taboo) **arse** *informal* a person or thing that is a nuisance ▷ *vb* **5** to cause (a person) distress, hurt, grief, anxiety, etc **6** *informal* to annoy; irritate ▷ See also **pains** [c13 from Old French *peine*, from Latin *poena* punishment, grief, from Greek *poinē* penalty]

pained (peɪnd) *adj* having or expressing pain or distress, esp mental or emotional distress: *a pained expression*

painful ('peɪnfʊl) *adj* **1** causing pain; distressing: *a painful duty* **2** affected with pain: *a painful leg* **3** tedious or difficult **4** *informal* extremely bad: *a painful performance* > 'painfully *adv* > 'painfulness *n*

painkiller ('peɪn,kɪlə) *n* **1** an analgesic drug or agent **2** anything that relieves pain

painless ('peɪnlɪs) *adj* **1** not causing pain or distress **2** not affected by pain > 'painlessly *adv* > 'painlessness *n*

pains (peɪnz) *pl n* **1** care, trouble, or effort (esp in the phrases **take pains**, **be at pains to**) **2** painful sensations experienced during contractions in childbirth; labour pains

painstaking ('peɪnz,teɪkɪŋ) *adj* extremely careful, esp as to fine detail: *painstaking research* > 'pains,takingly *adv* > 'pains,takingness *n*

paint (peɪnt) *n* **1** a substance used for decorating or protecting a surface, esp a mixture consisting of a solid pigment suspended in a liquid, that when applied to a surface dries to form a hard coating **2** a dry film of paint on a surface **3** the solid pigment of a paint before it is suspended in liquid **4** *informal* face make-up, such as rouge **5** short for **greasepaint** ▷ *vb* **6** to make (a picture) of (a figure, landscape, etc) with paint applied to a surface such as canvas **7** to coat (a surface) with paint, as in decorating **8** (*tr*) to apply (liquid) onto (a surface): *her mother painted the cut with antiseptic* **9** (*tr*) to apply make-up onto (the face, lips, etc) **10** (*tr*) to describe vividly in words **11 paint the town red** *informal* to celebrate uninhibitedly; go on a spree [c13 from Old French *peint* painted, from *peindre* to paint, from Latin *pingere* to paint, adorn] > 'painty *adj*

paintball game ('peɪnt,bɔːl) *n* a game in which teams of players simulate a military skirmish, shooting each other with paint pellets that explode on impact, marking the players who have been shot

paintbox ('peɪnt,bɒks) *n* a box containing a tray of dry watercolour paints

paintbrush ('peɪnt,brʌʃ) *n* a brush used to apply paint

paint-by-numbers *adj* formulaic; showing no original thought or creativity [c20 from children's painting books in which the colours to be used are identified by numbers on the design to be painted]

Painted Desert *n* a section of the high plateau country of N central Arizona, along the N side of the Little Colorado River Valley: brilliant-coloured rocks; occupied largely by Navaho and Hopi Indians. Area: about 20 000 sq km (7500 sq miles)

painted lady *n* a migratory nymphalid butterfly, *Vanessa cardui*, with pale brownish-red mottled wings

painted woman *n* *old-fashioned, derogatory* a woman whose appearance suggests she is promiscuous

painter¹ ('peɪntə) *n* **1** a person who paints surfaces as a trade **2** an artist who paints pictures

painter² ('peɪntə) *n* a line attached to the bow of a boat for tying it up [c15 probably from Old French *penteur* strong rope]

painterly ('peɪntəlɪ) *adj* **1** having qualities peculiar to painting, esp the depiction of shapes by means of solid masses of colour, rather than by lines. Compare **linear** (sense 5) **2** of or characteristic of a painter; artistic

painter's colic *n* *pathol* another name for **lead colic** [c19 so called because it frequently affected people who worked with lead-based paints or similar substances]

painting ('peɪntɪŋ) *n* **1** the art or process of applying paints to a surface such as canvas, to make a picture or other artistic composition **2** a composition or picture made in this way **3** the act of applying paint to a surface with a brush

paint stripper *or* **remover** *n* a liquid, often caustic, used to remove paint from a surface

paintwork ('peɪnt,wɜːk) *n* a surface, such as wood or a car body, that is painted

pair¹ (pɛə) *n, pl* **pairs** *or functioning as singular or plural* **pair 1** two identical or similar things matched for use together: *a pair of socks* **2** two persons, animals, things, etc, used or grouped together: *a pair of horses; a pair of scoundrels* **3** an object considered to be two identical or similar things joined together: *a pair of trousers* **4** two people joined in love or marriage **5** a male and a female animal of the same species, esp such animals kept for breeding purposes **6** *parliamentary procedure* **a** two opposed members who both agree not to vote on a specified motion or for a specific period of time **b** the agreement so made **7** two playing cards of the same rank or denomination: *a pair of threes* **8** one member of a matching pair: *I can't find the pair to this glove* **9** *cricket* short for a **pair of spectacles** (see **spectacles** (sense 2)) **10** *rowing* See **pair-oar 11** *Brit and US dialect* a group or set of more than two **12** *logic, maths* **a** a set with two members **b** an ordered set with two members

P

▷ *vb* **13** (often foll by *off*) to arrange or fall into groups of twos **14** to group or be grouped in matching pairs: *to pair socks* **15** to join or be joined in marriage; mate or couple **16** (when *tr*, usually *passive*) parliamentary procedure to form or cause to form a pair: *18 members were paired for the last vote* ▷ See also **pairs** [c13 from Old French *paire*, from Latin *paria* equal (things), from *pār* equal]

> **USAGE** Like other collective nouns, *pair* takes a singular or a plural verb according to whether it is seen as a unit or as a collection of two things: *the pair are said to dislike each other; a pair of good shoes is essential*

pair² (per) *adj* a Scot word for **poor**

pair bond *n* the exclusive relationship formed between a male and a female, esp in some species of animals and birds during courtship and breeding > **pair bonding** *n*

pair-oar *n* rowing a racing shell in which two oarsmen sit one behind the other and pull one oar each. Also called: **pair** Compare **double scull**

pair production *n* the production of an electron and a positron from a gamma-ray photon in a strong field as that passes close to an atomic nucleus

pair royal *n* (in some card games) a set of three cards of the same denomination

pairs (pɛəz) *pl n* another name for **Pelmanism** (sense 2)

pair trawling *n* the act or practice of using two boats to trawl for fish

paisa ('paɪsɑ:) *n*, *pl* **-se** (-seɪ) a monetary unit of Bangladesh, Bhutan, India, Nepal, and Pakistan worth one hundredth of a rupee [from Hindi]

paisano (paɪ'sɑ:nəʊ; *Spanish* pai'sano) *n*, *pl* **-nos** (-nəʊz; *Spanish* -nos) *Southwestern US* (often a term of address) **1** *informal* a friend; pal **2** a fellow countryman [c20 via Spanish from French *paysan* PEASANT]

paisley ('peɪzlɪ) *n* **1** a pattern of small curving shapes with intricate detailing, usually printed in bright colours **2** a soft fine wool fabric traditionally printed with this pattern **3** a garment made of this fabric, esp a shawl popular in the late 19th century **4** (*modifier*) of or decorated with this pattern: *a paisley scarf* [c19 named after PAISLEY]

Paisley ('peɪzlɪ) *n* an industrial town in SW Scotland, the administrative centre of Renfrewshire: one of the world's chief centres for the manufacture of thread, linen, and gauze in the 19th century. Pop: 74 170 (2001)

paitrick ('petrɪk) *n* a Scot word for **partridge**

Paiute or **Piute** ('paɪ.u:t, paɪ'ju:t) *n* **1** (*pl* **-utes** or **-ute**) a member of either of two North American Indian peoples (**Northern Paiute** and **Southern Paiute**) of the Southwestern US, related to the Aztecs **2** the language of either of these peoples, belonging to the Shoshonean subfamily of the Uto-Aztecan family

pajamas (pə'dʒɑ:məz) *pl n* the US spelling of **pyjamas**

Pak (pæk) *Indian* ▷ *n* **1** Pakistan ▷ *n*, *adj* **2** Pakistani

pakahi ('pɑ:kəhi:) *n* *NZ* **a** acid land that is unsuitable for cultivation **b** (*as modifier*): *pakahi soil* [c19 from Māori]

pakapoo ('pækəpu:) *n*, *pl* **-poos** *Austral* and *NZ* **1** a Chinese lottery with betting slips marked with Chinese characters **2** **like a pakapoo ticket** untidy, incomprehensible [c19 from Chinese]

pak-choi cabbage ('pɑ:k'tʃɔɪ) *n* another name for **bok choy**

Pakeha ('pɑ:kɪ,hɑ:) *n* (in New Zealand) a person who is not of Māori ancestry, esp a White person [from Māori]

Pakeha Māori *n* (in the 19th century) a European who adopted the Māori way of life

Paki ('pækɪ) *Brit* *slang*, *offensive* ▷ *n*, *pl* **Pakis 1** a Pakistani or person of Pakistani descent **2** (loosely) a person from any part of the Indian subcontinent ▷ *adj* **3** Pakistani or of Pakistani descent **4** (loosely) denoting a person from the Indian subcontinent

Paki-bashing *n* *Brit* *slang* the activity of making vicious and unprovoked physical assaults upon Pakistani immigrants or people of Pakistani descent > **'Paki-,basher** *n*

pakihi ('pɑ:ki:hi:) *n* *NZ* an area of swampy infertile land [Māori]

pakirikiri ('pɑ:kɪrɪ,kɪrɪ:) *n* *NZ* another name for **blue cod**

Pakistan (,pɑ:kɪ'stɑ:n) *n* **1** a republic in S Asia, on the Arabian Sea: the Union of Pakistan, formed in 1947, comprised West and East Pakistan; East Pakistan gained independence as Bangladesh in 1971 and West Pakistan became Pakistan; a member of the Commonwealth from 1947, it withdrew from 1972 until 1989; contains the fertile plains of the Indus valley rising to mountains in the north and west. Official language: Urdu. Official religion: Muslim. Currency: rupee. Capital: Islamabad. Pop: 157 315 000 (2004 est). Area: 801 508 sq km (309 463 sq miles) **2** a former republic in S Asia consisting of the provinces of West Pakistan and East Pakistan (now Bangladesh), 1500 km (900 miles) apart: formed in 1947 from the predominantly Muslim parts of India

Pakistani (,pɑ:kɪ'stɑ:nɪ) *n* **1** a native or inhabitant of Pakistan ▷ *adj* **2** of or relating to Pakistan or its inhabitants

pakoko ('pɑ:kəʊkəʊ) *n* *NZ* another name for **bully²**

pakora (pə'kɔ:rə) *n* an Indian dish consisting of pieces of vegetable, chicken, etc, dipped in a spiced batter and deep-fried: served with a piquant sauce [c20 from Hindi]

pakthong (pæk'θʊŋ) *n* another name for **nickel silver**

pal (pæl) *informal* ▷ *n* **1** a close friend; comrade **2** an accomplice ▷ *vb* **pals, palling, palled 3** (*intr*; usually foll by *with* or *about*) to associate as friends ▷ See also **pal up** [c17 from English Gypsy: brother, ultimately from Sanskrit *bhrātar* BROTHER]

PAL (pæl) *n* acronym for phase alternation line: a colour-television broadcasting system used generally in Europe

Pal. *abbreviation for* Palestine

palace ('pælɪs) *n* (*capital when part of a name*) **1** the official residence of a reigning monarch or member of a royal family: *Buckingham Palace* **2** the official residence of various high-ranking church dignitaries or members of the nobility, as of an archbishop **3** a large and richly furnished building resembling a royal palace ▷ Related adjectives: **palatial, palatine** [c13 from Old French *palais*, from Latin *Palātium* PALATINE², the site of the palace of the emperors]

palace revolution *n* a coup d'état made by those already in positions of power, usually with little violence

paladin ('pælədɪn) *n* **1** one of the legendary twelve peers of Charlemagne's court **2** a knightly champion [c16 via French from Italian *paladino*, from Latin *palātinus* imperial official, from *Palātium* PALATINE²]

palaeanthropic (,pælɪæn'θrɒpɪk) *adj* relating to or denoting the earliest variety of man

Palaearctic (,pælɪ'ɑ:ktɪk) *adj* of or denoting a zoogeographical region consisting of Europe, Africa north of the Sahara, and most of Asia north of the Himalayas

palaeethnology (,pælɪɛθ'nɒlədʒɪ) *n* the study of prehistoric man > **palaeethnological** (,pælɪ,ɛθnə'lɒdʒɪkᵊl) *adj* > **,palaeeth'nologist** *n*

palaeo-, *before a vowel* **palae-** or *esp US* **paleo-**, **pale-** *combining form* old, ancient, or prehistoric: *palaeography* [from Greek *palaios* old]

palaeoanthropology (,pælɪəʊ,ænθrə'pɒlədʒɪ) *n* the branch of anthropology concerned with primitive man

palaeobotany (,pælɪəʊ'bɒtənɪ) *n* the study of fossil plants > **palaeobotanical** (,pælɪəʊbə'tænɪkᵊl) or **,palaeobo'tanic** *adj* > **,palaeo'botanist** *n*

Palaeocene ('pælɪəʊ,si:n) *adj* **1** of, denoting, or formed in the first epoch of the Tertiary period, which lasted for 10 million years ▷ *n* **2** **the** the Palaeocene epoch or rock series [c19 from French from *paléo*- PALAEO- + Greek *kainos* new, recent]

palaeoclimatology (,pælɪəʊ,klaɪmə'tɒlədʒɪ) *n* the study of climates of the geological past > **,palaeo,clima'tologist** *n*

palaeocurrent ('pælɪəʊ,kʌrənt) *n* geology an ancient current, esp of water, evidence of which has been preserved in sedimentary rocks as fossilized ripple marks, etc

palaeoecology (,pælɪəʊɪ'kɒlədʒɪ) *n* the study of fossil animals and plants in order to deduce their ecology and the environmental conditions in which they lived > **,palaeo,eco'logical** *adj* > **,palaeoe'cologist** *n*

palaeoethnobotany (,pælɪəʊ,ɛθnəʊ'bɒtənɪ) *n* the study of fossil seeds and grains to further archaeological knowledge, esp in the domestication of cereals

Palaeogene ('pælɪə,dʒi:n) *adj* **1** of or formed in the Palaeocene, Eocene, and Oligocene epochs ▷ *n* **2** **the** the Palaeogene period or system

palaeogeography (,pælɪəʊdʒɪ'ɒgrəfɪ) *n* the study of geographical features of the geological past > **,palaeoge'ographer** *n* > **palaeogeographical** (,pælɪəʊ,dʒi:əʊ'græfɪkᵊl) or **,palaeo,geo'graphic** *adj* > **,palaeo,geo'graphically** *adv*

palaeography (,pælɪ'ɒgrəfɪ) *n* **1** the study of the handwritings of the past, and often the manuscripts as well, so that they may be dated, read, etc, and may serve as historical and literary sources **2** a handwriting of the past > **palae'ographer** *n* > **palaeographic** (,pælɪəʊ'græfɪk) or **,palaeo'graphical** *adj*

palaeolith ('pælɪəʊ,lɪθ) *n* a stone tool dating to the Palaeolithic

Palaeolithic (,pælɪəʊ'lɪθɪk) *n* **1** the period of the emergence of primitive man and the manufacture of unpolished chipped stone tools, about 2.5 million to 3 million years ago until about 12 000 BC. See also **Lower Palaeolithic, Middle Palaeolithic, Upper Palaeolithic** ▷ *adj* **2** (*sometimes not capital*) of or relating to this period

Palaeolithic man *n* any of various primitive types of man, such as Neanderthal man and Java man, who lived in the Palaeolithic

palaeomagnetism (,pælɪəʊ'mægnɪ,tɪzəm) *n* the study of the fossil magnetism in rocks, used to determine the past configurations of the continents and to investigate the past shape and magnitude of the earth's magnetic field > **,palaeomag'netic** *adj*

palaeontography (,pælɪɒn'tɒgrəfɪ) *n* the branch of palaeontology concerned with the description of fossils [c19 from PALAEO- + ONTO- + -GRAPHY] > **palaeontographic** (,pælɪ,ɒntə'græfɪk) or **,palae,onto'graphical** *adj*

palaeontol. *abbreviation for* palaeontology

palaeontology (,pælɪɒn'tɒlədʒɪ) *n* **1** the study of fossils to determine the structure and evolution of extinct animals and plants and the age and conditions of deposition of the rock strata in which they are found. See also **palaeobotany, palaeozoology 2** another name for **palaeozoology** [c19 from PALAEO- + ONTO- + -LOGY] > **palaeontological** (,pælɪ,ɒntə'lɒdʒɪkᵊl) *adj* > **,palae,onto'logically** *adv* > **,palaeon'tologist** *n*

palaeopathology (,pælɪəʊpə'θɒlədʒɪ) *n* the study of diseases of ancient man and fossil animals > **palaeo,patho'logical** *adj* > **,palaeopa'thologist** *n*

Palaeozoic (,pælɪəʊ'zəʊɪk) *adj* **1** of, denoting, or relating to an era of geological time that began 600 million years ago with the Cambrian period and lasted about 375 million years until the end of the Permian period ▷ *n* **2** **the** the Palaeozoic era [c19 from PALAEO- + Greek *zōē* life + -IC]

palaeozoology (,pælɪəʊzu:'ɒlədʒɪ) *n* the study of fossil animals. Also called: **palaeontology**

> palaeozoological (ˌpælɪəʊˌzʊəˈlɒdʒɪkᵊl) *adj*
> ˌpalaeozoˈologist *n*

palaestra *or esp US* **palestra** (pəˈlɛstrə, -ˈliː-) *n, pl* **-tras** *or* **-trae** (-triː) (in ancient Greece or Rome) a public place devoted to the training of athletes [C16 via Latin from Greek *palaistra*, from *palaiein* to wrestle]

Palagi (paːˈlʌŋi) *n, pl* **-gi** NZ a Samoan name for European [from Samoan *papālagi*]

palais de danse *French* (palɛ də dɑ̃s) *n* a dance hall

palais glide (ˈpæleɪ) *n* a dance with high kicks and gliding steps in which performers link arms in a row [C20 from PALAIS DE DANSE]

palanquin *or* **palankeen** (ˌpælənˈkiːn) *n* a covered litter, formerly used in the Orient, carried on the shoulders of four men [C16 from Portuguese *palanquim*, from Prakrit *pallanka*, from Sanskrit *paryanka* couch]

palatable (ˈpælətəbᵊl) *adj* **1** pleasant to taste **2** acceptable or satisfactory: *a palatable suggestion* > ˌpalataˈbility *or* ˈpalatableness *n* > ˈpalatably *adv*

palatal (ˈpælətᵊl) *adj* **1** Also: **palatine** of or relating to the palate **2** *phonetics* of, relating to, or denoting a speech sound articulated with the blade of the tongue touching the hard palate ▷ *n* **3** Also called: **palatine** the bony plate that forms the palate **4** *phonetics* a palatal speech sound, such as the semivowel (j) > ˈpalatally *adv*

palatalize *or* **palatalise** (ˈpælətəˌlaɪz) *vb* (*tr*) to pronounce (a speech sound) with the blade of the tongue touching the palate > ˌpalataliˈzation *or* ˌpalataliˈsation *n*

palate (ˈpælɪt) *n* **1** the roof of the mouth, separating the oral and nasal cavities. See **hard palate, soft palate** Related adj: **palatine 2** the sense of taste: *she had no palate for the wine* **3** relish or enjoyment **4** *botany* (in some two-lipped corollas) the projecting part of the lower lip that closes the opening of the corolla [C14 from Latin *palātum*, perhaps of Etruscan origin]

🖝 USAGE Avoid confusion with **palette** or **pallet**

palatial (pəˈleɪʃəl) *adj* of, resembling, or suitable for a palace; sumptuous > paˈlatially *adv* > paˈlatialness *n*

palatinate (pəˈlætɪnɪt) *n* a territory ruled by a palatine prince or noble or count palatine

Palatinate (pəˈlætɪnɪt) *n* **1** **the** either of two territories in SW Germany, once ruled by the counts palatine. **Upper Palatinate** is now in Bavaria; **Lower** *or* **Rhine Palatinate** is now in Rhineland-Palatinate, Baden-Württemberg, and Hesse. German name: **Pfalz 2** a native or inhabitant of the Palatinate

palatine¹ (ˈpæləˌtaɪn) *adj* **1** (of an individual) possessing royal prerogatives in a territory **2** of, belonging to, characteristic of, or relating to a count palatine, county palatine, palatinate, or palatine **3** of or relating to a palace ▷ *n* **4** *feudal history* the lord of a palatinate **5** any of various important officials at the late Roman, Merovingian, or Carolingian courts **6** (in Colonial America) any of the proprietors of a palatine colony, such as Carolina [C15 via French from Latin *palātīnus* belonging to the palace, from *palātium*; see PALACE]

palatine² (ˈpæləˌtaɪn) *adj* **1** of or relating to the palate ▷ *n* **2** either of two bones forming the hard palate [C17 from French *palatin*, from Latin *palātum* palate]

Palatine¹ (ˈpæləˌtaɪn) *adj* **1** of or relating to the Palatinate ▷ *n* **2** a Palatinate

Palatine² (ˈpæləˌtaɪn) *n* **1** one of the Seven Hills of Rome: traditionally the site of the first settlement of Rome ▷ *adj* **2** of, relating to, or designating this hill

Palau (paːˈlaʊ) *or* **Belau** *n* **Republic of.** a republic comprising a group of islands in the W Pacific, in the W Caroline Islands; administratively part of the UN Trust Territory of the Pacific Islands 1947–87; entered into an agreement of free association with the US (1980); became fully

independent in 1994. Chief island: Babelthuap. Capital: Koror; new capital under construction on Babelthuap. Pop: 20 000 (2003 est). Area: 476 sq km (184 sq miles). Former name: **Pelew Islands**

palaver (pəˈlɑːvə) *n* **1** tedious or time-consuming business, esp when of a formal nature: *all the palaver of filling in forms* **2** loud and confused talk and activity; hubbub **3** (often used humorously) a conference **4** *now rare* talk intended to flatter or persuade **5** *W African* **a** an argument **b** trouble arising from an argument ▷ *vb* **6** (*intr*) (often used humorously) to have a conference **7** (*intr*) to talk loudly and confusedly **8** (*tr*) to flatter or cajole [C18 from Portuguese *palavra* talk, from Latin *parabola* PARABLE]

Palawan (*Spanish* paˈlavan) *n* an island of the SW Philippines between the South China Sea and the Sulu Sea: the westernmost island in the country; mountainous and forested. Capital: Puerto Princesa. Pop: 311 550 (latest est). Area: 11 785 sq km (4550 sq miles)

palazzo pants (pəˈlætsəʊ) *pl n* women's trousers with very wide legs [C20 *palazzo* from Italian, literally: PALACE]

pale¹ (peɪl) *adj* **1** lacking brightness of colour; whitish: *pale morning light* **2** (of a colour) whitish; produced by a relatively small quantity of colouring agent **3** dim or wan: *the pale stars* **4** feeble: *a pale effort* **5** *South African* a euphemism for **White** ▷ *vb* **6** to make or become pale or paler; blanch **7** (*intr*; often foll by *before*) to lose superiority or importance (in comparison to): *her beauty paled before that of her hostess* [C13 from Old French *palle*, from Latin *pallidus* pale, from *pallēre* to look wan] > ˈpalely *adv* > ˈpaleness *n*

pale² (peɪl) *n* **1** a wooden post or strip used as an upright member in a fence **2** an enclosing barrier, esp a fence made of pales **3** an area enclosed by a pale **4** a sphere of activity within which certain restrictions are applied **5** *heraldry* an ordinary consisting of a vertical stripe, usually in the centre of a shield **6** **beyond the pale** outside the limits of social convention ▷ *vb* **7** (*tr*) to enclose with pales [C14 from Old French *pal*, from Latin *pālus* stake; compare POLE¹]

palea (ˈpeɪlɪə) *or* **pale** *n, pl* **paleae** (ˈpeɪlɪˌiː) *or* **pales** *botany* the inner of two bracts surrounding each floret in a grass spikelet ▷ Compare **lemma 2** any small membranous bract or scale [C18 from Latin: straw, chaff; see PALLET¹] > **paleaceous** (ˌpeɪlɪˈeɪʃəs) *adj*

paleface (ˈpeɪlˌfeɪs) *n* a derogatory term for a White person, said to have been used by North American Indians

Palembang (paːˈlɛmbɑːŋ) *n* a port in W Indonesia, in S Sumatra; oil refineries; university (1955). Pop: 1 451 419 (2000)

Palencia (*Spanish* paˈlenθia) *n* a city in N central Spain: earliest university in Spain (1208); seat of Castilian kings (12th–13th centuries); communications centre. Pop: 81 378 (2003 est)

Palenque (*Spanish* paˈleŋke) *n* the site of an ancient Mayan city in S Mexico famous for its architectural ruins

paleo- *or before a vowel* **pale-** *combining form* variants (esp US) of **palaeo-**

Palermo (pəˈlɛəməʊ, -ˈlɜː-; *Italian* paˈlɛrmo) *n* the capital of Sicily, on the NW coast: founded by the Phoenicians in the 8th century BC Pop: 686 722 (2001)

Palestine (ˈpælɪˌstaɪn) *n* **1** Also called: **the Holy Land, Canaan** the area between the Jordan River and the Mediterranean Sea in which most of the biblical narrative is located **2** the province of the Roman Empire in this region **3** the former British mandatory territory created by the League of Nations in 1922 (but effective from 1920), and including all of the present territories of Israel and Jordan between whom it was partitioned by the UN in 1948

Palestine Liberation Organization *n* an organization founded in 1964 with the aim of

creating a state for Palestinians; it recognized the state of Israel in 1993 and Israel granted Palestinians autonomy in the Gaza Strip and West Bank. Abbreviation: PLO

Palestinian (ˌpælɪˈstɪnɪən) *adj* **1** of or relating to Palestine ▷ *n* **2** a native or inhabitant of the former British mandate, or their descendants, esp such Arabs now living in the Palestinian Administered Territories, Jordan, Lebanon, or Israel, or as refugees from Israeli-occupied territory

Palestinian Administered Territories *n* the Gaza Strip and the West Bank in Israel: these areas were granted autonomous status under the control of the Palestinian National Authority following the 1993 peace agreement between Israel and the Palestine Liberation Organization. Also called: **Palestinian Autonomous Areas**

Palestinian National Authority *n* the authority formed in 1994 to govern the Palestinian Administered Territories: it controls policy on health, education, social welfare, direct taxation, tourism, and culture and manages elections to the Palestinian Council. Abbreviation: PNA

palestra (pəˈlɛstrə, -ˈliː-) *n, pl* **-tras** *or* **-trae** (-triː) the usual US spelling of **palaestra**

paletot (ˈpæltəʊ) *n* **1** a loose outer garment **2** a woman's fitted coat often worn over a crinoline or bustle [C19 from French]

palette (ˈpælɪt) *n* **1** Also: **pallet** a flat piece of wood, plastic, etc, used by artists as a surface on which to mix their paints **2** the range of colours characteristic of a particular artist, painting, or school of painting: *a restricted palette* **3** the available range of colours or patterns that can be displayed by a computer on a visual display unit **4** either of the plates of metal attached by a strap to the cuirass in a suit of armour to protect the armpits [C17 from French, diminutive of *pale* shovel, from Latin *pala* spade]

🖝 USAGE Avoid confusion with **palate** or **pallet**

p

palette knife *or* **pallet knife** *n* **1** a round-ended spatula with a thin flexible blade used esp by artists for mixing, applying, and scraping off paint, esp oil paint **2** a knife with a round-ended flexible blade used in cookery for scraping out a mixture from a bowl, spreading icing, etc

palfrey (ˈpɔːlfrɪ) *n archaic* a light saddle horse, esp ridden by women [C12 from Old French *palefrei*, from Medieval Latin *palafredus*, from Late Latin *paraverēdus*, from Greek *para* beside + Latin *verēdus* light fleet horse, of Celtic origin]

Pali (ˈpɑːlɪ) *n* an ancient language of India derived from Sanskrit; the language of the Buddhist scriptures [C19 from Sanskrit *pāli-bhāsa*, from *pāli* canon + *bhāsa* language, of Dravidian origin]

palikar (ˈpælɪˌkɑː) *n* a Greek soldier in the war of independence against Turkey (1821–28) [C19 from Modern Greek *palikari* youth]

palilalia (ˌpælɪˈleɪlɪə) *n* a speech disorder in which a word or phrase is rapidly repeated [C20 from Greek *palin* again + *lalein* to babble]

palimony (ˈpælɪmənɪ) *n US* alimony awarded to a nonmarried partner after the break-up of a long-term relationship [C20 from a blend of *pal* + *alimony*]

palimpsest (ˈpælɪmpˌsɛst) *n* **1** a manuscript on which two or more successive texts have been written, each one being erased to make room for the next ▷ *adj* **2** (of a text) written on a palimpsest **3** (of a document) used as a palimpsest [C17 from Latin *palimpsestus* parchment cleaned for reuse, from Greek *palimpsēstos*, from *palin* again + *psēstos* rubbed smooth, from *psēn* to scrape]

palindrome (ˈpælɪnˌdrəʊm) *n* a word or phrase the letters of which, when taken in reverse order, give the same word or phrase, such as *able was I ere I saw Elba* [C17 from Greek *palindromos* running back again, from *palin* again + -DROME] > **palindromic** (ˌpælɪnˈdrɒmɪk) *adj*

paling ('peɪlɪŋ) n 1 a fence made of pales 2 pales collectively 3 a single pale 4 the act of erecting pales

palingenesis (ˌpælɪn'dʒɛnɪsɪs) n, pl -ses (-ˌsiːz) 1 Christianity spiritual rebirth through metempsychosis of Christian baptism 2 biology another name for **recapitulation** (sense 2) [c19 from Greek palin again + genesis birth, GENESIS] > **palingenetic** (ˌpælɪndʒə'nɛtɪk) adj > ˌpalinge'netically adv

palinka (pə'lɪŋkə) n a type of apricot brandy, originating in Central and Eastern Europe

palinode ('pælɪˌnəʊd) n 1 a poem in which the poet recants something he has said in a former poem 2 rare a recantation [c16 from Latin palinōdia repetition of a song, from Greek, from palin again + ōidē song, ODE]

palinopsia (ˌpælɪ'nɒpsɪə) or **palinopia** (ˌpælɪ'nəʊpɪə) n a visual disorder in which the patient perceives a prolonged afterimage [from Greek palin again + ōps eye]

palisade (ˌpælɪ'seɪd) n 1 a strong fence made of stakes driven into the ground, esp for defence 2 one of the stakes used in such a fence 3 botany a layer of elongated mesophyll cells containing many chloroplasts, situated below the outer epidermis of a leaf blade ▷ vb 4 (tr) to enclose with a palisade [c17 via French, from Old Provençal palissada, ultimately from Latin pālus stake; see PALE², POLE¹]

palisades (ˌpælɪ'seɪdz, 'pælɪˌseɪdz) pl n US and Canadian high cliffs in a line, often along a river, resembling a palisade

palish ('peɪlɪʃ) adj rather pale

Palk Strait (pɔːk, pɔːlk) n a channel between SE India and N Ceylon. Width: about 64 km (40 miles)

pall¹ (pɔːl) n 1 a cloth covering, usually black, spread over a coffin or tomb 2 a coffin, esp during the funeral ceremony 3 a dark heavy covering; shroud: the clouds formed a pall over the sky 4 a depressing or oppressive atmosphere: her bereavement cast a pall on the party 5 heraldry an ordinary consisting of a Y-shaped bearing 6 Christianity a a small square linen cloth with which the chalice is covered at the Eucharist b an archaic word for **pallium** (sense 2) 7 an obsolete word for **cloak** ▷ vb 8 (tr) to cover or depress with a pall [Old English pæll, from Latin: PALLIUM]

pall² (pɔːl) vb 1 (intr; often foll by on) to become or appear boring, insipid, or tiresome (to): history classes palled on me 2 to cloy or satiate, or become cloyed or satiated [c14 variant of APPAL]

Palladian¹ (pə'leɪdɪən) adj denoting, relating to, or having the neoclassical style of architecture created by Palladio [c18 after Andrea Palladio (1508–80), Italian architect] > **Pal'ladianˌism** n

Palladian² (pə'leɪdɪən) adj 1 of or relating to the goddess Pallas Athena 2 literary wise or learned [c16 from Latin Palladius, from Greek Pallas, an epithet applied to Athena, meaning perhaps "(spear) brandisher" or perhaps "virgin"]

palladic (pə'lædɪk, -'leɪ-) adj of or containing palladium in the trivalent or tetravalent state

palladium¹ (pə'leɪdɪəm) n a ductile malleable silvery-white element of the platinum metal group occurring principally in nickel-bearing ores: used as a hydrogenation catalyst and, alloyed with gold, in jewellery. Symbol: Pd; atomic no.: 46; atomic wt.: 106.42; valency: 2, 3, or 4; relative density: 12.02; melting pt.: 1555°C; boiling pt.: 2964°C [c19 named after the asteroid PALLAS, at the time (1803) a recent discovery]

palladium² (pə'leɪdɪəm) n something believed to ensure protection; safeguard [c17 after the PALLADIUM]

Palladium (pə'leɪdɪəm) n a statue of Pallas Athena, esp the one upon which the safety of Troy depended

palladous (pə'leɪdəs, 'pælədəs) adj of or containing palladium in the divalent state

Pallas ('pæləs) n astronomy the second largest asteroid (diameter 520 km), revolving around the sun in a period of 4.62 years

Pallas Athena or **Pallas** n another name for Athena

pallbearer ('pɔːlˌbɛərə) n a person who carries or escorts the coffin at a funeral

pallescent (pæ'lɛsənt) adj botany becoming paler in colour with increasing age

pallet¹ ('pælɪt) n 1 a straw-filled mattress or bed 2 any hard or makeshift bed [c14 from Anglo-Norman paillet, from Old French paille straw, from Latin palea straw]
> USAGE Avoid confusion with **palate** or **palette**

pallet² ('pælɪt) n 1 an instrument with a handle and a flat, sometimes flexible, blade used by potters for shaping 2 a standard-sized platform of box section open at two ends on which goods may be stacked. The open ends allow the entry of the forks of a lifting truck so that the palletized load can be raised and moved about easily 3 horology the locking lever that engages and disengages alternate end pawls with the escape wheel to give impulses to the balance 4 a variant spelling of **palette** (sense 1) 5 music a flap valve of wood faced with leather that opens to allow air from the wind chest to enter an organ pipe, causing it to sound [c16 from Old French palette a little shovel, from pale spade, from Latin pala spade]
> USAGE Avoid confusion with **palate** or **palette**

palletize or **palletise** ('pælɪˌtaɪz) vb (tr) to stack or transport on a pallet or pallets > ˌpalleti'zation or ˌpalleti'sation n

pallet knife n a variant spelling of **palette knife**

pallet truck n a powered truck with a mast, sometimes telescopic, on which slides a carriage which can be raised and lowered hydraulically. The carriage has extended forks which can be passed under a palletized load for stacking or moving to a new position. Also called: **stacking truck**

palliasse or esp US **paillasse** ('pælɪˌæs, ˌpælɪ'æs) n a straw-filled mattress; pallet [c18 from French paillasse, from Italian pagliaccio, ultimately from Latin palea PALLET¹]

palliate ('pælɪˌeɪt) vb (tr) 1 to lessen the severity of (pain, disease, etc) without curing or removing; alleviate; mitigate 2 to cause (an offence) to seem less serious by concealing evidence; extenuate [c16 from Late Latin palliāre to cover up, from Latin pallium a cloak, PALLIUM] > ˌpalli'ation n > 'palliˌator n

palliative ('pælɪətɪv) adj 1 serving to palliate; relieving without curing ▷ n 2 something that palliates, such as a sedative drug or agent > 'palliatively adv

pallid ('pælɪd) adj 1 lacking colour or brightness; wan: a pallid complexion 2 lacking vigour; vapid: a pallid performance [c17 from Latin pallidus, from pallēre to be PALE¹] > 'pallidly adv > 'pallidness or pal'lidity n

pallium ('pælɪəm) n, pl -lia (-lɪə) or -liums 1 a garment worn by men in ancient Greece or Rome, made by draping a large rectangular cloth about the body 2 chiefly RC Church a woollen vestment consisting of a band encircling the shoulders with two lappets hanging from it front and back: worn by the pope, all archbishops, and (as a mark of special honour) some bishops 3 Also called: **mantle** anatomy the cerebral cortex and contiguous white matter 4 zoology another name for **mantle** (sense 5) [c16 from Latin: cloak; related to Latin palla mantle]

pall-mall ('pæl'mæl) n obsolete 1 a game in which a ball is driven by a mallet along an alley and through an iron ring 2 the alley itself [c17 from obsolete French, from Italian pallamaglio, from palla ball + maglio mallet]

Pall Mall ('pæl 'mæl) n a street in central London,

noted for its many clubs

pallor ('pælə) n a pale condition, esp when unnatural: fear gave his face a deathly pallor [c17 from Latin: whiteness (of the skin), from pallēre to be PALE¹]

pally ('pælɪ) adj -lier, -liest informal on friendly or familiar terms

pally up vb (intr, adverb; often foll by with) informal to become friends (with)

palm¹ (pɑːm) n 1 the inner part of the hand from the wrist to the base of the fingers. Related adjs: **thenar**, **volar** 2 a corresponding part in animals, esp apes and monkeys 3 a linear measure based on the breadth or length of a hand, equal to three to four inches or seven to ten inches respectively 4 the part of a glove that covers the palm 5 a hard leather shield worn by sailmakers to protect the palm of the hand 6 a the side of the blade of an oar that faces away from the direction of a boat's movement during a stroke b the face of the fluke of an anchor 7 a flattened or expanded part of the antlers of certain deer 8 in the palm of one's hand at one's mercy or command ▷ vb (tr) 9 to conceal in or about the hand, as in sleight-of-hand tricks 10 to touch or soothe with the palm of the hand ▷ See also **palm off** [c14 paume, via Old French from Latin palma; compare Old English folm palm of the hand, Greek palamē]

palm² (pɑːm) n 1 any treelike plant of the tropical and subtropical monocotyledonous family Arecaceae (formerly Palmae or Palmaceae), usually having a straight unbranched trunk crowned with large pinnate or palmate leaves 2 a leaf or branch of any of these trees, a symbol of victory, success, etc 3 merit or victory 4 an emblem or insignia representing a leaf or branch worn on certain military decorations [Old English, from Latin palma, from the likeness of its spreading fronds to a hand; see PALM¹]

Palma (Spanish 'palma) n the capital of the Balearic Islands, on the SW coast of Majorca: a tourist centre. Pop: 367 277 (2003 est). Official name: **Palma de Mallorca**

palmaceous (pæl'meɪʃəs) adj of, relating to, or belonging to the palm family, Arecaceae (formerly Palmae or Palmaceae)

palmar ('pælmə) adj of or relating to the palm of the hand

palmary ('pælmərɪ) adj rare worthy of praise [c17 from Latin palmārius relating to the palm of victory; see PALM²]

Palmas ('pælməs) n a city in N Brazil, capital of Tocantins state. Pop: 391 000 (2005 est)

palmate ('pælmeɪt, -mɪt) or **palmated** adj 1 shaped like an open hand: palmate antlers 2 botany having more than three lobes or segments that spread out from a common point: palmate leaves 3 (of the feet of most water birds) having three toes connected by a web [c18 from Latin palmatus, from palma palm; see PALM²]

palmation (pæl'meɪʃən) n 1 the state of being palmate 2 a projection or division of a palmate structure

Palm Beach n a town in SE Florida, on an island between Lake Worth (a lagoon) and the Atlantic: major resort and tourist centre. Pop: 9759 (2003 est)

palm berry n another name for **açaí**

palm civet n any of various small civet-like arboreal viverrine mammals of the genera Paradoxurus, Hemigalus, etc, of Africa and S and SE Asia

palmcorder ('pɑːmˌkɔːdə) n a small camcorder which can be held in the palm of the hand

palmer ('pɑːmə) n 1 (in Medieval Europe) a pilgrim bearing a palm branch as a sign of his visit to the Holy Land 2 (in Medieval Europe) an itinerant monk 3 (in Medieval Europe) any pilgrim 4 any of various artificial angling flies characterized by hackles around the length of the body [c13 from Old French palmier, from Medieval Latin palmārius, from Latin palma palm]

Palmer Archipelago n a group of islands between South America and Antarctica: part of the British Antarctic Territory (formerly the British colony of the Falkland Islands and Dependencies). (Claims are suspended under the Antarctic Treaty). Former name: **Antarctic Archipelago**

Palmer Land n the S part of the Antarctic Peninsula

Palmer Peninsula n the former name (until 1964) for the **Antarctic Peninsula**

Palmerston ('pɑːməstən) n the former name (1869–1911) of **Darwin**[1]

Palmerston North n a city in New Zealand, in the S North Island on the Manawatu River. Pop: 78 100 (2004 est)

palmer worm n the hairy black and white caterpillar of the goldtail moth [c16 originally applied to various destructive caterpillars of migratory habits]

palmette (pæl'met) n archaeol an ornament or design resembling the palm leaf [c19 from French: a little PALM[2]]

palmetto (pæl'mɛtəʊ) n, pl -tos or -toes 1 any of several small chiefly tropical fan palms, esp any of the genus Sabal, of the southeastern US. See also **cabbage palmetto, saw palmetto** 2 any of various other fan palms such as palms of the genera Serenoa, Thrinax, and Chamaerops [c16 from Spanish palmito a little PALM[2]]

Palmira (Spanish pal'mira) n a city in W Colombia: agricultural trading centre. Pop: 253 000 (2005 est)

palmistry ('pɑːmɪstrɪ) n the process or art of interpreting character, telling fortunes, etc, by the configuration of lines, marks, and bumps on a person's hand. Also called: **chiromancy** [c15 pawmistry, from paume PALM[1]; the second element is unexplained] > **palmist** n

palmitate ('pælmɪˌteɪt) n any salt or ester of palmitic acid

palmitic acid (pæl'mɪtɪk) n a white crystalline solid that is a saturated fatty acid: used in the manufacture of soap and candles. Formula: $(C_{15}H_{31})COOH$. Systematic name: **hexadecanoic acid** [c19 from French palmitique; see PALM[2], -ITE[2], -IC]

palmitin ('pælmɪtɪn) n the colourless glyceride of palmitic acid, occurring in many natural oils and fats. Formula: $(C_{15}H_{31}COO)_3C_3H_5$. Also called: **tripalmitin** [c19 from French palmitine, probably from palmite pith of the palm tree; see PALM[2]]

palm off vb (tr, adverb; often foll by on) 1 to offer, sell, or spend fraudulently: to palm off a counterfeit coin 2 to divert in order to be rid of: I palmed the unwelcome visitor off on John

palm oil n a yellow butter-like oil obtained from the fruit of the oil palm, used as an edible fat and in soap

palm-oil chop n a W African dish made with meat and palm oil

Palm Springs n a city in the US, in California: a popular tourist resort. Pop: 45 228 (2003 est)

palm sugar n sugar obtained from the sap of certain species of palm trees

Palm Sunday n the Sunday before Easter commemorating Christ's triumphal entry into Jerusalem

palmtop computer ('pɑːmˌtɒp) n a computer that has a small screen and compressed keyboard and is small enough to be held in the hand, often used as a personal organizer. Often shortened to: **palmtop** Compare **laptop computer**

palm vaulting n a less common name for **fan vaulting**

palm wine n (esp in W Africa) the sap drawn from the palm tree, esp when allowed to ferment

palmy ('pɑːmɪ) adj palmier, palmiest 1 prosperous, flourishing, or luxurious: a palmy life 2 covered with, relating to, or resembling palms: a palmy beach

palmyra (pæl'maɪrə) n a tall tropical Asian palm, Borassus flabellifer, with large fan-shaped leaves

used for thatching and weaving; grown also for its edible seedlings [c17 from Portuguese palmeira palm tree (see PALM[2]); perhaps influenced by PALMYRA, city in Syria]

Palmyra (pæl'maɪrə) n 1 an ancient city in central Syria: said to have been built by Solomon. Biblical name: **Tadmor** 2 an island in the central Pacific, in the Line Islands: under US administration

Palo Alto n 1 ('pæləʊ 'æltəʊ) a city in W California, southeast of San Francisco: founded in 1891 as the seat of Stanford University. Pop: 57 233 (2003 est) 2 (Spanish 'palo 'alto) a battlefield in E Mexico, northwest of Monterrey, where the first battle (1846) of the Mexican War took place, in which the Mexicans under General Mariano Arista were defeated by the Americans under General Zachary Taylor

palo cortado ('pæləʊ kɔr'tɑdəʊ) n a rich, dry sherry [Spanish, literally: crossed stick (referring to the classification system in which butts of palo cortado are marked with a vertical line and one or more horizontal lines)]

palolo worm (pə'ləʊləʊ) n any of several polychaete worms of the family Eunicidae, esp Eunice viridis, of the S Pacific Ocean: reproductive segments are shed from the posterior end of the body when breeding [c20 palolo, from Samoan or Tongan]

Palomar ('pæləˌmɑː) n Mount a mountain in S California, northeast of San Diego: site of **Mount Palomar Observatory,** which has a large (200-inch) reflecting telescope. Height: 1871 m (6140 ft)

palomino (ˌpælə'miːnəʊ) n, pl -nos a golden horse with a cream or white mane and tail [American Spanish, probably: dovelike, from Latin palumbīnus, from palumbēs ring dove]

palooka (pə'luːkə) n US slang a stupid or clumsy boxer or other person [c20 origin uncertain]

Palos (Spanish 'palɔs) n a village and former port in SW Spain: starting point of Columbus' voyage of discovery to America (1492)

palp (pælp) or **palpus** ('pælpəs) n, pl palps or palpi ('pælpaɪ) 1 either of a pair of sensory appendages that arise from the mouthparts of crustaceans and insects 2 either of a pair of tactile organs arising from the head or anterior end of certain annelids and molluscs [c19 from French, from Latin palpus a touching] > **palpal** adj

palpable ('pælpəbºl) adj 1 (usually prenominal) easily perceived by the senses or the mind; obvious: the excuse was a palpable lie 2 capable of being touched; tangible 3 med capable of being discerned by the sense of touch: a palpable tumour [c14 from Late Latin palpābilis that may be touched, from Latin palpāre to stroke, touch] > ˌpalpa'bility or 'palpableness > 'palpably adv

palpate[1] ('pælpeɪt) vb (tr) med to examine (an area of the body) by the sense of touch and pressure [c19 from Latin palpāre to stroke] > pal'pation n

palpate[2] ('pælpeɪt) adj zoology of, relating to, or possessing a palp or palps

palpebral ('pælpɪbrəl) adj of or relating to the eyelid [c19 from Late Latin palpebrālis, from Latin palpebra eyelid; probably related to palpāre to stroke]

palpebrate adj ('pælpɪbrɪt, -ˌbreɪt) 1 having eyelids ▷ vb ('pælpɪˌbreɪt) 2 (intr) to wink or blink, esp repeatedly

palpitate ('pælpɪˌteɪt) vb (intr) 1 (of the heart) to beat with abnormal rapidity 2 to flutter or tremble [c17 from Latin palpitāre to throb, from palpāre to stroke] > 'palpitant adj > ˌpalpi'tation n

palsgrave ('pɔːlzˌɡreɪv) n archaic a German count palatine [c16 from Dutch, from Middle Dutch paltsgrave, from palts estate of a palatine + grave count] > palsgravine ('pɔːlzɡrəˌviːn) fem n

palstave ('pɔːlˌsteɪv) n archaeol a kind of celt, usually of bronze, made to fit into a split wooden handle rather than having a socket for the handle [c19 from Danish paalstav, from Old Norse, from páll spade + stafr STAFF[1]]

palsy ('pɔːlzɪ) pathol ▷ n, pl -sies 1 paralysis, esp of a specified type: cerebral palsy ▷ vb -sies, -sying, -sied (tr) 2 to paralyse [c13 palesi, from Old French paralisie, from Latin PARALYSIS] > 'palsied adj

palsy-walsy ('pælzɪˌwælzɪ) adj informal excessively friendly

palter ('pɔːltə) vb (intr) 1 to act or talk insincerely 2 to haggle [c16 of unknown origin] > 'palterer n

paltry ('pɔːltrɪ) adj -trier, -triest 1 insignificant; meagre 2 worthless or petty [c16 from Low Germanic palter, paltrig ragged] > 'paltrily adv > 'paltriness n

paludal (pə'ljuːdºl, 'pæljʊdºl) adj rare 1 of, relating to, or produced by marshes 2 malarial [c19 from Latin palus marsh; related to Sanskrit palvala pond]

paludism ('pæljʊˌdɪzəm) n pathol a rare word for **malaria** [c19 from Latin palus marsh]

Paludrine ('pæljʊdrɪn) n trademark proguanil hydrochloride, a synthetic antimalarial drug first produced in 1944

pal up vb (intr, adverb; often foll by with) informal to become friends (with): he palled up with the other boys

paly ('peɪlɪ) adj (usually postpositive) heraldry vertically striped [c15 from Old French palé, from Latin pālus stake; see PALE[2]]

palynology (ˌpælɪ'nɒlədʒɪ) n the study of living and fossil pollen grains and plant spores [c20 from Greek palunein to scatter + -LOGY] > palynological (ˌpælɪnə'lɒdʒɪkºl) adj > ˌpaly'nologist n

Pama-Nyungan ('pɑːmə'njʊŋən) adj 1 of or relating to the largest superfamily of languages within the phylum of languages spoken by the native Australians ▷ n 2 this phylum

Pamirs (pə'mɪəz) pl n the a mountainous area of central Asia, mainly in Tajikistan and partly in Kyrgyzstan, extending into China and Afghanistan: consists of a complex of high ranges, from which the Tian Shan projects to the north, the Kunlun and Karakoram to the east, and the Hindu Kush to the west; Kommunizma Peak is situated in the Tajik Pamirs. Highest peak: Kongur Shan, 7719 m (25 326 ft). Also called: **Pamir**

Pamlico Sound ('pæmlɪkəʊ) n an inlet of the Atlantic between the E coast of North Carolina and its chain of offshore islands. Length: 130 km (80 miles)

pampas ('pæmpəz) n (functioning as singular or more often plural) a the extensive grassy plains of temperate South America, esp in Argentina b (as modifier): pampas dwellers [c18 from American Spanish pampa (sing), from Quechua bamba plain] > pampean ('pæmpɪən, pæm'piːən) adj

pampas grass ('pæmpəs, -pəz) n any of various large grasses of the South American genus Cortaderia and related genera, widely cultivated for their large feathery silver-coloured flower branches

Pampeluna (ˌpæmpə'luːnə) n the former name of **Pamplona**

pamper ('pæmpə) vb (tr) 1 to treat with affectionate and usually excessive indulgence; coddle; spoil 2 archaic to feed to excess [c14 of Germanic origin; compare German dialect pampfen to gorge oneself] > 'pamperer n

pampero (pæm'pɛərəʊ; Spanish pam'pero) n, pl -ros (-rəʊz; Spanish -ros) a dry cold wind in South America blowing across the pampas from the south or southwest [c19 from American Spanish: (wind) of the PAMPAS]

pamphlet ('pæmflɪt) n 1 a brief publication generally having a paper cover; booklet 2 a brief treatise, often on a subject of current interest, published in pamphlet form [c14 pamflet, from Anglo-Latin panfletus, from Medieval Latin Pamphilus title of a popular 12th-century amatory poem from Greek Pamphilos masculine proper name]

pamphleteer (ˌpæmflɪ'tɪə) n 1 a person who writes or issues pamphlets, esp of a controversial nature ▷ vb 2 (intr) to write or issue pamphlets

pamphrey ('pæmfrɪ) n Ulster dialect a cabbage [of

p

Pamphylia (pæmˈfɪlɪə) *n* an area on the S coast of ancient Asia Minor

Pamplona (pæmˈpləʊnə; *Spanish* pamˈplona) *n* a city in N Spain in the foothills of the Pyrenees: capital of the kingdom of Navarre from the 11th century until 1841. Pop: 190 937 (2003 est). Former name: **Pampeluna**

pampoen (ˌpamˈpʊn) *n South African* **1** a pumpkin **2** *informal* a fool

pampootie (ˌpæmˈpuːtiː) *n* a rawhide slipper worn by men in the Aran Islands [c19 of uncertain origin]

pan¹ (pæn) *n* **1 a** a wide metal vessel used in cooking **b** (*in combination*): saucepan **2** Also called: **panful** the amount such a vessel will hold **3** any of various similar vessels used esp in industry, as for boiling liquids **4** a dish used by prospectors, esp gold prospectors, for separating a valuable mineral from the gravel or earth containing it by washing and agitating **5** either of the two dishlike receptacles on a balance **6** Also called: **lavatory pan** *Brit* the bowl of a lavatory **7 a** a natural or artificial depression in the ground where salt can be obtained by the evaporation of brine **b** a natural depression containing water or mud **8** *Caribbean* the indented top from an oil drum used as the treble drum in a steel band **9** See **hardpan, brainpan 10** a small ice floe **11** a slang word for **face** (sense 1a) **12** a small cavity containing priming powder in the locks of old guns **13** a hard substratum of soil **14** short for **pan loaf** ▷ *vb* **pans, panning, panned 15** (when *tr*, often foll by *off* or *out*) to wash (gravel) in a pan to separate particles of (valuable minerals) from it **16** (*intr*; often foll by *out*) (of gravel) to yield valuable minerals by this process **17** (*tr*) *informal* to criticize harshly: *the critics panned his new play* ▷ See also **pan out** [Old English *panne*; related to Old Saxon, Old Norse *panna*, Old High German *pfanna*]

pan² (pæn) *n* **1** the leaf of the betel tree **2** a preparation of this leaf which is chewed, together with betel nuts and lime, in India and the East Indies [c17 from Hindi, from Sanskrit *parna* feather, wing, leaf]

pan³ (pæn) *vb* **pans, panning, panned 1** to move (a film camera) or (of a film camera) to be moved so as to follow a moving object or obtain a panoramic effect ▷ *n* **2 a** the act of panning **b** (*as modifier*): *a pan shot* [c20 shortened from *panoramic*]

Pan (pæn) *n Greek myth* the god of fields, woods, shepherds, and flocks, represented as a man with a goat's legs, horns, and ears. Related adjs: **Pandean, Panic**

Pan. *abbreviation for* Panama

pan- *combining form* **1** all or every: *panchromatic* **2** including or relating to all parts or members: *Pan-African; pantheistic* [from Greek *pan*, neuter of *pas* all]

panacea (ˌpænəˈsɪə) *n* a remedy for all diseases or ills [c16 via Latin from Greek *panakeia* healing everything, from *pan* all + *akēs* remedy] ▷ ˌpanaˈcean *adj*

panache (pəˈnæʃ, -ˈnɑːʃ) *n* **1** a dashing manner; style; swagger: *he rides with panache* **2** a feathered plume on a helmet [c16 via French from Old Italian *pennacchio*, from Late Latin *pinnāculum* feather, from Latin *pinna* feather; compare Latin *pinnāculum* PINNACLE]

panada (pəˈnɑːdə) *n* a mixture of flour, water, etc, or of breadcrumbs soaked in milk, used as a thickening [c16 from Spanish, from *pan* bread, from Latin *pānis*]

Pan-African *adj* **1** of or relating to all African countries or the advocacy of political unity among African countries ▷ *n* **2** a supporter of the Pan-African movement > ˈPan-ˈAfricanˌism *n*

Pan-Africanist Congress *n* a South African political party, founded as a liberation movement in 1959. Abbreviation: **PAC**

Panaji (pɑːˈnɑːdʒiː) *n* a variant of **Panjim**

Panama (ˌpænəˈmɑː, ˈpænəˌmɑː) *n* **1** a republic in Central America, occupying the Isthmus of Panama: gained independence from Spain in 1821 and joined Greater Colombia; became independent in 1903, with the immediate area around the canal forming the Canal Zone under US jurisdiction; Panama assumed sovereignty over the Canal Zone in 1979 and full control in 1999. Official language: Spanish; English is also widely spoken. Religion: Roman Catholic majority. Currency: balboa. Capital: Panama City. Pop: 3 178 000 (2004 est). Area: 75 650 sq km (29 201 sq miles) **2 Isthmus of** an isthmus linking North and South America, between the Pacific and the Caribbean. Length: 676 km (420 miles). Width (at its narrowest point): 50 km (31 miles). Former name: (Isthmus of) **Darien 3 Gulf of** a wide inlet of the Pacific in Panama

Panama Canal *n* a canal across the Isthmus of Panama, linking the Atlantic and Pacific Oceans: extends from Colón on the Caribbean Sea southeast to Balboa on the Gulf of Panama; built by the US (1904–14), after an unsuccessful previous attempt (1880–89) by the French under de Lesseps. Length: 64 km (40 miles)

Panama Canal Zone *n* See **Canal Zone**

Panama City *n* the capital of Panama, near the Pacific entrance of the Panama Canal: developed rapidly with the building of the Panama Canal; seat of the University of Panama (1935). Pop: 950 000 (2005 est)

Panama hat *n* (*sometimes not capital*) a hat made of the plaited leaves of the jipijapa plant of Central and South America. Often shortened to: **panama** or **Panama**

Panamanian (ˌpænəˈmeɪnɪən) *adj* **1** of or relating to Panama or its inhabitants ▷ *n* **2** a native or inhabitant of Panama

Pan-American *adj* of, relating to, or concerning North, South, and Central America collectively or the advocacy of political or economic unity among American countries > ˈPan-Aˈmericanˌism *n*

Pan American Union *n* the secretariat and major official agency of the Organization of American States

pan and tilt head *n films, television* a mounting device on which a camera may be rotated in a horizontal plane (pan) or in a vertical plane (tilt)

Pan-Arabism (ˈærəˌbɪzəm) *n* the principle of, support for, or the movement towards Arab political union or cooperation > ˈPan-ˈArab *adj, n* > ˈPan-ˈArabic *adj*

panatella (ˌpænəˈtɛlə) *n* a long slender cigar [American Spanish *panetela* long slim biscuit, from Italian *panatella* small loaf, from *pane* bread, from Latin *pānis*]

Panathenaea (ˌpæˌnæθɪˈniːə) *n* (in ancient Athens) a summer festival on the traditional birthday of Athena

Panay (pɑːˈnaɪ) *n* an island in the central Philippines, the westernmost of the Visayan Islands. Pop: 2 595 315 (latest est). Area: 12 300 sq km (4750 sq miles)

pancake (ˈpænˌkeɪk) *n* **1 a** a thin flat cake made from batter and fried on both sides, often served rolled and filled with a sweet or savoury mixture **b** (*as modifier*): *pancake mix* **2** a Scot name for **drop scone 3** a stick or flat cake of compressed make-up **4** Also called: **pancake landing** an aircraft landing made by levelling out a few feet from the ground and then dropping onto it ▷ *vb* **5** to cause (an aircraft) to make a pancake landing or (of an aircraft) to make a pancake landing

Pancake Day *n* another name for **Shrove Tuesday**

pancake ice *n* thin slabs of newly formed ice in polar seas

pancetta (pænˈtʃɛtə; *Italian* panˈtʃetta) *n* a lightly spiced cured bacon from Italy [Italian, literally: little belly]

panchax (ˈpænˌtʃæks) *n* any of several brightly coloured tropical Asian cyprinodont fishes of the genus *Aplocheilus*, such as *A. panchax* (**blue panchax**)

[c19 from New Latin (former generic name), of obscure origin]

Panchayat (pənˈtʃɑːjət) *n* a village council in India [Hindi, from Sanskrit *panch* five, because such councils originally consisted of five members]

Panchen Lama (ˈpɑːntʃən) *n* one of the two Grand Lamas of Tibet, ranking below the Dalai Lama. Also called: **Tashi Lama** [from Tibetan *panchen*, literally: great jewel, from the title of the lama (in full: great jewel among scholars)]

panchromatic (ˌpænkrəʊˈmætɪk) *adj photog* (of an emulsion or film) made sensitive to all colours by the addition of suitable dyes to the emulsion. Compare **orthochromatic**. > **panchromatism** (pænˈkrəʊməˌtɪzəm) *n*

pancosmism (pænˈkɒzˌmɪzəm) *n* the philosophical doctrine that the material universe is all that exists [c19 see PAN-, COSMOS, -ISM]

pancratium (pænˈkreɪʃɪəm) *n, pl* -**tia** (-ʃɪə) (in ancient Greece) a wrestling and boxing contest [c17 via Latin from Greek *pankration*, from PAN- + *kratos* strength] > **pancratic** (pænˈkrætɪk) *adj*

pancreas (ˈpæŋkrɪəs) *n* a large elongated glandular organ, situated behind the stomach, that secretes insulin and pancreatic juice [c16 via New Latin from Greek *pankreas*, from PAN- + *kreas* flesh] > **pancreatic** (ˌpæŋkrɪˈætɪk) *adj*

pancreatic juice *n* the clear alkaline secretion of the pancreas that is released into the duodenum and contains several digestive enzymes

pancreatin (ˈpæŋkrɪətɪn) *n* the powdered extract of the pancreas of certain animals, such as the pig, used in medicine as an aid to digestion by virtue of the enzymes it contains

pancreatitis (ˌpæŋkrɪəˈtaɪtɪs) *n* inflammation of the pancreas

pancreozymin (ˌpæŋkrɪəʊˈzaɪmɪn) *n* another name for **cholecystokinin**

panda (ˈpændə) *n* **1** Also called: **giant panda** a large black-and-white herbivorous bearlike mammal, *Ailuropoda melanoleuca*, related to the raccoons and inhabiting the high mountain bamboo forests of China: family *Procyonidae* **2** **lesser** or **red panda** a closely related smaller animal resembling a raccoon, *Ailurus fulgens*, of the mountain forests of S Asia, having a reddish-brown coat and ringed tail [c19 via French from a native Nepalese word]

panda car *n Brit* a police patrol car, esp a blue and white one [c20 so called because it was originally white with black or blue markings, supposedly resembling the markings of the giant panda]

pandanaceous (ˌpændəˈneɪʃəs) *adj* of, relating to, or belonging to the *Pandanaceae*, an Old World tropical family of monocotyledonous plants including the screw pines

pandanus (pænˈdeɪnəs) *n, pl* -**nuses** any of various Old World tropical palmlike plants of the genus *Pandanus*, having large aerial prop roots and leaves that yield a fibre used for making mats, etc: family *Pandanaceae*. See also **screw pine** [c19 via New Latin from Malay *pandan*]

Pandarus (ˈpændərəs) *n* **1** *Greek myth* the leader of the Lycians, allies of the Trojans in their war with the Greeks. He broke the truce by shooting Menelaus with an arrow and was killed in the ensuing battle by Diomedes **2** (in medieval legend) the procurer of Cressida on behalf of Troilus

Pandean (pænˈdiːən) *adj* of or relating to the god Pan

pandect (ˈpændɛkt) *n* **1** a treatise covering all aspects of a particular subject **2** (*often plural*) the complete body of laws of a country; legal code [c16 via Late Latin from Greek *pandektēs* containing everything, from PAN- + *dektēs* receiver, from *dekhesthai* to receive]

Pandects of Justinian *pl n* another name for **Digest**

pandemic (pænˈdɛmɪk) *adj* **1** (of a disease) affecting persons over a wide geographical area;

extensively epidemic ▷ *n* **2** a pandemic disease [c17 from Late Latin *pandēmus,* from Greek *pandēmos* general, from PAN- + *demos* the people]

pandemonium (ˌpændɪˈməʊnɪəm) *n* **1** wild confusion; uproar **2** a place of uproar and chaos [c17 coined by Milton to designate the capital of hell in *Paradise Lost,* from PAN- + Greek *daimōn* DEMON] ▷ ˌpandeˈmoniˌac *or* pandemonic (ˌpændɪˈmɒnɪk) *adj*

pander (ˈpændə) *vb* **1** (*intr*; foll by *to*) to give gratification (to weaknesses or desires) **2** (archaic when *tr*) to act as a go-between in a sexual intrigue (for) ▷ *n also* **panderer 3** a person who caters for vulgar desires, esp in order to make money **4** a person who procures a sexual partner for another; pimp [C16 (n): from *Pandare* PANDARUS]

pandiculation (pænˌdɪkjʊˈleɪʃən) *n* **1** the act of stretching and yawning, esp on waking **2** a yawn [c17 from Latin *pandiculari,* from *pendere* to stretch]

pandit (ˈpʌndɪt; *spelling pron* ˈpændɪt) *n Hinduism* a variant of **pundit** (sense 3)

P & L *abbreviation for* profit and loss

P & O *abbreviation for* the Peninsular and Oriental Steam Navigation Company

pandora (pænˈdɔːrə) *n* **1** a handsome red sea bream, *Pagellus erythrinus,* of European coastal waters, caught for food in the Mediterranean **2** a marine bivalve mollusc of the genus *Pandora* that lives on the surface of sandy shores and has thin equal valves **3** *music* another word for **bandore** [after PANDORA]

Pandora (pænˈdɔːrə) *or* **Pandore** (pænˈdɔː, ˈpændɔː) *n Greek myth* the first woman, made out of earth as the gods' revenge on man for obtaining fire from Prometheus. Given a box (**Pandora's box**) that she was forbidden to open, she disobeyed out of curiosity and released from it all the ills that beset man, leaving only hope within [from Greek, literally: all-gifted]

pandore (ˈpændɔː) *n music* another word for **bandore**

pandour (ˈpændʊə) *n* one of an 18th-century force of Croatian soldiers in the Austrian service, notorious for their brutality [c18 via French from Hungarian *pandur,* from Croat: guard, probably from Medieval Latin *banderius* summoner, from *bannum* BAN¹]

pandowdy (pænˈdaʊdɪ) *n, pl* **-dies** *US* a deep-dish pie made from fruit, esp apples, with a cake topping: *apple pandowdy* [c19 of unknown origin]

p & p *Brit* ▷ *abbreviation for* postage and packing

pandurate (ˈpændjʊˌreɪt) *or* **panduriform** (pænˈdjʊərɪˌfɔːm) *adj* (of plant leaves) shaped like the body of a fiddle [c19 from Late Latin *pandūra* BANDORE]

pandy (ˈpændɪ) *chiefly Scot and Irish* ▷ *n, pl* **-dies 1** (in schools) a stroke on the hand with a strap as a punishment ▷ *vb* **-dies, -dying, -died 2** (*tr*) to punish with such strokes [c19 from Latin *pande* (*manum*) stretch out (the hand), from *pandere* to spread or extend]

pane¹ (peɪn) *n* **1** a sheet of glass in a window or door **2** a panel of a window, door, wall, etc **3** a flat section or face, as of a cut diamond **4** *philately* **a** any of the rectangular marked divisions of a sheet of stamps made for convenience in selling **b** a single page in a stamp booklet. See also **tête-bêche, se tenant** [c13 from Old French *pan* portion, from Latin *pannus* rag]

pane² (peɪn) *n, vb* a variant of **peen**

pané *French* (pane) *adj* (of fish, meat, etc) dipped or rolled in breadcrumbs before cooking

paneer (pəˈnɪə) *n* a soft white cheese, used in Indian cookery [c20 from Hindi *panīr* cheese]

panegyric (ˌpænɪˈdʒɪrɪk) *n* a formal public commendation; eulogy [c17 via French and Latin from Greek, from *panēguris* public gathering, from PAN- + *aguris* assembly] ▷ ˌpaneˈgyrical *adj* ▷ ˌpaneˈgyrically *adv* ▷ ˌpaneˈgyrist *n*

panegyrize *or* **panegyrise** (ˈpænɪdʒɪˌraɪz) *vb* to make a eulogy or eulogies (about)

panel (ˈpænəl) *n* **1** a flat section of a wall, door, etc **2** any distinct section or component of something formed from a sheet of material, esp of a car body, the spine of a book, etc **3** a piece of material inserted in a skirt, dress, etc **4 a** a group of persons selected to act as a team in a quiz, to judge a contest, to discuss a topic before an audience, etc **b** (*as modifier*): *a panel game* **5** a public discussion by such a group: *a panel on public health* **6** *law* **a** a list of persons summoned for jury service **b** the persons on a specific jury **7** *Scots law* a person indicted or accused of crime after appearing in court **8 a** a thin board used as a surface or backing for an oil painting **b** a painting done on such a surface **9** any picture with a length much greater than its breadth **10** See **instrument panel 11** (formerly, in Britain) **a** a list of patients insured under the National Health Insurance Scheme **b** a list of medical practitioners within a given area available for consultation by these patients **12 on the panel** *Brit informal* receiving sickness benefit, esp from the government ▷ *vb* **-els, -elling, -elled** *or US* **-els, -eling, -eled** (*tr*) **13** to furnish or decorate with panels **14** to divide into panels **15** *law* **a** to empanel (a jury) **b** (in Scotland) to bring (a person) to trial; indict [c13 from Old French: portion, from *pan* piece of cloth, from Latin *pannus*; see PANE¹]

panel beater *n* a person who beats out the bodywork of motor vehicles

panel heating *n* a system of space heating with panels that contain heating pipes or electrical conductors

panelling *or US* **paneling** (ˈpænlɪŋ) *n* **1** panels collectively, as on a wall or ceiling **2** material used for making panels

panellist *or US* **panelist** (ˈpænlɪst) *n* a member of a panel, esp on a radio or television programme

panel pin *n* a light slender nail with a narrow head

panel saw *n* a saw with a long narrow blade for cutting thin wood

panel truck *n US and Canadian* a small van used esp for delivery rounds. British equivalent: **delivery van**

panel van *n* **1** *Austral* a small van with two rear doors, esp one having windows and seats in the rear **2** *NZ* a small enclosed delivery van

panettone (pænəˈtəʊnɪ; *Italian* panetˈtoːne) *n, pl* **-nes** *or* **-ni** (-ni) a kind of Italian spiced brioche containing sultanas: traditionally eaten at Christmas in Italy [Italian, from *panetto* small loaf, from *pane* bread, from Latin *pānis*]

Pan-European *adj* of or relating to all European countries or the advocacy of political or economic unity among European countries

pang (pæŋ) *n* a sudden brief sharp feeling, as of loneliness, physical pain, or hunger [c16 variant of earlier *prange,* of Germanic origin]

panga (ˈpæŋɡə) *n* **1** a broad heavy knife of E Africa, used as a tool or weapon **2** *US* a small fishing boat first developed in Japan and now used chiefly in US and Central American waters [from a native E African word. The panga boat is so called because it resembles the knife in shape]

Pangaea *or* **Pangea** (pænˈdʒiːə) *n* the ancient supercontinent, comprising all the present continents joined together, which began to break up about 200 million years ago. See also **Laurasia, Gondwanaland** [c20 from Greek, literally: all-earth]

pangenesis (pænˈdʒɛnɪsɪs) *n* a former theory of heredity, that each body cell produces hereditary particles that circulate in the blood before collecting in the reproductive cells. See also **blastogenesis** (sense 1) ▷ pangenetic (ˌpændʒəˈnɛtɪk) *adj* ▷ ˌpangeˈnetically *adv*

Pan-Germanism *n* (esp in the 19th century) the movement for the unification of Germany

Pang-fou (ˈpæŋˈfuː) *n* a variant transliteration of the Chinese name for **Bengbu**

Pangloss (ˈpæŋglɒs) *n* a person who views a situation with unwarranted optimism ▷ Panˈglossian *adj* [c19 after Dr *Pangloss,* a character in Voltaire's *Candide* (1759)]

pangolin (pæŋˈgəʊlɪn) *n* any mammal of the order *Pholidota* found in tropical Africa, S Asia, and Indonesia, having a body covered with overlapping horny scales and a long snout specialized for feeding on ants and termites. Also called: **scaly anteater** [c18 from Malay *peng-gōling,* from *gōling* to roll over; from its ability to roll into a ball]

Pango Pango (ˈpɑːŋəʊ ˈpɑːŋəʊ) *n* the former name of **Pago Pago**

pangram (ˈpænˌgræm) *n* a sentence incorporating all the letters of the alphabet, such as *the quick brown fox jumps over the lazy dog*

panhandle¹ (ˈpænˌhændəl) *n* **1** (*sometimes capital*) (in the US) a narrow strip of land that projects from one state into another **2** (in a South African city) a plot of land without street frontage

panhandle² (ˈpænˌhændəl) *vb US and Canadian informal* to accost and beg from (passers-by), esp on the street [c19 probably a back formation from *panhandler* a person who begs with a pan] ▷ ˈpanˌhandler *n*

Panhellenic (ˌpænhɛˈlɛnɪk) *adj* of or relating to all the Greeks, all Greece, or Panhellenism

Panhellenism (ˌpænˈhɛlɪˌnɪzəm) *n* the principle of or support for the union of all Greeks or all Greece ▷ ˌPanˈhellenist *n* ▷ ˌPanˌhellenˈistic *adj*

panic (ˈpænɪk) *n* **1** a sudden overwhelming feeling of terror or anxiety, esp one affecting a whole group of people **2** (*modifier*) of or resulting from such terror: *panic measures* ▷ *vb* **-ics, -icking, -icked 3** to feel or cause to feel panic [c17 from French *panique,* from New Latin *pānicus,* from Greek *panikos* emanating from PAN, considered as the source of irrational fear] ▷ ˈpanicky *adj*

Panic (ˈpænɪk) *adj* of or relating to the god Pan

panic attack *n* an episode of acute and disabling anxiety associated with such physical symptoms as hyperventilation and sweating. See also **panic disorder**

panic bolt *n* a bolt on the inside esp of double doors that is released by pressure on a waist-high bar: used for emergency exits in theatres, shops, etc

panic button *n* **1** a button or switch that operates any of various safety devices, for use in an emergency **2** **hit** *or* **press the panic button** *informal* to react to a situation by demanding emergency action; become excited; panic

panic buying *n* the buying up of large quantities of a commodity which, it is feared, is likely to be in short supply

panic disorder *n psychiatry* a condition in which a person experiences recurrent panic attacks

panic grass *n* any of various grasses of the genus *Panicum,* such as millet, grown in warm and tropical regions for fodder and grain [C15 *panic,* from Latin *pānicum,* probably a back formation from *pānicula* PANICLE]

panicle (ˈpænɪkəl) *n* **1** a compound raceme, occurring esp in grasses **2** any branched inflorescence [c16 from Latin *pānicula* tuft, diminutive of *panus* thread, ultimately from Greek *penos* web; related to *penion* bobbin] ▷ ˈpanicled *adj*

panicmonger (ˈpænɪkˌmʌŋɡə) *n* a person who spreads panic

panic room *n* a secure room with a separate telephone line within a house, to which a person can flee if someone breaks in

panic stations *pl n informal* a state of alarm; panicky reaction: *when he realized he'd lost the keys it was panic stations*

panic-stricken *or* **panic-struck** *adj* affected by panic

paniculate (pəˈnɪkjʊˌleɪt, -lɪt) *or* **paniculated** *adj botany* growing or arranged in panicles: *a paniculate inflorescence* ▷ paˈnicuˌlately *adv*

panidiomorphic (pænˌɪdɪəʊˈmɔːfɪk) *adj* (of

p

igneous rocks) having well-developed crystals [C19 from PAN- + IDIOMORPHIC]

Panjabi (pʌnˈdʒɑːbɪ) *n, adj* a variant spelling of **Punjabi**

panjandrum (pænˈdʒændrəm) *n* a pompous self-important official or person of rank [C18 after a character, the *Grand Panjandrum*, in a nonsense work (1755) by Samuel Foote, English playwright and actor]

Panjim (ˈpɑːnˌʒɪm) or **Panaji** *n* the capital of the Indian state of Goa (formerly capital of the union territory of Goa, Daman, and Diu until 1987): a port on the Arabian Sea on the coast of Goa. Pop: 58 785 (2001)

pan loaf *n Irish and Scot dialect* a loaf of bread with a light crust all the way round. Often shortened to: **pan** Compare **batch¹** (sense 4)

panmixia (pænˈmɪksɪə) or **panmixis** (pænˈmɪksɪs) *n* (in population genetics) random mating within an interbreeding population [C20 from New Latin, from Greek PAN- + *mixis* act of mating] > **panmictic** (pænˈmɪktɪk) *adj*

Panmunjom (ˈpɑːnˈmʊnˈdʒɒm) *n* a village in the demilitarized zone of Korea: site of truce talks leading to the end of the Korean War (1950–53)

pannage (ˈpænɪdʒ) *n archaic* 1 pasturage for pigs, esp in a forest 2 the right to pasture pigs in a forest 3 payment for this 4 acorns, beech mast, etc, on which pigs feed [C13 from Old French *pasnage*, ultimately from Latin *pastion-, pastiō* feeding, from *pascere* to feed]

panne (pæn) *n* a lightweight velvet fabric [C19 via Old French, from Latin *pinna* wing, feather]

pannier (ˈpænɪə) *n* 1 a large basket, esp one of a pair slung over a beast of burden 2 one of a pair of bags slung either side of the back wheel of a motorcycle, bicycle, etc 3 (esp in the 18th century) **a** a hooped framework to distend a woman's skirt **b** one of two puffed-out loops of material worn drawn back onto the hips to reveal the underskirt [C13 from Old French *panier*, from Latin *pānārium* basket for bread, from *pānis* bread]

pannikin (ˈpænɪkɪn) *n chiefly Brit* a small metal cup or pan [C19 from PAN¹ + -KIN]

pannikin boss *n Austral informal* a person in charge of a few fellow workers

Pannonia (pəˈnəʊnɪə) *n* a region of the ancient world south and west of the Danube: made a Roman province in 6 AD

pannus (ˈpænəs) *n* an inflammatory fleshy lesion on the surface of the eye [C15 from Latin, literally cloth]

panocha (pəˈnəʊtʃə) or **penuche** *n* 1 a coarse grade of sugar made in Mexico 2 (in the US) a sweet made from brown sugar and milk, often with chopped nuts [Mexican Spanish, diminutive of Spanish *pan* bread, from Latin *pānis*]

panoply (ˈpænəplɪ) *n, pl* -plies 1 a complete or magnificent array 2 the entire equipment of a warrior [C17 via French from Greek *panoplia* complete armour, from PAN- + *hopla* armour, pl of *hoplon* tool] > **ˈpanoplied** *adj*

panoptic (pænˈɒptɪk) or **panoptical** *adj* taking in all parts, aspects, etc, in a single view; all-embracing: *a panoptic survey* [C19 from Greek *panoptēs* seeing everything, from PAN- + *optos* visible] > **panˈoptically** *adv*

panorama (ˌpænəˈrɑːmə) *n* 1 an extensive unbroken view, as of a landscape, in all directions 2 a wide or comprehensive survey: *a panorama of the week's events* 3 a large extended picture or series of pictures of a scene, unrolled before spectators a part at a time so as to appear continuous 4 another name for **cyclorama** [C18 from PAN- + Greek *horāma* view] > **panoramic** (ˌpænəˈræmɪk) *adj* > **ˌpanoˈramically** *adv*

panoramic sight *n* a type of artillery sight with a large field of view

pan out *vb* (*intr, adverb*) *informal* to work out; turn out; result

panpipes (ˈpænˌpaɪps) *pl n* (*often singular; often capital*) a number of reeds or whistles of graduated lengths bound together to form a musical wind instrument. Also called: **pipes of Pan, syrinx**

pan potentiometer *n* a control on a stereo sound mixing desk by means of which the relative levels in right- and left-hand channels can be adjusted and hence the apparent position of the recorded or broadcast sound source within the stereo panorama can be controlled. Often shortened to: **pan pot** [C20 from PAN(ORAMIC) + POTENTIOMETER]

panradiometer (ˌpænreɪdɪˈɒmɪtə) *n physics* an instrument used for measuring radiant heat independently of wavelength

Pan-Slavism *n* (esp in the 19th century) the movement for the union of the Slavic peoples, esp under the hegemony of tsarist Russia > **ˈPan-ˈSlavic** *adj*

pansophy (ˈpænsəfɪ) *n* universal knowledge [C17 from New Latin *pansophia*; see PAN-, -SOPHY] > **pansophic** (pænˈsɒfɪk) or **panˈsophical** *adj* > **panˈsophically** *adv*

pansy (ˈpænzɪ) *n, pl* -sies 1 any violaceous garden plant that is a variety of *Viola tricolor*, having flowers with rounded velvety petals, white, yellow, or purple in colour. See also **wild pansy** 2 *slang, offensive* an effeminate or homosexual man or boy 3 **a** a strong violet colour **b** (*as adjective*): *a pansy carpet* [C15 from Old French *pensée* thought, from *penser* to think, from Latin *pensāre*]

pant (pænt) *vb* 1 to breathe with noisy deep gasps, as when out of breath from exertion or excitement 2 to say (something) while breathing thus 3 (*intr; often foll by for*) to have a frantic desire (for); yearn 4 (*intr*) to pulsate; throb rapidly ▷ *n* 5 the act or an instance of panting 6 a short deep gasping noise; puff [C15 from Old French *pantaisier*, from Greek *phantasioun* to have visions, from *phantasia* FANTASY]

Pantagruel (pænˈtægruːɛl) *n* a gigantic prince, noted for his ironical buffoonery, in the satire *Gargantua and Pantagruel* (1534) by the French writer François Rabelais (?1494–1553) > **ˌPantagruˈelian** or **ˌPantagruˈelic** *adj* > **ˌPantaˈgruelˌism** *n* > **ˌPantaˈgruelist** *n*

pantalets or **pantalettes** (ˌpæntəˈlɛts) *pl n* 1 long drawers, usually trimmed with ruffles, extending below the skirts: worn during the early and mid 19th century 2 a pair of ruffles for the ends of such drawers [C19 diminutive of PANTALOONS]

pantaloon (ˌpæntəˈluːn) *n theatre* 1 (in pantomime) an absurd old man, the butt of the clown's tricks 2 (*usually capital*) (in commedia dell'arte) a lecherous old merchant dressed in pantaloons [C16 from French *Pantalon*, from Italian *Pantalone*, local nickname for a Venetian, probably from *San Pantaleone*, a fourth-century Venetian saint]

pantaloons (ˌpæntəˈluːnz) *pl n* 1 **a** *history* men's tight-fitting trousers, esp those fastening under the instep worn in the late 18th and early 19th centuries **b** children's trousers resembling these 2 *informal or facetious* any trousers, esp baggy ones

pantechnicon (pænˈtɛknɪkən) *n Brit* 1 a large van, esp one used for furniture removals 2 a warehouse where furniture is stored [C19 from PAN- + Greek *tekhnikon* relating to the arts, from *tekhnē* art; originally the name of a London bazaar, the building later being used as a furniture warehouse]

Pantelleria (*Italian* pantelleˈriːa) *n* an Italian island in the Mediterranean, between Sicily and Tunisia: of volcanic origin; used by the Romans as a place of banishment. Pop: 7316 (1991 est). Area: 83 sq km (32 sq miles). Ancient name: **Cossyra** (kəˈsaɪrə)

Pan-Teutonism *n* another name for **Pan-Germanism**

Panth (pʌnθ) *n* the Sikh community [from Punjabi: path]

pantheism (ˈpænθɪˌɪzəm) *n* 1 the doctrine that God is the transcendent reality of which man, nature, and the material universe are manifestations 2 any doctrine that regards God as identical with the material universe or the forces of nature 3 readiness to worship all or a large number of gods > **ˈpantheist** *n* > **ˌpantheˈistic** or **ˌpantheˈistical** *adj* > **ˌpantheˈistically** *adv*

pantheon (ˈpænθɪən, ˈpænθɪən) *n* 1 (esp in ancient Greece or Rome) a temple to all the gods 2 all the gods collectively of a religion 3 a monument or building commemorating a nation's dead heroes [C14 via Latin from Greek *Pantheion*, from PAN- + *-theios* divine, from *theos* god]

Pantheon (ˈpænθɪən, ˈpænθɪən) *n* a circular temple in Rome dedicated to all the gods, built by Agrippa in 27 BC, rebuilt by Hadrian 120–24 AD, and used since 609 AD as a Christian church

panther (ˈpænθə) *n, pl* -thers or -ther 1 another name for **leopard** (sense 1), esp the black variety (**black panther**) 2 *US and Canadian* any of various related animals, esp the puma [C14 from Old French *pantère*, from Latin *panthēra*, from Greek *panthēr*; perhaps related to Sanskrit *pundarīka* tiger]

panties (ˈpæntɪz) *pl n* a pair of women's or children's underpants

pantihose (ˈpæntɪˌhəʊz) *pl n chiefly US* a variant spelling of **pantyhose**

pantile (ˈpænˌtaɪl) *n* 1 a roofing tile, with an S-shaped cross section, laid so that the downward curve of one tile overlaps the upward curve of the adjoining tile 2 a tapering roofing tile with a semicircular cross section, laid alternately so that the convex side of one tile overlaps the concave side of adjoining tiles [C17 from PAN¹ + TILE]

pantisocracy (ˌpæntɪˈsɒkrəsɪ) *n* a community, social group, etc, in which all have rule and everyone is equal [C18 (coined by Robert Southey (1774–1843), English poet): from Greek, from PANTO- + *isos* equal + -CRACY]

panto (ˈpæntəʊ) *n, pl* -tos *Brit informal* short for **pantomime** (sense 1)

panto- or before a vowel **pant-** *combining form* all: *pantisocracy; pantofle; pantograph; pantomime* [from Greek *pant-, pas*]

pantofle, pantoffle (pænˈtɒf³l) or **pantoufle** (pænˈtuːf³l) *n archaic* a kind of slipper [C15 from French *pantoufle*, from Old Italian *pantofola*, perhaps from Medieval Greek *pantophellos* shoe made of cork, from PANTO- + *phellos* cork]

pantograph (ˈpæntəˌɡrɑːf) *n* 1 an instrument consisting of pivoted levers for copying drawings, maps, etc, to any desired scale 2 a sliding type of current collector, esp a diamond-shaped frame mounted on a train roof in contact with an overhead wire 3 a device consisting of a parallelogram of jointed rods used to suspend a studio lamp so that its height can be adjusted > **pantographer** (pænˈtɒɡrəfə) *n* > **pantographic** (ˌpæntəˈɡræfɪk) *adj* > **ˌpantoˈgraphically** *adv* > **panˈtography** *n*

pantomime (ˈpæntəˌmaɪm) *n* 1 (in Britain) **a** a kind of play performed at Christmas time characterized by farce, music, lavish sets, stock roles, and topical jokes. Sometimes shortened to: **panto b** (*as modifier*): *a pantomime horse* 2 a theatrical entertainment in which words are replaced by gestures and bodily actions 3 action without words as a means of expression 4 (in ancient Rome) an actor in a dumb show 5 *informal, chiefly Brit* a confused or farcical situation ▷ *vb* 6 another word for **mime** (sense 5) [C17 via Latin from Greek *pantomīmos*; see PANTO-, MIME] > **pantomimic** (ˌpæntəˈmɪmɪk) *adj* > **pantomimist** (ˈpæntəˌmaɪmɪst) *n*

pantothenic acid (ˌpæntəˈθɛnɪk) *n* an oily acid that is a vitamin of the B complex. occurs widely in animal and vegetable foods and is essential for cell growth. Formula: $C_9H_{17}NO_5$ [C20 from Greek *pantothen* from every side]

pantoum (pænˈtuːm) *n prosody* a verse form consisting of a series of quatrains in which the second and fourth lines of each verse are repeated as the first and third lines of the next [C19 via

French from Malay *pantun*]

pantry ('pæntrɪ) *n, pl* **-tries** a small room or cupboard in which provisions, cooking utensils, etc, are kept; larder [c13 via Anglo-Norman, from Old French *paneterie* store for bread, ultimately from Latin *pānis* bread]

pants (pænts) *pl n* **1** *Brit* an undergarment reaching from the waist to the thighs or knees **2** a garment shaped to cover the body from the waist to the ankles or knees with separate tube-shaped sections for both legs. Also called: **trousers 3 bore, scare,** etc, **the pants off** *informal* to bore, scare, etc, extremely ▷ *adj* **4** *Brit slang* inferior [c19 shortened from *pantaloons*; see PANTALOON]

pantsuit ('pænt,sju:t, -,su:t) *n US and Canadian* a woman's suit of a jacket or top and trousers. Also called (in Britain and certain other countries): **trouser suit**

panty girdle ('pæntɪ) *n* a foundation garment with a crotch, often of lighter material than a girdle

pantyhose ('pæntɪ,həʊz) *n US, Canadian, and NZ* a one-piece clinging garment covering the body from the waist to the feet, worn by women in place of stockings. Also called: **pantihose,** (esp Brit) **tights** [c20 from PANTIES + HOSE²]

pantywaist ('pæntɪ,weɪst) *n* **1** a child's undergarment consisting of a shirt and pants buttoned together at the waist **2** *US informal* a man or boy considered as childish, lacking in courage, etc [c20 from PANTIES + WAIST]

panzer ('pænzə; *German* 'pantsər) *n* **1** (*modifier*) of, relating to, or characteristic of the fast mechanized armoured units employed by the German army in World War II: *a panzer attack* **2** a vehicle belonging to a panzer unit, esp a tank **3** (*plural*) armoured troops [c20 from German, from Middle High German, from Old French *panciere* coat of mail, from Latin *pantex* PAUNCH]

panzootic (,pænzəʊ'ɒtɪk) *n vet science* a disease that affects all the animals in a geographical area

Pão de Açúcar (p[ˉə]un di a'sukar) *n* the Portuguese name for the **Sugar Loaf Mountain**

Paoting *or* **Pao-ting** ('paʊ'tɪŋ) *n* a variant transliteration of the Chinese name for **Baoding**

Paotow ('paʊ'taʊ) *n* a variant transliteration of the Chinese name for **Baotou**

pap¹ (pæp) *n* **1** any soft or semiliquid food, such as bread softened with milk, esp for babies or invalids; mash **2** *South African* porridge made from maize **3** worthless or oversimplified ideas; drivel: *intellectual pap* [c15 from Middle Low German *pappe*, via Medieval Latin from Latin *pappāre* to eat; compare Dutch *pap*, Italian *pappa*]

pap² (pæp) *n* **1** *Scot and northern English dialect* a nipple or teat **2 a** something resembling a breast or nipple, such as (formerly) one of a pair of rounded hilltops **b** (*capital as part of a name*): *the Pap of Glencoe* [c12 of Scandinavian origin, imitative of a sucking sound; compare Latin *papilla* nipple, Sanskrit *pippalaka*]

pap³ (pæp) *vb* **-ps, -ping, -ped** (*tr*) (of the paparazzi) to follow and photograph (a famous person) [c20 from PAPARAZZO]

papa¹ (pə'pɑː) *n old-fashioned* an informal word for **father** (sense 1) [c17 from French, a children's word for father; compare Late Latin *pāpa*, Greek *pappa*]

papa² ('pɑːpɑː) *n RC Church* another name for the **pope¹** (sense 1) [c16 from Italian]

papa³ ('pɑːpɑ) *n NZ rare.* a soft blue-grey clay of marine siltstone or sandstone [Māori]

Papa ('pɑːpɑː) *n communications* a code word for the letter *p*

papacy ('peɪpəsɪ) *n, pl* **-cies 1** the office or term of office of a pope **2** the system of government in the Roman Catholic Church that has the pope as its head [c14 from Medieval Latin *pāpātia*, from *pāpa* POPE¹]

papain (pə'peɪɪn, -'paɪɪn) *n* a proteolytic enzyme occurring in the unripe fruit of the papaya tree, *Carica papaya*: used as a meat tenderizer and in medicine as an aid to protein digestion [c19 from PAPAYA]

papal ('peɪp³l) *adj* of or relating to the pope or the papacy > **'papally** *adv*

papal cross *n* a cross with three crosspieces

Papal States *pl n* the temporal domain of the popes in central Italy from 756 AD until the unification of Italy in 1870. Also called: **States of the Church**

Papanicolaou test *or* **smear** (,pæpə'nɪkəlu:) *n* the full name for **Pap test**

paparazzo (,pæpə'rætsəʊ) *n, pl* **-razzi** (-'rætsi:) a freelance photographer who specializes in candid camera shots of famous people and often invades their privacy to obtain such photographs [c20 from Italian]

papauma (pɑː'pɑːu:mə) *n, pl* **papauma** *NZ* another name for **broadleaf** (sense 2) [Māori]

papaveraceous (pə,peɪvə'reɪʃəs) *adj* of, relating to, or belonging to the *Papaveraceae*, a family of plants having large showy flowers and a cylindrical seed capsule with pores beneath the lid: includes the poppies and greater celandine [c19 from New Latin, from Latin *papāver* POPPY]

papaverine (pə'peɪvə,ri:n, -rɪn) *n* a white crystalline almost insoluble alkaloid found in opium and used as an antispasmodic to treat coronary spasms and certain types of colic. Formula: $C_{20}H_{21}NO_4$ [c19 from Latin *papāver* POPPY]

papaw (pə'pɔ:) *or* **pawpaw** *n* **1** another name for **papaya 2** Also called: **custard apple a** a bush or small tree, *Asimina triloba,* of central North America, having small fleshy edible fruit: family *Annonaceae* **b** the fruit of this tree [c16 from Spanish PAPAYA]

papaya (pə'paɪə) *n* **1** a Caribbean evergreen tree, *Carica papaya,* with a crown of large dissected leaves and large green hanging fruit: family *Caricaceae* **2** the fruit of this tree, having a yellow sweet edible pulp and small black seeds ▷ Also called: **papaw, pawpaw** [c15 *papaye,* from Spanish *papaya,* from an American Indian language; compare Carib *ababai*] > **pa'payan** *adj*

Papeete (,pɑːpɪ'i:tɪ) *n* the capital of French Polynesia, on the NW coast of Tahiti: one of the largest towns in the S Pacific. Pop: 130 000 (2005 est)

paper ('peɪpə) *n* **1** a substance made from cellulose fibres derived from rags, wood, etc, often with other additives, and formed into flat thin sheets suitable for writing on, decorating walls, wrapping, etc. Related adj: **papyraceous 2** a single piece of such material, esp if written or printed on **3** (*usually plural*) documents for establishing the identity of the bearer; credentials **4** (*plural*) Also called: **ship's papers** official documents relating to the ownership, cargo, etc, of a ship **5** (*plural*) collected diaries, letters, etc **6** See **newspaper** or **wallpaper 7** *government* See **white paper, green paper, command paper 8** a lecture or short published treatise on a specific subject **9** a short essay, as by a student **10 a** a set of written examination questions **b** the student's answers **11** *commerce* See **commercial paper 12** *theatre slang* a free ticket **13 on paper** in theory, as opposed to fact: *it was a good idea on paper, but failed in practice* ▷ *adj* **14** made of paper: *paper cups do not last long* **15** thin like paper: *paper walls* **16** (*prenominal*) existing only as recorded on paper but not yet in practice: *paper profits; paper expenditure* **17** taking place in writing: *paper battles* ▷ *vb* **18** to cover (walls) with wallpaper **19** (*tr*) to cover or furnish with paper **20** (*tr*) *theatre slang* to fill (a performance) by giving away free tickets (esp in the phrase **paper the house**) ▷ See also **paper over** [c14 from Latin PAPYRUS] > **'paperer** *n*

paperback ('peɪpə,bæk) *n* **1** a book or edition with covers made of flexible card, sold relatively cheaply. Compare **hardback** ▷ *adj also* **paperbound, soft-cover 2** of or denoting a paperback or publication of paperbacks ▷ *vb* (*tr*) **3** to publish in paperback > **'paper,backer** *n*

paperbark ('peɪpə,bɑ:k) *n* **1** any of several Australian myrtaceous trees of the genus *Melaleuca,* esp *M. quinquenervia,* of swampy regions, having spear-shaped leaves and papery bark that can be peeled off in thin layers **2** the papery bark of any of these trees

paperboard ('peɪpə,bɔ:d) *n* **a** a thick cardboard made of compressed layers of paper pulp; pasteboard **b** (*as modifier*): *a paperboard box*

paperboy ('peɪpə,bɔɪ) *n* a boy employed to deliver newspapers, magazines, etc > **'paper,girl** *fem n*

paper chase *n* a former type of cross-country run in which a runner laid a trail of paper for others to follow

paperclip ('peɪpə,klɪp) *n* a clip for holding sheets of paper together, esp one made of bent wire

paper-cutter *n* a machine for cutting paper, usually a blade mounted over a table on which paper can be aligned

paper filigree *n* another name for **rolled paperwork**

paperhanger ('peɪpə,hæŋə) *n* **1** a person who hangs wallpaper as an occupation **2** *US slang* a counterfeiter > **'paper,hanging** *n*

paperknife ('peɪpə,naɪf) *n, pl* **-knives** a knife with a comparatively blunt blade, esp one of wood, bone, etc, for opening sealed envelopes

paperless ('peɪpəlɪs) *adj* of, relating to, or denoting a means of communication, record keeping, etc, esp electronic, that does not use paper: *the paperless office*

paper money *n* paper currency issued by the government or the central bank as legal tender and which circulates as a substitute for specie

paper mulberry *n* a small moraceous E Asian tree, *Broussonetia papyrifera,* the inner bark of which was formerly used for making paper in Japan. See also **tapa**

paper nautilus *n* any cephalopod mollusc of the genus *Argonauta,* esp *A. argo,* of warm and tropical seas, having a papery external spiral shell: order *Octopoda* (octopods). Also called: **argonaut** Compare **pearly nautilus**

paper over *vb* (*tr, adverb*) to conceal (something controversial or unpleasant)

paper tape *n* a strip of paper for recording information in the form of rows of either six or eight holes, some or all of which are punched to produce a combination used as a discrete code symbol, formerly used in computers, telex machines, etc. US equivalent: **perforated tape**

paper tiger *n* a nation, institution, etc, that appears powerful but is in fact weak or insignificant [c20 translation of a Chinese phrase first applied to the US]

paperweight ('peɪpə,weɪt) *n* a small heavy object placed on loose papers to prevent them from scattering

paperwork ('peɪpə,w3:k) *n* clerical work, such as the completion of forms or the writing of reports or letters

papery ('peɪpərɪ) *adj* like paper, esp in thinness, flimsiness, or dryness > **'paperiness** *n*

papeterie ('pæpətrɪ; *French* papetri) *n* a box or case for papers and other writing materials [c19 from French, from *papetier* maker of paper, from *papier* PAPER]

Paphian ('peɪfɪən) *adj* **1** of or relating to Paphos **2** of or relating to Aphrodite **3** *literary* of sexual love

Paphlagonia (,pæflə'gəʊnɪə) *n* an ancient country and Roman province in N Asia Minor, on the Black Sea

Paphos¹ ('peɪfɒs) *n* a village in SW Cyprus, near the sites of two ancient cities: famous as the centre of Aphrodite worship and traditionally the place at which she landed after her birth among the waves. Pop: 32 575 (1992 est)

Paphos² ('peɪfɒs), **Paphus** ('peɪfəs) *n Greek myth* the son of Pygmalion and Galatea, who succeeded his father on the throne of Cyprus

Papiamento (*Spanish* papja'mento) *n* a creolized

Spanish spoken in the Netherlands Antilles [Spanish, from *papia* talk]

papier collé (*French* papje kɔle) *n* a type of collage, usually of an abstract design [French, literally: glued paper]

papier-mâché (ˌpæpjeɪˈmæʃeɪ; *French* papjemaʃe) *n* **1** a hard strong substance suitable for painting on, made of paper pulp or layers of paper mixed with paste, size, etc, and moulded when moist ▷ *adj* **2** made of papier-mâché [c18 from French, literally: chewed paper]

papilla (pəˈpɪlə) *n, pl* -lae (-liː) **1** the small projection of tissue at the base of a hair, tooth, or feather **2** any other similar protuberance **3** any minute blunt hair or process occurring in plants [c18 from Latin: nipple; related to Latin *papula* pimple] > paˈpillary, ˈpapillate *or* ˈpapillose *adj*

papilloma (ˌpæpɪˈləʊmə) *n, pl* -mata (-mətə) *or* -mas *pathol* a benign tumour derived from epithelial tissue and forming a rounded or lobulated mass [c19 from PAPILLA + -OMA] > ˌpapilˈlomatous *adj* > ˌpapilˈlomaˈtosis *n*

papillon (ˈpæpɪˌlɒn) *n* a breed of toy spaniel with large ears [French: butterfly, from Latin *pāpiliō*]

papillote (ˈpæpɪˌləʊt) *n* **1** a paper frill around cutlets, etc **2** en papillote (*French* ɑ̃ papijɔt) (of food) cooked in oiled greaseproof paper or foil [c18 from French PAPILLON]

papist (ˈpeɪpɪst) *n, adj* (often capital) usually *disparaging* another term for **Roman Catholic** [c16 from French *papiste*, from Church Latin *pāpa* POPE[1]] > paˈpistical *or* paˈpistic *adj* > ˈpapistry *n*

papoose *or* **pappoose** (pəˈpuːs) *n* **1** an American Indian baby or child **2** a pouchlike bag used for carrying a baby, worn on the back [c17 from Algonquian *papoos*]

pappus (ˈpæpəs) *n, pl* pappi (ˈpæpaɪ) a ring of fine feathery hairs surrounding the fruit in composite plants, such as the thistle; aids dispersal of the fruits by the wind [c18 via New Latin, from Greek *pappos* grandfather, old man, old man's beard, hence: pappus, down] > ˈpappose *or* ˈpappous *adj*

pappy[1] (ˈpæpɪ) *adj* -pier, -piest resembling pap; mushy

pappy[2] (ˈpæpɪ) *n, pl* -pies US an informal word for **father**

paprika (ˈpæprɪkə, pæˈpriː-) *n* **1** a mild powdered seasoning made from a sweet variety of red pepper **2** the fruit or plant from which this seasoning is obtained [c19 via Hungarian from Serbian, from *papar* PEPPER]

Pap test *or* **smear** (pæp) *n med* **1** another name for **cervical smear** **2** a similar test for precancerous cells in other organs ▷ Also called: **Papanicolaou smear** [c20 named after George *Papanicolaou* (1883–1962), US anatomist, who devised it]

Papua (ˈpæpjʊə) *n* **1** Territory of a former territory of Australia, consisting of SE New Guinea and adjacent islands: now part of Papua New Guinea. Former name (1888–1906): British New Guinea **2** the W part of the island of New Guinea: formerly under Dutch rule, becoming a province of Indonesia in 1963. Capital: Jayapura. Pop: 2 220 934 (2000). Area: 416 990 sq km (161 000 sq miles). Former names (until 1962): Dutch New Guinea, Netherlands New Guinea Former Indonesian names: Irian Barat (1962-1973); Irian Jaya (1973-2001) Former English name: West Irian (translation of Irian Barat) **3** Gulf of an inlet of the Coral Sea in the SE coast of New Guinea

Papuan (ˈpæpjʊən) *adj* **1** of or relating to Papua or any of the languages spoken there ▷ *n* **2** a native or inhabitant of Papua New Guinea **3** any of several languages of Papua New Guinea that apparently do not belong to the Malayo-Polynesian family

Papua New Guinea *n* a country in the SW Pacific; consists of the E half of New Guinea, the Bismarck Archipelago, the W Solomon Islands, Trobriand Islands, D'Entrecasteaux Islands, Woodlark Island, and the Louisiade Archipelago;

administered by Australia from 1949 until 1975, when it became an independent member of the Commonwealth. Official language: English; Tok Pisin (English Creole) and Motu are widely spoken. Religion: Christian majority. Currency: kina. Capital: Port Moresby. Pop: 5 836 000 (2004 est). Area: 461 693 sq km (178 260 sq miles)

papule (ˈpæpjuːl) *or* **papula** (ˈpæpjʊlə) *n, pl* -ules *or* -ulae (-jʊˌliː) *pathol* a small solid usually round elevation of the skin [c19 from Latin *papula* pustule, pimple] > ˈpapular *adj* > ˌpapuˈliferous *adj*

papyraceous (ˌpæpɪˈreɪʃəs) *adj* of, relating to, made of, or resembling paper [c18 from PAPYRUS + -ACEOUS; see PAPER]

papyrology (ˌpæpɪˈrɒlədʒɪ) *n* the study of ancient papyri > **papyrological** (ˌpæpɪrəˈlɒdʒɪkəl) *adj* > ˌpapyˈrologist *n*

papyrus (pəˈpaɪrəs) *n, pl* -ri (-raɪ) *or* -ruses **1** a tall aquatic cyperaceous plant, *Cyperus papyrus*, of S Europe and N and central Africa with small green-stalked flowers arranged like umbrella spokes around the stem top **2** a kind of paper made from the stem pith of this plant, used by the ancient Egyptians, Greeks, and Romans **3** an ancient document written on this paper [c14 via Latin from Greek *papūros* reed used in making paper]

par (pɑː) *n* **1** an accepted level or standard, such as an average (esp in the phrase **up to par**) **2** a state of equality (esp in the phrase **on a par with**) **3** *finance* the established value of the unit of one national currency in terms of the unit of another where both are based on the same metal standard **4** *commerce* **a** See **par value** **b** the condition of equality between the current market value of a share, bond, etc, and its face value (the **nominal par**). This equality is indicated by **at par**, while **above** (or **below**) **par** indicates that the market value is above (or below) face value **5** *golf* an estimated standard score for a hole or course that a good player should make: *par for the course was 72* **6** **below** or **under par** not feeling or performing as well as normal **7** **par for the course** an expected or normal occurrence or situation ▷ *adj* **8** average or normal **9** (usually prenominal) *commerce* of or relating to par: *par value* [c17 from Latin *pār* equal, on a level; see PEER[1]]

par. *abbreviation for* **1** paragraph **2** parenthesis **3** parish

Par. *abbreviation for* Paraguay

par- *prefix* a variant of para-[1] before a vowel

para[1] (ˈpɑːrə) *n, pl* -ras *or* -ra a monetary unit of Serbia worth one hundredth of a dinar; formerly a monetary unit of Yugoslavia [c17 Serbo-Croat, via Turkish from Persian *pārah* piece, portion]

para[2] (ˈpærə) *n informal* **1** **a** a soldier in an airborne unit **b** an airborne unit **2** a paragraph

para[3] (ˈpɑːrɑː) *n, pl* para a New Zealand fern, *Marattia salicina*, with long heavy fronds. Also called: **horseshoe fern, king fern** [Māori]

Pará (*Portuguese* paˈra) *n* **1** a state of N Brazil, on the Atlantic: mostly dense tropical rainforest. Capital: Belém. Pop: 6 453 683 (2002). Area: 1 248 042 sq km (474 896 sq miles) **2** another name for **Belém** **3** an estuary in N Brazil into which flow the Tocantins River and a branch of the Amazon. Length: about 320 km (200 miles)

para-[1] *or before a vowel* **par-** *prefix* **1** beside; near: *parameter; parathyroid* **2** beyond: *parapsychology* **3** resembling: *paramnesia* **4** defective; abnormal: *paraesthesia* **5** subsidiary to: *paraphysis* **6** (usually in italics) denoting that an organic compound contains a benzene ring with substituents attached to atoms that are directly opposite across the ring (the 1,4- positions): *paradinitrobenzene; para-cresol*. Abbreviation: *p-* Compare **ortho-** (sense 4), **meta-** (sense 4) **7** denoting an isomer, polymer, or compound related to a specified compound: *paraldehyde; paracasein* **8** denoting the form of a diatomic substance in which the spins of the two constituent atoms are antiparallel: *parahydrogen*. Compare **ortho-** (sense 6) [from Greek *para* (prep)

alongside, beyond]

para-[2] *combining form* indicating an object that acts as a protection against something: *parachute; parasol* [via French from Italian *para-*, from *parare* to defend, shield against, ultimately from Latin *parāre* to prepare]

para-aminobenzoic acid *n biochem* an acid present in yeast and liver: used in the manufacture of dyes and pharmaceuticals. Formula: $C_6H_4(NH_2)COOH$

parabasis (pəˈræbəsɪs) *n, pl* -ses (-ˌsiːz) (in classical Greek comedy) an address from the chorus to the audience [c19 from Greek, from *parabanein* to step forward]

parabiosis (ˌpærəbaɪˈəʊsɪs) *n* **1** the natural union of two individuals, such as Siamese twins, so that they share a common circulation of the blood **2** a similar union induced for experimental or therapeutic purposes [c20 from PARA-[1] + Greek *biōsis* manner of life, from *bios* life] > **parabiotic** (ˌpærəbaɪˈɒtɪk) *adj*

parablast (ˈpærəˌblæst) *n* the yolk of an egg, such as a hen's egg, that undergoes meroblastic cleavage [c19 from PARA-[1] + -BLAST] > ˌparaˈblastic *adj*

parable (ˈpærəbəl) *n* **1** a short story that uses familiar events to illustrate a religious or ethical point. Related adjs: **parabolic, parabolical 2** any of the stories of this kind told by Jesus Christ [c14 from Old French *parabole*, from Latin *parabola* comparison, from Greek *parabolē* analogy, from *paraballein* to throw alongside, from PARA-[1] + *ballein* to throw] > **parabolist** (pəˈræbəlɪst) *n*

parabola (pəˈræbələ) *n* a conic section formed by the intersection of a cone by a plane parallel to its side. Standard equation: $y^2 = 4ax$, where $2a$ is the distance between focus and directrix [c16 via New Latin from Greek *parabolē* a setting alongside; see PARABLE]

parabolic[1] (ˌpærəˈbɒlɪk) *adj* **1** of, relating to, or shaped like a parabola **2** shaped like a paraboloid: *a parabolic mirror*

parabolic[2] (ˌpærəˈbɒlɪk) *or* **parabolical** *adj* of or resembling a parable > ˌparaˈbolically *adv*

parabolic aerial *n* a formal name for **dish aerial**

parabolize[1] *or* **parabolise** (pəˈræbəˌlaɪz) *vb* (tr) to explain by a parable

parabolize[2] *or* **parabolise** (pəˈræbəˌlaɪz) *vb* (tr) to shape like a parabola or paraboloid > paˌraboliˈzation *or* paˌraboliˈsation *n*

paraboloid (pəˈræbəˌlɔɪd) *n* a geometric surface whose sections parallel to two coordinate planes are parabolic and whose sections parallel to the third plane are either elliptical or hyperbolic. Equations $x^2/a^2 \pm y^2/b^2 = 2cz$ > paˌraboˈloidal *adj*

parabrake (ˈpærəˌbreɪk) *n* another name for **brake parachute**

paracasein (ˌpærəˈkeɪsɪɪn, -siːn) *n US* another name for **casein**

Paracel Islands (ˌpærəˈsɛl) *n* a group of uninhabited islets and reefs in the N South China Sea, the subject of territorial claims by China and Vietnam. Compare **Spratly Islands**

paracentesis (ˌpærəsɛnˈtiːsɪs) *n med* the surgical puncture of a body cavity in order to draw off excess fluid

paracetamol (ˌpærəˈsiːtəˌmɒl, -ˈsɛtə-) *n* a mild analgesic and antipyretic drug used as an alternative to aspirin. US name: **acetaminophen** [c20 from *para-acetamidophenol*]

parachronism (pəˈrækrəˌnɪzəm) *n* an error in dating, esp by giving too late a date. Compare **prochronism** [c17 from PARA-[1] + *-chronism*, as in ANACHRONISM]

parachute (ˈpærəˌʃuːt) *n* **1 a** a device used to retard the fall of a man or package from an aircraft, consisting of a large fabric canopy connected to a harness **b** (as modifier): *parachute troops*. Sometimes shortened to: **chute** See also **brake parachute** ▷ *vb* **2** (of troops, supplies, etc) to land or cause to land by parachute from an aircraft **3** (in an election) to bring in (a candidate, esp someone well known) from outside the constituency [c18 from French, from PARA-² + *chute* fall] > ˈparaˌchutist *n*

paraclete (ˈpærəˌkliːt) *n rare* a mediator or advocate

Paraclete (ˈpærəˌkliːt) *n Christianity* the Holy Ghost as comforter or advocate [c15 via Old French from Church Latin *Paraclētus,* from Late Greek *Paraklētos* advocate, from Greek *parakalein* to summon as a helper, from PARA-¹ + *kalein* to call]

parade (pəˈreɪd) *n* 1 an ordered, esp ceremonial, march, assembly, or procession, as of troops being reviewed: *on parade* 2 Also called: **parade ground** a place where military formations regularly assemble 3 a visible show or display: *to make a parade of one's grief* 4 a public promenade or street of shops 5 a successive display of things or people 6 the interior area of a fortification 7 a parry in fencing 8 **rain on someone's parade** to hinder someone's enjoyment; upset someone's plans 9 **on parade a** on display **b** showing oneself off ▷ *vb* 10 (when *intr,* often foll by *through* or *along*) to walk or march, esp in a procession (through): *to parade the streets* 11 (*tr*) to exhibit or flaunt: *he was parading his medals* 12 (*tr*) to cause to assemble in formation, as for a military parade 13 (*intr*) to walk about in a public place [c17 from French: a making ready, a setting out, a boasting display; compare Italian *parata,* Spanish *parada,* all ultimately from Latin *parāre* to prepare] > paˈrader *n*

paradiddle (ˈpærəˌdɪdəl) *n* a group of four drum beats produced by using alternate sticks in the pattern right-left-right-right or left-right-left-left [c20 of imitative origin]

paradigm (ˈpærəˌdaɪm) *n* 1 *grammar* the set of all the inflected forms of a word or a systematic arrangement displaying these forms 2 a pattern or model 3 a typical or stereotypical example (esp in the phrase **paradigm case**) 4 (in the philosophy of science) a very general conception of the nature of scientific endeavour within which a given enquiry is undertaken [c15 via French and Latin from Greek *paradeigma* pattern, from *paradeiknunai* to compare, from PARA-¹ + *deiknunai* to show] > paradigmatic (ˌpærədɪɡˈmætɪk) *adj*

paradigm shift *n* a radical change in underlying beliefs or theory [c20 coined by T.S. Kuhn (1922–96), US philosopher of science]

paradisal (ˌpærəˈdaɪsəl), **paradisiacal** (ˌpærədɪˈsaɪəkəl) or **paradisiac** (ˌpærəˈdɪsɪˌæk) *adj* of, relating to, or resembling paradise

paradise (ˈpærəˌdaɪs) *n* 1 heaven as the ultimate abode or state of the righteous 2 *Islam* the sensual garden of delights that the Koran promises the faithful after death 3 Also called: **limbo** (according to some theologians) the intermediate abode or state of the just prior to the Resurrection of Jesus, as in Luke 23:43 4 the place or state of happiness enjoyed by Adam before the first sin; the Garden of Eden 5 any place or condition that fulfils all one's desires or aspirations 6 a park in which foreign animals are kept [Old English, from Church Latin *paradīsus,* from Greek *paradeisos* garden, of Persian origin; compare Avestan *pairidaēza* enclosed area, from *pairi-* around + *daēza* wall]

paradise duck *n* a large duck, *Casarca variegata,* of New Zealand, having a brightly coloured plumage. Also called: **putangitangi**

paradise fish *n* any of several beautifully coloured labyrinth fishes of the genus *Macropodus,* esp *M. opercularis,* of S and SE Asia

parador (ˈpærədɔː; *Spanish* ˈparaðor) *n, pl* -**dors** or -**dores** a state run hotel in Spain [Spanish]

parados (ˈpærəˌdɒs) *n* a bank behind a trench or other fortification, giving protection from being fired on from the rear [c19 from French, from PARA-² + *dos* back, from Latin *dorsum;* compare PARASOL, PARAPET]

paradox (ˈpærəˌdɒks) *n* 1 a seemingly absurd or self-contradictory statement that is or may be true: *religious truths are often expressed in paradox* 2 a self-contradictory proposition, such as *I always tell lies* 3 a person or thing exhibiting apparently contradictory characteristics 4 an opinion that conflicts with common belief [c16 from Late Latin *paradoxum,* from Greek *paradoxos* opposed to existing notions, from PARA-¹ + *doxa* opinion] > ˌparaˈdoxical *adj* > ˌparaˈdoxically *adv*

paradoxical intention *n* (in psychotherapy) the deliberate practice of a neurotic habit or thought, undertaken in order to remove it

paradoxical sleep *n physiol* sleep that appears to be deep but that is characterized by a brain wave pattern similar to that of wakefulness, rapid eye movements, and heavier breathing

paradrop (ˈpærəˌdrɒp) *n* the delivery of personnel or equipment from an aircraft by parachute

paraesthesia or US **paresthesia** (ˌpærɛsˈθiːzɪə) *n pathol* an abnormal or inappropriate sensation in an organ, part, or area of the skin, as of burning, prickling, tingling, etc > **paraesthetic** or US **paresthetic** (ˌpærɛsˈθɛtɪk) *adj*

paraffin (ˈpærəfɪn) or *less commonly* **paraffine** (ˈpærəˌfiːn) *n* 1 Also called: **paraffin oil,** (esp US and Canadian) **kerosene** a liquid mixture consisting mainly of alkane hydrocarbons with boiling points in the range 150°–300°C, used as an aircraft fuel, in domestic heaters, and as a solvent 2 another name for **alkane** 3 See **paraffin wax** 4 See **liquid paraffin** ▷ *vb* (*tr*) 5 to treat with paraffin or paraffin wax [c19 from German, from Latin *parum* too little + *affinis* adjacent; so called from its chemical inertia]

paraffin wax *n* a white insoluble odourless waxlike solid consisting mainly of alkane hydrocarbons with melting points in the range 50°–60°C, used in candles, waterproof paper, and as a sealing agent. Also called: **paraffin**

paraformaldehyde (ˌpærəfɔːˈmældɪˌhaɪd) or **paraform** (ˈpærəˌfɔːm) *n* a white amorphous solid polymeric form of formaldehyde: used as a convenient source of formaldehyde and as a fumigant. Formula: $(CH_2O)n$, where *n* lies between 6 and 50

paragenesis (ˌpærəˈdʒɛnɪsɪs) or **paragenesia** (ˌpærədʒɪˈniːzɪə) *n* a characteristic association of minerals in a particular type of rock or ore deposit > **paragenetic** (ˌpærədʒɪˈnɛtɪk) *adj* > ˌparageˈnetically *adv*

paragliding (ˈpærəˌɡlaɪdɪŋ) *n* the sport of cross-country gliding using a specially designed parachute shaped like flexible wings. > ˈparaˌglider *n*

paragnathous (ˌpærəɡˈneɪθəs) *adj* (of certain vertebrates) having the upper and lower jaws of equal length

paragoge (ˌpærəˈɡəʊdʒɪ) or **paragogue** (ˈpærəˌɡɒɡ) *n* the addition of a sound or a syllable to the end of a word, such as *st* in *amongst* [c17 via Late Latin from Greek *paragōgē* an alteration, ultimately from *paragein* to lead past, change] > **paragogic** (ˌpærəˈɡɒdʒɪk) or ˌparaˈgogical *adj* > ˌparaˈgogically *adv*

paragon (ˈpærəɡən) *n* 1 a model of excellence; pattern: *a paragon of virtue* 2 a size of printer's type, approximately equal to 20 point ▷ *vb* (*tr*) 3 *archaic* **a** to equal or surpass **b** to compare **c** to regard as a paragon [c16 via French from Old Italian *paragone* comparison, from Medieval Greek *parakonē* whetstone, from Greek *parakonan* to sharpen against, from PARA-¹ + *akonan* to sharpen, from *akonē* whetstone]

paragraph (ˈpærəˌɡrɑːf, -ˌɡræf) *n* 1 (in a piece of writing) one of a series of subsections each usually devoted to one idea and each usually marked by the beginning of a new line, indentation, increased interlinear space, etc 2 *printing* the character ¶, used as a reference mark or to indicate the beginning of a new paragraph 3 a short article in a newspaper ▷ *vb* (*tr*) 4 to form into paragraphs 5 to express or report in a paragraph [c16 from Medieval Latin *paragraphus,*

from Greek *paragraphos* line drawing attention to part of a text, from *paragraphein* to write beside, from PARA-¹ + *graphein* to write] > **paragraphic** (ˌpærəˈɡræfɪk) or ˌparaˈgraphical *adj* > ˌparaˈgraphically *adv*

paragraphia (ˌpærəˈɡrɑːfɪə) *n psychiatry* the habitual writing of a different word or letter from the one intended, often the result of a mental disorder or brain injury [c20 from New Latin; see PARA-¹, -GRAPH]

Paraguay (ˈpærəˌɡwaɪ) *n* 1 an inland republic in South America: colonized by the Spanish from 1537, gaining independence in 1811; lost 142 500 sq km (55 000 sq miles) of territory and over half its population after its defeat in the war against Argentina, Brazil, and Uruguay (1865–70). It is divided by the Paraguay River into a sparsely inhabited semiarid region (Chaco) in the west, and a central region of wooded hills, tropical forests, and rich grasslands, rising to the Paraná plateau in the east. Official languages: Spanish and Guarani. Religion: Roman Catholic majority. Currency: guarani. Capital: Asunción. Pop: 6 018 000 (2004 est). Area: 406 750 sq km (157 047 sq miles) 2 a river in South America flowing south through Brazil and Paraguay to the Paraná River. Length: about 2400 km (1500 miles)

Paraguayan (ˌpærəˈɡwaɪən) *adj* 1 of or relating to Paraguay or its inhabitants ▷ *n* 2 a native or inhabitant of Paraguay

Paraguay tea *n* another name for **maté**

parahydrogen (ˌpærəˈhaɪdrədʒən) *n chem* the form of molecular hydrogen (constituting about 25 per cent of the total at normal temperatures) in which the nuclei of the two atoms in each molecule spin in opposite directions. Compare **orthohydrogen**

Paraíba (*Portuguese* paraˈiba) *n* 1 a state of NE Brazil, on the Atlantic: consists of a coastal strip, with hills and plains inland; irrigated agriculture. Capital: João Pessoa. Pop: 3 494 893 (2002). Area: 56 371 sq km (21 765 sq miles) 2 Also called: **Paraíba do Sul** (ˈduː sul) a river in SE Brazil, flowing southwest and then northeast to the Atlantic near Campos. Length: 1060 km (660 miles) 3 Also called: **Paraíba do Norte** (ˈduː ˈnɔrtə) a river in NE Brazil, in Paraíba state, flowing northeast and east to the Atlantic. Length: 386 km (240 miles) 4 the former name (until 1930) of **João Pessoa**

para-influenza virus *n* any of a group of viruses that cause respiratory infections with influenza-like symptoms, esp in children

parakeet or **parrakeet** (ˈpærəˌkiːt) *n* any of numerous small usually brightly coloured long-tailed parrots, such as *Psittacula krameri* (**ring-necked parakeet**), of Africa [c16 from Spanish *periquito* and Old French *paroquet* parrot, of uncertain origin]

parakelia or **parakeelya** (ˌpærəˈkiːljə) *n* a succulent herb of the genus *Calandrinia,* with purple flowers, that thrives in inland Australia [from a native Australian language]

paralalia (ˌpærəˈleɪlɪə) *n* any of various speech disorders, esp the production of a sound different from that intended

paralanguage (ˈpærəˌlæŋɡwɪdʒ) *n linguistics* nonverbal elements in speech, such as intonation, that may affect the meaning of an utterance

paraldehyde (pəˈrældɪˌhaɪd) *n* a colourless liquid substance that is a cyclic trimer of acetaldehyde: used in making dyestuffs and as a hypnotic and anticonvulsant drug. Formula: $(C_2H_4O)_3$

paralegal (ˌpærəˈliːɡəl) *n* 1 a person trained to undertake legal work but not qualified as a professional solicitor or barrister ▷ *adj* 2 of or designating such a person

paralexia (ˌpærəˈlɛksɪə) *n* a disorder of the ability to read in which words and syllables are meaninglessly transposed > ˌparaˈlexic *adj*

paralimnion (ˌpærəˈlɪmnɪɒn) *n ecology* the region of a lake floor between the shoreline or water's

p

edge and the zone of rooted vegetation [from PARA-[1] + Greek *limnē* lake]

paralinguistics (ˌpærəlɪŋˈɡwɪstɪks) *n* (*functioning as singular*) the study of paralanguage > ˌparalinˈguistic *adj*

paralipomena (ˌpærəlaɪˈpɒmənə) *pl n* **1** things added in a supplement to a work **2** *Old Testament* another name for the Books of **Chronicles** [c14 via late Latin from Greek *paraleipomena*, from PARA-[1] (on one side) + *leipein* to leave]

paralipsis (ˌpærəˈlɪpsɪs) *or* **paraleipsis** (ˌpærəˈlaɪpsɪs) *n, pl* **-ses** (-siːz) a rhetorical device in which an idea is emphasized by the pretence that it is too obvious to discuss, as in *there are many drawbacks to your plan, not to mention the cost* [c16 via Late Latin from Greek: neglect, from *paraleipein* to leave aside, from PARA-[1] + *leipein* to leave]

parallax (ˈpærəˌlæks) *n* **1** an apparent change in the position of an object resulting from a change in position of the observer **2** *astronomy* the angle subtended at a celestial body, esp a star, by the radius of the earth's orbit. **Annual** or **heliocentric parallax** is the apparent displacement of a nearby star resulting from its observation from the earth. **Diurnal** or **geocentric parallax** results from the observation of a planet, the sun, or the moon from the surface of the earth [c17 via French from New Latin *parallaxis*, from Greek: change, from *parallassein* to change, from PARA-[1] + *allassein* to alter] > **parallactic** (ˌpærəˈlæktɪk) *adj* > ˌparalˈlactically *adv*

parallel (ˈpærəˌlɛl) *adj* (when *postpositive*, usually foll by *to*) **1** separated by an equal distance at every point; never touching or intersecting: *parallel walls* **2** corresponding; similar: *parallel situations* **3** *music* **a** Also: **consecutive** (of two or more parts or melodies) moving in similar motion but keeping the same interval apart throughout: *parallel fifths* **b** denoting successive chords in which the individual notes move in parallel motion **4** *grammar* denoting syntactic constructions in which the constituents of one construction correspond to those of the other **5** *computing* operating on several items of information, instructions, etc, simultaneously. Compare **serial** (sense 6) ▷ *n* **6** *maths* one of a set of parallel lines, planes, etc **7** an exact likeness **8** a comparison **9** Also called: **parallel of latitude** any of the imaginary lines around the earth parallel to the equator, designated by degrees of latitude ranging from 0° at the equator to 90° at the poles **10 a** a configuration of two or more electrical components connected between two points in a circuit so that the same voltage is applied to each (esp in the phrase **in parallel**) **b** (*as modifier*): *a parallel circuit* ▷ Compare **series** (sense 6) **11** *printing* the character (∥) used as a reference mark **12** a trench or line lying in advance of and parallel to other defensive positions ▷ *vb* **-lels**, **-leling**, **-leled** (*tr*) **13** to make parallel **14** to supply a parallel to **15** to be a parallel to or correspond with: *your experience parallels mine* [c16 via French and Latin from Greek *parallēlos* alongside one another, from PARA-[1] + *allēlos* one another]

parallel bars *pl n gymnastics* **a** (*functioning as plural*) a pair of wooden bars on uprights, sometimes at different heights, for various exercises **b** (*functioning as singular*) an event in a gymnastic competition in which competitors exercise on such bars

parallelepiped, parallelopiped (ˌpærəˌlɛləˈpaɪpɛd) *or* **parallelepipedon** (ˌpærəˌlɛləˈpaɪpɪdən) *n* a geometric solid whose six faces are parallelograms [c16 from Greek *parallēlepipedon*; from *parallēlos* PARALLEL + *epipedon* plane surface, from EPI- + *pedon* ground]

parallel importing *n* the importing of certain goods, esp pharmaceutical drugs, by dealers who undersell local manufacturers

paralleling (ˈpærəˌlɛlɪŋ) *n* a form of trading in which companies buy highly priced goods in a market in which the prices are low in order to be able to sell them in a market in which the prices are higher

parallelism (ˈpærəlɛˌlɪzəm) *n* **1** the state of being parallel **2** *grammar* the repetition of a syntactic construction in successive sentences for rhetorical effect **3** *philosophy* the dualistic doctrine that mental and physical processes are regularly correlated but are not causally connected, so that, for example, pain always accompanies, but is not caused by, a pin-prick. Compare **interactionism, occasionalism.** > ˈparalˌlelist *n, adj*

parallelogram (ˌpærəˈlɛləˌɡræm) *n* a quadrilateral whose opposite sides are parallel and equal in length. See also **rhombus, rectangle, trapezium, trapezoid** [c16 via French from Late Latin, from Greek *parallēlogrammon*, from *parallēlos* PARALLEL + *grammē* line, related to *graphein* to write]

parallelogram rule *n maths, physics* a rule for finding the resultant of two vectors by constructing a parallelogram with two adjacent sides representing the magnitudes and directions of the vectors, the diagonal through the point of intersection of the vectors representing their resultant

parallel port *n computing* (on a computer) a socket that can be used for connecting devices that send and receive data at more than one bit at a time; often used for connecting printers

parallel processing *n* the performance by a computer system of two or more simultaneous operations

parallel resonance *n* the resonance that results when circuit elements are connected with their inductance and capacitance in parallel, so that the impedance of the combination rises to a maximum at the resonant frequency. Compare **series resonance**

parallel ruler *n engineering* a drawing instrument in which two parallel edges are connected so that they remain parallel, although the distance between them can be varied

parallel turn *n skiing* a turn, executed by shifting one's weight, in which the skis stay parallel

paralogism (pəˈrælədˌʒɪzəm) *n* **1** *logic, psychol* an argument that is unintentionally invalid. Compare **sophism 2** any invalid argument or conclusion [c16 via Late Latin from Greek *paralogismos*, from *paralogizesthai* to argue fallaciously, from PARA-[1] + -*logizesthai*, ultimately from *logos* word] > paˈralogist *n* > paˌraloˈgistic *adj*

Paralympian (ˌpærəˈlɪmpɪən) *n* a competitor in the Paralympics

Paralympic (ˌpærəˈlɪmpɪk) *adj* of or relating to the Paralympics

Paralympics (ˌpærəˈlɪmpɪks) *pl n* **the** a sporting event, modelled on the Olympic Games, held solely for disabled competitors. Also called: **the Parallel Olympics** [c20 PARALLEL + OLYMPICS]

paralyse *or US* **paralyze** (ˈpærəˌlaɪz) *vb* (*tr*) **1** *pathol* to affect with paralysis **2** *med* to render (a part of the body) insensitive to pain, touch, etc, esp by injection of an anaesthetic **3** to make immobile; transfix [c19 from French *paralyser*, from *paralysie* PARALYSIS] > ˌparalyˈsation *n or US* ˌparalyˈzation *n* > ˈparaˌlyser *or US* ˈparaˌlyzer *n*

paralysis (pəˈrælɪsɪs) *n, pl* **-ses** (-ˌsiːz) **1** *pathol* **a** impairment or loss of voluntary muscle function or of sensation (**sensory paralysis**) in a part or area of the body, usually caused by a lesion or disorder of the muscles or the nerves supplying them **b** a disease characterized by such impairment or loss; palsy **2** cessation or impairment of activity: *paralysis of industry by strikes* [c16 via Latin from Greek *paralusis*; see PARA-[1], -LYSIS]

paralysis agitans (ˈædʒɪˌtænz) *n* another name for **Parkinson's disease**

paralytic (ˌpærəˈlɪtɪk) *adj* **1** of, relating to, or of the nature of paralysis **2** afflicted with or subject to paralysis **3** *Brit informal* very drunk ▷ *n* **4** a person afflicted with paralysis > ˌparaˈlytically *adv*

paramagnetism (ˌpærəˈmæɡnɪˌtɪzəm) *n physics* the phenomenon exhibited by substances that have a relative permeability slightly greater than unity and a positive susceptibility. The effect is due to the alignment of unpaired spins of electrons in atoms of the material. Compare **diamagnetism, ferromagnetism.** > **paramagnetic** (ˌpærəmæɡˈnɛtɪk) *adj*

Paramaribo (ˌpærəˈmærɪˌbəʊ; *Dutch* paːraːˈmaːriːboː) *n* the capital and chief port of Surinam, 27 km (17 miles) from the Atlantic on the Surinam River: the only large town in the country. Pop: 261 000 (2005 est)

paramatta *or* **parramatta** (ˌpærəˈmætə) *n* a lightweight twill-weave fabric of wool formerly with silk or cotton, used for dresses, etc, now used esp for rubber-proofed garments [c19 named after *Parramatta*, New South Wales, Australia, where it was originally produced]

paramecium (ˌpærəˈmiːsɪəm) *n, pl* **-cia** (-sɪə) any freshwater protozoan of the genus *Paramecium*, having an oval body covered with cilia and a ventral ciliated groove for feeding: phylum *Ciliophora* (ciliates) [c18 New Latin, from Greek *paramēkēs* elongated, from PARA-[1] + *mēkos* length]

paramedic (ˌpærəˈmɛdɪk) *or* **paramedical** *n* **1** a person, such as a laboratory technician, who supplements the work of the medical profession **2** a member of an ambulance crew trained in a number of life-saving skills, including infusion and cardiac care ▷ *adj* **3** of or designating such a person

parament (ˈpærəmənt) *n, pl* **paraments** *or* **paramenta** (ˌpærəˈmɛntə) (*often plural*) an ecclesiastical vestment or decorative hanging [c14 from Old French *parament*, from Medieval Latin *paramentum*, from Latin *parāre* to prepare]

parameter (pəˈræmɪtə) *n* **1** one of a number of auxiliary variables in terms of which all the variables in an implicit functional relationship can be explicitly expressed. See **parametric equations 2** a variable whose behaviour is not being considered and which may for present purposes be regarded as a constant, as y in the partial derivative $\partial f(x,y)/\partial x$ **3** *statistics* a characteristic of the distribution of a population, such as its mean, as distinct from that of a sample. Compare **statistic 4** *informal* any constant or limiting factor: *a designer must work within the parameters of budget and practicality* [c17 from New Latin; see PARA-[1], -METER] > **parametric** (ˌpærəˈmɛtrɪk) *or* ˌparaˈmetrical *adj*

parametric amplifier *n* a type of high-frequency amplifier in which energy from a pumping oscillator is transferred to the input signal through a circuit with a varying parameter, usually a varying reactance

parametric equalizer *n* an electronic device for cutting or boosting selected frequencies by continuous narrowing or widening of the frequencies to be filtered. Compare **graphic equalizer**

parametric equations *pl n* a set of equations expressing a number of quantities as explicit functions of the same set of independent variables and equivalent to some direct functional relationship of these quantities: *a circle $x^2+y^2=r^2$ has parametric equations $x=r \cos \theta$ and $y=r \sin \theta$ in terms of the parameters r and θ*

parametric statistics *n* (*functioning as singular*) the branch of statistics concerned with data measurable on interval or ratio scales, so that arithmetic operations are applicable to them, enabling parameters such as the mean of the distribution to be defined

paramilitary (ˌpærəˈmɪlɪtərɪ, -trɪ) *adj* **1** denoting or relating to a group of personnel with military structure functioning either as a civil force or in support of military forces **2** denoting or relating to a force with military structure conducting armed operations against a ruling or occupying power ▷ *n* **3 a** a paramilitary force **b** a member of such a force

paramnesia (ˌpæræmˈniːzɪə) *n psychiatry* a

disorder of the memory or the faculty of recognition in which dreams may be confused with reality

paramo ('pærəˌməʊ) *n, pl* **-mos** a high plateau in the Andes between the tree line and the permanent snow line [c18 American Spanish, from Spanish: treeless plain]

paramorph ('pærəˌmɔːf) *n* **1** a mineral that has undergone paramorphism **2** a plant or animal that is classified on the basis of inadequate data and differs taxonomically from other members of the species in which it has been placed
> ˌpara'morphic *or* ˌpara'morphous *adj*

paramorphine (ˌpærə'mɔːfiːn) *n* another name for **thebaine**

paramorphism (ˌpærə'mɔːˌfɪzəm) *n* a process by which the crystalline structure of a mineral alters without any change in its chemical composition

paramount ('pærəˌmaʊnt) *adj* **1** of the greatest importance or significance; pre-eminent ▷ *n* **2** *rare* a supreme ruler [c16 via Anglo-Norman from Old French *paramont*, from *par* by + *-amont* above, from Latin *ad montem* to the mountain]
> ˌpara'mountcy *n* > ˌpara'mountly *adv*

paramour ('pærəˌmʊə) *n* **1** *now usually derogatory* a lover, esp an adulterous woman **2** an archaic word for **beloved** (sense 2) [c13 from Old French, literally: through love]

Paraná *n* **1** (parə'na) a state of S Brazil, on the Atlantic: consists of a coastal plain and a large rolling plateau with extensive forests. Capital: Curitiba. Pop: 9 798 006 (2002). Area: 199 555 sq km (77 048 sq miles) **2** (para'na) a city in E Argentina, on the Paraná River opposite Santa Fe: capital of Argentina (1853–1862). Pop: 305 000 (2005 est) **3** (*Portuguese* parə'na; *Spanish* para'na) a river in central South America, formed in S Brazil by the confluence of the Rio Grande and the Paranaíba River and flowing generally south to the Atlantic through the Río de la Plata estuary. Length: 2900 km (1800 miles)

Paraná pine (pa'ra:nə) *n* **1** a large pine tree, *Araucaria angustifolia*, of South America yielding softwood timber: family *Araucariaceae* **2** the wood of this tree

parang ('pɑːræŋ) *n* a short stout straight-edged knife used by the Dyaks of Borneo [c19 from Malay]

paranoia (ˌpærə'nɔɪə) *n* **1** a form of schizophrenia characterized by a slowly progressive deterioration of the personality, involving delusions and often hallucinations **2** a mental disorder characterized by any of several types of delusions, in which the personality otherwise remains relatively intact **3** *informal* intense fear or suspicion, esp when unfounded [c19 via New Latin from Greek: frenzy, from *paranoos* distraught, from PARA-¹ + *noos* mind] > **paranoiac** (ˌpærə'nɔɪɪk) *or* **paranoic** (ˌpærə'nəʊɪk) *adj, n*

paranoid ('pærəˌnɔɪd) *adj* **1** of, characterized by, or resembling paranoia **2** *informal* exhibiting undue suspicion, fear of persecution, etc ▷ *n* **3** a person who shows the behaviour patterns associated with paranoia

paranormal (ˌpærə'nɔːməl) *adj* **1** beyond normal explanation ▷ *n* **2** the paranormal happenings generally

paranymph ('pærəˌnɪmf) *n archaic* a bridesmaid or best man [c16 via Late Latin from Greek *paranumphos*, from PARA-¹ + *numphē* bride (literally: person beside the bride)]

parapara ('pɑːrɑːpɑːrɑː) *n, pl* **parapara** a small New Zealand tree, *Pisonia brunoniana*, with sticky fruit and leaves which can trap small birds. Also called: **bird-catching tree** [Māori]

paraparesis (ˌpærəpə'riːsɪs) *n* muscle weakness, esp of the legs, allowing limited movement; partial paralysis > **paraparetic** (ˌpærəpə'rɛtɪk) *adj*

parapente (ˌpærə'pɛntɪ) *n* **1** another name for **paraskiing 2** the form of parachute used in this sport

parapet ('pærəpɪt, -ˌpɛt) *n* **1** a low wall or railing along the edge of a balcony, roof, etc **2** Also called: **breastwork** a rampart, mound of sandbags, bank, etc, in front of a trench, giving protection from fire from the front [c16 from Italian *parapetto*, literally: chest-high wall, from PARA-² + *petto*, from Latin *pectus* breast]

paraph ('pæræf) *n* a flourish after a signature, originally to prevent forgery [c14 via French from Medieval Latin *paraphus*, variant of *paragraphus* PARAGRAPH]

paraphasia (ˌpærə'feɪzɪə) *n* a defect of speech in which the normal flow of words is interrupted by inappropriate words and phrases [c20 from Greek PARA-¹ + *-phasia*, from *phanai* to speak]

paraphernalia (ˌpærəfə'neɪlɪə) *pl n* (*sometimes functioning as singular*) **1** miscellaneous articles or equipment **2** *law* (formerly) articles of personal property given to a married woman by her husband before or during marriage and regarded in law as her possessions over which she has some measure of control [c17 via Medieval Latin from Latin *parapherna* personal property of a married woman, apart from her dowry, from Greek, from PARA-¹ + *phernē* dowry, from *pherein* to carry]

paraphilia (ˌpærə'fɪlɪə) *n* any abnormal sexual behaviour; sexual anomaly or deviation [c20 from PARA-¹ + *-philia*, from Greek *philos* loving]

paraphimosis (ˌpærəfɪ'məʊsɪs) *n* inability to retract the penis into the prepuce as a result of narrowing of the prepuce

paraphrase ('pærəˌfreɪz) *n* **1** an expression of a statement or text in other words, esp in order to clarify **2** the practice of making paraphrases ▷ *vb* **3** to put (something) into other words; restate (something) [c16 via French from Latin *paraphrasis*, from Greek, from *paraphrazein* to recount]
> **paraphrastic** (ˌpærə'fræstɪk) *adj*

paraphysis (pə'ræfɪsɪs) *n, pl* **-ses** (-ˌsiːz) any of numerous sterile cells occurring between the sex organs of mosses and algae and between the spore-producing bodies of basidiomycetous and ascomycetous fungi [c19 New Latin from Greek: subsidiary growth, from PARA-¹ + *phusis* growth]
> pa'raphysate *adj*

paraplegia (ˌpærə'pliːdʒə) *n pathol* paralysis of the lower half of the body, usually as the result of disease or injury of the spine. Compare **hemiplegia, quadriplegia** [c17 via New Latin from Greek: a blow on one side, from PARA-¹ + *plēssein* to strike]

paraplegic (ˌpærə'pliːdʒɪk) *adj* **1** *pathol* of, relating to, or afflicted with paraplegia ▷ *n* **2** *pathol* a person afflicted with paraplegia

parapodium (ˌpærə'pəʊdɪəm) *n, pl* **-dia** (-dɪə) **1** any of the paired unjointed lateral appendages of polychaete worms, used in locomotion, respiration, etc **2** any of various similar appendages of other invertebrates, esp certain molluscs [New Latin: from PARA-¹ + -PODIUM]

parapraxis (ˌpærə'præksɪs) *n psychoanal* a minor error in action, such as slips of the tongue, supposedly the result of repressed impulses. See also **Freudian slip** [c20 from PARA-¹ + Greek *praxis* a doing, deed]

parapsychology (ˌpærəsaɪ'kɒlədʒɪ) *n* the study of mental phenomena, such as telepathy, which are beyond the scope of normal physical explanation
> **parapsychological** (ˌpærəsaɪkə'lɒdʒɪkᵊl) *adj*
> ˌparapsy'chologist *n*

Paraquat ('pærəˌkwɒt) *n trademark* a yellow extremely poisonous soluble solid used in solution as a weedkiller

Pará rubber (pə'rɑː, 'pɑːrə) *n* a South American rubber obtained from any of various euphorbiaceous trees of the genus *Hevea*, esp *H. brasiliensis*. See also **rubber tree** [c19 from PARÁ]

parasailing ('pærəˌseɪlɪŋ) *n* a sport in which a water-skier wearing a parachute is towed by a speedboat, becomes airborne, and sails along in the air

parasang ('pærəˌsæŋ) *n* a Persian unit of distance equal to about 5.5 km or 3.4 miles [c16 via Latin and Greek from a Persian word related to modern Persian *farsang*]

parascending ('pærəˌsɛndɪŋ) *n* a sport in which a participant wears a parachute and becomes airborne by being towed by a vehicle into the wind and then descends by parachute

parascience ('pærəˌsaɪəns) *n* the study of subjects that are outside the scope of traditional science because they cannot be explained by accepted scientific theory or tested by conventional scientific methods

paraselene (ˌpærəsɪ'liːnɪ) *n, pl* **-nae** (-niː) *meteorol* a bright image of the moon on a lunar halo. Also called: **mock moon** Compare **parhelion** [c17 New Latin, from PARA-¹ + Greek *selēnē* moon]
> ˌparase'lenic *adj*

Parashah ('pærəʃɑː; *Hebrew* para'ʃa) *n, pl* **-shoth** (-ʃəʊt; *Hebrew* -'ʃɔt) *Judaism* **1** any of the sections of the Torah read in the synagogue **2** any of the subsections of the weekly lessons read on Sabbaths in the synagogue ▷ Also called (Yiddish): **Parsha** [from Hebrew, from *pārāsh* to divide, separate]

parasite ('pærəˌsaɪt) *n* **1** an animal or plant that lives in or on another (the host) from which it obtains nourishment. The host does not benefit from the association and is often harmed by it **2** a person who habitually lives at the expense of others; sponger **3** (formerly) a sycophant [c16 via Latin from Greek *parasitos* one who lives at another's expense, from PARA-¹ + *sitos* grain]
> **parasitic** (ˌpærə'sɪtɪk) *or* ˌpara'sitical *adj*
> ˌpara'sitically *adv*

parasite drag *n* the part of the drag on an aircraft that is contributed by nonlifting surfaces, such as fuselage, nacelles, etc. Also called: **parasite resistance**

parasiticide (ˌpærə'sɪtɪˌsaɪd) *n* **1** any substance capable of destroying parasites ▷ *adj* **2** destructive to parasites > ˌpara'siti'cidal *adj*

parasitic male *n zoology* a male animal that is much smaller than the female and is totally dependent on the female for its nutrition, such as the male of some species of deep-sea angler fish

parasitic oscillation *n* (in an electronic circuit) oscillation at any undesired frequency. Sometimes shortened to: **parasitic**

parasitism ('pærəsaɪˌtɪzəm) *n* **1** the relationship between a parasite and its host **2** the state of being infested with parasites **3** the state of being a parasite

parasitize *or* **parasitise** ('pærəsɪˌtaɪz, -saɪ-) *vb* (*tr*) **1** to infest or infect with parasites **2** to live on (another organism) as a parasite

parasitoid ('pærəsɪˌtɔːd) *n zoology* an animal, esp an insect, that is parasitic during the larval stage of its life cycle but becomes free-living when adult

parasitology (ˌpærəsaɪ'tɒlədʒɪ) *n* the branch of biology that is concerned with the study of parasites > **parasitological** (ˌpærəsaɪtᵊ'lɒdʒɪkᵊl) *adj*
> ˌparasit'ologist *n*

paraskiing ('pærəˌskiːɪŋ) *n* the sport of jumping off high mountains wearing skis and a light parachute composed of inflatable fabric tubes that form a semirigid wing. Also called: **parapente**

parasol ('pærəˌsɒl) *n* an umbrella used for protection against the sun; sunshade [c17 via French from Italian *parasole*, from PARA-² + *sole* sun, from Latin *sōl*]

parasol mushroom *n* any of several fungi of the basidiomycetous genus *Lepiota*, having an umbrella-shaped cap, white gills, and a slender brownish stem with a prominent white ring

parastatal (ˌpærə'steɪtᵊl) *n* **1** a state-owned organization, esp in Africa ▷ *adj* **2** of or relating to such an organization

parastichy (pə'ræstɪkɪ) *n, pl* **-chies 1** a hypothetical spiral line connecting the bases of a series of leaves on a stem **2** an arrangement of

p

leaves so connected ▷ Compare **orthostichy** [c19 from PARA-¹ + Greek *stikhia*, from *stikhos* row, rank] > pa'rastichous *adj*

parasuicide (ˌpærəˈsuːɪˌsaɪd) *n* **1** the deliberate infliction of injury on oneself or the taking of a drug overdose as an attempt at suicide which may not be intended to be successful **2** a person who commits such an act

parasymbiosis (ˌpærəˌsɪmbɪˈəʊsɪs) *n* the symbiotic relationship that occurs between certain species of fungi and lichens (which are themselves symbiotic associations between a fungus and an alga) > ˌpara'symbiont *n* > ˌparaˌsymbi'otic *adj*

parasympathetic (ˌpærəˌsɪmpəˈθɛtɪk) *adj anatomy, physiol* of or relating to the division of the autonomic nervous system that acts in opposition to the sympathetic system by slowing the heartbeat, constricting the bronchi of the lungs, stimulating the smooth muscles of the digestive tract, etc. Compare **sympathetic** (sense 4)

parasynapsis (ˌpærəsɪˈnæpsɪs) *n* another name for **synapsis** (sense 1) > ˌparasyn'aptic *adj*

parasynthesis (ˌpærəˈsɪnθɪsɪs) *n* formation of words by means of compounding a phrase and adding an affix, as for example *light-headed*, which is *light* + *head* with the affix *-ed* > **parasynthetic** (ˌpærəsɪnˈθɛtɪk) *adj*

parasyntheton (ˌpærəˈsɪnθətɒn) *n, pl* **-ta** (-tə) a word formed by parasynthesis; for example, *kind-hearted* [from Greek]

parataniwha (pɑːrɑːˈtɑːniːfɑː) *n, pl* **parataniwha** a New Zealand plant, *Elatostema rugosa*, with pink and red serrated leaves [Māori]

parataxis (ˌpærəˈtæksɪs) *n* the juxtaposition of clauses in a sentence without the use of a conjunction, as for example *None of my friends stayed — they all left early* [c19 New Latin from Greek, from *paratassein*, literally: to arrange side by side, from PARA-¹ + *tassein* to arrange] > **paratactic** (ˌpærəˈtæktɪk) *adj* > ˌpara'tactically *adv*

paratha (pəˈrɑːtə) *n* (in Indian cookery) a flat unleavened bread, resembling a small nan bread, that is fried on a griddle [from Hindi *parāthā*]

parathion (ˌpærəˈθaɪɒn) *n* a slightly water-soluble toxic oil, odourless and colourless when pure, used as an insecticide. Formula: $C_{10}H_{14}NO_5PS$ [c20 from PARA-¹ + THIO- + -ON]

parathyroid (ˌpærəˈθaɪrɔɪd) *adj* **1** situated near the thyroid gland **2** of or relating to the parathyroid glands ▷ *n* **3** See **parathyroid gland**

parathyroid gland *n* any one of the small egg-shaped endocrine glands situated near or embedded within the thyroid gland: they secrete parathyroid hormone

parathyroid hormone *n* the hormone secreted by the parathyroid glands that controls the level of calcium in the blood: a deficiency of the hormone often results in tetany. Also called: **parathormone** (ˌpærəˈθɔːməʊn)

paratonic (ˌpærəˈtɒnɪk) *adj botany* (of a plant movement) occurring in response to an external stimulus

paratroops (ˈpærəˌtruːps) *pl n* troops trained and equipped to be dropped by parachute into a battle area. Also called: **paratroopers, parachute troops**

paratyphoid (ˌpærəˈtaɪfɔɪd) *pathol* ▷ *adj* **1** resembling typhoid fever or its causative agent **2** of or relating to paratyphoid fever ▷ *n* **3** See **paratyphoid fever**

paratyphoid fever *n pathol* a disease resembling but less severe than typhoid fever, characterized by chills, headache, nausea, vomiting, and diarrhoea, caused by bacteria of the genus *Salmonella*

paravane (ˈpærəˌveɪn) *n* a torpedo-shaped device towed from the bow of a vessel so that the cables will cut the anchors of any moored mines [c20 from PARA-² + VANE]

par avion *French* (par avjɔ̃) *adv* by aeroplane: used in labelling mail sent by air

paraxial (pæˈræksɪəl) *adj physics* (of a light ray)

parallel to the axis of an optical system

parazoan (ˌpærəˈzəʊən) *n, pl* **-zoa** (-ˈzəʊə) any multicellular invertebrate of the group *Parazoa*, which consists of the sponges (phylum *Porifera*). Compare **metazoan** [c19 from *parazoa*, formed on the model of *protozoa* and *metazoa*, from PARA-¹ + Greek *zōon* animal]

parboil (ˈpɑːˌbɔɪl) *vb* (*tr*) **1** to boil until partially cooked, often before further cooking **2** to subject to uncomfortable heat [c15 from Old French *parboillir*, from Late Latin *perbullīre* to boil thoroughly (see PER-, BOIL¹); modern meaning due to confusion of *par-* with *part*]

parbuckle (ˈpɑːˌbʌkəl) *n* **1** a rope sling for lifting or lowering a heavy cylindrical object, such as a cask or tree trunk ▷ *vb* **2** (*tr*) to raise or lower (an object) with such a sling [c17 *parbunkel*: of uncertain origin]

Parcae (ˈpɑːsiː) *pl n, sing* **Parca** (ˈpɑːkə) **the** the Roman goddesses of fate. Greek counterparts: **the Moirai**

parcel (ˈpɑːsəl) *n* **1** something wrapped up; package **2** a group of people or things having some common characteristic **3** a quantity of some commodity offered for sale; lot **4** a distinct portion of land **5** an essential part of something (esp in the phrase **part and parcel**) ▷ *vb* **-cels, -celling, -celled** *or US* **-cels, -celing, -celed** (*tr*) **6** (often foll by *up*) to make a parcel of; wrap up **7** (often foll by *out*) to divide (up) into portions **8** *nautical* to bind strips of canvas around (a rope) ▷ *adv* **9** an archaic word for **partly** [c14 from Old French *parcelle*, from Latin *particula* PARTICLE]

parcel-gilt *adj* partly gilded, esp (of an item of silverware) having the inner surface gilded [c15 from *parcel* (in the obsolete adv sense: partly) + GILT¹]

parcenary (ˈpɑːsɪnərɪ) *n* joint heirship. Also called: **coparcenary** [c16 from Old French *parçonerie*, from *parçon* distribution; see PARCENER]

parcener (ˈpɑːsɪnə) *n* a person who takes an equal share with another or others; coheir. Also called: **coparcener** [c13 from Old French *parçonier*, from *parçon* distribution, from Latin *partītiō* a sharing, from *partīre* to divide]

parch (pɑːtʃ) *vb* **1** to deprive or be deprived of water; dry up: *the sun parches the fields* **2** (*tr; usually passive*) to make very thirsty: *I was parched after the run* **3** (*tr*) to roast (corn, etc) lightly [c14 of obscure origin]

Parcheesi (pɑːˈtʃiːzɪ) *n trademark* a modern board game derived from the ancient game of pachisi

parchment (ˈpɑːtʃmənt) *n* **1** the skin of certain animals, such as sheep, treated to form a durable material, as for bookbinding, or (esp formerly) manuscripts **2** a manuscript, bookbinding, etc, made of or resembling this material **3** a type of stiff yellowish paper resembling parchment [c13 from Old French *parchemin*, via Latin from Greek *pergamēnē*, from *Pergamēnos* of Pergamum (where parchment was made); the form of Old French *parchemin* was influenced by *parche* leather, from Latin *Parthica* (*pellis*) Parthian (leather)] > 'parchmenty *adj*

parclose (ˈpɑːˌkləʊz) *n* a screen or railing in a church separating off an altar, chapel, etc [c14 from Old French, noun use of past participle of *parclore* to close off; see PER-, CLOSE¹]

pard¹ (pɑːd) *n US* short for **pardner**

pard² (pɑːd) *n archaic* a leopard or panther [c13 via Old French from Latin *pardus*, from Greek *pardos*]

pardalote (ˈpɑːdəˌləʊt) *n* any of various small Australian songbirds of the genus *Pardalotus*, esp the diamond bird [c19 from New Latin, from Greek *pardalōtos* spotted like a leopard; see PARD²]

pardner (ˈpɑːdnə) *n US dialect* friend or partner: used as a term of address

pardon (ˈpɑːdən) *vb* (*tr*) **1** to excuse or forgive (a person) for (an offence, mistake, etc): *to pardon someone; to pardon a fault* ▷ *n* **2** forgiveness; allowance **3 a** release from punishment for an offence **b** the warrant granting such release **4** a

Roman Catholic indulgence ▷ *sentence substitute* **5** Also: **pardon me, I beg your pardon a** sorry; excuse me **b** what did you say? [c13 from Old French, from Medieval Latin *perdōnum*, from *perdōnāre* to forgive freely, from Latin *per* (intensive) + *dōnāre* to grant] > 'pardonable *adj* > 'pardonably *adv* > 'pardonless *adj*

pardoner (ˈpɑːdənə) *n* (before the Reformation) a person licensed to sell ecclesiastical indulgences

Pardubice (*Czech* ˈpardubitsɛ) *n* a city in the central Czech Republic, on the Elbe River: 13th-century cathedral; oil refinery. Pop: 163 000 (1993)

pare (pɛə) *vb* (*tr*) **1** to peel or cut (the outer layer) from (something) **2** to cut the edges from (the nails); trim **3** to decrease bit by bit [c13 from Old French *parer* to adorn, from Latin *parāre* to make ready] > 'parer *n*

paregoric (ˌpærɪˈgɒrɪk) *n* a medicine containing opium, benzoic acid, camphor (English paregoric) or ammonia (Scottish paregoric), and anise oil, formerly widely used to relieve diarrhoea and coughing in children [c17 (meaning: relieving pain): via Late Latin from Greek *parēgorikos* soothing, from *parēgoros* relating to soothing speech, from PARA-¹ (beside, alongside of) + *-ēgor-*, from *agoreuein* to speak in assembly, from *agora* assembly]

pareira (pəˈreərə) *n* the root of a South American menispermaceous climbing plant, *Chondrodendron tomentosum*, used as a diuretic, tonic, and as a source of curare [c18 from Portuguese *pareira brava*, literally: wild vine]

paren. *abbreviation for* parenthesis

parenchyma (pəˈrɛŋkɪmə) *n* **1** unspecialized plant tissue consisting of simple thin-walled cells with intervening air spaces: constitutes the greater part of fruits, stems, roots, etc **2** animal tissue that constitutes the essential or specialized part of an organ as distinct from the blood vessels, connective tissue, etc, associated with it **3** loosely-packed tissue filling the spaces between the organs in lower animals such as flatworms [c17 via New Latin from Greek *parenkhuma* something poured in beside, from PARA-¹ + *enkhuma* infusion] > **parenchymatous** (ˌpærɛŋˈkɪmətəs) *adj*

parent (ˈpɛərənt) *n* **1** a father or mother **2** a person acting as a father or mother; guardian **3** *rare* an ancestor **4** a source or cause **5 a** an organism or organization that has produced one or more organisms or organizations similar to itself **b** (*as modifier*): *a parent organism* **6** *physics, chem* **a** a precursor, such as a nucleus or compound, of a derived entity **b** (*as modifier*): *a parent nucleus; a parent ion* [c15 via Old French from Latin *parens* parent, from *parere* to bring forth] > 'parenthood *n*

parentage (ˈpɛərəntɪdʒ) *n* **1** ancestry **2** derivation from a particular origin **3** a less common word for **parenthood**

parental (pəˈrɛntəl) *adj* **1** of or relating to a parent or parenthood **2** *genetics* designating the first generation in a line, which gives rise to all succeeding (filial) generations > pa'rentally *adv*

parent company *n* a company that owns more than half the shares of another company

parenteral (pæˈrɛntərəl) *adj med* **1** (esp of the route by which a drug is administered) by means other than through the digestive tract, esp by injection **2** designating a drug to be injected [c20 from PARA-¹ + ENTERO- + -AL¹] > par'enterally *adv*

parenthesis (pəˈrɛnθɪsɪs) *n, pl* **-ses** (-ˌsiːz) **1** a phrase, often explanatory or qualifying, inserted into a passage with which it is not grammatically connected, and marked off by brackets, dashes, etc **2** Also called: **bracket** either of a pair of characters, (), used to enclose such a phrase or as a sign of aggregation in mathematical or logical expressions **3** an intervening occurrence; interlude; interval **4 in parenthesis** inserted as a parenthesis [c16 via Late Latin from Greek: something placed in besides, from *parentithenai*,

from PARA-¹ + EN-² + *tithenai* to put] > **parenthetic**
(ˌpærənˈθɛtɪk) or ˌparenˈthetical *adj*
> ˌparenˈthetically *adv*

parenthesize or **parenthesise** (pəˈrɛnθɪˌsaɪz) *vb*
(*tr*) **1** to place in parentheses **2** to insert as a parenthesis **3** to intersperse (a speech, writing, etc) with parentheses

parenting (ˈpɛərəntɪŋ) *n* the care and upbringing of a child

parentless (ˈpɛərəntˌlɪs) *adj* having no living parents; orphaned

parent metal *n engineering, metallurgy* the metal of components that are being welded by a molten filler metal

Parents Anonymous *n* (in Britain) an association of local voluntary self-help groups offering help through an anonymous telephone service to parents who fear they will injure their children, or who have other problems in managing their children

parent teacher association *n* a social group of the parents of children at a school and their teachers formed in order to foster better understanding between them and to organize activities on behalf of the school. Abbreviation: **PTA**

parera (ˈpɑːrɛrɑː) *n, pl* parera a New Zealand duck, *Anas superciliosa*, with grey-edged brown feathers. Also called: **grey duck** [Māori]

parergon (pəˈrɛɡɒn) *n, pl* -ga (-ɡə) work that is not one's main employment [c17 from Latin, from Greek, from PARA-¹ + *ergon* work]

paresis (pəˈriːsɪs, ˈpærɪsɪs) *n, pl* -ses (-ˌsiːz) *pathol* **1** incomplete or slight paralysis of motor functions **2** short for **general paresis** See **general paralysis of the insane** [c17 via New Latin from Greek: a relaxation, from *parienai* to let go, from PARA-¹ + *hienai* to release] > **paretic** (pəˈrɛtɪk) *adj*

paresthesia (ˌpærɛsˈθiːzɪə) *n pathol* the usual US spelling of **paraesthesia**. > **paresthetic** (ˌpærɛsˈθɛtɪk) *adj*

Pareto (*Italian* paˈrɛːto) *adj* denoting a law, mathematical formula, etc, originally used by Vilfredo Pareto (1848–1923), Italian sociologist and economist, to express the frequency distribution of incomes in a society

pareu (ˈpɑːreɪˌuː) *n* a rectangle of fabric worn by Polynesians as a skirt or loincloth [from Tahitian]

parev, pareve or **parve** (ˈpɑːrvə, ˈpɑːrəv) *adj Judaism* containing neither meat nor milk products and so fit for use with either meat or milk dishes. Compare **milchik, fleishik** See also **kashruth**

par excellence *French* (par ɛksɛlɑːs; *English* pɑːr ˈɛksələns) *adv* to a degree of excellence; beyond comparison: *she is the charitable lady par excellence* [literally: by (way of) excellence]

parfait (pɑːˈfeɪ) *n* a rich frozen dessert made from eggs and cream with ice cream, fruit, etc [from French: PERFECT]

parfleche (ˈpɑːflɛʃ) *n US and Canadian* **1** a sheet of rawhide that has been dried after soaking in lye and water to remove the hair **2** an object, such as a case, made of this [c19 from Canadian French, from French *parer* to ward off, protect + *flèche* arrow]

parget (ˈpɑːdʒɪt) *n* **1** Also called: **pargeting a** plaster, mortar, etc, used to line chimney flues or cover walls **b** plasterwork that has incised ornamental patterns **2** another name for **gypsum** (esp when used in building) ▷ *vb* (*tr*) **3** to cover or decorate with parget [c14 from Old French *pargeter* to throw over, from *par* PER- + *geter*, from Medieval Latin *jactāre* to throw]

parhelic circle *n meteorol* a luminous band at the same altitude as the sun, parallel to the horizon, caused by reflection of the sun's rays by ice crystals in the atmosphere

parhelion (pɑːˈhiːlɪən) *n, pl* -lia (-lɪə) one of several bright spots on the parhelic circle or solar halo, caused by the diffraction of light by ice crystals in the atmosphere, esp around sunset.

Also called: **mock sun, sundog** Compare **anthelion** [c17 via Latin from Greek *parēlion*, from PARA-¹ (beside) + *hēlios* sun] > **parhelic** (pɑːˈhiːlɪk, -ˈhɛlɪk) or **parheliacal** (ˌpɑːhɪˈlaɪəkˀl) *adj*

pari- *combining form* equal or equally; even (in number): *parisyllabic; paripinnate* [from Latin *par*]

pariah (pəˈraɪə, ˈpærɪə) *n* **1** a social outcast **2** (formerly) a member of a low caste in South India [c17 from Tamil *paraiyan* drummer, from *paral* drum; so called because members of the caste were the drummers at festivals]

pariah dog *n* another term for **pye-dog**

Parian (ˈpɛərɪən) *adj* **1** denoting or relating to a fine white marble mined in classical times in Paros **2** denoting or relating to a fine biscuit porcelain used mainly for statuary **3** of or relating to Paros ▷ *n* **4** a native or inhabitant of Paros **5** Parian marble **6** Parian porcelain

Paricutín (*Spanish* pariku'tin) *n* a volcano in W central Mexico, in Michoacán state, formed in 1943 after a week of earth tremors; grew to a height of 2500 m (8200 ft) in a year and buried the village of Paricutín

paries (ˈpɛərɪˌiːz) *n, pl* parietes (pəˈraɪɪˌtiːz) the wall of an organ or bodily cavity [c18 from Latin: wall]

parietal (pəˈraɪɪtˀl) *adj* **1** *anatomy, biology* of, relating to, or forming the walls or part of the walls of a bodily cavity or similar structure: *the parietal bones of the skull* **2** of or relating to the side of the skull **3** (of plant ovaries) having ovules attached to the walls **4** *US* living or having authority within a college ▷ *n* **5** a parietal bone [c16 from Late Latin *parietālis*, from Latin *pariēs* wall]

parietal bone *n* either of the two bones forming part of the roof and sides of the skull

parietal cell *n* any one of the cells in the lining of the stomach that produce hydrochloric acid

parietal lobe *n* the portion of each cerebral hemisphere concerned with the perception and interpretation of sensations of touch, temperature, and taste and with muscular movements

pari-mutuel (ˌpærɪˈmjuːtjʊəl) *n, pl* pari-mutuels or **paris-mutuels** (ˌpærɪˈmjuːtjʊəlz) **a** a system of betting in which those who have bet on the winners of a race share in the total amount wagered less a percentage for the management **b** (*as modifier*): *the pari-mutuel machine* [c19 from French, literally: mutual wager]

paring (ˈpɛərɪŋ) *n* (*often plural*) something pared or cut off

pari passu *Latin* (ˌpærɪ ˈpæsuː, ˈpɑːrɪ) *adv usually legal* with equal speed or progress; equably: often used to refer to the right of creditors to receive assets from the same source without one taking precedence

paripinnate (ˌpærɪˈpɪneɪt) *adj* (of pinnate leaves) having an even number of leaflets and no terminal leaflet. Compare **imparipinnate**

Paris¹ (ˈpærɪs; *French* pari) *n* **1** the capital of France, in the north on the River Seine: constitutes a department; dates from the 3rd century BC, becoming capital of France in 987; centre of the French Revolution; centres around its original site on an island in the Seine, the Île de la Cité, containing Notre Dame; university (1150). Pop: 2 125 246 (1999). Ancient name: Lutetia **2** Treaty of Paris **a** a treaty of 1783 between the US, Britain, France, and Spain, ending the War of American Independence **b** a treaty of 1763 signed by Britain, France, and Spain that ended their involvement in the Seven Years' War **c** a treaty of 1898 between Spain and the US bringing to an end the Spanish-American War [via French and Old French, from Late Latin (*Lūtētia*) *Parisiōrum* (marshes) of the *Parisii*, a tribe of Celtic Gaul]

Paris² (ˈpærɪs) *n Greek myth* a prince of Troy, whose abduction of Helen from her husband Menelaus started the Trojan War

Paris Club *n* an informal group of representatives

from IMF member nations whose governments or central banks have lent money to governments of other countries. compare **Group of Ten**

Paris Commune *n French history* the council established in Paris in the spring of 1871 in opposition to the National Assembly and esp to the peace negotiated with Prussia following the Franco-Prussian War. Troops of the Assembly crushed the Commune with great bloodshed

Paris green *n* an emerald-green poisonous insoluble substance used as a pigment and insecticide. It is a double salt of copper arsenite and copper acetate. Formula: $3Cu(AsO_2)_2.Cu(C_2H_3O_2)_2$

parish (ˈpærɪʃ) *n* **1** a subdivision of a diocese, having its own church and a clergyman. Related adj: **parochial 2** the churchgoers of such a subdivision **3** (in England and, formerly, Wales) the smallest unit of local government in rural areas **4** (in Louisiana) a unit of local government corresponding to a county in other states of the US **5** the people living in a parish **6** on the parish *history* receiving parochial relief [c13 from Old French *paroisse*, from Church Latin *parochia*, from Late Greek *paroikia*, from *paroikos* Christian, sojourner, from Greek: neighbour, from PARA-¹ (beside) + *oikos* house]

Parishad (ˈpʌrɪʃəd) *n* (in India) an assembly [Hindi]

parish clerk *n* a person designated to assist in various church duties

parish council *n* (in England and, formerly, Wales) the administrative body of a parish. See **parish** (sense 3)

parishioner (pəˈrɪʃənə) *n* a member of a particular parish

parish pump *adj* of only local interest; parochial

parish register *n* a book in which the births, baptisms, marriages, and deaths in a parish are recorded

Parisian (pəˈrɪzɪən) *adj* **1** of or relating to Paris or its inhabitants ▷ *n* **2** a native or inhabitant of Paris

parison (ˈpærɪsˀn) *n* an unshaped mass of glass before it is moulded into its final form [c19 from French *paraison*, from *parer* to prepare]

parisyllabic (ˌpærɪsɪˈlæbɪk) *adj* (of a noun or verb, in inflected languages) containing the same number of syllables in all or almost all inflected forms. Compare **imparisyllabic**

parity¹ (ˈpærɪtɪ) *n, pl* -ties **1** equality of rank, pay, etc **2** close or exact analogy or equivalence **3** *finance* **a** the amount of a foreign currency equivalent at the established exchange rate to a specific sum of domestic currency **b** a similar equivalence between different forms of the same national currency, esp the gold equivalent of a unit of gold-standard currency **4** equality between prices of commodities or securities in two separate markets **5** *physics* a property of a physical system characterized by the behaviour of the sign of its wave function when all spatial coordinates are reversed in direction. The wave function either remains unchanged (**even parity**) or changes in sign (**odd parity**) **b** a quantum number describing this property, equal to +1 for even parity systems and –1 for odd parity systems. Symbol: P See also **conservation of parity 6** *maths* a relationship between two integers. If both are odd or both even they have the same parity; if one is odd and one even they have different parity **7** (in the US) a system of government support for farm products [c16 from Late Latin *pāritās*; see PAR]

parity² (ˈpærɪtɪ) *n* **1** the condition or fact of having given birth **2** the number of children to which a woman has given birth [c19 from Latin *parere* to bear]

parity check *n* a check made of computer data to ensure that the total number of bits of value 1 (or 0) in each unit of information remains odd or even after transfer between a peripheral device and the memory or vice versa

park (pɑːk) *n* **1** a large area of land preserved in a natural state for recreational use by the public. See also **national park 2** a piece of open land in a town with public amenities **3** *NZ* an area, esp of mountain country, reserved for recreational purposes **4** a large area of land forming a private estate **5** *English law* an enclosed tract of land where wild beasts are protected, acquired by a subject by royal grant or prescription. Compare **forest** (sense 5) **6** an area designed and landscaped to accommodate a group of related enterprises, businesses, research establishments, etc: *science park* **7** *US and Canadian* See **amusement park 8** *US, Canadian, and NZ* See **car park 9** *US and Canadian* a playing field or sports stadium **10 the park** *Brit informal* a soccer pitch **11** a gear selector position on the automatic transmission of a motor vehicle that acts as a parking brake **12** the area in which the equipment and supplies of a military formation are assembled **13** a high valley surrounded by mountains in the western US ▷ *vb* **14** to stop and leave (a vehicle) temporarily **15** to manoeuvre (a motor vehicle) into a space for it to be left: *try to park without hitting the kerb* **16** *stock exchange* to register (securities) in the name of another or of nominees in order to conceal their real ownership **17** (*tr*) *informal* to leave or put somewhere: *park yourself in front of the fire* **18** (*intr*) *military* to arrange equipment in a park **19** (*tr*) to enclose in or as a park [c13 from Old French *parc*, from Medieval Latin *parricus* enclosure, from Germanic; compare Old High German *pfarrih* pen, Old English *pearruc* PADDOCK¹] > ˈparkˌlike *adj*

parka (ˈpɑːkə) *n* a warm hip-length weatherproof coat with a hood, originally worn by the Inuit [c19 from Aleutian: skin]

parkade (ˈpɑːkeɪd) *n Canadian* a building used as a car park [c20 from PARK + (ARC)ADE]

Parker Morris standard *n* (*often plural*) (in Britain) a set of minimum criteria for good housing construction, design, and facilities, recommended by the 1961 report of the Central Housing Advisory Committee chaired by Sir Parker Morris. Subsequent governments have urged private and local authority house-builders to achieve these standards

parkette (ˌpɑːkˈɛt) *n Canadian* a small public park

parkie (ˈpɑːkɪ) *n informal* a park keeper

parkin (ˈpɑːkɪn) *or* **perkin** *n* (in Britain and New Zealand) a moist spicy ginger cake usually containing oatmeal [c19 of unknown origin]

parking disc *n* See **disc** (sense 7a)

parking lot *n US and Canadian* an area or building reserved for parking cars. Also called (in Britain and certain other countries): **carpark**

parking meter *n* a timing device, usually coin-operated, that indicates how long a vehicle may be left parked

parking orbit *n* an orbit around the earth or moon in which a spacecraft can be placed temporarily in order to prepare for the next step in its programme

parking ticket *n* a summons served for a parking offence

Parkinson's disease (ˈpɑːkɪnsənz) *n* a progressive chronic disorder of the central nervous system characterized by impaired muscular coordination and tremor. Often shortened to: **Parkinson's** Also called: **Parkinsonism, Parkinson's syndrome, paralysis agitans, shaking palsy** [c19 named after James *Parkinson* (1755–1824), British surgeon, who first described it]

Parkinson's law *n* the notion, expressed facetiously as a law of economics, that work expands to fill the time available for its completion [c20 named after C. N. *Parkinson* (1909–93), British historian and writer, who formulated it]

park keeper *n* (in Britain) an official employed by a local authority to patrol and supervise a public park

parkland (ˈpɑːkˌlænd) *n* grassland with scattered trees

parkour (ˈpɑːkɔː) *n* the sport or activity of running through urban areas while performing various gymnastic manoeuvres over or on man-made obstacles such as walls and buildings. Also called: **free running** [c20 from French *parcour*, used by the creators of the activity to mean 'obstacle course']

park savanna *n* savanna grassland scattered with trees

parkway (ˈpɑːkˌweɪ) *n* (in the US and Canada) a wide road planted with trees, turf, etc

parky (ˈpɑːkɪ) *adj* **parkier, parkiest** (*usually postpositive*) *Brit informal* (of the weather) chilly; cold [c19 perhaps from PERKY]

parlance (ˈpɑːləns) *n* **1** a particular manner of speaking, esp when specialized; idiom: *political parlance* **2** *archaic* any discussion, such as a debate [c16 from Old French, from *parler* to talk, via Medieval Latin from Late Latin *parabola* speech, PARABLE; compare PARLEY]

parlando (pɑːˈlændəʊ) *adj, adv music* to be performed as though speaking [Italian: speaking, from *parlare* to speak]

parlay (ˈpɑːlɪ) *US and Canadian* ▷ *vb* (*tr*) **1** to stake (winnings from one bet) on a subsequent wager. Brit equivalent: **double up 2** to exploit (one's talent) to achieve worldly success ▷ *n* **3** a bet in which winnings from one wager are staked on another, or a series of such bets [c19 variant of *paroli*, via French from Neapolitan Italian *parolo*, from *paro* a pair, from Latin *pār* equal, PAR]

parley (ˈpɑːlɪ) *n* **1** a discussion, esp between enemies under a truce to decide terms of surrender, etc ▷ *vb* **2** (*intr*) to discuss, esp with an enemy under a truce **3** (*tr*) to speak (a foreign language) [c16 from French, from *parler* to talk, from Medieval Latin *parabolāre*, from Late Latin *parabola* speech, PARABLE] > ˈparleyer *n*

parleyvoo (ˌpɑːlɪˈvuː) *informal* ▷ *vb* (*intr*) **1** to speak French ▷ *n* **2** the French language **3** a Frenchman [c20 jocular respelling of *parlez-vous (français)? do you speak (French)?*]

parliament (ˈpɑːləmənt) *n* **1** an assembly of the representatives of a political nation or people, often the supreme legislative authority **2** any legislative or deliberative assembly, conference, etc **3** Also: **parlement** (in France before the Revolution) any of several high courts of justice in which royal decrees were registered [c13 from Anglo-Latin *parliamentum*, from Old French *parlement*, from *parler* to speak; see PARLEY]

Parliament (ˈpɑːləmənt) *n* **1** the highest legislative authority in Britain, consisting of the House of Commons, which exercises effective power, the House of Lords, and the sovereign **2** a similar legislature in another country **3** the two chambers of a Parliament **4** the lower chamber of a Parliament **5** any of the assemblies of such a body created by a general election and royal summons and dissolved before the next election

parliamentarian (ˌpɑːləmɛnˈtɛərɪən) *n* **1** an expert in parliamentary procedures, etc **2** (*sometimes capital*) *Brit* a Member of Parliament ▷ *adj* **3** of or relating to a parliament or parliaments

Parliamentarian (ˌpɑːləmɛnˈtɛərɪən) *n* **1** a supporter of Parliament during the English Civil War ▷ *adj* **2** of or relating to Parliament or its supporters during the English Civil War

parliamentarianism (ˌpɑːləmɛnˈtɛərɪəˌnɪzəm) *or* **parliamentarism** (ˌpɑːləˈmɛntəˌrɪzəm) *n* the system of parliamentary government

parliamentary (ˌpɑːləˈmɛntərɪ, -trɪ) *adj* (*sometimes capital*) **1** of or characteristic of a parliament or Parliament **2** proceeding from a parliament or Parliament **3** conforming to or derived from the procedures of a parliament or Parliament **4** having a parliament or Parliament **5** of or relating to Parliament or its supporters during the English Civil War

parliamentary agent *n* (in Britain) a person who is employed to manage the parliamentary business of a private group

Parliamentary Commissioner *or in full* **Parliamentary Commissioner for Administration** *n* (in Britain) the official name for **ombudsman** (sense 2)

parliamentary private secretary *n* (in Britain) a backbencher in Parliament who assists a minister, esp in liaison with backbenchers. Abbreviation: **PPS**

parliamentary secretary *n* (in Britain) a Member of Parliament appointed, usually as a junior minister, to assist a Minister of the Crown with departmental responsibilities

parlor car *n* (in the US and Canada) a comfortable railway coach with individual reserved seats

parlour *or US* **parlor** (ˈpɑːlə) *n* **1** *old-fashioned* a living room, esp one kept tidy for the reception of visitors **2** a reception room in a priest's house, convent, etc **3** a small room for guests away from the public rooms in an inn, club, etc **4** *chiefly US, Canadian, and NZ* a room or shop equipped as a place of business: *a billiard parlor* **5** *Caribbean* a small shop, esp one selling cakes and nonalcoholic drinks **6** Also called: **milking parlour** a building equipped for the milking of cows [c13 from Anglo-Norman *parlur*, from Old French *parleur* room in convent for receiving guests, from *parler* to speak; see PARLEY]

parlour game *n* an informal indoor game

parlous (ˈpɑːləs) *archaic or humorous* ▷ *adj* **1** dangerous or difficult **2** cunning ▷ *adv* **3** extremely [c14 *perlous*, variant of PERILOUS] > ˈparlously *adv* > ˈparlousness *n*

Parma *n* **1** (*Italian* ˈparma) a city in N Italy, in Emilia-Romagna: capital of the duchy of Parma and Piacenza from 1545 until it became part of Italy in 1860 (esp Parmesan cheese). Pop: 163 457 (2001) **2** (ˈpɑːmə) a city in NE Ohio, south of Cleveland. Pop: 83 861 (2003 est)

Parma ham *n* cured ham from Italy

Parmentier (ˈpɑːmənˌtjeɪ; *French* parmɑ̃tje) *adj* (of soups, etc) containing or garnished with potatoes [c19 named after A. *Parmentier* (1737–1813), French horticulturist]

Parmesan (ˌpɑːmɪˈzæn, ˈpɑːmɪˌzæn) *adj* **1** of or relating to Parma or its inhabitants ▷ *n* **2** a native or inhabitant of Parma

Parmesan cheese *n* a hard dry cheese made from skimmed milk, used grated, esp on pasta dishes and soups

Parmigiano Reggiano (ˌpɑːmɪˌdʒɑːnəʊ rɛˈdʒɑːnəʊ) *n, pl* **-nos** another name for **Parmesan cheese**

Parnaíba *or* **Parnahiba** (*Portuguese* parnaˈiba) *n* a river in NE Brazil, rising in the Serra das Mangabeiras and flowing generally northeast, to the Atlantic. Length: about 1450 km (900 miles)

Parnassian¹ (pɑːˈnæsɪən) *adj* of or relating to Mount Parnassus or poetry

Parnassian² (pɑːˈnæsɪən) *n* **1** one of a school of French poets of the late 19th century who wrote verse that emphasized metrical form and restricted emotion ▷ *adj* **2** of or relating to the Parnassians or their poetry [c19 from French *parnassien*, from *Parnasse* PARNASSUS; from *Le Parnasse contemporain*, title of an anthology produced by these poets] > Parˈnassianˌism *or* Parˈnasˌsism *n*

Parnassus (pɑːˈnæsəs) *n* **1 Mount** a mountain in central Greece, in NW Boeotia: in ancient times sacred to Dionysus, Apollo, and the Muses, with the Castalian Spring and Delphi on its slopes. Height: 2457 m (8061 ft). Modern Greek names: **Parnassós** (ˌparnaˈsɔs), **Liákoura 2 a** the world of poetry **b** a centre of poetic or other creative activity **3** a collection of verse or belles-lettres

Parnellite (ˈpɑːnəˌlaɪt) *n* **1** a follower or admirer of Charles Stewart Parnell, the Irish nationalist (1846–91) ▷ *adj* **2** of or relating to Parnell or his supporters

Parnell shout *n* NZ *informal* a social occasion where each person in a group pays for his or her own entertainment or meal [from *Parnell*, suburb of Auckland, where very independent people on low incomes were supposed to live]

parochial (pə'rəʊkɪəl) *adj* 1 narrow in outlook or scope; provincial 2 of or relating to a parish or parishes [c14 via Old French from Church Latin *parochiālis*, see PARISH] > pa'rochial,ism *n* > pa'rochi,ality *n* > pa'rochially *adv*

parochial church council *n* Church of England an elected body of lay representatives of the members of a parish that administers the affairs of the parish

parody ('pærədɪ) *n*, *pl* -dies 1 a musical, literary, or other composition that mimics the style of another composer, author, etc, in a humorous or satirical way 2 mimicry of someone's individual manner in a humorous or satirical way 3 something so badly done as to seem an intentional mockery; travesty ▷ *vb* -dies, -dying, -died 4 (*tr*) to make a parody of [c16 via Latin from Greek *paroidiā* satirical poem, from PARA-[1] + *ōidē* song] > **parodic** (pə'rɒdɪk) *or* pa'rodical *adj* > 'parodist *n*

paroecious (pə'riːʃəs) *or* **paroicous** (pə'rɔɪkəs) *adj* (of mosses and related plants) having the male and female reproductive organs at different levels on the same stem [c19 from Greek *paroikos* living nearby, from PARA-[1] (beside) + *oikos* house; compare PARISH]

parol ('pærəl, pə'rəʊl) *law* ▷ *n* 1 (formerly) the pleadings in an action when presented by word of mouth 2 an oral statement; word of mouth (now only in the phrase **by parol**) ▷ *adj* 3 a (of a contract, lease, etc) made orally or in writing but not under seal b expressed or given by word of mouth: *parol evidence* [c15 from Old French *parole* speech; see PAROLE]

parole (pə'rəʊl) *n* 1 a the freeing of a prisoner before his sentence has expired, on the condition that he is of good behaviour b the duration of such conditional release 2 a promise given by a prisoner, as to be of good behaviour if granted liberty or partial liberty 3 a variant spelling of **parol** 4 *US military* a password 5 *linguistics* language as manifested in the individual speech acts of particular speakers. Compare **langue**, **performance** (sense 7), **competence** (sense 5) 6 **on parole** a conditionally released from detention b *informal* (of a person) under scrutiny, esp for a recurrence of an earlier shortcoming ▷ *vb* (*tr*) 7 to place (a person) on parole [c17 from Old French, from the phrase *parole d'honneur* word of honour; *parole* from Late Latin *parabola* speech] > pa'rolable *adj* > parolee (pə,rəʊ'liː) *n*

paronomasia (,pærənəʊ'meɪzɪə) *n* *rhetoric* a play on words, esp a pun [c16 via Latin from Greek: a play on words, from *paronomazein* to make a change in naming, from PARA-[1] (beside) + *onomazein* to name, from *onoma* a name] > **paronomastic** (,pærənəʊ'mæstɪk) *adj* > ,parono'mastically *adv*

paronym ('pærənɪm) *n* *linguistics* a cognate word [c19 via Late Latin from Greek *paronumon*, from PARA-[1] (beside) + *onoma* a name] > ,paro'nymic *or* **paronymous** (pə'rɒnɪməs) *adj* > pa'ronymously *adv*

parore ('pɑːrəʊeɪ) *n*, *pl* **parore** a dark brownish-green fish, *Girella tricuspidata* of coastal and esturine waters in New Zealand's North Island and Australia. Also called: **luderick, mangrove fish** [Māori]

Páros ('pærɒs) *n* a Greek island in the S Aegean Sea, in the Cyclades: site of the discovery (1627) of the Parian Chronicle, a marble tablet outlining Greek history from before 1000 BC to about 354 BC (now at Oxford University). Pop: 12 853 (2001). Area: 166 sq km (64 sq miles)

parosmia (pæ'rɒzmɪə) *n* any disorder of the sense of smell [c19 from PARA-[1] + Greek *osmē* smell]

parotic (pə'rɒtɪk) *adj* situated near the ear [c19 from New Latin *paroticus*, from Greek PARA-[1] (near) + *-oticus*, from *ous* ear]

parotid (pə'rɒtɪd) *adj* 1 relating to or situated near the parotid gland ▷ *n* 2 See **parotid gland** [c17 via French, via Latin from Greek *parōtis*, from PARA-[1] (near) + *-ōtis*, from *ous* ear]

parotid gland *n* a large salivary gland, in man situated in front of and below each ear

parotitis (,pærə'taɪtɪs) *or* **parotiditis** (pə,rɒtɪ'daɪtɪs) *n* inflammation of the parotid gland. See also **mumps**. > **parotitic** (,pærə'tɪtɪk) *or* **parotiditic** (pə,rɒtɪ'dɪtɪk) *adj*

parotoid (pə'rɒtɔɪd) *n* 1 Also called: **parotoid gland** any of various warty poison glands on the head and back of certain toads and salamanders ▷ *adj* 2 resembling a parotid gland [c19 from Greek *parot(is)* (see PAROTID) + -OID]

-parous *adj combining form* giving birth to: *oviparous* [from Latin *-parus*, from *parere* to bring forth]

parousia (pə'ruːsɪə) *n* *Christianity* another term for the **Second Coming** [c19 from Greek: presence]

paroxetine (pæ'rɒksətiːn) *n* an antidepressant drug that acts by preventing the re-uptake after release of serotonin in the brain, thereby prolonging its action: used for treating depression, obsessive-compulsive disorders, and panic disorder. Formula: $C_{19}H_{20}FNO_3$

paroxysm ('pærək,sɪzəm) *n* 1 an uncontrollable outburst: *a paroxysm of giggling* 2 *pathol* a a sudden attack or recurrence of a disease b any fit or convulsion [c17 via French from Medieval Latin *paroxysmus* annoyance, from Greek *paroxusmos*, from *paroxunein* to goad, from PARA-[1] (intensifier) + *oxunein* to sharpen, from *oxus* sharp] > ,parox'ysmal *or* ,parox'ysmic *adj* > ,parox'ysmally *adv*

paroxytone (pə'rɒksɪ,təʊn) *adj* 1 (in the classical Greek language) of, relating to, or denoting words having an acute accent on the next to last syllable ▷ *n* 2 a paroxytone word ▷ Compare **oxytone** [c18 via New Latin from Greek *paroxutonos*, from PARA-[1] (beside) + *-oxutonos* OXYTONE] > **paroxytonic** (,pærɒksɪ'tɒnɪk) *adj*

parpend ('pɑːpənd) *or* **parpen** ('pɑːpən) *n* other names for **perpend**[1]

parquet ('pɑːkeɪ, -kɪ) *n* 1 a floor covering of pieces of hardwood fitted in a decorative pattern; parquetry 2 Also called: **parquet floor** a floor so covered 3 *US* the stalls of a theatre 4 the main part of the Paris Bourse, where officially listed securities are traded. Compare **coulisse** (sense 3) 5 (in France) the department of government responsible for the prosecution of crimes ▷ *vb* (*tr*) 6 to cover (a floor) with parquet [c19 from Old French: small enclosure, from *parc* enclosure; see PARK]

parquet circle *n* *US* the seating area of the main floor of a theatre that lies to the rear of the auditorium and underneath the balcony. Also called: **parterre**

parquetry ('pɑːkɪtrɪ) *n* a geometric pattern of inlaid pieces of wood, often of different kinds, esp as used to cover a floor or to ornament furniture. Compare **marquetry**

parr (pɑː) *n*, *pl* **parrs** *or* **parr** a salmon up to two years of age, with dark spots and transverse bands [c18 of unknown origin]

parra ('pærə) *n* *Austral informal* a tourist or non-resident on a beach [c20 possibly from *Parramatta*, a district of Sydney]

parrakeet ('pærə,kiːt) *n* a variant spelling of **parakeet**

parramatta (,pærə'mætə) *n* a variant spelling of **paramatta**

parrel *or* **parral** ('pærəl) *n* *nautical* a ring that holds the jaws of a boom to the mast but lets it slide up and down [c15 probably from obsolete *aparail* equipment, a variant of APPAREL]

parricide ('pærɪ,saɪd) *n* 1 the act of killing either of one's parents 2 a person who kills his parent [c16 from Latin *parricīdium* murder of a parent or relative, and from *parricīda* one who murders a relative, from *parri-* (element related to Greek *pēos* kinsman) + *-cīdium*, *-cīda* -CIDE] > ,parri'cidal *adj*

parritch ('pærɪtʃ, 'pɑːr-) *n* a Scot word for **porridge**

parrot ('pærət) *n* 1 any bird of the tropical and subtropical order *Psittaciformes*, having a short hooked bill, compact body, bright plumage, and an ability to mimic sounds. Related adj: **psittacine** 2 a person who repeats or imitates the words or actions of another unintelligently 3 **sick as a parrot** *usually facetious* extremely disappointed ▷ *vb* -rots, -roting, -roted 4 (*tr*) to repeat or imitate mechanically without understanding [c16 probably from French *paroquet*; see PARAKEET] > 'parrotry *n*

parrot-fashion *adv informal* without regard for meaning; by rote: *she learned it parrot-fashion*

parrot fever *or* **disease** *n* another name for **psittacosis**

parrotfish ('pærət,fɪʃ) *n*, *pl* -fish *or* -fishes 1 any brightly coloured tropical marine percoid fish of the family *Scaridae*, having parrot-like jaws 2 *Austral* any of various brightly coloured marine fish of the family *Labridae* 3 any of various similar fishes

parrot toadstool *n* See **wax cap**

parry ('pærɪ) *vb* -ries, -rying, -ried 1 to ward off (an attack) by blocking or deflecting, as in fencing 2 (*tr*) to evade (questions), esp adroitly ▷ *n*, *pl* -ries 3 an act of parrying, esp (in fencing) using a stroke or circular motion of the blade 4 a skilful evasion, as of a question [c17 from French *parer* to ward off, from Latin *parāre* to prepare]

parse (pɑːz) *vb* *grammar* 1 to assign constituent structure to (a sentence or the words in a sentence) 2 (*intr*) (of a word or linguistic element) to play a specified role in the structure of a sentence [c16 from Latin *pars* (*orātionis*) part (of speech)] > 'parsable *adj*

parsec ('pɑː,sɛk) *n* a unit of astronomical distance equal to the distance from earth at which stellar parallax would be 1 second of arc; equivalent to 3.0857×10^{16} m or 3.262 light years [c20 from PARALLAX + SECOND[2]]

Parsee *or* **Parsi** ('pɑːsiː) *n* 1 an adherent of a monotheistic religion of Zoroastrian origin, the practitioners of which were driven out of Persia by the Muslims in the eighth century AD. It is now found chiefly in western India ▷ *adj* 2 of or relating to the Parsees or their religion [c17 from Persian *Pārsī* a Persian, from Old Persian *Pārsa* PERSIA] > 'Parsee,ism *n*

parser ('pɑːzə) *n* *computing* a program or part of a program that interprets input to a computer by recognizing key words or analysing sentence structure

Parsha ('pɑːʃə; *Yiddish* 'parʃə) *n* the Yiddish word for **Parashah**

Parsifal ('pɑːsɪfªl, -,fɑːl) *or* **Parzival** *n* *german myth* the hero of a medieval cycle of legends about the Holy Grail. English eqivalent: **Percival**

parsimony ('pɑːsɪmənɪ) *n* extreme care or reluctance in spending; frugality; niggardliness [c15 from Latin *parcimōnia*, from *parcere* to spare] > **parsimonious** (,pɑːsɪ'məʊnɪəs) *adj* > ,parsi'moniously *adv*

parsley ('pɑːslɪ) *n* 1 a S European umbelliferous plant, *Petroselinum crispum*, widely cultivated for its curled aromatic leaves, which are used in cooking 2 any of various similar and related plants, such as fool's-parsley, stone parsley, and cow parsley [c14 *persely*, from Old English *petersilie* + Old French *persil*, *pereisl*, both ultimately from Latin *petroselīnum* rock parsley, from Greek *petroselinon*, from *petra* rock + *selinon* parsley]

parsley fern *n* 1 a small bright green tufted European fern, *Cryptogramma crispa*, that grows on acid scree and rock in uplands 2 any of several other plants with crisped foliage, resembling that of parsley

parsley piert (pɪət) *n* a small N temperate rosaceous plant, *Aphanes arvensis*, having fan-shaped leaves and small greenish flowers [c17 from French *perce pierre*, literally: break stone]

parsnip ('pɑːsnɪp) *n* 1 a strong-scented umbelliferous plant, *Pastinaca sativa*, cultivated for

p

its long whitish root **2** the root of this plant, eaten as a vegetable **3** any of several similar plants, esp the cow parsnip [c14 from Old French *pasnaie*, from Latin *pastināca*, from *pastināre* to dig, from *pastinum* two-pronged tool for digging; also influenced by Middle English *nepe* TURNIP]

parson ('pɑːsᵊn) *n* **1** a parish priest in the Church of England, formerly applied only to those who held ecclesiastical benefices **2** any clergyman **3** NZ a nonconformist minister [c13 from Medieval Latin *persōna* parish priest, representative of the parish, from Latin: personage; see PERSON] > **parsonic** (pɑː'sɒnɪk) *or* **par'sonical** *adj*

parsonage ('pɑːsᵊnɪdʒ) *n* the residence of a parson who is not a rector or vicar, as provided by the parish

parson bird *n* another name for **tui** [c19 so called because of its dark plumage with white neck feathers]

parson's nose *n* the fatty extreme end portion of the tail of a fowl when cooked. Also called: **pope's nose**

part (pɑːt) *n* **1** a piece or portion of a whole **2** an integral constituent of something: *dancing is part of what we teach* **3** **a** an amount less than the whole; bit: *they only recovered part of the money* **b** (*as modifier*): *an old car in part exchange for a new one* **4** one of several equal or nearly equal divisions: *mix two parts flour to one part water* **5** **a** an actor's role in a play **b** the speech and actions which make up such a role **c** a written copy of these **6** a person's proper role or duty: *everyone must do his part* **7** (*often plural*) region; area: *you're well known in these parts* **8** *anatomy* any portion of a larger structure **9** a component that can be replaced in a machine, engine, etc: *spare parts* **10** *US, Canadian and Austral* the line of scalp showing when sections of hair are combed in opposite directions. British equivalent: **parting** **11** *music* **a** one of a number of separate melodic lines making up the texture of music **b** one of such melodic lines, which is assigned to one or more instrumentalists or singers: *the viola part; the soprano solo part* **c** such a line performed from a separately written or printed copy. See **part song** **12** **for the most part** generally **13** **for one's part** as far as one is concerned **14** **in part** to some degree; partly **15** **of many parts** having many different abilities **16** **on the part of** on behalf of **17** **part and parcel** an essential ingredient **18** **play a part** **a** to pretend to be what one is not **b** (foll by *in*) to have something to do (with); be instrumental (in): *to play a part in the king's downfall* **19** **take in good part** to respond to (teasing) with good humour **20** **take part in** to participate in **21** **take someone's part** to support someone in an argument ▷ *vb* **22** to divide or separate from one another; take or come apart: *to part the curtains; the seams parted when I washed the dress* **23** to go away or cause to go away from one another; stop or cause to stop seeing each other: *the couple parted amicably* **24** (*intr;* foll by *from*) to leave; say goodbye (to) **25** (*intr;* foll by *with*) to relinquish, esp reluctantly: *I couldn't part with my teddy bear* **26** (*tr;* foll by *from*) to cause to relinquish, esp reluctantly: *he's not easily parted from his cash* **27** (*intr*) to split; separate: *the path parts here* **28** (*tr*) to arrange (the hair) in such a way that a line of scalp is left showing **29** (*intr*) a euphemism for **die¹** (sense 1) **30** (*intr*) *archaic* to depart **31** **part company** **a** to end a friendship or association, esp as a result of a quarrel; separate: *they were in partnership, but parted company last year* **b** (foll by *with*) to leave; go away from; be separated from ▷ *adv* **32** to some extent; partly ▷ See also **parts** [c13 via Old French from Latin *partīre* to divide, from *pars* a part]

part. *abbreviation for* **1** participle **2** particular

partake (pɑː'teɪk) *vb* **-takes, -taking, -took, -taken** (*mainly intr*) **1** (foll by *in*) to have a share; participate: *to partake in the excitement* **2** (foll by *of*) to take or receive a portion, esp of food or drink: *each partook of the food offered to him* **3** (foll by *of*) to suggest or have some of the quality (of): *music partaking of sadness* **4** (*tr*) *archaic* to share in [c16 back formation from *partaker*, earlier *part taker*, based on Latin *particeps* participant; see PART, TAKE] > **par'taker** *n*

> USAGE *Partake of* is sometimes wrongly used as if it were a synonym of *eat* or *drink*. Correctly, one can only *partake of* food or drink which is available for several people to share

partan ('pɑːtᵊn; *Scot* 'partᵊn) *n* a Scot word for **crab¹** (senses 1, 2) [c15 of Celtic origin]

parted ('pɑːtɪd) *adj* **1** *botany* divided almost to the base: *parted leaves* **2** *heraldry* showing two coats of arms divided by a vertical central line

parterre (pɑː'tɛə) *n* **1** a formally patterned flower garden **2** *Brit* *Irish* the pit in a theatre **3** *US* another name for **parquet circle** [c17 from French, from *par* along + *terre* ground]

part exchange *n* a transaction in which used goods are taken as partial payment for more expensive ones of the same type

parthenocarpy (pɑː'θiːnəʊˌkɑːpɪ) *n* the development of fruit without fertilization or formation of seeds [c20 from Greek *parthenos* virgin + *karpos* fruit] > **parˌtheno'carpic** *or* **parˌtheno'carpous** *adj*

parthenogenesis (ˌpɑːθɪnəʊ'dʒɛnɪsɪs) *n* **1** a type of reproduction, occurring in some insects and flowers, in which the unfertilized ovum develops directly into a new individual **2** human conception without fertilization by a male; virgin birth [c19 from Greek *parthenos* virgin + *genesis* birth] > **parthenogenetic** (ˌpɑːθɪˌnəʊdʒɪ'nɛtɪk) *adj* > **ˌpartheˌnoge'netically** *adv*

Parthenon ('pɑːθəˌnɒn, -nən) *n* the temple on the Acropolis in Athens built in the 5th century BC and regarded as the finest example of the Greek Doric order

Parthenopaeus (ˌpɑːθənəʊ'piːəs) *n* *Greek myth* one of the Seven against Thebes, son of Atalanta

Parthenope (pɑː'θɛnəpɪ) *n* *Greek myth* a siren, who drowned herself when Odysseus evaded the lure of the sirens' singing. Her body was said to have been cast ashore at what became Naples

Parthenos ('pɑːθɪˌnɒs) *n* an epithet meaning "Virgin", applied by the Greeks to several goddesses, esp Athena

parthenospore (pɑː'θiːnəʊˌspɔː) *n* another name for **azygospore**

Parthia ('pɑːθɪə) *n* a country in ancient Asia, southeast of the Caspian Sea, that expanded into a great empire dominating SW Asia in the 2nd century BC It was destroyed by the Sassanids in the 3rd century A.D

Parthian ('pɑːθɪən) *adj* **1** of or relating to Parthia, a country in ancient Asia, or its inhabitants ▷ *n* **2** a native or inhabitant of Parthia

Parthian shot *n* another term for **parting shot** [alluding to the custom of Parthian archers who shot their arrows backwards while retreating]

partial ('pɑːʃəl) *adj* **1** relating to only a part; not general or complete: *a partial eclipse* **2** biased: *a partial judge* **3** (*postpositive;* foll by *to*) having a particular liking (for) **4** *botany* **a** constituting part of a larger structure: *a partial umbel* **b** used for only part of the life cycle of a plant: *a partial habitat* **c** (of a parasite) not exclusively parasitic **5** *maths* designating or relating to an operation in which only one of a set of independent variables is considered at a time ▷ *n* **6** Also called: **partial tone** *music, acoustics* any of the component tones of a single musical sound, including both those that belong to the harmonic series of the sound and those that do not **7** *maths* a partial derivative [c15 from Old French *parcial*, from Late Latin *partiālis* incomplete, from Latin *pars* PART] > **'partially** *adv* > **'partialness** *n*

> USAGE See at **partly**

partial derivative *n* the derivative of a function of two or more variables with respect to one of the variables, the other or others being considered constant. Written $\partial f/\partial x$

partial eclipse *n* an eclipse, esp of the sun, in which the body is only partially hidden. Compare **total eclipse, annular eclipse**

partial fraction *n* *maths* one of a set of fractions into which a more complicated fraction can be resolved

partiality (ˌpɑːʃɪ'ælɪtɪ) *n, pl* **-ties** **1** favourable prejudice or bias **2** (usually foll by *for*) liking or fondness **3** the state or condition of being partial

partially sighted *adj* **a** unable to see properly so that even with corrective aids normal activities are prevented or seriously hindered **b** (*as collective noun;* preceded by *the*): *the partially sighted* > **partial sight** *n*

partial pressure *n* the pressure that a gas, in a mixture of gases, would exert if it alone occupied the whole volume occupied by the mixture

partial product *n* the result obtained when a number is multiplied by one digit of a multiplier

partial reinforcement *n* *psychol* the process of randomly rewarding an organism for making a response on only some of the occasions it makes it

partible ('pɑːtəbᵊl) *adj* (esp of property or an inheritance) divisible; separable [c16 from Late Latin *partibilis*, from *part-*, *pars* PART]

Participaction (pɑːˌtɪsɪ'pækʃən) *n* (in Canada) a non-profit-making organization set up to promote physical fitness [from PARTICIP(ATION) + ACTION]

participate (pɑː'tɪsɪˌpeɪt) *vb* (*intr;* often foll by *in*) to take part, be or become actively involved, or share (in) [c16 from Latin *participāre*, from *pars* PART + *capere* to take] > **par'ticipant** *adj, n* > **parˌtici'pation** *n* > **par'ticiˌpator** *n* > **par'ticipatory** *adj*

participating insurance *n* a system of insurance by which policyholders receive dividends from the company's profit or surplus

participle ('pɑːtɪsɪpᵊl, pɑː'tɪsɪpᵊl) *n* a nonfinite form of verbs, in English and other languages, used adjectivally and in the formation of certain compound tenses. See also **present participle, past participle** [c14 via Old French from Latin *participium*, from *particeps* partaker, from *pars* PART + *capere* to take] > **participial** (ˌpɑːtɪ'sɪpɪəl) *adj, n* > **ˌparti'cipially** *adv*

particle ('pɑːtɪkᵊl) *n* **1** an extremely small piece of matter; speck **2** a very tiny amount; iota: *it doesn't make a particle of difference* **3** a function word, esp (in certain languages) a word belonging to an uninflected class having suprasegmental or grammatical function: *the Greek particles "mēn" and "de" are used to express contrast; questions in Japanese are indicated by the particle "ka"; English "up" is sometimes regarded as an adverbial particle* **4** a common affix, such as *re-*, *un-*, or *-ness* **5** *physics* a body with finite mass that can be treated as having negligible size, and internal structure **6** See **elementary particle** **7** *RC Church* a small piece broken off from the Host at Mass **8** *archaic* a section or clause of a document [c14 from Latin *particula* a small part, from *pars* PART]

particle accelerator *n* a machine for accelerating charged elementary particles to very high energies, used for research in nuclear physics. See also **linear accelerator, cyclotron, betatron, synchrotron, synchrocyclotron**

particle beam *n* **1** a stream of energized particles produced by a particle accelerator **2** such a stream emitted by a particle beam weapon

particle beam weapon *n* a weapon that fires particle beams into the atmosphere or space

particle board *n* another name for **chipboard**

particle physics *n* the study of fundamental particles and their properties. Also called: **high-energy physics**

particle separation *n* *transformational grammar* a rule that moves the particle of a phrasal verb, thus deriving a sentence like *He looked the answer up* from a structure that also underlies *He looked up the answer*

parti-coloured or **party-coloured** ('pɑːtɪˌkʌləd) adj having different colours in different parts; variegated [C16 parti, from (obsolete) party of more than one colour, from Old French: striped, from Latin partīre to divide]

particular (pə'tɪkjʊlə) adj 1 (prenominal) of or belonging to a single or specific person, thing, category, etc; specific; special: the particular demands of the job; no particular reason 2 (prenominal) exceptional or marked: a matter of particular importance 3 (prenominal) relating to or providing specific details or circumstances: a particular account 4 exacting or difficult to please, esp in details; fussy 5 (of the solution of a differential equation) obtained by giving specific values to the arbitrary constants in a general equation 6 logic (of a proposition) affirming or denying something about only some members of a class of objects, as in some men are not wicked. Compare **universal** (sense 10) 7 property law denoting an estate that precedes the passing of the property into ultimate ownership. See also **remainder** (sense 3), **reversion** (sense 4) ▷ n 8 a separate distinct item that helps to form a generalization: opposed to general 9 (often plural) an item of information; detail: complete in every particular 10 logic another name for **individual** (sense 7a) 11 philosophy an individual object, as contrasted with a universal. See **universal** (sense 12b) 12 **in particular** especially, particularly, or exactly [C14 from Old French particuler, from Late Latin particulāris concerning a part, from Latin particula PARTICLE V]

particular average n insurance partial damage to or loss of a ship or its cargo affecting only the shipowner or one cargo owner. Abbreviation: PA Compare **general average**

particularism (pə'tɪkjʊləˌrɪzəm) n 1 exclusive attachment to the interests of one group, class, sect, etc, esp at the expense of the community as a whole 2 the principle of permitting each state or minority in a federation to further its own interests or retain its own laws, traditions, etc 3 theol the doctrine that divine grace is restricted to the elect > par'ticularist n, adj > parˌticular'istic adj

particularity (pəˌtɪkjʊ'lærɪtɪ) n, pl -ties 1 (often plural) a specific circumstance: the particularities of the affair 2 great attentiveness to detail; fastidiousness 3 the quality of being precise 4 the state or quality of being particular as opposed to general; individuality

particularize or **particularise** (pə'tɪkjʊləˌraɪz) vb 1 to treat in detail; give details (about) 2 (intr) to go into detail > parˌculari'zation or parˌticulari'sation n > par'ticularˌizer or par'ticularˌiser n

particularly (pə'tɪkjʊləlɪ) adv 1 very much; exceptionally: I wasn't particularly successful 2 in particular; specifically: pensioners, particularly the less well-off

Particulars of Claim pl n law (in England) the first reading made by the claimant in a county court action, showing the facts upon which he or she relies in support of a claim and the relief asked for

particulate (pɑː'tɪkjʊlɪt, -ˌleɪt) n 1 a substance consisting of separate particles ▷ adj 2 of or made up of separate particles 3 genetics of, relating to, or designating inheritance of characteristics, esp with emphasis on the role of genes

parting ('pɑːtɪŋ) n 1 Brit the line of scalp showing when sections of hair are combed in opposite directions. US, Canadian, and Austral equivalent: **part 2** the act of separating or the state of being separated 3 a departure or leave-taking, esp one causing a final separation b (as modifier): a parting embrace 4 a place or line of separation or division 5 chem a division of a crystal along a plane that is not a cleavage plane 6 a euphemism for **death** ▷ adj (prenominal) 7 literary departing: the parting day 8 serving to divide or separate

parting shot n a hostile remark or gesture

delivered while departing. Also called: Parthian shot

parting strip n a thin strip of wood, metal, etc, used to separate two adjoining materials

parti pris French (parti pri) n a preconceived opinion [C19 literally: side taken]

Parti Québécois (French parti) n (in Canada) a political party in Quebec, formed in 1968 and originally advocating the separation of Quebec from the rest of the country. Abbreviation: PQ

partisan[1] or **partizan** (ˌpɑːtɪ'zæn, 'pɑːtɪˌzæn) n 1 an adherent or devotee of a cause, party, etc 2 a a member of an armed resistance group within occupied territory, esp in Italy or the Balkans in World War II b (as modifier): partisan forces ▷ adj 3 of, relating to, or characteristic of a partisan 4 relating to or excessively devoted to one party, faction, etc; one-sided: partisan control [C16 via French, from Old Italian partigiano, from parte faction, from Latin pars PART] > ˌparti'sanship or ˌparti'zanship n

partisan[2] or **partizan** ('pɑːtɪzən) n a spear or pike with two opposing axe blades or spikes [C16 from French partizane, from Old Italian partigiana, from partigiano PARTISAN[1]]

partita (pɑː'tiːtə) n, pl -te (-teɪ) or -tas music a type of suite [Italian: divided (piece), from Latin partīre to divide]

partite ('pɑːtaɪt) adj 1 (in combination) composed of or divided into a specified number of parts: bipartite 2 (esp of plant leaves) divided almost to the base to form two or more parts [C16 from Latin partīre to divide]

partition (pɑː'tɪʃən) n 1 a division into parts; separation 2 something that separates, such as a large screen dividing a room in two 3 a part or share 4 a division of a country into two or more separate nations 5 property law a division of property, esp realty, among joint owners 6 maths any of the ways by which an integer can be expressed as a sum of integers 7 logic, maths a the division of a class into a number of disjoint and exhaustive subclasses b such a set of subclasses 8 biology a structure that divides or separates 9 rhetoric the second part of a speech where the chief lines of thought are announced ▷ vb (tr) 10 (often foll by off) to separate or apportion into sections: to partition a room off with a large screen 11 to divide (a country) into two or more separate nations 12 property law to divide (property, esp realty) among joint owners, by dividing either the property itself or the proceeds of sale [C15 via Old French from Latin partītiō, from partīre to divide] > par'titioner or par'titionist n

partition coefficient n chem the ratio of the concentrations of a substance in two heterogenous phases in equilibrium with each other

partitive ('pɑːtɪtɪv) adj 1 grammar indicating that a noun involved in a construction refers only to a part or fraction of what it otherwise refers to. The phrase some of the butter is a partitive construction; in some inflected languages it would be translated by the genitive case of the noun 2 serving to separate or divide into parts ▷ n 3 grammar a partitive linguistic element or feature [C16 from Medieval Latin partītīvus serving to divide, from Latin partīre to divide] > 'partitively adv

partlet ('pɑːtlɪt) n a woman's garment covering the neck and shoulders, worn esp during the 16th century [C16 a variant of Middle English patelet strip of cloth, from Middle French patelette]

partly ('pɑːtlɪ) adv to some extent; not completely

USAGE Partly and partially are to some extent interchangeable, but partly should be used when referring to a part or parts of something: the building is partly (not partially) of stone, while partially is preferred for the meaning to some extent: his mother is partially (not partly) sighted

partner ('pɑːtnə) n 1 an ally or companion: a partner in crime 2 a member of a partnership 3 one of a pair of dancers or players on the same side in a game: my bridge partner 4 either member of a couple in a relationship ▷ vb 5 to be or cause to be a partner (of) [C14 variant (influenced by PART) of PARCENER] > 'partnerless adj

partners ('pɑːtnəz) pl n nautical a wooden construction around an opening in a deck, as to support a mast

partnership ('pɑːtnəʃɪp) n 1 a a contractual relationship between two or more persons carrying on a joint business venture with a view to profit, each incurring liability for losses and the right to share in the profits b the deed creating such a relationship c the persons associated in such a relationship 2 the state or condition of being a partner

partnerships for peace n a subsidiary organization of NATO, comprising former Warsaw Pact countries that wish to be allied with NATO but have not been granted full NATO membership: established in 1994

part-off n Caribbean a screen used to divide off part of a room, such as the eating place of a parlour

part of speech n a class of words sharing important syntactic or semantic features; a group of words in a language that may occur in similar positions or fulfil similar functions in a sentence. The chief parts of speech in English are noun, pronoun, adjective, determiner, adverb, verb, preposition, conjunction, and interjection. Abbreviation: POS

parton ('pɑːtɒn) n physics a hypothetical elementary particle postulated as a constituent of neutrons and protons [from PART + -ON]

partook (pɑː'tʊk) vb the past tense of **partake**

partridge ('pɑːtrɪdʒ) n, pl -tridges or -tridge 1 any of various small Old World gallinaceous game birds of the genera Perdix, Alectoris, etc, esp P. perdix (**common** or **European partridge**): family Phasianidae (pheasants) 2 US and Canadian any of various other gallinaceous birds, esp the bobwhite and ruffed grouse [C13 from Old French perdriz, from Latin perdix, from Greek]

partridgeberry ('pɑːtrɪdʒˌbɛrɪ) n, pl -ries 1 Also called: **boxberry, twinberry** a creeping woody rubiaceous plant, Mitchella repens, of E North America with small white fragrant flowers and scarlet berries 2 the berry of the wintergreen 3 another name for **wintergreen** (sense 1)

partridge-wood n the dark striped wood of the tropical American leguminous tree, Andira inermis, used for cabinetwork

parts (pɑːts) pl n 1 personal abilities or talents: a man of many parts 2 short for **private parts**

Parts of Holland n See Holland[1] (sense 3)

Parts of Kesteven n See (Parts of) Kesteven

Parts of Lindsey n See (Parts of) Lindsey

part song n 1 a song composed in harmonized parts 2 (in more technical usage) a piece of homophonic choral music in which the topmost part carries the melody

part-time adj 1 for less than the entire time appropriate to an activity: a part-time job; a part-time waitress ▷ adv part time 2 on a part-time basis: he works part time ▷ Compare **full-time**. > ˌpart-'timer n

parturient (pɑː'tjʊərɪənt) adj 1 of or relating to childbirth 2 giving birth 3 producing or about to produce a new idea, etc [C16 via Latin parturīre, from parere to bring forth] > par'turiency n

parturient fever n another name for **milk fever**

parturifacient (pɑːˌtjʊərɪ'feɪʃənt) adj, n a medical word for **oxytocic** [C19 from Latin parturīre to be in travail + facere to make]

parturition (ˌpɑːtjʊ'rɪʃən) n the act or process of giving birth [C17 from Late Latin parturītiō, from parturīre to be in labour]

partway ('pɑːtˌweɪ) adv some of the way; partly: I stopped reading partway through the chapter

part work n Brit a series of magazines issued as

at weekly or monthly intervals, which are designed to be bound together to form a complete course or book

part-writing *n music* the aspect of composition concerned with the writing of parts, esp counterpoint

party ('pɑːtɪ) *n, pl* -ties **1 a** a social gathering for pleasure, often held as a celebration **b** (*as modifier*): *party spirit* **c** (*in combination*): *partygoer* **2** a group of people associated in some activity: *a rescue party* **3 a** (*often capital*) a group of people organized together to further a common political aim, such as the election of its candidates to public office **b** (*as modifier*): *party politics* **4** the practice of taking sides on public issues **5** a person, esp one who participates in some activity such as entering into a contract **6** the person or persons taking part in legal proceedings, such as plaintiff or prosecutor: *a party to the action* **7** *informal, humorous* a person: *he's an odd old party* ▷ *vb* -ties, -tying, -tied (*intr*) **8** *informal* to celebrate; revel ▷ *adj* **9** *heraldry* (of a shield) divided vertically into two colours, metals, or furs [c13 from Old French *partie* part, faction, from Latin *partīre* to divide; see PART]

party line *n* **1** a telephone line serving two or more subscribers **2** the policies or dogma of a political party, to which all members are expected to subscribe **3** *chiefly US* the boundary between adjoining property

party list *n* (*modifier*) of or relating to a system of voting in which people vote for a party rather than for a candidate. Parties are assigned the number of seats which reflects their share of the vote. See **proportional representation**

party man *n* a loyal member of a political party, esp one who is extremely loyal or devoted

party politics *pl n* politics conducted through, by, or for parties, as opposed to other interests or the public good

party pooper ('puːpə) *n informal* a person whose behaviour or personality spoils other people's enjoyment [c20 originally US]

party popper *n* a small plastic cylinder which, when a string is pulled, makes a small bang and fires thin paper streamers into the air

party wall *n property law* a wall separating two properties or pieces of land and over which each of the adjoining owners has certain rights

parulis (pə'ruːlɪs) *n, pl* -lides (-lɪˌdiːz) *pathol* another name for **gumboil** [c19 from PARA-¹ + Greek *oulon* gum]

parure (pə'rʊə) *n* a set of jewels or other ornaments [c15 from Old French *pareure* adornment, from *parer* to embellish, from Latin *parāre* to arrange]

par value *n* the value imprinted on the face of a share certificate or bond and used to assess dividend, capital ownership, or interest. Also called: **face value** Compare **market value, book value** (sense 2)

Parvati ('pʌrvətɪ) *n Hinduism* goddess consort of the god Siva, associated with mountains [from Sanskrit: the mountain-dwelling one]

parve ('pɑːvə) *adj* a variant of **parev**

parvenu ('pɑːvəˌnjuː) *n* **1** a person, esp a man, who, having risen socially or economically, is considered to be an upstart or to lack the appropriate refinement for his or her new position ▷ *adj* **2** of or characteristic of a parvenu [c19 from French, from *parvenir* to attain, from Latin *pervenīre*, from *per* through + *venīre* to come]

parvenue ('pɑːvəˌnjuː) *n* **1** a woman who, having risen socially or economically, is considered to be an upstart or to lack the appropriate refinement for her new position ▷ *adj* **2** of or characteristic of a parvenue [c19 see PARVENU]

parvifoliate (ˌpɑːvɪˈfəʊlɪˌeɪt) *adj* (of plants) having small leaves in comparison with the size of the stem

parvis or **parvise** ('pɑːvɪs) *n* a court or portico in front of a building, esp a church [c14 via Old

French from Late Latin *paradīsus* PARADISE]

parvovirus ('pɑːvəʊˌvaɪrəs) *n* any of a group of viruses characterized by their very small size, each of which is specific to a particular species, as for example canine parvovirus [c20 New Latin from Latin *parvus* little + VIRUS]

Parzival (*German* 'partsifal) *n* a variant of **Parsifal**

pas (pɑː; *French* pɑ) *n, pl* **pas** (pɑːz; *French* pɑ) **1** a dance step or movement, esp in ballet **2** *rare* the right to precede; precedence [c18 French, literally: step]

PA's *pl n mountaineering* a type of rock boot [c20 named after Pierre Allain, French climber]

Pasadena (ˌpæsə'diːnə) *n* a city in SW California, east of Los Angeles. Pop: 144 413 (2003 est)

Pasargadae (pæ'sɑːɡəˌdiː) *n* an ancient city in Persia, northeast of Persepolis in present-day Iran: built by Cyrus the Great

Pasay ('pɑːsaɪ) *n* a city in the Philippines, on central Luzon just south of Manila, on Manila Bay. Pop: 364 000 (2005 est). Also called: **Rizal**

pascal ('pæskəl) *n* the derived SI unit of pressure; the pressure exerted on an area of 1 square metre by a force of 1 newton; equivalent to 10 dynes per square centimetre or 1.45×10^{-4} pound per square inch. Symbol: Pa [c20 named after Blaise Pascal (1623–62), French philosopher, mathematician, and physicist]

Pascal ('pæsˌkæl, -kəl) *n* a high-level computer programming language developed as a teaching language: used for general-purpose programming

Pascal's triangle *n* a triangle consisting of rows of numbers; the apex is 1 and each row starts and ends with 1, other numbers being obtained by adding together the two numbers on either side in the row above: used to calculate probabilities [c17 named after Blaise Pascal (1623–62), French philosopher, mathematician, and physicist]

Pascal's wager *n philosophy* the argument that it is in one's rational self-interest to act as if God exists, since the infinite punishments of hell, provided they have a positive probability, however small, outweigh any countervailing advantage [c17 named after Blaise Pascal (1623–62), French philosopher, mathematician, and physicist]

Pasch (pɑːsk, pæsk) *n* an archaic name for **Passover** (sense 1) or **Easter** [c12 from Old French *pasche*, via Church Latin and Greek from Hebrew *pesakh* PESACH]

paschal ('pæskəl) *adj* **1** of or relating to Passover **2** of or relating to Easter

paschal flower *n* another name for **pasqueflower**

Paschal Lamb *n* **1** (*sometimes not capitals*) Old Testament the lamb killed and eaten on the first day of the Passover **2** Christ regarded as this sacrifice

pas de basque (ˌpɑː də 'bɑːsk; *French* pɑ də bask) *n, pl* **pas de basque** a dance step performed usually on the spot, consisting of one long and two short movements during which the weight is transferred from one foot to the other: used esp in reels and jigs [from French, literally: Basque step]

Pas-de-Calais (*French* pɑdkalɛ) *n* a department of N France, in Nord-Pas-de-Calais region, on the Straits of Dover (the **Pas de Calais**): the part of France closest to the British Isles. Capital: Arras. Pop: 1 451 307 (2003 est). Area: 6752 sq km (2633 sq miles)

pas de chat (*French* padʃa) *n, pl* **pas de chat** *ballet* a catlike leap [French: cat's step]

pas de deux (*French* padø) *n, pl* **pas de deux** *ballet* a sequence for two dancers [French: step for two]

pase ('pɑːseɪ) *n bullfighting* a movement of the cape or muleta by a matador to attract the bull's attention and guide its attack [from Spanish, literally: pass]

pash¹ (pæʃ) *n slang* infatuation [c20 from PASSION]

pash² (pæʃ) *obsolete or dialect* ▷ *vb* **1** to throw or be thrown and break or be broken to bits; smash ▷ *n* **2** a crushing blow [c17 (n): from earlier *passhen* to throw with violence, probably of imitative origin]

pasha or **pacha** ('pɑːʃə, 'pæʃə) *n* (*formerly*) a

provincial governor or other high official of the Ottoman Empire or the modern Egyptian kingdom: placed after a name when used as a title [c17 from Turkish *paşa*]

pashalik or **pashalic** ('pɑːʃəlɪk) *n* the province or jurisdiction of a pasha [c18 from Turkish]

pashka ('pæʃkə) *n* a rich Russian dessert made of cottage cheese, cream, almonds, currants, etc, set in a special wooden mould and traditionally eaten at Easter

pashm ('pæʃəm) *n* the underfur of various Tibetan animals, esp goats, used for cashmere shawls [from Persian, literally: wool]

pashmina (pæʃ'miːnə) *n* a scarf or shawl made of pashm [from Persian *pashmina*; see PASHM]

Pashto, Pushto ('pʌʃtəʊ) or **Pushtu** *n* **1** a language of Afghanistan and NW Pakistan, belonging to the East Iranian branch of the Indo-European family: since 1936 the official language of Afghanistan **2** *pl* -to or -tos, -tu or -tus a speaker of the Pashto language; a Pathan ▷ *adj* **3** denoting or relating to this language or a speaker of it

Pasiphaë¹ (pə'sɪfiː) *n Greek myth* the wife of Minos and mother (by a bull) of the Minotaur

Pasiphaë² (pə'sɪfiː) *n astronomy* a small outer satellite of the planet Jupiter

paso doble ('pæsəʊ 'dəʊbleɪ; *Spanish* 'paso 'doβle) *n, pl* **paso dobles** or **pasos dobles** (*Spanish* 'pasos 'doβles) **1** a modern ballroom dance in fast duple time **2** a piece of music composed for or in the rhythm of this dance [Spanish: double step]

PASOK ('pæsɒk) *n acronym for* Panhellenic Socialist Movement [c20 Modern Greek *Pa(nhellenion) So(sialistiko) K(enema)*]

pas op ('pɑːs ˌɒp) *interj South African* beware [Afrikaans]

paspalum (pæs'peɪləm) *n* any of various grasses of the genus *Paspalum* of Australia and New Zealand having wide leaves [from New Latin, from Greek *paspalos*, a variety of millet]

pasqueflower ('pɑːskˌflaʊə, 'pæsk-) *n* **1** a purple-flowered herbaceous ranunculaceous plant, *Anemone pulsatilla* (or *Pulsatilla vulgaris*), of N and Central Europe and W Asia **2** any of several related North American plants, such as *A. patens* ▷ Also called: **paschal flower, pulsatilla** [c16 from French *passefleur*, from *passer* to excel + *fleur* flower; changed to *pasqueflower* Easter flower, because it blooms at Easter]

pasquinade (ˌpæskwɪ'neɪd) or **pasquil** ('pæskwɪl) *n* **1** an abusive lampoon or satire, esp one posted in a public place ▷ *vb* -ades, -ading, -aded or -quils, -quilling, -quilled **2** (*tr*) to ridicule with pasquinade [c17 from Italian *Pasquino* name given to an ancient Roman statue disinterred in 1501, which was annually posted with satirical verses] ▷ ˌpasquin'ader *n*

pass (pɑːs) *vb* **1** to go onwards or move by or past (a person, thing, etc) **2** to run, extend, or lead through, over, or across (a place): *the route passes through the city* **3** to go through or cause to go through (an obstacle or barrier): *to pass a needle through cloth* **4** to move or cause to move onwards or over: *he passed his hand over her face* **5** (*tr*) to go beyond or exceed: *this victory passes all expectation* **6** to gain or cause to gain an adequate or required mark, grade, or rating in (an examination, course, etc): *the examiner passed them all* **7** (*often foll by away* or *by*) to elapse or allow to elapse: *we passed the time talking* **8 pass the time of day (with)** to spend time amicably (with), esp in chatting, with no particular purpose **9** (*intr*) to take place or happen: *what passed at the meeting?* **10** to speak or exchange or be spoken or exchanged: *angry words passed between them* **11** to spread or cause to spread: *we passed the news round the class* **12** to transfer or exchange or be transferred or exchanged: *the bomb passed from hand to hand* **13** (*intr*) to undergo change or transition: *to pass from joy to despair* **14** (*when tr*, often foll by *down*) to transfer or be transferred by inheritance: *the house passed to the younger son* **15** to agree to or sanction or to be agreed to or receive the sanction of a legislative body, person of authority, etc: *the assembly passed 10 resolutions* **16** (*tr*) (of a legislative measure) to undergo (a procedural stage) and be agreed: *the bill passed the committee stage* **17** (when *tr*, often foll by *on* or *upon*) to pronounce or deliver (judgment, findings, etc): *the court passed sentence* **18** to go or allow to go without comment or censure: *the intended insult passed unnoticed* **19** (*intr*) to opt not to exercise a right, as by not answering a question or not making a bid or a play in card games **20** *physiol* to discharge (urine, faeces, etc) from the body **21** **pass water** to urinate **22** (*intr*) to come to an end or disappear: *his anger soon passed* **23** (*intr;* usually foll by *for* or *as*) to be likely to be mistaken for or accepted as (someone or something else): *you could easily pass for your sister* **24** (*intr;* foll by *away, on,* or *over*) a euphemism for **die**[1] (sense 1) **25** (*tr*) *chiefly US* to fail to declare (a dividend) **26** (*intr;* usually foll by *on* or *upon*) *chiefly US* (of a court, jury, etc) to sit in judgment; adjudicate **27** *sport* to hit, kick, or throw (the ball) to another player **28** **bring to pass** *archaic* to cause to happen **29** **come to pass** to happen ▷ *n* **30** the act of passing **31** **a** a route through a range of mountains where the summit is lower or where there is a gap between peaks **b** (*capital as part of a name*): *the Simplon Pass* **32** a way through any difficult region **33** a permit, licence, or authorization to do something without restriction: *she has a pass to visit the museum on Sundays* **34** **a** a document allowing entry to and exit from a military installation **b** a document authorizing leave of absence **35** *Brit* **a** the passing of a college or university examination to a satisfactory standard but not as high as honours **b** (*as modifier*): *a pass degree* ▷ Compare **honours** (sense 2) **36** a dive, sweep, or bombing or landing run by an aircraft **37** a motion of the hand or of a wand as a prelude to or part of a conjuring trick **38** *informal* an attempt, in words or action, to invite sexual intimacy (esp in the phrase **make a pass at**) **39** a state of affairs or condition, esp a bad or difficult one (esp in the phrase **a pretty pass**) **40** *sport* the transfer of a ball from one player to another **41** *fencing* a thrust or lunge with a sword **42** *bridge* the act of passing (making no bid) **43** *bullfighting* a variant of **pase** **44** *archaic* a witty sally or remark ▷ *interj* **45** *bridge* a call indicating that a player has no bid to make ▷ See also **pass by, pass off, pass out, pass over, pass up** [C13 from Old French *passer* to pass, surpass, from Latin *passūs* step, PACE[1]]

pass. *abbreviation for* passive

passable (ˈpɑːsəbᵊl) *adj* **1** adequate, fair, or acceptable: *a passable speech* **2** (of an obstacle) capable of being passed or crossed **3** (of currency) valid for general circulation **4** (of a proposed law) able to be ratified or enacted > ˈ**passableness** *n*

passably (ˈpɑːsəblɪ) *adv* **1** fairly; somewhat **2** acceptably; well enough: *she sings passably*

passacaglia (ˌpæsəˈkɑːljə) *n* **1** an old Spanish dance in slow triple time **2** a slow instrumental piece characterized by a series of variations on a particular theme played over a repeated bass part. See also **chaconne** (sense 1) [C17 earlier *passacalle,* from Spanish *pasacalle* street dance, from *paso* step + *calle* street; the ending *-alle* was changed to *-aglia* to suggest an Italian origin]

passade (pæˈseɪd) *n* *dressage* the act of moving back and forth in the same place [C17 via French from Italian *passata,* from *passare* to PASS]

passage[1] (ˈpæsɪdʒ) *n* **1** a channel, opening, etc, through or by which a person or thing may pass **2** *music* a section or division of a piece, movement, etc **3** a way, as in a hall or lobby **4** a section of a written work, speech, etc, esp one of moderate length **5** a journey, esp by ship: *the outward passage took a week* **6** the act or process of passing from one place, condition, etc, to another: *passage of a gas through a liquid* **7** the permission, right, or freedom to pass: *to be denied passage through a country* **8** the enactment of a law or resolution by a legislative or deliberative body **9** an evacuation of the bowels **10** *rare* an exchange or interchange, as of blows, words, etc (esp in the phrase **passage of arms**) [C13 from Old French from *passer* to PASS]

passage[2] (ˈpæsɪdʒ, ˈpæsɑːʒ) *dressage* ▷ *n* **1** a sideways walk in which diagonal pairs of feet are lifted alternately **2** a cadenced lofty trot, the moment of suspension being clearly defined ▷ *vb* **3** to move or cause to move at a passage [C18 from French *passager,* variant of *passéger,* from Italian *passeggiare* to take steps, ultimately from Latin *passūs* step, PACE[1]]

passage hawk *or* **passager hawk** (ˈpæsɪdʒə) *n* a young hawk or falcon caught while on migration. Compare **eyas, haggard**[1] (sense 4)

passageway (ˈpæsɪdʒˌweɪ) *n* a way, esp one in or between buildings; passage

passage work *n* *music* scales, runs, etc, in a piece of music which have no structural significance but provide an opportunity for virtuoso display

Passamaquoddy Bay (ˌpæsəməˈkwɒdɪ) *n* an inlet of the Bay of Fundy between New Brunswick (Canada) and Maine (US) at the mouth of the St Croix River

passant (ˈpæsᵊnt) *adj* (*usually postpositive*) *heraldry* (of a beast) walking, with the right foreleg raised [C14 from Old French, present participle of *passer* to PASS]

passata (pəˈsɑːtə) *n* a sauce made from sieved tomatoes, often used in Italian cookery [Italian]

pass band *n* the band of frequencies that is transmitted with maximum efficiency through a circuit, filter, etc

passbook (ˈpɑːsˌbʊk) *n* **1** a book for keeping a record of withdrawals from and payments into a building society **2** another name for **bankbook** **3** a customer's book in which is recorded by a trader a list of credit sales to that customer **4** (formerly in South Africa) an official document serving to identify the bearer, his race, his residence, and his employment

pass by *vb* **1** (*intr*) to go or move past **2** (*tr, adverb*) to overlook or disregard: *to pass by difficult problems*

Passchendaele (ˈpæʃənˌdeɪl) *n* a village in NW Belgium, in West Flanders province: the scene of heavy fighting during the third battle of Ypres in World War I during which 245 000 British troops were lost

passé (ˈpɑːseɪ, ˈpæseɪ; *French* pɑse) *adj* **1** out-of-date: *passé ideas* **2** past the prime; faded: *a passé society beauty* [C18 from French, past participle of *passer* to PASS]

passel (ˈpæsᵊl) *n* *informal or dialect, chiefly US* a group or quantity of no fixed number [variant of PARCEL]

passementerie (pæsˈmɛntrɪ; *French* pasmɑ̃tri) *n* a decorative trimming of gimp, cord, beads, braid, etc [C16 from Old French *passement,* from *passer* to trim, PASS]

passenger (ˈpæsɪndʒə) *n* **1** **a** a person travelling in a car, train, boat, etc, not driven by him **b** (*as modifier*): *a passenger seat* **2** *chiefly Brit* a member of a group or team who is a burden on the others through not participating fully in the work [C14 from Old French *passager* passing, from PASSAGE[1]]

passenger pigeon *n* a gregarious North American pigeon, *Ectopistes migratorius:* became extinct at the beginning of the 20th century

passe-partout (ˌpæspɑːˈtuː; *French* paspartu) *n* **1** a mounting for a picture in which strips of strong gummed paper are used to bind together the glass, picture, and backing **2** the gummed paper used for this **3** a mat, often decorated, on which a picture is mounted **4** something that secures entry everywhere, esp a master key [C17 from French, literally: pass everywhere]

passepied (pɑːsˈpjeɪ) *n, pl* **-pieds** (-ˈpjeɪ) **1** a lively minuet of Breton origin, in triple time, popular in the 17th century **2** a piece of music composed for or in the rhythm of this dance [C17 from French: pass the foot]

passer-by *n, pl* **passers-by** a person that is passing or going by, esp on foot

passerine (ˈpæsəˌraɪn, -ˌriːn) *adj* **1** of, relating to, or belonging to the *Passeriformes,* an order of birds characterized by the perching habit: includes the larks, finches, crows, thrushes, starlings, etc ▷ *n* **2** any bird belonging to the order *Passeriformes* [C18 from Latin *passer* sparrow]

pas seul (*French* pɑ sœl) *n, pl* **pas seuls** (*French* pɑ sœl) a dance sequence for one person [French, literally: step on one's own]

passible (ˈpæsɪbᵊl) *adj* susceptible to emotion or suffering; able to feel [C14 from Medieval Latin *passibilis,* from Latin *patī* to suffer; see PASSION] > ˌ**passiˈbility** *n*

passifloraceous (ˌpæsɪflɔːˈreɪʃəs) *adj* of, relating to, or belonging to the *Passifloraceae,* a tropical and subtropical family of climbing plants including the passionflowers: the flowers have five petals and threadlike parts forming a dense mass (corona) around the central disc [C19 from New Latin *Passiflora,* the type genus (passionflower)]

passim *Latin* (ˈpæsɪm) *adv* here and there; throughout: used to indicate that what is referred to occurs frequently in the work cited

passing (ˈpɑːsɪŋ) *adj* **1** transitory or momentary: *a passing fancy* **2** cursory or casual in action or manner: *a passing reference* ▷ *adv* ▷ *adj* **3** *archaic* to an extreme degree *passing strange* ▷ *n* **4** a place where or means by which one may pass, cross, etc **5** a euphemism for **death** **6** **in passing** by the way; incidentally: *he mentioned your visit in passing*

passing bell *n* a bell rung to announce a death or a funeral. Also called: **death bell, death knell**

passing note *or US* **passing tone** *n* *music* a nonharmonic note through which a melody passes from one harmonic note to the next. Compare **auxiliary note**

passing shot *n* *tennis* a winning shot hit outside an opponent's reach

passion (ˈpæʃən) *n* **1** ardent love or affection **2** intense sexual love **3** a strong affection or enthusiasm for an object, concept, etc: *a passion for poetry* **4** any strongly felt emotion, such as love, hate, envy, etc **5** a state or outburst of extreme anger: *he flew into a passion* **6** the object of an intense desire, ardent affection, or enthusiasm **7** an outburst expressing intense emotion: *he burst into a passion of sobs* **8** *philosophy* **a** any state of the mind in which it is affected by something external, such as perception, desire, etc, as contrasted with action **b** feelings, desires or emotions, as contrasted with reason **9** the sufferings and death of a Christian martyr [C12 via French from Church Latin *passiō* suffering, from Latin *patī* to suffer]

Passion (ˈpæʃən) *n* **1** the sufferings of Christ from the Last Supper to his death on the cross **2** any of the four Gospel accounts of this **3** a musical setting of this: *the St Matthew Passion*

passional (ˈpæʃənᵊl) *adj* **1** of, relating to, or due to passion or the passions ▷ *n* **2** a book recounting the sufferings of Christian martyrs or saints

passionate (ˈpæʃənɪt) *adj* **1** manifesting or exhibiting intense sexual feeling or desire: *a passionate lover* **2** capable of, revealing, or characterized by intense emotion: *a passionate plea* **3** easily roused to anger; quick-tempered > ˈ**passionately** *adv* > ˈ**passionateness** *n*

passionflower (ˈpæʃənˌflaʊə) *n* any passifloraceous plant of the tropical American genus *Passiflora,* cultivated for their red, yellow, greenish, or purple showy flowers: some species have edible fruit. See also **granadilla** [C17 so called from the alleged resemblance between parts of the flower and the instruments of Christ's crucifixion]

passion fruit *n* the edible fruit of any of various passionflowers, esp granadilla

passionless (ˈpæʃənlɪs) *adj* **1** empty of emotion or feeling: *a passionless marriage* **2** calm and detached > ˈ**passionlessly** *adv* > ˈ**passionlessness** *n*

Passion play *n* a play depicting the Passion of Christ

Passion Sunday *n* the fifth Sunday in Lent (the second Sunday before Easter), when Passiontide begins

Passiontide ('pæʃən,taɪd) *n* the last two weeks of Lent, extending from Passion Sunday to Holy Saturday

Passion Week *n* 1 the week between Passion Sunday and Palm Sunday 2 (formerly) Holy Week; the week before Easter

passivate ('pæsɪ,veɪt) *vb* (*tr*) to render (a metal) less susceptible to corrosion by coating the surface with a substance, such as an oxide

passive ('pæsɪv) *adj* 1 not active or not participating perceptibly in an activity, organization, etc 2 unresisting and receptive to external forces; submissive 3 not working or operating 4 affected or acted upon by an external object or force 5 *grammar* denoting a voice of verbs in sentences in which the grammatical subject is not the logical subject but rather the recipient of the action described by the verb, as *was broken* in the sentence *The glass was broken by a boy.* Compare **active** (sense 5a) 6 *chem* (of a substance, esp a metal) apparently chemically unreactive, usually as a result of the formation of a thin protective layer that prevents further reaction 7 *electronics, telecomm* a containing no source of power and therefore capable only of attenuating a signal: *a passive network* b not capable of amplifying a signal or controlling a function: *a passive communications satellite* 8 *finance* (of a bond, share, debt, etc) yielding no interest ▷ *n* 9 *grammar* a the passive voice b a passive verb [c14 from Latin *passīvus* susceptible of suffering, from *patī* to undergo] > 'passively *adv* > pas'sivity *or* 'passiveness *n*

passive-aggressive *adj* *psychoanal* of or relating to a personality that harbours aggressive emotions while behaving in a calm or detached manner

passive euthanasia *n* a form of euthanasia in which medical treatment that will keep a dying patient alive for a time is withdrawn

passive obedience *n* 1 unquestioning obedience to authority 2 the surrender of a person's will to another person

passive resistance *n* resistance to a government, law, etc, made without violence, as by fasting, demonstrating peacefully, or refusing to cooperate

passive safety *n* the practice of taking measures to reduce the consequences of accidents, as opposed to attempting to avoid them altogether. Compare **active safety**

passive smoking *n* the inhalation of smoke from other people's cigarettes by a nonsmoker > **passive smoker** *n*

passive vocabulary *n* all the words, collectively, that a person can understand. Compare **active vocabulary**

passivism ('pæsɪ,vɪzəm) *n* 1 the theory, belief, or practice of passive resistance 2 the quality, characteristics, or fact of being passive > 'passivist *n, adj*

passkey ('pɑːs,kiː) *n* 1 any of various keys, esp a latchkey 2 another term for **master key** *or* **skeleton key**

pass law *n* (formerly, in South Africa) a law restricting the movement of Black Africans, esp from rural to urban areas

pass off *vb* (*adverb*) 1 to be or cause to be accepted or circulated in a false character or identity: *he passed the fake diamonds off as real* 2 (*intr*) to come to a gradual end; disappear: *eventually the pain passed off* 3 to emit (a substance) as a gas or vapour, or (of a substance) to be emitted in this way 4 (*intr*) to take place: *the meeting passed off without disturbance* 5 (*tr*) to set aside or disregard: *I managed to pass off his insult*

pass out *vb* (*adverb*) 1 (*intr*) *informal* to become

unconscious; faint 2 (*intr*) *Brit* (esp of an officer cadet) to qualify for a military commission; complete a course of training satisfactorily: *General Smith passed out from Sandhurst in 1933* 3 (*tr*) to distribute

pass over *vb* 1 (*tr, adverb*) to take no notice of; disregard: *they passed me over in the last round of promotions* 2 (*intr, preposition*) to disregard (something bad or embarrassing): *we shall pass over your former faults*

Passover ('pɑːs,əʊvə) *n* 1 Also called: **Pesach, Pesah, Feast of the Unleavened Bread** an eight-day Jewish festival beginning on Nisan 15 and celebrated in commemoration of the passing over or sparing of the Israelites in Egypt, when God smote the firstborn of the Egyptians (Exodus 12). Related adj: **paschal** 2 another term for the **Paschal Lamb** [c16 from *pass over*, translation of Hebrew *pesah*, from *pāsah* to pass over]

passport ('pɑːspɔːt) *n* 1 an official document issued by a government, identifying an individual, granting him permission to travel abroad, and requesting the protection of other governments for him 2 a licence granted by a state to a foreigner, allowing the passage of his person or goods through the country 3 another word for **sea letter** (sense 1) 4 a quality, asset, etc, that gains a person admission or acceptance [c15 from French *passeport*, from *passer* to PASS + PORT¹]

pass up *vb* (*tr, adverb*) 1 *informal* to let go by; ignore: *I won't pass up this opportunity* 2 to take no notice of (someone)

passus ('pæsəs) *n, pl* **-sus** *or* **-suses** (esp in medieval literature) a division or section of a poem, story, etc [c16 from Latin: step, PACE¹]

password ('pɑːs,wɜːd) *n* 1 a secret word, phrase, etc, that ensures admission or acceptance by proving identity, membership, etc 2 an action, quality, etc, that gains admission or acceptance 3 a sequence of characters used to gain access to a computer system

past (pɑːst) *adj* 1 completed, finished, and no longer in existence: *past happiness* 2 denoting or belonging to all or a segment of the time that has elapsed at the present moment: *the past history of the world* 3 denoting a specific unit of time that immediately precedes the present one: *the past month* 4 (*prenominal*) denoting a person who has held and relinquished an office or position; former: *a past president* 5 *grammar* denoting any of various tenses of verbs that are used in describing actions, events, or states that have been begun or completed at the time of utterance. Compare **aorist, imperfect** (sense 4), **perfect** (sense 8) ▷ *n* 6 **the past** the period of time or a segment of it that has elapsed: *forget the past* 7 the history, experience, or background of a nation, person, etc: *a soldier with a distinguished past* 8 an earlier period of someone's life, esp one that contains events kept secret or regarded as disreputable 9 *grammar* a a past tense b a verb in a past tense ▷ *adv* 10 at a specified or unspecified time before the present; ago: *three years past* 11 on or onwards: *I greeted him but he just walked past* ▷ *prep* 12 beyond in time: *it's past midnight* 13 beyond in place or position: *the library is past the church* 14 moving beyond; in a direction that passes: *he walked past me* 15 beyond or above the reach, limit, or scope of: *his foolishness is past comprehension* 16 beyond or above in number or amount: *to count past ten* 17 **past it** *informal* unable to perform the tasks one could do when one was younger 18 **not put it past someone** to consider someone capable of (the action specified) [c14 from *passed*, past participle of PASS]

▊ **USAGE** The past participle of *pass* is sometimes wrongly spelt *past*: *the time for recriminations has passed* (not *past*)

pasta ('pæstə) *n* any of several variously shaped edible preparations made from a flour and water dough, such as spaghetti [Italian, from Late Latin: PASTE¹]

paste¹ (peɪst) *n* 1 a mixture or material of a soft or malleable consistency, such as toothpaste 2 an adhesive made from water and flour or starch, used esp for joining pieces of paper 3 a preparation of food, such as meat, that has been powdered to a creamy mass, for spreading on bread, crackers, etc 4 any of various sweet doughy confections: *almond paste* 5 dough, esp when prepared with shortening, as for making pastry 6 a Also called: **strass** a hard shiny glass used for making imitation gems b an imitation gem made of this glass 7 the combined ingredients of porcelain. See also **hard paste, soft paste** ▷ *vb* 8 (often foll by *on* or *onto*) to attach by or as if by using paste: *he pasted posters onto the wall* 9 (usually foll by *with*) to cover (a surface) with paper, usually attached with an adhesive: *he pasted the wall with posters* [c14 via French from Late Latin *pasta* dough, from Greek *pastē* barley porridge, from *pastos*, from *passein* to sprinkle]

paste² (peɪst) *vb* (*tr*) *slang* to hit, esp with the fists; punch or beat soundly [c19 variant of BASTE³]

pasteboard ('peɪst,bɔːd) *n* 1 a stiff board formed from layers of paper or pulp pasted together, esp as used in bookbinding b (*as modifier*): *a pasteboard book cover* 2 *slang* a card or ticket ▷ *adj* 3 flimsy; insubstantial 4 sham; fake

pastel (pæst⁹l, pæˈstɛl) *n* 1 a a substance made of ground pigment bound with gum, used for making sticks for drawing b a crayon of this c a drawing done in such crayons 2 the medium or technique of pastel drawing 3 a pale delicate colour 4 a light prose work, esp a poetic one 5 another name for **woad** ▷ *adj* 6 (of a colour) pale; delicate: *pastel blue* [c17 via French from Italian *pastello*, from Late Latin *pastellus* woad compounded into a paste, diminutive of *pasta* PASTE¹] > 'pastelist *or* 'pastellist *n*

pastern ('pæstən) *n* 1 the part of a horse's foot between the fetlock and the hoof 2 Also called: **fetter bone** either of the two bones that constitute this part [c14 from Old French *pasturon*, from *pasture* a hobble, from Latin *pāstōrius* of a shepherd, from PASTOR]

paste-up *n* *printing* 1 an assembly of typeset matter, illustrations, etc, pasted on a sheet of paper or board and used as a guide or layout in the production of a publication 2 a sheet of paper or board on which are pasted artwork, typeset matter, etc, for photographing prior to making a printing plate; another name for **camera-ready copy** 3 another name for **collage** (senses 1, 2)

pasteurism ('pæstə,rɪzəm, -stjə-, 'pɑː-) *n* *med* 1 a method of securing immunity from rabies in a person who has been bitten by a rabid animal, by daily injections of progressively more virulent suspensions of the infected spinal cord of a rabbit that died of rabies 2 a similar method of treating patients with other viral infections by the serial injection of progressively more virulent suspensions of the causative virus ▷ Also called: **Pasteur treatment**

pasteurization *or* **pasteurisation** (,pæstərɑɪˈzeɪʃən, -stjə-, -,pɑː-) *n* the process of heating beverages, such as milk, beer, wine, or cider, or solid foods, such as cheese or crab meat, to destroy harmful or undesirable microorganisms or to limit the rate of fermentation by the application of controlled heat

pasteurize *or* **pasteurise** ('pæstə,rɑɪz, -stjə-, 'pɑː-) *vb* (*tr*) 1 to subject (milk, beer, etc) to pasteurization 2 *rare* to subject (a patient) to pasteurism

pasteurizer *or* **pasteuriser** ('pæstə,rɑɪzə, -stjə-, 'pɑː-) *n* 1 an apparatus for pasteurizing substances (esp milk) 2 a person who carries out pasteurization

pastiche (pæˈstiːʃ) *or* **pasticcio** (pæˈstɪtʃəʊ) *n* 1 a work of art that mixes styles, materials, etc 2 a work of art that imitates the style of another artist or period [c19 French *pastiche*, Italian *pasticcio*, literally: piecrust (hence, something blended), from Late Latin *pasta* PASTE[1]

pasticheur (ˌpæstiːˈʃɜː) *n* a person who creates or performs pastiches

pastille *or* **pastil** (ˈpæstɪl) *n* **1** a small flavoured or medicated lozenge for chewing **2** an aromatic substance burnt to fumigate the air **3** *med* a small coated paper disc formerly used to estimate the dose or intensity of radiation (esp of X-rays): it changes colour when exposed **4** a variant of **pastel** (sense 1) [C17 via French from Latin *pastillus* small loaf, from *pānis* bread]

pastime (ˈpɑːsˌtaɪm) *n* an activity or entertainment which makes time pass pleasantly: *golf is my favourite pastime* [C15 from PASS + TIME, on the model of French *passe-temps*]

pasting (ˈpeɪstɪŋ) *n slang* a thrashing; heavy defeat

pastis (pæˈstɪs, -ˈstiːs) *n* an anise-flavoured alcoholic drink [from French, of uncertain origin]

pastitsio (pæsˈtɪtsɪəʊ) *n* a Greek dish consisting of minced meat and macaroni topped with béchamel sauce [C20 from Modern Greek]

past life therapy *n* a form of hypnosis or meditation based on the belief that an individual's present problems are rooted in events that occurred before birth in this life

past master *n* **1** a person with talent for, or experience in, a particular activity: *a past master of tact* **2** a person who has held the office of master in a Freemasons' lodge, guild, etc

Pasto (Spanish ˈpasto) *n* a city in SE Colombia, at an altitude of 2590 m (8500 ft). Pop: 404 000 (2005 est)

pastor (ˈpɑːstə) *n* **1** a clergyman or priest in charge of a congregation **2** a person who exercises spiritual guidance over a number of people **3** an archaic word for **shepherd** (sense 1) **4** Also called: **rosy pastor** a S Asian starling, *Sturnus roseus*, having glossy black head and wings and a pale pink body [C14 from Latin: shepherd, from *pascere* to feed] ▷ **ˈpastorˌship** *n*

pastoral (ˈpɑːstərəl) *adj* **1** of, characterized by, or depicting rural life, scenery, etc **2** (of a literary work) dealing with an idealized form of rural existence in a conventional way **3** (of land) used for pasture **4** denoting or relating to the branch of theology dealing with the duties of a clergyman or priest to his congregation **5** of or relating to a clergyman or priest in charge of a congregation or his duties as such **6** of or relating to a teacher's responsibility for the personal, as the distinct from the educational, development of pupils **7** of or relating to shepherds, their work, etc ▷ *n* **8** a literary work or picture portraying rural life, esp the lives of shepherds in an idealizing way. See also **eclogue** **9** *music* a variant of **pastorale** **10** *Christianity* **a** a letter from a clergyman to the people under his charge **b** the letter of a bishop to the clergy or people of his diocese **c** Also called: **pastoral staff** the crosier or staff carried by a bishop as a symbol of his pastoral responsibilities [C15 from Latin, from PASTOR] ▷ **ˈpastoralˌism** *n* ▷ **ˈpastorally** *adv*

pastorale (ˌpæstəˈrɑːl) *n, pl* -rales *music* **1** a composition evocative of rural life, characterized by moderate compound duple or quadruple time and sometimes a droning accompaniment **2** a musical play based on a rustic story, popular during the 16th century [C18 Italian, from Latin: PASTORAL]

pastoralist (ˈpɑːstərəlɪst) *n Austral* a grazier or land-holder raising sheep, cattle, etc, on a large scale

pastorate (ˈpɑːstərɪt) *n* **1** the office or term of office of a pastor **2** a body of pastors; pastors collectively

past participle *n* a participial form of verbs used to modify a noun that is logically the object of a verb, also used in certain compound tenses and passive forms of the verb in English and other languages

past perfect *grammar* ▷ *adj* **1** denoting a tense of

verbs used in relating past events where the action had already occurred at the time of the action of a main verb that is itself in a past tense. In English this is a compound tense formed with *had* plus the past participle ▷ *n* **2 a** the past perfect tense **b** a verb in this tense

pastrami (pəˈstrɑːmɪ) *n* highly seasoned smoked beef, esp prepared from a shoulder cut [from Yiddish, from Romanian *pastramă*, from *păstra* to preserve]

pastry (ˈpeɪstrɪ) *n, pl* -tries **1** a dough of flour, water, shortening, and sometimes other ingredients **2** baked foods, such as tarts, made with this dough **3** an individual cake or pastry pie [C16 from PASTE[1]]

pastry cream *n* a creamy custard, often flavoured, used as a filling for éclairs, flans, etc. Also called: **pastry custard**

pasturage (ˈpɑːstjərɪdʒ) *n* **1** the right to graze or the business of grazing cattle **2** another word for **pasture**

pasture (ˈpɑːstʃə) *n* **1** land covered with grass or herbage and grazed by or suitable for grazing by livestock **2** a specific tract of such land **3** the grass or herbage growing on it ▷ *vb* **4** (*tr*) to cause (livestock) to graze or (of livestock) to graze (a pasture) [C13 via Old French from Late Latin *pāstūra*, from *pascere* to feed]

pasty[1] (ˈpeɪstɪ) *adj* pastier, pastiest **1** of or like the colour, texture, etc, of paste **2** (esp of the complexion) pale or unhealthy-looking ▷ *n, pl* pasties **3** either one of a pair of small round coverings for the nipples used by striptease dancers ▷ **ˈpastily** *adv* ▷ **ˈpastiness** *n*

pasty[2] (ˈpæstɪ) *n, pl* pasties a round of pastry folded over a filling of meat, vegetables, etc: *Cornish pasty* [C13 from Old French *pastée*, from Late Latin *pasta* dough]

PA system *n* See **public-address system**

pat[1] (pæt) *vb* pats, patting, patted **1** to hit (something) lightly with the palm of the hand or some other flat surface: *to pat a ball* **2** to slap (a person or animal) gently, esp on the back, as an expression of affection, congratulation, etc **3** (*tr*) to shape, smooth, etc, with a flat instrument or the palm **4** (*intr*) to walk or run with light footsteps **5 pat (someone) on the back** *informal* to congratulate or encourage (someone) ▷ *n* **6** a light blow with something flat **7** a gentle slap **8** a small mass of something: *a pat of butter* **9** the sound made by a light stroke or light footsteps **10 pat on the back** *informal* a gesture or word indicating approval or encouragement [C14 perhaps imitative]

pat[2] (pæt) *adv* **1** Also: **off pat** exactly or fluently memorized or mastered: *he recited it pat* **2** opportunely or aptly **3 stand pat a** *chiefly US and Canadian* to refuse to abandon a belief, decision, etc **b** (in poker, etc) to play without adding new cards to the hand dealt ▷ *adj* **4** exactly right for the occasion; apt: *a pat reply* **5** too exactly fitting; glib: *a pat answer to a difficult problem* **6** exactly right: *a pat hand in poker* [C17 perhaps adverbial use ("with a light stroke") of PAT[1]]

pat[3] (pæt) *n* **on one's pat** *Austral informal* alone; on one's own [C20 rhyming slang, from *Pat Malone*]

Pat (pæt) *n* an informal name for an Irishman [from *Patrick*]

patagium (pəˈteɪdʒɪəm) *n, pl* -gia (-dʒɪə) **1** a web of skin between the neck, limbs, and tail in bats and gliding mammals that functions as a wing **2** a membranous fold of skin connecting margins of a bird's wing to the shoulder [C19 New Latin from Latin, from Greek *patageion* gold border on a tunic]

Patagonia (ˌpætəˈɡəʊnɪə) *n* **1** the southernmost region of South America, in Argentina and Chile extending from the Andes to the Atlantic. Area: about 777 000 sq km (300 000 sq miles) **2** an arid tableland in the southernmost part of Argentina, rising towards the Andes in the west

Patagonian (ˌpætəˈɡəʊnɪən) *adj* **1** of or relating to

Patagonia or its inhabitants ▷ *n* **2** a native or inhabitant of Patagonia

Patagonian toothfish (ˈtuːθˌfɪʃ) *n* a large food fish, *Dissostichus eleginoides*, found in the cold deep waters of the southern Atlantic and Indian oceans. Also called: **Chilean sea bass**

pataka (ˈpɑːtɑːkɑː) *n, pl* pataka NZ a building on stilts, used for storing provisions [Māori]

patch (pætʃ) *n* **1 a** a piece of material used to mend a garment or to make patchwork, a sewn-on pocket, etc **b** (*as modifier*): *a patch pocket* **2** a small piece, area, expanse, etc **3 a** a small plot of land **b** its produce: *a patch of cabbages* **4** a district for which particular officials, such as social workers or policemen, have responsibility **5** *pathol* any discoloured area on the skin, mucous membranes, etc, usually being one sign of a specific disorder **6** *med* **a** a protective covering for an injured eye **b** any protective dressing **7** an imitation beauty spot, esp one made of black or coloured silk, worn by both sexes, esp in the 18th century **8** Also called: **flash** US an identifying piece of fabric worn on the shoulder of a uniform, on a vehicle, etc **9** a small contrasting section or stretch: *a patch of cloud in the blue sky* **10** a scrap; remnant **11** *computing* a small set of instructions to correct or improve a computer program **12** *Austral informal* the insignia of a motorcycle club or gang **13** a bad patch a difficult or troubled time **14 not a patch on** *informal* not nearly as good as ▷ *vb* **15** to mend or supply (a garment, etc) with a patch or patches **16** to put together or produce with patches **17** (of material) to serve as a patch to **18** (often foll by *up*) to mend hurriedly or in a makeshift way **19** (often foll by *up*) to make (up) or settle (a quarrel) **20** to connect (electric circuits) together temporarily by means of a patch board **21** (usually foll by *through*) to connect (a telephone call) by means of a patch board **22** *computing* to correct or improve (a program) by adding a small set of instructions [C16 *pacche*, perhaps from French *pieche* PIECE] ▷ **ˈpatchable** *adj* ▷ **ˈpatcher** *n*

patch board *or* **panel** *n* a device with a large number of sockets into which electrical plugs can be inserted to form many different temporary circuits: used in telephone exchanges, computer systems, etc. Also called: **plugboard**

patchouli, pachouli *or* **patchouly** (ˈpætʃʊlɪ, pəˈtʃuːlɪ) *n* **1** any of several Asiatic trees of the genus *Pogostemon*, the leaves of which yield a heavy fragrant oil: family *Lamiaceae* (labiates) **2** the perfume made from this oil [C19 from Tamil *paccilai*, from *paccu* green + *ilai* leaf]

patch pocket *n* a pocket on the outside of a garment

patch quilt *n* Irish a patchwork quilt

patch test *n* *med* a test to detect an allergic reaction by applying small amounts of a suspected substance to the skin and then examining the area for signs of irritation

patchwork (ˈpætʃˌwɜːk) *n* **1** needlework done by sewing pieces of different materials together **2** something, such as a theory, made up of various parts: *a patchwork of cribbed ideas*

patchy (ˈpætʃɪ) *adj* patchier, patchiest **1** irregular in quality, occurrence, intensity, etc: *a patchy essay* **2** having or forming patches ▷ **ˈpatchily** *adv* ▷ **ˈpatchiness** *n*

patd *abbreviation for* patented

pate (peɪt) *n* the head, esp with reference to baldness or (in facetious use) intelligence [C14 of unknown origin]

pâté (ˈpæteɪ; French pate) *n* **1** a spread of very finely minced liver, poultry, etc, served usually as an hors d'oeuvre **2** a savoury pie of meat or fish [from French: PASTE[1]]

pâté de foie gras (pate də fwa gra) *n, pl* pâtés de foie gras (pate də fwa gra) a smooth rich paste made from the liver of a specially fattened goose, considered a great delicacy [French: pâté of fat liver]

patella (pəˈtɛlə) *n, pl* **-lae** (-liː) **1** *anatomy* a small flat triangular bone in front of and protecting the knee joint. Nontechnical name: **kneecap 2** *biology* a cuplike structure, such as the spore-producing body of certain ascomycetous fungi **3** *archaeol* a small pan [C17 from Latin, from *patina* shallow pan] > pa**ˈtellar** *adj*

patellate (pəˈtɛlɪt, -ˌleɪt) *adj* having the shape of a patella. Also: **patelliform** (pəˈtɛlɪˌfɔːm)

paten (ˈpætən) *or* **patin, patine** (ˈpætɪn) *n* a plate, usually made of silver or gold, esp the plate on which the bread is placed in the Eucharist [C13 from Old French *patene*, from Medieval Latin, from Latin *patina* pan]

patency (ˈpeɪtənsɪ) *n* **1** the condition of being obvious **2** the state of a bodily passage, duct, etc, of being open or unobstructed **3** *phonetics* the degree to which the vocal tract remains unobstructed in the articulation of a speech sound. See also **closure** (sense 7)

patent (ˈpætənt, ˈpeɪtənt) *n* **1 a** a government grant to an inventor assuring him the sole right to make, use, and sell his invention for a limited period **b** a document conveying such a grant **2** an invention, privilege, etc, protected by a patent **3 a** an official document granting a right **b** any right granted by such a document **4** (in the US) **a** a grant by the government of title to public lands **b** the instrument by which such title is granted **c** the land so granted **5** a sign that one possesses a certain quality ▷ *adj* **6** open or available for inspection (esp in the phrases **letters patent, patent writ**) **7** (ˈpeɪtənt) obvious: *their scorn was patent to everyone* **8** concerning protection, appointment, etc, of or by a patent or patents **9** proprietary **10** (esp of a bodily passage or duct) being open or unobstructed **11** *biology* spreading out widely: *patent branches* **12** (of plate glass) ground and polished on both sides ▷ *vb* (tr) **13** to obtain a patent for **14** (in the US) to grant (public land or mineral rights) by a patent **15** *metallurgy* to heat (a metal) above a transformation temperature and cool it at a rate that allows cold working [C14 via Old French from Latin *patēre* to lie open; n use, short for *letters patent*, from Medieval Latin *litterae patentes* letters lying open (to public inspection)] > **ˈpatentable** *adj* > **ˌpatentaˈbility** *n*

USAGE The pronunciation "ˈpætənt" is heard in *letters patent* and *Patent Office* and is the usual US pronunciation for all senses. In Britain "ˈpætənt" is sometimes heard for senses 1, 2 and 3, but "ˈpeɪtənt" is commoner and is regularly used in collocations like *patent leather*

patentee (ˌpeɪtənˈtiː, ˌpæ-) *n* a person, group, company, etc, that has been granted a patent

patent fastener *n* (in Ireland) another name for **press stud**

patent leather *n* leather or imitation leather processed with lacquer to give a hard glossy surface

patent log *n* *nautical* any of several mechanical devices for measuring the speed of a vessel and the distance travelled, consisting typically of a trailing rotor that registers its rotations on a meter. Compare **chip log**

patently (ˈpeɪtəntlɪ) *adv* obviously: *he was patently bored*

patent medicine *n* a medicine protected by a patent and available without a doctor's prescription

Patent Office (ˈpætənt) *n* a government department that issues patents. Abbreviation: **Pat. Off**

patentor (ˌpeɪtənˈtɔː, ˌpæ-) *n* a person who or official body that grants a patent or patents

patent right *n* the exclusive right granted by a patent

Patent Rolls *pl n* (in Britain) the register of patents issued

patent still *n* a type of still in which the

distillation is continuous [so called because a still of this type was patented in 1830]

pater (ˈpeɪtə) *n* *Brit* a public school slang word for **father**: now chiefly used facetiously [from Latin]

paterfamilias (ˌpeɪtəfəˈmɪlɪˌæs) *n, pl* **patresfamilias** (ˌpɑːtreɪzfəˈmɪlɪˌæs) **1** the male head of a household **2** *Roman law* **a** the head of a household having authority over its members **b** the parental or other authority of another person [Latin: father of the family]

paternal (pəˈtɜːnəl) *adj* **1** relating to or characteristic of a father, esp in showing affection, encouragement, etc; fatherly **2** (prenominal) related through the father: *his paternal grandfather* **3** inherited or derived from the male parent [C17 from Late Latin *paternālis*, from Latin *pater* father] > pa**ˈternally** *adv*

paternalism (pəˈtɜːnəˌlɪzəm) *n* the attitude or policy of a government or other authority that manages the affairs of a country, company, community, etc, in the manner of a father, esp in usurping individual responsibility and the liberty of choice > pa**ˈternalist** *n, adj* > paˌternalˈistic *adj* > paˌternalˈistically *adv*

paternity (pəˈtɜːnɪtɪ) *n* **1 a** the fact or state of being a father **b** (as modifier): *a paternity suit was filed against the man* **2** descent or derivation from a father **3** authorship or origin: *the paternity of the theory is disputed* [C15 from Late Latin *paternitās*, from Latin *pater* father]

paternity leave *n* **1** a period of paid absence from work, in the UK currently two weeks, to which a man is legally entitled immediately after the birth of his child **2** a period of paid or unpaid absence from work granted to a man by his employer immediately after the birth of his child

paternity suit *n* *law* the US (and in Britain a nontechnical) term for **affiliation proceedings**

paternoster (ˌpætəˈnɒstə) *n* **1** *RC Church* the beads at the ends of each decade of the rosary marking the points at which the Paternoster is recited **2** any fixed form of words used as a prayer or charm **3** Also called: **paternoster line** a type of fishing tackle in which short lines and hooks are attached at intervals to the main line **4** a type of lift in which platforms are attached to continuous chains. The lift does not stop at each floor but passengers enter while it is moving [Latin, literally: our father (from the opening of the Lord's Prayer)]

Paternoster (ˌpætəˈnɒstə) *n* (sometimes not capital) *RC Church* **1** the Lord's Prayer, esp in Latin **2** the recital of this as an act of devotion [see PATERNOSTER]

Paterson (ˈpætəsən) *n* a city in NE New Jersey: settled by the Dutch in the late 17th century. Pop: 150 782 (2003 est)

Paterson's curse *n* *Austral* a purple-flowered noxious plant, *Echium plantagineum*, a close relative of **viper's bugloss**, naturalized in Australia and NZ where its harmfulness to livestock has prompted attempts to limit its spread. Also called: **Salvation Jane**

path (pɑːθ) *n, pl* **paths** (pɑːðz) **1** a road or way, esp a narrow trodden track **2** a surfaced walk, as through a garden **3** the course or direction in which something moves: *the path of a whirlwind* **4** a course of conduct: *the path of virtue* **5** *computing* the directions for reaching a particular file or directory, as traced hierarchically through each of the parent directories usually from the root; the file or directory and all parent directories are separated from one another in the path by slashes [Old English *pæth*; related to Old High German, German *Pfad*] > **ˈpathless** *adj*

path. (pæθ) *abbreviation for* **1** pathological **2** pathology

-path *n combining form* **1** denoting a person suffering from a specified disease or disorder: *neuropath* **2** denoting a practitioner of a particular method of treatment: *osteopath* [back formation from -PATHY]

Pathan (pəˈtɑːn) *n* a member of the Pashto-speaking people of Afghanistan, NW Pakistan, and elsewhere, most of whom are Muslim in religion [C17 from Hindi]

pathetic (pəˈθɛtɪk) *adj* **1** evoking or expressing pity, sympathy, etc **2** distressingly inadequate: *the old man sat huddled in front of a pathetic fire* **3** *Brit informal* ludicrously or contemptibly uninteresting or worthless: *the standard of goalkeeping in amateur football today is pathetic* **4** *obsolete* of or affecting the feelings ▷ *pl n* **5** pathetic sentiments [C16 from French *pathétique*, via Late Latin from Greek *pathetikos* sensitive, from *pathos* suffering; see PATHOS] > pa**ˈthetically** *adv*

pathetic fallacy *n* (in literature) the presentation of inanimate objects in nature as possessing human feelings

pathfinder (ˈpɑːθˌfaɪndə) *n* **1** a person who makes or finds a way, esp through unexplored areas or fields of knowledge **2** an aircraft or parachutist who indicates a target area by dropping flares, etc **3** a radar device used for navigation or homing onto a target > **ˈpathˌfinding** *n*

pathfinder prospectus *n* a prospectus regarding the flotation of a new company that contains only sufficient details to test the market reaction

pathic (ˈpæθɪk) *n* **1** a catamite **2** a person who suffers; victim ▷ *adj* **3** of or relating to a catamite **4** of or relating to suffering [C17 via Latin from Greek *pathikos* passive; see PATHOS]

pathname (ˈpɑːθˌneɪm) *n* *computing* the name of a file or directory together with its position in relation to other directories traced back in a line to the root; the names of the file and each of the parent directories are separated from one another by slashes

patho- *or before a vowel* **path-** *combining form* disease: *pathology* [from Greek *pathos* suffering; see PATHOS]

pathogen (ˈpæθədʒɛn) *or* **pathogene** (ˈpæθəˌdʒiːn) *n* any agent that can cause disease

pathogenesis (ˌpæθəˈdʒɛnɪsɪs) *or* **pathogeny** (pəˈθɒdʒɪnɪ) *n* the origin, development, and resultant effects of a disease > **pathogenetic** (ˌpæθəʊdʒɪˈnɛtɪk) *adj*

pathogenic (ˌpæθəˈdʒɛnɪk) *adj* able to cause or produce disease: *pathogenic bacteria*

pathognomonic (ˌpæθəɡnəˈmɒnɪk) *adj pathol* characteristic or indicative of a particular disease [C17 from Greek *pathognōmonikos* expert in judging illness, from PATHO- + *gnōmōn* judge] > ˌpathognoˈmonically *adv*

pathognomy (pəˈθɒɡnəmɪ) *n* study or knowledge of the passions or emotions or their manifestations [C18 from PATHO- + -*gnomy*, as in PHYSIOGNOMY]

pathological (ˌpæθəˈlɒdʒɪkəl) *or less commonly* **pathologic** *adj* **1** of or relating to pathology **2** relating to, involving, or caused by disease **3** *informal* compulsively motivated: *a pathological liar* > ˌpathoˈlogically *adv*

pathologize *or* **pathologise** (pəˈθɒləˌdʒaɪz) *vb* (tr) to represent (something) as a disease: *this pathologizing of parenthood*

pathology (pəˈθɒlədʒɪ) *n, pl* **-gies 1** the branch of medicine concerned with the cause, origin, and nature of disease, including the changes occurring as a result of disease **2** the manifestations of disease, esp changes occurring in tissues or organs **3** any variant or deviant condition from normal > pa**ˈthologist** *n*

pathos (ˈpeɪθɒs) *n* **1** the quality or power, esp in literature or speech, of arousing feelings of pity, sorrow, etc **2** a feeling of sympathy or pity [C17 from Greek: suffering; related to *penthos* sorrow]

pathway (ˈpɑːθˌweɪ) *n* **1** another word for **path** (senses 1, 2) **2** a route to or way of access to; way of reaching or achieving something **3** courses taken by a student to gain entry to a higher course or towards a final qualification **4** *biochem* a chain of reactions associated with a particular metabolic process

-pathy *n combining form* **1** indicating feeling, sensitivity, or perception: *telepathy* **2** indicating disease or a morbid condition: *psychopathy* **3** indicating a method of treating disease: *osteopathy* [from Greek *patheia* suffering; see PATHOS] > **-pathic** *adj combining form*

Patiala (ˌpʌtɪˈɑːlə) *n* a city in N India, in E Punjab: seat of the Punjabi University (1962). Pop: 302 870 (2001)

patience (ˈpeɪʃəns) *n* **1** tolerant and even tempered perseverance **2** the capacity for calmly enduring pain, trying situations, etc **3** *chiefly Brit* any of various card games for one player only, in which the cards may be laid out in various combinations as the player tries to use up the whole pack. US equivalent: **solitaire 4** *obsolete* permission; sufferance [C13 via Old French from Latin *patientia* endurance, from *patī* to suffer]

patient (ˈpeɪʃənt) *adj* **1** enduring trying circumstances with even temper **2** tolerant; understanding **3** capable of accepting delay with equanimity **4** persevering or diligent: *a patient worker* **5** *archaic* admitting of a certain interpretation ▷ *n* **6** a person who is receiving medical care **7** *rare* a person or thing that is the recipient of some action [C14 see PATIENCE] > **ˈpatiently** *adv*

patiki (pɑːˈteɪkiː) *n, pl* **patiki** NZ another name for **dab²** (sense 3) [Māori]

patin *or* **patine** (ˈpætɪn) *n* variants of **paten**

patina¹ (ˈpætɪnə) *n, pl* **-nas 1** a film of oxide formed on the surface of a metal, esp the green oxidation of bronze or copper. See also **verdigris** (sense 1) **2** any fine layer on a surface: *a patina of frost* **3** the sheen on a surface that is caused by much handling [C18 from Italian: coating, from Latin: PATINA²]

patina² (ˈpætɪnə) *n, pl* **-nae** (-ˌniː) a broad shallow dish used in ancient Rome [from Latin, from Greek *patanē* platter]

patio (ˈpætɪˌəʊ) *n, pl* **-os 1** an open inner courtyard, esp one in a Spanish or Spanish-American house **2** an area adjoining a house, esp one that is paved and used for outdoor activities [C19 from Spanish: courtyard]

patisserie (pəˈtiːsərɪ) *n* **1** a shop where fancy pastries are sold **2** such pastries [C18 French, from *pâtissier* pastry cook, ultimately from Late Latin *pasta* PASTE¹]

Patmos (ˈpætmɒs) *n* a Greek island in the Aegean, in the NW Dodecanese: St John's place of exile (about 95 AD), where he wrote the Apocalypse. Pop: 2984 (2001). Area: 34 sq km (13 sq miles)

Patna (ˈpætnə) *n* a city in NE India, capital of Bihar state, on the River Ganges: founded in the 5th century BC; university (1917); centre of a rice-growing region. Pop: 1 376 950 (2001)

Patna rice *n* a variety of long-grain rice, used for savoury dishes

Pat. Off. *abbreviation for* Patent Office

patois (ˈpætwɑː; *French* patwa) *n, pl* **patois** (ˈpætwɑːz; *French* patwa) **1** an unwritten regional dialect of a language, esp of French, usually considered substandard **2** the jargon of particular group [C17 from Old French: rustic speech, perhaps from *patoier* to handle awkwardly, from *patte* paw]

pat. pend. *abbreviation for* patent pending

Patras (pəˈtræs, ˈpætrəs) *n* a port in W Greece, in the NW Peloponnese on the **Gulf of Patras** (an inlet of the Ionian Sea): one of the richest cities in Greece until the 3rd century BC; under Turkish rule from 1458 to 1687 and from 1715 until the War of Greek Independence, which began here in 1821. Pop: 193 000 (2005 est). Modern Greek name: Pátrai (ˈpɑtrɛ)

patri- *combining form* father: *patricide; patrilocal* [from Latin *pater*, Greek *patēr* FATHER]

patrial (ˈpeɪtrɪəl) *n* (in Britain formerly) a person having by statute the right of abode in the United Kingdom, and so not subject to immigration control [C20 from Latin *patria* native land]

patriarch (ˈpeɪtrɪˌɑːk) *n* **1** the male head of a tribe or family. Compare **matriarch** (sense 2) **2** a very old or venerable man **3** *Old Testament* any of a number of persons regarded as the fathers of the human race, divided into the antediluvian patriarchs, from Adam to Noah, and the postdiluvian, from Noah to Abraham **4** *Old Testament* any of the three ancestors of the Hebrew people: Abraham, Isaac, or Jacob **5** *Old Testament* any of Jacob's twelve sons, regarded as the ancestors of the twelve tribes of Israel **6** *early Christian Church* the bishop of one of several principal sees, esp those of Rome, Antioch, and Alexandria **7** *Eastern Orthodox Church* the bishops of the four ancient principal sees of Constantinople, Antioch, Alexandria, and Jerusalem, and also of Russia, Romania, and Serbia, the bishop of Constantinople (the **ecumenical Patriarch**) being highest in dignity among these **8** *RC Church* **a** a title given to the pope **b** a title given to a number of bishops, esp of the Uniat Churches, indicating their rank as immediately below that of the pope **9** *Mormon Church* another word for **Evangelist** (sense 2) **10** *Eastern Christianity* the head of the Coptic, Armenian, Syrian Jacobite, or Nestorian Churches, and of certain other non-Orthodox Churches in the East **11** the oldest or most venerable member of a group, community, etc: *the patriarch of steam engines* **12** a person regarded as the founder of a community, tradition, etc [C12 via Old French from Church Latin *patriarcha*] > **ˌpatriˈarchal** *adj* > **ˌpatriˈarchally** *adv*

patriarchal cross *n* a cross with two high horizontal bars, the upper one shorter than the lower

patriarchate (ˈpeɪtrɪˌɑːkɪt) *n* **1** the office, jurisdiction, province, or residence of a patriarch **2** a family or people under male domination or government

patriarchy (ˈpeɪtrɪˌɑːkɪ) *n, pl* **-chies 1** a form of social organization in which a male is the head of the family and descent, kinship, and title are traced through the male line **2** any society governed by such a system

patriate (ˈpætrɪˌeɪt, ˈpeɪtrɪˌeɪt) *vb* (tr) to bring under the authority of an autonomous country, for example as in the transfer of the Canadian constitution from UK to Canadian responsibility > **ˌpatriˈation** *n*

patrician (pəˈtrɪʃən) *n* **1** a member of the hereditary aristocracy of ancient Rome. In the early republic the patricians held almost all the higher offices. Compare **plebs** (sense 2) **2** a high nonhereditary title awarded by Constantine and his eastern Roman successors for services to the empire **3** (in medieval Europe) **a** a title borne by numerous princes including several emperors from the 8th to the 12th centuries **b** a member of the upper class in numerous Italian republics and German free cities **4** an aristocrat **5** a person of refined conduct, tastes, etc ▷ *adj* **6** (esp in ancient Rome) of, relating to, or composed of patricians **7** aristocratic **8** oligarchic and often antidemocratic or nonpopular: *patrician political views* [C15 from Old French *patricien*, from Latin *patricius* noble, from *pater* father]

patriciate (pəˈtrɪʃɪɪt, -ˌeɪt) *n* **1** the dignity, position, or rank of a patrician **2** the class or order of patricians

patricide (ˈpætrɪˌsaɪd) *n* **1** the act of killing one's father **2** a person who kills his father > **ˌpatriˈcidal** *adj*

patriclinous (ˌpætrɪˈklaɪnəs) *or* **patroclinous, patroclinal** (ˌpætrəˈklaɪnəl) *adj* (of animals and plants) showing the characters of the male parent. Compare **matriclinous** [C20 from Latin *pater* father + *clināre* to incline]

patrilineal (ˌpætrɪˈlɪnɪəl) *or* **patrilinear** *adj* tracing descent, kinship, or title through the male line > **ˌpatriˈlineally** *or* **ˌpatriˈlinearly** *adv*

patrilocal (ˌpætrɪˈləʊkəl) *adj* having or relating to a marriage pattern in which the couple lives with the husband's family > **ˌpatriˈlocally** *adv*

patrimony (ˈpætrɪmənɪ) *n, pl* **-nies 1** an inheritance from one's father or other ancestor **2** the endowment of a church [C14 *patrimoyne*, from Old French, from Latin *patrimonium* paternal inheritance] > **patrimonial** (ˌpætrɪˈməʊnɪəl) *adj* > **ˌpatriˈmonially** *adv*

patriot (ˈpeɪtrɪət, ˈpæt-) *n* a person who vigorously supports his country and its way of life [C16 via French from Late Latin *patriōta*, from Greek *patriōtēs*, from *patris* native land; related to Greek *patēr* father; compare Latin *pater* father, *patria* fatherland] > **patriotic** (ˌpætrɪˈɒtɪk) *adj* > **ˌpatriˈotically** *adv*

Patriot (ˈpeɪtrɪət) *n* a US surface-to-air missile system with multiple launch stations and the capability to track multiple targets by radar

patriotism (ˈpætrɪəˌtɪzəm) *n* devotion to one's own country and concern for its defence. Compare **nationalism**

patristic (pəˈtrɪstɪk) *or* **patristical** *adj* of or relating to the Fathers of the Church, their writings, or the study of these > **paˈtristically** *adv* > **paˈtristics** *n* (functioning as singular)

Patroclus (pəˈtrɒkləs) *n* *Greek myth* a friend of Achilles, killed in the Trojan War by Hector. His death made Achilles return to the fight after his quarrel with Agamemnon

patrol (pəˈtrəʊl) *n* **1** the action of going through or around a town, neighbourhood, etc, at regular intervals for purposes of security or observation **2** a person or group that carries out such an action **3** a military detachment with the mission of security, gathering information, or combat with enemy forces **4** a division of a troop of Scouts or Guides ▷ *vb* **-trols, -trolling, -trolled 5** to engage in a patrol of (a place) [C17 from French *patrouiller*, from *patouiller* to flounder in mud, from *patte* paw] > **paˈtroller** *n*

patrol car *n* a police car with a radio telephone used for patrolling streets and motorways. See also **panda car**

patrolman (pəˈtrəʊlmən) *n, pl* **-men 1** *chiefly US* a man, esp a policeman, who patrols a certain area **2** *Brit* a man employed to patrol an area to help motorists in difficulty

patrology (pəˈtrɒlədʒɪ) *n* **1** the study of the writings of the Fathers of the Church **2** a collection of such writings [C17 from Greek *patr-, patēr* father + -LOGY] > **patrological** (ˌpætrəˈlɒdʒɪkəl) *adj* > **paˈtrologist** *n*

patrol wagon *n* *US, Austral, and NZ* a police van for transporting prisoners. Also called (Informal): **paddy wagon,** (US) **police wagon**

patron¹ (ˈpeɪtrən) *n* **1** a person, esp a man, who sponsors or aids artists, charities, etc; protector or benefactor **2** a customer of a shop, hotel, etc, esp a regular one **3** See **patron saint 4** (in ancient Rome) the protector of a dependant or client, often the former master of a freedman still retaining certain rights over him **5** *Christianity* a person or body having the right to present a clergyman to a benefice [C14 via Old French from Latin *patrōnus* protector, from *pater* father] > **patronal** (pəˈtrəʊnəl) *adj* > **ˈpatronly** *adj*

patron² *French* (patrɔ̃) *n* a man, who owns or manages a hotel, restaurant, or bar

patron³ (ˈpætərn) *n* *Irish* a variant spelling of **pattern²**

patronage (ˈpætrənɪdʒ) *n* **1 a** the support given or custom brought by a patron or patroness **b** the position of a patron **2** (in politics) **a** the practice of making appointments to office, granting contracts, etc **b** the favours so distributed **3 a** a condescending manner **b** any kindness done in a condescending way **4** *Christianity* the right to present a clergyman to a benefice

patroness (ˈpeɪtrənˌɛs) *n* **1** a woman who sponsors or aids artists, charities, etc; protector or benefactor **2** See **patron saint** [see PATRON]

p

> patronal (pəˈtrəʊnᵊl) adj > ˈpatronly adj

patronize or **patronise** (ˈpætrəˌnaɪz) vb **1** to behave or treat in a condescending way **2** (tr) to act as a patron or patroness by sponsoring or bringing trade to > ˈpatronˌizer or ˈpatronˌiser n

patronizing or **patronising** (ˈpætrəˌnaɪzɪŋ) adj having a superior manner; condescending > ˈpatronˌizingly or ˈpatronˌisingly adv

patronne French (patrɔn) n a woman who owns or manages a hotel, restaurant, or bar

patron saint n a saint regarded as the particular guardian of a country, church, trade, person, etc

patronymic (ˌpætrəˈnɪmɪk) adj **1** (of a name) derived from the name of its bearer's father or ancestor. In Western cultures, many surnames are patronymic in origin, as for example Irish names beginning with O' and English names ending with -son; in other cultures, such as Russian, a special patronymic name is used in addition to the surname ▷ n **2** a patronymic name [c17 via Late Latin from Greek patronumikos, from patēr father + onoma NAME]

patroon (pəˈtruːn) n (in the US) a Dutch land-holder in New Netherland and New York with manorial rights in the colonial era [c18 from Dutch: PATRON¹] > paˈtroonˌship n

patsy (ˈpætsɪ) n, pl -sies slang, chiefly US and Canadian **1** a person who is easily cheated, victimized, etc **2** a scapegoat [c20 of unknown origin]

pattée (ˈpæteɪ, ˈpætɪ) adj (often postpositive) (of a cross) having triangular arms widening outwards [from French patte paw]

patten (ˈpætᵊn) n a wooden clog or sandal on a raised wooden platform or metal ring [c14 from Old French patin, probably from patte paw]

patter¹ (ˈpætə) vb **1** (intr) to walk or move with quick soft steps **2** to strike with or make a quick succession of light tapping sounds **3** (tr) rare to cause to patter ▷ n **4** a quick succession of light tapping sounds, as of feet: the patter of mice [c17 from PAT¹]

patter² (ˈpætə) n **1** the glib rapid speech of comedians, salesmen, etc **2** quick idle talk; chatter **3** the jargon of a particular group; lingo ▷ vb **4** (intr) to speak glibly and rapidly **5** to repeat (prayers) in a mechanical or perfunctory manner [c14 from Latin pater in Pater Noster Our Father]

pattern¹ (ˈpætᵊn) n **1** an arrangement of repeated or corresponding parts, decorative motifs, etc: although the notes seemed random, a careful listener could detect a pattern **2** a decorative design: a paisley pattern **3** a style: various patterns of cutlery **4** a plan or diagram used as a guide in making something: a paper pattern for a dress **5** a standard way of moving, acting, etc: traffic patterns **6** a model worthy of imitation: a pattern of kindness **7** a representative sample **8** a wooden or metal shape or model used in a foundry to make a mould **9 a** the arrangement of marks made in a target by bullets **b** a diagram displaying such an arrangement ▷ vb (tr) **10** (often foll by after or on) to model **11** to arrange as or decorate with a pattern [c14 patron, from Medieval Latin patrōnus example, from Latin: PATRON¹]

pattern² or **patron** (ˈpætərn) n Irish an outdoor assembly with religious practices, traders' stalls, etc on the feast day of a patron saint [c18 variant of PATRON¹; see PATTERN¹]

patter song n music a humorous song or aria, the text of which consists of rapid strings of words

patty (ˈpætɪ) n, pl -ties **1** a small flattened cake of minced food **2** a small pie [c18 from French PÂTÉ]

pattypan squash or **pattypan** (ˈpætɪˌpæn) n chiefly US a small round flattish squash with a scalloped rim and thin, pale green skin [c17 PATTY + PAN¹]

patu (ˈpaːtuː) n, pl patus a short Māori club, now used ceremonially [Māori]

patulous (ˈpætjʊləs) adj **1** botany spreading widely or expanded: patulous branches **2** rare gaping [c17 from Latin patulus open, from patēre to lie

open] > ˈpatulously adv > ˈpatulousness n

patutuki (ˈpaːtuːˌtuːkɪ) n NZ another name for **blue cod**

Pau (French po) n a city in SW France: residence of the French kings of Navarre; tourist centre for the Pyrenees. Pop: 78 732 (1999)

PAU abbreviation for **Pan American Union**

paua (ˈpaːʊa) n an edible abalone, Haliotis iris, of New Zealand, having an iridescent shell used esp for jewellery [from Māori]

paucal (ˈpɔːkᵊl) grammar ▷ n **1** a grammatical number occurring in some languages for words in contexts where a few of their referents are described or referred to ▷ adj **2** relating to or inflected for this number [from Latin paucus few]

paucity (ˈpɔːsɪtɪ) n **1** smallness of quantity; insufficiency; dearth **2** smallness of number; fewness [c15 from Latin paucitās scarcity, from paucus few]

pauldron (ˈpɔːldrən) n either of two metal plates worn with armour to protect the shoulders [c15 from French espauleron, from espaule shoulder; see EPAULETTE]

Pauli exclusion principle n physics the principle that two identical fermions cannot occupy the same quantum state in a body such as an atom; sometimes shortened to **exclusion principle** [c20 from Wolfgang Pauli (1900–58), US physicist born in Austria]

Pauline (ˈpɔːlaɪn) adj relating to Saint Paul (died ?67 AD), the Christian missionary, martyr, and writer of many of the epistles in the New Testament, or to his doctrines

Paul Jones n an old-time dance in which partners are exchanged [c19 named after John Paul Jones (1747–92), Scots-born US naval commander]

paulownia (pɔːˈləʊnɪə) n any scrophulariaceous tree of the Japanese genus Paulownia, esp P. tomentosa, having large heart-shaped leaves and clusters of purplish or white flowers [c19 New Latin, named after Anna Paulovna, daughter of Paul I of Russia]

Paul Pry n a nosy person [c19 from a character in the play Paul Pry by John Poole (1825)]

Paumotu Archipelago (paʊˈməʊtuː) n another name for the **Tuamotu Archipelago**

paunch (pɔːntʃ) n **1** the belly or abdomen, esp when protruding **2** another name for **rumen 3** nautical a thick mat that prevents chafing ▷ vb (tr) **4** to stab in the stomach; disembowel [c14 from Anglo-Norman paunche, from Old French pance, from Latin panticēs (pl) bowels]

paunchy (ˈpɔːntʃɪ) adj -ier, -iest having a protruding belly or abdomen > ˈpaunchiness n

pauper (ˈpɔːpə) n **1** a person who is extremely poor **2** (formerly) a destitute person supported by public charity [c16 from Latin: poor] > ˈpauperˌism n

pauperize or **pauperise** (ˈpɔːpəˌraɪz) vb (tr) to make a pauper of; impoverish

pauropod (ˈpɔːrəˌpɒd) n a member of the Pauropoda, a class of minute myriapods less than 2 mm (1/20 in.) in size, having 8 to 10 pairs of legs and branched antennae

pause (pɔːz) vb (intr) **1** to cease an action temporarily; stop **2** to hesitate; delay: she replied without pausing ▷ n **3** a temporary stop or rest, esp in speech or action; short break **4** prosody another word for **caesura 5** Also called: fermata music a continuation of a note or rest beyond its normal length. Usual symbol: ⌢ **6** give pause to to cause to hesitate [c15 from Latin pausa pause, from Greek pausis, from pauein to halt] > ˈpausal adj > ˈpauser n > ˈpausing n, adj

pav (pæv) n Austral and NZ informal short for **pavlova**

pavage (ˈpeɪvɪdʒ) n **1** history a tax towards paving streets, or the right to levy such a tax **2** the act of paving

pavane or **pavan** (pəˈvɑːn, -ˈvæn, ˈpævᵊn) n **1** a slow and stately dance of the 16th and 17th centuries **2** a piece of music composed for or in

the rhythm of this dance, usually characterized by a slow stately triple time [c16 pavan, via French from Spanish pavana, from Old Italian padovana Paduan (dance), from Padova Padua]

pave (peɪv) vb (tr) **1** to cover (a road, path, etc) with a firm surface suitable for travel, as with paving stones or concrete **2** to serve as the material for a pavement or other hard layer: bricks paved the causeway **3** (often foll by with) to cover with a hard layer (of): shelves paved with marble **4** to prepare or make easier (esp in the phrase **pave the way**): to pave the way for future development [c14 from Old French paver, from Latin pavīre to ram down] > ˈpaver n

pavé (ˈpæveɪ) n **1** a paved surface, esp an uneven one **2** a style of setting gems so closely that no metal shows

pavement (ˈpeɪvmənt) n **1** a hard-surfaced path for pedestrians alongside and a little higher than a road. US and Canadian word: sidewalk **2** a paved surface, esp one that is a thoroughfare **3** the material used in paving **4** civil engineering the hard layered structure that forms a road carriageway, airfield runway, vehicle park, or other paved areas **5** geology a level area of exposed rock resembling a paved road. See **limestone pavement** [c13 from Latin pavīmentum a hard floor, from pavīre to beat hard]

Pavia (ˈpaːvɪə) n a town in N Italy, in Lombardy: noted for its Roman and medieval remains, including the tomb of St Augustine. Pop: 71 214 (2001). Latin name: Ticinum

pavid (ˈpævɪd) adj rare fearful; timid [c17 from Latin pavidus fearful, from pavēre to tremble with fear]

pavilion (pəˈvɪljən) n **1** Brit a building at a sports ground, esp a cricket pitch, in which players change **2** a summerhouse or other decorative shelter **3** a building or temporary structure, esp one that is open and ornamental, for housing exhibitions **4** a large ornate tent, esp one with a peaked top, as used by medieval armies **5** one of a set of buildings that together form a hospital or other large institution **6** one of four main facets on a brilliant-cut stone between the girdle and the culet ▷ vb (tr) literary **7** to place or set in or as if in a pavilion: pavilioned in splendour **8** to provide with a pavilion or pavilions [c13 from Old French pavillon canopied structure, from Latin pāpiliō butterfly, tent]

paving (ˈpeɪvɪŋ) n **1** a paved surface; pavement **2** material used for a pavement, such as paving stones, bricks, or asphalt ▷ adj **3** of or for a paved surface or pavement **4** preparatory, facilitating, enabling: paving legislation

paving stone n a concrete or stone slab for paving

paviour or US **pavior** (ˈpeɪvjə) n **1** a person who lays paving **2** a machine for ramming down paving **3** material used for paving [c15 from paver, from PAVE]

pavis or **pavise** (ˈpævɪs) n a large square shield, developed in the 15th century, at first portable but later heavy and set up in a permanent position [c14 from Old French pavais, from Italian pavese of Pavia, Italian city where these shields were originally made]

Pavlodar (Russian pəvlaˈdar) n a port in NE Kazakhstan on the Irtysh River: major industrial centre with an oil refinery. Pop: 303 000 (2005 est)

pavlova (pævˈləʊvə) n a meringue cake topped with whipped cream and fruit [c20 named after Anna Pavlova (1885–1931), Russian ballerina]

Pavlovian (pævˈləʊvɪən) adj **1** of or relating to the work of Ivan Pavlov (1849–1936), the Russian physiologist **2** (of a reaction or response) automatic; involuntary

Pavo (ˈpaːvəʊ) n, Latin genitive Pavonis (pəˈvəʊnɪs) a small constellation near the South Pole lying between Tucana and Ara [Latin: peacock]

pavonine (ˈpævəˌnaɪn) adj of or resembling a peacock or the colours, design, or iridescence of a peacock's tail [c17 from Latin *pāvōnīnus*, from *pāvō* peacock]

paw (pɔː) *n* **1** any of the feet of a four-legged mammal, bearing claws or nails **2** *informal* a hand, esp one that is large, clumsy, etc ▷ *vb* **3** to scrape or contaminate with the paws or feet **4** (*tr*) *informal* to touch or caress in a clumsy, rough, or overfamiliar manner; maul [c13 via Old French from Germanic; related to Middle Dutch *pōte*, German *Pfote*]

pawky ('pɔːkɪ) *adj* pawkier, pawkiest *Scot* having or characterized by a dry wit [c17 from Scottish *pawk* trick, of unknown origin] > **pawkily** *adv* > **pawkiness** *n*

pawl (pɔːl) *n* a pivoted lever shaped to engage with a ratchet wheel to prevent motion in a particular direction [c17 perhaps from Dutch *pal* pawl]

pawn[1] (pɔːn) *vb* (*tr*) **1** to deposit (an article) as security for the repayment of a loan, esp from a pawnbroker **2** to stake: *to pawn one's honour* ▷ *n* **3** an article deposited as security **4** the condition of being so deposited (esp in the phrase **in pawn**) **5** a person or thing that is held as a security, esp a hostage **6** the act of pawning [c15 from Old French *pan* security, from Latin *pannus* cloth, apparently because clothing was often left as a surety; compare Middle Flemish *paen* pawn, German *Pfand* pledge] > **pawnage** *n*

pawn[2] (pɔːn) *n* **1** a chessman of the lowest theoretical value, limited to forward moves of one square at a time with the option of two squares on its initial move: it captures with a diagonal move only. Abbreviation: P Compare **piece** (sense 12) **2** a person, group, etc, manipulated by another [c14 from Anglo-Norman *poun*, from Old French *pehon*, from Medieval Latin *pedō* infantryman, from Latin *pēs* foot]

pawnbroker ('pɔːn,brəʊkə) *n* a dealer licensed to lend money at a specified rate of interest on the security of movable personal property, which can be sold if the loan is not repaid within a specified period > **pawn,broking** *n*

Pawnee (pɔːˈniː) *n* **1** (*pl* -nees *or* -nee) a member of a confederacy of related North American Indian peoples, formerly living in Nebraska and Kansas, now chiefly in Oklahoma **2** the language of these peoples, belonging to the Caddoan family

pawnshop ('pɔːn,ʃɒp) *n* the premises of a pawnbroker

pawn ticket *n* a receipt for goods pawned

pawpaw ('pɔː,pɔː) *n* a variant of **papaw** *or* **papaya**

pax (pæks) *n* **1** *chiefly RC Church* **a** a greeting signifying Christian love transmitted from one to another of those assisting at the Eucharist; kiss of peace **b** a small metal or ivory plate, often with a representation of the Crucifixion, formerly used to convey the kiss of peace from the celebrant at Mass to those attending it, who kissed the plate in turn ▷ *interj* **2** *Brit school slang* a call signalling an end to hostilities or claiming immunity from the rules of a game: usually accompanied by a crossing of the fingers [Latin: peace]

Pax (pæks) *n* **1** the Roman goddess of peace. Greek counterpart: **Irene** **2** a period of general peace, esp one in which there is one dominant nation [Latin: peace]

PAX *abbreviation for* private automatic exchange

Pax Romana ('pæks rəʊˈmɑːnə) *n* the Roman peace; the long period of stability under the Roman Empire

pax vobiscum Latin (pæks vəʊˈbɪskʊm) peace be with you

paxwax ('pæks,wæks) *n* *dialect* a strong ligament in the neck of many mammals, which supports the head [c15 changed from c14 *fax wax*, probably from Old English *feax* hair of the head, *wax* growth]

pay[1] (peɪ) *vb* pays, paying, paid **1** to discharge (a debt, obligation, etc) by giving or doing something: *he paid his creditors* **2** (when *intr*, often foll by *for*) to give (money) to (a person) in return

for goods or services: *they pay their workers well; they pay by the hour* **3** to give or afford (a person) a profit or benefit: *it pays one to be honest* **4** (*tr*) to give or bestow (a compliment, regards, attention, etc) **5** (*tr*) to make (a visit or call) **6** (*intr*; often foll by *for*) to give compensation or make amends **7** (*tr*) to yield a return of: *the shares pay 15 per cent* **8** to give or do (something equivalent) in return; pay back: *he paid for the insult with a blow* **9** (*tr*; past tense and past participle **paid** *or* **payed**) *nautical* to allow (a vessel) to make leeway **10** *Austral informal* to acknowledge or accept (something) as true, just, etc **11** pay one's way **a** to contribute one's share of expenses **b** to remain solvent without outside help ▷ *n* **12** **a** money given in return for work or services; a salary or wage **b** (*as modifier*): *a pay slip; pay claim* **13** paid employment (esp in the phrase **in the pay of**) **14** (*modifier*) requiring the insertion of money or discs before or during use: *a pay phone; a pay toilet* **15** (*modifier*) rich enough in minerals to be profitably mined or worked: *pay gravel* ▷ See also **pay back, pay down, pay for, pay in, pay off, pay out, pay up** [c12 from Old French *payer*, from Latin *pācāre* to appease (a creditor), from *pāx* PEACE]

pay[2] (peɪ) *vb* pays, paying, payed (*tr*) *nautical* to caulk (the seams of a wooden vessel) with pitch or tar [c17 from Old French *peier*, from Latin *picāre*, from *pix* pitch]

payable ('peɪəbəl) *adj* **1** (often foll by *on*) to be paid: *payable on the third of each month* **2** that is capable of being paid **3** capable of being profitable **4** (of a debt) imposing an obligation on the debtor to pay, esp at once

pay-and-display *adj* denoting a car-parking system in which a motorist buys a permit to park for a specified period from a coin-operated machine and displays the permit on or near the windscreen of his or her car so that it can be seen by a parking attendant

pay back *vb* (*tr, adverb*) **1** to retaliate against: *to pay someone back for an insult* **2** to give or do (something equivalent) in return for a favour, insult, etc **3** to repay (a loan) ▷ *n* **payback** **4 a** the return on an investment **b** Also called: **payback period** the time taken for a project to cover its outlay **5 a** something done in order to gain revenge **b** (*as modifier*): *payback killings*

pay bed *n* an informal name for **amenity bed** *or* **private pay bed**

payday ('peɪ,deɪ) *n* the day on which wages or salaries are paid

pay dirt *n* **1** a deposit rich enough in minerals to be worth mining **2** strike *or* hit pay dirt *informal* to achieve one's objective

pay down *vb* (*adverb*) to pay (a sum of money) at the time of purchase as the first of a series of instalments

PAYE (in Britain and New Zealand) *abbreviation for* pay as you earn; a system by which income tax levied on wage and salary earners is paid by employers directly to the government

payee (peɪˈiː) *n* **1** the person to whom a cheque, money order, etc, is made out **2** a person to whom money is paid or due

payer ('peɪə) *n* **1** a person who pays **2** the person named in a commercial paper as responsible for its payment on redemption

pay for *vb* (*preposition*) **1** to make payment (of) for **2** (*intr*) to suffer or be punished, as for a mistake, wrong decision, etc: *in his old age he paid for the laxity of his youth*

pay in *vb* (*tr, adverb*) to hand (money, a cheque, etc) to a cashier for depositing in a bank, etc

paying guest *n* a euphemism for **lodger** Abbreviation: PG

payload ('peɪ,ləʊd) *n* **1** that part of a cargo earning revenue **2 a** the passengers, cargo, or bombs carried by an aircraft **b** the equipment carried by a rocket, satellite, or spacecraft **3** the explosive power of a warhead, bomb, etc, carried by a missile or aircraft: *a missile carrying a 50-megaton payload*

paymaster ('peɪ,mɑːstə) *n* an official of a government, business, etc, responsible for the payment of wages and salaries

payment ('peɪmənt) *n* **1** the act of paying **2** a sum of money paid **3** something given in return; punishment or reward

payment by results *n* a system of wage payment whereby all or part of the wage varies systematically according to the level of work performance of an employee

paynim ('peɪnɪm) *n* *archaic* **1** a heathen or pagan **2** a Muslim [c13 from Old French *paienime*, from Late Latin *pāgānismus* paganism, from *pāgānus* PAGAN]

pay off *vb* **1** (*tr, adverb*) to pay all that is due in wages, etc, and discharge from employment **2** (*tr, adverb*) to pay the complete amount of (a debt, bill, etc) **3** (*intr, adverb*) to turn out to be profitable, effective, etc: *the gamble paid off* **4** (*tr, adverb or intr, preposition*) to take revenge on (a person) or for (a wrong done): *to pay someone off for an insult* **5** (*tr, adverb*) *informal* to give a bribe to **6** (*intr, adverb*) *nautical* (of a vessel) to make leeway ▷ *n* **payoff** **7** the final settlement, esp in retribution **8** *informal* the climax, consequence, or outcome of events, a story, etc, esp when unexpected or improbable **9** the final payment of a debt, salary, etc **10** the time of such a payment **11** *informal* a bribe

payola (peɪˈəʊlə) *n* *informal, chiefly US* **1** a bribe given to secure special treatment, esp to a disc jockey to promote a commercial product **2** the practice of paying or receiving such bribes [c20 from PAY[1] + -*ola*, as in *Pianola*]

pay out *vb* (*adverb*) **1** to distribute (money); disburse **2** (*tr*) to release (a rope) gradually, hand over hand **3** (*tr*) to retaliate against ▷ *n* **payout** **4** a sum of money paid out

pay-per-click *n* a system of payment used on the internet in which an advertiser on a website pays the website owner according to the number of people who visit the advertiser's website via the hyperlinked advert on the owner's website

pay-per-view *n* **a** a system of television broadcasting by which subscribers pay for each programme they wish to receive **b** (*as modifier*): *a pay-per-view channel* ▷ Compare **free-to-air, pay television**

payphone ('peɪ,fəʊn) *n* a public telephone operated by coins or a phonecard

payroll ('peɪ,rəʊl) *n* **1** a list of employees, specifying the salary or wage of each **2 a** the total of these amounts or the actual money equivalent **b** (*as modifier*): *a payroll tax*

Paysandú (Spanish paisanˈdu) *n* a port in W Uruguay, on the Uruguay River: the third largest city in the country. Pop: 74 568 (1996 est)

Pays de la Loire (French pei də la lwar) *n* a region of W France, on the Bay of Biscay: generally low-lying, drained by the River Loire and its tributaries; agricultural

payt *abbreviation for* payment

pay television *n* a system by which television programmes are transmitted in scrambled form, unintelligible except to those who have paid for descrambling equipment. Also called: **subscription television** Compare **free-to-air, pay-per-view**

pay up *vb* (*adverb*) to pay (money) promptly, in full, or on demand

pazzazz *or* **pazazz** (pəˈzæz) *n* *informal* variants of **pizzazz**

Pb the chemical symbol for lead [from New Latin *plumbum*]

PB *abbreviation for* **1** Pharmacopoeia Britannica **2** Prayer Book **3** *athletics* personal best

PBX (in Britain) *abbreviation for* private branch exchange; a telephone system that handles the internal and external calls of a building, firm, etc

pc *abbreviation for* **1** per cent **2** postcard **3** *obsolete* (in prescriptions) post cibum [Latin: after meals] **4** parsec

PC *abbreviation for* **1** personal computer **2** Parish Council(lor) **3** Past Commander **4** (in Britain and Canada) Police Constable **5** politically correct **6** Prince Consort **7** (in Britain and Canada) **Privy Council(lor) 8** (in Canada) Progressive Conservative

P/C, p/c *or* **p.c.** *abbreviation for* **1** petty cash **2** price current

PCB *abbreviation for* **polychlorinated biphenyl**

PCC (in Britain) *abbreviation for* Press Complaints Commission

pcm *abbreviation for* pulse code modulation

PCOS *abbreviation for* **polycystic ovary syndrome**

PCP *n* **1** phenylcyclohexylpiperidine (phencyclidine); a depressant drug used illegally as a hallucinogen. Informal name: angel dust ▷ *abbreviation for* **2** *Pneumocystis carinii* pneumonia. See **pneumocystis**

PCR *abbreviation for* polymerase chain reaction: a technique for rapidly producing many copies of a fragment of DNA for diagnostic or research purposes

PCSO (in Britain) *abbreviation for* Police Community Support Officer

pct *US abbreviation for* per cent

PCV (in Britain) *abbreviation for* passenger carrying vehicle

pd *abbreviation for* **1** paid **2** Also: **PD** per diem **3** potential difference

Pd *the chemical symbol for* palladium

PD (in the US) *abbreviation for* Police Department

PDA *abbreviation for* personal digital assistant

PDF *computing abbreviation for* portable document format: a format in which documents may be viewed

pdl *abbreviation for* **poundal**

pdq *slang* ▷ *abbreviation for* pretty damn quick

PDR *abbreviation for* **price-dividend ratio**

P-D ratio *n* short for **price-dividend ratio**

PDSA (in Britain) *abbreviation for* People's Dispensary for Sick Animals

pe¹ (peɪ; *Hebrew* pe) *n* the 17th letter in the Hebrew alphabet (Đ or, at the end of a word, ף) transliterated as *p* or, when final, *ph* [from Hebrew *peh* mouth]

pe² *the internet domain name for* Peru

PE *abbreviation for* **1** physical education **2 potential energy 3** Presiding Elder **4** (esp in postal addresses) Prince Edward Island (Canadian Province) **5** Also: **p.e** printer's error **6** *statistics* probable error **7** Protestant Episcopal **8** (in South Africa) Port Elizabeth **9** ▷ *international car registration for* Peru

pea (pi:) *n* **1** an annual climbing leguminous plant, *Pisum sativum*, with small white flowers and long green pods containing edible green seeds: cultivated in temperate regions **2 a** the seed of this plant, eaten as a vegetable **b** (*as modifier*): *pea soup* **3** any of several other leguminous plants, such as the sweet pea, chickpea, and cowpea [C17 from PEASE (incorrectly assumed to be a plural)] > 'pea,like *adj*

pea-brain *n informal* a foolish or unintelligent person

peace (pi:s) *n* **1 a** the state existing during the absence of war **b** (*as modifier*): *peace negotiations* **2** (*modifier*) denoting a person or thing symbolizing support for international peace: *peace women* **3** (*often capital*) a treaty marking the end of a war **4** a state of harmony between people or groups; freedom from strife **5** law and order within a state; absence of violence or other disturbance: *a breach of the peace* **6** absence of mental anxiety (often in the phrase **peace of mind**) **7** a state of stillness, silence, or serenity **8 at peace a** in a state of harmony or friendship **b** in a state of serenity **c** dead: *the old lady is at peace now* **9 hold** *or* **keep one's peace** to keep silent **10 keep the peace** to maintain or refrain from disturbing law and order **11 make one's peace with** to become reconciled with **12 make peace** to bring hostilities to an end ▷ *vb* **13** (*intr*) obsolete except as

an imperative to be or become silent or still [C12 from Old French *pais*, from Latin *pāx*]

peaceable ('pi:səbᵊl) *adj* **1** inclined towards peace **2** tranquil; calm > 'peaceableness *n* > 'peaceably *adv*

Peace Corps *n* an agency of the US government that sends American volunteers to developing countries, where they work on educational and other projects: established in 1961

peace dividend *n* additional money available to a government from cuts in defence expenditure because of the end of a period of hostilities

peaceful ('pi:sful) *adj* **1** not in a state of war or disagreement **2** tranquil; calm **3** not involving violence: *peaceful picketing* **4** of, relating to, or in accord with a time of peace: *peaceful uses of atomic energy* **5** inclined towards peace > 'peacefully *adv* > 'peacefulness *n*

peacekeeping ('pi:s,ki:pɪŋ) *n* **a** the maintenance of peace, esp the prevention of further fighting between hostile forces in an area **b** (*as modifier*): *a UN peacekeeping force* > 'peace,keeper *n*

peacemaker ('pi:s,meɪkə) *n* a person who establishes peace, esp between others > 'peace,making *n*

peace offering *n* **1** something given to an adversary in the hope of procuring or maintaining peace **2** *Judaism* a sacrificial meal shared between the offerer and Jehovah to intensify the union between them

peace pipe *n* a long decorated pipe smoked by North American Indians on ceremonial occasions, esp as a token of peace. Also called: **calumet, pipe of peace**

Peace River *n* a river in W Canada, rising in British Columbia as the Finlay River and flowing northeast into the Slave River. Length: 1715 km (1065 miles)

peace sign *n* a gesture made with the palm of the hand outwards and the index and middle fingers raised in a V. See also **V-sign** (sense 2)

peacetime ('pi:s,taɪm) *n* **a** a period without war; time of peace **b** (*as modifier*): *a peacetime agreement*

peach¹ (pi:tʃ) *n* **1** a small rosaceous tree, *Prunus persica*, with pink flowers and rounded edible fruit: cultivated in temperate regions. See also **nectarine** (sense 1) **2** the soft juicy fruit of this tree, which has a downy reddish-yellow skin, yellowish-orange sweet flesh, and a single stone. See also **nectarine** (sense 2) **3 a** a pinkish-yellow to orange colour **b** (*as adjective*): *a peach dress* **4** *informal* a person or thing that is especially pleasing [C14 *peche*, from Old French, from Medieval Latin *persica*, from Latin *Persicum mālum* Persian apple]

peach² (pi:tʃ) *vb* (*intr except in obsolete uses*) *slang* to inform against an accomplice [C15 variant of earlier *apeche*, from French, from Late Latin *impedicāre* to entangle; see IMPEACH] > 'peacher *n*

peach-blow *n* **1 a** a delicate purplish-pink colour **b** (*as adjective*): *a peach-blow vase* **2** a glaze of this colour on Oriental porcelain [C19 from PEACH¹ + BLOW³]

peach brandy *n* (esp in S. Africa) a brandy made from fermented peaches

peach Melba *n* a dessert made of halved peaches, vanilla ice cream, and Melba sauce [C20 named after Dame Nellie *Melba*, stage name of *Helen Porter Mitchell* (1861–1931), Australian operatic soprano]

peachy ('pi:tʃɪ) *adj* **peachier, peachiest 1** of or like a peach, esp in colour or texture **2** *informal* excellent; fine > 'peachily *adv* > 'peachiness *n*

peacock ('pi:,kɒk) *n, pl* **-cocks** *or* **-cock 1** a male peafowl, having a crested head and a very large fanlike tail marked with blue and green eyelike spots. Related adj: **pavonine 2** another name for **peafowl 3** a vain strutting person ▷ *vb* **4** to display (oneself) proudly **5** *obsolete slang, Austral* to acquire (the best pieces of land) in such a way that the surrounding land is useless to others [C14 *pecok, pe-* from Old English *pāwa* (from Latin *pāvō* peacock) + COCK¹] > 'pea,cockish *adj* > 'pea,hen *fem n*

peacock blue *n* **a** a greenish-blue colour **b** (*as adjective*): *a peacock-blue car*

peacock butterfly *n* a European nymphalid butterfly, *Inachis io*, having reddish-brown wings each marked with a purple eyespot

peacock ore *n* another name for **bornite**

peacock's tail *n* a handsome brown seaweed, *Padina pavonia* (though coloured yellow-olive, red, and green) whose fan-shaped fronds have concentric bands of iridescent hairs

pea crab *n* any of various globular soft-bodied crabs of the genus *Pinnotheres* and related genera that live commensally in the mantles of certain bivalves

peafowl ('pi:,faʊl) *n, pl* **-fowls** *or* **-fowl 1** either of two large pheasants, *Pavo cristatus* (**blue peafowl**) of India and Ceylon and *P. muticus* (**green peafowl**) of SE Asia. The males (see **peacock** (sense 1)) have a characteristic bright plumage **2** a rare closely related African species, *Afropavo congensis* (**Congo peafowl**), both sexes of which are brightly coloured

peag *or* **peage** (pi:g) *n* less common words for **wampum** [shortened from Narraganset *wampompeag* WAMPUM]

pea green *n* **a** a yellowish-green colour **b** (*as adjective*): *a pea-green teapot*

pea jacket *or* **peacoat** ('pi:,kəʊt) *n* a sailor's short heavy double-breasted overcoat of navy wool [C18 from Dutch *pijjekker*, from *pij* coat of coarse cloth + *jekker* jacket]

peak (pi:k) *n* **1** a pointed end, edge, or projection: *the peak of a roof* **2** the pointed summit of a mountain **3** a mountain with a pointed summit **4** the point of greatest development, strength, etc: *the peak of his career* **5 a** a sharp increase in a physical quantity followed by a sharp decrease: *a voltage peak* **b** the maximum value of this quantity **c** (*as modifier*): *peak voltage* **6** Also called: **visor** a projecting piece on the front of some caps **7 a** See **widow's peak b** the pointed end of a beard **8** *nautical* **a** the extreme forward (**forepeak**) or aft (**afterpeak**) part of the hull **b** (of a fore-and-aft quadrilateral sail) the after uppermost corner **c** the after end of a gaff ▷ *vb* **9** (*tr*) *nautical* to set (a gaff) or tilt (oars) vertically **10** to form or reach or cause to form or reach a peak or maximum ▷ *adj* **11** of or relating to a period of highest use or demand, as for watching television, commuting, etc: *peak viewing hours; peak time* [C16 perhaps from PIKE², influenced by BEAK¹; compare Spanish *pico*, French *pic*, Middle Low German *pēk*] > 'peaky *adj*

Peak District *n* a region of N central England, mainly in N Derbyshire at the S end of the Pennines: consists of moors in the north and a central limestone plateau; many caves. Highest point: 727 m (2088 ft)

peaked (pi:kt) *adj* having a peak; pointed

peak load *n* the maximum load on an electrical power-supply system. Compare **base load**

peak programme meter *n* an instrument for assessing the maximum levels of an electrical sound signal. Abbreviations: **PPM, ppm**

peaky ('pi:kɪ) *adj* **-kier, -kiest** wan, emaciated, or sickly [C16 of uncertain origin]

peal¹ (pi:l) *n* **1** a loud prolonged usually reverberating sound, as of bells, thunder, or laughter **2** *bell-ringing* a series of changes rung in accordance with specific rules, consisting of not fewer than 5000 permutations in a ring of eight bells **3** (*not in technical usage*) the set of bells in a belfry ▷ *vb* **4** (*intr*) to sound with a peal or peals **5** (*tr*) to give forth loudly and sonorously **6** (*tr*) to ring (bells) in peals [C14 *pele*, variant of *apele* APPEAL]

peal² (pi:l) *n* a dialect name for a grilse or a young sea trout

pean¹ ('pi:ən) *n* a less common US spelling of **paean**

pean² (pi:n) *n heraldry* a fur of sable spotted with or [C16 of uncertain origin]

Peano's axioms (pɪˈɑːnəʊz) *pl n* a set of axioms

that yield the arithmetic of the natural numbers [named after Giuseppe *Peano* (1858–1932), Italian mathematician]

peanut ('piːˌnʌt) *n* **a** a leguminous plant, *Arachis hypogaea*, of tropical America: widely cultivated for its edible seeds. The seed pods are forced underground where they ripen. See also **hog peanut b** the edible nutlike seed of this plant, used for food and as a source of oil. Also called: **goober, goober pea,** (*Brit*) **groundnut,** (*Brit*) **monkey nut** ▷ See also **peanuts**

peanut butter *n* a brownish oily paste made from peanuts

peanut oil *n* oil that is made from peanut seeds and used for cooking, in soaps, and in pharmaceutical products

peanuts ('piːˌnʌts) *n slang* a trifling amount of money

pear (pɛə) *n* **1** a widely cultivated rosaceous tree, *Pyrus communis*, having white flowers and edible fruits **2** the sweet gritty-textured juicy fruit of this tree, which has a globular base and tapers towards the apex **3** the wood of this tree, used for making furniture **4 go pear-shaped** *informal* to go wrong: *the plan started to go pear-shaped* [Old English *pere*, ultimately from Latin *pirum*]

pea rifle *n* a small rifle

pearl[1] (pɜːl) *n* **1** a hard smooth lustrous typically rounded structure occurring on the inner surface of the shell of a clam or oyster: consists of calcium carbonate secreted in layers around an invading particle such as a sand grain; much valued as a gem. Related adjs: **margaric, margaritic 2** any artificial gem resembling this **3** See **mother-of-pearl 4** a person or thing that is like a pearl, esp in beauty or value **5** a pale greyish-white colour, often with a bluish tinge **6** a size of printer's type, approximately equal to 5 point ▷ *adj* **7** of, made of, or set with pearl or mother-of-pearl **8** having the shape or colour of a pearl ▷ *vb* **9** (*tr*) to set with or as if with pearls **10** to shape into or assume a pearl-like form or colour **11** (*intr*) to dive or search for pearls [c14 from Old French, from Vulgar Latin *pernula* (unattested), from Latin *perna* sea mussel]

pearl[2] (pɜːl) *n, vb* a variant spelling of **purl**[1] (senses 2, 3, 5)

pearl ash *n* the granular crystalline form of potassium carbonate

pearl barley *n* barley ground into small round grains, used in cooking, esp in soups and stews

pearler ('pɜːlə) *n* **1** a person who dives for or trades in pearls **2** a boat used while searching for pearls **3** *Austral informal* something impressive: *that shot was a real pearler* ▷ *adj* **4** *Austral informal* excellent; pleasing

pearl grey *n* **a** a light bluish-grey colour **b** (*as adjective*): *pearl-grey shoes*

Pearl Harbor *n* an almost landlocked inlet of the Pacific on the S coast of the island of Oahu, Hawaii: site of a US naval base attacked by the Japanese in 1941, resulting in the US entry into World War II

pearlite ('pɜːlaɪt) *n* **1** the lamellar structure in carbon steels and some cast irons that consists of alternate plates of pure iron and iron carbide **2** a variant spelling of **perlite**. ▷ **pearlitic** (pɜːˈlɪtɪk) *adj*

pearlized *or* **pearlised** ('pɜːlaɪzd) *adj* having or given a pearly lustre: *a pearlized lipstick*

pearl millet *n* a tall grass, *Pennisetum glaucum*, cultivated in Africa, E Asia, and the southern US as animal fodder and for its pearly white seeds, which are used as grain

pearl oyster *n* any of various tropical marine bivalves of the genus *Pinctada* and related genera: a major source of pearls

Pearl River *n* **1** a river in central Mississippi, flowing southwest and south to the Gulf of Mexico. Length: 789 km (490 miles) **2** the English name for the **Zhu Jiang**

pearlwort ('pɜːlˌwɜːt) *n* any caryophyllaceous plant of the genus *Sagina*, having small white flowers that are spherical in bud

pearly ('pɜːlɪ) *adj* **pearlier, pearliest 1** resembling a pearl, esp in lustre **2** of the colour pearl; pale bluish-grey **3** decorated with pearls or mother-of-pearl ▷ *n, pl* **pearlies** (in Britain) **4** a London costermonger who wears on ceremonial occasions a traditional dress of dark clothes covered with pearl buttons **5** (*plural*) the clothes or the buttons themselves ▷ '**pearliness** *n*

Pearly Gates *pl n* **1** *informal* the entrance to heaven **2** (*not capitals*) *Brit slang* teeth

pearly king *n* the male London costermonger whose ceremonial clothes display the most lavish collection of pearl buttons. See also **pearly** (sense 4)

pearly nautilus *n* any of several cephalopod molluscs of the genus *Nautilus*, esp *N. pompilius*, of warm and tropical seas, having a partitioned pale pearly external shell with brown stripes. Also called: **chambered nautilus** Compare **paper nautilus**

pearly queen *n* the female London costermonger whose ceremonial clothes display the most lavish collection of pearl buttons. See also **pearly** (sense 4)

pearmain ('pɛəˌmeɪn) *n* any of several varieties of apple having a red skin [c15 from Old French *permain* a type of pear, perhaps from Latin *Parmēnsis* of Parma]

Pearson's correlation coefficient *n* a statistic measuring the linear relationship between two variables in a sample and used as an estimate of the correlation in the whole population, given by $r = Cov(X, Y)/\sqrt{[(Var(X).Var(Y)]}$. In full: **Pearson's product moment correlation coefficient** [named after Karl *Pearson* (1857–1936), British mathematician]

peart (pɪət) *adj dialect* lively; spirited; brisk [c15 variant of PERT] > '**peartly** *adv* > '**peartness** *n*

peasant ('pɛzənt) *n* **1 a** a member of a class of low social status that depends on either cottage industry or agricultural labour as a means of subsistence **b** (*as modifier*): *peasant dress* **2** *informal* a person who lives in the country; rustic **3** *informal* an uncouth or uncultured person [c15 from Anglo-French, from Old French *paisant*, from *païs* country, from Latin *pāgus* rural area; see PAGAN]

peasantry ('pɛzəntrɪ) *n* **1** peasants as a class **2** conduct characteristic of peasants **3** the status of a peasant

peasanty ('pɛzəntɪ) *adj* **1** having qualities ascribed to traditional country life or people; simple or unsophisticated **2** crude, awkward, or uncouth

pease (piːz) *n, pl* **pease** an archaic or dialect word for **pea** [Old English *peose*, via Late Latin from Latin *pisa* peas, pl of *pisum*, from Greek *pison*]

pease-brose ('piːzˌbroz, -ˌbrəʊz) *n Scot* brose made from a meal of dried peas

peasecod *or* **peascod** ('piːzˌkɒd) *n archaic* the pod of a pea plant [c14 from PEASE + COD[2]]

pease pudding *n* (esp in Britain) a dish of split peas that have been soaked and boiled served with ham or pork

peashooter ('piːˌʃuːtə) *n* a tube through which pellets such as dried peas are blown, used as a toy weapon

peasouper (ˌpiːˈsuːpə) *n* **1** *informal, chiefly Brit* dense dirty yellowish fog **2** *Canadian* a disparaging name for a **French Canadian**

peat[1] (piːt) *n* **1 a** a compact brownish deposit of partially decomposed vegetable matter saturated with water: found in uplands and bogs in temperate and cold regions and used as a fuel (when dried) and as a fertilizer **b** (*as modifier*): *peat bog* **2** a piece of dried peat for use as fuel [c14 from Anglo Latin *peta*, perhaps from Celtic; compare Welsh *peth* thing] > '**peaty** *adj*

peat[2] (piːt) *n* **1** *archaic, derogatory* a person, esp a woman **2** *obsolete* a term of endearment for a girl or woman [c16 of uncertain origin]

peatland ('piːtˌlænd) *n* an area of land consisting of peat bogs, usually containing many species of flora and fauna

peat moss *n* any of various mosses, esp sphagnum, that grow in wet places in dense masses and decay to form peat. Also called: **bog moss** See also **sphagnum**

peat reek *n* **1** the smoke of a peat fire **2** whisky distilled over a peat fire

peau de soie ('pəʊ də swɑː; *French* po də swa) *n* a rich reversible silk or rayon fabric [literally: skin of silk]

peavey *or* **peavy** ('piːvɪ) *n, pl* **-veys** *or* **-vies** *US and Canadian* a wooden lever with a metal pointed end and a hinged hook, used for handling logs. Compare **cant hook** [c19 named after Joseph *Peavey*, American who invented it]

pebble ('pɛbəl) *n* **1 a** a small smooth rounded stone, esp one worn by the action of water **b** *geology* a rock fragment, often rounded, with a diameter of 4–64 mm and thus smaller than a cobble but larger than a granule **2 a** a transparent colourless variety of rock crystal, used for making certain lenses **b** such a lens **3** (*modifier*) *informal* (of a lens or of spectacles) thick, with a high degree of magnification or distortion **4 a** a grainy irregular surface, esp on leather **b** leather having such a surface **5** *informal, chiefly Austral* a troublesome or obstinate person or animal ▷ *vb* (*tr*) **6** to pave, cover, or pelt with pebbles **7** to impart a grainy surface to (leather) [Old English *papolstān*, from *papol*- (perhaps of imitative origin) + *stān* stone] > '**pebbly** *adj*

pebble dash *n Brit* a finish for external walls consisting of small stones embedded in plaster

pebble garden *n NZ* a small ornamental garden mainly composed of an arrangement of pebbles

pebbling ('pɛblɪŋ) *n* in curling the act of spraying the rink with drops of hot water to slow down the stone

pebi- ('pɛbɪ) *prefix computing* denoting 2[50]: pebibyte [c20 from PE(TA-) + BI(NARY)]

pec (pɛk) *n* (*usually plural*) *informal* short for **pectoral muscle**

pecan (pɪˈkæn, 'piːkən) *n* **1** a hickory tree, *Carya pecan* (or *C. illinoensis*), of the southern US, having deeply furrowed bark and edible nuts **2** the smooth oval nut of this tree, which has a sweet oily kernel [c18 from Algonquian *paccan*; related to Ojibwa *pagân* nut with a hard shell, Cree *pakan*]

peccable ('pɛkəbəl) *adj* liable to sin; susceptible to temptation [c17 via French from Medieval Latin *peccābilis*, from Latin *peccāre* to sin] > ˌpecca'bility *n*

peccadillo (ˌpɛkəˈdɪləʊ) *n, pl* **-loes** *or* **-los** a petty sin or trifling fault [c16 from Spanish *pecadillo*, from *pecado* sin, from Latin *peccātum*, from *peccāre* to transgress]

peccant ('pɛkənt) *adj rare* **1** guilty of an offence; corrupt **2** violating or disregarding a rule; faulty **3** producing disease; morbid [c17 from Latin *peccans*, from *peccāre* to sin] > '**peccancy** *n* > '**peccantly** *adv*

peccary ('pɛkərɪ) *n, pl* **-ries** *or* **-ry** either of two piglike artiodactyl mammals, *Tayassu tajacu* (**collared peccary**) or *T. albirostris* (**white-lipped peccary**) of forests of southern North America, Central and South America: family *Tayassuidae* [c17 from Carib]

peccavi (pɛˈkɑːviː) *n, pl* **-vis** a confession of guilt [c16 from Latin, literally: I have sinned, from *peccāre*]

pech (pɛx) *vb, n* a Scot word for **pant** [c15 of imitative origin]

Pechenga ('pɛtʃɪŋə) *n* a region of NW Russia, a former territory of N Finland, ceded by Soviet Russia to Finland in 1920 and taken back in 1944. Former name: **Petsamo** (1920–1944)

Pechora (Russian pɪˈtʃɔrə) *n* a river in N Russia, rising in the Ural Mountains and flowing north in a great arc to the **Pechora Sea** (the SE part of the Barents Sea). Length: 1814 km (1127 miles)

peck[1] (pɛk) *n* **1** a unit of dry measure equal to 8 quarts or one quarter of a bushel **2** a container

p

used for measuring this quantity **3** a large quantity or number [c13 from Anglo-Norman, of uncertain origin]

peck² (pɛk) *vb* **1** (when *intr*, sometimes foll by *at*) to strike with the beak or with a pointed instrument **2** (*tr*; sometimes foll by *out*) to dig (a hole) by pecking **3** (*tr*) (of birds) to pick up (corn, worms, etc) by pecking **4** (*intr*; often foll by *at*) to nibble or pick (at one's food) **5** (*tr*) to kiss (a person) quickly and lightly **6** (*intr*; foll by *at*) to nag ▷ *n* **7** a quick light blow, esp from a bird's beak **8** a mark made by such a blow **9** *informal* a quick light kiss [c14 of uncertain origin; compare PICK¹, Middle Low German *pekken* to jab with the beak]

pecker ('pɛkə) *n* **1** *Brit slang* spirits (esp in the phrase **keep one's pecker up**) **2** *informal* short for **woodpecker** **3** *US and Canadian slang* a slang word for **penis**

pecking order *n* **1** Also called: **peck order** a natural hierarchy in a group of gregarious birds, such as domestic fowl **2** any hierarchical order, as among people in a particular group

peckish ('pɛkɪʃ) *adj informal, chiefly Brit* feeling slightly hungry; having an appetite [c18 from PECK²]

Pecksniffian (pɛk'snɪfɪən) *adj* affecting benevolence or high moral principles [c19 after Seth *Pecksniff*, character in *Martin Chuzzlewit* (1843), a novel by the English novelist Charles Dickens (1812–70)]

pecorino (ˌpɛkə'riːnəʊ) *n* an Italian cheese made from ewes' milk [c20 from Italian, literally: of ewes, from *pecora* sheep, from Latin *pecus*]

Pecos ('peɪkəs; *Spanish* 'pekɔs) *n* a river in the southwestern US, rising in N central New Mexico and flowing southeast to the Rio Grande. Length: about 1180 km (735 miles)

Pécs (*Hungarian* pe:tʃ) *n* an industrial city in SW Hungary: university (1367). Pop: 158 942 (2003 est)

pectase ('pɛkteɪs) *n* an enzyme occurring in certain ripening fruits: involved in transforming pectin into a soluble form [c19 from PECTIN + -ASE]

pectate ('pɛkteɪt) *n* a salt or ester of pectic acid [c19 from PECTIC ACID + -ATE¹]

pecten ('pɛktɪn) *n*, *pl* **-tens** *or* **-tines** (-tɪˌniːz) **1** a comblike structure in the eye of birds and reptiles, consisting of a network of blood vessels projecting inwards from the retina, which it is thought to supply with oxygen **2** any other comblike part or organ **3** any scallop of the genus *Pecten,* which swim by expelling water from their shell valves in a series of snapping motions [c18 from Latin: a comb, from *pectere,* related to Greek *pekein* to comb]

pectic acid *n* a complex acid containing arabinose and galactose that occurs in ripe fruit, beets, and other vegetables. Formula: $C_{35}H_{50}O_{33}$

pectin ('pɛktɪn) *n biochem* any of the acidic hemicelluloses that occur in ripe fruit and vegetables: used in the manufacture of jams because of their ability to solidify to a gel when heated in a sugar solution (may be referred to on food labels as **E440(a)**) [c19 from Greek *pēktos* congealed, from *pegnuein* to set] > **'pectic** *or* **'pectinous** *adj*

pectinate ('pɛktɪˌneɪt) *or* **pectinated** *adj* shaped like a comb: *pectinate antennae* [c18 from Latin *pectinātus* combed; see PECTEN] > ˌpecti'nation *n*

pectize *or* **pectise** ('pɛktaɪz) *vb* to change into a jelly; gel [c19 from Greek *pēktos* solidified; see PECTIN] > **'pectizable** *or* **'pectisable** *adj* > ˌpecti'zation *or* ˌpecti'sation *n*

pectoral ('pɛktərəl) *adj* **1** of or relating to the chest, breast, or thorax: *pectoral fins* **2** worn on the breast or chest: *a pectoral medallion* **3** *rare* heartfelt or sincere ▷ *n* **4** a pectoral organ or part, esp a muscle or fin **5** a medicine or remedy for disorders of the chest or lungs **6** anything worn on the breast or chest for decoration or protection [c15 from Latin *pectorālis,* from *pectus* breast] > **'pectorally** *adv*

pectoral fin *n* either of a pair of fins, situated just behind the head in fishes, that help to control the direction of movement during locomotion

pectoral girdle *or* **arch** *n* a skeletal support to which the front or upper limbs of a vertebrate are attached

pectoral muscle *n* either of two large chest muscles (**pectoralis major** and **pectoralis minor**), that assist in movements of the shoulder and upper arm

pectose ('pɛkˌtəʊz) *n* an insoluble carbohydrate found in the cell walls of unripe fruit that is converted to pectin by enzymic processes

peculate ('pɛkjʊˌleɪt) *vb* to appropriate or embezzle (public money) [c18 from Latin *pecūlārī,* from *pecūlium* private property (originally, cattle); see PECULIAR] > ˌpecu'lation *n* > 'pecuˌlator *n*

peculiar (pɪ'kjuːlɪə) *adj* **1** strange or unusual; odd: *a peculiar individual; a peculiar idea* **2** distinct from others; special **3** (*postpositive*; foll by *to*) belonging characteristically or exclusively (to): *peculiar to North America* ▷ *n* **4** Also called: **arbitrary** *printing* a special sort, esp an accented letter **5** *Church of England* a church or parish that is exempt from the jurisdiction of the ordinary in whose diocese it lies [c15 from Latin *pecūliāris* concerning private property, from *pecūlium,* literally: property in cattle, from *pecus* cattle] > **pe'culiarly** *adv*

peculiarity (pɪˌkjuːlɪ'ærɪtɪ) *n*, *pl* **-ties** **1** a strange or unusual habit or characteristic **2** a distinguishing trait, etc that is characteristic of a particular person; idiosyncrasy **3** the state or quality of being peculiar

peculiar people *pl n* **1** (*sometimes capitals*) a small sect of faith healers founded in London in 1838, having no ministers or external organization **2** the Jews considered as God's elect

peculium (pɪ'kjuːlɪəm) *n Roman law* property that a father or master allowed his child or slave to hold as his own [c17 from Latin; see PECULIAR]

pecuniary (pɪ'kjuːnɪərɪ) *adj* **1** consisting of or relating to money **2** *law* (of an offence) involving a monetary penalty [c16 from Latin *pecūniāris,* from *pecūnia* money] > **pe'cuniarily** *adv*

pecuniary advantage *n law* financial advantage that is dishonestly obtained by deception and that constitutes a criminal offence

ped- *combining form* a variant (esp US) of **paedo-**

-ped *or* **-pede** *n combining form* foot or feet: *quadruped; centipede* [from Latin *pēs, ped-* foot]

pedagogics (ˌpɛdə'gɒdʒɪks, -'gəʊ-) *n* (*functioning as singular*) another word for **pedagogy**

pedagogue *or sometimes US* **pedagog** ('pɛdəˌgɒg) *n* **1** a teacher or educator **2** a pedantic or dogmatic teacher [c14 from Latin *paedagōgus,* from Greek *paidagōgos* slave who looked after his master's son, from *pais* boy + *agōgos* leader] > ˌpeda'gogic *or* ˌpeda'gogical *adj* > ˌpeda'gogically *adv* > 'peda,gogism *or* 'peda,goguism *n*

pedagogy ('pɛdəˌgɒgɪ, -ˌgɒdʒɪ, -ˌgəʊdʒɪ) *n* the principles, practice, or profession of teaching

pedal¹ ('pɛdəl) *n* **1 a** any foot-operated lever or other device, esp one of the two levers that drive the chain wheel of a bicycle, the foot brake, clutch control, or accelerator of a car, one of the levers on an organ controlling deep bass notes, or one of the levers on a piano used to create a muted effect or sustain tone **b** (*as modifier*): *a pedal cycle* ▷ *vb* **-als, -alling, -alled** *or US* **-als, -aling, -aled** **2** to propel (a bicycle, boat, etc) by operating the pedals **3** (*intr*) to operate the pedals of an organ, piano, etc, esp in a certain way **4** to work (pedals of any kind) [c17 from Latin *pedālis;* see PEDAL²]

pedal² ('piːdəl) *adj* of or relating to the foot or feet [c17 from Latin *pedālis,* from *pēs* foot]

pedalfer (pɪ'dælfə) *n* a type of zonal soil deficient in lime but containing deposits of aluminium and iron, found in wet areas, esp those with high temperatures. Compare **pedocal** [c20 PEDO-² + ALUM + -*fer,* from Latin *ferrum* iron]

pedalo ('pɛdəˌləʊ) *n, pl* **-los** *or* **-loes** a pleasure craft driven by pedal-operated paddle wheels [c20 from PEDAL¹]

pedal point ('pɛdəl) *n music* a sustained bass note, over which the other parts move bringing about changing harmonies. Often shortened to: **pedal**

pedal pushers *pl n* calf-length trousers or jeans worn by women

pedal steel guitar *n* a floor-mounted, multineck, lap steel guitar with each set of strings tuned to a different open chord and foot pedals to raise or lower the pitch

pedant ('pɛdənt) *n* **1** a person who relies too much on academic learning or who is concerned chiefly with insignificant detail **2** *archaic* a schoolmaster or teacher [c16 via Old French from Italian *pedante* teacher; perhaps related to Latin *paedagōgus* PEDAGOGUE]

pedantic (pɪ'dæntɪk) *adj* of, relating to, or characterized by pedantry > **pe'dantically** *adv*

pedantry ('pɛdəntrɪ) *n, pl* **-ries** the habit or an instance of being a pedant, esp in the display of useless knowledge or minute observance of petty rules or details

pedate ('pɛdeɪt) *adj* **1** (of a plant leaf) divided into several lobes arising at a common point, the lobes often being stalked and the lateral lobes sometimes divided into smaller lobes **2** *zoology* having or resembling a foot: *a pedate appendage* [c18 from Latin *pedātus* equipped with feet, from *pēs* foot] > **'pedately** *adv*

pedatifid (pɪ'dætɪfɪd, -'deɪ-) *adj* (of a plant leaf) pedately divided, with the divisions less deep than in a pedate leaf

peddle ('pɛdəl) *vb* **1** to go from place to place selling (goods, esp small articles) **2** (*tr*) to sell (illegal drugs, esp narcotics) **3** (*tr*) to advocate (ideas) persistently or importunately: *to peddle a new philosophy* **4** (*intr*) *archaic* to trifle [c16 back formation from PEDLAR]

peddler ('pɛdlə) *n* **1** a person who sells illegal drugs, esp narcotics **2** the usual US spelling of **pedlar**

-pede *n combining form* a variant of **-ped**

pederast *or sometimes* **paederast** ('pɛdəˌræst) *n* a man who practises pederasty

pederasty *or sometimes* **paederasty** ('pɛdəˌræstɪ) *n* homosexual relations between men and boys [c17 from New Latin *paederastia,* from Greek, from *pais* boy + *erastēs* lover, from *eran* to love] > ˌpeder'astic *or sometimes* ˌpaeder'astic *adj*

pedes ('piːdiːz) *n* the plural of **pes**

pedestal ('pɛdɪstəl) *n* **1** a base that supports a column, statue, etc, as used in classical architecture **2** a position of eminence or supposed superiority (esp in the phrases **place, put,** *or* **set on a pedestal**) **3 a** either of a pair of sets of drawers used as supports for a writing surface **b** (*as modifier*): *a pedestal desk* [c16 from French *piédestal,* from Old Italian *piedestallo,* from *pie* foot + *di* of + *stallo* a stall]

pedestrian (pɪ'dɛstrɪən) *n* **1 a** a person travelling on foot; walker **b** (*as modifier*): *a pedestrian precinct* ▷ *adj* **2** dull; commonplace: *a pedestrian style of writing* [c18 from Latin *pedester,* from *pēs* foot]

pedestrian crossing *n Brit* a path across a road marked as a crossing for pedestrians. See also **zebra crossing, pelican crossing** US and Canadian name: **crosswalk**

pedestrianize *or* **pedestrianise** (pɪ'dɛstrɪəˌnaɪz) *vb* (*tr*) to convert (a street) into an area for the use of pedestrians only, by excluding all motor vehicles > peˌdestriani'zation *or* peˌdestriani'sation *n*

Pedi ('pɛdɪ) *n* **1** Also called: **Northern Sotho** a member of a subgroup of the Sotho people resident in the Transvaal **2** the dialect of Sotho spoken by this people

pedi- *combining form* indicating the foot: *pedicure* [from Latin *pēs, ped-* foot]

pediatrician (ˌpiːdɪə'trɪʃən) *n* the US spelling of **paediatrician**

pediatrics (ˌpiːdɪˈætrɪks) *n* the US spelling of **paediatrics**

pedicab (ˈpɛdɪˌkæb) *n* a pedal-operated tricycle, available for hire, with an attached seat for one or two passengers

pedicel (ˈpɛdɪˌsɛl) *n* **1** the stalk bearing a single flower of an inflorescence **2** Also called: **peduncle** *biology* any short stalk bearing an organ or organism **3** the second segment of an insect's antenna [C17 from New Latin *pedicellus*, from Latin *pedīculus*, from *pēs* foot] > **pedicellate** (pɪˈdɪsɪˌleɪt) *adj*

pedicle (ˈpɛdɪkᵊl) *n* *biology* any small stalk; pedicel; peduncle [C17 from Latin *pedīculus* small foot; see PEDICEL]

pedicular (pɪˈdɪkjʊlə) *adj* **1** relating to, infested with, or caused by lice **2** *biology* of or relating to a stem, stalk, or pedicle [C17 from Latin *pedīculāris*, from *pedīculus*, diminutive of *pedis* louse]

pediculate (pɪˈdɪkjʊlɪt, -ˌleɪt) *adj* **1** of, relating to, or belonging to the *Pediculati*, a large order of teleost fishes containing the anglers ▷ *n* **2** any fish belonging to the order *Pediculati* [C19 from Latin *pedīculus* little foot; see PEDICEL]

pediculosis (pɪˌdɪkjʊˈləʊsɪs) *n* *pathol* the state of being infested with lice [C19 via New Latin from Latin *pedīculus* louse; see PEDICULAR] > **pediculous** (pɪˈdɪkjʊləs) *adj*

pedicure (ˈpɛdɪˌkjʊə) *n* professional treatment of the feet, either by a medical expert or a cosmetician [C19 via French from Latin *pēs* foot + *curāre* to care for]

pediform (ˈpɛdɪˌfɔːm) *adj* shaped like a foot

pedigree (ˈpɛdɪˌgriː) *n* **1 a** the line of descent of a purebred animal **b** (*as modifier*): *a pedigree bull* **2** a document recording this **3** a genealogical table, esp one indicating pure ancestry **4** derivation or background [C15 from Old French *pie de grue* crane's foot, alluding to the spreading lines used in a genealogical chart] > ˈ**pediˌgreed** *adj*

pediment (ˈpɛdɪmənt) *n* **1** a low-pitched gable, esp one that is triangular, as used in classical architecture **2** a gently sloping rock surface, formed through denudation under arid conditions [C16 from obsolete *periment*, perhaps workman's corruption of PYRAMID] > ˌ**pediˈmental** *adj*

pedipalp (ˈpɛdɪˌpælp) *n* either member of the second pair of head appendages of arachnids: specialized for feeding, locomotion, etc [C19 from New Latin *pedipalpi*, from Latin *pēs* foot + *palpus* palp]

pedlar *or esp US* **peddler, pedler** (ˈpɛdlə) *n* a person who peddles; hawker [C14 changed from *peder*, from *ped*, *pedde* basket, of obscure origin]

pedo-[1] *or before a vowel* **ped-** *combining form* variants (esp US) of **paedo-**

pedo-[2] *combining form* indicating soil: *pedocal* [from Greek *pedon*]

pedocal (ˈpɛdəˌkæl) *n* a type of zonal soil that is rich in lime and characteristic of relatively dry areas. Compare **pedalfer** [from PEDO-[2] + CAL(CIUM)]

pedology[1] (pɪˈdɒlədʒɪ) *n* a US spelling of **paedology**

pedology[2] (pɪˈdɒlədʒɪ) *n* the study of the formation, characteristics, and distribution of soils > **pedological** (ˌpiːdəˈlɒdʒɪkᵊl) *adj* > **peˈdologist** *n*

pedometer (pɪˈdɒmɪtə) *n* a device containing a pivoted weight that records the number of steps taken in walking and hence the distance travelled

pedophilia (ˌpiːdəʊˈfɪlɪə) *n* a variant spelling (esp US) of **paedophilia**

peduncle (pɪˈdʌŋkᵊl) *n* **1** the stalk of a plant bearing an inflorescence or solitary flower **2** *anatomy* a stalklike structure, esp a large bundle of nerve fibres within the brain **3** *pathol* a slender process of tissue by which a polyp or tumour is attached to the body **4** *biology* another name for **pedicel** (sense 2) [C18 from New Latin *pedunculus*, from Latin *pedīculus* little foot; see PEDICLE] > **peˈduncled** *or* **peduncular** (pɪˈdʌŋkjʊlə) *adj*

pedunculate (pɪˈdʌŋkjʊlɪt, -ˌleɪt) *or* **pedunculated** *adj* having, supported on, or growing from a peduncle > **peˌduncuˈlation** *n*

pedunculate oak *n* a large deciduous oak tree, *Quercus robur*, of Eurasia, having lobed leaves and stalked acorns. Also called: **common oak**

pee (piː) *informal* ▷ *vb* **pees, peeing, peed** **1** (*intr*) to urinate ▷ *n* **2** urine **3** the act of urinating [C18 a euphemism for PISS, based on the initial letter]

Peebles (ˈpiːbᵊlz) *n* a town in SE Scotland, in Scottish Borders. Pop: 8065 (2001)

Peeblesshire (ˈpiːbᵊlzˌʃɪə, -ʃə) *n* (until 1975) a county of SE Scotland, now part of Scottish Borders. Also called: **Tweeddale**

peek (piːk) *vb* **1** (*intr*) to glance quickly or furtively; peep ▷ *n* **2** a quick or furtive glance [C14 *pike*, related to Middle Dutch *kiken* to peek]

peekaboo (ˈpiːkəˌbuː) *n* **1** a game for young children, in which one person hides his face and suddenly reveals it and cries "peekaboo." ▷ *adj* **2** (of a garment) made of fabric that is almost transparent or patterned with small holes [C16 from PEEK + BOO]

peel[1] (piːl) *vb* **1** (*tr*) to remove (the skin, rind, outer covering, etc) of (a fruit, egg, etc) **2** (*intr*) (of paint, etc) to be removed from a surface, esp through weathering **3** (*intr*) (of a surface) to lose its outer covering of paint, etc esp through weathering **4** (*intr*) (of a person or part of the body) to shed skin in flakes or (of skin) to be shed in flakes, esp as a result of sunburn **5** *croquet* to put (another player's ball) through a hoop or hoops **6 keep one's eyes peeled** (*or* **skinned**) to watch vigilantly ▷ *n* **7** the skin or rind of a fruit, etc ▷ See also **peel off** [Old English *pilian* to strip off the outer layer, from Latin *pilāre* to make bald, from *pilus* a hair]

peel[2] (piːl) *n* a long-handled shovel used by bakers for moving bread, in an oven [C14 *pele*, from Old French, from Latin *pāla* spade, from *pangere* to drive in; see PALETTE]

peel[3] (piːl) *n* (in Britain) a fortified tower of the 16th century on the borders between England and Scotland, built to withstand raids [C14 (fence made of stakes): from Old French *piel* stake, from Latin *pālus*; see PALE[2], PALING]

peeler[1] (ˈpiːlə) *n* **1** a special knife or mechanical device for peeling vegetables, fruit, etc: *a potato peeler* **2** *US slang* a striptease dancer

peeler[2] (ˈpiːlə) *n* *Brit dated slang* another word for **policeman** [C19 from the founder of the police force, Sir Robert Peel (1788–1850), British Conservative statesman]

peeling (ˈpiːlɪŋ) *n* a strip of skin, rind, bark, etc, that has been peeled off: *a potato peeling*

Peelite (ˈpiːlaɪt) *n* **1** a follower or admirer of Sir Robert Peel, the British Conservative statesman (1788–1850) ▷ *adj* **2** of or relating to Peel or his supporters

peel off *vb* (*adverb*) **1** to remove or be removed by peeling **2** (*intr*) *slang* to undress **3** (*intr*) (of an aircraft) to turn away as by banking, and leave a formation **4** *slang* to go away or cause to go away

peely-wally *or* **peelie-wallie** (ˈpiːlɪˈwælɪ) *adj* *Scot urban dialect* off colour; pale and ill-looking: *he's a wee bit peely-wally this morning* [apparently a reduplicated form of WALLY[2] in the sense: faded]

peen (piːn) *n* **1** the end of a hammer head opposite the striking face, often rounded or wedge-shaped ▷ *vb* **2** (*tr*) to strike with the peen of a hammer or with a stream of metal shot in order to bend or shape (a sheet of metal) [C17 variant of *pane*, perhaps from French *panne*, ultimately from Latin *pinna* point]

Peenemünde (ˌpiːnəˈmʊndə) *n* a village in N Germany, in Mecklenburg-West Pomerania on the Baltic coast: site of a German rocket-development centre in World War II

peep[1] (piːp) *vb* (*intr*) **1** to look furtively or secretly, as through a small aperture or from a hidden place **2** to appear partially or briefly: *the sun peeped through the clouds* ▷ *n* **3** a quick or furtive look **4** the first appearance: *the peep of dawn* [C15 variant of PEEK]

peep[2] (piːp) *vb* (*intr*) **1** (esp of young birds) to utter shrill small noises **2** to speak in a thin shrill voice ▷ *n* **3** a peeping sound **4** *US* any of various small sandpipers of the genus *Calidris* (or *Erolia*) and related genera, such as the pectoral sandpiper [C15 of imitative origin]

peeper (ˈpiːpə) *n* **1** a person who peeps **2** (*often plural*) a slang word for **eye**[1] (sense 1)

peephole (ˈpiːpˌhəʊl) *n* a small aperture, such as one in the door of a flat for observing callers before opening

Peeping Tom *n* a man who furtively observes women undressing; voyeur [C19 after the tailor who, according to legend, peeped at Lady Godiva when she rode naked through Coventry]

peepshow (ˈpiːpˌʃəʊ) *n* **1** Also called: **raree show** a small box with a peephole through which a series of pictures, esp of erotic poses, can be seen **2** a booth from which a viewer can see a live nude model for a fee

peep sight *n* an adjustable rear gun sight with a narrow aperture through which the target and the front sight are aligned when aiming

peepul (ˈpiːpᵊl) *or* **pipal** *n* an Indian moraceous tree, *Ficus religiosa*, resembling the banyan: regarded as sacred by Buddhists. Also called: **bo tree** [C18 from Hindi *pīpal*, from Sanskrit *pippala*]

peer[1] (pɪə) *n* **1** a member of a nobility; nobleman **2** a person who holds any of the five grades of the British nobility: duke, marquess, earl, viscount, and baron. See also **life peer** **3 a** a person who is an equal in social standing, rank, age, etc **b** (*as modifier*): *peer pressure* **4** *archaic* a companion; mate [C14 (in sense 3): from Old French *per*, from Latin *pār* equal]

peer[2] (pɪə) *vb* (*intr*) **1** to look intently with or as if with difficulty: *to peer into the distance* **2** to appear partially or dimly: *the sun peered through the fog* [C16 from Flemish *pieren* to look with narrowed eyes]

peerage (ˈpɪərɪdʒ) *n* **1** the whole body of peers; aristocracy **2** the position, rank, or title of a peer **3** (esp in the British Isles) a book listing the peers and giving genealogical and other information about them

peeress (ˈpɪərɪs) *n* **1** the wife or widow of a peer **2** a woman holding the rank of a peer in her own right

peer group *n* a social group composed of individuals of approximately the same age

peerie[1] (ˈpiːrɪ) *n* *Scot* a spinning top [C19 perhaps from *peir* a Scot variant of *pear*, alluding to the top's shape]

peerie[2] (ˈpiːrɪ) *adj* *Orkney and Shetland dialect* small [C19 of uncertain origin; perhaps from Norwegian dialect *piren* niggardly, thin]

peerless (ˈpɪəlɪs) *adj* having no equals; matchless

peer of the realm *n, pl* **peers of the realm** (in Great Britain and Northern Ireland) any member of the nobility entitled to sit in the House of Lords

peer review *n* the evaluation by fellow specialists of research that someone has done in order to assess its suitability for publication or further development > **ˌpeer-reˈviewed** *adj*

peer-to-peer *adj* (of a computer network) designed so that computers can send information directly to one another without passing through a centralized server. Abbreviation: **P2P**

peetweet (ˈpiːtˌwiːt) *n* *US* another name for the **spotted sandpiper** [C19 imitative of its cry]

peeve (piːv) *informal* ▷ *vb* **1** (*tr*) to irritate; vex; annoy ▷ *n* **2** something that irritates; vexation: *it was a pet peeve of his* [C20 back formation from PEEVISH] > **peeved** *adj*

peevers (ˈpiːvərz) *or* **peever** *n* (*functioning as singular*) *Scot dialect* hopscotch [from *peever* (the stone used in the game), of obscure origin]

peevish (ˈpiːvɪʃ) *adj* **1** fretful or irritable: *a peevish child* **2** *obsolete* perverse [C14 of unknown origin] > ˈ**peevishly** *adv* > ˈ**peevishness** *n*

peewee (ˈpiːwiː) *n* **1** a variant spelling of **pewee** **2** a variant (esp Scot) of **peewit** **3** *Austral* another name for **magpie lark** **4** *Canadian* **a** an age level of

P

12 to 13 in amateur sport, esp ice hockey **b** (*as modifier*): *peewee hockey*

peewit ('pi:wɪt) *n* another name for **lapwing** [C16 imitative of its call]

peg (pɛg) *n* **1** a small cylindrical pin or dowel, sometimes slightly tapered, used to join two parts together **2** a pin pushed or driven into a surface: used to mark scores, define limits, support coats, etc **3** *music* any of several pins passing through the head (**peg box**) of a stringed instrument, which can be turned so as to tune strings wound around them. See also **pin** (sense 11) **4** Also called: **clothes peg** *Brit* a split or hinged pin for fastening wet clothes to a line to dry. US and Canadian equivalent: **clothespin** **5** *informal* a person's leg **6** *Northern English dialect* a tooth **7** *Brit* a small drink of wine or spirits, esp of brandy or whisky and soda **8** an opportunity or pretext for doing something: *a peg on which to hang a theory* **9** a mountaineering piton **10** *croquet* a post that a player's ball must strike to win the game **11** *angling* a fishing station allotted to an angler in a competition, marked by a peg in the ground **12** *informal* a level of self-esteem, importance, etc (esp in the phrases **bring** *or* **take down a peg**) **13** *informal* See **peg leg** **14** **off the peg** *chiefly Brit* (of clothes) ready to wear, as opposed to tailor-made ▷ *vb* **pegs, pegging, pegged 15** (*tr*) to knock or insert a peg into or pierce with a peg **16** (*tr*; sometimes foll by *down*) to secure with pegs: *to peg a tent* **17** *mountaineering* to insert or use pitons **18** (*tr*) to mark (a score) with pegs, as in some card games **19** (*tr*) *informal* to aim and throw (missiles) at a target **20** (*intr*; foll by *away, along, etc*) *chiefly Brit* to work steadily: *he pegged away at his job for years* **21** (*tr*) to stabilize (the price of a commodity, an exchange rate, etc) by legislation or market operations ▷ See also **peg down, peg out** [C15 from Low Germanic *pegge*]

Pegasus[1] ('pɛgəsəs) *n Greek myth* an immortal winged horse, which sprang from the blood of the slain Medusa and enabled Bellerophon to achieve many great deeds as his rider

Pegasus[2] ('pɛgəsəs) *n, Latin genitive* **Pegasi** ('pɛgə,saɪ) a constellation in the N hemisphere lying close to Andromeda and Pisces

pegboard ('pɛg,bɔːd) *n* **1** a board having a pattern of holes into which small pegs can be fitted, used for playing certain games or keeping a score **2** another name for **solitaire** (sense 1) **3** hardboard perforated by a pattern of holes in which articles may be pegged or hung, as for display

peg climbing *n* another name for **aid climbing**

peg down *vb* (*tr, adverb*) to make (a person) committed to a course of action or bound to follow rules: *you won't peg him down to any decision*

pegging ('pɛgɪŋ) *n* another name for **aid climbing**

peg leg *n informal* **1** an artificial leg, esp one made of wood **2** a person with an artificial leg

pegmatite ('pɛgmə,taɪt) *n* any of a class of exceptionally coarse-grained intrusive igneous rocks consisting chiefly of quartz and feldspar: often occurring as dykes among igneous rocks of finer grain [C19 from Greek *pegma* something joined together] > **pegmatitic** (,pɛgmə'tɪtɪk) *adj*

peg out *vb* (*adverb*) **1** (*intr*) *informal* to collapse or die **2** *croquet* **a** (*intr*) to win a game by hitting the peg **b** (*tr*) to cause (an opponent's ball) to hit the peg, rendering it out of the game **3** (*intr*) *cribbage* to score the point that wins the game **4** (*tr*) to mark or secure with pegs: *to peg out one's claims to a piece of land*

peg top *n* a child's spinning top, usually made of wood with a metal centre pin

peg-top *adj* (of skirts, trousers, etc) wide at the hips then tapering off towards the ankle

Pegu (pɛ'guː) *n* a city in S Myanmar: capital of a united Burma (16th century). Pop: 307 000 (2005 est)

Pehlevi ('peɪləvɪ) *n* a variant of **Pahlavi**[2]

PEI *abbreviation for* Prince Edward Island

peignoir ('peɪnwɑː) *n* a woman's dressing gown

or negligee [C19 from French, from *peigner* to comb, since the garment was worn while the hair was combed]

Peipus ('paɪpəs) *n* a lake in W Russia, on the boundary with Estonia: drains into the Gulf of Finland. Area: 3512 sq km (1356 sq miles). Russian name: **Chudskoye Ozero**

Peiraeus (paɪ'riːəs, pɪ'reɪ-) *n* a variant spelling of **Piraeus**

pejoration (,piːdʒə'reɪʃən) *n* **1** *linguistics* semantic change whereby a word acquires unfavourable connotations: *the English word "silly" changed its meaning from "holy" or "happy" by pejoration*. Compare **amelioration** (sense 3) **2** the process of worsening; deterioration

pejorative (pɪ'dʒɒrətɪv, 'piːdʒər-) *adj* **1** (of words, expressions, etc) having an unpleasant or disparaging connotation ▷ *n* **2** a pejorative word, expression, etc [C19 from French *péjoratif*, from Late Latin *pējōrātus*, past participle of *pējōrāre* to make worse, from Latin *pēior* worse] > **pe'joratively** *adv*

pekan ('pɛkən) *n* another name for **fisher** (sense 2) [C18 from Canadian French *pékan*, of Algonquian origin; compare Abnaki *pékané*]

peke (piːk) *n informal* a Pekingese dog

Pekin (piː'kɪn) *n* a breed of white or cream duck with a bright orange bill [C18 via French from PEKING]

Peking ('piː'kɪŋ) *n* the former English name of **Beijing**

Pekingese (,piːkɪŋ'iːz) *or* **Pekinese** (,piːkə'niːz) *n* **1** (*pl* **-ese**) a small breed of pet dog with a profuse straight coat, curled plumed tail, and short wrinkled muzzle **2** the dialect of Mandarin Chinese spoken in Beijing (formerly Peking), the pronunciation of which serves as a standard for the language **3** (*pl* **-ese**) a native or inhabitant of Beijing (formerly Peking) ▷ *adj* **4** of or relating to Beijing (formerly Peking) or its inhabitants

Peking man *n* an early type of man, *Homo erectus*, remains of which, of the Lower Palaeolithic age, were found in a cave near Peking (now Beijing), China, in 1927

Peking sauce *n* another name for **hoisin sauce**

pekoe ('piːkəʊ) *n* a high-quality tea made from the downy tips of the young buds of the tea plant [C18 from Chinese (Amoy) *peh ho*, from *peh* white + *ho* down]

pelage ('pɛlɪdʒ) *n* the coat of a mammal, consisting of hair, wool, fur, etc [C19 via French from Old French *pel* animal's coat, from Latin *pilus* hair]

pelagian (pɛ'leɪdʒɪən) *adj* of or inhabiting the open sea [C18 from Latin *pelagius*, from Greek *pelagios* of the sea, from *pelagos* the sea]

Pelagian (pɛ'leɪdʒɪən) *adj* **1** of or relating to the British monk Pelagius (?360–?420 AD), or his doctrines ▷ *n* **2** an adherent of the doctrines of Pelagius ▷ See also **Pelagianism**

Pelagian Islands (pɛ'leɪdʒɪən) *pl n* a group of Italian islands (Lampedusa, Linosa, and Lampione) in the Mediterranean, between Tunisia and Malta. Pop: 4500 (latest est). Area: about 27 sq km (11 sq miles). Italian name: **Isole Pelagie** ('iːzole pe'ladʒe)

Pelagianism (pɛ'leɪdʒɪə,nɪzəm) *n Christianity* a heretical doctrine, first formulated by the British monk Pelagius (?360–?420 AD), that rejected the concept of original sin and maintained that the individual takes the initial steps towards salvation by his own efforts and not by the help of divine grace

pelagic (pɛ'lædʒɪk) *adj* **1** of or relating to the open sea: *pelagic whaling* **2** (of marine life) living or occurring in the upper waters of open sea **3** (of geological formations) derived from material that has fallen to the bottom from the upper waters of the sea [C17 from Latin *pelagicus*, from *pelagus*, from Greek *pelagos* sea]

pelargonic acid (,pɛlɑː'gɒnɪk) *n* another name for **nonanoic acid** [C19 so named because it was originally derived from PELARGONIUM leaves]

pelargonium (,pɛlə'gəʊnɪəm) *n* any plant of the chiefly southern African geraniaceous genus *Pelargonium*, having circular or lobed leaves and red, pink, or white aromatic flowers: includes many cultivated geraniums [C19 via New Latin from Greek *pelargos* stork, on the model of GERANIUM; from the likeness of the seed vessels to a stork's bill]

Pelasgian (pɛ'læzdʒɪən) *n* **1** a member of any of the pre-Hellenic peoples (the **Pelasgi**) who inhabited Greece and the islands and coasts of the Aegean Sea before the arrival of the Bronze Age Greeks ▷ *adj also* **Pelasgic 2** of or relating to these peoples

pelecypod (pɪ'lɛsɪ,pɒd) *n, adj* another word for **bivalve** (senses 1, 2) [C19 from Greek *pelekus* hatchet + -POD]

Pelée (pə'leɪ) *n* **Mount** a volcano in the Caribbean, in N Martinique: erupted in 1902, killing every person but one in the town of Saint-Pierre. Height: 1463 m (4800 ft)

pelerine ('pɛlə,riːn) *n* a woman's narrow cape with long pointed ends in front [C18 from French *pèlerine*, feminine of *pèlerin* PILGRIM, that is, a pilgrim's cape]

Pele's hair ('peɪleɪz, 'piːliːz) *n* fine threads of volcanic glass formed from molten lava by the action of wind, explosion, etc [C20 translation of Hawaiian *lauoho-o Pele*, from Pele, name of the goddess of volcanoes]

Peleus ('pɛliəs, 'piːliəs) *n Greek myth* a king of the Myrmidons; father of Achilles

Pelew Islands (pi'luː) *pl n* a former name of (the Republic of) **Palau**

pelf (pɛlf) *n contemptuous* money or wealth, esp if dishonestly acquired; lucre [C14 from Old French *pelfre* booty; related to Latin *pilāre* to despoil]

pelham ('pɛləm) *n* a horse's bit for a double bridle, less severe than a curb but more severe than a snaffle [probably from the proper name *Pelham*]

Pelias ('piːlɪ,æs) *n Greek myth* a son of Poseidon and Tyro. He feared his nephew Jason and sent him to recover the Golden Fleece, hoping he would not return

pelican ('pɛlɪkən) *n* any aquatic bird of the tropical and warm water family *Pelecanidae*, such as *P. onocrotalus* (**white pelican**): order *Pelecaniformes*. They have a long straight flattened bill, with a distensible pouch for engulfing fish [Old English *pellican*, from Late Latin *pelicānus*, from Greek *pelekān*; perhaps related to Greek *pelekus* axe, perhaps from the shape of the bird's bill; compare Greek *pelekas* woodpecker]

pelican crossing *n* a type of road crossing marked by black-and-white stripes or by two rows of metal studs and consisting of a pedestrian-operated traffic-light system [C20 from pe(*destrian*) li(*ght*) con(*trolled*) crossing, with *-con* adapted to *-can* of *pelican*]

Pelion ('piːlɪən) *n* a mountain in NE Greece, in E Thessaly. In Greek mythology it was the home of the centaurs. Height: 1548 m (5079 ft). Modern Greek name: **Pílion**

pelisse (pɛ'liːs) *n* **1** a fur-trimmed cloak **2** a high-waisted loose coat, usually fur-trimmed, worn esp by women in the early 19th century [C18 via Old French from Medieval Latin *pellicia* cloak, from Latin *pellis* skin]

pelite ('piːlaɪt) *n* any argillaceous rock such as shale [C19 from Greek *pēlos* mud] > **pelitic** (pɪ'lɪtɪk) *adj*

Pella ('pɛlə) *n* an ancient city in N Greece: the capital of Macedonia under Philip II

pellagra (pə'leɪgrə, -'læ-) *n pathol* a disease caused by a dietary deficiency of nicotinic acid, characterized by burning or itching often followed by scaling of the skin, inflammation of the mouth, diarrhoea, mental impairment, etc [C19 via Italian from *pelle* skin + -*agra*, from Greek *agra* paroxysm] > **pel'lagrous** *adj*

Pelles ('pɛliːz) *n* (in Arthurian legend) the father

of Elaine and one of the searchers for the Holy Grail

pellet ('pɛlɪt) *n* **1** a small round ball, esp of compressed matter: *a wax pellet* **2 a** an imitation bullet used in toy guns **b** a piece of small shot **3** a stone ball formerly used as a catapult or cannon missile **4** Also called: **cast, casting** *ornithol* a mass of undigested food, including bones, fur, feathers, etc, that is regurgitated by certain birds, esp birds of prey **5** a small pill **6** a raised area on coins and carved or moulded ornaments ▷ *vb* (*tr*) **7** to strike with pellets **8** to make or form into pellets [C14 from Old French *pelote*, from Vulgar Latin *pilota* (unattested), from Latin *pila* ball]

pellicle ('pɛlɪkᵊl) *n* **1** a thin skin or film **2** the hard protective outer layer of certain protozoans, such as those of the genus *Paramecium* **3** *botany* **a** the thin outer layer of a mushroom cap **b** a growth on the surface of a liquid culture **4** *photog* the thin layer of emulsion covering a plate, film, or paper [C16 via French from Latin *pellicula*, from *pellis* skin] > **pellicular** (pɛ'lɪkjʊlə) *adj*

pellitory ('pɛlɪtərɪ, -trɪ) *n, pl* -ries **1** any of various urticaceous plants of the S and W European genus *Parietaria*, esp *P. diffusa* (**pellitory-of-the-wall** or **wall pellitory**), that grow in crevices and have long narrow leaves and small pink flowers **2** **pellitory of Spain** a small Mediterranean plant, *Anacyclus pyrethrum*, the root of which contains an oil formerly used to relieve toothache: family *Asteraceae* (composites) [C16 *peletre*, from Old French *piretre*, from Latin *pyrethrum*, from Greek *purethron*, from *pur* fire, from the hot pungent taste of the root]

pell-mell ('pɛl'mɛl) *adv* **1** in a confused headlong rush: *the hounds ran pell-mell into the yard* **2** in a disorderly manner: *the things were piled pell-mell in the room* ▷ *adj* **3** disordered; tumultuous: *a pell-mell rush for the exit* ▷ *n* **4** disorder; confusion [C16 from Old French *pesle-mesle*, jingle based on *mesler* to MEDDLE]

pellucid (pɛ'luːsɪd) *adj* **1** transparent or translucent **2** extremely clear in style and meaning; limpid [C17 from Latin *pellūcidus*, variant of *perlūcidus*, from *perlūcēre* to shine through, from *per* through + *lūcēre* to shine] > **pel'lucidly** *adv* > ˌpellu'cidity or pel'lucidness *n*

pellum ('pɛləm) *n Southwest English dialect* dust

Pelmanism ('pɛlmə.nɪzəm) *n* **1** a system of training to improve the memory **2** (*often not capital*) Also called: **pairs**, (*esp US*) **concentration** a memory card game in which a pack of cards is spread out face down and players try to turn up pairs with the same number [named after the *Pelman* Institute, founded in London in 1898]

pelmet ('pɛlmɪt) *n* an ornamental drapery or board fixed above a window to conceal the curtain rail [C19 probably from French *palmette* palm-leaf decoration on cornice moulding; see PALMETTE]

Peloponnese (ˌpɛləpə'niːs) *n* **the** the S peninsula of Greece, joined to central Greece by the Isthmus of Corinth: chief cities in ancient times were Sparta and Corinth, now Patras. Pop: 503 300 (2001). Area: 21 439 sq km (8361 sq miles). Medieval name: Morea Modern Greek name: Peloponnesos Also called: Peloponnesus

Peloponnesian (ˌpɛləpə'niːʃən) *adj* of or relating to the Peloponnese or its inhabitants

Peloponnesian War *n* a war fought for supremacy in Greece from 431 to 404 BC, in which Athens and her allies were defeated by the league centred on Sparta

Pelops ('piːlɒps) *n Greek myth* the son of Tantalus, who as a child was killed by his father and served up as a meal for the gods

peloria (pɛ'lɔːrɪə) *n* the abnormal production of actinomorphic flowers in a plant of a species that usually produces zygomorphic flowers [C19 via New Latin from Greek *pelōros*, from *pelōr* monster] > **peloric** (pɛ'lɒrɪk, -'lɔː-) *adj*

pelorus (pɪ'lɔːrəs) *n, pl* -ruses a sighting device used in conjunction with a magnetic compass or a gyrocompass for measuring the relative bearings of observed points [of uncertain origin, perhaps from Latin *Pelōrus* a dangerous Sicilian promontory]

pelota (pə'lɒtə) *n* any of various games played in Spain, Spanish America, SW France, etc, by two players who use a basket strapped to their wrists or a wooden racket to propel a ball against a specially marked wall [C19 from Spanish: ball, from Old French *pelote*; occ PELLET]

Pelotas (*Portuguese* pe'lɔtas) *n* a port in S Brazil, in Rio Grande do Sul on the Canal de São Gonçalo. Pop: 323 000 (2005 est)

peloton ('pɛlə.tɒn) *n cycle racing* the main field of riders in a road race [C20 French, literally: pack]

pelt[1] (pɛlt) *vb* **1** (*tr*) to throw (missiles) at (a person) **2** (*tr*) to hurl (insults) at (a person) **3** (*intr*; foll by *along, over*, etc) to move rapidly; hurry **4** (*intr*; often foll by *down*) to rain heavily ▷ *n* **5** a blow **6** speed (esp in the phrase **at full pelt**) [C15 of uncertain origin, perhaps from PELLET] > 'pelter *n*

pelt[2] (pɛlt) *n* **1** the skin of a fur-bearing animal, such as a mink, esp when it has been removed from the carcass **2** the hide of an animal, stripped of hair and ready for tanning [C15 perhaps back formation from PELTRY]

peltast ('pɛltæst) *n* (in ancient Greece) a lightly armed foot soldier [C17 from Latin *peltasta*, from Greek *peltastēs* soldier equipped with a *pelta*, a small leather shield]

peltate ('pɛlteɪt) *adj* (of leaves) having the stalk attached to the centre of the lower surface [C18 from Latin *peltātus* equipped with a *pelta*, a small shield; see PELTAST] > 'peltately *adv* > pel'tation *n*

Peltier effect ('pɛltɪ.eɪ) *n physics* the production of heat at one junction and the absorption of heat at the other junction of a thermocouple when a current is passed around the thermocouple circuit. The heat produced is additional to the heat arising from the resistance of the wires. Compare **Seebeck effect** [C19 named after Jean *Peltier* (1785–1845), French physicist, who discovered it]

Peltier element *n* an electronic device consisting of metal strips between which alternate strips of n-type and p-type semiconductors are connected. Passage of a current causes heat to be absorbed from one set of metallic strips and emitted from the other by the Peltier effect

Pelton wheel ('pɛltən) *n* a type of impulse turbine in which specially shaped buckets mounted on the perimeter of a wheel are struck by a fast-flowing water jet [C19 named after L. A. *Pelton* (1829–1908), US engineer who invented it]

peltry ('pɛltrɪ) *n, pl* -ries the pelts of animals collectively [C15 from Old French *peleterie* collection of pelts, from Latin *pilus* hair]

pelvic ('pɛlvɪk) *adj* of, near, or relating to the pelvis

pelvic fin *n* either of a pair of fins attached to the pelvic girdle of fishes that help to control the direction of movement during locomotion

pelvic floor *n* the muscular area in the lower part of the abdomen, attached to the pelvis

pelvic-floor exercises *pl n* another name for **Kegel exercises**

pelvic girdle or **arch** *n* the skeletal structure to which the lower limbs in man, and the hind limbs or corresponding parts in other vertebrates, are attached

pelvic inflammatory disease *n* inflammation of a woman's womb, Fallopian tubes, or ovaries as a result of infection with one of a group of bacteria. Abbreviation: PID

pelvimetry (pɛl'vɪmɪtrɪ) *n obstetrics* measurement of the dimensions of the female pelvis

pelvis ('pɛlvɪs) *n, pl* -vises or -ves (-viːz) **1** the large funnel-shaped structure at the lower end of the trunk of most vertebrates: in man it is formed by the hipbones and sacrum **2** the bones that form this structure **3** any anatomical cavity or structure shaped like a funnel or cup **4** short for

renal pelvis [C17 from Latin: basin, laver]

pelycosaur ('pɛlɪkəʊˌsɔː) *n* any extinct mammal-like reptile of the order *Pelycosauria*, of Upper Carboniferous to Lower Permian times, from which the therapsids are thought to have evolved [C19 from New Latin *Pelycosauria*, from Greek *pelyx* bowl, PELVIS, + -SAUR]

Pemba ('pɛmbə) *n* an island in the Indian Ocean, off the E coast of Africa north of Zanzibar: part of Tanzania; produces most of the world's cloves. Chief town: Chake Chake. Pop: 362 166 (2002). Area: 984 sq km (380 sq miles)

Pembroke ('pɛmbrʊk) *n* **1** a town in SW Wales, in Pembrokeshire on Milford Haven: 11th-century castle where Henry VII was born. Pop (with Pembroke Dock): 15 890 (2001) **2** the smaller variety of corgi, usually having a short tail

Pembrokeshire ('pɛmbrʊkˌʃɪə, -ʃə) *n* a county of SW Wales, on the Irish Sea and the Bristol Channel: formerly (1974–96) part of Dyfed: a hilly peninsula with a deeply indented coast: tourism, agriculture, oil refining. Administrative centre: Haverfordwest. Pop: 116 300 (2003 est). Area: 1589 sq km (614 sq miles)

Pembroke table *n* a small table with drop leaves and often one or more drawers [perhaps named after Mary Herbert, Countess of *Pembroke* (1561–1621), who originally ordered its design]

pemmican or **pemican** ('pɛmɪkən) *n* a small pressed cake of shredded dried meat, pounded into paste with fat and berries or dried fruits, used originally by American Indians and now chiefly for emergency rations [C19 from Cree *pimikân*, from *pimii* fat, grease]

pemphigus ('pɛmfɪɡəs, pɛm'faɪ-) *n pathol* any of a group of blistering skin diseases, esp a potentially fatal form (**pemphigus vulgaris**) characterized by large blisters on the skin, mucous membranes of the mouth, genitals, intestines, etc, which eventually rupture and form painful denuded areas from which critical amounts of bodily protein, fluid, and blood may be lost [C18 via New Latin from Greek *pemphix* bubble]

pen[1] (pɛn) *n* **1** an implement for writing or drawing using ink, formerly consisting of a sharpened and split quill, and now of a metal nib attached to a holder. See also **ballpoint, fountain pen 2** the writing end of such an implement; nib **3** style of writing **4** the pen **a** writing as an occupation **b** the written word: *the pen is mightier than the sword* **5** the long horny internal shell of a squid ▷ *vb* pens, penning, penned **6** (*tr*) to write or compose [Old English *pinne*, from Late Latin *penna* (quill) pen, from Latin: feather]

pen[2] (pɛn) *n* **1** an enclosure in which domestic animals are kept: *sheep pen* **2** any place of confinement **3** a dock for servicing submarines, esp one having a bombproof roof ▷ *vb* pens, penning, penned or pent **4** (*tr*) to enclose or keep in a pen [Old English *penn*, perhaps related to PIN]

pen[3] (pɛn) *n US and Canadian informal* short for **penitentiary** (sense 1)

pen[4] (pɛn) *n* a female swan [C16 of unknown origin]

PEN (pɛn) *n acronym for* International Association of Poets, Playwrights, Editors, Essayists, and Novelists

Pen. *abbreviation for* Peninsula

penal ('piːnᵊl) *adj* **1** of, relating to, constituting, or prescribing punishment **2** payable as a penalty: *a penal sum* **3** used or designated as a place of punishment: *a penal institution* [C15 from Late Latin *poenālis* concerning punishment, from *poena* penalty] > 'penally *adv*

penal code *n* the codified body of the laws in any legal system that relate to crime and its punishment

penalize or **penalise** ('piːnəˌlaɪz) *vb* (*tr*) **1** to impose a penalty on (someone), as for breaking a law or rule **2** to inflict a handicap or disadvantage on **3** *sport* to award a free stroke, point, or penalty against (a player or team) **4** to declare (an act) legally punishable; make subject to a penalty > ˌpenaliˈzation *or* ˌpenaliˈsation *n*

penal servitude *n English criminal law* (formerly) the imprisonment of an offender and his subjection to hard labour. It was substituted for transportation in 1853 and abolished in 1948. Compare **hard labour**

penalty (ˈpɛnəltɪ) *n, pl* -ties **1** a legal or official punishment, such as a term of imprisonment **2** some other form of punishment, such as a fine or forfeit for not fulfilling a contract **3** loss, suffering, or other unfortunate result of one's own action, error, etc **4** *sport, games* a handicap awarded against a player or team for illegal play, such as a free shot at goal by the opposing team, loss of points, etc [c16 from Medieval Latin *poenālitās* penalty; see PENAL]

penalty area *n soccer* a rectangular area in front of the goal, within which the goalkeeper may handle the ball and within which a penalty is awarded for a foul by the defending team

penalty box *n* **1** *soccer* another name for **penalty area** **2** *ice hockey* a bench for players serving time penalties

penalty corner *n hockey* a free hit from the goal line taken by the attacking side. Also called: **short corner**

penalty kick *n* **1** *soccer* a free kick at the goal from a point (**penalty spot**) within the penalty area and 12 yards (about 11 m) from the goal, with only the goalkeeper allowed to defend it: awarded to the attacking team after a foul within the penalty area by a member of the defending team **2** *rugby union* a kick awarded after a serious foul that can be aimed straight at the goal to score three points

penalty killer *n ice hockey* a good player who, when his team is short-handed because of a penalty, is sent onto the ice to prevent the other side from scoring

penalty point *n* **1** *Brit* an endorsement on a driving licence due to a motoring offence: *he also got eight penalty points on his licence* **2** a point awarded against a sports team or competitor for an infringement of the rules

penalty rates *pl n Austral and NZ* rates of pay, such as double time, paid to employees working outside normal working hours

penalty shoot-out *n* **1** *soccer* a method of deciding the winner of a drawn match, in which players from each team attempt to score with a penalty kick **2** a similar method of resolving a tie in hockey, ice hockey, polo, etc

penance (ˈpɛnəns) *n* **1** voluntary self-punishment to atone for a sin, crime, etc **2** a feeling of regret for one's wrongdoings **3** *Christianity* **a** a punishment usually consisting of prayer, fasting, etc, undertaken voluntarily as an expression of penitence for sin **b** a punishment of this kind imposed by church authority as a condition of absolution ▷ *vb* **4** (*tr*) (of ecclesiastical authorities) to impose a penance upon (a sinner) [c13 via Old French from Latin *paenitentia* repentance; related to Latin *poena* penalty]

Penang (pɪˈnæŋ) *n* **1** a state of Peninsular Malaysia: consists of the island of Penang and the province Wellesley on the mainland, which first united administratively in 1798 as a British colony. Capital: George Town. Pop: 1 313 449 (2000). Area: 1031 sq km (398 sq miles). Also called: Pulau Pinang **2** a forested island off the NW coast of Malaya, in the Strait of Malacca. Area: 293 sq km (113 sq miles). Former name (until about 1867): Prince of Wales Island **3** another name for **George Town**

penannular (pɛnˈænjʊlə) *adj* of or forming an almost complete ring [c19 from PENE- + ANNULAR]

penates (pəˈnɑːtiːz) *pl n* See **lares and penates** [Latin]

pence (pɛns) *n* a plural of **penny**

▌ **USAGE** Since the decimalization of British currency and the introduction

of the abbreviation **p,** as in *10p, 85p,* etc, the abbreviation has tended to replace *pence* in speech, as in *4p* (ˌfɔːˈpiː), *12p* (ˌtwelvˈpiː), etc

pencel, pensel *or* **pensil** (ˈpɛnsəl) *n* a small pennon, originally one carried by a knight's squire [c13 via Anglo-French from Old French *penoncel* a little PENNON]

penchant (ˈpɒnʃɒn) *n* a strong inclination or liking; bent or taste [c17 from French, from *pencher* to incline, from Latin *pendēre* to be suspended]

Penchi (ˈpɛnˈtʃiː) *n* a variant transliteration of the Chinese name for **Benxi**

pencil (ˈpɛnsəl) *n* **1 a** a thin cylindrical instrument used for writing, drawing, etc, consisting of a rod of graphite or other marking substance, usually either encased in wood and sharpened or held in a mechanical metal device **b** (*as modifier*): *a pencil drawing* **2** something similar in shape or function: *a styptic pencil; an eyebrow pencil* **3** a narrow set of lines or rays, such as light rays, diverging from or converging to a point **4** *archaic* an artist's fine paintbrush **5** *rare* an artist's individual style or technique in drawing ▷ *vb* -cils, -cilling, -cilled *or US* -cils, -ciling, -ciled (*tr*) **6** to draw, colour, or write with a pencil **7** to mark with a pencil **8** pencil in to note, arrange, include, etc provisionally or tentatively [c14 from Old French *pincel*, from Latin *pēnicillus* painter's brush, from *pēniculus* a little tail, from *pēnis* tail] > ˈpenciller *or US* ˈpenciler *n*

pencil crayon *n Canadian* a pencil containing a coloured marking substance; coloured pencil

pend (pɛnd) *vb* (*intr*) **1** to await judgment or settlement **2** *dialect* to hang; depend ▷ *n* **3** *Scot* an archway or vaulted passage [c15 from Latin *pendēre* to hang; related to Latin *pendere* to suspend]

pendant (ˈpɛndənt) *n* **1 a** an ornament that hangs from a piece of jewellery **b** a necklace with such an ornament **2** a hanging light, esp a chandelier **3** a carved ornament that is suspended from a ceiling or roof **4** something that matches or complements something else **5** Also called: **pennant** *nautical* a length of wire or rope secured at one end to a mast or spar and having a block or other fitting at the lower end ▷ *adj* **6** a variant spelling of **pendent** [c14 from Old French, from *pendre* to hang, from Latin *pendēre* to hang down; related to Latin *pendere* to hang, *pondus* weight, Greek *span* to pull]

pendent (ˈpɛndənt) *adj* **1** dangling **2** jutting **3** (of a grammatical construction) incomplete: *a pendent nominative is a construction having no verb* **4** a less common word for **pending** (senses 2, 3) ▷ *n* **5** a variant spelling of **pendant** [c15 from Old French *pendant,* from *pendre* to hang; see PENDANT] > ˈpendency *n* > ˈpendently *adv*

pendente lite (pɛnˈdɛntɪ ˈlaɪtɪ) *adj law* while a suit is pending [Latin, literally: with litigation pending]

pendentive (pɛnˈdɛntɪv) *n* any of four triangular sections of vaulting with concave sides, positioned at a corner of a rectangular space to support a circular or polygonal dome [c18 from French *pendentif,* from Latin *pendens* hanging, from *pendere* to hang]

pending (ˈpɛndɪŋ) *prep* **1** while waiting for or anticipating ▷ *adj* (*postpositive*) **2** not yet decided, confirmed, or finished: *what are the matters pending?* **3** imminent: *these developments have been pending for some time*

Pendolino (ˌpɛndəʊˈliːnəʊ) *n* an Italian high-speed tilting train, now used in several countries

pendragon (pɛnˈdrægən) *n* a supreme war chief or leader of the ancient Britons [Welsh, literally: head dragon] > penˈdragonˌship *n*

pen drive *n computing* another name for **key drive**

pendu (ˈbɛndu:) *adj Hinglish informal* culturally backward [c21 from Punjabi *pind* village]

pendule (ˈpɒndjʊl, ˈpɛn-) *n mountaineering* a manoeuvre by which a climber on a rope from above swings in a pendulum-like series of

movements to reach another line of ascent. Also called: **pendulum**

pendulous (ˈpɛndjʊləs) *adj* hanging downwards, esp so as to swing from side to side [c17 from Latin *pendulus,* from *pendēre* to hang down] > ˈpendulously *adv* > ˈpendulousness *n*

pendulum (ˈpɛndjʊləm) *n* **1** a body mounted so that it can swing freely under the influence of gravity. It is either a bob hung on a light thread (**simple pendulum**) or a more complex structure (**compound pendulum**) **2** such a device used to regulate a clockwork mechanism **3** something that changes its position, attitude, etc fairly regularly: *the pendulum of public opinion* [c17 from Latin *pendulus* PENDULOUS]

pene- *or before a vowel* **pen-** *prefix* almost: *peneplain* [from Latin *paene*]

Penelope (pəˈnɛləpɪ) *n Greek myth* the wife of Odysseus, who remained true to him during his long absence despite the importunities of many suitors

peneplain *or* **peneplane** (ˈpiːnɪˌpleɪn, ˌpiːnɪˈpleɪn) *n* a relatively flat land surface produced by a long period of erosion [c19 from PENE- + PLAIN[1]] > ˌpenepla'nation *n*

penetralia (ˌpɛnɪˈtreɪlɪə) *pl n* **1** the innermost parts **2** secret matters [c17 from Latin, from *penetrālis* inner, from *penetrāre* to PENETRATE] > ˌpene'tralian *adj*

penetrance (ˈpɛnɪtrəns) *n genetics* the percentage frequency with which a gene exhibits its effect [c20 from PENETR(ANT) + -ANCE, on the model of German *penetranz*]

penetrant (ˈpɛnɪtrənt) *adj* **1** sharp; penetrating ▷ *n* **2** *chem* a substance that lowers the surface tension of a liquid and thus causes it to penetrate or be absorbed more easily **3** a person or thing that penetrates

penetrate (ˈpɛnɪˌtreɪt) *vb* **1** to find or force a way into or through (something); pierce; enter **2** to diffuse through (a substance); permeate **3** (*tr*) to see through: *their eyes could not penetrate the fog* **4** (*tr*) (of a man) to insert the penis into the vagina of (a woman) **5** (*tr*) to grasp the meaning of (a principle, etc) **6** (*intr*) to be understood: *his face lit up as the new idea penetrated* [c16 from Latin *penetrāre;* related to *penitus* inner, and *penus* the interior of a house] > ˈpenetrable *adj* > ˌpenetra'bility *n* > ˈpenetrably *adv* > ˈpenetrative *adj* > ˈpeneˌtrator *n*

penetrating (ˈpɛnɪˌtreɪtɪŋ) *adj* tending to or able to penetrate: *a penetrating mind; a penetrating voice* > ˈpeneˌtratingly *adv*

penetration (ˌpɛnɪˈtreɪʃən) *n* **1** the act or an instance of penetrating **2** the ability or power to penetrate **3** keen insight or perception **4** *military* an offensive manoeuvre that breaks through an enemy's defensive position **5** Also called: **market penetration** the proportion of the total number of potential purchasers of a product or service who either are aware of its existence or actually buy it **6** another name for **depth of field**

penetrometer (ˌpɛnɪˈtrɒmɪtə) *n physics* an instrument used to measure the penetrating power of radiation, such as X-rays

Peneus (pɪˈniːəs) *n* the ancient name for the **Salambria**

pen friend *n* another name for **pen pal**

Penghu *or* **P'eng-hu** (ˈpɛŋˈhuː) *n* transliteration of the Chinese name for the **Pescadores**

pengö (ˈpɛŋɡɜː) *n, pl* -gös (formerly) the standard monetary unit of Hungary, replaced by the forint in 1946 [from Hungarian, from *pengeni* to sound]

Pengpu (ˈpɛŋˈpuː) *n* a variant transliteration of the Chinese name for **Bengbu**

penguin (ˈpɛŋɡwɪn) *n* **1** any flightless marine bird, such as *Aptenodytes patagonica* (king penguin) and *Pygoscelis adeliae* (**Adélie penguin**), of the order *Sphenisciformes* of cool southern, esp Antarctic, regions: they have wings modified as flippers, webbed feet, and feathers lacking barbs. See also **emperor penguin, king penguin 2** an obsolete name for **great auk** [c16 perhaps from Welsh *pen* gwyn, from *pen* head + *gwyn* white]

penicillate (ˌpɛnɪˈsɪlɪt, -eɪt) *adj biology* having or resembling one or more tufts of fine hairs: *a penicillate caterpillar* [C19 from Latin *pēnicillus* brush, PENCIL] > ˌpeniˈcillately *adv* > ˌpenicilˈlation *n*

penicillin (ˌpɛnɪˈsɪlɪn) *n* any of a group of antibiotics with powerful bactericidal action, used to treat many types of infections, including pneumonia, gonorrhoea, and infections caused by streptococci and staphylococci: originally obtained from the fungus *Penicillium*, esp *P. notatum*. Formula: R–C₉H₁₁N₂O₄S where R is one of several side chains [C20 from PENICILLIUM]

penicillium (ˌpɛnɪˈsɪlɪəm) *n, pl* -cilliums or -cillia (-ˈsɪlɪə) any ascomycetous saprotrophic fungus of the genus *Penicillium*, which commonly grow as a green or blue mould on stale food: some species are used in cheese-making and others as a source of penicillin [C19 New Latin, from Latin *pēnicillus* tuft of hairs; named from the tufted appearance of the sporangia of this fungus]

penile (ˈpiːnaɪl) *adj* of or relating to the penis

penillion or **pennillion** (pɪˈnɪlɪən) *pl n, sing* penill (pɪˈnɪl) the Welsh art or practice of singing poetry in counterpoint to a traditional melody played on the harp [from Welsh: verses, plural of *penill* verse, stanza]

peninsula (pɪˈnɪnsjʊlə) *n* a narrow strip of land projecting into a sea or lake from the mainland [C16 from Latin, literally: almost an island, from *paene* PENE- + *insula* island] > penˈinsular *adj*

> USAGE The noun *peninsula* is sometimes confused with the adjective *peninsular: the Iberian peninsula* (not *peninsular*)

Peninsula *n* the short for the **Iberian Peninsula**

Peninsular War *n* the war (1808–14) fought in the Iberian Peninsula by British, Portuguese, and Spanish forces against the French, resulting in the defeat of the French: part of the Napoleonic Wars

peninsulate (pɪˈnɪnsjʊˌleɪt) *vb* (*tr*) to cause (land) to become peninsular

penis (ˈpiːnɪs) *n, pl* -nises or -nes (-niːz) the male organ of copulation in higher vertebrates, also used for urine excretion in many mammals [C17 from Latin]

penis envy *n psychoanal* a Freudian concept in which envy of the penis is postulated as the cause for some of the characteristics found in women

penitent (ˈpɛnɪtənt) *adj* 1 feeling regret for one's sins; repentant ▷ *n* 2 a person who is penitent 3 *Christianity* a a person who repents his sins and seeks forgiveness for them b *RC Church* a person who confesses his sins to a priest and submits to a penance imposed by him [C14 from Church Latin *paenitēns* regretting, from *paenitēre* to repent, of obscure origin] > ˈpenitence *n* > ˈpenitently *adv*

penitential (ˌpɛnɪˈtɛnʃəl) *adj* 1 showing, or constituting penance ▷ *n* 2 *chiefly RC Church* a book or compilation of instructions for confessors 3 a less common word for **penitent** (senses 2, 3) > ˌpeniˈtentially *adv*

penitentiary (ˌpɛnɪˈtɛnʃərɪ) *n, pl* -ries 1 (in the US and Canada) a state or federal prison: in Canada, esp a federal prison for offenders convicted of serious crimes. Sometimes shortened to: **pen** 2 *RC Church* a a cleric appointed to supervise the administration of the sacrament of penance in a particular area b a priest who has special faculties to absolve particularly grave sins c a cardinal who presides over a tribunal that decides all matters affecting the sacrament of penance d this tribunal itself ▷ *adj* 3 another word for **penitential** (sense 1) 4 *US and Canadian* (of an offence) punishable by imprisonment in a penitentiary [C15 (meaning also: an officer dealing with penances): from Medieval Latin *poenitentiārius*, from Latin *paenitēns* PENITENT]

Penki (ˈpɛnˈtʃiː) *n* a variant transliteration of the Chinese name for **Benxi**

penknife (ˈpɛnˌnaɪf) *n, pl* -knives a small knife with one or more blades that fold into the handle; pocketknife [C15 so called because it was originally used for making and repairing quill pens]

penman (ˈpɛnmən) *n, pl* -men 1 a person skilled in handwriting 2 a person who writes by hand in a specified way: *a bad penman* 3 an author

penmanship (ˈpɛnmənʃɪp) *n* style or technique of writing by hand. Also called: calligraphy

Penn. or **Penna** *abbreviation for* Pennsylvania

penna (ˈpɛnə) *n, pl* -nae (-niː) *ornithol* any large feather that has a vane and forms part of the main plumage of a bird [Latin: feather] > **pennaceous** (pɛˈneɪʃəs) *adj*

pen name *n* an author's pseudonym. Also called: **nom de plume**

pennant (ˈpɛnənt) *n* 1 a type of pennon, esp one flown from vessels as identification or for signalling 2 *chiefly US, Canadian, and Austral* a a flag serving as an emblem of championship in certain sports b (*as modifier*): *pennant cricket* 3 *nautical* another word for **pendant** (sense 5) 4 same as **flag¹** (sense 10) [C17 probably a blend of PENDANT and PENNON]

pennate (ˈpɛneɪt) or **pennated** *adj biology* 1 having feathers, wings, or winglike structures 2 another word for **pinnate** [C19 from Latin *pennātus*, from *penna* wing]

penne (ˈpɛnɪ) *n* pasta in the form of short tubes [C20 Italian, literally: quills]

penni (ˈpɛnɪ) *n, pl* -niä (-nɪə) or -nis a former Finnish monetary unit worth one hundredth of a markka [Finnish, from Low German *pennig* PENNY]

penniless (ˈpɛnɪlɪs) *adj* very poor; almost totally without money > **ˈpennilessly** *adv* > **ˈpennilessness** *n*

pennillion (pɪˈnɪlɪən) *n* a variant spelling of **penillion**

Pennine Alps (ˈpɛnaɪn) *pl n* a range of the Alps between Switzerland and Italy. Highest peak: Monte Rosa, 4634 m (15 204 ft)

Pennines (ˈpɛnaɪnz) *pl n* a system of hills in England, extending from the Cheviot Hills in the north to the River Trent in the south: forms the watershed for the main rivers of N England. Highest peak: Cross Fell, 893 m (2930 ft). Also called: **the Pennine Chain**

Pennine Way *n* a long-distance footpath extending from Edale, Derbyshire, for 402 km (250 miles) to Kirk Yetholm, Scottish Borders

penninite (ˈpɛnɪˌnaɪt) *n* a bluish-green variety of chlorite occurring in the form of thick crystals [C20 from German *Pennin* Pennine (Alps) + -ITE¹]

pennon (ˈpɛnən) *n* 1 a long flag, often tapering and rounded, divided, or pointed at the end, originally a knight's personal flag 2 a small tapering or triangular flag borne on a ship or boat 3 a poetic word for **wing** [C14 via Old French ultimately from Latin *penna* feather]

Pennsylvania (ˌpɛnsɪlˈveɪnɪə) *n* a state of the northeastern US: almost wholly in the Appalachians, with the Allegheny Plateau to the west and a plain in the southeast; the second most important US state for manufacturing. Capital: Harrisburg. Pop: 12 365 455 (2003 est). Area: 116 462 sq km (44 956 sq miles). Abbreviations: **Pa, Penn, Penna**, (with zip code) **PA**

Pennsylvania Dutch *n* Also called: **Pennsylvania German** a dialect of German spoken in E Pennsylvania 2 the Pennsylvania Dutch (*functioning as plural*) a group of German-speaking people in E Pennsylvania, descended from 18th-century settlers from SW Germany and Switzerland

Pennsylvanian (ˌpɛnsɪlˈveɪnɪən) *adj* 1 of the state of Pennsylvania 2 (in North America) of, denoting, or formed in the upper of two divisions of the Carboniferous period (see also **Mississippian** (sense 2)), which lasted 30 million years, during which coal measures were formed ▷ *n* 3 an inhabitant or native of the state of Pennsylvania 4 the the Pennsylvanian period or rock system,

equivalent to the Upper Carboniferous of Europe

penny (ˈpɛnɪ) *n, pl* pennies or pence (pɛns) 1 Also called (formerly): new penny (in Britain) a bronze coin having a value equal to one hundredth of a pound. Symbol: p 2 (in Britain before 1971) a bronze or copper coin having a value equal to one twelfth of a shilling or one two-hundred-and-fortieth of a pound. Abbreviation: d 3 a former monetary unit of the Republic of Ireland worth one hundredth of a pound 4 (*pl* pennies) (in the US and Canada) a cent 5 a coin of similar value, as used in several other countries 6 (*used with a negative*) *informal, chiefly Brit* the least amount of money: *I don't have a penny* 7 a bad penny *informal, chiefly Brit* an objectionable person or thing (esp in the phrase **turn up like a bad penny**) 8 a pretty penny *informal* a considerable sum of money 9 spend a penny *Brit informal* to urinate 10 the penny dropped *informal, chiefly Brit* the explanation of something was finally realized 11 two a penny plentiful but of little value [Old English *penig, pening*; related to Old Saxon *penni(n)g*, Old High German *pfeni(n)c*, German *Pfennig*]

penny-a-liner *n* now rare a hack writer or journalist

penny arcade *n chiefly US* a public place with various coin-operated machines for entertainment; amusement arcade

Penny Black *n* the first adhesive postage stamp, issued in Britain in 1840; an imperforate stamp bearing the profile of Queen Victoria on a dark background

pennyboy (ˈpɛnɪˌbɔɪ) *n Irish slang* an employee whose duties include menial tasks, such as running errands

pennycress (ˈpɛnɪˌkrɛs) *n* any of several plants of the genus *Thlaspi* of temperate Eurasia and North America, typically having small white or mauve flowers and rounded or heart-shaped leaves: family *Brassicaceae* (crucifers)

penny-dreadful *n, pl* -fuls *Brit informal* a cheap, often lurid or sensational book or magazine

penny-farthing *n Brit* an early type of bicycle with a large front wheel and a small rear wheel, the pedals being attached to the front wheel. US name: **ordinary** [C20 so called because of the similarity between the relative sizes of the wheels and the relative sizes of the (old) penny and farthing coins]

penny-pinching *adj informal* excessively careful with money > **ˈpenny-ˌpincher** *n*

pennyroyal (ˌpɛnɪˈrɔɪəl) *n* 1 a Eurasian plant, *Mentha pulegium*, with hairy leaves and small mauve flowers, that yields an aromatic oil used in medicine: family *Lamiaceae* (labiates) 2 Also called: **mock pennyroyal** a similar and related plant, *Hedeoma pulegioides*, of E North America [C16 variant of Anglo-Norman *puliol real*, from Old French *pouliol* (from Latin *pūleium* pennyroyal) + *real* ROYAL]

penny shares *pl n stock exchange* securities with a low market price, esp less than 20p, enabling small investors to purchase a large number for a relatively small outlay

pennyweight (ˈpɛnɪˌweɪt) *n* a unit of weight equal to 24 grains or one twentieth of an ounce (Troy)

penny whistle *n* a type of flageolet with six finger holes, esp a cheap one made of metal. Also called: **tin whistle**

penny-wise *adj* 1 greatly concerned with saving small sums of money 2 penny-wise and pound-foolish careful about trifles but wasteful in large ventures

pennywort (ˈpɛnɪˌwɜːt) *n* 1 Also called: **navelwort** a crassulaceous Eurasian rock plant, *Umbilicus rupestris* (or *Cotyledon umbilicus*), with whitish-green tubular flowers and rounded leaves 2 a marsh plant, *Hydrocotyle vulgaris*, of Europe and North Africa, having circular leaves and greenish-pink flowers: family *Hydrocotylaceae* 3 a gentianaceous plant, *Obolaria virginica*, of E North America, with

p

fleshy scalelike leaves and small white or purplish flowers **4** any of various other plants with rounded penny-like leaves

pennyworth ('pɛnɪˌwɜːθ) *n* **1** the amount that can be bought for a penny **2** a small amount: *he hasn't got a pennyworth of sense*

penology (piːˈnɒlədʒɪ) *n* **1** the branch of the social sciences concerned with the punishment of crime **2** the science of prison management ▷ Also: poenology [C19 from Greek *poinē* punishment] > penological (ˌpiːnəˈlɒdʒɪkˀl) *adj* > ˌpenoˈlogically *adv* > peˈnologist *n*

pen pal *n* a person with whom one regularly exchanges letters, often a person in another country whom one has not met. Also called: pen friend

penpusher ('pɛnˌpʊʃə) *n* a person who writes a lot, esp a clerk involved with boring paperwork > 'penˌpushing *adj, n*

Penrith (pen'rɪθ) *n* a market town in NW England, in Cumbria. Pop: 14 471 (2001)

pensel *or* **pensil** ('pɛnsˀl) *n* variants of **pencel**

Penshurst Place ('pɛnzhɜːst) *n* a 14th-century mansion near Tunbridge Wells in Kent: birthplace of Sir Philip Sidney; gardens laid out from 1560

pensile ('pɛnsaɪl) *adj ornithol* designating or building a hanging nest: *pensile birds* [C17 from Latin *pensilis* hanging down, from *pendēre* to hang] > pensility (pɛnˈsɪlɪtɪ) *or* 'pensileness *n*

pension[1] ('pɛnʃən) *n* **1** a regular payment made by the state to people over a certain age to enable them to subsist without having to work **2** a regular payment made by an employer to former employees after they retire **3** a regular payment made to a retired person as the result of his or her contributions to a personal pension scheme **4** any regular payment made on charitable grounds, by way of patronage, or in recognition of merit, service, etc: *a pension paid to a disabled soldier* ▷ *vb* **5** (*tr*) to grant a pension to [C14 via Old French from Latin *pēnsiō* a payment, from *pendere* to pay] > 'pensionable *adj* > 'pensionless *adj*

pension[2] *French* (pãsjõ) *n* (in France and some other countries) **1** a relatively cheap boarding house **2** another name for **full board** [C17 French; extended meaning of *pension* grant; see PENSION[1]]

pensionary ('pɛnʃənərɪ) *adj* **1** constituting a pension **2** maintained by or receiving a pension ▷ *n, pl* -aries **3** a person whose service can be bought; hireling

pensioneer trustee (ˌpɛnʃəˈnɪə) *n* (in Britain) a person authorized by the Inland Revenue to oversee the management of a pension fund

pensioner ('pɛnʃənə) *n* **1** a person who is receiving a pension, esp an old-age pension from the state **2** a person dependent on the pay or bounty of another **3** *obsolete, Brit* another name for **gentleman-at-arms**

pension mortgage *n* an arrangement whereby a person takes out a mortgage and pays the capital repayment instalments into a pension fund and the interest to the mortgagee. The loan is repaid out of the tax-free lump sum proceeds of the pension plan on the borrower's retirement

pension off *vb* (*tr, adverb*) **1** to cause to retire from a post and pay a pension to **2** to discard, because old and worn: *to pension off submarines*

pensive ('pɛnsɪv) *adj* **1** deeply or seriously thoughtful, often with a tinge of sadness **2** expressing or suggesting pensiveness [C14 from Old French *pensif*, from *penser* to think, from Latin *pensāre* to consider; compare PENSION[1]] > 'pensively *adv* > 'pensiveness *n*

penstemon (pɛnˈstiːmən) *n* a variant (esp US) of **pentstemon**

penstock ('pɛnˌstɒk) *n* **1** a conduit that supplies water to a hydroelectric power plant **2** a channel bringing water from the head gates to a water wheel **3** a sluice for controlling water flow [C17 from PEN[2] + STOCK]

pent (pɛnt) *vb* a past tense and past participle of **pen**[2]

penta- *combining form* five: *pentagon; pentameter; pentaprism* [from Greek *pente* five]

pentachlorophenol (ˌpɛntəˌklɔːrəˈfiːnɒl) *n* a white crystalline water-insoluble compound used as a fungicide, herbicide, and preservative for wood. Formula: C_6Cl_5OH

pentacle ('pɛntəkˀl) *n* another name for **pentagram** [C16 from Italian *pentacolo* something having five corners; see PENTA-]

pentad ('pɛntæd) *n* **1** a group or series of five **2** the number or sum of five **3** a period of five years **4** *chem* a pentavalent element, atom, or radical **5** *meteorol* a period of five days [C17 from Greek *pentas* group of five]

pentadactyl (ˌpɛntəˈdæktɪl) *adj* (of the limbs of amphibians, reptiles, birds, and mammals) consisting of an upper arm or thigh, a forearm or shank, and a hand or foot bearing five digits

pentagon ('pɛntəˌgɒn) *n* a polygon having five sides > pentagonal (pɛnˈtægənˀl) *adj*

Pentagon ('pɛntəˌgɒn) *n* **1** the five-sided building in Arlington, Virginia, that houses the headquarters of the US Department of Defense **2** the military leadership of the US

pentagram ('pɛntəˌgræm) *n* **1** a star-shaped figure formed by extending the sides of a regular pentagon to meet at five points **2** such a figure used as a magical or symbolic figure by the Pythagoreans, black magicians, etc ▷ Also called: pentacle, pentangle

pentahedron (ˌpɛntəˈhiːdrən) *n, pl* -drons *or* -dra (-drə) a solid figure having five plane faces. See also **polyhedron**. > ˌpentaˈhedral *adj*

pentamerous (pɛnˈtæmərəs) *adj* consisting of five parts, esp (of flowers) having the petals, sepals, and other parts arranged in groups of five > penˈtamerˌism *n*

pentameter (pɛnˈtæmɪtə) *n* **1** a verse line consisting of five metrical feet **2** (in classical prosody) a verse line consisting of two dactyls, one stressed syllable, two dactyls, and a final stressed syllable ▷ *adj* **3** designating a verse line consisting of five metrical feet

pentamidine (pɛnˈtæmɪˌdiːn, -dɪn) *n* a drug used to treat protozoal infections, esp pneumonia caused by *Pneumocystis carinii* in patients with AIDS

pentane ('pɛnteɪn) *n* an alkane hydrocarbon having three isomers, esp the isomer with a straight chain of carbon atoms (*n*-pentane) which is a colourless flammable liquid used as a solvent. Formula: C_5H_{12}

pentangle ('pɛnˌtæŋgˀl) *n* another name for **pentagram**

pentangular (pɛnˈtæŋgjʊlə) *adj* having five angles

pentanoic acid (ˌpɛntəˈnəʊɪk) *n* a colourless liquid carboxylic acid with an unpleasant odour, used in making perfumes, flavourings, and pharmaceuticals. Formula: $CH_3(CH_2)_3COOH$. Also called: valeric acid [from PENTANE]

pentaprism ('pɛntəˌprɪzəm) *n* a five-sided prism that deviates light from any direction through an angle of 90°, typically used in single-lens reflex cameras between lens and viewfinder to present the image the right way round

pentaquark ('pɛntəˌkwaːk) *n physics* a subatomic particle thought to consist of four quarks and one antiquark [C21]

pentarchy ('pɛntaːkɪ) *n, pl* -chies **1** government by five rulers **2** a ruling body of five **3** a union or association of five kingdoms, provinces, etc, each under its own ruler **4** a country ruled by a body of five > penˈtarchical *adj*

pentastich ('pɛntəˌstɪk) *n* a poem, stanza, or strophe that consists of five lines

Pentateuch ('pɛntəˌtjuːk) *n* the first five books of the Old Testament regarded as a unity [C16 from Church Latin *pentateuchus*, from Greek PENTA- + *teukhos* tool (in Late Greek: scroll)] > ˌPentaˈteuchal *adj*

pentathlon (pɛnˈtæθlən) *n* an athletic contest consisting of five different events, based on a competition in the ancient Greek Olympics. Compare **decathlon** [C18 from Greek *pentathlon*, from PENTA- + *athlon* contest] > penˈtathlete *n*

pentatomic (ˌpɛntəˈtɒmɪk) *adj chem* having five atoms in the molecule

pentatonic scale (ˌpɛntəˈtɒnɪk) *n music* any of several scales consisting of five notes, the most commonly encountered one being composed of the first, second, third, fifth, and sixth degrees of the major diatonic scale

pentavalent (ˌpɛntəˈveɪlənt) *adj chem* having a valency of five. Also: quinquevalent

pentazocine (pɛnˈtæzəʊˌsiːn) *n* a powerful synthetic drug used in medical practice as a narcotic analgesic

Pentecost ('pɛntɪˌkɒst) *n* **1** a Christian festival occurring on Whit Sunday commemorating the descent of the Holy Ghost on the apostles **2** also called: Feast of Weeks, Shavuot *Judaism* the harvest festival celebrated fifty days after the second day of Passover on the sixth and seventh days of Sivan, and commemorating the giving the Torah on Mount Sinai [Old English, from Church Latin *pentēcostē*, from Greek *pentēkostē* fiftieth]

Pentecostal (ˌpɛntɪˈkɒstˀl) *adj* **1** (*usually prenominal*) of or relating to any of various Christian groups that emphasize the charismatic aspects of Christianity and adopt a fundamental attitude to the Bible **2** of or relating to Pentecost or the influence of the Holy Ghost ▷ *n* **3** a member of a Pentecostal Church > ˌPenteˈcostalˌism *n* > ˌPenteˈcostalist *n, adj*

Pentelikon (pɛnˈtɛlɪkɒn) *n* a mountain in SE Greece, near Athens: famous for its white marble, worked regularly from the 6th century BC, from which the chief buildings and sculpture in Athens are made. Height: 1109 m (3638 ft). Latin name: Pentelicus

pentene ('pɛntiːn) *n* a colourless flammable liquid alkene having several straight-chained isomeric forms, used in the manufacture of organic compounds. Formula: C_5H_{10}. Also called: amylene

Penthesileia *or* **Penthesilea** (ˌpɛnθəsɪˈleɪə) *n Greek myth* the daughter of Ares and queen of the Amazons, whom she led to the aid of Troy. She was slain by Achilles

Pentheus ('pɛnθiəs) *n Greek myth* the grandson of Cadmus and his successor as king of Thebes, who resisted the introduction of the cult of Dionysus. In revenge the god drove him mad and he was torn to pieces by a group of bacchantes, one of whom was his mother

penthouse ('pɛntˌhaʊs) *n* **1** a flat or maisonette built onto the top floor or roof of a block of flats **2** a construction on the roof of a building, esp one used to house machinery **3** a shed built against a building, esp one that has a sloping roof **4** *real tennis* the roofed corridor that runs along three sides of the court [C14 *pentis* (later *penthouse*, by folk etymology), from Old French *apentis*, from Late Latin *appendicium* appendage, from Latin *appendere* to hang from; see APPENDIX]

pentimento (ˌpɛntɪˈmɛntəʊ) *n, pl* -ti (-tiː) **1** the revealing of a painting or part of a painting that has been covered over by a later painting **2** the part of a painting thus revealed [C20 Italian, literally: correction]

pentito *Italian* (pen'tiːto) *n, pl* -ti (-tiː) *or* -ti (-tɪ) a person involved in organized crime who offers information to the police in return for immunity from prosecution [literally: penitent]

Pentland Firth ('pɛntlənd) *n* a channel between the mainland of N Scotland and the Orkney Islands: notorious for rough seas. Length: 32 km (20 miles). Width: up to 13 km (8 miles)

pentlandite ('pɛntlənˌdaɪt) *n* a brownish-yellow mineral consisting of an iron and nickel sulphide in cubic crystalline form: the principal ore of nickel. Formula: $(Fe,Ni)S$ [C19 from French; named after J. B. Pentland (1797–1873), Irish scientist who discovered it]

pentobarbital sodium (ˌpɛntəˈbɑːbɪˌtəʊn) *n* a barbiturate drug used in medicine as a sedative and hypnotic. Formula: $C_{11}H_{17}N_2O_3Na$. US equivalent: **sodium pentabarbital**

pentode ('pɛntəʊd) *n* **1** an electronic valve having five electrodes: a cathode, anode, and three grids **2** (*modifier*) (of a transistor) having three terminals at the base or gate [C20 from PENTA- + Greek *hodos* way]

pentomic (pɛnˈtɒmɪk) *adj* denoting or relating to the subdivision of an army division into five battle groups, esp for nuclear warfare [C20 from PENTA- + ATOMIC]

pentosan ('pɛntəˌsæn) *n biochem* any of a group of polysaccharides, having the general formula $(C_5H_8O_4)_n$: occur in plants, humus, etc [C20 from PENTOSE + -AN]

pentose ('pɛntəʊs) *n* any monosaccharide containing five atoms of carbon per molecule: occur mainly in plants and the nucleic acids [C20 from PENTA- + -OSE²]

pentose phosphate pathway *n* a sequence of metabolic reactions by which NADPH is synthesized, together with ribose phosphate, part of the synthesis of nucleic acids

Pentothal sodium ('pɛntəˌθæl) *n* a trademark for thiopental sodium

pentoxide (pɛntˈɒksaɪd) *n* an oxide of an element with five atoms of oxygen per molecule

pentstemon (pɛntˈstiːmən) *or esp US* **penstemon** *n* any scrophulariaceous plant of the North American genus *Penstemon* (or *Pentstemon*), having white, pink, red, blue, or purple flowers with five stamens, one of which is bearded and sterile [C18 New Latin, from PENTA- + Greek *stēmōn* thread (here: stamen)]

pent-up *adj* (**pent up** *when postpositive*) **1** not released; repressed: *pent-up emotions* **2** kept unwillingly: *I've been pent up in this office for over a year*

pentyl ('pɛntaɪl, -tɪl) *n* (*modifier*) of, consisting of, or containing the monovalent group $CH_3CH_2CH_2CH_2CH_2$-: *a pentyl group or radical*

pentyl acetate *n* a colourless combustible liquid used as a solvent for paints, in the extraction of penicillin, in photographic film, and as a flavouring. Formula: $CH_3COOC_5H_{11}$. Also called: **amyl acetate** Nontechnical name: **banana oil**

pentylenetetrazol (ˌpɛntɪliːnˈtɛtrəˌzɒl) *n* a white crystalline water-soluble substance with a bitter taste, used in medicine to stimulate the central nervous system. Formula: $C_6H_{10}N_4$ [C20 from *penta-methylene-tetrazole*]

penuche (pəˈnuːtʃɪ) *n* a variant of **panocha**

penuchle *or* **penuckle** ('piːnʌkəl) *n* less common spellings of **pinochle**

penult ('pɛnʌlt, pɪˈnʌlt) *or* **penultima** (pɪˈnʌltɪmə) *n* the last syllable but one in a word [C16 Latin *paenultima syllaba*, from *paene ultima* almost the last]

penultimate (pɪˈnʌltɪmɪt) *adj* **1** next to the last ▷ *n* **2** anything that is next to the last, esp a penult [C17 from Latin *paene* almost + ULTIMATE, on the model of Latin *paenultimus*]

penumbra (pɪˈnʌmbrə) *n, pl* -**brae** (-briː) *or* -**bras** **1** a fringe region of half shadow resulting from the partial obstruction of light by an opaque object **2** *astronomy* the lighter and outer region of a sunspot **3** *painting* the point or area in which light and shade blend ▷ Compare **umbra** [C17 via New Latin from Latin *paene* almost + *umbra* shadow] > pe'numbral *or* pe'numbrous *adj*

penurious (pɪˈnjʊərɪəs) *adj* **1** niggardly with money **2** lacking money or means **3** yielding little; scanty > pe'nuriously *adv* > pe'nuriousness *n*

penury ('pɛnjʊrɪ) *n* **1** extreme poverty **2** extreme scarcity [C15 from Latin *pēnūria* dearth, of obscure origin]

Penutian (pɪˈnjuːtɪən, -ʃən) *n* **1** a family of North American Indian languages of the Pacific coast **2** a phylum of languages of North and South America, including Araucanian, Chinook, Mayan, and Sahaptin

Penza (*Russian* 'pjɛnzə) *n* a city in W Russia:

manufacturing centre. Pop: 514 000 (2005 est)

Penzance (pɛnˈzæns) *n* a town in SW England, in SW Cornwall: the westernmost town in England; resort and fishing port. Pop: 20 255 (2001)

peon¹ ('piːən, 'piːɒn) *n* **1** a Spanish-American farm labourer or unskilled worker **2** (formerly in Spanish America) a debtor compelled to work off his debts **3** any very poor person [C19 from Spanish *peón* peasant, from Medieval Latin *pedō* man who goes on foot, from Latin *pēs* foot; compare Old French *paon* PAWN²]

peon² (pjuːn, 'piːən, 'piːɒn) *n* (in India, Sri Lanka, etc, esp formerly) **1** a messenger or attendant, esp in an office **2** a native policeman **3** a foot soldier [C17 from Portuguese *peão* orderly; see PEON¹]

peonage ('piːənɪdʒ) *or* **peonism** ('piːəˌnɪzəm) *n* **1** the state of being a peon **2** a system in which a debtor must work for his creditor until the debt is paid off

peony *or* **paeony** ('piːənɪ) *n, pl* -**nies 1** any of various ranunculaceous shrubs and plants of the genus *Paeonia*, of Eurasia and North America, having large pink, red, white, or yellow flowers **2** the flower of any of these plants [Old English *peonie*, from Latin *paeōnia*, from Greek *paiōnia*; related to *paiōnios* healing, from *paiōn* physician]

people ('piːpəl) *n* (*usually functioning as plural*) **1** persons collectively or in general **2** a group of persons considered together: *blind people* **3** (*pl* peoples) the persons living in a country and sharing the same nationality: *the French people* **4** one's family: *he took her home to meet his people* **5** persons loyal to someone powerful: *the king's people accompanied him in exile* **6** the people **a** the mass of persons without special distinction, privileges, etc **b** the body of persons in a country, esp those entitled to vote ▷ *vb* **7** (*tr*) to provide with or as if with people or inhabitants [C13 from Old French *pople*, from Latin *populus*; see POPULACE]

　　　　USAGE See at **person**

people carrier *n* another name for **multipurpose vehicle**

people mover *n* **1** any of various automated forms of transport for large numbers of passengers over short distances, such as a moving pavement, driverless cars, etc **2** another name for **multipurpose vehicle**

people's democracy *n* (in Communist ideology) a country or form of government in transition from bourgeois democracy to socialism. In this stage there is more than one class, the largest being the proletariat, led by the Communist Party, which is therefore the dominant power

people's front *n* a less common term for **popular front**

people skills *pl n* the ability to deal with, influence, and communicate with other people

people's panel *n* a group of people composed of members of the public, brought together to discuss, investigate, or decide on a particular matter

People's Party *n US history* the political party of the Populists

Peoria (pɪˈɔːrɪə) *n* a port in N central Illinois, on the Illinois River. Pop: 112 907 (2003 est)

pep (pɛp) *n* **1** high spirits, energy, or vitality ▷ *vb* **peps, pepping, pepped 2** (*tr; usually foll by up*) to liven by imbuing with new vigour [C20 short for PEPPER]

PEP (pɛp) *n acronym for* **1** personal equity plan: a method of saving in the UK with certain tax advantages, in which investments up to a fixed annual value can be purchased: replaced by the ISA in 1999 but arrangements for existing PEPs remain unchanged ▷ *abbreviation for* **2** political and economic planning

peperomia (ˌpɛpəˈrəʊmɪə) *n* any plant of the large genus *Peperomia* from tropical and subtropical America with slightly fleshy ornamental leaves, some of which are grown as pot plants: family *Piperaceae* [New Latin, from Greek *peperi* pepper + *homoios* similar + -IA]

peplos *or* **peplus** ('pɛpləs) *n, pl* -**loses** *or* -**luses** (in ancient Greece) the top part of a woman's attire, caught at the shoulders and hanging in folds to the waist. Also called: **peplum** [C18 from Greek, of obscure origin]

peplum ('pɛpləm) *n, pl* -**lums** *or* -**la** (-lə) **1** a flared ruffle attached to the waist of a jacket, bodice, etc **2** a variant of **peplos** [C17 from Latin: full upper garment, from Greek *peplos* shawl]

pepo ('piːpəʊ) *n, pl* -**pos** the fruit of any of various cucurbitaceous plants, such as the melon, squash, cucumber, and pumpkin, having a firm rind, fleshy watery pulp, and numerous seeds [C19 from Latin: pumpkin, from Greek *pepōn* edible gourd, from *peptein* to ripen]

pepper ('pɛpə) *n* **1** a woody climbing plant, *Piper nigrum*, of the East Indies, having small black berry-like fruits: family *Piperaceae* **2** the dried fruit of this plant, which is ground to produce a sharp hot condiment. See also **black pepper, white pepper 3** any of various other plants of the genus *Piper*. See **cubeb, betel, kava 4** Also called: **capsicum** any of various tropical plants of the solanaceous genus *Capsicum*, esp *C. frutescens*, the fruits of which are used as a vegetable and a condiment. See also **bird pepper, sweet pepper, red pepper, cayenne pepper 5** the fruit of any of these capsicums, which has a mild or pungent taste **6** the condiment made from the fruits of any of these plants **7** any of various similar but unrelated plants, such as water pepper ▷ *vb* (*tr*) **8** to season with pepper **9** to sprinkle liberally; dot: *his prose was peppered with alliteration* **10** to pelt with small missiles [Old English *piper*, from Latin, from Greek *peperi*; compare French *poivre*, Old Norse *piparr*]

pepper-and-salt *adj* **1** (of cloth) marked with a fine mixture of black and white **2** (of hair) streaked with grey

peppercorn ('pɛpəˌkɔːn) *n* **1** the small dried berry of the pepper plant (*Piper nigrum*) **2** something trifling

peppercorn rent *n* a rent that is very low or nominal

peppered moth *n* a European geometrid moth, *Biston betularia*, occurring in a pale grey speckled form in rural areas and a black form in industrial regions. See also **melanism** (sense 1)

peppergrass ('pɛpəˌgrɑːs) *n US and Canadian* **1** any of various temperate and tropical aquatic or marsh ferns of the genus *Marsilea*, having floating leaves consisting of four leaflets: family *Marsileaceae* **2** any of several plants of the genus *Lepidium*, esp *L. campestre*, of dry regions of Eurasia, having small white flowers and pungent seeds: family *Brassicaceae* (crucifers). Also called (in Britain and certain other countries): **pepperwort**

pepper mill *n* a small hand mill used to grind peppercorns

peppermint ('pɛpəˌmɪnt) *n* **1** a temperate mint plant, *Mentha piperita*, with purple or white flowers: cultivated for its downy leaves, which yield a pungent oil **2** the oil from this plant, which is used as a flavouring **3** a sweet flavoured with peppermint

pepperoni (ˌpɛpəˈrəʊnɪ) *n* a highly seasoned dry sausage of pork and beef spiced with pepper, used esp on pizza [C20 from Italian *peperoni*, plural of *peperone* cayenne pepper]

pepper pot *n* **1** a small container with perforations in the top for sprinkling pepper **2** a Caribbean stew of meat, rice, vegetables, etc, highly seasoned with cassareep

pepper tree *n* any of several evergreen anacardiaceous trees of the chiefly South American genus *Schinus*, esp *S. molle* (also called: **mastic tree**), having yellowish-white flowers and bright red ornamental fruits

peppertree ('pɛpəˌtriː) *n NZ* another name for **kawakawa**

pepperwort ('pɛpəˌwɜːt) *n* **1** any of various temperate and tropical aquatic or marsh ferns of

p

the genus *Marsilea*, having floating leaves consisting of four leaflets: family Marsileaceae **2** any of several plants of the genus *Lepidium*, esp L. *campestre*, of dry regions of Eurasia, having small white flowers and pungent seeds: family *Brassicaceae* (crucifers). Usual US and Canadian name: **peppergrass**

peppery ('pɛpərɪ) *adj* **1** flavoured with or tasting of pepper **2** quick-tempered; irritable **3** full of bite and sharpness: *a peppery speech* > **'pepperiness** *n*

pep pill *n informal* a tablet containing a stimulant drug

peppy ('pɛpɪ) *adj* -pier, -piest *informal* full of vitality; bouncy or energetic > **'peppily** *adv* > **'peppiness** *n*

pepsin *or* **pepsine** ('pɛpsɪn) *n* a proteolytic enzyme produced in the stomach in the inactive form pepsinogen, which, when activated by acid, splits proteins into peptones [C19 via German from Greek *pepsis,* from *peptein* to digest]

pepsinate ('pɛpsɪˌneɪt) *vb* (tr) **1** to treat (a patient) with pepsin **2** to mix or infuse (something) with pepsin

pepsinogen (pɛpˈsɪnədʒən) *n* the inactive precursor of pepsin produced by the stomach

pep talk *n informal* an enthusiastic talk designed to increase confidence, production, cooperation, etc

peptic ('pɛptɪk) *adj* **1** of, relating to, or promoting digestion **2** of, relating to, or caused by pepsin or the action of the digestive juices [C17 from Greek *peptikos* capable of digesting, from *pepsis* digestion, from *peptein* to digest]

peptic ulcer *n pathol* an ulcer of the mucous membrane lining those parts of the alimentary tract exposed to digestive juices. It can occur in the oesophagus, the stomach, the duodenum, the jejunum, or in parts of the ileum

peptidase ('pɛptɪˌdeɪs, -ˌdeɪz) *n* any of a group of proteolytic enzymes that hydrolyse peptides to amino acids

peptide ('pɛptaɪd) *n* any of a group of compounds consisting of two or more amino acids linked by chemical bonding between their respective carboxyl and amino groups. See also **peptide bond, polypeptide**

peptide bond *n biochem* a chemical amide linkage, –NH–CO–, formed by the condensation of the amino group of one amino acid with the carboxyl group of another

peptize *or* **peptise** ('pɛptaɪz) *vb* (tr) *chem* to disperse (a substance) into a colloidal state, usually to form a sol > **'peptizable** *or* **'peptisable** *adj* > **ˌpepti'zation** *or* **ˌpepti'sation** *n* > **'peptizer** *or* **'peptiser** *n*

peptone ('pɛptəʊn) *n biochem* any of a group of compounds that form an intermediary group in the digestion of proteins to amino acids. See also **proteose** [C19 from German *Pepton,* from Greek *pepton* something digested, from *peptein* to digest] > **peptonic** (pɛpˈtɒnɪk) *adj*

peptonize *or* **peptonise** ('pɛptəˌnaɪz) *vb* (tr) to hydrolyse (a protein) to peptones by enzymic action, esp by pepsin or pancreatic extract > ˌpeptoni'zation *or* ˌpeptoni'sation *n* > 'pepto,nizer *or* 'pepto,niser *n*

Péquiste (peɪˈkiːst) *n* (*sometimes not capital*) (in Canada) a member or supporter of the Parti Québécois [from the French pronunciation of PQ + -*iste*]

Pequot ('piːkwɒt) *n* **1** (*pl* -quot *or* -quots) a member of a North American Indian people formerly living in S New England **2** the language of this people, belonging to the Algonquian family [probably based on Narraganset *paquatanog* destroyers]

per (pɜː; *unstressed* pə) *determiner* **1** for every: *three pence per pound* ▷ *prep* **2** (esp in some Latin phrases) by; through **3 as per** according to: *as per specifications* **4 as per usual** *informal* as usual [C15 from Latin: by, for each]

PER (in Britain) *abbreviation for* Professional Employment Register

per- *prefix* **1** through: *pervade* **2** throughout: *perennial* **3** away, beyond: *perfidy* **4** completely, throughly: *perplex* **5** (intensifier): *perfervid* **6** indicating that a chemical compound contains a high proportion of a specified element: *peroxide; perchloride* **7** indicating that a chemical element is in a higher than usual state of oxidation: *permanganate; perchlorate* **8** (*not in technical usage*) a variant of **peroxy-** *persulphuric acid* [from Latin *per* through]

Pera ('pɪərə) *n* the former name of **Beyoğlu**

peracid (pɜːˈræsɪd) *n* **1** an acid, such as perchloric acid, in which the element forming the acid radical exhibits its highest valency **2** (*not in technical usage*) an acid, such as persulphuric acid, that contains the -OOH group. Recommended names: per'oxo acid, per'oxy acid > **peracidity** (ˌpɛrəˈsɪdɪtɪ) *n*

peradventure (ˌpɛrədˈvɛntʃə, ˌpɜːr-) *archaic* ▷ *adv* **1** by chance; perhaps ▷ *n* **2** chance, uncertainty, or doubt [C13 from Old French *par aventure* by chance]

Peraea *or* **Perea** (pəˈriːə) *n* a region of ancient Palestine, east of the River Jordan and the Dead Sea

Perak ('pɛərə, 'pɪərə, pɪˈræk) *n* a state of NW Peninsular Malaysia, on the Strait of Malacca: tin mining. Capital: Ipoh. Pop: 2 051 236 (2000). Area: 20 680 sq km (8030 sq miles)

perambulate (pəˈræmbjʊˌleɪt) *vb* **1** to walk about (a place) **2** (tr) to walk round in order to inspect [C16 from Latin *perambulāre* to traverse, from *per* through + *ambulāre* to walk] > **perˌambuˈlation** *n* > **perambulatory** (pəˈræmbjʊlətərɪ, -trɪ) *adj*

perambulator (pəˈræmbjʊˌleɪtə) *n* **1** a formal word for **pram¹ 2** a wheel-like instrument used by surveyors to measure distances

per annum (pər ˈænəm) *adv* every year or by the year

per ardua ad astra *Latin* (pɜːr ˈɑːdjʊə æd ˈæstrə) through difficulties to the stars: the motto of the RAF

P/E ratio *abbreviation for* price-earnings ratio

perborate (pəˈbɔːreɪt) *n* any of certain salts derived, or apparently derived, from perboric acid. Perborates are used as bleaches in washing powders. See **sodium perborate**

percale (pəˈkeɪl, -ˈkɑːl) *n* a close-textured woven cotton fabric, plain or printed, used esp for sheets [C17 via French from Persian *pargālah* piece of cloth]

percaline ('pɜːkəˌliːn, -lɪn) *n* a fine light cotton fabric, used esp for linings [C19 from French; see PERCALE]

per capita (pə ˈkæpɪtə) *adj, adv* of or for each person [Latin, literally: according to heads]

perceive (pəˈsiːv) *vb* **1** to become aware of (something) through the senses, esp the sight; recognize or observe **2** (tr; *may take a clause as object*) to come to comprehend; grasp [C13 from Old French *perçoivre,* from Latin *percipere* seize entirely, from PER- (thoroughly) + *capere* to grasp] > **per'ceivable** *adj* > **perˌceiva'bility** *n* > **per'ceivably** *adv* > **per'ceiver** *n*

perceived noise decibel *n* a unit for measuring perceived levels of noise by comparison with the sound pressure level of a reference sound judged equally noisy by a normal listener. Abbreviation: PNdB

per cent (pə ˈsɛnt) *adv* **1** Also: **per centum** in or for every hundred. Symbol: % ▷ *n also* **per'cent 2** a percentage or proportion **3** (*often plural*) securities yielding a rate of interest as specified: *he bought three percents* [C16 from Medieval Latin *per centum* out of every hundred]

percentage (pəˈsɛntɪdʒ) *n* **1** proportion or rate per hundred parts **2** *commerce* the interest, tax, commission, or allowance on a hundred items **3** any proportion in relation to the whole **4** *informal* profit or advantage

percentile (pəˈsɛntaɪl) *n* one of 99 actual or notional values of a variable dividing its

distribution into 100 groups with equal frequencies; the 90th percentile is the value of a variable such that 90% of the relevant population is below that value. Also called: **centile**

percept ('pɜːsɛpt) *n* **1** a concept that depends on recognition by the senses, such as sight, of some external object or phenomenon **2** an object or phenomenon that is perceived [C19 from Latin *perceptum,* from *percipere* to PERCEIVE]

perceptible (pəˈsɛptəbªl) *adj* able to be perceived; noticeable or recognizable > **perˌcepti'bility** *n* > **per'ceptibly** *adv*

perception (pəˈsɛpʃən) *n* **1** the act or the effect of perceiving **2** insight or intuition gained by perceiving **3** the ability or capacity to perceive **4** way of perceiving; awareness or consciousness; view: *advertising affects the customer's perception of a product* **5** the process by which an organism detects and interprets information from the external world by means of the sensory receptors **6** *law* the collection, receipt, or taking into possession of rents, crops, etc [C15 from Latin *perceptiō* comprehension; see PERCEIVE] > **per'ceptional** *adj*

perceptive (pəˈsɛptɪv) *adj* **1** quick at perceiving; observant **2** perceptual **3** able to perceive > **per'ceptively** *adv* > **per'ceptiveness** *or* ˌpercep'tivity *n*

perceptual (pəˈsɛptjʊəl) *adj* of or relating to perception > **per'ceptually** *adv*

perceptual defence *n psychol* the process by which it is thought that certain stimuli are either not perceived or are distorted due to their offensive, unpleasant, or threatening nature

perceptual mapping *n marketing* the use of a graph or map in the development of a new product, in which the proximity of consumers' images of the new product to those of an ideal product provide an indication of the new product's likely success

perch¹ (pɜːtʃ) *n* **1** a pole, branch, or other resting place above ground on which a bird roosts or alights **2** a similar resting place for a person or thing **3** another name for **rod** (sense 7) **4** a solid measure for stone, usually taken as 198 inches by 18 inches by 12 inches **5** a pole joining the front and rear axles of a carriage **6** a frame on which cloth is placed for inspection **7** *obsolete or dialect* a pole ▷ *vb* **8** (usually foll by *on*) to alight, rest, or cause to rest on or a perch: *the bird perched on the branch; the cap was perched on his head* **9** (tr) to inspect (cloth) on a perch [C13 *perche* stake, from Old French, from Latin *pertica* long staff] > 'percher *n*

perch² (pɜːtʃ) *n, pl* perch *or* perches **1** any freshwater spiny-finned teleost fish of the family *Percidae,* esp those of the genus *Perca,* such as P. *fluviatilis* of Europe and P. *flavescens* (**yellow perch**) of North America: valued as food and game fishes **2** any of various similar or related fishes. Related adj: **percoid** [C13 from Old French *perche,* from Latin *perca,* from Greek *perkē;* compare Greek *perkos* spotted]

perchance (pəˈtʃɑːns) *adv archaic or poetic* **1** perhaps; possibly **2** by chance; accidentally [C14 from Anglo-French *par chance;* see PER, CHANCE]

Percheron ('pɜːʃəˌrɒn) *n* a compact heavy breed of carthorse, grey or black in colour [C19 from French, from *le Perche,* region of NW France where the breed originated]

perchery ('pɜːtʃərɪ) *n, pl* -eries **a** a barn in which hens are allowed to move without restriction **b** (*as modifier*): *perchery eggs* [C20 from PERCH¹]

perchlorate (pəˈklɔːreɪt) *n* any salt or ester of perchloric acid. Perchlorate salts contain the ion ClO_4^-

perchloric acid (pəˈklɔːrɪk) *n* a colourless syrupy oxyacid of chlorine containing a greater proportion of oxygen than chloric acid. It is a powerful oxidizing agent and is used as a laboratory reagent. Formula: $HClO_4$. Systematic name: **chloric(VII) acid**

perchloride (pəˈklɔːraɪd) *n* a chloride that contains more chlorine than other chlorides of the same element

perchloroethylene (pəˌklɔːrəʊˈɛθɪliːn) *or* **perchloroethene** (pəˌklɔːrəʊˈɛθiːn) *n* a colourless liquid used as a dry-cleaning solvent. Formula: $CCl_2{:}CCl_2$

percipient (pəˈsɪpɪənt) *adj* 1 able to perceive 2 perceptive ▷ *n* 3 a person or thing that perceives [C17 from Latin *percipiens* observing, from *percipere* to grasp; see PERCEIVE] > per'cipience *n* > per'cipiently *adv*

Percival *or* **Perceval** ('pɜːsɪvəl) *n* (in Arthurian legend) a knight in King Arthur's court. German equivalent: **Parzival**

percoid ('pɜːkɔɪd) *or* **percoidean** (pɜːˈkɔɪdɪən) *adj* 1 of, relating to, or belonging to the *Percoidea*, a suborder of spiny-finned teleost fishes including the perches, sea bass, red mullet, cichlids, etc 2 of, relating to, or resembling a perch ▷ *n* 3 any fish belonging to the suborder *Percoidea* [C19 from Latin *perca* PERCH² + -OID]

percolate *vb* ('pɜːkəˌleɪt) 1 to cause (a liquid) to pass through a fine mesh, porous substance, etc, or (of a liquid) to pass through a fine mesh, porous substance, etc; trickle: *rain percolated through the roof* 2 to permeate; penetrate gradually: *water percolated the road* 3 (*intr*) *US informal* to become active or lively: *she percolated with happiness* 4 to make (coffee) or (of coffee) to be made in a percolator ▷ *n* ('pɜːkəlɪt, -ˌleɪt) 5 a product of percolation [C17 from Latin *percolāre*, from PER + *cōlāre* to strain, from *cōlum* a strainer; see COLANDER] > percolable ('pɜːkələbəl) *adj* > ˌperco'lation *n* > 'percolative *adj*

percolator ('pɜːkəˌleɪtə) *n* a kind of coffeepot in which boiling water is forced up through a tube and filters down through the coffee grounds into a container

per contra ('pɜː 'kɒntrə) *adv* on the contrary [from Latin]

percuss (pəˈkʌs) *vb* (*tr*) 1 to strike sharply, rapidly, or suddenly 2 *med* to tap on (a body surface) with the fingertips or a special hammer to aid diagnosis or for therapeutic purposes [C16 from Latin *percutere*, from *per-* through + *quatere* to shake] > per'cussor *n*

percussion (pəˈkʌʃən) *n* 1 the act, an instance, or an effect of percussing 2 *music* the family of instruments in which sound arises from the striking of materials with sticks, hammers, or the hands 3 *music* **a** instruments of this family constituting a section of an orchestra, band, etc **b** (*as modifier*): *a percussion ensemble* 4 *med* the act of percussing a body surface 5 the act of exploding a percussion cap [C16 from Latin *percussiō*, from *percutere* to hit; see PERCUSS]

percussion cap *n* a detonator consisting of a paper or thin metal cap containing material that explodes when struck and formerly used in certain firearms

percussion instrument *n* any of various musical instruments that produce a sound when their resonating surfaces are struck directly, as with a stick or mallet, or by leverage action. They may be of definite pitch (as a kettledrum or xylophone), indefinite pitch (as a gong or rattle), or a mixture of both (as various drums)

percussionist (pəˈkʌʃənɪst) *n music* a person who plays any of several percussion instruments, esp in an orchestra

percussion lock *n* a gunlock in which the hammer strikes a percussion cap

percussion tool *n* a power driven tool which operates by striking rapid blows: the power may be electricity or compressed air

percussive (pəˈkʌsɪv) *adj* of, caused by, or relating to percussion > per'cussively *adv* > per'cussiveness *n*

percutaneous (ˌpɜːkjuːˈteɪnɪəs) *adj med* effected through the skin, as in the absorption of an ointment

Perdido (*Spanish* perˈðiðo) *n* **Monte** ('monte). a mountain in NE Spain, in the central Pyrenees. Height: 3352 m (10 997 ft). French name: (Mont) **Perdu**

per diem ('pɜː 'daɪɛm, 'diːɛm) *adv* 1 every day or by the day ▷ *n* 2 **a** an allowance for daily expenses, usually those incurred while working **b** (*as modifier*): *a per-diem allowance* [from Latin]

perdition (pəˈdɪʃən) *n* 1 *Christianity* **a** final and irrevocable spiritual ruin **b** this state as one that the wicked are said to be destined to endure for ever 2 another word for **hell** 3 *archaic* utter disaster, ruin, or destruction [C14 from Late Latin *perditiō* ruin, from Latin *perdere* to lose, from PER- (away) + *dāre* to give]

perdu *or* **perdue** ('pɜːdjuː) *adj* 1 *obsolete* (of a soldier) placed on hazardous sentry duty 2 *obsolete* (of a soldier) placed in a hazardous ambush 3 (of a person or thing) hidden or concealed ▷ *n* 4 *obsolete* a soldier placed on hazardous sentry duty 5 *obsolete* a soldier placed in a hazardous ambush [C16 via French: lost, from *perdre* to lose, from Latin *perdere* to destroy]

Perdu (pɛrdy) *n* **Mont** the French name for (Monte) **Perdido**

perdurable (pəˈdjʊərəbəl) *adj rare* extremely durable [C13 from Late Latin *perdūrābilis*, from Latin *per-* (intensive) + *dūrābilis* long-lasting, from *dūrus* hard] > ˌperdura'bility *n* > 'perdurably *adv*

père *French* (pɛr; *English* pɛə) *n* an addition to a French surname to specify the father rather than the son of the same name: *Dumas père*. Compare **fils¹**

Perea (pəˈriːə) *n* a variant spelling of **Peraea**

Père David's deer *n* a large grey deer, *Elaphurus davidianus*, surviving only in captivity as descendants of a herd preserved in the Imperial hunting park near Beijing [C20 named after Father A. *David* (died 1900), French missionary]

peregrinate ('pɛrɪɡrɪˌneɪt) *vb* 1 (*intr*) to travel or wander about from place to place; voyage 2 (*tr*) to travel through (a place) ▷ *adj* 3 an obsolete word for **foreign** [C16 from Latin, from *peregrīnārī* to travel; see PEREGRINE] > 'peregriˌnator *n*

peregrination (ˌpɛrɪɡrɪˈneɪʃən) *n* 1 a voyage, esp an extensive one 2 the act or process of travelling

peregrine ('pɛrɪɡrɪn) *adj archaic* 1 coming from abroad 2 travelling or migratory; wandering [C14 from Latin *peregrīnus* foreign, from *pereger* being abroad, from *per* through + *ager* land (that is, beyond one's own land)]

peregrine falcon *n* a falcon, *Falco peregrinus*, occurring in most parts of the world, having a dark plumage on the back and wings and lighter underparts. See also **duck hawk**

Pereira (*Spanish* peˈrɛira) *n* a town in W central Colombia: cattle trading and coffee processing. Pop: 656 000 (2005 est)

pereira bark (pəˈrɛərə) *n* the bark of a South American apocynaceous tree, *Geissospermum vellosii*: source of a substance formerly used for treating malaria [named after Jonathan *Pereira* (1804–53), English pharmacologist]

peremptory (pəˈrɛmptəri) *adj* 1 urgent or commanding: *a peremptory ring on the bell* 2 not able to be remitted or debated; decisive 3 positive or assured in speech, manner, etc; dogmatic 4 *law* **a** admitting of no denial or contradiction; precluding debate **b** obligatory rather than permissive [C16 from Anglo-Norman *peremptorie*, from Latin *peremptōrius* decisive, from *perimere* to take away completely, from PER- (intensive) + *emere* to take] > per'emptorily *adv* > per'emptoriness *n*

Perendale ('pɛrənˌdeɪl) *n* NZ a Romney-Cheviot crossbreed of sheep [C20 named after Sir Geoffrey S. *Peren*, New Zealand agriculturist]

perennate ('pɛrɪˌneɪt, pəˈrɛneɪt) *vb* (*intr*) (of plants) to live from one growing season to another, usually with a period of reduced activity between seasons [C17 from Latin *perennātus*, from *perennāre*, from PER- (through) + *annus* year]

perennial (pəˈrɛnɪəl) *adj* 1 lasting throughout the year or through many years 2 everlasting; perpetual ▷ *n* 3 a woody or herbaceous plant that can continue its growth for at least two years. Compare **annual** (sense 3), **biennial** (sense 3) [C17 from Latin *perennis* continual, from *per* through + *annus* year] > per'ennially *adv*

perentie *or* **perenty** (pəˈrɛntɪ) *n, pl* -ties a large dark-coloured monitor lizard, *Varanus giganteus*, of central and west Australia which grows to 7 ft [from a native Australian language]

perestroika (ˌpɛrəˈstrɔɪkə) *n* the policy of reconstructing the economy, etc, of the former Soviet Union under the leadership of Mikhail Gorbachov [C20 Russian, literally: reconstruction]

perf. *abbreviation for* 1 perfect 2 perforated 3 perforation

perfect *adj* ('pɜːfɪkt) 1 having all essential elements 2 unblemished; faultless: *a perfect gemstone* 3 correct or precise: *perfect timing* 4 utter or absolute: *a perfect stranger* 5 excellent in all respects: *a perfect day* 6 *maths* exactly divisible into equal integral or polynomial roots: *36 is a perfect square* 7 *botany* **a** (of flowers) having functional stamens and pistils **b** (of plants) having all parts present 8 *grammar* denoting a tense of verbs used in describing an action that has been completed by the subject. In English this is a compound tense, formed with *have* or *has* plus the past participle 9 *music* **a** of or relating to the intervals of the unison, fourth, fifth, and octave **b** (of a cadence) ending on the tonic chord, giving a feeling of conclusion. Also: **full, final** Compare **imperfect** (sense 6) 10 *archaic* positive certain, or assured ▷ *n* ('pɜːfɪkt) 11 *grammar* **a** the perfect tense **b** a verb in this tense ▷ *vb* (pəˈfɛkt) (*tr*) 12 to make perfect; improve to one's satisfaction: *he is in Paris to perfect his French* 13 to make fully accomplished 14 *printing* to print the reverse side of (a printed sheet of paper) [C13 from Latin *perfectus*, from *perficere* to perform, from *per* through + *facere* to do] > 'perfectness *n*

USAGE For most of its meanings, the adjective *perfect* describes an absolute state, i.e. one that cannot be qualified; thus something is either *perfect* or *not perfect*, and cannot be *more perfect* or *less perfect*. However when *perfect* means excellent in all respects, a comparative can be used with it without absurdity: *the next day the weather was even more perfect*

perfect binding *n* See **adhesive binding**

perfect competition *n economics* a market situation in which there exists a homogeneous product, freedom of entry, and a large number of buyers and sellers none of whom individually can affect price

perfect game *n* 1 *baseball* a game in which no batter on the opposing team reaches first base 2 *tenpin bowling* a game in which a bowler scores twelve consecutive strikes

perfect gas *n* another name for **ideal gas**

perfectible (pəˈfɛktəbəl) *adj* capable of becoming or being made perfect > perˌfecti'bility *n*

perfection (pəˈfɛkʃən) *n* 1 the act of perfecting or the state or quality of being perfect 2 the highest degree of a quality, etc: *the perfection of faithfulness* 3 an embodiment of perfection [C13 from Latin *perfectiō* a completing, from *perficere* to finish]

perfectionism (pəˈfɛkʃəˌnɪzəm) *n* 1 *philosophy* the doctrine that man can attain perfection in this life 2 the demand for the highest standard of excellence

perfectionist (pəˈfɛkʃənɪst) *n* 1 a person who strives for or demands the highest standards of excellence in work, etc 2 a person who believes the doctrine of perfectionism ▷ *adj* 3 of or relating to perfectionism

perfective (pəˈfɛktɪv) *adj* 1 tending to perfect 2 *grammar* denoting an aspect of verbs in some languages, including English, used to express

p

that the action or event described by the verb is or was completed: *I lived in London for ten years* is perfective; *I have lived in London for ten years* is imperfective, since the implication is that I still live in London

perfectly ('pɜːfɪktlɪ) *adv* **1** completely, utterly, or absolutely **2** in a perfect way; extremely well

perfect number *n* an integer, such as 28, that is equal to the sum of all its possible factors, excluding itself

perfecto (pə'fɛktəʊ) *n, pl* **-tos** a large cigar that is tapered from both ends [Spanish, literally: perfect]

perfector or **perfecter** ('pɜːfɪktə) *n* **1** a person who completes or makes something perfect **2** *printing* a machine or press capable of printing both sides of the paper in a single operation

perfect participle *n* another name for **past participle**

perfect pitch *n* another name (not in technical usage) for **absolute pitch** (sense 1)

perfect rhyme *n* **1** Also called: **full rhyme** rhyme between words in which the stressed vowels and any succeeding consonants are identical although the consonants preceding the stressed vowels may be different, as between *part/hart* or *believe/conceive* **2** a rhyme between two words that are pronounced the same although differing in meaning, as in *bough/bow*

perfervid (pɜː'fɜːvɪd) *adj literary* extremely ardent, enthusiastic, or zealous [C19 from New Latin *perfervidus*, from Latin *per-* (intensive) + *fervidus* FERVID] > **per'fervidly** *adv* > **per'fervidness** *n*

perfidious (pə'fɪdɪəs) *adj* guilty, treacherous, or faithless; deceitful > **per'fidiously** *adv* > **per'fidiousness** *n*

perfidy ('pɜːfɪdɪ) *n, pl* **-dies** a perfidious act [C16 from Latin *perfidia*, from *perfidus* faithless, from *per* beyond + *fidēs* faith]

perfin ('pɜːfɪn) *n philately* the former name for **spif** [from *perf(orated with) in(itials)*]

perfing ('pɜːfɪŋ) *n NZ* the practice of taking early retirement, with financial compensation, from the police force [from *P(olice) E(arly) R(etirement) F(und)*]

perfoliate (pə'fəʊlɪɪt, -ˌeɪt) *adj* (of a leaf) having a base that completely encloses the stem, so that the stem appears to pass through it [C17 from New Latin *perfoliātus*, from Latin *per-* through + *folium* leaf] > **per,foli'ation** *n*

perforate *vb* ('pɜːfəˌreɪt) **1** to make a hole or holes in (something); penetrate **2** (*tr*) to punch rows of holes between (stamps, coupons, etc) for ease of separation ▷ *adj* ('pɜːfərɪt) **3** *biology* **a** pierced by small holes: *perforate shells* **b** marked with small transparent spots **4** *philately* another word for **perforated** (sense 2) [C16 from Latin *perforāre*, from *per-* through + *forāre* to pierce] > **perforable** ('pɜːfərəbᵊl) *adj* > '**perforative** or '**perforatory** *adj* > '**perfoˌrator** *n*

perforated ('pɜːfəˌreɪtɪd) *adj* **1** pierced with one or more holes **2** (esp of stamps) having perforations. Abbreviation: **perf**

perforated tape *n* a US name for **paper tape**

perforation (ˌpɜːfə'reɪʃən) *n* **1** the act of perforating or the state of being perforated **2** a hole or holes made in something **3 a** a method of making individual stamps, coupons, etc, easily separable by punching holes along their margins **b** the holes punched in this way. Abbreviation: **perf**

perforation gauge *n* a graduated scale for measuring perforations and roulettes of postage stamps

perforce (pə'fɔːs) *adv* by necessity; unavoidably [C14 from Old French *par force*; see PER, FORCE¹]

perform (pə'fɔːm) *vb* **1** to carry out or do (an action) **2** (*tr*) to fulfil or comply with: *to perform someone's request* **3** to present or enact (a play, concert, etc) before or otherwise entertain an audience: *the group performed Hamlet* **4** (*intr*) *informal* to accomplish sexual intercourse: *he performed well*

[C14 from Anglo-Norman *perfourmer* (influenced by *forme* FORM), from Old French *parfournir*, from *par-* PER- + *fournir* to provide; see FURNISH] > **per'formable** *adj* > **per'former** *n*

performance (pə'fɔːməns) *n* **1** the act, process, or art of performing **2** an artistic or dramatic production: *last night's performance was terrible* **3** manner or quality of functioning: *a machine's performance* **4** *informal* mode of conduct or behaviour, esp when distasteful or irregular: *what did you mean by that performance at the restaurant?* **5** *informal* any tiresome procedure: *what a performance dressing the children to play in the snow!* **6** any accomplishment **7** *linguistics* (in transformational grammar) the form of the human language faculty, viewed as concretely embodied in speakers. Compare **competence** (sense 5), **langue**, **parole** (sense 5)

performance appraisal *n* the assessment, at regular intervals, of an employee's performance at work

performance art *n* a theatrical presentation that incorporates various art forms, such as dance, sculpture, music, etc

performance bond *n* a bond given by a bank to a third party guaranteeing that if a specified customer fails to fulfil all the terms of a specified contract, the bank will be responsible for any loss sustained by the third party

performance indicator *n* a quantitative or qualitative measurement, or any other criterion, by which the performance, efficiency, achievement, etc of a person or organization can be assessed, often by comparison with an agreed standard or target

performance test *n psychol* a test designed to assess a person's manual ability

performative (pə'fɔːmətɪv) *adj linguistics, philosophy* **1 a** denoting an utterance that constitutes some act, esp the act described by the verb. For example, *I confess that I was there* is itself a confession, and so is performative in the narrower sense, while *I'd like you to meet ...* (effecting an introduction) is performative only in the looser sense. See also **locutionary act, illocution, perlocution b** (*as noun*): *that sentence is a performative* **2 a** denoting a verb that may be used as the main verb in such an utterance **b** (*as noun*): *"promise" is a performative* > **per'formatively** *adv*

performing (pə'fɔːmɪŋ) *adj* (of an animal) trained to perform tricks before an audience, as in a circus

performing arts *pl n* the arts that are primarily performed before an audience, such as dance and drama

perfume *n* ('pɜːfjuːm) **1** a mixture of alcohol and fragrant essential oils extracted from flowers, spices, etc, or made synthetically, used esp to impart a pleasant long-lasting scent to the body, stationery, etc. See also **cologne, toilet water 2** a scent or odour, esp a fragrant one ▷ *vb* (pə'fjuːm) **3** (*tr*) to impart a perfume to [C16 from French *parfum*, probably from Old Provençal *perfum*, from *perfumar* to make scented, from *per* through (from Latin) + *fumar* to smoke, from Latin *fumāre* to smoke]

perfumer (pə'fjuːmə) or **perfumier** (pə'fjuːmjeɪ) *n* a person who makes or sells perfume

perfumery (pə'fjuːmərɪ) *n, pl* **-eries 1** a place where perfumes are sold **2** a factory where perfumes are made **3** the process of making perfumes **4** perfumes in general

perfunctory (pə'fʌŋktərɪ) *adj* **1** done superficially, only as a matter of routine; careless or cursory **2** dull or indifferent [C16 from Late Latin *perfunctōrius* negligent, from *perfunctus* dispatched, from *perfungī* to fulfil; see FUNCTION] > **per'functorily** *adv* > **per'functoriness** *n*

perfuse (pə'fjuːz) *vb* (*tr*) **1** to suffuse or permeate (a liquid, colour, etc) through or over (something) **2** *surgery* to pass (a fluid) through organ tissue to ensure adequate exchange of oxygen and carbon monoxide [C16 from Latin *perfūsus* wetted, from

perfundere to pour over, from PER- + *fundere* to pour] > **per'fusion** *n* > **per'fusionist** *n* > **per'fusive** *adj* > **per'fused** *adj*

Pergamum ('pɜːgəməm) *n* an ancient city in NW Asia Minor, in Mysia: capital of a major Hellenistic monarchy of the same name that later became a Roman province

pergola ('pɜːgələ) *n* a horizontal trellis or framework, supported on posts, that carries climbing plants and may form a covered walk [C17 via Italian from Latin *pergula* projection from a roof, from *pergere* to go forward]

perhaps (pə'hæps; *informal* præps) *adv* **1 a** possibly; maybe **b** (*as sentence modifier*): *he'll arrive tomorrow, perhaps; perhaps you'll see him tomorrow* ▷ *sentence substitute* **2** it may happen, be so, etc; maybe [C16 *perhappes*, from *per* by + *happes* chance, HAP¹]

peri ('pɪərɪ) *n, pl* **-ris 1** (in Persian folklore) one of a race of beautiful supernatural beings **2** any beautiful fairy-like creature [C18 from Persian: fairy, from Avestan *pairikā* witch]

peri- *prefix* **1** enclosing, encircling, or around: *pericardium; pericarp; perigon* **2** near or adjacent: *perihelion* [from Greek *peri* around, near, about]

perianth ('pɛrɪˌænθ) *n* the outer part of a flower, consisting of the calyx and corolla [C18 from French *périanthe*, from New Latin, from PERI- + Greek *anthos* flower]

periapt ('pɛrɪˌæpt) *n rare* a charm or amulet [C16 via French from Greek *periapton*, from PERI- + *haptos* clasped, from *haptein* to fasten]

periastron (ˌpɛrɪ'æstrɒn) *n astronomy* the point in the orbit of a body around a star when it is nearest to the star, esp applied to double-star systems

periblem ('pɛrɪˌblɛm) *n botany* a layer of meristematic tissue in stems and roots that gives rise to the cortex [C19 via German from Greek *periblēma* protection, from *periballein* to throw around, from PERI- + *ballein* to throw]

pericarditis (ˌpɛrɪkɑː'daɪtɪs) *n* inflammation of the pericardium > **pericarditic** (ˌpɛrɪkɑː'dɪtɪk) *adj*

pericardium (ˌpɛrɪ'kɑːdɪəm) *n, pl* **-dia** (-dɪə) the membranous sac enclosing the heart [C16 via New Latin from Greek *perikardion*, from PERI- + *kardia* heart] > ˌ**peri'cardial** or ˌ**peri'cardiˌac** *adj*

pericarp ('pɛrɪˌkɑːp) *n* **1** the part of a fruit enclosing the seeds that develops from the wall of the ovary **2** a layer of tissue around the reproductive bodies of some algae and fungi [C18 via French from New Latin *pericarpium*] > ˌ**peri'carpial** or ˌ**peri'carpic** *adj*

pericentre or US **pericenter** ('pɛrɪˌsɛntə) *n* the point in an elliptical orbit that is nearest to the centre of mass of the system

perichaetial (ˌpɛrɪ'kiːtɪəl) *adj* denoting the leaves in mosses that surround the archegonia and, later, the base of the sporophyte

perichondrium (ˌpɛrɪ'kɒndrɪəm) *n, pl* **-dria** (-drɪə) the white fibrous membrane that covers the surface of cartilage [C18 New Latin, from PERI- + Greek *chondros* cartilage] > ˌ**peri'chondrial** *adj*

periclase ('pɛrɪˌkleɪs) *n* a mineral consisting of magnesium oxide in the form of isometric crystals or grains: occurs in metamorphosed limestone [C19 from New Latin *periclasia*, from Greek *peri* very + *klasis* a breaking, referring to its perfect cleavage] > **periclastic** (ˌpɛrɪ'klæstɪk) *adj*

Periclean (ˌpɛrɪ'kliːən) *adj* of or relating to Pericles (?495–429 BC), the Athenian statesman, or to the period when Athens was the intellectual and artistic leader of the Greek city-states

periclinal (ˌpɛrɪ'klaɪnᵊl) *adj* **1** of or relating to a pericline **2** *botany* **a** denoting or relating to cell walls that are parallel to the surface of a plant part, such as a meristem **b** (of chimeras) having one component completely enclosed by the other component

pericline ('pɛrɪˌklaɪn) *n* **1** a white translucent variety of albite in the form of elongated crystals **2** Also called: **dome** a dome-shaped formation of stratified rock with its slopes following the direction of folding [C19 from Greek *periklinēs* sloping on all sides, from PERI- + *klinein* to lean]

pericope (pəˈrɪkəpɪ) *n* a selection from a book, esp a passage from the Bible read at religious services [C17 via Late Latin from Greek *perikopē* piece cut out, from PERI- + *kopē* a cutting] > **pericopic** (ˌpɛrɪˈkɒpɪk) *adj*

pericranium (ˌpɛrɪˈkreɪnɪəm) *n*, *pl* **-nia** (-nɪə) the fibrous membrane covering the external surface of the skull [C16 New Latin, from Greek *perikranion*] > ˌperiˈcranial *adj*

pericycle (ˈpɛrɪˌsaɪkəl) *n* a layer of plant tissue beneath the endodermis: surrounds the conducting tissue in roots and certain stems [C19 from Greek *perikuklos*] > **pericyclic** (ˌpɛrɪˈsaɪklɪk, -ˈsɪk-) *adj*

pericynthion (ˌpɛrɪˈsɪnθɪən) *n* the point at which a spacecraft launched from earth into a lunar orbit is nearest the moon. Compare **perilune, apocynthion** [C20 from PERI- + *-cynthion*, from CYNTHIA]

periderm (ˈpɛrɪˌdɜːm) *n* the outer corky protective layer of woody stems and roots, consisting of cork cambium, phelloderm and cork [C19 from New Latin *peridermis*] > ˌperiˈdermal *or* ˌperiˈdermic *adj*

peridium (pəˈrɪdɪəm) *n*, *pl* **-ridia** (-ˈrɪdɪə) the distinct outer layer of the spore-bearing organ in many fungi [C19 from Greek *pēridion* a little wallet, from *pēra* leather bag, of obscure origin]

peridot (ˈpɛrɪˌdɒt) *n* a pale green transparent variety of the olivine chrysolite, used as a gemstone [C14 from Old French *peritot*, of unknown origin]

peridotite (ˌpɛrɪˈdəʊtaɪt) *n* a dark coarse-grained ultrabasic plutonic igneous rock consisting principally of olivine [C19 from French, from PERIDOT] > **peridotitic** (ˌpɛrɪdəʊˈtɪtɪk) *adj*

perigee (ˈpɛrɪˌdʒiː) *n* the point in its orbit around the earth when the moon or an artificial satellite is nearest the earth. Compare **apogee** (sense 1) [C16 via French from Greek *perigeion*, from PERI- + *gea* earth] > ˌperiˈgean *or* ˌperiˈgeal *adj*

periglacial (ˌpɛrɪˈgleɪʃəl) *adj* relating to a region bordering a glacier: *periglacial climate*

perigon (ˈpɛrɪgɒn) *n* an angle of 360°. Also called: **round angle** [C19 from PERI- + Greek *gonia* angle]

Perigordian (ˌpɛrɪˈgɔːdɪən) *adj* 1 of, relating to, or characteristic of an Upper Palaeolithic culture in Europe, esp in France ▷ *n* 2 **the** the Perigordian culture [C20 after *Périgord*, district in France]

Périgueux (ˌpɛrɪˈgɜː; French perigø) *n* a town in SW France, capital of the Dordogne: noted for its Roman remains, medieval cathedral, and pâté de foie gras. Pop: 30 193 (1999)

perigynous (pəˈrɪdʒɪnəs) *adj* 1 (of a flower) having a concave or flat receptacle with the gynoecium and other floral parts at the same level, as in the rose 2 of or relating to the parts of a flower arranged in this way [C19 from New Latin *perigynus*; see PERI-, -GYNOUS] > peˈrigyny *n*

perihelion (ˌpɛrɪˈhiːlɪən) *n*, *pl* **-lia** (-lɪə) the point in its orbit when a planet or comet is nearest the sun. Compare **aphelion** [C17 from New Latin *perihēlium*, from PERI- + Greek *hēlios* sun]

peril (ˈpɛrɪl) *n* exposure to risk or harm; danger or jeopardy [C13 via Old French from Latin *perīculum*]

perilous (ˈpɛrɪləs) *adj* very hazardous or dangerous: *a perilous journey* > ˈperilously *adv* > ˈperilousness *n*

perilune (ˈpɛrɪˌluːn) *n* the point in a lunar orbit when a spacecraft launched from the moon is nearest the moon. Compare **apolune, pericynthion** [C20 from PERI- + *-lune*, from Latin *lūna* moon]

perilymph (ˈpɛrɪˌlɪmf) *n* the fluid filling the space between the membranous and bony labyrinths of the internal ear

perimenopause (ˌpɛrɪˈmɛnəʊˌpɔːz) *n* the period leading up to the menopause during which some of the symptoms associated with menopause may be experienced > ˌperiˌmenoˈpausal *adj*

perimeter (pəˈrɪmɪtə) *n* 1 *maths* **a** the curve or line enclosing a plane area **b** the length of this curve or line 2 **a** any boundary around something, such as a field **b** (as modifier): *a perimeter fence; a perimeter patrol* 3 a medical instrument for measuring the limits of the field of vision [C16 from French *périmètre*, from Latin *perimetros*; see PERI-, -METER] > **perimetric** (ˌpɛrɪˈmɛtrɪk) *or* ˌperiˈmetrical *adj* > ˌperiˈmetrically *adv* > peˈrimetry *n*

perimorph (ˈpɛrɪˌmɔːf) *n* a mineral that encloses another mineral of a different type > ˌperiˈmorphic *or* ˌperiˈmorphous *adj* > ˌperiˈmorphism *n*

perimysium (ˌpɛrɪˈmɪzɪəm) *n*, *pl* **-ia** (-ɪə) *anatomy* the sheath of fibrous connective tissue surrounding the primary bundles of muscle fibres [C19 from PERI- + *-mysium*, from Greek *mus* muscle]

perinatal (ˌpɛrɪˈneɪtəl) *adj* of, relating to, or occurring in the period from about three months before to one month after birth

perineal gland *n* *zoology* one of a pair of glands that are situated near the anus in some mammals and secrete an odorous substance

perinephrium (ˌpɛrɪˈnɛfrɪəm) *n*, *pl* **-ria** (-rɪə) *anatomy* the fatty and connective tissue surrounding the kidney [C19 from PERI- + *-nephrium*, from Greek *nephros* kidney] > ˌperiˈnephric *adj*

perineum (ˌpɛrɪˈniːəm) *n*, *pl* **-nea** (-ˈniːə) 1 the region of the body between the anus and the genital organs, including some of the underlying structures 2 the nearly diamond-shaped surface of the human trunk between the thighs [C17 from New Latin, from Greek *perinaion*, from PERI- + *inein* to empty out] > ˌperiˈneal *adj*

perineuritis (ˌpɛrɪnjʊˈraɪtɪs) *n* inflammation of the perineurium > **perineuritic** (ˌpɛrɪnjʊˈrɪtɪk) *adj*

perineurium (ˌpɛrɪˈnjʊərɪəm) *n* the connective tissue forming a sheath around a single bundle of nerve fibres [C19 from New Latin, from PERI- + Greek *neuron* nerve] > ˌperiˈneurial *adj*

period (ˈpɪərɪəd) *n* 1 1 a portion of time of indefinable length: *he spent a period away from home* 2 **a** a portion of time specified in some way: *the Arthurian period; Picasso's blue period* **b** (as modifier): *period costume* 3 a nontechnical name for an occurrence of menstruation 4 *geology* a unit of geological time during which a system of rocks is formed: *the Jurassic period* 5 a division of time, esp of the academic day 6 *physics, maths* **a** the time taken to complete one cycle of a regularly recurring phenomenon; the reciprocal of frequency. Symbol: *T* **b** an interval in which the values of a periodic function follow a certain pattern that is duplicated over successive intervals: $\sin x = \sin (x + 2\pi)$, *where 2π is the period* 7 *astronomy* **a** the time required by a body to make one complete rotation on its axis **b** the time interval between two successive maxima or minima of light variation of a variable star 8 *chem* one of the horizontal rows of elements in the periodic table. Each period starts with an alkali metal and ends with a rare gas. Compare **group** (sense 11) 9 the punctuation mark (.) used at the end of a sentence that is not a question or exclamation, after abbreviations, etc. Also called: **full stop** 10 a complete sentence, esp a complex one with several clauses 11 *music* a passage or division of a piece of music, usually consisting of two or more contrasting or complementary musical phrases and ending on a cadence. Also called: **sentence** 12 (in classical prosody) a unit consisting of two or more cola 13 *rare* a completion or end [C14 *peryod*, from Latin *periodus*, from Greek *periodos* circuit, from PERI- + *hodos* way]

periodate (pɜːˈraɪəˌdeɪt) *n* any salt or ester of a periodic acid

period drama *n* a drama set in a particular historical period

periodic (ˌpɪərɪˈɒdɪk) *adj* 1 happening or recurring at intervals; intermittent 2 of, relating to, or resembling a period 3 having or occurring in repeated periods or cycles > ˌperiˈodically *adv* > **periodicity** (ˌpɪərɪəˈdɪsɪtɪ) *n*

periodic acid (ˌpɜːraɪˈɒdɪk) *n* any of various oxyacids of iodine containing a greater proportion of oxygen than iodic acid and differing from each other in water content, esp either of the crystalline compounds HIO_4 (**metaperiodic acid**) and H_5IO_6 (**paraperiodic acid**) [C19 from PER- + IODIC]

periodical (ˌpɪərɪˈɒdɪkəl) *n* 1 a publication issued at regular intervals, usually monthly or weekly ▷ *adj* 2 of or relating to such publications 3 published at regular intervals 4 periodic or occasional

periodic function (ˌpɪərɪˈɒdɪk) *n* *maths* a function, such as sin *x*, whose value is repeated at constant intervals

periodic law (ˌpɪərɪˈɒdɪk) *n* the principle that the chemical properties of the elements are periodic functions of their atomic weights (also called: **Mendeleev's law**) or, more accurately, of their atomic numbers

periodic sentence (ˌpɪərɪˈɒdɪk) *n* *rhetoric* a sentence in which the completion of the main clause is left to the end, thus creating an effect of suspense

periodic system (ˌpɪərɪˈɒdɪk) *n* the classification of the elements based on the periodic law

periodic table (ˌpɪərɪˈɒdɪk) *n* a table of the elements, arranged in order of increasing atomic number, based on the periodic law. Elements having similar chemical properties and electronic structures appear in vertical columns (groups)

periodic tenancy *n* *social welfare* the letting of a dwelling for a repeated short term, as by the week, month, or quarter, with no end date

periodization *or* **periodisation** (ˌpɪərɪədaɪˈzeɪʃən) *n* the act or process of dividing history into periods

period of revolution *n* *astronomy* the mean time taken for one body, such as a planet, to complete a revolution about another, such as the sun

periodontal (ˌpɛrɪəˈdɒntəl) *adj* of, denoting, or affecting the gums and other tissues surrounding the teeth: *periodontal disease*

periodontics (ˌpɛrɪəˈdɒntɪks) *n* (functioning as singular) the branch of dentistry concerned with diseases affecting the tissues and structures that surround teeth. Also called: **periodontology** [C19 from PERI- + *-odontics*, from Greek *odōn* tooth] > ˌperioˈdontic *adj* > ˌperioˈdontically *adv*

period piece *n* an object, a piece of music, a play, etc, valued for its quality of evoking a particular historical period: often one regarded as of little except historical interest

perionychium (ˌpɛrɪəˈnɪkɪəm) *n*, *pl* **-ia** (-ɪə) the skin that surrounds a fingernail or toenail [C19 New Latin, from Greek *onux* a nail]

periosteum (ˌpɛrɪˈɒstɪəm) *n*, *pl* **-tea** (-tɪə) a thick fibrous two-layered membrane covering the surface of bones [C16 New Latin, from Greek *periosteon*, from PERI- + *osteon* bone] > ˌperiˈosteal *adj*

periostitis (ˌpɛrɪɒˈstaɪtɪs) *n* inflammation of the periosteum > **periostitic** (ˌpɛrɪɒˈstɪtɪk) *adj*

periotic (ˌpɛrɪˈəʊtɪk, -ˈɒtɪk) *adj* 1 of or relating to the structures situated around the internal ear 2 situated around the ear [C19 from PERI- + *-otic*, from Greek *ous* ear]

peripatetic (ˌpɛrɪpəˈtɛtɪk) *adj* 1 itinerant 2 *Brit* employed in two or more educational establishments and travelling from one to another: *a peripatetic football coach* ▷ *n* 3 a peripatetic person [C16 from Latin *peripatēticus*, from Greek *peripatētikos*, from *peripatein* to pace to and fro] > ˌperipaˈtetically *adv*

Peripatetic (ˌpɛrɪpəˈtɛtɪk) *adj* 1 of or relating to the teachings of the Greek philosopher Aristotle (384–322 BC), who used to teach philosophy while walking about the Lyceum in ancient Athens ▷ *n* 2 a student of Aristotelianism

peripatus (pəˈrɪpətəs) *n* any of a genus of wormlike arthropods having a segmented body and short unjointed limbs: belonging to the phylum *Onychophora* [from New Latin, from Greek *peripatos* a pacing about; see PERIPATETIC]

peripeteia, peripetia (ˌpɛrɪpɪˈtaɪə, -ˈtɪə) or **peripety** (pəˈrɪpɪtɪ) *n* (esp in drama) an abrupt turn of events or reversal of circumstances [C16 from Greek, from PERI- + *piptein* to fall (to change suddenly, literally: to fall around)] > ˌperipeˈteian or ˌperipeˈtian *adj*

peripheral (pəˈrɪfərəl) *adj* **1** not relating to the most important part of something; incidental, minor, or superficial **2** of, relating to, or of the nature of a periphery **3** *anatomy* of, relating to, or situated near the surface of the body: *a peripheral nerve* > peˈripherally *adv*

peripheral device or **unit** *n computing* any device, such as a disk, printer, modem, or screen, concerned with input/output, storage, etc. Often shortened to: **peripheral**

periphery (pəˈrɪfərɪ) *n, pl* -eries **1** the outermost boundary of an area **2** the outside surface of something **3** *anatomy* the surface or outermost part of the body or one of its organs or parts [C16 from Late Latin *peripherīa*, from Greek, from PERI- + *pherein* to bear]

periphrasis (pəˈrɪfrəsɪs) *n, pl* -rases (-rəˌsiːz) **1** a roundabout way of expressing something; circumlocution **2** an expression of this kind [C16 via Latin from Greek, from PERI- + *phrazein* to declare]

periphrastic (ˌpɛrɪˈfræstɪk) *adj* **1** employing or involving periphrasis **2** expressed in two or more words rather than by an inflected form of one: used esp of a tense of a verb where the alternative element is an auxiliary verb. For example, *He does go* and *He will go* involve periphrastic tenses > ˌperiˈphrastically *adv*

periphyton (pəˈrɪfɪˌtɒn) *n* aquatic organisms, such as certain algae, that live attached to rocks or other surfaces [C20 from Greek, from PERI- + *phutos*, from *phuein* to grow]

peripteral (pəˈrɪptərəl) *adj* having a row of columns on all sides [C19 from PERI- + -*pteral*, from Greek *pteron* wing]

perique (pəˈriːk) *n* a strong highly-flavoured tobacco cured in its own juices and grown in Louisiana [C19 apparently from *Périque*, nickname of Pierre Chenet, American tobacco planter who first grew it in Louisiana]

perisarc (ˈpɛrɪˌsɑːk) *n* the outer chitinous layer secreted by colonial hydrozoan coelenterates, such as species of *Obelia* [C19 from PERI- + -*sarc*, from Greek *sarx* flesh] > ˌperiˈsarcal or ˌperiˈsarcous *adj*

periscope (ˈpɛrɪˌskəʊp) *n* any of a number of optical instruments that enable the user to view objects that are not in the direct line of vision, such as one in a submarine for looking above the surface of the water. They have a system of mirrors or prisms to reflect the light and often contain focusing lenses [C19 from Greek *periskopein* to look around; see PERI-, -SCOPE]

periscopic (ˌpɛrɪˈskɒpɪk) *adj* (of a lens) having a wide field of view > ˌperiˈscopically *adv*

perish (ˈpɛrɪʃ) *vb* (*intr*) **1** to be destroyed or die, esp in an untimely way **2** to rot: *leather perishes if exposed to bad weather* **3 perish the thought!** may it never be or happen thus ▷ *n* **4 do a perish** *Austral informal* to die or come near to dying of thirst or starvation [C13 from Old French *périr*, from Latin *perīre* to pass away entirely, from PER- (away) + *īre* to go]

perishable (ˈpɛrɪʃəbəl) *adj* **1** liable to rot or wither ▷ *n* **2** (*often plural*) a perishable article, esp food > ˌperishaˈbility or ˈperishableness *n* > ˈperishably *adv*

perished (ˈpɛrɪʃt) *adj informal* (of a person, part of the body, etc) extremely cold

perishing (ˈpɛrɪʃɪŋ) *adj* **1** *informal* (of weather, etc) extremely cold **2** *slang* (intensifier qualifying something undesirable): *it's a perishing nuisance!* > ˈperishingly *adv*

perisperm (ˈpɛrɪˌspɜːm) *n* the nutritive tissue surrounding the embryo in certain seeds, and developing from the nucellus of the ovule > ˌperiˈspermal *adj*

perispomenon (ˌpɛrɪˈspəʊməˌnɒn) *adj* **1** (of a Greek word) bearing a circumflex accent on the last syllable ▷ *n* **2** a word having such an accent [from Greek, from PERI- (around) + *spaein* to pull, draw]

perissodactyl (pəˌrɪsəʊˈdæktɪl) or **perissodactyle** (pəˌrɪsəʊˈdæktaɪl) *n* **1** any placental mammal of the order *Perissodactyla*, having hooves with an odd number of toes: includes horses, tapirs, and rhinoceroses ▷ *adj* **2** of, relating to, or belonging to the *Perissodactyla* [C19 from New Latin *perissodactylus*, from Greek *perissos* uneven + *daktulos* digit] > ˌperissoˈdactylous *adj*

peristalsis (ˌpɛrɪˈstælsɪs) *n, pl* -ses (-siːz) *physiol* the succession of waves of involuntary muscular contraction of various bodily tubes, esp of the alimentary tract, where it effects transport of food and waste products [C19 from New Latin, from PERI- + Greek *stalsis* compression, from *stellein* to press together] > ˌperiˈstaltic *adj* > ˌperiˈstaltically *adv*

peristome (ˈpɛrɪˌstəʊm) *n* **1** a fringe of pointed teeth surrounding the opening of a moss capsule **2** any of various parts surrounding the mouth of invertebrates, such as echinoderms and earthworms, and of protozoans [C18 from New Latin *peristoma*, from PERI- + Greek *stoma* mouth] > ˌperiˈstomal or ˌperiˈstomial *adj*

peristyle (ˈpɛrɪˌstaɪl) *n* **1** a colonnade that surrounds a court or building **2** an area that is surrounded by a colonnade [C17 via French from Latin *peristȳlum*, from Greek *peristulon*, from PERI- + *stulos* column] > ˌperiˈstylar *adj*

perithecium (ˌpɛrɪˈθiːsɪəm) *n, pl* -cia (-sɪə) *botany* a flask-shaped structure containing asci that are discharged from an apical pore; a type of ascocarp [C19 from New Latin, from PERI- + Greek *thēkē* case]

peritoneal dialysis a technique of dialysis used when haemodialysis is inappropriate; it makes use of the peritoneum as an autogenous semipermeable membrane

peritoneum (ˌpɛrɪtəˈniːəm) *n, pl* -nea (-ˈniːə) or -neums a thin translucent serous sac that lines the walls of the abdominal cavity and covers most of the viscera [C16 via Late Latin from Greek *peritonaion*, from *peritonos* stretched around, from PERI- + *tenein* to stretch] > ˌperitoˈneal *adj*

peritonitis (ˌpɛrɪtəˈnaɪtɪs) *n* inflammation of the peritoneum > peritonitic (ˌpɛrɪtəˈnɪtɪk) *adj*

peritrack (ˈpɛrɪˌtræk) *n* another name for **taxiway**

peritricha (pəˈrɪtrɪkə) *pl n, sing* peritrich (ˈpɛrɪˌtrɪk) **1** ciliate protozoans, of the order *Peritrichida*, in which the cilia are restricted to a spiral around the mouth **2** bacteria having the entire cell surface covered with flagella [C19 from New Latin, from PERI- + Greek *thrix* hair] > peˈritrichous *adj*

periwig (ˈpɛrɪˌwɪg) *n* a wig, such as a peruke [C16 *perwyke*, changed from French *perruque* wig, PERUKE]

periwinkle¹ (ˈpɛrɪˌwɪŋkəl) *n* **1** any of various edible marine gastropods of the genus *Littorina*, esp *L. littorea*, having a spirally coiled shell. Often shortened to: **winkle** [C16 of unknown origin]

periwinkle² (ˈpɛrɪˌwɪŋkəl) *n* **1** Also called (US): creeping myrtle, trailing myrtle any of several Eurasian apocynaceous evergreen plants of the genus *Vinca*, such as *V. minor* (**lesser periwinkle**) and *V. major* (**greater periwinkle**), having trailing stems and blue flowers **2 a** a light purplish-blue colour **b** (*as adjective*): *a periwinkle coat* [C14 *pervenke*, from Old English *pervince*, from Late Latin *pervinca*]

perjink (pərˈdʒɪŋk) *adj Scot* prim or finicky [C19 of unknown origin]

perjure (ˈpɜːdʒə) *vb* (*tr*) *criminal law* to render (oneself) guilty of perjury [C15 from Old French *parjurer*, from Latin *perjūrāre*, from PER- + *jūrāre* to make an oath, from *jūs* law] > ˈperjurer *n*

perjured (ˈpɜːdʒəd) *adj criminal law* **1 a** having sworn falsely **b** having committed perjury **2** involving or characterized by perjury: *perjured evidence*

perjury (ˈpɜːdʒərɪ) *n, pl* -juries *criminal law* the offence committed by a witness in judicial proceedings who, having been lawfully sworn or having affirmed, wilfully gives false evidence [C14 from Anglo-French *parjurie*, from Latin *perjūrium* a false oath; see PERJURE] > perjurious (pɜːˈdʒʊərɪəs) *adj* > perˈjuriously *adv*

perk¹ (pɜːk) *adj* **1** pert; brisk; lively ▷ *vb* **2** See **perk up** [C16 see PERK UP]

perk² (pɜːk) *vb informal* **1** (*intr*) (of coffee) to percolate **2** (*tr*) to percolate (coffee)

perk³ (pɜːk) *n Brit informal* short for **perquisite**

perkin (ˈpɜːkɪn) *n* a variant of **parkin**

Perkin's mauve (ˈpɜːkɪnz) *n* another name for **mauve** (sense 2) [C19 named after Sir William Henry *Perkin* (1838–1907), who first synthesized it]

perk up *vb* (*adverb*) **1** to make or become more cheerful, hopeful, or lively **2** to rise or cause to rise briskly: *the dog's ears perked up* **3** (*tr*) to make smarter in appearance: *she perked up her outfit with a bright scarf* **4** (*intr*) *Austral slang* to vomit [C14 *perk*, perhaps from Norman French *perquer*; see PERCH¹]

perky (ˈpɜːkɪ) *adj* perkier, perkiest **1** jaunty; lively **2** confident; spirited > ˈperkily *adv* > ˈperkiness *n*

Perl (pɜːl) *n* a computer language that is used for text manipulation, esp on the World Wide Web [C20 from p(ractical) e(xtraction and) r(eport) l(anguage)]

perlemoen (ˈpɛələˌmʊn) *n South African* another name for **abalone** [from Afrikaans, from Dutch *paarlemoer* mother of pearl]

Perlis (ˈpɛəlɪs, ˈpɜː-) *n* a state of NW Peninsular Malaysia, on the Andaman Sea: a dependency of Thailand until 1909. Capital: Kangar. Pop: 204 450 (2000). Area: 803 sq km (310 sq miles)

perlite or **pearlite** (ˈpɜːlaɪt) *n* a variety of obsidian consisting of masses of small pearly globules: used as a filler, insulator, and soil conditioner [C19 from French, from *perle* PEARL¹] > perlitic or pearlitic (pɜːˈlɪtɪk) *adj*

perlocution (ˌpɜːləˈkjuːʃən) *n philosophy* the effect that someone has by uttering certain words, such as frightening or persuading a person. Also called: perlocutionary act Compare illocution [C16 (in the obsolete sense: the action of speaking): from Medieval or New Latin *perlocūtiō*; see PER-, LOCUTION] > ˌperloˈcutionary *adj*

perm¹ (pɜːm) *n* **1** a hairstyle produced by treatment with heat, chemicals, etc which gives long-lasting waves, curls, or other shaping. Also called (esp formerly): permanent wave **2** the act of giving or receiving such a hairstyle ▷ *vb* **3** (*tr*) to give a perm to (hair)

perm² (pɜːm) *n* short for **permutation** (sense 4)

Perm (*Russian* pjermj) *n* a port in W Russia, on the Kama River: oil refinery; university (1916). Pop: 984 000 (2005 est.). Former name (1940–62): Molotov

perma- *prefix informal* indicating a fixed state: *a perma-tan; perma-grin*

permaculture (ˈpɜːməˌkʌltʃə) *n* the practice of producing food, energy, etc, using ways that do not deplete the earth's natural resources [C20 coined by Bill Mollison (born 1928), Australian ecologist, from perma(nent agri)culture]

permafrost (ˈpɜːməˌfrɒst) *n* ground that is permanently frozen, often to great depths, the surface sometimes thawing in the summer [C20 from PERMA(NENT) + FROST]

permalloy (pɜːˈmælɔɪ) *n* any of various alloys containing iron and nickel (45–80 per cent) and sometimes smaller amounts of chromium and molybdenum [C20 from PERM(EABILITY) + ALLOY]

permanence (ˈpɜːmənəns) *n* the state or quality of being permanent

permanency (ˈpɜːmənənsɪ) *n, pl* -cies **1** a person or thing that is permanent **2** another word for **permanence**

permanent (ˈpɜːmənənt) *adj* **1** existing or intended to exist for an indefinite period: *a* *permanent structure* **2** not expected to change for an indefinite time; not temporary: *a permanent condition* [c15 from Latin *permanens* continuing, from *permanēre* to stay to the end, from *per-* through + *manēre* to remain] > 'permanently *adv*

Permanent Court of Arbitration *n* the official name of the Hague Tribunal

permanent hardness *n chem* hardness of water that cannot be removed by boiling as it results mainly from the presence of calcium and magnesium chlorides and sulphates

permanent health insurance *n* a form of insurance that provides up to 75 per cent of a person's salary, until retirement, in case of prolonged illness or disability

permanent magnet *n* a magnet, often of steel, that retains its magnetization after the magnetic field producing it has been removed > permanent magnetism *n*

permanent press *n* **a** a chemical treatment for clothing that makes the fabric crease-resistant and sometimes provides a garment with a permanent crease or pleats **b** (*as modifier*): *permanent-press skirts*

permanent resident *n Canadian* an immigrant who has been given official residential status, often prior to being granted citizenship

permanent set *n engineering* the change in shape of a material that results when the load to which it is subjected causes the elastic limit to be exceeded and is then removed

permanent wave *n* another name (esp formerly) for **perm¹** (sense 1)

permanent way *n chiefly Brit* the track of a railway, including the ballast, sleepers, rails, etc

permanganate (pə'mæŋɡə,neɪt, -nɪt) *n* a salt of permanganic acid

permanganic acid (,pɜːmæn'ɡænɪk) *n* a monobasic acid known only in solution and in the form of permanganate salts. Formula: HMnO₄. Systematic name: manganic(VII) acid

perma-tan *n* a permanent year-round suntan

permeability (,pɜːmɪə'bɪlɪti) *n* **1** the state or quality of being permeable **2** a measure of the response of a medium to a magnetic field, expressed as the ratio of the magnetic flux density in the medium to the field strength; measured in henries per metre. Symbol: μ See also **relative permeability, magnetic constant 3** *civil engineering* the rate of diffusion of a fluid under pressure through soil **4** the rate at which gas diffuses through the surface of a balloon or airship, usually expressed in litres per square metre per day

permeability coefficient *n* the volume of an incompressible fluid that will flow in unit time through a unit cube of a porous substance across which a unit pressure difference is maintained

permeable ('pɜːmɪəbᵊl) *adj* capable of being permeated, esp by liquids [c15 from Late Latin *permeābilis*, from Latin *permeāre* to pervade; see PERMEATE] > 'permeableness *n* > 'permeably *adv*

permeance ('pɜːmɪəns) *n* **1** the act of permeating **2** the reciprocal of the reluctance of a magnetic circuit. Symbol: Λ > 'permeant *adj, n*

permeate ('pɜːmɪ,eɪt) *vb* **1** to penetrate or pervade (a substance, area, etc): *a lovely smell permeated the room* **2** to pass through or cause to pass through by osmosis or diffusion: *to permeate a membrane* [c17 from Latin *permeāre*, from *per-* through + *meāre* to pass] > ,perme'ation *n* > 'permeative *adj*

per mensem *Latin* ('pɜː 'mɛnsəm) *adv* every month or by the month

Permian ('pɜːmɪən) *adj* **1** of, denoting, or formed in the last period of the Palaeozoic era, between the Carboniferous and Triassic periods, which lasted for 60 000 000 years ▷ *n* **2** **the** the Permian period or rock system [c19 after PERM, Russia]

permie ('pɜːmɪ) *n* a person, esp an office worker, employed by a firm on a permanent basis. Compare **temp** [c20 diminutive of PERMANENT]

per mill *or* **mil** (pə 'mɪl) *adv* by the thousand or in

each thousand [c19 from PER + French or Latin *mille* thousand, on the model of PER CENT]

permissible (pə'mɪsəbᵊl) *adj* permitted; allowable > per,missi'bility *n* > per'missibly *adv*

permission (pə'mɪʃən) *n* authorization to do something

permissive (pə'mɪsɪv) *adj* **1** tolerant; lenient: *permissive parents* **2** indulgent in matters of sex: *a permissive society* **3** granting permission **4** *archaic* not obligatory > per'missively *adv* > per'missiveness *n*

permit *vb* (pə'mɪt) -mits, -mitting, -mitted **1** (*tr*) to grant permission to do something: *you are permitted to smoke* **2** (*tr*) to consent to or tolerate: *she will not permit him to come* **3** (when *intr*, often foll by *of*; when *tr*, often foll by an infinitive) to allow the possibility (of): *the passage permits of two interpretations; his work permits him to relax nowadays* ▷ *n* ('pɜːmɪt) **4** an official certificate or document granting authorization; licence **5** permission, esp written permission [c15 from Latin *permittere*, from *per-* through + *mittere* to send] > per'mitter *n*

permittivity (,pɜːmɪ'tɪvɪtɪ) *n, pl* -ties a measure of the response of a substance to an electric field, expressed as the ratio of its electric displacement to the applied field strength; measured in farads per metre. Symbol: ε See also **relative permittivity, electric constant**

permutate ('pɜːmjʊ,teɪt) *vb* to alter the sequence or arrangement (of); treat by permutation: *endlessly permutating three basic designs*

permutation (,pɜːmjʊ'teɪʃən) *n* **1** *maths* **a** an ordered arrangement of the numbers, terms, etc, of a set into specified groups: *the permutations of a, b, and c, taken two at a time, are ab, ba, ac, ca, bc, cb* **b** a group formed in this way. The number of permutations of *n* objects taken *r* at a time is $n!/(n-r)!$ Symbol: $_nP_r$ ▷ Compare **combination** (sense 6) **2** a combination of items made by reordering **3** an alteration; transformation **4** a fixed combination for selections of results on football pools. Usually shortened to: perm [c14 from Latin *permūtātiō*, from *permūtāre* to change thoroughly; see MUTATION] > ,permu'tational *adj*

permute (pə'mjuːt) *vb* (*tr*) **1** to change the sequence of **2** *maths* to subject to permutation [c14 from Latin *permūtāre*, from *per-* + *mūtāre* to change, alter] > per'mutable *adj* > per,muta'bility *or* per'mutableness *n* > per'mutably *adv*

Pernambuco (,pɜːnəm'bjuːkəʊ) *Portuguese* pernəm'buku) *n* **1** a state of NE Brazil, on the Atlantic: consists of a humid coastal plain rising to a high inland plateau. Capital: Recife. Pop: 8 084 667 (2002). Area: 98 280 sq km (37 946 sq miles) **2** the former name of **Recife**

pernicious (pə'nɪʃəs) *adj* **1** wicked or malicious: *pernicious lies* **2** causing grave harm; deadly [c16 from Latin *perniciōsus*, from *perniciēs* ruin, from PER- (intensive) + *nex* death] > per'niciously *adv* > per'niciousness *n*

pernicious anaemia *n* a form of anaemia characterized by lesions of the spinal cord, weakness, sore tongue, numbness in the arms and legs, diarrhoea, etc: associated with inadequate absorption of vitamin B₁₂

pernickety (pə'nɪkɪtɪ) *or US* **persnickety** *adj informal* **1** excessively precise and attentive to detail; fussy **2** (of a task) requiring close attention; exacting [c19 originally Scottish, of unknown origin] > per'nicketiness *or US* per'snicketiness *n*

Pernik (*Bulgarian* 'pɛrnik) *n* an industrial town in W Bulgaria, on the Struma River. Pop: 84 000 (2005 est). Former name (1949–62): Dimitrovo

Pernod ('pɛənəʊ; *French* pɛrno) *n trademark* an aniseed-flavoured apéritif from France

peroneal (,pɛrə'niːəl) *adj anatomy* of or relating to the fibula or the outer side of the leg [c19 from New Latin *peronē* fibula, from Greek: fibula]

Peronist (pə'rɒnɪst) *n* **1** a follower or admirer of Juan Domingo Peron, the Argentine soldier, statesman, and dictator (1895–1974) ▷ *adj* **2** of or

relating to Peron, his policies, or his supporters

perorate ('pɛrə,reɪt) *vb* (*intr*) **1** to speak at length, esp in a formal manner **2** to conclude a speech or sum up, esp with a formal recapitulation

peroration (,pɛrə'reɪʃən) *n rhetoric* the conclusion of a speech or discourse, in which points made previously are summed up or recapitulated, esp with greater emphasis [c15 from Latin *perōrātiō*, from *perōrāre*, from PER- (thoroughly) + *orāre* to speak]

perovskite (pɛ'rɒvskaɪt) *n* a yellow, brown, or greyish-black mineral form of calcium titanate with some rare-earth elements, which is used in certain high-temperature ceramic superconductors [c19 named after Count Lev Alekseevich Perovski (1792–1856), Russian statesman]

peroxidase (pə'rɒksɪ,deɪs, -,deɪz) *n* any of a group of enzymes that catalyse the oxidation of a compound by the decomposition of hydrogen peroxide or an organic peroxide. They generally consist of a protein combined with haem

peroxidation (pə,rɒksɪ'deɪʃən) *n* a type of reaction in which oxygen atoms are formed leading to the production of peroxides. It is stimulated in the body by certain toxins and infections

peroxide (pə'rɒksaɪd) *n* **1** short for **hydrogen peroxide**, esp when used for bleaching hair **2** any of a class of metallic oxides, such as sodium peroxide, Na₂O₂, that contain the divalent ion ⁻O-O⁻ **3** (*not in technical usage*) any of certain dioxides, such as manganese peroxide, MnO₂, that resemble peroxides in their formula but do not contain the ⁻O-O⁻ ion **4** any of a class of organic compounds whose molecules contain two oxygen atoms bound together. They tend to be explosive **5** (*modifier*) of, relating to, bleached with, or resembling peroxide ▷ *vb* **6** (*tr*) to bleach (the hair) with peroxide

peroxide blonde *n usually disparaging* a woman having hair that is bleached rather than naturally blonde and that looks harsh or unnatural

peroxisome (pə'rɒksɪ,səʊm) *n* a type of organelle present in most eukaryotic cells that carry out oxidative reactions, such as oxidation of alcohol in the liver

peroxy- *or esp for inorganic compounds* **peroxo-** *combining form* indicating the presence of the peroxide group, -O–O-: *peroxysulphuric acid*. Also (not in technical usage): per-

peroxysulphuric acid (pə,rɒksɪsʌl'fjʊərɪk) *n* a white hygroscopic crystalline unstable oxidizing acid. Formula: H₂SO₅. Also called (not in technical usage): persulphuric acid, Caro's acid

perp (pɜːp) *n US and Canad informal* a person who has committed a crime [c20 from PERPETRATE]

perpend¹ ('pɜːpənd) *or* **perpent** *n* a large stone that passes through a wall from one side to the other. Also called: parpend, perpend stone [c15 from Old French *parpain*, of uncertain origin]

perpend² (pə'pɛnd) *vb* an archaic word for **ponder** [c16 from Latin *perpendere* to examine, from PER- (thoroughly) + *pendere* to weigh]

perpendicular (,pɜːpən'dɪkjʊlə) *adj* **1** Also: normal at right angles to a horizontal plane **2** denoting, relating to, or having the style of Gothic architecture used in England during the 14th and 15th centuries, characterized by tracery having vertical lines, a four-centred arch, and fan vaulting **3** upright; vertical ▷ *n* **4** *geometry* a line or plane perpendicular to another **5** any instrument used for indicating the vertical line through a given point **6** *mountaineering* a nearly vertical face [c14 from Latin *perpendiculāris*, from *perpendiculum* a plumb line, from *per-* through + *pendēre* to hang] > perpendicularity (,pɜːpən,dɪkjʊ'lærɪtɪ) *n* > ,perpen'dicularly *adv*

perpetrate ('pɜːpɪ,treɪt) *vb* (*tr*) to perform or be responsible for (a deception, crime, etc) [c16 from Latin *perpetrāre*, from *per-* (thoroughly) + *patrāre* to perform, perhaps from *pater* father, leader in the

p

performance of sacred rites] > ˌperpeˈtration n > ˈperpeˌtrator n

> **USAGE** *Perpetrate* and *perpetuate* are sometimes confused: *he must answer for the crimes he has perpetrated* (not *perpetuated*); *the book helped to perpetuate* (not *perpetrate*) *some of the myths surrounding his early life*

perpetual (pəˈpɛtjʊəl) *adj* **1** (*usually prenominal*) eternal; permanent **2** (*usually prenominal*) seemingly ceaseless because often repeated: *your perpetual complaints* **3** *horticulture* blooming throughout the growing season or year ▷ *n* **4** (of a crop plant) continually producing edible parts: *perpetual spinach* **5** a plant that blooms throughout the growing season [c14 via Old French from Latin *perpetuālis* universal, from *perpes* continuous, from *per-* (thoroughly) + *petere* to go towards] > perˈpetually *adv*

perpetual check *n* *chess* a consecutive series of checks that the checked player cannot avoid, leading to a drawn game

perpetual debenture *n* a bond or debenture that can either never be redeemed or cannot be redeemed on demand

perpetual inventory *n* a form of stock control in which running records are kept of all acquisitions and disposals

perpetual motion *n* **1** Also called: **perpetual motion of the first kind** motion of a hypothetical mechanism that continues indefinitely without any external source of energy. It is impossible in practice because of friction **2** Also called: **perpetual motion of the second kind** motion of a hypothetical mechanism that derives its energy from a source at a lower temperature. It is impossible in practice because of the second law of thermodynamics

perpetuate (pəˈpɛtjʊˌeɪt) *vb* (*tr*) to cause to continue or prevail: *to perpetuate misconceptions* [c16 from Latin *perpetuāre* to continue without interruption, from *perpetuus* PERPETUAL] > perˌpetuˈation n

> **USAGE** See at **perpetrate**

perpetuity (ˌpɜːpɪˈtjuːɪtɪ) *n, pl* **-ties** **1** eternity **2** the state or quality of being perpetual **3** *property law* a limitation preventing the absolute disposal of an estate for longer than the period allowed by law **4** an annuity with no maturity date and payable indefinitely **5** **in perpetuity** for ever [c15 from Old French *perpetuite*, from Latin *perpetuitās* continuity; see PERPETUAL]

Perpignan (*French* pɛrpiɲã) *n* a town in S France: historic capital of Roussillon. Pop: 105 115 (1999)

perplex (pəˈplɛks) *vb* (*tr*) **1** to puzzle; bewilder; confuse **2** to complicate: *to perplex an issue* [c15 from obsolete *perplex* (adj) intricate, from Latin *perplexus* entangled, from *per-* (thoroughly) + *plectere* to entwine]

perplexity (pəˈplɛksɪtɪ) *n, pl* **-ties** **1** the state of being perplexed **2** the state of being intricate or complicated **3** something that perplexes

per pro (pɜː ˈprəʊ) *prep* by delegation to; through the agency of: used when signing documents on behalf of someone else [Latin: abbreviation of *per prōcūratiōnem*]

> **USAGE** See at **pp**

perp walk *n* *US informal* an arranged public appearance of a recently arrested criminal for the benefit of the media

perquisite (ˈpɜːkwɪzɪt) *n* **1** an incidental benefit gained from a certain type of employment, such as the use of a company car **2** a customary benefit received in addition to a regular income **3** a customary tip **4** something expected or regarded as an exclusive right ▷ Often (*informal*) shortened to: **perk** [c15 from Medieval Latin *perquīsitum* an acquired possession, from Latin *perquīrere* to seek earnestly for something, from *per-* (thoroughly) + *quaerere* to ask for, seek]

Perrier water *or* **Perrier** (ˈpɛrɪeɪ) *n* *trademark* a sparkling mineral water from the south of France

[c20 named after a spring *Source Perrier*, at Vergèze, France]

perron (ˈpɛrən) *n* an external flight of steps, esp one at the front entrance of a building [c14 from Old French, from *pierre* stone, from Latin *petra*]

perry (ˈpɛrɪ) *n, pl* **-ries** alcoholic drink made of pears, similar in taste to cider [c14 *pereye*, from Old French *peré*, ultimately from Latin *pirum* pear]

persalt (ˈpɜːˌsɔːlt) *n* any salt of a peracid

perse (pɜːs) *n* **a** a dark greyish-blue colour **b** (*as adjective*): *perse cloth* [c14 from Old French, from Medieval Latin *persus*, perhaps changed from Latin *Persicus* Persian]

per se (ˈpɜː ˈseɪ) *adv* by or in itself; intrinsically [Latin]

persecute (ˈpɜːsɪˌkjuːt) *vb* (*tr*) **1** to oppress, harass, or maltreat, esp because of race, religion, etc **2** to bother persistently [c15 from Old French *persecuter*, back formation from *persecuteur*, from Late Latin *persecūtor* pursuer, from *persequī* to take vengeance upon] > ˈperseˌcutive adj > ˈperseˌcutor n

persecution (ˌpɜːsɪˈkjuːʃən) *n* the act of persecuting or the state of being persecuted

persecution complex *n* *psychol* an acute irrational fear that other people are plotting one's downfall and that they are responsible for one's failures

persecutory (ˈpɜːsɪˌkjuːtərɪ) *adj* involving or characteristic of persecution

Perseid (ˈpɜːsiɪd) *n* any member of a meteor shower occurring annually around August 12th and appearing to radiate from a point in the constellation Perseus [c19 from Greek *Persēides* daughters of PERSEUS[1]]

Persephone (pəˈsɛfənɪ) *n* *Greek myth* a daughter of Zeus and Demeter, abducted by Hades and made his wife and queen of the underworld, but allowed part of each year to leave it. Roman counterpart: **Proserpina**

Persepolis (pəˈsɛpəlɪs) *n* the capital of ancient Persia in the Persian Empire and under the Seleucids: founded by Darius; sacked by Alexander the Great in 330 BC

Perseus[1] (ˈpɜːsɪəs) *n* *Greek myth* a son of Zeus and Danaë, who with Athena's help slew the Gorgon Medusa and rescued Andromeda from a sea monster

Perseus[2] (ˈpɜːsɪəs) *n, Latin genitive* **Persei** (ˈpɜːsɪˌaɪ) a conspicuous constellation in the N hemisphere lying between Auriga and Cassiopeia and crossed by the Milky Way. It contains the eclipsing binary, Algol, and a rich cluster of galaxies

perseverance (ˌpɜːsɪˈvɪərəns) *n* **1** continued steady belief or efforts, withstanding discouragement or difficulty; persistence **2** *Christianity* persistence in remaining in a state of grace until death > ˌperseˈverant adj

perseveration (pɜːˌsɛvəˈreɪʃən) *n* *psychol* **1** the tendency for an impression, idea, or feeling to dissipate only slowly and to recur during subsequent experiences **2** an inability to change one's method of working when transferred from one task to another

persevere (ˌpɜːsɪˈvɪə) *vb* (*intr; often foll by in*) to show perseverance [c14 from Old French *perseverer*, from Latin *persevērāre*, from *perseverus* very strict; see SEVERE] > ˌperseˈvering adj > ˌperseˈveringly adv

Pershing (ˈpɜːʃɪŋ) *n* a US ballistic missile capable of carrying a nuclear or conventional warhead [c20 after John Joseph Pershing (1860–1948), US general]

Persia (ˈpɜːʃə) *n* **1** the former name (until 1935) of **Iran 2** another name for **Persian Empire**

Persian (ˈpɜːʃən) *adj* **1** of or relating to ancient Persia or modern Iran, their inhabitants, or their languages ▷ *n* **2** a native, citizen, or inhabitant of modern Iran; an Iranian **3** a member of an Indo-European people of West Iranian speech who established a great empire in SW Asia in the 6th century BC **4** (loosely) the language of Iran or Persia in any of its ancient or modern forms, belonging to the West Iranian branch of the Indo-

European family. See also **Avestan, Old Persian, Pahlavi**[2]**, Farsi**

Persian blinds *pl n* another term for **persiennes**

Persian carpet *or* **rug** *n* a carpet or rug made in Persia or other countries of the Near East by knotting silk or wool yarn by hand onto a woven backing, characterized by rich colours and flowing or geometric designs

Persian cat *n* a long-haired variety of domestic cat with a stocky body, round face, short nose, and short thick legs

Persian Empire *n* the S Asian empire established by Cyrus the Great in the 6th century BC and overthrown by Alexander the Great in the 4th century BC. At its height it extended from India to Europe

Persian greyhound *n* another name for the **Saluki**

Persian Gulf *n* a shallow arm of the Arabian Sea between SW Iran and Arabia: linked with the Arabian Sea by the Strait of Hormuz and the Gulf of Oman; important for the oilfields on its shores. Area: 233 000 sq km (90 000 sq miles)

Persian lamb *n* **1** a black loosely curled fur obtained from the skin of the karakul lamb **2** a karakul lamb

Persian melon *n* another name for **winter melon**

persicaria (ˌpɜːsɪˈkɛərɪə) *n* another name for **red shank**

persiennes (ˌpɜːsɪˈɛnz) *pl n* outside window shutters having louvres to keep out the sun while maintaining ventilation. Also called: **Persian blinds** [c19 from French, from *persien* Persian]

persiflage (ˈpɜːsɪˌflɑːʒ) *n* light frivolous conversation, style, or treatment; friendly teasing [c18 via French, from *persifler* to tease, from *per-* (intensive) + *siffler* to whistle, from Latin *sībilāre* to whistle]

persimmon (pɜːˈsɪmən) *n* **1** any of several tropical trees of the genus *Diospyros*, typically having hard wood and large orange-red fruit: family *Ebenaceae* **2** the sweet fruit of any of these trees, which is edible when completely ripe ▷ See also **ebony** (sense 1) [c17 of Algonquian origin; related to Delaware *pasīmēnan* dried fruit]

Persis (ˈpɜːsɪs) *n* an ancient region of SW Iran: homeland of the Achaemenid dynasty

persist (pəˈsɪst) *vb* (*intr*) **1** (*often foll by in*) to continue steadfastly or obstinately despite opposition or difficulty **2** to continue to exist or occur without interruption: *the rain persisted throughout the night* [c16 from Latin *persistere*, from *per-* (intensive) + *sistere* to stand steadfast, from *stāre* to stand] > perˈsister n

persistence (pəˈsɪstəns) *or* **persistency** *n* **1** the quality of persisting; tenacity **2** the act of persisting; continued effort or existence **3** the continuance of an effect after the cause of it has stopped: *persistence of vision*

persistent (pəˈsɪstənt) *adj* **1** showing persistence **2** incessantly repeated; unrelenting: *your persistent questioning* **3** (of plant parts) remaining attached to the plant after the normal time of withering: *a fruit surrounded by a persistent perianth* **4** *zoology* **a** (of parts normally present only in young stages) present in the adult: *persistent gills in axolotls* **b** continuing to grow or develop after the normal period of growth: *persistent teeth* **5** (of a chemical, esp when used as an insecticide) slow to break down; not easily degradable > perˈsistently adv

persistent cruelty *n* *Brit law* conduct causing fear of danger to the life or health of a spouse (used in matrimonial proceedings before magistrates)

persistent organic pollutant *n* a toxin resulting from a manufacturing process, which remains in the environment for many years. Abbreviation: POP

persistent vegetative state *n* *med* an irreversible condition, resulting from brain damage, characterized by lack of consciousness, thought, and feeling, although reflex activities (such as breathing) continue. Abbreviation: PVS

persnickety (pəˈsnɪkɪtɪ) *adj* the US word for **pernickety**

person (ˈpɜːsˀn) *n, pl* **persons 1** an individual human being **2** the body of a human being, sometimes including his or her clothing: *guns hidden on his person* **3** a grammatical category into which pronouns and forms of verbs are subdivided depending on whether they refer to the speaker, the person addressed, or some other individual, thing, etc **4** a human being or a corporation recognized in law as having certain rights and obligations **5** *philosophy* a being characterized by consciousness, rationality, and a moral sense, and traditionally thought of as consisting of both a body and a mind or soul **6** *archaic* a character or role; guise **7 in person a** actually present: *the author will be there in person* **b** without the help or intervention of others [c13 from Old French *persone*, from Latin *persōna* mask, perhaps from Etruscan *phersu* mask]

> **USAGE** *People* is the word usually used to refer to more than one individual: *there were a hundred people at the reception. Persons* is rarely used, except in official English: *several persons were interviewed*

Person (ˈpɜːsˀn) *n Christianity* any of the three hypostases existing as distinct in the one God and constituting the Trinity. They are the **First Person**, the Father, the **Second Person**, the Son, and the **Third Person**, the Holy Ghost

-person *suffix forming nouns* sometimes used instead of -*man* and -*woman* or -*lady*: *chairperson; salesperson*

> **USAGE** See at **-man**

persona (pɜːˈsəʊnə) *n, pl* -**nae** (-niː) **1** (*often plural*) a character in a play, novel, etc **2** an assumed identity or character **3** (in Jungian psychology) the mechanism that conceals a person's true thoughts and feelings, esp in his adaptation to the outside world [Latin: mask]

personable (ˈpɜːsənəbˀl) *adj* pleasant in appearance and personality > ˈpersonableness *n* > ˈpersonably *adv*

personage (ˈpɜːsənɪdʒ) *n* **1** an important or distinguished person **2** another word for **person** (sense 1) *a strange personage* **3** *rare* a figure in literature, history, etc

persona grata *Latin* (pɜːˈsəʊnə ˈɡrɑːtə) *n, pl* **personae gratae** (pɜːˈsəʊniː ˈɡrɑːtiː) an acceptable person, esp a diplomat acceptable to the government of the country to which he or she is sent

personal (ˈpɜːsənˀl) *adj* **1** of or relating to the private aspects of a person's life: *personal letters; a personal question* **2** (*prenominal*) of or relating to a person's body, its care, or its appearance: *personal hygiene; great personal beauty* **3** belonging to or intended for a particular person and no-one else: *as a personal favour; for your personal use* **4** (*prenominal*) undertaken by an individual himself: *a personal appearance by a celebrity* **5** referring to, concerning, or involving a person's individual personality, intimate affairs, etc, esp in an offensive way: *personal remarks; don't be so personal* **6** having the attributes of an individual conscious being: *a personal God* **7** of or arising from the personality: *personal magnetism* **8** of, relating to, or denoting grammatical person **9** *law* of or relating to movable property, such as money. Compare **real**[1] (sense 8) ⊳ *n* **10** *law* an item of movable property

personal care *n* help given to elderly or infirm people with essential everyday activities such as washing, dressing, and meals

personal column *n* a newspaper column containing personal messages, advertisements by charities, requests for friendship, holiday companions, etc

personal computer *n* a small inexpensive computer used in word processing, playing computer games, etc

personal digital assistant *n* a palmtop computer for storing information.

Abbreviation: PDA

personal equation *n* **1** the variation or error in observation or judgment caused by individual characteristics **2** the allowance made for such variation

personal equity plan *n* the full name for **PEP**

personalism (ˈpɜːsənəˌlɪzəm) *n* **1** a philosophical movement that stresses the value of persons **2** an idiosyncratic mode of behaviour or expression > ˌpersonalˈistic *adj* > ˈpersonalist *n, adj*

personality (ˌpɜːsəˈnælɪtɪ) *n, pl* -**ties 1** *psychol* the sum total of all the behavioural and mental characteristics by means of which an individual is recognized as being unique **2** the distinctive character of a person that makes him socially attractive: *a salesman needs a lot of personality* **3** a well-known person in a certain field, such as sport or entertainment **4** a remarkable person: *the old fellow is a real personality* **5** the quality of being a unique person **6** the distinctive atmosphere of a place or situation **7** (*often plural*) a personal remark

personality cult *n* deliberately cultivated adulation of a person, esp a political leader

personality disorder *n psychiatry* any of a group of mental disorders characterized by a permanent disposition to behave in ways causing suffering to oneself or others

personality inventory *n psychol* a form of personality test in which the subject answers questions about himself. The results are used to determine dimensions of personality, such as extroversion

personality type *n psychol* a cluster of personality traits commonly occurring together

personalize or **personalise** (ˈpɜːsənəˌlaɪz) *vb* (*tr*) **1** to endow with personal or individual qualities or characteristics **2** to mark (stationery, clothing, etc) with a person's initials, name, etc **3** to take (a remark, etc) personally **4** another word for **personify**. > ˌpersonaliˈzation *or* ˌpersonaliˈsation *n*

personally (ˈpɜːsənəlɪ) *adv* **1** without the help or intervention of others: *I'll attend to it personally* **2** (*sentence modifier*) in one's own opinion or as regards oneself: *personally, I hate onions* **3** as if referring to oneself: *to take the insults personally* **4** as a person: *we like him personally, but professionally he's incompetent*

personal organizer *n* **1** a diary that stores personal records, appointments, notes, etc **2** a pocket-sized electronic device that performs the same functions

personal pension *n* **1** a private pension scheme in which an individual contributes part of his or her salary to a financial institution, which invests it so that a lump sum is available on retirement; this is then used to purchase an annuity **2** a pension derived from such a scheme

personal pronoun *n* a pronoun having a definite person or thing as an antecedent and functioning grammatically in the same way as the noun that it replaces. In English, the personal pronouns include *I, you, he, she, it, we,* and *they,* and are inflected for case

personal property *n law* movable property, such as furniture or money. Compare **real property** Also called: **personalty**

personal shopper *n* a person employed, esp by a shop, to accompany and advise customers on shopping trips or to select items for them

personal stereo *n* a very small audio cassette player designed to be worn attached to a belt and used with lightweight headphones

personal stylist *n* a person employed by a rich or famous client to offer advice on clothes, hairstyles, and other aspects of personal appearance

personalty (ˈpɜːsənəltɪ) *n, pl* -**ties** *law* another word for **personal property** [c16 from Anglo-French, from Late Latin *persōnālitās* personality]

persona non grata *Latin* (pɜːˈsəʊnə nɒn ˈɡrɑːtə) *n, pl* **personae non gratae** (pɜːˈsəʊniː nɒn ˈɡrɑːtiː) **1** an

unacceptable or unwelcome person **2** a diplomatic or consular officer who is not acceptable to the government or sovereign to whom he or she is accredited

personate[1] (ˈpɜːsəˌneɪt) *vb* (*tr*) **1** to act the part of (a character in a play); portray **2** a less common word for **personify 3** *criminal law* to assume the identity of (another person) with intent to deceive > ˌpersonˈation *n* > ˈpersonative *adj*

personate[2] (ˈpɜːsənɪt, -ˌneɪt) *adj* (of the corollas of certain flowers) having two lips in the form of a face [c18 from New Latin *persōnātus* masked, from Latin *persōna*; see **PERSON**]

personhood (ˈpɜːsənˌhʊd) *n chiefly US* the condition of being a person who is an individual with inalienable rights, esp under the 14th Amendment of the Constitution of the United States

personification (pɜːˌsɒnɪfɪˈkeɪʃən) *n* **1** the attribution of human characteristics to things, abstract ideas, etc, as for literary or artistic effect **2** the representation of an abstract quality or idea in the form of a person, creature, etc, as in art and literature **3** a person or thing that personifies **4** a person or thing regarded as an embodiment of a quality: *he is the personification of optimism*

personify (pɜːˈsɒnɪˌfaɪ) *vb* -**fies, -fying, -fied** (*tr*) **1** to attribute human characteristics to (a thing or abstraction) **2** to represent (an abstract quality) in human or animal form **3** (of a person or thing) to represent (an abstract quality), as in art or literature **4** to be the embodiment of > perˈsoniˌfiable *adj* > perˈsoniˌfier *n*

personned *adj* another word for **manned**

personnel (ˌpɜːsəˈnɛl) *n* **1** the people employed in an organization or for a service or undertaking. Compare **materiel 2 a** the office or department that interviews, appoints, or keeps records of employees. Also called: **human resources b** (*as modifier*): *a personnel officer* [c19 from French, ultimately from Late Latin *persōnālis* personal (adj); see **PERSON**]

person of colour *n* a person who is not white

perspective (pəˈspɛktɪv) *n* **1** a way of regarding situations, facts, etc, and judging their relative importance **2** the proper or accurate point of view or the ability to see it; objectivity: *try to get some perspective on your troubles* **3** the theory or art of suggesting three dimensions on a two-dimensional surface, in order to recreate the appearance and spatial relationships that objects or a scene in recession present to the eye **4** the appearance of objects, buildings, etc, relative to each other, as determined by their distance from the viewer, or the effects of this distance on their appearance **5** a view over some distance in space or time; vista; prospect **6** a picture showing perspective [c14 from Medieval Latin *perspectīva ars* the science of optics, from *perspicere* to inspect carefully, from *per-* (intensive) + *specere* to behold] > perˈspectively *adv*

Perspex (ˈpɜːspɛks) *n trademark* any of various clear acrylic resins, used chiefly as a substitute for glass

perspicacious (ˌpɜːspɪˈkeɪʃəs) *adj* **1** acutely perceptive or discerning **2** *archaic* having keen eyesight [c17 from Latin *perspicax*, from *perspicere* to look at closely; see **PERSPECTIVE**] > ˌperspiˈcaciously *adv* > perspicacity (ˌpɜːspɪˈkæsɪtɪ) *or* ˌperspiˈcaciousness *n*

perspicuity (ˌpɜːspɪˈkjuːɪtɪ) *n* **1** the quality of being perspicuous **2** another word for **perspicacity**

perspicuous (pəˈspɪkjʊəs) *adj* (of speech or writing) easily understood; lucid [c15 from Latin *perspicuus* transparent, from *perspicere* to explore thoroughly; see **PERSPECTIVE**] > perˈspicuously *adv* > perˈspicuousness *n*

perspiration (ˌpɜːspəˈreɪʃən) *n* **1** the act or process of insensibly eliminating fluid through the pores of the skin, which evaporates immediately **2** the sensible elimination of fluid through the pores of

P

the skin, which is visible as droplets on the skin **3** the salty fluid secreted through the pores of the skin; sweat

perspiratory (pəˈspaɪərətərɪ, -trɪ) *adj* of, relating to, or stimulating perspiration

perspire (pəˈspaɪə) *vb* to secrete or exude (perspiration) through the pores of the skin [C17 from Latin *perspīrāre* to blow, from *per-* (through) + *spīrāre* to breathe; compare INSPIRE] > perˈspiringly *adv*

persuade (pəˈsweɪd) *vb* (*tr; may take a clause as object or an infinitive*) **1** to induce, urge, or prevail upon successfully: *he finally persuaded them to buy it* **2** to cause to believe; convince: *even with the evidence, the police were not persuaded* [C16 from Latin *persuādēre*, from *per-* (intensive) + *suādēre* to urge, advise] > perˈsuadable *or* perˈsuasible *adj* > perˌsuadaˈbility *or* perˌsuasiˈbility *n* > perˈsuader *n*

persuasion (pəˈsweɪʒən) *n* **1** the act of persuading or of trying to persuade **2** the power to persuade **3** the state of being persuaded; strong belief **4** an established creed or belief, esp a religious one **5** a sect, party, or faction [C14 from Latin *persuāsiō*; see PERSUADE]

persuasive (pəˈsweɪsɪv) *adj* having the power or ability to persuade; tending to persuade: *a persuasive salesman* > perˈsuasively *adv* > perˈsuasiveness *n*

persulphuric acid *or US* **persulfuric acid** (ˌpɜːsʌlˈfjʊərɪk) *n* other names (not in technical usage) for **peroxysulphuric acid**

pert (pɜːt) *adj* **1** saucy, impudent, or forward **2** jaunty: *a pert little hat* **3** *obsolete* clever or brisk [C13 variant of earlier *apert*, from Latin *apertus* open, from *aperīre* to open; influenced by Old French *aspert*, from Latin *expertus* EXPERT] > 'pertly *adv* > 'pertness *n*

PERT (pɜːt) *n acronym for* programme evaluation and review technique

pertain (pəˈteɪn) *vb* (*intr; often foll by* to) **1** to have reference, relation, or relevance: *issues pertaining to women* **2** to be appropriate: *the product pertains to real user needs* **3** to belong (to) or be a part (of); be an adjunct, attribute, or accessory (of) [C14 from Latin *pertinēre*, from *per-* (intensive) + *tenēre* to hold]

Perth (pɜːθ) *n* **1** a town in central Scotland, in Perth and Kinross on the River Tay: capital of Scotland from the 12th century until the assassination of James I there in 1437. Pop: 43 450 (2001) **2** a city in SW Australia, capital of Western Australia, on the Swan River: major industrial centre; University of Western Australia (1911). Pop: 1 176 542 (2001)

Perth and Kinross (kɪnˈrɒs) *n* a council area of N central Scotland, corresponding mainly to the historical counties of Perthshire and Kinross-shire: part of Tayside Region from 1975 until 1996: chiefly mountainous, with agriculture, tourism, and forestry. Administrative centre: Perth. Pop: 135 990 (2003 est). Area: 5321 sq km (2019 sq miles)

Perthshire ('pɜːθʃɪə, -ʃə) *n* (until 1975) a county of central Scotland, now part of Perth and Kinross council area

pertinacious (ˌpɜːtɪˈneɪʃəs) *adj* **1** doggedly resolute in purpose or belief; unyielding **2** stubbornly persistent [C17 from Latin *pertināx*, from *per-* (intensive) + *tenāx* clinging, from *tenēre* to hold] > ˌpertiˈnaciously *adv* > pertinacity (ˌpɜːtɪˈnæsɪtɪ) *or* ˌpertiˈnaciousness *n*

pertinent ('pɜːtɪnənt) *adj* relating to the matter at hand; relevant [C14 from Latin *pertinēns*, from *pertinēre* to PERTAIN] > 'pertinence *n* > 'pertinently *adv*

perturb (pəˈtɜːb) *vb* (*tr; often passive*) **1** to disturb the composure of; trouble **2** to throw into disorder **3** *physics, astronomy* to cause (a planet, electron, etc) to undergo a perturbation [C14 from Old French *pertourber*, from Latin *perturbāre* to confuse, from *per-* (intensive) + *turbāre* to agitate, from *turba* confusion] > perˈturbable *adj* > perˈturbably *adv* > perˈturbing *adj* > perˈturbingly *adv*

perturbation (ˌpɜːtəˈbeɪʃən) *n* **1** the act of perturbing or the state of being perturbed **2** a cause of disturbance or upset **3** *physics* a secondary influence on a system that modifies simple behaviour, such as the effect of the other electrons on one electron in an atom **4** *astronomy* a small continuous deviation in the inclination and eccentricity of the orbit of a planet or comet, due to the attraction of neighbouring planets

pertussis (pəˈtʌsɪs) *n* the technical name for **whooping cough** [C18 New Latin, from Latin *per-* (intensive) + *tussis* cough] > perˈtussal *adj*

Peru (pəˈruː) *n* a republic in W South America, on the Pacific: the centre of the great Inca Empire when conquered by the Spanish in 1532; gained independence in 1824 by defeating Spanish forces with armies led by San Martín and Bolívar; consists of a coastal desert, rising to the Andes; an important exporter of minerals and a major fishing nation. Official languages: Spanish, Quechua, and Aymara. Official religion: Roman Catholic. Currency: nuevo sol. Capital: Lima. Pop: 27 567 000 (2004 est). Area: 1 285 215 sq km (496 222 sq miles)

Peru Current *n* another name for the **Humboldt Current**

Perugia (pəˈruːdʒə; *Italian* peˈruːdʒa) *n* **1** a city in central Italy, in Umbria: centre of the Umbrian school of painting (15th century); university (1308); Etruscan and Roman remains. Pop: 149 125 (2001). Ancient name: **Perusia 2 Lake** another name for (Lake) **Trasimene**

peruke (pəˈruːk) *n* a type of wig for men, fashionable in the 17th and 18th centuries. Also called: **periwig** [C16 from French *perruque*, from Italian *perrucca* wig, of obscure origin]

peruse (pəˈruːz) *vb* (*tr*) **1** to read or examine with care; study **2** to browse or read through in a leisurely way [C15 (meaning: to use up): from PER- (intensive) + USE] > peˈrusal *n* > peˈruser *n*

Peruvian (pəˈruːvɪən) *adj* **1** of or relating to Peru or its inhabitants ▷ *n* **2** a native or inhabitant of Peru

Peruvian bark *n* another name for **cinchona** (sense 2)

perv (pɜːv) *slang* ▷ *n* **1** a pervert **2** *Austral* an erotic glance or look ▷ *vb also* **perve** (*intr*) **3** *Austral* to give a person an erotic look ▷ See also **perv on**

pervade (pɜːˈveɪd) *vb* (*tr*) to spread through or throughout, esp subtly or gradually; permeate [C17 from Latin *pervādere*, from *per-* through + *vādere* to go] > perˈvader *n* > pervasion (pɜːˈveɪʒən) *n*

pervasive (pɜːˈveɪsɪv) *adj* pervading or tending to pervade [C18 from Latin *pervāsus*, past participle of *pervādere* to PERVADE] > perˈvasively *adv* > perˈvasiveness *n*

perverse (pəˈvɜːs) *adj* **1** deliberately deviating from what is regarded as normal, good, or proper **2** persistently holding to what is wrong **3** wayward or contrary; obstinate; cantankerous **4** *archaic* perverted [C14 from Old French *pervers*, from Latin *perversus* turned the wrong way] > perˈversely *adv* > perˈverseness *n*

perversion (pəˈvɜːʃən) *n* **1** any abnormal means of obtaining sexual satisfaction **2** the act of perverting or the state of being perverted **3** a perverted form or usage

perversity (pəˈvɜːsɪtɪ) *n, pl* -ties **1** the quality or state of being perverse **2** a perverse action, comment, etc

perversive (pəˈvɜːsɪv) *adj* perverting or tending to pervert

pervert *vb* (*tr*) (pəˈvɜːt) **1** to use wrongly or badly **2** to interpret wrongly or badly; distort **3** to lead into deviant or perverted beliefs or behaviour; corrupt **4** to debase ▷ *n* ('pɜːvɜːt) **5** a person who practises sexual perversion [C14 from Old French *pervertir*, from Latin *pervertere* to turn the wrong way, from *per-* (indicating deviation) + *vertere* to turn] > perˈverter *n* > perˈvertible *adj*

perverted (pəˈvɜːtɪd) *adj* **1** deviating greatly from what is regarded as normal or right; distorted **2**

of or practising sexual perversion **3** incorrectly interpreted > perˈvertedly *adv* > perˈvertedness *n*

pervious ('pɜːvɪəs) *adj* **1** able to be penetrated; permeable **2** receptive to new ideas; open-minded [C17 from Latin *pervius*, from *per-* (through) + *via* a way] > 'perviously *adv* > 'perviousness *n*

perv on *vb* (*tr, preposition*) *slang* to make unwanted sexual advances towards

pes (peɪz, piːz) *n, pl* **pedes** ('pɛdiːz) **1** the technical name for the human **foot 2** the corresponding part in higher vertebrates **3** any footlike part [C19 New Latin: foot]

PES *abbreviation for* Party of European Socialists: the Socialist, Democratic, and Labour parties of the European Union, founded in 1992

Pesach *or* **Pesah** ('peɪsɑːk; *Hebrew* 'pɛsax) *n* other words for **Passover** (sense 1) [from Hebrew *pesah*; see PASSOVER]

pesade (pɛˈsɑːd) *n dressage* a position in which the horse stands on the hind legs with the forelegs in the air [C18 from French, from *posade*, from Italian *posata* a halt, from *posare* to stop, from Latin *pausa* end]

Pesaro (*Italian* 'peːzaro) *n* a port and resort in E central Italy, in the Marches on the Adriatic. Pop: 91 086 (2001). Ancient name: **Pisaurum** (pɪˈsaʊrəm)

Pescadores (ˌpɛskəˈdɔːriːz) *pl n* a group of 64 islands in Formosa Strait, separated from Taiwan (to which it belongs) by the **Pescadores Channel.** Pop: 90 719 (2001 est). Area: 127 sq km (49 sq miles). Chinese names: **Penghu, P'eng-hu**

Pescara (*Italian* pesˈkaːra) *n* a city and resort in E central Italy, on the Adriatic. Pop: 116 286 (2001)

peseta (pəˈseɪtə; *Spanish* peˈseta) *n* the former standard monetary unit of Spain and Andorra, divided into 100 céntimos; replaced by the euro in 2002 [C19 from Spanish, diminutive of PESO]

pesewa (pɪˈseɪwɑː) *n* a Ghanaian monetary unit worth one hundredth of a cedi

Peshawar (pəˈʃɔːə) *n* a city in N Pakistan, at the E end of the Khyber Pass: one of the oldest cities in Pakistan and capital of the ancient kingdom of Gandhara; university (1950). Pop: 1 255 000 (2005 est)

Peshitta (pəˈʃiːtə) *or* **Peshito** (pəˈʃiːtəʊ) *n* the principal Syriac version of the Bible [C18 *Peshito*, from Syriac]

pesky ('pɛskɪ) *adj* **peskier, peskiest** *informal, chiefly US and Canadian* troublesome: *pesky flies* [C19 probably changed from *pesty*; see PEST] > 'peskily *adv* > 'peskiness *n*

peso ('peɪsəʊ; *Spanish* 'peso) *n, pl* -**sos** (-səʊz; *Spanish* -sos) **1** the standard monetary unit, comprising 100 centavos, of Argentina, Chile, Colombia, Cuba, the Dominican Republic, Mexico, and the Philippines; formerly also of Guinea-Bissau, where it was replaced by the CFA franc **2** the standard monetary unit of Uruguay, divided into 100 centesimos **3** another name for **piece of eight** [C16 from Spanish: weight, from Latin *pēnsum* something weighed out, from *pendere* to weigh]

pessary ('pɛsərɪ) *n, pl* -ries *med* **1** a device for inserting into the vagina, either as a support for the uterus or (**diaphragm pessary**) to deliver a drug, such as a contraceptive **2** a medicated vaginal suppository [C14 from Late Latin *pessārium*, from Latin *pessum*, from Greek *pessos* plug]

pessimism ('pɛsɪˌmɪzəm) *n* **1** the tendency to expect the worst and see the worst in all things **2** the doctrine of the ultimate triumph of evil over good **3** the doctrine that this world is corrupt and that man's sojourn in it is a preparation for some other existence [C18 from Latin *pessimus* worst, from *malus* bad] > 'pessimist *n* > ˌpessiˈmistic *or less commonly* ˌpessiˈmistical *adj* > ˌpessiˈmistically *adv*

pest (pɛst) *n* **1** a person or thing that annoys, esp by imposing itself when it is not wanted; nuisance **2 a** any organism that damages crops, injures or irritates livestock or man, or reduces the fertility of land **b** (*as modifier*): *pest control* **3** *rare* an epidemic disease or pestilence [C16 from Latin *pestis* plague, of obscure origin]

pester ('pɛstə) vb (tr) to annoy or nag continually [c16 from Old French empestrer to hobble (a horse), from Vulgar Latin impāstōriāre (unattested) to use a hobble, from pāstōria (unattested) a hobble, from Latin pāstōrius relating to a herdsman, from pastor herdsman] > 'pesterer n > 'pesteringly adv

pester power n the ability possessed by a child to nag a parent relentlessly until the parent succumbs and agrees to the child's request

pesthouse ('pɛst,haʊs) n obsolete a hospital for treating persons with infectious diseases. Also called: lazaretto

pesticide ('pɛstɪ,saɪd) n a chemical used for killing pests, esp insects and rodents > ,pesti'cidal adj

pestiferous (pɛ'stɪfərəs) adj 1 informal troublesome; irritating 2 breeding, carrying, or spreading infectious disease 3 corrupting; pernicious [c16 from Latin pestifer, from pestis contagious disease, PEST + ferre to bring] > pes'tiferously adv > pes'tiferousness n

pestilence ('pɛstɪləns) n 1 a any epidemic outbreak of a deadly and highly infectious disease, such as the plague b such a disease 2 an evil influence or idea

pestilent ('pɛstɪlənt) adj 1 annoying; irritating 2 highly destructive morally or physically; pernicious 3 infected with or likely to cause epidemic or infectious disease [c15 from Latin pestilens unwholesome, from pestis plague] > 'pestilently adv

pestilential (,pɛstɪ'lɛnʃəl) adj 1 dangerous or troublesome; harmful or annoying 2 of, causing, or resembling pestilence > ,pesti'lentially adv

pestle ('pɛsᵊl) n 1 a club-shaped instrument for mixing or grinding substances in a mortar 2 a tool for pounding or stamping ▷ vb 3 to pound (a substance or object) with or as if with a pestle [c14 from Old French pestel, from Latin pistillum; related to pinsāre to crush]

pesto ('pɛstəʊ) n a sauce for pasta, consisting of basil leaves, pine nuts, garlic, oil, and Parmesan cheese, all crushed together [Italian, shortened form of pestato, past participle of pestare to pound, crush]

pet¹ (pet) n 1 a tame animal kept in a household for companionship, amusement, etc 2 a person who is fondly indulged; favourite: teacher's pet ▷ adj 3 kept as a pet: a pet dog 4 of or for pet animals: pet food 5 particularly cherished; favourite: a pet theory; a pet hatred 6 familiar or affectionate: a pet name 7 pet day Scot and Irish a single fine day during a period of bad weather ▷ vb pets, petting, petted 8 (tr) to treat (a person, animal, etc) as a pet; pamper 9 (tr) to pat or fondle (an animal, child, etc) 10 (intr) informal (of two people) to caress each other in an erotic manner, as during lovemaking (often in the phrase heavy petting) [c16 origin unknown] > 'petter n

pet² (pet) n 1 a fit of sulkiness, esp at what is felt to be a slight; pique ▷ vb pets, petting, petted 2 (intr) to take offence; sulk [c16 of uncertain origin]

PET abbreviation for 1 positron emission tomography ▷ n acronym for 2 potentially exempt transfer: a procedure in the UK whereby gifting property and cash is tax-free, provided that the donor lives for at least seven years after the gift is made

Pet. Bible abbreviation for Peter

Peta abbreviation for People for the Ethical Treatment of Animals

peta- prefix denoting 10¹⁵: petametres. Symbol: P [c20 so named because it is the SI prefix after TERA-; on the model of PENTA-, the prefix after TETRA-]

petabyte ('pɛtə,baɪt) n computing 10¹⁵ or 2⁵⁰ bytes

petal ('pɛtᵊl) n any of the separate parts of the corolla of a flower: often brightly coloured [c18 from New Latin petalum, from Greek petalon leaf; related to petannunai to lie open] > 'petaline adj > 'petal-,like adj > 'petalled adj

-petal adj combining form seeking: centripetal [from New Latin -petus, from Latin petere to seek]

petaliferous (,pɛtə'lɪfərəs) or **petalous** adj bearing or having petals

petalody ('pɛtə,ləʊdɪ) n a condition in certain plants in which stamens or other parts of the flower assume the form and function of petals [c19 from Greek petalōdēs like a leaf, from petalon leaf] > petalodic (,pɛtə'lɒdɪk) adj

petaloid ('pɛtə,lɔɪd) adj biology resembling a petal, esp in shape: the petaloid pattern on a sea urchin

pétanque French (,peɪ'tāk; English petāk) n another name, esp in the South of France, for **boules** [French, from Provençal pèd tanco foot fixed (to the ground)]

petard (pɪ'tɑːd) n 1 (formerly) a device containing explosives used to breach a wall, doors, etc 2 hoist with one's own petard being the victim of one's own schemes 3 a type of explosive firework [c16 from French: firework, from péter to break wind, from Latin pēdere]

petasus ('pɛtəsəs) or **petasos** ('pɛtəsəs, -,sɒs) n a broad-brimmed hat worn by the ancient Greeks, such as one with wings on either side as traditionally worn by Mercury [c16 via Latin from Greek petasos]

petaurist (pə'tɔːrɪst) n another name for **flying phalanger** [c20 from Latin petaurista tightrope walker]

petcock ('pɛt,kɒk) n a small valve for checking the water level in a steam boiler or draining condensed steam from the cylinder of a steam engine [c19 from PET¹ or perhaps French pet, from péter to break wind + COCK¹]

petechia (pɪ'tiːkɪə) n, pl -chiae (-kɪ,iː) a minute discoloured spot on the surface of the skin or mucous membrane, caused by an underlying ruptured blood vessel [c18 via New Latin from Italian petecchia freckle, of obscure origin] > pe'techial adj

peter¹ ('piːtə) vb (intr; foll by out or away) to fall (off) in volume, intensity, etc, and finally cease: the cash petered out in three months [c19 of unknown origin]

peter² ('piːtə) bridge, whist ▷ vb (intr) 1 to play a high card before a low one in a suit, usually a conventional signal of a doubleton holding or of strength in that suit ▷ n 2 the act of petering [c20 perhaps a special use of PETER¹ (to fall off in power)]

peter³ ('piːtə) n slang 1 a safe, till, or cash box 2 a prison cell 3 the witness box in a courtroom 4 chiefly US a slang word for **penis** [C17 (meaning a case): from the name Peter]

Peter ('piːtə) n New Testament either of the two epistles traditionally ascribed to the apostle Peter (in full **The First Epistle** and **The Second Epistle of Peter**)

Peterborough ('piːtəbərə, -brə) n 1 a city in central England, in Peterborough unitary authority, N Cambridgeshire on the River Nene: industrial centre; under development as a new town since 1968. Pop: 136 292 (2001) 2 a unitary authority in central England, in Cambridgeshire. Pop: 158 800 (2003 est). Area: 402 sq km (155 sq miles) 3 **Soke of** a former administrative unit of E central England, generally considered part of Northamptonshire or Huntingdonshire: absorbed into Cambridgeshire in 1974 4 a city in SE Canada, in SE Ontario: manufacturing centre. Pop: 73 303 (2001) 5 a traditional type of wooden canoe formerly made in Peterborough, SE Ontario

Peterlee ('piːtə,liː) n a new town in Co Durham, founded in 1948. Pop: 29 936 (2001)

Peterloo Massacre (,piːtə'luː) n an incident at St Peter's Fields, Manchester, in 1819 in which a radical meeting was broken up by a cavalry charge, resulting in about 500 injuries and 11 deaths [c19 from St Peter's Fields + WATERLOO]

peterman ('piːtəmən) n, pl -men slang a burglar skilled in safe-breaking [c19 from PETER³]

Petermann Peak ('piːtəmən) n a mountain in E Greenland. Height: 2932 m (9645 ft)

Peter Pan n a youthful, boyish, or immature man [c20 after the main character in Peter Pan (1904), a play by J. M. Barrie]

Peter Pan collar n a collar on a round neck, having two rounded ends at the front

Peter Principle n the the theory, usually taken facetiously, that all members in a hierarchy rise to their own level of incompetence [c20 from the book The Peter Principle (1969) by Dr. Lawrence J. Peter and Raymond Hull, in which the theory was originally propounded]

Petersburg ('piːtəz,bɜːg) n a city in SE Virginia, on the Appomattox River: scene of prolonged fighting (1864–65) during the final months of the American Civil War. Pop: 33 091 (2003 est)

petersham ('piːtəʃəm) n 1 a thick corded ribbon used to stiffen belts, button bands, etc 2 a heavy woollen fabric used esp for coats 3 a kind of overcoat made of such fabric [c19 named after Viscount Petersham (died 1851), English army officer]

Peter's pence or **Peter pence** n 1 an annual tax, originally of one penny, formerly levied for the maintenance of the Papal See: abolished by Henry VIII in 1534 2 a voluntary contribution made by Roman Catholics in many countries for the same purpose [c13 referring to St PETER, considered as the first pope]

Peters' projection n a form of modified world map projection that attempts to reflect accurately the relative surface areas of landmasses, an approach which gives greater prominence (than do standard representations) to equatorial countries. Compare **Mercator projection** [c20 named after Arno Peters, German historian]

pethidine ('pɛθɪ,diːn) n a white crystalline water-soluble drug used as an analgesic. Formula: $C_{15}H_{21}NO_2.HCl$. Also called: pethidine hydrochloride [c20 perhaps a blend of PIPERIDINE + ETHYL]

pétillant French (petijā) adj (of wine) slightly effervescent [French, from pétiller to effervesce]

petiolate ('pɛtɪə,leɪt) or **petiolated** adj (of a plant or leaf) having a leafstalk. Compare **sessile** (sense 1)

petiole ('pɛtɪ,əʊl) n 1 the stalk by which a leaf is attached to the rest of the plant 2 zoology a slender stalk or stem, such as the connection between the thorax and abdomen of ants [c18 via French from Latin petiolus little foot, from pēs foot]

petiolule ('pɛtɪəʊl,juːl) n the stalk of any of the leaflets making up a compound leaf [c19 from New Latin petiolūlus, diminutive of Latin petiolus; see PETIOLE]

petit ('pɛtɪ) adj (prenominal) chiefly law of little or lesser importance; small: petit jury [c14 from Old French: little, of obscure origin]

petit bourgeois ('pɛtɪ 'bʊəʒwɑː; French pəti burʒwa) n, pl petits bourgeois ('pɛtɪ 'bʊəʒwɑːz; French pəti burʒwa) 1 Also called: petite bourgeoisie, petty bourgeoisie the section of the middle class with the lowest social status, generally composed of shopkeepers, lower clerical staff, etc 2 a member of this stratum ▷ adj 3 of, relating to, or characteristic of the petit bourgeois, esp indicating a sense of self-righteousness and a high degree of conformity to established standards of behaviour

petite (pə'tiːt) adj (of a woman) small, delicate, and dainty [c18 from French, feminine of petit small]

petit four ('pɛtɪ 'fɔː; French pəti fur) n, pl petits fours ('pɛtɪ 'fɔːz; French pəti fur) any of various very small rich sweet cakes and biscuits, usually decorated with fancy icing, marzipan, etc [French, literally: little oven]

petition (pɪ'tɪʃən) n 1 a written document signed by a large number of people demanding some form of action from a government or other authority 2 any formal request to a higher authority or deity; entreaty 3 law a formal

p

application in writing made to a court asking for some specific judicial action: *a petition for divorce* **4** the action of petitioning ▷ *vb* **5** (*tr*) to address or present a petition to (a person in authority, government, etc): *to petition Parliament* **6** (*intr*; foll by *for*) to seek by petition: *to petition for a change in the law* [C14 from Latin *petītiō*, from *petere* to seek] > pe'titionary *adj*

petitioner (pɪˈtɪʃənə) *n* **1** a person who presents a petition **2** *chiefly Brit* the plaintiff in a divorce suit

petitio principii (pɪˈtɪʃɪˌəʊ prɪnˈkɪpɪˌaɪ) *n logic* a form of fallacious reasoning in which the conclusion has been assumed in the premises; begging the question. Sometimes shortened to: **petitio** [C16 Latin, translation of Greek *to en arkhēi aiteisthai* an assumption at the beginning]

petit jury *n* a jury of 12 persons empanelled to determine the facts of a case and decide the issue pursuant to the direction of the court on points of law. Also called: **petty jury** Compare **grand jury**. > **petit juror** *n*

petit larceny *n* **1** (formerly in England) the stealing of property valued at 12 pence or under. Abolished 1827 **2** (in some states of the US) the theft of property having a value below a certain figure ▷ Also called: **petty larceny** Compare **grand larceny**. > **petit larcenist** *n*

petit mal (ˈpɛtɪ ˈmæl; French pəti mal) *n* a mild form of epilepsy characterized by periods of impairment or loss of consciousness for up to 30 seconds. Compare **grand mal** [C19 French: little illness]

petit point (ˈpɛtɪ ˈpɔɪnt; French pəti pwɛ̃) *n* **1** Also called: **tent stitch** a small diagonal needlepoint stitch used for fine detail **2** work done with such stitches, esp fine tapestry ▷ Compare **gros point** [French: small point]

petits pois (French pəti pwa) *pl n* small sweet fresh green peas [French: small peas]

pet parent *n* a person who looks after a pet animal

USAGE This term is considered by some people concerned with the rights of animals to be more acceptable than *owner*

Petra (ˈpɛtrə, ˈpiːtrə) *n* an ancient city in the south of present-day Jordan; capital of the Nabataean kingdom

Petrarchan (pəˈtrɑːkən) *adj* of or relating to Petrarch (Italian name *Francesco Petrarca*), the Italian lyric poet and scholar (1304–74)

Petrarchan sonnet *n* a sonnet form associated with the poet Petrarch, having an octave rhyming a b b a a b b a and a sestet rhyming either c d e c d e or c d c d c d. Also called: **Italian sonnet**

petrel (ˈpɛtrəl) *n* any oceanic bird of the order *Procellariiformes*, having a hooked bill and tubular nostrils: includes albatrosses, storm petrels, and shearwaters. See also **storm petrel** [C17 variant of earlier *pitteral*, associated by folk etymology with St *Peter*, because the bird appears to walk on water]

Petri dish (ˈpɛtrɪ) *n* a shallow circular flat-bottomed dish, often with a fitting cover, used in laboratories, esp for producing cultures of microorganisms [C19 named after J. R. *Petri* (1852–1921), German bacteriologist]

petrifaction (ˌpɛtrɪˈfækʃən) or **petrification** (ˌpɛtrɪfɪˈkeɪʃən) *n* **1** the act or process of forming petrified organic material **2** the state of being petrified

Petrified Forest *n* a national park in E Arizona, containing petrified coniferous trees about 170 000 000 years old

petrify (ˈpɛtrɪˌfaɪ) *vb* **-fies, -fying, -fied 1** (*tr*; often *passive*) to convert (organic material, esp plant material) into a fossilized form by impregnation with dissolved minerals so that the original appearance is preserved **2** to make or become dull, unresponsive, insensitive, etc; deaden **3** (*tr*; often *passive*) to stun or daze with horror, fear, etc [C16 from French *pétrifier*, ultimately from Greek *petra* stone, rock] > ˈpetriˌfier *n*

Petrine (ˈpiːtraɪn) *adj* **1** *New Testament* of or relating to St Peter (died ?67 AD), the Christian apostle regarded by Roman Catholics as the first pope, his position of leadership, or the epistles, etc, attributed to him **2** *RC Church* of or relating to the supremacy in the Church that the pope is regarded as having inherited from St Peter: *the Petrine claims*

petro- or before a vowel **petr-** *combining form* **1** indicating stone or rock: *petrology* **2** indicating petroleum, its products, etc: *petrochemical* **3** of or relating to a petroleum-producing country: *petrostate* [from Greek *petra* rock or *petros* stone]

petrochemical (ˌpɛtrəʊˈkɛmɪkəl) *n* **1** any substance, such as acetone or ethanol, obtained from petroleum or natural gas ▷ *adj* **2** of, concerned with, or obtained from petrochemicals or related to petrochemistry > ˌpetroˈchemically *adv*

petrochemistry (ˌpɛtrəʊˈkɛmɪstrɪ) *n* **1** the chemistry of petroleum and its derivatives **2** the branch of chemistry concerned with the chemical composition of rocks

petrodollar (ˈpɛtrəʊˌdɒlə) *n* money, paid in dollars, earned by a country for the exporting of petroleum

petrog. *abbreviation for* petrography

petroglyph (ˈpɛtrəˌglɪf) *n* a drawing or carving on rock, esp a prehistoric one [C19 via French from Greek *petra* stone + *gluphē* carving]

Petrograd (ˈpɛtrəʊˌgræd; Russian pɪtraˈgrat) *n* a former name (1914–24) of **Saint Petersburg**

petrography (pɛˈtrɒɡrəfɪ) *n* the branch of petrology concerned with the description and classification of rocks. Abbreviation: **petrog** > **petrographer** (pɛˈtrɒɡrəfɪk) or ˌpetroˈgraphical *adj* > ˌpetroˈgraphically *adv*

petrol (ˈpɛtrəl) *n* any one of various volatile flammable liquid mixtures of hydrocarbons, mainly hexane, heptane, and octane, obtained from petroleum and used as a solvent and a fuel for internal-combustion engines. Usually petrol also contains additives such as antiknock compounds and corrosion inhibitors. US and Canadian name: **gasoline** [C16 via French from Medieval Latin PETROLEUM]

petrol. *abbreviation for* petrology

petrolatum (ˌpɛtrəˈleɪtəm) *n* a translucent gelatinous substance obtained from petroleum; used as a lubricant and in medicine as an ointment base and protective dressing. Also called: **mineral jelly, petroleum jelly** [C19 from PETROL + Latin *-atum* -ATE[1]]

petrol bomb *n* **1** a home-made incendiary device, consisting of a bottle filled with petrol and stoppered with a wick, that is thrown by hand; Molotov cocktail ▷ *vb* **petrol-bomb** (*tr*) **2** to attack with petrol bombs > **petrol bomber** *n*

petrol engine *n* an internal-combustion engine that uses petrol as fuel

petroleum (pəˈtrəʊlɪəm) *n* a dark-coloured thick flammable crude oil occurring in sedimentary rocks around the Persian Gulf, in parts of North and South America, and below the North Sea, consisting mainly of hydrocarbons. Fractional distillation separates the crude oil into petrol, paraffin, diesel oil, lubricating oil, etc. Fuel oil, paraffin wax, asphalt, and carbon black are extracted from the residue [C16 from Medieval Latin, from Latin *petra* stone + *oleum* oil]

petroleum ether *n* a volatile mixture of the higher alkane hydrocarbons, obtained as a fraction of petroleum and used as a solvent

petroleum jelly *n* another name for **petrolatum**

petrolhead (ˈpɛtrəlˌhɛd) *n informal* a person who is excessively interested in or is devoted to travelling by car

petrolic (pɛˈtrɒlɪk) *adj* of, relating to, containing, or obtained from petroleum

petrology (pɛˈtrɒlədʒɪ) *n, pl* **-gies** the study of the composition, origin, structure, and formation of rocks. Abbreviation: **petrol** > **petrological**

(ˌpɛtrəˈlɒdʒɪkəl) *adj* > ˌpetroˈlogically *adv* > peˈtrologist *n*

petrol pump *n* a device at a filling station that is used to deliver petrol to the tank of a car and which displays the quantity, quality, and usually the cost of the petrol delivered

petrol station *n Brit* another term for **filling station**

petronel (ˈpɛtrəˌnɛl) *n* a firearm of large calibre used in the 16th and early 17th centuries, esp by cavalry soldiers [C16 from French, literally: of the breast, from *poitrine* breast, from Latin *pectus*]

Petropavlovsk (Russian pɪtra'pavləfsk) *n* a city in N Kazakhstan on the Ishim River. Pop: 190 000 (2005 est)

Petrópolis (Portuguese pe'trɒpulis) *n* a city in SE Brazil, north of Rio de Janeiro: resort. Pop: 280 000 (2005 est)

petrosal (pɛˈtrəʊsəl) *adj anatomy* of, relating to, or situated near the dense part of the temporal bone that surrounds the inner ear [C18 from Latin *petrōsus* full of rocks, from *petra* a rock, from Greek]

petrous (ˈpɛtrəs, ˈpiː-) *adj* **1** *anatomy* denoting the dense part of the temporal bone that surrounds the inner ear **2** *rare* like rock or stone [C16 from Latin *petrōsus* full of rocks]

Petrovsk (Russian pɪˈtrɒfsk) *n* the former name (until 1921) of **Makhachkala**

Petrozavodsk (Russian pɪtrəzaˈvɒtsk) *n* a city in NW Russia, capital of the Karelian Autonomous Republic, on Lake Onega: developed around ironworks established by Peter the Great in 1703; university (1940). Pop: 265 000 (2005 est

pe-tsai cabbage (ˈpeɪˈtsaɪ) *n* another name for **Chinese cabbage** (sense 1) [from Chinese (Beijing) *pe ts'ai*, literally: white vegetable]

Petsamo (Finnish ˈpɛtsamo) *n* the former name (1920–1944) for **Pechenga**

petticoat (ˈpɛtɪˌkəʊt) *n* **1** a woman's light undergarment in the form of an underskirt or including a bodice supported by shoulder straps **2** *informal* **a** a humorous or mildly disparaging name for a woman **b** (*as modifier*): *petticoat politics* [C15 see PETTY, COAT]

pettifog (ˈpɛtɪˌfɒɡ) *vb* **-fogs, -fogging, -fogged** (*intr*) to be a pettifogger

pettifogger (ˈpɛtɪˌfɒɡə) *n* **1** a lawyer of inferior status who conducts unimportant cases, esp one who is unscrupulous or resorts to trickery **2** any person who quibbles or fusses over details [C16 from PETTY + *fogger*, of uncertain origin, perhaps from *Fugger*, name of a family (C15–16) of German financiers] > ˈpettiˌfoggery *n*

pettifogging (ˈpɛtɪˌfɒɡɪŋ) *adj* **1** petty: *pettifogging details* **2** mean; quibbling: *pettifogging lawyers*

pettish (ˈpɛtɪʃ) *adj* peevish; petulant: *a pettish child* [C16 from PET[2]] > ˈpettishly *adv* > ˈpettishness *n*

pettitoes (ˈpɛtɪˌtəʊz) *pl n* pig's trotters, esp when used as food [C16 from Old French *petite oie*, literally: little goose (giblets of a goose)]

petty (ˈpɛtɪ) *adj* **-tier, -tiest 1** trivial; trifling; inessential: *petty details* **2** of a narrow-minded, mean, or small-natured disposition or character: *petty spite* **3** minor or subordinate in rank: *petty officialdom* **4** *law* of lesser importance [C14 from Old French PETIT] > ˈpettily *adv* > ˈpettiness *n*

petty cash *n* a small cash fund kept on a firm's premises for the payment of minor expenses

petty jury *n* a variant spelling of **petit jury** > **petty juror** *n*

petty larceny *n* a variant spelling of **petit larceny**

petty officer *n* a noncommissioned officer in a naval service, comparable in rank to a sergeant in an army or marine corps

petty sessions *n* (*functioning as singular or plural*) another term for **magistrates' court**

petulant (ˈpɛtjʊlənt) *adj* irritable, impatient, or sullen in a peevish or capricious way [C16 via Old French from Latin *petulāns* bold, from *petulāre* (unattested) to attack playfully, from *petere* to assail] > ˈpetulance or ˈpetulancy *n* > ˈpetulantly *adv*

petunia (pɪ'tjuːnɪə) *n* any solanaceous plant of the tropical American genus *Petunia*: cultivated for their white, pink, blue, or purple funnel-shaped flowers [C19 via New Latin from obsolete French *petun* variety of tobacco, from Tupi *petyn*]

petuntse or **petuntze** (pɪ'tʌntsɪ, -'tʊn-) *n* a fusible feldspathic mineral used in hard-paste porcelain; china stone [C18 from Chinese (Beijing) *pe tun tzu*, from *pe* white + *tun* heap + *tzu* offspring]

Petworth House ('pɛtwɜːθ) *n* a mansion in Petworth in Sussex: rebuilt (1688–96) for Charles Seymour, 6th Duke of Somerset; gardens laid out by Capability Brown; subject of paintings by Turner

pew (pjuː) *n* **1** (in a church) **a** one of several long benchlike seats with backs, used by the congregation **b** an enclosed compartment reserved for the use of a family or other small group **2** *Brit informal* a seat (esp in the phrase **take a pew**) [C14 *pywe*, from Old French *puye*, from Latin *podium* a balcony, from Greek *podion* supporting structure, from *pous* foot]

pewee or **peewee** ('piːwiː) *n* any of several small North American flycatchers of the genus *Contopus*, having a greenish-brown plumage [C19 imitative of its cry]

pewit ('piːwɪt) *n* another name for **lapwing** [C13 imitative of the bird's cry]

pewter ('pjuːtə) *n* **1 a** any of various alloys containing tin (80–90 per cent), lead (10–20 per cent), and sometimes small amounts of other metals, such as copper and antimony **b** (*as modifier*): *pewter ware; a pewter tankard* **2 a** a bluish-grey colour **b** (*as adjective*): *pewter tights* **3** plate or kitchen utensils made from pewter [C14 from Old French *peaultre*, of obscure origin; related to Old Provençal *peltre* pewter] > **'pewterer** *n*

peyote (peɪ'əʊtɪ, pɪ-) *n* another name for **mescal** (sense 1) [Mexican Spanish, from Nahuatl *peyotl*]

pf *the internet domain name for* French Polynesia

pF *symbol for* picofarad

pf. *abbreviation for* **1** perfect **2** Also: **pfg pfennig 3** preferred

pfa *abbreviation for* please find attached

Pfalz (pfalts) *n* the German name for the **Palatinate**

pfennig ('fɛnɪɡ; *German* 'pfɛnɪç) *n, pl* -nigs *or* -nige (*German* -nɪɡə) **1** a former German monetary unit worth one hundredth of a Deutschmark **2** (formerly) a monetary unit worth one hundredth of an East German ostmark [German: PENNY]

PFI (in Britain) *abbreviation for* **Private Finance Initiative**

Pforzheim (*German* 'pfɔrtshaɪm) *n* a city in SW Germany, in W Baden-Württemberg: centre of the German watch and jewellery industry. Pop: 119 046 (2003 est)

pg *the internet domain name for* Papua New Guinea

PG[1] *symbol for* a film certified for viewing by anyone, but which contains scenes that may be unsuitable for children, for whom parental guidance is necessary [C20 from abbreviation of *parental guidance*]

PG[2] *abbreviation for* **1** paying guest **2** postgraduate

pg. *abbreviation for* page

Pg. *abbreviation for* **1** Portugal **2** Portuguese

PGA *abbreviation for* Professional Golfers' Association

PGD *abbreviation for* preimplantation genetic diagnosis; a technique using in vitro fertilization to ensure that a baby does not possess a known genetic defect of either parent. After genetic analysis of the embryos so formed, only those free of defect are implanted in the mother's womb

PGR *abbreviation for* psychogalvanic response

ph *the internet domain name for* Philippines

pH *n* potential of hydrogen; a measure of the acidity or alkalinity of a solution equal to the common logarithm of the reciprocal of the concentration of hydrogen ions in moles per cubic decimetre of solution. Pure water has a pH of 7, acid solutions have a pH less than 7, and alkaline solutions a pH greater than 7

Ph *the chemical symbol for* phenyl group or radical

ph. *abbreviation for* phase

phacelia (fə'siːlɪə) *n* any plant of the mostly annual American genus *Phacelia*, esp *P. campanularia*, grown for its large, deep blue bell flowers: family *Hydrophyllaceae* [New Latin, from Greek *phakelos* cluster (from the habit of the flowers) + -IA]

Phaeacian (fiː'eɪʃən) *n Greek myth* one of a race of people inhabiting the island of Scheria visited by Odysseus on his way home from the Trojan War

Phaedra ('fiːdrə) *n Greek myth* the wife of Theseus, who falsely accused her stepson Hippolytus of raping her because he spurned her amorous advances

phaeic ('fiːɪk) *adj* (of animals) having dusky coloration; less dark than melanic [C19 from Greek *phaiós* dusky] > **'phaeism** *n*

Phaethon ('feɪəθɒn) *n* an asteroid (6.9 km in diameter) that has an orbit approaching close to the sun and releases fragments of dust that enter the earth's atmosphere as meteors

Phaëthon ('feɪəθɒn) *n Greek myth* the son of Helios (the sun god) who borrowed his father's chariot and nearly set the earth on fire by approaching too close to it. Zeus averted the catastrophe by striking him down with a thunderbolt

phaeton ('feɪt²n) *n* a light four-wheeled horse-drawn carriage with or without a top, usually having two seats [C18 from PHAËTHON]

phage (feɪdʒ) *n* short for **bacteriophage**

-phage *n combining form* indicating something that eats or consumes something specified: *bacteriophage* [from Greek *-phagos*; see PHAGO-] > **-phagous** *adj combining form*

phagedaena or **phagedena** (ˌfædʒɪ'diːnə) *n pathol* a rapidly spreading ulcer that destroys tissues as it increases in size [C17 via Latin from Greek, from *phagein* to eat]

phago- *or before a vowel* **phag-** *combining form* eating, consuming, or destroying: *phagocyte* [from Greek *phagein* to consume]

phagocyte ('fæɡəˌsaɪt) *n* an amoeboid cell or protozoan that engulfs particles, such as food substances or invading microorganisms > **phagocytic** (ˌfæɡə'sɪtɪk) *adj*

phagocytosis (ˌfæɡəsaɪ'təʊsɪs) *n* the process by which a cell, such as a white blood cell, ingests microorganisms, other cells, and foreign particles

phagomania (ˌfæɡəʊ'meɪnɪə) *n* a compulsive desire to eat > **ˌphago'maniˌac** *n*

-phagy *or* **-phagia** *n combining form* indicating an eating or devouring: *anthropophagy* [from Greek *-phagia*; see PHAGO-]

phalange ('fælændʒ) *n, pl* phalanges (fæ'lændʒiːz) *anatomy* another name for **phalanx** (sense 5) [C16 via French, ultimately from Greek PHALANX]

phalangeal (fə'lændʒɪəl) *adj anatomy* of or relating to a phalanx or phalanges

phalanger (fə'lændʒə) *n* any of various Australasian arboreal marsupials, such as *Trichosurus vulpecula* (**brush-tailed phalanger**), having dense fur and a long tail: family *Phalangeridae*. Also called (Austral and NZ): possum See also **flying phalanger** [C18 via New Latin from Greek *phalaggion* spider's web, referring to its webbed hind toes]

Phalangist (fə'lændʒɪst) *n* **a** a member of a Lebanese Christian paramilitary organization founded in 1936 and originally based on similar ideas to the fascist Falange in Spain **b** (*as modifier*): *Phalangist leaders*

phalanstery ('fælənstərɪ, -strɪ) *n, pl* -steries **1** (in Fourierism) **a** buildings occupied by a phalanx **b** a community represented by a phalanx **2** any similar association or the buildings occupied by such an association [C19 from French *phalanstère*, from *phalange* PHALANX, on the model of *monastère* MONASTERY]

phalanx ('fælæŋks) *n, pl* phalanxes *or* phalanges (fæ'lændʒiːz) **1** an ancient Greek and Macedonian battle formation of hoplites presenting long spears from behind a wall of overlapping shields **2** any closely ranked unit or mass of people: *the police formed a phalanx to protect the embassy* **3** a number of people united for a common purpose **4** (in Fourierism) a group of approximately 1800 persons forming a commune in which all property is collectively owned **5** *anatomy* any of the bones of the fingers or toes. Related adj: **phalangeal 6** *botany* **a** a bundle of stamens, joined together by their stalks (filaments) **b** a form of vegetative spread in which the advance is on a broad front, as in the common reed ▷ Compare **guerrilla** [C16 via Latin from Greek: infantry formation in close ranks, bone of finger or toe]

phalarope ('fæləˌrəʊp) *n* any aquatic shore bird of the family *Phalaropidae*, such as *Phalaropus fulicarius* (**grey phalarope**), of northern oceans and lakes, having a long slender bill and lobed toes: order *Charadriiformes* [C18 via French from New Latin *Phalaropus*, from Greek *phalaris* coot + *pous* foot]

phallic ('fælɪk) *adj* **1** of, relating to, or resembling a phallus: *a phallic symbol* **2** *psychoanal* **a** relating to a stage of psychosexual development during which a male child's interest is concentrated on the genital organs **b** designating personality traits, such as conceit and self-assurance, due to fixation at the phallic stage of development. Compare **anal** (sense 2), **oral** (sense 7), **genital** (sense 2) **c** (in Freudian theory) denoting a phase of early childhood in which there is a belief that both sexes possess a phallus **3** of or relating to phallicism

phallicism ('fælɪˌsɪzəm) *or* **phallism** *n* the worship or veneration of the phallus > **'phallicist** *or* **'phallist** *n*

phallocentric (ˌfæləʊ'sɛntrɪk) *adj* dominated by male attitudes [C20 from PHALLUS + -CENTRIC] > **ˌphallocen'tricity** *or* ˌphallo'centrism *n*

phalloidin (fə'lɔɪdɪn) *n* a peptide toxin, responsible for the toxicity of the death cap mushroom, *Amanita phalloides* [C20 New Latin, from PHALLUS + -OID + -IN]

phallus ('fæləs) *n, pl* -luses *or* -li (-laɪ) **1** another word for **penis 2** an image of the penis, esp as a religious symbol of reproductive power [C17 via Late Latin from Greek *phallos*]

-phane *n combining form* indicating something resembling a specified substance: *cellophane* [from Greek *phainein* to shine, (in passive) appear]

phanerocrystalline (ˌfænərəʊ'krɪstəlɪn, -ˌlaɪn) *adj* (of igneous and metamorphic rocks) having a crystalline structure in which the crystals are large enough to be seen with the naked eye [C19 from Greek *phaneros* visible + CRYSTALLINE]

phanerogam ('fænərəʊˌɡæm) *n* any plant of the former major division *Phanerogamae*, which included all seed-bearing plants; a former name for **spermatophyte**. Compare **cryptogam** [C19 from New Latin *phanerogamus*, from Greek *phaneros* visible + *gamos* marriage] > ˌphanero'gamic *or* phanerogamous (ˌfænə'rɒɡəməs) *adj*

phanerophyte ('fænərəˌfaɪt, fə'nɛrə-) *n* a tree or shrub that bears its perennating buds more than 25 cm above the level of the soil [C20 from Greek *phanero-* visible + -PHYTE]

Phanerozoic (ˌfænərə'zəʊɪk) *adj* **1** of or relating to that part of geological time represented by rocks in which the evidence of life is abundant, comprising the Palaeozoic, Mesozoic, and Cenozoic eras ▷ *n* **2 the** the Phanerozoic era ▷ Compare **Cryptozoic**

phantasm ('fæntæzəm) *n* **1** a phantom **2** an illusory perception of an object, person, etc **3** (in the philosophy of Plato) objective reality as distorted by perception [C13 from Old French *fantasme*, from Latin *phantasma*, from Greek; related to Greek *phantazein* to cause to be seen, from *phainein* to show] > **phan'tasmal** *or* phan'tasmic *adj* > **phan'tasmally** *or* phan'tasmically *adv*

phantasmagoria (ˌfæntæzməˈɡɔːrɪə) or **phantasmagory** (fænˈtæzməɡərɪ) n 1 psychol a shifting medley of real or imagined figures, as in a dream 2 films a sequence of pictures made to vary in size rapidly while remaining in focus 3 rare a shifting scene composed of different elements [c19 probably from French fantasmagorie production of phantasms, from PHANTASM + -agorie, perhaps from Greek ageirein to gather together] > **phantasmagoric** (ˌfæntæzməˈɡɒrɪk) or ˌphantasmaˈgorical adj > ˌphantasmaˈgorically adv

phantasy (ˈfæntəsɪ) n, pl -sies an archaic spelling of **fantasy**

phantom (ˈfæntəm) n 1 a an apparition or spectre b (as modifier): a phantom army marching through the sky 2 the visible representation of something abstract, esp as appearing in a dream or hallucination: phantoms of evil haunted his sleep 3 something apparently unpleasant or horrific that has no material form 4 med another name for **manikin** (sense 2b) [c13 from Old French fantosme, from Latin phantasma PHANTASM]

phantom limb n the illusion that a limb still exists following its amputation, sometimes with pain (**phantom limb pain**)

phantom pregnancy n the occurrence of signs of pregnancy, such as enlarged abdomen and absence of menstruation, when no embryo is present, due to hormonal imbalance. Also called: **false pregnancy, pseudopregnancy** Technical name: **pseudocyesis**

phantom withdrawal n the unauthorized removal of funds from a bank account using an automated teller machine

-phany n combining form indicating a manifestation: theophany [from Greek -phania, from phainein to show; see -PHANE] > **-phanous** adj combining form

phar., Phar., pharm. or **Pharm.** abbreviation for 1 pharmaceutical 2 pharmacist 3 pharmacopoeia 4 pharmacy

Pharaoh (ˈfɛərəʊ) n the title of the ancient Egyptian kings [Old English Pharaon, via Latin, Greek, and Hebrew ultimately from Egyptian pr-'o great house] > **Pharaonic** (feəˈrɒnɪk) adj

Pharaoh ant or **Pharaoh's ant** n a small yellowish-red ant, Monomorium pharaonis, of warm regions: accidentally introduced into many countries, infesting heated buildings

Pharaoh hound n a medium-sized powerful swift-moving short-haired breed of hound having a glossy tan coat, sometimes with white markings

Pharisaic (ˌfærɪˈseɪɪk) or **Pharisaical** adj 1 Judaism of, relating to, or characteristic of the Pharisees or Pharisaism 2 (often not capital) righteously hypocritical > ˌPhariˈsaically adv > ˌPhariˈsaicalness n

Pharisaism (ˈfærɪseɪˌɪzəm) or **Phariseeism** (ˈfærɪsiːˌɪzəm) n 1 Judaism the tenets and customs of the Pharisees 2 (often not capital) observance of the external forms of religion without genuine belief; hypocrisy

Pharisee (ˈfærɪˌsiː) n 1 Judaism a member of an ancient Jewish sect that was opposed to the Sadducees, teaching strict observance of Jewish tradition as interpreted rabbinically and believing in life after death and in the coming of the Messiah 2 (often not capital) a self-righteous or hypocritical person [Old English Farīsēus, ultimately from Aramaic perīshāiyā, pl of perīsh separated]

pharma (ˈfɑːmə) n pharmaceutical companies when considered together as an industry

pharmaceutical (ˌfɑːməˈsjuːtɪkəl) or less commonly **pharmaceutlc** adj of or relating to drugs or pharmacy [c17 from Late Latin pharmaceuticus, from Greek pharmakeus purveyor of drugs; see PHARMACY] > ˌpharmaˈceutically adv

pharmaceutics (ˌfɑːməˈsjuːtɪks) n 1 (functioning as singular) another term for **pharmacy** (sense 1) 2 (functioning as plural) pharmaceutical remedies

pharmacist (ˈfɑːməsɪst) or less commonly **pharmaceutist** (ˌfɑːməˈsjuːtɪst) n a person qualified to prepare and dispense drugs

pharmaco- combining form indicating drugs: pharmacology; pharmacopoeia [from Greek pharmakon drug, potion]

pharmacodynamics (ˌfɑːməkəʊdaɪˈnæmɪks) n (functioning as singular) the branch of pharmacology concerned with the action of drugs on the physiology or pathology of the body > ˌpharmacodyˈnamic adj

pharmacogenomics (ˌfɑːməkəʊdʒɪˈnɒmɪks) n (functioning as singular) the study of human genetic variability in relation to drug action and its application to medical treatment > ˌpharmacogeˈnomic adj

pharmacognosy (ˌfɑːməˈkɒɡnəsɪ) n the branch of pharmacology concerned with crude drugs of plant and animal origin [c19 from PHARMACO- + gnosy, from Greek gnosis knowledge] > ˌpharmaˈcognosist n > pharmacognostic (ˌfɑːməkɒɡˈnɒstɪk) adj

pharmacokinetics (ˌfɑːməkəʊkɪˈnɛtɪks, -kaɪ-) n the branch of pharmacology concerned with the way drugs are taken into, move around, and are eliminated from, the body > ˌpharmacokiˈnetic adj > ˌpharmacokiˈnetically adv > **pharmacokineticist** (ˌfɑːməkəʊkɪˈnɛtɪsɪst) n

pharmacol. abbreviation for pharmacology

pharmacology (ˌfɑːməˈkɒlədʒɪ) n the science of drugs, including their characteristics and uses > **pharmacological** (ˌfɑːməkəˈlɒdʒɪkəl) adj > ˌpharmacoˈlogically adv > ˌpharmaˈcologist n

pharmacopoeia or sometimes US **pharmacopeia** (ˌfɑːməkəˈpiːə) n an authoritative book containing a list of medicinal drugs with their uses, preparation, dosages, formulas, etc [c17 via New Latin from Greek pharmakopoiia art of preparing drugs, from PHARMACO- + -poiia, from poiein to make] > ˌpharmacoˈpoeial or ˌpharmacoˈpoeist adj > ˌpharmacoˈpoeist n

pharmacy (ˈfɑːməsɪ) n, pl -cies 1 Also called: **pharmaceutics** the practice or art of preparing and dispensing drugs 2 a dispensary [c14 from Medieval Latin pharmacia, from Greek pharmakeia making of drugs, from pharmakon drug]

pharming (ˈfɑːmɪŋ) n the practice of rearing or growing genetically-modified animals or plants in order to develop pharmaceutical products [c20 blend of PHARMACEUTICAL + FARMING]

Pharos (ˈfɛərɒs) n a large Hellenistic lighthouse built on an island off Alexandria in Egypt in about 280 BC and destroyed by an earthquake in the 14th century: usually included among the Seven Wonders of the World

Pharsalus (fɑːˈseɪləs) n an ancient town in Thessaly in N Greece. Several major battles were fought nearby, including Caesar's victory over Pompey (48 BC)

pharyngeal (ˌfærɪnˈdʒiːəl) or **pharyngal** (fəˈrɪŋɡəl) adj 1 of, relating to, or situated in or near the pharynx 2 phonetics pronounced or supplemented in pronunciation with an articulation in or constriction of the pharynx ▷ n 3 phonetics a pharyngeal speech sound [c19 from New Latin pharyngeus; see PHARYNX]

pharyngeal tonsil n the technical name for adenoids

pharyngitis (ˌfærɪnˈdʒaɪtɪs) n inflammation of the pharynx

pharyngo- or before a vowel **pharyng-** combining form pharynx: pharyngoscope

pharyngology (ˌfærɪŋˈɡɒlədʒɪ) n the branch of medical science concerned with the pharynx and its diseases > **pharyngological** (ˌfærɪŋɡəˈlɒdʒɪkəl) adj > ˌpharynˈgologist n

pharyngoscope (fəˈrɪŋɡəˌskəʊp) n a medical instrument for examining the pharynx > **pharyngoscopic** (fəˌrɪŋɡəˈskɒpɪk) adj > **pharyngoscopy** (ˌfærɪŋˈɡɒskəpɪ) n

pharyngotomy (ˌfærɪŋˈɡɒtəmɪ) n, pl -mies surgical incision into the pharynx

pharynx (ˈfærɪŋks) n, pl **pharynges** (fæˈrɪndʒiːz) or **pharynxes** the part of the alimentary canal between the mouth and the oesophagus. Compare **nasopharynx** Related adj: **pharyngeal** [c17 via New Latin from Greek pharunx throat; related to Greek pharanx chasm]

phascogale (ˈfæskəɡeɪl, fæsˈkaːɡəlɪ) n Austral another name for **tuan²**

phase (feɪz) n 1 any distinct or characteristic period or stage in a sequence of events or chain of development: there were two phases to the resolution; his immaturity was a passing phase 2 astronomy one of the recurring shapes of the portion of the moon or an inferior planet illuminated by the sun: the new moon, first quarter, full moon, and last quarter are the four principal phases of the moon 3 physics a the fraction of a cycle of a periodic quantity that has been completed at a specific reference time, expressed as an angle b (as modifier): a phase shift 4 physics a particular stage in a periodic process or phenomenon 5 in phase (of two waveforms) reaching corresponding phases at the same time 6 out of phase (of two waveforms) not in phase 7 chem a distinct state of matter characterized by homogeneous composition and properties and the possession of a clearly defined boundary 8 zoology a variation in the normal form of an animal, esp a colour variation, brought about by seasonal or geographical change 9 biology (usually in combination) a stage in mitosis or meiosis: prophase; metaphase 10 electrical engineering one of the circuits in a system in which there are two or more alternating voltages displaced by equal amounts in phase (sense 5). See also **polyphase** (sense 1) 11 (in systemic grammar) the type of correspondence that exists between the predicators in a clause that has two or more predicators; for example connection by to, as in I managed to do it, or -ing, as in we heard him singing ▷ vb (tr) 12 (often passive) to execute, arrange, or introduce gradually or in stages: a phased withdrawal 13 (sometimes foll by with) to cause (a part, process, etc) to function or coincide with (another part, process, etc): he tried to phase the intake and output of the machine; he phased the intake with the output 14 chiefly US to arrange (processes, goods, etc) to be supplied or executed when required [c19 from New Latin phases, pl of phasis, from Greek: aspect; related to Greek phainein to show] > **phaseless** adj > **phasic** or **phaseal** adj

phase-contrast microscope n a microscope that makes visible details of colourless transparent objects. It employs a method of illumination such that small differences of refractive index of the materials in the object cause differences of luminous intensity by interference

phased array n an array of radio antennae connected together to form a single antenna. The beam produced can be steered across the sky by adjusting the phases of the signals. The absence of moving parts enables the beams to be steered very rapidly, making it useful in radar

phase in vb (tr, adverb) to introduce in a gradual or cautious manner: the legislation will be phased in

phase modulation n a type of modulation, used in communication systems, in which the phase of a radio carrier wave is varied by an amount proportional to the instantaneous amplitude of the modulating signal

phase out vb 1 (tr, adverb) to discontinue or withdraw gradually ▷ n **phase-out** 2 the action or an instance of phasing out: a phase-out of conventional forces

phase rule n the principle that in any system in equilibrium the number of degrees of freedom is equal to the number of components less the number of phases plus two. See also **degree of freedom, component** (sense 4)

phase shift keying n See PSK

phase speed or **velocity** n physics the speed at which the phase of a wave is propagated, the product of the frequency times the wavelength. This is the quantity that is determined by methods using interference. In a dispersive medium it differs from the group speed. Also called: **wave speed**, **wave velocity**

phase-switching *n* a technique used in radio interferometry in which the signal from one of the two antennae is periodically reversed in phase before being multiplied by the signal from the other antenna

-phasia *n combining form* indicating speech disorder of a specified kind: *aphasia* [from Greek, from *phanai* to speak] > **-phasic** *adj* and *n combining form*

phasing ('feɪzɪŋ) *n electrical engineering* a tonal sweep achieved by varying the phase relationship of two similar audio signals by mechanical or electronic means

phasmid ('fæzmɪd) *n* **1** any plant-eating insect of the mainly tropical order *Phasmida*: includes the leaf insects and stick insects ▷ *adj* **2** of, relating to, or belonging to the order *Phasmida* [c19 from New Latin *Phasmida*, from Greek *phasma* spectre]

phasor ('feɪzɔ:) *n electrical engineering* a rotating vector representing a quantity, such as an alternating current or voltage, that varies sinusoidally

phat (fæt) *adj slang* terrific; superb [c20 from Black slang, a corruption of FAT]

phatic ('fætɪk) *adj* (of speech, esp of conversational phrases) used to establish social contact and to express sociability rather than specific meaning [c20 from Greek *phat(os)* spoken + -IC]

PHC *abbreviation for* Pharmaceutical Chemist

PhD *abbreviation for* Doctor of Philosophy. Also: **DPhil**

pheasant ('fɛzənt) *n* **1** any of various long-tailed gallinaceous birds of the family *Phasianidae*, esp *Phasianus colchicus* (**ring-necked pheasant**), having a brightly-coloured plumage in the male: native to Asia but introduced elsewhere **2** any of various other gallinaceous birds of the family *Phasianidae*, including the quails and partridges **3** *US and Canadian* any of several other gallinaceous birds, esp the ruffed grouse [c13 from Old French *fesan*, from Latin *phāsiānus*, from Greek *phasianos ornis* Phasian bird, named after the River *Phasis*, in Colchis]

pheasant's eye *n* **1** an annual ranunculaceous plant, *Adonis annua* (or *autumnalis*), with scarlet flowers and finely divided leaves: native to S Europe but naturalized elsewhere **2** a type of narcissus, *Narcissus poeticus*, that has white petals and a small red-ringed cup

Phebe ('fi:bɪ) *n* a variant spelling of **Phoebe**[1]

phellem ('fɛləm) *n botany* the technical name for **cork** (sense 4) [c20 from Greek *phellos* cork + PHLOEM]

phelloderm ('fɛləʊˌdɜ:m) *n* a layer of thin-walled cells produced by the inner surface of the cork cambium [c19 from Greek *phellos* cork + -DERM] > ˌphello'dermal *adj*

phellogen ('fɛlədʒən) *n botany* the technical name for **cork cambium** [c19 from Greek *phellos* cork + -GEN] > phellogenetic (ˌfɛləʊdʒɪ'nɛtɪk) or phellogenic (ˌfɛləʊ'dʒɛnɪk) *adj*

phenacaine ('fi:nəˌkeɪn, 'fɛn-) *n* a crystalline basic compound that is the hydrochloride of holocaine: used as a local anaesthetic in ophthalmic medicine. Formula: $C_{18}H_{22}N_2O_2HCl$ [c20 from PHENO- + ACETO- + COCAINE]

phenacetin (fɪ'næsɪtɪn) *n* a white crystalline solid formerly used in medicine to relieve pain and fever. Because of its kidney toxicity it has been superseded by paracetamol. Formula: $CH_3CONHC_6H_4OC_2H_5$. Also called: acetophenetidin [c19 from PHENETIDINE + ACETYL + -IN]

phenacite ('fɛnəˌsaɪt) or **phenakite** ('fɛnəˌkaɪt) *n* a colourless or white glassy mineral consisting of beryllium silicate in hexagonal crystalline form: occurs in veins in granite. Formula: Be_2SiO_4 [c19

from Greek *phenax* a cheat, because of its deceptive resemblance to quartz]

phenanthrene (fɪ'nænθri:n) *n* a colourless crystalline aromatic compound isomeric with anthracene: used in the manufacture of dyes, drugs, and explosives. Formula: $C_{14}H_{10}$ [c19 from PHENO- + ANTHRACENE]

phenazine ('fɛnəˌzi:n) *n* a yellow crystalline tricyclic compound that is the parent compound of many azine dyes and some antibiotics. Formula: $C_6H_4N_2C_6H_4$ [c19 from PHENO- + AZINE]

phencyclidine (fɛn'sɪklɪˌdi:n) *n* See **PCP**

phenetics (fɪ'nɛtɪks) *n* (*functioning as singular*) *biology* a system of classification based on similarities between organisms without regard to their evolutionary relationships [c20 from PHEN(OTYPE) + (GEN)ETICS] > phe'netic *adj*

phenetidine (fɪ'nɛtɪˌdi:n, -dɪn) *n* a liquid amine that is a derivative of phenetole, existing in three isomeric forms: used in the manufacture of dyestuffs. Formula: $H_2NC_6H_4OC_2H_5$ [c19 from PHENETOLE + -ID[3] + -INE[2]]

phenetole ('fɛnɪˌtəʊl, -ˌtɒl) *n* a colourless oily compound; phenyl ethyl ether. Formula: $C_6H_5OC_2H_5$ [c19 from PHENO- + ETHYL + -OLE[1]]

phenformin (fɛn'fɔ:mɪn) *n* a biguanide administered orally in the treatment of diabetes to lower blood concentrations of glucose; it has been largely superseded by metformin. Formula: $C_{10}H_{15}N_5$ [c20 from PHEN(YL) + FORM(ALDEHYDE) + -IN]

phenix ('fi:nɪks) *n* a US spelling of **phoenix**

pheno- or before a vowel **phen-** *combining form* **1** showing or manifesting: *phenotype* **2** indicating that a molecule contains benzene rings: *phenobarbital* [from Greek *pheno-* shining, from *phainein* to show; its use in a chemical sense is exemplified in *phenol*, so called because originally prepared from illuminating gas]

phenobarbital (ˌfi:nəʊ'ba:bɪtəl) *n* a white crystalline derivative of barbituric acid used as a sedative for treating insomnia and as an anticonvulsant in epilepsy. Formula: $C_{12}H_{12}N_2O_3$

phenocopy ('fi:nəʊˌkɒpɪ) *n*, *pl* -copies a noninheritable change in an organism that is caused by environmental influence during development but resembles the effects of a genetic mutation

phenocryst ('fi:nəˌkrɪst, 'fɛn-) *n* any of several large crystals that are embedded in a mass of smaller crystals in igneous rocks such as porphyry [c19 from PHENO- (shining) + CRYSTAL]

phenol ('fi:nɒl) *n* **1** Also called: **carbolic acid** a white crystalline soluble poisonous acidic derivative of benzene, used as an antiseptic and disinfectant and in the manufacture of resins, nylon, dyes, explosives, and pharmaceuticals; hydroxybenzene. Formula: C_6H_5OH **2** *chem* any of a class of weakly acidic organic compounds whose molecules contain one or more hydroxyl groups bound directly to a carbon atom in an aromatic ring

phenolate ('fi:nəˌleɪt) *vb* **1** (*tr*) Also: **carbolize** to treat or disinfect with phenol ▷ *n* **2** another name (not in technical usage) for **phenoxide**

phenolic (fɪ'nɒlɪk) *adj* of, containing, or derived from phenol

phenolic resin *n* any one of a class of resins derived from phenol, used in paints, adhesives, and as thermosetting plastics. See also **Bakelite**

phenology (fɪ'nɒlədʒɪ) *n* the study of recurring phenomena, such as animal migration, esp as influenced by climatic conditions [c19 from PHENO(MENON) + -LOGY] > phenological (ˌfi:nə'lɒdʒɪkəl) *adj* > phe'nologist *n*

phenolphthalein (ˌfi:nɒl'θeɪli:n, -lɪɪn, -'θæl-) *n* a colourless crystalline compound used in medicine as a laxative and in chemistry as an indicator. Formula: $C_{20}H_{14}O_4$

phenom (fɪ'nɒm) *n informal* a person or thing of outstanding abilities or qualities [c20 from PHENOM(ENON)]

phenomena (fɪ'nɒmɪnə) *n* a plural of **phenomenon**

phenomenal (fɪ'nɒmɪnəl) *adj* **1** of or relating to a phenomenon **2** extraordinary; outstanding; remarkable: *a phenomenal achievement* **3** *philosophy* known or perceived by the senses rather than the mind > phe'nomenally *adv*

phenomenalism (fɪ'nɒmɪnəˌlɪzəm) *n philosophy* the doctrine that statements about physical objects and the external world can be analysed in terms of possible or actual experiences, and that entities, such as physical objects, are only mental constructions out of phenomenal appearances. Compare **idealism** (sense 3), **realism** (sense 6) > phe'nomenalist *n*, *adj* > phe,nomenal'istically *adv*

phenomenology (fɪ,nɒmɪ'nɒlədʒɪ) *n philosophy* **1** the movement founded by Husserl that concentrates on the detailed description of conscious experience, without recourse to explanation, metaphysical assumptions, and traditional philosophical questions **2** the science of phenomena as opposed to the science of being > phenomenological (fɪ,nɒmɪnə'lɒdʒɪk[ə]l) *adj* > phe,nomeno'logically *adv* > phe,nome'nologist *n*

phenomenon (fɪ'nɒmɪnən) *n*, *pl* -ena (-ɪnə) or -enons **1** anything that can be perceived as an occurrence or fact by the senses **2** any remarkable occurrence or person **3** *philosophy* **a** the object of perception, experience, etc **b** (in the writings of Kant) a thing as it appears and is interpreted in perception and reflection, as distinguished from its real nature as a thing-in-itself. Compare **noumenon** [c16 via Late Latin from Greek *phainomenon*, from *phainesthai* to appear, from *phainein* to show]

USAGE Although *phenomena* is often treated as if it were singular, correct usage is to employ *phenomenon* with a singular construction and *phenomena* with a plural: *that is an interesting phenomenon* (not *phenomena*); *several new phenomena were recorded in his notes*

p

phenothiazine (ˌfi:nəʊ'θaɪəzi:n) *n* **1** a colourless to light yellow insoluble crystalline compound used as an anthelmintic for livestock and in insecticides. Formula: $C_{12}H_9NS$ **2** any of several drugs derived from phenothiazine and used as strong tranquillizers and in the treatment of schizophrenia

phenotype ('fi:nəʊˌtaɪp) *n* the physical and biochemical characteristics of an organism as determined by the interaction of its genetic constitution and the environment. Compare **genotype**. > phenotypic (ˌfi:nəʊ'tɪpɪk) or ˌpheno'typical *adj* > ˌpheno'typically *adv*

phenoxide (fɪ'nɒksaɪd) *n* any of a class of salts of phenol. They contain the ion $C_6H_5O^-$. Also called: **phenolate**

phenoxy resin (fɪ'nɒksɪ) *n chem* any of a class of resins derived from polyhydroxy ethers

phenyl ('fi:naɪl, 'fɛnɪl) *n* (*modifier*) of, containing, or consisting of the monovalent group C_6H_5, derived from benzene: *a phenyl group or radical*

phenylalanine (ˌfi:naɪl'æləni:n, ˌfɛnɪl-) *n* an aromatic essential amino acid; a component of proteins

phenylamine (ˌfi:naɪlə'mi:n, ˌfɛnɪl-) *n* another name for **aniline**

phenylbutazone (ˌfi:naɪl'bju:təˌzəʊn) *n* an anti-inflammatory drug used in the treatment of rheumatic diseases; it has been largely superseded by other NSAIDs [c20 from (*dioxodi*)*phenylbut*(*ylpyr*)*azo*(*lidi*)*ne*]

phenylethylamine (ˌfi:naɪlˌɛθɪlə'mi:n, ˌfɛnɪl-) *n* an amine that occurs naturally as a neurotransmitter in the brain, has properties similar to those of amphetamine, is an antidepressant, and is found in chocolate. Formula: $C_8H_{11}N$

phenylketonuria (ˌfi:naɪlˌki:tə'njʊərɪə) *n* a congenital metabolic disorder characterized by the abnormal accumulation of phenylalanine in the body fluids, resulting in various degrees of mental deficiency [C20 New Latin; see PHENYL, KETONE, -URIA]

phenytoin (ˌfɛnɪ'təʊɪn) n an anticonvulsant drug used in the management of epilepsy and in the treatment of abnormal heart rhythms. Formula: $C_{15}H_{11}N_2O_2Na$. Also called: **diphenylhydantoin sodium** [C20 from (di)pheny(lhydan)toin]

pheromone ('fɛrəˌməʊn) n a chemical substance, secreted externally by certain animals, such as insects, affecting the behaviour or physiology of other animals of the same species [C20 phero-, from Greek pherein to bear + (HOR)MONE]

phew (fju:) interj an exclamation of relief, surprise, disbelief, weariness, etc

phi (faɪ) n, pl phis the 21st letter in the Greek alphabet, Φ, φ, a consonant, transliterated as ph or f

phial ('faɪəl) n a small bottle for liquids; vial [C14 from Old French fiole, from Latin phiola saucer, from Greek phialē wide shallow vessel]

Phi Beta Kappa ('faɪ 'beɪtə 'kæpə, 'biːtə) n (in the US) **1** a national honorary society, founded in 1776, membership of which is based on high academic ability **2** a member of this society [from the initials of the Greek motto philosophia biou kubernētēs philosophy the guide of life]

phil. abbreviation for **1** philosophy **2** philharmonic

Phil. abbreviation for **1** Philippians **2** Philippines **3** Philadelphia **4** Philharmonic

Philadelphia (ˌfɪlə'dɛlfɪə) n a city and port in SE Pennsylvania, at the confluence of the Delaware and Schuylkill Rivers: the fourth largest city in the US; founded by Quakers in 1682; cultural and financial centre of the American colonies and the federal capital (1790–1800); scene of the Continental Congresses (1774–83) and the signing of the Declaration of Independence (1776). Pop: 1 479 339 (2003 est)

philadelphus (ˌfɪlə'dɛlfəs) n any shrub of the N temperate genus Philadelphus, cultivated for their strongly scented showy flowers: family Hydrangeaceae. See also **mock orange** (sense 1) [C19 New Latin, from Greek philadelphon mock orange, literally: loving one's brother]

Philae ('faɪliː) n an island in Upper Egypt, in the Nile north of the Aswan Dam: of religious importance in ancient times; almost submerged since the raising of the level of the dam

philander (fɪ'lændə) vb (intr; often foll by with) (of a man) to flirt with women [C17 from Greek philandros fond of men, from philos loving + anēr man; used as a name for a lover in literary works] > phi'landerer n, adj

philanthropic (ˌfɪlən'θrɒpɪk) or **philanthropical** adj showing concern for humanity, esp by performing charitable actions, donating money, etc > ˌphilan'thropically adv

philanthropy (fɪ'lænθrəpɪ) n, pl -pies **1** the practice of performing charitable or benevolent actions **2** love of mankind in general [C17 from Late Latin philanthrōpia, from Greek: love of mankind, from philos loving + anthrōpos man] > phi'lanthropist or philanthrope (ˈfɪlənˌθrəʊp) n

philately (fɪ'lætəlɪ) n the collection and study of postage stamps and all related material concerned with postal history [C19 from French philatélie, from PHILO- + Greek ateleia exemption from charges (here referring to stamps), from A-¹ + telos tax, payment] > philatelic (ˌfɪlə'tɛlɪk) adj > ˌphila'telically adv > phi'latelist n

-phile or **-phil** n combining form indicating a person or thing having a fondness or preference for something specified: bibliophile; Francophile [from Greek philos loving]

Phllem. Bible abbreviation for Philemon

Philemon¹ (faɪ'liːmɒn) n **1** New Testament **1** a Christian of Colossae whose escaped slave came to meet Paul **2** the book (in full **The Epistle of Paul the Apostle to Philemon**), asking Philemon to forgive the slave for escaping

Philemon² (faɪ'liːmɒn) n Greek myth a poor

Phrygian, who with his wife Baucis offered hospitality to the disguised Zeus and Hermes

philharmonic (ˌfɪlhɑː'mɒnɪk, ˌfɪlə-) adj **1** fond of music **2** (capital when part of a name) denoting an orchestra, choir, society, etc, devoted to the performance, appreciation, and study of music ▷ n **3** (capital when part of a name) a specific philharmonic choir, orchestra, or society [C18 from French philharmonique, from Italian filarmonico music-loving; see PHILO-, HARMONY]

philhellene (fɪl'hɛliːn) or **philhellenist** (fɪl'hɛlɪnɪst) n **1** a lover of Greece and Greek culture **2** European history a supporter of the cause of Greek national independence > philhellenic (ˌfɪlhɛ'liːnɪk) adj > philhellenism (fɪl'hɛlɪˌnɪzəm) n

-philia n combining form **1** indicating a tendency towards: haemophilia **2** indicating an abnormal liking for: necrophilia [from Greek philos loving] > -philiac n combining form > -philous or -philic adj combining form

philibeg ('fɪlɪˌbɛg) n a variant spelling of **filibeg**

Philippeville ('fɪlɪpˌvɪl) n the former name of Skikda

Philippi (fɪ'lɪpaɪ, 'fɪlɪ-) n an ancient city in NE Macedonia: scene of the victory of Antony and Octavian over Brutus and Cassius (42 BC)

Philippian (fɪ'lɪpɪən) adj **1** of or relating to the ancient Macedonian city of Philippi ▷ n **2** a native or inhabitant of Philippi

Philippians (fɪ'lɪpɪəns) n (functioning as singular) a book of the New Testament (in full **The Epistle of Paul the Apostle to the Philippians**)

philippic (fɪ'lɪpɪk) n a bitter or impassioned speech of denunciation; invective

Philippics (fɪ'lɪpɪks) pl n **1** Demosthenes' orations against Philip of Macedon **2** Cicero's orations against Antony

Philippine ('fɪlɪˌpiːn) adj another word for **Filipino** (sense 3)

Philippine mahogany ('fɪlɪˌpiːn) n any of various Philippine hardwood trees of the genus Shorea and related genera: family Dipterocarpaceae

Philippines ('fɪlɪˌpiːnz, ˌfɪlɪ'piːnz) n (functioning as singular) **Republic of the** a republic in SE Asia, occupying an archipelago of about 7100 islands (including Luzon, Mindanao, Samar, and Negros): became a Spanish colony in 1571 but ceded to the US in 1898 after the Spanish-American War; gained independence in 1946. The islands are generally mountainous and volcanic. Official languages: Filipino, based on Tagalog, and English. Religion: Roman Catholic majority. Currency: peso. Capital: Manila. Pop: 81 408 000 (2004 est). Area: 300 076 sq km (115 860 sq miles). Related word: Filipino

Philippine Sea n part of the NW Pacific Ocean, east and north of the Philippines

Philippopolis (ˌfɪlɪ'pɒpəlɪs) n transliteration of the Greek name for **Plovdiv**

Philistia (fɪ'lɪstɪə) n an ancient country on the coast of SW Palestine

Philistian (fɪ'lɪstɪən) adj of or relating to Philistia, an ancient country in Palestine, or its inhabitants

Philistine ('fɪlɪˌstaɪn) n **1** a person who is unreceptive to or hostile towards culture, the arts, etc; a smug boorish person **2** a member of the non-Semitic people who inhabited ancient Philistia ▷ adj **3** (sometimes not capital) boorishly uncultured **4** of or relating to the ancient Philistines > Philistinism ('fɪlɪstɪˌnɪzəm) n

Phillips curve n economics a curve that purports to plot the relationship between unemployment and inflation on the theory that as inflation falls unemployment rises and vice versa [C20 named after A. W. H. Phillips (1914–75), English economist who formulated the theory]

Phillips screw n trademark a screw having a cruciform slot into which a screwdriver with a cruciform point (**Phillips screwdriver** (Trademark)) fits

phillumenist (fɪ'ljuːmənɪst, -'luː-) n a person who collects matchbox labels [C20 from PHILO- + Latin

lumen light + -IST] > phil'lumeny n

philo- or before a vowel **phil-** combining form indicating a love of: philology; philanthropic [from Greek philos loving]

Philoctetes (ˌfɪlɒk'tiːtiːz, fɪ'lɒktɪˌtiːz) n Greek myth a hero of the Trojan War, in which he killed Paris with the bow and poisoned arrows given to him by Hercules

philodendron (ˌfɪlə'dɛndrən) n, pl -drons or -dra (-drə) any aroid evergreen climbing plant of the tropical American genus Philodendron: cultivated as house plants [C19 New Latin from Greek: lover of trees]

philogyny (fɪ'lɒdʒɪnɪ) n rare fondness for women. Compare **misogyny** [C17 from Greek philogunia, from PHILO- + gunē woman] > phi'logynist n > phi'logynous adj

philol. abbreviation for **1** philological **2** philology

philology (fɪ'lɒlədʒɪ) n **1** comparative and historical linguistics **2** the scientific analysis of written records and literary texts **3** (no longer in scholarly use) the study of literature in general [C17 from Latin philologia, from Greek: love of language] > philological (ˌfɪlə'lɒdʒɪkᵊl) adj > ˌphilo'logically adv > phi'lologist or less commonly phi'lologer n

philomel ('fɪləˌmɛl) or **philomela** (ˌfɪləʊ'miːlə) n poetic names for a **nightingale** [C14 philomene, via Medieval Latin from Latin philomēla, from Greek]

Philomela (ˌfɪləʊ'miːlə) n Greek myth an Athenian princess, who was raped and had her tongue cut out by her brother-in-law Tereus, and subsequently was transformed into a nightingale. See **Procne**

philoprogenitive (ˌfɪləʊprəʊ'dʒɛnɪtɪv) adj rare **1** fond of children **2** producing many offspring

philos. abbreviation for **1** philosopher **2** philosophical

philosopher (fɪ'lɒsəfə) n **1** a student, teacher, or devotee of philosophy **2** a person of philosophical temperament, esp one who is patient, wise, and stoical **3** (formerly) an alchemist or devotee of occult science **4** a person who establishes the ideology of a cult or movement: the philosopher of the revolution

philosopher kings pl n **1** (in the political theory of Plato) the elite whose education has given them true knowledge of the Forms and esp of the Form of the Good, thus enabling them alone to rule justly **2** informal any ideologically motivated elite

philosopher's stone n a stone or substance thought by alchemists to be capable of transmuting base metals into gold

philosophical (ˌfɪlə'sɒfɪkᵊl) or **philosophic** adj **1** of or relating to philosophy or philosophers **2** reasonable, wise, or learned **3** calm and stoical, esp in the face of difficulties or disappointments **4** (formerly) of or relating to science or natural philosophy > ˌphilo'sophically adv > ˌphilo'sophicalness n

philosophical logic n the branch of philosophy that studies the relationship between formal logic and ordinary language, esp the extent to which the former can be held accurately to represent the latter

philosophize or **philosophise** (fɪ'lɒsəˌfaɪz) vb **1** (intr) to make philosophical pronouncements and speculations **2** (tr) to explain philosophically > phiˌlosophi'zation or phiˌlosophi'sation n > phi'loso,phizer or phi'loso,phiser n

philosophy (fɪ'lɒsəfɪ) n, pl -phies **1** the academic discipline concerned with making explicit the nature and significance of ordinary and scientific beliefs and investigating the intelligibility of concepts by means of rational argument concerning their presuppositions, implications, and interrelationships; in particular, the rational investigation of the nature and structure of reality (metaphysics), the resources and limits of knowledge (epistemology), the principles and import of moral judgment (ethics), and the relationship between language and reality (semantics) **2** the particular doctrines relating to these issues of some specific individual or school: *the philosophy of Descartes* **3** the critical study of the basic principles and concepts of a discipline: *the philosophy of law* **4** *archaic or literary* the investigation of natural phenomena, esp alchemy, astrology, and astronomy **5** any system of belief, values, or tenets **6** a personal outlook or viewpoint **7** serenity of temper [c13 from Old French *filosofie,* from Latin *philosophia,* from Greek, from *philosophos* lover of wisdom]

-philous *or* **-philic** *adj combining form* indicating love of or fondness for: *heliophilous* [from Latin *-philus,* from Greek *-philos;* see -PHILE]

philtre *or US* **philter** ('fɪltə) *n* a drink supposed to arouse love, desire, etc [c16 from Latin *philtrum,* from Greek *philtron* love potion, from *philos* loving]

philtrum ('fɪltrəm) *n, pl* **philtra** the indentation above the upper lip [c17 from Latin, see PHILTRE]

phimosis (faɪ'məʊsɪs) *n* abnormal tightness of the foreskin, preventing its being retracted over the tip of the penis [c17 via New Latin from Greek: a muzzling, from *phimos* a muzzle]

phi-phenomenon ('faɪfɪˌnɒmɪnən) *n, pl* **-na** (-nə) *psychol* **1** the illusion that when two lights are rapidly turned on and off in succession something appears to move backwards and forwards between them while the lights stay stationary **2** a similar illusion in which one light appears to move smoothly backwards and forwards [c20 arbitrary use of Greek *phi*]

phishing ('fɪʃɪŋ) *n* the practice of using fraudulent e-mails and copies of legitimate websites to extract financial data from computer users for purposes of identity theft [c21 from *fishing* in the sense of catching the unwary by offering bait; computer-hacker slang often replaces *f* with *ph*]

phiz (fɪz) *n slang, chiefly Brit* the face or a facial expression: *an ugly phiz.* Also called: **phizog** ('fɪzɒg, fɪ'zɒg) [c17 colloquial shortening of PHYSIOGNOMY]

phlebectomy (flɪ'bɛktəmɪ) *n* the surgical excision of a vein or part of a vein

phlebitis (flɪ'baɪtɪs) *n* inflammation of a vein [c19 via New Latin from Greek; see PHLEBO-, -ITIS] > **phlebitic** (flɪ'bɪtɪk) *adj*

phlebo- *or before a vowel* **phleb-** *combining form* indicating a vein: *phlebotomy* [from Greek *phleps, phleb-* vein]

phlebography (flɪ'bɒgrəfɪ) *n* another name for **venography**

phlebosclerosis (ˌflɛbəʊsklɪ'rəʊsɪs) *n pathol* hardening and loss of elasticity of the veins. Also called: **venosclerosis**

phlebotomize *or* **phlebotomise** (flɪ'bɒtəˌmaɪz) *vb (tr) surgery* to perform phlebotomy on (a patient)

phlebotomy (flɪ'bɒtəmɪ) *n, pl* **-mies** surgical incision into a vein. Also called: **venesection** [c14 from Old French *flebothomie,* from Late Latin *phlebotomia,* from Greek] > **phlebotomic** (ˌflɛbə'tɒmɪk) *or* ˌphlebo'tomical *adj* > **phle'botomist** *n*

Phlegethon ('flɛgɪˌθɒn) *n Greek myth* a river of fire in Hades [c14 from Greek, literally: blazing, from *phlegethein* to flame, blaze]

phlegm (flɛm) *n* **1** the viscid mucus secreted by the walls of the respiratory tract **2** *archaic* one of the four bodily humours **3** apathy; stolidity; indifference **4** self-possession; imperturbability; coolness [c14 from Old French *fleume,* from Late Latin *phlegma,* from Greek: inflammation, from *phlegein* to burn] > **phlegmy** *adj*

phlegmatic (flɛg'mætɪk) *or* **phlegmatical** *adj* **1** having a stolid or unemotional disposition **2** not easily excited > **phleg'matically** *adv* > **phleg'maticalness** *or* **phleg'maticness** *n*

phloem ('fləʊɛm) *n* tissue in higher plants that conducts synthesized food substances to all parts of the plant [c19 via German from Greek *phloos* bark]

phlogistic (flɒ'dʒɪstɪk) *adj* **1** *pathol* of inflammation; inflammatory **2** *chem* of, concerned with, or containing phlogiston

phlogiston (flɒ'dʒɪstɒn, -tən) *n chem* a hypothetical substance formerly thought to be present in all combustible materials and to be released during burning [c18 via New Latin from Greek, from *phlogizein* to set alight; related to *phlegein* to burn]

phlogopite ('flɒgəˌpaɪt) *n* a brownish mica consisting of a hydrous silicate of potassium, magnesium, and aluminium, occurring principally in metamorphic limestones and ultrabasic rocks. Formula: $KMg_3AlSi_3O_{10}(OH)_2$. See also **mica** [c19 from Greek *phlogōpos* of fiery appearance, from *phlox* flame + *ōps* eye]

phlox (flɒks) *n, pl* **phlox** *or* **phloxes** any polemoniaceous plant of the chiefly North American genus *Phlox:* cultivated for their clusters of white, red, or purple flowers [c18 via Latin from Greek: a plant of glowing colour, literally: flame]

PHLS (in Britain) *abbreviation for* Public Health Laboratory Service

phlyctena *or* **phlyctaena** (flɪk'tiːnə) *n, pl* **-nae** (-niː) *pathol* a small blister, vesicle, or pustule [c17 via New Latin from Greek *phluktaina,* from *phluzein* to swell]

Phnom Penh *or* **Pnom Penh** (ˌnɒm 'pɛn) *n* the capital of Cambodia, a port in the south at the confluence of the Mekong and Tonle Sap Rivers: capital of the country since 1865; university (1960). Pop: 1 174 000 (2005 est)

-phobe *n combining form* indicating a person or thing that fears or hates: *Germanophobe; xenophobe* [from Greek *-phobos* fearing] > **-phobic** *adj combining form*

phobia ('fəʊbɪə) *n psychiatry* an abnormal intense and irrational fear of a given situation, organism, or object [c19 from Greek *phobos* fear]

-phobia *n combining form* indicating an extreme abnormal fear of or aversion to: *acrophobia; claustrophobia* [via Latin from Greek, from *phobos* fear] > **-phobic** *adj combining form*

phobic ('fəʊbɪk) *adj* **1** of, relating to, or arising from a phobia ▷ *n* **2** a person suffering from a phobia

Phobos ('fəʊbɒs) *n* the larger of the two satellites of Mars and the closer to the planet. Approximate diameter (although it has an irregular shape): 23 km. Compare **Deimos**

Phocaea (fəʊ'siːə) *n* an ancient port in Asia Minor, the northernmost of Ionian cities on the W coast of Asia Minor: an important maritime state (about 1000–600 BC)

phocine ('fəʊsaɪn) *adj* **1** of, relating to, or resembling a seal **2** of, relating to, or belonging to the *Phocinae,* a subfamily that includes the harbour seal and grey seal [c19 ultimately from Greek *phōkē* a seal]

Phocis ('fəʊsɪs) *n* an ancient district of central Greece, on the Gulf of Corinth: site of the Delphic oracle

phocomelia (ˌfəʊkəʊ'miːlɪə) *or* **phocomely** (fəʊ'kɒməlɪ) *n* a congenital deformity resulting from prenatal interference with the development of the fetal limbs, characterized esp by short stubby hands or feet attached close to the body [c19 via New Latin from Greek *phōkē* a seal + *melos* a limb] > ˌphoco'melic *adj*

phoebe ('fiːbɪ) *n* any of several greyish-brown North American flycatchers of the genus *Sayornis,* such as *S. phoebe* (**eastern phoebe**) [c19 imitative of the bird's call]

Phoebe[1] *or* **Phebe** ('fiːbɪ) *n* **1** *classical myth* a Titaness, who later became identified with Artemis (Diana) as goddess of the moon **2** *poetic* a personification of the moon

Phoebe[2] ('fiːbɪ) *n* the outermost satellite of the planet Saturn. It has retrograde motion and a dark surface

Phoebus ('fiːbəs) *n* **1** Also called: **Phoebus Apollo** *Greek myth* Apollo as the sun god **2** *poetic* a

personification of the sun [c14 via Latin from Greek *Phoibos* bright; related to *phaos* light]

Phoenicia (fə'nɪʃɪə, -'niː-) *n* an ancient maritime country extending from the Mediterranean Sea to the Lebanon Mountains, now occupied by the coastal regions of Lebanon and parts of Syria and Israel: consisted of a group of city-states, at their height between about 1200 and 1000 BC, that were leading traders of the ancient world

Phoenician (fə'niːʃən, -'nɪʃɪən) *n* **1** a member of an ancient Semitic people of NW Syria who dominated the trade of the ancient world in the first millennium BC and founded colonies throughout the Mediterranean **2** the extinct language of this people, belonging to the Canaanitic branch of the Semitic subfamily of the Afro-Asiatic family ▷ *adj* **3** of or relating to Phoenicia, the Phoenicians, or their language

phoenix *or US* **phenix** ('fiːnɪks) *n* **1** a legendary Arabian bird said to set fire to itself and rise anew from the ashes every 500 years **2** a person or thing of surpassing beauty or quality [Old English *fenix,* via Latin from Greek *phoinix;* identical in form with Greek *Phoinix* Phoenician; purple]

Phoenix[1] ('fiːnɪks) *n, Latin genitive* **Phoenices** ('fiːnɪˌsiːz) a constellation in the S hemisphere lying between Grus and Eridanus

Phoenix[2] ('fiːnɪks) *n* a city in central Arizona, capital city of the state, on the Salt River. Pop: 1 388 416 (2003 est)

Phoenix Islands *pl n* a group of eight coral islands in the central Pacific: administratively part of Kiribati. Area: 28 sq km (11 sq miles)

Pholus ('fəʊləs) *n* a large astronomical object, some 2000 km in diameter, discovered in 1991. Its elliptical orbit around the earth, between the orbits of Neptune and Saturn, has a period of 93 years. It has been classified as an asteroid although it lies outside the main asteroid belt

phon (fɒn) *n* a unit of loudness that measures the intensity of a sound by the number of decibels it is above a reference tone having a frequency of 1000 hertz and a root-mean-square sound pressure of 20×10^{-6} pascal [c20 via German from Greek *phōnē* sound, voice]

phon. *abbreviation for* **1** Also: **phonet** phonetics **2** phonology

phonate (fəʊ'neɪt) *vb (intr)* to articulate speech sounds, esp to cause the vocal cords to vibrate in the execution of a voiced speech sound [c19 from Greek *phōnē* voice] > **pho'nation** *n* > **phonatory** ('fəʊnətərɪ, -trɪ) *adj*

phone[1] (fəʊn) *n, vb* short for **telephone**

phone[2] (fəʊn) *n phonetics* a single uncomplicated speech sound [c19 from Greek *phōnē* sound, voice]

-phone *combining form* **1** *(forming nouns)* indicating voice, sound, or a device giving off sound: *microphone; telephone* **2** *(forming nouns and adjectives)* (a person) speaking a particular language: *Francophone* [from Greek *phōnē* voice, sound] > **-phonic** *adj combining form*

phonecam ('fəʊnˌkam) *n* a digital camera incorporated in a mobile phone

phonecard ('fəʊnˌkɑːd) *n* a card for use in a cardphone that operates for the number or duration of calls paid for in the purchase price of the card

phone-in *n* **a** a radio or television programme in which listeners' or viewers' questions, comments, etc, are telephoned to the studio and broadcast live **b** *(as modifier): a phone-in discussion*

phone-jack *vb (tr)* to steal the mobile phone from (a person) [c21 PHONE[1] + (HI)JACK] > **'phone-jacker** *n*

phoneme ('fəʊniːm) *n linguistics* one of the set of speech sounds in any given language that serve to distinguish one word from another. A phoneme may consist of several phonetically distinct articulations, which are regarded as identical by native speakers, since one articulation may be substituted for another without any change of meaning. Thus /p/ and /b/ are separate

p

phonemes in English because they distinguish such words as *pet* and *bet,* whereas the light and dark /l/ sounds in *little* are not separate phonemes since they may be transposed without changing meaning [c20 via French from Greek *phōnēma* sound, speech]

phonemic (fə'niːmɪk) *adj linguistics* **1** of or relating to the phoneme **2** relating to or denoting speech sounds that belong to different phonemes rather than being allophonic variants of the same phoneme. Compare **phonetic** (sense 2) **3** of or relating to phonemics > pho'nemically *adv*

phonemics (fə'niːmɪks) *n (functioning as singular)* that aspect of linguistics concerned with the classification, analysis, interrelation, and environmental changes of the phonemes of a language > pho'nemicist *n*

phonendoscope (fə'nɛndəˌskəʊp) *n* an instrument that amplifies small sounds, esp within the human body [c20 from PHONO- + ENDO- + -SCOPE]

phoner ('fəʊnə) *n informal* a person making a telephone call

phone sex *n* sexual activity carried out verbally by telephone

phonetic (fə'nɛtɪk) *adj* **1** of or relating to phonetics **2** denoting any perceptible distinction between one speech sound and another, irrespective of whether the sounds are phonemes or allophones. Compare **phonemic** (sense 2) **3** conforming to pronunciation: *phonetic spelling* [c19 from New Latin *phōnēticus,* from Greek *phōnētikos,* from *phōnein* to make sounds, speak] > pho'netically *adv*

phonetic alphabet *n* a list of the words used in communications to represent the letters of the alphabet, as in E for Echo, T for Tango

phonetician (ˌfəʊnɪ'tɪʃən) *n* a person skilled in phonetics or one who employs phonetics in his work

phonetics (fə'nɛtɪks) *n (functioning as singular)* the science concerned with the study of speech processes, including the production, perception, and analysis of speech sounds from both an acoustic and a physiological point of view. This science, though capable of being applied to language studies, technically excludes linguistic considerations. Compare **phonology**

phonetist ('fəʊnɪtɪst) *n* **1** another name for **phonetician 2** a person who advocates or uses a system of phonetic spelling

phoney *or esp US* **phony** ('fəʊnɪ) *informal* ▷ *adj* -nier, -niest **1** not genuine; fake **2** (of a person) insincere or pretentious ▷ *n, pl* -neys *or* -nies **3** an insincere or pretentious person **4** something that is not genuine; a fake [c20 origin uncertain] > 'phoneyness *or esp US* 'phoniness *n*

phonics ('fɒnɪks) *n (functioning as singular)* **1** an obsolete name for **acoustics** (sense 1) **2** a method of teaching people to read by training them to associate letters with their phonetic values > 'phonic *adj* > 'phonically *adv*

phono- *or before a vowel* **phon-** *combining form* indicating a sound or voice: *phonograph; phonology* [from Greek *phōnē* sound, voice]

phonochemistry (ˌfəʊnəʊ'kɛmɪstrɪ) *n* the branch of chemistry concerned with the chemical effects of sound and ultrasonic waves

phonogram ('fəʊnəˌɡræm) *n* **1** any written symbol standing for a sound, syllable, morpheme, or word **2** a sequence of written symbols having the same sound in a variety of different words, for example, *ough* in *bought, ought, brought* > ˌphono'gramic *or* ˌphono'grammic *adj*

phonograph ('fəʊnəˌɡrɑːf, -ˌɡræf) *n* **1** an early form of gramophone capable of recording and reproducing sound on wax cylinders **2** *US and Canadian* a device for reproducing the sounds stored on a record: now usually applied to the nearly obsolete type that uses a clockwork motor and acoustic horn. Also called: **gramophone, record player**

phonographic (ˌfəʊnə'ɡræfɪk) *adj* **1** of or relating to phonography **2** of or relating to the recording of music

phonography (fəʊ'nɒɡrəfɪ) *n* **1** a writing system that represents sounds by individual symbols. Compare **logography 2** the employment of such a writing system > pho'nographer *or* pho'nographist *n*

phonolite ('fəʊnəˌlaɪt) *n* a fine-grained volcanic igneous rock consisting of alkaline feldspars and nepheline [c19 via French from German *Phonolith;* see PHONO-, -LITE] > phonolitic (ˌfəʊnə'lɪtɪk) *adj*

phonology (fə'nɒlədʒɪ) *n, pl* -gies the study of the sound system of a language and of languages in general. Compare **syntax** (senses 1, 2), **semantics 2** such a sound system > phonological (ˌfəʊnə'lɒdʒɪkˀl, ˌfɒn-) *adj* >ˌphono'logically *adv* > pho'nologist *n*

phonometer (fə'nɒmɪtə) *n* an apparatus that measures the intensity of sound, esp one calibrated in phons > phonometric (ˌfəʊnə'mɛtrɪk) *or* ˌphono'metrical *adj*

phonon ('fəʊnɒn) *n physics* a quantum of vibrational energy in the acoustic vibrations of a crystal lattice [c20 from PHONO- + -ON]

phono plug ('fəʊnəʊ) *n electrical engineering* a type of coaxial connector, used esp in audio equipment

phonoscope ('fəʊnəˌskəʊp) *n* a device that renders visible the vibrations of sound waves

phonotactics ('fəʊnəʊˌtæktɪks) *n (functioning as singular) linguistics* the study of the possible arrangement of the sounds of a language in the words of that language [c20 from PHONO- + -tactics, on the model of *syntactic;* see SYNTAX]

phonotype ('fəʊnəˌtaɪp) *n printing* **1** a letter or symbol representing a sound **2** text printed in phonetic symbols > phonotypic (ˌfəʊnə'tɪpɪk) *or* ˌphono'typical *adj*

phonotypy ('fəʊnəˌtaɪpɪ) *n* the transcription of speech into phonetic symbols > 'phono,typist *or* 'phono,typer *n*

phony ('fəʊnɪ) *adj,* -nier, -niest, *n, pl* -nies a variant spelling (esp US) of **phoney.** > 'phoniness *n*

-phony *n combining form* indicating a specified type of sound: *cacophony; euphony* [from Greek *-phōnia,* from *phōnē* sound] > **-phonic** *adj combining form*

phony war *n* **1** (in wartime) a period of apparent calm and inactivity, esp the period at the beginning of World War II **2** (in peacetime) a contrived embattled atmosphere; mock war

phooey ('fuːɪ) *interj informal* an exclamation of scorn, contempt, disbelief, etc [c20 probably variant of PHEW]

-phore *n combining form* indicating a person or thing that bears or produces: *gonophore; semaphore* [from New Latin *-phorus,* from Greek *-phoros* bearing, from *pherein* to bear] > **-phorous** *adj combining form*

-phoresis *n combining form* indicating a transmission: *electrophoresis* [from Greek *phorēsis* being carried, from *pherein* to bear]

phoresy ('fɒrəsɪ) *n* an association in which one animal clings to another to ensure movement from place to place, as some mites use some insects [c20 from New Latin *phoresia,* from Greek *phorēsis,* from *pherein* to carry]

phormium ('fɔːmɪəm) *n* any plant of the New Zealand bulbous genus *Phormium,* with leathery evergreen leaves and red or yellow flowers in panicles [New Latin, from Greek *phormos* a basket (from a use for the fibres)]

phosgene ('fɒzdʒiːn) *n* a colourless easily liquefied poisonous gas, carbonyl chloride, with an odour resembling that of new-mown hay: used in chemical warfare as a lethal choking agent and in the manufacture of pesticides, dyes, and polyurethane resins. Formula: $COCl_2$ [c19 from Greek *phōs* light + *-gene,* variant of -GEN]

phosgenite ('fɒzdʒɪˌnaɪt) *n* a rare fluorescent secondary mineral consisting of lead chloro-carbonate in the form of greyish tetragonal crystals. Formula: $Pb_2(Cl_2CO_3)$

phosphatase ('fɒsfəˌteɪs, -ˌteɪz) *n* any of a group of enzymes that catalyse the hydrolysis of organic phosphates

phosphate ('fɒsfeɪt) *n* **1** any salt or ester of any phosphoric acid, esp a salt of orthophosphoric acid **2** *(often plural)* any of several chemical fertilizers containing phosphorous compounds [c18 from French *phosphat;* see PHOSPHORUS, -ATE[1]] > phosphatic (fɒs'fætɪk) *adj*

phosphatide ('fɒsfəˌtaɪd) *n* another name for **phospholipid**

phosphatidylcholine (ˌfɒsfətɪdaɪl'kəʊliːn) *n* the systematic name for **lecithin**

phosphatidylethanolamine (ˌfɒsfətɪdaɪlˌɛθə'nɒləmiːn) *n* the systematic name for **cephalin**

phosphatidylserine (ˌfɒsfətɪdaɪl'sɪəriːn) *n* any of a class of phospholipids occurring in biological membranes and fats

phosphatize *or* **phosphatise** ('fɒsfəˌtaɪz) *vb* **1** *(tr)* to treat with a phosphate or phosphates, as by applying a fertilizer **2** to change or be changed into a phosphate > phosphati'zation *or* ˌphosphati'sation *n*

phosphaturia (ˌfɒsfə'tjʊərɪə) *n pathol* an abnormally large amount of phosphates in the urine [c19 New Latin, from PHOSPHATE + -URIA] > ˌphospha'turic *adj*

phosphene ('fɒsfiːn) *n* the sensation of light caused by pressure on the eyelid of a closed eye or by other mechanical or electrical interference with the visual system [c19 from Greek *phōs* light + *phainein* to show]

phosphide ('fɒsfaɪd) *n* any compound of phosphorus with another element, esp a more electropositive element

phosphine ('fɒsfiːn) *n* a colourless flammable gas that is slightly soluble in water and has a strong fishy odour: used as a pesticide. Formula: PH_3

phosphite ('fɒsfaɪt) *n* any salt or ester of phosphorous acid

phospho- *or before a vowel* **phosph-** *combining form* containing phosphorus: *phosphocreatine* [from French, from *phosphore* PHOSPHORUS]

phosphocreatine (ˌfɒsfə'kriːəˌtiːn) *or* **phosphocreatin** *n* a compound of phosphoric acid and creatine found in vertebrate muscle

phospholipid (ˌfɒsfə'lɪpɪd) *n* any of a group of compounds composed of fatty acids, phosphoric acid, and a nitrogenous base: important constituents of all membranes. Also called: **phosphatide**

phosphonic acid (fɒs'fɒnɪk) *n* the systematic name for **phosphorous acid**

phosphoprotein (ˌfɒsfə'prəʊtiːn) *n* any of a group of conjugated proteins, esp casein, in which the protein molecule is bound to phosphoric acid

phosphor ('fɒsfə) *n* a substance, such as the coating on a cathode-ray tube, capable of emitting light when irradiated with particles or electromagnetic radiation [c17 from French, ultimately from Greek *phōsphoros* PHOSPHORUS]

phosphorate ('fɒsfəˌreɪt) *vb* **1** to treat or combine with phosphorus **2** *(tr) rare* to cause (a substance) to exhibit phosphorescence

phosphor bronze *n* any of various hard corrosion-resistant alloys containing copper, tin (2–8 per cent), and phosphorus (0.1–0.4 per cent): used in gears, bearings, cylinder casings, etc

phosphoresce (ˌfɒsfə'rɛs) *vb (intr)* to exhibit phosphorescence

phosphorescence (ˌfɒsfə'rɛsəns) *n* **1** *physics* **a** a fluorescence that persists after the bombarding radiation producing it has stopped **b** a fluorescence for which the average lifetime of the excited atoms is greater than 10^{-8} seconds **2** the light emitted in phosphorescence **3** the emission of light during a chemical reaction, such as bioluminescence, in which insufficient heat is evolved to cause fluorescence. Compare **fluorescence**

phosphorescent (ˌfɒsfəˈrɛsᵊnt) *adj* exhibiting or having the property of phosphorescence > ˌphosphoˈrescently *adv*

phosphoric (fɒsˈfɒrɪk) *adj* of or containing phosphorus in the pentavalent state

phosphoric acid *n* **1** a colourless solid tribasic acid used in the manufacture of fertilizers and soap. Formula: H_3PO_4. Systematic name: phosphoric(V) acid Also called: orthophosphoric acid **2** any oxyacid of phosphorus produced by reaction between phosphorus pentoxide and water. See also **metaphosphoric acid, pyrophosphoric acid, hypophosphoric acid**

phosphorism (ˈfɒsfəˌrɪzəm) *n* poisoning caused by prolonged exposure to phosphorus

phosphorite (ˈfɒsfəˌraɪt) *n* **1** a fibrous variety of the mineral apatite **2** any of various mineral deposits that consist mainly of calcium phosphate > **phosphoritic** (ˌfɒsfəˈrɪtɪk) *adj*

phosphoroscope (fɒsˈfɒrəˌskəʊp) *n* an instrument for measuring the duration of phosphorescence after the source of radiation causing it has been removed

phosphorous (ˈfɒsfərəs) *adj* of or containing phosphorus in the trivalent state

phosphorous acid *n* **1** a white or yellowish hygroscopic crystalline dibasic acid. Formula: H_3PO_3. Systematic name: phosphonic acid Also called: orthophosphorous acid **2** any oxyacid of phosphorus containing less oxygen than the corresponding phosphoric acid

phosphorus (ˈfɒsfərəs) *n* **1** an allotropic nonmetallic element occurring in phosphates and living matter. Ordinary phosphorus is a toxic flammable phosphorescent white solid; the red form is less reactive and nontoxic: used in matches, pesticides, and alloys. The radioisotope **phosphorus-32** (**radiophosphorus**), with a half-life of 14.3 days, is used in radiotherapy and as a tracer. Symbol: P; atomic no.: 15; atomic wt.: 30.973 762; valency: 3 or 5; relative density: 1.82 (white), 2.20 (red); melting pt.: 44.1°C (white); boiling pt.: 280°C (white) **2** a less common name for a **phosphor** [C17 via Latin from Greek *phōsphoros* light-bringing, from *phōs* light + *pherein* to bring]

Phosphorus (ˈfɒsfərəs) *n* a morning star, esp Venus

phosphorus pentoxide *n* a white odourless solid produced when phosphorus burns: has a strong affinity for water with which it forms phosphoric acids. Formula: P_2O_5 (commonly existing as the dimer P_4O_{10}). Also called: **phosphoric anhydride**

phosphorylase (fɒsˈfɒrɪˌleɪs, -ˌleɪz) *n* any of a group of enzymes that catalyse the hydrolysis of glycogen to glucose-1-phosphate [C20 from PHOSPHORUS + -YL + -ASE]

phosphorylation (ˌfɒsfɒrɪˈleɪʃən) *n* the chemical or enzymic introduction into a compound of a phosphoryl group (a trivalent radical of phosphorus and oxygen)

phossy jaw (ˈfɒsɪ) *n* a gangrenous condition of the lower jawbone caused by prolonged exposure to phosphorus fumes [C19 *phossy*, colloquial shortening of PHOSPHORUS]

phot (fɒt, fəʊt) *n* a unit of illumination equal to one lumen per square centimetre. 1 phot is equal to 10 000 lux [C20 from Greek *phos* light]

photic (ˈfəʊtɪk) *adj* **1** of or concerned with light **2** *biology* of or relating to the production of light by organisms **3** Also: **photobathic** designating the zone of the sea where photosynthesis takes place [C19 from PHOTO- + -IC]

photo (ˈfəʊtəʊ) *n, pl* **-tos** short for **photograph** (sense 1)

photo- *combining form* **1** of, relating to, or produced by light: *photosynthesis* **2** indicating a photographic process: *photolithography* [from Greek *phōs, phōt-* light]

photoactinic (ˌfəʊtəʊækˈtɪnɪk) *adj* emitting actinic radiation

photoactive (ˌfəʊtəʊˈæktɪv) *adj* (of a substance) capable of responding to light or other electromagnetic radiation

photo-ageing *n* premature wrinkling of the skin caused by overexposure to sunlight > ˌphotoˈaged *adj*

photoautotrophic (ˌfəʊtəʊˌɔːtəʊˈtrɒfɪk) *adj* (of plants) capable of using light as the energy source in the synthesis of food from inorganic matter. See also **photosynthesis**

photobathic (ˌfəʊtəʊˈbæθɪk) *adj* another word for **photic** (sense 3) [from PHOTO- + Greek *bathus* deep + -IC]

photobiology (ˌfəʊtəʊbaɪˈɒlədʒɪ) *n* the branch of biology concerned with the effect of light on living organisms > **photobiological** (ˌfəʊtəʊˌbaɪəˈlɒdʒɪkᵊl) *adj* > **photobiˈologist** *n*

photo call *n* a time arranged for photographers, esp press photographers, to take pictures of a celebrity, the cast of a play, etc, usually for publicity purposes

photocatalysis (ˌfəʊtəʊkəˈtælɪsɪs) *n, pl* **-ses** (-ˌsiːz) the alteration of the rate of a chemical reaction by light or other electromagnetic radiation

photocathode (ˌfəʊtəʊˈkæθəʊd) *n* a cathode that undergoes or is used for photoemission

photocell (ˈfəʊtəʊˌsɛl) *n* a device in which the photoelectric or photovoltaic effect or photoconductivity is used to produce a current or voltage when exposed to light or other electromagnetic radiation. They are used in exposure meters, burglar alarms, etc. Also called: **photoelectric cell, electric eye**

photochemical (ˌfəʊtəʊˈkɛmɪkᵊl) *adj* of or relating to photochemistry; involving the chemical effects of light > ˌphotoˈchemically *adv*

photochemistry (ˌfəʊtəʊˈkɛmɪstrɪ) *n* the branch of chemistry concerned with the chemical effects of light and other electromagnetic radiations. Also called: **actinochemistry** > ˌphotoˈchemist *n*

photochromic (ˌfəʊtəʊˈkrəʊmɪk) *adj* (of glass) changing colour with the intensity of incident light, used, for example, in sunglasses that darken as the sunlight becomes brighter

photochronograph (ˌfəʊtəʊˈkrɒnəˌgrɑːf, -ˌgræf) *n physics* an instrument for measuring very small time intervals by the trace made by a beam of light on a moving photographic film > **photochronography** (ˌfəʊtəʊkrəˈnɒgrəfɪ) *n*

photocompose (ˌfəʊtəʊkəmˈpəʊz) *vb* (*tr*) to set (type matter) by photocomposition > ˌphotocomˈposer *n*

photocomposition (ˌfəʊtəʊˌkɒmpəˈzɪʃən) *n printing* typesetting by exposing type characters onto photographic film or photosensitive paper in order to make printing plates. Also called: **photosetting, phototypesetting**

photoconduction (ˌfəʊtəʊkənˈdʌkʃən) *n* conduction of electricity resulting from the absorption of light. See **photoconductivity**

photoconductivity (ˌfəʊtəʊˌkɒndʌkˈtɪvɪtɪ) *n* the change in the electrical conductivity of certain substances, such as selenium, as a result of the absorption of electromagnetic radiation > **photoconductive** (ˌfəʊtəʊkənˈdʌktɪv) *adj* > ˌphotoconˈductor *n*

photocopier (ˈfəʊtəʊˌkɒpɪə) *n* an instrument using light-sensitive photographic materials to reproduce written, printed, or graphic work

photocopy (ˈfəʊtəʊˌkɒpɪ) *n, pl* **-copies 1** a photographic reproduction of written, printed, or graphic work. See also **microcopy** ▷ *vb* **-copies, -copying, -copied 2** to reproduce (written, printed, or graphic work) on photographic material

photocurrent (ˈfəʊtəʊˌkʌrənt) *n* an electric current produced by electromagnetic radiation in the photoelectric effect, photovoltaic effect, or photoconductivity

photodegradable (ˌfəʊtəʊdɪˈgreɪdəbᵊl) *adj* (of plastic) capable of being decomposed by prolonged exposure to light

photodiode (ˌfəʊtəʊˈdaɪəʊd) *n* a semiconductor diode, the conductivity of which is controlled by incident illumination

photodisintegration (ˌfəʊtəʊdɪˌsɪntɪˈgreɪʃən) *n* disintegration of an atomic nucleus as a result of its absorption of a photon, usually a gamma ray

photodynamic (ˌfəʊtəʊdaɪˈnæmɪk) *adj* **1** of or concerned with photodynamics **2** involving or producing an adverse or toxic reaction to light, esp ultraviolet light **3** *med* denoting a therapy for cancer in which a cytotoxic drug is activated by a laser beam

photodynamics (ˌfəʊtəʊdaɪˈnæmɪks) *n* (*functioning as singular*) the branch of biology concerned with the effects of light on the actions of plants and animals

photoelasticity (ˌfəʊtəʊɪlæˈstɪsɪtɪ) *n* the effects of stress, such as double refraction, on the optical properties of transparent materials

photoelectric (ˌfəʊtəʊɪˈlɛktrɪk) or **photoelectrical** *adj* of or concerned with electric or electronic effects caused by light or other electromagnetic radiation > ˌphotoeˈlectrically *adv* > **photoelectricity** (ˌfəʊtəʊɪlɛkˈtrɪsɪtɪ) *n*

photoelectric cell *n* another name for **photocell**

photoelectric effect *n* **1** the ejection of electrons from a solid by an incident beam of sufficiently energetic electromagnetic radiation **2** any phenomenon involving electricity and electromagnetic radiation, such as photoemission

photoelectric magnitude *n astronomy* the magnitude of a star determined using a photometer plus a filter to select light or other radiation of the desired wavelength

photoelectron (ˌfəʊtəʊɪˈlɛktrɒn) *n* an electron ejected from an atom, molecule, or solid by an incident photon

photoelectrotype (ˌfəʊtəʊɪˈlɛktrəʊˌtaɪp) *n* an electrotype mode using photography

photoemission (ˌfəʊtəʊɪˈmɪʃən) *n* the emission of electrons due to the impact of electromagnetic radiation, esp as a result of the photoelectric effect > ˌphotoeˈmissive *adj*

photoengrave (ˌfəʊtəʊɪnˈgreɪv) *vb* (*tr*) to reproduce (an illustration) by photoengraving > ˌphotoenˈgraver *n*

photoengraving (ˌfəʊtəʊɪnˈgreɪvɪŋ) *n* **1** a photomechanical process for producing letterpress printing plates **2** a plate made by this process **3** a print made from such a plate

photo finish *n* **1** a finish of a race in which contestants are so close that a photograph is needed to decide the result **2** any race or competition in which the winners or placed contestants are separated by a very small margin

Photofit (ˈfəʊtəʊˌfɪt) *n trademark* **a** a method of combining photographs of facial features, hair, etc, into a composite picture of a face: formerly used by the police to trace suspects from witnesses' descriptions **b** (*as modifier*): *a Photofit picture*

photoflash (ˈfəʊtəʊˌflæʃ) *n* another name for **flashbulb**

photoflood (ˈfəʊtəʊˌflʌd) *n* a highly incandescent tungsten lamp used as an artificial light source for indoor photography, television, etc. The brightness is obtained by operating with higher than normal current

photofluorography (ˌfəʊtəʊfluəˈrɒgrəfɪ) *n med* the process of taking a photograph (**photofluorogram**) of a fluoroscopic image: used in diagnostic screening

photog. *abbreviation for* **1** photograph **2** photographer **3** photographic **4** photography

photogelatine process (ˌfəʊtəʊˈdʒɛlətiːn) *n* another name for **collotype** (sense 1)

photogene (ˈfəʊtəʊˌdʒiːn) *n* another name for **afterimage** [C19 from Greek *phōtogenēs* light-produced. See PHOTO-, -GENE]

photogenic (ˌfəʊtəʊˈdʒɛnɪk) *adj* **1** (esp of a person) having features, colouring, and a general facial appearance that look attractive in photographs **2**

p

biology producing or emitting light: *photogenic bacteria* > ,photo'genically *adv*

photogeology (ˌfəʊtəʊdʒɪ'ɒlədʒɪ) *n* the study and identification of geological phenomena using aerial photographs

photogram ('fəʊtəˌgræm) *n* 1 a picture, usually abstract, produced on a photographic material without the use of a camera, as by placing an object on the material and exposing to light 2 *obsolete* a photograph, often of the more artistic kind rather than a mechanical record

photogrammetry (ˌfəʊtəʊ'græmɪtrɪ) *n* the process of making measurements from photographs, used esp in the construction of maps from aerial photographs and also in military intelligence, medical and industrial research, etc > photogrammetric (ˌfəʊtəʊgrə'mɛtrɪk) *adj* > ,photo'grammetrist *n*

photograph ('fəʊtəˌgrɑːf, -ˌgræf) *n* 1 an image of an object, person, scene, etc, in the form of a print or slide recorded by a camera on photosensitive material. Often shortened to: **photo** > *vb* 2 to take a photograph of (an object, person, scene, etc)

photographer (fə'tɒgrəfə) *n* a person who takes photographs, either as a hobby or a profession

photographic (ˌfəʊtə'græfɪk) *adj* 1 of or relating to photography: *a photographic society; photographic materials* 2 like a photograph in accuracy or detail 3 (of a person's memory) able to retain facts, appearances, etc, in precise detail, often after only a very short view of or exposure to them > ,photo'graphically *adv*

photography (fə'tɒgrəfɪ) *n* 1 the process of recording images on sensitized material by the action of light, X-rays, etc, and the chemical processing of this material to produce a print, slide, or cine film 2 the art, practice, or occupation of taking and printing photographs, making cine films, etc

photogravure (ˌfəʊtəʊgrə'vjʊə) *n* 1 any of various methods in which an intaglio plate for printing is produced by the use of photography 2 matter printed from such a plate ▷ Former name: **heliogravure** [C19 from PHOTO- + French *gravure* engraving]

photojournalism (ˌfəʊtəʊ'dʒɜːnᵊˌlɪzəm) *n* journalism in which photographs are the predominant feature > ,photo'journalist *n* > ,photo'journal'istic *adj*

photokinesis (ˌfəʊtəʊkɪ'niːsɪs, -kaɪ-) *n biology* the movement of an organism in response to the stimulus of light > photokinetic (ˌfəʊtəʊkɪ'nɛtɪk, -kaɪ-) *adj* > ,photoki'netically *adv*

photolithograph (ˌfəʊtəʊ'lɪθəˌgrɑːf, -ˌgræf) *n* 1 a picture printed by photolithography ▷ *vb* 2 (*tr*) to reproduce (pictures, text, etc) by photolithography

photolithography (ˌfəʊtəʊlɪ'θɒgrəfɪ) *n* 1 a lithographic printing process using photographically made plates. Often shortened to: **photolitho** (ˌfəʊtəʊ'laɪθəʊ) 2 *electronics* a process used in the manufacture of semiconductor devices, thin-film circuits, optical devices, and printed circuits in which a particular pattern is transferred from a photograph onto a substrate, producing a pattern that acts as a mask during an etching or diffusion process. See also **planar process.** > ,photoli'thographer *n* > photolithographic (ˌfəʊtəʊˌlɪθə'græfɪk) *adj* > ,photo,litho'graphically *adv*

photoluminescence (ˌfəʊtəʊˌluː'mɪ'nɛsəns) *n* luminescence resulting from the absorption of light or infrared or ultraviolet radiation > ,photo,lumi'nescent *adj*

photolysis (fəʊ'tɒlɪsɪs) *n* chemical decomposition caused by light or other electromagnetic radiation. Compare **radiolysis.** > photolytic (ˌfəʊtəʊ'lɪtɪk) *adj*

photomap ('fəʊtəʊˌmæp) *n* 1 a map constructed by adding grid lines, place names, etc, to one or more aerial photographs ▷ *vb* -maps, -mapping, -mapped 2 (*tr*) to map (an area) using aerial photography

photomechanical (ˌfəʊtəʊmɪ'kænɪkᵊl) *adj* 1 of or relating to any of various methods by which printing plates are made using photography ▷ *n* 2 a final paste-up of artwork or typeset matter or both for photographing and processing into a printing plate. Often shortened to: **mechanical** > ,photome'chanically *adv*

photomechanical transfer *n* a method of producing photographic prints or offset printing plates from paper negatives by a chemical transfer process rather than by exposure to light

photometer (fəʊ'tɒmɪtə) *n* an instrument used in photometry, usually one that compares the illumination produced by a particular light source with that produced by a standard source. See also **spectrophotometer**

photometry (fəʊ'tɒmɪtrɪ) *n* 1 the measurement of the intensity of light 2 the branch of physics concerned with such measurements > photometric (ˌfəʊtə'mɛtrɪk) *adj* > ,photo'metrically *adv* > pho'tometrist *n*

photomicrograph (ˌfəʊtəʊ'maɪkrəˌgrɑːf, -ˌgræf) *n* 1 a photograph of a microscope image. Sometimes called: **microphotograph** 2 a less common name for **microphotograph** (sense 1) > photomicrographer (ˌfəʊtəʊmaɪ'krɒgrəfə) *n* > photomicrographic (ˌfəʊtəʊˌmaɪkrə'græfɪk) *adj* > ,photo,micro'graphically *adv* > ,photomi'crography *n*

photomontage (ˌfəʊtəʊmɒn'tɑːʒ) *n* 1 the technique of producing a composite picture by combining several photographs: used esp in advertising 2 the composite picture so produced

photomosaic (ˌfəʊtəʊmə'zeɪɪk) *n* a large-scale detailed picture made up of many photographs. See also **mosaic** (sense 5)

photomultiplier (ˌfəʊtəʊ'mʌltɪˌplaɪə) *n* a device sensitive to electromagnetic radiation, consisting of a photocathode, from which electrons are released by incident photons, and an electron multiplier, which amplifies and produces a detectable pulse of current

photomural (ˌfəʊtəʊ'mjʊərəl) *n* a decoration covering all or part of a wall consisting of a single enlarged photograph or a montage

photon ('fəʊtɒn) *n* a quantum of electromagnetic radiation, regarded as a particle with zero rest mass and charge, unit spin, and energy equal to the product of the frequency of the radiation and the Planck constant

photonasty ('fəʊtəʊˌnæstɪ) *n, pl* -ties a nastic movement in response to a change in light intensity > ,photo'nastic *adj*

photonegative (ˌfəʊtəʊ'nɛgətɪv) *adj physics* (of a material) having an electrical conductivity that decreases with increasing illumination

photoneutron (ˌfəʊtəʊ'njuːtrɒn) *n* a neutron emitted from a nucleus as a result of photodisintegration

photonics (fəʊ'tɒnɪks) *n* (*functioning as singular*) the study and design of devices and systems, such as optical fibres, that depend on the transmission, modulation, or amplification of streams of photons

photonuclear (ˌfəʊtəʊ'njuːklɪə) *adj physics* of or concerned with a nuclear reaction caused by a photon

photo-offset *n printing* an offset process in which the plates are produced photomechanically

photo op *n* short for **photo opportunity**

photo opportunity *n* an opportunity, either preplanned or accidental, for the press to photograph a politician, celebrity, or event

photoperiod (ˌfəʊtəʊ'pɪərɪəd) *n* the period of daylight in every 24 hours, esp in relation to its effects on plants and animals. See also **photoperiodism.** > ,photo,peri'odic *adj* > ,photo,peri'odically *adv*

photoperiodism (ˌfəʊtəʊ'pɪərɪəˌdɪzəm) *n* the response of plants and animals by behaviour, growth, etc, to photoperiods

photophilous (fəʊ'tɒfələs) *adj* (esp of plants) growing best in strong light > pho'tophily *n*

photophobia (ˌfəʊtəʊ'fəʊbɪə) *n* 1 *pathol* abnormal sensitivity of the eyes to light, esp as the result of inflammation 2 *psychiatry* abnormal fear of or aversion to sunlight or well-lit places > ,photo'phobic *adj*

photophore ('fəʊtəˌfɔː) *n zoology* any light-producing organ in animals, esp in certain fishes

photopia (fəʊ'təʊpɪə) *n* the normal adaptation of the eye to light; day vision [C20 New Latin, from PHOTO- + -OPIA] > photopic (fəʊ'tɒpɪk, -'təʊ-) *adj*

photopolymer (ˌfəʊtəʊ'pɒlɪmə) *n* a polymeric material that is sensitive to light: used in printing plates, microfilms, etc

photopositive (ˌfəʊtəʊ'pɒzɪtɪv) *adj physics* (of a material) having an electrical conductivity that increases with increasing illumination

photorealism (ˌfəʊtəʊ'rɪəˌlɪzəm) *n* a style of painting and sculpture that depicts esp commonplace urban images with meticulously accurate detail > ,photo'realist *n, adj*

photoreceptor (ˌfəʊtəʊrɪ'sɛptə) *n zoology, physiol* a light-sensitive cell or organ that conveys impulses through the sensory neuron connected to it

photoreconnaissance (ˌfəʊtəʊrɪ'kɒnɪsəns) *n chiefly military* reconnaissance from the air by camera

photo refractive keratomy *n* laser eye surgery that involves scraping away the protective cells of the cornea before reshaping its surface to improve vision. Abbreviation: **PRK**

photo relief *n* a method of showing the configuration of the relief of an area by photographing a model of it that is illuminated by a lamp in the northwest corner

photorespiration (ˌfəʊtəʊˌrɛspə'reɪʃən) *n* (in plants) a reaction that occurs during photosynthesis in which oxygen is assimilated and used to oxidize carbohydrates, with the release of carbon dioxide: differs from normal respiration in that there is no production of energy in the form of ATP

photosensitive (ˌfəʊtəʊ'sɛnsɪtɪv) *adj* sensitive to electromagnetic radiation, esp light: *a photosensitive photographic film* > ,photo,sensi'tivity *n*

photosensitize *or* **photosensitise** (ˌfəʊtəʊ'sɛnsɪˌtaɪz) *vb* (*tr*) to make (an organism or substance) photosensitive > ,photo,sensiti'zation *or* ,photo,sensiti'sation *n*

photoset ('fəʊtəʊˌsɛt) *vb* -sets, -setting, -set (*tr*) to set (type matter) by photosetting > 'photo,setter *n*

photosetting ('fəʊtəʊˌsɛtɪŋ) *n printing* another word for **photocomposition**

photoshoot ('fəʊtəʊˌʃuːt) *n* a session in which a photographer takes pictures of someone for publication

photosphere ('fəʊtəʊˌsfɪə) *n* the visible surface of the sun, several hundred kilometres thick > photospheric (ˌfəʊtəʊ'sfɛrɪk) *adj*

photostat ('fəʊtəʊˌstæt) *n* 1 a machine or process used to make quick positive or negative photographic copies of written, printed, or graphic matter 2 any copy made by such a machine ▷ *vb* -stats, -statting *or* -stating, -statted *or* -stated 3 to make a photostat copy (of) > ,photo'static *adj*

photosynthate (ˌfəʊtəʊ'sɪnˌθeɪt) *n* any substance synthesized in photosynthesis, esp a sugar

photosynthesis (ˌfəʊtəʊ'sɪnθɪsɪs) *n* 1 (in plants) the synthesis of organic compounds from carbon dioxide and water (with the release of oxygen) using light energy absorbed by chlorophyll 2 the corresponding process in certain bacteria > photosynthetic (ˌfəʊtəʊsɪn'θɛtɪk) *adj* > ,photosyn'thetically *adv*

photosynthesize *or* **photosynthesise** (ˌfəʊtəʊ'sɪnθɪˌsaɪz) *vb* (of plants and some bacteria) to carry out photosynthesis

photosystem ('fəʊtəʊˌsɪstəm) *n botany* either of two pigment-containing systems, photosystem I or II, in which the light-dependent chemical reactions of photosynthesis occur in the chloroplasts of plants

phototaxis (ˌfəʊtəʊˈtæksɪs) *or* **phototaxy** *n* the movement of an entire organism in response to light > **phototactic** (ˌfəʊtəʊˈtæktɪk) *adj*

phototherapy (ˌfəʊtəʊˈθɛrəpɪ) *or* **phototherapeutics** (ˌfəʊtəʊˌθɛrəˈpjuːtɪks) *n* (*functioning as singular*) the use of light in the treatment of disease > ˌphotoˌtheraˈpeutic *adj* > ˌphotoˌtheraˈpeutically *adv*

photothermic (ˌfəʊtəʊˈθɜːmɪk) *or* **photothermal** *adj* of or concerned with light and heat, esp the production of heat by light > ˌphotoˈthermically *or* ˌphotoˈthermally *adv*

phototonus (fəʊˈtɒtənəs) *n* the condition of plants that enables them to respond to the stimulus of light [C19 from PHOTO- + Greek *tonos* TONE] > **phototonic** (ˌfəʊtəʊˈtɒnɪk) *adj*

phototopography (ˌfəʊtəʊtəˈpɒɡrəfɪ) *n* the preparation of topographic maps from photographs

phototoxic (ˌfəʊtəʊˈtɒksɪk) *adj* (of cosmetics, skin creams, etc) making the skin hazardously sensitive to sunlight

phototransistor (ˌfəʊtəʊtrænˈzɪstə) *n* a junction transistor, whose base signal is generated by illumination of the base. The emitter current, and hence collector current, increases with the intensity of the light

phototroph (ˈfəʊtəʊˌtrɒf) *n* an organism that obtains energy from sunlight for the synthesis of organic compounds > **phototrophic** (ˌfəʊtəʊˈtrɒfɪk) *adj*

phototropism (ˌfəʊtəʊˈtrəʊpɪzəm) *n* **1** the growth response of plant parts to the stimulus of light, producing a bending towards the light source **2** the response of animals to light: sometimes used as another word for **phototaxis** > ˌphotoˈtropic *adj*

phototropy (ˌfəʊtəʊˈtrəʊpɪ) *n chem* **1** an alteration in the colour of certain substances as a result of being exposed to light of different wavelengths **2** the reversible loss of colour of certain dyestuffs when illuminated at a particular wavelength

phototube (ˈfəʊtəʊˌtjuːb) *n* a type of photocell in which radiation falling on a photocathode causes electrons to flow to an anode and thus produce an electric current

phototype (ˈfəʊtəʊˌtaɪp) *printing* ⊳ *n* **1 a** a printing plate produced by photography **b** a print produced from such a plate ⊳ *vb* **2** (*tr*) to reproduce (an illustration) using a phototype > **phototypic** (ˌfəʊtəʊˈtɪpɪk) *adj* > ˌphotoˈtypically *adv*

phototypeset (ˈfəʊtəʊˌtaɪpˌsɛt) *vb* -sets, -setting, -set (*tr*) to set (type matter) by phototypesetting

phototypesetting (ˌfəʊtəʊˈtaɪpˌsɛtɪŋ) *n printing* another word for **photocomposition**

phototypography (ˌfəʊtəʊtaɪˈpɒɡrəfɪ) *n* any printing process involving the use of photography > **phototypographical** (ˌfəʊtəʊˌtaɪpəˈɡræfɪkəl) *adj* > ˌphotoˈtypographically *adv*

photovoltaic (ˌfəʊtəʊvɒlˈteɪɪk) *adj* of, concerned with, or producing electric current or voltage caused by electromagnetic radiation

photovoltaic effect *n* the effect observed when electromagnetic radiation falls on a thin film of one solid deposited on the surface of a dissimilar solid producing a difference in potential between the two materials

photozincography (ˌfəʊtəʊzɪŋˈkɒɡrəfɪ) *n* a photoengraving process using a printing plate made of zinc > **photozincograph** (ˌfəʊtəʊˈzɪŋkəˌɡrɑːf, -ˌɡræf) *n*

phrasal (ˈfreɪzᵊl) *adj* of, relating to, or composed of phrases > **'phrasally** *adv*

phrasal verb *n* (in English grammar) a phrase that consists of a verb plus an adverbial or prepositional particle, esp one the meaning of which cannot be deduced by analysis of the meaning of the constituents: *"take in" meaning "deceive" is a phrasal verb*

phrase (freɪz) *n* **1** a group of words forming an immediate syntactic constituent of a clause. Compare **clause** (sense 1), **noun phrase**, **verb phrase 2** a particular expression, esp an original one **3** *music* a small group of notes forming a coherent unit of melody **4** (in choreography) a short sequence of dance movements ⊳ *vb* (*tr*) **5** *music* to divide (a melodic line, part, etc) into musical phrases, esp in performance **6** to express orally or in a phrase [C16 from Latin *phrasis,* from Greek: speech, from *phrazein* to declare, tell]

phrase book *n* a book containing frequently used expressions and their equivalents in a foreign language, esp for the use of tourists

phrase marker *n linguistics* a representation, esp one in the form of a tree diagram, of the constituent structure of a sentence

phraseogram (ˈfreɪzɪəˌɡræm) *n* a symbol representing a phrase, as in shorthand

phraseograph (ˈfreɪzɪəˌɡrɑːf) *n* a phrase for which there exists a phraseogram > **phraseographic** (ˌfreɪzɪəˈɡræfɪk) *adj* > **phraseography** (ˌfreɪzɪˈɒɡrəfɪ) *n*

phraseologist (ˌfreɪzɪˈɒlədʒɪst) *n* a person who is interested in or collects phrases or who affects a particular phraseology

phraseology (ˌfreɪzɪˈɒlədʒɪ) *n, pl* -gies **1** the manner in which words or phrases are used **2** a set of phrases used by a particular group of people > **phraseological** (ˌfreɪzɪəˈlɒdʒɪkᵊl) *adj* > ˌphraseoˈlogically *adv*

phrase-structure grammar *n* a grammar in which relations among the words and morphemes of a sentence are described, but not deeper or semantic relations. Abbreviation: PSG Compare **transformational grammar**

phrase-structure rule *n generative grammar* a rule of the form A → X where A is a syntactic category label, such as *noun phrase* or *sentence,* and X is a sequence of such labels and/or morphemes, expressing the fact that A can be replaced by X in generating the constituent structure of a sentence. Also called: **rewrite rule** Compare **transformational rule**

phrasing (ˈfreɪzɪŋ) *n* **1** the way in which something is expressed, esp in writing; wording **2** *music* the division of a melodic line, part, etc, into musical phrases

phratry (ˈfreɪtrɪ) *n, pl* -tries *anthropol* a group of people within a tribe who have a common ancestor [C19 from Greek *phratria* clan, from *phratēr* fellow clansman; compare Latin *frāter* brother] > **'phratric** *adj*

phreaking (ˈfriːkɪŋ) *n* the act of gaining unauthorized access to telecommunication systems, esp to obtain free calls [C20 blend of FREAKING + PHONE]

phreatic (frɪˈætɪk) *adj geography* of or relating to ground water occurring below the water table. Compare **vadose** [C19 from Greek *phrear* a well]

phreatophyte (frɪˈætəfaɪt) *n* a plant having very long roots that reach down to the water table or the layer above it [C20 from Greek *phrear* a well + -PHYTE]

phrenetic (frɪˈnɛtɪk) *adj* an obsolete spelling of **frenetic.** > phre'netically *adv* > phre'neticness *n*

phrenic (ˈfrɛnɪk) *adj* **1 a** of or relating to the diaphragm **b** (*as noun*): *the phrenic* **2** *obsolete* of or relating to the mind [C18 from New Latin *phrenicus,* from Greek *phrēn* mind, diaphragm]

phrenitis (frɪˈnaɪtɪs) *n rare* **1** another name for **encephalitis 2** a state of frenzy; delirium [C17 via Late Latin from Greek: delirium, from *phrēn* mind, diaphragm + -ITIS] > **phrenitic** (frɪˈnɪtɪk) *adj*

phreno- *or before a vowel* **phren-** *combining form* **1** mind or brain; *phrenology* **2** of or relating to the diaphragm: *phrenic* [from Greek *phrēn* mind, diaphragm]

phrenology (frɪˈnɒlədʒɪ) *n* (formerly) the branch of science concerned with localization of function in the human brain, esp determination of the strength of the faculties by the shape and size of the skull overlying the parts of the brain thought to be responsible for them > **phrenological** (ˌfrɛnəˈlɒdʒɪkᵊl) *adj* > phre'nologist *n*

phrensy (ˈfrɛnzɪ) *n, pl* -sies, *vb* an obsolete spelling of **frenzy**

Phrixus (ˈfrɪksəs) *n Greek myth* the son of Athamas and Nephele who escaped the wrath of his father's mistress, Ino, by flying to Colchis on a winged ram with a golden fleece. See also **Helle, Golden Fleece**

phrygana (frɪˈɡɑːnə) *n* another name for **garigue,** used esp in Greece

Phrygia (ˈfrɪdʒɪə) *n* an ancient country of W central Asia Minor

Phrygian (ˈfrɪdʒɪən) *adj* **1** of or relating to ancient Phrygia, its inhabitants, or their extinct language **2** *music* of or relating to an authentic mode represented by the natural diatonic scale from E to E. See **Hypo- 3** *music* (of a cadence) denoting a progression that leads a piece of music out of the major key and ends on the dominant chord of the relative minor key ⊳ *n* **4** a native or inhabitant of ancient Phrygia **5** an ancient language of Phrygia, belonging to the Thraco-Phrygian branch of the Indo-European family: recorded in a few inscriptions

Phrygian cap *n* a conical cap of soft material worn during ancient times that became a symbol of liberty during the French Revolution

PHS (in the US) *abbreviation for* Public Health Service

PHSE (in England and Wales) *abbreviation for* personal, social, and health education

phthalate (ˈθælɪt, ˈfθæl-) *n* a salt or ester of phthalic acid. Esters are commonly used as plasticizers in PVC; when ingested they can cause kidney and liver damage

phthalein (ˈθeɪliːn, -lɪn, ˈθæl-, ˈfθæl-) *n* any of a class of organic compounds obtained by the reaction of phthalic anhydride with a phenol and used in dyes [C19 from *phthal-,* shortened form of NAPHTHALENE + -IN]

phthalic acid (ˈθælɪk, ˈfθæl-) *n* a soluble colourless crystalline acid used in the synthesis of dyes and perfumes; 1,2-benzenedicarboxylic acid. Formula: $C_6H_4(COOH)_2$ [C19 *phthalic,* from *phthal-* (see PHTHALEIN) + -IC]

phthalic anhydride *n* a white crystalline substance used mainly in producing dyestuffs. Formula: $C_6H_4(CO)_2O$

phthalocyanine (ˌθæləʊˈsaɪəˌniːn, ˌθeɪ-, ˌfθæl-) *n* **1** a cyclic blue-green organic pigment. Formula: $(C_6H_4C_2N)_4N_4H_4$ **2** any of a class of compounds derived by coordination of this compound with a metal atom. They are blue or green pigments used in printing inks, plastics, and enamels [C20 from *phthal-* (see PHTHALEIN) + CYANINE]

phthiriasis (θɪˈraɪəsɪs) *n pathol* the state or condition of being infested with lice; pediculosis [C16 via Latin from Greek, from *phtheir* louse]

phthisic (ˈθaɪsɪk, ˈfθaɪsɪk, ˈtaɪsɪk) *obsolete* ⊳ *adj* **1** relating to or affected with phthisis ⊳ *n* **2** another name for **asthma** [C14 from Old French *tisike,* from Latin *phthisicus,* from Greek *phthisikos;* see PHTHISIS] > **'phthisical** *adj*

phthisis (ˈθaɪsɪs, ˈfθaɪ-, ˈtaɪ-) *n* any disease that causes wasting of the body, esp pulmonary tuberculosis [C16 via Latin from Greek: a wasting away, from *phthinein* to waste away]

Phuket (ˌpuːˈkɛt) *n* **1** an island and province of S Thailand, in the Andaman Sea: mainly flat; suffered badly in the Indian Ocean tsunami of December 2004. Area: 534 sq km (206 sq miles) **2** the chief town of the island of Phuket; a popular tourist resort

phut (fʌt) *informal* ⊳ *n* **1** a representation of a muffled explosive sound ⊳ *adv* **2 go phut** to break down or collapse [C19 of imitative origin]

phyco- *combining form* seaweed: *phycology* [from Greek *phukos*]

p

phycobilin (ˌfaɪkəʊˈbaɪlɪn) *n biology* any of a class of red or blue-green pigments found in the red algae and cyanobacteria

phycobiont (ˌfaɪkəʊˈbaɪɒnt) *n botany* the algal constituent of a lichen. Compare **mycobiont**

phycology (faɪˈkɒlədʒɪ) *n* the study of algae > **phycological** (ˌfaɪkəˈlɒdʒɪkᵊl) *adj* > **phyˈcologist** *n*

phycomycete (ˌfaɪkəʊˈmaɪsiːt) *n* any of a primitive group of fungi, formerly included in the class *Phycomycetes* but now classified in different phyla: includes certain mildews and moulds > **ˌphycomyˈcetous** *adj*

phyla (ˈfaɪlə) *n* the plural of **phylum**

phylactery (fɪˈlæktərɪ) *n, pl* -**teries** 1 *Judaism* (usually plural) Also called: **Tefillah** either of the pair of blackened square cases containing parchments inscribed with biblical passages, bound by leather thongs to the head and left arm, and worn by Jewish men during weekday morning prayers 2 a reminder or aid to remembering 3 *archaic* an amulet or charm [c14 from Late Latin *phylactērium,* from Greek *phulaktērion* outpost, from *phulax* a guard]

phyle (ˈfaɪlɪ) *n, pl* -**lae** (-liː) a tribe or clan of an ancient Greek people such as the Ionians [c19 from Greek *phulē* tribe, clan] > **ˈphylic** *adj*

phyletic (faɪˈlɛtɪk) *or* **phylogenetic** (ˌfaɪləʊdʒɪˈnɛtɪk) *adj* of or relating to the evolution of a species or group of organisms [c19 from Greek *phuletikos* tribal] > **phyˈletically** *or* ˌphyloge**ˈnetically** *adv*

-phyll *or* **-phyl** *n combining form* leaf: *chlorophyll* [from Greek *phullon*]

phyllid (ˈfɪlɪd) *n botany* the leaf of a liverwort or moss

phyllite (ˈfɪlaɪt) *n* a compact lustrous metamorphic rock, rich in mica, derived from a shale or other clay-rich rock [c19 from PHYLL(O)- + -ITE[1]] > **phyllitic** (fɪˈlɪtɪk) *adj*

phyllo (ˈfiːləʊ) *n* a variant of **filo** [c20 from Greek: leaf]

phyllo- *or before a vowel* **phyll-** *combining form* leaf: *phyllopod* [from Greek *phullon* leaf]

phylloclade (ˈfɪləʊˌkleɪd) *or* **phylloclad** (ˈfɪləʊˌklæd) *n* other names for **cladode** [c19 from New Latin *phyllocladium,* from PHYLLO- + Greek *klados* branch]

phyllode (ˈfɪləʊd) *n* a flattened leafstalk that resembles and functions as a leaf [c19 from New Latin *phyllodium,* from Greek *phullōdēs* leaflike] > **phylˈlodial** *adj*

phylloid (ˈfɪlɔɪd) *adj* resembling a leaf

phyllome (ˈfɪləʊm) *n* a leaf or a leaflike organ > **phyllomic** (fɪˈlɒmɪk, -ˈləʊ-) *adj*

phylloplane (ˈfɪləʊˌpleɪn) *n ecology* the surface of a leaf considered as a habitat, esp for microorganisms. Also called: **phyllosphere**

phylloquinone (ˌfɪləʊkwɪˈnəʊn) *n* a viscous fat-soluble liquid occurring in plants: essential for the production of prothrombin, required in blood clotting. Formula: $C_{31}H_{46}O_2$. Also called: **vitamin K₁**

phyllosilicate (ˌfɪləʊˈsɪlɪkeɪt) *n* any of a class of silicate minerals, including talc, consisting of thin sheets

phyllosphere (ˈfɪləʊˌsfɪə) *n* another name for **phylloplane**

phyllotaxis (ˌfɪləˈtæksɪs) *or* **phyllotaxy** *n, pl* -**taxes** (-ˈtæksiːz) *or* -**taxies** 1 the arrangement of the leaves on a stem 2 the study of this arrangement in different plants > **ˌphylloˈtactic** *adj*

-phyllous *adj combining form* having leaves of a specified number or type: *monophyllous* [from Greek *-phullos* or a leaf]

phylloxera (ˌfɪlɒkˈsɪərə, fɪˈlɒksərə) *n, pl* -**rae** (-riː) *or* -**ras** any homopterous insect of the genus *Phylloxera,* such as *P. vitifolia* (or *Viteus vitifolii*) (**vine phylloxera**), typically feeding on plant juices, esp of vines: family *Phylloxeridae* [c19 from New Latin PHYLLO- + Greek *xēros* dry]

phylo- *or before a vowel* **phyl-** *combining form* tribe; race; phylum: *phylogeny* [from Greek *phulon* race]

phylogeny (faɪˈlɒdʒɪnɪ) *or* **phylogenesis**

(ˌfaɪləʊˈdʒɛnɪsɪs) *n, pl* -**nies** *or* -**geneses** (-ˈdʒɛnɪˌsiːz) *biology* the sequence of events involved in the evolution of a species, genus, etc. Compare **ontogeny** [c19 from PHYLO- + -GENY] > **phylogenic** (ˌfaɪləʊˈdʒɛnɪk) *or* **phylogenetic** (ˌfaɪləʊdʒɪˈnɛtɪk) *adj*

phylum (ˈfaɪləm) *n, pl* -**la** (-lə) 1 a major taxonomic division of living organisms that contain one or more classes. An example is the phylum *Arthropoda* (insects, crustaceans, arachnids, etc, and myriapods) 2 any analogous group, such as a group of related language families or linguistic stocks [c19 New Latin, from Greek *phulon* race]

phys. *abbreviation for* 1 physical 2 physician 3 physics 4 physiological 5 physiology

physalis (faɪˈseɪlɪs) *n* See **Chinese lantern, strawberry tomato** [New Latin, from Greek *physallis* a bladder (from the form of the calyx)]

physiatrics (ˌfɪzɪˈætrɪks) *n (functioning as singular) med, US* another name for **physiotherapy** [c19 from PHYSIO- + -IATRICS] > **ˌphysiˈatric** *or* **ˌphysiˈatrical** *adj*

physic (ˈfɪzɪk) *n* 1 *rare* a medicine or drug, esp a cathartic or purge 2 *archaic* the art or skill of healing 3 an archaic term for **physics** (sense 1) ▷ *vb* -**ics,** -**icking,** -**icked** 4 (*tr*) *archaic* to treat (a patient) with medicine [c13 from Old French *fisique,* via Latin, from Greek *phusikē,* from *phusis* nature] > **ˈphysicky** *adj*

physical (ˈfɪzɪkᵊl) *adj* 1 of or relating to the body, as distinguished from the mind or spirit 2 of, relating to, or resembling material things or nature: *the physical universe* 3 involving or requiring bodily contact: *rugby is a physical sport* 4 of or concerned with matter and energy 5 of or relating to physics 6 perceptible to the senses; apparent: *a physical manifestation* ▷ *n* 7 short for **physical examination** ▷ See also **physicals** > **ˈphysically** *adv* > **ˈphysicalness** *n*

physical anthropology *n* the branch of anthropology dealing with the genetic aspect of human development and its physical variations

physical chemistry *n* the branch of chemistry concerned with the way in which the physical properties of substances depend on and influence their chemical structure, properties, and reactions

physical education *n* training and practice in sports, gymnastics, etc, as in schools and colleges. Abbreviation: **PE**

physical examination *n med* the process of examining the body by means of sight, touch, percussion, or auscultation to diagnose disease or verify fitness

physical geography *n* the branch of geography that deals with the natural features of the earth's surface

physical handicap *n* loss of or failure to develop a specific bodily function or functions, whether of movement, sensation, coordination, or speech, but excluding mental impairments or disabilities > **physically handicapped** *adj*

physicalism (ˈfɪzɪkᵊˌlɪzəm) *n philosophy* the doctrine that all phenomena can be described in terms of space and time and that all meaningful statements are either analytic, as in logic and mathematics, or can be reduced to empirically verifiable assertions. See also **logical positivism, identity theory.** > **ˈphysicalist** *n, adj* > **ˌphysicalˈistic** *adj*

physicality (ˌfɪzɪˈkælɪtɪ) *n* 1 the state or quality of being physical 2 the physical characteristics of a person, object, etc

physical jerks *pl n Brit informal* See **jerk¹** (sense 6)

physical medicine *n* the branch of medicine devoted to the management of physical disabilities, as resulting from rheumatic disease, poliomyelitis, etc. See also **rehabilitation** (sense 2)

physicals (ˈfɪzɪkᵊlz) *pl n commerce* commodities that can be purchased and used, as opposed to those bought and sold in a futures market. Also called: **actuals**

physical science *n* any of the sciences concerned with nonliving matter, energy, and the physical properties of the universe, such as physics, chemistry, astronomy, and geology. Compare **life science**

physical therapy *n* another term for **physiotherapy**

physician (fɪˈzɪʃən) *n* 1 a person legally qualified to practise medicine, esp one specializing in areas of treatment other than surgery; doctor of medicine 2 *archaic* any person who treats diseases; healer [c13 from Old French *fisicien,* from *fisique* PHYSIC]

physicist (ˈfɪzɪsɪst) *n* a person versed in or studying physics

physicochemical (ˌfɪzɪkəʊˈkɛmɪkᵊl) *adj* of, concerned with, or relating to physical chemistry or both physics and chemistry > **ˌphysicoˈchemically** *adv*

physics (ˈfɪzɪks) *n (functioning as singular)* 1 the branch of science concerned with the properties of matter and energy and the relationships between them. It is based on mathematics and traditionally includes mechanics, optics, electricity and magnetism, acoustics, and heat. Modern physics, based on quantum theory, includes atomic, nuclear, particle, and solid-state studies. It can also embrace applied fields such as geophysics and meteorology 2 physical properties of behaviour: *the physics of the electron* 3 *archaic* natural science or natural philosophy [c16 from Latin *physica,* translation of Greek *ta phusika* natural things, from *phusis* nature]

physio (ˈfɪzɪəʊ) *n informal* short for **physiotherapy, physiotherapist**

physio- *or before a vowel* **phys-** *combining form* 1 of or relating to nature or natural functions: *physiology* 2 physical: *physiotherapy* [from Greek *phusio,* from *phusis* nature, from *phuein* to make grow]

physiocrat (ˈfɪzɪəʊˌkræt) *n* a follower of Quesnay's doctrines of government, believing that the inherent natural order governing society was based on land and its natural products as the only true form of wealth [c18 from French *physiocrate;* see PHYSIO-, -CRAT] > **physiocracy** (ˌfɪzɪˈɒkrəsɪ) *n* > **ˌphysioˈcratic** *adj*

physiognomy (ˌfɪzɪˈɒnəmɪ) *n* 1 a person's features or characteristic expression considered as an indication of personality 2 the art or practice of judging character from facial features 3 the outward appearance of something, esp the physical characteristics of a geographical region [c14 from Old French *phisonomie,* via Medieval Latin, from Late Greek *phusiognomia,* erroneous for Greek *phusiognōmonia,* from *phusis* nature + *gnōmōn* judge] > **physiognomic** (ˌfɪzɪəˈnɒmɪk) *or* ˌphysiog**ˈnomical** *adj* > **ˌphysiogˈnomically** *adv* > **ˌphysiˈognomist** *n*

physiography (ˌfɪzɪˈɒgrəfɪ) *n* another name for **geomorphology** *or* **physical geography** > **ˌphysiˈographer** *n* > **physiographic** (ˌfɪzɪəˈgræfɪk) *or* ˌphysio**ˈgraphical** *adj* > **ˌphysioˈgraphically** *adv*

physiol. *abbreviation for* 1 physiological 2 physiology

physiological (ˌfɪzɪəˈlɒdʒɪkᵊl) *adj* 1 of or relating to physiology 2 of or relating to normal healthful functioning; not pathological > **ˌphysioˈlogically** *adv*

physiological psychology *n* the branch of psychology concerned with the study and correlation of physiological and psychological events

physiology (ˌfɪzɪˈɒlədʒɪ) *n* 1 the branch of science concerned with the functioning of organisms 2 the processes and functions of all or part of an organism [c16 from Latin *physiologia,* from Greek] > **ˌphysiˈologist** *n*

physiotherapy (ˌfɪzɪəʊˈθɛrəpɪ) *n* the therapeutic use of physical agents or means, such as massage, exercises, etc. Also called: **physical therapy,** (informal) **physio,** (US) **physiatrics**

> ˌphysioˈtherapist *n*

physique (fɪˈziːk) *n* the general appearance of the body with regard to size, shape, muscular development, etc [c19 via French, from Latin *physique* (adj) natural, from Latin *physicus* physical]

physoclistous (ˌfaɪsəʊˈklɪstəs) *adj* (of fishes) having an air bladder that is not connected to the alimentary canal. Compare **physostomous** [c19 from Greek *phusa* bladder + -*clistous*, from *kleistos* closed]

physostigmine (ˌfaɪsəʊˈstɪɡmiːn) *or* **physostigmin** (ˌfaɪsəʊˈstɪɡmɪn) *n* an alkaloid found in the Calabar bean used esp in eye drops to reduce pressure inside the eyeball. Formula: $C_{15}H_{21}N_3O_2$. Also called: **eserine** [c19 from New Latin *Physostigma* genus name, from Greek *phusa* bladder + *stigma* mark]

physostomous (faɪˈsɒstəməs) *adj* (of fishes) having a duct connecting the air bladder to part of the alimentary canal. Compare **physoclistous** [c19 from Greek *phusa* bladder + -*stomous*, from *stoma* mouth]

-phyte *n combining form* indicating a plant of a specified type or habitat: *lithophyte; thallophyte* [from Greek *phuton* plant] > **-phytic** *adj combining form*

phyto- *or before a vowel* **phyt-** *combining form* indicating a plant or vegetation: *phytogenesis* [from Greek *phuton* plant, from *phuein* to make grow]

phytoalexin (ˌfaɪtəʊəˈlɛksɪn) *n botany* any of a group of substances produced by plants that inhibit the growth of pathogenic fungi that infect them [c20 from PHYTO- + Greek *alexein* to ward off]

phytochemical (ˌfaɪtəʊˈkɛmɪkəl) *adj* **1** of or relating to phytochemistry or phytochemicals ▷ *n* **2** a chemical that occurs naturally in a plant

phytochemistry (ˌfaɪtəʊˈkɛmɪstri) *n* the branch of chemistry concerned with plants, their chemical composition and processes > ˌphytoˈchemist *n*

phytochrome (ˈfaɪtəʊˌkrəʊm) *n botany* a blue-green pigment existing in two interchangeable forms, present in most plants, that mediates many light-dependent processes, including photoperiodism and the greening of leaves

phytoestrogen (ˌfaɪtəʊˈiːstrədʒən) *n* any of various plant compounds which have oestrogenic properties

phytogenesis (ˌfaɪtəʊˈdʒɛnɪsɪs) *or* **phytogeny** (faɪˈtɒdʒəni) *n* the branch of botany concerned with the origin and evolution of plants > **phytogenetic** (ˌfaɪtəʊdʒɪˈnɛtɪk) *adj* > ˌphytogeˈnetically *adv*

phytogenic (ˌfaɪtəʊˈdʒɛnɪk) *adj* derived from plants: *coal is a phytogenic substance*

phytogeography (ˌfaɪtəʊdʒɪˈɒɡrəfi) *n* the branch of botany that is concerned with the geographical distribution of plants > ˌphytogeˈographer *n* > ˌphytoˌgeoˈgraphic *or* ˌphytoˌgeoˈgraphical *adj*

phytography (faɪˈtɒɡrəfi) *n* the branch of botany that is concerned with the detailed description of plants > **phytographic** (ˌfaɪtəˈɡræfɪk) *adj*

phytohormone (ˌfaɪtəʊˈhɔːməʊn) *n* a hormone-like substance produced by a plant

phytology (faɪˈtɒlədʒi) *n* a rare name for **botany** (sense 1) > **phytological** (ˌfaɪtəˈlɒdʒɪkəl) *adj* > ˌphytoˈlogically *adv* > phyˈtologist *n*

phyton (ˈfaɪtɒn) *n* a unit of plant structure, usually considered as the smallest part of the plant that is capable of growth when detached from the parent plant [c20 from Greek. See -PHYTE]

phytopathology (ˌfaɪtəʊpəˈθɒlədʒi) *n* the branch of botany concerned with diseases of plants > **phytopathological** (ˌfaɪtəʊˌpæθəˈlɒdʒɪkəl) *adj* > ˌphytopaˈthologist *n*

phytophagous (faɪˈtɒfəɡəs) *adj* (esp of insects) feeding on plants > phytophagy (faɪˈtɒfədʒi) *n*

phytoplankton (ˌfaɪtəˈplæŋktən) *n* the photosynthesizing organisms in plankton, mainly unicellular algae and cyanobacteria. Compare **zooplankton.** > phytoplanktonic

(ˌfaɪtəplæŋkˈtɒnɪk) *adj*

phytoremediation (ˌfaɪtəʊriˌmiːdɪˈeɪʃən) *n* another name for **bioremediation**

phytosociology (ˌfaɪtəʊˌsəʊsɪˈɒlədʒi, -ˌsəʊʃɪ-) *n* the branch of ecology that is concerned with the origin, development, etc, of plant communities > phytosociological (ˌfaɪtəʊˌsəʊsɪəˈlɒdʒɪkəl, -ˌsəʊʃɪə-) *adj* > ˌphytoˌsocioˈlogically *adv* > ˌphytoˌsociˈologist *n*

phytotherapy (ˌfaɪtəʊˈθɛrəpi) *n* the use of plants and plant products for medicinal purposes

phytotoxin (ˌfaɪtəˈtɒksɪn) *n* a toxin, such as strychnine, that is produced by a plant. Compare **zootoxin.** > ˌphytoˈtoxic *adj*

phytotron (ˈfaɪtəʊˌtrɒn) *n* a building in which plants can be grown on a large scale, under controlled conditions [c20 from PHYTO- + -TRON, on the model of CYCLOTRON]

pi¹ (paɪ) *n, pl* **pis 1** the 16th letter in the Greek alphabet (Π, π), a consonant, transliterated as *p* **2** *maths* a transcendental number, fundamental to mathematics, that is the ratio of the circumference of a circle to its diameter. Approximate value: 3.141 592...; symbol: π [c18 (mathematical use): representing the first letter of Greek *periphereia* PERIPHERY]

pi² *or* **pie** (paɪ) *n, pl* **pies 1** a jumbled pile of printer's type **2** a jumbled mixture ▷ *vb* **pies, piing, pied** *or* **pies, pieing, pied** (*tr*) **3** to spill and mix (set type) indiscriminately **4** to mix up [c17 of uncertain origin]

pi³ (paɪ) *adj Brit slang* short for **pious** (senses 2, 3)

PI *abbreviation for* **1** Philippine Islands **2** private investigator

Piacenza (*Italian* pjaˈtʃɛntsa) *n* a town in N Italy, in Emilia-Romagna on the River Po. Pop: 95 594 (2001). Latin name: **Placentia** (pləˈsɛntɪə)

piacular (paɪˈækjʊlə) *adj* **1** making expiation for a sacrilege **2** requiring expiation [c17 from Latin *piāculum* propitiatory sacrifice, from *piāre* to appease]

piaffe (pɪˈæf) *n dressage* a passage done on the spot [c18 from French, from *piaffer* to strut]

pia mater (ˈpaɪə ˈmeɪtə) *n* the innermost of the three membranes (see **meninges**) that cover the brain and spinal cord [c16 from Medieval Latin, literally: pious mother, intended to translate Arabic *umm raqīqah* tender mother]

pianism (ˈpiːəˌnɪzəm) *n* technique, skill, or artistry in playing the piano > piˈanistic *adj*

pianissimo (pɪəˈnɪsɪˌməʊ) *adj, adv music* (to be performed) very quietly. Symbol: *pp* [c18 from Italian, superlative of *piano* soft]

pianist (ˈpɪənɪst) *n* a person who plays the piano

piano¹ (pɪˈænəʊ) *n, pl* **-anos** a musical stringed instrument resembling a harp set in a vertical or horizontal frame, played by depressing keys that cause hammers to strike the strings and produce audible vibrations. See also **grand piano, upright piano** [c19 short for PIANOFORTE]

piano² (ˈpjaːnəʊ) *adj, adv music* (to be performed) softly. Symbol: *p* [c17 from Italian, from Latin *plānus* flat; see PLAIN¹]

piano accordion *n* an accordion in which the right hand plays a piano-like keyboard. See **accordion.** > piano accordionist *n*

pianoforte (pɪˈænəʊˈfɔːti) *n* the full name for **piano¹** [c18 from Italian, originally (*gravecembalo col*) *piano e forte* (harpsichord with) soft and loud; see PIANO², FORTE²]

Pianola (pɪəˈnəʊlə) *n trademark* a type of mechanical piano in which the keys are depressed by air pressure from bellows, this air flow being regulated by perforations in a paper roll. Also called: **player piano**

piano nobile (ˈpjaːnəʊ ˈnəʊbɪli) *n architect* the main floor of a large house, containing the reception rooms: usually of lofty proportions [Italian: great floor]

piano player *n* **1** another name for **pianist 2** any of various devices for playing a piano automatically

piano roll *n* a perforated roll of paper actuating the playing mechanism of a Pianola. Also called: music roll

piano stool *n* a stool on which a pianist sits when playing a piano, esp one whose height is adjustable

piano trio *n* **1** an instrumental ensemble consisting of a piano, a violin, and a cello **2** a piece of music written for such an ensemble, usually having the form and commonest features of a sonata

piassava (ˌpiːəˈsɑːvə) *or* **piassaba** (ˌpiːəˈsɑːbə) *n* **1** either of two South American palm trees, *Attalea funifera* or *Leopoldinia piassaba* **2** the coarse fibre obtained from either of these trees, used to make brushes and rope [c19 via Portuguese from Tupi *piaçaba*]

piastre *or* **piaster** (pɪˈæstə) *n* **1** (formerly) the standard monetary unit of South Vietnam, divided into 100 cents **2** a fractional monetary unit of Egypt, Lebanon, and Syria worth one hundredth of a pound; formerly also used in the Sudan **3** another name for **kuruş 4** a rare word for **piece of eight** [c17 from French *piastre*, from Italian *piastra d'argento* silver plate; related to Italian *piastro* PLASTER]

Piauí (*Portuguese* pja'ui) *n* a state of NE Brazil, on the Atlantic: rises to a semiarid plateau, with the more humid Paranaíba valley in the west. Capital: Teresina. Pop: 2 898 223 (2002). Area: 250 934 sq km (96 886 sq miles)

Piave (*Italian* ˈpjaːve) *n* a river in NE Italy, rising near the border with Austria and flowing south and southeast to the Adriatic: the main line of Italian defence during World War I. Length: 220 km (137 miles)

piazza (pɪˈætsə, -ˈædzə; *Italian* ˈpjattsa) *n* **1** a large open square in an Italian town **2** *chiefly Brit* a covered passageway or gallery [c16 from Italian: marketplace, from Latin *platēa* courtyard, from Greek *plateia*; see PLACE]

pibroch (ˈpiːbrɒk; *Gaelic* ˈpiːbrɒx) *n* **1** a form of music for Scottish bagpipes, consisting of a theme and variations **2** a piece of such music [c18 from Gaelic *piobaireachd*, from *piobair* piper]

pic (pɪk) *n, pl* **pics** *or* **pix** *informal* a photograph, picture, or illustration [c20 shortened from PICTURE]

pica¹ (ˈpaɪkə) *n* **1** Also called: **em, pica em** a printer's unit of measurement, equal to 12 points or 0.166 ins **2** (formerly) a size of printer's type equal to 12 point **3** a typewriter type size having 10 characters to the inch [c15 from Anglo-Latin *pīca* list of ecclesiastical regulations, apparently from Latin *pīca* magpie, with reference to its habit of making collections of miscellaneous items; the connection between the original sense (ecclesiastical list) and the typography meanings is obscure]

pica² (ˈpaɪkə) *n pathol* an abnormal craving to ingest substances such as clay, dirt, or hair, sometimes occurring during pregnancy, in persons with chlorosis, etc [c16 from medical Latin, from Latin: magpie, being an allusion to its omnivorous feeding habits]

picador (ˈpɪkəˌdɔː) *n bullfighting* a horseman who pricks the bull with a lance in the early stages of a fight to goad and weaken it [c18 from Spanish, literally: pricker, from *picar* to prick; see PIQUE¹]

Picardy (ˈpɪkədi) *n* a region of N France: mostly low-lying; scene of heavy fighting in World War I. French name: **Picardie** (pikardi)

Picardy third *n music* a major chord used in the final chord of a piece of music in the minor mode. Also called: **tierce de Picardie** [translation of French *tierce de Picardie*, from its use in the church music of Picardy]

picaresque (ˌpɪkəˈrɛsk) *adj* **1** of or relating to a type of fiction in which the hero, a rogue, goes through a series of episodic adventures. It originated in Spain in the 16th century **2** of or involving rogues or picaroons [c19 via French from

Spanish *picaresco*, from *pícaro* a rogue]

picaroon *or* **pickaroon** (ˌpɪkəˈruːn) *n archaic* an adventurer or rogue [c17 from Spanish *picarón*, from *pícaro*]

picayune (ˌpɪkəˈjuːn) *adj also* **picayunish** *US and Canadian informal* **1** of small value or importance **2** mean; petty ▷ *n* **3** the half real, an old Spanish-American coin **4** *US* any coin of little value, esp a five-cent piece [c19 from French *picaillon* coin from Piedmont, from Provençal *picaioun*, of unknown origin] > ˌ**pica'yunishly** *adv* > ˌ**pica'yunishness** *n*

Piccadilly (ˌpɪkəˈdɪlɪ) *n* one of the main streets of London, running from Piccadilly Circus to Hyde Park Corner

piccalilli (ˈpɪkəˌlɪlɪ) *n* a pickle of mixed vegetables, esp onions, cauliflower, and cucumber, in a mustard sauce [C18 *piccalillo*, perhaps a coinage based on PICKLE]

piccanin (ˈpɪkəˌnɪn, ˌpɪkəˈnɪn) *n South African offensive* a Black African child [variant of PICCANINNY]

piccaninny *or esp US* **pickaninny** (ˌpɪkəˈnɪnɪ) *n, pl* **-nies** **1** *offensive* a small Black or Aboriginal child **2** (*modifier*) tiny: *a piccaninny fire won't last long* [c17 perhaps from Portuguese *pequenino* tiny one, from *pequeno* small]

piccolo (ˈpɪkəˌləʊ) *n, pl* **-los** a woodwind instrument, the smallest member of the flute family, lying an octave above that of the flute. See **flute** (sense 1) [c19 from Italian: small; compare English PETTY, French *petit*]

pice (paɪs) *n, pl* **pice** a former Indian coin worth one sixty-fourth of a rupee [c17 from Mahratti *paisā*]

piceous (ˈpɪsɪəs, ˈpaɪsɪəs) *adj* of, relating to, or resembling pitch [c17 from Latin *piceus*, from *pix* PITCH²]

pi character *n printing* any special character, such as an accent or mathematical symbol, which is not normally obtained in a standard type fount

pichiciego (ˌpɪtʃɪsɪˈeɪgəʊ) *n, pl* **-gos** **1** a very small Argentine armadillo, *Chlamyphorus truncatus*, with white silky hair and pale pink plates on the head and back **2** **greater pichiciego** a similar but larger armadillo, *Burmeisteria retusa* [c19 from Spanish, probably from Guarani *pichey* small armadillo + Spanish *ciego* blind]

pick¹ (pɪk) *vb* **1** to choose (something) deliberately or carefully, from or as if from a group or number; select **2** to pluck or gather (fruit, berries, or crops) from (a tree, bush, field, etc): *to pick hops; to pick a whole bush* **3** (*tr*) to clean or prepare (fruit, poultry, etc) by removing the indigestible parts **4** (*tr*) to remove loose particles from (the teeth, the nose, etc) **5** (esp of birds) to nibble or gather (corn, etc) **6** (when *intr*, foll by *at*) to nibble (at) fussily or without appetite **7** to separate (strands, fibres, etc), as in weaving **8** (*tr*) to provoke (an argument, fight, etc) deliberately **9** (*tr*) to steal (money or valuables) from (a person's pocket) **10** (*tr*) to open (a lock) with an instrument other than a key **11** to pluck the strings of (a guitar, banjo, etc) **12** (*tr*) to make (one's way) carefully on foot: *they picked their way through the rubble* **13** **pick and choose** to select fastidiously, fussily, etc **14** **pick someone's brains** to obtain information or ideas from someone ▷ *n* **15** freedom or right of selection (esp in the phrase **take one's pick**) **16** a person, thing, etc, that is chosen first or preferred: *the pick of the bunch* **17** the act of picking **18** the amount of a crop picked at one period or from one area **19** *printing* a speck of dirt or paper fibre or a blob of ink on the surface of set type or a printing plate ▷ See also **pick at, pick off, pick on, pick out, pick-up** [c15 from earlier *piken* to pick, influenced by French *piquer* to pierce; compare Middle Low German *picken*, Dutch *pikken*] > ˈ**pickable** *adj*

pick² (pɪk) *n* **1** a tool with a handle carrying a long steel head curved and tapering to a point at one or both ends, used for loosening soil, breaking rocks, etc **2** any of various tools used for picking, such as an ice pick or toothpick **3** a plectrum ▷ *vb* **4** (*tr*) to pierce, dig, or break up (a hard surface) with a pick **5** (*tr*) to form (a hole) in this way [c14 perhaps variant of PIKE²]

pick³ (pɪk) (in weaving) *vb* **1** (*tr*) to cast (a shuttle) ▷ *n* **2** one casting of a shuttle **3** a weft or filling thread [c14 variant of PITCH¹]

pickaback (ˈpɪkəˌbæk) *n, adv, adj, vb* another word for **piggyback**

pick and mix *or* **pick 'n' mix** *n* **1** a selection of sweets from which the customer can choose, paid for by weight ▷ *adj* **pick-and-mix** **2** allowing the user to choose items or ideas and combine them as he or she wishes: *a pick-and-mix selection of fabric and wallpapers*

pickaninny (ˌpɪkəˈnɪnɪ) *n, pl* **-nies** a variant spelling (esp US) of **piccaninny**

pickaroon (ˌpɪkəˈruːn) *n* a variant spelling of **picaroon**

pick at *vb* (*intr, preposition*) to make criticisms of in a niggling or petty manner

pickaxe *or US* **pickax** (ˈpɪkˌæks) *n* **1** a large pick or mattock ▷ *vb* **2** to use a pickaxe on (earth, rocks, etc) [c15 from earlier *pikois* (but influenced also by AXE), from Old French *picois*, from *pic* PICK²; compare also PIQUE¹]

picker (ˈpɪkə) *n* **1** a person or thing that picks, esp that gathers fruit, crops, etc **2** (in weaving) a person or the part of the loom that casts the shuttle

pickerel (ˈpɪkərəl, ˈpɪkrəl) *n, pl* **-el** *or* **-els** any of several North American freshwater game fishes, such as *Esox americanus* and *E. niger*: family *Esocidae* (pikes, walleye, etc) [c14 a small pike; diminutive of PIKE¹]

pickerelweed (ˈpɪkərəlˌwiːd, ˈpɪkrəl-) *n* any of several North American freshwater plants of the genus *Pontederia*, esp *P. cordata*, having arrow-shaped leaves and purple flowers: family *Pontederiaceae*

picket (ˈpɪkɪt) *n* **1** a pointed stake, post, or peg that is driven into the ground to support a fence, provide a marker for surveying, etc **2** an individual or group that stands outside an establishment to make a protest, to dissuade or prevent employees or clients from entering, etc **3** Also: **picquet** a small detachment of troops or warships positioned towards the enemy to give early warning of attack ▷ *vb* **4** to post or serve as pickets at (a factory, embassy, etc): *let's go and picket the shop* **5** to guard (a main body or place) by using or acting as a picket **6** (*tr*) to fasten (a horse or other animal) to a picket **7** (*tr*) to fence (an area, boundary, etc) with pickets [c18 from French *piquet*, from Old French *piquer* to prick; see PIKE²] > ˈ**picketer** *n*

picket fence *n* a fence consisting of pickets supported at close regular intervals by being driven into the ground, by interlacing with strong wire, or by nailing to horizontal timbers fixed to posts in the ground

picket line *n* a line of people acting as pickets

pickin (ˈpɪkɪn) *n W African* a small child [from Portuguese *pequeno*; see PICCANINNY]

pickings (ˈpɪkɪŋz) *pl n* (*sometimes singular*) money, profits, etc, acquired easily or by more or less dishonest means; spoils

pickle (ˈpɪkᵊl) *n* **1** (*often plural*) vegetables, such as cauliflowers, onions, etc, preserved in vinegar, brine, etc **2** any food preserved in this way **3** a liquid or marinade, such as spiced vinegar, for preserving vegetables, meat, fish, etc **4** *chiefly US and Canadian* a cucumber that has been preserved and flavoured in a pickling solution, such as brine or vinegar **5** *informal* an awkward or difficult situation: *to be in a pickle* **6** *Brit informal* a mischievous child ▷ *vb* (*tr*) **7** to preserve in a pickling liquid **8** to immerse (a metallic object) in a liquid, such as an acid, to remove surface scale [c14 perhaps from Middle Dutch *pekel*; related to German *Pökel* brine] > ˈ**pickler** *n*

pickled (ˈpɪkᵊld) *adj* **1** preserved in a pickling liquid **2** *informal* intoxicated; drunk

picklock (ˈpɪkˌlɒk) *n* **1** a person who picks locks, esp one who gains unlawful access to premises by this means **2** an instrument for picking locks

pick-me-up *n informal* a tonic or restorative, esp a special drink taken as a stimulant

pick 'n' mix *n* **1** a variant spelling of **pick and mix**

pick off *vb* (*tr, adverb*) to aim at and shoot one by one

pick on *vb* (*tr, preposition*) to select (someone) for something unpleasant, esp in order to bully, blame, or cause to perform a distasteful task

pick out *vb* (*tr, adverb*) **1** to select for use or special consideration, illustration, etc, as from a group **2** to distinguish (an object from its surroundings), as in painting: *she picked out the woodwork in white* **3** to perceive or recognize (a person or thing previously obscured): *we picked out his face among the crowd* **4** to distinguish (sense or meaning) from or as if from a mass of detail or complication **5** to play (a tune) tentatively, by or as if by ear

pickpocket (ˈpɪkˌpɒkɪt) *n* a person who steals from the pockets or handbags of others in public places

pick-up *n* **1** Also called: **pick-up arm, tone arm** the light balanced arm of a record player that carries the wires from the cartridge to the preamplifier **2** an electromagnetic transducer that converts the vibrations of the steel strings of an electric guitar or other amplified instrument into electric signals **3** another name for **cartridge** (sense 3) **4** Also called: **pick-up truck** a small truck with an open body and low sides, used for light deliveries **5** *informal, chiefly US* an ability to accelerate rapidly: *this car has good pick-up* **6** *informal* a casual acquaintance, usually one made with sexual intentions **7** *informal* **a** a stop to collect passengers, goods, etc **b** the people or things collected **8** *slang* a free ride in a motor vehicle **9** *informal* an improvement **10** *slang* a pick-me-up ▷ *adj* **11** *US and Canadian* organized, arranged, or assembled hastily and without planning: *a pick-up band; pick-up games* ▷ *vb* **pick up** (*adverb*) **12** (*tr*) to gather up in the hand or hands **13** (*tr*) to acquire, obtain, or purchase casually, incidentally, etc **14** (*tr*) to catch (a disease): *she picked up a bad cold during the weekend* **15** (*intr*) to improve in health, condition, activity, etc: *the market began to pick up* **16** (*reflexive*) to raise (oneself) after a fall or setback **17** (*tr*) to notice or sense: *she picked up a change in his attitude* **18** to resume where one left off; return to: *we'll pick up after lunch; they picked up the discussion* **19** (*tr*) to learn gradually or as one goes along **20** (*tr*) to take responsibility for paying (a bill): *he picked up the bill for dinner* **21** (*tr*) *informal* to reprimand: *he picked her up on her table manners* **22** (*tr*) to collect or give a lift to (passengers, hitchhikers, goods, etc) **23** (*tr*) *informal* to become acquainted with, esp with a view to having sexual relations **24** (*tr*) *informal* to arrest **25** to increase (speed): *the cars picked up down the straight* **26** (*tr*) to receive (electrical signals, a radio signal, sounds, etc), as for transmission or amplification **27** **pick up the pieces** to restore a situation to normality after a crisis or collapse

Pickwickian (pɪkˈwɪkɪən) *adj* **1** of, relating to, or resembling Mr Pickwick in *The Pickwick Papers*, a novel by English novelist Charles Dickens (1812–70), esp in being naive or benevolent **2** (of the use or meaning of a word, etc) odd or unusual

picky (ˈpɪkɪ) *adj* **pickier, pickiest** *informal* fussy; finicky; choosy > ˈ**pickily** *adv* > ˈ**pickiness** *n*

picnic (ˈpɪknɪk) *n* **1** a trip or excursion to the country, seaside, etc, on which people bring food to be eaten in the open air **2** **a** any informal meal eaten outside **b** (*as modifier*): *a picnic lunch* **3** *informal, chiefly Austral* a troublesome situation or experience **4** **no picnic** *informal* a hard or disagreeable task ▷ *vb* **-nics, -nicking, -nicked** **5** (*intr*) to eat a picnic [c18 from French *piquenique*, of unknown origin] > ˈ**picnicker** *n*

picnic races *pl n Austral* horse races for amateur

riders held in rural areas

pico- prefix denoting 10⁻¹²: picofarad. Symbol: p [from Spanish pico small quantity, odd number, peak]

Pico de Aneto (Spanish 'piko de a'neto) n See Aneto

Pico de Teide (Spanish 'piko de 'teiðe) n See Teide

picofarad ('pi:kəʊˌfærəd, -æd) n a million millionth of a farad; 10⁻¹² farad. Symbol: pF

picoline ('pɪkəˌliːn, -lɪn) n a liquid derivative of pyridine found in bone oil and coal tar; methylpyridine. Formula: C₅H₄N(CH₃) [C19 from Latin pic-, pix PITCH² + -OL² + -INE²] > **picolinic** (ˌpɪkə'lɪnɪk) adj

picong ('pɪkɒŋ) n Caribbean any teasing or satirical banter, originally a verbal duel in song [from Spanish picón mocking, from picar to pierce; compare PICADOR]

picornavirus ('pɪˌkɔːnəˌvaɪrəs) n any one of a group of small viruses that contain RNA; the group includes polioviruses, rhinoviruses, coxsackie viruses, and the virus that causes foot-and-mouth disease [C20 from PICO + RNA + VIRUS]

picosecond ('pi:kəʊˌsɛkənd, 'paɪkəʊ-) n a million millionth of a second; 10⁻¹² second

picot ('pi:kəʊ) n any of a pattern of small loops, as on lace [C19 from French: small point, from pic point]

picotee (ˌpɪkə'ti:) n a type of carnation having pale petals edged with a darker colour, usually red [C18 from French picoté marked with points, from PICOT]

picquet ('pɪkɪt) n a variant spelling of **picket** (sense 3)

picrate ('pɪkreɪt) n 1 any salt or ester of picric acid, such as sodium picrate 2 a charge-transfer complex formed by picric acid

picric acid ('pɪkrɪk) n a toxic sparingly soluble crystalline yellow acid used as a dye, antiseptic, and explosive. Formula: C₆H₂OH(NO₂)₃. Systematic name: **2,4,6-trinitrophenol** See also **lyddite**

picrite ('pɪkraɪt) n a coarse-grained ultrabasic igneous rock consisting of olivine and augite with small amounts of plagioclase feldspar

picro- or before a vowel **picr-** combining form bitter: picrotoxin [from Greek pikros]

picrotoxin (ˌpɪkrə'tɒksɪn) n a bitter poisonous crystalline compound formerly used as an antidote for barbiturate poisoning. Formula: C₃₀H₃₄O₁₃

Pict (pɪkt) n a member of any of the peoples who lived in Britain north of the Forth and Clyde in the first to the fourth centuries AD: later applied chiefly to the inhabitants of NE Scotland. Throughout Roman times the Picts carried out border raids [Old English Peohtas; later forms from Late Latin Pictī painted men, from pingere to paint]

Pictish ('pɪktɪʃ) n 1 the language of the Picts, of which few records survive. Its origins are much disputed and it was extinct by about 900 AD ▷ adj 2 of or relating to the Picts

pictogram ('pɪktəˌgræm) n another word for **pictograph**

pictograph ('pɪktəˌgrɑːf, -ˌgræf) n 1 a picture or symbol standing for a word or group of words, as in written Chinese 2 a chart on which symbols are used to represent values, such as population levels or consumption [C19 from Latin pictus, from pingere to paint] > **pictographic** (ˌpɪktə'græfɪk) adj > **pictography** (pɪk'tɒgrəfɪ) n

Pictor ('pɪktə) n, Latin genitive **Pictoris** (pɪk'tɔːrɪs) a faint constellation in the S hemisphere lying between Dorado and Carina [Latin: painter]

pictorial (pɪk'tɔːrɪəl) adj 1 relating to, consisting of, or expressed by pictures 2 (of books, newspapers, etc) containing pictures 3 of or relating to painting or drawing 4 (of language, style, etc) suggesting a picture; vivid; graphic ▷ n 5 a a magazine, newspaper, etc, containing many pictures b (capital when part of a name): the Sunday Pictorial [C17 from Late Latin pictōrius, from

Latin pictor painter, from pingere to paint] > **pic'torially** adv

picture ('pɪktʃə) n 1 a a visual representation of something, such as a person or scene, produced on a surface, as in a photograph, painting, etc b (as modifier): picture gallery; picture postcard. Related adj: **pictorial** 2 a mental image or impression: a clear picture of events 3 a verbal description, esp one that is vivid 4 a situation considered as an observable scene: the political picture 5 a person or thing that bears a close resemblance to another: he was the picture of his father 6 a person, scene, etc, considered as typifying a particular state or quality: the picture of despair 7 a beautiful person or scene: you'll look a picture 8 a complete image on a television screen, comprising two interlaced fields 9 a a motion picture; film b (as modifier): picture theatre 10 the pictures chiefly Brit and Austral a cinema or film show 11 another name for **tableau vivant** 12 get the picture informal to understand a situation 13 in the picture informed about a given situation ▷ vb (tr) 14 to visualize or imagine 15 to describe or depict, esp vividly 16 (often passive) to put in a picture or make a picture of: they were pictured sitting on the rocks [C15 from Latin pictūra painting, from pingere to paint]

picture card n another name for **court card**

picturegoer ('pɪktʃəˌgəʊə) n Brit old-fashioned a person who goes to the cinema, esp frequently

picture hat n a decorated hat with a very wide brim, esp as worn by women in paintings by Gainsborough and Reynolds

picture house n chiefly Brit an old-fashioned name for **cinema** (sense 1a)

picture messaging n 1 the practice of sending and receiving photographs by mobile phone 2 the practice of communicating by mobile phone using graphics or pictures rather than text

picture moulding n 1 the edge around a framed picture 2 Also called: **picture rail** the moulding or rail near the top of a wall from which pictures can be hung

picture palace n Brit an old-fashioned name for **cinema** (sense 1a)

picture phone n a mobile phone that can take, send, and receive photographs

picturesque (ˌpɪktʃə'rɛsk) adj 1 visually pleasing, esp in being striking or vivid: a picturesque view 2 having a striking or colourful character, nature, etc 3 (of language) graphic; vivid [C18 from French pittoresque (but also influenced by PICTURE), from Italian pittoresco, from pittore painter, from Latin pictor] > ˌpictur'esquely adv > ˌpictur'esqueness n

picture tube n another name for **television tube**

picture window n a large window having a single pane of glass, usually placed so that it overlooks a view

picture writing n 1 any writing system that uses pictographs 2 a system of artistic expression and communication using pictures or symbolic figures

picul ('pɪkəl) n a unit of weight, used in China, Japan, and SE Asia, equal to approximately 60 kilograms or 133 pounds [C16 from Malay pīkul a grown man's load]

PID abbreviation for **pelvic inflammatory disease**

piddle ('pɪdəl) vb 1 (intr) informal to urinate 2 (when tr, often foll by away) to spend (one's time) aimlessly; fritter [C16 origin unknown] > 'piddler n

piddling ('pɪdlɪŋ) adj informal petty; trifling; trivial > 'piddlingly adv

piddock ('pɪdək) n any marine bivalve of the family Pholadidae, boring into rock, clay, or wood by means of sawlike shell valves. See also **shipworm** [C19 origin uncertain]

pidgin ('pɪdʒɪn) n a language made up of elements of two or more other languages and used for contacts, esp trading contacts, between the speakers of other languages. Unlike creoles, pidgins do not constitute the mother tongue of any speech community [C19 perhaps from Chinese

pronunciation of English business]

pidgin English n a pidgin in which one of the languages involved is English

pi-dog n a variant spelling of **pye-dog**

pie¹ (paɪ) n 1 a baked food consisting of a sweet or savoury filling in a pastry-lined dish, often covered with a pastry crust 2 have a (or one's) finger in the pie a to have an interest in or take part in some activity b to meddle or interfere 3 pie in the sky illusory hope or promise of some future good; false optimism [C14 of obscure origin]

pie² (paɪ) n an archaic or dialect name for **magpie** [C13 via Old French from Latin pīca magpie; related to Latin pīcus woodpecker]

pie³ (paɪ) n, vb printing a variant spelling of **pi²**

pie⁴ (paɪ) n a very small former Indian coin worth one third of a pice [C19 from Hindi pāī, from Sanskrit pādikā a fourth]

pie⁵ or **pye** (paɪ) n history a book for finding the Church service for any particular day [C15 from Medieval Latin pica almanac; see PICA¹]

pie⁶ (paɪ) adj be pie on NZ informal to be keen on [from Māori pai ana]

piebald ('paɪˌbɔːld) adj 1 marked or spotted in two different colours, esp black and white: a piebald horse ▷ n 2 a black-and-white pied horse [C16 PIE² + BALD; see also PIED]

pie cart n NZ a mobile van selling warmed-up food and drinks

piece (pi:s) n 1 an amount or portion forming a separate mass or structure; bit: a piece of wood 2 a small part, item, or amount forming part of a whole, esp when broken off or separated: a piece of bread 3 a length by which a commodity is sold, esp cloth, wallpaper, etc 4 an instance or occurrence: a piece of luck 5 slang a girl or woman regarded as an object of sexual attraction: a nice piece 6 an example or specimen of a style or type, such as an article of furniture: a beautiful piece of Dresden china 7 informal an opinion or point of view: to state one's piece 8 a literary, musical, or artistic composition 9 a coin having a value as specified: fifty-pence piece 10 a small object, often individually shaped and designed, used in playing certain games, esp board games: chess pieces 11 a a firearm or cannon b (in combination): fowling-piece 12 any chessman other than a pawn 13 US and Canadian a short time or distance: down the road a piece 14 Scot and English dialect a a slice of bread or a sandwich b a packed lunch taken to work, school, etc 15 (usually plural) Austral and NZ fragments of fleece wool. See also **oddment** (sense 2) 16 give someone a piece of one's mind informal to criticize or censure someone frankly or vehemently 17 go to pieces a (of a person) to lose control of oneself; have a breakdown b (of a building, organization, etc) to disintegrate 18 nasty piece of work Brit informal a cruel or mean person 19 of a piece of the same kind; alike 20 piece of cake informal something easily obtained or achieved ▷ vb (tr) 21 (often foll by together) to fit or assemble piece by piece 22 (often foll by up) to patch or make up (a garment) by adding pieces 23 textiles to join (broken threads) during spinning ▷ See also **piece out** [C13 pece, from Old French, of Gaulish origin; compare Breton pez piece, Welsh peth portion]

pièce de résistance French (pjɛs də rezistãs) n 1 the principal or most outstanding item in a series or creative artist's work 2 the main dish of a meal [lit: piece of resistance]

piece-dyed adj (of fabric) dyed after weaving. Compare **yarn-dyed**

piece goods pl n goods, esp fabrics, made in standard widths and lengths. Also called: **yard goods**

piecemeal ('pi:sˌmi:l) adv 1 by degrees; bit by bit; gradually 2 in or into pieces or piece from piece: to tear something piecemeal ▷ adj 3 fragmentary or unsystematic: a piecemeal approach [C13 pecemele, from PIECE + -mele, from Old English mælum quantity taken at one time]

p

piece of eight *n*, *pl* **pieces of eight** a former Spanish coin worth eight reals; peso

piece out *vb* (*tr, adverb*) **1** to extend by adding pieces **2** to cause to last longer by using only a small amount at a time: *to piece out rations*

piecer ('piːsə) *n* *textiles* a person who mends, repairs, or joins something, esp broken threads on a loom

piece rate *n* a fixed rate paid according to the quantity produced

piecework ('piːsˌwɜːk) *n* work paid for according to the quantity produced. Compare **timework**

pie chart *n* a circular graph divided into sectors proportional to the magnitudes of the quantities represented

piecrust table ('paɪˌkrʌst) *n* a round table, ornamented with carved moulding suggestive of a pie crust

pied (paɪd) *adj* having markings of two or more colours [c14 from PIE²; an allusion to the magpie's black-and-white colouring]

pied-à-terre (ˌpjeɪtɑːˈtɛə) *n*, *pl* **pieds-à-terre** (ˌpjeɪtɑːˈtɛə) a flat, house, or other lodging for secondary or occasional use [French, literally: foot on (the) ground]

piedmont ('piːdmɒnt) *adj* (*prenominal*) (of glaciers, plains, etc) formed or situated at the foot of a mountain or mountain range [from Italian *piémonte* mountain foot]

Piedmont ('piːdmɒnt) *n* **1** a region of NW Italy: consists of the upper Po Valley; mainly agricultural. Chief town: Turin. Pop: 4 231 334 (2003 est). Area: 25 399 sq km (9807 sq miles). Italian name: **Piemonte 2** a low plateau of the eastern US, between the coastal plain and the Appalachian Mountains

piedmontite *or* **piemontite** ('piːdmɒnˌtaɪt, -mən-) *n* a dark red mineral occurring in metamorphic rocks: a complex hydrated silicate containing calcium, aluminium, iron, and manganese. Formula: $Ca_2(Al,Fe,Mn)_3(SiO_4)_3OH$ [c19 from PIEDMONT in Italy]

pie-dog *n* a variant spelling of **pye-dog**

Pied Piper *n* **1** Also called: **the Pied Piper of Hamelin** (in German legend) a piper who rid the town of Hamelin of rats by luring them away with his music and then, when he was not paid for his services, lured away its children **2** (*sometimes not capitals*) a person who entices others to follow him

pied-piping *n* *transformational grammar* the principle that a noun phrase may take with it the rest of a prepositional phrase or a larger noun phrase in which it is contained, when moved in a transformation. For example, when the interrogative pronoun is moved to initial position, other words are moved too, as in *to whom did you speak?*

pied shag *n* a large New Zealand seabird, *Phalacrocorax varius*, with a white throat and underparts. Also called: **karuhiruhi**

pied wagtail *n* a British songbird, *Motacilla alba yarrellii*, with a black throat and back, long black tail, and white underparts and face: family *Motacillidae* (wagtails and pipits)

pie-eyed *adj* a slang term for **drunk** (sense 1)

pieman ('paɪmən) *n*, *pl* **-men** *Brit obsolete* a seller of pies

Piemonte (*Italian* pjeˈmonte) *n* the Italian name for **Piedmont** (sense 1)

pier (pɪə) *n* **1** a structure with a deck that is built out over water, and used as a landing place, promenade, etc **2** a pillar that bears heavy loads, esp one of rectangular cross section **3** the part of a wall between two adjacent openings **4** another name for **buttress** (sense 1) [c12 *per*, from Anglo-Latin *pera* pier supporting a bridge]

pierce (pɪəs) *vb* (*mainly tr*) **1** to form or cut (a hole) in (something) with or as if with a sharp instrument **2** to thrust into or penetrate sharply or violently: *the thorn pierced his heel* **3** to force (a way, route, etc) through (something) **4** (of light)

to shine through or penetrate (darkness) **5** (*also intr*) to discover or realize (something) suddenly or (of an idea) to become suddenly apparent **6** (of sounds or cries) to sound sharply through (the silence) **7** to move or affect (a person's emotions, bodily feelings, etc) deeply or sharply: *the cold pierced their bones* **8** (*intr*) to penetrate or be capable of penetrating: *piercing cold* [c13 *percen*, from Old French *percer*, ultimately from Latin *pertundere*, from *per* through + *tundere* to strike] > **'pierceable** *adj* > **'piercer** *n*

piercing ('pɪəsɪŋ) *adj* **1** (of a sound) sharp and shrill **2** (of eyes or a look) intense and penetrating **3** (of an emotion) strong and deeply affecting **4** (of cold or wind) intense or biting ▷ *n* **5** the art or practice of piercing body parts for the insertion of jewellery **6** an instance of the piercing of a body part > **'piercingly** *adv*

pier glass *n* a tall narrow mirror, usually one of a pair or set, designed to hang on the wall between windows, usually above a pier table

Pieria (paɪˈɪərɪə) *n* a region of ancient Macedonia, west of the Gulf of Salonika: site of the Pierian Spring

Pierian (paɪˈɪərɪən) *adj* **1** of or relating to the Muses or artistic or poetic inspiration **2** of or relating to Pieria

Pierian Spring *n* a sacred fountain in Pieria, in Greece, fabled to inspire those who drank from it

Pierides (paɪˈɪərɪˌdiːz) *pl n* *Greek myth* **1** another name for the Muses (see **Muse**) **2** nine maidens of Thessaly, who were defeated in a singing contest by the Muses and turned into magpies for their effrontery

pieridine (paɪˈɛərɪˌdaɪn) *adj* of, relating to, or belonging to the *Pieridae*, a family of butterflies including the whites and brimstones

pieris ('paɪərɪs) *n* any plant of a genus, *Pieris*, of American and Asiatic shrubs, esp *P. formosa forrestii*, grown for the bright red colour of its young foliage: family *Ericaceae* [New Latin, from Greek *Pierides*, a name for the Muses]

Pierre (pɪə) *n* a city in central South Dakota, capital of the state, on the Missouri River. Pop: 13 939 (2003 est)

Pierrot ('pɪərəʊ; *French* pjɛro) *n* **1** a male character from French pantomime with a whitened face, white costume, and pointed hat **2** (*usually not capital*) a clown or masquerader so made up

pier table *n* a side table designed to stand against a wall between windows

Piesporter ('piːzˌpɔːtə) *n* any of various white wines from the area around the village of Piesport in the Moselle valley in Germany

pietà (pɪeˈtɑː) *n* a sculpture, painting, or drawing of the dead Christ, supported by the Virgin Mary [Italian: pity, from Latin *pietās* PIETY]

Pietermaritzburg (ˌpiːtəˈmærɪtsˌbɜːg) *n* a city in E South Africa, the capital of KwaZulu/Natal: founded in 1839 by the Boers: gateway to Natal's mountain resorts. Pop: 223 519 (2001)

pietism ('paɪɪˌtɪzəm) *n* **1** a less common word for **piety 2** excessive, exaggerated, or affected piety or saintliness > **'pietist** *n* > **ˌpieˈtistic** *or* **ˌpieˈtistical** *adj*

Pietism ('paɪɪˌtɪzəm) *n* *history* a reform movement in the German Lutheran Churches during the 17th and 18th centuries that strove to renew the devotional ideal > **'Pietist** *n*

piet-my-vrou ('piːtˌmeɪˈfrəʊ) *n* *South African* a cuckoo, *Notococcyx solitarius*, having a red breast [from Afrikaans *piet* Peter + *my* my + *vrou* wife: onomatopoeic, based on the bird's three clear notes]

piety ('paɪɪtɪ) *n*, *pl* **-ties 1** dutiful devotion to God and observance of religious principles **2** the quality or characteristic of being pious **3** a pious action, saying, etc **4** *now rare* devotion and obedience to parents or superiors [c13 *piete*, from Old French, from Latin *pietās* piety, dutifulness, from *pius* PIOUS]

piezo- (paɪˈiːzəʊ-, piːˈeɪzəʊ-, 'piːtsəʊ-) *combining form*

pressure: *piezometer* [from Greek *piezein* to press]

piezochemistry (paɪˌiːzəʊˈkɛmɪstrɪ) *n* the study of chemical reactions at high pressures

piezoelectric crystal (paɪˌiːzəʊɪˈlɛktrɪk) *n* a crystal, such as quartz, that produces a potential difference across its opposite faces when under mechanical stress. See also **piezoelectric effect**

piezoelectric effect *or* **piezoelectricity** (paɪˌiːzəʊɪlɛkˈtrɪsɪtɪ) *n* *physics* **a** the production of electricity or electric polarity by applying a mechanical stress to certain crystals **b** the converse effect in which stress is produced in a crystal as a result of an applied potential difference > **piˌezoeˈlectrically** *adv*

piezomagnetic effect (paɪˌiːzəʊmægˈnɛtɪk) *or* **piezomagnetism** (paɪˌiːzəʊˈmægnɪtɪzəm) *n* *physics* **a** the production of a magnetic field by applying a mechanical stress to certain crystals **b** the converse effect in which stress is produced in a crystal as a result of an applied magnetic field > **piˌezomagˈnetically** *adj*

piezometer (ˌpaɪɪˈzɒmɪtə) *n* any instrument for the measurement of pressure (**piezometry**), esp very high pressure, or for measuring the compressibility of materials under pressure > **piezometric** (paɪˌiːzəʊˈmɛtrɪk) *adj* > **piˌezoˈmetrically** *adv*

piffle ('pɪfᵊl) *informal* ▷ *n* **1** nonsense: *to talk piffle* ▷ *vb* **2** (*intr*) to talk or behave feebly [c19 origin uncertain]

piffling ('pɪflɪŋ) *adj* worthless, trivial

pig (pɪg) *n* **1** any artiodactyl mammal of the African and Eurasian family *Suidae*, esp *Sus scrofa* (**domestic pig**), typically having a long head with a movable snout, a thick bristle-covered skin, and, in wild species, long curved tusks **2** a domesticated pig weighing more than 120 pounds (54 kg) **3** *informal* a dirty, greedy, or bad-mannered person **4** the meat of swine; pork **5** *derogatory* a slang word for **policeman 6 a** a mass of metal, such as iron, copper, or lead, cast into a simple shape for ease of storing or transportation **b** a mould in which such a mass of metal is formed **7** *Brit informal* something that is difficult or unpleasant **8** an automated device propelled through a duct or pipeline to clear impediments or check for faults, leaks, etc **9 a pig in a poke** something bought or received without prior sight or knowledge **10 make a pig of oneself** *informal* to overindulge oneself **11 on the pig's back** *Irish and NZ* successful; established: *he's on the pig's back now* ▷ Related adjective (for senses 1, 2): **porcine** ▷ *vb* **pigs, pigging, pigged 12** (*intr*) (of a sow) to give birth **13** (*intr*) Also: **pig it** *informal* to live in squalor **14** (*tr*) *informal* to devour (food) greedily ▷ See also **pig out** [c13 *pigge*, of obscure origin]

pig bed *n* a bed of sand in which pig iron is cast

pig dog *n* *NZ* a dog bred for hunting wild pigs in the bush

pigeon¹ ('pɪdʒɪn) *n* **1** any of numerous birds of the family *Columbidae*, having a heavy body, small head, short legs, and long pointed wings: order *Columbiformes*. See **rock dove 2** *slang* a victim or dupe [c14 from Old French *pijon* young dove, from Late Latin *pīpiō* young bird, from *pīpīre* to chirp]

pigeon² ('pɪdʒɪn) *n* *Brit informal* concern or responsibility (often in the phrase **it's his, her**, etc, **pigeon**) [c19 altered from PIDGIN]

pigeon breast *n* a deformity of the chest characterized by an abnormal protrusion of the breastbone, caused by rickets or by obstructed breathing during infancy. Also called: **chicken breast**

pigeon hawk *n* the North American variety of the merlin

pigeon-hearted *or* **pigeon-livered** *adj* of a timid or fearful disposition

pigeonhole ('pɪdʒɪnˌhəʊl) *n* **1** a small compartment for papers, letters, etc, as in a bureau **2** a hole or recess in a dovecote for pigeons to nest in **3** *informal* a category or classification ▷ *vb* (*tr*) **4** to put aside or defer **5** to classify or categorize, esp in a rigid manner

pigeon pea *n* another name for **dhal**

pigeon-toed *adj* having the toes turned inwards

pigeonwing ('pɪdʒɪn,wɪŋ) *n chiefly US* a fancy step in dancing in which the feet are clapped together

pigface ('pɪg,feɪs) *n Austral* a creeping succulent plant of the genus *Carpobrotus*, having bright-coloured flowers and red fruits and often grown for ornament: family *Aizoaceae*

pig fern *n NZ* giant bracken

pigfish ('pɪg,fɪʃ) *n, pl* **-fish** or **-fishes** **1** Also called: **hogfish** any of several grunts, esp *Orthopristis chrysopterus*, of the North American Atlantic coast **2** any of several wrasses, such as *Achoerodus gouldii* (**giant pigfish**), that occur around the Great Barrier Reef

piggery ('pɪgərɪ) *n, pl* **-geries 1** a place where pigs are kept and reared **2** great greediness; piggishness

piggin ('pɪgɪn) *n* a small wooden bucket or tub. Also called: **pipkin** [c16 origin unknown]

piggish ('pɪgɪʃ) *adj* **1** like a pig, esp in appetite or manners **2** *informal, chiefly Brit* obstinate or mean > **'piggishly** *adv* > **'piggishness** *n*

piggy ('pɪgɪ) *n, pl* **-gies 1** a child's word for a pig, esp a piglet **2 piggy in the middle a** a children's game in which one player attempts to retrieve a ball thrown over him or her by at least two other players **b** a situation in which a person or group is caught up in a disagreement between other people or groups **3** a child's word for toe or, sometimes, finger ▷ *adj* **-gier, -giest 4** another word for **piggish**

piggyback ('pɪgɪ,bæk) or **pickaback** *n* **1** a ride on the back and shoulders of another person **2** a system whereby a vehicle, aircraft, etc, is transported for part of its journey on another vehicle, such as a flat railway wagon, another aircraft, etc ▷ *adv* **3** on the back and shoulders of another person **4** on or as an addition to something else ▷ *adj* **5** of or for a piggyback: *a piggyback ride; piggyback lorry trains* **6** of or relating to a type of heart transplant in which the transplanted heart functions in conjunction with the patient's own heart ▷ *vb* (*tr*) **7** to give (a person) a piggyback on one's back and shoulders **8** to transport (one vehicle) on another **9** (*intr; often foll by on*) to exploit an existing resource, system, or product **10** (*tr*) to attach to or mount on (an existing piece of equipment or system)

piggy bank *n* a child's coin bank shaped like a pig with a slot for coins

pig-headed *adj* stupidly stubborn > ,pig-'headedly *adv* > ,pig-'headedness *n*

pig iron *n* crude iron produced in a blast furnace and poured into moulds in preparation for making wrought iron, steels, alloys, etc

Pig Island *n NZ informal* New Zealand

Pig Islander *n NZ informal* a New Zealander

pig-jump *vb* (*intr*) (of a horse) to jump from all four legs

Pig Latin *n* a secret language used by children in which any consonants at the beginning of a word are placed at the end, followed by -ay; for example *cathedral* becomes *athedralcay*

piglet ('pɪglɪt) *n* a young pig

pigmeat ('pɪg,miːt) *n* a less common name for **pork, ham¹** (sense 2) or **bacon** (sense 1)

pigment ('pɪgmənt) *n* **1** a substance occurring in plant or animal tissue and producing a characteristic colour, such as chlorophyll in green plants and haemoglobin in red blood **2** any substance used to impart colour **3** a powder that is mixed with a liquid to give a paint, ink, etc [c14 from Latin *pigmentum*, from *pingere* to paint] > **'pigmentary** *adj*

pigmentation (,pɪgmən'teɪʃən) *n* **1** coloration in plants, animals, or man caused by the presence of pigments **2** the deposition of pigment in animals, plants, or man

Pigmy ('pɪgmɪ) *n, pl* **-mies** a variant spelling of **Pygmy**

pignut ('pɪg,nʌt) *n* **1** Also called: **hognut a** the bitter nut of any of several North American hickory trees, esp *Carya glabra* (**brown hickory**) **b** any of the trees bearing such a nut **2** another name for **earthnut**

pig out *vb* (*intr, adverb*) *slang* to gorge oneself

pigpen ('pɪg,pen) *n US and Canadian* **1** a pen for pigs; sty **2** a dirty or untidy place. Also called: **pigsty**

pig-root *vb* (*intr*) *Austral and NZ* another term for **pig-jump**

pigs (pɪgz) *interj Austral slang* an expression of derision or disagreement. Also: **pig's arse, pig's bum**

Pigs (pɪgz) *n* **Bay of** See **Bay of Pigs**

pig's ear *n* something that has been badly or clumsily done; a botched job (esp in the phrase **make a pig's ear of** (**something**))

pig's fry *n* the heart, liver, lights, and sweetbreads of a pig cooked, esp fried, together

pigskin ('pɪg,skɪn) *n* **1** the skin of the domestic pig **2** leather made of this skin **3** *US and Canadian informal* a football ▷ *adj* **4** made of pigskin

pigstick ('pɪg,stɪk) *vb* (*intr*) (esp in India) to hunt and spear wild boar, esp from horseback

pigsticker ('pɪg,stɪkə) *n* **1** a person who hunts wild boar **2** *slang* a large sharp hunting knife

pigsticking ('pɪg,stɪkɪŋ) *n* the sport of hunting wild boar

pigsty ('pɪg,staɪ) *or US and Canadian* **pigpen** *n, pl* **-sties 1** a pen for pigs; sty **2** *Brit* a dirty or untidy place

pigswill ('pɪg,swɪl) *n* waste food or other edible matter fed to pigs. Also called: **pig's wash**

pigtail ('pɪg,teɪl) *n* **1** a bunch of hair or one of two bunches on either side of the face, worn loose or plaited **2** a twisted roll of tobacco > **'pig,tailed** *adj*

pigweed ('pɪg,wiːd) *n* **1** Also called: **redroot** any of several coarse North American amaranthaceous weeds of the genus *Amaranthus*, esp *A. retroflexus*, having hairy leaves and green flowers **2** a US name for **fat hen**

pihoihoi ('piː,hɔɪ'vɔɪ) *n, pl* **pihoihoi** a New Zealand pipit, *Anthus novaeseelandiae* [Māori]

pika ('paɪkə) *n* any burrowing lagomorph mammal of the family *Ochotonidae* of mountainous regions of North America and Asia, having short rounded ears, a rounded body, and rudimentary tail. Also called: **cony** [c19 from Tungusic *piika*]

pikau ('piː,kaʊ) *n NZ* a pack, knapsack, or rucksack [Māori]

pike¹ (paɪk) *n, pl* **pike** or **pikes 1** any of several large predatory freshwater teleost fishes of the genus *Esox*, esp *E. lucius* (**northern pike**), having a broad flat snout, strong teeth, and an elongated body covered with small scales: family *Esocidae* **2** any of various similar fishes [c14 short for *pikefish*, from Old English *pīc* point, with reference to the shape of its jaw]

pike² (paɪk) *n* **1** a medieval weapon consisting of an iron or steel spearhead joined to a long pole, the pikestaff **2** a point or spike ▷ *vb* **3** (*tr*) to stab or pierce using a pike [Old English *pīc* point, of obscure origin]

pike³ (paɪk) *n* short for **turnpike** (sense 1)

pike⁴ (paɪk) *n Northern English dialect* a pointed or conical hill [Old English *pīc*, of obscure origin]

pike⁵ (paɪk), **piked** (paɪkt) *adj* (of the body position of a diver) bent at the hips but with the legs straight [c20 of obscure origin]

pikelet ('paɪklɪt) *n* a dialect word for a **crumpet** (sense 1) [c18 from Welsh *bara pyglyd* pitchy bread]

pikeman ('paɪkmən) *n, pl* **-men** (formerly) a soldier armed with a pike

pikeperch ('paɪk,pɜːtʃ) *n, pl* **-perch** or **-perches** any of various pikelike freshwater teleost fishes of the genera *Stizostedion* (or *Lucioperca*), such as *S. lucioperca* of Europe: family *Percidae* (perches)

piker ('paɪkə) *n slang* **1** *Austral* a wild bullock **2** *Austral and NZ* a useless person; failure **3** *US, Austral, and NZ* a lazy person; shirker **4** a mean

person [c19 perhaps related to **PIKE³**]

Pikes Peak *n* a mountain in central Colorado, in the Rockies. Height: 4300 m (14 109 ft)

pikestaff ('paɪk,stɑːf) *n* the wooden handle of a pike

pikey ('paɪkɪ) *n Brit slang derogatory* **1** a gypsy or vagrant **2** a member of the underclass [perhaps from **TURNPIKE**]

piking ('paɪkɪŋ) *n* **1** the sport of fishing for pike **2** *Brit slang* the practice of deriving sexual pleasure from watching strangers have sex in parked cars and other secluded but public places

pilaster (pɪ'læstə) *n* a shallow rectangular column attached to the face of a wall [c16 from French *pilastre*, from Latin *pīla* pillar] > **pi'lastered** *adj*

Pilates (pɪ'lɑːtiːz) *n* a system of gentle exercise performed lying down that stretches and lengthens the muscles, designed to improve posture, flexibility, etc [c20 named after Joseph *Pilates* (1880–1967), its German inventor]

Pilatus (*German* pi'laːtʊs) *n* a mountain in central Switzerland, in Unterwalden canton: derives its name from the legend that the body of Pontius Pilate lay in a former lake on the mountain. Height: 2122 m (6962 ft)

pilau (pɪ'laʊ), **pilaf, pilaff** ('pɪlæf), **pilao** (pɪ'laʊ), **pilaw** (pɪ'lɔː) *or* **pulao** (pʊ'laʊ) *n* a dish originating from the East, consisting of rice flavoured with spices and cooked in stock, to which meat, poultry, or fish may be added [c17 from Turkish *pilāw*, from Persian]

pilch (pɪltʃ) *n Brit archaic* **1** an outer garment, originally one made of skin **2** an infant's outer wrapping, worn over the napkin [c17 from Old English *pylce* a garment made of skin and fur, from Late Latin *pellicia*, from Latin *pellis* fur]

pilchard ('pɪltʃəd) *n* **1** a European food fish, *Sardina* (or *Clupea*) *pilchardus*, with a rounded body covered with large scales: family *Clupeidae* (herrings) **2** a related fish, *Sardinops neopilchardus*, of S Australian waters [c16 *pylcher*, of obscure origin]

Pilcomayo (*Spanish* pilko'majo) *n* a river in S central South America, rising in W central Bolivia and flowing southeast, forming the border between Argentina and Paraguay, to the Paraguay River at Asunción. Length: about 1600 km (1000 miles)

pile¹ (paɪl) *n* **1** a collection of objects laid on top of one another or of other material stacked vertically; heap; mound **2** *informal* a large amount of money (esp in the phrase **make a pile**) **3** (*often plural*) *informal* a large amount: *a pile of work* **4** a less common word for **pyre 5** a large building or group of buildings **6** short for **voltaic pile 7** *physics* a structure of uranium and a moderator used for producing atomic energy; nuclear reactor **8** *metallurgy* an arrangement of wrought-iron bars that are to be heated and worked into a single bar **9** the point of an arrow ▷ *vb* **10** (*often foll by up*) to collect or be collected into or as if into a pile: *snow piled up in the drive* **11** (*intr; foll by in, into, off, out, etc*) to move in a group, esp in a hurried or disorganized manner: *to pile off the bus* **12 pile arms** to prop a number of rifles together, muzzles together and upwards, butts forming the base **13 pile it on** *informal* to exaggerate ▷ See also **pile up** [c15 via Old French from Latin *pīla* stone pier]

pile² (paɪl) *n* **1** a long column of timber, concrete, or steel that is driven into the ground to provide a foundation for a vertical load (a bearing pile) or a group of such columns to resist a horizontal load from earth or water pressure (a sheet pile) **2** *heraldry* an ordinary shaped like a wedge, usually displayed point-downwards ▷ *vb* (*tr*) **3** to drive (piles) into the ground **4** to provide or support (a structure) with piles [Old English *pīl*, from Latin *pīlum*]

pile³ (paɪl) *n* **1** *textiles* **a** the yarns in a fabric that stand up or out from the weave, as in carpeting, velvet, flannel, etc **b** one of these yarns **2** soft fine hair, fur, wool, etc [c15 from Anglo-Norman

p

pyle, from Latin *pilus* hair]

pilea ('pɪlɪə) *n* any plant of the tropical annual or perennial genus *Pilea,* esp *P. muscosa,* the artillery or gunpowder plant, which releases a cloud of pollen when shaken; some others are grown for their ornamental foliage: family *Urticaceae* [New Latin, from Greek *pilos* cap (from the shape of the segments of the perianth)]

pileate ('paɪlɪɪt, -ˌeɪt, 'pɪl-) *or* **pileated** ('paɪlɪˌeɪtɪd, 'pɪl-) *adj* **1** (of birds) having a crest **2** *botany* having a pileus [c18 from Latin *pīleātus* wearing a felt cap, from PILEUS]

pile cap *n* a reinforced or mass concrete connecting beam cast around the head of a group of piles enabling it to act as a single unit to support the imposed load

pile-driver *n* **1** a machine that drives piles into the ground either by repeatedly allowing a heavy weight to fall on the head of the pile or by using a steam hammer **2** *informal* a forceful punch or kick

pileous ('paɪlɪəs, 'pɪl-) *adj biology* **1** hairy **2** of or relating to hair [c19 ultimately from Latin *pilus* a hair]

piles (paɪlz) *pl n* a nontechnical name for **haemorrhoids** [c15 from Latin *pilae* balls (referring to the appearance of external piles)]

pile shoe *n* an iron casting shaped to a point and fitted to a lower end of a wooden or concrete pile. Also called: **shoe**

pileum ('paɪlɪəm, 'pɪl-) *n, pl* **-lea** (-lɪə) the top of a bird's head from the base of the bill to the occiput [c19 New Latin, from Latin PILEUS]

pile up *vb* (*adverb*) **1** to gather or be gathered in a pile; accumulate **2** *informal* to crash or cause to crash ▷ *n* **pile-up 3** *informal* a multiple collision of vehicles

pileus ('paɪlɪəs, 'pɪl-) *n, pl* **-lei** (-lɪˌaɪ) the upper cap-shaped part of a mushroom or similar spore-producing body [c18 (botanical use): New Latin, from Latin: felt cap]

pilewort ('paɪlˌwɜːt) *n* any of several plants, such as lesser celandine, thought to be effective in treating piles

pilfer ('pɪlfə) *vb* to steal (minor items), esp in small quantities [c14 *pylfre* (n) from Old French *pelfre* booty; see PELF] > **'pilferer** *n* > **'pilfering** *n*

pilferage ('pɪlfərɪdʒ) *n* **1** the act or practice of stealing small quantities or articles **2** the amount so stolen

pilgarlic (pɪl'gɑːlɪk) *n* **1** *obsolete* a bald head or a man with a bald head **2** *dialect* a pitiable person [c16 literally: peeled garlic]

pilgrim ('pɪlgrɪm) *n* **1** a person who undertakes a journey to a sacred place as an act of religious devotion **2** any wayfarer [c12 from Provençal *pelegrin,* from Latin *peregrīnus* foreign, from *per* through + *ager* field, land; see PEREGRINE]

Pilgrim ('pɪlgrɪm) *n* See **Canterbury Pilgrims** (sense 2)

pilgrimage ('pɪlgrɪmɪdʒ) *n* **1** a journey to a shrine or other sacred place **2** a journey or long search made for exalted or sentimental reasons ▷ *vb* **3** (*intr*) to make a pilgrimage

Pilgrimage of Grace *n* a rebellion in 1536 in N England against the Reformation and Henry VIII's government

Pilgrim Fathers *or* **Pilgrims** *pl n* **the** the English Puritans who sailed on the Mayflower to New England, where they founded Plymouth Colony in SE Massachusetts (1620)

pili¹ (pɪ'liː) *n, pl* **-lis 1** a burseraceous Philippine tree, *Canarium ovatum,* with edible seeds resembling almonds **2** Also called: **pili nut** the seed of this tree [from Tagalog]

pili² ('paɪlɪ) *pl n, sing* **pilus** ('paɪləs) *bacteriol* short curled hairlike processes on the surface of certain bacteria that are involved in conjugation and the attachment of the bacteria to other cells [c20 from Latin: hairs]

piliferous (paɪ'lɪfərəs) *adj* **1** (esp of plants or their parts) bearing or ending in a hair or hairs **2** designating the outer layer of root epidermis,

which bears the root hairs [c19 from Latin *pilus* hair + -FEROUS. Compare PILE³]

piliform ('pɪlɪˌfɔːm) *adj botany* resembling a long hair

piling ('paɪlɪŋ) *n* **1** the act of driving piles **2** a number of piles **3** a structure formed of piles

Pilion ('pɪljən) *n* transliteration of the Modern Greek name for **Pelion**

pill¹ (pɪl) *n* **1** a small spherical or ovoid mass of a medicinal substance, intended to be swallowed whole **2** **the** (*sometimes capital*) *informal* an oral contraceptive **3** something unpleasant that must be endured (esp in the phrase **bitter pill to swallow**) **4** *slang* a ball or disc **5** a small ball of matted fibres that forms on the surface of a fabric through rubbing **6** *slang* an unpleasant or boring person ▷ *vb* **7** (*tr*) to give pills to **8** (*tr*) to make pills of **9** (*intr*) **a** to form into small balls **b** (of a fabric) to form small balls of fibre on its surface through rubbing **10** (*tr*) *slang* to blackball ▷ See also **pills** [c15 from Middle Flemish *pille,* from Latin *pilula* a little ball, from *pila* ball]

pill² (pɪl) *vb* **1** *archaic or dialect* to peel or skin (something) **2** *archaic* to pillage or plunder (a place) **3** *obsolete* to make or become bald [Old English *pilian,* from Latin *pilāre* to strip]

pillage ('pɪlɪdʒ) *vb* **1** to rob (a town, village, etc) of (booty or spoils), esp during a war ▷ *n* **2** the act of pillaging **3** something obtained by pillaging; booty [c14 via Old French from *piller* to despoil, probably from *peille* rag, from Latin *pīleus* felt cap] > **'pillager** *n*

pillar ('pɪlə) *n* **1** an upright structure of stone, brick, metal, etc, that supports a superstructure or is used for ornamentation **2** something resembling this in shape or function: *a pillar of stones; a pillar of smoke* **3** a tall, slender, usually sheer rock column, forming a separate top **4** a prominent supporter: *a pillar of the Church* **5** **from pillar to post** from one place to another ▷ *vb* **6** (*tr*) to support with or as if with pillars [c13 from Old French *pilier,* from Latin *pīla;* see PILE¹]

pillar box *n* **1** (in Britain) a red pillar-shaped public letter box situated on a pavement ▷ *adj* **pillar-box 2** characteristic of a pillar box (in the phrase **pillar-box red**)

Pillars of Hercules *pl n* the two promontories at the E end of the Strait of Gibraltar: the Rock of Gibraltar on the European side and the Jebel Musa on the African side; according to legend, formed by Hercules

pill beetle *n* a very common beetle, *Byrrhus pilula,* typical of the family *Byrrhidae,* that can feign death by withdrawing legs and antennae into grooves underneath the oval body

pillbox ('pɪlˌbɒks) *n* **1** a box for pills **2** a small enclosed fortified emplacement, usually made of reinforced concrete **3** a small round hat, now worn esp by women

pill bug *n* any of various woodlice of the genera *Armadillidium* and *Oniscus,* capable of rolling up into a ball when disturbed

pillie ('pɪli) *n Austral informal* a pilchard

pillion ('pɪljən) *n* **1** a seat or place behind the rider of a motorcycle, scooter, horse, etc ▷ *adv* **2** on a pillion: *to ride pillion* [c16 from Gaelic; compare Scottish *pillean,* Irish *pillín* couch; related to Latin *pellis* skin]

pilliwinks ('pɪlɪˌwɪŋks) *pl n* a medieval instrument of torture for the fingers and thumbs [c14 of uncertain origin]

pillock ('pɪlək) *n Brit slang* a stupid or annoying person [c14 from Scandinavian dialect *pillicock* penis]

pillory ('pɪlərɪ) *n, pl* **-ries 1** a wooden framework into which offenders were formerly locked by the neck and wrists and exposed to public abuse and ridicule **2** exposure to public scorn or abuse ▷ *vb* **-ries, -rying, -ried** (*tr*) **3** to expose to public scorn or ridicule **4** to punish by putting in a pillory [c13 from Anglo-Latin *pillorium,* from Old French *pilori,* of uncertain origin; related to Provençal *espillori*]

pillow ('pɪləʊ) *n* **1** a cloth case stuffed with feathers, foam rubber, etc, used to support the head, esp during sleep **2** Also called: **cushion** a padded cushion or board on which pillow lace is made **3** anything like a pillow in shape or function ▷ *vb* (*tr*) **4** to rest (one's head) on or as if on a pillow **5** to serve as a pillow for [Old English *pylwe,* from Latin *pulvīnus* cushion; compare German *Pfühl*]

pillow block *n machinery* a block that supports a journal bearing. Also called: **plummer block**

pillowcase ('pɪləʊˌkeɪs) *or* **pillowslip** ('pɪləʊˌslɪp) *n* a removable washable cover of cotton, linen, nylon, etc, for a pillow

pillow fight *n* a mock fight in which participants thump each other with pillows

pillow lace *n* lace made by winding thread around bobbins on a padded cushion or board. Compare **point lace**

pillow lava *n* lava that has solidified under water, having a characteristic structure comprising a series of close-fitting pillow-shaped masses

pillow sham *n chiefly US* a decorative cover for a bed pillow

pillow talk *n* intimate conversation in bed

pills (pɪlz) *pl n* a slang word for **testicles**

pillwort ('pɪlˌwɜːt) *n* a small Eurasian water fern, *Pilularia globulifera,* with globular spore-producing bodies and grasslike leaves [c19 from PILL¹ + WORT]

pilocarpine (ˌpaɪləʊˈkɑːpaɪn, -pɪn) *or* **pilocarpin** (ˌpaɪləʊˈkɑːpɪn) *n* an alkaloid extracted from the leaves of the jaborandi tree, formerly used to induce sweating. Formula: $C_{11}H_{16}N_2O_2$ [c19 from New Latin *Pilocarpus* genus name, from Greek *pilos* hair + *karpos* fruit]

pilomotor (ˌpaɪləʊˈməʊtə) *adj physiol* causing movement of hairs: *pilomotor nerves*

Pílos ('pɪlɒs) *n* transliteration of the Modern Greek name for **Pylos**

pilose ('paɪləʊz) *or* **pilous** *adj biology* covered with fine soft hairs: *pilose leaves* [c18 from Latin *pilōsus,* from *pilus* hair] > **pilosity** (paɪˈlɒsɪtɪ) *n*

pilot ('paɪlət) *n* **1 a** a person who is qualified to operate an aircraft or spacecraft in flight **b** (*as modifier*): *pilot error* **2 a** a person who is qualified to steer or guide a ship into or out of a port, river mouth, etc **b** (*as modifier*): *a pilot ship* **3** a person who steers a ship **4** a person who acts as a leader or guide **5** *machinery* a guide, often consisting of a tongue or dowel, used to assist in joining two mating parts together **6** *machinery* a plug gauge for measuring an internal diameter **7** *films* a colour test strip accompanying black-and-white rushes from colour originals **8** an experimental programme on radio or television **9** See **pilot film 10** (*modifier*) used in or serving as a test or trial: *a pilot project* **11** (*modifier*) serving as a guide: *a pilot beacon* ▷ *vb* (*tr*) **12** to act as pilot of **13** to control the course of **14** to guide or lead (a project, people, etc) [c16 from French *pilote,* from Medieval Latin *pilotus,* ultimately from Greek *pēdon* oar; related to Greek *pous* foot]

pilotage ('paɪlətɪdʒ) *n* **1** the act of piloting an aircraft or ship **2** a pilot's fee **3** the navigation of an aircraft by the observation of ground features and use of charts

pilot balloon *n* a meteorological balloon used to observe air currents

pilot bird *n* a warbler of forest floors in SE Australia, *Pycnoptilus floccosus,* named from its alleged habit of accompanying the superb lyrebird

pilot biscuit *n* another term for **hardtack**

pilot cloth *n* a type of thick blue cloth used esp to make sailor's coats

pilot engine *n* a locomotive that leads one or more other locomotives at the head of a train of coaches or wagons

pilot film *n* a film of short duration serving as a guide to a projected series

pilot fish *n* **1** a small carangid fish, *Naucrates ductor,* of tropical and subtropical seas, marked with dark vertical bands: often accompanies sharks and other large fishes **2** any of various similar or related fishes

pilot house *n nautical* an enclosed structure on the bridge of a vessel from which it can be navigated; wheelhouse

piloting ('paɪlətɪŋ) *n* **1** the navigational handling of a ship near land using buoys, soundings, landmarks, etc, or the finding of a ship's position by such means **2** the occupation of a pilot

pilot lamp *n* a small light in an electric circuit or device that lights up when the circuit is closed or when certain conditions prevail

pilot light *n* **1** a small auxiliary flame that ignites the main burner of a gas appliance when the control valve opens **2** a small electric light used as an indicator

pilot officer *n* the most junior commissioned rank in the British Royal Air Force and in certain other air forces

pilot plant *n* a small-scale industrial plant in which problems can be identified and solved before the full-scale plant is built

pilot study *n* a small-scale experiment or set of observations undertaken to decide how and whether to launch a full-scale project

pilot whale *n* any of several black toothed whales of the genus *Globicephala*, such as *G. melaena*, that occur in all seas except polar seas: family *Delphinidae*. Also called: **black whale, blackfish**

pilous ('paɪləs) *adj* a variant of **pilose**

Pils (pɪlz, pɪls) *n* a type of lager-like beer [C20 abbrev of PILSNER]

Pilsen ('pɪlzən) *n* the German name for **Plzeň**

Pilsner ('pɪlznə) *or* **Pilsener** *n* a type of pale beer with a strong flavour of hops [named after PILSEN, where it was originally brewed]

Piltdown man ('pɪlt͵daʊn) *n* an advanced hominid postulated from fossil bones found in Sussex in 1912, but shown by modern dating methods in 1953 to be a hoax, which was perpetrated by a student museum assistant who was refused a wage

pilule ('pɪlju:l) *n* a small pill [C16 via French from Latin *pilula* little ball, from *pila* ball] > '**pilular** *adj*

pimento (pɪ'mɛntəʊ) *n, pl* **-tos** another name for **allspice** *or* **pimiento** [C17 from Spanish *pimiento* pepper plant, from Medieval Latin *pigmenta* spiced drink, from Latin *pigmentum* PIGMENT]

pi meson *n* another name for **pion**

pimiento (pɪ'mjɛntəʊ, -'mɛn-) *n, pl* **-tos** a Spanish pepper, *Capsicum annuum*, with a red fruit used raw in salads, cooked as a vegetable, and as a stuffing for green olives. Also called: **pimento** [variant of PIMENTO]

pimentón (͵pi:mjɛn'tɒn) *n* smoked chilli powder [from Spanish]

pimp[1] (pɪmp) *n* **1** a man who solicits for a prostitute or brothel and lives off the earnings **2** a man who procures sexual gratification for another; procurer; pander ▷ *vb* **3** (*intr*) to act as a pimp [C17 of unknown origin]

pimp[2] (pɪmp) *slang, chiefly Austral and NZ* ▷ *n* **1** a spy or informer ▷ *vb* **2** (*intr*; often foll by *on*) to inform (on) [of unknown origin]

pimpernel ('pɪmpə͵nɛl, -nəl) *n* **1** any of several plants of the primulaceous genus *Anagallis*, such as the scarlet pimpernel, typically having small star-shaped flowers **2** any of several similar and related plants, such as *Lysimachia nemorum* (**yellow pimpernel**) [C15 from Old French *pimpernelle*, ultimately from Latin *piper* PEPPER; compare Old English *pipeneale*]

pimple ('pɪmpəl) *n* **1** a small round usually inflamed swelling of the skin **2** any of the bumps on the surface of a table tennis bat [C14 related to Old English *piplian* to break out in spots; compare Latin *papula* pimple] > '**pimpled** *adj* > '**pimply** *adj* > '**pimpliness** *n*

pin (pɪn) *n* **1** **a** a short stiff straight piece of wire pointed at one end and either rounded or having a flattened head at the other: used mainly for fastening pieces of cloth, paper, etc, esp temporarily **b** (*in combination*): *pinhole* **2** short for **cotter pin, hairpin, panel pin, rolling pin** *or* **safety pin** **3** an ornamental brooch, esp a narrow one **4** a badge worn fastened to the clothing by a pin **5** something of little or no importance (esp in the phrases **not care** *or* **give a pin** (**for**)) **6** a peg or dowel **7** anything resembling a pin in shape, function, etc **8** (in various bowling games) a usually club-shaped wooden object set up in groups as a target **9** Also called: **cotter pin, safety pin** a clip on a hand grenade that prevents its detonation until removed or released **10** *nautical* **a** See **belaying pin** **b** the axle of a sheave **c** the sliding closure for a shackle **11** *music* a metal tuning peg on a piano, the end of which is inserted into a detachable key by means of which it is turned **12** *surgery* a metal rod, esp of stainless steel, for holding together adjacent ends of fractured bones during healing **13** *chess* a position in which a piece is pinned against a more valuable piece or the king **14** *golf* the flagpole marking the hole on a green **15** **a** the cylindrical part of a key that enters a lock **b** the cylindrical part of a lock where this part of the key fits **16** *wrestling* a position in which a person is held tight or immobile, esp with both shoulders touching the ground **17** a dovetail tenon used to make a dovetail joint **18** (in Britain) a miniature beer cask containing 4½ gallons **19** (*usually plural*) *informal* a leg **20** **be put to the pin on one's collar** *Irish* to be forced to make an extreme effort ▷ *vb* **pins, pinning, pinned** (*tr*) **21** to attach, hold, or fasten with or as if with a pin or pins **22** to transfix with a pin, spear, etc **23** (foll by *on*) *informal* to place (the blame for something): *he pinned the charge on his accomplice* **24** *chess* to cause (an enemy piece) to be effectively immobilized by attacking it with a queen, rook, or bishop so that moving it would reveal a check or expose a more valuable piece to capture **25** Also: **underpin** to support (masonry), as by driving in wedges over a beam ▷ See also **pin down** [Old English *pinn*; related to Old High German *pfinn*, Old Norse *pinni* nail]

PIN (pɪn) *n acronym for* personal identification number: a number used by a holder of a cash card or credit card used in EFTPOS

p-i-n *abbreviation for* p-type, intrinsic, n-type: a form of construction of semiconductor devices

pinaceous (paɪ'neɪʃəs) *adj* of, relating to, or belonging to the *Pinaceae*, a family of conifers with needle-like leaves: includes pine, spruce, fir, larch, and cedar [C19 via New Latin from Latin *pīnus* a pine]

piña cloth ('pi:njə) *n* a fine fabric made from the fibres of the pineapple leaf [C19 from Spanish *piña* pineapple]

piña colada ('pi:njə kə'lɑ:də) *n* a drink consisting of pineapple juice, coconut, and rum [C20 from Spanish, literally: strained pineapple]

pinafore ('pɪnə͵fɔ:) *n* **1** *chiefly Brit* an apron, esp one with a bib **2** *chiefly Brit* short for **pinafore dress** **3** *chiefly US* an overdress buttoning at the back [C18 from PIN + AFORE]

pinafore dress *n Brit* a sleeveless dress worn over a blouse or sweater. Often shortened to: **pinafore** US and Canadian name: **jumper**

Pinar del Río (*Spanish* pi'nar ðɛl 'rrio) *n* a city in W Cuba: tobacco industry. Pop: 158 000 (2005 est)

pinaster (paɪ'næstə, pɪ-) *n* a Mediterranean pine tree, *Pinus pinaster*, with paired needles and prickly cones. Also called: **maritime** (*or* **cluster**) **pinaster** [C16 from Latin: wild pine, from *pīnus* pine]

piñata (͵pɪn'jata) *n* a papier-mâché party decoration filled with sweets, hung up during parties, and struck with a stick until it breaks open [Spanish, from Italian *pignatta*, probably from dialect *pigna*, from Latin *pinea* pine cone]

pinball ('pɪn͵bɔ:l) *n* **a** a game in which the player shoots a small ball through several hazards on a table, electrically operated machine, etc **b** (*as modifier*): *a pinball machine*

pince-nez ('pæns͵neɪ, 'pɪns-; *French* pɛ̃sne) *n, pl* **pince-nez** eyeglasses that are held in place only by means of a clip over the bridge of the nose [C19 French, literally: pinch-nose]

pincer movement ('pɪnsə) *n* a military tactical movement in which two columns of an army follow a curved route towards each other with the aim of isolating and surrounding an enemy. Also called: **envelopment**

pincers ('pɪnsəz) *pl n* **1** Also called: **pair of pincers** a gripping tool consisting of two hinged arms with handles at one end and, at the other, curved bevelled jaws that close on the workpiece: used esp for extracting nails **2** the pair or pairs of jointed grasping appendages in lobsters and certain other arthropods [C14 from Old French *pinceour*, from Old French *pincier* to PINCH]

pinch (pɪntʃ) *vb* **1** to press (something, esp flesh) tightly between two surfaces, esp between a finger and the thumb (see **nip**[1]) **2** to confine, squeeze, or painfully press (toes, fingers, etc) because of lack of space: *these shoes pinch* **3** (*tr*) to cause stinging pain to: *the cold pinched his face* **4** (*tr*) to make thin or drawn-looking, as from grief, lack of food, etc **5** (usually foll by *on*) to provide (oneself or another person) with meagre allowances, amounts, etc **6** **pinch pennies** to live frugally because of meanness or to economize **7** (*tr*) *nautical* to sail (a sailing vessel) so close to the wind that her sails begin to luff and she loses way **8** (*intr*; sometimes foll by *out*) (of a vein of ore) to narrow or peter out **9** (usually foll by *off, out*, or *back*) to remove the tips of (buds, shoots, etc) to correct or encourage growth **10** (*tr*) *informal* to steal or take without asking **11** (*tr*) *informal* to arrest ▷ *n* **12** a squeeze or sustained nip **13** the quantity of a substance, such as salt, that can be taken between a thumb and finger **14** a very small quantity **15** a critical situation; predicament; emergency: *if it comes to the pinch we'll have to manage* **16** (usually preceded by *the*) sharp, painful, or extreme stress, need, etc: *feeling the pinch of poverty* **17** See **pinch bar** **18** *slang* a robbery **19** *slang* a police raid or arrest **20** **at a pinch** if absolutely necessary **21** **with a pinch** *or* **grain of salt** without wholly believing; sceptically [C16 probably from Old Norman French *pinchier* (unattested); related to Old French *pincier* to pinch; compare Late Latin *punctiāre* to prick]

P

pinch bar *n* a crowbar with a lug formed on it to provide a fulcrum

pinchbeck ('pɪntʃ͵bɛk) *n* **1** an alloy of copper and zinc, used as imitation gold **2** a spurious or cheap imitation; sham ▷ *adj* **3** made of pinchbeck **4** sham, spurious, or cheap [C18 (the alloy), C19 (something spurious): after Christopher *Pinchbeck* (?1670–1732), English watchmaker who invented it]

pinchcock ('pɪntʃ͵kɒk) *n* a clamp used to compress a flexible tube to control the flow of fluid through it

pinch effect *n* the constriction of a beam of charged particles, caused by a force on each particle due to its motion in the magnetic field generated by the movement of the other particles

pinch-hit *vb* **-hits, -hitting, -hit** (*intr*) **1** *baseball* to bat as a substitute for the scheduled batter **2** *US and Canadian informal* to act as a substitute **3** *cricket* (of a batsman in a limited-overs match) to bat aggressively at the start of an innings in order to take advantage of fielding restrictions > **pinch hitter** *n*

pinchpenny ('pɪntʃ͵pɛnɪ) *adj* **1** niggardly; miserly ▷ *n, pl* **-nies** **2** a miserly person; niggard

pinch point *n* a traffic-calming measure in which the road narrows to one lane, with a sign indicating which oncoming driver should give way

pin curl *n* a small section of hair wound in a circle and secured with a hairpin to set it in a curl

pincushion ('pɪn͵kʊʃən) *n* a small well-padded

cushion in which pins are stuck ready for use

pindan ('pɪnˌdæn) *n* **1** a desert region of Western Australia **2** the vegetation growing in this region [from a native Australian language]

Pindaric (pɪn'dærɪk) *adj* **1** of, relating to, or resembling the style of the Greek lyric poet Pindar (?518–?438 BC) **2** *prosody* having a complex metrical structure, either regular or irregular ▷ *n* **3** See **Pindaric ode**

Pindaric ode *n* a form of ode associated with Pindar consisting of a triple unit or groups of triple units, with a strophe and an antistrophe of identical structure followed by an epode of a different structure. Often shortened to: **Pindaric**

pindling ('pɪndlɪŋ) *adj dialect* **1** *Western Brit* peevish or fractious **2** *US* sickly or puny [C19 perhaps changed from *spindling*]

pin down *vb* (*tr, adverb*) **1** to force (someone) to make a decision or carry out a promise **2** to define clearly: *he had a vague suspicion that he couldn't quite pin down* **3** to confine to a place: *the fallen tree pinned him down*

Pindus ('pɪndəs) *n* a mountain range in central Greece between Epirus and Thessaly. Highest peak: Mount Smólikas, 2633 m (8639 ft). Modern Greek name: **Píndhos** ('pɪndɒs)

pine¹ (paɪn) *n* **1** any evergreen resinous coniferous tree of the genus *Pinus*, of the N hemisphere, with long needle-shaped leaves and brown cones: family *Pinaceae*. See also **longleaf pine, nut pine, pitch pine, Scots pine 2** any other tree or shrub of the family *Pinaceae* **3** the wood of any of these trees **4** any of various similar but unrelated plants, such as ground pine and screw pine [Old English *pīn*, from Latin *pīnus* pine]

pine² (paɪn) *vb* **1** (*intr; often foll by for* or an infinitive) to feel great longing or desire; yearn **2** (*intr; often foll by away*) to become ill, feeble, or thin through worry, longing, etc **3** (*tr*) *archaic* to mourn or grieve for [Old English *pīnian* to torture, from *pīn* pain, from Medieval Latin *pēna*, from Latin *poena* PAIN]

pineal ('pɪnɪəl, paɪ'niːəl) *adj* **1** resembling a pine cone **2** of or relating to the pineal gland [C17 via French from Latin *pīnea* pine cone]

pineal eye *n* an outgrowth of the pineal gland that forms an eyelike structure on the top of the head in certain cold-blooded vertebrates

pineal gland *or* **body** *n* a pea-sized organ in the brain, situated beneath the posterior part of the corpus callosum, that secretes melatonin into the bloodstream. Technical names: **epiphysis, epiphysis cerebri**

pineapple ('paɪnˌæpˀl) *n* **1** a tropical American bromeliaceous plant, *Ananas comosus*, cultivated in the tropics for its large fleshy edible fruit **2** the fruit of this plant, consisting of an inflorescence clustered around a fleshy axis and surmounted by a tuft of leaves **3** *military slang* a hand grenade [C14 *pinappel* pine cone; C17 applied to the fruit because of its appearance]

pineapple tree *n* another name for **neinei**

pineapple weed *n* an Asian plant, *Matricaria matricarioides*, naturalized in Europe and North America, having greenish-yellow flower heads, and smelling of pineapple when crushed: family *Asteraceae* (composites)

pine cone *n* the seed-producing structure of a pine tree. See **cone** (sense 3a)

pine end *n dialect* the gable or gable end of a building

pine marten *n* a marten, *Martes martes*, of N European and Asian coniferous woods, having dark brown fur with a creamy-yellow patch on the throat. See also **sweet marten**

pinene ('paɪniːn) *n* either of two isomeric terpenes, found in many essential oils and constituting the main part part of oil of turpentine. The commonest structural isomer (α-pinene) is used in the manufacture of camphor, solvents, plastics, and insecticides. Formula: $C_{10}H_{16}$ [C20 from PINE¹ + -ENE]

pine needle *n* any of the fine pointed leaves of a pine

pine nut *or* **kernel** *n* the edible seed of certain pine trees

pinery ('paɪnərɪ) *n, pl* -neries **1** a place, esp a hothouse, where pineapples are grown **2** a forest of pine trees, esp one cultivated for timber

Pines (paɪnz) *n* **Isle of** the former name of the (Isle of) **Youth**

pine tar *n* a brown or black semisolid or viscous substance, produced by the destructive distillation of pine wood, used in roofing compositions, paints, medicines, etc

pinetum (paɪ'niːtəm) *n, pl* -ta (-tə) an area of land where pine trees and other conifers are grown [C19 from Latin, from *pīnus* PINE¹]

pin-eyed *adj* (of flowers, esp primulas) having the stigma in the mouth of the corolla, on the end of a long style with the stamens lower in the tube. Compare **thrum-eyed**

pinfall ('pɪnˌfɔːl) *n wrestling* another name for **fall** (sense 48)

pinfeather ('pɪnˌfɛðə) *n ornithol* a feather emerging from the skin and still enclosed in its horny sheath

pinfish ('pɪnˌfɪʃ) *n, pl* -fish *or* -fishes a small porgy, *Lagodon rhomboides*, occurring off the SE North American coast of the Atlantic. Also called: **sailor's choice** [so named because it has spines]

pinfold ('pɪnˌfəʊld) *n* **1 a** a pound for stray cattle **b** a fold or pen for sheep or cattle ▷ *vb* **2** (*tr*) to gather or confine in a pinfold [Old English *pundfald*, from POUND³ + FOLD²]

ping (pɪŋ) *n* **1** a short high-pitched resonant sound, as of a bullet striking metal or a sonar echo **2** *computing* a system for testing whether internet systems are responding and how long in milliseconds it takes them to respond ▷ *vb* **3** (*intr*) to make such a noise **4** (*tr*) *computing* to send a test message to (a computer or server) in order to check whether it is responding or how long it takes it to respond [C19 of imitative origin] > '**pinging** *adj*

pinger ('pɪŋə) *n* a device that makes a pinging sound, esp one that can be preset to ring at a particular time

pingo ('pɪŋɡəʊ) *n, pl* -gos a mound of earth or gravel formed through pressure from a layer of water trapped between newly frozen ice and underlying permafrost in Arctic regions [C20 from Inuktitut]

Ping-Pong ('pɪŋˌpɒŋ) *n trademark* another name for **table tennis** Also called: **ping pong**

pinguid ('pɪŋɡwɪd) *adj* fatty, oily, or greasy; soapy [C17 from Latin *pinguis* fat, rich] > **pin'guidity** *n*

pinhead ('pɪnˌhɛd) *n* **1** the head of a pin **2** something very small **3** *informal* a stupid or contemptible person

pinheaded ('pɪnˌhɛdɪd) *adj informal* stupid or silly > **pin'headedness** *n*

pinhole ('pɪnˌhəʊl) *n* **1** a small hole made with or as if with a pin **2** *archery* the exact centre of an archery target, in the middle of the gold zone

pinhole camera *n* a camera with a pinhole as an aperture instead of a lens

pinion¹ ('pɪnjən) *n* **1** *chiefly poetic* a bird's wing **2** the part of a bird's wing including the flight feathers ▷ *vb* **3** to hold or bind (the arms) of (a person) so as to restrain or immobilize him **4** to confine or shackle **5** to make (a bird) incapable of flight by removing that part of (the wing) from which the flight feathers grow [C15 from Old French *pignon* wing, from Latin *pinna* wing]

pinion² ('pɪnjən) *n* a cogwheel that engages with a larger wheel or rack, which it drives or by which it is driven [C17 from French *pignon* cogwheel, from Old French *peigne* comb, from Latin *pecten* comb; see PECTEN]

Piniós (pi'njɒs) *n* transliteration of the Modern Greek name for the **Salambria**

pinite ('pɪnaɪt, 'paɪ-) *n* a greyish-green or brown mineral containing amorphous aluminium and

potassium sulphates [C19 from German *Pinit*, named after the *Pini* mine, Schneeberg, Saxony]

pin joint *n* a mechanical joint that will transmit axial load but will not transmit torque

pink¹ (pɪŋk) *n* **1** any of a group of colours with a reddish hue that are of low to moderate saturation and can usually reflect or transmit a large amount of light; a pale reddish tint **2** pink cloth or clothing: *dressed in pink* **3** any of various Old World plants of the caryophyllaceous genus *Dianthus*, such as *D. plumarius* (**garden pink**), cultivated for their fragrant flowers. See also **carnation** (sense 1) **4** any of various plants of other genera, such as the moss pink **5** the flower of any of these plants **6** the highest or best degree, condition, etc (esp in the phrases **in the pink of health, in the pink**) **7 a** a huntsman's scarlet coat **b** a huntsman who wears a scarlet coat ▷ *adj* **8** of the colour pink **9** *Brit informal* left-wing **10** *US derogatory* **a** sympathetic to or influenced by Communism **b** leftist or radical, esp half-heartedly **11** *informal* of or relating to homosexuals or homosexuality: *the pink vote* **12** (of a huntsman's coat) scarlet or red ▷ *vb* **13** (*intr*) another word for **knock** (sense 7) [C16 (the flower), C18 (the colour): perhaps a shortening of PINKEYE] > '**pinkish** *adj* > '**pinkness** *n* > '**pinky** *adj*

pink² (pɪŋk) *vb* (*tr*) **1** to prick lightly with a sword or rapier **2** to decorate (leather, cloth, etc) with a perforated or punched pattern **3** to cut with pinking shears [C14 perhaps of Low German origin; compare Low German *pinken* to peck]

pink³ (pɪŋk) *n* a sailing vessel with a narrow overhanging transom [C15 from Middle Dutch *pinke*, of obscure origin]

pink-collar *adj* of, relating to, or designating low-paid occupations traditionally associated with female workers. Compare **blue-collar, white-collar**

pink elephants *pl n* a facetious name applied to hallucinations caused by drunkenness

pinkeye ('pɪŋkˌaɪ) *n* **1** Also called: **acute conjunctivitis** an acute contagious inflammation of the conjunctiva of the eye, characterized by redness, discharge, etc: usually caused by bacterial infection **2** Also called: **infectious keratitis** a similar condition affecting the cornea of horses and cattle [C16 partial translation of obsolete Dutch *pinck oogen* small eyes]

pink-footed goose *n* a Eurasian goose, *Anser brachyrhynchus*, having a reddish-brown head, pink legs, and a pink band on its black beak

pink gin *n* a mixture of gin and bitters

pinkie *or* **pinky** ('pɪŋkɪ) *n, pl* -ies *Scot, US, and Canadian* the little finger [C19 from Dutch *pinkje*, diminutive of PINK¹; compare PINKEYE]

pinking shears *pl n* scissors with a serrated edge on one or both blades, producing a wavy edge to material cut, thus preventing fraying

pink noise *n* noise containing a mixture of frequencies, but excluding higher frequencies

pinko ('pɪŋkəʊ) *n, pl* -os *or* -oes *chiefly US derogatory* a person regarded as mildly left-wing

pinkroot ('pɪŋkˌruːt) *n* **1** any of several loganiaceous plants of the genus *Spigelia*, esp *S. marilandica*, of the southeastern US, having red-and-yellow flowers and pink roots **2** the powdered root of this plant, used as a vermifuge **3** a fungal disease of onions and related plants resulting in stunted growth and shrivelled pink roots

pink salmon *n* **1** any salmon having pale pink flesh, esp *Oncorhynchus gorbuscha*, of the Pacific Ocean **2** the flesh of such a fish

pink slip *n US informal* a notice of redundancy issued to an employee

Pinky bar *n trademark NZ* a chocolate-covered marshmallow bar

pin money *n* **1** an allowance by a husband to his wife for personal expenditure **2** money saved or earned to be used for incidental expenses

pinna ('pɪnə) *n, pl* -nae (-niː) *or* -nas **1** any leaflet of a pinnate compound leaf **2** *zoology* a feather, wing, fin, or similarly shaped part **3** another name for **auricle** (sense 2) [c18 via New Latin from Latin: wing, feather, fin]

pinnace ('pɪnɪs) *n* any of various kinds of ship's tender [c16 from French *pinace*, apparently from Old Spanish *pinaza*, literally: something made of pine, ultimately from Latin *pīnus* pine]

pinnacle ('pɪnək²l) *n* **1** the highest point or level, esp of fame, success, etc **2** a towering peak, as of a mountain **3** a slender upright structure in the form of a cone, pyramid, or spire on the top of a buttress, gable, or tower ▷ *vb* (*tr*) **4** to set on or as if on a pinnacle **5** to furnish with a pinnacle or pinnacles **6** to crown with a pinnacle [c14 via Old French from Late Latin *pinnāculum* a peak, from Latin *pinna* wing]

pinnate ('pɪneɪt, 'pɪnɪt) *or* **pinnated** *adj* **1** like a feather in appearance **2** (of compound leaves) having the leaflets growing opposite each other in pairs on either side of the stem [c18 from Latin *pinnātus*, from *pinna* feather] > **'pinnately** *adv* > **pin'nation** *n*

pinnati- *combining form* pinnate or pinnately: *pinnatifid*

pinnatifid (pɪ'nætɪfɪd) *adj* (of leaves) pinnately divided into lobes reaching more than halfway to the midrib > **pin'natifidly** *adv*

pinnatipartite (ˌpɪˌnætɪ'pɑːtaɪt) *adj* (of leaves) pinnately divided into lobes reaching just over halfway to the midrib

pinnatiped (pɪ'nætɪˌpɛd) *adj* (of birds) having lobate feet

pinnatisect (pɪ'nætɪˌsɛkt) *adj* (of leaves) pinnately divided almost to the midrib but not into separate leaflets

pinner ('pɪnə) *n* **1** a person or thing that pins **2** a small dainty apron **3** a cap with two long flaps pinned on

pinniped ('pɪnɪˌpɛd) *or* **pinnipedian** (ˌpɪnɪ'piːdɪən) *adj* **1** of, relating to, or belonging to the *Pinnipedia*, an order of aquatic placental mammals having a streamlined body and limbs specialized as flippers: includes seals, sea lions, and the walrus ▷ *n* **2** any pinniped animal ▷ Compare **fissiped** [c19 from New Latin *pinnipēs*, from Latin *pinna* feather, fin + *pēs* foot]

pinnule ('pɪnjuːl) *or* **pinnula** ('pɪnjʊlə) *n, pl* **pinnules** *or* **pinnulae** ('pɪnjʊˌliː) **1** any of the lobes of a leaflet of a pinnate compound leaf, which is itself pinnately divided **2** *zoology* any feather-like part, such as any of the arms of a sea lily [c16 from Latin *pinnula*, diminutive of *pinna* feather] > **'pinnular** *adj*

pinny ('pɪnɪ) *n, pl* **-nies** a child's or informal name for **pinafore** (sense 1)

pinochle, penuchle, penuckle *or* **pinocle** ('piːnʌk²l) *n* **1** a card game for two to four players similar to bezique **2** the combination of queen of spades and jack of diamonds in this game [c19 of unknown origin]

pinole (pɪ'nəʊlɪ) *n* (in the southwestern United States) flour made of parched ground corn, mesquite beans, sugar, etc [from American Spanish, from Nahuatl]

Pinotage ('pɪnətɑːʒ) *n* **1** a red grape variety of South Africa, a cross between the Pinot Noir and the Hermitage **2** any of the red wines made from this grape

Pinot Grigio ('piːnəʊ 'griːdʒəʊ) *n* **1** a variety of grape, grown in Italy for wine-making **2** any of the white Italian wines made from this grape [Italian *grigio* grey]

Pinot Noir ('piːnəʊ nwɑː) *n* **1** a variety of black grape, grown esp for wine-making **2** any of the red wines made from this grape [French]

PIN pad *n* a small keypad at a point of sale on which someone making a purchase using a credit or debit card types his or her PIN to confirm the purchase

pinpoint ('pɪnˌpɔɪnt) *vb* (*tr*) **1** to locate or identify exactly: *to pinpoint a problem; to pinpoint a place on a map* ▷ *n* **2** an insignificant or trifling thing **3** the point of a pin **4** (*modifier*) exact: *a pinpoint aim*

pinprick ('pɪnˌprɪk) *n* **1** a slight puncture made by or as if by a pin **2** a small irritation ▷ *vb* **3** (*tr*) to puncture with or as if with a pin

pin rail *n nautical* a strong wooden rail or bar containing holes for belaying pins to which lines are fastened on sailing vessels. Compare **fife rail**

pins and needles *n* (*functioning as singular*) *informal* **1** a tingling sensation in the fingers, toes, legs, etc, caused by the return of normal blood circulation after its temporary impairment **2** on pins and needles in a state of anxious suspense or nervous anticipation

Pinsk (*Russian* pinsk) *n* a city in SW Belarus: capital of a principality (13th–14th centuries). Pop: 134 000 (2005 est)

pinstripe ('pɪnˌstraɪp) *n* (in textiles) **a** a very narrow stripe in fabric or the fabric itself, used esp for men's suits **b** (*as modifier*): *a pinstripe suit*

pinswell ('pɪnˌswɛl) *n Southwest English dialect* a small boil

pint (paɪnt) *n* **1** a unit of liquid measure of capacity equal to one eighth of a gallon. 1 Brit pint is equal to 0.568 litre, 1 US pint to 0.473 litre **2** a unit of dry measure of capacity equal to one half of a quart. 1 US dry pint is equal to one sixty-fourth of a US bushel or 0.5506 litre **3** a measure having such a capacity **4** *Brit informal* **a** a pint of beer **b** a drink of beer: *he's gone out for a pint* [c14 from Old French *pinte*, of uncertain origin; perhaps from Medieval Latin *pincta* marks used in measuring liquids, ultimately from Latin *pingere* to paint; compare Middle Low German, Middle Dutch *pinte*]

pinta¹ ('pɪntə) *n* a tropical infectious skin disease caused by the bacterium *Treponema carateum* and characterized by the formation of papules and loss of pigmentation in circumscribed areas. Also called: **mal de pinto** [c19 from American Spanish, from Spanish: spot, ultimately from Latin *pictus* painted, from *pingere* to paint]

pinta² ('paɪntə) *n informal* a pint of milk [c20 phonetic rendering of *pint of*]

Pinta ('pɪntə) *n* **the** one of the three ships commanded by Columbus on his first voyage to America (1492)

pintadera (ˌpɪntə'dɛərə) *n* a decorative stamp, usually made of clay, found in the Neolithic of the E Mediterranean and in many American cultures [from Spanish, literally: an instrument for making decorations on bread, from *pintado* mottled, from *pintar* to PAINT]

pintado petrel (pɪn'tɑːdəʊ) *n* another name for **Cape pigeon** [c19 Portuguese: past participle of *pintar* to paint, referring to the mottled coloration]

pintail ('pɪnˌteɪl) *n, pl* **-tails** *or* **-tail** a greyish-brown duck, *Anas acuta*, with slender pointed wings and a pointed tail

Pinteresque (ˌpɪntər'ɛsk) *adj* reminiscent of the plays of Harold Pinter, the English dramatist (born 1930), noted for their equivocal and halting dialogue

pintle ('pɪnt²l) *n* **1** a pin or bolt forming the pivot of a hinge **2** the link bolt, hook, or pin on a vehicle's towing bracket **3** the needle or plunger of the injection valve of an oil engine [Old English *pintel* penis]

pinto ('pɪntəʊ) *US and Canadian* ▷ *adj* **1** marked with patches of white; piebald ▷ *n, pl* **-tos** **2** a pinto horse [c19 from American Spanish (originally: painted, spotted), ultimately from Latin *pingere* to paint]

pinto bean *n* a variety of kidney bean that has mottled seeds and is grown for food and fodder in the southwestern US

pint-size *or* **pint-sized** *adj informal* very small; tiny

Pintubi ('pɪntəbɪ) *n* **1** (*pl* **-bi** *or* **-bis**) an Aboriginal people of the southern border area of Western Australia and the Northern Territory **2** the language of this people

pin tuck *n* a narrow ornamental fold used esp on shirt fronts and dress bodices

pin-up *n* **1** *informal* **a** a picture of a sexually attractive person, esp when partially or totally undressed **b** (*as modifier*): *a pin-up magazine* **2** *slang* a person who has appeared in such a picture **3** a photograph of a famous personality **4** (*modifier*) *US* designed to be hung from a wall: *a pin-up lamp*

pinwheel ('pɪnˌwiːl) *n* **1** another name for **Catherine wheel** (sense 1) **2** a cogwheel whose teeth are formed by small pins projecting either axially or radially from the rim of the wheel **3** *US and Canadian* a toy consisting of plastic or paper vanes attached to a stick in such a manner that they revolve like the sails of a windmill. Also called (in Britain and certain other countries): **windmill, whirligig**

pinwork ('pɪnˌwɜːk) *n* (in needlepoint lace) the fine raised stitches

pinworm ('pɪnˌwɜːm) *n* a parasitic nematode worm, *Enterobius vermicularis*, infecting the colon, rectum, and anus of humans: family *Oxyuridae*. Also called: **threadworm**

pin wrench *n* a wrench fitted with a cylindrical pin that registers in a hole in the part to be rotated, used to improve the application of the turning moment

pinxit *Latin* ('pɪŋksɪt) he (or she) painted it: an inscription sometimes found on paintings following the artist's name

piny ('paɪnɪ) *adj* **pinier, piniest** of, resembling, or covered with pine trees

Pinyin ('pɪn'jɪn) *n* a system of romanized spelling developed in China in 1958: used to transliterate Chinese characters into the Roman alphabet

piolet (pjəʊ'leɪ) *n* a type of ice axe [c19 from French (Savoy) dialect *piola* axe]

pion ('paɪɒn) *or* **pi meson** *n physics* a meson having a positive or negative charge and a rest mass 273.13 times that of the electron, or no charge and a rest mass 264.14 times that of the electron [c20 from Greek letter PI¹ + ON]

pioneer (ˌpaɪə'nɪə) *n* **1 a** a colonist, explorer, or settler of a new land, region, etc **b** (*as modifier*): *a pioneer wagon* **2** an innovator or developer of something new **3** *military* a member of an infantry group that digs entrenchments, makes roads, etc **4** *ecology* the first species of plant or animal to colonize an area of bare ground ▷ *vb* **5** to be a pioneer (in or of) **6** (*tr*) to initiate, prepare, or open up: *to pioneer a medical programme* [c16 from Old French *paonier* infantryman, from *paon* PAWN²; see also PEON¹]

Pioneer¹ (ˌpaɪə'nɪə) *n* a total abstainer from alcoholic drink, esp a member of the **Pioneer Total Abstinence Association,** a society devoted to abstention

Pioneer² (ˌpaɪə'nɪə) *n* any of a series of US spacecraft that studied the solar system, esp **Pioneer 10,** which made the first flyby of Jupiter (1973), and **Pioneer 11,** which made the first flyby of Saturn (1979)

piopio ('piːɒpiːɒ) *n, pl* **piopio** a New Zealand thrush, *Turnagra capensis*, thought to be extinct [Māori, of imitative origin]

pious ('paɪəs) *adj* **1** having or expressing reverence for a god or gods; religious; devout **2** marked by reverence **3** marked by false reverence; sanctimonious **4** sacred; not secular **5** *archaic* having or expressing devotion for one's parents or others [c17 from Latin *pius*, related to *piāre* to expiate] > **'piously** *adv* > **'piousness** *n*

pip¹ (pɪp) *n* **1** the seed of a fleshy fruit, such as an apple or pear **2** any of the segments marking the surface of a pineapple **3** a rootstock or flower of the lily of the valley or certain other plants [c18 short for PIPPIN]

pip² (pɪp) *n* **1** a short high-pitched sound, a sequence of which can act as a time signal, esp on radio **2** a radar blip **3 a** a spot or single device, such as a spade, diamond, heart, or club on a playing card **b** any of the spots on dice or dominoes **4** *informal* the emblem worn on the

p

shoulder by junior officers in the British Army, indicating their rank. Also called: **star** ▷ *vb* **pips, pipping, pipped** **5** (of a young bird) **a** (*intr*) to chirp; peep **b** to pierce (the shell of its egg) while hatching **6** (*intr*) to make a short high-pitched sound [C16 (in the sense: spot or speck); C17 (vb); C20 (in the sense: short high-pitched sound): of obscure, probably imitative origin; senses 1 and 5 are probably related to PEEP[2]]

pip[3] (pɪp) *n* **1** a contagious disease of poultry characterized by the secretion of thick mucus in the mouth and throat **2** *facetious slang* a minor human ailment **3** *Brit, Austral, NZ and S African slang* a bad temper or depression (esp in the phrase **give (someone) the pip**) **4** **get** *or* **have the pip** *NZ informal* to sulk ▷ *vb* **pips, pipping, pipped** **5** *Brit slang* to cause to be annoyed or depressed [C15 from Middle Dutch *pippe*, ultimately from Latin *pituita* phlegm; see PITUITARY]

pip[4] (pɪp) *vb* **pips, pipping, pipped** (*tr*) *Brit slang* **1** to wound or kill, esp with a gun **2** to defeat (a person), esp when his success seems certain (often in the phrase **pip at the post**) **3** to blackball or ostracize [C19 (originally in the sense: to blackball): probably from PIP[2]]

pipa (ˈpiːpə) *n* a tongueless South American toad, *Pipa pipa*, that carries its young in pits in the skin of its back [C18 from Surinam dialect, probably of African origin]

pipage (ˈpaɪpɪdʒ) *n* **1** pipes collectively **2** conveyance by pipes **3** the money charged for such conveyance

pipal (ˈpaɪpᵊl) *n* a variant of **peepul**

pipe[1] (paɪp) *n* **1** a long tube of metal, plastic, etc, used to convey water, oil, gas, etc **2** a long tube or case **3** **a** an object made in any of various shapes and sizes, consisting of a small bowl with an attached tubular stem, in which tobacco or other substances are smoked **b** (*as modifier*): *a pipe bowl* **4** Also called: **pipeful** the amount of tobacco that fills the bowl of a pipe **5** *zoology, botany* any of various hollow organs, such as the respiratory passage of certain animals **6** **a** any musical instrument whose sound production results from the vibration of an air column in a simple tube **b** any of the tubular devices on an organ, in which air is made to vibrate either directly, as in a flue pipe, or by means of a reed **7** an obsolete three-holed wind instrument, held in the left hand while played and accompanied by the tabor. See **tabor** **8** **the pipes** See **bagpipes** **9** a shrill voice or sound, as of a bird **10** **a** a boatswain's pipe **b** the sound it makes **11** (*plural*) *informal* the respiratory tract or vocal cords **12** *metallurgy* a conical hole in the head of an ingot, made by escaping gas as the metal cools **13** a cylindrical vein of rich ore, such as one of the vertical diamond-bearing veins at Kimberley, South Africa **14** Also called: **volcanic pipe** a vertical cylindrical passage in a volcano through which molten lava is forced during eruption **15** *US slang* something easy to do, esp a simple course in college **16** **put that in your pipe and smoke it** *informal* accept that fact if you can ▷ *vb* **17** to play (music) on a pipe **18** (*tr*) to summon or lead by a pipe: *to pipe the dancers* **19** to utter (something) shrilly **20** **a** to signal orders to (the crew) by a boatswain's pipe **b** (*tr*) to signal the arrival or departure of: *to pipe the admiral aboard* **21** (*tr*) to convey (water, gas, etc) by a pipe or pipes **22** (*tr*) to provide with pipes **23** (*tr*) to trim (an article, esp of clothing) with piping **24** (*tr*) to force (cream, icing, etc) through a shaped nozzle to decorate food ▷ See also **pipe down, pipe up** [Old English *pīpe* (n), *pīpian* (vb), ultimately from Latin *pīpāre* to chirp] > ˈ**pipeless** *adj* > ˈ**pipy** *adj*

pipe[2] (paɪp) *n* **1** a large cask for wine, oil, etc **2** a measure of capacity for wine equal to four barrels. 1 pipe is equal to 126 US gallons or 105 Brit gallons **3** a cask holding this quantity with its contents [C14 via Old French (in the sense: tube, tubular vessel), ultimately from Latin *pīpāre* to chirp; compare PIPE[1]]

pipe bomb *n* a small explosive device hidden in a pipe or drain, detonated by means of a timer

pipeclay (ˈpaɪpˌkleɪ) *n* **1** a fine white pure clay, used in the manufacture of tobacco pipes and pottery and for whitening leather and similar materials ▷ *vb* **2** (*tr*) to whiten with pipeclay

pipe cleaner *n* a short length of thin wires twisted so as to hold tiny tufts of yarn: used to clean the stem of a tobacco pipe

piped music *n* light popular music prerecorded and played through amplifiers in a shop, restaurant, factory, etc, as background music. See also **Muzak**

pipe down *vb* (*intr, adverb*) *informal* to stop talking, making noise, etc

pipe dream *n* a fanciful or impossible plan or hope [alluding to dreams produced by smoking an opium pipe]

pipefish (ˈpaɪpˌfɪʃ) *n, pl* **-fish** *or* **-fishes** any of various teleost fishes of the genera *Nerophis*, *Syngnathus*, etc, having a long tubelike snout and an elongated body covered with bony plates: family *Syngnathidae*. Also called: **needlefish**

pipefitting (ˈpaɪpˌfɪtɪŋ) *n* **1** **a** the act or process of bending, cutting to length, and joining pipes **b** the branch of plumbing involving this **2** the threaded gland nuts, unions, adaptors, etc, used for joining pipes > ˈ**pipeˌfitter** *n*

pipe jacking *n* a method of laying underground pipelines by assembling the pipes at the foot of an access shaft and pushing them through the ground

pipeline (ˈpaɪpˌlaɪn) *n* **1** a long pipe, esp underground, used to transport oil, natural gas, etc, over long distances **2** a medium of communication, esp a private one **3** **in the pipeline** in the process of being completed, delivered, or produced ▷ *vb* (*tr*) **4** to convey by pipeline **5** to supply with a pipeline

pipe major *n* the noncommissioned officer, generally of warrant officer's rank, who is responsible for the training, duty, and discipline of a military or civilian pipe band

pip-emma (ˈpɪpˈɛmə) *adv old-fashioned* in the afternoon; p.m. Compare **ack-emma** [World War I phonetic alphabet for P, M]

pipe organ *n* another name for **organ** (the musical instrument). Compare **reed organ**

piper (ˈpaɪpə) *n* **1** a person who plays a pipe or bagpipes **2** **pay the piper and call the tune** to bear the cost of an undertaking and control it

piperaceous (ˌpɪpəˈreɪʃəs) *adj* of, relating to, or belonging to the *Piperaceae*, a family of pungent tropical shrubs and climbing flowering plants: includes pepper, betel, and cubeb [C17 via New Latin from Latin *piper* PEPPER]

piperazine (pɪˈpɛrəˌziːn, -zɪn) *n* a white crystalline deliquescent heterocyclic nitrogen compound used as an insecticide, corrosion inhibitor, and veterinary anthelmintic. Formula: $C_4H_{10}N_2$

piperidine (pɪˈpɛrɪˌdiːn, -dɪn) *n* a colourless liquid heterocyclic compound with a peppery ammoniacal odour: used in making rubbers and curing epoxy resins. Formula: $C_5H_{11}N$

piperine (ˈpɪpəˌraɪn, -rɪn) *n* a white crystalline insoluble alkaloid that is the active ingredient of pepper, used as a flavouring and as an insecticide. Formula: $C_{17}H_{19}NO_3$ [C19 from Latin *piper* PEPPER]

pipe roll *n history* an annual record of the accounts of a sheriff or other minister of the crown kept at the British Exchequer from the 12th to the 19th centuries. Also called: **the Great Roll of the Exchequer** [C17 from PIPE[1] and ROLL; perhaps from documents being rolled into a pipe shape]

piperonal (ˈpɪpərəʊˌnæl) *n* a white fragrant aldehyde used in flavourings, perfumery, and suntan lotions. Formula: $C_8H_6O_3$. Also called: **heliotropin**

pipes of Pan *pl n* another term for **panpipes**

pipestone (ˈpaɪpˌstəʊn) *n* a variety of consolidated red clay used by North American Indians to make tobacco pipes

pipette (pɪˈpɛt) *n* **1** a calibrated glass tube drawn to a fine bore at one end, filled by sucking liquid into the bulb, and used to transfer or measure known volumes of liquid ▷ *vb* **2** (*tr*) to transfer or measure out (a liquid) using a pipette [C19 via French: little pipe, from *pipe* PIPE[1]]

pipe up *vb* (*intr, adverb*) **1** to commence singing or playing a musical instrument: *the band piped up* **2** to speak up, esp in a shrill voice

pipewort (ˈpaɪpˌwɜːt) *n* a perennial plant, *Eriocaulon septangulare*, of wet places in W Republic of Ireland, the Scottish Hebrides, and the eastern US, having a twisted flower stalk and a greenish-grey scaly flower head: family *Eriocaulaceae*

pipi (ˈpɪpiː) *n, pl* **pipi** *or* **pipis** any of various shellfishes, esp *Plebidonax deltoides* of Australia or *Mesodesma novae-zelandiae* of New Zealand [Māori]

piping (ˈpaɪpɪŋ) *n* **1** pipes collectively, esp pipes formed into a connected system, as in the plumbing of a house **2** a cord of icing, whipped cream, etc, often used to decorate desserts and cakes **3** a thin strip of covered cord or material, used to edge hems, etc **4** the sound of a pipe or a set of bagpipes **5** the art or technique of playing a pipe or bagpipes **6** a shrill voice or sound, esp a whistling sound ▷ *adj* **7** making a shrill sound **8** *archaic* relating to the pipe (associated with peace), as opposed to martial instruments, such as the fife or trumpet ▷ *adv* **9** **piping hot** extremely hot

pipistrelle (ˌpɪpɪˈstrɛl) *n* any of numerous small brownish insectivorous bats of the genus *Pipistrellus*, occurring in most parts of the world: family *Vespertilionidae* [C18 via French from Italian *pipistrello*, from Latin *vespertīliō* a bat, from *vesper* evening, because of its nocturnal habits]

pipit (ˈpɪpɪt) *n* any of various songbirds of the genus *Anthus* and related genera, having brownish speckled plumage and a long tail: family *Motacillidae*. Also called: **titlark** [C18 probably of imitative origin]

pipiwharauroa (ˈpiːpiːˌfærəuːˌrɔːə) *n NZ* a Pacific migratory bird with a metallic green-gold plumage. Also called: **shining cuckoo**

pipkin (ˈpɪpkɪn) *n* **1** a small metal or earthenware vessel **2** another name for **piggin** [C16 perhaps a diminutive of PIPE[2]; see -KIN]

pippin (ˈpɪpɪn) *n* **1** any of several varieties of eating apple with a rounded oblate shape **2** the seed of any of these fruits [C13 from Old French *pepin*, of uncertain origin]

pipsissewa (pɪpˈsɪsəwə) *n* any of several ericaceous plants of the Asian and American genus *Chimaphila*, having jagged evergreen leaves and white or pinkish flowers. Also called: **wintergreen** [C19 from Cree *pipisisikweu*, literally: it breaks it into pieces, so called because it was believed to be efficacious in treating bladder stones]

pipsqueak (ˈpɪpˌskwiːk) *n informal* a person or thing that is insignificant or contemptible [C20 from PIP[2] + SQUEAK]

piquant (ˈpiːkənt, -kɑːnt) *adj* **1** having an agreeably pungent or tart taste **2** lively or stimulating to the mind [C16 from French (literally: prickling), from *piquer* to prick, goad; see PIQUE[1]] > ˈ**piquancy** *or less commonly* ˈ**piquantness** *n* > ˈ**piquantly** *adv*

pique[1] (piːk) *n* **1** a feeling of resentment or irritation, as from having one's pride wounded ▷ *vb* **piques, piquing, piqued** (*tr*) **2** to cause to feel resentment or irritation **3** to excite or arouse **4** (foll by *on* or *upon*) to pride or congratulate (oneself) [C16 from French, from *piquer* to prick, sting; see PICK[1]]

pique[2] (piːk) *piquet* ▷ *n* **1** a score of 30 points made by a player from a combination of cards held before play begins and from play while his opponent's score is nil ▷ *vb* **2** to score a pique (against) [C17 from French *pic*, of uncertain origin]

piqué (ˈpiːkeɪ) *n* a close-textured fabric of cotton,

silk, or spun rayon woven with lengthwise ribs [c19 from French *piqué* pricked, from *piquer* to prick]

piquet (pɪˈkɛt, -ˈkeɪ) *n* a card game for two people playing with a reduced pack and scoring points for card combinations and tricks won [c17 from French, of unknown origin; compare PIQUE²]

piquillo (Spanish piˈkiʎo) *n, pl* **-quillos** a variety of sweet red pepper grown in the Ebro River Valley in N Spain [c21 Spanish]

Pir (pɪr) *n* a title given to Sufi masters [Persian]

piracy (ˈpaɪrəsɪ) *n, pl* **-cies** 1 *Brit* robbery on the seas within admiralty jurisdiction 2 a felony, such as robbery or hijacking, committed aboard a ship or aircraft 3 the unauthorized use or appropriation of patented or copyrighted material, ideas, etc [c16 from Anglo-Latin *pirātia*, from Late Greek *peirāteia*; see PIRATE]

Piraeus or **Peiraeus** (paɪˈriːəs, pɪˈreɪ-) *n* a port in SE Greece, adjoining Athens: the country's chief port; founded in the 5th century BC as the port of Athens. Pop: 169 622 (1991). Modern Greek name: Piraiévs (ˌpɪrɛˈɛfs)

piragua (pɪˈrɑːgwə, -ˈræg-) *n* another word for **pirogue** [c17 via Spanish from Carib: dugout canoe]

piranha or **piraña** (pɪˈrɑːnjə) *n* any of various small freshwater voracious fishes of the genus *Serrasalmus* and related genera, of tropical America, having strong jaws and sharp teeth: family *Characidae* (characins) [c19 via Portuguese from Tupi: fish with teeth, from *pirá* fish + *sainha* tooth]

pirate (ˈpaɪrɪt) *n* 1 a person who commits piracy 2 a a vessel used by pirates b (*as modifier*): *a pirate ship* 3 a person who illicitly uses or appropriates someone else's literary, artistic, or other work 4 a a person or group of people who broadcast illegally b (*as modifier*): *a pirate radio station* ▷ *vb* 5 (*tr*) to use, appropriate, or reproduce (artistic work, ideas, etc) illicitly [c15 from Latin *pīrāta*, from Greek *peirātēs* one who attacks, from *peira* an attempt, attack] > **piratical** (paɪˈrætɪkəl) or **piˈratic** *adj* > **piˈratically** *adv*

piri-piri (ˌpɪrɪˈpɪrɪ) *n* a hot sauce, of Portuguese colonial origin, made from red chilli peppers [from a Bantu language: literally, pepper]

Pirithoüs (paɪˈrɪθəʊəs) *n Greek myth* a prince of the Lapiths, who accomplished many great deeds with his friend Theseus

pirn (pɜːn; *Scot* pɪrn) *n Scot* 1 a reel or bobbin 2 (in weaving) the spool of a shuttle 3 a fishing reel [c15 of uncertain origin]

pirog (pɪˈrɒg) *n, pl* **-rogi** (-ˈrɒgɪ) a large pie filled with meat, vegetables, etc [from Russian: pie]

pirogue (pɪˈrəʊg) or **piragua** *n* any of various kinds of dugout canoes [c17 via French from Spanish PIRAGUA]

pirouette (ˌpɪrʊˈɛt) *n* 1 a body spin, esp in dancing, on the toes or the ball of the foot ▷ *vb* 2 (*intr*) to perform a pirouette [c18 from French, from Old French *pirouet* spinning top; related to Italian *pirolo* little peg]

pirozhki or **piroshki** (pɪˈrɒʃkɪ) *pl n, sing* **pirozhok** (ˈpɪrəˌʒɒk) small triangular pastries filled with meat, vegetables, etc [c20 from Russian, from *pirozhók*, diminutive of PIROG]

Pisa (ˈpiːzə; *Italian* ˈpiːsa) *n* a city in Tuscany, NW Italy, near the mouth of the River Arno: flourishing maritime republic (11th–12th centuries), contains a university (1343), a cathedral (1063), and the Leaning Tower (begun in 1174 and about 5 m (17 ft) from perpendicular); tourism. Pop: 89 694 (2001)

pis aller *French* (piz ale) *n* a last resort; stopgap [literally: (at) the worst going]

piscary (ˈpɪskərɪ) *n, pl* **-ries** 1 a place where fishing takes place 2 the right to fish in certain waters [c15 from Latin *piscārius* fishing, from *piscis* a fish]

piscatorial (ˌpɪskəˈtɔːrɪəl) or **piscatory** (ˈpɪskətərɪ, -trɪ) *adj* 1 of or relating to fish, fishing, or fishermen 2 devoted to fishing [c19 from Latin *piscātōrius*, from *piscātor* fisherman]

> **ˌpiscaˈtorially** *adv*

Pisces (ˈpaɪsiːz, ˈpɪ-) *n, Latin genitive* Piscium (ˈpaɪsɪəm) 1 *astronomy* a faint extensive zodiacal constellation lying between Aquarius and Aries on the ecliptic 2 *astrology* a Also called: the Fishes the twelfth sign of the zodiac, symbol ♓, having a mutable water classification and ruled by the planets Jupiter and Neptune. The sun is in this sign between about Feb 19 and March 20 b a person born when the sun is in this sign 3 a a taxonomic group that comprises all fishes. See fish (sense 1) b a taxonomic group that comprises the bony fishes only. See teleost ▷ *adj* 4 *astrology* born under or characteristic of Pisces ▷ Also (for senses 2b, 4): Piscean (ˈpaɪsɪən) [c14 Latin: the fishes]

pisci- *combining form* fish: *pisciculture* [from Latin *piscis*]

pisciculture (ˈpɪsɪˌkʌltʃə) *n* the rearing and breeding of fish under controlled conditions > **ˌpisciˈcultural** *adj* > **ˌpisciˈculturally** *adv* > **ˌpisciˈculturist** *n, adj*

piscina (pɪˈsiːnə) *n, pl* **-nae** (-niː) or **-nas** *RC Church* a stone basin, with a drain, in a church or sacristy where water used at Mass is poured away [c16 from Latin: fish pond, from *piscis* a fish] > **piscinal** (ˈpɪsɪnəl) *adj*

piscine (ˈpɪsaɪn) *adj* of, relating to, or resembling a fish

Piscis Austrinus (ˈpɪsɪs ɒˈstraɪnəs, ˈpaɪ-) *n, Latin genitive* Piscis Austrini (ɒˈstraɪnaɪ) a small constellation in the S hemisphere lying between Aquarius and Grus and containing the first-magnitude star Fomalhaut [Latin: the Southern Fish]

piscivorous (pɪˈsɪvərəs) *adj* feeding on fish: *piscivorous birds*

pisé (ˈpiːzeɪ) *n* rammed earth or clay used to make floors or walls. Also called: **pisé de terre** [c18 French, from past participle of *piser*, from Latin *pisare* to beat, pound]

Pisgah (ˈpɪzgə) *n Mount Old Testament* the mountain slopes to the northeast of the Dead Sea, from one of which, Mount Nebo, Moses viewed Canaan

pish (pʃ, pɪʃ) *interj* 1 an exclamation of impatience or contempt ▷ *vb* 2 to make this exclamation at (someone or something)

pishogue (pɪˈʃəʊg) *n Irish* sorcery; witchcraft [from Irish *piseog, pisreog*]

Pishpek (pɪʃˈpɛk) *n* a variant transliteration of the Kyrgyz name for **Bishkek**

pisiform (ˈpɪsɪˌfɔːm) *adj* 1 *zoology, botany* resembling a pea ▷ *n* 2 a small pealike bone on the ulnar side of the carpus [c18 via New Latin from Latin *pīsum* pea + *forma* shape]

pismire (ˈpɪsˌmaɪə) *n* an archaic or dialect word for an **ant** [c14 (literally: urinating ant, from the odour of formic acid characteristic of an ant hill): from PISS + obsolete *mire* ant, of Scandinavian origin; compare Old Norse *maurr*, Middle Low German *mire* ant]

pisolite (ˈpaɪsəʊˌlaɪt) *n* a sedimentary rock, commonly a limestone, consisting of pea-sized concentric formations (**pisoliths**) within a fine matrix [c18 from New Latin *pisolithus* pea stone, from Greek *pisos* pea + *lithos* -LITE] > **pisolitic** (ˌpaɪsəʊˈlɪtɪk) *adj*

piss (pɪs) *slang* ▷ *vb* 1 (*intr*) to urinate 2 (*tr*) to discharge as or in one's urine: *to piss blood* ▷ *n* 3 an act of urinating 4 urine 5 *Austral* beer 6 on the piss drinking alcohol, esp in large quantities 7 piece of piss something easily obtained or achieved 8 take the piss to tease or make fun of someone or something 9 piss all over to be far superior to: *a version that pisses all over the original* [c13 from Old French *pisser*, probably of imitative origin]

piss about or **around** *vb* (*adverb*) *slang* 1 (*intr*) to behave in a casual or silly way 2 (*tr*) to waste the time of

pissant (ˈpɪsænt) *US informal* ▷ *n* 1 an

insignificant or contemptible person ▷ *adj* 2 insignificant or contemptible [c17 from PISS + ANT]

piss artist *n slang* 1 a boastful or incompetent person 2 a person who drinks heavily and gets drunk frequently

pissed (pɪst) *adj* 1 *Brit, Austral, and NZ slang* intoxicated; drunk 2 *US slang* annoyed, irritated, or disappointed

pisser (ˈpɪsə) *n slang* 1 someone or something that pisses 2 a disappointment or nuisance

pisshead (ˈpɪsˌhɛd) *n slang* a drunkard

piss off *vb* (*adverb*) *slang* 1 (*tr; often passive*) to annoy, irritate, or disappoint 2 (*intr*) *chiefly Brit* to go away; depart, often used to dismiss a person

pissoir (ˈpiːswɑː; *French* piswar) *n* a public urinal, usu. enclosed by a wall or screen [French, from *pisser* to urinate]

piss-poor *adj slang* of a contemptibly low standard or quality; pathetic

piss-up *n slang, chiefly Brit* a drinking session

pistachio (pɪˈstɑːʃɪˌəʊ) *n, pl* **-os** 1 an anacardiaceous tree, *Pistacia vera*, of the Mediterranean region and W Asia, with small hard-shelled nuts 2 Also called: **pistachio nut** the nut of this tree, having an edible green kernel 3 the sweet flavour of the pistachio nut, used esp in ice creams ▷ *adj* 4 of a yellowish-green colour [c16 via Italian and Latin from Greek *pistakion* pistachio nut, from *pistakē* pistachio tree, from Persian *pistah*]

pistareen (ˌpɪstəˈriːn) *n* a Spanish coin, used in the US and the West Indies until the 18th century [c18 perhaps changed from PESETA]

piste (piːst) *n* 1 a trail, slope, or course for skiing 2 a rectangular area for fencing bouts [c18 via Old French from Old Italian *pista*, from *pistare* to tread down]

pistil (ˈpɪstɪl) *n* the female reproductive part of a flower, consisting of one or more separate or fused carpels; gynoecium [c18 from Latin *pistillum* PESTLE]

pistillate (ˈpɪstɪlɪt, -ˌleɪt) *adj* (of plants) 1 having pistils but no anthers 2 having or producing pistils

Pistoia (*Italian* pisˈtɔːja) *n* a city in N Italy, in N Tuscany: scene of the defeat and death of Catiline in 62 BC Pop: 84 274 (2001)

pistol (ˈpɪstəl) *n* 1 a short-barrelled handgun 2 hold a pistol to a person's head to threaten a person in order to force him to do what one wants ▷ *vb* **-tols, -tolling, -tolled** or *US* **-tols, -toling, -toled** 3 (*tr*) to shoot with a pistol [c16 from French *pistole*, from German, from Czech *píšťala* pistol, pipe; related to Russian *pischal* shepherd's pipes]

pistole (pɪˈstəʊl) *n* any of various gold coins of varying value, formerly used in Europe [c16 from Old French, shortened from *pistolet*, literally: little PISTOL]

pistoleer (ˌpɪstəˈlɪə) *n obsolete* a person, esp a soldier, who is armed with or fires a pistol

pistol grip *n* a a handle shaped like the butt of a pistol b (*as modifier*): *a pistol-grip camera*

pistol-whip *vb* **-whips, -whipping, -whipped** (*tr*) to beat or strike with a pistol barrel

piston (ˈpɪstən) *n* a disc or cylindrical part that slides to and fro in a hollow cylinder. In an internal-combustion engine it is forced to move by the expanding gases in the cylinder head and is attached by a pivoted connecting rod to a crankshaft or flywheel, thus converting reciprocating motion into rotation [c18 via French from Old Italian *pistone*, from *pistare* to pound, grind, from Latin *pinsere* to crush, beat]

piston ring *n* a split ring, usually made of cast iron, that fits into a groove on the rim of a piston to provide a spring-loaded seal against the cylinder wall

piston rod *n* 1 the rod that connects the piston of a reciprocating steam engine to the crosshead 2 a less common name for a **connecting rod**

p

piston slap *n* the characteristic sound of a seriously worn piston in a cylinder (usually of the engine of a motor car)

pit[1] (pɪt) *n* **1** a large, usually deep opening in the ground **2 a** a mine or excavation with a shaft, esp for coal **b** the shaft in a mine **c** (*as modifier*): *pit pony; pit prop* **3** a concealed danger or difficulty **4 the pit** hell **5** Also called: **orchestra pit** the area that is occupied by the orchestra in a theatre, located in front of the stage **6** an enclosure for fighting animals or birds, esp gamecocks **7** *anatomy* **a** a small natural depression on the surface of a body, organ, structure, or part; fossa **b** the floor of any natural bodily cavity: *the pit of the stomach* **8** *pathol* a small indented scar at the site of a former pustule; pockmark **9** any of various small areas in a plant cell wall that remain unthickened when the rest of the cell becomes lignified, esp the vascular tissue **10** a working area at the side of a motor-racing track for servicing or refuelling vehicles **11** a section on the floor of a commodity exchange devoted to a special line of trading **12** a rowdy card game in which players bid for commodities **13** an area of sand or other soft material at the end of a long-jump approach, behind the bar of a pole vault, etc, on which an athlete may land safely **14** the ground floor of the auditorium of a theatre **15** *Brit* a slang word for **bed** (sense 1) *or* **bedroom** (sense 1) **16** another word for **pitfall** (sense 2) ▷ *vb* **pits, pitting, pitted 17** (*tr; often foll by against*) to match in opposition, esp as antagonists **18** to mark or become marked with pits **19** (*tr*) to place or bury in a pit ▷ See also **pits** [Old English *pytt,* from Latin *puteus;* compare Old French *pet,* Old High German *pfuzzi*]

pit[2] (pɪt) *chiefly US and Canadian* ▷ *n* **1** the stone of a cherry, plum, etc ▷ *vb* **pits, pitting, pitted 2** (*tr*) to extract the stone from (a fruit) [C19 from Dutch: kernel; compare PITH]

pit[3] (pɪt) *vb* a Scot word for **put**

pita (ˈpiːtə) *n* **1** any of several agave plants yielding a strong fibre. See also **istle 2** a species of pineapple, *Ananas magdalenae,* the leaves of which yield a white fibre **3** Also called: **pita fibre** the fibre obtained from any of these plants, used in making cordage and paper [C17 via Spanish from Quechua]

pitahaya (ˌpɪtəˈhaɪə) *n* **1** any giant cactus of Central America and the SW United States, esp the saguaro **2** Also called: **dragon fruit** the edible red pulpy fruit of such cacti, which has a mild sweet flavour [C18 Mexican Spanish, from Haitian Creole]

pitapat (ˌpɪtəˈpæt) *adv* **1** with quick light taps or beats ▷ *vb* **-pats, -patting, -patted 2** (*intr*) to make quick light taps or beats ▷ *n* **3** such taps or beats

pit bull terrier *n* a dog resembling the Staffordshire bull terrier but somewhat larger: developed for dog-fighting; it is not recognized by kennel clubs and is regarded as dangerous. It is not allowed in some countries, including the UK. Also called: **American pit bull terrier**

Pitcairn Island (pɪtˈkɛən, ˈpɪtkɛən) *n* an island in the S Pacific: forms with the islands of Ducie, Henderson and Oeno (all uninhabited) a UK Overseas Territory; Pitcairn itself was uninhabited until the landing in 1790 of the mutineers of H.M.S. *Bounty* and their Tahitian companions. Pop: 47 (2004 est). Area: 4.6 sq km (1.75 sq miles)

pitch[1] (pɪtʃ) *vb* **1** to hurl or throw (something); cast; fling **2** (*usually tr*) to set up (a camp, tent, etc) **3** (*tr*) to place or thrust (a stake, spear, etc) into the ground **4** (*intr*) to move vigorously or irregularly to and fro or up and down **5** (*tr*) to aim or fix (something) at a particular level, position, style, etc: *if you advertise privately you may pitch the price too low* **6** (*tr*) to aim to sell (a product) to a specified market or on a specified basis **7** (*intr*) to slope downwards **8** (*intr*) to fall forwards or downwards **9** (*intr*) (of a vessel) to dip and raise its bow and stern alternately **10** *cricket* to bowl (a ball) so that it bounces on a certain part of the wicket, or (of a ball) to bounce on a certain part of the wicket **11** (*intr*) (of a missile, aircraft, etc) to deviate from a stable flight attitude by movement of the longitudinal axis about the lateral axis. Compare **yaw** (sense 1), **roll** (sense 14) **12** (*tr*) (in golf) to hit (a ball) steeply into the air, esp with backspin to minimize roll **13** (*tr*) *music* **a** to sing or play accurately (a note, interval, etc) **b** (*usually passive*) (of a wind instrument) to specify or indicate its basic key or harmonic series by its size, manufacture, etc **14** (*tr*) *cards* to lead (a suit) and so determine trumps for that trick **15** *baseball* **a** (*tr*) to throw (a baseball) to a batter **b** (*intr*) to act as pitcher in a baseball game **16** *Southwest English dialect* (used with *it* as subject) to snow without the settled snow melting **17 in there pitching** *US and Canadian informal* taking part with enthusiasm **18 pitch a tale** (*or* **yarn**) to tell a story, usually of a fantastic nature ▷ *n* **19** the degree of elevation or depression **20 a** the angle of descent of a downward slope **b** such a slope **21** the extreme height or depth **22** *mountaineering* a section of a route between two belay points, sometimes equal to the full length of the rope but often shorter **23** the degree of slope of a roof, esp when expressed as a ratio of height to span **24** the distance between corresponding points on adjacent members of a body of regular form, esp the distance between teeth on a gearwheel or between threads on a screw thread **25** the distance between regularly spaced objects such as rivets, bolts, etc **26** the pitching motion of a ship, missile, etc **27 a** the distance a propeller advances in one revolution, assuming no slip **b** the blade angle of a propeller or rotor **28** the distance between the back rest of a seat in a passenger aircraft and the back of the seat in front of it **29** *music* **a** the auditory property of a note that is conditioned by its frequency relative to other notes: *high pitch; low pitch* **b** an absolute frequency assigned to a specific note, fixing the relative frequencies of all other notes. The fundamental frequencies of the notes A–G, in accordance with the frequency A = 440 hertz, were internationally standardized and accepted in 1939. See also **concert pitch** (sense 1), **international pitch 30** *cricket* the rectangular area between the stumps, 22 yards long and 10 feet wide; the wicket **31** *geology* the inclination of the axis of an anticline or syncline or of a stratum or vein from the horizontal **32** another name for **seven-up 33** the act or manner of pitching a ball, as in cricket **34** *chiefly Brit* a vendor's station, esp on a pavement **35** *slang* a persuasive sales talk, esp one routinely repeated **36** *chiefly Brit* (in many sports) the field of play **37** Also called: **pitch shot** *golf* an approach shot in which the ball is struck in a high arc **38 make a pitch for** *US and Canadian slang* **a** to give verbal support to **b** to attempt to attract (someone) sexually or romantically **39 queer someone's pitch** *Brit informal* to upset someone's plans ▷ See also **pitch in, pitch into, pitch on** [C13 *picchen;* possibly related to PICK[1]]

pitch[2] (pɪtʃ) *n* **1** any of various heavy dark viscid substances obtained as a residue from the distillation of tars. See also **coal-tar pitch 2** any of various similar substances, such as asphalt, occurring as natural deposits **3** any of various similar substances obtained by distilling certain organic substances so that they are incompletely carbonized **4** crude turpentine obtained as sap from pine trees ▷ Related adjective: **piceous** ▷ *vb* **5** (*tr*) to apply pitch to (something) [Old English *pic,* from Latin *pix*]

pitch accent *n* (in languages such as Ancient Greek or modern Swedish) an accent in which emphatic syllables are pronounced on a higher musical pitch relative to other syllables. Also called: **tonic accent**

pitch and putt *n* a type of miniature golf in which the holes are usually between 50 to 100 metres in length

pitch-and-toss *n* a game of skill and chance in which the player who pitches a coin nearest to a mark has the first chance to toss all the coins, winning those that land heads up

pitchbend (ˈpɪtʃˌbɛnd) *n* an electronic device that enables a player to bend the pitch of a note being sounded on a synthesizer, usually with a pitch wheel, strip, or lever

pitch-black *adj* **1** extremely dark; unlit: *the room was pitch-black* **2** of a deep black colour

pitchblende (ˈpɪtʃˌblɛnd) *n* a blackish mineral that is a type of uraninite and occurs in veins, frequently associated with silver: the principal source of uranium and radium. Formula: UO_2 [C18 partial translation of German *Pechblende,* from *Pech* PITCH[2] (from its black colour) + BLENDE]

pitch circle *n* an imaginary circle passing through the teeth of a gearwheel, concentric with the gearwheel, and having a radius that would enable it to be in contact with a similar circle around a mating gearwheel

pitch-cone angle *n* (in a bevel gear) the apex angle of the truncated cone (pitch cone) which forms the reference surface on which the teeth of a bevel gear are cut

pitch cylinder *n* an imaginary cylinder passing through, and coaxial with, the threads of a screw so that its intersection with opposite flanks of any groove is equal to half the thread pitch

pitch-dark *adj* extremely or completely dark

pitched battle *n* **1** a battle ensuing from the deliberate choice of time and place, engaging all the planned resources **2** any fierce encounter, esp one with large numbers

pitcher[1] (ˈpɪtʃə) *n* **1** a large jug, usually rounded with a narrow neck and often of earthenware, used mainly for holding water **2** *botany* any of the urn-shaped leaves of the pitcher plant [C13 from Old French *pichier,* from Medieval Latin *picārium,* variant of *bicārium* BEAKER]

pitcher[2] (ˈpɪtʃə) *n* **1** *baseball* the player on the fielding team who pitches the ball to the batter **2** a granite stone or sett used in paving

pitcher plant *n* any of various insectivorous plants of the genera *Sarracenia*, *Darlingtonia*, *Nepenthes*, and *Cephalotus*, having leaves modified to form pitcher-like organs that attract and trap insects, which are then digested. See also **huntsman's-cup**

pitchfork (ˈpɪtʃˌfɔːk) *n* **1** a long-handled fork with two or three long curved tines for lifting, turning, or tossing hay ▷ *vb* (*tr*) **2** to use a pitchfork on (something) **3** to thrust (someone) unwillingly into a position

pitch in *vb* (*intr, adverb*) **1** to cooperate or contribute **2** to begin energetically

pitching tool *n* a masonry chisel for rough work

pitching wedge *n golf* a club with a face angle of more than 50°, used for short, lofted pitch shots

pitch into *vb* (*intr, preposition*) *informal* **1** to assail physically or verbally **2** to get on with doing (something)

Pitch Lake *n* a deposit of natural asphalt in the Caribbean, in SW Trinidad. Area: 46 hectares (114 acres)

pitchman (ˈpɪtʃmən) *n, pl* **-men** *US and Canadian* **1** an itinerant pedlar of small merchandise who operates from a stand at a fair, etc **2** any high-pressure salesman or advertiser

pitchometer (pɪtʃˈɒmɪtə) *n* an instrument embodying a clinometer, for measuring the pitch of a ship's propeller

pitch on *or* **upon** *vb* (*intr, preposition*) to determine or decide

pitch pine *n* **1** any of various coniferous trees of the genus *Pinus*, esp *P. rigida*, of North America, having red-brown bark and long lustrous light brown cones: valued as a source of turpentine and pitch **2** the wood of any of these trees

pitch pipe *n* a small pipe, esp one having a reed

like a harmonica, that sounds a note or notes of standard frequency. It is used for establishing the correct starting note for unaccompanied singing

pitchstone ('pɪtʃˌstəʊn) *n* a dark glassy acid volcanic rock similar in composition to granite, usually intruded as dykes, sills, etc [c18 translation of German *Pechstein*]

pitchy ('pɪtʃɪ) *adj* **pitchier, pitchiest 1** full of or covered with pitch **2** resembling pitch > 'pitchiness *n*

piteous ('pɪtɪəs) *adj* **1** exciting or deserving pity **2** *archaic* having or expressing pity > 'piteously *adv* > 'piteousness *n*

pitfall ('pɪtˌfɔːl) *n* **1** an unsuspected difficulty or danger **2** a trap in the form of a concealed pit, designed to catch men or wild animals [Old English *pytt* PIT¹ + *fealle* trap]

pith (pɪθ) *n* **1** the soft fibrous tissue lining the inside of the rind in fruits such as the orange and grapefruit **2** the essential or important part, point, etc **3** weight; substance **4** Also called: **medulla** *botany* the central core of unspecialized cells surrounded by conducting tissue in stems **5** the soft central part of a bone, feather, etc ▷ *vb* (*tr*) **6** to destroy the brain and spinal cord of (a laboratory animal) by piercing or severing **7** to kill (animals) by severing the spinal cord **8** to remove the pith from (a plant) [Old English *pitha*; compare Middle Low German *pedik*, Middle Dutch *pitt(e)*]

pithead ('pɪtˌhɛd) *n* the top of a mine shaft and the buildings, hoisting gear, etc, situated around it

pithecanthropus (ˌpɪθɪkænˈθrəʊpəs, -ˈkænθrə-) *n, pl* -pi (-ˌpaɪ) any primitive apelike man of the former genus *Pithecanthropus,* now included in the genus *Homo.* See **Java man, Peking man** [c19 New Latin, from Greek *pithēkos* ape + *anthrōpos* man] > ˌpithe'canthroˌpine *or* ˌpithe'canthroˌpoid *adj*

pith helmet *n* a lightweight hat made of pith that protects the wearer from the sun. Also called: **topee, topi**

pithos ('pɪθɒs, 'paɪ-) *n, pl* -thoi (-θɔɪ) a large ceramic container for oil or grain [from Greek]

pithy ('pɪθɪ) *adj* **pithier, pithiest 1** terse and full of meaning or substance **2** of, resembling, or full of pith > 'pithily *adv* > 'pithiness *n*

pitiable ('pɪtɪəbəl) *adj* exciting or deserving pity or contempt > 'pitiableness *n* > 'pitiably *adv*

pitiful ('pɪtɪfʊl) *adj* **1** arousing or deserving pity **2** arousing or deserving contempt **3** *archaic* full of pity or compassion > 'pitifully *adv* > 'pitifulness *n*

pitiless ('pɪtɪlɪs) *adj* having or showing little or no pity or mercy > 'pitilessly *adv* > 'pitilessness *n*

Pitjantjatjara (ˌpɪtʃəntʃəˈtʃærə) *or* **Pitjantjara** (ˌpɪtʃənˈdʒærə) *n* **1** (*pl* -ra *or* -ras) an Aboriginal people of the desert area of South Australia **2** the language of this people

pitman ('pɪtmən) *n, pl* -men *chiefly Scot and northern English* a person who works down a mine, esp a coal miner

piton ('piːtɒn; *French* pitɔ̃) *n mountaineering* a metal spike that may be driven into a crevice of rock or into ice and used to secure a rope [c20 from French: ringbolt]

Pitot-static tube ('piːtəʊˈstætɪk) *n* combined Pitot and static pressure tubes placed in a fluid flow to measure the total and static pressures. The difference in pressures, as recorded on a manometer or airspeed indicator, indicates the fluid velocity. Also called: **Pitot tube**

Pitot tube ('piːtəʊ) *n* **1** a small tube placed in a fluid with its open end upstream and the other end connected to a manometer. It measures the total pressure of the fluid **2** short for **Pitot-static tube,** esp one fitted to an aircraft [c18 named after its inventor, Henri *Pitot* (1695–1771), French physicist]

pits (pɪts) *pl n slang* **the** the worst possible person, place, or thing [c20 perhaps shortened from *armpits*]

pitsaw ('pɪtˌsɔː) *n* a large saw formerly used for cutting logs into planks, operated by two men, one standing on top of the log and the other in a pit underneath it

pit-sawn *adj* (of timber, esp formerly) sawn into planks by hand in a saw-pit

pit stop *n* **1** *motor racing* a brief stop made at a pit by a racing car for repairs, refuelling, etc **2** *informal* any stop made during a car journey for refreshment, rest, or refuelling

pitta¹ ('pɪtə) *n* another name for **pitta bread**

pitta² ('pɪtə) *n* any of various small brightly coloured ground-dwelling tropical birds of the genus *Pitta* [c19 from Telugu]

pitta bread *or* **pitta** ('pɪtə) *n* a flat rounded slightly leavened bread, originally from the Middle East, with a hollow inside like a pocket, which can be filled with food. Also called: **Arab bread, Greek bread** [from Modern Greek: a cake]

pittance ('pɪtⁿns) *n* a small amount or portion, esp a meagre allowance of money [c16 from Old French *pietance* ration, ultimately from Latin *pietās* duty]

pitter-patter ('pɪtəˌpætə) *n* **1** the sound of light rapid taps or pats, as of raindrops ▷ *vb* **2** (*intr*) to make such a sound ▷ *adv* **3** with such a sound: *the rain fell pitter-patter on the window*

pittosporum (pɪˈtɒspərəm) *n* any of various trees and shrubs of the *Pittosporum* genus of Australasia, Asia, and Africa, having small fragrant flowers [New Latin, from Greek *pitta* pitch (from the resinous coating of the seeds) + *spora* seed]

Pittsburgh ('pɪtsbɜːg) *n* a port in SW Pennsylvania, at the confluence of the Allegheny and Monongahela Rivers, which form the Ohio River: settled around Fort Pitt in 1758; developed rapidly with the discovery of iron deposits and one of the world's richest coalfields; the largest river port in the US and an important industrial centre, formerly with large steel mills. Pop: 325 337 (2003 est)

Pitt Street Farmer *n Austral slang* another name for **Collins Street Farmer** [c20 after a principal business street in Sydney, Australia]

pituitary (pɪˈtjuːɪtərɪ, -trɪ) *n, pl* -taries **1** See **pituitary gland, pituitary extract** ▷ *adj* **2** of or relating to the pituitary gland **3** *archaic* of or relating to phlegm or mucus [c17 from Late Latin *pītuītārius* slimy, from *pītuīta* phlegm]

pituitary extract *n* a preparation of the pituitary gland, used in medicine for the therapeutic effects of its hormones

pituitary gland *or* **body** *n* the master endocrine gland, attached by a stalk to the base of the brain. Its two lobes (see **adenohypophysis** and **neurohypophysis**) secrete hormones affecting skeletal growth, development of the sex glands, and the functioning of the other endocrine glands. Also called: **hypophysis, hypophysis cerebri**

pituri ('pɪtʃərɪ) *n, pl* -ris an Australian solanaceous shrub, *Duboisia hopwoodii,* the leaves of which are the source of a narcotic used by the native Australians [c19 from a native Australian name]

pit viper *n* any venomous snake of the New World family *Crotalidae,* having a heat-sensitive organ in a pit on each side of the head: includes the rattlesnakes

pity ('pɪtɪ) *n, pl* pities **1** sympathy or sorrow felt for the sufferings of another **2** have (*or* take) pity on to have sympathy or show mercy for **3** something that causes regret or pity **4** an unfortunate chance: *what a pity you can't come* **5** more's the pity it is highly regrettable (that) ▷ *vb* pities, pitying, pitied **6** (*tr*) to feel pity for [c13 from Old French *pité,* from Latin *pietās* duty] > 'pitying *adj* > 'pityingly *adv*

pityriasis (ˌpɪtəˈraɪəsɪs) *n* **1** any of a group of skin diseases characterized by the shedding of dry flakes of skin **2** a similar skin disease of certain domestic animals [c17 via New Latin from Greek *pituriasis* scurfiness, from *pituron* bran]

più (pjuː) *adv music* (*in combination*) more (quickly, softly, etc): *più allegro; più mosso; più lento* [Italian, from Latin *plus* more]

piupiu ('piːuːˌpiːuː) *n* a skirt made from the leaves of the New Zealand flax, worn by Māoris on ceremonial occasions [Māori]

Piura (*Spanish* 'pjura) *n* a city in NW Peru: the oldest colonial city in Peru, founded by Pizarro in 1532; commercial centre of an agricultural district. Pop: 357 000 (2005 est)

Piute ('paɪuːt, paɪ'uːt) *n* a variant spelling of **Paiute**

pivot ('pɪvət) *n* **1** a short shaft or pin supporting something that turns; fulcrum **2** the end of a shaft or arbor that terminates in a bearing **3** a person or thing upon which progress, success, etc, depends **4** the person or position from which a military formation takes its reference, as when altering position ▷ *vb* **5** (*tr*) to mount on or provide with a pivot or pivots **6** (*intr*) to turn on or as if on a pivot [c17 from Old French; perhaps related to Old Provençal *pua* tooth of a comb]

pivotal ('pɪvətəl) *adj* **1** of, involving, or acting as a pivot **2** of crucial importance > 'pivotally *adv*

pivot bridge *n* another name for **swing bridge**

pivot grammar *n psychol* a loose grammar said to govern two-word utterances by children

piwakawaka (piːwɑːkɑːwɑːkɑː) *n, pl* piwakawaka a New Zealand fantail, *Rhipidura Fuliginosa* [Māori]

pix¹ (pɪks) *pl n informal* photographs; prints

pix² (pɪks) *n* a less common spelling of **pyx**

pixel ('pɪksəl) *n* any of a number of very small picture elements that make up a picture, as on a visual display unit [c20 from *pix* pictures + *el(ement)*]

pixelation (ˌpɪksɪˈleɪʃən) *n* a video technique in which an image is blurred by being overlaid with a grid of squares, usually to disguise the identity of a person

pixie *or* **pixy** ('pɪksɪ) *n, pl* pixies (in folklore) a fairy or elf [c17 of obscure origin]

pixilated *or* **pixillated** ('pɪksɪˌleɪtɪd) *adj chiefly US* **1** eccentric or whimsical **2** *slang* drunk [c20 from PIXIE + -lated, as in stimulated, titillated, etc] > ˌpixiˈlation *or* ˌpixilˈlation *n*

pize (paɪz) *vb* (*tr*) *Yorkshire dialect* to strike (someone a blow) [of obscure origin]

pizz. *music abbreviation for* pizzicato

pizza ('piːtsə) *n* a dish of Italian origin consisting of a baked disc of dough covered with cheese and tomatoes, usually with the addition of mushrooms, anchovies, sausage, or ham [c20 from Italian, perhaps from Vulgar Latin *picea* (unattested), from Latin *piceus* relating to PITCH²; perhaps related to Modern Greek *pitta* cake]

pizzazz *or* **pizazz** (pəˈzæz) *n informal* an attractive combination of energy and style; sparkle, vitality, glamour. Also called: **pazzazz, pazazz, pzazz** [c20 origin obscure]

pizzeria (ˌpiːtsəˈriːə) *n* a place where pizzas are made, sold, or eaten [c20 from Italian, from PIZZA + -eria -ERY]

pizzicato (ˌpɪtsɪˈkɑːtəʊ) *music* ▷ *adj, adv* **1** (in music for the violin family) to be plucked with the finger ▷ *n* **2** the style or technique of playing a normally bowed stringed instrument in this manner [c19 from Italian: pinched, from *pizzicare* to twist, twang]

pizzle ('pɪzəl) *n archaic or dialect* the penis of an animal, esp a bull [c16 of Germanic origin; compare Low German *pēsel,* Flemish *pēzel,* Middle Dutch *pēze* sinew]

pk¹ *pl* pks *abbreviation for* **1** pack **2** park **3** peak

pk² *the internet domain name for* Pakistan

PK 1 *abbreviation for* psychokinesis **2** ▷ *international car registration for* Pakistan

pkg. *pl* pkgs *abbreviation for* package

pkt *abbreviation for* packet

PKU *abbreviation for* phenylketonuria

pl¹ *abbreviation for* **1** place **2** plate **3** plural

pl² *the internet domain name for* Poland

PL 1 (in transformational grammar) *abbreviation for* plural **2** ▷ *international car registration for* Poland

Pl. (in street names) *abbreviation for* Place

PL/1 *n* programming language 1: a high-level computer programming language designed for mathematical and scientific purposes [c20 *p(rogramming) l(anguage)* 1]

PLA *abbreviation for* Port of London Authority

plaas (plɑːs) *n South African* a farm [Afrikaans]

placable ('plækəbᵊl) *adj* easily placated or appeased [c15 via Old French from Latin *plācābilis*, from *plācāre* to appease; related to *placēre* to please] > ˌplacaˈbility *or* 'placableness *n* > 'placably *adv*

placard ('plækɑːd) *n* 1 a printed or written notice for public display; poster 2 a small plaque or card ▷ *vb* (*tr*) 3 to post placards on or in 4 to publicize or advertise by placards 5 to display as a placard [c15 from Old French *plaquart*, from *plaquier* to plate, lay flat; see PLAQUE]

placate (plə'keɪt) *vb* (*tr*) to pacify or appease [c17 from Latin *plācāre*; see PLACABLE] > pla'cation *n*

placatory (plə'keɪtərɪ, 'plækətərɪ, -trɪ) *or less commonly* **placative** (plə'keɪtɪv, 'plækətɪv) *adj* placating or intended to placate

place (pleɪs) *n* 1 a particular point or part of space or of a surface, esp that occupied by a person or thing 2 a geographical point, such as a town, city, etc 3 a position or rank in a sequence or order 4 a an open square lined with houses of a similar type in a city or town b (*capital when part of a street name*): *Grosvenor Place* 5 space or room 6 a house or living quarters 7 a country house with grounds 8 any building or area set aside for a specific purpose 9 a passage in a book, play, film, etc: *to lose one's place* 10 proper or appropriate position or time: *he still thinks a woman's place is in the home* 11 right or original position: *put it back in its place* 12 suitable, appropriate, or customary surroundings (esp in the phrases **out of place, in place**) 13 right, prerogative, or duty: *it is your place to give a speech* 14 appointment, position, or job: *a place at college* 15 position, condition, or state: *if I were in your place* 16 a a space or seat, as at a dining table b (*as modifier*): *place mat* 17 *maths* the relative position of a digit in a number. See also **decimal place** 18 any of the best times in a race 19 *horse racing* a *Brit* the first, second, or third position at the finish b *US and Canadian* the first or usually the second position at the finish c (*as modifier*): *a place bet* 20 *theatre* one of the three unities. See **unity** (sense 8) 21 *archaic* an important position, rank, or role 22 **all over the place** in disorder or disarray 23 **another place** *Brit parliamentary procedure* a (in the House of Commons) the House of Lords b (in the House of Lords) the House of Commons 24 **give place (to)** to make room (for) or be superseded (by) 25 **go places** *informal* a to travel b to become successful 26 **in place of** a instead of; in lieu of: *go in place of my sister* b in exchange for: *he gave her it in place of her ring* 27 **know one's place** to be aware of one's inferior position 28 **pride of place** the highest or foremost position 29 **put someone in his (or her) place** to humble someone who is arrogant, conceited, forward, etc 30 **take one's place** to take up one's usual or specified position 31 **take the place of** to be a substitute for 32 **take place** to happen or occur 33 **the other place** *facetious* a (at Oxford University) Cambridge University b (at Cambridge University) Oxford University ▷ *vb* (*mainly tr*) 34 to put or set in a particular or appropriate place 35 to find or indicate the place of 36 to identify or classify by linking with an appropriate context: *to place a face* 37 to regard or view as being: *to place prosperity above sincerity* 38 to make (an order, a bet, etc) 39 to find a home or job for (someone) 40 to appoint to an office or position 41 (often foll by *with*) to put under the care (of) 42 to direct or aim carefully 43 (*passive*) *Brit* to cause (a racehorse, greyhound, athlete, etc) to arrive in first, second, third, or sometimes fourth place 44 (*intr*) *US and Canadian* (of a racehorse, greyhound, etc) to finish among the first three in a contest, esp in second position 45

to invest (funds) 46 to sing (a note) with accuracy of pitch 47 to insert (an advertisement) in a newspaper, journal, etc [c13 via Old French from Latin *platēa* courtyard, from Greek *plateia*, from *platus* broad; compare French *plat* flat]

placebo (plə'siːbəʊ) *n, pl* **-bos** *or* **-boes** 1 *med* an inactive substance or other sham form of therapy administered to a patient usually to compare its effects with those of a real drug or treatment, but sometimes for the psychological benefit to the patient through his believing he is receiving treatment. See also **control group, placebo effect** 2 something said or done to please or humour another 3 *RC Church* a traditional name for the vespers of the office for the dead [c13 (in the ecclesiastical sense): from Latin *Placebo Domino* I shall please the Lord (from the opening of the office for the dead); c19 (in the medical sense)]

placebo effect *n med* a positive therapeutic effect claimed by a patient after receiving a placebo believed by him to be an active drug. See **control group**

place card *n* a card placed on a dinner table before a seat, as at a formal dinner, indicating who is to sit there

place kick *football* ▷ *n* 1 a kick in which the ball is placed in position before it is kicked ▷ *vb* **place-kick** 2 to kick (a ball) using a place kick ▷ Compare **drop kick, punt²**

placeless ('pleɪsˌlɪs) *adj* not rooted in a specific place or community

placeman ('pleɪsmən) *n, pl* **-men** *Brit derogatory* a person who holds a public office, esp for private profit and as a reward for political support

placement ('pleɪsmənt) *n* 1 the act of placing or the state of being placed 2 arrangement or position 3 the process or business of finding employment

place name *n* the name of a geographical location, such as a town or area

placenta (plə'sɛntə) *n, pl* **-tas** *or* **-tae** (-tiː) 1 the vascular organ formed in the uterus during pregnancy, consisting of both maternal and embryonic tissues and providing oxygen and nutrients for the fetus and transfer of waste products from the fetal to the maternal blood circulation. See also **afterbirth** 2 the corresponding organ or part in certain mammals 3 *botany* a the part of the ovary of flowering plants to which the ovules are attached b the mass of tissue in nonflowering plants that bears the sporangia or spores [c17 via Latin from Greek *plakoeis* flat cake, from *plax* flat]

placental (plə'sɛntᵊl) *or* **placentate** *adj* (esp of animals) having a placenta: *placental mammals*. See also **eutherian**

placentation (ˌplæsɛn'teɪʃən) *n* 1 *botany* the way in which ovules are attached in the ovary 2 *zoology* a the way in which the placenta is attached in the uterus b the process of formation of the placenta

place of safety order *n social welfare, law* (in Britain) under the Children and Young Persons Act 1969, an order granted by a justice to a person or agency granting authority to detain a child or young person and take him or her to a place of safety for not more than 28 days, because of the child's actual or likely ill-treatment or neglect, etc

placer ('plæsə) *n* a surface sediment containing particles of gold or some other valuable mineral b (*in combination*): *placer-mining* [c19 from American Spanish: deposit, from Spanish *plaza* PLACE]

place setting *n* the set of items of cutlery, crockery, and glassware laid for one person at a dining table

placet ('pleɪsɛt) *n* a vote of expression of assent by saying the word *placet* [c16 from Latin, literally: it pleases]

place-value *adj* denoting a series in which successive digits represent successive powers of the base

placid ('plæsɪd) *adj* having a calm appearance or

nature [c17 from Latin *placidus* peaceful; related to *placēre* to please] > **placidity** (plə'sɪdɪtɪ) *or* 'placidness *n* > 'placidly *adv*

placing ('pleɪsɪŋ) *n stock exchange* a method of issuing securities to the public using an intermediary, such as a stockbroking firm

placket ('plækɪt) *n dressmaking* 1 a piece of cloth sewn in under a closure with buttons, hooks and eyes, zips, etc 2 the closure itself [c16 perhaps from Middle Dutch *plackaet* breastplate, from Medieval Latin *placca* metal plate]

placoderm ('plækəˌdɜːm) *n* any extinct bony-plated fishlike vertebrate of the class *Placodermi*, of Silurian to Permian times: thought to have been the earliest vertebrates with jaws [c19 from Greek *plac-, plax* a flat plate + -DERM]

placoid ('plækɔɪd) *adj* 1 platelike or flattened 2 (of the scales of sharks and other elasmobranchs) toothlike; composed of dentine with an enamel tip and basal pulp cavity [c19 from Greek *plac-, plax* flat]

plafond (plə'fɒn; *French* plafɔ̃) *n* 1 a ceiling, esp one having ornamentation 2 a card game, a precursor of contract bridge [c17 from French, literally: ceiling, maximum, from *plat* flat + *fond* bottom, from Latin *fundus* bottom]

plagal ('pleɪɡᵊl) *adj* 1 (of a cadence) progressing from the subdominant to the tonic chord, as in the *Amen* of a hymn 2 (of a mode) commencing upon the dominant of an authentic mode, but sharing the same final as the authentic mode. Plagal modes are designated by the prefix *Hypo-* before the name of their authentic counterparts: *the Hypodorian mode* ▷ Compare **authentic** (sense 5) [c16 from Medieval Latin *plagālis*, from *plaga*, perhaps from Greek *plagos* side]

plage (plɑːʒ) *n astronomy* a bright patch in the sun's chromosphere [French, literally: beach, strand]

plagiarism ('pleɪdʒəˌrɪzəm) *n* 1 the act of plagiarizing 2 something plagiarized > 'plagiarist *n* > ˌplagia'ristic *adj*

plagiarize *or* **plagiarise** ('pleɪdʒəˌraɪz) *vb* to appropriate (ideas, passages, etc) from (another work or author) > 'plagiaˌrizer *or* 'plagiaˌriser *n*

plagiary ('pleɪdʒərɪ) *n, pl* **-ries** *archaic* a person who plagiarizes or a piece of plagiarism [c16 from Latin *plagiārus* plunderer, from *plagium* kidnapping; related to *plaga* snare]

plagio- *combining form* slanting, inclining, or oblique: *plagiotropism* [from Greek *plagios*, from *plagos* side]

plagioclase ('pleɪdʒɪəʊˌkleɪz) *n* a series of feldspar minerals consisting of a mixture of sodium and calcium aluminium silicates in triclinic crystalline form: includes albite, oligoclase, and labradorite > **plagioclastic** (ˌpleɪdʒɪəʊ'klæstɪk) *adj*

plagioclimax (ˌpleɪdʒɪəʊ'klaɪmæks) *n ecology* the climax stage of a community, influenced by man or some other outside factor

plagiotropism (ˌpleɪdʒɪəʊ'trɒpɪzəm) *n* the growth of a plant at an angle to the vertical in response to a stimulus > ˌplagio'tropic *adj*

plague (pleɪɡ) *n* 1 any widespread and usually highly contagious disease with a high fatality rate 2 an infectious disease of rodents, esp rats, transmitted to man by the bite of the rat flea (*Xenopsylla cheopis*) 3 See **bubonic plague** 4 something that afflicts or harasses 5 *informal* an annoyance or nuisance 6 a pestilence, affliction, or calamity on a large scale, esp when regarded as sent by God 7 *archaic* used to express annoyance, disgust, etc: *a plague on you* ▷ *vb* **plagues, plaguing, plagued** (*tr*) 8 to afflict or harass 9 to bring down a plague upon 10 *informal* to annoy [c14 from Late Latin *plāga* pestilence, from Latin: a blow; related to Greek *plēgē* a stroke, Latin *plangere* to strike] > 'plaguer *n*

plaguy *or* **plaguey** ('pleɪɡɪ) *archaic, informal* ▷ *adj* 1 disagreeable or vexing ▷ *adv* 2 disagreeably or annoyingly > 'plaguily *adv*

plaice (pleɪs) *n, pl* **plaice** *or* **plaices** 1 a European flatfish, *Pleuronectes platessa,* having an oval brown body marked with red or orange spots and valued as a food fish: family *Pleuronectidae* **2** *US and Canadian* any of various other fishes of the family *Pleuronectidae,* esp *Hippoglossoides platessoides* [C13 from Old French *plaiz,* from Late Latin *platessa* flatfish, from Greek *platus* flat]

plaid (plæd, pleɪd) *n* **1 a** a long piece of cloth of a tartan pattern, worn over the shoulder as part of Highland costume **2 a** a crisscross weave or cloth **b** (*as modifier*): *a plaid scarf* [C16 from Scottish Gaelic *plaide,* of obscure origin]

Plaid Cymru (ˌplaɪd ˈkʌmrɪ) *n* the Welsh nationalist party [C20 Welsh, literally: party of Wales]

plain¹ (pleɪn) *adj* **1** flat or smooth; level **2** not complicated; clear: *the plain truth* **3** not difficult; simple or easy: *a plain task* **4** honest or straightforward **5** lowly, esp in social rank or education **6** without adornment or show: *a plain coat* **7** (of fabric) without pattern or of simple untwilled weave **8** not attractive **9** not mixed; simple: *plain vodka* **10** *knitting* or done in plain ▷ *n* **11** a level or almost level tract of country, esp an extensive treeless region **12** a simple stitch in knitting made by putting the right needle into a loop on the left needle, passing the wool round the right needle, and pulling it through the loop, thus forming a new loop **13** (in billiards) **a** the unmarked white ball, as distinguished from the spot balls **b** the player using this ball **14** (in Ireland) short for **plain porter,** a light porter *two pints of plain, please* ▷ *adv* **15** (intensifier): *just plain tired* ▷ See also **plains** [C13 from Old French: simple, from Latin *plānus* level, distinct, clear] > **'plainly** *adv* > **'plainness** *n*

plain² (pleɪn) *vb* a dialect or poetic word for **complain** [C14 *pleignen,* from Old French *plaindre* to lament, from Latin *plangere* to beat]

plainchant (ˈpleɪnˌtʃɑːnt) *n* another name for **plainsong** [C18 from French, rendering Medieval Latin *cantus plānus*; see PLAIN¹]

plain chocolate *n* chocolate with a slightly bitter flavour and dark colour. Compare **milk chocolate**

plain clothes *pl n* **a** ordinary clothes, as distinguished from uniform, as worn by a police detective on duty **b** (*as modifier*): *a plain-clothes policeman*

plain flour *n* flour to which no raising agent has been added

plain-laid *adj* (of a cable or rope) made of three strands twisted together from left to right

plains (pleɪnz) *pl n chiefly US* extensive tracts of level or almost level treeless countryside; prairies

plain sailing *n* **1** *informal* smooth or easy progress **2** *nautical* sailing in a body of water that is unobstructed; clear sailing. Compare **plane sailing**

Plains Indian *n* a member of any of the North American Indian peoples formerly living in the Great Plains of the US and Canada

plainsman (ˈpleɪnzmən) *n, pl* **-men** a person who lives in a plains region, esp in the Great Plains of North America

Plains of Abraham *n* (*functioning as singular*) a field in E Canada between Quebec City and the St Lawrence River: site of an important British victory (1759) in the Seven Years' War, which cost the French their possession of Canada

plainsong (ˈpleɪnˌsɒŋ) *n* the style of unison unaccompanied vocal music used in the medieval Church, esp in Gregorian chant. Also called: **plainchant** [C16 translation of Medieval Latin *cantus plānus*]

plain-spoken *adj* candid; frank; blunt

plaint (pleɪnt) *n* **1** *archaic* a complaint or lamentation **2** *law* a statement in writing of grounds of complaint made to a court of law and asking for redress of the grievance [C13 from Old French *plainte,* from Latin *planctus* lamentation, from *plangere* to beat]

plain text *n telecomm* a message set in a directly readable form rather than in coded groups

plaintiff (ˈpleɪntɪf) *n* (formerly) a person who brings a civil action in a court of law. Now replaced by **claimant** Compare **defendant** (sense 1) [C14 from legal French *plaintif,* from Old French *plaintif* (adj), from *plainte* PLAINT]

plaintive (ˈpleɪntɪv) *adj* expressing melancholy; mournful [C14 from Old French *plaintif* grieving, from *plainte* PLAINT] > **'plaintively** *adv* > **'plaintiveness** *n*

plain turkey *n Austral* a bustard

plaister (ˈpleɪstə) *n Scot* plaster

plait (plæt) *n* **1** a length of hair, ribbon, etc, that has been plaited **2** (in Britain) a loaf of bread of several twisting or intertwining parts **3** a rare spelling of **pleat** ▷ *vb* **4** (*tr*) to intertwine (strands or strips) in a pattern [C15 *pleyt,* from Old French *pleit,* from Latin *plicāre* to fold; see PLY²]

plan (plæn) *n* **1** a detailed scheme, method, etc, for attaining an objective **2** (*sometimes plural*) a proposed, usually tentative idea for doing something **3** a drawing to scale of a horizontal section through a building taken at a given level; a view from above an object or an area in orthographic projection. Compare **ground plan** (sense 1), **elevation** (sense 5) **4** an outline, sketch, etc **5** (in perspective drawing) any of several imaginary planes perpendicular to the line of vision and between the eye and object depicted ▷ *vb* **plans, planning, planned 6** to form a plan (for) or make plans (for) **7** (*tr*) to make a plan of (a building) **8** (*tr; takes a clause as object or an infinitive*) to have in mind as a purpose; intend [C18 via French from Latin *plānus* flat; compare PLANE¹, PLAIN¹]

planar (ˈpleɪnə) *adj* **1** of or relating to a plane **2** lying in one plane; flat [C19 from Late Latin *plānāris* on level ground, from Latin *plānus* flat] > **planarity** (pleɪˈnærɪtɪ)

planarian (pləˈnɛərɪən) *n* any free-living turbellarian flatworm of the mostly aquatic suborder *Tricladida,* having a three-branched intestine [C19 from New Latin *Plānāria* type genus, from Late Latin *plānārius* level, flat; see PLANE¹]

planar process *n* a method of producing diffused junctions in semiconductor devices. A pattern of holes is etched into an oxide layer formed on a silicon substrate, into which impurities are diffused through the holes

planation (pleɪˈneɪʃən) *n* the erosion of a land surface until it is basically flat

planchet (ˈplɑːntʃɪt) *n* a piece of metal ready to be stamped as a coin, medal, etc; flan [C17 from French: little board, from *planche* PLANK¹]

planchette (plɑːnˈʃɛt) *n* a heart-shaped board on wheels, on which messages are written under supposed spirit guidance [C19 from French: little board, from *planche* PLANK¹]

Planck constant or **Planck's constant** *n* a fundamental constant equal to the energy of any quantum of radiation divided by its frequency. It has a value of $6.62606876 \times 10^{-34}$ joule seconds. Symbol: *h* See also **Dirac constant** [C20 after Max Planck (1858–1947), German physicist]

Planck's law *n physics* a law that is the basis of quantum theory, which states that the energy of electromagnetic radiation is confined to indivisible packets (quanta), each of which has an energy equal to the product of the Planck constant and the frequency of the radiation [C20 after Max Planck (1858–1947), German physicist]

plane¹ (pleɪn) *n* **1** *maths* a flat surface in which a straight line joining any two of its points lies entirely on that surface **2** a flat or level surface **3** a level of existence, performance, attainment, etc **4 a** short for **aeroplane b** a wing or supporting surface of an aircraft or hydroplane ▷ *adj* **5** level or flat **6** *maths* (of a curve, figure, etc) lying entirely in one plane ▷ *vb* (*intr*) **7** to fly without moving wings or using engines; glide **8** (of a boat) to rise partly and skim over the water when moving at a certain speed **9** to travel by aeroplane [C17 from Latin *plānum* level surface]

> **'planeness** *n*

plane² (pleɪn) *n* **1** a tool with an adjustable sharpened steel blade set obliquely in a wooden or iron body, for levelling or smoothing timber surfaces, cutting mouldings or grooves, etc **2** a flat tool, usually metal, for smoothing the surface of clay or plaster in a mould ▷ *vb* (*tr*) **3** to level, smooth, or cut (timber, wooden articles, etc) using a plane or similar tool **4** (*often foll by off*) to remove using a plane [C14 via Old French from Late Latin *plāna* plane, from *plānāre* to level]

plane³ (pleɪn) *n* See **plane tree**

plane angle *n* an angle between two intersecting lines

plane chart *n* a chart used in plane sailing, in which the lines of latitude and longitude are straight and parallel

plane geometry *n* the study of the properties of and relationships between plane curves, figures, etc

plane polarization *n* a type of polarization in which the electric vector of waves of light or other electromagnetic radiation is restricted to vibration in a single plane

planer (ˈpleɪnə) *n* **1** a machine with a cutting tool that makes repeated horizontal strokes across the surface of a workpiece: used to cut flat surfaces into metal **2** a machine for planing wood, esp one in which the cutting blades are mounted on a rotating drum **3** *printing* a flat piece of wood used to level type in a chase **4** any person or thing that planes

plane sailing *n nautical* navigation without reference to the earth's curvature. Compare **plain sailing**

plane spotter *n* a person who observes, photographs, and catalogues aircraft as a hobby

plane surveying *n* the surveying of areas of limited size, making no corrections for the earth's curvature

planet (ˈplænɪt) *n* **1** Also called: **major planet** any of the nine celestial bodies, Mercury, Venus, Earth, Mars, Jupiter, Saturn, Uranus, Neptune, or Pluto, that revolve around the sun in elliptical orbits and are illuminated by light from the sun **2** Also called: **extrasolar planet** any other celestial body revolving around a star, illuminated by light from that star **3** *astrology* any of the planets of the solar system, excluding the earth but including the sun and moon, each thought to rule one or sometimes two signs of the zodiac. See also **house** (sense 9) [C12 via Old French from Late Latin *planēta,* from Greek *planētēs* wanderer, from *planaein* to wander]

plane table *n* **1** a surveying instrument consisting of a drawing board mounted on adjustable legs, and used in the field for plotting measurements directly ▷ *vb* **plane-table 2** to survey (a plot of land) using a plane table

planetarium (ˌplænɪˈtɛərɪəm) *n, pl* **-iums** or **-ia** (-ɪə) **1** an instrument for simulating the apparent motions of the sun, moon, and planets against a background of stars by projecting images of these bodies onto the inside of a domed ceiling **2** a building in which such an instrument is housed **3** a model of the solar system, sometimes mechanized to show the relative motions of the planets

planetary (ˈplænɪtərɪ, -trɪ) *adj* **1** of or relating to a planet **2** mundane; terrestrial **3** wandering or erratic **4** *astrology* under the influence of one of the planets **5** (of a gear, esp an epicyclic gear) having an axis that rotates around that of another gear **6** (of an electron) having an orbit around the nucleus of an atom ▷ *n, pl* **-taries 7** a train of planetary gears

planetary nebula *n* an expanding shell of gas surrounding a dying star, formed from matter ejected from the star's outer layers; the gas is ionized by the remaining hot stellar core, emitting light in the process [C18 named from its (occasional) resemblance to a planetary disc]

p

planetesimal hypothesis (ˌplænɪˈtɛsɪməl) *n* the discredited theory that the close passage of a star to the sun caused many small bodies (**planetesimals**) to be drawn from the sun, eventually coalescing to form the planets [C20 *planetesimal,* from PLANET + INFINITESIMAL]

planetoid (ˈplænɪˌtɔɪd) *n* another name for **asteroid** (sense 1) > ˌplaneˈtoidal *adj*

planetology (ˌplænɪˈtɒlədʒɪ) *n astronomy* the study of the origin, composition, and distribution of matter in the planets

plane tree *or* **plane** *n* any tree of the genus *Platanus,* having ball-shaped heads of fruits and leaves with pointed lobes: family *Platanaceae.* The hybrid *P. × acerifolia* (**London plane**) is frequently planted in towns. Also called: **platan** [C14 *plane,* from Old French, from Latin *platanus,* from Greek *platanos,* from *platos* wide, referring to the leaves]

planet-struck *or* **planet-stricken** *adj astrology* affected by the influence of a planet, esp malignly

planet wheel *or* **gear** *n* any one of the wheels of an epicyclic gear train that orbits the central axis of the train

planet Zog *n Brit informal* a place or situation that is far removed from reality or what is currently happening: *those of you who've been on planet Zog for the last ten years*

planform (ˈplænˌfɔːm) *n* the outline or silhouette of an object, esp an aircraft, as seen from above

plangent (ˈplændʒənt) *adj* **1** having a loud deep sound **2** resonant and mournful in sound [C19 from Latin *plangere* to beat (esp the breast, in grief); see PLAIN²] > ˈplangency *n* > ˈplangently *adv*

planimeter (plæˈnɪmɪtə) *n* a mechanical integrating instrument for measuring the area of an irregular plane figure, such as the area under a curve, by moving a point attached to an arm around the perimeter of the figure

planimetry (plæˈnɪmɪtrɪ) *n* the measurement of plane areas > **planimetric** (ˌplænɪˈmɛtrɪk) *or* ˌplaniˈmetrical *adj*

planish (ˈplænɪʃ) *vb* (*tr*) to give a final finish to (metal) by hammering or rolling to produce a smooth surface [C16 from Old French *planir* to smooth out, from Latin *plānus* flat, PLAIN¹] > ˈplanisher *n*

planisphere (ˈplænɪˌsfɪə) *n* a projection or representation of all or part of a sphere on a plane surface, such as a polar projection of the celestial sphere onto a chart [C14 from Medieval Latin *plānisphaerium,* from Latin *plānus* flat + Greek *sphaira* globe] > **planispheric** (ˌplænɪˈsfɛrɪk) *adj*

plank¹ (plæŋk) *n* **1** a stout length of sawn timber **2** something that supports or sustains **3** one of the policies in a political party's programme **4 walk the plank** to be forced by pirates to walk to one's death off the end of a plank jutting out over the water from the side of a ship *n* **5** *Brit slang* a stupid person; idiot ▷ *vb* (*tr*) **6** to cover or provide (an area) with planks **7** to beat (meat) to make it tender **8** *chiefly US and Canadian* to cook or serve (meat or fish) on a special wooden board [C13 from Old Norman French *planke,* from Late Latin *planca* board, from *plancus* flat-footed; probably related to Greek *plax* flat surface]

plank² (plæŋk) *vb* (*tr*) *Scot* to hide; cache [C19 a variant of *plant*]

planking (ˈplæŋkɪŋ) *n* **1** a number of planks **2** the act of covering or furnishing with planks

plank-sheer *n nautical* a plank or timber covering the upper ends of the frames of a wooden vessel [C14 *plancher,* from Old French *planchier,* from *planche* plank, from Latin *planca*; spelling influenced by PLANK¹, SHEER¹]

plankton (ˈplæŋktən) *n* the organisms inhabiting the surface layer of a sea or lake, consisting of small drifting plants and animals, such as diatoms. Compare **nekton** [C19 via German from Greek *planktos* wandering, from *plazesthai* to roam] > **planktonic** (plæŋkˈtɒnɪk) *adj*

planned economy *n* another name for **command economy**

planned obsolescence *n* the policy of deliberately limiting the life of a product in order to encourage the purchaser to replace it. Also called: **built-in obsolescence**

planner (ˈplænə) *n* **1** a person who makes plans, esp for the development of a town, building, etc **2** a chart for recording future appointments, etc

planning blight *n* the harmful effects of uncertainty about likely restrictions on the types and extent of future development in a particular area on the quality of life of its inhabitants and the normal growth of its business and community enterprises

planning permission *n* (in Britain) formal permission that must be obtained from a local authority before development or a change of use of land or buildings

plano- *or sometimes before a vowel* **plan-** *combining form* indicating flatness or planeness: *plano-concave* [from Latin *plānus* flat, level]

plano-concave (ˌpleɪnəʊˈkɒnkeɪv) *adj* (of a lens) having one side concave and the other side plane

plano-convex (ˌpleɪnəʊˈkɒnvɛks) *adj* (of a lens) having one side convex and the other side plane

planogamete (ˌplænəgəˈmiːt) *n* a motile gamete, such as a spermatozoon [C19 from Greek *planos* wandering (see PLANET) + GAMETE]

planography (pləˈnɒgrəfɪ) *n printing* any process, such as lithography, for printing from a flat surface > **planographic** (ˌpleɪnəˈgræfɪk) *adj* > ˌplanoˈgraphically *adv*

planometer (plæˈnɒmɪtə) *n* a flat metal plate used for directly testing the flatness of metal surfaces in accurate metalwork > **planometric** (ˌpleɪnəˈmɛtrɪk) *adj* > ˌplanoˈmetrically *adv* > plaˈnometry *n*

planosol (ˈpleɪnəˌsɒl) *n* a type of intrazonal soil of humid or subhumid uplands having a strongly leached upper layer overlying a clay hardpan [C20 from Latin PLANO- + *solum* soil]

plant¹ (plɑːnt) *n* **1** any living organism that typically synthesizes its food from inorganic substances, possesses cellulose cell walls, responds slowly and often permanently to a stimulus, lacks specialized sense organs and nervous system, and has no powers of locomotion **2** such an organism that is green, terrestrial, and smaller than a shrub or tree; a herb **3** a cutting, seedling, or similar structure, esp when ready for transplantation **4** *informal* a thing positioned secretly for discovery by another, esp in order to incriminate an innocent person **5** *billiards, snooker* a position in which the cue ball can be made to strike an intermediate which then pockets another ball ▷ *vb* (*tr*) **6** (often foll by *out*) to set (seeds, crops, etc) into (ground) to grow **7** to place firmly in position **8** to establish; found **9** to implant in the mind **10** *slang* to deliver (a blow) **11** *informal* to position or hide, esp in order to deceive or observe **12** to place (young fish, oysters, spawn, etc) in (a lake, river, etc) in order to stock the water ▷ See also **plant out** [Old English, from Latin *planta* a shoot, cutting] > ˈplantable *adj* > ˈplantˌlike *adj*

plant² (plɑːnt) *n* **1 a** the land, buildings, and equipment used in carrying on an industrial, business, or other undertaking or service **b** (*as modifier*): *plant costs* **2** a factory or workshop **3** mobile mechanical equipment for construction, road-making, etc [C20 special use of PLANT¹]

plant agreement *n* a collective agreement at plant level within industry

plantain¹ (ˈplæntɪn) *n* any of various N temperate plants of the genus *Plantago,* esp *P. major* (**great plantain**), which has a rosette of broad leaves and a slender spike of small greenish flowers: family *Plantaginaceae.* See also **ribwort** [C14 *plauntein,* from Old French *plantein,* from Latin *plantāgō,* from *planta* sole of the foot]

plantain² (ˈplæntɪn) *n* **1** a large tropical musaceous plant, *Musa paradisiaca* **2** the green-skinned banana-like fruit of this plant, eaten as a staple food in many tropical regions [C16 from Spanish *platano* plantain, PLANE TREE]

plantain-eater *n* another name for **touraco**

plantain lily *n* any of several Asian plants of the liliaceous genus *Hosta,* having broad ribbed leaves and clusters of white, blue, or lilac flowers. Also called: **day lily**

plantar (ˈplæntə) *adj* of, relating to, or occurring on the sole of the foot or a corresponding part: *plantar warts* [C18 from Latin *plantāris,* from *planta* sole of the foot]

plantation (plænˈteɪʃən) *n* **1** an estate, esp in tropical countries, where cash crops such as rubber, oil palm, etc, are grown on a large scale **2** a group of cultivated trees or plants **3** (formerly) a colony or group of settlers **4** *rare* the planting of seeds, shoots, etc

planter (ˈplɑːntə) *n* **1** the owner or manager of a plantation **2** a machine designed for rapid, uniform, and efficient planting of seeds in the ground **3** a colonizer or settler **4** a decorative pot or stand for house plants

planter's punch *n* a cocktail consisting of rum with lime or lemon juice and sugar

plantigrade (ˈplæntɪˌgreɪd) *adj* **1** walking with the entire sole of the foot touching the ground, as, for example, man and bears ▷ *n* **2** a plantigrade animal [C19 via French from New Latin *plantigradus,* from Latin *planta* sole of the foot + *gradus* a step]

plant kingdom *n* a category of living organisms comprising all plants but excluding the algae, fungi, and bacteria. Compare **animal kingdom, mineral kingdom**

plant louse *n* **1** another name for an **aphid 2** jumping plant louse any small active cicada-like insect of the homopterous family *Psyllidae* (or *Chermidae*), having hind legs adapted for leaping, and feeding on plant juices

plantocracy (plɑːnˈtɒkrəsɪ) *n, pl* -cies a ruling social class composed of planters

plant out *vb* (*tr, adverb*) to set (a seedling that has been raised in a greenhouse, frame, or other sheltered place) to grow out in open ground

plantsman (ˈplɑːntsmən) *or feminine* **plantswoman** *n, pl* -men *or* -women an experienced gardener who specializes in collecting rare or interesting plants

planula (ˈplænjʊlə) *n, pl* -lae (-ˌliː) the ciliated free-swimming larva of hydrozoan coelenterates such as the hydra [C19 from New Latin: a little plane, from Latin *plānum* level ground] > ˈplanular *adj*

plaque (plæk, plɑːk) *n* **1** an ornamental or commemorative inscribed tablet or plate of porcelain, wood, etc **2** a small flat brooch or badge, as of a club, etc **3** *pathol* any small abnormal patch on or within the body, such as the typical lesion of psoriasis **4** short for **dental plaque 5** *bacteriol* a clear area within a bacterial or tissue culture caused by localized destruction of the cells by a bacteriophage or other virus [C19 from French, from *plaquier* to plate, from Middle Dutch *placken* to beat (metal) into a thin plate]

plash¹ (plæʃ) *vb, n* a less common word for **splash** [Old English *plæsc,* probably imitative; compare Dutch *plas*]

plash² (plæʃ) *vb* another word for **pleach** [C15 from Old French *plassier,* from *plais* hedge, woven fence, from Latin *plectere* to plait; compare PLEACH]

plashy (ˈplæʃɪ) *adj* plashier, plashiest **1** wet or marshy **2** splashing or splashy

-plasia *or* **-plasy** *n combining form* indicating growth, development, or change: *hypoplasia* [from New Latin, from Greek *plasis* a moulding, from *plassein* to mould]

plasm (ˈplæzəm) *n* **1** protoplasm of a specified type: *germ plasm* **2** a variant of **plasma**

-plasm *n combining form* (in biology) indicating the material forming cells: *protoplasm; cytoplasm* [from Greek *plasma* something moulded; see PLASMA] > -plasmic *adj combining form*

plasma ('plæzmə) *or* **plasm** *n* **1** the clear yellowish fluid portion of blood or lymph in which the red blood cells, white blood cells, and platelets are suspended **2** short for **blood plasma 3** a former name for **protoplasm** *or* **cytoplasm 4** *physics* **a** a hot ionized material consisting of nuclei and electrons. It is sometimes regarded as a fourth state of matter and is the material present in the sun, most stars, and fusion reactors **b** the ionized gas in an electric discharge or spark, containing positive ions and electrons and a small number of negative ions together with un-ionized material **5** a green slightly translucent variety of chalcedony, used as a gemstone **6** a less common term for **whey** [c18 from Late Latin: something moulded, from Greek, from *plassein* to mould] > plasmatic (plæz'mætɪk) *or* 'plasmic *adj*

plasma engine *n* an engine that generates thrust by reaction to the emission of a jet of plasma

plasmagel ('plæzmə,dʒɛl) *n* another name for **ectoplasm** (sense 1)

plasmagene ('plæzmə,dʒiːn) *n biology* any gene other than those carried in the nucleus of a eukaryotic cell, such as a mitochondrial gene > plasmagenic (,plæzmə'dʒɛnɪk) *adj*

plasmalemma (,plæzmə'lɛmə) *or* **plasma membrane** *n* other names for **cell membrane**

plasmapheresis (,plæzmə'fɛrəsɪs) *n* (in blood transfusion) a technique for removing healthy or infected plasma by separating it from the red blood cells by settling or using a centrifuge and retransfusing the red blood cells into the donor or patient [c20 from PLASM + Greek *aphairesis* taking away]

plasmasol ('plæzmə,sɒl) *n* another name for **endoplasm**

plasma torch *n* an electrical device for converting a gas into a plasma, used for melting metal

plasmid ('plæzmɪd) *n* a small circle of bacterial DNA that is independent of the main bacterial chromosome. Plasmids often contain genes for drug resistances and can be transmitted between bacteria of the same and different species: used in genetic engineering [c20 from PLASM + -ID[1]]

plasmin ('plæzmɪn) *n* a proteolytic enzyme that causes fibrinolysis in blood clots

plasminogen (plæz'mɪnədʒən) *n biochem* a zymogen found in blood that gives rise to plasmin on activation

plasmo- *or before a vowel* **plasm-** *combining form* of, relating to, or resembling plasma: *plasmolysis* [from Greek *plasma*; see PLASMA]

plasmodesma (,plæzmə'dɛzmə) *or* **plasmodesm** ('plæzmə,dɛzəm) *n, pl* -desmata (-'dɛzmətə) *or* -desms *botany* any of various very fine cytoplasmic threads connecting the cytoplasm of adjacent cells via minute holes in the cell walls [c20 from PLASMO- + Greek *desma* bond]

plasmodium (plæz'məʊdɪəm) *n, pl* -dia (-dɪə) **1** an amoeboid mass of protoplasm, containing many nuclei: a stage in the life cycle of certain organisms, esp the nonreproductive stage of the slime moulds **2** any parasitic sporozoan protozoan of the genus *Plasmodium*, such as *P. falciparum* and *P. vivax*, which cause malaria [c19 New Latin; see PLASMA, -ODE[1]] > plas'modial *adj*

plasmoid ('plæz,mɔɪd) *n physics* a section of a plasma having a characteristic shape

plasmolyse *or US* **plasmolyze** ('plæzmə,laɪz) *vb* to subject (a cell) to plasmolysis or (of a cell) to undergo plasmolysis

plasmolysis (plæz'mɒlɪsɪs) *n* the shrinkage of protoplasm away from the cell walls that occurs as a result of excessive water loss, esp in plant cells (see **exosmosis**) > plasmolytic (,plæzmə'lɪtɪk) *adj* > ,plasmo'lytically *adv*

plasmon ('plæzmɒn) *n genetics* the sum total of plasmagenes in a cell [c20 from German, from Greek *plasma*. See PLASMA]

plasmosome ('plæzmə,səʊm) *n* another name for **nucleolus**

Plassey ('plæsɪ) *n* a village in NE India, in W Bengal: scene of Clive's victory (1757) over Siraj-ud-daula, which established British supremacy over India

-plast *n combining form* indicating an organized living cell or particle of living matter: *protoplast* [from Greek *plastos* formed, from *plassein* to form]

plaster ('plɑːstə) *n* **1** a mixture of lime, sand, and water, sometimes stiffened with hair or other fibres, that is applied to the surface of a wall or ceiling as a soft paste that hardens when dry **2** *Brit, Austral, and NZ* an adhesive strip of material, usually medicated, for dressing a cut, wound, etc **3** short for **mustard plaster** *or* **plaster of Paris** ▷ *vb* **4** to coat (a wall, ceiling, etc) with plaster **5** (*tr*) to apply like plaster: *she plastered make-up on her face* **6** (*tr*) to cause to lie flat or to adhere **7** (*tr*) to apply a plaster cast to **8** (*tr*) *slang* to strike or defeat with great force [Old English, from Medieval Latin *plastrum* medicinal salve, building plaster, via Latin from Greek *emplastron* curative dressing, from EM- + *plassein* to form] > 'plasterer *n* > 'plastery *adj*

plasterboard ('plɑːstə,bɔːd) *n* a thin rigid board, in the form of a layer of plaster compressed between two layers of fibreboard, used to form or cover walls

plaster cast *n* **1** *surgery* a cast made of plaster of Paris. See **cast** (sense 40) **2** a copy or mould of a sculpture or other object cast in plaster of Paris

plastered ('plɑːstəd) *adj slang* intoxicated; drunk

plastering ('plɑːstərɪŋ) *n* a coating or layer of plaster

plaster of Paris *n* **1** a white powder that sets to a hard solid when mixed with water, used for making sculptures and casts, as an additive for lime plasters, and for making casts for setting broken limbs. It is usually the hemihydrate of calcium sulphate, $2CaSO_4.H_2O$ **2** the hard plaster produced when this powder is mixed with water: a fully hydrated form of calcium sulphate ▷ Sometimes shortened to: **plaster** [c15 from Medieval Latin *plastrum parisiense*, originally made from the gypsum of *Paris*]

plastic ('plæstɪk, 'plɑːs-) *n* **1** any one of a large number of synthetic usually organic materials that have a polymeric structure and can be moulded when soft and then set, esp such a material in a finished state containing plasticizer, stabilizer, filler, pigments, etc. Plastics are classified as thermosetting (such as Bakelite) or thermoplastic (such as PVC) and are used in the manufacture of many articles and in coatings, artificial fibres, etc. Compare **resin** (sense 2) **2** short for **plastic money** ▷ *adj* **3** made of plastic **4** easily influenced; impressionable: *the plastic minds of children* **5** capable of being moulded or formed **6** *fine arts* **a** of or relating to moulding or modelling: *the plastic arts* **b** produced or apparently produced by moulding: *the plastic draperies of Giotto's figures* **7** having the power to form or influence: *the plastic forces of the imagination* **8** *biology* of or relating to any formative process; able to change, develop, or grow: *plastic tissues* **9** of or relating to plastic surgery **10** *slang* superficially attractive yet unoriginal or artificial: *plastic food* [c17 from Latin *plasticus* relating to moulding, from Greek *plastikos*, from *plassein* to form] > 'plastically *adv*

-plastic *adj combining form* growing or forming: *neoplastic* [from Greek *plastikos*; see PLASTIC]

plastic bomb *n* a bomb consisting of a putty-like explosive charge fitted with a detonator and timing device

plastic bullet *n* a solid PVC cylinder, 10 cm long and 38 mm in diameter, fired by police or military forces to regain control in riots. Formal name: baton round

Plasticine ('plæstɪ,siːn) *n trademark* a soft coloured material used, esp by children, for modelling

plasticity (plæ'stɪsɪtɪ) *n* **1** the quality of being plastic or able to be moulded **2** (in pictorial art) the quality of depicting space and form so that they appear three-dimensional

plasticize *or* **plasticise** ('plæstɪ,saɪz) *vb* to make or become plastic, as by the addition of a plasticizer > ,plastici'zation *or* ,plastici'sation *n*

plasticizer *or* **plasticiser** ('plæstɪ,saɪzə) *n* any of a number of substances added to materials in order to modify their physical properties. Their uses include softening and improving the flexibility of plastics and preventing dried paint coatings from becoming too brittle

plasticky ('plæstɪkɪ) *adj* made of or resembling plastic

plastic money *n* credit cards, used instead of cash (c20 from the cards being made of plastic)

plastic surgery *n* the branch of surgery concerned with therapeutic or cosmetic repair or re-formation of missing, injured, or malformed tissues or parts. Also called: anaplasty > plastic surgeon *n*

plastid ('plæstɪd) *n* any of various small particles in the cytoplasm of the cells of plants and some animals that contain pigments (see **chromoplast**), starch, oil, protein, etc [c19 via German from Greek *plastēs* sculptor, from *plassein* to form]

plastometer (plæ'stɒmɪtə) *n* an instrument for measuring plasticity > plastometric (,plæstəʊ'mɛtrɪk) *adj* > plas'tometry *n*

plastron ('plæstrən) *n* the bony plate forming the ventral part of the shell of a tortoise or turtle [c16 via French from Italian *piastrone*, from *piastra* breastplate, from Latin *emplastrum* PLASTER] > 'plastral *adj*

-plasty *n combining form* indicating plastic surgery involving a bodily part, tissue, or a specified process: *rhinoplasty; neoplasty* [from Greek *-plastia*; see -PLAST]

plat[1] (plæt) *n* a small area of ground; plot [c16 (also occurring in Middle English in place names): originally variant of PLOT[2]]

plat[2] (plæt) *n, vb* plats, platting, platted *dialect* a variant spelling of **plait** [c16 variant of PLAIT]

Plata (Spanish 'plata) *n* **Río de la** ('rio de la) an estuary on the SE coast of South America, between Argentina and Uruguay, formed by the Uruguay and Paraná Rivers. Length: 275 km (171 miles). Width: (at its mouth) 225 km (140 miles). Also called: La Plata English name: (River) **Plate**

Plataea (plə'tiːə) *n* an ancient city in S Boeotia, traditionally an ally of Athens: scene of the defeat of a great Persian army by the Greeks in 479 BC

platan ('plætˀn) *n* another name for **plane tree** [c14 from Latin *platanus*, from Greek *platanos*; see PLANE TREE]

plat du jour ('plɑː də 'ʒʊə; *French* pla dy ʒur) *n, pl* plats du jour ('plɑːz də 'ʒʊə; *French* pla dy ʒur) the specially prepared or recommended dish of the day on a restaurant's menu [French, literally: dish of the day]

plate (pleɪt) *n* **1 a** a shallow usually circular dish made of porcelain, earthenware, glass, etc, on which food is served or from which food is eaten **b** (*as modifier*): *a plate rack* **2 a** Also called: **plateful** the contents of a plate or the amount a plate will hold **b** *Austral and NZ* a plate of cakes, sandwiches, etc, brought by a guest to a party: *everyone was asked to bring a plate* **3** an entire course of a meal: *a cold plate* **4** any shallow or flat receptacle, esp for receiving a collection in church **5** flat metal of uniform thickness obtained by rolling, usually having a thickness greater than about three millimetres **6** a thin coating of metal usually on another metal, as produced by electrodeposition, chemical action, etc **7** metal or metalware that has been coated in this way, esp with gold or silver: *Sheffield plate* **8** dishes, cutlery, etc, made of gold or silver **9** a sheet of metal, plastic, rubber, etc, having a printing surface produced by a process such as stereotyping, moulding, or photographic deposition **10** a print taken from such a sheet or from a woodcut, esp when appearing in a book **11** a thin flat sheet of a substance, such as metal or glass **12** armour

p

made of overlapping or articulated pieces of thin metal **13** *photog* **a** a sheet of glass, or sometimes metal, coated with photographic emulsion on which an image can be formed by exposure to light **b** (*as modifier*): *a plate camera* **14** an orthodontic device, esp one used for straightening children's teeth **15** an informal word for **denture** (sense 1) **16** *anatomy* any flat platelike structure or part **17 a** a cup or trophy awarded to the winner of a sporting contest, esp a horse race **b** a race or contest for such a prize **18** any of the rigid layers of the earth's lithosphere of which there are believed to be at least 15. See also **plate tectonics 19** *electronics* **a** *chiefly US* the anode in an electronic valve **b** an electrode in an accumulator or capacitor **20** a horizontal timber joist that supports rafters or studs **21** a light horseshoe for flat racing **22** a thin cut of beef from the brisket **23** See **plate rail 24** Also called: **Communion plate** *RC Church* a flat plate held under the chin of a communicant in order to catch any fragments of the consecrated Host **25** *archaic* a coin, esp one made of silver **26 on a plate** in such a way as to be acquired without further trouble: *he was handed the job on a plate* **27 on one's plate** waiting to be done or dealt with: *he has a lot on his plate at the moment* ▷ *vb* (*tr*) **28** to coat (a surface, usually metal) with a thin layer of other metal by electrolysis, chemical reaction, etc **29** to cover with metal plates, as for protection **30** *printing* to make a stereotype or electrotype from (type or another plate) **31** to form (metal) into plate, esp by rolling **32** to give a glossy finish to (paper) by calendering **33** to grow (microorganisms) in a culture medium ▷ See also **plate up** [c13 from Old French: thin metal sheet, something flat, from Vulgar Latin *plattus* (unattested); related to Greek *platus* flat]

Plate (pleɪt) *n* **River** the English name for the (Río de la) **Plata**

plate armour *n* armour made of thin metal plates, which superseded mail during the 14th century

plateau (ˈplætəʊ) *n, pl* **-eaus** *or* **-eaux** (-əʊz) **1** a wide mainly level area of elevated land **2** a relatively long period of stability; levelling off ▷ *vb* (*intr*) **3** to remain at a stable level for a relatively long period [c18 from French, from Old French *platel* something flat, from *plat* flat; see PLATE]

Plateau (ˈplætəʊ) *n* a state of central Nigeria, formed in 1976 from part of Benue-Plateau State: tin mining. Capital: Jos. Pop (including Nassarawa state): 3 671 498 (1995 est.). Area (including Nassarawa state): 58 030 sq km (22 405 sq miles)

plated (ˈpleɪtɪd) *adj* **1 a** coated with a layer of metal **b** (*in combination*): *gold-plated* **2** (of a fabric) knitted in two different yarns so that one appears on the face and the other on the back

plate glass *n* glass formed into a thin sheet by rolling, used for windows

platelayer (ˈpleɪtˌleɪə) *n* *Brit* a workman who lays and maintains railway track. US and Canadian equivalent: **trackman**

platelet (ˈpleɪtlɪt) *n* a minute cell occurring in the blood of vertebrates and involved in clotting of the blood. Formerly called: **thrombocyte** [c19 a small PLATE]

platemark (ˈpleɪtˌmɑːk) *n, vb* another name for **hallmark** (senses 1, 4)

platen (ˈplætᵊn) *n* **1** a flat plate in a printing press that presses the paper against the type **2** the roller on a typewriter, against which the keys strike **3** the worktable of a machine tool, esp one that is slotted to enable T-bolts to be used [c15 from Old French *platine*, from *plat* flat; see PLATE]

plater (ˈpleɪtə) *n* **1** a person or thing that plates **2** *horse racing* **a** a mediocre horse entered chiefly for minor races **b** a blacksmith who shoes racehorses with the special type of light shoe used for racing

plate rail *n* *railways* an early flat rail with an

extended flange on its outer edge to retain wheels on the track. Sometimes shortened to: **plate**

plate tectonics *n* (*functioning as singular*) *geology* the study of the structure of the earth's crust and mantle with reference to the theory that the earth's lithosphere is divided into large rigid blocks (**plates**) that are floating on semifluid rock and are thus able to interact with each other at their boundaries, and to the associated theories of continental drift and seafloor spreading

plate up *vb* (*adverb*) to put food on a plate, ready for serving

platform (ˈplætfɔːm) *n* **1** a raised floor or other horizontal surface, such as a stage for speakers **2** a raised area at a railway station, from which passengers have access to the trains **3** See **drilling platform, production platform 4** the declared principles, aims, etc, of a political party, an organization, or an individual **5** a level raised area of ground **6 a** the thick raised sole of some high-heeled shoes **b** (*as modifier*): *platform shoes* **7** a vehicle or level place on which weapons are mounted and fired **8** a specific type of computer hardware or computer operating system [c16 from French *plateforme*, from *plat* flat + *forme* form, layout]

platform game *n* a type of computer game that is played by moving a figure on the screen through a series of obstacles and problems

platform rocker *n* *US and Canadian* a rocking chair supported on a stationary base

platform ticket *n* a ticket for admission to railway platforms but not for travel

platina (ˈplætɪnə, pləˈtiːnə) *n* an alloy of platinum and several other metals, including palladium, osmium, and iridium [c18 from Spanish: silvery element, from *plata* silver, from Provençal: silver plate]

plating (ˈpleɪtɪŋ) *n* **1** a coating or layer of material, esp metal **2** a layer or covering of metal plates

platinic (pləˈtɪnɪk) *adj* of or containing platinum, esp in the tetravalent state

platiniferous (ˌplætɪˈnɪfərəs) *adj* platinum-bearing

platiniridium (ˌplætɪnɪˈrɪdɪəm) *n* any alloy of platinum and iridium: used in jewellery, electrical contacts, and hypodermic needles

platinize *or* **platinise** (ˈplætɪˌnaɪz) *vb* (*tr*) to coat with platinum > ˌplatiniˈzation *or* ˌplatiniˈsation *n*

platino-, platini- *or before a vowel* **platin-** *combining form* of, relating to, containing, or resembling platinum: *platinotype*

platinocyanic acid (ˌplætɪnəʊsaɪˈænɪk) *n* a hypothetical tetrabasic acid known only in the form of platinocyanide salts. Formula: $H_2Pt(CN)_4$

platinocyanide (ˌplætɪnəʊˈsaɪəˌnaɪd, -nɪd) *n* any salt containing the divalent complex cation $[Pt(CN)_4]^{2-}$

platinoid (ˈplætɪˌnɔɪd) *adj* containing or resembling platinum: *a platinoid metal*

platinotype (ˈplætɪnəʊˌtaɪp) *n* an obsolete process for producing photographic prints using paper coated with an emulsion containing platinum salts, the resulting image in platinum black being more permanent and of a richer tone than the usual silver image

platinous (ˈplætɪnəs) *adj* of or containing platinum, esp in the divalent state

platinum (ˈplætɪnəm) *n* **1** a ductile malleable silvery-white metallic element, very resistant to heat and chemicals. It occurs free and in association with other platinum metals, esp in osmiridium: used in jewellery, laboratory apparatus, electrical contacts, dentistry, electroplating, and as a catalyst. Symbol: Pt; atomic no.: 78; atomic wt.: 195.08; valency: 1–4; relative density: 21.45; melting pt.: 1769°C; boiling pt.: 3827±100°C **2** a medium to light grey colour **b** (*as adjective*): *a platinum carpet* [c19 New Latin, from PLATINA, on the model of other metals with the suffix *-um*]

platinum black *n* *chem* a black powder consisting of very finely divided platinum metal. It is used as a catalyst, esp in hydrogenation reactions

platinum-blond *or feminine* **platinum-blonde** *adj* **1** (of hair) of a pale silver-blond colour **2 a** having hair of this colour **b** (*as noun*): *she was a platinum blonde*

platinum disc *n* **a** (in Britain) an album certified to have sold 300 000 copies or a single certified to have sold 600 000 copies **b** (in the US) an album or single certified to have sold one million copies. Compare **gold disc, silver disc**

platinum metal *n* any of the group of precious metallic elements consisting of ruthenium, rhodium, palladium, osmium, iridium, and platinum

platitude (ˈplætɪˌtjuːd) *n* **1** a trite, dull, or obvious remark or statement; a commonplace **2** staleness or insipidity of thought or language; triteness [c19 from French, literally: flatness, from *plat* flat] > ˌplatiˈtudinous *adj*

platitudinize *or* **platitudinise** (ˌplætɪˈtjuːdɪˌnaɪz) *vb* (*intr*) to speak or write in platitudes > ˌplatiˈtudiˌnizer *or* ˌplatiˈtudiˌniser *n*

Plato (ˈpleɪtəʊ) *n* a crater in the NW quadrant of the moon, about 100 km in diameter, that has a conspicuous dark floor

Platonic (pləˈtɒnɪk) *adj* **1** of or relating to the Greek philosopher Plato (?427–?347 BC) or his teachings **2** (*often not capital*) free from physical desire: *Platonic love* > Plaˈtonically *adv*

Platonic solid *n* any of the five possible regular polyhedra: cube, tetrahedron, octahedron, icosahedron, and dodecahedron. Also called (esp formerly): **Platonic body** [c17 named after Plato (?427–?347 BC), Greek philosopher, who was the first to list them]

Platonism (ˈpleɪtəˌnɪzəm) *n* **1** the teachings of the Greek philosopher Plato (?427–?347 BC) and his followers, esp the philosophical theory that the meanings of general words are real existing abstract entities (Forms) and that particular objects have properties in common by virtue of their relationship with these Forms. Compare **nominalism, conceptualism, intuitionism 2** the realist doctrine that mathematical entities have real existence and that mathematical truth is independent of human thought **3** See **Neo-Platonism**. > ˈPlatonist *n*

platoon (pləˈtuːn) *n* **1** *military* a subunit of a company usually comprising three sections of ten to twelve men: commanded by a lieutenant **2** a group or unit of people, esp one sharing a common activity, characteristic, etc [c17 from French *peloton* little ball, group of men, from *pelote* ball; see PELLET]

Plattdeutsch (*German* ˈplatdɔɪtʃ) *n* another name for **Low German** [literally: flat (that is, low) German]

Platte (plæt) *n* a river system of the central US, formed by the confluence of the **North Platte** and **South Platte** at North Platte, Nebraska: flows generally east to the Missouri River. Length: 499 km (310 miles)

platteland (ˈplatəˌlant) *n* **the** (in South Africa) the country districts or rural areas [c20 from Afrikaans, from Dutch *plat* flat + *land* country]

platter (ˈplætə) *n* **1** a large shallow usually oval dish or plate, used for serving food **2** a course of a meal, usually consisting of several different foods served on the same plate: *a seafood platter* [c14 from Anglo-Norman *plater*, from *plat* dish, from Old French *plat* flat; see PLATE]

platy[1] (ˈpleɪtɪ) *adj* **platier, platiest** of, relating to, or designating rocks the constituents of which occur in flaky layers: *platy fracture* [c19 from PLATE + -Y[1]]

platy[2] (ˈplætɪ) *n, pl* **platy, platys** *or* **platies** any of various small brightly coloured freshwater cyprinodont fishes of the Central American genus *Xiphophorus*, esp *X. maculatus* [c20 shortened from New Latin *Platypoecilus* former genus name, from

PLATY- + *-poecilus,* from Greek *poikilos* spotted]

platy- *combining form* indicating something flat: *platyhelminth* [from Greek *platus* flat]

platyhelminth (ˌplætɪˈhɛlmɪnθ) *n* any invertebrate of the phylum *Platyhelminthes* (the flatworms) [C19 from New Latin *Platyhelmintha* flatworm, from PLATY- + Greek *helmins* worm] > ˌ**platyhelˈminthic** *adj*

platykurtic (ˌplætɪˈkɜːtɪk) *adj statistics* (of a distribution) having kurtosis B_2 less than 3, less heavily concentrated about the mean than a normal distribution. Compare **leptokurtic, mesokurtic** [C20 from PLATY- + Greek *kurtos* arched, bulging + -IC]

platypus (ˈplætɪpəs) *n, pl* **-puses** See **duck-billed platypus** [C18 New Latin, from PLATY- + *-pus,* from Greek *pous* foot]

platyrrhine (ˈplætɪˌraɪn) *or* **platyrrhinian** (ˌplætɪˈrɪnɪən) *adj* **1** (esp of New World monkeys) having widely separated nostrils opening to the side of the face **2** (of humans) having an unusually short wide nose ▷ *n* **3** an animal or person with this characteristic ▷ Compare **catarrhine** [C19 from New Latin *platyrrhinus,* from PLATY- + *-rrhinus,* from Greek *rhis* nose]

plaudit (ˈplɔːdɪt) *n (usually plural)* **1** an expression of enthusiastic approval or approbation **2** a round of applause [C17 shortened from earlier *plauditē,* from Latin: applaud!, from *plaudere* to APPLAUD]

Plauen (*German* ˈplauən) *n* a city in E central Germany, in Saxony: textile centre. Pop: 70 070 (2003 est)

plausible (ˈplɔːzəbᵊl) *adj* **1** apparently reasonable, valid, truthful, etc: *a plausible excuse* **2** apparently trustworthy or believable: *a plausible speaker* [C16 from Latin *plausibilis* worthy of applause, from *plaudere* to APPLAUD] > ˌ**plausiˈbility** *or* ˈ**plausibleness** *n* > ˈ**plausibly** *adv*

plausive (ˈplɔːsɪv) *adj* **1** expressing praise or approval; applauding **2** *obsolete* plausible

play (pleɪ) *vb* **1** to occupy oneself in (a sport or diversion); amuse oneself in (a game) **2** *(tr)* to contend against (an opponent) in a sport or game: *Ed played Tony at chess and lost* **3** to fulfil or cause to fulfil (a particular role) in a team game: *he plays defence; he plays in the defence* **4** *(tr)* to address oneself to (a ball) in a game: *play the ball not the man* **5** *(intr;* often foll by *about* or *around)* to behave carelessly, esp in a way that is unconsciously cruel or hurtful; trifle or dally (with): *to play about with a young girl's affections* **6** (when *intr,* often foll by *at)* to perform or act the part (of) in or as in a dramatic production; assume or simulate the role (of): *to play the villain; just what are you playing at?* **7** to act out or perform (a dramatic production) **8** to give a performance in (a place) or (of a performance) to be given in a place **9** to have the ability to perform on (a musical instrument): *David plays the harp* **10** to perform (on a musical instrument) as specified: *he plays out of tune* **11** *(tr)* **a** to reproduce (a tune, melody, piece of music, note, etc) on an instrument **b** to perform works by (a specific composer): *to play Brahms* **12** to discharge or cause to discharge: *he played the water from the hose onto the garden* **13** to operate, esp to cause (a record player, radio, etc) to emit sound or (of a record player, radio, etc) to emit (sound): *he played a record; the radio was playing loudly* **14** to move or cause to move freely, quickly, or irregularly: *lights played on the scenery* **15** *(tr) stock exchange* to speculate or operate aggressively for gain in (a market) **16** *(tr) angling* to attempt to tire (a hooked fish) by alternately letting out and reeling in line and by using the rod's flexibility **17** to put (a card, counter, piece, etc) into play **18** to gamble (money) on a game **19** **play ball** *informal* to cooperate **20** **play fair** (or **false**) (often foll by *with*) to prove oneself fair (or unfair) in one's dealings **21** **play by ear** See **ear¹** (sense 19) **22** **play for time** to delay the outcome of some activity so as to gain time to one's own advantage **23** **play into the hands of** to act directly to the advantage of (an opponent) **24** **play the fool** See **fool¹** (sense 7) **25** **play the game** See **game¹** (sense 22) ▷ *n* **26** a dramatic composition written for performance by actors on a stage, on television, etc; drama **27** **a** the performance of a dramatic composition **b** *(in combination)*: *playreader* **28** **a** games, exercise, or other activity undertaken for pleasure, diversion, etc, esp by children **b** *(in combination)*: *playroom* **c** *(as modifier)*: *play dough* **29** manner of action, conduct, or playing: *fair play* **30** the playing or conduct of a game or the period during which a game is in progress: *rain stopped play* **31** *US and Canadian* a move or manoeuvre in a game: *a brilliant play* **32** the situation of a ball that is within the defined area and being played according to the rules (in the phrases **in play, out of play**) **33** a turn to play: *it's my play* **34** the act of playing for stakes; gambling **35** action, activity, or operation: *the play of the imagination* **36** freedom of or scope or space for movement: *too much play in the rope* **37** light, free, or rapidly shifting motion: *the play of light on the water* **38** fun, jest, or joking: *I only did it in play* **39** **make a play for** *informal* **a** to make an obvious attempt to gain **b** to attempt to attract or seduce ▷ See also **play along, playback, play down, play off, play on, play out, play up, play with** [Old English *plega* (n), *plegan* (vb); related to Middle Dutch *pleyen*] > ˈ**playable** *adj*

playa (ˈplɑːjə; *Spanish* ˈplaja) *n* (in the US) a temporary lake, or its dry often salty bed, in a desert basin [Spanish: shore, from Late Latin *plagia,* from Greek *plagios* slanting, from *plagos* side; compare French *plage* beach]

playable (ˈpleɪəbᵊl) *adj* able to be played or played up: *a simple bagatelle, playable by anybody; I doubt if our pitch is playable* > ˌ**playaˈbility** *n*

play-act *vb* **1** *(intr)* to pretend or make believe **2** *(intr)* to behave in an overdramatic or affected manner **3** to act in or as in (a play) > ˈ**play-ˌacting** *n* > ˈ**play-ˌactor** *n*

play along *vb (adverb)* **1** *(intr;* usually foll by *with)* to cooperate (with), esp as a temporary measure **2** *(tr)* to manipulate as if in a game, esp for one's own advantage: *he played the widow along until she gave him her money*

playback (ˈpleɪˌbæk) *n* **1** the act or process of reproducing a recording, esp on magnetic tape **2** the part of a tape recorder serving to reproduce or used for reproducing recorded material **3** *(modifier)* of or relating to the reproduction of signals from a recording: *the playback head of a tape recorder* ▷ *vb* **play back** *(adverb)* **4** to reproduce (recorded material) on (a magnetic tape) by means of a tape recorder

playbill (ˈpleɪˌbɪl) *n* **1** a poster or bill advertising a play **2** the programme of a play

playbook (ˈpleɪˌbʊk) *n* **1** a book containing a range of possible set plays **2** a notional range of possible tactics in any sphere of activity

playboy (ˈpleɪˌbɔɪ) *n* a man, esp one of private means, who devotes himself to the pleasures of nightclubs, expensive holiday resorts, female company, etc

play-centre *n NZ* a regular meeting of small children arranged by their parents or a welfare agency to give them an opportunity of supervised creative play. Also called (esp in Britain): **playgroup**

play down *vb (tr, adverb)* to make little or light of; minimize the importance of

player (ˈpleɪə) *n* **1** a person who participates in or is skilled at some game or sport **2** a person who plays a game or sport professionally **3** a person who plays a musical instrument **4** an actor **5** *informal* a participant, esp a powerful one, in a particular field of activity: *a leading city player* **6** See **record player** **7** the playing mechanism in a Pianola

player piano *n* a mechanical piano; Pianola

playful (ˈpleɪfʊl) *adj* **1** full of high spirits and fun: *a playful kitten* **2** good-natured and humorous: *a playful remark* > ˈ**playfully** *adv* > ˈ**playfulness** *n*

playgoer (ˈpleɪˌɡəʊə) *n* a person who goes to theatre performances, esp frequently

playground (ˈpleɪˌɡraʊnd) *n* **1** an outdoor area for children's play, esp one having swings, slides, etc, or adjoining a school **2** a place or region particularly popular as a sports or holiday resort **3** a sphere of activity: *reading was his private playground*

playgroup (ˈpleɪˌɡruːp) *n* a regular meeting of small children arranged by their parents or a welfare agency to give them an opportunity of supervised creative play. See also **preschool, playschool**

playhouse (ˈpleɪˌhaʊs) *n* **1** a theatre where live dramatic performances are given **2** a toy house, small room, etc, for children to play in

playing card *n* one of a pack of 52 rectangular stiff cards, used for playing a variety of games, each card having one or more symbols of the same kind (diamonds, hearts, clubs, or spades) on the face, but an identical design on the reverse. See also **suit** (sense 4)

playing field *n chiefly Brit* a field or open space used for sport

playlet (ˈpleɪlɪt) *n* a short play

playlist (ˈpleɪˌlɪst) *n* **1** a list of records chosen for playing, as on a radio station ▷ *vb* **2** *(tr)* to put (a song or record) on a playlist

play-lunch *n NZ* a schoolchild's mid-morning snack

playmaker (ˈpleɪˌmeɪkə) *n sport* a player whose role is to create scoring opportunities for his or her team-mates

playmate (ˈpleɪˌmeɪt) *or* **playfellow** *n* a friend or partner in play or recreation: *childhood playmates*

play off *vb (adverb)* **1** *(tr;* usually foll by *against)* to deal with or manipulate as if in playing a game: *to play one person off against another* **2** *(intr)* to take part in a play-off ▷ *n* **play-off** **3** *sport* an extra contest to decide the winner when two or more competitors are tied **4** *chiefly US and Canadian* a contest or series of games to determine a championship, as between the winners of two competitions

play on *vb (intr)* **1** *(adverb)* to continue to play **2** *(preposition)* Also: **play upon** to exploit or impose upon (the feelings or weakness of another) to one's own advantage **3** *(adverb) cricket* to hit the ball into one's own wicket

play on words *n* another term for **pun¹** (sense 1)

play out *vb (adverb)* **1** *(tr)* to finish: *let's play the game out if we aren't too late* **2** *(tr;* often *passive) informal* to use up or exhaust **3** *(tr)* to release gradually: *he played the rope out* **4** *(intr)* to happen or turn out: *Let's wait and see how things play out*

playpen (ˈpleɪˌpɛn) *n* a small enclosure, usually portable, in which a young child can be left to play in safety

playroom (ˈpleɪˌruːm, -ˌrʊm) *n* a recreation room, esp for children

playschool (ˈpleɪˌskuːl) *n* an informal nursery group taking preschool children in half-day sessions. Also called: **playgroup**

playsuit (ˈpleɪˌsuːt, -ˌsjuːt) *n* a woman's or child's outfit, usually comprising shorts and a top

play-the-ball *n rugby league* a method for bringing the ball back into play after a tackle, in which the tackled player is allowed to stand up and kick or heel the ball behind him or her to a team-mate

plaything (ˈpleɪˌθɪŋ) *n* **1** a toy **2** a person regarded or treated as a toy: *he thinks she is just his plaything*

playtime (ˈpleɪˌtaɪm) *n* a time for play or recreation, esp the school break

play up *vb (adverb)* **1** *(tr)* to emphasize or highlight: *to play up one's best features* **2** *Brit informal* to behave irritatingly (towards) **3** *(intr) Brit informal* (of a machine, car, etc) to function erratically: *the car is playing up again* **4** *Brit informal* to hurt; give (one) pain or trouble: *my back's playing me up again* **5** **play up to** **a** to support (another actor) in a performance **b** to try to gain favour with by flattery

play with *vb (intr, preposition)* **1** to consider without giving deep thought to or coming to a conclusion concerning: *we're playing with the idea of emigrating* **2** to behave carelessly with: *to play with a girl's affections* **3** to fiddle or mess about with: *he's just playing with his food*

playwright (ˈpleɪˌraɪt) *n* a person who writes plays

plaza (ˈplɑːzə; *Spanish* ˈplaθa) *n* **1** an open space or square, esp in Spain or a Spanish-speaking country **2** *chiefly US and Canadian* **a** a modern complex of shops, buildings, and parking areas **b** (*capital when part of a name*): *Rockefeller Plaza* [C17 from Spanish, from Latin *platēa* courtyard, from Greek *plateia*; see PLACE]

plc *or* **PLC** *abbreviation for* public limited company. See also **limited** (sense 5)

plea (pliː) *n* **1** an earnest entreaty or request: *a plea for help* **2** **a** *law* something alleged or pleaded by or on behalf of a party to legal proceedings in support of his claim or defence **b** *criminal law* the answer made by an accused to the charge: *a plea of guilty* **c** (in Scotland and formerly in England) a suit or action at law **3** an excuse, justification, or pretext: *he gave the plea of a previous engagement* [C13 from Anglo-Norman *plai*, from Old French *plaid* lawsuit, from Medieval Latin *placitum* court order (literally: what is pleasing), from Latin *placēre* to please]

plea bargaining *n* an agreement between the prosecution and defence, sometimes including the judge, in which the accused agrees to plead guilty to a lesser charge in return for more serious charges being dropped

pleach (pliːtʃ) *vb* *chiefly Brit* to interlace the stems or boughs of (a tree or hedge). Also: **plash** [C14 *plechen*, from Old North French *plechier*, from Latin *plectere* to weave, plait; compare PLASH[2]]

plead (pliːd) *vb* **pleads, pleading; pleaded, plead** (plɛd) *or esp Scot and US* **pled** (plɛd) **1** (when *intr*, often foll by *with*) to appeal earnestly or humbly (to) **2** (*tr; may take a clause as object*) to give as an excuse; offer in justification or extenuation: *to plead ignorance; he pleaded that he was insane* **3** (*intr*; often foll by *for*) to provide an argument or appeal (for): *her beauty pleads for her* **4** *law* to declare oneself to be (guilty or not guilty) in answer to the charge **5** *law* to advocate (a case) in a court of law **6** (*intr*) *law* **a** to file pleadings **b** to address a court as an advocate [C13 from Old French *plaidier*, from Medieval Latin *placitāre* to have a lawsuit, from Latin *placēre* to please; see PLEA] > ˈ**pleadable** *adj* > ˈ**pleader** *n*

pleading (ˈpliːdɪŋ) *n* *law* **1** the act of presenting a case in court, as by a lawyer on behalf of his client **2** the art or science of preparing the formal written statements of the parties to a legal action. See also **pleadings**

pleadings (ˈpliːdɪŋz) *pl n* *law* (formerly) the formal written statements presented alternately by the claimant and defendant in a lawsuit setting out the respective matters relied upon. Official name: **statements of case**

pleasance (ˈplɛzəns) *n* **1** a secluded part of a garden laid out with trees, walks, etc **2** *archaic* enjoyment or pleasure [C14 *plesaunce*, from Old French *plaisance*, from *plaisant* pleasant, from *plaisir* to PLEASE]

pleasant (ˈplɛzᵊnt) *adj* **1** giving or affording pleasure; enjoyable **2** having pleasing or agreeable manners, appearance, habits, etc **3** *obsolete* merry and lively [C14 from Old French *plaisant*, from *plaisir* to PLEASE] > ˈ**pleasantly** *adv* > ˈ**pleasantness** *n*

Pleasant Island *n* the former name of **Nauru**

pleasantry (ˈplɛzᵊntrɪ) *n, pl* **-ries** **1** (*often plural*) an agreeable or amusing remark, often one made in order to be polite: *they exchanged pleasantries* **2** an agreeably humorous manner or style **3** *rare* enjoyment; pleasantness: *a pleasantry of life* [C17 from French *plaisanterie*, from *plaisant* PLEASANT]

please (pliːz) *vb* **1** to give satisfaction, pleasure, or contentment to (a person); make or cause (a person) to be glad **2** to be the will of or have the will (to): *if it pleases you; the court pleases* **3** **if you please** if you will or wish, sometimes used in ironic exclamation **4** **pleased with** happy because of **5** **please oneself** to do as one likes ▷ *adv* **6** (*sentence modifier*) used in making polite requests and in pleading, asking for a favour, etc: *please don't tell the police where I am* **7** **yes please** a polite formula for accepting an offer, invitation, etc [C14 *plese*, from Old French *plaisir*, from Latin *placēre* to please, satisfy] > ˈ**pleasable** *adj* > **pleased** *adj* > **pleasedly** (ˈpliːzɪdlɪ) *adv* > ˈ**pleaser** *n*

pleasing (ˈpliːzɪŋ) *adj* giving pleasure; likable or gratifying > ˈ**pleasingly** *adv* > ˈ**pleasingness** *n*

pleasurable (ˈplɛʒərəbᵊl) *adj* enjoyable, agreeable, or gratifying > ˈ**pleasurableness** *n* > ˈ**pleasurably** *adv*

pleasure (ˈplɛʒə) *n* **1** an agreeable or enjoyable sensation or emotion: *the pleasure of hearing good music* **2** something that gives or affords enjoyment or delight: *his garden was his only pleasure* **3** **a** amusement, recreation, or enjoyment **b** (*as modifier*): *a pleasure boat; pleasure ground* **4** *euphemistic* sexual gratification or enjoyment: *he took his pleasure of her* **5** a person's preference or choice ▷ *vb* **6** (when *intr*, often foll by *in*) to give pleasure to or take pleasure (in) [C14 *plesir*, from Old French; related to Old French *plaisir* to PLEASE] > ˈ**pleasureful** *adj* > ˈ**pleasureless** *adj*

pleasure principle *n* *psychoanal* the idea that psychological processes and actions are governed by the gratification of needs. It is seen as the governing process of the id, whereas the reality principle is the governing process of the ego. See also **hedonism**

pleat (pliːt) *n* **1** any of various types of fold formed by doubling back fabric and pressing, stitching, or steaming into place. See also **box pleat, inverted pleat, kick pleat, knife pleat, sunburst pleats** ▷ *vb* **2** (*tr*) to arrange (material, part of a garment, etc) in pleats [C16 variant of PLAIT]

pleater (ˈpliːtə) *n* an attachment on a sewing machine that makes pleats

pleb (plɛb) *n* **1** short for **plebeian** **2** *Brit informal, often derogatory* a common vulgar person ▷ See also **plebs**

plebby (ˈplɛbɪ) *adj* **-bier, -biest** *Brit informal, often derogatory* common or vulgar: *a plebby party* [C20 shortened from PLEBEIAN]

plebe (pliːb) *n* *informal* a member of the lowest class at the US Naval Academy or Military Academy; freshman [C19 shortened from PLEBEIAN]

plebeian (pləˈbiːən) *adj* **1** of, relating to, or characteristic of the common people, esp those of Rome **2** lacking refinement; vulgar: *plebeian tastes* ▷ *n* **3** one of the common people, esp one of the Roman plebs **4** a person who is coarse or lacking in discernment [C16 from Latin *plēbēius* belonging to the people, from *plēbs* the common people of ancient Rome] > **pleˈbeian,ism** *n*

plebiscite (ˈplɛbɪˌsaɪt, -sɪt) *n* **1** a direct vote by the electorate of a state, region, etc, on some question of usually national importance, such as union with another state or acceptance of a government programme **2** any expression or determination of public opinion on some matter ▷ See also **referendum** [C16 from Old French *plēbiscite*, from Latin *plēbiscītum* decree of the people, from *plēbs* the populace + *scītum*, from *scīscere* to decree, approve, from *scīre* to know] > **plebiscitary** (pləˈbɪsɪtərɪ) *adj*

plebs (plɛbz) *n* **1** (*functioning as plural*) the common people; the masses **2** (*functioning as singular or plural*) common people of ancient Rome. Compare **patrician** [C17 from Latin: the common people of ancient Rome]

plectognath (ˈplɛktɒgˌnæθ) *n* **1** any spiny-finned marine fish of the mainly tropical order *Plectognathi* (or *Tetraodontiformes*), having a small mouth, strong teeth, and small gill openings: includes puffers, triggerfish, trunkfish, sunfish, etc ▷ *adj* **2** of, relating to, or belonging to the order *Plectognathi* [C19 via New Latin from Greek *plektos* twisted + *gnathos* jaw]

plectrum (ˈplɛktrəm) *n, pl* **-trums** *or* **-tra** (-trə) any implement for plucking a string, such as a small piece of plastic, wood, etc, used to strum a guitar, or the quill that plucks the string of a harpsichord [C17 from Latin *plēctrum* quill, plectrum, from Greek *plektron*, from *plessein* to strike]

pled (plɛd) *vb* *US or (esp in legal usage) Scot* a past tense and past participle of **plead**

pledge (plɛdʒ) *n* **1** a formal or solemn promise or agreement, esp to do or refrain from doing something **2** **a** collateral for the payment of a debt or the performance of an obligation **b** the condition of being collateral (esp in the phrase **in pledge**) **3** a sign, token, or indication: *the gift is a pledge of their sincerity* **4** an assurance of support or goodwill, conveyed by drinking to a person, cause, etc; toast: *we drank a pledge to their success* **5** a person who binds himself, as by becoming bail or surety for another **6** **take** *or* **sign the pledge** to make a vow to abstain from alcoholic drink ▷ *vb* **7** to promise formally or solemnly: *he pledged allegiance* **8** (*tr*) to bind or secure by or as if by a pledge: *they were pledged to secrecy* **9** to give, deposit, or offer (one's word, freedom, property, etc) as a guarantee, as for the repayment of a loan **10** to drink a toast to (a person, cause, etc) [C14 from Old French *plege*, from Late Latin *plebium* gage, security, from *plebīre* to pledge, of Germanic origin; compare Old High German *pflegan* to look after, care for] > ˈ**pledgable** *adj*

pledgee (plɛdʒˈiː) *n* **1** a person to whom a pledge is given **2** a person to whom property is delivered as a pledge

pledget (ˈplɛdʒɪt) *n* a small flattened pad of wool, cotton, etc, esp for use as a pressure bandage to be applied to wounds or sores [C16 of unknown origin]

pledgor, pledgeor (plɛdʒˈɔː) *or* **pledger** (ˈplɛdʒə) *n* a person who gives or makes a pledge

-plegia *n combining form* indicating a specified type of paralysis: *paraplegia* [from Greek, from *plēgē* stroke, from *plēssein* to strike] > **-plegic** *adj and n combining form*

pleiad (ˈplaɪəd) *n* a brilliant or talented group, esp one with seven members [C16 originally French *Pléiade*, name given by Pierre de Ronsard (1524–85) to himself and six other poets after a group of Alexandrian Greek poets who were called this after the PLEIADES[1]]

Pleiad (ˈplaɪəd) *n* one of the Pleiades (stars or daughters of Atlas)

Pleiades[1] (ˈplaɪəˌdiːz) *pl n* *Greek myth* the seven daughters of Atlas, placed as stars in the sky either to save them from the pursuit of Orion or, in another account, after they had killed themselves for grief over the death of their half-sisters the Hyades

Pleiades[2] (ˈplaɪəˌdiːz) *pl n* a young conspicuous open star cluster approximately 370 light years away in the constellation Taurus, containing several thousand stars only six or seven of which are visible to the naked eye. Compare **Hyades[1]**

plein-air (ˌpleɪnˈɛə; *French* plɛnɛr) *adj* of or in the manner of various French 19th-century schools of painting, esp impressionism, concerned with the observation of light and atmosphere effects outdoors [C19 from French phrase *en plein air* in the open (literally: full) air] > **plein-airist** (ˌpleɪnˈɛərɪst) *n*

pleio- *combining form* a variant of **plio-**

Pleiocene (ˈplaɪəʊˌsiːn) *adj, n* a variant spelling of **Pliocene**

pleiotropism (plaɪˈɒtrəˌpɪzəm) *n* *genetics* the condition of a gene of affecting more than one characteristic of the phenotype

Pleistocene (ˈplaɪstəˌsiːn) *adj* **1** of, denoting, or formed in the first epoch of the Quaternary period, which lasted for about 1 600 000 years. It was characterized by extensive glaciations of the

N hemisphere and the evolutionary development of man ▷ n 2 **the** the Pleistocene epoch or rock series [C19 from Greek *pleistos* most + *kainos* recent]

plenary ('pliːnərɪ, 'plɛn-) *adj* 1 full, unqualified, or complete: *plenary powers; plenary indulgence* 2 (of assemblies, councils, etc) attended by all the members ▷ *n, pl* **-ries** 3 a book of the gospels or epistles and homilies read at the Eucharist [C15 from Late Latin *plēnārius*, from Latin *plēnus* full; related to Middle English *plener*; see PLENUM] > '**plenarily** *adv*

plenipotent (plə'nɪpətənt) *adj* a less common word for **plenipotentiary**

plenipotentiary (ˌplɛnɪpə'tɛnʃərɪ) *adj* 1 (esp of a diplomatic envoy) invested with or possessing full power or authority 2 conferring full power or authority 3 (of power or authority) full; absolute ▷ *n, pl* **-aries** 4 a person invested with full authority to transact business, esp a diplomat authorized to represent a country. See also **envoy**[1] (sense 1) [C17 from Medieval Latin *plēnipotentiārius*, from Latin *plēnus* full + *potentia* POWER]

plenish ('plɛnɪʃ) *vb (tr) Scot* to fill, stock, or resupply [C15 from Old French *pleniss-*, from *plenir*, from Latin *plēnus* full] > '**plenisher** *n* > '**plenishment** *n*

plenitude ('plɛnɪˌtjuːd) *n* 1 abundance; copiousness 2 the condition of being full or complete [C15 via Old French from Latin *plēnitūdō*, from *plēnus* full]

plenteous ('plɛntɪəs) *adj* 1 ample; abundant: *a plenteous supply of food* 2 producing or yielding abundantly: *a plenteous grape harvest* [C13 *plenteus*, from Old French *plentivous*, from *plentif* abundant, from *plenté* PLENTY] > '**plenteously** *adv* > '**plenteousness** *n*

plentiful ('plɛntɪfʊl) *adj* 1 ample; abundant 2 having or yielding an abundance: *a plentiful year* > '**plentifully** *adv* > '**plentifulness** *n*

plenty ('plɛntɪ) *n, pl* **-ties** 1 (often foll by *of*) a great number, amount, or quantity; lots: *plenty of time; there are plenty of cars on display here* 2 generous or ample supplies of wealth, produce, or resources: *the age of plenty* 3 **in plenty** existing in abundance: *food in plenty* ▷ *determiner* 4 **a** very many; ample: *plenty of people believe in ghosts* **b** (*as pronoun*): *there's plenty more; that's plenty, thanks* ▷ *adv* 5 *not standard, chiefly US* (intensifier): *he was plenty mad* 6 *informal* more than adequately; abundantly: *the water's plenty hot enough* [C13 from Old French *plenté*, from Late Latin *plēnitās* fullness, from Latin *plēnus* full]

Plenty ('plɛntɪ) *n* **Bay of** a large bay of the Pacific on the NE coast of the North Island, New Zealand

plenum ('pliːnəm) *n, pl* **-nums** *or* **-na** (-nə) 1 an enclosure containing gas at a higher pressure than the surrounding environment 2 a fully attended meeting or assembly, esp of a legislative body 3 (esp in the philosophy of the Stoics) space regarded as filled with matter. Compare **vacuum** (sense 1) 4 the condition or quality of being full [C17 from Latin: space filled by matter, from *plēnus* full]

plenum system *n* a type of air-conditioning system in which air is passed into a room at a pressure greater than atmospheric pressure

pleo- *combining form* a variant of **plio-** *pleochroism; pleomorphism*

pleochroism (plɪ'ɒkrəʊˌɪzəm) *n* a property of certain crystals of absorbing light to an extent that depends on the orientation of the electric vector of the light with respect to the optic axes of the crystal. The effect occurs in uniaxial crystals (**dichroism**) and esp in biaxial crystals (**trichroism**) [C19 PLEO- + *-chroism*, from Greek *khrōs* skin colour] > **pleochroic** (ˌpliːə'krəʊɪk) *adj*

pleomorphism (ˌpliːə'mɔːˌfɪzəm) *or* **pleomorphy** ('pliːəˌmɔːfɪ) *n* 1 the occurrence of more than one different form in the life cycle of a plant or animal 2 the occurrence of more than one different form of crystal of one chemical compound; polymorphism > ˌ**pleo'morphic** *adj*

pleonasm ('pliːəˌnæzəm) *n rhetoric* 1 the use of more words than necessary or an instance of this, such as *a tiny little child* 2 a word or phrase that is superfluous [C16 from Latin *pleonasmus*, from Greek *pleonasmos* excess, from *pleonazein* to be redundant] > ˌ**pleo'nastic** *adj* > ˌ**pleo'nastically** *adv*

pleopod ('pliːəˌpɒd) *n* another name for **swimmeret** [C19 from Greek *plein* to swim + *pous* foot]

plerion ('plɪərɪən) *n* a filled-centre supernova remnant in which radiation is emitted by the centre as well as the shell [from New Latin, from Greek *plerome* a filling + -ION]

plesiosaur ('pliːsɪəˌsɔː) *n* any of various extinct marine reptiles of the order *Sauropterygia*, esp any of the suborder *Plesiosauria*, of Jurassic and Cretaceous times, having a long neck, short tail, and paddle-like limbs. See also **ichthyosaur**. Compare **dinosaur, pterosaur** [C19 from New Latin *plēsiosaurus*, from Greek *plēsios* near + *sauros* a lizard]

plessor ('plɛsə) *n* another name for **plexor**

plethora ('plɛθərə) *n* 1 superfluity or excess; overabundance 2 *pathol obsolete* a condition caused by dilation of superficial blood vessels, characterized esp by a reddish face [C16 via Medieval Latin from Greek *plēthōrē* fullness, from *plēthein* to grow full] > **plethoric** (plɛ'θɒrɪk) *adj* > **ple'thorically** *adv*

plethysmograph (plə'θɪzməˌgrɑːf, -ˌgræf, -'θɪs-) *n* a device for measuring the fluctuations in volume of a bodily organ or part, such as those caused by variations in the amount of blood it contains [C19 from Greek *plēthusmos* enlargement + *graphein* to write]

pleugh *or* **pleuch** (pluː, pluːx) *n, vb* a Scot word for **plough**

pleura ('plʊərə) *n, pl* **pleurae** ('plʊəriː) 1 the thin transparent serous membrane enveloping the lungs and lining the walls of the thoracic cavity 2 the plural of **pleuron** [C17 via Medieval Latin from Greek: side, rib] > '**pleural** *adj*

pleurisy ('plʊərɪsɪ) *n* inflammation of the pleura, characterized by pain that is aggravated by deep breathing or coughing [C14 from Old French *pleurisie*, from Late Latin *pleurisis*, from Greek *pleuritis*, from *pleura* side] > **pleuritic** (plʊ'rɪtɪk) *adj, n*

pleurisy root *n* 1 the root of the butterfly weed, formerly used as a cure for pleurisy 2 another name for **butterfly weed**

pleuro- *or before a vowel* **pleur-** *combining form* 1 of or relating to the side: *pleurodont; pleurodynia* 2 indicating the pleura: *pleurotomy* [from Greek *pleura* side]

pleurocarpous (ˌplʊərəʊ'kɑːpəs) *adj* (of mosses) having mainly horizontal trailing stems and the reproductive parts borne laterally ▷ Compare **acrocarpous**

pleurocentesis (ˌplʊərəʊsɛn'tiːsɪs) *n* another name for **thoracentesis**

pleurodont ('plʊərəʊˌdɒnt) *adj* 1 (of the teeth of some reptiles) having no roots and being fused by their lateral sides only to the inner surface of the jawbone. See also **acrodont** (sense 1) 2 having pleurodont teeth: *pleurodont lizards* ▷ *n* 3 an animal having pleurodont teeth

pleurodynia (ˌplʊərəʊ'daɪnɪə) *n* pain in the muscles between the ribs [C19 from New Latin, from PLEURO- + Greek *-odynia*, from *odynē* pain]

pleuron ('plʊərɒn) *n, pl* **pleura** ('plʊərə) the part of the cuticle of arthropods that covers the lateral surface of a body segment [C18 from Greek: side]

pleuropneumonia (ˌplʊərəʊnjuː'məʊnɪə) *n* the combined disorder of pleurisy and pneumonia

pleurotomy (plʊ'rɒtəmɪ) *n, pl* **-mies** surgical incision into the pleura, esp to drain fluid, as in pleurisy

pleuston ('pluːstən, -stɒn) *n* a mass of small organisms, esp algae, floating at the surface of shallow pools [C20 from Greek *pleusis* sailing, from *plein* to sail; for form, compare PLANKTON]

pleustonic (pluː'stɒnɪk) *adj* 1 of or relating to pleuston 2 denoting a marine organism held at the surface of the water by a float, such as the Portuguese man-of-war

Pleven (*Bulgarian* 'plɛvɛn) *or* **Plevna** (*Bulgarian* 'plɛvna) *n* a town in N Bulgaria: taken by Russia from the Turks in 1877 after a siege of 143 days. Pop: 102 000 (2005 est)

plew, plu *or* **plue** (pluː) *n* (formerly in Canada) a beaver skin used as a standard unit of value in the fur trade [from Canadian French *pelu* (adj) hairy, from French *poilu*, from *poil* hair, from Latin *pilus*]

plexiform ('plɛksɪˌfɔːm) *adj* like or having the form of a network or plexus; intricate or complex

Plexiglas ('plɛksɪˌglɑːs) *n trademark US* a transparent plastic, polymethylmethacrylate, used for combs, plastic sheeting, etc

plexor ('plɛksə) *or* **plessor** *n med* a small hammer with a rubber head for use in percussion of the chest and testing reflexes [C19 from Greek *plēxis* a stroke, from *plēssein* to strike]

plexus ('plɛksəs) *n, pl* **-uses** *or* **-us** 1 any complex network of nerves, blood vessels, or lymphatic vessels 2 an intricate network or arrangement [C17 New Latin, from Latin *plectere* to braid, PLAIT]

pliable ('plaɪəbᵊl) *adj* easily moulded, bent, influenced, or altered > ˌ**plia'bility** *or* '**pliableness** *n* > '**pliably** *adv*

pliant ('plaɪənt) *adj* 1 easily bent; supple: *a pliant young tree* 2 easily modified; adaptable; flexible: *a pliant system* 3 yielding readily to influence; compliant [C14 from Old French, from *plier* to fold, bend; see PLY[2]] > '**pliancy** *or* '**pliantness** *n* > '**pliantly** *adv*

plica ('plaɪkə) *n, pl* **plicae** ('plaɪsiː) 1 Also called: **fold** *anatomy* a folding over of parts, such as a fold of skin, muscle, peritoneum, etc 2 *pathol* a condition of the hair characterized by matting, filth, and the presence of parasites [C17 from Medieval Latin: a fold, from Latin *plicāre* to fold; see PLY[2]] > '**plical** *adj*

plicate ('plaɪkeɪt) *or* **plicated** *adj* having or arranged in parallel folds or ridges; pleated: *a plicate leaf; plicate rock strata* [C18 from Latin *plicātus* folded, from *plicāre* to fold] > '**plicately** *adv* > '**plicateness** *n*

P

plication (plaɪ'keɪʃən) *or* **plicature** ('plɪkətʃə) *n* 1 the act of folding or the condition of being folded or plicate 2 a folded part or structure, esp a fold in a series of rock strata 3 *surgery* the act or process of suturing together the walls of a hollow organ or part to reduce its size

plié ('pliːeɪ) *n* a classic ballet practice posture with back erect and knees bent [French: bent, from *plier* to bend]

plier ('plaɪə) *n* a person who plies a trade

pliers ('plaɪəz) *pl n* a gripping tool consisting of two hinged arms with usually serrated jaws that close on the workpiece [C16 from PLY[1]]

plight[1] (plaɪt) *n* a condition of extreme hardship, danger, etc [C14 *plit*, from Old French *pleit* fold, PLAIT; probably influenced by Old English *pliht* peril, PLIGHT[2]]

plight[2] (plaɪt) *vb (tr)* 1 to give or pledge (one's word): *he plighted his word to attempt it* 2 to promise formally or pledge (allegiance, support, etc): *to plight aid* 3 **plight one's troth** **a** to make a promise of marriage **b** to give one's solemn promise ▷ *n* 4 *archaic or dialect* a solemn promise, esp of engagement; pledge [Old English *pliht* peril; related to Old High German, German *Pflicht* duty] > '**plighter** *n*

plimsoll *or* **plimsole** ('plɪmsəl) *n Brit* a light rubber-soled canvas shoe worn for various sports. Also called: **gym shoe, sandshoe** [C20 so called because of the resemblance of the rubber sole to a Plimsoll line]

Plimsoll line ('plɪmsəl) *n* another name for **load line** [C19 named after Samuel *Plimsoll* (1824–98), MP, who advocated its adoption]

Plinian ('plɪnɪən) *adj geology* (of a volcanic eruption) characterized by repeated explosions [C20 named after Pliny the Younger (Latin name *Gaius Plinius Caecilius Secundus*. ?62–?113 AD), Roman writer and administrator, who described such eruptions]

plink (plɪŋk) *n* 1 a short sharp often metallic sound as of a string on a musical instrument being plucked or a bullet striking metal ▷ *vb* 2 (*intr*) to make such a noise 3 to hit (a target, such as a tin can) by shooting or to shoot at such a target [c20 of imitative origin] > '**plinking** *n, adj*

plinth (plɪnθ) *n* 1 Also called: **socle** the rectangular slab or block that forms the lowest part of the base of a column, statue, pedestal, or pier 2 Also called: **plinth course** the lowest part of the wall of a building that appears above ground level, esp one that is formed of a course of stone or brick 3 a flat block on either side of a doorframe, where the architrave meets the skirting 4 a flat base on which a structure or piece of equipment is placed [c17 from Latin *plinthus*, from Greek *plinthos* brick, shaped stone]

plio-, pleo- *or* **pleio-** *combining form* greater in size, extent, degree, etc; more: *Pliocene* [from Greek *pleiōn* more, from *polus* much, many]

Pliocene *or* **Pleiocene** (ˈplaɪəʊˌsiːn) *adj* 1 of, denoting, or formed in the last epoch of the Tertiary period, which lasted for three million years, during which many modern mammals appeared ▷ *n* 2 **the** the Pliocene epoch or rock series [c19 PLIO- + -*cene*, from Greek *kainos* recent]

plissé (ˈpliːseɪ, ˈplɪs-) *n* 1 fabric with a wrinkled finish, achieved by treatment involving caustic soda: *cotton plissé* 2 such a finish on a fabric [French *plissé* pleated, from *plisser* to pleat; see PLY²]

PLO *abbreviation for* **Palestine Liberation Organization**

ploat (pləʊt) *vb* (*tr*) *Northeastern English dialect* 1 to thrash; beat soundly 2 to pluck (a fowl) [from Dutch or Flemish *ploten* to pluck the feathers or fur from]

Płock (pwɒtsk) *n* a town in central Poland, on the River Vistula: several Polish kings are buried in the cathedral; oil refining, petrochemical works. Pop: 130 000 (2005 est)

plod (plɒd) *vb* **plods, plodding, plodded** 1 to make (one's way) or walk along (a path, road, etc) with heavy usually slow steps 2 (*intr*) to work slowly and perseveringly ▷ *n* 3 the act of plodding 4 the sound of slow heavy steps 5 *Brit slang* a policeman [c16 of imitative origin] > '**plodding** *adj* > '**ploddingly** *adv* > '**ploddingness** *n*

plodder (ˈplɒdə) *n* a person who plods, esp one who works in a slow and persevering manner

plodge (plɒdʒ) *Northeastern English dialect* ▷ *vb* 1 (*intr*) to wade in water, esp the sea ▷ *n* 2 the act of wading [of imitative origin; related to PLOD]

Ploeşti (*Romanian* ploˈjeʃti) *n* a city in SE central Romania: centre of the Romanian petroleum industry. Pop: 204 000 (2005 est)

-ploid *adj and n combining form* indicating a specific multiple of a single set of chromosomes: *diploid* [from Greek *-pl(oos)* -fold + -OID] > **-ploidy** *n combining form*

plonk¹ (plɒŋk) *vb* 1 (often foll by *down*) to drop or be dropped, esp heavily or suddenly: *he plonked the money on the table* ▷ *n* 2 the act or sound of plonking ▷ *interj* 3 an exclamation imitative of this sound

plonk² (plɒŋk) *n Brit, Austral, and NZ informal* alcoholic drink, usually wine, esp of inferior quality [c20 perhaps from French *blanc* white, as in *vin blanc* white wine]

plonker (ˈplɒŋkə) *n slang* a stupid person [c20 from PLONK¹]

plonking (ˈplɒŋkɪŋ) *adj* foolish, clumsy, or inept: *his plonking response to the princess's death*

plonko (ˈplɒŋkəʊ) *n, pl* **plonkos** *Austral slang* an alcoholic, esp one who drinks wine [c20 from PLONK²]

plook (pluːk) *n Scot* a variant spelling of **plouk**

plop (plɒp) *n* 1 the characteristic sound made by an object dropping into water without a splash ▷ *vb* **plops, plopping, plopped** 2 to fall or cause to

fall with the sound of a plop: *the stone plopped into the water* ▷ *interj* 3 an exclamation imitative of this sound: *to go plop* [c19 imitative of the sound]

plosion (ˈpləʊʒən) *n phonetics* the sound of an abrupt break or closure, esp the audible release of a stop. Also called: **explosion**

plosive (ˈpləʊsɪv) *phonetics* ▷ *adj* 1 articulated with or accompanied by plosion ▷ *n* 2 a plosive consonant; stop [c20 from French, from *explosif* EXPLOSIVE]

plot¹ (plɒt) *n* 1 a secret plan to achieve some purpose, esp one that is illegal or underhand: *a plot to overthrow the government* 2 the story or plan of a play, novel, etc 3 *military* a graphic representation of an individual or tactical setting that pinpoints an artillery target 4 *chiefly US* a diagram or plan, esp a surveyor's map 5 **lose the plot** *informal* to lose one's ability or judgment in a given situation ▷ *vb* **plots, plotting, plotted** 6 to plan secretly (something illegal, revolutionary, etc); conspire 7 (*tr*) to mark (a course, as of a ship or aircraft) on a map 8 (*tr*) to make a plan or map of 9 **a** to locate and mark (one or more points) on a graph by means of coordinates **b** to draw (a curve) through these points 10 (*tr*) to construct the plot of (a literary work) [c16 from PLOT², influenced in use by COMPLOT]

plot² (plɒt) *n* 1 a small piece of land: *a vegetable plot* ▷ *vb* **plots, plotting, plotted** 2 (*tr*) to arrange or divide (land) into plots [Old English: piece of land, plan of an area]

plotter (ˈplɒtə) *n* 1 an instrument for plotting lines or angles on a chart 2 a person who plots; conspirator

plough *or esp US* **plow** (plaʊ) *n* 1 an agricultural implement with sharp blades, attached to a horse, tractor, etc, for cutting or turning over the earth 2 any of various similar implements, such as a device for clearing snow 3 a plane with a narrow blade for cutting grooves in wood 4 (in agriculture) ploughed land 5 **put one's hand to the plough** to begin or undertake a task ▷ *vb* 6 to till (the soil) with a plough 7 to make (furrows or grooves) in (something) with or as if with a plough 8 (when *intr*, usually foll by *through*) to move (through something) in the manner of a plough: *the ship ploughed the water* 9 (*intr*; foll by *through*) to work at slowly or perseveringly 10 (*intr*; foll by *into* or *through*) (of a vehicle) to run uncontrollably into something in its path: *the plane ploughed into the cottage roof* 11 (*tr*; foll by *in, up, under*, etc) to turn over (a growing crop, manure, etc) into the earth with a plough 12 (*intr*) *Brit slang* to fail an examination [Old English *plōg* plough land; related to Old Norse *plogr*, Old High German *pfluoc*] > '**plougher** *or esp US* '**plower** *n*

Plough (plaʊ) *n* **the** the group of the seven brightest stars in the constellation Ursa Major. Also called: **Charles's Wain.** Usual US name: **the Big Dipper**

plough back *vb* (*tr, adverb*) to reinvest (the profits of a business) in the same business

ploughboy *or esp US* **plowboy** (ˈplaʊˌbɔɪ) *n* 1 a boy who guides the animals drawing a plough 2 any country boy

ploughman *or esp US* **plowman** (ˈplaʊmən) *n, pl* **-men** 1 a man who ploughs, esp using horses 2 any farm labourer > '**ploughmanship** *or esp US* '**plowmanship** *n*

ploughman's lunch *n* a snack lunch, served esp in a pub, consisting of bread and cheese with pickle

ploughman's spikenard *n* a European plant, *Inula conyza*, with tubular yellowish flower heads surrounded by purple bracts: family *Asteraceae* (composites). Also called: **fleawort**

Plough Monday *n* the first Monday after Epiphany, which in N and E England used to be celebrated with a procession of ploughmen drawing a plough from house to house

ploughshare *or esp US* **plowshare** (ˈplaʊˌʃeə) *n* the horizontal pointed cutting blade of a

mouldboard plough

ploughstaff *or esp US* **plowstaff** (ˈplaʊˌstɑːf) *n* 1 Also called: **ploughtail** one of the handles of a plough 2 a spade-shaped tool used to clean the ploughshare and mouldboard

plouk *or* **plook** (pluːk) *n Scot* a pimple [c15 of uncertain origin] > '**plouky** *or* '**plooky** *adj*

Plovdiv (*Bulgarian* ˈplɒvdif) *n* a city in S Bulgaria on the Maritsa River: the second largest town in Bulgaria; conquered by Philip II of Macedonia in 341 BC; capital of Roman Thracia; commercial centre of a rich agricultural region. Pop: 339 000 (2005 est). Greek name: **Philippopolis**

plover (ˈplʌvə) *n* 1 any shore bird of the family *Charadriidae*, typically having a round head, straight bill, and large pointed wings: order *Charadriiformes* 2 any of similar and related birds, such as the Egyptian plover (see **crocodile bird**) and the upland plover 3 **green plover** another name for **lapwing** [c14 from Old French *plovier* rainbird, from Latin *pluvia* rain]

plow (plaʊ) *n, vb* the usual US spelling of **plough** > '**plower** *n*

plowter *or* **plouter** (ˈplaʊtər) *Scot* ▷ *vb* (*intr*) 1 to work or play in water or mud; dabble 2 to potter ▷ *n* 3 the act of plowtering [c19 of uncertain origin]

ploy (plɔɪ) *n* 1 a manoeuvre or tactic in a game, conversation, etc; stratagem; gambit 2 any business, job, hobby, etc, with which one is occupied: *angling is his latest ploy* 3 *chiefly Brit* a frolic, escapade, or practical joke [c18 originally Scot and northern English, perhaps from obsolete n sense of EMPLOY meaning an occupation]

PLP (in Britain) *abbreviation for* **Parliamentary Labour Party**

PLR *abbreviation for* **Public Lending Right**

plu *or* **plue** (pluː) *n* variant spellings of **plew**

PLU *text messaging abbreviation for* **people like us**

pluck (plʌk) *vb* 1 (*tr*) to pull off (feathers, fruit, etc) from (a fowl, tree, etc) 2 (when *intr*, foll by *at*) to pull or tug 3 (*tr*; foll by *off, away*, etc) *archaic* to pull (something) forcibly or violently (from something or someone) 4 (*tr*) to sound (the strings) of (a musical instrument) with the fingers, a plectrum, etc 5 (*tr*) another word for **strip¹** (sense 7) 6 (*tr*) *slang* to fleece or swindle ▷ *n* 7 courage, usually in the face of difficulties or hardship 8 a sudden pull or tug 9 the heart, liver, and lungs, esp of an animal used for food [Old English *pluccian, plyccan*; related to German *pflücken*] > '**plucker** *n*

pluck up *vb* (*tr, adverb*) 1 to pull out; uproot 2 to muster (courage, one's spirits, etc)

plucky (ˈplʌkɪ) *adj* **pluckier, pluckiest** having or showing courage in the face of difficulties, danger, etc > '**pluckily** *adv* > '**pluckiness** *n*

plug (plʌg) *n* 1 a piece of wood, cork, or other material, often cylindrical in shape, used to stop up holes and gaps or as a wedge for taking a screw or nail 2 such a stopper used esp to close the waste pipe of a bath, basin, or sink while it is in use and removed to let the water drain away 3 a device having one or more pins to which an electric cable is attached: used to make an electrical connection when inserted into a socket 4 Also called: **volcanic plug** a mass of solidified magma filling the neck of an extinct volcano 5 See **sparking plug** 6 **a** a cake of pressed or twisted tobacco, esp for chewing **b** a small piece of such a cake 7 *angling* a weighted artificial lure with one or more sets of hooks attached, used in spinning 8 a seedling with its roots encased in potting compost, grown in a tray with compartments for each individual plant 9 *informal* a recommendation or other favourable mention of a product, show, etc, as on television, on radio, or in newspapers 10 *slang* a shot, blow, or punch (esp in the phrase **take a plug at**) 11 *informal* the mechanism that releases water to flush a lavatory (esp in the phrase **pull the plug**) 12 *chiefly US* an old horse 13 **pull the plug on** *informal* to put a stop to ▷ *vb* **plugs, plugging, plugged** **14** (*tr*) to stop up or secure (a hole, gap, etc) with or as if with a plug **15** (*tr*) to insert or use (something) as a plug: *to plug a finger into one's ear* **16** (*tr*) *informal* to make favourable and often-repeated mentions of (a song, product, show, etc), esp on television, on radio, or in newspapers **17** (*tr*) *slang* to shoot with a gun: *he plugged six rabbits* **18** (*tr*) *slang* to punch or strike **19** (*intr; foll by along, away*, etc) *informal* to work steadily or persistently [C17 from Middle Dutch *plugge*; related to Middle Low German *plugge*, German *Pflock*] > ˈ**plugger** *n*

plug and play *or* **plug'n'play** *n* **1** *computing* a feature of hardware that enables computers to automatically detect and configure hardware devices without the need for intervention ▷ *adj* **plug-and-play** **2** capable of detecting the addition of a new input or output device and automatically activating the appropriate control software. Abbreviation: **PnP**

plugboard (ˈplʌɡˌbɔːd) *n* another name for **patch board**

plug compatible *adj computing* (of peripheral devices) designed to be plugged into computer systems produced by different manufacturers

plug gauge *n engineering* an accurately machined plug used for checking the diameter of a hole. Compare **ring gauge**

plugged-in *adj slang* up-to-date; abreast of the times

plughole (ˈplʌɡˌhəʊl) *n* a hole, esp in a bath, basin, or sink, through which waste water drains and which can be closed with a plug

plug in *vb* **1** (*tr, adverb*) to connect (an electrical appliance) with a power source by means of an electrical plug ▷ *n* **plug-in** **2** a device that can be connected by means of a plug **3** *computing* a module or piece of software that can be added to a system to provide extra functions or features, esp software that enhances the capabilities of a web browser **4** *computing* (*as modifier*): *plug-in memory cards*

plug-ugly *adj* **1** *informal* extremely ugly ▷ *n, pl* **-lies** **2** *US slang* a city tough; ruffian [C19 origin obscure; originally applied to ruffians in New York who attempted to exert political pressure]

plum¹ (plʌm) *n* **1** a small rosaceous tree, *Prunus domestica*, with white flowers and an edible oval fruit that is purple, yellow, or green and contains an oval stone. See also **greengage, damson** **2** the fruit of this tree **3** a raisin, as used in a cake or pudding **4 a** a dark reddish-purple colour **b** (*as adjective*): *a plum carpet* **5** *informal* **a** something of a superior or desirable kind, such as a financial bonus **b** (*as modifier*): *a plum job* [Old English *plūme*; related to Latin *prunum*, German *Pflaume*] > ˈ**plumˌlike** *adj*

plum² (plʌm) *adj, adv* a variant spelling of **plumb** (senses 3–6)

plumage (ˈpluːmɪdʒ) *n* the layer of feathers covering the body of a bird [C15 from Old French, from *plume* feather, from Latin *plūma* down]

plumate (ˈpluːmeɪt, -mɪt) *or* **plumose** *adj zoology, botany* **1** of, relating to, or possessing one or more feathers or plumes **2** resembling a plume; covered with small hairs: *a plumate seed* [C19 from Latin *plumātus* covered with feathers; see PLUME]

plumb (plʌm) *n* **1** a weight, usually of lead, suspended at the end of a line and used to determine water depth or verticality **2** the perpendicular position of a freely suspended plumb line (esp in the phrases **out of plumb, off plumb**) ▷ *adj also* **plum** **3** (*prenominal*) *informal, chiefly US* (intensifier): *a plumb nuisance* ▷ *adv also* **plum** **4** in a vertical or perpendicular line **5** *informal, chiefly US* (intensifier): *plumb stupid* **6** *informal* exactly; precisely (also in the phrase **plumb on**) ▷ *vb* **7** (*tr; often foll by up*) to test the alignment of or adjust to the vertical with a plumb line **8** (*tr*) to undergo or experience (the worst extremes of misery, sadness, etc): *to plumb the depths of despair* **9** (*tr*) to understand or master (something obscure): *to plumb a mystery* **10** to connect or join (a device such as a tap) to a water pipe or drainage system [C13 from Old French *plomb* (unattested) lead line, from Old French *plon* lead, from Latin *plumbum* lead] > ˈ**plumbable** *adj*

plumbaginaceous (plʌmˌbædʒɪˈneɪʃəs) *adj* of, relating to, or belonging to the *Plumbaginaceae*, a family of typically coastal plants having flowers with a brightly coloured calyx and five styles: includes leadwort, thrift, and sea lavender

plumbago (plʌmˈbeɪɡəʊ) *n, pl* **-gos** **1** any plumbaginaceous plant of the genus *Plumbago*, of warm regions, having clusters of blue, white, or red flowers. See also **leadwort** **2** another name for **graphite** [C17 from Latin: lead ore, leadwort, translation of Greek *polubdaina* lead ore, from *polubdos* lead]

plumb bob *n* the weight, usually of lead, at the end of a plumb line; plummet

plumbeous (ˈplʌmbɪəs) *adj* made of or relating to lead or resembling lead in colour [C16 from Latin *plumbeus* leaden, from *plumbum* lead]

plumber (ˈplʌmə) *n* a person who installs and repairs pipes, fixtures, etc, for water, drainage, and gas [C14 from Old French *plommier* worker in lead, from Late Latin *plumbārius*, from Latin *plumbum* lead]

plumbery (ˈplʌmərɪ) *n, pl* **-eries** **1** the workshop of a plumber **2** another word for **plumbing** (sense 1)

plumbic (ˈplʌmbɪk) *adj* of or containing lead in the tetravalent state

Plumbicon (ˈplʌmbɪˌkɒn) *n trademark* a development of the vidicon television camera tube in which the photosensitive material is lead oxide

plumbiferous (plʌmˈbɪfərəs) *adj* (of ores, rocks, etc) containing or yielding lead

plumbing (ˈplʌmɪŋ) *n* **1** Also called: **plumbery** the trade or work of a plumber **2** the pipes, fixtures, etc, used in a water, drainage, or gas installation **3** the act or procedure of using a plumb to gauge depth, a vertical, etc

plumbism (ˈplʌmˌbɪzəm) *n* chronic lead poisoning [C19 from Latin *plumbum* lead]

plumb line *n* **1** a string with a metal weight at one end that, when suspended, points directly towards the earth's centre of gravity and so is used to determine verticality, the depth of water, etc **2** another name for **plumb rule**

plumbous (ˈplʌmbəs) *adj* of or containing lead in the divalent state [C17 from Late Latin *plumbōsus* full of lead, from Latin *plumbum* lead]

plumb rule *n* a plumb line attached to a narrow board, used by builders, surveyors, etc

plumbum (ˈplʌmbəm) *n* an obsolete name for **lead²** (the metal) [from Latin]

plume (pluːm) *n* **1** a feather, esp one that is large or ornamental **2** a feather or cluster of feathers worn esp formerly as a badge or ornament in a headband, hat, etc **3** *biology* any feathery part, such as the structure on certain fruits and seeds that aids dispersal by wind **4** something that resembles a plume: *a plume of smoke* **5** a token or decoration of honour; prize **6** *geology* a rising column of hot, low viscosity material within the earth's mantle, which is believed to be responsible for linear oceanic island chains and flood basalts. Also called **mantle plume** ▷ *vb* (*tr*) **7** to adorn or decorate with feathers or plumes **8** (of a bird) to clean or preen (itself or its feathers) **9** (foll by *on* or *upon*) to pride or congratulate (oneself) [C14 from Old French, from Latin *plūma* downy feather] > ˈ**plumeless** *adj* > ˈ**plumeˌlike** *adj*

plume moth *n* **1** one of a family (*Pterophoridae*) of slender-bodied micro moths with narrow wings, each usually divided into two, three, or four "plumes". The type is the white *Pterophorus pentadactylus* **2** **many-plumed moth** an unrelated species, *Alucita hexadactyla*

plummer block (ˈplʌmə) *n* another name for **pillow block**

plummet (ˈplʌmɪt) *vb* **-mets, -meting, -meted** **1** (*intr*) to drop down; plunge ▷ *n* **2** another word for **plumb bob** **3** a lead plumb used by anglers to determine the depth of water [C14 from Old French *plommet* ball of lead, from *plomb* lead, from Latin *plumbum*]

plummy (ˈplʌmɪ) *adj* **-mier, -miest** **1** of, full of, or resembling plums **2** *Brit informal* (of speech) having a deep tone and a refined and somewhat drawling articulation **3** *Brit informal* choice; desirable

plumose (ˈpluːməʊs, -məʊz) *adj* another word for **plumate** [C17 from Latin *plūmōsus* feathery] > ˈ**plumosely** *adv* > **plumosity** (pluːˈmɒsɪtɪ) *n*

plump¹ (plʌmp) *adj* **1** well filled out or rounded; fleshy or chubby: *a plump turkey* **2** bulging, as with contents; full: *a plump wallet* **3** (of amounts of money) generous; ample: *a plump cheque* ▷ *vb* **4** (often foll by *up* or *out*) to make or become plump: *to plump up a pillow* [C15 (meaning: dull, rude), C16 (in current senses): perhaps from Middle Dutch *plomp* dull, blunt] > ˈ**plumply** *adv* > ˈ**plumpness** *n*

plump² (plʌmp) *vb* **1** (often foll by *down, into*, etc) to drop or fall suddenly and heavily: *to plump down on the sofa* **2** (*intr*; foll by *for*) to give support (to) or make a choice (of) one out of a group or number ▷ *n* **3** a heavy abrupt fall or the sound of this ▷ *adv* **4** suddenly or heavily: *he ran plump into the old lady* **5** straight down; directly: *the helicopter landed plump in the middle of the field* ▷ *adj, adv* **6** in a blunt, direct, or decisive manner [C14 probably of imitative origin; compare Middle Low German *plumpen*, Middle Dutch *plompen*]

plump³ (plʌmp) *n archaic or dialect* a group of people, animals, or things; troop; cluster [C15 of uncertain origin]

plumper (ˈplʌmpə) *n* a pad carried in the mouth by actors to round out the cheeks

plum pudding *n* (in Britain) a dark brown rich boiled or steamed pudding made with flour, suet, sugar, and dried fruit

plumule (ˈpluːmjuːl) *n* **1** the embryonic shoot of seed-bearing plants **2** a down feather of young birds that persists in some adults [C18 from Late Latin *plūmula* a little feather]

plumy (ˈpluːmɪ) *adj* **plumier, plumiest** **1** plumelike; feathery **2** consisting of, covered with, or adorned with feathers

plunder (ˈplʌndə) *vb* **1** to steal (valuables, goods, sacred items, etc) from (a town, church, etc) by force, esp in time of war; loot **2** (*tr*) to rob or steal (choice or desirable things) from (a place): *to plunder an orchard* ▷ *n* **3** anything taken by plundering or theft; booty **4** the act of plundering; pillage [C17 probably from Dutch *plunderen* (originally: to plunder household goods); compare Middle High German *plunder* bedding, household goods] > ˈ**plunderable** *adj* > ˈ**plunderer** *n* > ˈ**plunderous** *adj*

plunderage (ˈplʌndərɪdʒ) *n* **1** *maritime law* **a** the embezzlement of goods on board a ship **b** the goods embezzled **2** the act of plundering

plunge (plʌndʒ) *vb* **1** (usually foll by *into*) to thrust or throw (something, oneself, etc): *they plunged into the sea* **2** to throw or be thrown into a certain state or condition: *the room was plunged into darkness* **3** (usually foll by *into*) to involve or become involved deeply (in): *he plunged himself into a course of Sanskrit* **4** (*intr*) to move or dash violently or with great speed or impetuosity **5** (*intr*) to descend very suddenly or steeply: *the ship plunged in heavy seas; a plunging neckline* **6** (*intr*) *informal* to speculate or gamble recklessly, for high stakes, etc ▷ *n* **7** a leap or dive as into water **8** *informal* a swim; dip **9** *chiefly US* a place where one can swim or dive, such as a swimming pool **10** a headlong rush: *a plunge for the exit* **11** a pitching or tossing motion **12** **take the plunge** *informal* **a** to resolve to do something dangerous or irrevocable **b** to get married [C14 from Old French *plongier*, from Vulgar Latin *plumbicāre* (unattested) to sound with a plummet, from Latin *plumbum* lead]

P

plunge bath *n* a bath large enough to immerse the whole body or to dive into

plunger ('plʌndʒə) *n* **1** a rubber suction cup fixed to the end of a rod, used to clear blocked drains **2** a device or part of a machine that has a plunging or thrusting motion; piston **3** *informal* a reckless gambler

plunk (plʌŋk) *vb* **1** to pluck (the strings) of (a banjo, harp, etc) or (of such an instrument) to give forth a sound when plucked **2** (often foll by *down*) to drop or be dropped, esp heavily or suddenly ▷ *n* **3** the act or sound of plunking **4** *informal* a hard blow ▷ *interj* **5** an exclamation imitative of the sound of something plunking ▷ *adv* **6** *informal* exactly; squarely: *plunk into his lap* [c20 imitative]

Plunket baby ('plʌŋkət) *n* NZ *informal* a baby brought up in infancy under the dietary recommendations of the Plunket Society

Plunket nurse *n* NZ a child-care nurse appointed by the Plunket Society

Plunket Society *n* the Royal New Zealand Society for the Health of Women and Children [named after Sir William Lee *Plunket* (1864–1920), Governor General of New Zealand at the time of its founding (1907)]

pluperfect (pluː'pɜːfɪkt) *adj, n* grammar another term for **past perfect** [c16 from the Latin phrase *plūs quam perfectum* more than perfect]

plur. *abbreviation for* **1** plural **2** plurality

plural ('plʊərəl) *adj* **1** containing, involving, or composed of more than one person, thing, item, etc: *a plural society* **2** denoting a word indicating that more than one referent is being referred to or described ▷ *n* **3** *grammar* **a** the plural number **b** a plural form [c14 from Old French *plurel*, from Late Latin *plūrālis* concerning many, from Latin *plūs* more] > **'plurally** *adv*

pluralism ('plʊərə,lɪzəm) *n* **1** the holding by a single person of more than one ecclesiastical benefice or office **2** *sociol* a theory of society as several autonomous but interdependent groups which either share power or continuously compete for power **3** the existence in a society of groups having distinctive ethnic origin, cultural forms, religions, etc **4** a theory that views the power of employers as being balanced by the power of trade unions in industrial relations such that the interests of both sides can be catered for **5** *philosophy* **a** a metaphysical doctrine that reality consists of more than two basic types of substance. Compare **monism** (sense 2), **dualism** (sense 2) **b** the metaphysical doctrine that reality consists of independent entities rather than one unchanging whole. Compare **monism** (sense 2), **absolutism** (sense 2b) > **pluralist** *n, adj* > ,plural'istic *adj*

plurality (plʊə'rælɪtɪ) *n, pl* -ties **1** the state of being plural or numerous **2** *maths* a number greater than one **3** *US and Canadian* the excess of votes or seats won by the winner of an election over the runner-up when no candidate or party has more than 50 per cent. British equivalent: relative majority **4** a large number **5** the greater number; majority **6** another word for **pluralism** (sense 1)

pluralize *or* **pluralise** ('plʊərə,laɪz) *vb* **1** (intr) to hold more than one ecclesiastical benefice or office at the same time **2** to make or become plural > ,plurali'zation *or* ,plurali'sation *n* > 'plural,izer *or* 'plural,iser *n*

plural voting *n* **1** a system that enables an elector to vote more than once in an election **2** (in Britain before 1948) a system enabling certain electors to vote in more than one constituency

pluri- *combining form* denoting several: *pluriliteral; pluripresence* [from Latin *plur-, plus* more, *plures* several]

pluriliteral (,plʊrɪ'lɪtərəl) *adj* (in Hebrew grammar) containing more than three letters in the root

pluripotent (,plʊrɪ'pəʊtˀnt) *adj* biology capable of differentiating into different types of body cell

pluripresence (,plʊrɪ'prɛzəns) *n* theol presence in more than one place at the same time

plurry ('plʌrɪ) *adj* Austral slang a euphemism for **bloody⁴**

plus (plʌs) *prep* **1** increased by the addition of: *four plus two* (written 4 + 2) **2** with or with the addition of: *a good job, plus a new car* ▷ *adj* **3** (prenominal) Also: **positive** indicating or involving addition: *a plus sign* **4** another word for **positive** (senses 8, 9) **5** on the positive part of a scale or coordinate axis: *a value of +x* **6** indicating the positive side of an electrical circuit **7** involving positive advantage or good: *a plus factor* **8** (postpositive) *informal* having a value above that which is stated or expected: *she had charm plus* **9** (postpositive) slightly above a specified standard on a particular grade or percentage: *he received a B+ rating on his essay* **10** botany designating the strain of fungus that can only undergo sexual reproduction with a minus strain ▷ *n* **11** short for **plus sign** **12** a positive quantity **13** *informal* something positive or to the good **14** a gain, surplus, or advantage ▷ Mathematical symbol: + [c17 from Latin: more; compare Greek *pleiōn*, Old Norse *fleiri* more, German *viel* much]

> USAGE *Plus*, *together with*, and *along with* do not create compound subjects in the way that *and* does: the number of the verb depends on that of the subject to which *plus*, *together with*, or *along with* is added: *this task, plus all the others, was* (not *were*) *undertaken by the government; the doctor, together with the nurses, was* (not *were*) *waiting for the patient*

plus fours *pl n* men's baggy knickerbockers reaching below the knee, now only worn for hunting, golf, etc [c20 so called because the trousers are made with four inches of material to hang over at the knee]

plush (plʌʃ) *n* **1 a** a fabric with a cut pile that is longer and softer than velvet **b** (as modifier): *a plush chair* ▷ *adj* **2** Also: **plushy** informal lavishly appointed; rich; costly [c16 from French *pluche*, from Old French *peluchier* to pluck, ultimately from Latin *pilus* a hair, PILE³] > 'plushly *adv* > 'plushness *n*

plus sign *n* the symbol +, indicating addition or positive quantity

plus size *n* **a** a clothing size designed for people who are above the average size **b** (as modifier): *plus-size underwear*

Pluto¹ ('pluːtəʊ) *n* classical myth the god of the underworld; Hades

Pluto² ('pluːtəʊ) *n* the smallest planet and the farthest known from the sun. Discovered in 1930 by Clyde Tombaugh (1906–97), it has one known satellite, Charon. Mean distance from sun: 5907 million km; period of revolution around sun: 248.6 years; period of axial rotation: 6.4 days; diameter and mass: 18 and 0.3 per cent that of earth respectively [Latin, from Greek *Ploutōn*, literally: the rich one]

PLUTO ('pluːtəʊ) *n* the code name of pipelines laid under the English Channel to supply fuel to the Allied forces landing in Normandy in 1944 [c20 from *p(ipe)l(ine) u(nder) t(he) o(cean)*]

plutocracy (pluː'tɒkrəsɪ) *n, pl* -cies **1** the rule or control of society by the wealthy **2** a state or government characterized by the rule of the wealthy **3** a class that exercises power by virtue of its wealth [c17 from Greek *ploutokratia* government by the rich, from *ploutos* wealth + *-kratia* rule, power] > plutocratic (,pluːtə'krætɪk) *or* ,pluto'cratical *adj* > ,pluto'cratically *adv*

plutocrat ('pluːtə,kræt) *n* a member of a plutocracy

pluton ('pluːtɒn) *n* any mass of igneous rock that has solidified below the surface of the earth [c20 back formation from PLUTONIC]

Plutonian (pluː'təʊnɪən) *adj* of or relating to Pluto (the god) or the underworld; infernal

plutonic (pluː'tɒnɪk) *adj* (of igneous rocks) derived from magma that has cooled and solidified below the surface of the earth. Also: **abyssal** [c20 named after PLUTO¹]

plutonium (pluː'təʊnɪəm) *n* a highly toxic metallic transuranic element. It occurs in trace amounts in uranium ores and is produced in a nuclear reactor by neutron bombardment of uranium-238. The most stable and important isotope, **plutonium-239**, readily undergoes fission and is used as a reactor fuel in nuclear power stations and in nuclear weapons. Symbol: Pu; atomic no.: 94; half-life of ^{239}Pu: 24 360 years; valency: 3, 4, 5, or 6; relative density (alpha modification): 19.84; melting pt.: 640°C; boiling pt.: 3230°C [c20 named after the planet *Pluto* because Pluto lies beyond Neptune and plutonium was discovered soon after NEPTUNIUM]

Plutus ('pluːtəs) *n* the Greek god of wealth [from Greek *ploutos* wealth]

pluvial ('pluːvɪəl) *adj* **1** of, characterized by, or due to the action of rain; rainy: *pluvial insurance* ▷ *n* **2** geology of or relating to rainfall or precipitation **3** a climate characterized by persistent heavy rainfall, esp one occurring in unglaciated regions during the Pleistocene epoch [c17 from Latin *pluviālis* rainy, from *pluvia* rain]

pluviometer (,pluːvɪ'ɒmɪtə) *n* an obsolete word for **rain gauge**. > pluviometric (,pluːvɪə'mɛtrɪk) *adj* > ,pluvio'metrically *adv* > ,pluvi'ometry *n*

Pluviôse French (plyvjoz) *n* the rainy month: the fifth month of the French revolutionary calendar, extending from Jan 21 to Feb 19 [c19 *pluviose*, c15 *pluvious*; see PLUVIOUS]

pluvious ('pluːvɪəs) *or* **pluviose** *adj* of or relating to rain; rainy [c15 from Late Latin *pluviōsus* full of rain, from *pluvia* rain, from *pluere* to rain]

ply¹ (plaɪ) *vb* plies, plying, plied (mainly tr) **1** to carry on, pursue, or work at (a job, trade, etc) **2** to manipulate or wield (a tool) **3** to sell (goods, wares, etc), esp at a regular place **4** (usually foll by *with*) to provide (with) or subject (to) repeatedly or persistently: *he plied us with drink the whole evening; to ply a horse with a whip; he plied the speaker with questions* **5** (intr) to perform or work steadily or diligently: *to ply with a spade* **6** (also intr) (esp of a ship) to travel regularly along (a route) or in (an area): *to ply between Dover and Calais; to ply the trade routes* [c14 *plye*, short for *aplye* to APPLY]

ply² (plaɪ) *n, pl* plies **1 a** a layer, fold, or thickness, as of cloth, wood, yarn, etc **b** (in combination): *four-ply* **2** a thin sheet of wood glued to other similar sheets to form plywood **3** one of the strands twisted together to make rope, yarn, etc ▷ *vb* (tr) **4** to twist together (two or more single strands) to make yarn [c15 from Old French *pli* fold, from *plier* to fold, from Latin *plicāre*]

Plymouth ('plɪməθ) *n* **1** a port in SW England, in Plymouth unitary authority, SW Devon, on **Plymouth Sound** (an inlet of the English Channel): Britain's chief port in Elizabethan times; the last port visited by the Pilgrim Fathers in the *Mayflower* before sailing to America; naval base; university (1992). Pop: 243 795 (1992) **2** a unitary authority in SW England, in Devon. Pop: 241 500 (2003 est). Area: 76 sq km (30 sq miles) **3** a city in SE Massachusetts, on **Plymouth Bay**: the first permanent European settlement in New England; founded by the Pilgrim Fathers. Pop: 54 109 (2003 est)

Plymouth Brethren *pl n* a religious sect founded *c.* 1827, strongly Puritanical in outlook and prohibiting many secular occupations for its members. It combines elements of Calvinism, Pietism, and millenarianism, and has no organized ministry

Plymouth Colony *n* the Puritan colony founded by the Pilgrim Fathers in SE Massachusetts (1620). See also **Mayflower**

Plymouth Rock *n* **1** a heavy American breed of domestic fowl bred for meat and laying **2** a boulder on the coast of Massachusetts:

traditionally thought to be the landing place of the Pilgrim Fathers (1620). See also **Mayflower**

plyometrics (ˌplaɪəʊˈmɛtrɪks) *pl n* (*functioning as singular*) a system of exercise in which the muscles are repeatedly stretched and suddenly contracted [C20 from Greek *plio* more + METRIC]
> ˌplyoˈmetric *adj*

plywood (ˈplaɪˌwʊd) *n* a structural board consisting of an odd number of thin layers of wood glued together under pressure, with the grain of one layer at right angles to the grain of the adjoining layer

Plzeň (*Czech* ˈplzɛnj) *n* an industrial city in the Czech Republic. Pop: 163 000 (2005 est). German name: Pilsen

pm¹ *abbreviation for* premium

pm² *the internet domain name for* St Pierre and Miquelon

Pm *the chemical symbol for* promethium

PM *abbreviation for* **1** Prime Minister **2** Past Master (of a fraternity) **3** Paymaster **4** Postmaster **5** *military* Provost Marshal

p.m., P.M., pm *or* **PM** *abbreviation for* **1** (indicating the time period from midday to midnight) post meridiem. Compare **a.m.** [Latin: after noon] **2** post-mortem (examination)

PMG *abbreviation for* **1** Paymaster General **2** Postmaster General **3** *military* Provost Marshal General

PMI *abbreviation for* private medical insurance

PMS *abbreviation for* **premenstrual syndrome**

PMT *abbreviation for* **1** **photomechanical transfer 2** premenstrual tension

pn *the internet domain name for* Pitcairn Island

PN, P/N *or* **pn** *abbreviation for* **promissory note**

PNdB *abbreviation for* perceived noise decibel

pneuma (ˈnjuːmə) *n philosophy* a person's vital spirit, soul, or creative energy. Compare **psyche** [C19 from Greek: breath, spirit, wind; related to *pnein* to blow, breathe]

pneumatic (njʊˈmætɪk) *adj* **1** of or concerned with air, gases, or wind. Compare **hydraulic 2** (of a machine or device) operated by compressed air or by a vacuum: *a pneumatic drill; pneumatic brakes* **3** containing compressed air: *a pneumatic tyre* **4** of or concerned with pneumatics **5** *theol* **a** of or relating to the soul or spirit **b** of or relating to the Holy Ghost or other spiritual beings **6** (of the bones of birds) containing air spaces which reduce their weight as an adaptation to flying **7** *informal* (of a woman) well rounded, esp with a large bosom ▷ *n* **8** short for **pneumatic tyre** [C17 from Late Latin *pneumaticus* of air or wind, from Greek *pneumatikos* of air or breath, from PNEUMA]
> pneuˈmatically *adv*

pneumatic conveyor *n engineering* a tube through which powdered or granular material, such as cement, grain, etc is transported by a flow of air

pneumatics (njʊˈmætɪks) *n* (*functioning as singular*) the branch of physics concerned with the mechanical properties of gases, esp air. Also called: aerometry, pneumodynamics

pneumatic trough *n chem* a shallow dishlike vessel filled with a liquid, usually water, and used in collecting gases by displacement of liquid from a filled jar held with its open end under the surface of the liquid

pneumatic tyre *n* a rubber tyre filled with air under pressure, used esp on motor vehicles

pneumato- *combining form* air; breath or breathing; spirit: *pneumatophore; pneumatology* [from Greek *pneuma, pneumat-*, breath; see PNEUMA]

pneumatology (ˌnjuːməˈtɒlədʒɪ) *n* **1** the branch of theology concerned with the Holy Ghost and other spiritual beings **2** an obsolete name for **psychology** (the science) **3** an obsolete term for **pneumatics.** > pneumatological (ˌnjuːmətəˈlɒdʒɪkəl) *adj* > ˌpneumaˈtologist *n*

pneumatolysis (ˌnjuːməˈtɒlɪsɪs) *n* a type of metamorphism in which hot gases from solidifying magma react with surrounding rock

pneumatometer (ˌnjuːməˈtɒmɪtə) *n* an instrument for measuring the pressure exerted by air being inhaled or exhaled during a single breath. Compare **spirometer.** > ˌpneumaˈtometry *n*

pneumatophore (njuːˈmætəʊˌfɔː) *n* **1** a specialized root of certain swamp plants, such as the mangrove, that branches upwards, rising above ground, and undergoes gaseous exchange with the atmosphere **2** a polyp in coelenterates of the order *Siphonophora*, such as the Portuguese man-of-war, that is specialized as a float

pneumectomy (njuːˈmɛktəmɪ) *n, pl* -mies *surgery* another word for **pneumonectomy**

pneumo-, pneumono- *or before a vowel* **pneum-, pneumon-** *combining form* of or related to a lung or the lungs; respiratory: *pneumoconiosis; pneumonitis* [from Greek *pneumōn* lung or *pneuma* breath]

pneumobacillus (ˌnjuːməʊbəˈsɪləs) *n, pl* -li (-laɪ) a rod-shaped bacterium that occurs in the respiratory tract, esp the Gram-negative *Klebsiella pneumoniae*, which causes pneumonia

pneumococcus (ˌnjuːməʊˈkɒkəs) *n, pl* -cocci (-ˈkɒkaɪ) a spherical bacterium that occurs in the respiratory tract, esp the Gram-positive *Diplococcus pneumoniae*, which causes pneumonia
> ˌpneumoˈcoccal *adj*

pneumoconiosis (ˌnjuːməʊˌkəʊnɪˈəʊsɪs) *or* **pneumonoconiosis** (ˌnjuːmənəʊˌkəʊnɪˈəʊsɪs) *n* any disease of the lungs or bronchi caused by the inhalation of metallic or mineral particles: characterized by inflammation, cough, and fibrosis [C19 shortened from *pneumonoconiosis*, from PNEUMO- + -coniosis, from Greek *konis* dust]

pneumocystis (ˌnjuːməʊˈsɪstɪs) *n* any protozoan of the genus *Pneumocystis*, esp *P. carinii*, which is a cause of pneumonia in people whose immune defences have been lowered by drugs or a disease

pneumodynamics (ˌnjuːməʊdaɪˈnæmɪks) *n* (*functioning as singular*) another name for **pneumatics**

pneumoencephalogram (ˌnjuːməʊɛnˈsɛfələˌgræm) *n* See **encephalogram** > pneumoencephalography (ˌnjuːməʊɛnˌsɛfəˈlɒgrəfɪ) *n*

pneumogastric (ˌnjuːməʊˈgæstrɪk) *adj anatomy* **1** of or relating to the lungs and stomach **2** a former term for **vagus**

pneumograph (ˈnjuːməˌgrɑːf, -ˌgræf) *n med* an instrument for making a record (**pneumogram**) of respiratory movements

pneumonectomy (ˌnjuːməʊˈnɛktəmɪ) *or* **pneumectomy** (njuːˈmɛktəmɪ) *n, pl* -mies the surgical removal of a lung or part of a lung [C20 from Greek *pneumōn* lung + -ECTOMY]

pneumonia (njuːˈməʊnɪə) *n* inflammation of one or both lungs, in which the air sacs (alveoli) become filled with liquid, which renders them useless for breathing. It is usually caused by bacterial (esp pneumococcal) or viral infection [C17 New Latin from Greek from *pneumōn* lung]

pneumonic (njuːˈmɒnɪk) *adj* **1** of, relating to, or affecting the lungs; pulmonary **2** of or relating to pneumonia [C17 from New Latin *pneumonicus*, from Greek, from *pneumon* lung]

pneumonitis (ˌnjuːmɒnˈaɪtɪs) *n* inflammation of the lungs

pneumothorax (ˌnjuːməʊˈθɔːˌræks) *n* **1** the abnormal presence of air between the lung and the wall of the chest (pleural cavity), resulting in collapse of the lung **2** *med* the introduction of air into the pleural cavity to collapse the lung: a former treatment for tuberculosis

PNG *international car registration for* Papua New Guinea

PNI *abbreviation for* psychoneuroimmunology

p-n junction *n electronics* a boundary between a p-type and n-type semiconductor that functions as a rectifier and is used in diodes and junction transistors

Pnom Penh (ˈnɒm ˈpɛn) *n* a variant spelling of **Phnom Penh**

PnP *abbreviation for* **plug'n'play**

po (pəʊ) *n, pl* **pos** *Brit* an informal word for **chamber pot** [C19 from POT¹]

Po¹ *the chemical symbol for* polonium

Po² (pəʊ) *n* a river in N Italy, rising in the Cottian Alps and flowing northeast to Turin, then east to the Adriatic: the longest river in Italy. Length: 652 km (405 miles). Latin name: Padus

PO *abbreviation for* **1** Post Office **2** Personnel Officer **3** petty officer **4** Pilot Officer **5** Also: p.o. postal order

poaceous (pəʊˈeɪʃəs) *adj* of, relating to, or belonging to the plant family *Poaceae* (grasses) [C18 via New Latin from Greek *poa* grass]

poach¹ (pəʊtʃ) *vb* **1** to catch (game, fish, etc) illegally by trespassing on private property **2** to encroach on or usurp (another person's rights, duties, etc) or steal (an idea, employee, etc) **3** *tennis, badminton* to take or play (shots that should belong to one's partner) **4** to break up (land) into wet muddy patches, as by riding over it, or (of land) to become broken up in this way **5** (*intr*) (of the feet, shoes, etc) to sink into heavy wet ground [C17 from Old French *pocher*, of Germanic origin; compare Middle Dutch *poken* to prod; see POKE¹]

poach² (pəʊtʃ) *vb* to simmer (eggs, fish, etc) very gently in water, milk, stock, etc [C15 from Old French *pochier* to enclose in a bag (as the yolks are enclosed by the whites); compare POKE²]

poacher¹ (ˈpəʊtʃə) *n* **1** a person who illegally hunts game, fish, etc, on someone else's property **2** poacher turned gamekeeper someone whose occupation or behaviour is the opposite of what it previously was, such as a burglar who now advises on home security

poacher² (ˈpəʊtʃə) *n* a metal pan with individual cups for poaching eggs

POB *abbreviation for* Post Office Box

pochard (ˈpəʊtʃəd) *n, pl* -chards *or* -chard any of various diving ducks of the genera *Aythya* and *Netta*, esp *A. ferina* of Europe, the male of which has a grey-and-black body and a reddish head [C16 of unknown origin]

pochette (pəˈʃɛt) *n* an envelope-shaped handbag used by women and men [C20 from French: little pocket]

pock (pɒk) *n* **1** any pustule resulting from an eruptive disease, esp from smallpox **2** another word for **pockmark** (sense 1) [Old English *pocc*; related to Middle Dutch *pocke*, perhaps to Latin *bucca* cheek] > ˈpocky *adj*

pocket (ˈpɒkɪt) *n* **1** a small bag or pouch in a garment for carrying small articles, money, etc **2** any bag or pouch or anything resembling this **3 a** a cavity or hollow in the earth, etc, such as one containing gold or other ore **b** the ore in such a place **4** a small enclosed or isolated area: *a pocket of resistance* **5** *billiards, snooker* any of the six holes with pouches or nets let into the corners and sides of a billiard table **6** a position in a race in which a competitor is hemmed in **7** *Australian rules football* a player in one of two side positions at the ends of the ground: *back pocket* **8** *South African* a bag or sack of vegetables or fruit **9** in one's pocket under one's control **10** in *or* out of pocket having made a profit or loss, as after a transaction **11** line one's pockets to make money, esp by dishonesty when in a position of trust **12** (*modifier*) suitable for fitting in a pocket: *a pocket edition* ▷ *vb* -ets, -eting, -eted (*tr*) **13** to put into one's pocket **14** to take surreptitiously or unlawfully; steal **15** (*usually passive*) to enclose or confine in or as if in a pocket **16** to receive (an insult, injury, etc) without retaliating **17** to conceal or keep back (feelings): *he pocketed his pride and accepted help* **18** *billiards, snooker* to drive (a ball) into a pocket **19** *US* (esp of the President) to retain (a bill) without acting on it in order to prevent it from becoming law. See also **pocket veto 20** to hem in (an opponent), as in racing [C15 from Anglo-Norman *poket* a little bag, from *poque* bag, from Middle Dutch *poke* POKE², bag; related to French *poche* pocket] > ˈpocketable *adj* > ˈpocketless *adj*

p

pocket battleship *n* a small heavily armoured and armed battle cruiser specially built to conform with treaty limitations on tonnage and armament, esp any of those built by Germany in the 1930s

pocketbike ('pɒkɪt,baɪk) *n* another name for **minimoto**

pocket billiards *n* (*functioning as singular*) billiards **1** another name for **pool²** (sense 5) **2** any game played on a table in which the object is to pocket the balls, esp snooker and pool

pocketbook ('pɒkɪt,bʊk) *n* US and Canadian a small bag or case for money, papers, etc, carried by a handle or in the pocket

pocket borough *n* (before the Reform Act of 1832) an English borough constituency controlled by one person or family who owned the land. Compare **rotten borough**

pocket drive *or* **keyring drive** *n computing* a small portable memory device that can be plugged into the USB port of many different types of computer

pocketful ('pɒkɪtfʊl) *n, pl* **-fuls 1** as much as a pocket will hold **2** *informal* a large amount: *it cost him a pocketful of money*

pocket gopher *n* the full name for **gopher** (sense 1)

pocketknife ('pɒkɪt,naɪf) *n, pl* **-knives** a small knife with one or more blades that fold into the handle; penknife

pocket money *n* **1** *Brit* a small weekly sum of money given to children by parents as an allowance **2** money for day-to-day spending, incidental expenses, etc

pocket mouse *n* any small mouselike rodent with cheek pouches, of the genus *Perognathus*, of desert regions of W North America: family *Heteromyidae*

pocket veto *n US* **1** the action of the President in retaining unsigned a bill passed by Congress within the last ten days of a session and thus causing it to die **2** any similar action by a state governor or other chief executive

pockies ('pɒkɪz) *pl n Scot dialect* woollen mittens

pockmark ('pɒk,mɑːk) *n* **1** Also called: **pock** a pitted scar left on the skin after the healing of a smallpox or similar pustule **2** any pitting of a surface that resembles or suggests such scars ▷ *vb* **3** (*tr*) to scar or pit (a surface) with pockmarks

pockmarked ('pɒk,mɑːkd) *adj* abounding in pockmarks

poco ('pəʊkəʊ; Italian 'pɔːko) *or* **un poco** *adj, adv music* (*in combination*) a little; to a small degree: *poco rit; un poco meno mosso* [from Italian: little, from Latin *paucus* few, scanty]

poco a poco *adv* (*in combination*) *music* little by little: *poco a poco rall* [Italian]

pococurante (,pəʊkəʊkjʊ'rænti) *n* **1** a person who is careless or indifferent ▷ *adj* **2** indifferent or apathetic [c18 from Italian, from *poco* little + *curante* caring] > ,pococu'ranteism *or* ,pococu'rantism *n*

pod¹ (pɒd) *n* **1 a** the fruit of any leguminous plant, consisting of a long two-valved case that contains seeds and splits along both sides when ripe **b** the seedcase as distinct from the seeds **2** any similar fruit **3** a streamlined structure attached by a pylon to an aircraft and used to house a jet engine (**podded engine**), fuel tank, armament, etc **4** an enclosed cabin suspended from a cable or a big wheel, for carrying passengers ▷ *vb* **pods, podding, podded 5** (*tr*) to remove the pod or shell from (peas, beans, etc) **6** (*intr*) (of a plant) to produce pods [c17 perhaps back formation from earlier *podware* bagged vegetables, probably from *pod*, variant of COD² + WARE¹]

pod² (pɒd) *n* a small group of animals, esp seals, whales, or birds [c19 of unknown origin]

pod³ (pɒd) *n* **1** a straight groove along the length of certain augers and bits **2** the socket that holds the bit in a boring tool [c16 of unknown origin]

POD *abbreviation for* pay on delivery

-pod *or* **-pode** *n combining form* indicating a certain type or number of feet: *arthropod; tripod* [from Greek *-podos* footed, from *pous* foot]

podagra (pə'dægrə) *n* gout of the foot or big toe [c15 via Latin from Greek, from *pous* foot + *agra* a trap] > po'dagral, po'dagric, po'dagrical *or* po'dagrous *adj*

podcast ('pɒd,kɑːst) *n* **1** an audio file similar to a radio broadcast, which can be downloaded and listened to on a computer, iPod, etc ▷ *vb* **-casts, -casting, -cast** *or* **-casted 2** (*intr*) to create such files and make them available for downloading **3** (*tr*) to make (music, interviews, etc) available using this format > 'pod,caster *n* > 'pod,casting *n*

poddie ('pɒdɪ) *n Brit informal* a user of or enthusiast for the iPod, a portable digital music player [c21]

poddle ('pɒdᵊl) *vb* (*intr*) *informal* (often foll by *along, round,* etc) to move or travel in a leisurely manner; amble [c19 variant of PADDLE²]

poddy ('pɒdɪ) *n, pl* **-dies** *Austral* **1** a handfed calf or lamb **2** any creature at an early stage of growth: *poddy mullet* [perhaps from *poddy* (adj) fat]

poddy-dodger ('pɒdɪ,dɒdʒə) *n Austral informal* a cattle thief who steals unbranded calves

podesta (pɒ'dɛstə; Italian pode'sta) *n* **1** (in modern Italy) a subordinate magistrate in some towns **2** (in Fascist Italy) the chief magistrate of a commune **3** (in medieval Italy) **a** any of the governors of the Lombard cities appointed by Frederick Barbarossa **b** a chief magistrate in any of various republics, such as Florence [c16 from Italian: power, from Latin *potestās* ability, power, from *posse* to be able]

podge (pɒdʒ) *or* **pudge** (pʌdʒ) *n informal* a short chubby person

Podgorica *or* **Podgoritsa** (*Russian* 'pɔdgɔ,ri:tsa) *n* a city in Serbia and Montenegro, the capital of Montenegro: under Turkish rule (1474–1878). Pop: 230 000 (2005 est). Former name (1946–92): Titograd

podgy ('pɒdʒɪ) *adj* **podgier, podgiest** short and fat; chubby > 'podgily *adv* > 'podginess *n*

podiatry (pɒ'daɪətrɪ) *n* another word for **chiropody** [c20 from Greek *pous* foot] > **podiatric** (,pəʊdɪ'ætrɪk) *adj* > po'diatrist *n*

podium ('pəʊdɪəm) *n, pl* **-diums** *or* **-dia** (-dɪə) **1** a small raised platform used by lecturers, orchestra conductors, etc; dais **2** a plinth that supports a colonnade or wall **3** a low wall surrounding the arena of an ancient amphitheatre **4** *zoology* **a** the terminal part of a vertebrate limb **b** any footlike organ, such as the tube foot of a starfish [c18 from Latin: platform, balcony, from Greek *podion* little foot, from *pous* foot]

-podium *n combining form* a part resembling a foot: *pseudopodium* [from New Latin: footlike; see PODIUM]

Podolsk (*Russian* pa'dɔljsk) *n* an industrial city in W Russia, near Moscow. Pop: 177 000 (2005 est)

podophyllin *or* **podophylin resin** (,pɒdəʊ'fɪlɪn) *n* a bitter yellow resin obtained from the dried underground stems of the May apple and mandrake: used to treat warts and formerly as a cathartic [c19 from New Latin *Podophyllum* genus of herbs including the May apple, from *podo-*, from Greek *pous* foot + *phullon* leaf]

-podous *adj combining form* having feet of a certain kind or number: *cephalopodous*

pod person *n, pl* **pod people** *informal* a person who behaves in a strange esp mechanical way, as if not fully human [c20 from the science-fiction film *Invasion of the Body Snatchers* (1956; remade 1978) in which individual humans are replaced by alien replicas grown in giant pods]

podzol ('pɒdzɒl) *or* **podsol** ('pɒdsɒl) *n* a type of soil characteristic of coniferous forest regions having a greyish-white colour in its upper leached layers [c20 from Russian: ash ground, from *pod* ground + *zola* ashes] > pod'zolic *or* pod'solic *adj*

podzolization (,pɒdzɒlaɪ'zeɪʃən), **podsolization** (,pɒdsɒlaɪ'zeɪʃən), **podzolisation** *or* **podsolisation** *n* the process by which the upper layer of a soil becomes acidic through the leaching of bases which are deposited in the lower horizons

podzolize ('pɒdzɒ,laɪz), **podsolize** ('pɒdsɒ,laɪz), **podzolise** *or* **podsolise** *vb* (*usually passive*) to make into or form a podzol

POE *abbreviation for* **1** *military* port of embarkation **2** port of entry

poem ('pəʊɪm) *n* **1** a composition in verse, usually characterized by concentrated and heightened language in which words are chosen for their sound and suggestive power as well as for their sense, and using such techniques as metre, rhyme, and alliteration **2** a literary composition that is not in verse but exhibits the intensity of imagination and language common to it: *a prose poem* **3** anything resembling a poem in beauty, effect, etc [c16 from Latin *poēma*, from Greek, variant of *poiēma* something composed, created, from *poiein* to make]

poenology (piː'nɒlədʒɪ) *n* a variant spelling of **penology**

poep (pʊp) *n South African slang* **1** an emission of intestinal gas from the anus **2** a mean or despicable person

poepol ('pʊpɒl) *n South African slang* **1** the anus **2** a foolish or despicable person [Afrikaans]

poesy ('pəʊɪzɪ) *n, pl* **-sies 1** an archaic word for **poetry 2** *poetic* the art of writing poetry **3** *archaic or poetic* a poem or verse, esp one used as a motto [c14 via Old French from Latin *poēsis*, from Greek, from *poiēsis* poetic art, creativity, from *poiein* to make]

poet ('pəʊɪt) *or sometimes when feminine* **poetess** *n* **1** a person who writes poetry **2** a person with great imagination and creativity [c13 from Latin *poēta*, from Greek *poiētēs* maker, poet, from *poiein* to make]

poetaster (,pəʊɪ'tæstə, -'teɪ-) *n* a writer of inferior verse [c16 from Medieval Latin; see POET, -ASTER]

poetic (pəʊ'ɛtɪk) *or* **poetical** *adj* **1** of or relating to poetry **2** characteristic of poetry, as in being elevated, sublime, etc **3** characteristic of a poet **4** recounted in verse > po'etically *adv*

poeticize (pəʊ'ɛtɪ,saɪz), **poetize** ('pəʊɪ,taɪz), **poeticise** *or* **poetise** *vb* **1** (*tr*) to put into poetry or make poetic **2** (*intr*) to speak or write poetically

poetic justice *n* fitting retribution; just deserts

poetic licence *n* justifiable departure from conventional rules of form, fact, logic, etc, as in poetry

poetics (pəʊ'ɛtɪks) *n* (*usually functioning as singular*) **1** the principles and forms of poetry or the study of these, esp as a form of literary criticism **2** a treatise on poetry

poet laureate *n, pl* **poets laureate** *Brit* the poet appointed as court poet of Britain who is given a post as an officer of the Royal Household. The first was Ben Jonson in 1616

poetry ('pəʊɪtrɪ) *n* **1** literature in metrical form; verse **2** the art or craft of writing verse **3** poetic qualities, spirit, or feeling in anything **4** anything resembling poetry in rhythm, beauty, etc [c14 from Medieval Latin *poētria*, from Latin *poēta* POET]

po-faced *adj* (of a person) wearing a disapproving stern expression [c20 possibly from PO + POKER-FACED]

pogey *or* **pogy** ('pəʊgɪ) *n, pl* **pogeys** *or* **pogies** *Canadian slang* **1** financial or other relief given to the unemployed by the government; dole **2** unemployment insurance **3 a** the office distributing relief to the unemployed **b** (*as modifier*): *pogey clothes* [c20 from earlier *pogie* workhouse, of unknown origin]

pogge (pɒg) *n* **1** Also called: **armed bullhead** a European marine scorpaenoid fish, *Agonus cataphractus*, of northern European waters, with a large head, long thin tail, and body completely covered with bony plates: family *Agonidae* **2** any other fish of the family *Agonidae* [c18 of unknown origin]

pogo (ˈpəʊgəʊ) *vb* pogos, pogoing, pogoed (*intr*) to jump up and down in one spot, as in a punk dance of the 1970s [c20 from POGO STICK; from the motion] > ˈpogoer *n*

pogonia (pəˈgəʊnɪə) *n* any orchid of the chiefly American genus *Pogonia,* esp the snakesmouth, having pink or white fragrant flowers [c19 New Latin, from Greek *pōgōnias* bearded, from *pōgōn* a beard]

pogo stick *n* a stout pole with a handle at the top, steps for the feet and a spring at the bottom, so that the user can spring up, down, and along on it [c20 of uncertain origin]

pogrom (ˈpɒgrəm) *n* an organized persecution or extermination of an ethnic group, esp of Jews [c20 via Yiddish from Russian: destruction, from *po-* like + *grom* thunder]

Pogson ratio (ˈpɒdʒsən) *n* the brightness ratio of two celestial objects that differ by one magnitude. On the Pogson scale a difference of 5 magnitudes is defined as a difference of 100 in the intensities of two stars; therefore a difference of 1 magnitude is equal to the fifth root of 100, i.e. 2.512 [c19 named after N. R. Pogson (1829–91), British astronomer]

pogy (ˈpəʊgɪ, ˈpɒgɪ) *n* 1 *pl* pogies *or* pogy another name for the **porgy** 2 *pl* pogies a variant spelling of **pogey** [c19 perhaps from Algonquian *pohegan* menhaden]

Pohai (ˌpəʊˈhaɪ) *n* a variant transliteration of the Chinese name for **Bohai**

pohiri (ˈpɒhiːriː) *n* a variant spelling of **powhiri**

pohutukawa (pəˌhuːtəˈkɑːwə) *n* a myrtaceous New Zealand tree, *Metrosideros excelsa,* with red flowers and hard red wood [from Māori]

poi¹ (pɔɪ, ˈpəʊɪ) *n* a Hawaiian dish made of the root of the taro baked, pounded to a paste, and fermented [c19 from Hawaiian]

poi² (pɔɪ) *n* NZ a ball of woven flax swung rhythmically in poi dances [Māori]

poi dance *n* NZ a women's formation dance that involves singing and manipulating a poi

-poiesis *n combining form* indicating the act of making or producing something specified: *haematopoiesis* [from Greek, from *poiēsis* a making; see POESY] > **-poietic** *adj combining form*

poignant (ˈpɔɪnjənt, -nənt) *adj* 1 sharply distressing or painful to the feelings 2 to the point; cutting or piercing: *poignant wit* 3 keen or pertinent in mental appeal: *a poignant subject* 4 pungent in smell [c14 from Old French, from Latin *pungens* pricking, from *pungere* to sting, pierce, grieve] > ˈpoignancy *or* ˈpoignance *n* > ˈpoignantly *adv*

poikilocyte (ˈpɔɪkɪləʊˌsaɪt) *n* an abnormally shaped red blood cell [c19 from Greek *poikilos* various + -CYTE]

poikilothermic (ˌpɔɪkɪləʊˈθɜːmɪk) *or* **poikilothermal** (ˌpɔɪkɪləʊˈθɜːməl) *adj* (of all animals except birds and mammals) having a body temperature that varies with the temperature of the surroundings. Compare **homoiothermic** [c19 from Greek *poikilos* various + THERMAL] > ˌpoikiloˈthermism *or* ˌpoikiloˈthermy *n*

poilu (ˈpwɑːluː; *French* pwaly) *n* an infantryman in the French Army, esp one in the front lines in World War I [c20 from French, literally: hairy (that is, virile), from *poil* hair, from Latin *pilus* a hair]

poinciana (ˌpɔɪnsɪˈɑːnə) *n* any tree of the tropical leguminous genera *Caesalpinia* (formerly *Poinciana*) having large orange or red flowers. See **royal poinciana** [c17 New Latin, named after M. de Poinci, 17th-century governor of the French Antilles]

poind (pɪnd) *vb* (*tr*) *Scots law* 1 to take (property of a debtor) in execution or by way of distress; distrain 2 to impound (stray cattle, etc) [c15 from Scots, variant of Old English *pyndan* to impound]

poinsettia (pɔɪnˈsɛtɪə) *n* a euphorbiaceous shrub,

Euphorbia (or *Poinsettia*) *pulcherrima,* of Mexico and Central America, widely cultivated for its showy scarlet bracts, which resemble petals [c19 New Latin, from the name of J. P. Poinsett (1799–1851), US Minister to Mexico, who introduced it to the US]

point (pɔɪnt) *n* 1 a dot or tiny mark 2 a location, spot, or position 3 any dot or mark used in writing or printing, such as a decimal point or a full stop 4 short for **vowel point** 5 the sharp tapered end of a pin, knife, etc 6 a pin, needle, or other object having such a point 7 *maths* **a** a geometric element having no dimensions and whose position in space is located by means of its coordinates **b** a location: *point of inflection* 8 a promontory, usually smaller than a cape 9 a specific condition or degree 10 a moment: *at that point he left the room* 11 an important or fundamental reason, aim, etc: *the point of this exercise is to train new teachers* 12 an essential element or thesis in an argument: *you've made your point; I take your point* 13 a suggestion or tip 14 a detail or item 15 an important or outstanding characteristic, physical attribute, etc: *he has his good points* 16 a distinctive characteristic or quality of an animal, esp one used as a standard in judging livestock 17 (*often plural*) any of the extremities, such as the tail, ears, or feet, of a domestic animal 18 *ballet* (*often plural*) the tip of the toes 19 a single unit for measuring or counting, as in the scoring of a game 20 *Australian rules football* an informal name for **behind** (sense 11) 21 *printing* a unit of measurement equal to one twelfth of a pica, or approximately 0.01384 inch. There are approximately 72 points to the inch 22 *finance* **a** a unit of value used to quote security and commodity prices and their fluctuations **b** a percentage unit sometimes payable by a borrower as a premium on a loan 23 *navigation* **a** one of the 32 marks on the circumference of a compass card indicating direction **b** the angle of 11°15′ between two adjacent marks **c** a point on the horizon indicated by such a mark 24 *cricket* **a** a fielding position at right angles to the batsman on the off side and relatively near the pitch **b** a fielder in this position 25 any of the numbers cast in the first throw in craps with which one neither wins nor loses by throwing them: 4, 5, 6, 8, 9, or 10 26 either of the two electrical contacts that make or break the current flow in the distributor of an internal-combustion engine 27 *Brit* (*often plural*) a junction of railway tracks in which a pair of rails can be moved so that a train can be directed onto either of two lines. US and Canadian equivalent: **switch** 28 (*often plural*) a piece of ribbon, cord, etc, with metal tags at the end: used during the 16th and 17th centuries to fasten clothing 29 *backgammon* a place or position on the board 30 *Brit* **a** short for **power point** **b** an informal name for **socket** (sense 2) 31 an aggressive position adopted in bayonet or sword drill 32 *military* the position at the head of a body of troops, or a person in this position 33 the position of the body of a pointer or setter when it discovers game 34 *boxing* a mark awarded for a scoring blow, knockdown, etc 35 any diacritic used in a writing system, esp in a phonetic transcription, to indicate modifications of vowels or consonants 36 *jewellery* a unit of weight equal to 0.01 carat 37 the act of pointing 38 *ice hockey* the position just inside the opponents' blue line 39 **beside the point** not pertinent; irrelevant 40 **case in point** a specific, appropriate, or relevant instance or example 41 **in point of** in the matter of; regarding 42 **make a point of a** to make (something) one's regular habit **b** to do (something) because one thinks it important 43 **not to put too fine a point on it** to speak plainly and bluntly 44 **on** (*or* **at**) **the point of** at the moment immediately before a specified condition, action, etc, is expected to begin: *on the point of leaving the room* 45 **score points off** to gain an advantage at someone else's expense 46

stretch a point a to make a concession or exception not usually made **b** to exaggerate 47 **to the point** pertinent; relevant 48 **up to a point** not completely ▷ *vb* 49 (usually foll by *at* or *to*) to indicate the location or direction of by or as by extending (a finger or other pointed object) towards it: *he pointed to the front door; don't point that gun at me* 50 (*intr*; usually foll by *at* or *to*) to indicate or identify a specific person or thing among several: *he pointed at the bottle he wanted; all evidence pointed to Donald as the murderer* 51 (*tr*) to direct or cause to go or face in a specific direction or towards a place or goal: *point me in the right direction* 52 (*tr*) to sharpen or taper 53 (*intr*) (of gun dogs) to indicate the place where game is lying by standing rigidly with the muzzle turned in its direction 54 (*tr*) to finish or repair the joints of (brickwork, masonry, etc) with mortar or cement 55 (*tr*) *music* to mark (a psalm text) with vertical lines to indicate the points at which the music changes during chanting 56 to steer (a sailing vessel) close to the wind or (of a sailing vessel) to sail close to the wind 57 (*tr*) *phonetics* to provide (a letter or letters) with diacritics 58 (*tr*) to provide (a Hebrew or similar text) with vowel points ▷ See also **point off, point out, point up** [c13 from Old French: spot, from Latin *punctum* a point, from *pungere* to pierce; also influenced by Old French *pointe* pointed end, from Latin *pungere*]

point after *n* American football a score given for a successful kick between the goalposts and above the crossbar, following a touchdown

point-and-click *adj computing* of or relating to the way a computer mouse can be used to select and operate functions from a computer screen: *a bright and cheerful point-and-click interface*

point-blank *adj* 1 **a** aimed or fired at a target so close that it is unnecessary to make allowance for the drop in the course of the projectile **b** permitting such aim or fire without loss of accuracy: *at point-blank range* 2 plain or blunt: *a point-blank question* ▷ *adv* 3 directly or straight 4 plainly or bluntly [c16 from POINT + BLANK (in the sense: centre spot of an archery target)]

point d'appui *French* (pwɛ̃ dapwi) *n,* *pl* **points d'appui** (pwɛ̃ dapwi) 1 a support or prop 2 (formerly) the base or rallying point for a military unit

point defect *n* an imperfection in a crystal, characterized by one unoccupied lattice position or one interstitial atom, molecule, or ion

Point de Galle (pɔɪnt də ˈgɑːlə) *n* a former name of **Galle**

point-device *obsolete* ▷ *adj* 1 very correct or perfect; precise ▷ *adv* 2 to perfection; perfectly; precisely [c14 perhaps from old French *à point devis* to the point arranged]

point duty *n* 1 the stationing of a policeman or traffic warden at a road junction to control and direct traffic 2 the position at the head of a military patrol, regarded as being the most dangerous

pointe (pɔɪnt) *n ballet* the tip of the toe (esp in the phrase **on pointes**) [from French: point]

Pointe-à-Pitre (*French* pwɛ̃tapitr) *n* the chief port of Guadeloupe, on SW Grande-Terre Island in the Caribbean. Pop: 20 948 (1999)

pointed (ˈpɔɪntɪd) *adj* 1 having a point 2 cutting or incisive: *a pointed wit* 3 obviously directed at or intended for a particular person or aspect: *pointed criticism* 4 emphasized or made conspicuous: *pointed ignorance* 5 (of an arch or style of architecture employing such an arch) Gothic 6 *music* (of a psalm text) marked to show changes in chanting 7 (of Hebrew text) with vowel points marked > ˈpointedly *adv* > ˈpointedness *n*

pointed arch *n* another name for **lancet arch**

Pointe-Noire (*French* pwɛ̃nwar) *n* a port in S Congo-Brazzaville, on the Atlantic: the country's chief port and former capital (1950–58). Pop: 638 000 (2005 est)

pointer (ˈpɔɪntə) *n* 1 a person or thing that points 2 an indicator on a measuring instrument 3 a

p

long rod or cane used by a lecturer to point to parts of a map, blackboard, etc **4** one of a breed of large swift smooth-coated dogs, usually white with black, liver, or lemon markings: when on shooting expeditions it points to the bird with its nose, body, and tail in a straight line **5** a helpful piece of information or advice

Pointers ('pɔɪntəz) *pl n* **the** the two brightest stars in the Plough (Dubhe and Merak), which lie in the direction pointing towards the Pole Star and are therefore used to locate it

point estimate *n statistics* a specific value assigned to a parameter of a population on the basis of sampling statistics. Compare **interval estimate**

point group *n crystallog* another term for **crystal class**

point guard *n basketball* **a** the position of the player responsible for directing the team's attacking play **b** a player in this position

pointillism ('pwæntɪ,lɪzəm, -tiː,ɪzəm, 'pɔɪn-) *n* the technique of painting elaborated from impressionism, in which dots of unmixed colour are juxtaposed on a white ground so that from a distance they fuse in the viewer's eye into appropriate intermediate tones. Also called: **divisionism** [C19 from French, from *pointiller* to mark with tiny dots, from *pointille* little point, from Italian *puntiglio*, from *punto* POINT] > **pointillist** *n, adj*

pointing ('pɔɪntɪŋ) *n* **1** the act or process of repairing or finishing joints in brickwork, masonry, etc, with mortar **2 a** the insertion of marks to indicate the chanting of a psalm or the vowels in a Hebrew text **b** the sequence of marks so inserted

point lace *n* lace made by a needle with buttonhole stitch on a paper pattern. Also called: **needlepoint** Compare **pillow lace**

pointless ('pɔɪntlɪs) *adj* **1** without a point **2** without meaning, relevance, or force **3** *sport* without a point scored > **pointlessly** *adv* > **pointlessness** *n*

point man *n chiefly US* **1** *military* a soldier who walks at the front of an infantry patrol in combat **2** the leader or spokesperson of a campaign or organization

point off *vb (tr, adverb)* to mark off from the right-hand side (a number of decimal places) in a whole number to create a mixed decimal: *point off three decimal places in 12345 and you get 12.345*

point of honour *n, pl* **points of honour** a circumstance, event, etc, that involves the defence of one's principles, social honour, etc

point of inflection *n, pl* **points of inflection** *maths* a stationary point on a curve at which the tangent is horizontal or vertical and where tangents on either side have the same sign

point of no return *n* **1** a point at which an irreversible commitment must be made to an action, progression, etc **2** a point in a journey at which, if one continues, supplies will be insufficient for a return to the starting place

point of order *n, pl* **points of order** a question raised in a meeting or deliberative assembly by a member as to whether the rules governing procedures are being breached

point of sale *n* (in retail distribution) the place at which a sale is made. Abbreviation: **POS**

point-of-sale terminal *n* (in retail distribution) a device used to record and process information relating to sales. Abbreviation: **POST**

point of view *n, pl* **points of view 1** a position from which someone or something is observed **2** a mental viewpoint or attitude **3** the mental position from which a story is observed or narrated: *the omniscient point of view*

point out *vb (tr, adverb)* to indicate or specify

pointsman ('pɔɪnts,mæn, -mən) *n, pl* **-men 1** a person who operates railway points. US and Canadian equivalent: **switchman 2** a policeman or traffic warden on point duty

point source *n optics* a source of light or other radiation that can be considered to have negligible dimensions

points system *n Brit* a system used to assess applicants' eligibility for local authority housing, based on (points awarded for) such factors as the length of time the applicant has lived in the area, how many children are in the family, etc

point system *n* **1** *printing* a system of measurement using the **point** (see sense 21) as its unit **2** a system for evaluation of achievement, as in education or industry, based on awarding points **3** any system of writing or printing, such as Braille, that uses protruding dots

point-to-point *n* **1** *Brit* **a** a steeplechase organized by a recognized hunt or other body, usually restricted to amateurs riding horses that have been regularly used in hunting **b** (*as modifier*): *a point-to-point race* ▷ *adj* **2** (of a route) from one place to the next **3** (of a radiocommunication link) from one point to another, rather than broadcast

point up *vb (tr, adverb)* to emphasize, esp by identifying: *he pointed up the difficulties we would encounter*

pointy ('pɔɪntɪ) *adj* **pointier, pointiest** having a sharp point or points; pointed

poise¹ (pɔɪz) *n* **1** composure or dignity of manner **2** physical balance or assurance in movement or bearing **3** the state of being balanced or stable; equilibrium; stability **4** the position of hovering **5** suspense or indecision ▷ *vb* **6** to be or cause to be balanced or suspended **7** (*tr*) to hold, as in readiness: *to poise a lance* **8** (*tr*) a rare word for **weigh¹** [C16 from Old French *pois* weight, from Latin *pēnsum*, from *pendere* to weigh]

poise² (pwɑːz, pɔɪz) *n* the cgs unit of viscosity; the viscosity of a fluid in which a tangential force of 1 dyne per square centimetre maintains a difference in velocity of 1 centimetre per second between two parallel planes 1 centimetre apart. It is equivalent to 0.1 newton second per square metre. Symbol: P [C20 named after Jean Louis Marie *Poiseuille* (1799–1869), French physician]

poised (pɔɪzd) *adj* **1** self-possessed; dignified; exhibiting composure **2** balanced and prepared for action: *a skier poised at the top of the slope*

poison ('pɔɪzᵊn) *n* **1** any substance that can impair function, cause structural damage, or otherwise injure the body. Related adj: **toxic 2** something that destroys, corrupts, etc: *the poison of fascism* **3** a substance that retards a chemical reaction or destroys or inhibits the activity of a catalyst **4** a substance that absorbs neutrons in a nuclear reactor and thus slows down the reaction. It may be added deliberately or formed during fission **5 what's your poison?** *informal* what would you like to drink? ▷ *vb* (*tr*) **6** to give poison to (a person or animal) esp with intent to kill **7** to add poison to **8** to taint or infect with or as if with poison **9** (foll by *against*) to turn (a person's mind) against: *he poisoned her mind against me* **10** to retard or stop (a chemical or nuclear reaction) by the action of a poison **11** to inhibit or destroy (the activity of a catalyst) by the action of a poison [C13 from Old French *puison* potion, from Latin *pōtiō* a drink, esp a poisonous one, from *pōtāre* to drink] > **poisoner** *n*

poison dogwood *or* **elder** *n* other names for **poison sumach**

poison gas *n* a gaseous substance, such as chlorine, phosgene, or lewisite, used in warfare to kill or harm

poison hemlock *n* the US name for **hemlock** (sense 1)

poison ivy *n* any of several North American anacardiaceous shrubs or vines of the genus *Rhus* (or *Toxicodendron*), esp *R. radicans*, which has small green flowers and whitish berries that cause an itching rash on contact. See also **sumach** (sense 1)

poison oak *n* **1** either of two North American anacardiaceous shrubs, *Rhus toxicodendron* or *R.*

diversiloba, that are related to the poison ivy and cause a similar rash. See also **sumach** (sense 1) **2** (*not in technical use*) another name for **poison ivy**

poisonous ('pɔɪzənəs) *adj* **1** having the effects or qualities of a poison **2** capable of killing or inflicting injury; venomous **3** corruptive or malicious > **poisonously** *adv* > **poisonousness** *n*

poison-pen letter *n* a letter written in malice, usually anonymously, and intended to abuse, frighten, or insult the recipient

poison pill *n finance* a tactic used by a company fearing an unwelcome takeover bid, in which the value of the company is automatically reduced, as by the sale of an issue of shares having an option unfavourable to the bidders, if the bid is successful

poison sumach *n* an anacardiaceous swamp shrub, *Rhus* (or *Toxicodendron*) *vernix* of the southeastern US, that has greenish-white berries and causes an itching rash on contact. Also called: **poison dogwood, poison elder.** See also **sumach**

Poisson distribution ('pwɑːsᵊn) *n statistics* a distribution that represents the number of events occurring randomly in a fixed time at an average rate λ; symbol $P_0(\lambda)$. For large n and small p with $np = \lambda$ it approximates to the binomial distribution $Bi(n,p)$ [C19 named after Siméon Denis *Poisson* (1781–1840), French mathematician]

Poisson's ratio *n* a measure of the elastic properties of a material expressed as the ratio of the fractional contraction in breadth to the fractional increase in length when the material is stretched. Symbol: μ or ν

Poitiers (*French* pwatje) *n* a city in S central France: capital of the former province of Poitou until 1790; scene of the battle (1356) in which the English under the Black Prince defeated the French; university (1432). Pop: 83 448 (1999)

poitín (pɒ'tiːn) *n* the Irish Gaelic spelling of **poteen**

Poitou (*French* pwatu) *n* a former province of W central France, on the Atlantic. Chief town: Poitiers

Poitou-Charentes (*French* pwatuʃarãt) *n* a region of W central France, on the Bay of Biscay: mainly low-lying

poitrine (,pwa'triːn) *n* a woman's bosom [French, literally: breast, chest]

poke¹ (pəʊk) *vb* **1** (*tr*) to jab or prod, as with the elbow, the finger, a stick, etc **2** (*tr*) to make (a hole, opening, etc) by or as by poking **3** (when *intr*, often foll by *at*) to thrust (at) **4** (*tr*) *informal* to hit with the fist; punch **5** (usually foll by *in, out, out of, through*, etc) to protrude or cause to protrude: *don't poke your arm out of the window* **6** (*tr*) to stir (a fire, pot, etc) by poking **7** (*intr*) to meddle or intrude **8** (*intr; often foll by about or around*) to search or pry **9** (*intr; often foll by along*) to loiter, potter, dawdle, etc **10** (*tr*) *slang* (of a man) to have sexual intercourse with **11 poke fun at** to mock or ridicule **12 poke one's nose into** See **nose** (sense 17) ▷ *n* **13** a jab or prod **14** short for **slowpoke 15** *informal* a blow with one's fist; punch **16** *slang* sexual intercourse [C14 from Low German and Middle Dutch *poken* to thrust, prod, strike]

poke² (pəʊk) *n* **1** *dialect* a pocket or bag **2 a pig in a poke** See **pig** (sense 9) [C13 from Old Northern French *poque*, of Germanic origin; related to Old English *pocca* bag, Old Norse *poki* POUCH, Middle Dutch *poke* bag; compare POACH²]

poke³ (pəʊk) *n* **1** Also called: **poke bonnet** a woman's bonnet with a brim that projects at the front, popular in the 18th and 19th centuries **2** the brim itself [C18 from POKE¹ (in the sense: to thrust out, project)]

poke⁴ (pəʊk) *n* short for **pokeweed**

pokeberry ('pəʊkbəri) *n, pl* **-berries 1** Also called: **inkberry** the berry of the pokeweed **2** another name for the **pokeweed**

pokelogan ('pəʊk,ləʊgən) *n Canadian* another name for **bogan** [C19 from Ojibwa *pokenogun*]

poker[1] ('pəʊkə) n 1 a metal rod, usually with a handle, for stirring a fire 2 a person or thing that pokes

poker[2] ('pəʊkə) n a card game of bluff and skill in which bets are made on the hands dealt, the highest-ranking hand (containing the most valuable combinations of sequences and sets of cards) winning the pool [C19 probably from French *poque* similar card game]

poker dice n 1 a dice marked on its six faces with the pictures of the playing cards from ace to nine 2 a gambling game, based on poker hands, played with five such dice

poker face n *informal* a face without expression, as that of a poker player attempting to conceal the value of his cards

poker-faced adj *informal* having a deliberately expressionless face

poker machine n *Austral and NZ* a fruit machine. Often shortened to: **pokie**

pokerwork ('pəʊkə,wɜːk) n 1 the art of decorating wood or leather by burning a design with a heated metal point; pyrography 2 artefacts decorated in this way

pokeweed ('pəʊk,wiːd), **pokeberry** or **pokeroot** n a tall North American plant, *Phytolacca americana*, that has small white flowers, juicy purple berries, and a poisonous purple root used medicinally: family *Phytolaccaceae*. Sometimes shortened to: poke Also called: inkberry [C18 *poke*, shortened from Algonquian *puccoon* plant used in dyeing, from *pak* blood]

pokie or **pokey** ('pəʊkɪ) n *Austral and NZ informal* short for **poker machine**

poky or **pokey** ('pəʊkɪ) adj pokier, pokiest 1 *informal* (esp of rooms) small and cramped 2 without speed or energy; slow ▷ n 3 the *chiefly US and Canadian slang* prison [C19 from POKE[1] (in slang sense: to confine)] > 'pokily adv > 'pokiness n

POL *military abbreviation for* petroleum, oil, and lubricants

Pol. *abbreviation for* 1 Poland 2 Polish

Pola ('pɔːla) n the Italian name for **Pula**

Polack ('pəʊlæk) n *derogatory slang* a Pole or a person of Polish descent [C16 from Polish *Polak* Pole]

polacre (pəʊ'lɑːkə) or **polacca** (pəʊ'lækə) n a three-masted sailing vessel used in the Mediterranean [C17 from either French *polacre* or Italian *polacca* Pole or Polish; origin unknown]

Poland ('pəʊlənd) n a republic in central Europe, on the Baltic: first united in the 10th century; dissolved after the third partition effected by Austria, Russia, and Prussia in 1795; re-established independence in 1918; invaded by Germany in 1939; ruled by a Communist government from 1947 to 1989, when a multiparty system was introduced. It consists chiefly of a low undulating plain in the north, rising to a low plateau in the south, with the Sudeten and Carpathian Mountains along the S border. Official language: Polish. Religion: Roman Catholic majority. Currency: zloty. Capital: Warsaw. Pop: 38 551 000 (2004 est). Area: 311 730 sq km (120 359 sq miles). Polish name: Polska

polar ('pəʊlə) adj 1 situated at or near, coming from, or relating to either of the earth's poles or the area inside the Arctic or Antarctic Circles: *polar regions* 2 having or relating to a pole or poles 3 pivotal or guiding in the manner of the Pole Star 4 directly opposite, as in tendency or character 5 *chem* a Also: **heteropolar** (of a molecule or compound) being or having a molecule in which there is an uneven distribution of electrons and thus a permanent dipole moment: *water has polar molecules* b (of a crystal or substance) being or having a crystal that is bound by ionic bonds: *sodium chloride forms polar crystals*

polar axis n the fixed line in a system of polar coordinates from which the polar angle, θ, is measured anticlockwise

polar bear n a white carnivorous bear, *Thalarctos maritimus*, of coastal regions of the North Pole

polar body n *physiol* a tiny cell containing little cytoplasm that is produced with the ovum during oogenesis when the oocyte undergoes meiosis

polar circle n a term for either the **Arctic Circle** or **Antarctic Circle**

polar coordinates *pl n* a pair of coordinates for locating a point in a plane by means of the length of a radius vector, *r*, which pivots about the origin to establish the angle, θ, that the position of the point makes with a fixed line. Usually written (r, θ). See also **Cartesian coordinates, spherical coordinates**

polar distance n the angular distance of a star, planet, etc, from the celestial pole; the complement of the declination. Also called: codeclination

polar equation n an equation in polar coordinates

polar front n *meteorol* a front dividing cold polar air from warmer temperate or tropical air

Polari (pə'lɑːrɪ) or **Parlyaree** (pɑː'ljɑːrɪ) n an English slang that is derived from the Lingua Franca of Mediterranean ports; brought to England by sailors from the 16th century onwards. A few words survive, esp in male homosexual slang [C19 from Italian *parlare* to speak]

polarimeter (,pəʊlə'rɪmɪtə) n 1 an instrument for measuring the amount of polarization of light 2 an instrument for measuring the rotation of the plane of polarization of light as a result of its passage through a liquid or solution. See **optical activity**. > polarimetric (,pəʊlərɪ'mɛtrɪk) adj > ,polar'imetry n

Polaris (pə'lɑːrɪs) n 1 Also called: the Pole Star, the North Star the brightest star in the constellation Ursa Minor, situated slightly less than 1° from the north celestial pole. It is a Cepheid variable, with a period of four days. Visual magnitude: 2.08–2.17; spectral type: F8Ib 2 a a type of US two-stage intermediate-range ballistic missile, usually fired by a submerged submarine b (as modifier): *a Polaris submarine* [shortened from Medieval Latin *stella polāris* polar star]

polariscope (pəʊ'lærɪ,skəʊp) n an instrument for detecting polarized light or for observing objects under polarized light, esp for detecting strain in transparent materials. See **photoelasticity**

polarity (pəʊ'lærɪtɪ) n, pl -ties 1 the condition of having poles 2 the condition of a body or system in which it has opposing physical properties at different points, esp magnetic poles or electric charge 3 the particular state of a part of a body or system that has polarity: *an electrode with positive polarity* 4 the state of having or expressing two directly opposite tendencies, opinions, etc

polarization or **polarisation** (,pəʊləraɪ'zeɪʃən) n 1 the condition of having or giving polarity 2 *physics* the process or phenomenon in which the waves of light or other electromagnetic radiation are restricted to certain directions of vibration, usually specified in terms of the electric field vector

polarize or **polarise** ('pəʊlə,raɪz) vb 1 to acquire or cause to acquire polarity 2 to acquire or cause to acquire polarization: *to polarize light* 3 to cause people to adopt extreme opposing positions: *to polarize opinion* > 'polar,izable or 'polar,isable adj

polarizer or **polariser** ('pəʊlə,raɪzə) n a person or a device that causes polarization

polar lights *pl n* the aurora borealis in the N hemisphere or the aurora australis in the S hemisphere

polarography (,pəʊlə'rɒgrəfɪ) n a technique for analysing and studying ions in solution by using an electrolytic cell with a very small cathode and obtaining a graph (**polarogram**) of the current against the potential to determine the concentration and nature of the ions. Because the cathode is small, polarization occurs and each type of anion is discharged at a different potential. The apparatus (**polarograph**) usually employs a dropping-mercury cathode > polarographic (,pəʊlərə'græfɪk) adj

Polaroid ('pəʊlə,rɔɪd) *trademark* ▷ n 1 a type of plastic sheet that can polarize a transmitted beam of normal light because it is composed of long parallel molecules. It only transmits plane-polarized light if these molecules are parallel to the plane of polarization and, since reflected light is partly polarized, it is often used in sunglasses to eliminate glare 2 Polaroid Land Camera any of several types of camera yielding a finished print by means of a special developing and processing technique that occurs inside the camera and takes only a few seconds to complete 3 (plural) sunglasses with lenses made from Polaroid plastic ▷ adj 4 of, relating to, using, or used in a Polaroid Land Camera: *Polaroid film*

polar orbit n the orbit of a satellite that passes over the poles of a planet

polar sequence n *astronomy* a series of stars in the vicinity of the N celestial pole whose accurately determined magnitudes serve as the standard for visual and photographic magnitudes of stars

polar wander n *geology* the movement of the earth's magnetic poles with respect to the geographic poles

polder ('pəʊldə, 'pɒl-) n a stretch of land reclaimed from the sea or a lake, esp in the Netherlands [C17 from Middle Dutch *polre*]

pole[1] (pəʊl) n 1 a long slender usually round piece of wood, metal, or other material 2 the piece of timber on each side of which a pair of carriage horses are hitched 3 another name for **rod** (sense 7) 4 *horse racing, chiefly US and Canadian* a the inside lane of a racecourse b (as modifier): *the pole position* c one of a number of markers placed at intervals of one sixteenth of a mile along the side of a racecourse 5 *nautical* a any light spar b the part of a mast between the head and the attachment of the uppermost shrouds 6 under bare poles *nautical* (of a sailing vessel) with no sails set 7 up the pole *Brit, Austral, and NZ informal* a slightly mad b mistaken; on the wrong track ▷ vb 8 (tr) to strike or push with a pole 9 (tr) a to set out (an area of land or garden) with poles b to support (a crop, such as hops or beans) on poles 10 (tr) to deoxidize (a molten metal, esp copper) by stirring it with green wood 11 to punt (a boat) [Old English *pāl*, from Latin *pālus* a stake, prop; see PALE[2]]

pole[2] (pəʊl) n 1 either of the two antipodal points where the earth's axis of rotation meets the earth's surface. See also **North Pole, South Pole** 2 *astronomy* short for **celestial pole** 3 *physics* a either of the two regions at the extremities of a magnet to which the lines of force converge or from which they diverge b either of two points or regions in a piece of material, system, etc, at which there are opposite electric charges, as at the two terminals of a battery 4 *maths* an isolated singularity of an analytical function 5 *biology* a either end of the axis of a cell, spore, ovum, or similar body b either end of the spindle formed during the metaphase of mitosis and meiosis 6 *physiol* the point on a neuron from which the axon or dendrites project from the cell body 7 either of two mutually exclusive or opposite actions, opinions, etc 8 *geometry* the origin in a system of polar or spherical coordinates 9 any fixed point of reference 10 poles apart (or asunder) having widely divergent opinions, tastes, etc 11 from pole to pole throughout the entire world [C14 from Latin *polus* end of an axis, from Greek *polos* pivot, axis, pole; related to Greek *kuklos* circle]

Pole (pəʊl) n a native, inhabitant, or citizen of Poland or a speaker of Polish

poleaxe or *US* **poleax** ('pəʊl,æks) n 1 another term for **battle-axe** (sense 1) 2 a former naval weapon with an axe blade on one side of the

p

handle and a spike on the other **3** an axe used by butchers to slaughter animals ▷ *vb* **4** (*tr*) to hit or fell with or as if with a poleaxe [C14 *pollax* battle-axe, from POLL + AXE]

polecat ('pəʊl,kæt) *n*, *pl* **-cats** or **-cat 1** Also called (formerly): **foumart** a dark brown musteline mammal, *Mustela putorius*, of woodlands of Europe, Asia, and N Africa, that is closely related to but larger than the weasel and gives off an unpleasant smell. See also **sweet marten 2** any of various related animals, such as the **marbled polecat**, *Vormela peregusna* **3** *US* a nontechnical name for **skunk** (sense 1) [C14 *polcat*, perhaps from Old French *pol* cock, from Latin *pullus*, + CAT¹; from its habit of preying on poultry]

pole dancing *n* a form of entertainment in which a scantily dressed woman dances erotically, turning on and posing against a vertically fixed pole on a stage > **pole dancer** *n*

pole horse *n* a horse harnessed alongside the shaft (pole) of a vehicle. Also called: **poler**

pole house *n* NZ a timber house built on a steep section and supported by heavy debarked logs in long piles

poleis ('pɒlaɪs) *n* the plural of **polis¹**

polemarch ('pɒlɪ,mɑːk) *n* (in ancient Greece) a civilian official, originally a supreme general [C16 from Greek *polemarchos*, from *polemos* war + *archos* ruler]

polemic (pə'lɛmɪk) *adj* also **po'lemical 1** of or involving dispute or controversy ▷ *n* **2** an argument or controversy, esp over a doctrine, belief, etc **3** a person engaged in such an argument or controversy [C17 from Medieval Latin *polemicus*, from Greek *polemikos* relating to war, from *polemos* war] > **po'lemically** *adv* > **polemicist** (pə'lɛmɪsɪst) *or* **polemist** ('pɒlɪmɪst) *n*

polemics (pə'lɛmɪks) *n* (*functioning as singular*) the art or practice of dispute or argument, as in attacking or defending a doctrine or belief

polemoniaceous (,pɒlɪˌməʊnɪ'eɪʃəs) *adj* of, relating to, or belonging to the *Polemoniaceae*, a chiefly North American family of plants that includes phlox and Jacob's ladder [C19 from New Latin *Polemōnium* type genus, from Greek *polemōnion* a plant, perhaps valerian]

polenta (pəʊ'lɛntə) *n* a thick porridge made in Italy, usually from maize [C16 via Italian from Latin: pearl barley, perhaps from Greek *palē* pollen]

pole piece *n electrical engineering* a piece of ferromagnetic material forming an extension of the magnetic circuit in an electric motor, etc, used to concentrate the magnetic field where it will be most effective

pole position *n* **1** (in motor racing) the starting position on the inside of the front row, generally considered the best one **2** an advantageous starting position

poler ('pəʊlə) *n* **1** another name for **pole horse 2** a person or thing that poles, esp a punter

pole star *n* a guiding principle, rule, standard, etc

Pole Star *n* the the star closest to the N celestial pole at any particular time. At present this is Polaris, but it will eventually be replaced by some other star owing to precession of the earth's axis

pole vault *n* **1** the a field event in which competitors attempt to clear a high bar with the aid of an extremely flexible long pole **2** a single attempt in the pole vault ▷ *vb* **pole-vault 3** (*intr*) to perform a pole vault or compete in the pole vault > **'pole-ˌvaulter** *n*

poley ('pəʊlɪ) *adj Austral* (of cattle) hornless or polled

poleyn ('pəʊleɪn) *n* a piece of armour for protecting the knee. Also called: **kneecap** [from Old French *polain*]

Polglish ('pəʊlglɪʃ) *n* informal Polish containing a high proportion of words of English origin [C20 from a blend of POLISH + ENGLISH]

police (pə'liːs) *n* **1 a** (often preceded by *the*) the organized civil force of a state, concerned with maintenance of law and order, the detection and prevention of crime, etc **b** (*as modifier*): *a police inquiry* **2** (*functioning as plural*) the members of such a force collectively **3** any organized body with a similar function: *security police* **4** *archaic* **a** the regulation and control of a community, esp in regard to the enforcement of law, the prevention of crime, etc **b** the department of government concerned with this ▷ *vb* (*tr*) **5** to regulate, control, or keep in order by means of a police or similar force **6** to observe or record the activity or enforcement of: *a committee was set up to police the new agreement on picketing* **7** *US* to make or keep (a military camp, etc) clean and orderly [C16 via French from Latin *polītīa* administration, government; see POLITY]

police court *n* **1** another name for **magistrates' court 2** (in Scotland, formerly) a burgh court with limited jurisdiction, presided over by lay magistrates or a stipendiary magistrate: replaced in 1975 by the **district court**

police dog *n* a dog, often an Alsatian, trained to help the police, as in tracking

policeman (pə'liːsmən) *or feminine* **policewoman** *n*, *pl* **-men** *or* **-women** a member of a police force, esp one holding the rank of constable

policeman's helmet *n* a Himalayan balsaminaceous plant, *Impatiens glandulifera*, with large purplish-pink flowers, introduced into Britain

Police Motu *n* a pidginized version of the Motu language, used as a lingua franca in Papua, originally chiefly by the police. Also called: **Hiri Motu**

police officer *n* a member of a police force, esp a constable; policeman. Often (esp as form of address) shortened to: **officer**

police procedural *n* a novel, film, or television drama that deals realistically with police work

police state *n* a state or country in which a repressive government maintains control through the police

police station *n* the office or headquarters of the police force of a district

police wagon *n* *US* another term for **patrol wagon**

policy¹ ('pɒlɪsɪ) *n*, *pl* **-cies 1** a plan of action adopted or pursued by an individual, government, party, business, etc **2** wisdom, prudence, shrewdness, or sagacity **3** *Scot* (*often plural*) the improved grounds surrounding a country house [C14 from Old French *policie*, from Latin *polītīa* administration, POLITY]

policy² ('pɒlɪsɪ) *n*, *pl* **-cies** a document containing a contract of insurance [C16 from Old French *police* certificate, from Old Italian *polizza*, from Latin *apodixis* proof, from Greek *apodeixis* demonstration, proof]

policyholder ('pɒlɪsɪˌhəʊldə) *n* a person or organization in whose name an insurance policy is registered

policy science *n* a branch of the social sciences concerned with the formulation and implementation of policy in bureaucracies, etc

polio ('pəʊlɪəʊ) *n* short for **poliomyelitis**

poliomyelitis (,pəʊlɪəʊ,maɪə'laɪtɪs) *n* an acute infectious viral disease, esp affecting children. In its paralytic form (**acute anterior poliomyelitis**) the brain and spinal cord are involved, causing weakness, paralysis, and wasting of muscle. Often shortened to: **polio** Also called: **infantile paralysis** [C19 New Latin, from Greek *polios* grey + *muelos* marrow]

polis¹ ('pɒlɪs) *n*, *pl* **poleis** ('pɒlaɪs) an ancient Greek city-state [from Greek: city]

polis² ('pɒlɪs) *n Scot and Irish* the police or a police officer [C19 a variant pronunciation of *police*]

polish ('pɒlɪʃ) *vb* **1** to make or become smooth and shiny by rubbing, esp with wax or an abrasive **2** (*tr*) to make perfect or complete **3** to make or become elegant or refined ▷ *n* **4** a finish or gloss **5** the act of polishing or the condition of having been polished **6** a substance used to produce a smooth and shiny, often protective surface **7** elegance or refinement, esp in style, manner, etc ▷ See also **polish off**, **polish up** [C13 *polis*, from Old French *polir*, from Latin *polīre* to polish] > **'polishable** *adj* > **'polisher** *n*

Polish ('pəʊlɪʃ) *adj* **1** of, relating to, or characteristic of Poland, its people, or their language ▷ *n* **2** the official language of Poland, belonging to the West Slavonic branch of the Indo-European family

Polish Corridor *n* the strip of land through E Pomerania providing Poland with access to the sea (1919–39), given to her in 1919 in the Treaty of Versailles, and separating East Prussia from the rest of Germany. It is now part of Poland

polished ('pɒlɪʃt) *adj* **1** accomplished: *a polished actor* **2** impeccably or professionally done: *a polished performance* **3** (of rice) having had the outer husk removed by milling

Polish Lowland sheepdog *n* a strongly-built medium-sized sheepdog of a Polish breed with a long thick shaggy coat that covers the eyes

Polish notation *n* a logical notation that dispenses with the need for brackets by writing the logical constants as operators preceding their arguments

polish off *vb* (*tr*, *adverb*) *informal* **1** to finish or process completely **2** to dispose of or kill

polish up *vb* (*adverb*) **1** to make or become smooth and shiny by polishing **2** (when *intr*, foll by *on*) to study or practise until adept at; improve: *polish up your spelling; he's polishing up on his German*

Politburo ('pɒlɪtˌbjʊərəʊ) *n* **1** the executive and policy-making committee of a Communist Party **2** the supreme policy-making authority in most Communist countries [C20 from Russian: contraction of *Politicheskoe Buro* political bureau]

polite (pə'laɪt) *adj* **1** showing regard for others, in manners, speech, behaviour, etc; courteous **2** cultivated or refined: *polite society* **3** elegant or polished: *polite letters* [C15 from Latin *polītus* polished; see POLISH] > **po'litely** *adv* > **po'liteness** *n*

politesse (,pɒlɪ'tɛs) *n* formal or genteel politeness [C18 via French from Italian *politezza*, ultimately from Latin *polīre* to POLISH]

politic ('pɒlɪtɪk) *adj* **1** artful or shrewd; ingenious: *a politic manager* **2** crafty or unscrupulous; cunning: *a politic old scoundrel* **3** sagacious, wise, or prudent, esp in statesmanship: *a politic choice* **4** an archaic word for **political** ▷ See also **body politic**, **politics** [C15 from Old French *politique*, from Latin *polīticus* concerning civil administration, from Greek *politikos*, from *politēs* citizen, from *polis* city] > **'politicly** *adv*

political (pə'lɪtɪkᵊl) *adj* **1** of or relating to the state, government, the body politic, public administration, policy-making, etc **2 a** of, involved in, or relating to government policy-making as distinguished from administration or law **b** of or relating to the civil aspects of government as distinguished from the military **3** of, dealing with, or relating to politics: *a political person* **4** of, characteristic of, or relating to the parties and the partisan aspects of politics **5** organized or ordered with respect to government: *a political unit* > **po'litically** *adv*

political economy *n* the former name for **economics** (sense 1)

politically correct *adj* demonstrating progressive ideals, esp by avoiding vocabulary that is considered offensive, discriminatory, or judgmental, esp concerning race and gender. Abbreviation: PC > **political correctness** *n*

political prisoner *n* someone imprisoned for holding, expressing, or acting in accord with particular political beliefs

political science *n* (esp as an academic subject) the study of the state, government, and politics: one of the social sciences > **political scientist** *n*

politician (,pɒlɪ'tɪʃən) *n* **1** a person actively

engaged in politics, esp a full-time professional member of a deliberative assembly **2** a person who is experienced or skilled in the art or science of politics, government, or administration; statesman **3** *disparaging, chiefly US* a person who engages in politics out of a wish for personal gain, as realized by holding a public office

politicize or **politicise** (pəˈlɪtɪˌsaɪz) *vb* **1** (*tr*) to render political in tone, interest, or awareness **2** (*intr*) to participate in political discussion or activity > poˌliticiˈzation or poˌliticiˈsation *n*

politicking (ˈpɒlɪˌtɪkɪŋ) *n* **1** political activity, esp seeking votes **2** activity directed towards acquiring power and influence, achieving one's own goals, etc > ˈpoliˌticker *n*

politico (pəˈlɪtɪˌkəʊ) *n, pl* **-cos** an informal word for a **politician** (senses 1, 3) [C17 from Italian or Spanish]

politico- *combining form* denoting political or politics: *politicoeconomic*

politics (ˈpɒlɪtɪks) *n* **1** (*functioning as singular*) the practice or study of the art and science of forming, directing, and administrating states and other political units; the art and science of government; political science **2** (*functioning as singular*) the complex or aggregate of relationships of people in society, esp those relationships involving authority or power **3** (*functioning as plural*) political activities or affairs: *party politics* **4** (*functioning as singular*) the business or profession of politics **5** (*functioning as singular or plural*) any activity concerned with the acquisition of power, gaining one's own ends, etc: *company politics are frequently vicious* **6** (*functioning as plural*) opinions, principles, sympathies, etc, with respect to politics: *his conservative politics* **7** (*functioning as plural*) **a** the policy-formulating aspects of government as distinguished from the administrative, or legal **b** the civil functions of government as distinguished from the military

polity (ˈpɒlɪtɪ) *n, pl* **-ties 1** a form of government or organization of a state, church, society, etc; constitution **2** a politically organized society, state, city, etc **3** the management of public or civil affairs **4** political organization [C16 from Latin *polītīa*, from Greek *politeia* citizenship, civil administration, from *politēs* citizen, from *polis* city]

polje (ˈpəʊljɛ) *n geography* a large elliptical depression in karst regions, sometimes containing a marsh or small lake [Serbo-Croat, literally: field; related to FLOOR]

polka (ˈpɒlkə) *n, pl* **-kas 1** a 19th-century Bohemian dance with three steps and a hop, in fast duple time **2** a piece of music composed for or in the rhythm of this dance ▷ *vb* **-kas, -kaing, -kaed 3** (*intr*) to dance a polka [C19 via French from Czech *pulka* half-step, from *pul* half]

polka dot *n* **1** one of a pattern of small circular regularly spaced spots on a fabric **2 a** a fabric or pattern with such spots **b** (*as modifier*): *a polka-dot dress* [C19 of uncertain origin]

poll (pəʊl) *n* **1** the casting, recording, or counting of votes in an election; a voting **2** the result or quantity of such a voting: *a heavy poll* **3** Also called: **opinion poll a** a canvassing of a representative sample of a large group of people on some question in order to determine the general opinion of the group **b** the results or record of such a canvassing **4** any counting or enumeration: *a poll of the number of men with long hair* **5** short for **poll tax 6** a list or enumeration of people, esp for taxation or voting purposes **7** the striking face of a hammer **8** the occipital or back part of the head of an animal ▷ *vb* (*mainly tr*) **9** to receive (a vote or quantity of votes): *he polled 10 000 votes* **10** to receive, take, or record the votes of: *he polled the whole town* **11** to canvass (a person, group, area, etc) as part of a survey of opinion **12** *chiefly US* to take the vote, verdict, opinion, etc, individually of each member (of a jury, conference, etc) **13** (*sometimes intr*) to cast (a vote) in an election **14** *computing* (in data transmission

when several terminals share communications channels) to check each channel rapidly to establish which are free, or to call for data from each terminal in turn **15** to clip or shear **16** to remove or cut short the horns of (cattle) [C13 (in the sense: a human head) and C17 (in the modern sense: a counting of heads, votes): from Middle Low German *polle* hair of the head, head, top of a tree; compare Swedish *pull* crown of the head]

pollack or **pollock** (ˈpɒlək) *n, pl* **-lacks, -lack** or **-locks, -lock** a gadoid food fish, *Pollachius pollachius*, that has a dark green back and a projecting lower jaw and occurs in northern seas, esp the North Atlantic Ocean [C17 from earlier Scottish *podlok*, of obscure origin]

pollan (ˈpɒlən) *n* any of several varieties of the whitefish *Coregonus pollan* that occur in lakes in Northern Ireland [C18 probably from Irish *poll* lake]

pollard (ˈpɒləd) *n* **1** an animal, such as a sheep or deer, that has either shed its horns or antlers or has had them removed **2** a tree that has had its top cut off to encourage the formation of a crown of branches ▷ *vb* **3** (*tr*) to convert into a pollard; poll [C16 hornless animal; see POLL]

polled (pəʊld) *adj* **1** (of animals, esp cattle) having the horns cut off or being naturally hornless **2** *archaic* shorn of hair; bald

pollen (ˈpɒlən) *n* a fine powdery substance produced by the anthers of seed-bearing plants, consisting of numerous fine grains containing the male gametes [C16 from Latin: powder; compare Greek *palē* pollen] > **pollinic** (pəˈlɪnɪk) *adj*

pollen analysis *n* another name for **palynology**

pollen basket *n* the part of the hind leg of a bee that is specialized for carrying pollen, typically consisting of a trough bordered by long hairs. Technical name: **corbicula**

pollen count *n* a measure of the pollen present in the air over a 24-hour period, often published to enable sufferers from hay fever to predict the severity of their attacks

pollen tube *n* a hollow tubular outgrowth that develops from a pollen grain after pollination, grows down the style to the ovule, and conveys male gametes to the egg cell

pollex (ˈpɒlɛks) *n, pl* **-lices** (-lɪˌsiːz) the first digit of the forelimb of amphibians, reptiles, birds, and mammals, such as the thumb of man and other primates [C19 from Latin: thumb, big toe] > **pollical** (ˈpɒlɪkᵊl) *adj*

pollinate (ˈpɒlɪˌneɪt) *vb* (*tr*) to transfer pollen from the anthers to the stigma of (a flower) > ˌpolliˈnation or ˈpolliˌnator *n*

polling (ˈpəʊlɪŋ) *n* **1 a** the casting or registering of votes at an election **b** (*as modifier*): *polling day* **2** the conducting of a public opinion poll **3** *computing* the automatic interrogation of terminals by a central controlling machine to determine if they are ready to receive or transmit messages

polling booth *n* a semienclosed space in which a voter stands to mark a ballot paper during an election

polling station *n* a building, such as a school, designated as the place to which voters go during an election to cast their votes

polliniferous or **polleniferous** (ˌpɒlɪˈnɪfərəs) *adj* **1** producing pollen: *polliniferous plants* **2** specialized for carrying pollen: *the polliniferous legs of bees*

pollinium (pəˈlɪnɪəm) *n, pl* **-ia** (-ɪə) a mass of cohering pollen grains, produced by plants such as orchids and transported as a whole during pollination [C19 New Latin; see POLLEN]

pollinosis or **pollenosis** (ˌpɒlɪˈnəʊsɪs) *n pathol* a technical name for **hay fever**

polliwog or **pollywog** (ˈpɒlɪˌwɒg) *n* **1** *Brit dialect, US,* and *Canadian* another name for **tadpole 2** *informal* a sailor who has not crossed the equator. Compare **shellback** [C15 *polwygle*; see POLL, WIGGLE]

pollster (ˈpəʊlstə) *n* a person who conducts opinion polls

poll tax *n* **1** a tax levied per head of adult population **2** an informal name for (the former) **community charge**

pollucite (ˈpɒljuˌsaɪt, pəˈluːˌsaɪt) *n* a colourless rare mineral consisting of a hydrated caesium aluminium silicate, often containing some rubidium. It occurs in coarse granite, esp in Manitoba, and is an important source of caesium. Formula: $CsAlSi_2O_6.\frac{1}{2}H_2O$ [C19 from Latin *polluc-*, stem of *Pollux* + -ITE¹; originally called *pollux*, alluding to Castor and Pollux, since it was associated with another mineral called *castor* or *castorite*]

pollutant (pəˈluːtᵊnt) *n* a substance that pollutes, esp a chemical or similar substance that is produced as a waste product of an industrial process

pollute (pəˈluːt) *vb* (*tr*) **1** to contaminate, as with poisonous or harmful substances **2** to make morally corrupt or impure; sully **3** to desecrate or defile [C14 *polute*, from Latin *polluere* to defile] > **polˈluter** *n*

polluted (pəˈluːtɪd) *adj* **1** made unclean or impure; contaminated **2** *US slang* intoxicated; drunk

pollution (pəˈluːʃən) *n* **1** the act of polluting or the state of being polluted **2** harmful or poisonous substances introduced into an environment

Pollux (ˈpɒləks) *n* **1** the brightest star in the constellation Gemini, lying close to the star **Castor**. Visual magnitude: 1.15; spectral type: KoIII; distance: 34 light years **2** *classical myth* See **Castor and Pollux**

polly (ˈpɒlɪ) *n, pl* **-lies** an informal word for **politician**

Pollyanna (ˌpɒlɪˈænə) *n* a person who is constantly or excessively optimistic [C20 after the chief character in *Pollyanna* (1913), a novel by Eleanor Porter (1868–1920), US writer]

polo (ˈpəʊləʊ) *n* **1** a game similar to hockey played on horseback using long-handled mallets (**polo sticks**) and a wooden ball **2** any of several similar games, such as one played on bicycles **3** short for **water polo 4** Also called: **polo neck a** a collar on a garment, worn rolled over to fit closely round the neck **b** a garment, esp a sweater, with such a collar [C19 from Balti (dialect of Kashmir): ball, from Tibetan *pulu*]

Polokwane (ˌpɒləˈkwɑːnɪ) *n* a town in NE South Africa, the capital of Limpopo province: commercial and agricultural centre. Pop: 90 398 (2001). Former name: **Pietersburg**

polonaise (ˌpɒləˈneɪz) *n* **1** a ceremonial marchlike dance in three-four time from Poland **2** a piece of music composed for or in the rhythm of this dance **3** a woman's costume with a tight bodice and an overskirt drawn back to show a decorative underskirt [C18 from French *danse polonaise* Polish dance]

polonium (pəˈləʊnɪəm) *n* a very rare radioactive element that occurs in trace amounts in uranium ores. The isotope **polonium-210** is produced artificially and is used as a lightweight power source in satellites and to eliminate static electricity in certain industries. Symbol: Po; atomic no.: 84; half-life of most stable isotope, ²⁰⁹Po: 103 years; valency: −2, 0, 2, 4, or 6; relative density (alpha modification): 9.32; melting pt.: 254°C; boiling pt.: 962°C [C19 New Latin, from Medieval Latin *Polōnia* Poland; named in honour of the Polish nationality of its discoverer, Marie Curie]

polony (pəˈləʊnɪ) *n, pl* **-nies** *Brit* another name for **bologna sausage** [C16 perhaps from BOLOGNA]

polo shirt *n* a knitted cotton short-sleeved shirt with a collar and three-button opening at the neck

Polska (ˈpɒlska) *n* the Polish name for **Poland**

Poltava (*Russian* palˈtavə) *n* a city in E Ukraine: scene of the victory (1709) of the Russians under Peter the Great over the Swedes under Charles XII;

p

centre of an agricultural region. Pop: 319 000 (2005 est)

poltergeist ('pɒltə,gaɪst) *n* a spirit believed to manifest its presence by rappings and other noises and also by acts of mischief, such as throwing furniture about [C19 from German, from *poltern* to be noisy + *Geist* GHOST]

poltroon (pɒl'truːn) *n* **1** an abject or contemptible coward ▷ *adj* **2** a rare word for **cowardly** [C16 from Old French *poultron*, from Old Italian *poltrone* lazy good-for-nothing, apparently from *poltrīre* to lie indolently in bed, from *poltro* bed]

poly ('pɒlɪ) *n*, *pl* **polys 1** *informal* short for **polytechnic** ▷ *adj* **2** *informal* short for **polyester 3** *informal* short for **polythene**

poly- *combining form* **1** more than one; many or much: *polyhedron* **2** having an excessive or abnormal number or amount: *polycythaemia* [from Greek *polus* much, many; related to Old English *fela* many]

polyadelphous (,pɒlɪə'dɛlfəs) *adj* **1** (of stamens) having united filaments so that they are arranged in three or more groups **2** (of flowers) having polyadelphous stamens [C19 from New Latin, from POLY- + *-adelphous* from Greek *adelphos* brother]

polyadic (,pɒlɪ'ædɪk) *adj logic, maths* (of a relation, operation, etc) having several argument places, as ... moves ... from ... to ..., which might be represented as $Mpox_1y_1z_1t_1x_2y_2z_2t_2$ where *p* names a person, *o* an object, and each *t* a time, and each *<x,y,z>* the coordinates of a place [C20 modelled on MONADIC]

polyamide (,pɒlɪ'æmaɪd, -mɪd) *n* any one of a class of synthetic polymeric materials containing recurring -CONH- groups. See also **nylon**

polyandry ('pɒlɪ,ændrɪ) *n* **1** the practice or condition of being married to more than one husband at the same time. Compare **polygamy 2** the practice in animals of a female mating with more than one male during one breeding season **3** the condition in flowers of having a large indefinite number of stamens ▷ Compare **polygyny** [C18 from Greek *poluandria*, from POLY- + *-andria* from *anēr* man] > ,poly'androus *adj*

polyanthus (,pɒlɪ'ænθəs) *n*, *pl* **-thuses 1** any of several hybrid garden primroses, esp *Primula polyantha*, which has brightly coloured flowers **2** polyanthus narcissus a Eurasian amaryllidaceous plant, *Narcissus tazetta*, having clusters of small yellow or white fragrant flowers [C18 New Latin, Greek: having many flowers]

polyarchy ('pɒlɪ,ɑːkɪ) *n*, *pl* **-chies** a political system in which power is dispersed [C17 from POLY- + -ARCHY]

polyatomic (,pɒlɪə'tɒmɪk) *adj* (of a molecule) containing more than two atoms

poly bag ('pɒlɪ) *n Brit informal* a polythene bag, esp one used to store or protect food or household articles

polybasic (,pɒlɪ'beɪsɪk) *adj* (of an acid) having two or more replaceable hydrogen atoms per molecule

polybasite (,pɒlɪ'beɪsaɪt, pə'lɪbə,saɪt) *n* a grey to black mineral consisting of a sulphide of silver, antimony, and copper in the form of platelike monoclinic crystals. It occurs in veins of silver ore. Formula: $(Ag,Cu)_{16}Sb_2S_{11}$ [C19 from POLY- + BASE[1] + -ITE[2]]

polycarbonate (,pɒlɪ'kɑːbə,neɪt, -nɪt) *n* any of a class of strong transparent thermoplastic resins used in moulding materials, laminates, etc

polycarboxylate (,pɒlɪ'kɑːbɒk,sɪleɪt) *n* a salt or ester of a polycarboxylic acid. Polycarboxylate esters are used in certain detergents

polycarboxylic acid (,pɒlɪ'kɑːbɒk,sɪlɪk) *n* a type of carboxylic acid containing two or more carboxyl groups

polycarpellary (,pɒlɪkɑː'pɛlərɪ) *adj* (of a plant gynoecium) having or consisting of many carpels

polycarpic (,pɒlɪ'kɑːpɪk) *or* **polycarpous** *adj* (of a plant) able to produce flowers and fruit several times in successive years or seasons > ,poly'carpy *n*

polycarpous (,pɒlɪ'kɑːpəs) *or* **polycarpic** *adj* (of a plant) having a gynoecium consisting of many distinct carpels

polycentrism (,pɒlɪ'sɛntrɪzəm) *n* (formerly) the fact, principle, or advocacy of the existence of more than one guiding or predominant ideological or political centre in a political system, alliance, etc, in the Communist world

polychaete (,pɒlɪ,kiːt) *n* **1** any marine annelid worm of the class *Polychaeta*, having a distinct head and paired fleshy appendages (parapodia) that bear bristles (chaetae or setae) and are used in swimming: includes the lugworms, ragworms, and sea mice ▷ *adj* also **polychaetous 2** of, relating to, or belonging to the class *Polychaeta* [C19 from New Latin, from Greek *polukhaitēs*: having much hair; see CHAETA]

polychasium (,pɒlɪ'keɪzɪəm) *n*, *pl* **-sia** (-zɪə) *botany* a cymose inflorescence in which three or more branches arise from each node [C20 from New Latin, from POLY- + *-chasium* as in DICHASIUM]

polychlorinated biphenyl (,pɒlɪ'klɔːrɪ,neɪtɪd) *n* any of a group of compounds in which chlorine atoms replace the hydrogen atoms in biphenyl: used in industry in electrical insulators and in the manufacture of plastics; a toxic pollutant that can become concentrated in animal tissue. Abbreviation: PCB

polychromatic (,pɒlɪkrəʊ'mætɪk), **polychromic** (,pɒlɪ'krəʊmɪk) *or* **polychromous** *adj* **1** having various or changing colours **2** (of light or other electromagnetic radiation) containing radiation with more than one wavelength > polychromatism (,pɒlɪ'krəʊmə,tɪzəm) *n*

polychrome ('pɒlɪ,krəʊm) *adj* **1** having various or changing colours; polychromatic **2** made with or decorated in various colours ▷ *n* **3** a work of art or artefact in many colours

polychromy ('pɒlɪ,krəʊmɪ) *n* decoration in many colours, esp in architecture or sculpture

polyclinic (,pɒlɪ'klɪnɪk) *n* a hospital or clinic able to treat a wide variety of diseases: general hospital

polyconic projection (,pɒlɪ'kɒnɪk) *n* a type of conic projection in which the parallels are not concentric and all meridians except the central one are curved lines. It is neither equal-area nor conformal, but is suitable for maps of areas or countries of great longitudinal extent

polycotton ('pɒlɪkɒtᵊn) *n* a fabric made from a mixture of polyester and cotton

polycotyledon (,pɒlɪ,kɒtɪ'liːdᵊn) *n* any of various plants, esp gymnosperms, that have or appear to have more than two cotyledons > ,poly,coty'ledonous *adj*

polycrystal ('pɒlɪ,krɪstᵊl) *n* an object composed of randomly oriented crystals, formed by rapid solidification

polycyclic (,pɒlɪ'saɪklɪk) *adj* **1** (of a molecule or compound) containing or having molecules that contain two or more closed rings of atoms **2** *biology* having two or more rings or whorls: *polycyclic shells; a polycyclic stele* ▷ *n* **3** a polycyclic compound: *anthracene is a polycyclic*

polycystic (,pɒlɪ'sɪstɪk) *adj med* containing many cysts: *a polycystic ovary*

polycystic ovary syndrome *n* a hormonal disorder in which the Graafian follicles in the ovary fail to develop completely so that they are unable to ovulate, remaining as multiple cysts that distend the ovary. The results can include reduced fertility, obesity, and hirsutism. Abbreviation: PCOS

polycythaemia *or esp US* **polycythemia** (,pɒlɪsaɪ'θiːmɪə) *n* an abnormal condition of the blood characterized by an increase in the number of red blood cells. It can occur as a primary disease of unknown cause (**polycythaemia vera** or **erythraemia**) or in association with respiratory or circulatory diseases [C19 from POLY- + CYTO- + -HAEMIA]

polydactyl (,pɒlɪ'dæktɪl) *adj also* polydactylous **1** (of man and other vertebrates) having more than the normal number of digits ▷ *n* **2** a human or other vertebrate having more than the normal number of digits [C19 via French from Greek *poludactulos* many-toed; see DACTYL]

polydemic (,pɒlɪ'dɛmɪk) *adj ecology rare* growing in or inhabiting more than two regions [C20 from POLY- + ENDEMIC]

Polydeuces (,pɒlɪ'djuːsiːz) *n* the Greek name of **Pollux**. See **Castor and Pollux**

polydipsia (,pɒlɪ'dɪpsɪə) *n pathol* excessive thirst [C18 New Latin, from POLY- + *-dipsia*, from Greek *dipsa* thirst] > ,poly'dipsic *adj*

poly-drug *adj* involving or taking more than one kind of illegal drug: *a poly-drug user*

polyembryony (,pɒlɪ'ɛmbrɪənɪ) *n* the production of more than one embryo from a single fertilized egg cell: occurs in certain plants and parasitic hymenopterous insects > polyembryonic (,pɒlɪ,ɛmbrɪ'ɒnɪk) *adj*

polyene ('pɒlɪ,iːn) *n* a chemical compound containing a chain of alternating single and double carbon-carbon bonds

polyester (,pɒlɪ'ɛstə) *n* any of a large class of synthetic materials that are polymers containing recurring -COO- groups: used as plastics, textile fibres, and adhesives

polyethene (,pɒlɪ'ɛθiːn) *n* the systematic name for **polythene**

polyethylene (,pɒlɪ'ɛθɪ,liːn) *n* another name for **polythene**

polygala (pə'lɪgələ) *n* any herbaceous plant or small shrub of the polygalaceous genus *Polygala*. See also **milkwort** [C18 New Latin, from Greek *polugalon*, from POLY- + *gala* milk]

polygalaceous (,pɒlɪgə'leɪʃəs, pə,lɪg-) *adj* of, relating to, or belonging to the *Polygalaceae*, a family of plants having flowers with two large outer petal-like sepals, three small sepals, and three to five petals: includes milkwort

polygamy (pə'lɪgəmɪ) *n* **1** the practice of having more than one wife or husband at the same time. Compare **polyandry, polygyny 2 a** the condition of having male, female, and hermaphrodite flowers on the same plant **b** the condition of having these different types of flower on separate plants of the same species **3** the practice in male animals of having more than one mate during one breeding season [C16 via French from Greek *polugamia* from POLY- + -GAMY] > po'lygamist *n* > po'lygamous *adj* > po'lygamously *adv*

polygene ('pɒlɪ,dʒiːn) *n* any of a group of genes that each produce a small quantitative effect on a particular characteristic of the phenotype, such as height

polygenesis (,pɒlɪ'dʒɛnɪsɪs) *n* **1** *biology* evolution of a polyphyletic organism or group **2** the hypothetical descent of the different races of man from different ultimate ancestors ▷ Compare **monogenesis**. > polygenetic (,pɒlɪdʒɪ'nɛtɪk) *adj* > ,polyge'netically *adv*

polygenic (,pɒlɪ'dʒɛnɪk) *adj* of, relating to, or controlled by polygenes: *polygenic inheritance*

polyglot ('pɒlɪ,glɒt) *adj* **1** having a command of many languages **2** written in, composed of, or containing many languages ▷ *n* **3** a person with a command of many languages **4** a book, esp a Bible, containing several versions of the same text written in various languages **5** a mixture or confusion of languages [C17 from Greek *poluglōttos* literally: many-tongued, from POLY- + *glōtta* tongue] > ,poly'glotism *or* ,poly'glottism *n*

polygon ('pɒlɪ,gɒn) *n* a closed plane figure bounded by three or more straight sides that meet in pairs in the same number of vertices, and do not intersect other than at these vertices. The sum of the interior angles is $(n-2) \times 180°$ for n sides; the sum of the exterior angles is 360°. A **regular polygon** has all its sides and angles equal. Specific polygons are named according to the number of sides, such as triangle, pentagon, etc [C16 via Latin from Greek *polugōnon* figure with

many angles] > **polygonal** (pə'lɪgənᵊl) adj
> po'lygonally adv

polygonaceous (ˌpɒlɪgə'neɪʃəs, pəˌlɪgə-) adj of, relating to, or belonging to the *Polygonaceae*, a chiefly N temperate family of plants having a sheathing stipule (ocrea) clasping the stem and small inconspicuous flowers: includes dock, sorrel, buckwheat, knotgrass, and rhubarb

polygonum (pə'lɪgənəm) n any polygonaceous plant of the genus *Polygonum*, having stems with knotlike joints and spikes of small white, green, or pink flowers. See also **knotgrass, bistort, prince's feather** (sense 2) [c18 New Latin, from Greek *polugonon* knotgrass, from *polu-* POLY- + *-gonon*, from *gonu* knee]

polygraph ('pɒlɪˌgrɑːf, -ˌgræf) n 1 an instrument for the simultaneous electrical or mechanical recording of several involuntary physiological activities, including blood pressure, skin resistivity, pulse rate, respiration, and sweating, used esp as a would-be lie detector 2 a device for producing copies of written, printed, or drawn matter [c18 from Greek *polugraphos* writing copiously] > **polygraphic** (ˌpɒlɪ'græfɪk) adj > ˌpoly'graphically adv

polygyny (pə'lɪdʒɪnɪ) n 1 the practice or condition of being married to more than one wife at the same time. Compare **polygamy** 2 the practice in animals of a male mating with more than one female during one breeding season 3 the condition in flowers of having many carpels ▷ Compare **polyandry** [c18 from POLY- + -*gyny*, from Greek *gunē* a woman] > po'lygynist n
> po'lygynous adj

polyhedral angle (ˌpɒlɪ'hiːdrəl) n a geometric configuration formed by the intersection of three or more planes, such as the faces of a polyhedron, that have a common vertex. See also **solid angle**

polyhedron (ˌpɒlɪ'hiːdrən) n, pl -drons or -dra (-drə) a solid figure consisting of four or more plane faces (all polygons), pairs of which meet along an edge, three or more edges meeting at a vertex. In a **regular polyhedron** all the faces are identical regular polygons making equal angles with each other. Specific polyhedrons are named according to the number of faces, such as tetrahedron, icosahedron, etc [c16 from Greek *poluedron*, from POLY- + *hedron* side, base]
> ˌpoly'hedral adj

polyhydric (ˌpɒlɪ'haɪdrɪk) adj another word for **polyhydroxy**, esp when applied to alcohols

polyhydroxy (ˌpɒlɪhaɪ'drɒksɪ) adj (of a chemical compound) containing two or more hydroxyl groups per molecule. Also: polyhydric

Polyhymnia (ˌpɒlɪ'hɪmnɪə) n Greek myth the Muse of singing, mime, and sacred dance [Latin, from Greek *Polumnia* full of songs; see POLY-, HYMN]

polyisoprene (ˌpɒlɪ'aɪsəˌpriːn) n any of various polymeric forms of isoprene, occurring in rubbers

polymath ('pɒlɪˌmæθ) n a person of great and varied learning [c17 from Greek *polumathēs* having much knowledge] > ˌpoly'mathic adj > polymathy (pə'lɪməθɪ) n

polymer ('pɒlɪmə) n a naturally occurring or synthetic compound, such as starch or Perspex, that has large molecules made up of many relatively simple repeated units. Compare **copolymer, oligomer.** > polymerism (pə'lɪməˌrɪzəm, 'pɒlɪmə-) n

polymerase (pə'lɪməreɪz) n any enzyme that catalyses the synthesis of a polymer, esp the synthesis of DNA or RNA

polymeric (ˌpɒlɪ'merɪk) adj of, concerned with, or being a polymer: *a polymeric compound* [c19 from Greek *polumerēs* having many parts]

polymerization or **polymerisation** (pəˌlɪməraɪ'zeɪʃən, ˌpɒlɪmeraɪ-) n the act or process of forming a polymer or copolymer, esp a chemical reaction in which a polymer is formed

polymerize or **polymerise** ('pɒlɪməˌraɪz, pə'lɪmə-) vb to react or cause to react to form a polymer

polymerous (pə'lɪmərəs) adj 1 (of flowers) having the petals, sepals, and other parts arranged in whorls of many parts 2 biology having or being composed of many parts

polymorph ('pɒlɪˌmɔːf) n 1 a species of animal or plant that exhibits polymorphism 2 any of the crystalline forms of a chemical compound that exhibits polymorphism 3 Also called: polymorphonuclear leucocyte any of a group of white blood cells that have lobed nuclei and granular cytoplasm and function as phagocytes; they include neutrophils, basophils, and eosinophils [c19 from Greek *polumorphos* having many forms]

polymorphic function n computing a function in a computer program that can deal with a number of different types of data

polymorphism (ˌpɒlɪ'mɔːfɪzəm) n 1 biology **a** the occurrence of more than one form of individual in a single species within an interbreeding population **b** the occurrence of more than one form in the individual polyps of a coelenterate colony 2 the existence or formation of different types of crystal of the same chemical compound

polymorphonuclear (ˌpɒlɪˌmɔːfəʊ'njuːklɪə) adj (of a leucocyte) having a lobed or segmented nucleus. See also **polymorph** (sense 3)

polymorphous (ˌpɒlɪ'mɔːfəs) or **polymorphic** adj 1 having, taking, or passing through many different forms or stages 2 (of a substance) exhibiting polymorphism 3 (of an animal or plant) displaying or undergoing polymorphism

polymyxin (ˌpɒlɪ'mɪksɪn) n any of several polypeptide antibiotics active against Gram-negative bacteria, obtained from the soil bacterium *Bacillus polymyxa* [New Latin *Bacillus polymyxa*; see POLY-, MYXO-, -IN]

Polynesia (ˌpɒlɪ'niːʒə, -ʒɪə) n one of the three divisions of islands in the Pacific, the others being Melanesia and Micronesia: includes Samoa, Society, Marquesas, Mangareva, Tuamotu, Cook, and Tubuai Islands, and Tonga [c18 via French from POLY- + Greek *nēsos* island]

Polynesian (ˌpɒlɪ'niːʒən, -ʒɪən) adj 1 of or relating to Polynesia, its people, or any of their languages ▷ n 2 a member of the people that inhabit Polynesia, generally of Caucasoid features with light skin and wavy hair 3 a branch of the Malayo-Polynesian family of languages, including Māori and Hawaiian and a number of other closely related languages of the S and central Pacific

polyneuritis (ˌpɒlɪnjʊ'raɪtɪs) n inflammation of many nerves at the same time

Polynices (ˌpɒlɪ'naɪsiːz) n Greek myth a son of Oedipus and Jocasta, for whom the Seven Against Thebes sought to regain Thebes. He and his brother Eteocles killed each other in single combat before its walls

polynomial (ˌpɒlɪ'nəʊmɪəl) adj 1 of, consisting of, or referring to two or more names or terms ▷ n 2 **a** a mathematical expression consisting of a sum of terms each of which is the product of a constant and one or more variables raised to a positive or zero integral power. For one variable, x, the general form is given by: $a_0x^n + a_1x^{n-1} + ... + a_{n-1}x + a_n$, where a_0, a_1, etc, are real numbers **b** Also called: multinomial any mathematical expression consisting of the sum of a number of terms 3 biology a taxonomic name consisting of more than two terms, such as *Parus major minor* in which *minor* designates the subspecies

polynuclear (ˌpɒlɪ'njuːklɪə) or **polynucleate** adj having many nuclei; multinuclear

polynucleotide (ˌpɒlɪ'njuːklɪəˌtaɪd) n biochem a molecular chain of nucleotides chemically bonded by a series of ester linkages between the phosphoryl group of one nucleotide and the hydroxyl group of the sugar in the adjacent nucleotide. Nucleic acids consist of long chains of polynucleotides

polynya ('pɒlənˌjɑː) n a stretch of open water surrounded by ice, esp near the mouths of large rivers, in arctic seas [c19 from Russian, from *poly* open, hollowed-out]

polyonymous (ˌpɒlɪ'ɒnɪməs) adj having or known by several different names

polyp ('pɒlɪp) n 1 zoology one of the two forms of individual that occur in coelenterates. It usually has a hollow cylindrical body with a ring of tentacles around the mouth. Compare **medusa** (sense 2) 2 Also called: polypus pathol a small vascularized growth arising from the surface of a mucous membrane, having a rounded base or a stalklike projection [c16 *polip*, from French *polype* nasal polyp, from Latin *pōlypus* sea animal, nasal polyp, from Greek *polupous* having many feet]
> 'polypous or 'polypoid adj

polypary ('pɒlɪpərɪ) or **polyparium** (ˌpɒlɪ'pɛərɪəm) n, pl -paries or -paria (-'pɛərɪə) the common base and connecting tissue of a colony of coelenterate polyps, esp coral [c18 from New Latin *polypārium*; see POLYP]

polypeptide (ˌpɒlɪ'peptaɪd) n any of a group of natural or synthetic polymers made up of amino acids chemically linked together; this class includes the proteins. See also **peptide**

polypetalous (ˌpɒlɪ'petələs) adj (of flowers) having many distinct or separate petals. Compare **gamopetalous**

polyphagia (ˌpɒlɪ'feɪdʒə) n 1 **a** an abnormal desire to consume excessive amounts of food, esp as the result of a neurological disorder **b** an insatiable appetite 2 the habit of certain animals, esp certain insects, of feeding on many different types of food [c17 New Latin, from Greek, from *poluphagos* eating much; see POLY-, -PHAGY]
> polyphagous (pə'lɪfəgəs) adj

polyphase ('pɒlɪˌfeɪz) adj 1 Also: multiphase (of an electrical system, circuit, or device) having, generating, or using two or more alternating voltages of the same frequency, the phases of which are cyclically displaced by fractions of a period. See also **single-phase, two-phase, three-phase** 2 having more than one phase

Polyphemus (ˌpɒlɪ'fiːməs) n Greek myth a cyclops who imprisoned Odysseus and his companions in his cave. To escape, Odysseus blinded him

polyphone ('pɒlɪˌfəʊn) n a letter or character having more than one phonetic value, such as English *c*, pronounced (k) before *a, o,* or *u* or (s) before *e* or *i*

polyphonic (ˌpɒlɪ'fɒnɪk) adj 1 music composed of relatively independent melodic lines or parts; contrapuntal 2 many-voiced 3 phonetics of, relating to, or denoting a polyphone
> poly'phonically adv

polyphonic prose n a rhythmically free prose employing poetic devices, such as assonance and alliteration

polyphony (pə'lɪfənɪ) n, pl -nies 1 polyphonic style of composition or a piece of music utilizing it 2 the use of polyphones in a writing system [c19 from Greek *poluphōnia* diversity of tones, from POLY- + *phōnē* speech, sound] > po'lyphonous adj
> po'lyphonously adv

polyphosphoric acid (ˌpɒlɪfɒs'fɒrɪk) n 1 any one of a series of oxyacids of phosphorus with the general formula $H_{n+2}P_nO_{3n+1}$. The first member is pyrophosphoric acid ($n = 2$) and the series includes the highly polymeric metaphosphoric acid. The higher acids exist in an equilibrium mixture 2 a glassy or liquid mixture of orthophosphoric and polyphosphoric acids: used industrially as a dehydrating agent, catalyst, and oxidizing agent

polyphyletic (ˌpɒlɪfaɪ'letɪk) adj biology relating to or characterized by descent from more than one ancestral group of animals or plants [c19 from POLY- + PHYLETIC] > ˌpolyphy'letically adv

polyphyodont (ˌpɒlɪ'faɪəʊˌdɒnt) adj having many successive sets of teeth, as fishes and other lower vertebrates. Compare **diphyodont** [c19 from Greek *poluphuēs* manifold (from *polu-* POLY- + *phuē* growth) + -ODONT]

p

polypill ('pɒlɪ,pɪl) *n* a proposed medication intended to reduce the likelihood of heart attacks and strokes, containing doses of different drugs to lower blood cholesterol, control blood pressure, and reduce the clotting tendency of the blood

polyploid ('pɒlɪ,plɔɪd) *adj* **1** (of cells, organisms, etc) having more than twice the basic (haploid) number of chromosomes ▷ *n* **2** an individual or cell of this type > **,poly'ploidal** *or* **,poly'ploidic** *adj* > **'poly,ploidy** *n*

polypod ('pɒlɪ,pɒd) *adj also* **polypodous** (pə'lɪpədəs) **1** (esp of insect larvae) having many legs or similar appendages ▷ *n* **2** an animal of this type

polypody ('pɒlɪ,pəʊdɪ) *n, pl* **-dies 1** any of various ferns of the genus *Polypodium*, esp *P. vulgare*, having deeply divided leaves and round naked sori: family *Polypodiaceae* **2** any fern of the family *Polypodiaceae*, all having opaque leaves that are divided in most species [c15 from Latin *polypodium*, from Greek, from POLY- + *pous* foot]

polypoid ('pɒlɪ,pɔɪd) *adj* **1** of, relating to, or resembling a polyp **2** (of a coelenterate) having the body in the form of a polyp

polypropylene (,pɒlɪ'prəʊpɪ,li:n) *n* any of various tough flexible synthetic thermoplastic materials made by polymerizing propylene and used for making moulded articles, laminates, bottles, pipes, and fibres for ropes, bristles, upholstery, and carpets. Systematic name: **polypropene**

polyprotodont (,pɒlɪ'prəʊtəʊ,dɒnt) *n* any marsupial of the group *Polyprotodontia*, characterized by four or more upper incisor teeth on each side of the jaw: includes the opossums and bandicoots. Compare **diprotodont** [c19 from POLY- + PROTO- + -ODONT]

polyptych ('pɒlɪptɪk) *n* an altarpiece consisting of more than three panels, set with paintings or carvings, and usually hinged for folding. Compare **diptych, triptych** [c19 via Late Latin from Greek *poluptuchon* something folded many times, from POLY- + *ptuchē* a fold]

polypus ('pɒlɪpəs) *n, pl* **-pi** (-paɪ) *pathol* another word for **polyp** (sense 2) [c16 via Latin from Greek: POLYP]

polyrhythm ('pɒlɪ,rɪðəm) *n music* a style of composition in which each part exhibits different rhythms

polyrhythmic (,pɒlɪ'rɪðmɪk) *adj music* of or relating to polyrhythm; characterized by different rhythms

polyribosome (,pɒlɪ'raɪbə,səʊm) *n biochem* an assemblage of ribosomes associated with a messenger RNA molecule, involved in peptide synthesis. Also called: **polysome**

polysaccharide (,pɒlɪ'sækə,raɪd, -rɪd) *or* **polysaccharose** (,pɒlɪ'sækə,rəʊz, -,rəʊs) *n* any one of a class of carbohydrates whose molecules contain linked monosaccharide units: includes starch, inulin, and cellulose. General formula: $(C_6H_{10}O_5)_n$. See also **oligosaccharide**

polysemy (,pɒlɪ'si:mɪ, pə'lɪsəmɪ) *n* the existence of several meanings in a single word. Compare **monosemy** [c20 from New Latin *polysēmia*, from Greek *polusēmos* having many meanings, from POLY- + *sēma* a sign] > **,poly'semous** *adj*

polysepalous (,pɒlɪ'sɛpələs) *adj* (of flowers) having distinct separate sepals. Compare **gamosepalous**

polysome ('pɒlɪ,səʊm) *n* another name for **polyribosome**

polysomic (,pɒlɪ'səʊmɪk) *adj* of, relating to, or designating a basically diploid chromosome complement, in which some but not all the chromosomes are represented more than twice [c20 from POLY- + -SOME³ + -IC]

polystichous (,pɒlɪ'staɪkəs) *adj* (of plant parts) arranged in a number of rows

polystyrene (,pɒlɪ'staɪri:n) *n* a synthetic thermoplastic material obtained by polymerizing styrene; used as a white rigid foam (**expanded polystyrene**) for insulating and packing and as a glasslike material in light fittings and water tanks

polysulphide (,pɒlɪ'sʌlfaɪd) *n* any sulphide of a metal containing divalent anions in which there are chains of sulphur atoms, as in the polysulphides of sodium, Na_2S_2, Na_2S_3, etc

polysyllabic (,pɒlɪsɪ'læbɪk) *adj* consisting of more than two syllables > **,polysyl'labically** *adv*

polysyllable ('pɒlɪ,sɪləb⁰l) *n* a word consisting of more than two syllables

polysyllogism (,pɒlɪ'sɪlə,dʒɪzəm) *n* a chain of syllogisms in which the conclusion of one syllogism serves as a premise for the next

polysyndeton (,pɒlɪ'sɪndɪtən) *n* **1** *rhetoric* the use of several conjunctions in close succession, esp where some might be omitted, as in *he ran and jumped and laughed for joy* **2** Also called: **syndesis** *grammar* a sentence containing more than two coordinate clauses [c16 POLY- + -*syndeton*, from Greek *sundetos* bound together]

polysynthetic (,pɒlɪsɪn'θɛtɪk) *adj* denoting languages, such as Inuktitut, in which single words may express the meaning of whole phrases or clauses by virtue of multiple affixes. Compare **synthetic** (sense 3), **analytic** (sense 3), **agglutinative** (sense 2) > **polysynthesis** (,pɒlɪ'sɪnθɪsɪs) *n* > **,poly'synthesism** *n* > **,polysyn'thetically** *adv*

polytechnic (,pɒlɪ'tɛknɪk) *n* **1** *Brit* a college offering advanced full- and part-time courses, esp vocational courses, in many fields at and below degree standard ▷ *adj* **2** of or relating to technical training [c19 via French from Greek *polutekhnos* skilled in many arts. See TECHNIC]

polytene ('pɒlɪ,ti:n) *adj* denoting a type of giant-size chromosome consisting of many replicated genes in parallel, found esp in *Drosophila* larvae [c20 from POLY- + Greek *taenia* band]

polytetrafluoroethylene (,pɒlɪ,tɛtrə,flʊərəʊ'ɛθɪ,li:n) *n* a white thermoplastic material with a waxy texture, made by polymerizing tetrafluoroethylene. It is nonflammable, resists chemical action and radiation, and has a high electrical resistance and an extremely low coefficient of friction. It is used for making gaskets, hoses, insulators, bearings, and for coating metal surfaces in chemical plants and in nonstick cooking vessels. Abbreviation: PTFE. Also called (trademark): **Teflon**

polytheism ('pɒlɪθi:,ɪzəm, ,pɒlɪ'θi:ɪzəm) *n* the worship of or belief in more than one god > **'poly,theist** *n* > **,polythe'istic** *adj* > **,polythe'istically** *adv*

polythene ('pɒlɪ,θi:n) *n* any one of various light thermoplastic materials made from ethylene with properties depending on the molecular weight of the polymer. The common forms are a waxy flexible plastic (**low-density polythene**) and a tougher rigid more crystalline form (**high-density polythene**). Polythene is used for packaging, moulded articles, pipes and tubing, insulation, textiles, and coatings on metal. Systematic name: **polyethene** Also called: **polyethylene**

polytonality (,pɒlɪtəʊ'nælɪtɪ) *or* **polytonalism** *n music* the simultaneous use of more than two different keys or tonalities > **,poly'tonal** *adj* > **,poly'tonally** *adv* > **,poly'tonalist** *n*

polytrophic (,pɒlɪ'trɒfɪk) *adj* (esp of bacteria) obtaining food from several different organic sources

polytunnel ('pɒlɪ,tʌn⁰l) *n* a large tunnel made of polythene and used as a greenhouse

polytypic (,pɒlɪ'tɪpɪk) *or* **polytypical** *adj* **1** existing in, consisting of, or incorporating several different types or forms **2** *biology* (of a taxonomic group) having many subdivisions, esp (of a species) having many subspecies and geographical races

polyunsaturated (,pɒlɪʌn'sætʃə,reɪtɪd) *adj* of or relating to a class of animal and vegetable fats, the molecules of which consist of long carbon chains with many double bonds. Polyunsaturated compounds are less likely to be converted into cholesterol in the body. They are widely used in margarines and in the manufacture of paints and varnishes. See also **monounsaturated**

polyurethane (,pɒlɪ'jʊərə,θeɪn) *or* **polyurethan** (,pɒlɪ'jʊərə,θæn) *n* a class of synthetic materials made by copolymerizing an isocyanate and a polyhydric alcohol and commonly used as a foam (**polyurethane foam**) for insulation and packing, as fibres and hard inert coatings, and in a flexible form (**polyurethane rubber**) for diaphragms and seals

polyuria (,pɒlɪ'jʊərɪə) *n pathol, physiol* the state or condition of discharging abnormally large quantities of urine, often accompanied by a need to urinate frequently > **,poly'uric** *adj*

polyvalent (,pɒlɪ'veɪlənt, ,pə'lɪvələnt) *adj* **1** *chem* having more than one valency **2** (of a vaccine) **a** effective against several strains of the same disease-producing microorganism, antigen, or toxin **b** produced from cultures containing several strains of the same microorganism > **,poly'valency** *n*

polyvinyl (,pɒlɪ'vaɪnɪl, -'vaɪn⁰l) *n* (*modifier*) designating a plastic or resin formed by polymerization of a vinyl derivative

polyvinyl acetate *n* a colourless odourless tasteless resin used in emulsion paints, adhesives, sealers, a substitute for chicle in chewing gum, and for sealing porous surfaces. Abbreviation: PVA

polyvinyl chloride *n* the full name of PVC

polyvinylidene chloride (,pɒlɪvaɪ'nɪlɪ,di:n) *n* any one of a class of thermoplastic materials formed by the polymerization of vinylidene chloride: used in packaging and for making pipes and fittings for chemical equipment. Also called: **saran**

polyvinyl resin *n* any of a class of thermoplastic resins that are made by polymerizing or copolymerizing a vinyl compound. The commonest type is PVC

Polyxena (pɒ'lɪksɪnə) *n Greek myth* a daughter of King Priam of Troy, who was sacrificed on the command of Achilles' ghost

polyzoan (,pɒlɪ'zəʊən) *n, adj* another word for **bryozoan** [c19 from New Latin, *Polyzoa* class name, from POLY- + -*zoan*, from Greek *zoion* an animal]

polyzoarium (,pɒlɪzəʊ'ɛərɪəm) *n, pl* **-ia** (-ɪə) a colony of bryozoan animals or its supporting skeletal framework > **,polyzo'arial** *adj*

polyzoic (,pɒlɪ'zəʊɪk) *adj zoology* **1** (of certain colonial animals) having many zooids or similar polyps **2** producing or containing many sporozoites

pom (pɒm) *n slang, Austral and NZ* short for **pommy**

POM *abbreviation for* prescription-only medicine *or* medication. Compare **OTC**

pomace ('pʌmɪs) *n* **1** the pulpy residue of apples or similar fruit after crushing and pressing, as in cider-making **2** any pulpy substance left after crushing, mashing, etc [c16 from Medieval Latin *pōmācium* cider, from Latin *pōmum* apple]

pomaceous (pɒ'meɪʃəs) *adj* of, relating to, or bearing pomes, such as the apple, pear, and quince trees [c18 from New Latin *pōmāceus*, from Latin *pōmum* apple]

pomade (pə'mɑ:d, -'meɪd) *n* **1** a perfumed oil or ointment put on the hair, as to make it smooth and shiny ▷ *vb* **2** (*tr*) to put pomade on ▷ Also: **pomatum** (pə'meɪtəm) [c16 from French *pommade*, from Italian *pomata* (originally made partly from apples), from Latin *pōmum* apple]

pomander (pəʊ'mændə) *n* **1** a mixture of aromatic substances in a sachet or an orange, formerly carried as scent or as a protection against disease **2** a container for such a mixture [c15 from Old French *pome d'ambre*, from Medieval Latin *pōmum ambrae* apple of amber]

pombe ('pɒmbɛ) *n E African* any alcoholic drink [Swahili]

pome (pəʊm) *n* the fleshy fruit of the apple and related plants, consisting of an enlarged receptacle enclosing the ovary and seeds [c15 from Old French, from Late Latin *pōma* apple, pl (assumed to be sing) of Latin *pōmum* apple]

pomegranate ('pɒmɪˌɡrænɪt, 'pɒmˌɡrænɪt) *n* **1** an Asian shrub or small tree, *Punica granatum*, cultivated in semitropical regions for its edible fruit: family *Punicaceae* **2** the many-chambered globular fruit of this tree, which has tough reddish rind, juicy red pulp, and many seeds [c14 from Old French *pome grenate*, from Latin *pōmum* apple + *grenate*, from Latin *grānātum*, from *grānātus* full of seeds]

pomelo ('pɒmɪˌləʊ) *n, pl* **-los 1** a tropical rutaceous tree, *Citrus maxima* (or *C. decumana*), grown widely in oriental regions for its large yellow grapefruit-like edible fruit **2** the fruit of this tree **3** *chiefly US* another name for **grapefruit** ▷ Also called: **shaddock** [c19 from Dutch *pompelmoes*, perhaps from *pompoen* big + Portuguese *limão* a lemon]

Pomerania (ˌpɒməˈreɪnɪə) *n* a region of N central Europe, extending along the S coast of the Baltic Sea from Stralsund to the Vistula River: now chiefly in Poland, with a small area in NE Germany. German name: **Pommern**. Polish name: **Pomorze**

Pomeranian (ˌpɒməˈreɪnɪən) *adj* **1** of or relating to Pomerania or its inhabitants ▷ *n* **2** a native or inhabitant of Pomerania, esp a German **3** a breed of toy dog of the spitz type with a long thick straight coat

pomfret[1] ('pʌmfrɪt, 'pɒm-) *or* **pomfret-cake** *n* a small black rounded confection of liquorice. Also called: **Pontefract cake** [c19 from *Pomfret*, earlier form of **PONTEFRACT**, where the cake was originally made]

pomfret[2] ('pɒmfrɪt) *n* **1** any of various fishes of the genus *Stromateidae* of the Indian and Pacific oceans: valued as food fishes **2** any of various scombroid fishes, esp *Brama raii*, of northern oceans: valued as food fishes [c18 perhaps from a diminutive form of Portuguese *pampo*]

pomiculture ('pɒmɪˌkʌltʃə) *n* the cultivation of fruit [c19 from Latin *pōmum* apple, fruit + **CULTURE**]

pomiferous (pɒˈmɪfərəs) *adj* (of the apple, pear, etc) producing pomes or pomelike fruits [c17 from Latin *pomifer* fruit-bearing]

pommel ('pʌməl, 'pɒm-) *n* **1** the raised part on the front of a saddle **2** a knob at the top of a sword or similar weapon ▷ *vb* **-mels, -melling, -melled** *or US* **-mels, -meling, -meled 3** a less common word for **pummel** [c14 from Old French *pomel* knob, from Vulgar Latin *pōmellum* (unattested) little apple, from Latin *pōmum* apple]

Pommern ('pɒmərn) *n* the German name for **Pomerania**

pommy ('pɒmɪ) *n, pl* **-mies** (*sometimes capital*) *slang* a mildly offensive word used by Australians and New Zealanders for an English person. Sometimes shortened to: **pom** [c20 of uncertain origin. Among a number of explanations are: (1) based on a blend of **IMMIGRANT** and **POMEGRANATE** (alluding to the red cheeks of English immigrants); (2) from the abbreviation *POME*, Prisoner of Mother England (referring to convicts)]

pomo ('pəʊməʊ) *adj informal* short for **postmodern**

pomology (pɒˈmɒlədʒɪ) *n* the branch of horticulture that is concerned with the study and cultivation of fruit [c19 from New Latin *pōmologia*, from Latin *pōmum* apple, fruit] > **pomological** (ˌpɒməˈlɒdʒɪkʰl) *adj* > **pomo'logically** *adv* > **pom'ologist** *n*

Pomona[1] (pəˈməʊnə) *n* another name for **Mainland** (in Orkney)

Pomona[2] (pəˈməʊnə) *n* the Roman goddess of fruit trees

Pomorze (pɔˈmɔːʒɛ) *n* the Polish name for **Pomerania**

pomosexual (ˌpəʊməʊˈsɛksjʊəl) *informal* ▷ *adj* **1** of or relating to a person who does not wish his or her sexuality to be put into a conventional category ▷ *n* **2** such a person [c20 from POMO + (HOMO)SEXUAL]

pomp (pɒmp) *n* **1** stately or magnificent display; ceremonial splendour **2** vain display, esp of dignity or importance **3** *obsolete* a procession or pageant [c14 from Old French *pompe*, from Latin *pompa* procession, from Greek *pompē*; related to Greek *pompein* to send]

pompadour ('pɒmpəˌdʊə) *n* an early 18th-century hairstyle for women, having the front hair arranged over a pad to give it greater height and bulk [c18 named after its originator Jeanne Antoinette Poisson, the Marquise de Pompadour (1721–64), mistress of Louis XV of France]

pompano ('pɒmpəˌnəʊ) *n, pl* **-no** *or* **-nos 1** any of several deep-bodied carangid food fishes of the genus *Trachinotus*, esp *T. carolinus*, of American coastal regions of the Atlantic **2** a spiny-finned food fish, *Palometa simillima*, of North American coastal regions of the Pacific: family *Stromateidae* (butterfish, etc) [c19 from Spanish *pámpano* type of fish, of uncertain origin]

Pompeii (pɒmˈpeɪiː) *n* an ancient city in Italy, southeast of Naples: buried by an eruption of Vesuvius (79 AD); excavation of the site, which is extremely well preserved, began in 1748

Pompeiian (pɒmˈpeɪən, -ˈpiː-) *adj* **1** of or relating to Pompeii or its inhabitants ▷ *n* **2** a native or inhabitant of Pompeii

Pompey ('pɒmpɪ) *n* an informal name for **Portsmouth**

pompilid ('pɒmpɪlɪd) *n* another name for the **spider-hunting wasp** [c20 from New Latin *pompilus*, from Greek *pompilos* a fish that accompanies ships, from *pempein* to send, escort]

pompom ('pɒmpɒm) *or* **pompon** *n* **1** a ball of tufted silk, wool, feathers, etc, worn on a hat for decoration **2 a** the small globelike flower head of certain cultivated varieties of dahlia and chrysanthemum **b** (*as modifier*): *pompom dahlia* [c18 from French, from Old French *pompe* knot of ribbons, of uncertain origin]

pom-pom ('pɒmpɒm) *n* an automatic rapid-firing, small-calibre cannon, esp a type of anti-aircraft cannon used in World War II. Also called: **pompom** [c19 of imitative origin]

pomposity (pɒmˈpɒsɪtɪ) *n, pl* **-ties 1** vain or ostentatious display of dignity or importance **2** the quality of being pompous **3** ostentatiously lofty style, language, etc **4** a pompous action, remark, etc

pompous ('pɒmpəs) *adj* **1** exaggeratedly or ostentatiously dignified or self-important **2** ostentatiously lofty in style: *a pompous speech* **3** *rare* characterized by ceremonial pomp or splendour > **'pompously** *adv* > **'pompousness** *n*

'pon (pɒn) *prep poetic* or *archaic* ▷ *contraction of* upon

ponce (pɒns) *derogatory slang, chiefly Brit* ▷ *n* **1** a man given to ostentatious or effeminate display in manners, speech, dress, etc **2** another word for **pimp**[1] ▷ *vb* **3** (*intr; often foll by* around *or* about) to act like a ponce [c19 from Polari, from Spanish *pu(n)to* male prostitute or French *pront* prostitute]

Ponce (*Spanish* 'pɔnθe) *n* a port in S Puerto Rico, on the Caribbean: the second largest town on the island; settled in the 16th century. Pop: 185 930 (2003 est)

poncey *or* **poncy** ('pɒnsɪ) *derogatory slang, chiefly Brit* ▷ *adj* **-cier, -ciest** ostentatious, pretentious, or effeminate

poncho ('pɒntʃəʊ) *n, pl* **-chos** a cloak of a kind originally worn in South America, made of a rectangular or circular piece of cloth, esp wool, with a hole in the middle to put the head through [c18 from American Spanish, from Araucanian *pantho* woollen material]

pond (pɒnd) *n* **a** a pool of still water, often artificially created **b** (*in combination*): *a fishpond* [c13 *ponde* enclosure; related to POUND[3]]

ponder ('pɒndə) *vb* (*when intr, sometimes foll by* on *or* over) to give thorough or deep consideration (to); meditate (upon) [c14 from Old French *ponderer*, from Latin *ponderāre* to weigh, consider, from *pondus* weight; related to *pendere* to weigh]

ponderable ('pɒndərəbʰl) *adj* **1** able to be evaluated or estimated; appreciable **2** capable of being weighed or measured ▷ *n* **3** (*often plural*) something that can be evaluated or appreciated; a substantial thing > **pondera'bility** *n* > **'ponderably** *adv*

ponderous ('pɒndərəs) *adj* **1** of great weight; heavy; huge **2** (esp of movement) lacking ease or lightness; awkward, lumbering, or graceless **3** dull or laborious: *a ponderous oration* [c14 from Latin *ponderōsus* of great weight, from *pondus* weight] > **'ponderously** *adv* > **'ponderousness** *or* **ponderosity** (ˌpɒndəˈrɒsɪtɪ) *n*

pond hockey *n Canadian* ice hockey played on a frozen pond

Pondicherry (ˌpɒndɪˈtʃɛrɪ) *n* **1** a Union Territory of SE India: transferred from French to Indian administration in 1954 and made a Union Territory in 1962. Capital: Pondicherry. Pop: 973 829 (2001 est). Area: 479 sq km (185 sq miles) **2** a port in SE India, capital of the Union Territory of Pondicherry, on the Coromandel Coast. Pop: 220 749 (2001)

pond life *n* **1** the animals that live in ponds **2** stupid or despicable people

pond lily *n* another name for **water lily**

Pondo ('pɒndəʊ) *n* **1** (*pl* **-do** *or* **-dos**) a member of a Negroid people of southern Africa, living chiefly in Pondoland **2** the language of this people, belonging to the Bantu grouping of the Niger-Congo family, and closely related to Xhosa

pondok ('pɒndɒk) *or* **pondokkie** (pɒnˈdɒkɪ) *n* (in southern Africa) a crudely made house built of tin sheet, reeds, etc [c20 from Malay *pondók* leaf house]

Pondoland ('pɒndəʊˌlænd) *n* an area in SE central South Africa: inhabited chiefly by the Pondo people

pond scum *n* a greenish layer floating on the surface of stagnant waters, consisting of various freshwater algae

pond-skater *n* any of various heteropterous insects of the family *Gerrididae*, esp *Gerris lacustris* (**common pond-skater**), having a slender hairy body and long hairy legs with which they skim about on the surface of ponds. Also called: **water strider, water skater**

pond snail *n* a general term for the freshwater snails: often specifically for the **great pond snail** (*Limnaea stagnalis*) and others of that genus. *L. truncatula* is a host of the liver fluke

pondweed ('pɒndˌwiːd) *n* **1** any of various water plants of the genus *Potamogeton*, which grow in ponds and slow streams: family *Potamogetonaceae* **2** Also called: **waterweed** *Brit* any of various unrelated water plants, such as Canadian pondweed, mare's-tail, and water milfoil, that have thin or much divided leaves

pone[1] (pəʊn) *n Southern US* **1** Also called: **pone bread, corn pone** bread made of maize **2** a loaf or cake of this [c17 from Algonquian; compare Delaware *apán* baked]

pone[2] (pəʊn, 'pəʊnɪ) *n cards* the player to the right of the dealer, or the nondealer in two-handed games [c19 from Latin: put!, that is, play, from *ponere* to put]

pong (pɒŋ) *Brit informal* ▷ *n* **1** a disagreeable or offensive smell; stink ▷ *vb* **2** (*intr*) to give off an unpleasant smell; stink [c20 perhaps from Romany *pan* to stink] > **'pongy** *adj*

ponga ('pɒŋə) *n* a tall tree fern, *Cyathea dealbata*, of New Zealand, with large feathery leaves [Māori]

pongee (pɒnˈdʒiː, 'pɒndʒiː) *n* **1** a thin plain-weave silk fabric from China or India, left in its natural colour **2** a cotton or rayon fabric similar to or in imitation of this, but not necessarily in the natural colour [c18 from Mandarin Chinese (Peking) *pen-chī* woven at home, on one's own loom, from *pen* own + *chi* loom]

p

pongid ('pɒŋgɪd, 'pɒndʒɪd) *n* **1** any primate of the family *Pongidae*, which includes the gibbons and the great apes ▷ *adj* **2** of, relating to, or belonging to the family *Pongidae* [from New Latin *Pongo* type genus, from Kongo *mpongi* ape]

pongo ('pɒŋgəʊ) *n, pl* **-gos 1** an anthropoid ape, esp an orang-utan or (formerly) a gorilla **2** *military slang* a soldier or marine [c17 from Kongo *mpongo*]

poniard ('pɒnjəd) *n* **1** a small dagger with a slender blade ▷ *vb* **2** (*tr*) to stab with a poniard [c16 from Old French *poignard* dagger, from *poing* fist, from Latin *pugnus*; related to Latin *pugnāre* to fight]

pons (pɒnz) *n, pl* **pontes** ('pɒnti:z) **1** a bridge of connecting tissue **2** short for **pons Varolii** [Latin: bridge]

pons asinorum (ˌæsɪ'nɔːrəm) *n* the geometric proposition that the angles opposite the two equal sides of an isosceles triangle are equal [Latin: bridge of asses, referring originally to the fifth proposition of the first book of Euclid, which was considered difficult for students to learn]

pons Varolii (və'rəʊlɪˌaɪ) *n, pl* **pontes Varolii** ('pɒnti:z) a broad white band of connecting nerve fibres that bridges the hemispheres of the cerebellum in mammals. Sometimes shortened to: **pons** [c16 New Latin, literally: bridge of Varoli, after Costanzo Varoli (?1543–75), Italian anatomist]

pont (pɒnt) *n* (in South Africa) a river ferry, esp one that is guided by a cable from one bank to the other [c17 from Dutch: ferryboat, PUNT¹; reintroduced through Afrikaans in 19th or 20th century]

Ponta Delgada (*Portuguese* 'pontə ðɛl'gaðə) *n* a port in the E Azores, on S São Miguel Island: chief commercial centre of the archipelago. Pop: 65 853 (2001)

Pontchartrain ('pɒntʃəˌtreɪn) *n* **Lake** a shallow lagoon in SE Louisiana, linked with the Gulf of Mexico by a narrow channel, the **Rigolets**: resort and fishing centre. Area: 1620 sq km (625 sq miles)

Pontefract ('pɒntɪˌfrækt) *n* an industrial town in N England, in Wakefield unitary authority, West Yorkshire: castle (1069), in which Richard II was imprisoned and murdered (1400). Pop: 28 250 (2001)

Pontefract cake *n* another name for **pomfret'**

Pontevedra (*Spanish* pɒnte'βeðra) *n* a port in NW Spain: takes its name from a 12-arched Roman bridge, the Pons Vetus. Pop: 77 993 (2003 est)

pontianak (ˌpɒntɪ'ɑːnæk) *n* (in Malay folklore) a female vampire; the ghost of a woman who has died in childbirth [from Malay]

Pontianak (ˌpɒntɪ'ɑːnæk) *n* a port in Indonesia, on W coast of Borneo almost exactly on the equator. Pop: 464 534 (2000)

Pontic ('pɒntɪk) *adj* denoting or relating to the Black Sea [c15 from Latin *Ponticus*, from Greek, from *Pontos* PONTUS]

pontifex ('pɒntɪˌfɛks) *n, pl* **pontifices** (pɒn'tɪfɪˌsiːz) (in ancient Rome) any of the senior members of the Pontifical College, presided over by the **Pontifex Maximus** [c16 from Latin, perhaps from Etruscan but influenced by folk etymology as if meaning literally: bridge-maker, from *pons* bridge + *-fex* from *facere* to make]

pontiff ('pɒntɪf) *n* a former title of the pagan high priest at Rome, later used of popes and occasionally of other bishops, and now confined exclusively to the pope [c17 from French *pontife*, from Latin PONTIFEX]

pontifical (pɒn'tɪfɪk³l) *adj* **1** of, relating to, or characteristic of a pontiff, the pope, or a bishop **2** having an excessively authoritative manner; pompous ▷ *n* **3** *RC Church, Church of England* a book containing the prayers and ritual instructions for ceremonies restricted to a bishop ▷ See also **pontificals**. ▷ pon'tifically *adv*

Pontifical College *n RC Church* **1** a major theological college under the direct control of the Roman Curia **2** the council of priests, being the chief hieratic body of the Church

Pontifical Mass *n RC Church, Church of England* a solemn celebration of Mass by a bishop

pontificals (pɒn'tɪfɪk³lz) *pl n chiefly RC Church* the insignia and special vestments worn by a bishop, esp when celebrating High Mass

pontificate *vb* (pɒn'tɪfɪˌkeɪt) (*intr*) **1** Also (less commonly): **pontify** ('pɒntɪˌfaɪ) to speak or behave in a pompous or dogmatic manner **2** to serve or officiate as a pontiff, esp in celebrating a Pontifical Mass ▷ *n* (pɒn'tɪfɪkɪt) **3** the office or term of office of a pontiff, now usually the pope

pontil ('pɒntɪl) *n* a less common word for **punty** [c19 from French, apparently from Italian *puntello*; see PUNTY]

pontine ('pɒntaɪn) *adj* **1** of or relating to bridges **2** of or relating to the pons Varolii [c19 from Latin *pons* bridge]

Pontine Marshes ('pɒntaɪn) *pl n* an area of W Italy, southeast of Rome: formerly malarial swamps, drained in 1932–34 after numerous attempts since 160 BC had failed. Italian name: Agro Pontino ('ɑːgro pon'tiːno)

pontonier (ˌpɒntə'nɪə) *n military obsolete* a person in charge of or involved in building a pontoon bridge [c19 from French *pontonnier*, from Latin *pontō* ferry boat, PONTOON¹]

pontoon¹ (pɒn'tuːn) *n* **1 a** a watertight float or vessel used where buoyancy is required in water, as in supporting a bridge, in salvage work, or where a temporary or mobile structure is required in military operations **b** (*as modifier*): *a pontoon bridge* **2** *nautical* a float, often inflatable, for raising a vessel in the water [c17 from French *ponton*, from Latin *pontō* punt, floating bridge, from *pōns* bridge]

pontoon² (pɒn'tuːn) *n* **1** Also called (esp US): **twenty-one, vingt-et-un** a gambling game in which players try to obtain card combinations worth 21 points **2** (in this game) the combination of an ace with a ten or court card when dealt to a player as his first two cards [c20 probably an alteration of French *vingt-et-un*, literally: twenty-one]

Pontus ('pɒntəs) *n* an ancient region of NE Asia Minor, on the Black Sea: became a kingdom in the 4th century BC; at its height under Mithridates VI (about 115–63 BC), when it controlled all Asia Minor; defeated by the Romans in the mid-1st century BC

Pontus Euxinus (juːk'saɪnəs) *n* the Latin name of the **Black Sea**

Pontypool (ˌpɒntɪ'puːl) *n* an industrial town in E Wales, in Torfaen county borough: famous for lacquered ironware in the 18th century. Pop: 35 447 (2001)

Pontypridd (ˌpɒntɪ'priːð) *n* an industrial town in S Wales, in Rhondda Cynon Taff county borough. Pop: 29 781 (2001)

pony ('pəʊnɪ) *n, pl* **ponies 1** any of various breeds of small horse, usually under 14.2 hands **2 a** a small drinking glass, esp for liqueurs **b** the amount held by such a glass **3** anything small of its kind **4** *Brit slang* a sum of £25, esp in bookmaking **5** Also called: **trot** *US slang* a literal translation used by students, often illicitly, in preparation for foreign language lessons or examinations; crib ▷ See also **pony up** [c17 from Scottish *powney*, perhaps from obsolete French *poulenet* a little colt, from *poulain* colt, from Latin *pullus* young animal, foal]

pony express *n* (in the American West) a system of mail transport that employed relays of riders and mounts, esp that operating from Missouri to California in 1860–61

ponytail ('pəʊnɪˌteɪl) *n* a hairstyle in which the hair is pulled tightly into a band or ribbon at the back of the head into a loose hanging fall

pony trekking *n* the act of riding ponies cross-country, esp as a pastime

pony up *vb* (*adverb*) *US informal* to give the money required

ponzu ('pɒnˌzuː) *n* a type of Japanese dipping sauce made from orange juice, sake, sugar, soy sauce, and red pepper [c21 from Japanese]

poo (puː) *interj, n, v* another spelling of **pooh**

pooch (puːtʃ) *n* a slang word for **dog** (sense 1) [of unknown origin]

pood (puːd) *n* a unit of weight, used in Russia, equal to 36.1 pounds or 16.39 kilograms [c16 from Russian *pud*, probably from Old Norse *pund* POUND²]

poodle ('puːd³l) *n* **1** a breed of dog, with varieties of different sizes, having curly hair, which is often clipped from ribs to tail for showing: originally bred to hunt waterfowl **2** a person who is servile; lackey [c19 from German *Pudel*, short for *Pudelhund*, from *pudeln* to splash + *Hund* dog; the dogs were formerly trained as water dogs; see PUDDLE, HOUND¹]

poodle-faker *n slang, old-fashioned* a young man or newly commissioned officer who makes a point of socializing with women; ladies' man

poof (pʊf, puːf) *or* **poove** *n Brit derogatory slang* a male homosexual [c20 from French *pouffe* puff] ▷ 'poofy *adj*

poofter ('pʊftə, 'puːf-) *n derogatory slang* **1** a man who is considered effeminate or homosexual **2** *NZ* a contemptible person [c20 expanded form of POOF]

pooh (puː) *interj* **1** an exclamation of disdain, contempt, or disgust ▷ *n* **2** a childish word for **faeces** ▷ *vb* **3** a childish word for **defecate**

Pooh-Bah ('puː'bɑː) *n* a pompous self-important official holding several offices at once and fulfilling none of them [c19 after the character, the Lord-High-Everything-Else, in *The Mikado* (1885), a light opera by Gilbert and Sullivan]

pooh-pooh ('puː'puː) *vb* (*tr*) to express disdain or scorn for; dismiss or belittle

pook (pʊk) *n Southwest English dialect* a haycock

pool¹ (puːl) *n* **1** a small body of still water, usually fresh; small pond **2** a small isolated collection of liquid spilt or poured on a surface; puddle: *a pool of blood* **3** a deep part of a stream or river where the water runs very slowly **4** an underground accumulation of oil or gas, usually forming a reservoir in porous sedimentary rock **5** See **swimming pool** [Old English *pōl*; related to Old Frisian *pōl*, German *Pfuhl*]

pool² (puːl) *n* **1** any communal combination of resources, funds, etc: *a typing pool* **2** the combined stakes of the betters in many gambling sports or games; kitty **3** *commerce* a group of producers who conspire to establish and maintain output levels and high prices, each member of the group being allocated a maximum quota; price ring **4** *finance, chiefly US* **a** a joint fund organized by security-holders for speculative or manipulative purposes on financial markets **b** the persons or parties involved in such a combination **5** any of various billiard games in which the object is to pot all the balls with the cue ball, esp that played with 15 coloured and numbered balls; pocket billiards ▷ *vb* (*tr*) **6** to combine (investments, money, interests, etc) into a common fund, as for a joint enterprise **7** *commerce* to organize a pool of (enterprises) **8** *Austral informal* to inform on or incriminate (someone) ▷ See also **pools** [c17 from French *poule*, literally: hen used to signify stakes in a card game, from Medieval Latin *pulla* hen, from Latin *pullus* young animal]

Poole (puːl) *n* **1** a port and resort in S England, in Poole unitary authority, Dorset, on **Poole Harbour**; seat of Bournemouth University (1992). Pop: 144 800 (2001) **2** a unitary authority in S England, in Dorset. Pop: 137 500 (2003 est). Area: 37 sq km (14 sq miles)

Pool Malebo ('puːl mə'liːbəʊ) *n* the Congolese name for **Stanley Pool**

poolroom ('puːlˌruːm, -ˌrʊm) *n US and Canadian* a hall or establishment where pool, billiards, etc, are played

pools (puːlz) *pl n Brit* an organized nationwide principally postal gambling pool betting on the

result of football matches. Also called: **football
pools** [C20 from POOL² (in the sense: a gambling
kitty)]

pool table *n* a billiard table on which pool is
played

poon¹ (puːn) *n* **1** any of several trees of the SE
Asian genus *Calophyllum* having lightweight hard
wood and shiny leathery leaves: family *Clusiaceae*
2 the wood of any of these trees, used to make
masts and spars [C17 from Singhalese *pūnu*]

poon² (puːn) *n Austral slang* a stupid or ineffectual
person [C20 from English dialect]

Poona *or* **Pune** (ˈpuːnə) *n* a city in W India, in W
Maharashtra: under British rule served as the
seasonal capital of the Bombay Presidency. Pop:
2 540 069 (2001)

poonce (puːns) *Austral slang* ▷ *n* **1** a male
homosexual ▷ *vb* (*intr*) **2** to behave effeminately
[C20 perhaps a blend of POOF and PONCE]

poontang (ˈpuːntæŋ) *n taboo slang* **1** the female
pudenda **2** a woman considered as a sexual object
3 sexual intercourse [possibly from F: *putain*
prostitute]

poop¹ (puːp) *nautical* ▷ *n* **1** a raised structure at the
stern of a vessel, esp a sailing ship **2** See **poop
deck** ▷ *vb* **3** (*tr*) (of a wave or sea) to break over the
stern of (a vessel) **4** (*intr*) (of a vessel) to ship a
wave or sea over the stern, esp repeatedly [C15
from Old French *pupe*, from Latin *puppis* poop,
ship's stern]

poop² (puːp) *vb US and Canadian slang* **1** (*tr; usually
passive*) to cause to become exhausted; tire: *he was
pooped after the race* **2** (*intr; usually foll by out*) to
give up or fail, esp through tiredness: *he pooped out
of the race* [C14 *poupen* to blow, make a sudden
sound, perhaps of imitative origin]

poop³ (puːp) *n US and Canadian slang* **a**
information; the facts **b** (*as modifier*): *a poop sheet*
[of unknown origin]

poop⁴ (puːp) *informal* ▷ *vb* (*intr*) **1** to defecate ▷ *n* **2**
faeces; excrement [perhaps related to POOP²]

poop deck *n nautical* the deck on top of the poop

pooper-scooper *n* a device used to remove dogs'
excrement from public areas [C20 POOP⁴ + -ER¹ +
SCOOPER]

Poopó (*Spanish* pooˈpo) *n* **Lake** a lake in SW
Bolivia, at an altitude of 3688 m (12 100 ft): fed by
the Desaguadero River. Area: 2540 sq km (980 sq
miles)

poor (puə, pɔː) *adj* **1 a** lacking financial or other
means of subsistence; needy **b** (*as collective noun;
preceded by the*): *the poor* **2** characterized by or
indicating poverty: *the country had a poor economy* **3**
deficient in amount; scanty or inadequate: *a poor
salary* **4** (*when postpositive, usually foll by in*) badly
supplied (with resources, materials, etc): *a region
poor in wild flowers* **5** lacking in quality; inferior **6**
giving no pleasure; disappointing or disagreeable:
a poor play **7** (*prenominal*) deserving of pity; unlucky:
poor John is ill again **8 poor man's (something)** a
(cheaper) substitute for (something) [C13 from Old
French *povre*, from Latin *pauper*; see PAUPER,
POVERTY] ▷ ˈpoorness *n*

poor box *n* a box, esp one in a church, used for
the collection of alms or money for the poor

poorhouse (ˈpuəˌhaʊs, ˈpɔː-) *n* (formerly) a
publicly maintained institution offering
accommodation to the poor

poor law *n English history* a law providing for the
relief or support of the poor from public, esp
parish, funds

poorly (ˈpuəlɪ, ˈpɔː-) *adv* **1** in a poor way or
manner; badly ▷ *adj* **2** (*usually postpositive*) *informal*
in poor health; rather ill: *he's poorly today*

poor man's orange *n NZ informal, obsolete* a
grapefruit

poor mouth *Irish* ▷ *n* **1** unjustified complaining,
esp to excite sympathy: *she always has the poor mouth*
▷ *vb* **poor-mouth** (*tr*) **2** *informal* to speak of
disparagingly; decry

poor rate *n English history* a rate or tax levied by
parishes for the relief or support of the poor

poor relation *n* a person or thing considered
inferior to another or others: *plastic is a poor relation
of real leather*

poort (puət) *n* (in South Africa) a steep narrow
mountain pass, usually following a river or
stream [C19 from Afrikaans, from Dutch: gateway;
see PORT⁴]

poortith (ˈpuːrˌtɪθ) *n Scot* a variant of **puirtith**

poor White *n often offensive* **a** a poverty-stricken
and underprivileged White person, esp in the
southern US and South Africa **b** (*as modifier*): *poor
White trash*

Pooterish (ˈpuːtərɪʃ) *adj* characteristic of or
resembling the fictional character Pooter, esp in
being bourgeois, genteel, or self-important [C20
from Charles *Pooter*, the hero of *Diary of a Nobody*
(1892), by George and Weedon Grossmith]

pootle (ˈpuːtᵊl) *vb* (*intr*) *Brit informal* to travel or go
in a relaxed or leisurely manner [C20 from *p(oodle)*
to travel + (T)OOTLE²]

poove (puːv) *n Brit derogatory slang* a variant of
poof

pop¹ (pɒp) *vb* **pops, popping, popped** **1** to make or
cause to make a light sharp explosive sound **2** to
burst open or cause to burst open with such a
sound **3** (*intr; often foll by in, out, etc*) *informal* to
come (to) or go (from) rapidly or suddenly; to pay a
brief or unexpected visit (to) **4** (*intr*) (esp of the
eyes) to protrude: *her eyes popped with amazement* **5**
to shoot or fire at (a target) with a firearm **6** (*tr*)
to place or put with a sudden movement: *she
popped some tablets into her mouth* **7** (*tr*) *informal* to
pawn: *he popped his watch yesterday* **8** (*tr*) *slang* to
take (a drug) in pill form or as an injection: *pill
popping* **9 pop one's clogs** See **clog** (sense 9) **10
pop the question** *informal* to propose marriage ▷ *n*
11 a light sharp explosive sound; crack **12** *informal*
a flavoured nonalcoholic carbonated beverage **13**
informal a try; attempt: *have a pop at goal* **14** *informal*
an instance of criticism: *Townsend has had a pop at
modern bands* **15 a pop** *informal* each: *30 million shares
at 7 dollars a pop* ▷ *adv* **16** with a popping sound
▷ *interj* **17** an exclamation denoting a sharp
explosive sound ▷ See also **pop off, pop-up** [C14 of
imitative origin]

pop² (pɒp) *n* **1 a** music of general appeal, esp
among young people, that originated as a
distinctive genre in the 1950s. It is generally
characterized by a strong rhythmic element and
the use of electrical amplification **b** (*as modifier*):
pop music; a pop record; a pop group **2** *informal* a piece
of popular or light classical music ▷ *adj* **3** *informal*
short for **popular**

pop³ (pɒp) *n* **1** an informal word for **father** **2**
informal a name used in addressing an old or
middle-aged man

POP *abbreviation for* **1** point of presence: a device
that enables access to the internet **2** *internet* post
office protocol: a protocol which brings e-mail to
and from a mail server **3** Post Office Preferred
(size of envelopes, etc) **4** persistent organic
pollutant

pop. *abbreviation for* **1** popular **2** popularly **3**
population

pop art *n* a movement in modern art that
imitates the methods, styles, and themes of
popular culture and mass media, such as comic
strips, advertising, and science fiction

popcorn (ˈpɒpˌkɔːn) *n* **1** a variety of maize having
hard rounded kernels that puff up when heated **2**
the puffed edible kernels of this plant [C19 so
called because of the noise the grains make when
they swell up and burst on heating]

popcorn movie *n* a film that appeals to a mass
audience

pope¹ (pəʊp) *n* **1** (*often capital*) the bishop of Rome
as head of the Roman Catholic Church. Related
adj: **papal 2** *Eastern Orthodox Churches* **a** a title
sometimes given to a parish priest **b** a title
sometimes given to the Greek Orthodox patriarch
of Alexandria **3** a person assuming or having a
status or authority resembling that of a pope [Old

English *papa*, from Church Latin: bishop, esp of
Rome, from Late Greek *papas* father-in-God, from
Greek *pappas* father]

pope² (pəʊp) *n* another name for **ruffe** (the fish)

popedom (ˈpəʊpdəm) *n* **1** the office or dignity of
a pope **2** the tenure of office of a pope **3** the
dominion of a pope; papal government

Popemobile (ˈpəʊpməˌbiːl) *n informal* a small
open-top car used by the Pope to move amongst
crowds [C20 POPE + -MOBILE]

popera (ˈpɒpərə, ˈpɒprə) *n* music drawing on
opera or classical music and aiming for popular
appeal [C20 from POP² (sense 1) + OPERA]

popery (ˈpəʊpərɪ) *n* a derogatory name for **Roman
Catholicism**

pope's eye *n* **1** (in sheep and cows) a gland in the
middle of the thigh surrounded by fat ▷ *adj*
popeseye **2** (in Scotland) denoting a cut of steak

pope's nose *n* another name for **parson's nose**

popette (pɒˈpet) *n informal* a young female fan or
performer of pop music [C20 POP² + -ETTE (sense 2)]

popeyed (ˈpɒpˌaɪd) *adj* **1** having bulging
prominent eyes **2** staring in astonishment;
amazed

popgun (ˈpɒpˌɡʌn) *n* a toy gun that fires a pellet
or cork by means of compressed air and makes a
popping sound

popinjay (ˈpɒpɪnˌdʒeɪ) *n* **1** a conceited, foppish, or
excessively talkative person **2** an archaic word for
parrot 3 the figure of a parrot used as a target
[C13 *papeniai*, from Old French *papegay* a parrot,
from Spanish *papagayo*, from Arabic *babaghā*]

popish (ˈpəʊpɪʃ) *adj derogatory* belonging to or
characteristic of Roman Catholicism
▷ ˈpopishly *adv*

Popish Plot *n* a supposed conspiracy (1678) to
murder Charles II of England and replace him
with his Catholic brother James: in reality a
fabrication by the informer Titus Oates

poplar (ˈpɒplə) *n* **1** any tree of the salicaceous
genus *Populus*, of N temperate regions, having
triangular leaves, flowers borne in catkins, and
light soft wood. See also **aspen, balsam poplar,
Lombardy poplar, white poplar 2** any of various
trees resembling the true poplars, such as the
tulip tree **3** the wood of any of these trees [C14
from Old French *poplier*, from *pouple*, from Latin
pōpulus]

poplin (ˈpɒplɪn) *n* **a** a strong fabric, usually of
cotton, in plain weave with fine ribbing, used for
dresses, children's wear, etc **b** (*as modifier*): *a poplin
shirt* [C18 from French *papeline*, perhaps from
Poperinge, a centre of textile manufacture in
Flanders]

popliteal (pɒpˈlɪtɪəl, ˌpɒplɪˈtiːəl) *adj* of, relating to,
or near the part of the leg behind the knee [C18
from New Latin *popliteus* the muscle behind the
knee joint, from Latin *poples* the ham of the knee]

popmobility (ˌpɒpməʊˈbɪlɪtɪ) *n* a form of exercise
that combines aerobics in a continuous dance
routine, performed to pop music [C20 POP² +
MOBILITY]

Popocatépetl (ˌpɒpəˈkætəpetᵊl, -ˌkætəˈpetᵊl;
Spanish popokaˈtepetl) *n* a volcano in SE central
Mexico, southeast of Mexico City. Height: 5452 m
(17 887 ft)

pop off *vb* (*intr, adverb*) *informal* **1** to depart suddenly
or unexpectedly **2** to die, esp suddenly or
unexpectedly: *he popped off at the age of sixty* **3** to
speak out angrily or indiscreetly: *he popped off at his
boss and got fired*

popover (ˈpɒpˌəʊvə) *n* **1** *Brit* an individual
Yorkshire pudding, often served with roast beef **2**
US and Canadian a light puffy hollow muffin made
from a batter mixture **3** a simple garment for
women or girls that is put on by being slipped
over the head

poppadom *or* **poppadum** (ˈpɒpədəm) *n* a thin
round crisp Indian bread, fried or roasted and
served with curry, etc [from Hindi]

popper (ˈpɒpə) *n* **1** a person or thing that pops **2**
Brit an informal name for **press stud 3** *chiefly US*

and Canadian a container for cooking popcorn in **4** *slang* an amyl nitrite capsule, which is crushed and its contents inhaled by drug users as a stimulant

Popperian (pɒˈpɪərɪən) *adj* **1** of or relating to Sir Karl Popper, the Austrian-born British philosopher (1902-94) ▷ *n* **2** a follower or admirer of Popper

poppet (ˈpɒpɪt) *n* **1** a term of affection for a small child or sweetheart **2** Also called: poppet valve a mushroom-shaped valve that is lifted from its seating against a spring by applying an axial force to its stem: commonly used as an exhaust or inlet valve in an internal-combustion engine **3** *nautical* a temporary supporting brace for a vessel hauled on land or in a dry dock [C14 early variant of PUPPET]

poppet head *n* the framework above a mining shaft that supports the winding mechanism

poppied (ˈpɒpɪd) *adj* **1** covered with poppies **2** of or relating to the effects of poppies, esp in inducing drowsiness or sleep

popping crease *n cricket* a line four feet in front of and parallel with the bowling crease, at or behind which the batsman stands [C18 from POP¹ (in the obsolete or dialect sense: to hit) + CREASE¹]

popple (ˈpɒpᵊl) *vb (intr)* **1** (of boiling water or a choppy sea) to heave or toss; bubble **2** (often foll by *along*) (of a stream or river) to move with an irregular tumbling motion: *the small rivulet poppled along over rocks and stones for half a mile* [C14 of imitative origin; compare Middle Dutch *popelen* to bubble, throb]

poppy (ˈpɒpɪ) *n, pl* **-pies 1** any of numerous papaveraceous plants of the temperate genus *Papaver*, having red, orange, or white flowers and a milky sap: see **corn poppy, Iceland poppy, opium poppy 2** any of several similar or related plants, such as the California poppy, prickly poppy, horned poppy, and Welsh poppy **3** *obsolete* any of the drugs, such as opium, that are obtained from these plants **4 a** a strong red to reddish-orange colour **b** (*as adjective*): *a poppy dress* **5** a less common name for **poppyhead** (sense 2) **6** an artificial red poppy flower worn to mark Remembrance Sunday [Old English *popæg*, ultimately from Latin *papāver*]

poppy² (ˈpɒpɪ) *adj* **-pier, -piest** of or relating to pop music

poppycock (ˈpɒpɪˌkɒk) *n informal* senseless chatter; nonsense [C19 from Dutch dialect *pappekak*, literally: soft excrement, from *pap* soft + *kak* dung; see PAP¹]

Poppy Day *n* an informal name for **Remembrance Sunday**

poppyhead (ˈpɒpɪˌhɛd) *n* **1** the hard dry seed-containing capsule of a poppy. See also **capsule** (sense 3a) **2** a carved ornament, esp one used on the top of the end of a pew or bench in Gothic church architecture

poppy seed *n* the small grey seeds of one type of poppy flower, used esp on loaves and as a cake filling

pop shop *n* a slang word for a **pawnshop**

Popsicle (ˈpɒpsɪkᵊl) *n trademark US and Canadian* an ice lolly

popster (ˈpɒpstə) *n informal* a pop star [C20 POP² + -STER]

popsy (ˈpɒpsɪ) *n, pl* **-sies** *old-fashioned, Brit slang* an attractive young woman [C19 diminutive formed from *pop*, shortened from POPPET; originally a nursery term]

populace (ˈpɒpjʊləs) *n* (*sometimes functioning as plural*) **1** the inhabitants of an area **2** the common people; masses [C16 via French from Italian *popolaccio* the common herd, from *popolo* people, from Latin *populus*]

popular (ˈpɒpjʊlə) *adj* **1** appealing to the general public; widely favoured or admired **2** favoured by an individual or limited group: *I'm not very popular with her* **3** connected with, representing, or prevailing among the general public; common:

popular discontent **4** appealing to or comprehensible to the layman: *a popular lecture on physics* ▷ *n* **5** (*usually plural*) cheap newspapers with mass circulation; the popular press. Also shortened to: **pops** [C15 from Latin *populāris* belonging to the people, democratic, from *populus* people] > **popularity** (ˌpɒpjʊˈlærɪtɪ) *n*

popular etymology *n linguistics* another name for **folk etymology**

popular front *n* (*often capital*) any of the left-wing groups or parties that were organized from 1935 onwards to oppose the spread of fascism

popularize *or* **popularise** (ˈpɒpjʊləˌraɪz) *vb (tr)* **1** to make popular; make attractive to the general public **2** to make or cause to become easily understandable or acceptable > ˌpopulariˈzation *or* ˌpopulariˈsation *n* > ˈpopularˌizer *or* ˈpopularˌiser *n*

popularly (ˈpɒpjʊləlɪ) *adv* **1** by the public as a whole; generally or widely **2** usually; commonly: *his full name is Robert, but he is popularly known as Bob* **3** in a popular manner

popular music *n* music having wide appeal, esp characterized by lightly romantic or sentimental melodies. See also **pop²**

popular sovereignty *n* (in the pre-Civil War US) the doctrine that the inhabitants of a territory should be free from federal interference in determining their own domestic policy, esp in deciding whether or not to allow slavery

populate (ˈpɒpjʊˌleɪt) *vb (tr)* **1** (*often passive*) to live in; inhabit **2** to provide a population for; colonize [C16 from Medieval Latin *populāre* to provide with inhabitants, from Latin *populus* people]

population (ˌpɒpjʊˈleɪʃən) *n* **1** (*sometimes functioning as plural*) all the persons inhabiting a country, city, or other specified place **2** the number of such inhabitants **3** (*sometimes functioning as plural*) all the people of a particular race or class in a specific area: *the Chinese population of San Francisco* **4** the act or process of providing a place with inhabitants; colonization **5** *ecology* a group of individuals of the same species inhabiting a given area **6** *astronomy* either of two main groups of stars classified according to age and location. **Population I** consists of younger metal-rich hot white stars, many occurring in galactic clusters and forming the arms of spiral galaxies. Stars of **population II** are older, the brightest being red giants, and are found in the centre of spiral and elliptical galaxies in globular clusters **7** Also called: **universe** *statistics* the entire finite or infinite aggregate of individuals or items from which samples are drawn

population control *n* a policy of attempting to limit the growth in numbers of a population, esp in poor or densely populated parts of the world, by programmes of contraception or sterilization

population explosion *n* a rapid increase in the size of a population caused by such factors as a sudden decline in infant mortality or an increase in life expectancy

population pyramid *n* a pyramid-shaped diagram illustrating the age distribution of a population: the youngest are represented by a rectangle at the base, the oldest by one at the apex

populism (ˈpɒpjʊˌlɪzəm) *n* a political strategy based on a calculated appeal to the interests or prejudices of ordinary people

populist (ˈpɒpjʊlɪst) *adj* **1** appealing to the interests or prejudices of ordinary people ▷ *n* **2** a person, esp a politician, who appeals to the interests or prejudices of ordinary people

Populist (ˈpɒpjʊlɪst) *n* **1** *US history* a member of the People's Party, formed largely by agrarian interests to contest the 1892 presidential election. The movement gradually dissolved after the 1904 election ▷ *adj also* **Populistic 2** of, characteristic of, or relating to the People's Party, the Populists, or any individual or movement with similar aims > ˈPopulism *n*

populist shop steward *n* a shop steward who operates in a delegate role, putting the immediate

interests of his members before union principles and policies

populous (ˈpɒpjʊləs) *adj* containing many inhabitants; abundantly populated [C15 from Late Latin *populōsus*] > ˈpopulously *adv* > ˈpopulousness *n*

pop-up *adj* **1** (of an appliance) characterized by or having a mechanism that pops up: *a pop-up toaster* **2** (of a book) having pages that rise when opened to simulate a three-dimensional form **3** *computing* (of a menu on a computer screen, etc) suddenly appearing when an option is selected ▷ *vb* **pop up 4** (*intr, adverb*) to appear suddenly from below ▷ *n* **5** *computing* something that appears over or above the open window on a computer screen

porae (ˈpɒrɑːə) *n, pl* **porae** a large edible sea fish, *Nemadactylus douglasi*, of New Zealand waters [Māori]

porangi (ˈpɔːræŋɪ) *adj NZ informal* crazy; mad [Māori]

porbeagle (ˈpɔːˌbiːgᵊl) *n* any of several voracious sharks of the genus *Lamna*, esp *L. nasus*, of northern seas: family *Isuridae*. Also called: **mackerel shark** [C18 from Cornish *porgh-bugel*, of obscure origin]

porcelain (ˈpɔːslɪn, -leɪn, ˈpɔːsə-) *n* **1** a more or less translucent ceramic material, the principal ingredients being kaolin and petuntse (hard paste) or other clays, ground glassy substances, soapstone, bone ash, etc **2** an object made of this or such objects collectively **3** (*modifier*) of, relating to, or made from this material: *a porcelain cup* [C16 from French *porcelaine*, from Italian *porcellana* cowrie shell, porcelain (from its shell-like finish), literally: relating to a sow (from the resemblance between a cowrie shell and a sow's vulva), from *porcella* little sow, from *porca* sow, from Latin; see PORK] > **porcellaneous** (ˌpɔːsəˈleɪnɪəs) *adj*

porcelain clay *n* another name for **kaolin**

porch (pɔːtʃ) *n* **1** a low structure projecting from the doorway of a house and forming a covered entrance **2** *US and Canadian* an exterior roofed gallery, often partly enclosed; veranda [C13 from French *porche*, from Latin *porticus* portico]

porcine (ˈpɔːsaɪn) *adj* of, connected with, or characteristic of pigs [C17 from Latin *porcīnus*, from *porcus* pig]

porcino (pɔːˈtʃiːnəʊ) *n, pl* **porcini** (pɔːˈtʃiːnɪ) an edible saprotrophic basidiomycetous woodland fungus, *Boletus edulis*, with a brown shining cap covering white spore-bearing tubes and having a rich nutty flavour: family *Boletineae*. Also called: **cep** [Italian, from Latin *porcīnus*, from *porcus* pig]

porcupine (ˈpɔːkjʊˌpaɪn) *n* any of various large hystricomorph rodents of the families *Hystricidae*, of Africa, Indonesia, S Europe, and S Asia, and *Erethizontidae*, of the New World. All species have a body covering of protective spines or quills [C14 *porc despyne* pig with spines, from Old French *porc espin*; see PORK, SPINE] > ˈporcuˌpinish *adj* > ˈporcuˌpiny *adj*

porcupine fish *n* any of various plectognath fishes of the genus *Diodon* and related genera, of temperate and tropical seas, having a body that is covered with sharp spines and can be inflated into a globe: family *Diodontidae*. Also called: **globefish**

porcupine grass *n Austral* another name for **spinifex** (sense 2)

porcupine provisions *pl n finance* provisions, such as poison pills or staggered directorships, made in the bylaws of a company to deter takeover bids. Also called: **shark repellents**

pore¹ (pɔː) *vb (intr)* **1** (foll by *over*) to make a close intent examination or study (of a book, map, etc): *he pored over the documents for several hours* **2** (foll by *over, on,* or *upon*) to think deeply (about): *he pored on the question of their future* **3** (foll by *over, on,* or *upon*) *rare* to look earnestly or intently (at); gaze fixedly (upon) [C13 *pouren*; perhaps related to PEER²]

■ **USAGE** See at **pour**

pore² (pɔː) *n* **1** *anatomy, zoology* any small opening in the skin or outer surface of an animal **2** *botany*

any small aperture, esp that of a stoma through which water vapour and gases pass **3** any other small hole, such as a space in a rock, soil, etc [c14 from Late Latin *porus*, from Greek *poros* passage, pore]

porgy ('pɔːgɪ) *n, pl* -gy *or* -gies **1** Also called: pogy any of various sparid fishes, many of which occur in American Atlantic waters. See also **scup, sheepshead 2** any of various similar or related fishes [c18 from Spanish *pargo*, from Latin *phager* type of fish, from Greek *phagros* sea bream]

Pori (Finnish 'pɔrɪ) *n* a port in SW Finland, on the Gulf of Bothnia. Pop: 76 189 (2003 est). Swedish name: Björneborg

poriferan (pɔːˈrɪfərən) *n* **1** any invertebrate of the phylum *Porifera*, which comprises the sponges ▷ *adj also* **poriferous 2** of, relating to, or belonging to the phylum *Porifera* [c19 from New Latin *porifer* bearing pores]

poriferous (pɔːˈrɪfərəs) *adj* **1** *biology* having many pores **2** another word for **poriferan** (sense 2)

porina (pɒˈraɪnə) *n* NZ **a** the larva of a moth which causes damage to grassland **b** (*as modifier*): *porina infestation* [from New Latin]

Porirua (ˌpɒrɪˈruːə) *n* a city in New Zealand, on the North Island just north of Wellington. Pop: 50 600 (2004 est)

porism ('pɔːrɪzəm) *n* a type of mathematical proposition considered by Euclid, the 3rd century BC Greek mathematician, the meaning of which is now obscure. It is thought to be a proposition affirming the possibility of finding such conditions as will render a certain problem indeterminate or capable of innumerable solutions [c14 from Late Latin *porisma*, from Greek: deduction, from *porizein* to deduce, carry; related to Greek *poros* passage] > **porismatic** (ˌpɔːrɪzˈmætɪk) *adj*

pork (pɔːk) *n* the flesh of pigs used as food [c13 from Old French *porc*, from Latin *porcus* pig]

pork barrel *n slang, chiefly US* a bill or project requiring considerable government spending in a locality to the benefit of the legislator's constituents who live there [c20 term originally applied to the Federal treasury considered as a source of lucrative grants]

porker ('pɔːkə) *n* a pig, esp a young one weighing between 40 and 67 kg, fattened to provide meat such as pork chops

pork pie *n* **1** a pie filled with minced seasoned pork **2** See **porky²**

porkpie hat ('pɔːkˌpaɪ) *n* a hat with a round flat crown and a brim that can be turned up or down

pork pig *n* a pig, typically of a lean type, bred and used principally for pork

pork scratchings *pl n* small pieces of crisply cooked pork crackling, eaten cold as an appetizer with drinks

porky¹ ('pɔːkɪ) *adj* porkier, porkiest **1** belonging to or characteristic of pork: *a porky smell* **2** *informal* fat; obese > **'porkiness** *n*

porky² ('pɔːkɪ) *n, pl* porkies *Brit slang* a lie. Also called: pork pie [from rhyming slang *pork pie* lie]

porn (pɔːn) *or* **porno** ('pɔːnəʊ) *n, adj informal* short for **pornography** *or* **pornographic**

pornocracy (pɔːˈnɒkrəsɪ) *n* government or domination of government by whores [c19 from Greek, from *pornē* a prostitute, harlot + -CRACY]

pornography (pɔːˈnɒgrəfɪ) *n* **1** writings, pictures, films, etc, designed to stimulate sexual excitement **2** the production of such material ▷ Sometimes (informal) shortened to: **porn** *or* **porno** [c19 from Greek *pornographos* writing of harlots, from *pornē* a harlot + *graphein* to write] > **por'nographer** *n* > **pornographic** (ˌpɔːnəˈgræfɪk) *adj* > **porno'graphically** *adv*

poromeric (ˌpɔːrəˈmɛrɪk) *adj* **1** (of a plastic) permeable to water vapour ▷ *n* **2** a substance having this characteristic, esp one based on polyurethane and used in place of leather in making shoe uppers [c20 from PORO(SITY) + (POLY)MER + -IC]

porosity (pɔːˈrɒsɪtɪ) *n, pl* -ties **1** the state or condition of being porous **2** *geology* the ratio of the volume of space to the total volume of a rock [c14 from Medieval Latin *porōsitās*, from Late Latin *porus* PORE²]

porous ('pɔːrəs) *adj* **1** permeable to water, air, or other fluids **2** *biology, geology* having pores; poriferous **3** easy to cross or penetrate: *the porous border into Thailand; the most porous defence in the league* [c14 from Medieval Latin *porōsus*, from Late Latin *porus* PORE²] > **'porously** *adv* > **'porousness** *n*

porphyria (pɔːˈfɪrɪə) *n* a hereditary disease of body metabolism, producing abdominal pain, mental confusion, etc [c19 from New Latin, from *porphyrin* a purple substance excreted by patients suffering from this condition, from Greek *porphura* purple]

porphyrin ('pɔːfɪrɪn) *n* any of a group of pigments occurring widely in animal and plant tissues and having a heterocyclic structure formed from four pyrrole rings linked by four methylene groups [c20 from Greek *porphura* purple, referring to its colour]

porphyritic (ˌpɔːfɪˈrɪtɪk) *adj* **1** (of rocks) having large crystals in a fine groundmass of minerals **2** consisting of porphyry

porphyrogenite (ˌpɔːfəˈrɒdʒɪˌnaɪt) *n* (*sometimes capital*) a prince born after his father has succeeded to the throne [c17 via Medieval Latin from Late Greek *porphurogenētos* born in the purple, from Greek *porphuros* purple]

porphyroid ('pɔːfɪˌrɔɪd) *adj* **1** (of metamorphic rocks) having a texture characterized by large crystals set in a finer groundmass ▷ *n* **2** a metamorphic rock having this texture

porphyropsin (ˌpɔːfɪˈrɒpsɪn) *n* a purple pigment occurring in the retina of the eye of certain freshwater fishes [c20 from Greek *porphura* purple + -OPSIS + -IN, on the model of RHODOPSIN]

porphyry ('pɔːfɪrɪ) *n, pl* -ries **1** any igneous rock with large crystals embedded in a finer groundmass of minerals **2** *obsolete* a reddish-purple rock consisting of large crystals of feldspar in a finer groundmass of feldspar, hornblende, etc [c14 *porfurie*, from Late Latin *porphyrītēs*, from Greek *porphurítēs* (*lithos*) purple (stone), from *porphuros* purple]

porpoise ('pɔːpəs) *n, pl* -poises *or* -poise **1** any of various small cetacean mammals of the genus *Phocaena* and related genera, having a blunt snout and many teeth: family *Delphinidae* (or *Phocaenidae*) **2** (*not in technical use*) any of various related cetaceans, esp the dolphin [c14 from French *pourpois*, from Medieval Latin *porcopiscus* (from Latin *porcus* pig + *piscis* fish), replacing Latin *porcus marīnus* sea pig]

porrect (pəˈrɛkt) *adj botany* extended forwards [c20 from Latin *porrectus*, from *porrigere* to stretch out]

porridge ('pɒrɪdʒ) *n* **1** a dish made from oatmeal or another cereal, cooked in water or milk to a thick consistency **2** *slang* a term in prison (esp in the phrase **do porridge**) [c16 variant (influenced by Middle English *porray* pottage) of POTTAGE]

porringer ('pɒrɪndʒə) *n* a small dish, often with a handle, for soup, porridge, etc [c16 changed from Middle English *potinger, poteger,* from Old French *potager,* from *potage* soup, contents of a pot; see POTTAGE]

Porsena ('pɔːsɪnə) *or* **Porsenna** (pɔːˈsɛnə) *n* Lars (laːz). 6th century BC, a legendary Etruscan king, alleged to have besieged Rome in a vain attempt to reinstate Tarquinius Superbus on the throne

port¹ (pɔːt) *n* **1** a town or place alongside navigable water with facilities for the loading and unloading of ships **2** See **port of entry** [Old English, from Latin *portus* harbour, port]

port² (pɔːt) *n* **1** Also called (formerly): larboard **a** the left side of an aircraft or vessel when facing the nose or bow **b** (*as modifier*): *the port bow.* Compare **starboard** (sense 1) ▷ *vb* **2** to turn or be turned towards the port [c17 origin uncertain]

port³ (pɔːt) *n* a sweet fortified dessert wine [c17 after *Oporto*, Portugal, from where it came originally]

port⁴ (pɔːt) *n* **1** *nautical* **a** an opening in the side of a ship, fitted with a watertight door, for access to the holds **b** See **porthole** (sense 1) **2** a small opening in a wall, armoured vehicle, etc, for firing through **3** an aperture, esp one controlled by a valve, by which fluid enters or leaves the cylinder head of an engine, compressor, etc **4** *electronics* a logic circuit for the input and ouput of data **5** *chiefly Scot* a gate or portal in a town or fortress [Old English, from Latin *porta* gate]

port⁵ (pɔːt) *military* ▷ *vb* **1** (*tr*) to carry (a rifle, etc) in a position diagonally across the body with the muzzle near the left shoulder ▷ *n* **2** this position [c14 from Old French, from *porter* to carry, from Latin *portāre*]

port⁶ (pɔːt) *vb* (*tr*) *computing* to change (programs) from one system to another [c20 probably from PORT⁴]

port⁷ (pɔːt) *n Austral* (esp in Queensland) a suitcase or school case [c20 shortened from PORTMANTEAU]

Port. *abbreviation for* **1** Portugal **2** Portuguese

porta ('pɔːtə) *n anatomy* an aperture in an organ, such as the liver, esp one providing an opening for blood vessels [c14 from Latin: gate, entrance]

portable ('pɔːtəbªl) *adj* **1** able to be carried or moved easily, esp by hand **2** (of software, files, etc) able to be transferred from one type of computer system to another **3** *archaic* able to be endured; bearable ▷ *n* **4** an article designed to be readily carried by hand, such as a television, typewriter, etc [c14 from Late Latin *portābilis,* from Latin *portāre* to carry] > ˌporta'bility *n* > 'portably *adv*

Port Adelaide *n* the chief port of South Australia, near Adelaide on St Vincent Gulf. Pop: 101 225 (1998 est)

Portadown (ˌpɔːtəˈdaʊn) *n* a town in S Northern Ireland, in the district of Armagh. Pop: 21 299 (1991)

portage ('pɔːtɪdʒ; French pɔrtaʒ) *n* **1** the act of carrying; transport **2** the cost of carrying or transporting **3** the act or process of transporting boats, supplies, etc, overland between navigable waterways **4** the route overland used for such transport ▷ *vb* **5** to transport (boats, supplies, etc) overland between navigable waterways [c15 from French, from Old French *porter* to carry]

Portakabin ('pɔːtəˌkæbɪn) *n trademark* a portable building quickly set up for use as a temporary office, etc

portal ('pɔːtªl) *n* **1** an entrance, gateway, or doorway, esp one that is large and impressive **2** any entrance or access to a place **3** *computing* an internet site providing links to other sites ▷ *adj* **4** *anatomy* **a** of or relating to a portal vein: *hepatic portal system* **b** of or relating to a porta [c14 via Old French from Medieval Latin *portāle,* from Latin *porta* gate, entrance]

portal frame *n civil engineering, building trades* a frame, usually of steel, consisting of two uprights and a cross beam at the top: the simplest structural unit in a framed building or a doorway

portal-to-portal *adj* of or relating to the period between the actual times workers enter and leave their mine, factory, etc: *portal-to-portal pay*

portal vein *n* any vein connecting two capillary networks, esp in the liver (**hepatic portal vein**)

portamento (ˌpɔːtəˈmɛntəʊ) *n, pl* -ti (-tɪ) *music* a smooth slide from one note to another in which intervening notes are not separately discernible. Compare **glissando** [c18 from Italian: a carrying, from Latin *portāre* to carry]

Port Arthur *n* **1** a former penal settlement (1833–70) in Australia, on the S coast of the Tasman Peninsula, Tasmania **2** the former name of **Lüshun**

portative ('pɔːtətɪv) *adj* **1** a less common word for **portable 2** concerned with the act of carrying

[c14 from French, from Latin *portāre* to carry]

portative organ *n music* a small portable organ with arm-operated bellows popular in medieval times

Port-au-Prince ('pɔːtəʊ'prɪns; *French* pɔrtoprɛ̃s) *n* the capital and chief port of Haiti, in the south on the Gulf of Gonaïves: founded in 1749 by the French; university (1944). Pop: 2 090 000 (2005 est)

Port Blair (bleə) *n* the capital of the Indian Union Territory of the Andaman and Nicobar Islands, a port on the SE coast of South Andaman Island: a former penal colony. Pop: 100 186 (2001)

portcullis (pɔːt'kʌlɪs) *n* an iron or wooden grating suspended vertically in grooves in the gateway of a castle or fortified town and able to be lowered so as to bar the entrance [c14 *port colice,* from Old French *porte coleïce* sliding gate, from *porte* door, entrance + *coleïce,* from *couler* to slide, flow, from Late Latin *cōlāre* to filter]

Porte (pɔːt) *n* short for **Sublime Porte**; the court or government of the Ottoman Empire [c17 shortened from French *Sublime Porte* High Gate, rendering the Turkish title *Babi Ali,* the imperial gate, which was regarded as the seat of government]

porte-cochere (,pɔːtkɒ'ʃeə) *n* 1 a large covered entrance for vehicles leading into a courtyard 2 a large roof projecting over a drive to shelter travellers entering or leaving vehicles [c17 from French: carriage entrance, from *porte* gateway + *coche* coach]

Port Elizabeth *n* a port in S South Africa, on Algoa Bay: motor-vehicle manufacture, fruit canning; resort. Pop: 237 502 (2001)

portend (pɔː'tɛnd) *vb* (*tr*) 1 to give warning of; predict or foreshadow 2 *obsolete* to indicate or signify; mean [c15 from Latin *portendere* to indicate, foretell; related to *prōtendere* to stretch out]

portent ('pɔːtɛnt) *n* 1 a sign or indication of a future event, esp a momentous or calamitous one; omen 2 momentous or ominous significance: *a cry of dire portent* 3 a miraculous occurrence; marvel [c16 from Latin *portentum* sign, omen, from *portendere* to PORTEND]

portentous (pɔː'tɛntəs) *adj* 1 of momentous or ominous significance 2 miraculous, amazing, or awe-inspiring; prodigious 3 self-important or pompous > por'tentously *adv* > por'tentousness *n*

porter[1] ('pɔːtə) *n* 1 a person employed to carry luggage, parcels, supplies, etc, esp at a railway station or hotel 2 (in hospitals) a person employed to move patients from place to place 3 *US and Canadian* a railway employee who waits on passengers, esp in a sleeper 4 *E African* a manual labourer [c14 from Old French *portour,* from Late Latin *portātōr,* from Latin *portāre* to carry]

porter[2] ('pɔːtə) *n* 1 *chiefly Brit* a person in charge of a gate or door; doorman or gatekeeper 2 a person employed by a university or college as a caretaker and doorkeeper who also answers enquiries 3 a person in charge of the maintenance of a building, esp a block of flats 4 Also called: **ostiary** *RC Church* a person ordained to what was formerly the lowest in rank of the minor orders [c13 from Old French *portier,* from Late Latin *portārius* doorkeeper, from Latin *porta* door]

porter[3] ('pɔːtə) *n Brit* a dark sweet ale brewed from black malt [c18 shortened from *porter's ale,* apparently because it was a favourite beverage of porters]

porterage ('pɔːtərɪdʒ) *n* 1 the work of carrying supplies, goods, etc, done by porters 2 the charge made for this

portered ('pɔːtəd) *adj* (of an apartment block) serviced by a caretaker

porterhouse ('pɔːtə,haʊs) *n* 1 Also called: **porterhouse steak** a thick choice steak of beef cut from the middle ribs or sirloin 2 (formerly) a place in which porter, beer, etc, and sometimes chops and steaks, were served [c19 (sense 1): said

to be named after a porterhouse or chophouse in New York]

portfire ('pɔːt,faɪə) *n* (formerly) a slow-burning fuse used for firing rockets and fireworks and, in mining, for igniting explosives [c17 from French *porte-feu,* from *porter* to carry + *feu* fire]

portfolio (pɔːt'fəʊlɪəʊ) *n, pl* -os 1 a flat case, esp of leather, used for carrying maps, drawings, etc 2 the contents of such a case, such as drawings, paintings, or photographs, that demonstrate recent work: *an art student's portfolio* 3 such a case used for carrying ministerial or state papers 4 the responsibilities or role of the head of a government department: *the portfolio for foreign affairs* 5 Minister without portfolio a cabinet minister who is not responsible for any government department 6 the complete investments held by an individual investor or by a financial organization [c18 from Italian *portafoglio,* from *portāre* to carry + *foglio* leaf, paper, from Latin *folium* leaf]

portfolio employment *n* the practice of working for several employers simultaneously rather than working full-time for a single employer

portfolio worker *n* a person in portfolio employment

Port-Gentil (*French* pɔrʒãti) *n* the chief port of Gabon, in the west near the mouth of the Ogooué River: oil refinery. Pop: 80 841 (1993)

Port Harcourt ('hɑːkət, -kɔːt) *n* a port in S Nigeria, capital of Rivers state on the Niger delta: the nation's second largest port; industrial centre. Pop: 942 000 (2005 est)

porthole ('pɔːt,həʊl) *n* 1 a small aperture in the side of a vessel to admit light and air, usually fitted with a watertight glass or metal cover, or both. Sometimes shortened to: **port** 2 an opening in a wall or parapet through which a gun can be fired; embrasure

portico ('pɔːtɪkəʊ) *n, pl* -coes *or* -cos 1 a covered entrance to a building; porch 2 a covered walkway in the form of a roof supported by columns or pillars, esp one built on to the exterior of a building [c17 via Italian from Latin *porticus* PORCH]

portière (,pɔːtɪ'ɛə; *French* pɔrtjɛr) *n* a curtain hung in a doorway [c19 via French from Medieval Latin *portāria,* from Latin *porta* door] > ,porti'èred *adj*

Porțile de Fier (pɔr'tsiːle de 'fjɛr) *n* the Romanian name for the **Iron Gate**

portion ('pɔːʃən) *n* 1 a part of a whole; fraction 2 a part allotted or belonging to a person or group 3 an amount of food served to one person; helping 4 *law* a share of property, esp one coming to a child from the estate of his parents **b** the property given by a woman to her husband at marriage; dowry 5 a person's lot or destiny ▷ *vb* (*tr*) 6 to divide up; share out 7 to give a share to (a person); assign or allocate 8 *law* to give a dowry or portion to (a person); endow [c13 via Old French from Latin *portiō* portion, allocation; related to *pars* PART] > 'portionless *adj*

Port Jackson *n* an inlet of the Pacific on the coast of SE Australia, forming a fine natural harbour: site of the city of Sydney, spanned by Sydney Harbour Bridge

Port Jackson willow *or* **wattle** *n* an Australian acacia tree, *Acacia cyanophylla,* introduced in the 19th century into South Africa, where it is now regarded as a pest

Portland ('pɔːtlənd) *n* 1 Isle of a rugged limestone peninsula in SW England, in Dorset, connected to the mainland by a narrow isthmus and by Chesil Bank: the lighthouse of **Portland Bill** lies at the S tip; famous for the quarrying of **Portland stone**, a fine building material. Pop (town): 12 000 (latest est) 2 an inland port in NW Oregon, on the Willamette River: the largest city in the state; shipbuilding and chemical industries. Pop: 538 544 (2003 est) 3 a port in SW Maine, on Casco Bay: the largest city in the state; settled by the

English in 1632, destroyed successively by French, Indian, and British attacks, and rebuilt; capital of Maine (1820–32). Pop: 63 635 (2003 est)

Portland cement *n* a cement that hardens under water and is made by heating a slurry of clay and crushed chalk or limestone to clinker in a kiln [c19 named after the Isle of PORTLAND, because its colour resembles that of the stone quarried there]

Portlaoise (,pɔːt'liːʃə) *n* a town in central Republic of Ireland, county town of Laois: site of a top-security prison. Pop: 12 127 (2002)

Port Louis ('luːɪs, 'luːɪ) *n* the capital and chief port of Mauritius, on the NW coast on the Indian Ocean. Pop: 146 876 (2002 est)

portly ('pɔːtlɪ) *adj* -lier, -liest 1 stout or corpulent 2 *archaic* stately; impressive [c16 from PORT[5] (in the sense: deportment, bearing)] > 'portliness *n*

Port Lyautey (ljəʊ'teɪ) *n* the former name (1932–56) of **Kénitra**

portmanteau (pɔːt'mæntəʊ) *n, pl* -teaus *or* -teaux (-təʊz) 1 (formerly) a large travelling case made of stiff leather, esp one hinged at the back so as to open out into two compartments 2 (*modifier*) embodying several uses or qualities: *the heroine is a portmanteau figure of all the virtues* [c16 from French: cloak carrier, from *porter* to carry + *manteau* cloak, MANTLE]

portmanteau word *n* another name for **blend** (sense 7) [c19 from the idea that two meanings are packed into one word]

Port Moresby ('mɔːzbɪ) *n* the capital and chief port of Papua New Guinea, on the SE coast on the Gulf of Papua: important Allied base in World War II. Pop: 290 000 (2005 est)

Portnet ('pɔːtnɛt) *n South African* the South African Port Authority

Port Nicholson ('nɪkəlsən) *n* 1 the first British settlement in New Zealand, established on Wellington Harbour in 1840: grew into Wellington 2 the former name for Wellington Harbour [c19 named after Capt. John *Nicholson,* Australian naval officer]

Porto ('portu) *n* the Portuguese name for **Oporto**

Porto Alegre (*Portuguese* 'portu a'lɛgri) *n* a port in S Brazil, capital of the Rio Grande do Sul state: the country's chief inland port; the chief commercial centre of S Brazil, with two universities (1936 and 1948). Pop: 3 795 000 (2005 est)

Portobello (,pɔːtəʊ'bɛləʊ) *n* a small port in Panama, on the Caribbean northeast of Colón: the most important port in South America in colonial times; declined with the opening of the Panama Canal. Pop: 3026 (1990 est)

port of call *n* 1 any port where a ship stops, excluding its home port 2 any place visited on a traveller's itinerary

port of entry *n law* an airport, harbour, etc, where customs officials are stationed to supervise the entry into and exit from a country of persons and merchandise

Port of Spain *n* the capital and chief port of Trinidad and Tobago, on the W coast of Trinidad. Pop: 56 000 (2005 est)

Porto Novo ('pɔːtəʊ 'nəʊvəʊ) *n* the capital of Benin, in the southwest on a coastal lagoon: formerly a centre of Portuguese settlement and the slave trade. Pop: 253 000 (2005 est)

Porto Rican ('pɔːtə 'riːkən) *adj, n* a former name for **Puerto Rican**

Porto Rico ('pɔːtə 'riːkəʊ) *n* the former name (until 1932) of **Puerto Rico**

Porto Velho (*Portuguese* 'portu 'vɛʎu) *n* a city in W Brazil, capital of the federal territory of Rondônia on the Madeira River. Pop: 301 000 (2005 est)

Port Phillip Bay *or* **Port Phillip** ('fɪlɪp) *n* a bay in SE Australia, which forms the harbour of Melbourne

portrait ('pɔːtrɪt, -treɪt) *n* 1 a a painting, drawing, sculpture, photograph, or other likeness of an individual, esp of the face **b** (*as modifier*): *a portrait gallery* 2 a verbal description or picture, esp of a person's character ▷ *adj* 3 *printing* (of a publication or an illustration in a publication) of greater height than width. Compare **landscape** (sense 5a)

portraitist ('pɔːtrɪtɪst, -treɪ-) *n* an artist, photographer, etc, who specializes in portraits

portraiture ('pɔːtrɪtʃə) *n* **1** the practice or art of making portraits **2 a** another term for **portrait** (sense 1) **b** portraits collectively **3** a verbal description

portray (pɔːˈtreɪ) *vb* (*tr*) **1** to represent in a painting, drawing, sculpture, etc; make a portrait of **2** to make a verbal picture of; depict in words **3** to play the part of (a character) in a play or film [c14 from Old French *portraire* to depict, from Latin *prōtrahere* to drag forth, bring to light, from PRO-¹ + *trahere* to drag] > por'trayable *adj* > por'trayal *n* > por'trayer *n*

portress ('pɔːtrɪs) *n* a female porter, esp a doorkeeper

Port Royal *n* **1** a fortified town in SE Jamaica, at the entrance to Kingston harbour: capital of Jamaica in colonial times **2** the former name (until 1710) of **Annapolis Royal 3** (*French* pɔr rwajal) an educational institution about 27 km (17 miles) west of Paris that flourished from 1638 to 1704, when it was suppressed by papal bull as it had become a centre of Jansenism. Its teachers were noted esp for their work on linguistics: their *Grammaire générale et raisonnée* exercised much influence

Port Said ('saːiːd, saɪd) *n* a port in NE Egypt, at the N end of the Suez Canal: founded in 1859 when the Suez Canal was begun; became the largest coaling station in the world and later an oil-bunkering port; damaged in the Arab-Israeli wars of 1967 and 1973. Pop: 546 000 (2005 est)

Port-Salut ('pɔː səˈluː; *French* pɔrsaly) *n* a mild semihard whole-milk cheese of a round flat shape. Also called: Port du Salut [c19 named after the Trappist monastery at *Port du Salut* in NW France where it was first made]

Portsmouth ('pɔːtsməθ) *n* **1** a port in S England, in Portsmouth unitary authority, Hampshire, on the English Channel: Britain's chief naval base; university (1992). Pop: 187 056 (2001). Informal name: Pompey **2** a unitary authority in S England, in Hampshire. Pop: 188 700 (2003 est). Area: 37 sq km (14 sq miles) **3** a port in SE Virginia, on the Elizabeth River: naval base; shipyards. Pop: 99 617 (2003 est)

Port Sudan *n* the chief port of the Sudan, in the NE on the Red Sea. Pop: 499 000 (2005 est)

Port Talbot ('tɔːlbət, 'tæl-) *n* a port in SE Wales, in Neath Port Talbot county borough on Swansea Bay: established as a coal port in the mid-19th century; large steelworks; ore terminal. Pop: 35 633 (2001)

Portugal ('pɔːtjʊgᵊl) *n* a republic in SW Europe, on the Atlantic: became an independent monarchy in 1139 and expelled the Moors in 1249 after more than four centuries of Muslim rule; became a republic in 1910; under the dictatorship of Salazar from 1932 until 1968, when he was succeeded by Dr Caetano, who was overthrown by a junta in 1974; constitutional government restored in 1976. Portugal is a member of the European Union. Official language: Portuguese. Religion: Roman Catholic majority. Currency: euro. Capital: Lisbon. Pop: 10 072 000 (2004 est). Area: 91 831 sq km (35 456 sq miles)

Portuguese (,pɔːtjʊˈgiːz) *n* **1** the official language of Portugal, its overseas territories, and Brazil: the native language of approximately 110 million people. It belongs to the Romance group of the Indo-European family and is derived from the Galician dialect of Vulgar Latin **2** (*pl* -guese) a native, citizen, or inhabitant of Portugal ▷ *adj* **3** relating to, denoting, or characteristic of Portugal, its inhabitants, or their language

Portuguese East Africa *n* a former name (until 1975) of **Mozambique**

Portuguese Guinea *n* the former name (until 1974) of **Guinea-Bissau**

Portuguese Guinean *adj* **1** of or relating to Portuguese Guinea, a former name for Guinea-Bissau, or its inhabitants ▷ *n* **2** a native or inhabitant of Portuguese Guinea

Portuguese India *n* a former Portuguese overseas province on the W coast of India, consisting of Goa, Daman, and Diu: established between 1505 and 1510; annexed by India in 1961

Portuguese man-of-war *n* any of several large complex colonial hydrozoans of the genus *Physalia*, esp *P. physalis*, having an aerial float and long stinging tentacles: order *Siphonophora*. Sometimes shortened to: man-of-war

Portuguese Timor *n* a former name for **East Timor**

Portuguese water dog *n* a robust dog of a Portuguese breed that has a wavy coat, often with the hindquarters and tail clipped, and is an excellent swimmer and diver

Portuguese West Africa *n* a former name (until 1975) of **Angola**

portulaca (,pɔːtjʊˈlækə, -ˈleɪkə) *n* any portulacaceous plant of the genus *Portulaca*, such as rose moss and purslane, of tropical and subtropical America, having yellow, pink, or purple showy flowers [c16 from Latin: PURSLANE]

portulacaceous (,pɔːtjʊləˈkeɪʃəs) *adj* of, relating to, or belonging to the *Portulacaceae*, a cosmopolitan family of mainly fleshy-leaved flowering plants common in the US

port wine stain *n* a type of haemangioma, seen as a purplish birthmark, often large and on the face or neck

POS *abbreviation for* **1** point of sale **2** part of speech

pos. *abbreviation for* **1** position **2** positive

posada Spanish (poˈsaða) *n*, *pl -das* (-ðas) an inn in a Spanish-speaking country [literally: place for stopping]

pose¹ (pəʊz) *vb* **1** to assume or cause to assume a physical attitude, as for a photograph or painting **2** (*intr*; often foll by *as*) to pretend to be or present oneself (as something one is not) **3** (*intr*) to affect an attitude or play a part in order to impress others **4** (*tr*) to put forward, ask, or assert: *to pose a question* ▷ *n* **5** a physical attitude, esp one deliberately adopted for or represented by an artist or photographer **6** a mode of behaviour that is adopted for effect [c14 from Old French *poser* to set in place, from Late Latin *pausāre* to cease, put down (influenced by Latin *pōnere* to place)]

pose² (pəʊz) *vb* (*tr*) **1** *rare* to puzzle or baffle **2** *archaic* to question closely [c16 from obsolete *appose*, from Latin *appōnere* to put to, set against; see OPPOSE]

Poseidon (pɒˈsaɪdᵊn) *n* **1** *Greek myth* the god of the sea and of earthquakes; brother of Zeus, Hades, and Hera. He is generally depicted in art wielding a trident. Roman counterpart: Neptune **2** a US submarine-launched ballistic missile

Posen ('pəʊzən) *n* the German name for **Poznań**

poser¹ ('pəʊzə) *n* **1** a person who poses **2** *informal* a person who likes to be seen in trendsetting clothes in fashionable bars, discos, etc

poser² ('pəʊzə) *n* a baffling or insoluble question

poseur (pəʊˈzɜː) *n* a person who strikes an attitude or assumes a pose in order to impress others [c19 from French, from *poser* to POSE¹]

posey ('pəʊzɪ) *or* **poserish** ('pəʊzərɪʃ) *adj informal* (of a place) for, characteristic of, or full of posers; affectedly trendy

posh (pɒʃ) *informal, chiefly Brit* ▷ *adj* **1** smart, elegant, or fashionable; exclusive: *posh clothes* **2** upper-class or genteel ▷ *adv* **3** in a manner associated with the upper class: *to talk posh* [c19 often said to be an acronym of the phrase *port out, starboard home*, the most desirable location for a cabin in British ships sailing to and from the East, being the north-facing or shaded side; but more likely to be a development of obsolete slang *posh* a dandy] > 'poshness *n*

posho ('pɒʃɔ) *n E African* **1** corn meal **2** payment of workers in foodstuffs rather than money [from Swahili]

posit ('pɒzɪt) *vb* (*tr*) **1** to assume or put forward as fact or the factual basis for an argument; postulate **2** to put in position ▷ *n* **3** a fact, idea, etc, that is posited; assumption [c17 from Latin *pōnere* to place, position]

positif ('pɒsɪtɪf) *n* (on older organs) a manual controlling soft stops [from French: positive]

position (pəˈzɪʃən) *n* **1** the place, situation, or location of a person or thing: *he took up a position to the rear* **2** the appropriate or customary location: *the telescope is in position for use* **3** the arrangement or disposition of the body or a part of the body: *the corpse was found in a sitting position* **4** the manner in which a person or thing is placed; arrangement **5** *military* an area or point occupied for tactical reasons **6** mental attitude; point of view; stand: *what's your position on this issue?* **7** social status or standing, esp high social standing **8** a post of employment; job **9** the act of positing a fact or viewpoint **10** something posited, such as an idea, proposition, etc **11** *sport* the part of a field or playing area where a player is placed or where he generally operates **12** *music* **a** the vertical spacing or layout of the written notes in a chord. Chords arranged with the three upper voices close together are in **close position**. Chords whose notes are evenly or widely distributed are in **open position**. See also **root position b** one of the points on the fingerboard of a stringed instrument, determining where a string is to be stopped **13** (in classical prosody) **a** the situation in which a short vowel may be regarded as long, that is, when it occurs before two or more consonants **b** make position (of a consonant, either on its own or in combination with other consonants, such as x in Latin) to cause a short vowel to become metrically long when placed after it **14** *finance* the market commitment of a dealer in securities, currencies, or commodities: *a long position; a short position* **15** in a position (foll by an infinitive) able (to): *I'm not in a position to reveal these figures* ▷ *vb* (*tr*) **16** to put in the proper or appropriate place; locate **17** *sport* to place (oneself or another player) in a particular part of the field or playing area **18** to put (someone or something) in a position (esp in relation to others) that confers a strategic advantage: *he's trying to position himself for a leadership bid* **19** *marketing* to promote (a product or service) by tailoring it to the needs of a specific market or by clearly differentiating it from its competitors (eg in terms of price or quality) **20** *rare* to locate or ascertain the position of [c15 from Late Latin *positiō* a positioning, affirmation, from *pōnere* to place, lay down] > po'sitional *adj*

positional notation *n* the method of denoting numbers by the use of a finite number of digits, each digit having its value multiplied by its place value, as in 936 = (9 × 100) + (3 × 10) + 6

position angle *n* the direction in which one object lies relative to another on the celestial sphere, measured in degrees from north in an easterly direction

position audit *n commerce* a systematic assessment of the current strengths and weaknesses of an organization as a prerequisite for future strategic planning

position effect *n* the effect on the phenotype of interacting genes when their relative positions on the chromosome are altered, as by inversion

positioning (pəˈzɪʃᵊnɪŋ) *n* the position held by a product brand in the opinion of consumers, in comparison with its competitors' brands

positive ('pɒzɪtɪv) *adj* **1** characterized by or expressing certainty or affirmation: *a positive answer* **2** composed of or possessing actual or specific qualities; real: *a positive benefit* **3** tending to emphasize what is good or laudable; constructive: *he takes a very positive attitude when*

p

correcting pupils' mistakes **4** tending towards progress or improvement; moving in a beneficial direction **5** *philosophy* **a** a constructive rather than sceptical **b** (of a concept) denoting the presence rather than the absence of some property **6** independent of circumstances; absolute or unqualified **7** (*prenominal*) *informal* (intensifier): *a positive delight* **8** *maths* **a** having a value greater than zero: *a positive number* **b** designating, consisting of, or graduated in one or more quantities greater than zero: *positive direction* **9** *maths* **a** measured in a direction opposite to that regarded as negative **b** having the same magnitude as but opposite sense to an equivalent negative quantity **10** *grammar* denoting the usual form of an adjective as opposed to its comparative or superlative form **11** *biology* indicating movement or growth towards a particular stimulus **12** *physics* **a** (of an electric charge) having an opposite polarity to the charge of an electron and the same polarity as the charge of a proton **b** (of a body, system, ion, etc) having a positive electric charge; having a deficiency of electrons: *a positive ion* **c** (of a point in an electric circuit) having a higher electric potential than some other point with an assigned zero potential **13** short for **electropositive** **14** (of a lens) capable of causing convergence of a parallel beam of light **15** *med* (of the results of an examination or test) indicating the existence or presence of a suspected disorder or pathogenic organism **16** *med* (of the effect of a drug or therapeutic regimen) beneficial or satisfactory **17** short for **Rh positive** **18** (of a machine part) having precise motion with no hysteresis or backlash **19** *chiefly US* (of a government) directly involved in activities beyond the minimum maintenance of law and order, such as social welfare or the organization of scientific research **20** *economics* of or denoting an analysis that is free of ethical, political, or value judgments **21** *astrology* of, relating to, or governed by the group of signs of the zodiac that belong to the air and fire classifications, which are associated with a self-expressive spontaneous nature ▷ *n* **22** something that is positive **23** *maths* a quantity greater than zero **24** *photog* a print or slide showing a photographic image whose colours or tones correspond to those of the original subject **25** *grammar* the positive degree of an adjective or adverb **26** a positive object, such as a terminal or plate in a voltaic cell **27** *music* **a** Also called: **positive organ** a medieval nonportable organ with one manual and no pedals. Compare **portative organ** **b** a variant spelling of **positif** ▷ Compare **negative** [C13 from Late Latin *positīvus* positive, agreed on an arbitrary basis, from *pōnere* to place] > **'positiveness** *or* **,posi'tivity** *n*

positive discrimination *or* **action** *n* the provision of special opportunities in employment, training, etc for a disadvantaged group, such as women, ethnic minorities, etc. US equivalent: **affirmative action**

positive feedback *n* See **feedback** (sense 1)

positively ('pɒzɪtɪvlɪ) *adv* **1** in a positive manner **2** (intensifier): *he disliked her: in fact, he positively hated her* ▷ *sentence substitute* **3** unquestionably; absolutely

positive polarity *n grammar* the grammatical characteristic of a word or phrase, such as *delicious* or *rather*, that may normally only be used in a semantically or syntactically positive or affirmative context

positive vetting *n* the checking of a person's background, political affiliation, etc, to assess his suitability for a position that may involve national security

positivism ('pɒzɪtɪ,vɪzəm) *n* **1** a strong form of empiricism, esp as established in the philosophical system of Auguste Comte, the French mathematician and philosopher (1798–1857), that rejects metaphysics and theology as seeking knowledge beyond the scope of experience, and holds that experimental investigation and observation are the only sources of substantial knowledge. See also **logical positivism** **2** Also called: **legal positivism** the jurisprudential doctrine that the legitimacy of a law depends on its being enacted in proper form, rather than on its content. Compare **natural law** (sense 3) **3** the quality of being definite, certain, etc > **'positivist** *n, adj* > **,positiv'istic** *adj* > **,positiv'istically** *adv*

positron ('pɒzɪ,trɒn) *n physics* the antiparticle of the electron, having the same mass but an equal and opposite charge. It is produced in certain decay processes and in pair production, annihilation occurring when it collides with an electron [C20 from *posi(tive + elec)tron*]

positron emission tomography *n* a technique for assessing brain activity and function by recording the emission of positrons from radioactively labelled substances, such as glucose or dopamine

positronium (,pɒzɪ'trəʊnɪəm) *n physics* a short-lived entity consisting of a positron and an electron bound together. It decays by annihilation to produce two or three photons [C20 from POSITRON + -IUM]

posology (pə'sɒlədʒɪ) *n* the branch of medicine concerned with the determination of appropriate doses of drugs or agents [C19 from French *posologie*, from Greek *posos* how much] > **posological** (,pɒsə'lɒdʒɪkᵊl) *adj*

poss (pɒs) *vb* (*tr*) to wash (clothes) by agitating them with a long rod, pole, etc [of uncertain origin]

poss. *abbreviation for* **1** possession **2** possessive **3** possible **4** possibly

posse ('pɒsɪ) *n* **1** *US* short for **posse comitatus**, the able-bodied men of a district assembled together and forming a group upon whom the sheriff may call for assistance in maintaining law and order **2** *law* possibility (esp in the phrase **in posse**) **3** *slang* a Jamaican street gang in the US **4** *informal* a group of friends or associates [C16 from Medieval Latin (n): power, strength, from Latin (vb): to be able, have power]

posse comitatus (,kɒmɪ'tɑːtəs) *n* the formal legal term for **posse** (sense 1) [Medieval Latin: strength (manpower) of the county]

posser ('pɒsə) *n* a short stick used for stirring clothes in a washtub

possess (pə'zɛs) *vb* (*tr*) **1** to have as one's property; own **2** to have as a quality, faculty, characteristic, etc: *to possess good eyesight* **3** to have knowledge or mastery of: *to possess a little French* **4** to gain control over or dominate: *whatever possessed you to act so foolishly?* **5** (foll by *of*) to cause to be the owner or possessor: *I am possessed of the necessary information* **6** (often foll by *with*) to cause to be influenced or dominated (by): *the news possessed him with anger* **7** to have sexual intercourse with **8** *now rare* to keep control over or maintain (oneself or one's feelings) in a certain state or condition: *possess yourself in patience until I tell you the news* **9** *archaic* to gain or seize [C15 from Old French *possesser*, from Latin *possidēre* to own, occupy; related to Latin *sedēre* to sit] > **pos'sessor** *n*

possessed (pə'zɛst) *adj* **1** (foll by *of*) owning or having **2** (*usually postpositive*) under the influence of a powerful force, such as a spirit or strong emotion **3** a less common word for **self-possessed**

possession (pə'zɛʃən) *n* **1** the act of possessing or state of being possessed: *in possession of the crown* **2** anything that is owned or possessed **3** (*plural*) wealth or property **4** the state of being controlled or dominated by or as if by evil spirits **5** the physical control or occupancy of land, property, etc, whether or not accompanied by ownership: *to take possession of a house* **6** a territory subject to a foreign state or to a sovereign prince: *colonial possessions* **7** *sport* control of the ball, puck, etc, as exercised by a player or team: *he lost possession*

possession order *n* (in Britain) a court order that entitles a landlord legally to evict a tenant or squatter and regain possession of the property

possessive (pə'zɛsɪv) *adj* **1** of or relating to possession or ownership **2** having or showing an excessive desire to possess, control, or dominate: *a possessive mother* **3** *grammar* **a** another word for **genitive** (sense 1) **b** denoting an inflected form of a noun or pronoun used to convey the idea of possession, association, etc, as *my* or *Harry's* ▷ *n* **4** *grammar* **a** the possessive case **b** a word or speech element in the possessive case > **pos'sessively** *adv* > **pos'sessiveness** *n*

possessory (pə'zɛsərɪ) *adj* **1** of, relating to, or having possession **2** *law* arising out of, depending upon, or concerned with possession: *a possessory title*

posset ('pɒsɪt) *n* a drink of hot milk curdled with ale, beer, etc, flavoured with spices, formerly used as a remedy for colds [C15 *poshoote*, of unknown origin]

possibility (,pɒsɪ'bɪlɪtɪ) *n, pl* **-ties** **1** the state or condition of being possible **2** anything that is possible **3** a competitor, candidate, etc, who has a moderately good chance of winning, being chosen, etc **4** (*often plural*) a future prospect or potential: *my new house has great possibilities*

possible ('pɒsɪbᵊl) *adj* **1** capable of existing, taking place, or proving true without contravention of any natural law **2** capable of being achieved: *it is not possible to finish in three weeks* **3** having potential or capabilities for favourable use or development: *the idea is a possible money-spinner* **4** that may or may not happen or have happened; feasible but less than probable: *it is possible that man will live on Mars* **5** *logic* (of a statement, formula, etc) capable of being true under some interpretation, or in some circumstances. Usual symbol: *Mp* or ◇*p*, where *p* is the given expression ▷ *n* **6** another word for **possibility** (sense 3) [C14 from Latin *possibilis* that may be, from *posse* to be able, have power]

> USAGE Although it is very common to talk about something being *very possible* or *more possible*, these uses are generally thought to be incorrect, since *possible* describes an absolute state, and therefore something can only be *possible* or *not possible*: *it is very likely* (not *very possible*) *that he will resign; it has now become easier* (not *more possible*) *to obtain an entry visa*

possible world *n logic* (in modal logic) a semantic device formalizing the notion of what the world might have been like. A statement is necessarily true if and only if it is true in every possible world

possibly ('pɒsɪblɪ) *sentence substitute, adv* **1** **a** perhaps or maybe **b** (*as sentence modifier*): *possibly he'll come* ▷ *adv* **2** by any chance; at all: *he can't possibly come*

possie *or* **pozzy** ('pɒzɪ) *n Austral and NZ informal* a place; position: *if we're early for the film we'll get a good possie at the back*

possum ('pɒsəm) *n* **1** an informal name for **opossum** (sense 1) **2** *Austral and NZ* any of various Australasian arboreal marsupials, such as *Trichosurus vulpecula* (**brush-tailed phalanger**), having dense fur and a long tail: family *Phalangeridae*. Also called: **phalanger** **3** **play possum** to pretend to be dead, ignorant, asleep, etc, in order to deceive an opponent

post¹ (pəʊst) *n* **1** a length of wood, metal, etc, fixed upright in the ground to serve as a support, marker, point of attachment, etc **2** *horse racing* **a** either of two upright poles marking the beginning (**starting post**) and end (**winning post**) of a racecourse **b** the finish of a horse race **3** any of the main upright supports of a piece of furniture, such as a four-poster bed ▷ *vb* (*tr*) **4** (sometimes foll by *up*) to fasten or put up (a notice) in a public place **5** to announce by means of or as if by means of a poster: *to post banns* **6** to

publish (a name) on a list [Old English, from Latin *postis;* related to Old High German *first* ridgepole, Greek *pastas* colonnade]
post[2] (pəʊst) *n* **1** a position to which a person is appointed or elected; appointment; job **2** a position or station to which a person, such as a sentry, is assigned for duty **3** a permanent military establishment **4** *Brit* either of two military bugle calls (**first post** and **last post**) ordering or giving notice of the time to retire for the night **5** See **trading post** (senses 1, 2) ▷ *vb* **6** (*tr*) to assign to or station at a particular place or position **7** *chiefly Brit* to transfer to a different unit or ship on taking up a new appointment, etc [C16 from French *poste,* from Italian *posto,* ultimately from Latin *pōnere* to place]
post[3] (pəʊst) *n* **1** *chiefly Brit* letters, packages, etc, that are transported and delivered by the Post Office; mail **2** *chiefly Brit* a single collection or delivery of mail **3** *Brit* an official system of mail delivery **4** an item of electronic mail made publicly available **5** (formerly) any of a series of stations furnishing relays of men and horses to deliver mail over a fixed route **6** a rider who carried mail between such stations **7** *Brit* another word for **pillar box** **8** *Brit* short for **post office** **9** a size of writing or printing paper, 15¼ by 19 inches or 16½ by 21 inches (**large post**) **10** any of various book sizes, esp 5¼ by 8¼ inches (**post octavo**) and 8¼ by 10¼ inches (**post quarto**) **11** **by return of post** *Brit* by the next mail in the opposite direction ▷ *vb* **12** (*tr*) *chiefly Brit* to send by post. US and Canadian word: **mail** **13** (*tr*) to make (electronic mail) publicly available **14** (*tr*) *book-keeping* **a** to enter (an item) in a ledger **b** (often foll by *up*) to compile or enter all paper items in (a ledger) **15** (*tr*) to inform of the latest news (esp in the phrase **keep someone posted**) **16** (*intr*) (of a rider) to rise from and reseat oneself in a saddle in time with the motions of a trotting horse; perform a rising trot **17** (*intr*) (formerly) to travel with relays of post horses **18** *archaic* to travel or dispatch with speed; hasten ▷ *adv* **19** with speed; rapidly **20** by means of post horses [C16 via French from Italian *poste,* from Latin *posita* something placed, from *pōnere* to put, place]
POST *abbreviation for* point of sales terminal
post- *prefix* **1** after in time or sequence; following; subsequent: *postgraduate* **2** behind; posterior to: *postorbital* [from Latin, from *post* after, behind]
postage (ˈpəʊstɪdʒ) *n* **a** the charge for delivering a piece of mail **b** (*as modifier*): *postage charges*
postage due stamp *n* a stamp affixed by a Post Office to a letter, parcel, etc, indicating that insufficient or no postage has been prepaid and showing the amount to be paid by the addressee on delivery
postage meter *n* *chiefly US and Canadian* a postal franking machine. Also called: **postal meter**
postage stamp *n* **1** a printed paper label with a gummed back for attaching to mail as an official indication that the required postage has been paid **2** a mark directly printed or embossed on an envelope, postcard, etc, serving the same function
postal (ˈpəʊstᵊl) *adj* of or relating to a Post Office or to the mail-delivery service > ˈ**postally** *adv*
postal card *n* *US* another term for **postcard**
postal code *n* *Canadian* a code of letters and digits used as part of a postal address to aid the sorting of mail. Also called (in Britain and certain other countries): **postcode**. US equivalent zip code
postal note *n* *Austral and NZ* the usual name for **postal order**
postal order *n* a written order for the payment of a sum of money, to a named payee, obtainable and payable at a post office
post-and-rail fence *n* a fence constructed of upright wooden posts with horizontal timber slotted through it
post-and-rail tea *n* *Austral informal* (in the 19th century) a coarse tea in which floating particles resembled a post-and-rail fence
postaxial (pəʊstˈæksɪəl) *adj* *anatomy* **1** situated or occurring behind the axis of the body **2** of or relating to the posterior part of a vertebrate limb
postbag (ˈpəʊstˌbæg) *n* **1** *chiefly Brit* another name for **mailbag** **2** the mail received by a magazine, radio programme, public figure, etc
post-bellum (ˈpəʊstˈbɛləm) *adj* (*prenominal*) of or during the period after a war, esp the American Civil War [C19 Latin *post* after + *bellum* war]
postbox (ˈpəʊstˌbɒks) *n* *chiefly Brit* a box into which mail is put for collection by the postal service. Also called: **letter box**
postboy (ˈpəʊstˌbɔɪ) *n* **1** a man or boy who brings the post round to offices **2** another name for **postilion**
postbus (ˈpəʊstˌbʌs) *n* (in Britain, esp in rural districts) a vehicle carrying the mail that also carries passengers
post captain *n* *history* (formerly) a naval officer holding a commission as a captain, as distinct from an officer with the courtesy title of captain
postcard (ˈpəʊstˌkɑːd) *n* a card, often bearing a photograph, picture, etc, on one side, (**picture postcard**), for sending a message by post without an envelope. Also called (US): **postal card**
postcava (pəʊstˈkɑːvə, -ˈkeɪvə) *n* *anatomy* the inferior vena cava [C19 New Latin; see POST-, VENA CAVA] > **postˈcaval** *adj*
post chaise *n* a closed four-wheeled horse-drawn coach used as a rapid means for transporting mail and passengers in the 18th and 19th centuries [C18 from POST[3] + CHAISE]
postcode (ˈpəʊstˌkəʊd) *n* *Brit and Austral* a code of letters and digits used as part of a postal address to aid the sorting of mail. Also called: **postal code**. US equivalent: **zip code**
postcode discrimination *n* discrimination on the basis of the area where someone lives, with relation to employment, credit rating, etc
postcode lottery *n* *Brit* a situation in which the standard of medical care, education, etc, received by the public varies from area to area, depending on the funding policies of various health boards, local authorities, etc
postcode prescribing *n* *Brit* the practice of prescribing more or less expensive and effective medical treatments to patients depending on where they live in a country, and which treatments their health board is willing and able to provide
postcoital (pəʊstˈkəʊɪtəl) *adj* of or relating to the period after sexual intercourse
post-colonial *adj* existing or occurring since a colony gained independence: *post-colonial Nigeria*
Postcomm (ˈpəʊstˌkɒm) *n* (in Britain) the Postal Services Commission, a body set up to look after the interests of postal service users
post-consumer *adj* **a** (of a consumer item) having been discarded for disposal or recovery **b** having been recycled
post-cyclic *adj* *transformational grammar* denoting rules that apply only after the transformations of a whole cycle. Compare **cyclic** (sense 6), **last-cyclic**
postdate (pəʊstˈdeɪt) *vb* (*tr*) **1** to write a future date on (a document), as on a cheque to prevent it being paid until then **2** to assign a date to (an event, period, etc) that is later than its previously assigned date of occurrence **3** to be or occur at a later date than
postdiluvian (ˌpəʊstdɪˈluːvɪən, -daɪ-) *adj* *also* **postdiluvial** **1** existing or occurring after the biblical Flood ▷ *n* **2** a person or thing existing after the biblical Flood [C17 from POST- + *diluvian,* from Latin *diluvium* deluge, flood]
postdoctoral (pəʊstˈdɒktərəl) *adj* of, relating to, or designating studies, research, or professional work above the level of a doctorate
postelection (ˌpəʊstɪˈlɛkʃən) *adj* happening or existing after an election
poster (ˈpəʊstə) *n* **1** a large printed picture, used for decoration **2** a placard or bill posted in a public place as an advertisement
poster boy *or* **poster girl** *n* **1** a person who appears on a poster **2** a person who typifies or represents a particular characteristic, cause, opinion, etc: *a poster girl for late motherhood* ▷ Also called: **poster child**
poste restante (ˈpəʊst rɪˈstænt; *French* pɔst rɛstɑ̃t) *n* **1** (not in the US and Canada) an address on mail indicating that it should be kept at a specified post office until collected by the addressee **2** the mail-delivery service or post-office department that handles mail having this address ▷ US and Canadian equivalent: **general delivery** [French, literally: mail remaining]
posterior (pɒˈstɪərɪə) *adj* **1** situated at the back of or behind something **2** coming after or following another in a series **3** coming after in time **4** *zoology* (of animals) of or near the hind end **5** *botany* (of a flower) situated nearest to the main stem **6** *anatomy* dorsal or towards the spine ▷ Compare **anterior** ▷ *n* **7** the buttocks; rump **8** *statistics* a posterior probability [C16 from Latin: latter, from *posterus* coming next, from *post* after] > **posˈteriorly** *adv*
posterior probability *n* *statistics* the probability assigned to some parameter or to an event on the basis of its observed frequency in a sample, and calculated from a prior probability by Bayes' theorem. Compare **prior probability** See also **empirical** (sense 5)
posterity (pɒˈstɛrɪtɪ) *n* **1** future or succeeding generations **2** all of one's descendants [C14 from French *postérité,* from Latin *posteritās* future generations, from *posterus* coming after, from *post* after]
postern (ˈpɒstən) *n* **1** a back door or gate, esp one that is for private use ▷ *adj* **2** situated at the rear or the side [C13 from Old French *posterne,* from Late Latin *posterula (jānua)* a back (entrance), from *posterus* coming behind; see POSTERIOR, POSTERITY]
poster paint *or* **colour** *n* a gum-based opaque watercolour paint used for writing posters, etc
post exchange *n* *US* a government-subsidized shop operated mainly for military personnel. Abbreviation: **PX**
postexilian (ˌpəʊstɪgˈzɪlɪən) *or* **postexilic** *adj* *Old Testament* existing or occurring after the Babylonian exile of the Jews (587–539 BC)
post-fascist *adj* **1** of or relating to various right-wing political parties in Europe which espouse a modified form of fascism and which take part in constitutional politics ▷ *n* **2** a member or supporter of such a party
postfeminist (pəʊstˈfɛmɪnɪst) *adj* **1** resulting from or including the beliefs and ideas of feminism **2** differing from or showing moderation of these beliefs and ideas ▷ *n* **3** a person who believes in or advocates any of the ideas that have developed from the feminist movement
postfix *vb* (pəʊstˈfɪks) **1** (*tr*) to add or append at the end of something; suffix ▷ *n* (ˈpəʊstˌfɪks) **2** a less common word for **suffix**
post-Fordism (ˌpəʊstˈfɔːdɪzəm) *n* the idea that modern industrial production has moved away from mass production in huge factories, as pioneered by Henry Ford, the US car manufacturer (1863–1947), towards specialized markets based on small flexible manufacturing units > ˌ**post-ˈFordist** *adj*
post-free *adv* ▷ *adj* **1** *Brit* with the postage prepaid; post-paid **2** free of postal charge
postglacial (pəʊstˈgleɪsɪəl) *adj* formed or occurring after a glacial period, esp after the Pleistocene epoch
postgraduate (pəʊstˈgrædjʊɪt) *n* **1** a student who has obtained a degree from a university, etc, and is pursuing studies for a more advanced qualification **2** (*modifier*) of or relating to such a student or to his studies ▷ Also (US and Canadian): **graduate**
posthaste (ˈpəʊstˈheɪst) *adv* **1** with great haste; as fast as possible ▷ *n* **2** *archaic* great haste

post hoc ('pəʊst 'hɒk) *n logic* the fallacy of assuming that temporal succession is evidence of causal relation [from Latin, short for *Post hoc ergo propter hoc* after this, therefore on account of this]

post horn *n* a simple valveless natural horn consisting of a long tube of brass or copper, either straight or coiled; formerly often used to announce the arrival of a mailcoach

post horse *n* (formerly) a horse kept at an inn or post house for use by postriders or for hire to travellers

post house *n* (formerly) a house or inn where horses were kept for postriders or for hire to travellers

posthumous ('pɒstjʊməs) *adj* **1** happening or continuing after one's death **2** (of a book, etc) published after the author's death **3** (of a child) born after the father's death [c17 from Latin *postumus* the last, but modified as though from Latin *post* after + *humus* earth, that is, after the burial] > **'posthumously** *adv*

posthypnotic suggestion (ˌpəʊsthɪp'nɒtɪk) *n* a suggestion made to the subject while in a hypnotic trance, to be acted upon at some time after emerging from the trance

postical ('pɒstiːk³l) or **posticous** (pɒ'stiːkəs, -'staɪ-) *adj* (of the position of plant parts) behind another part; posterior ▷ Compare **antical** [c19 from Latin *postīcus* that is behind, from *post* after]

postiche (pɒ'stiːʃ) *adj* **1** (of architectural ornament) inappropriately applied; sham **2** false or artificial; spurious ▷ *n* **3** another term for **hairpiece** (sense 2) **4** an imitation, counterfeit, or substitute **5** anything that is false; sham or pretence [c19 from French, from Italian *apposticcio* (n), from Late Latin *appositīcius* (adj); see APPOSITE]

postie ('pəʊstɪ) *n Scot, Austral, and NZ informal* a postman

postil ('pɒstɪl) *n* **1** a commentary or marginal note, as in a Bible **2** a homily or collection of homilies ▷ *vb* **-tils, -tiling, -tiled** or **-tils, -tilling, -tilled 3** *obsolete* to annotate (a biblical passage) [c15 (postille): from Old French *postille* from Medieval Latin *postilla,* perhaps from *post illa* (*verba textus*), after these words in the text, often the opening phrase of such an annotation]

postilion or **postillion** (pɒ'stɪljən) *n* a person who rides the near horse of the leaders in order to guide a team of horses drawing a coach [c16 from French *postillon,* from Italian *postiglione,* from *posta* POST[3]]

postimpressionism (ˌpəʊstɪm'preʃəˌnɪzəm) *n* a movement in painting in France at the end of the 19th century, begun by Paul Cézanne (1839–1906) and exemplified by Paul Gauguin (1848–1903), Vincent Van Gogh (1853–90), and Henri Matisse (1869–1954), which rejected the naturalism and momentary effects of impressionism but adapted its use of pure colour to paint subjects with greater subjective emotion > **ˌpostim'pressionist** *n, adj* > **ˌpostim,pression'istic** *adj*

postindustrial (ˌpəʊstɪn'dʌstrɪəl) *adj* characteristic of, relating to, or denoting work or a society that is no longer based on heavy industry

posting[1] ('pəʊstɪŋ) *n* a wrestling attack in which the opponent is hurled at the post in one of the corners of the ring

posting[2] ('pəʊstɪŋ) *n* **1** an appointment to a position or post, usually in another town or country **2** an electronic mail message sent to a bulletin board, website, etc, and intended for access by every user

Post-it Note *n trademark* a small square of sticky paper on which notes can be written

postliminy (pəʊst'lɪmɪnɪ) or **postliminium** (ˌpəʊstlɪ'mɪnɪəm) *n, pl* **-inies** or **-inia** (-ɪnɪə) *international law* the right by which persons and property seized in war are restored to their former status on recovery [c19 (in this sense): from Latin *postlīminium* a return behind one's threshold, from *līmen* threshold]

postlude ('pəʊstluːd) *n* **1** *music* a final or concluding piece or movement **2** a voluntary played at the end of a Church service [c19 from POST- + -*lude,* from Latin *lūdus* game; compare PRELUDE]

postman ('pəʊstmən) or *feminine* **postwoman** *n, pl* **-men** or **-women** a person who carries and delivers mail as a profession

postman's knock *n* a children's party game in which a kiss is exchanged for a pretend letter

postmark ('pəʊstˌmɑːk) *n* **1** any mark stamped on mail by postal officials, such as a simple obliteration, date mark, or indication of route. See also **cancellation** ▷ *vb* **2** (*tr*) to put such a mark on mail

postmaster ('pəʊstˌmɑːstə) *n* **1** Also (feminine): **postmistress** an official in charge of a local post office **2** the person responsible for managing the electronic mail at a site

postmaster general *n, pl* **postmasters general** the executive head of the postal service in certain countries

postmenopausal (ˌpəʊstmɛnəʊ'pɔːz³l) *adj* existing or taking place after the menopause

postmeridian (ˌpəʊstmə'rɪdɪən) *adj* after noon; in the afternoon or evening [c17 from Latin *postmerīdiānus* in the afternoon; see POST-, MERIDIAN]

post meridiem ('pəʊst mə'rɪdɪəm) the full form of **p.m.** [c17 Latin: after noon]

post mill *n* a windmill built round a central post on which the whole mill can be turned so that the sails catch the wind

postmillennial (ˌpəʊstmɪ'lɛnɪəl) *adj* existing or taking place after the millennium

postmillennialism (ˌpəʊstmɪ'lɛnɪəˌlɪzəm) *n* the doctrine or belief that the Second Coming of Christ will be preceded by the millennium > **ˌpostmil'lennialist** *n*

postmodern (pəʊst'mɒdən) *adj* (in the arts, architecture, etc) characteristic of a style and school of thought that rejects the dogma and practices of any form of modernism; in architecture, contrasting with international modernism and featuring elements from several periods, esp the Classical, often with ironic use of decoration > **post'modern ism** *n* > **post'modernist** *n, adj*

postmortem (pəʊst'mɔːtəm) *adj* **1** (*prenominal*) occurring after death ▷ *n* **2** analysis or study of a recently completed event: *a postmortem on a game of chess* **3** See **postmortem examination** [c18 from Latin, literally: after death]

postmortem examination *n* dissection and examination of a dead body to determine the cause of death. Also called: **autopsy, necropsy**

postnasal drip (pəʊst'neɪz³l) *n med* a mucus secretion from the rear part of the nasal cavity into the nasopharynx, usually as the result of a cold or an allergy

postnatal (pəʊst'neɪt³l) *adj* existing or taking place after giving birth

Postnet ('pəʊstnɛt) *n South African* an official postal service in South Africa

post-obit (pəʊst'əʊbɪt, -'ɒbɪt) *chiefly law* ▷ *n* **1** Also called: **post-obit bond** a bond given by a borrower, payable after the death of a specified person, esp one given to a moneylender by an expectant heir promising to repay when his interest falls into possession ▷ *adj* **2** taking effect after death [c18 from Latin *post obitum* after death]

post office *n* a building or room where postage stamps are sold and other postal business is conducted

Post Office *n* a government department or authority in many countries responsible for postal services and often telecommunications

post office box *n* a private numbered place in a post office, in which letters received are kept until called for

postoperative (pəʊst'ɒpərətɪv, -'ɒprətɪv) *adj* of, relating to, or occurring in the period following a surgical operation > **post'operatively** *adv*

postorbital (pəʊst'ɔːbɪt³l) *adj anatomy* situated behind the eye or the eye socket

post-paid *adv, adj* with the postage prepaid

postpartum (pəʊst'pɑːtəm) *adj med* following childbirth [Latin: after the act of giving birth]

postpone (pəʊst'pəʊn, pə'spəʊn) *vb* (*tr*) **1** to put off or delay until a future time **2** to put behind in order of importance; defer [c16 from Latin *postpōnere* to put after, neglect, from POST- + *ponere* to place] > **post'ponable** *adj* > **post'ponement** *n* > **post'poner** *n*

postposition (ˌpəʊstpə'zɪʃən) *n* **1** placement of a modifier or other speech element after the word that it modifies or to which it is syntactically related **2** a word or speech element so placed > **ˌpostpo'sitional** *adj* > **ˌpostpo'sitionally** *adv*

postpositive (pəʊst'pɒzɪtɪv) *adj* **1** (of an adjective or other modifier) placed after the word modified, either immediately after, as in *two men abreast,* or as part of a complement, as in *those men are bad* ▷ *n* **2** a postpositive modifier > **post'positively** *adv*

postprandial (pəʊst'prændɪəl) *adj* of or relating to the period immediately after lunch or dinner: *a postprandial nap*

postproduction (ˌpəʊstprə'dʌkʃən) *n* **a** the work on a film or a television programme, such as editing, dubbing, etc, that takes place after shooting or videotaping is completed **b** (*as modifier*): *postproduction costs*

post-Reformation *adj* happening or existing in the period or age after the Reformation

post-Revolutionary *adj* of or relating to the period or age after a revolution

postrider ('pəʊstˌraɪdə) *n* (formerly) a person who delivered post on horseback

post road *n* a road or route over which post is carried and along which post houses were formerly sited

post-rock *n* **1** a type of music that often varies from traditional rock in terms of form and instrumentation ▷ *adj* **2** of or relating to this type of music

postscript ('pəʊsˌskrɪpt, 'pəʊst-) *n* **1** a message added at the end of a letter, after the signature **2** any supplement, as to a document or book [c16 from Late Latin *postscribere* to write after, from POST- + *scribere* to write]

postseason (pəʊst'siːz³n) *chiefly US* ▷ *adj* **1** of or relating to the period after the end of a regular sporting season ▷ *n* **2** the period after the end of a regular sporting season: *home run drought in the postseason*

poststructuralism (pəʊst'strʌktʃərəˌlɪzəm) *n* an approach to literature that, proceeding from the tenets of structuralism, maintains that, as words have no absolute meaning, any text is open to an unlimited range of interpretations > **post'structuralist** *n, adj*

post town *n* a town having a main Post Office branch

post-traumatic stress disorder *n* a psychological condition, characterized by anxiety, withdrawal, and a proneness to physical illness, that may follow a traumatic experience. Abbreviation: **PTSD**

postulant ('pɒstjʊlənt) *n* a person who makes a request or application, esp a candidate for admission to a religious order [c18 from Latin *postulāns* asking, from *postulāre* to ask, demand] > **'postulancy** or **'postulantˌship** *n*

postulate *vb* ('pɒstjʊˌleɪt) (*tr; may take a clause as object*) **1** to assume to be true or existent; take for granted **2** to ask, demand, or claim **3** to nominate (a person) to a post or office subject to approval by a higher authority ▷ *n* ('pɒstjʊlɪt) **4** something taken as self-evident or assumed as the basis of an argument **5** a necessary condition or prerequisite **6** a fundamental principle **7** *logic, maths* an unproved and indemonstrable statement that should be taken for granted: used as an initial premise or underlying hypothesis in a process of reasoning [C16 from Latin *postulāre* to ask for, require; related to *pōscere* to request] > ˌpostuˈlation *n*

postulator ('pɒstjʊˌleɪtə) *n* RC Church a person, usually a priest, deputed to prepare and present a plea for the beatification or canonization of some deceased person

posture ('pɒstʃə) *n* **1** a position or attitude of the limbs or body **2** a characteristic manner of bearing the body; carriage: *to have good posture* **3** the disposition of the parts of a visible object **4** a mental attitude or frame of mind **5** a state, situation, or condition **6** a false or affected attitude; pose ▷ *vb* **7** to assume or cause to assume a bodily position or attitude **8** (*intr*) to assume an affected or unnatural bodily or mental posture; pose [C17 via French from Italian *postura*, from Latin *positūra*, from *pōnere* to place] > 'postural *adj* > 'posturer *n*

posturize or **posturise** ('pɒstʃəˌraɪz) *vb* a less common word for **posture** (senses 7, 8)

postviral syndrome (ˌpəʊstˈvaɪrəl) *n* another name for **myalgic encephalopathy** Abbreviation: PVS

postvocalic (ˌpəʊstvəˈkælɪk) *adj* phonetics following a vowel

post-war *adj* happening or existing after a war: *the early post-war years*

posy ('pəʊzɪ) *n, pl* -**sies** **1** a small bunch of flowers or a single flower; nosegay **2** archaic a brief motto or inscription, esp one on a trinket or a ring [C16 variant of POESY]

pot[1] (pɒt) *n* **1** a container made of earthenware, glass, or similar material; usually round and deep, often having a handle and lid, used for cooking and other domestic purposes **2** short for **flowerpot, teapot 3** the amount that a pot will hold; potful **4** a chamber pot, esp a small one designed for a baby or toddler **5** a handmade piece of pottery **6** a large mug or tankard, as for beer **7** Austral any of various measures used for serving beer **8** informal a cup or trophy, esp of silver, awarded as a prize in a competition **9** the money or stakes in the pool in gambling games, esp poker **10** (*often plural*) informal a large amount, esp of money **11** a wicker trap for catching fish, esp crustaceans: *a lobster pot* **12** billiards, snooker a shot by which a ball is pocketed **13** chiefly Brit short for **chimneypot 14** US informal a joint fund created by a group of individuals or enterprises and drawn upon by them for specified purposes **15** hunting See **pot shot 16** See **potbelly 17** go to pot to go to ruin; deteriorate ▷ *vb* pots, potting, potted (*mainly tr*) **18** to set (a plant) in a flowerpot to grow **19** to put or preserve (goods, meat, etc) in a pot **20** to cook (food) in a pot **21** to shoot (game) for food rather than for sport **22** to shoot (game birds or animals) while they are on the ground or immobile rather than flying or running **23** (*also intr*) to shoot casually or without careful aim at (an animal, etc) **24** to sit (a baby or toddler) on a chamber pot **25** (*also intr*) to shape clay as a potter **26** billiards, snooker to pocket (a ball) **27** informal to capture or win; secure ▷ See also **pot on** [Late Old English *pott*, from Medieval Latin *pottus* (unattested), perhaps from Latin *pōtus* a drink; compare Middle Low German *pot*, Old Norse *pottr*]

pot[2] (pɒt) *n* a Scot and northern English dialect a deep hole or pothole **b** (*capital when part of a name*): *Pen-y-Ghent Pot* [C14 perhaps identical with POT[1] but possibly of Scandinavian origin; compare Swedish dialect *putt* water hole, pit]

pot[3] (pɒt) *n* slang cannabis used as a drug in any form, such as leaves (marijuana or hemp) or resin (hashish) [C20 perhaps shortened from Mexican Indian *potiguaya*]

pot[4] (pɒt) *n* informal short for **potentiometer**

potable ('pəʊtəb³l) *adj* a less common word for **drinkable** ▷ *n* **2** something fit to drink; a beverage [C16 from Late Latin *pōtābilis* drinkable, from Latin *pōtāre* to drink] > ˌpota'bility *n*

potae ('pɒtaɪ) *n* NZ a hat [Māori]

potage French (pɔtaʒ; English pəʊˈtɑːʒ) *n* any thick soup [C16 from Old French; see POTTAGE]

potager ('pɒtɪdʒə) *n* a small kitchen garden [C17 from French *potagère* vegetable garden]

potamic (pəˈtæmɪk) *adj* of or relating to rivers [C19 from Greek *potamos* river]

potamology (ˌpɒtəˈmɒlədʒɪ) *n* obsolete the scientific study of rivers [C19 from Greek *potamos* river + -LOGY]

potash ('pɒtæʃ) *n* **1** another name for **potassium carbonate**, esp the form obtained by leaching wood ash **2** another name for **potassium hydroxide 3** potassium chemically combined in certain compounds: *chloride of potash* [C17 pot ashes, translation of obsolete Dutch *potaschen*; so called because originally obtained by evaporating the lye of wood ashes in pots]

potash alum *n* the full name for **alum** (sense 1)

potassium (pəˈtæsɪəm) *n* a light silvery element of the alkali metal group that is highly reactive and rapidly oxidizes in air; occurs principally in carnallite and sylvite. It is used when alloyed with sodium as a cooling medium in nuclear reactors and its compounds are widely used, esp in fertilizers. Symbol: K; atomic no.: 19; atomic wt.: 39.0983; valency: 1; relative density: 0.862; melting pt.: 63.71°C; boiling pt.: 759°C [C19 New Latin *potassa* potash] > po'tassic *adj*

potassium-argon dating *n* a technique for determining the age of minerals based on the occurrence in natural potassium of a small fixed amount of radioisotope ^{40}K that decays to the stable argon isotope ^{40}Ar with a half-life of 1.28×10^9 years. Measurement of the ratio of these isotopes thus gives the age of the mineral. Compare **radiocarbon dating, rubidium-strontium dating**

potassium bitartrate *n* another name (not in technical usage) for **potassium hydrogen tartrate**

potassium bromide *n* a white crystalline soluble substance with a bitter saline taste used in making photographic papers and plates and in medicine as a sedative. Formula: KBr

potassium carbonate *n* a white odourless substance used in making glass and soft soap and as an alkaline cleansing agent. Formula: K_2CO_3

potassium chlorate *n* a white crystalline soluble substance used in fireworks, matches, and explosives, and as a disinfectant and bleaching agent. Formula: $KClO_3$

potassium chloride *n* a white soluble crystalline substance used as a fertilizer and in medicine to prevent potassium deficiency. Formula: KCl

potassium cyanide *n* a white poisonous granular soluble solid substance used in photography and in extracting gold from its ores. Formula: KCN

potassium dichromate *n* an orange-red crystalline soluble solid substance that is a good oxidizing agent and is used in making chrome pigments and as a bleaching agent. Formula: $K_2Cr_2O_7$

potassium ferrocyanide *n* a yellow soluble crystalline compound used in case-hardening steel and making dyes and pigments. Formula: $K_4Fe(CN)_6$. Also called: potassium hexacyanoferrate (II), yellow prussiate of potash

potassium hydrogen tartrate *n* a colourless or white soluble crystalline salt used in baking powders, soldering fluxes, and laxatives. Formula: $KHC_4H_4O_6$. Also called (not in technical usage): potassium bitartrate, cream of tartar

potassium hydroxide *n* a white deliquescent alkaline solid used in the manufacture of soap, liquid shampoos, and detergents. Formula: KOH. Also called: caustic potash See also **lye**

potassium nitrate *n* a colourless or white crystalline compound used in gunpowders, pyrotechnics, fertilizers, and as a preservative for foods, esp as a curing salt for ham, sausages, etc (E252). Formula: KNO_3. Also called: saltpetre, nitre

potassium permanganate *n* a dark purple

poisonous odourless soluble crystalline solid, used as a bleach, disinfectant, and antiseptic. Formula: $KMnO_4$. Systematic name: potassium manganate(VII)

potassium sulphate *n* a soluble substance usually obtained as colourless crystals of the decahydrate: used in making glass and as a fertilizer. Formula: K_2SO_4

potation (pəʊˈteɪʃən) *n* **1** the act of drinking **2** a drink or draught, esp of alcoholic drink [C15 from Latin *pōtātiō* a drinking, from *pōtāre* to drink]

potato (pəˈteɪtəʊ) *n, pl* -toes **1** Also called: Irish potato, white potato **a** a solanaceous plant, *Solanum tuberosum*, of South America: widely cultivated for its edible tubers **b** the starchy oval tuber of this plant, which has a brown or red skin and is cooked and eaten as a vegetable **2** any of various similar plants, esp the sweet potato **3** hot potato slang a delicate or awkward matter [C16 from Spanish *patata* white potato, from Taino *batata* sweet potato]

potato beetle *n* another name for the **Colorado beetle**

potato blight *n* a devastating disease of potatoes produced by the oomycete *Phytophthora infestans* and the cause of the Irish potato famine of the mid-19th century

potato chip *n* **1** (*usually plural*) another name for **chip** (sense 4) **2** (*usually plural*) US and Canadian a very thin slice of potato fried and eaten cold as a snack. Also called (in eg Britain): **crisp**

potato crisp *n* (*usually plural*) another name for **crisp** (sense 10)

potatory ('pəʊtətərɪ, -trɪ) *adj* rare of, relating to, or given to drinking [C19 from Late Latin *pōtātōrius* concerning drinking, from Latin *pōtāre* to drink]

pot-au-feu (French pɔtofø) *n* **1** a traditional French stew of beef and vegetables **2** the large earthenware casserole in which this is cooked [literally: pot on the fire]

potbelly ('pɒtˌbelɪ) *n, pl* -lies **1** a protruding or distended belly **2** a person having such a belly **3** US and Canadian a small bulbous stove in which wood or coal is burned > 'pot,bellied *adj*

potboiler ('pɒtˌbɔɪlə) *n* informal a literary or artistic work of little merit produced quickly in order to make money

pot-bound *adj* (of a pot plant) having grown to fill all the available root space and therefore lacking room for continued growth

potboy ('pɒtˌbɔɪ) or **potman** ('pɒtmən) *n, pl* -boys or -men chiefly Brit (esp formerly) a youth or man employed at a public house to serve beer, etc

potch (pɒtʃ) *n* chiefly Austral slang inferior quality opal used in jewellery for mounting precious opals [C20 of uncertain origin]

pot cheese *n* US a type of coarse dry cottage cheese

poteen or **poitín** (pɒˈtiːn) *n* (in Ireland) illicit spirit, often distilled from potatoes [C19 from Irish *poitín* little pot, from *pota* pot]

potency ('pəʊtnsɪ) or **potence** *n, pl* -tencies or -tences **1** the state or quality of being potent **2** latent or inherent capacity for growth or development [C16 from Latin *potentia* power, from *posse* to be able]

potent[1] ('pəʊt³nt) *adj* **1** possessing great strength; powerful **2** (of arguments, etc) persuasive or forceful **3** influential or authoritative **4** tending to produce violent physical or chemical effects: *a potent poison* **5** (of a male) capable of having sexual intercourse [C15 from Latin *potēns* able, from *posse* to be able] > 'potently *adv* > 'potentness *n*

potent[2] ('pəʊt³nt) *adj* heraldry (of a cross) having flat bars across the ends of the arms [C17 from obsolete *potent* a crutch, from Latin *potentia* power]

potentate ('pəʊt³nˌteɪt) *n* a person who possesses great power or authority, esp a ruler or monarch [C14 from Late Latin *potentātus* ruler, from Latin: rule, command, from *potens* powerful, from *posse* to be able]

potential (pəˈtenʃəl) *adj* **1 a** possible but not yet

p

actual **b** (*prenominal*) capable of being or becoming but not yet in existence; latent **2** *grammar* (of a verb or form of a verb) expressing possibility, as English *may* and *might* **3** an archaic word for **potent**[1] ▷ *n* **4** latent but unrealized ability or capacity: *Jones has great potential as a sales manager* **5** *grammar* a potential verb or verb form **6** short for **electric potential** [c14 from Old French *potencial,* from Late Latin *potentiālis,* from Latin *potentia* power] > po'**tentially** *adv*

potential difference *n* the difference in electric potential between two points in an electric field; the work that has to be done in transferring unit positive charge from one point to the other, measured in volts. Symbol: *U, ΔV or Δφ.* Abbreviation: **pd**. Compare **electromotive force**

potential divider *n* a tapped or variable resistor or a chain of fixed resistors in series, connected across a source of voltage and used to obtain a desired fraction of the total voltage. Also called: **voltage divider**

potential energy *n* the energy of a body or system as a result of its position in an electric, magnetic, or gravitational field. It is measured in joules (SI units), electronvolts, ergs, etc. Symbol: E_p, V, U or φ. Abbreviation: **PE**

potentiality (pəˌtɛnʃɪˈælɪtɪ) *n, pl* -**ties** **1** latent or inherent capacity or ability for growth, fulfilment, etc **2** a person or thing that possesses such a capacity

potential well *n physics* a localized region in a field of force in which the potential has a deep minimum

potentiate (pəˈtɛnʃɪˌeɪt) *vb* (*tr*) **1** to cause to be potent **2** *med* to increase (the individual action or effectiveness) of two drugs by administering them in combination with each other

potentilla (ˌpəʊtˀnˈtɪlə) *n* any rosaceous plant or shrub of the N temperate genus *Potentilla,* having five-petalled flowers. See also **cinquefoil** (sense 1), **silverweed** (sense 1), **tormentil** [c16 New Latin, from Medieval Latin: garden valerian, from Latin *potēns* powerful, **POTENT**[1]]

potentiometer (pəˌtɛnʃɪˈɒmɪtə) *n* **1** an instrument for determining a potential difference or electromotive force by measuring the fraction of it that balances a standard electromotive force **2** a device with three terminals, two of which are connected to a resistance wire and the third to a brush moving along the wire, so that a variable potential can be tapped off: used in electronic circuits, esp as a volume control. Sometimes shortened to: **pot** > po,tenti'**ometry** *n*

potentiometric (pəˌtɛnʃɪəˈmɛtrɪk) *adj chem* (of a titration) having the end point determined by a change in potential of an electrode immersed in the solution

potful (ˈpɒtfʊl) *n* the amount held by a pot

pothead (ˈpɒtˌhɛd) *n slang* a habitual user of cannabis

pothecary (ˈpɒθɪkərɪ) *n, pl* -**caries** an archaic or Brit dialect variant of **apothecary**

potheen (pɒˈtiːn, pɒˈθiːn) *n* a rare variant of **poteen**

pother (ˈpɒðə) *n* **1** a commotion, fuss, or disturbance **2** a choking cloud of smoke, dust, etc ▷ *vb* **3** to make or be troubled or upset [c16 of unknown origin]

potherb (ˈpɒtˌhɜːb) *n* any plant having leaves, flowers, stems, etc, that are used in cooking for seasoning and flavouring or are eaten as a vegetable

pothole (ˈpɒtˌhəʊl) *n* **1** *geography* **a** a deep hole in limestone areas resulting from action by running water. See also **sinkhole** (sense 1) **b** a circular hole in the bed of a river produced by abrasion **2** a deep hole, esp one produced in a road surface by wear or weathering

potholing (ˈpɒtˌhəʊlɪŋ) *n Brit* a sport in which participants explore underground caves > 'pot,**holer** *n*

pothook (ˈpɒtˌhʊk) *n* **1** a curved or S-shaped hook

used for suspending a pot over a fire **2** a long hook used for lifting hot pots, lids, etc **3** an S-shaped mark, often made by children when learning to write

pothouse (ˈpɒtˌhaʊs) *n Brit* (formerly) a small tavern or pub

pothunter (ˈpɒtˌhʌntə) *n* **1** a person who hunts for food or for profit without regard to the rules of sport **2** *informal* a person who enters competitions for the sole purpose of winning prizes > 'pot,**hunting** *n, adj*

potiche (pɒˈtiːʃ) *n, pl* -**tiches** (-ˈtiːʃɪz, -ˈtiːʃ) a tall vase or jar, as of porcelain, with a round or polygonal body that narrows towards the neck and a detached lid or cover [French, from *pot* pot; compare **POTTAGE**]

potion (ˈpəʊʃən) *n* **1** a drink, esp of medicine, poison, or some supposedly magic beverage **2** a rare word for **beverage** [c13 via Old French from Latin *pōtiō* a drink, especially a poisonous one, from *pōtāre* to drink]

Potiphar (ˈpɒtɪfə) *n Old Testament* one of Pharaoh's officers, who bought Joseph as a slave (Genesis 37:36)

potlatch (ˈpɒtˌlætʃ) *n* **1** *anthropol* a competitive ceremonial activity among certain North American Indians, esp the Kwakiutl, involving a lavish distribution of gifts and the destruction of property to emphasize the wealth and status of the chief or clan **2** *US and Canadian informal* a wild party or revel [c19 from Chinook, from Nootka *patshatl* a giving, present]

pot liquor *n chiefly US* the broth in which meat, esp pork or bacon, and vegetables have been cooked

pot luck *n informal* **1 a** whatever food happens to be available without special preparation **b** (*as modifier*): *a pot-luck dinner* **2** whatever is available (esp in the phrase **take pot luck**)

potman (ˈpɒtmən) *n, pl* -**men** *chiefly Brit* another word for **potboy**

pot marigold *n* a Central European and Mediterranean plant, *Calendula officinalis,* grown for its rayed orange-and-yellow showy flowers, the petals of which were formerly used to colour food: family *Asteraceae* (composites). See also **calendula**

Potomac (pəˈtəʊmək) *n* a river in the E central US, rising in the Appalachian Mountains of West Virginia: flows northeast, then generally southeast to Chesapeake Bay. Length (from the confluence of headstreams): 462 km (287 miles)

potometer (pəˈtɒmɪtə) *n* an apparatus that measures the rate of water uptake by a plant or plant part [from Latin *pōtāre* to drink + **-METER**]

pot on *vb* (*tr, adverb*) to transfer (a plant) to a larger flowerpot

potoroo (ˌpɒtəˈruː) *n* another name for **kangaroo rat** [from a native Australian language]

Potosí (*Spanish* potoˈsi) *n* a city in S Bolivia, at an altitude of 4066 m (13 340 ft): one of the highest cities in the world; developed with the discovery of local silver in 1545; tin mining; university (1571). Pop: 144 000 (2005 est)

potpie (ˈpɒtˌpaɪ) *n* a meat and vegetable stew with a pie crust on top

pot plant *n* a plant grown in a flowerpot, esp indoors

potpourri (ˌpəʊˈpʊərɪ) *n, pl* -**ris** **1** a collection of mixed flower petals dried and preserved in a pot to scent the air **2** a collection of unrelated or disparate items; miscellany **3** a medley of popular tunes **4** a stew of meat and vegetables [c18 from French, literally: rotten pot, translation of Spanish *olla podrida* miscellany]

pot roast *n* meat, esp beef, that is browned and cooked slowly in a covered pot with very little water, often with vegetables added

Potsdam (ˈpɒtsdæm; *German* ˈpɔtsdam) *n* a city in Germany, the capital of Brandenburg on the Havel River: residence of Prussian kings and German emperors and scene of the **Potsdam Conference** of 1945, at which the main Allied powers agreed on a

plan to occupy Germany at the end of the Second World War. Pop: 144 979 (2003 est)

potsherd (ˈpɒtˌʃɜːd) or **potshard** (ˈpɒtˌʃɑːd) *n* a broken fragment of pottery [c14 from **POT**[1] + *schoord* piece of broken crockery; see **SHARD**]

pot shot *n* **1** a chance shot taken casually, hastily, or without careful aim **2** a shot fired to kill game in disregard of the rules of sport **3** a shot fired at quarry within easy range, often from an ambush

pot still *n* a type of still used in distilling whisky in which heat is applied directly to the pot in which the wash is contained

potstone (ˈpɒtˌstəʊn) *n* an impure massive variety of soapstone, formerly used for making cooking vessels

pottage (ˈpɒtɪdʒ) *n* a thick meat or vegetable soup [c13 from Old French *potage* contents of a pot, from *pot* **POT**[1]]

potted (ˈpɒtɪd) *adj* **1** placed or grown in a pot **2** cooked or preserved in a pot: *potted shrimps* **3** *informal* summarized or abridged: *a potted version of a novel*

potter[1] (ˈpɒtə) *n* a person who makes pottery

potter[2] (ˈpɒtə) *or esp US and Canadian* **putter** *chiefly Brit* ▷ *vb* **1** (*intr; often foll by about or around*) to busy oneself in a desultory though agreeable manner **2** (*intr; often foll by along or about*) to move with little energy or direction: *to potter about town* **3** (*tr; usually foll by away*) to waste (time): *to potter the day away* ▷ *n* **4** the act of pottering [c16 (in the sense: to poke repeatedly): from Old English *potian* to thrust; see **PUT**] > 'potterer *or esp US and Canadian* 'putterer *n*

Potteresque (ˌpɒtəˈrɛsk) *adj* resembling or suggestive of scenes and situations described in the Harry Potter novels of UK writer JK Rowling (born 1965)

Potteries (ˈpɒtərɪz) *pl n* (*sometimes functioning as singular*) **the** a region of W central England, in Staffordshire, in which the china and earthenware industries are concentrated

potter's field *n* **1** *US* a cemetery where the poor or unidentified are buried at the public expense **2** *New Testament* the land bought by the Sanhedrin with the money paid for the betrayal of Jesus (which Judas had returned to them) to be used as a burial place for strangers and the friendless poor (Acts 1:19; Matthew 27:7)

potter's wheel *n* a device with a horizontal rotating disc, on which clay is shaped into pots, bowls, etc, by hand

potter wasp *n* any of various solitary wasps of the genus *Eumenes,* which construct vaselike cells of mud or clay, in which they lay their eggs: family *Vespidae*

pottery (ˈpɒtərɪ) *n, pl* -**teries** **1** articles, vessels, etc, made from earthenware and dried and baked in a kiln **2** a place where such articles are made **3** the craft or business of making such articles ▷ Related adjective: **fictile** [c13 from Old French *poterie,* from *potier* potter, from *pot* **POT**[1]]

potting shed (ˈpɒtɪŋ) *n* a building in which plants are set in flowerpots and in which empty pots, potting compost, etc, are stored

pottle (ˈpɒtˀl) *n* **1** *archaic* a liquid measure equal to half a gallon **2** *NZ* a plastic or cardboard container for foods such as yoghurt, fruit salad, or cottage cheese [c14 *potel,* from Old French: a small **POT**[1]]

potto (ˈpɒtəʊ) *n, pl* -**tos** **1** a short-tailed prosimian primate, *Perodicticus potto,* having vertebral spines protruding through the skin in the neck region, native to tropical forests in West and Central Africa: family *Lorisidae* **2** **golden potto** another name for **angwantibo** **3** another name for **kinkajou** [c18 of West African origin; compare Wolof *pata* type of tail-less monkey]

Pott's disease (pɒts) *n* a disease of the spine, usually caused by tubercular infection and characterized by weakening and gradual disintegration of the vertebrae and the intervertebral discs [c18 named after Percivall *Pott*

(1714–88), English surgeon]

Pott's fracture *n* a fracture of the lower part of the fibula, usually with dislocation of the ankle [C18 see POTT'S DISEASE]

potty[1] ('pɒtɪ) *adj* -tier, -tiest *Brit informal* **1** foolish or slightly crazy **2** trivial or insignificant **3** (foll by *about* or *on*) very keen (about) [C19 perhaps from POT[1]] > **'pottiness** *n*

potty[2] ('pɒtɪ) *n, pl* -ties a child's word for chamber pot

pottymouth ('pɒtɪˌmaʊθ) *n informal* a person who habitually uses foul language

pot-walloper or **potwaller** ('pɒtˌwɒlə) *n* (in some English boroughs) a man entitled to the franchise before 1832 by virtue of possession of his own fireplace [C18 from POT[1] + *wallop* to boil furiously, from Old English *weallan* to boil]

pouch (paʊtʃ) *n* **1** a small flexible baglike container: *a tobacco pouch* **2** a saclike structure in any of various animals, such as the abdominal receptacle marsupium in marsupials or the cheek fold in rodents **3** *anatomy* any sac, pocket, or pouchlike cavity or space in an organ or part **4** another word for **mailbag 5** a Scot word for **pocket** ⊳ *vb* **6** (*tr*) to place in or as if in a pouch **7** to arrange or become arranged in a pouchlike form **8** (*tr*) (of certain birds and fishes) to swallow [C14 from Old Norman French *pouche*, from Old French *poche* bag; see POKE[2]] > **'pouchy** *adj*

pouched (paʊtʃt) *adj* having a pouch or pouches

pouf or **pouffe** (puːf) *n* **1** a large solid cushion, usually cylindrical or cubic in shape, used as a seat **2 a** a woman's hair style, fashionable esp in the 18th century, in which the hair is piled up in rolled puffs **b** a pad set in the hair to make such puffs **3** a stuffed pad worn under panniers **4** (puf, puːf) *Brit derogatory slang* less common spellings of **poof** [C19 from French; see PUFF]

Poujadism ('puːʒɑːdɪzəm) *n* a conservative reactionary movement to protect the business interests of small traders [C20 named after Pierre *Poujade* (born 1920), French publisher and bookseller who founded such a movement in 1954] > **'Poujadist** *n, adj*

poulard or **poularde** ('puːlɑːd) *n* a hen that has been spayed for fattening. Compare **capon** [C18 from Old French *pollarde*, from *polle* hen; see PULLET]

poult[1] (pəʊlt) *n* the young of a gallinaceous bird, esp of domestic fowl [C15 syncopated variant of *poulet* PULLET]

poult[2] (pult) *n* a fine plain-weave fabric of silk, rayon, nylon, etc, with slight ribs across it. Also called: **poult-de-soie** [C20 from French; of unknown origin; compare PADUASOY]

poulterer ('pəʊltərə) *n Brit* another word for a **poultryman** [C17 from obsolete *poulter*, from Old French *pouletier*, from *poulet* PULLET]

poultice ('pəʊltɪs) *n* **1** Also called: **cataplasm** *med* a local moist and often heated application for the skin consisting of substances such as kaolin, linseed, or mustard, used to improve the circulation, treat inflamed areas, etc **2** *Austral slang* a large sum of money, esp a debt [C16 from earlier *pultes*, from Latin *puls* a thick porridge]

poultry ('pəʊltrɪ) *n* domestic fowls collectively [C14 from Old French *pouletrie*, from *pouletier* poultry-dealer]

poultryman ('pəʊltrɪmən) or **poulterer** *n, pl* -trymen or -terers **1** Also called: **chicken farmer** a person who rears domestic fowls, esp chickens, for their eggs or meat **2** a dealer in poultry, esp one who sells the dressed carcasses

pounce[1] (paʊns) *vb* **1** (*intr*; often foll by *on* or *upon*) to spring or swoop, as in capturing prey ⊳ *n* **2** the act of pouncing; a spring or swoop **3** the claw of a bird of prey [C17 apparently from Middle English *punson* pointed tool; see PUNCHEON[2]] > **'pouncer** *n*

pounce[2] (paʊns) *vb* (*tr*) to emboss (metal) by hammering from the reverse side [C15 *pounsen*, from Old French *poinçonner* to stamp; perhaps the same as POUNCE[1]]

pounce[3] (paʊns) *n* **1** a very fine resinous powder, esp of cuttlefish bone, formerly used to dry ink or sprinkled over parchment or unsized writing paper to stop the ink from running **2** a fine powder, esp of charcoal, that is tapped through perforations in paper corresponding to the main lines of a design in order to transfer the design to another surface **3** (*as modifier*): *a pounce box* ⊳ *vb* (*tr*) **4** to dust (paper) with pounce **5** to transfer (a design) by means of pounce [C18 from Old French *ponce*, from Latin *pūmex* PUMICE] > **'pouncer** *n*

pouncet box ('paʊnsɪt) *n* a box with a perforated top used for containing perfume [C16 *pouncet*, perhaps alteration of *pounced* punched, perforated; see POUNCE[1]]

pound[1] (paʊnd) *vb* **1** (when *intr*, often foll by *on* or *at*) to strike heavily and often **2** (*tr*) to beat to a pulp; pulverize **3** (*tr*) to instil by constant drilling: *to pound Latin into him* **4** (*tr*; foll by *out*) to produce, as by typing heavily **5** to walk (the pavement, street, etc) repeatedly: *he pounded the pavement looking for a job* **6** (*intr*) to throb heavily ⊳ *n* **7** a heavy blow; thump **8** the act of pounding [Old English *pūnian*; related to Dutch *puin* rubble] > **'pounder** *n*

pound[2] (paʊnd) *n* **1** an avoirdupois unit of weight that is divided into 16 ounces and is equal to 0.453 592 kilograms. Abbreviation: **lb 2** a troy unit of weight divided into 12 ounces equal to 0.373 242 kilograms. Abbreviation: **lb tr** or **lb t 3** an apothecaries' unit of weight, used in the US, that is divided into 5760 grains and is equal to one pound troy **4** (*not in technical usage*) a unit of force equal to the mass of 1 pound avoirdupois where the acceleration of free fall is 32.174 feet per second per second. Abbreviation: **lbf 5 a** the standard monetary unit of the United Kingdom, the Channel Islands, the Isle of Man, and various UK overseas territories, divided into 100 pence. Official name: **pound sterling b** (*as modifier*): *a pound coin* **6** the standard monetary unit of the following countries **a** Cyprus: divided into 100 cents **b** Egypt: divided into 100 piastres **c** Lebanon: divided into 100 piastres **d** Syria: divided into 100 piastres **7** another name for **lira** (sense 2) **8** Also called: **pound Scots** a former Scottish monetary unit originally worth an English pound but later declining in value to 1 shilling 8 pence **9** the former standard monetary unit of the Republic of Ireland, divided into 100 pence; replaced by the euro in 2002. Also called: **punt 10** a former monetary unit of the Sudan replaced by the dinar in 1992 [Old English *pund*, from Latin *pondō* pound; related to German *Pfund* pound, Latin *pondus* weight]

pound[3] (paʊnd) *n* **1** an enclosure, esp one maintained by a public authority, for keeping officially removed vehicles or distrained goods or animals, esp stray dogs **2** a place where people are confined **3 a** a trap for animals **b** a trap or keepnet for fish. See **pound net** ⊳ *vb* **4** (*tr*) to confine in or as if in a pound; impound, imprison, or restrain [C14 from Late Old English *pund-* as in *pundfeald* PINFOLD]

poundage[1] ('paʊndɪdʒ) *n* **1** a tax, charge, or other payment of so much per pound of weight **2** a tax, charge, or other payment of so much per pound sterling **3** a weight expressed in pounds

poundage[2] ('paʊndɪdʒ) *n agriculture* **a** confinement of livestock within a pound **b** the fee required for freeing a head of livestock from a pound

poundal ('paʊndᵊl) *n* the fps unit of force; the force that imparts an acceleration of 1 foot per second per second to a mass of 1 pound. 1 poundal is equivalent to 0.1382 newton or 1.382×10^4 dynes. Abbreviation: **pdl** [C19 from POUND[2] + QUINTAL]

pound cake *n* a rich fruit cake originally made with a pound each of butter, sugar, and flour

pound cost averaging *n stock exchange* a method of accumulating capital by investing a fixed sum in a particular security at regular intervals, in order to achieve an average purchase price below the arithmetic average of the market prices on the purchase dates

-pounder ('paʊndə) *n* (*in combination*) **1** something weighing a specified number of pounds: *a 200-pounder* **2** something worth a specified number of pounds: *a ten-pounder* **3** a gun that discharges a shell weighing a specified number of pounds: *a two-pounder*

pound net *n* a fishing trap having an arrangement of standing nets directing the fish into an enclosed net

pound of flesh *n* something that is one's legal right but is an unreasonable demand (esp in the phrase **to have one's pound of flesh**) [from Shakespeare's *The Merchant of Venice* (1596), Act IV, scene i]

pound sterling *n* the official name for the standard monetary unit of the United Kingdom. See **pound**[2] (sense 5)

pour (pɔː) *vb* **1** to flow or cause to flow in a stream **2** (*tr*) to issue, emit, etc, in a profuse way **3** (*intr*; often foll by *down*) Also: **pour with rain** to rain heavily: *it's pouring down outside* **4** (*intr*) to move together in large numbers; swarm **5** (*intr*) to serve tea, coffee, etc: *shall I pour?* **6 it never rains but it pours** events, esp unfortunate ones, come together or occur in rapid succession **7 pour cold water on** *informal* to be unenthusiastic about or discourage **8 pour oil on troubled waters** to try to calm a quarrel, etc ⊳ *n* **9** a pouring, downpour, etc [C13 of unknown origin]

■ USAGE The verbs *pour* and *pore* are sometimes confused: *she poured cream over her strudel; she pored (not poured) over the manuscript*

pourboire *French* (purbwar) *n* a tip; gratuity [literally: for drinking]

pour encourager les autres *French* (pur ākuraʒe lez otrə) in order to encourage the others: often used ironically

pourparler *French* (purparle; *English* pʊəˈpɑːleɪ) *n* an informal or preliminary conference [literally: for speaking]

pourpoint ('pʊəˌpɔɪnt) *n* a man's stuffed quilted doublet of a kind worn between the Middle Ages and the 17th century [C15 from Old French, from *pourpoindre* to stick, from *pour-* variant of *par-*, from Latin *per* through + *poindre* to pierce, from Latin *pungere* to puncture]

pour point *n chem* the lowest temperature at which a mineral oil will flow under specified conditions

pousse-café *French* (puskafe) *n* **1** a drink of liqueurs of different colours in unmixed layers **2** any liqueur taken with coffee at the end of a meal [literally: coffee-pusher]

poussette (puːˈsɛt) *n* **1** a figure in country dancing in which couples hold hands and move up or down the set to change positions ⊳ *vb* **2** (*intr*) to perform such a figure [C19 from French, from *pousser* to push]

poussin (*French* pusẽ) *n* a young chicken reared for eating [from French]

pou sto ('puː ˈstəʊ) *n, pl* **pou stos** *literary* **1** a place upon which to stand **2** a basis of operation [Greek: where I may stand, from Archimedes' saying that he could move the earth if given a place to stand]

pout[1] (paʊt) *vb* **1** to thrust out (the lips), as when sullen, or (of the lips) to be thrust out **2** (*intr*) to swell out; protrude **3** (*tr*) to utter with a pout ⊳ *n* **4** (*sometimes* **the pouts**) a fit of sullenness **5** the act or state of pouting [C14 of uncertain origin; compare Swedish dialect *puta* inflated, Danish *pude* PILLOW] > **'poutingly** *adv* > **'pouty** *adj*

pout[2] (paʊt) *n, pl* **pout** or **pouts 1** short for **horned pout** or **eelpout 2** any of various gadoid food fishes, esp the bib (also called **whiting pout**) **3** any of certain other stout-bodied fishes [Old English *-pūte* as in *ǣlepūte* eelpout; related to Dutch *puit* frog]

p

pouter ('paʊtə) n **1** a person or thing that pouts **2** a breed of domestic pigeon with a large crop capable of being greatly puffed out

poutine (puːˈtiːn) n Canadian a dish of chipped potatoes topped with curd cheese and a tomato-based sauce [from Canadian French]

poverty ('pɒvətɪ) n **1** the condition of being without adequate food, money, etc **2** scarcity or dearth: *a poverty of wit* **3** a lack of elements conducive to fertility in land or soil [c12 from Old French *poverté*, from Latin *paupertās* restricted means, from *pauper* POOR]

poverty-stricken adj suffering from extreme poverty

poverty trap n the situation of being unable to escape poverty because of being dependent on state benefits, which are reduced by the same amount as any extra income gained

pow[1] (paʊ) interj an exclamation imitative of a collision, explosion, etc

pow[2] (paʊ) n Scot the head or a head of hair [a Scot variant of POLL]

pow[3] (paʊ) n Scot a creek or slow stream [c15 from earlier Scots *poll*]

POW abbreviation for prisoner of war

powan ('paʊən) n **1** a freshwater whitefish, *Coregonus clupeoides*, occurring in some Scottish lakes **2** any of certain similar related fishes, such as the vendace ▷ Also called: lake herring [c17 Scottish variant of POLLAN]

powder ('paʊdə) n **1** a solid substance in the form of tiny loose particles **2** any of various preparations in this form, such as gunpowder, face powder, or soap powder **3** fresh loose snow, esp when considered as skiing terrain **4** take a powder US and Canadian slang to run away or disappear ▷ vb **5** to turn into powder; pulverize **6** (tr) to cover or sprinkle with or as if with powder [c13 from Old French *poldre*, from Latin *pulvis* dust] > 'powderer n > 'powdery adj

powder blue n **a** a dusty pale blue colour **b** (as adjective): *a powder-blue coat*

powder burn n a superficial burn of the skin caused by a momentary intense explosion, esp of gunpowder

powder compact n See compact (sense 11)

powder flask n a small flask or case formerly used to carry gunpowder

powder horn n a powder flask consisting of the hollow horn of an animal

powder keg n **1** a small barrel used to hold gunpowder **2** informal a potential source or scene of violence, disaster, etc

powder metallurgy n the science and technology of producing solid metal components from metal powder by compaction and sintering

powder monkey n (formerly) a boy who carried powder from the magazine to the guns on warships

powder puff n a soft pad or ball of fluffy material used for applying cosmetic powder to the skin

powder room n euphemistic a lavatory for women in a restaurant, department store, etc

powdery mildew n **1** a plant disease characterized by a superficial white powdery growth on stems and leaves, caused by parasitic ascomycetous fungi of the family *Erysiphaceae*: affects the rose, aster, apple, vine, oak, etc **2** any of the fungi causing this disease ▷ Compare downy mildew

power ('paʊə) n **1** ability or capacity to do something **2** (often plural) a specific ability, capacity, or faculty **3** political, financial, social, etc, force or influence **4** control or dominion or a position of control, dominion, or authority **5** a state or other political entity with political, industrial, or military strength **6** a person who exercises control, influence, or authority: *he's a power in the state* **7** a prerogative, privilege, or liberty **8 a** legal authority to act, esp in a specified capacity, for another **b** the document conferring such authority **9 a** a military force **b** military potential **10** maths **a** the value of a number or quantity raised to some exponent **b** another name for **exponent** (sense 4) **11** statistics the probability of rejecting the null hypothesis in a test when it is false. The power of a test of a given null depends on the particular alternative hypothesis against which it is tested **12** physics, engineering a measure of the rate of doing work expressed as the work done per unit time. It is measured in watts, horsepower, etc. Symbol: *P* **13 a** the rate at which electrical energy is fed into or taken from a device or system. It is expressed, in a direct-current circuit, as the product of current and voltage and, in an alternating-current circuit, as the product of the effective values of the current and voltage and the cosine of the phase angle between them. It is measured in watts **b** (as modifier): *a power amplifier* **14** the ability to perform work **15 a** mechanical energy as opposed to manual labour **b** (as modifier): *a power mower* **16** a particular form of energy: *nuclear power* **17 a** a measure of the ability of a lens or optical system to magnify an object, equal to the reciprocal of the focal length. It is measured in dioptres **b** another word for **magnification 18** informal a large amount or quantity: *a power of good* **19** (plural) the sixth of the nine orders into which the angels are traditionally divided in medieval angelology **20 in one's power** (often foll by an infinitive) able or allowed (to) **21 in (someone's) power** under the control or sway of (someone) **22 the powers that be** the established authority or administration ▷ vb (tr) **23** to give or provide power to **24** to fit (a machine) with a motor or engine **25** (intr) slang to travel with great speed or force ▷ See also **power down, power up** [c13 from Anglo-Norman *poer*, from Vulgar Latin *potēre* (unattested), from Latin *posse* to be able]

power amplifier n electronics an amplifier that is usually the final amplification stage in a device and is designed to give the required power output

power-assisted adj (of the steering or brakes in a motor vehicle) helped by mechanical power

powerboat ('paʊəˌbəʊt) n a boat propelled by an inboard or outboard motor

powerboating ('paʊəˌbəʊtɪŋ) n the sport of driving powerboats in racing competitions

power brand n a brand of product that is a household name associated with a successful company

power broker n a person with power and influence, esp one who operates behind the scenes

power cut n a temporary interruption or reduction in the supply of electrical power to a particular area. Sometimes shortened to: cut

power dive n **1** a steep dive by an aircraft with its engines at high power ▷ vb **power-dive 2** to cause (an aircraft) to perform a power dive or (of an aircraft) to perform a power dive

power down vb (tr, adverb) to shut down (a computer system) in a methodical way, concluding by switching the power off

power dressing n a style of dressing in severely tailored suits, adopted by some women executives to project an image of efficiency

power drill n a hand tool with a rotating chuck driven by an electric motor and designed to take an assortment of tools for drilling, grinding, polishing, etc

power factor n (in an electrical circuit) the ratio of the power dissipated to the product of the input volts times amps

power forward n basketball **a** the position of one of the two players responsible for blocking shots and catching rebounds **b** a player in this position

powerful ('paʊəfʊl) adj **1** having great power, force, potency, or effect **2** extremely effective or efficient in action: *a powerful drug; a powerful lens* **3** dialect large or great: *a powerful amount of trouble* ▷ adv **4** dialect extremely; very: *he ran powerful fast* > 'powerfully adv > 'powerfulness n

powerhouse ('paʊəˌhaʊs) n **1** an electrical generating station or plant **2** informal a forceful or powerful person or thing

power kiting n an activity in which a person, sitting in a small buggy or wearing skis, etc, is propelled by the wind power generated by a large kite to which he or she is attached by ropes > power kite n

powerless ('paʊəlɪs) adj without power or authority > 'powerlessly adv > 'powerlessness n

powerlifting ('paʊəˌlɪftɪŋ) n a form of weightlifting in which contestants compete in the dead lift, squat, and bench press > 'power,lifter n

power line n a set of conductors used to transmit and distribute electrical energy. Sometimes shortened to: line

power lunch n a high-powered business meeting conducted over lunch

power nap n a short sleep taken during the working day with the intention of improving the quality of work later in the day

power of appointment n property law authority to appoint persons either from a particular class (**special power**) or selected by the donee of the power (**general power**) to take an estate or interest in property

power of attorney n **1** legal authority to act for another person in certain specified matters **2** the document conferring such authority ▷ Also called: letter of attorney

power pack n a device for converting the current from a supply into direct or alternating current at the voltage required by a particular electrical or electronic device

power plant n **1** the complex, including machinery, associated equipment, and the structure housing it, that is used in the generation of power, esp electrical power **2** the equipment supplying power to a particular machine or for a particular operation or process

power play n **1** behaviour or tactics intended to magnify a person's influence or power **2** the use of brute strength or force of numbers in order to achieve an objective

power point n **1** an electrical socket mounted on or recessed into a wall **2** such a socket, esp one installed before the introduction of 13 ampere ring mains, that is designed to provide a current of up to 15 amperes for supplying heaters, etc, rather than lights

power politics n (functioning as singular) (in international affairs) the threat or use of force as an instrument of national policy

power series n a mathematical series whose terms contain ascending positive integral powers of a variable, such as $a_0 + a_1x + a_2x^2 + ...$

power set n maths, logic a set the elements of which are all the subsets of a given set

power-sharing n a political arrangement in which opposing groups in a society participate in government

power station n an electrical generating station

power steering n a form of steering used on vehicles, where the torque applied to the steering wheel is augmented by engine power. Also called: power-assisted steering

power structure n **1** the structure or distribution of power and authority in a community **2** the people and groups who are part of such a structure

power tool n a tool powered by electricity

power up vb **1** (tr, adverb) to switch on the power to (a computer system) **2** to begin to make good use of or take full advantage of

power walking n walking at a brisk pace while pumping the arms as part of an aerobic exercise routine

power yoga n a form of yoga involving aerobic exercises and constant strenuous movement

powfagged ('paʊˌfægd) adj Northern English dialect exhausted

powhiri (ˌpəʊˈfiːrɪ) *n* NZ a Māori ceremony of welcome, esp to a marae [Māori]

powwow (ˈpaʊˌwaʊ) *n* **1** a talk, conference, or meeting **2** a magical ceremony of certain North American Indians, usually accompanied by feasting and dancing **3** (among certain North American Indians) a medicine man **4** a meeting of or negotiation with North American Indians ▷ *vb* **5** (*intr*) to hold a powwow [c17 from Algonquian; related to Natick *pauwau* one who practises magic, Narraganset *powwaw*]

Powys (ˈpaʊɪs) *n* a county in E Wales, formed in 1974 from most of Breconshire, Montgomeryshire, and Radnorshire. Administrative centre: Llandrindod Wells. Pop: 129 300 (2003 est). Area: 5077 sq km (1960 sq miles)

pox (pɒks) *n* **1** any disease characterized by the formation of pustules on the skin that often leave pockmarks when healed **2** (usually preceded by *the*) an informal name for **syphilis 3** a pox on (someone *or* something) (*interjection*) *archaic* an expression of intense disgust or aversion for (someone *or* something) [c15 changed from *pocks,* plural of POCK]

poxy (ˈpɒksɪ) *adj* poxier, poxiest *slang* **1** having or having had syphilis **2** rotten; lousy

Poyang Lake *or* **P'o-yang** (ˈpɔːˈjæŋ) *n* a lake in E China, in N Jiangxi province, connected by canal with the Yangtze River: the second largest lake in China. Area (at its greatest): 2780 sq km (1073 sq miles)

Poynting theorem (ˈpɔɪntɪŋ) *n* the theorem that the rate of flow of electromagnetic energy through unit area is equal to the **Poynting vector,** i.e. the cross product of the electric and magnetic field intensities [c19 named after John Henry *Poynting* (1852–1914), English physicist]

Poznań (*Polish* ˈpɔznajn) *n* a city in W Poland, on the Warta River: the centre of Polish resistance to German rule (1815–1918, 1939–45). Pop: 661 000 (2005 est). German name: Posen

Pozsony (ˈpoʒonj) *n* the Hungarian name for **Bratislava**

pozzuolana (ˌpɒtswəˈlɑːnə) *or* **pozzolana** (ˌpɒtsəˈlɑːnə) *n* **1** a type of porous volcanic ash used in making hydraulic cements **2** any of various artificial substitutes for this ash used in cements ▷ Also called: puzzolana [c18 from Italian: of POZZUOLI]

Pozzuoli (*Italian* potˈtswɔːli) *n* a port in SW Italy, in Campania on the **Gulf of Pozzuoli** (an inlet of the Bay of Naples): in a region of great volcanic activity; founded in the 6th century BC by the Greeks. Pop: 78 754 (2001)

pozzy (ˈpɒzɪ) *n, pl* pozzies a variant spelling of **possie**

pp *abbreviation for* **1** past participle **2** (in formal correspondence) per pro [Latin *per procurationem*: by delegation to] **3** privately printed **4** *music symbol for* pianissimo: an instruction to play very quietly

▎ USAGE In formal correspondence, when Brenda Smith is signing on behalf of Peter Jones, she should write *Peter Jones* pp (or *per pro*) *Brenda Smith,* not the other way about

pp *or* **PP** *abbreviation for* **1** parcel post **2** prepaid **3** post-paid **4** (in prescriptions) post prandium [Latin: after a meal]

PP *abbreviation for* **1** Parish Priest **2** past President

pp *abbreviation for* pages

P2P *abbreviation for* **peer-to-peer**

PPARC (in Britain) *abbreviation for* Particle Physics and Astronomy Research Council

ppd *abbreviation for* **1** post-paid **2** prepaid

PPE *abbreviation for* **1** philosophy, politics, and economics: a university course **2** personal protective equipment: clothing and equipment used to ensure personal safety in the workplace

ppm *abbreviation for* **1** *chem* parts per million **2** Also: PPM peak programme meter

PPP *abbreviation for* **1** purchasing power parity: a rate of exchange between two currencies that gives them equal purchasing powers in their own economies **2** private-public partnership: an agreement in which a private company commits skills or capital to a public-sector project for a financial return

ppr *or* **p.pr.** *abbreviation for* present participle

PPS *abbreviation for* **1** parliamentary private secretary **2** Also: pps post postscriptum [(for sense 2) Latin: after postscript; additional postscript]

PPTA (in New Zealand) *abbreviation for* Post-primary Teachers Association

pq *abbreviation for* previous question

PQ (in Canada) *abbreviation for* **1** (esp in postal addresses) Province of Quebec **2** Parti Québécois

PQE *or* **Pqe** *abbreviation for* post-qualification experience

pr *abbreviation for* **1** (*pl* prs) pair **2** paper **3** (in prescriptions) per rectum [Latin: through the rectum; to be inserted into the anus] **4** power

pr *the internet domain name for* Puerto Rico

Pr *the chemical symbol for* praseodymium

PR *abbreviation for* **1** proportional representation **2** public relations **3** Puerto Rico

Pr. *abbreviation for* **1** Priest **2** Prince

pracharak (prəˈtʃɑːrək) *n* (in India) a person appointed to propagate a cause through personal contact, meetings, public lectures, etc [Hindi]

practicable (ˈpræktɪkəbəl) *adj* **1** capable of being done; feasible **2** usable [c17 from French *praticable,* from *pratiquer* to practise; see PRACTICAL]
> ˌpractica'bility *or* 'practicableness *n*
> 'practicably *adv*

▎ USAGE See at **practical**

practical (ˈpræktɪkəl) *adj* **1** of, involving, or concerned with experience or actual use; not theoretical **2** of or concerned with ordinary affairs, work, etc **3** adapted or adaptable for use **4** of, involving, or trained by practice **5** being such for all useful or general purposes; virtual ▷ *n* **6** an examination in the practical skills of a subject: *a science practical* [c17 from earlier *practic,* from French *pratique,* via Late Latin from Greek *praktikos,* from *prassein* to experience, negotiate, perform]
> ˌpracti'cality *or* 'practicalness *n*

▎ USAGE A distinction is usually made between *practical* and *practicable. Practical* refers to a person, idea, project, etc, as being more concerned with or relevant to practice than theory: *he is a very practical person; the idea had no practical application. Practicable* refers to a project or idea as being capable of being done or put into effect: *the plan was expensive, yet practicable*

practical joke *n* a prank or trick usually intended to make the victim appear foolish > practical joker *n*

practically (ˈpræktɪkəlɪ, -klɪ) *adv* **1** virtually; almost: *it has rained practically every day* **2** in actuality rather than in theory: *what can we do practically to help?*

practical reason *or* **reasoning** *n philosophy, logic* **1** the faculty by which human beings determine how to act **2** reasoning concerning the relative merits of actions **3** the principles governing arguments which issue in actions or intentions to act

practice (ˈpræktɪs) *n* **1** a usual or customary action or proceeding: *it was his practice to rise at six; he made a practice of stealing stamps* **2** repetition or exercise of an activity in order to achieve mastery and fluency **3** the condition of having mastery of a skill or activity through repetition (esp in the phrases **in practice, out of practice**) **4** the exercise of a profession: *he set up practice as a lawyer* **5** the act of doing something: *he put his plans into practice* **6** the established method of conducting proceedings in a court of law ▷ *vb* **7** the US spelling of **practise** [c16 from Medieval Latin *practicāre* to practise, from Greek *praktikē* practical

science, practical work, from *prattein* to do, act]

practise *or* US **practice** (ˈpræktɪs) *vb* **1** to do or cause to do repeatedly in order to gain skill **2** (*tr*) to do (something) habitually or frequently: *they practise ritual murder* **3** to observe or pursue (something, such as a religion): *to practise Christianity* **4** to work at (a profession, job, etc): *he practises medicine* **5** (foll by *on* or *upon*) to take advantage of (someone, someone's credulity, etc) [c15 see PRACTICE]

practised *or* US **practiced** (ˈpræktɪst) *adj* **1** expert; skilled; proficient **2** acquired or perfected by practice

practitioner (prækˈtɪʃənə) *n* **1** a person who practises a profession or art **2** *christian Science* a person authorized to practise spiritual healing [c16 from *practician,* from Old French *praticien,* from *pratiquer* to PRACTISE]

Prader-Willi syndrome (ˌprɑːdəˈvɪlɪ) *n* a congenital condition characterized by obsessive eating, obesity, mental retardation, and small genitalia [c20 after Andreas *Prader* (born 1919) and H. *Willi* (born 1920), Swiss paediatricians]

Pradesh (prəˈdeɪʃ) *n Indian* a state, esp a state in the Union of India [Hindi]

Prado (ˈprɑːdəʊ) *n* an art gallery in Madrid housing an important collection of Spanish paintings

prae- *prefix* an archaic variant of **pre-**

praedial *or* **predial** (ˈpriːdɪəl) *adj* **1** of or relating to land, farming, etc **2** attached to or occupying land [c16 from Medieval Latin *praediālis,* from Latin *praedium* farm, estate] > ˌpraedi'ality *or* ˌpredi'ality *n*

praefect (ˈpriːfɛkt) *n* a variant spelling of **prefect** (senses 4–7) > praefectorial (ˌpriːfɛkˈtɔːrɪəl) *adj*

praemunire (ˌpriːmjʊˈnaɪərɪ) *n English history* **1** a writ charging with the offence of resorting to a foreign jurisdiction, esp to that of the Pope, in a matter determinable in a royal court **2** the statute of Richard II defining this offence [c14 from the Medieval Latin phrase (in the text of the writ) *praemūnīre faciās,* literally: that you cause (someone) to be warned in advance, from Latin *praemūnīre* to fortify or protect in front, from *prae* in front + *mūnīre* to fortify; in Medieval Latin the verb was confused with Latin *praemonēre* to forewarn]

praenomen (priːˈnəʊmɛn) *n, pl* -nomina (-ˈnɒmɪnə) *or* -nomens an ancient Roman's first or given name. See also **agnomen, cognomen, nomen** [c18 from Latin, from *prae-* before + *nōmen* NAME] > praenominal (priːˈnɒmɪnəl) *adj* > prae'nominally *adv*

Praesepe (praɪˈsiːpɪ) *n* an open cluster of several hundred stars in the constellation Cancer, visible to the naked eye as a hazy patch of light

praesidium (prɪˈsɪdɪəm) *n* a variant spelling of **presidium**

praetor *or* **pretor** (ˈpriːtə, -tɔː) *n* (in ancient Rome) any of several senior magistrates ranking just below the consuls [c15 from Latin: one who leads the way, probably from *praeīre,* from *prae-* before + *īre* to go] > prae'torial *or* pre'torial *adj* > 'praetorship *or* 'pretorship *n*

praetorian *or* **pretorian** (priːˈtɔːrɪən) *adj* **1** of or relating to a praetor ▷ *n* **2** a person holding praetorian rank; a praetor or ex-praetor

Praetorian *or* **Pretorian** (priːˈtɔːrɪən) *adj* **1** of or relating to the Praetorian Guard **2** (*sometimes not capital*) resembling the Praetorian Guard, esp with regard to corruption ▷ *n* **3** a member of the Praetorian Guard

Praetorian Guard *n* **1** the bodyguard of the Roman emperors, noted for its political corruption, which existed from 27 BC to 312 A.D **2** a member of this bodyguard

pragmatic (prægˈmætɪk) *adj* **1** advocating behaviour that is dictated more by practical consequences than by theory or dogma **2** *philosophy* of or relating to pragmatism **3** involving everyday or practical business **4** of or concerned with the affairs of a state or community **5** *rare* interfering or meddlesome;

p

officious ▷ Also (for senses 3, 5): **pragmatical** [c17 from Late Latin *prāgmaticus,* from Greek *prāgmatikos* from *pragma* act, from *prattein* to do] > prag,mati'cality *n* > prag'matically *adv*

pragmatics (præg'mætɪks) *n* (*functioning as singular*) **1** the study of those aspects of language that cannot be considered in isolation from its use **2** the study of the relation between symbols and those who use them

pragmatic sanction *n* an edict, decree, or ordinance issued with the force of fundamental law by a sovereign

pragmatism ('prægmə,tɪzəm) *n* **1** action or policy dictated by consideration of the immediate practical consequences rather than by theory or dogma **2** *philosophy* **a** the doctrine that the content of a concept consists only in its practical applicability **b** the doctrine that truth consists not in correspondence with the facts but in successful coherence with experience. See also **instrumentalism.** > 'pragmatist *n, adj* > ,pragma'tistic *adj*

Prague (prɑ:g) *n* the capital and largest city of the Czech Republic, on the Vltava River: a rich commercial centre during the Middle Ages; site of Charles University (1348) and a technical university (1707); scene of defenestrations (1419 and 1618) that contributed to the outbreak of the Hussite Wars and the Thirty Years' War respectively. Pop: 1 164 000 (2005 est). Czech name: **Praha**

Praha ('praha) *n* the Czech name for **Prague**

Praia ('praɪə) *n* the capital of Cape Verde; a port and submarine cable station. Pop: 115 000 (2005 est)

Prairial *French* (prɛrial) *n* the month of meadows: the ninth month of the French Revolutionary calendar, extending from May 21 to June 19 [c18 from French *prairie* meadow]

prairie ('prɛərɪ) *n* (*often plural*) a treeless grassy plain of the central US and S Canada. Compare **pampas, steppe, savanna** [c18 from French, from Old French *prairie,* from Latin *prātum* meadow]

prairie chicken, fowl, grouse *or* **hen** *n* either of two mottled brown-and-white grouse, *Tympanuchus cupido* or *T. pallidicinctus,* of North America

prairie crocus *n* *Canadian* a spring flower of the buttercup family

prairie dog *n* any of several gregarious sciurine rodents of the genus *Cynomys,* such as *C. ludovicianus,* that live in large complex burrows in the prairies of North America. Also called: **prairie marmot**

prairie-dogging *n* *informal* (in an open-plan office) the practice of looking over the top of one's partition in order to discover the source of or reason for a commotion [c20 after the actions of a PRAIRIE DOG, which stands on its hind legs to get a better view of something]

prairie oyster *n* **1** a drink consisting of raw unbeaten egg, vinegar or Worcester sauce (**Worcester oyster**), salt, and pepper: a supposed cure for a hangover **2** the testicles of a bull calf cooked and eaten

Prairie Provinces *pl n* the Canadian provinces of Manitoba, Saskatchewan, and Alberta, which lie in the N Great Plains region of North America: the chief wheat and petroleum producing area of Canada

prairie schooner *n* *chiefly US* a horse-drawn covered wagon similar to but smaller than a Conestoga wagon, used in the 19th century to cross the prairies of North America

prairie soil *n* a soil type occurring in temperate areas formerly under prairie grasses and characterized by a black A horizon, rich in plant foods

prairie turnip *n* another name for **breadroot**

prairie wolf *n* another name for **coyote** (sense 1)

praise (preɪz) *n* **1** the act of expressing commendation, admiration, etc **2** the extolling

of a deity or the rendering of homage and gratitude to a deity **3** the condition of being commended, admired, etc **4** *archaic* the reason for praise **5 sing someone's praises** to commend someone highly ▷ *vb* (*tr*) **6** to express commendation, admiration, etc, for **7** to proclaim or describe the glorious attributes of (a deity) with homage and thanksgiving [c13 from Old French *preisier,* from Late Latin *pretiāre* to esteem highly, from Latin *pretium* prize; compare PRIZE², PRECIOUS] > 'praiser *n*

praiseworthy ('preɪz,wɜːðɪ) *adj* deserving of praise; commendable > 'praise,worthily *adv* > 'praise,worthiness *n*

prajna ('prʊdʒnə, -njɑ:) *n* wisdom or understanding considered as the goal of Buddhist contemplation [from Sanskrit *prajñā,* from *prajānāti* he knows]

Prakrit ('prɑ:krɪt) *n* any of the vernacular Indic languages as distinguished from Sanskrit: spoken from about 300 BC to the Middle Ages. See also **Pali** [c18 from Sanskrit *prākṛta* original, from *pra-* before + *kr* to do, make + *-ta* indicating a participle] > Pra'kritic *adj*

praline ('prɑ:li:n) *n* **1** a confection of nuts with caramelized sugar, used in desserts and as a filling for chocolates **2** Also called: **sugared almond** a sweet consisting of an almond encased in sugar [c18 from French, named after César de Choiseul, comte de Plessis-*Praslin* (1598–1675), French field marshal whose chef first concocted it]

pralltriller ('prɑːl,trɪlə) *n* **1** an ornament used in 18th-century music consisting of an inverted mordent with an added initial upper note **2** another word for **inverted mordent** [German: bouncing trill]

pram¹ (præm) *n* *Brit* a cot-like four-wheeled carriage for a baby. US and Canadian term: **baby carriage** [c19 shortened and altered from PERAMBULATOR]

pram² (prɑ:m) *n* *nautical* a light tender with a flat bottom and a bow formed from the ends of the side and bottom planks meeting in a small raised transom [c16 from Middle Dutch *prame;* related to Old Frisian *prām*]

prana ('prɑ:nə) *n* (in Oriental medicine, martial arts, etc) cosmic energy believed to come from the sun and connecting the elements of the universe [from Sanskrit, literally: life-force]

prance (prɑ:ns) *vb* **1** (*intr*) to swagger or strut **2** (*intr*) to caper, gambol, or dance about **3** (*intr*) **a** (of a horse) to move with high lively springing steps **b** to ride a horse that moves in this way **4** (*tr*) to cause to prance ▷ *n* **5** the act or an instance of prancing [c14 *praunce;* perhaps related to German *prangen* to be in full splendour; compare Danish (dialect) *pransk* lively, spirited, used of a horse] > 'prancer *n* > 'prancingly *adv*

prandial ('prændɪəl) *adj* facetious of or relating to a meal [c19 from Latin *prandium* meal, luncheon] > 'prandially *adv*

prang (præŋ) *chiefly Brit slang* ▷ *n* **1** an accident or crash in an aircraft, car, etc **2** an aircraft bombing raid **3** an achievement ▷ *vb* **4** to crash or damage (an aircraft, car, etc) **5** to damage (a town, etc) by bombing [c20 possibly imitative of an explosion; perhaps related to Malay *perang* war, fighting]

prank¹ (præŋk) *n* a mischievous trick or joke, esp one in which something is done rather than said [c16 of unknown origin] > 'prankish *adj*

prank² (præŋk) *vb* **1** (*tr*) to dress or decorate showily or gaudily **2** (*intr*) to make an ostentatious display [c16 from Middle Dutch *pronken;* related to German *Prunk* splendour, *prangen* to be in full splendour]

prankster ('præŋkstə) *n* a practical joker

prase (preɪz) *n* a light green translucent variety of chalcedony [c14 from French, from Latin *prasius* a leek-green stone, from Greek *prasios,* from *prason* a leek]

praseodymium (,preɪzɪəʊ'dɪmɪəm) *n* a malleable ductile silvery-white element of the lanthanide series of metals. It occurs principally in monazite and bastnaesite and is used with other rare earths in carbon-arc lights and as a pigment in glass. Symbol: Pr; atomic no.: 59; atomic wt.: 140.90765; valency: 3; relative density: 6.773; melting pt.: 931°C; boiling pt.: 3520°C [c20 New Latin, from Greek *prasios* of a leek-green colour + DIDYMIUM]

prat (præt) *n* *slang* an incompetent or ineffectual person: often used as a term of abuse [c20 probably special use of C16 *prat* buttocks, of unknown origin]

prate (preɪt) *vb* **1** (*intr*) to talk idly and at length; chatter **2** (*tr*) to utter in an idle or empty way ▷ *n* **3** idle or trivial talk; prattle; chatter [c15 of Germanic origin; compare Middle Dutch *prāten,* Icelandic and Norwegian *prata,* Danish *prate*] > 'prater *n* > 'pratingly *adv*

pratfall ('præt,fɔ:l) *n* *US and Canadian slang* a fall upon one's buttocks [c20 from C16 *prat* buttocks (of unknown origin) + FALL]

pratincole ('prætɪŋ,kəʊl, 'preɪ-) *n* any of various swallow-like shore birds of the southern Old World genus *Glareola* and related genera, esp *G. pratincola,* having long pointed wings, short legs, and a short bill: family *Glareolidae,* order *Charadriiformes* [c18 from New Latin *pratincola* field-dwelling, from Latin *prātum* meadow + *incola* inhabitant]

pratique ('præti:k, præ'ti:k) *n* formal permission given to a vessel to use a foreign port upon satisfying the requirements of local health authorities [c17 from French, from Medieval Latin *practica* PRACTICE]

Prato (*Italian* 'prɑ:to) *n* a walled city in central Italy, in Tuscany: woollen industry. Pop: 172 499 (2001). Official name: **Prato in Toscana** (in tos'ka:na)

prattle ('præt⁹l) *vb* **1** (*intr*) to talk in a foolish or childish way; babble **2** (*tr*) to utter in a foolish or childish way ▷ *n* **3** foolish or childish talk [c16 from Middle Low German *pratelen* to chatter; see PRATE] > 'prattler *n* > 'prattlingly *adv*

prau (praʊ) *n* another word for **proa**

prawn (prɔ:n) *n* **1** any of various small edible marine decapod crustaceans of the genera *Palaemon, Penaeus,* etc, having a slender flattened body with a long tail and two pairs of pincers **2 come the raw prawn** *Austral informal* to attempt deception [c15 of obscure origin] > 'prawner *n*

prawn cracker *n* a puffy savoury crisp made from rice flour and prawn flavouring, served with Chinese food

praxis ('præksɪs) *n, pl* **praxises** *or* **praxes** ('præksiːz) **1** the practice and practical side of a profession or field of study, as opposed to the theory **2** a practical exercise **3** accepted practice or custom [c16 via Medieval Latin from Greek: deed, action, from *prassein* to do]

pray (preɪ) *vb* **1** (when *intr,* often foll by *for;* when *tr, usually takes a clause as object*) to utter prayers (to God or other object of worship): *we prayed to God for the sick child* **2** (when *tr, usually takes a clause as object or an infinitive*) to make an earnest entreaty (to or for); beg or implore: *she prayed to be allowed to go; leave, I pray you* **3** (*tr*) *rare* to accomplish or bring by praying: *to pray a soul into the kingdom* ▷ *interj* **4** *archaic* I beg you; please: *pray, leave us alone* [c13 from Old French *preier,* from Latin *precārī* to implore, from *prex* an entreaty; related to Old English *fricgan,* Old High German *frāgēn* to ask, Old Norse *fregna* to enquire]

prayer¹ (preə) *n* **1 a** a personal communication or petition addressed to a deity, esp in the form of supplication, adoration, praise, contrition, or thanksgiving **b** any other form of spiritual communion with a deity **2** a similar personal communication that does not involve adoration, addressed to beings venerated as being closely associated with a deity, such as angels or saints **3** the practice of praying: *prayer is our solution to human* *problems* **4** (*often plural*) a form of devotion, either public or private, spent mainly or wholly praying: *morning prayers* **5** (*capital when part of a recognized name*) a form of words used in praying: *the Lord's Prayer* **6** an object or benefit prayed for **7** an earnest request, petition, or entreaty **8** *law* a request contained in a petition to a court for the relief sought by the petitioner **9** *slang* a chance or hope: *she doesn't have a prayer of getting married* [C13 *preiere*, from Old French, from Medieval Latin *precāria*, from Latin *precārius* obtained by begging, from *prex* prayer] > **'prayerless** *adj*

prayer² ('preɪə) *n* a person who prays

prayer beads (preə) *pl n RC Church* the beads of the rosary

prayer book (preə) *n* **1** *ecclesiast* a book containing the prayers used at church services or recommended for private devotions **2** *Church of England* (*often capitals*) another name for **Book of Common Prayer**

prayerful ('preəfʊl) *adj* inclined to or characterized by prayer > **'prayerfully** *adv* > **'prayerfulness** *n*

prayer meeting (preə) *n chiefly Protestantism* a religious meeting at which the participants offer up prayers to God

prayer rug (preə) *n* the small carpet on which a Muslim kneels and prostrates himself while saying his prayers. Also called: **prayer mat**

prayer shawl (preə) *n Judaism* another word for **tallit**

prayer wheel (preə) *n Buddhism* (*esp in Tibet*) a wheel or cylinder inscribed with or containing prayers, each revolution of which is counted as an uttered prayer, so that such prayers can be repeated by turning it

praying mantis *or* **mantid** *n* another name for **mantis**

PRB *abbreviation for* (after the signatures of Pre-Raphaelite painters) Pre-Raphaelite Brotherhood

pre- *prefix* before in time, rank, order, position, etc: *predate; pre-eminent; premeditation; prefrontal; preschool* [from Latin *prae-*, from *prae* before, beforehand, in front]

preach (pri:tʃ) *vb* **1** to make known (religious truth) or give religious or moral instruction or exhortation in (sermons) **2** to advocate (a virtue, action, etc), esp in a moralizing way [C13 from Old French *prechier*, from Church Latin *praedicāre*, from Latin: to proclaim in public; see PREDICATE] > **'preachable** *adj*

preacher ('pri:tʃə) *n* **1** a person who has the calling and function of preaching the Christian Gospel, esp a Protestant clergyman **2** a person who preaches

Preacher ('pri:tʃə) *n the Bible* the author of Ecclesiastes or the book of Ecclesiastes

preacher curl *n* a weightlifting exercise for the biceps in which a barbell is lifted by flexing the elbows, with the upper arms resting on an angled bench [C20 from the resemblance of the exerciser using the bench to a preacher leaning over the pulpit]

preachify ('pri:tʃɪˌfaɪ) *vb* **-fies, -fying, -fied** (*intr*) *informal* to preach or moralize in a tedious manner > **'preachiˌfying** *n*

preachment ('pri:tʃmənt) *n* **1** the act of preaching **2** a tedious or pompous sermon or discourse

preachy ('pri:tʃɪ) *adj* **preachier, preachiest** *informal* inclined to or marked by preaching

preacquisition profit (ˌpri:ækwɪ'zɪʃən) *n* the retained profit of a company earned before a takeover and therefore not eligible for distribution as a dividend to the shareholders of the acquiring company

preadamite (pri:'ædəˌmaɪt) *n* **1** a person who believes that there were people on earth before Adam **2** a person assumed to have lived before Adam ▷ *adj also* **preadamic** (ˌpri:ə'dæmɪk) **3** of or relating to a preadamite

preadaptation (ˌpri:ædəp'teɪʃən) *n biology* the possession by a species or other group of characteristics that may favour survival in a changed environment, such as the limblike fins of crossopterygian fishes, which are preadaptation to terrestrial life

preadolescent (ˌpri:ædə'lɛsᵊnt) *n* **1** a person who has not yet reached adolescence ▷ *adj* **2** of or relating to the period before adolescence

preamble (pri:'æmbᵊl) *n* **1** a preliminary or introductory statement, esp attached to a statute or constitution setting forth its purpose **2** a preliminary or introductory conference, event, fact, etc [C14 from Old French *préambule*, from Late Latin *praeambulum* walking before, from Latin *prae-* before + *ambulāre* to walk]

preamplifier (pri:'æmplɪˌfaɪə) *n* an electronic amplifier used to improve the signal-to-noise ratio of an electronic device. It boosts a low-level signal to an intermediate level before it is transmitted to the main amplifier. Sometimes shortened to: **preamp**

prearranged (ˌpri:ə'reɪndʒd) *adj* having been arranged beforehand: *a pre-arranged meeting*

preaxial (pri:'æksɪəl) *adj anatomy* **1** situated or occurring in front of the axis of the body **2** of or relating to the anterior part of a vertebrate limb > **pre'axially** *adv*

prebend ('prɛbənd) *n* **1** the stipend assigned by a cathedral or collegiate church to a canon or member of the chapter **2** the land, tithe, or other source of such a stipend **3** a less common word for **prebendary 4** *Church of England* the office, formerly with an endowment, of a prebendary [C15 from Old French *prébende*, from Medieval Latin *praebenda* pension, stipend, from Latin *praebēre* to offer, supply, from *prae* forth + *habēre* to have, offer] > **prebendal** (prɪ'bɛndᵊl) *adj*

prebendary ('prɛbəndərɪ, -drɪ) *n, pl* **-daries 1** a canon or member of the chapter of a cathedral or collegiate church who holds a prebend **2** *Church of England* an honorary canon with the title of prebendary

prebiotic (ˌpri:baɪ'ɒtɪk) *adj* occurring or existing before the emergence of life

prebuttal (pri:'bʌtᵊl) *n informal* a prepared response to an anticipated criticism [C20 PRE- + (RE)BUTTAL]

Precambrian *or* **Pre-Cambrian** (pri:'kæmbrɪən) *adj* **1** of, denoting, or formed in the earliest geological era, which lasted for about 4 000 000 000 years before the Cambrian period ▷ *n* **2 the** the Precambrian era. See **Archaeozoic, Proterozoic**

precancel (pri:'kænsᵊl) *vb* **-cels, -celling, -celled** *or US* **-cels, -celing, -celed 1** (*tr*) to cancel (postage stamps) before placing them on mail ▷ *n* **2** a precancelled stamp > **pre,cancel'lation** *n*

precancerous *adj* (*esp of cells*) displaying characteristics that may develop into cancer

precarious (prɪ'kɛərɪəs) *adj* **1** liable to failure or catastrophe; insecure; perilous **2** *archaic* dependent on another's will [C17 from Latin *precārius* obtained by begging (hence, dependent on another's will), from *prex* PRAYER¹] > **pre'cariously** *adv* > **pre'cariousness** *n*

precast *adj* ('pri:ˌkɑ:st) **1** (*esp of concrete when employed as a structural element in building*) cast in a particular form before being used ▷ *vb* (pri:'kɑ:st) **-casts, -casting, -cast 2** (*tr*) to cast (concrete) in a particular form before use

precatory ('prɛkətərɪ, -trɪ) *adj rare* of, involving, or expressing entreaty; supplicatory. Also: **precative** ('prɛkətɪv) [C17 from Late Latin *precātōrius* relating to petitions, from Latin *precārī* to beg, PRAY]

precaution (prɪ'kɔ:ʃən) *n* **1** an action taken to avoid a dangerous or undesirable event **2** caution practised beforehand; circumspection [C17 from French, from Late Latin *praecautiō*, from Latin *praecavēre* to guard against, from *prae* before + *cavēre* to beware] > **pre'cautionary** *or* **pre'cautional** *adj* > **pre'cautious** *adj*

precautionary principle *n* the precept that an action should not be taken if the consequences are uncertain and potentially dangerous

precede (prɪ'si:d) *vb* **1** to go or be before (someone or something) in time, place, rank, etc **2** (*tr*) to preface or introduce [C14 via Old French from Latin *praecēdere* to go before, from *prae* before + *cēdere* to move]

precedence ('prɛsɪdəns) *or* **precedency** *n* **1** the act of preceding or the condition of being precedent **2** the ceremonial order or priority to be observed by persons of different stations on formal occasions: *the officers are seated according to precedence* **3** a right to preferential treatment: *I take precedence over you*

precedent *n* ('prɛsɪdənt) **1** *law* a judicial decision that serves as an authority for deciding a later case **2** an example or instance used to justify later similar occurrences ▷ *adj* (prɪ'si:dᵊnt, 'prɛsɪdənt) **3** preceding

precedented ('prɛsɪˌdɛntɪd) *adj* (of a decision, etc) supported by having a precedent

precedential (ˌprɛsɪ'dɛnʃəl) *adj* **1** of, involving, or serving as a precedent **2** having precedence > **ˌprece'dentially** *adv*

preceding (prɪ'si:dɪŋ) *adj* (*prenominal*) going or coming before; former

precentor (prɪ'sɛntə) *n* **1** a cleric who directs the choral services in a cathedral **2** a person who leads a congregation or choir in the sung parts of church services [C17 from Late Latin *praecentor* leader of the music, from *prae* before + *canere* to sing] > **precentorial** (ˌpri:sɛn'tɔ:rɪəl) *adj* > **pre'centorˌship** *n*

precept ('pri:sɛpt) *n* **1** a rule or principle for action **2** a guide or rule for morals; maxim **3** a direction, esp for a technical operation **4** *law* **a** a writ or warrant **b** a written order to a sheriff to arrange an election, the empanelling of a jury, etc **c** (in England) an order to collect money under a rate [C14 from Latin *praeceptum* maxim, injunction, from *praecipere* to admonish, from *prae* before + *capere* to take]

preceptive (prɪ'sɛptɪv) *adj* **1** of, resembling, or expressing a precept or precepts **2** didactic > **pre'ceptively** *adv*

preceptor (prɪ'sɛptə) *n* **1** *US* a practising physician giving practical training to a medical student **2** the head of a preceptory **3** *rare* a tutor or instructor > **pre'ceptorate** *n* > **preceptorial** (ˌpri:sɛp'tɔ:rɪəl) *or* **pre'ceptoral** *adj* > **pre'ceptorˌship** *n* > **pre'ceptress** *fem n*

preceptory (prɪ'sɛptərɪ) *n, pl* **-ries** (formerly) a subordinate house or community of the Knights Templars

precess (prɪ'sɛs) *vb* to undergo or cause to undergo precession

precession (prɪ'sɛʃən) *n* **1** the act of preceding **2** See **precession of the equinoxes 3** the motion of a spinning body, such as a top, gyroscope, or planet, in which it wobbles so that the axis of rotation sweeps out a cone [C16 from Late Latin *praecessiō* a going in advance, from Latin *praecēdere* to PRECEDE] > **pre'cessional** *adj* > **pre'cessionally** *adv*

precession of the equinoxes *n* the slightly earlier occurrence of the equinoxes each year due to the slow continuous westward shift of the equinoctial points along the ecliptic by 50 seconds of arc per year. It is caused by the precession of the earth's axis around the ecliptic pole, with a period of 25 800 years

pre-Christian *adj* of or referring to the period of history prior to the establishment of Christianity

pre-Christmas *adj* of or relating to the period prior to Christmas: *the pre-Christmas rush*

precinct ('pri:sɪŋkt) *n* **1 a** an enclosed area or building marked by a fixed boundary such as a wall **b** such a boundary **2** an area in a town, often closed to traffic, that is designed or reserved for a particular purpose: *a shopping precinct; pedestrian precinct* **3** *US* **a** a district of a city for administrative or police purposes **b** the police

p

responsible for such a district **4** *US* a polling or electoral district [c15 from Medieval Latin *praecinctum* (something) surrounded, from Latin *praecingere* to gird around, from *prae* before, around + *cingere* to gird]

precincts ('priːsɪŋkts) *pl n* the surrounding region or area

preciosity (ˌprɛʃɪˈɒsɪtɪ) *n, pl* -ties fastidiousness or affectation, esp in speech or manners

precious ('prɛʃəs) *adj* **1** beloved; dear; cherished **2** very costly or valuable **3** held in high esteem, esp in moral or spiritual matters **4** very fastidious or affected, as in speech, manners, etc **5** *informal* worthless: *you and your precious ideas!* ▷ *adv* **6** *informal* (intensifier): *there's precious little left* [c13 from Old French *precios,* from Latin *pretiōsus* valuable, from *pretium* price, value] > 'preciously *adv* > 'preciousness *n*

precious coral *n* another name for **red coral**

precious metal *n* any of the metals gold, silver, or platinum

precious stone *n* any of certain rare minerals, such as diamond, ruby, sapphire, emerald, or opal, that are highly valued as gemstones

precipice ('prɛsɪpɪs) *n* **1 a** the steep sheer face of a cliff or crag **b** the cliff or crag itself **2** a precarious situation [c16 from Latin *praecipitium* steep place, from *praeceps* headlong] > 'precipiced *adj*

precipitant (prɪˈsɪpɪtənt) *adj* **1** hasty or impulsive; rash **2** rushing or falling rapidly or without heed **3** abrupt or sudden ▷ *n* **4** *chem* a substance or agent that causes a precipitate to form > pre'cipitance *or* pre'cipitancy *n* > pre'cipitantly *adv*

precipitate *vb* (prɪˈsɪpɪˌteɪt) **1** (*tr*) to cause to happen too soon or sooner than expected; bring on **2** to throw or fall from or as from a height **3** to cause (moisture) to condense and fall as snow, rain, etc, or (of moisture, rain, etc) to condense and fall thus **4** *chem* to undergo or cause to undergo a process in which a dissolved substance separates from solution as a fine suspension of solid particles ▷ *adj* (prɪˈsɪpɪtɪt) **5** rushing ahead **6** done rashly or with undue haste **7** sudden and brief ▷ *n* (prɪˈsɪpɪtɪt) **8** *chem* a precipitated solid in its suspended form or after settling or filtering [c16 from Latin *praecipitāre* to throw down headlong, from *praeceps* headlong, steep, from *prae* before, in front + *caput* head] > pre'cipitable *adj* > pre,cipita'bility *n* > pre'cipitately *adv* > pre'cipitateness *n* > pre'cipitative *adj* > pre'cipi,tator *n*

precipitation (prɪˌsɪpɪˈteɪʃən) *n* **1** *meteorol* **a** rain, snow, sleet, dew, etc, formed by condensation of water vapour in the atmosphere **b** the deposition of these on the earth's surface **c** the amount precipitated **2** the production or formation of a chemical precipitate **3** the act of precipitating or the state of being precipitated **4** rash or undue haste **5** *spiritualism* the appearance of a spirit in bodily form; materialization

precipitation hardening *n metallurgy* a process in which alloys are strengthened by the formation, in their lattice, of a fine dispersion of one component when the metal is quenched from a high temperature and aged at an intermediate temperature

precipitin (prɪˈsɪpɪtɪn) *n immunol* an antibody that causes precipitation when mixed with its specific antigen

precipitous (prɪˈsɪpɪtəs) *adj* **1** resembling a precipice or characterized by precipices **2** very steep **3** hasty or precipitate > pre'cipitously *adv* > pre'cipitousness *n*

USAGE The use of *precipitous* to mean *hasty* is thought by some people to be incorrect

precis *or* **précis** ('preɪsiː) *n, pl* precis *or* précis ('preɪsiːz) **1** a summary of the essentials of a text; abstract ▷ *vb* **2** (*tr*) to make a precis of [c18 from French: PRECISE]

precise (prɪˈsaɪs) *adj* **1** strictly correct in amount or value: *a precise sum* **2** designating a certain thing and no other; particular: *this precise location* **3** using or operating with total accuracy: *precise instruments* **4** strict in observance of rules, standards, etc: *a precise mind* [c16 from French *précis,* from Latin *praecīdere* to curtail, from *prae* before + *caedere* to cut] > pre'ciseness *n*

precisely (prɪˈsaɪslɪ) *adv* **1** in a precise manner ▷ *sentence substitute* **2** exactly: used to confirm a statement by someone else

precisian (prɪˈsɪʒən) *n* a punctilious observer of rules or forms, esp in the field of religion > pre'cisianism *n*

precision (prɪˈsɪʒən) *n* **1** the quality of being precise; accuracy **2** (*modifier*) characterized by or having a high degree of exactness: *precision grinding; a precision instrument* [c17 from Latin *praecīsiō* a cutting off; see PRECISE] > pre'cisionism *n* > pre'cisionist *n*

preclinical (priːˈklɪnɪkəl) *adj med* **1** of, relating to, or occurring during the early phases of a disease before accurate diagnosis is possible **2** of, relating to, or designating an early period of scientific study by a medical student before practical experience with patients > pre'clinically *adv*

preclude (prɪˈkluːd) *vb* (*tr*) **1** to exclude or debar **2** to make impossible, esp beforehand [c17 from Latin *praeclūdere* to shut up, from *prae* in front, before + *claudere* to close] > pre'cludable *adj* > preclusion (prɪˈkluːʒən) *n* > preclusive (prɪˈkluːsɪv) *adj* > pre'clusively *adv*

precocial (prɪˈkəʊʃəl) *adj* **1** (of the young of some species of birds after hatching) covered with down, having open eyes, and capable of leaving the nest within a few days of hatching ▷ *n* **2** a precocial bird ▷ Compare **altricial** [c19 see PRECOCIOUS]

precocious (prɪˈkəʊʃəs) *adj* **1** ahead in development, such as the mental development of a child **2** *botany* (of plants, fruit, etc) flowering or ripening early [c17 from Latin *praecox* early maturing, from *prae* early + *coquere* to ripen] > pre'cociously *adv* > pre'cociousness *or* precocity (prɪˈkɒsɪtɪ) *n*

precognition (ˌpriːkɒgˈnɪʃən) *n psychol* the alleged ability to foresee future events. See also **clairvoyance, clairaudience** [c17 from Late Latin *praecognitiō* foreknowledge, from *praecognoscere* to foresee, from *prae* before + *cognoscere* to know, ascertain] > precognitive (priːˈkɒgnɪtɪv) *adj*

pre-Columbian *adj* of or relating to the Americas before they were discovered by Columbus

preconceive (ˌpriːkənˈsiːv) *vb* (*tr*) to form an idea of beforehand; conceive of ahead in time

preconception (ˌpriːkənˈsɛpʃən) *n* **1** an idea or opinion formed beforehand **2** a bias; prejudice

preconcert (ˌpriːkɒnˈsɜːt, -kɒnˈsət) *adj* of or relating to the period immediately before a performance or concert

precondition (ˌpriːkənˈdɪʃən) *n* **1** a necessary or required condition; prerequisite ▷ *vb* **2** (*tr*) *psychol* to present successively two stimuli to (an organism) without reinforcement so that they become associated; if a response is then conditioned to the second stimulus on its own, the same response will be evoked by the first stimulus

preconize *or* **preconise** ('priːkəˌnaɪz) *vb* (*tr*) **1** to announce or commend publicly **2** to summon publicly **3** (of the pope) to approve the appointment of (a nominee) to one of the higher dignities in the Roman Catholic Church [c15 from Medieval Latin *praecōnīzāre* to make an announcement, from Latin *praecō* herald] > ˌpreconiˈzation *or* ˌpreconiˈsation *n*

preconscious (priːˈkɒnʃəs) *adj* **1** *psychol* prior to the development of consciousness ▷ *n* **2** *psychoanal* mental contents or activity not immediately in consciousness but readily brought there ▷ Compare **subconscious, unconscious** > pre'consciously *adv* > pre'consciousness *n*

precontract *n* (priːˈkɒntrækt) **1** a contract or arrangement made beforehand, esp a betrothal ▷ *vb* (ˌpriːkənˈtrækt) **2** to betroth or enter into a betrothal by previous agreement **3** to make (an agreement, etc) by prior arrangement

precook (priːˈkʊk) *vb* (*tr*) to cook (food) beforehand

precritical (priːˈkrɪtɪkəl) *adj* of, relating to, or occurring during the period preceding a crisis or a critical state or condition: *a precritical phase of a disease*

precursor (prɪˈkɜːsə) *n* **1** a person or thing that precedes and shows or announces someone or something to come; harbinger **2** a predecessor or forerunner **3** a chemical substance that gives rise to another more important substance [c16 from Latin *praecursor* one who runs in front, from *praecurrere,* from *prae* in front + *currere* to run]

precursory (prɪˈkɜːsərɪ) *or* **precursive** *adj* **1** serving as a precursor **2** preliminary or introductory

pred. *abbreviation for* predicate

predacious *or* **predaceous** (prɪˈdeɪʃəs) *adj* **1** (of animals) habitually hunting and killing other animals for food **2** preying on others [c18 from Latin *praeda* plunder; compare PREDATORY] > pre'daciousness, pre'daceousness *or* predacity (prɪˈdæsɪtɪ) *n*

predate (priːˈdeɪt) *vb* (*tr*) **1** to affix a date to (a document, paper, etc) that is earlier than the actual date **2** to assign a date to (an event, period, etc) that is earlier than the actual or previously assigned date of occurrence **3** to be or occur at an earlier date than; precede in time

predation (prɪˈdeɪʃən) *n* a relationship between two species of animal in a community, in which one (the predator) hunts, kills, and eats the other (the prey)

predator ('prɛdətə) *n* **1** any carnivorous animal **2** a predatory person or thing

predatory ('prɛdətərɪ, -trɪ) *adj* **1** *zoology* another word for **predacious** (sense 1) **2** of, involving, or characterized by plundering, robbing, etc [c16 from Latin *praedātōrius* rapacious, from *praedārī* to pillage, from *praeda* booty] > 'predatorily *adv* > 'predatoriness *n*

predatory pricing *n commerce* offering goods or services at such a low price that competitors are forced out of the market

predecease (ˌpriːdɪˈsiːs) *vb* **1** to die before (some other person) ▷ *n* **2** *rare* earlier death

predecessor ('priːdɪˌsɛsə) *n* **1** a person who precedes another, as in an office **2** something that precedes something else **3** an ancestor; forefather [c14 via Old French from Late Latin *praedēcessor,* from *prae* before + *dēcēdere* to go away, from *dē* away + *cēdere* to go]

predella (prɪˈdɛlə; Italian preˈdɛlla) *n, pl* -le (-liː; Italian -le) **1** a painting or sculpture or a series of small paintings or sculptures in a long narrow strip forming the lower edge of an altarpiece or the face of an altar step or platform **2** a platform in a church upon which the altar stands [c19 from Italian: stool, step, probably from Old High German *bret* board]

predeposit (ˌpriːdɪˈpɒzɪt) *vb* (*tr*) to deposit beforehand or for future use

predestinarian (ˌpriːdɛstɪˈnɛərɪən) *theol* ▷ *n* **1** a person who believes in divine predestination ▷ *adj* **2** of or relating to predestination or characterizing those who believe in it > ˌpredestiˈnarianism *n*

predestinate *vb* (priːˈdɛstɪˌneɪt) **1** (*tr*) another word for **predestine** ▷ *adj* (priːˈdɛstɪnɪt, -ˌneɪt) **2** predestined or foreordained **3** *theol* subject to predestination; decided by God from all eternity

predestination (priːˌdɛstɪˈneɪʃən) *n* **1** *theol* **a** the act of God foreordaining every event from eternity **b** the doctrine or belief, esp associated with Calvin, that the final salvation of some of mankind is foreordained from eternity by God **2** the act of predestining or the state of being predestined

predestine (prɪˈdɛstɪn) or **predestinate** vb (tr) **1** to foreordain; determine beforehand **2** theol (of God) to decree from eternity (any event, esp the final salvation of individuals) [C14 from Latin praedestināre to resolve beforehand, from destināre to determine, DESTINE] > pre'destinable adj

predeterminate (ˌpriːdɪˈtɜːmɪnɪt, -ˌneɪt) adj determined beforehand; predetermined > ˌprede'terminately adv

predetermine (ˌpriːdɪˈtɜːmɪn) vb (tr) **1** to determine beforehand **2** to influence or incline towards an opinion beforehand; bias > ˌprede,termi'nation n > ˌprede'terminative adj > ˌprede'terminer n

predial (ˈpriːdɪəl) adj a variant spelling of **praedial**

predicable (ˈprɛdɪkəbəl) adj **1** capable of being predicated or asserted ▷ n **2** a quality, attribute, etc, that can be predicated **3** logic obsolete one of the five Aristotelian classes of predicates (**the five heads of predicables**), namely genus, species, difference, property, and relation [C16 from Latin praedicābilis, from praedicāre to assert publicly; see PREDICATE, PREACH] > ˌpredica'bility or 'predicableness n

predicament (prɪˈdɪkəmənt) n **1** a perplexing, embarrassing, or difficult situation **2** (ˈprɛdɪkəmənt) logic obsolete one of Aristotle's ten categories of being **3** archaic a condition, circumstance, state, position, etc [C14 from Late Latin praedicāmentum what is predicated, from praedicāre to announce, assert; see PREDICATE]

predicant (ˈprɛdɪkənt) adj **1** of or relating to preaching ▷ n **2** a member of a religious order founded for preaching, esp a Dominican **3** (ˌprɛdɪˈkænt) a variant spelling of **predikant** [C17 from Latin praedicāns preaching, from praedicāre to say publicly; see PREDICATE]

predicate vb (ˈprɛdɪˌkeɪt) (mainly tr) **1** (also intr; when tr, may take a clause as object) to proclaim, declare, or affirm **2** to imply or connote **3** (foll by on or upon) to base or found (a proposition, argument, etc) **4** logic **a** to assert or affirm (a property, characteristic, or condition) of the subject of a proposition **b** to make (a term, expression, etc) the predicate of a proposition ▷ n (ˈprɛdɪkɪt) **5** grammar **a** the part of a sentence in which something is asserted or denied of the subject of a sentence; one of the two major components of a sentence, the other being the subject **b** (as modifier): a predicate adjective **6** logic **a** an expression that is derived from a sentence by the deletion of a name **b** a property, characteristic, or attribute that may be affirmed or denied of something. The categorial statement all men are mortal relates two predicates, is a man and is mortal **c** the term of a categorial proposition that is affirmed or denied of its subject. In this example all men is the subject, and mortal is the predicate **d** a function from individuals to truth values, the truth set of the function being the extension of the predicate ▷ adj (ˈprɛdɪkɪt) **7** of or relating to something that has been predicated [C16 from Latin praedicāre to assert publicly, from prae in front, in public + dīcere to say] > ˌpredi'cation n

predicate calculus n the system of symbolic logic concerned not only with relations between propositions as wholes but also with the representation by symbols of individuals and predicates in propositions and with quantification over individuals. Also called: functional calculus. See also **propositional calculus**

predicative (prɪˈdɪkətɪv) adj **1** grammar relating to or occurring within the predicate of a sentence: a predicative adjective. Compare **attributive 2** logic (of a definition) given in terms that do not require quantification over entities of the same type as that which is thereby defined. Compare **impredicative**. > pre'dicatively adv

predicator (ˈprɛdɪˌkeɪtə) n (in systemic grammar) the part of a sentence or clause containing the verbal group; one of the four or five major

components into which clauses can be divided, the others being subject, object, adjunct, and (in some versions of the grammar) complement

predicatory (ˈprɛdɪˌkeɪtərɪ, ˌprɛdɪˈkeɪtərɪ) adj of, relating to, or characteristic of preaching or a preacher [C17 from Late Latin praedicātōrius, from praedicāre to proclaim]

predict (prɪˈdɪkt) vb (tr; may take a clause as object) to state or make a declaration about in advance, esp on a reasoned basis; foretell [C17 from Latin praedīcere to mention beforehand, from prae before + dīcere to say] > pre'dictable adj > pre,dicta'bility or pre'dictableness n > pre'dictably adv

prediction (prɪˈdɪkʃən) n **1** the act of predicting **2** something predicted; a forecast, prophecy, etc

predictive (prɪˈdɪktɪv) adj **1** of, relating to, or making predictions **2** text messaging (of mobile phone technology) enabling mobile phones to predict the word being entered in a text message from the first few letters: predictive texting > pre'dictively adv

predictor (prɪˈdɪktə) n **1** a person or thing that predicts **2** an instrument, used in conjunction with an anti-aircraft gun, that determines the speed, distance, height, and direction of hostile aircraft **3** statistics a more modern term for **independent variable**

predigest (ˌpriːdaɪˈdʒɛst, -dɪ-) vb (tr) to treat (food) artificially to aid subsequent digestion in the body > ˌpredi'gestion n

predikant or **predicant** (ˌprɛdɪˈkænt) n a minister in the Dutch Reformed Church, esp in South Africa [from Dutch, from Old French predicant, from Late Latin praedicāns preaching, from praedicāre to PREACH]

predilection (ˌpriːdɪˈlɛkʃən) n a predisposition, preference, or bias [C18 from French prédilection, from Medieval Latin praedīligere to prefer, from Latin prae before + dīligere to love]

predispose (ˌpriːdɪˈspəʊz) vb (tr) **1** (often foll by to or towards) to incline or make (someone) susceptible to something beforehand **2** chiefly law to dispose of (property, etc) beforehand; bequeath > ˌpredis'posal n

predisposition (ˌpriːdɪspəˈzɪʃən) n **1** the condition of being predisposed **2** med susceptibility to a specific disease. Compare **diathesis**

prednisolone (prɛdˈnɪsəˌləʊn) n a steroid drug derived from prednisone and having the same uses as cortisone [C20 altered from PREDNISONE]

prednisone (ˈprɛdnɪˌsəʊn) n a steroid drug derived from cortisone and having the same uses [C20 perhaps from PRE(GNANT) + -D(IE)N(E) + (CORT)ISONE]

predominant (prɪˈdɒmɪnənt) adj **1** having superiority in power, influence, etc, over others **2** prevailing; prominent > pre'dominance or pre'dominancy n

predominantly (prɪˈdɒmɪnəntlɪ) adv for the most part; mostly; mainly

predominate (prɪˈdɒmɪˌneɪt) vb **1** (intr; often foll by over) to have power, influence, or control **2** (intr) to prevail or preponderate **3** (tr) rare to dominate or have control over ▷ adj (prɪˈdɒmɪnɪt) **4** another word for **predominant** [C16 from Medieval Latin praedominārī, from Latin prae before + dominārī to bear rule, domineer] > pre'dominately adv > pre,domi'nation n > pre'domi,nator n

pre-echo (priːˈɛkəʊ) n **1** something that has preceded and anticipated something else; precursor **2** a fault in an audio recording in which a sound that is to come is heard too early: on tape sometimes caused by print-through

pre-eclampsia (ˌpriːɪˈklæmpsɪə) n pathol a toxic condition of pregnancy characterized by high blood pressure, protein in the urine, abnormal weight gain, and oedema. Compare **eclampsia**

pre-election n (modifier) existing or occurring before an election

pre-embryo (priːˈɛmbrɪəʊ) n the structure formed after fertilization of an ovum but before differentiation of embryonic tissue

preemie or **premie** (ˈpriːmɪ) n slang, chiefly US and Canadian a premature infant [C20 altered from PREMATURE]

pre-eminent (prɪˈɛmɪnənt) adj extremely eminent or distinguished; outstanding > pre-'eminence n > pre-'eminently adv

pre-empt (prɪˈɛmpt) vb **1** (tr) to acquire in advance of or to the exclusion of others; appropriate **2** (tr) chiefly US to occupy (public land) in order to acquire a prior right to purchase **3** (intr) bridge to make a high opening bid, often on a weak hand, to shut out opposition bidding > pre-'emptor n > pre-'emptory adj

pre-emption (prɪˈɛmpʃən) n **1** law the purchase of or right to purchase property in advance of or in preference to others **2** international law the right of a government to intercept and seize for its own purposes goods or property of the subjects of another state while in transit, esp in time of war [C16 from Medieval Latin praeemptiō, from praeemere to buy beforehand, from emere to buy]

pre-emptive (prɪˈɛmptɪv) adj **1** of, involving, or capable of pre-emption **2** bridge (of a high bid) made to shut out opposition bidding **3** military designed to reduce or destroy an enemy's attacking strength before it can use it: a pre-emptive strike > pre-'emptively adv

preen¹ (priːn) vb **1** (of birds) to maintain (feathers) in a healthy condition by arrangement, cleaning, and other contact with the bill **2** to dress or array (oneself) carefully; primp **3** (usually foll by on) to pride or congratulate (oneself) [C14 preinen, probably from prunen to PRUNE³, influenced by prenen to prick, pin (see PREEN²); suggestive of the pricking movement of the bird's beak] > 'preener n

preen² (priːn) n Scot a pin, esp a decorative one [Old English prēon a pin; related to Middle High German pfrieme awl, Dutch priem bodkin]

pre-exilian (ˌpriːɪɡˈzɪlɪən) or **pre-exilic** adj Old Testament prior to the Babylonian exile of the Jews (586–538 BC)

pre-exist adj occuring or existing previously > ˌpre-ex'istence n

pref. abbreviation for **1** preface **2** preference **3** preferred **4** prefix

prefab (ˈpriːˌfæb) n **a** a building that is prefabricated, esp a small house **b** (as modifier): a prefab house

prefabricate (priːˈfæbrɪˌkeɪt) vb (tr) to manufacture sections of (a building), esp in a factory, so that they can be easily transported to and rapidly assembled on a building site > pre'fabri,cated adj > pre,fabri'cation n

preface (ˈprɛfɪs) n **1** a statement written as an introduction to a literary or other work, typically explaining its scope, intention, method, etc; foreword **2** anything introductory **3** RC Church a prayer of thanksgiving and exhortation serving as an introduction to the canon of the Mass ▷ vb (tr) **4** to furnish with a preface **5** to serve as a preface to [C14 from Medieval Latin praefātia, from Latin praefātiō a saying beforehand, from praefārī to utter in advance, from prae before + fārī to say] > 'prefacer n

prefatory (ˈprɛfətərɪ, -trɪ) or **prefatorial** (ˌprɛfəˈtɔːrɪəl) adj of, involving, or serving as a preface; introductory [C17 from Latin praefārī to say in advance; see PREFACE] > 'prefatorily or ˌprefa'torially adv

prefect (ˈpriːfɛkt) n **1** (in France, Italy, etc) the chief administrative officer in a department **2** (in France, etc) the head of a police force **3** Brit a schoolchild appointed to a position of limited power over his fellows **4** (in ancient Rome) any of several magistrates or military commanders **5** Also called: **prefect apostolic** RC Church an official having jurisdiction over a missionary district that has no ordinary **6** RC Church one of two senior masters in a Jesuit school or college (the **prefect of studies** and the **prefect of discipline** or **first prefect**) **7** RC Church a cardinal in charge of a congregation of the Curia ▷ Also (for senses 4–7): **praefect** [C14 from Latin *praefectus* one put in charge, from *praeficere* to place in authority over, from *prae* before + *facere* to do, make] > **prefectorial** (ˌpriːfɛkˈtɔːrɪəl) *adj*

prefecture ('priːfɛkˌtjʊə) *n* **1** the office, position, or area of authority of a prefect **2** the official residence of a prefect in France, Italy, etc > pre'fectural *adj*

prefer (prɪˈfɜː) *vb* **-fers, -ferring, -ferred 1** (when *tr, may take a clause as object or an infinitive*) to like better or value more highly: *I prefer to stand* **2** *law* to give preference, esp to one creditor over others **3** (*esp of the police*) to put (charges) before a court, judge, magistrate, etc, for consideration and judgment **4** (*tr; often passive*) to advance in rank over another or others; promote [C14 from Latin *praeferre* to carry in front, prefer, from *prae* in front + *ferre* to bear] > pre'ferrer *n*

> USAGE Normally, *to* is used after *prefer* and *preferable*, not *than*: *I prefer Brahms to Tchaikovsky; a small income is preferable to no income at all.* However, *than* or *rather than* should be used to link infinitives: *I prefer to walk than/rather than to catch the train*

preferable ('prɛfərəbəl, 'prɛfrəbəl) *adj* preferred or more desirable > ˌprefera'bility *or* 'preferableness *n*

> USAGE Since *preferable* already means *more desirable*, one should not say something is *more preferable* or *most preferable*. See also at **prefer**

preferably ('prɛfərəblɪ, 'prɛfrəblɪ) *adv* ideally; by preference; if one had a choice

preference ('prɛfərəns, 'prɛfrəns) *n* **1** the act of preferring **2** something or someone preferred **3** *law* **a** the settling of the claims of one or more creditors before or to the exclusion of those of the others **b** a prior right to payment, as of a dividend or share in the assets of a company in the event of liquidation **4** *commerce* the granting of favour or precedence to particular foreign countries, as by levying differential tariffs

preference shares *pl n Brit and Austral* shares representing part of the capital issued by a company and entitling their holders to priority with respect to both net profit and net assets. Preference shares usually carry a definite rate of dividend that is generally lower than that declared on ordinary shares. US and Canadian name: **preferred stock**. Compare **ordinary shares, preferred ordinary shares**

preferential (ˌprɛfəˈrɛnʃəl) *adj* **1** showing or resulting from preference **2** giving, receiving, or originating from preference in international trade > preferentiality (ˌprɛfəˌrɛnʃɪˈælɪtɪ) *n* > ˌprefer'entially *adv*

preferential voting *n* a system of voting in which the electors signify their choices, as of candidates, in order of preference

preferment (prɪˈfɜːmənt) *n* **1** the act of promoting or advancing to a higher position, office, etc **2** the state of being preferred for promotion or social advancement **3** the act of preferring

preferred ordinary shares *pl n Brit* shares issued by a company that rank between preference shares and ordinary shares in the payment of dividends. Compare **preference shares**

preferred stock *n US and Canadian* shares representing part of the capital issued by a company and entitling their holders to priority with respect to both net profit and net assets. Preferred stock usually carries a definite rate of dividend that is generally lower than that declared on common stock. Also called (in eg Britain, Australia): **preference shares**

prefiguration (ˌpriːfɪɡəˈreɪʃən) *n* **1** the act of prefiguring **2** something that prefigures, such as a prototype > pre'figurative *adj* > pre'figuratively *adv* > pre'figurativeness *n*

prefigure (priːˈfɪɡə) *vb* (*tr*) **1** to represent or

suggest in advance **2** to imagine or consider beforehand > pre'figurement *n*

prefix *n* ('priːfɪks) **1** *grammar* an affix that precedes the stem to which it is attached, as for example *un-* in *unhappy*. Compare **suffix** (sense 1) **2** something coming or placed before ▷ *vb* (priːˈfɪks, 'priːfɪks) (*tr*) **3** to put or place before **4** *grammar* to add (a morpheme) as a prefix to the beginning of a word > prefixal ('priːfɪksəl, priːˈfɪks-) *adj* > 'prefixally *adv* > prefixion (priːˈfɪkʃən) *n*

preflight ('priːˌflaɪt) *adj* of or relating to the period just prior to a plane taking off

preformation (ˌpriːfɔːˈmeɪʃən) *n* **1** the act of forming in advance; previous formation **2** *biology* the theory, now discredited, that an individual develops by simple enlargement of a fully differentiated egg cell. Compare **epigenesis** (sense 1)

prefrontal (priːˈfrʌntəl) *adj* situated in, involving, or relating to the foremost part of the frontal lobe of the brain

preggers ('prɛɡəz) *adj chiefly Brit* an informal word for **pregnant** (sense 1)

preggy ('prɛɡɪ) *adj NZ* an informal word for **pregnant** (sense 1)

preglacial (priːˈɡleɪsɪəl) *adj* formed or occurring before a glacial period, esp before the Pleistocene epoch

pregnable ('prɛɡnəbəl) *adj* capable of being assailed or captured [C15 *prenable*, from Old French *prendre* to take, from Latin *prehendere* to lay hold of, catch] > ˌpregna'bility *n*

pregnancy ('prɛɡnənsɪ) *n, pl* **-cies 1** the state or condition of being pregnant **2** the period from conception to childbirth

pregnant ('prɛɡnənt) *adj* **1** carrying a fetus or fetuses within the womb **2** full of meaning or significance **3** inventive or imaginative **4** prolific or fruitful [C16 from Latin *praegnāns* with child, from *prae* before + (*g*)*nascī* to be born] > 'pregnantly *adv*

preheat (priːˈhiːt) *vb* (*tr*) to heat (an oven, grill, pan, etc) beforehand

prehensile (prɪˈhɛnsaɪl) *adj* adapted for grasping, esp by wrapping around a support: *a prehensile tail* [C18 from French *préhensile*, from Latin *prehendere* to grasp] > prehensility (ˌpriːhɛnˈsɪlɪtɪ) *n*

prehension (prɪˈhɛnʃən) *n* **1** the act of grasping **2** apprehension by the senses or the mind

prehistoric (ˌpriːhɪˈstɒrɪk) *or* **prehistorical** *adj* of or relating to man's development before the appearance of the written word > ˌprehis'torically *adv*

prehistory (priːˈhɪstərɪ) *n, pl* **-ries 1** the prehistoric period **2** the study of this period, relying entirely on archaeological evidence > prehistorian (ˌpriːhɪˈstɔːrɪən) *n*

prehominid (priːˈhɒmɪnɪd) *n* any of various extinct manlike primates. See also **australopithecine**

pre-ignition (ˌpriːɪɡˈnɪʃən) *n* ignition of all or part of the explosive charge in an internal-combustion engine before the exact instant necessary for correct operation

preindustrial (ˌpriːɪnˈdʌstrɪəl) *adj* of or relating to a society, age, etc, before industrialization

prejudge (priːˈdʒʌdʒ) *vb* (*tr*) to judge beforehand, esp without sufficient evidence > pre'judger *n* > pre'judgment *or* pre'judgement *n*

prejudice ('prɛdʒʊdɪs) *n* **1** an opinion formed beforehand, esp an unfavourable one based on inadequate facts **2** the act or condition of holding such opinions **3** intolerance of or dislike for people of a specific race, religion, etc **4** disadvantage or injury resulting from prejudice **5** in (*or* to) the prejudice of to the detriment of **6** without prejudice *law* without dismissing or detracting from an existing right or claim ▷ *vb* (*tr*) **7** to cause to be prejudiced **8** to disadvantage or injure by prejudice [C13 from Old French *préjudice*, from Latin *praejūdicium* a preceding judgment, disadvantage, from *prae* before + *jūdicium* trial, sentence, from *jūdex* a judge]

prejudicial (ˌprɛdʒʊˈdɪʃəl) *adj* causing prejudice; detrimental or damaging > ˌpreju'dicially *adv*

prelacy ('prɛləsɪ) *n, pl* **-cies 1** Also called: **prelature** ('prɛlɪtʃə) **a** the office or status of a prelate **b** prelates collectively **2** Also called: **prelatism** ('prɛləˌtɪzəm) *often derogatory* government of the Church by prelates

prelapsarian (ˌpriːlæpˈsɛərɪən) *adj* characteristic of or relating to the human state or time before the Fall: *prelapsarian innocence*

prelate ('prɛlɪt) *n* a Church dignitary of high rank, such as a cardinal, bishop, or abbot [C13 from Old French *prélat*, from Church Latin *praelātus*, from Latin *praeferre* to hold in special esteem, PREFER] > prelatic (prɪˈlætɪk) *or* pre'latical *adj*

prelatism ('prɛləˌtɪzəm) *n* government of the Church by prelates; episcopacy > 'prelatist *n*

prelect (prɪˈlɛkt) *vb* (*intr*) *rare* to lecture or discourse in public [C17 from Late Latin *praelegere* to instruct by reading, lecture, from *prae* in front of, in public + *legere* to read, choose] > pre'lection *n* > pre'lector *n*

prelexical (priːˈlɛksɪkəl) *adj transformational grammar* denoting or applicable at a stage in the formation of a sentence at which words and phrases have not yet replaced all of the underlying grammatical and semantic material of that sentence in the speaker's mind

prelibation (ˌpriːlaɪˈbeɪʃən) *n rare* an advance taste or sample; foretaste [C16 from Late Latin *praelībātiō* a tasting beforehand, offering of the first fruits, from Latin *prae* before + *lībāre* to taste]

prelim. *abbreviation for* preliminary

preliminaries (prɪˈlɪmɪnərɪz) *pl n* the full word for **prelims**

preliminary (prɪˈlɪmɪnərɪ) *adj* **1** (*usually prenominal*) occurring before or in preparation; introductory ▷ *n, pl* **-naries 2** a preliminary event or occurrence **3** an eliminating contest held before the main competition [C17 from New Latin *praelīmināris*, from Latin *prae* before + *līmen* threshold] > pre'liminarily *adv*

prelims ('priːlɪmz, prəˈlɪmz) *pl n* **1** Also called: **front matter** the pages of a book, such as the title page and contents, before the main text **2** the first public examinations taken for the bachelor's degree in some universities **3** (in Scotland) the school examinations taken as practice before public examinations [C19 a contraction of PRELIMINARIES]

prelingually deaf (priːˈlɪŋɡwəlɪ) *adj* **a** deaf from birth or having acquired deafness before learning to speak **b** (*as collective noun; preceded by the*): *the prelingually deaf*

preliterate (priːˈlɪtərɪt) *adj* relating to a society that has not developed a written language > preliteracy (priːˈlɪtərəsɪ) *n*

preloved ('priːˌlʌvd) *adj Austral informal* previously owned or used; second-hand

prelude ('prɛljuːd) *n* **1 a** a piece of music that precedes a fugue, or forms the first movement of a suite, or an introduction to an act in an opera, etc **b** (*esp for piano*) a self-contained piece of music **2** something serving as an introduction or preceding event, occurrence, etc ▷ *vb* **3** to serve as a prelude to (something) **4** (*tr*) to introduce by a prelude [C16 (*n*) from Medieval Latin *praelūdium*, from *prae* before + *-lūdium* entertainment, from Latin *lūdus* play; (*vb*) from Late Latin *praelūdere* to play beforehand, rehearse, from *lūdere* to play] > preluder (prɪˈljuːdə, 'prɛljʊdə) *n* > pre'ludial *adj* > prelusion (prɪˈljuːʒən) *n* > prelusive (prɪˈljuːsɪv) *or* prelusory (prɪˈljuːsərɪ) *adj* > pre'lusively *or* pre'lusorily *adv*

prem (prɛm) *n informal* a premature infant

prem. *abbreviation for* premium

premarital (priːˈmærɪtəl) *adj* (*esp of sexual relations*) occurring before marriage. Compare **extramarital**

premature (ˌprɛməˈtjʊə, 'prɛməˌtjʊə) *adj* **1** occurring or existing before the normal or expected time **2** impulsive or hasty: *a premature judgment* **3** (of an infant) weighing less than 2500 g (5½ lbs) and usually born before the end of the full period of gestation [C16 from Latin *praemātūrus*, very early, from *prae* in advance + *mātūrus* ripe] > ˌprema'turely *adv* > ˌprema'tureness or ˌprema'turity *n*

premaxilla (ˌpriːmæk'sɪlə) *n, pl* -lae (-liː) either of two bones situated in the upper jaw between the maxillary bones > ˌpremax'illary *adj*

premed (priː'mɛd) *informal* ▷ *adj* **1** short for **premedical** ▷ *n also* **premedic 2** short for **premedication 3** a premedical student

premedical (priː'mɛdɪkəl) *adj* **1** of or relating to a course of study prerequisite for entering medical school **2** of or relating to a person engaged in such a course of study: *a premedical student* > pre'medically *adv*

premedication (ˌpriːmɛdɪ'keɪʃən) *n surgery* any drugs administered to sedate and otherwise prepare a patient for general anaesthesia

premeditate (prɪ'mɛdɪˌteɪt) *vb* to plan or consider (something, such as a violent crime) beforehand > pre'mediˌtatedly *adv* > pre'mediˌtative *adj* > pre'mediˌtator *n*

premeditation (prɪˌmɛdɪ'teɪʃən) *n* **1** *law* prior resolve to do some act or to commit a crime **2** the act of premeditating

premenstrual (priː'mɛnstrʊəl) *adj* **1** of or occurring before a menstrual period **2** of or occuring before the menarche

premenstrual syndrome *or* **tension** *n* a group of symptoms, including nervous tension and fluid retention, any of which may be experienced as a result of hormonal changes in the days before a menstrual period starts. Abbreviations: PMS, PMT

premie ('priːmɪ) *n* a variant spelling of **preemie**

premier ('prɛmjə) *n* **1** another name for **prime minister 2** any of the heads of governments of the Canadian provinces and the Australian states **3** (*plural*) *Austral* the winners of a premiership ▷ *adj* (*prenominal*) **4** first in importance, rank, etc **5** first in occurrence; earliest [C15 from Old French: first, from Latin *prīmārius* principal, from *prīmus* first]

premier danseur *French* (prəmje dɑ̃sœr) *or feminine* **première danseuse** (prəmjɛr dɑ̃søz) *n, pl premiers danseurs or feminine premières danseuses* the principal dancer in a ballet company [C19 literally: first dancer]

premiere ('prɛmɪˌɛə, 'prɛmɪə) *n* **1** the first public performance of a film, play, opera, etc **2** the leading lady in a theatre company ▷ *vb* **3** to give or be the first public performance of [C19 from French, feminine of *premier* first]

premiership ('prɛmjəʃɪp) *n* **1** the office of premier **2 a** a championship competition held among a number of sporting clubs **b** a victory in such a championship

premillenarian (ˌpriːmɪlɪ'nɛəriən) *n* **1** a believer in or upholder of the doctrines of premillennialism ▷ *adj* **2** of or relating to premillennialism > ˌpremille'narianism *n*

premillennial (ˌpriːmɪ'lɛnɪəl) *adj* of or relating to the period preceding the millennium

premillennialism (ˌpriːmɪ'lɛnɪəˌlɪzəm) *n* the doctrine or belief that the millennium will be preceded by the Second Coming of Christ > ˌpremil'lennialist *n*

premise *n* ('prɛmɪs) **1** *Also:* **premiss** *logic* a statement that is assumed to be true for the purpose of an argument from which a conclusion is drawn ▷ *vb* (prɪ'maɪz, 'prɛmɪs) **2** (*when tr, may take a clause as object*) to state or assume (a proposition) as a premise in an argument, theory, etc [C14 from Old French *prémisse*, from Medieval Latin *praemissa* sent on before, from Latin *praemittere* to dispatch in advance, from *prae* before + *mittere* to send]

premises ('prɛmɪsɪz) *pl n* **1** a piece of land together with its buildings, esp considered as a place of business **2** *law* **a** (in a deed, etc) the

matters referred to previously; the aforesaid; the foregoing **b** the introductory part of a grant, conveyance, etc **3** *law* (in the US) the part of a bill in equity that states the names of the parties, details of the plaintiff's claims, etc

premium ('priːmɪəm) *n* **1** an amount paid in addition to a standard rate, price, wage, etc; bonus **2** the amount paid or payable, usually in regular instalments, for an insurance policy **3** the amount above nominal or par value at which something sells **4 a** an offer of something free or at a specially reduced price as an inducement to buy a commodity or service **b** (*as modifier*): *a premium offer* **5** a prize given to the winner of a competition; award **6** *US* an amount sometimes charged for a loan of money in addition to the interest **7** great value or regard: *to put a premium on someone's services* **8** a fee, now rarely required, for instruction or apprenticeship in a profession or trade **9 at a premium a** in great demand or of high value, usually because of scarcity **b** above par [C17 from Latin *praemium* prize, booty, reward]

Premium Savings Bonds *pl n* (in Britain) bonds issued by the Treasury since 1956 for purchase by the public. No interest is paid but there is a monthly draw for cash prizes of various sums. Also called: **premium bonds**

premolar (priː'məʊlə) *adj* **1** situated before a molar tooth ▷ *n* **2** any one of eight bicuspid teeth in the human adult, two situated on each side of both jaws between the first molar and the canine

premonish (prɪ'mɒnɪʃ) *vb* (*tr*) *rare* to admonish beforehand; forewarn

premonition (ˌprɛmə'nɪʃən) *n* **1** an intuition of a future, usually unwelcome, occurrence; foreboding **2** an early warning of a future event; forewarning [C16 from Late Latin *praemonitiō*, from Latin *praemonēre* to admonish beforehand, from *prae* before + *monēre* to warn, advise] > premonitory (prɪ'mɒnɪtərɪ, -trɪ) *adj*

Premonstratensian (ˌpriːˌmɒnstrə'tɛnsɪən) *n* **a** a member of a religious order founded at Prémontré in N France in 1120 by St Norbert (about 1080–1134) **b** (*as modifier*): *a Premonstratensian canon* [C17 from Medieval Latin (*locus*) *praemonstrātus* the place foreshown, because it was said to have been prophetically pointed out by St Norbert]

premorse (prɪ'mɔːs) *adj biology* appearing as though the end had been bitten off: *a premorse leaf* [C18 from Latin *praemorsus* bitten off in front, from *praemordēre*, from *prae* in front + *mordēre* to bite]

premunition (ˌpriːmjʊ'nɪʃən) *n med* a state of immunity acquired as the result of a persistent latent infection [C15 (in the sense: to protect beforehand): from Latin *praemūnitiō*, from *praemūnīre*, from *prae* before + *mūnīre* to fortify]

prenatal (priː'neɪtəl) *adj* **1** occurring or present before birth; during pregnancy ▷ *n* **2** *informal* a prenatal examination ▷ *Also:* **antenatal** > pre'natally *adv*

prenomen (priː'nəʊmɛn) *n, pl* -nomina (-'nɒmɪnə) *or* -nomens *US* a less common spelling of **praenomen**

prenominal (priː'nɒmɪnəl) *adj* **1** placed before a noun, esp (of an adjective or sense of an adjective) used only before a noun **2** of or relating to a praenomen

prenotion (priː'nəʊʃən) *n* a rare word for **preconception**

prentice ('prɛntɪs) *n* an archaic word for **apprentice**

prenup ('priːˌnʌp) *n Informal* a prenuptial agreement

prenuptial (priː'nʌpʃəl, -tʃəl) *adj* occurring or existing before marriage: *a prenuptial agreement*

prenuptial agreement *n* a contract made between a man and woman before they marry, agreeing on the distribution of their assets in the event of divorce

preoccupation (priːˌɒkjʊ'peɪʃən) *or* **preoccupancy** (priː'ɒkjʊpənsɪ) *n* **1** the state of being preoccupied, esp mentally **2** something

that holds the attention or preoccupies the mind

preoccupied (priː'ɒkjʊˌpaɪd) *adj* **1** engrossed or absorbed in something, esp one's own thoughts **2** already or previously occupied **3** *biology* (of a taxonomic name) already used to designate a genus, species, etc

preoccupy (priː'ɒkjʊˌpaɪ) *vb* -pies, -pying, -pied (*tr*) **1** to engross the thoughts or mind of **2** to occupy before or in advance of another [C16 from Latin *praeoccupāre* to capture in advance, from *prae* before + *occupāre* to seize, take possession of]

preordain (ˌpriːɔː'deɪn) *vb* (*tr*) to ordain, decree, or appoint beforehand > preordination (ˌpriːɔːdɪ'neɪʃən) *n*

prep (prɛp) *n* **1** *informal* short for **preparation** (sense 5) *or* (*chiefly US*) **preparatory school** ▷ *vb* **preps, prepping, prepped 2** (*tr*) to prepare (a patient) for a medical operation or procedure

prep. *abbreviation for* **1** preparation **2** preparatory **3** preposition

prepacked (priː'pækt) *adj* (of food, grain, etc) packed in advance of sale

preparation (ˌprɛpə'reɪʃən) *n* **1** the act or process of preparing **2** the state of being prepared; readiness **3** (*often plural*) a measure done in order to prepare for something; provision: *to make preparations for something* **4** something that is prepared, esp a medicinal formulation **5** (esp in a boarding school) **a** homework **b** the period reserved for this. Usually shortened to: **prep 6** *music* **a** the anticipation of a dissonance so that the note producing it in one chord is first heard in the preceding chord as a consonance **b** a note so employed **7** (*often capital*) the preliminary prayers at Mass or divine service

preparative (prɪ'pærətɪv) *adj* **1** serving to prepare; preparatory ▷ *n* **2** something that prepares > pre'paratively *adv*

preparatory (prɪ'pærətərɪ, -trɪ) *adj* **1** serving to prepare **2** introductory or preliminary **3** occupied in preparation **4** preparatory to as a preparation to; before: *a drink preparatory to eating* > pre'paratorily *adv*

preparatory school *n* **1** (in Britain) a private school, usually single-sex and for children between the ages of 6 and 13, generally preparing pupils for public school **2** (in the US) a private secondary school preparing pupils for college ▷ Often shortened to: **prep school**

prepare (prɪ'pɛə) *vb* **1** to make ready or suitable in advance for a particular purpose or for some use, event, etc: *to prepare a meal; to prepare to go* **2** to put together using parts or ingredients; compose or construct **3** (*tr*) to equip or outfit, as for an expedition **4** (*tr*) *music* to soften the impact of (a dissonant note) by the use of preparation **5 be prepared** (*foll by an infinitive*) to be willing and able (to do something): *I'm not prepared to reveal these figures* [C15 from Latin *praeparāre*, from *prae* before + *parāre* to make ready] > pre'parer *n*

preparedness (prɪ'pɛərɪdnɪs) *n* the state of being prepared or ready, esp militarily ready for war > pre'paredly *adv*

prepared piano *n* a piano in which some strings have been damped by having objects placed between them or tuned differently from the rest for specific tonal effect. This process was pioneered by US composer John Cage (1912–92)

prepay (priː'peɪ) *vb* -pays, -paying, -paid (*tr*) to pay for in advance > pre'payable *adj* > pre'payment *n*

prepense (prɪ'pɛns) *adj* (*postpositive*) (usually in legal contexts) arranged in advance; premeditated (esp in the phrase **malice prepense**) [C18 from Anglo-Norman *purpensé*, from Old French *purpenser* to consider in advance, from *penser* to think, from Latin *pēnsāre* to weigh, consider]

preponderance (prɪ'pɒndərəns) *or* **preponderancy** (prɪ'pɒndərənsɪ) *n* the quality of being greater in weight, force, influence, etc: *the preponderance of right-handed people*

preponderant (prɪ'pɒndərənt) *adj* greater in weight, force, influence, etc > pre'ponderancy *n*

p

> pre'ponderantly adv

preponderate (prɪˈpɒndəˌreɪt) vb (intr) **1** (often foll by over) to be more powerful, important, numerous, etc (than) **2** to be of greater weight than something else [c17 from Late Latin praeponderāre to be of greater weight, from pondus weight] > pre'ponderately adv > pre'ponder,ating adj > pre,ponder'ation n

prepone (priːˈpəʊn) vb (tr) Indian to bring forward to an earlier time [c20 PRE- + (POST)PONE]

preposition (ˌprɛpəˈzɪʃən) n a word or group of words used before a noun or pronoun to relate it grammatically or semantically to some other constituent of a sentence. Abbreviation: prep [c14 from Latin praepositiō a putting before, from pōnere to place] > ˌprepoˈsitional adj > ˌprepoˈsitionally adv

> USAGE The practice of ending a sentence with a preposition (Venice is a place I should like to go to) was formerly regarded as incorrect, but is now acceptable and is the preferred form in many contexts

prepositive (priːˈpɒzɪtɪv) adj **1** (of a word or speech element) placed before the word governed or modified ▷ n **2** a prepositive element > pre'positively adv

prepositor (priːˈpɒzɪtə) or **prepostor** (priːˈpɒstə) n Brit rare a prefect in any of certain public schools [c16 from Latin praepositus placed before]

prepossess (ˌpriːpəˈzɛs) vb (tr) **1** to preoccupy or engross mentally **2** to influence in advance for or against a person or thing; prejudice; bias **3** to make a favourable impression on beforehand

prepossessing (ˌpriːpəˈzɛsɪŋ) adj creating a favourable impression; attractive > ˌprepos'sessingly adv > ˌprepos'sessingness n

prepossession (ˌpriːpəˈzɛʃən) n **1** the state or condition of being prepossessed **2** a prejudice or bias, esp a favourable one

preposterous (prɪˈpɒstərəs) adj contrary to nature, reason, or sense; absurd; ridiculous [c16 from Latin praeposterus reversed, from prae in front, before + posterus following] > pre'posterously adv > pre'posterousness n

prepotency (prɪˈpəʊtənsɪ) n **1** the state or condition of being prepotent **2** genetics the ability of one parent to transmit more characteristics to its offspring than the other parent **3** botany the ability of pollen from one source to bring about fertilization more readily than that from other sources

prepotent (prɪˈpəʊtənt) adj **1** greater in power, force, or influence **2** biology showing prepotency [c15 from Latin praepotens very powerful, from posse to be able] > pre'potently adv

preppy ('prɛpɪ) informal ▷ adj **1** characteristic of or denoting a fashion style of neat, understated, and often expensive clothes; young but classic: suggesting that the wearer is well off, upper class, and conservative ▷ n, pl -pies **2** a person exhibiting such style [c20 originally US, from preppy a person who attends or has attended a preparatory school before college]

preprandial (priːˈprændɪəl) adj of or relating to the period immediately before lunch or dinner: enjoy a preprandial drink

preproduction (ˌpriːprəˈdʌkʃən) n **1** preliminary work on or trial production of a play, industrial prototype, etc ▷ adj **2** (of a period, model, etc) preliminary; trial

prep school n informal See **preparatory school**

prepubescent (ˌpriːpjuːˈbɛsənt) n **1** a person who has not yet reached puberty ▷ adj **2** not yet having reached puberty

prepublication (ˌpriːpʌblɪˈkeɪʃən) adj of or relating to the time, processes, sales, etc, before publication of a book, newspaper, etc

prepuce ('priːpjuːs) n **1** the retractable fold of skin covering the tip of the penis. Nontechnical name: **foreskin 2** a similar fold of skin covering the tip of the clitoris [c14 from Latin praepūtium] > preputial (priːˈpjuːʃəl) adj

prequel ('priːkwəl) n a film or book about an earlier stage of a story or a character's life, released because the later part of it has already been successful [c20 from PRE- + (se)quel]

Pre-Raphaelite (ˌpriːˈræfəlaɪt) n **1** a member of the **Pre-Raphaelite Brotherhood,** an association of British painters and writers including Dante Gabriel Rossetti (1828–82), Holman Hunt (1827–1910), and Sir John Everett Millais (1829–96), founded in 1848 to combat the shallow conventionalism of academic painting and revive the fidelity to nature and the vivid realistic colour that they considered typical of Italian painting before Raphael (1483–1520) ▷ adj **2** of, in the manner of, or relating to Pre-Raphaelite painting and painters > ˌPre-'Raphael,itism n

prereading (priːˈriːdɪŋ) adj **1** of or relating to the period before reading a text, book, etc

prerecorded (ˌpriːrɪˈkɔːdəd) adj having been recorded (on tape, video, etc) beforehand: a pre-recorded message

prerequisite (priːˈrɛkwɪzɪt) adj **1** required as a prior condition ▷ n **2** something required as a prior condition

prerogative (prɪˈrɒɡətɪv) n **1** an exclusive privilege or right exercised by a person or group of people holding a particular office or hereditary rank **2** any privilege or right **3** a power, privilege, or immunity restricted to a sovereign or sovereign government ▷ adj **4** having or able to exercise a prerogative [c14 from Latin praerogātīva privilege, earlier: group with the right to vote first, from prae before + rogāre to ask, beg for]

pre-Roman adj of or relating to the period before the founding of ancient Rome

Pres. abbreviation for President

presa ('prɛsa:) n, pl -se (-seɪ) music a sign or symbol used in a canon, round, etc, to indicate the entry of each part. Usual signs: +, :S:, or ✕ [Italian, literally: a taking up, from prendere to take, from Latin prehendere to grasp]

presage n ('prɛsɪdʒ) **1** an intimation or warning of something about to happen; portent; omen **2** a sense of what is about to happen; foreboding **3** archaic a forecast or prediction ▷ vb ('prɛsɪdʒ, prɪˈseɪdʒ) **4** (tr) to have a presentiment of **5** (tr) to give a forewarning of; portend **6** (intr) to make a prediction [c14 from Latin praesāgium presentiment, from praesāgīre to perceive beforehand, from sāgīre to perceive acutely] > pre'sageful adj > pre'sagefully adv > pre'sager n

presale ('priːseɪl) n the practice of arranging the sale of a product before it is available

Presb. abbreviation for Presbyterian

presbyopia (ˌprɛzbɪˈəʊpɪə) n a progressively diminishing ability of the eye to focus, noticeable from middle to old age, caused by loss of elasticity of the crystalline lens [c18 New Latin, from Greek presbus old man + ōps eye] > presbyopic (ˌprɛzbɪˈɒpɪk) adj

presbyter ('prɛzbɪtə) n **1 a** an elder of a congregation in the early Christian Church **b** (in some Churches having episcopal politics) an official who is subordinate to a bishop and has administrative, teaching, and sacerdotal functions **2** (in some hierarchical Churches) another name for **priest 3** (in the Presbyterian Church) **a** a teaching elder **b** a ruling elder [c16 from Late Latin, from Greek presbuteros an older man, from presbus old man]

presbyterate (ˌprɛzˈbɪtərɪt, -ˌreɪt) n **1** the status or office of a presbyter **2** a group of presbyters

presbyterial (ˌprɛzbɪˈtɪərɪəl) adj of or relating to a presbyter or presbytery. Also: **presbyteral** (prɛzˈbɪtərəl) > ˌpresbyˈterially adv

presbyterian (ˌprɛzbɪˈtɪərɪən) adj **1** of, relating to, or designating Church government by presbyters or lay elders ▷ n **2** an upholder of this type of Church government > ˌpresbyˈterianism n > ˌpresbyˌterianˈistic adj

Presbyterian (ˌprɛzbɪˈtɪərɪən) adj **1** of or relating to any of various Protestant Churches governed by presbyters or lay elders and adhering to various modified forms of Calvinism ▷ n **2** a member of a Presbyterian Church > ˌPresbyˈterianism n

presbytery ('prɛzbɪtərɪ, -trɪ) n, pl -teries **1** Presbyterian Church a local Church court composed of ministers and elders **b** the congregations or churches within the jurisdiction of any such court **2** the part of a cathedral or church east of the choir, in which the main altar is situated; sanctuary **3** presbyters or elders collectively **4** government of a church by presbyters or elders **5** RC Church the residence of a parish priest [c15 from Old French presbiterie, from Church Latin presbyterium, from Greek presbyterion; see PRESBYTER]

preschool or **pre-school** (priːˈskuːl) adj **a** (of a child) under the age at which compulsory education begins **b** (of services) for or relating to preschool children

prescience ('prɛsɪəns) n knowledge of events before they take place; foreknowledge [c14 from Latin praescīre to foreknow, from prae before + scīre to know] > 'prescient adj > 'presciently adv

prescientific (ˌpriːsaɪənˈtɪfɪk) adj of or relating to the period before the development of modern science and its methods

prescind (prɪˈsɪnd) vb rare **1** (intr; usually foll by from) to withdraw attention (from something) **2** (tr) to isolate, remove, or separate, as for special consideration [c17 from Late Latin praescindere to cut off in front, from Latin prae before + scindere to split]

prescribe (prɪˈskraɪb) vb **1** to lay down as a rule or directive **2** law to claim or acquire (a right, title, etc) by prescription **3** law to make or become invalid or unenforceable by lapse of time **4** med to recommend or order the use of (a drug or other remedy) [c16 from Latin praescrībere to write previously, from prae before + scrībere to write] > pre'scriber n

prescript n ('priːskrɪpt) **1** something laid down or prescribed ▷ adj (prɪˈskrɪpt, 'priːskrɪpt) **2** prescribed as a rule [c16 from Latin praescriptum something written down beforehand, from praescrībere to PRESCRIBE]

prescriptible (prɪˈskrɪptəbəl) adj **1** subject to prescription **2** depending on or derived from prescription > preˌscriptiˈbility n

prescription (prɪˈskrɪpʃən) n **1 a** written instructions from a physician, dentist, etc, to a pharmacist stating the form, dosage strength, etc, of a drug to be issued to a specific patient **b** the drug or remedy prescribed **2** (modifier) (of drugs) available legally only with a doctor's prescription **3 a** written instructions from an optician specifying the lenses needed to correct defects of vision **b** (as modifier): prescription glasses **4** the act of prescribing **5** something that is prescribed **6** a long established custom or a claim based on one **7** law **a** the uninterrupted possession of property over a stated period of time, after which a right or title is acquired (**positive prescription**) **b** the barring of adverse claims to property, etc, after a specified period of time has elapsed, allowing the possessor to acquire title (**negative prescription**) **c** the right or title acquired in either of these ways [c14 from legal Latin praescriptiō an order, prescription; see PRESCRIBE]

prescriptive (prɪˈskrɪptɪv) adj **1** making or giving directions, rules, or injunctions **2** sanctioned by long-standing usage or custom **3** derived from or based upon legal prescription: a prescriptive title > pre'scriptively adv > pre'scriptiveness n

prescriptivism (prɪˈskrɪptɪˌvɪzəm) n ethics the theory that moral utterances have no truth value but prescribe attitudes to others and express the conviction of the speaker. Compare **descriptivism, emotivism**

preseason ('priːˌsiːzən) n **a** the period immediately before the official season for a particular sport begins **b** (as modifier): a series of *preseason friendly matches*

presell (priːˈsɛl) *vb (tr)* **-sells, -selling, -sold** **1** to promote (a product, entertainment, etc) with publicity in advance of its appearance **2** to prepare (the public) for a product, entertainment, etc, with advance publicity **3** to agree a sale of (a product) before it is available **4** to sell (a book) before its publication date

presence (ˈprɛzəns) *n* **1** the state or fact of being present **2** the immediate proximity of a person or thing **3** personal appearance or bearing, esp of a dignified nature **4** an imposing or dignified personality **5** an invisible spirit felt to be nearby **6** *electronics* a recording control that boosts mid-range frequencies **7** (of a recording) a quality that gives the impression that the listener is in the presence of the original source of the sound **8** *obsolete* assembly or company **9** *obsolete* short for **presence chamber** [C14 via Old French from Latin *praesentia* a being before, from *praeesse* to be before, from *prae* before + *esse* to be]

presence chamber *n* the room in which a great person, such as a monarch, receives guests, assemblies, etc

presence of mind *n* the ability to remain calm and act constructively during times of crisis

presenile dementia (priːˈsiːnaɪl) *n* a form of dementia, of unknown cause, starting before a person is old

present[1] (ˈprɛzᵊnt) *adj* **1** (*prenominal*) in existence at the moment in time at which an utterance is spoken or written **2** (*postpositive*) being in a specified place, thing, etc: *the murderer is present in this room* **3** (*prenominal*) now in consideration or under discussion: *the present topic; the present author* **4** *grammar* denoting a tense of verbs used when the action or event described is occurring at the time of utterance or when the speaker does not wish to make any explicit temporal reference **5** *archaic* readily available; instant: *present help is at hand* **6** *archaic* mentally alert; attentive ▷ *n* **7** **the present** the time being; now **8** *grammar* **a** the present tense **b** a verb in this tense **9** **at present** at the moment; now **10** **for the present** for the time being; temporarily ▷ See also **presents** [C13 from Latin *praesens*, from *praeesse* to be in front of, from *prae-* before, in front + *esse* to be]

present[2] *vb* (prɪˈzɛnt) (*mainly tr*) **1** to introduce (a person) to another, esp to someone of higher rank **2** to introduce to the public: *to present a play* **3** to introduce and compere (a radio or television show) **4** to show; exhibit: *he presented a brave face to the world* **5** to put forward; submit: *she presented a proposal for a new book* **6** to bring or suggest to the mind: *to present a problem* **7** to give or award: *to present a prize* **8** to endow with or as if with a gift or award: *to present a university with a foundation scholarship* **9** to offer formally: *to present one's compliments* **10** to offer or hand over for action or settlement: *to present a bill* **11** to represent or depict in a particular manner: *the actor presented Hamlet as a very young man* **12** to salute someone with (one's weapon) (usually in the phrase **present arms**) **13** to aim or point (a weapon) **14** to nominate (a clergyman) to a bishop for institution to a benefice in his diocese **15** to lay (a charge, etc) before a court, magistrate, etc, for consideration or trial **16** to bring a formal charge or accusation against (a person); indict **17** *chiefly US* (of a grand jury) to take notice of (an offence) from personal knowledge or observation, before any bill of indictment has been drawn up **18** (*intr*) *med* to seek treatment for a particular symptom or problem: *she presented with postnatal depression* **19** (*intr*) *informal* to produce a favourable, etc impression: *she presents well in public; he presents as harmless but has poisoned his family* **20** **present oneself** to appear, esp at a specific time and place ▷ *n* (ˈprɛzᵊnt) **21** anything that is presented; a gift **22** **make someone a present of something** to give someone something: *I'll make you a present of a new car* [C13 from Old French *presenter*, from Latin *praesentāre* to exhibit, offer, from *praesens* PRESENT[1]]

presentable (prɪˈzɛntəbᵊl) *adj* **1** fit to be presented or introduced to other people **2** fit to be displayed or offered > **preˈsentableness** *or* **preˌsentaˈbility** *n* > **preˈsentably** *adv*

presentation (ˌprɛzənˈteɪʃən) *n* **1** the act of presenting or state of being presented **2** the manner of presenting, esp the organization of visual details to create an overall impression: *the presentation of the project is excellent but the content poor* **3** the method of presenting: *his presentation of the facts was muddled* **4** a verbal report presented with illustrative material, such as slides, graphs, etc: *a presentation on the company results* **5** **a** an offering or bestowal, as of a gift **b** (*as modifier*): *a presentation copy of a book* **6** a performance or representation, as of a play **7** the formal introduction of a person, as into society or at court; debut **8** the act or right of nominating a clergyman to a benefice **9** *med* the position of a baby relative to the birth canal at the time of birth **10** *commerce* another word for **presentment** (sense 4) **11** *television* linking material between programmes, such as announcements, trailers, or weather reports **12** an archaic word for **gift** **13** *philosophy* a sense datum **14** (*often capital*) another name for (feast of) **Candlemas.** > **ˌpresenˈtational** *adj*

presentationism (ˌprɛzənˈteɪʃəˌnɪzəm) *n* *philosophy* the theory that objects are identical with our perceptions of them. Compare **representationalism.** > **ˌpresenˈtationist** *n, adj*

presentative (prɪˈzɛntətɪv) *adj* **1** *philosophy* **a** able to be known or perceived immediately **b** capable of knowing or perceiving in this way **2** subject to or conferring the right of ecclesiastical presentation > **preˈsentativeness** *n*

present-day *n* (*modifier*) of the modern day; current: *I don't like present-day fashions*

presentee (ˌprɛzənˈtiː) *n* **1** a person who is presented, as at court **2** a person to whom something is presented

presenteeism (ˌprɛzənˈtiːɪzəm) *n* the practice of persistently working longer hours and taking fewer holidays than the terms of one's employment demand, esp as a result of fear of losing one's job [C20 a play on ABSENTEEISM]

presenter (prɪˈzɛntə) *n* **1** a person who presents something or someone **2** *radio, television* a person who introduces a show, links items, interviews guests, etc; compere

presentient (prɪˈsɛnʃənt, -ˈzɛn-, priː-) *adj* characterized by or experiencing a presentiment [C19 from Latin *praesentiens* present participle of *praesentire*, from *prae-* PRE- + *sentire* to feel]

presentiment (prɪˈzɛntɪmənt) *n* a sense of something about to happen; premonition [C18 from obsolete French, from *pressentir* to sense beforehand; see PRE-, SENTIMENT]

presently (ˈprɛzəntlɪ) *adv* **1** in a short while; soon **2** at the moment **3** an archaic word for **immediately**

presentment (prɪˈzɛntmənt) *n* **1** the act of presenting or state of being presented; presentation **2** something presented, such as a picture, play, etc **3** *law, chiefly US* a statement on oath by a grand jury of something within their own knowledge or observation, esp the commission of an offence when the indictment has been laid before them **4** *commerce* the presenting of a bill of exchange, promissory note, etc

present participle *n* a participial form of verbs used adjectivally when the action it describes is contemporaneous with that of the main verb of a sentence and also used in the formation of certain compound tenses. In English this form ends in *-ing*. Compare **gerund**

present perfect *adj, n* *grammar* another term for **perfect** (senses 8, 11)

presents (ˈprɛzənts) *pl n* *law* used in a deed or document to refer to itself: *know all men by these presents*

present value *n* the current capital value of a future income or outlay or of a series of such incomes or outlays. It is computed by the process of discounting at a predetermined rate of interest

preservative (prɪˈzɜːvətɪv) *n* **1** something that preserves or tends to preserve, esp a chemical added to foods to inhibit decomposition ▷ *adj* **2** tending or intended to preserve

preserve (prɪˈzɜːv) *vb* (*mainly tr*) **1** to keep safe from danger or harm; protect **2** to protect from decay or dissolution; maintain: *to preserve old buildings* **3** to maintain possession of; keep up: *to preserve a façade of indifference* **4** to prevent from decomposition or chemical change **5** to prepare (food), as by freezing, drying, or salting, so that it will resist decomposition **6** to make preserves of (fruit, etc) **7** to rear and protect (game) in restricted places for hunting or fishing **8** (*intr*) to maintain protection and favourable conditions for game in preserves ▷ *n* **9** something that preserves or is preserved **10** a special area or domain: *archaeology is the preserve of specialists* **11** (*usually plural*) fruit, etc, prepared by cooking with sugar **12** areas where game is reared for private hunting or fishing [C14 via Old French, from Late Latin *praeservāre* literally: to keep safe in advance, from Latin *prae-* before + *servāre* to keep safe] > **preˈservable** *adj* > **preˌservaˈbility** *n* > **preˈservably** *adv* > **preservation** (ˌprɛzəˈveɪʃən) *n* > **preˈserver** *n*

preset (prɪˈsɛt) *vb* **-sets, -setting, -set** (*tr*) **1** to set (a timing device) so that something begins to operate at the time specified ▷ *n* **2** *electronics* **a** control, such as a variable resistor, that is not as accessible as the main controls and is used to set initial conditions

preshrunk (priːˈʃrʌŋk) *adj* (of fabrics, garments, etc) having undergone a shrinking process during manufacture so that further shrinkage will not occur

preside (prɪˈzaɪd) *vb* (*intr*) **1** to sit in or hold a position of authority, as over a meeting **2** to exercise authority; control **3** to occupy a position as an instrumentalist: *he presided at the organ* [C17 via French from Latin *praesidēre* to superintend, from *prae* before + *sedēre* to sit] > **preˈsider** *n*

presidency (ˈprɛzɪdənsɪ) *n, pl* **-cies** **1** **a** the office, dignity, or term of a president **b** (*often capital*) the office of president of a republic, esp the office of the President of the US **2** *Mormon Church* **a** a local administrative council consisting of a president and two executive members **b** (*often capital*) the supreme administrative body composed of the Prophet and two councillors

president (ˈprɛzɪdənt) *n* **1** (*often capital*) the chief executive or head of state of a republic, esp of the US **2** (in the US) the chief executive officer of a company, corporation, etc **3** a person who presides over an assembly, meeting, etc **4** the chief executive officer of certain establishments of higher education [C14 via Old French from Late Latin *praesidens* ruler; see PRESIDE] > **presidential** (ˌprɛzɪˈdɛnʃəl) *adj* > **ˌpresiˈdentially** *adv* > **ˈpresidentˌship** *n*

president-elect *n* a person who has been elected president but has not yet entered office

presidio (prɪˈsɪdɪˌəʊ; *Spanish* preˈsiðjo) *n, pl* **-sidios** (-ˈsɪdɪˌəʊz; *Spanish* -ˈsiðjos) a military post or establishment, esp in countries under Spanish control [C19 from Spanish: garrison, from Latin *praesidium* a guard, protection; see PRESIDE]

presidium *or* **praesidium** (prɪˈsɪdɪəm) *n, pl* **-iums** *or* **-ia** (-ɪə) **1** (*often capital*) (in Communist countries) a permanent committee of a larger body, such as a legislature, that acts for it when it is in recess **2** a collective presidency, esp of a nongovernmental organization [C20 from Russian *prezidium*, from Latin *praesidium*, from *praesidēre* to superintend; see PRESIDE]

presignify (priːˈsɪgnɪˌfaɪ) *vb* **-fies, -fying, -fied** (*tr*) to signify beforehand; foreshadow; foretell

press[1] (prɛs) *vb* **1** to apply or exert weight, force, or steady pressure on: *he pressed the button on the*

P

camera **2** (*tr*) to squeeze or compress so as to alter in shape or form **3** to apply heat or pressure to (clothing) so as to smooth out or mark with creases; iron **4** to make (objects) from soft material by pressing with a mould, form, etc, esp to make gramophone records from plastic **5** (*tr*) to hold tightly or clasp, as in an embrace **6** (*tr*) to extract or force out (juice) by pressure (from) **7** (*tr*) *weightlifting* to lift (a weight) successfully with a press: *he managed to press 280 pounds* **8** (*tr*) to force, constrain, or compel **9** to importune or entreat (a person) insistently; urge: *they pressed for an answer* **10** to harass or cause harassment **11** (*tr*) to plead or put forward strongly or importunately: *to press a claim* **12** (*intr*) to be urgent **13** (*tr; usually passive*) to have little of: *we're hard pressed for time* **14** (when *intr*, often foll by *on* or *forward*) to hasten or advance or cause to hasten or advance in a forceful manner **15** (*intr*) to crowd; throng; push **16** (*tr*) (formerly) to put to death or subject to torture by placing heavy weights upon **17** (*tr*) *archaic* to trouble or oppress **18** **press charges** to bring charges against a person ▷ *n* **19** any machine that exerts pressure to form, shape, or cut materials or to extract liquids, compress solids, or hold components together while an adhesive joint is formed **20** See **printing press** **21** the art or process of printing **22** *at* or *in* (the) **press** being printed **23** *to* (the) **press** to be printed: *when is this book going to press?* **24** **the press a** news media and agencies collectively, esp newspapers **b** (*as modifier*): *a press matter; press relations* **25** **the press** those who work in the news media, esp newspaper reporters and photographers **26** the opinions and reviews in the newspapers, etc: *the play received a poor press* **27** the act of pressing or state of being pressed **28** the act of crowding, thronging, or pushing together **29** a closely packed throng of people; crowd; multitude **30** urgency or hurry in business affairs **31** a cupboard, esp a large one used for storing clothes or linen **32** a wood or metal clamp or vice to prevent tennis rackets, etc, from warping when not in use **33** *weightlifting* a lift in which the weight is raised to shoulder level and then above the head [C14 *pressen*, from Old French *presser*, from Latin *pressāre*, from *premere* to press]

press² (prɛs) *vb* (*tr*) **1** to recruit (men) by forcible measures for military service **2** to use for a purpose other than intended, (esp in the phrase **press into service**) ▷ *n* **3** recruitment into military service by forcible measures, as by a press gang [C16 back formation from *prest* to recruit soldiers; see PREST²; also influenced by PRESS¹]

press agency *n* another name for **news agency**

press agent *n* a person employed to obtain favourable publicity, such as notices in newspapers, for an organization, actor, etc. Abbreviation: **PA**

press box *n* an area reserved for reporters, as in a sports stadium

Pressburg ('prɛsbʊrk) *n* the German name for **Bratislava**

press conference *n* an interview for press and television reporters given by a politician, film star, etc

press fit *n* *engineering* a type of fit for mating parts, usually tighter than a sliding fit, used when the parts do not have to move relative to each other

press gallery *n* an area set apart for newspaper reporters, esp in a legislative assembly

press gang *n* **1** (formerly) a detachment of men used to press civilians for service in the navy or army ▷ *vb* **press-gang** (*tr*) **2** to force (a person) to join the navy or army by a press gang **3** to induce (a person) to perform a duty by forceful persuasion: *his friends press-ganged him into joining the committee*

pressie *or* **prezzie** ('prɛzɪ) *n* an informal word for **present²** (sense 21)

pressing ('prɛsɪŋ) *adj* **1** demanding immediate attention **2** persistent or importunate ▷ *n* **3** a large specified number of gramophone records produced at one time from a master record **4** a component formed in a press **5** *football* the tactic of trying to stay very close to the opposition when they are in possession of the ball > 'pressingly *adv* > 'pressingness *n*

pressman ('prɛsmən, -ˌmæn) *n, pl* -men **1** a person who works for the press **2** a person who operates a printing press

pressmark ('prɛsˌmɑːk) *n* *library science* a location mark on a book indicating a specific bookcase [C19 from PRESS¹ (in the sense: cupboard) + MARK¹]

press of sail *n* *nautical* the most sail a vessel can carry under given conditions. Also called: **press of canvas**

pressor ('prɛsə, -sɔː) *adj* *physiol* relating to or producing an increase in blood pressure [C19 from Latin *premere* to press]

press release *n* an official announcement or account of a news item circulated to the press

pressroom ('prɛsˌruːm, -ˌrʊm) *n* the room in a printing establishment that houses the printing presses

press stud *n* a fastening device consisting of one part with a projecting knob that snaps into a hole on another like part, used esp in closures in clothing. Also called: **popper, snap fastener**

press-up *n* an exercise in which the body is alternately raised from and lowered to the floor by the arms only, the trunk being kept straight with the toes and hands resting on the floor. Also called (US and Canadian): **push-up**

pressure ('prɛʃə) *n* **1** the state of pressing or being pressed **2** the exertion of force by one body on the surface of another **3** a moral force that compels: *to bring pressure to bear* **4** an urgent claim or demand or series of urgent claims or demands: *to work under pressure* **5** a burdensome condition that is hard to bear: *the pressure of grief* **6** the normal force applied to a unit area of a surface, usually measured in pascals (newtons per square metre), millibars, torr, or atmospheres. Symbol: *p* or *P* **7** short for **atmospheric pressure** *or* **blood pressure** ▷ *vb* **8** (*tr*) to constrain or compel, as by the application of moral force **9** another word for **pressurize** [C14 from Late Latin *pressūra* a pressing, from *premere* to press] > 'pressureless *adj*

pressure cabin *n* the pressurized cabin of an aircraft or spacecraft

pressure-cook *vb* to cook (food) in a pressure cooker

pressure cooker *n* **1** a strong hermetically sealed pot in which food may be cooked quickly under pressure at a temperature above the normal boiling point of water **2** NZ *informal* a trainee student attending a shortened qualifying course

pressure drag *n* the part of the total drag of a body moving through a gas or liquid caused by the components of the pressures at right angles to the surface of the body

pressure gauge *n* any instrument for measuring fluid pressure. See also **Bourdon gauge, manometer**

pressure gradient *n* **1** the change of pressure per unit distance. See **adverse pressure gradient, favourable pressure gradient 2** *meteorol* the decrease in atmospheric pressure per unit of horizontal distance, shown on a synoptic chart by the spacing of the isobars

pressure group *n* a group of people who seek to exert pressure on legislators, public opinion, etc, in order to promote their own ideas or welfare

pressure head *n* *physics* a more formal name for **head** (sense 24a)

pressure point *n* any of several points on the body above an artery that, when firmly pressed, will control bleeding from the artery at a point farther away from the heart

pressure suit *n* an inflatable suit worn by a person flying at high altitudes or in space, to provide protection from low pressure

pressure ulcer *or* **pressure sore** *n* another term for **bedsore**

pressure vessel *n* *engineering* a vessel designed for containing substances, reactions, etc, at pressures above atmospheric pressure

pressurize *or* **pressurise** ('prɛʃəˌraɪz) *vb* (*tr*) **1** to increase the pressure in (an enclosure, such as an aircraft cabin) in order to maintain approximately atmospheric pressure when the external pressure is low **2** to increase pressure on (a fluid) **3** to make insistent demands of (someone); coerce > ˌpressuriˈzation *or* ˌpressuriˈsation *n* > 'pressuˌrizer *or* 'pressuˌriser *n*

pressurized-water reactor *n* a nuclear reactor using water as coolant and moderator at a pressure that is too high to allow boiling to take place inside the reactor. The fuel is enriched uranium oxide cased in zirconium. Abbreviation: **PWR**

presswork ('prɛsˌwɜːk) *n* **1** the operation of a printing press **2** the matter printed by a printing press

prest¹ (prɛst) *adj* *obsolete* prepared for action or use; ready [C13 via Old French from Late Latin *praestus* ready to hand; see PRESTO]

prest² (prɛst) *n* *obsolete* a loan of money [C16 originally, loan money offered as an inducement to recruits, from Old French: advance pay in the army, from *prester* to lend, from Latin *praestāre* to provide, from *prae* before + *stāre* to stand]

Prester John ('prɛstə) *n* a legendary Christian priest and king, believed in the Middle Ages to have ruled in the Far East, but identified in the 14th century with the king of Ethiopia [C14 *Prestre Johan*, from Medieval Latin *presbyter Iohannes* Priest John]

prestidigitation (ˌprɛstɪˌdɪdʒɪˈteɪʃən) *n* another name for **sleight of hand** [C19 from French: quick-fingeredness, from Latin *praestigiae* feats of juggling, tricks, probably influenced by French *preste* nimble, and Latin *digitus* finger; see PRESTIGE] > ˌprestiˈdigiˌtator *n*

prestige (prɛˈstiːʒ) *n* **1** high status or reputation achieved through influence, wealth, etc; renown **b 2 a** the power to influence or impress; glamour **b** (*modifier*) *a prestige car* [C17 via French from Latin *praestigiae* feats of juggling, tricks; apparently related to Latin *praestringere* to bind tightly, blindfold, from *prae* before + *stringere* to draw tight, bind]

prestige pricing *n* *marketing* the practice of giving a product a high price to convey the idea that it must be of high quality or status

prestigious (prɛˈstɪdʒəs) *adj* **1** having status or glamour; impressive or influential **2** *rare* characterized by or using deceit, cunning, or illusion; fraudulent > presˈtigiously *adv* > presˈtigiousness *n*

prestissimo (prɛˈstɪsɪˌməʊ) *music* ▷ *adj, adv* **1** to be played as fast as possible ▷ *n, pl* -mos **2** a piece or passage directed to be played in this way [C18 from Italian: very quickly, from *presto* fast]

presto ('prɛstəʊ) *adj, adv* **1** *music* to be played very fast ▷ *adv* **2** immediately, suddenly, or at once (esp in the phrase **hey presto**) ▷ *n, pl* -tos **3** *music* a movement or passage directed to be played very quickly [C16 from Italian: fast, from Late Latin *praestus* (adj) ready to hand, Latin *praestō* (adv) present]

Preston ('prɛstən) *n* a city in NW England, administrative centre of Lancashire, on the River Ribble: developed as a weaving centre (17th–18th centuries); university (1992). Pop: 184 836 (2001)

Prestonpans (ˌprɛstənˈpænz) *n* a small town and resort in SE Scotland, in East Lothian on the Firth of Forth: scene of the battle (1745) in which the Jacobite army of Prince Charles Edward defeated government forces under Sir John Cope. Pop: 7153 (2001)

prestress (ˌpriːˈstrɛs) *vb* (*tr*) to apply tensile stress to (the steel cables, wires, etc, of a precast concrete part) before the load is applied

prestressed concrete *n* concrete that contains steel wires, cables, etc, that are prestressed within their elastic limit to counteract the stresses that will occur under load
Prestwich ('prɛstwɪtʃ) *n* a town in NW England, in Bury unitary authority, Greater Manchester. Pop: 31 693 (2001)
Prestwick ('prɛstwɪk) *n* a town in SW Scotland, in South Ayrshire on the Firth of Clyde; international airport, golf course; tourism. Pop: 14 934 (2001)
presumable (prɪ'zju:məbᵊl) *adj* able to be presumed or taken for granted
presumably (prɪ'zju:məblɪ) *adv* (*sentence modifier*) one presumes or supposes that: *presumably he won't see you, if you're leaving tomorrow*
presume (prɪ'zju:m) *vb* **1** (when *tr, often takes a clause as object*) to take (something) for granted; assume **2** (when *tr, often foll by an infinitive*) to take upon oneself (to do something) without warrant or permission; dare: *do you presume to copy my work?* **3** (*intr;* foll by *on* or *upon*) to rely or depend: *don't presume on his agreement* **4** *law* to take as proved until contrary evidence is produced [C14 via Old French from Latin *praesūmere* to take in advance, from *prae* before + *sūmere* to ASSUME] > **presumedly** (prɪ'zju:mɪdlɪ) *adv* > **pre'sumer** *n* > **pre'suming** *adj* > **pre'sumingly** *adv*
presumption (prɪ'zʌmpʃən) *n* **1** the act of presuming **2** bold or insolent behaviour or manners **3** a belief or assumption based on reasonable evidence **4** a ground or basis on which to presume **5** *law* an inference of the truth of a fact from other facts proved, admitted, or judicially noticed [C13 via Old French from Latin *praesumptiō* a using in advance, anticipation, from *praesūmere* to take beforehand; see PRESUME]
presumptive (prɪ'zʌmptɪv) *adj* **1** based on presumption or probability **2** affording reasonable ground for belief **3** of or relating to embryonic tissues that become differentiated into a particular tissue or organ: *presumptive epidermis* > **pre'sumptively** *adv* > **pre'sumptiveness** *n*
presumptuous (prɪ'zʌmptjʊəs) *adj* **1** characterized by presumption or tending to presume; bold; forward **2** an obsolete word for **presumptive.** > **pre'sumptuously** *adv* > **pre'sumptuousness** *n*
presuppose (,pri:sə'pəʊz) *vb* (*tr*) **1** to take for granted; assume **2** to require or imply as a necessary prior condition **3** *philosophy, logic, linguistics* to require (a condition) to be satisfied as a precondition for a statement to be either true or false or for a speech act to be felicitous. *Have you stopped beating your wife?* presupposes that the person addressed has a wife and has beaten her > **presupposition** (,pri:sʌpə'zɪʃən) *n*
preteen (pri:'ti:n) *n* a boy or girl approaching his or her teens
pretence *or US* **pretense** (prɪ'tɛns) *n* **1** the act of pretending **2** a false display; affectation **3** a claim, esp a false one, to a right, title, or distinction **4** make-believe or feigning **5** a false claim or allegation; pretext **6** a less common word for **pretension** (sense 3)
pretend (prɪ'tɛnd) *vb* **1** (when *tr, usually takes a clause as object or an infinitive*) to claim or allege (something untrue) **2** (*tr; may take a clause as object or an infinitive*) to make believe, as in a play: *you pretend to be Ophelia* **3** (*intr;* foll by *to*) to present a claim, esp a dubious one: *to pretend to the throne* **4** (*intr;* foll by *to*) *obsolete* to aspire as a candidate or suitor (for) ▷ *adj* **5** fanciful; make-believe; simulated: *a pretend gun* [C14 from Latin *praetendere* to stretch forth, feign, from *prae* in front + *tendere* to stretch]
pretender (prɪ'tɛndə) *n* **1** a person who pretends or makes false allegations **2** a person who mounts a claim, as to a throne or title
pretension (prɪ'tɛnʃən) *n* **1** (*often plural*) a false or unsupportable claim, esp to merit, worth, or importance **2** a specious or unfounded allegation; pretext **3** the state or quality of being pretentious
pretensive (prɪ'tɛnsɪv) *adj Caribbean* pretentious
pretentious (prɪ'tɛnʃəs) *adj* **1** making claim to distinction or importance, esp undeservedly **2** having or creating a deceptive outer appearance of great worth; ostentatious > **pre'tentiously** *adv* > **pre'tentiousness** *n*
preter- *prefix* beyond, more than, or exceeding: *preternatural* [from Latin *praeter-*, from *praeter*]
preterhuman (,pri:tə'hju:mən) *adj rare* beyond what is human
preterite *or US* **preterit** ('prɛtərɪt) *grammar* ▷ *n* **1** a tense of verbs used to relate past action, formed in English by inflection of the verb, as *jumped, swam* **2** a verb in this tense ▷ *adj* **3** denoting this tense [C14 from Late Latin *praeteritum* (*tempus*) past (time, tense), from Latin *praeterīre* to go by, from PRETER- + *īre* to go]
preterition (,prɛtə'rɪʃən) *n* **1** the act of passing over or omitting **2** *Roman law* the failure of a testator to name one of his children in his will, thus invalidating it **3** (in Calvinist theology) the doctrine that God passed over or left unpredestined those not elected to final salvation [C17 from Late Latin *praeteritiō* a passing over]
preteritive (prɪ'tɛrɪtɪv) *adj* (of a verb) having only past tense forms
preterm (,pri:'tɜ:m) *adj* **1** (of a baby) born prematurely ▷ *adv* **2** prematurely
pretermit (,pri:tə'mɪt) *vb* **-mits, -mitting, -mitted** (*tr*) *rare* **1** to overlook intentionally; disregard **2** to fail to do; neglect; omit [C16 from Latin *praetermittere* to let pass, from PRETER- + *mittere* to send, release] > **pretermission** (,pri:tə'mɪʃən) *n* > **,preter'mitter** *n*
preternatural (,pri:tə'nætʃrəl) *adj* **1** beyond what is ordinarily found in nature; abnormal **2** another word for **supernatural** [C16 from Medieval Latin *praeternātūrālis*, from Latin *praeter natūram* beyond the scope of nature] > **,preter'naturally** *adv* > **,preter'naturalism** *n* > **,preter'naturalness** *or* **,preter,natu'rality** *n*
pretest (pri:'tɛst) *vb* (*tr*) **1** to test (something) before presenting it to its intended public or client ▷ *n* ('pri:tɛst) **2** the act or instance of pretesting
pretext ('pri:tɛkst) *n* **1** a fictitious reason given in order to conceal the real one **2** a specious excuse; pretence [C16 from Latin *praetextum* disguise, from *praetexere* to weave in front, disguise; see TEXTURE]
pretonic (pri:'tɒnɪk) *adj* denoting or relating to the syllable before the one bearing the primary stress in a word
pretor ('pri:tə) *n* a variant spelling of **praetor**
Pretoria (prɪ'tɔ:rɪə) *n* a city in N South Africa, the administrative capital of South Africa; formerly capital of Transvaal province: two universities (1873, 1930); large steelworks. Pop: 525 384 (2001). Also called: **Tshwane**
prettify ('prɪtɪ,faɪ) *vb* **-fies, -fying, -fied** (*tr*) to make pretty, esp in a trivial fashion; embellish > **,prettifi'cation** *n* > **'pretti,fier** *n*
pretty ('prɪtɪ) *adj* **-tier, -tiest** **1** pleasing or appealing in a delicate or graceful way **2** dainty, neat, or charming **3** *informal, often ironic* excellent, grand, or fine: *here's a pretty mess!* **4** *informal* lacking in masculinity; effeminate; foppish **5** *Scot* vigorous or brave **6** an archaic word for **elegant** **7** **a pretty penny** *informal* a large sum of money **8** **sitting pretty** *informal* well placed or established financially, socially, etc ▷ *n, pl* **-ties** **9** a pretty person or thing ▷ *adv* **10** *informal* fairly or moderately; somewhat **11** *informal* quite or very ▷ *vb* **-ties, -tying, -tied** **12** (*tr;* often foll by *up*) to make pretty; adorn [Old English *prættig* clever; related to Middle Low German *prattich* obstinate, Dutch *prettig* glad, Old Norse *prettugr* cunning] > **'prettily** *adv* > **'prettiness** *n*
pretty-pretty *adj informal* excessively or ostentatiously pretty
pretzel ('prɛtsəl) *n* a brittle savoury biscuit, in the form of a knot or stick, glazed and salted on the outside, eaten esp in Germany and the US [C19 from German, from Old High German *brezitella;* perhaps related to Medieval Latin *bracellus* bracelet, from Latin *bracchium* arm]
Preussen ('prɔysən) *n* the German name for **Prussia**
prevail (prɪ'veɪl) *vb* (*intr*) **1** (often foll by *over* or *against*) to prove superior; gain mastery: *skill will prevail* **2** to be or appear as the most important feature; be prevalent **3** to exist widely; be in force **4** (often foll by *on* or *upon*) to succeed in persuading or inducing [C14 from Latin *praevalēre* to be superior in strength, from *prae* beyond + *valēre* to be strong] > **pre'vailer** *n*
prevailing (prɪ'veɪlɪŋ) *adj* **1** generally accepted; widespread: *the prevailing opinion* **2** most frequent or conspicuous; predominant: *the prevailing wind is from the north* > **pre'vailingly** *adv*
prevalent ('prɛvələnt) *adj* **1** widespread or current **2** superior in force or power; predominant [C16 (in the sense: powerful): from Latin *praevalens* very strong, from *praevalēre:* see PREVAIL] > **'prevalence** *or* **'prevalentness** *n* > **'prevalently** *adv*
prevaricate (prɪ'værɪ,keɪt) *vb* (*intr*) to speak or act falsely or evasively with intent to deceive [C16 from Latin *praevāricārī* to walk crookedly, from *prae* beyond + *vāricare* to straddle the legs; compare Latin *vārus* bent] > **pre,vari'cation** *n* > **pre'vari,cator** *n*
prevenient (prɪ'vi:nɪənt) *adj* coming before; anticipating or preceding [C17 from Latin *praevenīre* to precede, PREVENT] > **pre'veniently** *adv*
prevent (prɪ'vɛnt) *vb* **1** (*tr*) to keep from happening, esp by taking precautionary action **2** (*tr; often foll by from*) to keep (someone from doing something); hinder; impede **3** (*intr*) to interpose or act as a hindrance **4** (*tr*) *archaic* to anticipate or precede [C15 from Latin *praevenīre*, from *prae* before + *venīre* to come] > **pre'ventable** *or* **pre'ventible** *adj* > **pre,venta'bility** *or* **pre,venti'bility** *n* > **pre'ventably** *or* **pre'ventibly** *adv*

P

preventer (prɪ'vɛntə) *n* **1** a person or thing that prevents **2** *nautical* a rope or other piece of gear rigged to prevent a sail from gybing
prevention (prɪ'vɛnʃən) *n* **1** the act of preventing **2** a hindrance, obstacle, or impediment
preventive (prɪ'vɛntɪv) *adj* **1** tending or intended to prevent or hinder **2** *med* **a** tending to prevent disease; prophylactic **b** of or relating to the branch of medicine concerned with prolonging life and preventing disease **3** (in Britain) of, relating to, or belonging to the customs and excise service or the coastguard ▷ *n* **4** something that serves to prevent or hinder **5** *med* any drug or agent that tends to prevent or protect against disease **6** another name for **contraceptive** ▷ Also (except for sense 3): **preventative** (prɪ'vɛntətɪv) > **pre'ventively** *adv* > **pre'ventiveness** *n*
preverbal (,pri:'vɜ:bᵊl) *adj* **1** being before the development of speech: *preverbal infants* **2** *grammar* coming before the verb
preview *or US* **prevue** ('pri:vju:) *n* **1** an advance or preliminary view or sight **2** an advance showing before public presentation of a film, art exhibition, etc, usually before an invited audience of celebrities and journalists **3** a public performance of a play before the official first night ▷ *vb* **4** (*tr*) to view in advance
preview monitor *n* (in a television studio control room) a picture monitor used for inspecting a picture source before it is switched to transmission
previous ('pri:vɪəs) *adj* **1** (*prenominal*) existing or coming before something else in time or position; prior **2** (*postpositive*) *informal* taking place or done too soon; premature **3** **previous to** before; prior to [C17 from Latin *praevius* leading the way, from *prae* before + *via* way] > **'previously** *adv* > **'previousness** *n*
previous question *n* **1** (in the House of Commons) a motion to drop the present topic under debate, put in order to prevent a vote **2** (in

the House of Lords and US legislative bodies) a motion to vote on a bill or other question without delay ▷ See also **closure** (sense 4)

previse (prɪˈvaɪz) *vb (tr) rare* **1** to predict or foresee **2** to notify in advance [C16 from Latin *praevidēre* to foresee, from *prae* before + *vidēre* to see]

prevision (prɪˈvɪʒən) *n rare* **1** the act or power of foreseeing; prescience **2** a prophetic vision or prophecy

prevocalic (ˌpriːvəʊˈkælɪk) *adj* (of a consonant) coming immediately before a vowel > ˌ**prevoˈcalically** *adv*

prewar (ˌpriːˈwɔː, ˈpriːˌwɔː) *adj* of or occurring in the period before a war, esp before World War I or II

prewash (priːˈwɒʃ) *vb* **1** to give a preliminary wash to (clothes), esp in a washing machine ▷ *n* (ˈpriːwɒʃ) **2** a preliminary wash, esp in a washing machine

prey (preɪ) *n* **1** an animal hunted or captured by another for food **2** a person or thing that becomes the victim of a hostile person, influence, etc **3** **bird** *or* **beast of prey** a bird or animal that preys on others for food **4** an archaic word for **booty** ▷ *vb (intr; often foll by* on *or* upon*)* **5** to hunt or seize food by killing other animals **6** to make a victim (of others), as by profiting at their expense **7** to exert a depressing or obsessive effect (on the mind, spirits, etc); weigh heavily (upon) [C13 from Old French *preie*, from Latin *praeda* booty; see PREDATORY] > ˈ**preyer** *n*

prezzie (ˈprɛzɪ) *n* a variant of **pressie,** an informal word for **present**² (sense 21)

Priam (ˈpraɪəm) *n Greek myth* the last king of Troy, killed at its fall. He was father by Hecuba of Hector, Paris, and Cassandra

priapic (praɪˈæpɪk, -ˈeɪ-) *or* **priapean** (ˌpraɪəˈpiːən) *adj* **1** *(sometimes capital)* of or relating to Priapus **2** a less common word for **phallic**

priapism (ˈpraɪəˌpɪzəm) *n pathol* prolonged painful erection of the penis, caused by neurological disorders, obstruction of the penile blood vessels, etc [C17 from Late Latin *priāpismus*, ultimately from Greek PRIAPUS]

Priapus (praɪˈeɪpəs) *n* **1** (in classical antiquity) the god of the male procreative power and of gardens and vineyards **2** *(often not capital)* a representation of the penis

Pribilof Islands (ˈprɪbɪləf) *pl n* a group of islands in the Bering Sea, off SW Alaska, belonging to the US: the breeding ground of the northern fur seal. Area: about 168 sq km (65 sq miles). Also called: **Fur Seal Islands**

price (praɪs) *n* **1** the sum in money or goods for which anything is or may be bought or sold **2** the cost at which anything is obtained **3** the cost of bribing a person **4** a sum of money offered or given as a reward for a capture or killing **5** value or worth, esp high worth **6** *gambling* another word for **odds** **7** **at any price** whatever the price or cost **8** **at a price** at a high price **9** **beyond** *(or* **without)** **price** invaluable or priceless **10** **the price of (one)** *Irish* what (one) deserves, esp a fitting punishment: *it's just the price of him* **11** **what price (something)?** what are the chances of (something) happening now? ▷ *vb (tr)* **12** to fix or establish the price of **13** to ascertain or discover the price of **14** **price out of the market** to charge so highly for as to prevent the sale, hire, etc, of [C13 *pris*, from Old French, from Latin *pretium* price, value, wage] > ˈ**pricer** *n*

price break *n* a reduction in price, esp for bulk purchase

Price Commission *n* (in Britain) a commission established by the government in 1973 with authority to control prices as a measure against inflation. It was abolished in 1980

price control *n* the establishment and maintenance of maximum price levels for basic goods and services by a government, esp during periods of war or inflation

price discrimination *n economics* the setting of different prices to be charged to different consumers or in different markets for the same goods or services

price-dividend ratio *n* the ratio of the price of a share on a stock exchange to the dividends per share paid in the previous year, used as a measure of a company's potential as an investment. Abbreviations: **P-D ratio, PDR**

price-earnings ratio *n* the ratio of the price of a share on a stock exchange to the earnings per share, used as a measure of a company's future profitability. Abbreviation: **P/E ratio**

price-fixing *n* **1** the setting of prices by agreement among producers and distributors **2** another name for **price control** *or* **resale price maintenance**

price leadership *n marketing* the setting of the price of a product or service by a dominant firm at a level that competitors can match, in order to avoid a price war

priceless (ˈpraɪslɪs) *adj* **1** of inestimable worth; beyond valuation; invaluable **2** *informal* extremely amusing or ridiculous > ˈ**pricelessly** *adv* > ˈ**pricelessness** *n*

price ring *n* a group of traders formed to maintain the prices of their goods

prices and incomes policy *n* voluntary or statutory regulation of the level of increases in prices and incomes

price-sensitive *adj* likely to affect the price of property, esp shares and securities: *price-sensitive information*

price support *n* government maintenance of specified price levels at a minimum above market equilibrium by subsidy or by purchase of the market surplus at the guaranteed levels

price tag *n* **1** a ticket or label on an article for sale showing its price **2** the cost, esp of something not usually priced: *the price tag on a top footballer*

price war *n* a period of intense competition among enterprises, esp retail enterprises, in the same market, characterized by repeated price reductions rather than advertising, brand promotion, etc

pricey *or* **pricy** (ˈpraɪsɪ) *adj* **pricier, priciest** an informal word for **expensive**

prick (prɪk) *vb (mainly tr)* **1** **a** to make (a small hole) in (something) by piercing lightly with a sharp point **b** to wound in this manner **2** *(intr)* to cause or have a piercing or stinging sensation **3** to cause to feel a sharp emotional pain: *knowledge of such poverty pricked his conscience* **4** to puncture or pierce **5** to mark, delineate, or outline by dots or punctures **6** *(also intr; usually foll by* up*)* to rise or raise erect; point: *the dog pricked his ears up at his master's call* **7** *(usually foll by* out *or* off*)* to transplant (seedlings) into a larger container **8** *(often foll by* off*) navigation* to measure or trace (a course, distance, etc) on a chart with dividers **9** *archaic* to rouse or impel; urge on **10** *(intr) archaic* to ride fast on horseback; spur a horse on **11** **prick up one's ears** to start to listen attentively; become interested ▷ *n* **12** the act of pricking or the condition or sensation of being pricked **13** a mark made by a sharp point; puncture **14** a sharp emotional pain resembling the physical pain caused by being pricked: *a prick of conscience* **15** a taboo slang word for **penis** **16** *slang, derogatory* an obnoxious or despicable man **17** an instrument or weapon with a sharp point, such as a thorn, goad, bee sting, etc **18** the footprint or track of an animal, esp a hare **19** *obsolete* a small mark caused by pricking a surface; dot; point **20** **kick against the pricks** to hurt oneself by struggling against something in vain [Old English *prica* point, puncture; related to Dutch *prik*, Icelandic *prik* short stick, Swedish *prick* point, stick]

pricker (ˈprɪkə) *n* **1** a person or thing that pricks **2** *US* a thorn; prickle

pricket (ˈprɪkɪt) *n* **1** a male deer in the second year of life having unbranched antlers **2** a sharp metal spike on which to stick a candle **3** a candlestick having such a spike [C14 *priket*, from *prik* PRICK]

prickle (ˈprɪkᵊl) *n* **1** *botany* a pointed process arising from the outer layer of a stem, leaf, etc, and containing no woody or conducting tissue. Compare **thorn** (sense 1) **2** a pricking or stinging sensation ▷ *vb* **3** to feel or cause to feel a stinging sensation **4** *(tr)* to prick, as with a thorn [Old English *pricel*; related to Middle Low German *prekel*, German *Prickel*]

prickly (ˈprɪklɪ) *adj* **-lier, -liest** **1** having or covered with prickles **2** stinging or tingling **3** bad-tempered or irritable **4** full of difficulties; knotty: *a prickly problem* > ˈ**prickliness** *n*

prickly ash *n* a North American rutaceous shrub or small tree, *Zanthoxylum americanum*, having prickly branches, feathery aromatic leaves, and bark used as a remedy for toothache. Also called: **toothache tree**

prickly heat *n* a nontechnical name for **miliaria**

prickly pear *n* **1** any of various tropical cacti of the genus *Opuntia*, having flattened or cylindrical spiny joints and oval fruit that is edible in some species. See also **cholla, nopal** (sense 2) **2** the fruit of any of these plants

prickly poppy *n* an annual papaveraceous plant, *Argemone mexicana*, of tropical America, having prickly stems and leaves and large yellow or white flowers

prick song *n obsolete* **a** a piece of written vocal music **b** vocal music sung from a copy [C16 from *pricked song, prickt song*, from PRICK (in the sense: to mark out, notate)]

pride (praɪd) *n* **1** a feeling of honour and self-respect; a sense of personal worth **2** excessive self-esteem; conceit **3** a source of pride **4** satisfaction or pleasure taken in one's own or another's success, achievements, etc (esp in the phrase **take (a) pride in**) **5** the better or most superior part of something; flower **6** the most flourishing time **7** a group (of lions) **8** the mettle of a horse; courage; spirit **9** *archaic* sexual desire, esp in a female animal **10** *archaic* display, pomp, or splendour **11** **pride of place** the most important position ▷ *vb* **12** *(tr; foll by* on *or* upon*)* to take pride in (oneself) for **13** *(intr)* to glory or revel (in) [Old English *prȳda*; related to Latin *prodesse* to be useful, Old Norse *prūthr* stately; see PROUD] > ˈ**prideful** *adj* > ˈ**pridefully** *adv*

Pride's Purge (praɪd) *n* the expulsion from the Long Parliament of members hostile to the army by Thomas Pride (died 1658) in 1648

prie-dieu (priːˈdjɜː) *n* a piece of furniture consisting of a low surface for kneeling upon and a narrow front surmounted by a rest for the elbows or for books, for use when praying [C18 from French, from *prier* to pray + *Dieu* God]

prier *or* **pryer** (ˈpraɪə) *n* a person who pries

priest (priːst) *or feminine* **priestess** *n* **1** *Christianity* a person ordained to act as a mediator between God and man in administering the sacraments, preaching, blessing, guiding, etc **2** (in episcopal Churches) a minister in the second grade of the hierarchy of holy orders, ranking below a bishop but above a deacon **3** a minister of any religion **4** *Judaism* a descendant of the family of Aaron who has certain privileges in the synagogue service **5** (in some non-Christian religions) an official who offers sacrifice on behalf of the people and performs other religious ceremonies **6** *(sometimes capital)* a variety of fancy pigeon having a bald pate with a crest or peak at the back of the head **7** *angling* a small club used to kill fish caught ▷ *vb (tr)* **8** to make a priest; ordain ▷ Related adjective: **hieratic** [Old English *prēost*, apparently from PRESBYTER; related to Old High German *prēster*, Old French *prestre*] > ˈ**priestˌlike** *adj*

priestcraft (ˈpriːstˌkrɑːft) *n* **1** the art and skills involved in the work of a priest **2** *derogatory* the influence of priests upon politics or the use by them of secular power

priest-hole *or* **priest's hole** *n* a secret chamber

in certain houses in England, built as a hiding place for Roman Catholic priests when they were proscribed in the 16th and 17th centuries

priesthood ('priːstˌhʊd) *n* **1** the state, order, or office of a priest **2** priests collectively

priestly ('priːstlɪ) *adj* -lier, -liest of, relating to, characteristic of, or befitting a priest > 'priestliness *n*

priest-ridden *adj* dominated or governed by or excessively under the influence of priests

prig¹ (prɪg) *n* a person who is smugly self-righteous and narrow-minded [c18 of unknown origin] > 'priggery or 'priggishness *n* > 'priggish *adj* > 'priggishly *adv* > 'priggism *n*

prig² (prɪg) *Brit slang, archaic* ▷ *vb* prigs, prigging, prigged **1** another word for **steal** ▷ *n* **2** another word for **thief** [c16 of unknown origin]

prill (prɪl) *vb* **1** (*tr*) to convert (a material) into a granular free-flowing form ▷ *n* **2** prilled material [c18 originally a Cornish copper-mining term, of obscure origin]

prim (prɪm) *adj* primmer, primmest **1** affectedly proper, precise, or formal ▷ *vb* prims, primming, primmed **2** (*tr*) to make prim **3** to purse (the mouth) primly or (of the mouth) to be so pursed [c18 of unknown origin] > 'primly *adv* > 'primness *n*

prima ballerina ('priːmə) *n* a leading female ballet dancer [from Italian, literally: first ballerina]

primacy ('praɪməsɪ) *n, pl* -cies **1** the state of being first in rank, grade, etc **2** *Christianity* the office, rank, or jurisdiction of a primate or senior bishop or (in the Roman Catholic Church) the pope

prima donna ('priːmə 'dɒnə) *n, pl* prima donnas **1** a female operatic star; diva **2** *informal* a temperamental person [c19 from Italian: first lady]

primaeval (praɪ'miːvᵊl) *adj* a variant spelling of **primeval**

prima facie ('praɪmə 'feɪʃɪ) at first sight; as it seems at first [c15 from Latin, from *prīmus* first + *faciēs* FACE]

prima-facie evidence *n law* evidence that is sufficient to establish a fact or to raise a presumption of the truth of a fact unless controverted

primage ('praɪmɪdʒ) *n* NZ tax added to customs duty

primal ('praɪməl) *adj* **1** first or original **2** chief or most important [c17 from Medieval Latin *prīmālis*, from Latin *prīmus* first]

primal therapy *n psychol* a form of psychotherapy in which patients are encouraged to scream abusively about their parents and agonizingly about their own suffering in infancy. Also called: **primal scream therapy, scream therapy** [c20 from the book *The Primal Scream* (1970) by Arthur Janov, US psychologist, who originated the treatment]

primaquine ('praɪməˌkwiːn) *n* a synthetic drug used in the treatment of malaria. Formula: $C_{15}H_{21}N_3O$ [c20 from *prima-*, from Latin *prīmus* first + QUIN(OLIN)E]

primarily ('praɪmərəlɪ) *adv* **1** principally; chiefly; mainly **2** at first; originally

primary ('praɪmərɪ) *adj* **1** first in importance, degree, rank, etc **2** first in position or time, as in a series **3** fundamental; basic **4** being the first stage; elementary **5** (*prenominal*) of or relating to the education of children up to the age of 11 **6** (of the flight feathers of a bird's wing) growing from the manus **7 a** being the part of an electric circuit, such as a transformer or induction coil, in which a changing current induces a current in a neighbouring circuit: *a primary coil* **b** (of a current) flowing in such a circuit. Compare **secondary 8 a** (of a product) consisting of a natural raw material; unmanufactured **b** (of production or industry) involving the extraction or winning of such products. Agriculture, fishing, forestry, hunting, and mining are primary industries. Compare **secondary** (sense 7), **tertiary** (sense 3) **9**

chem **a** (of an organic compound) having a functional group attached to a carbon atom that is attached to at least two hydrogen atoms **b** (of an amine) having only one organic group attached to the nitrogen atom; containing the group NH_2 **c** (of a salt) derived from a tribasic acid by replacement of one acidic hydrogen atom with a metal atom or electropositive group **10** *linguistics* **a** derived from a word that is not a derivation but the ultimate form itself. *Lovable* is a primary derivative of *love* **b** (of Latin, Greek, or Sanskrit tenses) referring to present or future time. Compare **historic** (sense 3) **11** *geology* relating to magmas that have not experienced fractional crystallization or crystal contamination ▷ *n, pl* -ries **12** a person or thing that is first in rank, occurrence, etc **13** (in the US) **a** a preliminary election in which the voters of a state or region choose a party's convention delegates, nominees for office, etc. See also **closed primary, direct primary, open primary b** a local meeting of voters registered with one party to nominate candidates, select convention delegates, etc. Full name: **primary election 14** See **primary colour 15** any of the flight feathers growing from the manus of a bird's wing **16** a primary coil, winding, inductance, or current in an electric circuit **17** *astronomy* a celestial body around which one or more specified secondary bodies orbit: *the sun is the primary of the earth* [c15 from Latin *prīmārius* of the first rank, principal, from *prīmus* first]

primary accent *or* **stress** *n linguistics* the strongest accent in a word or breath group, as that on the first syllable of *agriculture*. Compare **secondary accent**

primary cell *n* an electric cell that generates an electromotive force by the direct and usually irreversible conversion of chemical energy into electrical energy. It cannot be recharged efficiently by an electric current. Also called: **voltaic cell.** Compare **secondary cell**

primary colour *n* **1** Also called: **additive primary** any of three spectral colours (usually red, green, and blue) that can be mixed to match any other colour, including white light but excluding black **2** Also called: **subtractive primary** any one of the spectral colours cyan, magenta, or yellow that can be subtracted from white light to match any other colour. An equal mixture of the three produces a black pigment **3** Also called: **psychological primary** any one of the colours red, yellow, green, or blue. All other colours look like a mixture of two or more of these colours and they play a unique role in the processing of colour by the visual system ▷ See also **secondary colour, complementary colour**

primary effect *n psychol* the process whereby the first few items on a list are learnt more rapidly than the middle items

primary election *n* See **primary** (sense 13)

primary mirror *n* the mirror that collects and focuses the incoming light in a reflecting telescope

primary processes *pl n psychoanal* unconscious, irrational thought processes, such as condensation or displacement, governed by the pleasure principle. Compare **secondary processes**

primary qualities *pl n* (in empiricist philosophy) those properties of objects that are directly known by experience, such as size, shape, and number

primary school *n* **1** (in Britain) a school for children below the age of 11. It is usually divided into an infant and a junior section **2** (in the US and Canada) a school equivalent to the first three or four grades of elementary school, sometimes including a kindergarten

primary stress *n linguistics* another term for **primary accent**

primate¹ ('praɪmeɪt) *n* **1** any placental mammal of the order *Primates*, typically having flexible hands and feet with opposable first digits, good eyesight, and, in the higher apes, a highly

developed brain: includes lemurs, lorises, monkeys, apes, and man ▷ *adj* **2** of, relating to, or belonging to the order *Primates* [c18 from New Latin *primates*, plural of *prīmās* principal, from *prīmus* first] > primatial (praɪ'meɪʃəl) *adj*

primate² ('praɪmeɪt) *n* **1** another name for **archbishop 2 Primate of all England** the Archbishop of Canterbury **3 Primate of England** the Archbishop of York [c13 from Old French, from Latin *prīmās* principal, from *prīmus* first]

primatology (ˌpraɪmə'tɒlədʒɪ) *n* the branch of zoology that is concerned with the study of primates > ˌprima'tologist *n*

prime (praɪm) *adj* **1** (*prenominal*) first in quality or value; first-rate **2** (*prenominal*) fundamental; original **3** (*prenominal*) first in importance, authority, etc; chief **4** *maths* **a** having no factors except itself or one: *$x^2 + x + 3$ is a prime polynomial* **b** (foll by *to*) having no common factors (with): *20 is prime to 21* **5** *finance* having the best credit rating: *prime investments* ▷ *n* **6** the time when a thing is at its best **7** a period of power, vigour, etc, usually following youth (esp in the phrase **the prime of life**) **8** the beginning of something, such as the spring **9** *maths* short for **prime number 10** *linguistics* a semantically indivisible element; minimal component of the sense of a word **11** *music* **a** unison **b** the tonic of a scale **12** *chiefly RC Church* the second of the seven canonical hours of the divine office, originally fixed for the first hour of the day, at sunrise **13** the first of eight basic positions from which a parry or attack can be made in fencing ▷ *vb* **14** to prepare (something); make ready **15** (*tr*) to apply a primer, such as paint or size, to (a surface) **16** (*tr*) to fill (a pump) with its working fluid before starting, in order to improve the sealing of the pump elements and to expel air from it before starting **17** (*tr*) to increase the quantity of fuel in the float chamber of (a carburettor) in order to facilitate the starting of an engine **18** (*tr*) to insert a primer into (a gun, mine, charge, etc) preparatory to detonation or firing **19** (*intr*) (of a steam engine or boiler) to operate with or produce steam mixed with large amounts of water **20** (*tr*) to provide with facts, information, etc, beforehand; brief [(adj) c14 from Latin *prīmus* first; (n) c13 from Latin *prīma* (*hora*) the first (hour); (vb) c16 of uncertain origin, probably connected with n] > 'primely *adv* > 'primeness *n*

prime cost *n* the portion of the cost of a commodity that varies directly with the amount of it produced, principally comprising materials and labour. Also called: **variable cost** Compare **overheads**

prime focus *n* the focal point of the objective lens or primary mirror of a telescope

prime meridian *n* the 0° meridian from which the other meridians or lines of longitude are calculated, usually taken to pass through Greenwich

prime minister *n* **1** the head of a parliamentary government **2** the chief minister of a sovereign or a state > prime ministership or prime ministry *n*

prime mover *n* **1** the original or primary force behind an idea, enterprise, etc **2 a** the source of power, such as fuel, wind, electricity, etc, for a machine **b** the means of extracting power from such a source, such as a steam engine, electric motor, etc **3** (in the philosophy of Aristotle) that which is the cause of all movement

Prime Mover *n* (usually preceded by *the*) *philosophy* God, esp when considered as a first cause

prime number *n* an integer that cannot be factorized into other integers but is only divisible by itself or 1, such as 2, 3, 5, 7, and 11. Sometimes shortened to: **prime.** Compare **composite number**

primer¹ ('praɪmə) *n* **1** an introductory text, such as a school textbook **2** *printing* See **long primer, great primer** [c14 via Anglo-Norman from Medieval Latin *prīmārius* (*liber*) a first (book), from Latin *prīmārius* PRIMARY]

primer² ('praɪmə) *n* **1** a person or thing that

p

primes **2** a device, such as a tube containing explosive, for detonating the main charge in a gun, mine, etc **3** a substance, such as paint, applied to a surface as a base, sealer, etc. Also called (for senses 2, 3): **priming** [c15 see PRIME (vb)]

prime rate *n* the lowest commercial interest rate charged by a bank at a particular time

primero (prɪˈmɛərəʊ) *n chiefly Brit* a 16th- and 17th-century card game [c16 from Spanish *primera* card game, from *primero* first, from Latin *prīmārius* chief]

primers (ˈprɪməz) *pl n NZ informal* the youngest class in a primary school

prime time *n* **1** the peak viewing time on television, for which advertising rates are the highest ▷ *adj* **primetime 2** occurring during or designed for prime time: *a primetime drama*

primeval or **primaeval** (praɪˈmiːvəl) *adj* of or belonging to the first age or ages, esp of the world [c17 from Latin *prīmaevus* youthful, from *prīmus* first + *aevum* age] > pri'**mevally** or pri'**maevally** *adv*

prime vertical *n astronomy* the great circle passing through the observer's zenith and meeting the horizon due east and west

primigravida (ˌpraɪmɪˈɡrævɪdə) *n, pl* **-das** or **-dae** (-ˌdiː) *obstetrics* a woman who is pregnant for the first time [c19 New Latin, from Latin *prima* first + *gravida* GRAVID (woman)]

primine (ˈpraɪmɪn) *n botany, now rare* the integument surrounding an ovule or the outer of two such integuments. Compare **secundine** [c19 via French from Latin *prīmus* first]

priming (ˈpraɪmɪŋ) *n* **1** something used to prime **2** a substance, used to ignite an explosive charge

primipara (praɪˈmɪpərə) *n, pl* **-ras** or **-rae** (-ˌriː) *obstetrics* a woman who has borne only one child. Also written: **Para I** [c19 from Latin, from *prīmus* first + *parere* to bring forth] > **primiparity** (ˌprɪmɪˈpærɪtɪ) *n* > pri'**miparous** *adj*

primitive (ˈprɪmɪtɪv) *adj* **1** of or belonging to the first or beginning; original **2** characteristic of an early state, esp in being crude or uncivilized: *a primitive dwelling* **3** *anthropol* denoting or relating to a preliterate and nonindustrial social system **4** *biology* **a** of, relating to, or resembling an early stage in the evolutionary development of a particular group of organisms: *primitive amphibians* **b** another word for **primordial** (sense 3) **5** showing the characteristics of primitive painters; untrained, childlike, or naive **6** *geology* pertaining to magmas that have experienced only small degrees of fractional crystallization or crystal contamination **7** *obsolete* of, relating to, or denoting rocks formed in or before the Palaeozoic era **8** *obsolete* denoting a word from which another word is derived, as for example *hope*, from which *hopeless* is derived **9** *Protestant theol* of, relating to, or associated with a minority group that breaks away from a sect, denomination, or Church in order to return to what is regarded as the original simplicity of the Gospels ▷ *n* **10** a primitive person or thing **11 a** an artist whose work does not conform to traditional, academic, or avant-garde standards of Western painting, such as a painter from an African or Oceanic civilization **b** a painter of the pre-Renaissance era in European painting **c** a painter of any era whose work appears childlike or untrained. Also called (for senses 11a, 11c): **naive 12** a work by such an artist **13** a word or concept from which another word or concept is derived **14** *maths* a curve, function, or other form from which another is derived [c14 from Latin *prīmitīvus* earliest of its kind, primitive, from *prīmus* first] > '**primitively** *adv* > '**primitiveness** *n*

primitivism (ˈprɪmɪtɪˌvɪzəm) *n* **1** the condition of being primitive **2** the notion that the value of primitive cultures is superior to that of the modern world **3** the principles, characteristics, etc, of primitive art and artists > '**primitivist** *n, adj* > ˌprimitiv'**istic** *adj*

Primitivo (ˌprɪmɪˈtiːvəʊ) *n, pl* **-vos 1** a black grape

grown in the Puglia region of Italy, used for making wine **2** a strong red wine made from this grape [c21 from Italian, literally: primitive, probably because the grape tends to ripen earlier than other grapes]

primo (ˈpriːməʊ) *n, pl* **-mos** or **-mi** (-mɪ) *music* the upper or right-hand part in a piano duet. Compare **secondo** [Italian: first, from Latin *prīmus*]

primogenitor (ˌpraɪməʊˈdʒɛnɪtə) *n* **1** a forefather; ancestor **2** an earliest parent or ancestor, as of a race [c17 alteration of PROGENITOR after PRIMOGENITURE]

primogeniture (ˌpraɪməʊˈdʒɛnɪtʃə) *n* **1** the state of being a first-born **2** *law* the right of an eldest son to succeed to the estate of his ancestor to the exclusion of all others. Compare **ultimogeniture** [c17 from Medieval Latin *prīmōgenitūra* birth of a first child, from Latin *prīmō* at first + Late Latin *genitūra* a birth] > **primogenitary** (ˌpraɪməʊˈdʒɛnɪtərɪ, -trɪ) *adj*

primordial (praɪˈmɔːdɪəl) *adj* **1** existing at or from the beginning; earliest; primeval **2** constituting an origin; fundamental **3** *biology* of or relating to an early stage of development: *primordial germ cells* ▷ *n* **4** an elementary or basic principle [c14 from Late Latin *prīmōrdiālis* original, from Latin *prīmus* first + *ōrdīrī* to begin] > pri'**mordiality** *n* > pri'**mordially** *adv*

primordium (praɪˈmɔːdɪəm) *n, pl* **-dia** (-dɪə) *biology* an organ or part in the earliest stage of development

primp (prɪmp) *vb* to dress (oneself), esp in fine clothes; prink [c19 probably from PRIM]

primrose (ˈprɪmˌrəʊz) *n* **1** any of various temperate primulaceous plants of the genus *Primula*, esp *P. vulgaris* of Europe, which has pale yellow flowers **2** short for **evening primrose 3** Also called: **primrose yellow** a light to moderate yellow, sometimes with a greenish tinge ▷ *adj* **4** of, relating to, or abounding in primroses **5** of the colour primrose **6** pleasant or gay [c15 from Old French *primerose*, from Medieval Latin *prīma rosa* first rose]

primrose path *n* (often preceded by *the*) a pleasurable way of life

primula (ˈprɪmjʊlə) *n* any primulaceous plant of the N temperate genus *Primula*, having white, yellow, pink, or purple funnel-shaped flowers with five spreading petals: includes the primrose, oxlip, cowslip, and polyanthus [c18 New Latin, from Medieval Latin *prīmula* (*vēris*) little first one (of the spring)]

primulaceous (ˌprɪmjʊˈleɪʃəs) *adj* of, relating to, or belonging to the *Primulaceae*, a family of plants having funnel-shaped or bell-shaped flowers: includes primrose, moneywort, pimpernel, and loosestrife

primum mobile *Latin* (ˈpraɪmʊm ˈməʊbɪlɪ) *n* **1** a prime mover **2** *astronomy* the outermost empty sphere in the Ptolemaic system that was thought to revolve around the earth from east to west in 24 hours carrying with it the inner spheres of the planets, sun, moon, and fixed stars [c15 from Medieval Latin: first moving (thing)]

primus (ˈpraɪməs) *n Scottish Episcopal Church* the presiding bishop in the Synod [from Latin: first]

Primus (ˈpraɪməs) *n trademark* a portable paraffin cooking stove, used esp by campers. Also called: **Primus stove**

primus inter pares *Latin* (ˈpraɪməs ˌɪntə ˈpɑːrɪz) first among equals

prince (prɪns) *n* **1** (in Britain) a son of the sovereign or of one of the sovereign's sons **2** a nonreigning male member of a sovereign family **3** the monarch of a small territory, such as Monaco, usually called a *principality*, that was at some time subordinate to an emperor or king **4** any sovereign; monarch **5** a nobleman in various countries, such as Italy and Germany **6** an outstanding member of a specified group: *a merchant prince* **7** *US and Canadian informal* a generous and charming man [c13 via Old French

from Latin *princeps* first man, ruler, chief] > '**prince,like** *adj*

Prince Albert *n* a man's double-breasted frock coat worn esp in the early 20th century

prince consort *n* the husband of a female sovereign, who is himself a prince

princedom (ˈprɪnsdəm) *n* **1** the dignity, rank, or position of a prince **2** a land ruled by a prince; principality

princedoms (ˈprɪnsdəmz) *pl n* (*often capital*) another term for **principalities**

Prince Edward Island *n* an island in the Gulf of St Lawrence that constitutes the smallest Canadian province. Capital: Charlottetown. Pop: 137 864 (2004 est). Area: 5656 sq km (2184 sq miles). Abbrevs: PE, PEI

Prince Edward Islander *n* a native or inhabitant of Prince Edward Island

princeling (ˈprɪnslɪŋ) *n* **1** Also called: **princekin** a young prince **2** Also called: **princelet** the ruler of an insignificant territory; petty or minor prince

princely (ˈprɪnslɪ) *adj* **-lier, -liest 1** generous or lavish **2** of, belonging to, or characteristic of a prince ▷ *adv* **3** in a princely manner > '**princeliness** *n*

Prince of Darkness *n* another name for **Satan**

Prince of Peace *n Bible* the future Messiah (Isaiah 9:6): held by Christians to be Christ

Prince of Wales[1] *n* the eldest son and heir apparent of the British sovereign

Prince of Wales[2] *n* **Cape** a cape in W Alaska, on the Bering Strait opposite the coast of the extreme northeast of Russia: the westernmost point of North America

Prince of Wales Island *n* **1** an island in N Canada, in Nunavut. Area: about 36 000 sq km (14 000 sq miles) **2** an island in SE Alaska, the largest island in the Alexander Archipelago. Area: about 4000 sq km (1500 sq miles) **3** an island in NE Australia, in N Queensland in the Torres Strait **4** the former name (until about 1867) of the island of **Penang**

prince regent *n* a prince who acts as regent during the minority, disability, or absence of the legal sovereign

prince royal *n* the eldest son of a monarch

Prince Rupert (ˈruːpət) *n* a port in W Canada, on the coast of British Columbia: one of the W termini of the Canadian National transcontinental railway. Pop: 14 643 (2001)

Prince Rupert's drop *n* a glass bead in the shape of a teardrop, a by-product of the glass-making process, formed by molten glass falling into water. The body of the drop can withstand great force, for example a hammer blow, but the whole will explode if the tail is nipped or the surface scored [c17 thought to have been introduced to England by Prince Rupert, the German-born nephew of Charles I of England]

prince's feather *n* **1** an amaranthaceous garden plant, *Amaranthus hybridus hypochondriacus*, with spikes of bristly brownish-red flowers **2** a tall tropical polygonaceous plant, *Polygonum orientale*, with hanging spikes of pink flowers

princess (prɪnˈsɛs) *n* **1** (in Britain) a daughter of the sovereign or of one of the sovereign's sons **2** a nonreigning female member of a sovereign family **3** the wife and consort of a prince **4** any very attractive or outstanding woman **5** Also called: **princess dress, princess line** a style of dress with a fitted bodice and an A-line skirt that is shaped by seams from shoulder to hem without a seam at the waistline

princess royal *n* **1** the eldest daughter of a British or (formerly) a Prussian sovereign: a title not always conferred **2** (*capitals*) the title of Princess Anne

Princeton (ˈprɪnstən) *n* a town in central New Jersey: settled by Quakers in 1696; an important educational centre, seat of Princeton University (founded at Elizabeth in 1747 and moved here in 1756); scene of the battle (1777) during the War of

American Independence in which Washington's troops defeated the British on the university campus. Pop: 13 577 (2003 est)

principal ('prɪnsɪpəl) *adj* (*prenominal*) **1** first in importance, rank, value, etc; chief **2** denoting or relating to capital or property as opposed to interest, etc ▷ *n* **3** a person who is first in importance or directs some event, action, organization, etc **4** (in Britain) a civil servant of an executive grade who is in charge of a section **5** *law* **a** a person who engages another to act as his agent **b** an active participant in a crime **c** the person primarily liable to fulfil an obligation **6** the head of a school or other educational institution **7** (in Scottish schools) a head of department **8** *finance* **a** capital or property, as contrasted with the income derived from it **b** the original amount of a debt on which interest is calculated **9** a main roof truss or rafter **10** *music* **a** the chief instrumentalist in a section of the orchestra **b** one of the singers in an opera company **c** either of two types of open diapason organ stops, one of four-foot length and pitch and the other of eight-foot length and pitch **11** the leading performer in a play [C13 via Old French from Latin *principālis* chief, from *princeps* chief man, PRINCE] > **'principalship** *n*

▪ USAGE See at principle

principal axis *n* **1** the line passing through the optical centre and centres of curvature of the faces of a lens or a curved mirror **2** any of three mutually perpendicular axes about which the moment of inertia of a body is maximum

principal boy *n* the leading male role in a pantomime, played by a woman

principal focus *n* another name for **focal point**

principalities (ˌprɪnsɪˈpælɪtɪ) *pl n* (*often capital*) the seventh of the nine orders into which the angels are divided in medieval angelology. Also called: **princedoms**

principality (ˌprɪnsɪˈpælɪtɪ) *n, pl* -ties **1 a** a territory ruled by a prince **b** a territory from which a prince draws his title **2** the dignity or authority of a prince [C14 (in the sense: pre-eminence): via Old French from Latin *principālis* PRINCIPAL]

principally ('prɪnsɪpəlɪ) *adv* mainly or most importantly

principal nursing officer *n* a grade of nurse concerned with administration in the British National Health Service

principal parts *pl n* **1** *grammar* the main inflected forms of a verb, from which all other inflections may be deduced. In English they are generally considered to consist of the third person present singular, present participle, past tense, and past participle **2** the sides and interior angles of a triangle

principate ('prɪnsɪˌpeɪt) *n* **1** a state ruled by a prince **2** a form of rule in the early Roman Empire in which some republican forms survived

Príncipe ('prɪnsɪpɪ; *Portuguese* 'prĩsipə) *n* an island in the Gulf of Guinea, off the W coast of Africa: part of São Tomé e Príncipe. Area: 150 sq km (58 sq miles)

principium (prɪnˈsɪpɪəm) *n, pl* -ia (-ɪə) (*usually plural*) a principle, esp a fundamental one [C17 Latin: an origin, beginning]

principle ('prɪnsɪpəl) *n* **1** a standard or rule of personal conduct: *a man of principle* **2** (*often plural*) a set of such moral rules: *he'd stoop to anything; he has no principles* **3** adherence to such a moral code; morality: *it's not the money but the principle of the thing; torn between principle and expediency* **4** a fundamental or general truth or law: *first principles* **5** the essence of something: *the male principle* **6** a source or fundamental cause; origin: *principle of life* **7** a rule or law concerning a natural phenomenon or the behaviour of a system: *the principle of the conservation of mass* **8** an underlying or guiding theory or belief: *the hereditary principle; socialist principles* **9** *chem* a constituent of a substance that gives the

substance its characteristics and behaviour: *bitter principle* **10** **in principle** in theory or essence **11** **on principle** because of or in demonstration of a principle [C14 from Latin *principium* beginning, basic tenet]

▪ USAGE *Principle* and *principal* are often confused: *the principal* (not *principle*) *reason for his departure; the plan was approved in principle* (not *in principal*)

Principle ('prɪnsɪpəl) *n* *christian Science* another word for **God**

principled ('prɪnsɪpəld) *adj* **a** having high moral principles **b** (*in combination*): *high-principled*

principle of economy *n* the another name for **Ockham's razor**

principle of indifference *n* the principle that, in the absence of any reason to expect one event rather than another, all the possible events should be assigned the same probability. See **mathematical probability**

principle of least action *n* the principle that motion between any two points in a conservative dynamical system is such that the action has a minimum value with respect to all paths between the points that correspond to the same energy. Also called: **Maupertuis principle**

prink (prɪŋk) *vb* **1** to dress (oneself, etc) finely; deck out **2** (*intr*) to preen oneself [C16 probably changed from PRANK² (to adorn, decorate)] > **'prinker** *n*

print (prɪnt) *vb* **1** to reproduce (text, pictures, etc), esp in large numbers, by applying ink to paper or other material by one of various processes **2** to produce or reproduce (a manuscript, a book, data, etc) in print, as for publication **3** to write (letters, etc) in the style of printed matter **4** to mark or indent (a surface) by pressing (something) onto it **5** to produce a photographic print from (a negative) **6** (*tr*) to implant or fix in the mind or memory **7** (*tr*) to make (a mark or indentation) by applying pressure ▷ *n* **8** printed matter such as newsprint **9** a printed publication such as a newspaper or book **10** **in print a** in printed or published form **b** (of a book, etc) offered for sale by the publisher **11** **out of print** no longer available from a publisher **12** a design or picture printed from an engraved plate, wood block, or other medium **13** printed text, esp with regard to the typeface used: *small print* **14** a positive photographic image in colour or black and white produced, usually on paper, from a negative image on film. Compare **slide** (sense 13) **15 a** a fabric with a printed design **b** (*as modifier*): *a print dress* **16 a** a mark or indentation made by pressing something onto a surface **b** a stamp, die, etc, that makes such an impression **c** the surface subjected to such an impression **17** See **fingerprint** ▷ See also **print out** [C13 *priente*, from Old French: something printed, from *preindre* to make an impression, from Latin *premere* to press]

printable ('prɪntəbəl) *adj* **1** capable of being printed or of producing a print **2** suitable for publication > **ˌprintaˈbility** *or* **'printableness** *n*

printed circuit *n* an electronic circuit in which certain components and the connections between them are formed by etching a metallic coating or by electrodeposition on one or both sides of a thin insulating board. Also called: **printed circuit board** *or* **card**

printer ('prɪntə) *n* **1** a person or business engaged in printing **2** a machine or device that prints **3** *computing* an output device for printing results on paper

printer's devil *n* an apprentice or errand boy in a printing establishment

printery ('prɪntərɪ) *n, pl* -eries **1** *chiefly US* an establishment in which printing is carried out **2** an establishment in which fabrics are printed

printhead ('prɪntˌhɛd) *n* *computing* a component in a printer that forms a printed character

printing ('prɪntɪŋ) *n* **1 a** the process, business, or art of producing printed matter **b** (*as modifier*):

printing ink **2** printed text **3** Also called: **impression** all the copies of a book or other publication printed at one time **4** a form of writing in which letters resemble printed letters

printing press *n* any of various machines used for printing

printmaker ('prɪntˌmeɪkə) *n* a person who makes print, esp a craftsman or artist in this field

print out *vb* (*tr, adverb*) **1** (of a computer output device, such as a line printer) to produce (printed information) ▷ *n* **print-out 2** such printed information

print shop *n* a place in which printing is carried out

print-through *n* the unwanted transfer of a recorded magnetic field pattern from one turn of magnetic tape to the preceding or succeeding turn on a reel, causing distortion

print unions *pl n* the trade unions within the printing industry

printwheel ('prɪntˌwiːl) *n* another name for **daisywheel**

prion¹ ('praɪən) *n* any of various dovelike petrels of the genus *Pachyptila* of the southern oceans that have a serrated bill [C19 New Latin, from Greek *priōn* a saw]

prion² ('priːɒn) *n* a protein in the brain, an abnormal form of which is thought to be the transmissable agent responsible for certain spongiform encephalopathies, such as BSE, scrapie, Creutzfeldt-Jakob disease, and kuru [C20 altered from *pro(teinaceous)* in(*fectious particle*)]

prior¹ ('praɪə) *adj* **1** (*prenominal*) previous; preceding **2** **prior to** before; until ▷ *n* **3** *statistics* a prior probability [C18 from Latin: previous]

prior² ('praɪə) *n* **1** the superior of a house and community in certain religious orders **2** the deputy head of a monastery or abbey, ranking immediately below the abbot **3** (*formerly*) a chief magistrate in medieval Florence and other Italian republics [C11 from Late Latin: head, from Latin (*adj*): previous, from Old Latin *pri* before]

priorate ('praɪərɪt) *n* the office, status, or term of office of a prior

prioress ('praɪərɪs) *n* a nun holding an office in her convent corresponding to that of a prior in a male religious order

prioritize *or* **prioritise** (praɪˈɒrɪˌtaɪz) *vb* (*tr*) **1** to arrange (items to be attended to) in order of their relative importance **2** to give priority to or establish as a priority > **ˌprioritiˈzation** *or* **ˌprioritiˈsation** *n*

priority (praɪˈɒrɪtɪ) *n, pl* -ties **1** the condition of being prior; antecedence; precedence **2** the right of precedence over others **3** something given specified attention: *my first priority*

prior probability *n* *statistics* the probability assigned to a parameter or to an event in advance of any empirical evidence, often subjectively or on the assumption of the principle of indifference. Compare **posterior probability**

priory ('praɪərɪ) *n, pl* -ories a religious house governed by a prior, sometimes being subordinate to an abbey [C13 from Medieval Latin *priōria*; see PRIOR²]

Pripet ('priːpɪt) *n* a river in E Europe, rising in NW Ukraine and flowing northeast into Belarus across the **Pripet Marshes** (the largest swamp in Europe), then east into the Dnieper River. Length: about 800 km (500 miles). Russian name: **Pripyat** ('prɪpjət)

prisage ('praɪzɪdʒ) *n* a customs duty levied until 1809 upon wine imported into England [C16 from Anglo-French, from Old French *prise* a taking or requisitioning, duty, from *prendre* to take; see PRISE]

prise *or* **prize** (praɪz) *vb* (*tr*) **1** to force open by levering **2** to extract or obtain with difficulty: *they had to prise the news out of him* ▷ *n* **3** *rare or dialect* a tool involving leverage in its use or the leverage so employed ▷ US and Canadian equivalent: **pry** [C17 from Old French *prise* a taking, from *prendre* to

P

take, from Latin *prehendere*; see PRIZE[1]]

prisere ('praɪ,sɪə) *n ecology* a primary sere or succession from bare ground to the community climax [C20 PRI(MARY) + SERE[2]]

prism ('prɪzəm) *n* **1** a transparent polygonal solid, often having triangular ends and rectangular sides, for dispersing light into a spectrum or for reflecting and deviating light. They are used in spectroscopes, binoculars, periscopes, etc **2** a form of crystal with faces parallel to the vertical axis **3** *maths* a polyhedron having parallel, polygonal, and congruent bases and sides that are parallelograms [C16 from Medieval Latin *prisma*, from Greek: something shaped by sawing, from *prizein* to saw]

prismatic (prɪz'mætɪk) *adj* **1** concerned with, containing, or produced by a prism **2** exhibiting bright spectral colours: *prismatic light* **3** *crystallog* another word for **orthorhombic**
> pris'matically *adv*

prismatoid ('prɪzmə,tɔɪd) *n* a polyhedron whose vertices lie in either one of two parallel planes. Compare **prism** (sense 3), **prismoid** [C19 from Greek *prismatoeidēs* shaped like a prism; see PRISM, -OID]
> ,prisma'toidal *adj*

prismoid ('prɪzmɔɪd) *n* a prismatoid having an equal number of vertices in each of the two parallel planes and whose sides are trapeziums or parallelograms [C18 from French *prismoïde*; see PRISM, -OID] > pris'moidal *adj*

prison ('prɪz³n) *n* **1** a public building used to house convicted criminals and accused persons remanded in custody and awaiting trial. See also **jail, penitentiary, reformatory** **2** any place of confinement or seeming confinement [C12 from Old French *prisun*, from Latin *prēnsiō* a capturing, from *prehendere* to lay hold of]

prisoner ('prɪzənə) *n* **1** a person deprived of liberty and kept in prison or some other form of custody as a punishment for a crime, while awaiting trial, or for some other reason **2** a person confined by any of various restraints *prisoners of time* **3** **take no prisoners** *informal* to be uncompromising and resolute in one's actions **4** **take (someone) prisoner** to capture and hold (someone) as a prisoner, esp as a prisoner of war

prisoner of war *n* a person, esp a serviceman, captured by an enemy in time of war. Abbreviation: POW

prisoner's base *n* a children's game involving two teams, members of which chase and capture each other to increase the number of children in their own base

prissy ('prɪsɪ) *adj* -sier, -siest fussy and prim, esp in a prudish way [C20 probably from PRIM + SISSY]
> 'prissily *adv* > 'prissiness *n*

Priština (*Serbo-Croat* 'priːʃtina) *n* a city in S Serbia and Montenegro, the capital of Kosovo: under Turkish control until 1912; severely damaged in the Kosovo conflict of 1999; nearby is the 14th-century Gračanica monastery. Pop: 261 000 (2005 est)

pristine ('prɪstaɪn, -tiːn) *adj* **1** of or involving the earliest period, state, etc; original **2** pure; uncorrupted **3** fresh, clean, and unspoiled: *his pristine new car* [C15 from Latin *pristinus* primitive; related to *prīmus* first, PRIME]

▪ USAGE The use of *pristine* to mean *fresh, clean, and unspoiled* is considered by some people to be incorrect

prithee ('prɪðɪ) *interj archaic* pray thee; please [C16 shortened from *I pray thee*]

prittle-prattle ('prɪt³l,præt³l) *n* foolish or idle talk; babble [C16 reduplication of PRATTLE]

priv. *abbreviation for* **1** private **2** privative

privacy ('praɪvəsɪ, 'prɪvəsɪ) *n* **1** the condition of being private or withdrawn; seclusion **2** the condition of being secret; secrecy **3** *philosophy* the condition of being necessarily restricted to a single person

Privatdocent (*German* pri'vaːtdo'tsɛnt) *n* (esp in German-speaking countries) a university lecturer

who formerly received fees from his students rather than a university salary [German, from *privat* PRIVATE + *docent* (for *Dozent* lecturer) from Latin *docēre* to teach]

private ('praɪvɪt) *adj* **1** not widely or publicly known: *they had private reasons for the decision* **2** confidential; secret: *a private conversation* **3** not for general or public use: *a private bathroom* **4** (*prenominal*) individual; special: *my own private recipe* **5** (*prenominal*) having no public office, rank, etc: *a private man* **6** (*prenominal*) denoting a soldier of the lowest military rank: *a private soldier* **7** of, relating to, or provided by a private individual or organization, rather than by the state or a public body: *the private sector; private housing* **8** (of a place) retired; sequestered; not overlooked **9** (of a person) reserved; uncommunicative **10** in private in secret; confidentially ▷ *n* **11** a soldier of the lowest rank, sometimes separated into qualification grades, in many armies and marine corps: *private first class* [C14 from Latin *prīvātus* belonging to one individual, withdrawn from public life, from *prīvāre* to deprive, bereave]
> 'privately *adv*

private bar *n Brit* the saloon or lounge bar of a public house. Also called: the private. Compare **public bar**

private bill *n* a bill presented to Parliament or Congress on behalf of a private individual, corporation, etc

private company *n* a limited company that does not issue shares for public subscription and whose owners do not enjoy an unrestricted right to transfer their shareholdings. Compare **public company**

private detective *n* an individual privately employed to investigate a crime, keep watch on a suspected person, or make other inquiries. Also called: private investigator

private enterprise *n* **1** economic activity undertaken by private individuals or organizations under private ownership. Compare **public enterprise** **2** another name for **capitalism**

privateer (,praɪvə'tɪə) *n* **1** an armed, privately owned vessel commissioned for war service by a government **2** Also called: privateersman a commander or member of the crew of a privateer ▷ *vb* **3** a competitor, esp in motor racing, who is privately financed rather than sponsored by a manufacturer **4** (*intr*) to serve as a privateer

private eye *n informal* a private detective

Private Finance Initiative *n* (in Britain) a government scheme to encourage private investment in public projects. Abbreviation: PFI

private health insurance *n* insurance against the need for medical treatment as a private patient

private hotel *n* **1** a residential hotel or boarding house in which the proprietor has the right to refuse to accept a guest as a guest, esp a person arriving by chance **2** *Austral and NZ* a hotel not having a licence to sell alcoholic liquor

private income *n* an income from sources other than employment, such as investment. Also called: private means

private language *n philosophy* a language that is not merely secret or accidentally limited to one user, but that cannot in principle be communicated to another

private law *n* the branch of law that deals with the rights and duties of private individuals and the relations between them. Compare **public law**

private life *n* the social or family life or personal relationships of an individual, esp of a person in the public eye, such as a politician or celebrity

private member *n* a member of a legislative assembly, such as the House of Commons, not having an appointment in the government

private member's bill *n* a public bill introduced in the House of Commons or the legislative assemblies of Canada, Australia, or New Zealand by a private member

private parts or **privates** ('praɪvɪts) *pl n* euphemistic terms for **genitals**

private patient *n Brit* a patient receiving medical treatment not paid for by the National Health Service

private pay bed *n* (in Britain) a bed in a National Health Service hospital, reserved for private patients who pay a consultant acting privately for treatment and who are charged by the health service for use of hospital facilities. Often shortened to: pay bed Compare **amenity bed**

private practice *n Brit* medical practice that is not part of the National Health Service

private press *n* a printing establishment primarily run as a pastime

private property *n* land or belongings owned by a person or group and kept for their exclusive use

private school *n* a school under the financial and managerial control of a private body or charitable trust, accepting mostly fee-paying pupils

private secretary *n* **1** a secretary entrusted with the personal and confidential matters of a business executive **2** a civil servant who acts as aide to a minister or senior government official. Compare **parliamentary private secretary**

private sector *n* the part of a country's economy that consists of privately owned enterprises. Compare **public sector**

private treaty *n* a sale of property for a price agreed directly between seller and buyer

private view *n* a preview, esp of an art exhibition, for specially invited guests

private viewdata *n* an interactive video text system with restricted access

privation (praɪ'veɪʃən) *n* **1** loss or lack of the necessities of life, such as food and shelter **2** hardship resulting from this **3** the state of being deprived **4** *logic obsolete* the absence from an object of what ordinarily or naturally belongs to such objects [C14 from Latin *prīvātiō* deprivation]

privative ('prɪvətɪv) *adj* **1** causing privation **2** expressing lack or negation, as for example the English suffix *-less* and prefix *un-* **3** *logic obsolete* (of a proposition) that predicates a logical privation [C16 from Latin *prīvātīvus* indicating loss, negative] > 'privatively *adv*

privatization issue *n* an issue of shares available for purchase by members of the public when a publicly owned organization is transferred to the private sector

privatize or **privatise** ('praɪvɪ,taɪz) *vb* (*tr*) to transfer (the production of goods or services) from the public sector of an economy into private ownership and operation > ,privati'zation or ,privati'sation *n*

privet ('prɪvɪt) *n* **a** any oleaceous shrub of the genus *Ligustrum*, esp *L. vulgare* or *L. ovalifolium*, having oval dark green leaves, white flowers, and purplish-black berries **b** (*as modifier*): *a privet hedge* [C16 of unknown origin]

privet hawk *n* a hawk moth, *Sphinx ligustri*, with a mauve-and-brown striped body: frequents privets

privilege ('prɪvɪlɪdʒ) *n* **1** a benefit, immunity, etc, granted under certain conditions **2** the advantages and immunities enjoyed by a small usually powerful group or class, esp to the disadvantage of others: *one of the obstacles to social harmony is privilege* **3** any of the fundamental rights guaranteed to the citizens of a country by its constitution **4 a** the right of a lawyer to refuse to divulge information obtained in confidence from a client **b** the right claimed by any of certain other functionaries to refuse to divulge information: *executive privilege* **5** the rights and immunities enjoyed by members of most legislative bodies, such as freedom of speech, freedom from arrest in civil cases during a session, etc **6** *US stock exchange* a speculative contract permitting its purchaser to make optional purchases or sales of securities at a specified time over a limited period of time. See also **call** (sense 61), **put** (sense 20), **spread** (sense 24c), **straddle** (sense 9) ▷ *vb* (*tr*) **7** to bestow a privilege or privileges upon **8** (foll by *from*) to free or exempt [C12 from Old French *privilège*, from Latin *prīvilēgium* law relevant to rights of an individual, from *prīvus* an individual + *lēx* law]

privileged (ˈprɪvɪlɪdʒd) *adj* **1** enjoying or granted as a privilege or privileges **2** *law* **a** not actionable as a libel or slander **b** (of a communication, document, etc) that a witness cannot be compelled to divulge **3** *nautical* (of a vessel) having the right of way

privily (ˈprɪvɪlɪ) *adv archaic or literary* in a secret way

privity (ˈprɪvɪtɪ) *n, pl* **-ties 1** a legally recognized relationship existing between two parties, such as that between lessor and lessee and between the parties to a contract: *privity of estate; privity of contract* **2** secret knowledge that is shared [C13 from Old French *priveté*]

privy (ˈprɪvɪ) *adj* privier, priviest **1** (*postpositive*; foll by *to*) participating in the knowledge of something secret **2** *archaic* secret, hidden, etc **3** *archaic* of or relating to one person only ▷ *n, pl* **privies 4** a lavatory, esp an outside one **5** *law* a person in privity with another. See **privity** (sense 1) [C13 from Old French *privé* something private, from Latin *prīvātus* PRIVATE]

privy chamber *n* **1** a private apartment inside a royal residence **2** *archaic* a private room reserved for the use of a specific person or group

privy council *n* **1** the council of state of a monarch or noble, esp formerly **2** *archaic* a private or secret council

Privy Council *n* the private council of the British sovereign, consisting of all current and former ministers of the Crown and other distinguished subjects, all of whom are appointed for life. See also **Judicial Committee of the Privy Council** ▷ **Privy Counsellor** *n*

privy purse *n* (*often capitals*) **1 a** (in Britain) an allowance voted by Parliament for the private expenses of the monarch: part of the civil list **b** (in other countries) a similar sum of money for the monarch **2** an official of the royal household responsible for dealing with the monarch's private expenses. Full name: **Keeper of the Privy Purse**

privy seal *n* (*often capitals*) (in Britain) a seal affixed to certain documents issued by royal authority: of less rank and importance than the great seal

prix fixe (*French* pri fiks) *n, pl* prix fixes (fiks) a fixed price charged for one of a set number of meals offered on a menu. Compare **à la carte, table d'hôte**

Prix Goncourt (*French* gɔ̃kur) *n* an annual prize for a work of French fiction [C20 after the Académie *Goncourt*, which awards the prizes, founded by the will of Edmond Goncourt (1822–96), French writer]

prize¹ (praɪz) *n* **1 a** a reward or honour for victory or for having won a contest, competition, etc **b** (*as modifier*): *prize jockey; prize essay* **2** something given to the winner of any game of chance, lottery, etc **3** something striven for **4** any valuable property captured in time of war, esp a vessel [C14 from Old French *prise* a capture, from Latin *prehendere* to seize; influenced also by Middle English *prise* reward; see PRICE]

prize² (praɪz) *vb* (*tr*) to esteem greatly; value highly [C15 *prise*, from Old French *preisier* to PRAISE]

prize³ (praɪz) *vb, n* a variant spelling of **prise**

prize court *n law* a court having jurisdiction to determine how property captured at sea in wartime is to be distributed

prizefight (ˈpraɪzˌfaɪt) *n* a boxing match for a prize or purse, esp one of the fights popular in the 18th and 19th centuries ▷ **ˈprizeˌfighter** *n* ▷ **ˈprizeˌfighting** *n*

prize money *n* **1** any money offered, paid, or received as a prize **2** (formerly) a part of the

money realized from the sale of a captured vessel

prize ring *n* **1** the enclosed area or ring used by prizefighters **2** the prize ring the sport of prizefighting

prizewinner (ˈpraɪzˌwɪnə) *n* a person, animal, or thing that wins a prize ▷ **ˈprizeˌwinning** *adj*

PRK *abbreviation for* photo refractive keratomy

prn (in prescriptions) *abbreviation for* pro re nata [Latin: as the situation demands; whenever needed]

pro¹ (prəʊ) *adv* **1** in favour of a motion, issue, course of action, etc. Compare **anti** ▷ *prep* **2** in favour of ▷ *n, pl* **pros 3** (*usually plural*) an argument or vote in favour of a proposal or motion. See also **pros and cons 4** (*usually plural*) a person who votes in favour of a proposal, motion, etc ▷ Compare **con²** [from Latin *prō* (prep) in favour of]

pro² (prəʊ) *n, pl* **pros, adj 1** *informal* short for **professional 2** ▷ *an internet domain name for* a professional practitioner **3** *slang* a prostitute [C19 by shortening]

PRO *abbreviation for* **1** Public Records Office **2** public relations officer

pro-¹ *prefix* **1** in favour of; supporting: *pro-Chinese* **2** acting as a substitute for: *proconsul; pronoun* [from Latin *prō* (adv and prep). In compound words borrowed from Latin, *prō-* indicates: forward, out (*project*); forward and down (*prostrate*); away from a place (*prodigal*); onward in time or space (*proceed*); extension outwards (*propagate*); before in time or place (*provide, protect*); on behalf of (*procure*); acting as a substitute for (*pronominal*); and sometimes intensive force (*promiscuous*)]

pro-² *prefix* before in time or position; anterior; forward: *prophase; procephalic; prognathous* [from Greek *pro* (prep) before (in time, position, rank, etc)]

proa (ˈprəʊə) or **prau** *n* any of several kinds of canoe-like boats used in the South Pacific, esp one equipped with an outrigger and sails [C16 from Malay *parāhū* a boat]

proabortion (ˌprəʊəˈbɔːʃən) *adj* in favour of the medical provision of abortion

proaction (prəʊˈækʃən) *n* action that initiates change as opposed to reaction to events [C20 from PRO-² + (RE)ACTION]

proactive (prəʊˈæktɪv) *adj* **1** tending to initiate change rather than reacting to events **2** *psychol* of or denoting a mental process that affects a subsequent process [C20 from PRO-² + (RE)ACTIVE]

proactive inhibition or **interference** *n psychol* the tendency for earlier memories to interfere with the retrieval of material learned later. Compare **retroactive inhibition**

pro-am (ˈprəʊˈæm) *adj* **1** (of a golf tournament, snooker tournament, etc) involving both professional and amateur players ▷ *n* **2** a sporting tournament involving both professional and amateur players

pro-American *adj* **1** in favour of or supporting America, its people, culture, etc ▷ *n* **2** a person who is in favour of or supports America, its people, culture, etc

prob. *abbreviation for* **1** probable **2** probably

probabilism (ˈprɒbəbɪˌlɪzəm) *n* **1** *philosophy* the doctrine that although certainty is impossible, probability is a sufficient basis for belief and action **2** the principle of Roman Catholic moral theology that in a situation in which authorities differ as to what is the right course of action it is permissible to follow any course which has the support of some authority ▷ **ˈprobabilist** *n, adj* ▷ **ˌprobabilˈistic** *adj* ▷ **ˌprobabilˈistically** *adv*

probability (ˌprɒbəˈbɪlɪtɪ) *n, pl* **-ties 1** the condition of being probable **2** an event or other thing that is probable **3** *statistics* a measure or estimate of the degree of confidence one may have in the occurrence of an event, measured on a scale from zero (impossibility) to one (certainty). It may be defined as the proportion of favourable outcomes to the total number of possibilities if these are indifferent (**mathematical probability**),

or the proportion observed in a sample (**empirical probability**), or the limit of this as the sample size tends to infinity (**relative frequency**), or by more subjective criteria (**subjective probability**)

probability density function *n statistics* a function representing the relative distribution of frequency of a continuous random variable from which parameters such as its mean and variance can be derived and having the property that its integral from *a* to *b* is the probability that the variable lies in this interval. Its graph is the limiting case of a histogram as the amount of data increases and the class intervals decrease in size. Also called: **density function**. Compare **cumulative distribution function, frequency distribution**

probability function *n statistics* the function the values of which are probabilities of the distinct outcomes of a discrete random variable

probable (ˈprɒbəbəl) *adj* **1** likely to be or to happen but not necessarily so **2** most likely: *the probable cause of the accident* ▷ *n* **3** a person who is probably to be chosen for a team, event, etc [C14 via Old French from Latin *probābilis* that may be proved, from *probāre* to prove]

probable cause *n law* reasonable grounds for holding a belief, esp such as will justify bringing legal proceedings against a person or will constitute a defence to a charge of malicious prosecution

probably (ˈprɒbəblɪ) *adv* **1** (*sentence modifier; not used with a negative or in a question*) in all likelihood or probability: *I'll probably see you tomorrow* ▷ *sentence substitute* **2** I believe such a thing or situation may be the case

proband (ˈprəʊbænd) *n* another name (esp US) for **propositus** (sense 2) [C20 from Latin *probandus*, gerundive of *probāre* to test]

probang (ˈprəʊbæŋ) *n surgery* a long flexible rod, often with a small sponge at one end, for inserting into the oesophagus, as to apply medication [C17 variant, apparently by association with PROBE, of *provang*, name coined by W. Rumsey (1584–1660), Welsh judge, its inventor; of unknown origin]

probate (ˈprəʊbɪt, -beɪt) *n* **1** the act or process of officially proving the authenticity and validity of a will **2 a** the official certificate stating a will to be genuine and conferring on the executors power to administer the estate **b** the probate copy of a will **3** (in the US) all matters within the jurisdiction of a probate court **4** (*modifier*) of, relating to, or concerned with probate: *probate value; a probate court* ▷ *vb* **5** (*tr*) *chiefly US and Canadian* to establish officially the authenticity and validity of (a will) [C15 from Latin *probāre* to inspect]

probation (prəˈbeɪʃən) *n* **1** a system of dealing with offenders by placing them under the supervision of a probation officer **2** on probation **a** under the supervision of a probation officer **b** undergoing a test period **3** a trial period, as for a teacher, religious novitiate, etc **4** the act of proving or testing **5** a period during which a new employee may have his employment terminated on the grounds of unsuitability ▷ **proˈbational** or **proˈbationary** *adj* ▷ **proˈbationally** *adv*

probationary assistant *n NZ* a teacher in the first probationary years. Abbreviation: **PA**

probationer (prəˈbeɪʃənə) *n* a person on probation

probation officer *n* an officer of a court who supervises offenders placed on probation and assists and befriends them

probative (ˈprəʊbətɪv) or **probatory** (ˈprəʊbətərɪ, -trɪ) *adj* **1** serving to test or designed for testing **2** providing proof or evidence [C15 from Late Latin *probātivus* concerning proof] ▷ **probatively** *adv*

probe (prəʊb) *vb* **1** (*tr*) to search into or question closely **2** to examine (something) with or as if with a probe ▷ *n* **3** something that probes, examines, or tests **4** *surgery* a slender and usually

p

flexible instrument for exploring a wound, sinus, etc **5** a thorough inquiry, such as one by a newspaper into corrupt practices **6** *electronics* a lead connecting to or containing a measuring or monitoring circuit used for testing **7** *electronics* a conductor inserted into a waveguide or cavity resonator to provide coupling to an external circuit **8** any of various devices that provide a coupling link, esp a flexible tube extended from an aircraft to link it with another so that it can refuel **9** See **space probe** [C16 from Medieval Latin *proba* investigation, from Latin *probāre* to test] > 'probeable *adj* > 'prober *n*

probiotic (ˌprəʊbaɪˈɒtɪk) *n* **1** a harmless bacterium that helps to protect the body from harmful bacteria **2** ▷ *n* a substance that encourages the growth of natural healthy bacteria in the gut ▷ *adj* **3** of or relating to probiotics: *probiotic yogurt* [C20 from PRO-¹ + (ANTI)BIOTIC]

probity ('prəʊbɪtɪ) *n* confirmed integrity; uprightness [C16 from Latin *probitās* honesty, from *probus* virtuous]

problem ('prɒbləm) *n* **1 a** any thing, matter, person, etc, that is difficult to deal with, solve, or overcome **b** (*as modifier*): *a problem child* **2** a puzzle, question, etc, set for solution **3** *maths* a statement requiring a solution usually by means of one or more operations or geometric constructions **4** (*modifier*) designating a literary work that deals with difficult moral questions: *a problem play* [C14 from Late Latin *problēma*, from Greek: something put forward; related to *proballein* to throw forwards, from PRO-² + *ballein* to throw]

problematic (ˌprɒbləˈmætɪk) *or* **problematical** *adj* **1** having the nature or appearance of a problem; questionable **2** *logic obsolete* (of a proposition) asserting that a property may or may not hold. Compare **apodeictic** (sense 2), **assertoric** > ˌproblemˈatically *adv*

pro bono publico *Latin* ('prəʊ 'bəʊnəʊ 'pʊblɪkəʊ) for the public good

proboscidean *or* **proboscidian** (ˌprəʊbɒˈsɪdɪən) *adj* **1** of, relating to, or belonging to the *Proboscidea*, an order of massive herbivorous placental mammals having tusks and a long trunk: contains the elephants ▷ *n* **2** any proboscidean animal

proboscis (prəʊˈbɒsɪs) *n*, *pl* **-cises** *or* **-cides** (-sɪˌdiːz) **1** a long flexible prehensile trunk or snout, as of an elephant **2** the elongated mouthparts of certain insects, adapted for piercing or sucking food **3** any similar part or organ **4** *informal, facetious* a person's nose, esp if large [C17 via Latin from Greek *proboskis* trunk of an elephant, from *boskein* to feed]

proboscis monkey *n* an Old World monkey, *Nasalis larvatus*, of Borneo, with an elongated bulbous nose

pro-British *adj* in favour of or supporting Britain, its people, culture, etc

probusiness (prəʊˈbɪznɪs) *adj* in favour of or supporting the practices of business

proc. *abbreviation for* **1** procedure **2** proceedings

procaine ('prəʊkeɪn, prəʊˈkeɪn) *n* a colourless or white crystalline water-soluble substance used, as the hydrochloride, as a local anaesthetic; 2-diethylaminoethyl-4-amino benzoate. Formula: $NH_2C_6H_4COOC_2H_4N(C_2H_5)_2$. See also **Novocaine** [C20 from PRO-¹ + (CO)CAINE]

procambium (prəʊˈkæmbɪəm) *n* undifferentiated plant tissue, just behind the growing tip in stems and roots, that develops into conducting tissues [C19 from PRO-² + CAMBIUM] > proˈcambial *adj*

procapitalist (prəʊˈkæpɪtəlɪst) *adj* in favour of or supporting capitalist policies and ideologies

procarp ('prəʊkɑːp) *n* a female reproductive organ in red algae [C19 from New Latin *procarpium*, from PRO-² + *-carpium*, from Greek *karpos* fruit]

procaryote (prəʊˈkærɪɒt) *n* a variant spelling of **prokaryote**

procathedral (ˌprəʊkəˈθiːdrəl) *n* a church serving as a cathedral

procedural agreement *n* regulations agreed between the parties to collective bargaining, defining the bargaining units, bargaining scope, procedures for collective bargaining, and the facilities to be provided to trade union representatives

procedure (prəˈsiːdʒə) *n* **1** a way of acting or progressing in a course of action, esp an established method **2** the established mode or form of conducting the business of a legislature, the enforcement of a legal right, etc **3** *computing* another name for **subroutine**. > proˈcedural *adj* > proˈcedurally *adv*

proceed (prəˈsiːd) *vb* (*intr*) **1** (often foll by *to*) to advance or carry on, esp after stopping **2** (often foll by *with*) to undertake and continue (something or to do something): *he proceeded with his reading* **3** (often foll by *against*) to institute or carry on a legal action **4** to emerge or originate; arise: *evil proceeds from the heart* ▷ See also **proceeds** [C14 from Latin *prōcēdere* to advance, from PRO-¹ + *cēdere* to go] > proˈceeder *n*

proceeding (prəˈsiːdɪŋ) *n* **1** an act or course of action **2 a** the institution of a legal action **b** any step taken in a legal action **3** (*plural*) the minutes of the meetings of a club, society, etc **4** (*plural*) legal action; litigation **5** (*plural*) the events of an occasion, meeting, etc

proceeds ('prəʊsiːdz) *pl n* **1** the profit or return derived from a commercial transaction, investment, etc **2** the result, esp the revenue or total sum, accruing from some undertaking or course of action, as in commerce

proceleusmatic (ˌprɒsɪluːsˈmætɪk) *prosody* ▷ *adj* **1** denoting or consisting of a metrical foot of four short syllables ▷ *n* **2** a proceleusmatic metrical foot [C18 from Late Latin *proceleusmaticus*, from Greek *prokeleusmatikos*, from *prokeleuein* to drive on, from PRO-² + *keleuein* to give orders]

procephalic (ˌprəʊsɪˈfælɪk) *adj* *anatomy* of or relating to the anterior part of the head

process¹ ('prəʊsɛs) *n* **1** a series of actions that produce a change or development: *the process of digestion* **2** a method of doing or producing something **3** a forward movement **4** the course of time **5 a** a summons, writ, etc, commanding a person to appear in court **b** the whole proceedings in an action at law **6** a natural outgrowth or projection of a part, organ, or organism **7** a distinct subtask of a computer system which can be regarded as proceeding in parallel with other subtasks of the system **8** (*modifier*) relating to the general preparation of a printing forme or plate by the use, at some stage, of photography **9** (*modifier*) denoting a film, film scene, shot, etc, made by techniques that produce unusual optical effects ▷ *vb* (*tr*) **10** to subject to a routine procedure; handle **11** to treat or prepare by a special method, esp to treat (food) in order to preserve it: *to process cheese* **12 a** to institute legal proceedings against **b** to serve a process on **13** *photog* **a** to develop, rinse, fix, wash, and dry (exposed film, etc) **b** to produce final prints or slides from (undeveloped film) **14** *computing* to perform mathematical and logical operations on (data) according to programmed instructions in order to obtain the required information **15** to prepare (food) using a food processor [C14 from Old French *procès*, from Latin *prōcessus* an advancing, from *prōcēdere* to PROCEED]

process² (prəˈsɛs) *vb* (*intr*) to proceed in or as if in a procession [C19 back formation from PROCESSION]

process camera *n* *printing* a large camera used in the photographic processes involved in the printing industry

process colour *n* *printing* any of the four colours (cyan, magenta, yellow, and black) used in process printing

process engineering *n* the branch of

engineering concerned with industrial processes, esp continuous ones, such as the production of petrochemicals > process engineer *n*

procession (prəˈsɛʃən) *n* **1** the act of proceeding in a regular formation **2** a group of people or things moving forwards in an orderly, regular, or ceremonial manner **3** a hymn, litany, etc, sung in a procession **4** *Christianity* the emanation of the Holy Spirit ▷ *vb* **5** (*intr*) *rare* to go in procession [C12 via Old French from Latin *prōcessiō* a marching forwards]

processional (prəˈsɛʃənəl) *adj* **1** of, relating to, or suitable for a procession ▷ *n* **2** *Christianity* **a** a book containing the prayers, hymns, litanies, and liturgy prescribed for processions **b** a hymn, litany, etc, used in a procession > proˈcessionally *adv*

processionary (prəˈsɛʃənərɪ) *adj* **1** of, relating to, or moving in a procession ▷ *n* **2** a processionary moth

processionary moth *n* a moth of the family *Thaumetopoeidae*, esp the **oak processionary moth** (*Thaumetopoea processionea*), the larvae of which leave the communal shelter nightly for food in a V-shaped procession

processor ('prəʊsɛsə) *n* **1** *computing* another name for **central processing unit** **2** a person or thing that carries out a process

process printing *n* a method of making reproductions of a coloured picture, usually by using four halftone plates for different coloured inks

process-server *n* a sheriff's officer who serves legal documents such as writs for appearance in court

procès-verbal *French* (prɔsɛverbal) *n*, *pl* **-baux** (-bo) a written record of an official proceeding; minutes [C17 from French: see PROCESS¹, VERBAL]

pro-Chinese *adj* in favour of or supporting China, its people, culture, etc

pro-choice *adj* (of an organization, pressure group, etc) supporting the right of a woman to have an abortion. Compare **pro-life**

prochronism ('prəʊkrəˌnɪzəm) *n* an error in dating that places an event earlier than it actually occurred. Compare **parachronism** [C17 from PRO-² + Greek *khronos* time + -ISM, by analogy with ANACHRONISM]

proclaim (prəˈkleɪm) *vb* (*tr*) **1** (*may take a clause as object*) to announce publicly **2** (*may take a clause as object*) to show or indicate plainly **3** to praise or extol [C14 from Latin *prōclāmāre* to shout aloud] > proˈclaimer *n* > proclamation (ˌprɒkləˈmeɪʃən) *n* > proclamatory (prəˈklæmətərɪ, -trɪ) *adj*

proclitic (prəˈklɪtɪk) *adj* **1** relating to or denoting a monosyllabic word or form having no stress or accent and pronounced as a prefix of the following word, as in English *'t* for *it* in *'twas* **b** (in classical Greek) relating to or denoting a word that throws its accent onto the following word ▷ *n* **2** a proclitic word or form ▷ Compare **enclitic** [C19 from New Latin *proclīticus*, from Greek *proklinein* to lean forwards; formed on the model of ENCLITIC]

proclivity (prəˈklɪvɪtɪ) *n*, *pl* **-ties** a tendency or inclination [C16 from Latin *prōclīvitās*, from *prōclīvis* steep, from PRO-¹ + *clīvus* a slope]

Procne ('prɒknɪ) *n* *Greek myth* a princess of Athens, who punished her husband for raping her sister Philomela by feeding him the flesh of their son. She was changed at her death into a swallow. See **Philomela**

pro-Communist *adj* **1** in favour of or supporting Communist policies and ideologies etc ▷ *n* **2** a person who is pro-Communist

proconsul (prəʊˈkɒnsəl) *n* **1** an administrator or governor of a colony, occupied territory, or other dependency **2** (in ancient Rome) the governor of a senatorial province [C14 from Latin, from *prō consule* (someone acting) for the consul. See PRO-², CONSUL] > proconsular (prəʊˈkɒnsjʊlə) *adj* > proˈconsulate *or* proˈconsulship *n*

procrastinate (prəʊˈkræstɪˌneɪt, prə-) *vb* (*usually intr*) to put off or defer (an action) until a later time; delay [c16 from Latin *prōcrāstināre* to postpone until tomorrow, from PRO-¹ + *crās* tomorrow] > pro,crastiˈnation *n* > proˈcrastiˌnator *n*

procreate (ˈprəʊkrɪˌeɪt) *vb* **1** to beget or engender (offspring) **2** (*tr*) to bring into being [c16 from Latin *prōcreāre,* from PRO-¹ + *creāre* to create] > ˈprocreant *or* ˈprocreˌative *adj* > ˌprocreˈation *n* > ˈprocreˌator *n*

Procrustean (prəʊˈkrʌstɪən) *adj* tending or designed to produce conformity by violent or ruthless methods

Procrustes (prəʊˈkrʌstiːz) *n Greek myth* a robber, who put travellers in his bed, stretching or lopping off their limbs so that they fitted it [c16 from Greek *Prokroustēs* the stretcher, from *prokrouein* to extend by hammering out]

procryptic (prəʊˈkrɪptɪk) *adj* (of animals) having protective coloration [c19 from PRO-² + Greek *kruptein* to conceal] > proˈcryptically *adv*

procto- *or before a vowel* **proct-** *combining form* indicating the anus or rectum: *proctology* [from Greek *prōktos*]

proctology (prɒkˈtɒlədʒɪ) *n* the branch of medical science concerned with the rectum > proctological (ˌprɒktəˈlɒdʒɪkᵊl) *adj* > procˈtologist *n*

proctor (ˈprɒktə) *n* **1** a member of the teaching staff of any of certain universities having the duties of enforcing discipline **2** *US* (in a college or university) a supervisor or monitor who invigilates examinations, enforces discipline, etc **3** (formerly) an agent, esp one engaged to conduct another's case in a court **4** (formerly) an agent employed to collect tithes **5** *Church of England* one of the elected representatives of the clergy in Convocation and the General Synod ▷ *vb* **6** (*tr*) *US* to invigilate (an examination) [c14 syncopated variant of PROCURATOR] > proctorial (prɒkˈtɔːrɪəl) *adj* > procˈtorially *adv*

proctoscope (ˈprɒktəˌskəʊp) *n* a medical instrument for examining the rectum > proctoscopic (ˌprɒktəˈskɒpɪk) *adj* > proctoscopy (prɒkˈtɒskəpɪ) *n*

procumbent (prəʊˈkʌmbənt) *adj* **1** Also: **prostrate** (of stems) growing along the ground **2** leaning forwards or lying on the face [c17 from Latin *prōcumbere* to fall forwards; compare INCUMBENT]

procuration (ˌprɒkjʊˈreɪʃən) *n* **1** the act of procuring **2** *law* **a** the appointment of an agent, procurator, or attorney **b** the office, function, or authority of such an official **c** the formal written authority given to such an official. See also **power of attorney 3** *criminal law* the offence of procuring women for immoral purposes **4** *archaic* the management of another person's affairs

procurator (ˈprɒkjʊˌreɪtə) *n* **1** (in ancient Rome) a civil official of the emperor's administration, often employed as the governor of a minor province or as a financial agent **2** *rare* a person engaged and authorized by another to manage his affairs [c13 from Latin: a manager, from *prōcūrāre* to attend to] > ˈprocuracy (ˈprɒkjʊrəsɪ) *or* ˈprocuˌratorship *n* > procuratorial (ˌprɒkjʊərəˈtɔːrɪəl) *or* procuratory (ˈprɒkjʊrətərɪ, -trɪ) *adj*

procurator fiscal *n* (in Scotland) a legal officer who performs the functions of public prosecutor and coroner

procuratory (ˈprɒkjʊrətərɪ) *n law* authorization to act on behalf of someone else

procure (prəˈkjʊə) *vb* **1** (*tr*) to obtain or acquire; secure **2** to obtain (women or girls) to act as prostitutes [c13 from Latin *prōcūrāre* to look after, from PRO-¹ + *cūrāre* to care for] > proˈcurable *adj* > proˈcurance *or* proˈcural *n*

procurement (prəˈkjʊəmənt) *n* **1** the act or an instance of procuring **2** *commerce* **a** the act of buying **b** (*as modifier*): *procurement cost; procurement budget*

procurer (prəˈkjʊərə) *or feminine* **procuress** (prəˈkjʊərɪs) *n* a person who procures, esp one who procures women or girls as prostitutes

Procyon (ˈprəʊsɪən) *n* the brightest star in the constellation Canis Minor, a binary with a very faint companion. Visual magnitude: 0.34; spectral type: F5IV; distance: 114 light years [c17 via Latin from Greek *Prokuōn* literally: before the Dog, from PRO-² + *kuōn* dog; so named because it rises just before Sirius, the Dog Star]

prod (prɒd) *vb* prods, prodding, prodded **1** to poke or jab with or as if with a pointed object **2** (*tr*) to rouse or urge to action ▷ *n* **3** the act or an instance of prodding **4** a sharp or pointed object **5** a stimulus or reminder [c16 of uncertain origin] > ˈprodder *n*

Prod (prɒd) *n derogatory slang* another word for **Protestant**

prod. *abbreviation for* **1** produce **2** produced **3** product

prodigal (ˈprɒdɪgᵊl) *adj* **1** recklessly wasteful or extravagant, as in disposing of goods or money **2** lavish in giving or yielding: *prodigal of compliments* ▷ *n* **3** a person who spends lavishly or squanders money [c16 from Medieval Latin *prōdigālis* wasteful, from Latin *prōdigus* lavish, from *prōdigere* to squander, from PRO-¹ + *agere* to drive] > ˌprodiˈgality *n* > ˈprodigally *adv*

prodigious (prəˈdɪdʒəs) *adj* **1** vast in size, extent, power, etc **2** wonderful or amazing **3** *obsolete* threatening [c16 from Latin *prōdigiōsus* marvellous, from *prōdigium,* see PRODIGY] > proˈdigiously *adv* > proˈdigiousness *n*

prodigy (ˈprɒdɪdʒɪ) *n, pl* -gies **1** a person, esp a child, of unusual or marvellous talents **2** anything that is a cause of wonder and amazement **3** something monstrous or abnormal **4** an archaic word for **omen** [c16 from Latin *prōdigium* an unnatural happening, from PRO-¹ + -*igium,* probably from *āio* I say]

prodrome (ˈprəʊdrəʊm) *n med* any symptom that signals the impending onset of a disease [c19 via French from New Latin *prodromus,* from Greek *prodromos* forerunner, from PRO-² + *dramein* to run] > proˈdromal *or* prodromic (prəʊˈdrɒmɪk) *adj*

prodrug (ˈprəʊˌdrʌg) *n* a compound that is itself biologically inactive but is metabolized in the body to produce an active therapeutic drug

produce *vb* (prəˈdjuːs) **1** to bring (something) into existence; yield **2** to bring forth (a product) by mental or physical effort; make: *she produced a delicious dinner for us* **3** (*tr*) to give birth to **4** (*tr*) to manufacture (a commodity): *this firm produces cartons* **5** (*tr*) to give rise to: *her joke produced laughter* **6** (*tr*) to present to view: *to produce evidence* **7** to bring before the public: *he produced two plays and a film last year* **8** to conceive and create the overall sound of (a record) and supervise its arrangement, recording, and mixing **9** (*tr*) *geometry* to extend (a line) ▷ *n* (ˈprɒdjuːs) **10** anything that is produced; product **11** agricultural products regarded collectively: *farm produce* [c15 from Latin *prōdūcere* to bring forward, from PRO-¹ + *dūcere* to lead] > proˈducible *adj* > proˌduciˈbility *n*

producer (prəˈdjuːsə) *n* **1** a person or thing that produces **2** *Brit* a person responsible for the artistic direction of a play, including interpretation of the script, preparation of the actors, and overall design **3** *US and Canadian* a person who organizes the stage production of a play, including the finance, management, etc **4** the person who takes overall administrative responsibility for a film or television programme. Compare **director** (sense 4) **5** the person who supervises the arrangement, recording, and mixing of a record **6** *economics* a person or business enterprise that generates goods or services for sale. Compare **consumer** (sense 1) **7** *chem* an apparatus or plant for making producer gas **8** (*often plural*) *ecology* an organism, esp a green plant, that builds up its own tissues from simple inorganic compounds. See also **consumer** (sense 3), **decomposer**

producer gas *n* a mixture of carbon monoxide and nitrogen produced by passing air over hot coke, used mainly as a fuel. Also called: **air gas.** See also **water gas**

producer goods *or* **producer's goods** *pl n* other terms for **capital goods**

product (ˈprɒdʌkt) *n* **1** something produced by effort, or some mechanical or industrial process **2** the result of some natural process **3** a result or consequence **4** a substance formed in a chemical reaction **5** *maths* **a** the result of the multiplication of two or more numbers, quantities, etc **b** Also called: **set product** another name for **intersection** (sense 3) **6** See **Cartesian product** [c15 from Latin *prōductum* (something) produced, from *prōdūcere* to bring forth]

product differentiation *n commerce* the real or illusory distinction between competing products in a market

production (prəˈdʌkʃən) *n* **1** the act of producing **2** anything that is produced; product **3** the amount produced or the rate at which it is produced **4** *economics* the creation or manufacture for sale of goods and services with exchange value **5** any work created as a result of literary or artistic effort **6** the organization and presentation of a film, play, opera, etc **7** *Brit* the artistic direction of a play **8 a** the supervision of the arrangement, recording, and mixing of a record **b** the overall sound quality or character of a recording: *the material is very strong but the production is poor* **9** (*modifier*) manufactured by a mass-production process: *a production model of a car* **10 make a production (out) of** *informal* to make an unnecessary fuss about > proˈductional *adj*

production line *n* a factory system in which parts or components of the end product are transported by a conveyor through a number of different sites at each of which a manual or machine operation is performed on them without interrupting the flow of production

production platform *n* (in the oil industry) a platform from which development wells are drilled that also houses a processing plant and other equipment necessary to keep an oilfield in production

productive (prəˈdʌktɪv) *adj* **1** producing or having the power to produce; fertile **2** yielding favourable or effective results **3** *economics* **a** producing or capable of producing goods and services that have monetary or exchange value: *productive assets* **b** of or relating to such production: *the productive processes of an industry* **4** (*postpositive; foll by of*) resulting in: *productive of good results* **5** denoting an affix or combining form used to produce new words > proˈductively *adv* > proˈductiveness *n*

productivity (ˌprɒdʌkˈtɪvɪtɪ) *n* **1** the output of an industrial concern in relation to the materials, labour, etc, it employs **2** the state of being productive

productivity bargaining *n* the process of reaching an agreement (**productivity agreement**) through collective bargaining whereby the employees of an organization agree to changes which are intended to improve productivity in return for an increase in pay or other benefits

product liability *n* the liability to the public of a manufacturer or trader for selling a faulty product

product life cycle *n marketing* the four stages (introduction, growth, maturity, and decline) into one of which the sales of a product fall during its market life

product line *n marketing* a group of related products marketed by the same company

product placement *n* the practice of a company paying for its product to be placed in a prominent position in a film or television programme as a form of advertising

proem (ˈprəʊɛm) *n* an introduction or preface, such as to a work of literature [c14 from Latin *prooemium* introduction, from Greek *prooimion,* from

p

PRO-² + *hoimē* song] > **proemial** (prəʊˈiːmɪəl) *adj*

proenzyme (prəʊˈɛnzaɪm) *n* the inactive form of an enzyme; zymogen

proestrus (prəʊˈɛstrəs, -ˈiːstrəs) *n* the usual US spelling of **pro-oestrus**

pro-European *adj* 1 having enthusiasm or admiration for the European Union ▷ *n* 2 a person who admires the European Union

prof (prɒf) *n informal* short for **professor**

Prof. *abbreviation for* Professor

profane (prəˈfeɪn) *adj* 1 having or indicating contempt, irreverence, or disrespect for a divinity or something sacred 2 not designed or used for religious purposes; secular 3 not initiated into the inner mysteries or sacred rites 4 vulgar, coarse, or blasphemous: *profane language* ▷ *vb* (*tr*) 5 to treat or use (something sacred) with irreverence 6 to put to an unworthy or improper use [C15 from Latin *profānus* outside the temple, from PRO-¹ + *fānum* temple] > **profanation** (ˌprɒfəˈneɪʃən) *n* > **profanatory** (prəˈfænətərɪ, -trɪ) *adj* > **proˈfanely** *adv* > **proˈfaneness** *n* > **proˈfaner** *n*

profanity (prəˈfænɪtɪ) *n, pl* **-ties** 1 the state or quality of being profane 2 vulgar or irreverent action, speech, etc

profascist (prəʊˈfæʃɪst) *adj* in favour of or supporting Fascism

profeminist (prəʊˈfɛmɪnɪst) *adj* in favour of or supporting feminism

profess (prəˈfɛs) *vb* 1 to affirm or announce (something, such as faith); acknowledge: *to profess ignorance; to profess a belief in God* 2 to claim (something, such as a feeling or skill, or to be or do something), often insincerely or falsely: *to profess to be a skilled driver* 3 to receive or be received into a religious order, as by taking vows [C14 from Latin *profitērī* to confess openly, from PRO-¹ + *fatērī* to confess]

professed (prəˈfɛst) *adj* (*prenominal*) 1 avowed or acknowledged 2 alleged or pretended 3 professing to be qualified as: *a professed philosopher* 4 having taken vows of a religious order > **professedly** (prəˈfɛsɪdlɪ) *adv*

profession (prəˈfɛʃən) *n* 1 an occupation requiring special training in the liberal arts or sciences, esp one of the three learned professions, law, theology, or medicine 2 the body of people in such an occupation 3 the act of professing; avowal; declaration 4 a Also called: **profession of faith** a declaration of faith in a religion, esp as made on entering the Church of that religion or an order belonging to it b the faith or the religion that is the subject of such a declaration [C13 from Medieval Latin *professiō* the taking of vows upon entering a religious order, from Latin: public acknowledgment; see PROFESS]

professional (prəˈfɛʃənˀl) *adj* 1 of, relating to, suitable for, or engaged in as a profession 2 engaging in an activity for gain or as a means of livelihood 3 extremely competent in a job, etc 4 undertaken or performed for gain or by people who are paid ▷ *n* 5 a person who belongs to or engages in one of the professions 6 a person who engages for his livelihood in some activity also pursued by amateurs 7 a person who engages in an activity with great competence 8 an expert player of a game who gives instruction, esp to members of a club by whom he is hired > **proˈfessionally** *adv*

professional association *n* a body of persons engaged in the same profession, formed usually to control entry into the profession, maintain standards, and represent the profession in discussions with other bodies

professional foul *n football* a deliberate foul committed as a last-ditch tactic to prevent an opponent from scoring

professionalism (prəˈfɛʃənəˌlɪzəm) *n* 1 the methods, character, status, etc, of a professional 2 the pursuit of an activity for gain or livelihood > **proˈfessionalist** *n, adj*

professionalize or **professionalise**

(prəˈfɛʃənəˌlaɪz) *vb* (*tr*) to impose a professional structure or status on (something) > **proˌfessionaliˈzation** or **proˌfessionaliˈsation** *n*

professor (prəˈfɛsə) *n* 1 the principal lecturer or teacher in a field of learning at a university or college; a holder of a university chair 2 *chiefly US and Canadian* any teacher in a university or college. See also **associate professor, assistant professor, full professor** 3 a person who claims skill and instructs others in some sport, occupation, etc 4 a person who professes his opinions, beliefs, etc [C14 from Medieval Latin: one who has made his profession in a religious order, from Latin: a public teacher; see PROFESS] > **professorial** (ˌprɒfɪˈsɔːrɪəl) *adj* > **ˌprofesˈsorially** *adv*

professoriate (ˌprɒfɪˈsɔːrɪɪt) or **professorate** (prəˈfɛsərɪt) *n* 1 a group of professors 2 Also called (esp Brit): **professorship** (prəˈfɛsəʃɪp) the rank or position of university professor

proffer (ˈprɒfə) *vb* 1 (*tr*) to offer for acceptance; tender ▷ *n* 2 the act of proffering [C13 from Old French *proffrir*, from PRO-¹ + *offrir* to offer] > **ˈprofferer** *n*

proficient (prəˈfɪʃənt) *adj* 1 having great facility (in an art, occupation, etc); skilled ▷ *n* 2 an archaic word for an **expert** [C16 from Latin *prōficere* to make progress, from PRO-¹ + *facere* to make] > **proˈficiency** *n* > **proˈficiently** *adv*

profile (ˈprəʊfaɪl) *n* 1 a side view, outline, or representation of an object, esp of a human face or head 2 a view or representation of an object, esp a building, in contour or outline 3 a short biographical sketch of a subject 4 a graph, table, or list of scores representing the extent to which a person, field, or object exhibits various tested characteristics or tendencies: *a population profile* 5 a vertical section of soil from the ground surface to the parent rock showing the different horizons 6 a a vertical section of part of the earth's crust showing the layers of rock b a representation of such a section 7 the outline of the shape of a river valley either from source to mouth (**long profile**) or at right angles to the flow of the river (**cross profile**) ▷ *vb* (*tr*) 8 to draw, write, or make a profile of 9 to cut out a shape from a blank (as of steel) with a cutter [C17 from Italian *profilo*, from *profilare* to sketch lightly, from PRO-¹ + Latin *filum* thread] > **profilist** (ˈprəʊfɪlɪst) *n*

profile component *n Brit education* attainment targets in different subjects brought together for the general assessment of a pupil

profile drag *n* the sum of the surface friction drag and the form drag for a body moving subsonically through a fluid

profiler (ˈprəʊfaɪlə) *n* a person or device that creates a profile, esp someone with psychological training who assists police investigations by identifying the likely characteristics of the perpetrator of a particular crime

profit (ˈprɒfɪt) *n* 1 (*often plural*) excess of revenues over outlays and expenses in a business enterprise over a given period of time, usually a year 2 the monetary gain derived from a transaction 3 a income derived from property or an investment, as contrasted with capital gains b the ratio of this income to the investment or principal 4 *economics* a the income or reward accruing to a successful entrepreneur and held to be the motivating factor of all economic activity in a capitalist economy b (*as modifier*): *the profit motive* 5 a gain, benefit, or advantage ▷ *vb* 6 to gain or cause to gain profit [C14 from Latin *prōfectus* advance, from *prōficere* to make progress; see PROFICIENT] > **ˈprofiter** *n* > **ˈprofitless** *adj*

profitable (ˈprɒfɪtəbˀl) *adj* affording gain, benefit, or profit > **ˈprofitably** *adv* > **ˈprofitableness** or **ˌprofitaˈbility** *n*

profit and loss *n book-keeping* an account compiled at the end of a financial year showing that year's revenue and expense items and indicating gross and net profit or loss

profit centre *n* a unit or department of a

company that is responsible for its costs and its profits

profiteer (ˌprɒfɪˈtɪə) *n* 1 a person who makes excessive profits, esp by charging exorbitant prices for goods in short supply ▷ *vb* 2 (*intr*) to make excessive profits > **ˌprofiˈteering** *n*

profiterole (ˌprɒfɪtəˈrəʊl, ˈprɒfɪtəˌrəʊl, prəˈfɪtəˌrəʊl) *n* a small case of choux pastry with a sweet or savoury filling [C16 from French, literally: a small profit, (related to the gifts, etc, given to a servant), from *profiter* to PROFIT]

profit-sharing *n* a system in which a portion of the net profit of a business is distributed to its employees, usually in proportion to their wages or their length of service

profit taking *n* selling commodities, securities, etc, at a profit after a rise in market values or before an expected fall in values

profit warning *n* a public announcement made by a company to shareholders and others warning that profits for a stated period will be much lower than had been expected

profligate (ˈprɒflɪgɪt) *adj* 1 shamelessly immoral or debauched 2 wildly extravagant or wasteful ▷ *n* 3 a profligate person [C16 from Latin *prōflīgātus* corrupt, from *prōflīgāre* to overthrow, from PRO-¹ + *flīgere* to beat] > **profligacy** (ˈprɒflɪgəsɪ) *n* > **ˈprofligately** *adv*

profluent (ˈprɒflʊənt) *adj* flowing smoothly or abundantly [C15 from Latin *prōfluere* to flow along]

pro-form *n* a word having grammatical function but assuming the meaning of an antecedent word or phrase for which it substitutes: *the word "does" is a pro-form for "understands Greek" in "I can't understand Greek but he does"*

pro forma (prəʊ ˈfɔːmə) *adj* 1 prescribing a set form or procedure ▷ *adv* 2 performed in a set manner [Latin: for form's sake]

pro forma invoice *n* an invoice issued before an order is placed or before the goods are delivered giving all the details and the cost of the goods

profound (prəˈfaʊnd) *adj* 1 penetrating deeply into subjects or ideas: *a profound mind* 2 showing or requiring great knowledge or understanding: *a profound treatise* 3 situated at or extending to a great depth 4 reaching to or stemming from the depths of one's nature: *profound regret* 5 intense or absolute: *profound silence* 6 thoroughgoing; extensive: *profound changes* ▷ *n* 7 *archaic or literary* a great depth; abyss [C14 from Old French *profund*, from Latin *profundus* deep, from PRO-¹ + *fundus* bottom] > **proˈfoundly** *adv* > **proˈfoundness** or **profundity** (prəˈfʌndɪtɪ) *n*

profuse (prəˈfjuːs) *adj* 1 plentiful, copious, or abundant: *profuse compliments* 2 (*often foll by in*) free or generous in the giving (of): *profuse in thanks* [C15 from Latin *profundere* to pour lavishly] > **proˈfusely** *adv* > **proˈfuseness** or **proˈfusion** *n*

prog¹ (prɒg) *vb* **progs, progging, progged** 1 (*intr*) *Brit slang or dialect* to prowl about for or as if for food or plunder ▷ *n* 2 *Brit slang or dialect* food obtained by begging 3 *Canadian dialect* a Newfoundland word for **food** [C17 of unknown origin]

prog² (prɒg) *Brit slang, archaic* ▷ *n* 1 short for **proctor** (sense 1) ▷ *vb* **progs, progging, progged** 2 (*tr*) (of a proctor) to discipline (a student)

prog³ (prɒg) *n informal* short for **programme**, esp a television programme

prog. *abbreviation for* 1 programme 2 progress 3 progressive

Prog. *abbreviation for* Progressive (Party, etc)

progenitive (prəʊˈdʒɛnɪtɪv) *adj* capable of bearing offspring > **proˈgenitiveness** *n*

progenitor (prəʊˈdʒɛnɪtə) *n* 1 a direct ancestor 2 an originator or founder of a future development; precursor [C14 from Latin: ancestor, from PRO-¹ + *genitor* parent, from *gignere* to beget]

progeny (ˈprɒdʒɪnɪ) *n, pl* **-nies** 1 the immediate descendant or descendants of a person, animal, etc 2 a result or outcome [C13 from Latin *prōgeniēs* lineage; see PROGENITOR]

progeria (prəʊˈdʒɪərɪə) *n med* premature old age, a rare condition occurring in children and characterized by small stature, absent or greying hair, wrinkled skin, and other signs of old age [c20 from PRO-² + Greek *gēras* old age]

pro-German *adj* in favour of or supporting Germany, its people, culture, etc: *pro-German sentiment in Britain*

progestational (ˌprəʊdʒɛˈsteɪʃənəl) *adj physiol* **1** of or relating to the phase of the menstrual cycle, lasting approximately 14 days, during which the uterus is prepared for pregnancy by the secretion of progesterone from the corpus luteum **2** preceding gestation; before pregnancy

progesterone (prəʊˈdʒɛstəˌrəʊn) *n* a steroid hormone, secreted mainly by the corpus luteum in the ovary, that prepares and maintains the uterus for pregnancy. Formula: $C_{21}H_{30}O_2$. Also called: corpus luteum hormone [c20 from PRO-¹ + GE(STATION) + STER(OL) + -ONE]

progestogen (prəʊˈdʒɛstədʒən) *or* **progestin** (prəˈdʒɛstɪn) *n* any of a group of steroid hormones that have progesterone-like activity, used in oral contraceptives and in treating gynaecological disorders [c20 from PROGEST(ERONE) + -O- + -GEN]

proglottis (prəʊˈɡlɒtɪs) *or* **proglottid** *n, pl* -glottides (-ˈɡlɒtɪˌdiːz) any of the segments that make up the body of a tapeworm. Each contains reproductive organs and separates from the worm when filled with fertilized eggs [c19 from Greek *proglōssis, proglōttis* point of the tongue, from PRO-² + *glōssa, glōtta* (so called because of its shape)] > proˈglottic *or* ˌproglotˈtidean *adj*

prognathous (prɒɡˈneɪθəs) *or* **prognathic** (prɒɡˈnæθɪk) *adj* having a projecting lower jaw [c19 from PRO-² + Greek *gnathos* jaw] > prognathism (ˈprɒɡnəˌθɪzəm) *n*

prognosis (prɒɡˈnəʊsɪs) *n, pl* -noses (-ˈnəʊsiːz) **1** *med* **a** a prediction of the course or outcome of a disease or disorder **b** the chances of recovery from a disease **2** any forecast or prediction [c17 via Latin from Greek: knowledge beforehand]

prognostic (prɒɡˈnɒstɪk) *adj* **1** of, relating to, or serving as a prognosis **2** foretelling or predicting ▷ *n* **3** *med* any symptom or sign used in making a prognosis **4** a sign or forecast of some future occurrence [c15 from Old French *pronostique*, from Latin *prognōsticum*, from Greek *prognōstikon*, from *progignōskein* to know in advance]

prognosticate (prɒɡˈnɒstɪˌkeɪt) *vb* **1** to foretell (future events) according to present signs or indications; prophesy **2** (*tr*) to foreshadow or portend [c16 from Medieval Latin *prognōsticāre* to predict] > progˌnostiˈcation *n* > progˈnosticative *adj* > progˈnostiˌcator *n*

program *or sometimes* **programme** (ˈprəʊɡræm) *n* **1** a sequence of coded instructions fed into a computer, enabling it to perform specified logical and arithmetical operations on data ▷ *vb* -grams, -gramming, -grammed *or* -grammes, -gramming, -grammed **2** (*tr*) to feed a program into (a computer) **3** (*tr*) to arrange (data) into a suitable form so that it can be processed by a computer **4** (*intr*) to write a program

program generator *n* a computer program that can be used to help to create other computer programs

programmable *or* **programable** (ˈprəʊˈɡræməbəl) *adj* (esp of a device or operation) capable of being programmed for automatic operation or computer processing > proˌgrammaˈbility *n*

programmatic (ˌprəʊɡrəˈmætɪk) *adj* **1** of or relating to programme music **2** of or relating to a programme

programme *or US* **program** (ˈprəʊɡræm) *n* **1** a written or printed list of the events, performers, etc, in a public performance **2** a performance or series of performances, often presented at a scheduled time, esp on radio or television **3** a specially arranged selection of things to be done: *what's the programme for this afternoon?* **4** a plan,

schedule, or procedure **5** a syllabus or curriculum ▷ *vb* -grammes, -gramming, -grammed *or US* -grams, -graming, -gramed **6** to design or schedule (something) as a programme ▷ *n, vb* **7** *computing* a variant spelling of **program** [c17 from Late Latin *programma*, from Greek: written public notice, from PRO-² + *graphein* to write]

programmed camera *n photog* a camera with electronic facilities for setting both aperture and shutter speed automatically on the basis of a through-the-lens light value and a given film speed

programmed cell death *n* another name for **apoptosis**

programmed learning *n* a teaching method in which the material to be learnt is broken down into easily understandable parts on which the pupil is able to test himself

programme evaluation and review technique *n* a method of planning, controlling, and checking the times taken to finish important parts of complex operations, such as making aircraft, ships, or bridges. Acronym: PERT. Compare **critical path analysis**

programme music *n* music that is intended to depict or evoke a scene or idea. Compare **absolute music**

programme of study *n Brit education* the prescribed syllabus that pupils must be taught at each key stage in the National Curriculum

programmer (ˈprəʊɡræmə) *n* a person who writes a program so that data may be processed by a computer

programming language *n* a simple language system designed to facilitate the writing of computer programs. See **high-level language, low-level language, machine code**

program statement *n* a single instruction in a computer program

program trading *n* trading on international stock exchanges using a computer program to exploit differences between stock index futures and actual share prices on world equity markets

progress *n* (ˈprəʊɡrɛs) **1** movement forwards, esp towards a place or objective **2** satisfactory development, growth, or advance: *she is making progress in maths* **3** advance towards completion, maturity, or perfection: *the steady onward march of progress* **4** (*modifier*) of or relating to progress: *a progress report* **5** *biology* increasing complexity, adaptation, etc, during the development of an individual or evolution of a group **6** *Brit* a stately royal journey **7 in progress** taking place; under way ▷ *vb* (prəˈɡrɛs) **8** (*intr*) to move forwards or onwards, as towards a place or objective **9** to move towards or bring nearer to completion, maturity, or perfection [c15 from Latin *prōgressus* a going forwards, from *prōgredī* to advance, from PRO-¹ + *gradī* to step]

progress chaser *n* a person employed to make sure at each stage, esp of a manufacturing process, that a piece of work is on schedule and is delivered to the customer on time > **progress chasing** *n*

progression (prəˈɡrɛʃən) *n* **1** the act of progressing; advancement **2** the act or an instance of moving from one thing or unit in a sequence to the next **3** *maths* a sequence of numbers in which each term differs from the succeeding term by a constant relation. See also **arithmetic progression, geometric progression, harmonic progression 4** *music* movement, esp of a logical kind, from one note to the next (**melodic progression**) or from one chord to the next (**harmonic progression**) **5** *astrology* one of several calculations, based on the movement of the planets, from which it is supposed that one can find the expected developments in a person's birth chart and the probable trends of circumstances for a year in his life > proˈgressional *adj* > proˈgressionally *adv*

progressionist (prəˈɡrɛʃənɪst) *or* **progressist**

(prəˈɡrɛsɪst) *n rare* an advocate of social, political, or economic progress; a member of a progressive political party > proˈgressionism *n*

progressive (prəˈɡrɛsɪv) *adj* **1** of or relating to progress **2** proceeding or progressing by steps or degrees **3** (*often capital*) favouring or promoting political or social reform through government action, or even revolution, to improve the lot of the majority: *a progressive policy* **4** denoting or relating to an educational system that allows flexibility in learning procedures, based on activities determined by the needs and capacities of the individual child, the aim of which is to integrate academic with social development **5** (of a tax or tax system) graduated so that the rate increases relative to the amount taxed. Compare **regressive** (sense 2) **6** (esp of a disease) advancing in severity, complexity, or extent **7** (of a dance, card game, etc) involving a regular change of partners after one figure, one game, etc **8** denoting an aspect of verbs in some languages, including English, used to express prolonged or continuous activity as opposed to momentary or habitual activity: *a progressive aspect of the verb "to walk" is "is walking."* ▷ *n* **9** a person who advocates progress, as in education, politics, etc **10 a** the progressive aspect of a verb in this aspect > proˈgressively *adv* > proˈgressiveness *n* > proˈgressivism *n* > proˈgressivist *n*

Progressive (prəˈɡrɛsɪv) *n* **1** *US history* a member or supporter of a Progressive Party **2** *Canadian history* a member or supporter of a chiefly agrarian reform movement advocating the nationalization of railways, low tariffs, an end to party politics, and similar measures: important in the early 1920s ▷ *adj* **3** of, relating to, or characteristic of a Progressive Party, Progressive movement, or Progressives

Progressive Conservative *n* (in Canada) a member or supporter of the Progressive Conservative Party

Progressive Conservative Party *n* (in Canada) a major political party with conservative policies

progressive dinner *n Austral and NZ* a meal in which each course is served at the home of a different person

Progressive Federal Party *n South African* a political party, formed in 1977 by a merger between the Progressive Party and members of the United Party, supporting qualified franchise for all South Africans irrespective of race, colour, or creed. See also **National Party, United Party**

Progressive Party *n* **1** a US political party, made up chiefly of dissident Republicans, that nominated Theodore Roosevelt as its presidential candidate in 1912 and supported primaries, progressive labour legislation, and other reforms **2** a US political party, composed mostly of farmers, socialists, and unionists, that nominated Robert La Follette for president in 1924 and supported public ownership of railways and of public utilities and other reforms **3** a US political party, composed chiefly of dissident Democrats, that nominated Henry Wallace for president in 1948 and supported the nationalization of key industries, advocated social reforms, and opposed the Cold War **4** (in South Africa) the former name for the **Progressive Federal Party**

progress payment *n* an instalment of a larger payment made to a contractor for work carried out up to a specified stage of the job

prog rock *or* **progressive rock** *n* a style of rock music originating in the 1970s and characterized by large-scale compositions, often on epic themes, in which musicians display instrumental virtuosity

prohibit (prəˈhɪbɪt) *vb* (*tr*) **1** to forbid by law or other authority **2** to hinder or prevent [c15 from Latin *prohibēre* to prevent, from PRO-¹ + *habēre* to hold] > proˈhibiter *or* proˈhibitor *n*

prohibition (ˌprəʊɪˈbɪʃən) *n* **1** the act of prohibiting or state of being prohibited **2** an order or decree that prohibits **3** (*sometimes capital*) (esp in the US) a policy of legally forbidding the manufacture, transportation, sale, or consumption of alcoholic beverages except for medicinal or scientific purposes **4** *law* an order of a superior court (in Britain the High Court) forbidding an inferior court to determine a matter outside its jurisdiction > ˌprohiˈbitionary *adj*

Prohibition (ˌprəʊɪˈbɪʃən) *n* the period (1920–33) when the manufacture, sale, and transportation of intoxicating liquors was banned by constitutional amendment in the US > ˌProhiˈbitionist *n*

prohibitionist (ˌprəʊɪˈbɪʃənɪst) *n* (*sometimes capital*) a person who favours prohibition, esp of alcoholic beverages > ˌprohiˈbitionism *n*

prohibitive (prəˈhɪbɪtɪv) *or less commonly* **prohibitory** (prəˈhɪbɪtərɪ, -trɪ) *adj* **1** prohibiting or tending to prohibit **2** (esp of prices) tending or designed to discourage sale or purchase > proˈhibitively *adv* > proˈhibitiveness *n*

project *n* (ˈprɒdʒɛkt) **1** a proposal, scheme, or design **2 a** a task requiring considerable or concerted effort, such as one by students **b** the subject of such a task **3** *US* short for **housing project** ⊳ *vb* (prəˈdʒɛkt) **4** (*tr*) to propose or plan **5** (*tr*) to predict; estimate; extrapolate: *we can project future needs on the basis of the current birth rate* **6** (*tr*) to throw or cast forwards **7** to jut or cause to jut out **8** (*tr*) to send forth or transport in the imagination: *to project oneself into the future* **9** (*tr*) to cause (an image) to appear on a surface **10** to cause (one's voice) to be heard clearly at a distance **11** *psychol* **a** (*intr*) (esp of a child) to believe that others share one's subjective mental life **b** to impute to others (one's hidden desires and impulses), esp as a means of defending oneself. Compare **introject 12** (*tr*) *geometry* to draw a projection of **13** (*intr*) to communicate effectively, esp to a large gathering [c14 from Latin *prōicere* to throw down, from PRO-¹ + *iacere* to throw]

projectile (prəˈdʒɛktaɪl) *n* **1** an object or body thrown forwards **2** any self-propelling missile, esp one powered by a rocket or the rocket itself **3** any object that can be fired from a gun, such as a bullet or shell ⊳ *adj* **4** capable of being or designed to be hurled forwards **5** projecting or thrusting forwards **6** *zoology* another word for **protrusile** [c17 from New Latin *prōjectilis* jutting forwards]

projection (prəˈdʒɛkʃən) *n* **1** the act of projecting or the state of being projected **2** an object or part that juts out **3** See **map projection 4** the representation of a line, figure, or solid on a given plane as it would be seen from a particular direction or in accordance with an accepted set of rules **5** a scheme or plan **6** a prediction based on known evidence and observations **7 a** the process of showing film on a screen **b** the image or images shown **8** *psychol* **a** the belief, esp in children, that others share one's subjective mental life **b** the process of projecting one's own hidden desires and impulses. See also **defence mechanism 9** the mixing by alchemists of powdered philosopher's stone with molten base metals in order to transmute them into gold > proˈjectional *adj*

projectionist (prəˈdʒɛkʃənɪst) *n* a person responsible for the operation of film projection machines

projection room *n* a small room in a cinema in which the film projectors are operated

projection television *n* a television receiver in which a very bright picture on a small cathode-ray tube screen is optically projected onto a large screen

projective (prəˈdʒɛktɪv) *adj* relating to or concerned with projection: *projective geometry* > proˈjectively *adv*

projective geometry *n* the branch of geometry concerned with the properties of solids that are invariant under projection and section

projective test *n* any psychological test, such as the Rorschach test, in which the subject is asked to respond to vague material. It is thought that unconscious ideas are thus projected, which, when the responses are interpreted, reveal hidden aspects of the subject's personality

projector (prəˈdʒɛktə) *n* **1** an optical instrument that projects an enlarged image of individual slides onto a screen or wall. Full name: **slide projector 2** an optical instrument in which a strip of film is wound past a lens at a fixed speed so that the frames can be viewed as a continuously moving sequence on a screen or wall. Full name: **film** *or* **cine projector 3** a device for projecting a light beam **4** a person who devises projects

projet (ˈprɒʒeɪ) *n diplomacy* a draft of a proposed treaty; plan or proposition [c19 via French from Latin *prōjectum* something projecting]

prokaryon (prəʊˈkærɪɒn) *n* the nucleus of a prokaryote

prokaryote *or* **procaryote** (prəʊˈkærɪɒt) *n* any organism having cells in each of which the genetic material is in a single DNA chain, not enclosed in a nucleus. Bacteria and archaeans are prokaryotes. Compare **eukaryote** [from PRO-² + KARYO- + -*ote* as in *zygote*] > **prokaryotic** *or* **procaryotic** (prəʊˌkærɪˈɒtɪk) *adj*

Prokopyevsk (*Russian* praˈkɒpjɪfsk) *n* a city in S Russia: the chief coal-mining centre of the Kuznetsk Basin. Pop: 216 000 (2005 est)

prolactin (prəʊˈlæktɪn) *n* a gonadotrophic hormone secreted by the anterior lobe of the pituitary gland. In mammals it stimulates the secretion of progesterone by the corpus luteum and initiates and maintains lactation. Also called: **luteotrophin, luteotrophic hormone**. See also **follicle-stimulating hormone, luteinizing hormone**

prolamine (ˈprəʊləˌmiːn, -mɪn, prəʊˈlæmiːn) *n* any of a group of simple plant proteins, including gliadin, hordein, and zein [c20 from PROL(INE) + AM(MONIA) + -INE²]

prolapse (ˈprəʊlæps, prəʊˈlæps) *pathol* ⊳ *n* **1** Also called: **prolapsus** (prəʊˈlæpsəs) the sinking or falling down of an organ or part, esp the womb. Compare **proptosis** ⊳ *vb* (*intr*) **2** (of an organ, etc) to sink from its normal position [c17 from Latin *prōlābī* to slide along, from PRO-¹ + *lābī* to slip]

prolate (ˈprəʊleɪt) *adj* having a polar diameter of greater length than the equatorial diameter. Compare **oblate¹** [c17 from Latin *prōferre* to enlarge] > ˈprolately *adv* > ˈprolateness *n*

prole (prəʊl) *n, adj derogatory slang, chiefly Brit* short for **proletarian**

proleg (ˈprəʊˌlɛg) *n* any of the short paired unjointed appendages on each abdominal segment of a caterpillar and any of certain other insect larvae [c19 from PRO-¹ + LEG]

prolegomenon (ˌprəʊlɛˈgɒmɪnən) *n, pl* -**na** (-nə) (*often plural*) a preliminary discussion, esp a formal critical introduction to a lengthy text [c17 from Greek, from *prolegein*, from PRO-² + *legein* to say] > ˌproleˈgomenal *adj*

prolepsis (prəʊˈlɛpsɪs) *n, pl* -**ses** (-siːz) **1** a rhetorical device by which objections are anticipated and answered in advance **2** use of a word after a verb in anticipation of its becoming applicable through the action of the verb, as *flat* in *hammer it flat* [c16 via Late Latin from Greek: anticipation, from *prolambanein* to anticipate, from PRO-² + *lambanein* to take] > proˈleptic *adj*

proletarian (ˌprəʊlɪˈtɛərɪən) *or less commonly* **proletary** (ˈprəʊlɪtərɪ, -trɪ) *adj* **1** of, relating, or belonging to the proletariat ⊳ *n, pl* -**tarians** *or* -**taries 2** a member of the proletariat [c17 from Latin *prōlētārius* one whose only contribution to the state was his offspring, from *prōlēs* offspring] > ˌproleˈtarianism *n* > ˌproleˈtarianness *n*

proletariat (ˌprəʊlɪˈtɛərɪət) *n* **1** all wage-earners collectively **2** the lower or working class **3** (in Marxist theory) the class of wage-earners, esp

industrial workers, in a capitalist society, whose only possession of significant material value is their labour **4** (in ancient Rome) the lowest class of citizens, who had no property [c19 via French from Latin *prōlētārius* PROLETARIAN]

pro-life *adj* (of an organization, pressure group, etc) supporting the right to life of the unborn; against abortion, experiments on embryos, etc > ˌpro-ˈlifer *n*

proliferate (prəˈlɪfəˌreɪt) *vb* **1** to grow or reproduce (new parts, cells, etc) rapidly **2** to grow or increase or cause to grow or increase rapidly [c19 from Medieval Latin *prōlifer* having offspring, from Latin *prōlēs* offspring + *ferre* to bear] > proˈliferative *adj*

proliferation (prəˌlɪfəˈreɪʃən) *n* **1** rapid growth or reproduction of new parts, cells, etc **2** rapid growth or increase in numbers **3** a great number: *done up in a proliferation of fancy frills*

proliferous (prəˈlɪfərəs) *adj* **1** (of plants) producing many side branches or offshoots and normally reproducing vegetatively by buds or by plantlets produced in the inflorescence **2** (of certain animals) reproducing by means of buds, etc [c17 from Medieval Latin *prōlifer* having offspring]

prolific (prəˈlɪfɪk) *adj* **1** producing fruit, offspring, etc, in abundance **2** producing constant or successful results **3** (often foll by *in* or *of*) rich or fruitful [c17 from Medieval Latin *prōlificus,* from Latin *prōlēs* offspring] > proˈlifically *adv* > proˈlificness *or* proˈlificacy *n*

proline (ˈprəʊliːn, -lɪn) *n* a nonessential amino acid that occurs in protein [c20 from PYRROLIDINE]

prolix (ˈprəʊlɪks, prəʊˈlɪks) *adj* **1** (of a speech, book, etc) so long as to be boring; verbose **2** indulging in prolix speech or writing; long-winded [c15 from Latin *prōlixus* stretched out widely, from PRO-¹ + *līquī* to flow] > proˈlixity *or less commonly* proˈlixness *n* > proˈlixly *adv*

prolocutor (prəʊˈlɒkjʊtə) *n* a chairman, esp of the lower house of clergy in a convocation of the Anglican Church [c15 from Latin: advocate, from PRO-¹ + *loquī* to speak] > proˈlocutorˌship *n*

PROLOG *or* **Prolog** (ˈprəʊlɒg) *n* a computer programming language based on mathematical logic [c20 from *pro(gramming in) log(ic)*]

prologue *or often US* **prolog** (ˈprəʊlɒg) *n* **1 a** the prefatory lines introducing a play or speech **b** the actor speaking these lines **2** a preliminary act or event **3** (in early opera) **a** an introductory scene in which a narrator summarizes the main action of the work **b** a brief independent play preceding the opera, esp one in honour of a patron ⊳ *vb* -**logues, -loguing, -logued** *or* -**logs, -loging, -loged 4** (*tr*) to introduce or preface with or as if with a prologue [c13 from Latin *prologus,* from Greek *prologos,* from PRO-² + *logos* discourse]

prolong (prəˈlɒŋ) *vb* (*tr*) to lengthen in duration or space; extend [c15 from Late Latin *prōlongāre* to extend, from Latin PRO-¹ + *longus* long] > **prolongation** (ˌprəʊlɒŋˈgeɪʃən) *n* > proˈlonger *n* > proˈlongment *n*

prolonge (prəˈlɒndʒ) *n* (formerly) a specially fitted rope used as part of the towing equipment of a gun carriage [c19 from French, from *prolonger* to PROLONG]

prolusion (prəˈluːʒən) *n* **1** a preliminary written exercise **2** an introductory essay, sometimes of a slight or tentative nature [c17 from Latin *prōlūsiō* preliminary exercise, from *prōlūdere* to practise beforehand, from PRO-¹ + *lūdere* to play] > prolusory (prəˈluːzərɪ) *adj*

prom (prɒm) *n* **1** *Brit* short for **promenade** (sense 1) *or* **promenade concert 2** *US and Canadian informal* short for **promenade** (sense 3)

PROM (prɒm) *n computing* ⊳ *acronym for* programmable read only memory

promenade (ˌprɒməˈnɑːd) *n* **1** *chiefly Brit* a public walk, esp at a seaside resort **2** a leisurely walk, esp one in a public place for pleasure or display **3** *US and Canadian* a ball or formal dance at a high school or college **4** a marchlike step in dancing **5** a marching sequence in a square or country dance ▷ *vb* **6** to take a promenade in or through (a place) **7** (*intr*) *dancing* to perform a promenade **8** (*tr*) to display or exhibit (someone or oneself) on or as if on a promenade [c16 from French, from *promener* to lead out for a walk, from Late Latin *prōmināre* to drive (cattle) along, from PRO-¹ + *mināre* to drive, probably from *mināri* to threaten] > ˌprome'nader *n*

promenade concert *n* a concert at which some of the audience stand rather than sit. Often shortened to: **prom**

promenade deck *n* an upper covered deck of a passenger ship for the use of the passengers

promethazine (prəʊ'mɛθəˌziːn) *n* an antihistamine drug used to treat allergies and to prevent vomiting, esp in motion sickness [c20 from PRO(PYL) + (*di*)*meth*(*ylamine*) + (PHENOTHI)AZINE]

Promethean (prə'miːθɪən) *adj* **1** of or relating to Prometheus **2** creative, original, or life-enhancing ▷ *n* **3** a person who resembles Prometheus

Prometheus (prə'miːθɪəs) *n Greek myth* a Titan, who stole fire from Olympus to give to mankind and in punishment was chained to a rock, where an eagle tore at his liver until Hercules freed him

promethium (prə'miːθɪəm) *n* a radioactive element of the lanthanide series artificially produced by the fission of uranium. Symbol: Pm; atomic no.: 61; half-life of most stable isotope, ¹⁴⁵Pm: 17.7 years; valency: 3; melting pt.: 1042°C; boiling pt.: 2460°C (approx.) [c20 New Latin from PROMETHEUS]

promilitary (prəʊ'mɪlɪtərɪ, -'mɪlɪtrɪ) *adj* in favour of or supporting military organizations, operations, or action

prominence ('prɒmɪnəns) *n* **1** the state or quality of being prominent **2** something that is prominent, such as a protuberance **3** relative importance or consequence **4** *astronomy* an eruption of incandescent gas from the sun's surface that can reach an altitude of several hundred thousand kilometres. Prominences are visible during a total eclipse. When viewed in front of the brighter solar disc, they are called filaments

prominent ('prɒmɪnənt) *adj* **1** jutting or projecting outwards **2** standing out from its surroundings; noticeable **3** widely known; eminent [c16 from Latin *prōminēre* to jut out, from PRO-¹ + *ēminēre* to project] > 'prominently *adv* > 'prominentness *n*

prominent moth *n* any moth of the family *Notodontidae* characterized by tufts of scales on the back edge of the forewing that stand up prominently at rest and give the group its name. It includes the puss moth and buff-tip as well as those with *prominent* in the name

promiscuity (ˌprɒmɪ'skjuːɪtɪ) *n* **1** promiscuous sexual behaviour **2** indiscriminate mingling, mixture, or confusion, as of parts or elements

promiscuous (prə'mɪskjʊəs) *adj* **1** indulging in casual and indiscriminate sexual relationships **2** consisting of a number of dissimilar parts or elements mingled in a confused or indiscriminate manner **3** indiscriminate in selection **4** casual or heedless [c17 from Latin *prōmiscuus* indiscriminate, from PRO-¹ + *miscēre* to mix] > pro'miscuously *adv* > pro'miscuousness *n*

promise ('prɒmɪs) *vb* **1** (often foll by *to*; when *tr*, may take a clause as object or an infinitive) to give an assurance of (something to someone); undertake (to do something) in the future: *I promise that I will come* **2** (*tr*) to undertake to give (something to someone): *he promised me a car for my birthday* **3** (when *tr*, takes an infinitive) to cause one to expect that in the future one is likely (to be or do something): *she promises to be a fine soprano* **4** (usually passive) to engage to be married; betroth: *I'm promised to Bill* **5** (*tr*) to assure (someone) of the authenticity or inevitability of something (often

in the parenthetic phrase **I promise you,** used to emphasize a statement): *there'll be trouble, I promise you* ▷ *n* **6** an undertaking or assurance given by one person to another agreeing or guaranteeing to do or give something, or not to do or give something, in the future **7** indication of forthcoming excellence or goodness: *a writer showing considerable promise* **8** the thing of which an assurance is given [c14 from Latin *prōmissum* a promise, from *prōmittere* to send forth] > 'promiser *n*

Promised Land *n* **1** *Old Testament* the land of Canaan, promised by God to Abraham and his descendants as their heritage (Genesis 12:7) **2** heaven, esp when considered as the goal towards which Christians journey in their earthly lives **3** any longed-for place where one expects to find greater happiness or fulfilment

promisee (ˌprɒmɪ'siː) *n contract law* a person to whom a promise is made. Compare **promisor**

promising ('prɒmɪsɪŋ) *adj* showing promise of favourable development or future success > 'promisingly *adv*

promisor (ˌprɒmɪ'sɔː, 'prɒmɪˌsɔː) *n contract law* a person who makes a promise. Compare **promisee**

promissory ('prɒmɪsərɪ) *adj* **1** containing, relating to, or having the nature of a promise **2** *insurance* stipulating how the provisions of an insurance contract will be fulfilled after it has been signed

promissory note *n chiefly US commerce* a document, usually negotiable, containing a signed promise to pay a stated sum of money to a specified person at a designated date or on demand. Also called: **note, note of hand**

promo ('prəʊməʊ) *n, pl* **-mos a** *informal* something that is used to promote a product, esp a videotape film used to promote a pop record **b** (*as modifier*): *a promo video* [c20 shortened from *promotion*]

promonarchist (prəʊ'mɒnəkɪst) *adj* in favour of or supporting the monarchy

promontory ('prɒməntərɪ, -trɪ) *n, pl* **-ries 1** a high point of land, esp of rocky coast, that juts out into the sea **2** *anatomy* any of various projecting structures [c16 from Latin *prōmunturium* headland; related to *prōminēre*; see PROMINENT]

promote (prə'məʊt) *vb* (*tr*) **1** to further or encourage the progress or existence of **2** to raise to a higher rank, status, degree, etc **3** to advance (a pupil or student) to a higher course, class, etc **4** to urge the adoption of; work for: *to promote reform* **5** to encourage the sale of (a product) by advertising or securing financial support **6** *chess* to exchange (a pawn) for any piece other than a king when the pawn reaches the 8th rank [c14 from Latin *prōmovēre* to push onwards, from PRO-¹ + *movēre* to move] > pro'motable *adj* > pro'motion *n* > pro'motional *adj*

promoter (prə'məʊtə) *n* **1** a person or thing that promotes **2** a person who helps to organize, develop, or finance an undertaking **3** a person who organizes and finances a sporting event, esp a boxing match **4** *chem* a substance added in small amounts to a catalyst to increase its activity **5** *genetics* a sequence of nucleotides, associated with a structural gene, that must bind with messenger RNA polymerase before transcription can proceed

promotive (prə'məʊtɪv) *adj* tending to promote > pro'motiveness *n*

prompt (prɒmpt) *adj* **1** performed or executed without delay **2** quick or ready to act or respond ▷ *adv* **3** *informal* punctually ▷ *vb* **4** (*tr*) to urge (someone to do something) **5** to remind (an actor, singer, etc) of lines forgotten during a performance **6** (*tr*) to refresh the memory of **7** (*tr*) to give rise to by suggestion: *his affairs will prompt discussion* ▷ *n* **8** *commerce* **a** the time limit allowed for payment of the debt incurred by purchasing goods or services on credit **b** the contract specifying this time limit **c** Also called: **prompt**

note a memorandum sent to a purchaser to remind him of the time limit and the sum due **9** the act of prompting **10** anything that serves to remind **11** an aid to the operator of a computer in the form of a question or statement that appears on the screen showing that the equipment is ready to proceed and indicating the options available [c15 from Latin *promptus* evident, from *prōmere* to produce, from PRO-¹ + *emere* to buy] > 'promptly *adv* > 'promptness *n*

promptbook ('prɒmptˌbʊk) *n* the production script of a play containing notes, cues, etc

prompter ('prɒmptə) *n* **1** a person offstage who reminds the actors of forgotten lines or cues **2** a person, thing, etc, that prompts

promptitude ('prɒmptɪˌtjuːd) *n* the quality of being prompt; punctuality

prompt side *n theatre* the side of the stage where the prompter is, usually to the actor's left in Britain and to his right in the United States

promulgate ('prɒməlˌgeɪt) *vb* (*tr*) **1** to put into effect (a law, decree, etc), esp by formal proclamation **2** to announce or declare officially **3** to make widespread ▷ Also (archaic): **promulge** (prəʊ'mʌldʒ) [c16 from Latin *prōmulgāre* to bring to public knowledge; probably related to *provulgāre* to publicize, from PRO-¹ + *vulgāre* to make common, from *vulgus* the common people] > ˌpromul'gation *n* > 'promulˌgator *n*

promycelium (ˌprəʊmaɪ'siːlɪəm) *n, pl* **-lia** (-lɪə) *botany* a short tubular outgrowth from certain germinating fungal spores that produces spores itself and then dies [c19 New Latin from PRO-¹ + MYCELIUM] > ˌpromy'celial *adj*

pron. *abbreviation for* **1** pronominal **2** pronoun **3** pronounced **4** pronunciation

pronate (prəʊ'neɪt) *vb* (*tr*) to turn (a limb, hand, or foot) so that the palm or sole is directed downwards [c19 from Late Latin *prōnāre* to bend forwards, bow] > pro'nation *n*

pronator (prəʊ'neɪtə) *n* any muscle whose contractions produce or affect pronation

prone (prəʊn) *adj* **1** lying flat or face downwards; prostrate **2** sloping or tending downwards **3** having an inclination to do something [c14 from Latin *prōnus* bent forward, from PRO-¹] > 'pronely *adv* > 'proneness *n*

-prone *adj combining form* liable or disposed to suffer: *accident-prone*

pronephros (prəʊ'nɛfrɒs) *n, pl* **-roi** (-rɔɪ) *or* **-ra** (-rə) the first-formed anterior part of the embryonic kidney in vertebrates, which remains functional in the larvae of the lower vertebrates. See also **mesonephros, metanephros** [c19 New Latin, from PRO-¹ + Greek *nephros* kidney] > pro'nephric *adj*

prong (prɒŋ) *n* **1** a sharply pointed end of an instrument, such as on a fork **2** any pointed projecting part ▷ *vb* **3** (*tr*) to prick or spear with or as if with a prong [c15 related to Middle Low German *prange* a stake, Gothic *anaprangan* to afflict] > pronged *adj*

pronghorn ('prɒŋˌhɔːn) *n* a ruminant mammal, *Antilocapra americana*, inhabiting rocky deserts of North America and having small branched horns: family *Antilocapridae*. Also called: **American antelope**

prong key *n* a key or spanner with two prongs or projections which engage corresponding holes in the face of a nut or component to be turned for tightening, adjustment, etc

pronominal (prəʊ'nɒmɪnəl) *adj* relating to or playing the part of a pronoun [c17 from Late Latin *prōnōminālis*, from *prōnōmen* a PRONOUN] > pro'nominally *adv*

pronominalize *or* **pronominalise** (prəʊ'nɒmɪnəˌlaɪz) *vb* (*tr*) to make (a word) into or treat as a pronoun > proˌnominali'zation *or* proˌnominali'sation *n*

pronotum (prəʊ'nəʊtəm) *n* the notum of the prothorax of an insect [c19 PRO-² + NOTUM]

pronoun ('prəʊˌnaʊn) *n* one of a class of words that serves to replace a noun phrase that has already been or is about to be mentioned in the sentence or context. Abbreviation: **pron** [c16 from Latin *prōnōmen*, from PRO-¹ + *nōmen* noun]

pronounce (prə'naʊns) *vb* **1** to utter or articulate (a sound or sequence of sounds) **2** (*tr*) to utter or articulate (sounds or words) in the correct way **3** (*tr; may take a clause as object*) to proclaim officially and solemnly: *I now pronounce you man and wife* **4** (when *tr*, may take a clause as object) to declare as one's judgment: *to pronounce the death sentence upon someone* **5** (*tr*) to make a phonetic transcription of (sounds or words) [c14 from Latin *prōnuntiāre* to announce, from PRO-¹ + *nuntiāre* to announce] ▷ **pro'nounceable** *adj* ▷ **pro'nouncer** *n*

pronounced (prə'naʊnst) *adj* **1** strongly marked or indicated **2** (of a sound) articulated with vibration of the vocal cords; voiced ▷ **pronouncedly** (prə'naʊnsɪdlɪ) *adv*

pronouncement (prə'naʊnsmənt) *n* **1** an official or authoritative statement or announcement **2** the act of pronouncing, declaring, or uttering formally

pronto ('prɒntəʊ) *adv informal* at once; promptly [c20 from Spanish: quick, from Latin *promptus* PROMPT]

pronuclear¹ (ˌprəʊ'njuːklɪə) *adj* in favour of or supporting the use of nuclear power ▷ **pro'nuclearist** *n, adj*

pronuclear² (ˌprəʊ'njuːklɪə) *adj* of or relating to a pronucleus

pronucleus (ˌprəʊ'njuːklɪəs) *n, pl* -**clei** (-klɪˌaɪ) the nucleus of a mature ovum or spermatozoan before fertilization

pronunciamento (prəˌnʌnsɪə'mɛntəʊ) *n, pl* -**tos 1** an edict, proclamation, or manifesto, esp one issued by rebels in a Spanish-speaking country **2** an authoritarian announcement [c19 from Spanish: pronouncement]

pronunciation (prəˌnʌnsɪ'eɪʃən) *n* **1** the act, instance, or manner of pronouncing sounds **2** the supposedly correct manner of pronouncing sounds in a given language **3** a phonetic transcription of a word

pro-oestrus (prəʊ'iːstrəs, -'ɛstrəs) *or US* **proestrus** *n* the period in the oestrous cycle that immediately precedes oestrus

proof (pruːf) *n* **1** any evidence that establishes or helps to establish the truth, validity, quality, etc, of something **2** *law* the whole body of evidence upon which the verdict of a court is based **3** *maths, logic* a sequence of steps or statements that establishes the truth of a proposition. See also **direct** (sense 17), **induction** (senses 4, 8) **4** the act of testing the truth of something (esp in the phrase **put to the proof**) **5** *Scots law* trial before a judge without a jury **6** *printing* a trial impression made from composed type, or a print-out (from a laser printer, etc) for the correction of errors **7** (in engraving, etc) a print made by an artist or under his supervision before he hands the plate over to a professional printer **8** *photog* a trial print from a negative **9 a** the alcoholic strength of proof spirit **b** the strength of a beverage or other alcoholic liquor as measured on a scale in which the strength of proof spirit is 100 degrees ▷ *adj* **10** (*usually postpositive; foll by against*) able to resist; impervious (to): *the roof is proof against rain* **11** having the alcoholic strength of proof spirit **12** of proved strength or impenetrability: *proof armour* ▷ *vb* **13** (*tr*) to take a proof from (type matter, a plate, etc) **14** to proofread (text) or inspect (a print, etc), as for approval **15** to render (something) proof, esp to waterproof [c13 from Old French *preuve* a test, from Late Latin *proba*, from Latin *probāre* to test]

-proof *adj* ▷ *vb combining form* secure against (damage by); (make) impervious to: *waterproof; mothproof; childproof* [from PROOF (adj)]

proofread ('pruːfˌriːd) *vb* -**reads**, -**reading**, -**read** (-ˌrɛd) to read (copy or printer's proofs) to detect and mark errors to be corrected ▷ '**proofˌreader** *n*

proof spirit *n* **1** (in Britain and Canada) a mixture

of alcohol and water or an alcoholic beverage that contains 49.28 per cent of alcohol by weight, 57.1 per cent by volume at 51°F: up until 1980 used as a standard of alcoholic liquids **2** (in the US) a similar standard mixture containing 50 per cent of alcohol by volume at 60°F

proof stress *n engineering* the equivalent of yield stress in materials which have no clearly defined yield point

proof theory *n* the branch of logic that studies the syntactic properties of formal theories, esp the syntactic characterization of deductive validity

prop¹ (prɒp) *vb* **props, propping, propped** (when *tr*, often foll by *up*) **1** (*tr*) to support with a rigid object, such as a stick **2** (*tr; usually also foll by against*) to place or lean **3** (*tr*) to sustain or support **4** (*intr*) *Austral and NZ* to stop suddenly or unexpectedly ▷ *n* **5** something that gives rigid support, such as a stick **6** a person or thing giving support, as of a moral or spiritual nature **7** *rugby* either of the forwards at either end of the front row of a scrum [c15 related to Middle Dutch *proppe* vine prop; compare Old High German *pfropfo* shoot, German *Pfropfen* stopper]

prop² (prɒp) *n* short for **property** (sense 8)

prop³ (prɒp) *n* an informal word for **propeller**

propaedeutic (ˌprəʊpɪ'djuːtɪk) *n* **1** (*often plural*) preparatory instruction basic to further study of an art or science ▷ *adj also* **propaedeutical 2** of, relating to, or providing such instruction [c19 from Greek *propaideuein* to teach in advance, from PRO-² + *paideuein* to rear]

propagable ('prɒpəgəbªl) *adj* capable of being propagated ▷ ˌpropaga'bility *or* 'propagableness *n*

propaganda (ˌprɒpə'gændə) *n* **1** the organized dissemination of information, allegations, etc, to assist or damage the cause of a government, movement, etc **2** such information, allegations, etc [c18 from Italian, use of *propāgandā* in the New Latin title *Sacra Congregatio de Propaganda Fide* Sacred Congregation for Propagating the Faith] ▷ ˌpropa'gandism *n* ▷ ˌpropa'gandist *n, adj*

Propaganda (ˌprɒpə'gændə) *n RC Church* a congregation responsible for directing the work of the foreign missions and the training of priests for these

propagandize *or* **propagandise** (ˌprɒpə'gændaɪz) *vb* **1** (*tr*) to spread by propaganda **2** (*tr*) to subject to propaganda **3** (*intr*) to spread or organize propaganda

propagate ('prɒpəˌgeɪt) *vb* **1** *biology* to reproduce or cause to reproduce; breed **2** (*tr*) *horticulture* to produce (plants) by layering, grafting, cuttings, etc **3** (*tr*) to promulgate; disseminate **4** *physics* to move through, cause to move through, or transmit, esp in the form of a wave: *to propagate sound* **5** (*tr*) to transmit (characteristics) from one generation to the next [c16 from Latin *propāgāre* to increase (plants) by cuttings, from *propāgēs* a cutting, from *pangere* to fasten] ▷ ˌpropa'gation *n* ▷ ˌpropa'gational *adj* ▷ 'propagative *adj*

propagator ('prɒpəˌgeɪtə) *n* **1** a person or thing that propagates **2** a shallow box with a heating element and cover used for germinating seeds or rooting cuttings

propagule ('prɒpəˌgjuːl) *or* **propagulum** (prəʊ'pægjʊləm) *n* a plant part, such as a bud, that becomes detached from the rest of the plant and grows into a new plant [c20 from PROPAG(ATE) + -ULE]

propane ('prəʊpeɪn) *n* a colourless flammable gaseous alkane found in petroleum and used as a fuel. Formula: $CH_3CH_2CH_3$ [c19 from PROPIONIC ACID + -ANE]

propanedioic acid (ˌprəʊpeɪndaɪ'əʊɪk) *n* a colourless crystalline compound occurring in sugar beet. Formula: $C_3H_4O_4,CH_2(COOH)_2$. Also called: malonic acid [c20 from PROPANE + DI-¹ + -O- + -IC]

propanoic acid (ˌprəʊpə'nəʊɪk) *n* a colourless liquid carboxylic acid used in inhibiting the

growth of moulds in bread. Formula: CH_3CH_2COOH. Former name: propionic acid [c20 from PROPANE + -O- + -IC]

proparoxytone (ˌprəʊpə'rɒksɪˌtəʊn) *adj* **1** (in Ancient Greek) of, relating to, or denoting words having an acute accent on the third syllable from the end ▷ *n* **2** a proparoxytone word ▷ Compare **paroxytone** [c18 from Greek *proparoxutonos*; see PRO-², PAROXYTONE]

pro patria *Latin* ('prəʊ 'pætrɪˌɑː) for one's country

propel (prə'pɛl) *vb* -**pels**, -**pelling**, -**pelled** (*tr*) to impel, drive, or cause to move forwards [c15 from Latin *prōpellere* to drive onwards, from PRO-¹ + *pellere* to drive]

propellant *or* **propellent** (prə'pɛlənt) *n* **1** something that provides or causes propulsion, such as the explosive charge in a gun or the fuel in a rocket **2** the gas used to carry the liquid droplets in an aerosol spray

propellent (prə'pɛlənt) *adj* able or tending to propel

propeller (prə'pɛlə) *n* **1** a device having blades radiating from a central hub that is rotated to produce thrust to propel a ship, aircraft, etc **2** a person or thing that propels

propeller shaft *n* the shaft that transmits power from the gearbox to the differential gear in a motor vehicle or from the engine to the propeller in a ship or aircraft

propelling pencil *n* a pencil consisting of a metal or plastic case containing a replaceable lead. As the point is worn away the lead can be extended, usually by turning part of the case

propend (prəʊ'pɛnd) *vb* (*intr*) *obsolete* to be inclined or disposed [c16 from Latin *prōpendēre* to hang forwards]

propene ('prəʊpiːn) *n* a colourless gaseous alkene obtained by cracking petroleum: used in synthesizing many organic compounds. Formula: $CH_3CH:CH_2$. Also called: propylene

propensity (prə'pɛnsɪtɪ) *n, pl* -**ties 1** a natural tendency or disposition **2** *obsolete* partiality [c16 from Latin *prōpensus* inclined to, from *prōpendēre* to PROPEND]

proper ('prɒpə) *adj* **1** (*usually prenominal*) appropriate or suited for some purpose: *in its proper place* **2** correct in behaviour or conduct **3** excessively correct in conduct; vigorously moral **4** up to a required or regular standard **5** (*immediately postpositive*) (of an object, quality, etc) referred to or named specifically so as to exclude anything not directly connected with it: *his claim is connected with the deed proper* **6** (*postpositive; foll by to*) belonging to or characteristic of a person or thing **7** (*prenominal*) *Brit informal* (intensifier): *I felt a proper fool* **8** (*usually postpositive*) (of heraldic colours) considered correct for the natural colour of the object or emblem depicted: *three martlets proper* **9** *maths, logic* (of a relation) distinguished from a weaker relation by excluding the case where the relata are identical. For example, every set is a subset of itself, but a **proper subset** must exclude at least one member of the containing set. See also **strict** (sense 6) **10** *archaic* pleasant or good ▷ *adv* **11** *Brit dialect* (intensifier): *he's proper stupid* **12** good and proper *informal* thoroughly: *to get drunk good and proper* ▷ *n* **13** the parts of the Mass that vary according to the particular day or feast on which the Mass is celebrated. Compare **ordinary** (sense 10) [c13 via Old French from Latin *prōprius* special] ▷ 'properly *adv* ▷ 'properness *n*

properdin ('prəʊpədɪn) *n immunol* a protein present in blood serum that, acting with complement, is involved in the destruction of alien cells, such as bacteria

proper fraction *n* a fraction in which the numerator has a lower absolute value than the denominator, as ½ or $x/(3 + x^2)$

proper motion *n* the very small continuous change in the direction of motion of a star relative to the sun. It is determined from its radial and tangential motion

proper noun *or* **name** *n* the name of a person, place, or object, as for example *Iceland, Patrick,* or *Uranus*. Compare **common noun**. Related adj: **onomastic**

propertied ('prɒpətɪd) *adj* owning land or property

proper time *n* time measured by a clock that has the same motion as the observer. Any clock in motion relative to the observer, or in a different gravitational field, will not, according to the theory of relativity, measure proper time

property ('prɒpətɪ) *n, pl* **-ties** **1** something of value, either tangible, such as land, or intangible, such as patents, copyrights, etc **2** *law* the right to possess, use, and dispose of anything **3** possessions collectively or the fact of owning possessions of value **4 a** a piece of land or real estate, esp used for agricultural purposes **b** (*as modifier*): *property rights* **5** *chiefly Austral* a ranch or station, esp a small one **6** a quality, attribute, or distinctive feature of anything, esp a characteristic attribute such as the density or strength of a material **7** *logic obsolete* another name for **proprium** **8** any movable object used on the set of a stage play or film. Usually shortened to: **prop** [c13 from Old French *propriété*, from Latin *proprietās* something personal, from *proprius* one's own]

property bond *n* a bond issued by a life-assurance company, the premiums for which are invested in a property-owning fund

property centre *n* a service for buying and selling property, including conveyancing, provided by a group of local solicitors. In full: **solicitors' property centre**

property man *n* a member of the stage crew in charge of the stage properties. Usually shortened to: **propman**

prophage ('prəʊfeɪdʒ) *n* a virus that exists in a bacterial cell and undergoes division with its host without destroying it. Compare **bacteriophage** [c20 by contraction from French *probactériophage;* see PRO-², BACTERIOPHAGE]

prophase ('prəʊ,feɪz) *n* **1** the first stage of mitosis, during which the nuclear membrane disappears and the nuclear material resolves itself into chromosomes. See also **metaphase, anaphase, telophase 2** the first stage of meiosis, divided into leptotene, zygotene, pachytene, diplotene, and diakinesis phases

prophecy ('prɒfɪsɪ) *n, pl* **-cies 1 a** a message of divine truth revealing God's will **b** the act of uttering such a message **2** a prediction or guess **3** the function, activity, or charismatic endowment of a prophet or prophets [c13 ultimately from Greek *prophētēs* PROPHET]

prophesy ('prɒfɪ,saɪ) *vb* **-sies, -sying, -sied 1** to reveal or foretell (something, esp a future event) by or as if by divine inspiration **2** (*intr*) *archaic* to give instruction in religious subjects [C14 *prophecien*, from PROPHECY] > 'prophe,siable *adj* > 'prophe,sier *n*

prophet ('prɒfɪt) *n* **1** a person who supposedly speaks by divine inspiration, esp one through whom a divinity expresses his will. Related adj: **vatic 2** a person who predicts the future: *a prophet of doom* **3** a spokesman for a movement, doctrine, etc **4** *Christian Science* a seer in spiritual matters **b** the vanishing of material sense to give way to the conscious facts of spiritual truth [c13 from Old French *prophète*, from Latin *prophēta*, from Greek *prophētēs* one who declares the divine will, from PRO-² + *phanai* to speak] > 'prophetess *fem n* > 'prophet-,like *adj*

Prophet ('prɒfɪt) *n* **the 1** the principal designation of Mohammed as the founder of Islam **2** a name for Joseph Smith as founder of the Mormon Church

prophetic (prə'fetɪk) *adj* **1** of or relating to a prophet or prophecy **2** containing or of the nature of a prophecy; predictive > pro'phetically *adv*

Prophets ('prɒfɪts) *pl n* the books constituting the second main part of the Hebrew Bible, which in Jewish tradition is subdivided into the **Former Prophets,** Joshua, Judges, I-II Samuel, and I-II Kings, and the **Latter Prophets,** comprising those books which in Christian tradition are alone called the **Prophets** and which are divided into **Major Prophets** and **Minor Prophets.** Compare **Law of Moses, Hagiographa**

prophylactic (,prɪʊfɪ'læktɪk) *adj* **1** protecting from or preventing disease **2** protective or preventive ▷ *n* **3** a prophylactic drug or device, esp a condom [c16 via French from Greek *prophulaktikos*, from *prophulassein* to guard by taking advance measures, from PRO-² + *phulax* a guard]

prophylaxis (,prɒfɪ'læksɪs) *n* the prevention of disease or control of its possible spread

propinquity (prə'pɪŋkwɪtɪ) *n* **1** nearness in place or time **2** nearness in relationship [c14 from Latin *propinquitās* closeness, from *propinquus* near, from *prope* near by]

propionate ('prəʊpɪə,neɪt) *n* any ester or salt of propionic acid

propionic acid (,prəʊpɪ'ɒnɪk) *n* the former name for **propanoic acid** [c19 from Greek *pro*- first + *pionic* from *piōn* fat, because it is first in order of the fatty acids]

propitiate (prə'pɪʃɪ,eɪt) *vb* (*tr*) to appease or make well disposed; conciliate [c17 from Latin *propitiāre* to appease, from *propitius* gracious] > pro'pitiable *adj* > pro,piti'ation *n* > pro,piti'atious *adj* > pro'pitiative *adj* > pro'piti,ator *n*

propitiatory (prə'pɪʃɪətərɪ) *adj* **1** designed or intended to propitiate; conciliatory; expiatory ▷ *n* **2** the mercy seat > pro'pitiatorily *adv*

propitious (prə'pɪʃəs) *adj* **1** favourable; auguring well **2** gracious or favourably inclined [c15 from Latin *propitius* well disposed, from *prope* close to] > pro'pitiously *adv* > pro'pitiousness *n*

propjet ('prɒp,dʒet) *n* another name for turboprop

propman ('prɒp,mæn) *n, pl* **-men** short for **property man**

propolis ('prɒpəlɪs) *n* a greenish-brown resinous aromatic substance collected by bees from the buds of trees for use in the construction of hives. Also called: **bee glue, hive dross** [c17 via Latin from Greek: suburb, bee glue, from *pro*- before + *polis* city]

propone (prə'pon, -'pəʊn) *vb Scot* to propose or put forward, esp before a court [c14 from Latin *prōpōnere* to PROPOSE]

proponent (prə'pəʊnənt) *n* **1** a person who argues in favour of something **2** *law* a person who seeks probate of a will [c16 from Latin *prōpōnere* to PROPOSE]

Propontis (prə'pɒntɪs) *n* the ancient name for (the Sea of) **Marmara**

proportion (prə'pɔ:ʃən) *n* **1** the relationship between different things or parts with respect to comparative size, number, or degree; relative magnitude or extent; ratio **2** the correct or desirable relationship between parts of a whole; balance or symmetry **3** a part considered with respect to the whole **4** (*plural*) dimensions or size: *a building of vast proportions* **5** a share, part, or quota **6** *maths* a relationship that maintains a constant ratio between two variable quantities: *x increases in direct proportion to y* **7** *maths* a relationship between four numbers or quantities in which the ratio of the first pair equals the ratio of the second pair ▷ *vb* (*tr*) **8** to adjust in relative amount, size, etc **9** to cause to be harmonious in relationship of parts [c14 from Latin *prōportiō* (a translation of Greek *analogia*), from phrase *prō portiōne*, literally: for (its, his, one's) PORTION] > pro'portionable *adj* > pro,portiona'bility *n* > pro'portionably *adv* > pro'portionment *n*

proportional (prə'pɔ:ʃən°l) *adj* **1** of, involving, or being in proportion **2** *maths* having or related by a constant ratio ▷ *n* **3** *maths* an unknown term in a proportion: *in a/b = c/x, x is the fourth proportional* > pro,portion'ality *n* > pro'portionally *adv*

proportional counter *n* an instrument for detecting and measuring the intensity of ionizing radiation. It is similar to a Geiger counter but operates at a lower potential difference such that the magnitude of the discharge is directly proportional to the number of gas molecules ionized by the detected particle. This may permit the identification of the particle or the determination of its energy

proportional font *n computing* a font type in which the width of letters and symbols varies depending on the letter or symbol

proportional representation *n* representation of parties in an elective body in proportion to the votes they win. Abbreviation: PR. Compare **first-past-the-post**. See also **Additional Member System, Alternative Vote, party list, Single Transferable Vote**

proportional spacing *n* a feature of some typewriters and other output devices whereby the space allotted to each character is determined by the width of the character

proportionate *adj* (prə'pɔ:ʃənɪt) **1** being in proper proportion ▷ *vb* (prə'pɔ:ʃə,neɪt) **2** (*tr*) to make proportionate > pro'portionately *adv* > pro'portionateness *n*

proposal (prə'pəʊz°l) *n* **1** the act of proposing **2** something proposed, as a plan **3** an offer, esp of marriage

propose (prə'pəʊz) *vb* **1** (when *tr, may take a clause as object*) to put forward (a plan, motion, etc) for consideration or action **2** (*tr*) to nominate, as for a position **3** (*tr*) to plan or intend (to do something): *I propose to leave town now* **4** (*tr*) to announce the drinking of (a toast) to (the health of someone, etc) **5** (*intr; often foll by to*) to make an offer of marriage (to someone) [c14 from Old French *proposer*, from Latin *prōpōnere* to display, from PRO-¹ + *pōnere* to place] > pro'posable *adj* > pro'poser *n*

proposition (,prɒpə'zɪʃən) *n* **1** a proposal or topic presented for consideration **2** *philosophy* **a** the content of a sentence that affirms or denies something and is capable of being true or false **b** the meaning of such a sentence: *I am warm* always expresses the same proposition whoever the speaker is. Compare **statement** (sense 8) **3** *maths* a statement or theorem, usually containing its proof **4** *informal* a person or matter to be dealt with: *he's a difficult proposition* **5** an invitation to engage in sexual intercourse ▷ *vb* **6** (*tr*) to propose a plan, deal, etc, to, esp to engage in sexual intercourse [C14 *proposicioun*, from Latin *prōpositiō* a setting forth; see PROPOSE] > ,propo'sitional *adj* > ,propo'sitionally *adv*

propositional attitude *n logic, philosophy* a relation between a person and a proposition, such as belief, desire, intention, etc

propositional calculus *n* the system of symbolic logic concerned only with the relations between propositions as wholes, taking no account of their internal structure. Compare **predicate calculus**

propositional function *n* another name for **open sentence**

propositus (prə'pɒzɪtəs) *or feminine* **proposita** (prə'pɒzɪtə) *n, pl* **-ti** (-,taɪ) *or feminine* **-tae** (-ti:) **1** *law* the person from whom a line of descent is traced **2** *med* Also called: (esp US): **proband** the first patient to be investigated in a family study, to whom all relationships are referred [from New Latin, from Latin *prōpōnere* to set forth; see PROPOUND]

propound (prə'paʊnd) *vb* (*tr*) **1** to suggest or put forward for consideration **2** *English law* **a** to produce (a will or similar instrument) to the proper court or authority in order for its validity to be established **b** (of an executor) to bring (an action to obtain probate) in solemn form [C16 *propone*, from Latin *prōpōnere* to set forth, from PRO-¹ + *pōnere* to place] > pro'pounder *n*

propr *abbreviation for* proprietor

propraetor or **propretor** (prəʊˈpriːtə) n (in ancient Rome) a citizen, esp an ex-praetor, granted a praetor's imperium to be exercised outside Rome, esp in the provinces [Latin, from *prō praetōre* one who acts for a praetor]

propranolol (prəʊˈprænəˌlɒl) n a drug used in the treatment of angina pectoris, arrhythmia, hypertension, and some forms of tremor. Formula: $C_{16}H_{21}NO_2$ [C20 from PRO(PYL) + *pr(op)anol* (from PROPANE + -OL) + -OL]

proprietary (prəˈpraɪətərɪ, -trɪ) adj 1 of, relating to, or belonging to property or proprietors 2 privately owned and controlled 3 med of or denoting a drug or agent manufactured and distributed under a trade name. Compare **ethical** (sense 3) ▷ n, pl -taries 4 med a proprietary drug or agent 5 a proprietor or proprietors collectively 6 a right to property b property owned 7 Also called: lord proprietary (in Colonial America) an owner, governor, or grantee of a proprietary colony [C15 from Late Latin *proprietārius* an owner, from *proprius* one's own] > proˈprietarily adv

proprietary colony n US history any of various colonies, granted by the Crown in the 17th century to a person or group of people with full governing rights

proprietary name n a name that is a trademark

proprietor (prəˈpraɪətə) n 1 an owner of an unincorporated business enterprise 2 a person enjoying exclusive right of ownership to some property 3 US history a governor or body of governors of a proprietary colony > proˈprietorship n > proprietorial (prəˌpraɪəˈtɔːrɪəl) adj > proˈprietress or proˈprietrix fem n

propriety (prəˈpraɪətɪ) n, pl -ties 1 the quality or state of being appropriate or fitting 2 conformity to the prevailing standard of behaviour, speech, etc 3 (plural) the proprieties the standards of behaviour considered correct by polite society [C15 from Old French *propriété*, from Latin *proprietās* a peculiarity, from *proprius* one's own]

proprioceptor (ˌprəʊprɪəˈsɛptə) n physiol any receptor (as in the gut, blood vessels, muscles, etc) that supplies information about the state of the body. Compare **exteroceptor, interoceptor** [C20 from *proprio-*, from Latin *proprius* one's own + RECEPTOR] > ˌproprioˈceptive adj

proprium (ˈprəʊprɪəm) n logic obsolete Also called: property an attribute that is not essential to a species but is common and peculiar to it [C16 Latin, neuter sing of *proprius* proper, own]

prop root n a root that grows from and supports the stem above the ground in plants such as mangroves

proptosis (prɒpˈtəʊsɪs) n, pl -ses (-siːz) pathol the forward displacement of an organ or part, such as the eyeball. See also **exophthalmos**. Compare **prolapse** [C17 via Late Latin from Greek, from *propiptein* to fall forwards]

propulsion (prəˈpʌlʃən) n 1 the act of propelling or the state of being propelled 2 a propelling force [C15 from Latin *prōpellere* to PROPEL] > **propulsive** (prəˈpʌlsɪv) or proˈpulsory adj

propyl (ˈprəʊpɪl) n (modifier) of, consisting of, or containing the monovalent group of atoms C_3H_7-: a propyl group or radical [C19 from PROP(IONIC ACID) + -YL]

propylaeum (ˌprɒpɪˈliːəm) or **propylon** (ˈprɒpɪˌlɒn) n, pl -laea (-ˈliːə) or -lons, -la a portico, esp one that forms the entrance to a temple [C18 via Latin from Greek *propulaion* before the gate, from PRO-² + *pulē* gate]

propylene (ˈprəʊpɪˌliːn) n another name for **propene** [C19 from PROPYL + -ENE]

propylene glycol n a colourless viscous hydroscopic sweet-tasting compound used as an antifreeze and brake fluid. Formula: $CH_3CH(OH)CH_2OH$. Systematic name: 1,2-dihydroxypropane

propylite (ˈprɒpɪˌlaɪt) n geology an altered andesite or similar rock containing calcite, chlorite, etc, produced by the action of hot water

[C20 from *propylon* (see PROPYLAEUM) + -ITE¹; so named because it is associated with the start of the Tertiary volcanic era]

propylthiouracil (ˌprəʊpɪlˌθaɪəʊˈjʊərəsɪl) n a white crystalline water-insoluble substance with an intensely bitter taste, used in medicine to treat hyperthyroidism. Formula: $C_7H_2N_2OS$ [from PROPYL + THIO- + *uracil* (URO-¹ + AC(ETIC) + -il -ILE)]

pro rata (ˈprəʊ ˈrɑːtə) in proportion [Medieval Latin]

prorate (prəʊˈreɪt, ˈprəʊreɪt) vb chiefly US and Canadian to divide, assess, or distribute (something) proportionately [C19 from PRO RATA] > proˈratable adj > proˈration n

proreform (ˌprəʊrɪˈfɔːm) adj in favour of or supporting reform, esp within politics

prorogue (prəˈrəʊg) vb to discontinue the meetings of (a legislative body) without dissolving it [C15 from Latin *prorogāre* literally: to ask publicly, from *prō-* in public + *rogāre* to ask] > prorogation (ˌprəʊrəˈgeɪʃən) n

prosaic (prəʊˈzeɪɪk) adj 1 lacking imagination 2 having the characteristics of prose [C16 from Late Latin *prōsaicus*, from Latin *prōsa* PROSE] > proˈsaically adv > proˈsaicness n

prosaism (prəʊˈzeɪɪzəm) or **prosaicism** (prəʊˈzeɪɪˌsɪzəm) n 1 prosaic quality or style 2 a prosaic expression, thought, etc > proˈsaist n

pros and cons pl n the various arguments in favour of and against a motion, action, etc [C16 from Latin *prō* for + *con*, from *contrā* against]

proscenium (prəˈsiːnɪəm) n, pl -nia (-nɪə) or -niums 1 the arch or opening separating the stage from the auditorium together with the area immediately in front of the arch 2 (in ancient theatres) the stage itself [C17 via Latin from Greek *proskēnion*, from *pro-* before + *skēnē* scene]

prosciutto (prəʊˈʃuːtəʊ; Italian proˈʃutto) n cured ham from Italy: usually served as an hors d'oeuvre [Italian, literally: dried beforehand, from *pro-* PRE- + *asciutto* dried]

proscribe (prəʊˈskraɪb) vb (tr) 1 to condemn or prohibit 2 to outlaw; banish; exile 3 (in ancient Rome) to outlaw (a citizen) by posting his name in public [C16 from Latin *prōscrībere* to put up a written public notice, from *prō-* in public + *scrībere* to write] > proˈscriber n

proscription (prəʊˈskrɪpʃən) n 1 the act of proscribing or the state of being proscribed 2 denunciation, prohibition, or exclusion 3 outlawry or ostracism [C14 from Latin *prōscriptiō*; see PROSCRIBE] > proˈscriptive adj > proˈscriptively adv > proˈscriptiveness n

prose (prəʊz) n 1 spoken or written language as in ordinary usage, distinguished from poetry by its lack of a marked metrical structure 2 a passage set for translation into a foreign language 3 commonplace or dull discourse, expression, etc 4 RC Church a hymn recited or sung after the gradual at Mass 5 (modifier) written in prose 6 (modifier) matter-of-fact ▷ vb 7 to write or say (something) in prose 8 (intr) to speak or write in a tedious style [C14 via Old French from Latin phrase *prōsa ōrātiō* straightforward speech, from *prorsus* prosaic, from *prōvertere* to turn forwards, from PRO-¹ + *vertere* to turn] > ˈproseˌlike adj

prosector (prəʊˈsɛktə) n a person who prepares or dissects anatomical subjects for demonstration [C19 from Latin, from *prōsecare* to cut up; probably on the model of French *prosecteur*]

prosecute (ˈprɒsɪˌkjuːt) vb 1 (tr) to bring a criminal action against (a person) for some offence 2 (intr) a to seek redress by legal proceedings b to institute or conduct a prosecution 3 (tr) to engage in or practise (a profession or trade) 4 (tr) to continue to do (a task, etc) [C15 from Latin *prōsecuī* to follow, from *prō-* forward + *sequī* to follow] > ˈproseˌcutable adj

prosecuting attorney n US law (in some states) an officer in a judicial district appointed to conduct criminal prosecutions on behalf of the state and people

prosecution (ˌprɒsɪˈkjuːʃən) n 1 the act of prosecuting or the state of being prosecuted 2 a the institution and conduct of legal proceedings against a person b the proceedings brought in the name of the Crown to put an accused on trial 3 the lawyers acting for the Crown to put the case against a person. Compare **defence** (sense 6) 4 the following up or carrying on of something begun, esp with a view to its accomplishment or completion

prosecutor (ˈprɒsɪˌkjuːtə) n a person who institutes or conducts legal proceedings, esp in a criminal court

proselyte (ˈprɒsɪˌlaɪt) n 1 a person newly converted to a religious faith or sect; a convert, esp a gentile converted to Judaism ▷ vb 2 a less common word for **proselytize** [C14 from Church Latin *prosēlytus*, from Greek *prosēlutos* recent arrival, convert, from *proserchesthai* to draw near] > proselytism (ˈprɒsɪlɪˌtɪzəm) n > proselytic (ˌprɒsɪˈlɪtɪk) adj

proselytize or **proselytise** (ˈprɒsɪlɪˌtaɪz) vb to convert (someone) from one religious faith to another > ˌproselytiˈzation or ˌproselytiˈsation n > ˈproselytˌizer or ˈproselytˌiser n

prosencephalon (ˌprɒsɛnˈsɛfəlɒn) n, pl -la (-lə) the part of the brain that develops from the anterior portion of the neural tube. Compare **mesencephalon, rhombencephalon** Nontechnical name: forebrain [C19 from New Latin, from Greek *prosō* forward + *enkephalos* brain] > prosencephalic (ˌprɒsɛnsɪˈfælɪk) adj

prosenchyma (prɒsˈɛŋkɪmə) n a plant tissue consisting of long narrow cells with pointed ends: occurs in conducting tissue [C19 from New Latin, from Greek *pros-* towards + *enkhuma* infusion; compare PARENCHYMA] > prosenchymatous (ˌprɒsɛnˈkaɪmətəs) adj

prose poem n a prose composition characterized by a poetic style

Proserpina (prəʊˈsɜːpɪnə) n the Roman goddess of the underworld. Greek counterpart: Persephone

prosimian (prəʊˈsɪmɪən) n 1 any primate of the primitive suborder *Prosimii*, including lemurs, lorises, and tarsiers ▷ adj 2 of, relating to, or belonging to the *Prosimii* ▷ Compare **anthropoid** (sense 4) [C19 via New Latin from PRO-² + Latin *sīmia* ape]

prosit German (ˈproːzɪt) interj good health! cheers! [German, from Latin, literally: may it prove beneficial]

proslavery (ˌprəʊˈsleɪvərɪ) adj in favour of or supporting slavery

prosody (ˈprɒsədɪ) n 1 the study of poetic metre and of the art of versification, including rhyme, stanzaic forms, and the quantity and stress of syllables 2 a system of versification 3 the patterns of stress and intonation in a language [C15 from Latin *prosōdia* accent of a syllable, from Greek *prosōidia* song set to music, from *pros* towards + *ōidē*, from *aoidē* song; see ODE] > prosodic (prəˈsɒdɪk) adj > ˈprosodist n

prosoma (prəʊˈsəʊmə) n, pl -mas or -mata (-mətə) zoology the head and thorax of an arachnid

prosopagnosia (ˌprɒsəpægˈnəʊsɪə) n an inability to recognize faces [C20 from Greek *prosōpon* face + AGNOSIA]

prosopography (ˌprɒsəˈpɒgrəfɪ) n 1 a description of a person's life and career 2 the study of such descriptions as part of history, esp Roman history [C16 from New Latin *prosopographia*, from Greek *prosōpon* face, person + -GRAPHY] > ˌprosoˈpographer n > prosopographical (ˌprɒsəpəˈgræfɪkᵊl) adj > ˌprosopoˈgraphically adv

prosopopoeia or **prosopopeia** (ˌprɒsəpəˈpiːə) n 1 rhetoric another word for **personification** 2 a figure of speech that represents an imaginary, absent, or dead person speaking or acting [C16 via Latin from Greek *prosōpopoiia* dramatization, from *prosōpon* face + *poiein* to make] > ˌprosopoˈpoeial or ˌprosopoˈpeial adj

pro-Soviet *adj* in favour of or supporting anything of, characteristic of, or relating to the former Soviet Union, its people, or its government

prospect *n* ('prɒspɛkt) **1** (*sometimes plural*) a probability or chance for future success, esp as based on present work or aptitude: *a good job with prospects* **2** a vision of the future; what is foreseen; expectation: *she was excited at the prospect of living in London; unemployment presents a grim prospect* **3** a view or scene, esp one offering an extended outlook **4** a prospective buyer, project, etc **5** a survey or observation **6** *mining* **a** a known or likely deposit of ore **b** the location of a deposit of ore **c** a sample of ore for testing **d** the yield of mineral obtained from a sample of ore ▷ *vb* (prə'spɛkt) **7** (when *intr*, often foll by *for*) to explore (a region) for gold or other valuable minerals **8** (*tr*) to work (a mine) to discover its profitability **9** (*intr*; often foll by *for*) to search (for) [c15 from Latin *prōspectus* distant view, from *prōspicere* to look into the distance, from *prō-* forward + *specere* to look] > **pro'spectless** *adj*

prospective (prə'spɛktɪv) *adj* **1** looking towards the future **2** (*prenominal*) anticipated or likely > **pro'spectively** *adv*

prospector (prə'spɛktə) *n* a person who searches for the natural occurrence of gold, petroleum, etc

prospectus (prə'spɛktəs) *n*, *pl* -tuses **1** a formal statement giving details of a forthcoming event, such as the publication of a book or an issue of shares **2** a pamphlet or brochure giving details of courses, as at a college or school [c18 Latin, literally: distant view; see PROSPECT]

prosper ('prɒspə) *vb* (*usually intr*) to thrive, succeed, etc, or cause to thrive, succeed, etc in a healthy way [c15 from Latin *prosperāre* to succeed, from *prosperus* fortunate, from PRO-¹ + *spēs* hope]

prosperity (prɒ'spɛrɪtɪ) *n* the condition of prospering; success or wealth

prosperity gospel *n* a modern version of, according to some, perversion of the gospel according to which the full blessings of God available to those who approach Him in faith and obedience include wealth, health and power

prosperous ('prɒspərəs) *adj* **1** flourishing; prospering **2** rich; affluent; wealthy **3** favourable or promising > **'prosperously** *adv* > **'prosperousness** *n*

prostaglandin (ˌprɒstə'glændɪn) *n* any of a group of potent hormone-like compounds composed of essential fatty acids and found in all mammalian tissues, esp human semen. Prostaglandins stimulate the muscles of the uterus and affect the blood vessels; they are used to induce abortion or birth [c20 from *prosta*(te) *gland* + -IN; it was originally believed to be secreted by the prostate gland]

prostate ('prɒsteɪt) *n* **1** Also called: prostate gland a gland in male mammals that surrounds the neck of the bladder and urethra and secretes a liquid constituent of the semen ▷ *adj* **2** Also: prostatic (prɒ'stætɪk) of or relating to the prostate gland. See also PSA [c17 via Medieval Latin from Greek *prostatēs* something standing in front (of the bladder), from *pro-* in front + *histanai* to cause to stand]

prostatectomy (ˌprɒstə'tɛktəmɪ) *n*, *pl* -mies surgical removal of all or a part of the prostate gland

prostatitis (ˌprɒstə'taɪtɪs) *n* inflammation of the prostate gland

prosternum (prəʊ'stɜ:nəm) *n*, *pl* -na (-nə) or -nums the sternum of the prothorax of an insect

prosthesis ('prɒsθɪsɪs, prɒs'θi:sɪs) *n*, *pl* -ses (-ˌsi:z) **1** *surgery* **a** the replacement of a missing bodily part with an artificial substitute **b** an artificial part such as a limb, eye, or tooth **2** *linguistics* another word for **prothesis** [c16 via Late Latin from Greek: an addition, from *prostithenai* to add, from *pros-* towards + *tithenai* to place] > **prosthetic** (prɒs'θɛtɪk) *adj* > **pros'thetically** *adv*

prosthetic group *n* the nonprotein component of a conjugated protein, such as the lipid group in a lipoprotein

prosthetics (prɒs'θɛtɪks) *n* (*functioning as singular*) the branch of surgery concerned with prosthesis

prosthodontics (ˌprɒsθə'dɒntɪks) *n* (*functioning as singular*) the branch of dentistry concerned with the artificial replacement of missing teeth [c20 from PROSTH(ESIS) + -ODONT + -ICS] > ˌprostho'dontist *n*

prostitute ('prɒstɪˌtju:t) *n* **1** a woman who engages in sexual intercourse for money **2** a man who engages in such activity, esp in homosexual practices **3** a person who offers his talent or work for unworthy purposes ▷ *vb* (*tr*) **4** to offer (oneself or another) in sexual intercourse for money **5** to offer (a person, esp oneself, or a person's talent) for unworthy purposes [c16 from Latin *prōstituere* to expose to prostitution, from *prō-* in public + *statuere* to cause to stand] > ˌprosti'tution *n* > 'prosti,tutor *n*

prostomium (prəʊ'stəʊmɪəm) *n*, *pl* -mia (-mɪə) the lobe at the head end of earthworms and other annelids: bears tentacles, palps, etc, or forms part of a sucker or proboscis [via New Latin from Greek *prostomion* mouth] > **pro'stomial** *adj*

prostrate *adj* ('prɒstreɪt) **1** lying with the face downwards, as in submission **2** exhausted physically or emotionally **3** helpless or defenceless **4** (of a plant) growing closely along the ground ▷ *vb* (prɒ'streɪt) (*tr*) **5** to bow or cast (oneself) down, as in submission **6** to lay or throw down flat, as on the ground **7** to make helpless or defenceless **8** to make exhausted [c14 from Latin *prōsternere* to throw to the ground, from *prō-* before + *sternere* to lay low] > **pros'tration** *n*

prostyle ('prəʊstaɪl) *adj* **1** (of a building) having a row of columns in front, esp as in the portico of a Greek temple ▷ *n* **2** a prostyle building, portico, etc [c17 from Latin *prostȳlos*, from Greek: with pillars in front, from PRO-² + *stulos* pillar]

prosumer (prə'sju:mə) *n* an amateur user of electronic equipment that is of a standard suitable for professional use [c21 PROFESSIONAL + CONSUMER]

prosy ('prəʊzɪ) *adj* prosier, prosiest **1** of the nature of or similar to prose **2** dull, tedious, or long-winded > **'prosily** *adv* > **'prosiness** *n*

Prot. *abbreviation for* Protestant

prot- *combining form* a variant of **proto-** before a vowel

protactinium (ˌprəʊtæk'tɪnɪəm) *n* a toxic radioactive metallic element that occurs in uranium ores and is produced by neutron irradiation of thorium. Symbol: Pa; atomic no.: 91; half-life of the most stable isotope, ²³¹Pa: 32 500 years; valency: 4 or 5; relative density: 15.37 (calc.); melting pt.: 1572°C. Former name: protoactinium

protagonist (prəʊ'tægənɪst) *n* **1** the principal character in a play, story, etc **2** a supporter, esp when important or respected, of a cause, political party, etc [c17 from Greek *prōtagōnistēs*, from *prōtos* first + *agōnistēs* actor] > **pro'tagonism** *n*

protamine ('prəʊtəˌmi:n) *n* any of a group of basic simple proteins that occur, in association with nucleic acids, in the sperm of some fish [c19 from German: see PROTO-, AMINE]

protandrous (prəʊ'tændrəs) *adj* **1** (of hermaphrodite or monoecious plants) maturing the anthers before the stigma **2** (of hermaphrodite animals) producing male gametes before female gametes. Compare **protogynous** > **pro'tandry** *n*

protanopia (ˌprəʊtə'nəʊpɪə) *n* a form of colour blindness characterized by a tendency to confuse reds and greens and by a loss of sensitivity to red light [c20 New Latin, from PROTO- + AN- + -OPIA] > **protanopic** (ˌprəʊtə'nɒpɪk) *adj*

protasis ('prɒtəsɪs) *n*, *pl* -ses (-si:z) **1** *logic*, *grammar* the antecedent of a conditional statement, such as *it rains* in *if it rains the game will be cancelled*. Compare **apodosis** **2** (in classical drama) the introductory part of a play [c17 via Latin from Greek: a proposal, from *pro-* before + *teinein* to extend] > **protatic** (prɒ'tætɪk) *adj*

protea ('prəʊtɪə) *n* any shrub or small tree of the genus *Protea*, of tropical and southern Africa, having flowers with coloured bracts arranged in showy heads: family *Proteaceae* [c20 from New Latin, from PROTEUS, referring to the large number of different forms of the plant] > **proteaceous** (ˌprəʊtɪ'eɪʃəs) *adj*

protean (prəʊ'ti:ən, 'prəʊtɪən) *adj* readily taking on various shapes or forms; variable [c16 from PROTEUS]

protease ('prəʊtɪˌeɪs) *n* any enzyme involved in proteolysis [c20 from PROTEIN + -ASE]

protease inhibitor *n* any one of a class of antiviral drugs that impair the growth and replication of HIV by inhibiting the action of protease produced by the virus: used in the treatment of AIDS

protect (prə'tɛkt) *vb* (*tr*) **1** to defend from trouble, harm, attack, etc **2** *economics* to assist (domestic industries) by the imposition of protective tariffs on imports **3** *commerce* to provide funds in advance to guarantee payment of (a note, draft, etc) [c16 from Latin *prōtegere* to cover before, from PRO-¹ + *tegere* to cover]

protectant (prə'tɛktənt) *n* a chemical substance that affords protection, as against frost, rust, insects, etc

protection (prə'tɛkʃən) *n* **1** the act of protecting or the condition of being protected **2** something that protects **3 a** the imposition of duties or quotas on imports, designed for the protection of domestic industries against overseas competition, expansion of domestic employment, etc **b** Also called: protectionism the system, policy, or theory of such restrictions. Compare **free trade** **4** a document that grants protection or immunity from arrest or harassment to a person, esp a traveller **5** *mountaineering* security on a climb provided by running belays, etc **6** *informal* **a** Also called: protection money money demanded by gangsters for freedom from molestation **b** freedom from molestation purchased in this way > pro'tection,ism *n* > pro'tectionist *n*, *adj*

protection ratio *n* the minimum acceptable ratio between the amplitudes of a wanted radio or television broadcast signal and any interfering signal

protective (prə'tɛktɪv) *adj* **1** giving or capable of giving protection **2** *economics* of, relating to, or intended for protection of domestic industries ▷ *n* **3** something that protects **4** a condom > **pro'tectively** *adv* > **pro'tectiveness** *n*

protective coloration *n* the coloration of an animal that enables it to blend with its surroundings and therefore escape the attention of predators

protective tariff *n* a tariff levied on imports to protect the domestic economy rather than to raise revenue

protector (prə'tɛktə) *n* **1** a person or thing that protects **2** *history* a person who exercised royal authority during the minority, absence, or incapacity of the monarch > **pro'tectoral** *adj* > **pro'tectress** *fem n*

Protector (prə'tɛktə) *n* short for **Lord Protector**, the title borne by Oliver Cromwell (1653–58) and by Richard Cromwell (1658–59) as heads of state during the period known as the **Protectorate**

protectorate (prə'tɛktərɪt) *n* **1 a** a territory largely controlled by but not annexed to a stronger state **b** the relation of a protecting state to its protected territory **2** the office or period of office of a protector

protectory (prə'tɛktərɪ) *n*, *pl* -ries an institution for the care of homeless, delinquent, or destitute children

protégé *or feminine* **protégée** ('prəʊtɪˌʒeɪ) *n* a person who is protected and aided by the patronage of another person [c18 from French *protéger* to PROTECT]

p

protein ('prəʊtiːn) *n* any of a large group of nitrogenous compounds of high molecular weight that are essential constituents of all living organisms. They consist of one or more chains of amino acids linked by peptide bonds and are folded into a specific three-dimensional shape maintained by further chemical bonding [C19 via German from Greek *prōteios* primary, from *protos* first + -IN] > ,protein'aceous, pro'teinic *or* pro'teinous *adj*

proteinase ('prəʊtɪ,neɪs, -,neɪz) *n* another name for **endopeptidase**

proteinuria (,prəʊtɪ'njʊərɪə) *n med* another name for **albuminuria**

pro tempore *Latin* ('prəʊ 'tɛmpərɪ) *adv, adj* for the time being. Often shortened to: **pro tem** ('prəʊ 'tɛm)

proteolysis (,prəʊtɪ'ɒlɪsɪs) *n* the hydrolysis of proteins into simpler compounds by the action of enzymes: occurs esp during digestion [C19 from New Latin, from proteo- (from PROTEIN) + -LYSIS] > proteolytic (,prəʊtɪə'lɪtɪk) *adj*

proteome ('prəʊtɪ,əʊm) *n* the full complement of proteins that occur within a cell, tissue, or organism [C20 from PROTE[IN] + -OME]

proteomics (,prəʊtɪ'ɒmɪks) *n (functioning as singular)* the branch of biochemistry concerned with the structure and analysis of the proteins occurring in living organisms

proteose ('prəʊtɪ,əʊs, -,əʊz) *n now rare* any of a group of compounds formed during proteolysis that are less complex than metaproteins but more so than peptones. Also called (esp US): **albumose** [C20 from PROTEIN + -OSE²]

protero- *combining form* anterior or former in time, place, order, etc: *proterozoic* [from Greek *proteros* fore]

Proterozoic (,prɒtərəʊ'zəʊɪk) *n* **1** the later of two divisions of the Precambrian era, during which the earliest plants and animals are assumed to have lived. Compare **Archaeozoic** ▷ *adj* **2** of or formed in the late Precambrian era

protest *n* ('prəʊtɛst) **1 a** public, often organized, dissent or manifestation of such dissent **b** (*as modifier*): *a protest march* **2** a declaration or objection that is formal or solemn **3** an expression of disagreement or complaint: *without a squeak of protest* **4 a** a formal notarial statement drawn up on behalf of a creditor and declaring that the debtor has dishonoured a bill of exchange or promissory note **b** the action of drawing up such a statement **c** a formal declaration by a taxpayer disputing the legality or accuracy of his assessment **5** a statement made by the master of a vessel attesting to the circumstances in which his vessel was damaged or imperilled **6** the act of protesting **7 under protest** having voiced objections; unwillingly ▷ *vb* (prə'tɛst) **8** (when *intr*, foll by *against, at, about, etc*; when *tr*, *may take a clause as object*) to make a strong objection (to something, esp a supposed injustice or offence) **9** (when *tr*, *may take a clause as object*) to assert or affirm in a formal or solemn manner **10** (when *tr*, *may take a clause as object*) to put up arguments against; disagree; complain; object: *"I'm okay," she protested; he protested that it was not his turn to wash up* **11** (*tr*) *chiefly US* to object forcefully to: *leaflets protesting Dr King's murder* **12** (*tr*) to declare formally that a (bill of exchange or promissory note) has been dishonoured [C14 from Latin *prōtestārī* to make a formal declaration, from *prō-* before + *testārī* to assert] > pro'testant *adj, n* > pro'tester *or* pro'testor *n* > pro'testingly *adv*

Protestant ('prɒtɪstənt) *n* **a** an adherent of Protestantism **b** (*as modifier*): *the Protestant Church*

Protestant Episcopal Church *n* the full title of the Episcopal Church

Protestantism ('prɒtɪstən,tɪzəm) *n* **1** the religion or religious system of any of the Churches of Western Christendom that are separated from the Roman Catholic Church and adhere substantially to principles established by Luther, Calvin, etc, in the Reformation **2** the Protestant Churches collectively **3** adherence to the principles of the Reformation

protestation (,prəʊtɛs'teɪʃən) *n* **1** the act of protesting **2** something protested about **3** a strong declaration

Proteus ('prəʊtɪəs) *n Greek myth* a prophetic sea god capable of changing his shape at will

Proteus syndrome *n pathol* a condition caused by malfunction in cell growth, in which bone and flesh tissue overgrow in localized areas of the body

prothalamion (,prəʊθə'leɪmɪən) *or* **prothalamium** *n, pl* -mia (-mɪə) a song or poem in celebration of a marriage [C16 from Greek *pro-* before + *thalamos* marriage; coined by Edmund Spenser, on the model of EPITHALAMION]

prothallus (prəʊ'θæləs) *or* **prothallium** (prəʊ'θælɪəm) *n, pl* -li (-laɪ) *or* -lia (-lɪə) *botany* the small flat free-living gametophyte that bears the reproductive organs of ferns, horsetails, and club mosses. It is either a green disc on the soil surface or it is colourless and subterranean [C19 from New Latin, from *pro-* before + Greek *thallus* a young shoot] > pro'thallic *or* pro'thallial *adj*

prothesis ('prɒθɪsɪs) *n* **1** a process in the development of a language by which a phoneme or syllable is prefixed to a word to facilitate pronunciation: *Latin "scala" gives Spanish "escala" by prothesis* **2** *Eastern Orthodox Church* the solemn preparation of the Eucharistic elements before consecration [C16 via Late Latin from Greek: a setting out in public, from *pro-* forth + *thesis* a placing] > prothetic (prə'θɛtɪk) *adj* > pro'thetically *adv*

prothonotary (,prəʊθə'nəʊtərɪ, -trɪ, prəʊ'θɒnə-) *or* **protonotary** *n, pl* -taries (formerly) a chief clerk in certain law courts [C15 from Medieval Latin *prōthonotārius*, from *prōtho-* PROTO- + Late Latin *notārius* NOTARY] > prothonotarial (prəʊ,θɒnə'tɛərɪəl) *or* pro,tono'tarial *adj*

prothorax (prəʊ'θɔːræks) *n, pl* -thoraxes *or* -thoraces (-'θɔːrə,siːz) the first segment of the thorax of an insect, which bears the first pair of walking legs. See also **mesothorax, metathorax**

prothrombin (prəʊ'θrɒmbɪn) *n biochem* a zymogen found in blood that gives rise to thrombin on activation. See also **phylloquinone**

protist ('prəʊtɪst) *n* (in some classification systems) any organism belonging to the kingdom *Protista*, originally including bacteria, protozoans, algae, and fungi, regarded as distinct from plants and animals. It was later restricted to protozoans, unicellular algae, and simple fungi. See also **protoctist** [C19 from New Latin *Protista* most primitive organisms, from Greek *prōtistos* the very first, from *prōtos* first]

protium ('prəʊtɪəm) *n* the most common isotope of hydrogen, having a mass number of 1 [C20 New Latin, from PROTO- + -IUM]

proto- *or sometimes before a vowel* **prot-** *combining form* **1** indicating the first in time, order, or rank: *protomartyr* **2** primitive, ancestral, or original: *prototype* **3** indicating the reconstructed earliest stage of a language: *Proto-Germanic* **4** indicating the first in a series of chemical compounds: *protoxide* **5** indicating the parent of a chemical compound or an element: *protactinium* [from Greek *prōtos* first, from *pro* before; see PRO-²]

protoactinium (,prəʊtəʊæk'tɪnɪəm) *n* the former name of **protactinium**

protochordate (,prəʊtəʊ'kɔːdeɪt) *n* **1** any chordate animal of the subphyla *Hemichordata* (acorn worms), *Urochordata* (tunicates), and *Cephalochordata* (lancelets) ▷ *adj* **2** of or relating to protochordates

protocol ('prəʊtə,kɒl) *n* **1** the formal etiquette and code of behaviour, precedence, and procedure for state and diplomatic ceremonies **2** a memorandum or record of an agreement, esp one reached in international negotiations, a meeting, etc **3 a** an amendment to a treaty or convention **b** an annexe appended to a treaty to deal with subsidiary matters or to render the treaty more lucid **c** a formal international agreement or understanding on some matter **4** *philosophy* In full: **protocol statement** a statement that is immediately verifiable by experience. See **logical positivism 5** *computing* the set form in which data must be presented for handling by a particular computer configuration, esp in the transmission of information between different computer systems [C16 from Medieval Latin *prōtocollum*, from Late Greek *prōtokollon* sheet glued to the front of a manuscript, from PROTO- + *kolla* glue]

protocist (prəʊ'tɒktɪst) *n* (in modern biological classifications) any unicellular or simple multicellular organism belonging to the kingdom *Protoctista*, which includes protozoans, algae, and slime moulds [C19 from New Latin *protoctista*, perhaps from Greek *prototokos* first born]

protogalaxy (,prəʊtəʊ'gæləksɪ) *n, pl* -axies a cloud of gas in the early stages of its evolution into a galaxy

protogenic (,prəʊtəʊ'dʒɛnɪk) *adj chem* (of a compound) able to donate a hydrogen ion (proton) in a chemical reaction

Proto-Germanic *n* the prehistoric unrecorded language that was the ancestor of all Germanic languages

protogynous (prəʊ'tɒdʒɪnəs) *adj* (of plants and hermaphrodite animals) producing female gametes before male ones. Compare **protandrous** > pro'togyny *n*

protohistory (,prəʊtəʊ'hɪstərɪ, -'hɪstrɪ) *n* the period or stage of human development or of a particular culture immediately prior to the emergence of writing > protohistoric (,prəʊtəʊhɪ'stɒrɪk) *adj*

protohuman (,prəʊtəʊ'hjuːmən) *n* **1** any of various prehistoric primates that resembled modern man ▷ *adj* **2** of or relating to any of these primates

Proto-Indo-European *n* the prehistoric unrecorded language that was the ancestor of all Indo-European languages

protolanguage (,prəʊtəʊ'læŋgwɪdʒ) *n* an extinct and unrecorded language reconstructed by comparison of its recorded or living descendants. Also called: **Ursprache**

protolithic (,prəʊtəʊ'lɪθɪk) *adj* of or referring to the earliest Stone Age

protomartyr (,prəʊtəʊ'mɑːtə) *n* **1** St Stephen as the first Christian martyr **2** the first martyr to lay down his life in any cause

protomorphic (,prəʊtəʊ'mɔːfɪk) *adj biology* primitive in structure; primordial

proton ('prəʊtɒn) *n* a stable, positively charged elementary particle, found in atomic nuclei in numbers equal to the atomic number of the element. It is a baryon with a charge of $1.602176462 \times 10^{-19}$ coulomb, a rest mass of $1.672\,62159 \times 10^{-27}$ kilogram, and spin ½ [C20 from Greek *prōtos* first]

protonema (,prəʊtə'niːmə) *n, pl* -nemata (-'niːmətə) a branched threadlike structure that grows from a moss spore and eventually develops into the moss plant [C19 from New Latin, from PROTO- + Greek *nema* thread] > ,proto'nemal *or* protonematal (,prəʊtə'niːmətˀl, -'nɛmətˀl) *adj*

protonic (prəʊ'tɒnɪk) *adj chem* (of a solvent, such as water) able to donate hydrogen ions to solute molecules

proton microscope *n* a powerful type of microscope that uses a beam of protons, giving high resolution and sharp contrast

proton number *n* another name for **atomic number**. Symbol: *Z*

Proto-Norse *n* the North Germanic language of Scandinavia up to about 700 A.D. See also **Old Norse**

proton-pump inhibitor *n* any of a group of drugs used to treat excessive secretion of acid in the stomach and any resulting ulcers. They block the enzyme (proton pump) in the cells of the gastric glands that secrete hydrochloric acid

protopathic (ˌprəʊtəˈpæθɪk) *adj physiol* **1** of or relating to a sensory nerve that perceives only coarse stimuli, such as pain **2** of or relating to such perception [c20 from PROTO- + Greek *pathos* suffering, disease + -IC] > protopathy (prəˈtɒpəθɪ) *n*

protophilic (ˌprəʊtəˈfɪlɪk) *adj chem* having or involving an affinity for hydrogen ions (protons)

protoplanet (ˈprəʊtəʊˌplænɪt) *n* a planet in its early stages of evolution by the process of accretion

protoplasm (ˈprəʊtəˌplæzəm) *n biology* the living contents of a cell, differentiated into cytoplasm and nucleoplasm [c19 from New Latin, from PROTO- + Greek *plasma* form] > ˌprotoˈplasmic *adj*

protoplast (ˈprəʊtəˌplæst) *n* a unit consisting of the living parts of a cell, including the protoplasm and cell membrane but not the vacuoles or (in plants) the cell wall [c16 from Late Latin *prōtoplastus* the first-formed, from Greek *prōtoplastos*, from PROTO- + *plassein* to shape] > ˌprotoˈplastic *adj*

protoporphyrin (ˌprəʊtəʊˈpɔːfɪrɪn) *n* a type of porphyrin that, when combined with an iron atom, forms haem, the oxygen-bearing prosthetic group of the red blood pigment haemoglobin

Protosemitic (ˌprəʊtəʊsɪˈmɪtɪk) *n* the hypothetical parent language of the Semitic group of languages

protostar (ˈprəʊtəʊˌstɑː) *n* a cloud of interstellar gas and dust that gradually collapses, forming a hot dense core, and evolves into a star once nuclear fusion can occur in the core

protostele (ˈprəʊtəˌstiːl, -ˌstiːlɪ) *n* a simple type of stele with a central core of xylem surrounded by a cylinder of phloem: occurs in most roots and the stems of ferns, etc > ˌprotoˈstelic *adj*

prototherian (ˌprəʊtəʊˈθɪərɪən) *adj* **1** of, relating to, or belonging to the *Prototheria*, a subclass of mammals that includes the monotremes ▷ *n* **2** any prototherian mammal; a monotreme ▷ Compare **eutherian, metatherian** [c19 New Latin, from PROTO- + Greek *theria* wild animals]

prototrophic (ˌprəʊtəˈtrɒfɪk) *adj* **1** (esp of bacteria) feeding solely on inorganic matter **2** (of cultured bacteria, fungi, etc) having no specific nutritional requirements

prototype (ˈprəʊtəˌtaɪp) *n* **1** one of the first units manufactured of a product, which is tested so that the design can be changed if necessary before the product is manufactured commercially **2** a person or thing that serves as an example of a type **3** *biology* the ancestral or primitive form of a species or other group; an archetype > ˌprotoˈtypal, **prototypic** (ˌprəʊtəˈtɪpɪk) or ˌprotoˈtypical *adj*

protoxide (prəʊˈtɒksaɪd) *n* the oxide of an element that contains the smallest amount of oxygen of any of its oxides

protoxylem (ˌprəʊtəˈzaɪləm) *n* the first-formed xylem tissue, consisting of extensible thin-walled cells thickened with rings or spirals of lignin. Compare **metaxylem**

protozoan (ˌprəʊtəˈzəʊən) *n, pl* -zoa (-ˈzəʊə) or -zoans **1** Also called: protozoon (ˌprəʊtəˈzəʊɒn) ▷ *pl* -zoa any of various minute unicellular organisms formerly regarded as invertebrates of the phylum *Protozoa* but now usually classified in certain phyla of protoctists. Protozoans include flagellates, ciliates, sporozoans, amoebas, and foraminifers ▷ *adj also* protozoic **2** of or relating to protozoans [c19 via New Latin from Greek PROTO- + *zoion* animal]

protozoology (ˌprəʊtəʊzəʊˈɒlədʒɪ) *n* the branch of biology concerned with the study of protozoans > protozoological (ˌprəʊtəʊˌzəʊəˈlɒdʒɪkᵊl) *adj* > ˌprotozoˈologist *n*

protract (prəˈtrækt) *vb (tr)* **1** to lengthen or extend (a speech, etc); prolong in time **2** (of a muscle) to draw, thrust, or extend (a part, etc) forwards **3** to plot or draw using a protractor and

scale [c16 from Latin *prōtrahere* to prolong, from PRO-¹ + *trahere* to drag] > proˈtractive *adj*

protracted (prəˈtræktɪd) *adj* extended or lengthened in time; prolonged: *a protracted legal battle* > proˈtractedly *adv* > proˈtractedness *n*

protractile (prəˈtræktaɪl) *or less commonly* **protractible** *adj* able to be extended or protruded: *protractile muscle*

protraction (prəˈtrækʃən) *n* **1** the act or process of protracting **2** the state or condition of being protracted **3** a prolongation or protrusion **4** an extension of something in time or space **5** something that is extended in time or space **6** the irregular lengthening of a syllable that is usually short

protractor (prəˈtræktə) *n* **1** an instrument for measuring or drawing angles on paper, usually a flat semicircular transparent plastic sheet graduated in degrees **2** a person or thing that protracts **3** a surgical instrument for removing a bullet from the body **4** *anatomy* a former term for extensor

protrude (prəˈtruːd) *vb* **1** to thrust or cause to thrust forwards or outwards **2** to project or cause to project from or as if from a surface [c17 from Latin, from PRO-² + *trudere* to thrust] > proˈtrudable *adj* > proˈtrudent *adj*

protrusile (prəˈtruːsaɪl) *adj zoology* capable of being thrust forwards: *protrusile jaws*. Also: projectile

protrusion (prəˈtruːʒən) *n* **1** something that protrudes **2** the state or condition of being protruded **3** the act or process of protruding

protrusive (prəˈtruːsɪv) *adj* **1** tending to project or jut outwards **2** a less common word for **obtrusive** **3** *archaic* causing propulsion > proˈtrusively *adv* > proˈtrusiveness *n*

protuberant (prəˈtjuːbərənt) *adj* swelling out from the surrounding surface; bulging [c17 from Late Latin *prōtūberāre* to swell, from PRO-¹ + *tūber* swelling] > proˈtuberance *or* proˈtuberancy *n* > proˈtuberantly *adv*

protuberate (prəˈtjuːbəˌreɪt) *vb (intr) rare* to swell out or project from the surrounding surface; bulge out

protyle (ˈprəʊtaɪl) *or* **protyl** (ˈprəʊtɪl) *n* a hypothetical primitive substance from which the chemical elements were supposed to have been formed [c19 from Greek *prōt-* PROTO- + *hylē* substance]

proud (praʊd) *adj* **1** (foll by *of*, an infinitive, or a clause) pleased or satisfied, as with oneself, one's possessions, achievements, etc, or with another person, his or her achievements, qualities, etc **2** feeling honoured or gratified by or as if by some distinction **3** having an inordinately high opinion of oneself; arrogant or haughty **4** characterized by or proceeding from a sense of pride: *a proud moment* **5** having a proper sense of self-respect **6** stately or distinguished **7** bold or fearless **8** (of a surface, edge, etc) projecting or protruding from the surrounding area **9** (of animals) restive or excited, esp sexually; on heat ▷ *adv* **10** do (someone) proud **a** to entertain (someone) on a grand scale: *they did us proud at the hotel* **b** to honour or distinguish (a person): *his honesty did him proud* [Late Old English *prūd*, from Old French *prud*, *prod* brave, from Late Latin *prōde* useful, from Latin *prōdesse* to be of value, from *prōd-*, variant of *prō-* for + *esse* to be] > ˈproudly *adv* > ˈproudness *n*

proud flesh *n* a non-technical name for **granulation tissue** [c14 from PROUD (in the sense: swollen, protruding)]

prounion (prəʊˈjuːnjən) *adj* **1** in favour of or supporting the constitutional union between two or more countries **2** in favour of or supporting the trades union movement

Proustian (ˈpruːstɪən) *adj* **1** of or relating to Marcel Proust, the French novelist (1871–1922), his works, or his style ▷ *n* **2** an admirer of Marcel Proust's works

proustite (ˈpruːstaɪt) *n* a red mineral consisting of silver arsenic sulphide in hexagonal crystalline form. Formula: Ag₃AsS₃ [c19 from French, named after Joseph Louis *Proust* (1754–1826), French chemist]

prov. *abbreviation for* **1** province **2** provincial **3** provisional

Prov. *abbreviation for* **1** Bible Proverbs **2** Province **3** Provost

prove (pruːv) *vb* proves, proving, proved; proved *or* proven (*mainly tr*) **1** (*may take a clause as object or an infinitive*) to establish or demonstrate the truth or validity of; verify, esp by using an established sequence of procedures or statements **2** to establish the quality of, esp by experiment or scientific analysis **3** *law* to establish the validity and genuineness of (a will) **4** to show (oneself) able or courageous **5** (*copula*) to be found or shown (to be): *this has proved useless; he proved to be invaluable* **6** *printing* to take a trial impression of (type, etc) **7** (*intr*) (of dough) to rise in a warm place before baking **8** *archaic* to undergo [c12 from Old French *prover*, from Latin *probāre* to test, from *probus* honest] > ˈprovable *adj* > ˌprovaˈbility *n* > ˈprovably *adv*

proven (ˈpruːvᵊn) *vb* **1** a past participle of **prove 2** See **not proven** ▷ *adj* **3** tried; tested: *a proven method* > ˈprovenly *adv*

provenance (ˈprɒvɪnəns) *or chiefly US* **provenience** (prəʊˈviːnɪəns) *n* a place of origin, esp that of a work of art or archaeological specimen [c19 from French, from *provenir*, from Latin *prōvenīre* to originate, from *venīre* to come]

Provençal (ˌprɒvɒnˈsɑːl; *French* prɔvɑ̃sal) *adj* **1** relating to, denoting, or characteristic of Provence, its inhabitants, their dialect of French, or their Romance language ▷ *n* **2** a language of Provence, closely related to Catalan, French, and Italian, belonging to the Romance group of the Indo-European family. It was important in the Middle Ages as a literary language, and attempts have been made since the 19th century to revive its literary status. See also **langue d'oc 3** a native or inhabitant of Provence

Provençale (ˌprɒvɒnˈsɑːl; *French* prɔvɑ̃sal) *adj* (of dishes) prepared with garlic, oil, and often tomatoes

Provence (*French* prɔvɑ̃s) *n* a former province of SE France, on the Mediterranean, and the River Rhône: forms part of the administrative region of Provence-Alpes-Côte d'Azur

provender (ˈprɒvɪndə) *n* **1** any dry feed or fodder for domestic livestock **2** food in general [c14 from Old French *provendre*, from Late Latin *praebenda* grant, from Latin *praebēre* to proffer; influenced also by Latin *prōvidēre* to look after]

proventriculus (ˌprəʊvɛnˈtrɪkjʊləs) *n, pl* -triculi (-ˈtrɪkjʊˌlaɪ) **1** the first part of the stomach of birds, the gizzard **2** the thick muscular stomach of crustaceans and insects; gizzard [c19 from New Latin, from Latin PRO-¹ + *ventriculus* little belly, from *venter* belly] > ˌproven'tricular *adj*

proverb (ˈprɒvɜːb) *n* **1** a short, memorable, and often highly condensed saying embodying, esp with bold imagery, some commonplace fact or experience **2** a person or thing exemplary in respect of a characteristic: *Antarctica is a proverb for extreme cold* **3** *ecclesiast* a wise saying or admonition providing guidance ▷ *vb (tr)* **4** to utter or describe (something) in the form of a proverb **5** to make (something) a proverb [c14 via Old French from Latin *prōverbium*, from *verbum* word]

proverbial (prəˈvɜːbɪəl) *adj* **1** (*prenominal*) commonly or traditionally referred to, esp as being an example of some peculiarity, characteristic, etc **2** of, connected with, embodied in, or resembling a proverb > proˈverbially *adv*

Proverbs (ˈprɒvɜːbz) *n* (*functioning as singular*) a book of the Old Testament consisting of the proverbs of various Israelite sages including Solomon

p

provide (prə'vaɪd) *vb* (*mainly tr*) **1** to put at the disposal of; furnish or supply **2** to afford; yield: *this meeting provides an opportunity to talk* **3** (*intr; often foll by for or against*) to take careful precautions (over): *he provided against financial ruin by wise investment* **4** (*intr; foll by for*) to supply means of support (to), esp financially: *he provides for his family* **5** (in statutes, documents, etc) to determine (what is to happen in certain contingencies), esp by including a proviso condition **6** to confer and induct into ecclesiastical offices **7** *now rare* to have or get in store: *in summer many animals provide their winter food* [c15 from Latin *prōvidēre* to provide for, from *prō-* beforehand + *vidēre* to see] > pro'vider *n*

providence ('prɒvɪdəns) *n* **1 a** *Christianity* God's foreseeing protection and care of his creatures **b** such protection and care as manifest by some other force **2** a supposed manifestation of such care and guidance **3** the foresight or care exercised by a person in the management of his affairs or resources

Providence[1] ('prɒvɪdəns) *n Christianity* God, esp as showing foreseeing care and protection of his creatures [c14 via French from Latin *prōvidēntia*, from *prōvidēre* to provide; see PROVIDE, -ENCE]

Providence[2] ('prɒvɪdəns) *n* a port in NE Rhode Island, capital of the state, at the head of Narragansett Bay: founded by Roger Williams in 1636. Pop: 176 365 (2003 est)

provident ('prɒvɪdənt) *adj* **1** providing for future needs **2** exercising foresight in the management of one's affairs or resources **3** characterized by or proceeding from foresight [c15 from Latin *prōvidens* foreseeing, from *prōvidēre* to PROVIDE] > 'providently *adv*

provident club *n Brit* a hire-purchase system offered by some large retail organizations

providential (ˌprɒvɪ'dɛnʃəl) *adj* relating to, characteristic of, or presumed to proceed from or as if from divine providence > ˌprovi'dentially *adv*

provident society *n* another name for **friendly society**

providing (prə'vaɪdɪŋ) *or* **provided** *conj* (*subordinating; sometimes foll by that*) on the condition or understanding (that): *I'll play, providing you pay me*

province ('prɒvɪns) *n* **1** a territory governed as a unit of a country or empire **2** a district, territory, or region **3** (*plural; usually preceded by the*) those parts of a country lying outside the capital and other large cities and regarded as outside the mainstream of sophisticated culture **4** *ecology* a subdivision of a region, characterized by a particular fauna and flora **5** an area or branch of learning, activity, etc **6** the field or extent of a person's activities or office **7** *RC Church, Church of England* an ecclesiastical territory, usually consisting of several dioceses, and having an archbishop or metropolitan at its head **8** a major administrative and territorial subdivision of a religious order **9** *history* a region of the Roman Empire outside Italy ruled by a governor from Rome [c14 from Old French, from Latin *prōvincia* conquered territory]

Provincetown ('prɒvɪnsˌtaʊn) *n* a village in SE Massachusetts, at the tip of Cape Cod: scene of the first landing place of the Pilgrims (1620) and of the signing of the Mayflower Compact (1620). Pop: 3472 (2003 est)

provincewide ('prɒvɪnsˌwaɪd) *Canadian* ▷ *adj* **1** covering or available to the whole of a province: *a provincewide referendum* ▷ *adv* **2** throughout a province: *an advertising campaign to go provincewide*

provincial (prə'vɪnʃəl) *adj* **1** of or connected with a province **2** characteristic of or connected with the provinces; local **3** having attitudes and opinions supposedly common to people living in the provinces; rustic or unsophisticated; limited **4** *NZ* denoting a football team representing a province, one of the historical administrative areas of New Zealand ▷ *n* **5** a person lacking the

sophistications of city life; rustic or narrow-minded individual **6** a person coming from or resident in a province or the provinces **7** the head of an ecclesiastical province **8** the head of a major territorial subdivision of a religious order > provinciality (prəˌvɪnʃɪ'ælɪtɪ) *n* > pro'vincially *adv*

Provincial Council *n* (formerly) a council administering any of the New Zealand provinces

provincialism (prə'vɪnʃəˌlɪzəm) *n* **1** narrowness of mind or outlook; lack of sophistication **2** a word or attitude characteristic of a provincial **3** attention to the affairs of one's province rather than the whole nation **4** the state or quality of being provincial ▷ Also called: **localism**

provincial police *n* (in Canada) the police force of a province, esp Ontario or Quebec

proving ground *n* a place or situation in which something new, such as equipment or a theory, can be tested

provirus ('prəʊˌvaɪrəs) *n* the inactive form of a virus in a host cell

provision (prə'vɪʒən) *n* **1** the act of supplying or providing food, etc **2** something that is supplied or provided **3** preparations made beforehand (esp in the phrase **make provision for**) **4** (*plural*) food and other necessities, esp for an expedition **5** (*plural*) food obtained for a household **6** a demand, condition, or stipulation formally incorporated in a document; proviso **7** the conferring of and induction into ecclesiastical offices ▷ *vb* **8** (*tr*) to supply with provisions [c14 from Latin *prōvīsiō* a providing; see PROVIDE] > pro'visioner *n*

provisional (prə'vɪʒənᵊl) *or less commonly* **provisionary** (prə'vɪʒənᵊrɪ) *adj* **1** subject to later alteration; temporary or conditional: *a provisional decision* ▷ *n* **2** a postage stamp surcharged during an emergency to alter the stamp's denomination or significance until a new or regular issue is printed > pro'visionally *adv*

Provisional (prə'vɪʒənᵊl) *adj* **1** of, designating, or relating to the unofficial factions of the IRA and Sinn Féin that became increasingly dominant following a split in 1969. The Provisional movement remained committed to a policy of terrorism until its ceasefires of the mid-1990s ▷ *n* **2** Also called: **Provo** a member of the Provisional IRA or Sinn Féin ▷ Compare **Official**

proviso (prə'vaɪzəʊ) *n, pl* **-sos** *or* **-soes 1** a clause in a document or contract that embodies a condition or stipulation **2** a condition or stipulation [c15 from Medieval Latin phrase *prōvīsō quod* it being provided that, from Latin *prōvīsus* provided]

provisory (prə'vaɪzərɪ) *adj* **1** containing a proviso; conditional **2** another word for **provisional** > pro'visorily *adv*

provitamin (prəʊ'vɪtəmɪn) *n* a substance, such as carotene, that is converted into a vitamin in animal tissues

Provo ('prəʊvəʊ) *n, pl* **-vos** another name for a **Provisional** (sense 2)

provocateur (prəˌvɒkə'tɜː) *n* a person who deliberately behaves controversially in order to provoke argument or other strong reactions

provocation (ˌprɒvə'keɪʃən) *n* **1** the act of provoking or inciting **2** something that causes indignation, anger, etc **3** *English criminal law* words or conduct that incite a person to attack another

provocative (prə'vɒkətɪv) *adj* acting as a stimulus or incitement, esp to anger or sexual desire; provoking: *a provocative look; a provocative remark* > pro'vocatively *adv* > pro'vocativeness *n*

provoke (prə'vəʊk) *vb* (*tr*) **1** to anger or infuriate **2** to cause to act or behave in a certain manner; incite or stimulate **3** to promote (certain feelings, esp anger, indignation, etc) in a person **4** *obsolete* to summon [c15 from Latin *prōvocāre* to call forth, from *vocāre* to call] > pro'voking *adj* > pro'vokingly *adv*

provolone (ˌprəʊvə'ləʊnɪ) *n* a mellow, pale yellow, soft, and sometimes smoked cheese, made of

cows' milk: usually moulded in the shape of a pear [Italian, from *provola*, apparently from Medieval Latin *probula* cheese made from buffalo milk]

provost ('prɒvəst) *n* **1** an appointed person who superintends or presides **2** the head of certain university colleges or schools **3** (in Scotland) the chairman and civic head of certain district councils or (formerly) of a burgh council. Compare **convener** (sense 2) **4** *Church of England* the senior dignitary of one of the more recent cathedral foundations **5** *RC Church* **a** the head of a cathedral chapter in England and some other countries **b** (formerly) the member of a monastic community second in authority under the abbot **6** (in medieval times) an overseer, steward, or bailiff in a manor **7** *obsolete* a prison warder **8** (prə'vəʊ) *Brit and Canadian military* a military policeman [Old English *profost*, from Medieval Latin *prōpositus* placed at the head (of), from Latin *praepōnere* to place first, from *prae-* before + *pōnere* to put]

provost court (prə'vəʊ) *n* a military court for trying people charged with minor offences in an occupied area

provost guard (prə'vəʊ) *n* (esp in the US) a detachment under command of the provost marshal

provost marshal (prə'vəʊ) *n* the officer in charge of military police and thus responsible for military discipline in a large camp, area, or city

prow (praʊ) *n* the bow of a vessel [c16 from Old French *proue*, from Latin *prora*, from Greek *prōra*; related to Latin *pro* in front]

prowar ('prəʊ'wɔː) *adj* in favour of or supporting war

prowess ('praʊɪs) *n* **1** outstanding or superior skill or ability **2** bravery or fearlessness, esp in battle [c13 from Old French *proesce*, from *prou* good; see PROUD]

prowl (praʊl) *vb* **1** (when *intr*, often foll by *around* or *about*) to move stealthily around (a place) as if in search of prey or plunder ▷ *n* **2** the act of prowling **3 on the prowl a** moving around stealthily **b** zealously pursuing members of the opposite sex [c14 *prollen*, of unknown origin] > 'prowler *n*

prox. *abbreviation for* proximo (next month)

proxemics (prɒk'siːmɪks) *n* (*functioning as singular*) the study of spatial interrelationships in humans or in populations of animals of the same species

Proxima ('prɒksɪmə) *n* a flare star in the constellation Centaurus that is the nearest star to the sun. It is a red dwarf of very low magnitude. Distance: 4.3 light years. Also called: **Proxima Centauri**. See also **Rigil Kent**

proximal ('prɒksɪməl) *adj* **1** *anatomy* situated close to the centre, median line, or point of attachment or origin. Compare **distal 2** another word for **proximate**. > 'proximally *adv*

proximate ('prɒksɪmɪt) *or* **proximal** *adj* **1** next or nearest in space or time **2** very near; close **3** immediately preceding or following in a series **4** a less common word for **approximate** [c16 from Late Latin *proximāre* to draw near, from Latin *proximus* next, from *prope* near] > 'proximately *adv* > 'proximateness *n* > ˌproxi'mation *n*

proxime accessit ('prɒksɪmɪ æk'sɛsɪt) *n* the person coming next after the winner in a competitive examination or an academic prize giving; runner-up [Latin: he came next]

proximity (prɒk'sɪmɪtɪ) *n* **1** nearness in space or time **2** nearness or closeness in a series [c15 from Latin *proximitās* closeness; see PROXIMATE]

proximity fuse *n* an electronically triggered device designed to detonate an explosive charge in a missile, etc, at a predetermined distance from the target

proximity talks *pl n* a diplomatic process whereby an impartial representative acts as go-between for two opposing parties who are willing to attend the same conference but unwilling to meet face to face

proximo ('prɒksɪməʊ) *adv now rare except when abbreviated in formal correspondence* in or during the next or coming month: *a letter of the seventh proximo.* Abbreviation: **prox.** Compare **instant, ultimo** [c19 from Latin: in or on the next, from *proximus* next]

proxy ('prɒksɪ) *n, pl* **proxies** **1** a person authorized to act on behalf of someone else; agent: *to vote by proxy* **2** the authority, esp in the form of a document, given to a person to act on behalf of someone else **3** *computing* short for **proxy server** [c15 *prokesye*, contraction of *procuracy*, from Latin *prōcūrātiō* procuration; see PROCURE]

proxy server *n computing* a computer that acts as an intermediary between a client machine and a server, caching information to save access time

Prozac ('prəʊzæk) *n trademark* fluoxetine; a drug that prolongs the action of serotonin in the brain; used as an antidepressant

PRP *abbreviation for* **1** performance-related pay **2** profit-related pay

prs *abbreviation for* pairs

PRT *abbreviation for* **1** *text messaging* party **2** personal rapid transit **3** petroleum revenue tax

prude (pru:d) *n* a person who affects or shows an excessively modest, prim, or proper attitude, esp regarding sex [c18 from French, from *prudefemme*, from Old French *prode femme* respectable woman; see PROUD] > '**prudish** *adj* > '**prudishly** *adv* > '**prudishness** *or* '**prudery** *n*

prudence ('pru:dəns) *n* **1** caution in practical affairs; discretion or circumspection **2** care taken in the management of one's resources **3** consideration for one's own interests **4** the condition or quality of being prudent

prudent ('pru:dᵊnt) *adj* **1** discreet or cautious in managing one's activities; circumspect **2** practical and careful in providing for the future **3** exercising good judgment or common sense [c14 from Latin *prūdēns* far-sighted, contraction of *prōvidens* acting with foresight; see PROVIDENT] > '**prudently** *adv*

prudential (pru:'dɛnʃəl) *adj* **1** characterized by or resulting from prudence **2** exercising prudence or sound judgment > **pru'dentially** *adv*

pruinose ('pru:ɪˌnəʊs, -ˌnəʊz) *adj botany* coated with a powdery or waxy bloom [c19 from Latin *pruīnōsus* frost-covered, from *pruīna* hoarfrost]

prune¹ (pru:n) *n* **1** a purplish-black partially dried fruit of any of several varieties of plum tree **2** *slang, chiefly Brit* a dull, uninteresting, or foolish person [c14 from Old French *prune*, from Latin *prūnum* plum, from Greek *prounon*]

prune² (pru:n) *vb* **1** to remove (dead or superfluous twigs, branches, etc) from (a tree, shrub, etc), esp by cutting off **2** to remove (anything undesirable or superfluous) from (a book, etc) [c15 from Old French *proignier* to clip, probably from *provigner* to prune vines, from *provain* layer (of a plant), from Latin *propāgo* a cutting] > '**prunable** *adj* > '**pruner** *n*

prune³ (pru:n) *vb* an archaic word for **preen**¹

prunella¹ (pru:'nɛlə), **prunelle** (pru:'nɛl) *or* **prunello** (pru:'nɛləʊ) *n* a strong fabric, esp a twill-weave worsted, used for gowns and the uppers of some shoes [c17 perhaps from PRUNELLE, with reference to the colour of the cloth]

prunella² (pru:'nɛlə) *n* See **selfheal** [New Latin, altered from *brunella*, from German *Braüne* quinsy, which it was thought to cure]

prunelle (pru:'nɛl) *n* a green French liqueur made from sloes [c18 from French: a little plum, from *prune* PRUNE¹]

pruning hook *n* a tool with a curved steel blade terminating in a hook, used for pruning

prurient ('prʊərɪənt) *adj* **1** unusually or morbidly interested in sexual thoughts or practices **2** exciting or encouraging lustfulness; erotic [c17 from Latin *prūrīre* to itch, to lust after] > '**prurience** *n* > '**pruriently** *adv*

prurigo (prʊə'raɪgəʊ) *n* a chronic inflammatory disease of the skin characterized by the formation of papules and intense itching [c19 from Latin: an itch] > **pruriginous** (prʊə'rɪdʒɪnəs) *adj*

pruritus (prʊə'raɪtəs) *n pathol* **1** any intense sensation of itching **2** any of various conditions characterized by intense itching [c17 from Latin: an itching; see PRURIENT] > **pruritic** (prʊə'rɪtɪk) *adj*

prusik ('prʌsɪk) *n mountaineering* **1** Also: **prusik knot** a sliding knot that locks under pressure and can be used to form a loop (**prusik loop**) in which a climber can place his foot in order to stand or ascend a rope ▷ *vb* **-siks, -siking, -siked** (*intr*) **2** to climb (up a standing rope) using prusik loops [c20 named after Dr *Prusik*, Austrian climber who devised the knot]

Prussia ('prʌʃə) *n* a former German state in N and central Germany, extending from France and the Low Countries to the Baltic Sea and Poland: developed as the chief military power of the Continent, leading the North German Confederation from 1867–71, when the German Empire was established; dissolved in 1947 and divided between East and West Germany, Poland, and the former Soviet Union. Area: (in 1939) 294 081 sq km (113 545 sq miles). German name: **Preussen**

Prussian ('prʌʃən) *adj* **1** of, relating to, or characteristic of Prussia or its people, esp of the Junkers and their formal military tradition ▷ *n* **2** a German native or inhabitant of Prussia **3** a member of a Baltic people formerly inhabiting the coastal area of the SE Baltic **4** See **Old Prussian**

Prussian blue *n* **1** any of a number of blue pigments containing ferrocyanide or ferricyanide complexes **2 a** the blue or deep greenish-blue colour of this pigment **b** (*as adjective*): *a Prussian-blue carpet*

Prussianism ('prʌʃəˌnɪzəm) *n* the ethos of the Prussian state and aristocracy, esp militarism and stern discipline

Prussianize *or* **Prussianise** ('prʌʃəˌnaɪz) *vb* (*tr*) to make Prussian in character, esp with respect to military matters > ˌ**Prussiani'zation** *or* ˌ**Prussiani'sation** *n*

prussiate ('prʌʃɪɪt) *n* any cyanide, ferrocyanide, or ferricyanide

prussic acid ('prʌsɪk) *n* the weakly acidic extremely poisonous aqueous solution of hydrogen cyanide [c18 from French *acide prussique* Prussian acid, so called because obtained from Prussian blue]

Prut (*Russian* prut) *n* a river in E Europe, rising in SW Ukraine and flowing generally southeast, forming part of the border between Romania and Moldova, to join the River Danube. Length: 853 km (530 miles)

PRW *text messaging abbreviation for* parents are watching

pry¹ (praɪ) *vb* **pries, prying, pried** **1** (*intr; often foll by into*) to make an impertinent or uninvited inquiry (about a private matter, topic, etc) ▷ *n, pl* **pries** **2** the act of prying **3** a person who pries [c14 of unknown origin]

pry² (praɪ) *vb* **pries, prying, pried** **1** to force open by levering **2** *US and Canadian* to extract or obtain with difficulty: *they had to pry the news out of him.* equivalent term (in Britain and other countries): **prise** [c14 of unknown origin]

pryer ('praɪə) *n* a variant spelling of **prier**

prytaneum (ˌprɪtə'ni:əm) *n, pl* **-nea** (-'ni:ə) the public hall of a city in ancient Greece [Latin, from Greek *prutaneion*, from *prutanis, prutaneus*]

Przemyśl (*Polish* 'pʃɛmɪʃl) *n* a city in SE Poland, near the border with Ukraine on the San River: a fortress in the early Middle Ages; belonged to Austria (1722–1918). Pop: 67 000 (latest est)

Przewalski's horse (ˌpɜ:ʒə'vælskɪz) *n* a wild horse, *Equus przewalskii*, of W Mongolia, having an erect mane and no forelock: extinct in the wild, only a few survive in captivity [c19 named after the Russian explorer Nikolai Mikhailovich *Przewalski* (1839–88), who discovered it]

ps *the internet domain name for* Palestinian Territories

PS *abbreviation for* **1** Passenger Steamer **2** phrase structure **3** Police Sergeant **4** Also: **ps** postscript **5** private secretary **6** prompt side

Ps. *or* **Psa.** *Bible abbreviation for* Psalm

PSA *abbreviation for* **1** prostatic specific antigen: an enzyme secreted by the prostate gland, increased levels of which are found in the blood of patients with cancer of the prostate **2** (in New Zealand) Public Service Association

psalm (sɑ:m) *n* **1** (*often capital*) any of the 150 sacred songs, lyric poems, and prayers that together constitute a book (Psalms) of the Old Testament **2** a musical setting of one of these poems **3** any sacred song or hymn [Old English, from Late Latin *psalmus*, from Greek *psalmos* song accompanied on the harp, from *psallein* to play (the harp)] > '**psalmic** *adj*

psalmist ('sɑ:mɪst) *n* the composer of a psalm or psalms, esp (when *capital* and preceded by *the*) David, traditionally regarded as the author of The Book of Psalms

psalmody ('sɑ:mədɪ, 'sæl-) *n, pl* **-dies** **1** the act of singing psalms or hymns **2** the art or practice of the setting to music or singing of psalms [c14 via Late Latin from Greek *psalmōidia* singing accompanied by a harp, from *psalmos* (see PSALM) + *ōidē* ODE] > '**psalmodist** *n* > **psalmodic** (sɑ:'mɒdɪk, sæl-) *adj*

Psalms (sɑ:mz) *n* (*functioning as singular*) the collection of 150 psalms in the Old Testament, the full title of which is **The Book of Psalms**

Psalter ('sɔ:ltə) *n* **1** another name for **Psalms**, esp in the version in the Book of Common Prayer **2** a translation, musical, or metrical version of the Psalms **3** a devotional or liturgical book containing a version of Psalms, often with a musical setting [Old English *psaltere*, from Late Latin *psaltērium*, from Greek *psaltērion* stringed instrument, from *psallein* to play a stringed instrument]

psalterium (sɔ:l'tɪərɪəm) *n, pl* **-teria** (-'tɪərɪə) the third compartment of the stomach of ruminants, between the reticulum and abomasum. Also called: **omasum** [c19 from Latin *psaltērium* PSALTER; from the similarity of its folds to the pages of a book]

psaltery ('sɔ:ltərɪ) *n, pl* **-teries** *music* an ancient stringed instrument similar to the lyre, but having a trapezoidal sounding board over which the strings are stretched [Old English: see PSALTER]

psammite ('sæmaɪt) *n* a rare name for **sandstone** [c19 from Greek *psammos* sand] > **psammitic** (sæ'mɪtɪk) *adj*

p's and q's *pl n* behaviour within social conventions; manners (esp in the phrase **to mind one's p's and q's**) [altered from *p(lea)se* and (*than*)*k-you's*]

PSBR (in Britain) *abbreviation for* public sector borrowing requirement: the excess of government expenditure over receipts (mainly from taxation) that has to be financed by borrowing from the banks or the public

psephite ('si:faɪt) *n* any rock, such as a breccia, that consists of large fragments embedded in a finer matrix [c19 via French from Greek *psēphos* a pebble] > **psephitic** (si:'fɪtɪk) *adj*

psephology (sɛ'fɒlədʒɪ) *n* the statistical and sociological study of elections [c20 from Greek *psephos* pebble, vote + -LOGY, from the ancient Greeks' custom of voting with pebbles] > **psephological** (ˌsɛfə'lɒdʒɪkᵊl) *adj* > ˌ**psepho'logically** *adv* > **pse'phologist** *n*

pseud (sju:d) *n* **1** *informal* a false, artificial, or pretentious person ▷ *adj* **2** another word for **pseudo**

pseud. *abbreviation for* pseudonym

pseudaxis (sju:'dæksɪs) *n botany* another name for **sympodium**

Pseudepigrapha (ˌsju:dɪ'pɪgrəfə) *pl n* various

p

Jewish writings from the first century BC to the first century AD that claim to have been divinely revealed but which have been excluded from the Greek canon of the Old Testament. Also called (in the Roman Catholic Church): **Apocrypha** [C17 from Greek *pseudepigraphos* falsely entitled, from PSEUDO- + *epigraphein* to inscribe] > **Pseudepigraphic** (ˌsjuːdɛpɪˈɡræfɪk), **ˌPseudepiˈgraphical** or **ˌPseudeˈpigraphous** *adj*

pseudo ('sjuːdəʊ) *adj informal* not genuine; pretended

pseudo- *or sometimes before a vowel* **pseud-** *combining form* **1** false, pretending, or unauthentic: *pseudo-intellectual* **2** having a close resemblance to: *pseudopodium* [from Greek *pseudēs* false, from *pseudein* to lie]

pseudoarthrosis (ˌsjuːdəʊɑːˈθrəʊsɪs) *or* **pseudarthrosis** (ˌsjuːdɑːˈθrəʊsɪs) *n, pl* -ses (-siːz) a joint formed by fibrous tissue bridging the gap between the two fragments of bone of an old fracture that have not united. Nontechnical names: **false joint**, **false ankylosis**. Also called: **nearthrosis**

pseudocarp ('sjuːdəʊˌkɑːp) *n* a fruit, such as the strawberry or apple, that includes parts other than the ripened ovary. Also called: **false fruit**, **accessory fruit** > ˌpseudoˈcarpous *adj*

pseudo-colour *n* an artificial colour

pseudocopulation (ˌsjuːdəʊˌkɒpjʊˈleɪʃən) *n botany* pollination of plants, esp orchids, by male insects while attempting to mate with flowers that resemble the female insect

pseudocyesis (ˌsjuːdəʊsaɪˈiːsɪs) *n, pl* -ces (-siːz) the technical name for **phantom pregnancy**

pseudoephedrine (ˌsjuːdəʊˈɛfɪˌdriːn, -ˌdrɪn) *n* a drug similar in action to ephedrine, used extensively as a decongestant

pseudohermaphroditism (ˌsjuːdəʊhɜːˈmæfrədaɪˌtɪzəm) *n* the congenital condition of having the organs of reproduction of one sex and the external genitalia, usually malformed, of the opposite sex. Compare **hermaphroditism**

pseudo-intransitive *adj* denoting an occurrence of a normally transitive verb in which a direct object is not explicitly stated or forms the subject of the sentence, as in *Margaret is cooking* or *these apples cook well*

pseudomonas (sjuːˈdɒmənəs) *n, pl* **pseudomonades** (ˌsjuːdəʊˈmɒnədiːz) any of a genus of rodlike Gram-negative bacteria that live in soil and decomposing organic matter: many species are pathogenic to plants and a few are pathogenic to man [C20 from New Latin, from PSEUDO- + Greek *monas* unit]

pseudomorph ('sjuːdəʊˌmɔːf) *n* a mineral that has an uncharacteristic crystalline form as a result of assuming the shape of another mineral that it has replaced > ˌpseudoˈmorphic *or* ˌpseudoˈmorphous *adj* > ˌpseudoˈmorphism *n*

pseudomutuality (ˌsjuːdəʊˌmjuːtjʊˈælɪtɪ) *n, pl* -ties *psychol* a relationship between two persons in which conflict of views or opinions is solved by simply ignoring it

pseudonym ('sjuːdəˌnɪm) *n* a fictitious name adopted, esp by an author [C19 via French from Greek *pseudōnumon*] > ˌpseudoˈnymity *n*

pseudonymous (sjuːˈdɒnɪməs) *adj* **1** having or using a false or assumed name **2** writing or having been written under a pseudonym > pseuˈdonymously *adv*

pseudopodium (ˌsjuːdəʊˈpəʊdɪəm) *n, pl* -dia (-dɪə) a temporary projection from the cell of an amoeboid protozoan, leucocyte, etc, used for feeding and locomotion

pseudopregnancy ('sjuːdəʊˌprɛgnənsɪ) *n* another name for **phantom pregnancy**

pseudoscalar (ˌsjuːdəʊˈskeɪlə) *n maths* a variable quantity that has magnitude but not direction and is an odd function of the coordinates. Compare **pseudovector**. **scalar** (sense 1), **tensor** (sense 2), **vector** (sense 1)

pseudoscience (ˌsjuːdəʊˈsaɪəns) *n* a discipline or approach that pretends to be or has a close resemblance to science > ˌpseudoˌscienˈtific *adj*

pseudovector (ˌsjuːdəʊˈvɛktə) *n maths* a variable quantity, such as angular momentum, that has magnitude and orientation with respect to an axis. The components are even functions of the coordinates. Also called: **axial vector.** Compare **pseudoscalar, scalar** (sense 1), **tensor** (sense 2), **vector** (sense 1)

psf *abbreviation for* pounds per square foot

PSG *abbreviation for* phrase-structure grammar

pshaw (pʃɔː) *interj becoming rare* an exclamation of disgust, impatience, disbelief, etc

psi¹ *abbreviation for* pounds per square inch

psi² (psaɪ) *n* **1** the 23rd letter of the Greek alphabet (Ψ, ψ), a composite consonant, transliterated as *ps* **2 a** paranormal or psychic phenomena collectively **b** (*as modifier*): *psi powers*

psia *abbreviation for* pounds per square inch, absolute

psid *abbreviation for* pounds per square inch, differential

psig *abbreviation for* pounds per square inch, gauge

psilocybin (ˌsɪləˈsaɪbɪn, ˌsaɪlə-) *n* a crystalline phosphate ester that is the active principle of the hallucinogenic fungus *Psilocybe mexicana*. Formula: $C_{12}H_{17}N_2O_4P$ [C20 from New Latin *Psilocybe* (from Greek *psilos* bare + *kubē* head) + -IN]

psilomelane (sɪˈlɒmɪˌleɪn) *n* a common black to grey secondary mineral consisting of hydrated basic oxide of manganese and barium: a source of manganese. Formula: $BaMn_9O_{16}(OH)_4$. Also called **romanicite** [C19 from Greek *psilos* bare + *melas* black]

psi particle *n* See **J/psi particle**

PSIS (in New Zealand) *abbreviation for* Public Service Investment Society, New Zealand's largest credit union

psittacine ('sɪtəˌsaɪn, -sɪn) *adj* of, relating to, or resembling a parrot [C19 from Late Latin *psittacīnus*, from Latin *psittacus* a parrot]

psittacosis (ˌsɪtəˈkəʊsɪs) *n* a disease of parrots, caused by the obligate intracellular parasite *Chlamydia psittaci*, that can be transmitted to man, in whom it produces inflammation of the lungs and pneumonia. Also called: **parrot fever**, **ornithosis** [C19 from New Latin, from Latin *psittacus* a parrot, from Greek *psittakos*; see -OSIS]

PSK *abbreviation for* phase shift keying: a digital data modulation system in which binary data signals switch the phase of a radio frequency carrier

Pskov (*Russian* pskɔf) *n* **1** a city in NW Russia, on the Velikaya River: one of the oldest Russian cities, at its height in the 13th and 14th centuries. Pop: 203 000 (2005 est) **2 Lake** the S part of Lake Peipus in NW Russia, linked to the main part by a channel 24 km (15 miles) long. Area: about 1000 sq km (400 sq miles)

PSL *abbreviation for* private sector liquidity: a measure of the money supply. See **M4, M5**

PSNI *abbreviation for* Police Service of Northern Ireland, established in 2000

psoas ('səʊəs) *n* either of two muscles of the loins that aid in flexing and rotating the thigh [C17 from New Latin, from Greek *psoai* (pl)]

psoralea (səˈreɪlɪə) *n* any plant of the tropical and subtropical leguminous genus *Psoralea*, having curly leaves, white or purple flowers, and short one-seeded pods. See **breadroot** [C19 via New Latin from Greek *psōraleos* mangy, from *psōra* mange, an allusion to the glandular dots of the plant]

psoriasis (səˈraɪəsɪs) *n* a skin disease characterized by the formation of reddish spots and patches covered with silvery scales: tends to run in families [C17 via New Latin from Greek: itching disease, from *psōra* itch] > **psoriatic** (ˌsɔːrɪˈætɪk) *adj*

PSS *or* **pss.** *abbreviation for* postscripts

psst (pst) *interj* an exclamation of beckoning, esp one made surreptitiously

PST (in the US and Canada) *abbreviation for* **Pacific Standard Time**

PSTN *abbreviation for* public switched telephone network: the conventional message switched telephone network

PSV (in Britain) *abbreviation for* public service vehicle (now called passenger carrying vehicle)

psych *or* **psyche** (saɪk) *vb* (*tr*) *informal* to psychoanalyse. See also **psych out, psych up** [C20 shortened from PSYCHOANALYSE]

psyche ('saɪkɪ) *n* the human mind or soul [C17 from Latin, from Greek *psukhē* breath, soul; related to Greek *psukhein* to breathe]

Psyche ('saɪkɪ) *n Greek myth* a beautiful girl loved by Eros (Cupid), who became the personification of the soul

psychedelia (ˌsaɪkəˈdɛlɪə, -ˈdiːlɪə) *n* (*functioning as singular or plural*) psychedelic objects, dress, music, etc

psychedelic *or* **psychodelic** (ˌsaɪkɪˈdɛlɪk) *adj* **1** relating to or denoting new or altered perceptions or sensory experiences, as through the use of hallucinogenic drugs **2** denoting any of the drugs, esp LSD, that produce these effects **3** *informal* (of painting, fabric design, etc) having the vivid colours and complex patterns popularly associated with the visual effects of psychedelic states [C20 from PSYCHE + Greek *delos* visible] > ˌpsycheˈdelically *or* ˌpsychoˈdelically *adv*

psychiatric (ˌsaɪkɪˈætrɪk) *or* **psychiatrical** *adj* of or relating to mental disorders or psychiatry > ˌpsychiˈatrically *adv*

psychiatric social worker *n social welfare* (in Britain) a qualified person who works with mentally disordered people and their families, based in a psychiatric hospital, child guidance clinic, or social services department area team, and who may also be an approved social worker

psychiatry (saɪˈkaɪətrɪ) *n* the branch of medicine concerned with the diagnosis and treatment of mental disorders > psyˈchiatrist *n*

psychic ('saɪkɪk) *adj* **1 a** outside the possibilities defined by natural laws, as mental telepathy **b** (of a person) sensitive to forces not recognized by natural laws **2** mental as opposed to physical; psychogenic **3** *bridge* (of a bid) based on less strength than would normally be required to make the bid ▷ *n* **4** a person who is sensitive to parapsychological forces or influences [C19 from Greek *psukhikos* of the soul or life] > 'psychical *adj* > 'psychically *adv*

psychic determinism *n psychol* the assumption, made esp by Sigmund Freud, the Austrian psychiatrist (1856–1939), that mental processes do not occur by chance but that a cause can always be found for them

psycho ('saɪkəʊ) *n, pl* -chos, *adj* an informal word for **psychopath** or **psychopathic**

psycho- *or sometimes before a vowel* **psych-** *combining form* indicating the mind or psychological or mental processes: *psychology; psychogenesis; psychosomatic* [from Greek *psukhē* spirit, breath]

psychoacoustics (ˌsaɪkəʊəˈkuːstɪks) *n* (*functioning as singular*) *psychol* the study of the relationship between sounds and their physiological and psychological effects

psychoactive (ˌsaɪkəʊˈæktɪv) *adj* capable of affecting mental activity: *a psychoactive drug*

psychoanal. *abbreviation for* psychoanalysis

psychoanalyse *or US* **psychoanalyze** (ˌsaɪkəʊˈænəˌlaɪz) *vb* (*tr*) to examine or treat (a person) by psychoanalysis > ˌpsychoˈanaˌlyser *or US* ˌpsychoˈanaˌlyzer *n*

psychoanalysis (ˌsaɪkəʊəˈnælɪsɪs) *n* a method of studying the mind and treating mental and emotional disorders based on revealing and investigating the role of the unconscious mind > **psychoanalyst** (ˌsaɪkəʊˈænəlɪst) *n* > **psychoanalytic** (ˌsaɪkəʊˌænəˈlɪtɪk) *or* ˌpsychoˌanaˈlytical *adj* > ˌpsychoˌanaˈlytically *adv*

psychobabble ('saɪkəʊˌbæbᵊl) *n informal* the jargon of psychology, esp as used and popularized in various types of psychotherapy

psychobilly ('saɪkəˌbɪlɪ) *n, pl* -lies **a** loud frantic rockabilly music **b** (*as modifier*): *a psychobilly track*

psychobiography (ˌsaɪkəʊbaɪˈɒɡrəfɪ) *n* a biography that pays particular attention to a person's psychological development ⊳ psychobiographical (ˌsaɪkəʊbaɪəˈɡræfɪkᵊl) *adj*

psychobiology (ˌsaɪkəʊbaɪˈɒlədʒɪ) *n psychol* the attempt to understand the psychology of organisms in terms of their biological functions and structures > psychobiological (ˌsaɪkəʊˌbaɪəˈlɒdʒɪkᵊl) *adj* > ˌpsychobio'logically *adv* > ˌpsychobi'ologist *n*

psychochemical (ˌsaɪkəʊˈkɛmɪkᵊl) *n* **1** any of various chemical compounds whose primary effect is the alteration of the normal state of consciousness ⊳ *adj* **2** of or relating to such chemical compounds

psychodrama ('saɪkəʊˌdrɑːmə) *n* **1** *psychiatry* a form of group therapy in which individuals act out, before an audience, situations from their past **2** a film, television drama, etc, in which the psychological development of the characters is emphasized > psychodramatic (ˌsaɪkəʊdrəˈmætɪk) *adj*

psychodynamics (ˌsaɪkəʊdaɪˈnæmɪks) *n* (*functioning as singular*) *psychol* the study of interacting motives and emotions > ˌpsychody'namic *adj* > ˌpsychody'namically *adv*

psychogalvanic response (ˌsaɪkəʊɡælˈvænɪk) *n* another name for **galvanic skin response** Abbreviation: PGR

psychogenesis (ˌsaɪkəʊˈdʒɛnɪsɪs) *n psychol* the study of the origin and development of personality, human behaviour, and mental processes > psychogenetic (ˌsaɪkəʊdʒɪˈnɛtɪk) *adj* > ˌpsychoge'netically *adv*

psychogenic (ˌsaɪkəʊˈdʒɛnɪk) *adj psychol* (esp of disorders or symptoms) of mental, rather than organic, origin > ˌpsycho'genically *adv*

psychogeriatric (ˌsaɪkəʊdʒɛrɪˈætrɪk) *adj* **1** *med* (of an old person) no longer in touch with everyday realities; exhibiting delusions; mentally incompetent ⊳ *n* **2 a** *derogatory* a confused old person **b** an impersonal label for a patient, as a unit, requiring institutional services appropriate for a mentally disordered old person ⊳ See also **confused elderly, geriatric, senile**

psychogeriatrics (ˌsaɪkəʊdʒɛrɪˈætrɪks) *n* (*functioning as singular*) *med* the branch of health care concerned with the study, diagnosis, and sometimes treatment of mentally disordered old people. Compare **geriatrics**

psychognosis (saɪˈkɒɡnəsɪs) *n psychol* **1** the use of hypnosis to study mental phenomena **2** the study of personality by observation of outward bodily signs > psychognostic (ˌsaɪkɒɡˈnɒstɪk) *adj*

psychographics (ˌsaɪkəʊˈɡræfɪks) *pl n* (*functioning as singular*) the study and grouping of people according to their attitudes and tastes, esp for market research

psychohistory (ˌsaɪkəʊˈhɪstərɪ, -ˈhɪstrɪ) *n, pl* -ries biography based on psychological theories of personality development

psychokinesis (ˌsaɪkəʊkɪˈniːsɪs, -kaɪ-) *n* **1** (in parapsychology) alteration of the state of an object by mental influence alone, without any physical intervention **2** *psychiatry* a state of violent uncontrolled motor activity [c20 from PSYCHO- + Greek *kinēsis* motion] > psychokinetic (ˌsaɪkəʊkɪˈnɛtɪk) *adj*

psychol. *abbreviation for* **1** psychological **2** psychology

psycholinguistics (ˌsaɪkəʊlɪŋˈɡwɪstɪks) *n* (*functioning as singular*) the psychology of language, including language acquisition by children, the mental processes underlying adult comprehension and production of speech, language disorders, etc > ˌpsycho'linguist *n* > ˌpsycholin'guistic *adj*

psychological (ˌsaɪkəˈlɒdʒɪkᵊl) *adj* **1** of or relating to psychology **2** of or relating to the mind or mental activity **3** having no real or objective basis; arising in the mind: *his backaches are all psychological* **4** affecting the mind > ˌpsycho'logically *adv*

psychological block *n* See **block** (sense 21)

psychological moment *n* the most appropriate time for producing a desired effect: *he proposed to her at the psychological moment*

psychological operations *pl n* another term for **psychological warfare**

psychological primary *n* one of a set of perceived colours (red, yellow, blue, green, black, and white) that can be used to characterize all other perceived colours

psychological warfare *n* the military application of psychology, esp to propaganda and attempts to influence the morale of enemy and friendly groups in time of war

psychologism (saɪˈkɒləˌdʒɪzəm) *n* **1** the belief in the importance and relevance of psychology for other sciences **2** the belief that psychology is the basis for all other natural and social sciences > psyˌcholo'gistic *adj*

psychologize *or* **psychologise** (saɪˈkɒləˌdʒaɪz) *vb* (*intr*) **1** to make interpretations of behaviour and mental processes **2** to carry out investigation in the field of psychology

psychology (saɪˈkɒlədʒɪ) *n, pl* -gies **1** the scientific study of all forms of human and animal behaviour, sometimes concerned with the methods through which behaviour can be modified. See also **analytical psychology, clinical psychology, comparative psychology, educational psychology, experimental psychology 2** *informal* the mental make-up or structure of an individual that causes him or her to think or act in the way he or she does > psy'chologist *n*

psychomachia (ˌsaɪkəʊˈmækɪə) *or* **psychomachy** ('saɪkəʊˌmækɪ) *n* conflict of the soul [c17 from Late Latin *psȳchomachia*, title of a poem by Prudentius (about 400), from Greek *psukhē* spirit + *makhē* battle]

psychometric (ˌsaɪkəʊˈmɛtrɪk) *or* **psychometrical** *adj* of or relating to psychometrics or psychometry > ˌpsycho'metrically *adv*

psychometrics (ˌsaɪkəʊˈmɛtrɪks) *n* (*functioning as singular*) **1** the branch of psychology concerned with the design and use of psychological tests **2** the application of statistical and mathematical techniques to psychological testing

psychometry (saɪˈkɒmɪtrɪ) *n psychol* **1** measurement and testing of mental states and processes. See also **psychometrics 2** (in parapsychology) the supposed ability to deduce facts about events by touching objects related to them > psychometrician (ˌsaɪkəʊməˈtrɪʃən) *or* psy'chometrist *n*

psychomotor (ˌsaɪkəʊˈməʊtə) *adj* of, relating to, or characterizing movements of the body associated with mental activity

psychoneuroimmunology (ˌsaɪkəʊˌnjʊərəʊˌɪmjʊˈnɒlədʒɪ) *n* the study of the effects of psychological factors on the immune system. Abbreviation: PNI

psychoneurosis (ˌsaɪkəʊnjʊˈrəʊsɪs) *n, pl* -roses (-ˈrəʊsiːz) another word for **neurosis** > psychoneurotic (ˌsaɪkəʊnjʊˈrɒtɪk) *adj*

psychopath ('saɪkəʊˌpæθ) *n* a person afflicted with a personality disorder characterized by a tendency to commit antisocial and sometimes violent acts and a failure to feel guilt for such acts. Also called: sociopath > ˌpsycho'pathic *adj* > ˌpsycho'pathically *adv*

psychopathic disorder *n law* (in England, according to the Mental Health Act 1983) a persistent disorder or disability of mind which results in abnormally aggressive or seriously irresponsible conduct on the part of the person concerned. See also **mental disorder**

psychopathic personality *n psychiatry* an antisocial personality characterized by the failure to develop any sense of moral responsibility and the capability of performing violent or antisocial acts

psychopathology (ˌsaɪkəʊpəˈθɒlədʒɪ) *n* the scientific study of mental disorders > psychopathological (ˌsaɪkəʊˌpæθəˈlɒdʒɪkᵊl) *adj* > ˌpsychopa'thologist *n*

psychopathy (saɪˈkɒpəθɪ) *n psychiatry* **1** another name for **psychopathic personality 2** any mental disorder or disease

psychopharmacology (ˌsaɪkəʊˌfɑːməˈkɒlədʒɪ) *n* the study of drugs that affect the mind > psychopharmacological (ˌsaɪkəʊˌfɑːməkəˈlɒdʒɪkᵊl) *adj* > ˌpsychoˌpharma'cologist *n*

psychophysics (ˌsaɪkəʊˈfɪzɪks) *n* (*functioning as singular*) the branch of psychology concerned with the relationship between physical stimuli and the effects they produce in the mind > ˌpsycho'physical *adj*

psychophysiology (ˌsaɪkəʊˌfɪzɪˈɒlədʒɪ) *n* the branch of psychology concerned with the physiological basis of mental processes > psychophysiological (ˌsaɪkəʊˌfɪzɪəˈlɒdʒɪkᵊl) *adj* > ˌpsychoˌphysi'ologist *n*

psychoprophylaxis (ˌsaɪkəʊˌprəʊfɪˈlæksɪs) *n* a method of preparing women for natural childbirth by means of special breathing and relaxation

psychosexual (ˌsaɪkəʊˈsɛksjʊəl) *adj* of or relating to the mental aspects of sex, such as sexual fantasies > ˌpsycho,sexu'ality *n* > ˌpsycho'sexually *adv*

psychosis (saɪˈkəʊsɪs) *n, pl* -choses (-ˈkəʊsiːz) any form of severe mental disorder in which the individual's contact with reality becomes highly distorted. Compare **neurosis** [c19 New Latin, from PSYCHO- + -OSIS]

psychosocial (ˌsaɪkəʊˈsəʊʃəl) *adj* of or relating to processes or factors that are both social and psychological in origin

psychosomatic (ˌsaɪkəʊsəˈmætɪk) *adj* of or relating to disorders, such as stomach ulcers, thought to be caused or aggravated by psychological factors such as stress

psychosurgery (ˌsaɪkəʊˈsɜːdʒərɪ) *n* any surgical procedure on the brain, such as a frontal lobotomy, to relieve serious mental disorders > psychosurgical (ˌsaɪkəʊˈsɜːdʒɪkᵊl) *adj*

psychosynthesis (ˌsaɪkəʊˈsɪnθɪsɪs) *n* a form of psychotherapy intended to release the patient's full potential by focusing on the positive rather than the negative

psychotherapy (ˌsaɪkəʊˈθɛrəpɪ) *or less commonly* **psychotherapeutics** (ˌsaɪkəʊˌθɛrəˈpjuːtɪks) *n* the treatment of nervous disorders by psychological methods > ˌpsychoˌthera'peutic *adj* > ˌpsychoˌthera'peutically *adv* > ˌpsycho'therapist *n*

psychotic (saɪˈkɒtɪk) *psychiatry* ⊳ *adj* **1** of, relating to, or characterized by psychosis ⊳ *n* **2** a person suffering from psychosis > psy'chotically *adv*

psychotomimetic (saɪˌkɒtəʊmɪˈmɛtɪk) *adj* (of drugs such as LSD and mescaline) capable of inducing psychotic symptoms

psychotropic (ˌsaɪkəʊˈtrɒpɪk) *adj* another word for **psychoactive**

psych out *vb* (*mainly tr, adverb*) *informal* **1** to guess correctly the intentions of (another); outguess **2** to analyse or solve (a problem, etc) psychologically **3** to intimidate or frighten **4** (*intr, adverb*) to lose control psychologically; break down

psychro- *combining form* cold: *psychrometer* [from Greek *psukhros*]

psychrometer (saɪˈkrɒmɪtə) *n* a type of hygrometer consisting of two thermometers, one of which has a dry bulb and the other a bulb that is kept moist and ventilated. The difference between the readings of the thermometers gives an indication of atmospheric humidity. Also called: wet-and-dry-bulb thermometer

psychrophilic (ˌsaɪkrəʊˈfɪlɪk) *adj* (esp of bacteria) showing optimum growth at low temperatures

p

psych up vb (tr, adverb) informal to get (oneself or another) into a state of psychological readiness for an action, performance, etc

psyllid ('sɪlɪd) or **psylla** ('sɪlə) n any homopterous insect of the family Psyllidae, which comprises the jumping plant lice. See **plant louse** (sense 2) [C19 from Greek psulla flea]

psyllium ('sɪlɪəm) n a grain, Plantago psafra, the husks of which are used medicinally as a laxative and to reduce blood cholesterol levels [C16 Latin, from Greek psulla flea, due to the resemblance of the seeds to fleas]

psyops ('saɪˌɒps) pl n short for **psychological operations**

pt abbreviation for **1** part **2** past tense **3** patient **4** payment **5** point **6** port **7** pro tempore **8** ▷ the internet domain name for Portugal

Pt (in place names) abbreviation for **1** Point **2** Port **3** ▷ the chemical symbol for platinum

PT abbreviation for **1** physical therapy **2** physical training **3** postal telegraph **4** pupil teacher **5** (in Britain, formerly) purchase tax **6** prothrombin time

pt. abbreviation for pint

pta symbol for peseta

PTA abbreviation for Parent-Teacher Association

Ptah (ptɑː, tɑː) n (in ancient Egypt) a major god worshipped as the creative power, esp at Memphis

ptarmigan ('tɑːmɪɡən) n, pl **-gans** or **-gan** any of several arctic and subarctic grouse of the genus Lagopus, esp L. mutus, which has a white winter plumage **2** (sometimes capital) a created domestic fancy pigeon with ruffled or curled feathers on the wings and back [C16 changed (perhaps influenced by Greek pteron wing) from Scottish Gaelic tarmachan, diminutive of tarmach, of obscure origin]

PT boat n patrol torpedo boat, the former US term for an **MTB**

Pte military abbreviation for private

pteridology (ˌtɛrɪ'dɒlədʒɪ) n the branch of botany concerned with the study of ferns and related plants [C19 from pterido-, from Greek pteris fern + -LOGY] > **pteridological** (ˌtɛrɪdəʊ'lɒdʒɪkəl) adj > ˌpteri'dologist n

pteridophyte ('tɛrɪdəʊˌfaɪt) n (in traditional classification) any plant of the division Pteridophyta, reproducing by spores and having vascular tissue, roots, stems, and leaves: includes the ferns, horsetails, and club mosses. In modern classifications these plants are placed in separate phyla [C19 from pterido-, from Greek pteris fern + -PHYTE] > **pteridophytic** (ˌtɛrɪdəʊ'fɪtɪk) or **pteridophytous** (ˌtɛrɪ'dɒfɪtəs) adj

pteridosperm ('tɛrɪdəˌspɜːm) n any extinct seed-producing fernlike plant of the group Pteridospermae. Also called: **seed fern** [C19 from Greek pteris a fern + -SPERM]

ptero- combining form wing, feather, or a part resembling a wing: pterodactyl [from Greek pteron wing, feather]

pterodactyl (ˌtɛrə'dæktɪl) n any extinct flying reptile of the genus Pterodactylus and related genera, having membranous wings supported on an elongated fourth digit. See also **pterosaur** [C19 from PTERO- + Greek daktulos finger]

pteropod ('tɛrəˌpɒd) n any small marine gastropod mollusc of the group or order Pteropoda, in which the foot is expanded into two winglike lobes for swimming and the shell is absent or thin-walled. Also called: **sea butterfly**

pterosaur ('tɛrəˌsɔː) n any extinct flying reptile of the order Pterosauria, of Jurassic and Cretaceous times: included the pterodactyls. Compare **dinosaur, plesiosaur**

-pterous or **-pteran** adj combining form indicating a specified number or type of wings: dipterous [from Greek -pteros, from pteron wing]

pterygial (tə'rɪdʒɪəl) adj zoology of or relating to a fin or wing [from Greek pterux wing]

pterygoid process ('tɛrɪˌɡɔɪd) n anatomy either of two long bony plates extending downwards from each side of the sphenoid bone within the skull [C18 pterygoid, from Greek pterugoeidēs, from pterux wing; see -OID]

pteryla ('tɛrɪlə) n, pl **-lae** (-ˌliː) ornithol any of the tracts of skin that bear contour feathers, arranged in lines along the body of a bird [C19 from New Latin, from Greek pteron feather + hulē wood, forest]

PTFE abbreviation for polytetrafluoroethylene

ptg abbreviation for printing

ptisan (tɪ'zæn) n **1** grape juice drained off without pressure **2** a variant spelling of **tisane** [C14 from Old French tisane, from Latin ptisana, from Greek ptisanē barley groats]

PTN abbreviation for public telephone network: the telephone network provided in Britain by British Telecom

PTO or **pto** abbreviation for please turn over

ptochocracy (təʊ'kɒkrəsɪ) n, pl **-cies** government by the poor [C18 from Greek, from ptochos poor + -CRACY]

Ptolemaeus (ˌtɒlɪ'miːəs) n a crater in the SE quadrant of the moon, about 140 kilometres (90 miles) in diameter

Ptolemaic (ˌtɒlɪ'meɪɪk) adj **1** of or relating to the 2nd century AD Greek astronomer, mathematician and geographer Ptolemy (Latin name Claudius Ptolemaeus) or to his conception of the universe **2** of or relating to the Macedonian dynasty that ruled Egypt from the death of Alexander the Great (323 BC) to the death of Cleopatra (30 BC)

Ptolemaic system n the theory of planetary motion developed by Ptolemy from the hypotheses of earlier philosophers, stating that the earth lay at the centre of the universe with the sun, the moon, and the known planets revolving around it in complicated orbits. Beyond the largest of these orbits lay a sphere of fixed stars. See also **epicycle** (sense 1). Compare **Copernican system**

Ptolemaist (ˌtɒlɪ'meɪɪst) n a believer in or adherent of the Ptolemaic system of the universe

ptomaine or **ptomain** ('təʊmeɪn) n any of a group of amines, such as cadaverine or putrescine, formed by decaying organic matter [C19 from Italian ptomaina, from Greek ptoma corpse, from piptein to fall]

ptomaine poisoning n a popular term for **food poisoning**. Ptomaines were once erroneously thought to be a cause of food poisoning

ptosis ('təʊsɪs) n, pl **ptoses** ('təʊsiːz) prolapse or drooping of a part, esp the eyelid [C18 from Greek: a falling] > **ptotic** ('tɒtɪk) adj

pts abbreviation for **1** parts **2** payments **3** points **4** ports

PTSD abbreviation for post-traumatic stress disorder

Pty Austral, NZ, and South African ▷ abbreviation for proprietary: used to denote a private limited company

ptyalin ('taɪəlɪn) n biochem an amylase secreted in the saliva of man and other animals [C19 from Greek ptualon saliva, from ptuein to spit]

ptyalism ('taɪəˌlɪzəm) n excessive secretion of saliva [C17 from Greek ptualismos, from ptualizein to produce saliva, from ptualon saliva]

p-type adj **1** (of a semiconductor) having a density of mobile holes in excess of that of conduction electrons **2** associated with or resulting from the movement of holes in a semiconductor: p-type conductivity. Compare **n-type**

Pu the chemical symbol for plutonium

pub (pʌb) n **1** chiefly Brit a building with a bar and one or more public rooms licensed for the sale and consumption of alcoholic drink, often also providing light meals. Formal name: **public house 2** Austral and NZ a hotel ▷ vb **pubs, pubbing, pubbed 3** (intr) informal to visit a pub or pubs (esp in the phrase **go pubbing**)

pub. abbreviation for **1** public **2** publication **3** published **4** publisher **5** publishing

pub-crawl informal, chiefly Brit ▷ n **1** a drinking tour of a number of pubs or bars ▷ vb **2** (intr) to make such a tour > 'pubˌcrawler n

pube ('pjuːb) n informal a pubic hair

puberty ('pjuːbətɪ) n the period at the beginning of adolescence when the sex glands become functional and the secondary sexual characteristics emerge. Also called: pubescence Related adj: **hebetic** [C14 from Latin pūbertās maturity, from pūber adult] > 'pubertal adj

puberulent (pjʊ'bɛrjʊlənt) adj biology covered with very fine down; finely pubescent [C19 from Latin pūber]

pubes ('pjuːbiːz) n, pl **pubes** ('pjuːbiːz) **1** the region above the external genital organs, covered with hair from the time of puberty **2** the pubic bones **3** the plural of **pubis** ▷ pl n ('pjuːbz) **4** informal pubic hair [from Latin]

pubescent (pjuː'bɛsᵊnt) adj **1** arriving or having arrived at puberty **2** (of certain plants and animals or their parts) covered with a layer of fine short hairs or down [C17 from Latin pūbēscere to reach manhood, from pūber adult] > pu'bescence n

pub grub n informal food served in a pub

pubic ('pjuːbɪk) adj of or relating to the pubes or pubis: pubic hair

pubis ('pjuːbɪs) n, pl **-bes** (-biːz) one of the three sections of the hipbone that forms part of the pelvis [C16 shortened from New Latin os pūbis bone of the PUBES]

public ('pʌblɪk) adj **1** of, relating to, or concerning the people as a whole **2** open or accessible to all: public gardens **3** performed or made openly or in the view of all: public proclamation **4** (prenominal) well-known or familiar to people in general: a public figure **5** (usually prenominal) maintained at the expense of, serving, or for the use of a community: a public library **6** open, acknowledged, or notorious: a public scandal **7** **go public a** (of a private company) to issue shares for subscription by the public **b** to reveal publicly hitherto confidential information ▷ n **8** the community or people in general **9** a part or section of the community grouped because of a common interest, activity, etc: the racing public [C15 from Latin pūblicus, changed from pōplicus of the people, from populus people]

public-address system n a system of one or more microphones, amplifiers, and loudspeakers for increasing the sound level of speech or music, used in auditoriums, public gatherings, etc. Sometimes shortened to: **PA system**

publican ('pʌblɪkən) n **1** (in Britain) a person who keeps a public house **2** (in ancient Rome) a public contractor, esp one who farmed the taxes of a province [C12 from Old French publicain, from Latin pūblicānus tax gatherer, from pūblicum state revenues]

public assistance n US payment given to individuals by government agencies on the basis of need

publication (ˌpʌblɪ'keɪʃən) n **1** the act or process of publishing a printed work **2** any printed work offered for sale or distribution **3** the act or an instance of making information public **4** the act of disseminating defamatory matter, esp by communicating it to a third person See **libel, slander**. Archaic word: publishment [C14 via Old French from Latin pūblicātiō confiscation of an individual's property, from pūblicāre to seize and assign to public use]

public bar n Brit a bar in a public house usually serving drinks at a cheaper price than in the saloon bar. Also called: **the public**. Compare **private bar**

public bill n (in Parliament) a bill dealing with public policy that usually applies to the whole country. Compare **private bill, hybrid bill**

public company n a limited company whose shares may be purchased by the public and traded freely on the open market and whose share capital is not less than a statutory minimum; public limited company. Compare **private company**

public convenience *n* a public lavatory, esp one in a public place

public corporation *n* (in Britain) an organization established to run a nationalized industry or state-owned enterprise. The chairman and board members are appointed by a government minister, and the government has overall control

public debt *n chiefly US* **1** the total financial obligations incurred by all governmental bodies of a nation **2** another name for **national debt**

public defender *n* (in the US) a lawyer engaged at public expense to represent indigent defendants

public domain *n* **1** *US* lands owned by a state or by the federal government **2** the status of a published work or invention upon which the copyright or patent has expired or which has not been patented or subject to copyright. It may thus be freely used by the public **3** **in the public domain** able to be discussed and examined freely by the general public

public enemy *n* a notorious person, such as a criminal, who is regarded as a menace to the public

public enterprise *n* economic activity by governmental organizations. Compare **private enterprise** (sense 1)

public expenditure *n* spending by central government, local authorities, and public corporations

public footpath *n* a footpath along which the public has right of way

public gallery *n* the gallery in a chamber of Parliament reserved for members of the public who wish to listen to the proceedings. Also called: **strangers' gallery**

public goods *pl n* services such as national defence, law enforcement, and road building, that are for the benefit of, and available to, all members of the public

public health inspector *n* (in Britain) a former name for **Environmental Health Officer**

public holiday *n* a holiday observed over the whole country

public house *n* **1** *Brit* the formal name for **pub** **2** *US and Canadian* an inn, tavern, or small hotel

public-interest group *n* the usual US and Canadian name for **pressure group**

publicist ('pʌblɪsɪst) *n* **1** a person who publicizes something, esp a press or publicity agent **2** a journalist **3** *rare* a person learned in public or international law

publicity (pʌ'blɪsɪtɪ) *n* **1 a** the technique or process of attracting public attention to people, products, etc, as by the use of the mass media **b** (*as modifier*): *a publicity agent* **2** public interest resulting from information supplied by such a technique or process **3** information used to draw public attention to people, products, etc **4** the state of being public [C18 via French from Medieval Latin *pūblicitās*; see PUBLIC]

publicize *or* **publicise** ('pʌblɪˌsaɪz) *vb* (*tr*) to bring to public notice; advertise

public law *n* **1** a law that applies to the public of a state or nation **2** the branch of law that deals with relations between a state and its individual members. Compare **private law**

Public Lending Right *n* the right of authors to receive payment when their books are borrowed from public libraries. Abbreviation: **PLR**

public-liability insurance *n* (in Britain) a form of insurance that pays compensation to a member of the public suffering injury or damage as a result of the policyholder or his employees failing to take reasonable care

public limited company *n* another name for **public company**. Abbreviation: **plc** *or* **PLC**

publicly ('pʌblɪklɪ) *adv* **1** in a public manner; without concealment; openly **2** in the name or with the consent of the public

public nuisance *n* **1** *law* an illegal act causing

harm to members of a particular community rather than to any individual **2** *informal* a person who is generally considered objectionable

public opinion *n* the attitude of the public, esp as a factor in determining the actions of government

public ownership *n* ownership by the state; nationalization

public prosecutor *n law* an official in charge of prosecuting important cases

Public Record Office *n* an institution in which official records are stored and kept available for inspection by the public

public relations *n* (*functioning as singular or plural*) **1 a** the practice of creating, promoting, or maintaining goodwill and a favourable image among the public towards an institution, public body, etc **b** the methods and techniques employed **c** (*as modifier*): *the public relations industry* **2** the condition of the relationship between an organization and the public **3** the professional staff employed to create, promote, or maintain a favourable relationship between an organization and the public. Abbreviation: **PR**

public school *n* **1** (in England and Wales) a private independent fee-paying secondary school **2** (in the US) any school that is part of a free local educational system

public sector *n* the part of an economy that consists of state-owned institutions, including nationalized industries and services provided by local authorities. Compare **private sector**

public servant *n* **1** an elected or appointed holder of a public office **2** *Austral and NZ* a member of the **public service** (sense 3). British equivalent: civil servant

public service *n* **1 a** government employment **b** the management and administration of the affairs of a political unit, esp the civil service **2 a** a service provided for the community **b** (*as modifier*): *a public-service announcement* **3** *Austral and NZ* the service responsible for the public administration of the government of a country. It excludes the legislative, judicial, and military branches. Members of the public service have no official political allegiance and are not generally affected by changes of governments. British equivalent: civil service

public-service corporation *n US* a private corporation that provides services to the community, such as telephone service, public transport

public speaking *n* the art or practice of making speeches to large audiences ▷ **public speaker** *n*

public spending *n* expenditure by central government, local authorities, and public enterprises

public-spirited *adj* having or showing active interest in public welfare or the good of the community

public transport *n* a system of buses, trains, etc, running on fixed routes, on which the public may travel

public utility *n* an enterprise concerned with the provision to the public of essentials, such as electricity or water. Also called (US): **public-service corporation**

public works *pl n* engineering projects and other constructions, financed and undertaken by a government for the community

publish ('pʌblɪʃ) *vb* **1** to produce and issue (printed or electronic matter) for distribution and sale **2** (*intr*) to have one's written work issued for publication **3** (*tr*) to announce formally or in public **4** (*tr*) to communicate (defamatory matter) to someone other than the person defamed: *to publish a libel* [C14 from Old French *puplier*, from Latin *pūblicāre* to make PUBLIC] ▷ **publishable** *adj* ▷ **publishing** *n*

publisher ('pʌblɪʃə) *n* **1** a company or person engaged in publishing periodicals, books, music, etc **2** *US and Canadian* the proprietor of a

newspaper or his representative

púcán ('puːkaːn) *n Irish* a traditional Connemara open sailing boat [Irish Gaelic]

puccoon (pə'kuːn) *n* **1** Also called: **alkanet** any of several North American boraginaceous plants of the genus *Lithospermum*, esp *L. canescens*, that yield a red dye. See also **gromwell 2** any of several other plants that yield a reddish dye, esp the bloodroot (**red puccoon**) **3** the dye from any of these plants [C17 of Algonquian origin; see POKEWEED]

puce (pjuːs) *n* **a** a colour varying from deep red to dark purplish-brown **b** (*as adjective*): *a puce carpet* [C18 shortened from French *couleur puce* flea colour, from Latin *pūlex* flea]

puck¹ (pʌk) *n* **1** a small disc of hard rubber used in ice hockey **2** a stroke at the ball in hurling **3** *Irish slang* a sharp blow ▷ *vb* (*tr*) **4** to strike (the ball) in hurling **5** *Irish slang* to strike hard; punch [C19 of unknown origin]

puck² (pʌk) *n* (*often capital*) a mischievous or evil spirit. Also called: Robin Goodfellow [Old English *pūca*, of obscure origin] ▷ '**puckish** *adj*

pucka ('pʌkə) *adj* a less common spelling of **pukka**

pucker ('pʌkə) *vb* **1** to gather or contract (a soft surface such as the skin of the face) into wrinkles or folds, or (of such a surface) to be so gathered or contracted ▷ *n* **2** a wrinkle, crease, or irregular fold [C16 perhaps related to POKE², from the creasing into baglike wrinkles]

puckerood (ˌpʌkə'ruːd) *adj NZ informal* ruined; exhausted [from Māori *pakaru* to shatter]

puck hog *n ice hockey informal* a player who is reluctant to pass the puck to other members of his or her team

pud (pʊd) *n Brit informal* short for **pudding**

pudding ('pʊdɪŋ) *n* **1** a sweetened usually cooked dessert made in many forms and of various ingredients, such as flour, milk, and eggs, with fruit, etc **2** a savoury dish, usually soft and consisting partially of pastry or batter: *steak-and-kidney pudding* **3** the dessert course in a meal **4** a sausage-like mass of seasoned minced meat, oatmeal, etc, stuffed into a prepared skin or bag and boiled [C13 *poding*; compare Old English *puduc* a wart, Low German *puddek* sausage] ▷ '**puddingy** *adj*

pudding club *n slang* the state of being pregnant (esp in the phrase **in the pudding club**)

pudding stone *n* a conglomerate rock in which there is a difference in colour or composition between the pebbles and the matrix

puddle ('pʌdᵊl) *n* **1** a small pool of water, esp of rain **2** a small pool of any liquid **3** a worked mixture of wet clay and sand that is impervious to water and is used to line a pond or canal **4** *rowing* the patch of eddying water left by the blade of an oar after completion of a stroke ▷ *vb* **5** (*tr*) to make (clay, etc) into puddle **6** (*tr*) to subject (iron) to puddling **7** (*intr*) to dabble or wade in puddles, mud, or shallow water **8** (*intr*) to mess about [C14 *podel*, diminutive of Old English *pudd* ditch, of obscure origin] ▷ '**puddler** *n* ▷ '**puddly** *adj*

puddling ('pʌdlɪŋ) *n* **1** a process for converting pig iron into wrought iron by heating it with ferric oxide in a furnace to oxidize the carbon **2** *building trades* the process of making a puddle

puddock ('pʌdək) *n* a Scot variant of **paddock²**

pudency ('pjuːdᵊnsɪ) *n* modesty, shame, or prudishness [C17 from Late Latin *pudentia*, from Latin *pudēre* to feel shame]

pudendum (pjuː'dɛndəm) *n, pl* **-da** (-də) (*often plural*) the human external genital organs collectively, esp of a female [C17 from Late Latin, from Latin *pudenda* the shameful (parts), from *pudēre* to be ashamed] ▷ pu'dendal *or* pudic ('pjuːdɪk) *adj*

pudge (pʌdʒ) *n informal* a variant of **podge** [C19 of uncertain origin; see PUDGY]

pudgy ('pʌdʒɪ) *adj* pudgier, pudgiest a variant spelling (esp US) of **podgy** [C19 of uncertain origin; compare earlier *pudsy* plump, perhaps from Scottish *pud* stomach, plump child] ▷ '**pudgily** *adv* ▷ '**pudginess** *n*

p

Pudsey ('pʌdzɪ) *n* a town in N England, in Leeds unitary authority, West Yorkshire. Pop: 32 391 (2001)

pudu ('puː,duː) *n* a diminutive Andean antelope, *Pudu pudu,* some 35 cm (13 to 14 in.) tall at the shoulder, with short straight horns and reddish-brown spotted coat [c19 its native name]

Puebla (*Spanish* 'pweβla) *n* **1** an inland state of S central Mexico, situated on the Anáhuac Plateau. Capital: Puebla. Pop: 5 070 346 (2000 est). Area: 33 919 sq km (13 096 sq miles) **2** a city in S Mexico, capital of Puebla state: founded in 1532; university (1537). Pop: 1 880 000 (2005 est). Full name: **Puebla de Zaragoza** (de θara'ɣoθa)

pueblo ('pweblaʊ; *Spanish* 'pweβlo) *n, pl* **-los** (-laʊz; *Spanish* -los) **1** a communal village, built by certain Indians of the southwestern US and parts of Latin America, consisting of one or more flat-roofed stone or adobe houses **2** (in Spanish America) a village or town **3** (in the Philippines) a town or township [c19 from Spanish: people, from Latin *populus*]

Pueblo¹ ('pweblaʊ) *n, pl* **-lo** or **-los** a member of any of the North American Indian peoples who live in pueblos, including the Tanoans, Zuñi, and Hopi

Pueblo² ('pweblaʊ) *n* a city in Colorado: a centre of the steel industry. Pop: 103 648 (2003 est)

puerile ('pjʊəraɪl) *adj* **1** exhibiting silliness; immature; trivial **2** of or characteristic of a child [c17 from Latin *puerīlis* childish, from *puer* a boy] > '**puerilely** *adv* > **puerility** (pjʊə'rɪlɪtɪ) *n*

puerilism ('pjʊərɪ,lɪzəm) *n psychiatry* immature or childish behaviour by an adult

puerperal (pjuː'ɜːpərəl) *adj* of, relating to, or occurring during the puerperium [c18 from New Latin *puerperālis* relating to childbirth; see PUERPERIUM]

puerperal fever *n* a serious, formerly widespread, form of blood poisoning caused by infection contracted during childbirth

puerperal psychosis *n* a mental disorder sometimes occurring in women after childbirth, characterized by deep depression, delusions of the child's death, and homicidal feelings towards the child

puerperium (pjʊə'pɪərɪəm) *n* the period following childbirth, lasting approximately six weeks, during which the uterus returns to its normal size and shape [c17 from Latin: childbirth, from *puerperus* relating to a woman in labour, from *puer* boy + *parere* to bear]

Puerto Rican ('pwɜːtəʊ 'riːkən, 'pwɛə-) *adj* **1** of or relating to Puerto Rico or its inhabitants ▷ *n* **2** a native or inhabitant of Puerto Rico

Puerto Rico ('pwɜːtəʊ 'riːkəʊ, 'pwɛə-) *n* an autonomous commonwealth (in association with the US) occupying the smallest and easternmost of the Greater Antilles in the Caribbean: one of the most densely populated areas in the world; ceded by Spain to the US in 1899. Currency: US dollar. Capital: San Juan. Pop: 3 897 000 (2004 est). Area: 9104 sq km (3515 sq miles). Former name (until 1932): **Porto Rico.** Abbreviation: **PR**

puff (pʌf) *n* **1** a short quick draught, gust, or emission, as of wind, smoke, air, etc, esp a forceful one **2** the amount of wind, smoke, etc, released in a puff **3** the sound made by or associated with a puff **4** an instance of inhaling and expelling the breath as in smoking **5** a swelling **6** a light aerated pastry usually filled with cream, jam, etc **7** a powder puff **8** exaggerated praise, as of a book, product, etc, esp through an advertisement **9** a piece of clothing fabric gathered up so as to bulge in the centre while being held together at the edges **10** a loose piece of hair wound into a cylindrical roll, usually over a pad, and pinned in place in a coiffure **11** a less common word for **quilt** (sense 1) **12** one's breath (esp in the phrase **out of puff**) **13** *derogatory slang* a male homosexual **14** a dialect word for **puffball** ▷ *vb* **15** to blow or breathe or cause to blow or breathe in short quick draughts or blasts

16 (*tr; often foll by out; usually passive*) to cause to be out of breath **17** to take puffs or draws at (a cigarette, cigar, or pipe) **18** to move with or by the emission of puffs: *the steam train puffed up the incline* **19** (*often foll by up, out, etc*) to swell, as with air, pride, etc **20** (*tr*) to praise with exaggerated empty words, often in advertising **21** (*tr*) to apply (cosmetic powder) from a powder puff to (the face) **22** to increase the price of (a lot in an auction) artificially by having an accomplice make false bids [Old English *pyffan*; related to Dutch German *puffen,* Swiss *pfuffen,* Norwegian *puffa,* all of imitative origin]

puff adder *n* **1** a large venomous African viper, *Bitis arietans,* that is yellowish-grey with brown markings and inflates its body when alarmed **2** another name for **hognose snake**

puffball ('pʌf,bɔːl) *n* any of various basidiomycetous saprotrophic fungi of the genera *Calvatia* and *Lycoperdon,* having a round fruiting body that discharges a cloud of brown spores when mature

puffbird ('pʌf,bɜːd) *n* any of various brownish tropical American birds of the family *Bucconidae,* having a large head: order *Piciformes* (woodpeckers, etc) [c19 so called because of its habit of puffing out its feathers]

puffer ('pʌfə) *n* **1** a person or thing that puffs **2** Also called: **globefish** any marine plectognath fish of the family *Tetraodontidae,* having an elongated spiny body that can be inflated to form a globe

puffery ('pʌfərɪ) *n, pl* **-eries** *informal* exaggerated praise, esp in publicity or advertising

puffin ('pʌfɪn) *n* any of various northern diving birds of the family *Alcidae* (auks, etc), esp *Fratercula arctica* (**common** or **Atlantic puffin**), having a black-and-white plumage and a brightly coloured vertically flattened bill: order *Charadriiformes* [c14 perhaps of Cornish origin]

puffin crossing *n* a UK pedestrian road crossing with traffic lights signalling red to stop the traffic flow when pedestrians are seen on the crossing by infrared detectors. The green signal reappears when no pedestrians are seen on the crossing [c20 p(edestrian) u(ser) f(riendly) in(telligent) crossing]

puff pastry or *US* **puff paste** *n* a dough rolled in thin layers incorporating fat to make a rich flaky pastry for pies, rich pastries, etc

puff piece *n* a flattering newspaper or magazine article about a person or an organization

puff-puff *n Brit* a children's name for a steam locomotive or railway train

puffy ('pʌfɪ) *adj* **puffier, puffiest 1** short of breath **2** swollen or bloated: *a puffy face* **3** pompous or conceited **4** blowing in gusts > '**puffily** *adv* > '**puffiness** *n*

pug¹ (pʌg) *n* **1** Also called: **carlin** a small compact breed of dog with a smooth coat, lightly curled tail, and a short wrinkled nose **2** any of several small geometrid moths, mostly of the genus *Eupithecia,* with slim forewings held outstretched at rest [c16 of uncertain origin] > '**puggish** *adj*

pug² (pʌg) *vb* **pugs, pugging, pugged** (*tr*) **1** to mix or knead (clay) with water to form a malleable mass or paste, often in a **pug mill 2** to fill or stop with clay or a similar substance **3** (of cattle) to trample (the ground) into consolidated mud [c19 of uncertain origin]

pug³ (pʌg) *n* a slang name for **boxer** (sense 1) [c20 shortened from PUGILIST]

Puget Sound ('pjuːdʒɪt) *n* an inlet of the Pacific in NW Washington. Length: about 130 km (80 miles)

pugging ('pʌgɪŋ) *n* material such as clay, mortar, sawdust, sand, etc, inserted between wooden flooring and ceiling to reduce the transmission of sound. Also called: **pug**

puggree, pugree ('pʌgrɪ) or **puggaree, pugaree** ('pʌgərɪ) *n* **1** the usual Indian word for **turban 2** a scarf, usually pleated, around the crown of some hats, esp sun helmets [c17 from

Hindi *pagrī,* from Sanskrit *parikara*]

puggy ('pʌgɪ) *adj* **-gier, -giest** *NZ* sticky, claylike [probably from PUG²]

pugilism ('pjuːdʒɪ,lɪzəm) *n* the art, practice, or profession of fighting with the fists; boxing [c18 from Latin *pugil* a boxer; related to *pugnus* fist, *pugna* a fight] > '**pugilist** *n* > ,**pugi'listic** *adj* > ,**pugi'listically** *adv*

Puglia ('puːʎʎa) *n* the Italian name for **Apulia**

pugnacious (pʌg'neɪʃəs) *adj* readily disposed to fight; belligerent [c17 from Latin *pugnāx*] > **pug'naciously** *adv* > **pugnacity** (pʌg'næsɪtɪ) or **pug'naciousness** *n*

pug nose *n* a short stubby upturned nose [c18 from PUG¹] > '**pug-,nosed** *adj*

Pugwash conferences ('pʌg,wɒʃ) *pl n* international peace conferences of scientists held regularly to discuss world problems: Nobel peace prize 1995 awarded to Joseph Rotblat, one of the founders of the conferences, secretary-general (1957–73), and president from 1988 [c20 from *Pugwash,* Nova Scotia, where the first conference was held]

puha ('puːhaː) *n NZ* another name for **sow thistle** [Māori]

puh-leeze (,pə'liːz) *interj* a humorous spelling of the emphatic pronunciation of *please,* suggesting the speaker's exasperation

puir (puːr, pyr) *adj* a Scot word for **poor**

puirtith or **poortith** ('puːr,tɪθ, 'pyr-) *n Scot* poverty [c16 from Old French *pouerteit, poverteit;* compare POVERTY]

puisne ('pjuːnɪ) *adj* (esp of a subordinate judge) of lower rank [c16 from Anglo-French, from Old French *puisné* born later, from *puis* at a later date, from Latin *posteā* afterwards + *né* born, from *naistre* to be born, from Latin *nascī*]

puissance ('pjuːɪsᵊns, 'pwiːsɑːns) *n* **1** a competition in showjumping that tests a horse's ability to jump a limited number of large obstacles **2** *archaic* or *poetic* power [c15 from Old French; see PUISSANT]

puissant ('pjuːɪsᵊnt) *adj archaic* or *poetic* powerful [c15 from Old French, ultimately from Latin *potēns* mighty, from *posse* to have power] > '**puissantly** *adv*

puja ('puːdʒa) *n Hinduism* a ritual in honour of the gods, performed either at home or in the mandir (temple) [from Sanskrit: worship]

puka ('puːkaː) *n, pl* **puka** *NZ* another name for **broadleaf** (sense 2) [Māori]

pukatea ('puːkaːtɛa) *n* an aromatic New Zealand tree, *Laurelia novaezealandaei,* valued for its high-quality timber [Māori]

puke (pjuːk) *slang* ▷ *vb* **1** to vomit ▷ *n* **2** the act of vomiting **3** the matter vomited [c16 probably of imitative origin; compare German *spucken* to spit]

pukeko ('pʊkəkəʊ) *n, pl* **-kos** a wading bird, *Porphyrio melanotus,* of New Zealand, with a brightly coloured plumage [Māori]

pukka or **pucka** ('pʌkə) *adj* (esp in India) **1** properly or perfectly done, constructed, etc: *a pukka road* **2** genuine: *pukka sahib* [c17 from Hindi *pakkā* firm, from Sanskrit *pakva*]

puku ('puːkuː) *n NZ* the belly or stomach [Māori]

pul (puːl) *n, pl* **puls** or **puli** ('puːlɪ) an Afghan monetary unit worth one hundredth of an afghani [via Persian from Turkish: small coin, from Late Greek *phollis* bag for money, from Latin *follis* bag]

pula ('puːlə) *n* the standard monetary unit of Botswana, divided into 100 thebe

Pula (*Serbo-Croat* 'puːla) *n* a port in NW Croatia at the S tip of the Istrian Peninsula: made a Roman military base in 178 BC; became the main Austro-Hungarian naval station and passed to Italy in 1919, to Yugoslavia in 1947, and is now in independent Croatia. Pop: 62 300 (1991). Latin name: **Pietas Julia** (paɪ'ɛɪtas 'juːlɪə) Italian name: **Pola**

pulao (pʊ'laʊ) *n* a variant of **pilau**

Pulau Pinang ('pʊlaʊ pɪ'næŋ) *n* another name for **Penang**

pulchritude ('pʌlkrɪˌtjuːd) *n formal or literary* physical beauty [C15 from Latin *pulchritūdō*, from *pulcher* beautiful] > ˌpulchri'tudinous *adj*

pule (pjuːl) *vb* (*intr*) to cry plaintively; whimper [C16 perhaps of imitative origin] > 'puler *n*

puli ('pjuːlɪ, 'pʊlɪ) *n* a breed of Hungarian sheepdog having a very long dense coat, usually black, that hangs in strands with a ropey or corded appearance [Hungarian, literally: leader]

Pulitzer prize ('pʊlɪtsə) *n* one of a group of prizes established by Hungarian-born US newspaper publisher Joseph Pulitzer (1847–1911) and awarded yearly since 1917 for excellence in American journalism, literature, and music

pulk (pʌlk) *n* a sledge that is pulled by dogs while a person skis behind to steer and brake [C19 from Finnish *pulkka*, from Sami *pulkke*]

pull (pʊl) *vb* (*mainly tr*) **1** (*also intr*) to exert force on (an object) so as to draw it towards the source of the force **2** to exert force on so as to remove; extract: *to pull a tooth* **3** to strip of feathers, hair, etc; pluck **4** to draw the entrails from (a fowl) **5** to rend or tear **6** to strain (a muscle, ligament, or tendon) injuriously **7** (usually foll by *off*) *informal* to perform or bring about: *to pull off a million-pound deal* **8** (often foll by *on*) *informal* to draw out (a weapon) for use: *he pulled a knife on his attacker* **9** *informal* to attract: *the pop group pulled a crowd* **10** (*also intr*) *slang* to attract (a sexual partner) **11** (*intr*; usually foll by *on* or *at*) to drink or inhale deeply: *to pull at one's pipe; pull on a bottle of beer* **12** to put on or make (a grimace): *to pull a face* **13** (*also intr*; foll by *away*, *out*, *over*, etc) to move (a vehicle) or (of a vehicle) be moved in a specified manner: *he pulled his car away from the roadside* **14** *printing* to take (a proof) from type **15** to withdraw or remove: *the board decided to pull their support* **16** *sport* to hit (a ball) so that it veers away from the direction in which the player intended to hit it (to the left for a right-handed player) **17** *cricket* to hit (a ball pitched straight or on the off side) to the leg side **18** *hurling* to strike (a fast-moving ball) in the same direction as it is already moving **19** (*also intr*) to row (a boat) or take a stroke of (an oar) in rowing **20** to be rowed by: *a racing shell pulls one, two, four, or eight oars* **21** (of a rider) to restrain (a horse), esp to prevent it from winning a race **22** (*intr*) (of a horse) to resist strongly the attempts of a rider to rein in or check it **23** **pull a fast one** *slang* to play a sly trick **24** **pull apart** *or* **to pieces** to criticize harshly **25** **pull your head in** *Austral informal* be quiet! **26** **pull (one's) punches** **a** *informal* to restrain the force of one's criticisms or actions **b** *boxing* to restrain the force of one's blows, esp when deliberately losing after being bribed, etc **27** **pull one's weight** *informal* to do one's fair or proper share of a task **28** **pull strings** *informal* to exercise personal influence, esp secretly or unofficially **29** **pull (someone's) leg** *informal* to make fun of, fool, or tease (someone) ▷ *n* **30** an act or an instance of pulling or being pulled **31** the force or effort used in pulling: *the pull of the moon affects the tides on earth* **32** the act or an instance of taking in drink or smoke **33** something used for pulling, such as a knob or handle **34** *informal* special advantage or influence: *his uncle is chairman of the company, so he has quite a lot of pull* **35** *informal* the power to attract attention or support **36** a period of rowing **37** a single stroke of an oar in rowing **38** the act of pulling the ball in golf, cricket, etc **39** the act of checking or reining in a horse **40** the amount of resistance in a bowstring, trigger, etc ▷ See also **pull about, pull back, pull down, pull in, pull off, pull on, pull out, pull over, pull through, pull together, pull up** [Old English *pullian*; related to Icelandic *pūla* to beat] > 'puller *n*

pull about *vb* (*tr, adverb*) to handle roughly

pull back *vb* (*adverb*) **1** to return or be returned to a rearward position by pulling: *the army pulled back* ▷ *n* **pullback** **2** the act of pulling back **3** a device for restraining the motion of a mechanism, etc, or for returning it to its original position

pull down *vb* (*tr, adverb*) to destroy or demolish: *the old houses were pulled down*

pullet ('pʊlɪt) *n* a young hen of the domestic fowl, less than one year old [C14 from Old French *poulet* chicken, from Latin *pullus* a young animal or bird]

pulley ('pʊlɪ) *n* **1** a wheel with a grooved rim in which a rope, chain, or belt can run in order to change the direction or point of application of a force applied to the rope, etc **2** a number of such wheels pivoted in parallel in a block, used to raise heavy loads **3** a wheel with a flat, convex, or grooved rim mounted on a shaft and driven by or driving a belt passing around it [C14 *poley*, from Old French *polie*, from Vulgar Latin *polidium* (unattested), apparently from Late Greek *polidion* (unattested) a little pole, from Greek *polos* axis]

pull in *vb* (*adverb*) **1** (*intr*; often foll by *to*) to reach a destination: *the train pulled in at the station* **2** (*intr*) Also: **pull over** (of a motor vehicle, driver, etc) **a** to draw in to the side of the road in order to stop or to allow another vehicle to pass **b** to stop (at a café, lay-by, etc) **3** (*tr*) to draw or attract: *his appearance will pull in the crowds* **4** (*tr*) *slang* to arrest **5** (*tr*) to earn or gain (money) ▷ *n* **pull-in** **6** *Brit* a roadside café, esp for lorry drivers

Pullman ('pʊlmən) *n, pl* **-mans** a luxurious railway coach, esp a sleeping car. Also called: **Pullman car** [C19 named after George M. *Pullman* (1831–97), the US inventor who first manufactured such coaches]

pull off *vb* (*tr*) **1** to remove (clothing) forcefully **2** (*adverb*) to succeed in performing (a difficult feat) **3** (*intr*) (of a motor vehicle, driver, etc) to move to the side of the road and stop **4** (*intr*) (of a motor vehicle, driver, etc) to start to move

pull on *vb* (*tr, adverb*) to don (clothing)

pullorum disease (pʊ'lɔːrəm) *n* an acute serious bacterial disease of very young birds, esp chickens, characterized by a whitish diarrhoea: caused by *Salmonella pullorum*, transmitted during egg production. Also called: **bacillary white diarrhoea** [Latin *pullōrum* of chickens, from *pullus* chicken]

pull out *vb* (*adverb*) **1** (*tr*) to extract **2** (*intr*) to depart: *the train pulled out of the station* **3** *military* to withdraw or escape or be withdrawn or rescued, as from a difficult situation **4** (*intr*) (of a motor vehicle, driver, etc) **a** to draw away from the side of the road **b** to draw out from behind another vehicle to overtake **5** (*intr*) to abandon a position or situation, esp a dangerous or embarrassing one **6** (foll by *of*) to level out or cause to level out (from a dive) ▷ *n* **pull-out** **7** an extra leaf of a book that folds out **8** a removable section of a magazine, etc **9** a flight manoeuvre during which an aircraft levels out after a dive **10** a withdrawal from a position or situation, esp a dangerous or embarrassing one

pullover ('pʊlˌəʊvə) *n* a garment, esp a sweater, that is pulled on over the head

pull over *vb* (*intr*) **1** (*intr*) (of a motor vehicle, driver, etc) to halt at the side of the road **2** (*tr*) (of a police officer) to instruct (the driver of a motor vehicle) to halt at the side of the road

pull through *vb* **1** Also: **pull round** to survive or recover or cause to survive or recover, esp after a serious illness or crisis ▷ *n* **pull-through** **2** a weighted cord with a piece of cloth at the end used to clean the bore of a firearm

pull together *vb* **1** (*intr, adverb*) to cooperate or work harmoniously **2** **pull oneself together** *informal* to regain one's self-control or composure

pullulate ('pʌljʊˌleɪt) *vb* (*intr*) **1** (of animals, etc) to breed rapidly or abundantly; teem; swarm **2** (of plants or plant parts) to sprout, bud, or germinate [C17 from Latin *pullulāre* to sprout, from *pullulus* a baby animal, from *pullus* young animal] > ˌpullu'lation *n*

pull up *vb* (*adverb*) **1** (*tr*) to remove by the roots **2** (often foll by *with* or *on*) to move level (with) or ahead (of) or cause to move level (with) or ahead (of), esp in a race **3** to stop **4** (*tr*) to rebuke ▷ *n* **pull-up** **5** an exercise in which the body is raised up by the arms pulling on a horizontal bar fixed above the head **6** *Brit old-fashioned* a roadside café

pullus ('pʊləs) *n* a technical term for a chick or young bird [C18 from Latin, from *pullulare* to sprout]

pulmonary ('pʌlmənərɪ, -mənrɪ, 'pʊl-) *adj* **1** of, or relating to or affecting the lungs **2** having lungs or lunglike organs [C18 from Latin *pulmōnārius*, from *pulmō* a lung; related to Greek *pleumōn* a lung]

pulmonary artery *n* either of the two arteries that convey oxygen-depleted blood from the heart to the lungs

pulmonary vein *n* any one of the four veins that convey oxygen-rich blood from the lungs to the heart

pulmonate ('pʌlmənɪt, 'pʊl-) *adj* **1** having lungs or lunglike organs **2** of, relating to, or belonging to the *Pulmonata*, a mostly terrestrial subclass or order of gastropod molluscs, including snails and slugs, in which the mantle is adapted as a lung ▷ *n* **3** any pulmonate mollusc [C19 from New Latin *pulmōnātus*]

pulmonic (pʌl'mɒnɪk, pʊl-) *adj* **1** of or relating to the lungs; pulmonary ▷ *n* **2** *rare* **a** a person with lung disease **b** a drug or remedy for lung disease [C17 from French *pulmonique*, from Latin *pulmō* a lung; see PULMONARY]

Pulmotor ('pʌlˌməʊtə, 'pʊl-) *n trademark* an apparatus for pumping oxygen into the lungs during artificial respiration

pulp (pʌlp) *n* **1** soft or fleshy plant tissue, such as the succulent part of a fleshy fruit **2** a moist mixture of cellulose fibres, as obtained from wood, from which paper is made **3** **a** a magazine or book containing trite or sensational material, and usually printed on cheap rough paper **b** (*as modifier*): *a pulp novel* **4** *dentistry* the soft innermost part of a tooth, containing nerves and blood vessels **5** any soft soggy mass or substance **6** *mining* pulverized ore, esp when mixed with water ▷ *vb* **7** to reduce (a material or solid substance) to pulp or (of a material or solid substance) to be reduced to pulp **8** (*tr*) to remove the pulp from (fruit) [C16 from Latin *pulpa*] > 'pulper *n*

pulpit ('pʊlpɪt) *n* **1** a raised platform, usually surrounded by a barrier, set up in churches as the appointed place for preaching, leading in prayer, etc **2** any similar raised structure, such as a lectern **3** a medium for expressing an opinion, such as a column in a newspaper **4** (usually preceded by *the*) **a** the preaching of the Christian message **b** the clergy or their message and influence [C14 from Latin *pulpitum* a platform]

pulpitum ('pʊlpɪtəm) *n* (in many cathedrals and large churches) a stone screen which divides the nave and the choir, often supporting a gallery or loft [C19 from Latin *pulpitum* a platform]

pulpwood ('pʌlpˌwʊd) *n* pine, spruce, or any other soft wood used to make paper

pulpy ('pʌlpɪ) *adj* **pulpier, pulpiest** having a soft or soggy consistency > 'pulpily *adv* > 'pulpiness *n*

pulque ('pʊlkɪ; *Spanish* 'pulke) *n* a light alcoholic drink from Mexico made from the juice of various agave plants, esp the maguey [C17 from Mexican Spanish, apparently from Nahuatl, from *puliuhqui* decomposed, since it will only keep for a day]

pulsar ('pʌlˌsɑː) *n* any of a number of very small extremely dense objects first observed in 1967, which rotate very rapidly and emit very regular pulses of polarized radiation, esp radio waves. They are thought to be neutron stars formed following supernova explosions [C20 from *puls(ating st)ar*, on the model of QUASAR]

pulsate (pʌl'seɪt) *vb* (*intr*) **1** to expand and contract with a rhythmic beat; throb **2** *physics* to vary in intensity, magnitude, size, etc: *the current was pulsating* **3** to quiver or vibrate [C18 from Latin *pulsāre* to push] > **pulsative** ('pʌlsətɪv) *adj* > 'pulsatively *adv*

pulsatile ('pʌlsəˌtaɪl) *adj* beating rhythmically;

p

pulsating or throbbing > **pulsatility** (ˌpʌlsəˈtɪlɪtɪ) n

pulsatilla (ˌpʌlsəˈtɪlə) n another name for **pasqueflower** [c16 from Medieval Latin, from *pulsāta* beaten (by the wind)]

pulsating star n a type of variable star, the variation in brightness resulting from expansion and subsequent contraction of the star

pulsation (pʌlˈseɪʃən) n 1 the act of pulsating 2 *physiol* a rhythmic beating or pulsing esp of the heart or an artery

pulsator (pʌlˈseɪtə) n 1 a device that stimulates rhythmic motion of a body; a vibrator 2 any pulsating machine, device, or part

pulsatory (ˈpʌlsətərɪ, -trɪ) adj 1 of or relating to pulsation 2 throbbing or pulsating

pulse[1] (pʌls) n 1 *physiol* a the rhythmic contraction and expansion of an artery at each beat of the heart, often discernible to the touch at points such as the wrists b a single pulsation of the heart or arteries 2 *physics, electronics* a a transient sharp change in voltage, current, or some other quantity normally constant in a system b one of a series of such transient disturbances, usually recurring at regular intervals and having a characteristic geometric shape c (*as modifier*): *a pulse generator*. Less common name: **impulse** 3 a recurrent rhythmic series of beats, waves, vibrations, etc b any single beat, wave, etc, in such a series 4 bustle, vitality, or excitement: *the pulse of a city* 5 the feelings or thoughts of a group or society as they can be measured: *the pulse of the voters* 6 **keep one's finger on the pulse** to be well-informed about current events ▷ vb 7 (*intr*) to beat, throb, or vibrate [c14 *pous*, from Latin *pulsus* a beating, from *pellere* to beat] > **pulseless** adj

pulse[2] (pʌls) n 1 the edible seeds of any of several leguminous plants, such as peas, beans, and lentils 2 the plant producing any of these seeds [c13 *pols*, from Old French, from Latin *puls* pottage of pulse]

pulse code modulation n *electronics* a form of pulse modulation in which the information is carried by coded groups of pulses. Abbreviation: **pcm**

pulse height analyser n *electronics* a multichannel analyser that sorts pulses into selected amplitude ranges

pulsejet (ˈpʌlsˌdʒɛt) n a type of ramjet engine in which air is admitted through movable vanes that are closed by the pressure resulting from each intermittent explosion of the fuel in the combustion chamber, thus causing a pulsating thrust. Also called: **pulsejet engine, pulsojet** (ˈpʌlsəʊˌdʒɛt)

pulse modulation n *electronics* 1 a type of modulation in which a train of pulses is used as the carrier wave, one or more of its parameters, such as amplitude, being modulated or modified in order to carry information 2 the modulation of a continuous carrier wave by means of pulses

pulsimeter (pʌlˈsɪmɪtə) n *med* an instrument for measuring the strength and rate of the pulse. Also called: **pulsometer**

pulsometer (pʌlˈsɒmɪtə) n 1 another name for **pulsimeter** 2 a vacuum pump that operates by steam being condensed and water admitted alternately in two chambers

pulverable (ˈpʌlvərəbᵊl) adj able to be pulverized

pulverize or **pulverise** (ˈpʌlvəˌraɪz) vb 1 to reduce (a substance) to fine particles, as by crushing or grinding, or (of a substance) to be so reduced 2 (*tr*) to destroy completely; defeat or injure seriously [c16 from Late Latin *pulverizare* or French *pulvériser*, from Latin *pulverum*, from *pulvis* dust] > ˌpulverˈizable or ˌpulverˈisable adj > ˌpulveriˈzation or ˌpulveriˈsation n > ˈpulverˌizer or ˈpulverˌiser n

pulverulent (pʌlˈvɛrʊlənt) adj consisting of, covered with, or crumbling to dust or fine particles [c17 from Latin *pulverulentus*, from *pulvis* dust] > pulˈverulence n

pulvillus (pʌlˈvɪləs) n, pl -li (-laɪ) a small pad between the claws at the end of an insect's leg [c18 from Latin, from *pulvīnulus*, diminutive of *pulvinus* cushion]

pulvinate (ˈpʌlvɪˌneɪt) or **pulvinated** adj 1 *architect* (of a frieze) curved convexly; having a swelling 2 *botany* a shaped like a cushion b (of a leafstalk) having a pulvinus [c19 from Latin *pulvīnātus* cushion-shaped]

pulvinus (pʌlˈvaɪnəs) n, pl -ni (-naɪ) a swelling at the base of a leafstalk: changes in its turgor pressure cause changes in the position of the leaf [c19 from Latin: cushion]

puma (ˈpjuːmə) n a large American feline mammal, *Felis concolor*, that resembles a lion, having a plain greyish-brown coat and long tail. Also called: **cougar, mountain lion** [c18 via Spanish from Quechuan]

pumice (ˈpʌmɪs) n 1 Also called: **pumice stone** a light porous acid volcanic rock having the composition of rhyolite, used for scouring and, in powdered form, as an abrasive and for polishing ▷ vb 2 (*tr*) to rub or polish with pumice [c15 *pomys*, from Old French *pomis*, from Latin *pūmex*] > **pumiceous** (pjuːˈmɪʃəs) adj

pumice country n NZ volcanic farmland in the North Island

pummel (ˈpʌməl) vb -mels, -melling, -melled or US -mels, -meling, -meled (*tr*) to strike repeatedly with or as if with the fists. Also (less commonly): **pommel** [c16 see POMMEL]

pump[1] (pʌmp) n 1 any device for compressing, driving, raising, or reducing the pressure of a fluid, esp by means of a piston or set of rotating impellers 2 *biology* a mechanism for the active transport of ions, such as protons, calcium ions, and sodium ions, across cell membranes: *a sodium pump* ▷ vb 3 (when *tr*, usually foll by *from, out, into, away*, etc) to raise or drive (air, liquid, etc, esp into or from something) with a pump or similar device 4 (*tr*; usually foll by *in* or *into*) to supply in large amounts: *to pump capital into a project* 5 (*tr*) to deliver (shots, bullets, etc) repeatedly with great force 6 to operate (something, esp a handle or lever) in the manner of a pump or (of something) to work in this way: *to pump the pedals of a bicycle* 7 (*tr*) to obtain (information) from (a person) by persistent questioning 8 (*intr*; usually foll by *from* or *out of*) (of liquids) to flow freely in large spurts: *oil pumped from the fissure* [c15 from Middle Dutch *pumpe* pipe, probably from Spanish *bomba*, of imitative origin]

pump[2] (pʌmp) n 1 a low-cut low-heeled shoe without fastenings, worn esp for dancing 2 a type of shoe with a rubber sole, used in games such as tennis; plimsoll [c16 of unknown origin]

pump-action adj 1 (of a shotgun or other repeating firearm) operated by a slide-action mechanism feeding ammunition from a magazine under the barrel into the breech 2 spraying or dispensing liquid by means of a pump rather than using a propellant

pumped storage n (in hydroelectric systems) a method of using power at a period of low demand to pump water back up to a high storage reservoir so that it can be released to generate electricity at a period of peak demand

pumpernickel (ˈpʌmpəˌnɪkᵊl) n a slightly sour black bread, originating in Germany, made of coarse rye flour [c18 from German, of uncertain origin]

pump gun n a repeating gun operated by a slide-action mechanism feeding ammunition from a magazine under the barrel into the breech

pump iron vb (*intr*) *slang* to exercise with weights; do body-building exercises

pumpkin (ˈpʌmpkɪn) n 1 any of several creeping cucurbitaceous plants of the genus *Cucurbita*, esp C. *pepo* of North America and C. *maxima* of Europe 2 a the large round fruit of any of these plants, which has a thick orange rind, pulpy flesh, and numerous seeds b (*as modifier*): *pumpkin pie* 3 (*often capital*) *chiefly US* a term of endearment [c17 from

earlier *pumpion*, from Old French *pompon*, from Latin *pepo*, from Greek *pepōn*, from *pepōn* ripe, from *peptein* to ripen]

pumpking or **pumpkin holder** (ˈpʌmpkɪn) n *computing* a person involved in a web-based project who has temporary but exclusive authority to make changes to the master source code [c20 PUMP(KIN) + KING; from an original practice involving a stuffed pumpkin which was passed to this person]

pumpkinseed (ˈpʌmpkɪnˌsiːd) n 1 the seed of the pumpkin 2 a common North American freshwater sunfish, *Lepomis gibbosus*, with brightly coloured markings: family *Centrarchidae*

pump priming n 1 the act or process of introducing fluid into a pump to improve the sealing of the pump parts on starting and to expel air from it 2 US government expenditure designed to stimulate economic activity in stagnant or depressed areas 3 another term for **deficit financing**

pump room n a building or room at a spa in which the water from a mineral spring may be drunk

pun[1] (pʌn) n 1 the use of words or phrases to exploit ambiguities and innuendoes in their meaning, usually for humorous effect; a play on words. An example is: "Ben Battle was a soldier bold, And used to war's alarms: But a cannonball took off his legs, So he laid down his arms." (Thomas Hood) ▷ vb puns, punning, punned 2 (*intr*) to make puns [c17 possibly from Italian *puntiglio* point of detail, wordplay; see PUNCTILIO]

pun[2] (pʌn) vb puns, punning, punned (*tr*) Brit to pack (earth, rubble, etc) by pounding [c16 dialectal variant of POUND[1]] > **punner** n

puna *Spanish* (ˈpuna) n 1 a high cold dry plateau, esp in the Andes 2 another name for **mountain sickness** [c17 from American Spanish, from Quechuan]

Punakha or **Punaka** (ˈpuːnəkə) n a town in W central Bhutan: a former capital of the country

punce (pʌns) *Northern English dialect* ▷ n 1 a kick ▷ vb **punce, puncing, punced** 2 to kick

punch[1] (pʌntʃ) vb 1 to strike blows (at), esp with a clenched fist 2 (*tr*) *Western US* to herd or drive (cattle), esp for a living 3 (*tr*) to poke or prod with a stick or similar object 4 **punch above one's weight** to do something that is considered to be beyond one's ability ▷ n 5 a blow with the fist 6 *informal* telling force, point, or vigour: *his arguments lacked punch* 7 **pull (one's) punches** See **pull** (sense 26) [c15 perhaps a variant of POUNCE[2]] > ˈpuncher n

punch[2] (pʌntʃ) n 1 a tool or machine for piercing holes in a material 2 any of various tools used for knocking a bolt, rivet, etc, out of a hole 3 a tool or machine used for stamping a design on something or shaping it by impact 4 the solid die of a punching machine for cutting, stamping, or shaping material 5 *computing* a device, such as a card punch or tape punch, used for making holes in a card or paper tape 6 See **centre punch** ▷ vb 7 (*tr*) to pierce, cut, stamp, shape, or drive with a punch [c14 shortened from *puncheon*, from Old French *ponçon*; see PUNCHEON[2]]

punch[3] (pʌntʃ) n any mixed drink containing fruit juice and, usually, alcoholic liquor, generally hot and spiced [c17 perhaps from Hindi *pānch*, from Sanskrit *pañca* five; the beverage originally included five ingredients]

Punch (pʌntʃ) n the main character in the traditional children's puppet show **Punch and Judy**

punchbag (ˈpʌntʃˌbæg) n Also called (US and Canadian): **punching bag** a suspended stuffed bag that is punched for exercise, esp boxing training

punchball (ˈpʌntʃˌbɔːl) n 1 a stuffed or inflated ball, supported by a flexible rod, that is punched for exercise, esp boxing training 2 US a game resembling baseball in which a light ball is struck with the fist

punchboard (ˈpʌntʃˌbɔːd) n a board full of holes

containing slips of paper, used in a gambling game in which a player attempts to push out a slip marked with a winning number

punchbowl ('pʌntʃ,bəʊl) *n* **1** a large bowl for serving punch, lemonade, etc, usually with a ladle and often having small drinking glasses hooked around the rim **2** *Brit* a bowl-shaped depression in the land

punch-drunk *adj* **1** demonstrating or characteristic of the behaviour of a person who has suffered repeated blows to the head, esp a professional boxer **2** dazed; stupefied

punched card *or esp US* **punch card** *n* (formerly) a card on which data can be coded in the form of punched holes. In computing, there were usually 80 columns and 12 rows, each column containing a pattern of holes representing one character. Sometimes shortened to: **card**

punched tape *or sometimes US* **perforated tape** *n* other terms for **paper tape**

puncheon¹ ('pʌntʃən) *n* **1** a large cask of variable capacity, usually between 70 and 120 gallons **2** the volume of such a cask used as a liquid measure [C15 *poncion*, from Old French *ponchon*, of uncertain origin]

puncheon² ('pʌntʃən) *n* **1** a short wooden post that is used as a vertical strut **2** a less common name for **punch²** (sense 1) [C14 *ponson*, from Old French *ponçon*, from Latin *punctiō* a puncture, from *pungere* to prick]

Punchinello (,pʌntʃɪ'nɛləʊ) *n*, *pl* -los *or* -loes **1** a type of clown from Italian burlesque or puppet shows, the prototype of Punch **2** (*sometimes not capital*) any grotesque or absurd character [C17 from earlier *Polichinello*, from Italian (Neapolitan dialect) *Polecenella*, from Italian *pulcino* chicken, ultimately from Latin *pullus* young animal]

punch line *n* the culminating part of a joke, funny story, etc, that gives it its humorous or dramatic point

punch-up *n Brit informal* a fight, brawl, or violent argument

punchy ('pʌntʃɪ) *adj* punchier, punchiest **1** an informal word for **punch-drunk 2** *informal* incisive or forceful: *a punchy article* > 'punchily *adv* > 'punchiness *n*

punctate ('pʌŋkteɪt) *or* **punctated** *adj* having or marked with minute spots, holes, or depressions [C18 from New Latin *punctātus*, from Latin *punctum* a point] > punc'tation *n*

punctilio (pʌŋk'tɪlɪ,əʊ) *n*, *pl* -os **1** strict attention to minute points of etiquette **2** a petty formality or fine point of etiquette [C16 from Italian *puntiglio* small point, from *punto* point, from Latin *punctum* point]

punctilious (pʌŋk'tɪlɪəs) *adj* **1** paying scrupulous attention to correctness in etiquette **2** attentive to detail > punc'tiliously *adv* > punc'tiliousness *n*

punctual ('pʌŋktjʊəl) *adj* **1** arriving or taking place at an arranged time; prompt **2** (of a person) having the characteristic of always keeping to arranged times, as for appointments, meetings, etc **3** *obsolete* precise; exact; apposite **4** *maths* consisting of or confined to a point in space [C14 from Medieval Latin *punctuālis* concerning detail, from Latin *punctum* point] > ,punctu'ality *n* > 'punctually *adv*

punctuate ('pʌŋktjʊ,eɪt) *vb* (*mainly tr*) **1** (*also intr*) to insert punctuation marks into (a written text) **2** to interrupt or insert at frequent intervals: *a meeting punctuated by heckling* **3** to give emphasis to [C17 from Medieval Latin *punctuāre* to prick, from Latin *punctum* a prick, from *pungere* to puncture] > 'punctu,ator *n*

punctuation (,pʌŋktjʊ'eɪʃən) *n* **1** the use of symbols not belonging to the alphabet of a writing system to indicate aspects of the intonation and meaning not otherwise conveyed in the written language **2** the symbols used for this purpose **3** the act or an instance of punctuating

punctuation mark *n* any of the signs used in

punctuation, such as a comma or question mark

puncture ('pʌŋktʃə) *n* **1** a small hole made by a sharp object **2** a perforation and loss of pressure in a pneumatic tyre, made by sharp stones, glass, etc **3** the act of puncturing or perforating ▷ *vb* **4** (*tr*) to pierce (a hole) in (something) with a sharp object **5** to cause (something pressurized, esp a tyre) to lose pressure by piercing, or (of a tyre, etc) to be pierced and collapse in this way **6** (*tr*) to depreciate (a person's self-esteem, pomposity, etc) [C14 from Latin *punctūra*, from *pungere* to prick] > 'puncturable *adj* > 'puncturer *n*

puncture vine *n* a tropical or subtropical prostrate vine, *Tribulus terrestris*, with yellow flowers and a hard, spiny fruit which breaks into five sections at maturity

pundit ('pʌndɪt) *n* **1** an expert **2** (formerly) a learned person **3** Also called: pandit a Brahman learned in Sanskrit and, esp in Hindu religion, philosophy or law [C17 from Hindi *pandit*, from Sanskrit *pandita* learned man, from *pandita* learned]

punditry ('pʌndɪtrɪ) *n* the expressing of expert opinions

Pune ('puːnə) *n* another name for **Poona**

pung (pʌŋ) *n Eastern US and Canadian* a horse-drawn sleigh with a boxlike body on runners [C19 shortened from Algonquian *tom-pung*; compare TOBOGGAN]

punga ('pʌŋə) *n* a variant spelling of **ponga**

pungent ('pʌndʒənt) *adj* **1** having an acrid smell or sharp bitter flavour **2** (of wit, satire, etc) biting; caustic **3** *biology* ending in a sharp point: *a pungent leaf* [C16 from Latin *pungens* piercing, from *pungere* to point] > 'pungency *n* > 'pungently *adv*

Punic ('pjuːnɪk) *adj* **1** of or relating to ancient Carthage or the Carthaginians **2** characteristic of the treachery of the Carthaginians ▷ *n* **3** the language of the ancient Carthaginians; a late form of Phoenician [C15 from Latin *Pūnicus*, variant of *Poenicus* Carthaginian, from Greek *Phoinix*]

Punic Wars *pl n* three wars (264–241 BC, 218–201 BC, and 149–146 BC), in which Rome crushed Carthaginian power, destroying Carthage itself

punish ('pʌnɪʃ) *vb* **1** to force (someone) to undergo a penalty or sanction, such as imprisonment, fines, death, etc, for some crime or misdemeanour **2** (*tr*) to inflict punishment for (some crime, etc) **3** (*tr*) to use or treat harshly or roughly, esp as by overexertion: *to punish a horse* **4** (*tr*) *informal* to consume (some commodity) in large quantities: *to punish the bottle* [C14 *punisse*, from Old French *punir*, from Latin *pūnīre* to punish, from *poena* penalty] > 'punisher *n* > 'punishing *adj* > 'punishingly *adv*

punishable ('pʌnɪʃəb²l) *adj* liable to be punished or deserving of punishment > ,punisha'bility *n*

punishment ('pʌnɪʃmənt) *n* **1** a penalty or sanction given for any crime or offence **2** the act of punishing or state of being punished **3** *informal* rough treatment **4** *psychol* any aversive stimulus administered to an organism as part of training

punitive ('pjuːnɪtɪv) *or less commonly* **punitory** ('pjuːnɪtərɪ, -trɪ) *adj* relating to, involving, or with the intention of inflicting punishment: *a punitive expedition* [C17 from Medieval Latin *pūnītīvus* concerning punishment, from Latin *pūnīre* to punish] > 'punitively *adv* > 'punitiveness *n*

Punjab (pʌn'dʒɑː, 'pʌndʒɑːb) *n* **1** (formerly) a province in NW British India: divided between India and Pakistan in 1947 **2** a state of NW India: reorganized in 1966 as a Punjabi-speaking state, a large part forming the new state of Haryana; mainly agricultural. Capital: Chandigarh. Pop: 24 289 296 (2001). Area: 50 255 sq km (19 403 sq miles) **3** a province of W Pakistan: created in 1947. Capital: Lahore. Pop: 82 710 000 (2003 est). Area: 205 344 sq km (127 595 sq miles)

Punjabi *or* **Panjabi** (pʌn'dʒɑːbɪ) *n* **1** a member of the chief people of the Punjab **2** the state language of the Punjab, belonging to the Indic branch of the Indo-European family ▷ *adj* **3** of or

relating to the Punjab, its people, or their language

Punjab States *pl n* (formerly) a group of states in NW India, amalgamated in 1956 with Punjab state

punk¹ (pʌŋk) *n* **1 a** a youth movement of the late 1970s, characterized by anti-Establishment slogans and outrageous clothes and hairstyles **b** an adherent of punk **c** short for **punk rock d** (*as modifier*): *a punk record* **2** an inferior, rotten, or worthless person or thing **3** worthless articles collectively **4** a petty criminal or hoodlum **5** *obsolete* a young male homosexual; catamite **6** *obsolete* a prostitute ▷ *adj* **7** inferior, rotten, or worthless [C16 via Polari from Spanish *pu(n)ta* prostitute, *pu(n)to* male prostitute] > 'punkish *adj*

punk² (pʌŋk) *n* **1** dried decayed wood that smoulders when ignited: used as tinder **2** any of various other substances that smoulder when ignited, esp one used to light fireworks [C18 of uncertain origin]

punka *or* **punkah** ('pʌŋkə) *n* a fan made of a palm leaf or leaves [C17 from Hindi *pankhā*, from Sanskrit *paksaka* fan, from *paksa* wing]

punk rock *n* a fast abrasive style of rock music of the late 1970s, characterized by aggressive or offensive lyrics and performance. Sometimes shortened to: punk > punk rocker *n*

punnet ('pʌnɪt) *n chiefly Brit* a small basket for fruit, such as strawberries [C19 perhaps diminutive of dialect *pun* POUND²]

punster ('pʌnstə) *n* a person who is fond of making puns, esp one who makes a tedious habit of this

punt¹ (pʌnt) *n* **1** an open flat-bottomed boat with square ends, propelled by a pole. See **quant¹** ▷ *vb* **2** to propel (a boat, esp a punt) by pushing with a pole on the bottom of a river, etc [Old English *punt* shallow boat, from Latin *pontō* punt, PONTOON¹]

punt² (pʌnt) *n* **1** a kick in certain sports, such as rugby, in which the ball is released and kicked before it hits the ground **2** any long high kick ▷ *vb* **3** to kick (a ball, etc) using a punt [C19 perhaps a variant of English dialect *bunt* to push, perhaps a nasalized variant of BUTT³]

punt³ (pʌnt) *chiefly Brit* ▷ *vb* **1** (*intr*) to gamble; bet ▷ *n* **2** a gamble or bet, esp against the bank, as in roulette, or on horses **3** Also called: **punter** a person who bets **4** take a punt at *Austral and NZ informal* to have an attempt or try at (something) [C18 from French *ponter* to punt, from *ponte* bet laid against the banker, from Spanish *punto* point, from Latin *punctum*]

punt⁴ (pʊnt) *n* (formerly) the Irish pound [Irish Gaelic: pound]

Punta Arenas (Spanish 'punta a'renas) *n* a port in S Chile, on the Strait of Magellan: the southernmost city in the world. Pop: 118 000 (2005 est). Former name: Magallanes

punter¹ ('pʌntə) *n* a person who punts a boat

punter² ('pʌntə) *n* a person who kicks a ball

punter³ ('pʌntə) *n* **1** a person who places a bet **2** *informal* any member of the public, esp when a customer: *the punters flock into the sales* **3** *slang* a prostitute's client **4** *slang* a victim of a con man

punty ('pʌntɪ) *n*, *pl* -ties a long iron rod used in the finishing process of glass-blowing. Also called: pontil [C17 see PONTIL]

puny ('pjuːnɪ) *adj* -nier, -niest **1** having a small physique or weakly constitution **2** paltry; insignificant [C16 from Old French *puisne* PUISNE] > 'punily *adv* > 'puniness *n*

pup (pʌp) *n* **1 a** a young dog, esp when under one year of age; puppy **b** the young of various other animals, such as the seal **2** in pup (of a bitch) pregnant **3** *informal, chiefly Brit contemptuous* a conceited young man (esp in the phrase **young pup**) **4** sell (someone) a pup to swindle (someone) by selling him something worthless **5** the night's a pup *Austral slang* it's early yet ▷ *vb* pups, pupping, pupped **6** (of dogs, seals, etc) to give birth to (young) [C18 back formation from PUPPY]

pupa ('pju:pə) *n*, *pl* -pae (-pi:) *or* -pas an insect at the immobile nonfeeding stage of development between larva and adult, when many internal changes occur. See **coarctate, exarate, obtect** [C19 via New Latin, from Latin: a doll, puppet]
> 'pupal *adj*

puparium (pju:'pɛərɪəm) *n*, *pl* -ia (-ɪə) a hard barrel-shaped case enclosing the pupae of the housefly and other dipterous insects
> pu'parial *adj*

pupate (pju:'peɪt) *vb* (*intr*) (of an insect larva) to develop into a pupa > pu'pation *n*

pupil¹ ('pju:pᵊl) *n* **1** a student who is taught by a teacher, esp a young student **2** *civil and Scots law* a boy under 14 or a girl under 12 who is in the care of a guardian [C14 from Latin *pupillus* an orphan, from *pūpus* a child]

pupil² ('pju:pᵊl) *n* the dark circular aperture at the centre of the iris of the eye, through which light enters [C16 from Latin *pūpilla*, diminutive of *pūpa* girl, puppet; from the tiny reflections in the eye]

pupillage *or US* **pupilage** ('pju:pɪlɪdʒ) *n* **1** the condition of being a pupil or duration for which one is a pupil **2** (in England) the period spent by a newly called barrister in the chambers of a member of the bar

pupillary¹ *or* **pupilary** ('pju:pɪlərɪ) *adj* of or relating to a pupil or a legal ward [C17 from PUPIL¹ + -ARY] > ,pupil'larity *or* ,pupi'larity *n*

pupillary² *or* **pupilary** ('pju:pɪlərɪ) *adj* of or relating to the pupil of the eye [C18 from Latin *pūpilla* PUPIL²]

pupiparous (pju:'pɪpərəs) *adj* (of certain dipterous flies) producing young that have already reached the pupa stage at the time of hatching [C19 from New Latin *pupiparus*, from PUPA + *parere* to bring forth]

puppet ('pʌpɪt) *n* **1 a** a small doll or figure of a person or animal moved by strings attached to its limbs or by the hand inserted in its cloth body **b** (*as modifier*): *a puppet theatre* **2 a** a person, group, state, etc, that appears independent but is in fact controlled by another **b** (*as modifier*): *a puppet government* [C16 *popet*, perhaps from Old French *poupette* little doll, ultimately from Latin *pūpa* girl, doll]

puppeteer (,pʌpɪ'tɪə) *n* a person who manipulates puppets

puppetry ('pʌpɪtrɪ) *n* **1** the art of making and manipulating puppets and presenting puppet shows **2** unconvincing or specious presentation

Puppis ('pʌpɪs) *n*, *Latin genitive* **Puppis** a constellation in the S hemisphere lying between Vela and Canis Major, a section of which is crossed by the Milky Way [Latin: the ship, the POOP of a ship]

puppy ('pʌpɪ) *n*, *pl* -pies **1** a young dog; pup **2** *informal, contemptuous* a brash or conceited young man; pup [C15 *popi*, from Old French *popée* doll; compare PUPPET] > 'puppy,hood *n* > 'puppyish *adj*

puppy fat *n* fatty tissue that develops in childhood or adolescence and usually disappears by maturity

puppy love *n* another term for **calf love**

pup tent *n* another name for **shelter tent**

Purana (pʊ'rɑ:nə) *n* any of a class of Sanskrit writings not included in the Vedas, characteristically recounting the birth and deeds of Hindu gods and the creation, destruction, or recreation of the universe [C17 from Sanskrit: ancient, from *purā* formerly] > Pu'ranic *adj*

Purbeck marble *or* **stone** ('pɜ:bɛk) *n* a fossil-rich limestone that takes a high polish: used for building, etc [C15 named after *Purbeck*, Dorset, where it is quarried]

purblind ('pɜ:,blaɪnd) *adj* **1** partly or nearly blind **2** lacking in insight or understanding; obtuse [C13 see PURE, BLIND; compare PARBOIL]

purchasable ('pɜ:tʃɪsəbᵊl) *adj* **1** able to be bribed or corrupted **2** able to be bought
> ,purchasa'bility *n*

purchase ('pɜ:tʃɪs) *vb* (*tr*) **1** to obtain (goods, etc) by payment **2** to obtain by effort, sacrifice, etc: *to purchase one's freedom* **3** to draw, haul, or lift (a load) with the aid of mechanical apparatus **4** to acquire (an estate) other than by inheritance ▷ *n* **5** something that is purchased, esp an article bought with money **6** the act of buying **7** acquisition of an estate by any lawful means other than inheritance **8** a rough measure of the mechanical advantage achieved by a lever **9** a firm foothold, grasp, etc, as for climbing or levering something **10** a means of achieving some influence, advantage, etc [C13 from Old French *porchacier* to strive to obtain, from *por-* for + *chacier* to CHASE¹] > 'purchaser *n*

purchase ledger *n* *commerce* a record of a company's purchases of goods and services showing the amounts paid and due

purchase tax *n* *Brit* a tax levied on nonessential consumer goods and added to selling prices by retailers

purdah *or* **purda** ('pɜ:də) *n* **1** the custom in some Muslim and Hindu communities of keeping women in seclusion, with clothing that conceals them completely when they go out **2** a screen in a Hindu house used to keep the women out of view **3** a veil worn by Hindu women of high caste **4** *informal* hiding or isolation: *the Treasury is currently locked in pre-budget purdah* [C19 from Hindi *parda* veil, from Persian *pardah*]

purdonium (pɜ:'dəʊnɪəm) *n* a type of coal scuttle having a slanted cover that is raised to open it, and an inner removable metal container for the coal [C19 named after its inventor, a Mr *Purdon*]

pure (pjʊə) *adj* **1** not mixed with any extraneous or dissimilar materials, elements, etc: *pure nitrogen* **2** free from tainting or polluting matter; clean; wholesome: *pure water* **3** free from moral taint or defilement: *pure love* **4** (*prenominal*) (intensifier): *pure stupidity; a pure coincidence* **5** (of a subject, etc) studied in its theoretical aspects rather than for its practical applications: *pure mathematics; pure science*. Compare **applied** **6** (of a vowel) pronounced with more or less unvarying quality without any glide; monophthongal **7** (of a consonant) not accompanied by another consonant **8** of supposedly unmixed racial descent **9** *genetics, biology* breeding true for one or more characteristics; homozygous **10** *music* **a** (of a sound) composed of a single frequency without overtones **b** (of intervals in the system of just intonation) mathematically accurate in respect to the ratio of one frequency to another [C13 from Old French *pur*, from Latin *pūrus* unstained]
> 'pureness *n*

purebred *adj* ('pjʊə'brɛd) **1** denoting a pure strain obtained through many generations of controlled breeding for desirable traits ▷ *n* ('pjʊə,brɛd) **2** a purebred animal. Compare **grade** (sense 9), **crossbred** (sense 2)

pure culture *n* *bacteriol* a culture containing a single species of microorganism

puree *or* **puri** ('pu:rɪ) *n* an unleavened flaky Indian bread, that is deep-fried in ghee and served hot [Hindi]

purée ('pjʊəreɪ) *n* **1** a smooth thick pulp of cooked and sieved fruit, vegetables, meat, or fish ▷ *vb* -rées, -réeing, -réed **2** (*tr*) to make (cooked foods) into a purée [C19 from French *purer* to PURIFY]

pure laine (pjʊə 'lɛn) *n* (in Quebec) a person belonging to a long-established family of French descent [French, literally: pure wool]

Pure Land sects *pl n* Mahayana Buddhist sects venerating the Buddha as the compassionate saviour

pure line *n* a breed or strain of animals or plants in which certain characters appear in successive generations as a result of inbreeding or self-fertilization

purely ('pjʊəlɪ) *adv* **1** in a pure manner **2** entirely: *purely by chance* **3** in a chaste or innocent manner

purfle ('pɜ:fᵊl) *n* *also* **purfling 1** a ruffled or curved ornamental band, as on clothing, furniture, etc ▷ *vb* **2** (*tr*) to decorate with such a band or bands [C14 from Old French *purfiler* to decorate with a border, from *filer* to spin, from *fil* thread, from Latin *filum*]

purgation (pɜ:'geɪʃən) *n* the act of purging or state of being purged; purification

purgative ('pɜ:gətɪv) *med* ▷ *n* **1** a drug or agent for purging the bowels ▷ *adj* **2** causing evacuation of the bowels; cathartic > 'purgatively *adv*

purgatorial (,pɜ:gə'tɔ:rɪəl) *adj* **1** serving to purify from sin **2** of, relating to, or like purgatory
> ,purga'torially *adv*

purgatory ('pɜ:gətərɪ, -trɪ) *n* **1** *chiefly RC Church* a state or place in which the souls of those who have died in a state of grace are believed to undergo a limited amount of suffering to expiate their venial sins and become purified of the remaining effects of mortal sin **2** a place or condition of suffering or torment, esp one that is temporary [C13 from Old French *purgatoire*, from Medieval Latin *pūrgātōrium*, literally: place of cleansing, from Latin *pūrgāre* to PURGE]

purge (pɜ:dʒ) *vb* **1** (*tr*) to rid (something) of (impure or undesirable elements) **2** (*tr*) to rid (a state, political party, etc) of (dissident or troublesome people) **3** (*tr*) to empty (the bowels) by evacuation of faeces **b** to cause (a person) to evacuate his bowels **4 a** to clear (a person) of a charge **b** to free (oneself) of guilt, as by atonement: *to purge contempt* **5** (*intr*) to be cleansed or purified ▷ *n* **6** the act or process of purging **7** the elimination of opponents or dissidents from a state, political party, etc **8** a purgative drug or agent; cathartic [C14 from Old French *purger*, from Latin *pūrgāre* to purify]
> 'purger *n*

Puri ('pʊəri:, pʊə'ri:) *n* a port in E India, in Orissa on the Bay of Bengal: 12th-century temple of Jagannath. Pop: 157 610 (2001)

Purification of the Virgin Mary *n* the *Christianity* **1** the presentation of Jesus in the Temple after the completion of Mary's purification (Luke 2:22) **2** Also called: **Candlemas** the feast commemorating this (Feb 2)

purificator ('pjʊərɪfɪ,keɪtə) *n* *Christianity* a small white linen cloth used to wipe the chalice and paten and also the lips and fingers of the celebrant at the Eucharist

purifier ('pjʊərɪ,faɪə) *n* a device or substance that frees something of extraneous, contaminating, or debasing matter

purify ('pjʊərɪ,faɪ) *vb* -fies, -fying, -fied **1** to free (something) of extraneous, contaminating, or debasing matter **2** (*tr*) to free (a person, etc) from sin or guilt **3** (*tr*) to make clean, as in a ritual, esp the churching of women after childbirth [C14 from Old French *purifier*, from Late Latin *pūrificāre* to cleanse, from *pūrus* pure + *facere* to make]
> ,purifi'cation *n* > purificatory ('pjʊərɪfɪ,keɪtərɪ) *adj*

Purim ('pʊərɪm; *Hebrew* pu:'ri:m) *n* a Jewish holiday celebrated on Adar 14, in February or March, and in Adar Sheni in leap years, to commemorate the deliverance of the Jews from the massacre planned for them by Haman (Esther 9) [Hebrew *pūrīm*, plural of *pūr* lot; from the casting of lots by Haman]

purine ('pjʊəri:n) *or* **purin** ('pjʊərɪn) *n* **1** a colourless crystalline solid that can be prepared from uric acid. Formula: $C_5H_4N_4$ **2** Also called: **purine base** any of a number of nitrogenous bases, such as guanine and adenine, that are derivatives of purine and constituents of nucleic acids and certain coenzymes [C19 from German *Purin*; see PURE, URIC, -INE²]

puriri (pu:'ri:ri:) *n*, *pl* -ris a forest tree, *Vitex lucens*, of New Zealand, having red berries and glossy green leaves and yielding a durable dark brown timber

purism ('pjʊə,rɪzəm) *n* insistence on traditional canons of correctness of form or purity of style or content, esp in language, art, or music > 'purist *adj, n* > pu'ristic *adj* > pu'ristically *adv*

puritan ('pjʊərɪtᵊn) n **1** a person who adheres to strict moral or religious principles, esp one opposed to luxury and sensual enjoyment ▷ adj **2** characteristic of a puritan [C16 from Late Latin *pūritās* PURITY] > 'puritan,ism n

Puritan ('pjʊərɪtᵊn) (in the late 16th and 17th centuries) n **1** any of the more extreme English Protestants, most of whom were Calvinists, who wished to purify the Church of England of most of its ceremony and other aspects that they deemed to be Catholic ▷ adj **2** of, characteristic of, or relating to the Puritans > 'Puritan,ism n

puritanical (,pjʊərɪ'tænɪkᵊl) or less commonly **puritanic** adj *usually disparaging* strict in moral or religious outlook, esp in shunning sensual pleasures **2** (*sometimes capital*) of or relating to a puritan or the Puritans > ,puri'tanically adv > ,puri'tanicalness n

purity ('pjʊərɪtɪ) n **1** the state or quality of being pure **2** *physics* a measure of the amount of a single-frequency colour in a mixture of spectral and achromatic colours

purl¹ ('pɜːl) n **1** Also called: purl stitch a knitting stitch made by doing a plain stitch backwards **2** a decorative border, as of lace **3** gold or silver wire thread ▷ vb **4** to knit (a row or garment) in purl stitch **5** to edge (something) with a purl ▷ Also (for senses 2, 3, 5): pearl [C16 from dialect *pirl* to twist into a cord]

purl² ('pɜːl) vb **1** (*intr*) (of a stream, etc) to flow with a gentle curling or rippling movement and a murmuring sound ▷ n **2** a curling movement of water; eddy **3** a murmuring sound, as of a shallow stream [C16 related to Norwegian *purla* to bubble]

purler¹ ('pɜːlə) n *informal* a headlong or spectacular fall (esp in the phrase **come a purler**)

purler² ('pɜːlə) n *Austral slang* something outstanding in its class [of unknown origin]

purlieu ('pɜːljuː) n **1** *English history* land on the edge of a forest that was once included within the bounds of the royal forest but was later separated although still subject to some of the forest laws, esp regarding hunting **2** (*usually plural*) a neighbouring area; outskirts **3** (*often plural*) a place one frequents **4** *rare* a district or suburb, esp one that is poor or squalid [C15 *purlewe*, from Anglo-French *puralé* a going through (influenced also by Old French *lieu* place), from Old French *puraler* to traverse, from *pur* through + *aler* to go]

purlin or **purline** ('pɜːlɪn) n a horizontal beam that provides intermediate support for the common rafters of a roof construction [C15 of uncertain origin]

purloin (pɜː'lɔɪn) vb to take (something) dishonestly; steal [C15 from Old French *porloigner* to put at a distance, from *por-* for + *loin* distant, from Latin *longus* long] > pur'loiner n

purple ('pɜːpᵊl) n **1** any of various colours with a hue lying between red and blue and often highly saturated; a nonspectral colour **2** a dye or pigment producing such a colour **3** cloth of this colour, often used to symbolize royalty or nobility **4** (*usually preceded by the*) high rank; nobility **5 a** the official robe of a cardinal **b** the rank, office, or authority of a cardinal as signified by this **6** the purple bishops collectively ▷ adj **7** of the colour purple **8** (of writing) excessively elaborate or full of imagery: *purple prose* **9** noble or royal [Old English, from Latin *purpura* purple dye, from Greek *porphura* the purple fish (*Murex*)] > 'purpleness n > 'purplish adj 'purply adj

purple emperor n any of several Old World nymphalid butterflies of the genus *Apatura*, esp *A. iris*, having mottled purple-and-brown wings

purple-fringed orchid or **orchis** n either of two North American orchids, *Habenaria psychodes* or *H. fimbriata*, having purple fringed flowers

purple gallinule n a long-toed purple aquatic bird, *Porphyrio porphyrio* (or *Porphyrula martinica*), of the southern US and Europe, with red legs and red bill: family *Rallidae* (rails, etc)

purple heart n **1** any of several tropical American leguminous trees of the genus *Peltogyne* **2** the decorative purple heartwood of any of these trees **3** *informal, chiefly Brit* a heart-shaped purple tablet consisting mainly of amphetamine

Purple Heart n a decoration awarded to members of the US Armed Forces for a wound incurred in action

purple medic n another name for **alfalfa**

purple patch n **1** Also called: purple passage a section in a piece of writing characterized by rich, fanciful, or ornate language **2** *slang* a period of success, good fortune, etc

purport vb (pɜː'pɔːt) (*tr*) **1** to claim (to be a certain thing, etc) by manner or appearance, esp falsely **2** (esp of speech or writing) to signify or imply ▷ n ('pɜːpɔːt) **3** meaning; significance **4** purpose; object; intention [C15 from Anglo-French: contents, from Old French *porporter* to convey, from *por-* forth + *porter* to carry, from Latin *portāre*]

purported (pɜː'pɔːtɪd) adj alleged; supposed; rumoured: *a purported two million dollar deal* > pur'portedly adv

purpose ('pɜːpəs) n **1** the reason for which anything is done, created, or exists **2** a fixed design, outcome, or idea that is the object of an action or other effort **3** fixed intention in doing something; determination: *a man of purpose* **4** practical advantage or use: *to work to good purpose* **5** that which is relevant or under consideration (esp in the phrase **to** or **from the purpose**) **6** *archaic* purport **7** **on purpose** intentionally ▷ vb (*tr*) **8** to intend or determine to do (something) [C13 from Old French *porpos*, from *porposer* to plan, from Latin *prōpōnere* to PROPOSE]

purpose-built adj made to serve a specific purpose

purposeful ('pɜːpəsfʊl) adj **1** having a definite purpose in view **2** fixed in one's purpose; determined > 'purposefully adv > 'purposefulness n

▮ USAGE *Purposefully* is sometimes wrongly used where *purposely* is meant: *he had purposely* (not *purposefully*) *left the door unlocked*

purposeless ('pɜːpəslɪs) adj having no fixed plan or intention > 'purposelessly adv > 'purposelessness n

purposely ('pɜːpəslɪ) adv for a definite reason; on purpose

▮ USAGE See at **purposeful**

purposive ('pɜːpəsɪv) adj **1** relating to, having, or indicating conscious intention **2** serving a purpose; useful > 'purposively adv > 'purposiveness n

purpura ('pɜːpjʊrə) n *pathol* any of several blood diseases causing purplish spots or patches on the skin due to subcutaneous bleeding [C18 via Latin from Greek *porphura* a shellfish yielding purple dye] > 'purpuric adj

purpure ('pɜːpjʊə) n, adj (*usually postpositive*) *heraldry* purple [Old English from Latin *purpura* PURPLE]

purpurin ('pɜːpjʊrɪn) n a red crystalline compound used as a stain for biological specimens; 1,2,4-trihydroxyanthraquinone. Formula: $C_{14}H_5O_2(OH)_3$ [C19 from Latin *purpura* PURPLE + -IN]

purr (pɜː) vb **1** (*intr*) (esp of cats) to make a low vibrant sound, usually considered as expressing pleasure, etc **2** (*tr*) to express (pleasure, etc) by this sound ▷ n **3** a purring sound [C17 of imitative origin; compare French *ronronner* to purr, German *schnurren*, Dutch *snorren*]

purse (pɜːs) n **1** a small bag or pouch, often made of soft leather, for carrying money, esp coins **2** *US and Canadian* a woman's handbag **3** anything resembling a small bag or pouch in form or function **4** wealth; funds **5** a sum of money that is offered, esp as a prize ▷ vb **6** (*tr*) to contract (the mouth, lips, etc) into a small rounded shape [Old English *purs*, probably from Late Latin *bursa* bag, ultimately from Greek: leather]

purser ('pɜːsə) n an officer aboard a passenger ship, merchant ship, or aircraft who keeps the accounts and attends to the welfare of the passengers

purse seine n a large net towed, usually by two boats, that encloses a school of fish and is then closed at the bottom by means of a line resembling the string formerly used to draw shut the neck of a money pouch or purse

purse strings pl n control of finance or expenditure (esp in such phrases as **hold** or **control the purse strings**)

purslane ('pɜːslɪn, -leɪn) n **1** a weedy portulacaceous plant, *Portulaca oleracea*, with small yellow flowers and fleshy leaves, which are used in salads and as a potherb **2** any of various similar or related plants, such as sea purslane and water purslane [C14 *purcelane*, from Old French *porcelaine*, from Late Latin *porcillāgō*, from Latin *porcillāca*, variant of *portulāca*]

pursuance (pə'sjuːəns) n the carrying out or pursuing of an action, plan, etc

pursuant (pə'sjuːənt) adj **1** (*usually postpositive*; often foll by to) *chiefly law* in agreement or conformity **2** *archaic* pursuing [C17 related to Middle English *poursuivant* following after, from Old French; see PURSUE] > pur'suantly adv

pursue (pə'sjuː) vb -sues, -suing, -sued (*mainly tr*) **1** (*also intr*) to follow (a fugitive, etc) in order to capture or overtake **2** (esp of something bad or unlucky) to follow closely or accompany: *ill health pursued her* **3** to seek or strive to attain (some object, desire, etc) **4** to follow the precepts of (a plan, policy, etc) **5** to apply oneself to (one's studies, hobbies, etc) **6** to follow persistently or seek to become acquainted with **7** to continue to discuss or argue (a point, subject, etc) [C13 from Anglo-Norman *pursiwer*, from Old French *poursivre*, from Latin *prōsequī* to follow after] > pur'suer n

pursuit (pə'sjuːt) n **1 a** the act of pursuing, chasing, or striving after **b** (*as modifier*): *a pursuit plane* **2** an occupation, hobby, or pastime **3** (in cycling) a race in which the riders set off at intervals along the track and attempt to overtake each other [C14 from Old French *poursieute*, from *poursivre* to prosecute, PURSUE]

pursuivant ('pɜːsɪvənt) n **1** the lowest rank of heraldic officer **2** *history* a state or royal messenger **3** *history* a follower or attendant [C14 from Old French, from *poursivre* to PURSUE]

pursy ('pɜːsɪ) adj **1** short-winded **2** *archaic* fat; overweight [C15 alteration of earlier *pursive*, from Anglo-French *porsif*, ultimately from Latin *pulsāre* to PULSATE]

purtenance ('pɜːtɪnəns) n *archaic* the inner organs, viscera [C14 from Old French *pertinance* something that belongs; see APPURTENANCE]

purulent ('pjʊərʊlənt) adj of, relating to, or containing pus [C16 from Latin *pūrulentus*, from PUS] > 'purulence or 'purulency n > 'purulently adv

Purús (Spanish pu'rus; Portuguese pu'rus) n a river in NW central South America, rising in SE Peru and flowing northeast to the Amazon. Length: about 3200 km (2000 miles)

purvey vb (pə'veɪ) (*tr*) **1** to sell or provide (commodities, esp foodstuffs) on a large scale **2** to publish or make available (lies, scandal, etc) ▷ n ('pɜːvɪ) **3** *Scot* the food and drink laid on at a wedding reception, etc [C13 from Old French *porveeir*, from Latin *prōvidēre* to PROVIDE]

purveyance (pə'veɪəns) n **1** *history* the collection or requisition of provisions for a sovereign **2** *rare* the act of purveying **3** *rare* that which is purveyed

purveyor (pə'veɪə) n **1** (*often plural*) a person, organization, etc, that supplies food and provisions **2** a person who spreads, repeats, or sells (information, lies, etc) **3** a person or thing that habitually provides or supplies a particular thing or quality: *a purveyor of humour* **4** *history* an officer providing or exacting provisions, lodging, etc, for a sovereign

purview ('pɜːvjuː) n **1** the scope of operation or concern of something **2** the breadth or range of

p

outlook or understanding **3** *law* the body of a statute, containing the enacting clauses [C15 from Anglo-Norman *purveu*, from *porveeir* to furnish; see PURVEY]

pus (pʌs) *n* the yellow or greenish fluid product of inflammation, composed largely of dead leucocytes, exuded plasma, and liquefied tissue cells [C16 from Latin *pūs*; related to Greek *puon* pus]

Pusan (ˈpuːˈsæn) *n* a port in SE South Korea, on the Korea Strait: the second largest city and chief port of the country; industrial centre; two universities. Pop: 3 527 000 (2005 est)

Puseyism (ˈpjuːzɪˌɪzəm) *n* a derogatory term for the **Oxford Movement,** used by its contemporary opponents [C19 after Edward Bouverie *Pusey* (1800–82), British ecclesiastic, a leader of the Oxford Movement] > ˈ**Puseyite** *n, adj*

push (pʊʃ) *vb* **1** (when *tr*, often foll by *off, away*, etc) to apply steady force to (something) in order to move it **2** to thrust (one's way) through something, such as a crowd, by force **3** (when *intr*, often foll by *for*) to apply oneself vigorously (to achieving a task, plan, etc) **4** (*tr*) to encourage or urge (a person) to some action, decision, etc **5** (when *intr*, often foll by *for*) to be an advocate or promoter (of): *to push for acceptance of one's theories* **6** (*tr*) to use one's influence to help (a person): *to push one's own candidate* **7** to bear upon (oneself or another person) in order to achieve more effort, better results, etc **8 a** (*tr*) to take undue risks, esp through overconfidence, thus risking failure: *to push one's luck* **b** (*intr*) to act overconfidently **9** *sport* to hit (a ball) with a stiff pushing stroke **10** (*tr*) *informal* to sell (narcotic drugs) illegally **11** (*intr*; foll by *out, into*, etc) (esp of geographical features) to reach or extend: *the cliffs pushed out to the sea* **12** (*tr*) to overdevelop (a photographic film), usually by the equivalent of up to two stops, to compensate for underexposure or increase contrast **13 push up (the) daisies** *slang* to be dead and buried ▷ *n* **14** the act of pushing; thrust **15** a part or device that is pressed to operate some mechanism **16** *informal* ambitious or enterprising drive, energy, etc **17** *informal* a special effort or attempt to advance, as of an army in a war: *to make a push* **18** *informal* a number of people gathered in one place, such as at a party **19** *Austral slang* a group or gang, esp one considered to be a clique **20** *sport* a stiff pushing stroke **21 at a push** *informal* with difficulty; only just **22 the push** *informal, chiefly Brit* dismissal, esp from employment **23 when push comes to shove** *informal* when matters become critical; when a decision needs to be made ▷ See also **push about, push along, push in, push off, push on, push through** [C13 from Old French *pousser*, from Latin *pulsāre*, from *pellere* to drive]

push about *or* **around** *vb* (*tr, adverb*) *slang* to bully; keep telling (a person) what to do in a bossy manner

push along *vb* (*intr, adverb*) *informal* to go away

pushball (ˈpʊʃˌbɔːl) *n chiefly US and Canadian* a game in which two teams try to push a heavy ball towards opposite goals

push-bike *n Brit* an informal name for **bicycle**

push button *n* **1** an electrical switch operated by pressing a button, which closes or opens a circuit **2** (*modifier*) **push-button a** operated by a push button: *a push-button radio* **b** initiated as simply as by pressing a button: *push-button warfare*

pushcart (ˈpʊʃˌkɑːt) *n chiefly US and Canadian* a handcart, typically having two wheels and a canvas roof, used esp by street vendors. Also called: **barrow**

pushchair (ˈpʊʃˌtʃɛə) *n* a usually collapsible chair-shaped carriage in which a small child may be wheeled. Also called: **baby buggy, buggy**. US and Canadian word: **stroller**. Austral words: **pusher, stroller**

pushed (pʊʃt) *adj* (often foll by *for*) *informal* short (of) or in need (of time, money, etc)

pusher (ˈpʊʃə) *n* **1** *informal* a person who sells illegal drugs, esp narcotics such as heroin and morphine **2** *informal* an actively or aggressively ambitious person **3 a** a type of aircraft propeller placed behind the engine **b** a type of aircraft using such a propeller **4** a person or thing that pushes **5** *Brit* a rakelike implement used by small children to push food onto a spoon **6** *Austral* the usual name for **pushchair**

push fit *n engineering* another name for **sliding fit**

push in *vb* (*intr, adverb*) to force one's way into a group of people, queue, etc

pushing (ˈpʊʃɪŋ) *adj* **1** enterprising, resourceful, or aggressively ambitious **2** impertinently self-assertive ▷ *adv* **3** almost or nearly (a certain age, speed, etc): *pushing fifty* > ˈ**pushingly** *adv* > ˈ**pushingness** *n*

Pushkin (ˈpʊʃkɪn) *n* a town in NW Russia: site of the imperial summer residence and Catherine the Great's palace. Pop: 97 000 (latest est). Former name: **Tsarskoye Selo** (1708–1937)

push money *n* a cash inducement provided by a manufacturer or distributor for a retailer or his staff, to reward successful selling

push off *vb* (*adverb*) **1** Also: **push out** to move into open water, as by being cast off from a mooring **2** (*intr*) *informal* to go away; leave

push on *vb* (*intr, adverb*) to resume one's course; carry on one's way steadily; press on

pushover (ˈpʊʃˌəʊvə) *n informal* **1** something that is easily achieved or accomplished **2** a person, team, etc, that is easily taken advantage of or defeated

pushpin (ˈpʊʃˌpɪn) *n US and Canadian* a pin with a small ball-shaped head

push polling *n* the use of loaded questions in a supposedly objective telephone opinion poll during a political campaign in order to bias voters against an opposing candidate

push-pull *n* (*modifier*) using two similar electronic devices, such as matched valves, made to operate 180° out of phase with each other. The outputs are combined to produce a signal that replicates the input waveform: *a push-pull amplifier*

pushrod (ˈpʊʃˌrɒd) *n* a metal rod transmitting the reciprocating motion that operates the valves of an internal-combustion engine having the camshaft in the crankcase

push-start *vb* (*tr*) **1** to start (a motor vehicle) by pushing it while it is in gear, thus turning the engine ▷ *n* **2** the act or process of starting a vehicle in this way

push through *vb* (*tr*) to compel to accept: *the bill was pushed through Parliament*

Pushto (ˈpʌʃtəʊ) *or* **Pushtu** (ˈpʌʃtuː) *n, adj* variant spellings of **Pashto**

push-up *n US and Canadian* an exercise in which the body is alternately raised from and lowered to the floor by the arms only, the trunk being kept straight with the toes and hands resting on the floor. Also called (in Britain and certain other countries): **press-up**

pushy (ˈpʊʃɪ) *adj* **pushier, pushiest** *informal* **1** offensively assertive or forceful **2** aggressively or ruthlessly ambitious > ˈ**pushily** *adv* > ˈ**pushiness** *n*

pusillanimous (ˌpjuːsɪˈlænɪməs) *adj* characterized by a lack of courage or determination [C16 from Late Latin *pusillanimis* from Latin *pusillus* weak + *animus* courage] > **pusillanimity** (ˌpjuːsɪləˈnɪmɪtɪ) *n* > ˌ**pusilˈlanimously** *adv*

puss[1] (pʊs) *n* **1** an informal name for a **cat.** See also **pussy**[1] (sense 1) **2** *slang* a girl or woman **3** an informal name for a **hare** [C16 related to Middle Low German *pūs*, Dutch *poes*, Lithuanian *puz*]

puss[2] (pʊs) *n slang* **1** the face **2** *Irish* a gloomy or sullen expression [C17 from Irish *pus*]

puss moth *n* a large pale prominent moth, *Cerura vinula*, whose larvae feed on willow and poplar, and are bright green with a masklike red head and claspers modified as "tails" that are protruded and raised in a state of alarm: family *Notodontidae*

pussy[1] (ˈpʊsɪ) *n, pl* **pussies 1** Also called: **puss, pussycat** (ˈpʊsɪˌkæt) an informal name for a **cat 2** a furry catkin, esp that of the pussy willow **3** a rare word for **tipcat 4** *taboo slang* the female pudenda **5** *taboo slang* a woman considered as a sexual object **6** *taboo slang, chiefly US* an ineffectual or timid person [C18 from PUSS[1]]

> USAGE Though possibly not quite as taboo for most people as the c... word, many still consider this item out of bounds in normal conversation and writing

pussy[2] (ˈpʌsɪ) *adj* **-sier, -siest** containing pus

pussycat (ˈpʊsɪˌkæt) *n* **1** an informal or child's name for a **cat**[1] (sense 1) **2** *Brit informal* an endearing or gentle person

pussyfoot (ˈpʊsɪˌfʊt) *informal* ▷ *vb* (*intr*) **1** to move about stealthily or warily like a cat **2** to avoid committing oneself ▷ *n, pl* **-foots 3** a person who pussyfoots

pussy willow (ˈpʊsɪ) *n* **1** a willow tree that produces silvery silky catkins, esp *Salix caprea* or *S. cinerea* in Britain or *S. discolor* in North America **2** any of various similar willows

pustulant (ˈpʌstjʊlənt) *adj* **1** causing the formation of pustules ▷ *n* **2** an agent causing such formation

pustulate *vb* (ˈpʌstjʊˌleɪt) **1** to form or cause to form into pustules ▷ *adj* (ˈpʌstjʊlɪt, -ˌleɪt) **2** covered with pustules > ˌ**pustuˈlation** *n*

pustule (ˈpʌstjuːl) *n* **1** a small inflamed elevated area of skin containing pus **2** any small distinct spot resembling a pimple or blister [C14 from Latin *pustula* a blister, variant of *pūsula*; compare Greek *phusallis* bladder, *phusa* bellows] > **pustular** (ˈpʌstjʊlə) *adj*

put (pʊt) *vb* **puts, putting, put** (*mainly tr*) **1** to cause to be (in a position or place): *to put a book on the table* **2** to cause to be (in a state, relation, etc): *to put one's things in order* **3** (foll by *to*) to cause (a person) to experience the endurance or suffering (of): *to put to death; to put to the sword* **4** to set or commit (to an action, task, or duty), esp by force: *he put him to work* **5** to render, transform, or translate: *to put into English* **6** to set (words) in a musical form (esp in the phrase **put to music**) **7** (foll by *at*) to estimate: *he put the distance at fifty miles* **8** (foll by *to*) to utilize (for the purpose of): *he put his knowledge to good use* **9** (foll by *to*) to couple a female animal (with a male) for the purpose of breeding: *the farmer put his heifer to the bull* **10** to state; express: *to put it bluntly* **11** to set or make (an end or limit): *he put an end to the proceedings* **12** to present for consideration in anticipation of an answer or vote; propose: *he put the question to the committee; I put it to you that one day you will all die* **13** to invest (money) in; give (support) to: *he put five thousand pounds into the project* **14** to impart: *to put zest into a party* **15** to throw or cast **16 not know where to put oneself** to feel awkward or embarrassed **17 put paid to** to destroy irrevocably and utterly: *the manager's disfavour put paid to their hopes for promotion* **18 stay put** to refuse to leave; keep one's position ▷ *n* **19** a throw or cast, esp in putting the shot **20** Also called: **put option** *stock exchange* an option to sell a stated amount of securities at a specified price during a specified limited period. Compare **call** (sense 58) ▷ See also **put about, put across, put aside, put away, put back, put by, put down, put forth, put forward, put in, put off, put on, put on to, put out, put over, put through, put up, put upon** [C12 *puten* to push; related to Old English *potian* to push, Norwegian, Icelandic *pota* to poke]

put about *vb* (*adverb*) **1** *nautical* to change course or cause to change course: *we put about and headed for home* **2** (*tr*) to make widely known: **3** (*tr; usually passive*) to disconcert or disturb

put across *vb* (*tr*) **1** (*adverb*) to communicate in a comprehensible way: *he couldn't put things across very well* **2 put one across** *informal* to get (someone) to accept or believe a claim, excuse, etc, by deception: *they put one across their teacher*

putamen (pju:'teɪmɛn) *n, pl* **-tamina** (-'tæmɪnə) the hard endocarp or stone of fruits such as the peach, plum, and cherry [C19 from Latin: clippings, from *putāre* to prune]

putangitangi (pu:ˌtɑ:ᵊŋgi:'tɑ:ᵊŋgi:) *n, pl* **putangitangi** NZ another name for **paradise duck** [Māori]

put aside *vb* (*tr, adverb*) **1** to move (an object, etc) to one side, esp in rejection **2** to store up; save: *to put money aside for a rainy day* **3** to ignore or disregard: *let us put aside our differences*

putative ('pju:tətɪv) *adj* **1** (*prenominal*) commonly regarded as being: *the putative father* **2** (*prenominal*) considered to exist or have existed; inferred **3** *grammar* denoting a mood of the verb in some languages used when the speaker does not have direct evidence of what he is asserting, but has inferred it on the basis of something else [C15 from Late Latin *putātīvus* supposed, from Latin *putāre* to consider] > **'putatively** *adv*

put away *vb* (*tr, adverb*) **1** to return (something) to the correct or proper place: *he put away his books* **2** to save: *to put away money for the future* **3** to lock up in a prison, mental institution, etc: *they put him away for twenty years* **4** to eat or drink, esp in large amounts **5** to put to death, because of old age or illness: *the dog had to be put away*

put back *vb* (*tr, adverb*) **1** to return to its former place **2** to move to a later time or date: *the wedding was put back a fortnight* **3** to delay or impede the progress of: *the strike put back production severely*

put by *vb* (*tr, adverb*) to set aside (money, goods, etc) to be kept for the future; store; save

put down *vb* (*tr, adverb*) **1** to make a written record of **2** to repress: *to put down a rebellion* **3** to consider; account: *they put him down for an ignoramus* **4** to attribute: *I put the mistake down to his inexperience* **5** to put to death, because of old age or illness: *the vet put the cat down* **6** to table on the agenda: *the MPs put down a motion on the increase in crime* **7** to put (a baby) to bed **8** to dismiss, reject, or humiliate ▷ *n* **put-down 9** a cruelly crushing remark

put forth *vb* (*tr, adverb*) *formal* **1** to present; propose **2** (of a plant) to produce or bear (leaves, branches, shoots, etc)

put forward *vb* (*tr, adverb*) **1** to propose; suggest **2** to offer the name of; nominate

put in *vb* (*adverb*) **1** (*intr*) *nautical* to bring a vessel into port, esp for a brief stay: *we put in for fresh provisions* **2** (often foll by *for*) to apply or cause to apply (for a job, in a competition, etc) **3** (*tr*) to submit: *he put in his claims form* **4** to intervene with (a remark) during a conversation **5** (*tr*) to devote (time, effort, etc) to a task: *he put in three hours overtime last night* **6** (*tr*) to establish or appoint: *he put in a manager* **7** (*tr*) *cricket* to cause (a team, esp the opposing one) to bat ▷ *n* **put-in 8** *rugby* the act of throwing the ball into a scrum

putlog ('pʌtˌlɒg) *or* **putlock** *n* a short horizontal beam that with others supports the floor planks of a scaffold [C17 changed (through influence of LOG[1]) from earlier *putlock*, probably from PUT (past participle) + LOCK[1]]

put off *vb* **1** (*tr, adverb*) to postpone or delay: *they have put off the dance until tomorrow* **2** (*tr, adverb*) to evade (a person) by postponement or delay: *they tried to put him off, but he came anyway* **3** (*tr, adverb*) to confuse; disconcert: *he was put off by her appearance* **4** (*tr, preposition*) to cause to lose interest in or enjoyment of: *the accident put him off driving* **5** (*intr, adverb*) *nautical* to be launched off from shore or from a ship: *we put off in the lifeboat towards the ship* **6** (*tr, adverb*) *archaic* to remove (clothes) ▷ *n* **putoff 7** *chiefly US* a pretext or delay

put on *vb* (*tr, mainly adverb*) **1** to clothe oneself in: *to put on a coat* **2** (*usually passive*) to adopt (an attitude or feeling) insincerely: *his misery was just put on* **3** to present or stage (a play, show, etc) **4** to increase or add: *she put on weight; the batsman put on fifty runs before lunch* **5** to cause (an electrical device) to function **6** (*also preposition*) to wager (money) on a horse race, game, etc: *he put ten pounds on the favourite* **7** (*also preposition*) to impose as a burden or levy: *to put a tax on cars* **8** *cricket* to cause (a bowler) to bowl **9 put (someone) on a** to connect (a person) by telephone **b** *slang* to mock or tease ▷ *n* **put-on** *slang, chiefly US and Canadian* **10** a hoax or piece of mockery **11** an affected manner or mode of behaviour

put on to *vb* (*tr, preposition*) **1** to connect by telephone **2** to inform (someone) of (a person's location or activities): *I put the police on to him* **3** to tell (a person) about (someone or something beneficial): *can you put me on to a cheap supermarket?*

put out *vb* (*tr, adverb*) **1** (*often passive*) **a** to annoy; anger **b** to confound or disturb; confuse **2** to extinguish or douse (a fire, light, etc): *he put out the fire* **3** to poke forward: *to put out one's tongue* **4** to be or present a source of inconvenience or annoyance to (a person): *I hope I'm not putting you out* **5** to issue or publish; broadcast: *the authorities put out a leaflet* **6** to render unconscious **7** to dislocate: *he put out his shoulder in the accident* **8** to show or exert: *the workers put out all their energy in the campaign* **9** to pass, give out (work to be done) at different premises **10** to lend (money) at interest **11** *cricket* to dismiss (a player or team) **12** *baseball* to cause (a batter or runner) to be out by a fielding play ▷ *n* **putout 13** *baseball* a play in which the batter or runner is put out

put over *vb* (*tr, adverb*) **1** *informal* to communicate (facts, information, etc) comprehensibly: *he puts his thoughts over badly* **2** *chiefly US* to postpone; defer: *the match was put over a week.* Brit equivalent: **put off 3 put (a fast) one over on** *informal* to get (someone) to accept or believe a claim, excuse, etc, by deception: *he put one over on his boss*

put-put ('pʌtˌpʌt) *informal* ▷ *n* **1** a light chugging or popping sound, as made by a petrol engine **2** a vehicle powered by an engine making such a sound ▷ *vb* **-puts, -putting, -putted 3** (*intr*) to make or travel along with such a sound

Putrajaya ('pu:trəˌdʒeɪə) *n* officially the capital of Malaysia since 1999, in the SW Malay Peninsula; a high-tech garden city, construction of which began in 1995 and is expected to be complete in about 2010, when the population is planned to be over 300 000; government functions are being transferred in stages from Kuala Lumpur, starting in 1999

putrefy ('pju:trɪˌfaɪ) *vb* **-fies, -fying, -fied** (of organic matter) to decompose or rot with an offensive smell [C15 from Old French *putrefier* + Latin *putrefacere*, from *puter* rotten + *facere* to make] > **putrefaction** (ˌpju:trɪ'fækʃən) *n* > **ˌputre'factive** *or* **putrefacient** (ˌpju:trɪ'feɪʃənt) *adj* > **'putreˌfiable** *adj* > **'putreˌfier** *n*

putrescent (pju:'trɛsᵊnt) *adj* **1** becoming putrid; rotting **2** characterized by or undergoing putrefaction [C18 from Latin *putrescere* to become rotten] > **pu'trescence** *n*

putrescible (pju:'trɛsɪbᵊl) *adj* **1** liable to become putrid ▷ *n* **2** a putrescible substance [C18 from Latin *putrescere* to decay] > **puˌtresci'bility** *n*

putrescine (pju:'trɛsi:n, -ɪn) *n* a colourless crystalline amine produced by decaying animal matter; 1,4-diaminobutane. Formula: $H_2N(CH_2)_4NH_2$ [C20 from Latin *putrescere* + -INE[2]]

putrid ('pju:trɪd) *adj* **1** (of organic matter) in a state of decomposition, usually giving off a foul smell: *putrid meat* **2** morally corrupt or worthless **3** sickening; foul: *a putrid smell* **4** *informal* deficient in quality or value: *a putrid film* [C16 from Latin *putridus* rotten, from *putrēre* to be rotten] > **pu'tridity** *or* **'putridness** *n* > **'putridly** *adv*

putsch (pʊtʃ) *n* a violent and sudden uprising; political revolt, esp a coup d'état [C20 from German: from Swiss German: a push, of imitative origin]

putt (pʌt) *golf* ▷ *n* **1** a stroke on the green with a putter to roll the ball into or near the hole ▷ *vb* **2** to strike (the ball) in this way [C16 of Scottish origin; related to PUT]

puttee *or* **putty** ('pʌtɪ) *n, pl* **-tees** *or* **-ties** (*usually plural*) a strip of cloth worn wound around the legs from the ankle to the knee, esp as part of a military uniform in World War I [C19 from Hindi *paṭṭī*, from Sanskrit *paṭṭikā*, from *paṭṭa* cloth]

putter[1] ('pʌtə) *n golf* **1** a club for putting, usually having a solid metal head **2** a golfer who putts

putter[2] ('pʌtə) *US and Canadian* ▷ *vb* **1** (*intr*; often foll by *about* or *around*) to busy oneself in a desultory though agreeable manner **2** (*intr*; often foll by *along* or *about*) to move with little energy or direction: *to putter about town* **3** (*tr*; usually foll by *away*) to waste (time): ▷ *n* **4** the act of puttering ▷ Equivalent term (in Britain and certain other countries): **potter** [C16 (in the sense: to poke repeatedly): from Old English *potian* to thrust; see PUT]

putter[3] ('pʊtə) *n* **1** a person who puts: *the putter of a question* **2** a person who puts the shot

put through *vb* (*tr, mainly adverb*) **1** to carry out to a conclusion: *he put through his plan* **2** (*also preposition*) to organize the processing of: *she put through his application to join the organization* **3** to connect by telephone **4** to make (a telephone call)

putting green ('pʌtɪŋ) *n* **1** (on a golf course) the area of closely mown grass at the end of a fairway where the hole is **2** an area of smooth grass with several holes for putting games

putto ('pʊtəʊ) *n, pl* **-ti** (-tɪ) a representation of a small boy, a cherub or cupid, esp in baroque painting or sculpture. See also **amoretto** [from Italian, from Latin *putus* boy]

putty ('pʌtɪ) *n, pl* **-ties 1** a stiff paste made of whiting and linseed oil that is used to fix glass panes into frames and to fill cracks or holes in woodwork, etc **2** any substance with a similar consistency, function, or appearance **3** a mixture of lime and water with sand or plaster of Paris used on plaster as a finishing coat **4** (*as modifier*): *a putty knife* **5** See **putty powder 6** a person who is easily influenced or persuaded: *he's putty in her hands* **7 a** a colour varying from a greyish-yellow to a greyish-brown or brownish-grey **b** (*as adjective*): *putty-coloured* **8 up to putty** *Austral informal* worthless or useless ▷ *vb* **-ties, -tying, -tied 9** (*tr*) to fix, fill, or coat with putty [C17 from French *potée* a potful]

putty powder *n* a powder, either tin oxide or tin and lead oxide, used for polishing glassware, metal, etc

Putumayo (*Spanish* putu'majo) *n* a river in NW South America, rising in S Colombia and flowing southeast as most of the border between Colombia and Peru, entering the Amazon in Brazil: scene of the Putumayo rubber scandal (1910–11) during the rubber boom, in which many Indians were enslaved and killed by rubber exploiters. Length: 1578 km (980 miles). Brazilian name: **Içá**

put up *vb* (*adverb, mainly tr*) **1** to build; erect: *to put up a statue* **2** to accommodate or be accommodated at: *can you put me up for tonight?* **3** to increase (prices) **4** to submit or present (a plan, case, etc) **5** to offer: *to put a house up for sale* **6** to provide or supply; give: *to put up a good fight* **7** to provide (money) for; invest in: *they put up five thousand for the new project* **8** to preserve or can (jam, etc) **9** to pile up (long hair) on the head in any of several styles **10** (*also intr*) to nominate or be nominated as a candidate, esp for a political or society post: *he put his wife up as secretary; he put up for president* **11** *archaic* to return (a weapon) to its holder, as a sword to its sheath: *put up your pistol!* **12 put up to a** to inform or instruct (a person) about (tasks, duties, etc) **b** to urge or goad (a person) on to; incite to **13 put up with** *informal* to endure; tolerate ▷ *adj* **put-up 14** dishonestly or craftily prearranged or conceived (esp in the phrase **put-up job**)

put upon *vb* (*intr, preposition, usually passive*) **1** to presume on (a person's generosity, good nature, etc); take advantage of: *he's always being put upon* **2** to impose hardship on; maltreat

P

putz (pʌts) *n US slang* a despicable or stupid person [from Yiddish *puts* ornament]

Puy de Dôme (pwi də dom) *n* **1** a department of central France in Auvergne region. Capital: Clermont-Ferrand. Pop: 609 817 (2003 est). Area: 8016 sq km (3094 sq miles) **2** a mountain in central France, in the Auvergne Mountains: a volcanic plug. Height: 1485 m (4872 ft)

Puy de Sancy (*French* pwi də sãsi) *n* a mountain in S central France: highest peak of the Monts Dore. Height: 1886 m (6188 ft)

puy lentil (pwi:) *n* a greyish-green variety of lentil that retains its shape after cooking [c20 named after *Le Puy*, in Haute-Loire, France]

puzzle ('pʌz²l) *vb* **1** to perplex or be perplexed **2** (*intr*; foll by *over*) to attempt the solution (of); ponder (about): *he puzzled over her absence* **3** (*tr*; usually foll by *out*) to solve by mental effort: *he puzzled out the meaning of the inscription* ▷ *n* **4** a person or thing that puzzles **5** a problem that cannot be easily or readily solved **6** the state or condition of being puzzled **7** a toy, game, or question presenting a problem that requires skill or ingenuity for its solution. See **jigsaw puzzle**, **Chinese puzzle** [c16 of unknown origin] > 'puzzling *adj*

puzzlement ('pʌz²lmənt) *n* the state or condition of being puzzled; perplexity

puzzler ('pʌzlə) *n* a person or thing that puzzles

puzzolana (ˌpʊtsə'lɑːnə) *n* a variant of **pozzuolana**

PVA *abbreviation for* polyvinyl acetate

PVC *abbreviation for* polyvinyl chloride; a synthetic thermoplastic material made by polymerizing vinyl chloride. The properties depend on the added plasticizer. The flexible forms are used in hosepipes, insulation, shoes, garments, etc Rigid PVC is used for moulded articles

PVR *abbreviation for* personal(ized) video recorder: a device for recording and replaying television programmes and films etc that uses a hard disk rather than videocassettes or DVDs and has various computer functions

PVS *abbreviation for* **1** persistent vegetative state **2** postviral syndrome

Pvt. *military abbreviation for* private

pw *the internet domain name for* Palau

PW *abbreviation for* policewoman

PWA *abbreviation for* person with AIDS

PWR *abbreviation for* pressurized-water reactor

pwt *abbreviation for* pennyweight

PX *US military abbreviation for* Post Exchange

py *the internet domain name for* Paraguay

PY *international car registration for* Paraguay

py- *combining form* variant of **pyo-** before a vowel

pya (pjɑː, pɪˈɑː) *n* a monetary unit of Myanmar worth one hundredth of a kyat [from Burmese]

pyaemia or **pyemia** (paɪˈiːmɪə) *n* blood poisoning characterized by pus-forming microorganisms in the blood [c19 from New Latin, from Greek *puon* pus + *haima* blood] > py'aemic or py'emic *adj*

pyat, pyot or **pyet** ('paɪət) *Scot* ▷ *n* **1** the magpie ▷ *adj* **2** pied [Middle English *piot*, from PIE²]

pycnidium (pɪk'nɪdɪəm) *n, pl* -ia (-ɪə) a small flask-shaped structure containing spores that occurs in ascomycetes and certain other fungi [c19 from New Latin, from Greek *puknos* thick]

pycno- or before a vowel **pycn-** *combining form* indicating thickness or density: *pycnometer* [via New Latin from Greek *puknos* thick]

pycnometer (pɪk'nɒmɪtə) *n* a small glass bottle of known volume for determining the relative density of liquids and solids by weighing > pycnometric (ˌpɪknə'mɛtrɪk) *adj*

Pydna ('pɪdnə) *n* a town in ancient Macedonia: site of a major Roman victory over the Macedonians, resulting in the downfall of their kingdom (168 BC)

pye (paɪ) *n* a variant spelling of **pie⁵**

pye-dog, pie-dog or **pi-dog** *n* an ownerless half-wild Asian dog [c19 Anglo-Indian *pye, paë,*

from Hindi *pāhī* outsider]

pyelitis (ˌpaɪə'laɪtɪs) *n* inflammation of the pelvis of the kidney. Compare **pyelonephritis**. > pyelitic (ˌpaɪə'lɪtɪk) *adj*

pyelo- or before a vowel **pyel-** *combining form* denoting the renal pelvis: *pyelonephritis* [from Greek *puelos* trough, pan; in the sense: pelvis]

pyelography (ˌpaɪə'lɒɡrəfɪ) *n med* the branch of radiology concerned with examination of the kidney and associated structures by means of an X-ray picture called a **pyelogram** ('paɪələʊˌɡræm). Also called: **urography** > pyelographic (ˌpaɪələʊ'ɡræfɪk) *adj*

pyelonephritis (ˌpaɪələʊnɪ'fraɪtɪs) *n* inflammation of the kidney and renal pelvis. Compare **pyelitis**

pygidium (paɪ'dʒɪdɪəm, -'ɡɪd-) *n, pl* -ia (-ɪə) the terminal segment, division, or other structure in certain annelids, arthropods, and other invertebrates [c19 from New Latin, from Greek *pugē* rump] > py'gidial *adj*

Pygmalion (pɪɡ'meɪlɪən) *n Greek myth* a king of Cyprus, who fell in love with the statue of a woman he had sculpted and which his prayers brought to life as Galatea

pygmy or **pigmy** ('pɪɡmɪ) *n, pl* -mies **1** an abnormally undersized person **2** something that is a very small example of its type **3** a person of little importance or significance **4** (*modifier*) of very small stature or size [c14 *pigmeis* the Pygmies, from Latin *Pygmaeus* a Pygmy, from Greek *pugmaios* undersized, from *pugmē* fist] > **pygmaean** or **pygmean** (pɪɡ'miːən) *adj*

Pygmy or **Pigmy** ('pɪɡmɪ) *n, pl* -mies a member of one of the dwarf peoples of Equatorial Africa, noted for their hunting and forest culture

pygmy chimpanzee *n* another name for **bonobo**

pygmy glider *n* a small arboreal marsupial, *Acrobates pygmaeus*, of Australia and New Guinea moving with gliding leaps using folds of skin between the hind limbs and forelimbs

pygmy possum *n* any of various small Australasian marsupials, esp the burramys

pyinkado (pjɪŋ'kɑːdəʊ) *n* **1** a leguminous tree, *Xylia xylocarpa* (or *dolabriformis*), native to India and Myanmar **2** the heavy durable timber of this tree, used for construction [c19 from Burmese]

pyjama or *US* **pajama** (pə'dʒɑːmə) *n* (*modifier*) **1** of or forming part of pyjamas: *pyjama top* **2** requiring pyjamas to be worn: *a pyjama party* ▷ See also **pyjamas** [c19 via Persian or Urdu from Persian *pāē, pāÿ* foot, leg + *jāmah* clothing, garment]

pyjamas or *US* **pajamas** (pə'dʒɑːməz) *pl n* **1** loose-fitting nightclothes comprising a jacket or top and trousers **2** full loose-fitting ankle-length trousers worn by either sex in various Eastern countries **3** women's flared trousers or trouser suit used esp for leisure wear

pyknic ('pɪknɪk) *adj* (of a physical type) characterized by a broad squat fleshy physique with a large chest and abdomen [c20 from Greek *puknos* thick]

pylon ('paɪlən) *n* **1** a large vertical steel tower-like structure supporting high-tension electrical cables **2** a post or tower for guiding pilots or marking a turning point in a race **3** a streamlined aircraft structure for attaching an engine pod, external fuel tank, etc, to the main body of the aircraft **4** a monumental gateway, such as one at the entrance to an ancient Egyptian temple **5** a temporary artificial leg [c19 from Greek *pulōn* a gateway]

pylorectomy (ˌpaɪlɔː'rɛktəmɪ) *n, pl* -mies the surgical removal of all or part of the pylorus, often including the adjacent portion of the stomach (**partial gastrectomy**)

pylorus (paɪ'lɔːrəs) *n, pl* -ri (-raɪ) the small circular opening at the base of the stomach through which partially digested food (chyme) passes to the duodenum [c17 via Late Latin from Greek *pulōros* gatekeeper, from *pulē* gate + *ouros* guardian] > py'loric *adj*

Pylos ('paɪlɒs) *n* a port in SW Greece, in the SW Peloponnese; scene of a defeat of the Spartans by the Athenians (425 BC) during the Peloponnesian War and of the Battle of Navarino (see **Navarino**). Italian name: **Navarino**. Modern Greek name: **Pílos**

pyo- or before a vowel **py-** *combining form* denoting pus: *pyosis* [from Greek *puon*]

pyoderma (ˌpaɪəʊ'dɜːmə) *n pathol* any skin eruption characterized by pustules or the formation of pus

pyogenesis (ˌpaɪəʊ'dʒɛnɪsɪs) *n pathol* the formation of pus > ˌpyo'genic *adj*

pyoid ('paɪɔɪd) *adj* resembling pus

Pyongyang or **P'yŏng-yang** ('pjɒŋ'jæŋ) *n* the capital of North Korea, in the southwest on the Taedong River: industrial centre; university (1946). Pop: 3 284 000 (2005 est)

pyorrhoea or *esp US* **pyorrhea** (ˌpaɪə'rɪə) *n* inflammation of the gums characterized by the discharge of pus and loosening of the teeth; periodontal disease > ˌpyor'rhoeal, ˌpyor'rhoeic or *esp US* ˌpyor'rheal, ˌpyor'rheic *adj*

pyosis (paɪ'əʊsɪs) *n pathol* the formation of pus

pyr- *combining form* a variant of **pyro-** before a vowel

pyracantha (ˌpaɪrə'kænθə) *n* any rosaceous shrub of the genus *Pyracantha*, esp the firethorn, widely cultivated for ornament [c17 from Greek *purakantha* name of a shrub, from PYRO- + *akantha* thorn]

pyralid ('pɪrəlɪd) *n* **1** any moth of the mostly tropical family *Pyralidae*, typically having narrow forewings and broad fringed hind wings: includes the bee moths and the corn borer ▷ *adj* **2** of, relating to, or belonging to the family *Pyralidae* [c19 via New Latin from Greek *puralis*: a mythical winged insect believed to live in fire, from *pur* fire]

pyramid ('pɪrəmɪd) *n* **1** a huge masonry construction that has a square base and, as in the case of the ancient Egyptian royal tombs, four sloping triangular sides **2** an object, formation, or structure resembling such a construction **3** *maths* a solid having a polygonal base and triangular sides that meet in a common vertex **4** *crystallog* a crystal form in which three planes intersect all three axes of the crystal **5** *anatomy* any pointed or cone-shaped bodily structure or part **6** *finance* a group of enterprises containing a series of holding companies structured so that the top holding company controls the entire group with a relatively small proportion of the total capital invested **7** *chiefly US* the series of transactions involved in pyramiding securities **8** (*plural*) a game similar to billiards with fifteen coloured balls ▷ *vb* **9** to build up or be arranged in the form of a pyramid **10** *chiefly US* to speculate in (securities or property) by increasing purchases on additional margin or collateral derived from paper profits associated with high prices of securities and property in a boom **11** *finance* to form (companies) into a pyramid [c16 (earlier *pyramis*): from Latin *pyramis*, from Greek *puramis*, probably from Egyptian] > **pyramidal** (pɪ'ræmɪd²l), ˌpyra'midical or ˌpyra'midic *adj* > py'ramidally or ˌpyra'midically *adv*

pyramidal orchid *n* a chalk-loving orchid, *Anacamptis pyramidalis*, bearing a dense cone-shaped spike of purplish-pink flowers with a long curved spur

pyramidal peak *n geology* a sharp peak formed where the ridges separating three or more cirques intersect; horn

pyramid selling *n* a practice adopted by some manufacturers of advertising for distributors and selling them batches of goods. The first distributors then advertise for more distributors who are sold subdivisions of the original batches at an increased price. This process continues until the final distributors are left with a stock that is unsaleable except at a loss

Pyramus and Thisbe ('pɪrəməs, 'θɪzbɪ) *n* (in Greek legend) two lovers of Babylon: Pyramus, wrongly supposing Thisbe to be dead, killed himself and she, encountering him in his death throes, did the same

pyran ('paɪræn, paɪ'ræn) *n* an unsaturated heterocyclic compound having a ring containing five carbon atoms and one oxygen atom and two double bonds. It has two isomers depending on the position of the saturated carbon atom relative to the oxygen [C20 from PYRO- + -AN]

pyranometer (ˌpaɪrə'nɒmɪtə) *n physics* another name for **solarimeter**

pyrargyrite (paɪ'rɑːdʒɪˌraɪt) *n* a dark red to black mineral consisting of silver antimony sulphide in hexagonal crystalline form: occurs in silver veins and is an important ore of silver. Formula: Ag_3SbS_3 [C19 from German *Pyrargyrit*, from PYRO- + Greek *arguros* silver]

pyrazole ('paɪrəˌzəʊl) *n* a crystalline soluble basic heterocyclic compound; 1,2-diazole. Formula: $C_3H_4N_2$ [C19 from German, from PYRROLE + inserted -*az*- (see AZO-)]

pyre (paɪə) *n* a heap or pile of wood or other combustible material, esp one used for cremating a corpse [C17 from Latin *pyra*, from Greek *pura* hearth, from *pur* fire]

pyrene[1] ('paɪriːn) *n* a solid polynuclear aromatic hydrocarbon extracted from coal tar. Formula: $C_{16}H_{10}$ [C19 from PYRO- + -ENE]

pyrene[2] ('paɪriːn) *n botany* any of several small hard stones that occur in a single fruit and contain a single seed each [C19 from New Latin *pyrena*, from Greek *purēn*]

Pyrenean (ˌpɪrə'niːən) *adj* of or relating to the Pyrenees or their inhabitants

Pyrenean mountain dog *n* a large heavily built dog of an ancient breed originally used to protect sheep from wild animals: it has a long thick white coat with a dense ruff. Also called: **Great Pyrenees**

Pyrenees (ˌpɪrə'niːz) *pl n* a mountain range between France and Spain, extending from the Bay of Biscay to the Mediterranean. Highest peak: Pico de Aneto, 3404 m (11 168 ft)

Pyrénées-Atlantiques (*French* pirenez-atlãtik) *or* **Pyrénées** *n* a department of SW France in Aquitaine region. Capital: Pau. Pop: 614 174 (2003 est). Area: 7712 sq km (3008 sq miles). Former name: **Basses-Pyrénées**

Pyrénées-Orientales (*French* pirenezɔrjãtal) *n* a department of S France, in Languedoc-Roussillon region. Capital: Perpignan. Pop: 411 447 (2003 est). Area: 4144 sq km (1616 sq miles)

pyrenoid ('paɪrəˌnɔɪd) *n* any of various small protein granules that occur in certain algae, mosses, and protozoans and are involved in the synthesis of starch [C19 from PYRENE[2] + -OID]

pyrethrin (paɪ'riːθrɪn) *n* **1** Also called: **pyrethrin I** an oily water-insoluble compound used as an insecticide. Formula: $C_{21}H_{28}O_3$ **2** Also called: **pyrethrin II** a compound of similar chemical structure and action, also found in pyrethrum. Formula: $C_{22}H_{28}O_5$ [C19 from PYRETHRUM + -IN]

pyrethroid (paɪ'riːθrɔɪd) *n* **1** any of various chemical compounds having similar insecticidal properties to pyrethrin ▷ *adj* **2** of or relating to such compounds

pyrethrum (paɪ'riːθrəm) *n* **1** any of several cultivated Eurasian chrysanthemums, such as *Chrysanthemum coccineum* and *C. roseum*, with white, pink, red, or purple flowers **2** any insecticide prepared from the dried flowers of any of these plants, esp *C. roseum* [C16 via Latin from Greek *purethron* feverfew, probably from *puretos* fever; see PYRETIC]

pyretic (paɪ'rɛtɪk) *adj pathol* of, relating to, or characterized by fever. Compare **antipyretic** [C18 from New Latin *pyreticus*, from Greek *puretos* fever, from *pur* fire]

Pyrex ('paɪrɛks) *n trademark* **a** any of a variety of borosilicate glasses that have low coefficients of expansion, making them suitable for heat-resistant glassware used in cookery and chemical apparatus **b** (*as modifier*): *a Pyrex dish*

pyrexia (paɪ'rɛksɪə) *n* a technical name for **fever** [C18 from New Latin, from Greek *purexis*, from *puressein* to be feverish, from *pur* fire] > **py'rexial** *or* **py'rexic** *adj*

pyrgeometer (ˌpɜːdʒɪ'ɒmɪtə) *n physics* an instrument for measuring the loss of heat by radiation from the earth's surface

pyrheliometer (pəˌhiːlɪ'ɒmɪtə) *n* an instrument for measuring the intensity of the sun's radiant energy > pyrheliometric (pəˌhiːlɪə'mɛtrɪk) *adj*

pyridine ('pɪrɪˌdiːn) *n* a colourless hygroscopic liquid with a characteristic odour. It is a basic heterocyclic compound containing one nitrogen atom and five carbon atoms in its molecules and is used as a solvent and in preparing other organic chemicals. Formula: C_5H_5N [C19 from PYRO- + -ID[3] + -INE[2]]

pyridoxal (ˌpɪrɪ'dɒksəl) *n biochem* a naturally occurring derivative of pyridoxine that is a precursor of a coenzyme (**pyridoxal phosphate**) involved in several enzymic reactions. Formula: $(CH_2OH)(CHO)C_5HN(OH)(CH_3)$

pyridoxamine (ˌpɪrɪ'dɒksəmiːn) *n biochem* a metabolic form of pyridoxine

pyridoxine (ˌpɪrɪ'dɒksiːn) *n biochem* a derivative of pyridine that is a precursor of the compounds pyridoxal and pyridoxamine. Also called: **vitamin B_6** [C20 from PYRID(INE) + OX(YGEN) + -INE[2]]

pyriform ('pɪrɪˌfɔːm) *adj* (esp of organs of the body) pear-shaped [C18 from New Latin *pyriformis*, from *pyri*-, erroneously from Latin *pirum* pear + -*formis* -FORM]

pyrimidine (paɪ'rɪmɪˌdiːn) *n* **1** a liquid or crystalline organic compound with a penetrating odour; 1,3-diazine. It is a weakly basic soluble heterocyclic compound and can be prepared from barbituric acid. Formula: $C_4H_4N_2$ **2** Also called: **pyrimidine base** any of a number of similar compounds having a basic structure that is derived from pyrimidine, including cytosine, thymine, and uracil, which are constituents of nucleic acids [C20 variant of PYRIDINE]

pyrite ('paɪraɪt) *n* a yellow mineral, found in igneous and metamorphic rocks and in veins. It is a source of sulphur and is used in the manufacture of sulphuric acid. Composition: iron sulphide. Formula: FeS_2. Crystal structure: cubic. Also called: **iron pyrites, pyrites** Nontechnical name: **fool's gold** [C16 from Latin *pyrites* flint, from Greek *puritēs* (*lithos*) fire (stone), that is, capable of withstanding or striking fire, from *pur* fire] > pyritic (paɪ'rɪtɪk) *or* **py'ritous** *adj*

pyrites (paɪ'raɪtiːz; *in combination* 'paɪraɪts) *n, pl* -tes **1** another name for **pyrite 2** any of a number of other disulphides of metals, esp of copper and tin

pyro- *or before a vowel* **pyr-** *combining form* **1** denoting fire, heat, or high temperature: *pyromania; pyrometer* **2** caused or obtained by fire or heat: *pyroelectricity* **3** *chem* **a** denoting a new substance obtained by heating another: *pyroboric acid is obtained by heating boric acid* **b** denoting an acid or salt with a water content intermediate between that of the ortho- and meta- compounds: *pyro-phosphoric acid* **4** *mineralogy* **a** having a property that changes upon the application of heat: *pyromorphite* **b** having a flame-coloured appearance: *pyroxylin*

pyrocatechol (ˌpaɪrəʊ'kætɪˌtʃɒl, -kɒl) *or* **pyrocatechin** (ˌpaɪrəʊ'kætɪkɪn) *n* another name for **catechol**

pyrochemical (ˌpaɪrəʊ'kɛmɪkəl) *adj* of, concerned with, being, producing, or resulting from chemical changes at high temperatures > ˌpyro'chemically *adv*

pyroclastic (ˌpaɪrəʊ'klæstɪk) *adj* (of rocks) formed from the solid fragments ejected during a volcanic eruption

pyroconductivity (ˌpaɪrəʊˌkɒndʌ'tɪvɪtɪ) *n* conductivity that can be induced in certain solids by heating them

pyroelectric (ˌpaɪrəʊɪ'lɛktrɪk) *adj* **1** of, concerned

with, or exhibiting pyroelectricity ▷ *n* **2** a pyroelectric substance

pyroelectricity (ˌpaɪrəʊɪlɛk'trɪsɪtɪ, -ˌiːlɛk-) *n* the development of opposite charges at the ends of the axis of certain hemihedral crystals, such as tourmaline, as a result of a change in temperature

pyrogallate (ˌpaɪrəʊ'gæleɪt) *n* any salt or ester of pyrogallol

pyrogallol (ˌpaɪrəʊ'gælɒl) *n* a white lustrous crystalline soluble phenol with weakly acidic properties; 1,2,3-trihydroxybenzene: used as a photographic developer and for absorbing oxygen. Formula: $C_6H_3(OH)_3$ [C20 from PYRO- + GALL(IC)[2] + -OL[1]] > ˌpyro'gallic *adj*

pyrogen ('paɪrəʊˌdʒɛn) *n* any of a group of substances that cause a rise in temperature in an animal body

pyrogenic (ˌpaɪrəʊ'dʒɛnɪk) *or* **pyrogenous** (paɪ'rɒdʒɪnəs) *adj* **1** produced by or producing heat **2** *pathol* causing or resulting from fever **3** *geology* less common words for **igneous**

pyrognostics (ˌpaɪrɒg'nɒstɪks) *pl n* the characteristics of a mineral, such as fusibility and flame coloration, that are revealed by the application of heat [C19 from PYRO- + -gnostics, from Greek *gnōsis* knowledge]

pyrography (paɪ'rɒgrəfɪ) *n, pl* -phies **1** the art or process of burning designs on wood or leather with heated tools or a flame **2** a design made by this process > py'rographer *n* > pyrographic (ˌpaɪrəʊ'græfɪk) *adj*

pyroligneous (ˌpaɪrəʊ'lɪgnɪəs) *or* **pyrolignic** *adj* (of a substance) produced by the action of heat on wood, esp by destructive distillation [C18 from French *pyroligneux*, from PYRO- + *ligneux* LIGNEOUS]

pyroligneous acid *n* the crude reddish-brown acidic liquid obtained by the distillation of wood and containing acetic acid, methanol, and acetone. Also called: **wood vinegar**

pyrolusite (ˌpaɪrəʊ'luːsaɪt) *n* a blackish fibrous or soft powdery mineral consisting of manganese dioxide in tetragonal crystalline form. It occurs in association with other manganese ores and is an important source of manganese. Formula: MnO_2 [C19 from PYRO- + Greek *lousis* a washing + -ITE[1], from its use in purifying glass]

pyrolyse *or US* **pyrolyze** ('paɪrəʊˌlaɪz) *vb* (*tr*) to subject to pyrolysis > 'pyro,lyser *or* 'pyro,lyzer *n*

pyrolysis (paɪ'rɒlɪsɪs) *n* **1** the application of heat to chemical compounds in order to cause decomposition **2** chemical decomposition of compounds caused by high temperatures > pyrolytic (ˌpaɪrəʊ'lɪtɪk) *adj*

pyromagnetic (ˌpaɪrəʊmæg'nɛtɪk) *adj* a former term for **thermomagnetic**

pyromancy ('paɪrəʊˌmænsɪ) *n* divination by fire or flames > 'pyro,mancer *n* > ˌpyro'mantic *adj*

pyromania (ˌpaɪrəʊ'meɪnɪə) *n psychiatry* the uncontrollable impulse and practice of setting things on fire > ˌpyro'mani,ac *n* > pyromaniacal (ˌpaɪrəʊmə'naɪəkəl) *adj*

pyrometallurgy (ˌpaɪrəʊmɛ'tælədʒɪ, -'mɛtəˌlɜːdʒɪ) *n* the branch of metallurgy involving processes performed at high temperatures, including sintering, roasting, smelting, casting, refining, alloying, and heat treatment

pyrometer (paɪ'rɒmɪtə) *n* an instrument for measuring high temperatures, esp by measuring the brightness (**optical pyrometer**) or total quantity (**radiation pyrometer**) of the radiation produced by the source. Other types include the resistance thermometer and the thermocouple > pyrometric (ˌpaɪrəʊ'mɛtrɪk) *or* ˌpyro'metrical *adj* > ˌpyro'metrically *adv* > py'rometry *n*

pyromorphite (ˌpaɪrəʊ'mɔːfaɪt) *n* a green, yellow, brown, or grey secondary mineral that consists of lead chloro-phosphate in the form of hexagonal crystals. Formula: $Pb_5Cl(PO_4)_3$ [C19 from German *Pyromorphit*, from PYRO- + Greek *morphē* form + -ITE[1], an allusion to the fact that it assumes a crystalline form when heated]

P

pyrone ('paɪrəʊn, paɪ'rəʊn) *n* **1** either of two heterocyclic compounds that have a ring containing five carbon atoms and one oxygen atom with two double bonds and a second oxygen atom attached to a carbon atom in either the *ortho*-position (**alpha pyrone**) or the *para*-position (**gamma pyrone**) **2** any one of a class of compounds that are substituted derivatives of a pyrone

pyrope ('paɪrəʊp) *n* a deep yellowish-red garnet that consists of magnesium aluminium silicate and is used as a gemstone. Formula: $Mg_3Al_2(SiO_4)_3$ [C14 (used loosely a red gem; modern sense C19): from Old French *pirope*, from Latin *pyrōpus* bronze, from Greek *purōpus* fiery-eyed, from *pur* fire + *ōps* eye]

pyrophoric (ˌpaɪrəʊ'fɒrɪk) *adj* **1** (of a chemical) igniting spontaneously on contact with air **2** (of an alloy) producing sparks when struck or scraped: *lighter flints are made of pyrophoric alloy* [C19 from New Latin *pyrophorus*, from Greek *purophoros* fire-bearing, from *pur* fire + *pherein* to bear]

pyrophosphate (ˌpaɪrəʊ'fɒsfeɪt) *n* any salt or ester of pyrophosphoric acid

pyrophosphoric acid (ˌpaɪrəʊfɒs'fɒrɪk) *n* a crystalline soluble solid acid formed by the reaction between one molecule of phosphorus pentoxide and two water molecules. Formula: $H_4P_2O_7$. See also **polyphosphoric acid**

pyrophotometer (ˌpaɪrəʊfəʊ'tɒmɪtə) *n* a type of pyrometer in which the temperature of an incandescent body is determined by photometric measurement of the light it emits > ˌpyropho'tometry *n*

pyrophyllite (ˌpaɪrəʊ'fɪlaɪt) *n* a white, silvery, or green micaceous mineral that consists of hydrated aluminium silicate in monoclinic crystalline form and occurs in metamorphic rocks. Formula: $Al_2Si_4O_{10}(OH)_2$

pyrosis (paɪ'rəʊsɪs) *n pathol* a technical name for **heartburn** [C18 from New Latin, from Greek: a burning, from *puroun* to burn, from *pur* fire]

pyrostat ('paɪrəʊˌstæt) *n* **1** a device that activates an alarm or extinguisher in the event of a fire **2** a thermostat for use at high temperatures > ˌpyro'static *adj*

pyrosulphate (ˌpaɪrəʊ'sʌlfeɪt) *n* any salt of pyrosulphuric acid. Also called: **disulphate**

pyrosulphuric acid (ˌpaɪrəʊsʌl'fjʊərɪk) *n* a fuming liquid acid made by adding sulphur trioxide to concentrated sulphuric acid. Formula: $H_2S_2O_7$. Also called: **disulphuric acid** See also **fuming sulphuric acid**

pyrotechnics (ˌpaɪrəʊ'tɛknɪks) *n* **1** (*functioning as singular*) the art or craft of making fireworks **2** (*functioning as singular or plural*) a firework display **3** (*functioning as singular or plural*) brilliance of display, as in the performance of music: *keyboard pyrotechnics* ▷ Also called: **pyrotechnic** > ˌpyro'technic *or* ˌpyro'technical *adj*

pyroxene (paɪ'rɒksiːn) *n* any of a group of silicate minerals having the general formula $ABSi_2O_6$, where A is usually calcium, sodium, magnesium, or iron, and B is usually magnesium, iron, chromium, manganese, or aluminium. Pyroxenes occur in basic igneous rocks and some metamorphic rocks, and have colours ranging from white to dark green or black. They may be monoclinic (clinopyroxenes) or orthorhombic (orthopyroxenes) in crystal structure. Examples are augite (the most important pyroxene), diopside, enstatite, hypersthene, and jadeite [C19 PYRO- + -*xene* from Greek *xenos* foreign, because it was mistakenly thought to have originated elsewhere when found in igneous rocks] > pyroxenic (ˌpaɪrɒk'sɛnɪk) *adj*

pyroxenite (paɪ'rɒksɪˌnaɪt) *n* a very dark coarse-grained ultrabasic rock consisting entirely of pyroxene minerals

pyroxylin (paɪ'rɒksɪlɪn) *n* a yellow substance obtained by nitrating cellulose with a mixture of nitric and sulphuric acids; guncotton: used to make collodion, plastics, lacquers, and adhesives [C19 from PYRO- + XYL(O)- + -IN]

Pyrrha ('pɪrə) *n Greek myth* the wife of Deucalion, saved with him from the flood loosed upon mankind by Zeus

pyrrhic[1] ('pɪrɪk) *prosody* ▷ *n* **1** a metrical foot of two short or unstressed syllables ▷ *adj* **2** of or relating to such a metrical foot **3** (of poetry) composed in pyrrhics [C16 via Latin, from Greek *purrhikhē*, traditionally said to be named after its inventor *Purrhikhos*]

pyrrhic[2] ('pɪrɪk) *n* **1** a war dance of ancient Greece ▷ *adj* **2** of or relating to this dance [C17 Latin from Greek *purrhikhios* belonging to the *purrhikhē* war dance performed in armour; see PYRRHIC[1]]

Pyrrhic victory *n* a victory in which the victor's losses are as great as those of the defeated. Also called: **Cadmean victory** [named after *Pyrrhus* (319–272 BC), king of Epirus (306–272), who defeated the Romans at Asculum in 279 BC but suffered heavy losses]

Pyrrhonism ('pɪrənɪzəm) *n* the sceptical philosophy of Pyrrho, the Greek philosopher (?365–?275 BC) > 'Pyrrhonist *n, adj*

pyrrhotite ('pɪrəˌtaɪt) *or* **pyrrhotine** ('pɪrəˌtiːn, -ˌtaɪn, -tɪn) *n* a common bronze-coloured magnetic mineral consisting of ferrous sulphide in hexagonal crystalline form. Formula: FeS [C19 from Greek *purrhotēs* redness, from *purrhos* fiery, from *pur* fire]

pyrrhuloxia (ˌpɪrə'lɒksɪə) *n* a grey-and-pink crested bunting, *Pyrrhuloxia sinuata*, of Central and SW North America, with a short parrot-like bill [from New Latin *Pyrrhula* genus of the finches (from Greek *purrhoulas* a flame-coloured bird, from *purrhos* red, from *pur* fire) + *Loxia* genus of the crossbills, from Greek *loxos* oblique]

Pyrrhus ('pɪrəs) *n* another name for **Neoptolemus**

pyrrole ('pɪrəʊl, pɪ'rəʊl) *n* a colourless insoluble toxic liquid having a five-membered ring containing one nitrogen atom, found in many naturally occurring compounds, such as chlorophyll. Formula: C_4H_5N. Also called: **azole** [C19 from Greek *purrhos* red, from *pur* fire + -OLE[1]] > pyrrolic (pɪ'rɒlɪk) *adj*

pyrrolidine (pɪ'rɒlɪˌdiːn) *n* an almost colourless liquid occurring in tobacco leaves and made commercially by hydrogenating pyrrole. It is a strongly alkaline heterocyclic base with molecules that contain a ring of four carbon atoms and one nitrogen atom. Formula: C_4H_9N

pyruvic acid (paɪ'ruːvɪk) *n* a colourless pleasant-smelling liquid formed as an intermediate in the metabolism of proteins and carbohydrates, helping to release energy to the body; 2-oxopropanoic acid. Formula: $CH_3COCOOH$ [C19 *pyruvic* from PYRO- + Latin *ūva* grape]

Pythagoras (paɪ'θægərəs) *n* a deep crater in the NE quadrant of the moon, 136 kilometres in diameter

Pythagoras' theorem *n* the theorem that in a right-angled triangle the square of the length of the hypotenuse equals the sum of the squares of the other two sides

Pythagorean (paɪˌθægə'riːən) *adj* **1** of or relating to Pythagoras, the Greek philosopher and mathematician (?580–?500 BC) **2** *music* denoting the diatonic scale of eight notes arrived at by Pythagoras and based on a succession of fifths ▷ *n* **3** a follower of Pythagoras

Pythagoreanism (paɪˌθægə'riːəˌnɪzəm) *n* the teachings of Pythagoras and his followers, esp that the universe is essentially a manifestation of mathematical relationships

Pythia ('pɪθɪə) *n Greek myth* the priestess of Apollo at Delphi, who transmitted the oracles

Pythian ('pɪθɪən) *adj also* **Pythic 1** of or relating to Delphi or its oracle ▷ *n* **2** the priestess of Apollo at the oracle of Delphi **3** an inhabitant of ancient Delphi [C16 via Latin *Pȳthius* from Greek *Puthios* of Delphi]

Pythian Games *pl n* (in ancient Greece) the second most important Panhellenic festival, celebrated in the third year of each Olympiad near Delphi. The four-year period between celebrations was known as a **Pythiad** ('pɪθɪˌæd)

Pythias ('pɪθɪˌæs) *n* See **Damon and Pythias**

python ('paɪθən) *n* any large nonvenomous snake of the family *Pythonidae* of Africa, S Asia, and Australia, such as *Python reticulatus* (**reticulated python**). They can reach a length of more than 20 feet and kill their prey by constriction [C16 New Latin, after PYTHON] > pythonic (paɪ'θɒnɪk) *adj*

Python ('paɪθən) *n Greek myth* a dragon, killed by Apollo at Delphi

Pythonesque (ˌpaɪθə'nɛsk) *adj* denoting a kind of humour that is absurd and unpredictable; zany; surreal [C20 named after the British television show *Monty Python's Flying Circus*, first broadcast in 1969]

pythoness ('paɪθəˌnɛs) *n* **1** a woman, such as Apollo's priestess at Delphi, believed to be possessed by an oracular spirit **2** a female soothsayer [C14 *phitonesse*, ultimately from Greek *Puthōn* PYTHON]

pyuria (paɪ'jʊərɪə) *n pathol* any condition characterized by the presence of pus in the urine [C19 from New Latin, from Greek *puon* pus + *ouron* urine]

pyx *or less commonly* **pix** (pɪks) *n* **1** Also called: **pyx chest** the chest in which coins from the British mint are placed to be tested for weight, etc **2** *Christianity* any receptacle in which the Eucharistic Host is kept [C14 from Latin *pyxis* small box, from Greek, from *puxos* box tree]

pyxidium (pɪk'sɪdɪəm) *or* **pyxis** ('pɪksɪs) *n, pl* -**ia** (-ɪə) *or* **pyxides** ('pɪksɪˌdiːz) the dry fruit of such plants as the plantain: a capsule whose upper part falls off when mature so that the seeds are released [C19 via New Latin from Greek *puxidion* a little box, from *puxis* box, PYX]

pyxie ('pɪksɪ) *n* a creeping evergreen shrub, *Pyxidanthera barbulata*, of the eastern US with small white or pink star-shaped flowers: family *Diapensiaceae* [C19 shortened from New Latin *Pyxidanthera*, from PYXIS + ANTHER]

pyxis ('pɪksɪs) *n, pl* **pyxides** ('pɪksɪˌdiːz) **1** a small box used by the ancient Greeks and Romans to hold medicines, etc **2** a rare word for **pyx 3** another name for **pyxidium** [C14 via Latin from Greek: box]

Pyxis ('pɪksɪs) *n, Latin genitive* **Pyxidis** ('pɪksɪdɪs) an inconspicuous constellation close to Puppis that was originally considered part of the more extensive constellation Argo

PYY₃₋₃₆ *abbreviation for* peripheral hormone peptide YY: a hormone that regulates hunger. After food enters the stomach it is secreted into the blood by cells lining the colon and the ileum

pzazz (pə'zæz) *n informal* a variant of **pizzazz**

Qq

q or **Q** (kjuː) *n, pl* **q's, Q's** or **Qs** 1 the 17th letter and 13th consonant of the modern English alphabet 2 a speech sound represented by this letter, in English usually a voiceless velar stop, as in *unique* and *quick*

q *symbol for* quintal

Q *symbol for* 1 *chess* queen 2 question 3 *physics* heat *text messaging* ▷ *abbreviation for* 4 queue

q. *abbreviation for* 1 quart 2 quarter 3 quarterly

Q. *abbreviation for* 1 quartermaster 2 *pl* Qq, qq Also: q quarto 3 Queen 4 question

qa *the internet domain name for* Qatar

QA *international car registration for* Qatar

qabalah (kəˈbɑːlə) *n* a variant spelling of **kabbalah**. ▷ qabalism (ˈkæbəˌlɪzəm) *n* > 'qabalist *n* > ˌqaba'listic *adj*

Qabis (ˈkɑːbɪs) *n* the Arabic name for **Gabès**

Qaddish (ˈkædɪʃ) *n, pl* **Qaddishim** a variant spelling of **Kaddish**

qadi (ˈkɑːdɪ, ˈkeɪdɪ) *n, pl* **-dis** a variant spelling of **cadi**

Qairwan (kaɪəˈwɑːn) *n* a variant of **Kairouan**

QANTAS (ˈkwɒntəs) *n* the Australian national airline [acronym of Queensland *and* Northern Territory Aerial Services, its original name: founded 1920]

Qaraghandy (*Kazakh* karaɣanˈdɪ) *n* a variant transliteration of the Kazakh name for **Karaganda**

QARANC *abbreviation for* Queen Alexandra's Royal Army Nursing Corps

qat (kæt, kɑːt) *n* a variant spelling of **khat**

Qatar or **Katar** (kæˈtɑː) *n* a state in E Arabia, occupying a peninsula in the Persian Gulf: under Persian rule until the 19th century; became a British protectorate in 1916; declared independence in 1971; exports petroleum and natural gas. Official language: Arabic. Official religion: (Sunni) Muslim. Currency: riyal. Capital: Doha. Pop: 619 000 (2004 est). Area: about 11 000 sq km (4250 sq miles)

Qatari or **Katari** (kæˈtɑːrɪ) *adj* 1 of or relating to Qatar or its inhabitants ▷ *n* 2 a native or inhabitant of Qatar

Qattara Depression (kəˈtɑːrə) *n* an arid basin in the Sahara, in NW Egypt, impassable to vehicles. Area: about 18 000 sq km (7000 sq miles). Lowest point: 133 m (435 ft) below sea level

qawwali (kəˈvɑːlɪ) *n* an Islamic religious song, esp in Asia

QB 1 *abbreviation for* Queen's Bench 2 *chess symbol for* queen's bishop

QBP *chess symbol for* queen's bishop's pawn

QC *abbreviation for* 1 Queen's Counsel 2 (esp in postal addresses) Quebec

QCA (in Britain) *abbreviation for* Qualifications and Curriculum Authority

QCD *abbreviation for* quantum chromodynamics

q.e. *abbreviation for* quod est [Latin: which is]

QED *abbreviation for* 1 quod erat demonstrandum [Latin: which was to be shown or proved] 2 **quantum electrodynamics**

QEF *abbreviation for* quod erat faciendum [Latin: which was to be done]

Qeshm (ˈkɛʃəm) or **Qishm** *n* 1 the largest island in the Persian Gulf: part of Iran. Area: 1336 sq km (516 sq miles) 2 the chief town of this island

QF *abbreviation for* quick-firing

Q factor *n* 1 a measure of the relationship between stored energy and rate of energy dissipation in certain electrical components, devices, etc, thus indicating their efficiency 2 Also called: Q value the heat released in a nuclear reaction, usually expressed in millions of electronvolts for each individual reaction. Symbol: Q [c20 short for *quality factor*]

QFD *abbreviation for* **quantum flavourdynamics**

Q fever *n* an acute disease characterized by fever and pneumonia, transmitted to man by the rickettsia *Coxiella burnetii* [c20 from *q(uery)* fever (the cause being unknown when it was named)]

qi (tʃiː) *n* a variant of **chi²**

qibla (ˈkɪblə) *n* a variant of **kiblah**

qigong (ˈtʃɪˈɡɒŋ) or **chi kung** *n* a system of breathing and exercise designed to benefit both physical and mental health [c20 from Chinese *qi* energy + *gong* exercise]

qindar (ˈkɪntɑː) or **qintar** (kɪnˈtɑː) *n, pl* **qindarka** (-ˈdɑːkə) or **-tarka** (-ˈtɑːkə) an Albanian monetary unit worth one hundredth of a lek

Qingdao (ˈtʃɪŋˈdaʊ), **Tsingtao** or **Chingtao** *n* a port in E China, in E Shandong province on Jiazhou Bay, developed as a naval base and fort in 1891. Shandong university (1926). Pop: 2 431 000 (2005 est)

Qinghai, Tsinghai or **Chinghai** (ˈtʃɪŋˈhaɪ) *n* 1 a province of NW China: consists largely of mountains and high plateaus. Capital: Xining. Pop: 5 340 000 (2003 est). Area: 721 000 sq km (278 400 sq miles) 2 the Pinyin transliteration of the Chinese name for **Koko Nor**

qintar (kɪnˈtɑː) *n* a variant spelling of **qindar**

Qiqihar, Chichihaerh, Ch'i-ch'i-haerh or **Tsitsihar** (ˈtʃiːˌtʃiːˈhɑː) *n* a city in NE China, in Heilongjiang province on the Nonni River. Pop: 1 452 000 (2005 est)

Qishm (ˈkɪʃəm) *n* a variant of **Qeshm**

QKt *chess symbol for* queen's knight

QKtP *chess symbol for* queen's knight's pawn

ql *abbreviation for* quintal

q.l. (in prescriptions) *abbreviation for* quantum libet [Latin: as much as you please]

Qld or **QLD** *abbreviation for* Queensland

QM *abbreviation for* Quartermaster

q.m. (in prescriptions) *abbreviation for* quaque mane [Latin: every morning]

QMC *abbreviation for* Quartermaster Corps

Q-methodology *n* a statistical methodology used by psychologists to identify alternative world-views, opinions, interpretations, etc in terms of statistically independent patterns of response recognized by clustering together individuals whose orderings of items, typically attitude statements, are similar. Compare **R-methodology**

QMG *abbreviation for* Quartermaster General

QMS *abbreviation for* Quartermaster Sergeant

QMV *abbreviation for* **Qualified Majority Voting**

qn (in prescriptions) *abbreviation for* quaque nocte [Latin: every night]

QN *chess symbol for* queen's knight

QNP *chess symbol for* queen's knight's pawn

Qom (kɒm), **Qum** or **Kum** *n* a city in NW central Iran: a place of pilgrimage for Shiite Muslims. Pop: 1 045 000 (2005 est)

Qomolangma (ˈtʃəʊməʊˌlɑːŋmə) *n* a Chinese name for (Mount) **Everest**

qoph (kʊf, kɒf; *Hebrew* kɔf) *n* a variant of **koph**

qorma (ˈkɔːmə) *n* a variant spelling of **korma**

QP *chess symbol for* queen's pawn

qqv *abbreviation for* quae vide (denoting a cross-reference to more than one item). Compare **qv** [New Latin: which (words, items, etc) see]

QR¹ *abbreviation for* Queen's Regulations

QR² *chess symbol for* queen's rook

qr. *pl* **qrs** *abbreviation for* 1 quarter 2 quarterly 3 quire

QRP *chess symbol for* queen's rook's pawn

qs *abbreviation for* 1 (in prescriptions) quantum sufficit [Latin: as much as will suffice] 2 quarter section (of land)

QS *abbreviation for* **quarter sessions**

Q-ship *n* a merchant ship with concealed guns, used to decoy enemy ships into the range of its weapons [named from *q(uery)*]

QSM (in New Zealand) *abbreviation for* Queen's Service Medal

QSO *abbreviation for* 1 *astronomy* **quasi-stellar object** 2 (in New Zealand) Queen's Service Order

Q-sort *n* a psychological test requiring subjects to sort items relative to one another along a dimension such as "agree"/"disagree" for analysis by Q-methodological statistics

qt *pl* **qt** or **qts** *abbreviation for* quart

q.t. *abbreviation for informal* 1 ▷ *abbreviation for* quiet 2 **on the q.t** secretly

qto *abbreviation for* quarto

QTS (in Britain) *abbreviation for* Qualified Teacher Status

qty *abbreviation for* quantity

qua (kweɪ, kwɑː) *prep* in the capacity of; by virtue of being [c17 from Latin, ablative singular (feminine) of *qui* who]

quack¹ (kwæk) *vb* (intr) 1 (of a duck) to utter a harsh guttural sound 2 to make a noise like a duck ▷ *n* 3 the harsh guttural sound made by a duck [c17 of imitative origin; related to Dutch *kwakken*, German *quacken*]

quack² (kwæk) *n* 1 a an unqualified person who claims medical knowledge or other skills b (as modifier): *a quack doctor* 2 *Brit, Austral, and NZ informal* a doctor; physician or surgeon ▷ *vb* 3 (intr) to act in the manner of a quack [c17 short for QUACKSALVER] > 'quackish *adj*

1321

quackery ('kwækərɪ) *n, pl* -eries the activities or methods of a quack

quack grass *n* another name for **couch grass** [C19 a variant of QUICK GRASS]

quacksalver ('kwæk,sælvə) *n* an archaic word for **quack²** [C16 from Dutch, from *quack,* apparently: to hawk + *salf* SALVE¹]

quad¹ (kwɒd) *n* short for **quadrangle** (sense 2)

quad² (kwɒd) *n printing* a block of type metal used for spacing

quad³ (kwɒd) *n* a variant spelling of **quod** (prison)

quad⁴ (kwɒd) *n* short for **quadruplet** (sense 1)

quad⁵ (kwɒd) *adj, n* **1** short for **quadraphonic** or **quadraphonics** ▷ *adj* **2** *anatomy* short for **quadriceps**

quad. *abbreviation for* **1** quadrangle **2** quadrilateral

quad bike *or* **quad** *n* a vehicle like a motorcycle with four large wheels, designed for agricultural, sporting, and other off-road uses

quadr- *combining form* a variant of **quadri-** before a vowel

quadragenarian (,kwɒdrədʒɪ'nɛərɪən) *n* **1** a person who is between 40 and 49 years old ▷ *adj* **2** being from 40 to 49 years old [C19 from Latin *quadrāgēnārius* consisting of forty, from *quādrāgintā* forty]

Quadragesima (,kwɒdrə'dʒɛsɪmə) *n* **1** Also called: Quadragesima Sunday the first Sunday in Lent **2** *obsolete* the forty days of Lent [C16 from Medieval Latin *quadrāgēsima dies* the fortieth day]

Quadragesimal (,kwɒdrə'dʒɛsɪməl) *adj* of, relating to, or characteristic of Lent or the season of Lent

quadrangle ('kwɒd,ræŋgəl) *n* **1** *geometry* a plane figure consisting of four points connected by four lines. In a **complete quadrangle,** six lines connect all pairs of points **2** a rectangular courtyard, esp one having buildings on all four sides. Often shortened to: **quad 3** the building surrounding such a courtyard [C15 from Late Latin *quadrangulum* figure having four corners] > **quadrangular** (kwɒ'dræŋgjʊlə) *adj*

quadrant ('kwɒdrənt) *n* **1** *geometry* **a** a quarter of the circumference of a circle **b** the area enclosed by two perpendicular radii of a circle and its circumference **c** any of the four sections into which a plane is divided by two coordinate axes **2** a piece of a mechanism in the form of a quarter circle, esp one used as a cam or a gear sector **3** an instrument formerly used in astronomy and navigation for measuring the altitudes of stars, consisting of a graduated arc of 90° and a sighting mechanism attached to a movable arm [C14 from Latin *quadrāns* a quarter] > **quadrantal** (kwɒ'dræntəl) *adj*

Quadrantid ('kwɒd,dræntɪd) *n* any member of a meteor shower occurring annually around Jan 3 and appearing to radiate from a point in the constellation Boötes

quadraphonics *or* **quadrophonics** (,kwɒdrə'fɒnɪks) *n (functioning as singular)* a system of sound recording and reproduction that uses four independent loudspeakers to give directional sources of sound. The speakers are fed by four separate amplified signals > **quadra'phonic** or **quadro'phonic** *adj* > **quadraphony** or **quadrophony** (kwɒ'drɒfənɪ) *n*

quadrat ('kwɒdrət) *n* **1** *ecology* an area of vegetation, often one square metre, marked out for study of the plants in the surrounding area **2** the frame used to mark out such an area [C14 (meaning "a square"): variant of QUADRATE]

quadrate *n* ('kwɒdrɪt, -reɪt) **1** a cube, square, or a square or cubelike object **2** one of a pair of bones of the upper jaw of fishes, amphibians, reptiles, and birds that articulates with the lower jaw. In mammals it forms the incus ▷ *adj* ('kwɒdrɪt, -reɪt) **3** of or relating to this bone **4** square or rectangular ▷ *vb* (kwɒ'dreɪt) **5** (*tr*) to make square or rectangular **6** (often foll by *with*) to conform or cause to conform [C14 from Latin *quadrāre* to make square]

quadratic (kwɒ'drætɪk) *maths* ▷ *n* **1** Also called: quadratic equation an equation containing one or more terms in which the variable is raised to the power of two, but no terms in which it is raised to a higher power ▷ *adj* **2** of or relating to the second power

quadrature ('kwɒdrətʃə) *n* **1** *maths* the process of determining a square having an area equal to that of a given figure or surface **2** the process of making square or dividing into squares **3** *astronomy* a configuration in which two celestial bodies, usually the sun and the moon or a planet, form an angle of 90° with a third body, usually the earth **4** *electronics* the relationship between two waves that are 90° out of phase

quadrella (kwɒ'drɛlə) *n Austral* four nominated horseraces in which the punter bets on selecting the four winners

quadrennial (kwɒ'drɛnɪəl) *adj* **1** occurring every four years **2** relating to or lasting four years ▷ *n* **3** a period of four years > **quad'rennially** *adv*

quadrennium (kwɒ'drɛnɪəm) *n, pl* -niums or -nia (-nɪə) a period of four years [C17 from Latin *quadriennium,* from QUADRI- + *annus* year]

quadri- *or before a vowel* **quadr-** *combining form* four: *quadrilateral; quadrilingual; quadrisyllabic* [from Latin; compare *quattuor* four]

quadric ('kwɒdrɪk) *maths* ▷ *adj* **1** having or characterized by an equation of the second degree, usually in two or three variables **2** of the second degree ▷ *n* **3** a quadric curve, surface, or function

quadricentennial (,kwɒdrɪsen'tɛnɪəl) *n* **1** a 400th anniversary ▷ *adj* **2** of, relating to, or celebrating a 400th anniversary

quadriceps ('kwɒdrɪ,sɛps) *n, pl* -cepses (-,sɛpsɪz) *or* -ceps *anatomy* a large four-part muscle of the front of the thigh, which extends the leg [C19 New Latin, from QUADRI- + *-ceps* as in BICEPS] > **quadricipital** (,kwɒdrɪ'sɪpɪtəl) *adj*

quadrifid ('kwɒdrɪfɪd) *adj botany* divided into four lobes or other parts: *quadrifid leaves*

quadriga (kwɒ'driːgə) *n, pl* -gas *or* -gae (-dʒiː) (in the classical world) a two-wheeled chariot drawn by four horses abreast [C18 from Latin, from earlier *quadrijugae* a team of four, from QUADRI- + *jugum* yoke]

quadrilateral (,kwɒdrɪ'lætərəl) *adj* **1** having or formed by four sides ▷ *n* **2** Also called: tetragon a polygon having four sides. A **complete quadrilateral** consists of four lines and their six points of intersection

quadrille¹ (kwɒ'drɪl, kwə-) *n* **1** a square dance of five or more figures for four or more couples **2** a piece of music for such a dance, alternating between simple duple and compound duple time [C18 via French from Spanish *cuadrilla,* diminutive of *cuadro* square, from Latin *quadra*]

quadrille² (kwɒ'drɪl, kwə-) *n* an old card game for four players [C18 from French, from Spanish *cuartillo,* from *cuarto* fourth, from Latin *quartus,* influenced by QUADRILLE¹]

quadrillion (kwɒ'drɪljən) *n* **1** (in Britain) the number represented as one followed by 24 zeros (10^{24}). US and Canadian word: **septillion 2** (in the US and Canada) the number represented as one followed by 15 zeros (10^{15}) ▷ *determiner* **3** (preceded by *a* or a numeral) amounting to this number: *a quadrillion atoms* **b** (*as pronoun*) *a quadrillion* [C17 from French *quadrillon,* from QUADRI- + *-illion,* on the model of *million*] > **quad'rillionth** *adj*

quadrinomial (,kwɒdrɪ'nəʊmɪəl) *n* an algebraic expression containing four terms

quadripartite (,kwɒdrɪ'pɑːtaɪt) *adj* **1** divided into or composed of four parts **2** maintained by or involving four participants or groups of participants

quadriplegia (,kwɒdrɪ'pliːdʒɪə, -dʒə) *n pathol* paralysis of all four limbs, usually as the result of injury to the spine. Also called: tetraplegia Compare hemiplegia, paraplegia [C20 from QUADRI- + Greek *plēgē* a blow, from *plēssein* to strike]

quadriplegic (,kwɒdrɪ'pliːdʒɪk) *adj* **1** *pathol* of, relating to, or afflicted with qudriplegia ▷ *n* **2** *pathol* a person afflicted with quadriplegia

quadripole ('kwɒdrɪ,pəʊl) *n physics* an electric circuit with two input and two output terminals

quadrisect ('kwɒdrɪ,sɛkt) *vb* to divide into four parts, esp into four equal parts > ,quadri'section *n*

quadrivalent (,kwɒdrɪ'veɪlənt) *adj chem* another word for **tetravalent.** > ,quadri'valency *or* ,quadri'valence *n*

quadrivial (kwɒ'drɪvɪəl) *adj* **1** having or consisting of four roads meeting at a point **2** (of roads or ways) going in four directions **3** of or relating to the quadrivium

quadrivium (kwɒ'drɪvɪəm) *n, pl* -ia (-ɪə) (in medieval learning) the higher division of the seven liberal arts, consisting of arithmetic, geometry, astronomy, and music. Compare **trivium** [from Medieval Latin, from Latin: crossroads, meeting of four ways, from QUADRI- + *via* way]

quadroon (kwɒ'druːn) *n* the offspring of a Mulatto and a White; a person who is one-quarter Black [C18 from Spanish *cuarterón,* from *cuarto* quarter, from Latin *quartus*]

quadrophonics (,kwɒdrə'fɒnɪks) *n* a variant spelling of **quadraphonics**

quadrumanous (kwɒ'druːmənəs) *adj* (of monkeys and apes) having all four feet specialized for use as hands [C18 from New Latin *quadrumanus,* from QUADRI- + Latin *manus* hand]

quadruped ('kwɒdrʊ,pɛd) *n* **1** an animal, esp a mammal, that has all four limbs specialized for walking ▷ *adj* **2** having four feet [C17 from Latin *quadrupēs,* from *quadru-* (see QUADRI-) + *pēs* foot] > **quadrupedal** (kwɒ'druːpɪdəl, ,kwɒdrʊ'pɛdəl) *adj*

quadruple ('kwɒdrʊpəl, kwɒ'druːpəl) *vb* **1** to multiply by four or increase fourfold ▷ *adj* **2** four times as much or as many; fourfold **3** consisting of four parts ▷ *n* **4** a quantity or number four times as great as another [C16 via Old French from Latin *quadruplus,* from *quadru-* (see QUADRI-) + *-plus* -fold] > **'quadruply** *adv*

quadruplet ('kwɒdrʊplɪt, kwɒ'druːplɪt) *n* **1** one of four offspring born at one birth. Often shortened to: **quad 2** a group or set of four similar things **3** *music* a group of four notes to be played in a time value of three

quadruple time *n* musical time in which there are four beats in each bar

quadruplex ('kwɒdrʊ,plɛks, kwɒ'druːplɛks) *adj* **1** consisting of four parts; fourfold **2** denoting a type of television video tape recorder having four transversely rotating heads [C19 from Latin, from *quadru-* (see QUADRI-) + *-plex* -fold] > **quadruplicity** (,kwɒdrʊ'plɪsɪtɪ) *n*

quadruplicate *adj* (kwɒ'druːplɪkɪt, -,keɪt) **1** fourfold or quadruple ▷ *vb* (kwɒ'druːplɪ,keɪt) **2** to multiply or be multiplied by four ▷ *n* (kwɒ'druːplɪkɪt, -,keɪt) **3** a group or set of four things [C17 from Latin *quadruplicāre* to increase fourfold] > **quad,rupli'cation** *n*

quadrupole ('kwɒdrʊ,pəʊl) *n physics* a set of four associated positive and negative electric charges or two associated magnetic dipoles

quaere ('kwɪərɪ) *rare* ▷ *n* **1** a query or question ▷ *interj* **2** ask or inquire: used esp to introduce a question [C16 Latin, imperative of *quaerere* to inquire]

quaestor ('kwiːstə, -tɔː) *or sometimes US* **questor** ('kwɛstə) *n* any of several magistrates of ancient Rome, usually a financial administrator [C14 from Latin, from *quaerere* to inquire] > **quaestorial** (kwɛ'stɔːrɪəl) *adj* > **'quaestor,ship** *n*

quaff (kwɒf, kwɑːf) *vb* to drink heartily or in one draught [C16 perhaps of imitative origin; compare Middle Low German *quassen* to eat or drink excessively] > **'quaffable** *adj* > **'quaffer** *n*

quag (kwæg, kwɒg) *n* another word for **quagmire** [C16 perhaps related to QUAKE; compare Middle Low German *quabbe*]

quagga ('kwægə) *n, pl* -gas *or* -ga a recently

extinct member of the horse family (*Equidae*), *Equus quagga*, of southern Africa: it had a sandy brown colouring with zebra-like stripes on the head and shoulders [c18 from obsolete Afrikaans, from Khoikhoi *q̆agga*; compare Xhosa *i-qwara* something striped]

quaggy ('kwægɪ, 'kwɒgɪ) *adj* -gier, -giest **1** resembling a marsh or quagmire; boggy **2** yielding, soft, or flabby > 'quagginess *n*

quagmire ('kwæg,maɪə, 'kwɒg-) *n* **1** a soft wet area of land that gives way under the feet; bog **2** an awkward, complex, or embarrassing situation [c16 from QUAG + MIRE]

quahog ('kwɑː,hɒg) *n* an edible clam, *Venus* (or *Mercenaria*) *mercenaria*, native to the Atlantic coast of North America, having a large heavy rounded shell. Also called: hard-shell clam, hard-shell, round clam Compare **soft-shell clam** [c18 from Narraganset, short for *poquauhock*, from *pohkeni* dark + *hogki* shell]

quaich or **quaigh** (kwex, kweɪx) *n*, *pl* quaichs or quaighs *Scot* a small shallow drinking cup, usually with two handles [from Scottish Gaelic *cuach* cup]

Quai d'Orsay (French ke dɔrsɛ) *n* the quay along the S bank of the Seine, Paris, where the French foreign office is situated

quail[1] (kweɪl) *n*, *pl* quails or quail **1** any small Old World gallinaceous game bird of the genus *Coturnix* and related genera, having a rounded body and small tail: family *Phasianidae* (pheasants) **2** any of various similar and related American birds, such as the bobwhite [c14 from Old French *quaille*, from Medieval Latin *quaccula*, probably of imitative origin]

quail[2] (kweɪl) *vb* (*intr*) to shrink back with fear; cower [c15 perhaps from Old French *quailler*, from Latin *coāgulāre* to curdle]

quaint (kweɪnt) *adj* **1** attractively unusual, esp in an old-fashioned style: *a quaint village* **2** odd, peculiar, or inappropriate: *a quaint sense of duty* [c13 (in the sense: clever): from Old French *cointe*, from Latin *cognitus* known, from *cognoscere* to ascertain] > 'quaintly *adv* > 'quaintness *n*

quair (kwer, kweə) *n* *Scot* a book [a variant of QUIRE[1]]

quake (kweɪk) *vb* (*intr*) **1** to shake or tremble with or as with fear **2** to convulse or quiver, as from instability ▷ *n* **3** the act or an instance of quaking **4** *informal* short for **earthquake** [Old English *cwacian*; related to Old English *cweccan* to shake, Old Irish *bocaim*, German *wackeln*]

Quaker ('kweɪkə) *n* **1** a member of the Religious Society of Friends, a Christian sect founded by the English religious leader George Fox (1624–91) about 1650, whose central belief is the doctrine of the Inner Light. Quakers reject sacraments, ritual, and formal ministry, hold meetings at which any member may speak, and have promoted many causes for social reform ▷ *adj* **2** of, relating to, or designating the Religious Society of Friends or its religious beliefs or practices [c17 originally a derogatory nickname, alluding either to their alleged ecstatic fits, or to George Fox's injunction to "*quake* at the word of the Lord"] > 'Quakeress *fem n* > 'Quakerish *adj* > 'Quakerism *n*

Quaker gun *n* a dummy gun, as of wood [alluding to the Quakers' traditional pacifism]

Quaker meeting *n* a gathering of the Quakers for worship, characterized by periods of silence and by members speaking as moved by the Spirit

quaking ('kweɪkɪŋ) *adj* unstable or unsafe to walk on, as a bog or quicksand: *a quaking bog; quaking sands*

quaking grass *n* any grass of the genus *Briza*, of N temperate regions and South America, having delicate flower branches that shake in the wind

quaky ('kweɪkɪ) *adj* quakier, quakiest inclined to quake; shaky; tremulous > 'quakily *adv* > 'quakiness *n*

quale ('kwɑːlɪ, 'kweɪ-) *n*, *pl* -lia (-lɪə) *philosophy* an essential property or quality [c17 Latin, neuter singular of *qualis* of what kind]

qualification (ˌkwɒlɪfɪ'keɪʃən) *n* **1** an ability, quality, or attribute, esp one that fits a person to perform a particular job or task: *he has no qualifications to be a teacher* **2** a condition that modifies or limits; restriction **3** the act of qualifying or state of being qualified

qualified ('kwɒlɪ,faɪd) *adj* **1** having the abilities, qualities, attributes, etc, necessary to perform a particular job or task **2** limited, modified, or restricted; not absolute

Qualified Majority Voting *n* a voting system, used by the EU Council of Ministers, enabling certain resolutions to be passed without unanimity. Abbreviation: QMV

qualifier ('kwɒlɪ,faɪə) *n* **1** a person or thing that qualifies, esp a contestant in a competition who wins a preliminary heat or contest and so earns the right to take part in the next round **2** a preliminary heat or contest **3** *grammar* another word for **modifier** (sense 1)

qualify ('kwɒlɪ,faɪ) *vb* -fies, -fying, -fied **1** to provide or be provided with the abilities or attributes necessary for a task, office, duty, etc: *his degree qualifies him for the job; he qualifies for the job, but would he do it well?* **2** (*tr*) to make less strong, harsh, or violent; moderate or restrict **3** (*tr*) to modify or change the strength or flavour of **4** (*tr*) *grammar* another word for **modify** (sense 3) **5** (*tr*) to attribute a quality to; characterize **6** (*intr*) to progress to the final stages of a competition, as by winning preliminary contests [c16 from Old French *qualifier*, from Medieval Latin *quālificāre* to characterize, from Latin *quālis* of what kind + *facere* to make] > 'quali,fiable *adj* > qualificatory ('kwɒlɪfɪkətərɪ, -,keɪ-) *adj*

qualitative ('kwɒlɪtətɪv, -,teɪ-) *adj* involving or relating to distinctions based on quality or qualities. Compare **quantitative** > 'qualitatively *adv*

qualitative analysis *n* See **analysis** (sense 4)

qualitative identity *n* *logic* the relation that holds between two relata that have properties in common. This term is used to distinguish many uses of the words *identical* or *same* in ordinary language from strict identity or numerical identity

quality ('kwɒlɪtɪ) *n*, *pl* -ties **1** a distinguishing characteristic, property, or attribute **2** the basic character or nature of something **3** a trait or feature of personality **4** degree or standard of excellence, esp a high standard **5** (formerly) high social status or the distinction associated with it **6** musical tone colour; timbre **7** *logic* the characteristic of a proposition that is dependent on whether it is affirmative or negative **8** *phonetics* the distinctive character of a vowel, determined by the configuration of the mouth, tongue, etc, when it is articulated and distinguished from the pitch and stress with which it is uttered **9** (*modifier*) having or showing excellence or superiority: *a quality product* [c13 from Old French *qualité*, from Latin *quālitās* state, nature, from *quālis* of what sort]

quality control *n* control of the relative quality of a manufactured product, usually by statistical sampling techniques

quality factor *n* a property of ionizing radiations that affects their ability to cause biological effects. For weakly ionizing radiations such as gamma rays it has value 1 whilst for alpha rays it is about 20. Former name: relative biological effectiveness

qualm (kwɑːm) *n* **1** a sudden feeling of sickness or nausea **2** a pang or sudden feeling of doubt, esp concerning moral conduct; scruple **3** a sudden sensation of misgiving or unease [Old English *cwealm* death or plague; related to Old High German *qualm* despair, Dutch *kwalm* smoke, stench] > 'qualmish *adj* > 'qualmishly *adv* > 'qualmishness *n*

quamash ('kwɒmæʃ, kwə'mæʃ) *n* another name for **camass** (sense 1)

quandary ('kwɒndrɪ, -dərɪ) *n*, *pl* -ries a situation or circumstance that presents problems difficult to solve; predicament; dilemma [c16 of uncertain origin; perhaps related to Latin *quandō* when]

quandong, quandang ('kwɒn,dɒn) or **quantong** ('kwɒn,tɒn) *n* **1** Also called: native peach **a** a small Australian santalaceous tree, *Fusarya acuminata* (or *Fusanus acuminatus*) **b** the edible fruit or nut of this tree, used in preserves **2** silver quandong **a** an Australian tree, *Elaeocarpus grandis*: family *Elaeocarpaceae* **b** the pale easily worked timber of this tree **3** *Austral informal* a person who takes advantage of other people's generosity [from a native Australian language]

quango ('kwæŋgəʊ) *n*, *pl* -gos a semipublic government-financed administrative body whose members are appointed by the government [c20 qu(asi-)a(utonomous) n(on)g(overnmental) o(rganization)]

quangocracy (kwæŋ'gɒkrəsɪ) *n*, *pl* -cies **1** the control or influence ascribed to quangos **2** quangos collectively

quant[1] (kwɒnt) *n* **1** a long pole for propelling a boat, esp a punt, by pushing on the bottom of a river or lake ▷ *vb* **2** to propel (a boat) with a quant [c15 probably from Latin *contus* a pole, from Greek *kontos*]

quant[2] (kwɒnt) *n* *informal* a highly paid computer specialist with a degree in a quantitative science, employed by a financial house to predict the future price movements of securities, commodities, currencies, etc [c20 from QUANTITATIVE]

quanta ('kwɒntə) *n* the plural of **quantum**

quantal ('kwɒntəl) *adj* **1** of or relating to a quantum or an entity that is quantized **2** denoting something that is capable of existing in only one of two states

quantifier ('kwɒntɪ,faɪə) *n* **1** *logic* **a** a symbol including a variable that indicates the degree of generality of the expression in which that variable occurs, as $(\exists x)$ in $(\exists x)Fx$, rendered "something is an F", (x) in $(x)(Fx{\rightarrow}Gx)$, rendered "all Fs are Gs" **b** any other symbol with an analogous interpretation: *the existential quantifier*, $(\exists x)$, *corresponds to the words "there is something, x, such that ..."* **2** *grammar* a word or phrase in a natural language having this role, such as *some*, *all*, or *many* in English

quantify ('kwɒntɪ,faɪ) *vb* -fies, -fying, -fied (*tr*) **1** to discover or express the quantity of **2** *logic* to specify the quantity of (a term) by using a quantifier, such as *all*, *some*, or *no* [c19 from Medieval Latin *quantificāre*, from Latin *quantus* how much + *facere* to make] > 'quantifiable *adj* > ,quantifi'cation *n*

quantitative ('kwɒntɪtətɪv, -,teɪ-) or **quantitive** *adj* **1** involving or relating to considerations of amount or size. Compare **qualitative** **2** capable of being measured **3** *prosody* denoting or relating to a metrical system, such as that in Latin and Greek verse, that is based on the relative length rather than stress of syllables > 'quantitatively or 'quantitively *adv*

quantitative analysis *n* See **analysis** (sense 4)

quantity ('kwɒntɪtɪ) *n*, *pl* -ties **1 a** a specified or definite amount, weight, number, etc **b** (*as modifier*): *a quantity estimate* **2** the aspect or property of anything that can be measured, weighed, counted, etc **3** a large or considerable amount **4** *maths* an entity having a magnitude that may be denoted by a numerical expression **5** *physics* a specified magnitude or amount; the product of a number and a unit **6** *logic* the characteristic of a proposition dependent on whether it is a universal or particular statement, considering all or only part of a class **7** *prosody* the relative duration of a syllable or the vowel in it [c14 from Old French *quantité*, from Latin *quantitās* extent, amount, from *quantus* how much]

▆ **USAGE** The use of a plural noun after

q

quantity of as in *a large quantity of bananas* was formerly considered incorrect, but is now acceptable

quantity surveyor *n* a person who estimates the cost of the materials and labour necessary for a construction job

quantity theory *n economics* a theory stating that the general price level varies directly with the quantity of money in circulation and the velocity with which it is circulated, and inversely with the volume of production expressed by the total number of money transactions

quantize *or* **quantise** ('kwɒntaɪz) *vb* (tr) **1** *physics* to restrict (a physical quantity) to one of a set of values characterized by quantum numbers **2** *maths* to limit (a variable) to values that are integral multiples of a basic unit > ˌquanti'zation *or* ˌquanti'sation *n*

quantometer (kwɒn'tɒmɪtə) *n engineering* a spectroscopic instrument for measuring the percentage of different metals present in a sample

quantum ('kwɒntəm) *n*, *pl* **-ta** (-tə) **1** *physics* **a** the smallest quantity of some physical property, such as energy, that a system can possess according to the quantum theory **b** a particle with such a unit of energy **2** amount or quantity, esp a specific amount **3** (*often used with a negative*) the least possible amount that can suffice: *there is not a quantum of evidence for your accusation* **4** something that can be quantified or measured **5** (*modifier*) loosely, sudden, spectacular, or vitally important: *a quantum improvement* [C17 from Latin *quantus* (adj) how much]

quantum chromodynamics *n physics* a theory describing the strong interaction in terms of quarks and gluons, with the colour of quarks used as an analogue of charge and the gluon as an analogue of the photon. Abbreviation: QCD [C20 *chromodynamics* from CHROMO- (referring to quark colour) + DYNAMICS, modelled on QUANTUM ELECTRODYNAMICS]

quantum computer *n* a type of computer which uses the ability of quantum systems to be in many different states at once, thus allowing it to perform many different computations simultaneously

quantum cryptography *n* a method of coding information based on quantum mechanics, which is said to be unbreakable

quantum efficiency *n* **1** *physics* the number of electrons released by a photocell per photon of incident radiation of a given energy **2** *chem* the number of chemical species that undergo reaction per photon of absorbed radiation of a given energy

quantum electrodynamics *n physics* a relativistic quantum mechanical theory concerned with electromagnetic interactions. Abbreviation: QED

quantum electronics *n* the application of quantum mechanics and quantum optics to the study and design of electronic devices

quantum field theory *n physics* quantum mechanical theory concerned with elementary particles, which are represented by fields whose normal modes of oscillation are quantized

quantum flavourdynamics *n* a gauge theory of the electromagnetic and weak interactions. Also called: **electroweak theory** Abbreviation: QFD [C20 *flavourdynamics* from FLAVOUR (referring to quark flavour) + DYNAMICS, modelled on QUANTUM ELECTRODYNAMICS]

quantum gravity *n physics* a theory of the gravitational interaction that involves quantum mechanics to explain the force

quantum leap *or* **jump** *n* a sudden highly significant advance; breakthrough [C20 from its use in physics meaning the sudden jump of an electron, atom, etc from one energy level to another]

quantum mechanics *n* (*functioning as singular*) the branch of mechanics, based on the quantum

theory used for interpreting the behaviour of elementary particles and atoms, which do not obey Newtonian mechanics

quantum meruit Latin ('mɛruːɪt) as much as he has earned: denoting a payment for goods or services in partial fulfilment of a contract or for those supplied when no price has been agreed

quantum number *n physics* one of a set of integers or half-integers characterizing the energy states of a particle or system of particles. A function of the number multiplied by a fixed quantity gives the observed value of some specified physical quantity possessed by the system

quantum state *n physics* a state of a system characterized by a set of quantum numbers and represented by an eigenfunction. The energy of each state is precise within the limits imposed by the uncertainty principle but may be changed by applying a field of force. States that have the same energy are called **degenerate**. See also **energy level**

quantum statistics *n* (*functioning as singular*) *physics* statistics concerned with the distribution of a number of identical elementary particles, atoms, ions, or molecules among possible quantum states

quantum teleportation *n physics* a process by which a change in the quantum state of one subatomic particle in an entangled pair occurs instantly in its twin, wherever it may be

quantum theory *n* a theory concerning the behaviour of physical systems based on Planck's idea that they can only possess certain properties, such as energy and angular momentum, in discrete amounts (quanta). The theory later developed in several equivalent mathematical forms based on De Broglie's theory (see **wave mechanics**) and on the Heisenberg uncertainty principle

quaquaversal (ˌkwɑːkwəˈvɜːsəl) *adj geology* directed outwards in all directions from a common centre: *the quaquaversal dip of a pericline* [C18 from Latin *quāquā* in every direction + *versus* towards]

quarantine ('kwɒrənˌtiːn) *n* **1** a period of isolation or detention, esp of persons or animals arriving from abroad, to prevent the spread of disease, usually consisting of the maximum known incubation period of the suspected disease **2** the place or area where such detention is enforced **3** any period or state of enforced isolation ▷ *vb* **4** (*tr*) to isolate in or as if in quarantine [C17 from Italian *quarantina* period of forty days, from *quaranta* forty, from Latin *quadrāgintā*]

quarantine flag *n nautical* the yellow signal flag for the letter Q, flown alone from a vessel to indicate that there is no disease aboard and to request pratique or, with a second signal flag, to indicate that there is disease aboard. Also called: **yellow flag, yellow jack**

quare (kweə) *adj Irish dialect* **1** remarkable or strange: *a quare fellow* **2** great or good: *you're in a quare mess* [probably variant of QUEER]

quark[1] (kwɑːk) *n physics* any of a set of six hypothetical elementary particles together with their antiparticles thought to be fundamental units of all baryons and mesons but unable to exist in isolation. The magnitude of their charge is either two thirds or one third of that of the electron [C20 coined by James Joyce (1882–1941), Irish novelist and short-story writer, in the novel *Finnegans Wake*, and given special application in physics]

quark[2] (kwɑːk) *n* a type of low-fat soft cheese [from German]

quarrel[1] ('kwɒrəl) *n* **1** an angry disagreement; argument **2** a cause of disagreement or dispute; grievance ▷ *vb* **-rels, -relling, -relled** *or US* **-rels, -reling, -reled** (*intr; often foll by with*) **3** to engage in a disagreement or dispute; argue **4** to find fault; complain [C14 from Old French *querele*, from

Latin *querēlla* complaint, from *querī* to complain] > 'quarreller *or US* 'quarreler *n*

quarrel[2] ('kwɒrəl) *n* **1** an arrow having a four-edged head, fired from a crossbow **2** a small square or diamond-shaped pane of glass, usually one of many in a fixed or casement window and framed with lead [C13 from Old French *quarrel* pane, from Medieval Latin *quadrellus*, diminutive of Latin *quadrus* square]

quarrelsome ('kwɒrəlsəm) *adj* inclined to quarrel or disagree; belligerent > 'quarrelsomely *adv* > 'quarrelsomeness *n*

quarrian *or* **quarrion** ('kwɒrɪən) *n* a cockatiel, *Leptolophus hollandicus*, of scrub and woodland regions of inland Australia, that feeds on seeds and grasses [C20 probably from a native Australian language]

quarrier ('kwɒrɪə) *n* another word for **quarryman**

quarry[1] ('kwɒrɪ) *n, pl* **-ries 1** an open surface excavation for the extraction of building stone, slate, marble, etc, by drilling, blasting, or cutting **2** a copious source of something, esp information ▷ *vb* **-ries, -rying, -ried 3** to extract (stone, slate, etc) from or as if from a quarry **4** (*tr*) to excavate a quarry in **5** to obtain (something, esp information) diligently and laboriously: *he was quarrying away in the reference library* [C15 from Old French *quarriere*, from *quarre* square-shaped stone, from Latin *quadrāre* to make square]

quarry[2] ('kwɒrɪ) *n, pl* **-ries 1** an animal, bird, or fish that is hunted, esp by other animals; prey **2** anything pursued or hunted [C14 *quarre* entrails offered to the hounds, from Old French *cuirée* what is placed on the hide, from *cuir* hide, from Latin *corium* leather; probably also influenced by Old French *coree* entrails, from Latin *cor* heart]

quarry[3] ('kwɒrɪ) *n, pl* **-ries 1** a square or diamond shape **2** something having this shape **3** another word for **quarrel**[2] [C16 from Old French *quarré*; see QUARREL[2]]

quarryman ('kwɒrɪmən) *n, pl* **-men** a man who works in or manages a quarry

quarry tile *n* a square or diamond-shaped unglazed floor tile [C20 from QUARRY[3]]

quart[1] (kwɔːt) *n* **1** a unit of liquid measure equal to a quarter of a gallon or two pints. 1 US quart (0.946 litre) is equal to 0.8326 U.K. quart. 1 U.K. quart (1.136 litres) is equal to 1.2009 US quarts **2** a unit of dry measure equal to 2 pints or one eighth of a peck [C14 from Old French *quarte*, from Latin *quartus* fourth]

quart[2] *n* **1** (kɑːt) *piquet* a sequence of four cards in the same suit **2** (kart) *fencing* a variant spelling of **quarte** [C17 from French *quarte* fourth]

quartan ('kwɔːtᵊn) *adj* (esp of a malarial fever) occurring every third day [C13 from Latin *febris quartāna* fever occurring every fourth day, reckoned inclusively]

quarte French (kart) *n* the fourth of eight basic positions from which a parry or attack can be made in fencing [C18 from French, fem of *quart* a quarter]

quarter ('kwɔːtə) *n* **1** one of four equal or nearly equal parts of an object, quantity, amount, etc **2** Also called: **fourth** the fraction equal to one divided by four (1/4) **3** *US and Canadian* a quarter of a dollar; 25-cent piece **4** a unit of weight equal to a quarter of a hundredweight. 1 US quarter is equal to 25 pounds; 1 Brit quarter is equal to 28 pounds **5** short for **quarter-hour 6** a fourth part of a year; three months **7** *astronomy* **a** one fourth of the moon's period of revolution around the earth **b** either of two phases of the moon, **first quarter** or **last quarter** when half of the lighted surface is visible from the earth **8** *informal* a unit of weight equal to a quarter of a pound or 4 ounces **9** *Brit* a unit of capacity for grain, etc, usually equal to 8 UK bushels **10** *sport* one of the four periods into which certain games are divided **11** *nautical* the part of a vessel's side towards the stern, usually aft of the aftermost mast: *the port quarter* **12** *nautical* the general direction along the water in the quadrant between the beam of a vessel and its stern: *the wind was from the port quarter* **13** a region or district of a town or city: *the Spanish quarter* **14** a region, direction, or point of the compass **15** (*sometimes plural*) an unspecified person or group of people: *to get word from the highest quarter* **16** mercy or pity, as shown to a defeated opponent (*esp in the phrases* **ask for** *or* **give quarter**) **17** any of the four limbs, including the adjacent parts, of the carcass of a quadruped or bird: *a hind quarter of beef* **18** *vet science* the side part of the wall of a horse's hoof **19** the part of a shoe or boot covering the heel and joining the vamp **20** *heraldry* one of four more or less equal quadrants into which a shield may be divided **21** *military slang* short for **quartermaster** ▷ *vb* **22** (*tr*) to divide into four equal or nearly equal parts **23** (*tr*) to divide into any number of parts **24** (*tr*) (*esp formerly*) to dismember (a human body): *to be drawn and quartered* **25** to billet or be billeted in lodgings, esp (of military personnel) in civilian lodgings **26** (*intr*) (of gun dogs or hounds) to range over an area of ground in search of game or the scent of quarry **27** (*intr*) *nautical* (of the wind) to blow onto a vessel's quarter: *the wind began to quarter* **28** (*tr*) *heraldry* **a** to divide (a shield) into four separate bearings with a cross **b** to place (one set of arms) in diagonally opposite quarters to another ▷ *adj* **29** being or consisting of one of four equal parts: *a quarter pound of butter* ▷ See also **quarters** [c13 from Old French *quartier*, from Latin *quartārius* a fourth part, from *quartus* fourth]

quarterage ('kwɔːtərɪdʒ) *n* **1** an allowance or payment made quarterly **2** *rare* shelter or lodging

quarterback ('kwɔːtəˌbæk) *n US and Canadian* **1** a player in American or Canadian football, positioned usually behind the centre, who directs attacking play **2** Monday-morning quarterbacking wisdom after the event, esp by spectators

quarter-bound *adj* (of a book) having a binding consisting of two types of material, the better type being used on the spine

quarter crack *n vet science* a sand crack on the inside of the forefoot of a horse

quarter day *n* any of four days in the year when certain payments become due. In England, Wales, and Northern Ireland these are Lady Day, Midsummer's Day, Michaelmas, and Christmas. In Scotland they are Candlemas, Whit Sunday, Lammas, and Martinmas

quarterdeck ('kwɔːtəˌdɛk) *n nautical* the after part of the weather deck of a ship, traditionally the deck on a naval vessel for official or ceremonial use

quartered ('kwɔːtəd) *adj* **1** *heraldry* (of a shield) divided into four sections, each having contrasting arms or having two sets of arms, each repeated in diagonally opposite corners **2** (of a log) sawn into four equal parts along two diameters at right angles to each other; quartersawn

quarterfinal ('kwɔːtəˌfaɪnəl) *n* the round before the semifinal in a competition

quarter grain *n* the grain of quartersawn timber

quarter horse *n* a small powerful breed of horse, originally bred for sprinting in quarter-mile races in Virginia in the late 18th century

quarter-hour *n* **1** a period of 15 minutes **2** any of the points on the face of a timepiece that mark 15 minutes before or after the hour, and sometimes 30 minutes after ▷ ˌquarter-ˈhourly *adv, adj*

quartering ('kwɔːtərɪŋ) *n* **1** *military* the allocation of accommodation to service personnel **2** *heraldry* **a** the marshalling of several coats of arms on one shield, usually representing intermarriages **b** any coat of arms marshalled in this way

quarterlife crisis ('kwɔːtəˌlaɪf) *n* a crisis that may be experienced in one's twenties, involving anxiety over the direction and quality of one's life

quarterlight ('kwɔːtəˌlaɪt) *n Brit* a small pivoted window in the door of a car for ventilation

quarterly ('kwɔːtəlɪ) *adj* **1** occurring, done, paid, etc, at intervals of three months **2** of, relating to, or consisting of a quarter ▷ *n, pl* -lies **3** a periodical issued every three months ▷ *adv* **4** once every three months **5** *heraldry* into or in quarters: *a shield divided quarterly*

quartermaster ('kwɔːtəˌmɑːstə) *n* **1** an officer responsible for accommodation, food, and equipment in a military unit **2** a rating in the navy, usually a petty officer, with particular responsibility for steering a ship and other navigational duties

quarter-miler *n* an athlete who specializes in running the quarter mile or the 400 metres

quartern ('kwɔːtən) *n* **1** a fourth part of certain weights or measures, such as a peck or a pound **2** Also called: **quartern loaf** *Brit* **a** a type of loaf 4 inches square, used esp for making sandwiches **b** any loaf weighing 1600 g when baked [c13 from Old French *quarteron*, from *quart* a quarter]

quarter note *n US and Canadian music* a note having the time value of a quarter of a semibreve Also called: **crotchet**

quarter-phase *adj* another term for **two-phase**

quarter plate *n* a photographic plate measuring 3¼ × 4¼ inches (8.3 × 10.8 cm)

quarter round *n architect* another name for **ovolo**

quarters ('kwɔːtəz) *pl n* **1** housing or accommodation, esp as provided for military personnel and their families **2** the stations assigned to military personnel, esp to each crew member of a warship: *general quarters* **3** (in India) housing provided by an employer or by the government **4** (*functioning as singular*) *military slang* short for **quartermaster**

quartersaw ('kwɔːtəˌsɔː) *vb* -saws, -sawing, -sawed, -sawed *or* -sawn (*tr*) to saw (timber) into quarters along two diameters of a log at right angles to each other

quarter section *n US and Canadian* a land measure, used in surveying, with sides half a mile long; 160 acres

quarter sessions *n* (*functioning as singular or plural*) **1** (in England and Wales, formerly) a criminal court held four times a year before justices of the peace or a recorder, empowered to try all but the most serious offences and to hear appeals from petty sessions. Replaced in 1972 by **crown courts**. Compare **assizes 2** (in Scotland, formerly) a court held by justices of the peace four times a year, empowered to hear appeals from justice of the peace courts and to deal with some licensing matters: abolished in 1975

quarterstaff ('kwɔːtəˌstɑːf) *n, pl* -staves (-ˌsteɪvz, -ˌstɑːvz) **1** a stout iron-tipped wooden staff about 6ft. long, formerly used in England as a weapon **2** the use of such a staff in fighting, sport, or exercise [c16 of uncertain origin]

quarter tone *n music* a quarter of a whole tone; a pitch interval corresponding to 50 cents measured on the well-tempered scale

quartet *or* **quartette** (kwɔːˈtɛt) *n* **1** a group of four singers or instrumentalists or a piece of music composed for such a group. See **string quartet 2** any group of four: *a quartet of fast bowlers* [c18 from Italian *quartetto*, diminutive of *quarto* fourth]

quartic ('kwɔːtɪk) *adj, n* another word for **biquadratic** [c19 from Latin *quartus* fourth]

quartile ('kwɔːtaɪl) *n* **1** *statistics* one of three actual or notional values of a variable dividing its distribution into four groups with equal frequencies ▷ *adj* **2** *statistics* denoting or relating to a quartile **3** *astrology* denoting an aspect of two heavenly bodies when their longitudes differ by 90° **4** a quarter part of a distribution [c16 from Medieval Latin *quartīlis*, from Latin *quartus* fourth]

quarto ('kwɔːtəʊ) *n, pl* -tos **1** a book size resulting from folding a sheet of paper, usually crown or demy, into four leaves or eight pages, each one quarter the size of the sheet. Often written: 4to, 4° **2** (formerly) a size of cut paper 10 in. by 8 in.

(25.4 cm by 20.3 cm) [c16 from New Latin phrase *in quartō* in quarter]

quartz (kwɔːts) *n* **1** a colourless mineral often tinted by impurities, found in igneous, sedimentary, and metamorphic rocks. It is used in the manufacture of glass, abrasives, and cement, and also as a gemstone; the violet-purple variety is amethyst, the brown variety is cairngorm, the yellow variety is citrine, and the pink variety is rose quartz. Composition: silicon dioxide. Formula: SiO_2. Crystal structure: hexagonal **2** short for **quartz glass** [c18 from German *Quarz*, of Slavic origin]

quartz clock *or* **watch** *n* a clock or watch that is operated by the vibrations of a quartz crystal controlled by a microcircuit

quartz crystal *n* a thin plate or rod cut in certain directions from a piece of piezoelectric quartz and accurately ground so that it vibrates at a particular frequency

quartz glass *n* a colourless glass composed of almost pure silica, resistant to very high temperatures and transparent to near-ultraviolet radiation. Also called: **silica glass, nitreous silica**. Sometimes shortened to: **quartz**

quartziferous (kwɔːtˈsɪfərəs) *adj* containing or composed of quartz

quartz-iodine lamp *or* **quartz lamp** *n* a type of tungsten-halogen lamp containing small amounts of iodine and having a quartz envelope, operating at high temperature and producing an intense light for use in car headlamps, etc

quartzite ('kwɔːtsaɪt) *n* **1** a very hard metamorphic rock consisting of a mosaic of intergrown quartz crystals **2** a white or grey sandstone composed of quartz

quasar ('kweɪzɑː, -sɑː) *n* any of a class of extragalactic objects that emit an immense amount of energy in the form of light, infrared radiation, etc, from a compact source. They are extremely distant and their energy generation is thought to involve a supermassive black hole located in the centre of a galaxy [c20 *quas(i-stell)ar (object)*]

quash (kwɒʃ) *vb* (*tr*) **1** to subdue forcefully and completely; put down; suppress **2** to annul or make void (a law, decision, etc) **3** to reject (an indictment, writ, etc) as invalid [c14 from Old French *quasser*, from Latin *quassāre* to shake]

Quashi *or* **Quashie** ('kwɑːʃɪ) *n Caribbean* an unsophisticated or gullible male Black peasant: *I'm not a Quashi that anyone can fool* [from Twi]

quasi ('kweɪzaɪ, -saɪ, 'kwɑːzɪ) *adv* as if; as it were [from Latin, literally: as if]

quasi- *combining form* **1** almost but not really; seemingly: *a quasi-religious cult* **2** resembling but not actually being; so-called: *a quasi-scholar*

quasi-contract *n* an implied contract which arises without the express agreement of the parties

quasi-judicial *adj* denoting or relating to powers and functions similar to those of a judge, such as those exercised by an arbitrator, administrative tribunal, etc

Quasimodo (ˌkwɔːzɪˈməʊdəʊ) *n* **1** another name for **Low Sunday** [from the opening words of the Latin introit for that day, *quasimodo geniti infantes* as new-born babies] **2** a character in Victor Hugo's novel *Notre-Dame de Paris* (1831), a grotesque hunchbacked bellringer of the cathedral of Notre Dame

quasi-quotation *n logic* a metalinguistic device for referring to the form of an expression containing variables without referring to the symbols for those variables. Thus while *"not p"* refers to the expression consisting of the word *not* followed by the letter *p*, the quasi-quotation ⌈ *not p* ⌉ refers to the form of any expression consisting of the word *not* followed by any value of the variable *p*. Usual symbol: ⌈ ⌉ (**corners**)

quasi-stellar object *n* a member of any of several classes of astronomical bodies, including **quasars** (strong radio sources) and **quasi-stellar**

q

galaxies (no traceable radio emission), both of which have exceptionally large red shifts. Abbreviation: QSO

quass (kvɑːs, kwæːs) *n* a variant of **kvass**

quassia ('kwɒʃə) *n* **1** any tree of the tropical American simaroubaceous genus *Quassia*, having bitter bark and wood **2** the bark and wood of *Quassia amara* and of a related tree, *Picrasma excelsa*, used in furniture making **3** a bitter compound extracted from this bark and wood, formerly used as a tonic and anthelmintic, now used in insecticides [c18 from New Latin, named after Graman *Quassi*, a slave who discovered (1730) the medicinal value of the root]

quatercentenary (ˌkwætəsɛn'tiːnərɪ) *n, pl* -naries a 400th anniversary or the year or celebration marking it [c19 from Latin *quater* four times + CENTENARY] > ˌquatercen'tennial *adj, n*

quaternary (kwə'tɜːnərɪ) *adj* **1** consisting of fours or by fours **2** fourth in a series **3** *chem* containing or being an atom bound to four other atoms or groups: *a quaternary ammonium compound* **4** *maths* having four variables > *n, pl* -naries **5** the number four or a set of four [c15 from Latin *quaternārius* each containing four, from *quaternī* by fours, distributive of *quattuor* four]

Quaternary (kwə'tɜːnərɪ) *adj* **1** of, denoting, or formed in the most recent period of geological time, which succeeded the Tertiary period nearly two million years ago > *n* **2 the** the Quaternary period or rock system, divided into Pleistocene and Holocene (Recent) epochs or series

quaternary ammonium compound *n* a type of ionic compound that can be regarded as derived from ammonium compounds by replacing the hydrogen atoms with organic groups

quaternion (kwə'tɜːnɪən) *n* **1** *maths* a generalized complex number consisting of four components, *x* = $x_0 + x_1 i + x_2 j + x_3 k$, where *x*, $x_0...x_3$ are real numbers and $i^2 = j^2 = k^2 = -1$, $ij = -ji = k$, etc **2** another word for **quaternary** (sense 5) [c14 from Late Latin *quaterniōn*, from Latin *quaternī* four at a time]

quaternity (kwə'tɜːnɪtɪ) *n, pl* -ties a group of four, esp a concept of God as consisting of four persons [c16 from Late Latin *quaternitās*, from Latin *quaternī* by fours; see QUATERNARY]

Quathlamba (kwa't'lɑːmbaː) *n* the Sotho name for the **Drakensberg**

quatrain ('kwɒtreɪn) *n* a stanza or poem of four lines, esp one having alternate rhymes [c16 from French, from *quatre* four, from Latin *quattuor*]

quatre ('kætrə; *French* katrə) *n* a playing card with four pips [French: four]

Quatre Bras (*French* katrə bra) *n* a village in Belgium near Brussels; site of a battle in June 1815 where Wellington defeated the French under Marshal Ney, immediately preceding the battle of Waterloo

quatrefoil ('kætrəˌfɔɪl) *n* **1** a leaf composed of four leaflets **2** *architect* a carved ornament having four foils arranged about a common centre, esp one used in tracery [c15 from Old French, from *quatre* four + *-foil* leaflet; compare TREFOIL]

quattrocento (ˌkwætrəʊ'tʃɛntəʊ; *Italian* kwattro'tʃɛnto) *n* the 15th century, esp in reference to Renaissance Italian art and literature [Italian, shortened from *milquattrocento* 1400]

quaver ('kweɪvə) *vb* **1** to say or sing (something) with a trembling voice **2** (*intr*) (esp of the voice) to quiver, tremble, or shake **3** (*intr*) *rare* to sing or play quavers or ornamental trills > *n* **4** *music* a note having the time value of an eighth of a semibreve. Usual US and Canadian name: **eighth note 5** a tremulous sound or note [c15 (in the sense: to vibrate, QUIVER[1]): from *quaven* to tremble, of Germanic origin; compare Low German *quabbeln* to tremble] > 'quaverer *n* > 'quavering *adj* > 'quaveringly *adv* > 'quavery *adj*

quay (kiː) *n* a wharf, typically one built parallel to the shoreline. Compare **pier** (sense 1) [c14 *keye*, from Old French *kai*, of Celtic origin; compare

Cornish *kē* hedge, fence, Old Breton *cai* fence]

quayage ('kiːɪdʒ) *n* **1** a system of quays **2** a charge for the use of a quay

quayside ('kiːˌsaɪd) *n* the edge of a quay along the water

quazzy ('kwæzɪ) *adj* quazzier, quazziest *Southwest English dialect* unwell

qubit ('kjuːbɪt) *n computing* a quantum bit [c20 from QU(ANTUM) + BIT[4]]

Que. *abbreviation for* Quebec

quean (kwiːn) *n* **1** *archaic* **a** a boisterous, impudent, or disreputable woman **b** a prostitute; whore **2** *Scot* a young unmarried woman or girl [Old English *cwene*; related to Old Saxon, Old High German *quena*, Gothic *qino*, Old Norse *kona*, Greek *gunē* woman. Compare QUEEN]

queasy ('kwiːzɪ) *adj* -sier, -siest **1** having the feeling that one is about to vomit; nauseous **2** feeling or causing uneasiness: *a queasy conscience* [c15 of uncertain origin] > 'queasily *adv* > 'queasiness *n*

Quebec (kwɪ'bɛk, kə-, kɛ-) *n* **1** a province of E Canada: the largest Canadian province; a French colony from 1608 to 1763, when it passed to Britain; lying mostly on the Canadian Shield, it has vast areas of forest and extensive tundra and is populated mostly in the plain around the St Lawrence River. Capital: Quebec. Pop: 7 542 760 (2004 est). Area: 1 540 680 sq km (594 860 sq miles). Abbreviation: **PQ 2** a port in E Canada, capital of the province of Quebec, situated on the St Lawrence River: founded in 1608 by Champlain; scene of the battle of the Plains of Abraham (1759), by which the British won Canada from the French. Pop: 169 076 (2001) **3** *communications* a code word for the letter *q*

Quebecker or **Quebecer** (kwɪ'bɛkə, kə-, kɛ-) *n* a native or inhabitant of the province of Quebec

Québécois (*French* kebekwa) *n, pl* -cois (-kwa) a native or inhabitant of the province of Quebec, esp a French-speaking one

quebracho (keɪ'brɑːtʃəʊ; *Spanish* ke'βratʃo) *n, pl* -chos (-tʃəʊz; *Spanish* -tʃos) **1** either of two anacardiaceous South American trees, *Schinopsis lorentzii* or *S. balansae*, having a tannin-rich hard wood used in tanning and dyeing **2** an apocynaceous South American tree, *Aspidosperma quebrachoblanco*, whose bark yields alkaloids used in medicine and tanning **3** the wood or bark of any of these trees **4** any of various other South American trees having hard wood [c19 from American Spanish, from *quiebracha*, from *quebrar* to break (from Latin *crepāre* to rattle) + *hacha* axe (from French *hache*)]

Quechua, Kechua ('kɛtʃwə) or **Quichua** *n* **1** (*pl* -uas or -ua) a member of any of a group of South American Indian peoples of the Andes, including the Incas **2** the language or family of languages spoken by these peoples, possibly distantly related to the Tupī-Guaraní family > 'Quechuan, 'Kechuan or 'Quichuan *adj, n*

queen (kwiːn) *n* **1** a female sovereign who is the official ruler or head of state **2** the wife or widow of a king **3** a woman or a thing personified as a woman considered the best or most important of her kind: *a beauty queen; the queen of ocean liners* **4** *slang* an effeminate male homosexual **5 a** the only fertile female in a colony of social insects, such as bees, ants, and termites, from the eggs of which the entire colony develops **b** (*as modifier*): *a queen bee* **6** an adult female cat **7** one of four playing cards in a pack, one for each suit, bearing the picture of a queen **8** a chess piece, theoretically the most powerful piece, able to move in a straight line in any direction or diagonally, over any number of squares > *vb* **9** *chess* to promote (a pawn) to a queen when it reaches the eighth rank **10** (*tr*) to crown as queen **11** (*intr*) *informal* (of a gay man) to flaunt one's homosexuality **12** (*intr*) to reign as queen **13 queen it** (often foll by *over*) *informal* to behave in an overbearing manner [Old English *cwēn*; related

to Old Saxon *quān* wife, Old Norse *kvæn*, Gothic *qēns* wife]

Queen-Anne *n* **1** a style of furniture popular in England about 1700–20 and in America about 1720–70, characterized by the use of unencumbered curves, walnut veneer, and the cabriole leg > *adj* **2** in or of this style **3** denoting or relating to a style of architecture popular in England during the early 18th century, characterized by red-brick construction with classical ornamentation

Queen Anne's Bounty *n Church of England* **1** a fund formed by Queen Anne in 1704 for the augmentation of the livings of the poorer Anglican clergy. In 1948 the administrators of the fund were replaced by the Church Commissioners for England **2** the office or board administering this fund

Queen Anne's lace *n* another name for **cow parsley**

Queen Anne's War *n* those conflicts (1702–13) of the War of the Spanish Succession that were fought in North America

queen bee *n* **1** the fertile female bee in a hive **2** *informal* a woman in a position of dominance or ascendancy over her peers or associates

Queenborough in Sheppey ('kwiːnbərə, 'ʃɛpɪ) *n* a town in SE England, in Kent: formed in 1968 by the amalgamation of Queenborough, Sheerness, and Sheppey. Pop: 3471 (2001)

queencake ('kwiːnˌkeɪk) *n* a small light cake containing currants

Queen Charlotte Islands *pl n* a group of about 150 islands off the W coast of Canada: part of British Columbia. Pop: 5316 (1991). Area: 9596 sq km (3705 sq miles)

queen consort *n* the wife of a reigning king

queendom ('kwiːndəm) *n* a territory, state, people, or community ruled over by a queen

queen dowager *n* the widow of a king

Queen Elizabeth Islands *pl n* a group of islands off the N coast of Canada: the northernmost islands of the Canadian Arctic archipelago, lying N of latitude 74°N; part of Nunavut. Area: about 390 000 sq km (150 000 sq miles)

queenly ('kwiːnlɪ) *adj* -lier, -liest **1** resembling or appropriate to a queen **2** having the rank of queen > *adv* **3** in a manner appropriate to a queen > 'queenliness *n*

Queen Mab (mæb) *n* (in British folklore) a bewitching fairy who rules over men's dreams

Queen Maud Land (mɔːd) *n* the large section of Antarctica between Coats Land and Enderby Land: claimed by Norway in 1939. (Claims are suspended under the Antarctic Treaty of 1959)

Queen Maud Range *n* a mountain range in Antarctica, in S Ross Dependency, extending for about 800 km (500 miles)

queen mother *n* the widow of a former king who is also the mother of the reigning sovereign

queen of puddings *n* a pudding made of moist but firm breadcrumb and custard mixture topped with jam and meringue

queen olive *n* a variety of olive having large fleshy fruit suitable for pickling, esp one from around Seville in Spain

queen post *n* one of a pair of vertical posts that connect the tie beam of a truss to the principal rafters. Compare **king post**

queen regent *n* a queen who acts as regent

queen regnant *n* a queen who reigns on her own behalf

Queens (kwiːnz) *n* a borough of E New York City, on Long Island. Pop: 2 225 486 (2003 est)

Queen's Award *n* either of two awards instituted by royal warrant (1976) for a sustained increase in export earnings by a British firm (**Queen's Award for Export Achievement**) or for an advance in technology (**Queen's Award for Technological Achievement**)

Queen's Bench Division *n* (in England when the sovereign is female) one of the divisions of the

High Court of Justice. Also called (when the sovereign is male): **King's Bench**

Queensberry rules ('kwiːnzbərɪ, -brɪ) *pl n* **1** the code of rules followed in modern boxing, requiring the use of padded gloves, rounds of three minutes, and restrictions on the types of blows allowed **2** *informal* gentlemanly or polite conduct, esp in a dispute [c19 named after the ninth Marquess of *Queensberry*, who originated the rules in 1869]

Queen's Counsel *n* (in England when the sovereign is female) a barrister or advocate appointed Counsel to the Crown on the recommendation of the Lord Chancellor, entitled to sit within the bar of the court and to wear a silk gown. Also called (when the sovereign is male): **King's Counsel**

Queen's County *n* the former name of **Laois**

queen's English *n* (when the British sovereign is female) standard Southern British English

queen's evidence *n* *English law* (when the sovereign is female) evidence given for the Crown against his or her former associates in crime by an accomplice (esp in the phrase **turn queen's evidence**). Also called (when the sovereign is male): **king's evidence** US equivalent: **state's evidence**

Queen's Guide *n* (in Britain and the Commonwealth when the sovereign is female) a Guide who has passed the highest tests of proficiency

queen's highway *n* (in Britain when the sovereign is female) any public road or right of way

Queen's House *n* the a Palladian mansion in Greenwich, London: designed (1616–35) by Inigo Jones; now part of the National Maritime Museum; restored 1984–90

queen-size or **queen-sized** *adj* (of a bed, etc) larger or longer than normal size but smaller or shorter than king-size

Queensland ('kwiːnzˌlænd, -lənd) *n* a state of NE Australia: fringed on the Pacific side by the Great Barrier Reef; the Great Dividing Range lies in the east, separating the coastal lowlands from the dry Great Artesian Basin in the south. Capital: Brisbane. Pop: 3 840 111 (2003 est). Area: 1 727 500 km (667 000 sq miles)

Queensland arrowroot *n* another name for **tous-les-mois** (sense 2)

Queensland blue *n* *Austral* a pumpkin with a bluish skin

Queensland cane toad *n* *Austral* a toad, *Bufo marinus*, introduced into Queensland from Hawaii to control insect pests, becoming a pest itself

Queenslander ('kwiːnzˌlændə, -ləndə) *n* a native or inhabitant of Queensland

Queensland lungfish *n* a lungfish, *Neoceratodus forsteri*, reaching a length of six feet: occurs in Queensland rivers but introduced elsewhere

Queensland nut *n* another name for **macadamia**

Queen's proctor *n* (in England when the sovereign is female) an official empowered to intervene in divorce and certain other cases when it is alleged that material facts are being suppressed

Queen's Regulations *pl n* (in Britain and certain other Commonwealth countries when the sovereign is female) the code of conduct for members of the armed forces. Abbreviation: **QR**

Queen's Scout *n* (in Britain and the Commonwealth when the sovereign is female) a Scout who has passed the highest tests of endurance, proficiency, and skill. US equivalent: **Eagle Scout**

queen's shilling or when the sovereign was male **king's shilling** *n* **1** (until 1879) a shilling paid to new recruits to the British army **2 take the queen's shilling** *Brit archaic* to enlist in the army

Queen's speech *n* (in Britain and the Commonwealth when the sovereign is female) another name for the **speech from the throne**

Queenstown ('kwiːnzˌtaʊn) *n* the former name (1849–1922) of **Cóbh**

Queen Street Farmer *n* *NZ* a businessman who runs a farm, often for a tax loss [from *Queen Street*, the main business street in Auckland]

queen substance *n* a pheromone secreted by queen honeybees and consumed by the workers, in whom it causes suppression of egg-laying

Queensware ('kwiːnz,wɛə) or **Queen's ware** *n* a type of light white earthenware with a brilliant glaze developed from creamware by Josiah Wedgwood and named in honour of his patroness, Queen Charlotte

queer (kwɪə) *adj* **1** differing from the normal or usual in a way regarded as odd or strange **2** suspicious, dubious, or shady **3** faint, giddy, or queasy **4** *informal derogatory* homosexual **5** *informal* odd or unbalanced mentally; eccentric or slightly mad **6** *slang* worthless or counterfeit ▷ *n* **7** *informal derogatory* a homosexual, usually a male ▷ *vb* (*tr*) *informal* **8** to spoil or thwart (esp in the phrase **queer someone's pitch**) **9** to put in a difficult or dangerous position [c16 perhaps from German *quer* oblique, ultimately from Old High German *twẽrh*] > 'queerish *adj* > 'queerly *adv* > 'queerness *n*

USAGE Although the term *queer* meaning homosexual is still considered derogatory when used by non-homosexuals, it is now being used by homosexuals of themselves as a positive term, as in *queer politics, queer cinema*

queer-bashing *n* *Brit slang* the activity of making vicious and unprovoked verbal or physical assaults upon homosexuals or supposed homosexuals > 'queer-,basher *n*

queer fish *n* *Brit informal* an eccentric or odd person

queer street *n* (*sometimes capitals*) *informal* a difficult situation, such as debt or bankruptcy (in the phrase **in queer street**)

quell (kwɛl) *vb* (*tr*) **1** to suppress or beat down (rebellion, disorder, etc); subdue **2** to overcome or allay: *to quell pain* [Old English *cwellan* to kill; related to Old Saxon *quellian*, Old High German *quellen*, Old Norse *kvelja* to torment] > 'queller *n*

Quelpart ('kwɛl,pɑːt) *n* a former name of **Cheju**

quelquechose ('kɛlkə'ʃəʊz) *n* an insignificant thing; mere trifle [French, literally: something]

Quemoy (kɛ'mɔɪ) *n* an island in Formosa Strait, off the SE coast of China: administratively part of Taiwan. Pop (with associated islets): 53 237 (1996 est). Area: 130 sq km (50 sq miles)

quench (kwɛntʃ) *vb* (*tr*) **1** to satisfy (one's thirst, desires, etc); slake **2** to put out (a fire, flame, etc); extinguish **3** to put down or quell; suppress: *to quench a rebellion* **4** to cool (hot metal) by plunging it into cold water **5** *physics* to reduce the degree of (luminescence or phosphorescence) in (excited molecules or a material) by adding a suitable substance **6** *electronics* **a** to suppress (sparking) when the current is cut off in an inductive circuit **b** to suppress (an oscillation or discharge) in a component or device [Old English *ācwencan* to extinguish; related to Old Frisian *quinka* to vanish] > 'quenchable *adj* > 'quencher *n* > 'quenchless *adj*

quenelle (kə'nɛl) *n* a finely sieved mixture of cooked meat or fish, shaped into various forms and cooked in stock or fried as croquettes [c19 from French, from German *Knödel* dumpling, from Old High German *knodo* knot]

quercetin or **quercitin** ('kwɜːsɪtɪn) *n* a yellow crystalline pigment found naturally in the rind and bark of many plants. It is used in medicine to treat fragile capillaries. Formula: $C_{15}H_{10}O_7$; melting pt: 316–7°C. Also called: **flavin** [c19 from Latin *quercētum* an oak forest (from *quercus* an oak) + -IN] > **quercetic** (kwɜː'sɛtɪk, -'siː-) *adj*

Querétaro (*Spanish* ke'retaro) *n* **1** an inland state of central Mexico: economy based on agriculture and mining. Capital: Querétaro. Pop: 1 402 010

(2000). Area: 11 769 sq km (4544 sq miles) **2** a city in central Mexico, capital of Querétaro state: scene of the signing (1848) of the treaty ending the US-Mexican War and of the execution of Emperor Maximilian (1867). Pop: 913 000 (2005 est)

querist ('kwɪərɪst) *n* a person who makes inquiries or queries; questioner

quern (kwɜːn) *n* a stone hand mill for grinding corn [Old English *cweorn*; related to Old Frisian *quern*, Old High German *kurn*, Old Norse *kverna*, Gothic *quairnus* millstone]

quernstone ('kwɜːnˌstəʊn) *n* **1** another name for **millstone** (sense 1) **2** one of the two small circular stones used in a quern

querulous ('kwɛrʊləs, 'kwɛrjʊ-) *adj* **1** inclined to make whining or peevish complaints **2** characterized by or proceeding from a complaining fretful attitude or disposition: *a querulous tone* [c15 from Latin *querulus* from *querī* to complain] > 'querulously *adv* > 'querulousness *n*

query ('kwɪərɪ) *n*, *pl* -ries **1** a question, esp one expressing doubt, uncertainty, or an objection **2** a less common name for **question mark** ▷ *vb* -ries, -rying, -ried (*tr*) **3** to express uncertainty, doubt, or an objection concerning (something) **4** to express as a query: *"What's up now?" she queried* **5** *US* to put a question to (a person); ask [c17 from earlier *quere*, from Latin *quaere* ask!, from *quaerere* to seek, inquire]

query language *n* *computing* the instructions and procedures used to retrieve information from a database

quesadilla (ˌkeɪsə'diːljə, -'diːjə) *n* a toasted tortilla filled with cheese and sometimes other ingredients [c21 from Spanish, diminutive of *queso* cheese]

quest (kwɛst) *n* **1** the act or an instance of looking for or seeking; search: *a quest for diamonds* **2** (in medieval romance) an expedition by a knight or company of knights to accomplish some prescribed task, such as finding the Holy Grail **3** the object of a search; goal or target: *my quest is the treasure of the king* **4** *rare* a collection of alms ▷ *vb* (*mainly intr*) **5** (foll by *for* or *after*) to go in search (of) **6** to go on a quest **7** (of gun dogs or hounds) **a** to search for game **b** to bay when in pursuit of game **8** *rare* to collect alms **9** (*also tr*) *archaic* to go in search of (a thing); seek or pursue [c14 from Old French *queste*, from Latin *quaesita* sought, from *quaerere* to seek] > 'quester *n* > 'questing *adj* > 'questingly *adv*

question ('kwɛstʃən) *n* **1** a form of words addressed to a person in order to elicit information or evoke a response; interrogative sentence **2** a point at issue: *it's only a question of time until she dies; the question is how long they can keep up the pressure* **3** a difficulty or uncertainty; doubtful point: *a question of money; there's no question about it* **4 a** an act of asking **b** an investigation into some problem or difficulty **5** a motion presented for debate by a deliberative body **6 put the question** to require members of a deliberative assembly to vote on a motion presented **7** *law* a matter submitted to a court or other tribunal for judicial or quasi-judicial decision **8 question of fact** (in English law) that part of the issue before a court that is decided by the jury **9 question of law** (in English law) that part of the issue before a court that is decided by the judge **10 beg the question a** to avoid giving a direct answer by posing another question **b** to assume the truth of that which is intended to be proved. See **petitio principii 11 beyond (all) question** beyond (any) dispute or doubt **12 call in** or **into question a** to make (something) the subject of disagreement **b** to cast doubt upon the validity, truth, etc, of (something) **13 in question** under discussion: *this is the man in question* **14 out of the question** beyond consideration; unthinkable or impossible: *the marriage is out of the question* **15 pop the question** *informal* to propose marriage ▷ *vb* (*mainly tr*) **16** to

q

put a question or questions to (a person); interrogate **17** to make (something) the subject of dispute or disagreement **18** to express uncertainty about the validity, truth, etc, of (something); doubt [c13 via Old French from Latin *quaestiō*, from *quaerere* to seek] > 'question**er** *n*

> USAGE The *question whether* should be used rather than the *question of whether* or the *question as to whether*: this leaves open the question whether he acted correctly

questionable ('kwɛstʃənəbªl) *adj* **1** (esp of a person's morality or honesty) admitting of some doubt; dubious **2** of disputable value or authority: *a questionable text* > 'questionableness *or* ,questiona'bility *n* > 'questionably *adv*

questioning ('kwɛstʃənɪŋ) *adj* **1** proceeding from or characterized by a feeling of doubt or uncertainty **2** enthusiastic or eager for philosophical or other investigations; intellectually stimulated: *an alert and questioning mind* > 'questioningly *adv*

questionless ('kwɛstʃənlɪs) *adj* **1** blindly adhering, as to a principle or course of action; unquestioning **2** a less common word for **unquestionable**. > 'questionlessly *adv*

question mark *n* **1** the punctuation mark ?, used at the end of questions and in other contexts where doubt or ignorance is implied **2** this mark used for any other purpose, as to draw attention to a possible mistake, as in a chess commentary **3** an element of doubt or uncertainty

question master *n Brit* the chairman of a quiz or panel game

questionnaire (,kwɛstʃə'nɛə, ,kɛs-) *n* a set of questions on a form, submitted to a number of people in order to collect statistical information [c20 from French, from *questionner* to ask questions]

question time *n* (in parliamentary bodies of the British type) a period of time set aside each day for members to question government ministers

questor ('kwɛstə) *n US* a variant of **quaestor** > questorial (kwɛ'stɔːrɪəl) *adj* > 'questor,ship *n*

Quetta ('kwɛtə) *n* a city in W central Pakistan, at an altitude of 1650 m (5500 ft): a summer resort, military station, and trading centre. Pop: 744 000 (2005 est)

quetzal ('kɛtsəl) *or* **quezal** (kɛ'saːl) *n, pl* -zals *or* -zales (-'saːlɛs) **1** Also called: **resplendent trogon** a crested bird, *Pharomachrus mocinno*, of Central and N South America, which has a brilliant green, red, and white plumage and, in the male, long tail feathers: family *Trogonidae*, order *Trogoniformes* (trogons) **2** the standard monetary unit of Guatemala, divided into 100 centavos [via American Spanish from Nahuatl *quetzalli* brightly coloured tail feather]

Quetzalcoatl (,kɛtsəlkəʊ'ætªl) *n* a god of the Aztecs and Toltecs, represented as a feathered serpent

queue (kjuː) *chiefly Brit* ▷ *n* **1** a line of people, vehicles, etc, waiting for something: *a queue at the theatre* **2** *computing* a list in which entries are deleted from one end and inserted at the other **3** a pigtail **4 jump the queue** See **queue-jump** ▷ *vb* queues, queuing *or* queueing, queued **5** (*intr*; often foll by *up*) to form or remain in a line while waiting **6** *computing* to arrange (a number of programs) in a predetermined order for accessing by a computer ▷ *US and Canadian word*: **line** [c16 (in the sense: tail); c18 (in the sense: pigtail): via French from Latin *cauda* tail]

queue-jump *vb* (*intr*) **1** to take a place in a queue ahead of those already queuing; push in **2** to obtain prior consideration or some other advantage out of turn or unfairly. Also: **Jump the queue** > queue-**jumper** *n*

queuing theory *n* a mathematical approach to the rate at which components queue to be processed by a machine, instructions are accessed by a computer, orders need to be serviced, etc, to achieve the optimum flow

Quezon City ('keizɒn) *n* a city in the Philippines, on central Luzon adjoining Manila: capital of the Philippines from 1948 to 1976; seat of the University of the Philippines (1908). Pop: 2 173 831 (2000)

quibble ('kwɪbªl) *vb* (*intr*) **1** to make trivial objections; prevaricate **2** *archaic* to play on words; pun ▷ *n* **3** a trivial objection or equivocation, esp one used to avoid an issue **4** *archaic* a pun [c17 probably from obsolete *quib*, perhaps from Latin *quibus* (from *quī* who, which), as used in legal documents, with reference to their obscure phraseology] > 'quibbler *n* > 'quibbling *adj, n* > 'quibblingly *adv*

Quiberon (French kibrɔ̃) *n* a peninsula of NW France, on the S coast of Brittany: a naval battle was fought off its coast in 1759 during the Seven Years' War, in which the British defeated the French

quiche (kiːʃ) *n* an open savoury tart with a rich custard filling to which bacon, onion, cheese, etc, are added: *quiche Lorraine* [French, from German *Kuchen* cake]

Quichua ('kɪtʃwə) *n, pl* -uas *or* -ua a variant of **Quechua**

quick (kwɪk) *adj* **1** (of an action, movement, etc) performed or occurring during a comparatively short time: *a quick move* **2** lasting a comparatively short time; brief: *a quick flight* **3** accomplishing something in a time that is shorter than normal: *a quick worker* **4** characterized by rapidity of movement; swift or fast: *a quick walker* **5** immediate or prompt: *a quick reply* **6** (*postpositive*) eager or ready to perform (an action): *quick to criticize* **7** responsive to stimulation; perceptive or alert; lively: *a quick eye* **8** eager or enthusiastic for learning: *a quick intelligence* **9** easily excited or aroused: *a quick temper* **10** skilfully swift or nimble in one's movements or actions; deft: *quick fingers* **11** *archaic* **a** alive; living **b** (*as noun*) living people (esp in the phrase **the quick and the dead**) **12** *archaic or dialect* lively or eager: *a quick dog* **13** (of a fire) burning briskly **14** composed of living plants: *a quick hedge* **15** *dialect* (of sand) lacking firmness through being wet **16** quick with child *archaic* pregnant, esp being in an advanced state of pregnancy, when the movements of the fetus can be felt ▷ *n* **17** any area of living flesh that is highly sensitive to pain or touch, esp that under a toenail or fingernail or around a healing wound **18** the vital or most important part (of a thing) **19** short for **quickset** (sense 1) **20 cut (someone) to the quick** to hurt (someone's) feelings deeply; offend gravely ▷ *adv* *informal* **21** in a rapid or speedy manner; swiftly **22** soon: *I hope he comes quick* ▷ *interj* **23** a command requiring the hearer to perform an action immediately or in as short a time as possible [Old English *cwicu* living; related to Old Saxon *quik*, Old High German *queck*, Old Norse *kvikr* alive, Latin *vīvus* alive, Greek *bios* life] > 'quickly *adv* > 'quickness *n*

quick assets *pl n accounting* assets readily convertible into cash; liquid current assets

quick-change artist *n* an actor or entertainer who undertakes several rapid changes of costume during his performance

quicken ('kwɪkən) *vb* **1** to make or become faster; accelerate: *he quickened his walk; her heartbeat quickened with excitement* **2** to impart to or receive vigour, enthusiasm, etc; stimulate or be stimulated: *science quickens man's imagination* **3** to make or become alive; revive **4 a** (of an unborn fetus) to begin to show signs of life **b** (of a pregnant woman) to reach the stage of pregnancy at which movements of the fetus can be felt

quick fire *n* **1** rapid continuous gunfire, esp at a moving target ▷ *adj* **quick-fire 2** Also: **quick-firing** capable of or designed for quick fire **3** *informal* rapid or following one another in rapid succession: *quick-fire questions*

quick-freeze *vb* -freezes, -freezing, -froze, -frozen (*tr*) to preserve (food) by subjecting it to rapid refrigeration at temperatures of 0°C or lower

quick grass *n* another name for **couch grass** [c17 Scot and northern English variant of *couch grass*, from the earlier *quick living*; compare QUITCH GRASS]

quickie ('kwɪkɪ) *n informal* **1** Also called (esp Brit): **quick one** a speedily consumed alcoholic drink **2 a** anything made, done, produced, or consumed rapidly or in haste **b** (*as modifier*): *a quickie divorce; a quickie ceremony*

quicklime ('kwɪk,laɪm) *n* another name for **calcium oxide** [c15 from QUICK (in the archaic sense: living) + LIME[1]]

quick march *n* **1** a march at quick time or the order to proceed at such a pace ▷ *interj* **2** a command to commence such a march

quick response *n marketing* the rapid replenishment of a customer's stock by a supplier with direct access to data from the customer's point of sale

quicksand ('kwɪk,sænd) *n* a deep mass of loose wet sand that submerges anything on top of it

quickset ('kwɪk,sɛt) *chiefly Brit* ▷ *n* **1 a** a plant or cutting, esp of hawthorn, set so as to form a hedge **b** such plants or cuttings collectively **2** a hedge composed of such plants ▷ *adj* **3** composed of such plants [c15 from *quick* in the archaic sense live, growing + *set* to plant, set in the ground]

quicksilver ('kwɪk,sɪlvə) *n* **1** another name for **mercury** (sense 1) ▷ *adj* **2** rapid or unpredictable in movement or change: *a quicksilver temper* [Old English, from *cwicu* alive (see QUICK) + *seolfor* silver]

quickstep ('kwɪk,stɛp) *n* **1** a modern ballroom dance in rapid quadruple time **2** a piece of music composed for or in the rhythm of this dance ▷ *vb* -steps, -stepping, -stepped **3** (*intr*) to perform this dance

quick-tempered *adj* readily roused to anger; irascible

quickthorn ('kwɪk,θɔːn) *n* hawthorn, esp when planted as a hedge [c17 probably from *quick* in the sense "fast-growing": compare QUICKSET]

quick time *n military* the normal marching rate of 120 paces to the minute. Compare **double time** (senses 3, 4)

quick trick *n bridge* a high card almost certain to win a trick, usually an ace or a king: the unit in one of the systems of hand valuation

quick-witted *adj* having a keenly alert mind, esp as used to avert danger, make effective reply, etc > ,quick-'wittedly *adv* > ,quick-'wittedness *n*

quid[1] (kwɪd) *n* a piece of tobacco, suitable for chewing [Old English *cwidu* chewing resin; related to Old High German *quiti* glue, Old Norse *kvātha* resin; see CUD]

quid[2] (kwɪd) *n, pl* quid **1** *Brit* a slang word for **pound** (sterling) **2** (be) quids in *Brit slang* to be in a very favourable or advantageous position **3** not the full quid *Austral and NZ slang* mentally subnormal [c17 of obscure origin]

quidditch ('kwɪdɪtʃ) *n* an imaginary game in which players fly on broomsticks [c20 coined by the British novelist J.K. Rowling (born 1965) in the novel *Harry Potter and the Philosopher's Stone*]

quiddity ('kwɪdɪtɪ) *n, pl* -ties **1** *philosophy* the essential nature of something. Compare **haecceity 2** a petty or trifling distinction; quibble [c16 from Medieval Latin *quidditās*, from Latin *quid* what]

quidnunc ('kwɪd,nʌŋk) *n* a person eager to learn news and scandal; gossipmonger [c18 from Latin, literally: what now]

quid pro quo ('kwɪd prəʊ 'kwəʊ) *n, pl* quid pro quos **1** a reciprocal exchange **2** something given in compensation, esp an advantage or object given in exchange for another [c16 from Latin: something for something]

quiescent (kwɪ'ɛsªnt) *adj* quiet, inactive, or dormant [c17 from Latin *quiescere* to rest] > qui'escence *or* qui'escency *n* > qui'escently *adv*

quiescent tank *n* a tank, usually for sewage sludge, in which the sludge is allowed to remain for a time so that sedimentation can occur

quiet ('kwaɪət) *adj* **1** characterized by an absence or near absence of noise: *a quiet street* **2** characterized by an absence of turbulent motion or disturbance; peaceful, calm, or tranquil: *a quiet glade; the sea is quiet tonight* **3** free from activities, distractions, worries, etc; untroubled: *a quiet life; a quiet day at work* **4** marked by an absence of work, orders, etc; not busy: *the factory is very quiet at the moment* **5** private; not public; secret: *a quiet word with someone* **6** free from anger, impatience, or other extreme emotion: *a quiet disposition* **7** free from pretentiousness or vain display; modest or reserved: *quiet humour* **8** *astronomy* (of the sun) exhibiting a very low number of sunspots, solar flares, and other surface phenomena; inactive. Compare **active** (sense 8) ▷ *n* **9** the state of being silent, peaceful, or untroubled **10** **on the quiet** without other people knowing; secretly ▷ *vb* **11** a less common word for **quieten** [C14 from Latin *quiētus*, past participle of *quiēscere* to rest, from *quiēs* repose, rest] > 'quietness *n*

quieten ('kwaɪət⁸n) *vb* chiefly *Brit* **1** (often foll by *down*) to make or become calm, silent, etc; pacify or become peaceful **2** (*tr*) to allay (fear, doubts, etc)

quietism ('kwaɪə,tɪzəm) *n* **1** a form of religious mysticism originating in Spain in the late 17th century, requiring withdrawal of the spirit from all human effort and complete passivity to God's will **2** a state of passivity and calmness of mind towards external events > 'quietist *n, adj*

quietly ('kwaɪətlɪ) *adv* **1** in a quiet manner **2** **just quietly** *Austral* between you and me; confidentially

quietude ('kwaɪə,tjuːd) *n* the state or condition of being quiet, peaceful, calm, or tranquil

quietus (kwaɪ'iːtəs, -'eɪtəs) *n, pl* **-tuses 1** anything that serves to quash, eliminate, or kill: *to give the quietus to a rumour* **2** a release from life; death **3** the discharge or settlement of debts, duties, etc [C16 from Latin *quiētus est*, literally: he is at rest, QUIET]

quiff (kwɪf) *n Brit* a prominent tuft of hair, esp one brushed up above the forehead [C19 of unknown origin]

quill (kwɪl) *n* **1 a** any of the large stiff feathers of the wing or tail of a bird **b** the long hollow central part of a bird's feather; calamus **2** a bird's feather made into a pen for writing **3** any of the stiff hollow spines of a porcupine or hedgehog **4** a device, formerly usually made from a crow quill, for plucking a harpsichord string **5** *angling* a length of feather barb stripped of barbules and used for the body of some artificial flies **6** a small roll of bark, esp one of dried cinnamon **7** (in weaving) a bobbin or spindle **8** a fluted fold, as in a ruff **9** a hollow shaft that rotates upon an inner spindle or concentrically about an internal shaft ▷ *vb* (*tr*) **10** to wind (thread, yarn, etc) onto a spool or bobbin **11** to make or press fluted folds in (a ruff) [C15 (in the sense: hollow reed or pipe): of uncertain origin; compare Middle Low German *quiele* quill]

quillai (kɪ'laɪ) *n* another name for **soapbark** (sense 1) [C19 via American Spanish from Araucanian]

quillet ('kwɪlɪt) *n archaic* a quibble or subtlety [C16 from earlier *quillity*, perhaps an alteration of QUIDDITY]

quilling ('kwɪlɪŋ) *n* decorative craftwork in which a material such as glass, fabric, or paper is formed into small bands or rolls that form the basis of a design

quillon (*French* kijɔ̃) *n* (often plural) either half of the extended crosspiece of a sword or dagger [C19 from French, diminutive of *quille* bowling pin, ultimately from Old High German *kegil* club, stake]

quill pen *n* another name for **quill** (sense 2)

quillwort ('kwɪl,wɜːt) *n* any aquatic tracheophyte plant of the genus *Isoetes*, with quill-like leaves at the bases of which are spore-producing

structures: family *Isoetaceae*, phylum *Lycopodophyta* (club mosses, etc)

Quilmes (*Spanish* 'kilmes) *n* a city in E Argentina: a resort and suburb of Buenos Aires. Pop: 550 069 (1999 est)

quilt (kwɪlt) *n* **1** a thick warm cover for a bed, consisting of a soft filling sewn between two layers of material, usually with crisscross seams **2** a bedspread or counterpane **3** anything quilted or resembling a quilt ▷ *vb* (*tr*) **4** to stitch together (two pieces of fabric) with (a thick padding or lining) between them: *to quilt cotton and wool* **5** to create (a garment, covering, etc) in this way **6** to pad with material **7** *Austral informal* to strike; clout [C13 from Old French *coilte* mattress, from Latin *culcita* stuffed item of bedding] > 'quilter *n*

quilting ('kwɪltɪŋ) *n* **1** material used for making a quilt **2** the act or process of making a quilt **3** quilted work

quim (kwɪm) *n Brit taboo* the female genitals [C19 of uncertain origin]

Quimper (*French* kɛ̃pɛr) *n* a city in NW France: capital of Finistère department. Pop: 63 238 (1999)

quin (kwɪn) *n Brit* short for **quintuplet** (sense 2) US and Canadian word: quint

quinacrine ('kwɪnə,kriːn) *n* **1** another name for **mepacrine 2** quinacrine mustard a nitrogen mustard derived from mepacrine and used as a stain for chromosomes [C20 from QUIN(INE) + ACR(ID) + -INE²]

quinary ('kwaɪnərɪ) *adj* **1** consisting of fives or by fives **2** fifth in a series **3** (of a number system) having a base of five ▷ *n, pl* **-ries 4** a set of five [C17 from Latin *quīnārius* containing five, from *quīnī* five each]

quinate ('kwaɪneɪt) *adj botany* arranged in or composed of five parts: *quinate leaflets* [C19 from Latin *quīnī* five each]

quince (kwɪns) *n* **1** a small widely cultivated Asian rosaceous tree, *Cydonia oblonga*, with pinkish-white flowers and edible pear-shaped fruits **2** the acid-tasting fruit of this tree, much used in preserves **3 Japanese** or **flowering quince**. another name for **japonica** [C14 *qwince* plural of *quyn* quince, from Old French *coin*, from Latin *cotōneum*, from Greek *kudōnion* quince, Cydonian (apple)]

quincentenary (,kwɪnsɛn'tiːnərɪ) *n, pl* **-naries** a 500th anniversary or the year or celebration marking it [C19 irregularly from Latin *quinque* five + CENTENARY] > **quincentennial** (,kwɪnsɛn'tɛnɪəl) *adj, n*

quincuncial (kwɪn'kʌnʃəl) *adj* **1** consisting of or having the appearance of a quincunx **2** (of the petals or sepals of a five-membered corolla or calyx in the bud) arranged so that two members overlap another two completely and the fifth overlaps on one margin and is itself overlapped on the other > quin'cuncially *adv*

quincunx ('kwɪnkʌŋks) *n* **1** a group of five objects arranged in the shape of a rectangle with one at each of the four corners and the fifth in the centre **2** *botany* a quincuncial arrangement of sepals or petals in the bud **3** *astrology* an aspect of 150° between two planets [C17 from Latin: five twelfths, from *quinque* five + *uncia* twelfth; in ancient Rome, this was a coin worth five twelfths of an AS² and marked with five spots]

quindecagon (kwɪn'dɛkəgən) *n* a geometric figure having 15 sides and 15 angles [C16 from Latin *quindecim* fifteen + *-agon*, as in *decagon*]

quindecaplet (kwɪn'dɛkə,plɛt) *n* **1** a group of 15 **2** one of a group of 15 [C20 irregularly formed on the models of *quadruplet*, *quintuplet*, etc]

quindecennial (,kwɪndɪ'sɛnɪəl) *adj* **1** ▷ *n* occurring once every 15 years or over a period of 15 years **2** a 15th anniversary [C20 from Latin *quindecim* fifteen + *annus* year, on the model of *biennial*]

quine (kwəɪn) *n Scot* a variant of **quean** (sense 2)

quinella (kwɪ'nɛlə) *n Austral and NZ* a form of betting on a horse race in which the punter bets

on selecting the first and second place-winners in any order [from American Spanish *quiniela* a game of chance]

Qui Nhon ('kwiː 'njɒŋ) *n* a port in SE Vietnam, on the South China Sea. Pop: 163 385 (1992 est)

quinic acid ('kwɪnɪk) *n* a white crystalline soluble optically active carboxylic acid, found in cinchona bark, bilberries, coffee beans, and the leaves of certain other plants; 1,3,4,5-tetrahydroxycyclohexanecarboxylic acid. Formula: $C_6H_7(OH)_4COOH$

quinidine ('kwɪnɪ,diːn) *n* a crystalline alkaloid drug that is an optically active diastereoisomer of quinine: used to treat heart arrhythmias. Formula: $C_{20}H_{24}N_2O_2$

quinine (kwɪ'niːn; *US* 'kwaɪnaɪn) *n* a bitter crystalline alkaloid extracted from cinchona bark, the salts of which are used as a tonic, antipyretic, analgesic, etc, and in malaria therapy. Formula: $C_{20}H_{24}N_2O_2$ [C19 from Spanish *quina* cinchona bark, from Quechua *kina* bark]

quinnat salmon ('kwɪnæt) *n* another name for **Chinook salmon** [C19 from Salish *t'kwinnat*]

quino- or before a vowel **quin-** combining form indicating cinchona, cinchona bark, or quinic acid: *quinidine; quinol; quinoline* [see QUININE]

quinoa ('kiːnəʊə, kwɪ'nəʊə) *n* a grain high in nutrients traditionally grown as a staple food high in the Andes [Spanish]

quinol ('kwɪnɒl) *n* another name for **hydroquinone**

quinoline ('kwɪnə,liːn, -lɪn) *n* **1** an oily colourless insoluble basic heterocyclic compound synthesized by heating aniline, nitrobenzene, glycerol, and sulphuric acid: used as a food preservative and in the manufacture of dyes and antiseptics. Formula: C_9H_7N **2** any substituted derivative of quinoline

quinolone ('kwɪnə,ləʊn) *n* any of a group of synthetic antibiotics, including ciprofloxacin, that inactivate an enzyme required for the replication of certain microorganisms

quinone (kwɪ'nəʊn, 'kwɪnəʊn) *n* another name for **benzoquinone**

quinonoid ('kwɪnə,nɔɪd, kwɪ'nəʊnɔɪd) or **quinoid** *adj* of, resembling, or derived from quinone

quinquagenarian (,kwɪŋkwədʒɪ'nɛərɪən) *n* **1** a person between 50 and 59 years old ▷ *adj* **2** being between 50 and 59 years old **3** of or relating to a quinquagenarian [C16 from Latin *quinquāgēnārius* containing fifty, from *quinquāgēnī* fifty each]

Quinquagesima (,kwɪŋkwə'dʒɛsɪmə) *n* the Sunday preceding Ash Wednesday, the beginning of Lent. Also called: **Quinquagesima Sunday** [C14 via Medieval Latin from Latin *quinquāgēsima diēs* fiftieth day]

quinque- combining form five: *quinquevalent* [from Latin *quinque*]

quinquecentenary (,kwɪŋkwɪsɛn'tiːnərɪ) *n, pl* **-naries** another name for **quincentenary**

quinquefoliate (,kwɪŋkwɪ'fəʊliːt, -,eɪt) *adj* (of leaves) having or consisting of five leaflets

quinquennial (kwɪn'kwɛnɪəl) *adj* **1** occurring once every five years or over a period of five years ▷ *n* **2** another word for **quinquennium 3** a fifth anniversary > quin'quennially *adv*

quinquennium (kwɪn'kwɛnɪəm) *n, pl* **-nia** (-nɪə) a period or cycle of five years [C17 from Latin *quinque* five + *annus* year]

quinquepartite (,kwɪŋkwɪ'pɑːtaɪt) *adj* **1** divided into or composed of five parts **2** maintained by or involving five participants or groups of participants

quinquereme (,kwɪŋkwɪ'riːm) *n* an ancient Roman galley with five banks of oars on each side [C16 from Latin *quinquerēmis*, from QUINQUE- + *rēmus* oar]

quinquevalent (,kwɪŋkwɪ'veɪlənt, kwɪn'kwɛvələnt) *adj chem* another word for **pentavalent**. > ,quinque'valency or quinquevalence (,kwɪŋkwɪ'veɪləns, kwɪn'kwɛvələns) *n*

q

quinsy ('kwɪnzɪ) *n* inflammation of the tonsils and surrounding tissues with the formation of abscesses [c14 via Old French and Medieval Latin from Greek *kunankhē*, from *kuōn* dog + *ankhein* to strangle]

quint¹ *n* **1** (kwɪnt) an organ stop sounding a note a fifth higher than that normally produced by the key depressed **2** (kɪnt) *piquet* a sequence of five cards in the same suit [c17 from French *quinte*, from Latin *quintus* fifth]

quint² (kwɪnt) *n US and Canadian* short for **quintuplet**. Also called (in Britain and certain other countries): **quin**

quinta ('kɪntə) *n winemaking* a Portuguese vineyard where grapes for wine or port are grown [c20 from Portuguese, literally: a country estate, farm]

quintain ('kwɪntɪn) *n* (*esp in medieval Europe*) **1** a post or target set up for tilting exercises for mounted knights or foot soldiers **2** the exercise of tilting at such a target [c14 from Old French *quintaine*, from Latin: street in a Roman camp between the fifth and sixth maniples, from *quintus* fifth]

quintal ('kwɪnt³l) *n* **1** a unit of weight equal to 100 pounds **2** a unit of weight equal to 100 kilograms [c15 via Old French from Arabic *qintār*, possibly from Latin *centēnārius* consisting of a hundred]

quintan ('kwɪntən) *adj* (of a fever) occurring every fourth day [c17 from Latin *febris quintāna* fever occurring every fifth day, reckoned inclusively]

Quintana Roo (*Spanish* kin'tana 'rɔo) *n* a state of SE Mexico, on the E Yucatán Peninsula: hot, humid, forested, and inhabited chiefly by Maya Indians. Capital: Chetumal. Pop: 287 000 (2005 est). Area: 50 350 sq km (19 463 sq miles)

quinte French (kɛ̃t) *n* the fifth of eight basic positions from which a parry or attack can be made in fencing [c18 French, from Latin *quinta*, fem of *quintus* fifth, from *quinque* five]

quintessence (kwɪn'tɛsəns) *n* **1** the most typical representation of a quality, state, etc **2** an extract of a substance containing its principle in its most concentrated form **3** (in ancient and medieval philosophy) ether, the fifth and highest essence or element after earth, water, air, and fire, which was thought to be the constituent matter of the heavenly bodies and latent in all things [c15 via French from Medieval Latin *quinta essentia* the fifth essence, translation of Greek *pemptē ousia*]

quintessential (ˌkwɪntɪ'sɛnʃəl) *adj* most typically representative of a quality, state, etc; perfect > ˌquintes'sentially *adv*

quintet *or* **quintette** (kwɪn'tɛt) *n* **1** a group of five singers or instrumentalists or a piece of music composed for such a group **2** any group of five [c19 from Italian *quintetto*, from *quinto* fifth]

quintic ('kwɪntɪk) *adj maths* of or relating to the fifth degree: *a quintic equation*

quintile ('kwɪntaɪl) *n astrology* **1** an aspect of 72° between two heavenly bodies **2** a fifth part of a distribution [c17 from Latin *quintus* fifth]

quintillion (kwɪn'tɪljən) *n, pl* -**lions** *or* -**lion** **1** (in Britain, France, and Germany) the number represented as one followed by 30 zeros (10³⁰). US and Canadian word: **nonillion 2** (in the US and Canada) the number represented as one followed by 18 zeros (10¹⁸). Brit word: **trillion** [c17 from Latin *quintus* fifth + -*illion*, as in MILLION] > quin'tillionth *adj*

quintuple ('kwɪntjʊp³l, kwɪn'tjuːp³l) *vb* **1** to multiply by five ▷ *adj* **2** five times as much or as many; fivefold **3** consisting of five parts ▷ *n* **4** a quantity or number five times as great as another [c16 from French, from Latin *quintus*, on the model of QUADRUPLE]

quintuplet ('kwɪntjʊplɪt, kwɪn'tjuːplɪt) *n* **1** a group or set of five similar things **2** one of five offspring born at one birth. Often shortened to: **quin 3** *music* a group of five notes to be played in a time value of three, four, or some other value

quintuplicate *adj* (kwɪn'tjuːplɪkɪt) **1** fivefold or quintuple ▷ *vb* (kwɪn'tjuːplɪˌkeɪt) **2** to multiply or be multiplied by five ▷ *n* (kwɪn'tjuːplɪkɪt) **3** a group or set of five things > quinˌtupli'cation *n*

quinze (*French* kɛ̃z) *n* a card game with rules similar to those of vingt-et-un, except that the score aimed at is 15 rather than 21 [French: fifteen]

quip (kwɪp) *n* **1** a sarcastic or cutting remark; gibe **2** a witty or clever saying: *a merry quip* **3** *archaic* another word for **quibble** ▷ *vb* quips, quipping, quipped **4** (*intr*) to make a quip [c16 from earlier *quippy*, probably from Latin *quippe* indeed, to be sure]

quipster ('kwɪpstə) *n* a person inclined to make sarcastic or witty remarks

quipu *or* **quippu** ('kiːpuː, 'kwɪpuː) *n* a device of the Incas of Peru used to record information, consisting of an arrangement of variously coloured and knotted cords attached to a base cord [c17 from Spanish *quipo*, from Quechua *quipu*, literally: knot]

quire¹ (kwaɪə) *n* **1** a set of 24 or 25 sheets of paper; a twentieth of a ream **2 a** four sheets of paper folded once to form a section of 16 pages **b** a section or gathering **3** a set of all the sheets in a book [c15 *quayer*, from Old French *quaier*, from Latin *quaternī* four at a time, from *quater* four times]

quire² (kwaɪə) *n* an obsolete spelling of **choir**

Quirinal ('kwɪrɪn³l) *n* one of the seven hills on which ancient Rome was built

Quirinus (kwɪ'raɪnəs) *n Roman myth* a god of war, who came to be identified with the deified Romulus

Quirites (kwɪ'raɪtiːz) *pl n* the citizens of ancient Rome [from Latin: inhabitants of *Cures*, later applied generally to Roman citizens]

quirk (kwɜːk) *n* **1** an individual peculiarity of character; mannerism or foible **2** an unexpected twist or turn: *a quirk of fate* **3** a continuous groove in an architectural moulding **4** a flourish, as in handwriting [c16 of unknown origin] > 'quirkily *adv* > 'quirkiness *n*

quirt (kwɜːt) *US and South African* ▷ *n* **1** a whip with a leather thong at one end ▷ *vb* (*tr*) **2** to strike with a quirt [c19 from Spanish *cuerda* CORD]

quis custodiet ipsos custodes? Latin (kwɪs kʊs'tɐʊdɪˌɛt 'ɪpsɒs kʊs'tɐʊdiːz) who will guard the guards?

quisling ('kwɪzlɪŋ) *n* a traitor who aids an occupying enemy force; collaborator [c20 after Major Vidkun *Quisling* (1887–1945), Norwegian collaborator with the Nazis]

quist (kwɪst) *n, pl* **quists** *or* **quist** *West Midland and southwestern English dialect* a wood pigeon [of obscure origin]

quit (kwɪt) *vb* quits, quitting, quitted *or chiefly US* quit **1** (*tr*) to depart from; leave: *he quitted the place hastily* **2** to resign; give up (a job): *he quitted his job today* **3** (*intr*) (of a tenant) to give up occupancy of premises and leave them: *they received notice to quit* **4** to desist or cease from (something or doing something); break off: *quit laughing* **5** (*tr*) to pay off (a debt); discharge or settle **6** (*tr*) *archaic* to conduct or acquit (oneself); comport (oneself): *he quits himself with great dignity* ▷ *adj* **7** (*usually predicative; foll by of*) free (from); released (from): *he was quit of all responsibility for their safety* [c13 from Old French *quitter*, from Latin *quiētus* QUIET; see QUIETUS]

quitch grass (kwɪtʃ) *n* another name for **couch grass** Sometimes shortened to: **quitch** [Old English *cwice*; perhaps related to *cwicu* living, QUICK (with the implication that the grass cannot be killed); compare Dutch *kweek*, Norwegian *kvike*, German *Queckengras*]

quitclaim ('kwɪtˌkleɪm) *law* ▷ *n* **1** a formal renunciation of any claim against a person or of a right to land ▷ *vb* **2** (*tr*) **a** to renounce (a claim) formally **b** to declare (a person) free from liability [c14 from Anglo-French *quiteclame*, from *quite* QUIT + *clamer* to declare (from Latin *clamāre* to shout)]

quite (kwaɪt) *adv* **1** to the greatest extent; completely or absolutely: *you're quite right; quite the opposite* **2** (*not used with a negative*) to a noticeable or partial extent; somewhat: *she's quite pretty* **3** in actuality; truly: *he thought the bag was heavy, but it was quite light; it's quite the thing to do* **4** quite a *or* an (*not used with a negative*) of an exceptional, considerable, or noticeable kind: *quite a girl; quite a long walk* **5** quite something a remarkable or noteworthy thing or person ▷ *sentence substitute* **6** Also: quite so an expression used to indicate agreement or assent [c14 adverbial use of *quite* (adj) QUIT]

◆ USAGE ·See at **very**

Quito ('kiːtəʊ; *Spanish* 'kito) *n* the capital of Ecuador, in the north at an altitude of 2850 m (9350 ft), just south of the equator: the oldest capital in South America, existing many centuries before the Incan conquest in 1487; a cultural centre since the beginning of Spanish rule (1534); two universities. Pop: 1 514 000 (2005 est)

quitrent ('kwɪtˌrɛnt) *n* (formerly) a rent payable by a freeholder or copyholder to his lord that released him from liability to perform services

quits (kwɪts) *informal* ▷ *adj* (*postpositive*) **1** on an equal footing; even: *now we are quits* **2** call it quits to agree to end a dispute, contest, etc, agreeing that honours are even ▷ *interj* **3** an exclamation indicating willingness to give up

quittance ('kwɪt³ns) *n* **1** release from debt or other obligation **2** a receipt or other document certifying this [c13 from Old French, from *quitter* to release from obligation; see QUIT]

quitter ('kwɪtə) *n* a person who gives up easily; defeatist, deserter, or shirker

quittor ('kwɪtə) *n vet science* infection of the cartilages on the side of a horse's foot, characterized by inflammation and the formation of pus [c13 perhaps from Old French *cuiture* a boiling, from Latin *coctūra* a cooking, from *coquere* to cook]

quiver¹ ('kwɪvə) *vb* **1** (*intr*) to shake with a rapid tremulous movement; tremble ▷ *n* **2** the state, process, or noise of shaking or trembling [c15 from obsolete *cwiver* quick, nimble; compare QUAVER] > 'quiverer *n* > 'quivering *adj* > 'quiveringly *adv* > 'quivery *adj*

quiver² ('kwɪvə) *n* a case for arrows [c13 from Old French *cuivre*; related to Old English *cocer*, Old Saxon *kokari*, Old High German *kohhari*, Medieval Latin *cucurum*]

quiverful ('kwɪvəfʊl) *n* **1** the amount that a quiver can hold **2** *literary* a fair number or full complement: *a quiverful of children*

qui vive (ˌkiː 'viːv) *n* on the qui vive on the alert; attentive [c18 from French, literally: long live who?, sentry's challenge (equivalent to "To whose party do you belong?" or "Whose side do you support?")]

Quixote ('kwɪksət; *Spanish* ki'xote) *n* See **Don Quixote**

quixotic (kwɪk'sɒtɪk) *adj* preoccupied with an unrealistically optimistic or chivalrous approach to life; impractically idealistic [c18 after DON QUIXOTE] > quix'otically *adv* > quixotism ('kwɪksəˌtɪzəm) *n*

quiz (kwɪz) *n, pl* quizzes **1 a** an entertainment in which the general or specific knowledge of the players is tested by a series of questions, esp as a radio or television programme **b** (*as modifier*): *a quiz programme* **2** any set of quick questions designed to test knowledge **3** an investigation by close questioning; interrogation **4** *obsolete* a practical joke; hoax **5** *obsolete* a puzzling or eccentric individual **6** *obsolete* a person who habitually looks quizzically at others, esp through a small monocle ▷ *vb* quizzes, quizzing, quizzed (*tr*) **7** to investigate by close questioning; interrogate **8** *US and Canadian informal* to test or examine the knowledge of (a student or class) **9** (*tr*) *obsolete* to look quizzically at, esp through a small monocle [c18 of unknown origin] > 'quizzer *n*

quizmaster ('kwɪz,mɑːstə) *n* a person who puts questions to contestants on a quiz programme

quizzical ('kwɪzɪkəl) *adj* questioning and mocking or supercilious: *a quizzical look* > ˌquizzi'cality *n* > 'quizzically *adv*

Qum (kʊm) *n* a variant of **Qom**

Qumran ('kʊmrɑːn) *n* See **Khirbet Qumran**

Qungur ('kʊŋʊə) *n* a variant transliteration of the Chinese name for **Kongur Shan**

quod (kwɒd) *n chiefly Brit* a slang word for **jail** [c18 of uncertain origin; perhaps changed from *quad*, short for *quadrangle*]

quod erat demonstrandum (*Latin* 'kwɒd 'ɛræt ˌdɛmən'strændʊm) (at the conclusion of a proof, esp of a theorem in Euclidean geometry) which was to be proved. Abbreviation: **QED**

quodlibet ('kwɒdlɪ,bɛt) *n* **1** a light piece of music based on two or more popular tunes **2** a subtle argument, esp one prepared as an exercise on a theological topic [c14 from Latin, from *quod* what + *libet* pleases, that is, whatever you like] > ˌquodli'betical *adj* > ˌquodli'betically *adv*

quoin, coign *or* **coigne** (kwɔɪn, kɔɪn) *n* **1** an external corner of a wall **2** Also called: **cornerstone** a stone forming the external corner of a wall **3** another name for **keystone** (sense 1) **4** *printing* a metal or wooden wedge or an expanding mechanical device used to lock type up in a chase **5** a wedge used for any of various other purposes, such as (formerly) to adjust elevation in muzzle-loading cannon [c16 variant of COIN (corner)]

quoin post *n* the vertical post at the side of a lock gate, about which the gate swings

quoit (kɔɪt) *n* **1** a ring of iron, plastic, rope, etc, used in the game of quoits **2** *Austral slang* a variant spelling of **coit** [c15 of unknown origin]

quoits (kɔɪts) *pl n* (*usually functioning as singular*) a game in which quoits are tossed at a stake in the ground in attempts to encircle it

quokka ('kwɒkə) *n* a small wallaby, *Setonix brachyurus*, of Western Australia, occurring mostly on offshore islands [from a native Australian language]

quoll ('kwɒl) *n Austral* another name for **native cat** [c18 from a native Australian language]

quondam ('kwɒndæm) *adj* (*prenominal*) of an earlier time; former: *her quondam lover* [c16 from Latin *adv*: formerly]

Quonset hut ('kwɒnsɪt) *n trademark US* a military shelter made of corrugated steel sheet, having a semicircular cross section. Brit equivalent: **Nissen hut**

quorate ('kwɔː,reɪt) *adj Brit* constituting or having a quorum

Quorn (kwɔːn) *n trademark* a vegetable protein developed from a type of fungus and used in cooking as a meat substitute

quorum ('kwɔːrəm) *n* a minimum number of members in an assembly, society, board of directors, etc, required to be present before any valid business can be transacted: *the quorum is forty; we don't have a quorum* [c15 from Latin, literally: of whom, occurring in Latin commissions in the formula *quorum vos...duos* (etc) *volumus* of whom we wish that you be...two]

quot. *abbreviation for* quotation

quota ('kwəʊtə) *n* **1** the proportional share or part of a whole that is due from, due to, or allocated to a person or group **2** a prescribed number or quantity, as of items to be manufactured, imported, or exported, immigrants admitted to a country, or students admitted to a college [c17 from Latin *quota pars* how big a share?, from *quotus* of what number]

quotable ('kwəʊtəbəl) *adj* apt or suitable for quotation: *his remarks are not quotable in mixed company* > ˌquota'bility *n*

quota-hopping *n* (in the EU) the practice of obtaining the right to catch a part of a country's national quota for fish in European waters by buying licences from its fishermen > 'quota-ˌhopper *n*

quota sampling *n marketing* a method of conducting marketing research in which the sample is selected according to a quota-system based on such factors as age, sex, social class, etc

quotation (kwəʊ'teɪʃən) *n* **1** a phrase or passage from a book, poem, play, etc, remembered and spoken, esp to illustrate succinctly or support a point or an argument **2** the act or habit of quoting from books, plays, poems, etc **3** *commerce* a statement of the current market price of a security or commodity **4** an estimate of costs submitted by a contractor to a prospective client; tender **5** *stock exchange* registration granted to a company or governmental body, enabling the shares and other securities of the company or body to be officially listed and traded **6** *printing* a large block of type metal that is less than type-high and is used to fill up spaces in type pages

quotation mark *n* either of the punctuation marks used to begin or end a quotation, respectively " and " or ' and ' in English printing and writing. When double marks are used, single marks indicate a quotation within a quotation, and vice versa. Also called: **inverted comma**

quote (kwəʊt) *vb* **1** to recite a quotation (from a book, play, poem, etc), esp as a means of illustrating or supporting a statement **2** (*tr*) to put quotation marks round (a word, phrase, etc) **3** *stock exchange* to state (a current market price) of (a security or commodity) ▷ *n* **4** an informal word for **quotation** (senses 1–4) **5** (*often plural*) an informal word for **quotation mark** put it in quotes ▷ *interj* **6** an expression used parenthetically to indicate that the words that follow it form a quotation: *the president said, quote, I shall not run for office in November, unquote* [c14 from Medieval Latin *quotāre* to assign reference numbers to passages, from Latin *quot* how many]

quote-driven *adj* denoting an electronic market system, esp for stock exchanges, in which prices are determined by quotations made by market makers or dealers. Compare **order-driven**

quoth (kwəʊθ) *vb archaic* (used with all pronouns except *thou* and *you*, and with nouns) another word for **said¹** (sense 2) [Old English *cwæth*, third person singular of *cwethan* to say; related to Old Frisian *quetha* to say, Old Saxon, Old High German *quethan*; see BEQUEATH]

quotha ('kwəʊθə) *interj archaic* an expression of mild sarcasm, used in picking up a word or phrase used by someone else: *Art thou mad? Mad, quotha! I am more sane than thou* [c16 from *quoth* a quoth he]

quotidian (kwəʊ'tɪdɪən) *adj* **1** (esp of attacks of malarial fever) recurring daily **2** everyday; commonplace ▷ *n* **3** a malarial fever characterized by attacks that recur daily [c14 from Latin *quotīdiānus*, variant of *cottīdiānus* daily]

quotient ('kwəʊʃənt) *n* **1 a** the result of the division of one number or quantity by another **b** the integral part of the result of division **2** a ratio of two numbers or quantities to be divided [c15 from Latin *quotiens* how often]

quo vadis ('kwəʊ 'vɑːdɪs) where are you going? [Latin: from the Vulgate version of John 16:5]

quo warranto ('kwəʊ wɒ'ræntəʊ) *n law* a proceeding initiated to determine or (formerly) a writ demanding by what authority a person claims an office, franchise, or privilege [from Medieval Latin: by what warrant]

Qur'an (kʊ'rɑːn, -'ræn) *n* a variant of **Koran**

qv (denoting a cross reference) *abbreviation for* quod vide [New Latin: which (word, item, etc) see]

Qwaqwa ('kwɑːkwə) *n* (formerly) a Bantu homeland in N South Africa; the only Bantu homeland without exclaves: abolished in 1994. Also called: **Basotho-Qwaqwa** Former name (until 1972): **Basotho-Ba-Borwa**

qwerty *or* **QWERTY keyboard** ('kwɜːtɪ) *n* the standard English language typewriter keyboard layout with the characters q, w, e, r, t, and y positioned on the top row of alphabetic characters at the left side of the keyboard

qy *abbreviation for* query

q

r or **R** (ɑː) *n*, *pl* **r's**, **R's** or **Rs 1** the 18th letter and 14th consonant of the modern English alphabet **2** a speech sound represented by this letter, in English usually an alveolar semivowel, as in *red* **3** See **three Rs**

R *symbol for* **1** *chem* radical **2** *currency* **a** rand **b** rupee **3** Réaumur temperature (scale) **4** *physics, electronics* resistance **5** roentgen *or* röntgen **6** *chess* rook **7** Royal **8** *chem* gas constant **9** (in the US and Australia) **a** restricted exhibition (used to describe a category of film certified as unsuitable for viewing by anyone under the age of 18) **b** (*as modifier*): *an R film*

r. *abbreviation for* **1** rare **2** recto **3** Also: **r** rod (unit of length) **4** ruled **5** *cricket, baseball* run(s)

R. *abbreviation for* **1** rabbi **2** rector **3** Regina [Latin: Queen] **4** Republican **5** response (in Christian liturgy) **6** Rex [Latin: King] **7** River **8** Royal

R. *or* **r.** *abbreviation for* **1** registered (trademark) **2** right **3** river **4** rouble

Ra¹ *the chemical symbol for* radium

Ra² (rɑː) *or* **Re** *n* the ancient Egyptian sun god, depicted as a man with a hawk's head surmounted by a solar disc and serpent

RA *abbreviation for* **1** rear admiral **2** *astronomy* **right ascension 3** (in Britain) Royal Academician *or* Academy **4** (in Britain) Royal Artillery **5** ▷ *international car registration for* Argentina (officially Argentine Republic)

RAAF *abbreviation for* Royal Australian Air Force

Rabat (rəˈbɑːt) *n* the capital of Morocco, in the northwest on the Atlantic coast, served by the port of Salé: became a military centre in the 12th century and a Corsair republic in the 17th century. Pop: 673 000 (2003)

rabato *or* **rebato** (rəˈbɑːtəʊ) *n*, *pl* **-tos** a wired or starched collar, often of intricate lace, that stood up at the back and sides: worn in the 17th century [c16 from French *rabat* collar, with the ending *-o* added as if the word were from Italian]

Rabaul (rɑːˈbaʊl) *n* a port in Papua New Guinea, on NE New Britain Island, in the Bismarck Archipelago: capital of the Territory of New Guinea until 1941; almost surrounded by volcanoes. Pop: 17 022 (1990)

Rabbath Ammon (ˈræbəθ ˈæmən) *n Old Testament* the ancient royal city of the Ammonites, on the site of modern Amman

rabbet (ˈræbɪt) *or* **rebate** *n* **1** a recess, groove, or step, usually of rectangular section, cut into a surface or along the edge of a piece of timber to receive a mating piece **2** a joint made between two pieces of timber using a rabbet ▷ *vb* (*tr*) **3** to cut or form a rabbet in (timber) **4** to join (pieces of timber) using a rabbet [c13 from Old French *rabattre* to beat down]

rabbi (ˈræbaɪ) *n*, *pl* **-bis 1** (in Orthodox Judaism) a man qualified in accordance with traditional religious law to expound, teach, and rule in accordance with this law **2** the religious leader of a congregation; the minister of a synagogue **3**

the Rabbis the early Jewish scholars whose teachings are recorded in the Talmud ▷ See also **Rav** [Hebrew, from *rabh* master + -*ī* my]

rabbinate (ˈræbɪnɪt) *n* **1** the position, function, or tenure of office of a rabbi **2** rabbis collectively

rabbinic (rəˈbɪnɪk) *or* **rabbinical** *adj* of or relating to the rabbis, their teachings, writings, views, language, etc > rab'binically *adv*

Rabbinic (rəˈbɪnɪk) *or* **Rabbinical Hebrew** *n* the form of the Hebrew language used by the rabbis of the Middle Ages

rabbinics (rəˈbɪnɪks) *n* (*functioning as singular*) the study of rabbinic literature of the post-Talmudic period

rabbinism (ˈræbɪˌnɪzəm) *n* the teachings and traditions of the rabbis of the Talmudic period > 'rabbinist *n*, *adj* > ˌrabbi'nistic *adj*

rabbit (ˈræbɪt) *n*, *pl* **-bits** *or* **-bit 1** any of various common gregarious burrowing leporid mammals, esp *Oryctolagus cuniculus* of Europe and North Africa and the cottontail of America. They are closely related and similar to hares but are smaller and have shorter ears **2** the fur of such an animal **3** *Brit informal* a novice or poor performer at a game or sport ▷ *vb* **4** (*intr*; often foll by *on* or *away*) *Brit informal* to talk inconsequentially; chatter [c14 perhaps from Walloon *robett*, diminutive of Flemish *robbe* rabbit, of obscure origin: C20 in sense 4, from rhyming slang *rabbit and pork* talk]

rabbiter (ˈræbɪtə) *n chiefly Austral* a person who traps and sells rabbits

rabbit fever *n pathol* another name for **tularaemia**

rabbitfish (ˈræbɪtˌfɪʃ) *n*, *pl* **-fish** *or* **-fishes 1** a large chimaera, *Chimaera monstrosa*, common in European seas, with separate caudal and anal fins and a long whiplike tail **2** any of the spiny-finned tropical marine fishes of the family *Siganidae* of Indo-Pacific waters. They have a rabbit-like snout and spines on the pelvic or ventral fins

rabbiting (ˈræbɪtɪŋ) *n* the activity of hunting rabbits

rabbitoh *or* **rabbito** (ˈræbɪtˌəʊ) *n Austral informal* (formerly) an itinerant seller of rabbits for eating [c20 from such a seller's cry]

rabbit-proof fence *n* **a** a fence through which rabbits are unable to pass **b** *Austral informal* a boundary between certain Australian states, marked by such a fence

rabbit punch *n* a sharp blow to the back of the neck that can cause loss of consciousness or even death. Austral name: **rabbit killer**

rabbitry (ˈræbɪtrɪ) *n*, *pl* **-ries 1** a place where tame rabbits are kept and bred **2** the rabbits kept in such a place

rabble¹ (ˈræbəl) *n* **1** a disorderly crowd; mob **2** the *contemptuous* the common people [c14 (in the sense: a pack of animals): of uncertain origin; perhaps related to Middle Dutch *rabbelen* to chatter, rattle]

rabble² (ˈræbəl) *n* **1** Also called: **rabbler** an iron tool or mechanical device for stirring, mixing, or skimming a molten charge in a roasting furnace ▷ *vb* **2** (*tr*) to stir, mix, or skim (the molten charge) in a roasting furnace [c17 from French *râble*, from Latin *rutābulum* rake for a furnace, from *ruere* to rake, dig up]

rabble-rouser *n* a person who manipulates the passions of the mob; demagogue > 'rabble-ˌrousing *adj*, *n*

Rabelaisian (ˌræbəˈleɪzɪən, -ʒən) *adj* **1** of, relating to, or resembling the work of François Rabelais, the French writer (?1494–1553), esp by broad, often bawdy humour and sharp satire ▷ *n* **2** a student or admirer of Rabelais > ˌRabe'laisianism *n*

rabi (ˈrʌbɪ) *n* (in Pakistan, India, etc) a crop that is harvested at the end of winter. Compare **kharif** [Urdu: spring crop, from Arabic *rabī'* spring]

Rabia (rəˈbɪə) *n* either the third or the fourth month of the Muslim year, known as **Rabia I** and **Rabia II** respectively; the Muslim spring

rabid (ˈræbɪd, ˈreɪ-) *adj* **1** relating to or having rabies **2** zealous; fanatical; violent; raging [c17 from Latin *rabidus* frenzied, mad, from *rabere* to be mad] > **rabidity** (rəˈbɪdɪtɪ) *or* 'rabidness *n* > 'rabidly *adv*

rabies (ˈreɪbiːz) *n pathol* an acute infectious viral disease of the nervous system transmitted by the saliva of infected animals, esp dogs. It is characterized by excessive salivation, aversion to water, convulsions, and paralysis. Also called: **hydrophobia, lyssa** [c17 from Latin: madness, from *rabere* to rave] > **rabic** (ˈræbɪk) *or* **rabietic** (ˌreɪbɪˈetɪk) *adj*

RAC *abbreviation for* **1** Royal Automobile Club **2** Royal Armoured Corps

raccoon *or* **racoon** (rəˈkuːn) *n*, *pl* **-coons** *or* **-coon 1** any omnivorous mammal of the genus *Procyon*, esp *P. lotor* (**North American raccoon**), inhabiting forests of North and Central America and the Caribbean: family *Procyonidae*, order *Carnivora* (carnivores). Raccoons have a pointed muzzle, long tail, and greyish-black fur with black bands around the tail and across the face **2** the fur of the North American raccoon [c17 from Algonquian *ärähkun*, from *ärähkunèm* he scratches with his hands]

raccoon dog *n* **1** a canine mammal, *Nyctereutes procyonoides*, inhabiting woods and forests near rivers in E Asia. It has long yellowish-brown black-tipped hair and facial markings resembling those of a raccoon **2** Also called: **coonhound** an American breed of dog having a short smooth black coat with tan markings, bred to hunt raccoons

race¹ (reɪs) *n* **1** a contest of speed, as in running, swimming, driving, riding, etc **2** any competition or rivalry: *the race for the White House* **3** rapid or constant onward movement: *the race of time* **4** a rapid current of water, esp one through a narrow channel that has a tidal range greater at one end than the other **5** a channel of a stream, esp one for conducting water to or from a water wheel or other device for utilizing its energy: *a mill race* **6 a** a channel or groove that contains ball bearings or roller bearings or that restrains a sliding component **b** the inner or outer cylindrical ring in a ball bearing or roller bearing **7** *Austral and NZ* a narrow passage or enclosure in a sheep yard through which sheep pass individually, as to a sheep dip **8** *Austral* a wire tunnel through which footballers pass from the changing room onto a football field **9** *NZ* a line of containers coupled together, used in mining to transport coal **10** another name for **slipstream** (sense 1) **11** *archaic* the span or course of life **12** not in the race *Austral informal* given or having no chance ▷ *vb* **13** to engage in a contest of speed with (another) **14** to engage (oneself or one's representative) in a race, esp as a profession or pastime: *to race pigeons* **15** to move or go as fast as possible **16** to run (an engine, shaft, propeller, etc) or (of an engine, shaft, propeller, etc) to run at high speed, esp after reduction of the load or resistance ▷ See also **race off, races** [C13 from Old Norse *rās* running; related to Old English *rǣs* attack]

race² (reɪs) *n* **1** a group of people of common ancestry, distinguished from others by physical characteristics, such as hair type, colour of eyes and skin, stature, etc Principal races are Caucasoid, Mongoloid, and Negroid **2 the human race** human beings collectively **3** a group of animals or plants having common characteristics that distinguish them from other members of the same species, usually forming a geographically isolated group; subspecies **4** a group of people sharing the same interests, characteristics, etc: *the race of authors* [C16 from French, from Italian *razza*, of uncertain origin]

race³ (reɪs) *n* a ginger root [C15 from Old French *rais*, from Latin *rādīx* a root]

Race (reɪs) *n Cape* a cape at the SE extremity of Newfoundland, Canada

racecard ('reɪsˌkɑːd) *n* a card or booklet at a race meeting with the times of the races, names of the runners, etc, printed on it

racecourse ('reɪsˌkɔːs) *n* a long broad track, usually of grass, enclosed between rails, and with starting and finishing points marked upon it, over which horses are raced. Also called (esp US and Canadian): **racetrack**

racegoer ('reɪsˌɡəʊə) *n* one who attends a race meeting, esp a habitual frequenter of race meetings

racehorse ('reɪsˌhɔːs) *n* a horse specially bred for racing

raceme (rə'siːm) *n* an inflorescence in which the flowers are borne along the main stem, with the oldest flowers at the base. It can be simple, as in the foxglove, or compound (see **panicle**) [C18 from Latin *racēmus* bunch of grapes]

race meeting *n* a prearranged fixture for racing horses (or sometimes greyhounds) over a set course at set times

racemic (rə'siːmɪk, -'sɛm-) *adj chem* of, concerned with, or being a mixture of equal amounts of enantiomers and consequently having no optical activity [C19 from RACEME (as in *racemic acid*) + -IC] > **racemism** ('ræsɪˌmɪzəm, rə'siːmɪzəm) *n*

racemic acid *n* the optically inactive form of tartaric acid that is sometimes found in grape juice

racemize or **racemise** ('ræsɪˌmaɪz) *vb* to change or cause to change into a racemic mixture > ˌracemi'zation or ˌracemi'sation *n*

racemose ('ræsɪˌməʊs, -ˌməʊz) or **racemous** *adj* being or resembling a raceme [C17 from Latin *racēmōsus* clustering] > 'raceˌmosely or 'racemously *adv*

race off *vb* (tr, adverb) *Austral informal* to entice (a person) away with a view to seduction

racer ('reɪsə) *n* **1** a person, animal, or machine

that races **2** a turntable used to traverse a heavy gun **3** any of several long slender nonvenomous North American snakes of the colubrid genus *Coluber* and related genera, such as *C. lateralis* (**striped racer**)

race relations *n* **1** (*functioning as plural*) the relations between members of two or more human races, esp within a single community **2** (*functioning as singular*) the branch of sociology concerned with such relations

race riot *n* a riot among members of different races in the same community

races ('reɪsɪz) *pl n* **the** a series of contests of speed between horses (or sometimes greyhounds) over a set course at prearranged times; a race meeting

racetrack ('reɪsˌtræk) *n* **1** a circuit or course, esp an oval one, used for motor racing, speedway, etc **2** *chiefly US and Canadian* a long broad track, usually of grass, enclosed between rails, and with starting and finishing points marked upon it, over which horses are raced. Also called: **racecourse**

raceway ('reɪsˌweɪ) *n* **1** another word for **race¹** (sense 5) **2** a racetrack, esp one for banger racing **3** another word (esp US) for **race¹** (sense 6)

Rachel *n* ('reɪtʃəl) *Old Testament* the second and best-loved wife of Jacob; mother of Joseph and Benjamin (Genesis 29–35)

rachilla or **rhachilla** (rə'kɪlə) *n* (in grasses) the short stem of a spikelet that bears the florets [C19 from New Latin, diminutive of RACHIS]

rachiotomy (ˌreɪkɪ'ɒtəmɪ) *n* another name for **laminectomy**

rachis or **rhachis** ('reɪkɪs) *n, pl* **rachises, rhachises** or **rachides, rhachides** ('ræki,diːz, 'reɪ-) **1** *botany* the main axis or stem of an inflorescence or compound leaf **2** *ornithol* the shaft of a feather, esp the part that carries the barbs **3** another name for **spinal column** [C17 via New Latin from Greek *rhakhis* ridge] > **rachial, rhachial** ('reɪkɪəl) or **rachidial, rhachidial** (rə'kɪdɪəl) *adj*

rachitis (rə'kaɪtɪs) *n pathol* another name for **rickets** [C18 New Latin, from Greek *rhakitis*; see RACHIS] > **rachitic** (rə'kɪtɪk) *adj*

Rachmanism ('rækməˌnɪzəm) *n* extortion or exploitation by a landlord of tenants of dilapidated or slum property, esp when involving intimidation or use of racial fears to drive out sitting tenants whose rent is fixed at a low rate [C20 after Perec *Rachman* (1920–62), British property-owner born in Poland]

racial ('reɪʃəl) *adj* **1** denoting or relating to the division of the human species into races on grounds of physical characteristics **2** characteristic of any such group **3** relating to or arising from differences between the races: *racial harmony* **4** of or relating to a subspecies > 'racially *adv*

racialize or **racialise** ('reɪʃəˌlaɪz) *vb* (tr) to render racial in tone or content

racial profiling *n* government activity directed at a suspect or group of suspects based solely on race

racial unconscious *n psychol* another term for **collective unconscious**

racing ('reɪsɪŋ) *adj* **1** denoting or associated with horse races: *the racing fraternity; a racing man* ▷ *n* **2** the practice of engaging horses (or sometimes greyhounds) in contests of speed

racism ('reɪsɪzəm) or **racialism** ('reɪʃəˌlɪzəm) *n* **1** the belief that races have distinctive cultural characteristics determined by hereditary factors and that this endows some races with an intrinsic superiority over others **2** abusive or aggressive behaviour towards members of another race on the basis of such a belief > 'racist or racialist *n, adj*

rack¹ (ræk) *n* **1** a framework for holding, carrying, or displaying a specific load or object: *a plate rack; a hat rack; a hay rack; a luggage rack* **2** a toothed bar designed to engage a pinion to form a mechanism that will interconvert rotary and rectilinear motions **3** a framework fixed to an aircraft for carrying bombs, rockets, etc **4** (usually preceded

by *the*) an instrument of torture that stretched the body of the victim **5** a cause or state of mental or bodily stress, suffering, etc; anguish; torment (esp in the phrase **on the rack**) **6** *US and Canadian* (in pool, snooker, etc) **a** the triangular frame used to arrange the balls for the opening shot **b** the balls so grouped. Brit equivalent: **frame** ▷ *vb* (tr) **7** to torture on the rack **8** Also: **wrack** to cause great stress or suffering to: *guilt racked his conscience* **9** Also: **wrack** to strain or shake (something) violently, as by great physical force: *the storm racked the town* **10** to place or arrange in or on a rack: *to rack bottles of wine* **11** to move (parts of machinery or a mechanism) using a toothed rack **12** to raise (rents) exorbitantly; rack-rent **13 rack one's brains** to strain in mental effort, esp to remember something or to find the solution to a problem ▷ See also **rack up** [C14 *rekke*, probably from Middle Dutch *rec* framework; related to Old High German *recchen* to stretch, Old Norse *rekja* to spread out] > 'racker *n*

▷ USAGE See at **wrack¹**

rack² (ræk) *n* destruction; wreck (obsolete except in the phrase **go to rack and ruin**) [C16 variant of WRACK¹]

rack³ (ræk) *n* another word for **single-foot**, a gait of the horse [C16 perhaps based on ROCK²]

rack⁴ (ræk) *n* **1** a group of broken clouds moving in the wind ▷ *vb* **2** (*intr*) (of clouds) to be blown along by the wind [Old English *wræc* what is driven; related to Gothic *wraks* persecutor, Swedish *vrak* wreckage]

rack⁵ (ræk) *vb* (tr) **1** to clear (wine, beer, etc) as by siphoning it off from the dregs **2** to fill a container with (beer, wine, etc) [C15 from Old Provençal *arraca*, from *raca* dregs of grapes after pressing]

rack⁶ (ræk) *n* the neck or rib section of mutton, pork, or veal [Old English *hræce*; related to Old High German *rahho*, Danish *harke*, Swedish *harkla* to clear one's throat]

rack-and-pinion *n* **1** a device for converting rotary into linear motion and vice versa, in which a gearwheel (the pinion) engages with a flat toothed bar (the rack) ▷ *adj* **2** (of a type of steering gear in motor vehicles) having a track rod with a rack along part of its length that engages with a pinion attached to the steering column

racket¹ ('rækɪt) *n* **1** a noisy disturbance or loud commotion; clamour; din **2** gay or excited revelry, dissipation, etc **3** an illegal enterprise carried on for profit, such as extortion, fraud, prostitution, drug peddling, etc **4** *slang* a business or occupation: *what's your racket?* **5** *music* **a** a medieval woodwind instrument of deep bass pitch **b** a reed stop on an organ of deep bass pitch ▷ *vb* **6** (*intr*; often foll by *about*) now rare to go about gaily or noisily, in search of pleasure, excitement, etc [C16 probably of imitative origin; compare RATTLE¹]

racket² or **racquet** ('rækɪt) *n* **1** a bat consisting of an open network of nylon or other strings stretched in an oval frame with a handle, used to strike the ball in tennis, badminton, etc **2** a snowshoe shaped like a tennis racket ▷ *vb* **3** (tr) to strike (a ball, shuttlecock, etc) with a racket ▷ See also **rackets** [C16 from French *raquette*, from Arabic *rāhat* palm of the hand]

racketeer (ˌrækɪ'tɪə) *n* **1** a person engaged in illegal enterprises for profit ▷ *vb* **2** (*intr*) to operate a racket > ˌracke'teering *n*

racket press *n* a device consisting of a frame closed by a spring mechanism, for keeping taut the strings of a tennis racket, squash racket, etc

rackets ('rækɪts) *n* (*functioning as singular*) **a** a game similar to squash played in a large four-walled court by two or four players using rackets and a small hard ball **b** (*as modifier*): *a rackets court; a rackets championship*

racket-tail *n* any of several birds with a racket-shaped tail, such as certain hummingbirds and kingfishers

r

rackety ('rækɪtɪ) *adj* **1** noisy, rowdy, or boisterous **2** socially lively and, sometimes, mildly dissolute: *a rackety life*

rack off *vb* (*intr, adverb; usually imperative*) *Austral and NZ slang* to go away; depart

rack railway *n* a steep mountain railway having a middle rail fitted with a rack that engages a pinion on the locomotive to provide traction. Also called: **cog railway**

rack-rent *n* **1** a high rent that annually equals or nearly equals the value of the property upon which it is charged **2** any extortionate rent ▷ *vb* **3** to charge an extortionate rent for (property, land, etc) [C17 from RACK¹ (sense 12) + RENT¹] > **'rack-ˌrenter** *n*

rack saw *n* *building trades* a wide-toothed saw

rack up *vb* (*tr, adverb*) **1** to accumulate (points) **2** Also: **rack down** to adjust the vertical alignment of (the picture from a film projector or telecine machine) so that the upper or lower edges of the frame do not show

raclette (ræ'klɛt) *n* a Swiss dish of melted cheese served on boiled potatoes [C20 from French, from *racler* to scrape, because the cheese is traditionally melted and scraped onto a plate]

racon ('reɪkɒn) *n* another name for **radar beacon** [C20 from ra(dar) + (bea)con]

raconteur (ˌrækɒn'tɜː) *n* a person skilled in telling stories [C19 French, from *raconter* to tell]

racoon (rə'kuːn) *n*, *pl* **-coons** *or* **-coon** a variant spelling of **raccoon**

RACQ (in Australia) *abbreviation for* Royal Automobile Club of Queensland

racquet ('rækɪt) *n* a variant spelling of **racket²**

racy ('reɪsɪ) *adj* **racier, raciest** **1** (of a person's manner, literary style, etc) having a distinctively lively and spirited quality; fresh **2** having a characteristic or distinctive flavour: *a racy wine* **3** suggestive; slightly indecent; risqué: *a racy comedy* > **'racily** *adv* > **'raciness** *n*

rad¹ (ræd) *n* a former unit of absorbed ionizing radiation dose equivalent to an energy absorption per unit mass of 0.01 joule per kilogram of irradiated material. 1 rad is equivalent to 0.01 gray [C20 shortened from RADIATION]

rad² *symbol for* radian

rad. *abbreviation for* **1** radical **2** radius

RADA ('rɑːdə) *n* (in Britain) ▷ *acronym for* Royal Academy of Dramatic Art

radar ('reɪdɑː) *n* **1** a method for detecting the position and velocity of a distant object, such as an aircraft. A narrow beam of extremely high-frequency radio pulses is transmitted and reflected by the object back to the transmitter, the signal being displayed on a radarscope. The direction of the reflected beam and the time between transmission and reception of a pulse determine the position of the object. Former name: **radiolocation** **2** the equipment used in such detection [C20 ra(dio) d(etecting) a(nd) r(anging)]

radar astronomy *n* the use of radar to map the surfaces of the planets, their satellites, and other bodies

radar beacon *n* a device for transmitting a coded radar signal in response to a signal from an aircraft or ship. The coded signal is then used by the navigator to determine his position. Also called: **racon**

radarscope ('reɪdɑːˌskəʊp) *n* a cathode-ray oscilloscope on which radar signals can be viewed. In a **plan position indicator**, the target is represented by a blip on a radial line that rotates around a point, representing the antenna

radar trap *n* See **speed trap**

raddle¹ ('rædəl) *vb* (*tr*) another word for **interweave** [C17 from obsolete noun sense of *raddle* meaning a rod, wattle, or lath, from Old French *redalle* a stick, pole; of obscure origin]

raddle² ('rædəl) *vb* **1** (*tr*) chiefly *Brit* to paint (the face) with rouge ▷ *n* ▷ *vb* **2** another word for **ruddle** [C16 variant of RUDDLE]

raddled ('rædəld) *adj* (esp of a person) unkempt or run-down in appearance [C17 from RADDLE²]

radge (rædʒ) *Scot dialect* ▷ *adj* **1** angry or uncontrollable ▷ *n* **2** a person acting in such a way **3** a rage [variant of RAGE; perhaps influenced by Romany *raj*]

radial ('reɪdɪəl) *adj* **1** (of lines, bars, beams of light, etc) emanating from a common central point; arranged like the radii of a circle **2** of, like, or relating to a radius or ray **3** spreading out or developing uniformly on all sides **4** of or relating to the arms of a starfish or similar radiating structures **5** *anatomy* of or relating to the radius or forearm **6** *astronomy* (of velocity) in a direction along the line of sight of a celestial object and measured by means of the red shift (or blue shift) of the spectral lines of the object. Compare **tangential** (sense 2) ▷ *n* **7** a radial part or section **8** *zoology* **a** any of the basal fin rays of most bony fishes **b** a radial or radiating structure, such as any of the ossicles supporting the oral disc of a sea star **9** short for **radial tyre** *or* **radial drilling machine** [C16 from Medieval Latin *radiālis* from RADIUS] > **'radially** *adv*

radial drilling machine *n* a machine in which the drilling head is mounted to slide along a radial arm which can be rotated, raised, or lowered on a vertical mast to adjust the position of the drill above the workpiece. Often shortened to: **radial**

radial engine *n* an internal-combustion engine having a number of cylinders arranged about a central crankcase

radial keratotomy (ˌkɛrə'tɒtəmɪ) *n* an operation designed to improve short-sightedness in which a number of cuts are made around the cornea to change the shape of it [C20 from KERATO- + -TOMY]

radial paralysis *n* *vet science* paralysis of a forelimb as a result of loss of function of the radial nerve, usually following traumatic injury

radial-ply *adj* (of a motor tyre) having the fabric cords in the outer casing running radially to enable the sidewalls to be flexible. Compare **cross-ply**

radial symmetry *n* a type of structure of an organism or part of an organism in which a vertical cut through the axis in any of two or more planes produces two halves that are mirror images of each other. Compare **bilateral symmetry**

radial tyre *n* a motor-vehicle tyre having a radial-ply casing. Often shortened to: **radial**

radial velocity *n* the component of the velocity of an object, esp a celestial body, directed along a line from the observer to the object

radian ('reɪdɪən) *n* an SI unit of plane angle; the angle between two radii of a circle that cut off on the circumference an arc equal in length to the radius. 1 radian is equivalent to 57.296 degrees and $\pi/2$ radians equals a right angle. Symbol: rad [C19 from RADIUS]

radiance ('reɪdɪəns) *or* **radiancy** *n*, *pl* **-ances** *or* **-ancies** **1** the quality or state of being radiant **2** a measure of the amount of electromagnetic radiation leaving or arriving at a point on a surface. It is the radiant intensity in a given direction of a small element of surface area divided by the orthogonal projection of this area onto a plane at right angles to the direction. Symbol: L_e

radiant ('reɪdɪənt) *adj* **1** sending out rays of light; bright; shining **2** characterized by health, intense joy, happiness, etc: *a radiant countenance* **3** emitted or propagated by or as radiation; radiated: *radiant heat* **4** sending out heat by radiation: *a radiant heater* **5** *physics* (of a physical quantity in photometry) evaluated by **absolute** energy measurements: *radiant flux; radiant efficiency*. Compare **luminous** (sense 2) **6** a point or object that emits radiation, esp the part of a heater that gives out heat **7** *astronomy* the point in space from which a meteor shower appears to emanate [C15 from Latin *radiāre* to shine, from *radius* ray of light,

RADIUS] > **'radiantly** *adv*

radiant efficiency *n* the ratio of the power emitted by a source of radiation to the power consumed by it. Symbol: η_e

radiant energy *n* energy that is emitted or propagated in the form of particles or electromagnetic radiation. It is measured in joules. Symbol: Q_e

radiant exitance *n* the ability of a surface to emit radiation expressed as the radiant flux emitted per unit area at a specified point on the surface. Symbol: M_e

radiant flux *n* the rate of flow of energy as radiation. It is measured in watts. Symbol: Φ_e

radiant heat *n* heat transferred in the form of electromagnetic radiation rather than by conduction or convection; infrared radiation

radiant heating *n* a system of heating a building by radiant heat emitted from panels containing electrical conductors, hot water, etc

radiant intensity *n* a measure of the amount of radiation emitted from a point expressed as the radiant flux per unit solid angle leaving this source. Symbol: I_e

radiata pine (ˌreɪdɪ'ɑːtə) *n* a pine tree, *Pinus radiata*, native to the western USA. but grown in Australia, New Zealand, and elsewhere to produce building timber. Often shortened to: **radiata** [from New Latin]

radiate *vb* ('reɪdɪˌeɪt) **1** Also: **eradiate** to emit (heat, light, or some other form of radiation) or (of heat, light, etc) to be emitted as radiation **2** (*intr*) (of lines, beams, etc) to spread out from a centre or be arranged in a radial pattern **3** (*tr*) (of a person) to show (happiness, health, etc) to a great degree ▷ *adj* ('reɪdɪɪt, -ˌeɪt) **4** having rays; radiating **5** (of a capitulum) consisting of ray florets **6** (of animals or their parts) showing radial symmetry **7** adorned or decorated with rays: *a radiate head on a coin* [C17 from Latin *radiāre* to emit rays]

radiation (ˌreɪdɪ'eɪʃən) *n* **1** *physics* **a** the emission or transfer of radiant energy as particles, electromagnetic waves, sound, etc **b** the particles, etc, emitted, esp the particles and gamma rays emitted in nuclear decay **2** Also called: **radiation therapy** *med* treatment using a radioactive substance **3** *anatomy* a group of nerve fibres that diverge from their common source **4** See **adaptive radiation** **5** the act, state, or process of radiating or being radiated **6** *surveying* the fixing of points around a central plane table by using an alidade and measuring tape > **ˌradi'ational** *adj*

radiation belt *n* a region in the magnetosphere of a planet in which charged particles are trapped by the planet's magnetic field, an example being the earth's Van Allen belts

radiation pattern *n* the graphic representation of the strength and direction of electromagnetic radiation in the vicinity of a transmitting aerial. Also called: **antenna pattern**

radiation pyrometer *n* See **pyrometer**

radiation resistance *n* the resistive component of the impedance of a radio transmitting aerial that arises from the radiation of power

radiation sickness *n* *pathol* illness caused by overexposure of the body or a part of the body to ionizing radiations from radioactive material or X-rays. It is characterized by vomiting, diarrhoea, and in severe cases by sterility and cancer

radiative ('reɪdɪətɪv) *or* **radiatory** ('reɪdɪətərɪ, -trɪ) *adj* *physics* emitting or causing the emission of radiation: *a radiative collision*

radiator ('reɪdɪˌeɪtə) *n* **1** a device for heating a room, building, etc, consisting of a series of pipes through which hot water or steam passes **2** a device for cooling an internal-combustion engine, consisting of thin-walled tubes through which water passes. Heat is transferred from the water through the walls of the tubes to the airstream, which is created either by the motion of the vehicle or by a fan **3** *Austral and NZ* an electric fire **4** *electronics* the part of an aerial or transmission line that radiates electromagnetic waves **5** an electric space heater

radical ('rædɪkᵊl) *adj* **1** of, relating to, or characteristic of the basic or inherent constitution of a person or thing; fundamental: *a radical fault* **2** concerned with or tending to concentrate on fundamental aspects of a matter; searching or thoroughgoing: *radical thought; a radical re-examination* **3** favouring or tending to produce extreme or fundamental changes in political, economic, or social conditions, institutions, habits of mind, etc: *a radical party* **4** *med* (of treatment) aimed at removing the source of a disease: *radical surgery* **5** *slang, chiefly US* very good; excellent **6** of, relating to, or arising from the root or the base of the stem of a plant: *radical leaves* **7** *maths* of, relating to, or containing roots of numbers or quantities **8** *linguistics* of or relating to the root of a word ▷ *n* **9** a person who favours extreme or fundamental change in existing institutions or in political, social, or economic conditions **10** *maths* a root of a number or quantity, such as $^3\sqrt{5}$, $\sqrt{x}$ **11** Also: **radicle** *chem* **a** short for **free radical b** another name for **group** (sense 10) **12** *linguistics* another word for **root¹** (sense 9) **13** (in logographic writing systems such as that used for Chinese) a part of a character conveying lexical meaning [c14 from Late Latin *rādīcālis* having roots, from Latin *rādix* a root] > 'radicalness *n*

radical axis *n* a line from any point of which tangents to two given circles are of equal length. It is the line joining the points of intersection of two circles

radicalism ('rædɪkə,lɪzəm) *n* **1** the principles, desires, or practices of political radicals **2** a radical movement, esp in politics **3** the state or nature of being radical, esp in politics > ,radical'istic *adj* > ,radical'istically *adv*

radically ('rædɪkəlɪ) *adv* thoroughly; completely; fundamentally: *to alter radically*

radical sign *n* the symbol √ placed before a number or quantity to indicate the extraction of a root, esp a square root. The value of a higher root is indicated by a raised digit in front of the symbol, as in $^3\sqrt{}$

radicand ('rædɪ,kænd, ,rædɪ'kænd) *n* a number or quantity from which a root is to be extracted, usually preceded by a radical sign: 3 *is the radicand of* √3 [c20 from Latin *rādicandum*, literally: that which is to be rooted, from *rādīcāre* to take root, from *rādix* root]

radicchio (ræ'di:kɪəʊ) *n, pl* **-chios** an Italian variety of chicory, having purple leaves streaked with white that are eaten raw in salads

radicel ('rædɪ,sɛl) *n* a very small root; radicle [c19 from New Latin *radicella* a little root, from Latin *rādix* root]

radices ('reɪdɪ,si:z) *n* a plural of **radix**

radicle ('rædɪkᵊl) *n* **1** *botany* **a** part of the embryo of seed-bearing plants that develops into the main root **b** a very small root or rootlike part **2** *anatomy* any bodily structure resembling a rootlet, esp one of the smallest branches of a vein or nerve **3** *chem* a variant spelling of **radical** (sense 11) [c18 from Latin *rādicula* little root, from *rādix* root]

radii ('reɪdɪ,aɪ) *n* a plural of **radius**

radio ('reɪdɪəʊ) *n, pl* **-os 1** the use of electromagnetic waves, lying in the radio-frequency range, for broadcasting, two-way communications, etc **2** an electronic device designed to receive, demodulate, and amplify radio signals from sound broadcasting stations, etc **3** a similar device permitting both transmission and reception of radio signals for two-way communications **4** the broadcasting, content, etc, of sound radio programmes: *he thinks radio is poor these days* **5 a** the occupation or profession concerned with any aspect of the broadcasting of sound radio programmes: *he's in*

radio **b** (*modifier*) relating to, produced for, or transmitted by sound radio: *radio drama* **6** short for **radiotelegraph, radiotelegraphy** or **radiotelephone 7** (*modifier*) **a** of, relating to, employed in, or sent by radio signals: *a radio station* **b** of, concerned with, using, or operated by radio frequencies: *radio spectrum* **8** (*modifier*) (of a motor vehicle) equipped with a radio for communication: *radio car* ▷ *vb* **-os, -oing, -oed 9** to transmit (a message) to (a person, radio station, etc) by means of radio waves ▷ Also called (esp Brit): **wireless** [c20 short for *radiotelegraphy*]

radio- *combining form* denoting radio, broadcasting, or radio frequency: *radiogram* **2** indicating radioactivity or radiation: *radiochemistry; radiolucent* **3** indicating a radioactive isotope or substance: *radioactinium; radiothorium; radioelement* [from French, from Latin *radius* ray; see RADIUS]

radioactivate (,reɪdɪəʊ'æktɪ,veɪt) *vb* (*tr*) to make radioactive > ,radio,acti'vation *n*

radioactive (,reɪdɪəʊ'æktɪv) *adj* exhibiting, using, or concerned with radioactivity > ,radio'actively *adv*

radioactive dating *n* another term for **radiometric dating**

radioactive decay *n* disintegration of a nucleus that occurs spontaneously or as a result of electron capture. One or more different nuclei are formed and usually particles and gamma rays are emitted. Sometimes shortened to: **decay** Also called: **disintegration**

radioactive series *n physics* a series of nuclides each of which undergoes radioactive decay into the next member of the series, ending with a stable element, usually lead. See **uranium series, neptunium series, thorium series, actinium series**

radioactive tracer *n med* See **tracer** (sense 3)

radioactive waste *n* any waste material containing radionuclides. Also called: **nuclear waste**

radioactivity (,reɪdɪəʊæk'tɪvɪtɪ) *n* the spontaneous emission of radiation from atomic nuclei. The radiation can consist of alpha, beta, and gamma radiation

radio astronomy *n* a branch of astronomy in which a radio telescope is used to detect and analyse radio signals received on earth from radio sources in space

radioautograph (,reɪdɪəʊ'ɔ:tə,grɑ:f, -,græf) *n* another name for **autoradiograph**

radio beacon *n* a fixed radio transmitting station that broadcasts a characteristic signal by means of which a vessel or aircraft can determine its bearing or position. Sometimes shortened to: **beacon**

radio beam *n* a narrow beam of radio signals transmitted by a radio or radar beacon, radio telescope, or some other directional aerial, used for communications, navigation, etc. Sometimes shortened to: **beam**

radiobiology (,reɪdɪəʊbaɪ'ɒlədʒɪ) *n* the branch of biology concerned with the effects of radiation on living organisms and the study of biological processes using radioactive substances as tracers > **radiobiological** (,reɪdɪəʊ,baɪə'lɒdʒɪkᵊl) *adj* > ,radio,bio'logically *adv* > ,radiobi'ologist *n*

radiocarbon (,reɪdɪəʊ'kɑ:bᵊn) *n* a radioactive isotope of carbon, esp carbon-14. See **carbon** (sense 1)

radiocarbon dating *n* a technique for determining the age of organic materials, such as wood, based on their content of the radioisotope ^{14}C acquired from the atmosphere when they formed part of a living plant. The ^{14}C decays to the nitrogen isotope ^{14}N with a half-life of 5730 years. Measurement of the amount of radioactive carbon remaining in the material thus gives an estimate of its age. Also called: **carbon-14 dating**

radiochemistry (,reɪdɪəʊ'kɛmɪstrɪ) *n* the chemistry of radioactive elements and their compounds > ,radio'chemical *adj* > ,radio'chemist *n*

radiocommunication (,reɪdɪəʊkə,mju:nɪ'keɪʃən)

n communication by means of radio waves

radio compass *n* any navigational device that gives a bearing by determining the direction of incoming radio waves transmitted from a particular radio station or beacon. See also **goniometer** (sense 2)

radio control *n* remote control by means of radio signals from a transmitter

radio-controlled *adj* controlled remotely using radio signals from a transmitter

radioelement (,reɪdɪəʊ'ɛlɪmənt) *n* an element that is naturally radioactive

radio frequency *n* **1 a** a frequency or band of frequencies that lie in the range 10 kilohertz to 300 000 megahertz and can be used for radio communications and broadcasting. Abbreviations: rf, RF See also **frequency band b** (*as modifier*): *a radio-frequency amplifier* **2** the frequency transmitted by a particular radio station

radio galaxy *n* a galaxy that is a strong emitter of radio waves

radiogenic (,reɪdɪəʊ'dʒɛnɪk) *adj* produced or caused by radioactive decay: *a radiogenic element; radiogenic heat*

radiogoniometer (,reɪdɪəʊ,gəʊnɪ'ɒmɪtə) *n* a device used to detect the direction of radio waves, consisting of a coil that is free to rotate within two fixed coils at right angles to each other

radiogram ('reɪdɪəʊ,græm) *n* **1** *Brit* a unit comprising a radio and record player **2** a message transmitted by radiotelegraphy **3** another name for **radiograph**

radiograph ('reɪdɪəʊ,grɑ:f, -,græf) *n* an image produced on a specially sensitized photographic film or plate by radiation, usually by X-rays or gamma rays. Also called: **radiogram, shadowgraph**

radiography (,reɪdɪ'ɒgrəfɪ) *n* the production of radiographs of opaque objects for use in medicine, surgery, industry, etc > ,radi'ographer *n* > **radiographic** (,reɪdɪəʊ'græfɪk) *adj* > ,radio'graphically *adv*

radioimmunoassay ('reɪdɪəʊ,ɪmjʊnəʊ'æseɪ) *n* a sensitive immunological assay, making use of antibodies and radioactive labelling, for the detection and quantification of biologically important substances, such as hormone concentrations in the blood

radio interferometer *n* a type of radio telescope in which two or more aerials connected to the same receiver produce interference patterns that can be analysed to provide an image of the source of the radio waves

radioisotope (,reɪdɪəʊ'aɪsətəʊp) *n* an isotope that is radioactive > **radioisotopic** (,reɪdɪəʊ,aɪsə'tɒpɪk) *adj*

radiolarian (,reɪdɪəʊ'lɛərɪən) *n* any of various marine protozoans constituting the order *Radiolaria*, typically having a siliceous shell and stiff radiating cytoplasmic projections: phylum *Actinopoda* (actinopods) [c19 from New Latin *Radiolaria*, from Late Latin *radiolus* little sunbeam, from Latin *radius* ray, RADIUS]

radiolocation (,reɪdɪəʊlə'keɪʃən) *n* a former name for **radar**. > ,radiolo'cational *adj*

radiological (,reɪdɪə'lɒdʒɪkᵊl) *adj* **1** of, relating to, or concerning radiology or the equipment used in radiology **2** of, relating to, or involving radioactive materials: *radiological warfare* > ,radio'logically *adv*

radiology (,reɪdɪ'ɒlədʒɪ) *n* the use of X-rays and radioactive substances in the diagnosis and treatment of disease > ,radi'ologist *n*

radiolucent (,reɪdɪəʊ'lu:sᵊnt) *adj* almost transparent to electromagnetic radiation, esp X-rays

radioluminescence (,reɪdɪəʊ,lu:mɪ'nɛsᵊns) *n physics* luminescence that is induced by radiation from a radioactive material > ,radio,lumi'nescent *adj*

radiolysis (,reɪdɪ'ɒlɪsɪs) *n* chemical

r

decomposition caused by radiation, such as a beam of electrons or X-rays > **radiolytic** (ˌreɪdɪ'lɪtɪk) *adj*

radiometeorograph (ˌreɪdɪəʊ'miːtɪərəˌɡrɑːf, -ˌɡræf) *n* another name for **radiosonde**

radiometer (ˌreɪdɪ'ɒmɪtə) *n* any instrument for the detection or measurement of radiant energy > **radiometric** (ˌreɪdɪəʊ'mɛtrɪk) *adj* > **radi'ometry** *n*

radiometric dating *n* any method of dating material based on the decay of its constituent radioactive atoms, such as potassium-argon dating or rubidium-strontium dating. Also called: **radioactive dating**

radiomicrometer (ˌreɪdɪəʊmaɪ'krɒmɪtə) *n* an instrument for detecting and measuring small amounts of radiation, usually by a sensitive thermocouple

radio microphone *n* a microphone incorporating a radio transmitter so that the user can move around freely

radiomimetic (ˌreɪdɪəʊmɪ'mɛtɪk) *adj* (of drugs) producing effects similar to those produced by X-rays

radionics (ˌreɪdɪ'ɒnɪks) *n* (functioning as singular) a dowsing technique using a pendulum to detect the energy fields that are emitted by all forms of matter

radionuclide (ˌreɪdɪəʊ'njuːklaɪd) *n* a nuclide that is radioactive

radiopager (ˌreɪdɪəʊˌpeɪdʒə) *n* a small radio receiver fitted with a buzzer to alert a person to telephone their home, office, etc, to receive a message > '**radio,paging** *n*

radiopaque (ˌreɪdɪəʊ'peɪk) or **radio-opaque** *adj* not permitting X-rays or other radiation to pass through > **radiopacity** (ˌreɪdɪəʊ'pæsɪtɪ) or ,**radio-o'pacity** *n*

radiophone (ˈreɪdɪəʊˌfəʊn) *n* another name for **radiotelephone** (sense 1)

radiophonic (ˌreɪdɪəʊ'fɒnɪk) *adj* denoting or relating to music produced by electronic means > ,**radio'phonically** *adv* > **radiophony** (ˌreɪdɪ'ɒfənɪ) *n*

radio receiver *n* an apparatus that receives incoming modulated radio waves and converts them into sound

radioresistant (ˌreɪdɪəʊrɪ'sɪstənt) *adj med* resistant to the effects of radiation

radioscope (ˈreɪdɪəʊˌskəʊp) *n* an instrument, such as a fluoroscope, capable of detecting radiant energy

radioscopy (ˌreɪdɪ'ɒskəpɪ) *n* another word for **fluoroscopy**. > **radioscopic** (ˌreɪdɪəʊ'skɒpɪk) *adj* > ,**radio'scopically** *adv*

radiosensitive (ˌreɪdɪəʊ'sɛnsɪtɪv) *adj* affected by or sensitive to radiation > ,**radio'sensitively** *adv* > ,**radio,sensi'tivity** *n*

radiosonde (ˈreɪdɪəʊˌsɒnd) *n* an airborne instrument to send meteorological information back to earth by radio. Also called: **radiometeorograph** [C20 RADIO- + French *sonde* sounding line]

radio source *n* a celestial object, such as a supernova remnant or quasar, that is a source of radio waves

radio spectrum *n* the range of electromagnetic frequencies used in radio transmission, lying between 10 kilohertz and 300 000 megahertz

radio star *n* another name for **radio source**

radio station *n* **1** an installation consisting of one or more transmitters or receivers, etc, used for radiocommunications **2** a broadcasting organization

radiotelegram (ˌreɪdɪəʊ'tɛlɪˌɡræm) *n* a message transmitted by radiotelegraphy. Also called: **radiogram**

radiotelegraph (ˌreɪdɪəʊ'tɛlɪˌɡrɑːf, -ˌɡræf) *vb* **1** to send (a message) by radiotelegraphy ▷ *n* **2** a message sent by radiotelegraphy

radiotelegraphy (ˌreɪdɪəʊtɪ'lɛɡrəfɪ) *n* a type of telegraphy in which messages (usually in Morse code) are transmitted by radio waves; its use is no longer widespread as it has been superseded by

satellite technology. Also called: **wireless telegraphy** > **radiotelegraphic** (ˌreɪdɪəʊˌtɛlɪ'ɡræfɪk) *adj* > ,**radio,tele'graphically** *adv*

radiotelemetry (ˌreɪdɪəʊtɪ'lɛmɪtrɪ) *n* the use of radio waves for transmitting information from a distant instrument to a device that indicates or records the measurements. Sometimes shortened to: **telemetry**

radiotelephone (ˌreɪdɪəʊ'tɛlɪˌfəʊn) *n* **1** Also called: **radiophone, wireless telephone** a device for communication by means of radio waves rather than by transmitting along wires or cables ▷ *vb* **2** to telephone (a person) by radiotelephone ▷ Sometimes shortened to: **radio** > **radiotelephonic** (ˌreɪdɪəʊˌtɛlɪ'fɒnɪk) *adj* > **radiotelephony** (ˌreɪdɪəʊtɪ'lɛfənɪ) *n*

radio telescope *n* an instrument consisting of an antenna or system of antennas connected to one or more radio receivers, used in radio astronomy to detect and analyse radio waves from space

radioteletype (ˌreɪdɪəʊ'tɛlɪˌtaɪp) *n* **1** a teleprinter that transmits or receives information by means of radio waves rather than by cable or wire **2** a network of such devices widely used for communicating news, messages, information, etc. Abbreviations: RTT, RTTY

radiotherapy (ˌreɪdɪəʊ'θɛrəpɪ) *n* the treatment of disease, esp cancer, by means of alpha or beta particles emitted from an implanted or ingested radioisotope, or by means of a beam of high-energy radiation. Compare **chemotherapy** > **radiotherapeutic** (ˌreɪdɪəʊˌθɛrə'pjuːtɪk) *adj* > ,**radio,thera'peutically** *adv* > ,**radio'therapist** *n*

radiothermy (ˈreɪdɪəʊˌθɜːmɪ) *n med* the treatment of disease by means of heat generated by electromagnetic radiation

radiotoxic (ˌreɪdɪəʊ'tɒksɪk) *adj* of or denoting the toxic effects of radiation or radioactive substances

radio valve *n* another name for **valve** (sense 3)

radio wave *n* an electromagnetic wave of radio frequency

radio window *n* a gap in ionospheric reflection that allows radio waves, with frequencies in the range 10 000 to 40 000 megahertz, to pass from or into space

radish (ˈrædɪʃ) *n* **1** any of various plants of the genus *Raphanus*, esp *R. sativus* of Europe and Asia, cultivated for its edible root: family *Brassicaceae* (crucifers) **2** the root of this plant, which has a pungent taste and is eaten raw in salads **3** wild **radish** another name for **white charlock**. See **charlock** (sense 2) [Old English *rǣdīc*, from Latin *rādīx* root]

radium (ˈreɪdɪəm) *n* **a** a highly radioactive luminescent white element of the alkaline earth group of metals. It occurs in pitchblende, carnotite, and other uranium ores, and is used in radiotherapy and in luminous paints. Symbol: Ra; atomic no.: 88; half-life of most stable isotope, ^{226}Ra: 1620 years; valency: 2; relative density: 5; melting pt: 700°C; boiling pt: 1140°C **b** (as modifier): *radium needle* [C20 from Latin *radius* ray]

radium therapy *n* treatment of disease, esp cancer, by exposing affected tissues to radiation from radium

radius (ˈreɪdɪəs) *n, pl* **-dii** (-dɪˌaɪ) *or* **-diuses 1** a straight line joining the centre of a circle or sphere to any point on the circumference or surface **2** the length of this line, usually denoted by the symbol *r* **3** the distance from the centre of a regular polygon to a vertex (**long radius**) or the perpendicular distance to a side (**short radius**) **4** *anatomy* the outer and slightly shorter of the two bones of the human forearm, extending from the elbow to the wrist **5 a** corresponding bone in other vertebrates **6** any of the veins of an insect's wing **7** a group of ray florets, occurring in such plants as the daisy **8 a** any radial or radiating part, such as a spoke **b** (as modifier): *a radius arm* **9** the lateral displacement of a cam or eccentric wheel **10** a circular area of a size indicated by the

length of its radius: *the police stopped every lorry within a radius of four miles* **11** the operational limit of a ship, aircraft, etc [C16 from Latin: rod, ray, spoke]

radius of action *n military* the maximum distance that a ship, aircraft, or land vehicle can travel from its base and return without refuelling

radius of curvature *n* the absolute value of the reciprocal of the curvature of a curve at a given point; the radius of a circle the curvature of which is equal to that of the given curve at that point. See also **centre of curvature**

radius of gyration *n* a length that represents the distance in a rotating system between the point about which it is rotating and the point to or from which a transfer of energy has the maximum effect. Symbol: *k* or *r*. In a system with a moment of inertia *I* and mass *m*, $k^2 = I/m$

radius vector *n* **1** *maths* a line joining a point in space to the origin of polar or spherical coordinates **2** *astronomy* an imaginary line joining a satellite to the planet or star around which it is orbiting

radix (ˈreɪdɪks) *n, pl* **-dices** (-dɪˌsiːz) *or* **-dixes 1** *maths* any number that is the base of a number system or of a system of logarithms: *10 is the radix of the decimal system* **2** *biology* the root or point of origin of a part or organ **3** *linguistics* a less common word for **root[1]** (sense 9) [C16 from Latin *rādīx* root; compare Greek *rhadix* small branch, *rhiza* root]

radix point *n* a point, such as the decimal point in the decimal system, separating the integral part of a number from the fractional part

Radnorshire (ˈrædnəˌʃɪə, -ʃə) or **Radnor** *n* (until 1974) a county of E Wales, now part of Powys

Radom (*Polish* ˈradɔm) *n* a city in E Poland: under Austria from 1795 to 1815 and Russia from 1815 to 1918. Pop: 232 000 (2005 est)

radome (ˈreɪdəʊm) *n* a protective housing for a radar antenna made from a material that is transparent to radio waves [C20 RA(DAR) + DOME]

radon (ˈreɪdɒn) *n* a colourless radioactive element of the rare gas group, the most stable isotope of which, radon-222, is a decay product of radium. It is used as an alpha particle source in radiotherapy. Symbol: Rn; atomic no.: 86; half-life of ^{222}Rn: 3.82 days; valency: 0; density: 9.73 kg/m³; melting pt: −71°C; boiling pt: −61.7°C [C20 from RADIUM + -ON]

radula (ˈrædjʊlə) *n, pl* **-lae** (-ˌliː) a horny tooth-bearing strip on the tongue of molluscs that is used for rasping food [C19 from Late Latin: a scraping iron, from Latin *rādere* to scrape] > '**radular** *adj*

RAE (in Britain) *abbreviation for* Royal Aircraft Establishment

RAEC *abbreviation for* Royal Army Educational Corps

RAF (*Not standard* ræf) *abbreviation for* Royal Air Force

raff (ræf) *n archaic or dialect* **1** rubbish; refuse **2** rabble or riffraff [C14 perhaps from Old French *rafle* a snatching up; compare RAFFLE, RIFFRAFF]

Rafferty (ˈræfətɪ) or **Rafferty's rules** *pl n Austral and NZ slang* no rules at all [C20 of uncertain origin]

raffia or **raphia** (ˈræfɪə) *n* **1** Also called: **raffia palm** a palm tree, *Raphia ruffia*, native to Madagascar, that has large plumelike leaves, the stalks of which yield a useful fibre **2** the fibre obtained from this plant, used for tying, weaving, etc **3** any of several related palms or the fibre obtained from them [C19 from Malagasy]

raffinate (ˈræfɪˌneɪt) *n* the liquid left after a solute has been extracted by solvent extraction [C20 from French *raffiner* to refine + -ATE[1]]

raffinose (ˈræfɪˌnəʊz, -ˌnəʊs) *n biochem* a trisaccharide of fructose, glucose, and galactose that occurs in sugar beet, cotton seed, certain cereals, etc Formula: $C_{18}H_{32}O_{16}$ [C19 from French *raffiner* to refine + -OSE[2]]

raffish (ˈræfɪʃ) *adj* **1** careless or unconventional in dress, manners, etc; rakish **2** tawdry; flashy; vulgar [C19 see RAFF] > '**raffishly** adv > '**raffishness** n

raffle ('ræf²l) n **1 a** a lottery in which the prizes are goods rather than money **b** (as modifier): a raffle ticket ▷ vb **2** (tr; often foll by off) to dispose of (goods) in a raffle [C14 (a dice game): from Old French, of obscure origin] > '**raffler** n

rafflesia (ræ'fli:zɪə) n any of various tropical Asian parasitic leafless plants constituting the genus *Rafflesia*, esp *R. arnoldi*, the flowers of which grow up to 45 cm (18 inches) across, smell of putrid meat, and are pollinated by carrion flies: family *Rafflesiaceae* [C19 New Latin, named after Sir Stamford *Raffles* (1781–1826), British colonial administrator, who discovered it]

raft¹ (rɑːft) n **1** a buoyant platform of logs, planks, etc, used as a vessel or moored platform **2** a thick slab of reinforced concrete laid over soft ground to provide a foundation for a building ▷ vb **3** to convey on or travel by raft, or make a raft from [C15 from Old Norse *raptr* RAFTER] > '**rafting** n

raft² (rɑːft) n informal a large collection or amount: a raft of old notebooks discovered in a cupboard [C19 from RAFF]

rafter ('rɑːftə) n any one of a set of sloping beams that form the framework of a roof [Old English *ræfter*; related to Old Saxon *rehter*, Old Norse *raptr*, Old High German *rāvo*; see RAFT¹]

RAFVR abbreviation for Royal Air Force Volunteer Reserve

rag¹ (ræg) n **1 a** a small piece of cloth, such as one torn from a discarded garment, or such pieces of cloth collectively **b** (as modifier): a rag doll; a rag book; rag paper **2** a fragmentary piece of any material; scrap; shred **3** informal a newspaper or other journal, esp one considered as worthless, sensational, etc **4** informal an item of clothing **5** informal a handkerchief **6** Brit slang, esp naval a flag or ensign **7 lose one's rag** to lose one's temper suddenly ▷ See also **rags** [C14 probably back formation from RAGGED, from Old English *raggig*; related to Old Norse *rögg* tuft]

rag² (ræg) vb **rags, ragging, ragged** (tr) **1** to draw attention facetiously and persistently to the shortcomings or alleged shortcomings of (a person) **2** Brit to play rough practical jokes on ▷ n **3** Brit a boisterous practical joke, esp one on a fellow student **4** (in British universities) **a** a period, usually a week, in which various events are organized to raise money for charity, including a procession of decorated floats and tableaux **b** (as modifier): rag day [C18 of uncertain origin]

rag³ (ræg) jazz ▷ n **1** a piece of ragtime music ▷ vb **rags, ragging, ragged 2** (tr) to compose or perform in ragtime [C20 shortened from RAGTIME]

rag⁴ (ræg) n a roofing slate that is rough on one side [C13 of obscure origin]

raga ('rɑːgə) n (in Indian music) **1** any of several conventional patterns of melody and rhythm that form the basis for freely interpreted compositions. Each pattern is associated with different aspects of religious devotion **2** a composition based on one of these patterns [C18 from Sanskrit *rāga* tone, colour]

ragamuffin ('rægə,mʌfɪn) n **1** a ragged unkempt person, esp a child **2** another name for **ragga** [C14 *Ragamoffyn*, name of a demon in the poem *Piers Plowman* (1393); probably based on RAG¹]

rag-and-bone man n Brit a man who buys and sells discarded clothing, furniture, etc. Also called: **ragman, ragpicker** US equivalent: **junkman**

ragbag ('ræg,bæg) n **1** a bag for storing odd rags **2** a confused assortment; jumble: a ragbag of ideas **3** informal a scruffy or slovenly person [C19]

ragbolt ('ræg,bəʊlt) n a bolt that has angled projections on it to prevent it working loose once it has been driven home

Ragdoll ('ræg,dɒl) n a breed of large long-haired cat with blue eyes

rage (reɪdʒ) n **1** intense anger; fury **2** violent

movement or action, esp of the sea, wind, etc **3** great intensity of hunger, sexual desire, or other feelings **4** aggressive behaviour associated with a specified environment or activity: road rage; school rage **5** a fashion or craze (esp in the phrase **all the rage**) **6** Austral and NZ informal a dance or party ▷ vb **7** (intr) to feel or exhibit intense anger **8** (esp of storms, fires, etc) to move or surge with great violence **9** (esp of a disease or epidemic) to spread rapidly and uncontrollably **10** Austral and NZ informal to have a good time [C13 via Old French from Latin *rabiēs* madness]

ragga ('rægə) n a dance-orientated style of reggae. Also called: **ragamuffin** [C20 shortened from RAGAMUFFIN]

ragged ('rægɪd) adj **1** (of clothes) worn to rags; tattered **2** (of a person) dressed in shabby tattered clothes **3** having a neglected or unkempt appearance: ragged weeds **4** having a loose, rough, or uneven surface or edge; jagged **5** uneven or irregular: a ragged beat; a ragged shout [C13 probably from *ragge* RAG¹] > '**raggedly** adv > '**raggedness** n

ragged robin n a caryophyllaceous plant, *Lychnis flosculi*, native to Europe and Asia, that has pink or white flowers with ragged petals. Also called: **cuckooflower** See also **catchfly**

ragged school n (in Britain, formerly) a free elementary school for poor children

raggedy ('rægɪdɪ) adj informal somewhat ragged; tattered: a raggedy doll

raggle ('ræg²l) n chiefly Scot a thin groove cut in stone or brickwork, esp to hold the edge of a roof [C19 of obscure origin]

raggle-taggle ('ræg²l'tæg²l) adj motley or unkempt: a raggle-taggle Gypsy [augmented form of RAGTAG]

ragi, raggee or **raggy** ('rægɪ) n a cereal grass, *Eleusine coracana*, cultivated in Africa and Asia for its edible grain [C18 from Hindi]

raglan ('ræglən) n **1** a coat with sleeves that continue to the collar instead of having armhole seams ▷ adj **2** cut in this design: a raglan sleeve [C19 named after Fitzroy James Henry Somerset, 1st Baron *Raglan* (1788–1855), British field marshal, diplomatist, and politician]

ragman ('ræg,mæn) n, pl -men another name for **rag-and-bone man**

Ragman rolls ('rægmən) pl n history a set of parchment rolls of 1296 enumerating the Scottish nobles who owed allegiance to Edward I of England, important as the only full list of the nobility of Scotland in the later 13th century [C18 from obsolete *ragman* in the sense: statute, roll, list]

Ragnarök or **Ragnarok** ('rɑːgnə,rɒk) n Norse myth the ultimate destruction of the gods in a cataclysmic battle with evil, out of which a new order will arise. German equivalent: **Götterdämmerung** [Old Norse *ragnarökkr*, from *regin* the gods + *rökkr* twilight]

ragout (ræ'guː) n **1** a richly seasoned stew of meat or poultry and vegetables ▷ vb -**gouts** (-'guːz) -**gouting** (-'guːɪŋ) -**gouted** (-'guːd) **2** (tr) to make into a ragout [C17 from French, from *ragoûter* to stimulate the appetite again, from ra- RE- + *goûter* from Latin *gustāre* to taste]

rag-rolling n a decorating technique in which paint is applied with a roughly folded cloth in order to create a marbled effect

rags (rægz) pl n **1** torn, old, or shabby clothing **2** cotton or linen cloth waste used in the manufacture of rag paper **3 glad rags** informal best clothes; finery **4 from rags to riches** informal **a** from poverty to great wealth **b** (as modifier): a rags-to-riches tale

ragstone ('ræg,stəʊn) n a hard sandstone or limestone, esp when used for building. Also called: **rag** or **ragg** [C14 from RAG¹ + STONE]

ragtag ('ræg,tæg) n disparaging the common people; rabble (esp in the phrase **ragtag and bobtail**) [C19]

ragtime ('ræg,taɪm) n a style of jazz piano music,

developed by Scott Joplin around 1900, having a two-four rhythm base and a syncopated melody [C20 probably from RAGGED + TIME]

rag trade n informal the clothing business, esp the aspects concerned with the manufacture and sale of dresses

Ragusa (Italian ra'guːza) n **1** an industrial town in SE Sicily. Pop: 68 956 (2001) **2** the Italian name (until 1918) for **Dubrovnik**

ragweed ('ræg,wiːd) n any plant of the chiefly North American genus *Ambrosia*, such as *A. artemisiifolia* (**common ragweed**): family *Asteraceae* (composites). Their green tassel-like flowers produce large amounts of pollen, which causes hay fever. Also called: **ambrosia**

ragworm ('ræg,wɜːm) n any polychaete worm of the genus *Nereis*, living chiefly in burrows in sand or mud and having a flattened body with a row of fleshy parapodia along each side. US name: **clamworm**

ragwort ('ræg,wɜːt) n any of several plants of the genus *Senecio*, esp *S. jacobaea* of Europe, that have yellow daisy-like flowers: family *Asteraceae* (composites). See also **groundsel** (sense 1)

rah (rɑː) interj informal, chiefly US short for **hurrah**

rah-rah ('rɑː,rɑː) adj informal, chiefly US like or marked by boisterous and uncritical enthusiasm and excitement [C20 a reduplication of RAH]

rahui (,rɑː'huːɪ) n NZ a Māori prohibition [Māori]

rai (raɪ) n a type of Algerian popular music based on traditional Algerian music influenced by modern Western pop [C20 Arabic, literally: opinion]

raia ('rɑːjə, 'raɪə) n a less common variant of **rayah**

raid (reɪd) n **1** a sudden surprise attack: an air raid **2** a surprise visit by police searching for criminals or illicit goods: a fraud-squad raid ▷ See also **bear raid, dawn raid** ▷ vb **3** to make a raid against (a person, thing, etc) **4** to sneak into (a place) in order to take something, steal, etc: raiding the larder [C15 Scottish dialect, from Old English *rād* military expedition; see ROAD] > '**raider** n

rail¹ (reɪl) n **1** a horizontal bar of wood, metal, etc, supported by vertical posts, functioning as a fence, barrier, handrail, etc **2** a horizontal bar fixed to a wall on which to hang things: a picture rail **3** a horizontal framing member in a door or piece of panelling. Compare **stile**² **4** short for **railing 5** one of a pair of parallel bars laid on a prepared track, roadway, etc, that serve as a guide and running surface for the wheels of a railway train, tramcar, etc **6 a** short for **railway b** (as modifier): rail transport **7** nautical a trim for finishing the top of a bulwark **8 off the rails a** into or in a state of dysfunction or disorder **b** eccentric or mad ▷ vb (tr) **9** to provide with a rail or railings **10** (usually foll by in or off) to fence (an area) with rails [C13 from Old French *raille* rod, from Latin *rēgula* ruler, straight piece of wood] > '**railless** adj

rail² (reɪl) vb (intr; foll by at or against) to complain bitterly or vehemently: to rail against fate [C15 from Old French *railler* to mock, from Old Provençal *ralhar* to chatter, joke, from Late Latin *ragere* to yell, neigh] > '**railer** n

rail³ (reɪl) n any of various small wading birds of the genus *Rallus* and related genera: family *Rallidae*, order *Gruiformes* (cranes, etc). They have short wings, long legs, and dark plumage [C15 from Old French *raale*, perhaps from Latin *rādere* to scrape]

railcar ('reɪl,kɑː) n a passenger-carrying railway vehicle consisting of a single coach with its own power unit

railcard ('reɪl,kɑːd) n Brit an identity card that young people or pensioners in Britain can buy, which allows them to buy train tickets more cheaply

rail gauge n See **gauge** (sense 11)

railhead ('reɪl,hɛd) n **1** a terminal of a railway **2** the farthest point reached by completed track on an unfinished railway **3** military the point at which material and personnel are transferred

r

from rail to another conveyance **4** the upper part of a railway rail, on which the traffic wheels run
railing (ˈreɪlɪŋ) *n* **1** (*often plural*) a fence, balustrade, or barrier that consists of rails supported by posts **2** rails collectively or material for making rails
raillery (ˈreɪlərɪ) *n, pl* **-leries 1** light-hearted satire or ridicule; banter **2** an example of this, esp a bantering remark [C17 from French, from *railler* to tease, banter; see RAIL[2]]
rail rage *n* a sense of extreme frustration experienced by rail users when subjected to delays, cancellations, etc, sometimes resulting in aggressive behaviour towards railway employees
railroad (ˈreɪlˌrəʊd) *n* **1** the usual US word for **railway** ▷ *vb* **2** (*tr*) *informal* to force (a person) into (an action) with haste or by unfair means
railway (ˈreɪlˌweɪ) *or US* **railroad** *n* **1** a permanent track composed of a line of parallel metal rails fixed to sleepers, for transport of passengers and goods in trains **2** any track on which the wheels of a vehicle may run: *a cable railway* **3** the entire equipment, rolling stock, buildings, property, and system of tracks used in such a transport system **4** the organization responsible for operating a railway network **5** (*modifier*) of, relating to, or used on a railway or railways: *a railway engine; a railway strike*
railwayman (ˈreɪlˌweɪmən) *n, pl* **-men** a worker on a railway, esp one other than a driver
raiment (ˈreɪmənt) *n archaic or poetic* attire; clothing; garments [C15 shortened from *arrayment*, from Old French *areement*; see ARRAY]
rain (reɪn) *n* **1 a** precipitation from clouds in the form of drops of water, formed by the condensation of water vapour in the atmosphere **b** a fall of rain; shower **c** (*in combination*): *a raindrop*. Related adjs: **hyetal, pluvious 2** a large quantity of anything falling rapidly or in quick succession: *a rain of abuse* **3** (**come**) **rain or shine a** regardless of the weather **b** regardless of circumstances **4 right as rain** *Brit informal* perfectly all right; perfectly fit ▷ *vb* **5** (*intr*; with *it* as subject) to be the case that rain is falling **6** (often with *it* as subject) to fall or cause to fall like rain: *the lid flew off and popcorn rained on everyone* **7** (*tr*) to bestow in large measure: *to rain abuse on someone* **8 rain cats and dogs** *informal* to rain heavily; pour **9 rained off** cancelled or postponed on account of rain. US and Canadian term: **rained out** ▷ See also **rains** [Old English *regn*; related to Old Frisian *rein*, Old High German *regan*, Gothic *rign*] > ˈ**rainless** *adj*
rainband (ˈreɪnˌbænd) *n* a dark band in the solar spectrum caused by water in the atmosphere
rainbird (ˈreɪnˌbɜːd) *n* any of various birds, such as (in Britain) the green woodpecker, whose cry is supposed to portend rain
rainbow (ˈreɪnˌbəʊ) *n* **1** a bow-shaped display in the sky of the colours of the spectrum, caused by the refraction and reflection of the sun's rays through rain or mist **2 a** any similar display of bright colours **b** (*as modifier*): *a rainbow pattern* **3** an illusory hope: *to chase rainbows* **4** (*modifier*) of or relating to a political grouping together by several minorities, esp of different races: *the rainbow coalition*
Rainbow (ˈreɪnˌbəʊ) *n* a member of the Rainbow Guides, the youngest group of girls (aged 5-7 years) in The Guide Association
rainbow bird *n* an Australian bee-eater, *Merops ornatus*, with a brightly-coloured plumage. It feeds in flight and nests in sandy burrows
Rainbow Bridge *n* a natural stone bridge over a creek in SE Utah. Height: 94 m (309 ft). Span: 85 m (278 ft)
rainbow flag *n* a multi-coloured flag used as a symbol of peace; often used to represent gay and lesbian pride
rainbow lorikeet *n* a small Australasian parrot, *Trichoglossus haematodus*, with brightly-coloured plumage
rainbow nation *n South African* an epithet, alluding to its multiracial population, of **South Africa** [C20 coined by Nelson Mandela (born 1918), South African statesman, following the end of apartheid]
rainbow quartz *n mineralogy* another name for **iris** (sense 3)
rainbow trout *n* a freshwater trout of North American origin, *Salmo gairdneri*, having a body marked with many black spots and two longitudinal red stripes
rain check *n* **1** *US and Canadian* a ticket stub for a baseball or other game that allows readmission on a future date if the event is cancelled because of rain **2** the deferral of acceptance of an offer, esp, a voucher issued to a customer wishing to purchase a sale item that is temporarily out of stock, enabling him to buy it at the special price when next the item is available **3 take a rain check** *informal* to accept the postponement of an offer
raincoat (ˈreɪnˌkəʊt) *n* a coat made of a waterproof material
rainfall (ˈreɪnˌfɔːl) *n* **1** precipitation in the form of raindrops **2** *meteorol* the amount of precipitation in a specified place and time
rainforest (ˈreɪnˌfɒrɪst) *n* dense forest found in tropical areas of heavy rainfall. The trees are broad-leaved and evergreen, and the vegetation tends to grow in three layers (undergrowth, intermediate trees and shrubs, and very tall trees, which form a canopy). Also called: **selva**
rain gauge *n* an instrument for measuring rainfall or snowfall, consisting of a cylinder covered by a funnel-like lid. Also called: **pluviometer**
Rainier (ˈreɪnɪə, reɪˈnɪə, rə-) *n* **Mount** a mountain in W Washington State: the highest mountain in the state and in the Cascade Range. Height: 4392 m (14 410 ft)
rainmaker (ˈreɪnˌmeɪkə) *n* **1** (among American Indians) a professional practitioner of ritual incantations or other actions intended to cause rain to fall **2** *informal, chiefly US* an influential employee who creates a great deal of business or revenue for his or her firm > ˈ**rainˌmaking** *n*
rainout (ˈreɪnˌaʊt) *n* radioactive fallout or atmospheric pollution carried to the earth by rain
rainproof (ˈreɪnˌpruːf) *adj* **1** Also: **raintight** (of garments, materials, buildings, etc) impermeable to rainwater ▷ *vb* **2** (*tr*) to make rainproof
rains (reɪnz) *pl n* **the** the season of heavy rainfall, esp in the tropics
rain shadow *n* the relatively dry area on the leeward side of high ground in the path of rain-bearing winds
rainstorm (ˈreɪnˌstɔːm) *n* a storm with heavy rain
rain tree *n* a leguminous tree, *Samanea saman*, native to Central America and widely planted in the tropics for ornament. It has red-and-yellow feathery flowers and pinnate leaves whose leaflets close at the approach of rain
rainwater (ˈreɪnˌwɔːtə) *n* water from rain (as distinguished from spring water, tap water, etc)
rainwater pipe *n Brit* another name for **downpipe**
rainy (ˈreɪnɪ) *adj* **rainier, rainiest 1** characterized by a large rainfall: *a rainy climate* **2** wet or showery; bearing rain > ˈ**rainily** *adv* > ˈ**raininess** *n*
rainy day *n* a future time of need, esp financial
raise (reɪz) *vb* (*mainly tr*) **1** to move, cause to move, or elevate to a higher position or level; lift **2** to set or place in an upright position **3** to construct, build, or erect: *to raise a barn* **4** to increase in amount, size, value, etc: *to raise prices* **5** to increase in degree, strength, intensity, etc: *to raise one's voice* **6** to advance in rank or status; promote **7** to arouse or awaken from or as if from sleep or death **8** to stir up or incite; activate: *to raise a mutiny* **9 raise Cain** (*or* **the devil, hell, the roof** etc) **a** to create a boisterous disturbance **b** to react or protest heatedly **10** to give rise to; cause or provoke: *to raise a smile* **11** to put forward for consideration: *to raise a question* **12** to cause to assemble or gather together; collect: *to raise an army* **13** to grow or cause to grow: *to raise a crop* **14** to bring up; rear: *to raise a family* **15** to cause to be heard or known; utter or express: *to raise a shout; to raise a protest* **16** to bring to an end; remove: *to raise a siege; raise a ban* **17** to cause (dough, bread, etc) to rise, as by the addition of yeast **18** *poker* to bet more than (the previous player) **19** *bridge* to bid (one's partner's suit) at a higher level **20** *nautical* to cause (something) to seem to rise above the horizon by approaching: *we raised land after 20 days* **21** to establish radio communications with: *we managed to raise Moscow last night* **22** to obtain (money, funds, capital, etc) **23** to bring (a surface, a design, etc) into relief; cause to project **24** to cause (a blister, welt, etc) to form on the skin to expel (phlegm) by coughing **26** *phonetics* to modify the articulation of (a vowel) by bringing the tongue closer to the roof of the mouth **27** *maths* to multiply (a number) by itself a specified number of times: *8 is 2 raised to the power 3* **28 a** to institute (a suit or action at law) **b** to draw up (a summons) **29** *chiefly US and Canadian* to increase the amount payable on (a cheque, money order, etc) fraudulently **30** *curling* to push (a stone) towards the tee with another stone **31 raise an eyebrow a** Also: **raise one's eyebrows** to look quizzical or surprised **b** to give rise to doubt or disapproval **32 raise one's glass (to)** to drink the health of (someone); drink a toast (to) **33 raise one's hat** *old-fashioned* to take one's hat briefly off one's head as a greeting or mark of respect ▷ *n* **34** the act or an instance of raising **35** *chiefly US and Canadian* an increase, esp in salary, wages, etc; rise [C12 from Old Norse *reisa*; related to Old English *rǣran* to REAR[2]] > ˈ**raisable** *or* ˈ**raiseable** *adj* > ˈ**raiser** *n*
raised beach *n* a wave-cut platform raised above the shoreline by a relative fall in the water level
raised bog *n ecology* a bog of convex shape produced by growth of sphagnum and other bog plants in acid conditions and the subsequent build up of acid peat
raisin (ˈreɪzᵊn) *n* a dried grape [C13 from Old French: grape, ultimately from Latin *racēmus* cluster of grapes; compare Greek *rhax* berry, grape] > ˈ**raisiny** *adj*
raising (ˈreɪzɪŋ) *n transformational grammar* a rule that moves a constituent from an embedded clause into the main clause. See also **subject-raising, negative-raising**
raison d'être *French* (rɛzɔ̃ dɛtrə) *n, pl* ***raisons d'être*** (rɛzɔ̃ dɛtrə) reason or justification for existence
raita (ˈreɪtə, raɪˈiːtə) *n* an Indian dish of finely chopped cucumber, peppers, mint, etc, in yoghurt, served with curries [C20 from Hindi]
raj (rɑːdʒ) *n* (in India) government; rule [C19 from Hindi, from Sanskrit *rājya*, from *rājati* he rules]
Raj (rɑːdʒ) *n* **the** the British government in India before 1947
Rajab (rəˈdʒæb) *n* the seventh month of the Muslim year
rajah *or* **raja** (ˈrɑːdʒə) *n* **1** (in India, formerly) a ruler or landlord: sometimes used as a form of address or as a title preceding a name **2** a Malayan or Javanese prince or chieftain [C16 from Hindi *rājā*, from Sanskrit *rājan* king; see RAJ; compare Latin *rex* king]
RAJAR (ˈreɪdʒɑː) *n acronym for* Radio Joint Audience Research
Rajasthan (ˌrɑːdʒəˈstɑːn) *n* a state of NW India, bordering on Pakistan: formed in 1958; contains the Thar Desert in the west; now the largest state in India. Capital: Jaipur. Pop: 56 473 122 (2001). Area: 342 239 sq km (132 111 sq miles)
raja yoga (ˈrɑːdʒə) *n* (*sometimes capitals*) a form of yoga chiefly concerned with controlling and using the energy of the mind by meditation. Compare **hatha yoga** [C19 from Sanskrit *rājan* king + YOGA]
Rajkot (ˈrɑːdʒkəʊt) *n* a city in W India, in S Gujarat. Pop: 966 642 (2001)
Rajput *or* **Rajpoot** (ˈrɑːdʒpʊt) *n Hinduism* one of a

Hindu military caste claiming descent from the Kshatriya, the original warrior caste [c16 from Hindi, from Sanskrit *rājan* king; see RAJ]

Rajputana (ˌrɑːdʒpʊˈtɑːnə) *n* a former group of princely states in NW India: now mostly part of Rajasthan

Rajya Sabha (ˈrɑːdʒjə ˈsʌbə) *n* the upper chamber of India's Parliament. Compare **Lok Sabha** [c20 Hindi, *rajya* state + *sabha* assembly]

Rakata (rəˈkɑːtə) *n* another name for **Krakatoa**

rake¹ (reɪk) *n* **1** a hand implement consisting of a row of teeth set in a headpiece attached to a long shaft and used for gathering hay, straw, leaves, etc, or for smoothing loose earth **2** any of several mechanical farm implements equipped with rows of teeth or rotating wheels mounted with tines and used to gather hay, straw, etc **3** any of various implements similar in shape or function, such as a tool for drawing out ashes from a furnace **4** the act of raking **5** NZ a line of wagons coupled together as one unit, used on railways ▷ *vb* **6** to scrape, gather, or remove (leaves, refuse, etc) with or as if with a rake **7** to level or prepare (a surface, such as a flower bed) with a rake or similar implement **8** (*tr*; sometimes foll by *out*) to clear (ashes, clinker, etc) from (a fire or furnace) **9** (*tr*; foll by *up* or *together*) to gather (items or people) with difficulty, as from a scattered area or limited supply **10** (*tr*; often foll by *through*, *over* etc) to search or examine carefully **11** (when *intr*, foll by *against*, *along* etc) to scrape or graze: *the ship raked the side of the quay* **12** (*tr*) to direct (gunfire) along the length of (a target): *machine-guns raked the column* **13** (*tr*) to sweep (one's eyes) along the length of (something); scan ▷ See also **rake in, rake-off, rake up** [Old English *raca*; related to Old Norse *raka*, Old High German *rehho* a rake, Gothic *rikan* to heap up, Latin *rogus* funeral pile]

rake² (reɪk) *n* a dissolute man, esp one in fashionable society; roué [c17 short for RAKEHELL]

rake³ (reɪk) *vb* (*mainly intr*) **1** to incline from the vertical by a perceptible degree, esp (of a ship's mast or funnel) towards the stern **2** (*tr*) to construct with a backward slope ▷ *n* **3** the degree to which an object, such as a ship's mast, inclines from the perpendicular, esp towards the stern **4** *theatre* the slope of a stage from the back towards the footlights **5** *aeronautics* **a** the angle between the wings of an aircraft and the line of symmetry of the aircraft **b** the angle between the line joining the centroids of the section of a propeller blade and a line perpendicular to the axis **6** the angle between the working face of a cutting tool and a plane perpendicular to the surface of the workpiece **7** a slanting ledge running across a crag in the Lake District [c17 of uncertain origin; perhaps related to German *ragen* to project, Swedish *raka*]

rake⁴ (reɪk) *vb* (*intr*) **1** (of gun dogs or hounds) to hunt with the nose to the ground **2** (of hawks) **a** to pursue quarry in full flight **b** (often foll by *away*) to fly wide of the quarry, esp beyond the control of the falconer [Old English *racian* to go forward, of uncertain origin]

rakehell (ˈreɪkˌhɛl) *archaic* ▷ *n* **1** a dissolute man; rake ▷ *adj* *also* **rakehelly** **2** profligate; dissolute [c16 from RAKE¹ + HELL; but compare Middle English *rakel* rash]

rake in *vb* (*tr, adverb*) *informal* to acquire (money) in large amounts

rake-off *slang* ▷ *n* **1** a share of profits, esp one that is illegal or given as a bribe ▷ *vb* **rake off 2** (*tr, adverb*) to take or receive (such a share of profits)

raker (ˈreɪkə) *n* **1** a person who rakes **2** a raking implement **3** *Midland English dialect* a large lump of coal

rake up *vb* (*tr, adverb*) to revive, discover, or bring to light (something forgotten): *to rake up an old quarrel*

raki *or* **rakee** (rɑːˈkiː, ˈrækɪ) *n* a strong spirit distilled in Turkey, the former Yugoslavia, etc, from grain, usually flavoured with aniseed or

other aromatics [c17 from Turkish *rāqī*]

raking (ˈreɪkɪŋ) *n* *rugby* the offence committed when a player deliberately scrapes an opponent's leg, arm, etc with the studs of his or her boots

rakish¹ (ˈreɪkɪʃ) *adj* dissolute; profligate [c18 from RAKE² + -ISH] > ˈrakishly *adv* > ˈrakishness *n*

rakish² (ˈreɪkɪʃ) *adj* **1** dashing; jaunty: *a hat set at a rakish angle* **2** *nautical* (of a ship or boat) having lines suggestive of speed [c19 probably from RAKE³ (SENSE 1), with reference to the sloping masts of pirate ships]

rale *or* **râle** (rɑːl) *n* *med* an abnormal coarse crackling sound heard on auscultation of the chest, usually caused by the accumulation of fluid in the lungs [c19 from French *râle*, from *râler* to breathe with a rattling sound; compare RAIL³]

Raleigh (ˈrɔːlɪ, ˈrɑː-) *n* a city in E central North Carolina, capital of the state. Pop: 316 802 (2003 est)

rall. *music abbreviation for* rallentando

rallentando (ˌrælɛnˈtændəʊ) *adj, adv music* becoming slower. Abbreviation: **rall** Also: ritardando, ritenuto [c19 Italian, from *rallentare* to slow down]

ralline (ˈrælaɪn, -ɪn) *adj* of, relating to, or belonging to the *Rallidae*, a family of birds that includes the rails, crakes, and coots [c19 from New Latin *Rallus* RAIL³]

rally¹ (ˈrælɪ) *vb* -lies, -lying, -lied **1** to bring (a group, unit, etc) into order, as after dispersal, or (of such a group) to reform and come to order: *the troops rallied for a final assault* **2** (when *intr*, foll by *to*) to organize (supporters, etc) for a common cause or (of such people) to come together for a purpose **3** to summon up (one's strength, spirits, etc) or (of a person's health, strength, or spirits) to revive or recover **4** (*intr*) *stock exchange* to increase sharply after a decline: *steels rallied after a bad day* **5** (*intr*) *tennis, squash, badminton* to engage in a rally ▷ *n*, *pl* -lies **6** a large gathering of people for a common purpose, esp for some political cause: *the Nuremberg Rallies* **7** a marked recovery of strength or spirits, as during illness **8** a return to order after dispersal or rout, as of troops, etc **9** *stock exchange* a sharp increase in price or trading activity after a decline **10** *tennis, squash, badminton* an exchange of several shots before one player wins the point **11** a type of motoring competition over public and closed roads [c16 from Old French *rallier*, from RE- + *alier* to unite; see ALLY] > ˈrallier *n*

rally² (ˈrælɪ) *vb* -lies, -lying, -lied to mock or ridicule (someone) in a good-natured way; chaff; tease [c17 from Old French *railler* to tease; see RAIL²]

rallycross (ˈrælɪˌkrɒs) *n* a form of motor sport in which cars race over a one-mile circuit of rough grass with some hard-surfaced sections. See also **autocross, motocross**

rally round *vb* (*intr*) to come to the aid of (someone); offer moral or practical support

ram (ræm) *n* **1** an uncastrated adult sheep **2** a piston or moving plate, esp one driven hydraulically or pneumatically **3** the falling weight of a pile driver or similar device **4** short for **battering ram 5** Also called: rostrum, beak a pointed projection in the stem of an ancient warship for puncturing the hull of enemy ships **6** a warship equipped with a ram **7** *slang* a sexually active man ▷ *vb* **rams, ramming, rammed 8** (*tr*; usually foll by *into*) to force or drive, as by heavy blows: *to ram a post into the ground* **9** (of a moving object) to crash with force (against another object) or (of two moving objects) to collide in this way: *the ships rammed the enemy* **10** (*tr*; often foll by *in* or *down*) to stuff or cram (something into a hole, etc) **11** (*tr*; foll by *onto, against* etc) to thrust violently: *he rammed the books onto the desk* **12** (*tr*) to present (an idea, argument, etc) forcefully or aggressively (esp in the phrase **ram (something) down someone's throat**) **13** (*tr*) to drive (a charge) into a firearm [Old English *ramm*; related to Old High German *ram* ram, Old Norse *ramr* fierce, *rimma* to fight] > ˈrammer *n*

Ram (ræm) *n* **the** the constellation Aries, the first sign of the zodiac

RAM¹ (ræm) *n* *computing* ▷ *acronym for* random access memory: semiconductor memory in which all storage locations can be rapidly accessed in the same amount of time. It forms the main memory of a computer, used by applications to perform tasks while the device is operating

RAM² *abbreviation for* Royal Academy of Music

r.a.m. *abbreviation for* relative atomic mass

Rama (ˈrɑːmə) *n* (in Hindu mythology) any of Vishnu's three incarnations (the heroes Balarama, Parashurama, or Ramachandra) [from Sanskrit *Rāma* black, dark]

Ramachandra (ˌrɑːməˈtʃʌndrə) *n* (in Hindu mythology) an incarnation of Vishnu; the hero of the *Ramayana* and a character in the *Mahabharata*. See also **Rama**

Ramadan, Rhamadhan (ˌræməˈdɑːn) *or* **Ramazan** (ˌræməˈzɑːn) *n* **1** the ninth month of the Muslim year, lasting 30 days, during which strict fasting is observed from sunrise to sunset **2** the fast itself [c16 from Arabic, literally: the hot month, from *ramad* dryness]

ram-air turbine *n* a small air-driven turbine fitted to an aircraft to provide power in the event of a failure of the normal systems

Ramallah (rəˈmælə) *n* a town in the West Bank, serving as headquarters of the Palestinian National Authority. Pop: 51 000 (2005 est)

Raman effect (ˈrɑːmən) *n* a change in wavelength of light that is scattered by electrons within a material. The effect is used in **Raman spectroscopy** for studying molecules [c20 named after Sir Chandrasekhara *Raman* (1888–1970), Indian physicist]

Ramat Gan (rɑːˈmɑːt ˈɡɑːn) *n* a city in Israel, E of Tel Aviv. Pop: 126 500 (2003 est)

Ramayana (rɑːˈmaɪənə) *n* a Sanskrit epic poem, composed about 300 BC, recounting the feats of Ramachandra

ramble (ˈræmbəl) *vb* (*intr*) **1** to stroll about freely, as for relaxation, with no particular direction **2** (of paths, streams, etc) to follow a winding course; meander **3** (of plants) to grow in a random fashion **4** (of speech, writing, etc) to lack organization ▷ *n* **5** a leisurely stroll, esp in the countryside [c17 probably related to Middle Dutch *rammelen* to wander (of animals); see RAM]

rambler (ˈræmblə) *n* **1** a weak-stemmed plant, esp any of various cultivated hybrid roses that straggle over other vegetation **2** a person who rambles, esp one who takes country walks **3** a person who lacks organization in his speech or writing

rambling (ˈræmblɪŋ) *adj* **1** straggling or sprawling haphazardly; unplanned: *a rambling old house* **2** (of speech or writing) lacking a coherent plan; diffuse and disconnected **3** (of a plant, esp a rose) profusely climbing and straggling **4** nomadic; wandering

Ramboesque (ˌræmbəʊˈɛsk) *adj* looking or behaving like, or characteristic of, Rambo, a fictional film character noted for his mindless brutality [c20 after *Rambo, First Blood II*, released in Britain 1985] > ˈRamboˌism *n*

Rambouillet¹ (French rɑbujɛ) *n* a town in N France, in the Yvelines department: site of the summer residence of French presidents. Pop: 24 758 (1999)

Rambouillet² (ˈrɒmbʊˌjeɪ, ˈræmbʊˌleɪ; French rɑbujɛ) *n* a fine-woolled merino-like breed of sheep [c19 from RAMBOUILLET¹]

rambunctious (ræmˈbʌŋkʃəs) *adj* *informal* boisterous; unruly [c19 probably from Icelandic *ram-* (intensifying prefix) + *-bunctious*, from BUMPTIOUS] > ramˈbunctiously *adv* > ramˈbunctiousness *n*

rambutan (ræmˈbuːtəⁿn) *n* **1** a sapindaceous tree, *Nephelium lappaceum*, native to SE Asia, that has bright red edible fruit **2** the fruit of this tree [c18 from Malay, from *rambut* hair]

r

RAMC *abbreviation for* Royal Army Medical Corps

ramekin *or* **ramequin** ('ræmɪkɪn) *n* **1** a savoury dish made from a cheese mixture baked in a fireproof container **2** the container itself [C18 French *ramequin*, of Germanic origin]

ramen ('rɑːmən) *n* **1** a Japanese dish consisting of a clear broth containing thin white noodles and sometimes vegetables, meat, etc ▷ *pl n* **2** thin white noodles served in such a broth [Japanese, from Chinese *la* to pull + *mian* noodles]

ramentum (rə'mɛntəm) *n*, *pl* -ta (-tə) any of the thin brown scales that cover the stems and leaves of young ferns [C17 from Latin *rādere* to scrape] ▷ ramentaceous (,ræmɛn'teɪʃəs) *adj*

rami ('reɪmaɪ) *n* the plural of **ramus**

ramie *or* **ramee** ('ræmɪ) *n* **1** a woody urticaceous shrub of Asia, *Boehmeria nivea*, having broad leaves and a stem that yields a flaxlike fibre **2** the fibre from this plant, used in making fabrics, cord, etc [C19 from Malay *rami*]

ramification (,ræmɪfɪ'keɪʃən) *n* **1** the act or process of ramifying or branching out **2** an offshoot or subdivision **3** (*often plural*) a subsidiary consequence, esp one that complicates **4** a structure of branching parts

ramiform ('ræmɪ,fɔːm) *adj* having a branchlike shape [C19 from Latin *rāmus* branch + -FORM]

ramify ('ræmɪ,faɪ) *vb* -fies, -fying, -fied **1** to divide into branches or branchlike parts **2** (*intr*) to develop complicating consequences; become complex [C16 from French *ramifier*, from Latin *rāmus* branch + *facere* to make]

Ramillies ('ræmɪliːz; *French* ramiji) *n* a village in central Belgium where the Duke of Marlborough defeated the French in 1706

ramjet *or* **ramjet engine** ('ræm,dʒɛt) *n* **a** a type of jet engine in which fuel is burned in a duct using air compressed by the forward speed of the aircraft **b** an aircraft powered by such an engine. Also called: **athodyd**

rammel ('ræməl) *n* *Northern English dialect* discarded or waste matter

rammish ('ræmɪʃ) *adj* like a ram, esp in being lustful or foul-smelling ▷ 'rammishly *adv* ▷ 'rammishness *n*

rammle ('ræməl) *n* *Midland English dialect* a collection of items saved in case they become useful

rammy ('ræmɪ) *n* *Scot pl* -mies a noisy disturbance or free-for-all [C20 perhaps from earlier *Scot rammle* row, uproar]

ramose ('reɪməʊs, ræ'məʊs) *or* **ramous** ('reɪməs) *adj* having branches [C17 from Latin *rāmōsus*, from *rāmus* branch] ▷ 'ramosely *or* 'ramously *adv* ▷ ramosity (ræ'mɒsɪtɪ) *n*

ramp (ræmp) *n* **1** a sloping floor, path, etc, that joins two surfaces at different levels **2** a movable stairway by which passengers enter and leave an aircraft **3** the act of ramping **4** *Brit slang* a swindle, esp one involving exorbitant prices **5** another name for **sleeping policeman** ▷ *vb* **6** (*intr*; often foll by *about* or *around*) (esp of animals) to rush around in a wild excited manner **7** to act in a violent or threatening manner, as when angry (esp in the phrase **ramp and rage**) **8** (*tr*) *finance* to buy (a security) in the market with the object of raising its price and enhancing the image of the company behind it for financial gain ▷ See also **ramp down, ramp up** [C18 (n): from C13 *rampe*, from Old French *ramper* to crawl or rear, probably of Germanic origin; compare Middle Low German *ramp* cramp]

rampage *vb* (ræm'peɪdʒ) **1** (*intr*) to rush about in an angry, violent, or agitated fashion ▷ *n* ('ræmpeɪdʒ, ræm'peɪdʒ) **2** angry or destructive behaviour **3** on the rampage behaving violently or destructively [C18 from Scottish, of uncertain origin; perhaps based on RAMP] ▷ ram'pageous *adj* ▷ ram'pageously *adv* ▷ ram'pageousness *n* ▷ 'rampager *n*

rampant ('ræmpənt) *adj* **1** unrestrained or violent in behaviour, desire, opinions, etc **2** growing or developing unchecked **3** (*postpositive*) *heraldry* (of a beast) standing on the hind legs, the right foreleg raised above the left **4** (of an arch) having one abutment higher than the other [C14 from Old French *ramper* to crawl, rear; see RAMP] ▷ 'rampancy *n* ▷ 'rampantly *adv*

rampart ('ræmpɑːt) *n* **1** the surrounding embankment of a fort, often including any walls, parapets, walks, etc, that are built on the bank **2** anything resembling a rampart in form or function, esp in being a defence or bulwark **3** *Canadian* a steep rock wall in a river gorge ▷ *vb* **4** (*tr*) to provide with a rampart; fortify [C16 from Old French, from *remparer*, from RE- + *emparer* to take possession of, from Old Provençal *antparar*, from Latin *ante* before + *parāre* to prepare]

ramp down *vb* (*adverb*) **1** to decrease or cause to decrease **2** (*intr*) to decrease the effort involved in a process

rampion ('ræmpɪən) *n* **1** a campanulaceous plant, *Campanula rapunculus*, native to Europe and Asia, that has clusters of bluish flowers and an edible white tuberous root used in salads **2** any of several plants of the related genus *Phyteuma* that are native to Europe and Asia and have heads of blue flowers [C16 probably from Old French *raiponce*, from Old Italian *raponzo*, from *rapa* turnip, from Latin *rāpum* turnip; see RAPE²]

ramp up *vb* (*adverb*) **1** to increase or cause to increase **2** (*intr*) to increase the effort involved in a process

Rampur ('ræmpʊə) *n* a city in N India, in N Uttar Pradesh. Pop: 281 549 (2001)

ram raid *n* *informal* a raid in which a stolen car is driven through a shop window in order to steal goods from the shop ▷ ram raiding *n* ▷ ram raider *n*

ramrod ('ræm,rɒd) *n* **1** a rod for cleaning the barrel of a rifle or other small firearms **2** a rod for ramming in the charge of a muzzle-loading firearm

Ramsgate ('ræmz,geɪt) *n* a port and resort in SE England, in E Kent on the North Sea coast. Pop: 37 967 (2001)

ramshackle ('ræm,ʃæk²l) *adj* (esp of buildings) badly constructed or maintained; rickety, shaky, or derelict [C17 *ramshackled*, from obsolete *ransackle* to RANSACK]

ramshorn snail ('ræmz,hɔːn) *n* any of various freshwater snails of the genus *Planorbis* that are widely used in aquariums

ramsons ('ræmzənz, -sənz) *pl n* (*usually functioning as singular*) **1** a broad-leaved garlic, *Allium ursinum*, native to Europe and Asia **2** the bulbous root of this plant, eaten as a relish [Old English *hramesa*; related to Middle Low German *ramese* Norwegian *rams*]

ramstam ('ræm'stæm) *Scot* ▷ *adv* **1** headlong; hastily ▷ *adj* **2** headlong; precipitate [C18 perhaps from RAM + dialect *stam* to stamp]

ramtil ('ræmtɪl) *n* **1** an African plant, *Guizotia abyssinica*, grown in India: family *Asteraceae* (composites) **2** Also called: **Niger seed** the seed of this plant, used as a source of oil and a bird food [C19 from Hindi, from Sanskrit *rāma* black + *tila* sesame]

ramulose ('ræmjʊ,ləʊs) *or* **ramulous** ('ræmjʊləs) *adj* (of the parts or organs of animals and plants) having many small branches [C18 from Latin *rāmulōsus* full of branching veins, from *rāmulus* twig, from *rāmus* branch]

ramus ('reɪməs) *n*, *pl* -mi (-maɪ) **1** the barb of a bird's feather **2** either of the two parts of the lower jaw of a vertebrate **3** any part or organ that branches from another part [C19 from Latin: branch]

ran (ræn) *vb* the past tense of **run**

RAN *abbreviation for* Royal Australian Navy

Rancagua (*Spanish* raŋ'kagwa) *n* a city in central Chile. Pop: 217 000 (2005 est)

rance (rɑːns) *n* a type of red marble, often with white or blue graining, that comes from Belgium

[C19 apparently from French *ranche* rod, pole]

ranch (rɑːntʃ) *n* **1** a large tract of land, esp one in North America, together with the necessary personnel, buildings, and equipment, for rearing livestock, esp cattle **2 a** any large farm for the rearing of a particular kind of livestock or crop: *a mink ranch* **b** the buildings, land, etc, connected with it ▷ *vb* **3** (*intr*) to manage or run a ranch **4** (*tr*) to raise (animals) on or as if on a ranch [C19 from Mexican Spanish *rancho* small farm; see RANCHO]

rancher ('rɑːntʃə) *n* a person who owns, manages, or works on a ranch

rancherie ('rɑːntʃərɪ) *n* (in British Columbia, Canada) a settlement of North American Indians, esp on a reserve [from Spanish *ranchería*]

ranchero (rɑːn'tʃɛərəʊ) *n*, *pl* -ros *Southwestern US* another word for **rancher** [C19 from American Spanish]

Ranchi ('ræntʃi) *n* an industrial city in E India, between the coal and iron belts of the Chota Nagpur Plateau; the capital of Jharkhand from 2000. Pop: 846 454 (2001)

rancho ('rɑːntʃəʊ) *n*, *pl* -chos *Southwestern US* **1** a hut or group of huts for housing ranch workers **2** another word for **ranch** [C17 from Mexican Spanish: camp, from Old Spanish *ranchar* to be billeted, from Old French *ranger* to place]

rancid ('rænsɪd) *adj* **1** (of butter, bacon, etc) having an unpleasant stale taste or smell as the result of decomposition **2** (of a taste or smell) rank or sour; stale [C17 from Latin *rancidus* rank, from *rancēre* to stink] ▷ rancidity (ræn'sɪdɪtɪ) *or* 'rancidness *n*

rancour *or US* **rancor** ('ræŋkə) *n* malicious resentfulness or hostility; spite [C14 from Old French, from Late Latin *rancor* rankness] ▷ 'rancorous *adj* ▷ 'rancorously *adv* ▷ 'rancorousness *n*

rand[1] (rænd, rɒnt) *n* the standard monetary unit of the Republic of South Africa, divided into 100 cents [C20 from Afrikaans, shortened from WITWATERSRAND, referring to the gold-mining there; related to RAND²]

rand[2] (rænd) *n* **1** *shoemaking* a leather strip put in the heel of a shoe before the lifts are put on **2** *dialect* **a** a strip or margin; border **b** a strip of cloth; selvage [Old English; related to Old High German *rant* border, rim of a shield, Old Norse *rönd* shield, rim]

Rand (rænd) *n* the short for **Witwatersrand**

R & A *abbreviation for* Royal and Ancient (Golf Club, St Andrews)

randan[1] (ræn'dæn, 'rændæn) *n* a boat rowed by three people, in which the person in the middle uses two oars and the people fore and aft use one oar each [C19 of uncertain origin]

randan[2] (,ræn'dæn, 'ræn,dæn) *n* rowdy behaviour; a spree [C18 perhaps changed from RANDOM]

R & B *abbreviation for* rhythm and blues

R & D *abbreviation for* research and development

randem ('rændɛm) *adv* **1** with three horses harnessed together as a team ▷ *n* **2** a carriage or team of horses so driven [C19 probably from RANDOM + TANDEM]

Randers (*Danish* 'ranərs) *n* a port and industrial centre in Denmark, in E Jutland on **Randers Fjord** (an inlet of the Kattegat). Pop: 55 739 (2004 est)

randlord ('rænd,lɔːd) *n* *South African* a mining magnate during the 19th-century gold boom in Johannesburg

random ('rændəm) *adj* **1** lacking any definite plan or prearranged order; haphazard: *a random selection* **2** *statistics* **a** having a value which cannot be determined but only described probabilistically: *a random variable* **b** chosen without regard to any characteristics of the individual members of the population so that each has an equal chance of being selected: *random sampling* **3** *informal* (of a person) unknown: *some random guy waiting for a bus* ▷ *n* **4** at random in a purposeless fashion; not following any prearranged order [c14 from Old French *randon*, from *randir* to gallop, of Germanic origin; compare Old High German *rinnan* to run] > 'randomly *adv* > 'randomness *n*

random access *n* another name for **direct access**

random access memory *n* See **RAM**

randomize *or* **randomise** ('rændə,maɪz) *vb* (*tr*) to set up (a selection process, sample, etc) in a deliberately random way in order to enhance the statistical validity of any results obtained > ,randomi'zation *or* ,randomi'sation *n* > 'random,izer *or* 'random,iser *n*

random numbers *pl n* a sequence of numbers that do not form any progression, used to facilitate unbiased sampling of a population. A **random-number generator** is part of the software of most computers and many calculators

random rubble *n* masonry in which untooled stones are set without coursing

random variable *n* *statistics* a quantity that may take any of a range of values, either continuous or discrete, which cannot be predicted with certainty but only described probabilistically. Abbreviation: rv

random walk *n* 1 a mathematical model used to describe physical processes, such as diffusion, in which a particle moves in straight-line steps of constant length but random direction 2 *statistics* a route consisting of successive and connected steps in which each step is chosen by a random mechanism uninfluenced by any previous step

random walk theory *n* *stock exchange* the theory that the future movement of share prices does not reflect past movements and therefore will not follow a discernible pattern

R and R *US military abbreviation for* rest and recreation

randy ('rændɪ) *adj* randier, randiest 1 *informal, chiefly Brit* **a** sexually excited or aroused **b** sexually eager or lustful 2 *chiefly Scot* lacking any sense of propriety or restraint; reckless ▷ *n, pl* randies 3 *chiefly Scot* **a** a rude or reckless person **b** a coarse rowdy woman [c17 probably from obsolete *rand* to RANT] > 'randily *adv* > 'randiness *n*

ranee ('rɑːnɪ) *n* a variant spelling of **rani**

Ranelagh Gardens ('rænɪlə) *pl n* a public garden in Chelsea opened in 1742: a centre for members of fashionable society to meet and promenade. The gardens were closed in 1804. Also called: Ranelagh [named after the Earl of *Ranelagh*, in whose grounds they were sited]

Ranfurly Shield (ræn'fɜːlɪ) *n* (in New Zealand) the premier rugby trophy, competed for annually by provincial teams [c20 named after the Earl of *Ranfurly* (1856–1933), 15th Governor of New Zealand (1897–1904), who presented it to the New Zealand Rugby Football Union in 1902]

rang (ræŋ) *vb* the past tense of **ring²**

■ USAGE See at **ring²**

rangatira (,rʌŋgə'tɪərə) *n* NZ a Māori chief of either sex [Māori]

rangatiratanga (,rʌŋgətɪərə'tʌŋgə) *n* NZ the condition of being a Māori chief; sovereignty [Māori]

range (reɪndʒ) *n* 1 the limits within which a person or thing can function effectively: *the range of vision* 2 the limits within which any fluctuation takes place: *a range of values* 3 the total products of a manufacturer, designer, or stockist: *the new autumn range* 4 **a** the maximum effective distance of a projectile fired from a weapon **b** the distance between a target and a weapon 5 an area set aside for shooting practice or rocket testing 6 the total distance which a ship, aircraft, or land vehicle is capable of covering without taking on fresh fuel: *the range of this car is about 160 miles* 7 *physics* the distance that a particle of ionizing radiation, such as an electron or proton, can travel through a given medium, esp air, before ceasing to cause ionization 8 *maths, logic* **a** (of a function) the set of values that the function takes for all possible arguments. Compare **domain**

(sense 7a) **b** (of a variable) the set of values that a variable can take **c** (of a quantifier) the set of values that the variable bound by the quantifier can take 9 *statistics* a measure of dispersion obtained by subtracting the smallest from the largest sample values 10 the extent of pitch difference between the highest and lowest notes of a voice, instrument, etc 11 *US and Canadian* **a** an extensive tract of open land on which livestock can graze **b** (*as modifier*). *range cattle* 12 the geographical region in which a species of plant or animal normally grows or lives 13 a rank, row, or series of items 14 a series or chain of mountains 15 a large stove with burners and one or more ovens, usually heated by solid fuel 16 the act or process of ranging 17 *nautical* a line of sight taken from the sea along two or more navigational aids that mark a navigable channel 18 the extension or direction of a survey line, established by marking two or more points 19 a double-faced bookcase, as in a library 20 *range of significance philosophy, logic* the set of subjects for which a given predicate is intelligible ▷ *vb* 21 to establish or be situated in a line, row, or series 22 (*tr; often reflexive, foll by* with) to put into a specific category; classify: *she ranges herself with the angels* 23 (foll by on) to aim or point (a telescope, gun, etc) or (of a gun, telescope, etc) to be pointed or aimed 24 to establish the distance of (a target) from (a weapon) 25 (*intr*) (of a gun or missile) to have a specified range 26 (when *intr*, foll by *over*) to wander about (in) an area; roam (over) 27 (*intr*; foll by *over*) (of an animal or plant) to live or grow in its normal habitat 28 (*tr*) to put (cattle) to graze on a range 29 (*intr*) to fluctuate within specific limits: *their ages range from 18 to 21* 30 (*intr*) to extend or run in a specific direction 31 (*tr*) *nautical* to coil (an anchor rope or chain) so that it will pay out smoothly 32 (*intr*) *nautical* (of a vessel) to swing back and forth while at anchor 33 (*tr*) to make (lines of printers' type) level or even at the margin [c13 from Old French: row, from *ranger* to position, from *renc* line]

rangefinder ('reɪndʒ,faɪndə) *n* 1 an instrument for determining the distance of an object from the observer, esp in order to sight a gun or focus a camera 2 another word for **tacheometer**

rangeland ('reɪndʒ,lænd) *n* (*often plural*) land that naturally produces forage plants suitable for grazing but where rainfall is too low or erratic for growing crops

range light *n* *nautical* 1 one of a pattern of navigation lights, usually fixed ashore, used by vessels for manoeuvring in narrow channels at night 2 one of a distinctive pattern of lights shown at night on the masts of a powered vessel, such as a tugboat, to aid in identifying its size, number of barges in tow, etc

ranger ('reɪndʒə) *n* 1 (*sometimes capital*) an official in charge of a forest, park, estate, nature reserve, etc 2 *chiefly US* a person employed to patrol a State or national park or forest. Brit equivalent: warden 3 *US* one of a body of armed troops employed to police a State or district: *a Texas Ranger* 4 (in the US and certain other armies) a commando specially trained in making raids 5 a person who wanders about large areas of country; a rover

Ranger¹ *or* **Ranger Guide** ('reɪndʒə) *n* Brit a member of the senior branch of the Guides

Ranger² ('reɪndʒə) *n* any of a series of nine American lunar probes launched between 1961 and 1965, three of which transmitted to earth photographs of the moon

rangi (rɑːˀŋiː) *n* NZ the sky [from *Rangi*, the sky god of Māori mythology]

ranging pole *or* **rod** *n* a pole for marking positions in surveying. Also called: range pole, rod

rangiora (,rængɪ'ɔːrə, ,ræŋɪ-) *n* an evergreen shrub or small tree, *Brachyglottis repanda*, of New Zealand, having large ovate leaves and small greenish-white flowers: family Asteraceae

(composites) [Māori]

Rangoon (ræŋ'guːn) *n* the former name (until 1989) of **Yangon**

rangy ('reɪndʒɪ) *adj* rangier, rangiest 1 (of animals or people) having long slender limbs 2 adapted to wandering or roaming 3 allowing considerable freedom of movement; spacious; roomy [c19 from RANGE + -Y¹] > 'rangily *adv* > 'ranginess *n*

rani *or* **ranee** ('rɑːnɪ) *n* (in oriental countries, esp India) a queen or princess; the wife of a rajah [c17 from Hindi: queen, from Sanskrit *rājñī*, feminine of *rājan* RAJAH]

rank¹ (ræŋk) *n* 1 a position, esp an official one, within a social organization, esp the armed forces: *the rank of captain* 2 high social or other standing; status 3 a line or row of people or things 4 the position of an item in any ordering or sequence 5 *Brit* a place where taxis wait to be hired 6 a line of soldiers drawn up abreast of each other. Compare **file¹** (sense 5) 7 any of the eight horizontal rows of squares on a chessboard 8 (in systemic grammar) one of the units of description of which a grammar is composed. Ranks of English grammar are sentence, clause, group, word, and morpheme 9 *music* a set of organ pipes controlled by the same stop 10 *maths* (of a matrix) the largest number of linearly independent rows or columns; the number of rows (or columns) of the nonzero determinant of greatest order that can be extracted from the matrix 11 **break ranks** *military* to fall out of line, esp when under attack 12 **close ranks** to maintain discipline or solidarity, esp in anticipation of attack 13 **pull rank** to get one's own way by virtue of one's superior position or rank ▷ *vb* 14 (*tr*) to arrange (people or things) in rows or lines; range 15 to accord or be accorded a specific position in an organization, society, or group 16 (*tr*) to array (a set of objects) as a sequence, esp in terms of the natural arithmetic ordering of some measure of the elements: *to rank students by their test scores* 17 (*intr*) to be important; rate: *money ranks low in her order of priorities* 18 *chiefly US* to take precedence or surpass in rank: *the colonel ranks at this camp* [c16 from Old French *ranc* row, rank, of Germanic origin; compare Old High German *hring* circle]

rank² (ræŋk) *adj* 1 showing vigorous and profuse growth: *rank weeds* 2 highly offensive or disagreeable, esp in smell or taste 3 (*prenominal*) complete or absolute; utter: *a rank outsider* 4 coarse or vulgar; gross: *his language was rank* [Old English *ranc* straight, noble; related to Old Norse *rakkr* upright, Dutch, Swedish *rank* tall and thin, weak] > 'rankly *adv* > 'rankness *n*

rank and file *n* 1 the ordinary soldiers of an army, excluding the officers 2 the great mass or majority of any group or organization, as opposed to the leadership 3 (*modifier*) of, relating to, or characteristic of the rank and file: *rank-and-file opinion; rank-and-file support* > rank and filer *n*

ranker ('ræŋkə) *n* 1 a soldier in the ranks 2 a commissioned officer who entered service as a recruit, esp in the army

Rankine cycle ('ræŋkɪn) *n* the thermodynamic cycle in steam engines by which water is pumped into a boiler at one end and the steam is condensed at the other [c19 named after W. J. M. *Rankine* (1820–72), Scottish physicist]

Rankine scale *n* an absolute scale of temperature in which the unit of temperature is equal to that on the Fahrenheit scale and the zero value of temperature is equal to –459.67°F. Compare **Kelvin scale**

ranking ('ræŋkɪn) *adj* 1 *chiefly US and Canadian* prominent; high ranking 2 *Caribbean slang* possessed of style; fashionable; exciting ▷ *n* 3 a position on a scale; rating: *a ranking in a tennis tournament*

rankism ('ræənk,ɪzəm) *n* discrimination against people on the grounds of rank

r

rankle ('ræŋkəl) *vb* (*intr*) to cause severe and continuous irritation, anger, or bitterness; fester: *his failure to win still rankles* [C14 *ranclen*, from Old French *draoncler* to fester, from *draoncle* ulcer, from Latin *dracunculus* small serpent, from *dracō* serpent; see DRAGON]

rankshift ('ræŋkʃɪft) (in systemic grammar) *n* **1** a phenomenon in which a unit at one rank in the grammar has the function of a unit at a lower rank, as for example in the phrase *the house on the corner*, where the words *on the corner* shift down from the rank of group to the rank of word ▷ *vb* **2** to shift or be shifted from one linguistic rank to another

ransack ('rænsæk) *vb* (*tr*) **1** to search through every part of (a house, box, etc); examine thoroughly **2** to plunder; pillage [C13 from Old Norse *rann* house + *saka* to search, SEEK] > 'ransacker *n*

ransom ('rænsəm) *n* **1** the release of captured prisoners, property, etc, on payment of a stipulated price **2** the price demanded or stipulated for such a release **3** rescue or redemption of any kind **4 hold to ransom a** to keep (prisoners, property, etc) in confinement until payment for their release is made or received **b** to attempt to force (a person or persons) to comply with one's demands **5 a king's ransom** a very large amount of money or valuables ▷ *vb* (*tr*) **6** to pay a stipulated price and so obtain the release of (prisoners, property, etc) **7** to set free (prisoners, property, etc) upon receiving the payment demanded **8** to redeem; rescue: *Christ ransomed men from sin* [C14 from Old French *ransoun*, from Latin *redemptiō* a buying back, REDEMPTION] > 'ransomer *n*

rant (rænt) *vb* **1** to utter (something) in loud, violent, or bombastic tones **2** (*intr*) *chiefly Scot* to make merry; frolic ▷ *n* **3** loud, declamatory, or extravagant speech; bombast **4** *chiefly Scot* a wild revel **5** *Scot* an energetic dance or its tune [C16 from Dutch *ranten* to rave; related to German *ranzen* to gambol] > 'ranter *n* > 'ranting *adj*, *n* > 'rantingly *adv*

ranula ('rænjʊlə) *n* a saliva-filled cyst that develops under the tongue [C17 from Latin *rana* frog + *-ula* from Latin *-ulus*, small]

ranunculaceous (rə,nʌŋkjʊ'leɪʃəs) *adj* of, relating to, or belonging to the *Ranunculaceae*, a N temperate family of flowering plants typically having flowers with five petals and numerous anthers and styles. The family includes the buttercup, clematis, hellebore, and columbine

ranunculus (rə'nʌŋkjʊləs) *n*, *pl* **-luses** or **-li** (-,laɪ) any ranunculaceous plant of the genus *Ranunculus*, having finely divided leaves and typically yellow five-petalled flowers. The genus includes buttercup, crowfoot, spearwort, and lesser celandine [C16 from Latin: tadpole, from *rāna* a frog]

RAOC *abbreviation for* Royal Army Ordnance Corps

rap¹ (ræp) *vb* **raps**, **rapping**, **rapped 1** to strike (a fist, stick, etc) against (something) with a sharp quick blow; knock: *he rapped at the door* **2** (*intr*) to make a sharp loud sound, esp by knocking **3** (*tr*) to rebuke or criticize sharply **4** (*tr*; foll by *out*) to put (forth) in sharp rapid speech; utter in an abrupt fashion: *to rap out orders* **5** (*intr*) *slang* to talk, esp volubly **6** (*intr*) to perform a rhythmic monologue with a musical backing **7 rap over the knuckles** to reprimand ▷ *n* **8** a sharp quick blow or the sound produced by such a blow **9** a sharp rebuke or criticism **10** *slang* voluble talk; chatter: *stop your rap* **11 a** a fast, rhythmic monologue over a prerecorded instrumental track **b** (*as modifier*): *rap music* **12** *slang* a legal charge or case **13 beat the rap** *US and Canadian slang* to escape punishment or be acquitted of a crime **14 take the rap** *slang* to suffer the consequences of a mistake, misdeed, or crime, whether guilty or not [C14 probably of Scandinavian origin; compare Swedish *rappa* to beat] > 'rapping *n*

rap² (ræp) *n* (*used with a negative*) the least amount (esp in the phrase **not to care a rap**) [C18 probably from *ropaire* counterfeit coin formerly current in Ireland]

rap³ (ræp) *vb*, *n Austral informal* a variant spelling of **wrap** (senses 8, 14)

rapacious (rə'peɪʃəs) *adj* **1** practising pillage or rapine **2** greedy or grasping **3** (of animals, esp birds) subsisting by catching living prey [C17 from Latin *rapāx* grasping, from *rapere* to seize] > ra'paciously *adv* > rapacity (rə'pæsɪtɪ) or ra'paciousness *n*

Rapacki Plan (*Polish* ra'patski) *n* the denuclearization of Poland, Czechoslovakia, East Germany, and West Germany, proposed by Adam Rapacki (1909–70), the Polish foreign minister, in 1957

Rapallo (*Italian* ra'pallo) *n* a port and resort in NW Italy, in Liguria on the **Gulf of Rapallo** (an inlet of the Ligurian Sea): scene of the signing of two treaties after World War I. Pop: 29 159 (2001)

Rapa Nui ('rɑ:pɑ: 'nu:ɪ) *n* another name for **Easter Island**

rape¹ (reɪp) *n* **1** the offence of forcing a person, esp a woman, to submit to sexual intercourse against that person's will. See also **statutory rape 2** the act of despoiling a country in warfare; rapine **3** any violation or abuse: *the rape of justice* **4** *archaic* abduction: *the rape of the Sabine women* ▷ *vb* (*mainly tr*) **5** to commit rape upon (a person) **6** (*also intr*) to plunder or despoil (a place) in war **7** *archaic* to carry off by force; abduct [C14 from Latin *rapere* to seize]

rape² (reɪp) *n* a Eurasian plant, *Brassica napus*, that has bright yellow flowers and is cultivated for its seeds, which yield a useful oil, and as a fodder plant: family *Brassicaceae* (crucifers). Also called: **colza, cole** [C14 from Latin *rāpum* turnip]

rape³ (reɪp) *n* (*often plural*) the skins and stalks of grapes left after wine-making: used in making vinegar [C17 from French *râpe*, of Germanic origin; compare Old High German *raspōn* to scrape together]

rapeseed ('reɪp,si:d) *n* the seed of the rape plant

rapeseed oil *n* oil extracted from rapeseed, used as a lubricant, as a constituent of soaps, etc. Also called: **rape oil, colza oil**

Raphael ('ræfeɪəl) *n Bible* one of the archangels; the angel of healing and the guardian of Tobias (Tobit 3:17; 5–12). Feast day: Sept 29

raphe ('reɪfɪ) *n*, *pl* **-phae** (-fi:) **1** an elongated ridge of conducting tissue along the side of certain seeds **2** a longitudinal groove on the valve of a diatom **3** *anatomy* a connecting ridge, such as that between the two halves of the medulla oblongata [C18 via New Latin from Greek *rhaphē* seam, from *rhaptein* to sew together]

raphia ('ræfɪə) *n* a variant spelling of **raffia**

raphide ('reɪfaɪd) or **raphis** ('reɪfɪs) *n*, *pl* **raphides** ('ræfɪ,di:z) any of numerous needle-shaped crystals, usually of calcium oxalate, that occur in many plant cells as a metabolic product [C18 from French, from Greek *rhaphis* needle]

rapid ('ræpɪd) *adj* **1** (of an action or movement) performed or occurring during a short interval of time; quick: *a rapid transformation* **2** characterized by high speed: *rapid movement* **3** acting or moving quickly; fast: *a rapid worker* ▷ *n* See also **rapids** [C17 from Latin *rapidus* tearing away, from *rapere* to seize; see RAPE¹] > 'rapidly *adv* > rapidity (rə'pɪdɪtɪ) or 'rapidness *n*

rapid eye movement *n* movement of the eyeballs under closed eyelids during paradoxical sleep, which occurs while the sleeper is dreaming. Abbreviation: **REM**

rapid fire *n* **1** a fast rate of gunfire ▷ *adj* **rapid-fire 2 a** firing shots rapidly **b** denoting medium-calibre mounted guns designed for rapid fire **3** done, delivered, or occurring in rapid succession

rapids ('ræpɪdz) *pl n* part of a river where the current is very fast and turbulent

rapid transit chess *n* the US name for **lightning chess** [from the name of the New York City underground railway system]

rapier ('reɪpɪə) *n* **1** a long narrow two-edged sword with a guarded hilt, used as a thrusting weapon, popular in the 16th and 17th centuries **2** a smaller single-edged 18th-century sword, used principally in France [C16 from Old French *espee rapiere*, literally: rasping sword; see RASP¹] > 'rapier-,like *adj*

rapine ('ræpaɪn) *n* the seizure of property by force; pillage [C15 from Latin *rapīna* plundering, from *rapere* to snatch]

rapist ('reɪpɪst) *n* a person who commits rape

rap jumping *n* the sport of descending high buildings, attached to ropes and a pulley

rapparee (,ræpə'ri:) *n* **1** an Irish irregular soldier of the late 17th century **2** *obsolete* any plunderer or robber [C17 from Irish *rapairidhe* pike, probably from English RAPIER]

rappee (ræ'pi:) *n* a moist English snuff of the 18th and 19th centuries [C18 from French *tabac râpé*, literally: scraped tobacco, from *râper* to scrape; see RAPE³, RASP¹]

rappel (ræ'pɛl) *vb* **-pels**, **-pelling**, **-pelled**, *n* **1** another word for **abseil** ▷ *n* **2** (formerly) a drumbeat to call soldiers to arms [C19 from French, from *rappeler* to call back, from Latin *appellāre* to summon]

rappé pie or **rappe** ('ræpeɪ) *n Canadian* an Acadian dish of grated potatoes and pork or chicken [from Acadian French *tarte râpée* grated pie]

rapper ('ræpə) *n* **1** something used for rapping, such as a knocker on a door **2** a performer of rap music

rapport (ræ'pɔ:) *n* (*often foll by with*) a sympathetic relationship or understanding. See also **en rapport** [C15 from French, from *rapporter* to bring back, from RE- + *aporter*, from Latin *apportāre*, from *adto* + *portāre* to carry]

rapporteur (,ræpɔ:'tɜ:) *n* a person appointed by a committee to prepare reports of meetings or carry out an investigation [C18 from French, literally: recorder, reporter]

rapprochement *French* (raprɔʃmã) *n* a resumption of friendly relations, esp between two countries [C19 literally: bringing closer]

rapscallion (ræp'skæljən) *n* a disreputable person; rascal or rogue [C17 from earlier *rascallion*; see RASCAL]

rapt¹ (ræpt) *adj* **1** totally absorbed; engrossed; spellbound, esp through or as if through emotion: *rapt with wonder* **2** characterized by or proceeding from rapture: *a rapt smile* [C14 from Latin *raptus* carried away, from *rapere* to seize; see RAPE¹] > 'raptly *adv*

rapt² (ræpt) *adj* Also: **wrapped** *Austral and NZ informal* very pleased: delighted

raptor ('ræptə) *n* **1** another name for **bird of prey 2** *informal* a carnivorous bipedal dinosaur of the late Cretaceous period [C17 from Latin: plunderer, from *rapere* to take by force]

raptorial (ræp'tɔ:rɪəl) *adj zoology* **1** (of the feet of birds) adapted for seizing prey **2** (esp of birds) feeding on prey; predatory **3** of or relating to birds of prey [C19 from Latin *raptor* a robber, from *rapere* to snatch]

rapture ('ræptʃə) *n* **1** the state of mind resulting from feelings of high emotion; joyous ecstasy **2** (*often plural*) an expression of ecstatic joy **3** the act of transporting a person from one sphere of existence to another, esp from earth to heaven ▷ *vb* **4** (*tr*) *archaic or literary* to entrance; enrapture [C17 from Medieval Latin *raptūra*, from Latin *raptus* RAPT¹]

rapturous ('ræptʃərəs) *adj* experiencing or manifesting ecstatic joy or delight > 'rapturously *adv* > 'rapturousness *n*

RAR *abbreviation for* Royal Australian Regiment

rara avis ('rɛərə 'eɪvɪs) *n*, *pl* **rarae aves** ('rɛəri: 'eɪvi:z) an unusual, uncommon, or exceptional person or thing [Latin: rare bird]

rare¹ (rɛə) *adj* **1** not widely known; not frequently used or experienced; uncommon or unusual: *a rare word* **2** occurring seldom: *a rare appearance* **3** not widely distributed; not generally occurring: *a rare herb* **4** (of a gas, esp the atmosphere at high altitudes) having a low density; thin; rarefied **5** uncommonly great; extreme: *kind to a rare degree* **6** exhibiting uncommon excellence; superlatively good or fine: *rare skill* **7** highly valued because of its uncommonness: *a rare prize* [c14 from Latin *rārus* sparse] > **'rareness** *n*

rare² (rɛə) *adj* (of meat, esp beef) very lightly cooked [Old English *hrēr*; perhaps related to *hreaw* RAW]

rarebit ('rɛəbɪt) *n* another term for **Welsh rabbit** [c18 by folk etymology from (WELSH) RABBIT; see RARE², BIT]

rare earth *n* **1** any oxide of a lanthanide **2** Also called: **rare-earth element** another name for **lanthanide**

raree show ('rɛəriː) *n* **1** a street show or carnival **2** another name for **peepshow** [c17 *raree* from RARE¹]

rarefaction (ˌrɛərɪˈfækʃən) or **rarefication** (ˌrɛərɪfɪˈkeɪʃən) *n* the act or process of making less dense or the state of being less dense > ˌrareˈfactional, ˌrarefiˈcational or ˌrareˈfactive *adj*

rarefied ('rɛərɪˌfaɪd) *adj* **1** exalted in nature or character; lofty: *a rarefied spiritual existence* **2** current within only a small group; esoteric or exclusive **3** (of a gas, esp the atmosphere at high altitudes) having a low density; thin

rarefy ('rɛərɪˌfaɪ) *vb* **-fies, -fying, -fied** to make or become rarer or less dense; thin out [c14 from Old French *raréfier*, from Latin *rārefacere*, from *rārus* RARE¹ + *facere* to make] > **'rare,fiable** *adj* > **'rare,fier** *n*

rare gas *n* another name for **inert gas** (sense 1)

rarely ('rɛəlɪ) *adv* **1** hardly ever; seldom: *I'm rarely in town these days* **2** to an unusual degree; exceptionally **3** *dialect* uncommonly well; excellently: *he did rarely at market yesterday*

USAGE Since *rarely* means *hardly ever*, one should not say something *rarely ever happens*

rareripe ('rɛəˌraɪp) US > *adj* **1** ripening early > *n* **2** a fruit or vegetable that ripens early [c18 *rare*, variant of RATHE + RIPE]

raring ('rɛərɪŋ) *adj* ready; willing; enthusiastic (esp in the phrase **raring to go**) [c20 from *rare*, variant of REAR²]

rarity ('rɛərɪtɪ) *n*, *pl* **-ties 1** a rare person or thing, esp something interesting or valued because it is uncommon **2** the state or quality of being rare

rark up *vb* (*tr, adverb*) NZ *informal* to give (someone) a severe reprimand

Rarotonga (ˌrɛərəˈtɒŋgə) *n* an island in the S Pacific, in the SW Cook Islands: the chief island of the group. Chief settlement: Avarua. Pop: 12 188 (2001). Area: 67 sq km (26 sq miles)

RAS *abbreviation for* **1** Royal Agricultural Society **2** Royal Astronomical Society

rasbora (ræzˈbɔːrə) *n* any of the small cyprinid fishes constituting the genus *Rasbora* of tropical Asia and East Africa. Many species are brightly coloured and are popular aquarium fishes [from New Latin, from an East Indian language]

RASC *abbreviation for* (the former) Royal Army Service Corps, now called Royal Corps of Transport

rascal ('rɑːskəl) *n* **1** a disreputable person **2** a mischievous or impish rogue **3** an affectionate or mildly reproving term for a child or old man: *you little rascal* **4** *obsolete* a person of lowly birth > *adj* **5** (*prenominal*) *obsolete* **a** belonging to the mob or rabble **b** dishonest; knavish [c14 from Old French *rascaille* rabble, perhaps from Old Norman French *rasque* mud, filth]

rascality (rɑːˈskælɪtɪ) *n*, *pl* **-ties** mischievous, disreputable, or dishonest character, behaviour, or action

rascally ('rɑːskəlɪ) *adj* **1** dishonest or mean; base **2** *archaic* (esp of places) wretchedly unpleasant; miserable > *adv* **3** in a dishonest or mean fashion

rase (reɪz) *vb* a variant spelling of **raze**

rash¹ (ræʃ) *adj* **1** acting without due consideration or thought; impetuous **2** characterized by or resulting from excessive haste or impetuosity: *a rash word* [c14 from Old High German *rasc* hurried, clever; related to Old Norse *roskr* brave] > **'rashly** *adv* > **'rashness** *n*

rash² (ræʃ) *n* **1** *pathol* any skin eruption **2** a series of unpleasant and unexpected occurrences: *a rash of forest fires* [c18 from Old French *rasche*, from *raschier* to scratch, from Latin *rādere* to scrape] > **'rash,like** *adj*

rasher ('ræʃə) *n* a thin slice of bacon or ham [c16 of unknown origin]

Rashid (ræˈʃiːd) *n* a town in N Egypt, on the Nile delta. Pop: 52 015 (latest est). Former name: Rosetta

rash shirt or **rash vest** *n* a shirt worn by surfers as protection against sunburn, heat rash, etc. Also called (Austral): **rashie**

Rasht (ræʃt) or **Resht** *n* a city in NW Iran, near the Caspian Sea: agricultural and commercial centre in a rice-growing area. Pop: 586 000 (2005 est)

rasmalai ('rɑːsməˌlaɪ) *n* **1** an Indian dessert made from cheese, milk, and almonds **2** *Hinglish informal* a physically attractive woman [Hindi *ras* juice + *malai* skin formed on a hot liquid when it cools]

rasorial (rəˈsɔːrɪəl) *adj* (of birds such as domestic poultry) adapted for scratching the ground for food [c19 from New Latin *Rasores* such birds, from Latin *rādere* to scrape]

rasp¹ (rɑːsp) *n* **1** a harsh grating noise **2** a coarse file with rows of raised teeth > *vb* **3** (*tr*) to scrape or rub (something) roughly, esp with a rasp; abrade **4** to utter with or make a harsh grating noise **5** to irritate (one's nerves or senses); grate (upon) [c16 from Old French *raspe*, of Germanic origin; compare Old High German *raspōn* to scrape] > **'rasper** *n* > **'raspish** *adj*

rasp² (rɑːsp) *n* another name, now Scot or informal, for **raspberry**

raspatory ('rɑːspətərɪ, -trɪ) *n*, *pl* **-ies** a surgical instrument for abrading; surgeon's rasp [c16 from Medieval Latin *raspatorium*]

raspberry ('rɑːzbərɪ, -brɪ) *n*, *pl* **-ries 1** any of the prickly shrubs of the rosaceous genus *Rubus*, such as *R. strigosus* of E North America and *R. idaeus* of Europe, that have pinkish-white flowers and typically red berry-like fruits (drupelets). See also **bramble 2 a** the fruit of any such plant **b** (*as modifier*): *raspberry jelly* **3 black raspberry** Popular name: **blackcap a** a related plant, *Rubus occidentalis*, of E North America, that has black berry-like fruits **b** the fruit of this plant **4 a** a dark purplish-red colour **b** (*as adjective*): *a raspberry dress* **5** a spluttering noise made with the tongue and lips to express contempt (esp in the phrase **blow a raspberry**) [c17 from earlier *raspis* raspberry, of unknown origin + BERRY: c19 in sense 5, from rhyming slang *raspberry tart* fart]

rasping ('rɑːspɪŋ) or **raspy** *adj* (esp of a noise) harsh or grating; rough

raspings ('rɑːspɪŋz) *pl n* browned breadcrumbs for coating fish and other foods before frying, baking, etc

rasse ('ræsɪ, ræs) *n* a small civet, *Viverricula indica*, of S and SE Asia [c19 from Javanese *rase*]

Rasta ('ræstə) *n, adj* short for **Rastafarian**

Rastafarian (ˌræstəˈfɛərɪən) *n* **1** a member of an originally Jamaican religion that regards **Ras Tafari** (the former emperor of Ethiopia, Haile Selassie (1892–1975)) as God > *adj* **2** of, characteristic of, or relating to the Rastafarians

raster ('ræstə) *n* **1** a pattern of horizontal scanning lines traced by an electron beam, esp on a television screen > *vb* **2** to use web-based technology to turn a digital image into a large picture composed of a grid of black and white dots [c20 via German from Latin: rake, from *rādere* to scrape]

rat (ræt) *n* **1** any of numerous long-tailed murine rodents, esp of the genus *Rattus*, that are similar to but larger than mice and are now distributed all over the world. See also **brown rat, black rat 2** *informal* a person who deserts his friends or associates, esp in time of trouble **3** *informal* a worker who works during a strike; blackleg; scab **4** *slang, chiefly US* an informer; stool pigeon **5** *informal* a despicable person **6 smell a rat** to detect something suspicious > *vb* **rats, ratting, ratted 7** (*intr*; usually foll by *on*) *informal* **a** to divulge secret information (about); betray the trust (of) **b** to default (on); abandon: *he ratted on the project at the last minute* **8** to hunt and kill rats > See also **rats** [Old English *rætt*; related to Old Saxon *ratta*, Old High German *rato*] > **'rat,like** *adj*

rata ('rɑːtə) *n* either of two New Zealand myrtaceous forest trees, *Metrosideros robusta* or *M. lucida*, having crimson flowers and hard wood [c19 from Māori]

ratable or **rateable** ('reɪtəbəl) *adj* **1** able to be rated or evaluated **2** *Brit* (of property) liable to payment of rates > ˌrataˈbility, ˌrateaˈbility, 'rateableness or 'rateableness *n* > 'ratably or 'rateably *adv*

ratable value or **rateable value** *n Brit* (formerly) a fixed value assigned to a property by a local authority, on the basis of which variable annual rates are charged

ratafia (ˌrætəˈfiːə) or **ratafee** (ˌrætəˈfiː) *n* **1** any liqueur made from fruit or from brandy with added fruit **2** a flavouring essence made from almonds **3** *chiefly Brit* Also called: **ratafia biscuit** a small macaroon flavoured with almonds [c17 from West Indian Creole French]

ratal ('reɪtəl) *Brit* > *n* **1** the amount on which rates are assessed; ratable value > *adj* **2** of or relating to rates (local taxation) [c19 see RATE¹]

ratan (ræˈtæn) *n* a variant spelling of **rattan**

Ratana ('rɑːtɑːnɑː) *adj* **1** of or relating to the Ratana Church or the Māori Christian religious movement associated with it > *n* **2** the Ratana Church itself **3** *pl* **Ratana** a member of the Ratana Church [from the Church's founder, TW *Ratana* (1873–1939)]

rataplan (ˌrætəˈplæn) *n* a drumming sound [from French, of imitative origin]

rat-arsed *adj Brit slang* drunk

rat-a-tat-tat ('rætəˌtætˈtæt) or **rat-a-tat** ('rætəˈtæt) *n* the sound of knocking on a door

ratatouille (ˌrætəˈtwiː) *n* a vegetable casserole made of tomatoes, aubergines, peppers, etc, fried in oil and stewed slowly [c19 from French, from *touiller* to stir, from Latin *tudiculāre*, from *tudes* hammer]

ratbag ('rætˌbæg) *n slang* a despicable person [c20 from RAT + BAG]

ratbaggery ('rætˌbægərɪ) *n Austral slang* nonsense, eccentricity

ratbite fever or **disease** ('rætˌbaɪt) *n pathol* an acute infectious febrile disease caused by the bite of a rat infected with either of two pathogenic bacteria (*Streptobacillus moniliformis* or *Spirillum minus*)

rat-catcher *n* a person whose job is to destroy or drive away vermin, esp rats

ratchet ('rætʃɪt) *n* **1** a device in which a toothed rack or wheel is engaged by a pawl to permit motion in one direction only **2** the toothed rack or wheel forming part of such a device > **3** to operate using a ratchet **4** (usually foll by *up* or *down*) to increase or decrease, esp irreversibly: *electricity prices will ratchet up this year; Hitchcock ratchets up the tension once again* [c17 from French *rochet*, from Old French *rocquet* blunt head of a lance, of Germanic origin: compare Old High German *rocko* distaff]

ratchet effect *n economics* an effect that occurs when a price or wage increases as a result of temporary pressure but fails to fall back when the pressure is removed

rate¹ (reɪt) *n* **1** a quantity or amount considered in relation to or measured against another

r

quantity or amount: *a rate of 70 miles an hour* **2** **a** a price or charge with reference to a standard or scale: *rate of interest; rate of discount* **b** (*as modifier*): *a rate card* **3** a charge made per unit for a commodity, service, etc **4** See **rates** **5** the relative speed of progress or change of something variable; pace: *he works at a great rate; the rate of production has doubled* **6** **a** relative quality; class or grade **b** (*in combination*): *first-rate ideas* **7** *statistics* a measure of the frequency of occurrence of a given event, such as births and deaths, usually expressed as the number of times the event occurs for every thousand of the total population considered **8** a wage calculated against a unit of time **9** the amount of gain or loss of a timepiece **10** **at any rate** in any case; at all events; anyway ▷ *vb* (*mainly tr*) **11** (*also intr*) to assign or receive a position on a scale of relative values; rank: *he is rated fifth in the world* **12** to estimate the value of; evaluate: *we rate your services highly* **13** to be worthy of; deserve: *this hotel does not rate four stars* **14** to consider; regard: *I rate him among my friends* **15** *Brit* to assess the value of (property) for the purpose of local taxation **16** *slang* to think highly of: *the clients do not rate the new system* [C15 from Old French, from Medieval Latin *rata*, from Latin *prō ratā parte* according to a fixed proportion, from *ratus* fixed, from *rērī* to think, decide]

rate[2] (reɪt) *vb* (*tr*) to scold or criticize severely; rebuke harshly [C14 perhaps related to Swedish *rata* to chide]

rateable (ˈreɪtəbᵊl) *adj* a variant spelling of **ratable**

rate-cap (ˈreɪtˌkæp) *vb* (*tr*) **-caps, -capping, -capped** (formerly in Britain) to impose on (a local authority) an upper limit on the level of the rate it may levy > **ˈrate-ˌcapping** *n*

rateen (ræˈtiːn) *n* a variant spelling of **ratine**

ratel (ˈreɪtᵊl) *n* **1** a musteline mammal, *Mellivora capensis*, inhabiting wooded regions of Africa and S Asia. It has a massive body, strong claws, and a thick coat that is paler on the back and it feeds on honey and small animals. Also called: **honey badger** **2** *South African* a six-wheeled armoured vehicle [C18 from Afrikaans]

rate of exchange *n* See **exchange rate**

rate of return *n* *finance* the ratio of the annual income from an investment to the original investment, often expressed as a percentage

ratepayer (ˈreɪtˌpeɪə) *n* a person who pays local rates, esp a householder

rates (reɪts) *pl n* (in some countries) a tax levied on property by a local authority

ratfink (ˈrætˌfɪŋk) *n* *slang, chiefly US and Canadian* a contemptible or undesirable person [C20 from RAT + FINK]

ratfish (ˈrætˌfɪʃ) *n, pl* **-fish** *or* **-fishes** **1** another name for **rabbitfish** (sense 1) **2** a chimaera, *Hydrolagus colliei*, of the North Pacific Ocean, which has a long narrow tail

rath (raθ) *n* *Irish history* a circular enclosure surrounded by an earthen wall: used as a dwelling and stronghold in former times [C16 from Irish Gaelic]

ratha (rʌt) *n* (in India) a four-wheeled carriage drawn by horses or bullocks; chariot [Hindi]

rathe (reɪð) *or* **rath** (rɑːθ) *adj* *archaic or literary* **1** blossoming or ripening early in the season **2** eager or prompt [Old English *hrathe*; related to Old High German *hrado*, Old Norse *hrathr*]

rather (ˈrɑːðə) *adv* (*in senses 1-4, not used with a negative*) **1** relatively or fairly; somewhat: *it's rather dull* **2** to a significant or noticeable extent; quite: *she's rather pretty* **3** to a limited extent or degree: *I rather thought that was the case* **4** with better or more just cause: *this text is rather to be deleted than rewritten* **5** more readily or willingly; sooner: *I would rather not see you tomorrow* ▷ *sentence connector* **6** on the contrary: *it's not cold. Rather, it's very hot indeed* ▷ *sentence substitute* (ˈrɑːˈðɜː) **7** an expression of strong affirmation, often in answer to a question: *Is it worth seeing? Rather!* [Old English *hrathor* comparative of *hræth* READY, quick; related to Old Norse *hrathr*]

> USAGE Both *would* and *had* are used with *rather* in sentences such as *I would rather* (or *had rather*) *go to the film than to the play. Had rather* is less common and is now widely regarded as slightly old-fashioned

rathouse (ˈræthaʊs) *n* *Austral slang* a psychiatric hospital or asylum

ratify (ˈrætɪˌfaɪ) *vb* **-fies, -fying, -fied** (*tr*) to give formal approval or consent to [C14 via Old French from Latin *ratus* fixed (see RATE[1]) + *facere* to make] > **ˈratiˌfiable** *adj* > **ˌratifiˈcation** *n* > **ˈratiˌfier** *n*

ratine, rateen, ratteen (ræˈtiːn) *or* **ratiné** (ˈrætɪˌneɪ) *n* a coarse loosely woven cloth [C17 from French, from *ratine*, of obscure origin]

rating[1] (ˈreɪtɪŋ) *n* **1** a classification according to order or grade; ranking **2** (in certain navies) a sailor who holds neither commissioned nor warrant rank; an ordinary seaman **3** *sailing* a handicap assigned to a racing boat based on its dimensions, sail area, weight, draught, etc **4** the estimated financial or credit standing of a business enterprise or individual **5** *radio, television* a figure based on statistical sampling indicating what proportion of the total listening and viewing audience tune in to a specific programme or network

rating[2] (ˈreɪtɪŋ) *n* a sharp scolding or rebuke

ratio (ˈreɪʃɪˌəʊ) *n, pl* **-tios** **1** a measure of the relative size of two classes expressible as a proportion: *the ratio of boys to girls is 2 to 1* **2** *maths* a quotient of two numbers or quantities. See also **proportion** (sense 6) [C17 from Latin: a reckoning, from *rērī* to think; see REASON]

ratiocinate (ˌrætɪˈɒsɪˌneɪt) *vb* (*intr*) to think or argue logically and methodically; reason [C17 from Latin *ratiōcinārī* to calculate, from *ratiō* REASON] > **ˌratiˌociˈnation** *n* > **ˌratiˈocinative** *adj* > **ˌratiˈociˌnator** *n*

ration (ˈræʃən) *n* **1** **a** a fixed allowance of food, provisions, etc, esp a statutory one for civilians in time of scarcity or soldiers in time of war: *a tea ration* **b** (*as modifier*): *a ration book* **2** a sufficient or adequate amount: *you've had your ration of television for today* ▷ *vb* (*tr*) **3** (often foll by *out*) to distribute (provisions), esp to an army **4** to restrict the distribution or consumption of (a commodity) by (people): *the government has rationed sugar; sugar is short, so I'll have to ration you* ▷ See also **rations** [C18 via French from Latin *ratiō* calculation; see REASON]

rational (ˈræʃənᵊl) *adj* **1** using reason or logic in thinking out a problem **2** in accordance with the principles of logic or reason; reasonable **3** of sound mind; sane: *the patient seemed quite rational* **4** endowed with the capacity to reason; capable of logical thought: *man is a rational being* **5** *maths* expressible as a ratio of two integers or polynomials: *a rational number; a rational function* ▷ *n* **6** *maths* a rational number [C14 from Latin *ratiōnālis*, from *ratiō* REASON] > **ˈrationally** *adv* > **ˈrationalness** *n*

rationale (ˌræʃəˈnɑːl) *n* a reasoned exposition, esp one defining the fundamental reasons for a course of action, belief, etc [C17 from New Latin, from Latin *ratiōnālis*]

rationalism (ˈræʃənəˌlɪzəm) *n* **1** reliance on reason rather than intuition to justify one's beliefs or actions **2** *philosophy* **a** the doctrine that knowledge about reality can be obtained by reason alone without recourse to experience **b** the doctrine that human knowledge can all be encompassed within a single, usually deductive, system **c** the school of philosophy initiated by René Descartes, the French philosopher and mathematician (1596–1650), which held both the above doctrines **3** the belief that knowledge and truth are ascertained by rational thought and not by divine or supernatural revelation > **ˈrationalist** *n* > **ˌrationalˈistic** *adj* > **ˌrationalˈistically** *adv*

rationality (ˌræʃəˈnælɪtɪ) *n, pl* **-ties** **1** the state or quality of being rational or logical **2** the possession or utilization of reason or logic **3** a reasonable or logical opinion **4** *economics* the assumption that an individual will compare all possible combinations of goods and their prices when making purchases

rationalize *or* **rationalise** (ˈræʃənəˌlaɪz) *vb* **1** to justify (one's actions, esp discreditable actions, or beliefs) with plausible reasons, esp after the event **2** *psychol* to indulge, often unchallenged, in excuses for or explanations of (behaviour about which one feels uncomfortable or guilty) **3** to apply logic or reason to (something) **4** (*tr*) to eliminate unnecessary equipment, personnel, or processes from (a group of businesses, factory, etc), in order to make it more efficient **5** (*tr*) *maths* to eliminate one or more radicals without changing the value of (an expression) or the roots of (an equation) > **ˌrationaliˈzation** *or* **ˌrationaliˈsation** *n* > **ˈrationalˌizer** *or* **ˈrationalˌiser** *n*

rational number *n* any real number of the form *a*/*b*, where *a* and *b* are integers and *b* is not zero, as 7 or 7/3

rations (ˈræʃənz) *pl n* (*sometimes singular*) a fixed daily allowance of food, esp to military personnel or when supplies are limited. See also **iron rations**

ratio scale *n* *statistics* a scale of measurement of data which permits the comparison of differences of values; a scale having a fixed zero value. The distances travelled by a projectile, for instance, are measured on a ratio scale since it makes sense to talk of one projectile travelling twice as far as another. Compare **ordinal scale, interval scale, nominal scale**

Ratisbon (ˈrætɪzˌbɒn) *n* the former English name for **Regensburg**

ratite (ˈrætaɪt) *adj* **1** (of flightless birds) having a breastbone that lacks a keel for the attachment of flight muscles **2** of or denoting the flightless birds, formerly classified as a group (the *Ratitae*), that have a flat breastbone, feathers lacking vanes, and reduced wings ▷ *n* **3** a bird, such as an ostrich, kiwi, or rhea, that belongs to this group; a flightless bird [C19 from Latin *ratis* raft]

rat kangaroo *n* any of several ratlike kangaroos of the genera *Bettongia, Potorous, Aepyprymnus*, etc, found on the Australian mainland and in Tasmania

ratline *or* **ratlin** (ˈrætlɪn) *n* *nautical* any of a series of light lines tied across the shrouds of a sailing vessel for climbing aloft [C15 of unknown origin]

RATO (ˈreɪtəʊ) *n acronym for* rocket-assisted takeoff

ratoon *or* **rattoon** (ræˈtuːn) *n* **1** a new shoot that grows from near the root or crown of crop plants, esp the sugar cane, after the old growth has been cut back ▷ *vb* **2** to propagate or cause to propagate by such a growth [C18 from Spanish *retoño* young shoot, from RE- + *otoñar* to sprout in autumn, from *otoño* AUTUMN]

ratpack (ˈrætˌpæk) *n* *derogatory slang* those members of the press who give wide, often intrusive, coverage of the private lives of celebrities: *the royal ratpack*

rat race *n* a continual routine of hectic competitive activity: *working in the City is a real rat race*

rat-running *n* the practice of driving through residential side streets to avoid congested main roads > **ˈrat-ˌrun** *n* > **ˈrat-ˌrunner** *n*

rats (ræts) *interj* **1** an exclamation of rejection or disdain ▷ *adj* **2** *Austral slang* deranged; insane

ratsbane (ˈrætsˌbeɪn) *n* rat poison, esp arsenic oxide

Ratskeller *German* (ˈraːtskɛlər) *n* **1** the cellar of a town hall, esp one used as a beer hall or restaurant **2** any similar establishment, esp in the US [German: from *Rat(haus)* town hall + *Keller* cellar]

rat snake *n* any of various nonvenomous rodent-eating colubrid snakes, such as *Elaphe obsoleta* of North America and *Ptyas mucosus* of Asia

rat-tail *n* **1** another name for **grenadier** (the fish) **2 a** a horse's tail that has no hairs **b** a horse having such a tail **3** a style of spoon in which the line of the handle is prolonged in a tapering moulding along the back of the bowl **4** a kind of woodworking or metalworking file

rat tamer *n Austral* an informal name for **psychologist** *or* **psychiatrist**

rattan *or* **ratan** (ræ'tæn) *n* **1** any of the climbing palms of the genus *Calamus* and related genera, having tough stems used for wickerwork and canes **2** the stems of such plants collectively **3** a stick made from one of these stems [C17 from Malay *rōtan*]

rat-tat ('ræt,tæt) *n* a variant of **rat-a-tat-tat**

ratteen (ræ'ti:n) *n* a variant spelling of **ratine**

ratter ('rætə) *n* **1** a dog or cat that catches and kills rats **2** another word for **rat** (senses 3, 4)

rattish ('rætɪʃ) *adj* of, resembling, or infested with rats

rattle[1] ('rætᵊl) *vb* **1** to make or cause to make a rapid succession of short sharp sounds, as of loose pellets colliding when shaken in a container **2** to shake or cause to shake with such a sound: *the explosion rattled the windows* **3** to send, move, drive, etc, with such a sound: *the car rattled along the country road* **4** (*intr*; foll by *on*) to chatter idly; talk, esp at length: *he rattled on about his work* **5** (*tr*; foll by *off*, *out* etc) to recite perfunctorily or rapidly **6** (*tr*) *informal* to disconcert; make frightened or anxious ▷ *n* **7** a rapid succession of short sharp sounds **8** an object, esp a baby's toy, filled with small pellets that rattle when shaken **9** a series of loosely connected horny segments on the tail of a rattlesnake, vibrated to produce a rattling sound **10** any of various European scrophulariaceous plants having a capsule in which the seeds rattle, such as *Pedicularis palustris* (**red rattle**) and *Rhinanthus minor* (**yellow rattle**) **11** idle chatter **12** an idle chatterer **13** *med* another name for **rale** [C14 from Middle Dutch *ratelen*; related to Middle High German *razzen*, of imitative origin]

rattle[2] ('rætᵊl) *vb* (*tr*; often foll by *down*) to fit (a vessel or its rigging) with ratlines [C18 back formation from *rattling*, variant of RATLINE]

rattlebox ('rætᵊl,bɒks) *n* any of various tropical and subtropical leguminous plants that have inflated pods within which the seeds rattle

rattler ('rætlə) *n* **1** something that rattles **2** *chiefly US and Canadian* an informal name for **rattlesnake**

rattlesnake ('rætᵊl,sneɪk) *n* any of the venomous New World snakes constituting the genera *Crotalus* and *Sistrurus*, such as *C. horridus* (**black** or **timber rattlesnake**): family *Crotalidae* (pit vipers). They have a series of loose horny segments on the tail that are vibrated to produce a buzzing or whirring sound

rattlesnake plantain *n* any of various small temperate and tropical orchids of the genus *Goodyera*, having mottled or striped leaves and spikes of yellowish-white flowers

rattletrap ('rætᵊl,træp) *n informal* a broken-down old vehicle, esp an old car

rattling ('rætlɪŋ) *adv informal* (intensifier qualifying something good, fine, pleasant, etc): *a rattling good lunch*

rattly ('rætlɪ) *adj* **-tlier, -tliest** having a rattle; rattling

rattoon (ræ'tu:n) *n, vb* a variant spelling of **ratoon**

rat-trap *n* **1** a device for catching rats **2** *informal* a type of bicycle pedal having serrated steel foot pads and a toe clip

ratty ('rætɪ) *adj* **-tier, -tiest** **1** *Brit and NZ informal* irritable; annoyed **2** *informal* (of the hair) unkempt or greasy **3** *US and Canadian slang* shabby; dilapidated **4** *Austral slang* **a** angry **b** mad **5** of, like, or full of rats > '**rattily** *adv* > '**rattiness** *n*

raucous ('rɔ:kəs) *adj* (of voices, cries, etc) harshly or hoarsely loud [C18 from Latin *raucus* hoarse] > '**raucously** *adv* > '**raucousness** *or less commonly* **raucity** ('rɔ:sɪtɪ) *n*

raunch (rɔ:ntʃ) *n slang* **1** lack of polish or refinement; crudeness **2** *chiefly US* slovenliness or untidiness

raunchy ('rɔ:ntʃɪ) *adj* **-chier, -chiest** *slang* **1** openly sexual; lusty; earthy **2** *chiefly US* slovenly or untidy [C20 of unknown origin] > '**raunchily** *adv* > '**raunchiness** *n*

raupatu (,raʊ'pɑ:tu:) *n NZ* the confiscation or seizure of land [Māori]

raupo (rɑ:u:pɒ) *n, pl* **raupo** a New Zealand bulrush, *Typha orientalis*, with sword-shaped leaves, traditionally used for construction and decoration [Māori]

rauriki ('raʊrəki:) *n, pl* **-kis** NZ another name for **sow thistle** [Māori]

rauwolfia (rɔ:'wʊlfɪə, raʊ-) *n* **1** any tropical tree or shrub of the apocynaceous genus *Rauwolfia*, esp *R. serpentina* of SE Asia **2** the powdered root of *R. serpentina*: a source of various drugs, esp reserpine [C19 New Latin, named after Leonhard *Rauwolf* (died 1596), German botanist]

Rav (ræv; *Hebrew* rav) *n Judaism* **1** a rabbi who is a person's religious mentor, or one to whom questions are addressed for authoritative decision **2** the title preferred by many orthodox rabbis to distinguish them from the clergy of other brands of Judaism

ravage ('rævɪdʒ) *vb* **1** to cause extensive damage to ▷ *n* **2** (*often plural*) destructive action: *the ravages of time* [C17 from French, from Old French *ravir* to snatch away, RAVISH] > '**ravagement** *n*

RAVC *abbreviation for* Royal Army Veterinary Corps

rave[1] (reɪv) *vb* **1** to utter (something) in a wild or incoherent manner, as when mad or delirious **2** (*intr*) to speak in an angry uncontrolled manner **3** (*intr*) (of the sea, wind, etc) to rage or roar **4** (*intr*; foll by *over* or *about*) *informal* to write or speak (about) with great enthusiasm **5** (*intr*) *Brit slang* to enjoy oneself wildly or uninhibitedly ▷ *n* **6** *informal* **a** enthusiastic or extravagant praise **b** (*as modifier*): *a rave review* **7** *Brit slang* **a** Also called: **rave-up** a party **b** a professionally organized party for young people, with electronic dance music, sometimes held in a field or disused building **8** *Brit slang* a fad or fashion: *the latest rave* **9** a name given to various types of dance music, such as techno, that feature fast electronic rhythm [C14 *raven*, apparently from Old French *resver* to wander]

rave[2] (reɪv) *n* a vertical sidepiece on a wagon [C16 modification of dialect *rathe*, of uncertain origin]

ravel ('rævᵊl) *vb* **-els, -elling, -elled** *or US* **-els, -eling, -eled** **1** to tangle (threads, fibres, etc) or (of threads, fibres, etc) to become entangled **2** (often foll by *out*) to tease or draw out (the fibres of a fabric or garment) or (of a garment or fabric) to fray out in loose ends; unravel **3** (*tr*; usually foll by *out*) to disentangle or resolve: *to ravel out a complicated story* **4** to break up (a road surface) in patches or (of a road surface) to begin to break up; fret; scab **5** *archaic* to make or become confused or complicated ▷ *n* **6** a tangle or complication [C16 from Middle Dutch *ravelen*] > '**raveller** *n* > '**ravelly** *adj*

ravelin ('rævlɪn) *n fortifications* an outwork having two embankments at a salient angle [C16 from Italian *ravellino* a little bank, from *riva* bank, from Latin *rīpa*]

ravelment ('rævəlmənt) *n rare* a ravel or tangle

raven[1] ('reɪvᵊn) *n* **1** a large passerine bird, *Corvus corax*, having a large straight bill, long wedge-shaped tail, and black plumage: family *Corvidae* (crows). It has a hoarse croaking cry **2 a** a shiny black colour **b** (*as adjective*): *raven hair* [Old English *hræfn*; related to Old High German *hraban*, Old Norse *hrafn*]

raven[2] ('rævᵊn) *vb* **1** to seize or seek (plunder, prey, etc) **2** to eat (something) voraciously or greedily; be ravenous in eating [C15 from Old French *raviner* to attack impetuously; see RAVENOUS] > '**ravener** *n*

Raven ('reɪvᵊn) *n* a traditional trickster hero among the native peoples of the Canadian Pacific Northwest [from RAVEN[1]]

ravening ('rævənɪŋ) *adj* (esp of animals such as wolves) voracious; predatory > '**raveningly** *adv*

Ravenna (rə'vɛnə; *Italian* ra'venna) *n* a city and port in NE Italy, in Emilia-Romagna: capital of the Western Roman Empire from 402 to 476, of the Ostrogoths from 493 to 526, and of the Byzantine exarchate from 584 to 751; famous for its ancient mosaics. Pop: 134 631 (2001)

ravenous ('rævənəs) *adj* **1** famished; starving **2** rapacious; voracious [C16 from Old French *ravineux*, from Latin *rapīna* plunder, from *rapere* to seize] > '**ravenously** *adv* > '**ravenousness** *n*

raver ('reɪvə) *n* **1** *Brit slang* a person who leads a wild or uninhibited social life **2** *slang* a person who enjoys rave music, esp one who frequents raves

ravin ('rævɪn) *vb* an archaic spelling of **raven**[2]

ravine (rə'vi:n) *n* a deep narrow steep-sided valley, esp one formed by the action of running water [C15 from Old French: torrent, from Latin *rapīna* robbery, influenced by Latin *rapidus* RAPID, both from *rapere* to snatch]

raving ('reɪvɪŋ) *adj* **1 a** delirious; frenzied **b** (*as adv*): *raving mad* **2** *informal* (intensifier): *a raving beauty* ▷ *n* **3** (*usually plural*) frenzied, irrational, or wildly extravagant talk or utterances > '**ravingly** *adv*

ravioli (,rævɪ'əʊlɪ) *n* small squares of pasta containing a savoury mixture of meat, cheese, etc [C19 from Italian dialect, literally: little turnips, from Italian *rava* turnip, from Latin *rāpa*]

ravish ('rævɪʃ) *vb* (*tr*) **1** (*often passive*) to give great delight to; enrapture **2** to rape **3** *archaic* to carry off by force [C13 from Old French *ravir*, from Latin *rapere* to seize] > '**ravisher** *n* > '**ravishment** *n*

ravishing ('rævɪʃɪŋ) *adj* delightful; lovely; entrancing > '**ravishingly** *adv*

raw (rɔ:) *adj* **1** (of food) not cooked: *raw onion* **2** (*prenominal*) in an unfinished, natural, or unrefined state; not treated by manufacturing or other processes: *raw materials for making steel; raw brick* **3** (of the skin, a wound, etc) having the surface exposed or abraded, esp painfully **4** ignorant, inexperienced, or immature: *a raw recruit* **5** (*prenominal*) not selected or modified: *raw statistics* **6** frank or realistic: *a raw picture of the breakdown of a marriage* **7** (of spirits) undiluted **8** *chiefly US* coarse, vulgar, or obscene **9** *chiefly US* recently done; fresh: *raw paintwork* **10** (of the weather) harshly cold and damp **11** *informal* unfair; unjust (esp in the phrase **a raw deal**) ▷ *n* **12** **the raw** *Brit informal* a sensitive point: *his criticism touched me on the raw* **13** **in the raw** **a** *informal* without clothes; naked **b** in a natural or unmodified state: *life in the raw* [Old English *hreaw*; related to Old High German *hrao*, Old Norse *hrār* raw, Latin *cruor* thick blood, Greek *kreas* meat] > '**rawish** *adj* > '**rawly** *adv* > '**rawness** *n*

Rawalpindi (rɔ:l'pɪndɪ) *n* an ancient city in N Pakistan: interim capital of Pakistan (1959–67) during the building of Islamabad. Pop: 1 794 000 (2005 est)

rawaru ('rɑ:wɑ:ru:) *n, pl* **rawaru** NZ another name for **blue cod** [Māori]

rawboned ('rɔ:'bəʊnd) *adj* having a lean bony physique

rawhide ('rɔ:,haɪd) *n* **1** untanned hide **2** a whip or rope made of strips cut from such a hide

rawhide hammer *n* a hammer, used to avoid damaging a surface, having a head consisting of a metal tube from each end of which a tight roll of hide protrudes

rawinsonde ('reɪwɪn,sɒnd) *n* a hydrogen balloon carrying meteorological instruments and a radar target, enabling the velocity of winds in the atmosphere to be measured [C20 blend of *radar* + *wind* + *radiosonde*]

Rawlplug ('rɔ:lplʌg) *n trademark* a short fibre or plastic tube used to provide a fixing in a wall for a screw

rawmaish (ˌrɔːˈmeɪʃ) *n Irish* foolish or exaggerated talk; nonsense [c20 from Irish Gaelic *ráiméis*]

raw material *n* **1** material on which a particular manufacturing process is carried out **2** a person or thing regarded as suitable for some particular purpose: *raw material for the army*

raw milk *n* unpasteurized milk

raw silk *n* **1** untreated silk fibres reeled from the cocoon **2** fabric woven from such fibres

rax (ræks) *Scot* ⊳ *vb* **1** (*tr*) to stretch or extend **2** (*intr*) to reach out **3** (*tr*) to pass or give (something to a person) with the outstretched hand; reach: *rax me the salt* **4** (*tr*) to strain or sprain ⊳ *n* **5** the act of stretching or straining [Old English *raxan*]

ray[1] (reɪ) *n* **1** a narrow beam of light; gleam **2** a slight indication, esp of something anticipated or hoped for: *a ray of solace* **3** *maths* a straight line extending from a point **4** a thin beam of electromagnetic radiation or particles **5** any of the bony or cartilaginous spines of the fin of a fish that form the support for the soft part of the fin **6** any of the arms or branches of a starfish or other radiate animal **7** *astronomy* any of a number of bright streaks that radiate from the youngest lunar craters, such as Tycho; they are composed of crater ejecta not yet darkened, and extend considerable distances **8** *botany* any strand of tissue that runs radially through the vascular tissue of some higher plants. See **medullary ray** ⊳ *vb* **9** (of an object) to emit (light) in rays or (of light) to issue in the form of rays **10** (*intr*) (of lines, etc) to extend in rays or on radiating paths **11** (*tr*) to adorn (an ornament, etc) with rays or radiating lines [c14 from Old French *rai*, from Latin *radius* spoke, RADIUS]

ray[2] (reɪ) *n* any of various marine selachian fishes typically having a flattened body, greatly enlarged winglike pectoral fins, gills on the undersurface of the fins, and a long whiplike tail. They constitute the orders *Torpediniformes* (**electric rays**) and *Rajiformes* [c14 from Old French *raie*, from Latin *raia*]

ray[3] (reɪ) *n music* (in tonic sol-fa) the second degree of any major scale; supertonic [c14 see GAMUT]

Ray (reɪ) *n* **Cape** a promontory in SW Newfoundland, Canada

rayah (ˈrɑːjə, ˈraɪə) *n* (formerly) a non-Muslim subject of the Ottoman Empire. Also (less common): **raia** [c19 from Turkish *raiyya*, from Arabic *ra'iyah* herd, flock]

Raybans (ˈreɪˌbænz) *pl n trademark* a brand of sunglasses

ray floret *or* **flower** *n* any of the small strap-shaped flowers in the flower head of certain composite plants, such as the daisy. Compare **disc floret**

ray gun *n* (in science fiction) a gun that emits rays to paralyse, stun, or destroy

Rayleigh disc (ˈreɪlɪ) *n* a small light disc suspended in the path of a sound wave, used to measure the intensity of the sound by analysing the resulting deflection of the disc [named after John William Strutt (1842–1919), Lord *Rayleigh*, British physicist]

Rayleigh scattering *n* a process in which electromagnetic radiation is elastically deflected by particles of matter, without a change of frequency but with a phase change

rayless (ˈreɪlɪs) *adj* **1** dark; gloomy **2** lacking rays: *a rayless flower* > **ˈraylessly** *adv* > **ˈraylessness** *n*

raylet (ˈreɪlɪt) *n* a small ray

Raynaud's disease (ˈreɪnəʊz) *n* a disease, mainly affecting women, in which spasms in the blood vessels of the fingers or toes restrict blood flow to the affected part, which becomes pale, numb, and sometimes painful. Often shortened to: **Raynaud's** [named after Maurice *Raynaud* (1834–81), French physician who first described it]

rayon (ˈreɪɒn) *n* **1** any of a number of textile fibres made from wood pulp or other forms of cellulose **2** any fabric made from such a fibre **3** (*modifier*) consisting of or involving rayon: *a rayon shirt* [c20 from French, from Old French *rai* RAY[1]]

raze *or* **rase** (reɪz) *vb* (*tr*) **1** to demolish (a town, buildings, etc) completely; level (esp in the phrase **raze to the ground**) **2** to delete; erase **3** *archaic* to graze [c16 from Old French *raser* from Latin *rādere* to scrape] > **ˈrazer** *or* **ˈraser** *n*

razee (ˈræziː) *history* ⊳ *n, pl* **razees 1** a sailing ship that has had its upper deck or decks removed ⊳ *vb* **razees, razeeing, razeed** (*tr*) **2** to remove the upper deck or decks of (a sailing ship) [c19 from French *rasée* shaved close, from *raser* to RAZE]

razoo (rəˈzuː) *n Austral and NZ informal* an imaginary coin: *not a brass razoo; they took every last razoo* [c20 of uncertain origin]

razor (ˈreɪzə) *n* **1** a sharp implement used esp by men for shaving the face **2 on a razor's edge** *or* **razor-edge** in an acute dilemma ⊳ *vb* **3** (*tr*) to cut or shave with a razor [c13 from Old French *rasour*, from *raser* to shave; see RAZE]

razorbill (ˈreɪzəˌbɪl) *or* **razor-billed auk** *n* a common auk, *Alca torda*, of the North Atlantic, having a thick laterally compressed bill with white markings

razor blade *n* a small rectangular piece of metal sharpened on one or both long edges for use in a razor for shaving

razor-cut *vb* **-cuts, -cutting, -cut 1** (*tr*) to trim or shape (the hair) with a razor ⊳ *n* **razor cut 2** a fluffy hairstyle, usually tapering at the neck, trimmed by a razor

razor-shell *n* any of various sand-burrowing bivalve molluscs of the genera *Ensis* and *Solen*, which have a long tubular shell. US name: **razor clam**

razor wire *n* strong wire with pieces of sharp metal set across it at close intervals, used to make fences or barriers

razz (ræz) *US and Canadian slang* ⊳ *vb* **1** (*tr*) to make fun of; deride ⊳ *n* **2** short for **raspberry** (sense 5)

razzia (ˈræzɪə) *n, pl* **-zias** *history* a raid for plunder or slaves, esp one carried out by Moors in North Africa [c19 from French, from Arabic *ghaziah* war]

Razzie (ˈræzɪ) *n* any of several gold-plated ornamental raspberries awarded annually in the United States by the Golden Raspberry Award Foundation for films or acting performances in films considered to be the worst of the year

razzle (ˈræzəl) *n* **on the razzle** *or* **razz** *Brit informal* out enjoying oneself or celebrating, esp while drinking freely [c20 from RAZZLE-DAZZLE]

razzle-dazzle (ˈræzəlˈdæzəl) *or* **razzmatazz** (ˈræzməˌtæz) *n slang* noisy or showy fuss or activity [c19 rhyming compound based on DAZZLE]

Rb *the chemical symbol for* rubidium

RB *international car registration for* (Republic of) Botswana

RB- *abbreviation for* reconnaissance bomber: *RB-57*

RBE *abbreviation for* relative biological effectiveness (of radiation)

rc *abbreviation for* reinforced concrete

RC *abbreviation for* **1** Red Cross **2** Reserve Corps **3** Also: **R.C.** Roman Catholic **4** ⊳ *international car registration for* (Republic of) China

RCA *abbreviation for* **1** (formerly) Radio Corporation of America **2** Royal Canadian Academy **3** Royal College of Art **4** *international car registration for* Central African Republic

RCAF *abbreviation for* Royal Canadian Air Force

RCB(CG) *international car registration for* (Republic of) Congo-Brazzaville

rcd *abbreviation for* received

RCD *abbreviation for* **residual current device**

RCH *international car registration for* (Republic of) Chile

RCL *abbreviation for* Royal Canadian Legion

RCM *abbreviation for* Royal College of Music

RCMP *abbreviation for* Royal Canadian Mounted Police

RCN *abbreviation for* **1** Royal Canadian Navy **2** Royal College of Nursing

RCO *abbreviation for* Royal College of Organists

r-colour *or* **r-colouring** *n phonetics* an (r) quality imparted to certain vowels, usually by retroflexion > **ˈr-ˌcoloured** *adj*

RCP *abbreviation for* Royal College of Physicians

rcpt *abbreviation for* receipt

RCS *abbreviation for* **1** Royal College of Science **2** Royal College of Surgeons

rct *military abbreviation for* recruit

RCT *abbreviation for* Royal Corps of Transport

RCVS *abbreviation for* Royal College of Veterinary Surgeons

rd *abbreviation for* **1** rendered **2** rod (unit of length) **3** road **4** round **5** *physics* rutherford

rd *or* **RD** (on a cheque) *abbreviation for* refer to drawer

Rd *abbreviation for* Road

RD (in New Zealand) *abbreviation for* Rural Delivery

RDA *abbreviation for* **1** Recommended Daily *or* Dietary Amount *or* Allowance **2** (in England) Regional Development Agency

RDC (formerly, in Britain) *abbreviation for* Rural District Council

RDS *abbreviation for* radio data system: a system in which digital signals are transmitted with normal radio programme to effect automatic tuning of receivers and other functions

RDX *abbreviation for* Research Department Explosive; another name for **cyclonite**

re[1] (reɪ, riː) *n music* a variant spelling of **ray**[3]

re[2] (riː) *prep* with reference to [c18 from Latin *rē*, ablative case of *rēs* thing]

> **USAGE** *Re*, in contexts such as *re your letter, your remarks have been noted* or *he spoke to me re your complaint*, is common in business or official correspondence. In general English *with reference to* is preferable in the former case and *about* or *concerning* in the latter. Even in business correspondence, the use of *re* is often restricted to the letter heading

re[3] *the internet domain name for* Reunion Island

Re[1] (reɪ) *n* another name for **Ra**[2]

Re[2] *the chemical symbol for* rhenium

Re[3] *or* **re** *symbol for* rupee

RE *abbreviation for* **1** Reformed Episcopal **2** Religious Education **3** Right Excellent **4** Royal Engineers

re- *prefix* **1** indicating return to a previous condition, restoration, withdrawal, etc: *rebuild; renew; retrace; reunite* **2** indicating repetition of an action: *recopy; remarry* [from Latin]

> **USAGE** Verbs beginning with *re-* indicate repetition or restoration. It is unnecessary to add an adverb such as *back* or *again*: *This must not occur again* (not *recur again*); *we recounted the votes* (not *recounted the votes again*, which implies that the votes were counted three times, not twice)

're *contraction of* are: *we're; you're; they're*

reach (riːtʃ) *vb* **1** (*tr*) to arrive at or get to (a place, person, etc) in the course of movement or action: *to reach the office* **2** to extend as far as (a point or place): *to reach the ceiling; can you reach?* **3** (*tr*) to come to (a certain condition, stage, or situation): *to reach the point of starvation* **4** (*intr*) to extend in influence or operation: *the Roman conquest reached throughout England* **5** (*tr*) *informal* to pass or give (something to a person) with the outstretched hand: *to reach someone a book* **6** (*intr*; foll by *out, for,* or *after*) to make a movement (towards) as if to grasp or touch: *to reach for something on a shelf* **7** (*intr*; foll by *for* or *after*) to strive or yearn: *to reach for the impossible* **8** (*tr*) to make contact or communication with (someone): *we tried to reach him all day* **9** (*tr*) to strike, esp in fencing or boxing **10** (*tr*) to amount to (a certain sum): *to reach the five million mark* **11** (*intr*) *nautical* to sail on a tack with the wind on or near abeam ▷ *n* **12** the act of reaching **13** the extent or distance of reaching: *within reach of safety; beyond her reach* **14** the range of influence, power, jurisdiction, etc **15** an open stretch of water, esp on a river **16** *nautical* the direction or distance sailed by a vessel on one tack **17** a bar on the rear axle of a vehicle connecting it with some part at the front end **18** *television, radio* the percentage of the population selecting a broadcast programme or channel for more than a specified time during a day or week **19** *marketing* the proportion of a market that an advertiser hopes to reach at least once in a campaign [Old English *rǣcan*; related to Old Frisian *rēka*, Old High German *reihhen*] > **'reachable** *adj* > **'reacher** *n*

reach-me-down *n informal* **1 a** (*often plural*) a garment that is cheaply ready-made or second-hand **b** (*as modifier*): *reach-me-down finery* **2** (*plural*) trousers **3** (*modifier*) not original; derivative; stale

reacquire (ˌriːəˈkwaɪə) *vb* (*tr*) to get or gain (something) again which one has owned

react (rɪˈækt) *vb* **1** (*intr*; *foll by to, upon etc*) (of a person or thing) to act in response to another person, a stimulus, etc or (of two people or things) to act together in a certain way **2** (*intr*; *foll by against*) to act in an opposing or contrary manner **3** (*intr*) *physics* to exert an equal force in the opposite direction to an acting force **4** *chem* to undergo or cause to undergo a chemical reaction [C17 from Late Latin *reagere*, from RE- + Latin *agere* to drive, do]

re-act (riːˈækt) *vb* (*tr*) to act or perform again

reactance (rɪˈæktəns) *n* **1** the opposition to the flow of alternating current by the capacitance or inductance of an electrical circuit; the imaginary part of the impedance *Z*, $Z = R + iX$, where R is the resistance, $i = \sqrt{-1}$, and *X* is the reactance. It is expressed in ohms. Compare **resistance** (sense 3) **2** the opposition to the flow of an acoustic or mechanical vibration, usually due to inertia or stiffness. It is the magnitude of the imaginary part of the acoustic or mechanical impedance

reactant (rɪˈæktənt) *n* a substance that participates in a chemical reaction, esp a substance that is present at the start of the reaction. Compare **product** (sense 4)

reaction (rɪˈækʃən) *n* **1** a response to some foregoing action or stimulus **2** the reciprocal action of two things acting together **3** opposition to change, esp political change, or a desire to return to a former condition or system **4** a response indicating a person's feelings or emotional attitude **5** *med* **a** any effect produced by the action of a drug, esp an adverse effect. Compare **side effect** **b** any effect produced by a substance (allergen) to which a person is allergic the simultaneous equal and opposite force that acts on a body whenever it exerts a force on another body **7** short for **chemical reaction** or **nuclear reaction** **8** *stock exchange* a sharp fall in price interrupting a general rise > **re'actional** *adj*

> USAGE *Reaction* is used to refer both to an instant response (*her reaction was one of amazement*) and to a considered response in the form of a statement (*the Minister gave his reaction to the court's decision*). Some people think this second use is incorrect

reactionary (rɪˈækʃənərɪ, -ʃənrɪ) *or* **reactionist** *adj* **1** of, relating to, or characterized by reaction, esp against radical political or social change ▷ *n*, *pl* **-aries** *or* **-ists** **2** a person opposed to radical change > **re'actionism** *n*

reaction chamber *n engineering* the chamber in a rocket engine in which the reaction or combustion of fuel occurs

reaction engine *or* **motor** *n* an engine, such as a jet or rocket engine, that ejects gas at high velocity and develops its thrust from the ensuing reaction

reaction formation *n psychoanal* a defence mechanism by which a person at a conscious level condemns a repressed wish: thus, a latent homosexual may denounce homosexuality

reaction time *n physiol* another name for **latent time**

reaction turbine *n* a turbine in which the working fluid is accelerated by expansion in both the static nozzles and the rotor blades. Torque is produced by the momentum changes in the rotor and by reaction from fluid accelerating out of the rotor. Compare **impulse turbine**

reactivate (rɪˈæktɪˌveɪt) *vb* (*tr*) to make (something) active or functional again > **reˌactiˈvation** *n*

reactive (rɪˈæktɪv) *adj* **1** readily partaking in chemical reactions: *sodium is a reactive metal; free radicals are very reactive* **2** of, concerned with, or having a reactance **3** responsive to stimulus **4** (of mental illnesses) precipitated by an external cause: *reactive depression* > **re'actively** *adv* > **reactivity** (ˌriːækˈtɪvɪtɪ) *or* **re'activeness** *n*

reactor (rɪˈæktə) *n* **1** *chem* a substance, such as a reagent, that undergoes a reaction **2** short for **nuclear reactor** **3** a vessel, esp one in industrial use, in which a chemical reaction takes place **4** a coil of low resistance and high inductance that introduces reactance into a circuit **5** *med* a person sensitive to a particular drug or agent

read[1] (riːd) *vb* **reads, reading, read** (rɛd) **1** to comprehend the meaning of (something written or printed) by looking at and interpreting the written or printed characters **2** to be occupied in such an activity: *he was reading all day* **3** (when *tr*, often *foll by out*) to look at, interpret, and speak aloud (something written or printed): *he read to us from the Bible* **4** (*tr*) to interpret the significance or meaning of through scrutiny and recognition: *he read the sky and predicted rain; to read a map* **5** (*tr*) to interpret or understand the meaning of (signs, characters, etc) other than by visual means: *to read Braille* **6** (*tr*) to have sufficient knowledge of (a language) to understand the written or printed word: *do you read German?* **7** (*tr*) to discover or make out the true nature or mood of: *to read someone's mind* **8** to interpret or understand (something read) in a specified way, or (of something read) to convey a particular meaning or impression: *I read this speech as satire; this book reads well* **9** (*tr*) to adopt as a reading in a particular passage: *for "boon" read "bone"* **10** (*intr*) to have or contain a certain form or wording: *the sentence reads as follows* **11** to undertake a course of study in (a subject): *to read history; read for the bar* **12** to gain knowledge by reading: *he read about the war* **13** (*tr*) to register, indicate, or show: *the meter reads 100* **14** (*tr*) to bring or put into a specified condition by reading: *to read a child to sleep* **15** (*tr*) to hear and understand, esp when using a two-way radio: *we are reading you loud and clear* **16** *computing* to obtain (data) from a storage device, such as magnetic tape. Compare **write** (sense 16) **17** (*tr*) to understand (written or printed music) by interpretation of the notes on the staff and to be able to reproduce the musical sounds represented by these notes **18 read a lesson** *or* **lecture** *informal* to censure or reprimand, esp in a long-winded manner **19 read between the lines** to perceive or deduce a meaning that is hidden or implied rather than being openly stated **20 you wouldn't read about it** *Austral informal* an expression of dismay, disgust, or disbelief ▷ *n* **21** matter suitable for reading: *this new book is a very good read* **22** the act of reading ▷ See also **read in, read into, read out, read up** [Old English *rǣdan* to advise, explain; related to Old Frisian *rēda*, Old High German *rātan*, Gothic *garēdan*]

read[2] (rɛd) *vb* **1** the past tense and past participle of **read**[1] ▷ *adj* **2** having knowledge gained from books (esp in the phrases **widely read, well-read**) **3 take (something) as read** to take (something) for granted as a fact; understand or presume

readable (ˈriːdəbᵊl) *adj* **1** (of handwriting, etc) able to be read or deciphered; legible **2** (of style of writing) interesting, easy, or pleasant to read > **ˌreada'bility** *or* **'readableness** *n* > **'readably** *adv*

readdress (ˌriːəˈdrɛs) *vb* (*tr*) **1** to look at or discuss (an issue, situation, etc) from a new or different point of view **2** to put a forwarding address onto (a letter received)

reader (ˈriːdə) *n* **1** a person who reads **2** a person who is fond of reading **3 a** *chiefly Brit* at a university, a member of staff having a position between that of a senior lecturer and a professor **b** *US* a teaching assistant in a faculty who grades papers, examinations, etc, on behalf of a professor **4 a** a book that is part of a planned series for those learning to read **b** a standard textbook, esp for foreign-language learning **5** a person who reads aloud in public **6** a person who reads and assesses the merit of manuscripts submitted to a publisher **7** a person employed to read proofs and indicate errors by comparison with the original copy; proofreader **8** short for **lay reader** **9** *Judaism, chiefly Brit* another word for **cantor** (sense 1)

readership (ˈriːdəʃɪp) *n* **1** all the readers collectively of a particular publication or author: *a readership of five million; Dickens's readership* **2** *chiefly Brit* the office, position, or rank of university reader

readies (ˈrɛdɪz) *pl n informal* a variant of **ready** (sense 8): see **ready money**

readily (ˈrɛdɪlɪ) *adv* **1** promptly; eagerly; willingly **2** without difficulty or delay; easily or quickly

read in (riːd) *vb* (*adverb*) **1** to read (data) into a computer memory or storage device **2 read oneself in** *Church of England* to assume possession of a benefice by publicly reading the Thirty-nine Articles

readiness (ˈrɛdɪnɪs) *n* **1** the state of being ready or prepared, as for use or action **2 in readiness a** prepared and waiting: *all was in readiness for the guests' arrival* **b** in preparation for: *he tidied the house in readiness for the guests' arrival* **3** willingness or eagerness to do something **4** ease or promptness

reading (ˈriːdɪŋ) *n* **1 a** the act of a person who reads **b** (*as modifier*): *a reading room; a reading lamp* **2 a** ability to read **b** (*as modifier*): *the reading public; a child of reading age* **3** any matter that can be read; written or printed text **4** a public recital or rendering of a literary work **5** the form of a particular word or passage in a given text, esp where more than one version exists **6** an interpretation, as of a piece of music, a situation, or something said or written **7** knowledge gained from books: *a person of little reading* **8** a measurement indicated by a gauge, dial, scientific instrument, etc **9** *parliamentary procedure* **a** the formal recital of the body or title of a bill in a legislative assembly in order to begin one of the stages of its passage **b** one of the three stages in the passage of a bill through a legislative assembly. See **first reading, second reading, third reading** **10** the formal recital of something written, esp a will

Reading (ˈrɛdɪŋ) *n* **1** a town in S England, in Reading unitary authority, Berkshire, on the River Thames: university (1892). Pop: 232 662 (2001) **2** a unitary authority in S England, in Berkshire. Pop: 144 100 (2003 est). Area: 37 sq km (14 sq miles)

reading group *n* a group of people who meet regularly to discuss a book that they have all read

read into (riːd) *vb* (*tr, preposition*) to discern in or infer from a statement (meanings not intended by the speaker or writer)

readjust (ˌriːəˈdʒʌst) *vb* to adjust or adapt (oneself or something) again, esp after an initial failure > **ˌread'justable** *adj* > **ˌread'juster** *n* > **ˌread'justment** *n*

readmission (ˌriːədˈmɪʃən) *n* the act or an instance of readmitting or being readmitted

readmit (ˌriːədˈmɪt) *vb* **-mits, -mitting, -mitted** (*tr*) to allow (someone) to enter or be admitted again

read only memory *n* See **ROM**

read out (riːd) *vb* (*adverb*) **1** (*tr*) to read

r

(something) aloud **2** to retrieve information from a computer memory or storage device **3** *(tr) US and Canadian* to expel (someone) from a political party or other society ▷ *n* **read-out 4 a** the act of retrieving information from a computer memory or storage device **b** the information retrieved

read up (riːd) *vb (adverb; when intr, often foll by on)* to acquire information about (a subject) by reading intensively

read-write head (ˈriːdˈraɪt) *n computing* an electromagnet that can both read and write information on a magnetic medium such as magnetic tape or disk

ready (ˈrɛdɪ) *adj* **readier, readiest 1** in a state of completion or preparedness, as for use or action **2** willing or eager: *ready helpers* **3** prompt or rapid: *a ready response* **4** *(prenominal)* quick in perceiving; intelligent: *a ready mind* **5** *(postpositive; foll by to)* on the point (of) or liable (to): *ready to collapse* **6** *(postpositive)* conveniently near (esp in the phrase **ready to hand**) **7 make** *or* **get ready** to prepare (oneself or something) for use or action ▷ *n* **8** *informal* (often preceded by *the*) short for **ready money 9 at** *or* **to the ready a** poised for use or action: *with pen at the ready* **b** (of a rifle) in the position normally adopted immediately prior to aiming and firing ▷ *vb* **10** *(tr)* to put in a state of readiness; prepare [Old English *(ge)rǣde*; related to Old Frisian *rēde*, Old High German *reiti*, Old Norse *reithr* ready]

ready-made *adj* **1** made for purchase and immediate use by any customer: *a ready-made jacket* **2** extremely convenient or ideally suited: *a ready-made solution* **3** unoriginal or conventional: *ready-made phrases* ▷ *n* **4** a ready-made article, esp a garment

ready-mix *n* **1** *(modifier)* consisting of ingredients blended in advance, esp of food that is ready to cook or eat after addition of milk or water: *a ready-mix cake* **2** concrete that is mixed before or during delivery to a building site

ready money *or* **cash** *n* funds for immediate use; cash. Also called: **the ready, the readies**

ready reckoner *n* a table of numbers used to facilitate simple calculations, esp one for applying rates of discount, interest, charging, etc to different sums

ready-to-wear *adj* (**ready to wear** *when postpositive*) **1** (of clothes) not tailored for the wearer; of a standard size ▷ *n* **2** an article or suit of such clothes

ready-witted *adj* quick to learn or perceive

reaffirm (ˌriːəˈfɜːm) *vb (tr)* to affirm (a claim, etc) again; reassert > ˌ**reaffirˈmation** *n*

reafforest (ˌriːəˈfɒrɪst) *or* **reforest** *vb (tr)* to replant (an area that was formerly forested) > ˌ**reafˌforestˈation** *or* ˌ**reforestˈation** *n*

reagent (riːˈeɪdʒənt) *n* a substance for use in a chemical reaction, esp for use in chemical synthesis and analysis

reagin (ˈriədʒɪn) *n immunol* a type of antibody that is formed against an allergen and is attached to the cells of a tissue. The antigen–antibody reaction that occurs on subsequent contact with the allergen causes tissue damage, leading to the release of histamine and other substances responsible for an allergic reaction [c20 from German *reagieren* to react + -IN]

real[1] (ˈrɪəl) *adj* **1** existing or occurring in the physical world; not imaginary, fictitious, or theoretical; actual **2** *(prenominal)* true; actual; not false: *the real reason* **3** *(prenominal)* deserving the name; rightly so called: *a real friend; a real woman* **4** not artificial or simulated; genuine: *real sympathy; real fur* **5** (of food, etc) traditionally made and having a distinct flavour: *real ale; real cheese* **6** *philosophy* existent or relating to actual existence (as opposed to nonexistent, potential, contingent, or apparent) **7** *(prenominal) economics* (of prices, incomes, wages, etc) considered in terms of purchasing power rather than nominal currency value **8** *(prenominal)* denoting or relating to immovable property such as land and tenements: *real property*. Compare **personal 9** *physics* See **image** (sense 2) **10** *maths* involving or containing real numbers alone; having no imaginary part **11** *music* **a** (of the answer in a fugue) preserving the intervals as they appear in the subject **b** denoting a fugue as having such an answer. Compare **tonal** (sense 3) **12** *informal* (intensifier): *a real fool; a real genius* **13 the real thing** the genuine article, not an inferior or mistaken substitute ▷ *n* **14** short for **real number 15 the real** that which exists in fact; reality **16 for real** *slang* not as a test or trial; in earnest [c15 from Old French *réel*, from Late Latin *reālis*, from Latin *rēs* thing] > ˈ**realness** *n*

real[2] (reɪˈɑːl; *Spanish* reˈal) *n, pl* **reals** *or* **reales** (*Spanish* reˈales) a former small Spanish or Spanish-American silver coin [c17 from Spanish, literally: royal, from Latin *rēgālis*; see REGAL[1]]

real[3] (*Portuguese* reˈal) *n, pl* **reis** (rəjʃ) **1** the standard monetary unit of Brazil, divided into 100 centavos **2** a former coin of Portugal [ultimately from Latin *rēgālis* REGAL[1]]

real ale *or* **beer** *n* any beer which is allowed to ferment in the cask and which when served is pumped up without using carbon dioxide

real estate *n* another term for **real property**

realgar (rɪˈælɡə) *n* a rare orange-red soft mineral consisting of arsenic sulphide in monoclinic crystalline form. It occurs in Utah and Romania and as a deposit from hot springs. It is an important ore of arsenic and is also used as a pigment. Formula: AsS [c14 via Medieval Latin from Arabic *rahj al-ghar* powder of the mine]

realia (rɪˈeɪlɪə) *pl n* real-life facts and material used in teaching [c20 from neuter pl of Late Latin *reālis*; see REAL[1]]

realign (ˌriːəˈlaɪn) *vb (tr)* to change or put back to a new or former place or position

realignment (ˌriːəˈlaɪnmənt) *n* the act or instance of restoring or changing to a previous or different position

realism (ˈrɪəˌlɪzəm) *n* **1** awareness or acceptance of the physical universe, events, etc, as they are, as opposed to the abstract or ideal **2** awareness or acceptance of the facts and necessities of life; a practical rather than a moral or dogmatic view of things **3** a style of painting and sculpture that seeks to represent the familiar or typical in real life, rather than an idealized, formalized, or romantic interpretation of it **4** any similar school or style in other arts, esp literature **5** *philosophy* the thesis that general terms such as common nouns refer to entities that have a real existence separate from the individuals which fall under them. See also **universal** (sense 11b) Compare **Platonism, nominalism, conceptualism, naive realism 6** *philosophy* the theory that physical objects continue to exist whether they are perceived or not. Compare **idealism, phenomenalism 7** *logic, philosophy* the theory that the sense of a statement is given by a specification of its truth conditions, or that there is a reality independent of the speaker's conception of it that determines the truth or falsehood of every statement

realist (ˈrɪəlɪst) *n* **1** a person who is aware of and accepts the physical universe, events, etc, as they are; pragmatist **2** an artist or writer who seeks to represent the familiar or typical in real life rather than an idealized, formalized, or romantic interpretation **3** *philosophy* a person who accepts realism **4** *(modifier)* of, relating to, or characteristic of realism or realists in the arts, philosophy, etc: *a realist school*

realistic (ˌrɪəˈlɪstɪk) *adj* **1** showing awareness and acceptance of reality **2** practical or pragmatic rather than ideal or moral **3** (of a book, film, etc) depicting or emphasizing what is real and actual rather than abstract or ideal **4** of or relating to philosophical realism > ˌ**realˈistically** *adv*

reality (rɪˈælɪtɪ) *n, pl* **-ties 1** the state of things as they are or appear to be, rather than as one might wish them to be **2** something that is real **3** the state of being real **4** *philosophy* **a** that which exists, independent of human awareness **b** the totality of facts as they are independent of human awareness of them. See also **conceptualism** Compare **appearance** (sense 6) **5 in reality** actually; in fact

reality check *n* an occasion or opportunity to consider a matter realistically or honestly

reality fiction *n* a satirical parody of a reality TV show

reality principle *n psychoanal* control of behaviour by the ego to meet the conditions imposed by the external world

reality show *n* a television show in which members of the public or celebrities are filmed living their everyday lives or undertaking specific challenges

reality TV *n* television programmes focusing on members of the public living in conditions created especially by the programme makers

realize *or* **realise** (ˈrɪəˌlaɪz) *vb* **1** (*when tr, may take a clause as object*) to become conscious or aware of (something) **2** *(tr, often passive)* to bring (a plan, ambition, etc) to fruition; make actual or concrete **3** *(tr)* to give (something, such as a drama or film) the appearance of reality **4** *(tr)* (of goods, property, etc) to sell for or make (a certain sum): *this table realized £800* **5** *(tr)* to convert (property or goods) into cash **6** *(tr)* (of a musicologist or performer) **a** to expand or complete (a thorough-bass part in a piece of baroque music) by supplying the harmonies indicated in the figured bass **b** to reconstruct (a composition) from an incomplete set of parts **7** to sound or utter (a phoneme or other speech sound) in actual speech; articulate > ˈ**realˌizable** *or* ˈ**realˌisable** *adj* > ˈ**realˌizably** *or* ˈ**realˌisably** *adv* > ˌ**realiˈzation** *or* ˌ**realiˈsation** *n* > ˈ**realˌizer** *or* ˈ**realˌiser** *n*

real life *n* **a** actual human life, as lived by real people, esp contrasted with the lives of fictional or fantasy characters: *miracles don't happen in real life* **b** *(as modifier)*: *a real-life mystery*

reallocate (riːˈæləkeɪt) *vb (tr)* to assign or allot to a different purpose or person from the one originally intended > ˌ**realloˈcation** *n*

really (ˈrɪəlɪ) *adv* **1** in reality; in actuality; assuredly: *it's really quite harmless* **2** truly; genuinely: *really beautiful* ▷ *interj* **3** an exclamation of dismay, disapproval, doubt, surprise, etc **4 not really?** an exclamation of surprise or polite doubt

USAGE See at **very**

realm (rɛlm) *n* **1** a royal domain; kingdom (now chiefly in such phrases as **Peer of the Realm**) **2** a field of interest, study, etc: *the realm of the occult* [c13 from Old French *reialme*, from Latin *regimen* rule, influenced by Old French *reial* royal, from Latin *rēgālis* REGAL[1]]

real number *n* a number expressible as a limit of rational numbers. See **number** (sense 1)

real part *n* the term *a* in a complex number $a + ib$, where $i = \sqrt{-1}$

realpolitik (reɪˈɑːlpɒlɪˈtiːk) *n* a ruthlessly realistic and opportunist approach to statesmanship, rather than a moralistic one, esp as exemplified by Bismarck [c19 German: politics of realism]

real presence *n* the doctrine that the body of Christ is actually present in the Eucharist

real property *n* immovable property, esp land and buildings, including proprietary rights over land, such as mineral rights. Compare **personal property** Also called: **real estate**

real tennis *n* an ancient form of tennis played in a four-walled indoor court with various openings, a sloping-roofed corridor along three sides, and a buttress on the fourth side. Also called: **royal tennis**

real-time *adj* denoting or relating to a data-processing system in which a computer receives constantly changing data, such as information relating to air-traffic control, travel booking systems, etc, and processes it sufficiently rapidly to be able to control the source of the data

realtor ('rɪəltə, -ˌtɔː) *n* a US and Canadian word for an **estate agent**, esp an accredited one [c20 from a trademark]

realty ('rɪəltɪ) *n* another term for **real property**

real wages *pl n economics* wages evaluated with reference to their purchasing power rather than to the money actually paid. Compare **money wages**

ream¹ (riːm) *n* **1** a number of sheets of paper, formerly 480 sheets (**short ream**), now 500 sheets (**long ream**) or 516 sheets (**printer's ream** or **perfect ream**). One ream is equal to 20 quires **2** (*often plural*) *informal* a large quantity, esp of written matter: *he wrote reams* [c14 from Old French *raime*, from Spanish *rezma*, from Arabic *rizmah* bale]

ream² (riːm) *vb* (*tr*) **1** to enlarge (a hole) by use of a reamer **2** *US* to extract (juice) from (a citrus fruit) using a reamer [c19 perhaps from C14 *remen* to open up, from Old English *rȳman* to widen]

reamer ('riːmə) *n* **1** a steel tool with a cylindrical or tapered shank around which longitudinal teeth are ground, used for smoothing the bores of holes accurately to size **2** *US* a utensil with a conical projection used for extracting juice from citrus fruits; lemon squeezer

rean (riːn) *n* a variant spelling of **reen**

reanalysis (ˌriːə'næləsɪs) *n* the act or an instance of analysing again

reanimate (riː'ænɪmeɪt) *vb* (*tr*) **1** to refresh or enliven (something) again: *to reanimate their enervated lives* **2** to bring back to life

reap (riːp) *vb* **1** to cut or harvest (a crop), esp corn, from (a field or tract of land) **2** (*tr*) to gain or get (something) as a reward for or result of some action or enterprise [Old English *riopan*; related to Norwegian *ripa* to scratch, Middle Low German *repen* to card, ripple (flax)] > **'reapable** *adj*

reaper ('riːpə) *n* **1** a person who reaps or a machine for reaping **2** **the grim reaper** death

reappear (ˌriːə'pɪə) *vb* to appear again > ˌreap'pearance *n*

reapply (ˌriːə'plaɪ) *vb* -plies, -plying, -plied **1** (*tr*) to put or spread (something) on again: *reapply sunscreen frequently* **2** (*intr*; often foll by *for*) to put in an application or request again

reappoint (ˌriːə'pɔɪnt) *vb* (*tr*) to assign (a person, committee, etc) to a post or role again > ˌreap'pointment *n*

reappraisal (ˌriːə'preɪzəl) *n* the assessment or estimation again of the worth, value, or quality of a person or thing

reappraise (ˌriːə'preɪz) *vb* (*tr*) to assess the worth, value, or quality of (someone or something) again

rear¹ (rɪə) *n* **1** the back or hind part **2** the area or position that lies at the back: *a garden at the rear of the house* **3** the section of a military force or procession farthest from the front **4** an informal word for **buttocks** (see **buttock**) **5** **bring up the rear** to be at the back in a procession, race, etc **6** **in the rear** at the back **7** (*modifier*) of or in the rear: *the rear legs; the rear side* [c17 probably abstracted from REARWARD or REARGUARD]

rear² (rɪə) *vb* **1** (*tr*) to care for and educate (children) until maturity; bring up; raise **2** (*tr*) to breed (animals) or grow (plants) **3** (*tr*) to place or lift (a ladder, etc) upright **4** (*tr*) to erect (a monument, building, etc); put up **5** (*intr*; often foll by *up*) (esp of horses) to lift the front legs in the air and stand nearly upright **6** (*intr*; often foll by *up* or *over*) (esp of tall buildings) to rise high; tower **7** (*intr*) to start with anger, resentment, etc [Old English *rēran*; related to Old High German *rēren* to distribute, Old Norse *reisa* to RAISE] > **'rearer** *n*

rear admiral *n* an officer holding flag rank in any of certain navies, junior to a vice admiral

rearguard ('rɪəˌɡɑːd) *n* **1** a detachment detailed to protect the rear of a military formation, esp in retreat **2** an entrenched or conservative element, as in a political party **3** **rearguard action a** an action fought by a rearguard **b** a defensive action

undertaken to try to stop something happening or continuing [c15 from Old French *rereguarde* (modern French *arrière-garde*), from *rer*, from Latin *retro* back + *guarde* GUARD; compare VANGUARD]

rear light *or* **lamp** *n* a red light, usually one of a pair, attached to the rear of a motor vehicle. Also called: **tail-light, tail lamp**

rearm (riː'ɑːm) *vb* **1** to arm again **2** (*tr*) to equip (an army, a nation, etc) with better weapons > re'armament *n*

rearmost ('rɪəˌməʊst) *adj* nearest the rear; coming last

rearmouse ('rɪəˌmaʊs) *n, pl* -mice an archaic or dialect word for **bat** (the animal) [See REREMOUSE]

rearrange (ˌriːə'reɪndʒ) *vb* (*tr*) **1** to put (something) into a new order: *to rearrange the lighting* **2** to put (something) back in its original order after it has been displaced **3** to fix a new date or time for (something postponed): *to rearrange a match* > ˌrear'ranger *n* > ˌrear'rangement *n*

rear sight *n* the sight of a gun nearest to the breech

rear-view mirror *n* a mirror on a motor vehicle enabling the driver to see traffic coming behind him or her

rearward ('rɪəwəd) *adj, adv* **1** Also (for adverb only): **rearwards** towards or in the rear ▷ *n* **2** a position in the rear, esp the rear division of a military formation [C14 (as a noun: the part of an army positioned behind the main body of troops): from Anglo-French *rerewarde*, variant of *reregarde*; see REARGUARD]

Rea Silvia ('rɪə 'sɪlvɪə) *n* a variant spelling of **Rhea Silvia**

reason ('riːzªn) *n* **1** the faculty of rational argument, deduction, judgment, etc **2** sound mind; sanity **3** a cause or motive, as for a belief, action, etc **4** an argument in favour of or a justification for something **5** *philosophy* the intellect regarded as a source of knowledge, as contrasted with experience **6** *logic* grounds for a belief; a premise of an argument supporting that belief **7** **by reason of** because of **8** **in** *or* **within reason** within moderate or justifiable bounds **9** **it stands to reason** it is logical or obvious: *it stands to reason that he will lose* **10** **listen to reason** to be persuaded peaceably **11** **reasons of State** political justifications for an immoral act ▷ *vb* **12** (when *tr*, takes a clause as object) to think logically or draw (logical conclusions) from facts or premises **13** (*intr*; usually foll by *with*) to urge or seek to persuade by reasoning **14** (*tr*; often foll by *out*) to work out or resolve (a problem) by reasoning [c13 from Old French *reisun*, from Latin *ratiō* reckoning, from *rērī* to think] > **'reasoner** *n*

USAGE The expression *the reason is because...* should be avoided. Instead one should say either *this is because...* or *the reason is that...*

reasonable ('riːzənəbªl) *adj* **1** showing reason or sound judgment **2** having the ability to reason **3** having modest or moderate expectations; not making unfair demands **4** moderate in price; not expensive **5** fair; average: *reasonable weather* > **'reasonably** *adv* > **'reasonableness** *n*

reasoned ('riːzªnd) *adj* well thought-out or well presented: *a reasoned explanation* > **'reasonedly** *adv*

reasoning ('riːzənɪŋ) *n* **1** the act or process of drawing conclusions from facts, evidence, etc **2** the arguments, proofs, etc, so adduced

reassemble (ˌriːə'sɛmbªl) *vb* **1** to come or bring together again: *parliament is due to reassemble* **2** to fit or join (something) together again > ˌreas'sembly *n*

reassert (ˌriːə'sɜːt) *vb* (*tr*) to assert (rights, claims, etc) again: *he reasserted his belief*

reassess (ˌriːə'sɛs) *vb* (*tr*) to assess (something) again; re-evaluate

reassessment (ˌriːə'sɛsmənt) *n* the act or an instance of assessing again

reassign (ˌriːə'saɪn) *vb* (*tr*) to move (personnel,

resources, etc) to a new post, department, location, etc > ˌreas'signment *n*

reassortment (ˌriːə'sɔːtmənt) *n* the formation of a hybrid virus containing parts from the genomes of two distinct viruses in a mixed infection

reassure (ˌriːə'ʃʊə) *vb* (*tr*) **1** to relieve (someone) of anxieties; restore confidence to **2** another term for **reinsure**. > ˌreas'surance *n* > ˌreas'surer *n* > ˌreas'suringly *adv*

reast (riːst) *vb* a variant spelling of **reest**

Réaum. *abbreviation for* Réaumur (scale)

Réaumur ('reɪəˌmjʊə) *adj* indicating measurement on the Réaumur scale of temperature

Réaumur scale *n* a scale of temperature in which the freezing point of water is taken as 0° and the boiling point is 80° [c18 named after René Antoine Ferchault de *Réaumur* (1683–1757), French physicist, who introduced it]

reave¹ (riːv) *vb* reaves, reaving, reaved *or* reft (rɛft) *archaic* **1** to carry off (property, prisoners, etc) by force **2** (*tr*; foll by *of*) to deprive; strip. See also **reive** [Old English *rēafian*; related to Old High German *roubōn* to rob, Old Norse *raufa* to break open]

reave² (riːv) *vb* reaves, reaving, reaved *or* reft (rɛft) *archaic* to break or tear (something) apart; cleave [C13 *reven*, probably from REAVE¹ and influenced in meaning by RIVE]

reawaken (ˌriːə'weɪkən) *vb* **1** to emerge or rouse from sleep **2** to become or make aware of (something) again

reb (rɛb) *n* (*sometimes capital*) *US informal* a Confederate soldier in the American Civil War (1861–65). Also called: Johnny Reb [short for REBEL]

Reb (rɛb) *n Judaism* an honorific title, corresponding to *Mr*, for those who do not have rabbinic qualifications: usually followed by the person's forename: *Reb Dovid* [Yiddish, from Hebrew *rabbī* rabbi, master]

rebadge (riː'bædʒ) *vb* (*tr*) to relaunch (a product) under a new name, brand, or logo

rebarbative (rɪ'bɑːbətɪv) *adj* fearsome; forbidding [c19 from French *rébarbatif*, from Old French *rebarber* to repel (an enemy), to withstand (him) face to face, from RE- + *barbe* beard, from Latin *barba*]

rebate¹ (ˈriːbeɪt) **1** a refund of a fraction of the amount payable or paid, as for goods purchased in quantity; discount ▷ *vb* (rɪ'beɪt) (*tr*) **2** to deduct (a part) of a payment from (the total) **3** *archaic* to reduce or diminish (something or the effectiveness of something) [c15 from Old French *rabatre* to beat down, hence reduce, deduct, from RE- + *abatre* to put down; see ABATE] > re'batable *or* re'bateable *adj* > **'rebater** *n*

rebate² ('riːbeɪt, 'ræbɪt) *n, vb* another word for **rabbet**

rebato (rə'bɑːtəʊ) *n, pl* -tos a variant spelling of **rabato**

Rebbe ('rɛbə) *n Judaism* **1** the usually dynastic leader of a Chassidic sect **2** an individual's chosen spiritual mentor [Yiddish, from Hebrew *rabbī* rabbi]

rebbetzin ('rɛbətsən) *n Judaism* the wife of a rabbi [from Yiddish]

rebec *or* **rebeck** ('riːbɛk) *n* a medieval stringed instrument resembling the violin but having a lute-shaped body [c16 from Old French *rebebe*, from Arabic *rebāb*; perhaps also influenced by Old French *bec* beak]

Rebecca (rɪ'bɛkə) *n Old Testament* the sister of Laban, who became the wife of Isaac and the mother of Esau and Jacob (Genesis 24–27). Douay spelling: Rebekah

rebel *vb* (rɪ'bɛl) -bels, -belling, -belled (*intr*; often foll by *against*) **1** to resist or rise up against a government or other authority, esp by force of arms **2** to dissent from an accepted moral code or convention of behaviour, dress, etc **3** to show repugnance (towards) ▷ *n* ('rɛbªl) **4 a** a person who rebels **b** (*as modifier*): *a rebel soldier; a rebel leader*

r

5 a person who dissents from some accepted moral code or convention of behaviour, dress, etc [C13 from Old French *rebelle*, from Latin *rebellis* insurgent, from RE- + *bellum* war] > ˈ**rebeldom** *n*

rebellion (rɪˈbɛljən) *n* **1** organized resistance or opposition to a government or other authority **2** dissent from an accepted moral code or convention of behaviour, dress, etc [C14 via Old French from Latin *rebelliō* revolt (of those conquered); see REBEL]

rebellious (rɪˈbɛljəs) *adj* **1** showing a tendency towards rebellion **2** (of a problem, etc) difficult to overcome; refractory > **reˈbelliously** *adv* > **reˈbelliousness** *n*

rebellow (rɪˈbɛləʊ) *vb archaic or literary* to re-echo loudly

rebirth (riːˈbɜːθ) *n* **1** a revival or renaissance: *the rebirth of learning* **2** a second or new birth; reincarnation

rebirthing (riːˈbɜːθɪŋ) *n* a form of psychotherapy in which the subject supposedly "relives" the experience of being born, in order to confront and overcome traumas and anxieties stemming from birth

reboot (riːˈbuːt) *vb* to shut down and restart (a computer system) or (of a computer system) to shut down and restart

rebore *n* (ˈriːˌbɔː) **1** the process of boring out the cylinders of a worn reciprocating engine and fitting oversize pistons ▷ *vb* (riːˈbɔː) **2** (*tr*) to carry out this process

reborn (riːˈbɔːn) *adj* born or as if born again, esp in having undergone spiritual regeneration

rebound *vb* (rɪˈbaʊnd) (*tr*) **1** to spring back, as from a sudden impact **2** to misfire, esp so as to hurt the perpetrator: *the plan rebounded* ▷ *n* (ˈriːbaʊnd) **3** the act or an instance of rebounding **4** **on the rebound** **a** in the act of springing back **b** *informal* in a state of recovering from rejection, disappointment, etc: *he married her on the rebound from an unhappy love affair* [C14 from Old French *rebondir*, from RE- + *bondir* to BOUND[2]]

rebozo (rɪˈbəʊzəʊ; *Spanish* reˈβoθo) *n, pl* **-zos** (-zəʊz; *Spanish* -θos) a long wool or linen scarf covering the shoulders and head, worn by Latin American women [C19 from Spanish: shawl, from *rebozar* to muffle]

rebrand (riːˈbrænd) *vb* (*tr*) to change or update the image of (an organization or product)

rebuff (rɪˈbʌf) *vb* (*tr*) **1** to snub, reject, or refuse (a person offering help or sympathy, an offer of help, etc) abruptly or out of hand **2** to beat back (an attack); repel ▷ *n* **3** a blunt refusal or rejection; snub **4** any sudden check to progress or action [C16 from Old French *rebuffer*, from Italian *ribuffare*, from *ribuffo* a reprimand, from *ri-* RE- + *buffo* puff, gust, apparently of imitative origin]

rebuild (riːˈbɪld) *vb* **-builds, -building, -built** **1** to make, construct, or form again: *the cost of rebuilding the house* **2** (*tr*) to restore (a system or situation) to a previous condition: *his struggle to rebuild his life*

rebuke (rɪˈbjuːk) *vb* **1** (*tr*) to scold or reprimand (someone) ▷ *n* **2** a reprimand or scolding [C14 from Old Norman French *rebuker*, from RE- + Old French *buchier* to hack down, from *busche* log, of Germanic origin] > **reˈbukable** *adj* > **reˈbuker** *n*

rebus (ˈriːbəs) *n, pl* **-buses** **1** a puzzle consisting of pictures representing syllables and words; in such a puzzle the word *hear* might be represented by H followed by a picture of an ear **2** a heraldic emblem or device that is a pictorial representation of or pun on the name of the bearer [C17 from French *rébus*, from the Latin *rēbus* by things, from RES]

rebut (rɪˈbʌt) *vb* **-buts, -butting, -butted** (*tr*) to refute or disprove, esp by offering a contrary contention or argument [C13 from Old French *reboter*, from RE- + *boter* to thrust, BUTT[3]] > **reˈbuttable** *adj* > **reˈbuttal** *n*

rebutter (rɪˈbʌtə) *n* **1** *law* a defendant's pleading in reply to a claimant's surrejoinder **2** a person who rebuts

rec (rɛk) *n informal* short for **recreation** (ground)

recalcitrant (rɪˈkælsɪtrənt) *adj* **1** not susceptible to control or authority; refractory ▷ *n* **2** a recalcitrant person [C19 via French from Latin *recalcitrāre*, from RE- + *calcitrāre* to kick, from *calx* heel] > **reˈcalcitrance** *n*

recalculate (riːˈkælkjʊˌleɪt) *vb* (*tr*) to calculate (a total, sum, etc) again

recalesce (ˌriːkəˈlɛs) *vb* (*intr*) to undergo recalescence

recalescence (ˌriːkəˈlɛsəns) *n* a sudden spontaneous increase in the temperature of cooling iron resulting from an exothermic change in crystal structure occurring at a particular temperature [C19 from Latin *recalēscere* to grow warm again, from RE- + *calēscere*, from *calēre* to be hot] > ˌ**recaˈlescent** *adj*

recall (rɪˈkɔːl) *vb* (*tr*) **1** (*may take a clause as object*) to bring back to mind; recollect; remember **2** to order to return; call back permanently or temporarily: *to recall an ambassador* **3** to revoke or take back **4** to cause (one's thoughts, attention, etc) to return from a reverie or digression **5** *poetic* to restore or revive ▷ *n* **6** the act of recalling or state of being recalled **7** revocation or cancellation **8** the ability to remember things; recollection **9** *military* (esp formerly) a signal to call back troops, etc, usually a bugle call: *to sound the recall* **10** *US* the process by which elected officials may be deprived of office by popular vote > **reˈcallable** *adj*

recant (rɪˈkænt) *vb* to repudiate or withdraw (a former belief or statement), esp formally in public [C16 from Latin *recantāre* to sing again, from RE- + *cantāre* to sing; see CHANT] > **recantation** (ˌriːkænˈteɪʃən) *n* > **reˈcanter** *n*

recap *vb* (ˈriːˌkæp, riːˈkæp) **-caps, -capping, -capped,** *n* (ˈriːˌkæp) **1** *informal* short for **recapitulate** *or* **recapitulation** ▷ *n* (ˈriːˌkæp) **2** *Austral and NZ* another name for **retread** > **reˈcappable** *adj*

recapitulate (ˌriːkəˈpɪtjʊˌleɪt) *vb* **1** to restate the main points of (an argument, speech, etc); summarize **2** (*tr*) (of an animal) to repeat (stages of its evolutionary development) during the embryonic stages of its life **3** to repeat at some point during a piece of music (material used earlier in the same work) [C16 from Late Latin *recapitulāre*, literally: to put back under headings; see CAPITULATE] > ˌ**recaˈpitulative** *or* ˌ**recaˈpitulatory** *adj*

recapitulation (ˌriːkəˌpɪtjʊˈleɪʃən) *n* **1** the act of recapitulating, esp summing up, as at the end of a speech **2** Also called: **palingenesis** *biology* the apparent repetition in the embryonic development of an animal of the changes that occurred during its evolutionary history. Compare **caenogenesis** **3** *music* the repeating of earlier themes, esp when forming the final section of a movement in sonata form

recaption (riːˈkæpʃən) *n law* the process of taking back one's own wife, child, property, etc, without causing a breach of the peace [C17 from RE- + CAPTION (in the sense: seizure)]

recapture (riːˈkæptʃə) *vb* (*tr*) **1** to capture or take again **2** to recover, renew, or repeat (a lost or former ability, sensation, etc): *she soon recaptured her high spirits* **3** *US* (of the government) to take lawfully (a proportion of the profits of a public-service undertaking) ▷ *n* **4** the act of recapturing or fact of being recaptured **5** *US* the seizure by the government of a proportion of the profits of a public-service undertaking

recast (riːˈkɑːst) *vb* **-casts, -casting, -cast** (*tr*) **1** (often foll by *as*) to give (someone or something) a new role, function, or character: *recast themselves as moderate and kind* **2** (often foll by *as*) to cast (an actor or actress) again or in a different part **3** to cast new actors or actresses for a production of (a play, film, etc)

recce (ˈrɛkɪ) *n, vb* **-ces, -ceing, -ced** *or* **-ceed** a slang word for **reconnaissance** *or* **reconnoitre**

recd *or* **rec'd** *abbreviation for* received

recede (rɪˈsiːd) *vb* (*intr*) **1** to withdraw from a point or limit; go back: *the tide receded* **2** to become more distant: *hopes of rescue receded* **3** to slope backwards: *apes have receding foreheads* **4** **a** (of a man's hair) to cease to grow at the temples and above the forehead **b** (of a man) to start to go bald in this way **5** to decline in value or character **6** (usually foll by *from*) to draw back or retreat, as from a promise [C15 from Latin *recēdere* to go back, from RE- + *cēdere* to yield, CEDE]

re-cede (riːˈsiːd) *vb* (*tr*) to restore to a former owner

receipt (rɪˈsiːt) *n* **1** a written acknowledgment by a receiver of money, goods, etc, that payment or delivery has been made **2** the act of receiving or fact of being received **3** (*usually plural*) an amount or article received **4** *archaic* another word for **recipe** ▷ *vb* **5** (*tr*) to acknowledge payment of (a bill), as by marking it **6** *chiefly US* to issue a receipt for (money, goods, etc) [C14 from Old Norman French *receite*, from Medieval Latin *recepta*, from Latin *recipere* to RECEIVE]

receiptor (rɪˈsiːtə) *n chiefly US* a person who receipts

receivable (rɪˈsiːvəb(ə)l) *adj* **1** suitable for or capable of being received, esp as payment or legal tender **2** (of a bill, etc) awaiting payment: *accounts receivable* ▷ *n* **3** (*usually plural*) the part of the assets of a business represented by accounts due for payment

receive (rɪˈsiːv) *vb* (*mainly tr*) **1** to take (something offered) into one's hand or possession **2** to have (an honour, blessing, etc) bestowed **3** to accept delivery or transmission of (a letter, telephone call, etc) **4** to be informed of (news or information) **5** to hear and consent to or acknowledge (an oath, confession, etc) **6** (of a vessel or container) to take or hold (a substance, commodity, or certain amount) **7** to support or sustain (the weight of something); bear **8** to apprehend or perceive (ideas, etc) **9** to experience, undergo, or meet with: *to receive a crack on the skull* **10** (*also intr*) to be at home to (visitors) **11** to greet or welcome (visitors or guests), esp in formal style **12** to admit (a person) to a place, society, condition, etc: *he was received into the priesthood* **13** to accept or acknowledge (a precept or principle) as true or valid **14** to convert (incoming radio signals) into sounds, pictures, etc, by means of a receiver **15** (*also intr*) *tennis* to play at the other end from the server; be required to return (service) **16** (*also intr*) to partake of (the Christian Eucharist) **17** (*intr*) *chiefly Brit* to buy and sell stolen goods [C13 from Old French *receivre*, from Latin *recipere* to take back, from RE- + *capere* to take]

received (rɪˈsiːvd) *adj* generally accepted or believed: *received wisdom*

Received Pronunciation *n* the accent of standard Southern British English. Abbreviation: **RP**

receiver (rɪˈsiːvə) *n* **1** a person who receives something; recipient **2** a person appointed by a court to manage property pending the outcome of litigation, during the infancy of the owner, or after the owner(s) has been declared bankrupt or of unsound mind **3** *chiefly Brit* a person who receives stolen goods knowing that they have been stolen **4** the equipment in a telephone, radio, or television that receives incoming electrical signals or modulated radio waves and converts them into the original audio or video signals **5** the part of a telephone containing the earpiece and mouthpiece that is held by the telephone user **6** the equipment in a radar system, radio telescope, etc, that converts incoming radio signals into a useful form, usually displayed on the screen of a cathode-ray oscilloscope **7** an obsolete word for **receptacle** **8** *chem* a vessel in which the distillate is collected during distillation **9** *US sport* a player whose function is to receive the ball, esp a footballer who catches long passes **10** the metallic frame situated behind the breech of a gun to guide the round into the chamber

receivership (rɪ'siːvəʃɪp) *n law* **1** the office or function of a receiver **2** the condition of being administered by a receiver

receiving order *n Brit, obsolete* a court order appointing a receiver to manage the property of a debtor or bankrupt. Official name: **bankruptcy order**

recency effect ('riːsənsɪ) *n psychol* the phenomenon that when people are asked to recall in any order the items on a list, those that come at the end of the list are more likely to be recalled than the others

recension (rɪ'sɛnʃən) *n* **1** a critical revision of a literary work **2** a text revised in this way [C17 from Latin *recēnsiō*, from *recēnsēre* to survey, from RE- + *cēnsēre* to assess]

recent ('riːsᵊnt) *adj* having appeared, happened, or been made not long ago; modern, fresh, or new [C16 from Latin *recens* fresh; related to Greek *kainos* new] > **'recently** *adv* > **'recentness** *or* **'recency** *n*

Recent ('riːsᵊnt) *adj, n geology* another word for **Holocene**

recept ('riːsɛpt) *n psychol* an idea or image formed in the mind by repeated experience of a particular pattern of sensory stimulation [C20 from RE- + (CON)CEPT]

receptacle (rɪ'sɛptəkᵊl) *n* **1** an object that holds something; container **2** *botany* **a** the enlarged or modified tip of the flower stalk that bears the parts of the flower **b** the shortened flattened stem bearing the florets of the capitulum of composite flowers such as the daisy **c** the part of lower plants that bears the reproductive organs or spores [C15 from Latin *receptāculum* a store-place, from *receptāre* to receive again, from *recipere* to RECEIVE]

reception (rɪ'sɛpʃən) *n* **1** the act of receiving or state of being received **2** the manner in which something, such as a guest or a new idea, is received: *a cold reception* **3** a formal party for guests, such as one after a wedding **4** an area in an office, hotel, etc, where visitors or guests are received and appointments or reservations dealt with **5** short for **reception room** **6** the quality or fidelity of a received radio or television broadcast: *the reception was poor* **7** *Brit* **a** the first class in an infant school **b** a class in a school designed to receive new immigrants, esp those whose knowledge of English is poor **c** (*as modifier*): *a reception teacher* [C14 from Latin *receptiō* a receiving, from *recipere* to RECEIVE]

reception centre *n social welfare* (in Britain) **1** a place to which distressed people, such as vagrants, addicts, victims of a disaster, refugees, etc, go pending more permanent arrangements **2** a local-authority home where children are looked after in a family crisis or where long-term placement is arranged for a child whose family cannot provide a home

receptionist (rɪ'sɛpʃənɪst) *n* a person employed in an office, hotel, doctor's surgery, etc, to receive clients, guests, or patients, answer the telephone, and arrange appointments, etc

reception room *n* **1** a room in a private house suitable for entertaining guests, esp a lounge or dining room **2** a room in a hotel suitable for large parties, receptions, etc

receptive (rɪ'sɛptɪv) *adj* **1** able to apprehend quickly **2** tending to receive new ideas or suggestions favourably **3** able to hold or receive > **re'ceptively** *adv* > **receptivity** (ˌriːsɛp'tɪvɪtɪ) *or* **re'ceptiveness** *n*

receptor (rɪ'sɛptə) *n* **1** *physiol* a sensory nerve ending that changes specific stimuli into nerve impulses **2** any of various devices that receive information, signals, etc

recess *n* (rɪ'sɛs, 'riːsɛs) **1** a space, such as a niche or alcove, set back or indented **2** (*often plural*) a secluded or secret place: *recesses of the mind* **3** a cessation of business, such as the closure of Parliament during a vacation **4** *anatomy* a small cavity or depression in a bodily organ, part, or structure **5** *US and Canadian* a break between classes at a school ▷ *vb* (rɪ'sɛs) **6** (*tr*) to place or set (something) in a recess **7** (*tr*) to build a recess or recesses in (a wall, building, etc) [C16 from Latin *recessus* a retreat, from *recēdere* to RECEDE]

recession[1] (rɪ'sɛʃən) *n* **1** a temporary depression in economic activity or prosperity **2** the withdrawal of the clergy and choir in procession from the chancel at the conclusion of a church service **3** the act of receding **4** a part of a building, wall, etc, that recedes [C17 from Latin *recessio*; see RECESS]

recession[2] (riː'sɛʃən) *n* the act of restoring possession to a former owner [C19 from RE- + CESSION]

recessional (rɪ'sɛʃənᵊl) *adj* **1** of or relating to recession ▷ *n* **2** a hymn sung as the clergy and choir withdraw from the chancel at the conclusion of a church service

recessionary (rɪ'sɛʃənərɪ) *adj* of, caused by, or undergoing economic recession

recessive (rɪ'sɛsɪv) *adj* **1** tending to recede or go back; receding **2** *genetics* **a** (of a gene) capable of producing its characteristic phenotype in the organism only when its allele is identical **b** (of a character) controlled by such a gene. Compare **dominant** (sense 4) **3** *linguistics* (of stress) tending to be placed on or near the initial syllable of a polysyllabic word ▷ *n* **4** *genetics* **a** a recessive gene or character **b** an organism having such a gene or character > **re'cessively** *adv* > **re'cessiveness** *n*

Rechabite ('rɛkəˌbaɪt) *n* a total abstainer from alcoholic drink, esp a member of the **Independent Order of Rechabites**, a society devoted to abstention [C14 via Medieval Latin from Hebrew *Rēkābīm* descendants of *Rēkāb*. See Jeremiah 35:6]

RECHAR ('riːtʃɑː) *n* an EU funding programme providing grants for the reconversion or development of depressed mining areas [C20 from French *Re*conversion de Bassins *Char*bonniers, literally: reconversion of coal fields]

recharge (riː'tʃɑːdʒ) *vb* (*tr*) **1** to cause (an accumulator, capacitor, etc) to take up and store electricity again **2** to revive or renew (one's energies) (esp in **recharge one's batteries**) > **re'chargeable** *adj*

réchauffé *French* (reʃofe) *n* **1** warmed-up leftover food **2** old, stale, or reworked material [C19 from French *réchauffer* to reheat, from RE- + *chauffer* to warm; see CHAFE]

recherché (rə'ʃɛəʃeɪ; *French* rəʃɛrʃe) *adj* **1** known only to connoisseurs; choice or rare **2** studiedly refined or elegant [C18 from French: past participle of *rechercher* to make a thorough search for; see RESEARCH]

recidivism (rɪ'sɪdɪˌvɪzəm) *n* habitual relapse into crime [C19 from Latin *recidīvus* falling back, from RE- + *cadere* to fall] > **re'cidivist** *n, adj* > **reˌcidi'vistic** *or* **re'cidivous** *adj*

Recife (rɛ'siːfə) *n* a port at the easternmost point of Brazil on the Atlantic: capital of Pernambuco state; built partly on an island, with many waterways and bridges. Pop: 3 527 000 (2005 est). Former name: **Pernambuco**

recipe ('rɛsɪpɪ) *n* **1** a list of ingredients and directions for making something, esp a food preparation **2** *med* (formerly) a medical prescription **3** a method for achieving some desired objective: *a recipe for success* [C14 from Latin, literally: take (it)! from *recipere* to take, RECEIVE]

recipience (rɪ'sɪpɪəns) *n* **1** the act of receiving **2** the quality of being receptive; receptiveness

recipient (rɪ'sɪpɪənt) *n* **1** a person who or thing that receives ▷ *adj* **2** a less common word for **receptive** [C16 via French from Latin *recipiēns*, from *recipere* to RECEIVE]

reciprocal (rɪ'sɪprəkᵊl) *adj* **1** of, relating to, or designating something given by each of two people, countries, etc, to the other; mutual: *reciprocal friendship; reciprocal trade* **2** given or done in return: *a reciprocal favour* **3** (of a pronoun) indicating that action is given and received by each subject; for example, *each other* in the sentence *they started to shout at each other* **4** *maths* of or relating to a number or quantity divided into one **5** *navigation* denoting a course or bearing that is 180° from the previous or assumed one ▷ *n* **6** something that is reciprocal **7** Also called: **inverse** *maths* a number or quantity that when multiplied by a given number or quantity gives a product of one: *the reciprocal of 2 is 0.5* [C16 from Latin *reciprocus* alternating] > **reˌcipro'cality** *n* > **re'ciprocally** *adv*

reciprocate (rɪ'sɪprəˌkeɪt) *vb* **1** to give or feel in return **2** to move or cause to move backwards and forwards **3** (*intr*) to be correspondent or equivalent [C17 from Latin *reciprocāre*, from *reciprocus* RECIPROCAL] > **reˌcipro'cation** *n* > **re'ciprocative** *or* **re'reciproˌcatory** *adj* > **re'ciproˌcator** *n*

reciprocating engine *n* an engine in which one or more pistons move backwards and forwards inside a cylinder or cylinders

reciprocity (ˌrɛsɪ'prɒsɪtɪ) *n, pl* **-ities** **1** reciprocal action or relation **2** a mutual exchange of commercial or other privileges [C18 via French from Latin *reciprocus* RECIPROCAL]

reciprocity failure *n photog* a failure of the two exposure variables, light intensity and exposure time, to behave in a reciprocal fashion at very high or very low values

recision (rɪ'sɪʒən) *n* the act of cancelling or rescinding; annulment: *the recision of a treaty* [C17 from Latin *recīsiō*, from *recīdere* to cut back]

recital (rɪ'saɪtᵊl) *n* **1** a musical performance by a soloist or soloists. Compare **concert** (sense 1) **2** the act of reciting or repeating something learned or prepared **3** an account, narration, or description **4** a detailed statement of facts, figures, etc **5** (*often plural*) *law* the preliminary statement in a deed showing the reason for its existence and leading up to and explaining the operative part > **re'citalist** *n*

r

recitation (ˌrɛsɪ'teɪʃən) *n* **1** the act of reciting from memory, or a formal reading of verse before an audience **2** something recited

recitative[1] (ˌrɛsɪtə'tiːv) *n* a passage in a musical composition, esp the narrative parts in an oratorio, set for one voice with either continuo accompaniment only or full accompaniment, reflecting the natural rhythms of speech [C17 from Italian *recitativo*; see RECITE]

recitative[2] (rɪ'saɪtətɪv) *adj* of or relating to recital

recite (rɪ'saɪt) *vb* **1** to repeat (a poem, passage, etc) aloud from memory before an audience, teacher, etc **2** (*tr*) to give a detailed account of **3** (*tr*) to enumerate (examples, etc) [C15 from Latin *recitāre* to cite again, from RE- + *citāre* to summon; see CITE] > **re'citable** *adj* > **re'citer** *n*

reck (rɛk) *vb archaic* (*used mainly with a negative*) **1** to mind or care about (something): *to reck nought* **2** (*usually impersonal*) to concern or interest (someone) [Old English *reccan*; related to Old High German *ruohhen* to take care, Old Norse *rækja*, Gothic *rakjan*]

reckless ('rɛklɪs) *adj* having or showing no regard for danger or consequences; heedless; rash: *a reckless driver; a reckless attempt* [Old English *recceleās* (see RECK, -LESS); related to Middle Dutch *roekeloos*, Old High German *ruahhalōs*] > **'recklessly** *adv* > **'recklessness** *n*

Recklinghausen (*German* rɛklɪŋ'hauzən) *n* an industrial city in NW Germany, in North Rhine-Westphalia on the N edge of the Ruhr. Pop: 123 144 (2003 est)

reckon ('rɛkən) *vb* **1** to calculate or ascertain by calculating; compute **2** (*tr*) to include; count as part of a set or class: *I reckon her with the angels* **3** (*usually passive*) to consider or regard: *he is reckoned clever* **4** (*when tr, takes a clause as object*) to think or suppose; be of the opinion: *I reckon you don't know where to go next* **5** (*intr*; foll by *with*) to settle accounts (with) **6** (*intr*; foll by *with* or *without*) to take into account or fail to take into account: *the bully reckoned without John's big brother* **7** (*intr*; foll by *on* or *upon*) to rely or depend: *I reckon on your support in this crisis* **8** (*tr*) *slang* to regard as good: *I don't reckon your chances of success* **9** (*tr*) *informal* to have a high opinion of: *she was sensitive to bad reviews, even from people she did not reckon* **10** **to be reckoned with** of considerable importance or influence [Old English (*ge*)*recenian* recount; related to Old Frisian *rekenia*, Old High German *rehhanōn* to count]

reckoner (ˈrɛkənə) *n* any of various devices or tables used to facilitate reckoning, esp a ready reckoner

reckoning (ˈrɛkənɪŋ) *n* **1** the act of counting or calculating **2** settlement of an account or bill **3** a bill or account **4** retribution for one's actions (esp in the phrase **day of reckoning**) **5** *navigation* short for **dead reckoning**

reclaim (rɪˈkleɪm) *vb* (*tr*) **1** to claim back: *to reclaim baggage* **2** to convert (desert, marsh, waste ground, etc) into land suitable for growing crops **3** to recover (useful substances) from waste products **4** to convert (someone) from sin, folly, vice, etc **5** *falconry* to render (a hawk or falcon) tame ▷ *n* **6** the act of reclaiming or state of being reclaimed [C13 from Old French *réclamer*, from Latin *reclāmāre* to cry out, protest, from RE- + *clāmāre* to shout] > **reˈclaimable** *adj* > **reˈclaimant** *or* **reˈclaimer** *n*

reclamation (ˌrɛkləˈmeɪʃən) *n* **1** the conversion of desert, marsh, or other waste land into land suitable for cultivation **2** the recovery of useful substances from waste products **3** the act of reclaiming or state of being reclaimed

réclame *French* (reklam) *n* **1** public acclaim or attention; publicity **2** the capacity for attracting publicity

reclinate (ˈrɛklɪˌneɪt) *adj* (esp of a leaf or stem) naturally curved or bent backwards so that the upper part rests on the ground [C18 from Latin *reclīnātus* bent back]

recline (rɪˈklaɪn) *vb* to rest or cause to rest in a leaning position [C15 from Old French *recliner*, from Latin *reclīnāre* to lean back, from RE- + *clīnāre* to LEAN[1]] > **reˈclinable** *adj* > **reclination** (ˌrɛklɪˈneɪʃən) *n*

recliner (rɪˈklaɪnə) *n* a type of armchair having a back that can be adjusted to slope at various angles and, usually, a leg rest

recluse (rɪˈkluːs) *n* **1** a person who lives in seclusion **2** a person who lives in solitude to devote himself to prayer and religious meditation; a hermit, anchorite, or anchoress ▷ *adj* **3** solitary; retiring [C13 from Old French *reclus*, from Late Latin *reclūdere* to shut away, from Latin RE- + *claudere* to close] > **reclusion** (rɪˈkluːʒən) *n* > **reˈclusive** *adj*

recognition (ˌrɛkəgˈnɪʃən) *n* **1** the act of recognizing or fact of being recognized **2** acceptance or acknowledgment of a claim, duty, fact, truth, etc **3** a token of thanks or acknowledgment **4** formal acknowledgment of a government or of the independence of a country **5** *chiefly US and Canadian* an instance of a chairman granting a person the right to speak in a deliberative body, debate, etc [C15 from Latin *recognitiō*, from *recognoscere* to know again, from RE- + *cognoscere* to know, ascertain] > **recognitive** (rɪˈkɒgnɪtɪv) *or* **reˈcognitory** *adj*

recognizance *or* **recognisance** (rɪˈkɒgnɪzəns) *n* **1** *law* **a** a bond entered into before a court or magistrate by which a person binds himself to do a specified act, as to appear in court on a stated day, keep the peace, or pay a debt **b** a monetary sum pledged to the performance of such an act **2** an obsolete word for **recognition** [C14 from Old French *reconoissance*, from *reconoistre* to RECOGNIZE] > **reˈcognizant** *or* **reˈcognisant** *adj*

recognize *or* **recognise** (ˈrɛkəgˌnaɪz) *vb* (*tr*) **1** to perceive (a person, creature, or thing) to be the same as or belong to the same class as something previously seen or known; know again **2** to accept or be aware of (a fact, duty, problem, etc): *to recognize necessity* **3** to give formal acknowledgment of the status or legality of (a government, an accredited representative, etc) **4** *chiefly US and Canadian* to grant (a person) the right to speak in a deliberative body, debate, etc **5** to give a token of thanks for (a service rendered, etc) **6** to make formal acknowledgment of (a claim, etc) **7** to show approval or appreciation of (something good or pleasing) **8** to acknowledge or greet (a person), as when meeting by chance **9** (*intr*) *chiefly US* to enter into a recognizance [C15 from Latin *recognoscere* to know again, from RE- + *cognoscere* to know, ascertain] > **ˈrecogˌnizable** *or* **ˈrecogˌnisable** *adj* > **ˌrecogˌnizaˈbility** *or* **ˌrecogˌnisaˈbility** *n* > **ˈrecogˌnizably** *or* **ˈrecogˌnisably** *adv* > **ˈrecogˌnizer** *or* **ˈrecogˌniser** *n*

recognizee *or* **recognisee** (rɪˌkɒgnɪˈziː) *n law* the person to whom one entering into a recognizance is bound

recognizor *or* **recognisor** (rɪˌkɒgnɪˈzɔː) *n law* a person who enters into a recognizance

recoil *vb* (rɪˈkɔɪl) (*intr*) **1** to jerk back, as from an impact or violent thrust **2** (often foll by *from*) to draw back in fear, horror, or disgust: *to recoil from the sight of blood* **3** (foll by *on* or *upon*) to go wrong, esp so as to hurt the perpetrator **4** (of a nucleus, atom, molecule, or elementary particle) to change momentum as a result of the emission of a photon or particle ▷ *n* (rɪˈkɔɪl, ˈriːkɔɪl) **5** **a** the backward movement of a gun when fired **b** the distance moved **6** the motion acquired by a particle as a result of its emission of a photon or other particle **7** the act of recoiling [C13 from Old French *reculer*, from RE- + *cul* rump, from Latin *cūlus*] > **reˈcoiler** *n*

recoilless (rɪˈkɔɪllɪs) *adj* denoting a gun, esp an antitank weapon, in which the blast is vented to the rear so as to eliminate or reduce recoil

recollect (ˌrɛkəˈlɛkt) *vb* (when *tr, often takes a clause as object*) to recall from memory; remember [C16 from Latin *recolligere* to gather again, from RE- + *colligere* to COLLECT[1]] > **ˌrecolˈlective** *adj* > **ˌrecolˈlectively** *adv*

recollection (ˌrɛkəˈlɛkʃən) *n* **1** the act of recalling something from memory; the ability to remember **2** something remembered; a memory

recombinant (riːˈkɒmbɪnənt) *genetics* ▷ *adj* **1** produced by the combining of genetic material from more than one origin ▷ *n* **2** a chromosome, cell, organism, etc, the genetic makeup of which results from recombination

recombinant DNA *n* DNA molecules that are extracted from different sources and chemically joined together; for example DNA comprising an animal gene may be recombined with DNA from a bacterium

recombination (ˌriːkɒmbɪˈneɪʃən) *n* **1** *genetics* any of several processes by which genetic material of different origins becomes combined. It most commonly occurs between two sets of parental chromosomes during production of germ cells **2** *physics* the union of free electrons and holes in a semiconductor or of free ions and electrons in a plasma

recombine (ˌriːkəmˈbaɪn) *vb* to join together again

recommence (ˌriːkəˈmɛns) *vb* to begin or commence again > **ˌrecomˈmencement** *n*

recommend (ˌrɛkəˈmɛnd) *vb* (*tr*) **1** (*may take a clause as object or an infinitive*) to advise as the best course or choice; counsel: *to recommend prudence* **2** to praise or commend: *to recommend a new book* **3** to make attractive or advisable: *the trip has little to recommend it* **4** *archaic* to entrust (a person or thing) to someone else's care; commend [C14 via Medieval Latin from Latin RE- + *commendāre* to COMMEND] > **ˌrecomˈmendable** *adj* > **ˌrecomˈmender** *n*

recommendation (ˌrɛkəmɛnˈdeɪʃən) *n* **1** the act of recommending **2** something that recommends, esp a letter presenting someone as suitable for a job, etc **3** something that is recommended, such as a course of action

recommendatory (ˌrɛkəˈmɛndətərɪ, -trɪ) *adj* intended to or serving to recommend

recommit (ˌriːkəˈmɪt) *vb* **-mits, -mitting, -mitted** (*tr*) **1** to send (a bill) back to a committee for further consideration **2** to commit again > **ˌrecomˈmitment** *or* **ˌrecomˈmittal** *n*

recompense (ˈrɛkəmˌpɛns) *vb* **1** (*tr*) to pay or reward for service, work, etc **2** (*tr*) to compensate for loss, injury, etc ▷ *n* **3** compensation for loss, injury, etc: *to make recompense* **4** reward, remuneration, or repayment [C15 from Old French *recompenser*, from Latin RE- + *compensāre* to balance in weighing; see COMPENSATE] > **ˈrecomˌpensable** *adj* > **ˈrecomˌpenser** *n*

recompose (ˌriːkəmˈpəʊz) *vb* (*tr*) **1** to restore to composure or calmness **2** to arrange or compose again; reform > **recomposition** (ˌriːkɒmpəˈzɪʃən) *n*

reconcilable (ˈrɛkənˌsaɪləbᵊl, ˌrɛkənˈsaɪ-) *adj* able or willing to be reconciled > **ˌreconˌcilaˈbility** *or* **ˈreconˌcilableness** *n* > **ˈreconˌcilably** *adv*

reconcile (ˈrɛkənˌsaɪl) *vb* (*tr*) **1** (*often passive*; usually foll by *to*) to make (oneself or another) no longer opposed; cause to acquiesce in something unpleasant: *she reconciled herself to poverty* **2** to become friendly with (someone) after estrangement or to re-establish friendly relations between (two or more people) **3** to settle (a quarrel or difference) **4** to make (two apparently conflicting things) compatible or consistent with each other **5** to reconsecrate (a desecrated church, etc) [C14 from Latin *reconciliāre* to bring together again, from RE- + *conciliāre* to make friendly, CONCILIATE] > **ˈreconˌcilement** *n* > **ˈreconˌciler** *n* > **reconciliation** (ˌrɛkənˌsɪlɪˈeɪʃən) *n* > **reconciliatory** (ˌrɛkənˈsɪlɪətərɪ, -trɪ) *adj*

Reconciliation (ˌrɛkənˌsɪlɪˈeɪʃən) *n RC Church* a sacrament in which repentant sinners are absolved and gain reconciliation with God and the Church, on condition of confession of their sins to a priest and of performing a penance

recondite (rɪˈkɒndaɪt, ˈrɛkənˌdaɪt) *adj* **1** requiring special knowledge to be understood; abstruse **2** dealing with abstruse or profound subjects [C17 from Latin *reconditus* hidden away, from RE- + *condere* to conceal] > **reˈconditely** *adv* > **reˈconditeness** *n*

recondition (ˌriːkənˈdɪʃən) *vb* (*tr*) to restore to good condition or working order: *to recondition an engine*

reconfigure (ˌriːkənˈfɪgə) *vb* (*tr*) to rearrange the elements or settings of (a system, device, computer application, etc)

reconfirm (ˌriːkənˈfɜːm) *vb* (*tr*) to confirm (an arrangement, agreement, etc) again: *reconfirm your return flight on arrival*

reconnaissance *or* **reconnoissance** (rɪˈkɒnɪsəns) *n* **1** the act of reconnoitring **2** the process of obtaining information about the position, activities, resources, etc, of an enemy or potential enemy **3** a preliminary inspection of an area of land before an engineering survey is made [C18 from French, from Old French *reconoistre* to explore, RECOGNIZE]

reconnect (ˌriːkəˈnɛkt) *vb* to link or be linked together again > **ˌreconˈnection** *n*

reconnoitre *or US* **reconnoiter** (ˌrɛkəˈnɔɪtə) *vb* **1** to survey or inspect (an enemy's position, region of land, etc); make a reconnaissance (of) ▷ *n* **2** the act or process of reconnoitring; a reconnaissance [C18 from obsolete French *reconnoître* to inspect, explore; see RECOGNIZE] > **ˌreconˈnoitrer** *or US* **ˌreconˈnoiterer** *n*

reconsider (ˌriːkənˈsɪdə) *vb* **1** to consider (something) again, with a view to changing one's policy or course of action **2** (in a legislative assembly or similar body) to consider again (a bill or other matter) that has already been voted upon > **ˌreconˌsiderˈation** *n*

reconstitute (riːˈkɒnstɪˌtjuːt) *vb* (*tr*) **1** to restore (food, etc) to its former or natural state or a semblance of it, as by the addition of water to a concentrate: *reconstituted lemon juice* **2** to reconstruct; form again > **reconstituent** (ˌriːkənˈstɪtjʊənt) *adj, n* > **ˌreconstiˈtution** *n*

reconstruct (ˌriːkənˈstrʌkt) *vb (tr)* **1** to construct or form again; rebuild: *to reconstruct a Greek vase from fragments* **2** to form a picture of (a crime, past event, etc) by piecing together evidence or acting out a version of what might have taken place > **ˌreconˈstructible** *adj* > **ˌreconˈstruction** *n* > **ˌreconˈstructive** *or* **ˌreconˈstructional** *adj* > **ˌreconˈstructor** *n*

Reconstruction (ˌriːkənˈstrʌkʃən) *n US history* the period after the Civil War when the South was reorganized and reintegrated into the Union (1865–77)

reconvene (ˌriːkənˈviːn) *vb* to gather, call together, or summon again, esp for a formal meeting

reconvert (ˌriːkənˈvɜːt) *vb (tr)* **1** to change (something) back to a previous state or form **2** to bring (someone) back to his or her former religion **3** *property law* to convert back (property previously converted) into its original form, as land into money and vice versa. See also **conversion** (sense 5) > **reconversion** (ˌriːkənˈvɜːʃən) *n*

record *n* (ˈrɛkɔːd) **1** an account in permanent form, esp in writing, preserving knowledge or information about facts or events **2** a written account of some transaction that serves as legal evidence of the transaction **3** a written official report of the proceedings of a court of justice or legislative body, including the judgments given or enactments made **4** anything serving as evidence or as a memorial: *the First World War is a record of human folly* **5** *(often plural)* information or data on a specific subject collected methodically over a long period: *weather records* **6 a** the best or most outstanding amount, rate, height, etc, ever attained, as in some field of sport: *an Olympic record; a world record; to break the record for the long jump* **b** *(as modifier)*: *a record time* **7** the sum of one's recognized achievements, career, or performance: *the officer has an excellent record* **8** a list of crimes of which an accused person has previously been convicted, which are known to the police but may only be disclosed to a court in certain circumstances **9** **have a record** to be a known criminal; have a previous conviction or convictions **10** Also called: **gramophone record, disc** a thin disc of a plastic material upon which sound has been recorded. Each side has a spiral groove, which undulates in accordance with the frequency and amplitude of the sound. Records were formerly made from a shellac-based compound but were later made from vinyl plastics **11** the markings made by a recording instrument such as a seismograph **12** *computing* a group of data or piece of information preserved as a unit in machine-readable form **13** (in some computer languages) a data structure designed to allow the handling of groups of related pieces of information as though the group was a single entity **14** **for the record** for the sake of a strict factual account **15** **go on record** to state one's views publicly **16** See **off the record** **17** **on record** **a** stated in a public document **b** publicly known **18** **set** *or* **put the record straight** to correct an error or misunderstanding ▷ *vb* (rɪˈkɔːd) *(mainly tr)* **19** to set down in some permanent form so as to preserve the true facts of: *to record the minutes of a meeting* **20** to contain or serve to relate (facts, information, etc) **21** to indicate, show, or register: *his face recorded his disappointment* **22** to remain as or afford evidence of: *these ruins record the life of the Romans in Britain* **23** *(also intr)* to make a recording of (music, speech, etc) for reproduction, or for later broadcasting **24** *(also intr)* (of an instrument) to register or indicate (information) on a scale: *the barometer recorded a low pressure* [C13 from Old French *recorder* to call to mind, from Latin *recordārī* to remember, from RE- + *cor* heart] > **reˈcordable** *adj*

record-changer *n* a device in a record player for changing records automatically

recorded delivery *n* a Post Office service by which an official record of posting and delivery is obtained for a letter or package. Compare **registered post**

recorder (rɪˈkɔːdə) *n* **1** a person who records, such as an official or historian **2** something that records, esp an apparatus that provides a permanent record of experiments, etc **3** short for **tape recorder** **4** *music* a wind instrument of the flute family, blown through a fipple in the mouth end, having a reedlike quality of tone. There are four usual sizes: bass, tenor, treble, and descant **5** (in England) a barrister or solicitor of at least ten years' standing appointed to sit as a part-time judge in the crown court [sense 4 probably from *record (vb)* in the archaic sense "to sing"] > **reˈcorderˌship** *n*

recording (rɪˈkɔːdɪŋ) *n* **1 a** the act or process of making a record, esp of sound on a gramophone record or magnetic tape **b** *(as modifier)*: *recording studio; recording head* **2** the record or tape so produced **3** something that has been recorded, esp a radio or television programme

Recording Angel *n* an angel who supposedly keeps a record of every person's good and bad acts

record label *n* a company that produces and sells records, CDs, and recordings

record of achievement *n Brit* a statement of the personal and educational development of each pupil

record player *n* a device for reproducing the sounds stored on a record, consisting of a turntable, usually electrically driven, that rotates the record at a fixed speed of 33, 45, or (esp formerly) 78 revolutions a minute. A stylus vibrates in accordance with undulations in the groove in the record: these vibrations are converted into electric currents, which, after amplification, are recreated in the form of sound by one or more loudspeakers. See also **monophonic, quadraphonics, stereophonic**

reco-reco (ˈrɛkəʊˈrɛkəʊ) *n, pl* **reco-recos** a percussion instrument consisting of a ridged gourd or bamboo cane that is scraped with a piece of wood or metal [C20 from a native Brazilian language]

recount (rɪˈkaʊnt) *vb (tr)* to tell the story or details of; narrate [C15 from Old French *reconter*, from RE- + *conter* to tell, relate; see COUNT[1]] > **reˈcountal** *n*

re-count *vb* (riːˈkaʊnt) **1** to count (votes, etc) again ▷ *n* (ˈriːˌkaʊnt) **2** a second or further count, esp of votes in a closely contested election

recoup (rɪˈkuːp) *vb* **1** to regain or make good (a financial or other loss) **2** *(tr)* to reimburse or compensate (someone), as for a loss **3** *law* to keep back (something due), having rightful claim to do so; withhold; deduct [C15 from Old French *recouper* to cut back, from RE- + *couper* to cut, from *coper* to behead; see COUP[1]] > **reˈcoupable** *adj* > **reˈcoupment** *n*

recourse (rɪˈkɔːs) *n* **1** the act of resorting to a person, course of action, etc, in difficulty or danger (esp in the phrase **have recourse to**) **2** a person, organization, or course of action that is turned to for help, protection, etc **3** the right to demand payment, esp from the drawer or endorser of a bill of exchange or other negotiable instrument when the person accepting it fails to pay **4** **without recourse** a qualified endorsement on such a negotiable instrument, by which the endorser protects himself from liability to subsequent holders [C14 from Old French *recours*, from Late Latin *recursus* a running back, from RE- + *currere* to run]

recover (rɪˈkʌvə) *vb* **1** *(tr)* to find again or obtain the return of (something lost) **2** to regain (loss of money, position, time, etc); recoup **3** (of a person) to regain (health, spirits, composure, etc), as after illness, a setback, or a shock, etc **4** to regain (a former and usually better condition): *industry recovered after the war* **5** *law* **a** *(tr)* to gain (something) by the judgment of a court of law: *to recover damages* **b** *(intr)* to succeed in a lawsuit **6** *(tr)* to obtain (useful substances) from waste **7** *(intr)* (in fencing, swimming, rowing, etc) to make a recovery [C14 from Old French *recoverer*, from Latin *recuperāre* RECUPERATE] > **reˈcoverable** *adj* > **reˌcoveraˈbility** *n* > **reˈcoverer** *n*

re-cover (riːˈkʌvə) *vb (tr)* **1** to cover again **2** to provide (a piece of furniture, book, etc) with a new cover

recovered memory *n* the alleged recollection of traumatic events from childhood by a person undergoing psychotherapy. See also **false memory syndrome**

recovery (rɪˈkʌvərɪ) *n, pl* **-eries** **1** the act or process of recovering, esp from sickness, a shock, or a setback; recuperation **2** restoration to a former or better condition **3** the regaining of something lost **4** the extraction of useful substances from waste **5** *law* **a** the obtaining of a right, etc, by the judgment of a court **b** (in the US) the final judgment or verdict in a case **6** *fencing* a return to the position of guard after making an attack **7** *swimming, rowing* the action of bringing the arm, oar, etc, forward for another stroke **8** *golf* a stroke played from the rough or a bunker to the fairway or green

recovery stock *n stock exchange* a security that has fallen in price but is believed to have the ability to recover

recreant (ˈrɛkrɪənt) *archaic* ▷ *adj* **1** cowardly; faint-hearted **2** disloyal ▷ *n* **3** a disloyal or cowardly person [C14 from Old French, from *recroire* to surrender, from RE- + Latin *crēdere* to believe; compare MISCREANT] > **ˈrecreance** *or* **ˈrecreancy** *n* > **ˈrecreantly** *adv*

recreate (ˈrɛkrɪˌeɪt) *vb rare* to amuse (oneself or someone else) [C15 from Latin *recreāre* to invigorate, renew, from RE- + *creāre* to CREATE] > **ˈrecreative** *adj* > **ˈrecreatively** *adv* > **ˈrecreˌator** *n*

re-create (ˌriːkrɪˈeɪt) *vb* to create anew; reproduce > **ˌre-creˈator** *n*

recreation (ˌrɛkrɪˈeɪʃən) *n* **1** refreshment of health or spirits by relaxation and enjoyment **2** an activity or pastime that promotes this **3 a** an interval of free time between school lessons **b** *(as modifier)*: *recreation period*

re-creation *n* **1** the state or instance of creating again or anew: *the re-creation of the Russian Empire* **2** a simulation or re-enactment of a scene, place, time, etc: *a re-creation of a vineyard kitchen*

recreational (ˌrɛkrɪˈeɪʃənᵊl) *adj* **1** of, relating to, or used for recreation: *recreational facilities* **2** (of a drug) taken for pleasure rather than for medical reasons or because of an addiction

recreational vehicle *n chiefly US* a large vanlike vehicle equipped to be lived in. Abbreviation: **RV**

recreation ground *n* an open space for public recreation, esp one in a town, with swings and slides, etc, for children. Often (informal) shortened to: **rec**

recreation room *n US and Canadian* **1** the full name for **rec room** **2** a room in a hotel, hospital, etc, for entertainment and social gatherings

recrement (ˈrɛkrɪmənt) *n* **1** *physiol* any substance, such as bile, that is secreted from a part of the body and later reabsorbed instead of being excreted **2** waste matter; refuse; dross [C16 via Old French from Latin *recrēmentum* slag, filth, from RE- + *cernere* to sift] > **ˌrecreˈmental** *adj*

recriminate (rɪˈkrɪmɪˌneɪt) *vb (intr)* to return an accusation against someone or engage in mutual accusations [C17 from Medieval Latin *recrīmināre*, from Latin *crīminārī* to accuse, from *crīmen* an accusation; see CRIME] > **reˈcriminative** *or* **reˈcriminatory** *adj* > **reˈcrimiˌnator** *n*

recrimination (rɪˌkrɪmɪˈneɪʃən) *n* **1** the act or an instance of recriminating **2** *law* a charge made by an accused against his accuser; countercharge

rec room *n US and Canadian* a room in a house used by the family for relaxation and entertainment. In full: **recreation room**

r

recross (riː'krɒs) vb (tr) to move or go across (something) again: recross the river at the Ponte Solferino

recrudesce (ˌriːkruːˈdɛs) vb (intr) (of a disease, trouble, etc) to break out or appear again after a period of dormancy; recur [C19 from Latin recrūdēscere to become raw again, from RE- + crūdēscere to grow worse, from crūdus bloody, raw; see CRUDE] > ˌrecruˈdescence n > ˌrecruˈdescent adj

recruit (rɪˈkruːt) vb **1 a** to enlist (men) for military service **b** to raise or strengthen (an army, navy, etc) by enlistment **2** (tr) to enrol or obtain (members, support, etc) **3** to furnish or be furnished with a fresh supply; renew **4** archaic to recover (health, strength, spirits, etc) ▷ n **5** a newly joined member of a military service **6** any new member or supporter [C17 from French recrute literally: new growth, from recroître to grow again, from Latin recrēscere from RE- + crēscere to grow] > reˈcruitable adj > reˈcruiter n > reˈcruitment n

recrystallize or **recrystallise** (riːˈkrɪstəˌlaɪz) vb **1** chem to dissolve and subsequently crystallize (a substance) from the solution, as in purifying chemical compounds, or (of a substance) to crystallize in this way **2** to undergo or cause to undergo the process in which a deformed metal forms a new set of undeformed crystal grains > reˌcrystalliˈzation or reˌcrystalliˈsation n

rect or **rec't** abbreviation for receipt

recta (ˈrɛktə) n a plural of rectum

rectal (ˈrɛktəl) adj of or relating to the rectum > ˈrectally adv

rectangle (ˈrɛkˌtæŋgᵊl) n a parallelogram having four right angles. Compare **rhombus** [C16 from Medieval Latin rectangulum, from Latin rectus straight + angulus angle]

rectangular (rɛkˈtæŋgjʊlə) adj **1** shaped like a rectangle **2** having or relating to right angles **3** mutually perpendicular: rectangular coordinates **4** having a base or section shaped like a rectangle > recˌtanguˈlarity n > recˈtangularly adv

rectangular coordinates pl n the Cartesian coordinates in a system of mutually perpendicular axes

rectangular hyperbola n a hyperbola with perpendicular asymptotes

recti (ˈrɛktaɪ) n the plural of rectus

recti- or before a vowel **rect-** combining form straight or right: rectilinear; rectangle [from Latin rectus]

rectified spirit n chem a constant-boiling mixture of ethanol and water, containing 95.6 per cent ethanol

rectifier (ˈrɛktɪˌfaɪə) n **1** an electronic device, such as a semiconductor diode or valve, that converts an alternating current to a direct current by suppression or inversion of alternate half cycles **2** chem an apparatus for condensing a hot vapour to a liquid in distillation; condenser **3** a thing or person that rectifies

rectify (ˈrɛktɪˌfaɪ) vb -fies, -fying, -fied (tr) **1** to put right; correct; remedy **2** to separate (a substance) from a mixture or refine (a substance) by fractional distillation **3** to convert (alternating current) into direct current **4** maths to determine the length of (a curve) **5** to cause (an object) to assume a linear motion or characteristic [C14 via Old French from Medieval Latin rectificāre to adjust, from Latin rectus straight + facere to make] > ˈrectiˌfiable adj > ˌrectifiˈcation n

rectilinear (ˌrɛktɪˈlɪnɪə) or **rectilineal** adj **1** in, moving in, or characterized by a straight line or lines: the rectilinear propagation of light **2** consisting of, bounded by, or formed by a straight line or lines > ˌrectiˈlinearly or ˌrectiˈlineally adv

rectitude (ˈrɛktɪˌtjuːd) n **1** moral or religious correctness **2** correctness of judgment [C15 from Late Latin rectitūdō, from Latin rectus right, straight, from regere to rule]

recto (ˈrɛktəʊ) n, pl -tos **1** the front of a sheet of printed paper **2** the right-hand pages of a book, bearing the odd numbers. Compare **verso** (sense 1b) [C19 from Latin rectus right, in rectō foliō on the right-hand page]

rectocele (ˈrɛktəʊˌsiːl) n pathol a protrusion or herniation of the rectum into the vagina [C19 New Latin, from RECTUM + -CELE]

rector (ˈrɛktə) n **1** Church of England a clergyman in charge of a parish in which, as its incumbent, he would formerly have been entitled to the whole of the tithes. Compare **vicar 2** RC Church a cleric in charge of a college, religious house, or congregation **3** Protestant Episcopal Church, Scottish Episcopal Church a clergyman in charge of a parish **4** chiefly Brit the head of certain schools or colleges **5** (in Scotland) a high-ranking official in a university: now a public figure elected for three years by the students [C14 from Latin: director, ruler, from regere to rule] > rectorate n > rectorial (rɛkˈtɔːrɪəl) adj > rectorship n

rectory (ˈrɛktərɪ) n, pl -ries **1** the official house of a rector **2** Church of England the office and benefice of a rector

rectrix (ˈrɛktrɪks) n, pl rectrices (ˈrɛktrɪˌsiːz, rɛkˈtraɪsiːz) any of the large stiff feathers of a bird's tail, used in controlling the direction of flight [C17 from Late Latin, feminine of rector governor, RECTOR] > rectricial (rɛkˈtrɪʃəl) adj

rectum (ˈrɛktəm) n, pl -tums or -ta (-tə) the lower part of the alimentary canal, between the sigmoid flexure of the colon and the anus [C16 shortened from New Latin rectum intestinum the straight intestine]

rectus (ˈrɛktəs) n, pl -ti (-taɪ) anatomy a straight muscle, esp either of two muscles of the anterior abdominal wall (**rectus abdominis**) [C18 from New Latin rectus musculus]

recumbent (rɪˈkʌmbənt) adj **1** lying down; reclining **2** (of a part or organ) leaning or resting against another organ or the ground: a recumbent stem **3** (of a fold in a rock formation) in which the axial plane is nearly horizontal [C17 from Latin recumbere to lie back, from RE- + cumbere to lie] > reˈcumbence or reˈcumbency n > reˈcumbently adv

recumbent bicycle n a type of bicycle that is ridden in a reclining position

recuperate (rɪˈkuːpəˌreɪt, -ˈkjuː-) vb **1** (intr) to recover from illness or exhaustion **2** to recover (losses of money, etc) [C16 from Latin recuperāre to recover, from RE- + capere to gain, take] > reˌcuperˈation n > reˈcuperative adj

recuperator (rɪˈkuːpəˌreɪtə, -ˈkjuː-) n **1** a person that recuperates **2** a device employing springs or pneumatic power to return a gun to the firing position after the recoil **3** chemical engineering a system of flues that transfers heat from the hot gases leaving a furnace to the incoming air

recur (rɪˈkɜː) vb -curs, -curring, -curred (intr) **1** to happen again, esp at regular intervals **2** (of a thought, idea, etc) to come back to the mind **3** (of a problem, etc) to come up again **4** maths (of a digit or group of digits) to be repeated an infinite number of times at the end of a decimal fraction [C15 from Latin recurrere, from RE- + currere to run] > reˈcurring adj > reˈcurringly adv

recurrent (rɪˈkʌrənt) adj **1** happening or tending to happen again or repeatedly **2** anatomy (of certain nerves, branches of vessels, etc) turning back, so as to run in the opposite direction > reˈcurrently adv > reˈcurrence n

recurrent fever n another name for **relapsing fever**

recurring decimal n a rational number that contains a pattern of digits repeated indefinitely after the decimal point. Also called: **circulating decimal, repeating decimal**

recursion (rɪˈkɜːʃən) n **1** the act or process of returning or running back **2** logic, maths the application of a function to its own values to generate an infinite sequence of values. The **recursion formula** or **clause** of a definition specifies the progression from one term to the next, as given the base clause $f(0) = 0$, $f(n + 1) = f(n) + 3$ specifies the successive terms of the sequence $f(n) = 3n$ [C17 from Latin recursio, from recurrere RECUR] > reˈcursive adj

recursive function n logic, maths a function defined in terms of the repeated application of a number of simpler functions to their own values, by specifying a base clause and a recursion formula

recursive subroutine n computing a subroutine that can call itself as part of its execution

recurvate (rɪˈkɜːvɪt, -veɪt) adj rare bent back

recurve (rɪˈkɜːv) vb to curve or bend (something) back or down or (of something) to be so curved or bent [C16 from Latin recurvāre from RE- + curvāre to CURVE]

recusant (ˈrɛkjʊzənt) n **1** (in 16th to 18th century England) a Roman Catholic who did not attend the services of the Church of England, as was required by law **2** any person who refuses to submit to authority ▷ adj **3** (formerly, of Catholics) refusing to attend services of the Church of England **4** refusing to submit to authority [C16 from Latin recūsāns refusing, from recūsāre from RE- + causārī to dispute, from causa a CAUSE] > ˈrecusance or ˈrecusancy n

recuse (rəˈkjuːz, rɪˈkjuːz) vb US, Canadian, and South African (tr; reflexive) to remove from participation in a court case due to potential prejudice or partiality [C19 see RECUSANT]

recycle (riːˈsaɪkᵊl) vb (tr) **1** to pass (a substance) through a system again for further treatment or use **2** to reclaim (packaging or products with a limited useful life) for further use **3** to institute a different cycle of processes or events in (a machine, system, etc) **4** to repeat (a series of operations) ▷ n **5** the repetition of a fixed sequence of events > reˈcyclable or reˈcycleable adj

red¹ (rɛd) n **1** any of a group of colours, such as that of a ripe tomato or fresh blood, that lie at one end of the visible spectrum, next to orange, and are perceived by the eye when light in the approximate wavelength range 740–620 nanometres falls on the retina. Red is the complementary colour of cyan and forms a set of primary colours with blue and green. Related adjs: **rubicund, ruddy 2** a pigment or dye of or producing these colours **3** red cloth or clothing: dressed in red **4** a red ball in snooker, billiards, etc **5** (in roulette and other gambling games) one of two colours on which players may place even bets, the other being black **6** Also called: **inner** archery a red ring on a target, between the blue and the gold, scoring seven points **7** in the red informal in debit; owing money **8** see red informal to become very angry ▷ adj **redder, reddest 9** of the colour red **10** reddish in colour or having parts or marks that are reddish: red hair; red deer **11** having the face temporarily suffused with blood, being a sign of anger, shame, etc **12** (of the complexion) rosy; florid **13** (of the eyes) bloodshot **14** (of the hands) stained with blood, as after committing murder **15** bloody or violent: red revolution **16** (of wine) made from black grapes and coloured by their skins **17** denoting the highest degree of urgency in an emergency; used by the police and the army and informally (esp in the phrase **red alert**) ▷ vb **reds, redding, redded 18** another word for **redden** [Old English rēad; compare Old High German rōt, Gothic rauths, Latin ruber, Greek eruthros, Sanskrit rohita] > ˈredly adv > ˈredness n

red² (rɛd) vb reds, redding, red or redded (tr) a variant spelling of **redd¹**

Red (rɛd) informal ▷ adj **1** Communist, Socialist, or Soviet **2** radical, leftist, or revolutionary ▷ n **3** a member or supporter of a Communist or Socialist Party or a national of a state having such a government, esp the former Soviet Union **4** a radical, leftist, or revolutionary [C19 from the colour chosen to symbolize revolutionary socialism]

redact (rɪˈdækt) vb (tr) **1** to compose or draft (an edict, proclamation, etc) **2** to put (a literary work, etc) into appropriate form for publication; edit [c15 from Latin *redigere* to bring back, from *red-* RE- + *agere* to drive] > re'daction *n* > re'dactional *adj* > re'dactor *n*

red admiral *n* a nymphalid butterfly, *Vanessa atalanta*, of temperate Europe and Asia, having black wings with red and white markings. See also **white admiral**

red algae *pl n* the numerous algae that constitute the phylum *Rhodophyta*, which contain a red pigment in addition to chlorophyll. The group includes carrageen, dulse, and laver. Also called: **red seaweed**

redan (rɪ'dæn) *n* a fortification of two parapets at a salient angle [c17 from French, from earlier *redent* notching of a saw edge, from RE- + *dent* tooth, from Latin *dēns*]

Red Army Faction *n* another name for the **Baader-Meinhof Gang**

redback or **redback spider** *n* a small venomous Australian spider, *Latrodectus hasselti*, having long thin legs and, in the female, a red stripe on the back of its globular abdomen

red-backed shrike *n* a common Eurasian shrike, *Lanius collurio*, the male of which has a grey crown and rump, brown wings and back, and a black-and-white face

red bag *n* (in Britain) a fabric bag for a barrister's robes, presented by a Queen's Counsel to a junior in appreciation of good work in a case. See also **blue bag**

red bark *n* a kind of cinchona containing a high proportion of alkaloids

red beds *pl n* sequences of red sedimentary rocks, usually sandstones or shales, coloured by the oxidization of the iron in them

red-bellied black snake *n* a highly venomous Australian black snake, *Pseudechis porphyriacus*, with a reddish underside

red biddy *n informal* cheap red wine fortified with methylated spirits

red blood cell *n* another name for **erythrocyte**

red-blooded *adj informal* vigorous; virile > ,red-'bloodedness *n*

red book *n Brit* (*sometimes capitals*) a government publication bound in red, esp the Treasury's annual forecast of revenue, expenditure, growth, and inflation

redbreast ('rɛd,brɛst) *n* any of various birds having a red breast, esp the Old World robin (see **robin** (sense 1))

redbrick ('rɛd,brɪk) *n* (*modifier*) denoting, relating to, or characteristic of a provincial British university of relatively recent foundation, esp as distinguished from Oxford and Cambridge

Redbridge ('rɛd,brɪdʒ) *n* a borough of NE Greater London: includes part of Epping Forest. Pop: 245 100 (2003 est). Area: 56 sq km (22 sq miles)

Red Brigades *pl n* **the** a group of urban guerrillas, based in Italy, who kidnapped and murdered the former Italian prime minister Aldo Moro in 1978

redbud ('rɛd,bʌd) *n* an American leguminous tree, *Cercis canadensis*, that has heart-shaped leaves and small budlike pink flowers. Also called: **American Judas tree**

redbug ('rɛd,bʌg) *n US* another name for **chigger** (sense 1)

redcap ('rɛd,kæp) *n* 1 *Brit informal* a military policeman 2 *US and Canadian* a porter at an airport or station

Redcar and Cleveland ('rɛdkɑ:) *n* a unitary authority in NE England, in North Yorkshire: formerly (1975–96) part of Cleveland county. Pop: 139 100 (2003 est). Area: 240 sq km (93 sq miles)

red card *sport* ▷ *n* 1 a card of a red colour displayed by a referee to indicate that a player has been sent off ▷ *vb* **red-card** 2 (*tr*) to send off (a player)

red carpet *n* 1 a strip of red carpeting laid for important dignitaries to walk on when arriving or departing 2 **a** deferential treatment accorded to a person of importance **b** (*as modifier*): *the returning hero had a red-carpet reception*

red cedar *n* 1 any of several North American coniferous trees, esp *Juniperus virginiana*, a juniper that has fragrant reddish wood used for making pencils, and *Thuja plicata*, an arbor vitae 2 the wood of any of these trees

red cent *n* (*used with a negative*) *informal, chiefly US* a cent considered as a trivial amount of money (esp in the phrases **not have a red cent**, **not worth a red cent**, etc)

Red China *n* an unofficial name for (the People's Republic of) **China**

red clover *n* a leguminous plant, *Trifolium pratense*, native to Europe and Asia, frequently planted as a forage crop. It has fragrant red flowers and three-lobed compound leaves

redcoat ('rɛd,kəʊt) *n* (formerly) a British soldier [c16 from the colour of the uniform jacket]

red cod *n* a deep-sea fish, *Physiculus bachus*, of Australia and New Zealand, with a grey-and-pink body that turns red when it is removed from water

red coral *n* any of several corals of the genus *Corallium*, the skeletons of which are pinkish red in colour and used to make ornaments, etc. Also called: **precious coral**

red corpuscle *n* another name for **erythrocyte**

Red Crescent *n* a national branch of or the emblem of the Red Cross Society in a Muslim country

Red Cross *n* 1 an international humanitarian organization (**Red Cross Society**) formally established by the Geneva Convention of 1864. It was originally limited to providing medical care for war casualties, but its services now include liaison between prisoners of war and their families, relief to victims of natural disasters, etc 2 any national branch of this organization 3 the emblem of this organization, consisting of a red cross on a white background

redcurrant ('rɛd'kʌrənt) *n* 1 a N temperate shrub, *Ribes rubrum*, having greenish flowers and small edible rounded red berries: family *Grossulariaceae* 2 **a** the fruit of this shrub **b** (*as modifier*): *redcurrant jelly*

redd[1] (rɛd) *Scot and northern English dialect* ▷ *vb* **redds, redding, redd** or **redded** 1 (*tr; often foll by up*) to bring order to; tidy (up) ▷ *n* 2 the act or an instance of redding [c15 *redden* to clear, perhaps a variant of RID] > 'redder *n*

redd[2] (rɛd) *n* a hollow in sand or gravel on a river bed, scooped out as a spawning place by salmon, trout, or other fish [c17 (originally: spawn): of obscure origin]

red deer *n* a large deer, *Cervus elaphus*, formerly widely distributed in the woodlands of Europe and Asia. The coat is reddish brown in summer and the short tail is surrounded by a patch of light-coloured hair

Red Deer *n* 1 a town in S Alberta on the Red Deer River: trade centre for mixed farming, dairying region, and natural gas processing. Pop: 67 707 (2001) 2 a river in W Canada, in SW Alberta, flowing southeast into the South Saskatchewan River. Length: about 620 km (385 miles) 3 a river in W Canada, flowing east through **Red Deer Lake** into Lake Winnipegosis. Length: about 225 km (140 miles)

redden ('rɛdən) *vb* 1 to make or become red 2 (*intr*) to flush with embarrassment, anger, etc; blush

reddish ('rɛdɪʃ) *adj* somewhat red > 'reddishly *adv* > 'reddishness *n*

Redditch ('rɛdɪtʃ) *n* a town in W central England, in N Worcestershire: designated a new town in the mid-1960s; metal-working industries. Pop: 74 803 (2001)

reddle ('rɛdəl) *n, vb* a variant spelling of **ruddle**

red duster *n Brit* an informal name for the **Red Ensign**

red dwarf *n* one of a class of small cool main-sequence stars

rede (ri:d) *archaic* ▷ *n* 1 advice or counsel 2 an

explanation ▷ *vb* (*tr*) 3 to advise; counsel 4 to explain [Old English *rǣdan* to rule; see READ[1]]

red earth *n* a clayey zonal soil of tropical savanna lands, formed by extensive chemical weathering, coloured by iron compounds, and less strongly leached than laterite

redecorate (ri:'dɛkəˌreɪt) *vb* to paint or wallpaper (a room, house, etc) again > re,deco'ration *n*

redeem (rɪ'di:m) *vb* (*tr*) 1 to recover possession or ownership of by payment of a price or service; regain 2 to convert (bonds, shares, etc) into cash 3 to pay off (a promissory note, loan, etc) 4 to recover (something pledged, mortgaged, or pawned) 5 to convert (paper money) into bullion or specie 6 to fulfil (a promise, pledge, etc) 7 to exchange (trading stamps, coupons, etc) for goods 8 to reinstate in someone's estimation or good opinion; restore to favour: *he redeemed himself by his altruistic action* 9 to make amends for 10 to recover from captivity, esp by a money payment 11 *Christianity* (of Christ as Saviour) to free (mankind) from sin by his death on the Cross [c15 from Old French *redimer*, from Latin *redimere* to buy back, from *red-* RE- + *emere* to buy] > re'deemer *n*

redeemable (rɪ'di:məbəl) or **redemptible** (rɪ'dɛmptəbəl) *adj* (of bonds, shares, etc) 1 subject to cancellation by repayment at a specified date or under specified conditions 2 payable in or convertible into cash > re,deema'bility *n* > re'deemably *adv*

Redeemer (rɪ'di:mə) *n* **The** Jesus Christ as having brought redemption to mankind

redeeming (rɪ'di:mɪŋ) *adj* serving to compensate for faults or deficiencies in quality, etc: *one redeeming feature*

redefine (,ri:dɪ'faɪn) *vb* (*tr*) to define (something) again or differently

red emperor *n Austral* a brightly-coloured marine food fish, *Lutjanus sebae*, of the Great Barrier Reef

redemption (rɪ'dɛmpʃən) *n* 1 the act or process of redeeming 2 the state of being redeemed 3 *Christianity* **a** deliverance from sin through the incarnation, sufferings, and death of Christ **b** atonement for guilt 4 conversion of paper money into bullion or specie 5 **a** removal of a financial obligation by paying off a note, bond, etc **b** (*as modifier*): *redemption date* [c14 via Old French from Latin *redemptiō* a buying back; see REDEEM] > re'demptional, re'demptive or re'demptory *adj* > re'demptively *adv*

redemptioner (rɪ'dɛmpʃənə) *n history* an emigrant to Colonial America who paid for his passage by becoming an indentured servant

redemption yield *n stock exchange* the yield produced by a redeemable gilt-edged security taking into account the annual interest it pays and an annualized amount to account for any profit or loss when it is redeemed

Redemptorist (rɪ'dɛmptərɪst) *n RC Church* a member of a religious congregation founded in 1732 to do missionary work among the poor [c19 from French *redemptoriste*, from Old French or Latin *redemptor*, from Latin *redimere*, see REDEEM]

Red Ensign *n* the ensign of the British Merchant Navy, having the Union Jack on a red background at the upper corner of the vertical edge alongside the hoist. Compare **White Ensign, Blue Ensign**

redeploy (,ri:dɪ'plɔɪ) *vb* to assign new positions or tasks to (labour, troops, etc) > ,rede'ployment *n*

redesign (,ri:dɪ'zaɪn) *vb* (*tr*) 1 to change the design of (something) ▷ *n* 2 something that has been redesigned

redevelop (,ri:dɪ'vɛləp) *vb* (*tr*) 1 to rebuild or replan (a building, area, etc) 2 *photog* to develop (a negative or print) for a second time, in order to improve the contrast, colour, etc 3 to develop (something) again > ,rede'veloper *n* > ,rede'velopment *n*

redevelopment area *n* an urban area in which all or most of the buildings are demolished and rebuilt

redeye ('rɛd,aɪ) *n* 1 *US slang* inferior whiskey 2

r

Canadian slang a drink incorporating beer and tomato juice **3** another name for **rudd**

red-eye *n informal* **a** an aeroplane flight leaving late at night or arriving early in the morning **b** (*as modifier*): *a red-eye flight*

red eye *n photog* an undesirable effect that sometimes appears in flashlight portraits when light from the flash enters the eye and is reflected from the retina on to the film, producing a red colour

red-faced *adj* **1** flushed with embarrassment or anger **2** having a florid complexion > **red-facedly** (ˌrɛdˈfeɪsɪdlɪ, -ˈfeɪstlɪ) *adv*

redfin (ˈrɛdˌfɪn) *n* any of various small cyprinid fishes of the genus *Notropis*, esp *N. cornutus*. They have reddish fins and are popular aquarium fishes

red fir *n* **1** a North American coniferous tree, *Abies magnifica*, having reddish wood valued as timber: family *Pinaceae* **2** any of various other pinaceous trees that have reddish wood **3** the wood of any of these trees

red fire *n* any combustible material that burns with a bright red flame: used in flares and fireworks. The colour is usually produced by strontium salts

redfish (ˈrɛdˌfɪʃ) *n, pl* **-fish** *or* **-fishes 1** a male salmon that has recently spawned. Compare **blackfish** (sense 2) **2** any of several red European scorpaenid fishes of the genus *Sebastes*, esp *S. marinus*, valued as a food fish

red flag *n* **1** a symbol of socialism, communism, or revolution **2** a warning of danger or a signal to stop

Red Flag *n* **the** a socialist song, written by James Connell in 1889

redfoot (ˈrɛdˌfʊt) *n vet science* a fatal disease of newborn lambs of unknown cause in which the horny layers of the feet become separated, exposing the red laminae below

red fox *n* the common fox, *Vulpes vulpes*, which has a reddish-brown coat: family *Canidae*, order *Carnivora* (carnivores)

red giant *n* a giant star towards the end of its life, with a relatively low temperature of 2000–4000 K, that emits red light

red grouse *n* a reddish-brown grouse, *Lagopus scoticus*, of upland moors of Great Britain: an important game bird

Red Guard *n* a member of a Chinese youth movement that attempted to effect the Cultural Revolution (1965–71)

red gum *n* **1** any of several Australian myrtaceous trees of the genus *Eucalyptus*, esp *E. camaldulensis*, which has reddish wood. See also **blue gum 2** the hard red wood from this tree, used for making railway sleepers, posts, etc **3** another name for **sweet gum**

red-handed *adj* (*postpositive*) in the act of committing a crime or doing something wrong or shameful (esp in the phrase **catch red-handed**) [C19 (earlier, C15 *red hand*)] > ˌred-ˈhandedly *adv* > ˌred-ˈhandedness *n*

red hat *n* **1** the broad-brimmed crimson hat given to cardinals as the symbol of their rank and office **2** the rank and office of a cardinal

redhead (ˈrɛdˌhɛd) *n* **1** a person with red hair **2** a diving duck, *Aythya americana*, of North America, the male of which has a grey-and-black body and a reddish-brown head

red-headed *adj* **1** (of a person) having red hair **2** (of an animal) having a red head

red heat *n* **1** the temperature at which a substance is red-hot **2** the state or condition of being red-hot

red herring *n* **1** anything that diverts attention from a topic or line of inquiry **2** a herring cured by salting and smoking

red-hot *adj* **1** (esp of metal) heated to the temperature at which it glows red: *iron is red-hot at about 500°C* **2** extremely hot: *the stove is red-hot, so don't touch it* **3** keen, excited, or eager; enthusiastic

4 furious; violent: *red-hot anger* **5** very recent or topical: *red-hot information* **6** *Austral slang* extreme, unreasonable, or unfair: *the charges are red-hot*

red-hot poker *n* See **kniphofia**

redia (ˈriːdɪə) *n, pl* **-diae** (-dɪˌiː) a parasitic larva of flukes that has simple locomotory organs, pharynx, and intestine and gives rise either to other rediae or to a different larva (the cercaria) [C19 from New Latin, named after Francesco *Redi* (1629–97), Italian naturalist]

redial (riːˈdaɪəl, -daɪl) *vb* **-dials, -dialling, -dialled** to dial (a telephone number) again

Rediffusion (ˌriːdɪˈfjuːʒən) *n trademark Brit* a system by which radio or television programmes are relayed to subscribers from a receiver via cables

Red Indian *n* ▷ *adj* another name, now considered offensive, for **American Indian** [see REDSKIN]

redingote (ˈrɛdɪŋˌɡəʊt) *n* **1** a woman's coat with a close-fitting top and a full skirt **2** a man's or woman's full-skirted outer coat of the 18th and 19th centuries **3** a woman's light dress or coat of the 18th century, with an open-fronted skirt, revealing a decorative underskirt [C19 from French, from English *riding coat*]

redintegrate (rɛˈdɪntɪˌɡreɪt) *vb* **1** (*tr*) to make whole or complete again; restore to a perfect state; renew **2** (*intr*) *psychol* to engage in the process of redintegration [C15 from Latin *redintegrāre* to renew, from RE- + *integer* complete] > reˈdinteˌɡrative *adj*

redintegration (rɛˌdɪntɪˈɡreɪʃən) *n* **1** the act or process of making whole again; renewal **2** *psychol* the process of responding to a part of a situation in the same manner as one has responded to the whole situation, as in the case of a souvenir reminding one of a holiday

redirect (ˌriːdɪˈrɛkt, ˌriːdaɪ-) *vb* (*tr*) to direct (someone or something) to a different place or by a different route > ˌrediˈrection *n*

rediscover (ˌriːdɪˈskʌvə) *vb* (*tr*) to discover (something) again: *rediscover the joys of life*

rediscovery (ˌriːdɪˈskʌvərɪ) *n, pl* **-ies** the act, process, or an instance of discovering (something) again

redistribute (ˌriːdɪˈstrɪbjuːt) *vb* (*tr*) to distribute (something) again or differently > ˌrediˈstributive *adj*

redistribution (ˌriːdɪstrɪˈbjuːʃən) *n* the act or instance of distributing or the state or manner of being distributed again

redivivus (ˌrɛdɪˈvaɪvəs) *adj rare* returned to life; revived [C17 from Late Latin, from Latin *red-* RE- + *vīvus* alive]

red kangaroo *n* a large Australian kangaroo, *Macropus rufus*, the male of which has a reddish coat

red kowhai *n* another name for **kaka beak**

red lead (lɛd) *n* a bright-red poisonous insoluble oxide of lead usually obtained as a powder by heating litharge in air. It is used as a pigment in paints. Formula: Pb_3O_4. Also called: **minium**

red-lead ore (ˈrɛdˈlɛd) *n* another name for **crocoite**

redleg (ˈrɛdˌlɛɡ) *n Caribbean derogatory* a poor White

red-legged partridge *n* a partridge, *Alectoris rufa*, having a reddish tail, red legs and bill, and flanks barred with chestnut, black, and white: common on farmlands and heaths in SW Europe, including Britain

red-letter day *n* a memorably important or happy occasion [C18 from the red letters used in ecclesiastical calendars to indicate saints' days and feasts]

red light *n* **1** a signal to stop, esp a red traffic signal in a system of traffic lights **2** a danger signal **3** an instruction to stop or discontinue **4 a** a red lamp in a window of or outside a house indicating that it is a brothel **b** (*as modifier*): *a red-light district*

redline (ˈrɛdˌlaɪn) *vb* (*tr*) **1** (esp of a bank or group of banks) to refuse a loan to (a person or country) because of the presumed risks involved **2** to restrict people's access to goods or services on the basis of the area in which they live

red line *n* a point beyond which a person or group is not prepared to negotiate

red man *n archaic* a North American Indian [C18 see REDSKIN]

red matipo (mɑːtiːpɒ) *n* another name for **mapau** [Māori]

red meat *n* any meat that is dark in colour, esp beef and lamb. Compare **white meat**

red mercury *n* a supposedly radioactive substance that could be used in a bomb made from nuclear waste, widely believed to be part of a confidence trick in which gangsters sold useless material to terrorists in the early 1990s

red mist *n informal* a feeling of extreme anger that clouds one's judgment temporarily

red mullet *n* any of the marine percoid fishes constituting the family *Mullidae*, esp *Mullus surmuletus*, a food fish of European waters. They have a pair of long barbels beneath the chin and a reddish coloration. US name: **goatfish**

redneck (ˈrɛdˌnɛk) *n disparaging* **1** (in the southwestern US) a poor uneducated White farm worker **2** a person or institution that is extremely reactionary ▷ *adj* **3** reactionary and bigoted: *redneck laws*

red ned (nɛd) *n Austral slang* any cheap red wine

redo (riːˈduː) *vb* **-does, -doing, -did, -done** (*tr*) **1** to do over again **2** *informal* to redecorate, esp thoroughly: *we redid the house last summer*

red oak *n* **1** any of several deciduous oak trees, esp *Quercus borealis*, native to North America, having bristly leaves with triangular lobes and acorns with small cups **2** the hard cross-grained reddish wood of this tree

red ochre *n* any of various natural red earths containing ferric oxide: used as pigments

redolent (ˈrɛdəʊlənt) *adj* **1** having a pleasant smell; fragrant **2** (*postpositive; foll by of* or *with*) having the odour of; scented (with): *a room redolent of country flowers* **3** (*postpositive; foll by of* or *with*) reminiscent or suggestive (of): *a picture redolent of the 18th century* [C14 from Latin *redolens* smelling (of), from *redolēre* to give off an odour, from *red-* RE- + *olēre* to smell] > ˈredolence *or less commonly* ˈredolency *n* > ˈredolently *adv*

red osier *n* any of several willow trees that have red twigs used for basketwork

red-osier dogwood *n* a North American shrub, *Cornus stolonifera*, having bright or dark red wood, white flowers, and whitish fruit

redouble (rɪˈdʌbᵊl) *vb* **1** to make or become much greater in intensity, number, etc: *to redouble one's efforts* **2** to send back (sounds) or (of sounds) to be sent back; echo or re-echo **3** *bridge* to double (an opponent's double) ▷ *n* **4** the act of redoubling

redoubt (rɪˈdaʊt) *n* **1** an outwork or detached fieldwork defending a pass, hilltop, etc **2** a temporary defence work built inside a fortification as a last defensive position [C17 via French from obsolete Italian *ridotta*, from Medieval Latin *reductus* shelter, from Latin *redūcere* to withdraw, from RE- + *dūcere* to lead]

redoubtable (rɪˈdaʊtəbᵊl) *adj* **1** to be feared; formidable **2** worthy of respect [C14 from Old French, from *redouter* to dread, from RE- + *douter* to be afraid, DOUBT] > reˈdoubtableness *n* > reˈdoubtably *adv*

redound (rɪˈdaʊnd) *vb* **1** (*intr; foll by to*) to have an advantageous or disadvantageous effect (on): *brave deeds redound to your credit* **2** (*intr; foll by on* or *upon*) to recoil or rebound **3** (*intr*) *archaic* to arise; accrue: *wealth redounding from wise investment* **4** (*tr*) *archaic* to reflect; bring: *his actions redound dishonour upon him* [C14 from Old French *redonder*, from Latin *redundāre* to stream over, from *red-* RE- + *undāre* to rise in waves, from *unda* a wave]

redowa (ˈrɛdəvə, -wə) *n* a Bohemian folk dance

similar to the waltz [C19 via French and German from Czech *rejdovák*, from *rejdovati* to guide around]

redox ('riːdɒks) *n* (*modifier*) another term for **oxidation-reduction** [C20 from RED(UCTION) + OX(IDATION)]

red packet *n* (in Hong Kong, Malaysia, etc) **1** a sum of money folded inside red paper and given at the Chinese New Year to unmarried younger relatives **2** such a gift given at Chinese weddings by the parents to the bride and groom and by the bride and groom to unmarried younger relatives

red-pencil *vb* -cils, -cilling, -cilled *or US* -cils, -ciling, -ciled (*tr*) to revise or correct (a book, manuscript, etc)

red pepper *n* **1** any of several varieties of the pepper plant *Capsicum frutescens*, cultivated for their hot pungent red podlike fruits **2** the fruit of any of these plants **3** the ripe red fruit of the sweet pepper **4** another name for **cayenne pepper**

red pine *n* a coniferous tree, *Dacrydium cupressinum*, of New Zealand, having narrow sharp pointed leaves: family *Podocarpaceae*. Also called: **rimu**

Red Planet *n* the an informal name for **Mars²** (sense 1)

redpoll ('rɛd,pɒl) *n* either of two widely distributed finches, *Acanthis flammea* or *A. hornemanni* (**arctic** or **hoary redpoll**), having a greyish-brown plumage with a red crown and pink breast

Red Poll *or* **Polled** *n* a red hornless short-haired breed of beef and dairy cattle

redraft *n* ('riː,drɑːft) **1** a second draft **2** a bill of exchange drawn on the drawer or endorser of a protested bill by the holder for the amount of the protested bill plus costs and charges **3** a re-exported commodity ▷ *vb* (riː'drɑːft) (*intr*) **4** to make a second copy of; draft again: *to redraft proposals for a project*

red rag *n* a provocation; something that infuriates [so called because red objects supposedly infuriate bulls]

red rattle *n* See **rattle** (sense 10)

redraw (riː'drɔː) *vb* -draws, -drawing, -drew, -drawn (*tr*) to draw or draw up (something) again or differently

redress (rɪ'drɛs) *vb* (*tr*) **1** to put right (a wrong), esp by compensation; make reparation for: *to redress a grievance* **2** to correct or adjust (esp in the phrase **redress the balance**) **3** to make compensation to (a person) for a wrong ▷ *n* **4** the act or an instance of setting right a wrong; remedy or cure: *to seek redress of grievances* **5** compensation, amends, or reparation for a wrong, injury, etc **6** relief from poverty or want [C14 from Old French *redrecier* to set up again, from RE- + *drecier* to straighten; see DRESS] > re'dressable *or* re'dressible *adj* > re'dresser *or less commonly* re'dressor *n*

re-dress (riː'drɛs) *vb* (*tr*) to dress (something) again

Red River *n* **1** Also called: **Red River of the South** a river in the S central US, flowing east from N Texas through Arkansas into the Mississippi in Louisiana. Length: 1639 km (1018 miles) **2** a river in the northern US, flowing north as the border between North Dakota and Minnesota and into Lake Winnipeg, Canada. Length: 515 km (320 miles) **3** a river in SE Asia, rising in SW China in Yünnan province and flowing southeast across N Vietnam to the Gulf of Tongkin: the chief river of N Vietnam, with an extensive delta. Length: 500 km (310 miles). Vietnamese name: **Song Koi**

red roman *n South African* a marine food fish, *Chrisoblephus laticeps*

redroot ('rɛd,ruːt) *n* **1** a bog plant, *Lachnanthes tinctoria*, of E North America, having woolly yellow flowers and roots that yield a red dye: family *Haemodoraceae* **2** another name for **pigweed** (sense 1)

red rose *n English history* the emblem of the House of Lancaster. See also **Wars of the Roses**, **white rose**

red route *n* an urban through route where the penalties for illegal parking are severe and are immediately enforced

red run *n skiing* a run of some difficulty, suitable for intermediate skiers

red salmon *n* **1** any salmon having reddish flesh, esp the sockeye salmon **2** the flesh of such a fish, esp canned

Red Sea *n* a long narrow sea between Arabia and NE Africa, linked with the Mediterranean in the north by the Suez Canal and with the Indian Ocean in the south: occasionally reddish in appearance through algae. Area: 438 000 sq km (169 000 sq miles)

red seaweed *n* another term for **red algae**

red setter *n* a popular name for **Irish setter**

redshank ('rɛd,ʃæŋk) *n* either of two large common European sandpipers, *Tringa totanus* or *T. erythropus* (**spotted redshank**), having red legs

red shank *n* an annual polygonaceous plant, *Polygonum persicaria*, of N temperate regions, having red stems, narrow leaves, and oblong spikes of pink flowers. Also called: **persicaria**, **lady's-thumb**

redshift ('rɛd,ʃɪft) *n* a shift in the lines of the spectrum of an astronomical object towards a longer wavelength (the red end of an optical spectrum), relative to the wavelength of these lines in the terrestrial spectrum, usually as a result of the **Doppler effect** caused by the recession of the object. Compare: **blueshift**

redskin ('rɛd,skɪn) *n* an informal name, now considered offensive, for an **American Indian** [C17 so called because one particular tribe, the now extinct Beothuks of Newfoundland, painted themselves with red ochre]

red snapper *n* any of various marine percoid food fishes of the genus *Lutjanus*, esp *L. blackfordi*, having a reddish coloration, common in American coastal regions of the Atlantic: family *Lutjanidae* (snappers)

red spider *n* short for **red spider mite** (see **spider mite**)

Red Spot *n* See **Great Red Spot**

red squirrel *n* **1** a reddish-brown squirrel, *Sciurus vulgaris*, inhabiting woodlands of Europe and parts of Asia **2 American red squirrel** Also called: **chickaree** either of two reddish-brown squirrels, *Tamiasciurus hudsonicus* or *T. douglasii*, inhabiting forests of North America

redstart ('rɛd,stɑːt) *n* **1** any European songbird of the genus *Phoenicurus*, esp *P. phoenicurus*, in which the male has a black throat, orange-brown tail and breast, and grey back: family *Muscicapidae* (thrushes, etc) **2** any North American warbler of the genus *Setophaga*, esp *S. ruticilla* [Old English *rēad* RED¹ + *steort* tail; compare German *Rotsterz*]

red tape *n* obstructive official routine or procedure; time-consuming bureaucracy [C18 from the red tape used to bind official government documents]

red tide *n* a discoloration of sea water caused by an explosive growth in phytoplankton density: sometimes toxic to fish life and, through accumulation in shellfish, to humans

red-top *n* a tabloid newspaper characterized by sensationalism [C20 from the colour of the masthead on these publications]

reduce (rɪ'djuːs) *vb* (*mainly tr*) **1** (*also intr*) to make or become smaller in size, number, extent, degree, intensity, etc **2** to bring into a certain state, condition, etc: *to reduce a forest to ashes; to reduce someone to despair* **3** (*also intr*) to make or become slimmer; lose or cause to lose excess weight **4** to impoverish (esp in the phrase **in reduced circumstances**) **5** to bring into a state of submission to one's authority; subjugate: *the whole country was reduced after three months* **6** to bring down the price of (a commodity): *the shirt was reduced in the sale* **7** to lower the rank or status of; demote: *he was reduced from corporal to private; reduced to the ranks* **8** to set out systematically as an aid to understanding; simplify: *his theories have been reduced in a popular treatise* **9** *maths* to modify or simplify the form of (an expression or equation), esp by substitution of one term by another **10** *cookery* to make (a sauce, stock, etc) more concentrated by boiling away some of the water in it **11** to thin out (paint) by adding oil, turpentine, etc; dilute **12** (*also intr*) *chem* **a** to undergo or cause to undergo a chemical reaction with hydrogen or formation of a hydride **b** to lose or cause to lose oxygen atoms **c** to undergo or cause to undergo an increase in the number of electrons. Compare **oxidize** **13** *photog* to lessen the density of (a negative or print) by converting some of the blackened silver in the emulsion to soluble silver compounds by an oxidation process using a photographic reducer **14** *surgery* to manipulate or reposition (a broken or displaced bone, organ, or part) back to its normal site **15** (*also intr*) *biology* to undergo or cause to undergo meiosis [C14 from Latin *redūcere* to bring back, from RE- + *dūcere* to lead] > re'ducible *adj* > re,duci'bility *n* > re'ducibly *adv*

reduced level *n surveying* calculated elevation in relation to a particular datum

reducer (rɪ'djuːsə) *n* **1** *photog* a chemical solution used to lessen the density of a negative or print by oxidizing some of the blackened silver to soluble silver compounds. Compare **intensifier** (sense 3) **2** a pipe fitting connecting two pipes of different diameters **3** a person or thing that reduces

reducing agent *n chem* a substance that reduces another substance in a chemical reaction, being itself oxidized in the process. Compare **oxidizing agent**

reducing glass *n* a lens or curved mirror that produces an image smaller than the object observed

reductase (rɪ'dʌkteɪz) *n* any enzyme that catalyses a biochemical reduction reaction [C20 from REDUCTION + -ASE]

reductio ad absurdum (rɪ'dʌktɪəʊ æd æb'sɜːdəm) *n* **1** a method of disproving a proposition by showing that its inevitable consequences would be absurd **2** a method of indirectly proving a proposition by assuming its negation to be true and showing that this leads to an absurdity **3** application of a principle or proposed principle to an instance in which it is absurd [Latin, literally: reduction to the absurd]

reduction (rɪ'dʌkʃən) *n* **1** the act or process or an instance of reducing **2** the state or condition of being reduced **3** the amount by which something is reduced **4** a form of an original resulting from a reducing process, such as a copy on a smaller scale **5** a simplified form, such as an orchestral score arranged for piano **6** *maths* **a** the process of converting a fraction into its decimal form **b** the process of dividing out the common factors in the numerator and denominator of a fraction; cancellation > re'ductive *adj*

reduction division *n* another name for **meiosis**

reduction formula *n maths* a formula, such as sin (90° ± A) = cos A, expressing the values of a trigonometric function of any angle greater than 90° in terms of a function of an acute angle

reductionism (rɪ'dʌkʃə,nɪzəm) *n* **1** the analysis of complex things, data, etc, into less complex constituents **2** *often disparaging* any theory or method that holds that a complex idea, system, etc, can be completely understood in terms of its simpler parts or components > re'ductionist *n*, *adj* > re,duction'istic *adj*

redundancy (rɪ'dʌndənsɪ) *n*, *pl* -cies **1 a** the state or condition of being redundant or superfluous, esp superfluous in one's job **b** (*as modifier*): *a redundancy payment* **2** excessive proliferation or profusion, esp of superfluity **3** duplication of components in electronic or mechanical equipment so that operations can continue following failure of a part **4** repetition of information or inclusion of additional information to reduce errors in

r

telecommunication transmissions and computer processing

redundancy payment *n* a sum of money given by an employer to an employee who has been made redundant: usually calculated on the basis of the employee's rate of pay and length of service

redundant (rɪ'dʌndənt) *adj* **1** surplus to requirements; unnecessary or superfluous **2** verbose or tautological **3** deprived of one's job because it is no longer necessary for efficient operation: *he has been made redundant* **4** (of components, information, etc) duplicated or added as a precaution against failure, error, etc [c17 from Latin *redundans* overflowing, from *redundāre* to run back, stream over; see REDOUND] > re'dundantly *adv*

red underwing *n* a large noctuid moth, *Catocala nupta*, having dull forewings and hind wings coloured red and black

reduplicate *vb* (rɪ'dju:plɪ,keɪt) **1** to make or become double; repeat **2** to repeat (a sound or syllable) in a word or (of a sound or syllable) to be repeated, esp in forming inflections in certain languages ▷ *adj* (rɪ'dju:plɪkɪt) **3** doubled or repeated **4** (of petals or sepals) having the margins curving outwards > re'duplicative *adj*

reduplication (rɪ,dju:plɪ'keɪʃən) *n* **1** the process or an instance of redoubling **2** the state, condition, or quality of being redoubled **3** a thing that has been redoubled **4** repetition of a sound or syllable in a word, as in the formation of the Latin perfect *tetigi* from *tangere* "touch"

reduviid (rɪ'dju:vɪɪd) *n* **1** any hemipterous bug of the family *Reduviidae*, which includes the assassin bugs and the wheel bug ▷ *adj* **2** of, relating to, or belonging to the family *Reduviidae* [c19 from New Latin *Reduviidae*, from Latin *reduvia* a hangnail]

redware ('rɛd,wɛə) *n* another name for **kelp,** the seaweed

red water *n* **1** a disease of cattle caused by the protozoan *Babesia* (or *Piroplasma*) *bovis*, which destroys the red blood cells, characterized by the passage of red or blackish urine. It is transmitted by tick bites **2** any of various other animal diseases characterized by haematuria

redwing ('rɛd,wɪŋ) *n* **1** a small European thrush, *Turdus iliacus*, having a speckled breast, reddish flanks, and brown back **2** a North American oriole, *Agelaius phoeniceus*, the male of which has a black plumage with a red-and-yellow patch on each wing

redwood ('rɛd,wʊd) *n* a giant coniferous tree, *Sequoia sempervirens*, of coastal regions of California, having reddish fibrous bark and durable timber: family *Taxodiaceae*. The largest specimen is over 120 metres (360 feet) tall. See also **sequoia**

Redwood seconds *n* (*functioning as singular*) a scale of measurement of viscosity based on the time in seconds taken for fluid to flow through a standard orifice: accepted as standard in the UK in 1886. See also **Saybolt universal seconds, Engler degrees** [named after Sir B *Redwood* (1846–1919), English chemist who proposed it]

reebok ('ri:bʌk, -bɒk) *n, pl* **-boks** *or* **-bok** a variant spelling of **rhebok**

re-echo (ri:'ɛkəʊ) *vb* **-oes, -oing, -oed 1** to echo (a sound that is already an echo); resound **2** (*tr*) to repeat like an echo

reed (ri:d) *n* **1** any of various widely distributed tall grasses of the genus *Phragmites*, esp *P. communis*, that grow in swamps and shallow water and have jointed hollow stalks **2** the stalk, or stalks collectively, of any of these plants, esp as used for thatching **3** *music* **a** a thin piece of cane or metal inserted into the tubes of certain wind instruments, which sets in vibration the air column inside the tube **b** a wind instrument or organ pipe that sounds by means of a reed **4** one of the several vertical parallel wires on a loom that may be moved upwards to separate the warp threads **5** a small semicircular architectural moulding. See also **reeding 6** an ancient Hebrew

unit of length equal to six cubits **7** an archaic word for **arrow 8** broken reed a weak, unreliable, or ineffectual person ▷ *vb* (*tr*) **9** to fashion into or supply with reeds or reeding **10** to thatch using reeds [Old English *hreod*; related to Old Saxon *hriod*, Old High German *hriot*]

redbird ('ri:d,bɜ:d) *n* any of several birds that frequent reed beds, esp (in the US and Canada) the bobolink

reedbuck ('ri:d,bʌk) *n, pl* **-bucks** *or* **-buck** any antelope of the genus *Redunca*, of Africa south of the Sahara, having a buff-coloured coat and inward-curving horns

reed bunting *n* a common European bunting, *Emberiza schoeniclus*, that occurs near reed beds and has a brown streaked plumage with, in the male, a black head

reed grass *n* a tall perennial grass, *Glyceria maxima*, of rivers and ponds of Europe, Asia, and Canada

reeding ('ri:dɪŋ) *n* **1** a set of small semicircular architectural mouldings **2** the milling on the edges of a coin

reedling ('ri:dlɪŋ) *n* a titlike Eurasian songbird, *Panurus biarmicus*, common in reed beds: family *Muscicapidae* (Old World flycatchers, etc). It has a tawny back and tail and, in the male, a grey-and-black head. Also called: **bearded tit**

reed mace *n* **1** Also called (*popularly*): **bulrush, false bulrush, cat's-tail** a tall reedlike marsh plant, *Typha latifolia*, with straplike leaves and flowers in long brown sausage-shaped spikes: family *Typhaceae*. See also **bulrush** (sense 2) **2** a related and similar plant, *Typha angustifolia*

reed organ *n* **1** a wind instrument, such as the harmonium, accordion, or harmonica, in which the sound is produced by reeds, each reed producing one note only **2** a type of pipe organ, such as the regal, in which all the pipes are fitted with reeds

reed pipe *n* **1** a wind instrument, such as a clarinet or oboe, whose sound is produced by a vibrating reed **2** an organ pipe sounded by a vibrating reed

reed stop *n* an organ stop controlling a rank of reed pipes

re-educate *vb* (*tr*) to teach or show (someone) something new or in a different way > ,re-edu'cation *n*

reed warbler *n* any of various common Old World warblers of the genus *Acrocephalus*, esp *A. scirpaceus*, that inhabit marshy regions and have a brown plumage

reedy ('ri:dɪ) *adj* **reedier, reediest 1** (of a place, esp a marsh) abounding in reeds **2** of or like a reed **3** having a tone like a reed instrument; shrill or piping: *a reedy voice* > 'readily *adv* > 'readiness *n*

reef¹ (ri:f) *n* **1** a ridge of rock, sand, coral, etc, the top of which lies close to the surface of the sea **2** a ridge- or mound-like structure built by sedentary calcareous organisms (esp corals) and consisting mainly of their remains **3** a vein of ore, esp one of gold-bearing quartz [c16 from Middle Dutch *ref*, from Old Norse *rif* RIB¹, REEF²]

reef² (ri:f) *nautical* ▷ *n* **1** the part gathered in when sail area is reduced, as in a high wind ▷ *vb* **2** to reduce the area of (sail) by taking in a reef **3** (*tr*) to shorten or bring inboard (a spar) [c14 from Middle Dutch *rif*; related to Old Norse *rif* reef, RIB¹, German *reffen* to reef; see REEF¹]

Reef (ri:f) *n* **the 1** another name for the **Great Barrier Reef 2** another name for the **Witwatersrand**

reefer¹ ('ri:fə) *n* **1** *nautical* a person who reefs, such as a midshipman **2** another name for **reefing jacket 3** *slang* a hand-rolled cigarette, esp one containing cannabis [c19 from REEF²; applied to the cigarette because of its resemblance to the rolled reef of a sail]

reefer² ('ri:fə) *n* a ship, lorry, or other form of transport designed to carry refrigerated cargo [c20 shortened and adapted from *refrigerator*]

reefing jacket *n* a man's short double-breasted jacket of sturdy wool. Also called: **reefer**

reef knot *n* a knot consisting of two overhand knots turned opposite ways. Also called: **square knot**

reef point *n* *nautical* one of several short lengths of line stitched through a sail for tying a reef

reek (ri:k) *vb* **1** (*intr*) to give off or emit a strong unpleasant odour; smell or stink **2** (*intr*; often foll by *of*) to be permeated (by); be redolent (of): *the letter reeks of subservience* **3** (*tr*) to treat with smoke; fumigate **4** (*tr*) *chiefly dialect* to give off or emit (smoke, fumes, vapour, etc) ▷ *n* **5** a strong offensive smell; stink **6** *chiefly dialect* smoke or steam; vapour [Old English *rēocan*; related to Old Frisian *riāka* to smoke, Old High German *rouhhan*, Old Norse *rjūka* to smoke, steam] > 'reeking *adj* > 'reekingly *adv* > 'reeky *adj*

reel¹ (ri:l, rɪəl) *n* **1** any of various cylindrical objects or frames that turn on an axis and onto which film, magnetic tape, paper tape, wire, thread, etc, may be wound. US equivalent: **spool 2** *angling* a device for winding, casting, etc, consisting of a revolving spool with a handle, attached to a fishing rod **3** a roll of celluloid exhibiting a sequence of photographs to be projected ▷ *vb* (*tr*) **4** to wind (cotton, thread, etc) onto a reel **5** (foll by *in, out* etc) to wind or draw with a reel: *to reel in a fish* [Old English *hrēol*; related to Old Norse *hrǽll* weaver's rod, Greek *krekein* to weave] > 'reelable *adj* > 'reeler *n*

reel² (ri:l, rɪəl) *vb* (*mainly intr*) **1** to sway, esp under the shock of a blow or through dizziness or drunkenness **2** to whirl about or have the feeling of whirling about: *his brain reeled* ▷ *n* **3** a staggering or swaying motion or sensation [c14 *relen*, probably from REEL¹]

reel³ (ri:l, rɪəl) *n* **1** any of various lively Scottish dances, such as the **eightsome reel** and **foursome reel** for a fixed number of couples who combine in square and circular formations **2** a piece of music having eight quavers to the bar composed for or in the rhythm of this dance [c18 from REEL²]

re-elect *vb* (*tr*) to elect (a person, political party, etc) to an official post for a further term

re-election *n* **1** the election of a person or persons for a further term of office: *his re-election as party leader* **2 a** the state of being elected again: *not seeking re-election* **b** (*as modifier*): *a re-election campaign*

reel-fed *adj* *printing* involving or printing on a web of paper: *a reel-fed press*. Compare **sheet-fed**

reel man *n* *Austral and NZ* (formerly) the member of a beach life-saving team who controlled the reel on which the line was wound

reel off *vb* (*tr, adverb*) to recite or write fluently and without apparent effort: *to reel off items on a list*

reel of three *n* (in Scottish country dancing) a figure-of-eight movement danced by three people

reel-to-reel *adj* **1** (of magnetic tape) wound from one reel to another in use **2** (of a tape recorder) using magnetic tape wound from one reel to another, as opposed to cassettes

re-emerge *vb* (*intr*: often foll by *from*) to emerge or appear again; resurface: *to re-emerge as a threat*

re-emergence *n* the act or an instance of re-emerging

re-employ *vb* (*tr*) to take on (a previous employee) again

re-employment *n* the act or an instance of employing or being employed again

reen *or* **rean** (ri:n) *n* *Southwest English dialect* a ditch, esp a drainage channel [from earlier *rhine*, from Old English *ryne*]

re-enact *vb* (*tr*) to represent or perform (an event, etc) that has happened before

re-enactment *n* the acting out or repetition of a past event or situation

re-engage *vb* **1** (*intr*) to take part in or participate again: *re-engaged in terrorism* **2** (*tr*) to employ (someone) again

re-engineering *n* **a** the restructuring of a company or part of its operations, esp by utilizing information technology **b** (*as modifier*): *a massive re-engineering programme*

re-enter *vb* (*tr*) to enter (something or somewhere) again

re-entering angle *n* an interior angle of a polygon that is greater than 180°. Also called: **re-entrant angle**

re-entrant (riːˈɛntrənt) *adj* **1** (of an angle, esp in fortifications) pointing inwards. Compare **salient** (sense 2) **2** *maths* (of an angle in a polygon) greater than 180° and thus pointing inwards ▷ *n* **3** an angle or part that points inwards

re-entry (riːˈɛntrɪ) *n, pl* **-tries 1** the act of retaking possession of land, etc, under a right reserved in an earlier transfer of the property, such as a lease **2** the return of a spacecraft into the earth's atmosphere

re-entry vehicle *n* the portion of a ballistic missile that carries a nuclear warhead and re-enters the earth's atmosphere

re-equip *vb* **-quips, -quipping, -quipped** (*tr*) to furnish (someone or something) with new supplies, equipment, etc

reest *or* **reast** (riːst) *vb* (*intr*) *Northern English dialect* (esp of horses) to be noisily uncooperative [probably from Scottish *arreest* ARREST; perhaps related to RESTIVE]

re-establish *vb* (*tr*) to establish (something) again: *a fight to re-establish his authority* > **ˌre-esˈtablishment** *n*

re-evaluate *vb* (*tr*) to evaluate again or differently > **ˌre-eˌvaluˈation** *n*

reeve[1] (riːv) *n* **1** *English history* the local representative of the king in a shire (under the ealdorman) until the early 11th century. Compare **sheriff 2** (in medieval England) a manorial steward who supervised the daily affairs of the manor: often a villein elected by his fellows **3** *canadian government* (in certain provinces) a president of a local council, esp in a rural area **4** (formerly) a minor local official in any of several parts of England and the US [Old English *gerēva*; related to Old High German *ruova* number, array]

reeve[2] (riːv) *vb* **reeves, reeving; reeved** *or* **rove** (rəʊv) (*tr*) *nautical* **1** to pass (a rope or cable) through an eye or other narrow opening **2** to fasten by passing through or around something [C17 perhaps from Dutch *rēven* REEF[2]]

reeve[3] (riːv) *n* the female of the ruff (the bird) [C17 of uncertain origin]

re-examine (ˌriːɪgˈzæmɪn) *vb* (*tr*) **1** to examine again **2** *law* to examine (one's own witness) again upon matters arising out of his cross-examination > **ˌre-exˈaminable** *adj* > **ˌre-exˌamiˈnation** *n* > **ˌre-exˈaminer** *n*

re-experience *vb* (*tr*) to participate in or undergo (an event or experience) again

re-export *vb* (ˌriːɪkˈspɔːt, riːˈɛkspɔːt) **1** to export (imported goods, esp after processing) ▷ *n* (riːˈɛkspɔːt) **2** the act of re-exporting **3** a re-exported commodity > **ˌre-exporˈtation** *n* > **ˌre-exˈporter** *n*

ref (rɛf) *n informal* short for **referee**

ref. *abbreviation for* **1** referee **2** reference

reface (riːˈfeɪs) *vb* (*tr*) **1** to repair or renew the facing of (a wall) **2** to put a new facing on (a garment)

refashion (riːˈfæʃən) *vb* (*tr*) to give a new form to (something)

Ref. Ch. *abbreviation for* Reformed Church

refection (rɪˈfɛkʃən) *n* refreshment with food and drink [C14 from Latin *refectiō* a restoring, from *reficere* to remake, from RE- + *facere* to make]

refectory (rɪˈfɛktərɪ, -trɪ) *n, pl* **-tories** a communal dining hall in a religious, academic, or other institution [C15 from Late Latin *refectōrium*, from Latin *refectus* refreshed]

refectory table *n* a long narrow dining table supported by two trestles joined by a stretcher or set into a base

refer (rɪˈfɜː) *vb* **-fers, -ferring, -ferred** (often foll by *to*) **1** (*intr*) to make mention (of) **2** (*tr*) to direct the attention of (someone) for information, facts, etc: *the reader is referred to Chomsky, 1965* **3** (*intr*) to seek information (from): *I referred to Directory Enquiries; he referred to his notes* **4** (*intr*) to be relevant (to); pertain or relate (to): *this song refers to an incident in the Civil War* **5** (*tr*) to assign or attribute: *Cromwell referred his victories to God* **6** (*tr*) to hand over for consideration, reconsideration, or decision: *to refer a complaint to another department* **7** (*tr*) to hand back to the originator as unacceptable or unusable **8** (*tr*) *Brit* to fail (a student) in an examination **9** (*tr*) *Brit* to send back (a thesis) to a student for improvement **10 refer to drawer** a request by a bank that the payee consult the drawer concerning a cheque payable by that bank (usually because the drawer has insufficient funds in his account), payment being suspended in the meantime **11** (*tr*) to direct (a patient) for treatment to another doctor, usually a specialist **12** (*tr*) *social welfare* to direct (a client) to another agency or professional for a service [C14 from Latin *referre* to carry back, from RE- + *ferre* to BEAR[1]] > **referable** (ˈrɛfərəbəl) *or* **referrable** (rɪˈfɜːrəbəl) *adj* > **reˈferral** *n* > **reˈferrer** *n*

USAGE The common practice of adding *back* to *refer* is tautologous, since this meaning is already contained in the *re-* of *refer: this refers to* (not *back to*) *what has already been said*. However, when *refer* is used in the sense of passing a document or question for further consideration to the person from whom it was received, it may be appropriate to say *he referred the matter back*

referee (ˌrɛfəˈriː) *n* **1** a person to whom reference is made, esp for an opinion, information, or a decision **2** the umpire or judge in any of various sports, esp football and boxing, responsible for ensuring fair play according to the rules **3** a person who is willing to testify to the character or capabilities of someone **4** *law* See **Official Referee** ▷ *vb* **-ees, -eeing, -eed 5** to act as a referee (in); preside (over)

reference (ˈrɛfərəns, ˈrɛfrəns) *n* **1** the act or an instance of referring **2** something referred, esp proceedings submitted to a referee in law **3** a direction of the attention to a passage elsewhere or to another book, document, etc **4** a book or passage referred to **5** a mention or allusion: *this book contains several references to the Civil War* **6** *philosophy* **a** the relation between a word, phrase, or symbol and the object or idea to which it refers **b** the object referred to by an expression. Compare **sense** (sense 13) **7 a** a source of information or facts **b** (*as modifier*): *a reference book; a reference library* **8** a written testimonial regarding one's character or capabilities **9** a person referred to for such a testimonial **10 a** (foll by *to*) relation or delimitation, esp to or by membership of a specific class or group; respect or regard: *all people, without reference to sex or age* **b** (*as modifier*): *a reference group* **11 terms of reference** the specific limits of responsibility that determine the activities of an investigating body, etc **12 point of reference** a fact forming the basis of an evaluation or assessment; criterion ▷ *vb* (*tr*) **13** to furnish or compile a list of references for (an academic thesis, publication, etc) **14** to make a reference to; refer to: *he referenced Chomsky, 1956* ▷ *prep* **15** *business* with reference to: *reference your letter of the 9th inst.* Abbreviation: **re** > **ˈreferencer** *n* > **referential** (ˌrɛfəˈrɛnʃəl) *adj*

reference book *n* **1** a book, such as an encyclopedia, dictionary, etc, from which information may be obtained **2** *South African* another name for **passbook** (sense 4)

referendum (ˌrɛfəˈrɛndəm) *n, pl* **-dums** *or* **-da** (-də) **1** submission of an issue of public importance to the direct vote of the electorate **2** a vote on such a measure **3** a poll of the members of a club, union, or other group to determine their views on some matter **4** a diplomatic official's note to his government requesting instructions ▷ See also (for senses 1, 2) **plebiscite** [C19 from Latin: something to be carried back, from *referre* to REFER]

referent (ˈrɛfərənt) *n* the object or idea to which a word or phrase refers. Compare **sense** (sense 13) [C19 from Latin *referens*, from *referre* to REFER]

referred pain *n psychol* pain felt in the body at some place other than its actual place of origin

reffo (ˈrɛfəʊ) *n, pl* **reffos** *Austral slang* an offensive name for a European refugee after World War II

refill *vb* (riːˈfɪl) **1** to fill (something) again ▷ *n* (ˈriːˌfɪl) **2** a replacement for a consumable substance in a permanent container **3** a second or subsequent filling: *a refill at the petrol station* **4** *informal* another drink to replace one already drunk > **reˈfillable** *adj*

refinancing (ˌriːfɪˈnænsɪŋ) *n* a method of paying a debt by borrowing additional money thus creating a second debt in order to pay the first

refine (rɪˈfaɪn) *vb* **1** to make or become free from impurities, sediment, or other foreign matter; purify **2** (*tr*) to separate (a mixture) into pure constituents, as in an oil refinery **3** to make or become free from coarse characteristics; make or become elegant or polished **4** (*tr*; often foll by *out*) to remove (something impure or extraneous) **5** (*intr*; often foll by *on* or *upon*) to enlarge or improve (upon) by making subtle or fine distinctions **6** (*tr*) to make (language) more subtle or polished [C16 from RE- + FINE[1]] > **reˈfinable** *adj*

refined (rɪˈfaɪnd) *adj* **1** not coarse or vulgar; genteel, elegant, or polite **2** subtle; discriminating **3** freed from impurities; purified

refinement (rɪˈfaɪnmənt) *n* **1** the act of refining or the state of being refined **2** a fine or delicate point, distinction, or expression; a subtlety **3** fineness or precision of thought, expression, manners, etc; polish or cultivation **4** a device, change, adaptation, etc, designed to improve performance or increase efficiency

refiner (rɪˈfaɪnə) *n* a person, device, or substance that removes impurities, sediment, or other unwanted matter from something

refinery (rɪˈfaɪnərɪ) *n, pl* **-eries** a factory for the purification of some crude material, such as ore, sugar, oil, etc

refit *vb* (riːˈfɪt) **-fits, -fitting, -fitted 1** to make or be made ready for use again by repairing, re-equipping, or resupplying ▷ *n* (ˈriːˌfɪt) **2** a repair or re-equipping, as of a ship, for further use > **reˈfitment** *n*

reflate (riːˈfleɪt) *vb* to inflate or be inflated again [C20 back formation from REFLATION]

reflation (riːˈfleɪʃən) *n* **1** an increase in economic activity **2** an increase in the supply of money and credit designed to cause such an increase ▷ Compare **inflation** (sense 2) [C20 from RE- + *-flation*, as in INFLATION or DEFLATION]

reflect (rɪˈflɛkt) *vb* **1** to undergo or cause to undergo a process in which light, other electromagnetic radiation, sound, particles, etc, are thrown back after impinging on a surface **2** (of a mirror, etc) to form an image of (something) by reflection **3** (*tr*) to show or express: *his tactics reflect his desire for power* **4** (*tr*) to bring as a consequence: *the success of the project reflected great credit on all the staff* **5** (*intr*; foll by *on* or *upon*) to cause to be regarded in a specified way: *her behaviour reflects well on her* **6** (*intr*; foll by *on* or *upon*) to cast dishonour, discredit, etc (on): *his conduct reflects on his parents* **7** (*intr*; usually foll by *on*) to think, meditate, or ponder [C15 from Latin *reflectere* to bend back, from RE- + *flectere* to bend; see FLEX]

reflectance (rɪˈflɛktəns) *or* **reflection factor** *n* a measure of the ability of a surface to reflect light or other electromagnetic radiation, equal to the ratio of the reflected flux to the incident flux. Symbol: ρ Compare **transmittance, absorptance**

reflecting telescope *n* a type of telescope in which the initial image is formed by a concave mirror. Also called: reflector. Compare **refracting telescope**

reflection *or less commonly* **reflexion** (rɪˈflɛkʃən) *n* **1** the act of reflecting or the state of being reflected **2** something reflected or the image so produced, as by a mirror **3** careful or long consideration or thought **4** implicit or explicit attribution of discredit or blame **5** *maths* a transformation in which the direction of one axis is reversed or which changes the sign of one of the variables **6** *anatomy* the bending back of a structure or part upon itself > reˈflectional *or* reˈflexional *adj*

reflection density *n physics* a measure of the extent to which a surface reflects light or other electromagnetic radiation, equal to the logarithm to base ten of the reciprocal of the reflectance. Symbol: D Former name: **optical density**

reflective (rɪˈflɛktɪv) *adj* **1** characterized by quiet thought or contemplation **2** capable of reflecting: *a reflective surface* **3** produced by reflection > reˈflectively *adv*

reflectivity (ˌriːflɛkˈtɪvɪtɪ) *n* **1** *physics* a measure of the ability of a surface to reflect radiation, equal to the reflectance of a layer of material sufficiently thick for the reflectance not to depend on the thickness **2** Also called: **reflectiveness** the quality or capability of being reflective

reflectometer (ˌriːflɛkˈtɒmɪtə) *n physics* an instrument for measuring the ratio of the energy of a reflected wave to the incident wave in a system

reflector (rɪˈflɛktə) *n* **1** a person or thing that reflects **2** a surface or object that reflects light, sound, heat, etc **3** a small translucent red disc, strip, etc, with a reflecting backing on the rear of a road vehicle, which reflects the light of the headlights of a following vehicle **4** another name for **reflecting telescope 5** part of an aerial placed so as to increase the forward radiation of the radiator and decrease the backward radiation

reflet (rəˈfleɪ) *n* an iridescent glow or lustre, as on ceramic ware [C19 from French: a reflection, from Italian *riflesso*, from Latin *reflexus*, from *reflectere* to REFLECT]

reflex *n* (ˈriːflɛks) **1 a** an immediate involuntary response, esp one that is innate, such as coughing or removal of the hand from a hot surface, evoked by a given stimulus **b** (*as modifier*): *a reflex action*. See also **reflex arc 2 a** a mechanical response to a particular situation, involving no conscious decision **b** (*as modifier*): *a reflex response* **3** a reflection; an image produced by or as if by reflection **4** a speech element derived from a corresponding form in an earlier state of the language: *"sorrow" is a reflex of Middle English "sorwe"*. ⊳ *adj* (ˈriːflɛks) **5** *maths* (of an angle) between 180° and 360° **6** (*prenominal*) turned, reflected, or bent backwards ⊳ *vb* (rɪˈflɛks) **7** (*tr*) to bend, turn, or reflect backwards [C16 from Latin *reflexus* bent back, from *reflectere* to reflect] > reˈflexible *adj* > reˌflexiˈbility *n*

reflex arc *n physiol* the neural pathway over which impulses travel to produce a reflex action, consisting of at least one afferent (receptor) and one efferent (effector) neuron

reflex camera *n* a camera in which the image is composed and focused on a large ground-glass viewfinder screen. In a **single-lens reflex** the light enters through the camera lens and falls on the film when the viewfinder mirror is retracted. In a **twin-lens reflex** the light enters through a separate lens and is deflected onto the viewfinder screen

reflexion (rɪˈflɛkʃən) *n Brit* a less common spelling of **reflection**. > reˈflexional *adj*

reflexive (rɪˈflɛksɪv) *adj* **1** denoting a class of pronouns that refer back to the subject of a sentence or clause. Thus, in the sentence *that man thinks a great deal of himself*, the pronoun *himself* is reflexive **2** denoting a verb used transitively with the reflexive pronoun as its direct object, as the French *se lever* "to get up" (literally "to raise oneself") or English *to dress oneself* **3** *physiol* of or relating to a reflex **4** *logic, maths* (of a relation) holding between any member of its domain and itself: *"... is a member of the same family as ..."* is reflexive. Compare **irreflexive, nonreflexive** ⊳ *n* **5** a reflexive pronoun or verb > reˈflexively *adv* > reˈflexiveness *or* reflexivity (ˌriːflɛkˈsɪvɪtɪ) *n*

reflexology (ˌriːflɛkˈsɒlədʒɪ) *n* **1** a form of therapy practised as a treatment in alternative medicine in which the soles of the feet are massaged: designed to stimulate the blood supply and nerves and thus relieve tension **2** *psychol* the belief that behaviour can be understood in terms of combinations of reflexes > reflexˈologist *n*

refluent (ˈrɛfluənt) *adj rare* flowing back; ebbing [C18 from Latin *refluere* to flow back] > ˈrefluence *n*

reflux (ˈriːflʌks) *vb* **1** *chem* to boil or be boiled in a vessel attached to a condenser, so that the vapour condenses and flows back into the vessel ⊳ *n* **2** *chem* **a** an act of refluxing **b** (*as modifier*): *a reflux condenser* **3** the act or an instance of flowing back; ebb [C15 from Medieval Latin *refluxus*, from Latin *refluere* to flow back]

reflux oesophagitis (iːˌsɒfəˈdʒaɪtɪs) *n* inflammation of the gullet caused by regurgitation of stomach acids, producing heartburn: may be associated with a hiatus hernia

reforest (riːˈfɒrɪst) *vb* (*tr*) another word for **reafforest**

reform (rɪˈfɔːm) *vb* **1** (*tr*) to improve (an existing institution, law, practice, etc) by alteration or correction of abuses **2** to give up or cause to give up a reprehensible habit or immoral way of life **3** *chem* to change the molecular structure of (a hydrocarbon) to make it suitable for use as petrol by heat, pressure, and the action of catalysts ⊳ *n* **4** an improvement or change for the better, esp as a result of correction of legal or political abuses or malpractices **5** a principle, campaign, or measure aimed at achieving such change **6** improvement of morals or behaviour, esp by giving up some vice [C14 via Old French from Latin *reformāre* to form again] > reˈformable *adj* > reˈformative *adj* > reˈformer *n*

re-form (riːˈfɔːm) *vb* to form anew > ˌre-forˈmation *n*

reformation (ˌrɛfəˈmeɪʃən) *n* the act or an instance of reforming or the state of being reformed > ˌreforˈmational *adj*

Reformation (ˌrɛfəˈmeɪʃən) *n* a religious and political movement of 16th-century Europe that began as an attempt to reform the Roman Catholic Church and resulted in the establishment of the Protestant Churches

reformatory (rɪˈfɔːmətərɪ, -trɪ) *n, pl* -ries **1** Also called: **reform school** (formerly) a place of instruction where young offenders were sent for corrective training. Compare **approved school** ⊳ *adj* **2** having the purpose or function of reforming

Reform Bill *or* **Act** *n Brit history* any of several bills or acts extending the franchise or redistributing parliamentary seats, esp the acts of 1832 and 1867

Reformed (rɪˈfɔːmd) *adj* **1** of or designating a Protestant Church, esp the Calvinist as distinct from the Lutheran **2** of or designating Reform Judaism

reformism (rɪˈfɔːmɪzəm) *n* a doctrine or movement advocating reform, esp political or religious reform, rather than abolition > reˈformist *n, adj*

Reform Judaism *n* a movement in Judaism originating in the 19th century, which does not require strict observance of the law, but adapts the historical forms of Judaism to the contemporary world. Compare **Orthodox Judaism, Conservative Judaism**

reformulate (riːˈfɔːmjʊˌleɪt) *vb* to change or update (an idea, plan, etc already formulated) > ˌreformuˈlation *n*

refract (rɪˈfrækt) *vb* (*tr*) **1** to cause to undergo refraction **2** to measure the refractive capabilities of (the eye, a lens, etc) [C17 from Latin *refractus* broken up, from *refringere*, from RE- + *frangere* to break] > reˈfractable *adj*

refracting telescope *n* a type of telescope in which the image is formed by a set of lenses. Also called: **refractor**. Compare **reflecting telescope**

refraction (rɪˈfrækʃən) *n* **1** *physics* the change in direction of a propagating wave, such as light or sound, in passing from one medium to another in which it has a different velocity **2** the amount by which a wave is refracted **3** the ability of the eye to refract light **4** the determination of the refractive condition of the eye **5** *astronomy* the apparent elevation in position of a celestial body resulting from the refraction of light by the earth's atmosphere

refractive (rɪˈfræktɪv) *adj* **1** of or concerned with refraction **2** (of a material or substance) capable of causing refraction > reˈfractively *adv* > reˈfractiveness *or* refractivity (ˌriːfrækˈtɪvɪtɪ) *n*

refractive index *n physics* a measure of the extent to which radiation is refracted on passing through the interface between two media. It is the ratio of the sine of the angle of incidence to the sine of the angle of refraction, which can be shown to be equal to the ratio of the phase speed in the first medium to that in the second. In the case of electromagnetic radiation, esp light, it is usual to give values of the **absolute refractive index** of a medium, that is for radiation entering the medium from free space. Symbol: ν, μ

refractometer (ˌriːfrækˈtɒmɪtə) *n* any instrument for determining the refractive index of a substance > refractometric (rɪˌfræktəˈmɛtrɪk) *adj* > ˌrefracˈtometry *n*

refractor (rɪˈfræktə) *n* **1** an object or material that refracts **2** another name for **refracting telescope**

refractory (rɪˈfræktərɪ) *adj* **1** unmanageable or obstinate **2** *med* not responding to treatment **3** (of a material) able to withstand high temperatures without fusion or decomposition ⊳ *n, pl* -ries **4** a material, such as fireclay or alumina, that is able to withstand high temperatures: used to line furnaces, kilns, etc [C17 variant of obsolete *refractary*; see REFRACT] > reˈfractorily *adv* > reˈfractoriness *n*

refractory period *n* a period during which a nerve or muscle is incapable of responding to stimulation, esp immediately following a previous stimulation. In an **absolute refractory period** there is a total inability to respond; in an **effective** *or* **relative refractory period** there is a response to very large stimuli

refrain[1] (rɪˈfreɪn) *vb* (*intr*; usually foll by *from*) to abstain (from action); forbear [C14 from Latin *refrēnāre* to check with a bridle, from RE- + *frēnum* a bridle] > reˈfrainer *n* > reˈfrainment *n*

refrain[2] (rɪˈfreɪn) *n* **1** a regularly recurring melody, such as the chorus of a song **2** a much repeated saying or idea [C14 via Old French, ultimately from Latin *refringere* to break into pieces]

reframe (riːˈfreɪm) *verb* (*tr*) **1** to support or enclose (a picture, photograph, etc) in a new or different frame **2** to change the plans or basic details of (a policy, idea, etc): *reframe policy issues and problems* **3** to look at, present, or think of (beliefs, ideas, relationships, etc) in a new or different way **4** to change the focus or perspective of (a view) through a lens **5** to say (something) in a different way: *reframe the question*

refrangible (rɪˈfrændʒɪbəl) *adj* capable of being refracted [C17 from Latin *refringere* to break up, from RE- + *frangere* to break] > reˌfrangiˈbility *or* reˈfrangibleness *n*

refreeze (riːˈfriːz) *vb* -freezes, -freezing, -froze, -frozen to freeze or be frozen again after having defrosted

refresh (rɪˈfrɛʃ) *vb* **1** (*usually tr or reflexive*) to make or become fresh or vigorous, as through rest, drink, or food; revive or reinvigorate **2** (*tr*) to enliven (something worn or faded), as by adding new decorations **3** (*tr*) to stimulate (the memory) **4** (*tr*) to replenish, as with new equipment or stores **5** *computing* to display the latest updated version (of a web page or document); reload [c14 from Old French *refreschir*; see RE-, FRESH] > reˈ**freshful** *adj*

refresher (rɪˈfrɛʃə) *n* **1** something that refreshes, such as a cold drink **2** *English law* a fee, additional to that marked on the brief, paid to counsel in a case that lasts more than a day

refresher course *n* a short educational course for people to review their subject and developments in it

refreshing (rɪˈfrɛʃɪŋ) *adj* **1** able to or tending to refresh; invigorating **2** pleasantly different or novel > reˈ**freshingly** *adv*

refreshment (rɪˈfrɛʃmənt) *n* **1** the act of refreshing or the state of being refreshed **2** (*plural*) snacks and drinks served as a light meal

refresh rate *n computing* the frequency at which the image on a monitor is renewed

refrigerant (rɪˈfrɪdʒərənt) *n* **1** a fluid capable of changes of phase at low temperatures: used as the working fluid of a refrigerator **2** a cooling substance, such as ice or solid carbon dioxide **3** *med* an agent that provides a sensation of coolness or reduces fever ▷ *adj* **4** causing cooling or freezing

refrigerate (rɪˈfrɪdʒəˌreɪt) *vb* to make or become frozen or cold, esp for preservative purposes; chill or freeze [c16 from Latin *refrīgerāre* to make cold, from RE- + *frīgus* cold] > reˌ**frigerˈation** *n* > reˈ**frigerative** *adj* > reˈ**frigeratory** *adj, n*

refrigerator (rɪˈfrɪdʒəˌreɪtə) *n* a chamber in which food, drink, etc, are kept cool. Informal word: **fridge**

refringent (rɪˈfrɪndʒənt) *adj physics* of, concerned with, or causing refraction; refractive [c18 from Latin *refringere* to break up; see REFRACT] > reˈ**fringency** *or* reˈ**fringence** *n*

reft (rɛft) *vb* a past tense and past participle of **reave**

refuel (riːˈfjuːəl) *vb* **-els, -elling, -elled** *or US* **-els, -eling, -eled** to supply or be supplied with fresh fuel

refuge (ˈrɛfjuːdʒ) *n* **1** shelter or protection, as from the weather or danger **2** any place, person, action, or thing that offers or appears to offer protection, help, or relief: *accused of incompetence, he took refuge in lying* **3** another name for **traffic island**. ▷ *vb* **4** *archaic* to take refuge or give refuge to [c14 via Old French from Latin *refugium*, from *refugere* to flee away, from RE- + *fugere* to escape]

refugee (ˌrɛfjʊˈdʒiː) *n* **a** a person who has fled from some danger or problem, esp political persecution: *refugees from Rwanda* **b** (*as modifier*): *a refugee camp; a refugee problem* > ˌ**refuˈgeeism** *n*

refugee capital *n finance* money from abroad invested, esp for a short term, in the country offering the highest interest rate

refugium (rɪˈfjuːdʒɪəm) *n, pl* **-gia** (-dʒɪə) a geographical region that has remained unaltered by a climatic change affecting surrounding regions and that therefore forms a haven for relict fauna and flora [c20 Latin: refuge]

refulgent (rɪˈfʌldʒənt) *adj literary* shining, brilliant, or radiant [c16 from Latin *refulgēre* to shine brightly, from RE- + *fulgēre* to shine] > reˈ**fulgence** *or less commonly* reˈ**fulgency** *n* > reˈ**fulgently** *adv*

refund *vb* (rɪˈfʌnd) (*tr*) **1** to give back (money), as when an article purchased is unsatisfactory **2** to reimburse (a person) ▷ *n* (ˈriːˌfʌnd) **3** return of money to a purchaser or the amount so returned [c14 from Latin *refundere* to pour back, from RE- + *fundere* to pour] > reˈ**fundable** *adj* > reˈ**funder** *n*

re-fund (riːˈfʌnd) *vb* (*tr*) *finance* **1** to discharge (an old or matured debt) by new borrowing, as by a new bond issue **2** to replace (an existing bond issue) with a new one [c20 from RE- + FUND]

refurbish (riːˈfɜːbɪʃ) *vb* (*tr*) to make neat, clean, or complete, as by renovating, re-equipping, or restoring > reˈ**furbishing** *or* reˈ**furbishment** *n*

refusal (rɪˈfjuːzəl) *n* **1** the act or an instance of refusing **2** the opportunity to reject or accept; option

refuse[1] (rɪˈfjuːz) *vb* **1** (*tr*) to decline to accept (something offered): *to refuse a present; to refuse promotion* **2** to decline to give or grant (something) to (a person, organization, etc) **3** (when *tr*, *takes an infinitive*) to express determination not (to do something); decline: *he refuses to talk about it* **4** (of a horse) to be unwilling to take (a jump), as by swerving or stopping **5** (*tr*) (of a woman) to declare one's unwillingness to accept (a suitor) as a husband [c14 from Old French *refuser*, from Latin *refundere* to pour back; see REFUND] > reˈ**fusable** *adj* > reˈ**fuser** *n*

refuse[2] (ˈrɛfjuːs) *n* **a** anything thrown away; waste; rubbish **b** (*as modifier*): *a refuse collection* [c15 from Old French *refuser* to REFUSE[1]]

refusenik *or* **refusnik** (rɪˈfjuːznɪk) *n* **1** (formerly) a Jew in the Soviet Union who had been refused permission to emigrate **2** a person who refuses to cooperate with a system or comply with a law because of a moral conviction [c20 from REFUSE[1] + -NIK]

refutation (ˌrɛfjʊˈteɪʃən) *n* **1** the act or process of refuting **2** something that refutes; disproof

refute (rɪˈfjuːt) *vb* **1** (*tr*) to prove (a statement, theory, charge, etc) of (a person) to be false or incorrect; disprove **2** to deny (a claim, charge, allegation, etc) [c16 from Latin *refūtāre* to rebut] > **refutable** (ˈrɛfjʊtəbəl, rɪˈfjuː-) *adj* > **refutability** (ˌrɛfjʊtəˈbɪlɪtɪ, rɪˌfjuː-) *n* > ˈ**refutably** *adv* > reˈ**futer** *n*

> **USAGE** The use of *refute* to mean *deny* is thought by many people to be incorrect

Reg. *abbreviation for* **1** Regent **2** Regina

regain *vb* (rɪˈgeɪn) (*tr*) **1** to take or get back; recover **2** to reach again ▷ *n* (ˈriːˌgeɪn) **3** the process of getting something back, esp lost weight: *this regain was inevitable* > reˈ**gainable** *adj* > reˈ**gainer** *n*

regal[1] (ˈriːgəl) *adj* of, relating to, or befitting a king or queen; royal [c14 from Latin *rēgālis* from *rēx* king] > ˈ**regally** *adv*

regal[2] (ˈriːgəl) *n* (*sometimes plural*) a portable organ equipped only with small reed pipes, popular from the 15th century and recently revived for modern performance [c16 from French *régale*; of obscure origin]

regale (rɪˈgeɪl) *vb* (*tr*; usually foll by *with*) **1** to give delight or amusement to: *he regaled them with stories of his youth* **2** to provide with choice or abundant food or drink ▷ *n* **3** *archaic* **a** a feast **b** a delicacy of food or drink [c17 from French *régaler*, from *gale* pleasure; related to Middle Dutch *wale* riches; see also GALA] > reˈ**galement** *n*

regalia (rɪˈgeɪlɪə) *pl n* (*sometimes functioning as singular*) **1** the ceremonial emblems or robes of royalty, high office, an order, etc **2** any splendid or special clothes; finery [c16 from Medieval Latin: royal privileges, from Latin *rēgālis* REGAL[1]]

regality (riːˈgælɪtɪ) *n, pl* **-ties** **1** the state or condition of being royal; kingship or queenship; royalty **2** the rights or privileges of royalty **3** *Scot history* **a** jurisdiction conferred by the sovereign on a powerful subject **b** a territory under such jurisdiction

regard (rɪˈgɑːd) *vb* **1** to look closely or attentively at (something or someone); observe steadily **2** (*tr*) to hold (a person or thing) in respect, admiration, or affection: *we regard your work very highly* **3** (*tr*) to look upon or consider in a specified way: *she regarded her brother as her responsibility* **4** (*tr*) to relate to; concern; have a bearing on **5** to take notice of or pay attention to (something); heed: *he has never regarded the conventions* **6** **as regards** (*preposition*) in respect of; concerning ▷ *n* **7** a gaze; look **8** attention; heed: *he spends without regard to his bank balance* **9** esteem, affection, or respect **10** reference, relation, or connection (esp in the phrases **with regard to** *or* **in regard to**) **11** (*plural*) good wishes or greetings (esp in the phrase **with kind regards**, used at the close of a letter) **12** in this regard on this point [c14 from Old French *regarder* to look at, care about, from RE- + *garder* to GUARD] > reˈ**gardable** *adj*

regardant (rɪˈgɑːdənt) *adj* (*usually postpositive*) *heraldry* (of a beast) shown looking backwards over its shoulder [c15 from Old French; see REGARD]

regardful (rɪˈgɑːdfʊl) *adj* **1** (often foll by *of*) showing regard (for); heedful (of) **2** showing regard, respect, or consideration > reˈ**gardfully** *adv* > reˈ**gardfulness** *n*

regarding (rɪˈgɑːdɪŋ) *prep* in respect of; on the subject of

regardless (rɪˈgɑːdlɪs) *adj* **1** (usually foll by *of*) taking no regard or heed; heedless ▷ *adv* **2** in spite of everything; disregarding drawbacks: *to carry on regardless* > reˈ**gardlessly** *adv* > reˈ**gardlessness** *n*

regatta (rɪˈgætə) *n* an organized series of races of yachts, rowing boats, etc [c17 from obsolete Italian (Venetian dialect) *rigatta* contest, of obscure origin]

regd *abbreviation for* registered

regelate (ˈriːdʒɪˌleɪt) *vb physics* to undergo or cause to undergo regelation [c19 from RE- + stem of participle of Latin *gelāre* to freeze]

regelation (ˌriːdʒɪˈleɪʃən) *n* the rejoining together of two pieces of ice as a result of melting under pressure at the interface between them and subsequent refreezing

regency (ˈriːdʒənsɪ) *n, pl* **-cies** **1** government by a regent or a body of regents **2** the office of a regent or body of regents **3** a territory under the jurisdiction of a regent or body of regents [c15 from Medieval Latin *regentia*, from Latin *regere* to rule]

Regency (ˈriːdʒənsɪ) *n* (preceded by *the*) **1** (in the United Kingdom) the period (1811–20) during which the Prince of Wales (later George IV (1762–1830; king 1820–30)) acted as regent during his father's periods of insanity **2** (in France) the period of the regency of Philip, Duke of Orleans, during the minority (1715–23) of Louis XV (1710–74; king 1715–74) ▷ *adj* **3** characteristic of or relating to the Regency periods in France or the United Kingdom or to the styles of architecture, furniture, art, literature, etc, produced in them

regenerate *vb* (rɪˈdʒɛnəˌreɪt) **1** to undergo or cause to undergo moral, spiritual, or physical renewal or invigoration **2** to form or be formed again; come or bring into existence once again **3** to replace (lost or damaged tissues or organs) by new growth, or to cause (such tissues) to be replaced **4** *chem* to restore or be restored to an original physical or chemical state **5** (*tr*) *electronics* (in a digital system) to reshape (distorted incoming pulses) for onward transmission ▷ *adj* (rɪˈdʒɛnərɪt) **6** morally, spiritually, or physically renewed or reborn; restored or refreshed > reˈ**generable** *adj* > reˈ**generacy** *n* > reˈ**generative** *adj* > reˈ**generatively** *adv* > reˈ**generˌator** *n*

regeneration (rɪˌdʒɛnəˈreɪʃən) *n* **1** the act or process of regenerating or the state of being regenerated; rebirth or renewal **2** the regrowth by an animal or plant of an organ, tissue, or part that has been lost or destroyed **3** *electronics* the use of positive feedback to increase the amplification of a radio frequency stage

regenerative cooling *n* the process of cooling the walls of the combustion chamber of a rocket by circulating the propellant around the chamber before combustion

Regensburg (*German* ˈreːgənsbʊrk) *n* a city in SE Germany, in Bavaria on the River Danube: a free Imperial city from 1245 and the leading commercial city of S Germany in the 12th and 13th centuries; the Imperial Diet was held in the town hall from 1663 to 1806. Pop: 128 604 (2003 est). Former English name: **Ratisbon**

regent ('ri:dʒənt) *n* **1** the ruler or administrator of a country during the minority, absence, or incapacity of its monarch **2** (formerly) a senior teacher or administrator in any of certain universities **3** *US and Canadian* a member of the governing board of certain schools and colleges **4** *rare* any person who governs or rules ▷ *adj* **5** (*usually postpositive*) acting or functioning as a regent: *a queen regent* **6** *rare* governing, ruling, or controlling [c14 from Latin *regēns* ruling, from *regere* to rule] > ˈregental *adj* > ˈregentship *n*

regent bowerbird *or* **regent bird** *n* an Australian bowerbird, *Sericulus chrysocephalus*, the male of which has a showy yellow and velvety-black plumage [after the Prince Regent, the title of George IV (1762–1830) as regent of Great Britain and Ireland during the insanity of his father (1811–20)]

regent honeyeater *n* a large brightly-coloured Australian honeyeater, *Zanthomiza phrygia*

Regent's Park *n* a park in central London, laid out as Marylebone Park by John Nash; now known for the London Zoo, its open-air theatre, and Nash's curved terraces

reggae ('rɛgeɪ) *n* a type of West Indian popular music having four beats to the bar, the upbeat being strongly accented [c20 of West Indian origin]

Reggio di Calabria (*Italian* 'reddʒo di ka'la:brja) *n* a port in S Italy, in Calabria on the Strait of Messina: founded about 720 BC by Greek colonists. Pop: 180 353 (2001)

Reggio nell'Emilia (*Italian* 'reddʒo nelle'mi:lja) *n* a city in N central Italy, in Emilia-Romagna: founded in the 2nd century BC by Marcus Aemilius Lepidus; ruled by the Este family in the 15th–18th centuries. Pop: 141 877 (2001)

regicide ('rɛdʒɪˌsaɪd) *n* **1** the killing of a king **2** a person who kills a king [c16 from Latin *rēx* king + -CIDE] > ˌregiˈcidal *adj*

regime *or* **régime** (reɪ'ʒi:m) *n* **1** a system of government or a particular administration: *a fascist regime; the regime of Fidel Castro* **2** a social system or order **3** *med* another word for **regimen** (sense 1) [c18 from French, from Latin *regimen* guidance, from *regere* to rule]

regime change *n* the transition from one political regime to another, esp through concerted political or military action

regimen ('rɛdʒɪˌmɛn) *n* **1** Also called: **regime** a systematic way of life or course of therapy, often including exercise and a recommended diet **2** administration or rule [c14 from Latin: guidance]

regiment *n* ('rɛdʒɪmənt) **1** a military formation varying in size from a battalion to a number of battalions **2** a large number in regular or organized groups: *regiments of beer bottles* ▷ *vb* ('rɛdʒɪˌmɛnt) (*tr*) **3** to force discipline or order on, esp in a domineering manner **4** to organize into a regiment or regiments **5** to form into organized groups **6** to assign to a regiment [c14 via Old French from Late Latin *regimentum* government, from Latin *regere* to rule] > ˌregiˈmental *adj* > ˌregiˈmentally *adv* > ˌregimenˈtation *n*

regimentals (ˌrɛdʒɪˈmɛntəlz) *pl n* **1** the uniform and insignia of a regiment **2** military dress

regimental sergeant major *n* *military* the senior Warrant Officer I in a British or Commonwealth regiment or battalion, responsible under the adjutant for all aspects of duty and discipline of the warrant officers, NCOs, and men. Abbreviation: **RSM** See also **company sergeant major** See also **warrant officer**

Regin ('reɪgɪn) *n* *Norse myth* a dwarf smith, tutor of Sigurd, whom he encouraged to kill Fafnir for the gold he guarded

Regina¹ (rɪ'dʒaɪnə) *n* queen: now used chiefly in documents, inscriptions, etc. Compare **Rex**

Regina² (rɪ'dʒaɪnə) *n* a city in W Canada, capital and largest city of Saskatchewan: founded in 1882 as Pile O'Bones. Pop: 178 225 (2001)

region ('ri:dʒən) *n* **1** any large, indefinite, and continuous part of a surface or space **2** an area considered as a unit for geographical, functional, social, or cultural reasons **3** an administrative division of a country: *Tuscany is one of the regions of the Italian Republic* **4** a realm or sphere of activity or interest **5** range, area, or scope: *in what region is the price likely to be?* **6** (in Scotland from 1975 until 1996) any of the nine territorial divisions into which the mainland of Scotland was divided for purposes of local government; replaced in 1996 by council areas. See also **islands council** [c14 from Latin *regiō*, from *regere* to govern]

regional ('ri:dʒənᵊl) *adj* of, characteristic of, or limited to a region: *the regional dialects of English* > ˈregionally *adv*

regional enteritis *n* another name for **Crohn's disease**

regionalism ('ri:dʒənəˌlɪzəm) *n* **1** division of a country into administrative regions having partial autonomy **2** advocacy of such division **3** loyalty to one's home region; regional patriotism **4** the common interests of national groups, people, etc, living in the same part of the world **5** a word, custom, accent, or other characteristic associated with a specific region > ˈregionalist *n, adj*

régisseur *French* (reʒisœr) *n* an official in a dance company with varying duties, usually including directing productions [from *régir* to manage]

register ('rɛdʒɪstə) *n* **1** an official or formal list recording names, events, or transactions **2** the book in which such a list is written **3** an entry in such a list **4** a recording device that accumulates data, totals sums of money, etc: *a cash register* **5** a movable plate that controls the flow of air into a furnace, chimney, room, etc **6** *computing* one of a set of word-sized locations in the central processing unit in which items of data are placed temporarily before they are operated on by program instructions **7** *music* **a** the timbre characteristic of a certain manner of voice production. See **head voice, chest voice b** any of the stops on an organ as classified in respect of its tonal quality: *the flute register* **8** *printing* **a** the correct alignment of the separate plates in colour printing **b** the exact correspondence of lines of type, columns, etc, on the two sides of a printed sheet of paper **9** a form of a language associated with a particular social situation or subject matter, such as obscene slang, legal language, or journalese **10** the act or an instance of registering ▷ *vb* **11** (*tr*) to enter or cause someone to enter (an event, person's name, ownership, etc) on a register; formally record **12** to show or be shown on a scale or other measuring instrument: *the current didn't register on the meter* **13** to show or be shown in a person's face, bearing, etc: *his face registered surprise* **14** (*intr*) to have an effect; make an impression: *the news of her uncle's death just did not register* **15** to send (a letter, package, etc) by registered post **16** (*tr*) *printing* to adjust (a printing press, forme, etc) to ensure that the printed matter is in register **17** (*intr*; often foll by *with*) (of a mechanical part) to align (with another part) **18** *military* to bring (a gun) to bear on its target by adjustment according to the accuracy of observed single rounds [c14 from Medieval Latin *registrum*, from Latin *regerere* to transcribe, from RE- + *gerere* to bear] > ˈregisterer *n* > ˈregistrable *adj*

registered disabled *adj* *social welfare* (in Britain) **1** (of a handicapped person) on a local authority register under the Chronically Sick and Disabled Persons Act 1970 **2** on a register kept by the Manpower Services Commission for employment purposes, and holding a green identity card, thus qualifying for special services ▷ Also called: **registered handicapped**. See also **green card** (sense 3), **handicap register**

Registered General Nurse *n* (in Britain) a nurse who has completed a three-year training course in all aspects of nursing care to enable the nurse to be registered with the United Kingdom Central Council for Nursing, Midwifery, and Health Visiting. Abbreviation: RGN

registered post *n* **1** a Post Office service by which compensation is paid for loss or damage to mail for which a registration fee has been paid. Compare **recorded delivery 2** mail sent by this service

Registered Trademark *n* See **trademark** (sense 1)

register mark *n* *printing* any of several marks incorporated on to printing plates to assist in the accurate positioning of images during printing

register office *n* *Brit* a government office where civil marriages are performed and births, marriages, and deaths are recorded. Often called: **registry office**

register ton *n* the full name for **ton¹** (sense 7)

registrant ('rɛdʒɪstrənt) *n* a person who registers a trademark or patent

registrar (ˌrɛdʒɪ'strɑː, 'rɛdʒɪˌstrɑː) *n* **1** a person who keeps official records **2** an administrative official responsible for student records, enrolment procedure, etc, in a school, college, or university **3** *Brit and NZ* a hospital doctor senior to a houseman but junior to a consultant, specializing in either medicine (**medical registrar**) or surgery (**surgical registrar**) **4** *chiefly US* a person employed by a company to maintain a register of its security issues > ˈregistrarship *n*

registration (ˌrɛdʒɪ'streɪʃən) *n* **1 a** the act of registering or state of being registered **b** (*as modifier*): *a registration number* **2** an entry in a register **3** a group of people, such as students, who register at a particular time **4** a combination of organ or harpsichord stops used in the performance of a piece of music > ˌregis'trational *adj*

registration document *n* *Brit* a document giving identification details of a motor vehicle, including its manufacturer, date of registration, engine and chassis numbers, and owner's name. Compare **logbook** (sense 2)

registration number *n* a sequence of letters and numbers assigned to a motor vehicle when it is registered, usually indicating the year and place of registration, displayed on numberplates at the front and rear of the vehicle, and by which the vehicle may be identified

registration plate *n* *Austral and NZ* a plate mounted on the front and back of a motor vehicle bearing the registration number. Also called (US): **license plate**, (Canadian) **licence plate**, (Brit and South African) **numberplate**

registry ('rɛdʒɪstrɪ) *n, pl* -tries **1** a place where registers are kept, such as the part of a church where the bride and groom sign a register after a wedding **2** the registration of a ship's country of origin: *a ship of Liberian registry* **3** another word for **registration**

registry office *n* *Brit* a name often used for a **register office**

Regius professor ('ri:dʒɪəs) *n* *Brit* a person appointed by the Crown to a university chair founded by a royal patron [c17 *regius*, from Latin: royal, from *rex* king]

reglet ('rɛglɪt) *n* **1** a flat narrow architectural moulding **2** *printing* a strip of oiled wood used for spacing between lines of hot metal type. Compare **lead²** (sense 7) [c16 from Old French, literally: a little rule, from *regle* rule, from Latin *rēgula*]

regmaker ('rɛxˌmɑːkə) *n* *South African* a drink taken to relieve the symptoms of a hangover; a pick-me-up [Afrikaans]

regnal ('rɛgnəl) *adj* **1** of a sovereign, reign, or kingdom **2** designating a year of a sovereign's reign calculated from the date of his or her accession [c17 from Medieval Latin *rēgnālis*, from Latin *rēgnum* sovereignty; see REIGN]

regnant ('rɛgnənt) *adj* **1** (*postpositive*) reigning **2** prevalent; current [c17 from Latin *regnāre* to REIGN] > ˈregnancy *n*

rego ('rɛdʒəʊ) *n* *Austral slang* **a** the registration of a motor vehicle **b** a fee paid for this

regolith ('rɛgəlɪθ) *n* the layer of loose material covering the bedrock of the earth and moon, etc, comprising soil, sand, rock fragments, volcanic ash, glacial drift, etc [c20 from Greek *rhēgos* covering, blanket + *lithos* stone]

regorge (rɪ'gɔːdʒ) *vb* **1** (*tr*) to vomit up; disgorge **2** (*intr*) (esp of water) to flow or run back [c17 from French *regorger*; see GORGE]

regosol ('rɛgəˌsɒl) *n* a type of azonal soil consisting of unconsolidated material derived from freshly deposited alluvium or sands [c20 from Greek *rhēgos* covering, blanket + Latin *solum* soil]

Reg. prof. *abbreviation for* Regius professor

regrate (rɪ'greɪt) *vb* (*tr*) **1** to buy up (commodities) in advance so as to raise their price for profitable resale **2** to resell (commodities so purchased); retail **3** *building trades* to redress the surface of (hewn stonework) [c15 from Old French *regrater* perhaps from RE- + *grater* to scratch] > **re'grater** *n*

regress *vb* (rɪ'grɛs) **1** (*intr*) to return or revert, as to a former place, condition, or mode of behaviour **2** (*tr*) *statistics* to measure the extent to which (a dependent variable) is associated with one or more independent variables ▷ *n* ('riːgrɛs) **3** the act of regressing **4** movement in a backward direction; retrogression **5** *logic* a supposed explanation each stage of which requires to be similarly explained, as saying that knowledge requires a justification in terms of propositions themselves known to be true [c14 from Latin *regressus* a retreat, from *regredī* to go back, from RE- + *gradī* to go] > **re'gressor** *n*

regression (rɪ'grɛʃən) *n* **1** *psychol* the adoption by an adult or adolescent of behaviour more appropriate to a child, esp as a defence mechanism to avoid anxiety **2** *statistics* **a** the analysis or measure of the association between one variable (the dependent variable) and one or more other variables (the independent variables), usually formulated in an equation in which the independent variables have parametric coefficients, which may enable future values of the dependent variable to be predicted **b** (*as modifer*): *regression curve* **3** *astronomy* the slow movement around the ecliptic of the two points at which the moon's orbit intersects the ecliptic. One complete revolution occurs about every 19 years **4** *geology* the retreat of the sea from the land **5** the act of regressing

regressive (rɪ'grɛsɪv) *adj* **1** regressing or tending to regress **2** (of a tax or tax system) levied or graduated so that the rate decreases as the amount taxed increases. Compare **progressive** (sense 5) **3** of, relating to, or characteristic of regression > **re'gressively** *adv* > **re'gressiveness** *n*

regret (rɪ'grɛt) *vb* **-grets, -gretting, -gretted** (*tr*) **1** (*may take a clause as object or an infinitive*) to feel sorry, repentant, or upset about **2** to bemoan or grieve the death or loss of ▷ *n* **3** a sense of repentance, guilt, or sorrow, as over some wrong done or an unfulfilled ambition **4** a sense of loss or grief **5** (*plural*) a polite expression of sadness, esp in a formal refusal of an invitation [c14 from Old French *regrete*, of Scandinavian origin; compare Old Norse *grāta* to weep] > **re'gretful** *adj* > **re'gretfully** *adv* > **re'gretfulness** *n* > **re'grettable** *adj* > **re'grettably** *adv* > **re'gretter** *n*

> USAGE *Regretful* and *regretfully* are sometimes wrongly used where *regrettable* and *regrettably* are meant: *he gave a regretful smile; he smiled regretfully; this is a regrettable* (not *regretful*) *mistake; regrettably* (not *regretfully*), *I shall be unable to attend*

regroup (riː'gruːp) *vb* **1** to reorganize (military forces), esp after an attack or a defeat **2** (*tr*) to rearrange into a new grouping or groupings **3** (*intr*) to consider using different tactics after a setback in a contest or argument

regrow (riː'grəʊ) *vb* **-grows, -growing, -grew, -grown** to grow or be grown again after having been cut or having died or withered

regrowth (riː'grəʊθ) *n* **1** the growing back of hair, plants, etc **2** the resurgence of an industry, economy, etc

Regt *abbreviation for* **1** Regent **2** Regiment

regulable ('rɛgjʊləb^{ə}l) *adj* able to be regulated

regular ('rɛgjʊlə) *adj* **1** normal, customary, or usual **2** according to a uniform principle, arrangement, or order: *trees planted at regular intervals* **3** occurring at fixed or prearranged intervals: *to make a regular call on a customer* **4** following a set rule or normal practice; methodical or orderly **5** symmetrical in appearance or form; even: *regular features* **6** (*prenominal*) organized, elected, conducted, etc, in a proper or officially prescribed manner **7** (*prenominal*) officially qualified or recognized: *he's not a regular doctor* **8** (*prenominal*) (intensifier): *a regular fool* **9** *US and Canadian informal* likable, dependable, or nice (esp in the phrase **a regular guy**) **10** denoting or relating to the personnel or units of the permanent military services: *a regular soldier; the regular army* **11** (of flowers) having any of their parts, esp petals, alike in size, shape, arrangement, etc; symmetrical **12** (of the formation, inflections, etc, of a word) following the usual pattern of formation in a language **13** *maths* **a** (of a polygon) equilateral and equiangular **b** (of a polyhedron) having identical regular polygons as faces that make identical angles with each other **c** (of a prism) having regular polygons as bases **d** (of a pyramid) having a regular polygon as a base and the altitude passing through the centre of the base **e** another name for **analytic** (sense 5) **14** *botany* another word for **actinomorphic** **15** (*postpositive*) subject to the rule of an established religious order or community: *canons regular* **16** *US politics* of, selected by, or loyal to the leadership or platform of a political party: *a regular candidate; regular policies* **17** *crystallog* another word for **cubic** (sense 4) ▷ *n* **18** a professional long-term serviceman in a military unit **19** *informal* a person who does something regularly, such as attending a theatre or patronizing a shop **20** a member of a religious order or congregation, as contrasted with a secular **21** *US politics* a party member loyal to the leadership, organization, platform, etc, of his party [c14 from Old French *reguler*, from Latin *rēgulāris* of a bar of wood or metal, from *rēgula* ruler, model] > **ˌregu'larity** *n* > **'regularly** *adv*

regularize *or* **regularise** ('rɛgjʊləˌraɪz) *vb* (*tr*) to make regular; cause to conform > **ˌregulari'zation** *or* **ˌregulari'sation** *n*

regulate ('rɛgjʊˌleɪt) *vb* (*tr*) **1** to adjust (the amount of heat, sound, etc, of something) as required; control **2** to adjust (an instrument or appliance) so that it operates correctly **3** to bring into conformity with a rule, principle, or usage [c17 from Late Latin *rēgulāre* to control, from Latin *rēgula* a ruler] > **'regulative** *or* **'regulatory** *adj* > **'regulatively** *adv*

regulated tenancy *n social welfare* (in Britain) the letting of a dwelling by a nonresident private landlord, usually at a registered fair rent, from which the landlord cannot evict the tenant without a possession order from a court. Compare **assured tenancy**

regulation (ˌrɛgjʊ'leɪʃən) *n* **1** the act or process of regulating **2** a rule, principle, or condition that governs procedure or behaviour **3** a governmental or ministerial order having the force of law **4** *embryol* the ability of an animal embryo to develop normally after its structure has been altered or damaged in some way **5** (*modifier*) as required by official rules or procedure: *regulation uniform* **6** (*modifier*) normal; usual; conforming to accepted standards: *a regulation haircut* **7** *electrical engineering* the change in voltage occurring when a load is connected across a power supply, caused by internal resistance (for direct current) or internal impedance (alternating current)

regulator ('rɛgjʊˌleɪtə) *n* **1** a person or thing that regulates **2** the mechanism, including the hairspring and the balance wheel, by which the speed of a timepiece is regulated **3** a timepiece, known to be accurate, by which others are timed and regulated **4** any of various mechanisms or devices, such as a governor valve, for controlling fluid flow, pressure, temperature, voltage, etc **5** Also called: **regulator gene** a gene the product of which controls the synthesis of a product from another gene

regulo ('rɛgjʊləʊ) *n* any of a number of temperatures to which a gas oven may be set: *cook at regulo 4 for 40 minutes* [c20 from *Regulo*, trademark for a type of thermostatic control on gas ovens]

regulus ('rɛgjʊləs) *n, pl* **-luses** *or* **-li** (-ˌlaɪ) impure metal forming beneath the slag during the smelting of ores [c16 from Latin: a petty king, from *rēx* king; formerly used for *antimony*, because it combines readily with gold, thought of as the king of metals] > **'reguline** *adj*

Regulus ('rɛgjʊləs) *n* the brightest star in the constellation Leo. Visual magnitude: 1.3; spectral type: B8; distance: 69 light years

regurgitate (rɪ'gɜːdʒɪˌteɪt) *vb* **1** to vomit forth (partially digested food) **2** (of some birds and certain other animals) to bring back to the mouth (undigested or partly digested food with which to feed the young) **3** (*intr*) to be cast up or out, esp from the mouth **4** (*intr*) *med* (of blood) to flow backwards, in a direction opposite to the normal one, esp through a defective heart valve [c17 from Medieval Latin *regurgitāre*, from RE- + *gurgitāre* to flood, from Latin *gurges* gulf, whirlpool] > **re'gurgitant** *n, adj* > **reˌgurgi'tation** *n*

rehab ('riːhæb) *n* **1** short for **rehabilitation** **2** *NZ informal* short for **Rehabilitation Department**

rehabilitate (ˌriːə'bɪlɪˌteɪt) *vb* (*tr*) **1** to help (a person who has acquired a disability or addiction or who has just been released from prison) to readapt to society or a new job, as by vocational guidance, retraining, or therapy **2** to restore to a former position or rank **3** to restore the good reputation of [c16 from Medieval Latin *rehabilitāre* to restore, from RE- + Latin *habilitās* skill, ABILITY] > **ˌreha'bilitative** *adj*

rehabilitation (ˌriːəˌbɪlɪ'teɪʃən) *n* **1** the act or process of rehabilitating **2** *med* **a** the treatment of physical disabilities by massage, electrotherapy, or exercises **b** (*as modifier*): *rehabilitation centre*

Rehabilitation Department *n NZ* a government department set up after World War II to assist ex-servicemen. Often shortened to: **rehab**

rehash *vb* (riː'hæʃ) **1** (*tr*) to rework, reuse, or make over (old or already used material) ▷ *n* ('riːˌhæʃ) **2** something consisting of old, reworked, or reused material [c19 from RE- + HASH^{1} (to chop into pieces)]

rehearsal (rɪ'hɜːs^{ə}l) *n* **1** a session of practising a play, concert, speech etc, in preparation for public performance **2** the act of going through or recounting; recital: *rehearsal of his own virtues was his usual occupation* **3** **in rehearsal** being prepared for public performance

rehearse (rɪ'hɜːs) *vb* **1** to practise (a play, concert, etc), in preparation for public performance **2** (*tr*) to run through; recount; recite: *the official rehearsed the grievances of the committee* **3** (*tr*) to train or drill (a person or animal) for the public performance of a part in a play, show, etc [c16 from Anglo-Norman *rehearser*, from Old French *rehercier* to harrow a second time, from RE- + *herce* harrow] > **re'hearser** *n*

reheat *vb* (riː'hiːt) **1** to heat or be heated again: *to reheat yesterday's soup* **2** (*tr*) to add fuel to (the exhaust gases of an aircraft jet engine) to produce additional heat and thrust ▷ *n* ('riːˌhiːt) *also* **reheating** **3** *aeronautics* another name (esp Brit) for **afterburning** (sense 1) > **re'heater** *n*

rehoboam (ˌriːə'bəʊəm) *n* a wine bottle holding

the equivalent of six normal bottles (approximately 156 ounces) [C19 named after *Rehoboam*, a son of King Solomon, from Hebrew, literally: the nation is enlarged]

rehouse (riːˈhaʊz) *vb* (*tr*) to accommodate (someone or something) in a new house or building

Reich (raɪk; *German* raiç) *n* **1** the Holy Roman Empire (**First Reich**) **2** the Hohenzollern empire from 1871 to 1919 (**Second Reich**) **3** the Weimar Republic from 1919 to 1933 **4** the Nazi dictatorship from 1933 to 1945 (**Third Reich**) [German: kingdom]

Reichenberg (ˈraɪçənbɛrk) *n* the German name for **Liberec**

Reichsmark (ˈraɪks,mɑːk; *German* ˈraiçsmark) *n, pl* -**marks** *or* -**mark** the standard monetary unit of Germany between 1924 and 1948, divided into 100 **Reichspfennigs**

Reichsrat (*German* ˈraiçsrat) *n* **1** the bicameral parliament of the Austrian half of Austria-Hungary (1867–1918) **2** the council of representatives of state governments within Germany from 1919 to 1934

Reichstag (ˈraiks,tɑːg; *German* ˈraiçstak) *n* **1** Also called: **diet** (in medieval Germany) the estates or a meeting of the estates **2** the legislative assembly representing the people in the North German Confederation (1867–71) and in the German empire (1871–1919) **3** the sovereign assembly of the Weimar Republic (1919–33) **4** the building in Berlin in which this assembly met and from 1999 in which the German government meets: its destruction by fire on Feb 27, 1933 (probably by agents of the Nazi government) marked the end of Weimar democracy. It was restored in the 1990s following German reunification

reify (ˈriːɪ,faɪ) *vb* -**fies**, -**fying**, -**fied** (*tr*) to consider or make (an abstract idea or concept) real or concrete [C19 from Latin *rēs* thing; compare DEIFY] > ˌreifiˈcation *n* > ˌreifiˈcatory *adj* > ˈreiˌfier *n*

Reigate (ˈraɪgɪt, -geɪt) *n* a town in S England, in Surrey at the foot of the North Downs. Pop (including Redhill): 50 436 (2001)

reign (reɪn) *n* **1** the period during which a monarch is the official ruler of a country **2** a period during which a person or thing is dominant, influential, or powerful: *the reign of violence is over* > *vb* (*intr*) **3** to exercise the power and authority of a sovereign **4** to be accorded the rank and title of a sovereign without having ruling authority, as in a constitutional monarchy **5** to predominate; prevail: *a land where darkness reigns* **6** (*usually present participle*) to be the most recent winner of a competition, contest, etc: *the reigning heavyweight champion* [C13 from Old French *reigne*, from Latin *rēgnum* kingdom, from *rēx* king]

▮ USAGE *Reign* is sometimes wrongly written for *rein* in certain phrases: *he gave full rein* (not *reign*) *to his feelings; it will be necessary to rein in* (not *reign in*) *public spending*

reignite (ˌriːɪgˈnaɪt) *vb* **1** to catch fire or cause to catch fire again: *the burners reignited* **2** to flare up or cause to flare up again: *to reignite the war*

Reign of Terror *n* the period of Jacobin rule during the French Revolution, during which thousands of people were executed for treason (Oct 1793–July 1794)

reiki (ˈreɪkɪ) *n* a form of therapy in which the practitioner is believed to channel energy into the patient in order to encourage healing or restore wellbeing [Japanese, from *rei* universal + *ki* life force]

reimburse (ˌriːɪmˈbɜːs) *vb* (*tr*) to repay or compensate (someone) for (money already spent, losses, damages, etc) [C17 from RE- + *imburse*, from Medieval Latin *imbursāre* to put in a moneybag, from *bursa* PURSE] > ˌreimˈbursable *adj* > ˌreimˈbursement *n* > ˌreimˈburser *n*

reimport *vb* (ˌriːɪmˈpɔːt, riːˈɪmpɔːt) **1** (*tr*) to import (goods manufactured from exported raw

materials) > *n* (riːˈɪmpɔːt) **2** the act of reimporting **3** a reimported commodity > ˌreimporˈtation *n* > ˌreimˈporter *n*

reimpose (ˌriːɪmˈpəʊz) *vb* (*tr*) to establish previously imposed laws, controls, etc, again > ˌreimpoˈsition *n*

reimpression (ˌriːɪmˈprɛʃən) *n* a reprinting of a book without editorial changes or additions

Reims *or* **Rheims** (riːmz; *French* rɛ̃s) *n* a city in NE France: scene of the coronation of most French monarchs. Pop: 187 206 (1999)

rein (reɪn) *n* **1** (*often plural*) one of a pair of long straps, usually connected together and made of leather, used to control a horse, running from the side of the bit or the headstall to the hand of the rider, driver, or trainer **2** a similar device used to control a very young child **3** any form or means of control: *to take up the reins of government* **4** the direction in which a rider turns (in phrases such as **on a left** (*or* **right**) **rein, change the rein**) **5** something that restrains, controls, or guides **6** **give (a) free rein** to allow considerable freedom; remove restraints **7** **keep a tight rein on** to control carefully; limit: *we have to keep a tight rein on expenditure* **8** **on a long rein** with the reins held loosely so that the horse is relatively unconstrained **9** **shorten the reins** to take up the reins so that the distance between hand and bit is lessened, in order that the horse may be more collected > *vb* **10** (*tr*) to check, restrain, hold back, or halt with or as if with reins **11** to control or guide (a horse) with a rein or reins: *they reined left* > See also **rein in** [C13 from Old French *resne*, from Latin *retinēre* to hold back, from RE- + *tenēre* to hold; see RESTRAIN]

▮ USAGE See at **reign**

reincarnate *vb* (riːˈɪnkɑːneɪt) (*tr; often passive*) **1** to cause to undergo reincarnation; be born again > *adj* (ˌriːɪnˈkɑːnɪt) **2** born again in a new body

reincarnation (ˌriːɪnkɑːˈneɪʃən) *n* **1** the belief that on the death of the body the soul transmigrates to or is born again in another body **2** the incarnation or embodiment of a soul in a new body after it has left the old one at physical death **3** embodiment again in a new form, as of a principle or idea > ˌreincarˈnationist *n, adj*

reindeer (ˈreɪnˌdɪə) *n, pl* -**deer** *or* -**deers** a large deer, *Rangifer tarandus*, having large branched antlers in the male and female and inhabiting the arctic regions of Greenland, Europe, and Asia. It also occurs in North America, where it is known as a caribou [C14 from Old Norse *hreindȳri*, from *hreinn* reindeer + *dȳr* animal; related to Dutch *rendier*, German *Rentier*; see DEER]

Reindeer Lake *n* a lake in W Canada, in Saskatchewan and Manitoba: drains into the Churchill River via the **Reindeer River**. Area: 6390 sq km (2467 sq miles)

reindeer moss *n* any of various lichens of the genus *Cladonia*, esp *C. rangiferina*, which occur in arctic and subarctic regions, providing food for reindeer

reinfect (ˌriːɪnˈfɛkt) *vb* (*mainly tr*) to infect or contaminate again > ˌreinˈfection *n*

reinforce (ˌriːɪnˈfɔːs) *vb* (*tr*) **1** to give added strength or support to **2** to give added emphasis to; stress, support, or increase: *his rudeness reinforced my determination* **3** to give added support to (a military force) by providing more men, supplies, etc **4** *psychol* to reward an action or response of (a human or animal) so that it becomes more likely to occur again [C17 from obsolete *renforce*, from French *renforcer*; see RE- + *inforce* ENFORCE] > ˌreinˈforcement *n*

reinforced concrete *n* concrete with steel bars, mesh, etc, embedded in it to enable it to withstand tensile and shear stresses

reinforced plastic *n* plastic with fibrous matter, such as carbon fibre, embedded in it to confer additional strength

rein in *vb* (*adverb*) to stop (a horse) by pulling on the reins

reins (reɪnz) *pl n archaic* the kidneys or loins [C14 from Old French, from Latin *rēnēs* the kidneys]

reinsman (ˈreɪnzmən) *n, pl* -**men** *Austral and NZ* the driver in a trotting race

reinstall *or* **reinstal** (ˌriːɪnˈstɔːl) *vb* -**stalls**, -**stalling**, -**stalled** *or* -**stals** *or* -**stalling** *or* -**stalled** (*tr*) **1** to put in place and connect (machinery, equipment, etc) again **2** to install (computer software) again, usually to solve a technical problem **3** to put (someone) back in a position, rank, etc: *Trinidad reinstalled him against Honduras*

reinstate (ˌriːɪnˈsteɪt) *vb* (*tr*) to restore to a former rank or condition > ˌreinˈstatement *n* > ˌreinˈstator *n*

reinsure (ˌriːɪnˈʃʊə, -ˈʃɔː) *vb* (*tr*) **1** to insure again **2** (of an insurer) to obtain partial or complete insurance coverage from another insurer for (a risk on which a policy has already been issued) > ˌreinˈsurance *n* > ˌreinˈsurer *n*

reintegrate (riːˈɪntɪˌgreɪt) *vb* **1** (*tr*) to make or be made into a whole again: *to reintegrate inner divisions* **2** (*often foll by into*) to amalgamate or help to amalgamate (a group) with an existing community: *reintegrate young homeless people into society* > ˌreinteˈgration *n*

reinterpret (ˌriːɪnˈtɜːprɪt) *vb* (*tr*) to interpret (an idea, etc) in a new or different way > ˌreinˌterpreˈtation *n*

reintroduce (ˌriːɪntrəˈdjuːs) *vb* (*tr*) to introduce (something) again > ˌreintroˈduction *n*

reinvent (ˌriːɪnˈvɛnt) *vb* (*tr*) **1** to replace (a product, etc) with an entirely new version **2** to duplicate (something that already exists) in what is therefore a wasted effort (esp in the phrase **reinvent the wheel**)

reinvest (ˌriːɪnˈvɛst) *vb* to put back profits from a previous investment into the same enterprise

reinvestigate (ˌriːɪnˈvɛstɪˌgeɪt) *vb* to investigate (a crime, murder, problem, etc) again > ˌreinˌvestiˈgation *n*

reinvigorate (ˌriːɪnˈvɪgəˌreɪt) *vb* (*tr*) to put vitality and vigour back into (someone or something) > ˌreinˌvigoˈration *n*

reissue (ˌriːˈɪʃjuː) *vb* (*tr*) **1** to issue (a recording, book, etc) again > *n* **2** something, esp a recording or book, which has been issued again

reiterate (riːˈɪtəˌreɪt) *vb* (*tr; may take a clause as object*) to say or do again or repeatedly [C16 from Latin *reiterāre* to repeat, from RE- + *iterāre* to do again, from *iterum* again] > reˌiterˈation *n* > reˈiterative *adj* > reˈiteratively *adv*

Reithian *or* **Reithean** (ˈriːθɪən) *adj* of or relating to John, 1st Baron Reith, the British public servant and first director general of the BBC (1889–1971)

reive (riːv) *vb* (*intr*) *Scot and northern English dialect* to go on a plundering raid [variant of REAVE[1]] > ˈreiver *n*

reject *vb* (rɪˈdʒɛkt) (*tr*) **1** to refuse to accept, acknowledge, use, believe, etc **2** to throw out as useless or worthless; discard **3** to rebuff (a person) **4** (of an organism) to fail to accept (a foreign tissue graft or organ transplant) because of immunological incompatibility > *n* (ˈriːdʒɛkt) **5** something rejected as imperfect, unsatisfactory, or useless [C15 from Latin *rēicere* to throw back, from RE- + *jacere* to hurl] > reˈjectable *adj* > reˈjecter *or* reˈjector *n* > reˈjection *n* > reˈjective *adj*

rejig (riːˈdʒɪg) *vb* -**jigs**, -**jigging**, -**jigged** (*tr*) **1** to re-equip (a factory or plant) **2** to rearrange, alter, or manipulate, sometimes in a slightly unscrupulous way > *n* **3** the act or process of rejigging > reˈjigger *n*

rejoice (rɪˈdʒɔɪs) *vb* **1** (when *tr*, takes a clause as object or an infinitive; when *intr*, often foll by *in*) to feel or express great joy or happiness **2** (*tr*) *archaic* to cause to feel joy [C14 from Old French *resjoir*, from RE- + *joir* to be glad, from Latin *gaudēre* to rejoice] > reˈjoicer *n* > reˈjoicing *n*

rejoin[1] (riːˈdʒɔɪn) *vb* **1** to come again into company with (someone or something) **2** (*tr*) to put or join together again; reunite

rejoin² (rɪˈdʒɔɪn) *vb (tr)* 1 to say (something) in reply; answer, reply, or retort 2 *law* to answer (a claimant's reply) [C15 from Old French *rejoign-*, stem of *rejoindre*; see RE-, JOIN]

rejoinder (rɪˈdʒɔɪndə) *n* 1 a reply or response to a question or remark, esp a quick witty one; retort 2 *law* (in pleading) the answer made by a defendant to the claimant's reply [C15 from Old French *rejoindre* to REJOIN²]

rejuvenate (rɪˈdʒuːvɪˌneɪt) *vb (tr)* 1 to give new youth, restored vitality, or youthful appearance to 2 *(usually passive) geography* a to cause (a river) to begin eroding more vigorously to a new lower base level, usually because of uplift of the land b to cause (a land surface) to develop youthful features [C19 from RE- + Latin *juvenis* young] > **reˌjuveˈnation** *n* > **reˈjuveˌnator** *n*

rejuvenesce (rɪˌdʒuːvəˈnɛs) *vb* 1 to make or become youthful or restored to vitality 2 *biology* to convert (cells) or (of cells) to be converted into a more active form > **reˌjuveˈnescence** *n* > **reˌjuveˈnescent** *adj*

rekindle (riːˈkɪndᵊl) *vb* 1 to arouse or cause to be aroused again: *rekindle the romance in your relationship* 2 to set alight or start to burn again

rel. *abbreviation for* 1 relating 2 relative(ly)

relapse *vb* (rɪˈlæps) *(intr)* 1 to lapse back into a former state or condition, esp one involving bad habits 2 to become ill again after apparent recovery ▷ *n* (rɪˈlæps, ˈriːˌlæps) 3 the act or an instance of relapsing 4 the return of ill health after an apparent or partial recovery [C16 from Latin *relābī* to slip back, from RE- + *lābī* to slip, slide] > **reˈlapser** *n*

relapsing fever *n* any of various infectious diseases characterized by recurring fever, caused by the bite of body lice or ticks infected with spirochaetes of the genus *Borrelia*. Also called: **recurrent fever**

relata (rɪˈleɪtə) *n* the plural of **relatum**

relate (rɪˈleɪt) *vb* 1 *(tr)* to tell or narrate (a story, information, etc) 2 (often foll by *to*) to establish association (between two or more things) or (of something) to have relation or reference (to something else) 3 *(intr*; often foll by *to*) to form a sympathetic or significant relationship (with other people, things, etc) [C16 from Latin *relātus* brought back, from *referre* to carry back, from RE- + *ferre* to bear; see REFER] > **reˈlatable** *adj* > **reˈlater** *n*

related (rɪˈleɪtɪd) *adj* 1 connected; associated 2 connected by kinship or marriage 3 (in diatonic music) denoting or relating to a key that has notes in common with another key or keys > **reˈlatedness** *n*

relation (rɪˈleɪʃən) *n* 1 the state or condition of being related or the manner in which things are related 2 connection by blood or marriage; kinship 3 a person who is connected by blood or marriage; relative; kinsman 4 reference or regard (esp in the phrase **in** *or* **with relation to**) 5 the position, association, connection, or status of one person or thing with regard to another or others 6 the act of relating or narrating 7 an account or narrative 8 *law* the principle by which an act done at one time is regarded in law as having been done antecedently 9 *law* the statement of grounds of complaint made by a relator 10 *logic, maths* a an association between ordered pairs of objects, numbers, etc, such as *... is greater than ...* b the set of ordered pairs whose members have such an association 11 *philosophy* a **internal relation** a relation that necessarily holds between its relata, as *4 is greater than 2* b **external relation** a relation that does not so hold ▷ See also **relations** [C14 from Latin *relātiō* a narration, a relation (between philosophical concepts)]

relational (rɪˈleɪʃənᵊl) *adj* 1 *grammar* indicating or expressing syntactic relation, as for example the case endings in Latin 2 having relation or being related 3 *computing* based on data stored in a tabular form: *a relational database*

relations (rɪˈleɪʃənz) *pl n* 1 social, political, or personal connections or dealings between or among individuals, groups, nations, etc 2 family or relatives 3 *euphemistic* sexual intercourse

relationship (rɪˈleɪʃənʃɪp) *n* 1 the state of being connected or related 2 association by blood or marriage; kinship 3 the mutual dealings, connections, or feelings that exist between two parties, countries, people, etc: *a business relationship* 4 an emotional or sexual affair or liaison 5 *logic, maths* another name for **relation** (sense 10)

relationship marketing *n* a marketing strategy in which a company seeks to build long-term relationships with its customers by providing consistent satisfaction

relative (ˈrɛlətɪv) *adj* 1 having meaning or significance only in relation to something else; not absolute: *a relative value* 2 *(prenominal)* (of a scientific quantity) being measured or stated relative to some other substance or measurement: *relative humidity; relative density.* Compare **absolute** (sense 10) 3 *(prenominal)* comparative or respective: *the relative qualities of speed and accuracy* 4 *(postpositive*; foll by *to*) in proportion (to); corresponding (to): *earnings relative to production* 5 having reference (to); pertinent (to): *matters not relative to the topic under discussion* 6 *grammar* denoting or belonging to a class of words that function as subordinating conjunctions in introducing relative clauses. In English, relative pronouns and determiners include *who, which,* and *that*. Compare **demonstrative** (sense 5), **interrogative** (sense 3) 7 *grammar* denoting or relating to a clause (**relative clause**) that modifies a noun or pronoun occurring earlier in the sentence 8 (of a musical key or scale) having the same key signature as another key or scale: *C major is the relative major of A minor* ▷ *n* 9 a person who is related by blood or marriage; relation 10 a relative pronoun, clause, or grammatical construction [C16 from Late Latin *relātīvus* referring] > **ˈrelativeness** *n*

relative aperture *n photog* the ratio of the equivalent focal length of a lens to the effective aperture of the lens; written as *f/n*, *f:n*, or *fn*, where *n* is the numerical value of this ratio and is equivalent to the f-number

relative atomic mass *n* the ratio of the average mass per atom of the naturally occurring form of an element to one-twelfth the mass of an atom of carbon-12. Symbol: A_r Abbreviation: **r.a.m** Former name: **atomic weight**

relative density *n* the ratio of the density of a substance to the density of a standard substance under specified conditions. For liquids and solids the standard is usually water at 4°C or some other specified temperature. For gases the standard is often air or hydrogen at the same temperature and pressure as the substance. Symbol: *d*. See also **specific gravity, vapour density**

relative frequency *n* a the ratio of the actual number of favourable events to the total possible number of events; often taken as an estimate of probability b the proportion of the range of a random variable taking a given value or lying in a given interval

relative humidity *n* the mass of water vapour present in the air expressed as a percentage of the mass that would be present in an equal volume of saturated air at the same temperature. Compare **absolute humidity**

relatively (ˈrɛlətɪvlɪ) *adv* in comparison or relation to something else; not absolutely

relative majority *n Brit* the excess of votes or seats won by the winner of an election over the runner-up when no candidate or party has more than 50 per cent. Compare **absolute majority**

relative molecular mass *n* the sum of all the relative atomic masses of the atoms in a molecule; the ratio of the average mass per molecule of a specified isotopic composition of a substance to one-twelfth the mass of an atom of carbon-12. Symbol: M_r Abbreviation: **r.m.m** Former name: **molecular weight**

relative permeability *n* the ratio of the permeability of a medium to that of free space. Symbol: μ_r

relative permittivity *n* the ratio of the permittivity of a substance to that of free space. Symbol: ε_r. Also called: **dielectric constant**

relativism (ˈrɛlətɪˌvɪzəm) *n* any theory holding that truth or moral or aesthetic value, etc, is not universal or absolute but may differ between individuals or cultures. See also **historicism** > **ˈrelativist** *n, adj*

relativistic (ˌrɛlətɪˈvɪstɪk) *adj* 1 *physics* having or involving a speed close to that of light so that the behaviour is described by the theory of relativity rather than by Newtonian mechanics: *a relativistic electron; a relativistic velocity* 2 *physics* of, concerned with, or involving relativity 3 of or relating to relativism > **ˌrelativˈistically** *adv*

relativity (ˌrɛləˈtɪvɪtɪ) *n* 1 either of two theories developed by Albert Einstein, the **special theory of relativity**, which requires that the laws of physics shall be the same as seen by any two different observers in uniform relative motion, and the **general theory of relativity** which considers observers with relative acceleration and leads to a theory of gravitation 2 *philosophy* dependence upon some variable factor such as the psychological, social, or environmental context. See **relativism** 3 the state or quality of being relative

relativize *or* **relativise** (ˈrɛlətɪvaɪz) *vb* 1 to make or become relative 2 *(tr)* to apply the theory of relativity to > **ˌrelativiˈzation** *or* **ˌrelativiˈsation** *n*

relator (rɪˈleɪtə) *n* 1 a person who relates a story; narrator 2 *English law* a person who gives information upon which the attorney general brings an action 3 *US law* a person who institutes proceedings by criminal information or quo warranto

relatum (rɪˈleɪtəm) *n, pl* **-ta** (-tə) *logic* one of the objects between which a relation is said to hold

relaunch *vb* (riːˈlɔːntʃ) *(tr)* 1 to launch again 2 to start, set in motion, or make available again ▷ *n* (ˈriːˌlɔːntʃ) 3 another launching, or something that is relaunched

relax (rɪˈlæks) *vb* 1 to make (muscles, a grip, etc) less tense or rigid or (of muscles, a grip, etc) to become looser or less rigid 2 *(intr)* to take rest or recreation, as from work or effort: *on Sundays, she just relaxes; she relaxes by playing golf* 3 to lessen the force of (effort, concentration, etc) or (of effort) to become diminished 4 to make (rules or discipline) less rigid or strict or (of rules, etc) to diminish in severity 5 *(intr)* (of a person) to become less formal; unbend [C15 from Latin *relaxāre* to loosen, from RE- + *laxāre* to loosen, from *laxus* loose, LAX] > **reˈlaxable** *adj* > **reˈlaxed** *adj* > **relaxedly** (rɪˈlæksɪdlɪ) *adv*

relaxant (rɪˈlæksᵊnt) *n* 1 *med* a drug or agent that relaxes, esp one that relaxes tense muscles ▷ *adj* 2 of, relating to, or tending to produce relaxation

relaxation (ˌriːlækˈseɪʃən) *n* 1 rest or refreshment, as after work or effort; recreation 2 a form of rest or recreation: *his relaxation is cricket* 3 a partial lessening of a punishment, duty, etc 4 the act of relaxing or state of being relaxed 5 *physics* the return of a system to equilibrium after a displacement from this state 6 *maths* a method by which errors resulting from an approximation are reduced by using new approximations

relaxation oscillator *n electronics* a nonsinusoidal oscillator, the timing of which is controlled by the charge and discharge time constants of resistance and capacitance components

relaxer (rɪˈlæksə) *n* a person or thing that relaxes, esp a substance used to straighten curly hair

relaxin (rɪˈlæksɪn) *n* 1 a mammalian polypeptide hormone secreted by the corpus luteum during pregnancy, which relaxes the pelvic ligaments 2 a preparation of this hormone, used to facilitate childbirth [C20 from RELAX + -IN]

r

relay *n* ('riːleɪ) **1** a person or team of people relieving others, as on a shift **2** a fresh team of horses, dogs, etc, posted at intervals along a route to relieve others **3** the act of relaying or process of being relayed **4 a** short for **relay race** **b** one of the sections of a relay race **5** an automatic device that controls the setting of a valve, switch, etc, by means of an electric motor, solenoid, or pneumatic mechanism **6** *electronics* an electrical device in which a small change in current or voltage controls the switching on or off of circuits or other devices **7** *radio* **a** a combination of a receiver and transmitter designed to receive radio signals and retransmit them, in order to extend their range **b** (*as modifier*): *a relay station* ▷ *vb* (rɪ'leɪ) (*tr*) **8** to carry or spread (something, such as news or information) by relays **9** to supply or replace with relays **10** to retransmit (a signal) by means of a relay **11** *Brit* to broadcast (a performance) by sending out signals through a transmitting station [C15 *relaien*, from Old French *relaier* to leave behind, from RE- + *laier* to leave, ultimately from Latin *laxāre* to loosen; see RELAX]

relay fast *n* (esp in India) a form of protest in which a number of persons go without food by turns. Also called: **relay hunger strike**

relay language *n* a language, usually an internationally dominant one, which acts as a medium to translate other usually little-spoken languages

relay race *n* a race between two or more teams of contestants in which each contestant covers a specified portion of the distance

relearn (riː'lɜːn) *vb* **-learns, -learning, -learned** *or* **-learnt** (*tr*) to learn (something previously known) again

release (rɪ'liːs) *vb* (*tr*) **1** to free (a person, animal, etc) from captivity or imprisonment **2** to free (someone) from obligation or duty **3** to free (something) from (one's grip); let go or fall **4** to issue (a record, film, book, etc) for sale or circulation **5** to make (news or information) known or allow (news, information, etc) to be made known: *to release details of an agreement* **6** *law* to relinquish (a right, claim, title, etc) in favour of someone else **7** *ethology* to evoke (a response) through the presentation of a stimulus that produces the response innately ▷ *n* **8** the act of freeing or state of being freed, as from captivity, imprisonment, duty, pain, life, etc **9** the act of issuing for sale or publication **10** something issued for sale or public showing, esp a film or a record: *a new release from Bob Dylan* **11** a news item, document, etc, made available for publication, broadcasting, etc **12** *law* the surrender of a claim, right, title, etc, in favour of someone else **13** a control mechanism for starting or stopping an engine **14 a** the opening of the exhaust valve of a steam engine near the end of the piston stroke **b** the moment at which this valve opens **15** the electronic control regulating how long a note sounds after a synthesizer key has been released **16** the control mechanism for the shutter in a camera [C13 from Old French *relesser*, from Latin *relaxāre* to slacken; see RELAX] > **re'leaser** *n*

relegate ('rɛlɪˌgeɪt) *vb* (*tr*) **1** to move to a position of less authority, importance, etc; demote **2** (*usually passive*) *chiefly Brit* to demote (a football team, etc) to a lower division **3** to assign or refer (a matter) to another or others, as for action or decision **4** (foll by *to*) to banish or exile **5** to assign (something) to a particular group or category [C16 from Latin *relēgāre* to send away, from RE- + *lēgāre* to send] > **'releˌgatable** *adj* > **ˌrele'gation** *n*

relent (rɪ'lɛnt) *vb* (*intr*) **1** to change one's mind about some decided course, esp a harsh one; become more mild or amenable **2** (of the pace or intensity of something) to slacken **3** (of the weather) to become more mild [C14 from RE- + Latin *lentāre* to bend, from *lentus* flexible, tenacious]

relentless (rɪ'lɛntlɪs) *adj* **1** (of an enemy, hostile attitude, etc) implacable; inflexible; inexorable **2** (of pace or intensity) sustained; unremitting > **re'lentlessly** *adv* > **re'lentlessness** *n*

Relenza (rɪ'lɛnzə) *n trademark* a preparation of an antiviral drug, zanamivir, used in the treatment of influenza to reduce the duration and severity of the illness

relevant ('rɛlɪvənt) *adj* **1** having direct bearing on the matter in hand; pertinent **2** *linguistics* another word for **distinctive** (sense 2) [C16 from Medieval Latin *relevans*, from Latin *relevāre* to lighten, from RE- + *levāre* to raise, RELIEVE] > **'relevance** *or* **'relevancy** *n* > **'relevantly** *adv*

reliable (rɪ'laɪəbᵊl) *adj* able to be trusted; predictable or dependable > **reˌlia'bility** *or less commonly* **re'liableness** *n* > **re'liably** *adv*

reliance (rɪ'laɪəns) *n* **1** dependence, confidence, or trust **2** something or someone upon which one relies > **re'liant** *adj* > **re'liantly** *adv*

relic ('rɛlɪk) *n* **1** something that has survived from the past, such as an object or custom **2** something kept as a remembrance or treasured for its past associations; keepsake **3** (*usually plural*) a remaining part or fragment **4** *RC Church, Eastern Church* part of the body of a saint or something supposedly used by or associated with a saint, venerated as holy **5** *informal* an old or old-fashioned person or thing **6** (*plural*) *archaic* the remains of a dead person; corpse **7** *ecology* a less common term for **relict** (sense 1) [C13 from Old French *relique*, from Latin *reliquiae* remains, from *relinquere* to leave behind, RELINQUISH]

relict ('rɛlɪkt) *n* **1** *ecology* **a** a group of animals or plants that exists as a remnant of a formerly widely distributed group in an environment different from that in which it originated **b** (*as modifier*): *a relict fauna* **2** *geology* **a** a mountain, lake, glacier, etc, that is a remnant of a pre-existing formation after a destructive process has occurred **b** a mineral that remains unaltered after metamorphism of the rock in which it occurs **3** an archaic word for **widow** (sense 1) **4** an archaic word for **relic** (sense 6) [C16 from Latin *relictus* left behind, from *relinquere* to RELINQUISH]

relief (rɪ'liːf) *n* **1** a feeling of cheerfulness or optimism that follows the removal of anxiety, pain, or distress: *I breathed a sigh of relief* **2** deliverance from or alleviation of anxiety, pain, distress, etc **3 a** help or assistance, as to the poor, needy, or distressed **b** (*as modifier*): *relief work* **4** short for **tax relief** **5** something that affords a diversion from monotony **6** a person who replaces or relieves another at some task or duty **7** a bus, shuttle plane, etc, that carries additional passengers when a scheduled service is full **8** a road (**relief road**) carrying traffic round an urban area; bypass **9 a** the act of freeing a beleaguered town, fortress, etc: *the relief of Mafeking* **b** (*as modifier*): *a relief column* **10** Also called: **relievo, rilievo** *sculpture, architect* **a** the projection of forms or figures from a flat ground, so that they are partly or wholly free of it **b** a piece of work of this kind **11** a printing process, such as engraving, letterpress, etc, that employs raised surfaces from which ink is transferred to the paper **12** any vivid effect resulting from contrast: *comic relief* **13** variation in altitude in an area; difference between highest and lowest level: *a region of low relief* **14** *mechanical engineering* the removal of the surface material of a bearing area to allow the access of lubricating fluid **15** *law* redress of a grievance or hardship: *to seek relief through the courts* **16** *European history* a succession of payments made by an heir to a fief to his lord: the size of the relief was determined by the lord within bounds set by custom **17** **on relief** *US and Canadian* (of people) in receipt of government aid because of personal need [C14 from Old French, from *relever* to raise up; see RELIEVE]

relief map *n* a map that shows the configuration and height of the land surface, usually by means of contours

relief pitcher *n baseball* a pitcher who replaces a side's main pitcher during a game. Also called: **reliever**

relieve (rɪ'liːv) *vb* (*tr*) **1** to bring alleviation of (pain, distress, etc) to (someone) **2** to bring aid or assistance to (someone in need, a disaster area, etc) **3** to take over the duties or watch of (someone) **4** to bring aid or a relieving force to (a besieged town, city, etc) **5** to free (someone) from an obligation **6** to make (something) less unpleasant, arduous, or monotonous **7** to bring into relief or prominence, as by contrast **8** (foll by *of*) *informal* to take from: *the thief relieved him of his watch* **9** **relieve oneself** to urinate or defecate [C14 from Old French *relever*, from Latin *relevāre* to lift up, relieve, from RE- + *levāre* to lighten] > **re'lievable** *adj*

relieved (rɪ'liːvd) *adj* **1** (*postpositive*; often foll by *at*, *about*, etc) experiencing relief, esp from worry or anxiety **2** *mechanical engineering* having part of the surface cut away to avoid friction or wear

reliever (rɪ'liːvə) *n* a person or thing that relieves **2** *baseball* another name for **relief pitcher**

relievo (rɪl'jeɪvəʊ, rɪ'liːvəʊ) *n, pl* **-vos** another name for **relief** (sense 9) [from Italian, literally: raised work]

relight (riː'laɪt) *vb* **-lights, -lighting, -lighted** *or* **-lit** to ignite or cause to ignite again

religieuse *French* (rəliʒjøz) *n* a nun [C18 feminine of RELIGIEUX]

religieux *French* (rəliʒjø) *n, pl* ***-gieux*** (-ʒjø) a member of a monastic order or clerical body [C17 from Latin *religiōsus* religious]

religion (rɪ'lɪdʒən) *n* **1** belief in, worship of, or obedience to a supernatural power or powers considered to be divine or to have control of human destiny **2** any formal or institutionalized expression of such belief: *the Christian religion* **3** the attitude and feeling of one who believes in a transcendent controlling power or powers **4** *chiefly RC Church* the way of life determined by the vows of poverty, chastity, and obedience entered upon by monks, friars, and nuns: *to enter religion* **5** something of overwhelming importance to a person: *football is his religion* **6** *archaic* **a** the practice of sacred ritual observances **b** sacred rites and ceremonies [C12 via Old French from Latin *religiō* fear of the supernatural, piety, probably from *religāre* to tie up, from RE- + *ligāre* to bind]

religionism (rɪ'lɪdʒəˌnɪzəm) *n* extreme religious fervour > **re'ligionist** *n, adj*

religiose (rɪ'lɪdʒɪˌəʊs) *adj* affectedly or extremely pious; sanctimoniously religious > **re'ligiˌosely** *adv* > **religiosity** (rɪˌlɪdʒɪ'ɒsɪtɪ) *n*

religious (rɪ'lɪdʒəs) *adj* **1** of, relating to, or concerned with religion **2 a** pious; devout; godly **b** (*as collective noun*; preceded by *the*): *the religious* **3** appropriate to or in accordance with the principles of a religion **4** scrupulous, exact, or conscientious **5** *Christianity* of or relating to a way of life dedicated to religion by the vows of poverty, chastity, and obedience, and defined by a monastic rule ▷ *n* **6** *Christianity* a member of an order or congregation living by such a rule; a monk, friar, or nun > **re'ligiously** *adv* > **re'ligiousness** *n*

Religious Society of Friends *n* the official name for the **Quakers**

relinquish (rɪ'lɪŋkwɪʃ) *vb* (*tr*) **1** to give up (a task, struggle, etc); abandon **2** to surrender or renounce (a claim, right, etc) **3** to release; let go [C15 from French *relinquir*, from Latin *relinquere* to leave behind, from RE- + *linquere* to leave] > **re'linquisher** *n* > **re'linquishment** *n*

reliquary ('rɛlɪkwərɪ) *n, pl* **-quaries** a receptacle or repository for relics, esp relics of saints [C17 from Old French *reliquaire*, from *relique* RELIC]

relique (rə'liːk, 'rɛlɪk) *n* an archaic spelling of **relic**

reliquiae (rɪ'lɪkwɪˌiː) *pl n archaic* fossil remains of animals or plants [C19 from Latin: remains]

relish ('rɛlɪʃ) *vb* (*tr*) **1** to savour or enjoy (an experience) to the full **2** to anticipate eagerly; look forward to **3** to enjoy the taste or flavour of (food, etc); savour **4** to give appetizing taste or flavour to (food), by or as if by the addition of pickles or spices ▷ *n* **5** liking or enjoyment, as of something eaten or experienced (esp in the phrase **with relish**) **6** pleasurable anticipation: *he didn't have much relish for the idea* **7** an appetizing or spicy food added to a main dish to enhance its flavour **8** an appetizing taste or flavour **9** a zestful trace or touch: *there was a certain relish in all his writing* **10** *music* (in English lute, viol, and keyboard music of the 16th and 17th centuries) a trilling ornament, used esp at cadences [c16 from earlier *reles* aftertaste, from Old French: something remaining, from *relaisser* to leave behind; see RELEASE] > **'relishable** *adj*

relive (riːˈlɪv) *vb* (*tr*) to experience (a sensation, event, etc) again, esp in the imagination > **re'livable** *adj*

rellies (ˈrɛlɪz) *pl n* *Austral and NZ informal* relatives or relations

reload (riːˈləʊd) *vb* **1** (*tr*) to place (cargo, goods, etc) back on (a ship, lorry, etc) **2** to put ammunition into a firearm after having discharged it **3** *computing* to fetch the latest updated version (of a web page or document); refresh

relocate (ˌriːləʊˈkeɪt) *vb* **1** to move or be moved to a new place, esp (of an employee, a business, etc) to a new area or place of employment **2** (*intr*) (of an employee, a business, etc) to move for reasons of business to a new area or place of employment > **relo'cation** *n*

relocation costs or **expenses** *pl n* payment made by an employer or a government agency to cover removal expenses and other costs incurred by an employee who is required to take up employment elsewhere

relocator (ˌriːləʊˈkeɪtər) *n* *computing* a program designed to transfer files from one computer to another

relucent (rɪˈluːsənt) *adj* *archaic* bright; shining [c16 from Latin *relūcēre* to shine out, from RE- + *lūcēre* to shine, from *lūx* light]

reluct (rɪˈlʌkt) *vb* (*intr*) *archaic* **1** (often foll by *against*) to struggle or rebel **2** to object; show reluctance [c16 from Latin *reluctārī* to resist, from RE- + *luctārī* to struggle]

reluctance (rɪˈlʌktəns) or less commonly **reluctancy** *n* **1** lack of eagerness or willingness; disinclination **2** *physics* a measure of the resistance of a closed magnetic circuit to a magnetic flux, equal to the ratio of the magnetomotive force to the magnetic flux

reluctant (rɪˈlʌktənt) *adj* **1** not eager; unwilling; disinclined **2** *archaic* offering resistance or opposition [c17 from Latin *reluctārī* to resist; see RELUCT] > **re'luctantly** *adv*

reluctivity (ˌrɛlʌkˈtɪvɪtɪ) *n, pl* **-ties** *physics* a specific or relative reluctance of a magnetic material [c19 RELUCT + -*ivity* on the model of *conductivity*]

relume (rɪˈluːm) or **relumine** (rɪˈluːmɪn) *vb* (*tr*) *archaic* to light or brighten again; rekindle [c17 from Late Latin *relūmināre*, from Latin RE- + *illūmināre* to ILLUMINE]

rely (rɪˈlaɪ) *vb* **-lies**, **-lying**, **-lied** (*intr*; foll by *on* or *upon*) **1** to be dependent (on): *he relies on his charm* **2** to have trust or confidence (in): *you can rely on us* [c14 from Old French *relier* to fasten together, repair, from Latin *religāre* to tie back, from RE- + *ligāre* to tie]

REM[1] *abbreviation for* **rapid eye movement**

REM[2] or **rem** (rɛm) *n acronym for* roentgen equivalent man

remain (rɪˈmeɪn) *vb* (*mainly intr*) **1** to stay behind or in the same place: *to remain at home; only Tom remained* **2** (*copula*) to continue to be: *to remain cheerful* **3** to be left, as after use, consumption, the passage of time, etc: *a little wine still remained in the bottle* **4** to be left to be done, said, etc: *it remains to be pointed out*. See also **remains** [c14 from Old

French *remanoir*, from Latin *remanēre* to be left, from RE- + *manēre* to stay]

remainder (rɪˈmeɪndə) *n* **1** a part or portion that is left, as after use, subtraction, expenditure, the passage of time, etc: *the remainder of the milk; the remainder of the day* **2** *maths* **a** the amount left over when one quantity cannot be exactly divided by another: *for 10 ÷ 3, the remainder is 1* **b** another name for **difference** (sense 7b) **3** *property law* a future interest in property; an interest in a particular estate that will pass to one at some future date, as on the death of the current possessor **4** a number of copies of a book left unsold when demand slows or ceases, which are sold at a reduced price by the publisher ▷ *vb* **5** (*tr*) to sell (copies of a book) as a remainder [c15 from Anglo-French, from Old French *remaindre* (infinitive used as noun), variant of *remanoir*; see REMAIN]

remainderman (rɪˈmeɪndəˌmæn) *n, pl* **-men** *property law* the person entitled to receive a particular estate on its determination. Compare **reversioner**

remains (rɪˈmeɪnz) *pl n* **1** any pieces, scraps, fragments, etc, that are left unused or still extant, as after use, consumption, the passage of time, etc: *the remains of a meal; archaeological remains* **2** the body of a dead person; corpse **3** *Also called:* **literary remains** the unpublished writings of an author at the time of his death

remake *n* (ˈriːˌmeɪk) **1** something that is made again, esp a new version of an old film **2** the act of making again or anew ▷ *vb* (riːˈmeɪk) **-makes**, **-making**, **-made 3** (*tr*) to make again or anew

remand (rɪˈmɑːnd) *vb* (*tr*) **1** *law* (of a court or magistrate) to send (a prisoner or accused person) back into custody or admit him to bail, esp on adjourning a case for further inquiries to be made **2** to send back ▷ *n* **3** the sending of a prisoner or accused person back into custody (or sometimes admitting him to bail) to await trial or continuation of his trial **4** the act of remanding or state of being remanded **5 on remand** in custody or on bail awaiting trial or completion of one's trial [c15 from Medieval Latin *remandāre* to send back word, from Latin RE- + *mandāre* to command, confine; see MANDATE] > **re'mandment** *n*

remand centre *n* (in Britain) an institution to which accused persons are sent for detention while awaiting appearance before a court. Until 1967 remand centres were for young people between 14 and 21 years of age

remand home *n* (no longer in technical use) an institution to which juvenile offenders between 8 and 14 years may be remanded or committed for detention. See also **community home**

remanence (ˈrɛmənəns) *n* *physics* the ability of a material to retain magnetization, equal to the magnetic flux density of the material after the removal of the magnetizing field. *Also called:* **retentivity** [c17 from Latin *remanēre* to stay behind, REMAIN]

remanent (ˈrɛmənənt) *adj* *rare* remaining or left over

remark (rɪˈmɑːk) *vb* **1** (when *intr*, often foll by *on* or *upon*; when *tr*, may take a clause as object) to pass a casual comment (about); reflect in informal speech or writing **2** (*tr*; may take a clause as object) to perceive; observe; notice ▷ *n* **3** a brief casually expressed thought or opinion; observation **4** notice, comment, or observation: *the event passed without remark* **5** *engraving* a variant spelling of **remarque** [c17 from Old French *remarquer* to observe, from RE- + *marquer* to note, MARK[1]] > **re'marker** *n*

remarkable (rɪˈmɑːkəbəl) *adj* **1** worthy of note or attention: *a remarkable achievement* **2** unusual, striking, or extraordinary: *a remarkable sight* > **re'markableness** or **re,marka'bility** *n* > **re'markably** *adv*

remarque or **remark** (rɪˈmɑːk) *n* **1** a mark in the margin of an engraved plate to indicate the stage

of production of the plate. It is removed before the plate is finished **2** a plate so marked **3** a print or proof from a plate so marked [c19 from French; see REMARK]

remarry (riːˈmærɪ) *vb* **-ries**, **-rying**, **-ried** to marry again > **re'marriage** *n*

remaster (riːˈmɑːstə) *vb* (*tr*) to make a new master audio recording, now usually digital, from (an earlier recording), to produce compact discs or stereo records with improved sound reproduction

rematch *n* (ˈriːˌmætʃ) **1** *sport* a second or return match between contestants ▷ *vb* (riːˈmætʃ) **2** (*tr*) to match (two contestants) again

remblai (French rɑ̃blɛ) *n* earth used for an embankment or rampart [c18 from French, from *remblayer* to embank, from *emblayer* to pile up]

Rembrandtesque (ˌrɛmbrænˈtɛsk) *adj* reminiscent of Rembrandt (full name *Rembrandt Harmensz van Rijn*) the Dutch painter (1606–69)

REME (ˈriːmiː) *n acronym for* Royal Electrical and Mechanical Engineers

remedial (rɪˈmiːdɪəl) *adj* **1** affording a remedy; curative **2** denoting or relating to special teaching, teaching methods, or material for backward and slow learners: *remedial education* > **re'medially** *adv*

remediation (rɪˌmiːdɪˈeɪʃən) *n* the action of remedying something, esp the reversal or stopping of damage to the environment

remedy (ˈrɛmɪdɪ) *n, pl* **-dies 1** (usually foll by *for* or *against*) any drug or agent that cures a disease or controls its symptoms **2** (usually foll by *for* or *against*) anything that serves to put a fault to rights, cure defects, improve conditions, etc: *a remedy for industrial disputes* **3** the legally permitted variation from the standard weight or quality of coins; tolerance ▷ *vb* (*tr*) **4** to relieve or cure (a disease, illness, etc) by or as if by a remedy **5** to put to rights (a fault, error, etc); correct [c13 from Anglo-Norman *remedie*, from Latin *remedium* a cure, from *remedērī* to heal again, from RE- + *medērī* to heal; see MEDICAL] > **remediable** (rɪˈmiːdɪəbəl) *adj* > **re'mediably** *adv* > **'remediless** *adj*

remember (rɪˈmɛmbə) *vb* **1** to become aware of (something forgotten) again; bring back to one's consciousness; recall **2** to retain (an idea, intention, etc) in one's conscious mind: *to remember Pythagoras' theorem; remember to do one's shopping* **3** (*tr*) to give money, etc, to (someone), as in a will or in tipping **4** (*tr*; foll by *to*) to mention (a person's name) to another person, as by way of greeting or friendship: *remember me to your mother* **5** (*tr*) to mention (a person) favourably, as in prayer **6** (*tr*) to commemorate (a person, event, etc): *to remember the dead of the wars* **7 remember oneself** to recover one's good manners after a lapse; stop behaving badly [c14 from Old French *remembrer*, from Late Latin *rememorārī* to recall to mind, from Latin RE- + *memor* mindful; see MEMORY] > **re'memberer** *n*

remembrance (rɪˈmɛmbrəns) *n* **1** the act of remembering or state of being remembered **2** something that is remembered; reminiscence **3** a memento or keepsake **4** the extent in time of one's power of recollection **5 a** the act of honouring some past event, person, etc **b** (*as modifier*): *a remembrance service*

remembrancer (rɪˈmɛmbrənsə) *n* *archaic* a reminder, memento, or keepsake

Remembrancer (rɪˈmɛmbrənsə) *n* (in Britain) **1** any of several officials of the Exchequer esp one (**Queen's** or **King's Remembrancer**) whose duties include collecting debts due to the Crown **2** an official (**City Remembrancer**) appointed by the Corporation of the City of London to represent its interests to Parliament and elsewhere

Remembrance Sunday *n* *Brit* the second Sunday in November, which is the Sunday closest to November 11, the anniversary of the armistice of 1918 that ended World War I, on which the dead of both World Wars are commemorated. *Also called:* **Remembrance Day**

r

remex ('riːmɛks) *n, pl* **remiges** ('rɛmɪˌdʒiːz) any of the large flight feathers of a bird's wing [c18 from Latin: a rower, from *rēmus* oar] > **remigial** (rɪˈmɪdʒɪəl) *adj*

remind (rɪˈmaɪnd) *vb* (*tr; usually foll by of; may take a clause as object or an infinitive*) to cause (a person) to remember (something or to do something); make (someone) aware (of something he may have forgotten): *remind me to phone home*

reminder (rɪˈmaɪndə) *n* **1** something that recalls the past **2** a note to remind a person of something not done

remindful (rɪˈmaɪndfʊl) *adj* **1** serving to remind **2** (*postpositive*) bearing in mind; mindful

reminisce (ˌrɛmɪˈnɪs) *vb* (*intr*) to talk or write about old times, past experiences, etc

reminiscence (ˌrɛmɪˈnɪsəns) *n* **1** the act of recalling or narrating past experiences **2** (*often plural*) some past experience, event, etc, that is recalled or narrated; anecdote **3** an event, phenomenon, or experience that reminds one of something else **4** (in the philosophy of Plato) the doctrine that perception and recognition of particulars is possible because the mind has seen the universal forms of all things in a previous disembodied existence **5** *psychol* the ability to perform a task better when tested some time after the task has been learnt than when tested immediately after learning it

reminiscent (ˌrɛmɪˈnɪsənt) *adj* **1** (*postpositive; foll by of*) stimulating memories (of) or comparisons (with) **2** characterized by reminiscence **3** (of a person) given to reminiscing [c18 from Latin *reminiscī* to call to mind, from RE- + *mēns* mind] > ˌremiˈniscently *adv*

remise (rɪˈmaɪz) *vb* **1** (*tr*) *law* to give up or relinquish (a right, claim, etc); surrender **2** *fencing* to make a renewed thrust on the same lunge after the first has missed ▷ *n* **3** *fencing* a second thrust made on the same lunge after the first has missed **4** *obsolete* a hired carriage **5** *obsolete* a coach house [c17 from French *remettre* to put back, from Latin *remittere* to send back, from RE- + *mittere* to send]

remiss (rɪˈmɪs) *adj* (*postpositive*) **1** lacking in care or attention to duty; negligent **2** lacking in energy; dilatory [c15 from Latin *remissus* from *remittere* to release, from RE- + *mittere* to send] > reˈmissly *adv* > reˈmissness *n*

remissible (rɪˈmɪsəbˀl) *adj* able to be remitted [c16 from Latin *remissibilis*; see REMIT] > reˌmissiˈbility or reˈmissibleness *n*

remission (rɪˈmɪʃən) *or less commonly* **remittal** (rɪˈmɪtˀl) *n* **1** the act of remitting or state of being remitted **2** a reduction of the term of a sentence of imprisonment, as for good conduct: *he got three years' remission* **3** forgiveness for sin **4** discharge or release from penalty, obligation, etc **5** lessening of intensity; abatement, as in the severity of symptoms of a disease > reˈmissive *adj* > reˈmissively *adv*

remit *vb* (rɪˈmɪt) -mits, -mitting, -mitted (*mainly tr*) **1** (*also intr*) to send (money, payment, etc), as for goods or service, esp by post **2** *law* (esp of an appeal court) to send back (a case or proceeding) to an inferior court for further consideration or action **3** to cancel or refrain from exacting (a penalty or punishment) **4** (*also intr*) to relax (pace, intensity, etc) or (of pace or the like) to slacken or abate **5** to postpone; defer **6** *archaic* to pardon or forgive (crime, sins, etc) ▷ *n* ('riːmɪt, rɪˈmɪt) **7** the area of authority or responsibility of an individual or a group: *by taking that action, the committee has exceeded its remit* **8** *law* the transfer of a case from one court or jurisdiction to another, esp from an appeal court to an inferior tribunal **9** the act of remitting **10** something remitted **11** NZ a proposal from a branch of an organization put forward for discussion at the annual general meeting [c14 from Latin *remittere* to send back, release, RE- + *mittere* to send] > reˈmittable *adj* > reˈmittal *n*

remittance (rɪˈmɪtəns) *n* **1** payment for goods or services received or as an allowance, esp when sent by post **2** the act of remitting

remittance man *n* a man living abroad on money sent from home, esp in the days of the British Empire

remittee (rɪˌmɪtˈiː) *n* the recipient of a remittance; one to whom payment is sent

remittent (rɪˈmɪtˀnt) *adj* (of a fever or the symptoms of a disease) characterized by periods of diminished severity > reˈmittence or reˈmittency *n* > reˈmittently *adv*

remitter (rɪˈmɪtə) *n* **1** Also called: **remittor** a person who remits **2** *property law* the principle by which a person out of possession of land to which he had a good title is adjudged to regain this when he again enters into possession of the land

remix *vb* (riːˈmɪks) **1** to change the balance and separation of (a recording), usually to emphasize the rhythm section ▷ *n* ('riːˌmɪks) **2** a remixed version of a recording

remnant ('rɛmnənt) *n* **1** (*often plural*) a part left over after use, processing, etc **2** a surviving trace or vestige, as of a former era: *a remnant of imperialism* **3** a piece of material from the end of a roll, sold at a lower price ▷ *adj* **4** remaining; left over [c14 from Old French *remenant* remaining, from *remanoir* to REMAIN]

remodel *vb* (riːˈmɒdˀl) -els, -elling, -elled *or US* -els *or* -eling *or* -eled (*tr*) **1** to change or alter the structure, style, or form of (something): *expand and remodel the kitchen* **2** to model again in clay, wax, etc; remould ▷ *n* ('riːˌmɒdˀl) **3** something that has been remodelled

remonetize *or* **remonetise** (riːˈmʌnɪˌtaɪz) *vb* (*tr*) to reinstate as legal tender: *to remonetize silver* > reˌmonetiˈzation *or* reˌmonetiˈsation *n*

remonstrance (rɪˈmɒnstrəns) *n* **1** the act of remonstrating; protestation **2** a protest or reproof, esp a petition presented in protest against something

Remonstrance (rɪˈmɒnstrəns) *n history* **1** See **Grand Remonstrance 2** the statement of Arminian principles drawn up in 1610 in Gouda in the Netherlands

remonstrant (rɪˈmɒnstrənt) *n* **1** a person who remonstrates, esp one who signs a remonstrance ▷ *adj* **2** *rare* remonstrating or protesting

Remonstrant (rɪˈmɒnstrənt) *n* a Dutch supporter of the Arminian Remonstrance of 1610

remonstrate ('rɛmənˌstreɪt) *vb* (*intr*) **1** (*usually foll by with, against, etc*) to argue in protest or objection: *to remonstrate with the government* **2** *archaic* to show or point out [c16 from Medieval Latin *remonstrāre* to point out (errors), from Latin RE- + *monstrāre* to show] > ˌremonˈstration *n* > remonstrative (rɪˈmɒnstrətɪv) *adj* > ˈremonˌstrator *n*

remontant (rɪˈmɒntənt) *adj* **1** (esp of cultivated roses) flowering more than once in a single season ▷ *n* **2** a rose having such a growth [c19 from French: coming up again, from *remonter*; see REMOUNT]

remontoir *or* **remontoire** (ˌrɛmənˈtwɑː) *n* any of various devices used in watches, clocks, etc, to compensate for errors arising from the changes in the force driving the escapement [c19 from French: winding mechanism, from *remonter* to wind; see REMOUNT]

remora ('rɛmərə) *n* any of the marine spiny-finned fishes constituting the family *Echeneidae*. They have a flattened elongated body and attach themselves to larger fish, rocks, etc, by a sucking disc on the top of the head [c16 from Latin, from RE- + *mora* delay; an allusion to its alleged habit of delaying ships]

remorse (rɪˈmɔːs) *n* **1** a sense of deep regret and guilt for some misdeed **2** compunction; pity; compassion [c14 from Medieval Latin *remorsus* a gnawing, from Latin *remordēre* to bite again, from RE- + *mordēre* to bite] > reˈmorseful *adj* > reˈmorsefully *adv* > reˈmorsefulness *n*

remorseless (rɪˈmɔːslɪs) *adj* **1** without compunction, pity, or compassion **2** not abating in intensity; relentless: *a remorseless wind* > reˈmorselessly *adv* > reˈmorselessness *n*

remortgage (riːˈmɔːɡɪdʒ) *vb* to take out a new or different mortgage on a property

remote (rɪˈməʊt) *adj* **1** located far away; distant **2** far from any centre of population, society, or civilization; out-of-the-way **3** distant in time **4** distantly related or connected: *a remote cousin* **5** removed, as from the source or point of action **6** slight or faint (esp in the phrases **not the remotest idea, a remote chance**) **7** (of a person's manner) aloof or abstracted **8** operated from a distance; remote-controlled: *a remote monitor* [c15 from Latin *remōtus* far removed, from *removēre*, from RE- + *movēre* to move] > reˈmotely *adv* > reˈmoteness *n*

remote access *n computing* access to a computer from a physically separate terminal

remote control *n* control of a system or activity by a person at a different place, usually by means of radio or ultrasonic signals or by electrical signals transmitted by wire > reˈmote-conˈtrolled *adj*

remote sensing *n* the use of an instrument, such as a radar device or camera, to scan the earth or another planet from space in order to collect data about some aspect of it > **remote-sensing** *adj*

remote sensor *n* any instrument, such as a radar device or camera, that scans the earth or another planet from space in order to collect data about some aspect of it

rémoulade (ˌrɛməˈleɪd; *French* remulad) *n* a mayonnaise sauce flavoured with herbs, mustard, and capers, served with salads, cold meat, etc [c19 from French, from Picard dialect *ramolas* horseradish, from Latin *armoracea*]

remould *vb* (riːˈməʊld) (*tr*) **1** to mould again **2** to bond a new tread onto the casing of (a worn pneumatic tyre) ▷ *n* ('riːˌməʊld) **3** a tyre made by this process ▷ Also (for senses 2, 3): **retread**

remount *vb* (riːˈmaʊnt) **1** to get on (a horse, bicycle, etc) again **2** (*tr*) to mount (a picture, jewel, exhibit, etc) again ▷ *n* ('riːˌmaʊnt) **3** a fresh horse, esp (formerly) to replace one killed or injured in battle

removal (rɪˈmuːvˀl) *n* **1** the act of removing or state of being removed **2 a** a change of residence **b** (*as modifier*): *a removal company* **3** dismissal from office **4** *South African* the forced displacement of a community for political or social reasons

removalist (rɪˈmuːvəlɪst) *n Austral* a person or company that transports household effects to a new home

remove (rɪˈmuːv) *vb* (*mainly tr*) **1** to take away and place elsewhere **2** to displace (someone) from office; dismiss **3** to do away with (a grievance, cause of anxiety, etc); abolish **4** to clear (dirt, stains, or anything unwanted) to disappear; get rid of **5** *euphemistic* to assassinate; kill **6** (*intr*) *formal* to change the location of one's home or place of business: *the publishers have removed to Mayfair* ▷ *n* **7** the act of removing, esp (formal) a removal of one's residence or place of work **8** the degree of difference separating one person, thing, or condition from another: *only one remove from madness* **9** *Brit* (in certain schools) a class or form, esp one for children of about 14 years, designed to introduce them to the greater responsibilities of a more senior position in the school **10** (at a formal dinner, formerly) a dish to be changed while the rest of the course remains on the table [c14 from Old French *removoir*, from Latin *removēre*; see MOVE] > reˈmovable *adj* > reˌmovaˈbility or reˈmovableness *n* > reˈmovably *adv* > reˈmover *n*

removed (rɪˈmuːvd) *adj* **1** separated by distance or abstract distinction **2** (*postpositive*) separated by a degree of descent or kinship: *the child of a person's first cousin is his first cousin once removed* > **removedness** (rɪˈmuːvɪdnɪs) *n*

Remscheid (*German* ˈrɛmʃaɪt) *n* an industrial city

in W Germany, in North Rhine-Westphalia. Pop: 117 717 (2003 est)

Remuera tractor (ˌrɛmʊˈɛərə) *n NZ informal* a four-wheel drive recreational vehicle [from the name of a wealthy suburb of Auckland]

remunerate (rɪˈmjuːnəˌreɪt) *vb* (*tr*) to reward or pay for work, service, etc [c16 from Latin *remūnerārī* to reward, from RE- + *mūnerāre* to reward, from *mūnus* a gift; see MUNIFICENT] > reˌmuneraˈbility *n* > reˈmunerable *adj* > reˈmunerˌator *n*

remuneration (rɪˌmjuːnəˈreɪʃən) *n* **1** the act of remunerating **2** pay; recompense

remunerative (rɪˈmjuːnərətɪv) *adj* earning money or rewards; paying > reˈmuneratively *adv* > reˈmunerativeness *n*

Remus (ˈriːməs) *n Roman myth* the brother of Romulus

renaissance (rəˈneɪsəns; *US also* ˈrɛnəˌsɒns) *or* **renascence** *n* a revival or rebirth, esp of culture and learning [c19 from French, from Latin RE- + *nascī* to be born]

Renaissance (rəˈneɪsəns; *US also* ˈrɛnəˌsɒns) *n* **1 the** the period of European history marking the waning of the Middle Ages and the rise of the modern world: usually considered as beginning in Italy in the 14th century **2 a** the spirit, culture, art, science, and thought of this period. Characteristics of the Renaissance are usually considered to include intensified classical scholarship, scientific and geographical discovery, a sense of individual human potentialities, and the assertion of the active and secular over the religious and contemplative life **b** (*as modifier*): *Renaissance writers*. See also **Early Renaissance, High Renaissance** ▷ *adj* **3** of, characteristic of, or relating to the Renaissance, its culture, etc

Renaissance man *n* a man of any period who has a broad range of intellectual interests

renal (ˈriːnəl) *adj* of, relating to, resembling, or situated near the kidney [c17 from French, from Late Latin *rēnālis*, from Latin *rēnēs* kidneys, of obscure origin]

renal pelvis *n* a small funnel-shaped cavity of the kidney into which urine is discharged before passing into the ureter

rename (riːˈneɪm) *vb* (*tr*) to change the name of (someone or something)

renascence (rɪˈnæsəns, -ˈneɪ-) *n* a variant of **renaissance**

renascent (rɪˈnæsənt, -ˈneɪ-) *adj* becoming active or vigorous again; reviving: *renascent nationalism* [c18 from Latin *renascī* to be born again]

rencounter (rɛnˈkaʊntə) *archaic* ▷ *n also* **rencontre** (rɛnˈkɒntə) **1** an unexpected meeting **2** a hostile clash, as of two armies, adversaries, etc; skirmish ▷ *vb* **3** to meet (someone) unexpectedly [c16 from French *rencontre*, from *rencontrer*; see ENCOUNTER]

rend (rɛnd) *vb* rends, rending, rent **1** to tear with violent force or to be torn in this way; rip **2** (*tr*) to tear or pull (one's clothes, etc), esp as a manifestation of rage or grief **3** (*tr*) (of a noise or cry) to disturb (the air, silence, etc) with a shrill or piercing tone **4** (*tr*) to pain or distress (the heart, conscience, etc) [Old English *rendan*; related to Old Frisian *renda*] > ˈrendible *adj*

render (ˈrɛndə) *vb* (*tr*) **1** to present or submit (accounts, etc) for payment, approval, or action **2** to give or provide (aid, charity, a service, etc) **3** to show (obedience), as due or expected **4** to give or exchange, as by way of return or requital: *to render blow for blow* **5** to cause to become: *grief had rendered him simple-minded* **6** to deliver (a verdict or opinion) formally **7** to portray or depict (something), as in painting, music, or acting **8** *computing* to use colour and shading to make a digital image look three-dimensional and solid **9** to translate (something) into another language or form **10** (sometimes foll by *up*) to yield or give: *the tomb rendered up its secret* **11** (often foll by *back*) to return (something); give back **12** to cover the surface of (brickwork, stone, etc) with a coat of plaster **13** (often foll by *down*) to extract (fat) from (meat) by

melting **14** *nautical* **a** to reeve (a line) **b** to slacken (a rope, etc) **15** *history* (of a feudal tenant) to make (payment) in money, goods, or services to one's overlord ▷ *n* **16 a** a first thin coat of plaster applied to a surface **17** *history* a payment in money, goods, or services made by a feudal tenant to his lord [c14 from Old French *rendre*, from Latin *reddere* to give back (influenced by Latin *prendere* to grasp), from RE- + *dare* to give] > ˈrenderable *adj* > ˈrenderer *n*

rendering (ˈrɛndərɪŋ) *n* **1** the act or an instance of performing a play, piece of music, etc **2** a translation of a text from a foreign language **3** Also called: **rendering coat, render** a coat of plaster or cement mortar applied to a surface **4** a perspective drawing showing an architect's idea of a finished building, interior, etc

rendezvous (ˈrɒndɪˌvuː) *n, pl* **-vous** (-ˌvuːz) **1** a meeting or appointment to meet at a specified time and place **2** a place where people meet **3** an arranged meeting of two spacecraft ▷ *vb* **4** to meet or cause to meet at a specified time or place [c16 from French, from *rendez-vous!* present yourselves! from *se rendre* to present oneself; see RENDER]

rendition (rɛnˈdɪʃən) *n* **1** a performance of a musical composition, dramatic role, etc **2** a translation of a text **3** the act of rendering **4** *archaic* surrender [c17 from obsolete French, from Late Latin *redditiō* see RENDER]

rendzina (rɛnˈdziːnə) *n* a dark interzonal type of soil found in grassy or formerly grassy areas of moderate rainfall, esp on chalklands [c20 from Polish]

renegade (ˈrɛnɪˌgeɪd) *n* **1 a** a person who deserts his cause or faith for another; apostate; traitor **b** (*as modifier*): *a renegade priest* **2** any outlaw or rebel [c16 from Spanish *renegado*, from Medieval Latin *renegāre* to renounce, from Latin RE- + *negāre* to deny]

renegado (ˌrɛnɪˈgɑːdəʊ) *n, pl* **-dos** an archaic word for **renegade**

renege *or* **renegue** (rɪˈniːg, -ˈneɪg) *vb* **1** (*intr*; often foll by *on*) to go back (on one's promise, etc) ▷ *vb* ▷ *n* **2** *cards* other words for **revoke** [c16 (in the sense: to deny, renounce): from Medieval Latin *renegāre* to renounce; see RENEGADE] > reˈneger *or* reˈneguer *n*

renegotiate (ˌriːnɪˈgəʊʃɪˌeɪt) *vb* to negotiate again in order to alter or change previously agreed terms > ˌreneˌgotiˈation *n*

renew (rɪˈnjuː) *vb* (*mainly tr*) **1** to take up again **2** (*also intr*) to begin (an activity) again; recommence: *to renew an attempt* **3** to restate or reaffirm (a promise, etc) **4** (*also intr*) to make (a lease, licence, or contract) valid or effective for a further period **5** to extend the period of loan of (a library book) **6** to regain or recover (vigour, strength, activity, etc) **7** to restore to a new or fresh condition **8** to replace (an old or worn-out part or piece) **9** to replenish (a supply, etc) > reˈnewable *adj* > reˌnewaˈbility *n* > reˈnewer *n*

renewable energy *n* another name for **alternative energy**

renewables *pl n* sources of alternative energy, such as wind and wave power

renewal (rɪˈnjuːəl) *n* **1** the act of renewing or state of being renewed **2** something that is renewed

Renfrew (ˈrɛnfruː) *n* an industrial town in W central Scotland, in Renfrewshire, W of Glasgow. Pop: 20 251 (2001)

Renfrewshire (ˈrɛnfruːʃɪə, -ʃə) *n* **1** a council area of W central Scotland, on the River Clyde W of Glasgow: corresponds to part of the historical county of Renfrewshire; part of Strathclyde region from 1975 to 1996: agricultural and residential, with clothing and manufacturing industries in Paisley. Administrative centre: Paisley. Pop: 170 980 (2003 est). Area: 261 sq km (101 sq miles) **2** a former county of W central Scotland, on the Firth of Clyde: became part of Strathclyde region

in 1975; now covered by the council areas of Renfrewshire, East Renfrewshire, and Inverclyde

reni- *combining form* kidney or kidneys: *reniform* [from Latin *rēnēs*]

reniform (ˈrɛnɪˌfɔːm) *adj* having the shape or profile of a kidney: *a reniform leaf; a reniform mass of haematite*

renin (ˈriːnɪn) *n* a proteolytic enzyme secreted by the kidneys, which plays an important part in the maintenance of blood pressure [c20 from RENI- + -IN]

renitent (rɪˈnaɪtənt, ˈrɛnɪtənt) *adj rare* **1** reluctant; recalcitrant **2** not flexible [c18 from Latin *renītī* to strive afresh, from RE- + *nītī* to endeavour] > reˈnitence *or* reˈnitency *n*

renk (rɛŋk) *adj Northern English dialect* unpleasant; horrible

renminbi *or* **renminbi yuan** (ˌrɛnˌmɪnˈbiː) *n, pl* **renminbi** another name for the Chinese **yuan** [Chinese *renmin* people + *bi* currency]

Rennes (*French* rɛn) *n* a city in NW France: the ancient capital of Brittany. Pop: 206 229 (1999)

rennet (ˈrɛnɪt) *n* **1 a** the membrane lining the fourth stomach (abomasum) of a young calf **b** the stomach of certain other young animals **2** a substance, containing the enzyme rennin, prepared esp from the stomachs of calves and used for curdling milk in making cheese and junket [c15 related to Old English *gerinnan* to curdle, RUN]

rennin (ˈrɛnɪn) *n* an enzyme that occurs in gastric juice and is a constituent of rennet. It coagulates milk by converting caseinogen to casein. Also called: **chymosin** [c20 from RENNET + -IN]

Reno (ˈriːnəʊ) *n* a city in W Nevada, at the foot of the Sierra Nevada: noted as a divorce, wedding, and gambling centre by reason of its liberal laws. Pop: 193 882 (2003 est)

renosterveld (rɛˈnɒstəˌfɛlt, -ˌvɛlt) *n* **the** an area of high altitude in SW South Africa, having fertile ground [from Afrikaans *renoster(bos)*, a plant of the daisy family + VELD]

renounce (rɪˈnaʊns) *vb* **1** (*tr*) to give up (a claim or right), esp by formal announcement: *to renounce a title* **2** (*tr*) to repudiate: *to renounce Christianity* **3** (*tr*) to give up (some habit, pursuit, etc) voluntarily: *to renounce smoking* **4** (*intr*) *cards* to fail to follow suit because one has no cards of the suit led ▷ *n* **5** *rare* a failure to follow suit in a card game [c14 from Old French *renoncer*, from Latin *renuntiāre* to disclaim, from RE- + *nuntiāre* to announce, from *nuntius* messenger] > reˈnouncement *n* > reˈnouncer *n*

renovate (ˈrɛnəˌveɪt) *vb* (*tr*) **1** to restore (something) to good condition: *to renovate paintings* **2** to revive or refresh (one's spirits, health, etc) [c16 from Latin *renovāre*, from RE- + *novāre* to make new, from *novus* NEW] > ˌrenoˈvation *n* > ˈrenoˌvator *n*

renown (rɪˈnaʊn) *n* widespread reputation, esp of a good kind; fame [c14 from Anglo-Norman *renoun*, from Old French *renom*, from *renomer* to celebrate, from RE- + *nomer* to name, from Latin *nōmināre*]

renowned (rɪˈnaʊnd) *adj* having a widespread, esp good, reputation; famous

rensselaerite (ˈrɛnsələˌraɪt, ˌrɛnsəˈlɛəraɪt) *n* a white or yellow compact variety of talc, used for ornaments [c19 named after Stephen Van *Rensselaer* (1764–1839), American army officer and politician]

rent¹ (rɛnt) *n* **1** a payment made periodically by a tenant to a landlord or owner for the occupation or use of land, buildings, or by a user for the use of other property, such as a telephone **2** *economics* **a** that portion of the national income accruing to owners of land and real property **b** the return derived from the cultivation of land in excess of production costs **c** See **economic rent 3 for rent** *chiefly US and Canadian* available for use and occupation subject to the payment of rent ▷ *vb* **4** (*tr*) to grant (a person) the right to use one's property in return for periodic payments **5** (*tr*) to

r

occupy or use (property) in return for periodic payments **6** (*intr; often foll by at*) to be let or rented (for a specified rental) [C12 from Old French *rente* revenue, from Vulgar Latin *rendere* (unattested) to yield; see RENDER] > ˌrentaˈbility *n* > ˈrentable *adj*

rent[2] (rɛnt) *n* **1** a slit or opening made by tearing or rending; tear **2** a breach or division, as in relations ▷ *vb* **3** the past tense and past participle of **rend**

rent-a- *prefix* **1** denoting a rental service **2** *derogatory or facetious* denoting a person or group that performs a function as if hired from a rental service: *rent-a-mob*

rental (ˈrɛntəl) *n* **1 a** the amount paid by a tenant as rent **b** the amount paid by a user for the use of property: *telephone rental* **c** an income derived from rents received **2** property available for renting **3** a less common name for **rent-roll** ▷ *adj* **4** of or relating to rent or renting

rent boy *n* a young male prostitute

rent control *n* regulation by law of the rent a landlord can charge for domestic accommodation and of his right to evict tenants

rente *French* (rɑ̃t) *n* **1** annual income from capital investment; annuity **2** government securities of certain countries, esp France **3** the interest on such securities

renter (ˈrɛntə) *n* **1** a person who lets his property in return for rent, esp a landlord **2** a person who rents property from another; tenant **3** a distributor of films to cinemas for commercial showing

rent-free *adj* ▷ *adv* without payment of rent

rentier *French* (rɑ̃tje) *n* **a** a person whose income consists primarily of fixed unearned amounts, such as rent or bond interest **b** (*as modifier*): *the rentier class* [from *rente*; see RENT[1]]

rent-roll *n* **1** a register of lands and buildings owned by a person, company, etc, showing the rent due and total amount received from each tenant **2** the total income arising from rented property

renunciate (rɪˈnʌnsɪɪt) *n* **1** *Hinduism* another word for **sannyasi** **2** *Christianity* any religious devotee who renounces earthly pleasures and lives as an ascetic

renunciation (rɪˌnʌnsɪˈeɪʃən) *n* **1** the act or an instance of renouncing **2** a formal declaration renouncing something **3** *stock exchange* the surrender to another of the rights to buy new shares in a rights issue [C14 from Latin *renunciātiō* a declaration, from *renuntiāre* to report, RENOUNCE] > reˈnunciative *or* reˈnunciatory *adj*

renvoi (rɛnˈvɔɪ) *n* the referring of a dispute or other legal question to a jurisdiction other than that in which it arose [C17 from French: a sending back, from *renvoyer*, from RE- + *envoyer* to send; see ENVOY[1]]

reo (ˈriːəʊ) *n* NZ a language [Māori]

reoccupy (riːˈɒkjʊˌpaɪ) *vb* **-pies, -pying, -pied** (*tr*) to occupy (a building, area, etc) again > ˌreoccuˈpation *n*

reoccur (ˌriːəˈkɜː) *vb* **-curs, -curring, -curred** (*intr*) to happen, take place, or come about again > ˌreocˈcurrence *n*

reoffend (ˈriːəˌfɛnd) *vb* (*intr*) to commit another offence > ˈreofˌfender *n*

reopen (riːˈəʊpən) *vb* to open or cause to open again

reorder (riːˈɔːdə) *vb* (*tr*) **1** to request (something) to be supplied again or differently **2** to arrange, regulate, or dispose (articles) in their proper places again

reorganization *or* **reorganisation** (ˌriːɔːgənaɪˈzeɪʃən) *n* the act of organizing or the state of being organized again

reorganize *or* **reorganise** (riːˈɔːgəˌnaɪz) *vb* (*tr*) to change the way (something) is organized

reorient (riːˈɔːrɪənt) *vb* (*tr*) to adjust or align (something) in a new or different way > ˌreorienˈtation *n*

rep[1] *or* **repp** (rɛp) *n* a silk, wool, rayon, or cotton fabric with a transversely corded surface [C19 from French *reps*, perhaps from English *ribs*; see RIB[1]] > **repped** *adj*

rep[2] (rɛp) *n* *theatre* short for **repertory** (**company**)

rep[3] (rɛp) *n* short for **representative** (senses 2, 5)

rep[4] (rɛp) *n* *informal* short for **reputation**

Rep. *abbreviation for* **1** *US* Representative **2** *US* Republican **3** Republic

repack (riːˈpæk) *vb* (*tr*) to place or arrange (articles) in (a container) again or in a different way

repackage (riːˈpækɪdʒ) *vb* (*tr*) to wrap or put (something) in a package again

repaint (riːˈpeɪnt) *vb* to apply a new or fresh coat of paint

repair[1] (rɪˈpɛə) *vb* (*tr*) **1** to restore (something damaged or broken) to good condition or working order **2** to heal (a breach or division) in (something): *to repair a broken marriage* **3** to make good or make amends for (a mistake, injury, etc) ▷ *n* **4** the act, task, or process of repairing **5** a part that has been repaired **6** state or condition: *in good repair* [C14 from Old French *reparer*, from Latin *reparāre*, from RE- + *parāre* to make ready] > reˈpairable *adj* > reˈpairer *n*

repair[2] (rɪˈpɛə) *vb* (*intr*) **1** (usually foll by *to*) to go (to a place): *to repair to the country* **2** (usually foll by *to*) to have recourse (to) for help, etc: *to repair to one's lawyer* **3** (usually foll by *from*) *archaic* to come back; return ▷ *n archaic* **4** the act of going or returning **5** a haunt or resort [C14 from Old French *repairier*, from Late Latin *repatriāre* to return to one's native land, from Latin RE- + *patria* fatherland; compare REPATRIATE]

repairman (rɪˈpɛəˌmæn) *n, pl* **-men** a man whose job it is to repair machines, appliances, etc

repand (rɪˈpænd) *adj* *botany* having a wavy margin: *a repand leaf* [C18 from Latin *repandus* bent backwards, from RE- + *pandus* curved] > reˈpandly *adv*

reparable (ˈrɛpərəbəl, ˈrɛprə-) *adj* able to be repaired, recovered, or remedied: *a reparable loss* [C16 from Latin *reparābilis*, from *reparāre* to REPAIR[1]] > ˌreparaˈbility *n* > ˈreparably *adv*

reparation (ˌrɛpəˈreɪʃən) *n* **1** the act or process of making amends: *an injury admitting of no reparation* **2** (*usually plural*) compensation exacted as an indemnity from a defeated nation by the victors: esp the compensation demanded of Germany by the Treaty of Versailles after World War I **3** the act or process of repairing or state of having been repaired [C14 *reparacioun*, ultimately from Latin *reparāre* to REPAIR[1]] > **reparative** (rɪˈpærətɪv) *or* reˈparatory *adj*

repartee (ˌrɛpɑːˈtiː) *n* **1** a sharp, witty, or aphoristic remark made as a reply **2** terse rapid conversation consisting of such remarks **3** skill in making sharp witty replies or conversation [C17 from French *repartie*, from *repartir* to retort, from RE- + *partir* to go away]

repartition (ˌriːpɑːˈtɪʃən) *n* **1** distribution or allotment **2** the act or process of distributing afresh ▷ *vb* **3** (*tr*) to divide up again; reapportion or reallocate

repast (rɪˈpɑːst) *n* **1** a meal or the food provided at a meal: *a light repast* **2** *archaic* **a** food in general; nourishment **b** the act of taking food or refreshment ▷ *vb* **3** (*intr*) *archaic* to feed (on) [C14 from Old French, from *repaistre* to feed, from Late Latin *repāscere* to nourish again, from Latin RE- + *pāscere* to feed, pasture (of animals)]

repatriate *vb* (*tr*) (riːˈpætrɪˌeɪt) **1** to send back (a refugee, prisoner of war, etc) to the country of his birth or citizenship **2** to send back (a sum of money previously invested abroad) to its country of origin ▷ *n* (riːˈpætrɪɪt) **3** a person who has been repatriated [C17 from Late Latin *repatriāre* from Latin RE- + *patria* fatherland; compare REPAIR[2]] > reˌpatriˈation *n*

repay (rɪˈpeɪ) *vb* **-pays, -paying, -paid** **1** to pay back (money) to (a person); refund or reimburse **2** to make a return for (something) by way of compensation: *to repay kindness* > reˈpayable *adj* > reˈpayment *n*

repeal (rɪˈpiːl) *vb* (*tr*) **1** to annul or rescind officially (something previously ordered); revoke: *these laws were repealed* **2** *obsolete* to call back (a person) from exile ▷ *n* **3** an instance or the process of repealing; annulment [C14 from Old French *repeler*, from RE- + *apeler* to call, APPEAL] > reˈpealable *adj* > reˈpealer *n*

Repeal (rɪˈpiːl) *n* (esp in the 19th century) the proposed dissolution of the Union between Great Britain and Ireland

repeat (rɪˈpiːt) *vb* **1** (*when tr, may take a clause as object*) to say or write (something) again, either once or several times; restate or reiterate **2** to do or experience (something) again once or several times **3** (*intr*) to occur more than once: *the last figure repeats* **4** (*tr; may take a clause as object*) to reproduce (the words, sounds, etc) uttered by someone else; echo **5** (*tr*) to utter (a poem, speech, etc) from memory; recite **6** (*intr*) **a** (of food) to be tasted again after ingestion as the result of belching or slight regurgitation **b** to belch **7** (*tr; may take a clause as object*) to tell to another person (the words, esp secrets, imparted to one by someone else) **8** (*intr*) (of a clock) to strike the hour or quarter-hour just past, when a spring is pressed **9** (*intr*) *US* to vote (illegally) more than once in a single election **10** **repeat oneself** to say or do the same thing more than once, esp so as to be tedious ▷ *n* **11 a** the act or an instance of repeating **b** (*as modifier*): *a repeat performance* **12** a word, action, etc, that is repeated **13** an order made out for goods, provisions, etc, that duplicates a previous order **14** a duplicate copy of something; reproduction **15** *radio, television* a further broadcast of a programme, film, etc, which has been broadcast before **16** *music* a passage that is an exact restatement of the passage preceding it [C14 from Old French *repeter*, from Latin *repetere* to seek again, from RE- + *petere* to seek] > reˌpeataˈbility *n* > reˈpeatable *adj*

> USAGE Since *again* is part of the meaning of *repeat*, one should not say something is *repeated again*

repeated (rɪˈpiːtɪd) *adj* done, made, or said again and again; continual or incessant > reˈpeatedly *adv*

repeater (rɪˈpiːtə) *n* **1** a person or thing that repeats **2** Also called: **repeating firearm** a firearm capable of discharging several shots without reloading **3** a timepiece having a mechanism enabling it to strike the hour or quarter-hour just past, when a spring is pressed **4** *electrical engineering* a device that amplifies or augments incoming electrical signals and retransmits them, thus compensating for transmission losses **5** Also called: **substitute** *nautical* one of three signal flags hoisted with others to indicate that one of the top three is to be repeated

repeating decimal *n* another name for **recurring decimal**

repechage (ˌrɛpɪˈʃɑːʒ) *n* a heat of a competition, esp in rowing or fencing, in which eliminated contestants have another chance to qualify for the next round or the final [C19 from French *repêchage* literally: fishing out again, from RE- + *pêcher* to fish + -AGE]

repel (rɪˈpɛl) *vb* **-pels, -pelling, -pelled** (*mainly tr*) **1** to force or drive back (something or somebody, esp an attacker) **2** (*also intr*) to produce a feeling of aversion or distaste in (someone or something); be disgusting (to) **3** to push aside; dismiss: *he repelled the suggestion as wrong and impossible* **4** to be effective in keeping away, controlling, or resisting: *an aerosol spray that repels flies* **5** to have no affinity for; fail to mix with or absorb: *water and oil repel each other* **6** to disdain to accept (something); turn away from or spurn: *she repelled his advances* **7** (*also intr*) to exert an opposing force on (something): *an electric charge repels another charge of the same sign* [C15 from Latin *repellere*, from RE- + *pellere* to push, drive] > reˈpeller *n*

USAGE See at **repulse**

repellent (rɪˈpɛlənt) *adj* **1** giving rise to disgust or aversion; distasteful or repulsive **2** driving or forcing away or back; repelling ▷ *n also* **repellant** **3** something, esp a chemical substance, that repels: *insect repellent* **4** a substance with which fabrics are treated to increase their resistance to water > **reˈpellence** *or* **reˈpellency** *n* > **reˈpellently** *adv*

repent[1] (rɪˈpɛnt) *vb* to feel remorse (for); be contrite (about); show penitence (for): *he repents of his extravagance; he repented his words* [C13 from Old French *repentir* from RE- + *pentir* to be contrite, from Latin *paenitēre* to repent] > **reˈpenter** *n*

repent[2] (ˈriːpᵊnt) *adj botany* lying or creeping along the ground; reptant: *repent stems* [C17 from Latin *rēpere* to creep]

repentance (rɪˈpɛntəns) *n* **1** remorse or contrition for one's past actions or sins **2** an act or the process of being repentant; penitence

repentant (rɪˈpɛntənt) *adj* **1** reproaching oneself for one's past actions or sins; contrite **2** characterized by or proceeding from a sense of contrition: *a repentant heart; his repentant words* > **reˈpentantly** *adv*

repercussion (ˌriːpəˈkʌʃən) *n* **1** (*often plural*) a result or consequence, esp one that is somewhat removed from the action or event which precipitated it: *the repercussions of the war are still keenly felt* **2** a recoil after impact; a rebound **3** a reflection, esp of sound; echo or reverberation **4** *music* the reappearance of a fugal subject and answer after an episode [C16 from Latin *repercussiō*, from *repercutere* to strike back; see PERCUSSION] > ˌ**reperˈcussive** *adj*

reperepe (rɛpɛrɛpɛ) *n, pl* **reperepe** another name for **elephant fish** [Māori]

repertoire (ˈrɛpəˌtwɑː) *n* **1** all the plays, songs, operas, or other works collectively that a company, actor, singer, dancer, etc, has prepared and is competent to perform **2** the entire stock of things available in a field or of a kind: *the comedian's repertoire of jokes was becoming stale* **3** **in repertoire** denoting the performance of two or more plays, ballets, etc, by the same company in the same venue on different evenings over a period of time: *"Nutcracker" returns to Covent Garden over Christmas in repertoire with "Giselle"* [C19 from French, from Late Latin *repertōrium* inventory; see REPERTORY]

repertory (ˈrɛpətərɪ, -trɪ) *n, pl* **-ries** **1** the entire stock of things available in a field or of a kind; repertoire **2** a building or place where a stock of things is kept; repository **3** short for **repertory company** [C16 from Late Latin *repertōrium* storehouse, from Latin *reperīre* to obtain, from RE- + *parere* to bring forth] > ˌ**reperˈtorial** *adj*

repertory company *n* a theatrical company that performs plays from a repertoire, esp at its own theatre. US name: **stock company**

repertory society *n NZ* a group that supports amateur performances of plays by its members

repetend (ˈrɛpɪˌtɛnd, ˌrɛpɪˈtɛnd) *n* **1** *maths* the digit or series of digits in a recurring decimal that repeats itself **2** anything repeated [C18 from Latin *repetendum* what is to be repeated, from *repetere* to REPEAT]

répétiteur *French* (repetitœr) *n* a member of an opera company who accompanies rehearsals on the piano and coaches the singers > ***répétiteuse*** (repetitøz) *fem n*

repetition (ˌrɛpɪˈtɪʃən) *n* **1** the act or an instance of repeating; reiteration **2** a thing, word, action, etc, that is repeated **3** a replica or copy **4** *civil and Scots law* the recovery or repayment of money paid or received by mistake, as when the same bill has been paid twice

repetitious (ˌrɛpɪˈtɪʃəs) *adj* characterized by unnecessary repetition > ˌ**repeˈtitiously** *adv* > ˌ**repeˈtitiousness** *n*

repetitive (rɪˈpɛtɪtɪv) *adj* characterized by or given to unnecessary repetition; boring: *dull, repetitive work* > **reˈpetitively** *adv* > **reˈpetitiveness** *n*

repetitive strain *or* **stress injury** *n* a condition, characterized by arm or wrist pains, that can affect musicians, computer operators, etc, who habitually perform awkward hand movements. Abbreviation: **RSI**

rephrase (riːˈfreɪz) *vb* (*tr*) to phrase again, esp so as to express more clearly

repine (rɪˈpaɪn) *vb* (*intr*) to be fretful or low-spirited through discontent [C16 from RE- + PINE[2]]

repique (rɪˈpiːk) *piquet* ▷ *n* **1** a score of 30 points made from the cards held by a player before play begins ▷ *vb* **2** to score a repique against (someone) [from French *repiq*]

replace (rɪˈpleɪs) *vb* (*tr*) **1** to take the place of; supersede: *the manual worker is being replaced by the machine* **2** to substitute a person or thing for (another which has ceased to fulfil its function); put in place of: *to replace an old pair of shoes* **3** to put back or return; restore to its rightful place > **reˈplaceable** *adj* > **reˌplaceaˈbility** *n* > **reˈplacer** *n*

replacement (rɪˈpleɪsmənt) *n* **1** the act or process of replacing **2** a person or thing that replaces another **3** *geology* the growth of a mineral within another of different chemical composition by gradual simultaneous deposition and removal **4** a process of fossilization by gradual substitution of mineral matter for the original organic matter. Also called **petrification**

replant (riːˈplɑːnt) *vb* (*tr*) **1** to plant again: *she replanted the bulbs that the dog had dug up* **2** to reattach (a severed limb or part) by surgery

replantation (ˌriːplænˈteɪʃən) *n* the reattachment of (severed limbs or parts) by surgery

replay *n* (ˈriːˌpleɪ) **1** Also called: **action replay** *television* a showing again of a sequence of action, esp of part of a sporting contest immediately after it happens either in slow motion (a **slow-motion replay**) or at normal speed **2** a rematch ▷ *vb* (riːˈpleɪ) **3** to play again (a record, television sequence, sporting contest, etc)

replenish (rɪˈplɛnɪʃ) *vb* (*tr*) **1** to make full or complete again by supplying what has been used up or is lacking **2** to put fresh fuel on (a fire) [C14 from Old French *replenir*, from RE- + *plenir* to fill, from Latin *plēnus* full] > **reˈplenisher** *n* > **reˈplenishment** *n*

replete (rɪˈpliːt) *adj* (*usually postpositive*) **1** (often foll by *with*) copiously supplied (with); abounding (in) **2** having one's appetite completely or excessively satisfied by food and drink; stuffed; gorged; satiated [C14 from Latin *replētus*, from *replēre* to refill, from RE- + *plēre* to fill] > **reˈpletely** *adv* > **reˈpleteness** *n*

repletion (rɪˈpliːʃən) *n* **1** the state or condition of being replete; fullness, esp excessive fullness due to overeating **2** the satisfaction of a need or desire

replevin (rɪˈplɛvɪn) *law* ▷ *n* **1** the recovery of goods unlawfully taken, made subject to establishing the validity of the recovery in a legal action and returning the goods if the decision is adverse **2** (formerly) a writ of replevin ▷ *vb* **3** another word for **replevy** [C15 from Anglo-French, from Old French *replevir* to give security for, from RE- + *plevir* to PLEDGE]

replevy (rɪˈplɛvɪ) *law* ▷ *vb* **-plevies, -plevying, -plevied** (*tr*) **1** to recover possession of (goods) by replevin ▷ *n, pl* **-plevies** **2** another word for **replevin** [C15 from Old French *replevir*; see REPLEVIN] > **reˈpleviable** *or* **reˈplevisable** *adj*

replica (ˈrɛplɪkə) *n* an exact copy or reproduction, esp on a smaller scale [C19 from Italian, literally: a reply, from *replicare* to repeat, from Latin: to bend back, repeat]

replicate *vb* (ˈrɛplɪˌkeɪt) (*mainly tr*) **1** (*also intr*) to make or be a copy of; reproduce **2** to fold (something) over on itself; bend back **3** to reply to ▷ *adj* (ˈrɛplɪkɪt) **4** folded back on itself: *a replicate leaf* [C19 from Latin *replicātus* bent back; see REPLICA] > ˈ**replicative** *adj*

replication (ˌrɛplɪˈkeɪʃən) *n* **1** a reply or response **2** *law* (formerly) the plaintiff's reply to a defendant's answer or plea **3** *biology* the production of exact copies of complex molecules, such as DNA molecules, that occurs during growth of living organisms **4** repetition of a procedure, such as a scientific experiment, in order to reduce errors **5** a less common word for **replica** [C14 via Old French from Latin *replicātiō* a folding back, from *replicāre* to unroll; see REPLY]

replicon (ˈrɛplɪˌkɒn) *n genetics* a region of a DNA molecule that is replicated from a single origin [C20 from REPLIC(ATION) + -ON]

reply (rɪˈplaɪ) *vb* **-plies, -plying, -plied** (*mainly intr*) **1** to make answer (to) in words or writing or by an action; respond: *he replied with an unexpected move* **2** (*tr; takes a clause as object*) to say (something) in answer: *he replied that he didn't want to come* **3** *law* to answer a defendant's plea **4** to return (a sound); echo ▷ *n, pl* **-plies** **5** an answer made in words or writing or through an action; response **6** the answer made by a plaintiff or petitioner to a defendant's case [C14 from Old French *replier* to fold again, reply, from Latin *replicāre* to fold back, from RE- + *plicāre* to fold] > **reˈplier** *n*

repo (ˈriːpəʊ) *n informal* short for **1** repurchase agreement **2** **a** repossession of property **b** (*as modifier*): *a repo car*

repoint (ˌriːˈpɔɪnt) *vb* (*tr*) to repair the joints of (brickwork, masonry, etc) with mortar or cement

repone (rɪˈpəʊn) *vb* (*tr*) *Scots law* to restore (someone) to his former status, office, etc; rehabilitate [C16 from Latin *repōnere* to put back, replace]

repopulate (riːˈpɒpjʊˌleɪt) *vb* (*tr*) to provide a new population for (an area in which the population has declined)

report (rɪˈpɔːt) *n* **1** an account prepared for the benefit of others, esp one that provides information obtained through investigation and published in a newspaper or broadcast **2** a statement made widely known; rumour: *according to report, he is not dead* **3** an account of the deliberations of a committee, body, etc: *a report of parliamentary proceedings* **4** *Brit* a statement on the progress, academic achievement, etc, of each child in a school, written by teachers and sent to the parents or guardian annually or each term **5** a written account of a case decided at law, giving the main points of the argument on each side, the court's findings, and the decision reached **6** comment on a person's character or actions; reputation: *he is of good report here* **7** a sharp loud noise, esp one made by a gun ▷ *vb* (when *tr, may take a clause as object*; when *intr*, often foll by *on*) **8** to give an account (of); describe **9** to give an account of the results of an investigation (into): *to report on housing conditions* **10** (of a committee, legislative body, etc) to make a formal report on (a bill) **11** (*tr*) to complain about (a person), esp to a superior: *I'll report you to the teacher* **12** (*tr*) to reveal information about (a fugitive, escaped prisoner, etc) esp concerning his whereabouts **13** (*intr*) to present oneself or be present at an appointed place or for a specific purpose: *report to the manager's office* **14** (*intr*) to say or show that one is (in a certain state): *to report fit* **15** (*intr*; foll by *to*) to be responsible to and under the authority of: *the plant manager reports to the production controller* **16** (*intr*) to act as a reporter for a newspaper or for radio or television **17** *law* to take down in writing details of (the proceedings of a court of law) as a record or for publication [C14 from Old French, from *reporter* to carry back, from Latin *reportāre*, from RE- + *portāre* to carry] > **reˈportable** *adj*

reportage (rɪˈpɔːtɪdʒ, ˌrɛpɔːˈtɑːʒ) *n* **1** the act or process of reporting news or other events of general interest **2** a journalist's style of reporting **3** a technique of documentary film or photo journalism that tells a story entirely through pictures

reported clause *n grammar* a bound clause that reports what someone has said or thought, bound

r

to a main clause that contains a verb of saying or thinking

reportedly (rɪ'pɔːtɪdlɪ) *adv* according to rumour or report: *he is reportedly living in Australia*

reported speech *n* another term for **indirect speech**

reporter (rɪ'pɔːtə) *n* **1** a person who reports, esp one employed to gather news for a newspaper, news agency, or broadcasting organization **2** a person, esp a barrister, authorized to write official accounts of judicial proceedings **3** a person authorized to report the proceedings of a legislature **4** (in Scotland) *social welfare* an official who arranges and conducts children's panel hearings and who may investigate cases and decide on the action to be taken

reporter gene *n* a gene with an easily recognizable phenotype, used in analysing the regulation of gene structures

reportorial (ˌrɛpɔː'tɔːrɪəl) *adj chiefly US* of or relating to a newspaper reporter [C20 from REPORTER, influenced by EDITORIAL] > **repor'torially** *adv*

report stage *n* the stage preceding the third reading in the passage of a bill through Parliament, at which the bill, as amended in committee, is reported back to the chamber considering it

repose[1] (rɪ'pəʊz) *n* **1** a state of quiet restfulness; peace or tranquillity **2** dignified calmness of manner; composure ▷ *vb* **3** to place (oneself or one's body) in a state of quiet relaxation; lie or lay down at rest **4** (*intr*) to lie when dead, as in the grave **5** (*intr*; foll by *on*, *in*, etc) *formal* to take support (from) or be based (on): *your plan reposes on a fallacy* [C15 from Old French *reposer*, from Late Latin *repausāre* from RE- + *pausāre* to stop; see PAUSE] > **re'posal** *n* > **re'poser** *n* > **re'poseful** *adj* > **re'posefully** *adv* > **re'posefulness** *n*

repose[2] (rɪ'pəʊz) *vb* (*tr*) **1** to put (trust or confidence) in a person or thing **2** to place or put (an object) somewhere [C15 from Latin *repōnere* to store up, from RE- + *pōnere* to put] > **re'posal** *n*

reposit (rɪ'pɒzɪt) *vb* (*tr*) to put away, deposit, or store up [C17 from Latin *repositus* replaced, from *repōnere*; see REPOSE[2], POSIT]

reposition (ˌriːpə'zɪʃən) *n* **1** the act or process of depositing or storing **2** *surgery* the return of a broken or displaced organ, or part to its normal site **3** *archaic* the reinstatement of a person in a post or office ▷ *vb* (*tr*) **4** to place in a new position **5** to target (a product or brand) at a new market by changing its image

repository (rɪ'pɒzɪtərɪ, -trɪ) *n, pl* **-ries** **1** a place or container in which things can be stored for safety **2** a place where things are kept for exhibition; museum **3** a place where commodities are kept before being sold; warehouse **4** a place of burial; sepulchre **5** a receptacle containing the relics of the dead **6** a person to whom a secret is entrusted; confidant [C15 from Latin *repositōrium*, from *repōnere* to place]

repossess (ˌriːpə'zɛs) *vb* (*tr*) **1** to take back possession of (property), esp for nonpayment of money due under a hire-purchase agreement **2** to restore ownership of (something) to someone > **repossession** (ˌriːpə'zɛʃən) *n* > ˌ**repos'sessor** *n*

repot (riː'pɒt) *vb* **-pots, -potting, -potted** (*tr*) to put (a house plant) into a new usually larger pot

repoussé (rə'puːseɪ) *adj* **1** raised in relief, as a design on a thin piece of metal hammered through from the underside **2** decorated with such designs ▷ *n* **3** a design or surface made in this way **4** the technique of hammering designs in this way [C19 from French, from *repousser* to push back, from RE- + *pousser* to PUSH]

repp (rɛp) *n* a variant spelling of **rep**[1]

reprehend (ˌrɛprɪ'hɛnd) *vb* (*tr*) to find fault with; criticize [C14 from Latin *reprehendere* to hold fast, rebuke, from RE- + *prendere* to grasp] > ˌ**repre'hendable** *adj* > ˌ**repre'hender** *n*

reprehensible (ˌrɛprɪ'hɛnsəbᵊl) *adj* open to criticism or rebuke; blameworthy [C14 from Late Latin *reprehensibilis*, from Latin *reprehendere* to hold back, reprove; see REPREHEND] > ˌ**repreˌhensi'bility** *or* ˌ**repre'hensibleness** *n* > ˌ**repre'hensibly** *adv*

reprehension (ˌrɛprɪ'hɛnʃən) *n* the act or an instance of reprehending; reproof or rebuke > ˌ**repre'hensive** *or rarely* ˌ**repre'hensory** *adj* > ˌ**repre'hensively** *adv*

represent (ˌrɛprɪ'zɛnt) *vb* (*tr*) **1** to stand as an equivalent of; correspond to: *our tent represents home to us when we go camping* **2** to act as a substitute or proxy (for) **3** to act as or be the authorized delegate or agent for (a person, country, etc): *an MP represents his constituency* **4** to serve or use as a means of expressing: *letters represent the sounds of speech* **5** to exhibit the characteristics of; exemplify; typify: *romanticism in music is represented by Beethoven* **6** to present an image of through the medium of a picture or sculpture; portray **7** to bring clearly before the mind **8** to set forth in words; state or explain **9** to describe as having a specified character or quality; make out to be: *he represented her as a saint* **10** to act out the part of on stage; portray **11** to perform or produce (a play); stage [C14 from Latin *repraesentāre* to exhibit, from RE- + *praesentāre* to PRESENT[2]] > ˌ**repre'sentable** *adj* > ˌ**repreˌsenta'bility** *n*

re-present (ˌriːprɪ'zɛnt) *vb* (*tr*) to present again > **re-presentation** (ˌriːprɛzən'teɪʃən) *n*

representation (ˌrɛprɪzɛn'teɪʃən) *n* **1** the act or an instance of representing or the state of being represented **2** anything that represents, such as a verbal or pictorial portrait **3** anything that is represented, such as an image brought clearly to mind **4** the principle by which delegates act for a constituency **5** a body of representatives **6** *contract law* a statement of fact made by one party to induce another to enter into a contract **7** an instance of acting for another, on his authority, in a particular capacity, such as executor or administrator **8** a dramatic production or performance **9** (*often plural*) a statement of facts, true or alleged, esp one set forth by way of remonstrance or expostulation **10** *linguistics* an analysis of a word, sentence, etc, into its constituents: *phonetic representation*

representational (ˌrɛprɪzɛn'teɪʃənᵊl) *adj* **1** *fine arts* depicting or attempting to depict objects, scenes, figures, etc, directly as seen; naturalistic **2** of or relating to representation

representationalism (ˌrɛprɪzɛn'teɪʃənəˌlɪzəm) *or* **representationism** *n* **1** *philosophy* the doctrine that in perceptions of objects what is before the mind is not the object but a representation of it. Compare **presentationism, naive realism.** See also **barrier of ideas** **2** *fine arts* the practice or advocacy of attempting to depict objects, scenes, figures, etc, directly as seen > ˌ**represenˌtational'istic** *adj* > ˌ**represen'tationist** *n, adj*

representative (ˌrɛprɪ'zɛntətɪv) *n* **1** a person or thing that represents another or others **2** a person who represents and tries to sell the products or services of a firm, esp a travelling salesman. Often shortened to: **rep** **3** a typical example **4** a person representing a constituency in a deliberative, legislative, or executive body, esp (*cap*) a member of the **House of Representatives** (the lower house of Congress) **5** *NZ* a rugby player, football player, etc, chosen to represent a province in interprovincial sports ▷ *adj* **6** serving to represent; symbolic **7** **a** exemplifying a class or kind; typical: *a representative example of the species* **b** containing or including examples of all the interests, types, etc, in a group: *a representative collection* **8** acting as deputy or proxy for another or others **9** acting for or representing a constituency or the whole people in the process of government: *a representative council* **10** of, characterized by, or relating to the political principle of representation of the people: *representative government* **11** of or relating to a mental picture or representation > ˌ**repre'sentatively** *adv* > ˌ**repre'sentativeness** *n*

repress (rɪ'prɛs) *vb* (*tr*) **1** to keep (feelings, etc) under control; suppress or restrain: *to repress a desire* **2** to put into a state of subjugation: *to repress a people* **3** *psychoanal* to banish (thoughts and impulses that conflict with conventional standards of conduct) from one's conscious mind [C14 from Latin *reprimere* to press back, from RE- + *premere* to PRESS[1]] > **re'presser** *n* > **re'pressible** *adj*

repressed (rɪ'prɛst) *adj* (of a person) repressing feelings, instincts, desires, etc

repression *n* **1** the act or process of repressing or the condition of being repressed **2** *psychoanal* the subconscious rejection of thoughts and impulses that conflict with conventional standards of conduct. Compare **suppression** (sense 2)

repressive (rɪ'prɛsɪv) *adj* **1** acting to control, suppress, or restrain **2** subjecting people, a society, etc to a state of subjugation > **re'pressively** *adv* > **re'pressiveness** *n*

repressor (rɪ'prɛsə) *n biochem* a protein synthesized under the control of a repressor gene, which has the capacity to bind to the operator gene and thereby shut off the expression of the structural genes of an operon

reprieve (rɪ'priːv) *vb* (*tr*) **1** to postpone or remit the punishment of (a person, esp one condemned to death) **2** to give temporary relief to (a person or thing), esp from otherwise irrevocable harm: *the government has reprieved the company with a huge loan* ▷ *n* **3** a postponement or remission of punishment, esp of a person condemned to death **4** a warrant granting a postponement **5** a temporary relief from pain or harm; respite **6** the act of reprieving or the state of being reprieved [C16 from Old French *repris* (something) taken back, from *reprendre* to take back, from Latin *reprehendere*; perhaps also influenced by obsolete English *repreve* to reprove] > **re'prievable** *adj* > **re'priever** *n*

reprimand ('rɛprɪˌmɑːnd) *n* **1** a reproof or formal admonition; rebuke ▷ *vb* **2** (*tr*) to admonish or rebuke, esp formally; reprove [C17 from French *réprimande*, from Latin *reprimenda* (things) to be repressed; see REPRESS]

reprint *n* ('riːˌprɪnt) **1** a reproduction in print of any matter already published; offprint **2** a reissue of a printed work using the same type, plates, etc, as the original ▷ *vb* (riː'prɪnt) **3** (*tr*) to print again > **re'printer** *n*

reprisal (rɪ'praɪzᵊl) *n* **1** (*often plural*) retaliatory action against an enemy in wartime, such as the execution of prisoners of war, destruction of property, etc **2** the act or an instance of retaliation in any form **3** (formerly) the forcible seizure of the property or subjects of one nation by another [C15 from Old French *reprisaille*, from Old Italian *ripresaglia*, from *riprendere* to recapture, from Latin *reprehendere* to hold fast; see REPREHEND]

reprise (rɪ'priːz) *music* ▷ *n* **1** the repeating of an earlier theme ▷ *vb* **2** to repeat (an earlier theme) [C14 from Old French, from *reprendre* to take back, from Latin *reprehendere*; see REPREHEND]

repro ('riːprəʊ) *n, pl* **-pros** **1** short for **reproduction** (sense 2): *repro furniture* **2** short for **reproduction proof**

reproach (rɪ'prəʊtʃ) *vb* (*tr*) **1** to impute blame to (a person) for an action or fault; rebuke **2** *archaic* to bring disgrace or shame upon ▷ *n* **3** the act of reproaching **4** rebuke or censure; reproof: *words of reproach* **5** disgrace or shame: *to bring reproach upon one's family* **6** something that causes or merits blame, rebuke, or disgrace **7** **above** *or* **beyond reproach** perfect; beyond criticism [C15 from Old French *reprochier*, from Latin RE- + *prope* near] > **re'proachable** *adj* > **re'proachableness** *n* > **re'proachably** *adv* > **re'proacher** *n*

reproachful (rɪ'prəʊtʃfʊl) *adj* **1** full of or expressing reproach **2** *archaic* deserving of reproach; disgraceful > **re'proachfully** *adv* > **re'proachfulness** *n*

reprobate ('rɛprəʊ,beɪt) *adj* 1 morally unprincipled; depraved 2 *Christianity* destined or condemned to eternal punishment in hell ▷ *n* 3 an unprincipled, depraved, or damned person 4 a disreputable or roguish person: *the old reprobate* ▷ *vb* (*tr*) 5 to disapprove of; condemn 6 (of God) to destine, consign, or condemn to eternal punishment in hell [C16 from Late Latin *reprobātus* held in disfavour, from Latin RE- + *probāre* to APPROVE[1]] > **reprobacy** ('rɛprəbəsɪ) *n* > **'repro,bater** *n*

reprobation (,rɛprəʊ'beɪʃən) *n* 1 disapproval, blame, or censure 2 *Christianity* condemnation to eternal punishment in hell; rejection by God > **reprobative** ('rɛprəbətɪv) *or* **,repro'bationary** *adj* > **'reprobatively** *adv*

reprocess (riː'prəʊsɛs) *vb* (*tr*) 1 to treat or prepare (something) by a special method again 2 to subject to a routine procedure again

reprocessing (riː'prəʊsɛsɪŋ) *adj* of or relating to the treatment of materials in order to make them reusable: *reprocessing plant*

reproduce (,riːprə'djuːs) *vb* (*mainly tr*) 1 to make a copy, representation, or imitation of; duplicate 2 (*also intr*) *biology* to undergo or cause to undergo a process of reproduction 3 to produce or exhibit again 4 to bring back into existence again; re-create 5 to bring before the mind again (a scene, event, etc) through memory or imagination 6 (*intr*) to come out (well, badly, etc), when copied 7 to replace (damaged parts or organs) by a process of natural growth; regenerate 8 to cause (a sound or television recording) to be heard or seen > **,repro'ducible** *adj* > **,repro'ducibly** *adv* > **,repro,duci'bility** *n*

reproducer (,riːprə'djuːsə) *n* 1 a person or thing that makes reproductions 2 a complete sound reproduction system 3 another name for **loudspeaker**

reproduction (,riːprə'dʌkʃən) *n* 1 *biology* any of various processes, either sexual or asexual, by which an animal or plant produces one or more individuals similar to itself 2 **a** an imitation or facsimile of a work of art, esp of a picture made by photoengraving **b** (*as modifier*): *a reproduction portrait*. Sometimes shortened to: **repro** 3 the quality of sound from an audio system 4 the act or process of reproducing 5 the state of being reproduced 6 a revival of an earlier production, as of a play

reproduction proof *n* *printing* a proof of very good quality used for photographic reproduction to make a printing plate. Sometimes shortened to: **repro** *or* **repro proof**

reproductive (,riːprə'dʌktɪv) *adj* of, relating to, characteristic of, or taking part in reproduction > **,repro'ductively** *adv* > **,repro'ductiveness** *n*

reprography (rɪ'prɒgrəfɪ) *n* the art or process of copying, reprinting, or reproducing printed material > **reprographic** (,rɛprə'græfɪk) *adj* > **,repro'graphically** *adv*

reproof (rɪ'pruːf) *n* an act or expression of rebuke or censure. Also called: **reproval** (rɪ'pruːvᵊl) [C14 *reproffe*, from Old French *reprove*, from Late Latin *reprobāre* to disapprove of; see REPROBATE]

re-proof (riː'pruːf) *vb* (*tr*) 1 to treat (a coat, jacket, etc) so as to renew its texture, waterproof qualities, etc 2 to provide a new proof of (a book, galley, etc)

reprove (rɪ'pruːv) *vb* (*tr*) to speak disapprovingly to (a person); rebuke or scold [C14 from Old French *reprover*, from Late Latin *reprobāre*, from Latin RE- + *probāre* to examine, APPROVE[1]] > **re'provable** *adj* > **re'prover** *n* > **re'proving** *adj* > **re'provingly** *adv*

rept *abbreviation for* 1 receipt 2 report

reptant ('rɛptənt) *adj* *biology* creeping, crawling, or lying along the ground. Also: **repent** [C17 from Latin *reptāre* to creep]

reptile ('rɛptaɪl) *n* 1 any of the cold-blooded vertebrates constituting the class *Reptilia*, characterized by lungs, an outer covering of horny scales or plates, and young produced in amniotic eggs. The class today includes the tortoises, turtles, snakes, lizards, and crocodiles; in Mesozoic times it was the dominant group, containing the dinosaurs and related forms 2 a grovelling insignificant person ▷ *adj* 3 creeping, crawling, or squirming 4 grovelling or insignificant; mean; contemptible [C14 from Late Latin *reptilis* creeping, from Latin *rēpere* to crawl]

reptilian (rɛp'tɪlɪən) *adj* 1 of, relating to, resembling, or characteristic of reptiles 2 mean or treacherous; contemptible: *reptilian behaviour* ▷ *n* 3 a less common name for **reptile**

Repub. *abbreviation for* 1 Republic 2 Republican

republic (rɪ'pʌblɪk) *n* 1 a form of government in which the people or their elected representatives possess the supreme power 2 a political or national unit possessing such a form of government 3 a constitutional form in which the head of state is an elected or nominated president 4 any community or group that resembles a political republic in that its members or elements exhibit a general equality, shared interests, etc: *the republic of letters* [C17 from French *république*, from Latin *rēspublica* literally: the public thing, from *rēs* thing + *publica* PUBLIC]

republican (rɪ'pʌblɪkən) *adj* 1 of, resembling, or relating to a republic 2 supporting or advocating a republic ▷ *n* 3 a supporter or advocate of a republic

Republican (rɪ'pʌblɪkən) *adj* 1 of, belonging to, or relating to a Republican Party 2 of, belonging to, or relating to the Irish Republican Army ▷ *n* 3 a member or supporter of a Republican Party 4 a member or supporter of the Irish Republican Army

republicanism (rɪ'pʌblɪkə,nɪzəm) *n* 1 the principles or theory of republican government 2 support for a republic 3 (*often capital*) support for a Republican Party or for the Irish Republican Army

republicanize *or* **republicanise** (rɪ'pʌblɪkə,naɪz) *vb* (*tr*) to make republican > **re,publicani'zation** *or* **re,publicani'sation** *n*

Republican Party *n* 1 the more conservative of the two major political parties in the US: established around 1854. Compare **Democratic Party** 2 any of a number of political parties in other countries, usually so named to indicate their opposition to monarchy 3 *US history* another name for the **Democratic-Republican Party**

Republic of Ireland *n* See **Ireland[1]** (sense 2)

repudiate (rɪ'pjuːdɪ,eɪt) *vb* (*tr*) 1 to reject the authority or validity of; refuse to accept or ratify: *Congress repudiated the treaty that the President had negotiated* 2 to refuse to acknowledge or pay (a debt) 3 to cast off or disown (a son, lover, etc) [C16 from Latin *repudiāre* to put away, from *repudium* a separation, divorce, from RE- + *pudēre* to be ashamed] > **re'pudiable** *adj* > **re,pudi'ation** *n* > **re'pudiative** *adj* > **re'pudi,ator** *n*

repugn (rɪ'pjuːn) *vb* *archaic* to oppose or conflict (with) [C14 from Old French *repugner*, from Latin *repugnāre* to fight against, from RE- + *pugnāre* to fight]

repugnant (rɪ'pʌgnənt) *adj* 1 repellent to the senses; causing aversion 2 distasteful; offensive; disgusting 3 contradictory; inconsistent or incompatible [C14 from Latin *repugnāns* resisting; see REPUGN] > **re'pugnance** *or now rarely* **re'pugnancy** *n* > **re'pugnantly** *adv*

repulse (rɪ'pʌls) *vb* (*tr*) 1 to drive back or ward off (an attacking force); repel; rebuff 2 to reject with coldness or discourtesy: *she repulsed his advances* 3 to produce a feeling of aversion or distaste ▷ *n* 4 the act or an instance of driving back or warding off; rebuff 5 a cold discourteous rejection or refusal [C16 from Latin *repellere* to drive back, REPEL] > **re'pulser** *n*

> USAGE Some people think that the use of *repulse* in sentences such as *he was repulsed by what he saw* is incorrect and that the correct word is *repel*

repulsion (rɪ'pʌlʃən) *n* 1 a feeling of disgust or aversion 2 *physics* a force tending to separate two objects, such as the force between two like electric charges or magnetic poles

repulsive (rɪ'pʌlsɪv) *adj* 1 causing or occasioning repugnance; loathsome; disgusting or distasteful: *a repulsive sight* 2 tending to repel, esp by coldness and discourtesy 3 *physics* concerned with, producing, or being a repulsion > **re'pulsively** *adv* > **re'pulsiveness** *n*

repurchase (riː'pɜːtʃɪs) *vb* (*tr*) 1 to buy back or buy again goods, securities, assets, etc ▷ *n* 2 an act or instance of repurchasing

repurchase agreement *n* an agreement in which a security or asset is sold and later repurchased at an agreed price to raise ready money. Sometimes shortened to: **repo**

reputable ('rɛpjʊtəbᵊl) *adj* 1 having a good reputation; honoured, trustworthy, or respectable 2 (of words) acceptable as good usage; standard > **,reputa'bility** *n* > **'reputably** *adv*

reputation (,rɛpjʊ'teɪʃən) *n* 1 the estimation in which a person or thing is generally held; opinion 2 a high opinion generally held about a person or thing; esteem 3 notoriety or fame, esp for some specified characteristic 4 **have a reputation** to be known or notorious, esp for promiscuity, excessive drinking, or the like [C14 from Latin *reputātiō* a reckoning, from *reputāre* to calculate, meditate; see REPUTE] > **,repu'tationless** *adj*

repute (rɪ'pjuːt) *vb* 1 (*tr; usually passive*) to consider (a person or thing) to be as specified: *he is reputed to be intelligent* ▷ *n* 2 public estimation; reputation: *a writer of little repute* [C15 from Old French *reputer*, from Latin *reputāre* to think over, from RE- + *putāre* to think]

reputed (rɪ'pjuːtɪd) *adj* (*prenominal*) generally reckoned or considered; supposed or alleged: *he is the reputed writer of a number of romantic poems*

reputedly (rɪ'pjuːtɪdlɪ) *adv* according to general belief or supposition: *the reputedly excellent food*

request (rɪ'kwɛst) *vb* (*tr*) 1 to express a desire for, esp politely; ask for or demand: *to request a bottle of wine* ▷ *n* 2 **a** the act or an instance of requesting, esp in the form of a written statement; petition or solicitation: *a request for a song* **b** (*as modifier*): *a request programme* 3 **at the request of** in accordance with the specific demand or wish of (someone) 4 **by request** in accordance with someone's desire 5 **in request** in demand; popular: *he is in request in concert halls all over the world* 6 **on request** on the occasion of a demand or request: *application forms are available on request* [C14 from Old French *requeste*, from Vulgar Latin *requaerere* (unattested) to seek after; see REQUIRE, QUEST] > **re'quester** *n*

request stop *n* a point on a route at which a bus will stop only if signalled to do so. US equivalent: **flag stop**

Requiem ('rɛkwɪ,ɛm) *n* 1 *RC Church* a Mass celebrated for the dead 2 a musical setting of this Mass 3 any piece of music composed or performed as a memorial to a dead person or persons [C14 from Latin *requiēs* rest, from the opening of the introit, *Requiem aeternam dona eis* Rest eternal grant unto them]

requiem shark *n* any shark of the family *Carcharhinidae*, occurring mostly in tropical seas and characterized by a nictitating membrane and a heterocercal tail. The family includes the tiger shark and the soupfin [C17 French *requiem* probably assimilated from a native name]

requiescat (,rɛkwɪ'ɛskæt) *n* a prayer for the repose of the souls of the dead [Latin, from *requiescat in pace* may he rest in peace]

require (rɪ'kwaɪə) *vb* (*mainly tr; may take a clause as object or an infinitive*) 1 to have need of; depend upon; want 2 to impose as a necessity; make necessary: *this work requires precision* 3 (*also intr*) to make formal request (for); insist upon or demand, esp as an obligation 4 to call upon or oblige (a person) authoritatively; order or command: *to require someone to account for his actions* [C14 from Old

French *requerre*, from Vulgar Latin *requaerere* (unattested) to seek after, from Latin *requīrere* to seek to know, but also influenced by *quaerere* to seek] ▷ re'quirable *adj* ▷ re'quirer *n*

USAGE The use of *require to* as in *I require to see the manager* or *you require to complete a special form* is thought by many people to be incorrect: *I need to see the manager; you are required to complete a special form*

requirement (rɪˈkwaɪəmənt) *n* **1** something demanded or imposed as an obligation: *Latin is no longer a requirement for entry to university* **2** a thing desired or needed **3** the act or an instance of requiring

requisite (ˈrɛkwɪzɪt) *adj* **1** absolutely essential; indispensable ▷ *n* **2** something indispensable; necessity [C15 from Latin *requisītus* sought after, from *requīrere* to seek for, REQUIRE] ▷ ˈrequisitely *adv* ▷ ˈrequisiteness *n*

requisition (ˌrɛkwɪˈzɪʃən) *n* **1** a request or demand, esp an authoritative or formal one **2** an official form on which such a demand is made **3** the act of taking something over, esp temporarily for military or public use in time of emergency **4** a necessary or essential condition; requisite **5** a formal request by one government to another for the surrender of a fugitive from justice ▷ *vb* (*tr*) **6** to demand and take for use or service, esp by military or public authority **7** (*may take an infinitive*) to require (someone) formally to do (something): *to requisition a soldier to drive a staff officer's car* ▷ ˌrequiˈsitionary *adj*

requital (rɪˈkwaɪtəl) *n* **1** the act or an instance of requiting **2** a return or compensation for a good or bad action

requite (rɪˈkwaɪt) *vb* (*tr*) to make return to (a person for a kindness or injury); repay with a similar action [C16 RE- + obsolete *quite* to discharge, repay; see QUIT] ▷ reˈquitable *adj* ▷ reˈquitement *n* ▷ reˈquiter *n*

reradiation (ˌriːreɪdɪˈeɪʃən) *n* radiation resulting from the previous absorption of primary radiation

rerailing (riːˈreɪlɪŋ) *n* the replacement of existing rails on a railway line

reread (riːˈriːd) *vb* -reads, -reading, -read (*tr*) to read (something) again

re-record *vb* (*tr*) to make a recording of (something recorded before) again: *they had to re-record it in the studio*

re-recording *n* a new or different version of a piece of music recorded previously: *a re-recording of the song*

reredorter (ˈrɪədɔːtə) *n history* a privy at the back of a monastic dormitory

reredos (ˈrɪədɒs) *n* **1** a screen or wall decoration at the back of an altar, in the form of a hanging, tapestry, painting, or piece of metalwork or sculpture **2** another word for **fireback** (sense 1) [C14 from Old French *areredos*, from *arere* behind + *dos* back, from Latin *dorsum*]

reremai (ˈrɛrɛmaːiː) *n, pl* reremai NZ another name for **basking shark** [Māori]

reremouse or **rearmouse** (ˈrɪəmaʊs) *n, pl* -mice an archaic or dialect word for **bat** (the animal) [Old English *hrēremūs*, probably from *hrēran* to move + *mūs* MOUSE]

re-route (riːˈ) *vb* **1** to route or direct (traffic, a road, a river, etc) in a different direction **2** to change the direction of (a project, funds, etc)

rerun *vb* (riːˈrʌn) -runs, -running, -ran (*tr*) **1** to broadcast or put on (a film, play, series, etc) again **2** to run (a race, etc) again ▷ *n* (ˈriːˌrʌn) **3** a film, play, series, etc, that is broadcast or put on again; repeat **4** a race that is run again **5** *computing* the repeat of a part of a computer program

res Latin (reɪs) *n, pl* res a thing, matter, or object

res. *abbreviation for* **1** residence **2** resides **3** resigned **4** resolution

res adjudicata (ˈreɪs əˌdʒuːdɪˈkɑːtə) *n* another term for **res judicata**

resale (ˈriːˌseɪl, riːˈseɪl) *n* the selling again of something purchased ▷ reˈsalable or reˈsaleable *adj*

resale price maintenance *n* the practice by which a manufacturer establishes a fixed or minimum price for the resale of a brand product by retailers or other distributors. US equivalent: **fair trade** Abbreviation: rpm

reschedule (riːˈʃɛdjuːl; *also, esp US* -skɛdʒʊəl) *vb* (*tr*) **1** to change the time, date, or schedule of **2** to arrange a revised schedule for repayment of (a debt)

rescind (rɪˈsɪnd) *vb* (*tr*) to annul or repeal [C17 from Latin *rēscindere* to cut off, from *re-* (intensive) + *scindere* to cut] ▷ reˈscindable *adj* ▷ reˈscinder *n* ▷ reˈscindment *n*

rescissible (rɪˈsɪsəbəl) *adj* able to be rescinded

rescission (rɪˈsɪʒən) *n* **1** the act of rescinding **2** *law* the right to have a contract set aside if it has been entered into mistakenly, as a result of misrepresentation, undue influence, etc

rescissory (rɪˈsɪsərɪ) *adj* having the power to rescind

rescript (ˈriːˌskrɪpt) *n* **1** (in ancient Rome) an ordinance taking the form of a reply by the emperor to a question on a point of law **2** any official announcement or edict; a decree **3** something rewritten **4** the act or process of rewriting [C16 from Latin *rēscrīptum* a reply, from *rēscribere* to write back]

rescue (ˈrɛskjuː) *vb* -cues, -cuing, -cued (*tr*) **1** to bring (someone or something) out of danger, attack, harm, etc; deliver or save **2** to free (a person) from legal custody by force **3** *law* to seize (goods or property) by force ▷ *n* **4 a** the act or an instance of rescuing **b** (*as modifier*): *a rescue party* **5** the forcible removal of a person from legal custody **6** *law* the forcible seizure of goods or property [C14 *rescowen*, from Old French *rescourre*, from RE- + *escourre* to pull away, from Latin *excutere* to shake off, from *quatere* to shake] ▷ ˈrescuable *adj* ▷ ˈrescuer *n*

reseal (riːˈsiːl) *vb* (*tr*) to close (something) tightly or securely again ▷ reˈsealable *adj*

research (rɪˈsɜːtʃ, ˈriːsɜːtʃ) *n* **1** systematic investigation to establish facts or principles or to collect information on a subject ▷ *vb* **2** to carry out investigations into (a subject, problem, etc) [C16 from Old French *recercher* to seek, search again, from RE- + *cercher* to SEARCH] ▷ reˈsearchable *adj* ▷ reˈsearcher *n*

research and development *n* the part of a commercial company's activity concerned with applying the results of scientific research to develop new products and improve existing ones. Abbreviation: R & D

research quantum *n Austral* the standard by which the contribution to a university of individual academics is measured and on the basis of which universities receive government funding and academics are promoted

reseat (riːˈsiːt) *vb* (*tr*) **1** to show (a person) to a new seat **2** to put a new seat on (a chair, etc) **3** to provide new seats for (a hall, theatre, etc) **4** to re-form the seating of (a valve)

reseau (ˈrɛzəʊ) *n, pl* -seaux (-zəʊ, -zəʊz) or -seaus **1** a mesh background to a lace or other pattern **2** *astronomy* a network of fine lines cut into a glass plate used as a reference grid on star photographs **3** *photog* a screen covered in a regular pattern of minute coloured dots or lines, formerly used in colour photography [C19 from French, from Old French *resel* a little net, from *rais* net, from Latin *rēte*]

resect (rɪˈsɛkt) *vb* (*tr*) *surgery* to cut out part of (a bone, an organ, or other structure or part) [C17 from Latin *resecāre* to cut away, from RE- + *secāre* to cut]

resection (rɪˈsɛkʃən) *n* **1** *surgery* excision of part of a bone, organ, or other part **2** *surveying* a method of fixing the position of a point by making angular observations to three fixed points ▷ reˈsectional *adj*

reseda (ˈrɛsɪdə) *n* **1** any plant of the European genus *Reseda*, including mignonette and dyer's rocket, which has small spikes of grey-green flowers ▷ *adj* **2** of a greyish-green colour; mignonette [C18 from New Latin, from Latin: heal! from *resēdāre* to assuage, from RE- + *sēdāre* to soothe; see SEDATE[2]]

reselect (ˌriːsɪˈlɛkt) *vb* (*tr*) to choose (someone or something) again, esp to choose an existing office-holder as candidate for re-election ▷ ˌreseˈlection *n*

resell (riːˈsɛl) *vb* -sells, -selling, -sold (*tr*) to sell (something) one has previously bought; sell on ▷ reˈseller *n*

resemblance (rɪˈzɛmbləns) *n* **1** the state or quality of resembling; likeness or similarity in nature, appearance, etc **2** the degree or extent to which or the respect in which a likeness exists **3** something resembling something else; semblance; likeness ▷ reˈsemblant *adj*

resemble (rɪˈzɛmbəl) *vb* (*tr*) to possess some similarity to; be like [C14 from Old French *resembler*, from RE- + *sembler* to look like, from Latin *similis* like] ▷ reˈsembler *n*

resent (rɪˈzɛnt) *vb* (*tr*) to feel bitter, indignant, or aggrieved at [C17 from French *ressentir*, from RE- + *sentir* to feel, from Latin *sentīre* to perceive; see SENSE]

resentful (rɪˈzɛntfʊl) *adj* feeling or characterized by resentment ▷ reˈsentfully *adv* ▷ reˈsentfulness *n*

resentment (rɪˈzɛntmənt) *n* anger, bitterness, or ill will

reserpine (ˈrɛsəpɪn) *n* an insoluble alkaloid, extracted from the roots of the plant *Rauwolfia serpentina*, used medicinally to lower blood pressure and as a sedative and tranquillizer. Its main adverse effect is mental depression. Formula: $C_{33}H_{40}N_2O_9$ [C20 from German *Reserpin*, probably from the New Latin name of the plant]

reservation (ˌrɛzəˈveɪʃən) *n* **1** the act or an instance of reserving **2** something reserved, esp hotel accommodation, a seat on an aeroplane, in a theatre, etc **3** (*often plural*) a stated or unstated qualification of opinion that prevents one's wholehearted acceptance of a proposal, claim, statement, etc **4** an area of land set aside, esp (in the US) for American Indian peoples **5** *Brit* the strip of land between the two carriageways of a dual carriageway **6** the act or process of keeping back, esp for oneself; withholding **7** *law* a right or interest retained by the grantor in property granted, conveyed, leased, etc, to another: *a reservation of rent*

reserve (rɪˈzɜːv) *vb* (*tr*) **1** to keep back or set aside, esp for future use or contingency; withhold **2** to keep for oneself; retain: *I reserve the right to question these men later* **3** to obtain or secure by advance arrangement: *I have reserved two tickets for tonight's show* **4** to delay delivery of (a judgment), esp in order to allow time for full consideration of the issues involved ▷ *n* **5 a** something kept back or set aside, esp for future use or contingency **b** (*as modifier*): *a reserve stock* **6** the state or condition of being reserved: *I have plenty in reserve* **7** a tract of land set aside for the protection and conservation of wild animals, flowers, etc: *a nature reserve* **8** *Canadian* an area of land set aside, esp (in the US and Canada) for American or Canadian Indian peoples. Also called: **reservation 9** *Austral and NZ* an area of publicly owned land set aside for sport, recreation, etc **10** the act of reserving; reservation **11** a member of a team who only plays if a playing member drops out; a substitute **12** (*often plural*) **a** a part of an army or formation not committed to immediate action in a military engagement **b** that part of a nation's armed services not in active service **13** coolness or formality of manner; restraint, silence, or reticence **14** *finance* **a** a portion of capital not invested (a **capital reserve**) or a portion of profits not distributed (a **revenue** or **general reserve**) by a bank or business enterprise and held to meet legal requirements, future liabilities, or contingencies **b** (*often plural*) liquid assets held by an organization, government, etc, to meet expenses and liabilities **15 without reserve** without reservations; fully; wholeheartedly [c14 from Old French *reserver*, from Latin *reservāre* to save up, from RE- + *servāre* to keep] > re'servable *adj* > re'server *n*

re-serve (riːˈsɜːv) *vb* (*tr*) to serve again

reserve bank *n* one of the twelve banks forming part of the US Federal Reserve System

reserve currency *n* foreign currency that is acceptable as a medium of international payments and that is therefore held in reserve by many countries

reserved (rɪˈzɜːvd) *adj* **1** set aside for use by a particular person or people: *this table is reserved* **2** cool or formal in manner; restrained, silent, or reticent **3** destined; fated: *reserved for great things* **4** referring to matters that are the responsibility of the national parliament rather than a devolved regional assembly: *defence is a reserved issue* > reservedly (rɪˈzɜːvɪdlɪ) *adv* > re'servedness *n*

reserved list *n Brit* a list of retired naval, army, or air-force officers available for recall to active service in an emergency

reserved occupation *n Brit* in time of war, an occupation from which one will not be called up for military service

reserved word *n* a word in a programming language or computer system that has a fixed meaning and therefore cannot be redefined by a programmer

reserve-grade *adj Austral* denoting a sporting team of the second rank in a club

reserve price *n* the minimum price acceptable to the owner of property being auctioned or sold. Also called (esp Scot and US): **upset price**

reserve tranche *n* the quota of 25 per cent to which a member of the IMF has unconditional access. Prior to 1978 it was paid in gold and known as the **gold tranche**

reservist (rɪˈzɜːvɪst) *n* one who serves in the reserve formations of a nation's armed forces

reservoir (ˈrɛzəˌvwɑː) *n* **1** a natural or artificial lake or large tank used for collecting and storing water, esp for community water supplies or irrigation **2** a receptacle for storing gas, esp one attached to a stove **3** *biology* a vacuole or cavity in an organism, containing a secretion or some other fluid **4** *anatomy* another name for **cisterna 5** a place where a great stock of anything is accumulated **6** a large supply of something; reserve: *a reservoir of talent* [c17 from French *réservoir*, from *réserver* to RESERVE]

reset[1] *vb* (riːˈsɛt) **-sets, -setting, -set** (*tr*) **1** to set again (a broken bone, matter in type, a gemstone, etc) **2** to restore (a gauge, dial, etc) to zero **3** *Also:* **clear** to restore (the contents of a register or similar device) in a computer system to zero ▷ *n* (ˈriːˌsɛt) **4** the act or an instance of setting again **5** a thing that is set again **6** a plant that has been recently transplanted **7** a device for resetting instruments, controls, etc > re'setter *n*

reset[2] *Scot* ▷ *vb* (riːˈsɛt) **-sets, -setting, -set 1** to receive or handle goods knowing they have been stolen ▷ *n* (ˈriːˌsɛt) **2** the receiving of stolen goods [c14 from Old French *receter*, from Latin *receptāre*, from *recipere* to receive] > re'setter *n*

resettle (riːˈsɛtᵊl) *vb* to settle or cause to settle in a new or different place

resettlement (riːˈsɛtᵊlmənt) *n* **a** the act or instance of settling or being settled in another place **b** (*as modifier*): *resettlement procedures*

res gestae (ˈreɪs ˈdʒɛstiː) *pl n* **1** things done or accomplished; achievements **2** *law* incidental facts and circumstances that are admissible in evidence because they introduce or explain the matter in issue [Latin]

resh (reɪʃ; *Hebrew* reʃ) *n* the 20th letter in the Hebrew alphabet (ר), transliterated as *r* [from Hebrew, from *rōsh* head]

reshape (riːˈʃeɪp) *vb* (*tr*) to shape (something) again or differently

Resht (reʃt) *n* a variant of **Rasht**

reshuffle (riːˈʃʌfᵊl) *n* **1** an act of shuffling again **2** a reorganization, esp of jobs within a government or cabinet ▷ *vb* **3** to carry out a reshuffle (on)

reside (rɪˈzaɪd) *vb* (*intr*) *formal* **1** to live permanently or for a considerable time (in a place); have one's home (in): *he now resides in London* **2** (of things, qualities, etc) to be inherently present (in); be vested (in): *political power resides in military strength* [c15 from Latin *residēre* to sit back, from RE- + *sedēre* to sit] > re'sider *n*

residence (ˈrɛzɪdəns) *n* **1** the place in which one resides; abode or home **2** a large imposing house; mansion **3** the fact of residing in a place or a period of residing **4** the official house of the governor of any of various countries **5** the state of being officially present **6 in residence a** actually resident: *the royal standard indicates that the Queen is in residence* **b** designating a creative artist resident for a set period at a university, college, etc, whose role is to stimulate an active interest in the subject: *composer in residence* **7** the seat of some inherent quality, characteristic, etc

residency (ˈrɛzɪdənsɪ) *n, pl* **-cies 1** a variant of **residence 2** a regular series of concerts by a band or singer at one venue **3** *US and Canadian* the period, following internship, during which a physician undergoes further clinical training, usually in one medical speciality **4** (in India, formerly) the official house of the governor general at the court of a native prince

resident (ˈrɛzɪdənt) *n* **1** a person who resides in a place **2** *social welfare* an occupant of a welfare agency home. Former name: **inmate 3** (esp formerly) a representative of the British government in a British protectorate **4** (esp in the 17th century) a diplomatic representative ranking below an ambassador **5** (in India, formerly) a representative of the British governor general at the court of a native prince **6** a bird or other animal that does not migrate **7** *US and Canadian* a physician who lives in the hospital where he works while undergoing specialist training after completing his internship. Compare **house physician 8** *Brit and NZ* a junior doctor, esp a house officer, who lives in the hospital in which he works ▷ *adj* **9** living in a place; residing **10** living or staying at a place in order to discharge a duty, etc **11** (of qualities, characteristics, etc) existing or inherent (in) **12** (of birds and other animals) not in the habit of migrating > 'resident,ship *n*

resident commissioner *n* the representative of Puerto Rico in the US House of Representatives. He may speak but has no vote

residential (ˌrɛzɪˈdɛnʃəl) *adj* **1** suitable for or allocated for residence: *a residential area* **2** relating to or having residence > ˌresi'dentially *adv*

residential care *n social welfare* the provision by a welfare agency of a home with social-work supervision for people who need more than just housing accommodation, such as children in care or mentally handicapped adults

residential school *n* (in Canada) a boarding school maintained by the Canadian government for Indian and Inuit children from sparsely populated settlements

residentiary (ˌrɛzɪˈdɛnʃərɪ) *adj* **1** residing in a place, esp officially; resident **2** subject to an obligation to reside in an official residence: *a residentiary benefice* ▷ *n, pl* **-tiaries 3** a clergyman obliged to reside in the place of his official appointment

residents association *n* an organization composed of voluntary members living in a particular neighbourhood, which aims to improve the social and communal facilities of the neighbourhood and to conserve or improve its environmental advantages. See also **community association, tenants association**

residual (rɪˈzɪdjʊəl) *adj* **1** of, relating to, or designating a residue or remainder; remaining;

left over **2** (of deposits, soils, etc) formed by the weathering of pre-existing rocks and the removal of disintegrated material **3** of or relating to the payment of residuals ▷ *n* **4** something left over as a residue; remainder **5** *statistics* **a** the difference between the mean of a set of observations and one particular observation **b** the difference between the numerical value of one particular observation and the theoretical result **6** (*often plural*) payment made to an actor, actress, musician, etc, for subsequent use of film in which the person appears > re'sidually *adv*

residual current device *adv, n* a circuit-breaking device installed in electrical equipment to protect the operator from electrocution. Abbreviation: **RCD**

residual unemployment *n* the unemployment that remains in periods of full employment, as a result of those mentally, physically, or emotionally unfit to work

residuary (rɪˈzɪdjʊərɪ) *adj* **1** of, relating to, or constituting a residue; residual **2** *law* entitled to the residue of an estate after payment of debts and distribution of specific gifts

residue (ˈrɛzɪˌdjuː) *n* **1** matter remaining after something has been removed **2** *law* what is left of an estate after the discharge of debts and distribution of specific gifts [c14 from Old French *residu*, from Latin *residuus* remaining over, from *residēre* to stay behind, RESIDE]

residuum (rɪˈzɪdjʊəm) *n, pl* **-ua** (-jʊə) a more formal word for **residue**

resign (rɪˈzaɪn) *vb* **1** (when *intr*, often foll by *from*) to give up tenure of (a job, office, etc) **2** (*tr*) to reconcile (oneself) to; yield: *to resign oneself to death* **3** (*tr*) to give up (a right, claim, etc); relinquish [c14 from Old French *resigner*, from Latin *resignāre* to unseal, invalidate, destroy, from RE- + *signāre* to seal; see SIGN] > re'signer *n*

re-sign (riːˈsaɪn) *vb* to sign (a document, etc) again

resignation (ˌrɛzɪgˈneɪʃən) *n* **1** the act of resigning **2** a formal document stating one's intention to resign **3** a submissive unresisting attitude; passive acquiescence

resigned (rɪˈzaɪnd) *adj* characteristic of or proceeding from an attitude of resignation; acquiescent or submissive > resignedly (rɪˈzaɪnɪdlɪ) *adv* > re'signedness *n*

resile (rɪˈzaɪl) *vb* (*intr*) to spring or shrink back; recoil or resume original shape [c16 from Old French *resilir*, from Latin *resilīre* to jump back, from RE- + *salīre* to jump] > re'silement *n*

resilience (rɪˈzɪlɪəns) *n* **1** Also called: **resiliency** the state or quality of being resilient **2** *ecology* the ability of an ecosystem to return to its original state after being disturbed **3** *physics* the amount of potential energy stored in an elastic material when deformed

resilient (rɪˈzɪlɪənt) *adj* **1** (of an object or material) capable of regaining its original shape or position after bending, stretching, compression, or other deformation; elastic **2** (of a person) recovering easily and quickly from shock, illness, hardship, etc; irrepressible > re'siliently *adv*

resin (ˈrɛzɪn) *n* **1** any of a group of solid or semisolid amorphous compounds that are obtained directly from certain plants as exudations. They are used in medicine and in varnishes **2** any of a large number of synthetic, usually organic, materials that have a polymeric structure, esp such a substance in a raw state before it is moulded or treated with plasticizer, stabilizer, filler, etc. Compare **plastic** (sense 1) ▷ *vb* **3** (*tr*) to treat or coat with resin [c14 from Old French *resine*, from Latin *rēsina*, from Greek *rhētinē* resin from a pine] > 'resinous *adj* > 'resinously *adv* > 'resinousness *n*

resinate (ˈrɛzɪˌneɪt) *vb* (*tr*) to impregnate with resin

resiniferous (ˌrɛzɪˈnɪfərəs) *adj* yielding or producing resin

r

resinoid (ˈrɛzɪˌnɔɪd) *adj* **1** resembling, characteristic of, or containing resin ▷ *n* **2** any resinoid substance, esp a synthetic compound
resipiscence (ˌrɛsɪˈpɪsəns) *n literary* acknowledgment that one has been mistaken [C16 from Late Latin *resipiscentia*, from *resipiscere* to recover one's senses, from Latin *sapere* to know] > ˌ**resiˈpiscent** *adj*
res ipsa loquitur (reɪs ˌɪpsɑː ˈlɒkwɪtə) *law* the thing or matter speaks for itself [Latin]
resist (rɪˈzɪst) *vb* **1** to stand firm (against); not yield (to); fight (against) **2** (*tr*) to withstand the deleterious action of; be proof against: *to resist corrosion* **3** (*tr*) to oppose; refuse to accept or comply with: *to resist arrest; to resist the introduction of new technology* **4** (*tr*) to refrain from, esp in spite of temptation (esp in the phrases **cannot** *or* **could not resist** (**something**)) ▷ *n* **5** a substance used to protect something, esp a coating that prevents corrosion [C14 from Latin *resistere* to stand still, oppose, from RE- + *sistere* to stand firm] > **reˈsister** *n* > **reˈsistible** *adj* > **reˌsistiˈbility** *n* > **reˈsistibly** *adv*
resistance (rɪˈzɪstəns) *n* **1** the act or an instance of resisting **2** the capacity to withstand something, esp the body's natural capacity to withstand disease **3 a** the opposition to a flow of electric current through a circuit component, medium, or substance. It is the magnitude of the real part of the impedance and is measured in ohms. Symbol: *R* Compare **reactance** (sense 1) **b** (*as modifier*): *resistance coupling* **4** any force that tends to retard or oppose motion: *air resistance* **5** (in psychoanalytical theory) the tendency of a person to prevent the translation of repressed thoughts and ideas from the unconscious to the conscious and esp to resist the analyst's attempt to bring this about **6** *physics* the magnitude of the real part of the acoustic or mechanical impedance **7 line of least resistance** the easiest, but not necessarily the best or most honourable, course of action **8** See **passive resistance**
Resistance (rɪˈzɪstəns) *n* **the** an illegal organization fighting for national liberty in a country under enemy occupation, esp in France during World War II
resistance thermometer *n* an accurate type of thermometer in which temperature is calculated from the resistance of a coil of wire (usually of platinum) or of a semiconductor placed at the point at which the temperature is to be measured
resistance welding *n* a welding technique in which the parts to be joined are held together under pressure and heat is produced by passing a current through the contact resistance formed between the two surfaces
resistant (rɪˈzɪstənt) *adj* **1** characterized by or showing resistance; resisting **2 a** impervious to the action of corrosive substances, heat, etc: *a highly resistant surface* **b** (*in combination*): *a heat-resistant surface* ▷ *n* **3** a person or thing that resists
Resistencia (*Spanish* rɛsisˈtenθja) *n* a city in NE Argentina, on the Paraná River. Pop: 423 000 (2005 est)
resistive (rɪˈzɪstɪv) *adj* **1** another word for **resistant** **2** exhibiting electrical resistance
resistivity (ˌriːzɪsˈtɪvɪtɪ) *n* **1** the electrical property of a material that determines the resistance of a piece of given dimensions. It is equal to RA/l, where R is the resistance, A the cross-sectional area, and l the length, and is the reciprocal of conductivity. It is measured in ohms. Symbol: ρ Former name: **specific resistance** **2** the power or capacity to resist; resistance
resistless (rɪˈzɪstlɪs) *adj archaic* **1** unresisting **2** irresistible > **reˈsistlessly** *adv*
resistor (rɪˈzɪstə) *n* an electrical component designed to introduce a known value of resistance into a circuit
resit *vb* (riːˈsɪt) **-sits, -sitting, -sat** (*tr*) **1** to sit (an examination) again ▷ *n* (ˈriːsɪt) **2** an examination taken again by a person who has not been successful in a previous attempt
res judicata (ˈreɪs ˌdʒuːdɪˈkɑːtə) *or* **res adjudicata** *n law* a matter already adjudicated upon that cannot be raised again [Latin]
reskill (riːˈskɪl) *vb* (*tr*) to train (workers) to acquire new or improved skills > **reˈskilling** *n*
resnatron (ˈrɛznəˌtrɒn) *n* a tetrode used to generate high power at high frequencies [C20 from RESONATOR + -TRON]
resoluble (rɪˈzɒljʊbᵊl, ˈrɛzəl-) *adj* another word for **resolvable**
re-soluble (riːˈsɒljʊbᵊl) *adj* capable of being dissolved again > **re-ˈsolubleness** *or* **re-ˌsoluˈbility** *n* > **re-ˈsolubly** *adv*
resolute (ˈrɛzəˌluːt) *adj* **1** firm in purpose or belief **2** characterized by resolution; determined [C16 from Latin *resolutus*, from *resolvere* to RESOLVE] > ˈ**resoˌlutely** *adv* > ˈ**resoˌluteness** *n*
resolution (ˌrɛzəˈluːʃən) *n* **1** the act or an instance of resolving **2** the condition or quality of being resolute; firmness or determination **3** something resolved or determined; decision **4** a formal expression of opinion by a meeting, esp one agreed by a vote **5** a judicial decision on some matter; verdict; judgment **6** the act or process of separating something into its constituent parts or elements **7** *med* **a** return from a pathological to a normal condition **b** subsidence of the symptoms of a disease, esp the disappearance of inflammation without the formation of pus **8** *music* the process in harmony whereby a dissonant note or chord is followed by a consonant one **9** the ability of a television or film image to reproduce fine detail **10** *physics* another word for **resolving power**. > ˌ**resoˈlutioner** *or* ˌ**resoˈlutionist** *n*
resolutive (rɪˈzɒljʊtɪv) *adj* **1** capable of dissolving; causing disintegration **2** *law* denoting a condition the fulfilment of which terminates a contract or other legal obligation
resolvable (rɪˈzɒlvəbᵊl) *or* **resoluble** *adj* able to be resolved or analysed > **reˌsolvaˈbility, reˌsoluˈbility, reˈsolvableness** *or* **reˈsolubleness** *n*
resolve (rɪˈzɒlv) *vb* (*mainly tr*) **1** (*takes a clause as object or an infinitive*) to decide or determine firmly **2** to express (an opinion) formally, esp (of a public meeting) one agreed by a vote **3** (*also intr*; usually foll by *into*) to separate or cause to separate (into) (constituent parts or elements) **4** (*usually reflexive*) to change, alter, or appear to change or alter: *the ghost resolved itself into a tree* **5** to make up the mind of; cause to decide: *the tempest resolved him to stay at home* **6** to find the answer or solution to; solve: *to resolve a problem* **7** to explain away or dispel: *to resolve a doubt* **8** to bring to an end; conclude: *to resolve an argument* **9** *med* to cause (a swelling or inflammation) to subside, esp without the formation of pus **10** (*also intr*) to follow (a dissonant note or chord) or (of a dissonant note or chord) to be followed by one producing a consonance **11** *chem* to separate (a racemic mixture) into its optically active constituents **12** *physics* **a** to distinguish between (separate parts) of (an image) as in a microscope, telescope, or other optical instrument **b** to separate (two adjacent peaks) in a spectrum by means of a spectrometer **13** *maths* to split (a vector) into its components in specified directions **14** an obsolete word for **dissolve** ▷ *n* **15** something determined or decided; resolution **16** firmness of purpose; determination: *nothing can break his resolve* [C14 from Latin *resolvere* to unfasten, reveal, from RE- + *solvere* to loosen; see SOLVE] > **reˈsolver** *n*
resolved (rɪˈzɒlvd) *adj* fixed in purpose or intention; determined > **resolvedly** (rɪˈzɒlvɪdlɪ) *adv* > **reˈsolvedness** *n*
resolvent (rɪˈzɒlvənt) *adj* **1** serving to dissolve or separate something into its elements; resolving ▷ *n* **2** something that resolves; solvent **3** a drug or agent able to reduce swelling or inflammation
resolving power *n* **1** Also called: **resolution** *physics* **a** the ability of a microscope, telescope, or other optical instrument to produce separate images of closely placed objects **b** the ability of a spectrometer to separate two adjacent peaks in a spectrum **2** *photog* the ability of an emulsion to show up fine detail in an image
resonance (ˈrɛzənəns) *n* **1** the condition or quality of being resonant **2** sound produced by a body vibrating in sympathy with a neighbouring source of sound **3** the condition of a body or system when it is subjected to a periodic disturbance of the same frequency as the natural frequency of the body or system. At this frequency the system displays an enhanced oscillation or vibration **4** amplification of speech sounds by sympathetic vibration in the bone structure of the head and chest, resounding in the cavities of the nose, mouth, and pharynx **5** *electronics* the condition of an electrical circuit when the frequency is such that the capacitive and inductive reactances are equal in magnitude. In a series circuit there is then maximum alternating current whilst in a parallel circuit there is minimum alternating current **6** *med* the sound heard when percussing a hollow bodily structure, esp the chest or abdomen. Change in the quality of the sound often indicates an underlying disease or disorder **7** *chem* the phenomenon in which the electronic structure of a molecule can be represented by two or more hypothetical structures involving single, double, and triple chemical bonds. The true structure is considered to be an average of these theoretical structures **8** *physics* **a** the condition of a system in which there is a sharp maximum probability for the absorption of electromagnetic radiation or capture of particles **b** a type of elementary particle of extremely short lifetime. Resonances are regarded as excited states of more stable particles **c** a highly transient atomic state formed during a collision process [C16 from Latin *resonāre* to RESOUND]
resonant (ˈrɛzənənt) *adj* **1** (of sound) resounding or re-echoing **2** producing or enhancing resonance, as by sympathetic vibration **3** characterized by resonance > ˈ**resonantly** *adv*
resonant cavity *n* another name for **cavity resonator**
resonate (ˈrɛzəˌneɪt) *vb* **1** to resound or cause to resound; reverberate **2** (of a mechanical system, electrical circuit, chemical compound, etc) to exhibit or cause to exhibit resonance **3** (*intr*; often foll by *with*) to be understood or receive a sympathetic response: *themes which will resonate with voters* **4** (*intr*: foll by *with*) to be filled with [C19 from Latin *resonāre*] > ˌ**resoˈnation** *n*
resonator (ˈrɛzəˌneɪtə) *n* any body or system that displays resonance, esp a tuned electrical circuit or a conducting cavity in which microwaves are generated by a resonant current
resorb (rɪˈsɔːb) *vb* (*tr*) to absorb again [C17 from Latin *resorbēre*, from RE- + *sorbēre* to suck in; see ABSORB] > **reˈsorbent** *adj* > **reˈsorptive** *adj*
resorcinol (rɪˈzɔːsɪˌnɒl) *n* a colourless crystalline phenol with a sweet taste, used in making dyes, drugs, resins, and adhesives. Formula: $C_6H_4(OH)_2$; relative density: 1.27; melting pt: 111°C; boiling pt at 1 atm.: 276°C [C19 New Latin, from RESIN + ORCINOL] > **reˈsorcinal** *adj*
resorption (rɪˈsɔːpʃən) *n* **1** the process of resorbing or the state of being resorbed **2** *geology* the partial or complete remelting or dissolution of a mineral by magma, resulting from changes in temperature, pressure, or magma composition
resort (rɪˈzɔːt) *vb* (*intr*) **1** (usually foll by *to*) to have recourse (to) for help, use, etc: *to resort to violence* **2** to go, esp often or habitually; repair: *to resort to the beach* ▷ *n* **3** a place to which many people go for recreation, rest, etc: *a holiday resort* **4** the use of something as a means, help, or recourse **5** the act of going to a place, esp for recreation, rest, etc **6 last resort** the last possible course of action open to one [C14 from Old French *resortir* to come out again, from RE- + *sortir* to emerge] > **reˈsorter** *n*

re-sort (riːˈsɔːt) *vb* (*tr*) to sort again

resound (rɪˈzaʊnd) *vb* (*intr*) **1** to ring or echo with sound; reverberate: *the hall resounded with laughter* **2** to make a prolonged echoing noise: *the trumpet resounded* **3** (of sounds) to echo or ring **4** to be widely famous [C14 from Old French *resoner*, from Latin *resonāre* to sound again]

re-sound (riːˈsaʊnd) *vb* to sound or cause to sound again

resounding (rɪˈzaʊndɪŋ) *adj* **1** clear and emphatic; unmistakable: *a resounding vote of confidence* **2** full of or characterized by resonance; reverberating: *a resounding slap* > **reˈsoundingly** *adv*

resource (rɪˈzɔːs, -ˈsɔːs) *n* **1** capability, ingenuity, and initiative; quick-wittedness: *a man of resource* **2** (*often plural*) a source of economic wealth, esp of a country (mineral, land, labour, etc) or business enterprise (capital, equipment, personnel, etc) **3** a supply or source of aid or support; something resorted to in time of need **4** a means of doing something; expedient [C17 from Old French *ressourse* relief, from *resourdre* to rise again, from Latin *resurgere*, from RE- + *surgere* to rise] > **reˈsourceless** *adj* > **reˈsourcelessness** *n*

resourceful (rɪˈzɔːsfʊl, -ˈsɔːs-) *adj* ingenious, capable, and full of initiative, esp in dealing with difficult situations > **reˈsourcefully** *adv* > **reˈsourcefulness** *n*

respect (rɪˈspɛkt) *n* **1** an attitude of deference, admiration, or esteem; regard **2** the state of being honoured or esteemed **3** a detail, point, or characteristic; particular: *he differs in some respects from his son* **4** reference or relation (esp in the phrases **in respect of**, **with respect to**) **5** polite or kind regard; consideration: *respect for people's feelings* **6** (*often plural*) an expression of esteem or regard (esp in the phrase **pay one's respects**) ▷ *vb* (*tr*) **7** to have an attitude of esteem towards; show or have respect for: *to respect one's elders* **8** to pay proper attention to; not violate: *to respect Swiss neutrality* **9** to show consideration for; treat courteously or kindly **10** *archaic* to concern or refer to [C14 from Latin *rēspicere* to look back, pay attention to, from RE- + *specere* to look]

respectable (rɪˈspɛktəbᵊl) *adj* **1** having or deserving the respect of other people; estimable; worthy **2** having good social standing or reputation **3** having socially or conventionally acceptable morals, standards, etc: *a respectable woman* **4** relatively or fairly good; considerable: *a respectable salary* **5** fit to be seen by other people; presentable > **reˌspectaˈbility** *or less commonly* **reˈspectableness** *n* > **reˈspectably** *adv*

respecter (rɪˈspɛktə) *n* **1** a person who respects someone or something **2** **no respecter of persons** a person whose attitude and behaviour is uninfluenced by consideration of another's rank, power, wealth, etc

respectful (rɪˈspɛktfʊl) *adj* full of, showing, or giving respect > **reˈspectfully** *adv* > **reˈspectfulness** *n*

respecting (rɪˈspɛktɪŋ) *prep* concerning; regarding

respective (rɪˈspɛktɪv) *adj* **1** belonging or relating separately to each of several people or things; several: *we took our respective ways home* **2** an archaic word for **respectful**. > **reˈspectiveness** *n*

respectively (rɪˈspɛktɪvlɪ) *adv* (in listing a number of items or attributes that refer to another list) separately in the order given

respirable (ˈrɛspɪrəbᵊl) *adj* **1** able to be breathed **2** suitable or fit for breathing > **ˌrespiraˈbility** *n*

respiration (ˌrɛspəˈreɪʃən) *n* **1** the process in living organisms of taking in oxygen from the surroundings and giving out carbon dioxide (**external respiration**). In terrestrial animals this is effected by breathing air **2** the chemical breakdown of complex organic substances, such as carbohydrates and fats, that takes place in the cells and tissues of animals and plants, during which energy is released and carbon dioxide produced (**internal respiration**)

respirator (ˈrɛspəˌreɪtə) *n* **1** an apparatus for providing long-term artificial respiration **2** Also called: **gas mask** a device worn over the mouth and nose to prevent inhalation of noxious fumes or to warm cold air before it is breathed

respiratory (ˈrɛspərətərɪ, -trɪ) *or rarely* **respirational** (ˌrɛspəˈreɪʃənᵊl) *adj* of, relating to, or affecting respiration or the organs used in respiration

respiratory failure *n* a condition in which the respiratory system is unable to provide an adequate supply of oxygen or to remove carbon dioxide efficiently

respiratory quotient *n biology* the ratio of the volume of carbon dioxide expired to the volume of oxygen consumed by an organism, tissue, or cell in a given time

respiratory syncytial virus *n* a myxovirus causing infections of the nose and throat, esp in young children. It is thought to be involved in some cot deaths. Abbreviation: **RSV**

respiratory system *n* the specialized organs, collectively, concerned with external respiration: in humans and other mammals it includes the trachea, bronchi, bronchioles, lungs, and diaphragm

respire (rɪˈspaɪə) *vb* **1** to inhale and exhale (air); breathe **2** (*intr*) to undergo the process of respiration **3** *literary* to breathe again in a relaxed or easy manner, as after stress or exertion [C14 from Latin *rēspīrāre* to exhale, from RE- + *spīrāre* to breathe; see SPIRIT[1]]

respite (ˈrɛspɪt, -paɪt) *n* **1** a pause from exertion; interval of rest **2** a temporary delay **3** a temporary stay of execution; reprieve ▷ *vb* **4** (*tr*) to grant a respite to; reprieve [C13 from Old French *respit*, from Latin *respectus* a looking back; see RESPECT] > **ˈrespiteless** *adj*

respite care *n social welfare* occasional usually planned residential care for dependent old or handicapped people, to provide relief for their permanent carers

resplendent (rɪˈsplɛndənt) *adj* having a brilliant or splendid appearance [C15 from *rēsplendēre* to shine brightly, from RE- + *splendēre* to shine; see SPLENDOUR] > **reˈsplendence** *or* **reˈsplendency** *n* > **reˈsplendently** *adv*

respond (rɪˈspɒnd) *vb* **1** to state or utter (something) in reply **2** (*intr*) to act in reply; react **3** (*intr*; foll by *to*) to react favourably **4** an archaic word for **correspond** ▷ *n* **5** *architect* a pilaster or an engaged column that supports an arch or a lintel **6** *Christianity* a choral anthem chanted in response to a lesson read at a church service [C14 from Old French *respondre*, from Latin *rēspondēre* to return like for like, from RE- + *spondēre* to pledge; see SPOUSE, SPONSOR] > **reˈspondence** *or* **reˈspondency** *n* > **reˈsponder** *n*

respondent (rɪˈspɒndənt) *n* **1** *law* a person against whom a petition, esp in a divorce suit, or appeal is brought ▷ *adj* **2** a less common word for **responsive**

responsa (rɪˈspɒnsə) *n Judaism* **1** the plural of **responsum** **2** that part of rabbinic literature concerned with written rulings in answer to questions

response (rɪˈspɒns) *n* **1** the act of responding; reply or reaction **2** *bridge* a bid replying to a partner's bid or double **3** (*usually plural*) *Christianity* a short sentence or phrase recited or sung by the choir or congregation in reply to the officiant at a church service **4** *electronics* the ratio of the output to the input level, at a particular frequency, of a transmission line or electrical device **5** any pattern of glandular, muscular, or electrical reactions that arises from stimulation of the nervous system [C14 from Latin *rēsponsum* answer, from *rēspondēre* to RESPOND] > **reˈsponseless** *adj*

responser *or* **responsor** (rɪˈspɒnsə) *n* a radio or radar receiver used in conjunction with an interrogator to receive and display signals from a transponder

response time *n computing* the length of time taken by a system to respond to an instruction

response variable *n statistics* a more modern term for **dependent variable** (sense 2)

responsibility (rɪˌspɒnsəˈbɪlɪtɪ) *n, pl* **-ties** **1** the state or position of being responsible **2** a person or thing for which one is responsible **3** the ability or authority to act or decide on one's own, without supervision

responsible (rɪˈspɒnsəbᵊl) *adj* **1** (*postpositive*; usually foll by *for*) having control or authority (over) **2** (*postpositive*; foll by *to*) being accountable for one's actions and decisions (to): *to be responsible to one's commanding officer* **3** (of a position, duty, etc) involving decision and accountability **4** (often foll by *for*) being the agent or cause (of some action) **5** able to take rational decisions without supervision; accountable for one's own actions: *a responsible adult* **6** able to meet financial obligations; of sound credit [C16 from Latin *rēsponsus*, from *rēspondēre* to RESPOND] > **reˈsponsibleness** *n* > **reˈsponsibly** *adv*

responsive (rɪˈspɒnsɪv) *adj* **1** reacting or replying quickly or favourably, as to a suggestion, initiative, etc **2** (of an organism) reacting to a stimulus > **reˈsponsively** *adv* > **reˈsponsiveness** *n*

responsory (rɪˈspɒnsərɪ) *n, pl* **-ries** *Christianity* an anthem or chant consisting of versicles and responses and recited or sung after a lesson in a church service [C15 from Late Latin *rēsponsōrium*, from Latin *rēspondēre* to answer]

responsum (rɪˈspɒnsəm) *n, pl* **-sa** (-sə) *Judaism* a written answer from a rabbinic authority to a question submitted [Latin, literally: reply, RESPONSE]

respray *vb* (riːˈspreɪ) (*tr*) **1** to spray (a car, wheels, etc) with a new coat of paint ▷ *n* (ˈriːˌspreɪ) **2** the act or an instance of respraying

res publica (ˈreɪs ˈpʊblɪˌkɑː) *n* the state, republic, or commonwealth [Latin, literally: the public thing]

r

rest[1] (rɛst) *n* **1** **a** relaxation from exertion or labour **b** (*as modifier*): *a rest period* **2** repose; sleep **3** any relief or refreshment, as from worry or something troublesome **4** calm; tranquillity **5** death regarded as repose: *eternal rest* **6** cessation from motion **7** **at rest** **a** not moving; still **b** calm; tranquil **c** dead **d** asleep **8** a pause or interval **9** a mark in a musical score indicating a pause of specific duration **10** *prosody* a pause in or at the end of a line; caesura **11** a shelter or lodging: *a seaman's rest* **12** a thing or place on which to put something for support or to steady it; prop **13** *billiards, snooker* any of various special poles used as supports for the cue in shots that cannot be made using the hand as a support **14** **come to rest** to slow down and stop **15** **lay to rest** to bury (a dead person) **16** **set (someone's mind) at rest** to reassure (someone) or settle (someone's mind) ▷ *vb* **17** to take or give rest, as by sleeping, lying down, etc **18** to place or position (oneself, etc) for rest or relaxation **19** (*tr*) to place or position for support or steadying: *to rest one's elbows on the table* **20** (*intr*) to be at ease; be calm **21** to cease or cause to cease from motion or exertion; halt **22** to lie dead and buried **23** (*intr*) to remain without further attention or action **24** to direct (one's eyes) or (of one's eyes) to be directed **25** to depend or cause to depend; base; rely: *the whole argument rests on one crucial fact* **26** to place or be placed, as blame, censure, etc **27** (*intr*; foll by *with, on, upon*, etc) to be a responsibility (of) **28** *law* to finish the introduction of evidence in (a case) **29** **rest on one's laurels** See **laurel** (sense 9) **30** **rest on one's oars** **a** to stop rowing for a time **b** to stop doing anything for a time [Old English *ræst, reste*, of Germanic origin; related to Gothic *rasta* a mile, Old Norse *röst* mile] > **ˈrester** *n*

rest[2] (rɛst) *n* (usually preceded by *the*) **1** something left or remaining; remainder **2** the others: *the rest of the world* ▷ *vb* **3** (*copula*) to continue to be (as specified); remain: *rest assured*

[c15 from Old French *rester* to remain, from Latin *rēstāre*, from RE- + *stāre* to STAND]

restage (riːˈsteɪdʒ) *vb* (*tr*) **1** to produce or perform a new production of (a play) **2** to organize or carry out (an event) again, esp if it has been cancelled: *attempts have been made to restage the race*

rest area *n Austral and NZ* a motorists' stopping place, usually off a highway, equipped with tables, seats, etc

restart *vb* (riːˈstɑːt) **1** to start again ▷ *n* (ˈriːˌstɑːt) **2 a** the act or an instance of starting again: *the restart of the lap* **b** (*as modifier*): *a restart device*

restate (riːˈsteɪt) *vb* (*tr*) to state or affirm again or in a new way > re'statement *n*

restaurant (ˈrɛstəˌrɒŋ, ˈrɛstrɒŋ, -rɒnt) *n* a commercial establishment where meals are prepared and served to customers [c19 from French, from *restaurer* to RESTORE]

restaurant car *n Brit* a railway coach in which meals are served. Also called: **dining car**

restaurateur (ˌrɛstərəˈtɜː) *n* a person who owns or runs a restaurant [c18 via French from Late Latin *restaurātor* one who restores, from Latin *restaurāre* to RESTORE]

▌USAGE Although the spelling *restauranteur* occurs frequently, it is a misspelling and should be avoided

rest-cure *n* **1** a rest taken as part of a course of medical treatment, as for stress, anxiety, etc **2** an easy undemanding time or assignment: usually used with a negative: *it's no rest-cure, I can assure you*

restful (ˈrɛstfʊl) *adj* **1** giving or conducive to rest **2** being at rest; tranquil; calm > ˈrestfully *adv* > ˈrestfulness *n*

restharrow (ˈrɛstˌhærəʊ) *n* any of several Eurasian leguminous plants of the genus *Ononis*, such as *O. repens* and *O. spinosa*, with tough stems and roots [c16 from *rest* variant of ARREST (to hinder, stop) + HARROW[1]]

rest-home *n* an old people's home

restiform (ˈrɛstɪˌfɔːm) *adj* (esp of bundles of nerve fibres) shaped like a cord or rope; cordlike [c19 from New Latin *restiformis*, from Latin *restis* a rope + *forma* shape]

resting (ˈrɛstɪŋ) *adj* **1** not moving or working; at rest **2** *euphemistic* (of an actor) out of work **3** (esp of plant spores) undergoing a period of dormancy before germination **4** (of cells) not undergoing mitosis

resting place *n* a place where someone or something rests, esp (**last resting place**) the grave

restitution (ˌrɛstɪˈtjuːʃən) *n* **1** the act of giving back something that has been lost or stolen **2** *law* the act of compensating for loss or injury by reverting as far as possible to the position before such injury occurred **3** the return of an object or system to its original state, esp a restoration of shape after elastic deformation [c13 from Latin *rēstitūtiō*, from *rēstituere* to rebuild, from RE- + *statuere* to set up] > ˌresti'tutive *or* ˌresti'tutory *adj*

restive (ˈrɛstɪv) *adj* **1** restless, nervous, or uneasy **2** impatient of control or authority [c16 from Old French *restif* balky, from *rester* to remain] > 'restively *adv* > 'restiveness *n*

restless (ˈrɛstlɪs) *adj* **1** unable to stay still or quiet **2** ceaselessly active or moving: *the restless wind* **3** worried; anxious; uneasy **4** not restful; without repose > 'restlessly *adv* > 'restlessness *n*

rest mass *n* the mass of an object that is at rest relative to an observer. It is the mass used in Newtonian mechanics

resto (ˈrɛstəʊ) *n, pl* **restos** *Austral informal* a restored antique, vintage car, etc

restock (riːˈstɒk) *vb* to replenish stores or supplies

restoration (ˌrɛstəˈreɪʃən) *n* **1** the act of restoring or state of being restored, as to a former or original condition, place, etc **2** the replacement or giving back of something lost, stolen, etc **3** something restored, replaced, or reconstructed **4** a model or representation of an extinct animal, landscape of a former geological age, etc

Restoration (ˌrɛstəˈreɪʃən) *n Brit history* **a** the

re-establishment of the monarchy in 1660 or the reign of Charles II (1660–85) **b** (*as modifier*): *Restoration drama*

restorationism (ˌrɛstəˈreɪʃəˌnɪzəm) *n* belief in a future life in which human beings will be restored to a state of perfection and happiness > ˌresto'rationist *n, adj*

restorative (rɪˈstɒrətɪv) *adj* **1** tending to revive or renew health, spirits, etc ▷ *n* **2** anything that restores or revives, esp a drug or agent that promotes health or strength

restorative justice *n* a method of dealing with convicted criminals in which they are urged to accept responsibility for their offences through meeting victims, making amends to victims or the community, etc

restore (rɪˈstɔː) *vb* (*tr*) **1** to return (something, esp a work of art or building) to an original or former condition **2** to bring back to health, good spirits, etc **3** to return (something lost, stolen, etc) to its owner **4** to reintroduce or re-enforce: *to restore discipline* **5** to reconstruct (an extinct animal, former landscape, etc) [c13 from Old French, from Latin *rēstaurāre* to rebuild, from RE- + -*staurāre*, as in *instaurāre* to renew] > re'storable *adj* > re'storableness *n* > re'storer *n*

restrain (rɪˈstreɪn) *vb* (*tr*) **1** to hold (someone) back from some action, esp by force **2** to deprive (someone) of liberty, as by imprisonment **3** to limit or restrict [c14 *restreyne*, from Old French *restreindre*, from Latin *rēstringere* to draw back tightly, from RE- + *stringere* to draw, bind; see STRAIN[1]] > re'strainable *adj*

restrained (rɪˈstreɪnd) *adj* **1** (of a person or person's manner) calm and unemotional **2** (of clothes, décor, etc) subtle and tasteful > restrainedly (rɪˈstreɪnɪdlɪ) *adv*

restrainer (rɪˈstreɪnə) *n* **1** a person who restrains **2** a chemical, such as potassium bromide, added to a photographic developer in order to reduce the amount of fog on a film and to retard the development

restraining order *n US law* an order issued by a civil court to a potential abuser to keep away from those named in the order

restraint (rɪˈstreɪnt) *n* **1** the ability to control or moderate one's impulses, passions, etc: *to show restraint* **2** the act of restraining or the state of being restrained **3** something that restrains; restriction [c15 from Old French *restreinte*, from *restreindre* to RESTRAIN]

restraint of trade *n* action tending to interfere with the freedom to compete in business

restraint order *n* another name for **freezing injunction**

restrict (rɪˈstrɪkt) *vb* (often foll by *to*) to confine or keep within certain often specified limits or selected bounds [c16 from Latin *rēstrictus* bound up, from *rēstringere*; see RESTRAIN]

restricted (rɪˈstrɪktɪd) *adj* **1** limited or confined **2** not accessible to the general public or (*esp US*) out of bounds to military personnel **3** *Brit* denoting or in a zone in which a speed limit or waiting restrictions for vehicles apply > re'strictedly *adv* > re'strictedness *n*

restricted users group *n* a group of people who, with knowledge of a secret password, or by some other method, have access to restricted information stored in a computer. Abbreviation: **RUG**

restriction (rɪˈstrɪkʃən) *n* **1** something that restricts; a restrictive measure, law, etc **2** the act of restricting or the state of being restricted **3** *logic, maths* a condition that imposes a constraint on the possible values of a variable or on the domain of arguments of a function > re'strictionist *n, adj*

restriction enzyme *n* any of several enzymes produced by bacteria as a defence against viral infection and commonly used to cut DNA for genetic manipulation or diagnosis

restriction fragment *n genetics* a fragment of a

DNA molecule cleaved by a restriction enzyme. See also RFLP

restrictive (rɪˈstrɪktɪv) *adj* **1** restricting or tending to restrict **2** *grammar* denoting a relative clause or phrase that restricts the number of possible referents of its antecedent. The relative clause in *Americans who live in New York* is restrictive; the relative clause in *Americans, who are generally extrovert,* is nonrestrictive > re'strictively *adv* > re'strictiveness *n*

restrictive covenant *n law* a covenant imposing a restriction on the use of land for the purpose of preserving the enjoyment or value of adjoining land

restrictive practice *n Brit* **1** a trading agreement against the public interest **2** a practice of a union or other group tending to limit the freedom of other workers or employers

rest room *n* a room in a public building having lavatories, washing facilities, and sometimes couches

restructure (riːˈstrʌktʃə) *vb* (*tr*) to organize (a system, business, society, etc) in a different way: *radical attempts to restructure the economy* > re'structuring *n*

rest stop *n* the US name for **lay-by** (sense 1)

restump (riːˈstʌmp) *vb* (*tr*) *Austral* to provide (a building) with new stumps

resubmit (ˌriːsəbˈmɪt) *vb* -mits, -mitting, -mitted to submit again: *to rework and resubmit her designs*

result (rɪˈzʌlt) *n* **1** something that ensues from an action, policy, course of events, etc; outcome; consequence **2** a number, quantity, or value obtained by solving a mathematical problem **3** *US* a decision of a legislative body **4** (*often plural*) the final score or outcome of a sporting contest **5** a favourable result, esp a victory or success ▷ *vb* (*intr*) **6** (often foll by *from*) to be the outcome or consequence (of) **7** (foll by *in*) to issue or terminate (in a specified way, state, etc); end: *to result in tragedy* **8** *property law* (of an undisposed or partially disposed of interest in land) to revert to a former owner when the prior interests come to an end [c15 from Latin *resultāre* to rebound, spring from, from RE- + *saltāre* to leap]

resultant (rɪˈzʌltənt) *adj* **1** that results; resulting ▷ *n* **2** *maths, physics* a single vector that is the vector sum of two or more other vectors

resultant tone *n* a musical sound sometimes heard when two loud notes are sounded together, either lower in pitch than either (**differential tone**) or higher (**summational tone**)

resume (rɪˈzjuːm) *vb* **1** to begin again or go on with (something adjourned or interrupted) **2** (*tr*) to occupy again, take back, or recover: *to resume one's seat; to resume possession* **3** (*tr*) to assume (a title, office, etc) again: *to resume the presidency* **4** *archaic* to summarize; make a résumé of [c15 from Latin *resūmere* to take up again, from RE- + *sūmere* to take up] > re'sumable *adj* > re'sumer *n*

résumé (ˈrezjʊˌmeɪ) *n* **1** a short descriptive summary, as of events **2** *US and Canadian* another name for **curriculum vitae** [c19 from French, from *résumer* to RESUME]

resumption (rɪˈzʌmpʃən) *n* the act of resuming or beginning again [c15 via Old French from Late Latin *resumptiō*, from Latin *resūmere* to RESUME] > re'sumptive *adj* > re'sumptively *adv*

resupinate (rɪˈsjuːpɪnɪt) *adj botany* (of plant parts, esp the flowers of many orchids) reversed or inverted in position, so as to appear to be upside down [c18 from Latin *resupīnātus* bent back, from *resupīnāre*, from RE- + *supīnāre* to place on the back; see SUPINE] > reˌsupi'nation *n*

resupine (rɪˈsjuːpaɪn) *adj rare* lying on the back; supine [c17 from Latin *resupīnus* lying on the back]

resupply (ˌriːsəˈplaɪ) *vb* -plies, -plying, -plied (*tr*) to provide (with something) again

resurface (riːˈsɜːfɪs) *vb* **1** (*intr*) to arise or occur again: *the problem resurfaced* **2** (*intr*) to rise or cause to rise again to the surface **3** (*tr*) to supply (something) with a new surface

resurge (rɪˈsɜːdʒ) *vb* (*intr*) *rare* to rise again from or as if from the dead [C16 from Latin *resurgere* to rise again, reappear, from RE- + *surgere* to lift, arise, SURGE]

resurgent (rɪˈsɜːdʒənt) *adj* rising again, as to new life, vigour, etc: *resurgent nationalism* > reˈsurgence *n*

resurrect (ˌrɛzəˈrɛkt) *vb* **1** to rise or raise from the dead; bring or be brought back to life **2** (*tr*) to bring back into use or activity; revive: *to resurrect an ancient law* **3** (*tr*) to renew (one's hopes, etc) **4** (*tr*) *facetious* (formerly) to exhume and steal (a body) from its grave, esp in order to sell it

resurrection (ˌrɛzəˈrɛkʃən) *n* **1** a supposed act or instance of a dead person coming back to life **2** belief in the possibility of this as part of a religious or mystical system **3** the condition of those who have risen from the dead **4** the revival of something: *a resurrection of an old story* [C13 via Old French from Late Latin *resurrectiō*, from Latin *resurgere* to rise again; see RESURGE] > ˌresurˈrectional *or* ˌresurˈrectionary *adj*

Resurrection (ˌrɛzəˈrɛkʃən) *n christian theol* **1** the rising again of Christ from the tomb three days after his death **2** the rising again from the dead of all mankind at the Last Judgment

resurrectionism (ˌrɛzəˈrɛkʃəˌnɪzəm) *n* **1** belief that men will rise again from the dead, esp the Christian doctrine of the Resurrection of Christ and of all mankind at the Last Judgment **2** *facetious* (formerly) body snatching

resurrectionist (ˌrɛzəˈrɛkʃənɪst) *n* **1** *facetious* (formerly) a body snatcher **2** a member of an Anglican religious community founded in 1892 **3** a person who believes in the Resurrection

resurrection plant *n* any of several unrelated desert plants that form a tight ball when dry and unfold and bloom when moistened. The best-known examples are the crucifer *Anastatica hierochuntica* (also called **rose of Jericho**), club mosses of the genus *Selaginella*, and the composite *Asteriscus pygmoeus*

resuscitate (rɪˈsʌsɪˌteɪt) *vb* (*tr*) to restore to consciousness; revive [C16 from Latin *resuscitāre*, from RE- + *suscitāre* to raise, from *sub-* up from below + *citāre* to rouse, from *citus* quick] > reˈsuscitable *adj* > reˌsusciˈtation *n* > reˈsuscitative *adj*

resuscitator (rɪˈsʌsɪˌteɪtə) *n* **1** an apparatus for forcing oxygen or a mixture containing oxygen into the lungs **2** a person who resuscitates

resveratrol (rɪˈsvɛrəˌtrɒl) *n* a compound found in red grapes, mulberries, peanuts, and certain plants, used medicinally as an antioxidant and anti-inflammatory [C20 from RES(ORCINOL) + VERATR(INE) + -OL[1]]

ret (rɛt) *vb* **rets, retting, retted** (*tr*) to moisten or soak (flax, hemp, jute, etc) to promote bacterial action in order to facilitate separation of the fibres from the woody tissue by beating [C15 of Germanic origin; related to Middle Dutch *reeten*, Swedish *röta*, German *rösten*; see ROT[1]]

retable (rɪˈteɪbᵊl) *n* an ornamental screenlike structure above and behind an altar, esp one used as a setting for a religious picture or carving [C19 from French, from Spanish *retablo*, from Latin *retrō* behind + *tabula* board; see REAR[1], TABLE]

retail (ˈriːteɪl) *n* **1** the sale of goods individually or in small quantities to consumers. Compare **wholesale** (sense 1) ▷ *adj* **2** of, relating to, or engaged in such selling: *retail prices* ▷ *adv* **3** in small amounts or at a retail price ▷ *vb* **4** to sell or be sold in small quantities to consumers **5** (rɪˈteɪl) (*tr*) to relate (gossip, scandal, etc) in detail, esp persistently [C14 from Old French *retaillier* to cut off, from RE- + *taillier* to cut; see TAILOR] > ˈretailer *n*

retail price index *n* (in Britain) a list, based on government figures and usually published monthly, that shows the extent of change in the prices of a range of goods selected as being essential items in the budget of a normal household. Abbreviation: **RPI**

retail therapy *n jocular* the action of shopping for clothes, etc in order to cheer oneself up

retain (rɪˈteɪn) *vb* (*tr*) **1** to keep in one's possession **2** to be able to hold or contain **3** (of a person) to be able to remember (information, facts, etc) without difficulty **4** to hold in position **5** to keep for one's future use, as by paying a retainer or nominal charge **6** *law* to engage the services of (a barrister) by payment of a preliminary fee **7** (in selling races) to buy back a winner that one owns when it is auctioned after the race **8** (of racehorse trainers) to pay an advance fee to (a jockey) so as to have prior or exclusive claims upon his services throughout the season [C14 from Old French *retenir*, from Latin *retinēre* to hold back, from RE- + *tenēre* to hold] > reˈtainable *adj* > reˈtainment *n*

retained object *n grammar* a direct or indirect object of a passive verb. The phrase *the drawings* in the sentence *Harry was given the drawings* is a retained object

retainer (rɪˈteɪnə) *n* **1** *history* a supporter or dependant of a person of rank, esp a soldier **2** a servant, esp one who has been with a family for a long time **3** a clip, frame, or similar device that prevents a part of a machine, engine, etc, from moving **4** a dental appliance for holding a loose tooth or prosthetic device in position **5** a fee paid in advance to secure first option on the services of a barrister, jockey, etc **6** a reduced rent paid for a flat, room, etc, during absence to reserve it for future use

retaining ring *n* another name for **circlip**

retaining wall *n* a wall constructed to hold back earth, loose rock, etc. Also called: **revetment**

retake *vb* (riːˈteɪk) **-takes, -taking, -took, -taken** (*tr*) **1** to take back or capture again: *to retake a fortress* **2** *films* to shoot again (a shot or scene) **3** to tape again (a recording) ▷ *n* (ˈriːˌteɪk) **4** *films* a rephotographed shot or scene **5** a retaped recording > reˈtaker *n*

retaliate (rɪˈtælɪˌeɪt) *vb* **1** (*intr*) to take retributory action, esp by returning some injury or wrong in kind **2** (*tr*) *rare* to avenge (an injury, wrong, etc) [C17 from Late Latin *retāliāre*, from Latin RE- + *tālis* of such kind] > reˌtaliˈation *n* > reˈtaliative *or* reˈtaliatory *adj* > reˈtaliˌator *n*

retard *vb* (rɪˈtɑːd) **1** (*tr*) to delay or slow down (the progress, speed, or development) of (something) ▷ *n* (ˈriːtɑːd) **2** *US offensive* a retarded person **3** *US offensive* a foolish person [C15 from Old French *retarder*, from Latin *retardāre*, from RE- + *tardāre* to make slow, from *tardus* sluggish; see TARDY]

retardant (rɪˈtɑːdᵊnt) *n* **1** a substance that reduces the rate of a chemical reaction ▷ *adj* **2** having a slowing effect

retardate (rɪˈtɑːdeɪt) *n psychol* a person who is retarded

retardation (ˌriːtɑːˈdeɪʃən) *or less commonly* **retardment** (rɪˈtɑːdmənt) *n* **1** the act of retarding or the state of being retarded **2** something that retards; hindrance **3** the rate of deceleration **4** *psychiatry* the slowing down of mental functioning and bodily movement > reˈtardative *or* reˈtardatory *adj*

retarded (rɪˈtɑːdɪd) *adj* underdeveloped, esp mentally and esp having an IQ of 70 to 85. See also **ESN, mental handicap, subnormal** (sense 2)

retarder (rɪˈtɑːdə) *n* **1** a person or thing that retards **2** a substance added to slow down the rate of a chemical change, such as one added to cement to delay its setting

retch (rɛtʃ, riːtʃ) *vb* **1** (*intr*) to undergo an involuntary spasm of ineffectual vomiting; heave **2** to vomit ▷ *n* **3** an involuntary spasm of ineffectual vomiting [Old English *hrǣcan*; related to Old Norse *hrǣkja* to spit]

retd *abbreviation for* **1** retired **2** retained **3** returned

rete (ˈriːtɪ) *n, pl* **retia** (ˈriːʃɪə, -tɪə) *anatomy* any network of nerves or blood vessels; plexus [C14 (referring to a metal network used with an astrolabe): from Latin *rēte* net] > ˈretial *adj*

retell (riːˈtɛl) *vb* **-tells, -telling, -told** (*tr*) to relate (a story, etc) again or differently

retene (ˈriːtiːn, ˈrɛt-) *n* a yellow crystalline hydrocarbon found in tar oils from pine wood and in certain fossil resins. Formula: $C_{18}H_{18}$ [C19 from Greek *rhētinē* resin]

retention (rɪˈtɛnʃən) *n* **1** the act of retaining or state of being retained **2** the capacity to hold or retain liquid **3** the capacity to remember **4** *pathol* the abnormal holding within the body of urine, faeces, etc, that are normally excreted **5** *commerce* a sum of money owed to a contractor but not paid for an agreed period as a safeguard against any faults found in the work carried out **6** (*plural*) *accounting* profits earned by a company but not distributed as dividends; retained earnings [C14 from Latin *retentiō*, from *retinēre* to RETAIN]

retentionist (rɪˈtɛnʃənɪst) *n* a person who advocates the retention of something, esp capital punishment

retentive (rɪˈtɛntɪv) *adj* having the capacity to retain or remember > reˈtentively *adv* > reˈtentiveness *n*

retentivity (ˌriːtɛnˈtɪvɪtɪ) *n* **1** the state or quality of being retentive **2** *physics* another name for **remanence**

retest (riːˈtɛst) *vb* (*tr*) to test (something) again or differently

rethink *vb* (riːˈθɪŋk) **-thinks, -thinking, -thought** **1** to think about (something) again, esp with a view to changing one's tactics or opinions ▷ *n* (ˈriːˌθɪŋk) **2** the act or an instance of thinking again

retiarius (ˌriːtɪˈɛərɪəs, ˌriːʃɪ-) *n, pl* **-arii** (-ˈɛərɪˌaɪ) (in ancient Rome) a gladiator armed with a net and trident [Latin, from *rēte* net]

retiary (ˈriːtɪərɪ, -ʃɪə-) *adj rare* of, relating to, or resembling a net or web [C17 from Latin RETIARIUS]

reticent (ˈrɛtɪsənt) *adj* not open or communicative; not saying all that one knows; taciturn; reserved [C19 from Latin *reticēre* to keep silent, from RE- + *tacēre* to be silent] > ˈreticence *n* > ˈreticently *adv*

reticle (ˈrɛtɪkᵊl) *or less commonly* **reticule** *n* a network of fine lines, wires, etc, placed in the focal plane of an optical instrument to assist measurement of the size or position of objects under observation. Also called: **graticule** [C17 from Latin *rēticulum* a little net, from *rēte* net]

reticulate (rɪˈtɪkjʊlɪt) *adj also* **reticular** (rɪˈtɪkjʊlə) **1** in the form of a network or having a network of parts: *a reticulate leaf* **2** resembling, covered with, or having the form of a net ▷ *vb* (rɪˈtɪkjʊˌleɪt) **3** to form or be formed into a net [C17 from Late Latin *rēticulātus* made like a net] > reˈticulately *adv* > reˌticuˈlation *n*

reticule (ˈrɛtɪˌkjuːl) *n* **1** (in the 18th and 19th centuries) a woman's small bag or purse, usually in the form of a pouch with a drawstring and made of net, beading, brocade, etc **2** a variant of **reticle** [C18 from French *réticule*, from Latin *rēticulum* RETICLE]

reticulocyte (rɪˈtɪkjʊləˌsaɪt) *n* an immature red blood cell containing a network of granules or filaments [C20 from RETICULUM + -CYTE]

reticuloendothelial (rɪˌtɪkjʊləʊˌɛndəʊˈθiːlɪəl) *adj physiol* denoting or relating to a bodily system that consists of all the cells able to ingest bacteria, colloidal particles, etc, with the exception of the leucocytes; it includes the lymphatic system and the spleen. See also **macrophage** [C20 from RETICULUM + ENDOTHELIAL]

reticulum (rɪˈtɪkjʊləm) *n, pl* **-la** (-lə) **1** any fine network, esp one in the body composed of cells, fibres, etc **2** the second compartment of the stomach of ruminants, situated between the rumen and psalterium [C17 from Latin: little net, from *rēte* net]

Reticulum (rɪˈtɪkjʊləm) *n, Latin genitive* **Reticuli** (rɪˈtɪkjʊˌlaɪ) a small constellation in the S hemisphere lying between Dorado and Hydrus

r

retiform ('riːtɪˌfɔːm, 'rɛt-) *adj rare* netlike; reticulate [C17 from Latin *rēte* net + *forma* shape]

retina ('rɛtɪnə) *n, pl* **-nas, -nae** (-ˌniː) the light-sensitive membrane forming the inner lining of the posterior wall of the eyeball, composed largely of a specialized terminal expansion of the optic nerve. Images focused here by the lens of the eye are transmitted to the brain as nerve impulses [C14 from Medieval Latin, perhaps from Latin *rēte* net] > **'retinal** *adj*

retinaculum (ˌrɛtɪ'nækjʊləm) *n, pl* **-la** (-lə) **1** connection or retention or something that connects or retains **2** *zoology* a small hook that joins the forewing and hind wing of a moth during flight [C18 (a surgical instrument used in castration): Latin, from *retinēre* to hold back] > **ˌreti'nacular** *adj*

retinal rivalry *n psychol* another name for **binocular rivalry**

retinene ('rɛtɪˌniːn) *or* **retinal** ('rɛtɪnəl) *n* the aldehyde form of the polyene retinol (vitamin A) that associates with the protein opsin to form the visual purple pigment rhodopsin [C20 from RETINA + -ENE]

retinite ('rɛtɪˌnaɪt) *n* any of various resins of fossil origin, esp one derived from lignite [C19 from French *rétinite*, from Greek *rhētinē* resin + -ITE[1]]

retinitis (ˌrɛtɪ'naɪtɪs) *n* inflammation of the retina [C20 from New Latin, from RETINA + -ITIS]

retinitis pigmentosa (ˌpɪgmən'təʊsə) *n* a degenerative hereditary disease of the human eye, characterized by pigmentary changes in the retina, night blindness, and eventual loss of vision [C19 *pigmentosa*, feminine of Latin *pigmentosus*]

retinol ('rɛtɪˌnɒl) *n* another name for **vitamin A** and **rosin oil** [C19 from Greek *rhētinē* resin + -OL[1]]

retinopathy (ˌrɛtɪ'nɒpəθɪ) *n* any of various noninflammatory diseases of the retina which may have serious effects on vision

retinoscopy (ˌrɛtɪ'nɒskəpɪ) *n ophthalmol* a procedure for detecting errors of refraction in the eye by means of an instrument (**retinoscope**) that reflects a beam of light from a mirror into the eye. Diagnosis is made by observing the areas of shadow and the direction in which the light moves when the mirror is rotated. Also called: **skiascopy, shadow test** > **retinoscopic** (ˌrɛtɪnə'skɒpɪk) *adj* > **ˌretino'scopically** *adv* > **ˌreti'noscopist** *n*

retinue ('rɛtɪˌnjuː) *n* a body of aides and retainers attending an important person, royalty, etc [C14 from Old French *retenue*, from *retenir* to RETAIN] > **'retiˌnued** *adj*

retiral (rɪ'taɪər[ə]l) *n Scot* the act of retiring from office, one's work, etc; retirement

retire (rɪ'taɪə) *vb (mainly intr)* **1** *(also tr)* to give up or to cause (a person) to give up his work, a post, etc, esp on reaching pensionable age (in Britain and Australia usually 65 for men, 60 for women) **2** to go away, as into seclusion, for recuperation, etc **3** to go to bed **4** to recede or disappear: *the sun retired behind the clouds* **5** to withdraw from a sporting contest, esp because of injury **6** *(also tr)* to pull back (troops, etc) from battle or an exposed position or (of troops, etc) to fall back **7** *(tr)* **a** to remove (bills, bonds, shares, etc) from circulation by taking them up and paying for them **b** to remove (money) from circulation [C16 from French *retirer*, from Old French RE- + *tirer* to pull, draw] > **re'tirer** *n*

retired (rɪ'taɪəd) *adj* **1 a** having given up one's work, office, etc, esp on completion of the normal period of service **b** *(as collective noun; preceded by the)*: *the retired* **2** withdrawn; secluded

retiree (rɪˌtaɪə'riː) *n chiefly US* a person who has retired from work

retirement (rɪ'taɪəmənt) *n* **1 a** the act of retiring from one's work, office, etc **b** *(as modifier)*: *retirement age* **2** the period of being retired from work: *she had many plans for her retirement* **3** seclusion from the world; privacy **4** the act of going away or retreating

retirement pension *n* a pension given to a person who has retired from regular employment, whether paid by the state, arising from the person's former employment, or the product of investment in a personal or stakeholder pension scheme

retirement relief *n* (formerly in Britain) relief from capital-gains tax given to persons at or over 50 when disposing of business assets

retiring (rɪ'taɪərɪŋ) *adj* shunning contact with others; shy; reserved > **re'tiringly** *adv*

retool (riː'tuːl) *vb* **1** to replace, re-equip, or rearrange the tools in (a factory, etc) **2** *chiefly US and Canadian* to revise or reorganize

retorsion (rɪ'tɔːʃən) *n rare* retaliatory action taken by a state whose citizens have been mistreated by a foreign power by treating the subjects of that power similarly; reprisal [C17 from French; see RETORT[1]]

retort[1] (rɪ'tɔːt) *vb* **1** (when *tr, takes a clause as object*) to utter (something) quickly, sharply, wittily, or angrily, in response **2** to use (an argument) against its originator; turn the tables by saying (something) ▷ *n* **3** a sharp, angry, or witty reply **4** an argument used against its originator [C16 from Latin *retorquēre* to twist back, from RE- + *torquēre* to twist, wrench] > **re'torter** *n*

retort[2] (rɪ'tɔːt) *n* **1** a glass vessel with a round bulb and long tapering neck that is bent down, used esp in a laboratory for distillation **2** a vessel in which large quantities of material may be heated, esp one used for heating ores in the production of metals or heating coal to produce gas ▷ *vb* **3** *(tr)* to heat in a retort [C17 from French *retorte*, from Medieval Latin *retorta*, from Latin *retorquēre* to twist back; see RETORT[1]]

retortion (rɪ'tɔːʃən) *n* **1** the act of retorting **2** a variant spelling of **retorsion**

retouch (riː'tʌtʃ) *vb (tr)* **1** to restore, correct, or improve (a painting, make-up, etc) with new touches **2** *photog* to alter (a negative or print) by painting over blemishes or adding details **3** to make small finishing improvements to **4** *archaeol* to detach small flakes from (a blank) in order to make a tool ▷ *n* **5** the art or practice of retouching **6** a detail that is the result of retouching **7** a photograph, painting, etc, that has been retouched **8** *archaeol* fine percussion to shape flakes of stone into usable tools > **re'touchable** *adj* > **re'toucher** *n*

retrace (rɪ'treɪs) *vb (tr)* **1** to go back over (one's steps, a route, etc) again: *we retraced the route we took last summer* **2** to go over (a past event) in the mind; recall **3** to go over (a story, account, etc) from the beginning > **re'traceable** *adj* > **re'tracement** *n*

re-trace (riː'treɪs) *vb (tr)* to trace (a map, drawing, etc) again

retract (rɪ'trækt) *vb* **1** *(tr)* to draw in (a part or appendage): *a snail can retract its horns; to retract the landing gear of an aircraft* **2** to withdraw (a statement, opinion, charge, etc) as invalid or unjustified **3** to go back on (a promise or agreement) **4** *(intr)* to shrink back, as in fear **5** *phonetics* to modify the articulation of (a vowel) by bringing the tongue back away from the lips [C16 from Latin *retractāre* to withdraw, from *tractāre* to pull, from *trahere* to drag] > **re'tractable** *or* **re'tractible** *adj* > **reˌtracta'bility** *or* **reˌtractibility** *n* > **retractation** (ˌriːtræk'teɪʃən) *n* > **re'tractive** *adj*

retractile (rɪ'træktaɪl) *adj* capable of being drawn in: *the retractile claws of a cat* > **retractility** (ˌriːtræk'tɪlɪtɪ) *n*

retraction (rɪ'trækʃən) *n* **1** the act of retracting or state of being retracted **2** the withdrawal of a statement, charge, etc

retractor (rɪ'træktə) *n* **1** *anatomy* any of various muscles that retract an organ or part **2** *surgery* an instrument for holding back the edges of a surgical incision or organ or part **3** a person or thing that retracts

retrain (riː'treɪn) *vb* **1** *(tr)* to teach (someone) a new skill so that he or she can do a job or find employment **2** *(intr)* to learn a new skill with a view to doing a job or finding employment

retral ('riːtrəl, 'rɛtrəl) *adj rare* at, near, or towards the back [C19 from Latin *retrō* backwards] > **'retrally** *adv*

retread *vb* (riː'trɛd) **-treads, -treading, -treaded** **1** *(tr)* another word for **remould** (sense 2) ▷ *n* ('riːˌtrɛd) **2** another word for **remould** (sense 3) **3** *Austral & NZ informal* a pensioner who has resumed employment, esp in a former profession **4** a film, piece of music, etc which is a superficially altered version of an earlier original

re-tread (riː'trɛd) *vb* **-treads, -treading, -trod, -trodden** *or* **-trod** *(tr)* to tread or walk over (one's steps) again

retreat (rɪ'triːt) *vb (mainly intr)* **1** *military* to withdraw or retire in the face of or from action with an enemy, either due to defeat or in order to adopt a more favourable position **2** to retire or withdraw, as to seclusion or shelter **3** (of a person's features) to slope back; recede **4** *(tr) chess* to move (a piece) back ▷ *n* **5** the act of retreating or withdrawing **6** *military* **a** a withdrawal or retirement in the face of the enemy **b** a bugle call signifying withdrawal or retirement, esp (formerly) to within a defended fortification **7** retirement or seclusion **8** a place, such as a sanatorium or monastery, to which one may retire for refuge, quiet, etc **9** a period of seclusion, esp for religious contemplation **10** an institution, esp a private one, for the care and treatment of the mentally ill, infirm, elderly, etc [C14 from Old French *retret*, from *retraire* to withdraw, from Latin *retrahere* to pull back; see RETRACT]

retrench (rɪ'trɛntʃ) *vb* **1** to reduce or curtail (costs); economize **2** *(tr)* to shorten, delete, or abridge **3** *(tr)* to protect by a retrenchment [C17 from Old French *retrenchier*, from RE- + *trenchier* to cut, from Latin *truncāre* to lop; see TRENCH] > **re'trenchable** *adj*

retrenchment (rɪ'trɛntʃmənt) *n* **1** the act of reducing expenditure in order to improve financial stability **2** an extra interior fortification to reinforce outer walls

retrial (riː'traɪəl) *n* a second or new trial, esp of a case that has already been adjudicated upon

retribution (ˌrɛtrɪ'bjuːʃən) *n* **1** the act of punishing or taking vengeance for wrongdoing, sin, or injury **2** punishment or vengeance [C14 via Old French from Church Latin *retribūtiō*, from Latin *retribuere* to repay, from RE- + *tribuere* to pay; see TRIBUTE] > **retributive** (rɪ'trɪbjʊtɪv) *or less commonly* **re'tributory** *adj* > **re'tributively** *adv*

retrieval (rɪ'triːv[ə]l) *n* **1** the act or process of retrieving **2** the possibility of recovery, restoration, or rectification (esp in the phrase **beyond retrieval**) **3** a computer filing operation that recalls records or other data from a file

retrieve (rɪ'triːv) *vb (mainly tr)* **1** to get or fetch back again; recover: *he retrieved his papers from various people's drawers* **2** to bring back to a more satisfactory state; revive **3** to extricate from trouble or danger; rescue or save **4** to recover or make newly available (stored information) from a computer system **5** *(also intr)* (of dogs) to find and fetch (shot game) **6** *tennis, squash, badminton* to return successfully (a shot difficult to reach) **7** to recall; remember ▷ *n* **8** the act of retrieving **9** the chance of being retrieved [C15 from Old French *retrover*, from RE- + *trouver* to find, perhaps from Vulgar Latin *tropāre* (unattested) to compose; see TROVER, TROUBADOUR] > **re'trievable** *adj* > **reˌtrieva'bility** *n* > **re'trievably** *adv*

retriever (rɪ'triːvə) *n* **1** one of a breed of large gun dogs that can be trained to retrieve game: see **golden retriever, labrador retriever, Chesapeake Bay retriever, curly-coated retriever, flat-coated retriever** **2** any dog used to retrieve shot game **3** a person or thing that retrieves

retro ('rɛtrəʊ) *n, pl* **-ros** **1** short for **retrorocket**

▷ *adj* **2** denoting something associated with or revived from the past: *retro dressing; retro fashion*

retro- *prefix* **1** back or backwards: *retroactive* **2** located behind: *retrolental* [from Latin *retrō* behind, backwards]

retroact (ˈrɛtrəʊˌækt) *vb* (*intr*) **1** to act in opposition **2** to influence or have reference to past events

retroaction (ˌrɛtrəʊˈækʃən) *n* **1** an action contrary or reciprocal to a preceding action **2** a retrospective action, esp a law affecting events prior to its enactment

retroactive (ˌrɛtrəʊˈæktɪv) *adj* **1** applying or referring to the past: *retroactive legislation* **2** effective or operative from a date or for a period in the past > ˌretroˈactively *adv* > ˌretroˈactiveness *or* ˌretroacˈtivity *n*

retroactive inhibition *or* **interference** *n psychol* the tendency for the retention of learned material or skills to be impaired by subsequent learning, esp by learning of a similar kind. Compare **proactive inhibition**

retrocede (ˌrɛtrəʊˈsiːd) *vb* **1** (*tr*) to give back; return **2** (*intr*) to go back or retire; recede > **retrocession** (ˌrɛtrəʊˈsɛʃən) *or* ˌretroˈcedence *n* > ˌretroˈcessive *or* ˌretroˈcedent *adj*

retrochoir (ˈrɛtrəʊˌkwaɪə) *n* the space in a large church or cathedral behind the high altar

retrofire (ˈrɛtrəʊˌfaɪə) *n* **1** the act of firing a retrorocket **2** the moment at which it is fired

retrofit (ˈrɛtrəʊˌfɪt) *vb* -fits, -fitting, -fitted (*tr*) to equip (a vehicle, piece of equipment, etc) with new parts, safety devices, etc, after manufacture

retroflex (ˈrɛtrəʊˌflɛks) *or* **retroflexed** *adj* **1** bent or curved backwards **2** *phonetics* of, relating to, or involving retroflexion [c18 from Latin *retrōflexus*, from *retrōflectere*, from RETRO- + *flectere* to bend]

retroflexion *or* **retroflection** (ˌrɛtrəʊˈflɛkʃən) *n* **1** the act or condition of bending or being bent backwards **2** *phonetics* the act of turning the tip of the tongue upwards and backwards towards the hard palate in the articulation of a vowel or a consonant

retrograde (ˈrɛtrəʊˌɡreɪd) *adj* **1** moving or bending backwards **2** (esp of order) reverse or inverse **3** tending towards an earlier worse condition; declining or deteriorating **4** *astronomy* **a** occurring or orbiting in a direction opposite to that of the earth's motion around the sun. Compare **direct** (sense 18) **b** occurring or orbiting in a direction around a planet opposite to the planet's rotational direction: *the retrograde motion of the satellite Phoebe around Saturn* **c** appearing to move in a clockwise direction due to the rotational period exceeding the period of revolution around the sun: *Venus has retrograde rotation* **5** *biology* tending to retrogress; degenerate **6** *music* of, concerning, or denoting a melody or part that is played backwards **7** *obsolete* opposed, contrary, or repugnant to ▷ *vb* (*intr*) **8** to move in a retrograde direction; retrogress **9** *US military* another word for **retreat** (sense 1) [c14 from Latin *retrōgradī* to go backwards, from *gradi* to walk, go] > ˌretrograˈdation *n* > ˈretroˌgradely *adv*

retrograde amnesia *n* amnesia caused by a trauma such as concussion, in which the memory loss relates to material learnt before the trauma. Compare **anterograde amnesia**

retrogress (ˌrɛtrəʊˈɡrɛs) *vb* (*intr*) **1** to go back to an earlier, esp worse, condition; degenerate or deteriorate **2** to move backwards; recede **3** *biology* to develop characteristics or features of lower or simpler organisms; degenerate [c19 from Latin *retrōgressus* having moved backwards, from *retrōgradī*; see RETROGRADE] > ˌretroˈgression *n* > ˌretroˈgressive *adj* > ˌretroˈgressively *adv*

retroject (ˌrɛtrəʊˈdʒɛkt) *vb* (*tr*) to throw backwards (opposed to *project*) [c19 from RETRO- + *-ject* as in PROJECT] > ˌretroˈjection *n*

retrolental (ˌrɛtrəʊˈlɛntᵊl) *adj* behind a lens, esp of the eye [c20 from RETRO- + *-lental*, from New Latin: LENS]

retro-operative *adj* affecting or operating on past events; retroactive

retropack (ˈrɛtrəʊˌpæk) *n* a system of retrorockets on a spacecraft

retropulsion (ˌrɛtrəʊˈpʌlʃən) *n med* an abnormal tendency to walk backwards: a symptom of Parkinson's disease

retrorocket (ˈrɛtrəʊˌrɒkɪt) *n* a small auxiliary rocket engine on a larger rocket, missile, or spacecraft, that produces thrust in the opposite direction to the direction of flight in order to decelerate the vehicle or make it move backwards. Often shortened to: retro

retrorse (rɪˈtrɔːs) *adj* (esp of plant parts) pointing backwards or in a direction opposite to normal [c19 from Latin *retrōrsus*, shortened form of *retrōversus* turned back, from RETRO- + *vertere* to turn] > reˈtrorsely *adv*

retrosexual (ˌrɛtrəʊˈsɛksjʊəl) *jocular* ▷ *n* **1** a heterosexual man who spends little time and money on his personal appearance ▷ *adj* **2** of or relating to such men [c20 from RETRO (sense 2) + (HETERO)SEXUAL]

retrospect (ˈrɛtrəʊˌspɛkt) *n* **1** the act of surveying things past (often in the phrase **in retrospect**) ▷ *vb archaic* **2** to contemplate (anything past); look back on (something) **3** (*intr*; often foll by *to*) to refer [c17 from Latin *retrōspicere* to look back, from RETRO- + *specere* to look]

retrospection (ˌrɛtrəʊˈspɛkʃən) *n* the act of recalling things past, esp in one's personal experience

retrospective (ˌrɛtrəʊˈspɛktɪv) *adj* **1** looking or directed backwards, esp in time; characterized by retrospection **2** applying to the past; retroactive ▷ *n* **3** an exhibition of an artist's life's work or a representative selection of it > ˌretroˈspectively *adv* > ˌretroˈspectiveness *n*

retroussé (rəˈtruːseɪ; *French* rətruse) *adj* (of a nose) turned up [c19 from French *retrousser* to tuck up; see TRUSS]

retroversion (ˌrɛtrəʊˈvɜːʃən) *n* **1** the act of turning or condition of being turned backwards **2** the condition of a part or organ, esp the uterus, that is turned or tilted backwards > ˈretroˌverse *adj* > ˈretroˌverted *adj*

Retrovir (ˈrɛtrəʊˌvɪə) *n trademark* a brand of the drug zidovudine

retrovirus (ˈrɛtrəʊˌvaɪrəs) *n* any of several viruses whose genetic specification is encoded in RNA rather than DNA and that are able to reverse the normal flow of genetic information from DNA to RNA by transcribing RNA into DNA: many retroviruses are known to cause cancer in animals > ˈretroˌviral *adj*

retry (riːˈtraɪ) *vb* -tries, -trying, -tried (*tr*) to try again (a case already determined); give a new trial to

retsina (rɛtˈsiːnə, ˈrɛtsɪnə) *n* a Greek wine flavoured with resin [Modern Greek, from Italian *resina* RESIN]

retune (riːˈtjuːn) *vb* (*tr*) **1** to tune (a musical instrument) differently or again **2** to tune (a radio, television, etc) to a different frequency

return (rɪˈtɜːn) *vb* **1** (*intr*) to come back to a former place or state **2** (*tr*) to give, take, or carry back; replace or restore **3** (*tr*) to repay or recompense, esp with something of equivalent value **4** (*tr*) to earn or yield (profit or interest) as an income from an investment or venture **5** (*intr*) to come back or revert in thought or speech: *I'll return to that later* **6** (*intr*) to recur or reappear **7** to answer or reply **8** (*tr*) to vote into office; elect **9** (*tr*) *law* (of a jury) to deliver or render (a verdict) **10** (*tr*) to send back or reflect (light or sound): *the canyon returned my shout* **11** (*tr*) to submit (a report, etc) about (someone or something) to someone in authority **12** (*tr*) *cards* to lead back (the suit led by one's partner) **13** (*tr*) *ball games* to hit, throw, or play (a ball) back **14** (*tr*) *architect* to turn (a part, decorative moulding, etc) away from its original direction **15** **return thanks** (of Christians) to say grace before a meal ▷ *n* **16** the act or an instance of coming back **17** something that is given or sent back, esp unsatisfactory merchandise returned to the maker or supplier or a theatre ticket sent back by a purchaser for resale **18** the act or an instance of putting, sending, or carrying back; replacement or restoration **19** (*often plural*) the yield, revenue, or profit accruing from an investment, transaction, or venture **20** the act or an instance of reciprocation or repayment (esp in the phrase **in return for**) **21** a recurrence or reappearance **22** an official report, esp of the financial condition of a company **23** **a** a form (a **tax return**) on which a statement concerning one's taxable income is made **b** the statement itself **24** (*often plural*) a statement of the votes counted at an election or poll **25** an answer or reply **26** *Brit* short for **return ticket** **27** *NZ informal* a second helping of food served at a table **28** *architect* **a** a part of a building that forms an angle with the façade **b** any part of an architectural feature that forms an angle with the main part **29** *law* a report by a bailiff or other officer on the outcome of a formal document such as a claim, summons, etc, issued by a court **30** *cards* a lead of a card in the suit that one's partner has previously led **31** *ball games* the act of playing or throwing a ball back **32** **by return (of post)** *Brit* by the next post back to the sender **33** **many happy returns (of the day)** a conventional greeting to someone on his or her birthday **34** **the point of no return** the point at which a person's commitment is irrevocable ▷ *adj* **35** of, relating to, or characterized by a return: *a return visit* **36** denoting a second, reciprocated occasion: *a return match* [c14 from Old French *retorner*; see RE-, TURN]

returnable (rɪˈtɜːnəbᵊl) *adj* **1** able to be taken, given, or sent back **2** required to be returned by law, as a claim to the court from which it issued > reˌturnaˈbility *n*

return crease *n cricket* one of two lines marked at right-angles to each bowling crease, from inside which a bowler must deliver the ball

returned soldier *n Austral and NZ* a soldier who has served abroad. Also (Austral): **returned man**

returnee (rɪˈtɜːˌniː) *n chiefly US and Canadian* a person who returns to his native country, esp after war service

returner (rɪˈtɜːnə) *n* **1** a person or thing that returns **2** a person who goes back to work after a break, esp a woman who has had children

returning officer *n* (in Britain, Canada, Australia, etc) an official in charge of conducting an election in a constituency or electoral district, who supervises the counting of votes and announces the results

return ticket *n Brit* a ticket entitling a passenger to travel to his destination and back again. US and Canadian equivalent: **round-trip ticket**

retuse (rɪˈtjuːs) *adj botany* having a rounded apex and a central depression: *retuse leaves* [c18 from Latin *retundere* to make blunt, from RE- + *tundere* to pound]

Reuben (ˈruːbɪn) *n Old Testament* **1** the eldest son of Jacob and Leah: one of the 12 patriarchs of Israel (Genesis 29:30) **2** the Israelite tribe descended from him **3** the territory of this tribe, lying to the northeast of the Dead Sea. Douay spelling: **Ruben**

reunify (riːˈjuːnɪˌfaɪ) *vb* -fies, -fying, -fied (*tr*) to bring together again (something, esp a country previously divided) > ˌreunifiˈcation *n*

reunion (riːˈjuːnjən) *n* **1** the act or process of coming together again **2** the state or condition of having been brought together again **3** a gathering of relatives, friends, or former associates

Réunion (riːˈjuːnjən; *French* reynjɔ̃) *n* an island in the Indian Ocean, in the Mascarene Islands: an overseas region of France, having been in French possession since 1642. A number of far-flung and uninhabited islands are also politically part of Réunion, some located on the opposite side of

Madagascar: Bassas da India, Europa, the Glorioso Islands (Îles Glorieuses), Juan de Nova, and Tromelin. Capital: Saint-Denis. Pop: 767 000 (2004 est). Area: 2510 sq km (970 sq miles)

reunionist (riːˈjuːnjənist) *n* a person who desires or works for reunion between the Roman Catholic Church and the Church of England > re'unionism *n* > re,union'istic *adj*

reunite (ˌriːjuːˈnaɪt) *vb* to bring or come together again > ˌreu'nitable *adj* > ˌreu'niter *n*

Reus (*Spanish* rɛus) *n* a city in NE Spain, northwest of Tarragona: became commercially important after the establishment of an English colony (about 1750). Pop: 94 407 (2003 est)

reusable (riːˈjuːzəbᵊl) *adj* able to be used more than once

reuse *vb* (riːˈjuːz) (*tr*) **1** to use again ▷ *n* (riːˈjuːs) **2** the act or process of using again

Reutlingen (*German* ˈrɔytlɪŋən) *n* a city in SW Germany, in Baden-Württemberg: founded in the 11th century; an Imperial free city from 1240 until 1802; textile industry. Pop: 112 346 (2003 est)

rev (rɛv) *informal* ▷ *n* **1** revolution per minute: *the engine was doing 5000 revs* ▷ *vb* revs, revving, revved **2** (*often foll by up*) to increase the speed of revolution of (an engine)

rev. *abbreviation for* **1** revenue **2** reverse(d) **3** review **4** revise(d) **5** revision **6** revolution **7** revolving

Rev. *abbreviation for* **1** *Bible* Revelation **2** Reverend

Reval (ˈreːval) *n* the German name for **Tallinn**

revalorize *or* **revalorise** (riːˈvælərˌraɪz) *vb* (*tr*) **1** to change the valuation of (assets) **2** to replace (a currency unit) by another > reˌvalori'zation *or* reˌvalori'sation *n*

revalue (riːˈvæljuː) *or US* **revaluate** *vb* **1** to adjust the exchange value of (a currency), esp upwards. Compare **devalue 2** (*tr*) to make a fresh valuation or appraisal of > reˌvalu'ation *n*

revamp (riːˈvæmp) *vb* (*tr*) **1** to patch up or renovate; repair or restore ▷ *n* **2** something that has been renovated or revamped **3** the act or process of revamping [C19 from RE- + VAMP²] > re'vamper *n* > re'vamping *n*

revanchism (rɪˈvæntʃɪzəm) *n* **1** a foreign policy aimed at revenge or the regaining of lost territories **2** desire or support for such a policy [C20 from French *revanche* REVENGE] > re'vanchist *n, adj*

rev counter *n Brit* an informal name for **tachometer**

Revd *abbreviation for* Reverend

reveal (rɪˈviːl) *vb* (*tr*) **1** (*may take a clause as object or an infinitive*) to disclose (a secret); divulge **2** to expose to view or show (something concealed) **3** (*of God*) to disclose (divine truths) either directly or through the medium of prophets, etc ▷ *n* **4** *architect* the vertical side of an opening in a wall, esp the side of a window or door between the frame and the front of the wall [C14 from Old French *reveler*, from Latin *revēlāre* to unveil, from RE- + *vēlum* a VEIL] > re'vealable *adj* > reˌveala'bility *n* > re'vealer *n* > re'vealment *n*

revealed religion *n* **1** religion based on the revelation by God to man of ideas that he would not have arrived at by his natural reason alone **2** religion in which the existence of God depends on revelation

revealing (rɪˈviːlɪŋ) *adj* **1** of significance or import: *a very revealing experience* **2** showing or designed to show more of the body than is usual or conventional: *a revealing costume* > re'vealingly *adv* > re'vealingness *n*

revegetate (riːˈvedʒɪˌteɪt) *vb* (*intr*) (of plants) to grow again and produce new tissue, esp to produce new growth on bare ground > reˌvege'tation *n*

reveille (rɪˈvælɪ) *n* **1** a signal, given by a bugle, drum, etc, to awaken soldiers or sailors in the morning **2** the hour at which this takes place ▷ Also called (esp US): **rouse** [C17 from French *réveillez!* awake! from RE- + Old French *esveillier* to be

wakeful, ultimately from Latin *vigilāre* to keep watch; see VIGIL]

revel (ˈrɛvᵊl) *vb* **-els, -elling, -elled** *or US* **-els, -eling, -eled** (*intr*) **1** (*foll by in*) to take pleasure or wallow: *to revel in success* **2** to take part in noisy festivities; make merry ▷ *n* **3** (*often plural*) an occasion of noisy merrymaking **4** a less common word for **revelry** [C14 from Old French *reveler* to be merry, noisy, from Latin *rebellāre* to revolt, REBEL] > 'reveller *n* > 'revelment *n*

revelation (ˌrɛvəˈleɪʃən) *n* **1** the act or process of disclosing something previously secret or obscure, esp something true **2** a fact disclosed or revealed, esp in a dramatic or surprising way **3** *Christianity* **a** God's disclosure of his own nature and his purpose for mankind, esp through the words of human intermediaries **b** something in which such a divine disclosure is contained, such as the Bible [C14 from Church Latin *revēlātiō* from Latin *revēlāre* to REVEAL] > ˌreve'lational *adj*

Revelation (ˌrɛvəˈleɪʃən) *n* (*popularly, often plural*) the last book of the New Testament, containing visionary descriptions of heaven, of conflicts between good and evil, and of the end of the world. Also called: the **Apocalypse**, the **Revelation of Saint John the Divine**

revelationist (ˌrɛvəˈleɪʃənist) *n* a person who believes that God has revealed certain truths to man

revelry (ˈrɛvᵊlrɪ) *n, pl* **-ries** noisy or unrestrained merrymaking

revenant (ˈrɛvɪnənt) *n* something, esp a ghost, that returns [C19 from French: ghost, from *revenir* to come back, from Latin *revenīre*, from RE- + *venīre* to come]

revenge (rɪˈvɛndʒ) *n* **1** the act of retaliating for wrongs or injury received; vengeance **2** something done as a means of vengeance **3** the desire to take vengeance or retaliate **4** a return match, regarded as a loser's opportunity to even the score ▷ *vb* (*tr*) **5** to inflict equivalent injury or damage for (injury received); retaliate in return for **6** to take vengeance for (oneself or another); avenge [C14 from Old French *revenger*, from Late Latin *revindicāre*, from RE- + *vindicāre* to VINDICATE] > re'vengeless *adj* > re'venger *n* > re'venging *adj* > re'vengingly *adv*

revengeful (rɪˈvɛndʒfʊl) *adj* full of or characterized by desire for vengeance; vindictive > re'vengefully *adv* > re'vengefulness *n*

revenue (ˈrɛvɪˌnjuː) *n* **1** the income accruing from taxation to a government during a specified period of time, usually a year **2 a** a government department responsible for the collection of government revenue **b** (*as modifier*): *revenue men* **3** the gross income from a business enterprise, investment, property, etc **4** a particular item of income **5** something that yields a regular financial return; source of income [C16 from Old French, from *revenir* to return, from Latin *revenīre*; see REVENANT] > 're,venued *adj*

revenue cutter *n* a small lightly armed boat used to enforce customs regulations and catch smugglers

revenuer (ˈrɛvɪˌnjuːə) *n US slang* a revenue officer or cutter

revenue tariff *n* a tariff for the purpose of producing public revenue. Compare **protective tariff**

reverb (ˈrɛvɜːb) *n* an electronic device that creates artificial acoustics

reverberate (rɪˈvɜːbəˌreɪt) *vb* **1** (*intr*) to resound or re-echo **2** to reflect or be reflected many times **3** (*intr*) to rebound or recoil **4** (*intr*) (of the flame or heat in a reverberatory furnace) to be deflected onto the metal or ore on the hearth **5** (*tr*) to heat, melt, or refine (a metal or ore) in a reverberatory furnace [C16 from Latin *reverberāre* to strike back, from RE- + *verberāre* to beat, from *verber* a lash] > re'verberant *or less commonly* re'verberative *adj* > re'verberantly *adv* > re'verber'ation *n*

reverberation time *n* a measure of the acoustic

properties of a room, equal to the time taken for a sound to fall in intensity by 60 decibels. It is usually measured in seconds

reverberator (rɪˈvɜːbəˌreɪtə) *n* **1** anything that produces or undergoes reverberation **2** another name for **reverberatory furnace**

reverberatory (rɪˈvɜːbərətərɪ, -trɪ) *adj* **1** characterized by, utilizing, or produced by reverberation ▷ *n, pl* **-ries 2** short for **reverberatory furnace**

reverberatory furnace *n* a metallurgical furnace having a curved roof that deflects heat onto the charge so that the fuel is not in direct contact with the ore

revere (rɪˈvɪə) *vb* (*tr*) to be in awe of and respect deeply; venerate [C17 from Latin *reverērī*, from RE- + *verērī* to fear, be in awe of] > re'verable *adj* > re'verer *n*

reverence (ˈrɛvərəns) *n* **1** a feeling or attitude of profound respect, usually reserved for the sacred or divine; devoted veneration **2** an outward manifestation of this feeling, esp a bow or act of obeisance **3** the state of being revered or commanding profound respect **4 saving your reverence** *archaic* a form of apology for using an obscene or taboo expression ▷ *vb* **5** (*tr*) to revere or venerate > 'reverencer *n*

Reverence (ˈrɛvərəns) *n* (*preceded by Your or His*) a title sometimes used to address or refer to a Roman Catholic priest

reverend (ˈrɛvərənd) *adj* **1** worthy of reverence **2** relating to or designating a clergyman or the clergy ▷ *n* **3** *informal* a clergyman [C15 from Latin *reverendus* fit to be revered; see REVERE]

Reverend (ˈrɛvərənd) *adj* a title of respect for a clergyman. Abbrevs: **Rev, Revd** *See also* **Very Reverend, Right Reverend, Most Reverend**

> **USAGE** *Reverend* with a surname alone (*Reverend Smith*), as a term of address ("*Yes, Reverend*"), or in the salutation of a letter (*Dear Rev Mr Smith*) are all generally considered to be wrong usage. Preferred are (*the*) *Reverend John Smith* or *Reverend Mr Smith* and *Dear Mr Smith*

Reverend Mother *n* a title of respect or form of address for the Mother Superior of a convent

reverent (ˈrɛvərənt, ˈrɛvrənt) *adj* feeling, expressing, or characterized by reverence [C14 from Latin *reverēns* respectful] > 'reverently *adv* > 'reverentness *n*

reverential (ˌrɛvəˈrɛnʃəl) *adj* resulting from or showing reverence: *a pilgrimage is a reverential act, performed by reverent people* > ˌreve'rentially *adv*

reverie *or* **revery** (ˈrɛvərɪ) *n, pl* **-eries 1** an act or state of absent-minded daydreaming: *to fall into a reverie* **2** a piece of instrumental music suggestive of a daydream **3** *archaic* a fanciful or visionary notion; daydream [C14 from Old French *resverie* wildness, from *resver* to behave wildly, of uncertain origin; see RAVE¹]

revers (rɪˈvɪə) *n, pl* **-vers** (-'vɪəz) (*usually plural*) the turned-back lining of part of a garment, esp a lapel or cuff [C19 from French, literally: REVERSE]

reversal (rɪˈvɜːsᵊl) *n* **1** the act or an instance of reversing **2** a change for the worse; reverse: *a reversal of fortune* **3** the state of being reversed **4** the annulment of a judicial decision, esp by an appeal court on grounds of error or irregularity

reversal film *n* photographic film that can be processed to produce a positive transparent image for direct projection, rather than a negative for printing

reverse (rɪˈvɜːs) *vb* (*mainly tr*) **1** to turn or set in an opposite direction, order, or position **2** to change into something different or contrary; alter completely: *reverse one's policy* **3** (*also intr*) to move or cause to move backwards or in an opposite direction: *to reverse a car* **4** to run (machinery, etc) in the opposite direction to normal **5** to turn inside out **6** *law* to revoke or set aside (a judgment, decree, etc); annul **7** (*often foll by out*) to print from plates so made that white lettering or design of (a page, text, display, etc) appears on a black or coloured background **8** **reverse arms** *military* to turn one's arms upside down, esp as a token of mourning **9** **reverse the charge(s)** to make a telephone call at the recipient's expense ▷ *n* **10** the opposite or contrary of something **11** the back or rear side of something **12** a change to an opposite position, state, or direction **13** **a** change for the worse; setback or defeat **14** **a** the mechanism or gears by which machinery, a vehicle, etc, can be made to reverse its direction **b** (*as modifier*): *reverse gear* **15** the side of a coin bearing a secondary design. Compare **obverse** (sense 5) **16** **a** printed matter in which normally black or coloured areas, esp lettering, appear white, and vice versa **b** (*as modifier*): *reverse plates* **17** **in reverse** in an opposite or backward direction **18** **the reverse of** emphatically not; not at all ▷ *adj* **19** opposite or contrary in direction, position, order, nature, etc; turned backwards **20** back to front; inverted **21** operating or moving in a manner contrary to that which is usual **22** denoting or relating to a mirror image [C14 from Old French, from Latin *reversus*, from *revertere* to turn back] > **re'versely** *adv* > **re'verser** *n*

reverse Apartheid *n* *S African* a perceived bias against Whites following the end of Apartheid

reverse-charge *adj* (*prenominal*) (of a telephone call) made at the recipient's expense. US equivalent: **collect**

reverse osmosis *n* a technique for purifying water, in which pressure is applied to force liquid through a semipermeable membrane in the opposite direction to that in normal osmosis

reverse takeover *n* *finance* the purchase of a larger company by a smaller company, esp of a public company by a private company

reverse transcriptase (træn'skrɪpteɪz) *n* an enzyme present in retroviruses that copies RNA into DNA, thus reversing the usual flow of genetic information in which DNA is copied into RNA

reverse video *n* *computing* a highlighting feature achieved by reversing the colours of normal characters and background on a visual display unit

reversi (rɪ'vɜːsɪ) *n* a game played on a draughtboard with 64 pieces, black on one side and white on the other. When pieces are captured they are turned over to join the capturing player's forces; the winner is the player who fills the board with pieces of his colour [C19 from French; see REVERSE]

reversible (rɪ'vɜːsəbᵊl) *adj* **1** capable of being reversed: *a reversible decision* **2** capable of returning to an original condition **3** *chem, physics* capable of assuming or producing either of two possible states and changing from one to the other: *a reversible reaction* **4** *thermodynamics* (of a change, process, etc) occurring through a number of intermediate states that are all in thermodynamic equilibrium **5** (of a fabric or garment) woven, printed, or finished so that either side may be used as the outer side ▷ *n* **6** a reversible garment, esp a coat > **re,versi'bility** *n* > **re'versibly** *adv*

reversing light *n* a light on the rear of a motor vehicle to warn others that the vehicle is being reversed

reversion (rɪ'vɜːʃən) *n* **1** a return to or towards an earlier condition, practice, or belief; act of reverting **2** the act of reversing or the state of being reversed; reversal **3** *biology* **a** the return of individuals, organs, etc, to a more primitive condition or type **b** the reappearance of primitive characteristics in an individual or group **4** *property law* **a** an interest in an estate that reverts to the grantor or his heirs at the end of a period, esp at the end of the life of a grantee **b** an estate so reverting **c** the right to succeed to such an estate **5** the benefit payable on the death of a life-insurance policyholder > **re'versionally** *adv* > **re'versionary** *or* **re'versional** *adj*

reversionary bonus *n* *insurance* a bonus added to the sum payable on death or at the maturity of a with-profits assurance policy

reversioner (rɪ'vɜːʃənə) *n* *property law* a person entitled to an estate in reversion. Compare **remainderman**

reverso (rɪ'vɜːsəʊ) *n, pl* **-sos** another name for **verso**

revert *vb* (rɪ'vɜːt) (*intr*; foll by *to*) **1** to go back to a former practice, condition, belief, etc: *she reverted to her old wicked ways* **2** to take up again or come back to a former topic **3** *biology* (of individuals, organs, etc) to return to a more primitive, earlier, or simpler condition or type **4** *US* to reply to someone: *we will revert to you with pricing and other details* **5** *property law* (of an estate or interest in land) to return to its former owner or his heirs when a grant, esp a grant for the lifetime of the grantee, comes to an end **6** **revert to type** to resume characteristics that were thought to have disappeared ▷ *n* ('riː,vɜːt) **7** a person who, having been converted, has returned to his former beliefs or Church [C13 from Latin *revertere* to return, from RE- + *vertere* to turn] > **re'verter** *n* > **re'vertible** *adj*

USAGE Since *back* is part of the meaning of *revert*, one should not say that someone *reverts back* to a certain type of behaviour

revest (riː'vɛst) *vb* (often foll by *in*) to restore (former power, authority, status, etc, to a person) or (of power, authority, etc) to be restored [C16 from Old French *revestir* to clothe again, from Latin RE- + *vestire* to clothe; see VEST]

revet (rɪ'vɛt) *vb* **-vets, -vetting, -vetted** to face (a wall or embankment) with stones [C19 from French *revêt*, from Old French *revestir* to reclothe; see REVEST]

revetment (rɪ'vɛtmənt) *n* **1** a facing of stones, sandbags, etc, to protect a wall, embankment, or earthworks **2** another name for **retaining wall** [C18 from French *revêtement* literally: a reclothing, from *revêtir*; see REVEST]

review (rɪ'vjuː) *vb* (*mainly tr*) **1** to look at or examine again: *to review a situation* **2** to look back upon (a period of time, sequence of events, etc); remember **3** to inspect, esp formally or officially: *the general reviewed his troops* **4** to read through or go over in order to correct **5** *law* to re-examine (a decision) judicially **6** to write a critical assessment of (a book, film, play, concert, etc), esp as a profession ▷ *n* **7** Also called: **reviewal** the act or an instance of reviewing **8** a general survey or report **9** a critical assessment of a book, film, play, concert, etc, esp one printed in a newspaper or periodical **10** **a** a publication containing such articles **b** (*capital when part of a name*): *the Saturday Review* **11** a second consideration; re-examination **12** a retrospective survey **13** a formal or official inspection **14** *US and Canadian* the process of rereading a subject or notes on it, esp in preparation for an examination. Also called (in Britain and certain other countries): **revision** **15** *law* judicial re-examination of a case, esp by a superior court **16** a less common spelling of **revue** [C16 from French, from *revoir* to see again, from Latin *re-* RE- + *vidēre* to see] > **re'viewable** *adj* > **re'viewer** *n*

review copy *n* a copy of a book sent by a publisher to a journal, newspaper, etc, to enable it to be reviewed

revile (rɪ'vaɪl) *vb* to use abusive or scornful language against (someone or something) [C14 from Old French *reviler*, from RE- + *vil* VILE] > **re'vilement** *n* > **re'viler** *n*

revise (rɪ'vaɪz) *vb* **1** (*tr*) to change, alter, or amend: *to revise one's opinion* **2** *Brit* to reread (a subject or notes on it) so as to memorize it, esp in preparation for an examination **3** (*tr*) to prepare a new version or edition of (a previously printed work) ▷ *n* **4** the act, process, or result of revising; revision [C16 from Latin *revīsere* to look back at, from RE- + *vīsere* to inspect, from *vidēre* to see; see REVIEW, VISIT] > **re'visable** *adj* > **re'visal** *n* > **re'viser** *n*

Revised Standard Version *n* a revision by American scholars of the American Standard Version of the Bible. The New Testament was published in 1946 and the entire Bible in 1953

Revised Version *n* a revision of the Authorized Version of the Bible prepared by two committees of British scholars, the New Testament being published in 1881 and the Old in 1885

revision (rɪ'vɪʒən) *n* **1** the act or process of revising **2** *Brit* the process of rereading a subject or notes on it, esp in preparation for an examination **3** a corrected or new version of a book, article, etc

revisionary (rɪ'vɪʒənərɪ) *adj* of or relating to a new or different version of something

revisionism (rɪ'vɪʒə,nɪzəm) *n* **1** (*sometimes capital*) **a** a moderate, nonrevolutionary version of Marxism developed in Germany around 1900 **b** (in Marxist-Leninist ideology) any dangerous departure from the true interpretation of the teachings of Karl Marx, the German founder of modern Communism (1818–83) **2** the advocacy of revision of some political theory, religious doctrine, historical or critical interpretation, etc **3** (*usually capital*) an ultra-nationalist form of Zionism that arose in Palestine in the 1940s > **re'visionist** *n, adj*

revisit (riː'vɪzɪt) *vb* (*tr*) **1** to visit again **2** to re-examine (a topic or theme) after an interval, with a view to making a fresh appraisal

revisory (rɪ'vaɪzərɪ) *adj* of, relating to, or having the power to revise

revitalize *or* **revitalise** (riː'vaɪtᵊ,laɪz) *vb* (*tr*) to restore vitality or animation to > **re,vitali'zation** *or* **re,vitali'sation** *n*

revival (rɪ'vaɪvᵊl) *n* **1** the act or an instance of reviving or the state of being revived **2** an instance of returning to life or consciousness **3** a renewed use, acceptance of, or interest in (past customs, styles, etc): *a revival of learning* **4** a new production of a play that has not been recently performed **5** a reawakening of faith or renewal of commitment to religion **6** an evangelistic meeting or service intended to effect such a reawakening in those present **7** the re-establishment of legal validity, as of a judgment, contract, etc

revivalism (rɪ'vaɪvə,lɪzəm) *n* **1** a movement, esp an evangelical Christian one, that seeks to reawaken faith **2** the tendency or desire to revive former customs, styles, etc

revivalist (rɪ'vaɪvəlɪst) *n* **1** a person who holds, promotes, or presides over religious revivals **2** a person who revives customs, ideas, etc ▷ *adj* **3** of, relating to, or characterizing revivalism or religious revivals > **re,vival'istic** *adj*

revive (rɪ'vaɪv) *vb* **1** to bring or be brought back to life, consciousness, or strength; resuscitate or be resuscitated **2** to give or assume new vitality; flourish again or cause to flourish again **3** to make or become operative or active again **4** to bring or come into use or currency again: *to revive a language* **5** (*tr*) to take up again **6** to bring or come back to mind **7** (*tr*) *theatre* to mount a new production of (an old play) [C15 from Old French *revivre* to live again, from Latin *revīvere*, from RE- + *vīvere* to live; see VIVID] > **re'vivable** *adj* > **re,viva'bility** *n* > **re'vivably** *adv* > **re'viver** *n* > **re'viving** *adj* > **re'vivingly** *adv*

revivify (rɪ'vɪvɪ,faɪ) *vb* **-fies, -fying, -fied** (*tr*) to give new life or spirit to; revive > **re,vivifi'cation** *n*

reviviscence (,rɛvɪ'vɪsəns, rɪ'vɪvɪsəns) *n* *rare* restoration to life or animation; revival [C17 from Latin, from *revīviscere* come back to life, related to *vīvere* to live; see REVIVE] > **,revi'viscent** *adj*

revocable ('rɛvəkəbᵊl) *or* **revokable** (rɪ'vəʊkəbᵊl) *adj* capable of being revoked; able to be cancelled > **,revoca'bility** *or* **re,voka'bility** *n* > **'revocably** *or* **re'vokably** *adv*

revocation (,rɛvə'keɪʃən) *n* **1** the act of revoking

r

or state of being revoked; cancellation **2 a** the cancellation or annulment of a legal instrument, esp a will **b** the withdrawal of an offer, power of attorney, etc > **revocatory** ('rɛvəkətərɪ, -trɪ) *adj*

revoice (riːˈvɔɪs) *vb* (*intr*) **1** to utter again; echo **2** to adjust the design of (an organ pipe or wind instrument) as after disuse or to conform with modern pitch

revoke (rɪˈvəʊk) *vb* **1** (*tr*) to take back or withdraw; cancel; rescind: *to revoke a law* **2** (*intr*) *cards* to break a rule of play by failing to follow suit when able to do so; renege ▷ *n* **3** *cards* the act of revoking; a renege [c14 from Latin *revocāre* to call back, withdraw, from RE- + *vocāre* to call] > **re'voker** *n*

revolt (rɪˈvəʊlt) *n* **1** a rebellion or uprising against authority **2 in revolt** in the process or state of rebelling ▷ *vb* **3** (*intr*) to rise up in rebellion against authority **4** (*usually passive*) to feel or cause to feel revulsion, disgust, or abhorrence [c16 from French *révolter* to revolt, from Old Italian *rivoltare* to overturn, ultimately from Latin *revolvere* to roll back, REVOLVE] > **re'volter** *n*

revolting (rɪˈvəʊltɪŋ) *adj* **1** causing revulsion; nauseating, disgusting, or repulsive **2** *informal* unpleasant or nasty > **re'voltingly** *adv*

revolute ('rɛvə,luːt) *adj* (*esp of the margins of a leaf*) rolled backwards and downwards [c18 from Latin *revolūtus* rolled back; see REVOLVE]

revolution (,rɛvəˈluːʃən) *n* **1** the overthrow or repudiation of a regime or political system by the governed **2** (*in Marxist theory*) the violent and historically necessary transition from one system of production in a society to the next, as from feudalism to capitalism **3** a far-reaching and drastic change, esp in ideas, methods, etc **4 a** movement in or as if in a circle **b** one complete turn in such a circle: *a turntable rotating at 33 revolutions per minute* **5 a** the orbital motion of one body, such as a planet or satellite, around another. Compare **rotation** (sense 5a) **b** one complete turn in such motion **6** a cycle of successive events or changes **7** *geology obsolete* a profound change in conditions over a large part of the earth's surface, esp one characterized by mountain building: *an orogenic revolution* [c14 via Old French from Late Latin *revolūtiō*, from Latin *revolvere* to REVOLVE]

revolutionary (,rɛvəˈluːʃənərɪ) *n, pl* **-aries 1** a person who advocates or engages in revolution ▷ *adj* **2** relating to or characteristic of a revolution **3** advocating or engaged in revolution **4** radically new or different **5** rotating or revolving > **,revo'lutionarily** *adv*

Revolutionary (,rɛvəˈluːʃənərɪ) *adj* **1** *chiefly US* of or relating to the conflict or period of the War of American Independence (1775–83) **2** of or relating to any of various other Revolutions, esp the **Russian Revolution** (1917) or the **French Revolution** (1789)

Revolutionary calendar *n* the calendar adopted by the French First Republic in 1793 and abandoned in 1805. Dates were calculated from Sept 22, 1792. The months were called Vendémiaire, Brumaire, Frimaire, Nivôse, Pluviôse, Ventôse, Germinal, Floréal, Prairial, Messidor, Thermidor, and Fructidor

Revolutionary Wars *pl n* the series of wars (1792–1802) fought against Revolutionary France by a combination of other powers, esp Britain, Austria, and Prussia

revolutionist (,rɛvəˈluːʃənɪst) *n* **1** a less common word for a **revolutionary** ▷ *adj* **2** of, characteristic of, or relating to revolution or revolutionaries

revolutionize *or* **revolutionise** (,rɛvəˈluːʃə,naɪz) *vb* (*tr*) **1** to bring about a radical change in: *science has revolutionized civilization* **2** to inspire or infect with revolutionary ideas: *they revolutionized the common soldiers* **3** to cause a revolution in (a country, etc) > **,revo'lution,izer** *or* **,revo'lution,iser** *n*

revolve (rɪˈvɒlv) *vb* **1** to move or cause to move around a centre or axis; rotate **2** (*intr*) to occur periodically or in cycles **3** to consider or be considered **4** (*intr*; foll by *around* or *about*) to be

centred or focused (upon) ▷ *n* **5** *theatre* a circular section of a stage that can be rotated by electric power to provide a scene change [c14 from Latin *revolvere*, from RE- + *volvere* to roll, wind] > **re'volvable** *adj* > **re'volvably** *adv*

revolver (rɪˈvɒlvə) *n* a pistol having a revolving multichambered cylinder that allows several shots to be discharged without reloading

revolving (rɪˈvɒlvɪŋ) *adj* denoting or relating to an engine, such as a radial aero engine, in which the cylinders revolve about a fixed shaft > **re'volvingly** *adv*

revolving credit *n* a letter of credit for a fixed sum, specifying that the beneficiary may make repeated use of the credit provided that the fixed sum is never exceeded

revolving door *n* **1** a door that rotates about a central vertical axis, esp one with four leaves arranged at right angles to each other, thereby excluding draughts **2 a** *informal* a tendency to change personnel on a frequent basis **b** (*as modifier*): *a revolving-door band* **3 a** *informal* the hiring of former government employees by private companies with which they had dealings when they worked for the government **b** (*as modifier*): *revolving-door consultancies*

revolving fund *n* a fund set up for a specific purpose and constantly added to by income from its investments

revue *or less commonly* **review** (rɪˈvjuː) *n* a form of light entertainment consisting of a series of topical sketches, songs, dancing, comic turns, etc [c20 from French; see REVIEW]

revulsion (rɪˈvʌlʃən) *n* **1** a sudden and unpleasant violent reaction in feeling, esp one of extreme loathing **2** the act or an instance of drawing back or recoiling from something **3** *obsolete* the diversion of disease or congestion from one part of the body to another by cupping, counterirritants, etc [c16 from Latin *revulsiō* a pulling away, from *revellere*, from RE- + *vellere* to pull, tear] > **re'vulsionary** *adj*

revulsive (rɪˈvʌlsɪv) *adj* **1** of or causing revulsion ▷ *n* **2** *med* a counterirritant > **re'vulsively** *adv*

Rev. Ver. *abbreviation for* Revised Version (of the Bible)

reward (rɪˈwɔːd) *n* **1** something given or received in return for a deed or service rendered **2** a sum of money offered, esp for help in finding a criminal or for the return of lost or stolen property **3** profit or return **4** something received in return for good or evil **5** *psychol* any pleasant event that follows a response and therefore increases the likelihood of the response recurring in the future ▷ *vb* **6** (*tr*) to give (something) to (someone), esp in gratitude for a service rendered [c14 from Old Norman French *rewarder* to regard, from RE- + *warder* to care for, guard, of Germanic origin; see WARD] > **re'wardable** *adj* > **re'warder** *n* > **re'wardless** *adj*

reward claim *n* *Austral history* a claim granted to a miner who discovered gold in a new area

rewarding (rɪˈwɔːdɪŋ) *adj* giving personal satisfaction; gratifying: *caring for the elderly is rewarding*

rewa-rewa ('reɪwəˈreɪwə) *n* a tall proteaceous tree of New Zealand, *Knightia excelsa*, yielding a beautiful reddish timber [c19 from Māori]

rewind *vb* (riːˈwaɪnd) **-winds, -winding, -wound 1** (*tr*) to wind back, esp a film or tape onto the original reel ▷ *n* ('riː,waɪnd, riːˈwaɪnd) **2** something rewound **3** the act of rewinding > **re'winder** *n*

rewire (riːˈwaɪə) *vb* (*tr*) to provide (a house, engine, etc) with new wiring > **re'wirable** *adj*

reword (riːˈwɜːd) *vb* (*tr*) to alter the wording of; express differently

rework (riːˈwɜːk) *vb* (*tr*) **1** to use again in altered form **2** to rewrite or revise **3** to reprocess for use again

reworked fossil (riːˈwɜːkt) *n* a fossil eroded from sediment and redeposited in younger sediment.

Also called: **derived fossil**

rewrite *vb* (riːˈraɪt) **-writes, -writing, -wrote, -written** (*tr*) **1** to write (written material) again, esp changing the words or form **2** *computing* to return (data) to a store when it has been erased during reading ▷ *n* ('riː,raɪt) **3** something rewritten

rewrite rule *n* *generative grammar* another name for **phrase-structure rule**

Rex (rɛks) *n* king: part of the official title of a king, now used chiefly in documents, legal proceedings, inscriptions on coins, etc. Compare **Regina¹** [Latin]

Rexine ('rɛksiːn) *n* *trademark* a form of artificial leather

Reye's syndrome (raɪz, reɪz) *n* a rare metabolic disease in children that can be fatal, involving damage to the brain, liver, and kidneys [c20 named after R D K *Reye* (1912–78) Australian paediatrician]

Reykjavik ('reɪkjə,viːk) *n* the capital and chief port of Iceland, situated in the southwest: its buildings are heated by natural hot water. Pop: 112 490 (2003 est)

Reynard ('rɛnəd, 'rɛnɑːd, 'reɪnəd, 'reɪnɑːd) *n* a name for a fox, used in medieval tales, fables, etc [from earlier *Renard, Renart*, hero of the French bestiary *Roman de Renart*: ultimately from the Old High German name *Reginhart*, literally: strong in counsel]

Reynolds number *n* a dimensionless number, $vρl/η$, where v is the fluid velocity, $ρ$ the density, $η$ the viscosity and l a dimension of the system. The value of the number indicates the type of fluid flow [c19 named after Osborne *Reynolds* (1842–1912), British physicist]

Reynosa (*Spanish* reˈnosa) *n* a city in E Mexico, in Tamaulipas state on the Rio Grande. Pop: 847 000 (2005 est)

rf *music abbreviation for* rinforzando. Also: **rfz**

Rf *the chemical symbol for* rutherfordium

RF *abbreviation for* **radio frequency**

RF- (*in the US Air Force*) *abbreviation for* reconnaissance fighter: *RF-4E*

RFC *abbreviation for* **1** Rugby Football Club **2** Royal Flying Corps

RFID *abbreviation for* radio-frequency identity (*or* identification): a technology that uses tiny computer chips to track items such as consumer commodities at a distance

RFLP *abbreviation for* restriction fragment length polymorphism: any variation in DNA between individuals revealed by restriction enzymes that cut DNA into fragments of different lengths in consequence of such variations. It is used forensically and in the diagnosis of hereditary disease

RG *international car registration for* (Republic of) Guinea

RGB *abbreviation for* red, green, blue: *RGB components of a colour; RGB signal*

RGN (*in Britain*) *abbreviation for* **Registered General Nurse**

RGS *abbreviation for* Royal Geographical Society

Rgt *abbreviation for* regiment

rh *or* **RH** *abbreviation for* right hand

Rh 1 *the chemical symbol for* rhodium **2** ▷ *abbreviation for* rhesus (esp in **Rh factor**)

RH 1 *abbreviation for* Royal Highness **2** *international car registration for* (Republic of) Haiti

RHA *abbreviation for* **1** Regional Health Authority **2** Royal Horse Artillery

rhabdomancy ('ræbdə,mænsɪ) *n* divination for water or mineral ore by means of a rod or wand; dowsing; divining [c17 via Late Latin from Late Greek *rhabdomanteia*, from *rhabdos* a rod + *manteia* divination] > **'rhabdo,mantist** *or* **'rhabdo,mancer** *n*

rhabdomyoma (,ræbdəʊmaɪˈəʊmə) *n, pl* **-mas** *or* **-mata** (-mətə) *pathol* a benign tumour of striated muscle [c19 from New Latin, from Greek *rhabdos* a rod + MYOMA]

rhachilla (rəˈkɪlə) *n* a variant spelling of **rachilla**

rhachis ('reɪkɪs) n, pl **rhachises** or **rhachides** ('ræki,di:z, 'reɪ-) a variant spelling of **rachis**

Rhadamanthus or **Rhadamanthys** (,rædə'mænθəs) n Greek myth one of the judges of the dead in the underworld ▷ ,Rhada'manthine adj

Rhaetia ('ri:ʃɪə) n an Alpine province of ancient Rome including parts of present-day Tyrol and E Switzerland

Rhaetian ('ri:ʃən) n **1** Also called: **Rhaeto-Romanic** ('ri:təʊrəʊ'mænɪk) a group of Romance languages or dialects spoken in certain valleys of the Alps, including Romansch, Ladin, and Friulian ▷ adj **2** denoting or relating to this group of languages **3** of or relating to Rhaetia

Rhaetian Alps pl n a section of the central Alps along E Switzerland's borders with Austria and Italy. Highest peak: Piz Bernina, 4049 m (13 284 ft)

Rhaetic or **Rhetic** ('ri:tɪk) adj **1** of or relating to a series of rocks formed in the late Triassic period ▷ n **2 the** the Rhaetic series

Rhamadhan (,ræmə'dɑ:n) n a variant spelling of **Ramadan**

rhamnaceous (ræm'neɪʃəs) adj of, relating to, or belonging to the *Rhamnaceae*, a widely distributed family of trees and shrubs having small inconspicuous flowers. The family includes the buckthorns [c19 from New Latin *Rhamnaceae*, from Greek *rhamnos* a thorn]

rhanja (rɑ:n'dʒɑ:) n Hinglish informal a male lover [after the male lover in a famous Punjabi love story]

rhapsodic (ræp'sɒdɪk) adj **1** of or like a rhapsody **2** lyrical or romantic ▷ rhap'sodically adv

rhapsodist ('ræpsədɪst) n **1** a person who speaks or writes rhapsodies **2** a person who speaks with extravagant enthusiasm **3** Also called: **rhapsode** ('ræpsəʊd) (in ancient Greece) a professional reciter of poetry, esp of Homer ▷ ,rhapso'distic adj

rhapsodize or **rhapsodise** ('ræpsə,daɪz) vb **1** to speak or write (something) with extravagant enthusiasm **2** (intr) to recite or write rhapsodies

rhapsody ('ræpsədɪ) n, pl **-dies 1** music a composition free in structure and highly emotional in character **2** an expression of ecstatic enthusiasm **3** (in ancient Greece) an epic poem or part of an epic recited by a rhapsodist **4** a literary work composed in an intense or exalted style **5** rapturous delight or ecstasy **6** obsolete a medley [c16 via Latin from Greek *rhapsōidia*, from *rhaptein* to sew together + *ōidē* song]

rhatany ('rætənɪ) n, pl **-nies 1** either of two South American leguminous shrubs, *Krameria triandra* or *K. argentea*, that have thick fleshy roots **2** the dried roots of such shrubs used as an astringent ▷ Also called: **krameria** [c19 from New Latin *rhatānia*, ultimately from Quechua *ratánya*]

rhd abbreviation for right-hand drive

rhea ('rɪə) n either of two large fast-running flightless birds, *Rhea americana* or *Pterocnemia pennata*, inhabiting the open plains of S South America: order *Rheiformes* (see **ratite**). They are similar to but smaller than the ostrich, having three-toed feet and a completely feathered body [c19 New Latin; arbitrarily named after RHEA[1]]

Rhea[1] ('rɪə) n Greek myth a Titaness, wife of Cronus and mother of several of the gods, including Zeus: a fertility goddess. Roman counterpart: **Ops**

Rhea[2] ('rɪə) n the second largest satellite of the planet Saturn

Rhea Silvia or **Rea Silvia** ('sɪlvɪə) n Roman myth the mother of Romulus and Remus by Mars. See also **Ilia**

rhebok or **reebok** ('ri:bʌk, -bɒk) n, pl **-boks** or **-bok** an antelope, *Pelea capreolus*, of southern Africa, having woolly brownish-grey hair [c18 Afrikaans, from Dutch *reebok* ROEBUCK]

Rheims (ri:mz) n French rēs) n a variant spelling of **Reims**

Rhein (rain) n the German name for the **Rhine**

Rheinland ('rainlant) n the German name for the **Rhineland**

Rheinland-Pfalz ('rainlant'pfalts) n the German name for **Rhineland-Palatinate**

rheme (ri:m) n linguistics the constituent of a sentence that adds most new information, in addition to what has already been said in the discourse. The rheme is usually, but not always, associated with the subject. Compare **theme** (sense 5) [c20 from Greek *rhēma* that which is said]

Rhemish ('ri:mɪʃ) adj of, relating to, or originating in Reims

Rhenish ('rɛnɪʃ, 'ri:-) adj **1** of or relating to the River Rhine or the lands adjacent to it, esp the Rhineland-Palatinate ▷ n **2** another word for **hock** (the wine)

rhenium ('ri:nɪəm) n a dense silvery-white metallic element that has a high melting point. It occurs principally in gadolinite and molybdenite and is used, alloyed with tungsten or molybdenum, in high-temperature thermocouples. Symbol: Re; atomic no: 75; atomic wt: 186.207; valency: –1 or 1–7; relative density: 21.02; melting pt: 3186°C; boiling pt: 5596°C (est) [c19 New Latin, from *Rhēnus* the Rhine]

rheo- combining form indicating stream, flow, or current: *rheometer; rheoscope* [from Greek *rheos* stream, anything flowing, from *rhein* to flow]

rheobase ('ri:əʊ,beɪs) n physiol the minimum nerve impulse required to elicit a response from a tissue

rheology (rɪ'ɒlədʒɪ) n the branch of physics concerned with the flow and change of shape of matter ▷ rheological (,ri:ə'lɒdʒɪkªl) adj ▷ rhe'ologist n

rheometer (rɪ'ɒmɪtə) n **1** med an instrument for measuring the velocity of the blood flow **2** another word for **galvanometer**. ▷ rheometric (,ri:ə'mɛtrɪk) adj ▷ rhe'ometry n

rheomorphism (,ri:ə'mɔ:fɪzəm) n geology the liquefaction of rock, which results in its flowing and intruding into surrounding rocks ▷ ,rheo'morphic adj

rheoreceptor ('ri:əri,sɛptə) n zoology a receptor in fish and some amphibians that responds to water currents

rheostat ('ri:ə,stæt) n a variable resistance, usually consisting of a coil of wire with a terminal at one end and a sliding contact that moves along the coil to tap off the current ▷ ,rheo'static adj

rheotaxis (,ri:ə'tæksɪs) n movement of an organism towards or away from a current of water ▷ ,rheo'tactik adj

rheotropism (rɪ'ɒtrə,pɪzəm) n growth of a plant or sessile animal in the direction of a current of water ▷ rheotropic (,ri:ə'trɒpɪk) adj

Rhesus ('ri:səs) n Greek myth a king of Thrace, who arrived in the tenth year of the Trojan War to aid Troy. Odysseus and Diomedes stole his horses because an oracle had said that if these horses drank from the River Xanthus, Troy would not fall

rhesus baby ('ri:səs) n a baby suffering from haemolytic disease at birth as its red blood cells (which are Rh positive) have been attacked in the womb by antibodies from its Rh negative mother. Technical name: **erythroblastosis fetalis** [c20 see RH FACTOR]

rhesus factor n See **Rh factor**

rhesus monkey n a macaque monkey, *Macaca mulatta*, of S Asia: used extensively in medical research [c19 New Latin, arbitrarily from Greek *Rhesos* RHESUS]

Rhetic ('ri:tɪk) adj, n a variant spelling of **Rhaetic**

rhetor ('ri:tə) n **1** a teacher of rhetoric **2** (in ancient Greece) an orator [c14 via Latin from Greek *rhētōr*; related to *rhēma* word]

rhetoric ('rɛtərɪk) n **1** the study of the technique of using language effectively **2** the art of using speech to persuade, influence, or please **3** excessive use of ornamentation and contrivance in spoken or written discourse **4** speech or discourse that pretends to significance but lacks true meaning [c14 via Latin from Greek *rhētorikē (tekhnē)* (the art of) rhetoric, from *rhētōr* RHETOR]

rhetorical (rɪ'tɒrɪkªl) adj **1** concerned with effect or style rather than content or meaning; bombastic **2** of or relating to rhetoric or oratory ▷ rhe'torically adv

rhetorical question n a question to which no answer is required: used esp for dramatic effect. An example is *Who knows?* (with the implication *Nobody knows*)

rhetorician (,rɛtə'rɪʃən) n **1** a teacher of the art of rhetoric **2** a stylish or eloquent writer or speaker **3** a person whose speech is pompous or extravagant

rheum (ru:m) n a watery discharge from the eyes or nose [c14 from Old French *reume*, ultimately from Greek *rheuma* bodily humour, stream, from *rhein* to flow]

rheumatic (ru:'mætɪk) adj **1** of, relating to, or afflicted with rheumatism ▷ n **2** a person afflicted with rheumatism [c14 ultimately from Greek *rheumatikos*, from *rheuma* a flow; see RHEUM] ▷ rheu'matically adv

rheumatic fever n a disease characterized by sore throat, fever, inflammation, and pain in the joints

rheumatics (ru:'mætɪks) n (functioning as singular) informal rheumatism

rheumatism ('ru:mə,tɪzəm) n any painful disorder of joints, muscles, or connective tissue. Compare **arthritis, fibrositis** [c17 from Latin *rheumatismus* catarrh, from Greek *rheumatismos*; see RHEUM]

rheumatoid ('ru:mə,tɔɪd) adj (of the symptoms of a disease) resembling rheumatism ▷ ,rheuma'toidally adv

rheumatoid arthritis n a chronic disease of the musculoskeletal system, characterized by inflammation and swelling of joints (esp joints in the hands, wrists, knees, and feet), muscle weakness, and fatigue

rheumatology (,ru:mə'tɒlədʒɪ) n the branch of medicine concerned with the study of rheumatic diseases ▷ rheumatological (,ru:mətə'lɒdʒɪkªl) adj ▷ ,rheuma'tologist n

rheumy ('ru:mɪ) adj **1** of the nature of rheum **2** literary damp and unhealthy: *the rheumy air*

rhexis ('rɛksɪs) n med the rupture of an organ or blood vessel [c17 from Greek *rhēxis* a bursting]

Rh factor n an agglutinogen commonly found in human blood: it may cause a haemolytic reaction, esp during pregnancy or following transfusion of blood that does not contain the agglutinogen. Full name: **rhesus factor** See also **Rh positive, Rh negative** [c20 named after the rhesus monkey, in which it was first discovered]

RHG abbreviation for Royal Horse Guards

rhigolene ('rɪgəʊ,li:n) n a volatile liquid obtained from petroleum and used as a local anaesthetic [c19 from Greek *rhigos* cold; see -OLE, -ENE]

rhinal ('raɪnªl) adj of or relating to the nose; nasal [c19 from Greek *rhis, rhin*]

Rhine (raɪn) n a river in central and W Europe, rising in SE Switzerland: flows through Lake Constance north through W Germany and west through the Netherlands to the North Sea. Length: about 1320 km (820 miles). Dutch name: Rijn French name: Rhin (rē) German name: Rhein

Rhineland ('raɪn,lænd, -lənd) n the region of Germany surrounding the Rhine. German name: Rheinland

Rhineland-Palatinate n a state of W Germany: formed in 1946 from the S part of the Prussian Rhine province, the Palatinate, and parts of Rhine-Hesse and Hesse-Nassau; part of West Germany until 1990: agriculture (with extensive vineyards) and tourism are important. Capital: Mainz. Pop: 4 059 000 (2003 est). Area: 19 832 sq km (7657 sq miles). German name: Rheinland-Pfalz

rhinencephalon (,raɪnɛn'sɛfə,lɒn) n, pl **-lons** or **-la** (-lə) anatomy the parts of the brain, in both cerebral hemispheres, that in the early stages of evolution were concerned with the sense of smell. It includes the olefactory bulb and tract and the

r

regions of the limbic system [c19 from RHINO- + ENCEPHALON] > **rhinencephalic** (ˌraɪnɛnsɪ'fælɪk) adj

Rhine Palatinate n See **Palatinate**

rhinestone ('raɪnˌstəʊn) n an imitation gem made of paste [c19 translation of French *caillou du Rhin*, referring to Strasbourg, where such gems were made]

Rhine wine n any of several wines produced along the banks of the Rhine, characteristically a white table wine such as Riesling

rhinitis (raɪ'naɪtɪs) n inflammation of the mucous membrane that lines the nose > **rhinitic** (raɪ'nɪtɪk) adj

rhino¹ ('raɪnəʊ) n, pl **-nos** or **-no** short for **rhinoceros**

rhino² ('raɪnəʊ) n Brit a slang word for **money** [c17 of unknown origin]

rhino- or before a vowel **rhin-** combining form indicating the nose or nasal: rhinology [from Greek *rhis*, *rhin*]

rhinoceros (raɪ'nɒsərəs, -'nɒsrəs) n, pl **-oses** or **-os** any of several perissodactyl mammals constituting the family *Rhinocerotidae* of SE Asia and Africa and having either one horn on the nose, like the **Indian rhinoceros** (*Rhinoceros unicornis*), or two horns, like the African **white rhinoceros** (*Diceros simus*) They have a very thick skin, massive body, and three digits on each foot [c13 via Latin from Greek *rhinokerōs*, from *rhis* nose + *keras* horn] > **rhinocerotic** (ˌraɪnəʊsɪ'rɒtɪk) adj

rhinoceros beetle n any of various scarabaeid beetles having one or more horns on the head, esp *Oryctes rhinoceros*, a serious pest on coconut plantations

rhinoceros bird n another name for the **oxpecker**

rhinology (raɪ'nɒlədʒɪ) n the branch of medical science concerned with the nose and its diseases > **rhinological** (ˌraɪnª'lɒdʒɪkªl) adj > **rhi'nologist** n

rhinoplasty ('raɪnəʊˌplæstɪ) n plastic surgery of the nose > ˌrhino'plastic adj

rhinoscopy (raɪ'nɒskəpɪ) n med examination of the nasal passages, esp with a special instrument called a **rhinoscope** ('raɪnəʊˌskəʊp) > **rhinoscopic** (ˌraɪnəʊ'skɒpɪk) adj

rhizo- or before a vowel **rhiz-** combining form root: rhizomorphous [from Greek *rhiza*]

rhizobium (raɪ'zəʊbɪəm) n, pl **-bia** (-bɪə) any rod-shaped bacterium of the genus *Rhizobium*, typically occurring in the root nodules of leguminous plants and able to fix atmospheric nitrogen. See also **nitrogen fixation** [c20 from RHIZO- + Greek *bios* life]

rhizocarpous (ˌraɪzəʊ'kɑːpəs) adj **1** (of plants) producing subterranean flowers and fruit **2** (of perennial plants) having roots that persist throughout the year but stems and leaves that wither at the end of the growing season

rhizocephalan (ˌraɪzəʊ'sɛfələn) n **1** any parasitic crustacean of the order *Rhizocephala*, esp *Sacculina carcini*, which has a saclike body and sends out absorptive processes into the body of its host, the crab: subclass *Cirripedia* (barnacles) ▷ adj also **rhizocephalous 2** of, relating to, or belonging to the order *Rhizocephala* [c19 from New Latin *Rhizocephala* (literally: root-headed), from RHIZO- + *-cephala* from Greek *kephalē* head]

rhizogenic (ˌraɪzəʊ'dʒɛnɪk), **rhizogenetic** (ˌraɪzəʊdʒə'nɛtɪk) or **rhizogenous** (raɪ'zɒdʒənəs) adj (of cells and tissues) giving rise to roots

rhizoid ('raɪzɔɪd) n any of various slender hairlike structures that function as roots in the gametophyte generation of mosses, ferns, and related plants > **rhi'zoidal** adj

rhizome ('raɪzəʊm) n a thick horizontal underground stem of plants such as the mint and iris whose buds develop new roots and shoots. Also called: **rootstock, rootstalk** [c19 from New Latin *rhizoma*, from Greek, from *rhiza* a root] > **rhizomatous** (raɪ'zɒmətəs, -'zəʊ-) adj

rhizomorph ('raɪzəʊˌmɔːf) n a rootlike structure of certain fungi, such as the honey fungus *Armillaria mellea*, consisting of a dense mass of hyphae

rhizomorphous (ˌraɪzəʊ'mɔːfəs) adj botany having the appearance of a root

rhizopod ('raɪzəʊˌpɒd) n **1** any protozoan of the phylum *Rhizopoda*, characterized by naked protoplasmic processes (pseudopodia). The group includes the amoebas ▷ adj **2** of, relating to, or belonging to the *Rhizopoda* > **rhizopodan** (raɪ'zɒpədən) adj, n > **rhi'zopodous** adj

rhizopus ('raɪzəʊpəs) n any zygomycetous fungus of the genus *Rhizopus*, esp *R. nigricans*, a bread mould [c19 New Latin, from RHIZO- + Greek *pous* foot]

rhizosphere ('raɪzəʊˌsfɪə) n the region of the soil in contact with the roots of a plant. It contains many microorganisms and its composition is affected by root activities

rhizotomy (raɪ'zɒtəmɪ) n, pl **-mies** surgical incision into the roots of spinal nerves, esp for the relief of pain

Rh negative n **1** blood that does not contain the Rh factor **2** a person having such blood

rho (rəʊ) n, pl **rhos** the 17th letter in the Greek alphabet (P, ρ), a consonant transliterated as *r* or *rh*

rhodamine ('rəʊdəˌmiːn, -mɪn) n any one of a group of synthetic red or pink basic dyestuffs used for wool and silk. They are made from phthalic anhydride and aminophenols [c20 from RHODO- + AMINE]

Rhode Island (rəʊd) n a state of the northeastern US, bordering on the Atlantic: the smallest state in the US; mainly low-lying and undulating, with an indented coastline in the east and uplands in the northwest. Capital: Providence. Pop: 1 076 164 (2003 est). Area: 2717 sq km (1049 sq miles). Abbreviations: **R.I,** (with zip code) **RI**

Rhode Island Red n a breed of domestic fowl, originating in America, characterized by a dark reddish-brown plumage and the production of brown eggs

Rhodes (rəʊdz) n **1** a Greek island in the SE Aegean Sea, about 16 km (10 miles) off the Turkish coast: the largest of the Dodecanese and the most easterly island in the Aegean. Capital: Rhodes. Pop: 117 007 (2001). Area: 1400 sq km (540 sq miles) **2** a port on this island, in the NE: founded in 408 BC; of great commercial and political importance in the 3rd century BC; suffered several earthquakes, notably in 225, when the Colossus was destroyed. Pop: 41 000 (latest est) ▷ Ancient Greek name: **Rhodos** Modern Greek name: **Ródhos**

Rhodes grass n a perennial grass, *Chloris gayana*, native to Africa but widely cultivated in dry regions for forage [c19 named after Cecil John Rhodes (1853–1902), British colonial financier and statesman]

Rhodesia (rəʊ'diːʃə, -zɪə) n a former name (1964–79) for **Zimbabwe**

Rhodesian (rəʊ'diːʃən, -zɪən) adj **1** of or relating to the former Rhodesia (now Zimbabwe) or its inhabitants ▷ n **2** a native or inhabitant of the former Rhodesia

Rhodesian Front n the governing party in Zimbabwe (then called Rhodesia) 1962–78

Rhodesian man n a type of early man, *Homo rhodesiensis* (or *H. sapiens rhodesiensis*), occurring in Africa in late Pleistocene times and resembling Neanderthal man in many features

Rhodesian ridgeback ('rɪdʒˌbæk) n a large short-haired breed of dog characterized by a ridge of hair growing along the back in the opposite direction to the rest of the coat. It was originally a hunting dog from South Africa

Rhodesoid (rəʊ'diːzɔɪd) adj relating to or resembling Rhodesian man

Rhodes scholarship n one of 72 scholarships founded by Cecil Rhodes, awarded annually on merit to Commonwealth and US students to study for two or sometimes three years at Oxford University > **Rhodes scholar** n

Rhodian ('rəʊdɪən) adj **1** of or relating to the island of Rhodes ▷ n **2** a native or inhabitant of Rhodes

rhodic ('rəʊdɪk) adj of or containing rhodium, esp in the tetravalent state

rhodinal ('rəʊdɪˌnæl) n another name for **citronellal**

rhodium ('rəʊdɪəm) n a hard corrosion-resistant silvery-white element of the platinum metal group, occurring free with other platinum metals in alluvial deposits and in nickel ores. It is used as an alloying agent to harden platinum and palladium. Symbol: Rh; atomic no: 45; atomic wt: 102.90550; valency: 2–6; relative density: 12.41; melting pt: 1963±3°C; boiling pt: 3697±100°C [c19 New Latin, from Greek *rhodon* rose, from the pink colour of its compounds]

rhodo- or before a vowel **rhod-** combining form rose or rose-coloured: rhododendron; rhodolite [from Greek *rhodon* rose]

rhodochrosite (ˌrəʊdəʊ'krəʊsaɪt) n a pink, red, grey, or brown mineral that consists of manganese carbonate in hexagonal crystalline form and occurs in ore veins. Formula: $MnCO_3$ [c19 from Greek *rhodokhrōs* of a rosy colour, from *rhodon* rose + *khrōs* colour]

rhododendron (ˌrəʊdə'dɛndrən) n any ericaceous shrub of the genus *Rhododendron*, native to S Asia but widely cultivated in N temperate regions. They are mostly evergreen and have clusters of showy red, purple, pink, or white flowers. Also called (US): **rosebay** See also **azalea** [c17 from Latin: oleander, from Greek, from *rhodon* rose + *dendron* tree]

rhododendron bug n See **lace bug**

rhodolite ('rəʊdəˌlaɪt) n a pale violet or red variety of garnet, used as a gemstone

rhodonite ('rəʊdəˌnaɪt) n a brownish translucent mineral consisting of manganese silicate in triclinic crystalline form with calcium, iron, or magnesium sometimes replacing the manganese. It occurs in metamorphic rocks, esp in New Jersey and Russia, and is used as an ornamental stone, glaze, and pigment. Formula: $MnSiO_3$ [c19 from German *Rhodonit*, from Greek *rhodon* rose + -ITE]

Rhodope Mountains ('rɒdəpɪ, rɒ'dəʊ-) pl n a mountain range in SE Europe, in the Balkan Peninsula extending along the border between Bulgaria and Greece. Highest peak: Golyam Perelik (Bulgaria), 2191 m (7188 ft)

rhodopsin (rəʊ'dɒpsɪn) n a red pigment in the rods of the retina in vertebrates. It is dissociated by light into retinene, the light energy being converted into nerve signals, and is re-formed in the dark. Also called: **visual purple** See also **iodopsin** [c20 from RHODO- + -OPSIS + -IN]

Rhodos ('rɒðɒs) n the Ancient Greek name for **Rhodes**

rhoicissus (ˌrəʊɪ'sɪsəs) n any plant of the climbing genus *Rhoicissus*, related to and resembling cissus, esp *R. rhomboidea* (grape ivy), grown for its shiny evergreen foliage: family *Vitaceae* [New Latin, from Greek *rhoia* pomegranate + CISSUS]

rhomb (rɒm) n another name for **rhombus**

rhombencephalon (ˌrɒmbɛn'sɛfəˌlɒn) n the part of the brain that develops from the posterior portion of the embryonic neural tube and comprises the cerebellum, pons, and the medulla oblongata. Compare **mesencephalon, prosencephalon** Nontechnical name: **hindbrain** [c20 from RHOMBUS + ENCEPHALON]

rhombic ('rɒmbɪk) adj **1** relating to or having the shape of a rhombus **2** crystallog another word for **orthorhombic**

rhombic aerial n a directional travelling-wave aerial, usually horizontal, consisting of two conductors each forming a pair of adjacent sides of a rhombus

rhombohedral (ˌrɒmbəʊ'hiːdrəl) adj **1** of or relating to a rhombohedron **2** crystallog another term for **trigonal** (sense 2)

rhombohedron (ˌrɒmbəʊˈhiːdrən) *n* a six-sided prism whose sides are parallelograms [C19 from RHOMBUS + -HEDRON]

rhomboid (ˈrɒmbɔɪd) *n* 1 a parallelogram having adjacent sides of unequal length ▷ *adj also* rhomˈboidal 2 having such a shape [C16 from Late Latin *rhomboides*, from Greek *rhomboeidēs* shaped like a RHOMBUS]

rhomboideus (rɒmˈbɔɪdɪəs) *n*, *pl* -dei (-dɪˌaɪ) *anatomy* either of two muscles that connect the spinal vertebrae to the scapulae [C19 New Latin, from Late Latin *rhomboides*: see RHOMBOID]

rhombus (ˈrɒmbəs) *n*, *pl* -buses *or* -bi (-baɪ) an oblique-angled parallelogram having four equal sides. Also called: rhomb Compare **square** (sense 1) [C16 from Greek *rhombos* something that spins; related to *rhembein* to whirl]

rhonchus (ˈrɒŋkəs) *n*, *pl* -chi (-kaɪ) a rattling or whistling respiratory sound resembling snoring, caused by secretions in the trachea or bronchi [C19 from Latin, from Greek *rhenkhos* snoring] > ˈrhonchal *or* ˈrhonchial *adj*

Rhondda (ˈrɒndə; *Welsh* ˈhrɔnða) *n* an urban area in S Wales, in Rhondda Cynon Taff county borough on two branches of the **Rhondda Valley**: developed into a major coal-mining centre after 1807 and grew to a population of 167 900 in 1924: the last coal mine closed in 1990. Pop: 59 947 (1991)

Rhondda Cynon Taff (ˈrɒndə ˈkʊnən ˈtæf) *n* a county borough in S Wales, created from part of Mid Glamorgan in 1996. Pop: 231 600 (2003 est). Area: 558 sq km (215 sq miles)

Rhône (rəʊn) *n* 1 a river in W Europe, rising in S Switzerland in the **Rhône glacier** and flowing to Lake Geneva, then into France through gorges between the Alps and Jura and south to its delta on the Gulf of Lions: important esp for hydroelectricity and for wine production along its valley. Length: 812 km (505 miles) 2 a department of E central France, in the Rhône-Alpes region. Capital: Lyon. Pop: 1 621 718 (2003 est). Area: 3233 sq km (1261 sq miles)

Rhône-Alpes (*French* ronalp) *n* a region of E France: mainly mountainous, rising to the edge of the Massif Central in the west and the French Alps in the east; drained by the Rivers Rhône, Saône, and Isère

rhotacism (ˈrəʊtəˌsɪzəm) *n* excessive use or idiosyncratic pronunciation of r [C19 from New Latin *rhōtacismus*, from Greek *rhōtakizein* (verb) from the letter *rho*] > ˈrhotacist *n* > ˌrhotaˈcistic *adj*

rhotic (ˈrəʊtɪk) *adj phonetics* denoting or speaking a dialect of English in which postvocalic rs are pronounced [from Greek *rho*, the letter r] > ˈrhoticity (ˈtɪsɪtɪ) *n*

Rh positive *n* 1 blood containing the Rh factor 2 a person having such blood

RHS *abbreviation for* 1 Royal Historical Society 2 Royal Horticultural Society 3 Royal Humane Society

rhubarb (ˈruːbɑːb) *n* 1 any of several temperate and subtropical plants of the polygonaceous genus *Rheum*, esp *R. rhaponticum* (**common garden rhubarb**), which has long green and red acid-tasting edible leafstalks, usually eaten sweetened and cooked 2 the leafstalks of this plant 3 a related plant, *Rheum officinale*, of central Asia, having a bitter-tasting underground stem that can be dried and used medicinally as a laxative or astringent 4 *US and Canadian slang* a heated discussion or quarrel ▷ *interj* ▷ *n*, *vb* 5 the noise made by actors to simulate conversation, esp by repeating the word *rhubarb* at random [C14 from Old French *reubarbe*, from Medieval Latin *reubarbum*, probably a variant of *rha barbarum* barbarian rhubarb, from *rha* rhubarb (from Greek, perhaps from *Rha* ancient name of the Volga) + Latin *barbarus* barbarian]

rhumb (rʌm) *n* short for **rhumb line**

rhumba (ˈrʌmbə, ˈrʊm-) *n*, *pl* -bas a variant spelling of **rumba**

rhumbatron (ˈrʌmbəˌtrɒn) *n* another name for

cavity resonator [C20 from RHUMBA + TRON, from the rhythmic variation of the waves]

rhumb line *n* 1 an imaginary line on the surface of a sphere, such as the earth, that intersects all meridians at the same angle 2 the course navigated by a vessel or aircraft that maintains a uniform compass heading ▷ Often shortened to: rhumb [C16 from Old Spanish *rumbo*, apparently from Middle Dutch *ruum* space, ship's hold, but also influenced by Latin RHOMBUS]

rhus (rʊs) *n* any shrub or small tree of the anacardiaceous genus *Rhus*, several species of which are cultivated as ornamentals for their foliage, which assumes brilliant colours in autumn ▷ See also **sumach**

rhyme *or archaic* **rime** (raɪm) *n* 1 identity of the terminal sounds in lines of verse or in words 2 a word that is identical to another in its terminal sound: *"while" is a rhyme for "mile"* 3 a verse or piece of poetry having corresponding sounds at the ends of the lines 4 any verse or piece of poetry 5 rhyme or reason sense, logic, or meaning: *this proposal has no rhyme or reason* ▷ *vb* 6 to use (a word) or (of a word) to be used so as to form a rhyme; be or make identical in sound 7 to render (a subject) into rhyme 8 to compose (verse) in a metrical structure ▷ See also **masculine rhyme, feminine rhyme, eye rhyme** [C12 from Old French *rime*, from *rimer* to rhyme, from Old High German *rīm* a number; spelling influenced by RHYTHM] > ˈrhymeless *or* ˈrimeless *adj*

rhyme royal *n prosody* a stanzaic form introduced into English verse by Chaucer, consisting of seven lines of iambic pentameter rhyming a b a b b c c

rhymester, rimester (ˈraɪmstə) *or* **rhymer, rimer** *n* a poet, esp one considered to be mediocre or mechanical in diction; poetaster or versifier

rhyming slang *n* slang in which a word is replaced by another word or phrase that rhymes with it; for example, *apples and pears* meaning *stairs*

rhynchocephalian (ˌrɪŋkəʊsɪˈfæliən) *adj* 1 of, relating to, or belonging to the *Rhyncocephalia*, an order of lizard-like reptiles common in the Mesozoic era but today represented only by the tuatara ▷ *n* 2 any reptile belonging to the order *Rhyncocephalia* [C19 from New Latin *Rhynchocephalia*, from Greek *rhunkhos* a snout + *kephalē* head]

rhynchophore (ˈrɪŋkəˌfɔː) *n* a member of the *Rhynchophora*, a former name for the superfamily of beetles (*Curculionoidea*) that comprises the weevils and bark beetles [C19 New Latin *rhyncophora*, from Greek *rhunkhos* a snout + -*phoros* bearing]

rhyolite (ˈraɪəˌlaɪt) *n* a fine-grained igneous rock consisting of quartz, feldspars, and mica or amphibole. It is the volcanic equivalent of granite [C19 *rhyo*- from Greek *rhuax* a stream of lava + LITE] > rhyolitic (ˌraɪəˈlɪtɪk) *adj*

rhythm (ˈrɪðəm) *n* 1 a the arrangement of the relative durations of and accents on the notes of a melody, usually laid out into regular groups (**bars**) of beats, the first beat of each bar carrying the stress b any specific arrangement of such groupings; time: *quadruple rhythm* 2 (in poetry) a the arrangement of words into a more or less regular sequence of stressed and unstressed or long and short syllables b any specific such arrangement; metre 3 (in painting, sculpture, architecture, etc) a harmonious sequence or pattern of masses alternating with voids, of light alternating with shade, of alternating colours, etc 4 any sequence of regularly recurring functions or events, such as the regular recurrence of certain physiological functions of the body, as the cardiac rhythm of the heartbeat [C16 from Latin *rhythmus*, from Greek *rhuthmos*; related to *rhein* to flow] > ˈrhythmless *adj*

rhythm and blues *n* (*functioning as singular*) any of various kinds of popular music derived from or influenced by the blues. Abbreviation: R & B

rhythmic (ˈrɪðmɪk) *or* **rhythmical** (ˈrɪðmɪkᵊl) *adj*

of, relating to, or characterized by rhythm, as in movement or sound; metrical, periodic, or regularly recurring > ˈrhythmically *adv* > rhythmicity (rɪðˈmɪsɪtɪ) *n*

rhythmic gymnastics *n* (*functioning as singular or plural*) a form of gymnastics involving movements using hand apparatus such as balls, hoops, and ribbons

rhythmics (ˈrɪðmɪks) *n* (*functioning as singular*) the study of rhythmic movement

rhythmist (ˈrɪðmɪst) *n rare* a person who has a good sense of rhythm

rhythm method *n* a method of controlling conception without the aid of a contraceptive device, by restricting sexual intercourse to those days in a woman's menstrual cycle on which conception is considered least likely to occur. See also **safe period**

rhythm section *n* those instruments in a band or group (usually piano, double bass, and drums) whose prime function is to supply the rhythm

rhyton (ˈraɪtɒn) *n*, *pl* -ta (-tə) (in ancient Greece) a horn-shaped drinking vessel with a hole in the pointed end through which to drink [C19 from Greek *rhuton*, from *rhutos* flowing; related to *rhein* to flow]

RI *abbreviation For* 1 Regina et Imperatrix [Latin: Queen and Empress] 2 Rex et Imperator [Latin: King and Emperor] 3 Rhode Island 4 Royal Institution 5 religious instruction 6 *international car registration for* (Republic of) Indonesia

R2I *abbreviation for* resistance to interrogation: a system used in military training to develop resistance to interrogation and torture techniques

ria (ˈriːə) *n* a long narrow inlet of the seacoast, being a former valley that was submerged by a rise in the level of the sea. Rias are found esp on the coasts of SW Ireland and NW Spain [C19 from Spanish, from *rio* river]

RIA *abbreviation for* Royal Irish Academy

RIAA curve *n electronics* a graphical representation, adopted as a worldwide standard, of the amplitude in relation to frequency response required for correct reproduction of microgroove disc recordings, compensating for the characteristics of the recording process [C20 Record Industry Association of America]

rial (ˈraɪəl) *n* 1 the standard monetary unit of Iran 2 the standard monetary unit of Oman, divided into 1000 baizas 3 another name for **riyal** [C14 from Persian, from Arabic *riyāl* RIYAL]

rialto (rɪˈæltəʊ) *n*, *pl* -tos a market or exchange [C19 after the RIALTO]

Rialto (rɪˈæltəʊ) *n* an island in Venice, Italy, linked with San Marco Island by the **Rialto Bridge** (1590) over the Grand Canal: the business centre of medieval and renaissance Venice

riant (ˈraɪənt) *adj rare* laughing; smiling; cheerful [C16 from French, from *rire* to laugh, from Latin *rīdēre*] > ˈriantly *adv*

rib¹ (rɪb) *n* 1 any of the 24 curved elastic arches of bone that together form the chest wall in man. All are attached behind to the thoracic part of the spinal column. Technical name: costa Compare **true rib, false ribs, floating rib** 2 the corresponding bone in other vertebrates 3 a cut of meat including one or more ribs 4 a part or element similar in function or appearance to a rib, esp a structural or supporting member or a raised strip or ridge 5 a structural member in a wing that extends from the leading edge to the trailing edge and maintains the shape of the wing surface 6 a projecting moulding or band on the underside of a vault or ceiling, which may be structural or ornamental 7 one of a series of raised rows in knitted fabric. See also **ribbing** (sense 3) 8 a raised ornamental line on the spine of a book where the stitching runs across it 9 any of the transverse stiffening timbers or joists forming the frame of a ship's hull 10 any of the larger veins of a leaf 11 a metal strip running along the top of the barrel of a shotgun or

r

handgun and guiding the alignment of the sights **12** a vein of ore in rock **13** a projecting ridge of a mountain; spur ▷ *vb* ribs, ribbing, ribbed (*tr*) **14** to furnish or support with a rib or ribs **15** to mark with or form into ribs or ridges **16** to knit plain and purl stitches alternately in order to make raised rows in (knitting) **17** *archaic* to enclose with or as if with ribs [Old English *ribb*; related to Old High German *rippi*, Old Norse *rif* REEF¹] ▷ 'ribless *adj* ▷ 'rib,like *adj*

rib² ('rɪb) *informal* ▷ *vb* ribs, ribbing, ribbed **1** (*tr*) to tease or ridicule ▷ *n* **2** a joke or hoax [c20 short for *rib-tickle* (vb)]

riba ('riːbə) *n* (in Islam) interest or usury, as forbidden by the Koran [c21 from Arabic *al-Riba*, literally: to excess or increase]

RIBA *abbreviation for* Royal Institute of British Architects

ribald ('rɪbəld) *adj* **1** coarse, obscene, or licentious, usually in a humorous or mocking way ▷ *n* **2** a ribald person [c13 from Old French *ribauld*, from *riber* to live licentiously, of Germanic origin] ▷ 'ribaldly *adv*

ribaldry ('rɪbəldrɪ) *n* ribald language or behaviour

riband *or* **ribband** ('rɪbənd) *n* **1** a ribbon, esp one awarded for some achievement. See also **blue riband 2** a flat rail attached to posts in a palisade [c14 variant of RIBBON]

ribbed and smoked sheet *n* another name for **smoked rubber**

ribbing ('rɪbɪŋ) *n* **1** a framework or structure of ribs **2** ribs collectively **3** a raised pattern in woven or knitted material, made in knitting by doing purl and plain stitches alternately

Ribble ('rɪbəl) *n* a river in NW England, flowing south and west through Lancashire to the Irish Sea. Length: 121 km (75 miles)

ribbon ('rɪbən) *n* **1** a narrow strip of fine material, esp silk, used for trimming, tying, etc **2** something resembling a ribbon; a long strip **3** a long thin flexible band of metal used as a graduated measure, spring, etc **4** a long narrow strip of ink-impregnated cloth for making the impression of type characters on paper in a typewriter or similar device **5** (*plural*) ragged strips or shreds (esp in the phrase **torn to ribbons**) **6** a small strip of coloured cloth signifying membership of an order or award of military decoration, prize, or other distinction **7** a small, usually looped, strip of coloured cloth worn to signify support for a charity or cause: *a red AIDS ribbon* ▷ *vb* (*tr*) **8** to adorn with a ribbon or ribbons **9** to mark with narrow ribbon-like marks **10** to reduce to ribbons; tear into strips [c14 *ryban*, from Old French *riban*, apparently of Germanic origin; probably related to RING¹, BAND²] ▷ 'ribbon-,like *or* 'ribbony *adj*

ribbon development *n Brit* the building of houses in a continuous row along a main road: common in England between the two World Wars

ribbonfish ('rɪbən,fɪʃ) *n, pl* **-fish** *or* **-fishes** any of various soft-finned deep-sea teleost fishes, esp *Regalecus glesne* (see **oarfish**), that have an elongated compressed body. They are related to the opah and dealfishes

ribbon microphone *n* a type of microphone in which the conductor is a thin ribbon of aluminium alloy moving perpendicularly in a magnetic field. It is strongly directional and can be used to reduce unwanted side noise

ribbon strip *n* another name for **ledger board** (sense 2)

ribbonwood ('rɪbən,wʊd) *n* a small evergreen malvaceous tree, *Hoheria populnea*, of New Zealand. Its wood is used in furniture making and the tough bark for making cord. Also called: **houhere, lacebark, thousand-jacket**

ribbon worm *n* another name for **nemertean** (sense 1)

ribcage ('rɪb,keɪdʒ) *n* the bony structure consisting of the ribs and their connective tissue that encloses and protects the lungs, heart, etc

Ribeirão Prêto (*Portuguese* riβəi'r[ˉə]u 'pretu) *n* a city in SE Brazil, in São Paulo state. Pop: 550 000 (2005 est)

ribgrass ('rɪb,grɑːs) *n* another name for **ribwort**

riboflavin *or* **riboflavine** (,raɪbəʊ'fleɪvɪn) *n* a yellow water-soluble vitamin of the B complex that occurs in green vegetables, germinating seeds, and in milk, fish, egg yolk, liver, and kidney. It is essential for the carbohydrate metabolism of cells. It is used as a permitted food colour, yellow or orange-yellow (**E101**). Formula: $C_{17}H_{20}N_4O_6$ Also called: vitamin B₂, lactoflavin [c20 from RIBOSE + FLAVIN]

ribonuclease (,raɪbəʊ'njuːkliː,eɪs, -,eɪz) *n* any of a group of enzymes that catalyse the hydrolysis of RNA [c20 from RIBONUCLE(IC ACID) + -ASE]

ribonucleic acid (,raɪbəʊnjuː'kliːɪk, -'kleɪ-) *n* the full name of **RNA** [c20 from RIBO(SE) + NUCLEIC ACID]

ribose ('raɪbəʊz, -bəʊs) *n biochem* a pentose sugar that is an isomeric form of arabinose and that occurs in RNA and riboflavin. Formula: $CH_2OH(CHOH)_3CHO$ [c20 changed from ARABINOSE]

ribosomal RNA *n biochem* a type of RNA thought to be transcribed from DNA in the nucleoli of cell nuclei, subsequently forming the component of ribosomes on which the translation of messenger RNA into protein chains is accomplished. Sometimes shortened to: **rRNA**

ribosome ('raɪbə,səʊm) *n* any of numerous minute particles in the cytoplasm of cells, either free or attached to the endoplasmic reticulum, that contain RNA and protein and are the site of protein synthesis [c20 from RIBO(NUCLEIC ACID) + -SOME³] ▷ 'ribo'somal *adj*

ribozyme ('raɪbə,zaɪm) *n* an RNA molecule capable of catalysing a chemical reaction, usually the cleavage of another RNA molecule [c20 from RIBO(NUCLEIC ACID) + (EN)ZYME]

rib-tickler *n* a very amusing joke or story

rib-tickling *adj* very amusing; causing laughter

ribwort ('rɪb,wɜːt) *n* a Eurasian plant, *Plantago lanceolata*, that has lancelike ribbed leaves, which form a rosette close to the ground, and a dense spike of small white flowers: family *Plantaginaceae*. Also called: **ribgrass** See also **plantain¹**

RIC *abbreviation for* Royal Institute of Chemistry

Ricardian (rɪ'kɑːdɪən) *adj* of or relating to David Ricardo, the British economist (1772–1823)

rice (raɪs) *n* **1** an erect grass, *Oryza sativa*, that grows in East Asia on wet ground and has drooping flower spikes and yellow oblong edible grains that become white when polished **2** the grain of this plant ▷ *vb* **3** (*tr*) *US and Canadian* to sieve (potatoes or other vegetables) to a coarse mashed consistency, esp with a ricer ▷ See also **Indian rice** [c13 *rys*, via French, Italian, and Latin from Greek *orūza*, of Oriental origin]

RICE (raɪs) *n acronym for* rest, ice, compression, elevation: the recommended procedure for controlling inflammation in injured limbs or joints

ricebird ('raɪs,bɜːd) *n* any of various birds frequenting rice fields, esp the Java sparrow

rice bowl *n* **1** a small bowl for eating rice out of, esp a decorative one made of china or porcelain **2** a fertile rice-producing region

rice grass *n* another name for **cord grass**

rice paper *n* **1** a thin semitransparent edible paper made from the straw of rice, on which macaroons and similar cakes are baked **2** a thin delicate Chinese paper made from an araliaceous plant, *Tetrapanax papyriferum* (**rice-paper plant**) of Taiwan, the pith of which is pared and flattened into sheets

ricer ('raɪsə) *n US and Canadian* a kitchen utensil with small holes through which cooked potatoes and similar soft foods are pressed to form a coarse mash

ricercare (,riːtʃə'kɑːreɪ) *or* **ricercar** ('riːtʃə,kɑː) *n, pl* **-cari** (-'kɑːriː) *or* **-cars** (in music of the 16th and

17th centuries) **1** an elaborate polyphonic composition making extensive use of contrapuntal imitation and usually very slow in tempo **2** an instructive composition to illustrate instrumental technique; étude [Italian, literally: to seek again]

rich (rɪtʃ) *adj* **1 a** well supplied with wealth, property, etc; owning much **b** (*as collective noun; preceded by the*): *the rich* **2** (when *postpositive*, usually foll by *in*) having an abundance of natural resources, minerals, etc: *a land rich in metals* **3** producing abundantly; fertile **4** (when *postpositive*, usually foll by *in* or *with*) well supplied with (desirable qualities): *a country rich with cultural interest* **5** of great worth or quality: *a rich collection of antiques* **6** luxuriant or prolific: *a rich growth of weeds* **7** expensively elegant, elaborate, or fine: *a rich display* **8** (of food) having a large proportion of flavoursome or fatty ingredients, such as spices, butter, or cream **9** having a full-bodied flavour: *a rich ruby port* **10** (of a smell) pungent or fragrant **11** (of colour) intense or vivid: *a rich red* **12** (of sound or a voice) full, mellow, or resonant **13** (of a fuel-air mixture) containing a relatively high proportion of fuel. Compare **weak** (sense 12) **14** very amusing, laughable, or ridiculous: *a rich joke; a rich situation* ▷ *n* **15** See riches [Old English *rīce* (originally of persons: great, mighty), of Germanic origin, ultimately from Celtic (compare Old Irish *rī* king)]

Richelieu River ('rɪʃə,ljɜː; *French* riʃəljø) *n* a river in E Canada, in S Quebec, rising in Lake Champlain and flowing north to the St Lawrence River. Length: 338 km (210 miles)

riches ('rɪtʃɪz) *pl n* wealth; an abundance of money, valuable possessions, or property

richly ('rɪtʃlɪ) *adv* **1** in a rich or elaborate manner: *a richly decorated carving* **2** fully and appropriately

Richmond ('rɪtʃmənd) *n* **1** a borough of Greater London, on the River Thames: formed in 1965 by the amalgamation of Barnes, Richmond, and Twickenham; site of Hampton Court Palace and the Royal Botanic Gardens at Kew. Pop: 179 200 (2003 est). Area: 55 sq km (21 sq miles). Official name: **Richmond-upon-Thames 2** a town in N England, in North Yorkshire: Norman castle. Pop: 8178 (2001) **3** a port in E Virginia, the state capital, at the falls of the James River: developed after the establishment of a trading post (1637); scene of the Virginia Conventions of 1774 and 1775; Confederate capital in the American Civil War. Pop: 194 729 (2003 est) **4** a county of SW New York City: coextensive with Staten Island borough; consists of Staten Island and several smaller islands

richness ('rɪtʃ,nɪs) *n* **1** the state or quality of being rich **2** *ecology* the number of individuals of a species in a given area

rich rhyme *n prosody* another term for **rime riche**

richt (rɪxt) *adj, adv, n* a Scot word for **right**

Richter scale ('rɪxtə) *n* a scale for expressing the magnitude of an earthquake in terms of the logarithm of the amplitude of the ground wave; values range from o to over 9. Compare **Mercalli scale**. See also **magnitude** (sense 5) [c20 named after Charles *Richter* (1900–85) US seismologist]

ricin ('raɪsɪn, 'rɪs-) *n biochem* a highly toxic protein, a lectin, derived from castor-oil seeds: used in experimental cancer therapy [c19 from New Latin *Ricinus* genus name, from Latin: castor-oil plant]

ricinoleic acid (,rɪsɪnəʊ'liːɪk, -'nəʊlɪɪk) *n* **1** an oily unsaturated carboxylic acid found, as the glyceride, in castor oil and used in the manufacture of soap and in finishing textiles; 12-hydroxy-9-octadecanoic acid. Formula: $C_{18}H_{34}O_3$ **2** the mixture of fatty acids obtained by hydrolysing castor oil [c19 from RICIN + OLEIC ACID]

rick¹ (rɪk) *n* **1** a large stack of hay, corn, peas, etc, built in the open in a regular-shaped pile, esp one with a thatched top ▷ *vb* **2** (*tr*) to stack or pile into ricks [Old English *hrēac*; related to Old Norse *hraukr*]

rick² (rɪk) *n* **1** a wrench or sprain, as of the back ▷ *vb* **2** (*tr*) to wrench or sprain (a joint, a limb, the back, etc) [C18 see WRICK]

ricker ('rɪkə) *n* a young kauri tree of New Zealand [from earlier use of the trunks as ships' rigging]

rickets ('rɪkɪts) *n* (*functioning as singular or plural*) *pathol* a disease mainly of children, characterized by softening of developing bone, and hence bow legs, malnutrition, and enlargement of the liver and spleen, caused by a deficiency of vitamin D [C17 of unknown origin]

rickettsia (rɪ'kɛtsɪə) *n, pl* **-siae** (-sɪˌiː) *or* **-sias** any of a group of parasitic bacteria that live in the tissues of ticks, mites, and other arthropods, and cause disease when transmitted to man and other animals [C20 named after Howard T *Ricketts* (1871–1910), US pathologist] > **rick'ettsial** *adj*

rickettsial disease *n* any of several acute infectious diseases caused by ticks, mites, or body lice infected with rickettsiae. The main types include typhus, spotted fever, Q fever, trench fever, and tsutsugamushi disease

rickety ('rɪkɪtɪ) *adj* **1** (of a structure, piece of furniture, etc) likely to collapse or break; shaky **2** feeble with age or illness; infirm **3** relating to, resembling, or afflicted with rickets [C17 from RICKETS] > **'ricketiness** *n*

rickey ('rɪkɪ) *n* a cocktail consisting of gin or vodka, lime juice, and soda water, served iced (esp in the phrase **a gin rickey**) [C19 of uncertain origin]

rickle ('rɪkᵊl) *n Scot* **1** an unsteady or shaky structure, esp a dilapidated building **2** a loose or disorganized heap [C16 perhaps of Scandinavian origin]

rickrack *or* **ricrac** ('rɪkˌræk) *n* a zigzag braid used for trimming [C20 dissimilated reduplication of RACK¹]

rickshaw ('rɪkʃɔː) *or* **ricksha** ('rɪkʃə) *n* **1** Also called: **jinrikisha** a small two-wheeled passenger vehicle drawn by one or two men, used in parts of Asia **2** Also called: **trishaw** a similar vehicle with three wheels, propelled by a man pedalling as on a tricycle ▷ See also **autorickshaw** [C19 shortened from JINRIKISHA]

ricochet ('rɪkəʃeɪ, 'rɪkəʃɛt) *vb* **-chets, -cheting** (-ʃeɪɪŋ) **-cheted** (-ʃeɪd) *or* **-chets, -chetting** (-ʃɛtɪŋ) **-chetted** (-ʃɛtɪd) **1** (*intr*) (esp of a bullet) to rebound from a surface or surfaces, usually with a characteristic whining or zipping sound ▷ *n* **2** the motion or sound of a rebounding object, esp a bullet **3** an object, esp a bullet, that ricochets [C18 from French, of unknown origin]

ricotta (rɪ'kɒtə) *n* a soft white unsalted cheese made from sheep's milk, used esp in making ravioli and gnocchi [C19 Italian, from Latin *recocta* recooked, from *recoquere*, from RE- + *coquere* to COOK]

RICS *abbreviation for* Royal Institution of Chartered Surveyors

rictus ('rɪktəs) *n, pl* **-tus** *or* **-tuses** **1** the GAPE or cleft of an open mouth or beak **2** a fixed or unnatural grin or grimace, as in horror or death [C18 from Latin, from *ringī* to gape] > **'rictal** *adj*

rid (rɪd) *vb* **rids, ridding, rid** *or* **ridded** (*tr*) **1** (foll by *of*) to relieve or deliver from something disagreeable or undesirable; make free (of): *to rid a house of mice* **2** **get rid of** to relieve or free oneself of (something or someone unpleasant or undesirable) [C13 (meaning: to clear land): from Old Norse *rythja*; related to Old High German *riutan* to clear land] > **'ridder** *n*

riddance ('rɪdᵊns) *n* the act of getting rid of something undesirable or unpleasant; deliverance or removal (esp in the phrase **good riddance**)

ridden ('rɪdᵊn) *vb* **1** the past participle of **ride** ▷ *adj* **2** (*in combination*) afflicted, affected, or dominated by something specified: *damp-ridden; disease-ridden*

riddle¹ ('rɪdᵊl) *n* **1** a question, puzzle, or verse so phrased that ingenuity is required for elucidation of the answer or meaning; conundrum **2** a person or thing that puzzles, perplexes, or confuses; enigma ▷ *vb* **3** to solve, explain, or interpret (a riddle or riddles) **4** (*intr*) to speak in riddles [Old English *rǣdelle, rǣdelse*, from *rǣd* counsel; related to Old Saxon *rādislo*, German *Rätsel*] > **'riddler** *n*

riddle² ('rɪdᵊl) *vb* (*tr*) **1** (usually foll by *with*) to pierce or perforate with numerous holes: *riddled with bullets* **2** to damage or impair **3** to put through a sieve; sift **4** to fill or pervade: *the report was riddled with errors* ▷ *n* **5** a sieve, esp a coarse one used for sand, grain, etc [Old English *hriddel* a sieve, variant of *hridder*; related to Latin *crībrum* sieve] > **'riddler** *n*

ride (raɪd) *vb* **rides, riding, rode, ridden** **1** to sit on and control the movements of (a horse or other animal) **2** (*tr*) to sit on and propel (a bicycle or similar vehicle) **3** (*intr*; often foll by *on* or *in*) to be carried along or travel on or in a vehicle: *she rides to work on the bus* **4** (*tr*) to travel over or traverse: *they rode the countryside in search of shelter* **5** (*tr*) to take part in by riding: *to ride a race* **6** to travel through or be carried across (sea, sky, etc): *the small boat rode the waves; the moon was riding high* **7** (*tr*) *US and Canadian* to cause to be carried: *to ride someone out of town* **8** (*intr*) to be supported as if floating: *the candidate rode to victory on his new policies* **9** (*intr*) (of a vessel) to lie at anchor **10** (*tr*) (of a vessel) to be attached to (an anchor) **11** (esp of a bone) to overlap or lie over (another structure or part) **12** *South African informal* **a** (*intr*) to drive a car **b** (*tr*) to transport (goods, farm produce, etc) by motor vehicle or cart **13** (*tr*) (esp of a male animal) to copulate with; mount **14** (*tr; usually passive*) to tyrannize over or dominate: *ridden by fear* **15** (*tr*) *informal* to persecute, esp by constant or petty criticism: *don't ride me so hard over my failure* **16** (*intr*) *informal* to continue undisturbed: *I wanted to change something, but let it ride* **17** (*tr*) to endure successfully; ride out **18** (*tr*) to yield slightly to (a blow or punch) in order to lessen its impact **19** (*intr*; often foll by *on*) (of a bet) to remain placed: *let your winnings ride on the same number* **20** (*intr*) *jazz* to play well, esp in freely improvising at perfect tempo **21** **ride roughshod over** to domineer over or act with complete disregard for **22** **ride to hounds** to take part in a fox hunt on horseback **23** **ride for a fall** to act in such a way as to invite disaster **24** **ride again** *informal* to return to a former activity or scene of activity **25** **riding high** confident, popular, and successful ▷ *n* **26** a journey or outing on horseback or in a vehicle **27** a path specially made for riding on horseback **28** transport in a vehicle, esp when given freely to a pedestrian; lift: *can you give me a ride to the station?* **29** a device or structure, such as a roller coaster at a fairground, in which people ride for pleasure or entertainment **30** **take for a ride** *informal* **a** to cheat, swindle, or deceive **b** to take (someone) away in a car and murder him ▷ See also **ride down, ride out, ride up** [Old English *rīdan*; related to Old High German *rītan*, Old Norse *rītha*] > **'ridable** *or* **'rideable** *adj*

Rideau Hall ('riːdəʊ) *n* (in Canada) the official residence of the Governor General, in Ottawa

ride down *vb* (*tr, adverb*) **1** to trample under the hooves of a horse **2** to catch up with or overtake by riding

rident ('raɪdᵊnt) *adj rare* laughing, smiling, or gay [C17 from Latin *rīdēre* to laugh; see RIANT]

ride out *vb* (*tr, adverb*) to endure successfully; survive (esp in the phrase **ride out the storm**)

rider ('raɪdə) *n* **1** a person or thing that rides, esp a person who rides a horse, a bicycle, or a motorcycle **2** an additional clause, amendment, or stipulation added to a legal or other document, esp (in Britain) a legislative bill at its third reading **3** *Brit* a statement made by a jury in addition to its verdict, such as a recommendation for mercy **4** any of various objects or devices resting on, surmounting, or strengthening something else **5** a small weight that can be slid along one arm of a chemical balance to make fine adjustments during weighing **6** *geology* a thin seam, esp of coal or mineral ore, overlying a thicker seam > **'riderless** *adj*

ride up *vb* (*intr, adverb*) to move or work away from the proper place or position: *her new skirt rode up uncomfortably*

ridge (rɪdʒ) *n* **1** a long narrow raised land formation with sloping sides esp one formed by the meeting of two faces of a mountain or of a mountain buttress or spur **2** any long narrow raised strip or elevation, as on a fabric or in ploughed land **3** *anatomy* any elongated raised margin or border on a bone, tooth, tissue membrane, etc **4** **a** the top of a roof at the junction of two sloping sides **b** (*as modifier*): *a ridge tile* **5** the back or backbone of an animal, esp a whale **6** *meteorol* an elongated area of high pressure, esp an extension of an anticyclone. Compare **trough** (sense 4) ▷ *vb* **7** to form into a ridge or ridges [Old English *hrycg*; related to Old High German *hrucki*, Old Norse *hryggr*] > **'ridgeˌlike** *adj* > **'ridgy** *adj*

ridgeling, ridgling ('rɪdʒlɪŋ) *or* **ridgel** ('rɪdʒəl) *n* **1** a domestic male animal with one or both testicles undescended, esp a horse **2** an imperfectly castrated male domestic animal [C16 perhaps from RIDGE, from the belief that the undescended testicles were near the animal's ridge or back]

ridgepole ('rɪdʒˌpəʊl) *n* **1** a timber laid along the ridge of a roof, to which the upper ends of the rafters are attached **2** the horizontal pole at the apex of a tent

ridgetree ('rɪdʒˌtriː) *n* another name for **ridgepole** (sense 1)

ridgeway ('rɪdʒˌweɪ) *n Brit* a road or track along a ridge, esp one of great antiquity

ridicule ('rɪdɪˌkjuːl) *n* **1** language or behaviour intended to humiliate or mock; derision ▷ *vb* **2** (*tr*) to make fun of, mock, or deride [C17 from French, from Latin *rīdiculus*, from *rīdēre* to laugh] > **'ridiˌculer** *n*

ridiculous (rɪ'dɪkjʊləs) *adj* worthy of or exciting ridicule; absurd, preposterous, laughable, or contemptible [C16 from Latin *rīdiculōsus*, from *rīdēre* to laugh] > **ri'diculously** *adv* > **ri'diculousness** *n*

riding¹ ('raɪdɪŋ) *n* **a** the art or practice of horsemanship **b** (*as modifier*): *a riding school*

riding² ('raɪdɪŋ) *n* **1** (*capital when part of a name*) any of the three former administrative divisions of Yorkshire: **North Riding, East Riding** and **West Riding** **2** (in Canada) a parliamentary constituency **3** (in New Zealand) a rural electorate for local government [from Old English *thriding*, from Old Norse *thrithjungr* a third. The *th*- was lost by assimilation to the *-t* or *-th* that preceded it, as in *west thriding*, etc]

riding breeches *pl n* tough breeches with padding inside the knees, worn for riding horses

riding crop *n* a short whip with a thong at one end and a handle for opening gates at the other

riding habit *n* a woman's dress worn for riding, usually with a full or a divided skirt

riding lamp *or* **light** *n* a light on a boat or ship showing that it is at anchor

ridotto (rɪ'dɒtəʊ) *n, pl* **-tos** an entertainment with music and dancing, often in masquerade: popular in 18th-century England [C18 from Italian: retreat, from Latin *reductus*, from *redūcere* to lead back]

riel ('riːəl) *n* the standard monetary unit of Cambodia, divided into 100 sen

Riemannian (*German* riː'mænɪən) *adj* of or relating to Georg Friedrich Bernhard Riemann, the German mathematician (1826–66)

Riemannian geometry *n* a branch of non-Euclidean geometry in which a line may have many parallels through a given point. It has a model on the surface of a sphere, with lines represented by great circles. Also called: **elliptic geometry**

riempie ('rɪmpɪ) *n South African* a leather thong or

r

lace used mainly to make chair seats [C19 (earlier *riem*): from Afrikaans, diminutive of *riem*, from Dutch: RIM]

Riesling (ˈriːzlɪŋ, ˈraɪz-) *n* **1** a white wine from the Rhine valley in Germany and from certain districts in other countries **2** the grape used to make this wine [C19 from German, from earlier *Rüssling*, of obscure origin]

Rievaulx Abbey (ˈriːvəʊ) *n* a ruined Cistercian abbey near Helmsley in Yorkshire: built in the 12th century and abandoned at the dissolution of the monasteries; landscaped in the 18th century

Rif, Riff (rɪf) *or* **Rifi** (ˈrɪfɪ) *n* **1** (*pl* **Rifs, Riffs, Rifis** *or* **Rif, Riff, Rifi**) a member of a Berber people, inhabiting the Atlas Mountains in Morocco **2** Also called: **Rifian, Riffian** (ˈrɪfɪən) the dialect of Berber spoken by this people **3** See **Er Rif**

rifampicin (rɪˈfæmpɪsɪn) *or US* **rifampin** (rɪˈfæmpɪn) *n* a drug used in the treatment of tuberculosis, meningitis, and leprosy [C20 from *rifam(y)cin*, from *Rififi*, nickname of the original culture, + -MYCIN, + inserted PI(PERAZINE)]

rife (raɪf) *adj* (*postpositive*) **1** of widespread occurrence; prevalent or current: *rumour was rife in the village* **2** very plentiful; abundant **3** (foll by *with*) abounding (in): *a land rife with poverty* [Old English *rīfe*; related to Old Norse *rīfr* generous, Middle Dutch *rīve*] > ˈ**rifely** *adv* > ˈ**rifeness** *n*

riff (rɪf) *music* ▷ *n* **1** (in jazz or rock music) a short series of chords ▷ *vb* **2** (*intr*) to play or perform riffs in jazz or rock music [C20 probably altered and shortened from REFRAIN[2]]

riffage (ˈrɪfɪdʒ) *n* (in jazz or rock music) the act or an instance of playing a short series of chords

riffle (ˈrɪfᵊl) *vb* **1** (when *intr*, often foll by *through*) to flick rapidly through (the pages of a book, magazine, etc), esp in a desultory manner **2** to shuffle (playing cards) by halving the pack and flicking the adjacent corners together **3** to make or become a riffle ▷ *n* **4** *US and Canadian* **a** a rapid in a stream **b** a rocky shoal causing a rapid **c** a ripple on water **5** *mining* a contrivance on the bottom of a sluice, containing transverse grooves for trapping particles of gold **6** the act or an instance of riffling [C18 probably from RUFFLE[1], influenced by RIPPLE[1]]

riffler (ˈrɪflə) *n* a file with a curved face for filing concave surfaces [C18 from French *rifloir*, from *rifler* to scratch]

riffola (ˌrɪˈfəʊlə) *n* *informal* the use of an abundance of dominant riffs

riffraff (ˈrɪfˌræf) *n* (*sometimes functioning as plural*) **1** worthless people, esp collectively; rabble **2** *dialect* worthless rubbish [C15 *rif and raf*, from Old French *rif et raf*; related to *rifler* to plunder, and *rafle* a sweeping up; see RIFLE[2], RAFFLE]

rifle[1] (ˈraɪfᵊl) *n* **1 a** a firearm having a long barrel with a spirally grooved interior, which imparts to the bullet spinning motion and thus greater accuracy over a longer range **b** (*as modifier*): *rifle fire* **2** (formerly) a large cannon with a rifled bore **3** one of the grooves in a rifled bore **4** (*plural*) **a** a unit of soldiers equipped with rifles **b** (*capital when part of a name*): *the Rifle Brigade* ▷ *vb* (*tr*) **5** to cut or mould spiral grooves inside the barrel of (a gun) **6** to throw or hit (a ball) with great speed [C18 from Old French *rifler* to scratch; related to Low German *rifeln* from *riefe* groove, furrow]

rifle[2] (ˈraɪfᵊl) *vb* (*tr*) **1** to search (a house, safe, etc) and steal from it; ransack **2** to steal and carry off: *to rifle goods from a shop* [C14 from Old French *rifler* to plunder, scratch, of Germanic origin] > ˈ**rifler** *n*

riflebird (ˈraɪfᵊlˌbɜːd) *n* any of various birds of paradise of the genera *Ptiloris* and *Craspedophora*, such as *C. magnifica* (**magnificent riflebird**) [from its call, compared to a whistling bullet]

rifle green *n* *Brit* **a** a dark olive green, as in the uniforms of certain rifle regiments **b** (*as adjective*): *rifle-green cloth*

rifle grenade *n* a grenade fired from a rifle

rifleman (ˈraɪfᵊlmən) *n, pl* **-men** **1** a person skilled in the use of a rifle, esp a soldier **2** Also called: **titipounamu** a wren, *Acanthisitta chloris*, of New Zealand: family *Xenicidae*. See also **bush wren**

rifle range *n* an area used for target practice with rifles

riflery (ˈraɪfᵊlrɪ) *n* *US* **1** rifle shots **2** the practice or skill of rifle marksmanship

rifling (ˈraɪflɪŋ) *n* **1** the cutting of spiral grooves on the inside of a firearm's barrel **2** the series of grooves so cut

rift[1] (rɪft) *n* **1** a gap or space made by cleaving or splitting; fissure **2** *geology* a long narrow zone of faulting resulting from tensional stress in the earth's crust **3** a gap between two cloud masses; break or chink: *he saw the sun through a rift in the clouds* **4** a break in friendly relations between people, nations, etc ▷ *vb* **5** to burst or cause to burst open; split [C13 from Old Norse; related to Danish *rift* cleft, Icelandic *ript* breach of contract]

rift[2] (rɪft) *n* *US* **1** a shallow or rocky part in a stream **2** the backwash from a wave that has just broken [C14 from Old Norse *rypta*; related to Icelandic *ropa* to belch]

rift valley *n* a long narrow valley resulting from the subsidence of land between two parallel faults, often associated with volcanism. The East African Rift Valley is an example

rig[1] (rɪɡ) *vb* **rigs, rigging, rigged** (*tr*) **1** *nautical* to equip (a vessel, mast, etc) with (sails, rigging, etc) **2** *nautical* to set up or prepare ready for use **3** to put the components of (an aircraft, etc) into their correct positions **4** to manipulate in a fraudulent manner, esp for profit: *to rig prices* ▷ *n* **5** *nautical* the distinctive arrangement of the sails, masts, and other spars of a vessel **6** In full: **drilling rig** the installation used in drilling for and exploiting natural oil and gas deposits **7** apparatus or equipment; gear **8** an amateur radio operator's transmitting and receiving set **9** *US and Canadian* a carriage together with one or more horses **10** *chiefly US and Canadian* an articulated lorry ▷ See also **rig down, rig out, rig up** [C15 from Scandinavian; related to Norwegian *rigga* to wrap]

rig[2] (rɪɡ) *n* *Scot and northern English dialect* a ridge or raised strip of unploughed land in a ploughed field [a variant of RIDGE]

Riga (ˈriːɡə) *n* the capital of Latvia, on the **Gulf of Riga** at the mouth of the Western Dvina on the Baltic Sea: a port and major trading centre since Viking times. Pop: 739 232 (2002 est)

rigadoon (ˌrɪɡəˈduːn) *or* **rigaudon** (*French* riɡodɔ̃) *n* **1** an old Provençal couple dance, light and graceful, in lively duple time **2** a piece of music for or in the rhythm of this dance [C17 from French, allegedly from its inventor *Rigaud*, a dancing master at Marseille]

rigamarole (ˈrɪɡəməˌrəʊl) *n* a variant of **rigmarole**

rigatoni (ˌrɪɡəˈtəʊnɪ) *n* macaroni in the form of short ridged often slightly curved pieces [C20 Italian, plural of *rigato*, from *rigare* to draw lines, make stripes, from *riga* a line, of Germanic origin]

rig down *vb* (*adverb*) *nautical* to disassemble and stow

Rigel (ˈraɪdʒəl, ˈraɪɡᵊl) *n* the brightest star, Beta Orionis, in the constellation Orion: a very luminous and extremely remote bluish-white supergiant, a double star. Visual magnitude: 0.12; spectral type: B8I [C16 from Arabic *rijl* foot; from its position in Orion's foot]

-rigged *adj* (*in combination*) (of a sailing vessel) having a rig of a certain kind: *ketch-rigged*

rigger (ˈrɪɡə) *n* **1** a workman who rigs vessels, etc **2** *rowing* a bracket on a racing shell or other boat to support a projecting rowlock **3** a person skilled in the use of pulleys, lifting gear, cranes, etc

rigging (ˈrɪɡɪŋ) *n* **1** the shrouds, stays, halyards, etc, of a vessel **2** the bracing wires, struts, and lines of a biplane, balloon, etc **3** any form of lifting gear, tackle, etc

rigging loft *n* **1** a loft or gallery in a boatbuilder's yard from which rigging can be fitted **2** a loft in a theatre from which scenery, etc, is raised and lowered

right (raɪt) *adj* **1** in accordance with accepted standards of moral or legal behaviour, justice, etc: *right conduct* **2** in accordance with fact, reason, or truth; correct or true **3** appropriate, suitable, fitting, or proper: *the right man for the job* **4** most favourable or convenient; preferred **5** in a satisfactory condition; orderly: *things are right again now* **6** indicating or designating the correct time: *the clock is right* **7** correct in opinion or judgment **8** sound in mind or body; healthy or sane **9** (*usually prenominal*) of, designating, or located near the side of something or someone that faces east when the front is turned towards the north. Related adj: **dextral** **10** (*usually prenominal*) worn on a right hand, foot, etc **11** (*sometimes capital*) of, designating, supporting, belonging to, or relating to the political or intellectual right (see sense 39) **12** (*sometimes capital*) conservative or reactionary: *the right wing of the party* **13** *geometry* **a** formed by or containing a line or plane perpendicular to another line or plane **b** having the axis perpendicular to the base: *a right circular cone* **c** straight: *a right line* **14** relating to or designating the side of cloth worn or facing outwards **15** *informal* (intensifier): *a right idiot* **16** **in one's right mind** sane **17** **she'll be right** *Austral and NZ informal* that's all right; not to worry **18** **the right side of** **a** in favour with: *you'd better stay on the right side of him* **b** younger than: *she's still on the right side of fifty* ▷ *adv* **19** **too right** *Austral and NZ informal* an exclamation of agreement **20** in accordance with correctness or truth; accurately **21** in the appropriate manner; properly **22** in a straight line; directly: *right to the top* **23** in the direction of the east from the point of view of a person or thing facing north **24** absolutely or completely; utterly **25** all the way: *the bus goes right to the city centre* **26** without delay; immediately or promptly: *I'll be right over* **27** exactly or precisely: *right here* **28** in a manner consistent with a legal or moral code; justly or righteously: *do right by me* **29** in accordance with propriety; fittingly or suitably: *it serves you right* **30** to good or favourable advantage; well **31** (esp in religious titles) most or very: *right reverend* **32** *informal or dialect* (intensifier): *I'm right glad to see you* **33** **right, left, and centre** on all sides; from every direction **34** **right off the bat** *informal* as the first in a series; to begin with ▷ *n* **35** any claim, title, etc, that is morally just or legally granted as allowable or due to a person: *I know my rights* **36** anything that accords with the principles of legal or moral justice **37** the fact or state of being in accordance with reason, truth, or accepted standards (esp in the phrase **in the right**) **38** *Irish* an obligation or duty: *you had a right to lock the door* **39** the right side, direction, position, area, or part: *the right of the army* **40** (*often capital and preceded by the*) the supporters or advocates of social, political, or economic conservatism or reaction, based generally on a belief that things are better left unchanged (opposed to *radical* or *left*) **41** *boxing* **a** a punch with the right hand **b** the right hand **42** *finance* **a** (*often plural*) the privilege of a company's shareholders to subscribe for new issues of the company's shares on advantageous terms **b** the negotiable certificate signifying this privilege **43** **by right** (*or* **rights**) properly: *by rights you should be in bed* **44** **in one's own right** having a claim or title oneself rather than through marriage or other connection **45** **to rights** consistent with justice, correctness, or orderly arrangement: *he put the matter to rights* ▷ *vb* (*mainly tr*) **46** (*also intr*) to restore to or attain a normal, esp an upright, position: *the raft righted in a few seconds* **47** to make (something) accord with truth or facts; correct **48** to restore to an orderly state or condition **49** to make reparation for (esp in the phrase **right a wrong**) ▷ *sentence substitute* **50** **a** indicating that a statement has been understood **b** asking whether a statement has been understood **c** indicating a subdividing point within a discourse ▷ *interj* **51** an expression of agreement or compliance [Old English *riht, reoht*; related to Old High German *reht*, Gothic *raihts*, Latin *rēctus*] > 'righter *n*

rightable ('raɪtəbᵊl) *adj* capable of being righted > 'rightably *adv* > 'rightableness *n*

right about *n* **1** a turn executed through 180° ▷ *adj* ▷ *adv* **2** in the opposite direction

right angle *n* **1** the angle between two radii of a circle that cut off on the circumference an arc equal in length to one quarter of the circumference; an angle of 90° or π/2 radians **2** at right angles perpendicular or perpendicularly. Related adj: **orthogonal**. > 'right-ˌangled *adj*

right-angled triangle *n* a triangle one angle of which is a right angle. US and Canadian name: right triangle

right ascension *n astronomy* the angular distance measured eastwards along the celestial equator from the vernal equinox to the point at which the celestial equator intersects a great circle passing through the celestial pole and the heavenly object in question. Symbol: α Compare **declination** (sense 1)

right away *adv* without delay; immediately or promptly

right-down *adv, adj* a variant of **downright**

righten ('raɪtᵊn) *vb* **1** (*tr*) to set right **2** to restore to or attain a normal or upright position

righteous ('raɪtʃəs) *adj* **1 a** characterized by, proceeding from, or in accordance with accepted standards of morality, justice, or uprightness; virtuous: *a righteous man* (*as collective noun; preceded by the*): *the righteous* **b** morally justifiable or right, esp from one's own point of view: *righteous indignation* [Old English *rihtwīs*, from RIGHT + WISE²] > 'righteously *adv* > 'righteousness *n*

right-footer *n informal* (esp in Ireland) a Protestant [See LEFT-FOOTER]

rightful ('raɪtfʊl) *adj* **1** in accordance with what is right; proper or just **2** (*prenominal*) having a legally or morally just claim: *the rightful owner* **3** (*prenominal*) held by virtue of a legal or just claim: *my rightful property* > 'rightfully *adv* > 'rightfulness *n*

right-hand *adj* (*prenominal*) **1** of, relating to, located on, or moving towards the right: *a right-hand bend; this car has right-hand drive* **2** for use by the right hand; right-handed **3** right-hand man one's most valuable assistant or supporter

right-handed *adj* **1** using the right hand with greater skill or ease than the left **2** performed with the right hand: *right-handed writing* **3** made for use by the right hand **4** worn on the right hand **5** turning from left to right; clockwise > ˌright-'handedly *adv* > ˌright-'handedness *n*

right-hander *n* **1** a blow with the right hand **2** a person who is right-handed

Right Honourable *adj* **1** (in Britain and certain Commonwealth countries) a title of respect for a Privy Councillor or an appeal-court judge **2** (in Britain) a title of respect for an earl, a viscount, a baron, or the Lord Mayor or Lord Provost of any of certain cities

rightish ('raɪtɪʃ) *adj* somewhat right, esp politically

rightist ('raɪtɪst) *adj* **1** of, tending towards, or relating to the political right or its principles; conservative, traditionalist, or reactionary ▷ *n* **2** a person who supports or belongs to the political right > 'rightism *n*

rightly ('raɪtlɪ) *adv* **1** in accordance with the facts; correctly **2** in accordance with principles of justice or morality **3** with good reason; justifiably **4** properly or suitably; appropriately **5** (*used with a negative*) *informal* with certainty; positively or precisely (usually in the phrases **I don't rightly know, I can't rightly say**)

right-minded *adj* holding opinions or principles that accord with what is right or with the opinions of the speaker > ˌright-'mindedly *adv* > ˌright-'mindedness *n*

rightness ('raɪtnɪs) *n* the state or quality of being right

righto or **right oh** ('raɪt'əʊ) *sentence substitute Brit informal* an expression of agreement or compliance

right off *adv* immediately; right away

right of search *n* the right of a belligerent to stop and search neutral merchant ships on the high seas in wartime

right of way *n, pl* rights of way **1** the right of one vehicle or vessel to take precedence over another, as laid down by law or custom **2 a** the legal right of someone to pass over another's land, acquired by grant or by long usage **b** the path or road used by this right **3** *US* the strip of land over which a power line, railway line, road, etc, extends

right on *interj* **1** *slang, chiefly US and Canadian* an exclamation of full agreement, concurrence, or compliance with the wishes, words, or actions of another ▷ *adj* **2** *informal* modern, trendy, and socially aware or relevant: *right-on green politics*

Right Reverend *adj* (in Britain) a title of respect for an Anglican or Roman Catholic bishop

rights issue *n stock exchange* an issue of new shares offered by a company to its existing shareholders on favourable terms. Also called: capitalization issue

rightsize ('raɪtˌsaɪz) *vb* to restructure (an organization) to cut costs and improve effectiveness without ruthlessly downsizing

right-thinking ('raɪtˌθɪŋkɪŋ) *adj* possessing reasonable and generally acceptable opinions

right triangle *n US and Canadian* a triangle one angle of which is a right angle. Also called (in Britain and certain other countries): right-angled triangle

rightward ('raɪtwəd) *adj* **1** situated on or directed towards the right ▷ *adv* **2** a variant of **rightwards**

rightwards ('raɪtwədz) or **rightward** *adv* towards or on the right

right whale *n* any large whalebone whale of the family *Balaenidae*. They are grey or black, have a large head, and, in most, no dorsal fin, and are hunted as a source of whalebone and oil. See also **bowhead** [C19 perhaps so named because it was *right* for hunting]

right wing *n* **1** (*often capitals*) the conservative faction of an assembly, party, etc **2** the part of an army or field of battle on the right from the point of view of one facing the enemy **3 a** the right-hand side of the field of play from the point of view of a team facing its opponent's goal **b** a player positioned in this area in any of various games **c** the position occupied by such a player ▷ *adj* right-wing **4** of, belonging to, or relating to the right wing > 'right-'winger *n*

Rigi ('riːgɪ) *n* a mountain in the Alps of N central Switzerland, between Lakes Lucerne, Zug, and Lauerz

rigid ('rɪdʒɪd) *adj* **1** not bending; physically inflexible or stiff **2** unbending; rigorously strict; severe **3** completely or excessively rigid [C16 from Latin *rigidus*, from *rigēre* to be stiff] > 'rigidly *adv* > ri'gidity or 'rigidness *n*

rigid designator *n logic* an expression that identifies the same individual in every possible world: for example, "Shakespeare" is a rigid designator since it is possible that Shakespeare might not have been a playwright but not that he might not have been Shakespeare

rigidify (rɪ'dʒɪdɪˌfaɪ) *vb* **-fies, -fying, -fied** to make or become rigid

Rigil Kent ('raɪdʒɪl 'kɛnt) *n astronomy* the star Alpha Centauri. Often shortened to: Rigil [from *Rigil Kentaurus*, from Arabic *al Rigil al Kentaurus* the Centaur's foot]

rigmarole ('rɪgməˌrəʊl) or **rigamarole** *n* **1** any long complicated procedure **2** a set of incoherent or pointless statements; garbled nonsense [C18 from earlier *ragman roll* a list, probably a roll used in a medieval game, wherein various characters were described in verse, beginning with *Ragemon le bon* Ragman the good]

rigor ('raɪɡɔː, 'rɪgə) *n* **1** *med* a sudden feeling of

chilliness, often accompanied by shivering: it sometimes precedes a fever **2** ('rɪgə) *pathol* rigidity of a muscle; muscular cramp **3** a state of rigidity assumed by some animals in reaction to sudden shock **4** the inertia assumed by some plants in conditions unfavourable to growth [see RIGOUR]

rigorism ('rɪgəˌrɪzəm) *n* **1** strictness in judgment or conduct **2** the religious cult of extreme self-denial **3** *RC theol* the doctrine that in cases of doubt in moral matters the stricter course must always be followed > 'rigorist *n* > ˌrigor'istic *adj*

rigor mortis ('rɪgə 'mɔːtɪs) *n pathol* the stiffness of joints and muscular rigidity of a dead body, caused by depletion of ATP in the tissues. It begins two to four hours after death and lasts up to about four days, after which the muscles and joints relax [C19 Latin, literally: rigidity of death]

rigorous ('rɪgərəs) *adj* **1** characterized by or proceeding from rigour; harsh, strict, severe **2** severely accurate **3** (esp of weather) extreme or harsh **4** *maths, logic* (of a proof) making the validity of the successive steps completely explicit > 'rigorously *adv* > 'rigorousness *n*

rigour or *US* **rigor** ('rɪgə) *n* **1** harsh but just treatment or action **2** a severe or cruel circumstance; hardship: *the rigours of famine* **3** strictness, harshness, or severity of character **4** strictness in judgment or conduct; rigorism **5** *maths, logic* logical validity or accuracy **6** *obsolete* rigidity [C14 from Latin *rigor*]

rig out *vb* **1** (*tr, adverb*; often foll by *with*) to equip or fit out (with) **2** to dress or be dressed ▷ *n* rigout **3** *informal* a person's clothing or costume, esp a bizarre outfit

rigsdaler ('rɪgzˌdɑːlə) *n* another word for **rix-dollar**

rig up *vb* (*tr, adverb*) to erect or construct, esp as a temporary measure: *cameras were rigged up to televise the event*

Rig-Veda (rɪg'veɪdə, -'viːdə) *n* a compilation of 1028 Hindu poems dating from 2000 BC or earlier [C18 from Sanskrit *rigveda*, from *ric* song of praise + VEDA]

Rijeka (rɪ'ɛkə; Serbo-Croat ri'jɛka) *n* a port in Croatia: an ancient town, changing hands many times before passing to Yugoslavia in 1947 until Croatia became independent in 1991. Pop: 135 000 (2005 est). Italian name: Fiume

rijksdaaler ('raɪksˌdɑːlə) *n* a variant of **rix-dollar**

Rijksmuseum ('raɪxsmjuːˌzɪəm) *n* a museum in Amsterdam housing the national art collection of the Netherlands

Rijn (rɛjn) *n* the Dutch name for the **Rhine**

rijsttafel ('raɪsˌtɑːfəl) *n* an Indonesian food consisting of a selection of rice dishes to which are added small pieces of a variety of other foods, such as meat, fish, fruit, pickles, and curry [from Dutch *rijst* rice + *tafel* table]

Rijswijk ('raɪsvaɪk; Dutch 'rɛjswɛjk) *n* a town in the SW Netherlands, in South Holland province on the SE outskirts of The Hague: scene of the signing (1697) of the **Treaty of Rijswijk** ending the War of the Grand Alliance. Pop: 48 000 (2003 est). English name: Ryswick

rikishi (rɪ'kɪʃɪ) *n, pl* rikishi a sumo wrestler [Japanese, literally: strong man]

Riksdag (Swedish 'riːksdag) *n* the Swedish parliament

Riksmål (Norwegian 'rɪksmɔl) *n* a former name for **Bokmål** [literally: language of the kingdom]

rile (raɪl) *vb* (*tr*) **1** to annoy or anger; irritate **2** *US and Canadian* to stir up or agitate (water, etc); roil or make turbid [C19 variant of ROIL]

Riley ('raɪlɪ) *n* the life of Riley a luxurious and carefree existence [C20 origin unknown]

rilievo *Italian* (ri'ljevo; *English* ˌrɪlɪ'eɪvəʊ) *n, pl* **-vi** (-vi; *English* -viː) another name for **relief** (sense 9)

rill (rɪl) *n* **1** a brook or stream; rivulet **2** a small channel or gulley, such as one formed during soil erosion **3** Also: **rille** one of many winding cracks on the moon [C15 from Low German *rille*; related to Dutch *ril*]

rillet (ˈrɪlɪt) *n* a little rill

rim (rɪm) *n* **1** the raised edge of an object, esp of something more or less circular such as a cup or crater **2** the peripheral part of a wheel, to which the tyre is attached **3** *basketball* the hoop from which the net is suspended ▷ *vb* **rims, rimming, rimmed** (*tr*) **4** to put a rim on (a pot, cup, wheel, etc) **5** *slang* to lick, kiss, or suck the anus of (one's sexual partner) **6** *ball games* (of a ball) to run around the edge of (a hole, basket, etc) [Old English *rima*; related to Old Saxon *rimi*, Old Norse *rimi* ridge]

RIM *international car registration for* (Islamic Republic of) Mauritania

rimaye (rɪˈmeɪ) *n* another name for **bergschrund** [c20 French, from Latin *rima* cleft]

rime¹ (raɪm) *n* **1** frost formed by the freezing of supercooled water droplets in fog onto solid objects ▷ *vb* **2** (*tr*) to cover with rime or something resembling rime [Old English *hrīm*; related to Dutch *rijm*, Middle High German *rīmeln* to coat with frost]

rime² (raɪm) *n, vb* an archaic spelling of **rhyme**

rimer (ˈraɪmə) *n* another name for **rhymester**

rime riche (ˈriːm ˈriːʃ) *n, pl* **rimes riches** (ˈriːmˈriːʃ) rhyme between words or syllables that are identical in sound, as in *command/demand, pair/pear* [French, literally: rich rhyme]

rimester (ˈraɪmstə) *n* a variant spelling of **rhymester**

rim-fire *adj* **1** (of a cartridge) having the primer in the rim of the base **2** (of a firearm) adapted for such cartridges ▷ Compare **centre-fire**

Rimini (ˈrɪmɪnɪ) *n* a port and resort in NE Italy, in Emilia-Romagna on the N Adriatic coast. Pop: 128 656 (2001). Ancient name: **Ariminum**

rimose (raɪˈməʊs, -ˈməʊz) *adj* (esp of plant parts) having the surface marked by a network of intersecting cracks [c18 from Latin *rīmōsus*, from *rīma* a split, crack] > ˈ**rimosely** *adv* > **rimosity** (raɪˈmɒsɪtɪ) *n*

rimrock (ˈrɪmˌrɒk) *n* rock forming the boundaries of a sandy or gravelly alluvial deposit

rimu (ˈriːmuː) *n* another name for **red pine** [from Māori]

rimy (ˈraɪmɪ) *adj* **rimier, rimiest** coated with rime

rind (raɪnd) *n* **1** a hard outer layer or skin on bacon, cheese, etc **2** the outer layer of a fruit or of the spore-producing body of certain fungi **3** the outer layer of the bark of a tree [Old English *rinde*; Old High German *rinta*, German *Rinde*]

rinderpest (ˈrɪndəˌpɛst) *n* an acute contagious viral disease of cattle, characterized by severe inflammation of the intestinal tract and diarrhoea [c19 German: cattle pest]

rinforzando (ˌriːnfɔːˈtsændəʊ) a less common term for **sforzando** [Italian, literally: reinforcing]

ring¹ (rɪŋ) *n* **1** a circular band usually of a precious metal, esp gold, often set with gems and worn upon the finger as an adornment or as a token of engagement or marriage **2** any object or mark that is circular in shape **3** a circular path or course **4** a group of people or things standing or arranged so as to form a circle **5** an enclosed space, usually circular in shape, where circus acts are performed **6** a square apron or raised platform, marked off by ropes, in which contestants box or wrestle **7 the ring** the sport of boxing **8** the field of competition or rivalry **9 throw one's hat in the ring** to announce one's intention to be a candidate or contestant **10** a group of people usually operating illegally and covertly: *a drug ring* **11** (esp at country fairs) an enclosure, often circular, where horses, cattle, and other livestock are paraded and auctioned **12** an area reserved for betting at a racecourse **13** a circular strip of bark cut from a tree or branch, esp in order to kill it **14** a single turn in a spiral **15** *geometry* the area of space lying between two concentric circles **16** *maths* a set that is subject to two binary operations, addition and multiplication, such that the set is an Abelian group under addition and is closed under multiplication, this latter operation being associative **17** *botany* short for **annual ring** **18** Also called: **closed chain** *chem* a closed loop of atoms in a molecule **19** *astronomy* any of the thin circular bands of small bodies orbiting a giant planet, esp Saturn. See also **Saturn²** (sense 1) **20 run rings around** *informal* to be greatly superior to; outclass completely ▷ *vb* **rings, ringing, ringed** (*tr*) **21** to surround with or as if with or form a ring; encircle **22** to mark (a bird) with a ring or clip for subsequent identification **23** to fit a ring in the nose of (a bull, pig, etc) so that it can be led easily **24** Also: **ringbark a** to cut away a circular strip of bark from (a tree or branch) in order to kill it **b** to cut a narrow or partial ring from (the trunk of a tree) in order to check or prevent vigorous growth **25** *Austral and NZ* to be the fastest shearer in a shearing shed (esp in the phrase **ring the shed**) [Old English *hring*; related to Old Norse *hringr*]

ring² (rɪŋ) *vb* **rings, ringing, rang, rung** **1** to emit or cause to emit a sonorous or resonant sound, characteristic of certain metals when struck **2** to cause (a bell) to emit a ringing sound by striking it once or repeatedly or (of a bell) to emit such a sound **3 a** (*tr*) to cause (a large bell, esp a church bell) to emit a ringing sound by pulling on a rope that is attached to a wheel on which the bell swings back and forth, being sounded by a clapper inside it. Compare **chime¹** (sense 6) **b** (*intr*) (of a bell) to sound by being swung in this way **4** (*intr*) (of a building, place, etc) to be filled with sound; echo: *the church rang with singing* **5** (*intr*; foll by *for*) to call by means of a bell, buzzer, etc **6** Also: **ring up** *chiefly Brit* to call (a person) by telephone **7** (*tr*) to strike or tap (a coin) in order to assess its genuineness by the sound produced **8** (*intr*) (of the ears) to have or give the sensation of humming or ringing **9** (*intr*) *electronics* (of an electric circuit) to produce a damped oscillatory wave after the application of a sharp input transition **10** *slang* to change the identity of (a stolen vehicle) by using the licence plate, serial number, etc, of another, usually disused, vehicle **11 ring a bell** to sound familiar; remind one of something, esp indistinctly **12 ring down the curtain a** to lower the curtain at the end of a theatrical performance **b** (foll by *on*) to put an end (to) **13 ring false** to give the impression of being false **14 ring the bell a** to do, say, or be the right thing **b** to reach the pinnacle of success or happiness **15 ring the changes** to vary the manner or performance of an action that is often repeated **16 ring true** to give the impression of being true: *that story doesn't ring true* ▷ *n* **17** the act of or a sound made by ringing **18** a sound produced by or suggestive of a bell **19** any resonant or metallic sound, esp one sustained or re-echoed **20** *informal, chiefly Brit* a telephone call: *he gave her a ring last night* **21** the complete set of bells in a tower or belfry: *a ring of eight bells.* See **peal¹** (sense 3) **22** an inherent quality or characteristic: *his explanation has the ring of sincerity* **23** *electronics* the damped oscillatory wave produced by a circuit that rings ▷ See also **ring back, ring in, ring off, ring out, ring up** [Old English *hringan*; related to Old High German *hringen* Old Norse *hringja*]

> USAGE *Rang* and *sang* are the correct forms of the past tenses of *ring* and *sing*, although *rung* and *sung* are still heard informally and dialectally: *he rung (rang) the bell*

ring back *vb* (*adverb*) to return a telephone call (to)

ringbark (ˈrɪŋˌbɑːk) *vb* another term for **ring¹** (sense 24)

ring binder *n* a loose-leaf binder fitted with metal rings that can be opened to allow perforated paper to be inserted

ringbolt (ˈrɪŋˌbəʊlt) *n* a bolt with a ring fitted through an eye attached to the bolt head

ringbone (ˈrɪŋˌbəʊn) *n* an abnormal bony growth affecting the pastern of a horse, often causing lameness

ring circuit *n* an electrical system in which distribution points are connected to the main supply in a continuous closed circuit

ringdove (ˈrɪŋˌdʌv) *n* **1** another name for **wood pigeon** **2** an Old World turtledove, *Streptopelia risoria*, having a greyish plumage with a black band around the neck

ring-dyke *n* a dyke having an approximately circular outcrop of rock

ringed (rɪŋd) *adj* **1** displaying ringlike markings **2** having or wearing a ring **3** formed by rings

ringed plover *n* a European shorebird, *Charadrius hiaticula*, with a greyish-brown back, white underparts with a black throat band, and orange legs: family *Charadriidae* (plovers)

ringent (ˈrɪndʒənt) *adj* (of the corolla of plants such as the snapdragon) consisting of two distinct gaping lips [c18 from Latin *ringī* to open the mouth wide]

ringer (ˈrɪŋə) *n* **1** a person or thing that rings a bell **2** Also called: **dead ringer** *slang* a person or thing that is almost identical to another **3** *slang* a stolen vehicle the identity of which has been changed by the use of the licence plate, serial number, etc, of another, usually disused, vehicle **4** *US* a contestant, esp a horse, entered in a competition under false representations of identity, record, or ability **5** *Austral and NZ* the fastest shearer in a shed **6** *Austral informal* the fastest or best at anything **7** a quoit thrown so as to encircle a peg **8** such a throw

Ringer's solution (ˈrɪŋəz) *n* a solution containing the chlorides of sodium, potassium, and calcium, used to correct dehydration and, in physiological experiments, as a medium for in vitro preparations

ring-fence *vb* **1** to assign (money, a grant, fund, etc) to one particular purpose, so as to restrict its use: *to ring-fence a financial allowance* **2** to oblige (a person or organization) to use money for a particular purpose ▷ *n* **ring fence** **3** an agreement, contract, etc, in which the use of money is restricted to a particular purpose

ring finger *n* the third finger, esp of the left hand, on which a wedding ring is traditionally worn

ring flash *n photog* a type of electronic flash in which the light source is arranged in a ring around the lens in order to produce a light without shadows

ring gauge *n engineering* a ring having an internal diameter of a specified size used for checking the diameter of a cylindrical object or part. Compare **plug gauge**

ringgit (ˈrɪŋɡɪt) *n* the standard monetary unit of Malaysia, divided into 100 sen [from Malay]

ring in *vb* (*adverb*) **1** (*intr*) *chiefly Brit* to report to someone by telephone **2** (*tr*) to accompany the arrival of with bells (esp in the phrase **ring in the new year**) **3** (*tr*) *Austral* to substitute (a horse) fraudulently for another horse in a race **4** (*tr*) *Austral and NZ informal* to recruit or include (a person) ▷ *n* **ring-in** **5** *Austral informal* a horse that serves as a substitute **6** *Austral and NZ informal* a person or thing that is not normally a member of a particular group; outsider

ringing tone *n Brit* a sequence of pairs of tones heard by the dialler on a telephone when the number dialled is ringing. Compare **engaged tone, dialling tone**

ringleader (ˈrɪŋˌliːdə) *n* a person who leads others in any kind of unlawful or mischievous activity

ringlet (ˈrɪŋlɪt) *n* **1** a lock of hair hanging down in a spiral curl **2** any of numerous butterflies of the genus *Erebia*, most of which occur in S Europe and have dark brown wings marked with small black-and-white eyespots: family *Satyridae* > ˈ**ringleted** *adj*

ring main *n* a domestic electrical supply in which outlet sockets are connected to the mains supply

ringmaster ('rɪŋˌmɑːstə) n the master of ceremonies in a circus

ring-necked adj (of animals, esp certain birds and snakes) having a band of distinctive colour around the neck

ring-necked pheasant n a common pheasant, *Phasianus colchicus*, originating in Asia. The male has a bright plumage with a band of white around the neck and the female is mottled brown

ring off vb (intr, adverb) chiefly Brit to terminate a telephone conversation by replacing the receiver

Ring of the Nibelung n 1 german myth a magic ring on which the dwarf Alberich placed a curse after it was stolen from him 2 the four great operas by Wagner, *Das Rheingold* (1869), *Die Walküre* (1870), *Siegfried* (1876), and *Götterdämmerung* (1876), based on this myth. Often shortened to: **The Ring**

ring out vb (adverb) 1 (tr) to accompany the departure of with bells (esp in the phrase **ring out the old year**) 2 (intr) to send forth a loud resounding noise

ring ouzel n a European thrush, *Turdus torquatus*, common in rocky areas. The male has a blackish plumage with a white band around the neck and the female is brown

ring road n a main road that bypasses a town or town centre. US names: **belt, beltway**

ring rot n a virulent bacterial disease of potatoes occurring in the vascular ring of the potato tuber. Also called: **potato ring rot**

ring-shout n a West African circle dance that has influenced jazz, surviving in the Black churches of the southern US

ringside ('rɪŋˌsaɪd) n 1 the area immediately surrounding an arena, esp the row of seats nearest a boxing or wrestling ring 2 a any place affording a close uninterrupted view b (as modifier): *a ringside seat*

ringster ('rɪŋstə) n a member of a ring controlling a market in antiques, art treasures, etc

ringtail ('rɪŋˌteɪl) n Also called: **ring-tailed cat** another name for **cacomistle** 2 Austral any of several possums having curling prehensile tails used to grasp branches while climbing. Also called: **ringtail possum**

ring-tailed adj (of an animal) having a tail marked with rings of a distinctive colour

ring taw n a game of marbles in which players attempt to knock other players' marbles out of a ring

ringtone ('rɪŋˌtəʊn) n a musical tune played by a mobile phone when a call is received

ring up vb (adverb) 1 chiefly Brit to make a telephone call (to) 2 (tr) to record on a cash register 3 (tr) to chronicle; record: *to ring up another success* 4 **ring up the curtain** a to begin a theatrical performance b (often foll by on) to make a start (on)

ringwomb ('rɪŋˌwuːm) n vet science a complication at lambing resulting from failure of the cervix to open

ringworm ('rɪŋˌwɜːm) n any of various fungal infections of the skin (esp the scalp) or nails, often appearing as itching circular patches. Also called: **tinea**

rink (rɪŋk) n 1 an expanse of ice for skating on, esp one that is artificially prepared and under cover 2 an area for roller skating on 3 a building or enclosure for ice skating or roller skating 4 bowls a strip of the green, usually about 5–7 metres wide, on which a game is played 5 curling the strip of ice on which the game is played, usually 41 by 4 metres 6 (in bowls and curling) the players on one side in a game [C14 (Scots): from Old French *renc* row, RANK¹]

rinkhals ('rɪŋkˌhals) n, pl -hals or -halses a venomous elapid snake, *Hemachatus hemachatus* of southern Africa, which spits venom at its enemies from a distance. Also called: **spitting snake** [Afrikaans, literally: ring neck]

rink rat n Canadian informal a young person who carries out chores at an ice-hockey rink in return for free skating time

rinse (rɪns) vb (tr) 1 to remove soap from (clothes, etc) by applying clean water in the final stage in washing 2 to wash lightly, esp without using soap 3 to give a light tint to (hair) ▷ n 4 the act or an instance of rinsing 5 hairdressing a liquid preparation put on the hair when wet to give a tint to it [C14 from Old French *rincer*, from Latin *recens* fresh, new] > 'rinsable or 'rinsible adj > ˌrinsa'bility or ˌrinsi'bility n > 'rinser n

rinsin' ('rɪnsɪn) adj slang excellent; wonderful

Rinzai ('rɪnzaɪ) n a Zen Buddhist school of Japan, characterized by the use of koans to lead to moments of insight and enlightenment

Rio Branco (Portuguese 'riu 'brəŋku) n 1 a city in W Brazil, capital of Acre state. Pop: 261 000 (2005 est) 2 a river in Brazil, flowing south to the Rio Negro. Length: 644 km (400 miles)

Río Bravo (Spanish 'rio 'braβo) n the Mexican name for the **Rio Grande**

Rio de Janeiro ('riːəʊ də dʒəˈnɪərəʊ) or **Rio** n 1 a port in SE Brazil, on Guanabara Bay: the country's chief port and its capital from 1763 to 1960; backed by mountains, notably Sugar Loaf Mountain; founded by the French in 1555 and taken by the Portuguese in 1567. Pop: 11 469 000 (2005 est). Related noun: **Carioca** 2 a state of E Brazil. Capital: Rio de Janeiro. Pop: 14 724 475 (2002). Area: 42 911 sq km (16 568 sq miles)

Río de la Plata ('riːəʊ də lɑː 'plaːtə) n See **Plata**

Río de Oro (Spanish 'rio ðe 'oro) n a former region of W Africa: comprised the S part of the Spanish Sahara (now Western Sahara)

Rio Grande n 1 ('riːəʊ 'grænd, 'grændɪ) a river in North America, rising in SW Colorado and flowing southeast to the Gulf of Mexico, forming the border between the US and Mexico. Length: about 3030 km (1885 miles). Mexican name: **Río Bravo** 2 (Portuguese 'riu 'grəndi) a port in SE Brazil, in SE Rio Grande do Sul state: serves as the port for Porto Alegre. Pop: 188 000 (2005 est)

Rio Grande do Norte (Portuguese 'riu 'grəndi du 'norti) n a state of NE Brazil, on the Atlantic: much of it is semiarid plateau. Capital: Natal. Pop: 2 852 784 (2002). Area: 53 014 sq km (20 469 sq miles)

Rio Grande do Sul (Portuguese 'riu 'grəndi du 'sul) n a state of S Brazil, on the Atlantic. Capital: Porto Alegre. Pop: 10 408 540 (2002). Area: 282 183 sq km (108 951 sq miles)

rioja (ri:'əʊxə) n a red or white wine, with a distinctive vanilla bouquet and flavour, produced around the Ebro river in central N Spain [C20 from *La Rioja*, the area where it is produced]

Río Negro ('riːəʊ 'neɪgrəʊ, 'nɛg-; Spanish 'rio 'neɣro) n See **Negro²**

riot ('raɪət) n 1 a a disturbance made by an unruly mob or (in law) three or more persons; tumult or uproar b (as modifier): *a riot gun; riot police; a riot shield* 2 boisterous activity; unrestrained revelry 3 an occasion of boisterous merriment 4 slang a person who occasions boisterous merriment 5 a dazzling or arresting display: *a riot of colour* 6 hunting the indiscriminate following of any scent by hounds 7 archaic wanton lasciviousness 8 **run riot** a to behave wildly and without restraint b (of plants) to grow rankly or profusely ▷ vb 9 (intr) to take part in a riot 10 (intr) to indulge in unrestrained revelry or merriment 11 (tr; foll by away) to spend (time or money) in wanton or loose living [C13 from Old French *riote* dispute, from *ruihoter* to quarrel, probably from *ruir* to make a commotion, from Latin *rugīre* to roar] > 'rioter n > 'rioting n

Riot Act n 1 criminal law (formerly in England) a statute of 1715 by which persons committing a riot had to disperse within an hour of the reading of the act by a magistrate 2 **read the riot act (to)** to warn or reprimand severely

riotous ('raɪətəs) adj 1 proceeding from or of the nature of riots or rioting 2 inciting to riot 3 characterized by wanton or lascivious revelry: *riotous living* 4 characterized by boisterous or unrestrained merriment: *riotous laughter* > 'riotously adv > 'riotousness n

riot shield n a large oblong curved transparent shield used by police controlling crowds

rip¹ (rɪp) vb rips, ripping, ripped 1 to tear or be torn violently or roughly; split or be rent 2 (tr; foll by off or out) to remove hastily, carelessly, or roughly 3 (intr) informal to move violently or precipitously; rush headlong 4 (intr; foll by into) informal to pour violent abuse (on); make a verbal attack (on) 5 (tr) to saw or split (wood) in the direction of the grain 6 (tr) informal computing to copy (music or software) without permission or making any payment 7 **let rip** to act or speak without restraint ▷ n 8 the place where something is torn; a tear or split 9 short for **ripsaw** ▷ See also **rip off, rip on, rip up** [C15 perhaps from Flemish *rippen*; compare Middle Dutch *rippen* to pull] > 'rippable adj

rip² (rɪp) n short for **riptide** (sense 1) [C18 perhaps from RIP¹]

rip³ (rɪp) n informal, archaic 1 something or someone of little or no value 2 an old worn-out horse 3 a dissolute character; reprobate [C18 perhaps altered from *rep*, shortened from REPROBATE]

RIP abbreviation for requiescat or requiescant in pace [Latin: may he, she, or they rest in peace]

riparian (raɪˈpɛərɪən) adj 1 of, inhabiting, or situated on the bank of a river 2 denoting or relating to the legal rights of the owner of land on a river bank, such as fishing or irrigation ▷ n 3 property law a person who owns land on a river bank [C19 from Latin *rīpārius*, from *rīpa* a river bank]

ripcord ('rɪpˌkɔːd) n 1 a cord that when pulled opens a parachute from its pack 2 a cord on the gas bag of a balloon that when pulled opens a panel, enabling gas to escape and the balloon to descend

ripe (raɪp) adj 1 (of fruit, grain, etc) mature and ready to be eaten or used; fully developed 2 mature enough to be eaten or used: *ripe cheese* 3 fully developed in mind or body 4 resembling ripe fruit, esp in redness or fullness: *a ripe complexion* 5 (postpositive; foll by for) ready or eager (to undertake or undergo an action) 6 (postpositive; foll by for) suitable; right or opportune: *the time is not yet ripe* 7 mature in judgment or knowledge 8 advanced but healthy (esp in the phrase **a ripe old age**) 9 slang a complete; thorough b excessive; exorbitant 10 slang slightly indecent; risqué [Old English *rīpe*; related to Old Saxon *rīpi*, Old High German *rīfi*, German *reif*] > 'ripely adv > 'ripeness n

ripen ('raɪpən) vb to make or become ripe > 'ripener n

ripieno (rɪˈpjɛnəʊ; Italian ri:'pje:no) n, pl -ni (-ni:) or -nos (in baroque concertos and concerti grossi) the full orchestra, as opposed to the instrumental soloists. Also called: **concerto** Compare **concertino** (sense 1) [C18 from Italian: from *ri-* RE- + *pieno*, from Latin *plēnus* full]

rip off 1 (tr) to tear violently or roughly (from) 2 (adverb) slang to steal from or cheat (someone) ▷ n rip-off 3 slang an article or articles stolen 4 slang a grossly overpriced article 5 slang the act of stealing or cheating

rip on verb (tr, adv) US slang to insult or criticize (someone) playfully; tease

Ripon ('rɪpən) n a city in N England, in North Yorkshire: cathedral (12th–16th centuries). Pop: 16 468 (2001)

riposte or **ripost** (rɪˈpɒst, rɪˈpəʊst) n 1 a swift sharp reply in speech or action 2 fencing a counterattack made immediately after a successful parry ▷ vb 3 (intr) to make a riposte [C18 from French, from Italian *risposta*, from *rispondere* to reply, RESPOND]

ripped (rɪpt) adj 1 torn: *ripped jeans* 2 informal denoting or having highly developed muscles, esp

r

abdominal muscles: *a ripped torso*

ripper ('rɪpə) *n* **1** a person who rips **2** a murderer who dissects or mutilates his victims' bodies **3** *informal, chiefly Austral and NZ* a fine or excellent person or thing

ripping ('rɪpɪŋ) *adj archaic, Brit slang* excellent; splendid > **'rippingly** *adv*

ripple[1] ('rɪpᵊl) *n* **1** a slight wave or undulation on the surface of water **2** a small wave or undulation in fabric, hair, etc **3** a sound reminiscent of water flowing quietly in ripples **4** *electronics* an oscillation of small amplitude superimposed on a steady value **5** *US and Canadian* another word for **riffle** (sense 4) **6** another word for **ripple mark** ▷ *vb* **7** (*intr*) to form ripples or flow with a rippling or undulating motion **8** (*tr*) to stir up (water) so as to form ripples **9** (*tr*) to make ripple marks **10** (*intr*) (of sounds) to rise and fall gently [C17 perhaps from RIP[1]] > **'rippler** *n* > **'rippling** *adj* > **'ripplingly** *adv* > **'ripply** *adj*

ripple[2] ('rɪpᵊl) *n* **1** a special kind of comb designed to separate the seed from the stalks in flax, hemp, or broomcorn ▷ *vb* **2** (*tr*) to comb with this tool [C14 of Germanic origin; compare Middle Dutch *repelen*, Middle High German *reffen* to ripple] > **'rippler** *n*

ripple control *n* the remote control of a switch by electrical impulses

ripple effect *n* the repercussions of an event or situation experienced far beyond its immediate location

ripple mark *n* one of a series of small wavy ridges of sand formed by waves on a beach, by a current in a sandy riverbed, or by wind on land: sometimes found fossilized on bedding planes of sedimentary rock

ripplet ('rɪplɪt) *n* a tiny ripple

rip-rap *n civil engineering* broken stones loosely deposited in water or on a soft bottom to provide a foundation and protect a riverbed or river banks from scour: used for revetments, embankments, breakwaters, etc [C19 reduplication of RAP[1]]

rip-roaring *adj informal* characterized by excitement, intensity, or boisterous behaviour

ripsaw ('rɪpˌsɔː) *n* a handsaw for cutting along the grain of timber

ripsnorter ('rɪpˌsnɔːtə) *n slang* a person or thing noted for intensity or excellence [C19 from RIP[1] + SNORTER] > **'ripˌsnorting** *adj*

riptide ('rɪpˌtaɪd) *n* **1** Also called: **rip, tide-rip** a stretch of turbulent water in the sea, caused by the meeting of currents or abrupt changes in depth **2** Also called: **rip current** a strong current, esp one flowing outwards from the shore, causing disturbance on the surface

Ripuarian (ˌrɪpjʊ'ɛərɪən) *adj* **1 a** of or relating to the group of Franks who lived during the 4th century near Cologne along the Rhine **b** of or designating their code of laws ▷ *n* **2** a Ripuarian Frank [C18 from Medieval Latin *Ripuārius*, perhaps from Latin *rīpa* a river bank]

rip up *vb* (*tr, adverb*) **1** to tear (paper) into small pieces **2** to annul, cancel, or unilaterally disregard **3** to dig up, dig into, or remove (a surface): *they are ripping up the street*

Rip Van Winkle ('rɪp væn 'wɪŋkᵊl) *n informal* **1** a person who is oblivious to changes, esp in social attitudes or thought **2** a person who sleeps a lot [C19 from a character who slept for 20 years, in a story (1819) by Washington Irving]

riroriro ('riːrəʊˌriːrəʊ) *n, pl* **-ros** another name for the **grey warbler** [Māori]

RISC (rɪsk) *n acronym for* reduced instruction set computer: a computer in which the set of instructions which it can perform has been reduced to the minimum, resulting in very fast data processing

rise (raɪz) *vb* **rises, rising, rose** (rəʊz) **risen** ('rɪzᵊn) (*mainly intr*) **1** to get up from a lying, sitting, kneeling, or prone position **2** to get out of bed, esp to begin one's day **3** to move from a lower to a higher position or place; ascend **4** to ascend or appear above the horizon: *the sun is rising* **5** to increase in height or level **6** to attain higher rank, status, or reputation: *he will rise in the world* **7** to be built or erected: *those blocks of flats are rising fast* **8** to become apparent; appear: *new troubles rose to afflict her* **9** to increase in strength, degree, intensity, etc: *her spirits rose* **10** to increase in amount or value: *house prices are always rising* **11** to swell up: *dough rises* **12** to become erect, stiff, or rigid: *the hairs on his neck rose in fear* **13** (of one's stomach or gorge) to manifest or feel nausea; retch **14** to become actively rebellious; revolt **15** to slope upwards: *the ground rises beyond the lake* **16** to return from the dead; be resurrected **17** to originate; come into existence **18** (of a session of a court, legislative assembly, etc) to come to an end; adjourn **19** *angling* (of fish) to come to the surface of the water, as when taking flies **20** (*tr*) *nautical* another term for **raise** (sense 20) **21** (often foll by *to*) *informal* to respond (to teasing, etc) or fall into a trap prepared for one ▷ *n* **22** the act or an instance of rising; ascent **23** an increase in height; elevation **24** an increase in rank, status, or position **25** an increase in amount, cost, or value **26** an increase in degree or intensity **27** *Brit* an increase in salary or wages. US and Canadian word: **raise 28** a piece of rising ground **29** an upward slope or incline **30** the appearance of the sun, moon, or other celestial body above the horizon **31** the vertical height of a step or of a flight of stairs **32** the vertical height of a roof above the walls or columns **33** the height of an arch above the impost level **34** *angling* the act or instance of fish coming to the surface of the water to take flies, etc **35** the beginning, origin, or source; derivation **36** *slang* an erection of the penis **37 get** *or* **take a rise out of** to provoke an angry or petulant reaction from **38 give rise to** to cause the development of; produce ▷ See also **rise above, rise to** [Old English *rīsan*; related to Old Saxon *rīsan*, Gothic *reisan*]

rise above *vb* (*intr, preposition*) to overcome or be unaffected by (something mean or contemptible)

risen ('rɪzᵊn) *vb* **1** the past participle of **rise** ▷ *adj* **2** restored from death; ascended into glory: *the risen Christ*

riser ('raɪzə) *n* **1** a person who rises, esp from bed: *an early riser* **2** the vertical part of a stair or step **3** a vertical pipe, esp one within a building

rise to *vb* (*intr, preposition*) to respond adequately to (the demands of something, esp a testing challenge)

risibility (ˌrɪzɪ'bɪlɪtɪ) *n, pl* **-ties 1** a tendency to laugh **2** hilarity; laughter

risible ('rɪzɪbᵊl) *adj* **1** having a tendency to laugh **2** causing laughter; ridiculous [C16 from Late Latin *rīsibilis*, from Latin *rīdēre* to laugh] > **'risibly** *adv*

rising ('raɪzɪŋ) *n* **1** an insurrection or rebellion; revolt **2** the yeast or leaven used to make dough rise in baking ▷ *adj* (*prenominal*) **3** increasing in rank, status, or reputation **4** increasing in maturity; growing up to adulthood: *the rising generation* ▷ *adv* **5** *informal* approaching the age of; nearly

rising damp *n* capillary movement of moisture from the ground into the walls of buildings. It results in structural damage up to a level of three feet

rising trot *n* a horse's trot in which the rider rises from the saddle every second beat. Compare **sitting trot**

risk (rɪsk) *n* **1** the possibility of incurring misfortune or loss **2** *insurance* **a** chance of a loss or other event on which a claim may be filed **b** the type of such an event, such as fire or theft **c** the amount of the claim should such an event occur **d** a person or thing considered with respect to the characteristics that may cause an insured event to occur **3 at risk a** vulnerable; likely to be lost or damaged **b** *social welfare* vulnerable to personal damage, to the extent that a welfare agency might take protective responsibility **4 no risk** *Austral informal* an expression of assent **5 take** *or* **run a risk** to proceed in an action without regard to the possibility of danger involved in it ▷ *vb* (*tr*) **6** to expose to danger or loss **7** to act in spite of the possibility of (injury or loss): *to risk a fall in climbing* [C17 from French *risque*, from Italian *risco*, from *rischiare* to be in peril, from Greek *rhiza* cliff (from the hazards of sailing along rocky coasts)] > **'risker** *n*

risk aversion *n* a strong disinclination to take risks

risk capital *n chiefly Brit* capital invested in an issue of ordinary shares, esp of a speculative enterprise. Also called: **venture capital**

risk factor *n med* a factor, such as a habit or an environmental condition, that predisposes an individual to develop a particular disease

risky ('rɪskɪ) *adj* **riskier, riskiest** involving danger; perilous > **'riskily** *adv* > **'riskiness** *n*

Risorgimento (rɪˌsɔːdʒɪ'mɛntəʊ) *n* the period of and the movement for the political unification of Italy in the 19th century [Italian, from *risorgere* to rise again, from Latin *resurgere*, from RE- + *surgere* to rise]

risotto (rɪ'zɒtəʊ) *n, pl* **-tos** a dish of rice cooked in stock and served variously with tomatoes, cheese, chicken, etc [C19 from Italian, from *riso* RICE]

risqué ('rɪskeɪ) *adj* bordering on impropriety or indecency: *a risqué joke* [C19 from French *risquer* to hazard, RISK]

Riss (rɪs) *n* the third major Pleistocene glaciation in Alpine Europe. See also **Günz, Mindel, Würm** [C20 named after the river *Riss*, a tributary of the Danube in Germany]

rissole ('rɪsəʊl) *n* a mixture of minced cooked meat coated in egg and breadcrumbs and fried. Compare **croquette** [C18 from French, probably ultimately from Latin *russus* red; see RUSSET]

risus sardonicus ('riːsəs sɑː'dɒnɪkəs) *n pathol* fixed contraction of the facial muscles resulting in a peculiar distorted grin, caused esp by tetanus. Also called: **trismus cynicus** ('trɪzməs 'sɪnɪkəs) [C17 New Latin, literally: sardonic laugh]

rit. *music abbreviation for* **1** ritardando **2** ritenuto

Ritalin ('rɪtəlɪn) *n trademark* a preparation of methylphenidate, a drug related to amphetamine, used to treat attention deficit disorder in children

ritardando (ˌrɪtɑː'dændəʊ) *adj, adv* another term for **rallentando** Abbreviation: **rit** [C19 from Italian, from *ritardare* to slow down]

rite (raɪt) *n* **1** a formal act or procedure prescribed or customary in religious ceremonies: *fertility rites; the rite of baptism* **2** a particular body of such acts or procedures, esp of a particular Christian Church: *the Latin rite* **3** a Christian Church: *the Greek rite* [C14 from Latin *rītus* religious ceremony]

ritenuto (ˌrɪtə'nuːtəʊ) *adj, adv music* **1** held back momentarily **2** another term for **rallentando** Abbreviation: **rit** [C19 from Italian, from past participle of *ritenere*, from Latin *retinēre* to hold back]

rite of passage *or* ***rite de passage*** (*French* rit də pɑsaʒ) *n* **1** a ceremony performed in some cultures at times when an individual changes his status, as at puberty and marriage **2** a significant event in a transitional period of someone's life

ritornello (ˌrɪtə'nɛləʊ) *n, pl* **-los** *or* **-li** (-liː) *music* **1** an orchestral passage between verses of an aria or song **2** a ripieno passage in a concerto grosso [C17 from Italian, literally: a little return, from *ritorno* a RETURN]

ritual ('rɪtjʊəl) *n* **1** the prescribed or established form of a religious or other ceremony **2** such prescribed forms in general or collectively **3** stereotyped activity or behaviour **4** *psychol* any repetitive behaviour, such as hand-washing, performed by a person with a compulsive personality disorder **5** any formal act, or procedure that is followed consistently ▷ *adj* **6** of, relating to, or characteristic of religious, social, or other rituals [C16 from Latin *rītuālis*, from *rītus*

RITE] > 'ritually *adv*

ritualism ('rɪtjʊəˌlɪzəm) *n* **1** emphasis, esp exaggerated emphasis, on the importance of rites and ceremonies **2** the study of rites and ceremonies, esp magical or religious ones > 'ritualist *n*

ritualistic (ˌrɪtjʊə'lɪstɪk) *adj* of, relating to, or suggestive of ritualism > ˌritual'istically *adv*

ritualize *or* **ritualise** ('rɪtjʊəˌlaɪz) *vb* **1** (*intr*) to engage in ritualism or devise rituals **2** (*tr*) to make (something) into a ritual

ritz (rɪts) *n* **put on the ritz** to assume a superior air or make an ostentatious display [from the luxury hotels created by the Swiss hotelier César Ritz (1850–1918)]

ritzy ('rɪtsɪ) *adj* ritzier, ritziest *slang* luxurious or elegant > 'ritzily *adv* > 'ritziness *n*

rivage ('rɪvɪdʒ) *n archaic* a bank, shore, or coast [c14 from Old French, from *rive* river bank, from Latin *rīpa*]

rival ('raɪv°l) *n* **1 a** a person, organization, team, etc, that competes with another for the same object or in the same field **b** (*as modifier*): *rival suitors; a rival company* **2** a person or thing that is considered the equal of another or others: *she is without rival in the field of economics* ▷ *vb* -vals, -valling, -valled *or US* -vals, -valing, -valed (*tr*) **3** to be the equal or near equal of: *an empire that rivalled Rome* **4** to try to equal or surpass; compete with in rivalry [c16 from Latin *rīvalis*, literally: one who shares the same brook, from *rīvus* a brook]

rivalry ('raɪvəlrɪ) *n, pl* -ries **1** the act of rivalling; competition **2** the state of being a rival or rivals > 'rivalrous *adj*

rive (raɪv) *vb* rives, riving, rived, rived *or* riven ('rɪv°n) (*usually passive*) **1** to split asunder: *a tree riven by lightning* **2** to tear apart: *riven to shreds* **3** *archaic* to break (the heart) or (of the heart) to be broken [c13 from Old Norse *rīfa*; related to Old Frisian *rīva*]

river ('rɪvə) *n* **1 a** a large natural stream of fresh water flowing along a definite course, usually into the sea, being fed by tributary streams **b** (*as modifier*): *river traffic; a river basin* **c** (*in combination*): *riverside; riverbed*. Related adjs: **fluvial, potamic 2** any abundant stream or flow: *a river of blood* **3 sell down the river** *informal* to deceive or betray [c13 from Old French *riviere*, from Latin *rīpārius* of a river bank, from *rīpa* bank] > 'riverless *adj*

river blindness *n* another name for **onchocerciasis**

river bugging *n* the activity or sport of rafting down fast-flowing rivers on a small inflatable single-seat craft, a **river bug**, that resembles an armchair

river horse *n* an informal name for the **hippopotamus**

riverine ('rɪvəˌraɪn) *adj* **1** of, like, relating to, or produced by a river **2** located or dwelling near a river; riparian

river red gum *n* a large Australian red gum tree, *Eucalyptus camaldulensis*, growing along river banks

Rivers ('rɪvəz) *n* a state of S Nigeria, in the Niger River Delta on the Gulf of Guinea. Capital: Port Harcourt. Pop: 4 103 372 (1995 est). Area: 21 850 sq km (8436 sq miles)

Riverside ('rɪvəˌsaɪd) *n* a city in SW California. Pop: 281 514 (2003 est)

rivet ('rɪvɪt) *n* **1** a short metal pin for fastening two or more pieces together, having a head at one end, the other end being hammered flat after being passed through holes in the pieces ▷ *vb* -ets, -eting, -eted (*tr*) **2** to join by riveting **3** to hammer in order to form into a head **4** (*often passive*) to cause to be fixed or held firmly, as in fascinated attention, horror, etc: *to be riveted to the spot* [c14 from Old French, from *river* to fasten, fix, of unknown origin] > 'riveter *n*

riveting ('rɪvɪtɪŋ) *adj* absolutely fascinating

Riviera (ˌrɪvɪ'ɛərə) *n* the Mediterranean coastal region between Cannes, France, and La Spezia, Italy: contains some of Europe's most popular resorts [c18 from Italian literally: shore,

ultimately from Latin *rīpa* bank, shore]

rivière (ˌrɪvɪ'ɛə) *n* a necklace the diamonds or other precious stones of which gradually increase in size up to a large centre stone [c19 from French: brook, RIVER]

rivulet ('rɪvjʊlɪt) *n* a small stream [c16 from Italian *rivoletto*, from Latin *rīvulus*, from *rīvus* stream]

rix-dollar ('rɪksˌdɒlə) *n* any of various former Scandinavian or Dutch small silver coins. Also called: rijksdaaler, rigsdaler [c16 partial translation of obsolete Dutch *rijksdaler*; *rijk* realm, kingdom]

Riyadh (rɪ'jɑːd) *n* the joint capital (with Mecca) of Saudi Arabia, situated in a central oasis: the largest city in the country. Pop: 5 514 000 (2005 est)

riyal (rɪ'jɑːl) *n* the standard monetary unit of Qatar, divided into 100 dirhams; Saudi Arabia, divided into 100 halala; and Yemen, divided into 100 fils [from Arabic *riyāl*, from Spanish *real* REAL[2]]

Rizal (Spanish ri'θal) *n* another name for **Pasay**

RL 1 abbreviation for Rugby League **2** ▷ *international car registration for* (Republic of) Lebanon

rly abbreviation for railway

rm abbreviation for **1** ream **2** room

RM abbreviation for **1** Royal Mail **2** Royal Marines **3** international car registration for (Republic of) Madagascar

RMA abbreviation for Royal Military Academy (Sandhurst)

RME abbreviation for **1** religious and moral education **2** rape *or* rapeseed methyl ester: a fuel derived from rapeseed oil

R-methodology *n* any statistical methodology in psychology that is contrasted with Q-methodology

RMM international car registration for (Republic of) Mali

r.m.m. abbreviation for relative molecular mass

rms abbreviation for root mean square

RMS abbreviation for **1** Royal Mail Service **2** Royal Mail Steamer

RMT abbreviation for National Union of Rail, Maritime and Transport Workers

Rn the chemical symbol for radon

RN 1 abbreviation for Royal Navy **2** ▷ *international car registration for* (Republic of) Niger

RNA *n biochem* ribonucleic acid; any of a group of nucleic acids, present in all living cells, that play an essential role in the synthesis of proteins. On hydrolysis they yield the pentose sugar ribose, the purine bases adenine and guanine, the pyrimidine bases cytosine and uracil, and phosphoric acid. See also **messenger RNA, transfer RNA, ribosomal RNA, DNA**

RNAS abbreviation for **1** Royal Naval Air Service(s) **2** Royal Naval Air Station

RNIB *Brit* abbreviation for Royal National Institute for the Blind

RNID *Brit* abbreviation for Royal National Institute for Deaf People

RNLI abbreviation for Royal National Lifeboat Institution

RNR abbreviation for Royal Naval Reserve

RNVR abbreviation for Royal Naval Volunteer Reserve

RNWMP (in Canada) abbreviation for Royal Northwest Mounted Police: a former name for the Royal Canadian Mounted Police

RNZ abbreviation for Radio New Zealand

RNZAF abbreviation for Royal New Zealand Air Force

RNZN abbreviation for Royal New Zealand Navy

ro the internet domain name for Romania

RO international car registration for Romania

roach[1] (rəʊtʃ) *n, pl* roaches *or* roach **1** a European freshwater cyprinid food fish, *Rutilus rutilus*, having a deep compressed body and reddish ventral and tail fins **2** any of various similar fishes [c14 from Old French *roche*, of obscure origin]

roach[2] (rəʊtʃ) *n* **1** short for **cockroach 2** *slang* the

butt of a cannabis cigarette

roach[3] (rəʊtʃ) *n nautical* **1** the amount by which the leech of a fore-and-aft sail projects beyond an imaginary straight line between the clew and the head **2** the curve at the foot of a square sail [c18 of unknown origin]

roach clip *n slang* a small clip resembling tweezers, used to hold the butt of a cannabis cigarette, in order to prevent burning one's fingers

roached (rəʊtʃt) *adj* arched convexly, as the back of certain breeds of dog, such as the whippet [c19 from ROACH[3] *or* roach (vb) to cut (a sail) into a roach]

road (rəʊd) *n* **1 a** an open way, usually surfaced with asphalt or concrete, providing passage from one place to another **b** (*as modifier*): *road traffic; a road map; a road sign* **c** (*in combination*): *the roadside* **2 a** a street **b** (*capital when part of a name*): *London Road* **3 a** *US* short for **railroad b** *Brit* one of the tracks of a railway **4** a way, path, or course: *the road to fame* **5** (*often plural*) Also called: roadstead *nautical* a partly sheltered anchorage **6** a drift or tunnel in a mine, esp a level one **7 hit the road** *slang* to start or resume travelling **8 on the road a** travelling, esp as a salesman **b** (of a theatre company, pop group, etc) on tour **c** leading a wandering life **9 take (to) the road** to begin a journey or tour **10 one for the road** *informal* a last alcoholic drink before leaving [Old English *rād*; related to *rīdan* to RIDE, and to Old Saxon *rēda*, Old Norse *reith*] > 'roadless *adj*

road agent *n US* (formerly) a bandit who robbed stagecoaches; highwayman

road allowance *n Canadian* land reserved by the government to be used for public roads

roadbed ('rəʊdˌbɛd) *n* **1** the material used to make a road **2** a layer of ballast that supports the sleepers of a railway track

roadblock ('rəʊdˌblɒk) *n* **1** a barrier set up across a road by the police or military, in order to stop a fugitive, inspect traffic, etc **2** a difficulty or obstacle to progress

road book *n* a book of maps, sometimes including a gazetteer

road-fund licence *n Brit* a licence showing that the tax payable in respect of a motor vehicle has been paid [c20 from the former *road fund* for the maintenance of public highways]

road hog *n informal* a selfish or aggressive driver

roadholding ('rəʊdˌhəʊldɪŋ) *n* the extent to which a motor vehicle is stable and does not skid, esp at high speeds, or on sharp bends or wet roads

roadhouse ('rəʊdˌhaʊs) *n* a pub, restaurant, etc, that is situated at the side of a road, esp a country road

road hump *n* the official name for **sleeping policeman**

roadie ('rəʊdɪ) *n informal* a person who transports and sets up equipment for a band or group

roadkill ('rəʊdˌkɪl) *n chiefly US* the remains of an animal or animals killed on the road by motor vehicles

road map *n* **1** a map intended for drivers, showing roads, distances, etc in a country or area **2** a plan or guide for future actions

road metal *n* crushed rock, broken stone, etc, used to construct a road

road movie *n* a genre of film in which the chief character is on the run or travelling in search of, or to escape from, himself

road pricing *n* the practice of charging motorists for using certain stretches of road, in order to reduce congestion

road rage *n* aggressive behaviour by a motorist in response to the actions of another road user

road rash *n US and Canadian informal* grazing of the skin as a result of falling off a bicycle, skateboard, etc, onto a hard surface

roadroller ('rəʊdˌrəʊlə) *n* a motor vehicle with heavy rollers for compressing road surfaces during road-making

r

roadrunner ('rəʊd,rʌnə) *n* a terrestrial crested bird, *Geococcyx californianus*, of Central and S North America, having a streaked plumage and long tail: family *Cuculidae* (cuckoos). Also called: chaparral cock

road show *n* **1 a** a radio show broadcast live from one of a number of towns or venues being visited by a disc jockey who is touring an area **b** the touring disc jockey and the personnel and equipment needed to present such a show **2** a group of entertainers on tour **3** any occasion when an organization attracts publicity while touring or visiting: *an antiques road show*

roadstead ('rəʊd,stɛd) *n* *nautical* another word for **road** (sense 5)

roadster ('rəʊdstə) *n* **1** an open car, esp one seating only two **2** a kind of bicycle

road tax *n* a tax paid, usually annually, on motor vehicles in use on the roads

road test *n* **1** a test to ensure that a vehicle is roadworthy, esp after repair or servicing, by driving it on roads **2** a test of something in actual use ▷ *vb* **road-test** (*tr*) **3** to test (a vehicle) in this way **4** to test (something) in a real and appropriate context

road train *n* *Austral* a line of linked trailers pulled by a truck, used for transporting stock, etc

roadway ('rəʊd,weɪ) *n* **1** the surface of a road **2** the part of a road that is used by vehicles

roadwork ('rəʊd,wɜːk) *n* sports training by running along roads

roadworks ('rəʊd,wɜːks) *pl n* repairs to a road or cable under a road, esp when forming a hazard or obstruction to traffic

roadworthy ('rəʊd,wɜːðɪ) *adj* **1** (of a motor vehicle) mechanically sound; fit for use on the roads ▷ *n, pl* **-ies** **2** *South African* a certificate of roadworthiness for a motor vehicle > '**road,worthiness** *n*

roam (rəʊm) *vb* **1** to travel or walk about with no fixed purpose or direction; wander ▷ *n* **2** the act of roaming [c13 origin unknown] > '**roamer** *n*

roan (rəʊn) *adj* **1** (of a horse) having a bay (**red roan**), chestnut (**strawberry roan**), or black (**blue roan**) coat sprinkled with white hairs ▷ *n* **2** a horse having such a coat **3** a soft unsplit sheepskin leather with a close tough grain, used in bookbinding, etc [c16 from Old French, from Spanish *roano*, probably from Gothic *rauths* red]

Roanoke Island ('rəʊə,nəʊk) *n* an island off the coast of North Carolina: site of the first attempted English settlement in America. Length: 19 km (12 miles). Average width: 5 km (3 miles)

roar (rɔː) *vb* (*mainly intr*) **1** (of lions and other animals) to utter characteristic loud growling cries **2** (*also tr*) (of people) to utter (something) with a loud deep cry, as in anger or triumph **3** to laugh in a loud hearty unrestrained manner **4** (of horses) to breathe with laboured rasping sounds. See **roaring** (sense 6) **5** (of the wind, waves, etc) to blow or break loudly and violently, as during a storm **6** (of a fire) to burn fiercely with a roaring sound **7** (of a machine, gun, etc) to operate or move with a loud harsh noise **8** (*tr*) to bring (oneself) into a certain condition by roaring: *to roar oneself hoarse* ▷ *n* **9** a loud deep cry, uttered by a person or crowd, esp in anger or triumph **10** a prolonged loud cry of certain animals, esp lions **11** any similar noise made by a fire, the wind, waves, artillery, an engine, etc **12** a loud unrestrained burst of laughter ▷ See also **roar up** [Old English *rārian*; related to Old High German *rērēn*, Middle Dutch *reren*] > '**roarer** *n*

roaring ('rɔːrɪŋ) *adj* **1** *informal* very brisk and profitable (esp in the phrase **a roaring trade**) **2** **the roaring days** *Austral* the period of the Australian goldrushes **3** *Irish derogatory informal* (intensifier): *a roaring communist* ▷ *adv* **4** noisily or boisterously (esp in the phrase **roaring drunk**) ▷ *n* **5** a loud prolonged cry **6** a debilitating breathing defect of horses characterized by rasping sounds with each breath: caused by inflammation of the respiratory tract or obstruction of the larynx. Compare **whistling.** > '**roaringly** *adv*

Roaring Forties *pl n* the *nautical* the areas of ocean between 40° and 50° latitude in the S Hemisphere, noted for gale-force winds

roarming ('rɔːmɪŋ) *adj* *Midland English dialect* severe: *a roarming cold*

roar up *vb* (*tr, adverb*) *Austral informal* to rebuke or reprimand (a person)

roast (rəʊst) *vb* (*mainly tr*) **1** to cook (meat or other food) by dry heat, usually with added fat and esp in an oven **2** to brown or dry (coffee, etc) by exposure to heat **3** *metallurgy* to heat (an ore) in order to produce a concentrate that is easier to smelt **4** to heat (oneself or something) to an extreme degree, as when sunbathing, sitting before the fire, etc **5** (*intr*) to be excessively and uncomfortably hot **6** *informal* to criticize severely ▷ *n* **7** something that has been roasted, esp meat [c13 from Old French *rostir*, of Germanic origin; compare Middle Dutch *roosten* to roast]

roaster ('rəʊstə) *n* **1** a person or thing that roasts **2** a roasting tin **3** a piece of food, such as a chicken or a potato, that is suitable for roasting

roasting ('rəʊstɪŋ) *informal* ▷ *adj* **1** extremely hot ▷ *n* **2** severe criticism

rob (rɒb) *vb* **robs, robbing, robbed** **1** to take something from (someone) illegally, as by force or threat of violence (*tr*) **2** to plunder (a house, shop, etc) **3** (*tr*) to deprive unjustly [c13 from Old French *rober*, of Germanic origin; compare Old High German *roubōn* to rob] > '**robber** *n*

robalo ('rɒbə,ləʊ, 'rəʊ-) *n, pl* **-los** *or* **-lo** any percoid fish of the family *Centropomidae*, occurring in warm and tropical (mostly marine) waters. Some of the larger species, such as the snooks, are important food fishes and many of the smaller ones are aquarium fishes [Spanish, probably changed from *lobaro* (unattested), from *lobo* wolf, from Latin *lupus*]

roband ('rɒbənd, 'rəʊbənd) *or* **robbin** *n* *nautical* a piece of marline used for fastening a sail to a spar [c18 probably related to Middle Dutch *rabant*, from *ra* sailyard + *bant* band]

Robben Island ('rɒbᵊn) *n* a small island in South Africa, 11 km (7 miles) off the Cape Peninsula: formerly used by the South African government to house political prisoners

robber crab *n* a terrestrial crab, *Birgus latro*, of the Indo-Pacific region, known for its habit of climbing coconut palms to feed on the nuts

robber fly *n* any of the predatory dipterous flies constituting the family *Asilidae*, which have a strong bristly body with piercing mouthparts and which prey on other insects. Also called: **bee killer, assassin fly**

robber trench *n* *archaeol* a trench that originally contained the foundations of a wall, the stones of which have been taken away

robbery ('rɒbərɪ) *n, pl* **-beries** **1** *criminal law* the stealing of property from a person by using or threatening to use force **2** the act or an instance of robbing

robbin ('rɒbɪn) *n* *nautical* another word for **roband**

robe (rəʊb) *n* **1** any loose flowing garment, esp the official vestment of a peer, judge, or academic **2** a dressing gown or bathrobe **3** *Austral informal* a wardrobe ▷ *vb* **4** to put a robe, etc, on (oneself or someone else); dress [c13 from Old French: of Germanic origin; compare Old French *rober* to ROB, Old High German *roub* booty]

robe-de-chambre *French* (rɔbdəʃɑ̃brə) *n, pl* ***robes-de-chambre*** (rɔbdəʃɑ̃brə) a dressing gown or bathrobe

Robertson screw ('rɒbətsᵊn) *n* *trademark* a screw having a square hole in the head into which a screwdriver with a square point (**Robertson screwdriver** (*Trademark*)) fits [c20 after its inventor P L Robertson (1896–1951), a Canadian industrialist]

robin ('rɒbɪn) *n* **1** Also called: **robin redbreast** a small Old World songbird, *Erithacus rubecula*, related to the thrushes: family *Muscicapidae*. The male has a brown back, orange-red breast and face, and grey underparts **2** a North American thrush, *Turdus migratorius*, similar to but larger than the Old World robin **3** any of various similar birds having a reddish breast [c16 arbitrary use of given name]

Robin Goodfellow ('rɒbɪn 'gʊd,fɛləʊ) *n* another name for **puck²**

robing room *n* a room in a palace, court, etc, where official robes of office are put on

Robin Hood *n* a legendary English outlaw of the reign of Richard I, who according to tradition lived in Sherwood Forest and robbed the rich to give to the poor

robinia (rə'bɪnɪə) *n* any tree of the leguminous genus *Robinia*, esp the locust tree (see **locust** (sense 2))

robin's-egg blue *n* *chiefly US* **a** a light greenish-blue colour **b** (*as adjective*): *a robin's-egg-blue dress*

Robinson Crusoe *n* the hero of Daniel Defoe's novel *Robinson Crusoe* (1719), who survived being shipwrecked on a desert island. The character is supposedly based on the Scottish sailor Alexander Selkirk (1676–1721), who was marooned on one of the islets of Juan Fernández

roble ('rəʊbleɪ) *n* **1** Also called: **white oak** an oak tree, *Quercus lobata*, of California, having leathery leaves and slender pointed acorns **2** any of several similar or related trees [c19 from Spanish: from Latin *rōbur* oak, strength]

roborant ('rəʊbərənt, 'rɒb-) *adj* **1** tending to fortify or increase strength ▷ *n* **2** a drug or agent that increases strength [c17 from Latin *roborāre* to strengthen, from *rōbur* an oak]

robot ('rəʊbɒt) *n* **1** any automated machine programmed to perform specific mechanical functions in the manner of a man **2** (*modifier*) not controlled by man; automatic: *a robot pilot* **3** a person who works or behaves like a machine; automaton **4** *South African* a set of traffic lights [c20 (used in RUR, a play by Karel Čapek) from Czech *robota* work; related to Old Slavonic *rabota* servitude, German *Arbeit* work] > **ro'botic** *adj* > '**robotism** *or* '**robotry** *n* > '**robot-,like** *adj*

robot bomb *n* another name for the **V-1**

robot dancing, robotics *or* **robotic dancing** *n* a dance of the 1980s characterized by jerky mechanical movements

robotics (rəʊ'bɒtɪks) *n* (*functioning as singular*) **1** the science or technology of designing, building, and using robots **2** another name for **robot dancing**

robotize *or* **robotise** ('rəʊbə,taɪz) *vb* (*tr*) **1** *chiefly US* to automate **2** to cause (a person) to be or become mechanical and lifeless, like a robot

Robson ('rɒbsən) *n* **Mount** a mountain in SW Canada, in E British Columbia: the highest peak in the Canadian Rockies. Height: 3954 m (12 972 ft)

robust (rəʊ'bʌst, 'rəʊbʌst) *adj* **1** strong in constitution; hardy; vigorous **2** sturdily built: *a robust shelter* **3** requiring or suited to physical strength: *a robust sport* **4** (esp of wines) having a rich full-bodied flavour **5** rough or boisterous **6** (of thought, intellect, etc) straightforward and imbued with common sense [c16 from Latin *rōbustus*, from *rōbur* an oak, strength] > **ro'bustly** *adv*

robusta (rəʊ'bʌstə) *n* **1** a species of coffee tree, *Coffea canephora* **2** coffee or coffee beans obtained from this plant [from Latin *rōbustus* strong]

robustious (rəʊ'bʌstʃəs) *adj* *archaic* **1** rough; boisterous **2** strong, robust, or stout > **ro'bustiously** *adv* > **ro'bustiousness** *n*

robustness (rəʊ'bʌstnɪs) *n* **1** the quality of being robust **2** *computing* the ability of a computer system to cope with errors during execution

roc (rɒk) *n* (in Arabian legend) a bird of enormous size and power [c16 from Arabic *rukhkh*, from Persian *rukh*]

ROC *abbreviation for* Royal Observer Corps

Roca ('rəʊkə) *n* **Cape.** a cape in SW central Portugal, near Lisbon: the westernmost point of continental Europe

rocaille (rɒ'kaɪ) *n* decorative rock or shell work,

esp as ornamentation in a rococo fountain, grotto, or interior [from French, from *roc* ROCK¹]

rocambole (ˈrɒkəmˌbəʊl) *n* a variety of sand leek whose garlic-like bulb is used for seasoning [c17 from French, from German *Rockenbolle*, literally: distaff bulb (with reference to its shape)]

Rochdale (ˈrɒtʃˌdeɪl) *n* **1** a town in NW England, in Rochdale unitary authority, Greater Manchester: former centre of the textile industry. Pop: 95 769 (2001) **2** a unitary authority in NW England, in Greater Manchester. Pop: 206 600 (2003 est). Area: 159 sq km (61 sq miles)

Roche limit (rɒʃ) *n astronomy* the distance from the centre of a body, such as a planet, at which the tidal forces are stronger than the mutual gravitational attraction between two adjacent orbiting objects [c19 named after E A Roche (1820–83), French mathematician]

Rochelle powder (rɒˈʃɛl) *n* another name for **Seidlitz powder** [c18 named after *La Rochelle*, French port]

Rochelle salt *n* a white crystalline double salt, sodium potassium tartrate, used in Seidlitz powder. Formula: $KNaC_4H_4O_6.4H_2O$

roche moutonnée (ˈrəʊʃ ˌmuːtəˈneɪ) *n, pl* roches moutonnées (ˈrəʊʃ ˌmuːtəˈneɪz) a rounded mass of rock smoothed and striated by ice that has flowed over it [c19 French, literally: fleecy rock, from *mouton* sheep]

Rochester (ˈrɒtʃɪstə) *n* **1** a city in SE England, in Medway unitary authority, Kent, on the River Medway. Pop: 27 123 (2001) **2** a city in NW New York State, on Lake Ontario. Pop: 215 093 (2003 est) **3** a city in the US, in Minnesota: site of the Mayo Clinic. Pop: 92 507 (2003 est)

rochet (ˈrɒtʃɪt) *n* a white surplice with tight sleeves, worn by bishops, abbots, and certain other Church dignitaries [c14 from Old French, from *roc* coat, outer garment, of Germanic origin; compare Old High German *roc* coat]

rock¹ (rɒk) *n* **1** *geology* any aggregate of minerals that makes up part of the earth's crust. It may be unconsolidated, such as a sand, clay, or mud, or consolidated, such as granite, limestone, or coal. See also **igneous, sedimentary, metamorphic 2** any hard mass of consolidated mineral matter, such as a boulder **3** *chiefly US, Canadian, and Austral* a stone **4** a person or thing suggesting a rock, esp in being dependable, unchanging, or providing firm foundation **5** *Brit* a hard sweet, typically a long brightly-coloured peppermint-flavoured stick, sold esp in holiday resorts **6** *slang* a jewel, esp a diamond **7** short for **rock salmon 8** (*plural*) *slang* the testicles **9** *slang* another name for **crack** (sense 29) **10** between a rock and a hard place having to choose between two equally unpleasant alternatives **11** on the rocks **a** in a state of ruin or destitution **b** (of drinks, esp whisky) served with ice [c14 from Old French *roche*, of unknown origin]

rock² (rɒk) *vb* **1** to move or cause to move from side to side or backwards and forwards **2** to reel or sway or cause (someone) to reel or sway, as with a violent shock or emotion **3** (*tr*) to shake or move (something) violently **4** (*intr*) to dance in the rock-and-roll style **5** *mining* to wash (ore) or (of ore) to be washed in a cradle **6** (*tr*) to roughen (a copper plate) with a rocker before engraving a mezzotint **7** rock the boat *informal* to create a disturbance in the existing situation ▷ *n* **8** a rocking motion **9** short for **rock and roll 10** Also called: rock music any of various styles of pop music having a heavy beat, derived from rock and roll ▷ See also **rock up** [Old English *roccian*; related to Middle Dutch, Old High German *rocken*, German *rücken*]

Rock (rɒk) *n* **1** the. an informal name for **Gibraltar 2** the. a Canadian informal name for **Newfoundland**

rockabilly (ˈrɒkəˌbɪlɪ) *n* **a** a fast, spare style of White rock music which originated in the mid-1950s in the US South **b** (*as modifier*): *a rockabilly number* [c20 from ROCK (AND ROLL) + (HILL)BILLY]

Rockall (ˈrɒkɔːl) *n* an uninhabited British island in the N Atlantic, 354 km (220 miles) W of the Outer Hebrides. Area: 0.07 ha (0.18 acres)

rock and roll *or* **rock'n'roll** *n* **1 a** a type of pop music originating in the 1950s as a blend of rhythm and blues and country and western. It is generally based upon the twelve-bar blues, the first and third beats in each bar being heavily accented **b** (*as modifier*): *the rock-and-roll era* **2** dancing performed to such music, with exaggerated body movements stressing the beat ▷ *vb* **3** (*intr*) to perform this dance > rock and roller *or* rock'n'roller *n*

rockaway (ˈrɒkəˌweɪ) *n US* a four-wheeled horse-drawn carriage, usually with two seats and a hard top

rock bass (bæs) *n* **1** a North American freshwater percoid fish, *Ambloplites rupestris*: an important food fish; family *Centrarchidae* (sunfishes, etc) **2** any similar or related fish

rock boot *n* a tight-fitting rock-climbing boot with a canvas or suede upper and smooth rubber sole, designed to give good grip on small holds

rock borer *n* any of various sea creatures that bore into rock, such as some sea urchins, sponges, annelid worms, barnacles, isopods, and molluscs

rock bottom *n* **a** the lowest possible level **b** (*as modifier*): *rock-bottom prices*

rock-bound *adj* hemmed in or encircled by rocks. Also (poetic): rock-girt

rock brake *n* any of various ferns of the genera *Pellaea* and *Cryptogramma*, which grow on rocky ground and have sori at the ends of the veins

rock cake *n* a small cake containing dried fruit and spice, with a rough surface supposed to resemble a rock

rock candy *n US and Canadian* a hard candy, typically a long brightly-coloured peppermint-flavoured stick. Also called (in Britain and certain other countries): rock

rock chopper *n Austral slang* a Roman Catholic [from the initials RC]

rock climb *n* **1** an instance of rock climbing or the route followed ▷ *vb* rock-climb (*intr*) **2** to practise rock climbing

rock climbing *n* the technique and sport of climbing on steep rock faces, usually with ropes and other equipment and as part of a team or pair

rock cod *n Austral* **1** any of various marine fishes found in rocky habitats in Australian waters NZ **2** another name for **blue cod**

rock cress *n* another name for **arabis**

rock crystal *n* a pure transparent colourless quartz, used in electronic and optical equipment. Formula: SiO_2

rock cycle *n* another name for **geological cycle**

rock dove *or* **pigeon** *n* a common dove, *Columba livia*, from which domestic and feral pigeons are descended. It has a pale grey plumage with black-striped wings

rocker (ˈrɒkə) *n* **1** any of various devices that transmit or operate with a rocking motion. See also **rocker arm 2** another word for **rocking chair 3** either of two curved supports on the legs of a chair or other article of furniture on which it may rock **4** a steel tool with a curved toothed cage, used to roughen the copper plate in engraving a mezzotint **5** *mining* another word for **cradle** (sense 9) **6 a** an ice skate with a curved blade **b** the curve itself **7** *skating* **a** a figure consisting of three interconnecting circles **b** a half turn in which the skater turns through 180°, so facing about while continuing to move in the same direction **8** a rock-music performer, fan, or song **9** *Brit* an adherent of a youth movement rooted in the 1950s, characterized by motorcycle trappings. Compare **mod¹ 10** off one's rocker *slang* crazy; demented

rocker arm *n* a lever that rocks about a pivot, esp a lever in an internal-combustion engine that transmits the motion of a pushrod or cam to a valve

rockery (ˈrɒkərɪ) *n, pl* -eries a garden constructed with rocks, esp one where alpine plants are grown. Also called: rock garden

rocket¹ (ˈrɒkɪt) *n* **1** a self-propelling device, esp a cylinder containing a mixture of solid explosives, used as a firework, distress signal, line carrier, etc **2 a** any vehicle propelled by a rocket engine, esp one used to carry a warhead, spacecraft, etc **b** (*as modifier*): *rocket propulsion; rocket launcher* **3** *Brit and NZ informal* a severe reprimand (esp in the phrase get a rocket) ▷ *vb* -ets, -eting, -eted **4** (*tr*) to propel (a missile, spacecraft, etc) by means of a rocket **5** (*intr*; foll by *off, away*, etc) to move off at high speed **6** (*intr*) to rise rapidly: *he rocketed to the top* [c17 from Old French *roquette*, from Italian *rochetto* a little distaff, from *rocca* distaff, of Germanic origin]

rocket² (ˈrɒkɪt) *n* **1** Also called: arugula a Mediterranean plant, *Eruca sativa*, having yellowish-white flowers and leaves used as a salad: family *Brassicaceae* (crucifers) **2** any of several plants of the related genus *Sisymbrium*, esp *S. irio* (**London rocket**), which grow on waste ground and have pale yellow flowers **3** yellow rocket any of several yellow-flowered plants of the related genus *Barbarea*, esp *B. vulgaris* **4** sea rocket any of several plants of the related genus *Cakile*, esp *C. maritima*, which grow along the seashores of Europe and North America and have mauve, pink, or white flowers **5** dame's rocket another name for **dame's violet** ▷ See also **dyer's rocket, wall rocket** [c16 from French *roquette*, from Italian *rochetta*, from Latin *ērūca* a caterpillar, hairy plant]

rocketeer (ˌrɒkɪˈtɪə) *n* an engineer or scientist concerned with the design, operation, or launching of rockets

rocket engine *n* a reaction engine in which a fuel and oxidizer are burnt in a combustion chamber, the products of combustion expanding through a nozzle and producing thrust. Also called: rocket motor

rocketry (ˈrɒkɪtrɪ) *n* the science and technology of the design, operation, maintenance, and launching of rockets

rocket science *n informal* an activity requiring considerable intelligence and ability (esp in the phrase not exactly rocket science) > rocket scientist *n*

rockfish (ˈrɒkˌfɪʃ) *n, pl* -fish *or* -fishes **1** any of various fishes that live among rocks, esp scorpaenid fishes of the genus *Sebastodes* and related genera, such as *S. caurinus* (**copper rockfish**) of North American Pacific coastal waters **2** *Brit* any of several coarse fishes when used as food, esp the dogfish or wolffish. Formerly called: rock salmon

rock flour *n* very finely powdered rock, produced when rocks are ground together (as along the faces of a moving fault or during the motion of glaciers) and are thus chemically unweathered

Rockford (ˈrɒkfəd) *n* a city in N Illinois, on the Rock River. Pop: 151 725 (2003 est)

rock garden *n* a garden featuring rocks or rockeries

Rockhampton (rɒkˈhæmptən, -ˈhæmtən) *n* a port in Australia, in E Queensland on the Fitzroy River. Pop: 59 475 (2001)

rockhopper (ˈrɒkˌhɒpə) *n* **1** a small penguin, *Eudyptes crestatus*, of Antarctica, the Falkland Islands, and New Zealand, with a yellow crest on each side of its head **2** *Austral informal* a fisherman who fishes from the rocks on the sea coast

Rockies (ˈrɒkɪz) *pl n* another name for the **Rocky Mountains**

rocking chair *n* a chair set on curving supports so that the sitter may rock backwards and forwards

rocking horse *n* a toy horse mounted on a pair of rockers on which a child can rock to and fro in a seesaw movement

rocking stone *n* a boulder so delicately poised that it can be rocked. Also called: logan, logan-stone

r

rockling ('rɒklɪŋ) *n, pl* **-lings** *or* **-ling** any small gadoid fish of the genera *Gaidropsarus, Ciliata,* etc (formerly all included in *Motella*), which have an elongated body with barbels around the mouth and occur mainly in the North Atlantic Ocean [C17 from ROCK¹ + -LING¹]

rock lobster *n* another name for the **spiny lobster**

rock mechanics *n (functioning as singular)* the study of the mechanical behaviour of rocks, esp their strength, elasticity, permeability, porosity, density, and reaction to stress

rock melon *n US, Austral, and NZ* another name for **cantaloupe**

rock'n'roll *n* a variant spelling of **rock and roll** > **rock'n'roller** *n*

rock oil *n* another name for **petroleum**

rockoon (rɒ'kuːn) *n* a rocket carrying scientific equipment for studying the upper atmosphere, fired from a balloon at high altitude [C20 from ROCKET¹ + BALLOON]

rock pigeon *n* another name for **rock dove**

rock plant *n* any plant that grows on rocks or in rocky ground

rock rabbit *n South African* another name for the **hyrax**

rockrose ('rɒk,rəʊz) *n* any of various cistaceous shrubs or herbaceous plants of the Eurasian genera *Helianthemum, Tuberaria,* and *Cistus,* cultivated for their yellow-white or reddish roselike flowers

rock salmon *n Brit* (formerly) any of several coarse fishes when used as food, esp the dogfish or wolffish: now known as **catfish** or **rockfish**

rock salt *n* another name for **halite**

rockshaft ('rɒk,ʃɑːft) *n* a shaft that rotates backwards and forwards rather than continuously, esp one used in the valve gear of a steam engine

rock snake *or* **python** *n* any large Australasian python of the genus *Liasis*

rock steady *n* a type of slow Jamaican dance music of the 1960s

rock tripe *n Canadian* any of various edible lichens, esp of the genus *Umbilicaria,* that grow on rocks and are used in the North as a survival food

rock up *vb (intr, adverb) South African* to arrive late or unannounced

rockweed ('rɒk,wiːd) *n* any of various seaweeds that grow on rocks exposed at low tide

rock wool *n* another name for **mineral wool**

rocky¹ ('rɒkɪ) *adj* **rockier, rockiest** **1** consisting of or abounding in rocks: *a rocky shore* **2** hard or unyielding: *rocky determination* **3** hard like rock: *rocky muscles* > **'rockily** *adv* > **'rockiness** *n*

rocky² ('rɒkɪ) *adj* **rockier, rockiest** **1** weak, shaky, or unstable **2** *informal* (of a person) dizzy; sickly; nauseated > **'rockily** *adv* > **'rockiness** *n*

Rocky Mountain goat *n* a sure-footed goat antelope, *Oreamnos americanus,* inhabiting the Rocky Mountains. It has thick white hair and black backward-curving horns

Rocky Mountains *or* **Rockies** *pl n* the chief mountain system of W North America, extending from British Columbia to New Mexico: forms the Continental Divide. Highest peak: Mount Elbert, 4399 m (14 431 ft). Mount McKinley (6194 m (20 320 ft)), in the Alaska Range, is not strictly part of the Rocky Mountains

Rocky Mountain spotted fever *n* an acute rickettsial disease characterized by high fever, chills, pain in muscles and joints, skin rash, etc. It is caused by the bite of a tick infected with the microorganism *Rickettsia rickettsii*

rococo (rə'kəʊkəʊ) *n (often capital)* **1** a style of architecture and decoration that originated in France in the early 18th century, characterized by elaborate but graceful, light, ornamentation, often containing asymmetrical motifs **2** an 18th-century style of music characterized by petite prettiness, a decline in the use of counterpoint, and extreme use of ornamentation **3** any florid or excessively ornamental style ▷ *adj* **4** denoting,

being in, or relating to the rococo **5** florid or excessively elaborate [C19 from French, from ROCAILLE, from *roc* ROCK¹]

rod (rɒd) *n* **1** a slim cylinder of metal, wood, etc; stick or shaft **2** a switch or bundle of switches used to administer corporal punishment **3** any of various staffs of insignia or office **4** power, esp of a tyrannical kind: *a dictator's iron rod* **5** a straight slender shoot, stem, or cane of a woody plant **6** See **fishing rod** **7** Also called: **pole, perch a** a unit of length equal to 5½ yards **b** a unit of square measure equal to 30¼ square yards **8** a straight narrow board marked with the dimensions of a piece of joinery, as the spacing of steps on a staircase **9** a metal shaft that transmits power in axial reciprocating motion: *piston rod, con(necting) rod.* Compare **shaft** (sense 5) **10** *surveying* another name (esp US) for **staff¹** (sense 8) **11** Also called: **retinal rod** any of the elongated cylindrical cells in the retina of the eye, containing the visual purple (rhodopsin), which are sensitive to dim light but not to colour. Compare **cone** (sense 5) **12** any rod-shaped bacterium **13** a slang word for **penis 14** *US* slang name for **pistol** (sense 1) **15** short for **hot rod** [Old English *rodd;* related to Old Norse *rudda* club, Norwegian *rudda, rydda* twig] > 'rod-like *adj*

rode¹ (rəʊd) *vb* the past tense of **ride**

rode² (rəʊd) *n nautical* an anchor rope or chain [C17 of unknown origin]

rode³ (rəʊd) *vb (intr)* (of the male woodcock) to perform a display flight at dusk during the breeding season [C18 in the sense "(of birds) to fly homeward in the evening"; of uncertain origin] > 'roding *n*

rodent ('rəʊd²nt) *n* **a** any of the relatively small placental mammals that constitute the order *Rodentia,* having constantly growing incisor teeth specialized for gnawing. The group includes porcupines, rats, mice, squirrels, marmots, etc **b** (*as modifier*): *rodent characteristics* [C19 from Latin *rōdere* to gnaw, corrode] > 'rodent-,like *adj*

rodenticide (rəʊ'dɛntɪ,saɪd) *n* a substance used for killing rats, mice, and other rodents

rodent operative *n Brit* a name sometimes used for an official (operative) employed by a local authority to destroy vermin

rodeo ('rəʊdɪ,əʊ) *n, pl* **-os** *chiefly US and Canadian* **1** a display of the skills of cowboys, including bareback riding, steer wrangling, etc **2** the rounding up of cattle for branding, counting, inspection, etc **3** an enclosure for cattle that have been rounded up [C19 from Spanish, from *rodear* to go around, from *rueda* a wheel, from Latin *rota*]

Ródhos ('rɒðɒs) *n* transliteration of the Modern Greek name for **Rhodes**

rodomontade (,rɒdəmɒn'teɪd, -'tɑːd) *literary* ▷ *n* **1 a** boastful words or behaviour; bragging **b** (*as modifier*): *rodomontade behaviour* ▷ *vb* **2** (*intr*) to boast, bluster, or rant [C17 from French, from Italian *rodomonte* a boaster, from *Rodomonte* the name of a braggart king of Algiers in epic poems by Boiardo and Ariosto]

roe¹ (rəʊ) *n* **1** Also called: **hard roe** the ovary of a female fish filled with mature eggs **2** Also called: **soft roe** the testis of a male fish filled with mature sperm **3** the ripe ovary of certain crustaceans, such as the lobster [C15 from Middle Dutch *roge,* from Old High German *roga;* related to Old Norse *hrogn*]

roe² (rəʊ) *n, pl* **roes** *or* **roe** short for **roe deer** [Old English *rā(ha),* related to Old High German *rēh(o),* Old Norse *rā*]

Roe (rəʊ) *n* Richard *law* (formerly) the defendant in a fictitious action, Doe versus Roe, to test a point of law. See also **Doe** (sense 1)

roebuck ('rəʊ,bʌk) *n, pl* **-bucks** *or* **-buck** the male of the roe deer

roe deer *n* a small graceful deer, *Capreolus capreolus,* of woodlands of Europe and Asia. The antlers are small and the summer coat is reddish-brown

roentgen *or* **röntgen** ('rɒntgən, -tjən, 'rɛnt-) *n* a

unit of dose of electromagnetic radiation equal to the dose that will produce in air a charge of 0.258×10^{-3} coulomb on all ions of one sign, when all the electrons of both signs liberated in a volume of air of mass one kilogram are stopped completely. Symbol: **R** or **r** [C20 named after German physicist W K Roentgen or Röntgen (1845–1923), who discovered X-rays]

roentgen equivalent man *n* the dose of ionizing radiation that produces the same effect in man as one roentgen of x- or gamma-radiation. Abbreviation: REM *or* rem

roentgenize, roentgenise, röntgenize *or* **röntgenise** ('rɒntgə,naɪz, -tjə-, 'rɛnt-) *vb (tr)* to bombard with X-rays > ,roentgeni'zation, ,roentgeni'sation, ,röntgeni'zation *or* ,röntgeni'sation *n*

roentgeno- *or* **röntgeno-** *combining form* indicating X-rays: *roentgenogram* [from ROENTGEN]

roentgenogram, röntgenogram ('rɒntgənə,græm, -tjə-, 'rɛnt-) *or* **roentgenograph, röntgenograph** *n chiefly US* an X-ray

roentgenology *or* **röntgenology** (,rɒntgə'nɒlədʒɪ, -tjə-, ,rɛnt-) *n* an obsolete name for **radiology** > roentgenological *or* röntgenological (,rɒntgənə'lɒdʒɪkᵊl, -tjə-, ,rɛnt-) *adj* > ,roentgeno'logically *or* ,röntgeno'logically *adv* > ,roentgen'ologist *or* ,röntgen'ologist *n*

roentgenopaque *or* **röntgenopaque** (,rɒntgənəʊ'peɪk, -tjən-, ,rɛnt-) *adj* (of a material) not allowing the transmission of X-rays

roentgenoscope *or* **röntgenoscope** ('rɒntgənəʊ,skəʊp, -tjə-, 'rɛnt-) *n* a less common name for **fluoroscope** > roentgenoscopic *or* röntgenoscopic (,rɒntgənəʊ'skɒpɪk, -tjə-,,rɛnt-) *adj* > roentgenoscopy *or* röntgenoscopy (,rɒntgə'nɒskəpɪ, -tjə-, ,rɛnt-) *n*

roentgenotherapy *or* **röntgenotherapy** (,rɒntgənə'θɛrəpɪ, -tjə-, ,rɛnt-) *n* the therapeutic use of X-rays

roentgen ray *n* a former name for **X-ray**

Roeselare ('ruːsəlɑːrə) *n* the Flemish name for **Roulers**

ROFL(OL) *text messaging abbreviation for* rolling on floor laughing (out loud)

rogallo (rə'gæləʊ) *n, pl* **-los** a flexible fabric delta wing, originally designed as a possible satellite retrieval vehicle but actually developed in the 1960s as the first successful hang-glider [C20 after Francis M *Rogallo,* the US engineer who designed it]

rogation (rəʊ'geɪʃən) *n (usually plural) Christianity* a solemn supplication, esp in a form of ceremony prescribed by the Church [C14 from Latin *rogātiō,* from *rogāre* to ask, make supplication]

Rogation Days *pl n* April 25 (the **Major Rogation**) and the Monday, Tuesday, and Wednesday before Ascension Day, observed by Christians as days of solemn supplication for the harvest and marked by processions, special prayers, and blessing of the crops

rogatory ('rɒgətərɪ, -trɪ) *adj (esp in legal contexts)* seeking or authorized to seek information [C19 from Medieval Latin *rogātōrius,* from Latin *rogāre* to ask]

roger ('rɒdʒə) *interj* **1** (used in signalling, telecommunications, etc) message received. Compare **wilco 2** an expression of agreement ▷ *vb* **3** *slang* (of a man) to copulate (with) [C20 from the name *Roger,* representing R for *received*]

USAGE The verb sense of this word was formerly considered to be taboo, and it was labelled as such in previous editions of *Collins English Dictionary.* However, it has now become acceptable in speech, although some older or more conservative people may object to its use

rognon *French* (rɔɲɔ̃) *n mountaineering* an isolated rock outcrop on a glacier [C20 literally: kidney]

rogue (rəʊg) *n* **1** a dishonest or unprincipled person, esp a man; rascal; scoundrel **2** *often jocular* a mischievous or wayward person, often a child; scamp **3** a crop plant which is inferior, diseased, or of a different, unwanted variety **4** **a** any inferior or defective specimen **b** (*as modifier*): *rogue heroin* **5** *archaic* a vagrant **6** **a** an animal of vicious character that has separated from the main herd and leads a solitary life **b** (*as modifier*): *a rogue elephant* ▷ *vb* **7** **a** (*tr*) to rid (a field or crop) of plants that are inferior, diseased, or of an unwanted variety **b** to identify and remove such plants [C16 of unknown origin; perhaps related to Latin *rogāre* to beg]

rogue dialler *n* a dial-up connection placed on a computer without the user's knowledge which, when the user tries to connect to the internet, automatically connects to a premium-rate phone number

roguery (ˈrəʊgərɪ) *n, pl* **-gueries** **1** behaviour characteristic of a rogue **2** a roguish or mischievous act

rogues' gallery *n* **1** a collection of photographs of known criminals kept by the police for identification purposes **2** a group of undesirable people

rogue state *n* a state that conducts its policy in a dangerously unpredictable way, disregarding international law or diplomacy

rogue trader *n* a person who makes deals without due regard for normal business practices and controls

roguish (ˈrəʊgɪʃ) *adj* **1** dishonest or unprincipled **2** mischievous or arch > **ˈroguishly** *adv* > **ˈroguishness** *n*

Rohypnol (ˌrəʊˈhɪpnɒl) *n* *trademark* a brand of the drug flunitrazepam used as a hypnotic: its ability to render someone unconscious and disoriented on awakening has been exploited by rapists

ROI *abbreviation for* **1** Republic of Ireland **2** *finance* return on investment

roil (rɔɪl) *vb* **1** (*tr*) to make (a liquid) cloudy or turbid by stirring up dregs or sediment **2** (*intr*) (esp of a liquid) to be agitated or disturbed **3** (*intr*) *dialect* to be noisy or boisterous **4** (*tr*) another word (now rare) for **rile** (sense 1) [C16 of unknown origin; compare RILE]

roily (ˈrɔɪlɪ) *adj* **roilier, roiliest** *rare* cloudy or muddy

roister (ˈrɔɪstə) *vb* (*intr*) **1** to engage in noisy merrymaking; revel **2** to brag, bluster, or swagger [C16 from Old French *rustre* lout, from *ruste* uncouth, from Latin *rusticus* rural; see RUSTIC] > **ˈroisterer** *n* > **ˈroisterous** *adj* > **ˈroisterously** *adv*

rojak (ˈrɒdʒak) *n* (in Malaysia) a salad dish served in chilli sauce [from Malay]

ROK *international car registration for* South Korea (Republic of Korea)

role *or* **rôle** (rəʊl) *n* **1** a part or character in a play, film, etc, to be played by an actor or actress **2** *psychol* the part played by a person in a particular social setting, influenced by his expectation of what is appropriate **3** usual or customary function: *what is his role in the organization?* [C17 from French *rôle* ROLL, an actor's script]

role model *n* a person regarded by others, esp younger people, as a good example to follow

role-playing *n* *psychol* activity in which a person imitates, consciously or unconsciously, a role uncharacteristic of himself. See also **psychodrama**

role-playing game *n* a game in which players assume the roles of fantasy characters

roll (rəʊl) *vb* **1** to move or cause to move along by turning over and over **2** to move or cause to move along on wheels or rollers **3** to flow or cause to flow onwards in an undulating movement: *billows of smoke rolled over the ground* **4** (*intr*) to extend in undulations: *the hills roll down to the sea* **5** (*intr*; usually foll by *around*) to move or occur in cycles **6** (*intr*) (of a planet, the moon, etc) to revolve in an orbit **7** (*intr*; foll by *on, by,* etc) to pass or elapse: *the years roll by* **8** to rotate or cause to rotate wholly or partially: *to roll one's eyes* **9** to curl, cause to curl, or admit of being curled, so as to form a ball, tube, or cylinder; coil **10** to make or form by shaping into a ball, tube, or cylinder: *to roll a cigarette* **11** (often foll by *out*) to spread or cause to spread out flat or smooth under or as if under a roller: *to roll the lawn; to roll pastry* **12** to emit, produce, or utter with a deep prolonged reverberating sound: *the thunder rolled continuously* **13** to trill or cause to be trilled: *to roll one's r's* **14** (*intr*) (of a vessel, aircraft, rocket, etc) to turn from side to side around the longitudinal axis. Compare **pitch**[1] (sense 11), **yaw** (sense 1) **15** to cause (an aircraft) to execute a roll or (of an aircraft) to execute a roll (sense 40) **16** (*intr*) to walk with a swaying gait, as when drunk; sway **17** (*intr*; often foll by *over*) (of an animal, esp a dog) to lie on its back and wriggle while kicking its legs in the air, without moving along **18** (*intr*) to wallow or envelop oneself (in) **19** (*tr*) to apply ink to (type, etc) with a roller or rollers **20** to throw (dice) **21** (*intr*) to operate or begin to operate: *the presses rolled* **22** (*intr*) *informal* to make progress; move or go ahead: *let the good times roll* **23** (*tr*) *informal, chiefly US and NZ* to rob (a helpless person, such as someone drunk or asleep) **24** (*tr*) *slang* to have sexual intercourse or foreplay with (a person) **25** **start** *or* **set the ball rolling** to open or initiate (an action, discussion, movement, etc) ▷ *n* **26** the act or an instance of rolling **27** anything rolled up in a cylindrical form: *a roll of newspaper* **28** an official list or register, esp of names: *an electoral roll* **29** a rounded mass: *rolls of flesh* **30** a strip of material, esp leather, fitted with pockets or pouches for holding tools, toilet articles, needles and thread, etc **31** a cylinder used to flatten something; roller **32** a small loaf of bread for one person: eaten plain, with butter, or as a light meal when filled with meat, cheese, etc **33** a flat pastry or cake rolled up with a meat (**sausage roll**), jam (**jam roll**), or other filling. See also **swiss roll** **34** a swell, ripple, or undulation on a surface: *the roll of the hills* **35** a swaying, rolling, or unsteady movement or gait **36** a deep prolonged reverberating sound: *the roll of thunder* **37** a rhythmic cadenced flow of words **38** a trilling sound; trill **39** a very rapid beating of the sticks on a drum **40** a flight manoeuvre in which an aircraft makes one complete rotation about its longitudinal axis without loss of height or change in direction **41** the angular displacement of a vessel, rocket, missile, etc, caused by rolling **42** a throw of dice **43** a bookbinder's tool having a brass wheel, used to impress a line or repeated pattern on the cover of a book **44** *slang* an act of sexual intercourse or petting (esp in the phrase **a roll in the hay**) **45** *US slang* an amount of money, esp a wad of paper money **46** **on a roll** *slang* experiencing continued good luck or success **47** **strike off the roll(s)** **a** to expel from membership **b** to debar (a solicitor) from practising, usually because of dishonesty ▷ See also **roll in, roll off, roll on, roll out, roll over, roll up** [C14 *rollen*, from Old French *roler*, from Latin *rotulus* a little wheel, from *rota* a wheel]

rollaway (ˈrəʊləˌweɪ) *n* (*modifier*) mounted on rollers so as to be easily moved, esp to be stored away after use

rollbar (ˈrəʊlˌbɑː) *n* a bar that reinforces the frame of a car, esp one used for racing, rallying, etc, to protect the driver if the car should turn over

roll call *n* **1** the reading aloud of an official list of names, those present responding when their names are read out **2** the time or signal for such a reading

rolled gold *n* a metal, such as brass, coated with a thin layer of gold, usually of above 9 carat purity. It is used in inexpensive jewellery. Also called (US): **filled gold**

rolled paperwork *n* a form of decoration on small objects, such as boxes, in which a design is made up of tiny rolls of paper cut crossways and laid together: popular in the 18th and 19th centuries. Also called: **curled paperwork, paper filigree**

rolled-steel joist *n* a steel beam, esp one with a cross section in the form of a letter H or I. Abbreviation: **RSJ**

roller (ˈrəʊlə) *n* **1** a cylinder having an absorbent surface and a handle, used for spreading paint **2** Also called: **garden roller** a heavy cast-iron cylinder or pair of cylinders on an axle to which a handle is attached; used for flattening lawns **3** a long heavy wave of the sea, advancing towards the shore. Compare **breaker**[1] (sense 2) **4** a hardened cylinder of precision-ground steel that forms one of the rolling components of a roller bearing or of a linked driving chain **5** a cylinder fitted on pivots, used to enable heavy objects to be easily moved **6** *printing* a cylinder, usually of hard rubber, used to ink a forme or plate before impression **7** a cylindrical tube or barrel onto which material is rolled for transport or storage **8** any of various other cylindrical devices that rotate about a cylinder **9** a small cylinder, esp one that is heated, onto which a woman's hair may be rolled to make it curl **10** *med* a bandage consisting of a long strip of muslin or cheesecloth rolled tightly into a cylindrical form before application **11** a band fastened around a horse's belly to keep a blanket in position **12** any of various Old World birds of the family *Coraciidae*, such as *Coracias garrulus* (**European roller**), that have a blue, green, and brown plumage, a slightly hooked bill, and an erratic flight: order *Coraciiformes* (kingfishers, etc) **13** (*often capital*) a variety of tumbler pigeon that performs characteristic backward somersaults in flight **14** a breed of canary that has a soft trilling song in which the notes are run together **15** a person or thing that rolls **16** *Austral* a man who rolls and trims fleeces after shearing **17** short for **roadroller** *or* **steamroller** **18** short for **roller caption**

rollerball (ˈrəʊləˌbɔːl) *n* a pen having a small moving nylon, plastic, or metal ball as a writing point

roller bearing *n* a bearing in which a shaft runs on a number of hardened-steel rollers held within a cage

Rollerblade (ˈrəʊləˌbleɪd) *n* *trademark* a type of roller skate in which the wheels are set in a single straight line under the boot

roller caption *n* *television* caption lettering that moves progressively up or across the picture, as for showing the credits at the end of a programme. Often shortened to: **roller**

roller chain *n* *engineering* a chain for transmitting power in which each link consists of two free-moving rollers held in position by pins connected to sideplates

roller coaster *n* another term for **big dipper**

roller derby *n* a race on roller skates, esp one involving aggressive tactics

roller skate *n* **1** a device having clamps and straps for fastening to a boot or shoe and four small wheels that enable the wearer to glide swiftly over a floor or other surface ▷ *vb* **roller-skate** **2** (*intr*) to move on roller skates > **roller skater** *n*

roller towel *n* **1** a towel with the two ends sewn together, hung on a roller **2** a continuous towel wound inside a roller enabling a clean section to be pulled out when required

roll film *n* a length of photographic film backed with opaque paper and rolled on a spool

rollick (ˈrɒlɪk) *vb* **1** (*intr*) to behave in a carefree, frolicsome, or boisterous manner ▷ *n* **2** a boisterous or carefree escapade or event [C19 of Scottish dialect origin, probably from ROMP + FROLIC]

rollicking[1] (ˈrɒlɪkɪŋ) *adj* boisterously carefree and swaggering

rollicking[2] (ˈrɒlɪkɪŋ) *n* *Brit informal* a very severe telling-off; dressing-down [C20 from ROLLICK (vb) (in former sense: to be angry, make a fuss);

perhaps influenced by BOLLOCKING]

roll in vb (mainly intr) **1** (adverb) to arrive in abundance or in large numbers **2** (adverb) informal to arrive at one's destination **3** (preposition) informal to abound or luxuriate in (wealth, money, etc) **4** (adverb; also tr) hockey to return (the ball) to play after it has crossed the touchline

rolling ('rəʊlɪŋ) adj **1** having gentle rising and falling slopes; undulating **2** progressing or spreading by stages or by occurrences in different places in succession, with continued or increasing effectiveness: three weeks of rolling strikes disrupted schools **3** subject to regular review and updating: a rolling plan for overseas development **4** deeply resounding; reverberating **5** slang extremely rich **6** that may be turned up or down: a rolling hat brim ▷ adv **7** slang swaying or staggering (in the phrase **rolling drunk**)

rolling bearing n any bearing in which the antifriction action depends on the rolling action of balls or rollers

rolling friction n engineering frictional resistance to rotation or energy losses in rolling bearings. Compare **sliding friction**

rolling hitch n a knot used for fastening one rope to another or to a spar, being easily released but jamming when the rope is pulled

rolling launch n marketing the process of introducing a new product into a market gradually. Compare **roll out** (sense 3)

rolling mill n **1** a mill or factory where ingots of heated metal are passed between rollers to produce sheets or bars of a required cross section and form **2** a machine having rollers that may be shaped to reduce ingots, etc, to a required cross section and form

rolling pin n a cylinder with handles at both ends, often of wood, used for rolling dough, pastry, etc, out flat

rolling stock n the wheeled vehicles collectively used on a railway, including the locomotives, passenger coaches, freight wagons, etc

rolling stone n a restless or wandering person

rollmop ('rəʊlˌmɒp) n a herring fillet rolled, usually around onion slices, and pickled in spiced vinegar [C20 from German Rollmops, from rollen to ROLL + Mops pug dog]

rollneck ('rəʊlˌnɛk) adj **1** (of a garment) having a high neck that may be rolled over ▷ n **2** a rollneck sweater or other garment

roll off vb (intr, adverb) electronics to exhibit gradually reduced response at the upper or lower ends of the working frequency range

roll of honour n a list of those who have died in war for their country, esp those from a particular locality or organization

roll on vb **1** Brit used to express the wish that an eagerly anticipated event or date will come quickly: roll on Saturday ▷ adj **roll-on 2** (of a deodorant, lip gloss, etc) dispensed by means of a revolving ball fitted into the neck of the container ▷ n **roll-on 3** a woman's foundation garment, made of elasticized material and having no fastenings **4** a liquid cosmetic, esp a deodorant, packed in a container having an applicator consisting of a revolving ball

roll-on/roll-off adj denoting a cargo ship or ferry designed so that vehicles can be driven straight on and straight off

roll out vb (tr, adverb) **1** to cause (pastry) to become flatter and thinner by pressure with a rolling pin **2** to show (a new type of aircraft) to the public for the first time **3** to launch (a new film, product, etc) in a series of stages over an area, each stage involving an increased number of outlets ▷ n **roll-out 4** a presentation to the public of a new aircraft, product, etc; a launch

roll over vb (adverb) **1** (intr) to overturn **2** See **roll** (sense 17) **3** slang to surrender **4** (tr) to allow (a loan, prize, etc) to continue in force for a further period ▷ n **rollover 5 a** an instance of such continuance of a loan, prize, etc **b** (as modifier): a

rollover jackpot

Rolls-Royce (ˌrəʊlzˈrɔɪs) n trademark **1** Also called (informal): **Rolls** a make of very high-quality, luxurious, and prestigious British car. The Rolls-Royce company is no longer British-owned **2** anything considered to be the very best of its kind [named after its designers, Charles Stewart Rolls (1877–1910), English pioneer motorist and aviator, and Sir (Frederick) Henry Royce (1863–1933), English engineer, who founded the Rolls-Royce Company (1906)]

roll-top desk n a desk having a slatted wooden panel that can be pulled down over the writing surface when not in use. Also called: **roll-top**

roll up vb (adverb) **1** to form or cause to form a cylindrical shape **2** (tr) to wrap (an object) round on itself or on an axis: to roll up a map **3** (intr) informal to arrive, esp in a vehicle ▷ n **roll-up 4** (intr) to proceed or develop **5** Brit informal a cigarette made by hand from loose tobacco and cigarette paper **6** Austral (in the 19th century) a mass meeting of workers on an issue of common concern **7** Austral archaic the attendance at any fixture: they had a good roll-up

rollway ('rəʊlˌweɪ) n **1** an incline down which logs are rolled for transportation **2** a series of rollers laid parallel to each other, over which heavy loads may be moved

roll-your-own n informal a hand-rolled cigarette

Rolodex ('rəʊləˌdɛks) n trademark chiefly US a small file for holding names, addresses, and telephone numbers, consisting of cards attached horizontally to a rotatable central cylinder

roly-poly ('rəʊlɪˈpəʊlɪ) adj **1** plump, buxom, or rotund ▷ n, pl **-lies 2** Brit a strip of suet pastry spread with jam, fruit, or a savoury mixture, rolled up, and baked or steamed as a pudding **3** a plump, buxom, or rotund person **4** Austral an informal name for **tumbleweed** [C17 apparently by reduplication from roly, from ROLL]

Rom (rɒm) n, pl **Roma** ('rɒmə) a male Gypsy [Romany]

ROM (rɒm) n computing ▷ acronym for read only memory: a storage device that holds data permanently and cannot in normal circumstances be altered by the programmer

rom. printing abbreviation for roman (type)

Rom. abbreviation for **1** Roman **2** Romance (languages) **3** Bible Romans **4** Romania(n)

Roma¹ ('rɔːma) n the Italian name for **Rome**

Roma² ('rəʊmə) n **1 a** another name for **Gypsy b** (as modifier): Roma gypsy musicians **2** another name for **Romany**

Romagna (Italian roˈmaɲɲa) n an area of N Italy: part of the Papal States up to 1860

Romaic (rəʊˈmeɪɪk) obsolete ▷ n **1** the modern Greek vernacular, esp Demotic ▷ adj **2** of or relating to Greek, esp Demotic [C19 from Greek Rhômaikos Roman, with reference to the Eastern Roman Empire]

romaine (rəʊˈmeɪn) n the usual US and Canadian name for **cos¹** (lettuce) [C20 from French, from romain Roman]

romaji ('rəʊmɑːdʒɪ) n the Roman alphabet as used to write Japanese

roman¹ ('rəʊmən) adj **1** of, relating to, or denoting a vertical style of printing type: the usual form of type for most printed matter. Compare **italic** ▷ n **2** roman type or print [C16 so called because the style of letters is that used in ancient Roman inscriptions]

roman² (French rɔmɑ̃) n a metrical narrative in medieval French literature derived from the chansons de geste

Roman ('rəʊmən) adj **1** of or relating to Rome or its inhabitants in ancient or modern times **2** of or relating to Roman Catholicism or the Roman Catholic Church **3** denoting, relating to, or having the style of architecture used by the ancient Romans, characterized by large-scale masonry domes, barrel vaults, and semicircular arches ▷ n **4** a citizen or inhabitant of ancient or

modern Rome **5** informal short for **Roman Catholic**

roman à clef French (rɔmɑ̃ a kle) n, pl **romans à clef** (rɔmɑ̃ a kle) a novel in which real people are depicted under fictitious names [literally: novel with a key]

Roman alphabet n the alphabet evolved by the ancient Romans for the writing of Latin, based upon an Etruscan form derived from the Greeks and ultimately from the Phoenicians. The alphabet serves for writing most of the languages of W Europe and many other languages

Roman arch n another name for **Norman arch**

Roman blind n a window blind consisting of a length of material which, when drawn up, gathers into horizontal folds from the bottom

Roman calendar n the lunar calendar of ancient Rome, replaced in 45 BC by the Julian calendar. It originally consisted of 10 months, with a special month intercalated between Feb 23 and 24

Roman candle n a firework that produces a continuous shower of sparks punctuated by coloured balls of fire [C19 so called from its having been originated in Italy]

Roman Catholic adj **1** of or relating to the Roman Catholic Church ▷ n **2** a member of this Church ▷ Often shortened to: **Catholic**

Roman Catholic Church n the Christian Church over which the pope presides, with administrative headquarters in the Vatican. Also called: **Catholic Church, Church of Rome**

Roman Catholicism n the beliefs, practices, and system of government of the Roman Catholic Church

romance n (rəˈmæns, ˈrəʊmæns) **1** a love affair, esp an intense but short-lived affair involving young people **2** love, esp romantic love idealized for its purity or beauty **3** a spirit of or inclination for adventure, excitement, or mystery **4** a mysterious, exciting, sentimental, or nostalgic quality, esp one associated with a place **5** a narrative in verse or prose, written in a vernacular language in the Middle Ages, dealing with strange and exciting adventures of chivalrous heroes **6** any similar narrative work dealing with events and characters remote from ordinary life **7** the literary genre represented by works of these kinds **8** (in Spanish literature) a short narrative poem, usually an epic or historical ballad **9** a story, novel, film, etc, dealing with love, usually in an idealized or sentimental way **10** an extravagant, absurd, or fantastic account or explanation **11** a lyrical song or short instrumental composition having a simple melody ▷ vb (rəˈmæns) **12** (intr) to tell, invent, or write extravagant or romantic fictions **13** (intr) to tell extravagant or improbable lies **14** (intr) to have romantic thoughts **15** (intr) (of a couple) to indulge in romantic behaviour **16** (tr) to be romantically involved with [C13 romauns, from Old French romans, ultimately from Latin Rōmānicus Roman] > ro'mancer n

Romance (rəˈmæns, ˈrəʊmæns) adj **1** denoting, relating to, or belonging to the languages derived from Latin, including Italian, Spanish, Portuguese, French, and Romanian **2** denoting a word borrowed from a Romance language: there are many Romance words in English ▷ n **3** this group of languages; the living languages that belong to the Italic branch of the Indo-European family

Roman collar n another name for **clerical collar**

Roman Empire n **1** the territories ruled by ancient Rome. At its height under Trajan, the Roman Empire included W and S Europe, Africa north of the Sahara, and SW Asia. In 395 AD it was divided by Theodosius into the **Eastern Roman Empire** whose capital was Byzantium and which lasted until 1453, and the **Western Roman Empire** which lasted until the sack of Rome in 476 **2** the government of Rome and its dominions by the emperors from 27 BC **3** the Byzantine Empire **4** the Holy Roman Empire

Romanes ('rɒmənɪs) *n* Romany; the language of the Gypsies [from Romany]

Romanesque (ˌrəʊmə'nɛsk) *adj* **1** denoting, relating to, or having the style of architecture used in W and S Europe from the 9th to the 12th century, characterized by the rounded arch, the groin vault, massive-masonry wall construction, and a restrained use of mouldings. See also **Norman** (sense 6) **2** denoting or relating to a corresponding style in painting, sculpture, etc [C18 see ROMAN, -ESQUE]

roman-fleuve *French* (rɔmɑ̃flœv) *n*, *pl* **romans-fleuves** (rɔmɑ̃flœv) a novel or series of novels dealing with a family or other group over several generations [literally: stream novel]

Roman holiday *n* entertainment or pleasure that depends on the suffering of others [C19 from Byron's poem *Childe Harold* (IV, 141)]

Romani ('rɒmənɪ, 'rəʊ-) *n*, *pl* **-nis** a variant spelling of **Romany**

Romania (rəʊ'meɪnɪə), **Rumania** or **Roumania** *n* a republic in SE Europe, bordering on the Black Sea: united in 1861; became independent in 1878; Communist government set up in 1945; became a socialist republic in 1965; a more democratic regime was installed after a revolution in 1989. It consists chiefly of a great central arc of the Carpathian Mountains and Transylvanian Alps, with the plains of Walachia, Moldavia, and Dobriya on the south and east and the Pannonian Plain in the west. Official language: Romanian. Religion: Romanian Orthodox (Christian) majority. Currency: leu. Capital: Bucharest. Pop: 22 280 000 (2004 est). Area: 237 500 sq km (91 699 sq miles)

Romanian (rəʊ'meɪnɪən), **Rumanian** or **Roumanian** *n* **1** the official language of Romania, belonging to the Romance group of the Indo-European family **2** a native, citizen, or inhabitant of Romania ▷ *adj* **3** relating to, denoting, or characteristic of Romania, its people, or their language

Romanic (rəʊ'mænɪk) *adj* another word for **Roman** or **Romance**

romanicite (rəʊ'mænɪˌsaɪt) *n* another name for **psilomelane**

Romanism ('rəʊməˌnɪzəm) *n* Roman Catholicism, esp when regarded as excessively or superstitiously ritualistic

Romanist ('rəʊmənɪst) *n* **1** a member of a Church, esp the Church of England, who favours or is influenced by Roman Catholicism **2** a Roman Catholic **3** a student of classical Roman civilization or law ▷ ˌRoman'istic *adj*

Romanize or **Romanise** ('rəʊməˌnaɪz) *vb* **1** (*tr*) to impart a Roman Catholic character to (a ceremony, practice, etc) **2** (*intr*) to be converted to Roman Catholicism **3** (*tr*) to transcribe or transliterate (a language) into the Roman alphabet **4** to make Roman in character, allegiance, style, etc ▷ ˌRomani'zation or ˌRomani'sation *n*

Roman law *n* **1** the system of jurisprudence of ancient Rome, codified under Justinian and forming the basis of many modern legal systems **2** another term for **civil law**

Roman mile *n* a unit of length used in ancient Rome, equivalent to about 1620 yards or 1481 metres

Roman nose *n* a nose having a high prominent bridge

Roman numerals *pl n* the letters used by the Romans for the representation of cardinal numbers, still used occasionally today. The integers are represented by the following letters: I (= 1), V (= 5), X (= 10), L (= 50), C (= 100), D (= 500), and M (= 1000). If a numeral is followed by another numeral of lower denomination, the two are added together; if it is preceded by one of lower denomination, the smaller numeral is subtracted from the greater. Thus VI = 6 (V + I), but IV = 4 (V − I). Other examples are XC (= 90), CL

(= 150), XXV (= 25), XLIV (= 44). Multiples of a thousand are indicated by a superior bar: thus, $\overline{V}$ = 5000, $\overline{X}$ = 10 000, $\overline{XD}$ = 490 000, etc

Romano (rəʊ'mɑːnəʊ) *n* a hard light-coloured sharp-tasting cheese, similar to Parmesan

Roman pace *n* an ancient Roman measure of length, equal to 5 Roman feet or about 58 inches (147 centimetres). See also **geometric pace**

Romans ('rəʊmənz) *n* (*functioning as singular*) a book of the New Testament (in full **The Epistle of Paul the Apostle to the Romans**), containing one of the fullest expositions of the doctrines of Saint Paul, written in 58 AD

Romansch or **Romansh** (rəʊ'mænʃ) *n* a group of Rhaetian dialects spoken in the Swiss canton of Graubünden; an official language of Switzerland since 1938. See also **Friulian, Ladin** [C17 from Romansch, literally: Romance language, from Latin *Rōmānicus* ROMANIC]

Roman snail *n* a large edible European snail, *Helix pomatia*, the usual *escargot* of menus, erroneously thought to have been introduced to northern Europe by the Romans

romantic (rəʊ'mæntɪk) *adj* **1** of, relating to, imbued with, or characterized by romance **2** evoking or given to thoughts and feelings of love, esp idealized or sentimental love: *a romantic woman; a romantic setting* **3** impractical, visionary, or idealistic: *a romantic scheme* **4** often euphemistic imaginary or fictitious: *a romantic account of one's war service* **5** (*often capital*) of or relating to a movement in European art, music, and literature in the late 18th and early 19th centuries, characterized by an emphasis on feeling and content rather than order and form, on the sublime, supernatural, and exotic, and the free expression of the passions and individuality ▷ *n* **6** a person who is romantic, as in being idealistic, amorous, or soulful **7** a person whose tastes in art, literature, etc, lie mainly in romanticism; romanticist **8** (*often capital*) a poet, composer, etc, of the romantic period or whose main inspiration or interest is romanticism [C17 from French *romantique*, from obsolete *romant* story, romance, from Old French *romans* ROMANCE] ▷ ro'mantically *adv*

romanticism (rəʊ'mæntɪˌsɪzəm) *n* **1** (*often capital*) the theory, practice, and style of the romantic art, music, and literature of the late 18th and early 19th centuries, usually opposed to classicism **2** romantic attitudes, ideals, or qualities ▷ ro'manticist *n*

romanticize or **romanticise** (rəʊ'mæntɪˌsaɪz) *vb* **1** (*intr*) to think or act in a romantic way **2** (*tr*) to interpret according to romantic precepts **3** to make or become romantic, as in style ▷ roˌmantici'zation or roˌmantici'sation *n*

Romany or **Romani** ('rɒmənɪ, 'rəʊ-) *n* **1** *pl* **-nies** or **-nis a** another name for a **Gypsy b** (*as modifier*): *Romany customs* **2** the language of the Gypsies, belonging to the Indic branch of the Indo-European family, but incorporating extensive borrowings from local European languages. Most of its 250 000 speakers are bilingual. It is extinct in Britain [C19 from Romany *romani* (adj) Gypsy, ultimately from Sanskrit *ḍomba* man of a low caste of musicians, of Dravidian origin]

romanza (rə'mænzə) *n* *music* a short instrumental piece of song-like character [from Italian]

romaunt (rə'mɔːnt) *n* *archaic* a verse romance [C16 from Old French; see ROMANTIC]

Rom. Cath. *abbreviation for* Roman Catholic

romcom ('rɒmˌkɒm) *n* *informal* a film or television comedy based around the romantic relationships of the characters [C20 ROM(ANTIC) + COM(EDY)]

Rome (rəʊm) *n* **1** the capital of Italy, on the River Tiber: includes the independent state of the Vatican City; traditionally founded by Romulus on the Palatine Hill in 753 BC, later spreading to six other hills east of the Tiber; capital of the Roman Empire; a great cultural and artistic

centre, esp during the Renaissance. Pop: 2 546 804 (2001). Italian name: **Roma 2** the Roman Empire **3** the Roman Catholic Church or Roman Catholicism

Romeo ('rəʊmɪəʊ) *n* **1** (*pl* **-os**) an ardent male lover **2** *communications* a code word for the letter *r* [from the hero of Shakespeare's *Romeo and Juliet* (1594)]

Romish ('rəʊmɪʃ) *adj* usually derogatory of, relating to, or resembling Roman Catholic beliefs or practices

Romney Marsh ('rɒmnɪ, 'rʌm-) *n* **1** a marshy area of SE England, on the Kent coast between New Romney and Rye: includes Dungeness **2** a type of hardy British sheep from this area, with long wool, bred for mutton

romp (rɒmp) *vb* (*intr*) **1** to play or run about wildly, boisterously, or joyfully **2 romp home** (*or* **in**) to win a race easily ▷ *n* **3** a noisy or boisterous game or prank **4** an instance of sexual activity between two or more people that is entered into light-heartedly and without emotional commitment: *naked sex romps* **5** Also called: **romper** *archaic* a playful or boisterous child, esp a girl **6** an easy victory [C18 probably variant of RAMP, from Old French *ramper* to crawl, climb] ▷ 'rompish *adj*

rompers ('rɒmpəz) *pl n* **1** a one-piece baby garment consisting of trousers and a bib with straps **2** NZ a type of costume worn by schoolgirls for games and gymnastics

romp through *vb* (*intr, preposition*) *informal* to progress quickly and easily through something

Romulus ('rɒmjʊləs) *n* *Roman myth* the founder of Rome, suckled with his twin brother Remus by a she-wolf after they were abandoned in infancy. Their parents were Rhea Silvia and Mars. Romulus later killed Remus in an argument over the new city

Roncesvalles ('rɒnsəˌvælz; *Spanish* rɔnθes'βaʎes) *n* a village in N Spain, in the Pyrenees: a nearby pass was the scene of the defeat of Charlemagne and death of Roland in 778. French name: Roncevaux (rɔ̃svo)

rondavel ('rɒndəˌvəl) *n* *South African* a circular often thatched building with a conical roof [of uncertain origin]

rondeau ('rɒndəʊ) *n*, *pl* **-deaux** (-dəʊ, -dəʊz) a poem consisting of 13 or 10 lines with two rhymes and having the opening words of the first line used as an unrhymed refrain. See also **roundel** [C16 from Old French, from *rondel* a little round, from *rond* ROUND]

rondel ('rɒndᵊl) *n* **1** a rondeau consisting of three stanzas of 13 or 14 lines with a two-line refrain appearing twice or three times **2** a figure in Scottish country dancing by means of which couples change position in the set [C14 from Old French, literally: a little circle, from *rond* ROUND]

rondelet ('rɒndəˌlɛt) *n* a brief rondeau, having five or seven lines and a refrain taken from the first line [C16 from Old French: a little RONDEL]

rondo ('rɒndəʊ) *n*, *pl* **-dos** a piece of music in which a refrain is repeated between episodes: often constitutes the form of the last movement of a sonata or concerto [C18 from Italian, from French RONDEAU]

Rondônia (*Portuguese* rõ'dɔnja) *n* a state of W Brazil: consists chiefly of tropical rainforest; a centre of the Amazon rubber boom until about 1912. Capital: Porto Velho. Pop: 1 431 777 (2002). Area: 243 043 sq km (93 839 sq miles). Former name (until 1956): Guaporé

rondure ('rɒndjʊə) *n* *literary* **1** a circle or curve **2** roundness or curvature [C17 from French *rondeur*, from *rond* ROUND]

rone (rəʊn; *Scot* ron) or **ronepipe** ('rəʊnˌpaɪp; *Scot* 'ronˌpaɪp) *n* *Scot* a drainpipe or gutter for carrying rainwater from a roof [C19 origin unknown]

Roneo ('rəʊnɪəʊ) *trademark* ▷ *vb* **-neos, -neoing, -neoed** (*tr*) **1** to duplicate (a document) from a stencil ▷ *n*, *pl* **-neos 2** a document reproduced by this process

r

ronggeng ('rɒŋgɛŋ) *n* a Malay traditional dance [Malay]

ronin ('rəʊnɪn) *n Japanese history* **1** a lordless samurai, esp one whose feudal lord had been deprived of his territory **2** such samurai collectively [Japanese]

ronnie ('rɒnɪ) *n Dublin dialect* a moustache [c20 from Ronald Colman (1891–1958), debonair moustached British film actor]

röntgen ('rɒntgən, -tjən, 'rɛnt-) *n* a variant spelling of **roentgen**

ronz (rɒnz) *abbreviation for NZ* rest of New Zealand (in relation to Auckland) > **'ronzer** *n*

roo (ru:) *n Austral informal* a kangaroo

rood (ru:d) *n* **1 a** a crucifix, esp one set on a beam or screen at the entrance to the chancel of a church **b** (*as modifier*): *rood beam; rood arch; rood screen* **2** the Cross on which Christ was crucified **3** a unit of area equal to one quarter of an acre or 0.10117 hectares **4** a unit of area equal to 40 square rods [Old English *rōd*; related to Old Saxon *rōda*, Old Norse *rōtha*]

Roodepoort ('ru:də,pʊət) *n* an industrial city in NE South Africa, in the Witwatersrand. Pop: 172 601 (2001)

rood screen *n* a partition of stone or wood, often richly carved and decorated, that separates the chancel from the main part of a church: it is surmounted by a crucifix (rood), and was an important feature of medieval churches, though in England many rood screens were destroyed at the Reformation

roof (ru:f) *n, pl* **roofs** (ru:fs, ru:vz) **1 a** a structure that covers or forms the top of a building **b** (*in combination*): *the rooftop* **c** (*as modifier*): *a roof garden* **2** the top covering of a vehicle, oven, or other structure: *the roof of a car* **3** *anatomy* any structure that covers an organ or part: *the roof of the mouth* **4** a highest or topmost point or part: *Mount Everest is the roof of the world* **5** a house or other shelter: *a poor man's roof* **6** *mountaineering* the underside of a projecting overhang **7 hit** (*or* **go through**) **the roof** *informal* **a** to get extremely angry; become furious **b** to rise or increase steeply **8 raise the roof a** to create a boisterous disturbance **b** to react or protest heatedly ▷ *vb* **9** (*tr*) to provide or cover with a roof or rooflike part [Old English *hrōf*; related to Middle Dutch, Old Norse *hrōf*] > **'roofer** *n* > **'roofless** *adj* > **'roof,like** *adj*

roof garden *n* a garden on a flat roof of a building

roofing ('ru:fɪŋ) *n* **1** material used to construct a roof **2** the act of constructing a roof

roof rack *n* a rack attached to the roof of a motor vehicle for carrying luggage, skis, etc

roofscape ('ru:f,skeɪp) *n* a view of the rooftops of a town, city, etc

rooftop ('ru:f,tɒp) *n* **1** the outside part of the roof of a building **2 shout from the rooftops** to proclaim (something) publicly

rooftree ('ru:f,tri:) *n* another name for **ridgepole**

rooibos tea ('rɔɪbɒs) *n South African* tea prepared from any of several species of *Borbonia* or *Aspalanthus*, believed to have tonic properties [from Afrikaans *rooi* red + *bos* bush]

rooikat ('rɔɪ,kæt) *n* a South African lynx, *Felis caracal* [Afrikaans *rooi* red + *kat* cat]

rooinek ('rʊɪnɛk, 'rɔɪ-) *n South African* a contemptuous name for an Englishman [c19 Afrikaans, literally: red neck]

rook[1] (rʊk) *n* **1** a large Eurasian passerine bird, *Corvus frugilegus*, with a black plumage and a whitish base to its bill: family *Corvidae* (crows) **2** *slang* a swindler or cheat, esp one who cheats at cards ▷ *vb* **3** (*tr*) *slang* to overcharge, swindle, or cheat [Old English *hrōc*; related to Old High German *hruoh*, Old Norse *hrōkr*]

rook[2] (rʊk) *n* a chesspiece that may move any number of unoccupied squares in a straight line, horizontally or vertically. Also called: **castle** [c14 from Old French *rok*, ultimately from Arabic *rukhkh*]

rookery ('rʊkərɪ) *n, pl* **-eries 1** a group of nesting rooks **2** a clump of trees containing rooks' nests **3 a** a breeding ground or communal living area of certain other species of gregarious birds or mammals, esp penguins or seals **b** a colony of any such creatures **4** *archaic* an overcrowded slum tenement building or area of housing

rookie ('rʊkɪ) *n informal* an inexperienced person or newcomer, esp a raw recruit in the army [c20 changed from RECRUIT]

rooky ('rʊkɪ) *adj* **rookier, rookiest** *literary* abounding in rooks

room (ru:m, rʊm) *n* **1** space or extent, esp unoccupied or unobstructed space for a particular purpose: *is there room to pass?* **2** an area within a building enclosed by a floor, a ceiling, and walls or partitions **3** (*functioning as singular or plural*) the people present in a room: *the whole room was laughing* **4** (foll by *for*) opportunity or scope: *room for manoeuvre* **5** (*plural*) a part of a house, hotel, etc that is rented out as separate accommodation; lodgings: *she got rooms in town* **6** a euphemistic word for **lavatory** (sense 1) ▷ *vb* **7** (*intr*) *chiefly US* to occupy or share a room or lodging: *where does he room?* [Old English *rūm*; related to Gothic, Old High German *rūm*] > **'roomer** *n*

roomette (ru:'mɛt, rʊ'mɛt) *n US and Canadian* a self-contained compartment in a railway sleeping car

roomful ('ru:mfʊl, 'rʊm-) *n, pl* **-fuls** a number or quantity sufficient to fill a room: *a roomful of furniture*

rooming house *n US and Canadian* a house having self-contained furnished rooms or flats for renting

roommate ('ru:m,meɪt, 'rʊm-) *n* a person with whom one shares a room or lodging

room service *n* service in a hotel providing meals, drinks, etc, in guests' rooms

room temperature *n* the normal temperature of a living room, usually taken as being around 20°C

roomy ('ru:mɪ, 'rʊmɪ) *adj* **roomier, roomiest** having ample room; spacious > **'roomily** *adv* > **'roominess** *n*

roorback ('rʊə,bæk) *n US* a false or distorted report or account, used to obtain political advantage [c19 after Baron von *Roorback*, invented author of an imaginary *Tour through the Western and Southern States* (1844), which contained a passage defaming James K Polk]

roost (ru:st) *n* **1** a place, perch, branch, etc, where birds, esp domestic fowl, rest or sleep **2** a temporary place to rest or stay **3 rule the roost** See **rule** (sense 20) ▷ *vb* **4** (*intr*) to rest or sleep on a roost **5** (*intr*) to settle down or stay **6 come home to roost** to have unfavourable repercussions [Old English *hrōst*; related to Old Saxon *hrost* loft, German *Rost* grid]

Roost (ru:st) *n* **the.** a powerful current caused by conflicting tides around the Shetland and Orkney Islands [c16 from Old Norse *röst*]

rooster ('ru:stə) *n chiefly US and Canadian* the male of the domestic fowl; a cock

root[1] (ru:t) *n* **1 a** the organ of a higher plant that anchors the rest of the plant in the ground, absorbs water and mineral salts from the soil, and does not bear leaves or buds **b** (loosely) any of the branches of such an organ **2** any plant part, such as a rhizome or tuber, that is similar to a root in structure, function, or appearance **3 a** the essential, fundamental, or primary part or nature of something: *your analysis strikes at the root of the problem* **b** (*as modifier*): *the root cause of the problem* **4** *anatomy* the embedded portion of a tooth, nail, hair, etc **5** origin or derivation, esp as a source of growth, vitality, or existence **6** (*plural*) a person's sense of belonging in a community, place, etc, esp the one in which he was born or brought up **7** an ancestor or antecedent **8** *Bible* a descendant **9** the form of a word that remains after removal of all affixes; a morpheme with lexical meaning that is not further subdivisible into other morphemes with lexical meaning. Compare **stem**[1] (sense 9) **10** *maths* a number or quantity that when multiplied by itself a certain number of times equals a given number or quantity: *3 is a cube root of 27* **11** Also called: **solution** *maths* a number that when substituted for the variable satisfies a given equation: *2 is a root of* $x^3 - 2x - 4 = 0$ **12** *music* (in harmony) the note forming the foundation of a chord **13** *Austral and NZ slang* sexual intercourse **14 root and branch a** (*adverb*) entirely; completely; utterly **b** (*adjective*) thorough; radical; complete ▷ Related adjective: **radical** ▷ *vb* **15** (*intr*) Also: **take root** to put forth or establish a root and begin to grow **16** (*intr*) Also: **take root** to become established, embedded, or effective **17** (*tr*) to fix or embed with or as if with a root or roots **18** *Austral and NZ slang* to have sexual intercourse (with) ▷ See also **root out, roots, root up** [Old English *rōt*, from Old Norse; related to Old English *wyrt* WORT] > **'rooter** *n* > **'root,like** *adj* > **'rooty** *adj* > **'rootiness** *n*

root[2] (ru:t) *vb* (*intr*) **1** (of a pig) to burrow in or dig up the earth in search of food, using the snout **2** (foll by *about, around, in* etc) *informal* to search vigorously but unsystematically [c16 changed (through influence of ROOT[1]) from earlier *wroot*, from Old English *wrōtan*; related to Old English *wrōt* snout, Middle Dutch *wrōte* mole] > **'rooter** *n*

root[3] *vb* (*intr*; usually foll by *for*) *informal* to give support to (a contestant, team, etc), as by cheering [c19 perhaps a variant of Scottish *rout* to make a loud noise, from Old Norse *rauta* to roar] > **'rooter** *n*

root-and-branch *adj* **1** on a large scale or without discrimination; wholesale: *root-and-branch reforms* ▷ *adv* **root and branch 2** entirely; completely; utterly: *Brazil needs reform root and branch*

root beer *n US and Canadian* an effervescent drink made from extracts of various roots and herbs

root canal *n* the passage in the root of a tooth through which its nerves and blood vessels enter the pulp cavity

root-canal therapy *n* another name for **root treatment**

root cap *n* a hollow cone of loosely arranged cells that covers the growing tip of a root and protects it during its passage through the soil

root climber *n* any of various climbing plants, such as the ivy, that adhere to a supporting structure by means of small roots growing from the side of the stem

root crop *n* a crop, as of turnips or beets, cultivated for the food value of its roots

rooted ('ru:tɪd) *adj* **1** having roots **2** deeply felt: *rooted objections* **3** *Austral slang* tired or defeated **4 get rooted!** *Austral taboo slang* an exclamation of contemptuous anger or annoyance, esp against another person

root ginger *n* the raw underground stem of the ginger plant used finely chopped or grated

root hair *n* any of the hollow hairlike outgrowths of the outer cells of a root, just behind the tip, that absorb water and salts from the soil

rooting compound *n horticulture* a substance, usually a powder, containing auxins in which plant cuttings are dipped in order to promote root growth

rootle ('ru:tᵊl) *vb* (*intr*) *Brit* another word for **root**[2]

rootless ('ru:tlɪs) *adj* having no roots, esp (of a person) having no ties with a particular place or community

rootlet ('ru:tlɪt) *n* a small root or branch of a root

root mean square *n* the square root of the average of the squares of a set of numbers or quantities: *the root mean square of 1, 2, and 4 is* $\sqrt{[(1^2 + 2^2 + 4^2)/3]} = \sqrt{7}$ Abbreviation: **rms**

root nodule *n* a swelling on the root of a leguminous plant, such as the pea or clover, that contains bacteria of the genus *Rhizobium*, capable of nitrogen fixation

root out *vb* (*tr, adverb*) to remove or eliminate completely: *we must root out inefficiency*

root position *n music* the vertical distribution of

the written notes of a chord in which the root of the chord is in the bass. See **position** (sense 12a), **inversion** (sense 5a)

roots (ruːts) *adj* (of popular music) going back to the origins of a style, esp in being genuine and unpretentious: *roots rock* ⊳ **'rootsy** *adj*

rootserver ('ruːt,sɜːvə) *n* any of a small number of important large servers on the internet that match addresses at the top-domain level

roots music *n* **1** another name for **world music 2** reggae, esp when regarded as authentic and uncommercialized

rootstock ('ruːt,stɒk) *n* **1** another name for **rhizome 2** another name for **stock** (sense 7) **3** *biology* a basic structure from which offshoots have developed

root treatment *n* *dentistry* a procedure, used for treating an abscess at the tip of the root of a tooth, in which the pulp is removed and a filling (**root filling**) inserted in the root canal. Also called: **root-canal therapy**

root up *vb* (*tr, adverb*) to tear or dig up by the roots

ropable *or* **ropeable** ('rəʊpəb³l) *adj* **1** capable of being roped **2** *Austral and NZ informal* **a** angry **b** wild or intractable: *a ropable beast*

rope (rəʊp) *n* **1 a** a fairly thick cord made of twisted and intertwined hemp or other fibres or of wire or other strong material **b** (*as modifier*): *a rope bridge; a rope ladder* **2** a row of objects fastened or united to form a line: *a rope of pearls; a rope of onions* **3** a quantity of material twisted or wound in the form of a cord **4** anything in the form of a filament or strand, esp something viscous or glutinous: *a rope of slime* **5 the rope a** a rope, noose, or halter used for hanging **b** death by hanging, strangling, etc **6 give (someone) enough rope to hang himself** to allow (someone) to accomplish his own downfall by his own foolish acts **7 know the ropes a** to have a thorough understanding of a particular sphere of activity **b** to be experienced in the ways of the world **8 on the ropes a** *boxing* driven against the ropes enclosing the ring by an opponent's attack **b** in a defenceless or hopeless position ⊳ *vb* **9** (*tr*) to bind or fasten with or as if with a rope **10** (*tr*; usually foll by *off*) to enclose or divide by means of a rope **11** (*intr*) to become extended in a long filament or thread **12** (when *intr*, foll by *up*) *mountaineering* to tie (climbers) together with a rope ⊳ See also **rope in** [Old English *rāp*; related to Old Saxon *rēp*, Old High German *reif*]

rope-a-dope *n* **a** a method of tiring out a boxing opponent by pretending to be trapped on the ropes while the opponent expends energy on punches that are blocked **b** (*as modifier*): *rope-a-dope strategy* [c20 coined by US boxer Muhammad Ali (born 1942)]

rope dancer *n* another name for a **tightrope walker**

rope in *vb* (*tr, adverb*) **1** *Brit* to persuade to take part in some activity **2** *US and Canadian* to trick or entice into some activity

rope's end *n* a short piece of rope, esp as formerly used for flogging sailors

ropewalk ('rəʊp,wɔːk) *n* a long narrow usually covered path or shed where ropes are made

ropey *or* **ropy** ('rəʊpɪ) *adj* **ropier, ropiest 1** *Brit informal* **a** inferior or inadequate **b** slightly unwell; below par **2** (of a viscous or sticky substance) forming strands or filaments **3** resembling a rope ⊳ **'ropily** *adv* ⊳ **'ropiness** *n*

rope yarn *n* the natural or synthetic fibres out of which rope is made

roque (rəʊk) *n* *US* a game developed from croquet, played on a hard surface with a resilient surrounding border from which the ball can rebound [c19 variant of CROQUET]

Roquefort ('rɒkfɔː) *n* a blue-veined cheese with a strong flavour, made from ewe's and goat's milk: matured in caves [c19 named after *Roquefort*, village in S France]

roquelaure ('rɒkə,lɔː) *n* a man's hooded knee-length cloak of the 18th and 19th centuries [c18 from French, named after the Duc de *Roquelaure* (1656–1738), French marshal]

roquet ('rəʊkɪ) *croquet* ⊳ *vb* **-quets** (-kɪz) **-queting** (-kɪɪŋ) **-queted** (-kɪd) **1** to drive one's ball against (another person's ball) in order to be allowed to croquet ⊳ *n* **2** the act of roqueting [c19 variant of CROQUET]

Roraima (*Portuguese* rɔ'raima) *n* a state of N Brazil; chiefly rainforest. Capital: Boa Vista. Pop: 346 871 (2002). Area: 230 104 sq km (89 740 sq miles)

ro-ro ('rəʊrəʊ) *adj acronym for* **roll-on/roll-off**

rorqual ('rɔːkwəl) *n* any of several whalebone whales of the genus *Balaenoptera*, esp *B. physalus*: family *Balaenopteridae*. They have a dorsal fin and a series of grooves along the throat and chest. Also called: **finback** [c19 from French, from Norwegian *rörhval*, from Old Norse *reytharhvalr*, from *reythr* (from *rauthr* red) + *hvalr* whale]

Rorschach test ('rɔːʃɑːk; *German* 'rɔrʃax) *n* *psychol* a personality test consisting of a number of unstructured ink blots presented for interpretation [c20 named after Hermann *Rorschach* (1884–1922), Swiss psychiatrist]

rort (rɔːt) *Austral informal* ⊳ *n* **1** a rowdy party or celebration **2** a dishonest scheme ⊳ *vb* **3** to take unfair advantage of something [c20 back formation from *rorty* (in the sense: good, splendid)] ⊳ **'rorty** *adj*

rorter ('rɔːtə) *n* *Austral informal* a small-scale confidence trickster

Rosa ('rəʊzə; *Italian* 'rɔːza) *n* **Monte** ('mɒntɪ; *Italian* 'monte) a mountain between Italy and Switzerland: the highest in the Pennine Alps. Height: 4634 m (15 204 ft)

rosace ('rəʊzeɪs) *n* **1** another name for **rose window 2** another name for **rosette** [c19 from French, from Latin *rosāceus* ROSACEOUS]

rosacea (rəʊ'zeɪʃə) *n* a chronic inflammatory disease causing the skin of the face to become abnormally flushed and sometimes pustular. Also called: **acne rosacea**

rosaceous (rəʊ'zeɪʃəs) *adj* **1** of, relating to, or belonging to the *Rosaceae*, a family of flowering plants typically having white, yellow, pink, or red five-petalled flowers. The family includes the rose, strawberry, blackberry, and many fruit trees such as apple, cherry, and plum **2** of the colour rose; rose-coloured; rosy [c18 from Latin *rosāceus* composed of roses, from *rosa* ROSE¹]

rosaniline (rəʊ'zænɪ,liːn, -lɪn) *or* **rosanilin** *n* a reddish-brown crystalline insoluble derivative of aniline used, in the form of its soluble hydrochloride, as a red dye. See also **fuchsin** [c19 from ROSE¹ + ANILINE]

rosarian (rəʊ'zɛərɪən) *n* a person who cultivates roses, esp professionally

Rosario (rəʊ'sɑːrɪəʊ; *Spanish* rɔ'sarjo) *n* an inland port in E Argentina, on the Paraná River: the second largest city in the country; industrial centre. Pop: 1 312 000 (2005 est)

rosarium (rəʊ'zɛərɪəm) *n, pl* **-sariums** *or* **-saria** (-'zɛərɪə) a rose garden [c19 New Latin]

rosary ('rəʊzərɪ) *n, pl* **-saries 1** *RC Church* **a** a series of prayers counted on a string of beads, usually consisting of five or 15 decades of Aves, each decade beginning with a Paternoster and ending with a Gloria **b** a string of 55 or 165 beads used to count these prayers as they are recited **2** (in other religions) a similar string of beads used in praying **3** a bed or garden of roses **4** an archaic word for a **garland** (of flowers, leaves, etc) [c14 from Latin *rosārium* rose garden, from *rosārius* of roses, from *rosa* ROSE¹]

rosbif (,rəʊs'biːf; *French* rɔsbif) *n* a term used in France for an English person [from French, from English *roast beef*, considered as being typically English]

Roscius ('rɒskɪəs, -sɪəs) *n* any actor [from Quintus Roscius Gallus (died 62 BC), Roman actor] ⊳ **'Roscian** *adj*

Roscommon (rɒs'kɒmən) *n* **1** an inland county

of N central Republic of Ireland, in Connacht. County town: Roscommon. Pop: 53 774 (2002). Area: 2463 sq km (951 sq miles) **2** a former name for **Galway** (sense 3)

rose¹ (rəʊz) *n* **1 a** any shrub or climbing plant of the rosaceous genus *Rosa*, typically having prickly stems, compound leaves, and fragrant flowers **b** (*in combination*): *rosebush; rosetree* **2** the flower of any of these plants **3** any of various similar plants, such as the rockrose and Christmas rose **4 a** a moderate purplish-red colour; purplish pink **b** (*as adjective*): *rose paint* **5** a rose, or a representation of one, as the national emblem of England **6** *jewellery* **a** a cut for a diamond or other gemstone, having a hemispherical faceted crown and a flat base **b** a gem so cut **7** a perforated cap fitted to the spout of a watering can or the end of a hose, causing the water to issue in a spray **8** a design or decoration shaped like a rose; rosette **9** Also called: **ceiling rose** *electrical engineering* a circular boss attached to a ceiling through which the flexible lead of an electric-light fitting passes **10** *history* See **red rose, white rose 11** bed of roses a situation of comfort or ease **12 under the rose** in secret; privately; sub rosa ⊳ *vb* **13** (*tr*) to make rose-coloured; cause to blush or redden [Old English, from Latin *rosa*, probably from Greek *rhodon* rose] ⊳ **'rose,like** *adj*

rose² (rəʊz) *vb* the past tense of **rise**

rosé ('rəʊzeɪ) *n* any pink wine, made either by removing the skins of red grapes after only a little colour has been extracted or by mixing red and white wines [c19 from French, literally: pink, from Latin *rosa* ROSE¹]

rose acacia *n* a leguminous shrub, *Robinia hispida*, of the southern US, having prickly branches bearing clusters of red scentless flowers. See also **locust** (sense 2)

rose apple *n* an ornamental myrtaceous tree, *Syzygium jambos*, of the East Indies, cultivated in the tropics for its edible fruit

roseate ('rəʊzɪ,eɪt) *adj* **1** of the colour rose or pink **2** excessively or idealistically optimistic ⊳ **'rose,ately** *adv*

Roseau ('rəʊzəʊ) *n* the capital of Dominica, a port on the SW coast: botanical gardens. Pop: 19 400 (2001 est)

rosebay ('rəʊz,beɪ) *n* **1** *US* any of several rhododendrons, esp *Rhododendron maximum* of E North America **2 rosebay willowherb** a perennial onagraceous plant, *Chamerion* (formerly *Epilobium*) *angustifolium*, that has spikes of deep pink flowers and is widespread in open places throughout N temperate regions **3** another name for **oleander**

rosebud ('rəʊz,bʌd) *n* **1** the bud of a rose **2** *literary* a pretty young woman

rose campion *n* a European caryophyllaceous plant, *Lychnis coronaria*, widely cultivated for its pink flowers. Its stems and leaves are covered with white woolly down. Also called: **dusty miller**

rose chafer *or* **beetle** *n* a British scarabaeid beetle, *Cetonia aurata*, that has a greenish-golden body with a metallic lustre and feeds on plants

rose-coloured *adj* **1** of the colour rose; rosy **2** See **rose-tinted 3** see through rose-coloured (*or* rose-tinted) glasses (*or* spectacles) to view in an excessively optimistic light

rose-cut *adj* (of a gemstone) cut with a hemispherical faceted crown and a flat base

rosefish ('rəʊz,fɪʃ) *n, pl* **-fish** *or* **-fishes 1** a red scorpaenid food fish, *Sebastes marinus*, of North Atlantic coastal waters **2** any of various other red fishes

rose geranium *n* a small geraniaceous shrub, *Pelargonium graveolens*, grown in North America for its pink flowers and fragrant leaves, used for scenting perfumes and cosmetics

rosehip ('rəʊz,hɪp) *n* the berry-like fruit of a rose plant. See **hip²**

rosella (rəʊ'zɛlə) *n* any of various Australian parrots of the genus *Platycercus*, such as *P. elegans* (**crimson rosella**), often kept as cage birds [c19

r

probably alteration of *Rose-hiller*, after *Rose Hill*, Parramatta, near Sydney]

rosemaling ('rəʊzəˌmɑːlɪŋ, -sə-) *n* a type of painted or carved decoration in Scandinavian peasant style consisting of floral motifs [c20 from Norwegian, literally: rose painting]

rose mallow *n* **1** Also called (US and Canadian): **marsh mallow** any of several malvaceous marsh plants of the genus *Hibiscus*, such as *H. moscheutos*, of E North America, having pink or white flowers and downy leaves **2** *US* another name for the **hollyhock**

rosemary ('rəʊzmərɪ) *n, pl* **-maries** an aromatic European shrub, *Rosmarinus officinalis*, widely cultivated for its grey-green evergreen leaves, which are used in cookery for flavouring and yield a fragrant oil used in the manufacture of perfumes: family *Lamiaceae* (labiates). It is the traditional flower of remembrance [c15 earlier *rosmarine*, from Latin *rōs* dew + *marīnus* marine; modern form influenced by folk etymology, as if ROSE¹ + MARY]

rose moss *n* a low-growing portulacaceous plant, *Portulaca grandiflora*, native to Brazil but widely cultivated as a garden plant for its brightly coloured flowers

rose of Jericho *n* another name for the **resurrection plant**

rose of Sharon *n* **1** Also called: **Aaron's beard** a creeping shrub, *Hypericum calycinum*, native to SE Europe but widely cultivated, having large yellow flowers: family *Hypericaceae* **2** Also called: **althaea** a Syrian malvaceous shrub, *Hibiscus syriacus* (or *Althaea frutex*), cultivated for its red or purplish flowers

roseola (rəʊˈziːələ) *n pathol* **1** a feverish condition of young children that lasts for some five days during the last two of which the patient has a rose-coloured rash. It is caused by the human herpes virus **2** any red skin eruption or rash [c19 from New Latin, diminutive of Latin *roseus* rosy] > ro'seolar *adj*

rose quartz *n* a rose-pink often translucent variety of quartz that is used for ornaments

rose-root *n* a Eurasian crassulaceous mountain plant, *Sedum rosea*, with fleshy pink-tipped leaves, a thick fleshy pinkish underground stem, and a cluster of yellow flowers. Also called: **midsummer-men**

rosery ('rəʊzərɪ) *n, pl* **-series** a bed or garden of roses

rose-tinted *adj* **1** Also: **rose-coloured** excessively optimistic **2 see through rose-tinted** (*or* **rose-coloured**) **glasses** (*or* **spectacles**) to view in an excessively optimistic light

rose topaz *n* a rose-pink form of topaz produced by heating yellow-brown topaz

Rosetta (rəʊˈzɛtə) *n* the former name of **Rashid**

Rosetta stone *n* a basalt slab discovered in 1799 at Rosetta, dating to the reign of Ptolemy V (196 BC) and carved with parallel inscriptions in Egyptian hieroglyphics, demotic characters, and Greek, which provided the key to the decipherment of ancient Egyptian texts

rosette (rəʊˈzɛt) *n* **1** a decoration or pattern resembling a rose, esp an arrangement of ribbons or strips formed into a rose-shaped design and worn as a badge or presented as a prize **2** another name for **rose window 3** a rose-shaped patch of colour, such as one of the clusters of spots marking a leopard's fur **4** *botany* a circular cluster of leaves growing from the base of a stem **5** any of various plant diseases characterized by abnormal leaf growth [c18 from Old French: a little ROSE¹]

rose-water *n* **1 a** scented water used as a perfume and in cooking, made by the distillation of rose petals or by impregnation with oil of roses **b** (*as modifier*): *rose-water scent* **2** (*modifier*) elegant or delicate, esp excessively so

rose window *n* a circular window, esp one that has ornamental tracery radiating from the centre

to form a symmetrical roselike pattern. Also called: **wheel window, rosette**

rosewood ('rəʊzˌwʊd) *n* **1** the hard dark wood of any of various tropical and subtropical leguminous trees, esp of the genus *Dalbergia*. It has a roselike scent and is used in cabinetwork **2** any of the trees yielding this wood

Rosh Chodesh (rɒʃ ˈxɔdɛʃ) *n Judaism* the first day of a new month, coinciding usually with the new moon, and also the preceding day if the previous month has 30 days, observed as a minor festival. See also **Jewish calendar** [from Hebrew, literally: the beginning of the new moon]

Rosh Hashanah *or* **Rosh Hashana** ('rɒʃ həˈʃɑːnə; *Hebrew* 'rɒʃ haʃaˈna) *n* the festival marking the Jewish New Year, celebrated on the first and second days of Tishri, and marked by penitential prayers and by the blowing of the shofar [from Hebrew *rōsh hasshānāh*, literally: beginning of the year, from *rōsh* head + *hash-shānāh* year]

Rosicrucian (ˌrəʊzɪˈkruːʃən) *n* **1** a member of a society professing esoteric religious doctrines, venerating the emblems of the rose and Cross as symbols of Christ's Resurrection and Redemption, and claiming various occult powers ▷ *adj* **2** of, relating to, or designating the Rosicrucians or Rosicrucianism [c17 from Latin *Rosae Crucis* Rose of the Cross, translation of the German name *Christian Rosenkreuz*, supposed founder of the society in the 15th century] > Rosi'crucianism *n*

Rosie Lee ('rəʊzɪ 'liː) *n Cockney rhyming slang* tea

rosin ('rɒzɪn) *n* **1** Also called: **colophony** a translucent brittle amber substance produced in the distillation of crude turpentine oleoresin and used esp in making varnishes, printing inks, and sealing waxes and for treating the bows of stringed instruments **2** (not in technical usage) another name for **resin** (sense 1) ▷ *vb* **3** (*tr*) to treat or coat with rosin [c14 variant of RESIN] > 'rosiny *adj*

Rosinante (ˌrɒzɪˈnæntɪ) *n* a worn-out emaciated old horse [c18 from Spanish, the name of Don Quixote's horse, from *rocin* old horse]

rosiner ('rɒzənə) *n Austral slang* a strong alcoholic drink [from English dialect sense of *rosin* to supply with liquor]

rosin oil *n* a yellowish fluorescent oily liquid obtained from certain resins, used in the manufacture of carbon black, varnishes, and lacquers. Also called: 'rosinol, retinol

rosinweed ('rɒzɪnˌwiːd) *n* any of several North American plants of the genus *Silphium* and related genera, esp the compass plant, having resinous juice, sticky foliage, and a strong smell: family *Asteraceae* (composites)

Roskilde (*Danish* 'rɒskilə) *n* a city in Denmark, on NE Zealand west of Copenhagen: capital of Denmark from the 10th century to 1443; scene of the signing (1658) of the **Peace of Roskilde** between Denmark and Sweden. Pop: 44 205 (2004 est)

ROSPA ('rɒspə) *n* (in Britain) ▷ *acronym for* Royal Society for the Prevention of Accidents

Ross and Cromarty (rɒs ənd 'krɒmətɪ) *n* (until 1975) a county of N Scotland, including the island of Lewis and many islets: now split between the Highland and Western Isles council areas

Ross Dependency *n* a section of Antarctica administered by New Zealand. (Claims are suspended under the Antarctic Treaty of 1959). Includes the coastal regions of Victoria Land and King Edward VII Land, the Ross Sea and islands, and the Ross Ice Shelf. Area: about 414 400 sq km (160 000 sq miles)

Ross Ice Shelf *n* the ice shelf forming the S part of the Ross Sea, between Victoria Land and Byrd Land. Also called: **Ross Barrier, Ross Shelf Ice**

Ross Island *n* an island in the W Ross Sea: contains the active volcano Mount Erebus

Rossiya (ra'siːjə) *n* transliteration of the Russian name for **Russia**

Ross Sea *n* a large arm of the S Pacific in

Antarctica, incorporating the Ross Ice Shelf and lying between Victoria Land and the Edward VII Peninsula

rostellum (rɒˈstɛləm) *n, pl* **-la** (-lə) *biology* a small beaklike process, such as the hooked projection from the top of the head in tapeworms or the outgrowth from the stigma of an orchid [c18 from Latin: a little beak, from *rōstrum* a beak] > ros'tellate *or* ros'tellar *adj*

roster¹ ('rɒstə) *n* **1** a list or register, esp one showing the order of people enrolled for duty ▷ *vb* **2** *marketing* the list of advertising agencies regularly used by a particular company **3** (*tr*) to place on a roster [c18 from Dutch *rooster* grating or list (the lined paper looking like a grid)]

roster² ('rɒstə) *n Northern English dialect* a rascal

rösti ('rɜːstɪ) *or* **rosti** ('rɒstɪ) *n* a Swiss dish consisting of grated potato formed into a cake, sometimes with onion, fried, and topped with cheese [c20 from Swiss German, literally: crisp and golden]

Rostock ('rɒstɒk) *n* a port in NE Germany, in Mecklenburg-West Pomerania on the Warnow estuary 13 km (8 miles) from the Baltic and its outport, Warnemünde: the chief port of the former East Germany; university (1419). Pop: 198 303 (2003 est)

Rostov *or* **Rostov-on-Don** ('rɒstɒv) *n* a port in S Russia, on the River Don 48 km (30 miles) from the Sea of Azov: industrial centre. Pop: 1 081 000 (2005 est)

rostral ('rɒstrəl) *adj* **1** *biology* of or like a beak or snout **2** adorned with the prows of ships: *a rostral column*

rostrate ('rɒsˌtreɪt) *adj biology* having a beak or beaklike process

rostrum ('rɒstrəm) *n, pl* **-trums** *or* **-tra** (-trə) **1** any platform, stage, or dais on which public speakers stand to address an audience **2** a platform or dais in front of an orchestra on which the conductor stands **3** another word for **ram** (sense 5) **4** the prow or beak of an ancient Roman ship **5** *biology, zoology* a beak or beaklike part [c16 from Latin *rōstrum* beak, ship's prow, from *rōdere* to nibble, gnaw; in plural, *rōstra*, orator's platform, because this platform in the Roman forum was adorned with the prows of captured ships]

rosy ('rəʊzɪ) *adj* **rosier, rosiest 1** of the colour rose or pink **2** having a healthy pink complexion: *rosy cheeks* **3** optimistic, esp excessively so: *a rosy view of social improvements* **4** full of health, happiness, or joy: *rosy slumbers* **5** resembling, consisting of, or abounding in roses > 'rosily *adv* > 'rosiness *n*

rosy finch *n* any of several finches of the genus *Leucosticte*, occurring in mountainous regions of North America and Asia. They have brown or grey plumage with pink patches on the wings, rump, and tail

rot¹ (rɒt) *vb* **rots, rotting, rotted 1** to decay or cause to decay as a result of bacterial or fungal action **2** (*intr*; usually foll by *off* or *away*) to fall or crumble (off) or break (away), as from natural decay, corrosive action, or long use **3** (*intr*) to become weak, debilitated, or depressed through inertia, confinement, etc; languish: *rotting in prison* **4** to become or cause to become morally corrupt or degenerate **5** (*tr*) *textiles* another word for **ret** ▷ *n* **6** the process of rotting or the state of being rotten **7** something decomposed, disintegrated, or degenerate. Related adj: **putrid 8** short for **dry rot 9** *pathol* any putrefactive decomposition of tissues **10** a condition in plants characterized by breakdown and decay of tissues, caused by bacteria, fungi, etc **11** *vet science* a contagious fungal disease of the feet of sheep characterized by inflammation, swelling, a foul smelling discharge, and lameness **12** (*also interjection*) nonsense; rubbish [Old English *rotian* (vb); related to Old Norse *rotna*. C13 (noun), from Scandinavian]

rot² *abbreviation for* rotation (of a mathematical function)

rota ('rəʊtə) *n chiefly Brit* a register of names

showing the order in which people take their turn to perform certain duties [C17 from Latin: a wheel]

Rota ('rəʊtə) *n* *RC Church* the supreme ecclesiastical tribunal for judging cases brought before the Holy See

rota bed *n* *social welfare* a bed in an old people's home, reserved for the regular respite care of dependent old people

rotachute ('rəʊtə,ʃuːt) *n* a device serving the same purpose as a parachute, in which the canopy is replaced by freely revolving rotor blades, used for the delivery of stores or recovery of missiles

Rotameter ('rəʊtə,miːtə) *n* *trademark* a device used for measuring the flow of a fluid. It consists of a small float supported in a tapering glass by the flow of the fluid, the height of the float indicating the rate of flow

rotan (rəʊ'tæn) (in Indonesia and Malaysia) *n* another name for **rattan** (sense 1)

rotaplane ('rəʊtə,pleɪn) *n* an aircraft that derives its lift from freely revolving rotor blades

Rotarian (rəʊ'tɛərɪən) *n* **1** a member of a Rotary Club ▷ *adj* **2** of or relating to Rotary Clubs or their members > **Ro'tarianism** *n*

rotary ('rəʊtərɪ) *adj* **1** of, relating to, or operating by rotation **2** turning or able to turn; revolving ▷ *n*, *pl* **-ries 3** a part of a machine that rotates about an axis **4** *US and Canadian* another term for **roundabout** (for traffic) [C18 from Medieval Latin *rotārius*, from Latin *rota* a wheel]

rotary clothesline *or* **clothes dryer** *n* an apparatus of radiating spokes that support lines on which clothes are hung to dry

Rotary Club *n* any of the local clubs that form **Rotary International**, an international association of professional and businessmen founded in the US in 1905 to promote community service

rotary engine *n* **1** an internal-combustion engine having radial cylinders that rotate about a fixed crankshaft **2** an engine, such as a turbine or wankel engine, in which power is transmitted directly to rotating components

rotary plough *or* **tiller** *n* an implement with a series of blades mounted on a power-driven shaft, used to break up soil or weeds

rotary press *n* a machine for printing from a revolving cylinder, or a plate attached to one, usually onto a continuous strip of paper

rotary pump *n* *engineering* a pump in which a liquid is displaced through a shaped stator by a shaped rotor

rotate *vb* (rəʊ'teɪt) **1** to turn or cause to turn around an axis, line, or point; revolve or spin **2** to follow or cause to follow a set order or sequence **3** (of a position, presidency, etc) to pass in turn from one eligible party to each of the other eligible parties **4** (of staff) to replace or be replaced in turn ▷ *adj* (rəʊ'teɪt) **5** *botany* designating a corolla the united petals of which radiate from a central point like the spokes of a wheel > **ro'tatable** *adj*

rotating (rəʊ'teɪtɪŋ) *adj* **1** revolving around a central axis, line, or point: *the rotating blades of a helicopter* **2** passing in turn to each of two or more eligible parties: *the rotating presidency of the EU*

rotation (rəʊ'teɪʃən) *n* **1** the act of rotating; rotary motion **2** a regular cycle of events in a set order or sequence **3** a planned sequence of cropping according to which the crops grown in successive seasons on the same land are varied so as to make a balanced demand on its resources of fertility **4** *maths* **a** a circular motion of a configuration about a given point or line, without a change in shape **b** a transformation in which the coordinate axes are rotated by a fixed angle about the origin **c** another name for **curl** (sense 11) Abbreviation (for sense 4C): **rot 5 a** the spinning motion of a body, such as a planet, about an internal axis. Compare **revolution** (sense 5a) **b** one complete turn in such motion > **ro'tational** *adj*

rotator (rəʊ'teɪtə) *n* **1** a person, device, or part that rotates or causes rotation **2** *anatomy* any of

various muscles that revolve a part on its axis

rotator cuff *anatomy* the structure around the shoulder joint consisting of the capsule of the joint along with the tendons of the adjacent muscles

rotatory ('rəʊtətərɪ, -trɪ) *or less commonly* **rotative** ('rəʊtətɪv) *adj* of, relating to, possessing, or causing rotation > **'rotatively** *adv*

Rotavator *or* **Rotovator** ('rəʊtə,veɪtə) *n* *trademark* a type of machine with rotating blades that will break up soil [C20 original form *Rotavator*, from *rota(ry)* *(culti)vator*]

rotavirus ('rəʊtə,vaɪrəs) *n* any member of a genus of viruses that cause worldwide endemic infections. They occur in birds and mammals, cause diarrhoea in children, and are usually transmitted in food prepared with unwashed hands

rote[1] (rəʊt) *n* **1** a habitual or mechanical routine or procedure **2 by rote** by repetition; by heart (often in the phrase **learn by rote**) [C14 origin unknown]

rote[2] (rəʊt) *n* an ancient violin-like musical instrument; crwth [C13 from Old French *rote*, of Germanic origin; related to Old High German *rotta*, Middle Dutch *rotte*]

rotenone ('rəʊtɪ,nəʊn) *n* a white odourless crystalline substance extracted from the roots of derris: a powerful insecticide. Formula: $C_{23}H_{22}O_6$; relative density: 1.27; melting pt: 163°C [C20 from Japanese *rōten* derris + -ONE]

ROTFL *text messaging* *abbreviation for* rolling on the floor laughing

rotgut ('rɒt,gʌt) *n* *facetious slang* alcoholic drink, esp spirits, of inferior quality

Rotherham ('rɒðərəm) *n* **1** an industrial town in N England, in Rotherham unitary authority, South Yorkshire. Pop: 117 262 (2001) **2** a unitary authority in N England, in South Yorkshire. Pop: 251 500 (2003 est). Area: 283 sq km (109 sq miles)

Rothesay ('rɒθsɪ) *n* a town in SW Scotland, in Argyll and Bute, on the E coast of the Isle of Bute. Pop: 5017 (2001)

roti ('rəʊtɪ, 'rʊtɪ) *n* (in India and the Caribbean) a type of unleavened bread [Hindi: bread]

rotifer ('rəʊtɪfə) *n* any minute aquatic multicellular invertebrate of the phylum *Rotifera*, having a ciliated wheel-like organ used in feeding and locomotion: common constituents of freshwater plankton. Also called: **wheel animalcule** [C18 from New Latin *Rotifera*, from Latin *rota* wheel + *ferre* to bear] > **rotiferal** (rəʊ'tɪfərəl) *or* **ro'tiferous** *adj*

rotisserie (rəʊ'tɪsərɪ) *n* **1** a rotating spit on which meat, poultry, etc, can be cooked **2** a shop or restaurant where meat is roasted to order [C19 from French, from Old French *rostir* to ROAST]

rotl ('rɒtəl) *n*, *pl* **rotls** *or* **artal** ('ɑːtəl) a unit of weight used in Muslim countries, varying in value between about one and five pounds [C17 from Arabic *ratl*, perhaps from Greek *litra* a pound]

rotogravure (,rəʊtəʊgrə'vjʊə) *n* **1** a printing process using a cylinder etched with many small recesses, from which ink is transferred to a moving web of paper, plastic, etc, in a rotary press **2** printed material produced in this way, esp magazines ▷ Often shortened to: **roto** [C20 from Latin *rota* wheel + GRAVURE]

roton ('rəʊtɒn) *n* *physics* a quantum of vortex motion

rotor ('rəʊtə) *n* **1** the rotating member of a machine or device, esp the armature of a motor or generator or the rotating assembly of a turbine. Compare **stator 2** a device having blades radiating from a central hub that is rotated to produce thrust to lift and propel a helicopter **3** the revolving arm of the distributor of an internal-combustion engine **4** a violent rolling wave of air occurring in the lee of a mountain or hill, in which the air rotates about a horizontal axis [C20 shortened form of ROTATOR]

Rotorua (,rəʊtə'ruːə) *n* a city in New Zealand, on

N central North Island at the SW end of Lake Rotorua: centre of forestry; noted for volcanic activity. Pop: 67 800 (2004 est)

rotovate *or* **rotavate** ('rəʊtə,veɪt) *vb* (*tr*) to break up the surface of (the earth, or an area of ground) using a Rotavator

rotten ('rɒtən) *adj* **1** affected with rot; decomposing, decaying, or putrid **2** breaking up, esp through age or hard use; disintegrating: *rotten ironwork* **3** morally despicable or corrupt **4** untrustworthy, disloyal, or treacherous **5** *informal* unpleasant, unfortunate, or nasty: *rotten luck; rotten weather* **6** *informal* unsatisfactory or poor: *rotten workmanship* **7** *informal* miserably unwell **8** *informal* distressed, uncomfortable, and embarrassed: *I felt rotten when I told him to go* **9** (of rocks, soils, etc) soft and crumbling, esp as a result of weathering **10** *slang, chiefly Austral and NZ* intoxicated; drunk ▷ *adv informal* **11** extremely; very much: *men fancy her rotten* [C13 from Old Norse *rottin*; related to Old English *rotian* to ROT[1]] > **'rottenly** *adv* > **'rottenness** *n*

rotten borough *n* (before the Reform Act of 1832) any of certain English parliamentary constituencies with only a very few electors. Compare **pocket borough**

rottenstone ('rɒtən,stəʊn) *n* a much-weathered limestone, rich in silica: used in powdered form for polishing metal

rotter ('rɒtə) *n* *slang, chiefly Brit* a worthless, unpleasant, or despicable person

Rotterdam ('rɒtə,dæm) *n* a port in the SW Netherlands, in South Holland province: the second largest city of the Netherlands and one of the world's largest ports; oil refineries, shipbuilding yards, etc Pop: 600 000 (2003 est)

Rottweiler ('rɒt,vaɪlə) *n* a breed of large robustly built dog with a smooth coat of black with dark tan markings on the face, chest, and legs. It was previously a docked breed [German, named after *Rottweil*, German city where the dog was originally bred]

rotund (rəʊ'tʌnd) *adj* **1** rounded or spherical in shape **2** plump **3** sonorous or grandiloquent; full in tone, style of speaking, etc [C18 from Latin *rotundus* wheel-shaped, round, from *rota* wheel] > **ro'tundity** *or* **ro'tundness** *n* > **ro'tundly** *adv*

rotunda (rəʊ'tʌndə) *n* a building or room having a circular plan, esp one that has a dome [C17 from Italian *rotonda*, from Latin *rotundus* round, from *rota* a wheel]

ROU *international car registration for* (Republic of) Uruguay

Roubaix (French rubɛ) *n* a city in N France near the Belgian border: forms, with Tourcoing, a large industrial conurbation. Pop: 96 984 (1999)

rouble *or* **ruble** ('ruːbəl) *n* **1** the standard monetary unit of Belarus and Russia, divided into 100 kopecks **2** the former standard monetary unit of Tajikistan, divided into 100 tanga [C16 from Russian *rubl* silver bar, from Old Russian *rublĭ* bar, block of wood, from *rubiti* to cut up]

rouche (ruːʃ) *n* a variant spelling of **ruche**

roucou ('ruː,kuː) *n* another name for **annatto** [C17 via French from Tupi *urucú*]

roué ('ruːeɪ) *n* a debauched or lecherous man; rake [C19 from French, literally: one broken on the wheel, from *rouer*, from Latin *rotāre* to revolve, from *rota* a wheel; with reference to the fate deserved by a debauchee]

Rouen (French rwā) *n* a city in N France, on the River Seine: the chief river port of France; became capital of the duchy of Normandy in 912; scene of the burning of Joan of Arc (1431); university (1964). Pop: 106 592 (1999)

rouge (ruːʒ) *n* **1** a red powder, used as a cosmetic for adding redness to the cheeks **2** short for **jeweller's rouge** ▷ *vb* (*tr*) **3** to apply rouge to [C18 from French: red, from Latin *rubeus*]

Rouge Croix (,ruːʒ 'krwɑː) *n* a pursuivant at the English college of arms

Rouge Dragon (,ruːʒ 'drægən) *n* a pursuivant at

r

the English college of arms

rouge et noir (ˈruːʒ eɪ ˈnwɑː; *French* ruʒ e nwar) *n* a card game in which the players put their stakes on any of two red and two black diamond-shaped spots marked on the table. Also called: **trente et quarante** [French, literally: red and black]

rough (rʌf) *adj* 1 (of a surface) not smooth; uneven or irregular 2 (of ground) covered with scrub, boulders, etc 3 denoting or taking place on uncultivated ground: *rough grazing; rough shooting* 4 shaggy or hairy 5 turbulent; agitated: *a rough sea* 6 (of the performance or motion of something) uneven; irregular 7 (of behaviour or character) rude, coarse, ill mannered, inconsiderate, or violent 8 harsh or sharp: *rough words* 9 *informal* severe or unpleasant: *a rough lesson* 10 (of work, a task, etc) requiring physical rather than mental effort 11 *informal* ill or physically upset: *he felt rough after an evening of heavy drinking* 12 unfair or unjust: *rough luck* 13 harsh or grating to the ear 14 harsh to the taste 15 without refinement, luxury, etc 16 not polished or perfected in any detail; rudimentary; not elaborate: *rough workmanship; rough justice* 17 not prepared or dressed: *rough gemstones* 18 (of a guess, estimate, etc) approximate 19 *Austral informal* (of a chance) not good 20 having the sound of *h*; aspirated 21 *rough on informal, chiefly Brit* a severe towards b unfortunate for (a person) 22 *the rough side of one's tongue* harsh words; a reprimand, rebuke, or verbal attack ▷ *n* 23 rough ground 24 a sketch or preliminary piece of artwork 25 an unfinished or crude state (esp in the phrase **in the rough**) 26 the rough *golf* the part of the course bordering the fairways where the grass is untrimmed 27 *tennis, squash, badminton* the side of a racket on which the binding strings form an uneven line 28 *informal* a rough or violent person; thug 29 the unpleasant side of something (esp in the phrase **take the rough with the smooth**) ▷ *adv* 30 in a rough manner; roughly 31 *sleep rough* to spend the night in the open; be without a home or without shelter ▷ *vb* 32 (*tr*) to make rough; roughen 33 (*tr*; foll by *out, in,* etc) to prepare (a sketch, report, piece of work, etc) in preliminary form 34 *rough it informal* to live without the usual comforts or conveniences of life ▷ See also **rough out, rough up** [Old English *rūh*; related to Old Norse *ruksa,* Middle Dutch *rūge, rūwe,* German *rauh*] ▷ ˈroughness *n*

roughage (ˈrʌfɪdʒ) *n* 1 the coarse indigestible constituents of food or fodder, which provide bulk to the diet and promote normal bowel function. See also **dietary fibre** 2 any rough or coarse material

rough-and-ready *adj* 1 crude, unpolished, or hastily prepared, but sufficient for the purpose 2 (of a person) without formality or refinement; rudely vigorous ▷ ˈrough-and-ˈreadiness *n*

rough-and-tumble *n* 1 a fight or scuffle without rules ▷ *adj* 2 characterized by roughness, disorderliness, and disregard for rules

rough breathing *n* (in Greek) the sign (ʽ) placed over an initial letter, or a second letter if the word begins with a diphthong, indicating that (in ancient Greek) it was pronounced with an *h*. Compare **smooth breathing**

roughcast (ˈrʌfˌkɑːst) *n* 1 a coarse plaster used to cover the surface of an external wall 2 any rough or preliminary form, model, etc ▷ *adj* 3 covered with or denoting roughcast ▷ *vb* -casts, -casting, -cast 4 to apply roughcast to (a wall, etc) 5 to prepare in rough 6 (*tr*) another word for **rough-hew**. ▷ ˈroughˌcaster *n*

rough collie *n* a large long-haired collie having a distinctive ruff and a long narrow head without a pronounced stop

rough-cut *n* a first edited version of a film with the scenes in sequence and the soundtrack synchronized

rough diamond *n* 1 an unpolished diamond 2

an intrinsically trustworthy or good person with uncouth manners or dress

rough-dry *adj* 1 (of clothes or linen) dried ready for pressing ▷ *vb* -dries, -drying, -dried 2 (*tr*) to dry (clothes or linen) without smoothing

roughen (ˈrʌfᵊn) *vb* to make or become rough

rough fish *n* a fish that is neither a sport fish nor useful as food or bait for sport fish

rough-hew *vb* -hews, -hewing, -hewed, -hewed or -hewn (*tr*) 1 to cut or hew (timber, stone, etc) roughly without finishing the surface 2 Also: **roughcast** to shape roughly or crudely

roughhouse (ˈrʌfˌhaʊs) *slang* ▷ *n* 1 rough, disorderly, or noisy behaviour ▷ *vb* 2 to treat (someone) in a boisterous or rough way

roughie[1] (ˈrʌfɪ) *n* a small food fish of the family *Arripididae,* found in southern and western Australian waters. Also called: **orange roughy, ruff, tommy rough**

roughie[2] *n Austral slang* 1 something unfair, esp a trick 2 (in horse racing) an outsider that wins

roughish (ˈrʌfɪʃ) *adj* somewhat rough

rough-legged buzzard *n* a buzzard, *Buteo lagopus,* of Europe, Asia, and North America, having feathers covering its legs

roughly (ˈrʌflɪ) *adv* 1 without being exact or fully authenticated; approximately: *roughly half the candidates were successful* 2 in a clumsy, coarse, or violent manner 3 in a crude or primitive manner: *a slab of roughly hewn stone*

rough music *n* (formerly) a loud cacophony created with tin pans, drums, etc, esp as a protest outside someone's house

roughneck (ˈrʌfˌnɛk) *n slang* 1 a rough or violent person; thug 2 a worker in an oil-drilling operation

rough out *vb* (*tr, adverb*) 1 See **rough** (sense 33) 2 *engineering* to machine (a workpiece, such as a casting or forging) with heavy cuts leaving a rough surface to be finished

rough passage *n* 1 a stormy sea journey 2 a difficult or testing time

rough puff pastry *n* a rich flaky pastry made with butter and used for pie-crusts, flans, etc

roughrider (ˈrʌfˌraɪdə) *n* a rider of wild or unbroken horses

roughshod (ˈrʌfˌʃɒd) *adj* 1 (of a horse) shod with rough-bottomed shoes to prevent sliding ▷ *adv* 2 *ride roughshod over* to domineer over or act with complete disregard for

rough sleeper *n* a homeless person who sleeps rough

rough spin *n NZ informal* unfair treatment

rough-spoken *adj* rude or uncouth in speech

rough stuff *n informal* violence

rough trade *n slang* (in homosexual use) a tough or violent sexual partner, casually picked up

rough up *vb* (*tr, adverb*) 1 *informal* to treat violently; beat up 2 to cause (feathers, hair, etc) to stand up by rubbing against the grain

roulade (ruːˈlɑːd) *n* 1 a slice of meat rolled, esp around a stuffing, and cooked 2 an elaborate run in vocal music [c18 from French, literally: a rolling, from *rouler* to ROLL]

rouleau (ˈruːləʊ) *n, pl* -leaux (-ləʊ, -ləʊz) or -leaus 1 a roll of paper containing coins 2 (*often plural*) a roll of ribbon [c17 from French, from *role* ROLL]

Roulers (ruːˈleəz; *French* ruleːr) *n* a city in NW Belgium, in West Flanders province: electronics. Pop: 55 273 (2004 est). Flemish name: **Roeselare**

roulette (ruːˈlɛt) *n* 1 a gambling game in which a ball is dropped onto a spinning horizontal wheel divided into 37 or 38 coloured and numbered slots, with players betting on the slot into which the ball will fall 2 a a toothed wheel for making a line of perforations b a tiny slit made by such a wheel on a sheet of stamps as an aid to tearing it apart 3 a curve generated by a point on one curve rolling on another ▷ *vb* (*tr*) 4 to use a roulette on (something), as in engraving, making stationery, etc [c18 from French, from *rouelle* a little wheel, from *roue* a wheel, from Latin *rota*]

Roumania (ruːˈmeɪnɪə) *n* a variant of **Romania**

Roumanian (ruːˈmeɪnɪən) *n, adj* a variant of **Romanian**

Roumelia (ruːˈmiːlɪə) *n* a variant spelling of **Rumelia**

round (raʊnd) *adj* 1 having a flat circular shape, as a disc or hoop 2 having the shape of a sphere or ball 3 curved; not angular 4 involving or using circular motion 5 (*prenominal*) complete; entire: *a round dozen* 6 *maths* a forming or expressed by an integer or whole number, with no fraction b expressed to the nearest ten, hundred, or thousand: *in round figures* 7 (of a sum of money) considerable; ample 8 fully depicted or developed, as a character in a book 9 full and plump: *round cheeks* 10 (of sound) full and sonorous 11 (of pace) brisk; lively 12 (*prenominal*) (of speech) candid; straightforward; unmodified: *a round assertion* 13 (of a vowel) pronounced with rounded lips ▷ *n* 14 a round shape or object 15 *in the round* a in full detail b *theatre* with the audience all round the stage 16 a session, as of a negotiation: *a round of talks* 17 a series, cycle, or sequence: *a giddy round of parties* 18 the daily round the usual activities of one's day 19 a stage of a competition: *he was eliminated in the first round* 20 (*often plural*) a series of calls, esp in a set order: *a doctor's rounds; a milkman's round* 21 a playing of all the holes on a golf course 22 a single turn of play by each player, as in a card game 23 one of a number of periods constituting a boxing, wrestling, or other match, each usually lasting three minutes 24 *archery* a specified number of arrows shot from a specified distance 25 a single discharge by a number of guns or a single gun 26 a bullet, blank cartridge, or other charge of ammunition 27 a number of drinks bought at one time for a group of people 28 a single slice of bread or toast or two slices making a single serving of sandwiches 29 a general outburst of applause, cheering, etc 30 movement in a circle or around an axis 31 *music* a part song in which the voices follow each other at equal intervals at the same pitch 32 a sequence of bells rung in order of treble to tenor. Compare **change** (sense 29) 33 a dance in which the dancers move in a circle 34 a cut of beef from the thigh between the rump and the shank 35 *go* or *make the rounds* a to go from place to place, as in making deliveries or social calls b (of information, rumour, etc) to be passed around, so as to be generally known ▷ *prep* 36 surrounding, encircling, or enclosing: *a band round her head* 37 on all or most sides of: *to look round one* 38 on or outside the circumference or perimeter of: *the stands round the racecourse* 39 situated at various points in: *a lot of shelves round the house* 40 from place to place in: *driving round Ireland* 41 somewhere in or near: *to stay round the house* 42 making a circuit or partial circuit about: *the ring road round the town* 43 reached by making a partial circuit about something: *the shop round the corner* 44 revolving round a centre or axis: *the earth's motion round its axis* 45 so as to have a basis in: *the story is built round a good plot* ▷ *adv* 46 on all or most sides: *the garden is fenced all round; the crowd gathered round* 47 on or outside the circumference or perimeter: *the racing track is two miles round* 48 in all directions from a point of reference: *he owns the land for ten miles round* 49 to all members of a group: *pass the food round* 50 in rotation or revolution: *the wheels turn round* 51 by a circuitous route: *the road to the farm goes round by the pond* 52 to a specific place: *she came round to see me* 53 *all year round* throughout the year; in every month ▷ *vb* 54 to make or become round 55 (*tr*) to encircle; surround 56 to move or cause to move with circular motion: *to round a bend* 57 (*tr*) a to pronounce (a speech sound) with rounded lips b to purse (the lips) ▷ See also **round down, round off, round on, round out, round up** [c13 from Old French *ront,* from Latin *rotundus* round, from *rota* a wheel] ▷ ˈroundness *n*

USAGE See at **around**

roundabout ('raʊndə,baʊt) n **1** Brit a revolving circular platform provided with wooden animals, seats, etc, on which people ride for amusement; merry-go-round **2** a road junction in which traffic streams circulate around a central island. US and Canadian name: **traffic circle 3** an informal name for **boring mill** ▷ adj **4** indirect or circuitous; devious ▷ adv, prep round about **5** on all sides: *spectators standing round about* **6** approximately: *at round about 5 o'clock*

round and round adv, prep following a circuitous or circular course for a comparatively long time, esp vainly

round angle n another name for **perigon**

round-arm adj, adv cricket denoting or using bowling with the arm held more or less horizontal

round clam n another name for the **quahog**

round dance n **1** a dance in which the dancers form a circle **2** a ballroom dance, such as the waltz, in which couples revolve

round down vb (tr, adverb) to lower (a number) to the nearest whole number or ten, hundred, or thousand below it. Compare **round up** (sense 2)

rounded ('raʊndɪd) adj **1** round or curved **2** having been made round or curved **3** full, mature, or complete **4** (of the lips) pursed, as in pronouncing the sound (u:) **5** (of a speech sound) articulated with rounded lips > 'roundedly adv > 'roundedness n

roundel ('raʊndəl) n **1** a form of rondeau consisting of three stanzas each of three lines with a refrain after the first and the third **2** a circular identifying mark in national colours on military aircraft **3** a small ornamental circular window, panel, medallion, plate, disc, etc **4** a round plate of armour used to protect the armpit **5** heraldry a charge in the shape of a circle **6** another word for **roundelay** (sense 1) [C13 from Old French rondel a little circle; see RONDEL]

roundelay ('raʊndɪ,leɪ) n **1** Also called: roundel a slow medieval dance performed in a circle **2** a song in which a line or phrase is repeated as a refrain [C16 from Old French rondelet a little rondel, from rondel; also influenced by LAY⁴]

rounder ('raʊndə) n **1** a run round all four bases after one hit in rounders **2** a tool or machine for rounding edges or surfaces

rounders ('raʊndəz) n (functioning as singular) Brit a ball game in which players run between posts after hitting the ball, scoring a **rounder** if they run round all four before the ball is retrieved

round file slang ▷ n **1** a wastepaper basket ▷ vb round-file **2** (tr) to throw into a wastepaper basket; discard; reject

round hand n a style of handwriting with large rounded curves. Compare **italic, copperplate** (sense 3)

Roundhead ('raʊnd,hɛd) n English history a supporter of Parliament against Charles I during the Civil War. Compare **Cavalier** [referring to their short-cut hair]

roundhouse ('raʊnd,haʊs) n **1** a circular building in which railway locomotives are serviced or housed, radial tracks being fed by a central turntable **2** boxing slang **a** a swinging punch or style of punching **b** (as modifier): a roundhouse style **3** pinochle, US a meld of all four kings and queens **4** an obsolete word for **jail 5** obsolete a cabin on the quarterdeck of a sailing ship

rounding ('raʊndɪŋ) n computing a process in which a number is approximated as the closest number that can be expressed using the number of bits or digits available

rounding error n computing an error introduced into a computation by the need to perform rounding

roundish ('raʊndɪʃ) adj somewhat round

roundlet ('raʊndlɪt) n literary a small circle [C14 from Old French rondelet, from Old French RONDEL]

roundly ('raʊndlɪ) adv **1** frankly, bluntly, or thoroughly: *to be roundly criticized* **2** in a round manner or so as to be round

round off vb (tr, adverb) **1** (often foll by with) to bring to a satisfactory conclusion; complete, esp agreeably: *we rounded off the evening with a brandy* **2** to make round or less jagged

round on vb (intr, preposition) to attack or reply to (someone) with sudden irritation or anger

round out vb (tr, adverb) **1** to make or become bigger or plumper; fill out, esp so as to be symmetrical **2** to round up (a number)

round robin n **1** a letter, esp a petition or protest, having the signatures in a circle in order to disguise the order of signing **2** any letter or petition signed by a number of people **3** US and Canadian a tournament, as in a competitive game or sport, in which each player plays against every other player

round-shouldered adj denoting a faulty posture characterized by drooping shoulders and a slight forward bending of the back

roundsman ('raʊndzmən) n, pl -men **1** Brit a person who makes rounds, as for inspection or to deliver goods **2** Austral and NZ a reporter covering a particular district or topic

round table n **a** a meeting of parties or people on equal terms for discussion **b** (as modifier): a round-table conference

Round Table n the **1** (in Arthurian legend) the table of King Arthur, shaped so that his knights could sit around it without any having precedence **2** Arthur and his knights collectively **3** one of an organization of clubs of young business and professional men who meet in order to further social and business activities and charitable work **4** (in New Zealand) an organization of businessmen supporting policies of the New Right

round-the-clock adj (or as adverb **round the clock**) throughout the day and night

round top n a platform round the masthead of a sailing ship

round tower n a freestanding circular stone belfry built in Ireland from the 10th century beside a monastery and used as a place of refuge

round trip n a trip to a place and back again, esp returning by a different route

roundtripping ('raʊnd,trɪpɪŋ) n finance a form of trading in which a company borrows a sum of money from one source and takes advantage of a short-term rise in interest rates to make a profit by lending it to another

round-trip ticket n US and Canadian a ticket entitling a passenger to travel to his destination and back again. British equivalent: return ticket

round up vb (tr, adverb) **1** to gather (animals, suspects, etc) together: *to round ponies up* **2** to raise (a number) to the nearest whole number or ten, hundred, or thousand above it. Compare **round down** ▷ n roundup **3** the act of gathering together livestock, esp cattle, so that they may be branded, counted, or sold **4** a collection of suspects or criminals by the police, esp in a raid **5** any similar act of collecting or bringing together: *a roundup of today's news*

roundwood ('raʊnd,wʊd) n forestry small pieces of timber (about 5–15 cm, or 2–6 in) in diameter; small logs

roundworm ('raʊnd,wɜːm) n any nematode worm, esp Ascaris lumbricoides, a common intestinal parasite of man and pigs

roup¹ (ruːp) n vet science any of various chronic respiratory diseases of birds, esp poultry [C16 of unknown origin] > 'roupy adj

roup² (raʊp) Scot and northern English dialect ▷ vb (tr) **1** to sell by auction ▷ n **2** an auction [C16 (originally: to shout): of Scandinavian origin; compare Icelandic raupa to boast]

rouse¹ (raʊz) vb **1** to bring (oneself or another person) out of sleep, unconsciousness, etc, or (of a person) to come to consciousness in this way **2** (tr) to provoke, stir, or excite: *to rouse someone's anger*

3 rouse oneself to become active or energetic **4** hunting to start or cause to start from cover: *to rouse game birds* **5** (intr) falconry (of hawks) to ruffle the feathers and cause them to stand briefly on end (a sign of contentment) **6** (raʊs) (intr; foll by on) Austral to speak scoldingly or rebukingly (to) ▷ n **7** chiefly US another term for **reveille** [C15 (in sense 5): origin obscure] > rousedness ('raʊzɪdnɪs) n

rouse² (raʊz) n archaic **1** an alcoholic drink, esp a full measure **2** another word for **carousal** [C17 probably a variant of CAROUSE (as in the phrase *drink a rouse*, erroneous for *drink carouse*); compare Danish *drikke en rus* to become drunk, German *Rausch* drunkenness]

rouseabout ('raʊzə,baʊt) n Austral and NZ an unskilled labourer in a shearing shed. Also called: roustabout

rouser ('raʊzə) n **a** a person or thing that rouses people, such as a stirring speech or compelling rock song **b** (in combination) rabble-rouser

rousing ('raʊzɪŋ) adj tending to rouse or excite; lively, brisk, or vigorous > 'rousingly adv

Roussillon (French rusijɔ̃) n a former province of S France: united with Aragon in 1172; passed to the French crown in 1659; now forms part of the region of Languedoc-Roussillon

roust (raʊst) vb (tr; often foll by out) to rout or stir, as out of bed [C17 perhaps an alteration of ROUSE¹]

roustabout ('raʊstə,baʊt) n **1** an unskilled labourer on an oil rig **2** Austral another word for **rouseabout 3** US and Canadian a labourer in a circus or fairground

rout¹ (raʊt) n **1** an overwhelming defeat **2** a disorderly retreat **3** a noisy rabble **4** law a group of three or more people proceeding to commit an illegal act **5** archaic a large party or social gathering ▷ vb **6** (tr) to defeat and cause to flee in confusion [C13 from Anglo-Norman rute, from Old French: disorderly band, from Latin ruptus broken, from rumpere to burst; see ROUTE]

rout² (raʊt) vb **1** to dig over or turn up (something), esp (of an animal) with the snout; root **2** (tr; usually foll by out or up) to get or find by searching **3** (tr; usually foll by out) to force or drive out: *they routed him out of bed at midnight* **4** (tr; often foll by out) to hollow or gouge out **5** (intr) to search, poke, or rummage [C16 variant of ROOT²]

route (ruːt) n **1** the choice of roads taken to get to a place **2** a regular journey travelled **3** (capital) US a main road between cities: *Route 66* **4** mountaineering the direction or course taken by a climb **5** med the means by which a drug or agent is administered or enters the body, such as by mouth or by injection: *oral route* ▷ vb routes, routing or routeing, routed (tr) **6** to plan the route of; send by a particular route [C13 from Old French rute, from Vulgar Latin rupta via (unattested), literally: a broken (established) way, from Latin ruptus broken, from rumpere to break, burst]

USAGE When forming the present participle or verbal noun from the verb to route it is preferable to retain the e in order to distinguish the word from routing, the present participle or verbal noun from rout¹, to defeat or rout², to dig, rummage: *the routeing of buses from the city centre to the suburbs*. The spelling routing in this sense is, however, sometimes encountered, esp in American English

routemarch ('ruːt,mɑːtʃ) n **1** military a long training march **2** informal any long exhausting walk ▷ vb **3** to go or send on a routemarch

router¹ ('raʊtə) n any of various tools or machines for hollowing out, cutting grooves, etc

router² ('ruːtə) n computing a device that allows packets of data to be moved efficiently between two points on a network

routh or **rowth** (raʊθ) Scot ▷ n **1** abundance ▷ adj **2** abundant; plentiful [C18 of uncertain origin]

routine (ruːˈtiːn) n **1** a usual or regular method of procedure, esp one that is unvarying **2** computing

r

a program or part of a program performing a specific function: *an input routine; an output routine* **3** a set sequence of dance steps **4** *informal* a hackneyed or insincere speech ▷ *adj* **5** of, relating to, or characteristic of routine [C17 from Old French, from *route* a customary way, ROUTE] > rou'tinely *adv*

roux (ruː) *n, pl* **roux** a mixture of equal amounts of fat and flour, heated, blended, and used as a basis for sauces [C19 from French: brownish, from Latin *russus* RUSSET]

rove¹ (rəʊv) *vb* **1** to wander about (a place) with no fixed direction; roam **2** (*intr*) (of the eyes) to look around; wander **3 have a roving eye** to show a widespread amorous interest in the opposite sex **4** (*intr*) *Australian rules football* to play as a rover ▷ *n* **5** the act of roving [C15 *roven* (in archery) to shoot at a target chosen at random (C16 to wander, stray), from Scandinavian; compare Icelandic *rāfa* to wander]

rove² (rəʊv) *vb* **1** (*tr*) to pull out and twist (fibres of wool, cotton, etc) lightly, as before spinning or in carding ▷ *n* **2** wool, cotton, etc, thus prepared [C18 of obscure origin]

rove³ (rəʊv) *n* a metal plate through which a rivet is passed and then clenched over [C15 from Scandinavian; compare Icelandic *ro*]

rove⁴ (rəʊv) *vb* a past tense and past participle of **reeve²**

rove beetle *n* any beetle of the family *Staphylinidae*, characterized by very short elytra and an elongated body: typically they are of carnivorous or scavenging habits

rove-over *adj prosody* (in sprung rhythm) denoting a metrical foot left incomplete at the end of one line and completed in the next

rover¹ ('rəʊvə) *n* **1** a person who roves; wanderer **2** *archery* a mark selected at random for use as a target **3** *croquet* a ball that has been driven through all the hoops but has not yet hit the winning peg **4** *Australian rules football* one of the three players in the ruck, usually smaller than the other two, selected for his agility in play **5** a small remote-controlled vehicle which roams over rough, esp extraterrestrial, terrain taking photographs, gathering rock and soil samples, etc [C15 from ROVE¹]

rover² ('rəʊvə) *n* a pirate or pirate ship [C14 probably from Middle Dutch or Middle Low German, from *roven* to rob]

rover³ ('rəʊvə) *n* a machine for roving wool, cotton, etc, or a person who operates such a machine [C18 from ROVE²]

Rover *or* **Rover Scout** *n* ('rəʊvə) *n Brit* the former name for **Venture Scout**

roving commission *n* authority or power given in a general area, without precisely defined terms of reference

row¹ (rəʊ) *n* **1** an arrangement of persons or things in a line: *a row of chairs* **2 a** *chiefly Brit* a street, esp a narrow one lined with identical houses **b** (*capital when part of a street name*): *Church Row* **3** a line of seats, as in a cinema, theatre, etc **4** *maths* a horizontal linear arrangement of numbers, quantities, or terms, esp in a determinant or matrix **5** a horizontal rank of squares on a chessboard or draughtboard **6 in a row** in succession; one after the other **7 a hard row to hoe** a difficult task or assignment [Old English *rāw, rǣw*; related to Old High German *rīga* line, Lithuanian *raiwe* strip]

row² (rəʊ) *vb* **1** to propel (a boat) by using oars **2** (*tr*) to carry (people, goods, etc) in a rowing boat **3** to be propelled by means of (oars or oarsmen) **4** (*intr*) to take part in the racing of rowing boats as a sport, esp in eights, in which each member of the crew pulls one oar. Compare **scull** (sense 6) **5** (*tr*) to race against in a boat propelled by oars ▷ *n* **6** an act, instance, period, or distance of rowing **7** an excursion in a rowing boat ▷ See also **row over** [Old English *rōwan*; related to Middle Dutch *roien*, Middle High German *rüejen*, Old Norse *rōa*, Latin

rēmus oar] > 'rower *n* > 'rowing *n*

row³ (raʊ) *n* **1** a noisy quarrel or dispute **2** a noisy disturbance; commotion: *we couldn't hear the music for the row next door* **3** a reprimand **4** give (someone) a row *informal* to scold (someone); tell off ▷ *vb* **5** (*intr*; often foll by *with*) to quarrel noisily **6** (*tr*) *archaic* to reprimand [C18 origin unknown]

rowan ('rəʊən, 'raʊ-) *n* another name for the (European) **mountain ash** [C16 from Scandinavian; compare Norwegian *rogn, raun*, Old Norse *reynir*]

rowboat ('rəʊ,bəʊt) *n US and Canadian* a small boat propelled by one or more pairs of oars. Also called (in Britain and other countries): **rowing boat**

rowdy ('raʊdɪ) *adj* **-dier, -diest 1** tending to create noisy disturbances; rough, loud, or disorderly ▷ *n, pl* **-dies 2** a person who behaves in a rough disorderly fashion [C19 originally US slang, perhaps related to ROW³] > 'rowdily *adv* > 'rowdiness *n*

rowdyism ('raʊdɪɪzəm) *n* rowdy behaviour or tendencies or a habitual pattern of rowdy behaviour: *the problem of rowdyism at football matches*

rowel ('raʊəl) *n* **1** a small spiked wheel attached to a spur **2** *vet science obsolete* a piece of leather or other material inserted under the skin of a horse to act as a seton and allow drainage ▷ *vb* **-els, -elling, -elled** *or US* **-els, -eling, -eled** (*tr*) **3** to goad (a horse) using a rowel **4** *vet science obsolete* to insert a rowel in (the skin of a horse) to allow drainage [C14 from Old French *roel* a little wheel, from *roe* a wheel, from Latin *rota*]

rowen ('raʊən) *n* another word for **aftermath** (sense 2) [C14 *reywayn*, corresponding to Old French *regain*, from RE- + *gain* rowen, from *gaignier* to till, earn; see GAIN¹]

row house (rəʊ) *n US and Canadian* a house that is part of a terrace. Also called (in Britain and certain other countries): **terraced house**

rowing boat ('rəʊɪŋ) *n chiefly Brit* a small boat propelled by one or more pairs of oars. Usual US and Canadian word: **rowboat**

rowing machine *n* a device with oars and a sliding seat resembling a sculling boat, used to provide exercise

rowlock ('rɒlək) *n* a swivelling device attached to the gunwale of a boat that holds an oar in place and acts as a fulcrum during rowing. Usual US and Canadian word: **oarlock**

row over (rəʊ) *vb* (*intr, adverb*) **1** to win a rowing race unopposed, by rowing the course ▷ *n* **rowover 2** the act of doing this

rowth (raʊθ) *n, adj Scot* a variant spelling of **routh**

Roxburghshire ('rɒksbərəʃɪə, -ʃə) *n* (until 1975) a county of SE Scotland, now part of Scottish Borders council area

Roy (rɔɪ) *n Austral slang* a trendy Australian male

royal ('rɔɪəl) *adj* **1** of, relating to, or befitting a king, queen, or other monarch; regal **2** (*prenominal; often capital*) established, chartered by, under the patronage or in the service of royalty: *the Royal Society of St George* **3** being a member of a royal family **4** above the usual or normal in standing, size, quality, etc **5** *informal* unusually good or impressive; first-rate **6** *nautical* just above the topgallant (in the phrase **royal mast**) ▷ *n* **7** (*sometimes capital*) *informal* a member of a royal family **8** Also called: **royal stag** a stag with antlers having 12 or more branches **9** *nautical* a sail set next above the topgallant, on a royal mast **10** a size of printing paper, 20 by 25 inches **11** Also called: **small royal** *chiefly Brit* a size of writing paper, 19 by 24 inches **12** any of various book sizes, esp 6¼ by 10 inches (**royal octavo**), 6¾ by 10¼ inches (**super royal octavo**), and (chiefly Brit) 10 by 12½ inches (**royal quarto**) and 10¼ by 13½ inches (**super royal quarto**) [C14 from Old French *roial*, from Latin *rēgālis*, fit for a king, from *rēx* king; compare REGAL¹] > 'royally *adv*

Royal Academy *n* a society founded by George III in 1768 to foster a national school of painting, sculpture, and design in England. Full name: **Royal Academy of Arts**

Royal Air Force *n* the air force of the United Kingdom. Abbreviation: **RAF**

Royal Air Force List *n Brit* an official list of all serving commissioned officers of the RAF and reserve officers liable for recall

Royal and Ancient Club *n* **the** a golf club, headquarters of the sport's ruling body, based in St Andrews, Scotland. Abbreviation: **R&A**

royal assent *n* (in Britain) the formal signing of an act of Parliament by the sovereign, by which it becomes law

royal blue *n* **a** a deep blue colour **b** (*as adjective*): *a royal-blue carpet*

Royal British Legion *n Brit* an organization founded in 1921 to provide services and assistance for former members of the armed forces

royal burgh *n* (in Scotland) a burgh that was established by a royal charter granted directly by the sovereign

Royal Canadian Mounted Police *n* the federal police force of Canada. Abbreviation: **RCMP**

Royal Commission *n* (in Britain) a body set up by the monarch on the recommendation of the prime minister to gather information about the operation of existing laws or to investigate any social, educational, or other matter. The commission has prescribed terms of reference and reports to the government on how any change might be achieved

royal duke *n* a duke who is also a royal prince, being a member of the royal family

Royal Engineers *pl n* a branch of the British army that undertakes the building of fortifications, mines, bridges, and other engineering works. Abbreviation: **RE**

royal fern *n* a fern, *Osmunda regalis*, of damp regions, having large fronds up to 2 metres (7 feet) in height, some of which are modified for bearing spores: family *Osmundaceae*

royal flush *n poker* a hand made up of the five top honours of a suit

Royal Highness *n* a title of honour used in addressing or referring to a member of a royal family

royal icing *n Brit* a hard white icing made from egg whites and icing sugar, used for coating and decorating cakes, esp fruit cakes

Royal Institution *n* a British society founded in 1799 for the dissemination of scientific knowledge

royalist ('rɔɪəlɪst) *n* **1** a supporter of a monarch or monarchy, esp a supporter of the Stuarts during the English Civil War **2** *informal* an extreme reactionary or conservative: *an economic royalist* ▷ *adj* **also** (*less commonly*) **royalistic 3** of, characteristic of, or relating to royalists > 'royalism *n*

royal jelly *n* a substance secreted by the pharyngeal glands of worker bees and fed to all larvae when very young and to larvae destined to become queens throughout their development

Royal Leamington Spa *n* the official name of **Leamington Spa**

Royal Marines *pl n Brit* a corps of soldiers specially trained in amphibious warfare. Abbreviation: **RM**

Royal Mint *n* a British organization having the sole right to manufacture coins since the 16th century. In 1968 it moved from London to Llantrisant in Wales

Royal National Theatre *n* a theatre complex in London, on the S bank of the Thames (opened 1976). The prefix Royal was added in 1988. It houses the Royal National Theatre Company

Royal Navy *n* the navy of the United Kingdom. Abbreviation: **RN**

royal palm *n* any of several palm trees of the genus *Roystonea*, esp *R. regia*, of tropical America, having a tall trunk with a tuft of feathery pinnate leaves

royal poinciana *n* a leguminous tree, *Delonix regia*, that is native to Madagascar but widely cultivated elsewhere, having clusters of large scarlet flowers and long pods. Also called: flamboyant

royal purple *n* **a** a deep reddish-purple colour, sometimes approaching a strong violet **b** (*as adjective*): *a royal-purple dress*

royal road *n* an easy or direct way of achieving a desired end: *the royal road to success*

Royal Scots Greys *pl n* **the**. a British cavalry regiment, the Second Dragoons. Also called: Greys, Scots Greys [c17 from their grey uniforms]

Royal Society *n* an association founded in England by Charles II in 1660 to promote research in the sciences

royal stag *n* See **royal** (sense 8)

Royal Standard *n* a flag bearing the arms of the British sovereign, flown only when she (or he) is present

royal tennis *n* another name for **real tennis**

royalty ('rɔɪəltɪ) *n*, *pl* **-ties** **1** the rank, power, or position of a king or queen **2 a** royal persons collectively **b** one who belongs to the royal family **3** any quality characteristic of a monarch; kingliness or regal dignity **4** a percentage of the revenue from the sale of a book, performance of a theatrical work, use of a patented invention or of land, etc, paid to the author, inventor, or proprietor

Royal Victorian Order *n* (in Britain) an order of chivalry founded by Queen Victoria in 1896, membership of which is conferred for special services to the sovereign. Abbreviation: VO

royal warrant *n* an authorization to a tradesman to supply goods to a royal household

Royal Worcester *n* Worcester china made after 1862

rozzer ('rɒzə) *n* Cockney slang a policeman [c19 of unknown origin]

RP abbreviation for **1** **Received Pronunciation 2** Reformed Presbyterian **3** Regius Professor **4** international car registration for (Republic of the) Philippines

RPC abbreviation for Royal Pioneer Corps

RPG abbreviation for **1** report program generator: a business-oriented computer programming language **2** rocket propelled grenade **3** role-playing game

RPI (in Britain) abbreviation for **retail price index**

rpm abbreviation for **1** revolutions per minute **2** resale price maintenance

rps abbreviation for revolutions per second

RPS (in Britain) abbreviation for Royal Photographic Society

rpt abbreviation for report

RPV abbreviation for remotely piloted vehicle

RQ abbreviation for **respiratory quotient**

RR abbreviation for **1** Right Reverend **2** (in the US and Canada) railroad **3** (in the US and Canada) rural route

-rrhagia *n combining form* (in pathology) an abnormal discharge or flow: *menorrhagia* [from Greek *-rrhagia* a bursting forth, from *rhēgnunai* to burst, break]

-rrhoea or esp US **-rrhea** *n combining form* (in pathology) a discharge or flow: *diarrhoea* [from New Latin, from Greek *-rrhoia*, from *rhoia* a flowing, from *rhein* to flow]

rRNA abbreviation for ribosomal RNA

RRP abbreviation for recommended retail price

RRSP (in Canada) abbreviation for Registered Retirement Savings Plan

Rs symbol for rupees

RS (in Britain) abbreviation for Royal Society

RSA abbreviation for **1** Republic of South Africa **2** Royal Scottish Academy **3** Royal Scottish Academician **4** Royal Society of Arts **5** (in New Zealand) Returned Services Association

RSC abbreviation for **1** Royal Shakespeare Company **2** Royal Society of Chemistry

RSFSR abbreviation for (formerly) Russian Soviet Federative Socialist Republic

RSG (in Britain) abbreviation for **1** rate support grant **2** civil defence Regional Seat of Government

RSGB abbreviation for Radio Society of Great Britain (amateur radio operators)

RSI abbreviation for **repetitive strain** or **stress injury**

RSJ abbreviation for rolled-steel joist

RSL abbreviation for **1** Royal Society of Literature **2** (in Australia) Returned Services League

RSM abbreviation for **1** **regimental sergeant major 2** Royal School of Music **3** Royal Society of Medicine **4** ▷ international car registration for (Republic of) San Marino

RSNO abbreviation for Royal Scottish National Orchestra

RSNZ abbreviation for Royal Society of New Zealand

RSPB (in Britain) abbreviation for Royal Society for the Protection of Birds

RSPCA (in Britain and Australia) abbreviation for Royal Society for the Prevention of Cruelty to Animals

RSS abbreviation for **a** Rich Site Summary: a way of allowing web users to receive news headlines and updates on their browser from selected websites as soon as they are published **b** (as modifier): *an RSS newsfeed*

RSV abbreviation for **1** Revised Standard Version (of the Bible) **2** respiratory syncytial virus

RSVP abbreviation for répondez s'il vous plaît [French: please reply]

rt abbreviation for right

RT abbreviation for radio telegraphy or radio telephony

RTA abbreviation for road traffic accident

RTC (in India) abbreviation for **1** Road Transport Corporation **2** Round Table Conference

RTE abbreviation for Radio Telefís Éireann [Irish Gaelic: Irish Radio and Television]

RTF computing abbreviation for rich text format: a standard file format allowing file transfer between different applications and operating systems

Rt Hon. abbreviation for Right Honourable

RTR abbreviation for Royal Tank Regiment

Rt Revd or **Rt Rev.** abbreviation for Right Reverend

RTT or **RTTY** abbreviation for radioteletype

ru the internet domain name for Russian Federation

Ru the chemical symbol for ruthenium

RU 1 abbreviation for Rugby Union **2** international car registration for Burundi

Ruanda-Urundi (rʊˈændəˈrʊndɪ) *n* a former territory of central Africa: part of German East Africa from 1890; a League of Nations mandate under Belgian administration from 1919; a United Nations trusteeship from 1946; divided into the independent states of Rwanda and Burundi in 1962

rub (rʌb) *vb* **rubs, rubbing, rubbed 1** to apply pressure and friction to (something) with a circular or backward and forward motion **2** to move (something) with pressure along, over, or against (a surface) **3** to chafe or fray **4** (*tr*) to bring into a certain condition by rubbing: *rub it clean* **5** (*tr*) to spread with pressure, esp in order to cause to be absorbed: *he rubbed ointment into his back* **6** (foll by *off, out, away*, etc) to remove or be removed by rubbing **7** bowls (of a bowl) to be slowed or deflected by an uneven patch on the green **8** (*tr*; often foll by *together*) to move against each other with pressure and friction (esp in the phrases **rub one's hands**, often a sign of glee, anticipation, or satisfaction, and **rub noses**, a greeting among the Inuit) **9 rub (someone's)nose in it** informal to remind (someone) unkindly of his failing or error **10 rub (up) the wrong way** to arouse anger (in); annoy **11 rub shoulders** (or) **elbows with** informal to mix with socially or associate with ▷ *n* **12** the act of rubbing **13** (preceded by *the*) an obstacle or difficulty (esp in the phrase **there's the rub**) **14** something that hurts the feelings or annoys; rebuke **15** bowls an uneven patch in the green **16** any roughness or unevenness of surface **17 a** golf an incident of accidental interference with the ball **b** informal a piece of good or bad luck ▷ See also **rub along, rub down, rub in, rub off, rub out, rub up** [c15 perhaps from Low German *rubben*, of obscure origin]

rubaboo ('rʌbəˌbuː) *n* Canadian a soup or stew made by boiling pemmican with, if available, flour and vegetables [c19 from Canadian French *rababou*, from Algonquian]

rubáiyát ('ruːbaɪˌjæt) *n* prosody (in Persian poetry) a verse form consisting of four-line stanzas [c19 from Arabic *rubā'iyah*, from *rubā'iy* consisting of four elements]

Rub' al Khali ('rʊb æl 'kɑːlɪ) *n* a desert in S Arabia, mainly in Saudi Arabia, extending southeast from Nejd to Hadramaut and northeast from Yemen to the United Arab Emirates. Area: about 777 000 sq km (300 000 sq miles). English names: Great Sandy Desert, Empty Quarter Also called: Ar Rimal

rub along *vb* (intr, adverb) Brit **1** to continue in spite of difficulties **2** to maintain an amicable relationship; not quarrel

rubato (ruːˈbɑːtəʊ) music ▷ *n*, *pl* **-tos 1** flexibility of tempo in performance ▷ *adj, adv* **2** to be played with a flexible tempo [c19 from the Italian phrase *tempo rubato*, literally: stolen time, from *rubare* to ROB]

rubber¹ ('rʌbə) *n* **1** Also called: India rubber, gum elastic, caoutchouc a cream to dark brown elastic material obtained by coagulating and drying the latex from certain plants, esp the tree *Hevea brasiliensis* **2** any of a large variety of elastomers produced by improving the properties of natural rubber or by synthetic means **3** chiefly Brit a piece of rubber or felt used for erasing something written, typed, etc; eraser **4** a coarse file **5** a cloth, pad, etc, used for polishing or buffing **6** a person who rubs something in order to smooth, polish, or massage **7** (often plural) chiefly US and Canadian a rubberized waterproof article, such as a mackintosh or overshoe **8** slang a male contraceptive; condom **9** (modifier) made of or producing rubber: *a rubber ball; a rubber factory* [c17 from RUB + -ER¹; the tree was so named because its product was used for rubbing out writing]

rubber² ('rʌbə) *n* **1** bridge, whist **a** a match of three games **b** the deal that wins such a match **2** a series of matches or games in any of various sports [c16 origin unknown]

rubber band *n* a continuous loop of thin rubber, used to hold papers, etc, together. Also called: elastic band

rubber bridge *n* a form of bridge in which fresh hands are dealt for each round and the aim is to win a rubber. Compare **duplicate bridge**

rubber cement *n* any of a number of adhesives made by dissolving rubber in a solvent such as benzene

rubber cheque *n* facetious a cheque that bounces

rubber goods *pl n* euphemistic contraceptives; condoms

rubberize or **rubberise** ('rʌbəˌraɪz) *vb* (tr) to coat or impregnate with rubber

rubber jaw *n* vet science a condition in which the mandible becomes demineralized and excessively mobile in animals with advanced renal disease

rubberneck ('rʌbəˌnɛk) slang ▷ *n* **1** a person who stares or gapes inquisitively, esp in a naive or foolish manner **2** a sightseer or tourist ▷ *vb* **3** (intr) to stare in a naive or foolish manner

rubber plant *n* **1** a moraceous plant, *Ficus elastica*, with glossy leathery leaves: a tall tree in India and Malaya, it is cultivated as a house plant in Europe and America **2** any of several tropical trees, the sap of which yields rubber. See also **rubber tree**

rubber stamp *n* **1** a device used for imprinting dates or commonly used phrases on forms, invoices, etc **2** automatic authorization of a payment, proposal, etc, without challenge **3** a person who makes such automatic authorizations; a cipher or person of little account ▷ *vb* **rubber-stamp** (tr) **4** to imprint (forms, invoices, etc) with a rubber stamp **5** informal to approve automatically

r

rubber tree *n* a tropical American euphorbiaceous tree, *Hevea brasiliensis*, cultivated throughout the tropics, esp in Malaya, for the latex of its stem, which is the major source of commercial rubber. See also **Pará rubber**

rubbery ('rʌbərɪ) *adj* having the texture of or resembling rubber, esp in flexibility or toughness

rubbing ('rʌbɪŋ) *n* an impression taken of an incised or raised surface, such as a brass plate on a tomb, by laying paper over it and rubbing with wax, graphite, etc

rubbing alcohol *n* a liquid usually consisting of 70 per cent denatured ethyl alcohol, used by external application as an antiseptic or rubefacient

rubbish ('rʌbɪʃ) *n* **1** worthless, useless, or unwanted matter **2** discarded or waste matter **3** foolish words or speech; nonsense ▷ *vb* **4** (*tr*) *informal* to criticize [C14 *robys*, of uncertain origin]

rubbish bin *n* a container for rubbish. NZ equivalent: **rubbish tin**

rubbishy ('rʌbɪʃɪ) *adj* worthless; of poor quality

rubbity ('rʌbətɪ) or **rubbidy** ('rʌbədɪ) *n, pl* **-ties** or **-dies** a pub [from rhyming slang *rubbity dub*]

rubble ('rʌbʰl) *n* **1** fragments of broken stones, bricks, etc **2** any fragmented solid material **3** *quarrying* the weathered surface layer of rock **4** Also called: **rubblework** masonry constructed of broken pieces of rock, stone, etc [C14 *robyl*; perhaps related to Middle English *rubben* to rub, or to RUBBISH] ▷ **'rubbly** *adj*

rubby ('rʌbɪ) *n, pl* **-bies** *Canadian slang* **1** rubbing alcohol, esp when mixed with cheap wine for drinking **2** a person who drinks such mixtures, esp a derelict alcoholic

rub down *vb* (*adverb*) **1** to dry or clean (a horse, athlete, oneself, etc) vigorously, esp after exercise **2** to make or become smooth by rubbing **3** (*tr*) to prepare (a surface) for painting by rubbing it with sandpaper ▷ *n* **rubdown 4** the act of rubbing down **5** the Hong Kong term for **dressing-down**

rube (ruːb) *n US and Canadian slang* an unsophisticated countryman [C20 probably from the name *Reuben*]

rubefy ('ruːbɪˌfaɪ) *vb* **-fies, -fying, -fied** (*tr*) to make red, esp (of a counterirritant) to make the skin go red [C19 from Latin *rubefacere*, from *rubeus* red + *facere* to make] ▷ **rubefacient** (ˌruːbɪˈfeɪʃənt) *adj, n* ▷ **rubefaction** (ˌruːbɪˈfækʃən) *n*

rubella (ruːˈbɛlə) *n* a mild contagious viral disease, somewhat similar to measles, characterized by cough, sore throat, skin rash, and occasionally vomiting. It can cause congenital defects if caught during the first three months of pregnancy. Also called: **German measles** [C19 from New Latin, from Latin *rubellus* reddish, from *rubeus* red]

rubellite ('ruːbɪˌlaɪt, ruːˈbɛl-) *n* a red transparent variety of tourmaline, used as a gemstone [C18 from Latin *rubellus* reddish]

Rubenesque (ˌruːbəˌnɛsk) *adj* (of a woman) having the physique associated with portraits of women by Sir Peter Paul Rubens (1577–1640), the Flemish painter; plump and attractive

rubeola (ruːˈbiːələ) *n* technical name for **measles** Compare **rubella** [C17 from New Latin, from Latin *rubeus* reddish, from *ruber* red] ▷ **ru'beolar** *adj*

rubescent (ruːˈbɛsənt) *adj literary* reddening; blushing [C18 from Latin *rubescere* to grow red, from *ruber* red] ▷ **ru'bescence** *n*

rubiaceous (ˌruːbɪˈeɪʃəs) *adj* of, relating to, or belonging to the *Rubiaceae*, a widely distributed family of trees, shrubs, and herbaceous plants that includes the coffee and cinchona trees, gardenia, madder, and bedstraws [C19 from New Latin *Rubiaceae*, from Latin *rubia* madder, from *rubeus* red]

Rubicon ('ruːbɪkən) *n* **1** a stream in N Italy: in ancient times the boundary between Italy and Cisalpine Gaul. By leading his army across it and marching on Rome in 49 BC, Julius Caesar broke the law that a general might not lead an army out of the province to which he was posted and so committed himself to civil war with the senatorial party **2** (*sometimes not capital*) a point of no return **3** a penalty in piquet by which the score of a player who fails to reach 100 points in six hands is added to his opponent's **4** **cross** (or **pass**) **the Rubicon** to commit oneself irrevocably to some course of action

rubicund ('ruːbɪkənd) *adj* of a reddish colour; ruddy; rosy [C16 from Latin *rubicundus*, from *rubēre* to be ruddy, from *ruber* red] ▷ **rubicundity** (ˌruːbɪˈkʌndɪtɪ) *n*

rubidium (ruːˈbɪdɪəm) *n* a soft highly reactive radioactive element of the alkali metal group; the 16th most abundant element in the earth's crust (310 parts per million), occurring principally in pollucite, carnallite, and lepidolite. It is used in electronic valves, photocells, and special glass. Symbol: Rb; atomic no: 37; atomic wt: 85.4678; half-life of ^{87}Rb: 5×10^{11} years; valency: 1, 2, 3, or 4; relative density: 1.532 (solid), 1.475 (liquid); melting pt: 39.48°C; boiling pt: 688°C [C19 from New Latin, from Latin *rubidus* dark red, with reference to the two red lines in its spectrum] ▷ **ru'bidic** *adj*

rubidium-strontium dating *n* a technique for determining the age of minerals based on the occurrence in natural rubidium of a fixed amount of the radioisotope ^{87}Rb which decays to the stable strontium isotope ^{87}Sr with a half-life of 4.7×10^{11} years. Measurement of the ratio of these isotopes thus gives the age of a mineral, for ages of up to about 4×10^9 years

rubiginous (ruːˈbɪdʒɪnəs) *adj* rust-coloured [C17 from Latin *rūbiginōsus*, from *rūbīgō* rust, from *ruber* red]

Rubik cube ('ruːbɪk) or **Rubik's cube** *n trademark* a puzzle consisting of a cube of six colours, each face of which is made up of nine squares, eight of which are individually rotatable. The aim is to swivel the squares until each face of the cube shows one colour only [C20 named after Professor Erno Rubik (born 1944), its Hungarian inventor]

rub in *vb* (*tr, adverb*) **1** to spread with pressure, esp in order to cause to be absorbed **2** **rub it in** *informal* to harp on (something distasteful to a person, of which he or she does not wish to be reminded)

rubious ('ruːbɪəs) *adj literary* of the colour ruby; dark red [C17 from RUBY + -OUS]

ruble ('ruːbʰl) *n* a variant spelling of **rouble**

rub off *vb* **1** to remove or be removed by rubbing **2** (*intr*; often foll by *on* or *onto*) to have an effect through close association or contact, esp so as to make similar: *her crude manners have rubbed off on you* ▷ *n* **rub-off 3** a resulting effect on something else; consequences: *a positive rub-off*

rub out *vb* (*tr, adverb*) **1** to remove or be removed with a rubber **2** *US slang* to murder **3** *Australian rules football* to suspend (a player)

rubric ('ruːbrɪk) *n* **1** a title, heading, or initial letter in a book, manuscript, or section of a legal code, esp one printed or painted in red ink or in some similarly distinguishing manner **2** a set of rules of conduct or procedure **3** a set of directions for the conduct of Christian church services, often printed in red in a prayer book or missal **4** instructions to a candidate at the head of the examination paper **5** an obsolete name for **red ochre** ▷ *adj* **6** written, printed, or marked in red [C15 *rubrike* red ochre, red lettering, from Latin *rubrīca* (*terra*) red (earth), ruddle, from *ruber* red] ▷ **'rubrical** *adj* ▷ **'rubrically** *adv*

rubricate ('ruːbrɪˌkeɪt) *vb* (*tr*) **1** to print (a book or manuscript) with red titles, headings, etc **2** to mark in red **3** to supply with or regulate by rubrics [C16 from Latin *rubricāre* to colour red, from *rubrīca* red earth; see RUBRIC] ▷ **ˌrubri'cation** *n* ▷ **'rubriˌcator** *n*

rubrician (ruːˈbrɪʃən) *n* an authority on liturgical rubrics

rubstone ('rʌbˌstəʊn) *n* a stone used for sharpening or smoothing, esp a whetstone

rub up *vb* (*adverb*) *chiefly Brit* **1** (when *intr*, foll by *on*) to refresh one's memory (of) **2** (*tr*) to smooth or polish

ruby ('ruːbɪ) *n, pl* **-bies 1** a deep red transparent precious variety of corundum: occurs naturally in Myanmar and Sri Lanka but is also synthesized. It is used as a gemstone, in lasers, and for bearings and rollers in watchmaking. Formula: Al_2O_3 **2 a** the deep-red colour of a ruby **b** (*as adjective*): *ruby lips* **3 a** something resembling, made of, or containing a ruby **b** (*as modifier*): *ruby necklace* **4** (*modifier*) denoting a fortieth anniversary: *our ruby wedding* **5** (formerly) a size of printer's type approximately equal to 5½ point [C14 from Old French *rubi*, from Latin *rubeus* reddish, from *ruber* red] ▷ **'ruby-ˌlike** *adj*

ruby glass *n* glass that has a deep rich red colour produced from oxides of various minerals, such as lead, copper, and iron

ruby silver *n* another name for **proustite** or **pyrargyrite**

ruby spinel *n* a red transparent variety of spinel, used as a gemstone

ruby-tail wasp *n* any of various brightly coloured wasps of the family *Chrysididae*, having a metallic sheen, which parasitize bees and other solitary wasps

RUC *abbreviation for* (the former) Royal Ulster Constabulary, now superseded by the Police Service of Northern Ireland

ruche or **rouche** (ruːʃ) *n* a strip of pleated or frilled lawn, lace, etc, used to decorate blouses, dresses, etc, or worn around the neck like a small ruff as in the 16th century [C19 from French, literally: beehive, from Medieval Latin *rūsca* bark of a tree, of Celtic origin]

ruching ('ruːʃɪŋ) *n* **1** material used for a ruche **2** ruche or ruches collectively

ruck[1] (rʌk) *n* **1** a large number or quantity; mass, esp of ordinary or undistinguished people or things **2** (in a race) a group of competitors who are well behind the leaders at the finish **3** *rugby* a loose scrum that forms around the ball when it is on the ground **4** *Australian rules football* the three players, two ruckmen and a rover, that do not have fixed positions but follow the ball closely ▷ *vb* **5** (*intr*) *rugby* to try to win the ball by advancing over it when it is on the ground, driving opponents backward in the process [C13 (meaning "heap of firewood"): perhaps from Scandinavian; compare Old Norse *hraukr* RICK[1]]

ruck[2] (rʌk) *n* **1** a wrinkle, crease, or fold ▷ *vb* **2** (usually foll by *up*) to become or make wrinkled, creased, or puckered [C18 from Scandinavian; related to Old Norse *hrukka*]

ruck[3] (rʌk) *n prison slang* a fight [C20 short for RUCKUS]

ruck[4] (rʌk) *n military slang* a rucksack

ruckle ('rʌkʰl) *n, vb Brit* another word for **ruck**[2]

ruckman ('rʌkˌmæn, -mən) *n, pl* **-men** *Australian rules football* a person who plays in the ruck

rucksack ('rʌkˌsæk) *n* a large bag, usually having two straps and a supporting frame, carried on the back and often used by climbers, campers, etc. US and Canadian name: **backpack** [C19 from German, literally: back sack]

ruckus ('rʌkəs) *n, pl* **-uses** *informal* an uproar; ruction [C20 from RUCTION + RUMPUS]

ruction ('rʌkʃən) *n informal* **1** an uproar; noisy or quarrelsome disturbance **2** (*plural*) a violent and unpleasant row: *there'll be ructions when she finds out* [C19 perhaps changed from INSURRECTION]

rudaceous (ruːˈdeɪʃəs) *adj* (of conglomerate, breccia, and similar rocks) composed of coarse-grained material. Compare **arenaceous** (sense 1), **argillaceous** [C20 from Latin *rudis* coarse, rough + -ACEOUS]

Ruda Śląska ('ruːdə 'ʃlɑnskə) *n* a town in SW Poland: coalmining. Pop: 159 665 (1999 est)

rudbeckia (rʌdˈbɛkɪə) *n* any plant of the North American genus *Rudbeckia*, cultivated for their showy flowers, which have golden-yellow rays and green or black conical centres: family *Asteraceae* (composites). See also **coneflower, black-eyed Susan** [C18 New Latin, named after Olaus Rudbeck (1630–1702), Swedish botanist]

rudd (rʌd) *n* a European freshwater cyprinid fish, *Scardinius erythrophthalmus*, having a compressed dark greenish body and reddish ventral and tail fins [C17 probably from dialect *rud* red colour, from Old English *rudu* redness]

rudder ('rʌdə) *n* 1 *nautical* a pivoted vertical vane that projects into the water at the stern of a vessel and can be controlled by a tiller, wheel, or other apparatus to steer the vessel 2 a vertical control surface attached to the rear of the fin used to steer an aircraft, in conjunction with the ailerons 3 anything that guides or directs [Old English *rōther*; related to Old French *rōther*, Old High German *ruodar*, Old Norse *rōthr*. See ROW²] > **'rudderless** *adj*

rudderhead ('rʌdə,hɛd) *n nautical* the top of the rudderpost, to which the steering apparatus may be fixed

rudderpost ('rʌdə,pəʊst) *n nautical* 1 Also called: **rudderstock** ('rʌdə,stɒk) a postlike member at the forward edge of a rudder 2 the part of the stern frame of a vessel to which a rudder is fitted

ruddle ('rʌdᵊl), **raddle** or **reddle** *n* 1 a red ochre, used esp to mark sheep ▷ *vb* 2 (*tr*) to mark (sheep) with ruddle [C16 diminutive formed from Old English *rudu* redness; see RUDD]

ruddock ('rʌdək) *n Brit* a dialect name for the **robin** (sense 1) [Old English *rudduc*; related to *rudu* redness; see RUDD]

ruddy ('rʌdɪ) *adj* **-dier, -diest** 1 (of the complexion) having a healthy reddish colour, usually resulting from an outdoor life 2 coloured red or pink: *a ruddy sky* ▷ *adv* ▷ *adj informal, chiefly Brit* 3 (intensifier) bloody; damned: *a ruddy fool* [Old English *rudig*, from *rudu* redness (see RUDD); related to Old High German *rot* RED¹, Swedish *rod*, Old Norse *rythga* to make rusty] > **'ruddily** *adv* > **'ruddiness** *n*

ruddy duck *n* a small duck, *Oxyura jamaicensis*, that inhabits marshes, ponds, etc, in North America and N South America and has a stiff upright tail. The male has a reddish-brown body and blue bill in the breeding season

rude (ru:d) *adj* 1 insulting or uncivil; discourteous; impolite: *he was rude about her hairstyle* 2 lacking refinement; coarse or uncouth 3 vulgar or obscene: *a rude joke* 4 unexpected and unpleasant: *a rude awakening to the facts* 5 roughly or crudely made: *we made a rude shelter on the island* 6 rough or harsh in sound, appearance, or behaviour 7 humble or lowly 8 (*prenominal*) robust or sturdy: *in rude health* 9 (*prenominal*) approximate or imprecise: *a rude estimate* [C14 via Old French from Latin *rudis* coarse, unformed] > **'rudely** *adv* > **'rudeness** or informal **'rudery** *n*

rude awakening *n* an occurrence of being made to face an unpleasant fact

ruderal ('ru:dərəl) *n* 1 a plant that grows on waste ground ▷ *adj* 2 growing in waste places [C19 from New Latin *rūderālis*, from Latin *rūdus* rubble]

Rudesheimer ('ru:dəs,haɪmə) *n* a white Rhine wine: named after the town of Rüdesheim on the Rhine

rudiment ('ru:dɪmənt) *n* 1 (*often plural*) the first principles or elementary stages of a subject 2 (*often plural*) a partially developed version of something 3 *biology* an organ or part in its earliest recognizable form, esp one in an embryonic or vestigial state [C16 from Latin *rudīmentum* a beginning, from *rudis* unformed; see RUDE]

rudimentary (,ru:dɪ'mɛntərɪ) or less commonly **rudimental** *adj* 1 basic; fundamental; not elaborated or perfected 2 incompletely developed; vestigial: *rudimentary leaves* > **,rudi'mentarily** or less commonly **,rudi'mentally** *adv*

rudish ('ru:dɪʃ) *adj* somewhat rude

Rudolf ('ru:dɒlf) *n* **Lake** the former name (until 1979) of (Lake) **Turkana**

rue¹ (ru:) *vb* **rues, ruing, rued** 1 to feel sorrow, remorse, or regret for (one's own wrongdoing, past events with unpleasant consequences, etc) ▷ *n* 2 *archaic* sorrow, pity, or regret [Old English *hrēowan*; related to Old Saxon *hreuwan*, Old High German *hriuwan*] > **'ruer** *n*

rue² (ru:) *n* any rutaceous plant of the genus *Ruta*, esp *R. graveolens*, an aromatic Eurasian shrub with small yellow flowers and evergreen leaves which yield an acrid volatile oil, formerly used medicinally as a narcotic and stimulant. Archaic name: **herb of grace** Compare **goat's-rue**, **meadow rue, wall rue** [C14 from Old French, from Latin *rūta*, from Greek *rhutē*]

rueful ('ru:fʊl) *adj* 1 feeling or expressing sorrow or repentance: *a rueful face* 2 inspiring sorrow or pity > **'ruefully** *adv* > **'ruefulness** *n*

rufescent (ru:'fɛsᵊnt) *adj botany* tinged with red or becoming red [C19 from Latin *rūfescere* to grow reddish, from *rūfus* red, auburn] > **ru'fescence** *n*

ruff¹ (rʌf) *n* 1 a circular pleated, gathered, or fluted collar of lawn, muslin, etc, often starched or wired, worn by both men and women in the 16th and 17th centuries 2 a natural growth of long or coloured hair or feathers around the necks of certain animals or birds 3 a an Old World shore bird, *Philomachus pugnax*, the male of which has a large erectile ruff of feathers in the breeding season: family *Scolopacidae* (sandpipers, etc), order *Charadriiformes* b the male of this bird. Compare **reeve³** [C16 back formation from RUFFLE¹] > **'ruff,like** *adj*

ruff² (rʌf) *n cards* 1 (*also verb*) another word for **trump¹** 2 an old card game similar to whist [C16 from Old French *roffle*; perhaps changed from Italian *trionfa* TRUMP¹]

ruff³ (rʌf) *n* another name for **roughie¹**

ruffe or **ruff** (rʌf) *n* a European freshwater teleost fish, *Acerina cernua*, having a single spiny dorsal fin: family *Percidae* (perches). Also called: **pope** [C15 perhaps an alteration of ROUGH (referring to its scales)]

ruffed grouse *n* a large North American grouse, *Bonasa umbellus*, having brown plumage with darker markings around the neck and a black-tipped fan-shaped tail

ruffian ('rʌfɪən) *n* a violent or lawless person; hoodlum or villain [C16 from Old French *rufien*, from Italian *ruffiano*, perhaps related to Langobardic *hruf* scurf, scabbiness] > **'ruffianism** *n* > **'ruffianly** *adj*

ruffle¹ ('rʌfᵊl) *vb* 1 to make, be, or become irregular or rumpled: *to ruffle a child's hair; a breeze ruffling the water* 2 to annoy, irritate, or be annoyed or irritated 3 (*tr*) to make into a ruffle; pleat 4 (of a bird) to erect (its feathers) in anger, display, etc 5 (*tr*) to flick (cards, pages, etc) rapidly with the fingers ▷ *n* 6 an irregular or disturbed surface 7 a strip of pleated material used for decoration or as a trim 8 *zoology* another name for **ruff¹** (sense 2) 9 annoyance or irritation [C13 of Germanic origin; compare Middle Low German *ruffelen* to crumple, Old Norse *hrufla* to scratch]

ruffle² ('rʌfᵊl) *n* 1 a low continuous drumbeat ▷ *vb* 2 (*tr*) to beat (a drum) with a low repetitive beat [C18 from earlier *ruff*, of imitative origin]

ruffle³ ('rʌfᵊl) *vb* (*intr*) *archaic* to behave riotously or arrogantly; swagger [C15 of obscure origin]

ruffler ('rʌflə) *n* 1 a person or thing that ruffles 2 an attachment on a sewing machine used for making frills

rufiyaa (ru:'fi:jɑ:) *n* the standard monetary unit of the Maldives, divided into 100 laari

rufous ('ru:fəs) *adj* reddish-brown [C18 from Latin *rūfus*]

rug (rʌg) *n* 1 a floor covering, smaller than a carpet and made of thick wool or of other material, such as an animal skin 2 *chiefly Brit* a blanket, esp one used as a wrap or lap robe for travellers 3 *slang* a wig 4 **pull the rug out from under** to betray, expose, or leave defenceless [C16 from Scandinavian; compare Norwegian *rugga*, Swedish *rugg* coarse hair. See RAG¹] > **'rug,like** *adj*

RUG *computing* abbreviation for **restricted users group**

ruga ('ru:gə) *n, pl* **-gae** (-dʒi:) (*usually plural*) *anatomy* a fold, wrinkle, or crease [C18 Latin]

Rugbeian ('rʌɡbɪən) *adj* 1 of or relating to Rugby School ▷ *n* 2 a person educated at Rugby School

rugby or **rugby football** ('rʌɡbɪ) *n* 1 a form of football played with an oval ball in which the handling and carrying of the ball is permitted. Also called: **rugger** 2 *Canadian* another name for **Canadian football** ▷ See also **rugby league, rugby union** [C19 named after the public school at Rugby, where it was first played]

Rugby ('rʌɡbɪ) *n* a town in central England, in E Warwickshire: famous public school, founded in 1567. Pop: 61 988 (2001)

rugby head *n NZ derogatory slang* a male follower of rugby culture

rugby league *n* a form of rugby football played between teams of 13 players

rugby union *n* a form of rugby football played between teams of 15 players

rugged ('rʌɡɪd) *adj* 1 having an uneven or jagged surface 2 rocky or steep: *rugged scenery* 3 (of the face) strong-featured or furrowed 4 rough, severe, or stern in character 5 without refinement or culture; rude: *rugged manners* 6 involving hardship; harsh: *a rugged life in the mountains* 7 difficult or hard: *a rugged test* 8 (of equipment, machines, etc) designed to withstand rough treatment or use in rough conditions 9 *chiefly US and Canadian* sturdy or strong; robust [C14 from Scandinavian; compare Swedish *rugga* to make rough] > **'ruggedly** *adv* > **'ruggedness** *n*

ruggedize or **ruggedise** ('rʌɡɪ,daɪz) *vb* (*tr*) to make durable, as for military use

rugger ('rʌɡə) *n chiefly Brit* an informal name for **rugby**

rugger bugger *n derogatory slang* a male follower of rugby culture

rugose ('ru:ɡəʊs, -ɡəʊz) or **rugous, rugate** ('ru:ɡeɪt, -ɡɪt) *adj* wrinkled: *rugose leaves* [C18 from Latin *rūgōsus*, from *rūga* a wrinkle] > **rugosely** *adv* > **rugosity** (ru:'ɡɒsɪtɪ) *n*

rug rat *n US and Canadian informal* a child not yet walking

Ruhr (rʊə; *German* ru:r) *n* the chief coalmining and industrial region of Germany: in North Rhine-Westphalia around the valley of the **River Ruhr** (a tributary of the Rhine 235 km (146 miles) long). German name: **Ruhrgebiet** ('ru:rgə,bi:t)

ruin ('ru:ɪn) *n* 1 destroyed or decayed building or town 2 the state or condition of being destroyed or decayed 3 loss of wealth, position, etc, or something that causes such loss; downfall 4 something that is severely damaged: *his life was a ruin* 5 a person who has suffered a downfall, bankruptcy, etc 6 loss of value or usefulness 7 *archaic* loss of her virginity by a woman outside marriage ▷ *vb* 8 (*tr*) to bring to ruin; destroy 9 (*tr*) to injure or spoil: *the town has been ruined with tower blocks* 10 (*intr*) *archaic or poetic* to fall into ruins; collapse [C14 from Old French *ruine*, from Latin *ruīna* a falling down, from *ruere* to fall violently] > **'ruinable** *adj* > **'ruiner** *n*

ruination (,ru:ɪ'neɪʃən) *n* 1 the act of ruining or the state of being ruined 2 something that causes ruin

ruinous ('ru:ɪnəs) *adj* causing, tending to cause, or characterized by ruin or destruction: *a ruinous course of action* > **'ruinously** *adv* > **'ruinousness** *n*

rule (ru:l) *n* 1 an authoritative regulation or direction concerning method or procedure, as for a court of law, legislative body, game, or other human institution or activity: *judges' rules; play according to the rules* 2 the exercise of governmental authority or control: *the rule of Caesar* 3 the period of time in which a monarch or government has power: *his rule lasted 100 days* 4 a customary form or procedure; regular course of action: *he made a* *morning swim his rule* **5** (usually preceded by *the*) the common order of things; normal condition: *violence was the rule rather than the exception* **6 a** prescribed method or procedure for solving a mathematical problem, or one constituting part of a computer program, usually expressed in an appropriate formalism **7** a formal expression of a grammatical regularity in a linguistic description of a language **8** any of various devices with a straight edge for guiding or measuring; ruler: *a carpenter's rule* **9 a** a printed or drawn character in the form of a long thin line **b** another name for **dash**[1] (sense 13) *en rule; em rule* **c** a strip of brass or other metal used to print such a line **10** *Christianity* a systematic body of prescriptions defining the way of life to be followed by members of a religious order **11** *law* an order by a court or judge **12 as a rule** normally or ordinarily ▷ *vb* **13** to exercise governing or controlling authority over (a people, political unit, individual, etc): *he ruled for 20 years; his passion for her ruled his life* **14** (when *tr*, *often takes a clause as object*) to decide authoritatively; decree: *the chairman ruled against the proposal* **15** (*tr*) to mark with straight parallel lines or make one straight line, as with a ruler: *to rule a margin* **16** (*tr*) to restrain or control: *to rule one's temper* **17** (*intr*) to be customary or prevalent: *chaos rules in this school* **18** (*intr*) to be pre-eminent or superior: *football rules in the field of sport* **19** (*tr*) *astrology* (of a planet) to have a strong affinity with certain human attributes, activities, etc, associated with (one or sometimes two signs of the zodiac): *Mars rules Aries* **20 rule the roost** (*or* **roast**) to be pre-eminent; be in charge [C13 from Old French *riule*, from Latin *rēgula* a straight edge; see REGULATE] > **'rulable** *adj*

rule of three *n* a mathematical rule asserting that the value of one unknown quantity in a proportion is found by multiplying the denominator of each ratio by the numerator of the other

rule of thumb *n* **a** a rough and practical approach, based on experience, rather than a scientific or precise one based on theory **b** (*as modifier*): *a rule-of-thumb decision*

rule out *vb* (*tr, adverb*) **1** to dismiss from consideration **2** to make impossible; preclude or prevent: *the rain ruled out outdoor games*

ruler ('ruːlə) *n* **1** a person who rules or commands **2** Also called: **rule** a strip of wood, metal, or other material, having straight edges graduated usually in millimetres or inches, used for measuring and drawing straight lines

Rules (ruːlz) *pl n* **1** short for **Australian Rules** (football) **2 the Rules** *English history* the neighbourhood around certain prisons (esp the Fleet and King's Bench prison) in which trusted prisoners were allowed to live under specified restrictions

ruling ('ruːlɪŋ) *n* **1** a decision of someone in authority, such as a judge **2** one or more parallel ruled lines ▷ *adj* **3** controlling or exercising authority: *the ruling classes* **4** prevalent or predominant

ruly ('ruːlɪ) *adj facetious* orderly; well-behaved; tidy [C20 back-formation from UNRULY]

rum[1] (rʌm) *n* spirit made from sugar cane, either coloured brownish-red by the addition of caramel or by maturation in oak containers, or left white [C17 perhaps shortened from C16 *rumbullion*, of uncertain origin]

rum[2] (rʌm) *adj* **rummer, rummest** *Brit slang* strange; peculiar; odd [C19 perhaps from Romany *rom* man] > **'rumly** *adv* > **'rumness** *n*

rum[3] (rʌm) *n* short for **rummy**[1]

Rumania (ruː'meɪnɪə) *n* a variant of **Romania**

Rumanian (ruː'meɪnɪən) *adj, n* a variant of **Romanian**

rumba *or* **rhumba** ('rʌmbə, 'rʊm-) *n* **1** a rhythmic and syncopated Cuban dance in duple time **2** a ballroom dance derived from this **3** a piece of music composed for or in the rhythm of this dance [C20 from Spanish: lavish display, of uncertain origin]

rumble ('rʌmbᵊl) *vb* **1** to make or cause to make a deep resonant sound: *thunder rumbled in the sky* **2** to move with such a sound: *the train rumbled along* **3** (*tr*) to utter with a rumbling sound: *he rumbled an order* **4** (*tr*) to tumble (metal components, gemstones, etc) in a barrel of smooth stone in order to polish them **5** (*tr*) *Brit informal* to find out about (someone or something): *the police rumbled their plans* **6** (*intr*) *US slang* to be involved in a gang fight ▷ *n* **7** a deep resonant sound **8** a widespread murmur of discontent **9** another name for **tumbler** (sense 4) **10** *US, Canadian, and NZ slang* a gang fight [C14 perhaps from Middle Dutch *rummelen*; related to German *rummeln, rumpeln*] > **'rumbler** *n* > **'rumbling** *adj* > **'rumblingly** *adv*

rumble seat *n US and Canadian* a folding outside seat at the rear of some early cars; dicky

rumble strip *n* one of a set of roughly surfaced strips set in a road on the approach to a junction or hazard, to alert drivers by means of a change in tyre noise

rumbustious (rʌm'bʌstjəs) *adj* boisterous or unruly [C18 probably a variant of ROBUSTIOUS] > **rum'bustiously** *adv* > **rum'bustiousness** *n*

Rumelia (ruː'miːlɪə) *n history* the possessions of the Ottoman Empire in the Balkan peninsula: including Macedonia, Albania, Thrace, and an autonomous province (**Eastern Rumelia**) ceded in 1885 to Bulgaria

rumen ('ruːmɛn) *n, pl* **-mens** *or* **-mina** (-mɪnə) the first compartment of the stomach of ruminants, behind the reticulum, in which food is partly digested before being regurgitated as cud [C18 from Latin: throat, gullet]

ruminant ('ruːmɪnənt) *n* **1** any artiodactyl mammal of the suborder *Ruminantia*, the members of which chew the cud and have a stomach of four compartments, one of which is the rumen. The group includes deer, antelopes, cattle, sheep, and goats **2** any other animal that chews the cud, such as a camel ▷ *adj* **3** of, relating to, or belonging to the suborder *Ruminantia* **4** (of members of this suborder and related animals, such as camels) chewing the cud; ruminating **5** meditating or contemplating in a slow quiet way

ruminate ('ruːmɪˌneɪt) *vb* **1** (of ruminants) to chew (the cud) **2** (when *intr*, often foll by *upon, on*, etc) to meditate or ponder (upon) [C16 from Latin *rūmināre* to chew the cud, from RUMEN] > **ˌrumi'nation** *n* > **'ruminative** *adj* > **'ruminatively** *adv* > **'rumiˌnator** *n*

rummage ('rʌmɪdʒ) *vb* **1** (when *intr*, often foll by *through*) to search (through) while looking for something, often causing disorder or confusion ▷ *n* **2** an act of rummaging **3** a jumble of articles **4** *obsolete* confusion or bustle [C14 (in the sense: to pack a cargo): from Old French *arrumage*, from *arrumer* to stow in a ship's hold, probably of Germanic origin] > **'rummager** *n*

rummage out *or* **up** *vb* (*tr*) to find by searching vigorously; turn out

rummage sale *n* **1** a sale of miscellaneous articles, usually cheap and predominantly secondhand, in aid of charity. Also called (in Britain and certain other countries): **jumble sale** **2** *US* a sale of unclaimed property or unsold stock

rummer ('rʌmə) *n* a drinking glass, typically having an ovoid bowl on a short stem [C17 from Dutch *roemer* a glass for drinking toasts, from *roemen* to praise]

rummy[1] ('rʌmɪ) *or* **rum** *n* a card game based on collecting sets and sequences [C20 perhaps from RUM[2]]

rummy[2] ('rʌmɪ) *adj* another word for **rum**[2]

rummy[3] ('rʌmɪ) *n, pl* **-mies** **1** *US and Canadian* a slang word for **drunkard** ▷ *adj* **2** of or like rum in taste or smell

rumour *or US* **rumor** ('ruːmə) *n* **1 a** information, often a mixture of truth and untruth, passed around verbally **b** (*in combination*): *a rumour-monger* **2** gossip or hearsay **3** *archaic* din or clamour **4** *obsolete* fame or reputation ▷ *vb* **5** (*tr; usually passive*) to pass around or circulate in the form of a rumour: *it is rumoured that the Queen is coming* **6** *literary* to make or cause to make a murmuring noise [C14 via Old French from Latin *rūmor* common talk; related to Old Norse *rymja* to roar, Sanskrit *rāut* he cries]

rump (rʌmp) *n* **1** the hindquarters of a mammal, not including the legs **2** the rear part of a bird's back, nearest to the tail **3** a person's buttocks **4** Also called: **rump steak** a cut of beef from behind the loin and above the round **5** an inferior remnant [C15 from Scandinavian; compare Danish *rumpe*, Icelandic *rumpr*, German *Rumpf* trunk of the body] > **'rumpless** *adj*

Rumpelstiltskin (ˌrʌmpᵊl'stɪltskɪn) *n* a dwarf in a German folktale who aids the king's bride on condition that she give him her first child or guess the dwarf's name. She guesses correctly and in his rage he destroys himself

rumple ('rʌmpᵊl) *vb* **1** to make or become wrinkled, crumpled, ruffled, or dishevelled ▷ *n* **2** a wrinkle, fold, or crease [C17 from Middle Dutch *rompelen*; related to Old English *gerumpen* creased, wrinkled] > **'rumply** *adj*

rumpo (rʌmpəʊ) *n slang* sexual intercourse

Rump Parliament *or* **the Rump** *n English history* the remainder of the Long Parliament after Pride's Purge. It sat from 1648–53

rumpus ('rʌmpəs) *n, pl* **-puses** a noisy, confused, or disruptive commotion [C18 of unknown origin]

rumpus room *n US, Canadian, and NZ* a room used for noisy activities, such as parties or children's games

rumpy-pumpy ('rʌmpɪ'pʌmpɪ) *n informal* sexual intercourse

Rum Rebellion *n Austral* the deposition of Governor William Bligh in 1808 by officers of the New South Wales Corps, caused by his interference in their trading activities, esp in the trafficking of rum

run (rʌn) *vb* **runs, running, ran, run** **1** (*intr*) **a** (of a two-legged creature) to move on foot at a rapid pace so that both feet are off the ground together for part of each stride **b** (of a four-legged creature) to move at a rapid gait; gallop or canter **2** (*tr*) to pass over (a distance, route, etc) in running: *to run a mile; run a race* **3** (*intr*) to run in or finish a race as specified, esp in a particular position: *John is running third* **4** (*tr*) to perform or accomplish by or as if by running: *to run an errand* **5** (*intr*) to flee; run away: *they took to their heels and ran* **6** (*tr*) to bring into a specified state or condition by running: *to run oneself to a standstill* **7** (*tr*) to track down or hunt (an animal): *to run a fox to earth* **8** (*intr*) to move about freely and without restraint: *the children are running in the garden* **9** (*intr; usually* foll by *to*) to go or have recourse, as for aid, assistance, etc: *he's always running to his mother when he's in trouble* **10** (*tr*) to set (animals) loose on (a field or tract of land) so as to graze freely **11** (*intr; often* foll by *over, round* or *up*) to make a short trip or brief informal visit: *I'll run over to your house this afternoon* **12** to move quickly and easily on wheels by rolling, or in any of certain other ways: *a ball running along the ground; a sledge running over snow* **13** to move or cause to move with a specified result or in a specified manner: *to run a ship aground; to run into a tree* **14** (often foll by *over*) to move or pass or cause to move or pass quickly: *to run a vacuum cleaner over the carpet; to run one's eyes over a page* **15** (*tr;* foll by *into, out of, through*, etc) to force, thrust, or drive: *she ran a needle into her finger* **16** (*tr*) to drive or maintain and operate (a vehicle) **17** (*tr*) to give a lift to (someone) in a vehicle; transport: *he ran her to the railway station* **18** to ply or cause to ply between places on a route: *the bus runs from Piccadilly to Golders Green* **19** to operate or be operated; function or cause to function: *the engine is running smoothly* **20** (*tr*) to perform or carry out: *to run tests* **21** (*tr*) to be in charge of; manage: *to run a company*

22 to extend or continue or cause to extend or continue in a particular direction, for a particular duration or distance, etc: *the road runs north; the play ran for two years; the months ran into years* **23** (*intr*) *law* **a** to have legal force or effect: *the lease runs for two more years* **b** to accompany; be an integral part of or adjunct to: *an easement runs with the land* **24** (*tr*) to be subjected to, be affected by, or incur: *to run a risk; run a temperature* **25** (*intr*; often foll by *to*) to be characterized (by); tend or incline: *her taste runs to extravagant hats; to run to fat* **26** (*intr*) to recur persistently or be inherent: *red hair runs in my family* **27** to cause or allow (liquids) to flow or (of liquids) to flow, esp in a manner specified: *water ran from the broken pipe; the well has run dry* **28** (*intr*) to melt and flow: *the wax grew hot and began to run* **29** *metallurgy* **a** to melt or fuse **b** (*tr*) to mould or cast (molten metal): *to run lead into ingots* **30** (*intr*) (of waves, tides, rivers, etc) to rise high, surge, or be at a specified height: *a high sea was running that night* **31** (*intr*) to be diffused: *the colours in my dress ran when I washed it* **32** (*intr*) (of stitches) to unravel or come undone or (of a garment) to have stitches unravel or come undone: *if you pull that thread the whole seam will run* **33** to sew (an article) with continuous stitches **34** (*intr*) (of growing vines, creepers, etc) to trail, spread, or climb: *ivy running over a cottage wall* **35** (*intr*) to spread or circulate quickly: *a rumour ran through the town* **36** (*intr*) to be stated or reported: *his story runs as follows* **37** to publish or print or be published or printed in a newspaper, magazine, etc: *they ran his story in the next issue* **38** (often foll by *for*) *chiefly US and Canadian* to be a candidate or present as a candidate for political or other office: *Anderson is running for president* **39** (*tr*) to get past or through; evade: *to run a blockade* **40** (*tr*) to deal in (arms, etc), esp by importing illegally: *he runs guns for the rebels* **41** *nautical* to sail (a vessel, esp a sailing vessel) or (of such a vessel) to be sailed with the wind coming from astern **42** (*intr*) (of fish) **a** to migrate upstream from the sea, esp in order to spawn **b** to swim rapidly in any area of water, esp during migration **43** (*tr*) *cricket* to score (a run or number of runs) by hitting the ball and running between the wickets **44** (*tr*) *billiards, snooker* to make (a number of successful shots) in sequence **45** (*tr*) *golf* to hit (the ball) so that it rolls along the ground **46** (*tr*) *bridge* to cash (all one's winning cards in a long suit) successively **47** **run a bath** to turn on the taps to fill a bath with water for bathing oneself **48** **run close** to compete closely with; present a serious challenge to: *he got the job, but a younger man ran him close* **49** **run for it** *informal* to attempt to escape from arrest, etc, by running **50** **be run off one's feet** to be extremely busy ▷ *n* **51** an act, instance, or period of running **52** a gait, pace, or motion faster than a walk: *she went off at a run* **53** a distance covered by running or a period of running: *a run of ten miles* **54** an act, instance, or period of travelling in a vehicle, esp for pleasure: *to go for a run in the car* **55** free and unrestricted access: *we had the run of the house and garden for the whole summer* **56** **a** a period of time during which a machine, computer, etc, operates **b** the amount of work performed in such a period **57** a continuous or sustained period: *a run of good luck* **58** a continuous sequence of performances: *the play had a good run* **59** *cards* a sequence of winning cards in one suit, usually more than five: *a run of spades* **60** tendency or trend: *the run of the market* **61** type, class, or category: *the usual run of graduates* **62** (usually foll by *on*) a continuous and urgent demand: *a run on butter; a run on the dollar* **63** a series of unravelled stitches, esp in stockings or tights; ladder **64** the characteristic pattern or direction of something: *the run of the grain on a piece of wood* **65** **a** a continuous vein or seam of ore, coal, etc **b** the direction in which it lies **66** **a** a period during which water or other liquid flows **b** the amount of such a flow **67** a pipe, channel, etc, through which water or other liquid flows **68** *US* a small stream **69** a steeply inclined pathway or course, esp a snow-covered one used for skiing and bobsleigh racing. See also **green run, blue run, red run, black run** **70** an enclosure for domestic fowls or other animals, in which they have free movement: *a chicken run* **71** (esp in Australia and New Zealand) a tract of land for grazing livestock **72** a track or area frequented by animals: *a deer run; a rabbit run* **73** a group of animals of the same species moving together **74** the migration of fish upstream in order to spawn **75** *nautical* **a** the tack of a sailing vessel in which the wind comes from astern **b** part of the hull of a vessel near the stern where it curves upwards and inwards **76** *military* **a** a mission in a warplane **b** short for **bombing run** **77** the movement of an aircraft along the ground during takeoff or landing **78** *music* a rapid scalelike passage of notes **79** *cricket* a score of one, normally achieved by both batsmen running from one end of the wicket to the other after one of them has hit the ball. Compare **extra** (sense 6), **boundary** (sense 2c) **80** *baseball* an instance of a batter touching all four bases safely, thereby scoring **81** *golf* the distance that a ball rolls after hitting the ground **82** **a run for (one's) money** *informal* **a** a strong challenge or close competition **b** pleasure derived from an activity **83** **in the long run** as the eventual outcome of a sequence of events, actions, etc; ultimately **84** **in the short run** as the immediate outcome of a series of events, etc **85** **on the run** **a** escaping from arrest; fugitive **b** in rapid flight; retreating: *the enemy is on the run* **c** hurrying from place to place: *she's always on the run* **86** **the runs** *slang* diarrhoea ▷ See also **runabout, run across, run after, run along, run around, run away, run down, run in, run into, run off, run on, run out, run over, run through, run to, run up, run with** [Old English *runnen*, past participle of *(ge)rinnan*; related to Old Frisian, Old Norse *rinna*, Old Saxon, Gothic, Old High German *rinnan*]

runabout ('rʌnəˌbaʊt) *n* **1** a small car, esp one for use in a town **2** a light aircraft **3** a light motorboat **4** a person who moves about constantly or busily ▷ *vb* **run about** **5** (*intr, adverb*) to move busily from place to place

run across *vb* (*intr, preposition*) to meet unexpectedly; encounter by chance

run after *vb* (*intr, preposition*) *informal* **1** to pursue (a member of the opposite sex) with persistent attention **2** to pursue (anything) persistently **3** to care for in an excessively attentive way

runagate ('rʌnəˌgeɪt) *n* *archaic* **a** a vagabond, fugitive, or renegade **b** (*as modifier*): *a runagate priest* [C16 variant (influenced by RUN) of RENEGADE]

run along *vb* (*intr, adverb*) (often said patronizingly) to go away; leave

runanga ('ruːnɑːᵊŋɑː) *n, pl* **runanga** NZ a Māori assembly or council [Māori]

run around *vb* (*intr, adverb*) *informal* **1** (often foll by *with*) to associate habitually (with) **2** to behave in a fickle or promiscuous manner ▷ *n* **run-around** **3** *informal* deceitful or evasive treatment of a person (esp in the phrase **give** *or* **get the run-around**) **4** *printing* an arrangement of printed matter in which the column width is narrowed to accommodate an illustration

run away *vb* (*intr, adverb*) **1** to take flight; escape **2** to go away; depart **3** (of a horse) to gallop away uncontrollably **4** **a** to abscond or elope with: *he ran away with his boss's daughter* **b** to make off with; steal **c** to escape from the control of: *his enthusiasm ran away with him* **d** to win easily or be assured of victory in (a competition): *he ran away with the race* ▷ *n* **runaway** **5** **a** a person or animal that runs away **b** (*as modifier*): *a runaway horse* **6** the act or an instance of running away **7** (*modifier*) occurring as a result of the act of eloping: *a runaway wedding* **8** (*modifier*) (of a race, victory, etc) easily won

runch (rʌntʃ) *n* *Scot and northern English* another name for **white charlock**. See **charlock** (sense 2) [C16 of obscure origin]

runcible spoon ('rʌnsɪbᵊl) *n* a forklike utensil with two broad prongs and one sharp curved prong [*runcible* coined by Edward Lear in a nonsense poem (1871)]

runcinate ('rʌnsɪnɪt, -ˌneɪt) *adj* (of a leaf) having a saw-toothed margin with the teeth or lobes pointing backwards [C18 from New Latin *runcīnātus*, from Latin *runcīnāre* to plane off, from *runcīna* a carpenter's plane]

Runcorn ('rʌŋˌkɔːn) *n* a town in NW England, in Halton unitary authority, N Cheshire, on the Manchester Ship Canal: port and industrial centre; designated a new town in 1964. Pop: 60 072 (2001)

rundale ('rʌnˌdeɪl) *n* (formerly) the name given, esp in Ireland and earlier in Scotland, to the system of land tenure in which each land-holder had several strips of land that were not contiguous. Also called (in Scotland): **runrig** [C16 *ryndale*, from RUN (vb) + *dale*, a northern variant of DOLE[1], in the sense "a portion"]

rundle ('rʌndᵊl) *n* **1** a rung of a ladder **2** a wheel, esp of a wheelbarrow [C14 variant of ROUNDEL]

rundlet ('rʌndlɪt) *n* *obsolete* a liquid measure, generally about 15 gallons [C14 see ROUNDLET]

run down *vb* (*mainly adverb*) **1** to cause or allow (an engine, battery, etc) to lose power gradually and cease to function or (of an engine, battery, etc) to do this **2** to decline or reduce in number or size: *the firm ran down its sales force* **3** (*tr, usually passive*) to tire, sap the strength of, or exhaust: *he was thoroughly run down and needed a holiday* **4** (*tr*) to criticize adversely; denigrate; decry **5** (*tr*) to hit and knock to the ground with a moving vehicle **6** *nautical* **a** (*tr*) to collide with and cause to sink **b** (*intr, preposition*) to navigate so as to move parallel to (a coast) **7** (*tr*) to pursue and find or capture: *to run down a fugitive* **8** (*tr*) to read swiftly or perfunctorily: *he ran down their list of complaints* ▷ *adj* **run-down** **9** tired; exhausted **10** worn-out, shabby, or dilapidated ▷ *n* **rundown** **11** a brief review, résumé, or summary **12** the process of a motor or mechanism coming gradually to a standstill after the source of power is removed **13** a reduction in number or size

rune (ruːn) *n* **1** any of the characters of an ancient Germanic alphabet, derived from the Roman alphabet, in use, esp in Scandinavia, from the 3rd century AD to the end of the Middle Ages. Each character was believed to have a magical significance **2** any obscure piece of writing using mysterious symbols **3** a kind of Finnish poem or a stanza in such a poem [Old English *rūn*, from Old Norse *rūn* secret; related to Old Saxon, Old High German, Gothic *runa*] > **'runic** *adj*

rung[1] (rʌŋ) *n* **1** one of the bars or rods that form the steps of a ladder **2** a crosspiece between the legs of a chair, etc **3** *nautical* a spoke on a ship's wheel or a handle projecting from the periphery **4** *dialect* a cudgel or staff [Old English *hrung*; related to Old High German *runga*, Gothic *hrugga*] > **'rungless** *adj*

rung[2] (rʌŋ) *vb* the past participle of **ring**[2]

USAGE See at **ring**[2]

run in *vb* (*adverb*) **1** to run (an engine) gently, usually for a specified period when it is new, in order that the running surfaces may become polished **2** (*tr*) to insert or include **3** (*intr*) (of an aircraft) to approach a point or target **4** (*tr*) *informal* to take into custody; arrest ▷ *n* **run-in** **5** *informal* an argument or quarrel: *a run-in with the boss* **6** an approach to the end of an event, etc: *the run-in to the championship* **7** *printing* matter inserted in an existing paragraph

run into *vb* (*preposition; mainly intr*) **1** (*also tr*) to collide with or cause to collide with **2** to encounter unexpectedly **3** (*also tr*) to be beset by or cause to be beset by: *the project ran into financial difficulties* **4** to extend to: *debts running into thousands*

runlet ('rʌnlɪt) *n* *archaic* a cask for wine, beer, etc [C14 from Old French *rondelet* ROUNDLET]

runnel ('rʌnᵊl) *n* *literary* a small stream [C16 from

r

Old English *rynele*; related to RUN]
runner ('rʌnə) *n* 1 a person who runs, esp an athlete 2 a messenger for a bank or brokerage firm 3 an employee of an art or antique dealer who visits auctions to bid on desired lots 4 a person engaged in the solicitation of business 5 a person on the run; fugitive 6 **a** a person or vessel engaged in smuggling; smuggler **b** (*in combination*): *a rum-runner* 7 a person who operates, manages, or controls something 8 **a** either of the strips of metal or wood on which a sledge runs **b** the blade of an ice skate 9 a roller or guide for a sliding component 10 a channel through which molten material enters a casting or moulding 11 the rotating element of a water turbine 12 another name for **running belay** 13 any of various carangid fishes of temperate and tropical seas, such as *Caranx crysos* (**blue runner**) of American Atlantic waters 14 *botany* **a** a slender stem with very long internodes, as of the strawberry, that arches down to the ground and propagates by producing roots and shoots at the nodes or tip **b** a plant that propagates in this way 15 a strip of lace, linen, etc, placed across a table, dressing table, etc for protection and decoration 16 a narrow rug or carpet, as for a passage 17 another word for **rocker** (on a rocking chair) 18 **do a runner** *slang* to run away in order to escape trouble or to avoid paying for something
runner bean *n* another name for **scarlet runner**
runner-up *n, pl* **runners-up** a contestant finishing a race or competition in second place
running ('rʌnɪŋ) *adj* 1 maintained continuously; incessant: *a running battle* 2 (*postpositive*) without interruption: *he lectured for two hours running* 3 denoting or relating to the scheduled operation of a public vehicle: *the running time of a train* 4 accomplished at a run: *a running jump* 5 (of a knot) sliding along the rope from which it is made, so as to form a noose which becomes smaller when the rope is pulled 6 (of a wound, sore, etc) discharging pus or a serous fluid 7 denoting or relating to operations for maintenance: *running repairs* 8 prevalent: *running prices* 9 repeated or continuous: *a running design* 10 (of certain plants, plant stems, etc) creeping along the ground 11 flowing: *running water* 12 (of handwriting) having the letters run together ▷ *n* 13 management or organization: *the running of a company* 14 operation or maintenance: *the running of a machine* 15 competition or a competitive situation (in the phrases **in the running, out of the running**) 16 **make the running** to set the pace in a competition or race 17 *rare* the power or ability to run
running belay *n mountaineering* the clipping of the rope through a karabiner attached to a sling, piton, nut, etc, secured to the mountain: used by a leading climber of a team to reduce the length of a possible fall. Also called: **runner**
running board *n* a footboard along the side of a vehicle, esp an early motorcar
running commentary *n* a continuous spoken description of an event while it is happening
running head *or* **title** *n printing* a heading printed at the top of every page or every other page of a book
running light *n nautical* one of several white, red, or green lights displayed by vessels operating at night
running mate *n* 1 *US* a candidate for the subordinate of two linked positions, esp a candidate for the vice-presidency 2 a horse that pairs another in a team
running repairs *pl n* repairs, as to a machine or vehicle, that are minor and can be made with little or no interruption in the use of the item
running rigging *n nautical* the wires and ropes used to control the operations of a sailing vessel. Compare **standing rigging**
running stitch *n* a simple form of hand stitching, consisting of small stitches that look the same on both sides of the fabric, usually used for gathering. Sometimes called: **gathering stitch**
runny ('rʌnɪ) *adj* **-nier, -niest** 1 tending to flow; liquid 2 (of the nose or nasal passages) exuding mucus
Runnymede ('rʌnɪˌmiːd) *n* a meadow on the S bank of the Thames near Windsor, where King John met his rebellious barons in 1215 and acceded to Magna Carta
run off *vb* (*adverb*) 1 (*intr*) to depart in haste 2 (*tr*) to produce quickly, as copies on a duplicating machine 3 to drain (liquid) or (of liquid) to be drained 4 (*tr*) to decide (a race) by a runoff 5 (*tr*) to get rid of (weight, etc) by running 6 (*intr*) (of a flow of liquid) to begin to dry up; cease to run 7 **run off with a** to steal; purloin **b** to elope with ▷ *n* **runoff** 8 **a** an extra race to decide the winner after a tie **b** a contest or election held after a previous one has failed to produce a clear victory for any one person 9 that portion of rainfall that runs into streams as surface water rather than being absorbed into ground water or evaporating 10 the overflow of a liquid from a container 11 *NZ* grazing land for store cattle
run-of-paper *adj* (of a story, advertisement, etc) placed anywhere in a newspaper, at the discretion of the editor
run-of-the-mill *adj* ordinary, average, or undistinguished in quality, character, or nature; not special or excellent
run on *vb* (*adverb*) 1 (*intr*) to continue without interruption 2 to write with linked-up characters 3 *printing* to compose text matter without indentation or paragraphing ▷ *n* **run-on** 4 *printing* **a** text matter composed without indenting **b** (*as modifier*): *run-on text matter* 5 **a** a word added at the end of a dictionary entry whose meaning can be easily inferred from the definition of the headword **b** (*as modifier*): *a run-on entry*
run out *vb* (*adverb*) 1 (*intr*; *often foll by of*) to exhaust (a supply of something) or (of a supply) to become exhausted 2 (*intr*) to expire; become no longer valid: *my passport has run out* 3 **run out on** *informal* to desert or abandon 4 (*tr*) *cricket* to dismiss (a running batsman) by breaking the wicket with the ball, or with the ball in the hand, while he is out of his ground ▷ *n* **run-out** 5 *cricket* dismissal of a batsman by running him out 6 *mechanical engineering* an imperfection of a rotating component so that not all parts revolve about their intended axes relative to each other
run over *vb* 1 (*tr, adverb*) to knock down (a person) with a moving vehicle 2 (*intr*) to overflow the capacity of (a container) 3 (*intr, preposition*) to examine hastily or make a rapid survey of 4 (*intr, preposition*) to exceed (a limit): *we've run over our time*
runt (rʌnt) *n* 1 the smallest and weakest young animal in a litter, esp the smallest piglet in a litter 2 *derogatory* an undersized or inferior person 3 a large pigeon, originally bred for eating [C16 origin unknown] > '**runtish** *adj* > '**runty** *adj* > '**runtiness** *n*
run through *vb* 1 (*tr, adverb*) to transfix with a sword or other weapon 2 (*intr, preposition*) to exhaust (money) by wasteful spending; squander 3 (*intr, preposition*) to practise or rehearse 4 (*intr, preposition*) to examine hastily ▷ *n* **run-through** 5 a practice or rehearsal 6 a brief survey
run time *n computing* the time during which a computer program is executed
run to *vb* (*intr, preposition*) to be sufficient for: *my income doesn't run to luxuries*
run up *vb* (*tr, adverb*) 1 to amass or accumulate; incur: *to run up debts* 2 to make by sewing together quickly: *to run up a dress* 3 to hoist: *to run up a flag* ▷ *n* **run-up** 4 an approach run by an athlete for a long jump, pole vault, etc 5 a preliminary or preparatory period: *the run-up to the election*
runway ('rʌnˌweɪ) *n* 1 a hard level roadway or other surface from which aircraft take off and on which they land 2 an enclosure for domestic animals; run 3 *forestry, US and Canadian* a chute for sliding logs down 4 a narrow ramp extending from the stage into the audience in a theatre, etc, esp as used by models in a fashion show
run with *vb* (*intr, preposition*) 1 to associate with habitually: *run with the pack* 2 to proceed with or put into action: *possible for us to run with this proposal*
RUOK *text messaging abbreviation for* are you OK?
rupee (ruːˈpiː) *n* the standard monetary unit of India, Nepal, and Pakistan (divided into 100 paise), Sri Lanka, Mauritius, and the Seychelles (divided into 100 cents) [C17 from Hindi *rupaīyā*, from Sanskrit *rūpya* coined silver, from *rūpa* shape, beauty]
Rupert[2] ('ruːpət) *n military derogatory slang* a junior army officer
Rupert's Land *n* (formerly, in Canada) the territories granted by Charles II to the Hudson's Bay Company in 1670 and ceded to the Canadian Government in 1870, comprising all the land watered by rivers flowing into Hudson Bay
rupiah (ruːˈpiːə) *n, pl* **-ah** *or* **-ahs** the standard monetary unit of Indonesia, divided into 100 sen [from Hindi: RUPEE]
rupicolous (ruːˈpɪkələs) *adj biology* living or growing on or among rocks [C19 from Latin *rūp(ēs)* crag + -I- + -COLOUS]
rupture ('rʌptʃə) *n* 1 the act of breaking or bursting or the state of being broken or burst 2 a breach of peaceful or friendly relations 3 *pathol* **a** the breaking or tearing of a bodily structure or part **b** another word for **hernia** ▷ *vb* 4 to break or burst or cause to break or burst 5 to affect or be affected with a rupture or hernia 6 to undergo or cause to undergo a breach in relations or friendship [C15 from Latin *ruptūra* a breaking, from *rumpere* to burst forth; see ERUPT] > '**rupturable** *adj*
rural ('rʊərəl) *adj* 1 of, relating to, or characteristic of the country or country life 2 living in or accustomed to the country 3 of, relating to, or associated with farming ▷ Compare **urban** [C15 via Old French from Latin *rūrālis*, from *rūs* the country] > '**ruralism** *n* > '**ruralist** *n* > **ru'rality** *n* > '**rurally** *adv*
rural dean *n chiefly Brit* a clergyman having authority over a group of parishes
rural delivery *n NZ* a mail service in a country area, often run by contractors for the Post Office
rural district *n* (in England and Wales from 1888 to 1974 and Northern Ireland from 1898 to 1973) a rural division of a county
ruralize *or* **ruralise** ('rʊərəˌlaɪz) *vb* 1 (*tr*) to make rural in character, appearance, etc 2 (*intr*) to go into the country to live > ˌ**rurali'zation** *or* ˌ**rurali'sation** *n*
rural science *or* **studies** *n Brit* the study and theory of agriculture, biology, ecology, and associated fields
Ruritania (ˌrʊərɪˈteɪnɪə, -njə) *n* 1 an imaginary kingdom of central Europe: setting of several novels by Anthony Hope, esp *The Prisoner of Zenda* (1894) 2 any setting of adventure, romance, and intrigue
Ruritanian (ˌrʊərɪˈteɪnɪən, -njən) *adj* 1 of or relating to Ruritania 2 involving adventure, romance, and intrigue ▷ *n* 3 a native or inhabitant of Ruritania
ruru ('ruːruː) *n NZ* another name for **mopoke** [Māori]
RUS *international car registration for* Russia
ruse (ruːz) *n* an action intended to mislead, deceive, or trick; stratagem [C15 from Old French: trick, esp to evade capture, from *ruser* to retreat, from Latin *recūsāre* to refuse]
Ruse ('ruːseɪ) *n* a city in NE Bulgaria, on the River Danube: the chief river port and one of the largest industrial centres in Bulgaria. Pop: 172 000 (2005 est)
rush[1] (rʌʃ) *vb* 1 to hurry or cause to hurry; hasten 2 to make a sudden attack upon (a fortress, position, person, etc) 3 (when *intr*, often foll by *at*, *in* or *into*) to proceed or approach in a reckless manner 4 **rush one's fences** to proceed with

precipitate haste **5** (*intr*) to come, flow, swell, etc, quickly or suddenly: *tears rushed to her eyes* **6** *slang* to cheat, esp by grossly overcharging **7** (*tr*) *US and Canadian* to make a concerted effort to secure the agreement, participation, etc, of (a person) **8** (*intr*) *American football* to gain ground by running forwards with the ball ▷ *n* **9** the act or condition of rushing **10** a sudden surge towards someone or something: *a gold rush* **11** a sudden surge of sensation, esp produced by a drug **12** a sudden demand ▷ *adj* (*prenominal*) **13** requiring speed or urgency: *a rush job* **14** characterized by much movement, business, etc: *a rush period* [C14 *ruschen*, from Old French *ruser* to put to flight, from Latin *recūsāre* to refuse, reject] > 'rusher *n*

rush² (rʌʃ) *n* **1** any annual or perennial plant of the genus *Juncus*, growing in wet places and typically having grasslike cylindrical leaves and small green or brown flowers: family *Juncaceae* Many species are used to make baskets **2** any of various similar or related plants, such as the woodrush, scouring rush, and spike-rush **3** something valueless; a trifle; straw: *not worth a rush* **4** short for **rush light** [Old English *risce, rysce*; related to Middle Dutch *risch*, Norwegian *rusk*, Old Slavonic *rozga* twig, rod] > 'rush,like *adj*

rushes (rʌʃɪz) *pl n* (*sometimes singular*) (in film-making) the initial prints of a scene or scenes before editing, usually prepared daily

rush hour *n* a period at the beginning and end of the working day when large numbers of people are travelling to or from work

rush light *or* **candle** *n* a narrow candle, formerly in use, made of the pith of various types of rush dipped in tallow

Rushmore ('rʌʃmɔː) *n* **Mount** a mountain in W South Dakota, in the Black Hills: a national memorial, with the faces of Washington, Lincoln, Jefferson, and Roosevelt carved into its side by Gutzon Borglum between 1927 and 1941. Height: 1841 m (6040 ft)

rushy ('rʌʃɪ) *adj* rushier, rushiest abounding in, covered with, or made of rushes > 'rushiness *n*

rus in urbe *Latin* (rʊs ɪn 'ɜːbɪ) the country in the town

rusk (rʌsk) *n* a light bread dough, sweet or plain, baked twice until it is brown, hard, and crisp: often given to babies [C16 from Spanish or Portuguese *rosca* screw, bread shaped in a twist, of unknown origin]

Russ (rʌs) *n, pl* Russ *or* Russes, *adj* an archaic word for **Russian** (person or language)

RUSS *international car registration for* Russia

Russ. *abbreviation for* Russia(n)

Russborough House ('rʌsbərə) *n* a mansion near Blessington in Co Wicklow, Republic of Ireland: built by Richard Castle and Francis Bindon for the 1st Earl of Miltown from 1740

Russell's paradox *n* *logic* the paradox discovered by British philosopher and mathematician Bertrand Russell (1872–1970) in the work of Gottlob Frege, that the class of all classes that are not members of themselves is a member of itself only if it is not, and is not only if it is. This undermines the notion of an all-inclusive universal class

russet ('rʌsɪt) *n* **1** brown with a yellowish or reddish tinge **2 a** a rough homespun fabric, reddish-brown in colour, formerly in use for clothing **b** (*as modifier*): *a russet coat* **3** any of various apples with rough brownish-red skins **4** abnormal roughness on fruit, caused by parasites, pesticides, or frost ▷ *adj* **5** (of tanned hide leather) dressed ready for staining **6** *archaic* simple; homely; rustic: *a russet life* **7** of the colour russet: *russet hair* [C13 from Anglo-Norman, from Old French *rosset*, from *rous*, from Latin *russus*; related to Latin *ruber* red] > 'russety *adj*

Russia ('rʌʃə) *n* (full name **Russian Federation**) **1** the largest country in the world, covering N Eurasia and bordering on the Pacific and Arctic Oceans and the Baltic, Black, and Caspian Seas:

originating from the principality of Muscovy in the 17th century, it expanded to become the Russian Empire; the Tsar was overthrown in 1917 and the Communist Russian Soviet Federative Socialist Republic was created; this merged with neighbouring Soviet Republics in 1922 to form the Soviet Union; on the disintegration of the Soviet Union in 1991 the Russian Federation was established as an independent state. Official language: Russian. Religion: nonreligious and Russian orthodox Christian. Currency: rouble. Capital: Moscow. Pop: 142 397 000 (2004 est). Area: 17 074 984 sq km (6 592 658 sq miles) **2** another name for the **Russian Empire 3** another name for the former **Soviet Union 4** another name for the former **Russian Soviet Federative Socialist Republic** ▷ Russian name: Rossiya

Russia leather *n* a smooth dyed leather made from calfskin and scented with birch tar oil, originally produced in Russia

Russian ('rʌʃən) *n* **1** the official language of Russia: an Indo-European language belonging to the East Slavonic branch **2** the official language of the former Soviet Union **3** a native or inhabitant of Russia ▷ *adj* **4** of, relating to, or characteristic of Russia, its people, or their language

Russian doll *n* any of a set of hollow wooden figures, each of which splits in half to contain the next smallest figure, down to the smallest. Also called: matryoshka, matrioshka

Russian dressing *n* mayonnaise or vinaigrette with chilli sauce, chopped gherkins, etc

Russian Empire *n* the tsarist empire in Asia and E Europe, overthrown by the Russian Revolution of 1917

Russian Federation *n* See **Russia**

Russianize *or* **Russianise** ('rʌʃə,naɪz) *vb* to make or become Russian in style, character, etc > ,Russiani'zation *or* ,Russiani'sation *n*

Russian Orthodox Church *n* the national Church of Russia, constituting a branch of the Eastern Church presided over by the Patriarch of Moscow

Russian Revolution *n* **1** Also called (reckoned by the Julian calendar): **February Revolution** the uprising in Russia in March 1917, during which the tsar abdicated and a provisional government was set up **2** Also called (reckoned by the Julian calendar): **October Revolution** the seizure of power by the Bolsheviks under Lenin in November 1917, transforming the uprising into a socialist revolution. This was followed by a period of civil war against counter-revolutionary armies (1918–22), which ended in eventual victory for the Bolsheviks

Russian roulette *n* **1** a game of chance in which each player in turn spins the cylinder of a revolver loaded with only one cartridge and presses the trigger with the barrel against his own head **2** any act which, if repeated several times, is likely to have disastrous consequences

Russian salad *n* a salad of cold diced cooked vegetables mixed with Russian dressing

Russian Soviet Federative Socialist Republic *n* (formerly) the largest administrative division of the Soviet Union. Abbreviation: RSFSR

Russian Turkestan *n* See **Turkestan**

Russian wolfhound *n* a less common name for **borzoi**

Russian Zone *n* another name for the **Soviet Zone**

Russify ('rʌsɪ,faɪ) *vb* -fies, -fying, -fied (*tr*) to cause to become Russian in character > ,Russifi'cation *n*

Russky *or* **Russki** ('rʌskɪ) *n, pl* -kies *or* -kis, *adj* *chiefly US* a slang word for **Russian** [C20]

Russo- ('rʌsəʊ-) *combining form* Russia or Russian: *Russo-Japanese*

Russo-Japanese War *n* a war (1904–05) between Russia and Japan, caused largely by rivalry over Korea and Manchuria. Russia suffered a series of major defeats

Russophile ('rʌsəʊ,faɪl) *or* **Russophil** *n* **1** an admirer of Russia or the former Soviet Union, its customs, political system, etc ▷ *adj* **2** showing admiration of Russia or the former Soviet Union

Russophobe ('rʌsəʊ,fəʊb) *n* a person who feels intense and often irrational hatred (**Russophobia**) for Russia, or esp the former Soviet Union, its political system, etc > ,Russo'phobic *adj*

russula ('rʌsjʊlə) *n, pl* -lae (-liː) *or* -las any fungus of the large basidiomycetous genus *Russula*, of typical toadstool shape and often brightly coloured, such as the yellow *R. ochroleuca* and *R. lutea*, the green *R. aeruginea*, the violet-pink *R. fragilis*, and the purple *R. atropurpurea*

rust (rʌst) *n* **1** a reddish-brown oxide coating formed on iron or steel by the action of oxygen and moisture **2** Also called: rust fungus *plant pathol* **a** any basidiomycetous fungus of the order *Uredinales*, parasitic on cereal plants, conifers, etc **b** any of various plant diseases characterized by reddish-brown discoloration of the leaves and stem, esp that caused by the rust fungi **3 a** a strong brown colour, sometimes with a reddish or yellowish tinge **b** (*as adjective*): *a rust carpet* **4** any corrosive or debilitating influence, esp lack of use ▷ *vb* **5** to become or cause to become coated with a layer of rust **6** to deteriorate or cause to deteriorate through some debilitating influence or lack of use [Old English *rūst*; related to Old Saxon, Old High German *rost*] > 'rustless *adj*

rust belt *n* an area where heavy industry is in decline, esp in the Midwest of the US

rust bucket *n* **1** *slang* something that is run-down or dilapidated, esp a very badly rusted car ▷ *adj* rustbucket **2** *informal* run-down or dilapidated: *rustbucket factories*

rustic ('rʌstɪk) *adj* **1** of, characteristic of, or living in the country; rural **2** having qualities ascribed to country life or people; simple; unsophisticated: *rustic pleasures* **3** crude, awkward, or uncouth **4** made of untrimmed branches: *a rustic seat* **5** denoting or characteristic of a style of furniture popular in England in the 18th and 19th centuries, in which the legs and feet of chairs, tables, etc, were made to resemble roots, trunks, and branches of trees **6** (of masonry) having a rusticated finish ▷ *n* **7** a person who comes from or lives in the country **8** an unsophisticated, simple, or clownish person from the country **9** Also called: rusticwork brick or stone having a rough finish [C16 from Old French *rustique*, from Latin *rūsticus*, from *rūs* the country] > 'rustically *adv* > rusticity (rʌ'stɪsɪtɪ) *n*

rusticana (,rʌstɪ'kɑːnə) *pl n* objects, such as agricultural implements, garden furniture, etc, relating to the countryside or made in imitation of rustic styles

rusticate ('rʌstɪ,keɪt) *vb* **1** to banish or retire to the country **2** to make or become rustic in style, behaviour, etc **3** (*tr*) *architect* to finish (an exterior wall) with large blocks of masonry that are separated by deep joints and decorated with a bold, usually textured, design **4** (*tr*) *Brit* to send down from university for a specified time as a punishment [C17 from Latin *rūsticārī*, from *rūs* the country] > ,rusti'cation *n* > 'rusti,cator *n*

rusticating ('rʌstɪ,keɪtɪŋ) *n* (in New Zealand) a wide type of weatherboarding used in older houses. Also called: rusticated

rustle¹ ('rʌsəl) *vb* **1** to make or cause to make a low crisp whispering or rubbing sound, as of dry leaves or paper **2** to move with such a sound ▷ *n* **3** such a sound or sounds [Old English *hrūxlian*; related to Gothic *hrukjan* to crow², Old Norse *hraukr* raven, crow¹] > 'rustling *adj, n* > 'rustlingly *adv*

rustle² ('rʌsəl) *vb* **1** *chiefly US and Canadian* to steal (cattle, horses, etc) **2** *US and Canadian informal* to move swiftly and energetically [C19 probably special use of RUSTLE¹ (in the sense: to move with quiet sound)]

rustler ('rʌslə) *n* **1** *chiefly US and Canadian* a cattle or horse thief **2** *US and Canadian informal* an

r

energetic or vigorous person

rustle up vb (tr, adverb) informal **1** to prepare (a meal, snack, etc) rapidly, esp at short notice **2** to forage for and obtain

rustproof ('rʌst,pruːf) adj treated against rusting

rusty ('rʌstɪ) adj rustier, rustiest **1** covered with, affected by, or consisting of rust: a rusty machine; a rusty deposit **2** of the colour rust **3** discoloured by age: a rusty coat **4** (of the voice) tending to croak **5** old-fashioned in appearance; seemingly antiquated: a rusty old gentleman **6** out of practice; impaired in skill or knowledge by inaction or neglect **7** (of plants) affected by the rust fungus > 'rustily adv > 'rustiness n

rut¹ (rʌt) n **1** a groove or furrow in a soft road, caused by wheels **2** any deep mark, hole, or groove **3** a narrow or predictable way of life, set of attitudes, etc; dreary or undeviating routine (esp in the phrase **in a rut**) ▷ vb ruts, rutting, rutted **4** (tr) to make a rut or ruts in [c16 probably from French route road]

rut² (rʌt) n **1** a recurrent period of sexual excitement and reproductive activity in certain male ruminants, such as the deer, that corresponds to the period of oestrus in females **2** another name for **oestrus** ▷ vb ruts, rutting, rutted **3** (intr) (of male ruminants) to be in a period of sexual excitement and activity [c15 from Old French rut noise, roar, from Latin rugītus, from rugīre to roar]

rutabaga (,ruːtə'beɪgə) n Also called (in Britain and certain other countries): swede **1** US and Canadian a Eurasian plant, Brassica napus (or B. napobrassica), cultivated for its bulbous edible root, which is used as a vegetable and as cattle fodder: family Brassicaceae (crucifers) **2** the root of this plant [c18 from Swedish dialect rotabagge, literally: root bag]

rutaceous (ruː'teɪʃəs) adj of, relating to, or belonging to the Rutaceae, a family of tropical and temperate flowering plants many of which have aromatic leaves. The family includes rue and citrus trees [c19 from New Latin Rutaceae, from Latin rūta RUE²]

ruth (ruːθ) n archaic **1** pity; compassion **2** repentance; remorse **3** grief or distress [c12 from rewen to RUE¹]

Ruth (ruːθ) n Old Testament **a** a Moabite woman, who left her own people to remain with her mother-in-law Naomi, and became the wife of Boaz; an ancestress of David **b** the book in which these events are recounted

Ruthenia (ruː'θiːnɪə) n a region of E Europe on the south side of the Carpathian Mountains: belonged to Hungary from the 14th century, to Czechoslovakia from 1918 to 1939, and was ceded to the former Soviet Union in 1945; in 1991 it became part of the newly independent Ukraine. Also called: Carpatho-Ukraine

Ruthenian (ruː'θiːnɪən) adj **1** of or relating to Ruthenia, its people, or their dialect of Ukrainian ▷ n **2** a dialect of Ukrainian **3** a native or inhabitant of Ruthenia

ruthenic (ruː'θɛnɪk) adj of or containing ruthenium, esp in a high valency state

ruthenious (ruː'θiːnɪəs) adj of or containing ruthenium in a divalent state

ruthenium (ruː'θiːnɪəm) n a hard brittle white element of the platinum metal group. It occurs free with other platinum metals in pentlandite and other ores and is used to harden platinum and palladium. Symbol: Ru; atomic no: 44; atomic wt: 101.07; valency: 0–8; relative density: 12.41; melting pt: 2334°C; boiling pt: 4150°C [c19 from Medieval Latin Ruthenia Russia, where it was first

discovered]

rutherford ('rʌðəfəd) n a unit of activity equal to the quantity of a radioactive nuclide required to produce one million disintegrations per second. Abbreviation: rd [c20 named after Ernest Rutherford, 1st Baron Rutherford (1871–1937), New Zealand-born British physicist]

rutherfordium (,rʌðə'fɔːdɪəm) n a transactinide element produced by bombarding californium-249 nuclei with carbon-12 nuclei. Symbol: Rf; atomic number: 104; atomic wt: 261. Name in the former Soviet Union: kurchatovium [c20 named after Ernest Rutherford, 1st Baron Rutherford (1871–1937), New Zealand-born British physicist]

ruthful ('ruːθfʊl) adj archaic full of or causing sorrow or pity > 'ruthfully adv > 'ruthfulness n

ruthless ('ruːθlɪs) adj feeling or showing no mercy; hardhearted > 'ruthlessly adv > 'ruthlessness n

rutilant ('ruːtɪlənt) adj rare of a reddish colour or glow [c15 from Latin rutilāns having a red glow, from rutilāre, from rutilus ruddy, red]

rutilated ('ruːtɪ,leɪtɪd) adj (of minerals, esp quartz) containing needles of rutile

rutile ('ruːtaɪl) n a black, yellowish, or reddish-brown mineral, found in igneous rocks, metamorphosed limestones, and quartz veins. It is a source of titanium. Composition: titanium dioxide. Formula: TiO₂. Crystal structure: tetragonal [c19 via French from German Rutil, from Latin rutilus red, glowing]

Rutland ('rʌtlənd) n an inland county of central England: the smallest of the historical English counties, it became part of Leicestershire in 1974 but was reinstated as an independent unitary authority in 1997: mainly agricultural. Administrative centre: Oakham. Pop: 35 700 (2003 est). Area: 394 sq km (152 sq miles)

ruttish ('rʌtɪʃ) adj **1** (of an animal) in a condition of rut **2** lascivious or salacious > 'ruttishly adv > 'ruttishness n

rutty ('rʌtɪ) adj -tier, -tiest full of ruts or holes: a rutty track > 'ruttily adv > 'ruttiness n

Ruwenzori (,ruːwɛn'zɔːrɪ) n a mountain range in central Africa, on the border between Uganda and the Democratic Republic of Congo (formerly Zaïre) between Lakes Edward and Albert: generally thought to be Ptolemy's "Mountains of the Moon". Highest peak: Mount Stanley, 5109 m (16 763 ft)

rv statistics abbreviation for random variable

RV abbreviation for **1** Revised Version (of the Bible) **2** chiefly US recreational vehicle

rw the internet domain name for Rwanda

RW abbreviation for **1** Right Worshipful **2** Right Worthy

RWA international car registration for Rwanda

Rwanda¹ (rʊ'ændə) n a republic in central Africa: part of German East Africa from 1899 until 1917, when Belgium took over the administration; became a republic in 1961 after a Hutu revolt against the Tutsi (1959); fighting between the ethnic groups broke out repeatedly after independence, culminating in the genocide of Tutsis by Hutus in 1994. Official languages: Rwanda, French, and English. Religion: Roman Catholic, African Protestant, Muslim, and animist. Currency: Rwanda franc. Capital: Kigali. Pop: 8 481 000 (2004 est). Area: 26 338 sq km (10 169 sq miles). Former name (until 1962): Ruanda

Rwanda² (rʊ'ændə) n one of the official languages of Rwanda, belonging to the Bantu group of the Niger-Congo family and closely related to Kirundi. Also called: Kinyarwanda

Rwandan (rʊ'ændən) adj **1** of or relating to

Rwanda or its inhabitants ▷ n **2** a native or inhabitant of Rwanda

rwd abbreviation for rear-wheel drive

Rwy or **Ry** abbreviation for railway

-ry suffix forming nouns a variant of **-ery**: dentistry

Ryazan (Russian rɪ'zanj) n a city in W central Russia: capital of a medieval principality; oil refineries and engineering industries. Pop: 523 000 (2005 est)

Rybinsk (Russian 'ribinsk) n a city in W central Russia, on the River Volga: an important river port, terminal of the Mariinsk Waterway (between Saint Petersburg and the Volga) at the SE end of the **Rybinsk Reservoir** (area: 4700 sq km (1800 sq miles)). Pop: 218 000 (2005 est). Former names: Shcherbakov (from the Revolution until 1957), Andropov (1984–91)

Rydal ('raɪdəl) n a village in NW England, in Cumbria on **Rydal Water** (a small lake). **Rydal Mount**, home of Wordsworth from 1813 to 1850, is situated here

Ryder Cup (raɪdə) n **the**. the trophy awarded in a professional golfing competition between teams representing Europe and the US [c20 named after Samuel Ryder (1859–1936), British businessman and golf patron]

rye¹ (raɪ) n **1** a tall hardy widely cultivated annual grass, Secale cereale, having soft bluish-green leaves, bristly flower spikes, and light brown grain. See also **wild rye 2** the grain of this grass, used in making flour and whiskey, and as a livestock food **3** Also called: rye whiskey whiskey distilled from rye. US whiskey must by law contain not less than 51 per cent rye **4** US short for **rye bread** [Old English ryge; related to Old Norse rugr, Old French rogga, Old Saxon roggo]

rye² (raɪ) n Gypsy dialect a gentleman [from Romany rai, from Sanskrit rājan king; see RAJAH]

Rye (raɪ) n a resort in SE England, in East Sussex: one of the Cinque Ports. Pop: 4195 (2001)

rye bread n any of various breads made entirely or partly from rye flour, often with caraway seeds

rye-brome n a grass, Bromus secalinus, native to Europe and Asia, having rough leaves and wheatlike ears. US names: cheat, chess

rye-grass n any of various grasses of the genus Lolium, esp L. perenne, native to Europe, N Africa, and Asia and widely cultivated as forage crops. They have a flattened flower spike and hairless leaves

Ryeland ('raɪlənd) n a breed of large hornless sheep having fine wool, originating from Herefordshire, England

Ryobu Shinto (riː'əʊbuː) n a fusion of Shinto and Buddhism, which flourished in Japan in the 13th century [from Japanese ryō bu literally: two parts]

ryokan (rɪ'əʊkən) n a traditional Japanese inn [Japanese]

ryot (raɪət) n (in India) a peasant or tenant farmer [c17 from Hindi ra'īyat, from Arabic ra'īyah flock, peasants, from ra'ā pasture]

Ryswick ('rɪzwɪk) n the English name for **Rijswijk**

Ryukyu Islands (rɪ'uːkjuː) pl n a chain of 55 islands in the W Pacific, extending almost 650 km (400 miles) from S Japan to N Taiwan: an ancient kingdom, under Chinese rule from the late 14th century, invaded by Japan in the early 17th century, under full Japanese sovereignty from 1879 to 1945, and US control from 1945 to 1972; now part of Japan again. They are subject to frequent typhoons. Chief town: Naha City (on Okinawa). Pop: 1 318 220 (2000). Area: 2196 sq km (849 sq miles). Japanese name: **Nansei-shoto**

Ss

s or **S** (ɛs) *n*, *pl* **s's**, **S's** or **Ss** **1** the 19th letter and 15th consonant of the modern English alphabet **2** a speech sound represented by this letter, usually an alveolar fricative, either voiceless, as in *sit*, or voiced, as in *dogs* **3 a** something shaped like an S **b** (*in combination*): *an S-bend in a road*

s *symbol for* second (of time)

S *symbol for* **1** satisfactory **2** Society **3** small (size) **4** South **5** *chem* sulphur **6** *physics* **a** entropy **b** siemens **c** strangeness **7** *currency* **a** (the former) schilling **b** sol **c** (the former) sucre **8** *international car registration for* Sweden

s. *abbreviation for* **1** see **2** semi- **3** shilling **4** singular **5** son **6** succeeded

S. *abbreviation for* **1** Saint **2** school **3** Sea **4** Signor **5** Society [Latin *socius*]

-s¹ or **-es** *suffix* forming the plural of most nouns: *boys; boxes* [from Old English *-as*, plural nominative and accusative ending of some masculine nouns]

-s² or **-es** *suffix* forming the third person singular present indicative tense of verbs: *he runs; she washes* [from Old English (northern dialect) *-es*, *-s*, originally the ending of the second person singular]

-s³ *suffix of nouns* forming nicknames and names expressing affection or familiarity: *Fats; Fingers; ducks* [special use of -s¹]

-'s *suffix* **1** forming the possessive singular of nouns and some pronouns: *man's; one's* **2** forming the possessive plural of nouns whose plurals do not end in -s: *children's* **3** forming the plural of numbers, letters, or symbols: *20's; p's and q's* **4** *informal* contraction of *is* or *has*: *he's here; John's coming; it's gone* **5** *informal* contraction of *us* with *let*: *let's* **6** *informal* contraction of *does* in some questions: *where's he live?; what's he do?* [senses 1, 2: assimilated contraction from Middle English *-es*, from Old English, masculine and neuter genitive singular; sense 3, equivalent to -s¹]

-s' *suffix* forming the possessive of plural nouns ending in the sound *s* or *z* and of some singular nouns: *girls'; for goodness' sake*

sa *the internet domain name for* Saudi Arabia

Sa *a former chemical symbol for* samarium

SA *abbreviation for* **1** Salvation Army **2** Sociedad Anónima [Spanish: limited company] **3** Société anonyme [French: limited company] **4** South Africa **5** South America **6** South Australia **7** *Sturmabteilung*: the Nazi terrorist militia, organized around 1924 **8** *international car registration for* Saudi Arabia

s.a. *abbreviation for* **1** semiannual **2** sex appeal **3** sine anno [Latin: without date]

Saar (sɑː; *German* zaːr) *n* **1** a river in W Europe, rising in the Vosges Mountains and flowing north to the Moselle River in Germany. Length: 246 km (153 miles). French name: **Sarre 2 the Saar** another name for **Saarland**

Saarbrücken (*German* zaːrˈbrʏkən) *n* an industrial city in W Germany, capital of Saarland state, on the Saar River. Pop: 181 860 (2003 est)

SAARC *abbreviation for* South Asian Association for Regional Cooperation

Saarland (*German* ˈzaːrlant) *n* a state of W Germany: formed in 1919; under League of Nations administration until 1935; occupied by France (1945–57); part of West Germany (1957–90): contains rich coal deposits and is a major industrial region. Capital: Saarbrücken. Pop: 1 060 000 (2003 est). Area: 2567 sq km (991 sq miles)

sab (sæb) *n informal* a person engaged in direct action to prevent a targeted activity, esp fox hunting, taking place [c20 shortened from SABOTEUR]

Saba (ˈsɑːbə) *n* **1** an island in the NE Caribbean, in the Netherlands Antilles. Pop: 2498 (2004 est). Area: 13 sq km (5 sq miles) **2** another name for **Sheba¹** (sense 1)

Sabadell (*Spanish* saβaˈðɛl) *n* a town in NE Spain, near Barcelona: textile manufacturing. Pop: 191 057 (2003 est)

sabadilla (ˌsæbəˈdɪlə) *n* **1** a tropical American liliaceous plant, *Schoenocaulon officinale* **2** the bitter brown seeds of this plant, which contain the alkaloids veratrine and veratridine and are used in insecticides [c19 from Spanish *cebadilla*, diminutive of *cebada* barley, from Latin *cibāre* to feed, from *cibus* food]

Sabaean or **Sabean** (səˈbiːən) *n* **1** an inhabitant or native of ancient Saba **2** the ancient Semitic language of Saba ▷ *adj* **3** of or relating to ancient Saba, its inhabitants, or their language [c16 from Latin *Sabaeus*, from Greek *Sabaios* belonging to Saba (Sheba)]

Sabah (ˈsɑːbɑː) *n* a state of Malaysia, occupying N Borneo and offshore islands in the South China and Sulu Seas: became a British protectorate in 1888; gained independence and joined Malaysia in 1963. Capital: Kota Kinabalu. Pop: 2 603 485 (2000). Area: 76 522 sq km (29 545 sq miles). Former name (until 1963): **North Borneo**

Sabaoth (sæˈbeɪɒθ, ˈsæbeɪɒθ) *n Bible* hosts, armies (esp in the phrase **the Lord of Sabaoth** in Romans 9:29) [c14 via Latin and Greek from Hebrew *çˈbāōth*, from *çābā*]

sabayon (ˌsæbaɪˈjɒn; *French* sabajɔ̃) *n* a dessert or sweet sauce made with egg yolks, sugar, and wine beaten together over heat till thick: served either hot or cold [c20 from French, alteration of Italian *zabione* ZABAGLIONE]

sabbat (ˈsæbæt, -ət) *n* another word for **Sabbath** (sense 4)

Sabbatarian (ˌsæbəˈtɛərɪən) *n* **1** a person advocating the strict religious observance of Sunday **2** a person who observes Saturday as the Sabbath ▷ *adj* **3** of or relating to the Sabbath or its observance [c17 from Late Latin *sabbatārius* a Sabbath-keeper] > ˌSabbaˈtarianism *n*

Sabbath (ˈsæbəθ) *n* **1** the seventh day of the week, Saturday, devoted to worship and rest from work in Judaism and in certain Christian Churches **2** Sunday, observed by Christians as the day of worship and rest from work in commemoration of Christ's Resurrection **3** (*not capital*) a period of rest **4** Also called: **sabbat**, **witches' Sabbath** a midnight meeting or secret rendezvous for practitioners of witchcraft, sorcery, or devil worship [Old English *sabbat*, from Latin *sabbatum*, from Greek *sabbaton*, from Hebrew *shabbāth*, from *shābath* to rest]

sabbath school *n* (*sometimes capitals*) *chiefly US* a school for religious instruction held on the Sabbath

sabbatical (səˈbætɪkªl) *adj* **1** denoting a period of leave granted to university staff, teachers, etc, esp approximately every seventh year: *a sabbatical year; sabbatical leave* **2** denoting a post that renders the holder eligible for such leave ▷ *n* **3** any sabbatical period [c16 from Greek *sabbatikos*; see SABBATH]

Sabbatical (səˈbætɪkªl) *adj also* **Sabbatic 1** of, relating to, or appropriate to the Sabbath as a day of rest and religious observance ▷ *n* **2** short for **sabbatical year**

sabbatical year *n* (*often capitals*) *Bible* a year during which the land was to be left uncultivated, debts annulled, etc, supposed to be observed every seventh year by the ancient Israelites according to Leviticus 25

SABC *abbreviation for* South African Broadcasting Corporation

Sabellian (səˈbɛlɪən) *n* **1** an extinct language or group of languages of ancient Italy, surviving only in a few inscriptions belonging to the Osco-Umbrian group **2** a member of any of the ancient peoples speaking this language, including the Sabines ▷ *adj* **3** of or relating to this language or its speakers [c17 from Latin *Sabellī* group of Italian tribes]

saber (ˈseɪbə) *n*, *vb* the US spelling of **sabre**

sabermetrics (ˌseɪbəˈmɛtrɪks) *n* (*functioning as singular*) the statistical and mathematical analysis of baseball records [c20 *saber* (from initials of *Society of American Baseball Research*) + *-metrics* as in ECONOMETRICS]

sabin (ˈsæbɪn, ˈseɪ-) *n physics* a unit of acoustic absorption equal to the absorption resulting from one square foot of a perfectly absorbing surface [c20 introduced by Wallace C *Sabine* (1868–1919), US physicist]

Sabine (ˈsæbaɪn) *n* **1** a member of an ancient Oscan-speaking people who lived in central Italy northeast of Rome ▷ *adj* **2** of, characteristic of, or relating to this people or their language

Sabin vaccine (ˈseɪbɪn) *n* a vaccine taken orally to immunize against poliomyelitis, developed by Albert Bruce Sabin (1906–93) in 1955

sabkha (ˈsæbxə, -kə) *n* a flat coastal plain with a salt crust, common in Arabia [c19 from Arabic]

sable (ˈseɪbªl) *n*, *pl* **-bles** or **-ble 1** a marten, *Martes zibellina*, of N Asian forests, with dark brown luxuriant fur. Related adj: **zibeline 2 a** the highly valued fur of this animal **b** (*as modifier*): *a sable coat*

3 *American* **sable** the brown, slightly less valuable fur of the American marten, *Martes americana* **4** the colour of sable fur: a dark brown to yellowish-brown colour ▷ *adj* **5** of the colour of sable fur **6** black; dark; gloomy **7** (*usually postpositive*) *heraldry* of the colour black [c15 from Old French, from Old High German *zobel*, of Slavic origin; related to Russian *sobol'*, Polish *sobol*]

Sable ('seɪbᵊl) *n* **Cape 1** a cape at the S tip of Florida: the southernmost point of continental US **2** the southernmost point of Nova Scotia, Canada

sable antelope *n* a large black E African antelope, *Hippotragus niger*, with long backward-curving horns

Sable Island pony *n* a variety of wild pony found on Sable Island, Nova Scotia

sabot ('sæbəʊ; *French* sabo) *n* **1** a shoe made from a single block of wood **2** a shoe with a wooden sole and a leather or cloth upper **3** a lightweight sleeve in which a subcalibre round is enclosed in order to make it fit the rifling of a firearm. After firing the sabot drops away **4** *Austral* a small sailing boat with a shortened bow [c17 from French, probably from Old French *savate* an old shoe, also influenced by *bot* BOOT¹; related to Italian *ciabatta* old shoe, Old Provençal *sabata*]

sabotage ('sæbə,tɑːʒ) *n* **1** the deliberate destruction, disruption, or damage of equipment, a public service, etc, as by enemy agents, dissatisfied employees, etc **2** any similar action or behaviour ▷ *vb* **3** (*tr*) to destroy, damage, or disrupt, esp by secret means [c20 from French, from *saboter* to spoil through clumsiness (literally: to clatter in sabots)]

saboteur (,sæbə'tɜː) *n* a person who commits sabotage [c20 from French; see SABOTAGE]

sabra ('sɑːbrə) *n* a native-born Israeli Jew [from Hebrew *Sabēr* prickly pear, common plant in the coastal areas of the country]

sabre *or US* **saber** ('seɪbə) *n* **1** a stout single-edged cavalry sword, having a curved blade **2** a sword used in fencing, having a narrow V-shaped blade, a semicircular guard, and a slightly curved hand **3** a cavalry soldier ▷ *vb* **4** (*tr*) to injure or kill with a sabre [c17 via French from German (dialect) *Sabel*, from Middle High German *sebel*, perhaps from Magyar *száblya*; compare Russian *sablya* sabre]

sabre-rattling *n, adj informal* seeking to intimidate by an aggressive display of military power

sabretache ('sæbə,tæʃ) *n* a leather case suspended from a cavalryman's saddle [c19 via French from German *Säbeltasche* sabre pocket]

sabre-toothed tiger *or* **cat** *n* any of various extinct Tertiary felines of the genus *Smilodon* and related genera, with long curved upper canine teeth

SABS *abbreviation for* South African Bureau of Standards

sabulous ('sæbjʊləs) *or* **sabulose** ('sæbjʊləʊs) *adj* **1** like sand in texture; gritty **2** *Also:* **sabuline** ('sæbjʊliːn) (of plants) growing in sand [c17 from Latin *sabulōsus*, from *sabulum* SAND] > **sabulosity** (,sæbjʊ'lɒsɪtɪ) *n*

sac (sæk) *n* a pouch, bag, or pouchlike part in an animal or plant [c18 from French, from Latin *saccus*; see SACK¹] > **sac,like** *adj*

SAC (*in Britain*) *abbreviation for* Special Area of Conservation

sacaton (,sækə'təʊn) *n* a coarse grass, *Sporobolus wrightii*, of the southwestern US and Mexico, grown for hay and pasture [American Spanish *zacatón*, from *zacate* coarse grass, from Nahuatl *zacatl*]

SACC *abbreviation for* South African Council of Churches

saccade (sə'kɑːd, -'keɪd) *n* **1** the movement of the eye when it makes a sudden change of fixation, as in reading **2** a sudden check given to a horse [c18 from French: a jerk on the reins of a horse]

saccate ('sækeɪt) *adj botany* in the form of a sac; pouched [c19 from New Latin *saccatus*, from *saccus*: see SACK¹]

saccharase ('sækə,reɪs) *n* another name for **invertase**

saccharate ('sækə,reɪt) *n* any salt or ester of saccharic acid

saccharic acid (sæ'kærɪk) *n* a white soluble solid dicarboxylic acid obtained by the oxidation of cane sugar or starch; 2,3,4,5-tetrahydroxy-hexanedioic acid. Formula: COOH(CHOH)₄COOH

saccharide ('sækə,raɪd, -rɪd) *n* any sugar or other carbohydrate, esp a simple sugar

saccharify, **saccharize**, **saccharise** ('sækə,raɪz) *vb* -fies, -fying, -fied (*tr*) to convert (starch) into sugar > sac,charifi'cation, ,sacchari'zation *or* ,sacchari'sation *n*

saccharimeter (,sækə'rɪmɪtə) *n* any instrument for measuring the strength of sugar solutions, esp a type of polarimeter for determining the concentration from the extent to which the solution rotates the plane of polarized light > ,saccha'rimetry *n*

saccharin ('sækərɪn) *n* a very sweet white crystalline slightly soluble powder used as a nonfattening sweetener. Formula: C₇H₅NO₃S [c19 from SACCHARO- + -IN]

saccharine ('sækə,raɪn, -,riːn) *adj* **1** excessively sweet; sugary: *a saccharine smile* **2** of, relating to, of the nature of, or containing sugar or saccharin > 'saccharinely *adv* > saccharinity (,sækə'rɪnɪtɪ) *n*

saccharo- *or before a vowel* **sacchar-** *combining form* sugar: *saccharomycete* [via Latin from Greek *sakkharon*, ultimately from Sanskrit *śarkarā* sugar]

saccharoid ('sækə,rɔɪd) *adj* **1** *Also:* **saccharoidal** *geology* having or designating a texture resembling that of loaf sugar: *saccharoid marble* ▷ *n* **2** *biochem* any of a group of polysaccharides that remotely resemble sugars, but are not sweet and are often insoluble

saccharometer (,sækə'rɒmɪtə) *n* a hydrometer used to measure the strengths of sugar solutions. It is usually calibrated directly to give a reading of concentration

saccharose ('sækə,rəʊz, -,rəʊs) *n* a technical name for **sugar** (sense 1)

saccular ('sækjʊlə) *adj* of or resembling a sac

sacculate ('sækjʊlɪt, -,leɪt) *or* **sacculated** *adj* of, relating to, or possessing a saccule, saccules, or a sacculus > saccu'lation *n*

saccule ('sækjuːl) *or* **sacculus** ('sækjʊləs) *n, pl* -cules *or* -li (liː) **1** a small sac **2** the smaller of the two parts of the membranous labyrinth of the internal ear. Compare **utricle** (sense 1) [c19 from Latin *sacculus* diminutive of *saccus* SACK¹]

sacculiform (sæ'kjʊlɪ,fɔːm) *adj biology* (of plant parts, etc) shaped like a small sac

sacerdotal (,sæsə'dəʊtᵊl) *adj* of, relating to, or characteristic of priests [c14 from Latin *sacerdōtālis*, from *sacerdōs* priest, from *sacer* sacred] > ,sacer'dotally *adv*

sacerdotalism (,sæsə'dəʊtᵊ,lɪzəm) *n* **1** the principles, methods, etc, of the priesthood **2** the belief that ordained priests are endowed with sacramental and sacrificial powers **3** exaggerated respect for priests **4** *derogatory* power over people's opinions and actions achieved by priests through sophistry or guile > ,sacer'dotalist *n*

sachem ('seɪtʃəm) *n* **1** *US* a leader of a political party or organization, esp of Tammany Hall **2** another name for **sagamore** [c17 from Narraganset *sāchim* chief] > **sachemic** (seɪ'tʃɛmɪk, 'seɪtʃə-) *adj*

sachet ('sæʃeɪ) *n* **1** a small sealed envelope, usually made of plastic or paper, for containing sugar, salt, shampoo, etc **2 a** a small soft bag containing perfumed powder, placed in drawers to scent clothing **b** the powder contained in such a bag [c19 from Old French: a little bag, from *sac* bag; see SACK¹]

Sachsen ('zaksən) *n* the German name for **Saxony**

sack¹ (sæk) *n* **1** a large bag made of coarse cloth, thick paper, etc, used as a container **2** *Also called:*

sackful the amount contained in a sack, sometimes used as a unit of measurement **3 a** a woman's loose tube-shaped dress **b** *Also called:* **sacque** a woman's full loose hip-length jacket, worn in the 18th and mid-20th centuries **4** *short for* **rucksack 5** *cricket, Austral* a run scored off a ball not struck by the batsman: allotted to the team as an extra and not to the individual batsman. Also called (in Britain and certain other countries): **bye 6 the sack** *informal* dismissal from employment **7** a slang word for **bed 8 hit the sack** *slang* to go to bed **9 rough as sacks** *NZ* uncouth ▷ *vb* (*tr*) **10** *informal* to dismiss from employment **11** to put into a sack or sacks [Old English *sacc*, from Latin *saccus* bag, from Greek *sakkos*; related to Hebrew *saq*] > 'sack,like *adj*

sack² (sæk) *n* **1** the plundering of a place by an army or mob, usually involving destruction, slaughter, etc **2** *American football* a tackle on a quarterback which brings him down before he has passed the ball ▷ *vb* **3** (*tr*) to plunder and partially destroy (a place) **4** *American football* to tackle and bring down a quarterback before he has passed the ball [c16 from French phrase *mettre à sac*, literally: to put (loot) in a sack, from Latin *saccus* SACK¹] > 'sacker *n*

sack³ (sæk) *n archaic except in trademarks* any dry white wine formerly imported into Britain from SW Europe [c16 *wyne seck*, from French *vin sec* dry wine, from Latin *siccus* dry]

sackable ('sækəbᵊl) *adj* of or denoting an offence, infraction of rules, etc, that is sufficently serious to warrant dismissal from an employment

sackbut ('sæk,bʌt) *n* a medieval form of trombone [c16 from French *saqueboute*, from Old French *saquer* to pull + *bouter* to push; see BUTT³; used in the Bible (Daniel 3) as a mistranslation of Aramaic *sabb'ka* stringed instrument]

sackcloth ('sæk,klɒθ) *n* **1** coarse cloth such as sacking **2** garments made of such cloth, worn formerly to indicate mourning or penitence **3 sackcloth and ashes** a public display of extreme grief, remorse, or repentance

sacking ('sækɪŋ) *n* coarse cloth used for making sacks, woven from flax, hemp, jute, etc

sack race *n* a race in which the competitors' legs and often bodies are enclosed in sacks > **sack racing** *n*

SACP *abbreviation for* South African Communist Party

sacral¹ ('seɪkrəl) *adj* of, relating to, or associated with sacred rites [c19 from Latin *sacrum* sacred object]

sacral² ('seɪkrəl) *adj* of or relating to the sacrum [c18 from New Latin *sacrālis*, from SACRUM]

sacrament ('sækrəmənt) *n* **1** an outward sign combined with a prescribed form of words and regarded as conferring some specific grace upon those who receive it. The Protestant sacraments are baptism and the Lord's Supper. In the Roman Catholic and Eastern Churches they are baptism, penance, confirmation, the Eucharist, holy orders, matrimony, and the anointing of the sick (formerly extreme unction) **2** (*often capital*) the Eucharist **3** the consecrated elements of the Eucharist, esp the bread **4** something regarded as possessing a sacred or mysterious significance **5** a symbol; pledge [c12 from Church Latin *sacrāmentum* vow, from Latin *sacrāre* to consecrate]

sacramental (,sækrə'mɛntᵊl) *adj* **1** of, relating to, or having the nature of a sacrament **2** bound by or as if by a sacrament ▷ *n* **3** *RC Church* a sacrament-like ritual action, such as the sign of the cross or the use of holy water > ,sacra'mentally *adv* > sacramentality (,sækrəmən'tælɪtɪ) *or* ,sacra'mentalness *n*

sacramentalism (,sækrə'mɛntᵊ,lɪzəm) *n* belief in or special emphasis upon the efficacy of the sacraments for conferring grace > ,sacra'mentalist *n*

Sacramentarian (,sækrəmɛn'tɛərɪən) *n* **1** any Protestant theologian, such as the Swiss

Reformation leader Ulrich Zwingli (1484–1531), who maintained that the bread and wine of the Eucharist were the body and blood of Christ only in a figurative sense and denied His real presence in these elements **2** one who believes in sacramentalism ▷ *adj* **3** of or relating to Sacramentarians **4** (*not capital*) of or relating to sacraments > ˌSacramenˈtarianism *n*

Sacramento (ˌsækrəˈmɛntəʊ) *n* **1** an inland port in N central California, capital of the state at the confluence of the American and Sacramento Rivers: became a boom town in the gold rush of the 1850s. Pop: 445 335 (2003 est) **2** a river in N California, flowing generally south to San Francisco Bay. Length: 615 km (382 miles)

sacrarium (sæˈkrɛərɪəm) *n*, *pl* -**craria** (-ˈkrɛərɪə) **1** the sanctuary of a church **2** *RC Church* a place near the altar of a church, similar in function to the piscina, where materials used in the sacred rites are deposited or poured away [C18 from Latin *sacrārium*, from *sacer* SACRED]

sacred (ˈseɪkrɪd) *adj* **1** exclusively devoted to a deity or to some religious ceremony or use; holy; consecrated **2** worthy of or regarded with reverence, awe, or respect **3** protected by superstition or piety from irreligious actions **4** connected with or intended for religious use: *sacred music* **5** dedicated to; in honour of [C14 from Latin *sacrāre* to set apart as holy, from *sacer* holy] > ˈsacredly *adv* ˈsacredness *n*

Sacred College *n* the collective body of the cardinals of the Roman Catholic Church

sacred cow *n informal* a person, institution, custom, etc, unreasonably held to be beyond criticism [alluding to the Hindu belief that cattle are sacred]

Sacred Heart *n RC Church* **1** the heart of Jesus Christ, a symbol of His love and sacrifice **2** a representation of this, usually bleeding, as an aid to devotion

sacred mushroom *n* **1** any of various hallucinogenic mushrooms, esp species of *Psilocybe* and *Amanita*, that have been eaten in rituals in various parts of the world **2** a mescal button, used in a similar way

sacred site *n Austral informal* a place of great significance

sacrifice (ˈsækrɪˌfaɪs) *n* **1** a surrender of something of value as a means of gaining something more desirable or of preventing some evil **2** a ritual killing of a person or animal with the intention of propitiating or pleasing a deity **3** a symbolic offering of something to a deity **4** the person, animal, or object surrendered, destroyed, killed, or offered **5** a religious ceremony involving one or more sacrifices **6** loss entailed by giving up or selling something at less than its value **7** *chess* the act or an instance of sacrificing a piece ▷ *vb* **8** to make a sacrifice (of); give up, surrender, or destroy (a person, thing, etc) **9** *chess* to permit or force one's opponent to capture (a piece) freely, as in playing a combination or gambit: *he sacrificed his queen and checkmated his opponent on the next move* [C13 via Old French from Latin *sacrificium*, from *sacer* holy + *facere* to make] > ˈsacriˌficeable *adj* ˈsacriˌficer *n*

sacrifice paddock *n* NZ a grassed area allowed to be grazed completely, to be cultivated and resown later

sacrificial (ˌsækrɪˈfɪʃəl) *adj* used in or connected with a sacrifice > ˌsacriˈficially *adv*

sacrificial anode *n metallurgy* an electropositive metal, such as zinc, that protects a more important electronegative part by corroding when attacked by electrolytic action

sacrilege (ˈsækrɪlɪdʒ) *n* **1** the misuse or desecration of anything regarded as sacred or as worthy of extreme respect: *to play Mozart's music on a kazoo is sacrilege* **2** the act or an instance of taking anything sacred for secular use [C13 from Old French *sacrilège*, from Latin *sacrilegium*, from *sacrilegus* temple-robber, from *sacra* sacred things +

legere to take] > sacrilegist (ˌsækrɪˈliːdʒɪst) *n*

sacrilegious (ˌsækrɪˈlɪdʒəs) *adj* **1** of, relating to, or involving sacrilege; impious **2** guilty of sacrilege > ˌsacriˈlegiously *adv* ˌsacriˈlegiousness *n*

sacring (ˈseɪkrɪŋ) *n archaic* the act or ritual of consecration, esp of the Eucharist or of a bishop [C13 from obsolete *sacren* to consecrate, from Latin *sacrāre*; see SACRED]

sacring bell *n chiefly RC Church* a small bell rung at the elevation of the Host and chalice during Mass

sacristan (ˈsækrɪstən) or **sacrist** (ˈsækrɪst, ˈseɪ-) *n* **1** a person who has charge of the contents of a church, esp the sacred vessels, vestments, etc **2** a less common word for **sexton** (sense 1) [C14 from Medieval Latin *sacristānus*, from *sacrista*, from Latin *sacer* holy]

sacristy (ˈsækrɪstɪ) *n*, *pl* -**ties** a room attached to a church or chapel where the sacred vessels, vestments, etc, are kept and where priests attire themselves [C17 from Medieval Latin *sacristia*; see SACRISTAN]

sacroiliac (ˌseɪkrəʊˈɪlɪˌæk, ˌsæk-) *anatomy* ▷ *adj* **1** of or relating to the sacrum and ilium, their articulation, or their associated ligaments ▷ *n* **2** the joint where these bones meet

sacrosanct (ˈsækrəʊˌsæŋkt) *adj* very sacred or holy; inviolable [C17 from Latin *sacrōsanctus* made holy by sacred rite, from *sacrō* by sacred rite, from *sacer* holy + *sanctus*, from *sancīre* to hallow] > ˌsacroˈsanctity or ˈsacroˌsanctness *n*

sacrum (ˈseɪkrəm, ˈsæk-) *n*, *pl* -**cra** (-krə) **1** (in man) the large wedge-shaped bone, consisting of five fused vertebrae, in the lower part of the back **2** the corresponding part in some other vertebrates [C18 from Latin *os sacrum* holy bone, because it was used in sacrifices, from *sacer* holy]

sad (sæd) *adj* **sadder**, **saddest** **1** feeling sorrow; unhappy **2** causing, suggestive, or expressive of such feelings: *a sad story* **3** unfortunate; unsatisfactory; shabby; deplorable: *her clothes were in a sad state* **4** *Brit informal* ludicrously contemptible; pathetic: *he's a sad, boring little wimp* **5** (of pastry, cakes, etc) not having risen fully; heavy **6** (of a colour) lacking brightness; dull or dark **7** *archaic* serious; grave ▷ *vb* **8** *NZ* to express sadness or displeasure strongly [Old English *sæd* weary; related to Old Norse *sathr*, Gothic *saths*, Latin *satur, satis* enough] > ˈsadly *adv* ˈsadness *n*

SAD *abbreviation for* **seasonal affective disorder**

sad case *n informal* a person considered to be ludicrously contemptible or pathetic

sadden (ˈsædən) *vb* to make or become sad

saddle (ˈsædəl) *n* **1** a seat for a rider, usually made of leather, placed on a horse's back and secured with a girth under the belly **2** a similar seat on a bicycle, tractor, etc, made of leather or steel **3** a back pad forming part of the harness of a packhorse **4** anything that resembles a saddle in shape, position, or function **5** a cut of meat, esp mutton, consisting of part of the backbone and both loins **6** the part of a horse or similar animal on which a saddle is placed **7** the part of the back of a domestic chicken that is nearest to the tail **8** *civil engineering* a block on top of one of the towers of a suspension bridge that acts as a bearing surface over which the cables or chains pass **9** *engineering* the carriage that slides on the bed of a lathe and supports the slide rest, tool post, or turret **10** the nontechnical name for **clitellum 11** another name for **col** (sense 1) **12** a raised piece of wood or metal for covering a doorsill **13** **in the saddle** in a position of control ▷ *vb* **14** (sometimes foll by *up*) to put a saddle on (a horse) **15** (*intr*) to mount into the saddle **16** (*tr*) to burden; charge: *I didn't ask to be saddled with this job* [Old English *sadol, sædel*; related to Old Norse *sothull*, Old High German *satul*] > ˈsaddleless *adj* ˈsaddle-ˌlike *adj*

saddleback (ˈsædəlˌbæk) *n* **1** a marking resembling a saddle on the backs of various animals **2** a breed of black pig with a white band across its back **3** a rare bird of New Zealand,

Philesturnus carunculatus, having a chestnut-coloured saddle-shaped marking across its back and wings **4** another name for **saddle roof 5** another name for **col** (sense 1)

saddle-backed *adj* **1** having the back curved in shape or concave like a saddle **2** having a saddleback

saddlebag (ˈsædəlˌbæg) *n* **1** a pouch or small bag attached to the saddle of a horse, bicycle, etc **2** (*plural*) *informal* rolls of fat protruding from the sides of a person's thighs

saddlebill (ˈsædəlˌbɪl) *n* a large black-and-white stork, *Ephippiorhynchus senegalensis*, of tropical Africa, having a heavy red bill with a black band around the middle and a yellow patch at the base. Also called: **jabiru** [C19 (as *saddle-bill stork*): so called because of the appearance of its bill]

saddle block *n surgery* a type of spinal anaesthesia producing sensory loss in the buttocks, inner sides of the thighs, and perineum

saddlebow (ˈsædəlˌbəʊ) *n* the pommel of a saddle

saddlecloth (ˈsædəlˌklɒθ) *n* a light cloth put under a horse's saddle, so as to prevent rubbing

saddle gall *n vet science* a raw area of skin, with loss of hair, on the back or behind the elbow of a horse caused by uneven pressure by the saddle or girth

saddle horse *n* a lightweight horse kept for riding only. Compare **carthorse** Also called: **saddler**

saddler (ˈsædlə) *n* a person who makes, deals in, or repairs saddles and other leather equipment for horses

saddle roof *n* a roof that has a ridge and two gables. Also called: **saddleback**

saddlery (ˈsædlərɪ) *n*, *pl* -**dleries 1** saddles, harness, and other leather equipment for horses collectively **2** the business, work, or place of work of a saddler

saddle soap *n* a soft soap containing neat's-foot oil used to preserve and clean leather

saddle-sore *adj* **1** sore after riding a horse **2** (of a horse or rider) having sores caused by the chafing of the saddle ▷ *n* **saddle sore 3** such a sore

saddle stitching *n* a method of binding in which the sections of a publication are inserted inside each other and secured through the middle fold with thread, or wire staples

saddletree (ˈsædəlˌtriː) *n* the frame of a saddle

saddo (ˈsædəʊ) *n*, *pl* -**dos** or -**does** *Brit slang* a socially inadequate or pathetic person [C20 from SAD (sense 4) + -O]

Sadducee (ˈsædjʊˌsiː) *n Judaism* a member of an ancient Jewish sect that was opposed to the Pharisees, denying the resurrection of the dead, the existence of angels, and the validity of oral tradition [Old English *saddūcēas*, via Latin and Greek from Late Hebrew *ṣāddûqî*, probably from *Sadoq* Zadok, high priest and supposed founder of the sect] > ˌSadduˈcean *adj* ˈSadduˌceeism *n*

sadhana (ˈsɑːdʌnə) *n Hinduism* one of a number of spiritual practices or disciplines which lead to perfection, these being contemplation, asceticism, worship of a god, and correct living [from Sanskrit: effective]

sadhe, sade or **tsade** (ˈsɑːdiː, ˈtsɑːdiː; *Hebrew* ˈtsɑːdiː) *n* the 18th letter in the Hebrew alphabet (צ or, at the end of a word ץ), transliterated as *s* or *ts* and pronounced more or less like English *s* or *ts* with pharyngeal articulation

sadhu or **saddhu** (ˈsɑːduː) *n* a Hindu wandering holy man [Sanskrit, from *sādhu* good]

sadiron (ˈsædˌaɪən) *n* a heavy iron pointed at both ends, for pressing clothes [C19 from SAD (in the obsolete sense: heavy) + IRON]

sadism (ˈseɪdɪzəm, ˈsæ-) *n* the gaining of pleasure or sexual gratification from the infliction of pain and mental suffering on another person. See also **algolagnia** Compare **masochism** [C19 from French, named after Comte Donatien Alphonse François de Sade, known as the *Marquis de Sade* (1740–1814), French soldier and writer of works

S

describing sexual perversion] ▷ **'sadist** *n* ▷ **sadistic** (sə'dɪstɪk) *adj* ▷ **sa'distically** *adv*

Sadler's Wells ('sædləz wɛlz) *n* (*functioning as singular*) a theatre in London. It was renovated in 1931 by Lilian Bayliss and became the home of the Sadler's Wells Opera Company and the Sadler's Wells Ballet (now the Royal Ballet) [named after the medicinal *wells* on the site and its owner Thomas *Sadler*, who founded the original theatre on the site]

sado ('sɑːdəʊ) *n* a variant of **chado**

sadomasochism (ˌseɪdəʊ'mæsəˌkɪzəm, ˌsædəʊ-) *n* **1** the combination of sadistic and masochistic elements in one person, characterized by both aggressive and submissive periods in relationships with others **2** sexual practice in which one partner adopts a sadistic role and the other a masochistic one. Abbreviations: **SM, S & M** Compare **sadism, masochism** ▷ ˌsadomaso'chistic *adj*

Sadowa ('sɑːdəʊvə) *n* a village in the Czech Republic, in NE Bohemia: scene of the decisive battle of the Austro-Prussian war (1866) in which the Austrians were defeated by the Prussians. Czech name: **Sadová** ('sadova:)

SADS (sædz) *n acronym for* sudden adult death syndrome: the sudden death of an apparently healthy adult, for which no cause can be found at postmortem [late C20 by analogy with SIDS (sudden infant death syndrome)]

sad sack *n US slang* an inept person who makes mistakes despite good intentions [C20 from a cartoon character created by G Baker, US cartoonist]

sae (se) *adv* a Scot word for **so¹** (sense 1)

SAE (in the US) *abbreviation for* Society of Automotive Engineers

s.a.e. *abbreviation for* stamped addressed envelope

Safar *or* **Saphar** (sə'fɑː) *n* the second month of the Muslim year [from Arabic]

safari (sə'fɑːrɪ) *n, pl* -**ris 1** an overland journey or hunting expedition, esp in Africa **2** the people, animals, etc, that go on the expedition [C19 from Swahili: journey, from Arabic *safarīya*, from *safara* to travel]

safari jacket *n* another name for **bush jacket**

safari park *n* an enclosed park in which lions and other wild animals are kept uncaged in the open and can be viewed by the public from cars, etc

safari suit *n* an outfit made of tough cotton, denim, etc, consisting of a bush jacket with matching trousers, shorts, or skirt

safe (seɪf) *adj* **1** affording security or protection from harm: *a safe place* **2** (*postpositive*) free from danger: *you'll be safe here* **3** secure from risk; certain; sound: *a safe investment; a safe bet* **4** worthy of trust; prudent: *a safe companion* **5** tending to avoid controversy or risk: *a safe player* **6** unable to do harm; not dangerous: *a criminal safe behind bars; water safe to drink* **7** *Brit informal* excellent **8 on the safe side** as a precaution ▷ *adv* **9** in a safe condition: *the children are safe in bed now* **10** **play safe** to act in a way least likely to cause danger, controversy, or defeat ▷ *n* **11** a strong container, usually of metal and provided with a secure lock, for storing money or valuables **12** a small ventilated cupboard-like container for storing food **13** *US and Canadian* a slang word for **condom** [C13 from Old French *salf*, from Latin *salvus*; related to Latin *salus* safety] ▷ **'safely** *adv* ▷ **'safeness** *n*

safe-blower *n* a person who uses explosives to open safes and rob them

safe-breaker *n* a person who breaks open and robs safes. Also called: **safe-cracker**

safe-conduct *n* **1** a document giving official permission to travel through a region, esp in time of war **2** the protection afforded by such a document ▷ *vb* (*tr*) **3** to conduct (a person) in safety **4** to give a safe-conduct to

safe-deposit *or* **safety-deposit** *n* **a** a place or building with facilities for the safe storage of money or valuables **b** (*as modifier*): *a safe-deposit box*

safeguard ('seɪfˌgɑːd) *n* **1** a person or thing that ensures protection against danger, damage, injury, etc **2** a document authorizing safe-conduct ▷ *vb* **3** (*tr*) to defend or protect

safe house *n* a place used secretly by undercover agents, terrorists, etc, as a meeting place or refuge

safekeeping ('seɪf'kiːpɪŋ) *n* the act of keeping or state of being kept in safety

safelight ('seɪfˌlaɪt) *n photog* a light that can be used in a room in which photographic material is handled, transmitting only those colours to which a particular type of film, plate, or paper is relatively insensitive

safe period *n informal* the period during the menstrual cycle when conception is considered least likely to occur. See also **rhythm method**

safe seat *n* a Parliamentary seat that at an election is sure to be held by the same party as held it before

safe sex *or* **safer sex** *n* sexual intercourse using physical protection, such as a condom, or nonpenetrative methods to prevent the spread of such diseases as AIDS

safe surfing *n* the practice of using security measures to protect one's computer while surfing the internet

safety ('seɪftɪ) *n, pl* -**ties 1** the quality of being safe **2** freedom from danger or risk of injury **3** a contrivance or device designed to prevent injury **4** *American football* **a** Also called: **safetyman** either of two players who defend the area furthest back in the field **b** a play in which the offensive team causes the ball to cross its own goal line and then grounds the ball behind that line, scoring two points for the opposing team. Compare **touchback**

safety belt *n* **1** another name for **seat belt 2** a belt or strap worn by a person working at a great height and attached to a fixed object to prevent him from falling

safety catch *n* a device to prevent the accidental operation of a mechanism, eg in a firearm or lift

safety chain *n* a chain on the fastening of a bracelet, watch, etc, to ensure that it cannot open enough to fall off accidentally. Also called: **guard**

safety curtain *n* a curtain made of fireproof material that can be lowered to separate the auditorium and stage in a theatre to prevent the spread of a fire

safety factor *n* another name for **factor of safety**

safety film *n* photographic film consisting of a nonflammable cellulose acetate or polyester base

safety fuse *n* **1** a slow-burning fuse for igniting detonators from a distance **2** an electrical fuse that protects a circuit from overloading

safety glass *n* glass made by sandwiching a layer of plastic or resin between two sheets of glass so that if broken the fragments will not shatter

Safety Islands *pl n* a group of three small French islands in the Atlantic, off the coast of French Guiana. French name: **Îles du Salut**

safety lamp *n* an oil-burning miner's lamp in which the flame is surrounded by a metal gauze to prevent it from igniting combustible gas. Also called: **Davy lamp**

safety match *n* a match that will light only when struck against a specially prepared surface

safety net *n* **1** a net used in a circus to catch high-wire and trapeze artistes if they fall **2** any means of protection from hardship or loss, such as insurance

safety pin *n* **1** a spring wire clasp with a covering catch, made so as to shield the point when closed and to prevent accidental unfastening **2** another word for **pin** (sense 9)

safety razor *n* a razor with a guard or guards fitted close to the cutting edge or edges so that deep cuts are prevented and the risk of accidental cuts reduced

safety touch *n Canadian football* a two-point play

safety valve *n* **1** a valve in a pressure vessel that allows fluid to escape when a predetermined level of pressure has been reached **2** a harmless outlet for emotion, energy, tension etc

saffian ('sæfɪən) *n* leather tanned with sumach and usually dyed a bright colour [C16 via Russian and Turkish from Persian *sakhtiyān* goatskin, from *sakht* hard]

safflower ('sæflaʊə) *n* **1** a thistle-like Eurasian annual plant, *Carthamus tinctorius*, having large heads of orange-yellow flowers and yielding a dye and an oil used in paints, medicines, etc: family *Asteraceae* (composites) **2** a red dye used for cotton and for colouring foods and cosmetics, or a drug obtained from the florets of this plant ▷ Also called: **false saffron** [C16 via Dutch *saffloer* or German *safflor* from Old French *saffleur*, from Early Italian *saffiore*, of uncertain origin. Influenced by SAFFRON, FLOWER]

saffron ('sæfrən) *n* **1** an Old World crocus, *Crocus sativus*, having purple or white flowers with orange stigmas **2** the dried stigmas of this plant, used to flavour or colour food **3** **meadow saffron** another name for **autumn crocus 4** **false saffron** another name for **safflower 5 a** an orange to orange-yellow colour **b** (*as adjective*): *a saffron dress* [C13 from Old French *safran*, from Medieval Latin *safranum*, from Arabic *za'farān*]

Safi (French safi) *n* a port in W Morocco, 170 km (105 miles) northwest of Marrakech, to which it is the nearest port. Pop: 470 000 (2003)

Safid Rud (sæ'fiːd 'ruːd) *n* a river in N Iran, flowing northeast to a delta on the Caspian Sea. Length: about 785 km (490 miles)

S.Afr. *abbreviation for* South Africa(n)

safranine *or* **safranin** ('sæfrənɪn, -ˌniːn) *n* any of a class of azine dyes, used for textiles and biological stains [C19 from French *safran* SAFFRON + -INE²]

safrole ('sæfrəʊl) *n* a colourless or yellowish oily water-insoluble liquid present in sassafras and camphor oils and used in soaps and perfumes. Formula: $C_{10}H_{10}O_2$ [C19 from (SAS)SAFR(AS) + -OLE¹]

saft (sæft) *adj* a Scot word for **soft**

sag (sæg) *vb* (*mainly intr*) **sags**, **sagging**, **sagged 1** (*also tr*) to sink or cause to sink in parts, as under weight or pressure: *the bed sags in the middle* **2** to fall in value: *prices sagged to a new low* **3** to hang unevenly; droop **4** (of courage, spirits, etc) to weaken; flag ▷ *n* **5** the act or an instance of sagging: *a sag in profits* **6** *nautical* the extent to which a vessel's keel sags at the centre. Compare **hog** (sense 6), **hogged 7 a** a marshy depression in an area of glacial till, chiefly in the US Middle West **b** (*as modifier*): *sag and swell topography* [C15 from Scandinavian; compare Swedish *sacka*, Dutch *zakken*, Norwegian dialect *sakka* to subside, Danish *sakke* to lag behind]

saga ('sɑːgə) *n* **1** any of several medieval prose narratives written in Iceland and recounting the exploits of a hero or a family **2** any similar heroic narrative **3** Also called: **saga novel** a series of novels about several generations or members of a family **4** any other artistic production said to resemble a saga **5** *informal* a series of events or a story stretching over a long period [C18 from Old Norse: a narrative; related to Old English *secgan* to SAY¹]

sagacious (sə'geɪʃəs) *adj* **1** having or showing sagacity; wise **2** *obsolete* (of hounds) having an acute sense of smell [C17 from Latin *sagāx*, from *sāgīre* to be astute] ▷ **sa'gaciously** *adv* ▷ **sa'gaciousness** *n*

sagacity (sə'gæsɪtɪ) *n* foresight, discernment, or keen perception; ability to make good judgments

sagamore ('sægəˌmɔː) *n* (among some North American Indians) a chief or eminent man. Also called: **sachem** [C17 from Abnaki *sāgimau*, literally: he overcomes]

Sagarmatha ('sɑːgɑːˌmɑːθə) *n* the Nepalese name for (Mount) **Everest**

sag bag *n* another name for **bean bag** (sense 2)

sage¹ (seɪdʒ) *n* **1** a man revered for his profound wisdom ▷ *adj* **2** profoundly wise or prudent **3** *obsolete* solemn [C13 from Old French, from Latin *sapere* to be sensible; see SAPIENT] > **'sagely** *adv* > **'sageness** *n*

sage² (seɪdʒ) *n* **1** a perennial Mediterranean plant, *Salvia officinalis*, having grey-green leaves and purple, blue, or white flowers: family *Lamiaceae* (labiates) **2** the leaves of this plant, used in cooking for flavouring **3** short for **sagebrush** [C14 from Old French *saulge*, from Latin *salvia*, from *salvus* safe, in good health (from the curative properties attributed to the plant)]

sagebrush ('seɪdʒ,brʌʃ) *n* any of several aromatic plants of the genus *Artemisia*, esp *A. tridentata*, a shrub of W North America, having silver-green leaves and large clusters of small white flowers: family *Asteraceae* (composites)

sage Derby *n* See Derby² (sense 4)

sage grouse *n* a large North American grouse, *Centrocercus urophasianus*, the males of which perform elaborate courtship displays [C19 so named because it lives among, and eats, SAGEBRUSH]

saggar *or* **sagger** ('sægə) *n* a clay box in which fragile ceramic wares are placed for protection during firing [C17 perhaps alteration of SAFEGUARD]

sagging moment *n* a bending moment that produces concave bending at the middle of a simple supported beam. Also called: **positive bending moment**

Saghalien (sə'gɑ:ljən) *n* a variant of **Sakhalin**

Sagitta (sə'gɪtə) *n, Latin genitive* **Sagittae** (sə'gɪti:) a small constellation in the N hemisphere lying between Cygnus and Aquila and crossed by the Milky Way [C16 from Latin, literally: an arrow]

sagittal ('sædʒɪtəl) *adj* **1** resembling an arrow; straight **2** of or relating to the sagittal suture **3** situated in a plane parallel to the sagittal suture > **'sagittally** *adv*

sagittal suture *n* a serrated line on the top of the skull that marks the junction of the two parietal bones

Sagittarius (,sædʒɪ'tɛərɪəs) *n, Latin genitive* **Sagittarii** (,sædʒɪ'tɛərɪ,aɪ) **1** *astronomy* a large conspicuous zodiacal constellation in the S hemisphere lying between Scorpius and Capricornus on the ecliptic and crossed by the Milky Way and containing the galactic centre **2** Also called: **the Archer** *astrology* **a** the ninth sign of the zodiac, symbol ♐, having a mutable fire classification and ruled by the planet Jupiter. The sun is in this sign between Nov 22 and Dec 21 **b** a person born when the sun is in this sign ▷ *adj* **3** *astrology* born under or characteristic of Sagittarius ▷ Also (for senses 2b, 3): **Sagittarian** (,sædʒɪ'tɛərɪən) [C14 from Latin: an archer, from *sagitta* an arrow]

sagittate ('sædʒɪ,teɪt) *or* **sagittiform** (sə'dʒɪtɪ,fɔ:m, 'sædʒ-) *adj* (esp of leaves) shaped like the head of an arrow [C18 from New Latin *sagittātus*, from Latin *sagitta* arrow]

sago ('seɪgəʊ) *n* a starchy cereal obtained from the powdered pith of a sago palm, used for puddings and as a thickening agent [C16 from Malay *sāgū*]

sago grass *n* *Austral* a tall tough grass, *Paspalidum globoideum*, grown as forage for cattle

sago palm *n* **1** any of various tropical Asian palm trees, esp any of the genera *Metroxylon*, *Arenga*, and *Caryota*, the trunks of which yield sago **2** any of several palmlike cycads that yield sago, esp *Cycas revoluta*

saguaro (sə'gwɑ:rəʊ, sə'wɑ:-) *or* **sahuaro** (sə'wɑ:rəʊ) *n, pl* **-ros** a giant cactus, *Carnegiea gigantea*, of desert regions of Arizona, S California, and Mexico, having white nocturnal flowers and edible red pulpy fruits [Mexican Spanish, variant of *sahuaro*, an Indian name]

Saguenay (,sægə'neɪ) *n* a river in SE Canada in S Quebec, rising as the Péribonca River on the central plateau and flowing south, then east to the St Lawrence. Length: 764 km (475 miles)

Sagunto (*Spanish* sa'ɣunto) *n* an industrial town in E Spain, near Valencia: allied to Rome and made a heroic resistance to the Carthaginian attack led by Hannibal (219–218 BC). Pop: 58 287 (2003 est). Ancient name: **Saguntum** (sə'gʌntəm)

Sahaptin (sɑ:'hæptɪn), **Sahaptan** (sɑ:'hæptən) *or* **Sahaptian** (sɑ:'hæptɪən) *n* **1** (*pl* **-tins, -tans, -tians** *or* **-tin, -tan, -tian**) a member of a North American Indian people of Oregon and Washington, including the Nez Percé **2** the language of this people ▷ Also: **Shahaptin** (ʃə'hæptɪn)

Sahara (sə'hɑ:rə) *n* a desert in N Africa, extending from the Atlantic to the Red Sea and from the Mediterranean to central Mali, Niger, Chad, and the Sudan: the largest desert in the world, occupying over a quarter of Africa; rises to over 3300 m (11 000 ft) in the central mountain system of the Ahaggar and Tibesti massifs; large reserves of iron ore, oil, and natural gas. Area: 9 100 000 sq km (3 500 000 sq miles). Average annual rainfall: less than 254 mm (10 in). Highest recorded temperature: 58°C (136.4°F)

Saharan (sə'hɑ:rən) *n* **1** a group of languages spoken in parts of Chad and adjacent countries, now generally regarded as forming a branch of the Nilo-Saharan family ▷ *adj* **2** relating to or belonging to this group of languages **3** of or relating to the Sahara

sahib (sɑ:hɪb) *or* **saheb** (sɑ:hɛb) *n* (in India) a form of address or title placed after a man's name or designation, used as a mark of respect [C17 from Urdu, from Arabic *çāhib*, literally: friend]

Sahitya Akademi (sɑ:'hɪtjə ə'kɑ:dəmɪ) *n* a body set up by the Government of India for cultivating literature in Indian languages and in English

saice (saɪs) *n* a variant spelling of **syce**

said¹ (sɛd) *adj* **1** (*prenominal*) (in contracts, pleadings, etc) named or mentioned previously; aforesaid ▷ *vb* **2** the past tense and past participle of **say**

said² ('sɑ:ɪd) *n* a variant of **sayyid**

Saida ('sɑ:ɪdə) *n* a port in SW Lebanon, on the Mediterranean: on the site of ancient Sidon; terminal of the Trans-Arabian pipeline from Saudi Arabia. Pop: 150 000 (2005 est)

saiga (saɪgə) *n* either of two antelopes, *Saiga tatarica* or *S. mongolica*, of the plains of central Asia, having an enlarged slightly elongated nose [C19 from Russian]

Saigon (saɪ'gɒn) *n* the former name (until 1976) of **Ho Chi Minh City**

sail (seɪl) *n* **1** an area of fabric, usually Terylene or nylon (formerly canvas), with fittings for holding it in any suitable position to catch the wind, used for propelling certain kinds of vessels, esp over water **2** a voyage on such a vessel: *a sail down the river* **3** a vessel with sails or such vessels collectively: *to travel by sail; we raised seven sail in the northeast* **4** a ship's sails collectively **5** something resembling a sail in shape, position, or function, such as the part of a windmill that is turned by the wind or the part of a Portuguese man-of-war that projects above the water **6** the conning tower of a submarine **7** **in sail** having the sail set **8** **make sail** **a** to run up the sail or to run up more sail **b** to begin a voyage **9** **set sail** **a** to embark on a voyage by ship **b** to hoist sail **10** **under sail** **a** with sail hoisted **b** under way ▷ *vb* (*mainly intr*) **11** to travel in a boat or ship: *we sailed to Le Havre* **12** to begin a voyage; set sail: *we sail at 5 o'clock* **13** (of a vessel) to move over the water: *the liner is sailing to the Caribbean* **14** (*tr*) to manoeuvre or navigate a vessel: *he sailed the schooner up the channel* **15** (*tr*) to sail over: *she sailed the Atlantic single-handed* **16** (often foll by *over, through*, etc) to move fast or effortlessly: *we sailed through customs; the ball sailed over the fence* **17** to move along smoothly; glide **18** (often foll by *in* or *into*) *informal* **a** to begin (something) with vigour **b** to make an attack (on) violently with words or physical force [Old English *segl*; related to Old Frisian *seil*, Old Norse *segl*, German *Segel*] > **'sailable** *adj* > **'sailless** *adj*

sailboard ('seɪl,bɔ:d) *n* the craft used for windsurfing, consisting of a moulded board like a surfboard, to which a mast bearing a single sail is attached by a swivel joint

sailboarding ('seɪl,bɔ:dɪŋ) *n* another name for **windsurfing**

sailcloth ('seɪl,klɒθ) *n* **1** any of various fabrics from which sails are made **2** a lighter cloth used for clothing, etc

sailer ('seɪlə) *n* a vessel, esp one equipped with sails, with specified sailing characteristics: *a good sailer*

sailfish ('seɪl,fɪʃ) *n, pl* **-fish** *or* **-fishes** **1** any of several large scombroid game fishes of the genus *Istiophorus*, such as *I. albicans* (**Atlantic sailfish**), of warm and tropical seas: family *Istiophoridae*. They have an elongated upper jaw and a long sail-like dorsal fin **2** another name for **basking shark**

sailing ('seɪlɪŋ) *n* **1** the practice, art, or technique of sailing a vessel **2** a method of navigating a vessel: *rhumb-line sailing* **3** an instance of a vessel's leaving a port: *scheduled for a midnight sailing*

sailing boat *or esp US and Canadian* **sailboat** ('seɪl,bəʊt) *n* a boat propelled chiefly by sail

sailing ship *n* a large sailing vessel

sailor ('seɪlə) *n* **1** any member of a ship's crew, esp one below the rank of officer **2** a person who sails, esp with reference to the likelihood of his becoming seasick: *a good sailor* **3** short for **sailor hat** *or* sailor suit > **'sailorly** *adj*

sailor hat *n* a hat with a flat round crown and fairly broad brim that is rolled upwards

sailor's-choice *n* any of various small percoid fishes of American coastal regions of the Atlantic, esp the grunt *Haemulon parra* and the pinfish

sailor suit *n* a child's suit, usually navy and white, with a collar that is squared off at the back like a sailor's

sailplane ('seɪl,pleɪn) *n* a high-performance glider

sain (seɪn) *vb* (*tr*) *archaic* to make the sign of the cross over so as to bless or protect from evil or sin [Old English *segnian*, from Latin *signare* to SIGN (with the cross)]

sainfoin ('sænfɔɪn) *n* a Eurasian perennial leguminous plant, *Onobrychis viciifolia*, widely grown as a forage crop, having pale pink flowers and curved pods [C17 from French, from Medieval Latin *sānum faenum* wholesome hay, referring to its former use as a medicine]

saint (seɪnt; *unstressed* sənt) *n* **1** a person who after death is formally recognized by a Christian Church, esp the Roman Catholic Church, as having attained, through holy deeds or behaviour, a specially exalted place in heaven and the right to veneration **2** a person of exceptional holiness or goodness **3** (*plural*) *Bible* the collective body of those who are righteous in God's sight ▷ *vb* **4** (*tr*) to canonize; recognize formally as a saint [C12 from Old French, from Latin *sanctus* holy, from *sancīre* to hallow] > **'saintdom** *n* > **'saintless** *adj* > **'saintlike** *adj*

Saint Agnes's Eve *n, usually abbreviated to* **St Agnes's Eve** the night of Jan 20, when according to tradition a woman can discover the identity of her future husband by performing certain rites

Saint Albans ('ɔ:lbənz) *n, usually abbreviated to* **St Albans** a city in SE England, in W Hertfordshire: founded in 948 AD around the Benedictine abbey first built in Saxon times on the site of the martyrdom (about 303 AD) of St Alban; present abbey built in 1077; Roman ruins. Pop: 82 429 (2001). Latin name: **Verulamium**

Saint Andrews *n, usually abbreviated to* **St Andrews** a city in E Scotland, in Fife on the North Sea: the oldest university in Scotland (1411); famous golf links. Pop: 14 209 (2001)

Saint Andrew's Cross *n, usually abbreviated to* **St Andrew's Cross 1** a diagonal cross with equal arms **2** a white diagonal cross on a blue ground [C18 so called because Saint Andrew, one of the twelve apostles of Jesus, is reputed to have been crucified on a cross of this shape]

S

Saint Anthony's Cross n, *usually abbreviated to* St Anthony's Cross another name for **tau cross**

Saint Anthony's fire n, *usually abbreviated to* St Anthony's fire *pathol* another name for **ergotism** or **erysipelas** [c16 so named because praying to *St Anthony* was believed to effect a cure]

Saint Augustine ('ɔːgəsˌtiːn) n, *usually abbreviated to* St Augustine a resort in NE Florida, on the Intracoastal Waterway: the oldest town in North America (1565); the northernmost outpost of the Spanish colonial empire for over 200 years. Pop: 11 915 (2003 est)

Saint Austell ('ɔːstəl) n, *usually abbreviated to* St Austell a town in SW England, in S Cornwall on **St Austell Bay** (an inlet of the English Channel): centre for the now-declining china clay industry; the Eden Project, a rainforest environment in the world's largest greenhouse, is nearby; administratively part of St Austell with Fowey 1968-74. Pop (with Fowey): 22 658 (2001)

Saint Bartholomew's Day Massacre n, *usually abbreviated to* St Bartholomew's Day Massacre the murder of Huguenots in Paris that began on Aug 24, 1572 on the orders of Charles IX, acting under the influence of his mother Catherine de' Medici

Saint Bernard n, *usually abbreviated to* St Bernard a large breed of dog with a dense red-and-white coat, formerly used as a rescue dog in mountainous areas [c19 so called because they were kept by the monks of the hospice at the Great SAINT BERNARD PASS]

Saint Bernard Pass n, *usually abbreviated to* St Bernard Pass either of two passes over the Alps: the **Great St Bernard Pass** 2472 m (8110 ft) high, east of Mont Blanc between Italy and Switzerland, or the **Little St Bernard Pass** 2157 m (7077 ft) high, south of Mont Blanc between Italy and France

Saint-Brieuc (*French* sɛ̃briø) n, *usually abbreviated to* St-Brieuc a market town in NW France, near the N coast of Brittany. Pop: 46 087 (1999)

Saint Catharines n, *usually abbreviated to* St Catharines an industrial city in S central Canada, in S Ontario on the Welland Canal. Pop: 129 170 (2001)

Saint Christopher n, *usually abbreviated to* St Christopher another name for **Saint Kitts**

Saint Christopher-Nevis n, *usually abbreviated to* St Christopher-Nevis the official name of **Saint Kitts-Nevis**

Saint Clair (klɛə) n, *usually abbreviated to* St Clair **Lake** a lake between SE Michigan and Ontario: linked with Lake Huron by the **St Clair River** and with Lake Erie by the Detroit River. Area: 1191 sq km (460 sq miles)

Saint-Cloud (*French* sɛ̃klu) n, *usually abbreviated to* St-Cloud a residential suburb of Paris: former royal palace; Sèvres porcelain factory. Pop: 28 157 (1999)

Saint Croix (krɔɪ) n, *usually abbreviated to* St Croix an island in the Caribbean, the largest of the Virgin Islands of the US: purchased from Denmark by the US in 1917. Chief town: Christiansted. Pop: 53 234 (2000). Area: 207 sq km (80 sq miles). Also called: Santa Cruz ('sæntə 'kruːz)

Saint Croix River n, *usually abbreviated to* St Croix River a river on the border between the northeast US and SE Canada, flowing from the Chiputneticook Lakes to Passamaquoddy Bay, forming the border between Maine, US, and New Brunswick, Canada. Length: 121 km (75 miles)

Saint David's n, *usually abbreviated to* St David's a town in SW Wales, in Pembrokeshire: its cathedral was a place of pilgrimage in medieval times. Pop: 1627 (2001)

Saint-Denis (*French* sɛ̃dni) n, *usually abbreviated to* St-Denis **1** a town in N France, on the Seine: 12th-century Gothic abbey church, containing the tombs of many French monarchs; an industrial suburb of Paris. Pop: 85 832 (1999) **2** the capital of the French overseas region of Réunion, a port on the N coast. Pop: 131 557 (1999)

sainted ('seɪntɪd) adj **1** canonized **2** like a saint in character or nature **3** hallowed or holy

Sainte Foy (seɪnt 'fɔɪ, sənt) n, *usually abbreviated to* Ste Foy a SW suburb of Quebec, on the St Lawrence River. Pop: 72 547 (2001)

Saint Elias Mountains pl n, *usually abbreviated to* St Elias Mountains a mountain range between SE Alaska and the SW Yukon, Canada. Highest peak: Mount Logan, 5959 m (19 550 ft)

Saint Elmo's fire ('ɛlməʊz) n, *usually abbreviated to* St Elmo's fire (not in technical usage) a luminous region that sometimes appears around church spires, the masts of ships, etc. It is a corona discharge in the air caused by atmospheric electricity. Also called: corposant [c16 so called because it was associated with *Saint Elmo* (a corruption, via *Sant'Ermo*, of *Saint Erasmus*, died 303) the patron saint of Mediterranean sailors]

Saint-Émilion (*French* sɛ̃temiljɔ̃) n a full-bodied red wine, similar to a Burgundy, produced around the town of Saint-Émilion in Bordeaux

Saint-Étienne (*French* sɛ̃tetjɛn) n, *usually abbreviated to* St-Étienne a town in E central France: a major producer of textiles and armaments. Pop: 180 210 (1999)

Saint Gall (*French* sɛ̃ gal) n, *usually abbreviated to* St Gall **1** a canton of NE Switzerland. Capital: St Gall. Pop: 455 200 (2002 est). Area: 2012 sq km (777 sq miles) **2** a town in NE Switzerland, capital of St Gall canton: an important educational centre in the Middle Ages. Pop: 72 626 (2000). German name: Sankt Gallen (zaŋkt 'galən)

Saint George's n, *usually abbreviated to* St George's the capital of Grenada, a port in the southwest. Pop: 3908 (2001)

Saint George's Channel n, *usually abbreviated to* St George's Channel a strait between Wales and Ireland, linking the Irish Sea with the Atlantic. Length: about 160 km (100 miles). Width: up to 145 km (90 miles)

Saint George's Cross n, *usually abbreviated to* St George's Cross a red Greek cross on a white background

Saint George's mushroom n an edible whitish basidiomycetous fungus, *Tricholoma gambosum*, with a floury smell [so named because it appears earlier than most fungi, around St George's day (23 April)]

Saint Gotthard ('gʊtəd) n, *usually abbreviated to* St Gotthard **1** a range of the Lepontine Alps in SE central Switzerland **2** a pass over the St Gotthard mountains, in S Switzerland. Height: 2114 m (6935 ft)

Saint Helena (ˌsɛntɪ'liːnə) n, *usually abbreviated to* St Helena a volcanic island in the SE Atlantic, forming a UK Overseas Territory with its dependencies Tristan da Cunha and Ascension, and the uninhabited Gough, Inaccessible, and Nightingale Islands: discovered by the Portuguese in 1502 and annexed by England in 1651; scene of Napoleon's exile and death. Capital: Jamestown. Pop: 5644 (2003 est). Area: 122 sq km (47 sq miles)

Saint Helens n, *usually abbreviated to* St Helens **1** a town in NW England, in St Helens unitary authority, Merseyside: glass industry. Pop: 102 629 (2001) **2** a unitary authority in NW England, in Merseyside. Pop: 176 700 (2003 est). Area: 130 sq km (50 sq miles) **3** a volcanic peak in S Washington state; it erupted in 1980 after lying dormant from 1857

Saint Helier ('hɛlɪə) n, *usually abbreviated to* St Helier a market town and resort in the Channel Islands, on the S coast of Jersey. Pop: 28 310 (2001)

sainthood ('seɪnthʊd) n **1** the state or character of being a saint **2** saints collectively

Saint James's Palace n, *usually abbreviated to* St James's Palace a palace in Pall Mall, London: a residence of British monarchs from 1697 to 1837

Saint John n, *in most cases usually abbreviated to* St John **1** a port in E Canada, at the mouth of the St John River: the largest city in New Brunswick; very often not abbreviated to 'St'. Pop: 90 762

(2001) **2** an island in the Caribbean, in the Virgin Islands of the US. Pop: 4197 (2000). Area: 49 sq km (19 sq miles) **3** Lake a lake in Canada, in S Quebec: drained by the Saguenay River. Area: 971 sq km (375 sq miles) **4** a river in E North America, rising in Maine, US, and flowing northeast to New Brunswick, Canada, then generally southeast to the Bay of Fundy. Length: 673 km (418 miles)

Saint John's n, *usually abbreviated to* St John's **1** a port in Canada, capital of Newfoundland and Labrador, on the E coast of the Avalon Peninsula. Pop: 122 709 (2001) **2** the capital of Antigua and Barbuda: a port on the NW coast of the island of Antigua. Pop: 24 226 (2000 est)

Saint John's bread n, *usually abbreviated to* St John's bread another name for **carob** (sense 2) [c16 so called because its beans were thought to be the "locusts" that JOHN THE BAPTIST ate in the desert]

Saint John's wort n, *usually abbreviated to* St John's wort **a** any of numerous shrubs or herbaceous plants of the temperate genus *Hypericum*, such as *H. perforatum*, having yellow flowers and glandular leaves: family Hypericaceae **b** a preparation of this plant often used to treat mild depression. See also **rose of Sharon** (sense 1), **tutsan** [c15 so named because it was traditionally gathered on *Saint John's Eve* (June 23) as a protection against evil spirits]

Saint Kilda ('kɪldə) n, *usually abbreviated to* St Kilda **1** a group of volcanic islands in the Atlantic, in the Outer Hebrides: uninhabited since 1930; bird sanctuary **2** Also called: Hirta the main island of this group

Saint Kitts (kɪts) n, *usually abbreviated to* St Kitts an island in the E Caribbean, in the Leeward Islands: part of the state of St Kitts-Nevis. Capital: Basseterre. Pop: 34 703 (2001). Area: 168 sq km (65 sq miles). Also called: Saint Christopher

Saint Kitts-Nevis n, *usually abbreviated to* St Kitts-Nevis an independent state in the E Caribbean; comprises the two islands of St Kitts and Nevis: with the island of Anguilla formed a colony (1882–1967) and a British associated state (1967–83); Anguilla formally separated from the group in 1983; gained full independence in 1983 as a member of the Commonwealth. Official language: English. Religion: Protestant majority. Currency: E Caribbean dollar. Capital: Basseterre. Pop: 42 000 (2003 est). Area: 262 sq km (101 sq miles)

Saint Laurent (*French* sɛ̃ lɔrɑ̃) n, *usually abbreviated to* St Laurent a W suburb of Montreal, Canada. Pop: 77 391 (2001)

Saint Lawrence n, *usually abbreviated to* St Lawrence **1** a river in SE Canada, flowing northeast from Lake Ontario, forming part of the border between Canada and the US, to the Gulf of St Lawrence: commercially one of the most important rivers in the world as the easternmost link of the St Lawrence Seaway. Length: 1207 km (750 miles). Width at mouth: 145 km (90 miles) **2** Gulf of a deep arm of the Atlantic off the E coast of Canada between Newfoundland and the mainland coasts of Quebec, New Brunswick, and Nova Scotia

Saint Lawrence Seaway n, *usually abbreviated to* St Lawrence Seaway an inland waterway of North America, passing through the Great Lakes, the St Lawrence River, and connecting canals and locks: one of the most important waterways in the world. Length: 3993 km (2480 miles)

Saint Leger ('lɛdʒə) n, *usually abbreviated to* St Leger the an annual horse race run at Doncaster since 1776: one of the classics of the flat-racing season

Saint Leonard ('lɛnəd) n, *usually abbreviated to* St Leonard a N suburb of Montreal, Canada. Pop: 69 604 (2001)

Saint-Lô (*French* sɛ̃lo) n, *usually abbreviated to* St-Lô a market town in NW France: a Calvinist stronghold in the 16th century. Pop: 20 090 (1999)

Saint Louis ('luɪs) n, *usually abbreviated to* St Louis a port in E Missouri, on the Mississippi River near its confluence with the Missouri: the largest city in the state; university; major industrial centre. Pop: 332 223 (2003 est)

Saint-Louis (*French* sɛ̃lwi) *n, usually abbreviated to* St-Louis a port in NW Senegal, on an island at the mouth of the Senegal River: the first French settlement in W Africa (1689); capital of Senegal until 1958. Pop: 183 000 (2005 est)

Saint Lucia ('luːʃə) *n, usually abbreviated to* St Lucia an island state in the Caribbean, in the Windward Islands group of the Lesser Antilles: a volcanic island; gained self-government in 1967 as a British Associated State; attained full independence within the Commonwealth in 1979. Official language: English. Religion: Roman Catholic majority. Currency: E Caribbean dollar. Capital: Castries. Pop: 150 000 (2004 est). Area: 616 sq km (238 sq miles)

Saint Luke's summer *n, usually abbreviated to* St Luke's summer a period of unusually warm weather in the autumn [referring to St Luke's feast-day, Oct 7 in the pre-Gregorian calendar (now Oct 18)]

saintly ('seɪntlɪ) *adj* -lier, -liest like, relating to, or suitable for a saint > 'saintlily *adv* > 'saintliness *n*

Saint Martin *n, usually abbreviated to* St Martin an island in the E Caribbean, in the Leeward Islands: administratively divided since 1648, the north belonging to France (as a dependency of Guadeloupe) and the south belonging to the Netherlands (as part of the Netherlands Antilles); salt industry. Pop: (French) 29 078 (1999); (Dutch) 33 119 (2004 est). Areas: (French) 52 sq km (20 sq miles); (Dutch) 33 sq km (13 sq miles). Dutch name: Sint Maarten

Saint Martin's summer *n, usually abbreviated to* St Martin's summer a period of unusually warm weather in the late autumn, esp early November [referring to St Martin's feast-day, Oct 31 in the pre-Gregorian calendar (now Nov 11)]

Saint-Maur-des-Fossés (*French* sɛ̃mordefose) *n, usually abbreviated to* St-Maur-des-Fossés a town in N France, on the River Marne: a residential suburb of SE Paris. Pop: 73 069 (1999)

Saint-Mihiel (*French* sɛ̃mjel) *n, usually abbreviated to* St-Mihiel a village in NE France, on the River Meuse: site of a battle in World War I, in which the American army launched its first offensive in France

Saint Moritz (məˈrɪts) *n, usually abbreviated to* St Moritz a village in E Switzerland, in Graubünden canton in the Upper Engadine, at an altitude of 1856 m (6089 ft): sports and tourist centre. Pop: 5589 (2000)

Saint-Nazaire (*French* sɛ̃nazɛr) *n, usually abbreviated to* St-Nazaire a port in NW France, at the mouth of the River Loire: German submarine base in World War II; shipbuilding. Pop: 65 874 (1999)

Saint-Ouen (*French* sɛ̃twɛ̃) *n, usually abbreviated to* St-Ouen a town in N France, on the Seine: an industrial suburb of Paris; famous flea market. Pop: 39 722 (1999)

Saint Paul *n, usually abbreviated to* St Paul a port in SE Minnesota, capital of the state, at the head of navigation of the Mississippi: now contiguous with Minneapolis (the Twin Cities). Pop: 280 404 (2003 est)

saintpaulia (sənt'pɔːlɪə) *n* another name for African violet [c20 New Latin, named after Baron W von *Saint Paul*, German soldier (died 1910), who discovered it]

Saint Paul's *n, usually abbreviated to* St Paul's a cathedral in central London, built between 1675 and 1710 to replace an earlier cathedral destroyed during the Great Fire (1666): regarded as Wren's masterpiece

Saint Peter's *n, usually abbreviated to* St Peter's the basilica of the Vatican City, built between 1506 and 1615 to replace an earlier church: the largest church in the world, 188 m (615 ft) long, and chief pilgrimage centre of Europe; designed by many architects, notably Bramante, Raphael, Sangallo,

Michelangelo, and Bernini

Saint Petersburg ('piːtəz,bɜːg) *n, usually abbreviated to* St Petersburg 1 a city and port in Russia, on the Gulf of Finland at the mouth of the Neva River: founded by Peter the Great in 1703 and built on low-lying marshes subject to frequent flooding; capital of Russia from 1712 to 1918; a cultural and educational centre, with a university (1819); a major industrial centre, with engineering, shipbuilding, chemical, textile, and printing industries. Pop: 5 315 000 (2005 est). Former names: Petrograd (1914–24), Leningrad (1924–91) 2 a city and resort in W Florida, on Tampa Bay. Pop: 247 610 (2003 est)

Saint-Pierre (*French* sɛ̃ pjɛr) *n, usually abbreviated to* St-Pierre a town on the coast of the French island of Martinique, destroyed by the eruption of Mont Pelée in 1902 with the loss of about 30 000 lives; later partly rebuilt

Saint Pierre and Miquelon (,mɪkəˈlɒn; *French* miklɔ̃) *n, usually abbreviated to* St Pierre and Miquelon an archipelago in the Atlantic, off the S coast of Newfoundland: an overseas department of France, the only remaining French possession in North America; consists of the islands of St Pierre, with most of the population, and Miquelon, about ten times as large; fishing industries. Capital: St Pierre. Pop: 6000 (2003 est). Area: 242 sq km (94 sq miles)

Saint Pölten ('pɜːltən) *n* See Sankt Pölten

Saint-Quentin (*French* sɛ̃kɑ̃tɛ̃) *n, usually abbreviated to* St-Quentin a town in N France, on the River Somme: textile industry. Pop: 59 066 (1999)

saint's day *n Christianity* a day in the church calendar commemorating a saint

Saint-Simonianism (sənts ɪ'məʊnɪə,nɪzəm) *or* **Saint-Simonism** (sənt'saɪmənɪzəm) *n* the socialist system advocated by the Comte de Saint-Simon (1760–1825), the French social philosopher > Saint-Si'monian *n, adj*

Saint Swithin's Day *n, usually abbreviated to* St Swithin's Day July 15, observed as a Church festival commemorating Saint Swithin. It is popularly supposed that if it rains on this day the rain will persist for the next 40 days

Saint Thomas *n, usually abbreviated to* St Thomas 1 an island in the E Caribbean, in the Virgin Islands of the US. Capital: Charlotte Amalie. Pop: 51 181 (2000). Area: 83 sq km (28 sq miles) 2 the former name (1921–37) of Charlotte Amalie

Saint Valentine's Day *n, usually abbreviated to* St Valentine's Day Feb 14, the day on which valentines are exchanged, originally connected with the pagan festival of Lupercalia

Saint Vincent *n, usually abbreviated to* St Vincent 1 Cape a headland at the SW extremity of Portugal: scene of several important naval battles, notably in 1797, when the British defeated the French and Spanish 2 Gulf a shallow inlet of SE South Australia, to the east of the Yorke Peninsula: salt industry

Saint Vincent and the Grenadines *n, usually abbreviated to* St Vincent and the Grenadines an island state in the Caribbean, in the Windward Islands of the Lesser Antilles: comprises the island of St Vincent and the Northern Grenadines; formerly a British associated state (1969–79); gained full independence in 1979 as a member of the Commonwealth. Official language: English. Religion: Protestant majority. Currency: Caribbean dollar. Capital: Kingstown. Pop: 121 000 (2004 est). Area: 389 sq km (150 sq miles)

Saint Vitus's dance ('vaɪtəsɪz) *n, usually abbreviated to* St Vitus's dance *pathol* a nontechnical name for Sydenham's chorea [c17 so called because sufferers traditionally prayed to *Saint Vitus* (3rd-century child martyr) for relief and were said to be cured by a visit to his shrine]

Saipan (saɪ'pæn) *n* an island in the W Pacific, administrative centre of the US associated territory of the Northern Mariana Islands; captured by the Americans and used as an air base

until the end of World War II. Pop: 62 392 (2000). Area: 180 sq km (70 sq miles)

sair (ser) *adj, adv* a Scot word for sore

Saïs ('seɪɪs) *n* (in ancient Egypt) a city in the W Nile delta; the royal capital of the 24th dynasty (about 730–715 BC) and the 26th dynasty (about 664–525 BC)

Saite ('seɪaɪt) *n* a native or inhabitant of the ancient Egyptian city of Saïs

saith (sɛθ) *vb* (used with *he, she,* or *it*) *archaic* a form of the present tense (indicative mood) of **say**

saithe (seɪθ) *n Brit* another name for **coalfish** [c19 from Old Norse *seithr* coalfish; compare Gaelic *saigh, saighean* coalfish, Irish *saoidhean* young of fish]

Saitic (seɪ'ɪtɪk) *adj* of or relating to the ancient Egyptian city of Saïs or its inhabitants

Saiva ('saɪvə, 'ʃaɪ-) *n* 1 a member of a branch of Hinduism devoted to the worship of Siva, but rejecting the notion of his incarnations ▷ *adj* 2 of or relating to Saivism or Saivites > 'Saivism *n* > 'Saivite *n*

sakai ('sakaɪ) *n* (in Malaysia) 1 a Malaysian aborigine 2 a wild or uncouth person [from Malay]

Sakai (sɑː'kaɪ) *n* a port in S Japan, on S Honshu on Osaka Bay: an industrial satellite of Osaka. Pop: 787 833 (2002 est)

sake[1] (seɪk) *n* 1 benefit or interest (esp in the phrase for (someone's *or* one's own) sake) 2 the purpose of obtaining or achieving (esp in the phrase for the sake of (something)) 3 used in various exclamations of impatience, urgency, etc: *for heaven's sake; for pete's sake* [c13 (in the phrase *for the sake of,* probably from legal usage): from Old English *sacu* lawsuit (hence, a cause); related to Old Norse *sok*, German *Sache* matter]

sake[2], **saké** *or* **saki** ('sækɪ) *n* a Japanese alcoholic drink made from fermented rice [c17 from Japanese]

saker ('seɪkə) *n* a large falcon, *Falco cherrug,* of E Europe and central Asia: used in falconry [c14 *sagre,* from Old French *sacre,* from Arabic *saqr*]

Sakhalin (*Russian* səxa'lin) *or* **Saghalien** *n* an island in the Sea of Okhotsk, off the SE coast of Russia north of Japan: fishing, forestry, and mineral resources (coal and petroleum). Capital: Yuzhno-Sakhalinsk. Pop: 546 500 (2002). Area: 76 000 sq km (29 300 sq miles). Japanese name (1905–24): Karafuto

Sakha Republic (*Russian* 'saxa) *or* **Yakutia** *n* an administrative division in E Russia, in NE Siberia on the Arctic Ocean: the coldest inhabited region of the world; it has rich mineral resources. Capital: Yakutsk. Pop: 948 100 (2002). Area: 3 103 200 sq km (1 197 760 sq miles). Former name: Yakut Republic

saki ('sɑːkɪ) *n* any of several small mostly arboreal New World monkeys of the genera *Pithecia* and *Chiropotes,* having long hair and a long bushy tail [c20 French, from Tupi *saqi*]

Saktas ('sæktəs) *n* a Hindu sect worshipping female goddesses represented by the vulva [c19 from Sanskrit. See SAKTI]

Sakti ('sæktɪ) *or* **Shakti** ('ʃaktɪ) *n Hinduism* 1 the female principle or organ of reproduction and generative power in general 2 this principle manifested in the consorts of the gods, esp Kali [c19 from Sanskrit *sákti* power]

Sakyamuni (,saːkjə'muːnɪ) *n* one of the titles of the Buddha, deriving from the name of Sakya where he was born [Sanskrit, literally: hermit of the Sākya tribe]

sal (sæl) *n* a pharmacological term for **salt** (sense 3) [Latin]

salaam (sə'lɑːm) *n* 1 a Muslim form of salutation consisting of a deep bow with the right palm on the forehead 2 a salutation signifying peace, used chiefly by Muslims ▷ *vb* 3 to make a salaam or salute (someone) with a salaam [c17 from Arabic *salām* peace, from the phrase *assalām 'alaikum* peace be to you]

S

salable ('seɪləbᵊl) *adj* the US spelling of **saleable**

salacious (sə'leɪʃəs) *adj* **1** having an excessive interest in sex **2** (of books, magazines, etc) erotic, bawdy, or lewd [c17 from Latin *salax* fond of leaping, from *salīre* to leap] > sa'laciously *adv* > sa'laciousness *or* salacity (sə'læsɪtɪ) *n*

salad ('sæləd) *n* **1** a dish of raw vegetables, such as lettuce, tomatoes, etc, served as a separate course with cold meat, eggs, etc, or as part of a main course **2** any dish of cold vegetables or fruit: *potato salad; fruit salad* **3** any green vegetable used in such a dish, esp lettuce [c15 from Old French *salade*, from Old Provençal *salada*, from *salar* to season with salt, from Latin *sal* salt]

salad bar *n* a counter in a restaurant or other place where food is sold at which a range of salads is displayed, often for self-service

salad days *pl n* a period of youth and inexperience [allusion to *Antony and Cleopatra* (1.v.73) by William Shakespeare: "my salad days When I was green in judgment, cold in blood"]

salad dressing *n* a sauce for salad, such as oil and vinegar or mayonnaise

salade (sə'lɑːd) *n* another word for **sallet**

salade niçoise (sæ'lɑːd niːˈswɑːz) *n* a cold dish consisting of hard-boiled eggs, anchovy fillets, olives, tomatoes, tuna fish, etc [c20 from French, literally salad of or from *Nice*, S France]

Salado (Spanish saˈlaðo) *n* **1** a river in N Argentina, rising in the Andes as the Juramento and flowing southeast to the Paraná River. Length: 2012 km (1250 miles) **2** a river in W Argentina, rising near the Chilean border as the Desaguadero and flowing south to the Colorado River. Length: about 1365 km (850 miles)

Salamanca (Spanish salaˈmaŋka) *n* a city in W Spain: a leading cultural centre of Europe till the end of the 16th century; market town. Pop: 157 906 (2003 es

salamander ('sælə,mændə) *n* **1** any of various urodele amphibians, such as *Salamandra salamandra* (**European fire salamander**) of central and S Europe (family *Salamandridae*). They are typically terrestrial, have an elongated body, and only return to water to breed **2** *chiefly US and Canadian* any urodele amphibian **3** a mythical reptile supposed to live in fire **4** an elemental fire-inhabiting being **5** any person or thing able to exist in fire or great heat **6** *metallurgy* a residue of metal and slag deposited on the walls of a furnace **7** a portable stove used to dry out a building under construction [c14 from Old French *salamandre*, from Latin *salamandra*, from Greek] > salamandrine (,sælə'mændrɪn) *adj*

Salambria (sə'læmbrɪə, ,sɑːlɑːm'brɪə) *n* a river in N Greece, in Thessaly, rising in the Pindus Mountains and flowing southeast and east to the Gulf of Salonika. Length: about 200 km (125 miles). Ancient name: Peneus Modern Greek name: Piniós

salami (sə'lɑːmɪ) *n* a highly seasoned type of sausage, usually flavoured with garlic [c19 from Italian, plural of *salame*, from Vulgar Latin *salāre* (unattested) to salt, from Latin *sal* salt]

Salamis ('sæləmɪs) *n* an island in the Saronic Gulf, Greece: scene of the naval battle in 480 BC, in which the Greeks defeated the Persians. Pop: 20 000 (latest est). Area: 95 sq km (37 sq miles)

sal ammoniac *n* another name for **ammonium chloride**

salaried ('sælərɪd) *adj* earning or yielding a salary: *a salaried worker; salaried employment*

salary ('sælərɪ) *n*, *pl* -ries **1** a fixed regular payment made by an employer, often monthly, for professional or office work as opposed to manual work. Compare **wage** (sense 1) > *vb* -ries, -rying, -ried **2** (*tr*) to pay a salary to [c14 from Anglo-Norman *salarie*, from Latin *salārium* the sum given to Roman soldiers to buy salt, from *sal* salt]

salaryman ('sælərɪ,mæn) *n*, *pl* -men (in Japan) an office worker

salchow ('sɔːlkəʊ) *n* a figure-skating jump made

from the inner backward edge of one foot with one, two, or three full turns in the air, returning to the outer backward edge of the opposite foot [c20 named after Ulrich *Salchow* (1877–1949), Swedish figure skater, who originated it]

Salduba (sæl'duːbə, 'sældəbə) *n* the pre-Roman (Celtiberian) name for **Zaragoza**

sale (seɪl) *n* **1** the exchange of goods, property, or services for an agreed sum of money or credit **2** the amount sold **3** the opportunity to sell; market: *there was no sale for luxuries* **4** the rate of selling or being sold: *a slow sale of synthetic fabrics* **5 a** an event at which goods are sold at reduced prices, usually to clear old stocks **b** (*as modifier*): *sale bargains* **6** an auction [Old English *sala*, from Old Norse *sala*. See also **SELL**]

Sale (seɪl) *n* **1** a town in NW England, in Trafford unitary authority, Greater Manchester: a residential suburb of Manchester. Pop: 55 234 (2001) **2** a city in SE Australia, in SE Victoria: centre of an agricultural region. Pop: 12 854 (2001)

Salé (French sale) *n* a port in NW Morocco, on the Atlantic adjoining Rabat. Pop: 880 000 (2003)

saleable *or* US **salable** ('seɪləbᵊl) *adj* fit for selling or capable of being sold > ,salea'bility, 'saleableness *or* US ,sala'bility, 'salableness *n* > 'saleably *or* US 'salably *adv*

sale and lease back *n* a system of raising capital for a business by selling the business property and then renting it from the new owner for an agreed period

Salem ('seɪləm) *n* **1** a city in S India, in Tamil Nadu: textile industries. Pop: 693 236 (2001) **2** a city in NE Massachusetts, on the Atlantic: scene of the execution of 19 people after the witch hunts of 1692. Pop: 42 067 (2003 est) **3** a city in the NW USA, the state capital of Oregon: food-processing. Pop: 142 914 (2003 est) **4** an Old Testament name for **Jerusalem** (Genesis 14:18; Psalms 76:2)

sale of work *n* *Brit* a sale of goods and handicrafts made by the members of a club, church congregation, etc, to raise money

sale or return *or* **sale and return** *n* an arrangement by which a retailer pays only for goods sold, returning those that are unsold to the wholesaler or manufacturer

salep ('sæləp) *n* the dried ground starchy tubers of various orchids, used for food and formerly as drugs [c18 via French and Turkish from Arabic *sahlab*, shortened from *khusy ath-tha'lab*, literally: fox's testicles, name of an orchid]

saleratus (,sælə'reɪtəs) *n* another name for **sodium bicarbonate**, esp when used in baking powders [c19 from New Latin *sal aerātus* aerated salt]

Salerno (Italian sa'lɛrno) *n* a port in SW Italy, in Campania on the **Gulf of Salerno**: first medical school of medieval Europe. Pop: 138 188 (2001)

saleroom ('seɪl,ruːm, -,rʊm) *n* *chiefly Brit* a room where objects are displayed for sale, esp by auction

salesclerk ('seɪlz,klɜːrk) *n* *US and Canadian* a shop assistant. Sometimes shortened to: **clerk**

sales forecast *n* a prediction of future sales of a product, either judgmental or based on previous sales patterns

Salesian (sə'liːzjən, -ʒən) *adj* **1** of or relating to the French ecclesiastic and theologian St Francis of Sales (1567–1622) or to the religious orders founded by him or by St John Bosco in his name. See also **Visitation** (sense 2) > *n* **2** a member of a Salesian order, esp a member of the Society of St Francis of Sales founded in Turin by St John Bosco (1854), and dedicated to all types of educational work [c19 from *Sales*]

salesman ('seɪlzmən) *n*, *pl* -men **1** Also called (fem): **saleswoman**, (fem) **salesgirl**, (fem) **saleslady**, **salesperson** a person who sells merchandise or services either in a shop or by canvassing in a designated area **2** short for **travelling salesman**

salesmanship ('seɪlzmənʃɪp) *n* **1** the technique,

skill, or ability of selling **2** the work of a salesman

sales pitch *or* **talk** *n* an argument or other persuasion used in selling

sales promotion *n* activities or techniques intended to create consumer demand for a product or service

sales resistance *n* opposition of potential customers to selling, esp aggressive selling

salesroom ('seɪlz,ruːm, -,rʊm) *n* a room in which merchandise on sale is displayed

sales tax *n* a tax levied on retail sales receipts and added to selling prices by retailers

sales trader *n* *stock exchange* a person employed by a market maker, or his firm, to find clients

salet ('sælɪt) *n* a variant spelling of **sallet**

saleyard ('seɪl,jɑːd) *n* *Austral and NZ* an area with pens for holding animals before auction

Salford ('sɔːlfəd, 'sɒl-) *n* **1** a city in NW England in Salford unitary authority, Greater Manchester, on the Manchester Ship Canal: a major centre of the cotton industry in the 19th century; extensive dock area, now redeveloped, includes the Lowry arts centre; university (1967). Pop: 72 750 (2001) **2** a unitary authority in NW England, in Greater Manchester. Pop: 216 500 (2003 est). Area: 97 sq km (37 sq miles)

Salian ('seɪlɪən) *adj* **1** denoting or relating to a group of Franks (the **Salii**) who settled in the Netherlands in the 4th century AD and later conquered large areas of Gaul, esp in the north > *n* **2** a member of this group

salic ('sælɪk, 'seɪ-) *adj* (of rocks and minerals) having a high content of silica and alumina [c20 from *s(ilica)* + *al(umina)* + -IC]

Salic *or* **Salique** ('sælɪk, 'seɪlɪk) *adj* of or relating to the Salian Franks or the Salic law

salicaceous (,sælɪ'keɪʃəs) *adj* of, relating to, or belonging to the *Salicaceae*, a chiefly N temperate family of trees and shrubs having catkins: includes the willows and poplars [c19 via New Latin from Latin *salix* a willow]

salicin *or* **salicine** ('sælɪsɪn) *n* a colourless or white crystalline water-soluble glucoside obtained from the bark of poplar trees and used as a medical analgesic. Formula: $C_{13}H_{18}O_7$ [c19 from French *salicine*, from Latin *salix* willow]

salicional (sə'lɪʃənəl) *or* **salicet** ('sælɪ,sɛt) *n* a soft-toned organ stop with a reedy quality [c19 from German, from Latin *salix* willow]

Salic law *n* *history* **1 a** the code of laws of the Salic Franks and other Germanic tribes **b** a law within this code excluding females from inheritance **2** a law excluding women from succession to the throne in certain countries, such as France and Spain

salicornia (,sælɪ'kɔːnɪə) *n* any chenopodiaceous plant of the genus *Salicornia*, of seashores and salt marshes: includes glasswort [c19 from Late Latin, perhaps from Latin *sal* salt + *cornu* a horn]

salicylate (sə'lɪsɪ,leɪt) *n* any salt or ester of salicylic acid

salicylic acid (,sælɪ'sɪlɪk) *n* a white crystalline slightly water-soluble substance with a sweet taste and bitter aftertaste, used in the manufacture of aspirin, dyes, and perfumes, and as a fungicide. Formula: $C_6H_4(OH)(COOH)$ [c19 from *salicyl* (via French from Latin *salix* a willow + -YL) + -IC]

salient ('seɪlɪənt) *adj* **1** prominent, conspicuous, or striking: *a salient feature* **2** (esp in fortifications) projecting outwards at an angle of less than 180°. Compare **re-entrant** (sense 1) **3** *geometry* (of an angle) pointing outwards from a polygon and hence less than 180°. Compare **re-entrant** (sense 2) **4** (esp of animals) leaping > *n* **5** *military* a projection of the forward line into enemy-held territory **6** a salient angle [c16 from Latin *salīre* to leap] > 'salience *or* 'saliency *n* > 'saliently *adv*

salientian (,seɪlɪ'ɛnʃɪən) *n, adj* another word for **anuran** [c19 from New Latin *Salientia*, literally: leapers, from Latin *salīre* to leap]

saliferous (sæˈlɪfərəs) *adj* (esp of rock strata) containing or producing salt [c19 from Latin *sal* SALT + *ferre* to bear]

salify (ˈsælɪˌfaɪ) *vb* -fies, -fying, -fied (*tr*) **1** to treat, mix with, or cause to combine with a salt **2** to convert (a substance) into a salt: *to salify ammonia by treatment with hydrochloric acid* [c18 from French *salifier*, from New Latin *salificāre*, from Latin *sal* salt + *facere* to make] > ˌsaliˈfiable *adj* > ˌsalifiˈcation *n*

salimeter (sæˈlɪmɪtə) *n* another word for **salinometer**. > salimetric (ˌsælɪˈmɛtrɪk) *adj* > salˈimetry *n*

salina (səˈlaɪnə) *n* a salt marsh, lake, or spring [c17 from Spanish, from Medieval Latin: salt pit, from Late Latin *salīnus* SALINE]

saline (ˈseɪlaɪn) *adj* **1** of, concerned with, consisting of, or containing common salt: *a saline taste* **2** *med* of or relating to a saline **3** of, concerned with, consisting of, or containing any chemical salt, esp a metallic salt resembling sodium chloride ▷ *n* **4** *med* an isotonic solution of sodium chloride in distilled water [c15 from Late Latin *salīnus*, from Latin *sal* salt] > salinity (səˈlɪnɪtɪ) *n*

salinometer (ˌsælɪˈnɒmɪtə) *n* a hydrometer for determining the amount of salt in a solution, usually calibrated to measure concentration. Also called: salimeter > salinometric (ˌsælɪnəˈmɛtrɪk) *adj* > ˌsaliˈnometry *n*

Salique (ˈsælɪk, ˈseɪlɪk) *adj* a variant spelling of **Salic**

Salisbury (ˈsɔːlzbərɪ, -brɪ) *n* **1** the former name (until 1982) of **Harare 2** a city in S Australia: an industrial suburb of N Adelaide. Pop: 112 344 (1998 est) **3** a city in S England, in SE Wiltshire: nearby Old Sarum was the site of an Early Iron Age hill fort; its cathedral (1220–58) has the highest spire in England. Pop: 43 355 (2001). Ancient name: Sarum Official name: New Sarum

Salisbury Plain *n* an open chalk plateau in S England, in Wiltshire: site of Stonehenge; military training area. Average height: 120 m (400 ft)

Salish (ˈseɪlɪʃ) *or* **Salishan** (ˈseɪlɪʃən, ˈsæl-) *n* **1** a family of North American Indian languages spoken in the northwestern US and W Canada **2** the Salish (*functioning as plural*) the peoples collectively who speak these languages, divided in Canada into the **Coast Salish** and the **Interior Salish**

saliva (səˈlaɪvə) *n* the secretion of salivary glands, consisting of a clear usually slightly acid aqueous fluid of variable composition. It moistens the oral cavity, prepares food for swallowing, and initiates the process of digestion. Related adj: **sialoid** [c17 from Latin, of obscure origin] > salivary (səˈlaɪvərɪ, ˈsælɪvərɪ) *adj*

salivary gland *n* any of the glands in mammals that secrete saliva. In man the chief salivary glands are the **parotid**, **sublingual** and **submaxillary** glands

salivate (ˈsælɪˌveɪt) *vb* **1** (*intr*) to secrete saliva, esp an excessive amount **2** (*tr*) to cause (a laboratory animal, etc) to produce saliva, as by the administration of mercury > ˌsaliˈvation *n*

sallee *or* **sally** (ˈsælɪ) *n Austral* **1** Also called: **snow gum** a SE Australian eucalyptus tree, *Eucalyptus pauciflora*, with a pale grey bark **2** any of various acacia trees [probably of native origin]

sallenders (ˈsæləndəz) *n vet science* a disease of the skin behind the tarsus (hock) of a horse

sallet, salet (ˈsælɪt) *or* **salade** *n* a light round helmet extending over the back of the neck; replaced the basinet in the 15th century [c15 from French *salade*, probably from Old Italian *celata*, from *celare* to conceal, from Latin]

sallow¹ (ˈsæləʊ) *adj* **1** (esp of human skin) of an unhealthy pale or yellowish colour ▷ *vb* **2** (*tr*) to make sallow [Old English *salu*; related to Old Norse *sol* seaweed (Icelandic *sōlr* yellowish), Old High German *salo*, French *sale* dirty] > ˈsallowish *adj* > ˈsallowly *adv* > ˈsallowness *n*

sallow² (ˈsæləʊ) *n* **1** any of several small willow trees, esp the Eurasian *Salix cinerea* (**common sallow**), which has large catkins that appear before the leaves **2** a twig or the wood of any of these trees [Old English *sealh*; related to Old Norse *selja*, Old High German *salaha*, Middle Low German *salwīde*, Latin *salix*] > ˈsallowy *adj*

sally¹ (ˈsælɪ) *n, pl* -lies **1** a sudden violent excursion, esp by besieged forces to attack the besiegers; sortie **2** a sudden outburst or emergence into action, expression, or emotion **3** an excursion or jaunt **4** a jocular retort ▷ *vb* -lies, -lying, -lied (*intr*) **5** to make a sudden violent excursion **6** (often foll by *forth*) to go out on an expedition, etc **7** to come, go, or set out in an energetic manner **8** to rush out suddenly [c16 from Old French *saillie*, from *saillir* to dash forwards, from Latin *salīre* to leap]

sally² (ˈsælɪ) *n, pl* -lies the lower part of a bell rope, where it is caught at handstroke, into which coloured wool is woven to make a grip [c19 perhaps from an obsolete or dialect sense of SALLY¹ leaping movement]

Sally (ˈsælɪ) *n, pl* -lies a member of the Salvation Army

Sally Army *n Brit informal* short for **Salvation Army**

Sally Lunn (lʌn) *n* a flat round cake made from a sweet yeast dough, usually served hot [c19 said to be named after an 18th-century English baker who invented it]

sallyport (ˈsælɪˌpɔːt) *n* an opening in a fortified place from which troops may make a sally

salmagundi *or* **salmagundy** (ˌsælməˈɡʌndɪ) *n* **1** a mixed salad dish of cooked meats, eggs, beetroot, etc, popular in 18th-century England **2** a miscellany; potpourri [c17 from French *salmigondis*, perhaps from Italian *salami conditi* pickled salami]

Salmanazar (ˌsælməˈnæzə) *n* a wine bottle holding the equivalent of twelve normal bottles (approximately 312 ounces) [c19 humorous allusion to an Assyrian king mentioned in the Bible (II Kings 17:3); compare JEROBOAM]

salmi *or* **salmis** (ˈsælmɪ) *n, pl* -mis (-mɪ) a ragout of game stewed in a rich brown sauce [c18 from French, shortened form of *salmigondis* SALMAGUNDI]

salmon (ˈsæmən) *n, pl* -ons *or* -on **1** any soft-finned fish of the family *Salmonidae*, esp *Salmo salar* of the Atlantic and *Oncorhynchus* species (sockeye, Chinook, etc) of the Pacific, which are important food fishes. They occur in cold and temperate waters and many species migrate to fresh water to spawn **2** *Austral* any of several unrelated fish, esp the Australian salmon **3** short for **salmon pink** [c13 from Old French *saumon*, from Latin *salmō*; related to Late Latin *salar* trout]

salmonberry (ˈsæmənbərɪ, -brɪ) *n, pl* -ries **1** a spineless raspberry bush, *Rubus spectabilis*, of North America, having reddish-purple flowers and large red or yellow edible fruits **2** the fruit of this plant [c19 so called from the colour of the berries]

salmonella (ˌsælməˈnɛlə) *n, pl* -lae (-ˌliː) any Gram-negative rod-shaped aerobic bacterium of the genus *Salmonella*, including *S. typhosa*, which causes typhoid fever, and many species (notably *S. enteritidis*) that cause food poisoning (**salmonellosis**): family *Enterobacteriaceae* [c19 New Latin, named after Daniel E *Salmon* (1850–1914), US veterinary surgeon]

salmonid (ˈsælmənɪd) *n* any fish of the family *Salmonidae*

salmon ladder *n* a series of steps in a river designed to enable salmon to bypass a dam and move upstream to their breeding grounds

salmonoid (ˈsælməˌnɔɪd) *adj* **1** of, relating to, or belonging to the *Salmonoidea*, a suborder of soft-finned teleost fishes having a fatty fin between the dorsal and tail fins: includes the salmon, whitefish, grayling, smelt, and char **2** of, relating to, or resembling a salmon ▷ *n* **3** any fish belonging to the suborder *Salmonoidea*, esp any of

the family *Salmonidae* (salmon, trout, char)

salmon pink *n* **a** a yellowish-pink colour, sometimes with an orange tinge **b** (*as adjective*): *a salmon-pink hat*. ▷ Sometimes shortened to: salmon

salmon trout *n* any of various large trout, esp the sea trout

salol (ˈsælɒl) *n* a white sparingly soluble crystalline compound with a slight aromatic odour, used as a preservative and to absorb light in sun-tan lotions, plastics, etc; phenyl salicylate. Formula: $C_6H_4(OH)COOC_6H_5$ [c19 from *salicyl* (see SALICYLIC ACID) + -OL]

Salome (səˈləʊmɪ) *n New Testament* the daughter of Herodias, at whose instigation she beguiled Herod by her seductive dancing into giving her the head of John the Baptist

salon (ˈsælɒn) *n* **1** a room in a large house in which guests are received **2** an assembly of guests in a fashionable household, esp a gathering of major literary, artistic, and political figures from the 17th to the early 20th centuries **3** a commercial establishment in which hairdressers, beauticians, etc, carry on their businesses: *beauty salon* **4 a** a hall for exhibiting works of art **b** such an exhibition, esp one showing the work of living artists [c18 from French, from Italian *salone*, augmented form of *sala* hall, of Germanic origin; compare Old English *sele* hall, Old High German *sal*, Old Norse *salr* hall]

Salonika *or* **Salonica** (səˈlɒnɪkə) *n* the English name for **Thessaloníki**

salon music *n sometimes derogatory* light classical music intended esp for domestic entertaining

saloon (səˈluːn) *n* **1** Also called: saloon bar *Brit* another word for **lounge** (sense 5) **2** a large public room on a passenger ship **3** any large public room used for a specific purpose: *a dancing saloon* **4** *chiefly US and Canadian* a place where alcoholic drink is sold and consumed **5** a closed two-door or four-door car with four to six seats. US, Canadian, and NZ name: sedan **6** an obsolete word for **salon** (sense 1) [c18 from French SALON]

saloop (səˈluːp) *n* an infusion of aromatic herbs or other plant parts, esp salep, formerly used as a tonic or cure [c18 changed from SALEP]

Salop (ˈsæləp) *n* a former name (1974–80) of **Shropshire**

salopettes (ˌsæləˈpɛts) *pl n* a garment worn for skiing, consisting of quilted trousers reaching to the chest and held up by shoulder straps [c20 from French]

Salopian (səˈləʊpjən) *n* **1** a native or inhabitant of Shropshire ▷ *adj* **2** of or relating to Shropshire or its inhabitants [from *Salop*, a former name of Shropshire]

salpa (ˈsælpə) *n, pl* -pas *or* -pae (-piː) any of various minute floating animals of the genus *Salpa*, of warm oceans, having a transparent barrel-shaped body with openings at either end: class *Thaliacea*, subphylum *Tunicata* (tunicates) [c19 from New Latin, from Latin: variety of stockfish, from Greek *salpē*] > salpiform (ˈsælpɪˌfɔːm) *adj*

salpicon (ˈsælpɪkən) *n* a mixture of chopped fish, meat, or vegetables in a sauce, used as fillings for croquettes, pastries, etc [c18 from French, from Spanish, from *salpicar* to sprinkle with salt]

salpiglossis (ˌsælpɪˈɡlɒsɪs) *n* any solanaceous plant of the Chilean genus *Salpiglossis*, some species of which are cultivated for their bright funnel-shaped flowers [c19 New Latin, from Greek *salpinx* trumpet + *glōssa* tongue]

salpingectomy (ˌsælpɪnˈdʒɛktəmɪ) *n, pl* -mies surgical removal of a Fallopian tube [c20 from SALPINX + -ECTOMY]

salpingitis (ˌsælpɪnˈdʒaɪtɪs) *n* inflammation of a Fallopian tube [c19 from SALPINX + -ITIS] > salpingitic (ˌsælpɪnˈdʒɪtɪk) *adj*

salpingo- *combining form* indicating the Fallopian tubes: *salpingo-oophorectomy* [c20 from SALPINX]

salpinx (ˈsælpɪŋks) *n, pl* salpinges (sælˈpɪndʒiːz) *anatomy* another name for the **Fallopian tube** or the **Eustachian tube** [C19 from Greek: trumpet] > salpingian (sæl'pɪndʒɪən) *adj*

salsa ('sælsə) *n* **1** a type of Latin American big-band dance music **2** a dance performed to this kind of music **3** *Mexican cookery* a spicy tomato-based sauce [C20 from Spanish: sauce]

salsify ('sælsɪfɪ) *n, pl* **-fies 1** Also called: **oyster plant, vegetable oyster** a Mediterranean plant, *Tragopogon porrifolius*, having grasslike leaves, purple flower heads, and a long white edible taproot: family *Asteraceae* (composites) **2** the root of this plant, which tastes of oysters and is eaten as a vegetable [C17 from French *salsifis*, from Italian *sassefrica*, from Late Latin *saxifrica*, from Latin *saxum* rock + *fricāre* to rub]

sal soda *n* the crystalline decahydrate of sodium carbonate

salt (sɔːlt) *n* **1** a white powder or colourless crystalline solid, consisting mainly of sodium chloride and used for seasoning and preserving food **2** (*modifier*) preserved in, flooded with, containing, or growing in salt or salty water: *salt pork; salt marshes* **3** *chem* any of a class of usually crystalline solid compounds that are formed from, or can be regarded as formed from, an acid and a base by replacement of one or more hydrogen atoms in the acid molecules by positive ions from the base **4** liveliness or pungency: *his wit added salt to the discussion* **5** dry or laconic wit **6** a sailor, esp one who is old and experienced **7** short for **saltcellar 8 rub salt into someone's wounds** to make someone's pain, shame, etc, even worse **9 salt of the earth** a person or group of people regarded as the finest of their kind **10 with a grain** (*or* **pinch**) **of salt** with reservations; sceptically **11 worth one's salt** efficient; worthy of one's pay ▷ *vb* (*tr*) **12** to season or preserve with salt **13** to scatter salt over (an icy road, path, etc) to melt the ice **14** to add zest to **15** (often foll by *down* or *away*) to preserve or cure with salt or saline solution **16** *chem* to treat with common salt or other chemical salt **17** to provide (cattle, etc) with salt **18** to give a false appearance of value to, esp to introduce valuable ore fraudulently into (a mine, sample, etc) ▷ *adj* **19** not sour, sweet, or bitter; salty **20** *obsolete* rank or lascivious (esp in the phrase **a salt wit**) ▷ See also **salt away, salt out, salts** [Old English *sealt;* related to Old Norse, Gothic *salt*, German *Salz*, Lettish *sāls*, Latin *sāl*, Greek *hals*] > 'saltish *adj* > 'saltless *adj* > 'salt,like *adj* > 'saltness *n*

SALT (sɔːlt) *n* acronym for Strategic Arms Limitation Talks *or* Treaty

Salta (*Spanish* 'salta) *n* a city in NW Argentina: thermal springs. Pop: 504 000 (2005 est)

saltant ('sæltənt) *adj* (of an organism) differing from others of its species because of a saltation [C17 from Latin *saltāns* dancing, from *saltāre*, from *salīre* to spring]

saltarello (,sæltə'rɛləʊ) *n, pl* **-li** (-lɪ) *or* **-los 1** a traditional Italian dance, usually in compound duple time **2** a piece of music composed for or in the rhythm of this dance [C18 from Italian, from *saltare* to dance energetically, from Latin; see SALTANT]

saltation (sæl'teɪʃən) *n* **1** *biology* an abrupt variation in the appearance of an organism, species, etc, usually caused by genetic mutation **2** *geology* the leaping movement of sand or soil particles carried in water or by the wind **3** a sudden abrupt movement or transition [C17 from Latin *saltātiō* a dance, from *saltāre* to leap about]

saltatorial (,sæltə'tɔːrɪəl) *or* **saltatory** *adj* **1** *biology* specialized for or characterized by jumping: *the saltatorial legs of a grasshopper* **2** of or relating to saltation [C17 *saltatory*, from Latin *saltātōrius* concerning dancing, from *saltātor* a dancer; see SALTANT]

salt away *or less commonly* **down** *vb* (*tr, adverb*) to hoard or save (money, valuables, etc)

salt bath *n metallurgy* a bath of molten salts in which steel can be immersed to soak to a uniform and accurately maintained temperature as part of the process of heat treatment. Different salts are used for different temperatures

saltbox ('sɔːlt,bɒks) *n* **1** a box for salt with a sloping lid **2** *US* a house that has two storeys in front and one storey at the back, with a gable roof that extends downwards over the rear

saltbush ('sɔːlt,bʊʃ) *n* any of various chenopodiaceous shrubs of the genus *Atriplex* that grow in alkaline desert regions

salt cake *n* an impure form of sodium sulphate obtained as a by-product in several industrial processes: used in the manufacture of detergents, glass, and ceramic glazes

saltcellar ('sɔːlt,sɛlə) *n* **1** a small container for salt used at the table **2** *Brit informal* either of the two hollows formed above the collarbones of very slim people [changed (through influence of cellar) from C15 *salt saler; saler* from Old French *saliere* container for salt, from Latin *salārius* belonging to salt, from *sal* salt]

saltchuck ('sɔːlt,tʃʌk) *n Canadian, chiefly W coast* any body of salt water [C20 from SALT + CHUCK[4]]

saltchucker ('sɔːlt,tʃʌkə) *n Canadian W coast informal* a saltwater angler

salt dome *or* **plug** *n* a domelike structure of stratified rocks containing a central core of salt: formed by the upward movement of a salt deposit

Salteaux *or* **Saulteaux** ('səʊtəʊ) *n* a member of a Native Canadian people of Manitoba [from Ojibwa]

salted ('sɔːltɪd) *adj* **1** seasoned, preserved, or treated with salt **2** *informal* experienced in an occupation

salter ('sɔːltə) *n* **1** a person who deals in or manufactures salt **2** a person who treats meat, fish, etc, with salt

saltern ('sɔːltən) *n* **1** another word for **saltworks 2** a place where salt is obtained from pools of evaporated sea water [Old English *saltærn*, from SALT + *ærn* house. Compare BARN[1], RANSACK]

saltfish ('sɔːltfɪʃ) *n Caribbean* salted cod

salt flat *n* a flat expanse of salt left by the total evaporation of a body of water

saltie ('sɔːltɪ) *n Austral informal* a saltwater crocodile

saltigrade ('sæltɪ,greɪd) *adj* (of animals) adapted for moving in a series of jumps [C19 from New Latin *Saltigradae*, name formerly applied to jumping spiders, from Latin *saltus* a leap + *gradī* to move]

Saltillo (*Spanish* sal'tiʎo) *n* a city in N Mexico, capital of Coahuila state: resort and commercial centre of a mining region. Pop: 698 000 (2005 est)

salting ('sɔːltɪŋ) *n* (*often plural*) an area of low ground regularly inundated with salt water; often taken to include its halophyte vegetation; a salt marsh

saltire *or less commonly* **saltier** ('sɔːl,taɪə) *n heraldry* an ordinary consisting of a diagonal cross on a shield [C14 *sawturoure*, from Old French *sauteour* cross-shaped barricade, from *saulter* to jump, from Latin *saltāre*]

salt lake *n* an inland lake of high salinity resulting from inland drainage in an arid area of high evaporation

Salt Lake City *n* a city in N central Utah, near the Great Salt Lake at an altitude of 1330 m (4300 ft): state capital; founded in 1847 by the Mormons as world capital of the Mormon Church; University of Utah (1850). Pop: 179 894 (2003 est)

salt lick *n* **1** a place where wild animals go to lick naturally occurring salt deposits **2** a block of salt or a salt preparation given to domestic animals to lick

salt marsh *n* an area of marshy ground that is intermittently inundated with salt water or that retains pools or rivulets of salt or brackish water, together with its characteristic halophytic vegetation

Salto (*Spanish* 'salto) *n* a port in NW Uruguay, on the Uruguay River. It is Uruguay's second largest

city. Pop: 105 000 (2005 est)

salt out *vb* (*adverb*) *chem* to cause (a dissolved substance) to come out of solution by adding an electrolyte

saltpan ('sɔːlt,pæn) *n* a shallow basin, usually in a desert region, containing salt, gypsum, etc, that was deposited from an evaporated salt lake

saltpetre *or US* **saltpeter** (,sɔːlt'piːtə) *n* **1** another name for **potassium nitrate 2** short for **Chile saltpetre** [C16 from Old French *salpetre*, from Latin *sal petrae* salt of rock]

salt pork *n* pork, esp the fat pork taken from the back, sides, and belly, that has been cured with salt

salts (sɔːlts) *pl n* **1** *med* any of various mineral salts, such as magnesium sulphate or sodium sulphate, for use as a cathartic **2** short for **smelling salts 3 like a dose of salts** *informal* very fast

saltus ('sæltəs) *n, pl* **-tuses** a break in the continuity of a sequence, esp the omission of a necessary step in a logical argument [Latin: a leap]

saltwater ('sɔːlt,wɔːtə) *adj* of, relating to, or inhabiting salt water, esp the sea: *saltwater fishes*

saltworks ('sɔːlt,wɜːks) *n* (*functioning as singular*) a place, building, or factory where salt is produced

saltwort ('sɔːlt,wɜːt) *n* **1** Also called: **glasswort, kali** any of several chenopodiaceous plants of the genus *Salsola*, esp *S. kali*, of beaches and salt marshes, which has prickly leaves, striped stems, and small green flowers. See also **barilla 2** another name for **sea milkwort**

salty ('sɔːltɪ) *adj* **saltier, saltiest 1** of, tasting of, or containing salt **2** (esp of humour) sharp; piquant **3** relating to life at sea > 'saltily *adv* > 'saltiness *n*

salubrious (sə'luːbrɪəs) *adj* conducive or favourable to health; wholesome [C16 from Latin *salūbris*, from *salūs* health] > sa'lubriously *adv* > sa'lubriousness *or* salubrity (sə'luːbrɪtɪ) *n*

Saluki (sə'luːkɪ) *n* a tall breed of hound with a smooth coat and long fringes on the ears and tail. Also called: **gazehound, gazelle hound, Persian greyhound** [C19 from Arabic *salūqīy* of Saluq, name of an ancient Arabian city]

salutary ('sæljʊtərɪ, -trɪ) *adj* **1** promoting or intended to promote an improvement or beneficial effect: *a salutary warning* **2** promoting or intended to promote health [C15 from Latin *salūtāris* wholesome, from *salūs* safety] > 'salutarily *adv* > 'salutariness *n*

salutation (,sæljʊ'teɪʃən) *n* **1** an act, phrase, gesture, etc, that serves as a greeting **2** a form of words used as an opening to a speech or letter, such as *Dear Sir* or *Ladies and Gentlemen* **3** the act of saluting [C14 from Latin *salūtātiō*, from *salūtāre* to greet; see SALUTE]

salutatory (sə'luːtətərɪ, -trɪ) *adj* of, relating to, or resembling a salutation > sa'lutatorily *adv*

salute (sə'luːt) *vb* **1** (*tr*) to address or welcome with friendly words or gestures of respect, such as bowing or lifting the hat; greet **2** (*tr*) to acknowledge with praise or honour: *we salute your gallantry* **3** *military* to pay or receive formal respect, as by presenting arms or raising the right arm ▷ *n* **4** the act of saluting **5** a formal military gesture of respect [C14 from Latin *salūtāre* to greet, from *salūs* wellbeing] > sa'luter *n*

salvable ('sælvəb[ə]l) *adj* capable of or suitable for being saved or salvaged [C17 from Late Latin *salvāre* to save, from Latin *salvus* safe] > ,salva'bility *or* 'salvableness *n* > 'salvably *adv*

Salvador ('sælvə,dɔː; *Portuguese* salva'dor) *n* a port in E Brazil, capital of Bahia state: founded in 1549 as capital of the Portuguese colony, which it remained until 1763; a major centre of the African slave trade in colonial times. Pop: 3 331 000 (2005 est). Former name: **Bahia** Official name: **São Salvador da Bahia de Todos os Santos** (sãu salva'dor 'də: ba'ia 'də: 'toːduʃ uʃ 'sɐntuʃ)

Salvadorian[1], Salvadorean (,sælvə'dɔːrɪən) *or* **Salvadoran** (,sælvə'dɔːrən) *n* **1** a native or inhabitant of El Salvador ▷ *adj* **2** of or relating to El Salvador, or its people, culture, etc

Salvadorian² (ˌsælvəˈdɔːrɪən) *n* **1** a native or inhabitant of Salvador ▷ *adj* **2** of or relating to Salvador or its inhabitants

salvage (ˈsælvɪdʒ) *n* **1** the act, process, or business of rescuing vessels or their cargoes from loss at sea **2 a** the act of saving any goods or property in danger of damage or destruction **b** (*as modifier*): *a salvage operation* **3** the goods or property so saved **4** compensation paid for the salvage of a vessel or its cargo **5** the proceeds from the sale of salvaged goods or property ▷ *vb* (*tr*) **6** to save or rescue (goods or property) from fire, shipwreck, etc **7** to gain (something beneficial) from a failure: *she salvaged little from the broken marriage* [C17 from Old French, from Medieval Latin *salvāgium*, from *salvāre* to SAVE¹] > **ˈsalvageable** *adj* > **ˈsalvager** *n*

salvation (sælˈveɪʃən) *n* **1** the act of preserving or the state of being preserved from harm **2** a person or thing that is the means of preserving from harm **3** *Christianity* deliverance by redemption from the power of sin and from the penalties ensuing from it **4** *Christian Science* the realization that Life, Truth, and Love are supreme and that they can destroy such illusions as sin, death, etc [C13 from Old French *sauvacion*, from Late Latin *salvātiō*, from Latin *salvātus* saved, from *salvāre* to SAVE¹] > **salˈvational** *adj*

Salvation Army *n* **a** a Christian body founded in 1865 by William Booth and organized on quasi-military lines for evangelism and social work among the poor **b** (*as modifier*): *the Salvation Army Hymn Book*

salvationist (sælˈveɪʃənɪst) *n* **1** a member of an evangelical sect emphasizing the doctrine of salvation **2** (*often capital*) a member of the Salvation Army ▷ *adj* **3** stressing the doctrine of salvation **4** (*often capital*) of or relating to the Salvation Army > **salˈvationism** *n*

Salvation Jane (dʒeɪn) *n Austral* another name, used in South Australia, for **Paterson's curse**

salva veritate *Latin* (ˈsælvə ˌvɛrɪˈtɑːteɪ) *adv philosophy* without affecting truth-value

salve¹ (sælv, sɑːv) *n* **1** an ointment for wounds, sores, etc **2** anything that heals or soothes ▷ *vb* (*tr*) **3** to apply salve to (a wound, sore, etc) **4** to soothe, comfort, or appease [Old English *sealf*; related to Old High German *salba*, Greek *elpos* oil, Sanskrit *sarpis* lard]

salve² (sælv) *vb* **1** a less common word for **salvage** **2** an archaic word for **save¹** (sense 3) [C18 from SALVAGE]

salver (ˈsælvə) *n* a tray, esp one of silver, on which food, letters, visiting cards, etc, are presented [C17 from French *salve*, from Spanish *salva* tray from which the king's taster sampled food, from Latin *salvāre* to SAVE¹]

salverform (ˈsælvəˌfɔːm) *adj* (of the corolla of the phlox and certain other flowers) consisting of a narrow tube with flat spreading terminal petals

salvia (ˈsælvɪə) *n* any herbaceous plant or small shrub of the genus *Salvia*, such as the sage, grown for their medicinal or culinary properties or for ornament: family *Lamiaceae* (labiates) [C19 from Latin: SAGE²]

salvo¹ (ˈsælvəʊ) *n*, *pl* -**vos** *or* -**voes** **1** a discharge of fire from weapons in unison, esp on a ceremonial occasion **2** concentrated fire from many weapons, as in a naval battle **3** an outburst, as of applause [C17 from Italian *salva*, from Old French *salve*, from Latin *salvē*! greetings! from *salvēre* to be in good health, from *salvus* safe]

salvo² (ˈsælvəʊ) *n*, *pl* -**vos** *rare* **1** an excuse or evasion **2** an expedient to save a reputation or soothe hurt feelings **3** (in legal documents) a saving clause; reservation [C17 from such Medieval Latin phrases as *salvō iure* the right of keeping safe, from Latin *salvus* safe]

Salvo (ˈsælvəʊ) *n*, *pl* -**vos** *Austral slang* a member of the Salvation Army

sal volatile (vɒˈlætɪlɪ) *n* **1** another name for **ammonium carbonate** **2** Also called: **spirits of ammonia**, (*archaic*) **hartshorn** a solution of ammonium carbonate in alcohol and aqueous ammonia, often containing aromatic oils, used as smelling salts [C17 from New Latin: volatile salt]

salvor *or* **salver** (ˈsælvə) *n* a person instrumental in salvaging a vessel or its cargo [C17 from SALVAGE + -OR¹]

salwar kameez (ˈsælwɑː ˌkæmiːz) *n* a long tunic worn over a pair of baggy trousers, usually worn by women, esp in Pakistan

Salween (ˈsælwiːn) *n* a river in SW Asia, rising in the Tibetan Plateau and flowing east and south through SW China and Myanmar to the Gulf of Martaban. Length: 2400 km (1500 miles)

Salyut (sælˈjuːt) *n* any of a series of seven Soviet space stations. The first was launched into earth orbit in April 1971 and the last was launched in April 1982. The Salyut programme led to the Mir space station [C20 Russian: salute]

Salzburg (ˈsæltsbɜːg; *German* ˈzaltsburk) *n* **1** a city in W Austria, capital of Salzburg province: 7th-century Benedictine abbey; a centre of music since the Middle Ages and birthplace of Mozart; tourist centre. Pop: 142 662 (2001) **2** a state of W Austria. Pop: 521 238 (2003 est). Area: 7154 sq km (2762 sq miles)

Salzgitter (*German* zalts'gɪtər) *n* an industrial city in central Germany, in SE Lower Saxony. Pop: 109 855 (2003 est)

sam (sæm) *vb* (*tr*) **sams, samming, sammed** *Northern English dialect* **sam hold of** to collect; gather up

SAM (sæm) *n* acronym for surface-to-air missile

Sam. *Bible abbreviation for* Samuel

S.Am. *abbreviation for* South America(n)

samadhi (sʌˈmɑːdi) *n Buddhism, Hinduism* a state of deep meditative contemplation which leads to higher consciousness [from Sanskrit: concentration, from *samā* together + *dhi* mind]

Samar (ˈsɑːmə) *n* an island in E central Philippines, separated from S Luzon by the San Bernardino Strait: the third largest island in the republic. Capital: Catbalogan. Pop: 1 140 000 (2005 est). Area: 13 080 sq km (5050 sq miles)

samara (səˈmɑːrə, ˈsæmərə) *n* a dry indehiscent one-seeded fruit with a winglike extension to aid dispersal: occurs in the ash, maple, etc. Also called: **key fruit** [C16 from New Latin, from Latin: seed of an elm]

Samara (*Russian* saˈmarə) *n* a port in SW Russia, on the River Volga: centre of an important industrial complex; oil refining. Pop: 1 168 000 (1999 est). Former name (1935–91): **Kuibyshev** *or* **Kuybyshev**

Samarang (səˈmɑːrɑːŋ) *n* a variant spelling of **Semarang**

Samaria (səˈmɛərɪə) *n* **1** the region of ancient Palestine that extended from Judaea to Galilee and from the Mediterranean to the River Jordan; the N kingdom of Israel **2** the capital of this kingdom; constructed northwest of Shechem in the 9th century BC

samariform (səˈmɑːrɪˌfɔːm) *adj botany* shaped like a samara; winged

Samaritan (səˈmærɪtən) *n* **1** a native or inhabitant of Samaria **2** short for **Good Samaritan 3** a member of a voluntary organization (**the Samaritans**) which offers counselling to people in despair, esp by telephone **4** the dialect of Aramaic spoken in Samaria ▷ *adj* **5** of or relating to Samaria > **Saˈmaritanism** *n*

samarium (səˈmɛərɪəm) *n* a silvery metallic element of the lanthanide series occurring chiefly in monazite and bastnaesite and used in carbon-arc lighting, as a doping agent in laser crystals, and as a neutron-absorber. Symbol: Sm; atomic no: 62; atomic wt: 150.36; valency: 2 or 3; relative density: 7.520; melting pt: 1074°C; boiling pt: 1794°C [C19 New Latin, from SAMARSKITE + -IUM]

Samarkand (ˈsæməˌkænd; *Russian* səmarˈkant) *n* a

city in E Uzbekistan: under Tamerlane it became the chief economic and cultural centre of central Asia, on trade routes from China and India (the "silk road"). Pop: 289 000 (2005 est). Ancient name: **Maracanda**

samarskite (səˈmɑːskaɪt) *n* a velvety black mineral of complex composition occurring in pegmatites: used as a source of uranium and certain rare earth elements [C19 named after Colonel von *Samarski*, 19th-century Russian inspector of mines]

Sama-Veda (ˈsɑːməˈveɪdə) *n Hinduism* the third Veda containing the rituals for sacrifices [C18 from Sanskrit *sāman* a chant + VEDA]

samba (ˈsæmbə) *n*, *pl* -**bas 1** a lively modern ballroom dance from Brazil in bouncy duple time **2** a piece of music composed for or in the rhythm of this dance ▷ *vb* -**bas, -baing, -baed 3** (*intr*) to perform such a dance [Portuguese, of African origin]

sambar *or* **sambur** (ˈsæmbə) *n*, *pl* -**bars, -bar** *or* -**burs, -bur** a S Asian deer, *Cervus unicolor*, with three-tined antlers [C17 from Hindi, from Sanskrit *śambarra*, of obscure origin]

sambo¹ (ˈsæmbəʊ) *n*, *pl* -**bos 1** *slang* an offensive word for **Black¹**: often used as a term of address **2** the offspring of a Black and a member of another race or a mulatto [C18 from American Spanish *zambo* a person of Black descent; perhaps related to Bantu *nzambu* monkey]

sambo² *or* **sambo wrestling** (ˈsæmbəʊ) *n* a type of wrestling based on judo that originated in Russia and now features in international competitions [C20 from Russian *sam(ozashchita) b(ez) o(ruzhiya)* self-defence without weapons] > **sambo wrestler** *n*

Sambre (*French* sɑːbrə) *n* a river in W Europe, rising in N France and flowing east into Belgium to join the Meuse at Namur. Length: 190 km (118 miles)

Sam Browne belt *n* a military officer's wide belt supported by a strap passing from the left side of the belt over the right shoulder [C20 named after Sir *Samuel J Browne* (1824–1901), British general, who devised such a belt]

same (seɪm) *adj* (usually preceded by *the*) **1** being the very one: *she is wearing the same hat she wore yesterday* **2 a** being the one previously referred to; aforesaid **b** (*as noun*): *a note received about same* **3 a** identical in kind, quantity, etc: *two girls of the same age* **b** (*as noun*): *we'd like the same, please* **4** unchanged in character or nature: *his attitude is the same as ever* **5** all the same **a** Also: just the same nevertheless; yet **b** immaterial: *it's all the same to me* ▷ *adv* **6** in an identical manner [C12 from Old Norse *samr*; related to Old English adverbial phrase *swā same* same likewise, Gothic *sama*, Latin *similis*, Greek *homos* same]

▎ USAGE The use of *same* exemplified in *if you send us your order for the materials, we will deliver same tomorrow* is common in business and official English. In general English, however, this use of the word is avoided: *may I borrow your book? I'll return it* (not *same*) *tomorrow*

samekh (ˈsɑːmək; *Hebrew* ˈsamɛx) *n* the 15th letter in the Hebrew alphabet (ס) transliterated as *s* [Hebrew, literally: a support]

sameness (ˈseɪmnɪs) *n* **1** the state or quality of being the same **2** lack of change; monotony

samey (ˈseɪmɪ) *adj informal* monotonous; repetitive; unvaried

samfoo (ˈsæmfuː) *n* a style of casual dress worn by Chinese women, consisting of a waisted blouse and trousers [from Chinese (Cantonese) *sam* dress + *foo* trousers]

Samhain (ˈsɑːwɪn, ˈsauɪn, ˈsauɪn) *n* an ancient Celtic festival held on Nov 1 to mark the beginning of winter and the beginning of a new year. It is also celebrated by modern pagans [from Irish, from Old Irish *samain*]

Sami (ˈsɑːmɪ) *n* **1** *pl* -**mi** *or* -**mis** a member of the

S

indigenous people of Lapland **2** the language of this people, belonging to the Finno-Ugric family ▷ *adj* **3** of or relating to this people or their language

USAGE The indigenous people of Lapland prefer to be called *Sami*, although *Lapp* is still in widespread use

Samian ('seɪmɪən) *adj* **1** of or relating to Samos or its inhabitants ▷ *n* **2** a native or inhabitant of Samos

Samian ware *n* **1** a fine earthenware pottery, reddish-brown or black in colour, found in large quantities on Roman sites **2** Also called: Arretine ware the earlier pottery from which this developed, an imitation of a type of Greek pottery, made during the first century BC at Arretium [C19 named after the island of SAMOS, source of a reddish-coloured earth resembling terra sigillata, similar to the earth from which the pottery was made]

samiel ('sæmjɛl) *n* another word for **simoom** [C17 from Turkish *samyeli*, from *sam* poisonous + *yel* wind]

samisen ('sæmɪ,sɛn) *n* a Japanese plucked stringed instrument with a long neck, an unfretted fingerboard, and a rectangular soundbox [Japanese, from Chinese *san-hsien*, from *san* three + *hsien* string]

samite ('sæmaɪt, 'seɪ-) *n* a heavy fabric of silk, often woven with gold or silver threads, used in the Middle Ages for clothing [C13 from Old French *samit*, from Medieval Latin *examitum*, from Greek *hexamiton*, from *hexamitos* having six threads, from *hex* six + *mitos* a thread]

samiti *or* **samithi** ('sʌmɪtɪ) *n* (in India) an association, esp one formed to organize political activity [Hindi]

samizdat (*Russian* səmiz'dat) *n* (in the former Soviet Union) **a** a system of clandestine printing and distribution of banned or dissident literature **b** (*as modifier*): *a samizdat publication* [C20 from Russian, literally: self-published]

Sammarinese (sə,mærɪ'ni:z) *adj*, *n* a variant of **San Marinese**

sammy ('sæmɪ) *n*, *pl* -mies *informal* (in South Africa) an Indian fruit and vegetable vendor who goes from house to house [C20 from the forename *Sammy*]

Samnite ('sæmnaɪt) (in ancient Italy) *n* **1** a member of an Oscan-speaking people of the S Apennines, who clashed repeatedly with Rome between 350 BC and 200 BC ▷ *adj* **2** of or relating to this people

Samnium ('sæmnɪəm) *n* an ancient country of central Italy inhabited by Oscan-speaking Samnites: corresponds to the present-day regions of Abruzzi, Molise, and part of Campania

Samoa (sə'məʊə) *n* **1** an independent state occupying four inhabited islands and five uninhabited islands in the S Pacific archipelago of the Samoa Islands: established as a League of Nations mandate under New Zealand administration in 1920 and a UN trusteeship in 1946; gained independence as Western Samoa in 1962 as the first fully independent Polynesian state; officially changed its name to Samoa in 1997; a member of the Commonwealth. Languages: Samoan and English. Religion: Christian. Currency: tala. Capital: Apia. Pop: 180 000 (2004 est). Area 2841 sq km (1097 sq miles) **2** Also called: Samoa Islands a group of islands in the S Pacific, northeast of Fiji: an independent kingdom until the mid 19th century, when it was divided administratively into **American Samoa** (in the east) and **German Samoa** (in the west); the latter was mandated to New Zealand in 1919 and gained full independence in 1962 as Western Samoa, now **Samoa** (sense 1). Area: 3038 sq km (1173 sq miles)

Samoan (sə'məʊən) *adj* **1** of or relating to Samoa, its people, or their language ▷ *n* **2** a member of

the people that inhabit Samoa **3** the language of Samoa, belonging to the Polynesian family of languages

Samos ('seɪmɒs) *n* a Greek island in the E Aegean Sea, off the SW coast of Turkey: a leading commercial centre of ancient Greece. Pop: 33 809 (2001). Area: 492 sq km (190 sq miles)

samosa (sə'məʊsə) *n*, *pl* -sas *or* -sa (in Indian cookery) a small triangular pastry case containing spiced vegetables or meat and served fried [C20 from Hindi]

Samothrace ('sæmə,θreɪs) *n* a Greek island in the NE Aegean Sea: mountainous. Pop: 2723 (2001)

samovar ('sæmə,vɑː, ,sæmə'vɑː) *n* (esp in Russia) a metal urn for making tea, in which the water is heated esp formerly by charcoal held in an inner container or nowadays more usually by electricity [C19 from Russian, from *samo-* self (related to SAME) + *varit'* to boil]

Samoyed (,sæmə'jɛd) *n* **1** (*pl* -yed *or* -yeds) a member of a group of peoples who migrated along the Russian Arctic coast and now live chiefly in the area of the N Urals: related to the Finns **2** the languages of these peoples, related to Finno-Ugric within the Uralic family **3** (sə'mɔɪɛd) a Siberian breed of dog of the spitz type, having a dense white or cream coat with a distinct ruff, and a tightly curled tail [C17 from Russian *Samoed*] > ,Samo'yedic *adj*

samp (sæmp) *n* South African crushed maize used for porridge [C17 from Narraganset *nasaump* softened by water]

sampan ('sæmpæn) *n* any small skiff, widely used in the Orient, that is propelled by oars or a scull [C17 from Chinese *san pan*, from *san* three + *pan* board]

samphire ('sæm,faɪə) *n* **1** Also called: rock samphire an umbelliferous plant, *Crithmum maritimum*, of Eurasian coasts, having fleshy divided leaves and clusters of small greenish-white flowers **2** golden samphire a Eurasian coastal plant, *Inula crithmoides*, with fleshy leaves and yellow flower heads: family *Asteraceae* (composites) **3** another name for **glasswort** (sense 1) **4** any of several other plants of coastal areas [C16 *sampiere*, from French *herbe de Saint Pierre* Saint Peter's herb; perhaps influenced by *camphire* CAMPHOR]

sample ('sɑːmpˀl) *n* **1 a** a small part of anything, intended as representative of the whole; specimen **b** (*as modifier*): *a sample bottle* **2** Also called: sampling *statistics* **a** a set of individuals or items selected from a population for analysis to yield estimates of, or to test hypotheses about, parameters of the whole population. A **biased sample** is one in which the items selected share some property which influences their distribution, while a **random sample** is devised to avoid any such interference so that its distribution is affected only by, and so can be held to represent, that of the whole population. See also **matched sample b** (*as modifier*): *sample distribution* ▷ *vb* **3** (*tr*) to take a sample or samples of **4** *music* **a** to take a short extract from (one record) and mix it into a different backing track **b** to record (a sound) and feed it into a computerized synthesizer so that it can be reproduced at any pitch [C13 from Old French *essample*, from Latin *exemplum* EXAMPLE]

sample point *n statistics* a single possible observed value of a variable; a member of the sample space of an experiment

sampler ('sɑːmplə) *n* **1** a person who takes samples **2** a piece of embroidery executed as an example of the embroiderer's skill in using a variety of stitches: often incorporating numbers, letters, and the name and age of the embroiderer in a decorative panel **3** *music* a piece of electronic equipment used for sampling **4** a recording comprising a collection of tracks from other albums, intended to stimulate interest in the featured products

sample space *n statistics* the set of possible outcomes of an experiment; the range of values of a random variable

sampling ('sɑːmplɪŋ) *n* **1** the process of selecting a random sample **2** a variant of **sample** (sense 2) **3** the process of taking a short extract from (a record) and mixing it into a different backing track **4** a process in which a continuous electrical signal is approximately represented by a series of discrete values, usually regularly spaced

sampling frame *n statistics* See **frame** (sense 13)

sampling statistic *n* any function of observed data, esp one used to estimate the corresponding parameter of the underlying distribution, such as the sample mean, sample variance, etc. Compare estimator (sense 2), **parameter** (sense 3)

samsara (səm'sɑːrə) *n* **1** *Hinduism* the endless cycle of birth, death, and rebirth **2** *Buddhism* the transmigration or rebirth of a person [Sanskrit, literally: a passing through, from *sam* altogether + *sarati* it runs]

samshu ('sæmʃuː, -ʃuː) *n* an alcoholic drink from China that is made from fermented rice and resembles sake [C17 perhaps modification of Chinese *shao chiu* spirits that will burn, from *shao* to burn + *chiu* spirits]

Samson ('sæmsən) *n* **1** a judge of Israel, who performed herculean feats of strength against the Philistine oppressors until he was betrayed to them by his mistress Delilah (Judges 13–16) **2** any man of outstanding physical strength

Samsun (*Turkish* 'samsun) *n* a port in N Turkey, on the Black Sea. Pop: 395 000 (2005 est). Ancient name: Amisus (əmi:səs)

Samuel ('sæmjʊəl) *n Old Testament* **1** a Hebrew prophet, seer, and judge, who anointed the first two kings of the Israelites (I Samuel 1–3; 8–15) **2** either of the two books named after him, I and II Samuel

samurai ('sæmʊ,raɪ, 'sæmjʊ-) *n*, *pl* -rai **1** the Japanese warrior caste that provided the administrative and fighting aristocracy from the 11th to the 19th centuries **2** a member of this aristocracy [C19 from Japanese]

samurai bond *n* a bond issued in Japan and denominated in yen, available for purchase by nonresidents of Japan. Compare **shogun bond**

san (sæn) *n old-fashioned informal* short for **sanatorium** (esp sense 3)

San[1] (sɑːn) *n* **1** an aboriginal people of southern Africa **2** a group of the Khoisan languages, spoken mostly by Bushmen

San[2] (sɑːn) *n* a river in E central Europe, rising in W Ukraine and flowing northwest across SE Poland to the Vistula River. Length: about 450 km (280 miles)

San'a *or* **Sanaa** (sɑː'nɑː) *n* the administrative capital of Yemen, on the central plateau at an altitude of 2350 m (7700 ft): formerly the capital of North Yemen. Pop: 1 621 000 (2005 est)

San Antonian (sæn æn'təʊnɪ,ən) *adj* **1** of or relating to San Antonio or its inhabitants ▷ *n* **2** a native or inhabitant of San Antonio

San Antonio (sæn æn'təʊnɪ,əʊ) *n* a city in S Texas: site of the Alamo; the leading town in Texas until about 1930. Pop: 1 214 725 (2003 est)

Sanatana Dharma (sa,natana 'darma:) *n* the name used by Hindus for Hinduism [from Sanskrit: the eternal way]

sanative ('sænətɪv) *adj* a less common word for **curative** [C15 from Medieval Latin *sānātīvus*, from Latin *sānāre* to heal, from *sānus* healthy]

sanatorium (,sænə'tɔːrɪəm) *or US* **sanitarium** *n*, *pl* -riums *or* -ria (-rɪə) **1** an institution for the medical care and recuperation of persons who are chronically ill **2** a health resort **3** Brit a room in a boarding school where sick pupils may be treated in isolation [C19 from New Latin, from Latin *sānāre* to heal]

sanbenito (,sænbə'ni:təʊ) *n*, *pl* -tos **1** a yellow garment bearing a red cross, worn by penitent heretics in the Inquisition **2** a black garment bearing flames and devils, worn by impenitent heretics at an auto-da-fé [c16 from Spanish *San Benito* Saint Benedict, an ironical allusion to its likeness to the Benedictine scapular]

San Bernardino (sæn ˌbɜːnəˈdiːnəʊ) *n* a city in SE California: founded in 1851 by Mormons from Salt Lake City. Pop: 195 357 (2003 est)

San Bernardino Pass *n* a pass over the Lepontine Alps in SE Switzerland. Highest point: 2062 m (6766 ft)

San Blas (ˈsaːn ˈblaːs) *n* **1 Isthmus of** the narrowest part of the Isthmus of Panama. Width: about 50 km (30 miles) **2 Gulf of** an inlet of the Caribbean on the N coast of Panama

Sancerre (sɒnˈsɛə; *French* sɑ̃sɛr) *n* a dry white wine produced in the Loire valley in France [French]

San Cristóbal (*Spanish* san kriˈstoβal) *n* **1** Also called: **Chatham Island** an island in the Pacific, in the Galápagos Islands. Area: 505 sq km (195 sq miles) **2** a city in SW Venezuela: founded in 1561 by Spanish conquistadores. Pop: 395 000 (2005 est)

sanctified (ˈsæŋktɪˌfaɪd) *adj* **1** consecrated or made holy **2** a less common word for **sanctimonious**

sanctify (ˈsæŋktɪˌfaɪ) *vb* **-fies, -fying, -fied** (*tr*) **1** to make holy **2** to free from sin; purify **3** to sanction (an action or practice) as religiously binding: *to sanctify a marriage* **4** to declare or render (something) productive or conductive to holiness, blessing, or grace **5** *obsolete* to authorize to be revered [c14 from Late Latin *sanctificāre*, from Latin *sanctus* holy + *facere* to make] > ˈsanctiˌfiable *adj* > ˌsanctifiˈcation *n*

sanctimonious (ˌsæŋktɪˈməʊnɪəs) *adj* affecting piety or making a display of holiness [c17 from Latin *sanctimonia* sanctity, from *sanctus* holy] > ˌsanctiˈmoniously *adv* > ˌsanctiˈmoniousness *n* > ˈsanctimony *n*

sanction (ˈsæŋkʃən) *n* **1** final permission; authorization **2** aid or encouragement **3** something, such as an ethical principle, that imparts binding force to a rule, oath, etc **4** the penalty laid down in a law for contravention of its provisions **5** (*often plural*) a coercive measure, esp one taken by one or more states against another guilty of violating international law ▷ *vb* (*tr*) **6** to give authority to; permit **7** to make authorized; confirm [c16 from Latin *sanctiō* the establishment of an inviolable decree, from *sancīre* to decree] > ˈsanctionable *adj* > ˈsanctioner *n* > ˈsanctionless *adj*

sanction mark *n* a mark on pieces of 19th-century French furniture signifying that the piece met the quality standards required by the Parisian guild of ebonists

sanctitude (ˈsæŋktɪˌtjuːd) *n* saintliness; holiness

sanctity (ˈsæŋktɪtɪ) *n*, *pl* **-ties 1** the condition of being sanctified; holiness **2** anything regarded as sanctified or holy **3** the condition of being inviolable; sacredness: *the sanctity of marriage* [c14 from Old French *saincteté*, from Latin *sanctitās*, from *sanctus* holy]

sanctuary (ˈsæŋktjʊərɪ) *n*, *pl* **-aries 1** a holy place **2** a consecrated building or shrine **3** *Old Testament* **a** the Israelite temple at Jerusalem, esp the holy of holies **b** the tabernacle in which the Ark was enshrined during the wanderings of the Israelites **4** the chancel, or that part of a sacred building surrounding the main altar **5 a** a sacred building where fugitives were formerly entitled to immunity from arrest or execution **b** the immunity so afforded **6** a place of refuge; asylum **7** a place, protected by law, where animals, esp birds, can live and breed without interference [c14 from Old French *sainctuarie*, from Late Latin *sanctuārium* repository for holy things, from Latin *sanctus* holy]

sanctuary lamp *n* *Christianity* a lamp, usually red, placed in a prominent position in the sanctuary of a church, that when lit indicates the presence of the Blessed Sacrament

sanctum (ˈsæŋktəm) *n*, *pl* **-tums, -ta** (-tə) **1** a sacred or holy place **2** a room or place of total privacy or inviolability [c16 from Latin, from *sanctus* holy]

sanctum sanctorum (sæŋkˈtɔːrəm) *n* **1** *Bible* another term for the **holy of holies 2** *often facetious* an especially private place [c14 from Latin, literally: holy of holies, rendering Hebrew *qōdesh haqqodāshīm*]

Sanctus (ˈsæŋktəs) *n* **1** *liturgy* the hymn that occurs immediately after the preface in the celebration of the Eucharist **2** a musical setting of this, usually incorporated into the Ordinary of the Roman Catholic Mass [c14 from the first word of the hymn, *Sanctus sanctus sanctus* Holy, holy, holy, from Latin *sancīre* to consecrate]

Sanctus bell *n* *chiefly RC Church* a bell rung as the opening words of the Sanctus are pronounced and also at other important points during Mass

sand (sænd) *n* **1** loose material consisting of rock or mineral grains, esp rounded grains of quartz, between 0.05 and 2 mm in diameter **2** (*often plural*) a sandy area, esp on the seashore or in a desert **3 a** a greyish-yellow colour **b** (*as adjective*): *sand upholstery* **4** the grains of sandlike material in an hourglass **5** *US informal* courage; grit **6 draw a line in the sand** to put a stop to or a limit on **7 the sands are running out** there is not much time left before death or the end ▷ *vb* **8** (*tr*) to smooth or polish the surface of with sandpaper or sand: *to sand a floor* **9** (*tr*) to sprinkle or cover with or as if with sand; add sand to **10** to fill or cause to fill with sand: *the channel sanded up* [Old English; related to Old Norse *sandr*, Old High German *sant*, Greek *hamathos*] > ˈsandˌlike *adj*

Sandakan (ˈsaːnˈdaːkaːn) *n* a port in Malaysia, on the NE coast of Sabah: capital (until 1947) of North Borneo. Pop: 347 334 (2000)

sandal (ˈsændᵊl) *n* **1** a light shoe consisting of a sole held on the foot by thongs, straps, etc **2** a strap passing over the instep or around the ankle to keep a low shoe on the foot [c14 from Latin *sandalium*, from Greek *sandalion* a small sandal, from *sandalon* sandal] > ˈsandalled *adj*

sandalwood (ˈsændᵊlˌwʊd) or **sandal** *n* **1** any of several evergreen hemiparasitic trees of the genus *Santalum*, esp *S. album* (**white sandalwood**), of S Asia and Australia, having hard light-coloured heartwood: family *Santalaceae* **2** the wood of any of these trees, which is used for carving, is burned as incense, and yields an aromatic oil used in perfumery **3** any of various similar trees or their wood, esp *Pterocarpus santalinus* (**red sandalwood**), a leguminous tree of SE Asia having dark red wood used as a dye [c14 *sandal*, from Medieval Latin *sandalum*, from Late Greek *sandanon*, from Sanskrit *candana* sandalwood]

Sandalwood Island *n* the former name for **Sumba**

sandarac or **sandarach** (ˈsændəˌræk) *n* **1** Also called: **sandarac tree** either of two coniferous trees, *Tetraclinis articulata* of N Africa or *Callistris endlicheri* of Australia, having hard fragrant dark wood: family *Cupressaceae* **2** a brittle pale yellow transparent resin obtained from the bark of this tree and used in making varnish and incense **3** Also called: **citron wood** the wood of this tree, used in building [c16 *sandaracha*, from Latin *sandaraca* red pigment, from Greek *sandarakē*]

sandbag (ˈsændˌbæg) *n* **1** a sack filled with sand used for protection against gunfire, floodwater, etc, or as ballast in a balloon, ship, etc **2** a bag filled with sand and used as a weapon ▷ *vb* **-bags, -bagging, -bagged** (*tr*) **3** to protect or strengthen with sandbags **4** to hit with or as if with a sandbag **5** *finance* to obstruct (an unwelcome takeover bid) by prolonging talks in the hope that an acceptable bidder will come forward > ˈsandˌbagger *n*

sandbank (ˈsændˌbæŋk) *n* a submerged bank of sand in a sea or river, that may be exposed at low tide

sand bar *n* a ridge of sand in a river or sea, built up by the action of tides, currents, etc, and often exposed at low tide

sandblast (ˈsændˌblaːst) *n* **1** a jet of sand or grit blown from a nozzle under air, water, or steam pressure ▷ *vb* (*tr*) **2** to clean, grind, or decorate (a surface) with a sandblast > ˈsandˌblaster *n*

sand-blind *adj* not completely blind; partially able to see. Compare **stone-blind** [c15 changed (through influence of SAND) from Old English *samblind* (unattested), from *sam-* half, SEMI- + BLIND] > ˈsand-ˌblindness *n*

sandbox (ˈsændˌbɒks) *n* **1** a container on a railway locomotive from which sand is released onto the rails to assist the traction **2** a box with sand shaped for moulding metal **3** a container of sand for small children to play in

sandbox tree *n* a tropical American euphorbiaceous tree, *Hura crepitans*, having small woody seed capsules, which explode when ripe to scatter the seeds: formerly used to hold sand for blotting ink

sandboy (ˈsændˌbɔɪ) *n* **happy** (or **jolly**) **as a sandboy** very happy; high-spirited

sand-cast *vb* **-casts, -casting, -cast** (*tr*) to produce (a casting) by pouring molten metal into a mould of sand > ˈsand-ˌcasting *n*

sand castle *n* a mass of sand moulded into a castle-like shape, esp as made by a child on the seashore

sand colic *n* *vet science* a form of colic caused by the ingestion of sand or eating sand-contaminated feeds and subsequent collection of sand in the gastrointestinal tract

sand crab *n* *Austral* another name for **blue swimmer**

sand crack *n* *vet science* a deep crack or fissure in the wall of a horse's hoof, often causing lameness. See also **toe crack, quarter crack**

sand dab *n* any of various small flatfishes of the genus *Citharichthys* that occur in American Pacific coastal waters and are important food fishes

sand dollar *n* any of various flattened disclike echinoderms of the order *Clypeasteroida*, of shallow North American coastal waters: class *Echinoidea* (sea urchins)

sand eel or **lance** *n* any silvery eel-like marine spiny-finned fish of the family *Ammodytidae* found burrowing in sand or shingle. Popular name: **launce**

sandek (ˈsanˌdɛk) *n* *Judaism* a man who holds a baby being circumcised [Hebrew]

sander (ˈsændə) *n* **1** a power-driven tool for smoothing surfaces, esp wood, plastic, etc, by rubbing with an abrasive disc **2** a person who uses such a device

sanderling (ˈsændəlɪŋ) *n* a small sandpiper, *Crocethia alba*, that frequents sandy shores [c17 perhaps from SAND + Old English *erthling, eorthling* EARTHLING]

sand flea *n* another name for the **chigoe** (sense 1), **sand hopper**

sandfly (ˈsændˌflaɪ) *n*, *pl* **-flies 1** any of various small mothlike dipterous flies of the genus *Phlebotomus* and related genera: the bloodsucking females transmit diseases including leishmaniasis: family *Psychodidae* **2** any of various similar and related flies

sandglass (ˈsændˌglaːs) *n* a less common word for **hourglass**

sandgrouse (ˈsændˌgraʊs) *n* any bird of the family *Pteroclididae*, of dry regions of the Old World, having very short feet, a short bill, and long pointed wings and tail: order *Columbiformes*

sandhi (ˈsændɪ) *n*, *pl* **-dhis** *linguistics* modification of the form or sound of a word under the influence of an adjacent word [from Sanskrit *samdhi* a placing together, from *sam* together + *dadhāti* he puts]

sandhog (ˈsændˌhɒg) *n* *chiefly US and Canadian* a person who works in underground or underwater construction projects

S

sand hopper *n* any of various small hopping amphipod crustaceans of the genus *Orchestia* and related genera, common in intertidal regions of seashores. Also called: **beach flea**, **sand flea**

Sandhurst (ˈsændˌhɜːst) *n* a village in S England, in Bracknell unitary authority, Berkshire: seat of the Royal Military Academy for the training of officer cadets in the British Army. Pop: 19 546 (2001)

San Diego (ˌsæn dɪˈeɪɡəʊ) *n* a port in S California, on the Pacific: naval base; two universities. Pop: 1 266 753 (2003 est)

Sandinista (ˌsændɪˈniːstə) *n* (in Nicaragua) **a** one of a left-wing group of revolutionaries who overthrew President Somoza in 1979 and formed a socialist coalition government. The Sandinistas were opposed militarily by the US-backed Contras during the 1980s and were defeated in a general election in 1990 **b** (*as modifier*): *the Sandinista revolution* [C20 from Spanish, named after Augusto César *Sandino* a Nicaraguan general and rebel leader, murdered in 1933]

sand lance *or* **launce** *n* another name for the **sand eel**

sand leek *n* a Eurasian alliaceous plant, *Allium scorodoprasum*, having reddish-pink flowers, purple bulbils, and a garlic-like bulb. See also **rocambole**

sand lizard *n* a small greyish-brown European lizard, *Lacerta agilis*, that has long clawed digits and, in the male, bright green underparts: family *Lacertidae*

sandlot (ˈsændˌlɒt) *n* US **1** an area of vacant ground used by children for playing baseball and other games **2** (*modifier*) denoting a game or sport played on a sandlot: *sandlot baseball*

S & M *abbreviation for* sadomasochism

sandman (ˈsændˌmæn) *n*, *pl* **-men** (in folklore) a magical person supposed to put children to sleep by sprinkling sand in their eyes

sand martin *n* a small brown European songbird, *Riparia riparia*, with white underparts: it nests in tunnels bored in sand, river banks, etc: family *Hirundinidae* (swallows and martins)

sand painting *n* a type of painting done by American Indians, esp in the healing ceremonies of the Navaho, using fine coloured sand on a neutral ground

sandpaper (ˈsændˌpeɪpə) *n* **1** (formerly) a strong paper coated with sand for smoothing and polishing **2** a common name for **glasspaper** ▷ *vb* **3** (*tr*) to polish or grind (a surface) with or as if with sandpaper

sandpiper (ˈsændˌpaɪpə) *n* **1** any of numerous N hemisphere shore birds of the genera *Tringa*, *Calidris*, etc, typically having a long slender bill and legs and cryptic plumage: family *Scolopacidae*, order *Charadriiformes* **2** any other bird of the family *Scolopacidae*, which includes snipes and woodcocks

sandpit (ˈsændˌpɪt) *n* **1** a shallow pit or container holding sand for children to play in **2** a pit from which sand is extracted

Sandringham (ˈsændrɪŋəm) *n* a village in E England, in Norfolk near the E shore of the Wash: site of **Sandringham House**, a residence of the royal family

sandshoe (ˈsændˌʃuː) *n* Brit and Austral a light canvas shoe with a rubber sole; plimsoll

sand shrimp *n* See **shrimp** (sense 4)

sandsoap (ˈsændˌsəʊp) *n* a gritty general-purpose soap

sandstone (ˈsændˌstəʊn) *n* any of a group of common sedimentary rocks consisting of sand grains consolidated with such materials as quartz, haematite, and clay minerals: used widely in building

sandstorm (ˈsændˌstɔːm) *n* a strong wind that whips up clouds of sand, esp in a desert

sand table *n* military a surface on which sand can be modelled into a relief map on which to demonstrate tactics

sand trap *n* another name (esp US) for **bunker** (sense 2)

sand viper *n* **1** a S European viper, *Vipera ammodytes*, having a yellowish-brown coloration with a zigzag pattern along the back **2** another name for **horned viper**

sand wasp *n* a solitary wasp of the subfamily *Sphecinae*, a subgroup of the digger wasps most of which nest in sandy ground

sand wedge *n* golf a club with a flanged sole and a face angle of more than 50°, used in bunker shots to cut through sand, get under the ball, and lift it clear

Sandwell (ˈsændwɛl) *n* a unitary authority in central England, in West Midlands. Pop: 285 000 (2003 est). Area: 86 sq km (33 sq miles)

sandwich (ˈsænwɪdʒ, -wɪtʃ) *n* **1** two or more slices of bread, usually buttered, with a filling of meat, cheese, etc **2** anything that resembles a sandwich in arrangement ▷ *vb* (*tr*) **3** to insert tightly between two other things **4** to put into a sandwich **5** to place between two dissimilar things [C18 named after John Montagu, 4th Earl of *Sandwich* (1718–92), who ate sandwiches rather than leave the gambling table for meals]

sandwich beam *n* a composite beam in which a viscoelastic layer is sandwiched between two elastic layers

sandwich board *n* one of two connected boards, usually bearing advertisements, that are hung over the shoulders in front of and behind a person

sandwich cake *n* a cake that is made up of two or more layers with a jam or other filling. Also called: **layer cake**

sandwich compound *n* chem any of a class of organometallic compounds whose molecules have a metal atom or ion bound between two plane parallel organic rings. See also **metallocene**

sandwich course *n* any of several courses consisting of alternate periods of study and industrial work

Sandwich Islands *pl n* the former name of **Hawaii**

sandwich man *n* a man who carries sandwich boards

sandwich tern *n* a European tern, *Sterna sandvicensis*, that has a yellow-tipped bill, whitish plumage, and white forked tail, and nests in colonies on beaches, etc [C18 from the town of *Sandwich* in Kent]

sandworm (ˈsændˌwɜːm) *n* any of various polychaete worms that live in burrows on sandy shores, esp the lugworm

sandwort (ˈsændˌwɜːt) *n* **1** any of numerous caryophyllaceous plants of the genus *Arenaria*, which grow in dense tufts on sandy soil and have white or pink solitary flowers **2** any of various related plants

sandy (ˈsændɪ) *adj* sandier, sandiest **1** consisting of, containing, or covered with sand **2** (esp of hair) reddish-yellow **3** resembling sand in texture ▷ ˈsandiness *n*

sand yacht *n* a wheeled boat with sails, built to be propelled over sand, esp beaches, by the wind

sandy blight *n* Austral a nontechnical name for any of various eye inflammations

sane (seɪn) *adj* **1** sound in mind; free from mental disturbance **2** having or showing reason, good judgment, or sound sense **3** obsolete healthy [C17 from Latin *sānus* healthy] ▷ ˈsanely *adv* ▷ ˈsaneness *n*

San Fernando (Spanish san fɛrˈnando) *n* **1** a port in Trinidad and Tobago, on Trinidad on the Gulf of Paria: the second-largest town in the country. Pop: 55 149 (2000) **2** an inland port in W Venezuela, on the Apure River. Pop: 84 180 (latest est). Official name: **San Fernando de Apure 3** a port in SW Spain, on the Isla de León SE of Cádiz; site of an arsenal (founded 1790) and of the most southerly observatory in Europe. Pop: 88 490 (2003 est)

Sanforized *or* **Sanforised** (ˈsænfəˌraɪzd) *adj* trademark (of a fabric) preshrunk using a patented process

San Franciscan (ˌsæn frænˈsɪskən) *n* **1** a native or inhabitant of San Francisco ▷ *adj* **2** of or relating to San Francisco or its inhabitants

San Francisco (ˌsæn frænˈsɪskəʊ) *n* a port in W California, situated around the Golden Gate: developed rapidly during the California gold rush; a major commercial centre and one of the world's finest harbours. Pop: 751 682 (2003 est)

San Francisco Bay *n* an inlet of the Pacific in W California, linked with the open sea by the Golden Gate strait. Length: about 80 km (50 miles). Greatest width: 19 km (12 miles).

sang[1] (sæŋ) *vb* the past tense of **sing**

■ USAGE See at **ring**[2]

sang[2] (sæŋ) *n* a Scot word for **song**

sangar (ˈsʌŋɡə) *n* military a breastwork of stone or sods [C19 from Pashto]

sangaree (ˌsæŋɡəˈriː) *n* a spiced drink similar to sangria [C18 from Spanish *sangría* a bleeding, from *sangre* blood, from Latin *sanguis*; see SANGUINE]

sanger (ˈsæŋə) *n* Austral slang a sandwich. Also called: **sango**

sang-froid (French sɑ̃frwa) *n* composure; self-possession; calmness [C18 from French, literally: cold blood]

Sangh (sʌŋɡ) *n* (in India) an association or union, esp a political or labour organization [Hindi]

Sangha (ˈsʌŋɡə) *n* **a** the Buddhist community **b** (in Theravada Buddhism) the monastic order [from Sanskrit: group, congregation]

sanghat (ˈsʌŋɡʌt) *n* Sikhism a fellowship or assembly, esp a local Sikh community or congregation [Punjabi]

Sangiovese (ˌsændʒəʊˈveɪzɪ) *n* **1** a black grape grown in the Tuscany region of Italy, used for making Chianti and other wines **2** a red wine made from this grape

Sango (ˈsɑːŋɡəʊ) *n* a language used in Chad, the Central African Republic, N Democratic Republic of Congo (formerly Zaïre), and the Congo, belonging to the Adamawa branch of the Niger-Congo family

sangoma (sæŋˈɡəʊmə, -ˈɡɔːmə) *n* South African a witch doctor, healer, or herbalist [from Zulu *isangoma*]

Sangrail, Sangraal (sæŋˈɡreɪl) *or* **Sangreal** (ˈsæŋɡriəl) *n* another name for the **Holy Grail** [C15 from Old French *Saint Graal*. See SAINT, HOLY GRAIL]

Sangre de Cristo Mountains (ˈsæŋɡrɪ də ˈkrɪstəʊ) *pl n* a mountain range in S Colorado and N New Mexico: part of the Rocky Mountains. Highest peak: Blanca Peak, 4364 m (14 317 ft)

sangria (sæŋˈɡriːə) *n* a Spanish drink of red wine, sugar, orange or lemon juice, and iced soda, sometimes laced with brandy [Spanish: a bleeding; see SANGAREE]

sanguinaria (ˌsæŋɡwɪˈnɛərɪə) *n* **1** the dried rhizome of the bloodroot, used as an emetic **2** another name for **bloodroot** (sense 1) [C19 from New Latin *herba sanguināria*, literally: the bloody herb]

sanguinary (ˈsæŋɡwɪnərɪ) *adj* **1** accompanied by much bloodshed **2** bloodthirsty **3** consisting of, flowing, or stained with blood [C17 from Latin *sanguinārius*] ▷ ˈsanguinarily *adv* ▷ ˈsanguinariness *n*

sanguine (ˈsæŋɡwɪn) *adj* **1** cheerful and confident; optimistic **2** (esp of the complexion) ruddy in appearance **3** blood-red **4** an obsolete word for **sanguinary** (sense 2) ▷ *n* **5** Also called: **red chalk** a red pencil containing ferric oxide, used in drawing [C14 from Latin *sanguineus* bloody, from *sanguis* blood] ▷ ˈsanguinely *adv* ▷ ˈsanguineness *or* sanˈguinity *n*

sanguineous (sæŋˈɡwɪnɪəs) *adj* **1** of, containing, relating to, or associated with blood **2** a less common word for **sanguine** (senses 1–3) ▷ sanˈguineousness *n*

sanguinolent (sæŋˈɡwɪnələnt) *adj* containing, tinged with, or mixed with blood [C15 from Latin *sanguinolentus*, from *sanguis* blood] ▷ sanˈguinolency *n*

Sanhedrin (ˈsænɪdrɪn) *n* Judaism **1** the supreme

judicial, ecclesiastical, and administrative council of the Jews in New Testament times, having 71 members **2** a similar tribunal of 23 members having less important functions and authority [c16 from Late Hebrew, from Greek *sunedrion* council, from *sun-* SYN- + *hedra* seat]

sanicle ('sænɪkᵊl) *n* any umbelliferous plant of the genus *Sanicula*, of most regions except Australia, having clusters of small white flowers and oval fruits with hooked bristles: formerly thought to have healing powers [c15 via Old French from Medieval Latin *sānicula*, probably from Latin *sānus* healthy]

sanidine ('sænɪˌdiːn, -dɪn) *n* an alkali feldspar that is a high-temperature glassy form of orthoclase in flat, tabular crystals, found in lavas and dykes. Formula: KAlSi₃O₈ [c19 from German, from Greek *sanis, sanidos* a board]

sanies ('seɪnɪˌiːz) *n pathol* a thin greenish foul-smelling discharge from a wound, ulcer, etc, containing pus and blood [c16 from Latin, of obscure origin]

San Ildefonso (*Spanish* san ilde'fɔnso) *n* a town in central Spain, near Segovia: site of the 18th-century summer palace of the kings of Spain. Also called: **La Granja**

sanitarian (ˌsænɪ'tɛərɪən) *adj* **1** of or relating to sanitation ▷ *n* **2** a sanitation expert

sanitarium (ˌsænɪ'tɛərɪəm) *n, pl* -riums *or* -ria (-rɪə) the US spelling of **sanatorium** [c19 from Latin *sānitās* health]

sanitary ('sænɪtərɪ, -trɪ) *adj* **1** of or relating to health and measures for the protection of health **2** conducive to or promoting health; free from dirt, germs, etc; hygienic [c19 from French *sanitaire*, from Latin *sānitās* health] > 'sanitarily *adv* > 'sanitariness *n*

sanitary belt *n* a belt for supporting a sanitary towel

sanitary engineering *n* the branch of civil engineering associated with the supply of water, disposal of sewage, and other public health services > sanitary engineer *n*

sanitary inspector *n* (in Britain) a former name for **Environmental Health Officer**

sanitary protection *n* sanitary towels and tampons, collectively

sanitary towel *or esp US* **napkin** *n* an absorbent pad worn externally by women during menstruation to absorb the menstrual flow

sanitation (ˌsænɪ'teɪʃən) *n* the study and use of practical measures for the preservation of public health

sanitize *or* **sanitise** ('sænɪˌtaɪz) *vb (tr)* **1** to make sanitary or hygienic, as by sterilizing **2** to omit unpleasant details from (a news report, document, etc) to make it more palatable to the recipients > ˌsaniti'zation *or* ˌsaniti'sation *n*

sanity ('sænɪtɪ) *n* **1** the state of being sane **2** good sense or soundness of judgment [c15 from Latin *sānitās* health, from *sānus* healthy]

sanjak ('sændʒæk) *n* (in the Turkish Empire) a subdivision of a vilayet [c16 from Turkish *sancâk*, literally: a flag]

San Jose (ˌsæn həʊ'zeɪ) *n* a city in W central California: a leading world centre of the fruit drying and canning industry. Pop: 898 349 (2003 est)

San José (*Spanish* saŋ xo'se) *n* the capital of Costa Rica, on the central plateau: a major centre of coffee production in the mid-19th century; University of Costa Rica (1843). Pop: 1 145 000 (2005 est)

San Jose scale *n* a small E Asian homopterous insect, *Quadraspidiotus perniciosus*, introduced into the US and other countries, where it has become a serious pest of fruit trees: family *Diaspididae* [c20 from its first being seen in the United States at *San Jose, California*]

San Juan (*Spanish* saŋ 'xwan) *n* **1** the capital and chief port of Puerto Rico, on the NE coast; University of Puerto Rico; manufacturing centre.

Pop: 433 733 (2003 est) **2** a city in W Argentina: almost completely destroyed by an earthquake in 1944. Pop: 455 000 (2005 est)

San Juan Bautista (*Spanish* saŋ 'xwan bau'tista) *n* the former name of **Villahermosa**

San Juan Islands (sæn 'wɑːn, 'hwɑːn) *pl n* a group of islands between NW Washington, US, and SE Vancouver Island, Canada: administratively part of Washington

San Juan Mountains *pl n* a mountain range in SW Colorado and N New Mexico: part of the Rocky Mountains. Highest peak: Uncompahgre Peak, 4363 m (14 314 ft)

sank (sæŋk) *vb* the past tense of **sink**

Sankhya ('sæŋkjə) *n* one of the six orthodox schools of Hindu philosophy, teaching an eternal interaction of spirit and matter [from Sanskrit *sāmkhya*, literally: based on calculation, from *samkhyāti* he reckons]

Sankt Pölten (*German* zaŋkt 'pœltən) *n, usually abbreviated to* St Pölten a city in NE Austria, the capital of Lower Austria state. Pop: 49 121 (2001)

San Luis Potosí (*Spanish* san 'lwis poto'si) *n* **1** a state of central Mexico: mainly high plateau; economy based on mining (esp silver) and agriculture. Capital: San Luis Potosí. Pop: 927 000 (2005 est). Area: 62 849 sq km (24 266 sq miles) **2** an industrial city in central Mexico, capital of San Luis Potosí state, at an altitude of 1850 m (6000 ft). Pop: 628 134 (2000 est)

San Marinese (ˌsæn ˌmærɪ'niːz) *or* **Sammarinese** (sə,mærɪ'niːz) *adj* **1** of or relating to San Marino or its inhabitants ▷ *n* **2** a native or inhabitant of San Marino

San Marino (ˌsæn mə'riːnəʊ) *n* a republic in S central Europe in the Apennines, forming an enclave in Italy: the smallest republic in Europe, according to tradition founded by St Marinus in the 4th century. Official language: Italian. Religion: Roman Catholic majority. Currency: euro. Capital: San Marino. Pop: 28 000 (2003 est). Area: 62 sq km (24 sq miles)

sannyasi, sanyasi (sʌn'jɑːsɪ) *or* **sannyasin** (sʌn'jɑːsɪn) *n* a Brahman who having attained the fourth and last stage of life as a beggar will not be reborn, but will instead be absorbed into the Universal Soul. Also called: renunciate [from Hindi: abandoning, from Sanskrit *samnyāsin*]

San Pedro Sula (*Spanish* san 'peðro 'sula) *n* a city in NW Honduras: the country's chief industrial centre. Pop: 610 000 (2005 est)

sanpro ('sæn,prəʊ) *n advertising* sanitary-protection products, collectively

San Remo (*Italian* san 'rɛːmo) *n* a port and resort in NW Italy, in Liguria on the slopes of the Maritime Alps; flower market. Pop: 50 608 (2001)

sans (sænz) *prep* an archaic word for **without** [c13 from Old French *sanz*, from Latin *sine* without, but probably also influenced by Latin *absentiā* in the absence of]

Sans. *or* **Sansk.** *abbreviation for* Sanskrit

San Salvador (sæn 'sælvə,dɔː; *Spanish* san salβa'ðor) *n* the capital of El Salvador, situated in the SW central part: became capital in 1841; ruined by earthquakes in 1854 and 1873; university (1841). Pop: 1 472 000 (2005 est)

San Salvador Island *n* an island in the central Bahamas: the first land in the New World seen by Christopher Columbus (1492). Area: 156 sq km (60 sq miles). Also called: **Watling Island**

sans-culotte (ˌsænzkjʊ'lɒt; *French* sākylɔt) *n* **1** (during the French Revolution) **a** (originally) a revolutionary of the poorer class **b** (later) any revolutionary, esp one having extreme republican sympathies **2** any revolutionary extremist [c18 from French, literally: without knee breeches, because the revolutionaries wore pantaloons or trousers rather than knee breeches] > ˌsans-cu'lottism *n* > ˌsans-cu'lottist *n*

San Sebastián (ˌsæn sə'bæstjən; *Spanish* san seβas'tjan) *n* a port and resort in N Spain on the Bay of Biscay: former summer residence of the

Spanish court. Pop: 181 811 (2003 est). Official name: Donostia-San Sebastián

sansevieria (ˌsænsɪ'vɪərɪə) *n* any herbaceous perennial plant of the liliaceous genus *Sansevieria*, of Old World tropical regions. Some are cultivated as house plants for their erect bayonet-like fleshy leaves of variegated green (mother-in-law's tongue); others yield useful fibre (bowstring hemp) [New Latin, named after Raimondo di Sangro (1710–71), Italian scholar and prince of *San Severo*]

Sanskrit ('sænskrɪt) *n* an ancient language of India, the language of the Vedas, of Hinduism, and of an extensive philosophical and scientific literature dating from the beginning of the first millennium BC. It is the oldest recorded member of the Indic branch of the Indo-European family of languages; recognition of the existence of the Indo-European family arose in the 18th century from a comparison of Sanskrit with Greek and Latin. Although it is used only for religious purposes, it is one of the official languages of India [c17 from Sanskrit *samskrta* perfected, literally: put together] > 'Sanskritist *n*

Sanskritic (sæn'skrɪtɪk) *adj* **1** of or relating to Sanskrit **2** denoting or belonging to those Indic languages that developed directly from Sanskrit, such as Pali, Hindi, Punjabi, and Bengali ▷ *n* **3** this group of languages

Sanson-Flamsteed projection ('sænsən'flæmsti:d) *n* another name for **sinusoidal projection** [devised by the cartographer *Sanson* in 1650, adapted by *Flamsteed* in 1729]

sans serif *or* **sanserif** (sæn'sɛrɪf) *n* a style of printer's typeface in which the characters have no serifs

San Stefano (ˌsæn stɪ'fɑːnəʊ) *n* a village in NW Turkey, near Istanbul on the Sea of Marmara: scene of the signing (1878) of the treaty ending the Russo-Turkish War. Turkish name: Yeşilköy

Santa ('sæntə) *n informal* short for **Santa Claus**

Santa Ana *n* **1** (*Spanish* 'santa 'ana) a city in NW El Salvador: the second largest city in the country; coffee-processing industry. Pop: 172 000 (2005 est) **2** ('sæntə 'ænə) a city in SW California: commercial and processing centre of a rich agricultural region. Pop: 342 510 (2003 est)

Santa Catalina ('sæntə ˌkætᵊ'liːnə) *n* an island in the Pacific, off the coast of SW California: part of Los Angeles county: resort. Area: 181 sq km (70 sq miles). Also called: Catalina Island

Santa Catarina (*Portuguese* 'santə kətə'rinə) *n* a state of S Brazil, on the Atlantic: consists chiefly of the Great Escarpment. Capital: Florianópolis. Pop: 5 527 707 (2002). Area: 95 985 sq km (37 060 sq miles)

Santa Clara (*Spanish* 'santa 'klara) *n* a city in W central Cuba: sugar and tobacco industries. Pop: 216 000 (2005 est)

Santa Claus ('sæntə ˌklɔːz) *n* the legendary patron saint of children, commonly identified with Saint Nicholas, who brings presents to children on Christmas Eve or, in some European countries, on Saint Nicholas' Day. Often shortened to: Santa Also called: Father Christmas

Santa Cruz ('sæntə 'kruːz; *Spanish* 'santa 'kruθ) *n* **1** a province of S Argentina, on the Atlantic: consists of a large part of Patagonia, with the forested foothills of the Andes in the west. Capital: Río Gallegos. Pop: 206 897 (2000 est). Area: 243 940 sq km (94 186 sq miles) **2** a city in E Bolivia: the second largest town in Bolivia. Pop: 1 352 000 (2005 est) **3** another name for **Saint Croix**

Santa Cruz de Tenerife ('sæntə 'kruːz də ˌtɛnə'riːf; *Spanish* 'santa 'kruθ de tene'rife) *n* a port and resort in the W Canary Islands, on NE Tenerife: oil refinery. Pop: 220 022 (2003 est)

Santa Fe *n* **1** ('sæntə 'feɪ) a city in N central New Mexico, capital of the state: one of the oldest European settlements in North America, founded in 1610 as the capital of the Kingdom of New

S

Mexico; developed trade with the US by the Santa Fe Trail in the early 19th century. Pop: 66 476 (2003 est) **2** (*Spanish* 'santa 'fe) an inland port in E Argentina, on the Salado River: University of the Littoral (1920). Pop: 492 000 (2005 est)

Santa Fean ('sæntə 'feiən) *adj* **1** of or relating to Santa Fe or its inhabitants ▷ *n* **2** a native or inhabitant of Santa Fe

Santa Fe Trail ('sæntə 'fei) *n* an important trade route in the western US from about 1821 to 1880, linking Independence, Missouri to Santa Fe, New Mexico

Santa Gertrudis ('sæntə gə'truːdɪs) *n* one of a breed of large red beef cattle developed in Texas

Santa Isabel (*Spanish* 'santa isa'βel) *n* the former name (until 1973) of **Malabo**

santalaceous (ˌsæntə'leɪʃəs) *adj* of, relating to, or belonging to the *Santalaceae*, a family of semiparasitic plants of Australia and Malaysia including sandalwood and quandong [C19 via New Latin from Late Greek *santalon* sandalwood]

Santa Maria¹ ('sæntə mə'riːə) *n* **the** the flagship of Columbus on his first voyage to America (1492)

Santa Maria² *n* **1** (*Portuguese* 'sæntə ma'ria) a city in S Brazil, in Rio Grande do Sul state. Pop: 252 000 (2005 est) **2** (*Spanish* 'santa ma'ria) an active volcano in SW Guatemala. Height: 3768 m (12 362 ft)

Santa Marta (*Spanish* 'santa 'marta) *n* a port in NW Colombia, on the Caribbean: the oldest city in Colombia, founded in 1525; terminus of the Atlantic railway from Bogotá (opened 1961). Pop: 454 000 (2005 est)

Santa Maura ('santa 'maura) *n* the Italian name for **Levkás**

Santander (*Spanish* santan'der) *n* a port and resort in N Spain, on an inlet of the Bay of Biscay: noted for its prehistoric collection from nearby caves; shipyards and an oil refinery. Pop: 184 778 (2003 est)

Santarém (*Portuguese* sənta'rɐ̃j) *n* a port in N Brazil, in Pará state where the Tapajós River flows into the Amazon. Pop: 190 000 (2005 est)

Santa Rosa de Copán (*Spanish* 'santa 'rɔsa de ko'pan) *n* a village in W Honduras: noted for the ruined Mayan city of Copán, which lies to the west

Santee (sæn'tiː) *n* a river in SE central South Carolina, formed by the union of the Congaree and Wateree Rivers: flows southeast to the Atlantic; part of the **Santee-Wateree-Catawba River System** an inland waterway 866 km (538 miles) long. Length: 230 km (143 miles)

Santeria (ˌsæntə'rɪə) *n* a Caribbean religion composed of elements from both traditional African religion and Roman Catholicism [American Spanish, literally: holiness]

Santiago (ˌsæntɪ'ɑːɡəʊ; *Spanish* san'tjaɣo) *n* **1** the capital of Chile, at the foot of the Andes: commercial and industrial centre; two universities. Pop: 5 623 000 (2005 est). Official name: **Santiago de Chile** (de 'tʃile) **2** a city in the N Dominican Republic. Pop: 479 000 (2005 est). Official name: **Santiago de los Caballeros** (de los kaβa'ʎeros)

Santiago de Compostela (*Spanish* de kompos'tela) *n* a city in NW Spain: place of pilgrimage since the 9th century and the most visited (after Jerusalem and Rome) in the Middle Ages; cathedral built over the tomb of the apostle St James. Pop: 92 339 (2003 est). Latin name: **Campus Stellae** ('kæmpəs 'stɛliː)

Santiago de Cuba (*Spanish* de 'kuβa) *n* a port in SE Cuba, on **Santiago Bay** (a large inlet of the Caribbean): capital of Cuba until 1589; university (1947); industrial centre. Pop: 456 000 (2005 est)

Santiago del Estero (*Spanish* del es'tero) *n* a city in N Argentina: the oldest continuous settlement in Argentina, founded in 1553 by Spaniards from Peru. Pop: 385 000 (2005 est)

Santo Domingo ('sæntəʊ də'mɪŋɡəʊ; *Spanish* 'santo ðo'miŋɡo) *n* **1** the capital and chief port of

the Dominican Republic, on the S coast: the oldest continuous European settlement in the Americas, founded in 1496; university (1538). Pop: 1 920 000 (2005 est). Former name (1936–61): **Ciudad Trujillo 2** the former name (until 1844) of the **Dominican Republic 3** another name (esp in colonial times) for **Hispaniola**

santolina (ˌsæntə'liːnə) *n* any plant of the evergreen Mediterranean genus *Santolina*, esp *S. chamaecyparissus*, grown for its silvery-grey felted foliage: family *Asteraceae* (composites) [New Latin, altered from SANTONICA]

santonica (sæn'tɒnɪkə) *n* **1** an oriental wormwood plant, *Artemisia cina* (or *maritima*) **2** the dried flower heads of this plant, formerly used as a vermifuge ▷ Also called: **wormseed** [C17 New Latin, from Late Latin *herba santonica* herb of the *Santones* (probably wormwood), from Latin *Santonī* a people of Aquitania]

santonin ('sæntənɪn) *n* a white crystalline soluble substance extracted from the dried flower heads of santonica and used in medicine as an anthelmintic. Formula: $C_{15}H_{18}O_3$ [C19 from SANTONICA + -IN]

Santos (*Portuguese* 'sɐ̃ntuʃ) *n* a port in S Brazil, in São Paulo state: the world's leading coffee port. Pop: 1 634 000 (2005 est)

sanyasi (sʌn'jɑːsɪ) *n* a variant of **sannyasi**

SANZAR ('sæn,zə) *n* *acronym for* South African, New Zealand, and Australian Rugby: an agreement between the rugby unions of these nations under which various competitions are held

São Francisco (*Portuguese* sãw frɐ̃'sisku) *n* a river in E Brazil, rising in SW Minas Gerais state and flowing northeast, then southeast to the Atlantic northeast of Aracajú. Length: 3200 km (1990 miles)

São Luís (*Portuguese* sãw 'lwis) or **São Luíz** ('lwiʒ) *n* a port in NE Brazil, capital of Maranhão state, on the W coast of São Luís Island: founded in 1612 by the French and taken by the Portuguese in 1615. Pop: 982 000 (2005 est)

São Miguel (*Portuguese* sãw mi'ɣɛl) *n* an island in the E Azores: the largest of the group. Pop: 131 609 (2001). Area: 854 sq km (333 sq miles)

Saône (*French* son) *n* a river in E France, rising in Lorraine and flowing generally south to join the Rhône at Lyon, as its chief tributary: canalized for 375 km (233 miles) above Lyon; linked by canals with the Rhine, Marne, Seine, and Loire Rivers. Length: 480 km (298 miles)

Saône-et-Loire (*French* sonelwar) *n* a department of central France, in Burgundy region. Capital: Mâcon. Pop: 543 848 (2003 est). Area: 8627 sq km (3365 sq miles)

São Paulo (*Portuguese* sãw 'paulu) *n* **1** a state of SE Brazil: consists chiefly of tableland draining west into the Paraná River. Capital: São Paulo. Pop: 38 177 742 (2002). Area: 247 239 sq km (95 459 sq miles) **2** a city in S Brazil, capital of São Paulo state: the largest city and industrial centre in Brazil, with one of the busiest airports in the world; three universities; rapidly expanding population. Pop: 25 000 (1874); 2 017 025 (1950); Pop: 18 333 000 (2005 est)

Saorstat Eireann ('sɛəstɑːt 'ɛərən) *n* the Gaelic name for the **Irish Free State**

São Salvador (*Portuguese* sãw salva'dor) *n* short for **São Salvador da Bahia de Todos os Santos**, the official name for **Salvador**

São Tomé e Príncipe (*Portuguese* sãw tu'mɛ 'ɛ: 'prĩsipə) *n* a republic in the Gulf of Guinea, off the W coast of Africa, on the Equator: consists of the islands of Principe and São Tomé; colonized by the Portuguese in the late 15th century; became independent in 1975. Official language: Portuguese. Religion: Roman Catholic majority. Currency: dobra. Capital: São Tomé. Pop: 164 000 (2004 est). Area: 1001 sq km (386 sq miles)

sap¹ (sæp) *n* **1** a solution of mineral salts, sugars, etc, that circulates in a plant **2** any vital body

fluid **3** energy; vigour **4** *slang* a gullible or foolish person **5** another name for **sapwood** ▷ *vb* **saps, sapping, sapped** (*tr*) **6** to drain of sap [Old English *sæp*; related to Old High German *safp*, German *Saft* juice, Middle Low German *sapp*, Sanskrit *sabar* milk juice] > **sapless** *adj*

sap² (sæp) *n* **1** a deep and narrow trench used to approach or undermine an enemy position, esp in siege warfare ▷ *vb* **saps, sapping, sapped 2** to undermine (a fortification, etc) by digging saps **3** (*tr*) to weaken [C16 *zappe*, from Italian *zappa* spade, of uncertain origin; perhaps from Old Italian (dialect) *zappo* a goat]

SAP (sæp) (in Britain) *acronym for* Standard Assessment Procedure, the recognized performance indicator for measuring energy efficiency in buildings

sapajou ('sæpə,dʒuː) *n* another name for **capuchin** (monkey) [C17 from French, of Tupi origin]

sapanwood ('sæpən,wʊd) *n* a variant spelling of **sappanwood**

sapele (sə'piːlɪ) *n* **1** any of several W African meliaceous trees of the genus *Entandrophragma*, esp *E. cylindricum*, yielding a hard timber resembling mahogany **2** the timber obtained from such a tree, used to make furniture [C20 West African name]

Saphar (sə'fɑː) *n* a variant spelling of **Safar**

saphead¹ ('sæp,hɛd) *n* *slang* a simpleton, idiot, or fool > **sap,headed** *adj*

saphead² ('sæp,hɛd) *n* *military* the end of a sap nearest to the enemy

saphena (sə'fiːnə) *n*, *pl* **-nae** (-niː) *anatomy* either of two large superficial veins of the legs [C14 via Medieval Latin from Arabic *sāfin*] > **sa'phenous** *adj*

sapid ('sæpɪd) *adj* **1** having a pleasant taste **2** agreeable or engaging [C17 from Latin *sapidus*, from *sapere* to taste] > **sapidity** (sə'pɪdɪtɪ) or **'sapidness** *n*

sapient ('seɪpɪənt) *adj* *often used ironically* wise or sagacious [C15 from Latin *sapere* to taste] > **'sapience** *n* > **'sapiently** *adv*

sapiential (ˌseɪpɪ'ɛnʃəl, ˌsæpɪ-) *adj* showing, having, or providing wisdom > **ˌsapi'entially** *adv*

sapindaceous (ˌsæpɪn'deɪʃəs) *adj* of, relating to, or belonging to the *Sapindaceae*, a tropical and subtropical family of trees, shrubs, and lianas including the soapberry, litchi, and supplejack [C19 via New Latin from Latin *sāpō* soap + *Indus* Indian]

Sapir-Whorf hypothesis *n* the theory that human languages determine the structure of the real world as perceived by human beings, rather than vice versa, and that this structure is different and incommensurable from one language to another [named after Edward *Sapir* (1884–1939), US anthropologist and linguist, and Benjamin Lee *Whorf* (1897–1943), US linguist]

sapling ('sæplɪŋ) *n* **1** a young tree **2** *literary* a youth

sapodilla (ˌsæpə'dɪlə) *n* **1** a large tropical American evergreen tree, *Achras zapota*, the latex of which yields chicle **2** Also called: **sapodilla plum** the edible brown rough-skinned fruit of this tree, which has a sweet yellowish pulp ▷ Also called: **naseberry, sapota** [C17 from Spanish *zapotillo*, diminutive of *zapote* sapodilla fruit, from Nahuatl *tsapotl*]

saponaceous (ˌsæpəʊ'neɪʃəs) *adj* resembling soap; soapy [C18 from New Latin *sāpōnāceus*, from Latin *sāpō* SOAP] > ˌsapo'naceousness *n*

saponaria (ˌsæpə'nɛərɪə) *n* See **soapwort** [New Latin, from Late Latin *saponarius* soapy]

saponify (sə'pɒnɪ,faɪ) *vb* **-fies, -fying, -fied** *chem* **1** to undergo or cause to undergo a process in which a fat is converted into a soap by treatment with alkali **2** to undergo or cause to undergo a reaction in which an ester is hydrolysed to an acid and an alcohol as a result of treatment with an alkali [C19 from French *saponifier*, from Latin *sāpō* SOAP] > sa'poni,fiable *adj* > sa'poni,fier *n* > sa,ponifi'cation *n*

saponin ('sæpənɪn) n any of a group of plant glycosides with a steroid structure that foam when shaken and are used in detergents [C19 from French *saponine*, from Latin *sāpō* SOAP]

saponite ('sæpə,naɪt) n a clay mineral consisting of hydrated magnesium aluminium silicate and occurring in metamorphic rocks such as serpentine [C19 from Swedish *saponit* (a rendering of German *Seifenstein* soapstone), from Latin *sāpō* SOAP]

sapor ('seɪpɔː, -pə) n rare the quality in a substance that is perceived by the sense of taste; flavour [C15 from Latin: SAVOUR] > ,sapo'rific or 'saporous adj

sapota (sə'pəʊtə) n 1 (in tropical America) any of various different fruits 2 another name for **sapodilla** [C16 from Spanish *zapote*, from Nahuatl *tsapotl*; see SAPODILLA]

sapotaceous (,sæpə'teɪʃəs) adj of, relating to, or belonging to the *Sapotaceae*, a family of leathery-leaved tropical plants: includes the gutta-percha and balata trees, sapodilla, and shea [C19 from New Latin *sapota* SAPOTA]

sappanwood or **sapanwood** ('sæpən,wʊd) n 1 a small leguminous tree, *Caesalpinia sappan*, of S Asia producing wood that yields a red dye 2 the wood of this tree [C16 *sapan*, via Dutch from Malay *sapang*]

sapper ('sæpə) n 1 a soldier who digs trenches 2 (in the British Army) a private of the Royal Engineers

Sapphic ('sæfɪk) adj 1 prosody denoting a metre associated with Sappho, the 6th century BC Greek lyric poetess of Lesbos, consisting generally of a trochaic pentameter line with a dactyl in the third foot 2 of or relating to Sappho or her poetry 3 lesbian ▷ n 4 prosody a verse, line, or stanza written in the Sapphic form

Sapphic ode n another term for **Horatian ode**

sapphire ('sæfaɪə) n 1 a any precious corundum gemstone that is not red, esp the highly valued transparent blue variety. A synthetic form is used in electronics and precision apparatus. Formula: Al_2O_3 b (as modifier): *a sapphire ring* 2 a the blue colour of sapphire b (as adjective): *sapphire eyes* [C13 *safir*, from Old French, from Latin *sapphīrus*, from Greek *sappheiros*, perhaps from Hebrew *sappīr*, ultimately perhaps from Sanskrit *śanipriya*, literally: beloved of the planet Saturn, from *śani* Saturn + *priya* beloved]

sapphirine ('sæfə,riːn, -rɪn) n 1 a rare blue or bluish-green mineral that consists of magnesium aluminium silicate in monoclinic crystalline form and occurs as small grains in some metamorphic rocks 2 a blue variety of spinel ▷ adj 3 relating to or resembling sapphire

sapphism ('sæfɪzəm) n a less common word for **lesbianism** [C19 after Sappho, 6th century BC, Greek lyric poetess of Lesbos, who is believed to have been a lesbian]

Sapporo ('sɑːpəʊ,rəʊ) n a city in N Japan, on W Hokkaido: commercial centre; university (1918). Pop: 1 822 992 (2002 est)

sappy ('sæpɪ) adj -pier, -piest 1 (of plants) full of sap 2 full of energy or vitality 3 slang silly or fatuous > 'sappily adv > 'sappiness n

sapraemia (sæ'priːmɪə) n pathol blood poisoning caused by toxins of putrefactive bacteria [C19 New Latin, from SAPRO- + -EMIA] > sa'praemic adj

sapro- or before a vowel **sapr-** combining form indicating dead or decaying matter: *saprogenic; saprolite* [from Greek *sapros* rotten]

saprobe ('sæprəʊb) n an organism, esp a fungus, that lives on decaying organisms; a saprotroph. See also **saprophyte** [C20 from Greek, from SAPRO- + *bios* life] > sap'robic adj

saprobiont (,sæprəʊ'baɪɒnt) n another name for **saprotroph**

saprogenic (,sæprəʊ'dʒɛnɪk) or **saprogenous** (sæ'prɒdʒɪnəs) adj 1 producing or resulting from decay: *saprogenic bacteria* 2 growing on decaying matter > saprogenicity (,sæprədʒə'nɪsɪtɪ) n

saprolite ('sæprəʊlɪt) n a deposit of earth, clay, silt, etc, formed by decomposition of rocks that has remained in its original site > ,sapro'litic adj

sapropel ('sæprə,pɛl) n an unconsolidated sludge consisting of the decomposed remains of aquatic organisms, esp algae, that accumulates at the bottoms of lakes and oceans [C20 from SAPRO- + -pel from Greek *pēlos* mud] > ,sapro'pelic adj

saprophagous (sæ'prɒfəgəs) adj (of certain animals) feeding on dead or decaying organic matter

saprophyte ('sæprəʊ,faɪt) n any plant that lives and feeds on dead organic matter using mycorrhizal fungi associated with its roots; a saprotrophic plant > saprophytic (,sæprəʊ'fɪtɪk) adj > ,sapro'phytically adv

saprotroph ('sæprəʊ,trɒf) n any organism, esp a fungus or bacterium, that lives and feeds on dead organic matter. Also called: saprobe, saprobiont > saprotrophic (,sæprəʊ'trɒfɪk) adj > ,sapro'trophically adv

saprozoic (,sæprəʊ'zəʊɪk) adj 1 (of animals or plants) feeding on dead organic matter 2 of or relating to nutrition in which the nutrient substances are derived from dead organic matter

sapsago ('sæpsə,gəʊ) n a hard greenish Swiss cheese made with sour skimmed milk and coloured and flavoured with clover [C19 changed from German *Schabziger*, from *schaben* to grate + dialect *Ziger* a kind of cheese]

sapsucker ('sæp,sʌkə) n either of two North American woodpeckers, *Sphyrapicus varius* or *S. thyroideus*, that have white wing patches and feed on the sap from trees

sapwood ('sæp,wʊd) n the soft wood, just beneath the bark in tree trunks, that consists of living tissue. Compare **heartwood**

SAR abbreviation for Special Administrative Region (of China)

sarabande or **saraband** ('særə,bænd) n 1 a decorous 17th-century courtly dance 2 music a piece of music composed for or in the rhythm of this dance, in slow triple time, often incorporated into the classical suite [C17 from French, from Spanish *zarabanda*, of uncertain origin]

Saracen ('særəsən) n 1 history a member of one of the nomadic Arabic tribes, esp of the Syrian desert, that harassed the borders of the Roman Empire in that region 2 a a Muslim, esp one who opposed the crusades b (in later use) any Arab ▷ adj 3 of or relating to Arabs of either of these periods, regions, or types 4 designating, characterizing, or relating to Muslim art or architecture [C13 from Old French *Sarrazin*, from Late Latin *Saracēnus*, from Late Greek *Sarakēnos*, perhaps from Arabic *sharq* sunrise, from *shāraqa* to rise] > Saracenic (,særə'sɛnɪk) or ,Sara'cenical adj

Saragossa (,særə'gɒsə) n the English name for **Zaragoza**

Sarah ('seərə) n Old Testament the wife of Abraham and mother of Isaac (Genesis 17:15–22)

Sarajevo (Serbo-Croat 'sarajɛvɔ) or **Serajevo** n the capital of Bosnia-Herzegovina: developed as a Turkish town in the 15th century; capital of the Turkish and Austro-Hungarian administrations in 1850 and 1878 respectively; scene of the assassination of Archduke Franz Ferdinand in 1914, precipitating World War I; besieged by Bosnian Serbs (1992–95). Pop: 603 000 (2005 est)

saran (sə'ræn) n any one of a class of thermoplastic resins based on vinylidene chloride, used in fibres, moulded articles, and coatings [C20 after *Saran*, trademark coined by the Dow Chemical Co]

sarangi (sɑː'rʌŋgɪ) n music a stringed instrument of India played with a bow [Hindi]

Saransk (Russian sa'ransk) n a city in W central Russia, capital of the Mordovian Republic: university (1957). Pop: 304 000 (2005 est)

Sarasvati (sʌ'rʌsvətɪ) n Hinduism a goddess of learning and eloquence

Saratov (Russian sa'ratəf) n an industrial city in

W Russia, on the River Volga: university (1919). Pop: 868 000 (2005 est)

Sarawak (sə'rɑːwək) n a state of Malaysia, on the NW coast of Borneo on the South China Sea: granted to Sir James Brooke by the Sultan of Brunei in 1841 as a reward for helping quell a revolt; mainly agricultural. Capital: Kuching. Pop: 2 071 506 (2000). Area: about 121 400 sq km (48 250 sq miles)

sarcasm ('sɑːkæzəm) n 1 mocking, contemptuous, or ironic language intended to convey scorn or insult 2 the use or tone of such language [C16 from Late Latin *sarcasmus*, from Greek *sarkasmos*, from *sarkazein* to rend the flesh, from *sarx* flesh]

sarcastic (sɑː'kæstɪk) adj 1 characterized by sarcasm 2 given to the use of sarcasm > sar'castically adv

sarcenet or **sarsenet** ('sɑːsnɪt) n a fine soft silk fabric formerly from Italy and used for clothing, ribbons, etc [C15 from Old French *sarzinet*, from *Sarrazin* SARACEN]

sarco- or before a vowel **sarc-** combining form indicating flesh: *sarcoma* [from Greek *sark-*, *sarx* flesh]

sarcocarp ('sɑːkəʊ,kɑːp) n botany 1 the fleshy mesocarp of such fruits as the peach or plum 2 any fleshy fruit

sarcoid ('sɑːkɔɪd) adj 1 of, relating to, or resembling flesh ▷ n 2 a tumour resembling a sarcoma

sarcolemma (,sɑːkəʊ'lɛmə) n, pl -mas, -mata (-mətə) the membrane covering a muscle fibre

sarcoma (sɑː'kəʊmə) n, pl -mata (-mətə) or -mas pathol a usually malignant tumour arising from connective tissue [C17 via New Latin from Greek *sarkōma* fleshy growth; see SARCO-, -OMA] > sar'coma,toid or sar'comatous adj

sarcomatosis (sɑː,kəʊmə'təʊsɪs) n pathol a condition characterized by the development of several sarcomas at various bodily sites [C19 see SARCOMA, -OSIS]

sarcomere ('sɑːkəʊ,mɪə) n any of the units that together comprise skeletal muscle

sarcophagus (sɑː'kɒfəgəs) n, pl -gi (-,gaɪ) or -guses a stone or marble coffin or tomb, esp one bearing sculpture or inscriptions [C17 via Latin from Greek *sarkophagos* flesh-devouring; from the type of stone used, which was believed to destroy the flesh of corpses]

sarcoplasm ('sɑːkəʊ,plæzəm) n the cytoplasm of a muscle fibre > ,sarco'plasmic adj

sarcous ('sɑːkəs) adj (of tissue) muscular or fleshy [C19 from Greek *sarx* flesh]

sard (sɑːd) or **sardius** ('sɑːdɪəs) n an orange, red, or brown variety of chalcedony, used as a gemstone. Formula: SiO_2. Also called: sardine [C14 from Latin *sarda*, from Greek *sardios* stone from Sardis]

sardar or **sirdar** (sə'dɑː) n (in India) 1 a title used before the name of Sikh men 2 a leader [Hindi, from Persian]

Sardegna (sar'deɲɲa) n the Italian name for **Sardinia**

sardine¹ (sɑː'diːn) n, pl -dines, -dine 1 any of various small marine food fishes of the herring family, esp a young pilchard. See also **sild** 2 like sardines very closely crowded together [C15 via Old French from Latin *sardīna*, diminutive of *sarda* a fish suitable for pickling]

sardine² ('sɑːdiːn, -dⁿn) n another name for **sard** [C14 from Late Latin *sardinus*, from Greek *sardinos lithos* Sardian stone, from *Sardeis* Sardis]

Sardinia (sɑː'dɪnɪə) n the second-largest island in the Mediterranean: forms, with offshore islands, an administrative region of Italy; ceded to Savoy by Austria in 1720 in exchange for Sicily and formed the Kingdom of Sardinia with Piedmont; became part of Italy in 1861. Capital: Cagliari. Pop: 1 637 639 (2003 est). Area: 24 089 sq km (9301 sq miles). Italian name: Sardegna

Sardinian (sɑː'dɪnɪən) adj 1 of or relating to

S

Sardinia, its inhabitants, or their language ▷ *n* **2** a native or inhabitant of Sardinia **3** the spoken language of Sardinia, sometimes regarded as a dialect of Italian but containing many loan words from Spanish

Sardis ('sɑːdɪs) *or* **Sardes** ('sɑːdiːz) *n* an ancient city of W Asia Minor: capital of Lydia

sardius ('sɑːdɪəs) *n* **1** *Old Testament* a precious stone, probably a ruby, set in the breastplate of the high priest **2** another name for **sard** [c14 via Late Latin from Greek *sardios*, from *Sardeis* Sardis]

sardonic (sɑːˈdɒnɪk) *adj* characterized by irony, mockery, or derision [c17 from French *sardonique*, from Latin *sardonius*, from Greek *sardonios* derisive, literally: of Sardinia, alteration of Homeric *sardanios* scornful (laughter or smile)] > sar'donically *adv* > sar'donicism *n*

sardonyx ('sɑːdənɪks) *n* a variety of chalcedony with alternating reddish-brown and white parallel bands, used as a gemstone. Formula: SiO_2 [c14 via Latin from Greek *sardonux*, perhaps from *sardion* SARDINE² + *onux* nail]

SARFU *abbreviation for* South African Rugby Football Union

sargasso *or* **sargasso weed** (sɑːˈɡæsəʊ) *n, pl* -sos another name for **gulfweed, sargassum** [c16 from Portuguese *sargaço*, of unknown origin]

Sargasso Sea *n* a calm area of the N Atlantic, between the Caribbean and the Azores, where there is an abundance of floating seaweed of the genus *Sargassum*

sargassum (sɑːˈɡæsəm) *or* **sargasso** (sɑːˈɡæsəʊ) *n* any floating brown seaweed of the genus *Sargassum*, such as gulfweed, of warm seas, having ribbon-like fronds containing air sacs [c18 from New Latin; see SARGASSO]

sarge (sɑːdʒ) *n informal* sergeant: used esp as a term of address

Sargodha (sɑːˈɡəʊdə) *n* a city in NE Pakistan: grain market. Pop: 556 000 (2005 est)

sari *or* **saree** ('sɑːrɪ) *n, pl* -ris *or* -rees the traditional dress of women of India, Pakistan, etc, consisting of a very long narrow piece of cloth elaborately swathed around the body [c18 from Hindi *sārī*, from Sanskrit *śātī*]

Sarie Marais ('sɑːrɪ mɑːˈreɪ) *n South African* a popular Afrikaans song

sarin ('særɪn) *n* isopropyl methylphosphono-fluoridate: used in chemical warfare as a lethal nerve gas producing asphyxia. Formula: $CH_3P(O)(F)OCH(CH_3)_2$ [c20 from German, from the surnames of its inventors, *S(chrader), A(mbrose), R(udinger)*, and *(van der L)in(de)*]

sark (sɑːk) *n Scot* a shirt or (formerly) chemise [Old English *serc*; related to Old Norse *serkr*]

Sark (sɑːk) *n* an island in the English Channel in the Channel Islands, consisting of **Great Sark** and **Little Sark**, connected by an isthmus: ruled by a hereditary Seigneur or Dame. Pop: 591 (2000). Area: 5 sq km (2 sq miles). French name: **Sercq**

Sarka ('zɑːkə) *n* a variant spelling of **Zarqa**

sarking ('sɑːkɪŋ, 'særkɪŋ) *n Scot, northern English, and NZ* a timber or felt cladding placed over the rafters of a roof before the tiles or slates are fixed in place [c15 from verbal use of SARK]

sarky ('sɑːkɪ) *adj* -kier, -kiest *Brit informal* sarcastic

Sarmatia (sɑːˈmeɪʃɪə) *n* the ancient name of a region between the Volga and Vistula Rivers now covering parts of Poland, Belarus, and SW Russia

Sarmatian (sɑːˈmeɪʃɪən) *n* **1** a native or inhabitant of Sarmatia, an ancient region of E Europe ▷ *adj* **2** of or relating to Sarmatia or its inhabitants

Sarmatic (sɑːˈmætɪk) *adj* of or relating to Sarmatia or its inhabitants

sarmentose (sɑːˈmɛntəʊs), **sarmentous** (sɑːˈmɛntəs) *or* **sarmentaceous** (ˌsɑːmənˈteɪʃəs) *adj* (of plants such as the strawberry) having stems in the form of runners [c18 from Latin *sarmentōsus* full of twigs, from *sarmentum* brushwood, from *sarpere* to prune]

sarmie ('sɑːmɪ) *n South African children's slang* a sandwich [c20 from Northern English SARNIE]

Sarnen (German 'zarnən) *n* a town in central Switzerland, capital of Obwalden demicanton: resort. Pop: 9145 (2000)

Sarnia ('sɑːnɪə) *n* an inland port in S central Canada, in SW Ontario at the S end of Lake Huron: oil refineries. Pop: 78 577 (2001)

sarnie ('sɑːnɪ) *n Brit informal* a sandwich [c20 probably from Northern or dialect pronunciation of first syllable of *sandwich*]

sarod (sæˈrəʊd) *n* an Indian stringed musical instrument that may be played with a bow or plucked [c19 from Hindi]

sarong (sɑːˈrɒŋ) *n* **1** a draped skirtlike garment worn by men and women in the Malay Archipelago, Sri Lanka, the Pacific islands, etc **2** a fashionable Western adaptation of this garment [c19 from Malay, literally: sheath]

Saronic Gulf (səˈrɒnɪk) *n* an inlet of the Aegean on the SE coast of Greece. Length: about 80 km (50 miles). Width: about 48 km (30 miles). Also called: (Gulf of) **Aegina**

saros ('seɪrɒs) *n* a cycle of about 18 years 11 days (6585.32 days) in which eclipses of the sun and moon occur in the same sequence and at the same intervals as in the previous such cycle [c19 from Greek, from Babylonian *šāru* 3600 (years); modern astronomical use apparently based on mistaken interpretation of *šāru* as a period of 18½ years] > saronic (səˈrɒnɪk) *adj*

Saros ('sɑːrɒs) *n* **Gulf of** an inlet of the Aegean in NW Turkey, north of the Gallipoli Peninsula. Length: 59 km (37 miles). Width: 35 km (22 miles)

sarpanch (səˈpʌntʃ) *n* the head of a panchayat [Urdu, from *sar* head + Sanskrit *panch* five; see PANCHAYAT]

Sarpedon (sɑːˈpiːdɒn) *n Greek myth* a son of Zeus and Laodameia, or perhaps Europa, and king of Lycia. He was slain by Patroclus while fighting on behalf of the Trojans

sarracenia (ˌsærəˈsiːnɪə) *n* any American pitcher plant of the genus *Sarracenia*, having single nodding flowers and leaves modified as pitchers that trap and digest insects: family *Sarraceniaceae* [c18 New Latin, named after D *Sarrazin*, 17th-century botanist of Quebec]

sarraceniaceous (ˌsærəˌsiːnɪˈeɪʃəs) *adj* of, relating to, or belonging to the *Sarraceniaceae*, an American family of pitcher plants

Sarre (sar) *n* the French name for the **Saar**

sarrusophone (səˈruːzəˌfəʊn) *n* a wind instrument resembling the oboe but made of brass [c19 named after *Sarrus*, French bandmaster, who invented it (1856)]

SARS¹ (sɑːz) *n acronym for* severe acute respiratory syndrome; a severe viral infection of the lungs characterized by high fever, a dry cough, and breathing difficulties. It is contagious, having an airborne mode of transmission

SARS² *abbreviation for* South African Revenue Service

sarsaparilla (ˌsɑːsəpəˈrɪlə, ˌsɑːspə-) *n* **1** any of various prickly climbing plants of the tropical American genus *Smilax* having large aromatic roots and heart-shaped leaves: family *Smilacaceae* **2** the dried roots of any of these plants, formerly used as a medicine **3** a nonalcoholic drink prepared from these roots **4** any of various plants resembling true sarsaparilla, esp the araliaceous plant *Aralia nudicaulis* (**wild sarsaparilla**), of North America [c16 from Spanish *sarzaparrilla*, from *zarza* a bramble, (from Arabic *šaras*) + -*parrilla*, from Spanish *parra* a climbing plant]

sarsen ('sɑːsᵊn) *n* **1** *geology* a boulder of silicified sandstone, probably of Tertiary age, found in large numbers in S England **2** such a stone used in a megalithic monument. Also called: greywether [c17 probably a variant of SARACEN]

sarsenet ('sɑːsnɪt) *n* a variant spelling of **sarcenet**

Sarthe (*French* sart) *n* a department of NW France,

in Pays de la Loire region. Capital: Le Mans. Pop: 536 857 (2003 est). Area: 6245 sq km (2436 sq miles)

sartor ('sɑːtə) *n* a humorous or literary word for **tailor** [c17 from Latin: a patcher, from *sarcīre* to patch]

sartorial (sɑːˈtɔːrɪəl) *adj* **1** of or relating to a tailor or to tailoring **2** *anatomy* of or relating to the sartorius [c19 from Late Latin *sartōrius* from SARTOR] > sar'torially *adv*

sartorius (sɑːˈtɔːrɪəs) *n, pl* -torii (-ˈtɔːrɪˌaɪ) *anatomy* a long ribbon-shaped muscle that aids in flexing the knee [c18 New Latin, from *sartorius musculus*, literally: tailor's muscle, because it is used when one sits in the cross-legged position in which tailors traditionally sat while sewing]

Sarum ('seərəm) *n* the ancient name of **Salisbury** (sense 3)

Sarum use *n* the distinctive local rite or system of rites used at Salisbury cathedral in late medieval times

Sarvodaya (sɑˈvəʊdəjə) *n* (in India) economic and social development and improvement of a community as a whole [Hindi, from *sarva* all + *udaya* rise]

SAS *abbreviation for* Special Air Service

Sasebo ('sɑːsəˌbəʊ) *n* a port in SW Japan, on NW Kyushu on Omura Bay: naval base. Pop: 242 474 (2002 est)

saser ('seɪzə) *n* a device for amplifying ultrasound, working on a similar principle to a laser [c20 *s(ound) a(mplification by) s(timulated) e(mission) of r(adiation)*]

sash¹ (sæʃ) *n* a long piece of ribbon, silk, etc, worn around the waist like a belt or over one shoulder, as a symbol of rank [c16 from Arabic *shāsh* muslin]

sash² (sæʃ) *n* **1** a frame that contains the panes of a window or door ▷ *vb* (*tr*) **2** to furnish with a sash, sashes, or sash windows [c17 originally plural *sashes*, variant of *shashes*, from CHASSIS]

sashay (sæˈʃeɪ) *vb* (*intr*) *informal* **1** to move, walk, or glide along casually **2** to move or walk in a showy way; parade [c19 from an alteration of *chassé*, a gliding dance step]

sash cord *n* a strong cord connecting a sash weight to a sliding sash

sashimi ('sæʃɪmɪ) *n* a Japanese dish of thin fillets of raw fish [c19 from Japanese *sashi* pierce + *mi* flesh]

sash saw *n* a small tenon saw used for cutting sashes

sash weight *n* a weight used to counterbalance the weight of a sliding sash in a sash window and thus hold it in position at any height

sash window *n* a window consisting of two sashes placed one above the other so that one or each can be slid over the other to open the window

sasin ('sæsɪn) *n* another name for the **blackbuck** [c19 of unknown origin]

sasine ('seɪsɪn, 'seɪ-) *n Scots law* the granting of legal possession of feudal property [c17 Scots variant of SEISIN]

Sask. *abbreviation for* Saskatchewan

Saskatchewan (sæsˈkætʃɪwən) *n* **1** a province of W Canada: consists of part of the Canadian Shield in the north and open prairie in the south; economy based chiefly on agriculture and mineral resources. Capital: Regina. Pop: 995 391 (2004 est). Area: 651 900 sq km (251 700 sq miles). Abbreviations: Sask, SK **2** a river in W Canada, formed by the confluence of the North and South Saskatchewan Rivers: flows east to Lake Winnipeg. Length: 596 km (370 miles)

Saskatchewanian (sæsˌkætʃəˈwɒnɪən) *n* **1** a native or inhabitant of Saskatchewan ▷ *adj* **2** of or relating to Saskatchewan or its inhabitants

saskatoon (ˌsæskəˈtuːn) *n* a species of serviceberry, *Amelanchier alnifolia*, of W Canada: noted for its succulent purplish berries [from Cree *misaskwatomin*, from *misaskwat* tree of many branches + *min* fruit]

Saskatoon (ˌsæskəˈtuːn) *n* a city in W Canada, in

S Saskatchewan on the South Saskatchewan River: oil refining; university (1907). Pop: 196 816 (2001)

sasquatch ('sæs,kwætʃ) *n* (in Canadian folklore) in British Columbia, a hairy beast or manlike monster said to leave huge footprints [from Salish]

sass (sæs) *US and Canadian informal* ▷ *n* **1** insolent or impudent talk or behaviour ▷ *vb* (*intr*) **2** to talk or answer back in such a way [c20 back formation from SASSY[1]]

sassaby ('sæsəbɪ) *n, pl* -bies an African antelope, *Damaliscus lunatus*, of grasslands and semideserts, having angular curved horns and an elongated muzzle: thought to be the swiftest hoofed mammal [c19 from Bantu *tshêsêbê*]

sassafras ('sæsə,fræs) *n* **1** an aromatic deciduous lauraceous tree, *Sassafras albidum*, of North America, having three-lobed leaves and dark blue fruits **2** the aromatic dried root bark of this tree, used as a flavouring, and yielding sassafras oil **3** *Austral* any of several unrelated trees having a similar fragrant bark [c16 from Spanish *sasafras*, of uncertain origin]

sassafras oil *n* a clear volatile oil that is extracted from the root of the sassafras tree and contains camphor, pinene, and safrole

Sassanid ('sæsənɪd) *n, pl* Sassanids or Sassanidae (sæ'sænɪ,diː) any member of the native dynasty that built and ruled an empire in Persia from 224 to 636 A.D ▷ Sa'ssanian *adj*

Sassari (*Italian* 'sassari) *n* a city in NW Sardinia, Italy: the second-largest city on the island; university (1565). Pop: 120 729 (2001)

Sassenach ('sæsə,næx; *Scot* -næx) *n Scot and occasionally Irish* an English person or a Lowland Scot [c18 from Scot Gaelic *Sasunnach*, Irish *Sasanach*, from Late Latin *saxonēs* Saxons]

sassy[1] ('sæsɪ) *adj* -sier, -siest *US informal* insolent, impertinent [c19 variant of SAUCY] ▷ 'sassily *adv* ▷ 'sassiness *n*

sassy[2] ('sæsɪ), **sasswood** ('sæs,wʊd) or **sassy wood** *n* **1** a W African leguminous tree, *Erythrophleum guineense*, with poisonous bark (**sassy bark**) and hard strong wood **2** the bark or wood of this tree or the alkaloid derived from them, which is sometimes used in medicine [c19 probably from a language of the Kwa family: compare Twi *sese* plane tree, Ewe *sesewu* a kind of timber tree]

sastra ('ʃaːstrə) *n* a variant spelling of **shastra**

sastruga (sə'struːgə, sæ-) or **zastruga** *n* one of a series of ridges on snow-covered plains, caused by the action of wind laden with ice particles [from Russian *zastruga* groove, from *za* by + *struga* deep place]

sat[1] (sæt) *vb* the past tense and past participle of **sit**

sat[2] (sʌt) *adj South African* **1** very tired; exhausted **2** drunk [Afrikaans]

SAT *abbreviation for* (in the US) Scholastic Aptitude Test

Sat. *abbreviation for* **1** Saturday **2** Saturn

Satan ('seɪt³n) *n* the devil, adversary of God, and tempter of mankind: sometimes identified with Lucifer (Luke 4:5–8) [Old English, from Late Latin, from Greek, from Hebrew: plotter, from *sātan* to plot against]

satang (sæ'tæŋ) *n, pl* -tang a monetary unit of Thailand worth one hundredth of a baht [from Thai *satān*]

satanic (sə'tænɪk) or now rarely **satanical** *adj* **1** of or relating to Satan **2** supremely evil or wicked; diabolic ▷ sa'tanically *adv* ▷ sa'tanicalness *n*

Satanism ('seɪt³,nɪzəm) *n* **1** the worship of Satan **2** a form of such worship which includes blasphemous or obscene parodies of Christian prayers, etc **3** a satanic disposition or satanic practices ▷ 'Satanist *n, adj*

satay, satai or **saté** ('sæteɪ) *n* barbecued spiced meat cooked on skewers usually made from the stems of coconut leaves [from Malay]

SATB *abbreviation for* soprano, alto, tenor, bass: a combination of voices in choral music

satchel ('sætʃəl) *n* a rectangular bag, usually made of leather or cloth and provided with a shoulder strap, used for carrying books, esp school books [c14 from Old French *sachel* a little bag, from Late Latin *saccellus*, from Latin *saccus* SACK[1]] ▷ 'satchelled *adj*

sate[1] (seɪt) *vb* (*tr*) **1** to satisfy (a desire or appetite) fully **2** to supply beyond capacity or desire [Old English *sadian*; related to Old High German *satōn*; see SAD, SATIATE]

sate[2] (sæt, seɪt) *vb archaic* a past tense and past participle of **sit**

sateen (sæ'tiːn) *n* a glossy linen or cotton fabric, woven in such a way that it resembles satin [c19 changed from SATIN, on the model of VELVETEEN]

satellite ('sæt³,laɪt) *n* **1** a celestial body orbiting around a planet or star: *the earth is a satellite of the sun* **2** Also called: **artificial satellite** a man-made device orbiting around the earth, moon, or another planet transmitting to earth scientific information or used for communication. See also **communications satellite** **3** a person, esp one who is obsequious, who follows or serves another **4** a country or political unit under the domination of a foreign power **5** a subordinate area or community that is dependent upon a larger adjacent town or city **6** (*modifier*) subordinate to or dependent upon another: *a satellite nation* **7** (*modifier*) of, used in, or relating to the transmission of television signals from a satellite to the house: *a satellite dish aerial* ▷ *vb* **8** (*tr*) to transmit by communications satellite [c16 from Latin *satelles* an attendant, probably of Etruscan origin]

satellite broadcasting *n* the transmission of television or radio programmes from an artificial satellite at a power suitable for direct reception in the home

satellite dish aerial *n* a parabolic aerial for reception from or transmission to an artificial satellite. Often shortened to: **dish aerial** or **dish**

satellite navigation system *n computing* a computer-operated system of navigation that uses signals from orbiting satellites and mapping data to pinpoint the user's position and plot a subsequent course

satellitium (,sæt³'lɪtɪəm, -'lɪʃɪəm) *n astrology* a group of three or more planets lying in one sign of the zodiac [c17 from Latin, literally: bodyguard, retinue, from *satelles* an attendant. See SATELLITE]

satem ('saːtəm, 'seɪ-) *adj* denoting or belonging to the group of Indo-European languages in which original velar stops became palatalized (k > s or ʃ). These languages belong to the Indic, Iranian, Armenian, Slavonic, Baltic, and Albanian branches and are traditionally regarded as the E group. Compare **centum** [from Avestan *satəm* hundred; chosen to exemplify the variation of initial *s* with initial *k* (as in *centum*) in Indo-European languages]

satiable ('seɪʃɪəb³l, 'seɪʃə-) *adj* capable of being satiated ▷ ,satia'bility *n* ▷ 'satiably *adv*

satiate ('seɪʃɪ,eɪt) *vb* (*tr*) **1** to fill or supply beyond capacity or desire, often arousing weariness **2** to supply to satisfaction or capacity [c16 from Latin *satiāre* to satisfy, from *satis* enough] ▷ ,sati'ation *n*

Saticon ('sætɪ,kɒn) *n trademark* a high-resolution television camera tube used when high definition is required [c20 from S(ELENIUM) + A(RSENIC) + T(ELLURIUM) (used in the tube screen) + ICON(OSCOPE)]

satiety (sə'taɪɪtɪ) *n* the state of being satiated [c16 from Latin *satietās*, from *satis* enough]

satin ('sætɪn) *n* **1** a fabric of silk, rayon, etc, closely woven to show much of the warp, giving a smooth glossy appearance **2** (*modifier*) of or like satin in texture: *a satin finish* [c14 via Old French from Arabic *zaitūnī* of Zaytūn, Arabic rendering of Chinese *Tseutung* (now *Tsinkiang*), port in southern China from which the cloth was probably first exported] ▷ 'satin-,like *adj* ▷ 'satiny *adj*

satin bowerbird *n* the largest Australian bowerbird, *Ptilonorhynchus violaceus*, the male of which has lustrous blue plumage

satinet or **satinette** (,sætɪ'nɛt) *n* a thin or imitation satin [c18 from French: small satin]

satinflower ('sætɪn,flaʊə) *n* another name for **greater stitchwort** (see **stitchwort**)

satinpod ('sætɪn,pɒd) *n* another name for **honesty** (the plant)

satin stitch *n* an embroidery stitch consisting of rows of flat stitches placed close together [c17 so called from the satin-like appearance of embroidery using this stitch]

satin walnut *n* the brown heartwood of the sweet gum tree, used for furniture, fittings, and panelling

satinwood ('sætɪn,wʊd) *n* **1** a rutaceous tree, *Chloroxylon swietenia*, that occurs in the East Indies and has hard wood with a satiny texture **2** the wood of this tree, used in veneering, cabinetwork, marquetry, etc **3** West Indian Satinwood another name for **yellowwood** (sense 2)

satire ('sætaɪə) *n* **1** a novel, play, entertainment, etc, in which topical issues, folly, or evil are held up to scorn by means of ridicule and irony **2** the genre constituted by such works **3** the use of ridicule, irony, etc, to create such an effect [c16 from Latin *satira* a mixture, from *satur* sated, from *satis* enough]

satirical (sə'tɪrɪk³l) or **satiric** *adj* **1** of, relating to, or containing satire **2** given to the use of satire ▷ sa'tirically *adv* ▷ sa'tiricalness *n*

satirist ('sætərɪst) *n* **1** a person who writes satire **2** a person given to the use of satire

satirize or **satirise** ('sætə,raɪz) *vb* to deride (a person or thing) by means of satire ▷ ,satiri'zation or ,satiri'sation *n* ▷ 'sati,rizer or 'sati,riser *n*

satisfaction (,sætɪs'fækʃən) *n* **1** the act of satisfying or state of being satisfied **2** the fulfilment of a desire **3** the pleasure obtained from such fulfilment **4** a source of fulfilment **5** reparation or compensation for a wrong done or received **6** RC Church, Church of England the performance by a repentant sinner of a penance **7** Christianity the atonement for sin by the death of Christ [c15 via French from Latin *satisfactionem*, from *satisfacere* to SATISFY]

satisfactory (,sætɪs'fæktərɪ, -trɪ) *adj* **1** adequate or suitable; acceptable: *a satisfactory answer* **2** giving satisfaction **3** constituting or involving atonement, recompense, or expiation for sin ▷ ,satis'factorily *adv* ▷ ,satis'factoriness *n*

satisfice ('sætɪs,faɪs) *vb* **1** (*intr*) to act in such a way as to satisfy the minimum requirements for achieving a particular result **2** (*tr*) obsolete to satisfy [c16 altered from SATISFY]

satisficing behaviour ('sætɪs,faɪsɪŋ) *n economics* the form of behaviour demonstrated by firms who seek satisfactory profits and satisfactory growth rather than maximum profits

satisfy ('sætɪs,faɪ) *vb* -fies, -fying, -fied (mainly tr) **1** (*also intr*) to fulfil the desires or needs of (a person) **2** to provide amply for (a need or desire) **3** to relieve of doubt; convince **4** to dispel (a doubt) **5** to make reparation to or for **6** to discharge or pay off (a debt) to (a creditor) **7** to fulfil the requirements of; comply with: *you must satisfy the terms of your lease* **8** maths, logic to fulfil the conditions of (a theorem, assumption, etc); to yield a truth by substitution of the given value: $x = 3$ satisfies $x^2 - 4x + 3 = 0$ [c15 from Old French *satisfier*, from Latin *satisfacere*, from *satis* enough + *facere* to make, do] ▷ 'satis,fiable *adj* ▷ 'satis,fier *n* ▷ 'satis,fying *adj* ▷ 'satis,fyingly *adv*

satori (sæ'tɔːrɪ) *n Zen Buddhism* the state of sudden indescribable intuitive enlightenment [from Japanese]

satrap ('sætrəp) *n* **1** (in ancient Persia) a provincial governor **2** a subordinate ruler, esp a despotic one [c14 from Latin *satrapa*, from Greek *satrapēs*, from Old Persian *khshathrapāvan*, literally: protector of the land]

S

satrapy ('sætrəpɪ) *n, pl* -trapies the province, office, or period of rule of a satrap

SATs (sæts) *pl n Brit education acronym for* **standard assessment tasks**, **standard assessment tests**, or **standard attainment tests** (now officially called **national tests**). See also **SAT**

sat sri akal (ˌsɑːt ˈsɪriː əˈkɑːl) *interj* a salutation used in India [Punjabi *eternal is the great timeless lord*]

satsuma (sætˈsuːmə) *n* **1** a small citrus tree, *Citrus nobilis* var *unshiu*, cultivated, esp in Japan, for its edible fruit **2** the fruit of this tree, which has a loose rind and easily separable segments [C19 originally from the province of *Satsuma*, Japan]

Satsuma (ˈsætsʊˌmɑː) *n* a former province of SW Japan, on S Kyushu: famous for its porcelain

Satsuma ware *n* **1** simple pottery made in Satsuma, Japan, from the late 16th century **2** ornamental glazed porcelain ware made in Satsuma, Japan, from the late 18th century

saturable ('sætʃərəbəl) *adj chem* capable of being saturated ▷ **satura'bility** *n*

saturant ('sætʃərənt) *chem n* **1** the substance that causes a solution, etc, to be saturated ▷ *adj* **2** (of a substance) causing saturation [C18 from Latin *saturāns*]

saturate *vb* ('sætʃəˌreɪt) **1** to fill, soak, or imbue totally **2** to make (a chemical compound, vapour, solution, magnetic material, etc) saturated or (of a compound, vapour, etc) to become saturated **3** (*tr*) *military* to bomb or shell heavily ▷ *adj* ('sætʃərɪt, -ˌreɪt) **4** a less common word for **saturated** [C16 from Latin *saturāre*, from *satur* sated, from *satis* enough] ▷ ˌsatu'rater or ˌsatu'rator *n*

saturated ('sætʃəˌreɪtɪd) *adj* **1** (of a solution or solvent) containing the maximum amount of solute that can normally be dissolved at a given temperature and pressure. See also **supersaturated 2** (of a colour) having a large degree of saturation **3** (of a chemical compound) **a** containing no multiple bonds and thus being incapable of undergoing additional reactions: *a saturated hydrocarbon* **b** containing no unpaired valence electrons **4** (of a fat, esp an animal fat) containing a high proportion of fatty acids having single bonds. See also **polyunsaturated, unsaturated 5** (of a vapour) containing the equilibrium amount of gaseous material at a given temperature and pressure. See also **supersaturated 6** (of a magnetic material) fully magnetized **7** extremely wet; soaked

saturation (ˌsætʃəˈreɪʃən) *n* **1** the act of saturating or the state of being saturated **2** *chem* the state of a chemical compound, solution, or vapour when it is saturated **3** *meteorol* the state of the atmosphere when it can hold no more water vapour at its particular temperature and pressure, the relative humidity then being 100 per cent **4** the attribute of a colour that enables an observer to judge its proportion of pure chromatic colour. See also **colour 5** *physics* the state of a ferromagnetic material in which it is fully magnetized. The magnetic domains are then all fully aligned **6** *electronics* the state of a valve or semiconductor device that is carrying the maximum current of which it is capable and is therefore unresponsive to further increases of input signal **7** the level beyond which demand for a product or service is not expected to increase ▷ *modifier* **8** denoting the maximum possible intensity of coverage of an area: *saturation bombing; a saturation release of a film*

saturation diving *n* a method of diving in which divers live in a complex of decompression chambers for up to 28 days, going to work via a diving bell, and only decompressing at the end of the period. Helium is substituted for nitrogen in the air supply to avoid the narcotic effects of nitrogen

saturation point *n* **1** the point at which no more (people, things, ideas, etc) can be absorbed, accommodated, used, etc **2** *chem* the point at which no more solute can be dissolved in a

solution or gaseous material absorbed in a vapour

Saturday ('sætədɪ) *n* the seventh and last day of the week: the Jewish Sabbath [Old English *sæternes dæg*, translation of Latin *Sāturnī diēs* day of Saturn; compare Middle Dutch *saterdach*, Dutch *zaterdag*]

Saturday night special *n US informal* a small handgun that is cheap and easy to buy

Saturn¹ ('sætɜːn) *n* the Roman god of agriculture and vegetation. Greek counterpart: **Cronus**

Saturn² ('sætɜːn) *n* **1** one of the **giant planets**, the sixth planet from the sun, around which revolve planar concentric rings (**Saturn's rings**) consisting of small frozen particles. The planet has at least 30 satellites. Mean distance from sun: 1425 million km; period of revolution around sun: 29.41 years; period of axial rotation: 10.23 hours; equatorial diameter and mass: 9.26 and 95.3 times that of the earth, respectively. See also **Titan² 2** a large US rocket used for launching various objects, such as a spaceprobe or an Apollo spacecraft, into space **3** the alchemical name for **lead²**

Saturnalia (ˌsætəˈneɪlɪə) *n, pl* -lia *or* -lias **1** an ancient Roman festival celebrated in December: renowned for its general merrymaking **2** (*sometimes not capital*) a period or occasion of wild revelry [C16 from Latin *Sāturnālis* relating to **Saturn¹**] ▷ **Satur'nalian** *adj*

Saturnian (sæˈtɜːnɪən) *adj* **1** of or connected with the Roman god Saturn, whose reign was thought of as a golden age **2** of or relating to the planet Saturn **3** *prosody* denoting a very early verse form in Latin in which the accent was one of stress rather than quantity, there being an equal number of main stresses in each line, regardless of the number of unaccented syllables ▷ *n* **4** a line in Saturnian metre

saturniid (sæˈtɜːnɪɪd) *n* **1** any moth of the mainly tropical family *Saturniidae*, typically having large brightly coloured wings: includes the emperor, cecropia, and luna moths ▷ *adj* **2** of, relating to, or belonging to the *Saturniidae*

saturnine ('sætəˌnaɪn) *adj* **1** having a gloomy temperament; taciturn **2** *archaic* **a** of or relating to lead **b** having or symptomatic of lead poisoning [C15 from French *saturnin*, from Medieval Latin *sāturnīnus* (unattested), from Latin *Sāturnus* Saturn, with reference to the gloomy influence attributed to the planet Saturn] ▷ 'satur,ninely *adv* ▷ saturninity (ˌsætəˈnɪnɪtɪ) *n*

saturnism ('sætəˌnɪzəm) *n pathol* another name for **lead poisoning** [C19 from New Latin *sāturnismus*; properties similar to those of lead were attributed to the planet]

satyagraha ('sɔːtjɑːˌgrɔːhɑː) *n* **1** the policy of nonviolent resistance adopted by Mahatma Gandhi from about 1919 to oppose British rule in India **2** any movement of nonviolent resistance [via Hindi from Sanskrit, literally: insistence on truth, from *satya* truth + *agraha* forceful]

satyagrahi ('sʌtɪ,grʌhiː) *n* an exponent of nonviolent resistance, esp as a form of political protest

satyr ('sætə) *n* **1** *Greek myth* one of a class of sylvan deities, represented as goatlike men who drank and danced in the train of Dionysus and chased the nymphs **2** a man who has strong sexual desires **3** a man who has satyriasis **4** any of various butterflies of the genus *Satyrus* and related genera, having dark wings often marked with eyespots: family *Satyridae* [C14 from Latin *satyrus*, from Greek *saturos*] ▷ **satyric** (səˈtɪrɪk) *or* sa'tyrical *adj* ▷ 'satyr-,like *adj*

satyriasis (ˌsætɪˈraɪəsɪs) *n* a neurotic condition in men in which the symptoms are a compulsion to have sexual intercourse with as many women as possible and an inability to have lasting relationships with them. Compare **nymphomania** [C17 via New Latin from Greek *saturiasis*; see **SATYR**, -**IASIS**]

satyrid (səˈtɪərɪd) *n* any butterfly of the family *Satyridae*, having typically brown or dark wings

with paler markings: includes the graylings, satyrs, browns, ringlets, and gatekeepers

satyr play *n* (in ancient Greek drama) a ribald play with a chorus of satyrs, presented at the Dionysian festival

sauce (sɔːs) *n* **1** any liquid or semiliquid preparation eaten with food to enhance its flavour **2** anything that adds piquancy **3** *US and Canadian* stewed fruit **4** *US dialect* vegetables eaten with meat **5** *informal* impudent language or behaviour ▷ *vb* (*tr*) **6** to prepare (food) with sauce **7** to add zest to **8** to make agreeable or less severe **9** *informal* to be saucy to [C14 via Old French from Latin *salsus* salted, from *salīre* to sprinkle with salt, from *sal* salt] ▷ 'sauceless *adj*

sauce boat *n* another term for **gravy boat**

saucebox ('sɔːsˌbɒks) *n informal* a saucy person

saucepan ('sɔːspən) *n* a metal or enamel pan with a long handle and often a lid, used for cooking food

saucer ('sɔːsə) *n* **1** a small round dish on which a cup is set **2** any similar dish [C14 from Old French *saussier* container for **SAUCE**] ▷ 'saucerful *n* ▷ 'saucerless *adj*

sauch *or* **saugh** (sɔːx) *n* a sallow or willow [C15 from Old English *salh*]

saucy ('sɔːsɪ) *adj* saucier, sauciest **1** impertinent **2** pert; jaunty: *a saucy hat* ▷ 'saucily *adv* ▷ 'sauciness *n*

Saudi ('sɔːdɪ, 'saʊ-) *or* **Saudi Arabian** *adj* **1** of or relating to Saudi Arabia or its inhabitants ▷ *n* **2** a native or inhabitant of Saudi Arabia

Saudi Arabia ('sɔːdɪ, 'saʊ-) *n* a kingdom in SW Asia, occupying most of the Arabian peninsula between the Persian Gulf and the Red Sea: founded in 1932 by Ibn Saud, who united Hejaz and Nejd; consists mostly of desert plateau; large reserves of petroleum and natural gas. Official language: Arabic. Official religion: (Sunni) Muslim. Currency: riyal. Capital: Riyadh (royal), Jidda (administrative). Pop: 24 919 000 (2004 est). Area: 2 260 353 sq km (872 722 sq miles)

sauerbraten ('saʊəˌbrɑːtən; *German* 'zaʊərˌbrɑːtən) *n* beef marinated in vinegar, sugar, and seasonings, and then braised [German, from *sauer* **SOUR** + *Braten* roast]

sauerkraut ('saʊəˌkraʊt) *n* finely shredded and pickled cabbage [German, from *sauer* **SOUR** + *Kraut* cabbage]

sauger ('sɔːgə) *n* a small North American pikeperch, *Stizostedion canadense*, with a spotted dorsal fin: valued as a food and game fish [C19 of unknown origin]

Saul (sɔːl) *n* **1** *Old Testament* the first king of Israel (?1020–1000 BC). He led Israel successfully against the Philistines, but was in continual conflict with the high priest Samuel. He became afflicted with madness and died by his own hand; succeeded by David **2** *New Testament* the name borne by Paul prior to his conversion (Acts 9: 1–30)

Sault Sainte Marie ('suː seɪnt məˈriː) *n, usually abbreviated to* **Sault Ste Marie 1** an inland port in central Canada, in Ontario on the St Mary's River, which links Lake Superior and Lake Huron, opposite Sault Ste Marie, Michigan: canal bypassing the rapids completed in 1895. Pop: 67 385 (2001) **2** an inland port in NE Michigan, opposite Sault Ste Marie, Ontario: canal around the rapids completed in 1855, enlarged and divided in 1896 and 1919 (popularly called **Soo Canals**). Pop: 14 184 (2003 est)

sauna ('sɔːnə) *n* **1** an invigorating bath originating in Finland in which the bather is subjected to hot steam, usually followed by a cold plunge or by being lightly beaten with birch twigs **2** the place in which such a bath is taken [C20 from Finnish]

saunter ('sɔːntə) *vb* (*intr*) **1** to walk in a casual manner; stroll ▷ *n* **2** a leisurely pace or stroll **3** a leisurely old-time dance [C17 (meaning: to wander aimlessly), C15 (to muse): of obscure origin] ▷ 'saunterer *n*

-saur *or* **-saurus** *n combining form* lizard: *dinosaur* [from New Latin *saurus*]

saurel ('sɔːrəl) *n* a US name for **horse mackerel** (sense 1) [c19 via French from Late Latin *saurus*, from Greek *sauros*, of obscure origin]

saurian ('sɔːrɪən) *adj* 1 of, relating to, or resembling a lizard 2 of, relating to, or belonging to the *Sauria*, a former suborder of reptiles (now called *Lacertilia*), which included the lizards ▷ *n* 3 a former name for lizard [c15 from New Latin *Sauria*, from Greek *sauros*]

saurischian (sɔːˈrɪskɪən) *adj* 1 of, relating to, or belonging to the *Saurischia*, an order of late Triassic to Cretaceous dinosaurs including the theropods and sauropods ▷ *n* 2 any dinosaur belonging to the order *Saurischia*; a lizard-hipped dinosaur [c19 from New Latin *Saurischia*, from *saurus* + ISCHIUM]

sauropod ('sɔːrəˌpɒd) *n* any herbivorous quadrupedal saurischian dinosaur of the suborder *Sauropoda*, of Jurassic and Cretaceous times, including the brontosaurus, diplodocus, and titanosaurs. They had small heads and long necks and tails and were partly amphibious [c19 from New Latin *sauropoda*, from Greek *sauros* lizard + *pous* foot] > **sauropodous** (sɔːˈrɒpədəs) *adj*

saury ('sɔːrɪ) *n, pl* -ries any teleost fish, such as the Atlantic *Scomberesox saurus* of the family *Scomberesocidae* of tropical and temperate seas, having an elongated body and long toothed jaws. Also called: skipper [c18 perhaps from Late Latin *saurus*; see SAUREL]

sausage ('sɒsɪdʒ) *n* 1 finely minced meat, esp pork or beef, mixed with fat, cereal or bread, and seasonings (**sausage meat**), and packed into a tube-shaped animal intestine or synthetic casing 2 an object shaped like a sausage 3 *aeronautics informal* a sausage-shaped balloon 4 not a sausage nothing at all [c15 from Old Norman French *saussiche*, from Late Latin *salsīcia*, from Latin *salsus* salted; see SAUCE] > **'sausage-,like** *adj*

sausage dog *n* an informal name for **dachshund**

sausage roll *n Brit* a roll of sausage meat in pastry

Saussurean (səʊsˈʊərɪən) *adj* of or relating to Ferdinand de Saussure, the Swiss linguist (1857–1913)

saut (sɔːt) *n, vb, adj* a Scot word for **salt**

sauté ('səʊteɪ) *vb* -tés, -téing *or* -téeing, -téed 1 to fry (food) quickly in a little fat ▷ *n* 2 a dish of sautéed food, esp meat that is browned and then cooked in a sauce ▷ *adj* 3 sautéed until lightly brown: *sauté potatoes* [c19 from French: tossed, from *sauter* to jump, from Latin *saltāre* to dance, from *salīre* to spring]

Sauternes (səʊˈtɜːn) *n* (*sometimes not capital*) a sweet white wine made in the southern Bordeaux district of France [c18 from *Sauternes*, the district where it is produced]

sauve qui peut French (sov ki pø) *n* a state of panic or disorder; rout [literally: save (himself) who can]

Sauvignon Blanc ('səʊvɪnjɒn 'blɒŋk) *n* 1 a white grape grown in the Bordeaux and Loire regions of France, New Zealand, and elsewhere, used for making wine 2 any of various white wines made from this grape

sav (sæv) *n Austral and NZ informal* short for **saveloy**

Sava ('sɑːvə) *or* **Save** (sɑːv) *n* a river in SE Europe, rising in NW Slovenia and flowing east and south to the Danube at Belgrade. Length: 940 km (584 miles)

savage ('sævɪdʒ) *adj* 1 wild; untamed: *savage beasts of the jungle* 2 ferocious in temper; vicious: *a savage dog* 3 uncivilized; crude: *savage behaviour* 4 (of peoples) nonliterate or primitive: *a savage tribe* 5 (of terrain) rugged and uncultivated 6 *obsolete* far from human habitation ▷ *n* 7 a member of a nonliterate society, esp one regarded as primitive 8 a crude or uncivilized person 9 a fierce or vicious person or animal ▷ *vb* (tr) 10 to criticize violently 11 to attack ferociously and wound: *the*

dog savaged the child [c13 from Old French *sauvage*, from Latin *silvāticus* belonging to a wood, from *silva* a wood] > **'savagedom** *n* > **'savagely** *adv* > **'savageness** *n*

Savage Island *n* another name for **Niue**

savagery ('sævɪdʒrɪ) *n, pl* -ries 1 an uncivilized condition 2 a savage act or nature 3 savages collectively

Savaii (sɑːˈvaɪiː) *n* the largest island in Samoa: mountainous and volcanic. Pop: 42 400 (2001). Area: 1174 sq km (662 sq miles)

savanna *or* **savannah** (səˈvænə) *n* open grasslands, usually with scattered bushes or trees, characteristic of much of tropical Africa [c16 from Spanish *zavana*, from Taino *zabana*]

Savannah (səˈvænə) *n* 1 a port in the US, in E Georgia, near the mouth of the Savannah River: port of departure of the *Savannah* for Liverpool (1819), the first steamship to cross the Atlantic. Pop: 127 573 (2003 est) 2 a river in the southeastern US, formed by the confluence of the Tugaloo and Seneca Rivers in NW South Carolina: flows southeast to the Atlantic. Length: 505 km (314 miles)

savant ('sævənt; *French* savɑ̃) *n* a man of great learning; sage [c18 from French, from *savoir* to know, from Latin *sapere* to be wise; see SAPIENT] > **'savante** *fem n*

savate (səˈvæt) *n* a form of boxing in which blows may be delivered with the feet as well as the hands [c19 from French, literally: old worn-out shoe; related to SABOT]

save¹ (seɪv) *vb* 1 (tr) to rescue, preserve, or guard (a person or thing) from danger or harm 2 to avoid the spending, waste, or loss of (money, possessions, etc) 3 (tr) to deliver from sin; redeem 4 (often foll by *up*) to set aside or reserve (money, goods, etc) for future use 5 (tr) to treat with care so as to avoid or lessen wear or degeneration: *use a good light to save your eyes* 6 (tr) to prevent the necessity for; obviate the trouble of: *good work now will save future revision* 7 (tr) *sport* to prevent (a goal) by stopping (a struck ball or puck) 8 (intr) *chiefly US* (of food) to admit of preservation; keep ▷ *n* 9 *sport* the act of saving a goal 10 *computing* an instruction to write information from the memory onto a tape or disk [c13 from Old French *salver*, via Late Latin from Latin *salvus* safe] > **'savable** *or* **'saveable** *adj* > **'savableness** *or* **'saveableness** *n* > **'saver** *n*

save² (seɪv) *archaic or literary* ▷ *prep* 1 (often foll by *for*) Also: saving with the exception of ▷ *conj* 2 but; except [c13 from Old French *sauf*, from Latin *salvō*, from *salvus* safe]

save-all *n* 1 a device to prevent waste or loss 2 *nautical* **a** a net used while loading a ship **b** a light sail set to catch wind spilling from another sail 3 *dialect* overalls or a pinafore 4 *Brit* a dialect word for **miser**

save as you earn *n* (in Britain) a savings scheme operated by the government, in which monthly contributions earn tax-free interest. Abbreviation: SAYE

saveloy ('sævɪˌlɔɪ) *n* a smoked sausage made from salted pork, well seasoned and coloured red with saltpetre [c19 probably via French from Italian *cervellato*, from *cervello* brain, from Latin *cerebellum*, diminutive of *cerebrum* brain]

savin *or* **savine** ('sævɪn) *n* 1 a small spreading juniper bush, *Juniperus sabina*, of Europe, N Asia, and North America 2 the oil derived from the shoots and leaves of this plant, formerly used in medicine to treat rheumatism, etc 3 another name for **red cedar** (sense 1) [c14 from Old French *savine*, from Latin *herba Sabīna* the Sabine plant]

saving ('seɪvɪŋ) *adj* 1 tending to save or preserve 2 redeeming or compensating (esp in the phrase **saving grace**) 3 thrifty or economical 4 *law* denoting or relating to an exception or reservation: *a saving clause in an agreement* ▷ *n* 5 preservation or redemption, esp from loss or danger 6 economy or avoidance of waste 7

reduction in cost or expenditure: *a saving of 100 dollars* 8 anything saved 9 (*plural*) money saved for future use 10 *law* an exception or reservation ▷ *prep* 11 with the exception of ▷ *conj* 12 except > **'savingly** *adv*

savings account *n* an account at a bank that accumulates interest

savings and loan association *n* a US name for a **building society**

savings bank *n* 1 a bank that accepts the savings of depositors and pays interest on them 2 a container, usually having a slot in the top, for saving coins

savings ratio *n economics* the ratio of personal savings to disposable income, esp using the difference between national figures for disposable income and consumer spending as a measure of savings

saviour *or US* **savior** ('seɪvjə) *n* a person who rescues another person or a thing from danger or harm [c13 *saveour*, from Old French, from Church Latin *Salvātor* the Saviour; see SAVE¹]

Saviour *or US* **Savior** ('seɪvjə) *n Christianity* Jesus Christ regarded as the saviour of men from sin

Savoie (*French* savwa) *n* 1 a department of E France, in Rhône-Alpes region. Capital: Chambéry. Pop: 386 246 (2003 est). Area: 6188 sq km (2413 sq miles) 2 the French name for **Savoy**

savoir-faire ('sævwɑːˈfɛə) *n* the ability to do the right thing in any situation [French, literally: knowing how to do]

savoir-vivre ('sævwɑːˈviːvrə) *n* familiarity with the customs of good society; breeding [French, literally: a knowing how to live]

Savona (*Italian* saˈvoːna) *n* a port in NW Italy, in Liguria on the Mediterranean: an important centre of the Italian iron and steel industry. Pop: 59 907 (2001)

savory ('seɪvərɪ) *n, pl* -vories 1 any of numerous aromatic plants of the genus *Satureja*, esp *S. montana* (**winter savory**) and *S. hortensis* (**summer savory**), of the Mediterranean region, having narrow leaves and white, pink, or purple flowers: family *Lamiaceae* (labiates) 2 the leaves of any of these plants, used as a potherb [c14 probably from Old English *sætherie*, from Latin *satureïa*, of obscure origin]

savour *or US* **savor** ('seɪvə) *n* 1 the quality in a substance that is perceived by the sense of taste or smell 2 a specific taste or smell: *the savour of lime* 3 a slight but distinctive quality or trace 4 the power to excite interest: *the savour of wit has been lost* 5 *archaic* reputation ▷ *vb* 6 (intr; often foll by *of*) to possess the taste or smell (of) 7 (intr; often foll by *of*) to have a suggestion (of) 8 (tr) to give a taste to; season 9 (tr) to taste or smell, esp appreciatively 10 (tr) to relish or enjoy [c13 from Old French *savour*, from Latin *sapor* taste, from *sapere* to taste] > **'savourless** *or US* **'savorless** *adj* > **'savorous** *adj*

savoury *or US* **savory** ('seɪvərɪ) *adj* 1 attractive to the sense of taste or smell 2 salty or spicy; not sweet: *a savoury dish* 3 pleasant 4 respectable ▷ *n, pl* -vouries 5 a savoury dish served as an hors d'oeuvre or dessert [c13 *savure*, from Old French *savouré*, from *savourer* to SAVOUR] > **'savourily** *or US* **'savorily** *adv* > **'savouriness** *or US* **'savoriness** *n*

savoy (səˈvɔɪ) *n* a cultivated variety of cabbage, *Brassica oleracea capitata*, having a compact head and wrinkled leaves [c16 named after the SAVOY region]

Savoy (səˈvɔɪ) *n* an area of SE France, bordering on Italy, mainly in the Savoy Alps: a duchy in the late Middle Ages and part of the Kingdom of Sardinia from 1720 to 1860, when it became part of France. French name: Savoie

Savoy Alps *pl n* a range of the Alps in SE France. Highest peak: Mont Blanc, 4807 m (15 772 ft)

Savoyard¹ (səˈvɔɪɑːd; *French* savwajar) *n* 1 a native of Savoy 2 the dialect of French spoken in Savoy ▷ *adj* 3 of or relating to Savoy, its inhabitants, or their dialect

S

Savoyard[2] (sə'vɔɪɑ:d) *n* **1** a person keenly interested in the operettas of Gilbert and Sullivan **2** a person who takes part in these operettas [c20 from the *Savoy* Theatre, built in London in 1881 by Richard D'Oyly Carte for the presentation of operettas by Gilbert and Sullivan]

savvy ('sævɪ) *slang* ▷ *vb* -vies, -vying, -vied **1** to understand or get the sense of (an idea, etc) **2** no savvy I don't (he doesn't, etc) understand ▷ *n* **3** comprehension ▷ *adj* -vier, -viest **4** *chiefly US* shrewd; well-informed [c18 corruption of Spanish *sabe(usted)* (you) know, from *saber* to know, from Latin *sapere* to be wise]

saw[1] (sɔ:) *n* **1** any of various hand tools for cutting wood, metal, etc, having a blade with teeth along one edge **2** any of various machines or devices for cutting by use of a toothed blade, such as a power-driven circular toothed wheel or toothed band of metal ▷ *vb* saws, sawing, sawed, sawed *or* sawn **3** to cut with a saw **4** to form by sawing **5** to cut as if wielding a saw: *to saw the air* **6** to move (an object) from side to side as if moving a saw [Old English *sagu*; related to Old Norse *sog*, Old High German *saga*, Latin *secāre* to cut, *secūris* axe] ▷ 'sawer ▷ 'saw,like *adj*

saw[2] (sɔ:) *vb* the past tense of **see**

saw[3] (sɔ:) *n* a wise saying, maxim, or proverb [Old English *sagu* a saying; related to SAGA]

SAW *abbreviation for* **surface acoustic wave**

sawbill ('sɔ:,bɪl) *n* **1** another name for **merganser** *or* **motmot 2** any of various hummingbirds of the genus *Ramphodon* [c19 so called because of their serrated bills]

sawbones ('sɔ:,bəʊnz) *n*, *pl* -bones *or* -boneses *slang* a surgeon or doctor

sawbuck ('sɔ:,bʌk) *n* **1** *US and Canadian* a sawhorse, esp one having an X-shaped supporting structure **2** *chiefly US and Canadian slang* a ten-dollar bill [c19 (in the sense: sawhorse) translated from Dutch *zaagbok*; (in the sense: ten-dollar bill) from the legs of a sawbuck forming the Roman numeral X]

sawder ('sɔ:də) *informal* ▷ *n* **1** flattery; compliments (esp in the phrase **soft sawder**) ▷ *vb* (*tr*) **2** to flatter [c19 metaphorical use of variant of SOLDER]

saw doctor *n* NZ a sawmill specialist who sharpens and services saw blades

sawdust ('sɔ:,dʌst) *n* particles of wood formed by sawing

sawfish ('sɔ:,fɪʃ) *n*, *pl* -fish *or* -fishes any sharklike ray of the family *Pristidae* of subtropical coastal waters and estuaries, having a serrated bladelike mouth

sawfly ('sɔ:,flaɪ) *n*, *pl* -flies any of various hymenopterous insects of the family *Tenthredinidae* and related families, the females of which have a sawlike ovipositor

sawhorse ('sɔ:,hɔ:s) *n* a stand for timber during sawing

sawmill ('sɔ:,mɪl) *n* **1** an industrial establishment where timber is sawn into planks, etc **2** a large sawing machine

sawn (sɔ:n) *vb* a past participle of **saw**

Sawney ('sɔ:nɪ) *n* **1** a derogatory word for **Scotsman 2** (*also not capital*) *informal* a fool [c18 a Scots variant of *Sandy*, short for *Alexander*]

sawn-off *or esp US* **sawed-off** *adj* **1** (*prenominal*) (of a shotgun) having the barrel cut short, mainly to facilitate concealment of the weapon **2** *informal* (of a person) small in stature

saw-off *n Canadian* **1** a deadlock or stalemate **2** a compromise

saw palmetto *n* any of several dwarf prickly palms, esp any of the genus *Sabal*, of the southeastern US

saw-pit *n* (esp formerly) a pit above which a log is sawn into planks with a large pitsaw

saw set *n* a tool used for setting the teeth of a saw, consisting of a type of clamp used to bend each tooth in turn at a slight angle to the plane of the saw to improve cutting, alternate teeth being

bent in the same direction

sawtooth ('sɔ:,tu:θ) *adj* **1** (of a waveform) having an amplitude that varies linearly with time between two values, the interval in one direction often being much greater than the other **2** having or generating such a waveform

saw-wort ('sɔ:,wɜ:t) *n* a perennial Old World plant, *Serratula tinctoria*, having serrated leaves that yield a yellow dye: family *Asteraceae* (composites)

sawyer ('sɔ:jə) *n* a person who saws timber for a living [c14 *sawier*, from SAW[1] + -*ier*, variant of -ER[1]]

sax[1] (sæks) *n* a tool resembling a small axe, used for cutting roofing slate [Old English *seax* knife; related to Old Saxon *sahs*, Old Norse *sax*]

sax[2] (sæks) *n informal* short for **saxophone**

saxatile ('sæksə,taɪl; *as specific name* sæk'sætɪlɪ) *adj* growing on or living among rocks [c17 from Latin *saxitilis*, from *saxum* rock]

Saxe (saks) *n* the French name for **Saxony**

saxe blue (saks) *n* **a** a light greyish-blue colour **b** (*as adjective*): *a saxe-blue dress* [c19 from French *Saxe* Saxony, source of a dye of this colour]

saxhorn ('sæks,hɔ:n) *n* a valved brass instrument used chiefly in brass and military bands, having a tube of conical bore and a brilliant tone colour. It resembles the tuba and constitutes a family of instruments related to the flugelhorn and cornet [c19 named after Adolphe *Sax* (see SAXOPHONE), who invented it (1845)]

saxicolous (sæk'sɪkələs) *adj* living on or among rocks: *saxicolous plants*. Also: **saxicole, saxatile** ('sæksə,taɪl) [c19 from New Latin *saxicolus*, from Latin *saxum* rock + *colere* to dwell]

saxifragaceous (,sæksɪfrə'geɪʃəs) *adj* of, relating to, or belonging to the *Saxifragaceae*, a chiefly arctic and alpine family of plants having a basal rosette or cushion of leaves and small but showy flowers: includes saxifrage

saxifrage ('sæksɪ,freɪdʒ) *n* any saxifragaceous plant of the genus *Saxifraga*, characterized by smallish white, yellow, purple, or pink flowers [c15 from Late Latin *saxifraga*, literally: rock-breaker (probably alluding to its ability to dissolve kidney stones), from Latin *saxum* rock + *frangere* to break]

Saxon ('sæksən) *n* **1** a member of a West Germanic people who in Roman times spread from Schleswig across NW Germany to the Rhine. Saxons raided and settled parts of S Britain in the fifth and sixth centuries AD. In Germany they established a duchy and other dominions, which changed and shifted through the centuries, usually retaining the name Saxony **2** a native or inhabitant of Saxony **3 a** the Low German dialect of Saxony **b** any of the West Germanic dialects spoken by the ancient Saxons or their descendants ▷ *adj* **4** of, relating to, or characteristic of the ancient Saxons, the Anglo-Saxons, or their descendants **5** of, relating to, or characteristic of Saxony, its inhabitants, or their Low German dialect ▷ See also **West Saxon, Anglo-Saxon** [c13 (replacing Old English *Seaxe*): via Old French from Late Latin *Saxon-, Saxo*, from Greek; of Germanic origin and perhaps related to the name of a knife used by the Saxons; compare SAW[1]]

Saxon blue *n* a dye made by dissolving indigo in a solution of sulphuric acid [c19 named after SAXONY, where it originated]

saxony ('sæksənɪ) *n* **1** a fine 3-ply yarn used for knitting and weaving **2** a fine woollen fabric used for coats, etc [c19 named after SAXONY, where it was produced]

Saxony ('sæksənɪ) *n* **1** a state in E Germany, formerly part of East Germany. Pop: 4 321 000 (2003 est) **2** a former duchy and electorate in SE and central Germany, whose territory changed greatly over the centuries **3** (in the early Middle Ages) any territory inhabited or ruled by Saxons ▷ Compare **Saxony-Anhalt, Lower Saxony** German name: Sachsen French name: Saxe

Saxony-Anhalt ('sæksənɪ 'ɑ:nhɑ:lt) *n* a state of E Germany: created in 1947 from the state of Anhalt

and those parts of Prussia formerly ruled by the duchy of Saxony: part of East Germany until 1990. Pop: 2 523 000 (2003 est)

saxophone ('sæksə,fəʊn) *n* a keyed wind instrument of mellow tone colour, used mainly in jazz and dance music. It is made in various sizes, has a conical bore, and a single reed. Often shortened to: **sax** [c19 named after Adolphe *Sax* (1814–94), Belgian musical-instrument maker, who invented it (1846)] ▷ **saxophonic** (,sæksə'fɒnɪk) *adj* ▷ **saxophonist** (sæk'sɒfənɪst) *n*

say[1] (seɪ) *vb* **says** (sɛz) **saying, said** (*mainly tr*) **1** to speak, pronounce, or utter **2** (*also intr*) to express (an idea) in words; tell: *we asked his opinion but he refused to say* **3** (*also intr; may take a clause as object*) to state (an opinion, fact, etc) positively; declare; affirm **4** to recite: *to say grace* **5** (*may take a clause as object*) to report or allege: *they say we shall have rain today* **6** (*may take a clause as object*) to take as an assumption; suppose: *let us say that he is lying* **7** (*may take a clause as object*) to convey by means of artistic expression: *the artist in this painting is saying that we should look for hope* **8** to make a case for: *there is much to be said for either course of action* **9** (*usually passive*) Irish to persuade or coax (someone) to do something: *If I hadn't been said by her, I wouldn't be in this fix* **10** go without saying to be so obvious as to need no explanation **11** I say! *chiefly Brit informal* an exclamation of surprise **12** not to say even; and indeed **13** that is to say in other words; more explicitly **14** to say nothing of as well as; even disregarding: *he was warmly dressed in a shirt and heavy jumper, to say nothing of a thick overcoat* **15** to say the least without the slightest exaggeration: *at the very least* ▷ *adv* **16** approximately: *there were, say,* 20 *people present* **17** for example: *choose a number, say, four* ▷ *n* **18** the right or chance to speak: *let him have his say* **19** authority, esp to influence a decision: *he has a lot of say in the company's policy* **20** a statement of opinion: *you've had your say, now let me have mine* ▷ *interj* **21** *US and Canadian informal* an exclamation to attract attention or express surprise, etc [Old English *secgan*; related to Old Norse *segja*, Old Saxon *seggian*, Old High German *sagēn*] ▷ 'sayer *n*

say[2] (seɪ) *n archaic* a type of fine woollen fabric [c13 from Old French *saie*, from Latin *saga*, plural of *sagum* a type of woollen cloak]

Sayan Mountains (sɑ:'jæn) *pl n* a mountain range in S central Russia, in S Siberia. Highest peak: Munku-Sardyk, 3437 m (11 457 ft)

Saybolt universal seconds (seɪ'bəʊlt) *n* (*functioning as singular*) a US measurement of viscosity similar in type to the British Redwood seconds [named after G M *Saybolt* (died 1924), US chemist, who proposed it]

SAYE *abbreviation for* **save as you earn**

saying ('seɪɪŋ) *n* a maxim, adage, or proverb

say-so *n informal* **1** an arbitrary assertion **2** an authoritative decision **3** the authority to make a final decision

sayyid, sayid ('saɪɪd) *or* **said** *n* **1** a Muslim claiming descent from Mohammed's grandson Husain **2** a Muslim honorary title [c17 from Arabic: lord]

sazerac ('sæzə,ræk) *n US* a mixed drink of whisky, Pernod, syrup, bitters, and lemon [c20 of uncertain origin]

sb *the internet domain name for* Solomon Islands

Sb *the chemical symbol for* antimony [from New Latin *stibium*]

sb. *abbreviation for* substantive

SBA *abbreviation for* standard beam approach: a radar navigation system that gives lateral guidance to aircraft when landing

SBE *abbreviation for* Southern British English

SBS *abbreviation for* **Special Boat Service**

SBU *abbreviation for* strategic business unit: a division within an organization responsible for marketing its own range of products

sc[1] *printing abbreviation for* small capitals

sc[2] *the internet domain name for* Seychelles

Sc *the chemical symbol for* scandium
SC *abbreviation for* **1** Signal Corps **2** South Carolina **3** (in Canada) Star of Courage
sc. *abbreviation for* **1** scene **2** scilicet
scab (skæb) *n* **1** the dried crusty surface of a healing skin wound or sore **2** a contagious disease of sheep, a form of mange, caused by a mite (*Psoroptes communis*) **3** a fungal disease of plants characterized by crusty spots on the fruits, leaves, etc **4** *derogatory* **a** Also called: **blackleg** a person who refuses to support a trade union's actions, esp one who replaces a worker who is on strike **b** (*as modifier*): *scab labour* **5** a despicable person ▷ *vb* **scabs, scabbing, scabbed** (*intr*) **6** to become covered with a scab **7** (of a road surface) to become loose so that potholes develop **8** to replace a striking worker [Old English *sceabb*; related to Old Norse *skabb*, Latin *scabiēs*, Middle Low German *schabbe* scoundrel, German *schäbig* SHABBY] > ˈ**scab,like** *adj*
scabbard (ˈskæbəd) *n* a holder for a bladed weapon such as a sword or bayonet; sheath [c13 *scauberc*, from Norman French *escaubers* (pl), of Germanic origin; related to Old High German *skār* blade and *bergan* to protect]
scabbard fish *n* any of various marine spiny-finned fishes of the family *Trichiuridae*, esp of the genus *Lepidopus*, having a long whiplike scaleless body and long sharp teeth: most common in warm waters
scabble (ˈskæbᵊl) *vb* (*tr*) to shape (stone) roughly [c17 from earlier *scapple*, from French *escapler* to shape (timber)]
scabby (ˈskæbɪ) *adj* **-bier, -biest 1** *pathol* having an area of the skin covered with scabs **2** *pathol obsolete* having scabies **3** *informal* despicable > ˈ**scabbily** *adv* > ˈ**scabbiness** *n*
scabby mouth *n Austral* another name for **orf**
scabies (ˈskeɪbiːz, -bɪˌiːz) *n* a contagious skin infection caused by the mite *Sarcoptes scabiei*, characterized by intense itching, inflammation, and the formation of vesicles and pustules [c15 from Latin: scurf, from *scabere* to scratch; see SHAVE] > **scabietic** (ˌskeɪbɪˈɛtɪk) *adj*
scabious¹ (ˈskeɪbɪəs) *adj* **1** having or covered with scabs **2** of, relating to, or resembling scabies [c17 from Latin *scabiōsus*, from SCABIES]
scabious² (ˈskeɪbɪəs) *n* **1** any plant of the genus *Scabiosa*, esp *S. atropurpurea*, of the Mediterranean region, having blue, red, or whitish dome-shaped flower heads: family *Dipsacaceae* **2** any of various similar plants of the related genus *Knautia* **3** **devil's bit scabious** a similar and related Eurasian marsh plant, *Succisa pratensis* [c14 from Medieval Latin *scabiōsa herba* the scabies plant, referring to its use in treating scabies]
scablands (ˈskæbˌlændz) *pl n* a type of terrain, found for example in the NW US, consisting of bare rock surfaces, with little or no soil cover and scanty vegetation, that have been deeply channelled by glacial flood waters
scabrid (ˈskæbrɪd) *adj* having a rough or scaly surface [c19 see SCABROUS] > **scabridity** (skəˈbrɪdɪtɪ) *n*
scabrous (ˈskeɪbrəs) *adj* **1** roughened because of small projections; scaly **2** indelicate, indecent, or salacious: *scabrous humour* **3** difficult to deal with; knotty [c17 from Latin *scaber* rough; related to SCABIES] > ˈ**scabrously** *adv* > ˈ**scabrousness** *n*
scad (skæd) *n, pl* **scad** *or* **scads** any of various carangid fishes of the genus *Trachurus*, esp the horse mackerel [c17 of uncertain origin; compare Swedish *skädde* flounder]
scads (skædz) *pl n informal* a large amount or number [c19 of uncertain origin]
Scafell Pike (skɔːˈfɛl) *n* a mountain in NW England, in Cumbria in the Lake District: the highest peak in England. Height: 977 m (3206 ft)
scaffold (ˈskæfəld, -fəʊld) *n* **1** a temporary metal or wooden framework that is used to support workmen and materials during the erection, repair, etc, of a building or other construction **2** a raised wooden platform on which plays are performed, tobacco, etc, is dried, or (esp formerly) criminals are executed ▷ *vb* (*tr*) **3** to provide with a scaffold **4** to support by means of a scaffold [c14 from Old French *eschaffaut*, from Vulgar Latin *catafalicum* (unattested); see CATAFALQUE] > ˈ**scaffolder** *n*
scaffolding (ˈskæfəldɪŋ) *n* **1** a scaffold or system of scaffolds **2** the building materials used to make scaffolds
scag¹ *or* **skag** (skæg) *n* a slang name for **heroin**
scag² (skæg) *South Wales and southwest English dialect* ▷ *n* **1** a tear in a garment or piece of cloth ▷ *vb* **scags, scagging, scagged 2** (*tr*) to make a tear in (cloth) [apparently related to Old Norse *skaga* to project]
scagliola (skælˈjəʊlə) *n* imitation marble made of glued gypsum with a polished surface of coloured stone or marble dust [c16 from Italian, diminutive of *scaglia* chip of marble, of Germanic origin; related to SHALE, SCALE²]
Scala (ˈskaːla) *n* **La** See **La Scala**
scalability (ˌskeɪləˈbɪlɪtɪ) *n* the ability of something, esp a computer system, to adapt to increased demands
scalable (ˈskeɪləbᵊl) *adj* **1** capable of being scaled or climbed **2** *computing* (of a network) able to be expanded to cope with increased use > ˈ**scalableness** *n* > ˈ**scalably** *adv*
scalade (skəˈleɪd) *or* **scalado** (skəˈleɪdəʊ) *n, pl* **-lades** *or* **-lados** short for **escalade** [c16 from Old Italian *scalada*, from *scala* a ladder; see SCALE³]
scalage (ˈskeɪlɪdʒ) *n* **1** *US* a percentage deducted from the price of goods liable to shrink or leak **2** *forestry, US and Canadian* the estimated amount of usable timber in a log [c19 from SCALE³ + -AGE]
scalar (ˈskeɪlə) *n* **1** a quantity, such as time or temperature, that has magnitude but not direction. Compare **vector** (sense 1), **tensor** (sense 2), **pseudoscalar, pseudovector 2** *maths* an element of a field associated with a vector space ▷ *adj* **3** having magnitude but not direction [c17 (meaning: resembling a ladder): from Latin *scālāris*, from *scāla* ladder]
scalare (skəˈlɛərɪ) *n* another name for **angelfish** (sense 2) [c19 from Latin *scālāris* of a ladder, SCALAR, referring to the runglike pattern on its body]
scalariform (skəˈlærɪˌfɔːm) *adj biology* resembling a ladder: *a scalariform cell* [c19 from New Latin *scālāriformis* from Latin *scālāris* of a ladder + -FORM]
scalar multiplication *n maths* an operation used in the definition of a vector space in which the product of a scalar and a vector is a vector, the operation is distributive over the addition of both scalars and vectors, and is associative with multiplication of scalars
scalar product *n* the product of two vectors to form a scalar, whose value is the product of the magnitudes of the vectors and the cosine of the angle between them. Written: ***A•B*** or ***AB***. Compare **vector product** Also called: **dot product**
scalawag (ˈskæləˌwæg) *n* a variant of **scallywag**
scald¹ (skɔːld) *vb* **1** to burn or be burnt with or as if with hot liquid or steam **2** (*tr*) to subject to the action of boiling water, esp so as to sterilize **3** (*tr*) to heat (a liquid) almost to boiling point **4** (*tr*) to plunge (tomatoes, peaches, etc) into boiling water briefly in order to skin them more easily ▷ *n* **5** the act or result of scalding **6** an abnormal condition in plants, characterized by discoloration and wrinkling of the skin of the fruits, caused by exposure to excessive sunlight, gases, etc [c13 via Old Norman French from Late Latin *excaldāre* to wash in warm water, from *calida* (*aqua*) warm (water), from *calēre* to be warm] > ˈ**scalder** *n*
scald² (skɔːld) *n* a variant spelling of **skald**
scald³ (skɔːld) *obsolete* ▷ *adj also* **scalled 1** scabby ▷ *n* **2** a scab or a skin disease producing scabs [c16 from SCALL]
scald-crow *n Irish* another name for **hooded crow**
scaldfish (ˈskɔːldˌfɪʃ, ˈskaːld-) *n, pl* **-fish** *or* **-fishes** a small European flatfish, *Arnoglossus laterna*, covered with large fragile scales: family *Bothidae* [c19 from SCALD³]
scale¹ (skeɪl) *n* **1** any of the numerous plates, made of various substances resembling enamel or dentine, covering the bodies of fishes **2** **a** any of the horny or chitinous plates covering a part or the entire body of certain reptiles and mammals **b** any of the numerous minute structures covering the wings of lepidoptera. Related adj: **squamous 3** a thin flat piece or flake **4** a thin flake of dead epidermis shed from the skin: excessive shedding may be the result of a skin disease **5** a specialized leaf or bract, esp the protective covering of a bud or the dry membranous bract of a catkin **6** See **scale insect 7** a flaky black oxide of iron formed on the surface of iron or steel at high temperatures **8** any oxide formed on a metal during heat treatment **9** another word for **limescale** ▷ *vb* **10** (*tr*) to remove the scales or coating from **11** to peel off or cause to peel off in flakes or scales **12** (*intr*) to shed scales **13** to cover or become covered with scales, incrustation, etc **14** (*tr*) to throw (a disc or thin flat object) edgewise through the air or along the surface of water **15** (*intr*) *Austral informal* to ride on public transport without paying a fare **16** (*tr*) *South African slang* to steal (something) [c14 from Old French *escale*, of Germanic origin; compare Old English *scealu* SHELL] > ˈ**scale,like** *adj*
scale² (skeɪl) *n* **1** (*often plural*) a machine or device for weighing **2** one of the pans of a balance **3** **tip the scales** **a** to exercise a decisive influence **b** (foll by *at*) to amount in weight (to) ▷ *vb* (*tr*) **4** to weigh with or as if with scales **5** to have a weight of [c13 from Old Norse *skāl* bowl, related to Old High German *scāla* cup, Old English *scealu* SHELL, SCALE¹]
scale³ (skeɪl) *n* **1** a sequence of marks either at regular intervals or else representing equal steps used as a reference in making measurements **2** a measuring instrument having such a scale **3** **a** the ratio between the size of something real and that of a model or representation of it: *the scale of the map was so large that we could find our house on it* **b** (*as modifier*): *a scale model* **4** a line, numerical ratio, etc, for showing this ratio **5** a progressive or graduated table of things, wages, etc, in order of size, value, etc: *a wage scale for carpenters* **6** an established measure or standard **7** a relative degree or extent: *he entertained on a grand scale* **8** *music* a group of notes taken in ascending or descending order, esp within the compass of one octave **9** *maths* the notation of a given number system: *the decimal scale* **10** a graded series of tests measuring mental development, etc **11** *obsolete* a ladder or staircase ▷ *vb* **12** to climb to the top of (a height) by or as if by a ladder **13** (*tr*) to make or draw (a model, plan, etc) according to a particular ratio of proportionate reduction **14** (*tr; usually foll by up or down*) to increase or reduce proportionately in size, etc **15** *US and Canadian* (in forestry) to estimate the board footage of (standing timber or logs) ▷ See also **scale back** [c15 via Italian from Latin *scāla* ladder; related to Old French *eschiele*, Spanish *escala*]
scale back *vb* (*adverb*) to reduce or make a reduction in the level of activity, extent, numbers, etc
scaleboard (ˈskeɪlˌbɔːd, ˈskæbəd) *n* a very thin piece of board, used for backing a picture, as a veneer, etc
scale insect *n* any small homopterous insect of the family *Coccidae* and related families, which typically live and feed on plants and secrete a protective scale around themselves. Many species, such as the San Jose scale, are important pests
scale leaf *n botany* **1** a modified leaf, often small and membranous, protecting buds, etc **2** any of the leaves of some conifers, such as cypresses, that are small and tightly pressed to the stem
scale moss *n* any of various leafy liverworts of

S

the order *Jungermanniales,* which resemble mosses

scalene ('skeɪliːn) *adj* **1** *maths* (of a triangle) having all sides of unequal length **2** *anatomy* of or relating to any of the scalenus muscles [c17 from Late Latin *scalēnus* with unequal sides, from Greek *skalēnos*]

scalenus (skə'liːnəs, skeɪ-) *n, pl* **-ni** (-naɪ) *anatomy* any one of the three muscles situated on each side of the neck extending from the cervical vertebrae to the first or second pair of ribs [c18 from New Latin; see SCALENE]

scaler ('skeɪlə) *n* **1** a person or thing that scales **2** Also called: **counter, scaling circuit** an electronic device or circuit that aggregates electric pulses and gives a single output pulse for a predetermined number of input pulses

Scales (skeɪlz) *n* **the** the constellation Libra, the seventh sign of the zodiac

scaling ladder *n* a ladder used to climb high walls, esp one used formerly to enter a besieged town, fortress, etc

scall (skɔːl) *n pathol* a former term for any of various diseases of the scalp characterized by itching and scab formation [c14 from Old Norse *skalli* bald head. Compare SKULL] > **scalled** *adj*

scallion ('skæljən) *n* any of various onions or similar plants, such as the spring onion, that have a small bulb and long leaves and are eaten in salads. Also called: **green onion** [c14 from Anglo-French *scalun,* from Latin *Ascalōnia (caepa)* Ascalonian (onion), from *Ascalo* Ascalon, a Palestinian port]

scallop ('skɒləp, 'skæl-) *n* **1** any of various marine bivalves of the family *Pectinidae,* having a fluted fan-shaped shell: includes free-swimming species (genus *Pecten*) and species attached to a substratum (genus *Chlamys*). See also **pecten** (sense 3) **2** the edible adductor muscle of certain of these molluscs **3** either of the shell valves of any of these molluscs **4** a scallop shell or similarly shaped dish, in which fish, esp shellfish, is cooked and served **5** one of a series of curves along an edge, esp an edge of cloth **6** the shape of a scallop shell used as the badge of a pilgrim, esp in the Middle Ages **7** *chiefly Austral* a potato cake fried in batter ▷ *vb* **8** (*tr*) to decorate (an edge) with scallops **9** to bake (food) in a scallop shell or similar dish **10** (*intr*) to collect scallops [c14 from Old French *escalope* shell, of Germanic origin; see SCALP] > **scalloper** *n* > **scalloping** *n*

scally ('skælɪ) *n, pl* **-lies** *Northwest English dialect* a rascal; rogue [c20 from SCALLYWAG]

scallywag ('skælɪˌwæg) *n* **1** *informal* a scamp; rascal **2** (*after the US Civil War*) a White Southerner who supported the Republican Party and its policy of Black emancipation. Scallywags were viewed as traitors by their fellow Southerners ▷ Also: **scalawag, scallawag** [c19 (originally undersized animal) of uncertain origin]

scaloppine *or* **scaloppini** (ˌskælə'piːnɪ) *pl n* escalopes of meat, esp veal, cooked in a rich sauce, usually of wine with seasonings [Italian: from *scaloppa* a fillet, probably from Old French *escalope* SCALLOP]

scalp (skælp) *n* **1** *anatomy* the skin and subcutaneous tissue covering the top of the head **2** (among North American Indians) a part of this removed as a trophy from a slain enemy **3** a trophy or token signifying conquest **4** *hunting, chiefly US* a piece of hide cut from the head of a victim as a trophy or as proof of killing in order to collect a bounty **5** *informal, chiefly US* a small speculative profit taken in quick transactions **6** *Scot dialect* a projection of bare rock from vegetation ▷ *vb* (*tr*) **7** to cut the scalp from **8** *informal, chiefly US* to purchase and resell (securities) quickly so as to make several small profits **9** *informal* to buy (tickets) cheaply and resell at an inflated price [c13 probably from Scandinavian; compare Old Norse *skalpr* sheath, Middle Dutch *schelpe,* Danish *skalp* husk] > 'scalper *n*

scalpel ('skælpəl) *n* a surgical knife with a short thin blade [c18 from Latin *scalpellum,* from *scalper* a knife, from *scalpere* to scrape] > **scalpellic** (skæl'pɛlɪk) *adj*

scalping ('skælpɪŋ) *n* a process in which the top portion of a metal ingot is machined away before use, thus removing the layer containing defects and impurities

scalp lock *n* a small tuft or plait of hair left on the shaven scalp by American Indian warriors as a challenge to enemies

scaly ('skeɪlɪ) *adj* scalier, scaliest **1** resembling or covered in scales **2** peeling off in scales > 'scaliness *n*

scaly anteater *n* another name for **pangolin**

scam (skæm) *slang* ▷ *n* **1** a stratagem for gain; a swindle ▷ *vb* scams, scamming, scammed **2** (*tr*) to swindle (someone) by means of a trick

Scamander (skə'mændə) *n* the ancient name for the **Menderes** (sense 2)

scambaiting ('skæmˌbeɪtɪŋ) *n computing slang* the practice of pretending to fall for fraudulent online schemes in order to waste the time of the perpetrators

scammer ('skæmə) *or* **scamster** *n slang* a person who perpetrates a scam; swindler

scammony ('skæmənɪ) *n, pl* **-nies 1** a twining Asian convolvulus plant, *Convolvulus scammonia,* having arrow-shaped leaves, white or purple flowers, and tuberous roots **2** a resinous juice obtained from the roots of this plant and having purgative properties **3** any of various similar medicinal resins or the plants that yield them [Old English, via Latin from Greek *skammōnia,* of obscure origin] > **scammoniate** (skæ'məʊnɪɪt) *adj*

scamp[1] (skæmp) *n* **1** an idle mischievous person; rascal **2** a mischievous child [c18 from *scamp* (vb) to be a highway robber, probably from Middle Dutch *schampen* to decamp, from Old French *escamper,* from *es-* EX-[1] + *-camper,* from Latin *campus* field] > 'scampish *adj*

scamp[2] (skæmp) *vb* a less common word for **skimp** > 'scamper *n*

scamper ('skæmpə) *vb* (*intr*) **1** to run about playfully **2** (often foll by *through*) to hurry quickly through (a place, task, book, etc) ▷ *n* **3** the act of scampering [c17 probably from *scamp* (vb); see SCAMP[1]] > 'scamperer *n*

scampi ('skæmpɪ) *n* (*usually functioning as singular*) large prawns, usually eaten fried in breadcrumbs [Italian: plural of *scampo* shrimp, of obscure origin]

scamster ('skæmstə) *n slang* a variant of **scammer**

scamto ('skæmtəʊ) *n South African* the argot of urban South African Blacks [c20 of uncertain origin]

scan (skæn) *vb* scans, scanning, scanned **1** (*tr*) to scrutinize minutely **2** (*tr*) to glance over quickly **3** (*tr*) *prosody* to read or analyse (verse) according to the rules of metre and versification **4** (*intr*) *prosody* to conform to the rules of metre and versification **5** (*tr*) *electronics* to move a beam of light, electrons, etc, in a predetermined pattern over (a surface or region) to obtain information, esp either to sense and transmit or to reproduce a television image **6** (*tr*) to examine data stored on (magnetic tape, etc), usually in order to retrieve information **7** to examine or search (a prescribed region) by systematically varying the direction of a radar or sonar beam **8** *physics* to examine or produce or be examined or produced by a continuous charge of some variable: *to scan a spectrum* **9** *med* to obtain an image of (a part of the body) by means of a scanner ▷ *n* **10** the act or an instance of scanning **11** *med* **a** the examination of a part of the body by means of a scanner: *a brain scan; ultrasound scan* **b** the image produced by a scanner [c14 from Late Latin *scandere* to scan (verse), from Latin: to climb] > 'scannable *adj*

scandal ('skænd³l) *n* **1** a disgraceful action or event: *his negligence was a scandal* **2** censure or outrage arising from an action or event **3** a person whose conduct causes reproach or disgrace **4** malicious talk, esp gossip about the private lives of other people **5** *law* a libellous action or statement ▷ *vb* (*tr*) *obsolete* **6** to disgrace **7** to scandalize [c16 from Late Latin *scandalum* stumbling block, from Greek *skandalon* a trap] > 'scandalous *adj* > 'scandalously *adv* > 'scandalousness *n*

scandalize *or* **scandalise** ('skændəˌlaɪz) *vb* (*tr*) to shock, as by improper behaviour > ˌscandali'zation *or* ˌscandali'sation *n* > 'scandalˌizer *or* 'scandalˌiser *n*

scandalmonger ('skænd³lˌmʌŋgə) *n* a person who spreads or enjoys scandal, gossip, etc

Scandaroon (ˌskændə'ruːn) *n* a large variety of fancy pigeon having a long thin body and an elongated neck and head [from *Scandaroon* the former name of *Ishenderon* a seaport in Turkey]

scandent ('skændənt) *adj* (of plants) having a climbing habit [c17 from Latin *scandere* to climb]

Scandian ('skændɪən) *n* another name for a **Scandinavian** [c17 from Latin *Scandia* Scandinavia]

scandic ('skændɪk) *adj* of or containing scandium

Scandinavia (ˌskændɪ'neɪvɪə) *n* **1** Also called: **the Scandinavian Peninsula** the peninsula of N Europe occupied by Norway and Sweden **2** the countries of N Europe, esp considered as a cultural unit and including Norway, Sweden, Denmark, and often Finland, Iceland, and the Faeroes

Scandinavian (ˌskændɪ'neɪvɪən) *adj* **1** of, relating to, or characteristic of Scandinavia, its inhabitants, or their languages ▷ *n* **2** a native or inhabitant of Scandinavia **3** Also called: **Norse** the northern group of Germanic languages, consisting of Swedish, Danish, Norwegian, Icelandic, and Faeroese

Scandinavian Shield *n* another name for **Baltic Shield**

scandium ('skændɪəm) *n* a rare light silvery-white metallic element occurring in minute quantities in numerous minerals. Symbol: Sc; atomic no: 21; atomic wt: 44.955910; valency: 3; relative density: 2.989; melting pt: 1541°C; boiling pt: 2836°C [c19 from New Latin, from Latin *Scandia* Scandinavia, where it was discovered]

scanner ('skænə) *n* **1** a person or thing that scans **2** a device, usually electronic, used to measure or sample the distribution of some quantity or condition in a particular system, region, or area **3** an aerial or similar device designed to transmit or receive signals, esp radar signals, inside a given solid angle of space, thus allowing a particular region to be scanned **4** any of various devices used in medical diagnosis to obtain an image of an internal organ or part. See **CAT scanner, nuclear magnetic resonance scanner, ultrasound scanner 5** *informal* a television outside broadcast vehicle **6** short for **optical scanner 7** *printing* an electronic device which scans artwork and illustrations and converts the images to digital form for manipulation, and incorporation into printed publications

scanning electron microscope *n* a type of electron microscope that produces a three-dimensional image

scansion ('skænʃən) *n* the analysis of the metrical structure of verse. See **quantity** (sense 7), **stress** (sense 4) [c17 from Latin: climbing up, from *scandere* to climb, SCAN]

scansorial (skæn'sɔːrɪəl) *adj zoology* specialized for, characterized by, or relating to climbing: *a scansorial bird* [c19 from Latin *scānsōrius,* from *scandere* to climb]

scant (skænt) *adj* **1** scarcely sufficient; limited: *he paid her scant attention* **2** (*prenominal*) slightly short of the amount indicated; bare: *a scant ten inches* **3** (*postpositive; foll by of*) having a short supply (of) ▷ *vb* (*tr*) **4** to limit in size or quantity **5** to provide with a limited or inadequate supply of **6** to treat in a slighting or inadequate manner ▷ *adv* **7** scarcely; barely [C14 from Old Norse *skamt*, from *skammr*/short; related to Old High German *scam*] > ˈscantly *adv* > ˈscantness *n*

scantling (ˈskæntlɪŋ) *n* **1** a piece of sawn timber, such as a rafter, that has a small cross section **2** the dimensions of a piece of building material or the structural parts of a ship, esp those in cross section **3** a building stone, esp one that is more than 6 feet in length **4** a small quantity or amount [C16 changed (through influence of SCANT and -LING¹) from earlier *scantillon*, a carpenter's gauge, from Old Norman French *escantillon*, ultimately from Latin *scandere* to climb; see SCAN]

scantlings (ˈskæntlɪŋz) *pl n* the structural casings of the internal gas paths in an aeroengine

scanty (ˈskæntɪ) *adj* scantier, scantiest **1** limited; barely enough; meagre **2** insufficient; inadequate **3** lacking fullness; small > ˈscantily *adv* > ˈscantiness *n*

Scapa Flow (ˈskæpə) *n* an extensive landlocked anchorage off the N coast of Scotland, in the Orkney Islands: major British naval base in both World Wars. Length: about 24 km (15 miles). Width: 13 km (8 miles)

scape¹ (skeɪp) *n* **1** a leafless stalk in plants that arises from a rosette of leaves and bears one or more flowers **2** *zoology* a stalklike part, such as the first segment of an insect's antenna [C17 from Latin *scāpus* stem, from (Doric) Greek *skapos*; see SHAFT] > ˈscapose *adj*

scape² or **'scape** (skeɪp) *vb, n* an archaic word for **escape**

-scape *suffix forming nouns* indicating a scene or view of something, esp a pictorial representation: *seascape* [abstracted from LANDSCAPE]

scapegoat (ˈskeɪpˌɡəʊt) *n* **1** a person made to bear the blame for others **2** *Old Testament* a goat used in the ritual of Yom Kippur (Leviticus 16); it was symbolically laden with the sins of the Israelites and sent into the wilderness to be destroyed ▷ *vb* **3** (*tr*) to make a scapegoat of [C16 from ESCAPE + GOAT, coined by William Tyndale to translate Biblical Hebrew *azāzēl* (probably) goat for Azazel, mistakenly thought to mean "goat that escapes"]

scapegrace (ˈskeɪpˌɡreɪs) *n* an idle mischievous person [C19 from SCAPE² + GRACE, alluding to a person who lacks God's grace]

scapewheel (ˈskeɪpˌwiːl) *n* a less common name for **escape wheel**

scaphocephalic (ˌskæfɪsɪˈfælɪk) *adj* **1** *anatomy* having a head that is abnormally long and narrow as a result of the two parietal bones on the top of the skull closing prematurely **2** an individual with such a head. Compare **dolichocephalic, brachycephalic** > ˌscaphoˈcephaly or ˈscaphoˌcephalism *n*

scaphoid (ˈskæfɔɪd) *adj anatomy* an obsolete word for **navicular** [C18 via New Latin from Greek *skaphoeidēs*, from *skaphē* boat]

scaphopod (ˈskæfəˌpɒd) *n* any marine mollusc of the class *Scaphopoda*, which includes the tusk (or tooth) shells [C20 from New Latin, from Greek *skaphē* boat + -POD]

scapolite (ˈskæpəˌlaɪt) *n* any of a group of colourless, white, grey, or violet fluorescent minerals consisting of sodium or calcium aluminium silicate, carbonate, and chloride in tetragonal crystalline form. They occur mainly in impure limestones and pegmatites. Also called: wernerite [C19 from German *Skapolith*, from Greek *skapos* rod + -LITE]

scapula (ˈskæpjʊlə) *n, pl* -lae (-liː) *or* -las **1** either of two large flat triangular bones, one on each side of the back part of the shoulder in man. Nontechnical name: shoulder blade **2** the corresponding bone in most vertebrates [C16 from Late Latin: shoulder]

scapular (ˈskæpjʊlə) *adj* **1** *anatomy* of or relating to the scapula ▷ *n* **2** part of the monastic habit worn by members of many Christian, esp Roman Catholic, religious orders, consisting of a piece of

woollen cloth worn over the shoulders, and hanging down in front and behind to the ankles **3** two small rectangular pieces of woollen cloth joined by tapes passing over the shoulders and worn under secular clothes in token of affiliation to a religious order **4** any of the small feathers that are attached to the humerus of a bird and lie along the shoulder ▷ Also called (for senses 2, 3): **scapulary**

scar¹ (skɑː) *n* **1** any mark left on the skin or other tissue following the healing of a wound **2** a permanent change in a person's character resulting from emotional distress: *his wife's death left its scars on him* **3** the mark on a plant indicating the former point of attachment of a part, esp the attachment of a leaf to a stem **4** a mark of damage; blemish ▷ *vb* scars, scarring, scarred **5** to mark or become marked with a scar **6** (*intr*) to heal leaving a scar [C14 via Late Latin from Greek *eskhara* scab]

scar² (skɑː) *n* **1** an irregular enlongated trench-like feature on a land surface that often exposes bedrock **2** a similar formation in a river or sea. Also called (Scot): scaur [C14 from Old Norse *sker* low reef, SKERRY]

scarab (ˈskærəb) *n* **1** any scarabaeid beetle, esp *Scarabaeus sacer* (**sacred scarab**), regarded by the ancient Egyptians as divine **2** the scarab as represented on amulets, etc, of ancient Egypt, or in hieroglyphics as a symbol of the solar deity [C16 from Latin *scarabaeus*; probably related to Greek *karabos* horned beetle]

scarabaeid (ˌskærəˈbiːɪd) or **scarabaean** (ˌskærəˈbiːən) *n* **1** any beetle of the family *Scarabaeidae*, including the sacred scarab and other dung beetles, the chafers, goliath beetles, and rhinoceros beetles ▷ *adj* **2** of, relating to, or belonging to the family *Scarabaeidae* [C19 from New Latin]

scarabaeoid (ˌskærəˈbiːɔɪd) *adj* **1** Also: scaraboid (ˈskærəˌbɔɪd) of, relating to, or resembling a scarabaeid **2** a former word for **lamellicorn**

scarabaeus (ˌskærəˈbiːəs) *n, pl* -baeuses *or* -baei (-ˈbiːaɪ) a less common name for **scarab**

Scaramouch or **Scaramouche** (ˈskærəˌmaʊtʃ, -ˌmuːtʃ) *n* a stock character who appears as a boastful coward in commedia dell'arte and farce [C17 via French from Italian *Scaramuccia*, from *scaramuccia* a SKIRMISH]

Scarborough (ˈskɑːbrə) *n* a fishing port and resort in NE England, in North Yorkshire on the North Sea: developed as a spa after 1660; ruined 12th-century castle. Pop: 38 364 (2001)

scarce (skeəs) *adj* **1** rarely encountered **2** insufficient to meet the demand **3** make oneself scarce *informal* to go away, esp suddenly ▷ *adv* **4** *archaic or literary* scarcely [C13 from Old Norman French *scars*, from Vulgar Latin *excarpsus* (unattested) plucked out, from Latin *excerpere* to select; see EXCERPT] > ˈscarceness *n*

scarcely (ˈskeəslɪ) *adv* **1** hardly at all; only just **2** *often used ironically* probably not or definitely not: *that is scarcely justification for your actions*

▋ USAGE See at **hardly**

scarcement (ˈskeəsmənt) *n* a ledge in a wall [C16 probably from obsolete sense of SCARCE to reduce + -MENT]

scarcity (ˈskeəsɪtɪ) *n, pl* -ties **1** inadequate supply; dearth; paucity **2** rarity or infrequent occurrence

scare (skeə) *vb* **1** to fill or be filled with fear or alarm **2** (*tr*; often foll by *away* or *off*) to drive (away) by frightening **3** (*tr*) *US and Canadian informal* (foll by *up*) **a** to produce (a meal) quickly from whatever is available **b** to manage to find (something) quickly or with difficulty: *brewers need to scare up more sales* ▷ *n* **4** a sudden attack of fear or alarm **5** a period of general fear or alarm ▷ *adj* **6** causing (needless) fear or alarm: *a scare story* [C12 from Old Norse *skirra*; related to Norwegian *skjerra*, Swedish dialect *skjarra*] > ˈscarer *n*

scarecrow (ˈskeəˌkrəʊ) *n* **1** an object, usually in the shape of a man, made out of sticks and old

clothes to scare birds away from crops **2** a person or thing that appears frightening but is not actually harmful **3** *informal* **a** an untidy-looking person **b** a very thin person

scaredy-cat (ˈskeədɪˌkæt) *n informal* someone who is easily frightened

scaremonger (ˈskeəˌmʌŋɡə) *n* a person who delights in spreading rumours of disaster > ˈscareˌmongering *n*

scare quotes *pl n* quotation marks placed around a word or phrase to indicate that it should not be taken literally or automatically accepted as true

scarf¹ (skɑːf) *n, pl* scarves (skɑːvz) *or* scarfs **1** a rectangular, triangular, or long narrow piece of cloth worn around the head, neck, or shoulders for warmth or decoration ▷ *vb* (*tr*) *rare* **2** to wrap with or as if with a scarf **3** to use as or in the manner of a scarf [C16 of uncertain origin; compare Old Norman French *escarpe*, Medieval Latin *scrippum* pilgrim's pack; see SCRIP²]

scarf² (skɑːf) *n, pl* scarfs **1** Also called: scarf joint, scarfed joint a lapped joint between two pieces of timber made by notching or grooving the ends and strapping, bolting, or gluing the two pieces together **2** the end of a piece of timber shaped to form such a joint **3** NZ a wedge-shaped cut made in a tree before felling, to determine the direction of the fall **4** *whaling* an incision made along a whale's body before stripping off the blubber ▷ *vb* (*tr*) **5** to join (two pieces of timber) by means of a scarf **6** to make a scarf on (a piece of timber) **7** to cut a scarf in (a whale) [C14 probably from Scandinavian; compare Norwegian *skarv*, Swedish *skarf*, Low German, Dutch *scherf* SCARF¹]

scarfskin (ˈskɑːfˌskɪn) *n* the outermost layer of the skin; epidermis or cuticle [C17 from SCARF¹ (in the sense: an outer covering)]

scarificator (ˈskeərɪfɪˌkeɪtə, ˈskærɪ-) *n* a surgical instrument for use in superficial puncturing of the skin or other tissue

scarify¹ (ˈskeərɪˌfaɪ, ˈskærɪ-) *vb* -fies, -fying, -fied (*tr*) **1** *surgery* to make tiny punctures or superficial incisions in (the skin or other tissue), as for inoculating **2** *agriculture* **a** to break up and loosen (soil) to a shallow depth **b** to scratch or abrade the outer surface of (seeds) to increase water absorption or hasten germination **3** to wound with harsh criticism [C15 via Old French from Latin *scarīfāre* to scratch open, from Greek *skariphasthai* to draw, from *skariphos* a pencil] > ˌscarifiˈcation *n* > ˈscariˌfier *n*

scarify² (ˈskeərɪˌfaɪ) *vb* -fies, -fying, -fied (*tr*) *informal* to make scared; frighten [C18 from SCARE + -IFY] > ˈscariˌfyingly *adv*

▋ USAGE *Scarify* is sometimes wrongly thought to mean the same as *scare*: *a frightening* (not *scarifying*) *film*

scarious (ˈskeərɪəs) or **scariose** (ˈskeərɪˌəʊs) *adj* (of plant parts) membranous, dry, and brownish in colour: *scarious bracts* [C19 from New Latin *scariōsus*, of uncertain origin]

scarlatina (ˌskɑːləˈtiːnə) *n* the technical name for **scarlet fever** [C19 from New Latin, from Italian *scarlattina*, diminutive of *scarlatto* SCARLET] > ˌscarlaˈtinal *adj*

scarlet (ˈskɑːlɪt) *n* **1** a vivid red colour, sometimes with an orange tinge **2** cloth or clothing of this colour ▷ *adj* **3** of the colour scarlet **4** sinful or immoral, esp unchaste [C13 from Old French *escarlate* fine cloth, of unknown origin]

scarlet fever *n* an acute communicable disease characterized by fever, strawberry-coloured tongue, and a typical rash starting on the neck and chest and spreading to the abdomen and limbs, caused by all group A haemolytic *Streptococcus* bacteria. Technical name: scarlatina

scarlet hat *n* another term for **red hat**

scarlet letter *n* (esp among US Puritans) a scarlet letter *A* formerly worn by a person convicted of adultery

scarlet pimpernel *n* a weedy primulaceous plant, *Anagallis arvensis*, of temperate regions,

S

having small red, purple, or white star-shaped flowers that close in bad weather. Also called: **shepherd's** (*or* **poor man's**) **weatherglass**

scarlet runner *n* a climbing perennial bean plant, *Phaseolus multiflorus* (or *P. coccineus*), of tropical America, having scarlet flowers: widely cultivated for its long green edible pods containing edible seeds. Also called: **runner bean, string bean**

scarlet tanager *n* an E North American tanager, *Piranga olivacea*, the male of which has a bright red head and body with black wings and tail

scarlet woman *n* **1** *New Testament* a sinful woman described in Revelation 17, interpreted as a figure either of pagan Rome or of the Roman Catholic Church regarded as typifying vice overlaid with gaudy pageantry **2** any sexually promiscuous woman, esp a prostitute

scarp (skɑːp) *n* **1** a steep slope, esp one formed by erosion or faulting; escarpment. See also **cuesta** **2** *fortifications* the side of a ditch cut nearest to and immediately below a rampart ▷ *vb* **3** (*tr; often passive*) to wear or cut so as to form a steep slope [C16 from Italian *scarpa*]

scarper ('skɑːpə) *Brit slang* ▷ *vb* (*intr*) **1** to depart in haste ▷ *n* **2** a hasty departure [C19 probably an adaptation of Italian *scappare* to escape; perhaps influenced by folk etymology *Scapa Flow* Cockney rhyming slang for *go*]

scart (skært) *Scot* ▷ *vb* **1** to scratch or scrape ▷ *n* **2** a scratch or scrape **3** a stroke of a pen **4** a small amount; scraping [C14 from earlier *scrat*]

Scart *or* **SCART** (skɑːt) *n electronics* **a** a 21-pin plug-and-socket system which carries picture, sound, and other signals, used especially in home entertainment systems **b** (*as modifier*): *a Scart cable* [C20 after Syndicat des Constructeurs des Appareils Radiorécepteurs et Téléviseurs, the company that designed it]

scarves (skɑːvz) *n* a plural of **scarf**

scary ('skɛərɪ) *adj* **scarier, scariest** *informal* **1** causing fear or alarm; frightening **2** easily roused to fear; timid

scat[1] (skæt) *vb* **scats, scatting, scatted** (*intr; usually imperative*) *informal* to go away in haste [C19 perhaps from a hiss + the word *cat*, used to frighten away cats]

scat[2] (skæt) *n* **1** a type of jazz singing characterized by improvised vocal sounds instead of words ▷ *vb* **scats, scatting, scatted** **2** (*intr*) to sing jazz in this way [C20 perhaps imitative]

scat[3] (skæt) *n* any marine and freshwater percoid fish of the Asian family *Scatophagidae*, esp *Scatophagus argus*, which has a beautiful coloration [C20 shortened from *Scatophagus*; see SCATO-]

scat[4] (skæt) *n* an animal dropping [C20 see SCATO-]

scathe (skeɪð) *vb* (*tr*) **1** *rare* to attack with severe criticism **2** *archaic or dialect* to injure ▷ *n* **3** *archaic or dialect* harm [Old English *sceatha*; related to Old Norse *skathi*, Old Saxon *scatho*] > '**scatheless** *adj*

scathing ('skeɪðɪŋ) *adj* **1** harshly critical; scornful: *a scathing remark* **2** damaging; painful > '**scathingly** *adv*

scato- *or before a vowel* **scat-** *combining form* dung or excrement: *scatophagous* [from Greek *skōr*, *skat-* dung]

scatological (ˌskætə'lɒdʒɪkᵊl) *or less commonly* **scatologic** (ˌskætə'lɒdʒɪk) *adj* **1** characterized by obscenity or preoccupation with obscenity, esp in the form of references to excrement **2** of or relating to the scientific study of excrement

scatology (skæ'tɒlədʒɪ) *n* **1** the scientific study of excrement, esp in medicine for diagnostic purposes, and in palaeontology of fossilized excrement **2** obscenity or preoccupation with obscenity, esp in the form of references to excrement > **sca'tologist** *n*

scatter ('skætə) *vb* **1** (*tr*) to throw about in various directions; strew **2** to separate and move or cause to separate and move in various directions; disperse **3** to deviate or cause to deviate in many directions, as in the diffuse reflection or refraction of light ▷ *n* **4** the act of scattering **5** a substance or a number of objects scattered about [C13 probably a variant of SHATTER] > '**scatterable** *adj* > '**scatterer** *n*

scatterbrain ('skætəˌbreɪn) *n* a person who is incapable of serious thought or concentration

scatterbrained ('skætəˌbreɪnd) *adj* exhibiting or characterized by lack of serious thought or concentration; disorganized; silly

scatter diagram *n statistics* a graph that plots along two axes at right angles to each other the relationship between two variable quantities, such as height and weight

scatter-gun *n* a shotgun

scattering ('skætərɪŋ) *n* **1** a small amount **2** *physics* the process in which particles, atoms, etc, are deflected as a result of collision

scatter pin *n* a small decorative pin usually worn in groups of two or three

scatter rug *n* a small rug used to cover a limited area

scattershot ('sk[ae]tə,ʃɒt) *adj* random; haphazard: *their approach to conservation is scattershot and unscientific*

scatty ('skætɪ) *adj* **-tier, -tiest** *Brit informal* **1** empty-headed, frivolous, or thoughtless **2** distracted (esp in **drive someone scatty**) [C20 from SCATTERBRAINED] > '**scattily** *adv* > '**scattiness** *n*

scaud (skɔːd) *vb, n* a Scot word for **scald**

scaup *or* **scaup duck** (skɔːp) *n* either of two diving ducks, *Aythya marila* (**greater scaup**) or *A. affinis* (**lesser scaup**), of Europe and America, having a black-and-white plumage in the male. Also called (US): **bluebill, broadbill** [C16 Scottish variant of SCALP]

scauper ('skɔːpə) *n* a variant spelling of **scorper**

scaur (skɔːr) *n* a Scot variant of **scar**

scavenge ('skævɪndʒ) *vb* **1** to search for (anything usable) among discarded material **2** (*tr*) to purify (a molten metal) by bubbling a suitable gas through it. The gas may be inert or may react with the impurities **3** to clean up filth from (streets, etc) **4** *chem* to act as a scavenger for (atoms, molecules, ions, radicals, etc)

scavenge pump *n engineering* an oil pump used in some internal-combustion engines to return oil from the crankcase to the oil tank

scavenger ('skævɪndʒə) *n* **1** a person who collects things discarded by others **2** any animal that feeds on decaying organic matter, esp on refuse **3** a substance added to a chemical reaction or mixture to counteract the effect of impurities **4** a person employed to clean the streets [C16 from Anglo-Norman *scawager*, from Old Norman French *escauwage* examination, from *escauwer* to scrutinize, of Germanic origin; related to Flemish *scauwen*] > '**scavengery** *n*

scavenger beetle *n* any beetle of the mostly aquatic family *Hydrophilidae*, having clubbed antennae and long palps, and usually feeding on decaying vegetation

scavenger hunt *n* a game in which players are required to collect an assortment of miscellaneous items: usually played outdoors

scavenge stroke *or* **scavenging stroke** *n* (in a reciprocating engine) the stroke of a piston in a four-stroke cycle that pushes the burnt gases out as exhaust. Also called: **exhaust stroke**

ScD *abbreviation for* Doctor of Science

SCE (in Scotland) *abbreviation for* Scottish Certificate of Education: either of two public examinations in specific subjects taken as school-leaving qualifications or as qualifying examinations for entry into a university, college, etc. See also **higher** (sense 2), **O grade**

scena ('ʃeɪnə) *n, pl* **-ne** (-ˌneɪ) **1** a scene in an opera, usually longer than a single aria **2** a dramatic vocal piece written in operatic style

scenario (sɪ'nɑːrɪˌəʊ) *n, pl* **-narios** **1** a summary of the plot of a play, etc, including information about its characters, scenes, etc **2** a predicted sequence of events: *let's try another scenario, involving the demise of democracy* [C19 via Italian from Latin *scēnārium*, from *scēna*; see SCENE] > **scenarist** ('siːnərɪst, sɪ'nɑː-) *n*

scend *or* **send** (sɛnd) *nautical* ▷ *vb* **scends, scending, scended** *or* **sends, sending, sent** **1** (of a vessel) to surge upwards in a heavy sea ▷ *n* **2** the upward heaving of a vessel pitching **3** the forward lift given a vessel by the sea [C17 perhaps from DESCEND or ASCEND]

scene (siːn) *n* **1** the place where an action or event, real or imaginary, occurs **2** the setting for the action of a play, novel, etc **3** an incident or situation, real or imaginary, esp as described or represented **4** **a** a subdivision of an act of a play, in which the time is continuous and the setting fixed **b** a single event, esp a significant one, in a play **5** *films* a shot or series of shots that constitutes a unit of the action **6** the backcloths, stage setting, etc, for a play or film set; scenery **7** the prospect of a place, landscape, etc **8** a display of emotion, esp an embarrassing one to the onlookers **9** *informal* the environment for a specific activity: *the fashion scene* **10** *informal* interest or chosen occupation: *classical music is not my scene* **11** *rare* the stage, esp of a theatre in ancient Greece or Rome **12** **behind the scenes** out of public view; privately [C16 from Latin *scēna* theatrical stage, from Greek *skēnē* tent, stage]

scene dock *or* **bay** *n* a place in a theatre where scenery is stored, usually near the stage

scenery ('siːnərɪ) *n, pl* **-eries** **1** the natural features of a landscape **2** *theatre* the painted backcloths, stage structures, etc, used to represent a location in a theatre or studio [C18 from Italian SCENARIO]

scenic ('siːnɪk, 'sɛn-) *adj* **1** of or relating to natural scenery **2** having beautiful natural scenery: *a scenic drive* **3** of or relating to the stage or stage scenery **4** (in painting) representing a scene, such as a scene of action or a historical event > '**scenically** *adv*

scenic railway *n* **1** a miniature railway used for amusement in a park, zoo, etc **2** a roller coaster

scenic reserve *n* NZ an area of natural beauty, set aside for public recreation

scenography (siː'nɒgrəfɪ) *n* **1** the art of portraying objects or scenes in perspective **2** scene painting, esp in ancient Greece [C17 via Latin from Greek *skēnographia* a drawing in perspective, from *skēnē* SCENE] > **sce'nographer** *n* > **scenographic** (ˌsiːnəʊ'græfɪk) *or* ˌ**sceno'graphical** *adj* > ˌ**sceno'graphically** *adv*

scent (sɛnt) *n* **1** a distinctive smell, esp a pleasant one **2** a smell left in passing, by which a person or animal may be traced **3** a trail, clue, or guide **4** an instinctive ability for finding out or detecting **5** another word (esp Brit) for **perfume** ▷ *vb* **6** (*tr*) to recognize or be aware of by or as if by the smell **7** (*tr*) to have a suspicion of; detect: *I scent foul play* **8** (*tr*) to fill with odour or fragrance **9** (*intr*) (of hounds, etc) to hunt by the sense of smell **10** to smell (at): *the dog scented the air* [C14 from Old French *sentir* to sense, from Latin *sentīre* to feel; see SENSE] > '**scented** *adj* > '**scentless** *adj* > '**scentlessness** *n*

scented orchid *n* a slender orchid, *Gymnadenia conopsea*, with fragrant pink flowers carried in a dense spike and having a three-lobed lip; found in calcareous turf. Also called: **fragrant orchid**

sceptic *or archaic and US* **skeptic** ('skɛptɪk) *n* **1** a person who habitually doubts the authenticity of accepted beliefs **2** a person who mistrusts people, ideas, etc, in general **3** a person who doubts the truth of religion, esp Christianity ▷ *adj* **4** of or relating to sceptics; sceptical [C16 from Latin *scepticus*, from Greek *skeptikos* one who reflects upon, from *skeptesthai* to consider] > '**scepticism** *or archaic and US* '**skepticism** *n*

Sceptic *or archaic and US* **Skeptic** ('skɛptɪk) *n* **1** a member of one of the ancient Greek schools of philosophy, esp that of Pyrrho (?365–?275 BC), who believed that real knowledge of things is impossible ▷ *adj* **2** of or relating to the Sceptics > 'Scepticism *or archaic and US* 'Skepticism *n*

sceptical *or archaic and US* **skeptical** ('skɛptɪkᵊl) *adj* **1** not convinced that something is true; doubtful **2** tending to mistrust people, ideas, etc, in general **3** of or relating to sceptics; sceptic > 'sceptically *or archaic and US* 'skeptically *adv*

sceptre *or US* **scepter** ('sɛptə) *n* **1** a ceremonial staff held by a monarch as the symbol of authority **2** imperial authority; sovereignty ▷ *vb* **3** (*tr*) to invest with authority [c13 from Old French *sceptre*, from Latin *scēptrum*, from Greek *skeptron* staff] > 'sceptred *or US* 'sceptered *adj*

SCG (in Australia) *abbreviation for* Sydney Cricket Ground

sch. *abbreviation for* school

Schadenfreude *German* ('ʃɑːdənfrɔydə) *n* delight in another's misfortune [German: from *Schaden* harm + *Freude* joy]

Schaerbeek (*Flemish* 'sxaːrbeːk) *n* a city in central Belgium: an industrial suburb of Brussels. Pop: 110 253 (2004 est)

Schaffhausen (*German* ʃaːfˈhauzən) *n* **1** a small canton of N Switzerland. Pop: 73 900 (2002 est). Area: 298 sq km (115 sq miles) **2** a town in N Switzerland, capital of Schaffhausen canton, on the Rhine. Pop: 33 628 (2000). French name: Schaffhouse

schappe ('ʃæpə) *n* a yarn or fabric made from waste silk [from German]

Schaumburg-Lippe (*German* 'ʃaumbʊrk'lɪpə) *n* a former state of NW Germany, between Westphalia and Hanover: part of Lower Saxony since 1946

schedule ('ʃɛdjuːl; *also, esp US* 'skɛdʒʊəl) *n* **1** a plan of procedure for a project, allotting the work to be done and the time for it **2** a list of items: *a schedule of fixed prices* **3** a list of times, esp of arrivals and departures; timetable **4** a list of tasks to be performed, esp within a set period **5** *law* a list or inventory, usually supplementary to a contract, will, etc **6** on schedule at the expected or planned time ▷ *vb* (*tr*) **7** to make a schedule of or place in a schedule **8** to plan to occur at a certain time [c14 earlier *cedule, sedule* via Old French from Late Latin *schedula* small piece of paper, from Latin *scheda* sheet of paper] > 'schedular *adj*

scheduled ('ʃɛdjuːld) *adj* **1** arranged or planned according to a programme, timetable, etc: *a scheduled meeting; a change to the scheduled programmes on TV tonight* **2** (of an aircraft or a flight) part of a regular service, not specially chartered **3** *Brit* (of a building, place of historic interest, etc) entered on a list of places to be preserved. See also **listed building**

scheduled castes *pl n* certain classes in Indian society officially granted special concessions. See **Harijan**

scheduled territories *pl n* the another name for **sterling area**

scheduler ('ʃɛdjuːlə; *US* 'skɛdʒʊələ) *n* **1** a person whose job is to allot times for television or radio programmes to be broadcast **2** *computing* a computer program designed to aid in scheduling tasks

scheelite ('ʃiːlaɪt) *n* a white, brownish, or greenish mineral, usually fluorescent, consisting of calcium tungstate in tetragonal crystalline form with some tungsten often replaced by molybdenum: occurs principally in contact metamorphic rocks and quartz veins, and is an important source of tungsten and purified calcium tungstate. Formula: $CaWO_4$ [c19 from German *Scheelit*, named after Karl Wilhelm Scheele (1742–86), Swedish chemist]

Scheldt (ʃɛlt, skɛlt) *n* a river in W Europe, rising in NE France and flowing north and northeast through W Belgium to Antwerp, then northwest to the North Sea in the SW Netherlands. Length: 435 km (270 miles). Flemish and Dutch name: Schelde ('sxɛldə) French name: **Escaut**

schema ('skiːmə) *n, pl* **-mata** (-mətə) **1** a plan, diagram, or scheme **2** (in the philosophy of Kant) a rule or principle that enables the understanding to apply its categories and unify experience: *universal succession is the schema of causality* **3** *psychol* a mental model of aspects of the world or of the self that is structured in such a way as to facilitate the processes of cognition and perception **4** *logic* an expression using metavariables that may be replaced by object language expressions to yield a well-formed formula. Thus *A – A is an axiom* schema for identity, representing the infinite number of axioms, *x = x, y = y, z = z*, etc [c19 from Greek: form]

schematic (skɪˈmætɪk, skiː-) *adj* **1** of or relating to the nature of a diagram, plan, or schema ▷ *n* **2** a schematic diagram, esp of an electrical circuit > sche'matically *adv*

schematism ('skiːməˌtɪzəm) *n* the general form, arrangement, or classification of something

schematize *or* **schematise** ('skiːməˌtaɪz) *vb* (*tr*) to form into or arrange in a scheme > ˌschemati'zation *or* ˌschemati'sation *n*

scheme (skiːm) *n* **1** a systematic plan for a course of action **2** a systematic arrangement of correlated parts; system **3** a secret plot **4** a visionary or unrealizable project **5** a chart, diagram, or outline **6** an astrological diagram giving the aspects of celestial bodies at a particular time **7** *chiefly Brit* a plan formally adopted by a commercial enterprise or governmental body, as for pensions, etc **8** *chiefly Scot* an area of housing that is laid out esp by a local authority; estate ▷ *vb* **9** (*tr*) to devise a system for **10** to form intrigues (for) in an underhand manner [c16 from Latin *schema*, from Greek *skhēma* form] > 'schemer *n*

schemie ('skiːmɪ) *n Scot informal derogatory* a resident of a housing scheme [c20]

scheming ('skiːmɪŋ) *adj* **1** given to making plots; cunning ▷ *n* **2** intrigues > 'schemingly *adv*

Schengen Convention *or* **Agreement** ('ʃɛŋən) *n* an agreement, signed in 1985, but not implemented until 1995, to abolish border controls within Europe: ten countries had acceded by 1995; the UK is not a signatory

scherzando (skɛəˈtsændəʊ) *music* ▷ *adj, adv* **1** to be performed in a light-hearted manner ▷ *n, pl* **-di** (-diː) *or* **-dos** **2** a movement, passage, etc, directed to be performed in this way [Italian, literally: joking. See SCHERZO]

scherzo ('skɛətsəʊ) *n, pl* **-zos** *or* **-zi** (-tsiː) a brisk lively movement, developed from the minuet, with a contrasting middle section (a trio). See **minuet** (sense 2) [Italian: joke, of Germanic origin; compare Middle High German *scherzen* to jest]

Schickard ('ʃɪkəd) *n* a large crater in the SW quadrant of the moon, about 227 kilometres (141 miles) in diameter

Schick test (ʃɪk) *n med* a skin test to determine immunity to diphtheria: a dilute diphtheria toxin is injected into the skin; within two or three days a red inflamed area will develop if no antibodies are present [c20 named after Bela *Schick* (1877–1967), US paediatrician]

Schiedam (*Dutch* sxiːˈdɑm) *n* a port in the SW Netherlands, in South Holland province west of Rotterdam: gin distilleries. Pop: 76 000 (2003 est)

Schiff base (ʃɪf) *n* the product of the chemical association of an aldehyde with a primary amine [c19 named after Hugo *Schiff* (1834–1915), German chemist]

schiller ('ʃɪlə) *n* an unusual iridescent or metallic lustre in some minerals caused by internal reflection from certain inclusions such as gas cavities or mineral intergrowths. Formula: $NaFe_3B_3Al_3(Al_3Si_6O_{27})(OH)_4$ [c19 from German *Schiller* iridescence, from Old High German *scilihen* to blink]

schilling ('ʃɪlɪŋ) *n* **1** the former standard monetary unit of Austria, divided into 100 groschen; replaced by the euro in 2002 **2** an old German coin of low denomination [c18 from German: SHILLING]

schipperke ('ʃɪpəkɪ, 'skɪp-) *n* a small Dutch breed of tailless dog with a foxy head, pricked ears, and usually a black coat [c19 from Dutch, literally: little boatman (from its use as a guard dog on canal barges). See SKIPPER¹]

schism ('skɪzəm, 'sɪz-) *n* **1** the division of a group into opposing factions **2** the factions so formed **3** division within or separation from an established Church, *cap* the Roman Catholic Church, not necessarily involving differences in doctrine [c14 from Church Latin *schisma*, from Greek *skhisma* a cleft, from *skhizein* to split]

schismatic (skɪzˈmætɪk, sɪz-) *or* **schismatical** *adj* **1** of, relating to, or promoting schism ▷ *n* **2** a person who causes schism or belongs to a schismatic faction > schis'matically *adv* > schis'maticalness *n*

schist (ʃɪst) *n* any metamorphic rock that can be split into thin layers because its micaceous minerals have become aligned in thin parallel bands [c18 from French *schiste*, from Latin *lapis schistos* stone that may be split, from Greek *skhizein* to split] > 'schistose *adj* > schistosity (ʃɪ'stɒsɪtɪ) *n*

schistosome ('ʃɪstəˌsəʊm) *n* any of various blood flukes of the chiefly tropical genus *Schistosoma*, which cause disease in man and domestic animals. Also called: bilharzia [c19 from New Latin *Schistosoma*; see SCHIST, -SOME³]

schistosomiasis (ˌʃɪstəsəʊˈmaɪəsɪs) *n* a disease caused by infestation of the body with blood flukes of the genus *Schistosoma*. Also called: bilharziasis

schizanthus (skɪtˈsænθəs) *n* any plant of the Chilean annual genus *Schizanthus*, some species of which are grown as pot or garden plants for their showy red, white, or yellow orchid-like flowers: family *Solanaceae*. Sometimes called: poor man's orchid [New Latin, from Greek *schizein* to cut + *anthos* flower (from the deeply divided corolla)]

schizo ('skɪtsəʊ) *offensive* ▷ *adj* **1** schizophrenic ▷ *n, pl* **-os** **2** a schizophrenic person

schizo- *or before a vowel* **schiz-** *combining form* indicating a cleavage, split, or division: *schizocarp; schizophrenia* [from Greek *skhizein* to split]

schizocarp ('skɪzəˌkɑːp) *n botany* a dry fruit that splits into two or more one-seeded portions at maturity > ˌschizo'carpous *or* ˌschizo'carpic *adj*

schizogenesis (ˌskɪtsəʊˈdʒɛnɪsɪs) *n* asexual reproduction by fission of the parent organism or part > schizogenetic (ˌskɪtsəʊdʒɪ'nɛtɪk) *adj*

schizogony (skɪt'sɒɡənɪ) *n* asexual reproduction in protozoans that is characterized by multiple fission

schizoid ('skɪtsɔɪd) *adj* **1** *psychol* denoting a personality disorder characterized by extreme shyness and oversensitivity to others **2** *informal* characterized by or showing conflicting or contradictory attitudes, ideas, etc ▷ *n* **3** a person who has a schizoid personality

schizomycete (ˌskɪtsəʊmaɪˈsiːt) *n* (formerly) any microscopic organism of the now obsolete class *Schizomycetes*, which included the bacteria > schizomycetic (ˌskɪtsəʊmaɪˈsɛtɪk) *or* ˌschizomy'cetous *adj*

schizont ('skɪtsɒnt) *n* a cell formed from a trophozoite during the asexual stage of the life cycle of sporozoan protozoans, such as the malaria parasite [c19 from SCHIZO- + -ont a being, from Greek *einai* to be]

schizophrenia (ˌskɪtsəʊˈfriːnɪə) *n* **1** any of a group of psychotic disorders characterized by progressive deterioration of the personality, withdrawal from reality, hallucinations, delusions, social apathy, emotional instability, etc. See **catatonia, hebephrenia, paranoia** **2** *informal* behaviour that appears to be motivated by contradictory or conflicting principles [c20 from SCHIZO- + Greek *phrēn* mind + -IA]

schizophrenic (ˌskɪtsəʊˈfrɛnɪk) *adj* **1** exhibiting symptoms of schizophrenia **2** *informal* experiencing or maintaining contradictory attitudes, emotions, etc ▷ *n* **3** a person who

S

suffers from schizophrenia

schizophrenogenic (ˌskɪtsəʊˌfriːnəʊˈdʒɛnɪk, -ˌfrɛnəʊ-) *adj* tending to cause schizophrenia

schizopod (ˈskɪtsəʊˌpɒd) *n* any of various shrimplike crustaceans of the former order *Schizopoda*, now separated into the orders *Mysidacea* (opossum shrimps) and *Euphausiacea*

schizothymia (ˌskɪtsəʊˈθaɪmɪə) *n psychiatry* the condition of being schizoid or introverted. It encompasses elements of schizophrenia but does not involve the same depth of psychological disturbance [c20 New Latin, from SCHIZO- + -*thymia*, from Greek *thumos* spirit] > ˌschizoˈthymic *adj*

schlemiel, schlemihl *or* **shlemiel** (ʃləˈmiːl) *n US slang* an awkward or unlucky person whose endeavours usually fail [Yiddish, from German, after the hero of a novel by Chamisso (1781–1838)]

schlep (ʃlɛp) *vb* schleps, schlepping, schlepped **1** to drag or lug (oneself or an object) with difficulty ▷ *n* **2** a stupid or clumsy person **3** an arduous journey or procedure [Yiddish, from German *schleppen*]

Schlesien (ˈʃleːzɪən) *n* the German name for **Silesia**

Schleswig (German ˈʃleːsvɪç) *n* **1** a fishing port in N Germany, in Schleswig-Holstein state: on an inlet of the Baltic. Pop: 24 288 (2003 est) **2** a former duchy, in the S Jutland Peninsula: annexed by Prussia in 1864; N part returned to Denmark after a plebiscite in 1920; S part forms part of the German state of Schleswig-Holstein. Danish name: **Slesvig**

Schleswig-Holstein (German ˈʃleːsvɪçˈhɔlʃtaɪn) *n* a state of N Germany, formerly in West Germany: drained chiefly by the River Elbe; mainly agricultural. Capital: Kiel. Pop: 2 823 000 (2003 est). Area: 15 658 sq km (6045 sq miles)

Schlieffen Plan (German ˈʃliːfən) *n* a plan intended to ensure German victory over a Franco-Russian alliance by holding off Russia with minimal strength and swiftly defeating France by a massive flanking movement through the Low Countries, devised by Alfred, Count von Schlieffen (1833–1913) in 1905

schlieren (ˈʃliərən) *n* **1** *physics* visible streaks produced in a transparent medium as a result of variations in the medium's density leading to variations in refractive index. They can be recorded by flash photography (**schlieren photography**) **2** streaks or platelike masses of mineral in a rock mass, that differ in texture or composition from the main mass [German, plural of *Schliere* streak] > ˈschlieric *adj*

schlock (ʃlɒk) *chiefly US slang* ▷ *n* **1** goods or produce of cheap or inferior quality; trash ▷ *adj* **2** cheap, inferior, or trashy [Yiddish: damaged merchandise, probably from German *Schlag* a blow; related to SLAY]

schlong (ʃlɒŋ) *n US* a slang word for **penis**

schlub (ʃlʌb) *n US slang* a coarse or contemptible person [Yiddish, of uncertain origin]

schlumbergera (ʃləmˈbɜːɡərə) *n* See **Christmas cactus**

schmaltz *or* **schmalz** (ʃmælts, ʃmɔːlts) *n* **1** excessive sentimentality, esp in music **2** *US* animal fat used in cooking [c20 from German (*Schmalz*) and Yiddish: melted fat, from Old High German *smalz*]

schmaltzy (ʃmæltsɪ, ʃmɔːltsɪ) *adj* -ier, -iest excessively sentimental

schmear *or* **schmeer** (ʃmɪə) *n US informal* a situation, matter, or affair (esp in the phrase **the whole schmear**) [c20 from Yiddish *shmirn* to smear or grease]

schmick (ʃmɪk) *adj Austral informal* excellent, elegant, or stylish [c20 of unknown origin]

Schmidt telescope *or* **camera** *n* a catadioptric telescope designed to produce a very sharp image of a large area of sky in one photographic exposure. It incorporates a thin specially shaped glass plate at the centre of curvature of a short-focus spherical primary mirror so that the resulting image, which is focused on a photographic plate, is free from spherical aberration, coma, and astigmatism [c20 named after B V *Schmidt* (1879–1935), Estonian-born German inventor]

Schmitt trigger *n electronics* a bistable circuit that gives a constant output when the input voltage is above a specified value [c20 named after O H *Schmitt* (born 1913), US scientist]

schmo *or* **shmo** (ʃməʊ) *n, pl* schmoes *or* shmoes *US slang* a dull, stupid, or boring person [from Yiddish *shmok*]

schmooze (ʃmuːz) *slang* ▷ *vb* **1** (*intr*) to chat or gossip **2** (*tr*) to chat to (someone) for the purposes of self-promotion or to gain some advantage ▷ *n* **3** a trivial conversation; chat [Yiddish, from *schmues* a chat, from Hebrew *shemuoth* reports]

schmuck (ʃmʌk) *n US slang* a stupid or contemptible person; oaf [from Yiddish *schmuck* penis, from German *Schmuck* decoration, from Middle High German *smucken* to press into]

schmutter (ˈʃmʌtə) *n slang* cloth or clothing [c20 from Yiddish *schmatte* rag, from Polish *szmata*]

schnapper (ˈʃnæpə) *n* a variant of **snapper** (senses 1, 2)

schnapps *or* **schnaps** (ʃnæps) *n* **1** a Dutch spirit distilled from potatoes **2** (in Germany) any strong spirit [c19 from German *Schnaps*, from *schnappen* to SNAP]

schnauzer (ˈʃnaʊtsə) *n* a wire-haired breed of dog of the terrier type, originally from Germany, having a greyish coat and distinctive beard, moustache, and eyebrows [c19 from German *Schnauze* SNOUT]

schnecken (ˈʃnɛkən) *pl n, sing* schnecke (ˈʃnɛkə) *chiefly US* a sweet spiral-shaped bread roll flavoured with cinnamon and nuts [German, plural of *Schnecke* SNAIL]

Schneider Trophy (ˈʃnaɪdə) *n* a trophy for air racing between seaplanes of any nation, first presented by Jacques Schneider in 1913; won outright by Britain in 1931

schnitzel (ˈʃnɪtsəl) *n* a thin slice of meat, esp veal. See also **Wiener schnitzel** [German: cutlet, from *schnitzen* to carve, *schnitzeln* to whittle]

schnook (ʃnʊk) *n US slang* a stupid or gullible person [from Yiddish *shnok*, variant of *shmok* SCHMO]

schnorkel (ˈʃnɔːkəl) *n, vb* a less common variant of **snorkel**

schnorrer (ˈʃnɔːrə) *n US slang* a person who lives off the charity of others; professional beggar [Yiddish, from German *Schnurrer* beggar (who played an instrument), from Middle High German *snurren* to hum]

schnozzle (ˈʃnɒzəl) *n chiefly US* a slang word for **nose** (sense 1) [alteration of Yiddish *shnoitsl*, diminutive of *shnoits*, from German *Schnauze* SNOUT]

schola cantorum (ˈskəʊlə kænˈtɔːrəm) *n, pl* scholae cantorum (ˈskəʊliː) a choir or choir school maintained by a church [Medieval Latin: school of singers]

scholar (ˈskɒlə) *n* **1** a learned person, esp in the humanities **2** a person, esp a child, who studies; pupil **3** a student of merit at an educational establishment who receives financial aid, esp from an endowment given for such a purpose **4** *South African* a school pupil [c14 from Old French *escoler*, via Late Latin from Latin *schola* SCHOOL¹] > ˈscholarly *adj* > ˈscholarliness *n*

scholarship (ˈskɒləʃɪp) *n* **1** academic achievement; erudition; learning **2 a** financial aid provided for a scholar because of academic merit **b** the position of a student who gains this financial aid **c** (*as modifier*): *a scholarship student* **3** the qualities of a scholar

scholar's mate *n chess* a simple mate by the queen on the f7 square, achievable by white's fourth move

scholastic (skəˈlæstɪk) *adj* **1** of, relating to, or befitting schools, scholars, or education **2** pedantic or precise **3** (*often capital*) characteristic of or relating to the medieval Schoolmen ▷ *n* **4** a student or pupil **5** a person who is given to quibbling or logical subtleties; pedant **6** (*often capital*) a disciple or adherent of scholasticism; Schoolman **7 a** a Jesuit student who is undergoing a period of probation prior to commencing his theological studies **b** the status and position of such a student **8** a formalist in art [c16 via Latin from Greek *skholastikos* devoted to learning, ultimately from *skholē* SCHOOL¹] > schoˈlastically *adv*

scholasticate (skəˈlæstɪˌkeɪt, -kɪt) *n RC Church* the state of being a scholastic, the period during which a Jesuit student is a scholastic, or an institution where scholastics pass this period [c19 from New Latin *scholasticātus*, from Latin *scholasticus* SCHOLASTIC]

scholasticism (skəˈlæstɪˌsɪzəm) *n* **1** (*sometimes capital*) the system of philosophy, theology, and teaching that dominated medieval western Europe and was based on the writings of the Church Fathers and (from the 12th century) Aristotle, the Greek philosopher (384–322 BC) **2** strict adherence to traditional doctrines

scholiast (ˈskəʊlɪˌæst) *n* a medieval annotator, esp of classical texts [c16 from Late Greek *skholiastēs*, from *skholiazein* to write a SCHOLIUM] > ˌscholiˈastic *adj*

scholium (ˈskəʊlɪəm) *n, pl* -lia (-lɪə) a commentary or annotation, esp on a classical text [c16 from New Latin, from Greek *skholion* exposition, from *skholē* SCHOOL¹]

school¹ (skuːl) *n* **1 a** an institution or building at which children and young people usually under 19 receive education **b** (*as modifier*): *school bus; school day* **c** (*in combination*): *schoolroom; schoolwork* **2** any educational institution or building **3** a faculty, institution, or department specializing in a particular subject: *a law school* **4** the staff and pupils of a school **5** the period of instruction in a school or one session of this: *he stayed after school to do extra work* **6** meetings held occasionally for members of a profession, etc **7** a place or sphere of activity that instructs: *the school of hard knocks* **8** a body of people or pupils adhering to a certain set of principles, doctrines, or methods **9** a group of artists, writers, etc, linked by the same style, teachers, or aims: *the Venetian school of painting* **10** a style of life: *a gentleman of the old school* **11** *informal* a group assembled for a common purpose, esp gambling or drinking ▷ *vb* (*tr*) **12** to train or educate in or as in a school **13** to discipline or control **14** an archaic word for **reprimand** [Old English *scōl*, from Latin *schola* school, from Greek *skholē* leisure spent in the pursuit of knowledge]

school² (skuːl) *n* **1** a group of porpoises or similar aquatic animals that swim together ▷ *vb* **2** (*intr*) to form such a group [Old English *scolu* SHOAL²]

school attendance officer *n* a former name for **Educational Welfare Officer**

school board *n* **1** (formerly in Britain) an elected board of ratepayers who provided local elementary schools between 1870 and 1902 **2** (in the US and Canada) a local board of education

schoolboy (ˈskuːlˌbɔɪ) *or feminine* **schoolgirl** *n* a child attending school

School Certificate *n* (in England and Wales between 1917 and 1951 and currently in New Zealand) a certificate awarded to school pupils who pass a public examination: the equivalent of O level. Abbreviation: SC

School Committee *n* (in New Zealand) a parent group selected to support a primary school

school crossing patrol *n* the official name for **lollipop man** *or* **lady**

schoolhouse (ˈskuːlˌhaʊs) *n* **1** a building used as a school, esp a rural school **2** a house attached to a school

schoolie (ˈskuːlɪ) *n* **1** *Austral slang* a schoolteacher or a high-school student **2** (in Australia) a holiday away from home in which large numbers of school leavers join together

Schoolies Week ('sku:li:z) *n* (in Australia) a week when large numbers of school leavers gather together for a holiday away from home after the end of their final exams

schooling ('sku:lɪŋ) *n* 1 education, esp when received at school 2 the process of teaching or being taught in a school 3 the training of an animal, esp of a horse for dressage 4 an archaic word for **reprimand**

school-leaver *n* a pupil who is about to leave or has recently left school, esp at the minimum school-leaving age > 'school-,leaving *adj*

schoolman ('sku:lmən) *n, pl* -men 1 (*sometimes capital*) a scholar versed in the learning of the Schoolmen 2 *rare, chiefly US* a professional educator or teacher

Schoolman ('sku:lmən) *n, pl* -men (*sometimes not capital*) a master in one of the schools or universities of the Middle Ages who was versed in scholasticism; scholastic

schoolmarm ('sku:l,mɑːm) *n informal* 1 a woman schoolteacher, esp when considered to be prim, prudish, or old-fashioned 2 *Brit* any woman considered to be prim, prudish, or old-fashioned [C19 from SCHOOL¹ + *marm*, variant of MA'AM. See MADAM] > 'school,marmish *adj*

schoolmaster ('sku:l,mɑːstə) *n* 1 a man who teaches in or runs a school 2 a person or thing that acts as an instructor 3 a food fish, *Lutjanus apodus*, of the warm waters of the Caribbean and Atlantic: family *Lutjanidae* (snappers) ▷ *vb* (intr) 4 to be a schoolmaster > 'school,mastering *n* > 'school,masterish *adj* > 'school,masterly *adj* > 'school,mastership *n*

schoolmate ('sku:l,meɪt) *or* **schoolfellow** *n* a companion at school; fellow pupil

school milk *n social welfare* (formerly, in Britain) a third of a pint of milk, originally provided free by the local education authority to all young pupils, then later given only to children who passed a needs or means test

schoolmistress ('sku:l,mɪstrɪs) *n* a woman who teaches in or runs a school > 'school,mistressy *adj*

school night *n* 1 any night of the week that precedes a day of school 2 *jocular* any night of the week that precedes a day of work

school of arts *n Austral* a public building in a small town, originally one used for adult education

school prawn *n Austral* a common olive-green prawn, *Metapenaeus macleayi*

Schools (sku:lz) *pl n* 1 **the** the medieval Schoolmen collectively 2 (at Oxford University) **a** the Examination Schools, the University building in which examinations are held **b** *informal* the Second Public Examination for the degree of Bachelor of Arts; finals

school shark *n Austral* an Australian shark resembling the tope, *Notogaleus australis*

school ship *n* a ship for training young men in seamanship, for a career in the regular or merchant navy

schoolteacher ('sku:l,ti:tʃə) *n* a person who teaches in a school > 'school,teaching *n*

school welfare officer *n* a former name for Educational Welfare Officer

school year *n* 1 a twelve-month period, (in Britain) usually starting in late summer and continuing for three terms until the following summer, during which pupils remain in the same class 2 the time during this period when the school is open

schooner ('sku:nə) *n* 1 a sailing vessel with at least two masts, with all lower sails rigged fore-and-aft, and with the main mast stepped aft 2 *Brit* a large glass for sherry 3 *US, Canadian, Austral, and NZ* a large glass for beer [C18 origin uncertain]

schooner rig *n nautical* a rig in which the mainmast is taller than the foremast

schorl (ʃɔːl) *n* a black tourmaline consisting of a

borosilicate of sodium, iron, and aluminium. Formula: $NaFe_3B_3Al_3(Al_2Si_6O_{27})(OH)_4$ [C18 from German *Schörl*, origin unknown] > schor'laceous *adj*

schottische (ʃɒ'tiːʃ) *n* 1 a 19th-century German dance resembling a slow polka 2 a piece of music composed for or in the manner of this dance [C19 from German *der schottische Tanz* the Scottish dance]

Schottky defect ('ʃɒtkɪ) *n physics* a crystal defect in which vacancies exist in the lattice [C20 named after Walter *Schottky* (1886–1976), German physicist]

Schottky effect *n physics* a reduction in the energy required to remove an electron from a solid surface in a vacuum when an electric field is applied to the surface

Schottky noise *n* another name for **shot noise**

Schouten Islands ('ʃaʊtᵊn) *pl n* a group of islands in the Pacific, off the N coast of Papua New Guinea. Pop: 25 490 (latest est). Area: 3185 sq km (1230 sq miles)

Schrödinger equation *n* an equation used in wave mechanics to describe a physical system. For a particle of mass *m* and potential energy V it is written $(ih/2\pi).(\partial\psi/\partial t) = (-h^2/8\pi^2 m)\nabla^2\psi + V\psi$, where $i = \sqrt{-1}$, h is the Planck constant, *t* the time, ∇^2 the Laplace operator, and ψ the wave function

schtick (ʃtɪk) *n* a variant form of **shtick**

schul (ʃuːl) *n* a variant spelling of **shul**

schuss (ʃʊs) *skiing* ▷ *n* 1 a straight high-speed downhill run ▷ *vb* 2 (intr) to perform a schuss [German: SHOT¹]

Schutzstaffel German ('ʃʊtsʃtafəl) *n, pl* -feln (-fəln) See SS

schwa *or* **shwa** (ʃwɑː) *n* 1 a central vowel represented in the International Phonetic Alphabet by (ə). The sound occurs in unstressed syllables in English, as in *around, mother,* and *sofa* 2 the symbol (ə) used to represent this sound [C19 via German from Hebrew *shewā*, a diacritic indicating lack of a vowel sound]

Schwaben ('ʃvaːbən) *n* the German name for Swabia

Schwarzschild radius ('ʃwɔːtsʃɪld; *German* 'ʃvartsʃɪlt) *n astronomy* the radius of a sphere (**Schwarzschild sphere**) surrounding a non-rotating uncharged black hole, from within which no information can escape because of gravitational forces [C20 named after Karl *Schwarzschild* (1873–1916), US astrophysicist]

Schwarzwald ('ʃvartsvalt) *n* the German name for the **Black Forest**

Schweinfurt (*German* 'ʃvainfʊrt) *n* a city in central Germany, in N Bavaria on the River Main. Pop: 54 601 (2003 est)

Schweiz (ʃvaits) *n* the German name for **Switzerland**

Schwerin (*German* ʃve'riːn) *n* a city in N Germany, in Mecklenburg-West Pomerania on **Lake Schwerin**. Pop: 97 694 (2003 est)

Schwyz (*German* ʃviːts) *n* 1 a canton of central Switzerland: played an important part in the formation of the Swiss confederation, to which it gave its name. Capital: Schwyz. Pop: 133 300 (2002 est). Area: 908 sq km (351 sq miles) 2 a town in E central Switzerland, capital of Schwyz canton: tourism. Pop: 13 802 (2000)

sci. *abbreviation for* 1 science 2 scientific

sciaenid (saɪ'iːnɪd) *or* **sciaenoid** *adj* 1 of, relating to, or belonging to the *Sciaenidae*, a family of mainly tropical and subtropical marine percoid fishes that includes the drums, grunts, and croakers ▷ *n* 2 any sciaenid fish [C19 from Latin *sciaena* a type of fish, from Greek *skiaina*]

sciamachy (saɪ'æməkɪ) *or* **sciomachy, skiamachy** (skaɪ'æməkɪ) *n, pl* -chies *rare* a fight with an imaginary enemy [C17 from Greek *skiamakhia* a mock fight, from *skia* a shadow + *makhesthai* to fight]

sciatic (saɪ'ætɪk) *adj* 1 *anatomy* of or relating to the hip or the hipbone 2 of, relating to, or

afflicted with sciatica [C16 from French *sciatique*, from Late Latin *sciaticus*, from Latin *ischiadicus* relating to pain in the hip, from Greek *iskhiadikos*, from *iskhia* hip joint]

sciatica (saɪ'ætɪkə) *n* a form of neuralgia characterized by intense pain and tenderness along the course of the body's longest nerve (**sciatic nerve**), extending from the back of the thigh down to the calf of the leg [C15 from Late Latin *sciatica*; see SCIATIC]

SCID *abbreviation for* severe combined immune deficiency; a serious condition in which babies are born with reduced numbers of T- and B-lymphocytes, which impairs their immune systems and makes them susceptible to severe infections and cancer

science ('saɪəns) *n* 1 the systematic study of the nature and behaviour of the material and physical universe, based on observation, experiment, and measurement, and the formulation of laws to describe these facts in general terms 2 the knowledge so obtained or the practice of obtaining it 3 any particular branch of this knowledge: *the pure and applied sciences* 4 any body of knowledge organized in a systematic manner 5 skill or technique 6 *archaic* knowledge [C14 via Old French from Latin *scientia* knowledge, from *scīre* to know]

science fiction *n* **a** a literary genre that makes imaginative use of scientific knowledge or conjecture **b** (*as modifier*): *a science fiction writer*

Science Museum *n* a museum in London, originating from 1852 and given its present name and site in 1899: contains collections relating to the history of science, technology, and industry

science park *n* an area usually linked with a university where scientific research and commercial development are carried on in cooperation

scienter (saɪ'entə) *adv law* knowingly; wilfully [from Latin]

sciential (saɪ'enʃəl) *adj* 1 of or relating to science 2 skilful or knowledgeable

scientific (,saɪən'tɪfɪk) *adj* 1 (prenominal) of, relating to, derived from, or used in science: *scientific equipment* 2 (prenominal) occupied in science: *scientific manpower* 3 conforming with the principles or methods used in science: *a scientific approach* > ,scien'tifically *adv*

scientific content analysis *n* the close analysis of the content of statements made to the police by suspects in an attempt to identify innocence or guilt

scientific method *n* a method of investigation in which a problem is first identified and observations, experiments, or other relevant data are then used to construct or test hypotheses that purport to solve it

scientific socialism *n* Marxist socialism. Compare **utopian socialism**

scientism ('saɪən,tɪzəm) *n* 1 the application of, or belief in, the scientific method 2 the uncritical application of scientific or quasi-scientific methods to inappropriate fields of study or investigation > ,scien'tistic *adj*

scientist ('saɪəntɪst) *n* a person who studies or practises any of the sciences or who uses scientific methods

Scientist ('saɪəntɪst) *n* 1 *Christian Science* Christ as supreme spiritual healer 2 short for **Christian Scientist**

Scientology (,saɪən'tɒlədʒɪ) *n trademark* the philosophy of the Church of Scientology, a nondenominational movement founded in the US in the 1950s, which emphasizes self-knowledge as a means of realizing full spiritual potential [C20 from Latin *scient(ia)* SCIENCE + -LOGY] > ,Scien'tologist *n*

sci-fi ('saɪ,faɪ) *n* short for **science fiction**

scilicet ('sɪlɪ,set) *adv* namely; that is: used esp in explaining an obscure text or an ambiguity, or supplying a missing word [Latin: shortened from

S

scīre licet it is permitted to know]

scilla ('sɪlə) *n* any liliaceous plant of the genus *Scilla*, of Old World temperate regions, having small bell-shaped flowers. See also **squill** (sense 3) [c19 via Latin from Greek *skilla*; compare SQUILL]

Scillonian (sɪ'ləʊnɪən) *adj* 1 of or relating to the Scilly Isles or their inhabitants ▷ *n* 2 a native or inhabitant of the Scilly Isles

Scilly Isles, Scilly Islands ('sɪlɪ) *or* **Scillies** ('sɪlɪz) *pl n* a group of about 140 small islands (only five inhabited) off the extreme SW coast of England: tourist centre. Capital: Hugh Town. Pop: 2100 (2003 est). Area: 16 sq km (6 sq miles)

scimitar *or rarely* **simitar** ('sɪmɪtə) *n* an oriental sword with a curved blade broadening towards the point [c16 from Old Italian *scimitarra*, probably from Persian *shimshīr*, of obscure origin]

scincoid ('sɪŋkɔɪd) *or* **scincoidian** *adj* 1 of, relating to, or resembling a skink ▷ *n* 2 any animal, esp a lizard, resembling a skink [c18 from New Latin *scincoidēs*, from Latin *scincus* a SKINK]

scindapsus (sɪn'dæpsəs) *n* any plant of the tropical Asiatic climbing genus *Scindapsus*, typically stem rooting, esp *S. aureus* and *S. pictus*, grown as greenhouse or house plants for their leathery heart-shaped variegated leaves: family *Araceae* [New Latin, from Greek *skindapsos* an ivy-like plant]

scintigraphy (,sɪn'tɪgrəfɪ) *n med* a diagnostic technique using a radioactive tracer and scintillation counter for producing pictures (**scintigrams**) of internal parts of the body [c20 from SCINTI(LLATION) + -GRAPHY]

scintilla (sɪn'tɪlə) *n* a minute amount; hint, trace, or particle [c17 from Latin: a spark]

scintillate ('sɪntɪ,leɪt) *vb* (*mainly intr*) 1 (*also tr*) to give off (sparks); sparkle; twinkle 2 to be animated or brilliant 3 *physics* to give off flashes of light as a result of the impact of particles or photons [c17 from Latin *scintillāre*, from *scintilla* a spark] > 'scintillant *adj* > 'scintillantly *adv*

scintillating ('sɪntɪ,leɪtɪŋ) *adj* 1 sparkling; twinkling 2 animated or brilliant > 'scintil,latingly *adv*

scintillation (,sɪntɪ'leɪʃən) *n* 1 the act of scintillating 2 a spark or flash 3 the twinkling of stars or radio sources, caused by rapid changes in the density of the earth's atmosphere, the interplanetary medium, or the interstellar medium producing uneven refraction of starlight 4 *physics* a flash of light produced when a material scintillates

scintillation counter *n* an instrument for detecting and measuring the intensity of high-energy radiation. It consists of a phosphor with which particles collide producing flashes of light that are detected by a photomultiplier and converted into pulses of electric current that are counted by electronic equipment

scintillator ('sɪntɪ,leɪtə) *n physics* a phosphor that produces scintillations

scintillometer (,sɪntɪ'lɒmɪtə) *n physics* a device for observing ionizing radiation by the scintillations it produces in a suitable material

scintillon (sɪn'tɪlən) *n* a luminescent body present in the cytoplasm of some dinoflagellates

sciolism ('saɪə,lɪzəm) *n rare* the practice of opinionating on subjects of which one has only superficial knowledge [c19 from Late Latin *sciolus* someone with a smattering of knowledge, from Latin *scīre* to know] > 'sciolist *n* > ,scio'listic *adj*

sciomachy (saɪ'ɒməkɪ) *n, pl* -chies a variant of sciamachy

sciomancy ('saɪə,mænsɪ) *n* divination with the help of ghosts [c17 via Latin from Greek *skia* ghost + -MANCY] > 'sciomancer *n* > ,scio'mantic *adj*

scion ('saɪən) *n* 1 a descendant, heir, or young member of a family 2 a shoot or twig of a plant used to form a graft [c14 from Old French *cion*, of Germanic origin; compare Old High German *chīnan* to sprout]

sciophyte ('saɪə,faɪt) *n now rare* any plant that grows best in the shade [c20 via Latin from Greek *skia* shade + -PHYTE] > sciophytic (,saɪə'fɪtɪk) *adj*

scire facias ('saɪərɪ 'feɪʃɪ,æs) *n law rare* 1 a judicial writ founded upon some record, such as a judgment, letters patent, etc, requiring the person against whom it is brought to show cause why the record should not be enforced or annulled 2 a proceeding begun by the issue of such a writ [c15 from legal Latin, literally: cause (him) to know]

scirrhous ('sɪrəs) *adj pathol* of or resembling a scirrhus; hard > scirrhosity (sɪ'rɒsɪtɪ) *n*

scirrhus ('sɪrəs) *n, pl* -rhi (-raɪ) *or* -rhuses *pathol* a hard cancerous growth composed of fibrous tissues. Also called: scirrhous carcinoma [c17 from New Latin, from Latin *scirros*, from Greek *skirros*, from *skiros* hard] > scirrhoid ('sɪrɔɪd) *adj*

scissel ('skɪsəl) *n* the waste metal left over from sheet metal after discs have been punched out of it [c19 from French *cisaille*, from *cisailler* to clip]

scissile ('sɪsaɪl) *adj* capable of being cut or divided [c17 from Latin *scissilis* that can be split, from *scindere* to cut]

scission ('sɪʃən) *n* the act or an instance of cutting, splitting, or dividing [c15 from Late Latin *scissiō*, from *scindere* to split]

scissor ('sɪzə) *n* 1 (*modifier*) of or relating to scissors: *a scissor blade* ▷ *vb* 2 to cut (an object) with scissors

scissors ('sɪzəz) *pl n* 1 Also called: pair of scissors a cutting instrument used for cloth, hair, etc, having two crossed pivoted blades that cut by a shearing action, with ring-shaped handles at one end 2 a wrestling hold in which a wrestler wraps his legs round his opponent's body or head, locks his feet together, and squeezes 3 any gymnastic or athletic feat in which the legs cross and uncross in a scissor-like movement 4 *athletics* a technique in high-jumping, now little used, in which the legs perform a scissor-like movement in clearing the bar [c14 *sisoures*, from Old French *cisoires*, from Vulgar Latin *cīsōria* (unattested), ultimately from Latin *caedere* to cut; see CHISEL] > 'scissor-,like *adj*

scissors kick *n* 1 a type of swimming kick used esp in the sidestroke, in which one leg is moved forward and the other bent back and they are then brought together again in a scissor-like action 2 *football* a kick in which the player leaps into the air raising one leg and brings up his other leg to kick the ball

scissure ('sɪʒə, 'sɪʃə) *n rare* a longitudinal cleft [c15 from Latin *scissūra* a rending, from Latin *scindere* to split]

sciurine ('saɪjʊrɪn, -,raɪn) *adj* 1 of, relating to, or belonging to the *Sciuridae*, a family of rodents inhabiting most parts of the world except Australia and southern South America: includes squirrels, marmots, and chipmunks ▷ *n* 2 any sciurine animal [c19 from Latin *sciūrus*, from Greek *skiouros* squirrel, from *skia* a shadow + *oura* a tail]

sciuroid ('saɪjʊrɔɪd, saɪ'jʊərɔɪd) *adj* 1 (of an animal) resembling a squirrel 2 (esp of the spikes of barley) shaped like a squirrel's tail [c19 from Latin *sciūrus* squirrel + -OID]

sclaff (sklæf) *golf* ▷ *vb* 1 to cause (the club) to hit (the ground behind the ball) when making a stroke ▷ *n* 2 a sclaffing stroke or shot Also: duff [c19 from Scottish *sclaf* to shuffle] > 'sclaffer *n*

sclera ('sklɪərə) *n* the firm white fibrous membrane that forms the outer covering of the eyeball. Also called: sclerotic [c19 from New Latin, from Greek *sklēros* hard]

sclere (sklɪə) *n zoology* a supporting anatomical structure, esp a sponge spicule

sclerenchyma (sklɪə'rɛŋkɪmə) *n* a supporting tissue in plants consisting of dead cells with very thick lignified walls [c19 from SCLERO- + PARENCHYMA] > sclerenchymatous (,sklɪərɛŋ'kɪmətəs) *adj*

sclerite ('sklɪəraɪt) *n zoology* 1 any of the hard chitinous plates that make up the exoskeleton of an arthropod 2 any calcareous or chitinous part, such as a spicule or plate [c19 from SCLERO- + -ITE¹] > scleritic (sklɪə'rɪtɪk) *adj*

scleritis (sklɪə'raɪtɪs) *or* **sclerotitis** (,sklɪərəʊ'taɪtɪs) *n pathol* inflammation of the sclera

sclero- *or before a vowel* **scler-** *combining form* 1 indicating hardness: *sclerosis* 2 of or relating to the sclera: *sclerotomy* [from Greek *sklēros* hard]

scleroderma (,sklɪərəʊ'dɜːmə), **sclerodermia** (,sklɪərəʊ'dɜːmɪə) *or* **scleriasis** (sklɪ'raɪəsɪs) *n* a chronic progressive disease most common among women, characterized by a local or diffuse thickening and hardening of the skin [c19 from New Latin *sclerōdermus*, from Greek, from *sklēros* hard + *derma* skin]

sclerodermatous (,sklɪərəʊ'dɜːmətəs) *adj* 1 (of animals) possessing a hard external covering of scales or plates 2 of or relating to scleroderma

scleroid ('sklɪərɔɪd) *adj* (of organisms and their parts) hard or hardened

scleroma (sklɪə'rəʊmə) *n, pl* -mata (-mətə) *or* -mas *pathol* any small area of abnormally hard tissue, esp in a mucous membrane [c17 from New Latin, from Greek, from *sklēroun* to harden, from *sklēros* hard]

sclerometer (sklɪə'rɒmɪtə) *n* an instrument that determines the hardness of a mineral or metal by means of a diamond point > sclerometric (,sklɪərə'mɛtrɪk) *adj*

sclerophyll ('sklɛrəʊ,fɪl) *n* a woody plant with small leathery evergreen leaves that is the dominant plant form in certain hot dry areas, esp the Mediterranean region [c20 from Greek *sklēros* hard + *phullon* a leaf] > sclerophyllous (sklɛ'rɒfɪləs) *adj*

scleroprotein (,sklɪərəʊ'prəʊtiːn) *n* any of a group of insoluble stable proteins such as keratin, elastin, and collagen that occur in skeletal and connective tissues. Also called: albuminoid

sclerosed ('sklɪərəʊst) *adj pathol* hardened; sclerotic

sclerosis (sklɪə'rəʊsɪs) *n, pl* -ses (-siːz) 1 *pathol* a hardening or thickening of organs, tissues, or vessels from chronic inflammation, abnormal growth of fibrous tissue, or degeneration of the myelin sheath of nerve fibres, or (esp on the inner walls of arteries) deposition of fatty plaques. Compare **arteriosclerosis, atherosclerosis, multiple sclerosis** 2 the hardening of a plant cell wall or tissue by the deposition of lignin [c14 via Medieval Latin from Greek *sklērōsis* a hardening] 3 a debilitating lack of progress or innovation within an institution or organization > scle'rosal *adj*

sclerotic (sklɪə'rɒtɪk) *adj* 1 of or relating to the sclera 2 of, relating to, or having sclerosis 3 *botany* characterized by the hardening and strengthening of cell walls ▷ *n* 4 another name for sclera [c16 from Medieval Latin *sclērōticus*, from Greek; see SCLEROMA]

sclerotin ('sklɛrəʊtɪn) *n* a protein in the cuticle of insects that becomes hard and dark

sclerotium (sklɪə'rəʊʃɪəm) *n, pl* -tia (-ʃɪə) a compact mass of hyphae, that is formed by certain fungi and gives rise to new fungal growth or spore-producing structures [c18 from New Latin, from Greek *sklēros* hard] > scle'rotioid *or* scle'rotial *adj*

sclerotize *or* **sclerotise** ('sklɛrə,taɪz) *vb* (*tr; usually passive*) *zoology* to harden and darken (an insect's cuticle) > ,scleroti'zation *or* ,scleroti'sation *n*

sclerotomy (sklɪə'rɒtəmɪ) *n, pl* -mies surgical incision into the sclera

sclerous ('sklɪərəs) *adj anatomy, pathol* hard; bony; indurated [c19 from Greek *sklēros* hard]

SCM (in Britain) *abbreviation for* 1 State Certified Midwife 2 Student Christian Movement

scody ('skəʊdɪ) *adj NZ informal* unkempt; dirty: *they lived in a scody student flat*

scoff¹ (skɒf) *vb* 1 (*intr; often foll by at*) to speak contemptuously (about); express derision (for);

mock **2** (*tr*) *obsolete* to regard with derision ▷ *n* **3** an expression of derision **4** an object of derision [C14 probably from Scandinavian; compare Old Frisian *skof* mockery, Danish *skof, skuf* jest] > 'scoffer *n* > 'scoffing *adj* > 'scoffingly *adv*

scoff[2] (skɒf) *informal, chiefly Brit* ▷ *vb* **1** to eat (food) fast and greedily; devour ▷ *n* **2** food or rations [C19 variant of *scaff* food; related to Afrikaans, Dutch *schoft* quarter of the day, one of the four daily meals]

scofflaw ('skɒflɔ:) *n US informal* a person who habitually flouts or violates the law, esp one who fails to pay debts or answer summonses

scold (skəʊld) *vb* **1** to find fault with or reprimand (a person) harshly; chide **2** (*intr*) to use harsh or abusive language ▷ *n* **3** a person, esp a woman, who constantly finds fault [C13 from Old Norse SKALD] > 'scoldable *adj* > 'scolder *n* > 'scolding *n* > 'scoldingly *adv*

scolecite ('skɒlɪ,saɪt, 'skəʊl-) *n* a white zeolite mineral consisting of hydrated calcium aluminium silicate in groups of radiating monoclinic crystals. Formula: $CaAl_2Si_3O_{10}.3H_2O$ [C19 *scolec-* from Greek *skōlēx* SCOLEX + -ITE[1]]

scolex ('skəʊlɛks) *n, pl* **scoleces** (skəʊ'li:si:z) *or* **scolices** ('skɒlɪ,si:z, 'skəʊ-) the headlike part of a tapeworm, bearing hooks and suckers by which the animal is attached to the tissues of its host [C19 from New Latin, from Greek *skōlēx* worm]

scoliosis (,skɒlɪ'əʊsɪs) *n pathol* an abnormal lateral curvature of the spine, of congenital origin or caused by trauma or disease of the vertebrae or hipbones. Compare **kyphosis, lordosis** [C18 from New Latin, from Greek: a curving, from *skolios* bent] > **scoliotic** (,skɒlɪ'ɒtɪk) *adj*

scollop[1] ('skɒləp) *n, vb* a variant of **scallop**

scollop[2] ('skɒləp) *n* (in Ireland) a rod, pointed at both ends, used to pin down thatch [C19 from Irish Gaelic *scolb*]

scolopendrid (,skɒlə'pɛndrɪd) *n* any centipede of the family *Scolopendridae*, including some large and poisonous species [C19 from New Latin *Scolopendridae*, from Latin *scolopendra*, from Greek *skolopendra* legendary sea-fish] > **scolopendrine** (,skɒlə'pɛndraɪn, -drɪn) *adj*

scolopendrium (skɒlə'pɛndrɪəm) *n* another name for **hart's-tongue** [C17 from New Latin, from Greek *scolopendrion*, from a fancied resemblance of the fern and its sori to a centipede]

scombroid ('skɒmbrɔɪd) *adj* **1** of, relating to, or belonging to the *Scombroidea*, a suborder of marine spiny-finned fishes having a spindle-shaped body and a forked powerful tail: includes the mackerels, tunnies, bonitos, swordfish, and sailfish ▷ *n* **2** any fish belonging to the suborder *Scombroidea* [C19 from Greek *skombros* a mackerel; see -OID]

sconce[1] (skɒns) *n* **1** a bracket fixed to a wall for holding candles or lights **2** a flat candlestick with a handle [C14 from Old French *esconse* hiding place, lantern, or from Late Latin *sconsa*, from *absconsa* dark lantern]

sconce[2] (skɒns) *n* a small protective fortification, such as an earthwork [C16 from Dutch *schans*, from Middle High German *schanze* bundle of brushwood]

sconce[3] (skɒns) (at Oxford and Cambridge Universities, esp formerly) *vb* (*tr*) **1** to challenge (a fellow student) on the grounds of a social misdemeanour to drink a large quantity of beer without stopping **2** *obsolete* to fine (a student) for some minor misdemeanour ▷ *n* **3** the act of sconcing **4** a mug or tankard used in sconcing [C17 of obscure origin]

sconce[4] (skɒns) *n archaic* **1** the head or skull **2** sense, brain, or wit [C16 probably jocular use of SCONCE[1]]

scone *n* **1** (skɒn, skəʊn) a light plain doughy cake made from flour with very little fat, cooked in an oven or (esp originally) on a griddle, usually split open and buttered **2** (skɒn) *Austral* a slang word for **head** (sense 1) **3** *Austral slang* **a** angry **b** insane [C16 Scottish, perhaps from Middle Low German *schonbrot*, Middle Dutch *schoonbrot* fine bread]

Scone (sku:n) *n* a parish in Perth and Kinross, E Scotland, consisting of the two villages of New Scone and Old Scone, formerly the site of the Pictish capital and the stone upon which medieval Scottish kings were crowned. The stone was removed to Westminster Abbey by Edward I in 1296; it was returned to Scotland in 1996 and placed in Edinburgh Castle. Scone Palace was rebuilt in the Neo-Gothic style in the 19th century

scooby doo (,sku:bɪ 'du:) *n rhyming slang* a clue: *I don't have a scooby doo what you're talking about.* Often shortened to **scooby** [C20 from *Scooby Doo*, a cartoon character on children's television]

scoop (sku:p) *n* **1** a utensil used as a shovel or ladle, esp a small shovel with deep sides and a short handle, used for taking up flour, corn, etc **2** a utensil with a long handle and round bowl used for dispensing liquids **3** a utensil with a round bowl and short handle, sometimes with a mechanical device to empty the bowl, for serving ice cream or mashed potato **4** anything that resembles a scoop in action, such as the bucket on a dredge **5** a spoonlike surgical instrument for scraping or extracting foreign matter, etc, from the body **6** the quantity taken up by a scoop **7** the act of scooping, dredging, etc **8** a hollow cavity **9** *slang* a large quick gain, as of money **10** a news story reported in one newspaper before all the others; an exclusive **11** any sensational piece of news ▷ *vb* (*mainly tr*) **12** (often foll by *up*) to take up and remove (an object or substance) with or as if with a scoop **13** (often foll by *out*) to hollow out with or as if with a scoop: *to scoop a hole in a hillside* **14** to win (a prize, award, or large amount of money) **15** to beat (rival newspapers) in uncovering a news item **16** *sport* to hit (the ball) on its underside so that it rises into the air [C14 via Middle Dutch *schōpe* from Germanic; compare Old High German *scephan* to ladle, German *schöpfen, Schaufel* SHOVEL, Dutch *schoep* vessel for baling] > 'scooper *n* > 'scoop,ful *n*

scoop neck *n* a rounded low-cut neckline on a woman's garment

scoosh (skuʃ) *Scot* ▷ *vb* **1** to squirt **2** (*intr*) (of liquid) to rush ▷ *n* **3** a squirt or rush of liquid **4** any fizzy drink [C19 of imitative origin]

scoot (sku:t) *vb* **1** to go or cause to go quickly or hastily; dart or cause to dart off or away **2** *Scot* to squirt ▷ *n* **3** the act of scooting **4** *Scot* a squirt [C19 probably of Scandinavian origin; compare SHOOT]

scooter ('sku:tə) *n* **1** a child's vehicle consisting of a low footboard on wheels, steered by handlebars. It is propelled by pushing one foot against the ground **2** See **motor scooter** **3** (in the US and Canada) another term for **ice yacht** > 'scooterist *n*

scop (skɒp) *n* (in Anglo-Saxon England) a bard or minstrel [Old English: related to Old Norse *skop, skaup*, Old High German *scof, scopf* poem]

scopa ('skəʊpə) *n, pl* **-pae** (-,pi:) a tuft of hairs on the abdomen or hind legs of bees, used for collecting pollen [C19 from Latin, used only in pl *scopae* twigs, brush]

SCOPA ('skəʊpə) (in South Africa) *n acronym for* Standing Committee on Public Accounts

scope (skəʊp) *n* **1** opportunity for exercising the faculties or abilities; capacity for action: *plenty of scope for improvement* **2** range of view, perception, or grasp; outlook **3** the area covered by an activity, topic, etc; range: *the scope of his thesis was vast* **4** *nautical* slack left in an anchor cable **5** *logic, linguistics* that part of an expression that is governed by a given operator: the scope of the negation in $PV-(q \wedge r)$ is $-(q \wedge r)$ **6** *informal* short for **telescope, microscope, oscilloscope**, etc **7** *archaic* purpose or aim ▷ *vb* (*tr*) **8** *informal* to look at or examine carefully ▷ See also **scope out** [C16 from Italian *scopo* goal, from Latin *scopus*, from Greek *skopos* target; related to Greek *skopein* to watch]

-scope *n combining form* indicating an instrument for observing, viewing, or detecting: *microscope; stethoscope* [from New Latin *-scopium*, from Greek *-skopion*, from *skopein* to look at] > **-scopic** *adj combining form*

scope out *vb* (*tr*) to assess the potential of an opportunity or suggestion: *a scoping-out study*

scoping study *n* a preliminary study to define the scope of a project

scopolamine (skə'pɒlə,mi:n, -mɪn, ,skəʊpə'læmɪn) *n* a colourless viscous liquid alkaloid extracted from certain plants, such as henbane: used in preventing travel sickness and as an anticholinergic, sedative, and truth serum. Formula: $C_{17}H_{21}NO_4$. Also called: **hyoscine**. See also **atropine** [C20 *scopol-* from New Latin *scopolia Japonica* Japanese belladonna (from which the alkaloid is extracted), named after G A *Scopoli* (1723–88), Italian naturalist, + AMINE]

scopoline ('skəʊpə,li:n, -lɪn) *n* a soluble crystalline alkaloid obtained from the decomposition of scopolamine and used as a sedative. Formula: $C_8H_{13}NO_2$. Also called: **oscine** [C19 from *scopol-* (as in SCOPOLAMINE) + -INE[2]]

scopula ('skɒpjʊlə) *n, pl* **-las, -lae** (-,li:) a small tuft of dense hairs on the legs and chelicerae of some spiders [C19 from Late Latin: a broom-twig, from *scōpa* thin twigs] > **scopulate** ('skɒpjʊ,leɪt, -lɪt) *adj*

Scopus ('skəʊpəs) *n* **Mount** a mountain in central Israel, east of Jerusalem: a N extension of the Mount of Olives; site of the Hebrew University (1925). Height: 834 m (2736 ft)

-scopy *n combining form* indicating a viewing or observation: *microscopy* [from Greek *-skopia*, from *skopein* to look at]

scorbutic (skɔ:'bju:tɪk) *adj* of, relating to, or having scurvy [C17 from New Latin *scorbūticus*, from Medieval Latin *scorbūtus*, probably of Germanic origin; compare Old English *sceorf* scurf, Middle Low German *scorbuk* scurvy] > scor'butically *adv*

scorch (skɔ:tʃ) *vb* **1** to burn or become burnt, so as to affect the colour, taste, etc, or to cause or feel pain **2** to wither or parch or cause to wither from exposure to heat **3** (*intr*) *informal* to be very hot: *it is scorching outside* **4** (*tr*) *informal* to criticize harshly **5** (*intr*) *Brit slang* to drive or ride very fast ▷ *n* **6** a slight burn **7** a mark caused by the application of too great heat **8** *horticulture* a mark or series of marks on fruit, vegetables, etc, caused by pests or insecticides [C15 probably from Old Norse *skorpna* to shrivel up] > 'scorching *adj*

scorched earth policy *n* **1** the policy in warfare of removing or destroying everything that might be useful to an invading enemy, esp by fire **2** *business* a manoeuvre by a company expecting an unwelcome takeover bid in which apparent profitability is greatly reduced by a reversible operation, such as borrowing at an exorbitant interest rate

scorcher ('skɔ:tʃə) *n* **1** a person or thing that scorches **2** something severe or caustic **3** *informal* a very hot day **4** *Brit informal* something remarkable

score (skɔ:) *n* **1** an evaluative usually numerical record of a competitive game or match **2** the total number of points made by a side or individual in a game or match **3** the act of scoring, esp a point or points **4** **the score** *informal* the actual situation; the true facts: *to know the score* **5** *US and Canadian* the result of a test or exam **6** a group or set of twenty: *three score years and ten* **7** (*usually plural*; foll by *of*) a great number; lots: *I have scores of things to do* **8** *music* **a** the written or printed form of a composition in which the instrumental or vocal parts appear on separate staves vertically arranged on large pages (**full score**) or in a condensed version, usually for piano (**short score**) or voices and piano (**vocal score**) **b** the incidental music for a film or play **c** the songs, music, etc, for a stage or film musical **9** a mark or notch, esp one made in keeping a tally **10** an account of amounts due **11** an amount recorded as due **12** a reason or account: *the book was rejected on the score of length* **13** a grievance **14 a** a line marking a division or boundary **b** (*as modifier*): *score line* **15** *informal* the victim of a theft or swindle **16** *dancing* notation indicating a dancer's moves **17** *over the score informal* excessive; unfair **18** settle or pay off a score **a** to avenge a wrong **b** to repay a debt ▷ *vb* **19** to gain (a point or points) in a game or contest **20** (*tr*) to make a total score of: *to score twelve* **21** to keep a record of the score (of) **22** (*tr*) to be worth (a certain amount) in a game **23** (*tr*) *US and Canadian* to evaluate (a test or exam) numerically; mark **24** (*tr*) to record by making notches in **25** to make (cuts, lines, etc) in or on **26** (*intr*) *slang* to obtain something desired, esp to purchase an illegal drug **27** (*intr*) *slang* (of a man) to be successful in seducing a person **28** (*tr*) **a** to set or arrange (a piece of music) for specific instruments or voices **b** to write the music for (a film, play, etc) **29** to achieve (success or an advantage): *your idea really scored with the boss* **30** (*tr*) *chiefly US and Canadian* to criticize harshly; berate **31** to accumulate or keep a record of (a debt) [Old English *scora*; related to Old Norse *skor* notch, tally, twenty] > 'scorer *n*

scoreboard ('skɔː,bɔːd) *n sport* a board for displaying the score of a game or match

scorecard ('skɔː,kɑːd) *n* **1** a card on which scores are recorded in various games, esp golf **2** a card identifying the players in a sports match, esp cricket or baseball

score draw *n* (esp in football) a result of a match in which both sides have scored an equal number of goals

score off *vb* (*intr, preposition*) to gain an advantage at someone else's expense

score out *vb* (*tr, adverb*) to delete or cancel by marking through with a line or lines; cross out

scoria ('skɔːrɪə) *n, pl* -riae (-rɪ,iː) **1** a rough cindery crust on top of solidified lava flows containing numerous vesicles **2** refuse obtained from smelted ore; slag [C17 from Latin: dross, from Greek *skōria*, from *skōr* excrement] > scoriaceous (,skɔːrɪ'eɪʃəs) *adj*

scorify ('skɔːrɪ,faɪ) *vb* -fies, -fying, -fied to remove (impurities) from metals by forming scoria > ,scorifi'cation *n* > 'scori,fier *n*

scoring ('skɔːrɪŋ) *n* **1** the act or practice of scoring **2** another name for **orchestration** (see **orchestrate**)

scorn (skɔːn) *n* **1** open contempt or disdain for a person or thing; derision **2** an object of contempt or derision **3** *archaic* an act or expression signifying contempt ▷ *vb* **4** to treat with contempt or derision **5** (*tr*) to reject with contempt [C12 *schornen*, from Old French *escharnir*, of Germanic origin; compare Old High German *scerōn* to behave rowdily, obsolete Dutch *schern* mockery] > 'scorner *n* > 'scornful *adj* > 'scornfully *adv* > 'scornfulness *n*

scorpaenid (skɔː'piːnɪd) *n* **1** any spiny-finned marine fish of the family *Scorpaenidae*, having sharp spines on the fins and a heavy armoured head: includes the scorpion fishes, rockfishes, and redfishes ▷ *adj* **2** of, relating to, or belonging to the family *Scorpaenidae* [via New Latin from Latin *scorpaena* a sea-scorpion; see SCORPION]

scorpaenoid (skɔː'piːnɔɪd) *adj* **1** of, relating to, or belonging to the *Scorpaenoidea*, a suborder of spiny-finned fishes having bony plates covering the head: includes the sculpins, scorpion fishes, gurnards, etc ▷ *n* **2** any fish belonging to the suborder *Scorpaenoidea*

scorper *or* **scauper** ('skɔːpə) *n* a kind of fine chisel with a square or curved tip used in wood engraving for clearing away large areas of the block or clearing away lines [C19 erroneously for *scauper* scalper, from Latin *scalper* knife]

Scorpio ('skɔːpɪ,əʊ) *n* **1** Also called: the Scorpion *astrology* **a** the eighth sign of the zodiac, symbol

♏, having a fixed water classification and ruled by the planets Mars and Pluto. The sun is in this sign between about Oct 23 and Nov 21 **b** a person born during a period when the sun is in this sign **2** *astronomy* another name for **Scorpius** ▷ *adj* **3** *astrology* born under or characteristic of Scorpio ▷ Also (for senses 1b, 3): Scorpionic (,skɔːpɪ'ɒnɪk) [Latin: SCORPION]

scorpioid ('skɔːpɪ,ɔɪd) *adj* **1** of, relating to, or resembling scorpions or the order (*Scorpionida*) to which they belong **2** *botany* (esp of a cymose inflorescence) having the main stem coiled during development

scorpion ('skɔːpɪən) *n* **1** any arachnid of the order *Scorpionida*, of warm dry regions, having a segmented body with a long tail terminating in a venomous sting **2** false scorpion any small nonvenomous arachnid of the order *Pseudoscorpionida* (or *Chelonethida*), which superficially resemble scorpions but lack the long tail. See **book scorpion** **3** any of various other similar arachnids, such as the whip scorpion, or other arthropods, such as the water scorpion **4** *Old Testament* a barbed scourge (I Kings 12:11) **5** *history* a war engine for hurling stones; ballista [C13 via Old French from Latin *scorpiō*, from Greek *skorpios*, of obscure origin]

Scorpion ('skɔːpɪən) *n* **the** the constellation Scorpio, the eighth sign of the zodiac

scorpion fish *n* any of various scorpaenid fishes of the genus *Scorpaena* and related genera, of temperate and tropical seas, having venomous spines on the dorsal and anal fins

scorpion fly *n* any of various insects of the family *Panorpidae*, of the N hemisphere, having a scorpion-like but nonvenomous tail in the males, long antennae, and a beaklike snout: order *Mecoptera*

scorpion grass *n* another name for **forget-me-not**

Scorpius ('skɔːpɪəs) *n, Latin genitive* Scorpii ('skɔːpɪ,aɪ) a large zodiacal constellation lying between Libra and Sagittarius and crossed by the Milky Way. It contains the first magnitude star Antares. Also called: Scorpio

Scot (skɒt) *n* **1** a native or inhabitant of Scotland **2** a member of a tribe of Celtic raiders from the north of Ireland who carried out periodic attacks against the British mainland coast from the 3rd century AD, eventually settling in N Britain during the 5th and 6th centuries

Scot. *abbreviation for* **1** Scotch (whisky) **2** Scotland **3** Scottish

scot and lot *n Brit history* a municipal tax paid by burgesses and others that came to be regarded as a qualification for the borough franchise in parliamentary elections (until the Reform Act of 1832) [C13 *scot* tax, from Germanic; compare Old Norse *skot*; related to Old French *escot* (French *écot*) + LOT (in the obsolete sense: tax)]

scotch¹ (skɒtʃ) *vb* (*tr*) **1** to put an end to; crush: *bad weather scotched our plans* **2** *archaic* to injure so as to render harmless **3** *obsolete* to cut or score ▷ *n* **4** *archaic* a gash; scratch **5** a line marked down, as for hopscotch [C15 of obscure origin]

scotch² (skɒtʃ) *vb* **1** (*tr*) to block, prop, or prevent from moving with or as if with a wedge ▷ *n* **2** a block or wedge to prevent motion [C17 of obscure origin]

Scotch¹ (skɒtʃ) *adj* **1** another word for **Scottish** ▷ *n* **2** the Scots or their language

> USAGE In the north of England and in Scotland, *Scotch* is not used outside fixed expressions such as *Scotch whisky*. The use of *Scotch* for *Scots* or *Scottish* is otherwise felt to be incorrect, esp when applied to people

Scotch² (skɒtʃ) *n* **1** Also called: Scotch whisky whisky distilled esp from fermented malted barley and made in Scotland **2** *Northeast English* a type of relatively mild beer

Scotch broth *n Brit* a thick soup made from

mutton, lamb, or beef stock, vegetables, and pearl barley

Scotch egg *n Brit* a hard-boiled egg enclosed in a layer of sausage meat, covered in egg and crumbs, and fried

Scotchman ('skɒtʃmən) *n, pl* -men (*regarded as bad usage by the Scots*) another word for **Scotsman**

Scotch mist *n* **1** a heavy wet mist **2** drizzle [C16 so called because it is common on Scottish hills]

Scotch pancake *n* another name for **drop scone**

Scotch snap *n music* a rhythmic pattern consisting of a short note followed by a long one. Also called: Scotch catch [C19 so named because it is characteristic of, though not exclusive to, Scottish dance music, esp that for strathspeys]

Scotch tape *n trademark chiefly US* a transparent or coloured adhesive tape made of cellulose or a similar substance

Scotch terrier *n* another name for **Scottish terrier**

Scotchwoman ('skɒtʃ,wʊmən) *n, pl* -women (*regarded as bad usage by the Scots*) another word for **Scotswoman**

Scotch woodcock *n* hot toast spread with anchovies or anchovy paste and topped with creamy scrambled eggs

scoter ('skəʊtə) *n, pl* -ters *or* -ter any sea duck of the genus *Melanitta*, such as *M. nigra* (**common scoter**), of northern regions. The male plumage is black with white patches around the head and eyes [C17 origin unknown]

scot-free *adv, adj* (*predicative*) without harm, loss, or penalty [C16 see SCOT AND LOT]

scotia ('skəʊʃə) *n* a deep concave moulding, esp one used on the base of an Ionic column between the two torus mouldings [C16 via Latin from Greek *skotia*, from *skotos* darkness (from the shadow in the cavity)]

Scotism ('skəʊtɪzəm) *n* the doctrines of John Duns Scotus, the Scottish scholastic theologian and Franciscan priest (?1265–1308), esp those holding that philosophy and theology are independent. See **haecceity**. > 'Scotist *n, adj* > Sco'tistic *adj*

Scotland ('skɒtlənd) *n* a country that is part of the United Kingdom, occupying the north of Great Britain: the English and Scottish thrones were united under one monarch in 1603 and the parliaments in 1707: a separate Scottish parliament was established in 1999. Scotland consists of the Highlands in the north, the central Lowlands, and hilly uplands in the south; has a deeply indented coastline, about 800 offshore islands (mostly in the west), and many lochs. Capital: Edinburgh. Pop: 5 057 400 (2003 est). Area: 78 768 sq km (30 412 sq miles). Related adjs: **Scots, Caledonian, Scottish**

Scotland Yard *n* the headquarters of the London police controlled directly by the British Home Office and hence having certain national responsibilities. Official name: New Scotland Yard

scotoma (skɒ'təʊmə) *n, pl* -mas *or* -mata (-mətə) **1** *pathol* a blind spot; a permanent or temporary area of depressed or absent vision caused by lesions of the visual system, viewing the sun directly (**eclipse scotoma**), squinting, etc **2** *psychol* a mental blind spot; inability to understand or perceive certain matters [C16 via Medieval Latin from Greek *skotōma* giddiness, from *skotoun* to make dark, from *skotos* darkness] > scotomatous (skɒ'tɒmətəs) *adj*

scotopia (skə'təʊpɪə, skəʊ-) *n* the ability of the eye to adjust for night vision [New Latin, from Greek *skotos* darkness + -OPIA] > scotopic (skə'tɒpɪk, skəʊ-) *adj*

Scots (skɒts) *adj* **1** of, relating to, or characteristic of Scotland, its people, their English dialects, or their Gaelic language ▷ *n* **2** any of the English dialects spoken or written in Scotland. See also **Lallans**

Scots Greys *pl n* **the** another name for (the) **Royal Scots Greys**

Scotsman ('skɒtsmən) *n, pl* -men a native or inhabitant of Scotland

Scots pine *or* **Scotch pine** *n* **1** a coniferous tree, *Pinus sylvestris*, of Europe and W and N Asia, having blue-green needle-like leaves and brown cones with a small prickle on each scale: a valuable timber tree **2** the wood of this tree ▷ Also called: Scots *or* Scotch fir

Scotswoman ('skɒts,wʊmən) *n, pl* -women a woman who is a native or inhabitant of Scotland

Scotticism ('skɒtɪ,sɪzəm) *n* a Scottish idiom, word, etc

Scottie *or* **Scotty** ('skɒtɪ) *n, pl* -ties **1** See **Scottish terrier 2** *informal* a Scotsman

Scottish ('skɒtɪʃ) *adj* **1** of, relating to, or characteristic of Scotland, its people, their Gaelic language, or their English dialect ▷ *n* **2** the (*functioning as plural*) the Scots collectively

Scottish Blackface *n* a common breed of hardy mountain sheep having horns and a black face, kept chiefly on the mainland of Scotland

Scottish Borders *n* a council area in SE Scotland, on the English border: created in 1996, it has the same boundaries as the former Borders Region: it is mainly hilly, with agriculture (esp sheep farming) the chief economic activity. Administrative centre: Newtown St Boswells. Pop: 108 280 (2003 est). Area: 4734 sq km (1827 sq miles)

Scottish Certificate of Education *n* See **SCE**

Scottish Fold *n* a breed of medium-sized short-haired cat with folded ears

Scottish Gaelic *n* the Goidelic language of the Celts of Scotland, spoken in the Highlands and Western Isles

Scottish National Party *n* a political party advocating the independence of Scotland, founded in 1934. Abbreviation: SNP > Scottish Nationalist *or informal* Scot Nat (næt) *n, adj*

Scottish terrier *n* a small but sturdy breed of terrier, having short legs and erect ears and tail and a longish, wiry, usually black coat. Often shortened to: Scottie Former name: Aberdeen terrier

Scottish topaz *n* a form of yellow transparent quartz

scoundrel ('skaʊndrəl) *n* a worthless or villainous person [c16 of unknown origin] > 'scoundrelly *adj*

scour[1] ('skaʊə) *vb* **1** to clean or polish (a surface) by washing and rubbing, as with an abrasive cloth **2** to remove dirt from or have the dirt removed from **3** (*tr*) to clear (a channel) by the force of water; flush **4** (*tr*) to remove by or as if by rubbing **5** (*intr*) (of livestock, esp cattle) to have diarrhoea **6** (*tr*) to cause (livestock) to purge their bowels **7** (*tr*) to wash (wool) to remove wax, suint, and other impurities ▷ *n* **8** the act of scouring **9** the place scoured, esp by running water **10** something that scours, such as a cleansing agent **11** (*often plural*) prolonged diarrhoea in livestock, esp cattle [c13 via Middle Low German *schüren*, from Old French *escurer*, from Late Latin *excūrāre* to cleanse, from *cūrāre*; see CURE] > 'scourer *n*

scour[2] (skaʊə) *vb* **1** to range over (territory), as in making a search **2** to move swiftly or energetically over (territory) [c14 from Old Norse *skūr*]

scourge (skɜːdʒ) *n* **1** a person who harasses, punishes, or causes destruction **2** a means of inflicting punishment or suffering **3** a whip used for inflicting punishment or torture ▷ *vb* (*tr*) **4** to whip; flog **5** to punish severely [c13 from Anglo-French *escorge*, from Old French *escorgier* (unattested) to lash, from *es-* EX-[1] + Latin *corrigia* whip] > 'scourger *n*

scouring rush *n* any of several horsetails, esp *Equisetum hyemale*, that have rough-ridged stems and were formerly used for scouring and polishing

scourings ('skaʊərɪŋz) *pl n* **1** the residue left after cleaning grain **2** residue that remains after scouring

scouse (skaʊs) *n Liverpool dialect* a stew made from left-over meat [c19 shortened from LOBSCOUSE]

Scouse (skaʊs) *Brit informal* ▷ *n* **1** Also called: Scouser a person who lives in or comes from Liverpool **2** the dialect spoken by such a person ▷ *adj* **3** of or from Liverpool; Liverpudlian [c20 from SCOUSE]

scout[1] (skaʊt) *n* **1** a person, ship, or aircraft sent out to gain information **2** *military* a person or unit despatched to reconnoitre the position of the enemy **3** *sport* a person employed by a club to seek new players **4** the act or an instance of scouting **5** (esp at Oxford University) a college servant. Compare **gyp**[3] **6** *obsolete* (in Britain) a patrolman of a motoring organization **7** *informal* a fellow or companion ▷ *vb* **8** to examine or observe (anything) in order to obtain information **9** (*tr*; sometimes foll by *out* or *up*) to seek **10** (*intr*) to act as a scout for a sports club **11** (*intr*; foll by *about* or *around*) to go in search (for) [c14 from Old French *ascouter* to listen to, from Latin *auscultāre* to AUSCULTATE] > 'scouter *n*

scout[2] (skaʊt) *vb archaic* to reject (a person or thing) with contempt [c17 from Old Norse *skúta* derision]

Scout (skaʊt) *n* (*sometimes not capital*) a boy or (in some countries) a girl who is a member of a worldwide movement (the **Scout Association**) founded as the Boy Scouts in England in 1908 by Lord Baden-Powell with the aim of developing character and responsibility. See also **Air Scout, Girl Scout, Guide, Sea Scout, Venture Scout**

scout car *n* a fast lightly armoured vehicle used for reconnaissance

Scouting ('skaʊtɪŋ) *n* **a** the activities, programmes, principles, etc, of the Scout Association **b** (*as modifier*): *the international Scouting movement*

Scout Leader *n* the leader of a troop of Scouts

scoutmaster ('skaʊt,mɑːstə) *n* a former name for **Scout Leader**

scow (skaʊ) *n* **1** an unpowered barge used for freight; lighter **2** (esp in the midwestern US) a sailing yacht with a flat bottom, designed to plane [c18 via Dutch *schouw* from Low German *schalde*, related to Old Saxon *skaldan* to push (a boat) into the sea]

scowl (skaʊl) *vb* **1** (*intr*) to contract the brows in a threatening or angry manner ▷ *n* **2** a gloomy or threatening expression [c14 probably from Scandinavian; compare Danish *skule* to look down, Old English *scūlēgede* squint-eyed]

scowler ('skaʊlə) *n* **1** a person who scowls **2** *Northern English dialect* a hooligan

scozza ('skɒzə) *n Austral slang* a rowdy person, esp one who drinks a lot of alcohol

SCP *abbreviation for* **single-cell protein**

SCQF (in Scotland) *abbreviation for* Scottish Credit and Qualifications Framework

SCR *abbreviation for* **1** (in British universities) senior common room **2** silicon controlled rectifier

scr. *abbreviation for* scruple (unit of weight)

scrabble ('skræbəl) *vb* **1** (*intr*; often foll by *about* or *at*) to scrape (at) or grope (for), as with hands or claws **2** to struggle (with) **3** (*intr*; often foll by *for*) to struggle to gain possession, esp in a disorderly manner **4** to scribble ▷ *n* **5** the act or an instance of scrabbling **6** a scribble **7** a disorderly struggle [c16 from Middle Dutch *shrabbelen*, frequentative of *shrabben* to scrape] > 'scrabbler *n*

Scrabble ('skræbəl) *n trademark* a board game in which words are formed by placing lettered tiles in a pattern similar to a crossword puzzle > 'Scrabbler *n*

scrag (skræg) *n* **1** a thin or scrawny person or animal **2** the lean end of a neck of veal or mutton **3** *informal* the neck of a human being ▷ *vb* scrags, scragging, scragged (*tr*) **4** *informal* to wring the neck of; throttle [c16 perhaps variant of CRAG; related to Norwegian *skragg*, German *Kragen* collar]

scraggly ('skræglɪ) *adj* -glier, -gliest untidy or irregular

scraggy ('skrægɪ) *adj* -gier, -giest **1** lean or scrawny **2** rough; unkempt > 'scraggily *adv* > 'scragginess *n*

scram[1] (skræm) *vb* scrams, scramming, scrammed (*intr*; *often imperative*) *informal* to go away hastily; get out [c20 shortened from SCRAMBLE]

scram[2] (skræm) *n* **1** an emergency shutdown of a nuclear reactor ▷ *vb* **2** (of a nuclear reactor) to shut down or be shut down in an emergency [c20 perhaps from SCRAM[1]]

scramb *or* **scram** (skræm) *vb* (*tr*) *Brit dialect* to scratch with nails or claws [from Dutch *schrammen*]

scramble ('skræmbəl) *vb* **1** (*intr*) to climb or crawl, esp by using the hands to aid movement **2** (*intr*) to proceed hurriedly or in a disorderly fashion **3** (*intr*; often foll by *for*) to compete with others, esp in a disordered manner: *to scramble for a prize* **4** (*intr*; foll by *through*) to deal with hurriedly and unsystematically **5** (*tr*) to throw together in a haphazard manner; jumble **6** (*tr*) to collect in a hurried or disorganized manner **7** (*tr*) to cook (eggs that have been whisked up with milk and seasoning) in a pan containing a little melted butter **8** *military* to order (a crew or aircraft) to take off immediately or (of a crew or aircraft) to take off immediately **9** (*tr*) to render (speech) unintelligible during transmission by means of an electronic scrambler ▷ *n* **10** the act of scrambling **11** a climb over rocks that involves the use of the hands but not ropes, etc **12** a disorderly struggle, esp to gain possession **13** *military* an immediate preparation for action, as of crew, aircraft, etc **14** *Brit* a motorcycle rally in which competitors race across rough open ground [c16 blend of SCRABBLE and RAMP]

scrambled egg *or* **eggs** *n slang* gold embroidery on the peak of a high-ranking military officer's cap

scrambler ('skræmblə) *n* **1** a plant that produces long weak shoots by which it grows over other plants **2** an electronic device that renders speech unintelligible during transmission, normal speech being restored at the receiving system

scramjet ('skræm,dʒɛt) *n* **1 a** a type of ramjet in which the forward motion of the craft forces oxygen to mix with fuel (usually hydrogen) at supersonic speeds within a duct in the engine **b** an aircraft powered by such an engine **2** (*modifier*) *scramjet technology* [c20 from s(*upersonic*) + c(*ombustion*) + RAMJET]

scran (skræn) *n* **1** *slang* food; provisions **2** bad scran to *Irish dialect* bad luck to [c18 of unknown origin]

scrannel ('skrænəl) *adj archaic* **1** thin **2** harsh [c17 probably from Norwegian *skran* lean. Compare SCRAWNY]

Scranton ('skræntən) *n* an industrial city in NE Pennsylvania: university (1888). Pop: 74 320 (2003 est)

scrap[1] (skræp) *n* **1** a small piece of something larger; fragment **2** an extract from something written **3 a** waste material or used articles, esp metal, often collected and reprocessed **b** (*as modifier*): *scrap iron* **4** (*plural*) pieces of discarded food ▷ *vb* scraps, scrapping, scrapped (*tr*) **5** to make into scrap **6** to discard as useless [c14 from Old Norse *skrap*; see SCRAPE]

scrap[2] (skræp) *informal* ▷ *n* **1** a fight or argument ▷ *vb* scraps, scrapping, scrapped **2** (*intr*) to quarrel or fight [c17 perhaps from SCRAPE]

scrapbook ('skræp,bʊk) *n* a book or album of blank pages in which to mount newspaper cuttings, pictures, etc

scrape (skreɪp) *vb* **1** to move (a rough or sharp object) across (a surface), esp to smooth or clean **2** (*tr*; often foll by *away* or *off*) to remove (a layer) by rubbing **3** to produce a harsh or grating sound by rubbing against (an instrument, surface, etc) **4** (*tr*) to injure or damage by rough contact: *to scrape*

S

one's knee **5** (*intr*) to be very economical or sparing in the use (of) (esp in the phrase **scrimp and scrape**) **6** (*intr*) to draw the foot backwards in making a bow **7** (*tr*) to finish (a surface) by use of a scraper **8** (*tr*) to make (a bearing, etc) fit by scraping **9** **bow and scrape** to behave with excessive humility ▷ *n* **10** the act of scraping **11** a scraped place **12** a harsh or grating sound **13** *informal* an awkward or embarrassing predicament **14** *informal* a conflict or struggle [Old English *scrapian;* related to Old Norse *skrapa,* Middle Dutch *schrapen,* Middle High German *schraffen*] > 'scrapable *adj* > 'scraper *n*

scrape in *vb* (*intr, adverb*) to succeed in entering with difficulty or by a narrow margin: *he only just scraped into university.* Also: **scrape into**

scraperboard ('skreɪpəˌbɔːd) *n* **1** thin card covered with a layer of white china clay and a black top layer of Indian ink, which can be scraped away with a special tool to leave a white line **2** a picture or design produced in this way

scrape through *vb* (*adverb*) **1** (*intr*) to manage or survive with difficulty **2** to succeed in with difficulty or by a narrow margin: *he scraped through by one mark*

scrape together *or* **up** *vb* (*tr, adverb*) to collect with difficulty: *to scrape together money for a new car*

scrapheap ('skræpˌhiːp) *n* **1** a pile of discarded material **2** **on the scrapheap** (of people or things) having outlived their usefulness

scrapie ('skreɪpɪ) *n* a disease of sheep and goats: one of a group of diseases (including BSE in cattle) that are caused by a protein prion, and result in spongiform encephalopathy [C20 from SCRAPE + -IE]

scraping ('skreɪpɪŋ) *n* **1** the act of scraping **2** a sound produced by scraping **3** (*often plural*) something scraped off, together, or up; a small amount

scrapple ('skræpᵊl) *n* *US* scraps of pork cooked with cornmeal and formed into a loaf [C19 from SCRAP[1]]

scrappy[1] ('skræpɪ) *adj* -pier, -piest fragmentary; disjointed > 'scrappily *adv* > 'scrappiness *n*

scrappy[2] ('skræpɪ) *adj* -pier, -piest *informal* pugnacious

scratch (skrætʃ) *vb* **1** to mark or cut (the surface of something) with a rough or sharp instrument **2** (often foll by *at, out, off,* etc) to scrape (the surface of something), as with claws, nails, etc **3** to scrape (the surface of the skin) with the nails, as to relieve itching **4** to chafe or irritate (a surface, esp the skin) **5** to make or cause to make a grating sound; scrape **6** (*tr;* sometimes foll by *out*) to erase by or as if by scraping **7** (*tr*) to write or draw awkwardly **8** (*intr;* sometimes foll by *along*) to earn a living, manage, etc, with difficulty **9** to withdraw (an entry) from a race, match, etc **10** (*intr*) *billiards, snooker* **a** to make a shot resulting in a penalty **b** to make a lucky shot **11** (*tr*) *US* to cancel (the name of a candidate) from a party ticket in an election **12** (*intr;* often foll by *for*) *Austral informal* to be struggling or in difficulty, esp in earning a living **13** to treat (a subject) superficially **14** **you scratch my back and I'll scratch yours** if you will help me, I will help you ▷ *n* **15** the act of scratching **16** a slight injury **17** a mark made by scratching **18** a slight grating sound **19** (in a handicap sport) **a** a competitor or the status of a competitor who has no allowance or receives a penalty **b** (*as modifier*): *a scratch player* **20** the time, initial score, etc, of such a competitor **21** **a** the line from which competitors start in a race **b** (formerly) a line drawn on the floor of a prize ring at which the contestants stood to begin or continue fighting **22** a withdrawn competitor in a race, etc **23** *billiards, snooker* **a** a shot that results in a penalty, as when the cue ball enters the pocket **b** a lucky shot **24** poultry food **25** **from scratch** *informal* from the very beginning **26** **up to scratch** (*usually used with a negative*) *informal* up to standard ▷ *adj* **27** *sport* (of a team) assembled hastily **28** (in a handicap sport) with no allowance or penalty **29** *informal* rough or haphazard ▷ See also **scratches, scratch together** [C15 via Old French *escrater* from Germanic; compare Old High German *krazzōn* (German *kratzen*); related to Old French *gratter* to GRATE[1]] > 'scratchy *adj* > 'scratchily *adv* > 'scratchiness *n*

scratchcard ('skrætʃˌkɑːd) *n* a ticket that reveals whether or not the holder is eligible for a prize when the surface is removed by scratching

scratcher ('skrætʃə) *n* a person, animal, or thing that scratches

scratches ('skrætʃɪz) *n* (*functioning as singular*) a disease of horses characterized by dermatitis in the region of the fetlock. Also called: **cracked heels, mud fever** [C16 so called because it makes the pastern appear to be scratched]

scratch file *n* *computing* a temporary store for use during the execution of a program

scratchie ('skrætʃɪ) *n* *Austral informal* a scratchcard

scratching ('skrætʃɪŋ) *n* a percussive effect obtained by rotating a gramophone record manually: a disc-jockey and dub technique

scratch pad *n* **1** *chiefly US and Canadian* a notebook, esp one with detachable leaves **2** *computing* a small semiconductor memory for temporary storage

scratchplate ('skrætʃˌpleɪt) *n* a plastic or metal plate attached to the front of a guitar to protect it from pick scratches

scratch sheet *n* *US and Canadian informal* another term for a **dope sheet**

scratch test *n* *med* a skin test to determine allergic sensitivity to various substances by placing the allergen to be tested over an area of lightly scratched skin. A positive reaction is typically indicated by the formation of a weal

scratch together *or* **up** *vb* (*tr, adverb*) to assemble with difficulty: *he scratched up a team for the football match*

scratch video *n* the technique or practice of recycling images from films or television to make collages

scraw (skrɑː) *n* *Irish* a sod from the surface of a peat bog or from a field [from Irish Gaelic *scraith*]

scrawl (skrɔːl) *vb* **1** to write or draw (signs, words, etc) carelessly or hastily; scribble ▷ *n* **2** careless or scribbled writing, drawing, or marks [C17 perhaps a blend of SPRAWL and CRAWL[1]] > 'scrawler *n* > 'scrawly *adj*

scrawny ('skrɔːnɪ) *adj* scrawnier, scrawniest **1** very thin and bony; scraggy **2** meagre or stunted: *scrawny vegetation* [C19 variant of dialect *scranny;* see SCRANNEL] > 'scrawnily *adv* > 'scrawniness *n*

scrawp (skrɑːp) *vb* *Midland English dialect* to scratch (the skin) to relieve itching

screak (skriːk) *dialect, chiefly US* ▷ *vb* **1** (*intr*) to screech or creak ▷ *n* **2** a screech or creak [C16 from Old Norse *skrækja.* See SCREECH[1], SHRIEK] > 'screaky *adj*

scream (skriːm) *vb* **1** to utter or emit (a sharp piercing cry or similar sound or sounds), esp as of fear, pain, etc **2** (*intr*) to laugh wildly **3** (*intr*) to speak, shout, or behave in a wild or impassioned manner **4** (*tr*) to bring (oneself) into a specified state by screaming: *she screamed herself hoarse* **5** (*intr*) to be extremely conspicuous: *these orange curtains scream, you need more restful colours in a bedroom* ▷ *n* **6** a sharp piercing cry or sound, esp one denoting fear or pain **7** *informal* a person or thing that causes great amusement [C13 from Germanic; compare Middle Dutch *schreem,* West Frisian *skrieme* to weep]

screamer ('skriːmə) *n* **1** a person or thing that screams **2** any goose-like aquatic bird, such as *Chauna torquata* (**crested screamer**), of the family *Anhimidae* of tropical and subtropical South America: order *Anseriformes* (ducks, geese, etc) **3** someone or something that raises screams of laughter or astonishment **4** *US and Canadian slang* a sensational headline **5** *Austral slang* **a** a person or thing that is excellent of its kind **b** See **two-pot screamer**

scream therapy *n* another name for **primal therapy**

scree (skriː) *n* an accumulation of weathered rock fragments at the foot of a cliff or hillside, often forming a sloping heap. Also called: **talus** [Old English *scrīthan* to slip; related to Old Norse *skrītha* to slide, German *schreiten* to walk]

screech[1] (skriːtʃ) *n* **1** a shrill, harsh, or high-pitched sound or cry ▷ *vb* **2** to utter with or produce a screech [C16 variant of earlier *scritch,* of imitative origin] > 'screecher *n*

screech[2] (skriːtʃ) *n* *Canadian* (esp in Newfoundland) a dark rum [perhaps special use of SCREECH[1]]

screech owl *n* **1** a small North American owl, *Otus asio,* having ear tufts and a reddish-brown or grey plumage **2** *Brit* any owl that utters a screeching cry

screechy ('skriːtʃɪ) *adj* -ier, -iest loud and shrill

screed (skriːd) *n* **1** a long or prolonged speech or piece of writing **2** a strip of wood, plaster, or metal placed on a surface to act as a guide to the thickness of the cement or plaster coat to be applied **3** a mixture of cement, sand, and water applied to a concrete slab, etc, to give a smooth surface finish **4** *Scot* a rent or tear or the sound produced by this [C14 probably variant of Old English *scrēade* SHRED]

screen (skriːn) *n* **1** a light movable frame, panel, or partition serving to shelter, divide, hide, etc **2** anything that serves to shelter, protect, or conceal **3** a frame containing a mesh that is placed over a window or opening to keep out insects **4** a decorated partition, esp in a church around the choir. See also **rood** (sense 1) **5** a sieve **6** a system for selecting people, such as candidates for a job **7** the wide end of a cathode-ray tube, esp in a television set, on which a visible image is formed **8** a white or silvered surface, usually fabric, placed in front of a projector to receive the enlarged image of a film or of slides **9** **the screen** the film industry or films collectively **10** *photog* a plate of ground glass in some types of camera on which the image of a subject is focused before being photographed **11** *printing* a glass marked with fine intersecting lines, used in a camera for making half-tone reproductions **12** men or ships deployed around and ahead of a larger military formation to warn of attack or protect from a specific threat **13** *sport, chiefly US and Canadian* a tactical ploy in which a player blocks an opponent's view **14** *psychoanal* anything that prevents a person from realizing his true feelings about someone or something **15** *electronics* See **screen grid** ▷ *vb* (*tr*) **16** (sometimes foll by *off*) to shelter, protect, or conceal **17** to sieve or sort **18** to test or check (an individual or group) so as to determine suitability for a task, etc **19** to examine for the presence of a disease, weapons, etc: *the authorities screened five hundred cholera suspects* **20** to provide with a screen or screens **21** to project (a film) onto a screen, esp for public viewing **22** (*intr*) to be shown at a cinema or on the television **23** *printing* to photograph (a picture) through a screen to render it suitable for half-tone reproduction **24** *sport, chiefly US and Canadian* to block the view of (an opposing player) [C15 from Old French *escren* (French *écran*); related to Old High German *skrank,* German *Schrank* cupboard] > 'screenable *adj* > 'screener *n* > 'screenˌful *n* > 'screenˌlike *adj*

screenager ('skriːnˌeɪdʒə) *n* *informal* a teenager who is fully conversant with and skilled in the use of computers and other electronic devices

screen grid *n* *electronics* an electrode placed between the control grid and anode of a valve and having a fixed positive potential relative to the grid. It acts as an electrostatic shield preventing capacitive coupling between grid and anode, thus increasing the stability of the device. Sometimes shortened to: screen See also **suppressor grid**

screenie ('skri:nɪ) n Austral informal short for **screensaver**

screenings ('skri:nɪŋz) pl n refuse separated by sifting

screening test n a simple test performed on a large number of people to identify those who have or are likely to develop a specified disease

screen memory n psychoanal a memory that is tolerable but allied to a distressing event and which is unconsciously used to hide the distressing memory

screenplay ('skri:n,pleɪ) n the script for a film, including instructions for sets and camera work

screen process n a method of printing using a fine mesh of silk, nylon, etc, treated with an impermeable coating except in the areas through which ink is subsequently forced onto the paper behind. Also called: silk-screen printing

screensaver ('skri:nseɪvər) n a computer program that reduces screen damage resulting from an unchanging display when a computer is switched on but not in use by blanking the screen or generating moving patterns, etc

screenshot ('skri:n,ʃɒt) n an image created by copying part or all of the display on a computer screen at a particular moment, for example in order to demonstrate the use of a piece of software

screen test n 1 a filmed audition of a prospective actor or actress to test suitability 2 the test film so made

screen trading n a form of trading on a market or exchange in which the visual display unit of a computer replaces personal contact as in floor trading

screenwriter ('skri:n,raɪtə) n a person who writes screenplays

screet (skri:t) Midland English dialect ▷ vb 1 to shed tears; weep ▷ n 2 the act or sound of crying

screigh or **screich** (skri:x) n, vb a Scot word for **screech** (sense 1)

screw (skru:) n 1 a device used for fastening materials together, consisting of a threaded and usually tapered shank that has a slotted head by which it may be rotated so as to cut its own thread as it bores through the material 2 Also called: screw-bolt a threaded cylindrical rod that engages with a similarly threaded cylindrical hole; bolt 3 a thread in a cylindrical hole corresponding with that on the bolt or screw with which it is designed to engage 4 anything resembling a screw in shape or spiral form 5 a twisting movement of or resembling that of a screw 6 Also called: screw-back billiards, snooker a a stroke in which the cue ball recoils or moves backward after striking the object ball, made by striking the cue ball below its centre b the motion resulting from this stroke 7 another name for **propeller** (sense 1) 8 slang a prison guard 9 Brit slang salary, wages, or earnings 10 Brit a small amount of salt, tobacco, etc, in a twist of paper 11 slang a person who is mean with money 12 slang an old, unsound, or worthless horse 13 (often plural) slang force or compulsion (esp in the phrase put the screws on) 14 slang sexual intercourse 15 have a screw loose informal to be insane 16 turn or tighten the screw slang to increase the pressure ▷ vb 17 (tr) to rotate (a screw or bolt) so as to drive it into or draw it out of a material 18 (tr) to cut a screw thread in (a rod or hole) with a tap or die or on a lathe 19 to turn or cause to turn in the manner of a screw 20 (tr) to attach or fasten with a screw or screws 21 (tr) informal to take advantage of; cheat 22 (tr; often foll by up) to distort or contort: he screwed his face into a scowl 23 Also: screw back to impart a screw to (a ball) 24 (tr, often foll by from or out of) to coerce or force out of; extort 25 slang to have sexual intercourse (with) 26 (tr) slang to burgle 27 have one's head screwed on (the right way) informal to

be wise or sensible ▷ See also **screw up** [c15 from French escroe, from Medieval Latin scrōfa screw, from Latin: sow, presumably because the thread of the screw is like the spiral of the sow's tail] > 'screwer n > 'screw₁like adj

USAGE The use of this otherwise utilitarian word in a sexual sense, though recorded in an 18th century slang dictionary, does not appear to have really taken off until well into the 20th. Although a classic example of the anatomical metaphor for the sex act seen from the male point of view, it can be used as a transitive verb by women, which suggests that the metaphor is all but dead

screwball ('skru:,bɔ:l) slang, chiefly US and Canadian ▷ n 1 an odd or eccentric person ▷ adj 2 odd; zany; eccentric

screw conveyor n engineering a duct along which material is conveyed by the rotational action of a spiral vane which lies along the length of the duct. Also called: worm conveyor

screwdriver ('skru:,draɪvə) n 1 a tool used for turning screws, usually having a handle of wood, plastic, etc, and a steel shank with a flattened square-cut tip that fits into a slot in the head of the screw 2 an alcoholic beverage consisting of orange juice and vodka

screwed (skru:d) adj 1 fastened by a screw or screws 2 having spiral grooves like a screw; threaded 3 twisted or distorted 4 Brit a slang word for **drunk**

screw eye n a wood screw with its shank bent into a ring

screw jack n a lifting device utilizing the mechanical advantage of a screw thread, the effort being applied through a bevel drive. Also called: jackscrew, jack

screw pile n a pile with a threaded tip that is screwed into the ground by a winch or capstan

screw pine n any of various pandanaceous plants of the Old World tropical genus Pandanus, having a spiral mass of pineapple-like leaves and heavy conelike fruits

screw plate n a steel plate with threaded holes used for making male screws

screw propeller n an early form of ship's propeller in which an Archimedes' screw is used to produce thrust by accelerating a flow of water > 'screw-pro'pelled adj

screw tap n another name for **tap²** (sense 6)

screw thread n the helical ridge on a screw formed by a die or lathe tool

screw top n 1 a lid with a threaded rim that is turned on the corresponding thread on the neck of a bottle or container to close it securely 2 a bottle or container having such a lid > 'screw-₁top or 'screw-₁topped adj

screw up vb (tr, adverb) 1 to twist out of shape or distort 2 to summon up or call upon: to screw up one's courage 3 (also intr) informal to mishandle or make a mess (of) 4 (often passive) informal to cause to become very anxious, confused, or nervous: he is really screwed up about his exams ▷ n **screw-up** 5 slang something mishandled or done badly

screwworm ('skru:,wɜ:m) n 1 the larva of a dipterous fly, Callitroga macellaria, that develops beneath the skin of living mammals often causing illness or death 2 the fly producing this larva: family Calliphoridae

screwy ('skru:ɪ) adj screwier, screwiest informal odd, crazy, or eccentric

scribble¹ ('skrɪbᵊl) vb 1 to write or draw in a hasty or illegible manner 2 to make meaningless or illegible marks (on) 3 derogatory or facetious to write poetry, novels, etc ▷ n 4 hasty careless writing or drawing 5 writing, esp literary matter, of poor quality 6 meaningless or illegible marks [c15 from Medieval Latin scrībillāre to write hastily, from Latin scrībere to write] > 'scribbly adj

scribble² ('skrɪbᵊl) vb (tr) to card (wool, etc) [c17

probably from Low German; compare schrubben SCRUB¹]

scribbler ('skrɪblə) n derogatory or facetious a writer of poetry, novels, journalism, etc

scribbly gum ('skrɪbᵊlɪ) n any species of the genus Eucalyptus with smooth white bark marked with random patterns made by wood-boring insects

scribe (skraɪb) n 1 a person who copies documents, esp a person who made handwritten copies before the invention of printing 2 a clerk or public copyist 3 Old Testament a recognized scholar and teacher of the Jewish Law 4 Judaism a man qualified to write certain documents in accordance with religious requirements 5 an author or journalist: used humorously 6 another name for **scriber** ▷ vb 7 to score a line on (a surface) with a pointed instrument, as in metalworking [(in the senses: writer, etc) c14 from Latin scrība clerk, from scrībere to write; c17 (vb): perhaps from INSCRIBE] > 'scribal adj

scriber ('skraɪbə) n a pointed steel tool used to score materials as a guide to cutting, etc. Also called: scribe

scrim (skrɪm) n an open-weave muslin or hessian fabric, used in upholstery, lining, building, and in the theatre to create the illusion of a solid wall or to suggest haziness, etc, according to the lighting [c18 origin unknown]

scrimmage ('skrɪmɪdʒ) n 1 a rough or disorderly struggle 2 American football the clash of opposing linemen at every down ▷ vb 3 (intr) to engage in a scrimmage 4 (tr) to put (the ball) into a scrimmage [c15 from earlier scrimish, variant of SKIRMISH] > 'scrimmager n

scrimp (skrɪmp) vb 1 (when intr, sometimes foll by on) to be very economical or sparing in the use (of) (esp in the phrase **scrimp and save**) 2 (tr) to treat meanly: he is scrimping his children 3 (tr) to cut too small ▷ adj 4 a less common word for **scant** [c18 Scottish, origin unknown] > 'scrimpy adj > 'scrimpily adv > 'scrimpiness n

scrimshank ('skrɪm,ʃæŋk) vb (intr) Brit military slang to shirk work [c19 of unknown origin]

scrimshaw ('skrɪm,ʃɔ:) n 1 the art of decorating or carving shells, ivory, etc, done by sailors as a leisure activity 2 a an article made in this manner b such articles collectively ▷ vb 3 to produce scrimshaw (from) [c19 origin uncertain, perhaps after a surname]

scrip¹ (skrɪp) n 1 a written certificate, list, etc 2 a small scrap, esp of paper with writing on it 3 finance a a certificate representing a claim to part of a share of stock b the shares allocated in a bonus issue [c18 in some senses, probably from SCRIPT; otherwise, short for subscription receipt]

scrip² (skrɪp) n archaic a small bag or wallet, as carried by pilgrims [c14 from Old French escreppe, variant of escarpe SCARF¹]

scrip³ (skrɪp) or **script** n informal a medical prescription [c20 short for PRESCRIPTION]

scrip issue n another name for **bonus issue**

scripophily (skrɪ'pɒfɪlɪ) n the hobby of collecting bonds and share certificates, esp those of historical interest [c20 from SCRIP¹ + -o- + -phily, from Greek philos loving] > scripophile ('skrɪpəʊ,faɪl) n

script (skrɪpt) n 1 handwriting as distinguished from print, esp cursive writing 2 the letters, characters, or figures used in writing by hand 3 any system or style of writing 4 written copy for the use of performers in films and plays 5 law a an original or principal document b (esp in England) a will or codicil or the draft for one 6 any of various typefaces that imitate handwriting 7 computing a series of instructions that is executed by a computer program 8 an answer paper in an examination 9 another word for **scrip³** ▷ vb 10 (tr) to write a script for [c14 from Latin scriptum something written, from scrībere to write]

scripter ('skrɪptə) n a person who writes scripts

S

for films, plays, or television dramas

script kiddie *n slang* a child or teenager who gains illegal access to computer systems, often by using hacking programs downloaded from the internet

scriptorium (skrɪp'tɔːrɪəm) *n, pl* **-riums** *or* **-ria** (-rɪə) a room, esp in a monastery, set apart for the writing or copying of manuscripts [from Medieval Latin]

scriptural ('skrɪptʃərəl) *adj* **1** *(often capital)* of, in accordance with, or based on Scripture **2** of or relating to writing > '**scripturally** *adv*

scripture ('skrɪptʃə) *n* a sacred, solemn, or authoritative book or piece of writing [c13 from Latin *scriptūra* written material, from *scrībere* to write]

Scripture ('skrɪptʃə) *n* **1** Also called: Holy Scripture, Holy Writ, the Scriptures *Christianity* the Old and New Testaments **2** any book or body of writings, esp when regarded as sacred by a particular religious group

scriptwriter ('skrɪpt,raɪtə) *n* a person who prepares scripts, esp for a film > '**script,writing** *n*

scrivener ('skrɪvnə) *n archaic* **1** a person who writes out deeds, letters, etc; copyist **2** a notary [c14 from *scrivein* clerk, from Old French *escrivain*, ultimately from Latin *scrība* SCRIBE]

scrobiculate (skrəʊ'bɪkjʊlɪt, -,leɪt) *or* **scrobiculated** *adj biology* having a surface covered with small round pits or grooves [c19 from Latin *scrobiculus* diminutive of *scrobis* a ditch]

scrod (skrɒd) *n US* a young cod or haddock, esp one split and prepared for cooking [c19 perhaps from obsolete Dutch *schrood,* from Middle Dutch *schrode* SHRED (n); the name perhaps refers to the method of preparing the fish for cooking]

scrofula ('skrɒfjʊlə) *n pathol (no longer in technical use)* tuberculosis of the lymphatic glands. Also called (formerly): **the king's evil** [c14 from Medieval Latin, from Late Latin *scrōfulae* swollen glands in the neck, literally: little sows (sows were thought to be particularly prone to the disease), from Latin *scrōfa* sow]

scrofulous ('skrɒfjʊləs) *adj* **1** of, relating to, resembling, or having scrofula **2** morally degraded > '**scrofulously** *adv* > '**scrofulousness** *n*

scroggin ('skrɒgɪn) *n NZ informal* a tramper's home-made high-calorie sweetmeat

scroll (skrəʊl) *n* **1** a roll of parchment, paper, etc, usually inscribed with writing **2** an ancient book in the form of a roll of parchment, papyrus, etc **3 a** a decorative carving or moulding resembling a scroll **b** *(as modifier): a scroll saw* **c** *(in combination): scrollwork* ▷ *vb* **4** *(tr)* to saw into scrolls **5** to roll up like a scroll **6** *computing* to move (text) from right to left or up and down on a screen in order to view text that cannot be contained within a single display image [c15 *scrowle,* from *scrowe,* from Old French *escroe* scrap of parchment, but also influenced by ROLL]

scroll saw *n* a saw with a narrow blade for cutting intricate ornamental curves in wood

scrollwork ('skrəʊl,wɜːk) *n* ornamental work in scroll-like patterns, esp when done with a scroll saw

scrome (skrəʊm) *vb Northern English dialect* **scromes, scroming, scromed** **1** *(intr)* to crawl or climb, esp using the hands to aid movement **2** to wriggle

scrooch (skruːtʃ) *vb Midland English dialect* to scratch (the skin) to relieve itching

Scrooge (skruːdʒ) *n* a mean or miserly person [c19 after a character in Dickens' story *A Christmas Carol* (1843)]

scroop (skruːp) *dialect* ▷ *vb* **1** *(intr)* to emit a grating or creaking sound ▷ *n* **2** such a sound [c18 of imitative origin]

scrophulariaceous (,skrɒfjʊ,lɛərɪ'eɪʃəs) *adj* of, relating to, or belonging to the *Scrophulariaceae,* a family of plants including figwort, snapdragon, foxglove, toadflax, speedwell, and mullein [c19 from New Latin *(herba) scrophularia* scrofula (plant),

from the use of such plants in treating scrofula]

scrorp (skrɒp) *n Midland English dialect* a deep scratch or weal

scrote (skrəʊt) *n slang* **1** *derogatory* a worthless fellow **2** another word for **scrotum**

scrotum ('skrəʊtəm) *n, pl* **-ta** (-tə) *or* **-tums** the pouch of skin containing the testes in most mammals [c16 from Latin] > '**scrotal** *adj*

scrouge (skraʊdʒ, skruːdʒ) *vb (tr) dialect* to crowd or press [c18 alteration of c16 *scruze* to squeeze, perhaps blend of SCREW + SQUEEZE]

scrounge (skraʊndʒ) *vb informal* **1** (when *intr,* sometimes foll by *around*) to search in order to acquire (something) without cost **2** to obtain or seek to obtain (something) by cadging or begging [c20 variant of dialect *scrunge* to steal, of obscure origin] > '**scrounger** *n*

scrub[1] (skrʌb) *vb* **scrubs, scrubbing, scrubbed** **1** to rub (a surface) hard, with or as if with a brush, soap, and water, in order to clean it **2** to remove (dirt), esp by rubbing with a brush and water **3** *(intr; foll by up)* (of a surgeon) to wash the hands and arms thoroughly before operating **4** *(tr)* to purify (a vapour or gas) by removing impurities **5** *(tr) informal* to delete or cancel **6** *(intr) horse racing slang* (of jockeys) to urge a horse forwards by moving the arms and whip rhythmically forwards and backwards alongside its neck ▷ *n* **7** the act of or an instance of scrubbing ▷ See also **scrub round** [c14 from Middle Low German *schrubben,* or Middle Dutch *schrobben*]

scrub[2] (skrʌb) *n* **1 a** vegetation consisting of stunted trees, bushes, and other plants growing in an arid area **b** *(as modifier): scrub vegetation* **2** an area of arid land covered with such vegetation **3 a** an animal of inferior breeding or condition **b** *(as modifier): a scrub bull* **4** a small or insignificant person **5** anything stunted or inferior **6** *sport, US and Canadian* a player not in the first team **7** the **scrub** *Austral informal* a remote place, esp one where contact with people can be avoided ▷ *adj* prenominal **8** small, stunted, or inferior **9** *sport, US and Canadian* **a** (of a player) not in the first team **b** (of a team) composed of such players **c** (of a contest) between scratch or incomplete teams [c16 variation of SHRUB[1]]

scrubber[1] ('skrʌbə) *n* **1** a person or thing that scrubs **2** an apparatus for purifying a gas **3** *Brit and Austral derogatory slang* a promiscuous woman

scrubber[2] ('skrʌbə) *n Austral* a domestic animal, esp a bullock, that has run wild in the bush [c19 from SCRUB[2]]

scrub bird *n* either of two fast-running wren-like passerine birds, *Atrichornis clamosus* or *A. rufescens,* that constitute the Australian family *Atrichornithidae*

scrubby ('skrʌbɪ) *adj* **-bier, -biest** **1** covered with or consisting of scrub **2** (of trees or vegetation) stunted in growth **3** *Brit informal* messy > '**scrubbiness** *n*

scrub fowl *or* **turkey** *n* another name for **megapode**

scrubland ('skrʌb,lænd) *n* an area of scrub vegetation

scrub round *vb (intr, preposition) informal* to waive; avoid or ignore: *we can scrub round the rules*

scrub turkey *n* **1** another name for **megapode** **2** *Austral* another name for **brush turkey**

scrub typhus *n* an acute febrile disease characterized by severe headache, skin rash, chills, and swelling of the lymph nodes, caused by the bite of mites infected with the microorganism *Rickettsia tsutsugamushi*: occurs mainly in Asia, Australia, and the islands of the western Pacific

scruff[1] (skrʌf) *n* the nape of the neck (esp in the phrase **by the scruff of the neck**) [c18 variant of *scuft,* perhaps from Old Norse *skoft* hair; related to Old High German *scuft*]

scruff[2] (skrʌf) *n* **1** *informal* an untidy scruffy person **2** *informal* a disreputable person, ruffian **3** another name for **scum** (sense 3)

scruffy ('skrʌfɪ) *adj* **scruffier, scruffiest** unkempt or shabby

scrum (skrʌm) *n* **1** *rugby* the act or method of restarting play after an infringement when the two opposing packs of forwards group together with heads down and arms interlocked and push to gain ground while the scrum half throws the ball in and the hookers attempt to scoop it out to their own team. A scrum is usually called by the referee (**set scrum**) but may be formed spontaneously (**loose scrum**) **2** *informal* a disorderly struggle ▷ *vb* **scrums, scrumming, scrummed** **3** *(intr; usually foll by down) rugby* to form a scrum [c19 shortened from SCRUMMAGE]

scrum half *n rugby* **1** a player who puts in the ball at scrums and tries to get it away to his three-quarter backs **2** this position in a team

scrummage ('skrʌmɪdʒ) *n, vb* **1** *rugby* another word for **scrum** **2** a variant of **scrimmage** [c19 variant of SCRIMMAGE] > '**scrummager** *n*

scrummie ('skrʌmɪ) *n chiefly South African, Austral and NZ informal* short for **scrum half**

scrummy ('skrʌmɪ) *adj* **-mier, -miest** *informal* delicious; lovely [c20 from SCRUMPTIOUS]

scrump (skrʌmp) *vb dialect* to steal (apples) from an orchard or garden [dialect variant of SCRIMP]

scrumple ('skrʌmpəl) *vb* (usually foll by *up*) to crumple or crush (something, esp a piece of paper) or (esp of a piece of paper) to become crumpled or crushed [c16 variant of CRUMPLE]

scrumptious ('skrʌmpʃəs) *adj informal* very pleasing; delicious [c19 probably changed from SUMPTUOUS] > '**scrumptiously** *adv* > '**scrumptiousness** *n*

scrumpy ('skrʌmpɪ) *n* a rough dry cider, brewed esp in the West Country [from *scrump,* variant of SCRIMP (in obsolete sense: withered), referring to the apples used]

scrunch (skrʌntʃ) *vb* **1** to crumple, crush, or crunch or to be crumpled, crushed, or crunched ▷ *n* **2** the act or sound of scrunching [c19 variant of CRUNCH]

scruncheon *or* **scrunchion** ('skrʌntʃən) *n Canadian* (in Newfoundland) a small crisp piece of fried pork fat [origin unknown]

scrunchie ('skrʌntʃɪ) *n* a loop of elastic covered loosely with fabric, used to hold the hair in a ponytail, etc

scruple ('skruːpəl) *n* **1** *(often plural)* a doubt or hesitation as to what is morally right in a certain situation **2** *archaic* a very small amount **3** a unit of weight equal to 20 grains (1.296 grams) **4** an ancient Roman unit of weight equivalent to approximately one twenty-fourth of an ounce ▷ *vb* **5** *(obsolete when tr)* to have doubts (about), esp for a moral reason [c16 from Latin *scrūpulus* a small weight, from *scrūpus* rough stone] > '**scrupleless** *adj*

scrupulous ('skruːpjʊləs) *adj* **1** characterized by careful observation of what is morally right **2** very careful or precise [c15 from Latin *scrūpulōsus* punctilious] > '**scrupulously** *adv* > '**scrupulousness** *n*

scrutable ('skruːtəbəl) *adj rare* open to or able to be understood by scrutiny [c17 from Latin *scrūtārī* to inspect closely; see SCRUTINY] > ,**scruta'bility** *n*

scrutator (skruː'teɪtə) *n* a person who examines or scrutinizes [from Latin, from *scrūtārī* to search]

scrutineer (,skruːtɪ'nɪə) *n* a person who examines, esp one who scrutinizes the conduct of an election poll

scrutinize *or* **scrutinise** ('skruːtɪ,naɪz) *vb (tr)* to examine carefully or in minute detail > '**scruti,nizer** *or* '**scruti,niser** *n*

scrutiny ('skruːtɪnɪ) *n, pl* **-nies** **1** close or minute examination **2** a searching look **3 a** (in the early Christian Church) a formal testing that catechumens had to undergo before being baptized **b** a similar examination of candidates for holy orders [c15 from Late Latin *scrūtinium* an investigation, from *scrūtārī* to search (originally referring to rag-and-bone men), from *scrūta* rubbish]

scry (skraɪ) *vb* **scries, scrying, scried** (*intr*) to divine, esp by crystal gazing [C16 from DESCRY]

SCSI ('skʌzɪ) *n* Small Computer Systems Interface: a system for connecting a computer to peripheral devices

scuba ('skju:bə) *n* **a** an apparatus used in skindiving, consisting of a cylinder or cylinders containing compressed air attached to a breathing apparatus **b** (*as modifier*): *scuba diving* [C20 from the initials of *self-contained underwater breathing apparatus*]

scud (skʌd) *vb* **scuds, scudding, scudded 1** (*intr*) (esp of clouds) to move along swiftly and smoothly **2** (*intr*) *nautical* to run before a gale **3** (*tr*) *Scot* to hit; slap ▷ *n* **4** the act of scudding **5** *meteorol* **a** a formation of low fractostratus clouds driven by a strong wind beneath rain-bearing clouds **b** a sudden shower or gust of wind **6** *Scot* a slap [C16 probably of Scandinavian origin; related to Norwegian *skudda* to thrust, Swedish *skudda* to shake]

Scud (skʌd) *n informal* a Soviet-made surface-to-surface missile, originally designed to carry nuclear warheads and with a range of 300 km; later modified to achieve greater range: used by Iraq in the Iran-Iraq War and in the Gulf Wars

scudo ('sku:dəʊ) *n*, *pl* -di (-di:) any of several former Italian coins [C17 from Italian: shield, from Latin *scūtum*]

scuff (skʌf) *vb* **1** to scrape or drag (the feet) while walking **2** to rub or scratch (a surface) or (of a surface) to become rubbed or scratched **3** (*tr*) *US* to poke at (something) with the foot ▷ *n* **4** the act or sound of scuffing **5** a rubbed place caused by scuffing **6** a backless slipper [C19 probably of imitative origin]

scuffle¹ ('skʌfəl) *vb* (*intr*) **1** to fight in a disorderly manner **2** to move by shuffling **3** to move in a hurried or confused manner ▷ *n* **4** a disorderly struggle **5** the sound made by scuffling or shuffling [C16 from Scandinavian; compare Swedish *skuff, skuffa* to push]

scuffle² ('skʌfəl) *n US* a type of hoe operated by pushing rather than pulling [C18 from Dutch *schoffel* SHOVEL]

scull (skʌl) *n* **1** a single oar moved from side to side over the stern of a boat to propel it **2** one of a pair of short-handled oars, both of which are pulled by one oarsman, esp in a racing shell **3** a racing shell propelled by an oarsman or oarsmen pulling two oars **4** (*plural*) a race between racing shells, each propelled by one, two, or four oarsmen pulling two oars **5** an act, instance, period, or distance of sculling ▷ *vb* **6** to propel (a boat) with a scull [C14 of unknown origin] > 'sculler *n*

scullery ('skʌlərɪ) *n*, *pl* -leries *chiefly Brit* a small room or part of a kitchen where washing up, vegetable preparation, etc is done [C15 from Anglo-Norman *squillerie*, from Old French *escuelerie*, from *escuele* a bowl, from Latin *scutella*, from *scutra* a flat tray]

scullion ('skʌljən) *n* **1** a mean or despicable person **2** *archaic* a servant employed to do rough household work in a kitchen [C15 from Old French *escouillon* cleaning cloth, from *escouve* a broom, from Latin *scōpa* a broom]

sculpin ('skʌlpɪn) *n*, *pl* -pin or -pins *US and Canadian* any of various fishes of the family *Cottidae* (bullheads and sea scorpions) [C17 of unknown origin]

sculpsit Latin ('skʌlpsɪt) he (or she) sculptured it: an inscription following the artist's name on a sculpture

sculpt (skʌlpt) *vb* **1** a variant of **sculpture** (senses 5–8) **2** (*intr*) to practise sculpture ▷ Also: **sculp** [C19 from French *sculpter*, from Latin *sculpere* to carve]

sculptor ('skʌlptə) *or feminine* **sculptress** *n* a person who practises sculpture

Sculptor ('skʌlptə) *n*, *Latin genitive* Sculptoris (skʌlp'tɔ:rɪs) a faint constellation in the S hemisphere between Phoenix and Cetus

sculpture ('skʌlptʃə) *n* **1** the art of making figures or designs in relief or in the round by carving wood, moulding plaster, etc, or casting metals, etc **2** works or a work made in this way **3** ridges or indentations as on a shell, formed by natural processes **4** the gradual formation of the landscape by erosion ▷ *vb* (*mainly tr*) **5** (*also intr*) to carve, cast, or fashion (stone, bronze, etc) three dimensionally **6** to portray (a person, etc) by means of sculpture **7** to form in the manner of sculpture, esp to shape (landscape) by erosion **8** to decorate with sculpture ▷ Also (for senses 5–8): **sculpt** [C14 from Latin *sculptūra* a carving; see SCULPT] > 'sculptural *adj* > 'sculpturally *adv*

sculpturesque (ˌskʌlptʃə'rɛsk) *adj* resembling sculpture > ˌsculptur'esquely *adv* > ˌsculptur'esqueness *n*

scum (skʌm) *n* **1** a layer of impure matter that forms on the surface of a liquid, often as the result of boiling or fermentation **2** the greenish film of algae and similar vegetation surface of a stagnant pond **3** Also called: **dross, scruff** the skin of oxides or impurities on the surface of a molten metal **4** waste matter **5** a worthless person or group of people ▷ *vb* **scums, scumming, scummed 6** (*tr*) to remove scum from **7** (*intr*) *rare* to form a layer of or become covered with scum [C13 of Germanic origin; related to Old High German *scūm*, Middle Dutch *schūm*, Old French *escume*; see SKIM] > 'scum,like *adj* > 'scummer *n*

scumbag ('skʌm,bæg) *n slang* an offensive or despicable person [C20 perhaps from earlier US sense: condom, from US slang *scum* semen + *bag*]

scumble ('skʌmbəl) *vb* **1** (in painting and drawing) to soften or blend (an outline or colour) with an upper coat of opaque colour, applied very thinly ▷ *n* **2** the upper layer of colour applied in this way **3** the technique or effects of scumbling [C18 probably from SCUM]

scummy ('skʌmɪ) *adj* -mier, -miest **1** of, resembling, consisting of, or covered with scum **2** dirty, unpleasant, or nasty

scuncheon ('skʌntʃən) *n* the inner part of a door jamb or window frame [C15 from Old French *escoinson*, from *coin* angle]

scundered ('skʌndəd) *adj Irish dialect* **1** embarrassed **2** same as **scunnered**

scunge (skʌndʒ) *Austral and NZ slang* ▷ *vb* **1** to borrow ▷ *n* **2** a dirty or worthless person **3** a person who borrows, esp habitually [C20 of unknown origin]

scungy ('skʌndʒɪ) *adj* scungier, scungiest *Austral and NZ informal* miserable; sordid; dirty [C20 of uncertain origin]

scunner ('skʌnə; *Scot* 'skʌnər) *dialect, chiefly Scot* ▷ *vb* **1** (*intr*) to feel aversion **2** (*tr*) to produce a feeling of aversion in ▷ *n* **3** a strong aversion (often in the phrase **take a scunner to**) **4** an object of dislike; nuisance [C14 from Scottish *skunner*, of unknown origin]

scunnered ('skʌnəd) *adj dialect, chiefly Scot* **1** annoyed, discontented, or bored **2** nauseated or disgusted, esp from a surfeit of food, drink, etc [C15 of unknown origin]

Scunthorpe ('skʌn,θɔ:p) *n* a town in E England, in North Lincolnshire unitary authority, Lincolnshire: developed rapidly after the discovery of local iron ore in the late 19th century; iron and steel industries have declined. Pop: 72 660 (2001)

scup (skʌp) *n* a common sparid fish, *Stenotomus chrysops*, of American coastal regions of the Atlantic. Also called: **northern porgy** [C19 from Narraganset *mishcup*, from *mishe* big + *kuppe* close together; from the form of the scales]

scupper¹ ('skʌpə) *n* **1** *nautical* a drain or spout allowing water on the deck of a vessel to flow overboard **2** an opening in the side of a building for draining off water **3** a drain in a factory floor for running off water from a sprinkler system [C15 *skopper*, of uncertain origin; perhaps related to SCOOP]

scupper² ('skʌpə) *vb* (*tr*) *Brit* **1** *slang* to overwhelm, ruin, or disable **2** to sink (one's ship) deliberately [C19 of unknown origin]

scuppernong ('skʌpə,nɒŋ) *n* **1** a sweet American wine, slightly golden, made from a variety of muscadine grape **2** another name for **muscadine** (sense 2), the variety from which this wine is made [C19 named after *Scuppernong* River in North Carolina where the grape grows]

scur (skɜ:) *n vet science* a small unattached growth of horn at the site of a normal horn in cattle

scurf (skɜ:f) *n* **1** another name for **dandruff 2** flaky or scaly matter adhering to or peeling off a surface [Old English *scurf*; related to Old Norse *skurfōtta* scurfy, Old High German *scorf*, Danish *skurv*] > 'scurfy *adj*

scurrilous ('skʌrɪləs) *adj* **1** grossly or obscenely abusive or defamatory **2** characterized by gross or obscene humour [C16 from Latin *scurrīlis* derisive, from *scurra* buffoon] > scurrility (skə'rɪlɪtɪ) or 'scurrilousness *n* > 'scurrilously *adv*

scurry ('skʌrɪ) *vb* -ries, -rying, -ried **1** to move about or proceed hurriedly **2** (*intr*) to whirl about ▷ *n*, *pl* -ries **3** the act or sound of scurrying **4** a brisk light whirling movement, as of snow **5** *horse racing* a short race or sprint [C19 probably shortened from *hurry-scurry*]

scurvy ('skɜ:vɪ) *n* **1** a disease caused by a lack of vitamin C, characterized by anaemia, spongy gums, bleeding beneath the skin, and, (in infants) malformation of bones and teeth. Related adj: **scorbutic** ▷ *adj* -vier, -viest **2** mean or despicable: *a scurvy knave* [C16 see SCURF] > 'scurvily *adv* > 'scurviness *n*

scurvy grass *n* any of various plants of the genus *Cochlearia*, esp *C. officinalis*, of Europe and North America, formerly used to treat scurvy: family *Brassicaceae* (crucifers)

scut (skʌt) *n* the short tail of animals such as the deer and rabbit [C15 probably of Scandinavian origin; compare Old Norse *skutr* end of a vessel, Icelandic *skott* tail]

scuta ('skju:tə) *n* the plural of **scutum**

scutage ('skju:tɪdʒ) *n* (in feudal society) a payment sometimes exacted by a lord from his vassal in lieu of military service [C15 from Medieval Latin *scūtāgium*, literally: shield dues, from Latin *scūtum* a shield]

Scutari *n* **1** ('sku:tərɪ, sku:'tɑ:rɪ) the former name of Üsküdar **2** (sku'tari) the Italian name for Shkodër

scutate ('skju:teɪt) *adj* **1** (of animals) having or covered with large bony or horny plates **2** *botany* shaped like a round shield or buckler: *a scutate leaf* [C19 from Latin *scūtātus* armed with a shield, from *scūtum* a shield] > scu'tation *n*

scutch¹ (skʌtʃ) *vb* **1** (*tr*) to separate the fibres from the woody part of (flax) by pounding ▷ *n* **2** the tool used for this. Also called: **scutcher** [C18 from obsolete French *escoucher*, from Vulgar Latin *excuticāre* (unattested) to beat out, from Latin EX-¹ + *quatere* to shake]

scutch² (skʌtʃ) *vb* (*tr*) *Northern English dialect* to strike with an open hand

scutcheon ('skʌtʃən) *n* **1** a variant of **escutcheon 2** any rounded or shield-shaped structure, esp a scute > 'scutcheonless *adj* > 'scutcheon-,like *adj*

scutch grass *n* another name for **Bermuda grass** and **couch grass**. Sometimes shortened to: **scutch** [variant of COUCH GRASS]

scute (skju:t) *n zoology* a horny or chitinous plate that makes up part of the exoskeleton in armadillos, turtles, fishes, etc [C14 (the name of a French coin; C19 in zoological sense): from Latin *scūtum* shield]

scutellation (ˌskju:tɪ'leɪʃən) *n zoology* **1** the way in which scales or plates are arranged in an animal **2** a covering of scales or scutella, as on a bird's leg [C19 New Latin, from *scutella*, plural of SCUTELLUM + -ATION]

scutellum (skju:'tɛləm) *n*, *pl* -la (-lə) *biology* **1** the last of three plates into which the notum of an insect's thorax is divided **2** one of the scales on the tarsus of a bird's leg **3** an outgrowth from a germinating grass seed that probably represents the cotyledon **4** any other small shield-shaped part or structure [C18 from New Latin: a little shield, from Latin *scūtum* a shield] > scu'tellar *adj* > scutellate ('skju:tɪˌleɪt, -lɪt) *adj*

scutiform ('skju:tɪˌfɔ:m) *adj* (esp of plant parts) shaped like a shield [C17 from New Latin *scūtiformis*, from Latin *scūtum* a shield + *forma* shape]

scutter ('skʌtə) *vb, n Brit* an informal word for **scurry** [C18 probably from SCUTTLE², with -ER¹ as in SCATTER]

scuttle¹ ('skʌtəl) *n* **1** See **coal scuttle 2** *dialect, chiefly Brit* a shallow basket, esp for carrying vegetables **3** the part of a motor-car body lying immediately behind the bonnet [Old English *scutel* trencher, from Latin *scutella* bowl, diminutive of *scutra* platter; related to Old Norse *skutill*, Old High German *scuzzila*, perhaps to Latin *scūtum* shield]

scuttle² ('skʌtəl) *vb* **1** (*intr*) to run or move about with short hasty steps ▷ *n* **2** a hurried pace or run [C15 perhaps from SCUD, influenced by SHUTTLE]

scuttle³ ('skʌtəl) *vb* **1** (*tr*) *nautical* to cause (a vessel) to sink by opening the seacocks or making holes in the bottom **2** (*tr*) to give up (hopes, plans, etc) ▷ *n* **3** *nautical* a small hatch or its cover [C15 (n): via Old French from Spanish *escotilla* a small opening, from *escote* opening in a piece of cloth, from *escotar* to cut out]

scuttlebutt ('skʌtəlˌbʌt) *n nautical* **1** a drinking fountain **2** (formerly) a cask of drinking water aboard a ship **3** *chiefly US slang* rumour or gossip [C19 from SCUTTLE³ + BUTT⁴]

scutum ('skju:təm) *n, pl* **-ta** (-tə) **1** the middle of three plates into which the notum of an insect's thorax is divided **2** another word for **scute 3** a large Roman shield [Latin: shield]

Scutum ('skju:təm) *n, Latin genitive* **Scuti** ('skju:taɪ) a small faint constellation in the S hemisphere lying between Sagittarius and Aquila and crossed by the Milky Way. Also called: **Scutum Sobieskii** (sɒ'bjɛski) [Latin, literally: the Shield]

scuzzy ('skʌzɪ) *adj* **-zier, -ziest** *slang, chiefly US* unkempt, dirty, or squalid [C20 perhaps from *disgusting* or perhaps from a blend of *scum* and *fuzz*]

Scylla ('sɪlə) *n* **1** *Greek myth* a sea nymph transformed into a sea monster believed to drown sailors navigating the Strait of Messina. She was identified with a rock off the Italian coast. Compare **Charybdis 2 between Scylla and Charybdis** in a predicament in which avoidance of either of two dangers means exposure to the other

scyphiform ('saɪfɪˌfɔ:m) *adj* shaped like a cup or goblet: *a scyphiform cell* [C19 from Greek *skuphos* cup + -FORM]

scyphistoma (saɪ'fɪstəmə) *n, pl* **-mae** (-ˌmi:) or **-mas** a sessile hydra-like individual representing the polyp stage of scyphozoans. It produces forms which become free-swimming jellyfish [C19 from Greek *skuphos* cup + STOMA]

scyphozoan (ˌsaɪfə'zəʊən) *n* **1** any marine medusoid coelenterate of the class *Scyphozoa;* a jellyfish ▷ *adj* **2** of, relating to, or belonging to the *Scyphozoa* [C19 via New Latin from Greek *skuphos* bowl + *zōion* animal]

scyphus ('saɪfəs) *n, pl* **-phi** (-faɪ) **1** an ancient Greek two-handled drinking cup without a footed base **2** *botany* a cuplike body formed at the end of the thallus in certain lichens [C18 from Latin: goblet, from Greek *skuphos*]

Scyros ('skɪrɒs) *n* a variant spelling of **Skyros**

scythe (saɪð) *n* **1** a manual implement for cutting grass, etc, having a long handle held with both hands and a curved sharpened blade that moves in a plane parallel to the ground ▷ *vb* **2** (*tr*) to cut (grass, etc) with a scythe [Old English *sigthe;* related to Old Norse *sigthr*, Old High German *segansa*] > 'scytheˌlike *adj*

Scythia ('sɪðɪə) *n* an ancient region of SE Europe

and Asia, north of the Black Sea: now part of Ukraine

Scythian ('sɪðɪən) *adj* **1** of or relating to ancient Scythia, its inhabitants, or their language ▷ *n* **2** a member of an ancient nomadic people of Scythia **3** the extinct language of this people, belonging to the East Iranian branch of the Indo-European family

sd¹ *abbreviation for* **1** sine die **2** sound **3** *philosophy* sense datum

sd² *the internet domain name for* Sudan

SD *abbreviation for* **1** South Dakota **2** Also: **sd** *statistics* **standard deviation 3** *international car registration for* Swaziland

S. Dak. *abbreviation for* South Dakota

SDI *abbreviation for* Strategic Defense Initiative. See **Star Wars**

SDK *computing abbreviation for* software development kit

SDLP (in Northern Ireland) *abbreviation for* **Social Democratic and Labour Party**

SDP *abbreviation for* **Social Democratic Party**

SDRs *abbreviation for* **special drawing rights**

SDSL *abbreviation for* symmetric digital subscriber line: a telephone line that carries data in the form of digital pulses, but not at the same time as voice messages are being sent

se *the internet domain name for* Sweden

Se *the chemical symbol for* selenium

SE *symbol for* southeast(ern)

sea (si:) *n* **1 a** (usually preceded by *the*) the mass of salt water on the earth's surface as differentiated from the land. Related adjs: **marine, maritime, thalassic b** (*as modifier*): *sea air* **2** (*capital when part of place name*) **a** one of the smaller areas of ocean: *the Irish Sea* **b** a large inland area of water: *the Caspian Sea* **3** turbulence or swell, esp of considerable size: *heavy seas* **4** (*capital when part of a name*) *astronomy* any of many huge dry plains on the surface of the moon. See also **mare² 5** anything resembling the sea in size or apparent limitlessness **6** the life or career of a sailor (esp in the phrase **follow the sea**) **7 at sea a** on the ocean **b** in a state of confusion **8 go to sea** to become a sailor **9 put (out) to sea** to embark on a sea voyage [Old English *sǣ;* related to Old Norse *sǣr,* Old Frisian *sē,* Gothic *saiws,* Old High German *sēo*]

sea anchor *n nautical* any device, such as a bucket or canvas funnel, dragged in the water to keep a vessel heading into the wind or reduce drifting

sea anemone *n* any of various anthozoan coelenterates, esp of the order *Actiniaria,* having a polypoid body with oral rings of tentacles. See also **actinia**

sea aster *n* a composite perennial plant of salt marshes, *Aster tripolium,* having yellow and purple flowers like those of the related Michaelmas daisy

sea bag *n* a canvas bag, closed by a line threaded through grommets at the top, used by a seaman for his belongings

sea bass (bæs) *n* any of various American coastal percoid fishes of the genus *Centropristes* and related genera, such as *C. striatus* (**black sea bass**), having an elongated body with a long spiny dorsal fin almost divided into two: family *Serranidae*

Seabee ('si:ˌbi:) *n* a member of the US Navy's Construction Battalions established to build airstrips [C20 from pronunciation of CB, for *Construction Battalion*]

sea beet *n* the wild form of *Beta vulgaris*. See **beet**

sea bird *n* a bird such as a gull, that lives on the sea

sea biscuit *n* another term for **hardtack**

seablite ('si:ˌblaɪt) *n* a prostrate annual plant of the goosefoot family, *Suaeda maritima,* of salt marshes, having fleshy alternate leaves and small green flowers [C18 SEA + *blite*, via Latin from Greek *bliton* ORACHE]

seaboard ('si:ˌbɔ:d) *n* **a** land bordering on the sea; the seashore **b** (*as modifier*): *seaboard towns*

seaborgium ('si:ˌbɔ:gɪəm) *n* a synthetic

transuranic element, synthesized and identified in 1974. Symbol: Sg; atomic no: 106 [C20 named after Glenn *Seaborg* (1912–99), US chemist and nuclear physicist]

seaborne ('si:ˌbɔ:n) *adj* **1** carried on or by the sea **2** transported by ship

sea bream *n* any sparid fish, esp *Pagellus centrodontus,* of European seas, valued as a food fish

sea breeze *n* a wind blowing from the sea to the land, esp during the day when the land surface is warmer

sea buckthorn *n* a thorny Eurasian shrub, *Hippophaë rhamnoides,* growing on sea coasts and having silvery leaves and orange fruits: family *Elaeagnaceae*

sea butterfly *n* another name for **pteropod**

sea captain *n* the master of a ship, usually a merchant ship

sea change *n* a seemingly magical change, as brought about by the action of the sea [coined by Shakespeare, in Ariel's song "Full Fathom Five" in *The Tempest* (1611)]

sea chest *n* a usually large firm chest used by a sailor for storing personal property

seacoast ('si:ˌkəʊst) *n* land bordering on the sea; a coast

seacock ('si:ˌkɒk) *n nautical* a valve in the hull of a vessel below the water line for admitting sea water or for pumping out bilge water

sea cow *n* **1** any sirenian mammal, such as a dugong or manatee **2** an archaic name for **walrus**

sea cucumber *n* any echinoderm of the class *Holothuroidea,* having an elongated body covered with a leathery skin and bearing a cluster of tentacles at the oral end. They usually creep on the sea bed or burrow in sand [C17 so named because of its cucumber-like shape]

seadog ('si:ˌdɒg) *n* another word for **fogbow** or **fogdog**

sea dog *n* an experienced or old sailor

Sea-Doo ('si:ˌdu:) *n trademark Canadian* a small self-propelled watercraft for one person

sea duck *n* any of various large diving ducks, such as the eider and the scoter, that occur along coasts

sea eagle *n* any of various fish-eating eagles that live near the sea, esp *Haliaetus albicilla* (**European sea eagle** or **white-tailed eagle**) having a brown plumage and white tail

sea-ear *n* another name for the **ormer** (sense 1)

sea elephant *n* another name for **elephant seal**

sea fan *n* any of various corals of the genus *Gorgonia* and related genera, having a treelike or fan-shaped horny skeleton: order *Gorgonacea* (gorgonians)

seafarer ('si:ˌfɛərə) *n* **1** a traveller who goes by sea **2** a less common word for **sailor**

seafaring ('si:ˌfɛərɪŋ) *adj* (*prenominal*) **1** travelling by sea **2** working as a sailor ▷ *n* **3** the act of travelling by sea **4** the career or work of a sailor

sea fir *n* another name for **hydroid** (sense 3)

sea-floor spreading ('si:ˌflɔ:) *n* a series of processes in which new oceanic lithosphere is created at oceanic ridges, spreads away from the ridges, and returns to the earth's interior along subduction zones. Also called: **ocean floor spreading**

sea foam *n* **1** foam formed on the surface of the sea **2** a former name for **meerschaum** (sense 1)

seafood ('si:ˌfu:d) *n* edible saltwater fish or shellfish

sea fret *n* a wet mist or haze coming inland from the sea

seafront ('si:ˌfrʌnt) *n* a built-up area facing the sea

sea-girt *adj literary* surrounded by the sea

seagoing ('si:ˌgəʊɪŋ) *adj* intended for or used at sea

sea gooseberry *n* any of various ctenophores of the genus *Pleurobrachia* and related genera, having a rounded body with longitudinal rows of cilia and hairlike tentacles

sea green *n* **a** a moderate green colour, sometimes with a bluish or yellowish tinge **b** (*as adjective*): *a sea-green carpet*

seagull ('si:ˌgʌl) *n* **1** a popular name for the **gull** (the bird) **2** *NZ* a casual wharf labourer who is not a trade-union member

sea hare *n* any of various marine gastropods of the order *Aplysiomorpha* (or *Anaspidea*), esp *Aplysia punctata*, having a soft body with an internal shell and two pairs of earlike tentacles

sea heath *n* a small tough perennial plant, *Frankenia laevis*, of Eurasian salt marshes, having minute leaves and pink flowers: family *Frankeniaceae*

Seahenge (ˌsiː'hɛndʒ) *n* a Bronze Age timber circle discovered off the coast of Norfolk in E England. Dating from 2050 BC, it is thought to have been used as a ceremonial site

sea holly *n* a European umbelliferous plant, *Eryngium maritimum*, of sandy shores, having spiny bluish-green stems and blue flowers

sea horse *n* **1** any marine teleost fish of the temperate and tropical genus *Hippocampus*, having a bony-plated body, a prehensile tail, and a horselike head and swimming in an upright position: family *Syngnathidae* (pipefishes) **2** an archaic name for the **walrus** **3** a fabled sea creature with the tail of a fish and the front parts of a horse

sea-island cotton *n* **1** a cotton plant, *Gossypium barbadense*, of the Sea Islands, widely cultivated for its fine long fibres **2** the fibre of this plant or the material woven from it

Sea Islands *pl n* a chain of islands in the Atlantic off the coasts of South Carolina, Georgia, and Florida

sea kale *n* a European coastal plant, *Crambe maritima*, with broad fleshy leaves and white flowers, cultivated for its edible asparagus-like shoots: family *Brassicaceae* (crucifers). Compare **kale**

seakale beet ('si:ˌkeɪl) *n* another name for **chard**

sea king *n* any of the greater Viking pirate chiefs who led raids on the coasts of early medieval Europe

seal¹ (si:l) *n* **1** a device impressed on a piece of wax, moist clay, etc, fixed to a letter, document, etc, as a mark of authentication **2** a stamp, ring, etc, engraved with a device to form such an impression **3** a substance, esp wax, so placed over an envelope, document, etc, that it must be broken before the object can be opened or used **4** any substance or device used to close or fasten tightly **5** a material, such as putty or cement, that is used to close an opening to prevent the passage of air, water, etc **6** a small amount of water contained in the trap of a drain to prevent the passage of foul smells **7** an agent or device for keeping something hidden or secret **8** anything that gives a pledge or confirmation **9** a decorative stamp often sold in aid of charity **10** *RC Church* Also called: **seal of confession** the obligation never to reveal anything said by a penitent in confession **11** set one's seal on (*or* to) **a** to mark with one's sign or seal **b** to endorse ▷ *vb* (*tr*) **12** to affix a seal to, as proof of authenticity **13** to stamp with or as if with a seal **14** to approve or authorize **15** (sometimes foll by *up*) to close or secure with or as if with a seal: *to seal one's lips; seal up a letter* **16** (foll by *off*) to enclose (a place) with a fence, wall, etc **17** to decide irrevocably **18** *Mormon Church* to make (a marriage or adoption) perpetually binding **19** to close tightly so as to render airtight or watertight **20** to paint (a porous material) with a nonporous coating **21** *Austral and NZ* to consolidate (a road surface) with bitumen, tar, etc [C13 *seel*, from Old French, from Latin *sigillum* little figure, from *signum* a sign] ▷ 'sealable *adj*

seal² (si:l) *n* **1** any pinniped mammal of the families *Otariidae* (see **eared seal**) and *Phocidae* (see **earless seal**) that are aquatic but come on shore to breed. Related adjs: **otarid, phocine** **2** any earless seal (family *Phocidae*), esp the common or harbour seal or the grey seal (*Halichoerus grypus*) **3** sealskin ▷ *vb* **4** (*intr*) to hunt for seals [Old English *seolh*; related to Old Norse *selr*, Old High German *selah*, Old Irish *selige* tortoise] > 'seal-ˌlike *adj*

sea lace *n* a brown seaweed, *Chorda filum*, that grows on stones under sandy bottoms and produces chordlike fronds up to 8.5 metres (28 ft) long

sea ladder *n* a rope ladder, set of steps, etc, by which a boat may be boarded at sea

sea lamprey *n* a common anadromous lamprey, *Petromyzon marinus*, a form of which occurs in the Great Lakes of N America and causes great losses of fish

sea lane *n* an established route for ships

sealant ('si:lənt) *n* **1** any substance, such as wax, used for sealing documents, bottles, etc **2** any of a number of substances used for stopping leaks, waterproofing wood, etc

sea lavender *n* any of numerous perennial plants of the plumbaginaceous genus *Limonium*, of temperate salt marshes, having spikes of white, pink, or mauve flowers, several species of which are grown as garden plants. See also **statice**

sea lawyer *n* *nautical slang* a contentious seaman

seal brown *n* **a** a dark brown colour often with a yellowish or greyish tinge **b** (*as adjective*): *a seal-brown dress*

sealed (si:ld) *vb* **1** the past participle of **seal¹** ▷ *adj* **2** *Austral and NZ* (of a road) having a hard surface; made-up

sealed-beam *adj* (esp of a car headlight) having a lens and prefocused reflector sealed in the lamp vacuum

sealed book *n* another term for **closed book**

sealed move *n* *chess* the last move before an adjournment, which is written down by the player making it, sealed in an envelope, and kept secret from his opponent until play is resumed

sealed orders *pl n* written instructions that are not to be read until a specified time

sealed unit *n* a hard disk that is permanently sealed to prevent damage to the read/write head. See also **Winchester disk**

sea legs *pl n* *informal* **1** the ability to maintain one's balance on board ship, esp in rough weather **2** the ability to resist seasickness, esp in rough weather

sealer¹ ('si:lə) *n* **1** a person or thing that seals **2** (formerly in Britain and currently in the US) an official who examines the accuracy of weights and measures **3** a coating of paint, varnish, etc, applied to a surface to prevent the absorption of subsequent coats

sealer² ('si:lə) *n* a person or ship occupied in hunting seals

sealery ('si:ləri) *n*, *pl* -eries **1** the occupation of hunting seals **2** any place where seals are regularly to be found, esp a seal rookery

sea letter *n* **1** Also called: **passport** a document issued to a merchant vessel, esp in wartime, authorizing it to leave a port or proceed freely **2** (formerly) a document issued to a vessel in port, describing its cargo, crew, etc

sea lettuce *n* any of various green seaweeds of the genus *Ulva*, which have edible wavy translucent fronds

sea level *n* the level of the surface of the sea with respect to the land, taken to be the mean level between high and low tide, and used as a standard base for measuring heights and depths

sea lily *n* any of various sessile echinoderms, esp of the genus *Ptilocrinus*, in which the body consists of a long stalk attached to a hard surface and bearing a central disc with delicate radiating arms: class *Crinoidea* (crinoids)

sealing wax *n* a hard material made of shellac, turpentine, and pigment that softens when heated. It is used for sealing documents, parcels, letters, etc

sea lion *n* any of various large eared seals, such as *Zalophus californianus* (**Californian sea lion**), of the N Pacific, often used as a performing animal

sea loch *n* another name for **loch** (sense 2)

Sea Lord *n* (in Britain) either of the two serving naval officers (**First** and **Second Sea Lords**) who sit on the admiralty board of the Ministry of Defence

seal-point *n* a popular variety of the Siamese cat, having a dark brown mask, paws, and tail, and a cream body

seal ring *n* another term for **signet ring**

sealskin ('si:lˌskɪn) *n* **1 a** the skin or pelt of a fur seal, esp when dressed with the outer hair removed and the underfur dyed dark brown **b** (*as modifier*): *a sealskin coat* **2** a garment made of this skin

Sealyham terrier ('si:liəm) *n* a short-legged wire-haired breed of terrier with a medium-length white coat. Often shortened to: **Sealyham** [named after *Sealyham*, village in S Wales, where it was bred in the 19th century]

seam (si:m) *n* **1** the line along which pieces of fabric are joined, esp by stitching **2** a ridge or line made by joining two edges **3** a stratum of coal, ore, etc **4** in a good seam *Northern English dialect* doing well, esp financially **5** a linear indentation, such as a wrinkle or scar **6** *surgery* another name for **suture** (sense 1b) **7** (*modifier*) *cricket* of or relating to a style of bowling in which the bowler utilizes the stitched seam round the ball in order to make it swing in flight and after touching the ground: *a seam bowler* **8** bursting at the seams full to overflowing ▷ *vb* **9** (*tr*) to join or sew together by or as if by a seam **10** *US* to make ridges in (knitting) using purl stitch **11** to mark or become marked with or as if with a seam or wrinkle [Old English; related to Old Norse *saumr*, Old High German *soum*]

seaman ('si:mən) *n*, *pl* -men **1** a rating trained in seamanship as opposed to electrical engineering, etc **2** a man who serves as a sailor **3** a person skilled in seamanship > 'seaman-ˌlike *adj* > 'seamanly *adj*, *adv*

seamanship ('si:mənʃɪp) *n* skill in and knowledge of the work of navigating, maintaining, and operating a vessel

seamark ('si:ˌmɑːk) *n* *nautical* an aid to navigation, such as a conspicuous object on a shore used as a guide

sea mat *n* a popular name for a **bryozoan**

seam bowler *or* **seamer** *n* *cricket* a fast bowler who makes the ball bounce on its seam so that it will change direction > seam bowling *n*

seamer ('si:mə) *n* **1** a person or thing that seams **2** another name for **seam bowler**

sea mew *n* another name for **mew** (sense 2)

sea mile *n* a unit of distance used in navigation, defined as the length of one minute of arc, measured along the meridian, in the latitude of the position. Its actual length varies slightly with latitude but is about 1853 metres (6080 feet). Symbol: M See also **nautical mile**

sea milkwort *n* a primulaceous plant, *Glaux maritima*, of estuary mud and seaside rocks of N temperate coasts, having trailing stems and small pink flowers. Also called: saltwort, black saltwort Compare **milkwort**

seamless ('si:mlɪs) *adj* **1** (of a garment) having no seams **2** continuous or flowing: *seamless output; a seamless performance*

seamount ('si:ˌmaʊnt) *n* a submarine mountain rising more than 1000 metres above the surrounding ocean floor. Compare **guyot**

sea mouse *n* any of several large polychaete worms of the genus *Aphrodite* and related genera, having a broad flattened body covered dorsally with a dense mat of iridescent hairlike chaetae [C16 so called because of its appearance]

seamstress ('sɛmstrɪs) *or rarely* **sempstress** ('sɛmpstrɪs) *n* a woman who sews and makes clothes, esp professionally

seamy ('si:mɪ) *adj* seamier, seamiest **1** showing

S

the least pleasant aspect; sordid **2** (esp of the inner side of a garment) showing many seams ▷ **'seaminess** *n*

Seanad Éireann ('ʃænəð 'eːrən) *n* (in the Republic of Ireland) the upper chamber of parliament; the Senate [from Irish, literally: senate of Ireland]

seance *or* **séance** ('seɪɑːns, -ɑːns) *n* **1** a meeting at which spiritualists attempt to receive messages from the spirits of the dead **2** a meeting of a society [C19 from French, literally: a sitting, from Old French *seoir* to sit, from Latin *sedēre*]

sea onion *n* another name for **sea squill**

sea otter *n* a large marine otter, *Enhydra lutris*, of N Pacific coasts, formerly hunted for its thick dark brown fur

sea pen *n* any of various anthozoan coelenterates of the genus *Pennatula* and related genera, forming fleshy feather-like colonies in warm seas: order *Pennatulacea*

sea perch *n* **1** any of various marine serranid fishes, such as the bass and stone bass, that have an elongated body with a very spiny dorsal fin and occur in all except polar seas **2** another name for **surfperch**

sea pink *n* another name for **thrift** (the plant)

seaplane ('siːˌpleɪn) *n* any aircraft that lands on and takes off from water. Also called (esp US): **hydroplane**

seaport ('siːˌpɔːt) *n* **1** a port or harbour accessible to seagoing vessels **2** a town or city located at such a place

sea power *n* **1** a nation that possesses great naval strength **2** the naval strength of a country or nation

sea purse *n* a tough horny envelope containing fertilized eggs, produced by the female of certain sharks and skates. Also called: **mermaid's purse**

sea purslane *n* a small chenopodiaceous shrub, *Halimione portulacoides*, of salt marshes in Eurasia and parts of Africa, having oval leaves and inconspicuous flowers

SEAQ ('siːˌæk) (in Britain) *n acronym for* Stock Exchange Automated Quotation: a computerized system that collects and displays the prices and transactions in securities

seaquake ('siːˌkweɪk) *n obsolete* an agitation and disturbance of the sea caused by an earthquake at the sea bed. It is now usually described as an earthquake

sear[1] (sɪə) *vb* (*tr*) **1** to scorch or burn the surface of **2** to brand with a hot iron **3** to cause to wither or dry up **4** *rare* to make callous or unfeeling ▷ *n* **5** a mark caused by searing ▷ *adj* **6** *poetic* dried up [Old English *sēarian* to become withered, from *sēar* withered; related to Old High German *sōrēn*, Greek *hauos* dry, Sanskrit *sōsa* drought]

sear[2] (sɪə) *n* the catch in the lock of a small firearm that holds the hammer or firing pin cocked [C16 probably from Old French *serre* a clasp, from *serrer* to hold firmly, from Late Latin *serāre* to bolt, from Latin *sera* a bar]

sea ranger *n Brit* a senior Guide training in seamanship. US equivalent: **mariner**

sea raven *n* a large fish, *Hemitripterus americanus*, of North American Atlantic coastal waters that inflates itself with air when caught: family *Cottidae* (bullheads and sea scorpions)

search (sɜːtʃ) *vb* **1** to look through (a place, records, etc) thoroughly in order to find someone or something **2** (*tr*) to examine (a person) for concealed objects by running one's hands over the clothing **3** to look at or examine (something) closely: *to search one's conscience* **4** (*tr*; foll by *out*) to discover by investigation **5** *surgery* **a** to explore (a bodily cavity) during a surgical procedure **b** to probe (a wound) **6** (*tr*) *military* to fire all over (an area) **7** *computing* to review (a file) to locate specific information **8** *archaic* to penetrate **9** **search me** *informal* I don't know ▷ *n* **10** the act or an instance of searching **11** the examination of a vessel by the right of search **12** *computing* **a** a review of a file to locate specific information **b** (*as*

modifier): *a search routine* **13** **right of search** *international law* the right possessed by the warships of a belligerent state in time of war to board and search merchant vessels to ascertain whether ship or cargo is liable to seizure [C14 from Old French *cerchier*, from Late Latin *circāre* to go around, from Latin *circus* CIRCLE] ▷ **'searchable** *adj* ▷ **'searcher** *n*

search dog *n* a dog trained to assist rescue workers in finding people buried under rubble by detection by smell

search engine *n computing* a service provided on the internet enabling users to search for items of interest

searching ('sɜːtʃɪŋ) *adj* keenly penetrating: *a searching look* ▷ **'searchingly** *adv* ▷ **'searchingness** *n*

searchlight ('sɜːtʃˌlaɪt) *n* **1** a device, consisting of a light source and a reflecting surface behind it, that projects a powerful beam of light in a particular direction **2** the beam of light produced by such a device

search order *n law* an injunction allowing a person to enter the premises of another to search for and take copies of evidence required for a court case, used esp in cases of infringement of copyright. Former name: **Anton Piller order**

search party *n* a group of people taking part in an organized search, as for a lost, missing, or wanted person

search warrant *n* a written order issued by a justice of the peace authorizing a constable or other officer to enter and search premises for stolen goods, drugs, etc

sea robin *n* any of various American gurnards of the genus *Prionotus* and related genera, such as *P. carolinus* (**northern sea robin**)

sea room *n* sufficient space to manoeuvre a vessel

sea salt *n* salt obtained by evaporation of sea water

seascape ('siːˌskeɪp) *n* a sketch, picture, etc, of the sea

sea scorpion *n* any of various northern marine scorpaenoid fishes of the family *Cottidae*, esp *Taurulus bubalis* (**long-spined sea scorpion**). They have a tapering body and a large head covered with bony plates and spines

Sea Scout *n* a Scout belonging to any of a number of Scout troops whose main activities are canoeing, sailing, etc, and who wear sailors' caps as part of their uniform

sea serpent *n* a huge legendary creature of the sea resembling a snake or dragon

sea shanty *n* same as **shanty**[2]

seashell ('siːˌʃɛl) *n* the empty shell of a marine mollusc

seashore ('siːˌʃɔː) *n* **1** land bordering on the sea **2** the land between the marks of high and low water

seasick ('siːˌsɪk) *adj* suffering from nausea and dizziness caused by the motion of a ship at sea ▷ **'sea,sickness** *n*

seaside ('siːˌsaɪd) *n* **a** any area bordering on the sea, esp one regarded as a resort **b** (*as modifier*): *a seaside hotel*

sea slater *n* a large (2.5 cm or 1 in.) nocturnal isopod, *Ligia oceanica*, that lives in cracks in rocks or walls around the high-water mark

sea slug *n* any of various shell-less marine gastropod molluscs, esp those of the order *Nudibranchia*. See **nudibranch**

sea snail *n* any small spiny-finned fish of the family *Liparidae*, esp *Liparis liparis*, of cold seas, having a soft scaleless tadpole-shaped body with the pelvic fins fused into a sucker. Also called: **snailfish**

sea snake *n* any venomous snake of the family *Hydrophiidae*, of tropical seas, that swims by means of a laterally compressed oarlike tail

season ('siːzən) *n* **1** one of the four equal periods into which the year is divided by the equinoxes and solstices, resulting from the apparent

movement of the sun north and south of the equator during the course of the earth's orbit around it. These periods (spring, summer, autumn, and winter) have their characteristic weather conditions in different regions, and occur at opposite times of the year in the N and S hemispheres **2** a period of the year characterized by particular conditions or activities: *the rainy season* **3** the period during which any particular species of animal, bird, or fish is legally permitted to be caught or killed: *open season on red deer* **4** a period during which a particular entertainment, sport, etc, takes place: *a season at the National Theatre; the football season; the tourist season* **5** (esp formerly) a period of fashionable social events in a particular place: *the London season* **6** any definite or indefinite period **7** any of the major periods into which the ecclesiastical calendar is divided, such as Lent, Advent, or Easter **8** (*sometimes capital*) Christmas (esp in the phrases **compliments of the season, Season's greetings**) **9** a period or time that is considered proper, suitable, or natural for something **10** **in good season** early enough **11** **in season a** (of game) permitted to be caught or killed **b** (of fresh food) readily available **c** Also: **in** *or* **on heat** (of some female mammals) sexually receptive **d** appropriate ▷ *vb* **12** (*tr*) to add herbs, salt, pepper, or spice to (food) **13** (*tr*) to add zest to **14** (in the preparation of timber) to undergo or cause to undergo drying **15** (*tr*; *usually passive*) to make or become mature or experienced: *seasoned troops* **16** (*tr*) to mitigate or temper: *to season one's admiration with reticence* [C13 from Old French *seson*, from Latin *satiō* a sowing, from *serere* to sow] ▷ **'seasoned** *adj* ▷ **'seasoner** *n* ▷ **'seasonless** *adj*

seasonable ('siːzənəbᵊl) *adj* **1** suitable for the season **2** taking place at the appropriate time ▷ **'seasonableness** *n* ▷ **'seasonably** *adv*

seasonal ('siːzənᵊl) *adj* of, relating to, or occurring at a certain season or certain seasons of the year: *seasonal labour* ▷ **'seasonally** *adv* ▷ **'seasonalness** *n*

seasonal affective disorder *n* a state of depression sometimes experienced by people in winter, thought to be related to lack of sunlight. Abbreviation: **SAD**

seasoning ('siːzənɪŋ) *n* **1** something that enhances the flavour of food, such as salt or herbs **2** another term (not now in technical usage) for **drying** (sense 2)

season ticket *n* a ticket for a series of events, number of journeys, etc, within a limited time, usually obtained at a reduced rate

sea spider *n* a small marine arachnid, having four pairs of legs and somewhat resembling a spider, unusual in that the male carries the eggs once they are laid and cares for the offspring

sea squill *or* **onion** *n* a Mediterranean liliaceous plant, *Urginea maritima*, having dense spikes of small white flowers, and yielding a bulb with medicinal properties

sea squirt *n* any minute primitive marine animal of the class *Ascidiacea*, most of which are sedentary, having a saclike body with openings through which water enters and leaves. See also **ascidian**

sea steps *pl n* projecting metal bars attached to a ship's side, used for boarding

sea swallow *n* a popular name for **tern**[1]

seat (siːt) *n* **1** a piece of furniture designed for sitting on, such as a chair or sofa **2** the part of a chair, bench, etc, on which one sits **3** a place to sit, esp one that requires a ticket: *I have two seats for the film tonight* **4** another name for **buttocks** (see **buttock**) **5** the part of a garment covering the buttocks **6** the part or area serving as the base of an object **7** the part or surface on which the base of an object rests **8** the place or centre in which something is located: *a seat of government* **9** a place of abode, esp a country mansion that is or was originally the chief residence of a family **10** a membership or the right to membership in a legislative or similar body **11** *chiefly Brit* a parliamentary constituency **12** membership in a stock exchange **13** the manner in which a rider sits on a horse **14** by the seat of one's pants by instinct rather than knowledge or experience **15** on seat W African informal (of officials) in the office rather than on tour or on leave: *the agricultural advisor will be on seat tomorrow* ▷ *vb* **16** (*tr*) to bring to or place on a seat; cause to sit down **17** (*tr*) to provide with seats **18** (*tr; often passive*) to place or centre: *the ministry is seated in the capital* **19** (*tr*) to set firmly in place **20** (*tr*) to fix or install in a position of power **21** (*tr*) to put a seat on or in (an item of furniture, garment, etc) **22** (*intr*) (of garments) to sag in the area covering the buttocks: *your thin skirt has seated badly* [Old English *gesete;* related to Old Norse *sæti,* Old High German *gasāzi,* Middle Dutch *gesaete*] > 'seatless *adj*

sea tangle *n* any of various brown seaweeds, esp any of the genus *Laminaria*

seat belt *n* **1** Also called: safety belt a belt or strap worn in a vehicle to restrain forward motion in the event of a collision **2** a similar belt or strap worn in an aircraft at takeoff and landing and in rough weather

-seater *n* a settee, vehicle, cinema, etc, having a number of seats as specified: *a forty-seater coach*

seating ('si:tɪŋ) *n* **1** the act of providing with a seat or seats **2 a** the provision of seats, as in a theatre, cinema, etc **b** (*as modifier*): *seating arrangements* **3** material used for covering or making seats

Seaton Valley ('si:tᵊn) *n* a region in NE England, in SE Northumberland: consists of a group of former coal-mining villages

sea trout *n* **1** a silvery marine variety of the brown trout that migrates to fresh water to spawn. Compare **brown trout 2** any of several marine sciaenid fishes of the genus *Cynoscion,* such as *C. nebulosus* (**spotted sea trout**) and the weakfish, of North American coastal waters

Seattle (sɪ'ætᵊl) *n* a port in W Washington, on the isthmus between Lake Washington and Puget Sound: the largest city in the state and chief commercial centre of the Northwest; two universities. Pop: 569 101 (2003 est)

sea urchin *n* any echinoderm of the class *Echinoidea,* such as *Echinus esculentus* (**edible sea urchin**), typically having a globular body enclosed in a rigid spiny test and occurring in shallow marine waters

sea vegetable *n* an edible seaweed

sea wall *n* a wall or embankment built to prevent encroachment or erosion by the sea or to serve as a breakwater > 'sea-,walled *adj*

seawan *or* **sewan** ('si:wən) *n* shell beads, usually unstrung, used by certain North American Indians as money; wampum [c18 from Narraganset *seawohn* loose]

seaward ('si:wəd) *adv* **1** a variant of **seawards** ▷ *adj* **2** directed or moving towards the sea **3** (esp of a wind) coming from the sea

seawards ('si:wədz) *or* **seaward** *adv* towards the sea

seaware ('si:,wɛə) *n* any of numerous large coarse seaweeds, esp when cast ashore and used as fertilizer [Old English *sǣwār,* from *sǣ* SEA + *wār* seaweed]

sea wasp *n* Austral another name for **box jellyfish**

seaway ('si:,weɪ) *n* **1** a waterway giving access to an inland port, navigable by ocean-going ships **2** a vessel's progress **3** a rough or heavy sea **4** a route across the sea

seaweed ('si:,wi:d) *n* **1** any of numerous multicellular marine algae that grow on the seashore, in salt marshes, in brackish water, or submerged in the ocean **2** any of certain other plants that grow in or close to the sea

seaworthy ('si:,w3:ðɪ) *adj* in a fit condition or ready for a sea voyage > 'sea,worthiness *n*

sea wrack *n* any of various seaweeds found on the shore, esp any of the larger species

sebaceous (sɪ'beɪʃəs) *adj* **1** of or resembling sebum, fat, or tallow; fatty **2** secreting fat or a greasy lubricating substance [c18 from Late Latin *sēbāceus,* from SEBUM]

sebaceous glands *pl n* the small glands in the skin that secrete sebum into hair follicles and onto most of the body surface except the soles of the feet and the palms of the hands

sebacic acid (sɪ'bæsɪk, -'beɪ-) *n* another name for **decanedioic acid**

Sebastopol (sɪ'bæstəpəl) *n* the English name for **Sevastopol**

sebi- *or* **sebo-** *combining form* fat or fatty matter: *sebiferous* [from Latin *sēbum* tallow]

sebiferous (sɪ'bɪfərəs) *adj* biology producing or carrying a fatty, oily, or waxlike substance

seborrhoea *or esp US* **seborrhea** (,sɛbə'rɪə) *n* any disease of the skin characterized by excessive secretion of sebum by the sebaceous glands and its accumulation on the skin surface > ,sebor'rhoeal, ,sebor'rhoeic *or esp US* ,sebor'rheal, ,sebor'rheic *adj*

sebum ('si:bəm) *n* the oily secretion of the sebaceous glands that acts as a lubricant for the hair and skin and provides some protection against bacteria [c19 from New Latin, from Latin: tallow]

sec¹ (sɛk) *adj* **1** (of wines) dry **2** (of champagne) of medium sweetness [c19 from French, from Latin *siccus*]

sec² (sɛk) *n informal* short for **second:** *wait a sec*

sec³ (sɛk) *abbreviation for* secant

SEC *abbreviation for* **Securities and Exchange Commission**

sec. *abbreviation for* **1** second (of time) **2** secondary **3** secretary **4** section **5** sector

SECAM ('si:,kæm) *n acronym for* séquentiel couleur à mémoire: a colour-television broadcasting system used in France, the former Soviet Union, and some other countries

secant ('si:kənt) *n* **1** (of an angle) a trigonometric function that in a right-angled triangle is the ratio of the length of the hypotenuse to that of the adjacent side; the reciprocal of cosine. Abbreviation: sec **2** a line that intersects a curve [c16 from Latin *secāre* to cut] > 'secantly *adv*

secateurs ('sɛkətəz, ,sɛkə'tɜ:z) *pl n chiefly Brit* a small pair of shears for pruning, having a pair of pivoted handles, sprung so that they are normally open, and usually a single cutting blade that closes against a flat surface [c19 plural of French *sécateur,* from Latin *secāre* to cut]

secco ('sɛkəʊ) *n, pl* -cos **1** wall painting done on dried plaster with tempera or pigments ground in limewater. Compare **fresco 2** any wall painting other than true fresco [c19 from Italian: dry, from Latin *siccus*]

secede (sɪ'si:d) *vb* (*intr; often foll by from*) (of a person, section, etc) to make a formal withdrawal of membership, as from a political alliance, church, organization, etc [c18 from Latin *sēcēdere* to withdraw, from *sē-* apart + *cēdere* to go] > se'ceder *n*

secern (sɪ's3:n) *vb* (*tr*) rare **1** (of a gland or follicle) to secrete **2** to distinguish or discriminate [c17 from Latin *sēcernere* to separate, from *sē-* apart + *cernere* to distinguish] > se'cernment *n*

secession (sɪ'sɛʃən) *n* **1** the act of seceding **2** (*often capital*) *chiefly US* the withdrawal in 1860–61 of 11 Southern states from the Union to form the Confederacy, precipitating the American Civil War [c17 from Latin *sēcessiō* a withdrawing, from *sēcēdere* to SECEDE] > se'cessional *adj* > se'cession,ism *n, adj*

sech (ʃɛk, sɛtʃ, 'sɛk'eɪtʃ) *n* hyperbolic secant; a hyperbolic function that is the reciprocal of cosh

seclude (sɪ'klu:d) *vb* (*tr*) **1** to remove from contact with others **2** to shut off or screen from view [c15 from Latin *sēclūdere* to shut off, from *sē-* + *claudere* to imprison]

secluded (sɪ'klu:dɪd) *adj* **1** kept apart from the company of others: *a secluded life* **2** sheltered; private > se'cludedly *adv* > se'cludedness *n*

seclusion (sɪ'klu:ʒən) *n* **1** the act of secluding or the state of being secluded **2** a secluded place [c17 from Medieval Latin *sēclūsiō;* see SECLUDE]

seclusive (sɪ'klu:sɪv) *adj* **1** tending to seclude **2** fond of seclusion > se'clusively *adv* > se'clusiveness *n*

second¹ ('sɛkənd) *adj* (*usually prenominal*) **1 a** coming directly after the first in numbering or counting order, position, time, etc; being the ordinal number of *two:* often written 2nd **b** (*as noun*): *the second in line* **2** rated, graded, or ranked between the first and third levels **3** alternate: *every second Thursday* **4** additional; extra: *a second opportunity* **5** resembling a person or event from an earlier period of history; unoriginal: *a second Wagner* **6** of lower quality; inferior: *belonging to the second class* **7** denoting the lowest but one forward ratio of a gearbox in a motor vehicle **8** music **a** relating to or denoting a musical part, voice, or instrument lower in pitch than another part, voice, or instrument (the first): *the second tenors* **b** of or relating to a part, instrument, or instrumentalist regarded as subordinate to another (the first): *the second flute* **9** at second hand by hearsay ▷ *n* **10** *Brit education* an honours degree of the second class, usually further divided into an upper and lower designation. Full term: second-class honours degree **11** the lowest but one forward ratio of a gearbox in a motor vehicle: *he changed into second on the bend* **12** (in boxing, duelling, etc) an attendant who looks after a competitor **13** a speech seconding a motion or the person making it **14** *music* **a** the interval between one note and another lying next above or below it in the diatonic scale **b** one of two notes constituting such an interval in relation to the other. See also **minor** (sense 4), **major** (sense 14), **interval** (sense 5) **15** (*plural*) goods of inferior quality **16** (*plural*) *informal* a second helping of food **17** (*plural*) the second course of a meal ▷ *vb* (*tr*) **18** to give aid or backing to **19** (in boxing, etc) to act as second to (a competitor) **20** to make a speech or otherwise express formal support for (a motion already proposed) ▷ *adv* **21** Also: secondly in the second place ▷ *sentence connector* **22** Also: secondly as the second point: linking what follows with the previous statement [c13 via Old French from Latin *secundus* coming next in order, from *sequī* to follow] > 'seconder *n*

second² ('sɛkənd) *n* **1 a** 1/60 of a minute of time **b** the basic SI unit of time: the duration of 9 192 631 770 periods of radiation corresponding to the transition between two hyperfine levels of the ground state of caesium-133. Symbol: s **2** 1/60 of a minute of angle. Symbol: ″ **3** a very short period of time; moment [c14 from Old French, from Medieval Latin *pars minūta secunda* the second small part (a minute being the first small part of an hour); see SECOND¹]

second³ (sɪ'kɒnd) *vb* (*tr*) *Brit* **1** to transfer (an employee) temporarily to another branch, etc **2** *military* to transfer (an officer) to another post, often retiring him to a staff or nonregimental position [c19 from French *en second* in second rank (or position)]

Second Advent *n* a less common term for the **Second Coming**

secondary ('sɛkəndərɪ, -drɪ) *adj* **1** one grade or step after the first; not primary **2** derived from or depending on what is primary, original, or first: *a secondary source* **3** below the first in rank, importance, etc; not of major importance **4** (*prenominal*) of or relating to the education of young people between the ages of 11 and 18: *secondary education* **5** (of the flight feathers of a bird's wing) growing from the ulna **6 a** being the part of an electric circuit, such as a transformer or induction coil, in which a current is induced by a changing current in a neighbouring coil: *a secondary coil* **b** (of a current) flowing in such a circuit. Compare **primary** (sense 7) **7** (of an industry) involving the manufacture

S

of goods from raw materials. Compare **primary** (sense 8b), **tertiary** (sense 2) **8** *geology* (of minerals) formed by the alteration of pre-existing minerals **9** *chem* **a** (of an organic compound) having a functional group attached to a carbon atom that is attached to one hydrogen atom and two other groups **b** (of an amine) having only two organic groups attached to a nitrogen atom; containing the group NH **c** (of a salt) derived from a tribasic acid by replacement of two acidic hydrogen atoms with metal atoms or electropositive groups **10** *linguistics* **a** derived from a word that is itself a derivation from another word. Thus, *lovably* comes from *lovable* and is a secondary derivative from *love* **b** (of a tense in Latin, Greek, or Sanskrit) another word for **historic** (sense 3) ▷ *n, pl* **-aries 11** a person or thing that is secondary **12** a subordinate, deputy, or inferior **13** a secondary coil, winding, inductance, or current in an electric circuit **14** *ornithol* any of the flight feathers that grow from the ulna of a bird's wing. See **primary** (sense 6) **15** *astronomy* a celestial body that orbits around a specified primary body: *the moon is the secondary of the earth* **16** *med* a cancerous growth in some part of the body away from the site of the original tumour **17** *American football* **a** (usually preceded by *the*) cornerbacks and safeties collectively **b** their area in the field **18** short for **secondary colour** > 'secondarily *adv* > 'secondariness *n*

secondary accent *or* **stress** *n phonetics* (in a system of transcribing utterances recognizing three levels of stress) the accent on a syllable of a word or breath group that is weaker than the primary accent but stronger than the lack of stress: *in the word "agriculture" the secondary accent falls on the third syllable*. Compare **primary accent**

secondary cell *n* an electric cell that can be recharged and can therefore be used to store electrical energy in the form of chemical energy. See also **accumulator** (sense 1) Compare **primary cell**

secondary colour *n* a colour formed by mixing two primary colours. Sometimes shortened to: **secondary**

secondary emission *n physics* the emission of electrons (**secondary electrons**) from a solid as a result of bombardment with a beam of electrons, ions, or metastable atoms: used in electron multipliers

secondary modern school *n Brit* (formerly) a secondary school offering a more technical or practical and less academic education than a grammar school

secondary picketing *n* the picketing by strikers of a place of work that supplies goods to or distributes goods from their employer > secondary picket *n*

secondary processes *pl n psychoanal* the logical conscious type of mental functioning, guided by external reality. Compare **primary processes**

secondary qualities *pl n* (in empiricist philosophy) those properties of objects that are explained in terms of the primary properties of their parts, such as heat in terms of the motion of molecules

secondary school *n* a school for young people, usually between the ages of 11 and 18

secondary sexual characteristic *n* any of various features distinguishing individuals of different sex but not directly concerned in reproduction. Examples are the antlers of a stag and the beard of a man

secondary stress *n* another term for **secondary accent**

second ballot *n* an electoral procedure in which if no candidate emerges as a clear winner in a first ballot, candidates at the bottom of the poll are eliminated and another ballot is held among the remaining candidates

second-best *adj* **1** next to the best **2** come off second best *informal* to be defeated in competition

▷ *n* second best **3** an inferior alternative

second chamber *n* the upper house of a bicameral legislative assembly

second childhood *n* dotage; senility (esp in the phrases **in his, her,** etc, **second childhood**)

second class *n* **1** the class or grade next in value, quality, etc, to the first ▷ *adj* **second-class** when prenominal **2** of the class or grade next to the best in quality, etc **3** shoddy or inferior **4** of or denoting the class of accommodation in a hotel or on a train, etc, lower in quality and price than first class **5 a** (in Britain) of or relating to mail that is processed more slowly than first-class mail **b** (in the US and Canada) of or relating to mail that consists mainly of newspapers, etc **6** *education* See **second¹** (sense 10) ▷ *adv* **7** by second-class mail, transport, etc

second-class citizen *n* a person whose rights and opportunities are treated as less important than those of other people in the same society

Second Coming *or less commonly* **Second Advent** *n* the prophesied return of Christ to earth at the Last Judgment

second cousin *n* the child of a first cousin of either of one's parents

second-degree burn *n pathol* See **burn¹** (sense 22)

seconde (sɪ'kɒnd; *French* səɡɔ̃d) *n* the second of eight positions from which a parry or attack can be made in fencing [C18 from French *seconde parade* the second parry]

secondee (sə,kɒn'di:) *n* a person who is seconded

Second Empire *n* **1 a** the imperial government of France under Napoleon III **b** the period during which this government functioned (1852–70) **2** the style of furniture and decoration of the Second Empire, reviving the Empire style, but with fussier ornamentation

second estate *n rare* the nobility collectively

second fiddle *n informal* **1 a** the second violin in a string quartet or one of the second violins in an orchestra **b** the musical part assigned to such an instrument **2** a secondary status **3** a person who has a secondary status

second floor *n* **1** *Brit* the storey of a building immediately above the first and two floors up from the ground. US and Canadian term: **third floor 2** *US and Canadian* the floor or storey of a building immediately above the ground floor. British equivalent: **first floor**

second generation *n* **1** offspring of parents born in a given country ▷ *modifier* **2** of an improved or refined stage of development in manufacture: *a second-generation robot*

second growth *or* **secondary growth** *n* natural regrowth of a forest after fire, cutting, or some other disturbance

second-guess *vb informal* **1** to criticize or evaluate with hindsight **2** to attempt to anticipate or predict (a person or thing) > 'second-'guesser *n*

second hand *n* a pointer on the face of a timepiece that indicates the seconds. Compare **hour hand, minute hand**

second-hand *adj* **1** previously owned or used **2** not from an original source or experience **3** dealing in or selling goods that are not new: *a second-hand car dealer* ▷ *adv* **4** from a source of previously owned or used goods: *he prefers to buy second-hand* **5** not directly: *he got the news second-hand*

second-homer *n* a person who owns another house in addition to their main home, often in an area where they are not native and used as a holiday home

Second International *n* **1 the** an international association of socialist parties and trade unions that began in Paris in 1889 and collapsed during World War I. The right-wing elements reassembled at Berne in 1919. See also **Labour and Socialist International 2** another name for the **Labour and Socialist International**

second language *n* **1** a language other than the mother tongue that a person or community uses

for public communication, esp in trade, higher education, and administration **2** a non-native language officially recognized and adopted in a multilingual country as a means of public communication

second lieutenant *n* an officer holding the lowest commissioned rank in the armed forces of certain nations

secondly ('sɛkəndlɪ) *adv* another word for **second¹**, usually used to precede the second item in a list of topics

second man *n* a person who assists the driver in crewing a locomotive

second mate *n* the next in command of a merchant vessel after the first mate. Also called: **second officer**

secondment (sɪ'kɒndmənt) *n Brit* a temporary transfer to another job or post within the same organization [C19 from French *en second* in second rank (or position)]

second mortgage *n* a mortgage incurred after a first mortgage and having second claim against the security

second name *n* another term for **surname** (sense 1)

second nature *n* a habit, characteristic, etc, not innate but so long practised or acquired as to seem so

secondo (sɛ'kɒndəʊ) *n, pl* **-di** (-di:) the left-hand part in a piano duet. Compare **primo** [Italian: SECOND¹]

second person *n* a grammatical category of pronouns and verbs used when referring to or describing the individual or individuals being addressed

second-rate *adj* **1** not of the highest quality; mediocre **2** second in importance, etc > 'second-'rater *n*

second reading *n* the second presentation of a bill in a legislative assembly, as to approve its general principles (in Britain), or to discuss a committee's report on it (in the US)

Second Republic *n* **1** the republican government of France from the deposition of Louis Philippe (1848) until the Second Empire (1852) **2** the period during which this form of government existed (1848–52)

second row *n* (*functioning as singular or plural*) *rugby union* **a** the forwards in the second row of a scrum **b** (*as modifier*): *a second-row forward*

second sight *n* the alleged ability to foresee the future, see actions taking place elsewhere, etc; clairvoyance > 'second-'sighted *adj* > 'second-'sightedness *n*

second-strike *adj* **1** (of a nuclear weapon) intended to be used in a counterattack in response to a nuclear attack **2** (of a strategy) based on the concept of surviving an initial nuclear attack with enough nuclear weaponry to retaliate

second string *n* **1** *chiefly Brit* an alternative course of action, etc, intended to come into use should the first fail (esp in the phrase **a second string to one's bow**) **2** a substitute or reserve player or team ▷ *adj* **second-string** *chiefly US and Canadian* **3** *sport* **a** being a substitute player **b** being the second-ranked player of a team in an individual sport **4** second-rate or inferior

second thought *n* (*usually plural*) a revised opinion or idea on a matter already considered

second wind (wɪnd) *n* **1** the return of the ability to breathe at a comfortable rate, esp following a period of exertion **2** renewed ability to continue in an effort

Second World War *n* another name for **World War II**

secrecy ('si:krɪsɪ) *n, pl* **-cies 1** the state or quality of being secret **2** the state of keeping something secret **3** the ability or tendency to keep things secret

secret ('si:krɪt) *adj* **1** kept hidden or separate from the knowledge of others. Related adj: **cryptic 2** known only to initiates: *a secret password* **3** hidden from general view or use: *a secret garden* **4** able or tending to keep things private or to oneself **5** operating without the knowledge of outsiders: *a secret society* **6** outside the normal range of knowledge ▷ *n* **7** something kept or to be kept hidden **8** something unrevealed; mystery **9** an underlying explanation, reason, etc, that is not apparent: *the secret of success* **10** a method, plan, etc, known only to initiates **11** *liturgy* a variable prayer, part of the Mass, said by the celebrant after the offertory and before the preface **12** in the secret. among the people who know a secret [C14 via Old French from Latin *sēcrētus* concealed, from *sēcernere* to sift; see SECERN] > 'secretly *adv*

secret agent *n* a person employed in espionage

secretagogue (sɪ'kriːtəgɒg) *n med* a substance that stimulates secretion > se,creta'gogic *adj*

secretaire (,sɛkrɪ'tɛə) *n* an enclosed writing desk, usually having an upper cabinet section [C19 from French *secrétaire*; see SECRETARY]

secretariat (,sɛkrɪ'tɛərɪət) *n* **1 a** an office responsible for the secretarial, clerical, and administrative affairs of a legislative body, executive council, or international organization **b** the staff of such an office **c** the building or rooms in which such an office is housed **2** a body of secretaries **3** a secretary's place of work; office **4** the position of a secretary [C19 via French from Medieval Latin *sēcrētāriātus*, from *sēcrētārius* SECRETARY]

secretary ('sɛkrətrɪ) *n, pl* -taries **1** a person who handles correspondence, keeps records, and does general clerical work for an individual, organization, etc **2** the official manager of the day-to-day business of a society or board **3** (in Britain) a senior civil servant who assists a government minister **4** (in the US and New Zealand) the head of a government administrative department **5** (in Britain) See **secretary of state 6** (in Australia) the head of a public service department **7** *diplomacy* the assistant to an ambassador or diplomatic minister of certain countries **8** another name for **secretaire** [C14 from Medieval Latin *sēcrētārius*, from Latin *sēcrētum* something hidden; see SECRET] > secretarial (,sɛkrɪ'tɛərɪəl) *adj* > 'secretaryship *n*

secretary bird *n* a large African long-legged diurnal bird of prey, *Sagittarius serpentarius*, having a crest and tail of long feathers and feeding chiefly on snakes: family *Sagittariidae*, order *Falconiformes* (hawks, falcons, etc) [C18 so called because its crest resembles a group of quill pens stuck behind the ear]

secretary-general *n, pl* secretaries-general a chief administrative official, as of the United Nations

secretary of state *n* **1** (in Britain) the head of any of several government departments **2** (in the US) the head of the government department in charge of foreign affairs (**State Department**) **3** (in certain US states) an official with various duties, such as keeping records

secrete[1] (sɪ'kriːt) *vb* (of a cell, organ, etc) to synthesize and release (a secretion) [C18 back formation from SECRETION] > se'cretor *n*

secrete[2] (sɪ'kriːt) *vb (tr)* to put in a hiding place [C18 variant of obsolete *secret* to hide away; see SECRET (n)]

secret history *n* a version of historical events which differs from the official or commonly accepted record and purports to be the true version. Also called: shadow history

secretin (sɪ'kriːtɪn) *n* a peptic hormone secreted by the mucosae of the duodenum and jejunum when food passes from the stomach [C20 from SECRETION + -IN]

secretion (sɪ'kriːʃən) *n* **1** a substance that is released from a cell, esp a glandular cell, and is synthesized in the cell **2** the process involved in producing and releasing such a substance from the cell [C17 from Medieval Latin *sēcrētiō*, from Latin: a separation; see SECERN] > se'cretionary *adj*

secretive ('siːkrɪtɪv, sɪ'kriːtɪv) *adj* **1** inclined to secrecy; reticent **2** another word for **secretory** > 'secretively *adv* > 'secretiveness *n*

secretory (sɪ'kriːtərɪ) *adj* of, relating to, or producing a secretion: *a secretory cell; secretory function*

secret police *n* a police force that operates relatively secretly to check subversion or political dissent

secret Santa *n* **a** a system whereby each member of a group chooses at random another member of the group for whom to buy a Christmas present at an agreed cost, so that each member buys one present and receives one present **b** a person chosen in this way to buy another person's Christmas present

secret service *n* **1** a government agency or department that conducts intelligence or counterintelligence operations **2** such operations

Secret Service *n* a US government agency responsible for the protection of the president, the suppression of counterfeiting, and certain other police activities

secret society *n* a society or organization that conceals its rites, activities, etc, from those who are not members

sect (sɛkt) *n* **1** a subdivision of a larger religious group (esp the Christian Church as a whole) the members of which have to some extent diverged from the rest by developing deviating beliefs, practices, etc **2** *often disparaging* **a** a schismatic religious body characterized by an attitude of exclusivity in contrast to the more inclusive religious groups called denominations or Churches **b** a religious group regarded as extreme or heretical **3** a group of people with a common interest, doctrine, etc; faction [C14 from Latin *secta* faction, following, from the stem of *sequī* to follow]

-sect *vb combining form* to cut or divide, esp into a specified number of parts: *trisect* [from Latin *sectus* cut, from *secāre* to cut; see SAW[1]]

sectarian (sɛk'tɛərɪən) *adj* **1** of, belonging or relating to, or characteristic of sects or sectaries **2** adhering to a particular sect, faction, or doctrine **3** narrow-minded, esp as a result of rigid adherence to a particular sect ▷ *n* **4** a member of a sect or faction, esp one who is bigoted in his adherence to its doctrines or in his intolerance towards other sects, etc > sec'tarian,ism *n*

sectarianize *or* **sectarianise** (sɛk'tɛərɪə,naɪz) *vb (tr)* to render sectarian

sectary ('sɛktərɪ) *n, pl* -taries **1** a member of a sect, esp a person who belongs to a religious sect that is regarded as heretical or schismatic **2** a person excessively devoted to a particular sect **3** a member of a Nonconformist denomination, esp one that is small [C16 from Medieval Latin *sectārius*, from Latin *secta* SECT]

sectile ('sɛktaɪl) *adj* able to be cut smoothly [C18 from Latin *sectilis*, from *secāre* to cut] > sectility (sɛk'tɪlɪtɪ) *n*

section ('sɛkʃən) *n* **1** a part cut off or separated from the main body of something **2** a part or subdivision of a piece of writing, book, etc: *the sports section of the newspaper* **3** one of several component parts **4** a distinct part or subdivision of a country, community, etc **5** *US and Canadian* an area one mile square (640 acres) in a public survey, esp in the western parts of the US and Canada **6** *NZ* a plot of land for building on, esp in a suburban area **7** the section of a railway track that is maintained by a single crew or is controlled by a particular signal box **8** the act or process of cutting or separating by cutting **9** a representation of a portion of a building or object exposed when cut by an imaginary vertical plane so as to show its construction and interior **10** *geometry* **a** a plane surface formed by cutting through a solid **b** the shape or area of such a plane surface. Compare **cross section** (sense 1) **11** *surgery* any procedure involving the cutting or

division of an organ, structure, or part, such as a Caesarian section **12** a thin slice of biological tissue, mineral, etc, prepared for examination by a microscope **13** a segment of an orange or other citrus fruit **14** a small military formation, typically comprising two or more squads or aircraft **15** *Austral and NZ* a fare stage on a bus, tram, etc **16** *music* **a** an extended division of a composition or movement that forms a coherent part of the structure: *the development section* **b** a division in an orchestra, band, etc, containing instruments belonging to the same class: *the brass section* **17** Also called: signature, gathering, gather, quire a folded printing sheet or sheets ready for gathering and binding ▷ *vb (tr)* **18** to cut or divide into sections **19** to cut through so as to reveal a section **20** (in drawing, esp mechanical drawing) to shade so as to indicate sections **21** *surgery* to cut or divide (an organ, structure, or part) **22** *Brit social welfare* to have (a mentally disturbed person) confined in a mental hospital under an appropriate section of the mental health legislation [C16 from Latin *sectiō*, from *secāre* to cut]

sectional ('sɛkʃənᵊl) *adj* **1** composed of several sections **2** of or relating to a section > 'sectionally *adv*

sectionalism ('sɛkʃənə,lɪzəm) *n* excessive or narrow-minded concern for local or regional interests as opposed to the interests of the whole > 'sectionalist *n, adj*

sectionalize *or* **sectionalise** ('sɛkʃənə,laɪz) *vb (tr)* **1** to render sectional **2** to divide into sections, esp geographically > ,sectionali'zation *or* ,sectionali'sation *n*

section mark *n printing* a mark (§) inserted into text matter to draw attention to a footnote or to indicate a section of a book, etc. Also called: section

sector ('sɛktə) *n* **1** a part or subdivision, esp of a society or an economy: *the private sector* **2** *geometry* either portion of a circle included between two radii and an arc. Area: $\frac{1}{2}r^2\theta$, where *r* is the radius and θ is the central angle subtended by the arc (in radians) **3** a measuring instrument consisting of two graduated arms hinged at one end **4** a part or subdivision of an area of military operations **5** *computing* the smallest addressable portion of the track on a magnetic tape, disk, or drum store [C16 from Late Latin: sector, from Latin: a cutter, from *secāre* to cut] > 'sectoral *adj*

sectorial (sɛk'tɔːrɪəl) *adj* **1** of or relating to a sector **2** *zoology* **a** adapted for cutting: *the sectorial teeth of carnivores* **b** designating a vein in the wing of an insect that links certain branches of the radius vein

secular ('sɛkjʊlə) *adj* **1** of or relating to worldly as opposed to sacred things; temporal **2** not concerned with or related to religion **3** not within the control of the Church **4** (of an education, etc) **a** having no particular religious affinities **b** not including compulsory religious studies or services **5** (of clerics) not bound by religious vows to a monastic or other order **6** occurring or appearing once in an age or century **7** lasting for a long time **8** *astronomy* occurring slowly over a long period of time: *the secular perturbation of a planet's orbit* ▷ *n* **9** a member of the secular clergy **10** another word for **layman** [C13 from Old French *seculer*, from Late Latin *saeculāris* temporal, from Latin: concerning an age, from *saeculum* an age] > 'secularly *adv*

secularism ('sɛkjʊlə,rɪzəm) *n* **1** *philosophy* a doctrine that rejects religion, esp in ethics **2** the attitude that religion should have no place in civil affairs **3** the state of being secular > 'secularist *n, adj* > ,secular'istic *adj*

secularity (,sɛkjʊ'lærɪtɪ) *n, pl* -ties **1** the state or condition of being secular **2** interest in or adherence to secular things **3** a secular concern or matter

secularize *or* **secularise** ('sɛkjʊlə,raɪz) *vb (tr)* **1** to change from religious or sacred to secular functions, etc **2** to dispense from allegiance to a religious order **3** *law* to transfer (property) from ecclesiastical to civil possession or use **4** *English legal history* to transfer (an offender) from the jurisdiction of the ecclesiastical courts to that of the civil courts for the imposition of a more severe punishment > ,seculari'zation *or* ,seculari'sation *n* > 'secular,izer *or* 'secular,iser *n*

secund (sɪ'kʌnd) *adj botany* having or designating parts arranged on or turned to one side of the axis [c18 from Latin *secundus* following, from *sequī* to follow; see SECOND[1]] > se'cundly *adv*

Secunderabad (sə'kʌndərə,bæd, -,bɑːd) *n* a former town in S central India, in N Andra Pradesh: one of the largest British military stations in India: now part of Hyderabad city

secundine ('sɛkən,daɪn, -dɪn) *n botany, now rare* one of the two integuments surrounding the ovule of a plant [c17 from Late Latin *secundīnae*, from Latin *secundus* following + -INE. See SECOND[1]]

secundines ('sɛkən,daɪnz, sɪ'kʌndɪnz) *pl n physiol* a technical word for **afterbirth** [c14 from Late Latin *secundīnae*, from Latin *secundus* following; see SECOND[1]]

secure (sɪ'kjʊə) *adj* **1** free from danger, damage, etc **2** free from fear, care, etc **3** in safe custody **4** not likely to fail, become loose, etc **5** able to be relied on; certain: *a secure investment* **6** *nautical* stowed away or made inoperative **7** *archaic* careless or overconfident ▷ *vb* **8** (*tr*) to obtain or get possession of: *I will secure some good seats* **9** (when *intr*, often foll by *against*) to make or become free from danger, fear, etc **10** (*tr*) to make fast or firm; fasten **11** (when *intr*, often foll by *against*) to make or become certain; guarantee: *this plan will secure your happiness* **12** (*tr*) to assure (a creditor) of payment, as by giving security **13** (*tr*) to make (a military position) safe from attack **14** *nautical* to make (a vessel or its contents) safe or ready by battening down hatches, stowing gear, etc **15** (*tr*) *nautical* to stow or make inoperative: *to secure the radio* [c16 from Latin *sēcūrus* free from care, from *sē-* without + *cūra* care] > se'curable *adj* > se'curely *adv* > se'curement *n* > se'cureness *n* > se'curer *n*

secure tenancy *n social welfare* (in Britain) the letting of a dwelling by a nonprivate landlord, usually a local council or housing association, under an agreement that allows security of tenure, subletting, improvements made to the property by the tenant without consequent rent increase, and the right to buy the dwelling at a discount after three years' occupancy

secure unit *n* an establishment providing secure accommodation, education and training, psychiatric help, etc for offenders and people who are mentally ill

Securities and Exchange Commission *n* a US federal agency established in 1934 to supervise and regulate issues of and transactions in securities and to prosecute illegal stock manipulations. Abbreviation: SEC

Securities and Investments Board *n* (from 1986 to 1997) a British regulatory body that oversaw London's financial markets, each of which has its own self-regulatory organization: replaced by the Financial Services Authority. Abbreviation: SIB

securitization *or* **securitisation** (sɪ,kjʊərɪtaɪ'zeɪʃən) *n finance* the use of such securities as eurobonds to enable investors to lend directly to borrowers with a minimum of risk but without using banks as intermediaries

security (sɪ'kjʊərɪtɪ) *n, pl* **-ties** **1** the state of being secure **2** assured freedom from poverty or want: *he needs the security of a permanent job* **3** a person or thing that secures, guarantees, etc **4** precautions taken to ensure against theft, espionage, etc: *the security in the government offices was not very good* **5** (*often plural*) **a** a certificate of creditorship or property carrying the right to receive interest or dividend, such as shares or bonds **b** the financial asset represented by such a certificate **6** the

specific asset that a creditor can claim title to in the event of default on an obligation **7** something given or pledged to secure the fulfilment of a promise or obligation **8** a person who undertakes to fulfil another person's obligation **9** the protection of data to ensure that only authorized personnel have access to computer files **10** *archaic* carelessness or overconfidence

security blanket *n* **1** a policy of temporary secrecy by police or those in charge of security, in order to protect a person, place, etc, threatened with danger, from further risk **2** a baby's blanket, soft toy, etc, to which a baby or young child becomes very attached, using it as a comforter **3** *informal* anything used or thought of as providing reassurance

Security Council *n* a permanent organ of the United Nations established to maintain world peace. It consists of five permanent members (China, France, Russia, the UK, and the US) and ten nonpermanent members

security guard *n* a person employed to protect buildings, people, etc, and to collect and deliver large sums of money

security of tenure *n* (in Britain) the right of a tenant to continue to occupy a dwelling or site unless the landlord obtains a court order for possession of the property or termination of the tenancy agreement

security risk *n* a person deemed to be a threat to state security in that he could be open to pressure, have subversive political beliefs, etc

securocrat (sɪ'kjʊərəʊ,kræt) *n* a military or police officer who has the power to influence government policy

secy *or* **sec'y** *abbreviation for* secretary

sedan (sɪ'dæn) *n* **1** *US, Canadian, and NZ* a closed two-door or four-door car with four to six seats. Also called (in Britain and certain other countries): saloon **2** short for **sedan chair** [c17 of uncertain origin; compare Latin *sēdēs* seat]

Sedan (*French* sədɑ̃; *English* sɪ'dæn) *n* a town in NE France, on the River Meuse: passed to France in 1642; a Protestant stronghold (16th–17th centuries); scene of a French defeat (1870) during the Franco-Prussian War and of a battle (1940) in World War II, which began the German invasion of France. Pop: 20 548 (1999)

sedan chair *n* a closed chair for one passenger, carried on poles by two bearers. It was commonly used in the 17th and 18th centuries. Sometimes shortened to: sedan

sedate[1] (sɪ'deɪt) *adj* **1** habitually calm and composed in manner; serene **2** staid, sober, or decorous [c17 from Latin *sēdāre* to soothe; related to *sedēre* to sit] > se'dately *adv* > se'dateness *n*

sedate[2] (sɪ'deɪt) *vb* (*tr*) to administer a sedative to [c20 back formation from SEDATIVE]

sedation (sɪ'deɪʃən) *n* **1** a state of calm or reduced nervous activity **2** the administration of a sedative

sedative ('sɛdətɪv) *adj* **1** having a soothing or calming effect **2** of or relating to sedation ▷ *n* **3** *med* a sedative drug or agent [c15 from Medieval Latin *sēdātīvus*, from Latin *sēdātus* assuaged; see SEDATE[1]]

sedentary ('sɛdᵊntərɪ, -trɪ) *adj* **1** characterized by or requiring a sitting position: *sedentary work* **2** tending to sit about without taking much exercise **3** (of animals) moving about very little, usually because of attachment to a rock or other surface **4** (of animals) not migratory [c16 from Latin *sedentārius*, from *sedēre* to sit] > 'sedentarily *adv* > 'sedentariness *n*

Seder ('seɪdə) *n Judaism* a ceremonial meal with prescribed ritual reading of the Haggadah observed in Jewish homes on the first night or first two nights of Passover [from Hebrew *sēdher* order]

sederunt (sɪ'derʊnt, sɪ'dɛərənt) *n* (in Scotland) **1** a sitting of an ecclesiastical assembly, court, etc **2**

the list of persons present [c17 from Latin *sēdērunt* they were sitting, from *sedēre* to sit]

sedge (sɛdʒ) *n* **1** any grasslike cyperaceous plant of the genus *Carex*, typically growing on wet ground and having rhizomes, triangular stems, and minute flowers in spikelets **2** any other plant of the family *Cyperaceae* [Old English *secg*; related to Middle High German *segge* sedge, Old English *sagu* SAW[1]] > 'sedgy *adj*

sedge fly *n* an angler's name for various caddis flies, notably the grey sedge, the murragh, and the cinnamon sedge

Sedgemoor ('sɛdʒ,mʊə) *n* a low-lying plain in SW England, in central Somerset: scene of the defeat (1685) of the Duke of Monmouth

sedge warbler *n* a European songbird, *Acrocephalus schoenobaenus*, of reed beds and swampy areas, having a streaked brownish plumage with white eye stripes: family *Muscicapidae* (Old World flycatchers, etc)

sedilia (sɛ'daɪlɪə) *n* (*functioning as singular*) the group of three seats, each called a **sedile** (sɛ'daɪlɪ), often recessed, on the south side of a sanctuary where the celebrant and ministers sit at certain points during High Mass [c18 from Latin, from *sedīle* a chair, from *sedēre* to sit]

sediment ('sɛdɪmənt) *n* **1** matter that settles to the bottom of a liquid **2** material that has been deposited from water, ice, or wind [c16 from Latin *sedimentum* a settling, from *sedēre* to sit] > sedimentous (,sɛdɪ'mɛntəs) *adj*

sedimentary (,sɛdɪ'mɛntərɪ) *adj* **1** characteristic of, resembling, or containing sediment **2** (of rocks) formed by the accumulation and consolidation of mineral and organic fragments that have been deposited by water, ice, or wind. Compare **igneous**, **metamorphic** > ,sedi'mentarily *adv*

sedimentation (,sɛdɪmɛn'teɪʃən) *n* **1** the process of formation of sedimentary rocks **2** the deposition or production of sediment **3** *chem, biochem* the process by which large molecules or macroscopic particles are concentrated in a centrifugal field in a centrifuge or ultracentrifuge

sedimentation tank *n* a tank into which sewage is passed to allow suspended solid matter to separate out

sedimentology (,sɛdɪmɛn'tɒlədʒɪ) *n* the branch of geology concerned with sedimentary rocks and deposits > ,sedimen'tologist *n*

sedition (sɪ'dɪʃən) *n* **1** speech or behaviour directed against the peace of a state **2** an offence that tends to undermine the authority of a state **3** an incitement to public disorder **4** *archaic* revolt [c14 from Latin *sēditiō* discord, from *sēd-* apart + *itiō* a going, from *īre* to go] > se'ditionary *n, adj*

seditious (sɪ'dɪʃəs) *adj* **1** of, like, or causing sedition **2** inclined to or taking part in sedition > se'ditiously *adv* > se'ditiousness *n*

Sedna ('sɛdnə) *n* a large planet-like object discovered in 2003, orbiting the sun but considerably beyond Pluto [c21 after the Inuit goddess of the ocean]

seduce (sɪ'djuːs) *vb* (*tr*) **1** to persuade to engage in sexual intercourse **2** to lead astray, as from the right action **3** to win over, attract, or lure [c15 from Latin *sēdūcere* to lead apart, from *sē-* apart + *dūcere* to lead] > se'ducible *or* se'duceable *adj*

seducer (sɪ'djuːsə) *or feminine* **seductress** (sɪ'dʌktrɪs) *n* a person who entices, allures, or seduces, esp one who entices another to engage in sexual intercourse

seduction (sɪ'dʌkʃən) *n* **1** the act of seducing or the state of being seduced **2** a means of seduction

seductive (sɪ'dʌktɪv) *adj* tending to seduce or capable of seducing; enticing; alluring > se'ductively *adv* > se'ductiveness *n*

sedulous ('sɛdjʊləs) *adj* constant or persistent in use or attention; assiduous; diligent [c16 from Latin *sēdulus*, of uncertain origin] > sedulity (sɪ'djuːlɪtɪ) *or* 'sedulousness *n* > 'sedulously *adv*

sedum ('siːdəm) *n* any crassulaceous rock plant of

the genus *Sedum*, having thick fleshy leaves and clusters of white, yellow, or pink flowers. See also **stonecrop, rose-root, orpine** [C15 from Latin: houseleek]

see[1] (siː) *vb* **sees, seeing, saw, seen** **1** to perceive with the eyes **2** (when *tr*, *may take a clause as object*) to perceive (an idea) mentally; understand: *I explained the problem but he could not see it* **3** (*tr*) to perceive with any or all of the senses: *I hate to see you so unhappy* **4** (*tr*; *may take a clause as object*) to be aware of in advance; foresee: *I can see what will happen if you don't help* **5** (when *tr*, *may take a clause as object*) to ascertain or find out (a fact); learn: *see who is at the door* **6** (when *tr*, *takes a clause as object*; when *intr*, foll by *to*) to make sure (of something) or take care (of something): *see that he gets to bed early* **7** (when *tr*, *may take a clause as object*) to consider, deliberate, or decide: *see if you can come next week* **8** (*tr*) to have experience of; undergo: *he had seen much unhappiness in his life* **9** (*tr*) to allow to be in a specified condition: *I cannot stand by and see a child in pain* **10** (*tr*) to be characterized by: *this period of history has seen much unrest* **11** (*tr*) to meet or pay a visit to: *to see one's solicitor* **12** (*tr*) to receive, esp as a guest or visitor: *the Prime Minister will see the deputation now* **13** (*tr*) to frequent the company of: *she is seeing a married man* **14** (*tr*) to accompany or escort: *I saw her to the door* **15** (*tr*) to refer to or look up: *for further information see the appendix* **16** (in gambling, esp in poker) to match (another player's bet) or match the bet of (another player) by staking an equal sum **17** **as far as I can see** to the best of my judgment or understanding **18** **see fit** (*takes an infinitive*) to consider proper, desirable, etc: *I don't see fit to allow her to come here* **19** **see (someone) hanged** *or* **damned first** *informal* to refuse absolutely to do what one has been asked **20** **see (someone) right** *Brit informal* to ensure fair treatment of (someone): *if he has cheated you, I'll see you right* **21** **see the light (of day)**. See **light**[1] (sense 24) **22** **see you, see you later,** *or* **be seeing you** an expression of farewell **23** **you see** *informal* a parenthetical filler phrase used to make a pause in speaking or add slight emphasis ▷ See also **see about, see into, see of, see off, see out, see over, see through** [Old English *sēon*; related to Old Norse *sjā*, Gothic *saihwan*, Old Saxon *sehan*] > 'seeable *adj*

see[2] (siː) *n* the diocese of a bishop, or the place within it where his cathedral or procathedral is situated. See also **Holy See** [C13 from Old French *sed*, from Latin *sēdēs* a seat; related to *sedēre* to sit]

see about *vb* (*intr, preposition*) **1** to take care of; look after: *he couldn't see about the matter because he was ill* **2** to investigate; enquire into: *to see about a new car*

Seebeck ('siːbɛk) *n philately* **1** any of a set of stamps issued (1890–99) in Nicaragua, Honduras, Ecuador, and El Salvador and named after Nicholas Frederick Seebeck, who provided them free to the respective governments **2** any of the reprints issued later for personal gain by Seebeck

Seebeck effect ('siːbɛk; *German* 'zeːbɛk) *n* the phenomenon in which a current is produced in a circuit containing two or more different metals when the junctions between the metals are maintained at different temperatures. Also called: **thermoelectric effect** Compare **Peltier effect** [C19 named after Thomas *Seebeck* (1770–1831), German physicist]

seed (siːd) *n* **1** *botany* a mature fertilized plant ovule, consisting of an embryo and its food store surrounded by a protective seed coat (testa). Related adj: **seminal** **2** the small hard seedlike fruit of plants such as wheat **3** (loosely) any propagative part of a plant, such as a tuber, spore, or bulb **4** such parts collectively **5** the source, beginning, or germ of anything: *the seeds of revolt* **6** *chiefly Bible* offspring or descendants: *the seed of Abraham* **7** an archaic or dialect term for **sperm** *or* **semen** **8** *sport* a seeded player **9** the egg cell or cells of the lobster and certain other animals **10** See **seed oyster** **11** *chem* a small crystal added to a supersaturated solution or supercooled liquid to induce crystallization **12** **go** *or* **run to seed** **a** (of plants) to produce and shed seeds **b** to lose vigour, usefulness, etc ▷ *vb* **13** to plant (seeds, grain, etc) in (soil): *we seeded this field with oats* **14** (*intr*) (of plants) to form or shed seeds **15** (*tr*) to remove the seeds from (fruit, etc) **16** (*tr*) *chem* to add a small crystal to (a supersaturated solution or supercooled liquid) in order to cause crystallization **17** (*tr*) to scatter certain substances, such as silver iodide, in (clouds) in order to cause rain **18** (*tr*) **a** to arrange (the draw of a tournament) so that outstanding teams or players will not meet in the early rounds **b** to distribute (players or teams) in this manner [Old English *sǣd*; related to Old Norse *sāth*, Gothic *sēths*, Old High German *sāt*] > 'seed,like *adj* > 'seedless *adj*

SEED *abbreviation for* Scottish Executive Education Department

seedbed ('siːd,bɛd) *n* **1** a plot of land in which seeds or seedlings are grown before being transplanted **2** the place where something develops: *the seedbed of discontent*

seedcake ('siːd,keɪk) *n* a sweet cake flavoured with caraway seeds and lemon rind or essence

seed capital *n finance* a small amount of capital required to finance the research necessary to produce a business plan for a new company

seed capsule *or* **seedcase** ('siːd,keɪs) *n* the part of a fruit enclosing the seeds; pericarp

seed coat *n* the nontechnical name for **testa**

seed coral *n* small pieces of coral used in jewellery, etc

seed corn *n* **1** the good quality ears or kernels of corn that are used as seed **2** assets or investments that are expected to provide profits in the future

seeder ('siːdə) *n* **1** a person or thing that seeds **2** a device used to remove seeds, as from fruit, etc **3** any of various devices for sowing grass seed or grain on the surface of the ground

seed fern *n* another name for **pteridosperm**

seed leaf *n* the nontechnical name for **cotyledon**

seedling ('siːdlɪŋ) *n* a very young plant produced from a seed

seed money *n* money used for the establishment of an enterprise

seed oyster *n* a young oyster, esp a cultivated oyster, ready for transplantation

seed pearl *n* a tiny pearl weighing less than a quarter of a grain

seed plant *n* any plant that reproduces by means of seeds: a gymnosperm or angiosperm

seed pod *n* a carpel or pistil enclosing the seeds of a plant, esp a flowering plant

seed potato *n* a potato tuber used for planting

seed vessel *n botany* a dry fruit, such as a capsule

seedy ('siːdɪ) *adj* **seedier, seediest** **1** shabby or unseemly in appearance: *seedy clothes* **2** (of a plant) at the stage of producing seeds **3** *informal* not physically fit; sickly > 'seedily *adv* > 'seediness *n*

seeing ('siːɪŋ) *n* **1** the sense or faculty of sight; vision **2** *astronomy* the quality of the observing conditions (especially the turbulence of the atmosphere) during an astronomical observation ▷ *conj* **3** (*subordinating*; often foll by *that*) in light of the fact (that); inasmuch as; since

USAGE The use of *seeing as how* as in *seeing as (how) the bus is always late, I don't need any reason to hurry* is generally thought to be incorrect or non-standard

seeing-eye dog *n* the US name for **guide dog**

see into *vb* (*intr, preposition*) **1** to examine or investigate **2** to discover the true nature of: *I can't see into your thoughts*

seek (siːk) *vb* **seeks, seeking, sought** (*mainly tr*) **1** (when *intr*, often foll by *for* or *after*) to try to find by searching; look for: *to seek a solution* **2** (*also intr*) to try to obtain or acquire: *to seek happiness* **3** to attempt (to do something); try: *I'm only seeking to help* **4** (*also intr*) to enquire about or request (something): *to seek help* **5** to go or resort to: *to seek the garden for peace* **6** an archaic word for **explore** [Old English *sēcan*; related to Old Norse *sōkja*, Gothic *sōkjan*, Old High German *suohhen*, Latin *sāgīre* to perceive by scent; see BESEECH] > 'seeker *n*

seek out *vb* (*tr, adverb*) to search hard for a specific person or thing and find: *she sought out her friend from amongst the crowd*

seel (siːl) *vb* (*tr*) **1** to sew up the eyelids of (a hawk or falcon) so as to render it quiet and tame **2** *obsolete* to close up the eyes of, esp by blinding [C15 *silen*, from Old French *ciller*, from Medieval Latin *ciliāre*, from Latin *cilium* an eyelid]

Seeland ('zeːlant) *n* the German name for **Zealand**

seelie ('siːlɪ) *pl n* **the** **1** good benevolent fairies ▷ *adj* **2** **a** of or belonging to the seelie **b** good and benevolent like the seelie: *seelie wights* [an earlier form of SILLY]

seem (siːm) *vb* (may take an infinitive) **1** (*copula*) to appear to the mind or eye; look: *this seems nice; the car seems to be running well* **2** to give the impression of existing; appear to be: *there seems no need for all this nonsense* **3** used to diminish the force of a following infinitive to be polite, more noncommittal, etc: *I can't seem to get through to you* [C12 perhaps from Old Norse *soma* to beseem, from *sæmr* befitting; related to Old English *sēman* to reconcile; see SAME] > 'seemer *n*

USAGE See at **like**[1]

seeming ('siːmɪŋ) *adj* **1** (*prenominal*) apparent but not actual or genuine: *seeming honesty* ▷ *n* **2** outward or false appearance > 'seemingness *n*

seemingly ('siːmɪŋlɪ) *adv* **1** in appearance but not necessarily in actuality: *with seemingly effortless ease* **2** (*sentence modifier*) apparently; as far as one knows: *seemingly, he had few friends left*

seemly ('siːmlɪ) *adj* **-lier, -liest** **1** proper or fitting **2** *obsolete* pleasing or handsome in appearance ▷ *adv* **3** *archaic* properly or decorously [C13 from Old Norse *sæomiligr*, from *sæmr* befitting] > 'seemliness *n*

seen (siːn) *vb* the past participle of **see**

see of *vb* (*tr, preposition*) to meet; be in contact with: *we haven't seen much of him since he got married*

see off *vb* (*tr, adverb*) **1** to be present at the departure of (a person making a journey) **2** *informal* to cause to leave or depart, esp by force

see out *vb* (*tr, adverb*) **1** to remain or endure until the end of: *we'll see the first half of the game out and then leave* **2** to be present at the departure of (a person from a house, room, etc)

see over *or* **round** *vb* (*intr, preposition*) to inspect by making a tour of: *she said she'd like to see over the house*

seep (siːp) *vb* **1** (*intr*) to pass gradually or leak through or as if through small openings; ooze ▷ *n* **2** a small spring or place where water, oil, etc, has oozed through the ground **3** another word for **seepage** [Old English *sīpian*; related to Middle High German *sīfen*, Swedish dialect *sipa*]

seepage ('siːpɪdʒ) *n* **1** the act or process of seeping **2** liquid or moisture that has seeped

seer[1] (sɪə) *n* **1** a person who can supposedly see into the future; prophet **2** a person who professes supernatural powers **3** a person who sees > 'seeress *fem n*

seer[2] (sɪə) *n* a variant spelling of **ser**

seersucker ('sɪə,sʌkə) *n* a light cotton, linen, or other fabric with a crinkled surface and often striped [C18 from Hindi *śīrśakar*, from Persian *shīr o shakkar*, literally: milk and sugar]

seesaw ('siː,sɔː) *n* **1** a plank balanced in the middle so that two people seated on the ends can ride up and down by pushing on the ground with their feet **2** the pastime of riding up and down on a seesaw **3** **a** an up-and-down or back-and-forth movement **b** (*as modifier*): *a seesaw movement* ▷ *vb* **4** (*intr*) to move up and down or back and forth in such a manner; oscillate [C17 reduplication of SAW[1], alluding to the movement from side to side, as in sawing]

seethe (siːð) *vb* **1** (*intr*) to boil or to foam as if

boiling **2** (*intr*) to be in a state of extreme agitation, esp through anger **3** (*tr*) to soak in liquid **4** (*tr*) *archaic* to cook or extract the essence of (a food) by boiling ▷ *n* **5** the act or state of seething [Old English *sēothan*; related to Old Norse *sjōtha*, Old High German *siodan* to seethe]
seething (ˈsiːðɪŋ) *adj* **1** boiling or foaming as if boiling **2** crowded and full of restless activity **3** in a state of extreme agitation, esp through anger > ˈ**seethingly** *adv*
see through *vb* **1** (*tr*) to help out in time of need or trouble: *I know you're short of money, but I'll see you through* **2** (*tr, adverb*) to remain with until the end or completion: *let's see the job through* **3** (*intr, preposition*) to perceive the true nature of: *I can see through your evasion* ▷ *adj* **see-through** **4** partly or wholly transparent or translucent, esp (of clothes) in a titillating way: *a see-through nightie*
sefer (ˈsɛfɛr, ˈseɪfɛr) *n Judaism* **1** In full: **sefer torah** the scrolls of the Law **2** any book of Hebrew religious literature [from Hebrew, literally: book]
Sefton (ˈsɛftᵊn) *n* a unitary authority in NW England, in Merseyside. Pop: 281 600 (2003 est). Area: 150 sq km (58 sq miles)
segment *n* (ˈsɛgmənt) **1** *maths* **a** a part of a line or curve between two points **b** a part of a plane or solid figure cut off by an intersecting line, plane, or planes, esp one between a chord and an arc of a circle **2** one of several parts or sections into which an object is divided; portion **3** *zoology* any of the parts into which the body or appendages of an annelid or arthropod are divided **4** *linguistics* a speech sound considered in isolation ▷ *vb* (sɛgˈmɛnt) **5** to cut or divide (a whole object) into segments [c16 from Latin *segmentum*, from *secāre* to cut] > **segmentary** (ˈsɛgməntərɪ, -trɪ) *adj*
segmental (sɛgˈmɛntᵊl) *adj* **1** of, like, or having the form of a segment **2** divided into segments **3** *linguistics* of, relating to, or constituting an isolable speech sound > segˈ**mentally** *adv*
segmentation (ˌsɛgmɛnˈteɪʃən) *n* **1** the act or an instance of dividing into segments **2** *embryol* another name for **cleavage** (sense 4) **3** *zoology* another name for **metamerism** (sense 1)
segmentation cavity *n* another name for **blastocoel**
segno (ˈsɛnjəʊ; *Italian* ˈseɲɲo) *n, pl* **-gni** (-njiː; *Italian* -ɲɲi) *music* a sign at the beginning or end of a section directed to be repeated. Symbol: 𝄋 *or* :S: [Italian: a sign, from Latin *signum*]
Segovia (sɪˈgəʊvɪə; *Spanish* seˈɣoβja) *n* a town in central Spain: site of a Roman aqueduct, still in use, and the fortified palace of the kings of Castile (the Alcázar). Pop: 55 640 (2003 est)
segregate (ˈsɛgrɪˌgeɪt) *vb* **1** to set or be set apart from others or from the main group **2** (*tr*) to impose segregation on (a racial or minority group) **3** *genetics, metallurgy* to undergo or cause to undergo segregation [c16 from Latin *sēgregāre*, from *sē-* apart + *grex* a flock] > **segregable** (ˈsɛgrɪgəbᵊl) *adj* > ˈ**segreˌgative** *adj* > ˈ**segreˌgator** *n*
segregation (ˌsɛgrɪˈgeɪʃən) *n* **1** the act of segregating or state of being segregated **2** *sociol* the practice or policy of creating separate facilities within the same society for the use of a minority group **3** *genetics* the separation at meiosis of the two members of any pair of alleles into separate gametes. See also **Mendel's laws** **4** *metallurgy* the process in which a component of an alloy or solid solution separates in small regions within the solid or on the solid's surface > ˌ**segreˈgational** *adj*
segregationist (ˌsɛgrɪˈgeɪʃənɪst) *n* a person who favours, advocates, or practises racial segregation
segue (ˈsɛgweɪ) *vb* **segues, segueing, segued** (*intr*) **1** (often foll by *into*) to proceed from one section or piece of music to another without a break **2** (*imperative*) play on without pause: a musical direction ▷ *n* **3** the practice or an instance of playing music in this way [from Italian: follows, from *seguire* to follow, from Latin *sequī*]
seguidilla (ˌsɛgɪˈdiːljə) *n* **1** a Spanish dance in a fast triple rhythm **2** a piece of music composed for or in the rhythm of this dance **3** *prosody* a stanzaic form consisting of four to seven lines and marked by a characteristic rhythm [Spanish: a little dance, from *seguida* a dance, from *seguir* to follow, from Latin *sequī*]
seicento (*Italian* seiˈtʃɛnto) *n* the 17th century with reference to Italian art and literature [Italian, shortened from *mille seicento* one thousand six hundred]
seiche (seɪʃ) *n* a periodic oscillation of the surface of an enclosed or semienclosed body of water (lake, inland sea, bay, etc) caused by such phenomena as atmospheric pressure changes, winds, tidal currents, and earthquakes [c19 from Swiss French, first used to describe rise and fall of water in Lake Geneva; of obscure origin]
Seidlitz powder *or* **powders** (ˈsɛdlɪts) *n* a laxative consisting of two powders, tartaric acid and a mixture of sodium bicarbonate and Rochelle salt (sodium potassium tartrate). Also called: **Rochelle powder** [c19 named after *Seidlitz*, a village in Bohemia with mineral springs having similar laxative effects]
seif dune (seɪf) *n* (in deserts, esp the Sahara) a long ridge of blown sand, often several miles long [*seif*, from Arabic: sword, from the shape of the dune]
seigneur (sɛˈnjɜː; *French* sɛɲœr) *n* **1** a feudal lord, esp in France **2** (in French Canada, until 1854) the landlord of an estate that was subdivided among peasants who held their plots by a form of feudal tenure [c16 from Old French, from Vulgar Latin *senior*, from Latin: an elderly man; see SENIOR] > **seiˈgneurial** *adj*
seigneury (ˈseɪnjərɪ) *n, pl* **-gneuries** the estate of a seigneur
seignior (ˈseɪnjə) *n* **1** a less common name for a **seigneur** **2** (in England) the lord of a seigniory [c14 from Anglo-French *segnour*; see SEIGNEUR] > **seigniorial** (seɪˈnjɔːrɪəl) *adj*
seigniorage (ˈseɪnjərɪdʒ) *n* **1** something claimed by a sovereign or superior as a prerogative, right, or due **2** a fee payable to a government for coining bullion **3** the difference in value between the cost of bullion and the face value of the coin made from it
seigniory (ˈseɪnjərɪ) *or* **signory** (ˈsiːnjərɪ) *n, pl* **-gniories** *or* **-gnories** **1** less common names for a **seigneury** **2** (in England) the fee or manor of a seignior; a feudal domain **3** the authority of a seignior or the relationship between him and his tenants **4** a body of lords
seik (siːk) *adj* a Scot word for **sick**
seine (seɪn) *n* **1** a large fishing net that hangs vertically in the water by means of floats at the top and weights at the bottom ▷ *vb* **2** to catch (fish) using this net [Old English *segne*, from Latin *sagēna*, from Greek *sagēnē*; related to Old High German *segina*, Old French *saïne*]
Seine (seɪn; *French* sɛn) *n* a river in N France, rising on the Plateau de Langres and flowing northwest through Paris to the English Channel: the second longest river in France, linked by canal with the Rivers Somme, Scheldt, Meuse, Rhine, Saône, and Loire. Length: 776 km (482 miles)
Seine-et-Marne (*French* sɛnemarn) *n* a department of N central France, in Île-de-France region. Capital: Melun. Pop: 1 232 467 (2003 est). Area: 5931 sq km (2313 sq miles)
Seine-Maritime (*French* sɛnmaritim) *n* a department of N France, in Haute-Normandie region. Capital: Rouen. Pop: 1 237 263 (2003 est). Area: 6342 sq km (2473 sq miles)
Seine-Saint-Denis (*French* sɛnsɛ̃dni) *n* a department of N central France, in Île-de-France region. Capital: Bobigny. Pop: 1 396 122 (2003 est). Area: 236 sq km (92 sq miles)
seise *or US* **seize** (siːz) *vb* to put into legal possession of (property, etc) [variant of SEIZE] > ˈ**seisable** *adj* > ˈ**seiser** *n*
seisin *or US* **seizin** (ˈsiːzɪn) *n property law* feudal possession of an estate in land [c13 from Old French *seisine*, from *seisir* to SEIZE]
seism (ˈsaɪzəm) *n* a less common name for **earthquake** [c19 from Greek *seismos*, from *seiein* to shake]
seismic (ˈsaɪzmɪk) *adj* **1** Also (less commonly): **seismical** (ˈsaɪzmɪkᵊl) relating to or caused by earthquakes or artificially produced earth tremors **2** of enormous proportions or having highly significant consequences: *seismic social change* > ˈ**seismically** *adv*
seismic array *n* a system of linked seismographs arranged in a regular geometric pattern to increase sensitivity to earthquake detection
seismicity (saɪzˈmɪsɪtɪ) *n* seismic activity; the phenomenon of earthquake activity or the occurrence of artificially produced earth tremors
seismic wave *n* an earth vibration generated by an earthquake or explosion
seismo- *or before a vowel* **seism-** *combining form* earthquake: *seismology* [from Greek *seismos*]
seismograph (ˈsaɪzməˌgrɑːf, -ˌgræf) *n* an instrument that registers and records the features of earthquakes. A **seismogram** (ˈsaɪzməˌgræm) is the record from such an instrument. Also called: **seismometer** > **seismographic** (ˌsaɪzməˈgræfɪk) *adj* > **seismographer** (saɪzˈmɒgrəfə) *n* > **seisˈmography** *n*
seismology (saɪzˈmɒlədʒɪ) *n* the branch of geology concerned with the study of earthquakes and seismic waves > **seismologic** (ˌsaɪzməˈlɒdʒɪk) *or* ˌ**seismoˈlogical** *adj* > ˌ**seismoˈlogically** *adv* > **seisˈmologist** *n*
seismonasty (ˈsaɪzməˌnæstɪ) *n botany* a nastic movement in response to shock, esp the rapid folding of the leaflets of the sensitive plant due to changes in turgor pressure caused by vibration [c20 from SEISMO- + -NASTY]
seismoscope (ˈsaɪzməˌskəʊp) *n* an obsolete instrument that indicates the occurrence of an earthquake. Compare **seismograph** > **seismoscopic** (ˌsaɪzməˈskɒpɪk) *adj*
sei whale (seɪ) *n* a rorqual, *Balaenoptera borealis* [c20 from Norwegian *seihval*, from *sei* coalfish (see SAITHE) + *hval* whale: so called because it follows coalfish in search of food]
seize (siːz) *vb* (*mainly tr*) **1** (also *intr*, foll by *on*) to take hold of quickly; grab: *she seized her hat and ran for the bus* **2** (sometimes foll by *on* or *upon*) to grasp mentally, esp rapidly: *she immediately seized his idea* **3** to take mental possession of: *alarm seized the crowd* **4** to take possession of rapidly and forcibly: *the thief seized the woman's purse* **5** to take legal possession of; take into custody **6** to take by force or capture: *the army seized the undefended town* **7** to take immediate advantage of: *to seize an opportunity* **8** *nautical* to bind (two ropes together or a piece of gear to a rope). See also **serve** (sense 19) **9** (*intr*; often foll by *up*) (of mechanical parts) to become jammed, esp because of excessive heat **10** (*passive*; usually foll by *of*) to be apprised of; conversant with **11** the usual US spelling of **seise** [c13 *saisen*, from Old French *saisir*, from Medieval Latin *sacīre* to position, of Germanic origin; related to Gothic *satjan* to SET[1]] > ˈ**seizable** *adj*
seizing (ˈsiːzɪŋ) *n nautical* a binding used for holding together two ropes, two spars, etc, esp by lashing with a separate rope
seizure (ˈsiːʒə) *n* **1** the act or an instance of seizing or the state of being seized **2** *pathol* a sudden manifestation or recurrence of a disease, such as an epileptic convulsion
sejant *or* **sejeant** (ˈsiːdʒənt) *adj* (*usually postpositive*) *heraldry* (of a beast) shown seated [c16 variant of *seant*, from Old French, from *seoir* to sit, from Latin *sedēre*]
Sejm (seɪm) *n* the unicameral legislature of Poland [Polish: assembly]
Sekondi (ˌsɛkənˈdiː) *n* a port in SW Ghana, 8 km (5 miles) northeast of Takoradi: linked administratively with Takoradi in 1946. Pop (with Takoradi): 335 000 (2005 est)
Sekt (zɛkt) *n* any of various German sparkling

wines [c20 from German, from Spanish *vino seco* dry wine]

sel (sɛl) *n* a Scot word for **self**

selachian (sɪˈleɪkɪən) *adj* **1** of, relating to, or belonging to the *Selachii* (or *Elasmobranchii*), a large subclass of cartilaginous fishes including the sharks, rays, dogfish, and skates ▷ *n* **2** any fish belonging to the subclass *Selachii*. Also: **elasmobranch** [c19 from New Latin *Selachii*, from Greek *selakhē* a shark; related to Greek *selas* brightness]

selaginella (ˌsɛlædʒɪˈnɛlə) *n* any club moss of the genus *Selaginella*, having stems covered in small pointed leaves and small spore-bearing cones: family **Selaginellaceae**. See also **resurrection plant** [c19 from New Latin, diminutive of Latin *selāgō* plant similar to the savin]

selah (ˈsiːlə) *n* a Hebrew word of unknown meaning occurring in the Old Testament psalms, and thought to be a musical direction [c16 from Hebrew]

Selangor (səˈlæŋə) *n* a state of Peninsular Malaysia, on the Strait of Malacca: established as a British protectorate in 1874, became a Federated Malay State in 1896 and part of Malaysia in 1946; tin producer. Capital: Shah Alam. Pop: 4 188 876 (2000). Area: 8203 sq km (3167 sq miles)

Selby (ˈsɛlbɪ) *n* an inland port in N England, in North Yorkshire, on the River Ouse: centre for a coalfield since 1983; agricultural products. Pop: 15 807 (2001)

seldom (ˈsɛldəm) *adv* not often; rarely [Old English *seldon*; related to Old Norse *sjāldan*, Old High German *seltan*]

select (sɪˈlɛkt) *vb* **1** to choose (someone or something) in preference to another or others ▷ *adj also* **selected 2** chosen in preference to another or others **3** of particular quality or excellence **4** limited as to membership or entry: *a select gathering* **5** careful in making a choice [c16 from Latin *sēligere* to sort, from *sē-* apart + *legere* to choose] > se'lectly *adv* > se'lectness *n*

selecta (sɪˈlɛktə) *n* slang a disc jockey [c20 phonetic rendering of SELECTOR]

select committee *n* (in Britain) a small committee composed of members of parliament, set up by either House of Parliament to investigate and report back on a specified matter of interest

selectee (sɪˌlɛkˈtiː) *n US* a person who is selected, esp for military service

selection (sɪˈlɛkʃən) *n* **1** the act or an instance of selecting or the state of being selected **2** a thing or number of things that have been selected **3** a range from which something may be selected: *this shop has a good selection of clothes* **4** *biology* the natural or artificial process by which certain organisms or characters are reproduced and perpetuated in the species in preference to others. See also **natural selection 5** a contestant in a race chosen as likely to win or come second or third **6** *Austral* **a** the act of free-selecting **b** a tract of land acquired by free-selection

selective (sɪˈlɛktɪv) *adj* **1** of or characterized by selection **2** tending to choose carefully or characterized by careful choice **3** *electronics* occurring at, operating at, or capable of separating out a particular frequency or band of frequencies > se'lectively *adv* > se'lectiveness *n*

selective attention *n psychol* the process by which a person can selectively pick out one message from a mixture of messages occurring simultaneously

selective service *n US* (formerly) compulsory military service under which men were conscripted selectively

selective synchronization *n* a sound-recording process that facilitates overdubs by feeding the recorded track to the performer straight from the recording head. Often shortened to: **sel-sync**

selectivity (sɪˌlɛkˈtɪvɪtɪ) *n* **1** the state or quality of being selective **2** the degree to which a radio

receiver or other circuit can respond to and separate the frequency of a desired signal from other frequencies by tuning **3** the principle that welfare services should go only to those whose need is greatest, as revealed by needs tests, means tests, etc

selectman (sɪˈlɛktmən) *n, pl* **-men** any of the members of the local boards of most New England towns

selector (sɪˈlɛktə) *n* **1** a person or thing that selects **2** a device used in automatic telephone switching that connects one circuit with any one of a number of other circuits **3** *Brit* a person who chooses the members of a sports team **4** *Austral* the holder of a tract of land acquired by free-selection

selectorate (sɪˈlɛktərɪt) *n* a body of people responsible for making a selection, esp members of a political party who select candidates for an election [c20 from SELECT + (ELECT)ORATE]

selenate (ˈsɛlɪˌneɪt) *n* any salt or ester formed by replacing one or both of the hydrogens of selenic acid with metal ions or organic groups [c19 from SELENIUM + -ATE¹]

Selene (sɪˈliːnɪ) *n* the Greek goddess of the moon. Roman counterpart: Luna

selenic (sɪˈliːnɪk) *adj* of or containing selenium, esp in the hexavalent state

selenic acid *n* a colourless crystalline soluble strong dibasic acid analogous to sulphuric acid. Formula: H_2SeO_4

selenious (sɪˈliːnɪəs) *or* **selenous** (sɪˈliːnəs) *adj* of or containing selenium in the divalent or tetravalent state

selenious acid *n* a white soluble crystalline strong dibasic acid analogous to sulphurous acid. Formula: H_2SeO_3

selenite (ˈsɛlɪˌnaɪt) *n* a colourless glassy variety of gypsum [c17 via Latin from Greek *selēnitēs lithos* moonstone, from *selēnē* moon; so called because it was believed to wax and wane with the moon]

selenium (sɪˈliːnɪəm) *n* a nonmetallic element that exists in several allotropic forms. It occurs free in volcanic areas and in sulphide ores, esp pyrite. The common form is a grey crystalline solid that is photoconductive, photovoltaic, and semiconducting: used in photocells, solar cells, and in xerography. Symbol: Se; atomic no: 34; atomic wt: 78.96; valency: –2, 4, or 6; relative density: 4.79 (grey); melting pt: 221°C (grey); boiling pt: 685°C (grey) [c19 from New Latin, from Greek *selēnē* moon; named by analogy to TELLURIUM (from Latin *tellus* earth)]

selenium cell *n* a photoelectric cell containing a strip of selenium between two metal electrodes

seleno- *or before a vowel* **selen-** *combining form* denoting the moon: *selenology* [from Greek *selēnē* moon]

selenodont (sɪˈliːnəˌdɒnt) *adj* **1** (of the teeth of certain mammals) having crescent-shaped ridges on the crowns, as in deer ▷ *n* **2** a mammal with selenodont teeth [c19 from SELENO- (moon-shaped) + -ODONT]

selenography (ˌsiːlɪˈnɒɡrəfɪ) *n* the branch of astronomy concerned with the description and mapping of the surface features of the moon > **selenograph** (sɪˈliːnəʊˌɡrɑːf, -ˌɡræf) *n* > ˌsele'nographer *or* ˌselle'nographist *n* > selenographic (sɪˌliːnəʊˈɡræfɪk) *or* se,leno'graphical *adj* > se,leno'graphically *adv*

selenology (ˌsiːlɪˈnɒlədʒɪ) *n* the branch of astronomy concerned with the moon, its physical characteristics, nature, origin, etc > selenological (sɪˌliːnəʊˈlɒdʒɪkᵊl) *adj* > sele'nologist *n*

selenomorphology (sɪˌliːnəʊmɔːˈfɒlədʒɪ) *n* the study of the lunar surface and landscape

Seleucia (sɪˈluːʃɪə) *n* **1** an ancient city in Mesopotamia, on the River Tigris: founded by Seleucus Nicator in 312 BC; became the chief city of the Seleucid empire; sacked by the Romans around 162 AD **2** an ancient city in SE Asia Minor, on the River Calycadnus (modern Goksu Nehri):

captured by the Turks in the 13th century; site of present-day Silifke (Turkey). Official name: **Seleucia Tracheotis** (ˌtrækɪˈəʊtɪs) *or* **Trachea** (trəˈkɪə) **3** an ancient port in Syria, on the River Orontes: the port of Antioch, of military importance during the wars between the Ptolemies and Seleucids; largely destroyed by earthquake in 526; site of present-day Samandağ (Turkey). Official name: **Seleucia Pieria** (paɪˈrɪə)

self (sɛlf) *n, pl* **selves** (sɛlvz) **1** the distinct individuality or identity of a person or thing **2** a person's usual or typical bodily make-up or personal characteristics: *she looked her old self again* **3** good **self** (*or* selves) *rare* a polite way of referring to or addressing a person (or persons), used following *your, his, her,* or *their* **4** one's own welfare or interests: *he only thinks of self* **5** an individual's consciousness of his own identity or being **6** *philosophy* (usually preceded by the) that which is essential to an individual, esp the mind or soul in Cartesian metaphysics; the ego **7** a bird, animal, etc, that is a single colour throughout, esp a self-coloured pigeon ▷ *pron* **8** *not standard* myself, yourself, etc: *seats for self and wife* ▷ *adj* **9** of the same colour or material: *a dress with a self belt*. See also **self-coloured 10** *obsolete* the same [Old English *seolf*; related to Old Norse *sjālfr*, Gothic *silba*, Old High German *selb*]

self- *combining form* **1** of oneself or of itself: *self-defence; self-rule* **2** by, to, in, due to, for, or from the self: *self-employed; self-inflicted; self-respect* **3** automatic or automatically: *self-propelled*

self-abnegation *n* the denial of one's own interests in favour of the interests of others > ˌself-'abneˌgating *adj*

self-absorbed *adj* preoccupied with one's own thoughts, emotions, life, etc

self-absorption *n* **1** preoccupation with oneself to the exclusion of others or the outside world **2** *physics* the process in which some of the radiation emitted by a material is absorbed by the material itself

self-abuse *n* **1** disparagement or misuse of one's own abilities, etc **2** a censorious term for **masturbation**

self-acting *adj* not requiring an external influence or control to function; automatic > ˌself-'action *n*

self-actualization *n psychol* the process of establishing oneself as a whole person, able to develop one's abilities and to understand oneself

self-addressed *adj* **1** addressed for return to the sender **2** directed to oneself: *a self-addressed remark*

self-adhesive *adj* (of a letter, label, etc) coated with an adhesive substance, esp where no moistening is needed

self-administered *adj* (of medicine, etc) given by oneself

self-advancement *n* the act or process of improving one's position, education, etc

self-advocacy *n social welfare* (esp in the US) **1 a** the practice of having mentally handicapped people speak for themselves and control their own affairs, rather than having nonhandicapped people automatically assume responsibility for them. See also **normalization b** (*as modifier*): *a self-advocacy group* **2** the act or condition of representing oneself, either generally in society or in formal proceedings, such as a court

self-aggrandizement *n* the act of increasing one's own power, importance, etc, esp in an aggressive or ruthless manner > ˌself-ag'granˌdizing *adj*

self-analysis *n* the act or process of analysing oneself

self-annealing *adj metallurgy* denoting certain metals, such as lead, tin, and zinc, that recrystallize at air temperatures and so may be cold-worked without strain-hardening

self-annihilation *n* the surrender of the self in mystical contemplation, union with God, etc

self-appointed *adj* having assumed authority

S

without the agreement of others: *a self-appointed critic*

self-assertion *n* the act or an instance of putting forward one's own opinions, etc, esp in an aggressive or conceited manner > ˌself-as'serting *adj* > ˌself-as'sertingly *adv* > ˌself-as'sertive *adj* > ˌself-as'sertively *adv* > ˌself-as'sertiveness *n*

self-assessment *n* **1** an evaluation of one's own abilities and failings **2** *finance* a system to enable taxpayers to assess their own tax liabilities

self-assurance *n* confidence in the validity, value, etc, of one's own ideas, opinions, etc

self-assured *adj* confident of one's own worth > ˌself-as'suredly *adv* > ˌself-as'suredness *n*

self-aware *adj* conscious of one's own feelings, character, etc

self-catering *adj* denoting accommodation in which the tenant or visitor provides and prepares his own food

self-censorship *n* the regulation of a group's actions and statements by its own members rather than an external agency

self-centred *adj* totally preoccupied with one's own concerns > ˌself-'centredly *adv* > ˌself-'centredness *n*

self-certification *n* (in Britain) a formal assertion by a worker to his employer that absence from work for up to seven days was due to sickness. From 1982 this replaced a doctor's certificate for the purposes of paying sickness benefit. See also **sick note**

self-cleaning *adj* (of an oven, filter, etc) having a mechanism to clean itself

self-coloured *adj* **1** having only a single and uniform colour: *self-coloured flowers; a self-coloured dress* **2** (of cloth, material, etc) **a** having the natural or original colour **b** retaining the colour of the thread before weaving

self-command *n* another term for **self-control**

self-compatible *adj* (of a plant) capable of self-fertilization > ˌself-com.pati'bility *n*

self-concept *n* *psychol* the whole set of attitudes, opinions, and cognitions that a person has of himself

self-confessed *adj* according to one's own testimony or admission: *a self-confessed liar*

self-confidence *n* confidence in one's own powers, judgment, etc > ˌself-'confident *adj* > ˌself-'confidently *adv*

self-congratulation *n* the state or an instance of congratulating or being pleased with oneself

self-conscious *adj* **1** unduly aware of oneself as the object of the attention of others; embarrassed **2** conscious of one's existence > ˌself-'consciously *adv* > ˌself-'consciousness *n*

self-contained *adj* **1** containing within itself all parts necessary for completeness **2** (of a flat) having its own kitchen, bathroom, and lavatory not shared by others and usually having its own entrance **3** able or tending to keep one's feelings, thoughts, etc, to oneself; reserved **4** able to control one's feelings or emotions in the presence of others > ˌself-con'tainedly *adv* > ˌself-con'tainedness *n*

self-control *n* the ability to exercise restraint or control over one's feelings, emotions, reactions, etc > ˌself-con'trolled *adj* > ˌself-con'trolling *adj*

self-correcting *adj* capable of correcting itself without external aid

self-critical *adj* critical of oneself: *his self-critical attitude*

self-criticism *n* unfavourable or severe judgement of oneself, one's abilities, one's actions, etc

self-deception *or* **self-deceit** *n* the act or an instance of deceiving oneself, esp as to the true nature of one's feelings or motives > ˌself-de'ceptive *adj*

self-defeating *adj* (of a plan, action, etc) unable to achieve the intended result

self-defence *n* **1** the act of defending oneself, one's actions, ideas, etc **2** boxing as a means of

defending the person (esp in the phrase **noble art of self-defence**) **3** *law* the right to defend one's person, family, or property against attack or threat of attack by the use of no more force than is reasonable > ˌself-de'fensive *adj*

self-delusion *n* the act or state of deceiving or deluding oneself

self-denial *n* the denial or sacrifice of one's own desires > ˌself-de'nying *adj* > ˌself-de'nyingly *adv*

self-deprecating *or* **self-depreciating** *adj* having a tendency to disparage oneself

self-destruct *vb* **1** (*intr*) to explode or disintegrate automatically as a result of pre-programming: *the missile self-destructed* **2** to destroy oneself, one's reputation, etc, through one's habits or actions: *I totally self-destructed with drugs* ▷ *n* **3** (*as modifier*): *hit the self-destruct button*

self-destruction *n* the act or an instance of self-destructing

self-determination *n* **1** the power or ability to make a decision for oneself without influence from outside **2** the right of a nation or people to determine its own form of government without influence from outside > ˌself-de'termined *adj* > ˌself-de'termining *adj*

self-development *n* the state or process of improving or developing oneself

self-directed *adj* (of study, learning, etc) regulated or conducted by oneself

self-discipline *n* the act of disciplining or power to discipline one's own feelings, desires, etc, esp with the intention of improving oneself > ˌself-'disciplined *adj*

self-dissociation *n* *chem* the splitting of the molecules of certain highly polar liquids, such as water and liquid ammonia, into ions

self-doubt *n* the act or state of doubting oneself

self-drive *adj* denoting or relating to a hired car that is driven by the hirer

self-educated *adj* **1** educated through one's own efforts without formal instruction **2** educated at one's own expense, without financial aid > ˌself-.edu'cation *n*

self-effacement *n* the act of making oneself, one's actions, etc, inconspicuous, esp because of humility or timidity

self-effacing *adj* tending to make oneself, one's actions, etc, inconspicuous, esp because of humility or timidity; modest > ˌself-ef'facingly *adv*

self-elected *adj* having been elected or appointed to a post, position, etc, by onself

self-employed *adj* earning one's living in one's own business or through freelance work, rather than as the employee of another > ˌself-em'ployment *n*

self-esteem *n* **1** respect for or a favourable opinion of oneself **2** an unduly high opinion of oneself; vanity

self-evident *adj* containing its own evidence or proof without need of further demonstration > ˌself-'evidence *n* > ˌself-'evidently *adv*

self-examination *n* scrutiny of one's own conduct, motives, desires, etc > ˌself-ex'amining *adj*

self-excited *adj* **1** (of an electrical machine) having the current for the magnetic field system generated by the machine itself or by an auxiliary machine coupled to it **2** (of an oscillator) generating its own energy and depending on resonant circuits for frequency determination

self-exculpatory *adj* intended to excuse oneself from blame or guilt

self-executing *adj* (of a law, treaty, or clause in a deed or contract, etc) coming into effect automatically at a specified time, no legislation or other action being needed for enforcement

self-existent *adj* *philosophy* existing independently of any other being or cause > ˌself-ex'istence *n*

self-explanatory *or less commonly* **self-explaining** *adj* understandable without explanation; self-evident

self-expression *n* the expression of one's own personality, feelings, etc, as in painting, poetry, or other creative activity > ˌself-ex'pressive *adj*

self-feeder *n* any machine or device capable of automatically supplying materials when and where they are needed, esp one for making measured quantities of food constantly available to farm livestock

self-fertilization *n* fertilization in a plant or animal by the fusion of male and female gametes produced by the same individual. Compare **cross-fertilization** (sense 1) > ˌself-'ferti.lized *adj* > ˌself-'ferti.lizing *or* ˌself-'fertile *adj*

self-financing *adj* (of a student, business, etc) financing oneself or itself without external grants or aid

self-forgetful *adj* forgetful of one's own interests > ˌself-for'getfully *adv* > ˌself-for'getfulness *n*

self-fulfilling *adj* (of an opinion or prediction) borne out because it is expected to be true or to happen: *a self-fulfilling prophecy*

self-fulfilment *n* the fulfilment of one's hopes, dreams, goals, etc

self-government *n* **1** the government of a country, nation, etc, by its own people **2** the state of being self-controlled **3** an archaic term for **self-control.** > ˌself-'governed *adj* > ˌself-'governing *adj*

self-harm *n* the practice of cutting or otherwise wounding oneself, usually considered as indicating psychological disturbance > ˌself-'harming *n*

self-hatred *n* a feeling of intense dislike for oneself: *feelings of self-hatred*

selfheal ('sɛlf.hi:l) *n* **1** a low-growing European herbaceous plant, *Prunella vulgaris*, with tightly clustered violet-blue flowers and reputedly having healing powers: family *Lamiaceae* (labiates) **2** any of several other plants thought to have healing powers. Also called: **allheal, heal-all**

self-healing *n* **a** the act or instance of healing onself **b** (*as modifier*): *the self-healing process*

self-help *n* **1** the act or state of providing the means to help oneself without relying on the assistance of others **2 a** the practice of solving one's problems by joining or forming a group designed to help those suffering from a particular problem **b** (*as modifier*): *a self-help group*

selfhood ('sɛlfhʊd) *n* **1** *philosophy* **a** the state of having a distinct identity **b** the individuality so possessed **2** a person's character **3** the quality of being egocentric

self-hypnosis *n* the state or act of hypnotizing oneself

self-identity *n* the conscious recognition of the self as having a unique identity

self-image *n* one's own idea of oneself or sense of one's worth

self-immolation *n* the act or an instance of setting fire to oneself

self-important *adj* having or showing an unduly high opinion of one's own abilities, importance, etc > ˌself-im'portantly *adv* > ˌself-im'portance *n*

self-imposed *adj* (of a task, role, or circumstance) having been imposed on oneself by oneself

self-improvement *n* the improvement of one's status, position, education, etc, by one's own efforts

self-incompatible *adj* (of a plant) incapable of self-fertilization because its own pollen is prevented from germinating on the stigma or the pollen tube is blocked before it reaches the egg cell > ˌself-.incom.pati'bility *n*

self-induced *adj* **1** induced or brought on by oneself or itself **2** *electronics* produced by self-induction

self-inductance *n* the inherent inductance of a circuit, given by the ratio of the electromotive force produced in the circuit by self-induction to the rate of change of current producing it. It is usually expressed in henries. Symbol: *L*. Also called: **coefficient of self-induction**

self-induction *n* the production of an

electromotive force in a circuit when the magnetic flux linked with the circuit changes as a result of a change in current in the same circuit. See also **self-inductance** Compare **mutual induction**. > ˌself-in'ductive *adj*

self-indulgent *adj* tending to indulge one's own desires, etc > ˌself-in'dulgence *n* > ˌself-in'dulgently *adv*

self-inflicted *adj* (of an injury) having been inflicted on oneself by oneself

self-insurance *n* the practice of insuring oneself or one's property by accumulating a reserve out of one's income or funds rather than by purchase of an insurance policy

self-interest *n* 1 one's personal interest or advantage 2 the act or an instance of pursuing one's own interest > ˌself-'interested *adj* > ˌself-'interestedness *n*

selfish ('sɛlfɪʃ) *adj* 1 chiefly concerned with one's own interest, advantage, etc, esp to the total exclusion of the interests of others 2 relating to or characterized by self-interest > 'selfishly *adv* > 'selfishness *n*

self-justification *n* the act or an instance of justifying or providing excuses for one's own behaviour, etc

self-justifying *adj* offering excuses for one's behaviour, often when they are not called for

self-knowledge *n* knowledge of one's own character, etc

selfless ('sɛlflɪs) *adj* having little concern for one's own interests > 'selflessly *adv* > 'selflessness *n*

self-liquidating *adj* 1 (of a loan, bill of exchange, etc) used to finance transactions whose proceeds are expected to accrue before the date of redemption or repayment 2 (of a business transaction, project, investment, etc) yielding proceeds sufficient to cover the initial outlay or to finance any recurrent outlays

self-loading *adj* (of a firearm) utilizing some of the force of the explosion to eject the empty shell and replace it with a new one. Also: autoloading See also **automatic** (sense 5), **semiautomatic** (sense 2) > ˌself-'loader *n*

self-love *n* the instinct or tendency to seek one's own well-being or to further one's own interest

self-made *adj* 1 having achieved wealth, status, etc, by one's own efforts 2 made by oneself

self-motivated *adj* motivitated or driven by oneself or one's own desires, without any external agency

self-mutilation *n* the act or an instance of mutilating oneself

self-opinionated *or less commonly* **self-opinioned** *adj* 1 having an unduly high regard for oneself or one's own opinions 2 clinging stubbornly to one's own opinions

self-parody *n* the act or an instance of mimicking oneself in a humorous or satirical way

self-perpetuating *adj* (of machine, emotion, idea, etc) continuing or prevailing without any external agency or intervention

self-pity *n* the act or state of pitying oneself, esp in an exaggerated or self-indulgent manner > ˌself-'pitying *adj* > ˌself-'pityingly *adv*

self-pollination *n* the transfer of pollen from the anthers to the stigma of the same flower or of another flower on the same plant. Compare **cross-pollination**. > ˌself-'pollinated *adj*

self-portrait *n* a portrait one draws or paints of oneself

self-possessed *adj* having control of one's emotions, etc > ˌself-pos'sessedly *adv* > ˌself-pos'session *n*

self-praise *n* the act or an instance of expressing commendation for oneself

self-preservation *n* the preservation of oneself from danger or injury, esp as a basic instinct

self-proclaimed *adj* proclaimed or described by oneself: *the self-proclaimed leader*

self-professed *adj* avowed or acknowledged by oneself

self-promotion *n* the act or practice of promoting one's own interests, profile, etc

self-pronouncing *adj* (in a phonetic transcription) of, relating to, or denoting a word that, except for additional diacritic marks of stress, may keep the letters of its ordinary orthography to represent its pronunciation

self-propelled *adj* (of a vehicle) provided with its own source of tractive power rather than requiring an external means of propulsion > ˌself-pro'pelling *adj*

self-protection *n* the act or an instance of protecting or defending oneself > ˌself-pro'tective *adj*

self-punishment *n* the act or an instance of punishing oneself

self-questioning *adj* doubting or questioning oneself or one's abilities

self-raising *adj* (of flour) having a raising agent, such as baking powder, already added

self-realization *n* the realization or fulfilment of one's own potential or abilities

self-regard *n* 1 concern for one's own interest 2 proper esteem for oneself

self-regarding *adj* 1 self-centred; egotistical 2 *philosophy* (of an action) affecting the interests of no-one other than the agent, and hence, according to John Stuart Mill, immune from moral criticism

self-regulating *adj* (of a business, society, etc) enforcing or upholding its own rules and laws without external agency of intervention

self-regulating organization *n* one of several British organizations set up in 1986 under the auspices of the Securities and Investment Board to regulate the activities of London investment markets. Abbreviation: SRO

self-reliance *n* reliance on one's own abilities, decisions, etc > ˌself-re'liant *adj* > ˌself-re'liantly *adv*

self-renunciation *n* the renunciation of one's own rights, claims, interest, etc, esp in favour of those of others > ˌself-re'nunciatory *adj*

self-replicate *vb* (*intr*) (of a computer virus, etc) to reproduce itself

self-reproach *n* the act of finding fault with or blaming oneself > ˌself-re'proachful *adj* > ˌself-re'proachfully *adv*

self-respect *n* a proper sense of one's own dignity and integrity > ˌself-re'spectful *or* ˌself-re'specting *adj*

self-restraint *n* restraint imposed by oneself on one's own feelings, desires, etc

self-righteous *adj* having or showing an exaggerated awareness of one's own virtuousness or rights > ˌself-'righteously *adv* > ˌself-'righteousness *n*

self-rule *n* another term for **self-government** (sense 1)

self-sacrifice *n* the sacrifice of one's own desires, interest, etc, for the sake of duty or for the well-being of others > ˌself-'sacrificing *adj* > ˌself-'sacrificingly *adv*

selfsame ('sɛlfˌseɪm) *adj* (*prenominal*) the very same

self-satisfied *adj* having or showing a complacent satisfaction with oneself, one's own actions, behaviour, etc > ˌself-'satisfaction *n*

self-sealing *adj* (esp of an envelope) designed to become sealed with the application of pressure only

self-seeking *n* 1 the act or an instance of seeking one's own profit or interest, esp exclusively ▷ *adj* 2 having or showing an exclusive preoccupation with one's own profit or interest: *a self-seeking attitude* > ˌself-'seeker *n*

self-service *adj* 1 of or denoting a shop, restaurant, petrol station, etc, where the customer serves himself ▷ *n* 2 the practice of serving oneself, as in a shop, etc

self-serving *adj* habitually seeking one's own advantage, esp at the expense of others

self-sown *adj* (of plants) growing from seed dispersed by any means other than by the agency

of man or animals. Also: self-seeded

self-starter *n* 1 the former name for a **starter** (sense 1) 2 a person who is strongly motivated and shows initiative, esp at work

self-styled *adj* (*prenominal*) claiming to be of a specified nature, quality, profession, etc: *a self-styled expert*

self-sufficient *or* **self-sufficing** *adj* able to provide for or support oneself without the help of others > ˌself-sufficiency *n* > ˌself-sufficiently *adv*

self-suggestion *n* another term for **autosuggestion**

self-supporting *adj* 1 able to support or maintain oneself without the help of others 2 able to stand up or hold firm without support, props, attachments, etc

self-talk *n* the act or practice of talking to oneself, either aloud or silently and mentally: *positive self-talk*

self-tanning *or* **self-tan** *n* **a** a cosmetic substance applied to the skin to simulate a suntan **b** (*as modifier*): *self-tanning lotion*

self-tapping *adj* (of a screw) cutting its own thread when screwed into a plain hole in a metal sheet

self-taught *adj* having learnt oneself without any external or formal instruction

self-tender *n* an offer by a company to buy back some or all of its shares from its shareholders, esp as a protection against an unwelcome takeover bid

self-treatment *n* the act or an instance of applying (medical) treatment to oneself

self-understanding *n* the ability to understand one's own actions

self-violence *n* *euphemistic* suicide

self-will *n* stubborn adherence to one's own will, desires, etc, esp at the expense of others > ˌself-'willed *adj*

self-winding *adj* (of a wrist watch) having a mechanism, activated by the movements of the wearer, in which a rotating or oscillating weight rewinds the mainspring

self-worth *n* respect for or a favourable opinion of oneself

Seljuk (sɛl'dʒuːk) *or* **Seljukian** (sɛl'dʒuːkɪən) *n* 1 a member of any of the pre-Ottoman Turkish dynasties ruling over large parts of Asia in the 11th, 12th, and 13th centuries AD ▷ *adj* 2 of or relating to these dynasties or to their subjects [C19 from Turkish]

selkie ('sɛlkɪ) *n Scot* a variant of **silkie**

Selkirk Mountains *pl n* a mountain range in SW Canada, in SE British Columbia. Highest peak: Mount Sir Sandford, 3533 m (11 590 ft)

Selkirk Rex *n* a breed of large curly-haired cat

Selkirkshire ('sɛlkɜːkˌʃɪə, -ʃə) *n* (until 1975) a county of SE Scotland, now part of Scottish Borders

sell (sɛl) *vb* sells, selling, sold 1 to dispose of or transfer or be disposed of or transferred to a purchaser in exchange for money or other consideration; put or be on sale 2 to deal in (objects, property, etc): *he sells used cars for a living* 3 (*tr*) to give up or surrender for a price or reward: *to sell one's honour* 4 to promote or facilitate the sale of (objects, property, etc): *publicity sells many products* 5 to induce or gain acceptance of: *to sell an idea* 6 (*intr*) to be in demand on the market: *these dresses sell well in the spring* 7 (*tr*) *informal* to deceive or cheat 8 (*tr*; foll by *on*) to persuade to accept or approve (of): *to sell a buyer on a purchase* 9 **sell down the river** *informal* to betray 10 **sell oneself a** to convince someone else of one's potential or worth **b** to give up one's moral or spiritual standards, etc 11 **sell short a** *informal* to disparage or belittle **b** *finance* to sell securities or goods without owning them in anticipation of buying them before delivery at a lower price ▷ *n* 12 the act or an instance of selling. Compare **hard sell, soft sell** 13 *informal* **a** a trick, hoax, or deception **b** *Irish* a great disappointment: *the service in the hotel was a*

S

sell ▷ See also **sell in, sell off, sell out, sell up** [Old English *sellan* to lend, deliver; related to Old Norse *selja* to sell, Gothic *saljan* to offer sacrifice, Old High German *sellen* to sell, Latin *cōnsilium* advice] > 'sellable *adj*

Sellafield ('sɛləˌfiːld) *n* the site of an atomic power station and nuclear reprocessing plant in NW England, in W Cumbria. Former name: Windscale

sell-by date *n* **1** a date printed on the packaging of perishable goods, indicating the date after which the goods should not be offered for sale **2** **past one's sell-by date** *informal* beyond one's prime

seller ('sɛlə) *n* **1** a person who sells **2** an article to be sold: *this item is always a good seller* **3** short for **selling race**

sellers' market *n* a market in which demand exceeds supply and sellers can influence prices

Sellers screw thread *n* a thread form in a system of standard sizes proposed by Sellers in 1884 and later accepted as standard in the USA, having a 60° flank angle with a flat top and foot [named after William *Sellers* (1824–1905), US engineer]

sell in *vb* (*adverb*) **1** (*tr*) to sell (new products) to a retail outlet to be sold to the public **2** (*intr*) to use the established system to one's advantage, rather than attempting to fight against it

selling-plater *n* **1** a horse that competes, or is only good enough to compete, in a selling race **2** a person or thing of limited ability or value

selling race *or* **plate** *n* a horse race in which the winner must be offered for sale at auction

sell off *vb* (*tr, adverb*) to sell (remaining or unprofitable items), esp at low prices

Sellotape ('sɛləˌteɪp) *n* **1** *trademark* a type of transparent adhesive tape made of cellulose or a similar substance ▷ *vb* **2** (*tr*) to seal or stick using adhesive tape

sell out *vb* (*adverb*) **1** Also (chiefly Brit): **sell up** to dispose of (supplies of something) completely by selling **2** (*tr*) *informal* to betray, esp through a secret agreement **3** (*intr*) *informal* to abandon one's principles, standards, etc ▷ *n* **sellout** **4** *informal* a performance for which all tickets are sold **5** a commercial success **6** *informal* a betrayal **7** *informal* a person who betrays their principles, standards, friends, etc

sell-through *n* **1** the ratio of the quantity of goods sold by a retailer to the quantity originally delivered to it wholesale **2** the sale of prerecorded video cassettes or DVDs, as opposed to their being available for hire only ▷ *adj* **3** (of prerecorded video cassettes or DVDs) sold in this way

sell up *vb* (*adverb*) *chiefly Brit* **1** (*tr*) to sell all (the possessions or assets) of (a bankrupt debtor) in order to discharge his debts as far as possible **2** (*intr*) to sell a business

selsyn ('sɛlsɪn) *n* another name for **synchro** [from SEL(F-) + SYN(CHRONOUS)]

sel-sync ('sɛlˌsɪŋk) *n* short for **selective synchronization**

Seltzer ('sɛltsə) *n* **1** a natural effervescent water with a high content of minerals **2** a similar synthetic water, used as a beverage. Also called: **Seltzer water** [C18 changed from German *Selterser Wasser* water from (*Nieder*) *Selters*, district where mineral springs are located, near Wiesbaden, Germany]

selva ('sɛlvə) *n* **1** dense equatorial forest, esp in the Amazon basin, characterized by tall broad-leaved evergreen trees, epiphytes, lianas, etc **2** a tract of such forest [C19 from Spanish and Portuguese, from Latin *silva* forest]

selvage *or* **selvedge** ('sɛlvɪdʒ) *n* **1** the finished nonfraying edge of a length of woven fabric **2** a similar strip of material allowed in fabricating a metal or plastic article, used esp for handling components during manufacture [C15 from SELF + EDGE; related to Dutch *selfegghe*, German *Selbende*] > 'selvaged *adj*

selves (sɛlvz) *n* **a** the plural of **self** **b** (*in combination*): *ourselves; yourselves; themselves*

semanteme (sɪˈmæntiːm) *n* another word for **sememe** (sense 2)

semantic (sɪˈmæntɪk) *adj* **1** of or relating to meaning or arising from distinctions between the meanings of different words or symbols **2** of or relating to semantics **3** *logic* concerned with the interpretation of a formal theory, as when truth tables are given as an account of the sentential connectives [C19 from Greek *sēmantikos* having significance, from *sēmainein* to signify, from *sēma* a sign] > se'mantically *adv*

semantics (sɪˈmæntɪks) *n* (*functioning as singular*) **1** the branch of linguistics that deals with the study of meaning, changes in meaning, and the principles that govern the relationship between sentences or words and their meanings **2** the study of the relationships between signs and symbols and what they represent **3** *logic* **a** the study of interpretations of a formal theory **b** the study of the relationship between the structure of a theory and its subject matter **c** (of a formal theory) the principles that determine the truth or falsehood of sentences within the theory, and the references of its terms > se'manticist *n*

semantic tableau *n logic* **1** a method of demonstrating the consistency or otherwise of a set of statements by constructing a diagrammatic representation of all the circumstances that satisfy the set of statements **2** the diagram so constructed

semaphore ('sɛməˌfɔː) *n* **1** an apparatus for conveying information by means of visual signals, as with movable arms or railway signals, flags, etc **2** a system of signalling by holding a flag in each hand and moving the arms to designated positions to denote each letter of the alphabet ▷ *vb* **3** to signal (information) by means of semaphore [C19 via French, from Greek *sēma* a signal + -PHORE] > **semaphoric** (ˌsɛməˈfɒrɪk) *or* ˌsema'phorical *adj* > ˌsema'phorically *adv*

Semarang *or* **Samarang** (səˈmɑːraːŋ) *n* a port in S Indonesia, in N Java on the Java Sea. Pop: 1 348 803 (2000)

semasiology (sɪˌmeɪsɪˈɒlədʒɪ) *n* another name for **semantics** [C19 from Greek *sēmasia* meaning, from *sēmainein* to signify + -LOGY] > **semasiological** (sɪˌmeɪsɪəˈlɒdʒɪkəl) *adj* > seˌmasio'logically *adv* > seˌmasi'ologist *n*

sematic (sɪˈmætɪk) *adj* (of the conspicuous coloration of certain animals) acting as a warning, esp to potential predators [C19 from Greek *sēma* a sign]

sematology (ˌsɛməˈtɒlədʒɪ) *n* another name for **semantics** [C19 from Greek *sēmat-*, *sēma* sign + -LOGY]

semblable ('sɛmbləbəl) *archaic* ▷ *adj* **1** resembling or similar **2** apparent rather than real ▷ *n* **3** something that resembles another thing **4** a resemblance [C14 from Old French, from *sembler* to seem; see SEMBLANCE] > 'semblably *adv*

semblance ('sɛmbləns) *n* **1** outward appearance, esp without any inner substance or reality **2** a resemblance or copy [C13 from Old French, from *sembler* to seem, from Latin *simulāre* to imitate, from *similis* like]

semé *or* **semée** ('sɛmeɪ; French səme) *adj* (*postpositive; usually foll by of*) *heraldry* dotted (with): *semé of fleurs-de-lys gules* [C16 from French, literally: sown, from *semer* to sow, from Latin *sēmināre*, from *sēmen* seed]

semei- *prefix* for words beginning thus, see the more common spelling in **semi-**

Semele ('sɛmɪlɪ) *n Greek myth* mother of Dionysus by Zeus

semelparous ('sɛməlˌpærəs) *adj* **1** Also: **hapaxanthic, monocarpic** (of a plant) producing flowers and fruit only once before dying **2** (of an animal) producing offspring only once during its lifetime > 'semel,parity *n*

sememe ('siːmiːm) *n linguistics* **1** the meaning of a morpheme **2** Also called: **semanteme** a minimum unit of meaning in terms of which it is sometimes proposed that meaning in general might be analysed [C20 (coined in 1933 by Leonard Bloomfield (1887–1949), US linguist): from Greek *sēma* a sign + -EME]

semen ('siːmɛn) *n* **1** the thick whitish fluid containing spermatozoa that is ejaculated from the male genital tract **2** another name for **sperm¹** [C14 from Latin: seed]

Semeru *or* **Semeroe** (səˈmɛruː) *n* a volcano in Indonesia: the highest peak in Java. Height: 3676 m (12 060 ft)

semester (sɪˈmɛstə) *n* **1** (in some universities) either of two divisions of the academic year, ranging from 15 to 18 weeks **2** (in German universities) a session of six months [C19 via German from Latin *sēmestris* half-yearly, from *sex* six + *mensis* a month] > se'mestral *adj*

semi ('sɛmɪ) *n, pl* semis **1** *Brit* short for **semidetached** (house) **2** short for **semifinal** **3** *US, Canadian, Austral, and NZ* short for **semitrailer**

semi- *prefix* **1** half: *semicircle*. Compare **demi-** (sense 1), **hemi-** **2** partially, partly, not completely, or almost: *semiprofessional; semifinal* **3** occurring twice in a specified period of time: *semiannual; semiweekly* [from Latin; compare Old English *sōm-*, *sām-* half, Greek *hēmi-*]

semiannual (ˌsɛmɪˈænjʊəl) *adj* **1** occurring every half-year **2** lasting for half a year > ˌsemi'annually *adv*

semiaquatic (ˌsɛmɪəˈkwætɪk) *adj* (of organisms, esp plants) occurring close to the water and sometimes within it

semiarid (ˌsɛmɪˈærɪd) *adj* characterized by scanty rainfall and scrubby vegetation, often occurring in continental interiors: *the semiarid regions of Australia* > ˌsemi'ridity *n*

semiautomatic (ˌsɛmɪˌɔːtəˈmætɪk) *adj* **1** partly automatic **2** (of a firearm) self-loading but firing only one shot at each pull of the trigger. Compare **automatic** (sense 5) ▷ *n* **3** a semiautomatic firearm > ˌsemiˌauto'matically *adv*

Semi-Bantu *n* **1** a group of languages of W Africa, mainly SE Nigeria and Cameroon, that were not traditionally classed as Bantu but that show certain essential Bantu characteristics. They are now classed with Bantu in the Benue-Congo branch of the Niger-Congo family ▷ *adj* **2** relating to or belonging to this group of languages

semibold (ˌsɛmɪˈbəʊld) *printing* ▷ *adj* **1** denoting a weight of typeface between medium and bold face **2** denoting matter printed in this ▷ *n* **3** semibold type

semibreve ('sɛmɪˌbriːv) *n music* a note, now the longest in common use, having a time value that may be divided by any power of 2 to give all other notes. Usual US and Canadian name: **whole note** See also **breve** (sense 2)

semicentennial (ˌsɛmɪsɛnˈtɛnɪəl) *adj* **1** (*prenominal*) of or relating to the 50th anniversary of some event **2** occurring once every 50 years ▷ *n* **3** a 50th anniversary

semicircle ('sɛmɪˌsɜːkəl) *n* **1 a** one half of a circle **b** half the circumference of a circle **2** anything having the shape or form of half a circle > **semicircular** (ˌsɛmɪˈsɜːkjʊlə) *adj* > ˌsemi'circularly *adv*

semicircular canal *n anatomy* any of the three looped fluid-filled membranous tubes, at right angles to one another, that comprise the labyrinth of the ear: concerned with the sense of orientation and equilibrium

semicolon (ˌsɛmɪˈkəʊlən) *n* the punctuation mark (;) used to indicate a pause intermediate in value or length between that of a comma and that of a full stop

semiconductor (ˌsɛmɪkənˈdʌktə) *n* **1** a substance, such as germanium or silicon, that has an electrical conductivity that increases with temperature and is intermediate between that of a metal and an insulator. The behaviour may be exhibited by the pure substance (**intrinsic semiconductor**) or as a result of impurities (**extrinsic semiconductor**) **2 a** a device, such as a transistor or integrated circuit, that depends on the properties of such a substance **b** (*as modifier*): *a semiconductor diode* ▷ ˌsemicon'duction *n*

semiconscious (ˌsɛmɪ'kɒnʃəs) *adj* not fully conscious ▷ ˌsemi'consciously *adv* ▷ ˌsemi'consciousness *n*

semidetached (ˌsɛmɪdɪ'tætʃt) *adj* **a** (of a building) joined to another on one side by a common wall **b** (*as noun*): *they live in a suburban semidetached*

semidetached binary *n* a pair of stars that are so close together that mass transfer occurs from one to the other

semidiurnal (ˌsɛmɪdaɪ'ɜːnəl) *adj* **1** of or continuing during half a day **2** occurring every 12 hours

semidome ('sɛmɪˌdəʊm) *n* a half-dome, esp one used to cover a semicircular apse

semielliptical (ˌsɛmɪɪ'lɪptɪkəl) *adj* shaped like one half of an ellipse, esp one divided along the major axis

semifinal (ˌsɛmɪ'faɪnəl) *n* **a** the round before the final in a competition **b** (*as modifier*): *the semifinal draw*

semifinalist (ˌsɛmɪ'faɪnəlɪst) *n* a player or team taking part in a semifinal

semifluid (ˌsɛmɪ'fluːɪd) *adj* also (*rarely*) semifluidic (ˌsɛmɪfluː'ɪdɪk) **1** having properties between those of a liquid and those of a solid ▷ *n* **2** a substance that has such properties because of high viscosity: *tar is a semifluid*. Also: semiliquid ▷ ˌsemiflu'idity *n*

semifreddo (ˌsɛmɪ'frɛdəʊ) *n*, *pl* -dos a partially frozen Italian dessert similar to ice cream [Italian, literally: half cold]

semiliterate (ˌsɛmɪ'lɪtərɪt) *adj* **1** hardly able to read or write **2** able to read but not to write

Sémillon ('seɪmiːjɒn; *French* semijɔ̃) *n* **1** a white grape grown in the Bordeaux area of France and in Australia, used for making wine **2** any of various white wines made from this grape [French]

semilunar (ˌsɛmɪ'luːnə) *adj* shaped like a crescent or half-moon

semilunar valve *n anatomy* either of two crescent-shaped valves, one in the aorta and one in the pulmonary artery, that prevent regurgitation of blood into the heart

seminal ('sɛmɪnəl) *adj* **1** potentially capable of development **2** highly original, influential and important **3** rudimentary or unformed **4** of or relating to semen: *seminal fluid* **5** *biology* of or relating to seed [c14 from Late Latin *sēminālis* belonging to seed, from Latin *sēmen* seed] ▷ ˌsemi'nality *n* ▷ 'seminally *adv*

seminar ('sɛmɪˌnɑː) *n* **1** a small group of students meeting regularly under the guidance of a tutor, professor, etc, to exchange information, discuss theories, etc **2** one such meeting or the place in which it is held **3** a higher course for postgraduates **4** any group or meeting for holding discussions or exchanging information [c19 via German from Latin *sēminārium* SEMINARY]

seminarian (ˌsɛmɪ'nɛərɪən) *n* a student at a seminary

seminary ('sɛmɪnərɪ) *n*, *pl* -naries **1** an academy for the training of priests, rabbis, etc **2** *US* another word for **seminar** (sense 1) **3** a place where something is grown [c15 from Latin *sēminārium* a nursery garden, from *sēmen* seed] ▷ ˌsemi'narial *adj*

semination (ˌsɛmɪ'neɪʃən) *n rare* the production, dispersal, or sowing of seed [c16 from Late Latin *sēminātiō*, from Latin *sēmināre* to sow, from *sēmen* seed]

seminiferous (ˌsɛmɪ'nɪfərəs) *adj* **1** containing, conveying, or producing semen: *the seminiferous tubules of the testes* **2** (of plants) bearing or producing seeds [c17 from Latin *sēmin-*, *sēmen* seed + connecting vowel + -FEROUS]

Seminole ('sɛmɪˌnəʊl) *n* **1** (*pl* -noles *or* -nole) a member of a North American Indian people consisting of Creeks who moved into Florida in the 18th century **2** the language of this people, belonging to the Muskhogean family [from Creek *simanó-li* fugitive, from American Spanish *cimarrón* runaway]

seminoma (ˌsɛmɪ'nəʊmə) *n pl* -mas *or* -mata (-mətə) *pathol* a malignant tumour of the testicle [c20 from French *seminome*, from Latin *sēmen* semen + -OMA]

semiochemical (ˌsɛmɪəʊ'kɛmɪkəl) *n* a chemical substance produced by an animal and used in communications, such as a pheromone [c20 *semio-* from Greek *sēmeion* a sign + CHEMICAL]

semiology *or* **semeiology** (ˌsɛmɪ'ɒlədʒɪ, ˌsiː'mɪ-) *n* another word for **semiotics** [c17 (in the sense "sign language"): from Greek *sēmeion* sign + -LOGY] ▷ semiologic (ˌsɛmɪə'lɒdʒɪk, ˌsiː-mɪ-), ˌsemio'logical, ˌsemeio'logic, ˌsemeio'logical *adj* ▷ ˌsemi'ologist *or* ˌsemei'ologist *n*

semiotic *or* **semeiotic** (ˌsɛmɪ'ɒtɪk, ˌsiː-mɪ-) *adj* **1** relating to signs and symbols, esp spoken or written signs **2** relating to semiotics **3** of, relating to, or resembling the symptoms of disease; symptomatic [c17 from Greek *sēmeiōtikos* taking note of signs, from *sēmeion* a sign]

semiotician (ˌsɛmɪə'tɪʃən) *n* a person who studies semiotics

semiotics *or* **semeiotics** (ˌsɛmɪ'ɒtɪks, ˌsiː-mɪ-) *n* (*functioning as singular*) **1** the study of signs and symbols, esp the relations between written or spoken signs and their referents in the physical world or the world of ideas. See also **semantics, syntactics, pragmatics 2** the scientific study of the symptoms of disease; symptomatology ▷ Also called: **semiology, semeiology**

Semipalatinsk (*Russian* sɪmɪpa'latinsk) *n* a city in NE Kazakhstan on the Irtysh River; an important communications centre. Pop: 282 000 (2005 est)

semipalmate (ˌsɛmɪ'pælmət) *or* **semipalmated** *adj* (of the feet of some birds) having the front three toes partly webbed

semiparasitic (ˌsɛmɪˌpærə'sɪtɪk) *adj* **1** (of plants, such as mistletoe) obtaining some food from a host but undergoing photosynthesis at the same time **2** (of bacteria or fungi) usually parasitic but capable of living as a saprotroph ▷ semiparasite (ˌsɛmɪ'pærəsaɪt) *n* ▷ semiparasitism (ˌsɛmɪ'pærəsɪˌtɪzəm) *n*

semipermeable (ˌsɛmɪ'pɜːmɪəbəl) *adj* (esp of a cell membrane) selectively permeable ▷ ˌsemiˌpermea'bility *n*

semipolar bond (ˌsɛmɪ'pəʊlə) *n chem* another name for **coordinate bond**

semiporcelain (ˌsɛmɪ'pɔːslɪn) *n* a durable porcellaneous stoneware; stone china

semipostal (ˌsɛmɪ'pəʊstəl) *adj philately, chiefly US* denoting stamps where all or part of the receipts from sale are given to some charitable cause

semiprecious (ˌsɛmɪ'prɛʃəs) *adj* (of certain stones) having commercial value, but less than a precious stone

semipro ('sɛmɪˌprəʊ) *adj, n, pl* -pros short for **semiprofessional**

semiprofessional (ˌsɛmɪprə'fɛʃənəl) *adj* **1** (of a person) engaged in an activity or sport part-time but for pay **2** (of an activity or sport) engaged in by semiprofessional people **3** of or relating to a person whose activities are professional in some respects: *a semiprofessional pianist* ▷ *n* **4** a semiprofessional person ▷ ˌsemipro'fessionally *adv*

semiquaver ('sɛmɪˌkweɪvə) *n music* a note having the time value of one-sixteenth of a semibreve. Usual US and Canadian name: **sixteenth note**

semirigid (ˌsɛmɪ'rɪdʒɪd) *adj* **1** partly but not wholly rigid **2** (of an airship) maintaining shape by means of a main supporting keel and internal gas pressure

semiskilled (ˌsɛmɪ'skɪld) *adj* partly skilled or trained but not sufficiently so to perform specialized work

semisolid (ˌsɛmɪ'sɒlɪd) *adj* **1 a** having a viscosity and rigidity intermediate between that of a solid and a liquid **b** partly solid ▷ *n* **2** a substance in this state

semisolus (ˌsɛmɪ'səʊləs) *n* an advertisement that appears on the same page as another advertisement but not adjacent to it

semisubmersible rig *n* (in the oil industry) a type of drilling platform that floats supported by underwater pontoons, with much of its structure below the water line for stability in high winds: usually used only for exploratory drilling for oil or gas. Sometimes shortened to: **semisubmersible**

Semite ('siːmaɪt) *or less commonly* **Shemite** *n* **1** a member of the group of Caucasoid peoples who speak a Semitic language, including the Jews and Arabs as well as the ancient Babylonians, Assyrians, and Phoenicians **2** another word for a **Jew** [c19 from New Latin *sēmita* descendant of Shem, via Greek *Sēm*, from Hebrew SHEM]

Semitic (sɪ'mɪtɪk) *or less commonly* **Shemitic** *n* **1** a branch or subfamily of the Afro-Asiatic family of languages that includes Arabic, Hebrew, Aramaic, Amharic, and such ancient languages as Akkadian and Phoenician ▷ *adj* **2** denoting, relating to, or belonging to this group of languages **3** denoting, belonging to, or characteristic of any of the peoples speaking a Semitic language, esp the Jews or the Arabs **4** another word for **Jewish**

Semitics (sɪ'mɪtɪks) *n* (*functioning as singular*) the study of Semitic languages and culture ▷ Semitist ('sɛmɪtɪst)

Semito-Hamitic ('sɛmɪtəʊhæ'mɪtɪk) *n* **1** a former name for the **Afro-Asiatic** family of languages ▷ *adj* **2** denoting or belonging to this family of languages

semitone ('sɛmɪˌtəʊn) *n* an interval corresponding to a frequency difference of 100 cents as measured in the system of equal temperament, and denoting the pitch difference between certain adjacent degrees of the diatonic scale (**diatonic semitone**) or between one note and its sharpened or flattened equivalent (**chromatic semitone**); minor second. Also called (US and Canadian): half step Compare **whole tone** ▷ semitonic (ˌsɛmɪ'tɒnɪk) *adj* ▷ ˌsemi'tonally *adv*

semitrailer (ˌsɛmɪ'treɪlə) *n* a type of trailer or articulated lorry that has wheels only at the rear, the front end being supported by the towing vehicle

semitropical (ˌsɛmɪ'trɒpɪkəl) *adj* **1** partly tropical **2** another word for **subtropical**. ▷ ˌsemi'tropics *pl n*

semivitreous (ˌsɛmɪ'vɪtrɪəs) *adj* **1** partially vitreous **2** *ceramics* not wholly impervious to liquid

semivocal (ˌsɛmɪ'vəʊkəl) *or* **semivocalic** (ˌsɛmɪvəʊ'kælɪk) *adj* of or relating to a semivowel

semivowel ('sɛmɪˌvaʊəl) *n phonetics* **1** a vowel-like sound that acts like a consonant, in that it serves the same function in a syllable carrying the same amount of prominence as a consonant relative to a true vowel, the nucleus of the syllable. In English and many other languages the chief semivowels are (w) in *well* and (j), represented as *y*, in *yell* **2** a frictionless continuant classified as one of the liquids; (l) or (r) ▷ Also called: glide

semiyearly (ˌsɛmɪ'jɪəlɪ) *adj* another word for **semiannual**

semmit ('sɪmɪt, 'sɛm-) *n Scot* a vest [c15 of unknown origin]

semolina (ˌsɛmə'liːnə) *n* the large hard grains of wheat left after flour has been bolted, used for puddings, soups, etc [c18 from Italian *semolino*, diminutive of *semola* bran, from Latin *simila* very fine wheat flour]

Sempach (*German* 'zɛmpax) *n* a village in central Switzerland, in Lucerne canton on **Lake Sempach**: scene of the victory (1386) of the Swiss over the Hapsburgs

semper fidelis Latin ('sɛmpə fɪ'deɪlɪs) always faithful

semper paratus *Latin* ('sɛmpə pə'rɑːtəs) always prepared

sempervivum (ˌsɛmpə'vaɪvəm) *n* See **houseleek** [New Latin, from Latin *sempervivus* ever-living, from *semper* always + *vivere* to live]

sempiternal (ˌsɛmpɪ't3ːnᵊl) *adj literary* everlasting; eternal [c15 from Old French *sempiternel*, from Late Latin *sempiternālis*, from Latin *sempiternus*, from *semper* always + *aeternus* ETERNAL] > ˌsempi'ternally *adv* > sempiternity (ˌsɛmpɪ't3ːnɪtɪ) *n*

semplice ('sɛmplɪtʃɪ) *adj, adv music* to be performed in a simple manner [Italian: simple, from Latin *simplex*]

sempre ('sɛmprɪ) *adv music* (preceding a tempo or dynamic marking) always; consistently. It is used to indicate that a specified volume, tempo, etc, is to be sustained throughout a piece or passage [Italian: always, from Latin *semper*]

sempstress ('sɛmpstrɪs) *n* a rare word for **seamstress**

Semtex ('sɛmtɛks) *n* a pliable plastic explosive originally produced in the Czech Republic [c20 originally a trade name]

sen (sɛn) *n, pl* **sen** a monetary unit of Brunei, worth one hundredth of a dollar, Cambodia, worth one hundredth of a riel, Indonesia, worth one hundredth of a rupiah, Malaysia, worth one hundredth of a ringgit, and formerly of Japan (where it is still used as a unit of account) [c19 ultimately from Chinese *ch'ien* coin]

SEN (in Britain) *abbreviation for* (formerly) State Enrolled Nurse

Sen. *or* **sen.** *abbreviation for* **1** senator **2** senior

sena ('seɪnɑː) *n* (in India) the army: used in the names of certain paramilitary political organizations [Hindi]

senarmontite (ˌsɛnɑː'mɒntaɪt) *n* a white or grey mineral consisting of antimony trioxide in cubic crystalline form. Formula: Sb₂O₃ [c19 named after Henri de *Sénarmont* (died 1862), French mineralogist]

senary ('siːnərɪ) *adj* of or relating to the number six; having six parts or units [c17 from Latin *sēnārius*, from *sēnī* six each, from *sex* SIX]

senate ('sɛnɪt) *n* **1** any legislative or governing body considered to resemble a Senate **2** the main governing body at some colleges and universities [c13 from Latin *senātus* council of the elders, from *senex* an old man]

Senate ('sɛnɪt) *n* (*sometimes not capital*) **1** the upper chamber of the legislatures of the US, Canada, Australia, and many other countries **2** the legislative council of ancient Rome. Originally the council of the kings, the Senate became the highest legislative, judicial, and religious authority in republican Rome **3** the ruling body of certain free cities in medieval and modern Europe

senator ('sɛnətə) *n* **1** (*often capital*) a member of a Senate or senate **2** any legislator or statesman

senatorial (ˌsɛnə'tɔːrɪəl) *adj* **1** of, relating to, befitting, or characteristic of a senator **2** composed of senators **3** *chiefly US* electing or entitled to representation by a senator: *senatorial districts* > ˌsena'torially *adv*

senatus consultum *Latin* (sə'nɑːtəs kən'sʊltəm) *n, pl* **senatus consulta** (kən'sʊltə) a decree of the Senate of ancient Rome, taking the form of advice to a magistrate

send¹ (sɛnd) *vb* **sends, sending, sent** **1** (*tr*) to cause or order (a person or thing) to be taken, directed, or transmitted to another place: *to send a letter; she sent the salesman away* **2** (*when intr*, foll by *for*; *when tr, takes an infinitive*) to dispatch a request or command (for something or to do something): *he sent for a bottle of wine; he sent to his son to come home* **3** (*tr*) to direct or cause to go to a place or point: *his blow sent the champion to the floor* **4** (*tr*) to bring to a state or condition: *this noise will send me mad* **5** (*tr*; often foll by *forth, out,* etc) to cause to issue; emit: *his cooking sent forth a lovely smell from the kitchen* **6** (*tr*)

to cause to happen or come: *misery sent by fate* **7** to transmit (a message) by radio, esp in the form of pulses **8** (*tr*) *slang* to move to excitement or rapture: *this music really sends me* **9** **send (someone) about his** *or* **her business** to dismiss or get rid of (someone) **10** **send (someone) packing** to dismiss or get rid of (someone) peremptorily ▷ *n* **11** another word for **swash** (sense 4) ▷ See also **send down, sendoff, send up** [Old English *sendan*; related to Old Norse *senda*, Gothic *sandjan*, Old High German *senten*] > **sendable** *adj* > **sender** *n*

send² (sɛnd) *vb* **sends, sending, sent**, *n* a variant spelling of **scend**

Sendai (sɛn'daɪ) *n* a city in central Japan, on NE Honshu: university (1907). Pop: 986 713 (2002 est)

sendal ('sɛndᵊl) *n* **1** a fine silk fabric used, esp in the Middle Ages, for ceremonial clothing, etc **2** a garment of such fabric [c13 from Old French *cendal*, from Medieval Latin *cendalum*; probably related to Greek *sindon* fine linen]

send down *vb* (*tr, adverb*) *Brit* **1** to expel from a university, esp permanently **2** *informal* to send to prison

sendoff ('sɛndˌɒf) *n informal* **1** a demonstration of good wishes to a person about to set off on a journey, new career, etc **2** a start, esp an auspicious one, to a venture ▷ *vb* **send off** (*tr, adverb*) **3** to cause to depart; despatch **4** *sport* (of the referee) to dismiss (a player) from the field of play for some offence **5** *informal* to give a sendoff to

send up *vb* (*tr, adverb*) **1** *slang* to send to prison **2** *Brit informal* to make fun of, esp by doing an imitation or parody of: *he sent up the teacher marvellously* ▷ *n* **send-up** **3** *Brit informal* a parody or imitation

Seneca ('sɛnɪkə) *n* **1** (*pl* **-cas** *or* **-ca**) a member of a North American Indian people formerly living south of Lake Ontario; one of the Iroquois peoples **2** the language of this people, belonging to the Iroquoian family [c19 from Dutch *Sennecaas* (plural), probably of Algonquian origin]

senecio (sɪ'niːʃɪəʊ) *n, pl* **-cios** any plant of the genus *Senecio*, including groundsels, ragworts, and cineraria: family *Asteraceae* (composites)

senega ('sɛnɪɡə) *n* **1** a milkwort plant, *Polygala senega*, of the eastern US, with small white flowers **2** the root of this plant, used as an expectorant ▷ Also called: **senega snakeroot, seneca snakeroot** [c18 variant of *Seneca* (the Indian tribe)]

Senegal (ˌsɛnɪ'ɡɔːl) *n* a republic in West Africa, on the Atlantic: made part of French West Africa in 1895; became fully independent in 1960; joined with The Gambia to form the Confederation of Senegambia (1982–89); mostly low-lying, with semidesert in the north and tropical forest in the southwest. Official language: French. Religion: Muslim majority. Currency: franc. Capital: Dakar. Pop: 10 339 000 (2004 est). Area: 197 160 sq km (76 124 sq miles)

Senegalese (ˌsɛnɪɡə'liːz) *adj* **1** of or relating to Senegal or its inhabitants ▷ *n* **2** a native or inhabitant of Senegal

Senegambia (ˌsɛnə'ɡæmbɪə) *n* a region of W Africa, between the Senegal and Gambia Rivers: now mostly in Senegal

Senegambia Confederation *n* an economic and political union (1982–89) between Senegal and The Gambia

senescent (sɪ'nɛsᵊnt) *adj* **1** growing old **2** characteristic of old age [c17 from Latin *senēscere* to grow old, from *senex* old] > **se'nescence** *n*

seneschal ('sɛnɪʃəl) *n* **1** a steward of the household of a medieval prince or nobleman who took charge of domestic arrangements, etc **2** *Brit* a cathedral official [c14 from Old French, from Medieval Latin *siniscalcus*, of Germanic origin; related to Old High German *senescalh* oldest servant, from *sene-* old + *scalh* a servant]

senile ('siːnaɪl) *adj* **1** of, relating to, or characteristic of old age **2** mentally or physically weak or infirm on account of old age **3** (of land

forms or rivers) at an advanced stage in the cycle of erosion. See **old** (sense 18) [c17 from Latin *senīlis*, from *senex* an old man] > **senilely** *adv* > senility (sɪ'nɪlɪtɪ) *n*

senile dementia *n* dementia starting in old age with no precipitating physical cause

senior ('siːnjə) *adj* **1** higher in rank or length of service **2** older in years: *senior citizens* **3** of or relating to adulthood, maturity, or old age: *senior privileges* **4** *education* **a** of, relating to, or designating more advanced or older pupils **b** of or relating to a secondary school **5** *US* of, relating to, or designating students in the fourth and final year at college ▷ *n* **6** a senior person **7** an elderly person **8 a** a senior pupil, student, etc **b** a fellow of senior rank in an English university [c14 from Latin: older, from *senex* old]

Senior ('siːnjə) *adj chiefly US* being the older: used to distinguish the father from the son with the same first name or names: *Charles Parker, Senior.* Abbreviations: **Sr, Sen**

senior aircraftman *n* a rank in the Royal Air Force comparable to that of a private in the army, though not the lowest rank in the Royal Air Force

senior citizen *n* an old age pensioner

senior common room *n* (in British universities, colleges, etc) a common room for the use of academic staff. Compare **junior common room**

seniority (ˌsiːnɪ'ɒrɪtɪ) *n, pl* **-ties 1** the state of being senior **2** precedence in rank, etc, due to senior status

senior management *n* another term for **top management**

senior moment *n jocular* a lapse of memory common in elderly people

senior service *n Brit* the Royal Navy

Senlac ('sɛnlæk) *n* a hill in Sussex: site of the Battle of Hastings in 1066

senna ('sɛnə) *n* **1** any of various tropical plants of the leguminous genus *Cassia*, esp *C. angustifolia* (**Arabian senna**) and *C. acutifolia* (**Alexandrian senna**), having typically yellow flowers and long pods **2 senna leaf** the dried leaflets of any of these plants, used as a cathartic and laxative ▷ See also **bladder senna** [c16 via New Latin from Arabic *sanā*]

Sennar (sɛnɑː, sɛ'nɑː) *n* **1** a region of the E Sudan, between the White Nile and the Blue Nile: a kingdom from the 16th to 19th centuries **2** a town in this region, on the Blue Nile: the nearby **Sennar Dam** (1925) supplies irrigation water to Gezira. Pop: 135 000 (2005 est)

sennet ('sɛnɪt) *n* a fanfare: used as a stage direction in Elizabethan drama [c16 probably variant of SIGNET (meaning "a sign")]

sennight *or* **se'nnight** ('sɛnaɪt) *n* an archaic word for **week** [Old English *seofan nihte*; see SEVEN, NIGHT]

sennit ('sɛnɪt) *n* **1** a flat braided cordage used on ships **2** plaited straw, grass, palm leaves, etc, as for making hats [c17 of unknown origin]

señor (sɛ'njɔː; *Spanish* se'ɲor) *n, pl* **-ñors** *or* **-ñores** (*Spanish* -'ɲores) a Spaniard or Spanish-speaking man: a title of address equivalent to *Mr* when placed before a name or *sir* when used alone [Spanish, from Latin *senior* an older man, SENIOR]

señora (sɛ'njɔːrə; *Spanish* se'ɲora) *n, pl* **-ras** (-rəz; *Spanish* -ras) a married Spanish or Spanish-speaking woman: a title of address equivalent to *Mrs* when placed before a name or *madam* when used alone

señorita (ˌsɛnjɔː'riːtə; *Spanish* seɲo'rita) *n, pl* **-tas** (-təz; *Spanish* -tas) an unmarried Spanish or Spanish-speaking woman: a title of address equivalent to *Miss* when placed before a name or *madam* or *miss* when used alone

sensate ('sɛnseɪt) *adj* **1** perceived by the senses **2** *obsolete* having the power of sensation [c16 from Late Latin *sensātus* endowed with sense, from Latin *sensus* SENSE] > **sensately** *adv*

sensation (sɛn'seɪʃən) *n* **1** the power of perceiving through the senses **2** a physical condition or experience resulting from the stimulation of one of the sense organs: *a sensation of warmth* **3** a general feeling or awareness: *a sensation of fear* **4** a state of widespread public excitement: *his announcement caused a sensation* **5** anything that causes such a state: *your speech was a sensation* [C17 from Medieval Latin *sensātiō*, from Late Latin *sensātus* SENSATE] > **sen'sationless** *adj*

sensational (sɛn'seɪʃənəl) *adj* **1** causing or intended to cause intense feelings, esp of curiosity, horror, etc: *sensational disclosures in the press* **2** *informal* extremely good: *a sensational skater* **3** of or relating to the faculty of sensation **4** *philosophy* of or relating to sensationalism > **sen'sationally** *adv*

sensationalism (sɛn'seɪʃənəˌlɪzəm) *n* **1** the use of sensational language, etc, to arouse an intense emotional response **2** such sensational matter itself **3** Also called: **sensualism** *philosophy* **a** the doctrine that knowledge cannot go beyond the analysis of experience **b** *ethics* the doctrine that the ability to gratify the senses is the only criterion of goodness **4** *psychol* the theory that all experience and mental life may be explained in terms of sensations and remembered images **5** *aesthetics* the theory of the beauty of sensuality in the arts ▷ Also called (for senses 3, 4): **sensationism** > **sen'sationalist** *n, adj* > **senˌsational'istic** *adj*

sensationalize *or* **sensationalise** (sɛn'seɪʃənəˌlaɪz) *vb* (*tr*) to cause (events, esp in newspaper reports) to seem more vivid, shocking, etc, than they really are

sense (sɛns) *n* **1** any of the faculties by which the mind receives information about the external world or about the state of the body. In addition to the five traditional faculties of sight, hearing, touch, taste, and smell, the term includes the means by which bodily position, temperature, pain, balance, etc, are perceived **2** such faculties collectively; the ability to perceive **3** a feeling perceived through one of the senses: *a sense of warmth* **4** a mental perception or awareness: *a sense of happiness* **5** moral discernment; understanding: *a sense of right and wrong* **6** (*sometimes plural*) sound practical judgment or intelligence: *he is a man without any sense* **7** reason or purpose: *what is the sense of going out in the rain?* **8** substance or gist; meaning: *what is the sense of this proverb?* **9** specific meaning; definition: *in what sense are you using the word?* **10** an opinion or consensus **11** *maths* one of two opposite directions measured on a directed line; the sign as contrasted with the magnitude of a vector **12** **make sense** to be reasonable or understandable **13** *logic, linguistics* **a** the import of an expression as contrasted with its referent. Thus *the morning star* and *the evening star* have the same reference, Venus, but different senses **b** the property of an expression by virtue of which its referent is determined **c** that which one grasps in understanding an expression **14** take leave of one's senses. See **leave**[2] (sense 8) ▷ *vb* (*tr*) **15** to perceive through one or more of the senses **16** to apprehend or detect without or in advance of the evidence of the senses **17** to understand **18** *computing* **a** to test or locate the position of (a part of computer hardware) **b** to read (data) [C14 from Latin *sēnsus*, from *sentīre* to feel]

sense datum *n philosophy* a sensation detached both from any information it may convey and from its putative source in the external world, such as the bare awareness of a red visual field. Sense data are held by some philosophers to be the immediate objects of experience providing certain knowledge from which knowledge of material objects is inferred. See also **representationalism** (sense 1), **apriorism**

senseless ('sɛnslɪs) *adj* **1** lacking in sense; foolish: *a senseless plan* **2** lacking in feeling; unconscious **3** lacking in perception; stupid > **'senselessly** *adv* > **'senselessness** *n*

sense organ *n* a structure in animals that is specialized for receiving external or internal stimuli and transmitting them in the form of nervous impulses to the brain

sensi (*Japanese* 'sɛnseɪ) *n* a teacher or instructor, esp of karate or judo [Japanese: teacher, leader]

sensibilia (ˌsɛnsɪ'bɪlɪə) *n* that which can be sensed [Latin, neuter plural of *sensibilis* SENSIBLE]

sensibility (ˌsɛnsɪ'bɪlɪtɪ) *n, pl* **-ties** **1** the ability to perceive or feel **2** (*often plural*) the capacity for responding to emotion, impression, etc **3** (*often plural*) the capacity for responding to aesthetic stimuli **4** mental responsiveness; discernment; awareness **5** (*usually plural*) emotional or moral feelings: *cruelty offends most people's sensibilities* **6** the condition of a plant of being susceptible to external influences, esp attack by parasites

sensible ('sɛnsɪbəl) *adj* **1** having or showing good sense or judgment: *a sensible decision* **2** (of clothing) serviceable; practical: *sensible shoes* **3** having the capacity for sensation; sensitive **4** capable of being apprehended by the senses **5** perceptible to the mind **6** (sometimes foll by *of*) having perception; aware: *sensible of your kindness* **7** readily perceived; considerable: *a sensible difference* ▷ *n* **8** Also called: **sensible note** a less common term for **leading note** [C14 from Old French, from Late Latin *sēnsibilis*, from Latin *sentīre* to sense] > **'sensibleness** *n* > **'sensibly** *adv*

sensible horizon *n* See **horizon** (sense 2a)

sensillum (sɛn'sɪləm) *n, pl* **-la** (-lə) a sense organ in insects, typically consisting of a receptor organ in the integument connected to sensory neurons [New Latin, diminutive of Latin *sensus* sense (Middle Latin: sense organ)]

sensitive ('sɛnsɪtɪv) *adj* **1** having the power of sensation **2** responsive to or aware of feelings, moods, reactions, etc **3** easily irritated; delicate: *sensitive skin* **4** affected by external conditions or stimuli **5** easily offended **6** of or relating to the senses or the power of sensation **7** capable of registering small differences or changes in amounts, quality, etc: *a sensitive instrument* **8** *photog* having a high sensitivity: *a sensitive emulsion* **9** connected with matters affecting national security, esp through access to classified information **10** (of a stock market or prices) quickly responsive to external influences and thus fluctuating or tending to fluctuate [C14 from Medieval Latin *sēnsitīvus*, from Latin *sentīre* to feel] > **'sensitively** *adv* > **'sensitiveness** *n*

sensitive plant *n* **1** a tropical American mimosa plant, *Mimosa pudica*, the leaflets and stems of which fold if touched **2** any similar plant, such as the leguminous plant *Cassia nictitans* of E North America **3** *informal* a person who is easily upset

sensitivity (ˌsɛnsɪ'tɪvɪtɪ) *n, pl* **-ties** **1** the state or quality of being sensitive **2** *physiol* the state, condition, or quality of reacting or being sensitive to an external stimulus, drug, allergen, etc **3** *electronics* the magnitude or time of response of an instrument, circuit, etc, to an input signal, such as a current **4** *photog* the degree of response of an emulsion to light or other actinic radiation, esp to light of a particular colour, expressed in terms of its speed

sensitize *or* **sensitise** ('sɛnsɪˌtaɪz) *vb* **1** to make or become sensitive **2** (*tr*) to render (an individual) sensitive to a drug, allergen, etc **3** (*tr*) *photog* to make (a material) sensitive to light or to other actinic radiation, esp to light of a particular colour, by coating it with a photographic emulsion often containing special chemicals, such as dyes > **ˌsensiti'zation** *or* **ˌsensiti'sation** *n* > **'sensiˌtizer** *or* **'sensiˌtiser** *n*

sensitometer (ˌsɛnsɪ'tɒmɪtə) *n* an instrument for measuring the sensitivity to light of a photographic material over a range of exposures > **ˌsensi'tometry** *n*

sensor ('sɛnsə) *n* anything, such as a photoelectric cell, that receives a signal or stimulus and responds to it [C19 from Latin *sēnsus* perceived, from *sentīre* to observe]

sensorimotor (ˌsɛnsərɪ'məʊtə) *or* **sensomotor** (ˌsɛnsə'məʊtə) *adj* of or relating to both the sensory and motor functions of an organism or to the nerves controlling them

sensorium (sɛn'sɔːrɪəm) *n, pl* **-riums** *or* **-ria** (-rɪə) **1** the area of the brain considered responsible for receiving and integrating sensations from the outside world **2** *physiol* the entire sensory and intellectual apparatus of the body [C17 from Late Latin, from Latin *sēnsus* felt, from *sentīre* to perceive]

sensor network *or* **wireless sensor network** *n computing* a network of tiny autonomous devices embedded in everyday objects or sprinkled on the ground, able to communicate using wireless links

sensory ('sɛnsərɪ) *or less commonly* **sensorial** (sɛn'sɔːrɪəl) *adj* **1** of or relating to the senses or the power of sensation **2** of or relating to those processes and structures within an organism that receive stimuli from the environment and convey them to the brain [C18 from Latin *sensōrius*, from *sentīre* to feel]

sensory deprivation *n psychol* an experimental situation in which all stimulation is cut off from the sensory receptors

sensual ('sɛnsjʊəl) *adj* **1** of or relating to any of the senses or sense organs; bodily **2** strongly or unduly inclined to gratification of the senses **3** tending to arouse the bodily appetites, esp the sexual appetite **4** of or relating to sensualism [C15 from Late Latin *sensuālis*, from Latin *sēnsus* SENSE. Compare French *sensuel*, Italian *sensuale*] > **'sensually** *adv* > **'sensualness** *n*

sensualism ('sɛnsjʊəˌlɪzəm) *n* **1** the quality or state of being sensual **2** another word for **sensationalism** (senses 3a, 3b)

sensuality (ˌsɛnsjʊ'ælɪtɪ) *n, pl* **-ties** **1** the quality or state of being sensual **2** excessive indulgence in sensual pleasures > **sensualist** ('sɛnsjʊəlɪst) *n*

sensum ('sɛnsəm) *n, pl* **-sa** (-sə) another word for **sense datum**

sensuous ('sɛnsjʊəs) *adj* **1** aesthetically pleasing to the senses **2** appreciative of or moved by qualities perceived by the senses **3** of, relating to, or derived from the senses [C17 apparently coined by Milton to avoid the unwanted overtones of SENSUAL; not in common use until C19 from Latin *sēnsus* SENSE + -OUS] > **'sensuously** *adv* > **'sensuousness** *n*

Sensurround ('sɛnsəˌraʊnd) *n trademark* a sound reproduction system used esp in cinemas, in which low-frequency output causes bodily sensations in the audience, resulting in a feeling of involvement in the film

sent[1] (sɛnt) *vb* the past tense and past participle of **send**[1] and **send**[2]

sent[2] (sɛnt) *n, pl* **-ti** a monetary unit of Estonia, worth one hundredth of a kroon [C19 ultimately from Chinese *ch'ien* coin]

sentence ('sɛntəns) *n* **1** a sequence of words capable of standing alone to make an assertion, ask a question, or give a command, usually consisting of a subject and a predicate containing a finite verb **2** the judgment formally pronounced upon a person convicted in criminal proceedings, esp the decision as to what punishment is to be imposed **3** an opinion, judgment, or decision **4** *music* another word for **period** (sense 11) **5** any short passage of scripture employed in liturgical use: *the funeral sentences* **6** *logic* a well-formed expression, without variables **7** *archaic* a proverb, maxim, or aphorism ▷ *vb* **8** (*tr*) to pronounce sentence on (a convicted person) in a court of law: *the judge sentenced the murderer to life imprisonment* [C13 via Old French from Latin *sententia* a way of thinking, from *sentīre* to feel] > **sentential** (sɛn'tɛnʃəl) *adj* > **sen'tentially** *adv*

sentence connector *n* a word or phrase that introduces a clause or sentence and serves as a transition between it and a previous clause or sentence, as for example *also* in *I'm buying eggs and*

S

also I'm looking for a dessert for tonight. It may be preceded by a coordinating conjunction such as *and* in the above example

sentence stress *n* the stress given to a word or words in a sentence, often conveying nuances of meaning or emphasis

sentence substitute *n* a word or phrase, esp one traditionally classified as an adverb, that is used in place of a finite sentence, such as *yes, no, certainly,* and *never*

sentencing circle *n* a method of dispensing justice amongst native Canadian peoples involving discussion between offenders, victims, and members of the community

sentential calculus *n logic* the formal theory the intended interpretation of which concerns the logical relations between sentences treated only as a whole and without regard to their internal structure

sentential function *n* another name for **open sentence**

sententious (sɛn'tɛnʃəs) *adj* **1** characterized by or full of aphorisms, terse pithy sayings, or axioms **2** constantly using aphorisms, etc **3** tending to indulge in pompous moralizing [c15 from Latin *sententiōsus* full of meaning, from *sententia;* see SENTENCE] > sen'tentiously *adv*
> sen'tentiousness *n*

sentience ('sɛnʃəns) *or* **sentiency** *n* **1** the state or quality of being sentient; awareness **2** sense perception not involving intelligence or mental perception; feeling

sentient ('sɛntɪənt) *adj* **1** having the power of sense perception or sensation; conscious ⊳ *n* **2** *rare* a sentient person or thing [c17 from Latin *sentiēns* feeling, from *sentīre* to perceive]
> 'sentiently *adv*

sentiment ('sɛntɪmənt) *n* **1** susceptibility to tender, delicate, or romantic emotion: *she has too much sentiment to be successful* **2** *(often plural)* a thought, opinion, or attitude **3** exaggerated, overindulged, or mawkish feeling or emotion **4** an expression of response to deep feeling, esp in art or literature **5** a feeling, emotion, or awareness: *a sentiment of pity* **6** a mental attitude modified or determined by feeling: *there is a strong revolutionary sentiment in his country* **7** a feeling conveyed, or intended to be conveyed, in words [c17 from Medieval Latin *sentīmentum,* from Latin *sentīre* to feel]

sentimental (ˌsɛntɪ'mɛntᵊl) *adj* **1** tending to indulge the emotions excessively **2** making a direct appeal to the emotions, esp to romantic feelings **3** relating to or characterized by sentiment > ˌsenti'mentally *adv*

sentimentalism (ˌsɛntɪ'mɛntᵊˌlɪzəm) *n* **1** the state or quality of being sentimental **2** an act, statement, etc, that is sentimental
> ˌsenti'mentalist *n*

sentimentality (ˌsɛntɪmɛn'tælɪtɪ) *n, pl* **-ties 1** the state, quality, or an instance of being sentimental **2** an act, statement, etc, that is sentimental

sentimentalize *or* **sentimentalise** (ˌsɛntɪ'mɛntᵊˌlaɪz) *vb* to make sentimental or behave sentimentally > ˌsentiˌmentali'zation *or* ˌsentiˌmentali'sation *n*

sentimental value *n* the value of an article in terms of its sentimental associations for a particular person

sentinel ('sɛntɪnᵊl) *n* **1** a person, such as a sentry, assigned to keep guard **2** *computing* a character used to indicate the beginning or end of a particular block of information ⊳ *vb* -nels, -nelling, -nelled *(tr)* **3** to guard as a sentinel **4** to post as a sentinel **5** to provide with a sentinel [c16 from Old French *sentinelle,* from Old Italian *sentinella,* from *sentina* watchfulness, from *sentire* to notice, from Latin]

sentry ('sɛntrɪ) *n, pl* **-tries 1** a soldier who guards or prevents unauthorized access to a place, keeps watch for danger, etc **2** the watch kept by a sentry [c17 perhaps shortened from obsolete

centrinel, c16 variant of SENTINEL]

sentry box *n* a small shelter with an open front in which a sentry may stand to be sheltered from the weather

Senussi *or* **Senusi** (sɛ'nu:sɪ) *n, pl* **-sis** a member of a zealous and aggressive Muslim sect of North Africa and Arabia, founded in 1837 by **Sidi Mohammed ibn Ali al Senussi** (?1787–1859)
> Se'nussian *or* Se'nusian *adj*

senza ('sɛntsɑ:) *prep music* without; omitting [Italian]

Seoul (səʊl) *n* the capital of South Korea, in the west on the Han River: capital of Korea from 1392 to 1910, then seat of the Japanese administration until 1945; became capital of South Korea in 1948; cultural and educational centre. Pop: 9 592 000 (2005 est)

SEPA *abbreviation for* Scottish Environment Protection Agency

sepal ('sɛpᵊl) *n* any of the separate parts of the calyx of a flower [c19 from New Latin *sepalum: sep-,* from Greek *skepē* a covering + *-alum,* from New Latin *petalum* PETAL] > 'sepalled *or* sepalous ('sɛpələs) *adj*

sepaloid ('si:pəˌlɔɪd) *or* **sepaline** *adj* (esp of petals) resembling a sepal in structure and function

-sepalous *adj combining form* having sepals of a specified type or number: *polysepalous* > **-sepaly** *n combining form*

separable ('sɛpərəbᵊl, 'sɛprəbᵊl) *adj* able to be separated, divided, or parted > ˌsepara'bility *or* 'separableness *n* > 'separably *adv*

separate *vb* ('sɛpəˌreɪt) **1** *(tr)* to act as a barrier between: *a range of mountains separates the two countries* **2** to put or force or be put or forced apart **3** to part or be parted from a mass or group **4** *(tr)* to discriminate between: *to separate the men from the boys* **5** to divide or be divided into component parts; sort or be sorted **6** to sever or be severed **7** *(intr)* (of a married couple) to cease living together by mutual agreement or after obtaining a decree of judicial separation ⊳ *adj* ('sɛprɪt, 'sɛpərɪt) **8** existing or considered independently: *a separate problem* **9** disunited or apart **10** set apart from the main body or mass **11** distinct, individual, or particular **12** solitary or withdrawn **13** *(sometimes capital)* designating or relating to a Church or similar institution that has ceased to have associations with an original parent organization [c15 from Latin *sēparāre,* from *sē-* apart + *parāre* to obtain] > 'separately *adv* > 'separateness *n*

separates ('sɛprɪts, 'sɛpərɪts) *pl n* women's outer garments that only cover part of the body and so are worn in combination with others, usually unmatching; skirts, blouses, jackets, trousers, etc. Compare **coordinates**

separate school *n* (in Canada) a school for a large religious minority financed by its rates and administered by its own school board but under the authority of the provincial department of education

separating funnel *n chem* a large funnel having a tap in its output tube, used to separate immiscible liquids

separation (ˌsɛpə'reɪʃən) *n* **1** the act of separating or state of being separated **2** the place or line where a separation is made **3** a gap that separates **4** *family law* the cessation of cohabitation between a man and wife, either by mutual agreement or under a decree of a court. See **judicial separation** Compare **divorce 5 a** the act of jettisoning a burnt-out stage of a multistage rocket **b** the instant at which such a stage is jettisoned

separation anxiety *n psychoanal* a state of distress felt at the prospect of being separated from a familiar or beloved person

separatist ('sɛpərətɪst, 'sɛprə-) *or* **separationist** *n* **a** a person who advocates or practises secession from an organization or group **b** *(as modifier): a separatist movement* > 'separaˌtism *n* > ˌsepara'tistic *adj*

Separatist ('sɛpərətɪst, 'sɛprə-) *n (sometimes not capital)* a person who advocates the secession of a province, esp Quebec, from Canada
> 'Separaˌtism *n*

separative ('sɛpərətɪv, 'sɛprə-) *adj* tending to separate or causing separation > 'separatively *adv* > 'separativeness *n*

separator ('sɛpəˌreɪtə) *n* **1** a person or thing that separates **2** a device for separating things into constituent parts, as milk into cream, etc
> 'separatory *adj*

separatrix ('sɛpəˌreɪtrɪks) *n, pl* separatrices (ˌsɛpə'reɪtrɪˌsi:z) another name for **solidus** (sense 1) [via New Latin from Late Latin, feminine of *sēparātor* one that separates]

Sephardi (sɪ'fɑ:di:) *n, pl* -dim (-dɪm) *Judaism* **1 a** a Jew of Spanish, Portuguese, or North African descent **b** (loosely) any Oriental Jew **2** the pronunciation of Hebrew used by these Jews, and of Modern Hebrew as spoken in Israel **3** *(modifier)* of or pertaining to the Sephardim, esp to their liturgy and ritual **4** *(modifier)* of or pertaining to the liturgy adopted by certain European, esp Chassidic, communities who believe it to be more authentic but nonetheless differing from the genuine Oriental liturgy ⊳ Compare **Ashkenazi** [c19 from Late Hebrew, from Hebrew *sepharad* a region mentioned in Obadiah 20, thought to have been Spain] > Se'phardic *adj*

sepia ('si:pɪə) *n* **1** a dark reddish-brown pigment obtained from the inky secretion of the cuttlefish **2** any cuttlefish of the genus *Sepia* **3** a brownish tone imparted to a photograph, esp an early one such as a calotype. It can be produced by first bleaching a print (after fixing) and then immersing it for a short time in a solution of sodium sulphide or of alkaline thiourea **4** a brownish-grey to dark yellowish-brown colour **5** a drawing or photograph in sepia ⊳ *adj* **6** of the colour sepia or done in sepia: *a sepia print* [c16 from Latin: a cuttlefish, from Greek; related to Greek *sēpein* to make rotten]

sepiolite ('si:pɪəˌlaɪt) *n* another name for **meerschaum** (sense 1) [c19 from German *Sepiolith,* from Greek *sēpion* bone of a cuttlefish; see SEPIA, -LITE]

sepmag ('sɛpˌmæg) *adj* designating a film or television programme for which the sound is recorded on separate magnetic material and run in synchronism with the picture [c20 from SEP(ARATE) + MAG(NETIC)]

sepoy ('si:pɔɪ) *n* (formerly) an Indian soldier in the service of the British [c18 from Portuguese *sipaio,* from Urdu *sipāhī,* from Persian: horseman, from *sipāh* army]

Sepoy Rebellion *or* **Mutiny** *n* the Indian Mutiny of 1857–58

seppuku (sɛ'pu:ku:) *n* another word for **hara-kiri** [from Japanese, from Chinese *ch'ieh* to cut + *fu* bowels]

sepsis ('sɛpsɪs) *n* the presence of pus-forming bacteria in the body [c19 via New Latin from Greek *sēpsis* a rotting; related to Greek *sēpein* to cause to decay]

sept (sɛpt) *n* **1** *anthropol* a clan or group that believes itself to be descended from a common ancestor **2** a branch of a tribe or nation, esp in medieval Ireland or Scotland [c16 perhaps variant of SECT]

Sept *abbreviation for* **1** September **2** Septuagint

septa ('sɛptə) *n* the plural of **septum**

septal ('sɛptᵊl) *adj* of or relating to a septum

septarium (sɛp'tɛərɪəm) *n, pl* -ia (-ɪə) a mass of mineral substance having cracks filled with another mineral, esp calcite [c18 from New Latin, from Latin SEPTUM] > sep'tarian *adj*

septate ('sɛpteɪt) *adj* divided by septa: *a septate plant ovary* [c19 from New Latin *septātus* having a SEPTUM]

septavalent (ˌsɛptə'veɪlənt) *adj chem* another word for **heptavalent** [c19 from SEPT(IVALENT) + (HEPT)AVALENT]

September (sɛpˈtɛmbə) *n* the ninth month of the year, consisting of 30 days [Old English, from Latin: the seventh (month) according to the original calendar of ancient Rome, from *septem* seven]

September Massacre *n* (during the French Revolution) the massacre of royalist prisoners and others in Paris between Sept 2 and 6, 1792

Septembrist (sɛpˈtɛmbrɪst) *n French history* a person who took part in the September Massacre

septenary (ˈsɛptɪnərɪ) *adj* **1** of or relating to the number seven **2** forming a group of seven **3** another word for **septennial** ▷ *n, pl* -**naries 4** the number seven **5** a group of seven things **6** a period of seven years **7** *prosody* a line of seven metrical feet [C16 from Latin *septēnārius*, from *septēnī* seven each, from *septem* seven]

septennial (sɛpˈtɛnɪəl) *adj* **1** occurring every seven years **2** relating to or lasting seven years [C17 from Latin *septennis*, from *septem* seven + *annus* a year] > sepˈtennially *adv*

septennium (sɛpˈtɛnɪəm) *n, pl* -**niums, -nia** (-nɪə) a period or cycle of seven years [C19 from Latin, from *septem* seven + -*ennium*, from *annus* year]

septentrion (sɛpˈtɛntrɪ,ɒn) *n archaic* the northern regions or the north [C14 from Latin *septentriōnēs*, literally: the seven ploughing oxen (the constellation of the Great Bear), from *septem* seven + *triōnēs* ploughing oxen] > sepˈtentrional *adj*

septet *or* **septette** (sɛpˈtɛt) *n* **1** *music* a group of seven singers or instrumentalists or a piece of music composed for such a group **2** a group of seven people or things [C19 from German, from Latin *septem* seven]

septi-¹ *or before a vowel* **sept-** *combining form* seven: *septivalent* [from Latin *septem*]

septi-² *combining form* septum: *septicidal*

septic (ˈsɛptɪk) *adj* **1** of, relating to, or caused by sepsis **2** of, relating to, or caused by putrefaction ▷ *n* **3** *Austral and NZ informal* short for **septic tank** [C17 from Latin *sēpticus*, from Greek *sēptikos*, from *sēptos* decayed, from *sēpein* to make rotten] > ˈseptically *adv* > sepˈticity (sɛpˈtɪsɪtɪ) *n*

septicaemia *or US* **septicemia** (,sɛptɪˈsiːmɪə) *n* a condition caused by pus-forming microorganisms in the blood. Nontechnical name: **blood poisoning** See also **bacteraemia, pyaemia** [C19 from New Latin, from Greek *sēptik(os)* SEPTIC + -AEMIA] > ,septiˈcaemic *or US* ,septiˈcemic *adj*

septicidal (,sɛptɪˈsaɪdᵊl) *adj botany* (of a dehiscence) characterized by splitting along the partitions of the seed capsule [C19 from SEPTI-² + -CIDAL] > ,septiˈcidally *adv*

septic tank *n* a tank, usually below ground, for containing sewage to be decomposed by anaerobic bacteria

septifragal (sɛpˈtɪfrəgᵊl) *adj* (of a dehiscence) characterized by breaking apart from a natural line of division in the fruit [C19 from SEPTI-² + -*fragal*, from Latin *frangere* to break]

septilateral (,sɛptɪˈlætərəl) *adj* having seven sides

septillion (sɛpˈtɪljən) *n, pl* -**lions** *or* -**lion 1** (in Britain, France, and Germany) the number represented as one followed by 42 zeros (10⁴²) **2** (in the US and Canada) the number represented as one followed by 24 zeros (10²⁴). Brit word: **quadrillion** [C17 from French, from *sept* seven + -*illion*, on the model of *million*] > sepˈtillionth *adj, n*

septime (ˈsɛptiːm) *n* the seventh of eight basic positions from which a parry or attack can be made in fencing [C19 from Latin *septimus* seventh, from *septem* seven]

septivalent (,sɛptɪˈveɪlənt) *or* **septavalent** (,sɛptəˈveɪlənt) *adj chem* another word for **heptavalent**

septuagenarian (,sɛptjuədʒɪˈnɛərɪən) *n* **1** a person who is from 70 to 79 years old ▷ *adj* **2** being between 70 and 79 years old **3** of or relating to a septuagenarian [C18 from Latin *septuāgēnārius*, from *septuāgēnī* seventy each, from *septuāgintā* seventy]

Septuagesima (,sɛptjuəˈdʒɛsɪmə) *n* the third

Sunday before Lent [C14 from Church Latin *septuāgēsima* (*dīes*) the seventieth (day); compare QUINQUAGESIMA]

Septuagint (ˈsɛptjuə,dʒɪnt) *n* the principal Greek version of the Old Testament, including the Apocrypha, believed to have been translated by 70 or 72 scholars [C16 from Latin *septuāgintā* seventy]

septum (ˈsɛptəm) *n, pl* -**ta** (-tə) **1** *biology, anatomy* a dividing partition between two tissues or cavities **2** a dividing partition or membrane between two cavities in a mechanical device [C18 from Latin *saeptum* wall, from *saepīre* to enclose; related to Latin *saepēs* a fence]

septuple (ˈsɛptjʊpᵊl) *adj* **1** seven times as much or many; sevenfold **2** consisting of seven parts or members ▷ *vb* **3** (*tr*) to multiply by seven [C17 from Late Latin *septuplus*, from *septem* seven; compare QUADRUPLE]

septuplet (sɛpˈtju:plɪt, ˈsɛptjʊplɪt) *n* **1** *music* a group of seven notes played in a time value of six, eight, etc **2** one of seven offspring produced at one birth **3** a group of seven things

septuplicate (sɛpˈtju:plɪkət) *n* **1** a group or set of seven things ▷ *adj* **2** having or being in seven parts; sevenfold

sepulchral (sɪˈpʌlkrəl) *adj* **1** suggestive of a tomb; gloomy **2** of or relating to a sepulchre > seˈpulchrally *adv*

sepulchre *or US* **sepulcher** (ˈsɛpəlkə) *n* **1** a burial vault, tomb, or grave **2** Also called: **Easter sepulchre** a separate alcove in some medieval churches in which the Eucharistic elements were kept from Good Friday until the Easter ceremonies ▷ *vb* **3** (*tr*) to bury in a sepulchre [C12 from Old French *sépulcre*, from Latin *sepulcrum*, from *sepelīre* to bury]

sepulture (ˈsɛpəltʃə) *n* **1** the act of placing in a sepulchre **2** an archaic word for **sepulchre** [C13 via Old French from Latin *sepultūra*, from *sepultus* buried, from *sepelīre* to bury]

seq. *abbreviation for* **1** sequel **2** sequens [Latin: the following (one)]

seqq. *abbreviation for* sequentia [Latin: the following (ones)]

sequacious (sɪˈkweɪʃəs) *adj* **1** logically following in regular sequence **2** ready to follow any leader; pliant [C17 from Latin *sequāx* pursuing, from *sequī* to follow] > seˈquaciously *adv* > sequacity (sɪˈkwæsɪtɪ) *n*

sequel (ˈsiːkwəl) *n* **1** anything that follows from something else; development **2** a consequence or result **3** a novel, play, etc, that continues a previously related story [C15 from Late Latin *sequēla*, from Latin *sequī* to follow]

sequela (sɪˈkwiːlə) *n, pl* -**lae** (-liː) (*often plural*) *med* **1** any abnormal bodily condition or disease related to or arising from a pre-existing disease **2** any complication of a disease [C18 from Latin: SEQUEL]

sequence (ˈsiːkwəns) *n* **1** an arrangement of two or more things in a successive order **2** the successive order of two or more things: *chronological sequence* **3** a sequentially ordered set of related things or ideas **4** an action or event that follows another or others **5 a** *cards* a set of three or more consecutive cards, usually of the same suit **b** *bridge* a set of two or more consecutive cards **6** *music* an arrangement of notes or chords repeated several times at different pitches **7** *maths* **a** an ordered set of numbers or other mathematical entities in one-to-one correspondence with the integers 1 to *n* **b** an ordered infinite set of mathematical entities in one-to-one correspondence with the natural numbers **8** a section of a film constituting a single continuous uninterrupted episode **9** *biochem* the unique order of amino acids in the polypeptide chain of a protein or of nucleotides in the polynucleotide chain of DNA or RNA **10** *RC Church* another word for **prose** (sense 4) ▷ *vb* (*tr*) **11** to arrange in a sequence **12** *biochem* to determine the order of the units comprising (a protein, nucleic acid, genome, etc) [C14 from Medieval

Latin *sequentia* that which follows, from Latin *sequī* to follow]

sequence of tenses *n grammar* the sequence according to which the tense of a subordinate verb in a sentence is determined by the tense of the principal verb, as in *I believe he is lying, I believed he was lying,* etc

sequencer (ˈsiːkwənsə) *n* **1** an electronic device that determines the order in which a number of operations occur **2** an electronic device that sorts information into the required order for data processing **3** a unit connected to a synthesizer, which is capable of memorizing sequences of notes

sequencing (ˈsiːkwənsɪŋ) *n biochem* **1** the procedure of determining the order of amino acids in the polypeptide chain of a protein (**protein sequencing**) or of nucleotides in a DNA section comprising a gene (**gene sequencing**) **2** Also called: **priority sequencing** *commerce* specifying the order in which jobs are to be processed, based on the allocation of priorities

sequent (ˈsiːkwənt) *adj* **1** following in order or succession **2** following as a result; consequent ▷ *n* **3** something that follows; consequence **4** *logic* a formal representation of an argument. The inference of A from A & B is written A & B ⊢ A. The sequent ⊢ A represents the derivation of A from no assumptions and thus indicates that A is a theorem [C16 from Latin *sequēns*, from *sequī* to follow] > ˈsequently *adv*

sequential (sɪˈkwɛnʃəl) *adj* **1** characterized by or having a regular sequence **2** another word for **sequent.** > sequentiality (sɪ,kwɛnʃɪˈælɪtɪ) *n* > seˈquentially *adv*

sequential access *n* a method of reaching and reading data from a computer file by reading through the file from the beginning. Compare **direct access**

sequential scanning *n* a system of scanning a television picture along the lines in numerical sequence. Compare **interlaced scanning**

sequester (sɪˈkwɛstə) *vb* (*tr*) **1** to remove or separate **2** (*usually passive*) to retire into seclusion **3** *law* to take (property) temporarily out of the possession of its owner, esp until the claims of creditors are satisfied or a court order is complied with **4** *international law* to requisition or appropriate (enemy property) [C14 from Late Latin *sequestrāre* to surrender for safekeeping, from Latin *sequester* a trustee] > seˈquestrable *adj*

sequestrant (sɪˈkwɛstrənt) *n chem* any substance used to bring about sequestration, often by chelation. They are used in horticulture to counteract lime in the soil

sequestrate (sɪˈkwɛstreɪt) *vb* (*tr*) **1** *law* a variant of **sequester** (sense 3) **2** *chiefly Scots law* **a** to place (the property of a bankrupt) in the hands of a trustee for the benefit of his creditors **b** to render (a person) bankrupt **3** *archaic* to seclude or separate [C16 from Late Latin *sequestrāre* to SEQUESTER] > sequestrator (ˈsiːkwɛs,treɪtə, sɪˈkwɛs,treɪtə) *n*

sequestration (,siːkwɛˈstreɪʃən) *n* **1** the act of sequestering or state of being sequestered **2** *law* the sequestering of property **3** *chem* the effective removal of ions from a solution by coordination with another type of ion or molecule to form complexes that do not have the same chemical behaviour as the original ions. See also **sequestrant**

sequestrum (sɪˈkwɛstrəm) *n, pl* -**tra** (-trə) *pathol* a detached piece of necrotic bone that often migrates to a wound, abscess, etc. See **sequester** [C19 from New Latin, from Latin: something deposited] > seˈquestral *adj*

sequin (ˈsiːkwɪn) *n* **1** a small piece of shiny often coloured metal foil or plastic, usually round, used to decorate garments, etc **2** Also called: **zecchino** any of various gold coins that were formerly minted in Italy, Turkey, and Malta [C17 via French from Italian *zecchino*, from *zecca* mint, from Arabic *sikkah* die for striking coins] > 'sequined *adj*

sequoia (sɪ'kwɔɪə) *n* either of two giant Californian coniferous trees, *Sequoia sempervirens* (**redwood**) or *Sequoiadendron giganteum* (formerly *Sequoia gigantea*) (**big tree** or **giant sequoia**): family *Taxodiaceae* [C19 New Latin, named after *Sequoya*, known also as George Guess, (?1770–1843), American Indian scholar and leader]

Sequoia National Park *n* a national park in central California, in the Sierra Nevada Mountains: established in 1890 to protect groves of giant sequoias, some of which are about 4000 years old. Area: 1556 sq km (601 sq miles)

ser *or* **seer** (sɪə) *n* a unit of weight used in India, usually taken as one fortieth of a maund [from Hindi]

sera ('sɪərə) *n* a plural of **serum**

sérac ('sɛræk) *n* a pinnacle of ice among crevasses on a glacier, usually on a steep slope [C19 from Swiss French: a variety of white cheese (hence the ice that it resembles) from Medieval Latin *serācium*, from Latin *serum* whey]

seraglio (sɛ'rɑːlɪˌəʊ) *or* **serail** (sə'raɪ, -'raɪl, -'reɪl) *n, pl* **-raglios** *or* **-rails 1** the harem of a Muslim house or palace **2** a sultan's palace, esp in the former Turkish empire **3** the wives and concubines of a Muslim [C16 from Italian *serraglio* animal cage, from Medieval Latin *serrāculum* bolt, from Latin *sera* a door bar; associated also with Turkish *seray* palace]

serai (sɛ'raɪ) *n* (in the East) a caravanserai or inn [C17 from Turkish *saray* palace, from Persian *sarāī* palace; see CARAVANSERAI]

Serajevo (*Serbo-Croat* 'sɛrajɛvɔ) *n* a variant of **Sarajevo**

Seram *or* **Ceram** (sɪ'ræm) *n* an island in Indonesia, in the Moluccas, separated from New Guinea by the **Ceram Sea**: mountainous and densely forested. Area: 17 150 sq km (6622 sq miles). Also called: **Serang** (sə'ræŋ)

serape (sə'rɑːpɪ) *n* **1** a blanket-like shawl often of brightly-coloured wool worn by men in Latin America **2** a large shawl worn around the shoulders by women as a fashion garment

seraph ('sɛrəf) *n, pl* **-aphs** *or* **-aphim** (-əfɪm) **1** *theol* a member of the highest order of angels in the celestial hierarchies, often depicted as the winged head of a child **2** *Old Testament* one of the fiery six-winged beings attendant upon Jehovah in Isaiah's vision (Isaiah 6) [C17 back formation from plural *seraphim*, via Late Latin from Hebrew]

seraphic (sɪ'ræfɪk) *or* **seraphical** *adj* **1** of or resembling a seraph **2** blissfully serene; rapt > se'raphically *adv*

Serapis ('sɛrəpɪs) *n* a Graeco-Egyptian god combining attributes of Apis and Osiris

Serb (sɜːb) *n, adj* another word for **Serbian** [C19 from Serbian *Srb*]

Serbia ('sɜːbɪə) *n* a constituent republic of the Union of Serbia and Montenegro: declared a kingdom in 1882; precipitated World War I by the conflict with Austria; became part of the Kingdom of the Serbs, Croats, and Slovenes (later called Yugoslavia) in 1918; with Montenegro formed the Federal Republic of Yugoslavia when the other constituent republics became independent in 1991–92; a new Union of Serbia and Montenegro formed in 2002; the autonomous region of Kosovo has been administered by the UN since the conflict of 1999. Capital: Belgrade. Pop: 7 479 437 (2002). Area: 88 361 sq km (34 109 sq miles). Former name: **Servia** Serbian name: **Srbija**

Serbia and Montenegro, Union of *n* a country in SE Europe, consisting of the republics of Serbia and Montenegro; replaced the Federal Republic of Yugoslavia in 2002; chiefly mountainous, with the Danube plains in the N. Official language: Serbian. Religion: Serbian Orthodox majority, with Roman Catholic and Muslim minorities. Currencies: new dinar and euro (in Montenegro and Kosovo). Capital: Belgrade. Pop: 10 519 000 (2004 est). Area: 102 173 sq km (39 449 sq miles)

Serbian ('sɜːbɪən) *or* **Serb** *adj* **1** of, relating to, or characteristic of Serbia, its people, or their dialect of Serbo-Croat ▷ *n* **2** the dialect of Serbo-Croat spoken in Serbia **3 a** a native or inhabitant of Serbia **b** a speaker of the Serbian dialect

Serbo-Croat *or* **Serbo-Croatian** *n* **1** the language of the Serbs and the Croats, belonging to the South Slavonic branch of the Indo-European family. The Serbian dialect is usually written in the Cyrillic alphabet, the Croatian in Roman. Also called: **Croato-Serb** ▷ *adj* **2** of or relating to this language

Sercq (sɛrk) *n* the French name for **Sark**

serdab ('sɜːdæb, sə'dæb) *n* a secret chamber in an ancient Egyptian tomb [C19 (earlier, in the sense: cellar): from Arabic: cellar, from Persian *sardāb* ice cellar, from *sard* cold + *āb* water]

sere¹ *or* **sear** (sɪə) *adj* **1** *archaic* dried up or withered ▷ *vb, n* **2** a rare spelling of **sear** (sense 1) [Old English *sēar*; see SEAR¹]

sere² (sɪə) *n* the series of changes occurring in the ecological succession of a particular community [C20 from SERIES]

serein (sə'reɪn) *n* fine rain falling from a clear sky after sunset, esp in the tropics [C19 via French, from Old French *serain* dusk, from Latin *sērus* late]

Seremban (sə'rɛmbən) *n* a town in Peninsular Malaysia, capital of Negri Sembilan state. Pop: 332 000 (2005 est)

serenade (ˌsɛrɪ'neɪd) *n* **1** a piece of music appropriate to the evening, characteristically played outside the house of a woman **2** a piece of music indicative or suggestive of this **3** an extended composition in several movements similar to the modern suite or divertimento ▷ *vb* **4** (*tr*) to play a serenade for (someone) **5** (*intr*) to play a serenade ▷ Compare **aubade** [C17 from French *sérénade*, from Italian *serenata*, from *sereno* peaceful, from Latin *serēnus* calm; also influenced in meaning by Italian *sera* evening, from Latin *sērus* late] > ˌsere'nader *n*

serenata (ˌsɛrɪ'nɑːtə) *n* **1** an 18th-century cantata, often dramatic in form **2** another word for **serenade** [C18 from Italian; see SERENADE]

serendipity (ˌsɛrən'dɪpɪtɪ) *n* the faculty of making fortunate discoveries by accident [C18 coined by Horace Walpole, from the Persian fairytale *The Three Princes of Serendip*, in which the heroes possess this gift] > ˌseren'dipitous *adj*

serene (sɪ'riːn) *adj* **1** peaceful or tranquil; calm **2** clear or bright: *a serene sky* **3** (*often capital*) honoured: used as part of certain royal titles: *His Serene Highness* [C16 from Latin *serēnus*] > se'renely *adv* > se'reneness *n*

serenity (sɪ'rɛnɪtɪ) *n, pl* **-ties 1** the state or quality of being serene **2** (*often capital*) a title of honour used of certain royal personages: preceded by *his*, *her*, etc

serf (sɜːf) *n* (esp in medieval Europe) an unfree person, esp one bound to the land. If his lord sold the land, the serf was passed on to the new landlord [C15 from Old French, from Latin *servus* slave; see SERVE] > 'serfdom *or* 'serfhood *n* > 'serf,like *adj*

serge (sɜːdʒ) *n* **1** a twill-weave woollen or worsted fabric used for clothing **2** a similar twilled cotton, silk, or rayon fabric [C14 from Old French *sarge*, from Vulgar Latin *sārica* (unattested), from Latin *sērica*, from Greek *sērikon* silk, from *sērikos* silken, from *sēr* silkworm]

sergeant ('sɑːdʒənt) *n* **1** a noncommissioned officer in certain armed forces, usually ranking above a corporal **2 a** (in Britain) a police officer ranking between constable and inspector **b** (in the US) a police officer ranking below a captain **3** See **sergeant at arms 4** a court or municipal officer who has ceremonial duties **5** (formerly) a tenant by military service, not of knightly rank **6** See **serjeant at law**. Also: **serjeant** [C12 from Old French *sergent*, from Latin *serviēns*, literally: serving, from *servīre* to SERVE] > **sergeancy** ('sɑːdʒənsɪ) *or* 'sergeantship *n*

sergeant at arms *n* **1** an officer of a legislative or fraternal body responsible for maintaining internal order **2** (formerly) an officer who served a monarch or noble, esp as an armed attendant ▷ Also called: **sergeant, serjeant at arms, serjeant**

sergeant at law *n* a variant spelling of **serjeant at law**

sergeant baker *n* a large brightly-coloured fish of the genus *Latropiscis*, found in temperate reef waters of Australasia [named after *Sergeant (William) Baker*, a Norfolk Island colonist]

sergeant major *n* **1** a noncommissioned officer of the highest rank or having specific administrative tasks in branches of the armed forces of various countries **2** a large damselfish, *Abudefduf saxatilis*, having a bluish-grey body marked with black stripes

Sergipe (*Portuguese* ser'ʒipi) *n* a state of NE Brazil: the smallest Brazilian state; a centre of resistance to Dutch conquest (17th century). Capital: Aracajú. Pop: 1 846 039 (2002). Area: 13 672 sq km (8492 sq miles)

Sergt *abbreviation for* Sergeant

serial ('sɪərɪəl) *n* **1** a novel, play, etc, presented in separate instalments at regular intervals **2** a publication, usually regularly issued and consecutively numbered ▷ *adj* **3** of, relating to, or resembling a series **4** published or presented as a serial **5** of or relating to such publication or presentation **6** *computing* of or operating on items of information, instructions, etc, in the order in which they occur. Compare **parallel** (sense 5) **7** of, relating to, or using the techniques of serialism **8** *logic, maths* (of a relation) connected, transitive, and asymmetric, thereby imposing an order on all the members of the domain, as *less than* on the natural numbers. See also **ordering** [C19 from New Latin *seriālis*, from Latin *seriēs* SERIES] > 'serially *adv*

serial correlation *n* *statistics* another name for **autocorrelation**

serialism ('sɪərɪəˌlɪzəm) *n* (in 20th-century music) the use of a sequence of notes in a definite order as a thematic basis for a composition and a source from which the musical material is derived. See also **twelve-tone**

serialize *or* **serialise** ('sɪərɪəˌlaɪz) *vb* (*tr*) to publish or present in the form of a serial > ˌseriali'zation *or* ˌseriali'sation *n*

serial killer *n* a person who carries out a series of murders

serial monogamy *n* the practice of having a number of long-term romantic or sexual partners in succession

serial number *n* any of the consecutive numbers assigned to machines, tools, books, etc

serial port *n* *computing* (on a computer) a socket that can be used for connecting devices that send data one bit at a time; often used for connecting the mouse or a modem

seriate ('sɪərɪɪt) *adj* forming a series > 'seriately *adv*

seriatim (ˌsɪərɪ'ætɪm, ˌsɛr-) *adv* in a series; one after another in regular order [C17 from Medieval Latin, from Latin *seriēs* SERIES]

sericeous (sɪ'rɪʃəs) *adj* *botany* **1** covered with a layer of small silky hairs: *a sericeous leaf* **2** silky [C18 from Late Latin *sēriceus* silken, from Latin *sēricus*; see SERGE]

sericin ('sɛrɪsɪn) *n* a gelatinous protein found on the fibres of raw silk [C19 from Latin *sēricum* silk + -IN]

sericulture ('sɛrɪˌkʌltʃə) *n* the rearing of silkworms for the production of raw silk [C19 via French; *seri-* from Latin *sēricum* silk, from Greek *sērikos* silken, from *sēr* a silkworm] > ˌseri'cultural *adj* > ˌseri'culturist *n*

seriema (ˌsɛrɪ'iːmə) *n* either of two cranelike South American birds, *Cariama cristata* or *Chunga burmeisteri*, having a crest just above the bill, rounded wings, and a long tail: family *Cariamidae*, order *Gruiformes* (cranes, rails, etc) [C19 from New Latin, from Tupi *çariama* crested]

series ('sɪəriːz, -rɪz) *n, pl* -ries **1** a group or connected succession of similar or related things, usually arranged in order **2** a set of radio or television programmes having the same characters and setting but different stories **3** a set of books having the same format, related content, etc, published by one firm **4** a set of stamps, coins, etc, issued at a particular time **5** *maths* the sum of a finite or infinite sequence of numbers or quantities. See also **geometric series** **6** *electronics* **a** a configuration of two or more components connected in a circuit so that the same current flows in turn through each of them (esp in the phrase **in series**) **b** (*as modifier*): *a series circuit*. Compare **parallel** (sense 10) **7** *rhetoric* a succession of coordinate elements in a sentence **8** *geology* a stratigraphical unit that is a subdivision of a system and represents the rocks formed during an epoch [c17 from Latin: a row, from *serere* to link]

series resonance *n* the resonance that results when circuit elements are connected with their inductance and capacitance in series, so that the impedance of the combination falls to a minimum at the resonant frequency. Compare **parallel resonance**

series-wound ('sɪəriːzˌwaʊnd, -rɪz-) *adj* (of a motor or generator) having the field and armature circuits connected in series. Compare **shunt-wound**

serif *or rarely* **seriph** ('sɛrɪf) *n printing* a small line at the extremities of a main stroke in a type character [c19 perhaps from Dutch *schreef* dash, probably of Germanic origin, compare Old High German *screvōn* to engrave]

serigraph ('sɛrɪˌɡræf, -ˌɡrɑːf) *n* a colour print made by an adaptation of the silk-screen process [c19 from *seri-*, from Latin *sēricum* silk + -GRAPH] > serigraphy (sə'rɪɡrəfɪ) *n*

serin ('sɛrɪn) *n* any of various small yellow-and-brown finches of the genus *Serinus*, esp *S. serinus*, of parts of Europe and North Africa. See also **canary** [c16 from French, perhaps from Old Provençal *sirena* a bee-eater, from Latin *sīrēn*, a kind of bird, from SIREN]

serine ('sɛriːn, 'sɪəriːn, -rɪn) *n* a sweet-tasting amino acid that is synthesized in the body and is involved in the synthesis of cysteine; 2-amino-3-hydroxypropanoic acid. Formula: $CH_2(OH)CH(NH_2)COOH$ [c19 from SERICIN + -INE²]

seringa (sə'rɪŋɡə) *n* **1** any of several euphorbiaceous trees of the Brazilian genus *Hevea*, that yield rubber **2** a deciduous simaroubaceous tree, *Kirkia acuminata*, of southern Africa with a graceful shape [c18 from Portuguese, variant of SYRINGA]

Seringapatam (sə,rɪŋɡəpə'tæm) *n* a small town in S India, in Karnataka on **Seringapatam Island** in the Cauvery River: capital of Mysore from 1610 to 1799, when it was besieged and captured by the British. Pop: 23 448 (2001)

seriocomic (,sɪərɪəʊ'kɒmɪk) *or less commonly* **seriocomical** *adj* mixing serious and comic elements > ˌserio'comically *adv*

serious ('sɪərɪəs) *adj* **1** grave in nature or disposition; thoughtful: *a serious person* **2** marked by deep feeling; in earnest; sincere: *is he serious or joking?* **3** concerned with important matters: *a serious conversation* **4** requiring effort or concentration: *a serious book* **5** giving rise to fear or anxiety; critical: *a serious illness* **6** *informal* worthy of regard because of substantial quantity or quality: *serious money; serious wine* **7** *informal* extreme or remarkable: *a serious haircut* [c15 from Late Latin *sēriōsus*, from Latin *sērius*; probably related to Old English *swær* gloomy, Gothic *swers* esteemed] > 'seriousness *n*

seriously ('sɪərɪəslɪ) *adv* **1** in a serious manner or to a serious degree **2** *informal* extremely or remarkably: *seriously tall*

serjeant ('sɑːdʒənt) *n* a variant spelling of **sergeant**

serjeant at arms *n* a variant spelling of **sergeant at arms**

serjeant at law *n* (formerly in England) a barrister of a special rank, to which he was raised by a writ under the Great Seal. Also called: serjeant, sergeant at law, sergeant

sermon ('sɜːmən) *n* **1 a** an address of religious instruction or exhortation, often based on a passage from the Bible, esp one delivered during a church service **b** a written version of such an address **2** a serious speech, esp one administering reproof [c12 via Old French from Latin *sermō* discourse, probably from *serere* to join together] > sermonic (sɜː'mɒnɪk) *or* ser'monical *adj*

sermonize *or* **sermonise** ('sɜːmə,naɪz) *vb* to talk to or address (a person or audience) as if delivering a sermon > 'sermon,izer *or* 'sermon,iser *n*

Sermon on the Mount *n New Testament* a major discourse delivered by Christ, including the Beatitudes and the Lord's Prayer (Matthew 5–7)

sero- *combining form* indicating a serum: *serotherapy*

seroconvert (,sɪərəʊkən'vɜːt) *vb* (*intr*) (of an individual) to produce antibodies specific to, and in response to the presence in the blood of, a particular antigen, such as a virus or vaccine > ,serocon'version *n*

serology (sɪ'rɒlədʒɪ) *n* the science concerned with serums > serologic (,sɪərə'lɒdʒɪk) *or* ,sero'logical *adj* > se'rologist *n*

seronegative (,sɪərəʊ'nɛɡətɪv) *adj* (of a person whose blood has been tested for a specific disease, such as AIDS) showing no serological reaction indicating the presence of the disease

seropositive (,sɪərəʊ'pɒzɪtɪv) *adj* (of a person whose blood has been tested for a specific disease, such as AIDS) showing a serological reaction indicating the presence of the disease

seropurulent (,sɪərəʊ'pjʊərələnt) *adj pathol* composed of or containing both serum and pus

serosa (sɪ'rəʊsə) *n* **1** another name for **serous membrane** **2** one of the thin membranes surrounding the embryo in an insect's egg [c19 from New Latin, from *serōsus* relating to SERUM]

serotherapy (,sɪərəʊ'θɛrəpɪ) *n* the treatment of disease by the injection of serum containing antibodies to the disease

serotine ('sɛrə,taɪn) *adj* **1** Also: serotinal (sɪ'rɒtɪnᵊl), serotinous *biology* produced, flowering, or developing late in the season ▷ *n* **2** either of two insectivorous bats, *Eptesicus serotinus* or *Vespertilio serotinus*: family Vespertilionidae [c16 from Latin *sērōtinus* late, from *sērus* late; applied to the bats because they fly late in the evening]

serotonin (,sɛrə'təʊnɪn) *n* a compound that occurs in the brain, intestines, and blood platelets and acts as a neurotransmitter, as well as inducing vasoconstriction and contraction of smooth muscle; 5-hydroxytryptamine (5HT) [from SERO- + TON(IC) + -IN]

serotype ('sɪərəʊ,taɪp) *n medicine* a category into which material, usually a bacterium, is placed based on its serological activity, esp in terms of the antigens it contains or the antibodies produced against it

serous ('sɪərəs) *adj* of, resembling, producing, or containing serum [c16 from Latin *serōsus*, from SERUM] > serosity (sɪ'rɒsɪtɪ) *or* 'serousness *n*

serous fluid *n* a thin watery fluid found in many body cavities, esp those lined with serous membrane

serous membrane *n* any of the smooth moist delicate membranes, such as the pleura or peritoneum, that line the closed cavities of the body and secrete a watery exudate

serow ('sɛrəʊ) *n* either of two antelopes, *Capricornis sumatraensis* and *C. crispus*, of mountainous regions of S and SE Asia, having a dark coat and conical backward-pointing horns [c19 from Lepcha *sā-ro* Tibetan goat]

Seroxat ('sɛ,rɒksæt) *n trademark* a drug that prolongs the action of serotonin in the brain; used to treat depression and social anxiety

Serpens ('sɜːpɛnz) *n, Latin genitive* Serpentis (sə'pɛntɪs) a faint extensive constellation situated in the N and S equatorial regions and divided into two parts, **Serpens Caput** (the head) lying between Ophiuchus and Boötes and **Serpens Cauda** (the tail) between Ophiuchus and Aquila [Latin: SERPENT]

serpent ('sɜːpənt) *n* **1** a literary or dialect word for **snake 2** *Old Testament* a manifestation of Satan as a guileful tempter (Genesis 3:1–5) **3** a sly, deceitful, or unscrupulous person **4** an obsolete wind instrument resembling a snake in shape, the bass form of the cornett **5** a firework that moves about with a serpentine motion when ignited [c14 via Old French from Latin *serpēns* a creeping thing, from *serpere* to creep; related to Greek *herpein* to crawl]

serpentine¹ ('sɜːpən,taɪn) *adj* **1** of, relating to, or resembling a serpent **2** twisting; winding ▷ *n* **3** *maths* a curve that is symmetric about the origin of and asymptotic to the *x*-axis [c14 from Late Latin *serpentīnus*, from *serpēns* SERPENT]

serpentine² ('sɜːpən,taɪn) *n* **1** a dark green or brown mineral with a greasy or silky lustre, found in igneous and metamorphic rocks. It is used as an ornamental stone; and one variety (chrysotile) is known as asbestos. Composition: hydrated magnesium silicate. Formula: $Mg_3Si_2O_5(OH)_4$. Crystal structure: monoclinic **2** any of a group of minerals having the general formula $(Mg,Fe)_3Si_2O_5(OH)_4$ [c15 *serpentyn*, from Medieval Latin *serpentīnum* SERPENTINE¹; referring to the snakelike patterns of these minerals]

serpigo (sɜː'paɪɡəʊ) *n pathol* any progressive skin eruption, such as ringworm or herpes [c14 from Medieval Latin, from Latin *serpere* to creep] > serpiginous (sɜː'pɪdʒɪnəs) *adj*

SERPS *or* **Serps** (sɜːps) *n* (in Britain) *acronym for* state earnings-related pension scheme

serpulid ('sɜːpjʊlɪd) *n* a marine polychaete worm of the family *Serpulidae*, which constructs and lives in a calcareous tube attached to stones or seaweed and has a crown of ciliated tentacles [c19 Latin, from *serpula* a little serpent]

serra ('sɛrə) *n, pl* -rae (-riː) *zoology* a sawlike part or organ [c19 from Latin: saw]

serranid (sə'rænɪd, 'sɛrə-) *or* **serranoid** ('sɛrə,nɔɪd) *n* **1** any of numerous mostly marine percoid fishes of the family *Serranidae*: includes the sea basses, sea perches, groupers, and jewfish ▷ *adj* **2** of or belonging to the family *Serranidae* [c19 from New Latin *Serranidae*, from *serrānus* genus name from Latin *serra* sawfish]

Serrano ham (sə'rɑːnəʊ) *n* cured ham from Spain

serrate *adj* ('sɛrɪt, -eɪt) **1** (of leaves) having a margin of forward pointing teeth **2** having a notched or sawlike edge ▷ *vb* (sə'reɪt) **3** (*tr*) to make serrate [c17 from Latin *serrātus* saw-shaped, from *serra* a saw]

serrated *adj* (sə'reɪtɪd) having a notched or sawlike edge

serration (sə'reɪʃən) *or less commonly* **serrature** ('sɛrətʃə) *n* **1** the state or condition of being serrated **2** a row of notches or toothlike projections on an edge **3** a single notch

serried ('sɛrɪd) *adj* in close or compact formation: *serried ranks of troops* [c17 from Old French *serré* close-packed, from *serrer* to shut up; see SEAR²]

serriform ('sɛrɪ,fɔːm) *adj biology* resembling a notched or sawlike edge [*serri-*, from Latin *serra* saw]

serrulate ('sɛrʊ,leɪt, -lɪt) *or* **serrulated** *adj* (esp of leaves) minutely serrate [c18 from New Latin *serrulātus*, from Latin *serrula* diminutive of *serra* a saw]

serrulation (,sɛrʊ'leɪʃən) *n* **1** any of the notches in a serrulate object **2** the condition of being serrulate

sertularian (,sɜːtjʊ'lɛərɪən) *n* any of various hydroid coelenterates of the genus *Sertularia*, forming feathery colonies of long branched stems

S

bearing stalkless paired polyps [C18 from New Latin *Sertulāria*, from Latin *sertula* diminutive of *serta* a garland]

serum ('sɪərəm) *n, pl* **-rums** *or* **-ra** (-rə) **1** See **blood serum** **2** antitoxin obtained from the blood serum of immunized animals **3** *physiol, zoology* clear watery fluid, esp that exuded by serous membranes **4** a less common word for **whey** [C17 from Latin: whey] > '**serumal** *adj*

serum albumin *n* a form of albumin that is the most abundant protein constituent of blood plasma. See also **albumin**

serum globulin *n* the blood serum component consisting of proteins with a larger molecular weight than serum albumin. See also **immunoglobulin**

serum hepatitis *n* a former name for **hepatitis B**

serum sickness *n* an allergic reaction, such as vomiting, skin rash, etc, that sometimes follows 2-3 weeks after an injection of a foreign serum

serval ('sɜːvəl) *n, pl* **-vals** *or* **-val** a slender feline mammal, *Felis serval,* of the African bush, having an orange-brown coat with black spots, large ears, and long legs [C18 via French from Late Latin *cervālis* staglike, from Latin *cervus* a stag]

servant ('sɜːvənt) *n* **1** a person employed to work for another, esp one who performs household duties **2** See **public servant** [C13 via Old French, from *servant* serving, from *servir* to SERVE] > '**servant-ˌlike** *adj*

serve (sɜːv) *vb* **1** to be in the service of (a person) **2** to render or be of service to (a person, cause, etc); help **3** (in a shop) to give (customers) information about articles for sale and to hand over articles purchased **4** (*tr*) to provide (guests, customers, etc) with food, drink, etc: *she served her guests with cocktails* **5** to distribute or provide (food, drink, etc) for guests, customers, etc: *do you serve coffee?* **6** (*tr; sometimes foll by up*) to present (food, drink, etc) in a specified manner: *cauliflower served with cheese sauce* **7** (*tr*) to provide with a regular supply of **8** (*tr*) to work actively for: *to serve the government* **9** (*tr*) to pay homage to: *to serve God* **10** to answer the requirements of; suit: *this will serve my purpose* **11** (*intr; may take an infinitive*) to have a use; function: *this wood will serve to build a fire* **12** to go through (a period of service, enlistment, imprisonment, etc) **13** (*intr*) (of weather, conditions, etc) to be favourable or suitable **14** (*tr*) Also: **service** (of a male animal) to copulate with (a female animal) **15** *sport* to put (the ball) into play **16** (*intr*) *RC Church* to act as server at Mass or other services **17** (*tr*) to deliver (a legal document, esp a writ or summons) to (a person) **18** to provide (a machine, etc) with an impulse or signal for control purposes or with a continuous supply of fuel, working material, etc **19** (*tr*) *nautical* to bind (a rope, spar, etc) with wire or fine cord to protect it from chafing, etc. See also **seize** (sense 8) **20** **serve (a person) right** *informal* to pay (a person) back, esp for wrongful or foolish treatment or behaviour ▷ *n* **21** *sport* short for **service** (sense 17) **22** *Austral* a portion or helping of food or drink [C13 from Old French *servir,* from Latin *servīre,* from *servus* a slave] > '**servable** *or* '**serveable** *adj*

server ('sɜːvə) *n* **1** a person who serves **2** *chiefly RC Church* a person who acts as acolyte or assists the priest at Mass **3** something that is used in serving food and drink **4** the player who serves in racket games **5** *computing* a computer or program that supplies data or resources to other machines on a network

Servia ('sɜːvɪə) *n* the former name of **Serbia**

Servian ('sɜːvɪən) *adj, n* a former word for **Serbian**

service¹ ('sɜːvɪs) *n* **1** an act of help or assistance **2** an organized system of labour and material aids used to supply the needs of the public: *telephone service; bus service* **3** the supply, installation, or maintenance of goods carried out by a dealer **4** the state of availability for use by the public (esp in the phrases **into** *or* **out of service**) **5** a periodic overhaul made on a car, machine, etc **6** the act or manner of serving guests, customers, etc, in a shop, hotel, restaurant, etc **7** a department of public employment and its employees: *civil service* **8** employment in or performance of work for another: *he has been in the service of our firm for ten years* **9** the work of a public servant **10 a** one of the branches of the armed forces **b** (*as modifier*): *service life* **11** the state, position, or duties of a domestic servant (esp in the phrase **in service**) **12** the act or manner of serving food **13** a complete set of dishes, cups, etc, for use at table **14** public worship carried out according to certain prescribed forms: *divine service* **15** the prescribed form according to which a specific kind of religious ceremony is to be carried out: *the burial service* **16** a unified collection of musical settings of the canticles and other liturgical items prescribed by the Book of Common Prayer as used in the Church of England **17** *sport* **a** the act, manner, or right of serving a ball **b** the game in which a particular player serves: *he has lost his service.* Often shortened to: **serve** **18** (in feudal law) the duty owed by a tenant to his lord **19** the serving of a writ, summons, etc, upon a person **20** *nautical* a length of tarred marline or small stuff used in serving **21** (of male animals) the act of mating **22** (*modifier*) of, relating to, or for the use of servants or employees ▷ *vb* (*tr*) **23** to make fit for use **24** to supply with assistance **25** to overhaul (a car, machine, etc) **26** (of a male animal) to mate with (a female) **27** *Brit* to meet interest and capital payments on (debt) ▷ See also **services** [C12 *servise,* from Old French, from Latin *servitium* condition of a slave, from *servus* a slave]

service² ('sɜːvɪs) *n* See **service tree**

serviceable ('sɜːvɪsəbəl) *adj* **1** capable of or ready for service; usable **2** capable of giving good service; durable **3** *archaic* diligent in service > ˌ**serviceaˈbility** *or* '**serviceableness** *n* > '**serviceably** *adv*

service area *n* **1** a place on a motorway providing garage services, restaurants, toilet facilities, etc **2** the area within which a satisfactory signal can be received from a given radio transmitter

serviceberry ('sɜːvɪsˌbɛrɪ) *n, pl* **-ries** **1** Also called: **shadbush** any of various North American rosaceous trees or shrubs of the genus *Amelanchier,* esp *A. canadensis,* which has white flowers and edible purplish berries **2** the fruit of any of these plants **3** the fruit of the service tree ▷ Also called (for senses 1, 2): **shadberry, Juneberry**

service ceiling *n* the height above sea level, measured under standard conditions, at which the rate of climb of an aircraft has fallen to a specified amount. Compare **absolute ceiling**

service charge *n* a percentage of a bill, as at a restaurant or hotel, added to the total to pay for service

service contract *n* a contract between an employer and a senior employee, esp a director, executive, etc

service flat *n Brit* a flat in which domestic services are provided by the management. Also called (esp Austral): **serviced flat**

service industry *n* an industry that provides services, such as transport or entertainment, rather than goods

service line *n* (in certain racket games) **1** the line at the back of the court behind which the server must stand when serving **2** a line indicating the boundary of a permissible service, as on the backwall of a squash court

serviceman ('sɜːvɪsˌmæn, -mən) *n, pl* **-men** **1** Also called (feminine): **servicewoman** a person who serves in the armed services of a country **2** a man employed to service and maintain equipment

service module *n* a section of an Apollo spacecraft housing the rocket engine, radar, fuel cells, etc, and jettisoned on re-entry into the earth's atmosphere. See also **lunar module, command module**

service road *n Brit* a relatively narrow road running parallel to a main road and providing access to houses, shops, offices, factories, etc, situated along its length

services ('sɜːvɪsɪz) *pl n* **1** work performed for remuneration **2** (usually preceded by *the*) the armed forces **3** (*sometimes singular*) *economics* commodities, such as banking, that are mainly intangible and usually consumed concurrently with their production. Compare **goods** (sense 2) **4** a system of providing the public with gas, water, etc

service station *n* **1** a place that supplies fuel, oil, etc, for motor vehicles and often carries out repairs, servicing, etc **2** a place that repairs and sometimes supplies mechanical or electrical equipment

service tree *n* **1** Also called: **sorb** a Eurasian rosaceous tree, *Sorbus domestica,* cultivated for its white flowers and brown edible apple-like fruits **2** **wild service tree** a similar and related Eurasian tree, *Sorbus torminalis* [*service,* from Old English *syrfe,* from Vulgar Latin *sorbea* (unattested), from Latin *sorbus* SORB]

servient tenement ('sɜːvɪənt) *n property law* the land or tenement over which an easement or other encumbrance is exercised by the dominant tenement. Compare **dominant tenement**

serviette (ˌsɜːvɪˈɛt) *n chiefly Brit* a small square of cloth or paper used while eating to protect the clothes, wipe the mouth and hands, etc [C15 from Old French, from *servir* to SERVE; formed on the model of OUBLIETTE]

servile ('sɜːvaɪl) *adj* **1** obsequious or fawning in attitude or behaviour; submissive **2** of or suitable for a slave **3** existing in or relating to a state of slavery **4** (when *postpositive,* foll by *to*) submitting or obedient [C14 from Latin *servīlis,* from *servus* slave] > '**servilely** *adv* > **servility** (sɜːˈvɪlɪtɪ) *or* '**servileness** *n*

servile work *n RC Church* work of a physical nature that is forbidden on Sundays and on certain holidays

serving ('sɜːvɪŋ) *n* a portion or helping of food or drink

servitor ('sɜːvɪtə) *n archaic* a person who serves another [C14 from Old French *servitour,* from Late Latin *servītor,* from Latin *servīre* to SERVE]

servitude ('sɜːvɪˌtjuːd) *n* **1** the state or condition of a slave; bondage **2** the state or condition of being subjected to or dominated by a person or thing: *servitude to drink* **3** *law* a burden attaching to an estate for the benefit of an adjoining estate or of some definite person. See also **easement** **4** short for **penal servitude** [C15 via Old French from Latin *servitūdō,* from *servus* a slave]

servlet ('sɜːvlɪt) *n computing* a small program that runs on a web server often accessing databases in response to client input

servo ('sɜːvəʊ) *adj* **1** (*prenominal*) of, relating to, forming part of, or activated by a servomechanism: *servo brakes* ▷ *n, pl* **-vos** **2** *informal* short for **servomechanism** [see SERVOMOTOR]

servomechanism ('sɜːvəʊˌmɛkəˌnɪzəm, ˌsɜːvəʊˈmɛk-) *n* a mechanical or electromechanical system for control of the position or speed of an output transducer. Negative feedback is incorporated to minimize discrepancies between the output state and the input control setting > **servomechanical** (ˌsɜːvəʊmɪˈkænɪkəl) *adj*

servomotor ('sɜːvəʊˌməʊtə) *n* any motor that supplies power to a servomechanism [C19 from French *servo-moteur,* from Latin *servus* slave + French *moteur* MOTOR]

servqual ('sɜːvˌkwɒl) *n marketing* the provision of high-quality products by an organization backed by a high level of service for consumers [C20 from SERV(ICE)¹ + QUAL(ITY)]

sesame ('sɛsəmɪ) *n* **1** a tropical herbaceous plant, *Sesamum indicum,* of the East Indies, cultivated, esp in India, for its small oval seeds: family *Pedaliaceae*

2 the seeds of this plant, used in flavouring bread and yielding an edible oil (**benne oil** or **gingili**). Also called: benne, gingili, til [C15 from Latin *sēsamum*, from Greek *sēsamon*, *sēsamē*, of Semitic origin; related to Arabic *simsim*]

sesamoid (ˈsɛsəˌmɔɪd) *adj anatomy* **1** of or relating to various small bones formed in tendons, such as the patella **2** of or relating to any of various small cartilages, esp those of the nose [C17 from Latin *sēsamoīdēs* like sesame (seed), from Greek]

sesh (sɛʃ) *n slang* short for **session**

Sesotho (sɪˈsuːtuː) *n* the dialect of Sotho spoken by the Basotho: an official language of Lesotho. Also called: **Southern Sotho** Former name: **Basuto**

sesqui- *prefix* **1** indicating one and a half: *sesquicentennial* **2** (in a chemical compound) indicating a ratio of two to three: *sesquioxide* [from Latin, contraction of SEMI- + *as* AS² + *-que* and]

sesquialtera (ˌsɛskwɪˈæltərə) *n music* **1** a mixture stop on an organ **2** another term for **hemiola** [C16 from Latin *sesqui-* half + *alter* second, other]

sesquicarbonate (ˌsɛskwɪˈkɑːbəˌneɪt, -nɪt) *n* a mixed salt consisting of a carbonate and a hydrogen carbonate, such as sodium sesquicarbonate, $Na_2CO_3.NaHCO_3.2H_2O$

sesquicentennial (ˌsɛskwɪsɛnˈtɛnɪəl) *adj* **1** of or relating to a period of 150 years ▷ *n* **2** a period or cycle of 150 years **3** a 150th anniversary or its celebration > ˌ**sesquicenˈtennially** *adv*

sesquioxide (ˌsɛskwɪˈɒksaɪd) *n* any of certain oxides whose molecules contain three atoms of oxygen for every two atoms of the element: *chromium sesquioxide*, Cr_2O_3

sesquipedalian (ˌsɛskwɪpɪˈdeɪlɪən) *or less commonly* **sesquipedal** (sɛsˈkwɪpədᵊl) *adj* **1** tending to use very long words **2** (of words or expressions) long and ponderous; polysyllabic ▷ *n* **3** a polysyllabic word [C17 from Latin *sēsquipedālis* of a foot and a half (coined by Horace in *Ars Poetica*), from SESQUI- + *pedālis* of the foot, from *pēs* foot] > ˌ**sesquipeˈdalianism** *n*

sesquiterpene (ˌsɛskwɪˈtɜːpiːn) *n* any of certain terpenes whose molecules contain one and a half times as many atoms as a normal terpene. Formula: $C_{15}H_{24}$

sessile (ˈsɛsaɪl) *adj* **1** (of flowers or leaves) having no stalk; growing directly from the stem **2** (of animals such as the barnacle) permanently attached to a substratum [C18 from Latin *sēssilis* concerning sitting, from *sedēre* to sit] > **sessility** (sɛˈsɪlɪtɪ) *n*

sessile oak *n* another name for the **durmast** (sense 1)

session (ˈsɛʃən) *n* **1** the meeting of a court, legislature, judicial body, etc, for the execution of its function or the transaction of business **2** a single continuous meeting of such a body **3** a series or period of such meetings **4** *education* **a** the time during which classes are held **b** a school or university term or year **5** *Presbyterian Church* the judicial and administrative body presiding over a local congregation and consisting of the minister and elders **6** a meeting of a group of musicians to record in a studio **7** a meeting of a group of people to pursue an activity **8** any period devoted to an activity **9** See **Court of Session** [C14 from Latin *sessiō* a sitting, from *sedēre* to sit] > ˈ**sessional** *adj* > ˈ**sessionally** *adv*

session musician *n* a studio musician, esp one who works freelance

sessions (ˈsɛʃənz) *pl n* the sittings or a sitting of justice in court. See **magistrates' court, quarter sessions**

sesterce (ˈsɛstɛːs) *or* **sestertius** (sɛˈstɜːtɪəs) *n* a silver or, later, bronze coin of ancient Rome worth a quarter of a denarius [C16 from Latin *sēstertius* a coin worth two and a half asses, from *sēmis* half + *tertius* a third]

sestertium (sɛˈstɜːtɪəm) *n, pl* **-tia** (-tɪə) an ancient Roman money of account equal to 1000 sesterces [C16 from Latin, from the phrase *mille sestertium* a thousand of sesterces; see SESTERCE]

sestet (sɛˈstɛt) *n* **1** *prosody* the last six lines of a Petrarchan sonnet **2** *prosody* any six-line stanza **3** another word for **sextet** (sense 1) [C19 from Italian *sestetto*, from *sesto* sixth, from Latin *sextus*, from *sex* six]

sestina (sɛˈstiːnə) *n* an elaborate verse form of Italian origin, normally unrhymed, consisting of six stanzas of six lines each and a concluding tercet. The six final words of the lines in the first stanza are repeated in a different order in each of the remaining five stanzas and also in the concluding tercet. Also called: **sextain** [C19 from Italian, from *sesto* sixth, from Latin *sextus*]

Sestos (ˈsɛstɒs) *n* a ruined town in NW Turkey, at the narrowest point of the Dardanelles: N terminus of the bridge of boats built by Xerxes in 481 BC for the crossing of his armies of invasion

set¹ (sɛt) *vb* **sets, setting, set** (*mainly tr*) **1** to put or place in position or into a specified state or condition: *to set a book on the table; to set someone free* **2** (*also intr*; foll by *to* or *on*) to put or be put (to); apply or be applied: *he set fire to the house; they set the dogs on the scent* **3** to put into order or readiness for use; prepare: *to set a trap; to set the table for dinner* **4** (*also intr*) to put, form, or be formed into a jelled, firm, fixed, or rigid state: *the jelly set in three hours* **5** (*also intr*) to put or be put into a position that will restore a normal state: *to set a broken bone* **6** to adjust (a clock or other instrument) to a position **7** to determine or establish: *we have set the date for our wedding* **8** to prescribe or allot (an undertaking, course of study, etc): *the examiners have set "Paradise Lost"* **9** to arrange in a particular fashion, esp an attractive one: *she set her hair; the jeweller set the diamonds in silver* **10** (of clothes) to hang or fit (well or badly) when worn **11** Also: **set to music** to provide music for (a poem or other text to be sung) **12** Also: **set up** *printing* to arrange or produce (type, film, etc) from (text or copy); compose **13** to arrange (a stage, television studio, etc) with scenery and props **14** to describe or present (a scene or the background to a literary work, story, etc) in words: *his novel is set in Russia* **15** to present as a model of good or bad behaviour (esp in the phrases **set an example, set a good example, set a bad example**) **16** (foll by *on* or *by*) to value (something) at a specified price or estimation of worth: *he set a high price on his services* **17** (foll by *at*) to price (the value of something) at a specified sum: *he set his services at £300* **18** (*also intr*) to give or be given a particular direction: *his course was set to the East* **19** (*also intr*) to rig (a sail) or (of a sail) to be rigged so as to catch the wind **20** (*intr*) (of the sun, moon, etc) to disappear beneath the horizon **21** to leave (dough, etc) in one place so that it may prove **22** to sharpen (a cutting blade) by grinding or honing the angle adjacent to the cutting edge **23** to displace alternate teeth of (a saw) to opposite sides of the blade in order to increase the cutting efficiency **24** to sink (the head of a nail) below the surface surrounding it by using a nail set **25** *computing* to give (a binary circuit) the value 1 **26** (of plants) to produce (fruits, seeds, etc) after pollination or (of fruits or seeds) to develop after pollination **27** to plant (seeds, seedlings, etc) **28** to place (a hen) on (eggs) for the purpose of incubation **29** (*intr*) (of a gun dog) to turn in the direction of game, indicating its presence **30** *Scot and Irish* to let or lease: *to set a house* **31** *bridge* to defeat (one's opponents) in their attempt to make a contract **32** a dialect word for **sit** **33** **set eyes on** to see ▷ *n* **34** the act of setting or the state of being set **35** a condition of firmness or hardness **36** bearing, carriage, or posture: *the set of a gun dog when pointing* **37** the fit or hang of a garment, esp when worn **38** the scenery and other props used in and identifying the location of a stage or television production, film, etc **39** Also called: **set width** *printing* **a** the width of the body of a piece of type **b** the width of the lines of type in a page or column **40** *nautical* **a** the cut of the sails or the arrangement of the sails, spars, rigging, etc, of a vessel **b** the direction from which a wind is blowing or towards which a tide or current is moving **41** *psychol* a temporary bias disposing an organism to react to a stimulus in one way rather than in others **42** a seedling, cutting, or similar part that is ready for planting: *onion sets* **43** a blacksmith's tool with a short head similar to a cold chisel set transversely onto a handle and used, when struck with a hammer, for cutting off lengths of iron bars **44** See **nail set** **45** the direction of flow of water **46** a mechanical distortion of shape or alignment, such as a bend in a piece of metal **47** the penetration of a driven pile for each blow of the drop hammer **48** a variant spelling of **sett** ▷ *adj* **49** fixed or established by authority or agreement: *set hours of work* **50** (*usually postpositive*) rigid or inflexible: *she is set in her ways* **51** conventional, artificial, or stereotyped, rather than spontaneous: *she made her apology in set phrases* **52** (*postpositive*; foll by *on* or *upon*) resolute in intention: *he is set upon marrying* **53** (of a book, etc) prescribed for students' preparation for an examination ▷ See also **set about, set against, set aside, set back, set down, set forth, set in, set off, set on, set out, set to, set up, set upon** [Old English *settan*, causative of *sittan* to SIT; related to Old Frisian *setta*, Old High German *sezzan*]

set² (sɛt) *n* **1** a number of objects or people grouped or belonging together, often forming a unit or having certain features or characteristics in common: *a set of coins; John is in the top set for maths* **2** a group of people who associate together, esp a clique: *he's part of the jet set* **3** *maths, logic* **a** Also called: **class** a collection of numbers, objects, etc, that is treated as an entity: {3, the moon} is the set the two members of which are the number 3 and the moon **b** (in some formulations) a class that can itself be a member of other classes **4** any apparatus that receives or transmits television or radio signals **5** *tennis, squash, badminton* one of the units of a match, in tennis one in which one player or pair of players must win at least six games: *Graf lost the first set* **6** **a** the number of couples required for a formation dance **b** a series of figures that make up a formation dance **7** **a** a band's or performer's concert repertoire on a given occasion: *the set included no new numbers* **b** a continuous performance: *the Who played two sets* ▷ *vb* **sets, setting, set** **8** (*intr*) (in square dancing and country dancing) to perform a sequence of steps while facing towards another dancer: *set to your partners* **9** (*usually tr*) to divide into sets: *in this school we set our older pupils for English* [C14 (in the obsolete sense: a religious sect): from Old French *sette*, from Latin *secta* SECT; later sense development influenced by the verb SET¹]

seta (ˈsiːtə) *n, pl* **-tae** (-tiː) **1** (in invertebrates and some plants) any bristle or bristle-like appendage **2** (in mosses) the stalk of the sporophyte that bears the capsule [C18 from Latin] > **setaceous** (sɪˈteɪʃəs) *adj* > **seˈtaceously** *adv* > ˈ**setal** *adj*

set about *vb* (*intr, preposition*) **1** to start or begin **2** to attack physically or verbally

set against *vb* (*tr, preposition*) **1** to balance or compare: *to set a person's faults against his virtues* **2** to cause to be hostile or unfriendly to

set aside *vb* (*tr, adverb*) **1** to reserve for a special purpose; put to one side **2** to discard, dismiss, or quash

set-aside *n* **a** (in the European Union) a scheme in which a proportion of farmland is taken out of production in order to reduce surpluses or maintain or increase prices of a specific crop **b** (*as modifier*): *set-aside land*

set back *vb* (*tr, adverb*) **1** to hinder; impede **2** *informal* to cost (a person) a specified amount ▷ *n* **setback** **3** anything that serves to hinder or impede **4** a recession in the upper part of a high building, esp one that increases the daylight at lower levels **5** Also called: **offset, setoff** a steplike

shelf where a wall is reduced in thickness
set chisel *n* another name for **cold chisel**
set down *vb (tr, adverb)* **1** to write down or record **2** to judge, consider, or regard: *he set him down as an idiot* **3** (foll by *to*) to ascribe; attribute: *his attitude was set down to his illness* **4** to reprove; rebuke **5** to snub; dismiss **6** *Brit* to allow (passengers) to alight from a bus, taxi, etc
se tenant *French* (sə tənɑ̃) *adj* **1** denoting two postage stamps of different face values and sometimes of different designs in an unseparated pair ▷ *n* **2** such a pair of stamps [literally: holding together]
set forth *vb (adverb) formal or archaic* **1** *(tr)* to state, express, or utter: *he set forth his objections* **2** *(intr)* to start out on a journey: *the expedition set forth on the first of July*
Seth (sɛθ) *n Old Testament* Adam's third son, given by God in place of the murdered Abel (Genesis 4:25)
SETI (ˈsɛtɪ) *n acronym for* Search for Extraterrestrial Intelligence; the attempt to detect signals, esp radiowaves or light, from an intelligent extraterrestrial source
setiferous (sɪˈtɪfərəs) *or* **setigerous** (sɪˈtɪdʒərəs) *adj biology* bearing bristles [C19 see SETA, -FEROUS, -GEROUS]
setiform (ˈsiːtɪˌfɔːm) *adj biology* shaped like a seta
set in *vb (intr, adverb)* **1** to become established: *the winter has set in* **2** (of wind) to blow or (of current) to move towards shore ▷ *adj* **set-in 3** (of a part) made separately and then added to a larger whole: *a set-in sleeve*
setline (ˈsɛtˌlaɪn) *n* any of various types of fishing line that consist of a long line suspended across a stream, between buoys, etc, and having shorter hooked and baited lines attached. See **trawl** (sense 2), **trotline**
set off *vb (adverb)* **1** *(intr)* to embark on a journey **2** *(tr)* to cause (a person) to act or do something, such as laugh or tell stories **3** *(tr)* to cause to explode **4** *(tr)* to act as a foil or contrast to, esp so as to improve: *that brooch sets your dress off well* **5** *(tr) accounting* to cancel a credit on (one account) against a debit on another, both of which are in the name of the same person, enterprise, etc **6** *(intr)* to bring a claim by way of setoff ▷ *n* **setoff 7** anything that serves as a counterbalance **8** anything that serves to contrast with or enhance something else; foil **9** another name for **setback** (sense 5) **10** a counterbalancing debt or claim offered by a debtor against a creditor **11** a cross claim brought by a debtor that partly offsets the creditor's claim. See also **counterclaim**
set-off *n printing* a fault in which ink is transferred from a heavily inked or undried printed sheet to the sheet next to it in a pile. Also called (esp Brit): **offset**
set on *vb (tr)* **1** *(preposition)* to cause to attack: *they set the dogs on him* **2** *(adverb)* to instigate or incite; urge: *he set the child on to demand food*
Seto Naikai (ˈsɛtəʊ ˈnaɪkaɪ) *n* transliteration of the Japanese name for the **Inland Sea**
setose (ˈsiːtəʊs) *adj biology* covered with setae; bristly [C17 from Latin *saetōsus*, from *saeta* a bristle]
set out *vb (adverb, mainly tr)* **1** to present, arrange, or display: *he set the flowers out in the vase* **2** to give a full account of; explain exactly: *he set out the matter in full* **3** to plan or lay out (a garden, etc) **4** *(intr)* to begin or embark on an undertaking, esp a journey
set piece *n* **1** a work of literature, music, etc, often having a conventional or prescribed theme, intended to create an impressive effect **2** a piece of scenery built to stand independently as part of a stage set **3** a display of fireworks **4** *sport* a rehearsed team manoeuvre, usually attempted in continuous games at a restart of play, esp when the other side has been penalized for improper play
set point *n tennis, squash, badminton* a point that would enable one side to win a set
setscrew (ˈsɛtˌskruː) *n* a screw that fits into the boss or hub of a wheel, coupling, cam, etc, and prevents motion of the part relative to the shaft on which it is mounted
set square *n* a thin flat piece of plastic, metal, etc, in the shape of a right-angled triangle, used in technical drawing
sett *or* **set** (sɛt) *n* **1** a small rectangular paving block made of stone, such as granite, used to provide a durable road surface. Compare **cobblestone 2** the burrow of a badger **3 a** a square in a pattern of tartan **b** the pattern itself [C19 variant of SET¹ (n)]
settee (sɛˈtiː) *n* a seat, for two or more people, with a back and usually with arms [C18 changed from SETTLE²]
setter (ˈsɛtə) *n* any of various breeds of large gun dog, having silky coats and plumed tails. See **English setter, Gordon setter, Irish setter** [C16 so called because they can be used to indicate where game is: see SET¹]
set theory *n* **1** *maths* the branch of mathematics concerned with the properties and interrelationships of sets **2** *logic* a theory constructed within first-order logic that yields the mathematical theory of classes, esp one that distinguishes sets from proper classes as a means of avoiding certain paradoxes
setting (ˈsɛtɪŋ) *n* **1** the surroundings in which something is set; scene **2** the scenery, properties, or background, used to create the location for a stage play, film, etc **3** *music* a composition consisting of a certain text and music provided or arranged for it **4** the metal mounting and surround of a gem: *diamonds in an antique gold setting* **5** the tableware, cutlery, etc, for a single place at table **6** any of a series of points on a scale or dial that can be selected to control the level as of temperature, speed, etc, at which a machine functions **7** a clutch of eggs in a bird's nest, esp a clutch of hen's eggs
setting lotion *n* a perfumed solution of gum or a synthetic resin in a solvent, used in hairdressing to make a set last longer
setting rule *n printing* a metal strip used in the hand-setting of type in a composing stick to separate the line being set from the previous one
settle¹ (ˈsɛtᵊl) *vb* **1** *(tr)* to put in order; arrange in a desired state or condition: *he settled his affairs before he died* **2** to arrange or be arranged in a fixed or comfortable position: *he settled himself by the fire* **3** *(intr)* to come to rest or a halt: *a bird settled on the hedge* **4** to take up or cause to take up residence: *the family settled in the country* **5** to establish or become established in a way of life, job, residence, etc **6** *(tr)* to migrate to and form a community; colonize **7** to make or become quiet, calm, or stable **8** *(intr)* to be cast or spread; come down: *fog settled over a wide area* **9** to make (a liquid) clear or (of a liquid) to become clear; clarify **10** to cause (sediment) to sink to the bottom, as in a liquid, or (of sediment) to sink thus **11** to subside or cause to subside and become firm or compact: *the dust settled* **12** (sometimes foll by *up*) to pay off or account for (a bill, debt, etc) **13** *(tr)* to decide, conclude, or dispose of: *to settle an argument* **14** *(intr; often foll by on or upon)* to agree or fix: *to settle upon a plan* **15** *(tr; usually foll by on or upon)* to secure (title, property, etc) to a person, as by making a deed of settlement, will, etc: *he settled his property on his wife* **16** to determine (a legal dispute, etc) by agreement of the parties without resort to court action (esp in the phrase **settle out of court**) ▷ See also **settle down, settle for, settle in, settle with** [Old English *setlan;* related to Dutch *zetelen;* see SETTLE²] ▷ ˈ**settleable** *adj*
settle² (ˈsɛtᵊl) *n* a seat, for two or more people, usually made of wood with a high back and arms, and sometimes having a storage space in the boxlike seat [Old English *setl;* related to Old Saxon, Old High German *sezzal*]
settle down *vb (adverb, mainly intr)* **1** *(also tr)* to make or become quiet and orderly **2** (often foll by *to*) to apply oneself diligently: *please settle down to work* **3** to adopt an orderly and routine way of life, take up a permanent post, etc, esp after marriage
settle for *vb (intr, preposition)* to accept or agree to in spite of dispute or dissatisfaction
settle in *vb (adverb)* to become or help to become adapted to and at ease in a new home, environment, etc
settlement (ˈsɛtᵊlmənt) *n* **1** the act or state of settling or being settled **2** the establishment of a new region; colonization **3** a place newly settled; colony **4** a collection of dwellings forming a community, esp on a frontier **5** a community formed by members of a group, esp of a religious sect **6** a public building used to provide educational and general welfare facilities for persons living in deprived areas **7** a subsidence of all or part of a structure **8 a** the payment of an outstanding account, invoice, charge, etc **b** *(as modifier)*: *settlement day* **9** an adjustment or agreement reached in matters of finance, business, etc **10** *law* **a** a conveyance, usually to trustees, of property to be enjoyed by several persons in succession **b** the deed or other instrument conveying such property **c** the determination of a dispute, etc, by mutual agreement without resorting to legal proceedings
settler (ˈsɛtlə) *n* a person who settles in a new country or a colony
settler's clock *n Austral* (formerly) an informal name for **kookaburra** [C19 so called because its laugh was heard at dawn and sunset]
settle with *vb (preposition)* **1** *(intr)* to pay a debt or bill to **2** *(intr)* to make an agreement with **3** to get one's revenge for (a wrong or injury) with (a person)
settlings (ˈsɛtlɪŋz) *pl n* any matter or substance that has settled at the bottom of a liquid; sediment; dregs
settlor (ˈsɛtlə) *n law* a person who settles property on someone
set to *vb (intr, adverb)* **1** to begin working **2** to start fighting ▷ *n* **set-to 3** *informal* a brief disagreement or fight
set-top box *n* a device which converts the signals from a digital television broadcast into a form which can be viewed on a standard television set
Setúbal (*Portuguese* səˈtuβal) *n* a port in SW Portugal, on **Setúbal Bay** south of Lisbon: an earthquake in 1755 destroyed most of the old town. Pop: 113 937 (2001)
set up *vb (adverb, mainly tr)* **1** *(also intr)* to put into a position of power, etc **2** *(also intr)* to begin or enable (someone) to begin (a new venture), as by acquiring or providing means, equipment, etc **3** to build or construct: *to set up a shed* **4** to raise, cause, or produce: *to set up a wail* **5** to advance or propose: *to set up a theory* **6** to restore the health of: *the sea air will set you up again* **7** to establish (a record) **8** *informal* to cause (a person) to be blamed, accused, etc **9** *informal* **a** to provide (drinks, etc) for: *set 'em up, Joe!* **b** to pay for the drinks of: *I'll set up the next round* **10** *printing* another term for **set¹** (sense 12) ▷ *n* **setup 11** *informal* the way in which anything is organized or arranged **12** *slang* an event the result of which is prearranged: *it's a setup* **13** a prepared arrangement of materials, machines, etc, for a job or undertaking **14** a station at which a surveying instrument, esp a theodolite, is set up **15** *films* the position of the camera, microphones, and performers at the beginning of a scene ▷ *adj* **set-up 16** physically well-built
set upon *vb (intr, preposition)* to attack: *three thugs set upon him*
set width *n* another name for **set¹** (sense 39)
Sevan (sɛˈvɑːn) *n* **Lake** a lake in Armenia at an altitude of 1914 m (6279 ft). Area: 1417 sq km (547 sq miles)
Sevastopol (*Russian* sɪvasˈtɔpəlj) *n* a port, resort, and naval base in S Ukraine, in the Crimea, on the Black Sea: captured and destroyed by British,

French, and Turkish forces after a siege of 11 months (1854–55) during the Crimean War; taken by the Germans after a siege of 8 months (1942) during World War II. Pop: 338 000 (2005 est.). English name: **Sebastopol**

seven ('sɛv'n) *n* **1** the cardinal number that is the sum of six and one and is a prime number. See also **number** (sense 1) **2** a numeral, 7, VII, etc, representing this number **3** the amount or quantity that is one greater than six **4** anything representing, represented by, or consisting of seven units, such as a playing card with seven symbols on it **5** Also called: **seven o'clock** seven hours after noon or midnight ▷ *determiner* **6 a** amounting to seven: *seven swans a-swimming* **b** (*as pronoun*): *you've eaten seven already* ▷ Related prefixes: **hepta-, septi-** ▷ See also **sevens** [Old English *seofon*; related to Gothic *sibun*, German *sieben*, Old Norse *sjau*, Latin *septem*, Greek *hepta*, Sanskrit *saptá*]

Seven against Thebes *pl n Greek myth* the seven members of an expedition undertaken to regain for Polynices, a son of Oedipus, his share in the throne of Thebes from his usurping brother Eteocles. The seven are usually listed as Polynices, Adrastus, Amphiaraus, Capaneus, Hippomedon, Tydeus, and Parthenopaeus. The campaign failed and the warring brothers killed each other in single combat before the Theban walls. See also **Adrastus**

seven deadly sins *pl n* a fuller name for the **deadly sins**

sevenfold ('sɛv'n,fəʊld) *adj* **1** equal to or having seven times as many or as much **2** composed of seven parts ▷ *adv* **3** by or up to seven times as many or as much

Seven Hills of Rome *pl n* the hills on which the ancient city of Rome was built: the Palatine, Capitoline, Quirinal, Caelian, Aventine, Esquiline, and Viminal

sevens ('sɛv'nz) *n* (*functioning as singular*) a Rugby Union match or series of matches played with seven players on each side

seven seas *pl n* the oceans of the world considered as the N and S Pacific, the N and S Atlantic, and the Arctic, Antarctic, and Indian Oceans

seven-segment display *n* an arrangement of seven bars forming a square figure of eight, used in electronic displays of alphanumeric characters: any letter or figure can be represented by illuminating selected bars

Seven Sleepers *pl n* seven Christian youths from Ephesus who were walled up in a cave by the Emperor Decius in 250 AD and, according to legend, slept for 187 years

seventeen ('sɛv'n'ti:n) *n* **1** the cardinal number that is the sum of ten and seven and is a prime number. See also **number** (sense 1) **2** a numeral, 17, XVII, etc, representing this number **3** the amount or quantity that is seven more than ten **4** something represented by, representing, or consisting of 17 units ▷ *determiner* **5 a** amounting to seventeen: *seventeen attempts* **b** (*as pronoun*): *seventeen were sold* [Old English *seofontīene*]

seventeenth ('sɛv'n'ti:nθ) *adj* **1** (*usually prenominal*) **a** coming after the sixteenth in numbering or counting order, position, time, etc; being the ordinal number of *seventeen*: often written 17th **b** (*as noun*): *the ship docks on the seventeenth* ▷ *n* **2 a** one of 17 approximately equal parts of something **b** (*as modifier*): *a seventeenth part* **3** the fraction equal to one divided by 17 (1/17)

seventeen-year locust *n* an E North American cicada, *Magicicada septendecim*, appearing in great numbers at infrequent intervals because its nymphs take 13 or 17 years to mature. Also called: **periodical cicada**

seventh ('sɛv'nθ) *adj* **1** (*usually prenominal*) **a** coming after the sixth and before the eighth in numbering or counting order, position, time, etc; being the ordinal number of *seven*: often written 7th **b** (*as noun*): *she left on the seventh; he was the*

seventh to arrive ▷ *n* **2 a** one of seven equal or nearly equal parts of an object, quantity, measurement, etc **b** (*as modifier*): *a seventh part* **3** the fraction equal to one divided by seven (1/7) **4** *music* **a** the interval between one note and another seven notes away from it counting inclusively along the diatonic scale **b** one of two notes constituting such an interval in relation to the other. See also **major** (sense 14), **minor** (sense 4), **interval** (sense 5) **c** short for **seventh chord** ▷ *adv* **5** Also: **seventhly** after the sixth person, position, event, etc ▷ *sentence connector* **6** Also: **seventhly** as the seventh point: linking what follows to the previous statements, as in a speech or argument

seventh chord *n music* a chord consisting of a triad with a seventh added above the root. See **dominant seventh chord, diminished seventh chord, major seventh chord, minor seventh chord**

Seventh-Day Adventist *n Protestant theol* a member of that branch of the Adventists which constituted itself as a separate body after the expected Second Coming of Christ failed to be realized in 1844. They are strongly Protestant, believe that Christ's coming is imminent, and observe Saturday instead of Sunday as their Sabbath

seventh heaven *n* **1** the final state of eternal bliss, esp according to Talmudic and Muslim eschatology **2** a state of supreme happiness [C19 so named from the belief that there are seven levels of heaven, the seventh and most exalted being the abode of God and the angels]

seventieth ('sɛv'ntiɪθ) *adj* **1** (*usually prenominal*) **a** being the ordinal number of *seventy* in numbering or counting order, position, time, etc: often written 70th **b** (*as noun*): *the seventieth in line* ▷ *n* **2 a** one of 70 approximately equal parts of something **b** (*as modifier*): *a seventieth part* **3** the fraction equal to one divided by 70 (1/70)

seventy ('sɛv'nti) *n, pl* **-ties 1** the cardinal number that is the product of ten and seven. See also **number** (sense 1) **2** a numeral, 70, LXX, etc, representing this number **3** (*plural*) the numbers 70–79, esp the 70th to the 79th year of a person's life or of a particular century **4** the amount or quantity that is seven times as big as ten **5** something represented by, representing, or consisting of 70 units ▷ *determiner* **6 a** amounting to seventy: *the seventy varieties of fabric* **b** (*as pronoun*): *to invite seventy to the wedding* [Old English *seofentig*]

seven-up *n* a card game in which the lead to each round determines the trump suit. Also called: **all fours, pitch**

Seven Wonders of the World *pl n* the seven structures considered by ancient and medieval scholars to be the most wondrous of the ancient world. The list varies, but generally consists of the Pyramids of Egypt, the Hanging Gardens of Babylon, Phidias' statue of Zeus at Olympia, the temple of Artemis at Ephesus, the mausoleum of Halicarnassus, the Colossus of Rhodes, and the Pharos (or lighthouse) of Alexandria

seven-year itch *n informal* a tendency towards infidelity, traditionally said to begin after about seven years of marriage

Seven Years' War *n* the war (1756–63) of Britain and Prussia, who emerged in the ascendant, against France and Austria, resulting from commercial and colonial rivalry between Britain and France and from the conflict in Germany between Prussia and Austria

sever ('sɛvə) *vb* **1** to put or be put apart; separate **2** to divide or be divided into parts **3** (*tr*) to break off or dissolve (a tie, relationship, etc) [C14 *severen*, from Old French *severer*, from Latin *sēparāre* to SEPARATE]

severable ('sɛvərəb'l) *adj* **1** able to be severed **2** *law* capable of being separated, as a clause in an agreement: *a severable contract*

several ('sɛvrəl) *determiner* **1 a** more than a few; an indefinite small number: *several people objected* **b**

(*as pronoun; functioning as plural*): *several of them know* ▷ *adj* **2** (*prenominal*) various; separate: *the members with their several occupations* **3** (*prenominal*) distinct; different: *three several times* **4** *law* capable of being dealt with separately; not shared. Compare **joint** (sense 15) [C15 via Anglo-French from Medieval Latin *sēparālis*, from Latin *sēpar*, from *sēparāre* to SEPARATE]

severally ('sɛvrəlɪ) *adv* **1** separately, individually, or distinctly **2** each in turn; respectively

severalty ('sɛvrəltɪ) *n, pl* **-ties 1** the state of being several or separate **2** (*usually preceded by in*) *property law* the tenure of property, esp land, in a person's own right and not jointly with another or others

severance ('sɛvərəns) *n* **1** the act of severing or state of being severed **2** a separation **3** *law* the division into separate parts of a joint estate, contract, etc

severance pay *n* compensation paid by an organization to an employee who leaves because, through no fault of his own, the job to which he was appointed ceases to exist, as during rationalization, and no comparable job is available to him

severe (sɪ'vɪə) *adj* **1** rigorous or harsh in the treatment of others; strict: *a severe parent* **2** serious in appearance or manner; stern **3** critical or dangerous: *a severe illness* **4** causing misery or discomfort by its harshness: *severe weather* **5** strictly restrained in appearance; austere: *a severe way of dressing* **6** hard to endure, perform, or accomplish: *a severe test* **7** rigidly precise or exact [C16 from Latin *sevērus*] ▷ **se'verely** *adv* ▷ **se'vereness** or **severity** (sɪ'vɛrɪtɪ) *n*

Severn ('sɛv'n) *n* **1** a river in E Wales and W England, rising in Powys and flowing northeast and east into England, then south to the Bristol Channel. Length: about 290 km (180 miles) **2** a river in SE central Canada, in Ontario, flowing northeast to Hudson Bay. Length: about 676 km (420 miles)

Severnaya Zemlya (*Russian* 'sjevɪrnəjə zɪm'lja) *n* an archipelago in the Arctic Ocean off the coast of N central Russia

Seveso (se'veɪsəʊ) *n* a town in N Italy, near Milan: evacuated in 1976 after contamination by a poisonous cloud of dioxin gas released from a factory

Seville (sə'vɪl) *n* a port in SW Spain, on the Guadalquivir River: chief town of S Spain under the Vandals and Visigoths (5th–8th centuries); centre of Spanish colonial trade (16th–17th centuries); tourist centre. Pop: 709 975 (2003 est.). Ancient name: **Hispalis** Spanish name: **Sevilla** (se'βiʎa)

Seville orange *n* **1** an orange tree, *Citrus aurantium*, of tropical and semitropical regions: grown for its bitter fruit, which is used to make marmalade **2** the fruit of this tree ▷ Also called: **bitter orange**

Sèvres (*French* sɛvrə) *n* porcelain ware manufactured at Sèvres, near Paris, from 1756, characterized by the use of clear colours and elaborate decorative detail

sew (səʊ) *vb* **sews, sewing, sewed; sewn** or **sewed 1** to join or decorate (pieces of fabric, etc) by means of a thread repeatedly passed through with a needle or similar implement **2** (*tr; often foll by on or up*) to attach, fasten, or close by sewing **3** (*tr*) to make (a garment, etc) by sewing ▷ See also **sew up** [Old English *sēowan*; related to Old Norse *sȳja*, Gothic *siujan*, Old High German *siuwen*, Latin *suere* to sew, Sanskrit *sīvjati* he sews]

sewage ('su:ɪdʒ) *n* waste matter from domestic or industrial establishments that is carried away in sewers or drains for dumping or conversion into a form that is not toxic [C19 back formation from SEWER[1]]

sewage farm *n* a place where sewage is treated, esp for use as manure

sewage gas *n* gas given off in the digestion of sewage consisting of approximately 66 per cent

S

methane and 34 per cent carbon dioxide

sewan ('si:wən) *n* a variant spelling of **seawan**

Seward Peninsula ('sju:əd) *n* a peninsula of W Alaska, on the Bering Strait. Length: about 290 km (180 miles)

sewellel (sɪ'wɛləl) *n* another name for **mountain beaver** (see **beaver¹** (sense 3)) [c19 probably from Chinook]

sewer¹ ('su:ə) *n* **1** a drain or pipe, esp one that is underground, used to carry away surface water or sewage ▷ *vb* **2** (*tr*) to provide with sewers [c15 from Old French *esseveur*, from *essever* to drain, from Vulgar Latin *exaquāre* (unattested), from Latin EX-¹ + *aqua* water]

sewer² ('səʊə) *n* a person or thing that sews

sewer³ ('su:ə) *n* (in medieval England) a servant of high rank in charge of the serving of meals and the seating of guests [c14 shortened from Anglo-French *asseour*, from Old French *asseoir* to cause to sit, from Latin *assidēre*, from *sedēre* to sit]

sewerage ('su:ərɪdʒ) *n* **1** an arrangement of sewers **2** the removal of surface water or sewage by means of sewers **3** another word for **sewage**

sewin *or* **sewen** ('sjʊən) *n* (in Wales and Ireland) another name for the **sea trout** [c16 origin unknown]

sewing ('səʊɪŋ) *n* **a** a piece of cloth, etc, that is sewn or to be sewn **b** (*as modifier*): *sewing basket*

sewing machine *n* any machine designed to sew material. It is now usually driven by electric motor but is sometimes operated by a foot treadle or by hand

sewn (səʊn) *vb* a past participle of **sew**

sewn binding *n bookbinding* a style of binding where the backs of the gathered sections are sewn together before being inserted into a cover

sew up *vb* (*tr, adverb*) **1** to fasten or mend completely by sewing **2** *US* to acquire sole use or control of **3** *informal* to complete or negotiate successfully: *to sew up a deal*

sex (sɛks) *n* **1** the sum of the characteristics that distinguish organisms on the basis of their reproductive function **2** either of the two categories, male or female, into which organisms are placed on this basis **3** short for **sexual intercourse 4** feelings or behaviour resulting from the urge to gratify the sexual instinct **5** sexual matters in general ▷ *modifier* **6** of or concerning sexual matters: *sex education; sex hygiene* **7** based on or arising from the difference between the sexes: *sex discrimination* ▷ *vb* **8** (*tr*) to ascertain the sex of [c14 from Latin *sexus*; compare *secāre* to divide]

sex- *combining form* six: *sexcentennial* [from Latin]

sexagenarian (ˌsɛksədʒɪ'neərɪən) *n* **1** a person from 60 to 69 years old ▷ *adj* **2** being from 60 to 69 years old **3** of or relating to a sexagenarian [c18 from Latin *sexāgēnārius*, from *sexāgēnī* sixty each, from *sexāgintā* sixty] > **sexagenary** (sɛk'sædʒɪnərɪ) *adj, n*

Sexagesima (ˌsɛksə'dʒɛsɪmə) *n* the second Sunday before Lent [c16 from Latin: sixtieth, from *sexāgintā* sixty]

sexagesimal (ˌsɛksə'dʒɛsɪməl) *adj* **1** relating to or based on the number 60: *sexagesimal measurement of angles* ▷ *n* **2** a fraction in which the denominator is some power of 60; a sixtieth

sexaholic (ˌsɛksə'hɒlɪk) *n* a person who is addicted to sex

sex-and-shopping *adj* (*prenominal*) (of a novel) belonging to a genre of novel in which the central character, a woman, has a number of sexual encounters, and the author mentions the name of many up-market products: *a sex-and-shopping blockbuster*

sexangular (sɛks'æŋɡjʊlə) *adj* another name for **hexagonal**. > **sex'angularly** *adv*

sex appeal *n* the quality or power of attracting the opposite sex

sexcentenary (ˌsɛksɛn'ti:nərɪ) *adj* **1** of or relating to 600 or a period of 600 years **2** of, relating to, or celebrating a 600th anniversary ▷ *n, pl* **-naries 3**

a 600th anniversary or its celebration [c18 from Latin *sexcentēnī* six hundred each]

sex change *n* **a** a change in a person's physical sexual characteristics to those of the opposite sex, often achieved by surgery **b** (*as modifier*): *a sex-change operation*

sex chromosome *n* either of the chromosomes determining the sex of animals. See also **X-chromosome, Y-chromosome**

sexed (sɛkst) *adj* **1** (*in combination*) having a specified degree of sexuality: *undersexed* **2** of, relating to, or having sexual differentiation

sexennial (sɛk'sɛnɪəl) *adj* **1** occurring once every six years or over a period of six years ▷ *n* **2** a sixth anniversary [c17 from Latin *sexennis* of six years, from *sex* six + *annus* a year] > **sex'ennially** *adv*

sexercise ('sɛksəˌsaɪz) *n* sexual activity, regarded as a way of keeping fit

sex hormone *n* an animal hormone affecting development and growth of reproductive organs and related parts

sexism ('sɛksɪzəm) *n* discrimination on the basis of sex, esp the oppression of women by men [c20 from SEX + -ISM, on the model of RACISM] > 'sexist *n, adj*

sexivalent *or* **sexavalent** (ˌsɛksɪ'veɪlənt) *adj chem* another word for **hexavalent**

sexless ('sɛkslɪs) *adj* **1** having or showing no sexual differentiation **2** having no sexual desires **3** sexually unattractive > 'sexlessly *adv* > 'sexlessness *n*

sex-limited *adj genetics* of or designating a character or the gene producing it that appears in one sex only

sex linkage *n genetics* the condition in which a particular gene is located on a sex chromosome, esp on the X-chromosome, so that the character controlled by the gene is associated with either of the sexes > 'sex,linked *adj*

sex object *n* a person viewed or treated as a means of obtaining sexual gratification

sexology (sɛk'sɒlədʒɪ) *n* the study of sexual behaviour in human beings > sex'ologist *n* > sexological (ˌsɛksə'lɒdʒɪkᵊl) *adj*

sexpartite (sɛks'pɑ:taɪt) *adj* **1** (esp of vaults, arches, etc) divided into or composed of six parts **2** maintained by or involving six participants or groups of participants

sexpert ('sɛkspɜːt) *n informal* a person who professes a knowledge of sexual matters [c20 a blend of SEX + EXPERT]

sexploitation (ˌsɛksplɔɪ'teɪʃən) *n* the commercial exploitation of sex in films and other media [c20 blend of SEX + EXPLOITATION]

sexpot ('sɛks,pɒt) *n slang* a person, esp a young woman, considered as being sexually very attractive

sex shop *n* **a** a shop selling aids purporting to increase the pleasurableness of sexual activity **b** a shop selling erotica and pornographic material

sex-starved *adj* deprived of sexual gratification

sext (sɛkst) *n chiefly RC Church* the fourth of the seven canonical hours of the divine office or the prayers prescribed for it: originally the sixth hour of the day (noon) [c15 from Church Latin *sexta hōra* the sixth hour]

Sext (sɛkst) *n RC Church* an official compilation of decretals issued by Boniface VIII in 1298 to supplement the five books of the Liber Extra. It forms part of the Corpus Juris Canonici. In full: **Liber Sextus**

sextain ('sɛksteɪn) *n* another word for **sestina** [c17 from obsolete French *sestine* SESTINA, but also influenced by obsolete *sixain* stanza of six lines]

sextan ('sɛkstən) *adj* (of a fever) marked by paroxysms that recur after an interval of five days [c17 from Medieval Latin *sextana* (*febris*) (fever) of the sixth (day)]

Sextans ('sɛkstənz) *n, Latin genitive* Sextantis (sɛk'tæntɪs) a faint constellation lying on the celestial equator close to Leo and Hydra [New Latin: SEXTANT]

sextant ('sɛkstənt) *n* **1** an optical instrument used in navigation and consisting of a telescope through which a sighting of a heavenly body is taken, with protractors for determining its angular distance above the horizon or from another heavenly body **2** a sixth part of a circle having an arc which subtends an angle of 60° [c17 from Latin *sextāns* one sixth of a unit]

sextet *or* **sextette** (sɛks'tɛt) *n* **1** *music* a group of six singers or instrumentalists or a piece of music composed for such a group **2** a group of six people or things [c19 variant of SESTET, with Latinization of *ses-*]

sex-text *vb* (*tr*) to send a text message of a sexual nature to (someone)

sex therapy *n* treatment by counselling, behaviour modification, etc, for psychosexual and physical problems in sexual intercourse > **sex therapist** *n*

sextile ('sɛkstaɪl) *n* **1** *statistics* one of five actual or notional values of a variable dividing its distribution into six groups with equal frequencies **2** *astrology, astronomy* an aspect or position of 60° between two planets or other celestial bodies [c16 from Latin *sextīlis* one sixth (of a circle), from *sextus* sixth]

sextillion (sɛks'tɪljən) *n, pl* **-lions** *or* **-lion 1** (in Britain, France, and Germany) the number represented as one followed by 36 zeros (10^{36}) **2** (in the US and Canada) the number represented as one followed by 21 zeros (10^{21}) [c17 from French, from SEX- + -*illion*, on the model of SEPTILLION] > **sex'tillionth** *adj, n*

sexto ('sɛkstəʊ) *n, pl* **-tos** another word for **sixmo** [c19 from Latin *sextus* sixth]

sextodecimo (ˌsɛkstəʊ'dɛsɪˌməʊ) *n, pl* **-mos** *bookbinding* another word for **sixteenmo** [c17 from Latin *sextusdecimus* sixteenth]

sexton ('sɛkstən) *n* **1** a person employed to act as caretaker of a church and its contents and graveyard, and often also as bell-ringer, gravedigger, etc **2** another name for the **burying beetle** [c14 from Old French *secrestein*, from Medieval Latin *sacristānus* SACRISTAN]

sex tourism *n* tourism with the intention of exploiting permissive or poorly enforced local laws concerning sex, esp sex with children

sextuple ('sɛkstjʊpᵊl) *n* **1** a quantity or number six times as great as another ▷ *adj* **2** six times as much or many; sixfold **3** consisting of six parts or members **4** (of musical time or rhythm) having six beats per bar [c17 Latin *sextus* sixth + *-uple*, as in QUADRUPLE]

sextuplet ('sɛkstjʊplɪt) *n* **1** one of six offspring born at one birth **2** a group of six things **3** *music* a group of six notes played in a time value of four

sextuplicate *n* (sɛks'tu:pləkɪt, -ˌkeɪt, -'tju:-, -'tʌp-) **1** a group or set of six things, esp identical copies ▷ *adj* (sɛks'tu:pləkɪt, -ˌkeɪt, -'tju:-, -'tʌp-) **2** six times as many, much, or often **3** *maths* raised to the sixth power ▷ *vb* (sɛks'tu:pləˌkeɪt, -'tju:-, -'tʌp-) **4** to multiply or become multiplied by six [c20 from SEXTU(PLE + DU)PLICATE]

sex-typed *adj* characterized as appropriate for or of one sex rather than the other > 'sex-ˌtyping *n*

sexual ('sɛksjʊəl) *adj* **1** of, relating to, or characterized by sex or sexuality **2** (of reproduction) characterized by the union of male and female gametes. Compare **asexual** (sense 2) [c17 from Late Latin *sexuālis*; see SEX] > 'sexually *adv*

sexual dimorphism *n biology* differences in appearance between the males and females of a species

sexual harassment *n* the persistent unwelcome directing of sexual remarks and looks, and unnecessary physical contact at a person, usually a woman, esp in the workplace

sexual intercourse *n* the act carried out for procreation or for pleasure in which, typically, the insertion of the male's erect penis into the female's vagina is followed by rhythmic thrusting usually culminating in orgasm; copulation;

coitus. Related adj: **venereal**

sexuality (ˌsɛksjʊˈælɪtɪ) *n* **1** the state or quality of being sexual **2** preoccupation with or involvement in sexual matters **3** the possession of sexual potency

sexualize *or* **sexualise** (ˈsɛksjʊəˌlaɪz) *vb* **1** to make or become sexual or sexually aware **2** to give or acquire sexual associations > ˌsexualiˈzation *or* ˌsexualiˈsation *n*

sexual reproduction *n* reproduction involving the fusion of a male and female haploid gamete

sexual selection *n* an evolutionary process in animals, in which selection by females of males with certain characters, such as large antlers or bright plumage, results in the preservation of these characters in the species

sex up *vb* (*tr, adverb*) *informal* to make (something) more interesting or exciting: *the BBC decided to sex up the book's title*

sex worker *n* a prostitute

sexy (ˈsɛksɪ) *adj* **sexier, sexiest** *informal* **1** provoking or intended to provoke sexual interest: *a sexy dress; a sexy book* **2** feeling sexual interest; aroused **3** interesting, exciting, or trendy: *a sexy project; a sexy new car* > ˈsexily *adv* > ˈsexiness *n*

Seychelles (seɪˈʃɛl, -ˈʃɛlz) *pl n* a group of volcanic islands in the W Indian Ocean: taken by the British from the French in 1744: became an independent republic within the Commonwealth in 1976, incorporating the British Indian Ocean Territory islands of Aldabra, Farquhar and Desroches. Languages: Creole, English, and French. Religion: Roman Catholic majority. Currency: rupee. Capital: Victoria. Pop: 81 000 (2003 est). Area: 455 sq km (176 sq miles)

Seyfert galaxy (ˈsaɪfət) *n* any of a class of spiral galaxies having a very bright nucleus, possibly corresponding to an active period in the lives of all spiral galaxies [c20 named after Carl K *Seyfert* (died 1960), US astronomer]

Seyhan (seɪˈhɑːn) *n* another name for **Adana**

sf, sf., sfz *or* **sfz.** *music abbreviation for* sforzando

SF *or* **sf** *abbreviation for* science fiction

SFA *abbreviation for* **1** Scottish Football Association **2** Sweet Fanny Adams. See **fanny adams**

Sfax (sfæks) *n* a port in E Tunisia, on the Gulf of Gabès: the second largest town in Tunisia; commercial centre of a phosphate region. Pop: 570 000 (2005 est)

sferics (ˈsfɛrɪks) *n* the usual US spelling of **spherics²**

SFO *abbreviation for* Serious Fraud Office: the department of the British government which investigates cases of serious financial fraud

sforzando (sfɔːˈtsɑːndəʊ) *or* **sforzato** (sfɔːˈtsɑːtəʊ) *music* ▷ *adj, adv* **1** to be played with strong initial attack. Abbreviation: sf ▷ *n* **2** a symbol, mark, etc, such as >, written above a note, indicating this [c19 from Italian, from *sforzare* to force, from ex-¹ + *forzare*, from Vulgar Latin *fortiāre* (unattested) to FORCE¹]

sfumato (sfuːˈmɑːtəʊ) *n* (in painting) a gradual transition between areas of different colour, avoiding sharp outlines [from Italian, from *sfumato* shaded off, from *sfumare* to shade off, from Latin ex-¹ + *fūmāre* to smoke]

SFW (in South Africa) *abbreviation for* Stellenbosch Farmers' Winery, South Africa's leading wine producer

SFX *pl n films, television* **1** short for **sound effects 2** short for **special effects** [c20 s(OUND), s(PECIAL) + a phonetic respelling of EFFECTS]

sg¹ *abbreviation for* specific gravity

sg² *the internet domain name for* Singapore

SG *abbreviation for* **1** (in transformational grammar) singular **2** solicitor general

sgd *abbreviation for* signed

SGHWR *abbreviation for* **steam-generating heavy-water reactor**

sgian-dhu (ˈskiːənˈduː, ˈskiːn-) *n Scot* a dirk carried in the stocking by Highlanders [Gaelic *sgian* knife + *dhu* black]

SGML *abbreviation for* standard generalized markup language: an international standard used in publishing for defining the structure and formatting of documents

SGP *international car registration for* Singapore

sgraffito (sgrɑˈfiːtəʊ) *n, pl* **-ti** (-tɪ) **1** a technique in mural or ceramic decoration in which the top layer of glaze, plaster, etc, is incised with a design to reveal parts of the ground **2** such a decoration **3** an object decorated in such a way [c18 from Italian, from *sgraffire* to scratch; see GRAFFITI]

's Gravenhage (sxrɑːvənˈhɑːxə) *n* a Dutch name for (The) **Hague**

Sgt *abbreviation for* Sergeant

Sgt Maj *abbreviation for* Sergeant Major

sh¹ (*spelling pron ʃʃʃ*) *interj* an exclamation to request silence or quiet

sh² *the internet domain name for* St Helena

SHA *navigation abbreviation for* sidereal hour angle

Shaanxi (ˈʃænˈʃiː) *or* **Shensi** *n* a province of NW China: one of the earliest centres of Chinese civilization; largely mountainous. Capital: Xi'an. Pop: 36 900 000 (2003 est). Area: 195 800 sq km (75 598 sq miles)

Shaba (ˈʃɑːbə) *n* the former name (1972–97) of **Katanga**

Shaban *or* **Shaaban** (ʃəˈbɑːn, ʃɑː-) *n* the eighth month of the Muslim year [from Arabic *sha'bān*]

shabash (ˈʃɑːˈbɑːʃ) *interj Indian* an expression meaning well done; bravo [Urdu]

Shabbat (ʃɑːˈbɑːt) *or* **Shabbos, Shabbes** (ˈʃɑːbəs) *n, pl* Shabbatot (ʃɑːbɑːˈtot) Shabbosos (ʃɑːˈbosəs) *or* Shabbosim (ʃɑːbosəm) *Judaism* another word for the **Sabbath** [from Hebrew *shabbāth*; see SABBATH]

shabby (ˈʃæbɪ) *adj* **-bier, -biest 1** threadbare or dilapidated in appearance **2** wearing worn and dirty clothes; seedy **3** mean, despicable, or unworthy: *shabby treatment* **4** dirty or squalid [c17 from Old English *sceabb* SCAB + -Y¹] > ˈshabbily *adv* > ˈshabbiness *n*

shabby-genteel *adj* preserving or aspiring to the forms and manners of gentility despite appearing shabby

Shabuoth (ʃəˈvuːəs, -əʊs; Hebrew ʃavuːˈɔt) *n* a variant spelling of **Shavuot**

Shacharis, Shaharith Hebrew (ˈʃaxəˌras) *or* **Shaharith** (ʃaxaˈrit) *n Judaism* the morning service

Shache (ˈʃæˈtʃeɪ), **Soche** *or* **So-ch'e** *n* a town in W China, in the W Xinjiang Uygur AR: a centre of the caravan trade between China, India, and Transcaspian areas. Also called: **Yarkand**

shack¹ (ʃæk) *n* **1** a roughly built hut **2** *South African* temporary accommodation put together by squatters ▷ *vb* **3** See **shack up** [c19 perhaps from dialect *shackly* ramshackle, from dialect *shack* to shake]

shack² (ʃæk) *vb Midland English dialect* to evade (work or responsibility)

shackle (ˈʃækəl) *n* **1** (*often plural*) a metal ring or fastening, usually part of a pair used to secure a person's wrists or ankles; fetter **2** (*often plural*) anything that confines or restricts freedom **3** a rope, tether, or hobble for an animal **4** a U-shaped bracket, the open end of which is closed by a bolt (**shackle pin**), used for securing ropes, chains, etc ▷ *vb* (*tr*) **5** to confine with or as if with shackles **6** to fasten or connect with a shackle [Old English *sceacel*; related to Dutch *schakel*, Old Norse *skokull* wagon pole, Latin *cingere* to surround] > ˈshackler *n*

shacko (ˈʃækəʊ) *n, pl* shackos *or* shackoes a variant spelling of **shako**

shack up *vb* (*intr, adverb*; usually foll by *with*) *slang* to live or take up residence, esp with a mistress or lover

shad (ʃæd) *n, pl* shad *or* shads **1** any of various herring-like food fishes of the genus *Alosa* and related genera, such as A. *alosa* (**allis shad**) of Europe, that migrate from the sea to freshwater to spawn: family *Clupeidae* (herrings) **2** any of various similar but unrelated fishes [Old English *sceadd*; related to Norwegian *skadd*, German *Schade*

shad, Old Irish *scatán* herring, Latin *scatēre* to well up]

shadberry (ˈʃædbərɪ, -brɪ) *n, pl* -ries another name for **serviceberry** (senses 1, 2) [c19 perhaps so called because they appear when SHAD fish are in the rivers to spawn]

shadbush (ˈʃædˌbʊʃ) *n* another name for **serviceberry** (sense 1)

shadchan Yiddish (ˈʃatxən, Hebrew ʃadˈxan) *n, pl* **shadchanim** (ʃatˈxɔnɪm), **shadchans** a Jewish marriage broker [from Hebrew *shadhkhān*, from *shiddēkh* to arrange a marriage]

shaddock (ˈʃædək) *n* another name for **pomelo** [c17 named after Captain *Shaddock*, who brought its seed from the East Indies to Jamaica in 1696]

shade (ʃeɪd) *n* **1** relative darkness produced by the blocking out of light **2** a place made relatively darker or cooler than other areas by the blocking of light, esp sunlight **3** a position of relative obscurity **4** something used to provide a shield or protection from a direct source of light, such as a lampshade **5** a darker area indicated in a painting, drawing, etc, by shading **6** a colour that varies slightly from a standard colour due to a difference in hue, saturation, or luminosity: *a darker shade of green* **7** a slight amount: *a shade of difference* **8** *literary* a ghost **9** an archaic word for **shadow 10** put in the shade to appear better than (another); surpass ▷ *vb* (*mainly tr*) **11** to screen or protect from heat, light, view, etc **12** to make darker or dimmer **13** to represent (a darker area) in (a painting, drawing, etc), by means of hatching, using a darker colour, etc **14** (*also intr*) to change or cause to change slightly **15** to lower (a price) slightly [Old English *sceadu*; related to Gothic *skadus*, Old High German *skato*, Old Irish *scáth* shadow, Greek *skotos* darkness, Swedish *skäddä* fog] > ˈshadeless *adj*

shades (ʃeɪdz) *pl n* **1** gathering darkness at nightfall **2** a slang word for **sunglasses 3** (*often capital*; preceded by *the*) a literary term for **Hades 4** (foll by *of*) undertones or suggestions: *shades of my father!*

shading (ˈʃeɪdɪŋ) *n* the graded areas of tone, lines, dots, etc, indicating light and dark in a painting or drawing

shadoof *or* **shaduf** (ʃəˈduːf) *n* a mechanism for raising water, consisting of a pivoted pole with a bucket at one end and a counterweight at the other, esp as used in Egypt and the Near East [c19 from Egyptian Arabic]

shadow (ˈʃædəʊ) *n* **1** a dark image or shape cast on a surface by the interception of light rays by an opaque body **2** an area of relative darkness **3** the dark portions of a picture **4** a hint, image, or faint semblance: *beyond a shadow of a doubt* **5** a remnant or vestige: *a shadow of one's past self* **6** a reflection **7** a threatening influence; blight: *a shadow over one's happiness* **8** a spectre **9** an inseparable companion **10** a person who trails another in secret, such as a detective **11** *med* a dark area on an X-ray film representing an opaque structure or part **12** (in Jungian psychology) the archetype that represents man's animal ancestors **13** *archaic or rare* protection or shelter **14** (*modifier*) *Brit* designating a member or members of the main opposition party in Parliament who would hold ministerial office if their party were in power: *shadow Chancellor; shadow cabinet* ▷ *vb* (*tr*) **15** to cast a shadow over **16** to make dark or gloomy; blight **17** to shade from light **18** to follow or trail secretly **19** (often foll by *forth*) to represent vaguely **20** *painting, drawing* another word for **shade** (sense 13) [Old English *sceadwe*, oblique case of *sceadu* SHADE; related to Dutch *schaduw*] > ˈshadower *n* > ˈshadowless *adj*

shadow bands *n* slow-moving waves of light and dark observed to move across light-coloured surfaces on the earth just before and after totality in a solar eclipse. They are thought to originate from the effects of irregular atmospheric refraction

shadow-box vb (intr) **1** boxing to practise blows and footwork against an imaginary opponent **2** to act or speak unconvincingly, without saying what one means, etc: he's just shadow-boxing > 'shadow-,boxing n

shadowgraph ('ʃædəʊˌɡrɑːf, -ˌɡræf) n **1** a silhouette made by casting a shadow, usually of the hands, on a lighted surface **2** another name for **radiograph**

shadow history n another name for **secret history**

shadow mask n television a perforated metal sheet mounted close to the phosphor-dotted screen in some colour television tubes. The holes are positioned so that each of the three electron beams strikes the correct phosphor dot producing the required colour mixture in the image

shadow play n a theatrical entertainment using shadows thrown by puppets or actors onto a lighted screen

shadow price n economics the calculated price of a good or service for which no market price exists

shadow test n med another name for **retinoscopy**

shadowy ('ʃædəʊɪ) adj **1** full of shadows; dark; shady **2** resembling a shadow in faintness; vague **3** illusory or imaginary **4** mysterious or secretive: a shadowy underworld figure > 'shadowiness n

Shadrach ('ʃædræk, 'ʃeɪ-) n Old Testament one of Daniel's three companions, who, together with Meshach and Abednego, was miraculously saved from destruction in Nebuchadnezzar's fiery furnace (Daniel 3:12–30)

shaduf (ʃə'duːf) n a variant spelling of **shadoof**

shady ('ʃeɪdɪ) adj shadier, shadiest **1** full of shade; shaded **2** affording or casting a shade **3** dim, quiet, or concealed **4** informal dubious or questionable as to honesty or legality > 'shadily adv > 'shadiness n

SHAEF (ʃeɪf) n (in World War II) acronym for Supreme Headquarters Allied Expeditionary Forces

shaft (ʃɑːft) n **1** the long narrow pole that forms the body of a spear, arrow, etc **2** something directed at a person in the manner of a missile: shafts of sarcasm **3** a ray, beam, or streak, esp of light **4** a rod or pole forming the handle of a hammer, axe, golf club, etc **5** a revolving rod that transmits motion or power: usually used of axial rotation. Compare **rod** (sense 9) **6** one of the two wooden poles by which an animal is harnessed to a vehicle **7** anatomy **a** the middle part (diaphysis) of a long bone **b** the main portion of any elongated structure or part **8** the middle part of a column or pier, between the base and the capital **9** a column, obelisk, etc, esp one that forms a monument **10** architect a column that supports a vaulting rib, sometimes one of a set **11** a vertical passageway through a building, as for a lift **12** a vertical passageway into a mine **13** ornithol the central rib of a feather **14** an archaic or literary word for **arrow 15** get the shaft US and Canadian slang to be tricked or cheated > vb **16** slang to have sexual intercourse with (a woman) **17** slang to trick or cheat [Old English sceaft; related to Old Norse skapt, German Schaft, Latin scāpus shaft, Greek skeptron SCEPTRE, Lettish skeps javelin]

shaft feather n archery one of the two fletchings on an arrow. Compare **cock feather**

shafting ('ʃɑːftɪŋ) n **1** an assembly of rotating shafts for transmitting power **2** the stock from which shafts are made **3** architect a set of shafts

shag¹ (ʃæɡ) n **1** a matted tangle, esp of hair, wool, etc **2** a napped fabric, usually a rough wool **3** shredded coarse tobacco > vb shags, shagging, shagged **4** (tr) to make shaggy [Old English sceacga; related to sceaga SHAW¹, Old Norse skegg beard, skagi tip, skōgr forest]

shag² (ʃæɡ) n **1** another name for the **green cormorant** (Phalacrocorax aristotelis) **2** like a shag on a rock Austral slang abandoned and alone [c16 special use of SHAG¹, with reference to its crest]

shag³ (ʃæɡ) Brit slang > vb shags, shagging, shagged **1** to have sexual intercourse with (a person) **2** (tr; often foll by out; usually passive) to exhaust; tire > n **3** an act of sexual intercourse [c20 of unknown origin]

USAGE Though still likely to cause offence to many older or more conservative people, this word has lost a lot of its shock value of late. It seems to have a jocular, relaxed connotation, which most of the other words in this field do not. No doubt its acceptability has been accelerated by its use in the title of an Austin Powers film. Interestingly, though advertisements for the film caused a large number of complaints to the British Advertising Standards Authority, they were not upheld

shagbark ('ʃæɡˌbɑːk) or **shellbark** n **1** a North American hickory tree, Carya ovata, having loose rough bark and edible nuts **2** the wood of this tree, used for tool handles, fuel, etc **3** the light-coloured hard-shelled nut of this tree [c18 so called because of the texture of its bark]

shaggable ('ʃæɡəbᵊl) adj Brit slang sexually attractive

shaggy ('ʃæɡɪ) adj -gier, -giest **1** having or covered with rough unkempt fur, hair, wool, etc: a shaggy dog **2** rough or unkempt **3** (in textiles) having a nap of long rough strands > 'shaggily adv > 'shagginess n

shaggy cap n an edible saprotrophic agaricaceous fungus, Coprinus comatus, having a white cap covered with shaggy scales

shaggy dog story n informal a long rambling joke ending in a deliberate anticlimax, such as a pointless punch line

shagreen (ʃæ'ɡriːn) n **1** the rough skin of certain sharks and rays, used as an abrasive **2** a rough grainy leather made from certain animal hides [c17 from French chagrin, from Turkish çagri rump; also associated through folk etymology with SHAG¹, GREEN]

shagroon (ʃæ'ɡruːn) n NZ history a nineteenth-century Australian settler in Canterbury [perhaps from Irish seachrán wandering]

shagtastic (ʃæɡ'tæstɪk) adj Brit slang **1** sexually attractive; sexy **2** excellent; wonderful [c20 from SHAG³ + (FAN)TASTIC]

shah (ʃɑː) n a ruler of certain Middle Eastern countries, esp (formerly) Iran [c16 from Persian: king] > 'shahdom n

shahada (ʃə'hɑːdə) n the Islamic declaration of faith, repeated daily by Muslims [from Arabic, literally: witnessing]

Shahaptin (ʃə'hæptɪn), **Shahaptan** (ʃə'hæptən) or **Shahaptian** (ʃə'hæptɪən) n variants of Sahaptin

Shahjahanpur (ʃɑːdʒəˌhɑːn'pʊə) n a city in N India, in central Uttar Pradesh: founded in 1647 in the reign of Shah Jahan. Pop: 297 932 (2001)

shahtoosh (ʃɑː'tuːʃ) n a soft wool that comes from the protected Tibetan antelope

Shaitan (ʃaɪ'tɑːn) n (in Muslim countries) **a** Satan **b** any evil spirit **c** a vicious person or animal [c17 from Arabic shaytān, from Hebrew śātān; see SATAN]

shake (ʃeɪk) vb shakes, shaking, shook, shaken ('ʃeɪkᵊn) **1** to move or cause to move up and down or back and forth with short quick movements; vibrate **2** to sway or totter or cause to sway or totter **3** to clasp or grasp (the hand) of (a person) in greeting, agreement, etc: he shook John by the hand; he shook John's hand; they shook and were friends **4** shake hands to clasp hands in greeting, agreement, etc **5** shake on it informal to shake hands in agreement, reconciliation, etc **6** to bring or come to a specified condition by or as if by shaking: he shook free and ran **7** (tr) to wave or brandish: he shook his sword **8** (tr; often foll by up) to rouse, stir, or agitate **9** (tr) to shock, disturb, or

upset: he was shaken by the news of her death **10** (tr) to undermine or weaken: the crisis shook his faith **11** to mix (dice) by rattling in a cup or the hand before throwing **12** (tr) Austral archaic slang to steal **13** (tr) US and Canadian informal to escape from: can you shake that detective? **14** music to perform a trill on (a note) **15** (tr) US informal to fare or progress; happen as specified: how's it shaking? **16** shake a leg informal to hurry: usually used in the imperative **17** shake in one's shoes to tremble with fear or apprehension **18** shake one's head to indicate disagreement or disapproval by moving the head from side to side **19** shake the dust from one's feet to depart gladly or with the intention not to return > n **20** the act or an instance of shaking **21** a tremor or vibration **22** the shakes informal a state of uncontrollable trembling or a condition that causes it, such as a fever **23** informal a very short period of time; jiffy: in half a shake **24** a shingle or clapboard made from a short log by splitting it radially **25** a fissure or crack in timber or rock **26** an instance of shaking dice before casting **27** music another word for trill' (sense 1) **28** a dance, popular in the 1960s, in which the body is shaken convulsively in time to the beat **29** an informal name for **earthquake 30** short for **milk shake 31** no great shakes informal of no great merit or value; ordinary > See also **shake down, shake off, shake up** [Old English sceacan; related to Old Norse skaka to shake, Old High German untscachōn to be driven] > 'shakable or 'shakeable adj

shake down vb (adverb) **1** to fall or settle or cause to fall or settle by shaking **2** (tr) US slang to extort money from, esp by blackmail or threats of violence **3** (tr) US slang to search thoroughly **4** (tr) informal, chiefly US to submit (a vessel, etc) to a shakedown test **5** (intr) to go to bed, esp to a makeshift bed **6** (intr) (of a person, animal, etc) to settle down > n **shakedown 7** US slang a swindle or act of extortion **8** US slang a thorough search **9** a makeshift bed, esp of straw, blankets, etc **10** informal, chiefly US **a** a voyage to test the performance of a ship or aircraft or to familiarize the crew with their duties **b** (as modifier): a shakedown run

shaken baby syndrome n a combination of physical injuries and conditions such as brain damage and broken bones, sometimes leading to death, caused by the vigorous shaking of an infant or young child

shake off vb (adverb) **1** to remove or be removed with or as if with a quick movement: she shook off her depression **2** (tr) to escape from; elude: they shook off the police

shake-out n the process of reducing the number of people in a workforce in order to lower the costs of a company

shaker ('ʃeɪkə) n **1** a person or thing that shakes **2** a container, often having a perforated top, from which something, such as a condiment, is shaken **3** a container in which the ingredients of alcoholic drinks are shaken together

Shakers ('ʃeɪkəz) pl n **the** an American millenarian sect, founded in 1747 as an offshoot of the Quakers, given to ecstatic shaking, advocating celibacy for its members, and practising common ownership of property

Shakespearean or **Shakespearian** (ʃeɪk'spɪərɪən) adj **1** of, relating to, or characteristic of William Shakespeare, the English dramatist and poet (1564–1616), or his works > n **2** a student of or specialist in Shakespeare's works

Shakespeareana ('ʃeɪkˌspɪərɪ'ɑːnə, ʃeɪkˌspɪər-) pl n collected writings or items relating to Shakespeare

Shakespearean sonnet n a sonnet form developed in 16th-century England and employed by Shakespeare, having the rhyme scheme a b a b c d c d e f e f g g. Also called: Elizabethan sonnet, English sonnet

shake up *vb* (*tr, adverb*) **1** to shake or agitate in order to mix **2** to reorganize drastically **3** to stir or rouse **4** to restore the shape of (a pillow, cushion, etc) **5** *informal* to disturb or shock mentally or physically ▷ *n* **shake-up 6** *informal* a radical or drastic reorganization

Shakhty (*Russian* ˈʃaxtɪ) *n* an industrial city in W Russia: the chief town of the E Donets Basin; a major coal-mining centre. Pop: 219 000 (2005 est)

shaking palsy *n* another name for **Parkinson's disease**

shako *or* **shacko** (ˈʃækəʊ) *n, pl* shakos, shakoes *or* shackos, shackoes a tall usually cylindrical military headdress, having a plume and often a peak, popular esp in the 19th century [c19 via French from Hungarian *csákó*, from Middle High German *zacke* a sharp point]

Shakta (ˈʃʌktə) *n Hinduism* a devotee of Sakti, the wife of Siva [from Sanskrit *śākta* concerning Sakti] > ˈShaktism *n* > ˈShaktist *n*

Shakti (ˈʃʌktɪ) *n* a variant of **Sakti**

shaky (ˈʃeɪkɪ) *adj* shakier, shakiest **1** tending to shake or tremble **2** liable to prove defective; unreliable **3** uncertain or questionable: *your arguments are very shaky* > ˈshakily *adv* > ˈshakiness *n*

shale (ʃeɪl) *n* a dark fine-grained laminated sedimentary rock formed by compression of successive layers of clay-rich sediment [Old English *scealu* SHELL; compare German *Schalstein* laminated limestone; see SCALE¹, SCALE²] > ˈshaly *adj*

shale oil *n* an oil distilled from shales and used as fuel

shall (ʃæl; *unstressed* ʃəl) *vb, past* should (takes an infinitive without *to* or an implied infinitive) **1** (esp with I or we as subject) used as an auxiliary to make the future tense: *we shall see you tomorrow.* Compare **will¹** (sense 1) **2** (with *you, he, she, it, they,* or a noun as subject) **a** used as an auxiliary to indicate determination on the part of the speaker, as in issuing a threat: *you shall pay for this!* **b** used as an auxiliary to indicate compulsion, now esp in official documents: *the Tenant shall return the keys to the Landlord* **c** used as an auxiliary to indicate certainty or inevitability: *our day shall come* **3** (with any noun or pronoun as subject, esp in conditional clauses or clauses expressing doubt) used as an auxiliary to indicate nonspecific futurity: *I don't think I shall ever see her again; he doubts whether he shall be in tomorrow* [Old English *sceal*; related to Old Norse *skal*, Old High German *zal*]

> USAGE The usual rule given for the use of *shall* and *will* is that where the meaning is one of simple futurity, *shall* is used for the first person of the verb and *will* for the second and third: *I shall go tomorrow; they will be there now.* Where the meaning involves command, obligation, or determination, the positions are reversed: *it shall be done; I will definitely go.* However, *shall* has come to be largely neglected in favour of *will,* which has become the commonest form of the future in all three persons

shalloon (ʃæˈluːn) *n* a light twill-weave woollen fabric used chiefly for coat linings, etc [c17 from Old French *chalon*, from the name of *Châlons-sur-Marne*, France, where it originated]

shallop (ˈʃæləp) *n* **1** a light boat used for rowing in shallow water **2** (formerly) a two-masted gaff-rigged vessel [c16 from French *chaloupe*, from Dutch *sloep* SLOOP]

shallot (ʃəˈlɒt) *n* **1** Also called: **scallion** an alliaceous plant, *Allium ascalonicum,* cultivated for its edible bulb **2** the bulb of this plant, which divides into small sections and is used in cooking for flavouring and as a vegetable [c17 from Old French *eschalotte*, from Old French *eschaloigne*, from Latin *Ascalōnia caepa* Ascalonian onion, from *Ascalon*, a Palestinian town]

shallow (ˈʃæləʊ) *adj* **1** having little depth **2**

lacking intellectual or mental depth or subtlety; superficial ▷ *n* **3** (*often plural*) a shallow place in a body of water; shoal ▷ *vb* **4** to make or become shallow [c15 related to Old English *sceald* shallow; see SHOAL¹] > ˈshallowly *adv* > ˈshallowness *n*

shalom aleichem *Hebrew* (ʃaˈlɒm aˈlexɛm; *English* ʃəˈlɒm əˈleɪxəm) *interj* peace be to you: used by Jews as a greeting or farewell. Often shortened to: **shalom**

shalt (ʃælt) *vb archaic or dialect* (used with the pronoun *thou* or its relative equivalent) a singular form of the present tense (indicative mood) of **shall**

shalwar (ˈʃælwaː) *n* a pair of loose-fitting trousers tapering to a narrow fit around the ankles, worn in the Indian subcontinent, often with a kameez [from Urdu and Persian *shalwār*]

sham (ʃæm) *n* **1** anything that is not what it purports or appears to be **2** something false, fake, or fictitious that purports to be genuine **3** a person who pretends to be something other than he is ▷ *adj* **4** counterfeit or false; simulated ▷ *vb* shams, shamming, shammed **5** to falsely assume the appearance of (something); counterfeit: *to sham illness* [c17 perhaps a Northern English dialect variant of SHAME] > ˈshammer *n*

shaman (ˈʃæmən) *n* **1** a priest of shamanism **2** a medicine man of a similar religion, esp among certain tribes of North American Indians [c17 from Russian *shaman*, from Tungusian *šaman,* from Pali *samana* Buddhist monk, ultimately from Sanskrit *śrama* religious exercise] > shamanic (ʃəˈmænɪk) *adj*

shamanism (ˈʃæməˌnɪzəm) *n* **1** the religion of certain peoples of northern Asia, based on the belief that the world is pervaded by good and evil spirits who can be influenced or controlled only by the shamans **2** any similar religion involving forms of spiritualism > ˈshamanist *n, adj* > ˌshamanˈistic *adj*

Shamash (ˈʃaːmæʃ) *n* the sun god of Assyria and Babylonia [from Akkadian: sun]

shamateur (ˈʃæməˌtɜː, -ˌtjʊə, -tə, -tʃə) *n* a sportsperson who is officially an amateur but accepts payment [c20 from a blend of SHAM + AMATEUR]

shamba (ˈʃamba) *n* (in E Africa) any field used for growing crops [Swahili]

shamble (ˈʃæmbəl) *vb* **1** (*intr*) to walk or move along in an awkward or unsteady way ▷ *n* **2** an awkward or unsteady walk [c17 from *shamble* (adj) ungainly, perhaps from the phrase *shamble legs* legs resembling those of a meat vendor's table; see SHAMBLES] > ˈshambling *adj, n*

shambles (ˈʃæmbəlz) *n* (*functioning as singular or plural*) **1** a place of great disorder: *the room was a shambles after the party* **2** a place where animals are brought to be slaughtered **3** any place of slaughter or carnage **4** *Brit dialect* a row of covered stalls or shops where goods, originally meat, are sold [c14 *shamble* table used by meat vendors, from Old English *sceamel* stool, from Late Latin *scamellum* a small bench, from Latin *scamnum* stool]

shambolic (ʃæmˈbɒlɪk) *adj informal* completely disorganized; chaotic [c20 irregularly formed from SHAMBLES]

shame (ʃeɪm) *n* **1** a painful emotion resulting from an awareness of having done something dishonourable, unworthy, degrading, etc **2** capacity to feel such an emotion **3** ignominy or disgrace **4** a person or thing that causes this **5** an occasion for regret, disappointment, etc: *it's a shame you can't come with us* **6** put to shame **a** to disgrace **b** to surpass totally ▷ *interj* **7** *South African informal* **a** an expression of sympathy **b** an expression of pleasure or endearment ▷ *vb* (*tr*) **8** to cause to feel shame **9** to bring shame on; disgrace **10** (*often foll by into*) to compel through a sense of shame: *he shamed her into making an apology* **11** name and shame See **name** (sense 17) [Old English *scamu*; related to Old Norse *skömm*, Old

High German *skama* > ˈshamable *or* ˈshameable *adj*

shamefaced (ˈʃeɪmˌfeɪst) *adj* **1** bashful or modest **2** showing a sense of shame [c16 alteration of earlier *shamefast*, from Old English *sceamfaest*; see SHAME, FAST¹] > shamefacedly (ʃeɪmˈfeɪsɪdlɪ, ˈʃeɪmˌfeɪstlɪ) *adv* > shameˈfacedness *n*

shameful (ˈʃeɪmfʊl) *adj* causing or deserving shame; scandalous > ˈshamefully *adv* > ˈshamefulness *n*

shameless (ˈʃeɪmlɪs) *adj* **1** having no sense of shame; brazen **2** done without shame; without decency or modesty > ˈshamelessly *adv* > ˈshamelessness *n*

shamina (ˈʃæˈmiːnə) *n* a wool blend of pashm and shahtoosh

shammes *or* **shammash** (ˈʃɑːməs; *Hebrew* ʃaˈmaʃ) *n, pl* shammosim *or* shammashim (*Hebrew* ʃaˈmɔsɪm) *Judaism* **1** an official acting as the beadle, sexton, and caretaker of a synagogue **2** the extra candle used on the Feast of Hanukkah to kindle the lamps or candles of the menorah [from Hebrew *shāmmāsh*, from Aramaic *shĕmāsh* to serve]

shammy (ˈʃæmɪ) *n, pl* -mies *informal* another word for **chamois** (sense 3) Also called: **shammy leather** [c18 variant, influenced by the pronunciation, of CHAMOIS]

Shamo (ˈʃɑːməʊ) *n* transliteration of the Chinese name for the **Gobi**

shampoo (ʃæmˈpuː) *n* **1** a liquid or cream preparation of soap or detergent to wash the hair **2** a similar preparation for washing carpets, etc **3** the process of shampooing ▷ *vb* -poos, -pooing, -pooed **4** (*tr*) to wash (the hair, etc) with such a preparation [c18 from Hindi *chāmpo*, from *chāmpnā* to knead] > shamˈpooer *n*

shamrock (ˈʃæmˌrɒk) *n* a plant having leaves divided into three leaflets, variously identified as the wood sorrel, red clover, white clover, and black medick: the national emblem of Ireland [c16 from Irish Gaelic *seamróg*, diminutive of *seamar* clover]

shamus (ˈʃɑːməs, ˈʃeɪ-) *n, pl* -muses US *slang* a police or private detective [probably from SHAMMES, influenced by Irish *Séamas* James]

Shan (ʃɑːn) *n* **1** (*pl* Shans *or* Shan) a member of a Mongoloid people living in Myanmar, Thailand, and SW China **2** the language or group of dialects spoken by the Shan, belonging to the Sino-Tibetan family and closely related to Thai

Shandong (ˈʃænˈdʌŋ) *or* **Shantung** *n* a province of NE China, on the Yellow Sea and the Gulf of Chihli: part of the earliest organized state of China (1520–1030 BC); consists chiefly of the fertile plain of the lower Yellow River, with mountains over 1500 m (5000 ft) high in the centre. Capital: Jinan. Pop: 91 250 000 (2003 est). Area: 153 300 sq km (59 189 sq miles)

shandrydan (ˈʃændrɪˌdæn) *n* **1** a two-wheeled cart or chaise, esp one with a hood **2** any decrepit old-fashioned conveyance [c19 of unknown origin]

shandy (ˈʃændɪ) *or US* **shandygaff** (ˈʃændɪˌgæf) *n, pl* -dies *or* -gaffs an alcoholic drink made of beer and ginger beer or lemonade [c19 of unknown origin]

Shang (ʃæŋ) *n* **1** the dynasty ruling in China from about the 18th to the 12th centuries BC ▷ *adj* **2** of or relating to the pottery produced during the Shang dynasty

Shangaan (ˈʃaŋgaːn) *n* a member of any of the Tsonga-speaking Bantu peoples settled in Mozambique and NE Transvaal, esp one who works in a gold mine

shanghai (ˈʃæŋhaɪ, ʃæŋˈhaɪ) *slang* ▷ *vb* -hais, -haiing, -haied (*tr*) **1** to kidnap (a man or seaman) for enforced service at sea, esp on a merchant ship **2** to force or trick (someone) into doing something, going somewhere, etc **3** *Austral and NZ* to shoot with a catapult ▷ *n* **4** *Austral and NZ* a catapult [c19 from the city of SHANGHAI; from the forceful methods formerly used to collect crews for voyages to the Orient]

Shanghai (ˈʃæŋˈhaɪ) *n* a port in E China, in SE

S

Jiangsu near the estuary of the Yangtze: the largest city in China and one of the largest ports in the world; a major cultural and industrial centre, with two universities. Pop: 12 665 000 (2005 est)

Shango ('ʃæŋgəʊ) *n* **a** a W African religious cult surviving in some parts of the Caribbean **b** (*as modifier*): *Shango ritual* [Yoruba]

Shangri-la (ˌʃæŋgrɪ'lɑ:) *n* a remote or imaginary utopia [C20 from the name of an imaginary valley in the Himalayas, from *Lost Horizon* (1933), a novel by James Hilton]

shank (ʃæŋk) *n* **1** *anatomy* the shin **2** the corresponding part of the leg in vertebrates other than man **3** a cut of meat from the top part of an animal's shank **4** the main part of a tool, between the working part and the handle **5** the part of a bolt between the thread and the head **6** the cylindrical part of a bit by which it is held in the drill **7** the ring or stem on the back of some buttons **8** the stem or long narrow part of a key, anchor, hook, spoon handle, nail, pin, etc **9** the band of a ring as distinguished from the setting **10 a** the part of a shoe connecting the wide part of the sole with the heel **b** the metal or leather piece used for this **11** *printing* the body of a piece of type, between the shoulder and the foot **12** *engineering* a ladle used for molten metal **13** *music* another word for **crook** (sense 6) ▷ *vb* **14** (*intr*) (of fruits, roots, etc) to show disease symptoms, esp discoloration **15** (*tr*) *golf* to mishit (the ball) with the foot of the shaft rather than the face of the club [Old English *scanca*; related to Old Frisian *schanke*, Middle Low German *schenke*, Danish, Swedish *skank* leg]

shanks's mare *or US and Canadian* **shanks's mare** ('ʃæŋksɪz) *n informal* one's own legs as a means of transportation [C18 from SHANK (in the sense: lower leg); probably with a pun on the surname *Shanks*]

Shannon ('ʃænən) *n* a river in the Republic of Ireland, rising in NW Co Cavan and flowing south to the Atlantic by an estuary 113 km (70 miles) long: the longest river in the Republic of Ireland. Length: 260 km (161 miles)

shanny ('ʃænɪ) *n, pl* -nies a European blenny, *Blennius pholis*, of rocky coastal waters [C19 of obscure origin]

Shansi ('ʃæn'si:) *n* a variant transliteration of the Chinese name for **Shanxi**

Shan State (ʃɑ:n, ʃæn) *n* an administrative division of E Myanmar: formed in 1947 from the joining of the Federation of Shan States with the Wa States; consists of the **Shan plateau** crossed by forested mountain ranges reaching over 2100 m (7000 ft). Pop: 4 416 000 (1994 est). Area: 149 743 sq km (57 816 sq miles)

shan't (ʃɑ:nt) *contraction of* shall not

Shantou *or* **Shantow** ('ʃæn'taʊ) *n* a port in SE China, in E Guangdong near the mouth of the Han River: became a treaty port in 1869. Pop: 1 356 000 (2005 est). Also called: Swatow

shantung (ʃæn'tʌŋ) *n* **1** a heavy silk fabric with a knobbly surface **2** a cotton or rayon imitation of this [C19 so called because it was first imported to Britain from SHANTUNG in China]

Shantung ('ʃæn'tʌŋ) *n* a variant transliteration of the Chinese name for **Shandong**

shanty¹ ('ʃæntɪ) *n, pl* -ties **1** a ramshackle hut; crude dwelling **2** *Austral and NZ* a public house, esp an unlicensed one **3** (formerly, in Canada) **a** a log bunkhouse at a lumber camp **b** the camp itself [C19 from Canadian French *chantier* cabin built in a lumber camp, from Old French *gantier* GANTRY]

shanty², **shantey** ('ʃæntɪ), **chanty** *or US* **chantey** ('ʃæntɪ, 'tʃæn-) *n, pl* -ties *or* -teys a song originally sung by sailors, esp a rhythmic one forming an accompaniment to work [C19 from French *chanter* to sing; see CHANT]

shantytown ('ʃæntɪˌtaʊn) *n* a town or section of a town or city inhabited by very poor people living in shanties, esp in a developing country

Shanxi ('ʃæn'ʃi:) *or* **Shansi** *n* a province of N China: China's richest coal reserves and much heavy industry. Capital: Taiyuan. Pop: 33 140 000 (2003 est). Area: 157 099 sq km (60 656 sq miles)

shape (ʃeɪp) *n* **1** the outward form of an object defined by outline **2** the figure or outline of the body of a person **3** a phantom **4** organized or definite form: *my plans are taking shape* **5** the form that anything assumes; guise **6** something used to provide or define form; pattern; mould **7** condition or state of efficiency: *to be in good shape* **8** out of shape **a** in bad physical condition **b** bent, twisted, or deformed **9** take shape to assume a definite form ▷ *vb* **10** (when *intr*, often foll by *into* or *up*) to receive or cause to receive shape or form **11** (*tr*) to mould into a particular pattern or form; modify **12** (*tr*) to plan, devise, or prepare: *to shape a plan of action* **13** an obsolete word for **appoint** [Old English *gesceap*, literally: that which is created, from *scieppan* to create; related to *sceap* sexual organs, Old Norse *skap* destiny, Old High German *scaf* form] > 'shapable *or* 'shapeable *adj* > 'shaper *n*

SHAPE (ʃeɪp) *n acronym for* Supreme Headquarters Allied Powers Europe

-shaped (ʃeɪpt) *adj combining form* having the shape of: *an L-shaped room; a pear-shaped figure*

shapeless ('ʃeɪplɪs) *adj* **1** having no definite shape or form: *a shapeless mass; a shapeless argument* **2** lacking a symmetrical or aesthetically pleasing shape: *a shapeless figure* > 'shapelessly *adv* > 'shapelessness *n*

shapely ('ʃeɪplɪ) *adj* -lier, -liest (esp of a woman's body or legs) pleasing or attractive in shape > 'shapeliness *n*

shape up *vb* (*intr, adverb*) **1** *informal* to proceed or develop satisfactorily **2** *informal* to develop a definite or proper form ▷ *n* shapeup **3** *US and Canadian* (formerly) a method of hiring dockers for a day or shift by having a union hiring boss select them from a gathering of applicants

shard (ʃɑ:d) *or* **sherd** *n* **1** a broken piece or fragment of a brittle substance, esp of pottery **2** *zoology* a tough sheath, scale, or shell, esp the elytra of a beetle [Old English *sceard*; related to Old Norse *skarth* notch, Middle High German *scharte* notch]

share¹ (ʃɛə) *n* **1** a part or portion of something owned, allotted to, or contributed by a person or group **2** (*often plural*) any of the equal parts, usually of low par value, into which the capital stock of a company is divided: ownership of shares carries the right to receive a proportion of the company's profits. See also **ordinary shares**, **preference shares 3** go shares *informal* to share (something) with another or others ▷ *vb* **4** (*tr*; often foll by *out*) to divide or apportion, esp equally **5** (when *intr*, often foll by *in*) to receive or contribute a portion of: *we can share the cost of the petrol; six people shared in the inheritance* **6** to join with another or others in the use of (something): *can I share your umbrella?* [Old English *scearu*; related to Old Norse *skor* amount, Old High German *scara* crowd; see SHEAR] > 'sharable *or* 'shareable *adj* > 'sharer *n*

share² (ʃɛə) *n* short for **ploughshare** [Old English *scear*; related to Old Norse *skeri*, Old High German *scaro*]

share certificate *n* a document issued by a company certifying ownership of one or more of its shares. US equivalent: stock certificate

sharecrop ('ʃɛəˌkrɒp) *vb* -crops, -cropping, -cropped *chiefly US* to cultivate (farmland) as a sharecropper

sharecropper ('ʃɛəˌkrɒpə) *n chiefly US* a farmer, esp a tenant farmer, who pays over a proportion of a crop or crops as rent

shared care *n social welfare* an arrangement between a welfare agency and a family with a dependent handicapped member, whereby the agency takes the handicapped person into a home for respite care or in emergencies

shared logic *n computing* the sharing of a central processing unit and associated software among several terminals

shared ownership *n* (in Britain) a form of house purchase whereby the purchaser buys a proportion of the dwelling, usually from a local authority or housing association, and rents the rest

shared resources *n* (*functioning as singular*) *computing* the sharing of peripherals among several terminals

sharefarmer ('ʃɛəˌfɑ:mə) *n chiefly Austral* a farmer who pays a fee to another in return for use of land to raise crops, etc

shareholder ('ʃɛəˌhəʊldə) *n* the owner of one or more shares in a company

share index *n* an index showing the movement of share prices. See **Financial Times Industrial Ordinary Share Index, Financial Times Stock Exchange 100 Index**

share market *n Austral and NZ* **1 a** a highly organized market facilitating the purchase and sale of securities and operated by professional stockbrokers and market makers according to fixed rules **b** a place where securities are regularly traded **c** (*as modifier*): *a share-market speculator* **2** the prices or trading activity of a share market: *the share market is buoyant*. Also called: stock exchange

share-milker *n* (in New Zealand) a person who lives on a dairy farm milking the owner's herd for an agreed share of the profits and, usually, building his own herd simultaneously

share of voice *n* the proportion of the total audience or readership commanded by a media group across its full range of publishing and broadcasting activities

share option *n* a scheme giving employees an option to buy shares in the company for which they work at a favourable price or discount

share premium *n Brit* the excess of the amount actually subscribed for an issue of corporate capital over its par value. Also called (esp US): capital surplus

Sharesave ('ʃɛəˌseɪv) *n* (in Britain) a system by which employees can invest, risk-free, in their company's shares

share shop *n* a stockbroker, bank, or other financial intermediary that handles the buying and selling of shares for members of the public, esp during a privatization issue

shareware ('ʃɛəˌwɛə) *n computing* software available to all users without the need for a licence and for which a token fee is requested

Shari ('ʃɑ:rɪ) *n* a variant spelling of **Chari** (the river)

sharia *or* **sheria** (ʃə'ri:ə) *n* the body of doctrines that regulate the lives of those who profess Islam [Arabic]

sharia-compliant *adj* (of a product or service) produced or offered in accordance with the doctrines of the sharia

sharif (ʃæ'ri:f) *n* a variant transliteration of **sherif**

shark¹ (ʃɑ:k) *n* any of various usually ferocious selachian fishes, typically marine with a long body, two dorsal fins, rows of sharp teeth, and between five and seven gill slits on each side of the head [C16 of uncertain origin] > 'shark,like *adj*

shark² (ʃɑ:k) *n* **1** a person who preys on or victimizes others, esp by swindling or extortion ▷ *vb* **2** *archaic* to obtain (something) by cheating or deception [C18 probably from German *Schurke* rogue; perhaps also influenced by SHARK¹]

shark bell *n chiefly Austral* a bell sounded to warn swimmers of the presence of sharks. Also: shark alarm

shark net *or* **mesh** *n chiefly Austral* **1** a net for catching sharks **2** a long piece of netting strung across a bay, inlet, etc, to exclude sharks

shark patrol *n chiefly Austral* a watch for sharks kept by an aircraft flying over beaches used by swimmers

shark repellents *pl n finance* another name for **porcupine provisions**

shark siren *n chiefly Austral* a siren sounded to warn swimmers of the presence of sharks

sharkskin (ˈʃɑːkˌskɪn) *n* a smooth glossy fabric of acetate rayon, used for sportswear, etc

sharksucker (ˈʃɑːkˌsʌkə) *n* an informal name for a **remora**

shark watcher *n informal* a business consultant who assists companies in identifying and preventing unwelcome takeover bids

Sharon (ˈʃærən) *n* **Plain of** a plain in W Israel, between the Mediterranean and the hills of Samaria, extending from Haifa to Tel Aviv

sharon fruit (ˈʃærən) *n* another name for **persimmon** (sense 2)

sharp (ʃɑːp) *adj* **1** having a keen edge suitable for cutting **2** having an edge or point; not rounded or blunt **3** involving a sudden change, esp in direction: *a sharp bend* **4** moving, acting, or reacting quickly, efficiently, etc: *sharp reflexes* **5** clearly defined **6** mentally acute; clever; astute **7** sly or artful; clever in an underhand way: *sharp practice* **8** bitter or harsh: *sharp words* **9** shrill or penetrating: *a sharp cry* **10** having an acrid taste **11** keen; biting: *a sharp wind; sharp pain* **12** *music* **a** (*immediately postpositive*) denoting a note that has been raised in pitch by one chromatic semitone: B *sharp* **b** (of an instrument, voice, etc) out of tune by being or tending to be too high in pitch. Compare **flat¹** (sense 23) **13** *phonetics* a less common word for **fortis** **14** *informal* **a** stylish **b** too smart **15** **at the sharp end** involved in the area of any activity where there is most difficulty, competition, danger, etc ▷ *adv* **16** in a sharp manner **17** exactly: *six o'clock sharp* **18** *music* **a** higher than a standard pitch **b** out of tune by being or tending to be too high in pitch: *she sings sharp.* Compare **flat¹** (sense 29) ▷ *n* **19** *music* **a** an accidental that raises the pitch of the following note by one chromatic semitone. Usual symbol: ♯ **b** a note affected by this accidental. Compare **flat¹** (sense 35) **20** a thin needle with a sharp point **21** *informal* a sharper **22** (*usually plural*) any medical instrument with sharp point or edge, esp a hypodermic needle ▷ *vb* **23** (*tr*) *music, US and Canadian* to raise the pitch of (a note), esp by one chromatic semitone. Usual equivalent in Britain and certain other countries: **sharpen** ▷ *interj* **24** *South African slang* an exclamation of full agreement or approval [Old English *scearp*; related to Old Norse *skarpr*, Old High German *scarpf*, Old Irish *cerb*, Lettish *skarbs*] ▷ **ˈsharply** *adv* ▷ **ˈsharpness** *n*

sharpbender (ˈʃɑːpˌbɛndə) *n informal* an organization that has been underperforming its competitors but suddenly becomes more successful, often as a result of new management or changes in its business strategy [c20 from the sharp upward bend in its sales or profits]

Shar Pei (ʃɑː ˈpeɪ) *n* a compact squarely-built dog of a Chinese breed, with loose wrinkled skin and a harsh bristly coat [c20 from Chinese *shā pí*, literally: sand skin]

sharpen (ˈʃɑːpən) *vb* **1** to make or become sharp or sharper **2** *music* to raise the pitch of (a note), esp by one chromatic semitone. Usual US and Canadian word: **sharp** ▷ **ˈsharpener** *n*

sharper (ˈʃɑːpə) *n* a person who cheats or swindles; fraud

Sharpeville (ˈʃɑːpvɪl) *n* a town in E South Africa: scene of riots in 1960 (when 69 demonstrators died), 1984, and 1985 (when 19 died)

sharp-eyed *adj* **1** having very good eyesight **2** observant or alert

sharpie (ˈʃɑːpɪ) *n Austral* a member of a teenage group having short hair and distinctive clothes. Compare **skinhead**

sharpish (ˈʃɑːpɪʃ) *adj* **1** fairly sharp ▷ *adv* **2** *informal* promptly; quickly

sharp-set *adj* **1** set to give an acute cutting angle **2** keenly hungry **3** keen or eager

sharpshooter (ˈʃɑːpˌʃuːtə) *n* an expert marksman, esp with a rifle ▷ **ˈsharpˌshooting** *n*

sharp-sighted *adj* having keen vision; sharp-eyed ▷ **ˌsharp-ˈsightedly** *adv* ▷ **ˌsharp-ˈsightedness** *n*

sharp-tongued *adj* bitter or critical in speech; sarcastic

sharp-witted *adj* having or showing a keen intelligence; perceptive ▷ **ˌsharp-ˈwittedly** *adv* ▷ **ˌsharp-ˈwittedness** *n*

shashlik or **shashlick** (ʃɑːʃˈlɪk, ˈʃɑːʃlɪk) *n* a type of kebab [from Russian, of Turkic origin; compare *shish kebab*]

Shasta daisy (ˈʃæstə) *n* a Pyrenean plant, *Chrysanthemum maximum*, widely cultivated for its large white daisy-like flowers: family *Asteraceae* (composites) [named after Mount *Shasta* in California]

shastra (ˈʃɑːstrə), **shaster** (ˈʃɑːstə) or **sastra** *n* any of the sacred writings of Hinduism [c17 from Sanskrit *śāstra*, from *śās* to teach]

shat (ʃæt) *vb taboo* a past tense and past participle of **shit**

Shatt-al-Arab (ˈʃætælˈærəb) *n* a river in SE Iraq, formed by the confluence of the Tigris and Euphrates Rivers: flows southeast as part of the border between Iraq and Iran to the Persian Gulf. Length: 193 km (120 miles)

shatter (ˈʃætə) *vb* **1** to break or be broken into many small pieces **2** (*tr*) to impair or destroy: *his nerves were shattered by the torture* **3** (*tr*) to dumbfound or thoroughly upset: *she was shattered by the news* **4** (*tr*) *informal* to cause to be tired out or exhausted **5** an obsolete word for **scatter** ▷ *n* **6** (*usually plural*) *obsolete* or *dialect* a fragment [c12 perhaps obscurely related to SCATTER] ▷ **ˈshatterer** *n* ▷ **ˈshattering** *adj* ▷ **ˈshatteringly** *adv*

shattered (ˈʃætɪd) *adj* **1** broken into many small pieces **2** impaired or destroyed **3** dumbfounded or thoroughly upset **4** *informal* tired out or exhausted

shatterproof (ˈʃætəˌpruːf) *adj* designed to resist shattering

shave (ʃeɪv) *vb* **shaves, shaving, shaved; shaved** or **shaven** (*mainly tr*) **1** (*also intr*) to remove (the beard, hair, etc) from (the face, head, or body) by scraping the skin with a razor **2** to cut or trim very closely **3** to reduce to shavings **4** to remove thin slices from (wood, etc) with a sharp cutting tool; plane or pare **5** to touch or graze in passing **6** *informal* to reduce (a price) by a slight amount **7** *US commerce* to purchase (a commercial paper) at a greater rate of discount than is customary or legal ▷ *n* **8** the act or an instance of shaving **9** any tool for scraping **10** a thin slice or shaving **11** an instance of barely touching something **12** **close shave** *informal* a narrow escape [Old English *sceafan*; related to Old Norse *skafa*, Gothic *skaban* to shave, Latin *scabere* to scrape] ▷ **ˈshavable** or **ˈshaveable** *adj*

shaveling (ˈʃeɪvlɪŋ) *n archaic* **1** *derogatory* a priest or clergyman with a shaven head **2** a young fellow; youth

shaven (ˈʃeɪvᵊn) *adj* **a** closely shaved or tonsured **b** (*in combination*): *clean-shaven*

shaver (ˈʃeɪvə) *n* **1** a person or thing that shaves **2** Also called: **electric razor, electric shaver** an electrically powered implement for shaving, having reciprocating or rotating blades behind a fine metal comb or pierced foil **3** *informal* a youngster, esp a young boy **4** *obsolete* a person who makes hard or extortionate bargains

Shavian (ˈʃeɪvɪən) *adj* **1** of, relating to, or like George Bernard Shaw (1856–1950), the Irish dramatist and critic, his works, ideas, etc ▷ *n* **2** an admirer of Shaw or his works ▷ **ˈShavianism** *n*

shaving (ˈʃeɪvɪŋ) *n* **1** a thin paring or slice, esp of wood, that has been shaved from something ▷ *modifier* **2** used when shaving the face, etc: *shaving cream*

Shavuot or **Shabuoth** (ʃəˈvuːəs, -əʊs; *Hebrew* ʃavuːˈɔt) *n* the Hebrew name for **Pentecost** (sense 2) [from Hebrew *shābhūʻōth*, plural of *shābhūāʻ* week]

shaw¹ (ʃɔː) *n archaic* or *dialect* a small wood; thicket; copse [Old English *sceaga*; related to Old Norse *skagi* tip, *skaga* to jut out, *skōgr* forest, *skegg* beard]

shaw² (ʃɔː) *Scot* ▷ *vb* **1** to show ▷ *n* **2** a show **3** the part of a potato plant that is above ground

shawl (ʃɔːl) *n* a piece of fabric or knitted or crocheted material worn around the shoulders by women or wrapped around a baby [c17 from Persian *shāl*]

shawl collar *n* a collar rolled back in a continuous and tapering line along the surplice neckline of a garment

shawlie (ˈʃɔːlɪ) *n Irish* a disparaging term for a working-class woman who wears a shawl

shawm (ʃɔːm) *n music* a medieval form of the oboe with a conical bore and flaring bell, blown through a double reed [c14 *shalmye*, from Old French *chalemie*, ultimately from Latin *calamus* a reed, from Greek *kalamos*]

Shawnee (ʃɔːˈniː) *n* (*pl* **-nees** or **-nee**) a member of a North American Indian people formerly living along the Tennessee River **2** the language of this people, belonging to the Algonquian family [c20 back formation from obsolete *Shawnese*, from Shawnee *Shaawanwaaki* people of the south, from *shaawanawa* south]

Shawwal (ʃəˈwɑːl) *n* the tenth month of the Muslim year [from Arabic]

shay (ʃeɪ) *n* a dialect word for **chaise** [c18 back formation from CHAISE, mistakenly thought to be plural]

Shcheglovsk (*Russian* ʃtʃɪgˈlɔfsk) *n* the former name (until 1932) of **Kemerovo**

Shcherbakov (*Russian* ʃtʃɪrbaˈkɔf) *n* a former name (from the Revolution until 1957) of **Rybinsk**

she (ʃiː) *pron* (*subjective*) **1** refers to a female person or animal: *she is a doctor; she's a fine mare* **2** refers to things personified as feminine, such as cars, ships, and nations **3** *Austral and NZ* an informal word for **it** (esp in the phrases **she's apples, she'll be right**, etc) ▷ *n* **4 a** a female person or animal **b** (*in combination*): *she-cat* [Old English *sīe*, accusative of *sēo*, feminine demonstrative pronoun]

▇ USAGE See at **me¹**

shea (ʃɪə) *n* **1** a tropical African sapotaceous tree, *Butyrospermum parkii*, with oily seeds **2** **shea butter** the white butter-like fat obtained from the seeds of this plant and used as food, to make soaps, etc [c18 from Bambara *si*]

sheading (ˈʃiːdɪŋ) *n* any of the six subdivisions of the Isle of Man [variant of *shedding*; see SHED²]

sheaf (ʃiːf) *n, pl* **sheaves** (ʃiːvz) **1** a bundle of reaped but unthreshed corn tied with one or two bonds **2** a bundle of objects tied together **3** the arrows contained in a quiver ▷ *vb* **4** (*tr*) to bind or tie into a sheaf [Old English *sceaf*, related to Old High German *skoub* sheaf, Old Norse *skauf* tail, Gothic *skuft* tuft of hair]

shear (ʃɪə) *vb* **shears, shearing, sheared** or *Austral and NZ* **shore; sheared** or **shorn** **1** (*tr*) to remove (the fleece or hair) of (sheep, etc) by cutting or clipping **2** to cut or cut through (something) with shears or a sharp instrument **3** *engineering* to cause (a part, member, shaft, etc) to deform or fracture or (of a part, etc) to deform or fracture as a result of excess torsion or transverse load **4** (*tr; often foll by of*) to strip or divest: *to shear someone of his power* **5** (when *intr,* foll by *through*) to move through (something) by or as if by cutting **6** *Scot* to reap (corn, etc) with a scythe or sickle ▷ *n* **7** the act, process, or an instance of shearing **8** a shearing of a sheep or flock of sheep, esp when referred to as an indication of age: *a sheep of two shears* **9** a form of deformation or fracture in which parallel planes in a body or assembly slide over one another **10** *physics* the deformation of a body, part, etc, expressed as the lateral displacement between two points in parallel planes divided by the distance between the planes **11** either one of the blades of a pair of shears, scissors, etc **12** a machine that cuts sheet material by passing a knife blade through it **13** a device for lifting heavy loads consisting of a tackle supported by a framework held steady by guy ropes ▷ See also **shears, shore** [Old English *sceran*; related to Old Norse *skera* to cut, Old Saxon, Old High German *skeran* to shear; see SHARE²] > ˈshearer *n*

shearing gang *n* NZ a group of itinerant workers who contract to shear, class, and bale a farmer's wool clip

shearing shed *n* NZ a farm building equipped with power machinery for sheepshearing and equipment for baling wool. Also called: **woolshed**

shearlegs (ˈʃɪəˌlɛgz) *n* a variant spelling of **sheerlegs**

shearling (ˈʃɪəlɪŋ) *n* **1** a young sheep after its first shearing **2** the skin of such an animal

shear pin *n* an easily replaceable pin inserted in a machine at a critical point and designed to shear and stop the machine if the load becomes too great

shears (ʃɪəz) *pl n* **1 a** large scissors, as for cutting cloth, jointing poultry, etc **b** a large scissor-like and usually hand-held cutting tool with flat blades, as for cutting hedges **2** any of various analogous cutting or clipping implements or machines **3** short for **sheerlegs 4 off the shears** *Austral informal* (of a sheep) newly shorn

shear strength *n* the degree to which a material or bond is able to resist shear

shear stress *n* the form of stress in a body, part, etc, that tends to produce cutting rather than stretching or bending

shear stud *n* a stud that transfers shear stress between metal and concrete in composite structural members in which the stud is welded to the metal component

shearwater (ˈʃɪəˌwɔːtə) *n* any of several oceanic birds of the genera *Puffinus*, such as *P. puffinus* (**Manx shearwater**), *Procellaria*, etc, specialized for an aerial or aquatic existence: family *Procellariidae*, order *Procellariiformes* (petrels) [c17 so named because their wings seem to clip the waves when they are flying low]

sheatfish (ˈʃiːtˌfɪʃ) *n, pl* -**fish** *or* -**fishes** another name for **European catfish** (see **silurid** (sense 1)) [c16 variant of *sheathfish*; perhaps influenced by German *Schaid* sheatfish; see SHEATH, FISH]

sheath (ʃiːθ) *n, pl* **sheaths** (ʃiːðz) **1** a case or covering for the blade of a knife, sword, etc **2** any similar close-fitting case **3** *biology* an enclosing or protective structure, such as a leaf base encasing the stem of a plant **4** the protective covering on an electric cable **5** a figure-hugging dress with a narrow tapering skirt **6** another name for **condom** ▷ *vb* **7** (*tr*) another word for **sheathe** [Old English *scēath*; related to Old Norse *skeithir*, Old High German *sceida* a dividing; compare Old English *scādan* to divide]

sheathbill (ˈʃiːθˌbɪl) *n* either of two pigeon-like shore birds, *Chionis alba* or *C. minor*, of antarctic and subantarctic regions, constituting the family *Chionididae*: order *Charadriiformes*. They have a white plumage and a horny sheath at the base of the bill

sheathe (ʃiːð) *vb* (*tr*) **1** to insert (a knife, sword, etc) into a sheath **2** (esp of cats) to retract (the claws) **3** to surface with or encase in a sheath or sheathing

sheathing (ˈʃiːðɪŋ) *n* **1** any material used as an outer layer, as on a ship's hull **2** boarding, etc, used to cover the wall studding or roof joists of a timber frame

sheath knife *n* a knife carried in or protected by a sheath

sheave¹ (ʃiːv) *vb* (*tr*) to gather or bind into sheaves

sheave² (ʃiːv) *n* a wheel with a grooved rim, esp one used as a pulley [c14 of Germanic origin; compare Old High German *scība* disc]

sheaves (ʃiːvz) *n* the plural of **sheaf**

Sheba¹ (ˈʃiːbə) *n* **1** Also called: **Saba** the ancient kingdom of the Sabeans: a rich trading nation

dealing in gold, spices, and precious stones (I Kings 10) **2** the region inhabited by this nation, located in the SW corner of the Arabian peninsula: modern Yemen

Sheba² (ˈʃiːbə) *n* **Queen of Sheba** *Old Testament* a queen of the Sabeans, who visited Solomon (I Kings 10:1–13)

shebang (ʃɪˈbæŋ) *n slang* **1** a situation, matter, or affair in the phrase **the whole shebang 2** a hut or shack [c19 of uncertain origin]

Shebat (ʃɛˈvat) *n* a variant spelling of **Shevat**

shebeen *or* **shebean** (ʃɪˈbiːn) *n* **1** *Irish, Scot and South African* a place where alcoholic drink is sold illegally **2** (in Ireland) alcohol, esp home-distilled whiskey, sold without a licence **3** (in South Africa) a place where Black African men engage in social drinking **4** (in the US and Ireland) weak beer [c18 from Irish Gaelic *síbín* beer of poor quality]

Shechem (ˈʃɛkəm, -ɛm) *n* the ancient name of **Nablus**

Shechina *or* **Shekinah** (ʃɛˈkaɪnə; *Hebrew* ʃəxiːˈna) *n Judaism* **1** the radiance in which God's immanent presence in the midst of his people, esp in the Temple, is visibly manifested **2** the divine presence itself as contrasted with the divine transcendence [c17 from Hebrew *shĕkhīnāh*, from *shākhan* to dwell]

shechita *or* **shechitah** (ʃəxiːtə, ˈʃxitə) *n* the Jewish method of killing animals for food [from Hebrew, literally: slaughter]

shed¹ (ʃɛd) *n* **1** a small building or lean-to of light construction, used for storage, shelter, etc **2** a large roofed structure, esp one with open sides, used for storage, repairing locomotives, sheepshearing, etc **3** a large retail outlet in the style of a warehouse **4** NZ another name for **freezing works 5** NZ **in the shed** at work **6** to abolish or get rid of (jobs, workers, etc) ▷ *vb* **sheds, shedding, shedded 7** (*tr*) NZ to store (hay or wool) in a shed [Old English *sced*; probably variant of *scead* shelter, SHADE] > ˈshedˌlike *adj*

shed² (ʃɛd) *vb* **sheds, shedding, shed** (*mainly tr*) **1** to pour forth or cause to pour forth: *to shed tears; shed blood* **2 shed** (*or* **throw**) **light on** *or* **upon** to clarify or supply additional information about **3** to cast off or lose: *the snake shed its skin; trees shed their leaves* **4** (of a lorry) to drop (its load) on the road by accident **5** to repel: *this coat sheds water* **6** (*also intr*) (in weaving) to form an opening between (the warp threads) in order to permit the passage of the shuttle **7** (*tr*) *dialect* to make a parting in (the hair) ▷ *n* **8** (in weaving) the space made by shedding **9** short for **watershed 10** *chiefly Scot* a parting in the hair [Old English *sceadan*; related to Gothic *skaidan*, Old High German *skeidan* to separate²; see SHEATH] > ˈshedable *or* ˈsheddable *adj*

shed³ (ʃɛd) *vb* **sheds, shedding, shed 1** (*tr*) to separate or divide off (some farm animals) from the remainder of a group: *a good dog can shed his sheep in a matter of minutes* ▷ *n* **2** (of a dog) the action of separating farm animals [from SHED²] > ˈshedding *n*

shed⁴ (ʃɛd) *n physics* a former unit of nuclear cross section equal to 10^{-52} square metre [c20 from SHED¹; so called by comparison to BARN² because of its smaller size]

she'd (ʃiːd) contraction of she had *or* she would

shedder (ˈʃɛdə) *n* **1** a person or thing that sheds **2** an animal, such as a llama, snake, or lobster, that moults **3** NZ a person who milks cows in a milking shed

shedful (ˈʃɛdfʊl) *n* **1** the quantity or amount contained in a shed **2** *informal* a lot: *a shedful of helpful hints*

shed hand *n chiefly Austral and NZ* a worker in a sheepshearing shed

shedload (ˈʃɛdˌləʊd) *n slang* a very large amount or number

shed out *vb* (*tr, adverb*) NZ to separate off (sheep that have lambed) and move them to better pasture

shed up *vb* (*tr, adverb*) NZ to store (hay) in a shed

sheen (ʃiːn) *n* **1** a gleaming or glistening brightness; lustre **2** *poetic* splendid clothing ▷ *adj* **3** *rare* shining and beautiful; radiant [Old English *sciene*; related to Old Norse *skjōni* white horse, Gothic *skauns* beautiful, Old High German *scōni* bright] > ˈsheeny *adj*

sheeny (ˈʃiːnɪ) *n, pl* **sheenies** *slang* a derogatory word for a Jew [c19 of unknown origin]

sheep (ʃiːp) *n, pl* **sheep 1** any of various bovid mammals of the genus *Ovis* and related genera, esp *O. aries* (**domestic sheep**), having transversely ribbed horns and a narrow face. There are many breeds of domestic sheep, raised for their wool and for meat. Related adj: **ovine 2 Barbary sheep** another name for **aoudad 3** a meek or timid person, esp one without initiative **4 separate the sheep from the goats** to pick out the members of any group who are superior in some respects [Old English *sceap*; related to Old Frisian *skēp*, Old Saxon *scāp*, Old High German *scāf*] > ˈsheepˌlike *adj*

SHEEP abbreviation for Sky High Earnings Expectations Possibly: applied to investments that appear to offer high returns but may be unreliable

sheepcote (ˈʃiːpˌkəʊt) *n chiefly Brit* another word for **sheepfold**

sheep-dip *n* **1** any of several liquid disinfectants and insecticides in which sheep are immersed to kill vermin and germs in their fleece **2** a deep trough containing such a liquid

sheepdog (ˈʃiːpˌdɒg) *n* **1** Also called: shepherd dog a dog used for herding sheep. See **Border collie 2** any of various breeds of dog reared originally for herding sheep. See **Old English sheepdog, Shetland sheepdog**

sheepdog trial *n* (*often plural*) a competition in which sheepdogs are tested in their tasks

sheepfold (ˈʃiːpˌfəʊld) *n* a pen or enclosure for sheep

sheepish (ˈʃiːpɪʃ) *adj* **1** abashed or embarrassed, esp through looking foolish or being in the wrong **2** resembling a sheep in timidity or lack of initiative > ˈsheepishly *adv* > ˈsheepishness *n*

sheep ked *or* **tick** *n* a wingless dipterous fly, *Melophagus ovinus*, that is an external parasite of sheep: family *Hippoboscidae*

sheeple (ˈʃiːpᵊl) *n* (*functioning as plural*) *informal* people who tend to follow the majority in matters of opinion, taste, etc [c20 from SHEEP + PEOPLE]

sheep measles *n* (*functioning as singular or plural*) a disease of sheep caused by infestation by the cysticerci of a dog tapeworm (*Taenia ovis*)

sheepo (ˈʃiːpəʊ) *n, pl* **sheepos** NZ a person employed to bring sheep to the catching pen in a shearing shed

sheep race *n* NZ a single-file walkway for sheep at the entrance to a sheep-dip

sheep's eyes *pl n* old-fashioned amorous or inviting glances

sheep's fescue *n* a temperate perennial tufted grass, *Festuca ovina*, with narrow inwardly rolled leaves [c18 so called because it is often used for sheep pastures]

sheepshank (ˈʃiːpˌʃæŋk) *n* a knot consisting of two hitches at the ends of a bight made in a rope to shorten it temporarily

sheepshead (ˈʃiːpsˌhɛd) *n, pl* -**head** *or* -**heads** any of several sparid fishes with strong crushing teeth, esp *Archosargus rhomboidalis*, of the American Atlantic, which is marked with dark bands

sheepshearing (ˈʃiːpˌʃɪərɪŋ) *n* **1** the act or process of shearing sheep **2** the season or an occasion of shearing sheep **3** a feast held on such an occasion > ˈsheepˌshearer *n*

sheepskin (ˈʃiːpˌskɪn) *n* **a** the skin of a sheep, esp when used for clothing, etc, or with the fleece removed and used for parchment **b** (as modifier): a *sheepskin coat*

sheep sorrel *or* **sheep's sorrel** *n* a polygonaceous plant, *Rumex acetosella*, of the N hemisphere, having slightly bitter-tasting leaves and small reddish flowers

sheep station *or* **run** *n Austral and NZ* a large sheep farm. Also called: **run**

sheep tick *n* **1** a tick, *Ixodes ricinus*, that is parasitic on sheep, cattle, and man and transmits the disease louping ill in sheep **2** another name for **sheep ked**

sheepwalk ('ʃiːpˌwɔːk) *n chiefly Brit* a tract of land for grazing sheep

sheer¹ (ʃɪə) *adj* **1** perpendicular; very steep: *a sheer cliff* **2** (of textiles) so fine as to be transparent **3** (*prenominal*) absolute; unmitigated: *sheer folly* **4** *obsolete* bright or shining ▷ *adv* **5** steeply or perpendicularly **6** completely or absolutely ▷ *n* **7** any transparent fabric used for making garments [Old English *scīr*; related to Old Norse *skīrr* bright, Gothic *skeirs* clear, Middle High German *schīr*] > 'sheerly *adv* > 'sheerness *n*

sheer² (ʃɪə) *vb* (foll by *off* or *away* (from)) **1** to deviate or cause to deviate from a course **2** (*intr*) to avoid an unpleasant person, thing, topic, etc ▷ *n* **3** the upward sweep of the deck or bulwarks of a vessel **4** *nautical* the position of a vessel relative to its mooring [C17 perhaps variant of *shear*]

sheerlegs *or* **shearlegs** ('ʃɪəˌlɛgz) *n* (*functioning as singular*) a device for lifting heavy weights consisting of two or more spars lashed together at the upper ends from which a lifting tackle is suspended. Also called: **shears** [C19 variant of *shear legs*]

Sheerness (ʃɪə'nɛs) *n* a port and resort in SE England, in N Kent at the junction of the Medway estuary and the Thames: administratively part of Queenborough in Sheppey since 1968

sheesh (ʃiːʃ) *interj informal* an exclamation of surprise or annoyance

sheet¹ (ʃiːt) *n* **1** a large rectangular piece of cotton, linen, etc, generally one of a pair used as inner bedclothes **2 a** a thin piece of a substance such as paper, glass, or metal, usually rectangular in form **b** (*as modifier*): *sheet iron* **3** a broad continuous surface; expanse or stretch: *a sheet of rain* **4** a newspaper, esp a tabloid **5** a piece of printed paper to be folded into a section for a book **6** a page of stamps, usually of one denomination and already perforated **7** any thin tabular mass of rock covering a large area ▷ *vb* **8** (*tr*) to provide with, cover, or wrap in a sheet **9** (*intr*) (of rain, snow, etc) to fall heavily [Old English *sciete*; related to *sceat* corner, lap, Old Norse *skaut*, Old High German *scōz* lap]

sheet² (ʃiːt) *n nautical* a line or rope for controlling the position of a sail relative to the wind [Old English *scēata* corner of a sail; related to Middle Low German *schōte* rope attached to a sail; see SHEET¹]

sheet anchor *n* **1** *nautical* a large strong anchor for use in emergency **2** a person or thing to be relied upon in an emergency [C17 from earlier *shute anker*, from *shoot* (obsolete) the sheet of a sail]

sheet bend *n* a knot used esp for joining ropes of different sizes. Also called: **becket bend, weaver's hitch**

sheet down *vb* (*intr, adverb*) (of rain) to fall heavily in sheets

sheet-fed *adj printing* involving or printing on separate sheets of paper. Compare **reel-fed**

sheeting ('ʃiːtɪŋ) *n* fabric from which sheets are made

sheet lightning *n* lightning that appears as a broad sheet, caused by the reflection of more distant lightning

sheet metal *n* metal in the form of a sheet, the thickness being intermediate between that of plate and that of foil

sheet music *n* **1** the printed or written copy of a short composition or piece, esp in the form of unbound leaves **2** music in its written or printed form

sheet pile *n civil engineering* one of a group of piles made of timber, steel, or prestressed concrete set close together to resist lateral pressure, as from earth or water. Compare **bearing pile**

Sheffer's stroke *n logic* a function of two sentences, equivalent to the negation of their conjunction, and written *p|q* (*p* and *q* are both not true) where *p,q*, are the arguments: *p|q* is false only when *p,q* are both true. It is possible to construct all truth functions out of this one alone [named after H. M. *Sheffer* (1883–1964), US philosopher]

Sheffield ('ʃɛfiːld) *n* **1** a city in N England, in Sheffield unitary authority, South Yorkshire on the River Don: important centre of steel manufacture and of the cutlery industry; Sheffield university (1905) and Sheffield Hallam University (1992). Pop: 439 866 (2001) **2** a unitary authority in N England, in South Yorkshire. Pop: 512 500 (2003 est). Area: 368 sq km (142 sq miles)

Sheffield Shield *n* (in Australia) the former name for the trophy of the annual interstate cricket competition [C19 named after Lord *Sheffield*, sponsor of a visiting English side in 1891–92, who inaugurated the Sheffield Shield competition in 1892]

sheikh *or* **sheik** (ʃeɪk) *n* (in Muslim countries) **a** the head of an Arab tribe, village, etc **b** a venerable old man **c** a high priest or religious leader, esp a Sufi master [C16 from Arabic *shaykh* old man]

sheikhdom *or* **sheikdom** ('ʃeɪkdəm) *n* the territory ruled by a sheikh

sheila ('ʃiːlə) *n Austral and NZ old-fashioned* an informal word for **girl** *or* **woman** [C19 from the girl's name *Sheila*]

shekel *or* **sheqel** ('ʃɛkʲl) *n* **1** the standard monetary unit of modern Israel, divided into 100 agorot **2** any of several former coins and units of weight of the Near East **3** (*often plural*) *informal* any coin or money [C16 from Hebrew *sheqel*]

Shekinah (ʃe'kaɪnə; *Hebrew* ʃəxi'na) *n Judaism* a variant spelling of **Shechina**

shelduck ('ʃɛlˌdʌk) *or masculine* **sheldrake** ('ʃɛlˌdreɪk) *n, pl* **-ducks, -duck** *or* **-drakes, -drake** any of various large usually brightly coloured gooselike ducks, such as *Tadorna tadorna* (**common shelduck**), of the Old World [C14 *shel*, probably from dialect *sheld* pied; related to Middle Dutch *schillede* variegated]

shelf (ʃɛlf) *n, pl* **shelves** (ʃɛlvz) **1** a thin flat plank of wood, metal, etc, fixed horizontally against a wall, etc, for the purpose of supporting objects **2** something resembling this in shape or function **3** the objects placed on a shelf, regarded collectively: *a shelf of books* **4** a projecting layer of ice, rock, etc, on land or in the sea. See also **continental shelf 5** *mining* a layer of bedrock hit when sinking a shaft **6** *archery* the part of the hand on which an arrow rests when the bow is grasped **7** See **off the shelf 8** on the **shelf** put aside or abandoned: used esp of unmarried women considered to be past the age of marriage ▷ *vb* **9** (*tr*) *Austral slang* to inform upon [Old English *scylfe* ship's deck; related to Middle Low German *schelf* shelf, Old English *scylf* crag] > 'shelf,like *adj*

shelf ice *n* a less common term for **ice shelf**

shelf life *n* the length of time a packaged food, chemical, etc, will last without deteriorating

shelf-stacker *n* a person whose job is to fill the shelves and displays in a supermarket or other shop with goods for sale

shell (ʃɛl) *n* **1** the protective calcareous or membranous outer layer of an egg, esp a bird's egg **2** the hard outer covering of many molluscs that is secreted by the mantle **3** any other hard outer layer, such as the exoskeleton of many arthropods **4** the hard outer layer of some fruits, esp of nuts **5** any hard outer case **6** a hollow artillery projectile filled with explosive primed to explode either during flight, on impact, or after penetration. Compare **ball¹** (sense 7a) **7** a small-arms cartridge comprising a hollow casing inside which is the primer, charge, and bullet **8** a pyrotechnic cartridge designed to explode in the air **9** *rowing* a very light narrow racing boat **10** the external structure of a building, esp one that is unfinished or one that has been gutted by fire **11** the basic structural case of something, such as a machine, vehicle, etc **12** *physics* **a** a class of electron orbits in an atom in which the electrons have the same principal quantum number and orbital angular momentum quantum number and differences in their energy are small compared with differences in energy between shells **b** an analogous energy state of nucleons in certain theories (**shell models**) of the structure of the atomic nucleus **13** the pastry case of a pie, flan, etc **14** a thin slab of concrete or a skeletal framework made of wood or metal that forms a shell-like roof **15** *Brit* (in some schools) a class or form **16** come (*or* bring) out of one's shell to become (or help to become) less shy and reserved ▷ *vb* **17** to divest or be divested of a shell, husk, pod, etc **18** to separate or be separated from an ear, husk, cob, etc **19** (*tr*) to bombard with artillery shells ▷ See also **shell out** [Old English *sciell*; related to Old Norse *skel* shell, Gothic *skalja* tile, Middle Low German *schelle* shell; see SCALE¹, SHALE] > 'shell-less *adj* > 'shell-,like *adj* > 'shelly *adj*

she'll (ʃiːl; *unstressed* ʃɪl) *contraction of* she will *or* she shall

shellac (ʃə'læk, 'ʃɛlæk) *n* **1** a yellowish resin secreted by the lac insect, esp a commercial preparation of this used in varnishes, polishes, and leather dressings **2** Also called: **shellac varnish** a varnish made by dissolving shellac in ethanol or a similar solvent **3** a gramophone record based on shellac ▷ *vb* **-lacs, -lacking, -lacked** (*tr*) **4** to coat or treat (an article) with a shellac varnish **5** *US slang* to defeat completely [C18 SHELL + LAC¹, translation of French *laque en écailles*, literally: lac in scales, that is, in thin plates] > 'shel'lacker *n*

shellacking (ʃə'lækɪŋ, 'ʃɛlækɪŋ) *n slang, chiefly US and Canadian* a complete defeat; a sound beating: *anyone who gives a shellacking to their bigger neighbours*

shellback ('ʃɛlˌbæk) *n* **1** *informal* a sailor who has crossed the equator. Compare **polliwog** (sense 2) **2** an experienced or old sailor

shellbark ('ʃɛlˌbɑːk) *n* another name for **shagbark** [C19 so called from the texture of its bark]

shell bean *n US* any of various bean plants that are cultivated for their edible seeds rather than for their pods

shell company *n business* **1** a near-defunct company, esp one with a stock-exchange listing, used as a vehicle for a thriving company **2** a company that has ceased to trade but retains its registration and is sold for a small sum to enable its new owners to avoid the cost and trouble of registering a new company

shellfire ('ʃɛlˌfaɪə) *n* the firing of artillery shells

shellfish ('ʃɛlˌfɪʃ) *n, pl* **-fish** *or* **-fishes** any aquatic invertebrate having a shell or shell-like carapace, esp such an animal used as human food. Examples are crustaceans such as crabs and lobsters and molluscs such as oysters

shell game *n* the US name for **thimblerig**

shell gland *n zoology* a gland in certain invertebrates that secretes the components required for forming the shell of an egg

shell jacket *n* an army officer's waist-length mess jacket

shell-like *adj* **1** resembling the empty shell of a mollusc ▷ *n* **2** *slang* an ear (esp in the phrase **a word in your shell-like**)

shell out *vb* (*adverb*) *informal* to pay out or hand over (money) [C19 from SHELL (in the sense: to remove from a pod or (figuratively) a purse)]

shell program *n computing* a basic low-cost computer program that provides a framework within which the user can develop the program to suit his personal requirements

shellproof ('ʃɛlˌpruːf) *adj* designed, intended, or able to resist shellfire

shell shock *n* loss of sight, memory, etc, resulting from psychological strain during prolonged engagement in warfare. Also called: **combat neurosis**

shell-shocked *adj* **1** suffering from shell shock **2** in a state of stunned confusion or shock; dazed

shell star *n astronomy* a type of star, usually of spectral type B to F, surrounded by a gaseous shell

shell suit *n* a lightweight tracksuit consisting of an inner cotton layer covered by a waterproof nylon layer

Shelta ('ʃɛltə) *n* a secret language used by some itinerant tinkers in Ireland and parts of Britain, based on systematically altered Gaelic [c19 from earlier *sheldrū*, perhaps an arbitrary alteration of Old Irish *bēlre* speech]

shelter ('ʃɛltə) *n* **1** something that provides cover or protection, as from weather or danger; place of refuge **2** the protection afforded by such a cover; refuge **3** the state of being sheltered ▷ *vb* **4** (*tr*) to provide with or protect by a shelter **5** (*intr*) to take cover, as from rain; find refuge **6** (*tr*) to act as a shelter for; take under one's protection [c16 of uncertain origin] > '**shelterer** *n* > '**shelterless** *adj*

shelter belt *n* a row of trees planted to protect an area from the wind

sheltered ('ʃɛltəd) *adj* **1** protected from wind or weather: *a sheltered garden* **2** protected from outside influences: *a sheltered upbringing* **3** (of buildings) specially designed to provide a safe environment for the elderly, handicapped, or disabled: *sheltered workshops for the blind.* See also **sheltered housing**

sheltered housing *n* accommodation designed esp for the elderly or infirm consisting of a group of individual premises, often with some shared facilities and a caretaker. Also called: **sheltered accommodation, sheltered homes**

shelter tent *n US* a military tent for two men

sheltie *or* **shelty** ('ʃɛltɪ) *n, pl* **-ties** another name for **Shetland pony** *or* **Shetland sheepdog** [c17 probably from Orkney dialect *sjalti,* from Old Norse *Hjalti* Shetlander, from *Hjaltland* Shetland]

shelve¹ (ʃɛlv) *vb* (*tr*) **1** to place on a shelf **2** to provide with shelves **3** to put aside or postpone from consideration **4** to dismiss or cause to retire [c16 from *shelves,* plural of SHELF] > '**shelver** *n*

shelve² (ʃɛlv) *vb* (*intr*) to slope away gradually; incline [c16 origin uncertain]

shelves (ʃɛlvz) *n* the plural of **shelf**

shelving ('ʃɛlvɪŋ) *n* **1** material for making shelves **2** a set of shelves; shelves collectively

Shem (ʃɛm) *n Old Testament* the eldest of Noah's three sons (Genesis 10:21). Douay spelling: **Sem** (sɛm)

Shema (ʃə'mɑː) *n* **1** the central statement of Jewish belief, the sentence "Hear, O Israel: the Lord is your God; the Lord is One" (Deuteronomy 6:4) **2** the section of the liturgy consisting of this and related biblical passages, Deuteronomy 6:4–9 and 11:13–21 and Numbers 15:37–41, recited in the morning and evening prayers and on retiring at night [Hebrew, literally: hear]

she-male *n informal* a male-to-female transsexual

Shembe ('ʃɛmbɛ) *n* (in South Africa) an African sect that combines Christianity with aspects of Bantu religion

Shemini Atseres ('ʃmini ɑ'tsɛrɛs) *or* **Shemini Atzereth** ('ʃəmini ɑ'tsɛrɛt) *n Judaism* the festival which follows upon Sukkoth on Tishri 22 (and 23 outside Israel), and includes Simchat Torah

Shemite ('ʃɛmaɪt) *n* another word for **Semite**

Shemitic (ʃə'mɪtɪk) *n, adj* another word for **Semitic**

Shemona Esrei *Hebrew* (ʃəmə'na ɛs'reɪ; *Yiddish* 'ʃmonə 'ɛsreɪ) *n Judaism* another name for **Amidah** [literally: eighteen (blessings)]

shemozzle (ʃɪ'mɒzəl) *n informal* a noisy confusion or dispute; uproar [c19 perhaps from Yiddish *shlimazl* misfortune]

Shenandoah National Park (ʃɛnən'dəʊə) *n* a national park in N Virginia: established in 1935 to protect part of the Blue Ridge Mountains. Area: 782 sq km (302 sq miles)

shenanigan (ʃɪ'nænɪgən) *n informal* **1** (*usually plural*) roguishness; mischief **2** an act of treachery; deception [c19 of unknown origin]

shend (ʃɛnd) *vb* **shends, shending, shent** (ʃɛnt) (*tr*) *archaic* **1** to put to shame **2** to chide or reproach **3** to injure or destroy [Old English *gescendan,* from *scand* SHAME]

Shensi ('ʃɛn'siː) *n* a variant transliteration of the Chinese name for **Shaanxi**

Shenyang ('ʃɛn'jæŋ) *n* a walled city in NE China in S Manchuria, capital of Liaoning province: capital of the Manchu dynasty from 1644–1912; seized by the Japanese in 1931. Pop: 4 916 000 (2005 est.). Former name: **Mukden**

she-oak *n* any of various Australian trees of the genus *Casuarina.* See **casuarina** [c18 *she* (in the sense: inferior) + OAK]

Sheol ('ʃiːəʊl, -ɒl) *n Old Testament* **1** the abode of the dead **2** (*often not capital*) hell [c16 from Hebrew *shĕ'ōl*]

shepherd ('ʃɛpəd) *n* **1** a person employed to tend sheep. Female equivalent: **shepherdess.** Related adjs: **bucolic, pastoral 2** a person, such as a clergyman, who watches over or guides a group of people ▷ *vb* (*tr*) **3** to guide or watch over in the manner of a shepherd **4** *Australian rules football* to prevent opponents from tackling (a member of one's own team) by blocking their path [from Old English *sceaphirde.* See SHEEP, HERD²]

Shepherd *n astronomy* a small moon of (eg) Saturn orbiting close to the rings and partly responsible for ring stability

shepherd dog *n* another term for **sheepdog** (sense 1)

shepherd's needle *n* a European umbelliferous plant, *Scandix pectenveneris,* with long needle-like fruits

shepherd's pie *n chiefly Brit* a baked dish of minced meat covered with mashed potato. Also called: **cottage pie**

shepherd's-purse *n* a plant, *Capsella bursa-pastoris,* having small white flowers and flattened triangular seed pods: family *Brassicaceae* (crucifers) [c15 compare Latin *bursa pastoris,* French *bourse-de-berger,* German *Hirtentasche,* Dutch *herdentasch*]

shepherd's weatherglass *n Brit* another name for the **scarlet pimpernel**

Sheppey ('ʃɛpɪ) *n* **Isle of** an island in SE England, off the N coast of Kent in the Thames estuary: separated from the mainland by **The Swale,** a narrow channel. Chief towns: Sheerness, Minster. Pop: 31 854 (latest est.). Area: 80 sq km (30 sq miles)

sherang (ʃə'ræŋ) *n* **head sherang** *Austral and NZ* the boss; person in authority: *who is the head sherang around here?*

sherardize *or* **sherardise** ('ʃɛrə,daɪz) *vb metallurgy* to coat (iron or steel) with zinc by heating in a container with zinc dust or (of iron or steel) to be coated in this way [c20 process named after *Sherard Cowper-Coles* (died 1936), English inventor] > ,**sherardi'zation** *or* ,**sherardi'sation** *n*

Sheraton ('ʃɛrətən) *adj* denoting furniture made by or in the style of Thomas Sheraton, the English furniture maker (1751–1806), characterized by lightness, elegance, and the extensive use of inlay

sherbet ('ʃɜːbət) *n* **1** a fruit-flavoured slightly effervescent powder, eaten as a sweet or used to make a drink: *lemon sherbet* **2** *US and Canadian* a water ice made from fruit juice, egg whites, milk, etc. Also called (in Britain and certain other countries): **sorbet 3** *Austral slang* beer **4** a cooling Oriental drink of sweetened fruit juice **5** *South African informal* a euphemistic word for **shit** [c17 from Turkish *şerbet,* from Persian *sharbat,* from Arabic *sharbah* drink, from *shariba* to drink]

Sherborne ('ʃɛːbɔːn) *n* a town in S England in Dorset: noted for its medieval abbey, ruined medieval castle, and Sherborne Castle, a mansion built by Sir Walter Raleigh in 1594. Pop: 9350 (2001)

Sherbrooke ('ʃɜː,brʊk) *n* a city in E Canada, in S Quebec: university. It is an industrial and

commercial centre. Pop: 127 354 (2001)

sherd (ʃɜːd) *n* a variant of **shard**

sheria (ʃə'riːə) *n* a variant spelling of **sharia**

sherif, shereef (ʃɛ'riːf) *or* **sharif** *n, pl* **ashraf** *Islam* **1** a descendant of Mohammed through his daughter Fatima **2** (formerly) the governor of Mecca **3** an honorific title accorded to any Muslim ruler [c16 from Arabic *sharīf* noble]

sheriff ('ʃɛrɪf) *n* **1** (in the US) the chief law-enforcement officer in a county: popularly elected, except in Rhode Island **2** (in England and Wales) the chief executive officer of the Crown in a county, having chiefly ceremonial duties. Related adj: **shrieval 3** (in Scotland) a judge in any of the sheriff courts **4** (in Australia) an administrative officer of the Supreme Court, who enforces judgments and the execution of writs, empanels juries, etc **5** (in New Zealand) an officer of the High Court [Old English *scīrgerēfa,* from *scīr* SHIRE¹ + *gerēfa* REEVE¹] > '**sheriffdom** *n*

sheriff court *n* (in Scotland) a court having jurisdiction to try summarily or on indictment all but the most serious crimes and to deal with most civil actions

sherpa ('ʃɜːpə) *n* an official who makes preparations for or assists a government representative or important delegate at a summit meeting or conference [c20 from SHERPA, a member of a people noted for providing assistance to mountaineers: from a pun on the different senses of SUMMIT]

Sherpa ('ʃɜːpə) *n, pl* **-pas** *or* **-pa** a member of a people of Mongolian origin living on the southern slopes of the Himalayas in Nepal, noted as mountaineers

sherry ('ʃɛrɪ) *n, pl* **-ries** a fortified wine, originally from the Jerez region in S Spain, usually drunk as an apéritif [c16 from earlier *sherris* (assumed to be plural), from Spanish *Xeres,* now *Jerez*]

's Hertogenbosch (*Dutch* shɛrto:xən'bɔs) *n* a city in the S Netherlands, capital of North Brabant province: birthplace of Hieronymus Bosch. Pop: 133 000 (2003 est.). Also called: **Den Bosch.** French name: **Bois-le-Duc**

sherwani (ʃɛə'wɑːnɪ) *n, pl* **-nis** a long coat closed up to the neck, worn by men in India [Hindi]

Sherwood Forest ('ʃɜː,wʊd) *n* an ancient forest in central England, in Nottinghamshire: formerly a royal hunting ground and much more extensive; famous as the home of Robin Hood

she's (ʃiːz) *contraction of* she is or she has

Shetland ('ʃɛtlənd) *n* Also called: **Shetland Islands** a group of about 100 islands (fewer than 20 inhabited), off the N coast of Scotland, which constitute an island authority of Scotland: a Norse dependency from the 8th century until 1472; noted for the breeding of Shetland ponies, knitwear manufacturing, and fishing; oil-related industries. Administrative centre: Lerwick. Pop: 21 870 (2003 est.). Area: 1426 sq km (550 sq miles). Official name (until 1974): **Zetland**

Shetland pony *n* a very small sturdy breed of pony with a long shaggy mane and tail. Also called: **sheltie**

Shetland sheepdog *n* a small dog similar in appearance to a rough collie. Also called: **sheltie**

Shetland wool *n* a fine loosely twisted wool yarn spun from the fleece of Shetland sheep and used esp for sweaters

sheuch *or* **sheugh** (ʃuːx, ʃʌx) *n Scot dialect* a ditch or trough [dialect variant of SOUGH²]

Sheva Brachoth *or* **Sheva Brochos** (*Hebrew* 'ʃɛvɑ brɑ'xot; *Yiddish* 'ʃɛvə 'brɔxəs) *pl n Judaism* **1** the seven blessings said during the marriage service and repeated at the celebration thereafter **2** any of the celebratory meals held on the seven days after a wedding [literally: seven blessings]

Shevat *or* **Shebat** (ʃɛ'vat) *n* (in the Jewish calendar) the eleventh month of the year according to biblical reckoning and the fifth month of the civil year [from Hebrew]

shew (ʃəʊ) *vb* **shews, shewing, shewed; shewn**

(ʃəʊn) *or* shewed an archaic spelling of **show** > 'shewer *n*

shewbread *or* **showbread** ('ʃəʊˌbrɛd) *n Old Testament* the loaves of bread placed every Sabbath on the table beside the altar of incense in the tabernacle or temple of ancient Israel (Exodus 25:30; Leviticus 24:5–9) [on the model of German *Schaubrot*, a translation of the Greek *artoi enōpioi*, a translation of the Hebrew *lechem pānīm*, literally: bread of the presence]

SHF *or* **shf** *radio abbreviation for* **superhigh frequency**

Shiah *or* **Shia** ('ʃiːə) *n* **1** one of the two main branches of Islam (the other being the Sunni), now mainly in Iran, which regards Mohammed's cousin Ali and his successors as the true imams **2** another name for **Shiite** ▷ *adj* **3** designating or characteristic of this sect or its beliefs and practices [c17 from Arabic *shī'ah* sect, from *shā'a* to follow]

shiai ('ʃiːaɪ) *n* a judo contest [Japanese]

shiatsu (ʃiː'ætsuː) *n* massage in which pressure is applied to the same points of the body as in acupuncture. Also called: **acupressure** [Japanese, from Chinese *chī* finger + *yā* pressure]

shibboleth ('ʃɪbəˌlɛθ) *n* **1** a belief, principle, or practice which is commonly adhered to but which is thought by some people to be inappropriate or out of date **2** a custom, phrase, or use of language that acts as a test of belonging to, or as a stumbling block to becoming a member of, a particular social class, profession, etc [c14 from Hebrew, literally: ear of grain; the word is used in the Old Testament by the Gileadites as a test word for the Ephraimites, who could not pronounce the sound *sh*]

shicker ('ʃɪkə) *n Austral archaic slang* alcoholic drink; liquor [via Yiddish from Hebrew]

shickered ('ʃɪkəd) *adj Austral and NZ slang* drunk; intoxicated

shidduch *Yiddish* ('ʃɪdəx) *n, pl* **shidduchim** (ʃɪ'duːxɪm) *Judaism* **1 a** an arranged marriage **b** the arrangement of a marriage **2** any negotiated agreement [from Hebrew: see SHADCHAN]

shied (ʃaɪd) *vb* the past tense and past participle of **shy¹** and **shy²**

shield (ʃiːld) *n* **1** any protection used to intercept blows, missiles, etc, such as a tough piece of armour carried on the arm **2** any similar protective device **3** Also called: **scutcheon**, **escutcheon** *heraldry* a pointed stylized shield used for displaying armorial bearings **4** anything that resembles a shield in shape, such as a prize in a sports competition **5** the protective outer covering of an animal, such as the shell of a turtle **6** *physics* a structure of concrete, lead, etc, placed around a nuclear reactor or other source of radiation in order to prevent the escape of radiation **7** a broad stable plateau of ancient Precambrian rocks forming the rigid nucleus of a particular continent. See **Baltic Shield**, **Canadian Shield 8** short for **dress shield 9** *civil engineering* a hollow steel cylinder that protects men driving a circular tunnel through loose, soft, or water-bearing ground **10** *the shield informal* **a** *Austral* short for the **Sheffield Shield b** *NZ* short for the **Ranfurly Shield** ▷ *vb* **11** (*tr*) to protect, hide, or conceal (something) from danger or harm [Old English *scield*; related to Old Norse *skjöldr*, Gothic *skildus*, Old High German *scilt* shield, Old English *sciell* SHELL] > 'shielder *n* > 'shield,like *adj*

shield bug *n* any shield-shaped herbivorous heteropterous insect of the superfamily *Pentamoidea*, esp any of the family *Pentatomidae*. Also called: **stink bug**

shield cricket *n Austral* the interstate cricket competition held for the Sheffield Shield

shield fern *n* any temperate woodland fern of the genus *Polystichum* having shield-shaped flaps covering the spore-producing bodies: family *Aspleniaceae*

shield match *n* **a** *Austral* a cricket match for the Sheffield Shield **b** *NZ* a rugby match for the Ranfurly Shield

Shield of David *n* another term for the **Star of David**

shield volcano *n* a broad volcano built up from the repeated nonexplosive eruption of basalt to form a low dome or shield, usually having a large caldera at the summit

shieling ('ʃiːlɪŋ) *or* **shiel** (ʃiːl) *n chiefly Scot* **1** a rough, sometimes temporary, hut or shelter used by people tending cattle on high or remote ground **2** pasture land for the grazing of cattle in summer [c16 from Middle English *shale* hut, of unknown origin]

shier¹ ('ʃaɪə) *adj* a comparative of **shy**

shier² *or* **shyer** ('ʃaɪə) *n* a horse that shies habitually

shiest ('ʃaɪɪst) *adj* a superlative of **shy**

shift (ʃɪft) *vb* **1** to move or cause to move from one place or position to another **2** (*tr*) to change for another or others **3** to change (gear) in a motor vehicle **4** (*intr*) (of a sound or set of sounds) to alter in a systematic way **5** (*intr*) to provide for one's needs (esp in the phrase **shift for oneself**) **6** (*intr*) to proceed by indirect or evasive methods **7** to remove or be removed, esp with difficulty: *no detergent can shift these stains* **8** (*intr*) slang to move quickly **9** (*tr*) *computing* to move (bits held in a store location) to the left or right ▷ *n* **10** the act or an instance of shifting **11** a group of workers who work for a specific period **12** the period of time worked by such a group **13** an expedient, contrivance, or artifice **14** the displacement of rocks, esp layers or seams in mining, at a geological fault **15** an underskirt or dress with little shaping [Old English *sciftan*; related to Old Norse *skipta* to divide, Middle Low German *schiften*, to separate] > 'shifter *n*

shifting cultivation *n* a land-use system, esp in tropical Africa, in which a tract of land is cultivated until its fertility diminishes, when it is abandoned until this is restored naturally

shifting spanner *n Austral and NZ* an adjustable spanner. Also called: **shifter**

shift key *n* a key on a typewriter or computer keyboard used to type capital letters and certain numbers and symbols

shiftless ('ʃɪftlɪs) *adj* lacking in ambition or initiative > 'shiftlessly *adv* > 'shiftlessness *n*

shiftwork ('ʃɪft,wɜːk) *n* a system of employment where an individual's normal hours of work are, in part, outside the period of normal day working and may follow a different pattern in consecutive periods of weeks

shifty ('ʃɪftɪ) *adj* **shiftier**, **shiftiest 1** given to evasions; artful **2** furtive in character or appearance **3** full of expedients; resourceful > 'shiftily *adv* > 'shiftiness *n*

shigella (ʃɪ'gɛlə) *n* any rod-shaped Gram-negative bacterium of the genus *Shigella*; some species cause dysentery [c20 named after K. *Shiga* (1870–1957), Japanese bacteriologist, who discovered it]

shih-tzu (ʃiː'tsuː) *n* a small dog of a breed derived from crossing the Pekingese and the Tibetan apso. It has a long straight dense coat and carries its tail curled over its back [from Chinese, literally: lion]

Shiism ('ʃiːɪzəm) *n Islam* the beliefs and practices of Shiah

shiitake (ʃɪ'tɑːkeɪ) *or* **shitake** *n, pl* **-take** a kind of mushroom widely used in Oriental cookery [c20 from Japanese *shii* tree + *take* mushroom]

Shiite ('ʃiːaɪt) *or* **Shiah** *Islam* ▷ *n* **1** an adherent of Shiah ▷ *adj* **2** of or relating to Shiah > Shiitic (ʃiː'ɪtɪk) *adj*

Shijiazhuang ('ʃiːdʒɑː'dʒwæŋ) *or* **Shihchiachuang**, **Shihkiachwang** (ʃiːtʃjɑː'tʃwæŋ) *n* a city in NE China, capital of Hebei province: textile manufacturing. Pop: 1 733 000 (2005 est)

shikar (ʃɪ'kɑː) *n* (in India) **1** hunting, esp big-game hunting ▷ *vb* **-kars**, **-karring**, **-karred 2** to hunt (game, esp big game) [c17 via Urdu from Persian]

shikari *or* **shikaree** (ʃɪ'kɑːrɪ) *n, pl* **-ris** *or* **-rees** (in India) a hunter

Shikoku ('ʃiːkəʊˌkuː) *n* the smallest of the four main islands of Japan, separated from Honshu by the Inland Sea: forested and mountainous. Pop: 4 137 000 (2002 est). Area: 17 759 sq km (6857 sq miles)

shiksa ('ʃɪksə) *n often derogatory* (used by Jews) **1** a non-Jewish girl **2** a Jewish girl who fails to live up to traditional Jewish standards [Yiddish *shikse*, feminine of *sheygets* non-Jewish youth, from Hebrew *sheqes* defect]

shill (ʃɪl) *n slang* a confidence trickster's assistant, esp a person who poses as an ordinary customer, gambler, etc, in order to entice others to participate [c20 perhaps shortened from *shillaber* a circus barker, of unknown origin]

shillelagh *or* **shillala** (ʃə'leɪlə, -lɪ; *Irish* ʃɪ'le:lə) *n* (in Ireland) a stout club or cudgel, esp one made of oak or blackthorn [c18 from Irish Gaelic *sail* cudgel + *éille* leash, thong]

shilling ('ʃɪlɪŋ) *n* **1** a former British and Australian silver or cupronickel coin worth one twentieth of a pound: not minted in Britain since 1970. Abbreviations: s, sh **2** the standard monetary unit of Kenya, Somalia, Tanzania, and Uganda: divided into 100 cents **3** an old monetary unit of the US varying in value in different states **4** (*in combination*) *Scot* an indication of the strength and character of a beer, referring to the price after duty that was formerly paid per barrel: *sixty-shilling*. Symbol: /- [Old English *scilling*; related to Old Norse *skillingr*, Gothic *skilliggs*, Old High German *skilling*]

shilling mark *n* another name for **slash** (sense 12) [so named because it was used to separate shillings from pence when writing amounts less than one pound before the introduction of decimal currency in Britain. For example, *three shillings and eleven pence* was written 3/11]

Shillong (ʃɪ'lɒŋ) *n* a city in NE India, capital of Meghalaya: situated on the **Shillong Plateau** at an altitude of 1520 m (4987 ft); destroyed by earthquake in 1897 and rebuilt. Pop: 132 876 (2001)

shillyshally ('ʃɪlɪˌʃælɪ) *informal* ▷ *vb* **-lies**, **-lying**, **-lied 1** (*intr*) to be indecisive, esp over unimportant matters; hesitate ▷ *adv* **2** in an indecisive manner ▷ *adj* **3** indecisive or hesitant ▷ *n, pl* **-lies 4** indecision or hesitation; vacillation [c18 from *shall I shall I*, by reduplication of *shall I*] > 'shilly,shallier *n*

Shiloh ('ʃaɪləʊ) *n* a town in central ancient Palestine, in Canaan on the E slope of Mount Ephraim: keeping place of the tabernacle and the ark; destroyed by the Philistines

shilpit ('ʃɪlpɪt) *adj Scot* puny; thin; weak-looking [c19 of unknown origin]

shily ('ʃaɪlɪ) *adv* a less common spelling of **shyly**

shim (ʃɪm) *n* **1** a thin packing strip or washer often used with a number of similar washers or strips to adjust a clearance for gears, etc **2** *physics* a thin strip of magnetic material, such as soft iron, used to adjust a magnetic field ▷ *vb* **shims**, **shimming**, **shimmed 3** (*tr*) to modify a load, clearance, or magnetic field by the use of shims

shimmer ('ʃɪmə) *vb* **1** (*intr*) to shine with a glistening or tremulous light ▷ *n* **2** a faint, glistening, or tremulous light [Old English *scimerian*; related to Middle Low German *schēmeren* to grow dark, Old Norse *skimi* brightness] > 'shimmering *adj* > 'shimmeringly *adv*

shimmery ('ʃɪmərɪ) *adj* **-merier**, **-meriest 1** shining with a glistening or tremulous light **2** glamorous; flashy

shimmy ('ʃɪmɪ) *n, pl* **-mies 1** an American ragtime dance with much shaking of the hips and shoulders **2** abnormal wobbling motion in a motor vehicle, esp in the front wheels or steering **3** an informal word for **chemise** ▷ *vb* **-mies**,

S

-mying, -mied (*intr*) **4** to dance the shimmy **5** to vibrate or wobble [C19 changed from CHEMISE, mistakenly assumed to be plural]

Shimonoseki (ˌʃɪmənəʊˈsɛkɪ) *n* a port in SW Japan, on SW Honshu: scene of the peace treaty (1895) ending the Sino-Japanese War; a heavy industrial centre. Pop: 246 924 (2002 est)

shin¹ (ʃɪn) *n* **1** the front part of the lower leg **2** the front edge of the tibia **3** *chiefly Brit* a cut of beef, the lower foreleg ▷ *vb* shins, shinning, shinned **4** (when *intr*, often foll by *up*) to climb (a pole, tree, etc) by gripping with the hands or arms and the legs and hauling oneself up **5** (*tr*) to kick (a person) in the shins [Old English *scinu*; related to Old High German *scina* needle, Norwegian dialect *skina* small disc]

shin² (ʃɪn) *n* the 22nd letter in the Hebrew alphabet (ש), transliterated as *sh* [from Hebrew *shīn*, literally: tooth]

Shinar (ˈʃaɪnɑː) *n Old Testament* the southern part of the valley of the Tigris and Euphrates, often identified with Sumer; Babylonia

shinbone (ˈʃɪnˌbəʊn) *n* the nontechnical name for **tibia** (sense 1)

shindig (ˈʃɪnˌdɪɡ) *n informal* **1** a noisy party, dance, etc **2** another word for **shindy** [C19 variant of SHINDY]

shindy (ˈʃɪndɪ) *n, pl* -dies *informal* **1** a quarrel or commotion (esp in the phrase **kick up a shindy**) **2** another word for **shindig** [C19 variant of SHINTY]

shine (ʃaɪn) *vb* shines, shining, shone **1** (*intr*) to emit light **2** (*intr*) to glow or be bright with reflected light **3** (*tr*) to direct the light of (a lamp, etc): *he shone the torch in my eyes* **4** (*tr; past tense and past participle* **shined**) to cause to gleam by polishing: *to shine shoes* **5** (*intr*) to be conspicuously competent; excel: *she shines at tennis* **6** (*intr*) to appear clearly; be conspicuous: *the truth shone out of his words* ▷ *n* **7** the state or quality of shining; sheen; lustre **8** (**come**) rain or shine **a** whatever the weather **b** regardless of circumstances **9** *informal* short for **moonshine** (whisky) **10** *informal* a liking or fancy (esp in the phrase **take a shine to**) [Old English *scīnan*; related to Old Norse *skīna*, Gothic *skeinan*, Old High German *scīnan* to shine, Greek *skia* shadow]

shiner (ˈʃaɪnə) *n* **1** something that shines, such as a polishing device **2** any of numerous small North American freshwater cyprinid fishes of the genus *Notropis* and related genera, such as *N. cornutus* (**common shiner**) and *Notemigonus crysoleucas* (**golden shiner**) **3** a popular name for the **mackerel** **4** *informal* a black eye **5** *NZ old-fashioned informal* a vagrant or tramp

shingle¹ (ˈʃɪŋɡ³l) *n* **1** a thin rectangular tile, esp one made of wood, that is laid with others in overlapping rows to cover a roof or a wall **2** a woman's short-cropped hairstyle **3** *US and Canadian* a small signboard or nameplate fixed outside the office of a doctor, lawyer, etc **4** a **shingle short** *Austral informal* unintelligent or mentally subnormal ▷ *vb* (*tr*) **5** to cover (a roof or a wall) with shingles **6** to cut (the hair) in a short-cropped style [C12 *scingle*, from Late Latin *scindula* a split piece of wood, from Latin *scindere* to split] > ˈshingler *n*

shingle² (ˈʃɪŋɡ³l) *n* **1** coarse gravel, esp the pebbles found on beaches **2** a place or area strewn with shingle [C16 of Scandinavian origin; compare Norwegian *singl* pebbles] > ˈshingly *adj*

shingle³ (ˈʃɪŋɡ³l) *vb* (*tr*) *metallurgy* to hammer or squeeze the slag out of (iron) after puddling in the production of wrought iron [C17 from Old French dialect *chingler* to whip, from *chingle* belt, from Latin *cingula* girdle; see CINGULUM]

shingles (ˈʃɪŋɡ³lz) *n* (*functioning as singular*) an acute viral disease affecting the ganglia of certain nerves, characterized by inflammation, pain, and skin eruptions along the course of the affected nerve. Technical names: **herpes zoster, zoster** [C14 from Medieval Latin *cingulum* girdle, rendering Greek *zōnē* ZONE]

shining cuckoo *n* another name for **pipiwharauroa**

shinju (ˈʃɪndʒuː) *n* (formerly, in Japan) a ritual double suicide of lovers

shinkin (ˈʃɪŋkɪn) *n South Wales dialect* a worthless person [Welsh, from the surname *Jenkin*, of Dutch origin]

shinleaf (ˈʃɪnˌliːf) *n, pl* -leaves the usual US name for **wintergreen** (sense 3)

Shinner (ˈʃɪnə) *n* (in Ireland) *informal* a supporter or member of Sinn Féin

shinplaster (ˈʃɪnˌplɑːstə) *n US, Canadian, and Austral* a promissory note on brittle paper, issued by an individual [C19 so called because of its resemblance to a sticking plaster]

shin splints *n* (*functioning as singular or plural*) a painful swelling of the front lower leg, associated with muscle or bone inflammation, and common among athletes and other sportspeople

Shinto (ˈʃɪntəʊ) *n* the indigenous religion of Japan, polytheistic in character and incorporating the worship of a number of ethnic divinities, from the chief of which the emperor is believed to be descended [C18 from Japanese: the way of the gods, from Chinese *shēn* gods + *tao* way] > ˈShintoism *n* > ˈShintoist *n, adj*

shinty (ˈʃɪntɪ) *or US and Canadian* **shinny** (ˈʃɪnɪ) *n, pl* -ties *or* -nies **1** a simple form of hockey of Scottish origin played with a ball and sticks curved at the lower end **2** the stick used in this game ▷ *vb* -ties, -tying, -tied *or US and Canadian* -nies, -nying, -nied (*intr*) **3** to play shinty [C17 possibly from Scottish Gaelic *sinteag* a pace, bound]

shiny (ˈʃaɪnɪ) *adj* shinier, shiniest **1** glossy or polished; bright **2** (of clothes or material) worn to a smooth and glossy state, as by continual rubbing > ˈshininess *n*

ship (ʃɪp) *n* **1** a vessel propelled by engines or sails for navigating on the water, esp a large vessel that cannot be carried aboard another, as distinguished from a boat **2** *nautical* a large sailing vessel with three or more square-rigged masts **3** the crew of a ship **4** short for **airship** or **spaceship** **5** *informal* any vehicle or conveyance **6** **when one's ship comes in** when one has become successful or wealthy ▷ *vb* **ships, shipping, shipped 7** to place, transport, or travel on any conveyance, esp aboard a ship: *ship the microscopes by aeroplane; can we ship tomorrow?* **8** (*tr*) *nautical* to take (water) over the side **9** to bring or go aboard a vessel: *to ship oars* **10** (*tr; often foll by off*) *informal* to send away, often in order to be rid of: *they shipped the children off to boarding school* **11** (*intr*) to engage to serve aboard a ship: *I shipped aboard a Liverpool liner* **12** *informal* (*tr*) to concede (a goal): *Celtic have shipped eight goals in three away matches* ▷ See also **ship out** [Old English *scip*; related to Old Norse *skip*, Old High German *skif* ship, *scipfī* cup] > ˈshippable *adj*

-ship *suffix forming nouns* **1** indicating state or condition: *fellowship* **2** indicating rank, office, or position: *lordship* **3** indicating craft or skill: *horsemanship; workmanship; scholarship* [Old English *-scipe*; compare SHAPE]

shipboard (ˈʃɪpˌbɔːd) *n* **1** (*modifier*) taking place, used, or intended for use aboard a ship: *a shipboard encounter* **2** on shipboard on board a ship

ship-broker *n* a person who acts for a shipowner by getting cargo and passengers for his ships and also handling insurance and other matters

shipbuilder (ˈʃɪpˌbɪldə) *n* a person or business engaged in the building of ships > ˈshipˌbuilding *n*

ship chandler *n* a person or business dealing in supplies for ships > ship chandlery *n*

Shipka Pass (ˈʃɪpkə) *n* a pass over the Balkan Mountains in central Bulgaria: scene of a bloody Turkish defeat in the Russo-Turkish War (1877–78). Height: 1334 m (4376 ft)

shipload (ˈʃɪpˌləʊd) *n* the quantity carried by a ship

shipmaster (ˈʃɪpˌmɑːstə) *or* **shipman** (ˈʃɪpmən) *n, pl* -masters *or* -men the master or captain of a ship

shipmate (ˈʃɪpˌmeɪt) *n* a sailor who serves on the same ship as another

shipment (ˈʃɪpmənt) *n* **1 a** goods shipped together as part of the same lot: *a shipment of grain* **b** (*as modifier*): *a shipment schedule* **2** the act of shipping cargo

ship money *n English history* a tax levied to finance the fitting out of warships: abolished 1640

ship of the line *n nautical* (formerly) a warship large enough to fight in the first line of battle

ship out *vb* (*adverb*) to depart or cause to depart by ship: *we shipped out at dawn; they shipped out the new recruits*

shipowner (ˈʃɪpˌəʊnə) *n* a person who owns or has shares in a ship or ships

shipper (ˈʃɪpə) *n* a person or company in the business of shipping freight

shippie (ˈʃɪpɪ) *n NZ slang* a prostitute who solicits at a port

shipping (ˈʃɪpɪŋ) *n* **1 a** the business of transporting freight, esp by ship **b** (*as modifier*): *a shipping magnate; shipping line* **2 a** ships collectively: *there is a lot of shipping in the Channel* **b** the tonnage of a number of ships: *shipping for this year exceeded that of last*

shipping agent *n* a person or company whose business is to prepare shipping documents, arrange shipping space and insurance, and deal with customs requirements

shipping clerk *n* a person employed by a company to arrange, receive, record, and send shipments of goods

shipping ton *n* the full name for **ton¹** (sense 5)

ship-rigged *adj* rigged as a full-rigged ship

ship's articles *or* **shipping articles** *pl n* a type of contract by which sailors agree to the conditions, payment, etc, for the ship in which they are going to work

ship's biscuit *n* another name for **hardtack**

ship's boy *n* a young man or boy employed to attend the needs of passengers or officers aboard ship

shipshape (ˈʃɪpˌʃeɪp) *adj* **1** neat; orderly ▷ *adv* **2** in a neat and orderly manner

ship's papers *pl n* the documents that are required by law to be carried by a ship for the purpose of ascertaining details of her ownership, nationality, destination, and cargo or to prove her neutrality

shipway (ˈʃɪpˌweɪ) *n* **1** the structure on which a vessel is built, then launched **2** a canal used by ships

shipworm (ˈʃɪpˌwɜːm) *n* any wormlike marine bivalve mollusc of the genus *Teredo* and related genera and family *Teredinidae*. They bore into wooden piers, ships, etc, by means of drill-like shell valves. See also **piddock**

shipwreck (ˈʃɪpˌrɛk) *n* **1** the partial or total destruction of a ship at sea **2** a wrecked ship or part of such a ship **3** ruin or destruction: *the shipwreck of all my hopes* ▷ *vb* (*tr*) **4** to wreck or destroy (a ship) **5** to bring to ruin or destruction [Old English *scipwræc*, from SHIP + *wræc* something driven by the sea; see WRACK²]

shipwright (ˈʃɪpˌraɪt) *n* an artisan skilled in one or more of the tasks required to build vessels

shipyard (ˈʃɪpˌjɑːd) *n* a place or facility for the building, maintenance, and repair of ships

shiralee (ˌʃɪrəˈliː) *n Austral history informal* a swag; swagman's bundle [C19 of unknown origin]

Shiraz¹ (ʃɪəˈrɑːz) *n* a city in SW Iran, at an altitude of 1585 m (5200 ft): an important Muslim cultural centre in the 14th century; university (1948); noted for fine carpets. Pop: 1 230 000 (2005 est)

Shiraz² (ʃɪəˈrɑːz) *n* the name used in Australia for the Syrah grape and wines [from SHIRAZ¹, where the wine supposedly originated]

shire¹ (ʃaɪə) *n* **1 a** one of the British counties **b** (*in combination*): *Yorkshire* **2** (in Australia) a rural district having its own local council **3** See **shire horse** **4** the Midland counties of England, esp

Northamptonshire and Leicestershire, famous for hunting, etc [Old English *scīr* office; related to Old High German *scīra* business]

shire² (ʃaɪə) *vb* (*tr*) *Ulster dialect* to refresh or rest: *let me get my head shired* [from Old English *scīr* clear]

Shire (ʃiːəreɪ) *or* **Shiré** *n* a river in E central Africa, flowing from Lake Malawi through Malawi and Mozambique to the Zambezi. Length: 596 km (370 miles)

Shire Highlands *or* **Shiré Highlands** *pl n* an upland area of S Malawi. Average height: 900 m (3000 ft)

shire horse *n* a large heavy breed of carthorse with long hair on the fetlocks. Often shortened to: **shire** [c19 so called because the breed was originally reared in the *Shires*. See SHIRE¹]

shirk¹ (ʃɜːk) *vb* 1 to avoid discharging (work, a duty, etc); evade ▷ *n* *also* **shirker** 2 a person who shirks [c17 probably from German *Schurke* rogue; see SHARK²]

shirk² (ʃiːk) *n Islam* **a** the fundamental sin of regarding anything as equal to Allah **b** any belief that is considered to be in opposition to Allah and Islam [from Arabic: association]

shirr (ʃɜː) *vb* 1 to gather (fabric) into two or more parallel rows to decorate a dress, blouse, etc, often using elastic thread 2 (*tr*) to bake (eggs) out of their shells ▷ *n* *also* **shirring** 3 a series of gathered rows decorating a dress, blouse, etc [c19 of unknown origin]

shirt (ʃɜːt) *n* 1 a garment worn on the upper part of the body, esp by men, usually of light material and typically having a collar and sleeves and buttoning up the front 2 short for **nightshirt** *or* **undershirt** 3 **keep your shirt on** *informal* refrain from losing your temper (often used as an exhortation to another) 4 **put** *or* **lose one's shirt on** *informal* to bet or lose all one has on (a horse, etc) [Old English *scyrte*; related to Old English *sceort* SHORT, Old Norse *skyrta* skirt, Middle High German *schurz* apron]

shirtdress (ʃɜːtˌdrɛs) *n* a dress that resembles a lengthened shirt, often worn with a belt

shirting (ʃɜːtɪŋ) *n* fabric used in making men's shirts

shirt-lifter *n derogatory slang* a homosexual

shirtsleeve (ʃɜːtˌsliːv) *n* 1 the sleeve of a shirt 2 **in one's shirtsleeves** not wearing a jacket

shirt-tail *n* the part of a shirt that extends below the waist

shirtwaister (ʃɜːtˌweɪstə) *or US and Canadian* **shirtwaist** *n* a woman's dress with a tailored bodice resembling a shirt

shirty (ʃɜːtɪ) *adj* **shirtier, shirtiest** *slang, chiefly Brit* bad-tempered or annoyed [c19 perhaps based on such phrases as *to get someone's shirt out* to annoy someone] > **shirtily** *adv* > **shirtiness** *n*

shisha (ʃiːʃə) *n* another name for **hookah** [c21 from Persian *shishe* a bottle]

shish kebab (ʃiːʃ kəˈbæb) *n* a dish consisting of small pieces of meat and vegetables threaded onto skewers and grilled [from Turkish *şiş kebab*, from *şiş* skewer; see KEBAB]

shiso (ʃiːsəʊ) *n* another name for **beefsteak plant** [Japanese]

shit (ʃɪt) *taboo* ▷ *vb* **shits, shitting; shitted, shit** *or* **shat** 1 to defecate 2 (usually foll by *on*) *slang* to give the worst possible treatment (to) ▷ *n* 3 faeces; excrement 4 rubbish; nonsense 5 an obnoxious or worthless person 6 cannabis resin or heroin 7 **in the shit** in trouble 8 **the shit hits the fan** the real trouble begins ▷ *interj* 9 an exclamation expressing anger, disgust, etc. Also (esp dialect): **shite** (ʃaɪt) [Old English *scite* (unattested) dung, *scītan* to defecate, of Germanic origin; related to Old English *scēadan* to separate, Old Norse *skíta* to defecate, Middle Dutch *schitte* excrement] > **shitty** *adj* > **shittily** *adv* > **shittiness** *n*

shitake (ʃiˈtɑːkeɪ) *n* a variant of **shiitake**

shithead (ʃɪtˌhɛd) *n taboo slang* a fool; idiot: used as a term of abuse

shitload (ʃɪtˌləʊd) *n taboo slang* a lot; large amount: *a shitload of money*

shit-stir *vb* (*intr*) *slang* to make trouble > **shit-ˌstirrer** *n*

shittah (ʃɪtə) *n, pl* **shittim** (ʃɪtɪm) *or* **shittahs** a tree mentioned in the Old Testament, thought to be either of two Asian acacias, *Acacia seyal* or *A. tortilis*, having close-grained yellow-brown wood [c17 from Hebrew *shittāh*; related to Egyptian *šout* acacia]

Shittim (ʃɪtɪm) *n Old Testament* the site to the east of the Jordan and northeast of the Dead Sea where the Israelites encamped before crossing the Jordan (Numbers 25:1–9)

shittim wood (ʃɪtɪm) *n Old Testament* a kind of wood, probably acacia, from which the Ark of the Covenant and parts of the tabernacle were made [c14 from Hebrew *shittīm*, plural of SHITTAH]

shiur (ʃiʊr, ʃiˈuːr) *n, pl* **shiurim** (ʃiʊˈrim, ʃiˈuːrim) a lesson, esp one in which a passage of the Talmud is studied together by a group of people [from Hebrew, literally: measurement]

shiv (ʃiv) *n* a variant spelling of **chiv**

Shiva (ʃiːvə, ʃɪvə) *n* a variant spelling of **Siva** > **Shivaism** *n* > **Shivaist** *n, adj*

shivah (ʃiːvə, ʃɪvə) *n Judaism* 1 the period of formal mourning lasting seven days from the funeral during which the mourner stays indoors and sits on a low stool 2 **sit shivah** to mourn [from Hebrew, literally: seven (days)]

shivaree (ʃɪvəˈriː) *n* Also called: **charivari** *n US and Canadian* 1 a discordant mock serenade to newlyweds, made with pans, kettles, etc 2 a confused noise; din

shive (ʃaɪv) *n* 1 a flat cork or bung for wide-mouthed bottles 2 an archaic word for **slice** [c13 from Middle Dutch or Middle Low German *schive*; see SHEAVE¹]

shiver¹ (ʃɪvə) *vb* (*intr*) 1 to shake or tremble, as from cold or fear 2 **a** (of a sail) to luff; flap or shake **b** (of a sailing vessel) to sail close enough to the wind to make the sails luff ▷ *n* 3 the act of shivering; a tremulous motion 4 **the shivers** an attack of shivering, esp through fear or illness [c13 *chiveren*, perhaps variant of *chevelen* to chatter (used of teeth), from Old English *ceafl* JOWL¹] > **shiverer** *n* > **shivering** *adj*

shiver² (ʃɪvə) *vb* 1 to break or cause to break into fragments ▷ *n* 2 a splintered piece [c13 of Germanic origin; compare Old High German *scivaro*, Middle Dutch *scheveren* to shiver, Old Norse *skífa* to split]

shivery (ʃɪvərɪ) *adj* 1 inclined to shiver or tremble 2 causing shivering, esp through cold or fear

Shizuoka (ʃiːzuːˈəʊkə) *n* a city in central Japan, on S Honshu: a centre for green tea; university (1949). Pop: 468 775 (2002 est)

Shkodër (*Albanian* ʃkodər) *n* a market town in NW Albania, on **Lake Shkodër**: an Illyrian capital in the first millennium BC. Pop: 83 700 (1991 est). Italian name: **Scutari**

shloshim (ʃləʃim, ʃlaʊʃim) *n Judaism* the period of thirty days' deep mourning following a death [from Hebrew, literally: thirty (days)]

Shluh (ʃəˈluː, ʃluː) *n* 1 (*pl* **Shluhs** *or* **Shluh**) a member of a Berber people inhabiting the Atlas Mountains in Morocco and Algeria 2 the dialect of Berber spoken by this people

SHM *abbreviation for* **simple harmonic motion**

shmatte *Yiddish* (ʃmɑtə) *n* 1 a rag 2 anything shabby 3 (*modifier*) clothes: a jocular use: *the shmatte trade*

shmo (ʃməʊ) *n, pl* **shmoes** a variant form of **schmo**

Shoah (ʃəʊə) *n* (in secular Judaism) a Hebrew word for **holocaust** (sense 2). See also **Churban** (sense 2) [literally: destruction]

shoal¹ (ʃəʊl) *n* 1 a stretch of shallow water 2 a sandbank or rocky area in a stretch of water, esp one that is visible at low water ▷ *vb* 3 to make or become shallow 4 (*intr*) *nautical* to sail into shallower water ▷ *adj also* **shoaly** 5 a less

common word for **shallow** 6 *nautical* (of the draught of a vessel) drawing little water [Old English *sceald* SHALLOW] > **shoaliness** *n*

shoal² (ʃəʊl) *n* 1 a large group of certain aquatic animals, esp fish 2 a large group of people or things ▷ *vb* 3 (*intr*) to collect together in such a group [Old English *scolu*; related to Middle Low German, Middle Dutch *schōle* SCHOOL²]

shoat *or* **shote** (ʃəʊt) *n* a piglet that has recently been weaned [c15 related to West Flemish *schote*]

shochet (ʃɒket, ʃɔːxet) *n, pl* **shochets, shochetim** (in Judaism) a person who has been specially trained and licensed to slaughter animals and birds in accordance with the laws of shechita [c19 from Hebrew, literally: slaughtering]

shock¹ (ʃɒk) *vb* 1 to experience or cause to experience extreme horror, disgust, surprise, etc: *the atrocities shocked us; she shocks easily* 2 to cause a state of shock in (a person) 3 to come or cause to come into violent contact; jar ▷ *n* 4 a sudden and violent jarring blow or impact 5 something that causes a sudden and violent disturbance in the emotions: *the shock of her father's death made her ill* 6 *pathol* a state of bodily collapse or near collapse caused by circulatory failure or sudden lowering of the blood pressure, as from severe bleeding, burns, fright, etc [c16 from Old French *choc*, from *choquier* to make violent contact with, of Germanic origin; related to Middle High German *schoc*] > **shockable** *adj* > **shockaˈbility** *n*

shock² (ʃɒk) *n* 1 a number of sheaves set on end in a field to dry 2 a pile or stack of unthreshed corn ▷ *vb* 3 (*tr*) to set up (sheaves) in shocks [c14 probably of Germanic origin; compare Middle Low German, Middle Dutch *schok* shock of corn, group of sixty]

shock³ (ʃɒk) *n* 1 a thick bushy mass, esp of hair ▷ *adj* 2 *rare* bushy; shaggy [c19 perhaps from SHOCK²]

shock absorber *n* any device designed to absorb mechanical shock, esp one fitted to a motor vehicle to damp the recoil of the suspension springs

shocker (ʃɒkə) *n informal* 1 a person or thing that shocks or horrifies 2 a sensational novel, film, or play

shockheaded (ʃɒkˌhɛdɪd) *adj* having a head of bushy or tousled hair

shock-horror *adj facetious* (esp of newspaper headlines) sensationalistic: *shock-horror stories about the British diet* [c20 SHOCK¹ + HORROR]

shocking (ʃɒkɪŋ) *adj* 1 causing shock, horror, or disgust 2 **shocking pink** a vivid or garish shade of pink 3 *informal* very bad or terrible: *shocking weather* > **shockingly** *adv* > **shockingness** *n*

shock jock *n informal* a radio disc jockey who is deliberately controversial or provocative

shockproof (ʃɒkˌpruːf) *adj* capable of absorbing shock without damage: *a shockproof watch*

shockstall (ʃɒkˌstɔːl) *n* the loss of lift and increase of drag experienced by transonic aircraft when strong shock waves on the wings cause the airflow to separate from the wing surfaces

shock therapy *or* **treatment** *n* the treatment of certain psychotic conditions by injecting drugs or by passing an electric current through the brain (**electroconvulsive therapy**) to produce convulsions or coma

shock troops *pl n* soldiers specially trained and equipped to carry out an assault

shock tube *n* an apparatus in which a gas is heated to very high temperatures by means of a shock wave, usually for spectroscopic investigation of the natures and reactions of the resulting radicals and excited molecules

shockumentary (ʃɒkjuːˈmɛntərɪ, -trɪ) *n, pl* -ies a television programme showing members of the public in shocking or violent situations [c20 a blend of SHOCK + DOCUMENTARY]

shock wave *n* 1 a region across which there is a rapid pressure, temperature, and density rise, usually caused by a body moving supersonically

S

in a gas or by a detonation. Often shortened to: shock. See also **sonic boom, shock tube** **2** a feeling of shock, horror, surprise, etc that affects many people as it spreads through a community **3** the effect created on a queue of moving cars in the lane of a motorway when one car brakes suddenly and the cars behind have to brake as well, causing cars to slow down, sometimes for miles behind the first braking car

shod (ʃɒd) *vb* the past participle of **shoe**

shoddy (ˈʃɒdɪ) *adj* **-dier, -diest** **1** imitating something of better quality **2** of poor quality; trashy **3** made of shoddy material ▷ *n, pl* **-dies** **4** a yarn or fabric made from wool waste or clippings **5** anything of inferior quality that is designed to simulate superior quality [c19 of unknown origin] > ˈ**shoddily** *adv* > ˈ**shoddiness** *n*

shoe (ʃuː) *n* **1** **a** one of a matching pair of coverings shaped to fit the foot, esp one ending below the ankle, having an upper of leather, plastic, etc, on a sole and heel of heavier leather, rubber, or synthetic material **b** (*as modifier*): *shoe cleaner* **2** anything resembling a shoe in shape, function, position, etc, such as a horseshoe **3** a band of metal or wood on the bottom of the runner of a sledge **4** (in baccarat, etc) a boxlike device for holding several packs of cards and allowing the cards to be dispensed singly **5** a base for the supports of a superstructure of a bridge, roof, etc **6** a metal collector attached to an electric train that slides along the third rail and picks up power for the motor **7** *engineering* a lining to protect from and withstand wear: see **brake shoe, pile shoe** **8** **be in (a person's) shoes** *informal* to be in (another person's) situation ▷ *vb* **shoes, shoeing, shod** (*tr*) **9** to furnish with shoes **10** to fit (a horse) with horseshoes **11** to furnish with a hard cover, such as a metal plate, for protection against friction or bruising [Old English *scōh;* related to Old Norse *skōr,* Gothic *skōhs,* Old High German *scuoh*]

shoebill (ˈʃuːˌbɪl) *n* a large wading bird, *Balaeniceps rex,* of tropical E African swamps, having a dark plumage, a large head, and a large broad bill: family *Balaenicipitidae,* order *Ciconiiformes* [c19 so named because of the shape of its bill]

shoeblack (ˈʃuːˌblæk) *n* (esp formerly) a person who shines boots and shoes

shoehorn (ˈʃuːˌhɔːn) *n* **1** a smooth curved implement of horn, metal, plastic, etc, inserted at the heel of a shoe to ease the foot into it ▷ *vb* **2** (*tr*) to cram (people or things) into a very small space

shoelace (ˈʃuːˌleɪs) *n* a cord or lace for fastening shoes

shoe leather *n* **1** leather used to make shoes **2** **save shoe leather** to avoid wearing out shoes, as by taking a bus rather than walking

shoemaker (ˈʃuːˌmeɪkə) *n* a person who makes or repairs shoes or boots > ˈ**shoeˌmaking** *n*

Shoemaker-Levy 9 (ˈʃuːˌmeɪkə liːvaɪ) *n* a comet that was captured into an orbit around Jupiter and later broke up, the fragments colliding with Jupiter in July 1995 [c20 after *Carolyn Shoemaker* (born 1929), and *Eugene Shoemaker* (1928–97), and *David Levy* (born 1948), US astronomers, who discovered the orbiting fragments]

shoer (ˈʃuːə) *n* *rare* a person who shoes horses; farrier

shoeshine (ˈʃuːʃaɪn) *n* **1** the act or an instance of polishing a pair of shoes **2** the appearance or shiny surface of polished shoes

shoestring (ˈʃuːˌstrɪŋ) *n* **1** another word for **shoelace** **2** *informal* **a** a very small or petty amount of money (esp in the phrase **on a shoestring**) **b** (*as modifier*): *a shoestring budget*

shoetree (ˈʃuːˌtriː) *n* a wooden or metal form inserted into a shoe or boot to stretch it or preserve its shape

shofar *or* **shophar** (ˈʃəʊfɑː; *Hebrew* ʃoˈfar) *n, pl* **-fars, -phars** *or* **-froth, -phroth** (*Hebrew* -ˈfrɔt) *Judaism* a ram's horn sounded in the synagogue daily during the month of Elul and repeatedly on Rosh Hashanah, and by the ancient Israelites as a warning, summons, etc [from Hebrew *shōphār* ram's horn]

shogun (ˈʃəʊˌɡuːn) *n* *Japanese history* **1** (from 794 AD) a chief military commander **2** (from about 1192 to 1867) any of a line of hereditary military dictators who relegated the emperors to a position of purely theoretical supremacy [c17 from Japanese, from Chinese *chiang chün* general, from *chiang* to lead + *chün* army] > ˈ**shoˌgunal** *adj*

shogunate (ˈʃəʊɡʊnɪt, -ˌneɪt) *n* *Japanese history* the office or rule of a shogun

shogun bond *n* a bond sold on the Japanese market by a foreign institution and denominated in a foreign currency. Compare **samurai bond**

shoji (ˈʃəʊʒiː, -dʒiː) *n, pl* **-ji** *or* **-jis** **1** a rice-paper screen in a sliding wooden frame, used in Japanese houses as a partition **2** any similar screen [c19 from Japanese, from *shō* to separate + *ji* a piece]

Sholapur (ˈʃəʊləˌpʊə) *n* a city in SW India, in S Maharashtra: major textile centre. Pop: 873 037 (2001)

Shona (ˈʃɒnə) *n* **1** (*pl* **-na** *or* **-nas**) a member of a Sotho people of S central Africa, living chiefly in Zimbabwe and Mozambique **2** the language of this people, belonging to the Bantu group of the Niger-Congo family

shone (ʃɒn; *US* ʃəʊn) *vb* the past tense and past participle of **shine**

shoneen (ˈʃoːniːn) *n* *Irish* an Irishman who imitates English ways [c19 from Irish Gaelic *Seoinín,* diminutive of *Seon* John (taken as typical English name)]

shongololo (ʃɒŋɡəˈləʊləʊ) *n, pl* **-los** a variant spelling of **songololo**

shonky (ˈʃɒŋkɪ) *adj* **-kier, -kiest** *Austral and NZ informal* **1** of dubious integrity or legality **2** unreliable; unsound [c19 perhaps from Yiddish *shonniker* or from SH(ODDY) + (W)ONKY]

shoo (ʃuː) *interj* **1** go away!: used to drive away unwanted or annoying people, animals, etc ▷ *vb* **shoos, shooing, shooed** **2** (*tr*) to drive away by or as if by crying "shoo." **3** (*intr*) to cry "shoo." [c15 imitative; related to Middle High German *schū,* French *shou,* Italian *scio*]

shoofly pie (ˈʃuːˌflaɪ) *n* *US* a dessert similar to treacle tart

shoogle (ˈʃʊɡᵊl) *dialect, chiefly Scot* ▷ *vb* **1** to shake, sway, or rock back and forth ▷ *n* **2** a rocking motion; shake [from dialectal *shog, shug;* apparently related to German *schaukeln* to shake] > ˈ**shoogly** *adj*

shoo-in *n* **1** a person or thing that is certain to win or succeed **2** a match or contest that is easy to win

shook[1] (ʃʊk) *n* **1** (in timber working) a set of parts ready for assembly, esp of a barrel **2** a group of sheaves piled together on end; shock [c18 of unknown origin]

shook[2] (ʃʊk) *vb* **1** the past tense of **shake** ▷ *adj* **2** *Austral and NZ informal* keen on; enthusiastic about

shool (ʃuːl) *n* a dialect word for **shovel**

shoon (ʃuːn) *n* *dialect, chiefly Scot* a plural of **shoe**

shoot (ʃuːt) *vb* **shoots, shooting, shot** **1** (*tr*) to hit, wound, damage, or kill with a missile discharged from a weapon **2** to discharge (a missile or missiles) from a weapon **3** to fire (a weapon) or (of a weapon) to be fired **4** to send out or be sent out as if from a weapon: *he shot questions at her* **5** (*intr*) to move very rapidly; dart **6** (*tr*) to slide or push into or out of a fastening: *to shoot a bolt* **7** to emit (a ray of light) or (of a ray of light) to be emitted **8** (*tr*) to go or pass quickly over or through: *to shoot rapids* **9** (*intr*) to hunt game with a gun for sport **10** (*tr*) to pass over (an area) in hunting game **11** to extend or cause to extend; project **12** (*tr*) to discharge down or as if down a chute **13** (*intr*) (of a plant) to produce (buds, branches, etc) **14** (*intr*) (of a seed) to germinate **15** to photograph or record (a sequence, subject, etc) **16** (*tr; usually passive*) to variegate or streak, as with colour **17** *sport* to hit or propel (the ball, etc) towards the goal **18** (*tr*) *sport, chiefly US and Canadian* to score (points, strokes, etc): *he shot 72 on the first round* **19** (*tr*) to plane (a board) to produce a straight edge **20** (*tr*) *mining* to detonate **21** (*tr*) to measure the altitude of (a celestial body) **22** (often foll by *up*) *slang* to inject (someone, esp oneself) with (a drug, esp heroin) **23** **shoot a line** See **line**[1] (sense 58) **24** **shoot from the hip** to speak bluntly or impulsively without concern for the consequences **25** **shoot one's bolt** See **bolt**[1] (sense 13) **26** **shoot oneself in the foot** *informal* to damage one's own cause inadvertently **27** **shoot one's mouth off** *slang* **a** to talk indiscreetly **b** to boast or exaggerate **28** **shoot the breeze** See **breeze**[1] (sense 5) ▷ *n* **29** the act of shooting **30** the action or motion of something that is shot **31** the first aerial part of a plant to develop from a germinating seed **32** any new growth of a plant, such as a bud, young branch, etc **33** *chiefly Brit* a meeting or party organized for hunting game with guns **34** an area or series of coverts and woods where game can be hunted with guns **35** a steep descent in a stream; rapid **36** *informal* a photographic assignment **37** *geology, mining* a narrow workable vein of ore **38** *obsolete* the reach of a shot **39** **the whole shoot** *slang* everything ▷ *interj* **40** *US and Canadian* an exclamation expressing disbelief, scepticism, disgust, disappointment, etc ▷ See also **shoot down, shoot out, shoot through, shoot up** [Old English *sceōtan;* related to Old Norse *skjōta,* Old High German *skiozan* to shoot, Old Slavonic *iskydati* to throw out]

shootaround (ˈʃuːtəˌraʊnd) *n* *basketball* an informal match or practice session

shoot down *vb* (*tr, adverb*) **1** to shoot callously **2** to cause to fall to earth by hitting with a missile **3** to defeat or disprove: *he shot down her argument*

shoot-'em-up *or* **shoot-em-up** *n* *informal* **1** a type of computer game, the object of which is to shoot as many enemies, targets, etc, as possible **2** a fast-moving film involving many gunfights, battles, etc

shooter (ˈʃuːtə) *n* **1** a person or thing that shoots **2** *slang* a gun **3** *cricket* a ball that unexpectedly travels low on pitching

shooting box *n* a small country house providing accommodation for a shooting party during the shooting season. Also called: **shooting lodge**

shooting brake *n* *Brit* a former name for **estate car**

shooting gallery *n* **1** an area, often enclosed, designed for target practice, shooting, etc **2** *slang* a house where heroin addicts inject themselves

shooting guard *n* *basketball* the player responsible for attempting long-range shots

shooting iron *n* *US slang* a firearm, esp a pistol

shooting script *n* *films* written instructions indicating to the cameraman the order of shooting

shooting star *n* an informal name for **meteor**

shooting stick *n* a device that resembles a walking stick, having a spike at one end and a folding seat at the other

shoot out *vb* (*tr, adverb*) **1** to fight to the finish by shooting (esp in the phrase **shoot it out**) ▷ *n* **shoot-out** **2** a conclusive gunfight

shoot through *vb* (*intr, adverb*) *informal, chiefly Austral* to leave; depart

shoot up *vb* (*adverb*) **1** (*intr*) to grow or become taller very fast **2** (*tr*) to hit with a number of shots **3** (*tr*) to spread terror throughout (a place) by lawless and wanton shooting **4** (*tr*) *slang* to inject (someone, esp oneself) with (a drug, esp heroin)

shop (ʃɒp) *n* **1** a place, esp a small building, for the retail sale of goods and services **2** an act or instance of shopping, esp household shopping: *the weekly shop* **3** a place for the performance of a specified type of work; workshop **4** **all over the shop** *informal* **a** in disarray: *his papers were all over the shop* **b** in every direction: *I've searched for it all* over the shop 5 shut up shop to close business at the end of the day or permanently 6 talk shop to speak about one's work, esp when meeting socially, sometimes with the effect of excluding those not similarly employed ▷ vb shops, shopping, shopped 7 (intr; often foll by for) to visit a shop or shops in search of (goods) with the intention of buying them 8 (tr) slang, chiefly Brit to inform on or betray, esp to the police [Old English sceoppa stall, booth; related to Old High German scopf shed, Middle Dutch schoppe stall]

shopaholic (ˌʃɒpəˈhɒlɪk) n informal a compulsive shopper [C20 from SHOP + -HOLIC]
> ˌshopaˈholism n

shop around vb (intr, adverb) informal 1 to visit a number of shops or stores to compare goods and prices 2 to consider a number of possibilities before making a choice

shop assistant n a person who serves in a shop

shop floor n 1 the part of a factory housing the machines and men directly involved in production 2 a workers, esp factory workers organized in a union b (as modifier): shop-floor protest

shophar (ˈʃəʊfɑː; Hebrew ʃɔˈfar) n, pl -phars or -phroth (Hebrew -ˈfrɔt) a variant spelling of **shofar**

shopkeeper (ˈʃɒpˌkiːpə) n a person who owns or manages a shop or small store > ˈshopˌkeeping n

shoplifter (ˈʃɒpˌlɪftə) n a person who steals goods from a shop during shopping hours

shoplifting (ˈʃɒpˌlɪftɪŋ) n the act of stealing goods from a shop during shopping hours

shopper (ˈʃɒpə) n a person who buys goods in a shop

shopping (ˈʃɒpɪŋ) n 1 a number or collection of articles purchased 2 the act or an instance of making purchases

shopping bag lady n another name for **bag lady**

shopping basket n the list of items an internet shopper chooses to buy at one time from a website

shopping cart n the usual US and Canadian word for **shopping basket**

shopping centre n 1 a purpose-built complex of shops, restaurants, etc, for the use of pedestrians 2 the area of a town where most of the shops are situated

shopping mall n a large enclosed shopping centre

shopping precinct n a pedestrian area containing shops, restaurants, etc, forming a single architectural unit and usually providing car-parking facilities

shopsoiled (ˈʃɒpˌsɔɪld) adj 1 worn, faded, tarnished, etc, from being displayed in a shop or store. US word: shopworn 2 no longer new or fresh

shop steward n a coworker elected by trade union members to represent them in discussions and negotiations with the management

shoptalk (ˈʃɒpˌtɔːk) n conversation concerning one's work, esp when carried on outside business hours

shopwalker (ˈʃɒpˌwɔːkə) n Brit a person employed by a departmental store to supervise sales personnel, assist customers, etc. US equivalent: floorwalker

shopworn (ˈʃɒpˌwɔːn) adj the US word for shopsoiled

shoran (ˈʃɔːræn) n a short-range radar system by which an aircraft, ship, etc, can accurately determine its position by the time taken for a signal to be sent to two radar beacons at known locations and be returned [C20 sho(rt) ra(nge) n(avigation)]

shore¹ (ʃɔː) n 1 the land along the edge of a sea, lake, or wide river. Related adj: littoral 2 a land, as opposed to water (esp in the phrase **on shore**) b (as modifier): shore duty 3 law the tract of coastland lying between the ordinary marks of high and low water 4 (often plural) a country: his native shores ▷ vb 5 (tr) to move or drag (a boat) onto a shore [C14 probably from Middle Low German, Middle

Dutch schōre; compare Old High German scorra cliff; see SHEAR]

shore² (ʃɔː) n 1 a prop, post, or beam used to support a wall, building, ship in dry dock, etc ▷ vb 2 (tr; often foll by up) to prop or make safe with or as if with a shore [C15 from Middle Dutch schōre; related to Old Norse skortha prop] > ˈshoring n

shore³ (ʃɔː) vb Austral and NZ a past tense of **shear**

shore bird n any of various birds that live close to water, esp any bird of the families Charadriidae or Scolopacidae (plovers, sandpipers, etc). Also called (Brit): wader

shore leave n naval 1 permission to go ashore. Compare **liberty** (sense 5) 2 time spent ashore during leave

shoreless (ˈʃɔːlɪs) adj 1 without a shore suitable for landing 2 poetic boundless; vast: the shoreless wastes

shoreline (ˈʃɔːˌlaɪn) n the edge of a body of water

shore patrol n US a naval unit serving the same function as the military police

shoreward (ˈʃɔːwəd) adj 1 near or facing the shore ▷ adv also shorewards 2 towards the shore

shoreweed (ˈʃɔːˌwiːd) n a tufty aquatic perennial, Littorella uniflora, of the plantain family, that forms underwater mats but usually flowers only on muddy margins

shorn (ʃɔːn) vb a past participle of **shear**

short (ʃɔːt) adj 1 of little length; not long 2 of little height; not tall 3 of limited duration 4 not meeting a requirement; deficient: the number of places laid at the table was short by four 5 (postpositive; often foll by of or on) lacking (in) or needful (of): I'm always short of money 6 concise; succinct 7 lacking in the power of retentiveness: a short memory 8 abrupt to the point of rudeness: the salesgirl was very short with him 9 finance not possessing the securities or commodities that have been sold under contract and therefore obliged to make a purchase before the delivery date b of or relating to such sales, which depend on falling prices for profit 10 phonetics a denoting a vowel of relatively brief temporal duration b classified as short, as distinguished from other vowels. Thus in English (ɪ) in bin, though of longer duration than (iː) in beat, is nevertheless regarded as a short vowel c (in popular usage) denoting the qualities of the five English vowels represented orthographically in the words pat, pet, pit, pot, put, and putt 11 prosody a denoting a vowel that is phonetically short or a syllable containing such a vowel. In classical verse short vowels are followed by one consonant only or sometimes one consonant plus a following l or r b (of a vowel or syllable in verse that is not quantitative) not carrying emphasis or accent; unstressed 12 (of pastry) crumbly in texture. See also **shortcrust pastry** 13 (of a drink of spirits) undiluted; neat 14 **have (someone) by the short and curlies** informal to have (someone) completely in one's power 15 **in short supply** scarce 16 **short and sweet** unexpectedly brief 17 **short for** an abbreviation for ▷ adv 18 abruptly: to stop short 19 briefly or concisely 20 rudely or curtly 21 finance without possessing the securities or commodities at the time of their contractual sale: to sell short 22 **caught** or **taken short** having a sudden need to urinate or defecate 23 **fall short** a to prove inadequate b (often foll by of) to fail to reach or measure up to (a standard) 24 **go short** not to have a sufficient amount, etc 25 **short of** except: nothing short of a miracle can save him now ▷ n 26 anything that is short 27 a drink of spirits as opposed to a long drink such as beer 28 phonetics, prosody a short vowel or syllable 29 finance a a short contract or sale b a short seller 30 a short film, usually of a factual nature 31 See **short circuit** (sense 1) 32 **for short** informal as an abbreviation: he is called Jim for short 33 **in short** a as a summary b in a few words ▷ vb 34 See **short circuit** (sense 2) ▷ See also **shorts** [Old English scort; related to Old Norse skortr a lack, skera to cut,

Old High German scurz short] > ˈshortness n

short account n 1 the aggregate of short sales on an open market, esp a stock market 2 the account of a stock-market speculator who sells short

short-acting adj (of a drug) quickly effective, but requiring regularly repeated doses for long-term treatment, being rapidly absorbed, distributed in the body, and excreted. Compare **intermediate-acting, long-acting**

shortage (ˈʃɔːtɪdʒ) n a deficiency or lack in the amount needed, expected, or due; deficit

short bill n a bill of exchange that is payable at sight, on demand, or within less than ten days

shortboard (ˈʃɔːtˌbɔːd) n a type of surfboard that is shorter than standard

shortbread (ˈʃɔːtˌbrɛd) n a rich crumbly biscuit made from dough with a large proportion of butter [C19 from SHORT (in the sense: crumbly)]

shortcake (ˈʃɔːtˌkeɪk) n 1 a kind of shortbread made from a rich biscuit dough 2 a dessert made of layers of shortcake filled with fruit and cream [C16 from SHORT (in the sense: crumbly)]

short-change vb (tr) 1 to give less than correct change to 2 slang to treat unfairly or dishonestly, esp by giving less than is deserved or expected > ˌshort-ˈchanger n

short circuit n 1 a faulty or accidental connection between two points of different potential in an electric circuit, bypassing the load and establishing a path of low resistance through which an excessive current can flow. It can cause damage to the components if the circuit is not protected by a fuse ▷ vb short-circuit 2 to develop or cause to develop a short circuit 3 (tr) to bypass (a procedure, regulation, etc) 4 (tr) to hinder or frustrate (plans, etc) ▷ Sometimes (for senses 1, 2) shortened to: short

short column n a column whose relative dimensions ensure that when it is overloaded it fails by crushing, rather than buckling

shortcoming (ˈʃɔːtˌkʌmɪŋ) n a failing, defect, or deficiency

short corner n hockey another name for **penalty corner**

short covering n 1 the purchase of securities or commodities by a short seller to meet delivery requirements 2 the securities or commodities purchased

shortcrust pastry (ˈʃɔːtˌkrʌst) n a basic type of pastry that is made with half the quantity of fat to flour, and has a crisp but crumbly texture. Also called: short pastry

short cut n 1 a route that is shorter than the usual one 2 a means of saving time or effort ▷ vb short-cut -cuts, -cutting, -cut 3 (intr) to use a short cut [C16 from CUT (in the sense: a direct route)]

short-dated adj (of a gilt-edged security) having less than five years to run before redemption. Compare **medium-dated, long-dated**

short-day adj (of plants) able to flower only if exposed to short periods of daylight (less than 12 hours), each followed by a long dark period. Compare **long-day**

short division n the division of numbers, usually integers, that can be worked out mentally rather than on paper

shorten (ˈʃɔːtən) vb 1 to make or become short or shorter 2 (tr) nautical to reduce the area of (sail) 3 (tr) to make (pastry, bread, etc) short, by adding butter or another fat 4 gambling to cause (the odds) to lessen or (of odds) to become less > ˈshortener n

shortening (ˈʃɔːtənɪŋ) n butter, lard, or other fat, used in a dough, cake mixture, etc, to make the mixture short

Shorter Catechism n chiefly Presbyterian Church the more widely used and influential of two catechisms of religious instruction drawn up in 1647

shortfall (ˈʃɔːtˌfɔːl) n 1 failure to meet a goal or a requirement 2 the amount of such a failure;

S

deficiency: *a shortfall of £30m*

short fuse *n informal* a quick temper

shorthand (ˈʃɔːtˌhænd) *n* **a** a system of rapid handwriting employing simple strokes and other symbols to represent words or phrases **b** (*as modifier*): *a shorthand typist*

short-handed *adj* **1** lacking the usual or necessary number of assistants, workers, etc **2** *sport, US and Canadian* with less than the full complement of players > ˌshort-ˈhandedness *n*

shorthand typist *n Brit* a person skilled in the use of shorthand and in typing. US and Canadian name: **stenographer**

short head *n horse racing* a distance shorter than the length of a horse's head

shorthold tenancy (ˈʃɔːtˌhəʊld) *n* (in Britain) the letting of a dwelling by a nonresident private landlord for a fixed term of between one and five years at a fair rent

shorthorn (ˈʃɔːtˌhɔːn) *n* a short-horned breed of cattle with several regional varieties. Also called: **Durham**

short hundredweight *n* the full name for **hundredweight** (sense 2)

shortie *or* **shorty** (ˈʃɔːtɪ) *n* **1** *informal* **a** *pl* **shorties** a person or thing that is extremely short **b** (*as modifier*): *a shortie nightdress* **2** a Scot name for **shortbread**

short jenny *n billiards* an in-off into a middle pocket. Compare **long jenny** [from *Jenny*, pet form of *Janet*]

short leg *n cricket* **a** a fielding position on the leg side near the batsman's wicket **b** a fielder in this position

short list *chiefly Brit* ▷ *n* **1** a list of suitable applicants for a job, post, etc, from which the successful candidate will be selected ▷ *vb* (*tr*) **short-list 2** to put (someone) on a short list

short-lived *adj* living or lasting only for a short time

shortly (ˈʃɔːtlɪ) *adv* **1** in a short time; soon **2** in a few words; briefly **3** in a curt or rude manner

short metre *n* a stanza form, used esp for hymns, consisting of four lines, the third of which has eight syllables, while the rest have six

Short money *n* (in Britain) the annual payment made to Opposition parties in the House of Commons to help them pay for certain services necessary to the carrying out of their parliamentary duties; established in 1975. Compare **Cranborne money** [named after the Rt Hon Edward Short MP, Leader of the House of Commons in 1975]

short odds *pl n* (in betting) an almost even chance

short order *n chiefly US and Canadian* **a** food that is easily and quickly prepared **b** (*as modifier*): *short-order counter*

short-range *adj* of small or limited extent in time or distance: *a short-range forecast; a short-range gun*

shorts (ʃɔːts) *pl n* **1** trousers reaching the top of the thigh or partway to the knee, worn by both sexes for sport, relaxing in summer, etc **2** *chiefly US and Canadian* men's underpants that usually reach mid-thigh. Usual Brit word: **pants 3** short-dated gilt-edged securities **4** short-term bonds **5** securities or commodities that have been sold short **6** timber cut shorter than standard lengths **7** a livestock feed containing a large proportion of bran and wheat germ **8** items needed to make up a deficiency

short selling *n finance* the practice of selling commodities, securities, currencies, etc that one does not have in the expectation that falling prices will enable one to buy them in at a profit before they have to be delivered

short shrift *n* **1** brief and unsympathetic treatment **2** (formerly) a brief period allowed to a condemned prisoner to make confession **3 make short shrift of** to dispose of quickly and unsympathetically

short-sighted *adj* **1** relating to or suffering from myopia **2** lacking foresight: *a short-sighted plan* > ˌshort-ˈsightedly *adv* > ˌshort-ˈsightedness *n*

short-spoken *adj* tending to be abrupt in speech

short-staffed *adj* lacking an adequate number of staff, assistants, etc

shortstop (ˈʃɔːtˌstɒp) *n baseball* **a** the fielding position to the left of second base viewed from home plate **b** the player at this position

short story *n* a prose narrative of shorter length than the novel, esp one that concentrates on a single theme

short straw *n* **draw the short straw** be the person (as in drawing lots) to whom an unwelcome task or fate falls

short subject *n chiefly US* a short film, esp one presented between screenings of a feature film

short-tailed shearwater *n Austral* a large Australian shearwater that migrates to the northern hemisphere in the southern winter

short-tempered *adj* easily moved to anger; irascible

short-term *adj* **1** of, for, or extending over a limited period **2** *finance* extending over, maturing within, or required within a short period of time, usually twelve months: *short-term credit; short-term capital*

short-termism *n* the tendency to focus attention on short-term gains, often at the expense of long-term success or stability

short-term memory *n psychol* that section of the memory storage system of limited capacity (approximately seven items) that is capable of storing material for a brief period of time. Compare **long-term memory**

short time *or* **short-time working** *n* a system of working, usually for a temporary period, when employees are required to work and be paid for fewer than their normal hours per week due to a shortage of work

short ton *n* the full name for **ton**¹ (sense 2)

short-waisted *adj* unusually short from the shoulders to the waist

short wave *n* **a** a radio wave with a wavelength in the range 10–100 metres **b** (*as modifier*): *a short-wave broadcast*

short-winded *adj* **1** tending to run out of breath, esp after exertion **2** (of speech or writing) terse or abrupt

Shosholoza (ˌʃəʊʃəʊˈləʊzə) *n South African* a popular Zulu choral song [from Zulu, literally: move forward]

Shoshone *or* **Shoshoni** (ʃəʊˈʃəʊnɪ) *n* **1** *pl* **-nes, -ne** *or* **-nis, -ni** a member of a North American Indian people of the southwestern US, related to the Aztecs **2** the language of this people, belonging to the Uto-Aztecan family

Shoshonean *or* **Shoshonian** (ʃəʊˈʃəʊnɪən, ʃəʊʃəˈniːən) *n* a subfamily of North American Indian languages belonging to the Uto-Aztecan family, spoken mainly in the southwestern US

shot¹ (ʃɒt) *n* **1** the act or an instance of discharging a projectile **2** (*pl* **shot**) a solid missile, such as an iron ball or a lead pellet, discharged from a firearm **3 a** small round pellets of lead collectively, as used in cartridges **b** metal in the form of coarse powder or small pellets **4** the distance that a discharged projectile travels or is capable of travelling **5** a person who shoots, esp with regard to his ability: *he is a good shot* **6** *informal* an attempt; effort **7** *informal* a guess or conjecture **8** any act of throwing or hitting something, as in certain sports **9** the launching of a rocket, missile, etc, esp to a specified destination: *a moon shot* **10 a** a single photograph: *I took 16 shots of the wedding* **b** a series of frames on cine film concerned with a single event **c** a length of film taken by a single camera without breaks, used with others to build up a full motion picture or television film **11** *informal* an injection, as of a vaccine or narcotic drug **12** *informal* **a** a glass of alcoholic drink, esp spirits **13**

sport a heavy metal ball used in the shot put **14** an explosive charge used in blasting **15** globules of metal occurring in the body of a casting that are harder than the rest of the casting **16** a unit of chain length equal to 75 feet (Brit) or 90 feet (US) **17 call the shots** *slang* to have control over an organization, course of action, etc **18 have a shot at** *informal* **a** to attempt **b** *Austral* to jibe at or vex **19 like a shot** very quickly, esp willingly **20 shot in the arm** *informal* anything that regenerates, increases confidence or efficiency, etc: *his arrival was a shot in the arm for the company* **21 shot in the dark** a wild guess **22 that's the shot** *Austral informal* that is the right thing to do ▷ *vb* **shots, shotting, shotted 23** (*tr*) to weight or load with shot [Old English *scot*; related to Old Norse *skot*, Old High German *scoz* missile; see SHOOT]

shot² (ʃɒt) *vb* **1** the past tense and past participle of **shoot** ▷ *adj* **2** (of textiles) woven to give a changing colour effect: *shot silk* **3** streaked with colour **4** *slang* exhausted **5 get shot** *or* **shut of** *slang* to get rid of

shot-blasting *n* the cleaning of metal, etc, by a stream of shot

shote (ʃəʊt) *n* a variant spelling of **shoat**

shotgun (ˈʃɒtˌɡʌn) *n* **1 a** a shoulder firearm with unrifled bore designed for the discharge of small shot at short range and used mainly for hunting small game **b** (*as modifier*): *shotgun fire* **2** *American football* an offensive formation in which the quarterback lines up for a snap unusually far behind the line of scrimmage ▷ *adj* **3** *chiefly US* involving coercion or duress: *a shotgun merger* **4** *chiefly US* involving or relying on speculative suggestions, etc: *a shotgun therapy* ▷ *vb* **-guns, -gunning, -gunned 5** (*tr*) *US* to shoot or threaten with or as if with a shotgun

shotgun wedding *n informal* a wedding into which one or both partners are coerced, usually because the woman is pregnant

shot hole *n* a drilled hole into which explosive is put for blasting

shot noise *or* **effect** *n* the inherent electronic noise arising in an electric current because of the discontinuous nature of conduction by electrons. Also called: **Schottky noise** (ˈʃɒtkɪ)

shot put *n* **1** an athletic event in which contestants hurl or put a heavy metal ball or shot as far as possible **2** a single put of the shot > ˈshot-ˌputter *n*

shott *or* **chott** (ʃɒt) *n* **1** a shallow temporary salt lake or marsh in the North African desert **2** the hollow in which it lies [c19 via French *chott* from Arabic *shatt*]

shotten (ˈʃɒtᵊn) *adj* **1** (of fish, esp herring) having recently spawned **2** *archaic* worthless or undesirable [c15 from obsolete past participle of SHOOT]

shot tower *n* a building formerly used in the production of shot, in which molten lead was graded and dropped from a great height into water, thus cooling it and forming the shot

should (ʃʊd) *vb* the past tense of **shall**: used as an auxiliary verb to indicate that an action is considered by the speaker to be obligatory (*you should go*) or to form the subjunctive mood with *I* or *we* (*I should like to see you; if I should be late, go without me*) [Old English *sceold*; see SHALL]

shoulder (ˈʃəʊldə) *n* **1** the part of the vertebrate body where the arm or a corresponding forelimb joins the trunk: the pectoral girdle and associated structures **2** the joint at the junction of the forelimb with the pectoral girdle **3** a cut of meat including the upper part of the foreleg **4** *printing* the flat surface of a piece of type from which the face rises **5** *tanning* the portion of a hide covering the shoulders and neck of the animal, usually including the cheeks **6** the part of a garment that covers the shoulder **7** anything that resembles a shoulder in shape or position **8** the strip of unpaved land that borders a road **9** *engineering* a substantial projection or abrupt change in shape or diameter designed to withstand thrust **10** *photog* the portion of the characteristic curve of a photographic material indicating the maximum density that can be produced on the material **11** *jewellery* the part of a ring where the shank joins the setting **12** **a shoulder to cry on** a person one turns to for sympathy with one's troubles **13** **give (someone) the cold shoulder** *informal* **a** to treat (someone) in a cold manner; snub **b** to ignore or shun (someone) **14** **put one's shoulder to the wheel** *informal* to work very hard **15** **rub shoulders with** See **rub** (sense 11) **16** **shoulder to shoulder** **a** side by side or close together **b** in a corporate effort ▷ *vb* **17** (*tr*) to bear or carry (a burden, responsibility, etc) as if on one's shoulders **18** to push (something) with or as if with the shoulder **19** (*tr*) to lift or carry on the shoulders **20** **shoulder arms** *military* to bring the rifle vertically close to the right side with the muzzle uppermost and held at the trigger guard [Old English *sculdor;* related to Old High German *sculterra*]

shoulder blade *n* the nontechnical name for **scapula**

shoulder pad *n* a small pad inserted to raise or give shape to the shoulder of a garment

shoulder patch *n* *US military* an emblem worn high on the arm as an insignia. Also called: **shoulder flash**

shoulder strap *n* a strap over one or both of the shoulders, as to hold up a garment or to support a bag, etc

shoulder surfing *n* *informal* a form of credit-card fraud in which the perpetrator stands behind and looks over the shoulder of the victim as he or she withdraws money from an automated teller machine, memorizes the card details, and later steals the card

shouldn't (ˈʃʊdᵊnt) *vb contraction of* should not

shouldst (ʃʊdst) *or* **shouldest** (ˈʃʊdɪst) *vb archaic or dialect* (used with the pronoun *thou* or its relative equivalent) a form of the past tense of **shall**

shouse (ʃaʊs) *Austral slang* ▷ *n* **1** a toilet; lavatory ▷ *adj* **2** unwell or in poor spirits [c20 shortening of *shithouse*]

shout (ʃaʊt) *n* **1** a loud cry, esp to convey emotion or a command **2** *informal, Brit, Austral, and NZ* **a** a round, esp of drinks **b** one's turn to buy a round of drinks **3** *informal* a greeting (to family, friends, etc) sent to a radio station for broadcasting **4** *informal* an occasion on which the members of an emergency service are called out on duty ▷ *vb* **5** to utter (something) in a loud cry; yell **6** (*intr*) to make a loud noise **7** (*tr*) *Austral and NZ informal* to treat (someone) to (something), esp a drink [c14 probably from Old Norse *skūta* taunt; related to Old Norse *skjōta* to SHOOT] > ˈ**shouter** *n*

shout down *vb* (*tr, adverb*) to drown, overwhelm, or silence by shouting or talking loudly

shouty (ˈʃaʊtɪ) *adj informal* characterized by or involving shouting: *a shouty youth; shouty conversation*

shove (ʃʌv) *vb* **1** to give a thrust or push to (a person or thing) **2** (*tr*) to give a violent push to; jostle **3** (*intr*) to push one's way roughly **4** (*tr*) *informal* to put (something) somewhere, esp hurriedly or carelessly: *shove it in the bin* ▷ *n* **5** the act or an instance of shoving ▷ See also **shove off** [Old English *scūfan;* related to Old Norse *skūfa* to push, Gothic *afskiuban* to push away, Old High German *skioban* to shove] > ˈ**shover** *n*

shove-halfpenny *n* *Brit* a game in which players try to propel old halfpennies or polished discs with the hand into lined sections of a wooden or slate board

shovel (ˈʃʌvᵊl) *n* **1** an instrument for lifting or scooping loose material, such as earth, coal, etc, consisting of a curved blade or a scoop attached to a handle **2** any machine or part resembling a shovel in action **3** Also called: **shovelful** the amount that can be contained in a shovel **4** short for **shovel hat** ▷ *vb* **-els, -elling, -elled** *or US* **-els, -eling, -eled** **5** to lift (earth, etc) with a shovel **6** (*tr*) to clear or dig (a path) with or as if with a shovel **7** (*tr*) to gather, load, or unload in a hurried or careless way: *he shovelled the food into his mouth and rushed away* [Old English *scofl;* related to Old High German *scūfla* shovel, Dutch *schoffel* hoe; see SHOVE] > ˈ**shoveller** *or US* ˈ**shoveler** *n*

shovel beak *n* *vet science* a deformity of the beak in intensively reared chicks. Also called: **mandibular disease**

shoveler (ˈʃʌvələ) *n* a duck, *Anas* (or *Spatula*) *clypeata,* of ponds and marshes, having a spoon-shaped bill, a blue patch on each wing, and in the male a green head, white breast, and reddish-brown body

shovel hat *n* a black felt hat worn by some clergymen, with a brim rolled up to resemble a shovel in shape

shovelhead (ˈʃʌvᵊlˌhɛd) *n* a common shark, *Sphyrna tiburo,* of the Atlantic and Pacific Oceans, having a shovel-shaped head: family *Sphyrnidae* (hammerheads)

shovelnose (ˈʃʌvᵊlˌnəʊz) *n* an American freshwater sturgeon, *Scaphirhynchus platorynchus,* having a broad shovel-like snout

shove off *vb* (*intr, adverb; often imperative*) **1** to move from the shore in a boat **2** *informal* to go away

show (ʃəʊ) *vb* **shows, showing, showed; shown** *or* **showed** **1** to make, be, or become visible or noticeable: *to show one's dislike* **2** (*tr*) to present to view; exhibit: *he showed me a picture* **3** (*tr*) to indicate or explain; prove: *to show that the earth moves round the sun* **4** (*tr*) to exhibit or present (oneself or itself) in a specific character: *to show oneself to be trustworthy* **5** (*tr; foll by* how *and an infinitive*) to instruct by demonstration: *show me how to swim* **6** (*tr*) to indicate or register: *a barometer shows changes in the weather* **7** (*tr*) to grant or bestow: *to show favour to someone* **8** (*intr*) to appear: *to show to advantage* **9** to exhibit, display, or offer (goods, etc) for sale: *three artists were showing at the gallery* **10** (*tr*) to allege, as in a legal document: *to show cause* **11** to present (a play, film, etc) or (of a play, etc) to be presented, as at a theatre or cinema **12** (*tr*) to guide or escort: *please show me to my room* **13** **show in** *or* **out** to conduct a person into or out of a room or building by opening the door for him **14** (*intr*) to win a place in a horse race, etc **15** to give a performance of riding and handling (a horse) to display its best points **16** (*intr*) *informal* to put in an appearance; arrive ▷ *n* **17** a display or exhibition **18** a public spectacle **19** an ostentatious or pretentious display **20** a theatrical or other entertainment **21** a trace or indication **22** *obstetrics* a discharge of blood at the onset of labour **23** *US, Austral, and NZ informal* a chance; opportunity (esp in the phrases **give someone a show, he's got no show of winning,** etc) **24** a sporting event consisting of contests in which riders perform different exercises to show their skill and their horses' ability and breeding **25** *slang, chiefly Brit* a thing or affair (esp in the phrases **good show, bad show,** etc) **26** *Austral and NZ mining* a slight indication of the presence of gold **27** a display of farm animals, with associated competitions **28** **for show** in order to attract attention **29** **run the show** *informal* to take charge of or manage an affair, business, etc **30** **steal the show** to draw the most attention or admiration, esp unexpectedly **31** **stop the show** *informal* **a** (of a stage act, etc) to receive so much applause as to interrupt the performance **b** to be received with great enthusiasm ▷ See also **show off, show up** [Old English *scēawian;* related to Old High German *scouwōn* to look, Old Norse *örskār* careful, Greek *thuoskoos* seer]

show bill *n* a poster advertising a play or show. Also called: **show card**

showboat (ˈʃəʊˌbəʊt) *n* **1** a paddle-wheel river steamer with a theatre and a repertory company ▷ *vb* **2** (*intr*) to perform or behave in a showy and flamboyant way

showbread (ˈʃəʊˌbrɛd) *n* a variant spelling of **shewbread**

show business *n* the entertainment industry, including theatre, films, television, and radio. Informal term: **show biz**

show card *n* **1** *commerce* a tradesman's advertisement mounted on card as a poster **2** another term for **show bill**

showcase (ˈʃəʊˌkeɪs) *n* **1** a glass case used to display objects in a museum or shop **2** a setting in which anything may be displayed to best advantage ▷ *vb* **3** (*tr*) to exhibit or display ▷ *adj* **4** displayed or meriting display as in a showcase

show copy *n* *films* a positive print of a film for use at an important presentation such as a premiere

showd (ʃaʊd) *Northeast Scot dialect* ▷ *vb* **1** (*intr*) to rock or sway to and fro **2** (*tr*) to rock (a baby in one's arms or in a pram) ▷ *n* **3** a rocking motion [from Old English *scūdan* to shake]

show day *n* (in Australia) a public holiday in a state on the date of its annual agricultural and industrial show

showdown (ˈʃəʊˌdaʊn) *n* **1** *informal* an action that brings matters to a head or acts as a conclusion or point of decision **2** *poker* the exposing of the cards in the players' hands on the table at the end of the game

shower[1] (ˈʃaʊə) *n* **1** a brief period of rain, hail, sleet, or snow **2** a sudden abundant fall or downpour, as of tears, sparks, or light **3** a rush; outpouring: *a shower of praise* **4** **a** a kind of bath in which a person stands upright and is sprayed with water from a nozzle **b** the room, booth, etc, containing such a bath. Full name: **shower bath** **5** *Brit slang* a derogatory term applied to a person or group, esp to a group considered as being slack, untidy, etc **6** *US, Canadian, Austral, and NZ* a party held to honour and present gifts to a person, as to a prospective bride **7** a large number of particles formed by the collision of a cosmic-ray particle with a particle in the atmosphere **8** *NZ* a light fabric cover thrown over a tea table to protect the food from flies, dust, etc ▷ *vb* **9** (*tr*) to sprinkle or spray with or as if with a shower: *shower the powder into the milk* **10** (often with *it* as subject) to fall or cause to fall in the form of a shower **11** (*tr*) to give (gifts, etc) in abundance or present (a person) with (gifts, etc): *they showered gifts on him* **12** (*intr*) to take a shower [Old English *scūr;* related to Old Norse *skūr,* Old High German *skūr* shower, Latin *caurus* northwest wind] > ˈ**showery** *adj*

shower[2] (ˈʃəʊə) *n* a person or thing that shows

showerproof (ˈʃaʊəˌpruːf) *adj* (of a garment, etc) resistant to or partly impervious to rain > ˈ**showerˌproofing** *n*

showgirl (ˈʃəʊˌgɜːl) *n* a girl who appears in variety shows, nightclub acts, etc, esp as a singer or dancer

showground (ˈʃəʊˌgraʊnd) *n* an open-air setting for agricultural displays, competitions, etc. Also called (Austral and NZ): **showgrounds**

show house *n* a house on a new estate that is decorated and furnished for prospective buyers to view

showing (ˈʃəʊɪŋ) *n* **1** a presentation, exhibition, or display **2** manner of presentation; performance **3** evidence

showjumping (ˈʃəʊˌdʒʌmpɪŋ) *n* the riding of

S

horses in competitions to demonstrate skill in jumping over or between various obstacles > 'show-jumper n

showman ('ʃəʊmən) n, pl -men **1** a person who presents or produces a theatrical show, etc **2** a person skilled at presenting anything in an effective manner > 'showmanship n

shown (ʃəʊn) vb a past participle of **show**

show off vb (adverb) **1** (tr) to exhibit or display so as to invite admiration **2** (intr) informal to behave in such a manner as to make an impression ▷ n **show-off 3** informal a person who makes a vain display of himself

show of hands n the raising of hands to indicate voting for or against a proposition

showpiece ('ʃəʊ,piːs) n **1** anything displayed or exhibited **2** anything prized as a very fine example of its type

showplace ('ʃəʊ,pleɪs) n a place exhibited or visited for its beauty, historic interest, etc

show pony n informal a person who tries to be the centre of attention; show-off

showroom ('ʃəʊ,ruːm, -,rʊm) n a room in which goods, such as cars, are on display

show stopper n informal a stage act, etc, that receives so much applause as to interrupt the performance

show trial n a trial conducted primarily to make a particular impression on the public or on other nations, esp one that demonstrates the power of the state over the individual

show up vb (adverb) **1** to reveal or be revealed clearly **2** (tr) to expose or reveal the faults or defects of by comparison **3** (tr) informal to put to shame; embarrass: *he showed me up in front of my friends* **4** (intr) informal to appear or arrive

showy ('ʃəʊɪ) adj showier, showiest **1** gaudy, flashy, or ostentatious **2** making a brilliant or imposing display > 'showily adv > 'showiness n

shoyu ('ʃəʊ,juː) n a Japanese variety of soy sauce [c18 Japanese]

shpt abbreviation for shipment

shrank (ʃræŋk) vb a past tense of **shrink**

shrapnel ('ʃræpnᵊl) n **1 a** a projectile containing a number of small pellets or bullets exploded before impact **b** such projectiles collectively **2** fragments from this or any other type of shell [c19 named after H. Shrapnel (1761–1842), English army officer, who invented it]

shred (ʃrɛd) n **1** a long narrow strip or fragment torn or cut off **2** a very small piece or amount; scrap ▷ vb shreds, shredding, shredded or shred **3** (tr) to tear or cut into shreds [Old English scread; related to Old Norse skrjöthr torn-up book, Old High German scrōt cut-off piece; see SCROLL, SHROUD, SCREED] > 'shredder n

Shreveport ('ʃriːv,pɔːt) n a city in NW Louisiana, on the Red River: centre of an oil and natural-gas region. Pop: 198 364 (2003 est)

shrew (ʃruː) n **1** Also called: shrewmouse any small mouse-like long-snouted mammal, such as *Sorex araneus* (**common shrew**), of the family *Soricidae*: order *Insectivora* (insectivores). See also **water shrew**. Related adj: **soricine 2** a bad-tempered or mean-spirited woman [Old English scrēawa; related to Old High German scrawaz dwarf, Icelandic skröggr old man, Norwegian skrugg dwarf]

shrewd (ʃruːd) adj **1** astute and penetrating, often with regard to business **2** artful and crafty: *a shrewd politician* **3** obsolete **a** piercing: *a shrewd wind* **b** spiteful [c14 from shrew (obsolete vb) to curse, from SHREW] > 'shrewdly adv > 'shrewdness n

shrewdie ('ʃruːdɪ) n Austral and NZ informal a shrewd person [c20 from SHREWD + -IE]

shrewish ('ʃruːɪʃ) adj (esp of a woman) bad-tempered and nagging > 'shrewishly adv > 'shrewishness n

shrew mole n any of several moles, such as *Uropsilus soricipes* of E Asia or *Neurotrichus gibbsi* of E North America, having a long snout and long tail

shrewmouse ('ʃruː,maʊs) n, pl -mice another name for **shrew,** esp the common shrew

Shrewsbury ('ʃrəʊzbərɪ, -brɪ, 'ʃruːz-) n a town in W central England, administrative centre of Shropshire, on the River Severn: strategically situated near the Welsh border; market town. Pop: 67 126 (2001)

shriek (ʃriːk) n **1** a shrill and piercing cry ▷ vb **2** to produce or utter (words, sounds, etc) in a shrill piercing tone [c16 probably from Old Norse skrækja to SCREECH¹] > 'shrieker n

shrieval ('ʃriːvᵊl) adj of or relating to a sheriff

shrievalty ('ʃriːvᵊltɪ) n, pl -ties **1** the office or term of office of a sheriff **2** the jurisdiction of a sheriff [c16 from SHRIEVE, on the model of mayoralty]

shrieve (ʃriːv) n an archaic word for **sheriff**

shrift (ʃrɪft) n archaic the act or an instance of shriving or being shriven. See also **short shrift** [Old English scrift, from Latin scriptum SCRIPT]

shrike (ʃraɪk) n **1** Also called: butcherbird any songbird of the chiefly Old World family *Laniidae*, having a heavy hooked bill and feeding on smaller animals which they sometimes impale on thorns, barbed wire, etc. See also **bush shrike** (sense 1) **2** any of various similar but unrelated birds, such as the cuckoo shrikes **3** shrike thrush or tit another name for **thickhead** (the bird) [Old English scrīc thrush; related to Middle Dutch schrīk corncrake; see SCREECH¹, SHRIEK]

shrill (ʃrɪl) adj **1** sharp and high-pitched in quality **2** emitting a sharp high-pitched sound ▷ vb **3** to utter (words, sounds, etc) in a shrill tone **4** (tr) rare to cause to produce a shrill sound [c14 probably from Old English scralletan; related to German schrill shrill, Dutch schrallen to shriek] > 'shrillness n > 'shrilly adv

shrimp (ʃrɪmp) n **1** any of various chiefly marine decapod crustaceans of the genus *Crangon* and related genera, having a slender flattened body with a long tail and a single pair of pincers **2** any of various similar but unrelated crustaceans, such as the opossum shrimp and mantis shrimp **3** Also called: freshwater shrimp any of various freshwater shrimplike amphipod crustaceans of the genus *Gammarus*, esp *G. pulex* **4** Also called: sand shrimp any of various shrimplike amphipod crustaceans of the genus *Gammarus*, esp *G. locusta*. See also **opossum shrimp 5** informal a diminutive person, esp a child ▷ vb **6** (intr) to fish for shrimps [c14 probably of Germanic origin; compare Middle Low German schrempen to shrink; see SCRIMP, CRIMP] > 'shrimper n

shrine (ʃraɪn) n **1** a place of worship hallowed by association with a sacred person or object **2** a container for sacred relics **3** the tomb of a saint or other holy person **4** a place or site venerated for its association with a famous person or event **5** RC Church a building, alcove, or shelf arranged as a setting for a statue, picture, or other representation of Christ, the Virgin Mary, or a saint ▷ vb **6** short for **enshrine** [Old English scrīn, from Latin scrīnium bookcase; related to Old Norse skrin, Old High German skrīni] > 'shrine,like adj

shrink (ʃrɪŋk) vb shrinks, shrinking; shrank or shrunk; shrunk or shrunken **1** to contract or cause to contract as from wetness, heat, cold, etc **2** to become or cause to become smaller in size **3** (intr; often foll by from) **a** to recoil or withdraw: *to shrink from the sight of blood* **b** to feel great reluctance (at): *to shrink from killing an animal* ▷ n **4** the act or an instance of shrinking **5** a slang word for **psychiatrist** [Old English scrincan; related to Old Norse skrokkr torso, Old Swedish skrunkin wrinkled, Old Norse hrukka a crease, Icelandic skrukka wrinkled woman] > 'shrinkable adj > 'shrinker n > 'shrinking adj > 'shrinkingly adv

shrinkage ('ʃrɪŋkɪdʒ) n **1** the act or fact of shrinking **2** the amount by which anything decreases in size, value, weight, etc **3** the loss in body weight during shipment and preparation of livestock for marketing as meat **4** the loss of merchandise in a retail store through theft or damage

shrink fit n engineering a tight fit of a collar or wheel boss on a shaft obtained by expanding the collar or boss by heating to enable it to be threaded onto the shaft and then allowing it to cool, or by freezing the shaft to reduce its diameter to enable it to be threaded into the collar or boss and then allowing the shaft temperature to rise

shrinking violet n informal a shy person

shrink-wrap vb -wraps, -wrapping, -wrapped (tr) to package (a product) in a flexible plastic wrapping designed to shrink about its contours to protect and seal it

shrive (ʃraɪv) vb shrives, shriving; shrove or shrived; shriven ('ʃrɪvᵊn) or shrived chiefly RC Church **1** to hear the confession of (a penitent) **2** (tr) to impose a penance upon (a penitent) and grant him sacramental absolution **3** (intr) to confess one's sins to a priest in order to obtain sacramental forgiveness [Old English scrīfan, from Latin scrībere to write] > 'shriver n

shrivel ('ʃrɪvᵊl) vb -els, -elling, -elled or US -els, -eling, -eled **1** to make or become shrunken and withered **2** to lose or cause to lose vitality [c16 probably of Scandinavian origin; compare Swedish dialect skryvla wrinkle]

shroff (ʃrɒf) n **1** (in China, Japan, etc, esp formerly) an expert employed to separate counterfeit money or base coin from the genuine **2** (in India) a moneychanger or banker ▷ vb **3** (tr) to test (money) and separate out the counterfeit and base [c17 from Portuguese xarrafo, from Hindi sarrāf moneychanger, from Arabic]

shroom (ʃruːm, ʃrʊm) slang ▷ n **1** short for **magic mushroom** ▷ vb (intr) **2** to take magic mushrooms for their intoxicating effects [c21 shortening of MUSHROOM] > 'shroomer n

Shropshire ('ʃrɒpʃɪə, -ʃə) n **1** a county of W central England: Telford and Wrekin became an independent unitary authority in 1998; mainly agricultural. Administrative centre: Shrewsbury. Pop (excluding Telford and Wrekin): 286 700 (2003 est). Area (excluding Telford and Wrekin): 3201 sq km (1236 sq miles) **2** a breed of medium-sized sheep having a dense fleece, originating from Shropshire and Staffordshire, England

shroud (ʃraʊd) n **1** a garment or piece of cloth used to wrap a dead body **2** anything that envelops like a garment: *a shroud of mist* **3** a protective covering for a piece of equipment **4** astronautics a streamlined protective covering used to protect the payload during a rocket-powered launch **5** nautical one of a pattern of ropes or cables used to stay a mast **6** any of a set of wire cables stretched between a smokestack or similar structure and the ground, to prevent side sway **7** Also called: shroud line any of a set of lines running from the canopy of a parachute to the harness ▷ vb **8** (tr) to wrap in a shroud **9** (tr) to cover, envelop, or hide **10** archaic to seek or give shelter [Old English scrūd garment; related to Old Norse skrūth gear] > 'shroudless adj

shroud-laid adj (of a rope) made with four strands twisted to the right, usually around a core

shrove (ʃrəʊv) vb a past tense of **shrive**

Shrovetide ('ʃrəʊv,taɪd) n the Sunday, Monday, and Tuesday before Ash Wednesday, formerly a time when confessions were made in preparation for Lent

Shrove Tuesday n the last day of Shrovetide; Pancake Day

shrub¹ (ʃrʌb) n a woody perennial plant, smaller than a tree, with several major branches arising from near the base of the main stem [Old English scrybb; related to Middle Low German schrubben coarse, uneven, Old Swedish skrubba to SCRUB¹] > 'shrub,like adj

shrub² (ʃrʌb) n **1** a mixed drink of rum, fruit juice, sugar, and spice **2** mixed fruit juice, sugar, and spice made commercially to be mixed with rum or other spirits [c18 from Arabic sharāb, variant of shurb drink; see SHERBET]

shrubbery ('ʃrʌbərɪ) *n, pl* **-beries** **1** a place where a number of shrubs are planted **2** shrubs collectively

shrubby ('ʃrʌbɪ) *adj* **-bier, -biest** **1** consisting of, planted with, or abounding in shrubs **2** resembling a shrub > **'shrubbiness** *n*

shrub layer *n* See **layer** (sense 2)

shrug (ʃrʌg) *vb* **shrugs, shrugging, shrugged** **1** to draw up and drop (the shoulders) abruptly in a gesture expressing indifference, contempt, ignorance, etc ▷ *n* **2** the gesture so made **3** a woman's short jacket or close-fitting cardigan [C14 of uncertain origin]

shrug off *vb* (*tr, adverb*) **1** to minimize the importance of; dismiss **2** to get rid of **3** to wriggle out of or push off (clothing)

shrunk (ʃrʌŋk) *vb* a past participle and past tense of **shrink**

shrunken ('ʃrʌŋk^{ə}n) *vb* **1** a past participle of **shrink** ▷ *adj* **2** (*usually prenominal*) reduced in size: *a shrunken head*

shtetl ('ʃtet^{ə}l) *n, pl* **shtetlach** ('ʃtetla:x) *or* **shtetls** (formerly) a small Jewish community in Eastern Europe [Yiddish, little town]

shtick (ʃtɪk) *or* **schtick** *n slang* a comedian's routine; act; piece [C20 from Yiddish *shtik* piece, from Middle High German *stücke*]

shtoom (ʃtʊm) *adj slang* silent; dumb (esp in the phrase **keep shtoom**) [from Yiddish, from German *stumm* silent]

S-HTTP *abbreviation for computing* secure hypertext transfer protocol: a way of transmitting individual messages securely over the internet

Shuar (ʃwa:) *n* **1** the name the Jivaro people of the Ecuadorian and Peruvian Amazon have for themselves **2** any of the languages spoken by the Shuar people. See **Jivaro** [from Shuar *shuar* people]

shuck (ʃʌk) *n* **1** the outer covering of something, such as the husk of a grain of maize, a pea pod, or an oyster shell ▷ *vb* (*tr*) **2** to remove the shucks from **3** *informal, chiefly US and Canadian* to throw off or remove (clothes, etc) [C17 American dialect, of unknown origin] > **'shucker** *n*

shucks (ʃʌks) *US and Canadian informal* ▷ *pl n* **1** something of little value (esp in the phrase **not worth shucks**) ▷ *interj* **2** an exclamation of disappointment, annoyance, etc

shudder ('ʃʌdə) *vb* **1** (*intr*) to shake or tremble suddenly and violently, as from horror, fear, aversion, etc ▷ *n* **2** the act of shuddering; convulsive shiver [C18 from Middle Low German *schōderen;* related to Old Frisian *skedda* to shake, Old High German *skutten* to shake] > **'shuddering** *adj* > **'shudderingly** *adv* > **'shuddery** *adj*

shuffle ('ʃʌf^{ə}l) *vb* **1** to walk or move (the feet) with a slow dragging motion **2** to change the position of (something), esp quickly or in order to deceive others **3** (*tr*) to mix together in a careless manner: *he shuffled the papers nervously* **4** to mix up (cards in a pack) to change their order **5** (*intr*) to behave in an awkward, evasive, or underhand manner; equivocate **6** (when *intr*, often foll by *into* or *out of*) to move or cause to move clumsily: *he shuffled out of the door* **7** (*intr*) to dance the shuffle ▷ *n* **8** the act or an instance of shuffling **9** a dance or dance step with short dragging movements of the feet [C16 probably from Low German *schüffeln;* see SHOVE] > **'shuffler** *n*

shuffleboard ('ʃʌf^{ə}l,bɔ:d) *n* **1** a game in which players push wooden or plastic discs with a long cue towards numbered scoring sections marked on a floor, esp a ship's deck **2** the marked area on which this game is played

shuffle off *vb* (*tr, adverb*) to thrust off or put aside: *shuffle off responsibility*

shuffle play *n* a facility on a compact disc player that randomly selects a track from one of a number of compact discs

shufty *or* **shufti** ('ʃʊftɪ, 'ʃʌftɪ) *n, pl* **-ties** *Brit slang* a look; peep [C20 from Arabic]

Shufu *or* **Sufu** ('ʃu:'fu:) *n* transliteration of the Chinese name for **Kashi**

shuggy ('ʃʌgɪ) *n, pl* **-gies** *Northeastern English dialect* a swing, as at a fairground [from *shog, shug* to shake; see SHOOGLE]

shul *or* **schul** (ʃu:l) *n* the Yiddish word for **synagogue** [Yiddish: synagogue, from Old High German *scuola* SCHOOL[1]]

Shulamite ('ʃu:lə,maɪt) *n Old Testament* an epithet of uncertain meaning applied to the bride in the Song of Solomon 6:13

Shulchan Aruch (ʃʊl'xɑn ɑr'ʊx, 'ʃʊlxən 'aʊrəx) *n* the main codification of Jewish law derived from the Talmud, compiled by the 16th-century rabbi, Joseph Caro

shun (ʃʌn) *vb* **shuns, shunning, shunned** (*tr*) to avoid deliberately; keep away from [Old English *scunian,* of obscure origin] > **'shunnable** *adj* > **'shunner** *n*

'shun (ʃʌn) *interj military* a clipped form of **attention** (sense 7)

shunt (ʃʌnt) *vb* **1** to turn or cause to turn to one side; move or be moved aside **2** *railways* to transfer (rolling stock) from track to track **3** *electronics* to divert or be diverted through a shunt **4** (*tr*) to evade by putting off onto someone else **5** (*tr*) *motor racing slang* to crash (a car) ▷ *n* **6** the act or an instance of shunting **7** a railway point **8** *electronics* a low-resistance conductor connected in parallel across a device, circuit, or part of a circuit to provide an alternative path for a known fraction of the current **9** *med* a channel that bypasses the normal circulation of the blood: a congenital abnormality or surgically induced **10** *Brit informal* a collision which occurs when a vehicle runs into the back of the vehicle in front [C13 perhaps from *shunen* to SHUN]

shunter ('ʃʌntə) *n* a small railway locomotive used for manoeuvring coaches rather than for making journeys

shunt-wound ('ʃʌnt,waʊnd) *adj electrical engineering* (of a motor or generator) having the field and armature circuits connected in parallel. Compare **series-wound**

shura *or* **shoora** ('ʃʊərə) *n* **1** *Islam* a consultative council or assembly **2** *Islam* the process of decision-making by consultation and deliberation [from Arabic *shūrā*, literally: consultation]

shush (ʃʊʃ) *interj* **1** be quiet! hush! ▷ *vb* **2** to silence or calm (someone) by or as if by saying "shush" [C20 reduplication of SH, influenced by HUSH[1]]

Shushan ('ʃu:ʃæn) *n* the Biblical name for **Susa**

shut (ʃʌt) *vb* **shuts, shutting, shut** **1** to move (something) so as to cover an aperture; close: *to shut a door* **2** to close (something) by bringing together the parts: *to shut a book* **3** (*tr; often foll by up*) to close or lock the doors of: *to shut up a house* **4** (*tr; foll by in, out, etc*) to confine, enclose, or exclude: *to shut a child in a room* **5** (*tr*) to prevent (a business, etc) from operating **6** **shut one's eyes to** to ignore deliberately **7** **shut the door on** **a** to refuse to think about **b** to render impossible ▷ *adj* **8** closed or fastened ▷ *n* **9** the act or time of shutting **10** the line along which pieces of metal are welded **11** **get shut** *or* **shot of** *slang* to get rid of ▷ See also **shutdown, shut-off, shutout, shut up** [Old English *scyttan;* related to Old Frisian *sketta* to shut in, Middle Dutch *schutten* to obstruct]

shutdown ('ʃʌt,daʊn) *n* **1** **a** the closing of a factory, shop, etc **b** (*as modifier*): *shutdown costs* ▷ *vb* **shut down** (*adverb*) **2** to cease or cause to cease operation **3** (*tr*) to close by lowering **4** (*tr*) (of fog) to descend and envelop **5** (*intr; foll by on or upon*) *informal* to put a stop to; clamp down on **6** (*tr*) to reduce the power level of (a nuclear reactor) to the lowest possible value

shuteye ('ʃʌt,aɪ) *n* an informal term for **sleep**

shut-in *n* **1** *chiefly US and Canadian* **a** a person confined indoors by illness **b** (*as modifier*): *a shut-in patient* **2** *psychiatry* a condition in which the person is highly withdrawn and unable to express his own feelings. See also **schizoid**

shut-off *n* **1** a device that shuts something off, esp a machine control **2** a stoppage or cessation ▷ *vb* **shut off** (*tr, adverb*) **3** to stem the flow of **4** to block off the passage through **5** to isolate or separate

shutout ('ʃʌt,aʊt) *n* **1** a less common word for a **lockout** **2** *sport* a game in which the opposing team does not score ▷ *vb* **shut out** (*tr, adverb*) **3** to keep out or exclude **4** to conceal from sight: *we planted trees to shut out the view of the road* **5** to prevent (an opponent) from scoring

shut-out bid *n bridge* a pre-emptive bid

shutter ('ʃʌtə) *n* **1** a hinged doorlike cover, often louvred and usually one of a pair, for closing off a window **2** **put up the shutters** to close business at the end of the day or permanently **3** *photog* an opaque shield in a camera that, when tripped, admits light to expose the film or plate for a predetermined period, usually a fraction of a second. It is either built into the lens system or lies in the focal plane of the lens (**focal-plane shutter**) **4** *photog* a rotating device in a film projector that permits an image to be projected onto the screen only when the film is momentarily stationary **5** *music* one of the louvred covers over the mouths of organ pipes, operated by the swell pedal **6** a person or thing that shuts ▷ *vb* (*tr*) **7** to close with or as if with a shutter or shutters **8** to equip with a shutter or shutters

shuttering ('ʃʌtərɪŋ) *n* another word (esp Brit) for **formwork**

shutter priority *n photog* an automatic exposure system in which the photographer selects the shutter speed and the camera then automatically sets the correct aperture. Compare **aperture priority**

shuttle ('ʃʌt^{ə}l) *n* **1** a bobbin-like device used in weaving for passing the weft thread between the warp threads **2** a small bobbin-like device used to hold the thread in a sewing machine or in tatting, knitting, etc **3** **a** a bus, train, aircraft, etc, that plies between two points, esp one that offers a frequent service over a short route **b** short for **space shuttle** **4** **a** the movement between various countries of a diplomat in order to negotiate with rulers who refuse to meet each other **b** (*as modifier*): *shuttle diplomacy* **5** *badminton* short for **shuttlecock** ▷ *vb* **6** to move or cause to move by or as if by a shuttle [Old English *scytel* bolt; related to Middle High German *schüzzel,* Swedish *skyttel.* See SHOOT, SHOT]

shuttle armature *n* a simple H-shaped armature used in small direct-current motors

shuttlecock ('ʃʌt^{ə}l,kɒk) *n* **1** a light cone consisting of a cork stub with feathered flights, struck to and fro in badminton and battledore. Often shortened to: **shuttle** **2** anything moved to and fro, as in an argument ▷ *vb* **3** to move or cause to move to and fro, like a shuttlecock [C16 from SHUTTLE + COCK[1]]

shut up *vb* (*adverb*) **1** (*tr*) to prevent all access to **2** (*tr*) to confine or imprison **3** *informal* to cease to talk or make a noise or cause to cease to talk or make a noise: often used in commands **4** (*intr*) (of horses in a race) to cease through exhaustion from maintaining a racing pace

shwa (ʃwa:) *n* a variant spelling of **schwa**

shwe-shwe *or* **shweshwe** ('ʃwɛʃwɛ) *n South African* an African cotton print fabric

shy[1] (ʃaɪ) *adj* **shyer, shyest** *or* **shier, shiest** **1** not at ease in the company of others **2** easily frightened; timid **3** (often foll by *of*) watchful or wary **4** *poker* (of a player) without enough money to back his bet **5** (of plants and animals) not breeding or producing offspring freely **6** (foll by *of*) *informal, chiefly US and Canadian* short (of) **7** (*in combination*) showing reluctance or disinclination: *workshy* ▷ *vb* **shies, shying, shied** (*intr*) **8** to move suddenly, as from fear: *the horse shied at the snake in the road* **9** (usually foll by *off* or *away*) to draw back; recoil ▷ *n, pl* **shies** **10** a sudden movement, as from fear [Old English *sceoh;* related to Old High

S

German *sciuhen* to frighten away, Dutch *schuw* shy, Swedish *skygg*] > 'shyer *n* > 'shyly *adv* > 'shyness *n*

shy² (ʃaɪ) *vb* **shies, shying, shied 1** to throw (something) with a sideways motion ▷ *n, pl* **shies 2** a quick throw **3** *informal* a gibe **4** *informal* an attempt; experiment **5** short for **cockshy** [c18 of Germanic origin; compare Old High German *sciuhen* to make timid, Middle Dutch *schüchteren* to chase away] > 'shyer *n*

Shylock ('ʃaɪˌlɒk) *n* a heartless or demanding creditor [c19 after *Shylock*, the name of the heartless usurer in Shakespeare's *The Merchant of Venice* (1596)]

shypoo (ʃaɪ'puː) *n Austral informal* **a** liquor of poor quality **b** a place where this is sold **c** (*as modifier*): *a shypoo shanty* [c20 of uncertain origin]

shyster ('ʃaɪstə) *n informal, chiefly US* a person, esp a lawyer or politician, who uses discreditable or unethical methods [c19 probably based on *Scheuster*, name of a disreputable 19th-century New York lawyer]

si¹ (siː) *n music* a variant of **te**

si² *the internet domain name for* Slovenia

Si¹ (ʃiː) *or* **Si Kiang** *n* a variant transliteration of the Chinese name for the **Xi**

Si² *the chemical symbol for* silicon

SI 1 *symbol for* Système International (d'Unités). See **SI unit 2** *NZ abbreviation for* South Island

sial ('saɪəl) *n* the silicon-rich and aluminium-rich rocks of the earth's continental upper crust, the most abundant individual rock being granite [c20 *si(licon)* + *al(uminium)*] > **sialic** ('saɪlɪk) *adj*

sialagogue *or* **sialogogue** ('saɪələˌɡɒɡ, saɪ'ælə,ɡɒɡ) *n med* any drug or agent that can stimulate the flow of saliva [c18 from New Latin *sialagōgus*, from Greek *sialon* saliva + -AGOGUE] > **sialagogic** *or* **sialogogic** (ˌsaɪələ'ɡɒdʒɪk) *adj*

Sialkot (sɪ'ælkɒt) *n* a city in NE Pakistan: shrine of Guru Nanak. Pop: 487 000 (2005 est)

sialoid ('saɪəˌlɔɪd) *adj* resembling saliva [from Greek *sialon* saliva + -OID]

Siam (saɪ'æm, 'saɪæm) *n* **1** the former name (until 1939 and 1945–49) of **Thailand 2 Gulf of** an arm of the South China Sea between the Malay Peninsula and Indochina

siamang ('saɪəˌmæŋ) *n* a large black gibbon, *Hylobates* (or *Symphalangus*) *syndactylus*, of Sumatra and the Malay Peninsula, having a large reddish-brown vocal sac beneath the chin and the second and third toes united [c19 from Malay]

Siamese (ˌsaɪə'miːz) *n, pl* **-mese 1** See **Siamese cat** ▷ *adj* **2** characteristic of, relating to, or being a Siamese twin ▷ *adj* ▷ *n* **3** another word for **Thai**

Siamese cat *n* a short-haired breed of cat with a tapering tail, blue eyes, and dark ears, mask, tail, and paws [so called because the breed is believed to have originated in SIAM]

Siamese fighting fish *n* a brightly coloured labyrinth fish, *Betta splendens*, of Thailand and Malaysia, having large sail-like fins: the males are very pugnacious

Siamese twins *pl n* non-technical name for **conjoined twins** [c19 named after a famous pair of conjoined twins, Chang and Eng (1811–74), who were born in SIAM]

Sian (ʃja:n) *n* a variant transliteration of the Chinese name for **Xi'an**

Siang (ʃja:ŋ) *n* a variant transliteration of the Chinese name for the **Xiang**

Siangtan ('ʃja:ŋ'ta:n) *n* a variant transliteration of the Chinese name for **Xiangtan**

sib (sɪb) *n* **1** a blood relative **2** a brother or sister; sibling **3** kinsmen collectively; kindred **4** any social unit that is bonded by kinship through one line of descent only [Old English *sibb*; related to Old Norse *sifjar* relatives, Old High German *sippa* kinship, Latin *suus* one's own; see GOSSIP]

SIB (in Britain) *abbreviation for* (the former) **Securities and Investments Board**

Siberia (saɪ'bɪərɪə) *n* a vast region of Russia and N Kazakhstan: extends from the Ural Mountains to the Pacific and from the Arctic Ocean to the

borders with China and Mongolia; colonized after the building of the Trans-Siberian Railway. Area: 13 807 037 sq km (5 330 896 sq miles)

Siberian (saɪ'bɪərɪən) *adj* **1** of or relating to Siberia or its inhabitants ▷ *n* **2** a native or inhabitant of Siberia

Siberian forest cat *n* a breed of powerfully-built long-haired cat, typically tabby with a white ruff and white paws

sibilant ('sɪbɪlənt) *adj phonetics* **1** relating to or denoting the consonants (s, z, ʃ, ʒ), all pronounced with a characteristic hissing sound **2** having a hissing sound: *the sibilant sound of wind among the leaves* ▷ *n* **3** a sibilant consonant [c17 from Latin *sībilāre* to hiss, of imitative origin; compare Greek *sizein* to hiss] > 'sibilance *or* 'sibilancy *n* > 'sibilantly *adv*

sibilate ('sɪbɪˌleɪt) *vb* to pronounce or utter (words or speech) with a hissing sound > ˌsibi'lation *n*

Sibiu (Romanian si'biu) *n* an industrial town in W central Romania: originally a Roman city, refounded by German colonists in the 12th century. Pop: 133 000 (2005 est). German name: Hermannstadt. Hungarian name: Nagyszeben

sibling ('sɪblɪŋ) *n* **1 a** a person's brother or sister **b** (*as modifier*): *sibling rivalry* **2** any fellow member of a sib [c19 specialized meaning of Old English *sibling* relative, from SIB; see -LING¹]

sibship ('sɪbʃɪp) *n* a group of children of the same parents

sibyl ('sɪbɪl) *n* **1** (in ancient Greece and Rome) any of a number of women believed to be oracles or prophetesses, one of the most famous being the sibyl of Cumae, who guided Aeneas through the underworld **2** a witch, fortune-teller, or sorceress [c13 ultimately from Greek *Sibulla*, of obscure origin] > **sibylline** ('sɪbɪˌlaɪn, sɪ'bɪlaɪn) *or* **sibyllic**, **sibylic** (sɪ'bɪlɪk) *adj*

Sibylline Books *pl n* (in ancient Rome) a collection of prophetic sayings, supposedly bought from the Cumaean sibyl, bearing upon Roman policy and religion

sic¹ (sɪk) *adv* so or thus: inserted in brackets in a written or printed text to indicate that an odd or questionable reading is what was actually written or printed [Latin]

sic² (sɪk) *vb* **sics, sicking, sicked** (*tr*) **1** to turn on or attack: used only in commands, as to a dog **2** to urge (a dog) to attack [c19 dialect variant of SEEK]

sic³ (sɪk) *determiner, adv* a Scot word for **such**

Sicanian (sɪ'keɪnɪən) *adj* another word for **Sicilian**

siccar ('sɪkər) *adj Scot* sure; certain. Also: **sicker** [Middle English, from Latin *sēcūrus* SECURE]

siccative ('sɪkətɪv) *n* a substance added to a liquid to promote drying: used in paints and some medicines [c16 from Late Latin *siccātīvus*, from Latin *siccāre* to dry up, from *siccus* dry]

sice (saɪs) *n* a variant spelling of **syce**

sicht (sɪxt) *n, vb* a Scot word for **sight**

Sichuan ('sɪtʃwɑ:n), **Szechuan** *or* **Szechwan** *n* a province of SW China: the most populous administrative division in the country, esp in the central Red Basin, where it is crossed by three main tributaries of the Yangtze. Capital: Chengdu. Pop: 81 000 000 (2003 est). Area: about 569 800 sq km (220 000 sq miles)

Sicilia (si'tʃiːlja) *n* the Latin and Italian name for **Sicily**

Sicilian (sɪ'sɪlɪən) *adj* **1** of or relating to Sicily or its inhabitants ▷ *n* **2** a native or inhabitant of Sicily

siciliano (sɪˌsɪlɪ'ɑ:nəʊ, ˌsɪtʃɪ'ljɑ:nəʊ) *n, pl* **-ianos 1** an old dance in six-beat or twelve-beat time **2** music composed for or in the rhythm of this dance [Italian: Sicilian]

Sicilian vespers *n* (*functioning as singular*) a revolt in 1282 against French rule in Sicily, in which the ringing of the vesper bells on Easter Monday served as the signal to massacre and drive out the French

Sicily ('sɪsɪlɪ) *n* the largest island in the Mediterranean, separated from the tip of SW Italy

by the Strait of Messina: administratively an autonomous region of Italy; settled by Phoenicians, Greeks, and Carthaginians before the Roman conquest of 241 BC; under Normans (12th–13th centuries); formed the **Kingdom of the Two Sicilies** with Naples in 1815; mountainous and volcanic. Capital: Palermo. Pop: 4 972 124 (2003 est). Area: 25 460 sq km (9830 sq miles). Latin names: Sicilia, Trinacria. Italian name: Sicilia

sick¹ (sɪk) *adj* **1** inclined or likely to vomit **2 a** suffering from ill health **b** (*as collective noun; preceded by the*): *the sick* **3 a** of, relating to, or used by people who are unwell: *sick benefits* **b** (*in combination*): *sickbed* **4** deeply affected with a mental or spiritual feeling akin to physical sickness: *sick at heart* **5** mentally, psychologically, or spiritually disturbed **6** *informal* delighting in or catering for the macabre or sadistic; morbid: *sick humour* **7** (often foll by *of*) *informal* Also: **sick and tired** disgusted or weary, esp because satiated: *I am sick of his everlasting laughter* **8** (often foll by *for*) weary with longing; pining: *I am sick for my own country* **9** pallid or sickly **10** not in working order **11** (of land) unfit for the adequate production of certain crops **12** look sick *slang* to be outclassed ▷ *n, vb* **13** an informal word for **vomit** ▷ See also **sick-out** [Old English *sēoc*; related to Old Norse *skjūkr*, Gothic *siuks*, Old High German *sioh*] > 'sickish *adj*

sick² (sɪk) *vb* a variant spelling of **sic²**

sickbay ('sɪkˌbeɪ) *n* a room or area for the treatment of the sick or injured, as on board a ship or at a boarding school

sick building syndrome *n* a group of symptoms, such as headaches, eye irritation, and lethargy, that may be experienced by workers in offices with limited ventilation

sick-dog *n Austral slang* **1** a calm and unruffled person ▷ *adj* **2** excellent

sicken ('sɪkən) *vb* **1** to make or become sick, nauseated, or disgusted **2** (*intr*; often foll by *for*) to show symptoms (of an illness)

sickener ('sɪkˀnə) *n* **1** something that induces sickness or nausea **2** a bright red basidiomycetous fungus of either of two species of *Russula*, notably the poisonous R. *emetica*

sickening ('sɪkənɪŋ) *adj* **1** causing sickness or revulsion **2** *informal* extremely annoying > 'sickeningly *adv*

sick headache *n* **1** a headache accompanied by nausea **2** a nontechnical name for **migraine**

sickie ('sɪkɪ) *n informal* a day of sick leave from work, whether for genuine sickness or not [c20 from SICK¹ + -IE]

sickle ('sɪkˀl) *n* an implement for cutting grass, corn, etc, having a curved blade and a short handle [Old English *sicol*, from Latin *sēcula*; related to *secāre* to cut]

sick leave *n* leave of absence from work through illness

sicklebill ('sɪkˀlˌbɪl) *n* any of various birds having a markedly curved bill, such as *Falculea palliata*, a Madagascan bird of the family *Vangidae*, *Hemignathus procerus*, a Hawaiian honey creeper, and certain hummingbirds and birds of paradise

sickle-cell anaemia *n* a hereditary haemolytic anaemia, occurring in Black populations, and caused by mutant haemoglobin. The red blood cells become sickle-shaped. It is characterized by fever, abdominal pain, jaundice, leg ulcers, etc

sickle feather *n* (*often plural*) any of the elongated tail feathers of certain birds, esp the domestic cock [c17 so called because of its shape]

sickle medick *n* a small Eurasian leguminous plant, *Medicago falcata*, having trifoliate leaves, yellow flowers, and sickle-shaped pods. Also called: **yellow medick**

sick list *n* a list of the sick, esp in the army or navy

sickly ('sɪklɪ) *adj* **-lier, -liest 1** disposed to frequent ailments; not healthy; weak **2** of, relating to, or caused by sickness **3** (of a smell, taste, etc) causing revulsion or nausea **4** (of light or colour) faint or feeble **5** mawkish; insipid: *sickly affectation* ▷ *adv* **6** in a sick or sickly manner > 'sickliness *n*

sickness ('sɪknɪs) *n* **1** an illness or disease **2** nausea or queasiness **3** the state or an instance of being sick

sickness benefit *n* **1** (formerly, in the British National Insurance scheme) a weekly payment made to a person who had been off work through illness for more than three days and less than six months; replaced by **incapacity benefit** in 1995 **2** (in New Zealand) a payment made by the Department of Social Welfare to a person unable to work owing to a medical condition

sick note *n Brit informal* a document given to an employer certifying that an employee's absence from work of more than four days was due to illness. If the absence is for more than seven days the note must be signed by a doctor. See also **self-certification**

sicko ('sɪkəʊ) *informal* ▷ *n, pl* **sickos 1** a person who is mentally disturbed or perverted ▷ *adj* **2** perverted or in bad taste: *sicko prurience* [c20 from SICK¹ (sense 5) + -O]

sick-out *US and Caribbean* ▷ *n* **1** a form of industrial action in which all workers in a factory, etc, report sick simultaneously ▷ *vb* **sick out 2** (*intr, adverb*) to take part in such action

sick pay *n* wages paid to an employee while he is on sick leave

sickroom ('sɪkˌruːm, -ˌrʊm) *n* **1** a room to which a person who is ill is confined **2** a room set aside, as in a school, for people who are taken ill

sic passim Latin ('sɪk 'pæsɪm) a phrase used in printed works to indicate that a word, spelling, etc, occurs in the same form throughout [literally: thus everywhere]

sic transit gloria mundi Latin ('sɪk 'trænsɪt 'glɔːrɪˌɑː 'mʊndiː) thus passes the glory of the world

Sicyon ('sɪsɪˌɒn, 'sɪsɪən) *n* an ancient city in S Greece, in the NE Peloponnese near Corinth: declined after 146 BC

sidalcea (sɪ'dælsɪə) *n* any plant of the mostly perennial N American genus *Sidalcea*, related to and resembling mallow, esp *S. malvaeflora*, grown for its spikes of lilac, pink, or red flowers: family *Malvaceae*. Also called: **Greek mallow** [New Latin, from Greek *sidē* a plant name + *alkea* a kind of mallow]

Siddhartha (sɪ'dɑːtə) *n* the personal name of the Buddha

siddhuism ('sɪ'duːɪzəm) *n Indian* any contrived metaphor or simile [c20 named after the Indian cricket commentator *Navjot Singh Siddhu*, renowned for using language of this kind]

siddur Hebrew (siː'duːr; English 'sɪdʊə) *n, pl* -**durim** (-duː'riːm) -**durs** *Judaism* the Jewish prayer book [literally: order]

side (saɪd) *n* **1** a line or surface that borders anything **2** *geometry* **a** any line segment forming part of the perimeter of a plane geometric figure **b** another name for **face** (sense 13) **3** either of two parts into which an object, surface, area, etc, can be divided, esp by a line, median, space, etc: *the right side and the left side*. Related adj: **lateral 4** either of the two surfaces of a flat object: *the right and wrong side of the cloth* **5** a surface or part of an object that extends vertically: *the side of a cliff* **6** either half of a human or animal body, esp the area around the waist, as divided by the median plane: *I have a pain in my side* **7** the area immediately next to a person or thing: *he stood at her side* **8** a district, point, or direction within an area identified by reference to a central point: *the south side of the city* **9** the area at the edge of a room, road, etc, as distinguished from the middle **10** aspect or part: *look on the bright side; his cruel side* **11** one of two or more contesting factions, teams, etc **12** a page in an essay, book, etc **13** a position, opinion, etc, held in opposition to another in a dispute **14** line of descent: *he gets his brains from his mother's side* **15** *informal* a television channel **16**

billiards, snooker spin imparted to a ball by striking it off-centre with the cue. US and Canadian equivalent: English **17** *Brit slang* insolence, arrogance, or pretentiousness: *to put on side* **18** **on one side** set apart from the rest, as provision for emergencies, etc, or to avoid muddling **19** **on the side a** apart from or in addition to the main object **b** as a sideline **c** *US* as a side dish **d** bit **on the side** See **bit** (sense 11) **20** **side by side a** close together **b** (foll by *with*) beside or near to **21** **take sides** to support one group, opinion, etc, as against another **22** on the weak, heavy, etc, side tending to be too weak, heavy, etc ▷ *adj* **23** being on one side; lateral **24** from or viewed as if from one side **25** directed towards one side **26** not main; subordinate or incidental: *side door; side road* ▷ *vb* **27** (*intr*; usually foll by *with*) to support or associate oneself with a faction, interest, etc **28** (*tr*) to provide with siding or sides **29** (*tr*; often foll by *away* or *up*) *Northern English dialect* to tidy up or clear (dishes, a table, etc) [Old English *sīde*; related to *sīd* wide, Old Norse *sītha* side, Old High German *sīta*]

side arms *pl n* weapons carried on the person, by sling, belt, or holster, such as a sword, pistol, etc

sideband ('saɪdˌbænd) *n* the frequency band either above (**upper sideband**) or below (**lower sideband**) the carrier frequency, within which fall the spectral components produced by modulation of a carrier wave. See also **single sideband transmission**

sideboard ('saɪdˌbɔːd) *n* a piece of furniture intended to stand at the side of a dining room, with drawers, cupboards, and shelves to hold silver, china, linen, etc

sideboards ('saɪdˌbɔːdz) *pl n* another term for **sideburns**

sideburns ('saɪdˌbɜːnz) *pl n* a man's whiskers grown down either side of the face in front of the ears. Also called: **sideboards, side whiskers,** (*Austral*) **sidelevers** [c19 variant of BURNSIDES]

sidecar ('saɪdˌkɑː) *n* **1** a small car attached on one side to a motorcycle, usually for one passenger, the other side being supported by a single wheel **2** a cocktail containing brandy with equal parts of Cointreau and lemon juice

side chain *n chem* a group of atoms bound to an atom, usually a carbon, that forms part of a larger chain or ring in a molecule

-sided *adj* (*in combination*) having a side or sides as specified: *three-sided; many-sided*

side deal *n* a transaction between two people for their private benefit, which is subsidiary to a contract negotiated by them on behalf of the organizations they represent

side dish *n* a portion of food served in addition to the main dish

side-dress *vb* (*tr*) to place fertilizers on or in the soil near the roots of (growing plants)

side drum *n* a small double-headed drum carried at the side with snares that produce a rattling effect

side effect *n* **1** any unwanted nontherapeutic effect caused by a drug. Compare **aftereffect** (sense 2) **2** any secondary effect, esp an undesirable one

side-foot *soccer* ▷ *n* **1** a shot or pass played with the side of the foot ▷ *vb* **2** (*tr*) to strike (a ball) with the side of the foot

sidekick ('saɪdˌkɪk) *n informal* a close friend or follower who accompanies another on adventures, etc

sidelight ('saɪdˌlaɪt) *n* **1** light coming from the side **2** a side window **3** either of the two navigational running lights used by vessels at night, a red light on the port and a green on the starboard **4** *Brit* either of two small lights on the front of a motor vehicle, used to indicate the presence of the vehicle at night rather than to assist the driver **5** additional or incidental information

sideline ('saɪdˌlaɪn) *n* **1** *sport* a line that marks the

side boundary of a playing area **2** a subsidiary interest or source of income **3** an auxiliary business activity or line of merchandise ▷ *vb* (*tr*) **4** to prevent (a player) from taking part in a game **5** to prevent (a person) from pursuing a particular activity, operation, career, etc

sidelines ('saɪdˌlaɪnz) *pl n* **1** *sport* the area immediately outside the playing area, where substitute players sit **2** the peripheral areas of any organization, etc

sidelong ('saɪdˌlɒŋ) *adj* (*prenominal*) **1** directed or inclining to one side **2** indirect or oblique ▷ *adv* **3** from the side; obliquely

sideman ('saɪdmən) *n, pl* -**men** a member of a dance band or a jazz group other than the leader

side meat *n US informal* salt pork or bacon [c19 so called because it comes from the side of the pig]

sidereal (saɪ'dɪərɪəl) *adj* **1** of, relating to, or involving the stars **2** determined with reference to one or more stars: *the sidereal day* [c17 from Latin *sīdereus*, from *sīdus* a star, a constellation] > si'dereally *adv*

sidereal day *n* See **day** (sense 5)

sidereal hour *n* a 24th part of a sidereal day

sidereal month *n* See **month** (sense 5)

sidereal period *n astronomy* the period of revolution of a body about another with respect to one or more distant stars

sidereal time *n* time based upon the rotation of the earth with respect to the distant stars, the **sidereal day** being the unit of measurement

sidereal year *n* See **year** (sense 5)

siderite ('saɪdəˌraɪt) *n* **1** Also called: **chalybite** a pale yellow to brownish-black mineral consisting chiefly of iron carbonate in hexagonal crystalline form. It occurs mainly in ore veins and sedimentary rocks and is an important source of iron. Formula: $FeCO_3$ **2** a meteorite consisting principally of metallic iron > **sideritic** (ˌsaɪdə'rɪtɪk) *adj*

sidero- *or before a vowel* **sider-** *combining form* indicating iron: *siderolite* [from Greek *sidēros*]

sideroad ('saɪdˌrəʊd) *n Canadian* (esp in Ontario) a road, usually north-south, going at right angles to concession roads

siderolite ('saɪdərəˌlaɪt) *n* a meteorite consisting of a mixture of iron, nickel, and such ferromagnesian minerals as olivine and pyroxene

siderophilin (ˌsɪdə'rɒfɪlɪn) *n* another name for **transferrin** [from SIDERO- + -PHIL(E) + -IN]

siderosis (ˌsaɪdə'rəʊsɪs) *n* **1** a lung disease caused by breathing in fine particles of iron or other metallic dust **2** an excessive amount of iron in the blood or tissues > **siderotic** (ˌsɪdə'rɒtɪk) *adj*

siderostat ('saɪdərəʊˌstæt) *n* an astronomical instrument consisting essentially of a plane mirror driven about two axes so that light from a celestial body, esp the sun, is reflected along a constant direction for a long period of time. See also **heliostat**. Compare **coelostat** [c19 from *sidero-*, from Latin *sidus* a star + -STAT, on the model of HELIOSTAT] > ˌsidero'static *adj*

side-saddle *n* **1** a riding saddle originally designed for women riders in skirts who sit with both legs on the near side of the horse ▷ *adv* **2** on or as if on a side-saddle: *to be riding side-saddle*

sideshow ('saɪdˌʃəʊ) *n* **1** a small show or entertainment offered in conjunction with a larger attraction, as at a circus or fair **2** a subordinate event or incident

sideslip ('saɪdˌslɪp) *n* **1** a sideways skid, as of a motor vehicle **2** a sideways and downward movement towards the inside of a turn by an aircraft in a sharp bank ▷ *vb* -**slips,** -**slipping,** -**slipped 3** another name for **slip¹** (sense 12)

sidesman ('saɪdzmən) *n, pl* -**men** *Church of England* a man elected to help the parish church warden

side-splitting *adj* **1** producing great mirth **2** (of laughter) uproarious or very hearty

sidestep ('saɪdˌstɛp) *vb* -**steps,** -**stepping,** -**stepped 1** to step aside from or out of the way of (something) **2** (*tr*) to dodge or circumvent ▷ *n*

side step 3 a movement to one side, as in dancing, boxing, etc > **'side,stepper** *n*

side street *n* a minor or unimportant street, esp one leading off a main thoroughfare

sidestroke ('saɪd,strəʊk) *n* a type of swimming stroke in which the swimmer lies sideways in the water paddling with his arms and making a scissors kick with his legs

sideswipe ('saɪd,swaɪp) *n* **1** a glancing blow or hit along or from the side **2** an unexpected criticism of someone or something while discussing another subject ▷ *vb* **3** to strike (someone) with such a blow > **'side,swiper** *n*

side tone *n* sound diverted from a telephone microphone to the earpiece so that a speaker hears his own voice at the same level and position as that of the respondent

sidetrack ('saɪd,træk) *vb* **1** to distract or be distracted from a main subject or topic ▷ *n* **2** *US and Canadian* a railway siding **3** the act or an instance of sidetracking; digression

side-valve engine *n* a type of internal-combustion engine in which the inlet and exhaust valves are in the cylinder block at the side of the pistons. Compare **overhead-valve engine**

sidewalk ('saɪd,wɔːk) *n US and Canadian* a hard-surfaced path for pedestrians alongside and a little higher than a road. Also called (in Britain and certain other countries): **pavement**

sidewall ('saɪd,wɔːl) *n* either of the sides of a pneumatic tyre between the tread and the rim

sideward ('saɪdwəd) *adj* **1** directed or moving towards one side ▷ *adv also* **sidewards 2** towards one side

sideways ('saɪd,weɪz) *adv* **1** moving, facing, or inclining towards one side **2** from one side; obliquely **3** with one side forward ▷ *adj* (*prenominal*) **4** moving or directed to or from one side **5** towards or from one side

sidewheel ('saɪd,wiːl) *n* one of the paddle wheels of a sidewheeler

sidewheeler ('saɪd,wiːlə) *n* a vessel, esp a river boat, propelled by two large paddle wheels, one on each side. Compare **stern-wheeler**

side whiskers *pl n* another name for **sideburns**

sidewinder ('saɪd,waɪndə) *n* **1** a North American rattlesnake, *Crotalus cerastes,* that moves forwards by a sideways looping motion **2** *boxing, US* a heavy swinging blow from the side **3** a US air-to-air missile using infrared homing aids in seeking its target

sidhe (ʃiː, 'ʃiːðɪ) *pl n* the inhabitants of fairyland; fairies [c18 from Irish Gaelic *aos sídhe* people of the fairy mound; compare BANSHEE]

Sidi-bel-Abbès (*French* sidibɛlabɛs) *n* a city in NW Algeria: headquarters of the Foreign Legion until Algerian independence (1962). Pop: 201 000 (2005 est)

siding ('saɪdɪŋ) *n* **1** a short stretch of railway track connected to a main line, used for storing rolling stock or to enable trains on the same line to pass **2** a short railway line giving access to the main line for freight from a factory, mine, quarry, etc **3** *US and Canadian* material attached to the outside of a building to make it weatherproof

sidle ('saɪdəl) *vb* (*intr*) **1** to move in a furtive or stealthy manner; edge along **2** to move along sideways ▷ *n* **3** a sideways movement [c17 back formation from obsolete *sideling* sideways] > **'sidler** *n*

Sidon ('saɪdᵊn) *n* the chief city of ancient Phoenicia: founded in the third millennium BC; wealthy through trade and the making of glass and purple dyes; now the Lebanese city of Saïda

Sidonian (saɪˈdəʊnɪən) *adj* **1** of or relating to the ancient Phoenician city of Sidon or its inhabitants ▷ *n* **2** a native or inhabitant of Sidon

Sidra ('sɪdrə) *n* **Gulf of** a wide inlet of the Mediterranean on the N coast of Libya

SIDS *abbreviation for* sudden infant death syndrome. See **cot death**

siècle French (sjɛklə) *n* a century, period, or era

siege (siːdʒ) *n* **1 a** the offensive operations carried out to capture a fortified place by surrounding it, severing its communications and supply lines, and deploying weapons against it **b** (*as modifier*): *siege warfare* **2** a persistent attempt to gain something **3** a long tedious period, as of illness, etc **4** *obsolete* a seat or throne **5 lay siege to** to besiege ▷ *vb* **6** (*tr*) to besiege or assail [c13 from Old French *sege* a seat, from Vulgar Latin *sēdicāre* (unattested) to sit down, from Latin *sedēre*]

siege mentality *n* a state of mind in which a person believes that he or she is being constantly oppressed or attacked

Siegen ('siːgən) *n* a city in NW Germany, in North Rhine-Westphalia: manufacturing centre; birthplace of Rubens. Pop: 107 768 (2003 est)

Siege Perilous *n* (in Arthurian legend) the seat at the Round Table that could be filled only by the knight destined to find the Holy Grail and that was fatal to anyone else [from SIEGE (in the archaic sense: a seat or throne)]

Siegfried ('siːɡfriːd; *German* 'ziːkfriːt) *n German myth* a German prince, the son of Sigmund and husband of Kriemhild, who, in the *Nibelungenlied,* assumes possession of the treasure of the Nibelungs by slaying the dragon that guards it, wins Brunhild for King Gunther, and is eventually killed by Hagen. Norse equivalent: Sigurd

Siegfried line *n* the line of fortifications built by the Germans prior to and during World War II opposite the Maginot line in France

Sieg Heil German (ziːk haɪl) hail to victory: a Nazi salute, often accompanied by the raising of the right arm

siemens ('siːmənz) *n, pl* siemens the derived SI unit of electrical conductance equal to 1 reciprocal ohm. Symbol: S. Formerly called: mho

Siena (sɪˈɛnə; *Italian* 'sjɛːna) *n* a walled city in central Italy, in Tuscany: founded by the Etruscans; important artistic centre (13th–14th centuries); university (13th century). Pop: 52 625 (2001)

sienna (sɪˈɛnə) *n* **1** a natural earth containing ferric oxide used as a yellowish-brown pigment when untreated (**raw sienna**) or a reddish-brown pigment when roasted (**burnt sienna**) **2** the colour of this pigment. See also **burnt sienna** [c18 from Italian *terra di Siena* earth of SIENA]

sierra (sɪˈɛərə) *n* a range of mountains with jagged peaks, esp in Spain or America [c17 from Spanish, literally: saw, from Latin *serra;* see SERRATE] > sɪˈerran *adj*

Sierra (sɪˈɛərə) *n communications* a code word for the letter s

Sierra Leone (sɪˈɛərə lɪˈəʊnɪ, lɪˈəʊn) *n* a republic in W Africa, on the Atlantic: became a British colony in 1808 and gained independence (within the Commonwealth) in 1961; declared a republic in 1971; became a one-party state in 1978; multiparty democracy restored in 1991 but military rule was imposed following a coup in 1992, which led to civil unrest; consists of coastal swamps rising to a plateau in the east. Official language: English. Religion: Muslim majority and animist. Currency: leone. Capital: Freetown. Pop: 5 169 000 (2004 est). Area: 71 740 sq km (27 699 sq miles)

Sierra Leonean (sɪˈɛərə lɪˈəʊnɪən) *adj* **1** of or relating to Sierra Leone or its inhabitants ▷ *n* **2** a native or inhabitant of Sierra Leone

Sierra Madre (*Spanish* 'sjɛrra 'maðre) *n* (*functioning as singular*) the main mountain system of Mexico, extending for 2500 km (1500 miles) southeast from the N border: consists of the **Sierra Madre Oriental** in the east, the **Sierra Madre Occidental** in the west, and the **Sierra Madre del Sur** in the south. Highest peak: Citlaltépetl, 5699 m (18 698 ft)

Sierra Morena (*Spanish* 'sjɛrra moˈrena) *n* (*functioning as singular*) a mountain range in SW Spain, between the Guadiana and Guadalquivir Rivers. Highest peak: Estrella, 1299 m (4262 ft)

Sierra Nevada *n* (*functioning as singular*) **1** (sɪˈɛərə nɪˈvɑːdə) a mountain range in E California, parallel to the Coast Ranges. Highest peak: Mount Whitney, 4418 m (14 495 ft) **2** (*Spanish* 'sjɛrra neˈβaða) a mountain range in SE Spain, mostly in Granada and Almería provinces. Highest peak: Cerro de Mulhacén, 3478 m (11 411 ft)

sies (sɪs, siːs) *interj South African informal* a variant of **sis²**

siesta (sɪˈɛstə) *n* a rest or nap, usually taken in the early afternoon, as in hot countries [c17 from Spanish, from Latin *sexta hōra* the sixth hour, that is, noon]

sieve (sɪv) *n* **1** a device for separating lumps from powdered material, straining liquids, grading particles, etc, consisting of a container with a mesh or perforated bottom through which the material is shaken or poured **2** *rare* a person who gossips and spreads secrets **3 memory** *or* **head like a sieve** a very poor memory ▷ *vb* **4** to pass or cause to pass through a sieve **5** (*tr;* often foll by *out*) to separate or remove (lumps, materials, etc) by use of a sieve [Old English *sife;* related to Old Norse *sef* reed with hollow stalk, Old High German *sib* sieve, Dutch *zeef*] > **'sieve,like** *adj*

sievert ('siːvət) *n* **1** the derived SI unit of dose equivalent, equal to 1 joule per kilogram. 1 sievert is equivalent to 100 rems. Symbol: Sv **2** (*formerly*) a unit of gamma radiation dose approximately equal to 8.4×10^{-2} gray [c20 named after Rolf *Sievert* (1896–1966), Swedish physicist]

sieve tube *n botany* an element of phloem tissue consisting of a longitudinal row of thin-walled elongated cells with perforations in their connecting walls through which food materials pass

sif (siːf) *adj South African slang* disgusting; sickening; nasty [c20 from *syphilitic*]

sifaka (sɪˈfɑːkə) *n* either of two large rare arboreal lemuroid primates, *Propithecus diadema* or *P. verreauxi,* of Madagascar, having long strikingly patterned or coloured fur: family *Indriidae* [from Malagasy]

sift (sɪft) *vb* **1** (*tr*) to sieve (sand, flour, etc) in order to remove the coarser particles **2** to scatter (something) over a surface through a sieve **3** (*tr*) to separate with or as if with a sieve; distinguish between **4** (*tr*) to examine minutely: *to sift evidence* **5** (*intr*) to move as if through a sieve [Old English *siftan;* related to Middle Low German *siften* to sift, Dutch *ziften;* see SIEVE] > **'sifter** *n*

siftings ('sɪftɪŋz) *pl n* material or particles separated out by or as if by a sieve

sig. *abbreviation for* signature

Sig. *abbreviation for* **1** (in prescriptions) signā [Latin: sign] **2** (in prescriptions) signature **3** signor **4** signore

sigh (saɪ) *vb* **1** (*intr*) to draw in and exhale audibly a deep breath as an expression of weariness, despair, relief, etc **2** (*intr*) to make a sound resembling this: *trees sighing in the wind* **3** (*intr;* often foll by *for*) to yearn, long, or pine **4** (*tr*) to utter or express with sighing ▷ *n* **5** the act or sound of sighing [Old English *sīcan,* of obscure origin] > **'sigher** *n*

sight (saɪt) *n* **1** the power or faculty of seeing; perception by the eyes; vision. Related adjs: **optical, visual 2** the act or an instance of seeing **3** the range of vision: *within sight of land* **4** range of mental vision; point of view; judgment: *in his sight she could do nothing wrong* **5** a glimpse or view (esp in the phrases **catch sight of, lose sight of**) **6** anything that is seen **7** (*often plural*) anything worth seeing; spectacle: *the sights of London* **8** *informal* anything unpleasant or undesirable to see: *his room was a sight!* **9** any of various devices or instruments used to assist the eye in making alignments or directional observations, esp such a device used in aiming a gun **10** an observation or alignment made with such a device **11** an opportunity for observation **12** *obsolete* insight or skill **13 a sight** *informal* a great deal: *she's a sight too* *good for him* **14 a sight for sore eyes** a person or thing that one is pleased or relieved to see **15 at** *or* **on sight a** as soon as seen **b** on presentation: *a bill payable at sight* **16 know by sight** to be familiar with the appearance of without having personal acquaintance: *I know Mr Brown by sight but we have never spoken* **17 not by a long sight** *informal* on no account; not at all **18 out of sight a** not visible *slang* **b** extreme or very unusual **c** (*as interj.*): *that's marvellous!* **19 set one's sights on** to have (a specified goal) in mind; aim for **20 sight unseen** without having seen the object at issue: *to buy a car sight unseen* ▷ *vb* **21** (*tr*) to see, view, or glimpse **22** (*tr*) **a** to furnish with a sight or sights **b** to adjust the sight of **23** to aim (a firearm) using the sight [Old English *sihth*; related to Old High German *siht*; see SEE[1]] > ˈ**sightable** *adj*

sight bill *or* **draft** *n* variants of **demand bill**

sighted (ˈsaɪtɪd) *adj* **1** not blind **2** (*in combination*) having sight of a specified kind: *short-sighted*

sighter (ˈsaɪtə) *n shooting, archery* any of six practice shots allowed to each competitor in a tournament

sightless (ˈsaɪtlɪs) *adj* **1** blind **2** invisible > ˈ**sightlessly** *adv* > ˈ**sightlessness** *n*

sightline (ˈsaɪtˌlaɪn) *n* an uninterrupted line of vision, as in a theatre, etc, or from a vehicle joining a road

sightly (ˈsaɪtlɪ) *adj* **-lier, -liest 1** pleasing or attractive to see **2** *US* providing a pleasant view > ˈ**sightliness** *n*

sight-read (ˈsaɪtˌriːd) *vb* **-reads, -reading, -read** (-ˌrɛd) to sing or play (music in a printed or written form) without previous preparation > ˈ**sight-ˌreader** *n* > ˈ**sight-ˌreading** *n*

sightscreen (ˈsaɪtˌskriːn) *n cricket* a large white screen placed near the boundary behind the bowler to help the batsman see the ball

sightsee (ˈsaɪtˌsiː) *vb* **-sees, -seeing, -saw, -seen** *informal* to visit the famous or interesting sights of (a place) > ˈ**sightˌseer** *n*

sightseeing (ˈsaɪtˌsiːɪŋ) *n informal* **a** the activity of visiting the famous or interesting sights of a place **b** (*as modifier*): *sightseeing trip*

sigil (ˈsɪdʒɪl) *n rare* **1** a seal or signet **2** a sign or image supposedly having magical power [C17 from Latin *sigillum* a little sign, from *signum* a SIGN] > **sigillary** (ˈsɪdʒɪlərɪ) *adj*

sigla (ˈsɪglə) *n* the list of symbols used in a book, usually collected together as part of the preliminaries [Latin: plural of *siglum*, diminutive of *signum* sign]

siglos (ˈsɪglɒs) *n, pl* **-loi** (-lɔɪ) a silver coin of ancient Persia worth one twentieth of a daric

sigma (ˈsɪgmə) *n* **1** the 18th letter in the Greek alphabet (Σ, σ or, when final, ς), a consonant, transliterated as *S* **2** *maths* the symbol Σ, indicating summation of the numbers or quantities indicated [Greek, of Semitic origin; related to Hebrew SAMEKH]

sigmate (ˈsɪgmɪt, -meɪt) *adj* shaped like the Greek letter sigma or the Roman *S* > **sigmation** (sɪgˈmeɪʃən) *n*

sigmoid (ˈsɪgmɔɪd) *adj also* **sigmoidal 1** shaped like the letter S **2** of or relating to the sigmoid colon of the large intestine ▷ *n* **3** See **sigmoid colon** [C17 from Greek *sigmoeidēs* sigma-shaped]

sigmoid colon *n* the S-shaped bend in the final portion of the large intestine that leads to the rectum. Also called: **sigmoid flexure**

sigmoid flexure *n zoology* an S-shaped curve, as in the necks of certain birds

sigmoidoscope (sɪgˈmɔɪdəˌskəʊp) *n* an instrument incorporating a light for the direct observation of the colon, rectum, and sigmoid flexure > **sigmoidoscopic** (sɪgˌmɔɪdəˈskɒpɪk) *adj* > **sigmoidoscopy** (ˌsɪgmɔɪdˈɒskəpɪ) *n*

Sigmund (ˈsɪgmənd, ˈsiːgmʊnd; *German* ˈziːkmʊnt) *n* **1** *Norse myth* the father of the hero Sigurd **2** Also called: **Siegmund** (*German* ˈziːkmʊnt) *German myth* king of the Netherlands, father of Siegfried

sign (saɪn) *n* **1** something that indicates or acts as a token of a fact, condition, etc, that is not immediately or outwardly observable **2** an action or gesture intended to convey information, a command, etc **3 a** a board, placard, etc, displayed in public and inscribed with words or designs intended to inform, warn, etc **b** (*as modifier*): *a sign painter* **4** an arbitrary or conventional mark or device that stands for a word, phrase, etc **5** *maths, logic* **a** any symbol indicating an operation: *a plus sign; an implication sign* **b** the positivity or negativity of a number, quantity, or expression: *subtraction from zero changes the sign of an expression* **6** an indication or vestige: *the house showed no signs of being occupied* **7** a portentous or significant event **8** an indication, such as a scent or spoor, of the presence of an animal **9** *med* any objective evidence of the presence of a disease or disorder. Compare **symptom** (sense 1) **10** *astrology* See **sign of the zodiac** ▷ *vb* **11** to write (one's name) as a signature to (a document, etc) in attestation, confirmation, ratification, etc **12** (*intr*; often foll by *to*) to make a sign; signal **13** to engage or be engaged by written agreement, as a player for a team, etc **14** (*tr*) to outline in gestures a sign over, esp the sign of the cross **15** (*tr*) to indicate by or as if by a sign; betoken **16** (*intr*) to use sign language ▷ See also **sign away, sign in, sign off, sign on, sign out, sign up** [C13 from Old French *signe*, from Latin *signum* a sign] > ˈ**signable** *adj*

signage (ˈsaɪnɪdʒ) *n* signs collectively, esp street signs or signs giving directions

signal (ˈsɪgnᵊl) *n* **1** any sign, gesture, token, etc, that serves to communicate information **2** anything that acts as an incitement to action: *the rise in prices was a signal for rebellion* **3 a** a variable parameter, such as a current or electromagnetic wave, by which information is conveyed through an electronic circuit, communications system, etc **b** the information so conveyed **c** (*as modifier*): *signal strength; a signal generator* ▷ *adj* **4** distinguished or conspicuous **5** used to give or act as a signal ▷ *vb* **-nals, -nalling, -nalled** *or US* **-nals, -naling, -naled 6** to communicate (a message, etc) to (a person) [C16 from Old French *seignal*, from Medieval Latin *signāle*, from Latin *signum* SIGN] > ˈ**signaller** *or US* ˈ**signaler** *n*

signal box *n* **1** a building containing manually operated signal levers for all the railway lines in its section **2** a control point for a large area of a railway system, operated electrically and semiautomatically

signal generator *n electrical engineering* an apparatus used to generate a signal consisting of a known oscillating voltage, usually between 1 microvolt and 1 volt, over a range of frequencies, to test electronic equipment

signalize *or* **signalise** (ˈsɪgnəˌlaɪz) *vb* (*tr*) **1** to make noteworthy or conspicuous **2** to point out carefully

signally (ˈsɪgnəlɪ) *adv* conspicuously or especially

signalman (ˈsɪgnᵊlmən) *n, pl* **-men 1** a railway employee in charge of the signals and points within a section **2** a man who sends and receives signals, esp in the navy

signalment (ˈsɪgnᵊlmənt) *n US* a detailed description of a person, for identification or use in police records [from French *signalement*, from *signaler* to distinguish]

signal-to-noise ratio *n* the ratio of one parameter, such as power of a wanted signal to the same parameter of the noise at a specified point in an electronic circuit, etc

signatory (ˈsɪgnətərɪ, -trɪ) *n, pl* **-ries 1** a person who has signed a document such as a treaty or contract or an organization, state, etc, on whose behalf such a document has been signed ▷ *adj* **2** having signed a document, treaty, etc [C17 from Latin *signātōrius* concerning sealing, from *signāre* to seal, from *signum* a mark]

signature (ˈsɪgnɪtʃə) *n* **1** the name of a person or a mark or sign representing his name, marked by himself or by an authorized deputy **2** the act of signing one's name **3 a** a distinctive mark, characteristic, etc, that identifies a person or thing **b** (*as modifier*): *a signature fragrance* **4** *music* See **key signature, time signature 5** *US* the part of a medical prescription that instructs a patient how frequently and in what amounts he should take a drug or agent. Abbreviations: **Sig, S 6** *printing* **a** a sheet of paper printed with several pages that upon folding will become a section or sections of a book **b** such a sheet so folded **c** a mark, esp a letter, printed on the first page of a signature [C16 from Old French, from Medieval Latin *signātūra*, from Latin *signāre* to sign]

signature tune *n Brit* a melody used to introduce or identify a television or radio programme, a dance band, a performer, etc. Also called (esp US and Canadian): **theme song**

sign away *vb* (*tr, adverb*) to dispose of or lose by or as if by signing a document

signboard (ˈsaɪnˌbɔːd) *n* a board carrying a sign or notice, esp one used to advertise a product, event, etc

signed minor *n maths* another name for **cofactor**

signed-ranks test *n statistics* See **Wilcoxon test**

signer (ˈsaɪnə) *n* **1** a person who signs something **2** a person who uses sign language to communicate with deaf people

signet (ˈsɪgnɪt) *n* **1** a small seal, esp one as part of a finger ring **2** a seal used to stamp or authenticate documents **3** the impression made by such a seal ▷ *vb* **4** (*tr*) to stamp or authenticate with a signet [C14 from Medieval Latin *signētum* a little seal, from Latin *signum* a SIGN]

signet ring *n* a finger ring bearing a signet

significance (sɪgˈnɪfɪkəns) *n* **1** consequence or importance **2** something signified, expressed, or intended **3** the state or quality of being significant **4** *statistics* **a** a measure of the confidence that can be placed in a result, esp a substantive causal hypothesis, as not being merely a matter of chance **b** (*as modifier*): *a significance level*. Compare **confidence level.** See also **hypothesis testing**

significance test *n statistics* (in hypothesis testing) a test of whether the alternative hypothesis achieves the predetermined significance level in order to be accepted in preference to the null hypothesis

significant (sɪgˈnɪfɪkənt) *adj* **1** having or expressing a meaning; indicative **2** having a covert or implied meaning; suggestive **3** important, notable, or momentous **4** *statistics* of or relating to a difference between a result derived from a hypothesis and its observed value that is too large to be attributed to chance and that therefore tends to refute the hypothesis [C16 from Latin *significāre* to SIGNIFY] > **sigˈnificantly** *adv*

significant figures *or esp US* **significant digits** *pl n* **1** the figures of a number that express a magnitude to a specified degree of accuracy, rounding up or down the final figure: *3.14159 to four significant figures is 3.142* **2** the number of such figures: *3.142 has four significant figures*. Compare **decimal place** (sense 2)

significant other *n US informal* a spouse or lover

signification (ˌsɪgnɪfɪˈkeɪʃən) *n* **1** something that is signified; meaning or sense **2** the act of signifying

significative (sɪgˈnɪfɪkətɪv) *adj* **1** (of a sign, mark, etc) symbolic **2** another word for **significant** > **sigˈnificatively** *adv* > **sigˈnificativeness** *n*

signify (ˈsɪgnɪˌfaɪ) *vb* **-fies, -fying, -fied** (when *tr*, *may take a clause as object*) **1** (*tr*) to indicate, show, or suggest **2** (*tr*) to imply or portend: *the clouds signified the coming storm* **3** (*tr*) to stand as a symbol, sign, etc (for) **4** (*intr*) *informal* to be significant or important [C13 from Old French *signifier*, from Latin *significāre*, from *signum* a sign, mark + *facere* to make] > ˈ**signiˌfiable** *adj* > ˈ**signiˌfier** *n*

sign in *vb* (*adverb*) **1** to sign or cause to sign a register, as at a hotel, club, etc **2** to make or become a member, as of a club

S

signing ('saɪnɪŋ) *n* a specific set of manual signs used to communicate with deaf people

sign language *n* **1** another word for **signing 2** any system of communication by manual signs or gestures

sign manual *n law* a person's signature in his own hand, esp that of a sovereign on an official document

sign off *vb* (*adverb*) **1** (*intr*) to announce the end of a radio or television programme, esp at the end of a day **2** (*intr*) *bridge* to make a conventional bid indicating to one's partner that one wishes the bidding to stop **3** (*tr*) to withdraw or retire from (an activity) **4** (*tr*) (of a doctor) to declare (someone) unfit for work, because of illness **5** (*intr*) *Brit* to terminate one's claim to unemployment benefit

sign of the cross *n chiefly RC Church* a gesture in which the right hand is moved from the forehead to the breast and from the left shoulder to the right to describe the form of a cross in order to invoke the grace of Christ

sign of the zodiac *n* any of the 12 equal areas, 30° wide, into which the zodiac can be divided, named after the 12 zodiacal constellations. In astrology, it is thought that a person's psychological type and attitudes to life can be correlated with the sign in which the sun lay at the moment of his birth, with the ascendant sign, and to a lesser extent with the signs in which other planets lay at this time. Also called: **sign, star sign, sun sign**. See also **planet** (sense 3), **house** (sense 9)

sign on *vb* (*adverb*) **1** (*tr*) to hire or employ **2** (*intr*) to commit oneself to a job, activity, etc **3** (*intr*) *Brit* to register as unemployed with the Department of Social Security

signor or **signior** ('si:njɔ:; *Italian* siɲ'ɲor) *n*, *pl* -**gnors** or -**gnori** (*Italian* -'ɲori) an Italian man: usually used before a name as a title equivalent to *Mr*

signora (si:n'jɔ:rə; *Italian* siɲ'ɲora) *n*, *pl* -**ras** or -**re** (*Italian* -re) a married Italian woman: a title of address equivalent to *Mrs* when placed before a name or *madam* when used alone [Italian, feminine of SIGNORE]

signore (si:n'jɔ:ri:; *Italian* siɲ'ɲore) *n*, *pl* -**ri** (-ri; *Italian* -ri) an Italian man: a title of respect equivalent to *sir* [Italian, ultimately from Latin *senior* an elder, from *senex* an old man]

signorina (ˌsi:njɔ:'ri:nə; *Italian* siɲɲo'rina) *n*, *pl* -**nas** or -**ne** (*Italian* -ne) an unmarried Italian woman: a title of address equivalent to *Miss* when placed before a name or *madam* or *miss* when used alone [Italian, diminutive of SIGNORA]

signory ('si:njəri) *n*, *pl* -**gnories** a variant spelling of **seigniory**

sign out *vb* (*adverb*) to sign (one's name) to indicate that one is leaving a place: *he signed out for the evening*

signpost ('saɪnˌpəʊst) *n* **1** a post bearing a sign that shows the way, as at a roadside **2** something that serves as a clue or indication; sign ▷ *vb* (*tr*; *usually passive*) **3** to mark with signposts **4** to indicate direction towards

sign test *n* a statistical test used to analyse the direction of differences of scores between the same or matched pairs of subjects under two experimental conditions

sign up *vb* (*adverb*) to enlist or cause to enlist, as for military service

Sigurd ('sɪgʊəd; *German* 'zi:gʊrt) *n Norse myth* a hero who killed the dragon Fafnir to gain the treasure of Andvari, won Brynhild for Gunnar by deception, and then was killed by her when she discovered the fraud. His wife was Gudrun. German counterpart: **Siegfried**

sik (sɪk) *adj Austral slang* excellent

sika ('si:kə) *n* a Japanese forest-dwelling deer, *Cervus nippon*, having a brown coat, spotted with white in summer, and a large white patch on the rump [from Japanese *shika*]

Sikang ('ʃi:'kæŋ) *n* a former province of W China: established in 1928 from part of W Sichuan and E Tibet; dissolved in 1955

Sikh (si:k) *n* **1** a member of an Indian religion that separated from Hinduism and was founded in the 16th century, that teaches monotheism and that has the Granth as its chief religious document, rejecting the authority of the Vedas ▷ *adj* **2** of or relating to the Sikhs or their religious beliefs and customs [C18 from Hindi, literally: disciple, from Sanskrit *śiksati* he studies] ▷ 'Sikhˌism *n*

Si Kiang ('ʃi:ˈkjæŋ, kaɪˈæŋ) *n* See **Xi**

Siking ('si:'kɪŋ) *n* a former name for **Xi'an**

Sikkim ('sɪkɪm) *n* a state of NE India. formerly an independent state: under British control (1861–1947); became an Indian protectorate in 1950 and an administrative division of India in 1975; lies in the Himalayas, rising to 8600 m (28 216 ft) at Kanchenjunga in the north. Capital: Gangtok. Pop: 540 493 (2001). Area: 7096 sq km (2740 sq miles)

Sikkimese (ˌsɪkɪ'mi:z) *adj* **1** of or relating to Sikkim or its inhabitants ▷ *n* **2** a native or inhabitant of Sikkim

silage ('saɪlɪdʒ) *n* any crop harvested while green for fodder and kept succulent by partial fermentation in a silo. Also called: **ensilage** [C19 alteration (influenced by SILO) of ENSILAGE]

Silastic (sɪ'læstɪk) *n trademark* a flexible inert silicone rubber, used esp in prosthetic medicine

sild (sɪld) *n* any of various small young herrings, esp when prepared and canned in Norway [Norwegian]

sile (saɪl) *vb* (*tr*) *Northern English dialect* to pour with rain [probably from Old Norse; compare Swedish and Norwegian dialect *sila* to pass through a strainer]

silence ('saɪləns) *n* **1** the state or quality of being silent **2** the absence of sound or noise; stillness **3** refusal or failure to speak, communicate, etc, when expected: *his silence on the subject of their promotion was alarming* **4** a period of time without noise **5** oblivion or obscurity ▷ *vb* (*tr*) **6** to bring to silence **7** to put a stop to; extinguish: *to silence all complaint* [C13 via Old French from Latin *silentium*, from *silēre* to be quiet. See SILENT]

silenced ('saɪlənst) *adj* (of a clergyman) forbidden to preach or perform his clerical functions: *a silenced priest*

silencer ('saɪlənsə) *n* **1** any device designed to reduce noise, esp the tubular device containing baffle plates in the exhaust system of a motor vehicle. US and Canadian name: **muffler 2** a tubular device fitted to the muzzle of a firearm to deaden the report **3** a person or thing that silences

silene (saɪ'li:nɪ) *n* any plant of the large perennial genus *Silene*, with mostly red or pink flowers; many, esp *S.* or *Agrostemma coeli-rosa*, are grown as garden plants: family *Caryophyllaceae*. See also **campion** [New Latin from Latin *silenus viscaria*]

silent ('saɪlənt) *adj* **1** characterized by an absence or near absence of noise or sound: *a silent house* **2** tending to speak very little or not at all **3** unable to speak **4** failing to speak, communicate, etc, when expected: *the witness chose to remain silent* **5** not spoken or expressed: *silent assent* **6** not active or in operation: *a silent volcano* **7** (of a letter) used in the conventional orthography of a word but no longer pronounced in that word: *the "k" in "know" is silent* **8** denoting a film that has no accompanying soundtrack, esp one made before 1927, when such soundtracks were developed ▷ *n* **9** a silent film [C16 from Latin *silēns*, from *silēre* to be quiet] ▷ 'silently *adv* ▷ 'silentness *n*

silent cop *n Austral informal* a small hemispherical traffic marker at an intersection

silent majority *n* a presumed moderate majority of the citizens who are too passive to make their views known

silent partner *n US and Canada* a partner in a business who does not play an active role, esp one who supplies capital. Also called (in Britain and certain other countries): **sleeping partner**

Silenus (saɪ'li:nəs) *n Greek myth* **1** chief of the satyrs and foster father to Dionysus: often depicted riding drunkenly on a donkey **2** (*often not capital*) one of a class of woodland deities, closely similar to the satyrs

silesia (saɪ'li:ʃə) *n* a twill-weave fabric of cotton or other fibre, used esp for pockets, linings, etc [C17 Latinized form of German *Schlesien* SILESIA]

Silesia (saɪ'li:ʃə) *n* a region of central Europe around the upper and middle Oder valley: mostly annexed by Prussia in 1742 but became almost wholly Polish in 1945; rich coal and iron-ore deposits. Polish name: **Śląsk**. Czech name: **Slezsko**. German name: **Schlesien**

Silesian (saɪ'li:ʃən) *adj* **1** of or relating to Silesia or its inhabitants ▷ *n* **2** a native or inhabitant of Silesia

silex ('saɪlɛks) *n* a type of heat-resistant glass made from fused quartz [C16 from Latin: hard stone, flint]

silhouette (ˌsɪlu:'ɛt) *n* **1** the outline of a solid figure as cast by its shadow **2** an outline drawing filled in with black, often a profile portrait cut out of black paper and mounted on a light ground ▷ *vb* **3** (*tr*) to cause to appear in silhouette [C18 named after Étienne de *Silhouette* (1709–67), French politician, perhaps referring to silhouettes as partial portraits, with a satirical allusion to Silhouette's brief career as controller general (1759)]

silica ('sɪlɪkə) *n* **1** the dioxide of silicon, occurring naturally as quartz, cristobalite, and tridymite. It is a refractory insoluble material used in the manufacture of glass, ceramics, and abrasives **2** short for **silica glass** [C19 New Latin, from Latin: SILEX]

silica gel *n* an amorphous form of silica capable of absorbing large quantities of water: used in drying gases and oils, as a carrier for catalysts and an anticaking agent for cosmetics

silica glass *n* another name for **quartz glass**

silicate ('sɪlɪkɪt, -ˌkeɪt) *n* a salt or ester of silicic acid, esp one of a large number of usually insoluble salts with polymeric negative ions having a structure formed of tetrahedrons of SiO_4 groups linked in rings, chains, sheets, or three dimensional frameworks. Silicates constitute a large proportion of the earth's minerals and are present in cement and glass

siliceous or **silicious** (sɪ'lɪʃəs) *adj* **1** of, relating to, or containing abundant silica: *siliceous deposits; a siliceous clay* **2** (of plants) growing in or needing soil rich in silica

silici- or before a vowel **silic-** *combining form* indicating silica or silicon: *silicify*

silicic (sɪ'lɪsɪk) *adj* of, concerned with, or containing silicon or an acid obtained from silicon

silicic acid *n* a white gelatinous substance obtained by adding an acid to a solution of sodium silicate. It has an ill-defined composition and is best regarded as hydrated silica, $SiO_2.nH_2O$

silicide ('sɪlɪˌsaɪd) *n* any one of a class of binary compounds formed between silicon and certain metals

siliciferous (ˌsɪlɪ'sɪfərəs) *adj* containing or yielding silicon or silica

silicify (sɪ'lɪsɪˌfaɪ) *vb* -**fies**, -**fying**, -**fied** to convert or be converted into silica: *silicified wood* ▷ siˌlicifi'cation *n*

silicium (sɪ'lɪsɪəm) *n* a rare name for **silicon**

silicle ('sɪlɪkəl) *n botany* a variant of **silicula**

silicon ('sɪlɪkən) *n* **a** a brittle metalloid element that exists in two allotropic forms; occurs principally in sand, quartz, granite, feldspar, and clay. It is usually a grey crystalline solid but is also found as a brown amorphous powder. It is used in transistors, rectifiers, solar cells, and alloys. Its compounds are widely used in glass manufacture, the building industry, and in the form of silicones. Symbol: Si; atomic no: 14; atomic wt: 28.0855; valency: 4; relative density: 2.33; melting pt: 1414°C; boiling pt: 3267°C **b** (*modifier; sometimes capital*) denoting an area of a country that contains a density of high-technology industry [C19 from SILICA, on the model of *boron, carbon*]

Silicon Alley *n* an area of New York City in which industries associated with information technology are concentrated

silicon carbide *n* an extremely hard bluish-black insoluble crystalline substance produced by heating carbon with sand at a high temperature and used as an abrasive and refractory material. Silicon carbide whiskers have a high tensile strength and are used in composites; very pure crystals are used as semiconductors. Formula: SiC

silicon chip *n* another term for **chip** (sense 8)

silicon-controlled rectifier *n* a semiconductor rectifier whose forward current between two electrodes, the anode and cathode, is initiated by means of a signal applied to a third electrode, the gate. The current subsequently becomes independent of the signal. It is a type of thyristor. Abbreviation: **SCR**

silicone (ˈsɪlɪˌkəʊn) *n chem* **a** any of a large class of polymeric synthetic materials that usually have resistance to temperature, water, and chemicals, and good insulating and lubricating properties, making them suitable for wide use as oils, water-repellents, resins, etc. Chemically they have alternate silicon and oxygen atoms with the silicon atoms bound to organic groups **b** (*as modifier*): *silicone rubber* ▷ See also **siloxane**

Silicon Fen *n* an area of Cambridgeshire, esp around the city of Cambridge, in which industries associated with information technology are concentrated

Silicon Glen *n* a collective term for the industries in Scotland associated with information technology, esp those concentrated in the central conurbation between Glasgow and Edinburgh

silicon rectifier *n electronics* a rectifier consisting of a semiconductor diode using crystalline silicon

Silicon Valley *n* **1** an industrial strip in W California, extending S of San Francisco, in which the US information technology industry is concentrated **2** any area in which industries associated with information technology are concentrated

silicosis (ˌsɪlɪˈkəʊsɪs) *n pathol* a form of pneumoconiosis caused by breathing in tiny particles of silica, quartz, or slate, and characterized by shortness of breath and fibrotic changes in the tissues of the lungs

silicula (sɪˈlɪkjʊlə), **silicle** (ˈsɪlɪkᵊl) *or* **silicule** (ˈsɪlɪkjʊl) *n, pl* **-liculae** (-ˈlɪkjʊliː), **-cles** *or* **-cules** ▷ *n botany* a short broad siliqua, occurring in such cruciferous plants as honesty and shepherd's-purse [C18 from Latin *silicula* a small pod; see SILIQUA]

siliculose (sɪˈlɪkjʊˌləʊs, -ˌləʊz) *adj* (of certain cruciferous plants such as honesty) producing siliculae [C18 from New Latin *siliculōsus*, from *silicula* a SILICLE]

siliqua (sɪˈliːkwə, ˈsɪlɪkwə) *or* **silique** (sɪˈliːk, ˈsɪlɪk) *n, pl* **-liquae** (-ˈliːkwiː) **-liquas** *or* **-liques** the long dry dehiscent fruit of cruciferous plants, such as the wallflower, consisting of two compartments separated by a central septum to which the seeds are attached [C18 via French from Latin *siliqua* a pod] > **siliquaceous** (ˌsɪlɪˈkweɪʃəs) *adj* > **siliquose** (ˈsɪlɪˌkwəʊs) *or* **siliquous** (ˈsɪlɪkwəs) *adj*

silk (sɪlk) *n* **1** the very fine soft lustrous fibre produced by a silkworm to make its cocoon **2 a** thread or fabric made from this fibre **b** (*as modifier*): *a silk dress* **3** a garment made of this **4** a very fine fibre produced by a spider to build its web, nest, or cocoon **5** the tuft of long fine styles on an ear of maize **6** *Brit* **a** the gown worn by a Queen's (or King's) Counsel **b** *informal* a Queen's (or King's) Counsel **c** **take silk** to become a Queen's (or King's) Counsel ▷ *vb* **7** (*intr*) *US and Canadian* (of maize) to develop long hairlike styles [Old English *sioluc*; compare Old Norse *silki*, Greek *sērikon*, Korean *sir*; all ultimately from Chinese *ssŭ* silk] > ˈ**silk**ˌ**like** *adj*

silkaline *or* **silkalene** (ˌsɪlkəˈliːn) *n* a fine smooth cotton fabric used for linings, etc [C20 from SILK + *-aline*, from *-oline* as in CRINOLINE]

silk cotton *n* another name for **kapok**

silk-cotton tree *n* any of several tropical bombacaceous trees of the genus *Ceiba*, esp *Ceiba pentandra*, having seeds covered with silky hairs from which kapok is obtained. Also called: **kapok tree**

silken (ˈsɪlkən) *adj* **1** made of silk **2** resembling silk in smoothness or gloss **3** dressed in silk **4** soft and delicate **5** *rare* luxurious or elegant

silk hat *n* a man's top hat covered with silk

silkie (ˈsɪlkɪ) *or* **selkie** *n* a Scot word for a **seal** (the animal) [from earlier Scot *selich*, Old English *seolh*]

silk-screen printing *n* another name for **screen process**

silkweed (ˈsɪlkˌwiːd) *n* another name for **milkweed** (sense 1) [C19 so called because the pods contain a silklike down]

silkworm (ˈsɪlkˌwɜːm) *n* **1** the larva of the Chinese moth *Bombyx mori*, that feeds on the leaves of the mulberry tree: widely cultivated as a source of silk **2** any of various similar or related larvae **3** **silkworm moth** the moth of any of these larvae

silky (ˈsɪlkɪ) *adj* **silkier, silkiest** **1** resembling silk in texture; glossy **2** made of silk **3** (of a voice, manner, etc) suave; smooth **4** *botany* covered with long fine soft hairs: *silky leaves* > ˈ**silkily** *adv* > ˈ**silkiness** *n*

silky oak *n* any of several trees of the Australian genus *Grevillea*, esp *G. robusta*, having divided leaves, smooth glossy wood, and showy clusters of orange, red, or white flowers: cultivated in the tropics as shade trees: family *Proteaceae*

silky terrier *n* another name for a **Sydney silky**

sill (sɪl) *n* **1** a shelf at the bottom of a window inside a room **2** a horizontal piece along the outside lower member of a window, that throws water clear of the wall below **3** the lower horizontal member of a window or door frame **4** a continuous horizontal member placed on top of a foundation wall in order to carry a timber framework **5** a flat usually horizontal mass of igneous rock, situated between two layers of older sedimentary rock, that was formed by an intrusion of magma [Old English *syll*; related to Old Norse *svill* sill, Icelandic *svoli* tree trunk, Old High German *swella* sill, Latin *solum* ground]

sillabub (ˈsɪləˌbʌb) *n* a variant spelling of **syllabub**

siller (ˈsɪlər) *Scot* ▷ *n* **1** silver **2** money ▷ *adj* **3** silver [a Scot variant of SILVER]

sillimanite (ˈsɪlɪməˌnaɪt) *n* a white, brown, or green fibrous mineral that consists of aluminium silicate in orthorhombic crystalline form and occurs in metamorphic rocks. Formula: Al_2SiO_5 [C19 named after Benjamin *Silliman* (1779–1864), US chemist]

silly (ˈsɪlɪ) *adj* **-lier, -liest** **1** lacking in good sense; absurd **2** frivolous, trivial, or superficial **3** feeble-minded **4** dazed, as from a blow **5** *obsolete* homely or humble ▷ *n* **6** (*modifier*) *cricket* (of a fielding position) near the batsman's wicket: *silly mid-on* **7** *pl* **-lies** Also called: **silly-billy** *informal* a foolish person [C15 (in the sense: pitiable, hence the later senses: foolish): from Old English *sǣlig* (unattested) happy, from *sǣl* happiness; related to Gothic *sēls* good] > ˈ**silliness** *n*

silly season *n Brit* a period, usually during the hot summer months, when journalists fill space reporting on frivolous events and activities

silo (ˈsaɪləʊ) *n, pl* **-los** **1** a pit, trench, horizontal container, or tower, often cylindrical in shape, in which silage is made and stored **2** a strengthened underground position in which missile systems are sited for protection against attack [C19 from Spanish, perhaps from Celtic]

Siloam (saɪˈləʊəm, sɪ-) *n Bible* a pool in Jerusalem where Jesus cured a man of his blindness (John 9)

siloxane (sɪˈlɒkseɪn) *n* any of a class of compounds containing alternate silicon and oxygen atoms with the silicon atoms bound to hydrogen atoms or organic groups. Many are highly complex polymers. See also **silicone** [C20 from SIL(ICON) + OX(YGEN) + (METH)ANE]

silt (sɪlt) *n* **1** a fine deposit of mud, clay, etc, esp one in a river or lake ▷ *vb* **2** (usually foll by *up*) to fill or become filled with silt; choke [C15 of Scandinavian origin; compare Norwegian, Danish *sylt* salt marsh; related to Old High German *sulza* salt marsh; see SALT] > **sil**ˈ**tation** *n* > ˈ**silty** *adj*

siltstone (ˈsɪltˌstəʊn) *n* a variety of fine sandstone formed from consolidated silt

Silures (saɪˈlʊəriːz) *pl n* a powerful and warlike tribe of ancient Britain, living chiefly in SE Wales, who fiercely resisted Roman invaders in the 1st century AD

Silurian (saɪˈlʊərɪən) *adj* **1** of, denoting, or formed in the third period of the Palaeozoic era, between the Ordovician and Devonian periods, which lasted for 25 million years, during which fishes first appeared **2** of or relating to the Silures ▷ *n* **3** **the** the Silurian period or rock system

silurid (saɪˈlʊərɪd) *n* **1** any freshwater teleost fish of the Eurasian family *Siluridae*, including catfish, such as *Silurus glanis* (**European catfish**), that have an elongated body, naked skin, and a long anal fin ▷ *adj* **2** of, relating to, or belonging to the family *Siluridae* [C19 from Latin *silūrus*, from Greek *silouros* a river fish]

silva (ˈsɪlvə) *n* a variant spelling of **sylva**

silvan (ˈsɪlvən) *adj* a variant spelling of **sylvan**

Silvanus *or* **Sylvanus** (sɪlˈveɪnəs) *n Roman myth* the Roman god of woodlands, fields, and flocks. Greek counterpart: **Pan** [Latin: from *silva* woodland]

silver (ˈsɪlvə) *n* **1 a** a very ductile malleable brilliant greyish-white element having the highest electrical and thermal conductivity of any metal. It occurs free and in argentite and other ores: used in jewellery, tableware, coinage, electrical contacts, and in electroplating. Its compounds are used in photography. Symbol: Ag; atomic no: 47; atomic wt: 107.8682; valency: 1 or 2; relative density: 10.50; melting pt: 961.93°C; boiling pt: 2163°C **b** (*as modifier*): *a silver coin*. Related adj: **argent** **2** coin made of, or having the appearance of, this metal **3** cutlery, whether made of silver or not **4** any household articles made of silver **5** *photog* any of a number of silver compounds used either as photosensitive substances in emulsions or as sensitizers **6 a** a brilliant or light greyish-white colour **b** (*as adjective*): *silver hair* **7** short for **silver medal** ▷ *adj* **8** well-articulated: *silver speech* **9** (*prenominal*) denoting the 25th in a series, esp an annual series: *a silver wedding anniversary* ▷ *vb* **10** (*tr*) to coat with silver or a silvery substance: *to silver a spoon* **11** to become or cause to become silvery in colour [Old English *siolfor*; related to Old Norse *silfr*, Gothic *silubr*, Old High German *silabar*, Old Slavonic *sirebro*] > ˈ**silverer** *n* > ˈ**silvering** *n*

silver age *n* **1** (in Greek and Roman mythology) the second of the world's major epochs, inferior to the preceding golden age and characterized by opulence and irreligion **2** the postclassical period of Latin literature, occupying the early part of the Roman imperial era, characterized by an overindulgence in elegance for its own sake and empty scholarly rhetoric

silverback (ˈsɪlvəˌbæk) *n* an older male gorilla with grey hair on its back

silver beet *n* a variety of beet, *Beta vulgaris cicla*, having large firm green leaves: staple cooked green vegetable in Australia and New Zealand

silver bell *n* any of various deciduous trees of the styracaceous genus *Halesia*, esp *H. carolina*, of North America and China, having white bell-shaped flowers. Also called: **snowdrop tree**

S

silver belly *n* NZ a freshwater eel

silver birch *n* a betulaceous tree, *Betula pendula*, of N temperate regions of the Old World, having silvery-white peeling bark. See also **birch** (sense 1)

silver bromide *n* a yellowish insoluble powder that darkens when exposed to light: used in making photographic emulsions. Formula: AgBr

silver certificate *n* (formerly) a banknote issued by the US Treasury to the public and redeemable in silver

silver chloride *n* a white insoluble powder that darkens on exposure to light because of the production of metallic silver: used in making photographic emulsions and papers. Formula: AgCl

silver disc *n* (in Britain) an album certified to have sold 60 000 copies or a single certified to have sold 200 000 copies. Compare **gold disc, platinum disc**

silver-eye *n* Austral and NZ another name for **white-eye**

silver fern *n* NZ 1 another name for **ponga** 2 a formalized spray of fern leaf, silver on a black background: the symbol of New Zealand sporting teams, esp the All Blacks

Silver Ferns *pl n* **the** the women's international netball team of New Zealand

silver fir *n* any of various fir trees the leaves of which have a silvery undersurface, esp *Abies alba*, an important timber tree of central and S Europe

silverfish ('sɪlvə,fɪʃ) *n, pl* **-fish** *or* **-fishes** 1 a silver variety of the goldfish *Carassius auratus* 2 any of various other silvery fishes, such as the moonfish *Monodactylus argenteus* 3 any of various small primitive wingless insects of the genus *Lepisma*, esp *L. saccharina*, that have long antennae and tail appendages and occur in buildings, feeding on food scraps, bookbindings, etc: order *Thysanura* (bristletails)

silver fox *n* 1 an American red fox in a colour phase in which the fur is black with long silver-tipped hairs 2 the valuable fur or pelt of this animal

silver frost *n* another name for **glaze ice**

silver-gilt *n* silver covered with a thin film of gold

silver goal *n* soccer (in certain competitions) a goal scored in a full half of extra time that is played if a match is drawn. This goal counts as the winner if it is the only goal scored in the full half or full period of extra time

silverhorn ('sɪlvə,hɔːn) *n* any of various usually darkish caddis flies of the family *Leptoceridae*, characterized by very long pale antennae. The larvae are a favourite food of trout

silver iodide *n* a yellow insoluble powder that darkens on exposure to light: used in photography and artificial rainmaking. Formula: AgI

silver lining *n* a comforting or hopeful aspect of an otherwise desperate or unhappy situation (esp in the phrase **every cloud has a silver lining**)

silver maple *n* a North American maple tree, *Acer saccharinum*, having five-lobed leaves that are green above and silvery-white beneath

silver medal *n* a medal of silver awarded to a competitor who comes second in a contest or race. Compare **gold medal, bronze medal**

silvern ('sɪlvən) *adj* archaic or poetic silver

silver nitrate *n* a white crystalline soluble poisonous substance used in making photographic emulsions, other silver salts, and as a medical antiseptic and astringent. Formula: AgNO₃. See also **lunar caustic**

silver plate *n* 1 a thin layer of silver deposited on a base metal 2 articles, esp tableware, made of silver plate ▷ *vb* **silver-plate** 3 (*tr*) to coat (a metal, object, etc) with silver, as by electroplating

silverpoint ('sɪlvə,pɔɪnt) *n* a drawing technique popular esp in the 15th and 16th centuries, using an instrument with a silver wire tip on specially prepared paper

silver screen *n* the informal 1 films collectively or the film industry 2 the screen onto which films are projected

silver service *n* (in restaurants) a style of serving food using a spoon and fork in one hand like a pair of tongs

silverside ('sɪlvə,saɪd) *n* 1 Brit and NZ a coarse cut of beef below the aitchbone and above the leg 2 Also called: **silversides** any small marine or freshwater teleost fish of the family *Atherinidae*, related to the grey mullets: includes the jacksmelt

silversmith ('sɪlvə,smɪθ) *n* a craftsman who makes or repairs articles of silver
> 'silver,smithing *n*

silver-spooned *adj* informal born into, of, or relating to a wealthy upper-class family [C20 from *born with a silver spoon in one's mouth*; see SPOON]

silver standard *n* a monetary system in which the legal unit of currency is defined with reference to silver of a specified fineness and weight and sometimes (esp formerly) freely redeemable for it

silver surfer *n* informal an older, esp retired, person who uses the internet

silvertail ('sɪlvə,teɪl) *n* Austral informal a rich and influential person

silver thaw *n* Canadian 1 a freezing rainstorm 2 another name for **glitter** (sense 7)

silver-tongued *adj* persuasive; eloquent: *silver-tongued salesman*

silverware ('sɪlvə,wɛə) *n* articles, esp tableware, made of or plated with silver

silverweed ('sɪlvə,wiːd) *n* 1 a rosaceous perennial creeping plant, *Potentilla anserina*, with silvery pinnate leaves and yellow flowers 2 any of various convolvulaceous shrubs of the genus *Argyreia*, of SE Asia and Australia, having silvery leaves and purple flowers

silvery ('sɪlvərɪ) *adj* 1 of or having the appearance of silver: *the silvery moon* 2 containing or covered with silver 3 having a clear ringing sound
> 'silveriness *n*

silver-Y moth *n* a brownish noctuid moth, *Plusia gamma*, having a light Y-shaped marking on each forewing; it migrates in large flocks. Often shortened to: **silver-Y**

silviculture ('sɪlvɪ,kʌltʃə) *n* the branch of forestry that is concerned with the cultivation of trees [C20 *silvi-*, from Latin *silva* woodland + CULTURE]
> ,silvi'cultural *adj* > ,silvi'culturist *n*

s'il vous plaît French (sil vu plɛ) if you please; please

sim (sɪm) *n* a computer game which simulates an activity such as playing a sport or flying an aircraft

sima ('saɪmə) *n* 1 the silicon-rich and magnesium-rich rocks of the earth's oceanic crust, the most abundant individual rock being basalt 2 the earth's continental lower crust, probably comprised of gabbro rather than basalt [C20 from SI(LICA) + MA(GNESIA)] > **simatic** (saɪˈmætɪk) *adj*

simar (sɪˈmɑː) *n* a variant spelling of **cymar**

simarouba *or* **simaruba** (,sɪməˈruːbə) *n* 1 any tropical American tree of the genus *Simarouba*, esp *S. amara*, having divided leaves and fleshy fruits: family Simaroubaceae 2 the medicinal bark of any of these trees [C18 from New Latin, from Carib *simaruba*]

simaroubaceous *or* **simarubaceous** (,sɪmaruːˈbeɪʃəs) *adj* of, relating to, or belonging to the Simaroubaceae, a mainly tropical family of trees and shrubs that includes ailanthus and quassia

simba ('sɪmbə) *n* an E African word for **lion** [Swahili]

Simbirsk (Russian sɪmˈbirsk) *n* a city in W central Russia on the River Volga: birthplace of Lenin (V. I. Ulyanov). Pop: 639 000 (2005 est). Former name (1924–91): **Ulyanovsk**

SIM Card *n* acronym for subscriber identity module card; a small card used in a mobile phone to store data about the network, telephone number, etc

Simchath Torah, Simhath Torah *or* **Simchas Torah** (sɪmˈxat tɔrˈɑː, ˈsɪmxɑs ˈtaʊrɔ) *n* a Jewish festival celebrated immediately after Sukkoth on Tishri 23 (in Israel, Tishri 22) to mark the completion of the annual cycle of Torah readings and its immediate recommencement [from Hebrew *śimhath tōrāh*, literally: celebration of the Torah]

Simeon ('sɪmɪən) *n* 1 a Old Testament the second son of Jacob and Leah b the tribe descended from him c the territory once occupied by this tribe in the extreme south of the land of Canaan 2 New Testament a devout Jew, who recognized the infant Jesus as the Messiah and uttered the canticle *Nunc Dimittis* over him in the Temple (Luke 2:25–35)

Simferopol (Russian simfɪˈrɔpəlj) *n* a city in S Ukraine on the S Crimean Peninsula: a Scythian town in the 1st century BC; seized by the Russians in 1736. Pop: 344 000 (2005 est)

simian ('sɪmɪən) *adj* 1 Also (rare): **simious** ('sɪmɪəs) of, relating to, or resembling a monkey or ape ▷ *n* 2 a monkey or ape [C17 from Latin *sīmia* an ape, probably from *sīmus* flat-nosed, from Greek *sīmos*]

similar ('sɪmɪlə) *adj* 1 showing resemblance in qualities, characteristics, or appearance; alike but not identical 2 geometry (of two or more figures) having corresponding angles equal and all corresponding sides in the same ratio. Compare **congruent** (sense 2) 3 maths (of two classes) equinumerous [C17 from Old French *similaire*, from Latin *similis*] > **similarity** (,sɪmɪˈlærɪtɪ) *n*
> 'similarly *adv*

USAGE As *should not be used after *similar*: Wilson held a similar position to Jones (not *a similar position as Jones*); the system is similar to the one in France (not *similar as in France*)

simile ('sɪmɪlɪ) *n* a figure of speech that expresses the resemblance of one thing to another of a different category, usually introduced by *as* or *like*. Compare **metaphor** [C14 from Latin *simile* something similar, from *similis* like]

similitude (sɪˈmɪlɪ,tjuːd) *n* 1 likeness; similarity 2 a thing or sometimes a person that is like or the counterpart of another 3 archaic a simile, allegory, or parable [C14 from Latin *similitūdō*, from *similis* like]

simitar ('sɪmɪtə) *n* a rare spelling of **scimitar**

Simla ('sɪmlə) *n* a city in N India, capital of Himachal Pradesh state: summer capital of India (1865–1939); hill resort and health centre. Pop: 142 161 (2001). Official name: **Shimla**

simmer ('sɪmə) *vb* 1 to cook (food) gently at or just below the boiling point 2 (*intr*) to be about to break out in rage or excitement ▷ *n* 3 the act, sound, or state of simmering [C17 perhaps of imitative origin; compare German *summen* to hum]

simmer dim ('sɪmər, -mə) *n* Scot the night-long twilight found in the Northern Isles around midsummer [Scottish form of SUMMER¹ + DIM]

simmer down *vb* (*adverb*) 1 (*intr*) informal to grow calmer or quieter, as after intense rage or excitement 2 (*tr*) to reduce the volume of (a liquid) by boiling slowly

simnel cake ('sɪmnˀl) *n* Brit a fruit cake containing a layer of marzipan, often coloured with saffron and topped with marzipan, traditionally eaten at Lent or Easter [C13 *simenel*, from Old French, from Latin *simila* fine flour, probably of Semitic origin; related to Greek *semidalis* fine flour]

simoniac (sɪˈməʊnɪ,æk) *n* a person who is guilty of practising simony > **simoniacal** (,saɪməˈnaɪəkˀl) *adj* > ,simo'niacally *adv*

Simon Peter *n* New Testament the full name of the apostle Peter, a combination of his original name and the name given him by Christ (Matthew 16:17–18)

simon-pure *adj* real; genuine; authentic [C19 from the phrase *the real Simon Pure*, name of a character in the play *A Bold Stroke for a Wife* (1717) by Susannah Centlivre (1669–1723) who is impersonated by another character in some scenes]

simony ('saɪmənɪ) *n Christianity* the practice, now usually regarded as a sin, of buying or selling spiritual or Church benefits such as pardons, relics, etc, or preferments [c13 from Old French *simonie,* from Late Latin *sīmōnia,* from the name of *Simon Magus,* a Samaritan sorceror of the 1st century AD] > 'simonist *n*

Simon Zelotes (zɪ'ləʊtiːz) *n* **Saint** one of the 12 apostles, who had probably belonged to the Zealot party before becoming a Christian (Luke 6:15). Owing to a misinterpretation of two similar Aramaic words he is also, but mistakenly, called *the Canaanite* (Matthew 10:4). Feast day: Oct 28 or May 10

simoom (sɪ'muːm) *or* **simoon** (sɪ'muːn) *n* a strong suffocating sand-laden wind of the deserts of Arabia and North Africa. Also called: **samiel** [from Arabic *samūm* poisonous, from *sam* poison, from Aramaic *sammā* poison]

simp (sɪmp) *n US slang* short for **simpleton**

simpatico (sɪm'pɑːtɪˌkəʊ, -'pæt-) *adj informal* **1** pleasant or congenial **2** of similar mind or temperament; compatible [Italian: from *simpatia* SYMPATHY]

simper ('sɪmpə) *vb* **1** (*intr*) to smile coyly, affectedly, or in a silly self-conscious way **2** (*tr*) to utter (something) in a simpering manner ▷ *n* **3** a simpering smile; smirk [c16 probably from Dutch *simper* affected] > 'simperer *n* > 'simpering *adj, n* > 'simperingly *adv*

simple ('sɪmp^əl) *adj* **1** not involved or complicated; easy to understand or do: *a simple problem* **2** plain; unadorned: *a simple dress* **3** consisting of one element or part only; not combined or complex: *a simple mechanism* **4** unaffected or unpretentious: *although he became famous, he remained a simple and well-liked man* **5** not guileful; sincere; frank: *her simple explanation was readily accepted* **6** of humble condition or rank: *the peasant was of simple birth* **7** weak in intelligence; feeble-minded **8** (*prenominal*) without additions or modifications; mere: *the witness told the simple truth* **9** (*prenomina*) ordinary or straightforward: *a simple case of mumps* **10** *chem* (of a substance or material) consisting of only one chemical compound rather than a mixture of compounds **11** *maths* **a** (of a fraction) containing only integers **b** (of an equation) containing variables to the first power only; linear **c** (of a root of an equation) occurring only once; not multiple **12** *biology* not divided into parts: *a simple leaf; a simple eye* **13** *music* relating to or denoting a time where the number of beats per bar may be two, three, or four ▷ *n archaic* **14** a simpleton; fool **15** a plant, esp a herbaceous plant, having medicinal properties [c13 via Old French from Latin *simplex* plain] > 'simpleness *n*

simple fraction *n* a fraction in which the numerator and denominator are both integers expressed as a ratio rather than a decimal. Also called: **common fraction, vulgar fraction**

simple fracture *n* a fracture in which the broken bone does not pierce the skin. Also called: **closed fracture.** Compare **compound fracture**

simple fruit *n* a fruit, such as a grape or cherry, that is formed from only one ovary

simple harmonic motion *n* a form of periodic motion of a particle, etc, in which the acceleration is always directed towards some equilibrium point and is proportional to the displacement from this point. Abbreviation: **SHM**

simple-hearted *adj* free from deceit; open; frank; sincere

simple interest *n* interest calculated or paid on the principal alone. Compare **compound interest**

simple machine *n* a simple device for altering the magnitude or direction of a force. The six basic types are the lever, wheel and axle, pulley, screw, wedge, and inclined plane

simple microscope *n* a microscope having a single lens; magnifying glass. Compare

compound microscope

simple-minded *adj* **1** stupid; foolish; feeble-minded **2** unsophisticated; artless > ˌsimple-'mindedly *adv* > ˌsimple-'mindedness *n*

simple sentence *n* a sentence consisting of a single main clause. Compare **compound sentence, complex sentence**

Simple Simon *n* a foolish man or boy; simpleton [c20 after the name of a character in a nursery rhyme]

simple tense *n grammar* a tense of verbs, in English and other languages, not involving the use of an auxiliary verb in addition to the main verb, as for example the past *he drowned* as opposed to the future *he will drown*

simpleton ('sɪmp^əltən) *n* a foolish or ignorant person

simplex ('sɪmplɛks) *adj* **1** permitting the transmission of signals in only one direction in a radio circuit, etc. Compare **duplex** ▷ *n* **2** *linguistics* a simple not a compound word **3** *geometry* the most elementary geometric figure in Euclidean space of a given dimension; a line segment in one-dimensional space or a triangle in two-dimensional space [c16 from Latin: simple, literally: one-fold, from *sim-* one + *plex,* from *plicāre* to fold; compare DUPLEX]

simplicidentate (ˌsɪmplɪsɪ'dɛnteɪt) *adj* **1** of, relating to, or belonging to the *Simplicidentata,* a former suborder including all the mammals now classified as rodents: used when lagomorphs were included in the order *Rodentia* ▷ *n* **2** any animal of this type

simplicity (sɪm'plɪsɪtɪ) *n* the quality or condition of being simple

simplify ('sɪmplɪˌfaɪ) *vb* **-fies, -fying, -fied** (*tr*) **1** to make less complicated, clearer, or easier **2** *maths* to reduce (an equation, fraction, etc) to a simpler form by cancellation of common factors, regrouping of terms in the same variable, etc [c17 via French from Medieval Latin *simplificāre,* from Latin *simplus* simple + *facere* to make] > ˌsimplifi'cation *n* > 'simplificative *adj* > 'simpliˌfier *n*

simplistic (sɪm'plɪstɪk) *adj* **1** characterized by extreme simplicity; naive **2** oversimplifying complex problems; making unrealistically simple judgments or analyses > 'simplism *n* > sim'plistically *adv*

> **USAGE** Since *simplistic* already has *too* as part of its meaning, it is tautologous to talk about something being *too simplistic* or *over-simplistic*

Simplon Pass ('sɪmplən) *n* a pass over the Lepontine Alps in S Switzerland, between Brig (Switzerland) and Iselle (Italy). Height: 2009 m (6590 ft)

simply ('sɪmplɪ) *adv* **1** in a simple manner **2** merely; only **3** absolutely; altogether; really: *a simply wonderful holiday* ▷ *sentence modifier* **4** frankly; candidly

Simpson Desert ('sɪmpsən) *n* an uninhabited arid region in central Australia, mainly in the Northern Territory. Area: about 145 000 sq km (56 000 sq miles)

simul ('sɪməl) *n* a shortened form of **simultaneous** (sense 2)

simulacrum (ˌsɪmjʊ'leɪkrəm) *n, pl* -**cra** (-krə) *archaic* **1** any image or representation of something **2** a slight, unreal, or vague semblance of something; superficial likeness [c16 from Latin: likeness, from *simulāre* to imitate, from *similis* like]

simulant ('sɪmjʊlənt) *adj* **1** simulating **2** (esp of plant parts) resembling another part in structure or function

simular ('sɪmjʊlə) *archaic* ▷ *n* **1** a person or thing that simulates or imitates; sham ▷ *adj* **2** fake; simulated

simulate *vb* ('sɪmjʊˌleɪt) (*tr*) **1** to make a pretence of; feign: *to simulate anxiety* **2** to reproduce the conditions of (a situation, etc), as in carrying out an experiment: *to simulate weightlessness* **3** to

assume or have the appearance of; imitate ▷ *adj* ('sɪmjʊlɪt, -ˌleɪt) **4** *archaic* assumed or simulated [c17 from Latin *simulāre* to copy, from *similis* like] > 'simulative *adj* > 'simulatively *adv*

simulated ('sɪmjʊˌleɪtɪd) *adj* **1** (of fur, leather, pearls, etc) being an imitation of the genuine article, usually made from cheaper material **2** (of actions, qualities, emotions, etc) imitated; feigned

simulation (ˌsɪmjʊ'leɪʃən) *n* **1** the act or an instance of simulating **2** the assumption of a false appearance or form **3** a representation of a problem, situation, etc, in mathematical terms, esp using a computer **4** *maths, statistics, computing* the construction of a mathematical model for some process, situation, etc, in order to estimate its characteristics or solve problems about it probabilistically in terms of the model **5** *psychiatry* the conscious process of feigning illness in order to gain some particular end; malingering

simulator ('sɪmjʊˌleɪtə) *n* **1** any device or system that simulates specific conditions or the characteristics of a real process or machine for the purposes of research or operator training: *space simulator* **2** a person who simulates

simulcast ('sɪməlˌkɑːst) *vb* **1** (*tr*) to broadcast (a programme, etc) simultaneously on radio and television ▷ *n* **2** a programme, etc, so broadcast [c20 from SIMUL(TANEOUS) + (BROAD)CAST]

simultaneous (ˌsɪməl'teɪnɪəs; *US* ˌsaɪməl'teɪnɪəs) *adj* **1** occurring, existing, or operating at the same time; concurrent ▷ *n* **2** *chess* a display in which one player plays a number of opponents at once, walking from board to board. Sometimes shortened to: **simul** [c17 formed on the model of INSTANTANEOUS from Latin *simul* at the same time, together] > ˌsimul'taneously *adv* > ˌsimul'taneousness *or* simultaneity (ˌsɪməltə'niːɪtɪ; *US* ˌsaɪməltə'niːɪtɪ) *n*

simultaneous equations *pl n* a set of equations that are all satisfied by the same values of the variables

sin[1] (sɪn) *n* **1** *theol* **a** a transgression of God's known will or any principle or law regarded as embodying this **b** the condition of estrangement from God arising from such transgression. See also **actual sin, mortal sin, original sin, venial sin** **2** any serious offence, as against a religious or moral principle **3** any offence against a principle or standard **4** live in sin *informal* (of an unmarried couple) to live together ▷ *vb* (*intr*) sins, sinning, sinned **5** *theol* to commit a sin **6** (usually foll by *against*) to commit an offence (against a person, principle, etc) [Old English *synn;* related to Old Norse *synth,* Old High German *suntea* sin, Latin *sons* guilty] > 'sinner *n*

sin[2] (sɪn) *prep, conj, adv* a Scot dialect word for **since**

sin[3] (siːn) *n* the 21st letter in the Hebrew alphabet (ש), transliterated as S

sin[4] (saɪn) *maths abbreviation for* sine

SIN *or* **S.I.N.** (in Canada) *abbreviation for* social insurance number

Sinai ('saɪnaɪ, 'saɪnɪˌaɪ) *n* **1** a mountainous peninsula of NE Egypt at the N end of the Red Sea, between the Gulf of Suez and the Gulf of Aqaba: occupied by Israel in 1967; fully restored by 1982 **2** **Mount** the mountain where Moses received the Law from God (Exodus 19–20): often identified as Jebel Musa, sometimes as Jebel Serbal, both on the S Sinai Peninsula

Sinaitic (ˌsaɪnɪ'ɪtɪk) *or* **Sinaic** (sɪ'neɪɪk) *adj* **1** of or relating to the Sinai Peninsula **2** of or relating to Mount Sinai

Sinaloa (ˌsiːnə'ləʊə, ˌsɪn-; *Spanish* sina'loa) *n* a state of W Mexico. Capital: Culiacán. Pop: 2 534 835 (2000). Area: 58 092 sq km (22 425 sq miles)

sinanthropus (sɪn'ænθrəpəs) *n* a primitive apelike man of the genus *Sinanthropus,* now considered a subspecies of *Homo erectus.* See also **Java man, Peking man** [c20 from New Latin, from Late Latin *Sīnae* the Chinese + *-anthropus,* from Greek *anthrōpos* man]

sinapism ('sɪnəˌpɪzəm) n a technical name for **mustard plaster** [C17 from Late Latin *sināpismus*, from Greek *sinapismos* application of mustard plaster, from *sinapi* mustard, of Egyptian origin]

Sinarquist ('sɪnɑːkɪst, -kwɪst) n (in Mexico) a member of a fascist movement in the 1930s and 1940s having links with the Nazis and the Falangists: hostile towards the US, Communism, Jews, organized labour, etc [C20 Mexican Spanish *sinarquista*, from Spanish *sin* without + *anarquista* anarchist] > **Sin'arquism** n

sin bin n 1 slang (in ice hockey, rugby, etc) an area off the field of play where a player who has committed a foul can be sent to sit for a specified period 2 Brit informal a special unit on a separate site from a school that disruptive schoolchildren attend until they can be reintegrated into their normal classes

since (sɪns) prep 1 during or throughout the period of time after: *since May it has only rained once* ▷ conj (subordinating) 2 (sometimes preceded by *ever*) continuously from or starting from the time when: *since we last met, important things have happened* 3 seeing that; because: *since you have no money, you can't come* ▷ adv 4 since that time: *he left yesterday and I haven't seen him since* [Old English *sīththan*, literally: after that; related to Old High German *sīd* since, Latin *sērus* late]

▆ USAGE See at **ago**

sincere (sɪn'sɪə) adj 1 not hypocritical or deceitful; open; genuine: *a sincere person; sincere regret* 2 archaic pure; unadulterated; unmixed 3 obsolete sound; whole [C16 from Latin *sincērus*] > **sin'cerely** adv > **sincerity** (sɪn'sɛrɪtɪ) or **sin'cereness** n

sinciput ('sɪnsɪˌpʌt) n, pl **sinciputs** or **sincipita** (sɪn'sɪpɪtə) anatomy the forward upper part of the skull [C16 from Latin: half a head, from SEMI- + *caput* head] > **sin'cipital** adj

Sind (sɪnd) n a province of SE Pakistan, mainly in the lower Indus valley: formerly a province of British India; became a province of Pakistan in 1947; divided in 1955 between Hyderabad and Khairpur; reunited as a province in 1970. Capital: Karachi. Pop: 34 240 000 (2003 est). Area: 140 914 sq km (54 407 sq miles)

Sindhi ('sɪndɪ) n 1 (pl -dhi or -dhis) a former inhabitant of Sind. The Muslim majority now lives in Pakistan while the Hindu minority has mostly moved to India 2 the language of this people, belonging to the Indic branch of the Indo-European family

sine¹ (saɪn) n (of an angle) **a** a trigonometric function that in a right-angled triangle is the ratio of the length of the opposite side to that of the hypotenuse **b** a function that in a circle centred at the origin of a Cartesian coordinate system is the ratio of the ordinate of a point on the circumference to the radius of the circle. Abbreviation: **sin** [C16 from Latin *sinus* a bend; in New Latin, *sinus* was mistaken as a translation of Arabic *jiba* sine (from Sanskrit *jīva*, literally: bowstring) because of confusion with Arabic *jaib* curve]

sine² ('saɪnɪ) prep (esp in Latin phrases or legal terms) lacking; without

sinecure ('saɪnɪˌkjʊə) n 1 a paid office or post involving minimal duties 2 a Church benefice to which no spiritual or pastoral charge is attached [C17 from Medieval Latin phrase (*beneficium*) *sine cūrā* (benefice) without cure (of souls), from Latin *sine* without + *cūra* cure, care] > **'sine,curism** n > **'sine,curist** n

sine curve n a curve of the equation y = sin x. Also called: **sinusoid**

sine die Latin ('saɪnɪ 'daɪɪ) adv, adj without a day fixed: *an adjournment sine die* [literally: without a day]

sine prole Latin ('saɪnɪ 'prəʊlɪ) adj, adv law without issue (esp in the phrase *demisit sine prole* (died without issue))

sine qua non Latin ('saɪnɪ kweɪ 'nɒn) n an essential condition or requirement [literally: without which not]

sinew ('sɪnjuː) n 1 anatomy another name for **tendon** 2 (often plural) **a** a source of strength or power **b** a literary word for **muscle** [Old English *sionu*; related to Old Norse *sin*, Old Saxon *sinewa*, Old High German *senawa* sinew, Lettish *pasainis* string] > **'sinewless** adj

sine wave n any oscillation, such as a sound wave or alternating current, whose waveform is that of a sine curve

sinewy ('sɪnjʊɪ) adj 1 consisting of or resembling a tendon or tendons 2 muscular; brawny 3 (esp of language, style, etc) vigorous; forceful 4 (of meat, etc) tough; stringy > **'sinewiness** n

sinfonia (ˌsɪnfə'nɪə) n, pl -nie (-'niːeɪ) 1 another word for **symphony** (senses 2, 3) 2 (capital when part of a name) a symphony orchestra [Italian]

sinfonietta (ˌsɪnfən'jɛtə, -fəʊn-) n 1 a short or light symphony 2 (capital when part of name) a small symphony orchestra [Italian: a little symphony, from SINFONIA]

sinful ('sɪnfʊl) adj 1 having committed or tending to commit sin: *a sinful person* 2 characterized by or being a sin: *a sinful act* > **'sinfully** adv > **'sinfulness** n

sing (sɪŋ) vb **sings, singing, sang, sung** 1 to produce or articulate (sounds, words, a song, etc) with definite and usually specific musical intonation 2 (when intr, often foll by *to*) to perform (a song) to the accompaniment (of): *to sing to a guitar* 3 (intr; foll by *of*) to tell a story or tale in song (about): *I sing of a maiden* 4 (intr; foll by *to*) to address a song (to) or perform a song (for) 5 (intr) to perform songs for a living, as a professional singer 6 (intr) (esp of certain birds and insects) to utter calls or sounds reminiscent of music 7 (when intr, usually foll by *of*) to tell (something) or give praise (to someone), esp in verse: *the poet who sings of the Trojan dead* 8 (intr) to make a whining, ringing, or whistling sound: *the kettle is singing; the arrow sang past his ear* 9 (intr) (of the ears) to experience a continuous ringing or humming sound 10 (tr) (esp in church services) to chant or intone (a prayer, psalm, etc) 11 (tr) to bring to a given state by singing: *to sing a child to sleep* 12 (intr) slang, chiefly US to confess or act as an informer 13 (intr) Austral (in Aboriginal witchcraft) to bring about a person's death by incantation. The same power can sometimes be used beneficently ▷ n 14 informal an act or performance of singing 15 a ringing or whizzing sound, as of bullets ▷ See also **sing along, sing out** [Old English *singan*; related to Old Norse *syngja* to sing, Gothic *siggwan*, Old High German *singan*] > **'singable** adj > **'singing** adj, n

▆ USAGE See at **ring²**

sing abbreviation for **singular**

sing along vb (intr, adverb) 1 to join in singing with a performer ▷ n **sing-along** 2 such a singsong

Singapore (ˌsɪŋə'pɔː, ˌsɪŋgə-) n 1 a republic in SE Asia, occupying one main island and over 50 small islands at the S end of the Malay Peninsula: established as a British trading post in 1819 and became part of the Straits Settlements in 1826; occupied by the Japanese (1942–45); a British colony from 1946, becoming self-governing in 1959; part of the Federation of Malaysia from 1963 to 1965, when it became an independent republic (within the Commonwealth). Official languages: Chinese, Malay, English, and Tamil. Religion: Buddhist, Taoist, traditional beliefs, and Muslim. Currency: Singapore dollar. Capital: Singapore. Pop: 4 315 000 (2004 est). Area: 646 sq km (250 sq miles) 2 the capital of the republic of Singapore: a major international port; administratively not treated as a city

Singaporean (ˌsɪŋə'pɔːrɪən, ˌsɪŋgə-) adj 1 of or relating to Singapore or its inhabitants ▷ n 2 a native or inhabitant of Singapore

singe (sɪndʒ) vb **singes, singeing, singed** 1 to burn or be burnt superficially; scorch: *to singe one's clothes* 2 (tr) to burn the ends of (hair, etc) 3 (tr) to

expose (a carcass) to flame to remove bristles or hair ▷ n 4 a superficial burn [Old English *sengan*; related to Middle High German *sengen* to singe, Dutch *sengel* spark, Norwegian *sengla* to smell of burning, Swedish *sjängla* to singe, Icelandic *sāngr*]

singer ('sɪŋə) n 1 a person who sings, esp one who earns a living by singing 2 a singing bird 3 an obsolete word for **poet**

singer-songwriter n a performer who writes his or her own songs

Singh (sɪŋ) n a title assumed by a Sikh when he becomes a full member of the community [from Hindi, from Sanskrit *sinhá* a lion]

Singhalese (ˌsɪŋə'liːz) n, pl -leses or -lese ▷ adj a variant spelling of **Sinhalese**

singing hinny n a type of currant cake popular in NE England which, when cooked on a griddle, makes a singing noise [*hinny* Scottish and N English variant of HONEY]

singing telegram n a greetings service in which a person is employed to present greetings by singing to the person celebrating

single ('sɪŋgᵊl) adj (usually prenominal) 1 existing alone; solitary: *upon the hill stood a single tower* 2 distinct from other things; unique or individual 3 composed of one part 4 designed for one user: *a single room; a single bed* 5 (also postpositive) unmarried 6 connected with the condition of being unmarried: *he led a single life* 7 (esp of combat) involving two individuals; one against one 8 sufficient for one person or thing only: *a single portion of food* 9 even one: *there wasn't a single person on the beach* 10 (of a flower) having only one set or whorl of petals 11 determined; single-minded: *a single devotion to duty* 12 (of the eye) seeing correctly: *to consider something with a single eye* 13 rare honest or sincere; genuine 14 archaic (of ale, beer, etc) mild in strength ▷ n 15 something forming one individual unit 16 an unmarried person 17 a gramophone record, CD, or cassette with a short recording, usually of pop music, on it 18 golf a game between two players 19 cricket a hit from which one run is scored 20 **a** Brit a pound note **b** US and Canadian a dollar note 21 See **single ticket** ▷ vb 22 (tr; usually foll by *out*) to select from a group of people or things; distinguish by separation: *he singled him out for special mention* 23 (tr) to thin out (seedlings) 24 short for **single-foot** ▷ See also **singles** [C14 from Old French *sengle*, from Latin *singulus* individual] > **'singleness** n

single-acting adj (of a reciprocating engine or pump) having a piston or pistons that are pressurized on one side only. Compare **double-acting** (sense 1)

single-action n (modifier) (of a firearm) requiring the hammer to be cocked by hand before firing

single-blind adj of or relating to an experiment, esp one to discover people's reactions to certain commodities, drugs, etc, in which the experimenters but not the subjects know the particulars of the test items during the experiment. Compare **double-blind**

single bond n chem a covalent bond formed between two atoms by the sharing of one pair of electrons

single-breasted adj (of a garment) having the fronts overlapping only slightly and with one row of fastenings

single-cell protein n protein that is produced by micro-organisms fermenting in liquid or gaseous petroleum fractions or other organic substances: used as a food supplement. Abbreviation: **SCP**

single cream n cream having a low fat content that does not thicken with beating

single-cross n genetics a hybrid of the first generation between two inbred lines

single-cut file n a file with teeth in one direction only: used for filing soft material

single-decker n Brit informal a bus with only one passenger deck

single density n computing a disk with the normal capacity for storage

singledom ('sɪŋg°ldəm) *n informal* the state of being unmarried or not involved in a long-term relationship

single-end *n Scot dialect* accommodation consisting of a single room

single-ended *adj electronics* (of an amplifier) having one side of the input and one side of the output connected to earth: used for an unbalanced signal

single entry *n* **a** a simple book-keeping system in which transactions are entered in one account only. Compare **double entry b** (*as modifier*): *a single-entry account*

single file *n* a line of persons, animals, or things ranged one behind the other, either stationary or moving

single-foot *n* **1** a rapid showy gait of a horse in which each foot strikes the ground separately, as in a walk ▷ *vb* **2** to move or cause to move at this gait

single-handed *adj* ▷ *adv* **1** unaided or working alone: *a single-handed crossing of the Atlantic* **2** having or operated by one hand or one person only > ˌsingle-'handedly *adv* > ˌsingle-'handedness *n*

single-lens reflex *n See* **reflex camera**

single market *n* a market consisting of a number of nations, esp those of the European Union, in which goods, capital, and currencies can move freely across borders without tariffs or restrictions

single-minded *adj* having but one aim or purpose; dedicated > ˌsingle-'mindedly *adv* > ˌsingle-'mindedness *n*

single parent *n* **a** a person who has a dependent child or dependent children and who is widowed, divorced, or unmarried **b** (*as modifier*): *a single-parent family*. Also called (NZ): **solo parent**

single-phase *adj* (of a system, circuit, or device) having, generating, or using a single alternating voltage

singles ('sɪŋg°lz) *pl n tennis, badminton* a match played with one person on each side

singles bar *n* a bar or club that is a social meeting place for single people

single-sex *adj* (of schools, etc) admitting members of one sex only; not coeducational

single sideband transmission *n* a method of transmitting radio waves in which either the upper or the lower sideband is transmitted, the carrier being either wholly or partially suppressed. This reduces the required bandwidth and improves the signal-to-noise ratio. Abbreviation: SSB

single-space *vb* (*tr*) to type (copy) without leaving a space between the lines

single-step *vb* -steps, -stepping, -stepped (*tr*) *computing* to perform a single instruction on (a program), generally under the control of a debug program

singlestick ('sɪŋg°lˌstɪk) *n* **1** a wooden stick used instead of a sword for fencing **2** fencing with such a stick **3** any short heavy stick

singlet ('sɪŋglɪt) *n* **1** *chiefly Brit and Austral* a man's sleeveless undergarment covering the body from the shoulders to the hips **2** *Austral* a similar sleeveless garment worn as outerwear. Also called (in Britain): **vest 3** *chiefly Brit* a garment worn with shorts by athletes, boxers, etc **4** NZ a black woollen outer garment worn by bushmen **5** *physics* a multiplet that has only one member **6** *chem* a chemical bond consisting of one electron [c18 from SINGLE, on the model of *doublet*]

single tax *n* US **1** a taxation system in which a tax on one commodity, usually land, is the only source of revenue **2** such a tax

single thread *n computing* the execution of an entire task from beginning to end without interruption

single ticket *n Brit* a ticket entitling a passenger to travel only to his destination, without returning. US and Canadian equivalent: **one-way ticket**. Compare **return ticket**

singleton ('sɪŋg°ltən) *n* **1** *bridge* an original holding of one card only in a suit **2** a single object, individual, etc, separated or distinguished from a pair or group **3** *maths* a set containing only one member **4** a person who is neither married nor in a relationship [c19 from SINGLE, on the model of SIMPLETON]

single-tongue *vb music* to play (any nonlegato passage) on a wind instrument by obstructing and uncovering the air passage through the lips with the tongue. Compare **double-tongue, triple-tongue**. > single tonguing *n*

single-track *adj* **1** (of a railway) having only a single pair of lines, so that trains can travel in only one direction at a time **2** (of a road) only wide enough for one vehicle **3** able to think about only one thing; one-track

Single Transferable Vote *n* (*modifier*) of or relating to a system of voting in which voters list the candidates in the order of preference. Any candidate achieving a predetermined proportion of the votes in a constituency is elected. Votes exceeding this amount and those cast for the bottom candidate are redistributed according to the stated preferences. Redistribution continues until all the seats are filled. Abbreviation: STV. See **proportional representation**

singletree ('sɪŋg°lˌtriː) *n* a variant, esp US and Austral, of **swingletree**

Singlish ('sɪŋglɪʃ) *n* a variety of English spoken in Singapore, incorporating elements of Chinese and Malay [c20 from a blend of SINGAPOREAN + ENGLISH]

singly ('sɪŋglɪ) *adv* **1** one at a time; one by one **2** apart from others; separately; alone

sing out *vb* (*tr, adverb*) to call out in a loud voice; shout

Sing Sing *n* a prison in New York State, in Ossining [variant of *Ossining*]

singsong ('sɪŋˌsɒŋ) *n* **1** an accent, metre, or intonation that is characterized by an alternately rising and falling rhythm, as in a person's voice, piece of verse, etc **2** *Brit* an informal session of singing, esp of popular or traditional songs ▷ *adj* **3** having a regular or monotonous rising and falling rhythm: *a singsong accent*

Singspiel *German* ('zɪŋʃpiːl) *n* a type of comic opera in German with spoken dialogue, popular during the late 18th and early 19th centuries [literally: singing play]

singular ('sɪŋgjʊlə) *adj* **1** remarkable; exceptional; extraordinary: *a singular feat* **2** unusual; odd: *a singular character* **3** unique **4** denoting a word or an inflected form of a word indicating that not more than one referent is being referred to or described **5** *logic* of or referring to a specific thing or person as opposed to something general ▷ *n* **6** *grammar* **a** the singular number **b** a singular form of a word [c14 from Latin *singulāris* SINGLE] > 'singularly *adv* > 'singularness *n*

singularity (ˌsɪŋgjʊ'lærɪtɪ) *n, pl* -ties **1** the state, fact, or quality of being singular **2** something distinguishing a person or thing from others **3** something remarkable or unusual **4** *maths* **a** a point at which a function is not differentiable although it is differentiable in a neighbourhood of that point. See also **pole²** (sense 4) **b** another word for **discontinuity 5** *astronomy* a hypothetical point in space-time at which matter is infinitely compressed to infinitesimal volume

singularize or **singularise** ('sɪŋgjʊləˌraɪz) *vb* (*tr*) **1** to make (a word, etc) singular **2** to make conspicuous > ˌsingulari'zation or ˌsingulari'sation *n*

singulary ('sɪŋgjʊlərɪ) *adj logic, maths* (of an operator) monadic

singultus (sɪŋ'gʌltəs) *n* a technical name for **hiccup** [c18 from Latin, literally: a sob]

sinh (ʃaɪn, sɪnʃ) *n* hyperbolic sine; a hyperbolic function, sinh $z = \frac{1}{2}(e^z - e^{-z})$, related to sine by the expression sinh $iz = i \sin z$, where $i = \sqrt{-1}$ [c20 from SIN(E)¹ + H(YPERBOLIC)]

Sinhailien (ʃɪn'haɪ'ljɛn) *n* a variant transliteration of the alternative name for **Lianyungang**

Sinhalese (ˌsɪnhə'liːz) or **Singhalese** *n* **1** pl, -leses or -lese a member of a people living chiefly in Sri Lanka, where they constitute the majority of the population **2** the language of this people, belonging to the Indic branch of the Indo-European family; the official language of Sri Lanka. It is written in a script of Indian origin ▷ *adj* **3** of or relating to this people or their language

Sinicism ('saɪnɪˌsɪzəm, 'sɪn-) *n rare* a Chinese custom or idiom [c19 from Medieval Latin *Sinicus* Chinese, from Late Latin *Sīnae* the Chinese, from Greek *Sinai*, from Arabic *Sīn* China]

Sining ('ʃiː'nɪŋ) *n* variant transliteration of the Chinese name for **Xining**

sinister ('sɪnɪstə) *adj* **1** threatening or suggesting evil or harm; ominous: *a sinister glance* **2** evil or treacherous, esp in a mysterious way **3** (*usually postpositive*) *heraldry* of, on, or starting from the left side from the bearer's point of view and therefore on the spectator's right **4** *archaic* located on the left side **5** *archaic* (of signs, omens, etc) unfavourable ▷ Compare **dexter¹** [c15 from Latin *sinister* on the left-hand side, considered by Roman augurs to be the unlucky one] > 'sinisterly *adv* > 'sinisterness *n*

sinistral ('sɪnɪstrəl) *adj* **1** of, relating to, or located on the left side, esp the left side of the body **2** a technical term for **left-handed 3** (of the shells of certain gastropod molluscs) coiling in a clockwise direction from the apex ▷ Compare **dextral** [c15 (in the obsolete sense: adverse, evil); c19 (in current senses): from Medieval Latin *sinistrālis*. See SINISTER] > 'sinistrally *adv*

sinistrodextral (ˌsɪnɪstrəʊ'dɛkstrəl) *adj* going or directed from left to right: *a sinistrodextral script* [See SINISTER, DEXTER¹]

sinistrorse (ˌsɪnɪ'strɔːs, ˌsɪnɪ'strɔːs) *adj* (of some climbing plants) growing upwards in a spiral from right to left, or clockwise. Compare **dextrorse** [c19 from Latin *sinistrōrsus* turned towards the left, from *sinister* on the left + *vertere* to turn] > ˌsinis'trorsal *adj* > 'sinis,trorsely *adv*

sinistrous ('sɪnɪstrəs) *adj archaic* **1** sinister or ill-omened **2** sinistral > 'sinistrously *adv*

Sinitic (sɪ'nɪtɪk) *n* **1** a branch of the Sino-Tibetan family of languages, consisting of the various languages or dialects of Chinese. Compare **Tibeto-Burman** ▷ *adj* **2** belonging or relating to this group of languages

sink (sɪŋk) *vb* sinks, sinking, sank; sunk or sunken **1** to descend or cause to descend, esp beneath the surface of a liquid or soft substance **2** (*intr*) to appear to move down towards or descend below the horizon **3** (*intr*) to slope downwards; dip **4** (*intr; often foll by in or into*) to pass into or gradually enter a specified lower state or condition: *to sink into apathy* **5** to make or become lower in volume, pitch, etc **6** to make or become lower in value, price, etc **7** (*intr*) to become weaker in health, strength, etc **8** to decline or cause to decline in moral value, worth, etc **9** (*intr*) to seep or penetrate **10** (*tr*) to suppress or conceal: *he sank his worries in drink* **11** (*tr*) to dig, cut, drill, bore, or excavate (a hole, shaft, etc) **12** (*tr*) to drive into the ground: *to sink a stake* **13** (*tr*; usually foll by *in* or *into*) **a** to invest (money) **b** to lose (money) in an unwise or unfortunate investment **14** (*tr*) to pay (a debt) **15** (*intr*) to become hollow; cave in: *his cheeks had sunk during his illness* **16** (*tr*) to hit, throw, or propel (a ball) into a hole, basket, pocket, etc: *he sank a 15-foot putt* **17** (*tr*) *Brit informal* to drink, esp quickly: *he sank three pints in half an hour* **18** sink or swim to take risks where the alternatives are loss and failure or security and success ▷ *n* **19** a fixed basin, esp in a kitchen, made of stone, earthenware, metal, etc, used for washing **20** See **sinkhole 21** another word for **cesspool 22** a place of vice or corruption **23** an area of ground below that of the surrounding land, where water collects **24** *physics* a device or part of a system at which energy is removed from the system: *a heat sink* ▷ *adj* **25** *informal* (of a housing estate or school) deprived or having low standards of achievement [Old English *sincan;* related to Old Norse *sökkva* to sink, Gothic *siggan,* Old High German *sincan,* Swedish *sjunka*] > **'sinkable** *adj*

sinkage ('sɪŋkɪdʒ) *n* *rare* the act of sinking or degree to which something sinks or has sunk

sinker ('sɪŋkə) *n* **1** a weight attached to a fishing line, net, etc, to cause it to sink in water **2** a person who sinks shafts, etc **3** *US* an informal word for **doughnut 4** **hook, line, and sinker** See **hook** (sense 18)

sinkhole ('sɪŋk,həʊl) *n* **1** Also called (esp Brit): **swallow hole** a depression in the ground surface, esp in limestone, where a surface stream disappears underground **2** a place into which foul matter runs

Sinkiang-Uighur Autonomous Region ('sɪn'kjæŋ 'wiːgʊə) *n* a variant transliteration of the Chinese name for the **Xinjiang Uygur Autonomous Region**

sink in *vb* (*intr, adverb*) to enter or penetrate the mind: *eventually the news sank in*

sinking ('sɪŋkɪŋ) *n* **a** a feeling in the stomach caused by hunger or uneasiness **b** (*as modifier*): *a sinking feeling*

sinking fund *n* a fund accumulated out of a business enterprise's earnings or a government's revenue and invested to repay a long-term debt or meet a depreciation charge

sinless ('sɪnlɪs) *adj* free from sin or guilt; innocent; pure > **'sinlessly** *adv* > **'sinlessness** *n*

Sinn Féin ('ʃɪn 'feːn) *n* an Irish republican political movement founded about 1905 and linked to the revolutionary Irish Republican Army: divided into a Provisional and an Official movement since a similar split in the IRA in late 1969 [C20 from Irish: we ourselves] > **Sinn Féiner** *n* > **Sinn Féinism** *n*

Sino- *combining form* Chinese: *Sino-Tibetan; Sinology* [from French, from Late Latin *Sīnae* the Chinese, from Late Greek *Sinai,* from Arabic *Sīn* China, probably from Chinese *Ch'in*]

Sinology (saɪ'nɒlədʒɪ, sɪ-) *n* the study of Chinese history, language, culture, etc > **Sinological** (,saɪnə'lɒdʒɪkəl, ,sɪn-) *adj* > **Si'nologist** *n* > **Sinologue** ('saɪnə,lɒg) *n*

Sinope (sə'nəʊpɪ) *n* *astronomy* a small outer satellite of the planet Jupiter

Sino-Tibetan ('saɪnəʊ-) *n* **1** a family of languages that includes most of the languages of China, as well as Tibetan, Burmese, and possibly Thai. Their most noticeable phonological characteristic is the phonemic use of tones ▷ *adj* **2** belonging or relating to this family of languages

sinsemilla (,sɪnsə'miːljə) *n* **1** a type of marijuana with a very high narcotic content **2** the plant from which it is obtained, a strain of *Cannabis sativa* [C20 from American Spanish, literally: without seed]

sin tax *n* *informal* a tax levied on something that is considered morally or medically harmful, such as alcohol or tobacco

sinter ('sɪntə) *n* **1** a whitish porous incrustation, usually consisting of silica, that is deposited from hot springs **2** the product of a sintering process **3** another name for **cinder** (sense 3) ▷ *vb* **4** (*tr*) to form large particles, lumps, or masses from (metal powders or powdery ores) by heating or pressure or both [C18 German: CINDER]

Sint Maarten (sɪnt 'maːrtə) *n* the Dutch name for **Saint Martin**

Sintra ('sɪntrə) *n* a town in central Portugal, near Lisbon, in the Sintra mountains: noted for its castles and palaces and the beauty of its setting: tourism. Former name: **Cintra**

sinuate ('sɪnjʊɪt, -,eɪt) *or* **sinuated** *adj* **1** Also: **sinuous** (of leaves) having a strongly waved margin **2** another word for **sinuous** [C17 from

Latin *sinuātus* curved; see SINUS, -ATE[1]] > **'sinuately** *adv*

Sinŭiju (sɪ,nuːɪ'dʒuː) *n* a port in North Korea, on the Yalu River opposite Andong, China: developed by the Japanese during their occupation (1910–45); industrial centre. Pop: 349 000 (2005 est)

sinuosity (,sɪnjʊ'ɒsɪtɪ) *or less commonly* **sinuation** *n, pl* **-osities** *or* **-ations 1** the quality of being sinuous **2** a turn, curve, or intricacy

sinuous ('sɪnjʊəs) *adj* **1** full of turns or curves; intricate **2** devious; not straightforward **3** supple; lithe ▷ Also: **sinuate** [C16 from Latin *sinuōsus* winding, from *sinus* a curve] > **'sinuously** *adv* > **'sinuousness** *n*

sinus ('saɪnəs) *n, pl* **-nuses 1** *anatomy* **a** any bodily cavity or hollow space **b** a large channel for venous blood, esp between the brain and the skull **c** any of the air cavities in the cranial bones **2** *pathol* a passage leading to a cavity containing pus **3** *botany* a small rounded notch between two lobes of a leaf, petal, etc **4** an irregularly shaped cavity [C16 from Latin: a curve, bay]

sinusitis (,saɪnə'saɪtɪs) *n* inflammation of the membrane lining a sinus, esp a nasal sinus

sinusoid ('saɪnə,sɔɪd) *n* **1** any of the irregular terminal blood vessels that replace capillaries in certain organs, such as the liver, heart, spleen, and pancreas **2** another name for **sine curve** ▷ *adj* **3** resembling a sinus [C19 from French *sinusoïde.* See SINUS, -OID]

sinusoidal (,saɪnə'sɔɪdᵊl) *adj* **1** *maths* of or relating to a sine curve **2** *physics* having a magnitude that varies as a sine curve > **sinus'oidally** *adv*

sinusoidal projection *n* an equal-area map projection on which all parallels are straight lines and all except the prime meridian are sine curves, often used to show tropical latitudes. Also called: **Sanson-Flamsteed projection**

Sion *n* **1** (*French* sjɔ̃) a town in SW Switzerland, capital of Valais canton, on the River Rhône. Pop: 27 171 (2000). Latin name: **Sedunum 2** (*saɪən*) a variant of **Zion**

Siouan ('suːən) *n* **1** a family of North American Indian languages including Sioux, probably related to Iroquoian ▷ *adj* **2** of or relating to the Sioux peoples or languages

Sioux (suː) *n* **1** *pl* **Sioux** (suː, suːz) a member of a group of North American Indian peoples formerly ranging over a wide area of the Plains from Lake Michigan to the Rocky Mountains **2** any of the Siouan languages [from French, shortened from *Nadowessioux,* from Chippewa *Nadoweisiw*]

sip (sɪp) *vb* **sips, sipping, sipped 1** to drink (a liquid) by taking small mouthfuls; drink gingerly or delicately ▷ *n* **2** a small quantity of a liquid taken into the mouth and swallowed **3** an act of sipping [C14 probably from Low German *sippen*] > **'sipper** *n*

siphon *or* **syphon** ('saɪfᵊn) *n* **1** a tube placed with one end at a certain level in a vessel of liquid and the other end outside the vessel below this level, so that atmospheric pressure forces the liquid through the tube and out of the vessel **2** See **soda siphon 3** *zoology* any of various tubular organs in different aquatic animals, such as molluscs and elasmobranch fishes, through which a fluid, esp water, passes ▷ *vb* **4** (often foll by *off*) to pass or draw off through or as if through a siphon [C17 from Latin *sīphō,* from Greek *siphōn* siphon] > **'siphonage** *n* > **'siphonal** *or* **siphonic** (saɪ'fɒnɪk) *adj*

siphon bottle *n* another name (esp US) for **soda siphon**

siphonophore ('saɪfənə,fɔː, saɪ'fɒnə-) *n* any marine colonial hydrozoan of the order *Siphonophora,* including the Portuguese man-of-war [C19 from New Latin *siphonophora,* from Greek *siphōnophoros* tube-bearing] > **siphonophorous** (,saɪfə'nɒfərəs) *adj*

siphonostele ('saɪfənə,stiːl) *n* *botany* the cylinder of conducting tissue surrounding a central core of pith in certain stems. See also **stele** (sense 3) [C19

from SIPHON + STELE] > **siphonostelic** (,saɪfənə'stiːlɪk) *adj*

Siple ('saɪpᵊl) *n* **Mount** a mountain in Antarctica, on the coast of Byrd Land. Height: 3100 m (10 171 ft)

sipper ('sɪpə) *n* *US informal* a drinking straw

sippet ('sɪpɪt) *n* a small piece of something, esp a piece of toast or fried bread eaten with soup or gravy [C16 used as diminutive of SOP; see -ET]

sippy cup *n* *US and Canadian* a plastic cup for young children which has a tight-fitting lid with a perforated spout

SIPS *abbreviation for* side impact protection system: bars built into certain cars to strengthen the bodywork

sir (sɜː) *n* **1** a formal or polite term of address for a man **2** *archaic* a gentleman of high social status [C13 variant of SIRE]

Sir (sɜː) *n* **1** a title of honour placed before the name of a knight or baronet: *Sir Walter Raleigh* **2** *archaic* a title placed before the name of a figure from ancient history

Siracusa (sira'kuːza) *n* the Italian name for **Syracuse**

sirdar ('sɜːdɑː) *n* **1** a general or military leader in Pakistan and India **2** (formerly) the title of the British commander in chief of the Egyptian Army **3** a variant spelling of **sardar** [from Hindi *sardār,* from Persian, from *sar* head + *dār* possession]

sire (saɪə) *n* **1** a male parent, esp of a horse or other domestic animal **2** a respectful term of address, now used only in addressing a male monarch **3** *obsolete* a man of high rank ▷ *vb* **4** (*tr*) (esp of a domestic animal) to father; beget [C13 from Old French, from Latin *senior* an elder, from *senex* an old man]

siren ('saɪərən) *n* **1** a device for emitting a loud wailing sound, esp as a warning or signal, typically consisting of a rotating perforated metal drum through which air or steam is passed under pressure **2** (*sometimes capital*) *Greek myth* one of several sea nymphs whose seductive singing was believed to lure sailors to destruction on the rocks the nymphs inhabited **3** **a** a woman considered to be dangerously alluring or seductive **b** (*as modifier*): *her siren charms* **4** any aquatic eel-like salamander of the North American family *Sirenidae,* having external gills, no hind limbs, and reduced forelimbs [C14 from Old French *sereine,* from Latin *sīrēn,* from Greek *seirēn*]

sirenian (saɪ'riːnɪən) *adj* **1** of, relating to, or belonging to the *Sirenia,* an order of aquatic herbivorous placental mammals having forelimbs modified as paddles, no hind limbs, and a horizontally flattened tail: contains only the dugong and manatees ▷ *n* **2** any animal belonging to the order *Sirenia*; a sea cow

Siret (sɪ'rɛt) *n* a river in SE Europe, rising in Ukraine and flowing southeast through E Romania to the Danube. Length: about 450 km (280 miles)

Sirius ('sɪrɪəs) *n* the brightest star in the sky after the sun, lying in the constellation Canis Major. It is a binary star whose companion, Sirius B, is a very faint white dwarf. Distance: 8.6 light years. Also called: **the Dog Star, Canicula, Sothis.** Related adjs: **canicular, cynic** [C14 via Latin from Greek *Seirios,* of obscure origin]

sirloin ('sɜː,lɔɪn) *n* a prime cut of beef from the loin, esp the upper part [C16 *surloyn,* from Old French *surlonge,* from *sur* above + *longe,* from *loigne* LOIN]

sirocco (sɪ'rɒkəʊ) *n, pl* **-cos 1** a hot oppressive and often dusty wind usually occurring in spring, beginning in N Africa and reaching S Europe **2** any hot southerly wind, esp one moving to a low pressure centre [C17 from Italian, from Arabic *sharq* east wind]

sironize *or* **sironise** ('saɪrə,naɪz) *vb* (*tr*) *Austral* to treat (a woollen fabric) chemically to prevent it from wrinkling after being washed [C20 from (C)SIRO + -*n*- + -IZE]

siroset (ˈsaɪrəʊˌsɛt) *adj Austral* of or relating to the chemical treatment of woollen fabrics to give a permanent-press effect, or a garment so treated

sirrah (ˈsɪrə) *n archaic* a contemptuous term used in addressing a man or boy [C16 probably variant of SIRE]

sirree (səˈriː) *interj* (*sometimes capital*) *US informal* an emphatic exclamation used with *yes* or *no*

sir-reverence *interj obsolete* an expression of apology used esp to introduce taboo or vulgar words or phrases [C16 short for *save your reverence*]

Sir Roger de Coverley *n* an English country dance performed to a traditional tune by two rows of dancers facing each other [C18 alteration of *Roger of Coverley* influenced by *Sir Roger de Coverley*, a fictitious character appearing in the *Spectator* essays by Addison and Steele]

sirup (ˈsɪrəp) *n US* a less common spelling of **syrup**

sirvente (səˈvɛnt) *n* a verse form employed by the troubadours of Provence to satirize moral or political themes [C19 via French from Provençal *sirventes* song of a servant (that is, of a lover serving his mistress), from *sirvent* a servant, from Latin *servīre* to SERVE]

sis[1] (sɪs) *n informal* short for **sister**

sis[2] *or* **sies** (sɪs, siːs) *interj South African informal* an exclamation of disgust [Afrikaans, possibly from Khoi]

SIS *abbreviation for* **1** (in Britain) Secret Intelligence Service. Also called: **MI6** **2** (in New Zealand) Security Intelligence Service

sisal (ˈsaɪsᵊl) *n* **1** a Mexican agave plant, *Agave sisalana*, cultivated for its large fleshy leaves, which yield a stiff fibre used for making rope **2** the fibre of this plant **3** any of the fibres of certain similar or related plants ▷ Also called: **sisal hemp** [C19 from Mexican Spanish, named after *Sisal*, a port in Yucatán, Mexico]

Sisera (ˈsɪsərə) *n* a defeated leader of the Canaanites, who was assassinated by Jael (Judges 4:17–21)

siskin (ˈsɪskɪn) *n* **1** a yellow-and-black Eurasian finch, *Carduelis spinus* **2** **pine siskin** a North American finch, *Spinus pinus*, having a streaked yellowish-brown plumage [C16 from Middle Dutch *sīseken*, from Middle Low German *sīsek*; related to Czech *čížek*, Russian *chizh*]

Sissinghurst Castle (ˈsɪsɪŋhɜːst) *n* a restored Elizabethan mansion near Cranbrook in Kent: noted for the gardens laid out in the 1930s by Victoria Sackville-West and Harold Nicolson

sissy *or* **cissy** (ˈsɪsɪ) *n, pl* **-sies** **1** an effeminate, weak, or cowardly boy or man ▷ *adj* **2** Also (informal or dialect): **ˈsissiˈfied** *or* **ˈcissiˈfied** effeminate, weak, or cowardly

sister (ˈsɪstə) *n* **1** a female person having the same parents as another person **2** See **half-sister**, **stepsister** **3** a female person who belongs to the same group, trade union, etc, as another or others **4** *informal* a form of address to a woman or girl, used esp by Blacks in the US **5** a senior nurse **6** *chiefly RC Church* a nun or a title given to a nun **7** a woman fellow member of a Church or religious body **8** (*modifier*) belonging to the same class, fleet, etc, as another or others: *a sister ship* **9** (*modifier*) *biology* denoting any of the cells or cell components formed by division of a parent cell or cell component: *sister nuclei* [Old English *sweostor*; related to Old Norse *systir*, Old High German *swester*, Gothic *swistar*]

sisterhood (ˈsɪstəˌhʊd) *n* **1** the state of being related as a sister or sisters **2** a religious body or society of sisters, esp a community, order, or congregation of nuns **3** the bond between women who support the Women's Movement

sister-in-law *n, pl* **sisters-in-law** **1** the sister of one's husband or wife **2** the wife of one's brother

sisterly (ˈsɪstəlɪ) *adj* of, resembling, or suitable to a sister, esp in showing kindness and affection > **ˈsisterliness** *n*

Sistine Chapel (ˈsɪstaɪn, -tiːn) *n* the chapel of the pope in the Vatican at Rome, built for Sixtus IV and decorated with frescoes by Michelangelo and others [Sistine, from Italian *Sistino* relating to *Sisto* Sixtus (Pope Sixtus IV)]

sistroid (ˈsɪstrɔɪd) *adj* contained between the convex sides of two intersecting curves. Compare **cissoid** (sense 2) [C20 from SISTRUM + -OID]

sistrum (ˈsɪstrəm) *n, pl* **-tra** (-trə) a musical instrument of ancient Egypt consisting of a metal rattle [C14 via Latin from Greek *seistron*, from *seiein* to shake]

Sisyphean (ˌsɪsɪˈfiːən) *adj* **1** relating to Sisyphus **2** actually or seemingly endless and futile

Sisyphus (ˈsɪsɪfəs) *n Greek myth* a king of Corinth, punished in Hades for his misdeeds by eternally having to roll a heavy stone up a hill: every time he approached the top, the stone escaped his grasp and rolled to the bottom

sit (sɪt) *vb* **sits, sitting, sat** (*mainly intr*) **1** (*also tr*; when *intr*, often foll by *down*, *in*, or *on*) to adopt or rest in a posture in which the body is supported on the buttocks and thighs and the torso is more or less upright: *to sit on a chair; sit a horse* **2** (*tr*) to cause to adopt such a posture **3** (of an animal) to adopt or rest in a posture with the hindquarters lowered to the ground **4** (of a bird) to perch or roost **5** (of a hen or other bird) to cover eggs to hatch them; brood **6** to be situated or located **7** (of the wind) to blow from the direction specified **8** to adopt and maintain a posture for one's portrait to be painted, etc **9** to occupy or be entitled to a seat in some official capacity, as a judge, elected representative, etc **10** (of a deliberative body) to be convened or in session **11** to remain inactive or unused: *his car sat in the garage for a year* **12** to rest or lie as specified: *the nut was sitting so awkwardly that he couldn't turn it* **13** (of a garment) to fit or hang as specified: *that dress sits well on you* **14** to weigh, rest, or lie as specified: *greatness sits easily on him* **15** (*tr*) *chiefly Brit* to take (an examination): *he's sitting his bar finals* **16** (usually foll by *for*) *chiefly Brit* to be a candidate (for a qualification): *he's sitting for a BA* **17** (*intr; in combination*) to look after a specified person or thing for someone else: *granny-sit* **18** (*tr*) to have seating capacity for **19** **sitting pretty** *informal* well placed or established financially, socially, etc **20** **sit tight** **a** to wait patiently; bide one's time **b** to maintain one's position, stand, or opinion firmly ▷ See also **sit back, sit down, sit-in, sit on, sit out, sit over, sit under, sit up** [Old English *sittan*; related to Old Norse *sitja*, Gothic *sitan*, Old High German *sizzen*, Latin *sedēre* to sit, Sanskrit *sīdati* he sits]

SIT *text messaging abbreviation for* stay in touch

Sita (ˈsiːtaː) *n Hinduism* goddess consort of the god Vishnu in the incarnation of Rama

sitar (sɪˈtɑː, ˈsɪtɑː) *n* a stringed musical instrument, esp of India, having a long neck, a rounded body, and movable frets. The main strings, three to seven in number, overlie other sympathetic strings, the tuning depending on the raga being performed [from Hindi *sitār*, literally: three-stringed] > **siˈtarist** *n*

sitatunga (ˌsɪtəˈtʊŋgə) *n* another name for **marshbuck**

sit back *vb* (*intr, adverb*) to relax, as when action should be taken: *many people just sit back and ignore the problems of today*

sitcom (ˈsɪtˌkɒm) *n* an informal term for **situation comedy**

sit down *vb* (*adverb*) **1** to adopt or cause (oneself or another) to adopt a sitting posture **2** (*intr*; foll by *under*) to suffer (insults, etc) without protests or resistance ▷ *n* **sit-down** **3** a form of civil disobedience in which demonstrators sit down in a public place as a protest or to draw attention to a cause **4** See **sit-down strike** ▷ *adj* **sit-down** **5** (of a meal, etc) eaten while sitting down at a table

sit-down money *n Austral informal* social security benefits

sit-down strike *n* a strike in which workers refuse to leave their place of employment until a settlement is reached

site (saɪt) *n* **1** **a** the piece of land where something was, is, or is intended to be located: *a building site; archaeological site* **b** (*as modifier*): *site office* **2** an internet location where information relating to a specific subject or group of subjects can be accessed ▷ *vb* **3** (*tr*) to locate, place, or install (something) in a specific place [C14 from Latin *situs* situation, from *sinere* to be placed]

sitella (sɪˈtɛlə) *n Austral* any of various small generally black-and-white birds of the genus *Neositta*, having a straight sharp beak and strong claws used to run up trees in search of insects: family *Sittidae* (nuthatches). Also called: **tree-runner** [C19 from New Latin, the diminutive of *sitta*, from Greek *sittē* nuthatch]

site map *n computing* a plan of a website showing its contents and where it can be viewed

sitfast (ˈsɪtˌfɑːst) *n* a sore on a horse's back caused by rubbing of the saddle [C17 from SIT + FAST[1] (in the sense: secure, fixed)]

sith (sɪθ) *adv, conj, prep* an archaic word for **since** [Old English *siththa*, short for *siththan* SINCE]

sithee (ˈsɪðɪ) *interj Northern English dialect* look here! listen!

sit-in *n* **1** a form of civil disobedience in which demonstrators occupy seats in a public place and refuse to move as a protest **2** another term for **sit-down strike** ▷ *vb* **sit in** (*intr, adverb*) **3** (often foll by *for*) to deputize (for) **4** (foll by *on*) to take part (in) as a visitor or guest: *we sat in on Professor Johnson's seminar* **5** to organize or take part in a sit-in

Sitka (ˈsɪtkə) *n* a town in SE Alaska, in the Alexander Archipelago on W Baranof Island: capital of Russian America (1804–67) and of Alaska (1867–1906). Pop: 8876 (2003 est)

sitkamer (ˈsɪtˌkɑːmə) *n South African* a sitting room [from Afrikaans *sit* sitting + *kamer* room]

sitka spruce (ˈsɪtkə) *n* a tall North American spruce tree, *Picea sitchensis*, having yellowish-green needle-like leaves: yields valuable timber [C19 from SITKA]

sitology (saɪˈtɒlədʒɪ) *n* the scientific study of food, diet, and nutrition [C19 from Greek *sitos* food, grain + -LOGY]

sit on *vb* (*intr, preposition*) **1** to be a member of (a committee, etc) **2** *informal* to suppress **3** *informal* to check or rebuke

sitosterol (saɪˈtɒstəˌrɒl) *n* a white powder or waxy white solid extracted from soya beans, consisting of a mixture of isomers of the formula $C_{29}H_{50}O$ with other sterols: used in cosmetics and medicine [C20 from Greek *sitos* food, grain + STEROL]

sit out *vb* (*adverb*) **1** (*tr*) to endure to the end: *I sat out the play although it was terrible* **2** (*tr*) to remain seated throughout (a dance, etc) **3** (*intr*) *chiefly Brit* to lean backwards over the side of a light sailing boat in order to carry the centre of gravity as far to windward as possible to reduce heeling. US and Canadian term: **hike out**

sit over *vb* (*intr, preposition*) *cards* to be seated in an advantageous position on the left of (the player)

Sitsang (ˈsiːˈtsæŋ) *n* a Chinese name for **Tibet**

sittella *n* a variant spelling of **sitella**

sitter (ˈsɪtə) *n* **1** a person or animal that sits **2** a person who is posing for his or her portrait to be painted, carved, etc **3** a broody hen or other bird that is sitting on its eggs to hatch them **4** (*in combination*) a person who looks after a specified person or thing for someone else: *flat-sitter* **5** short for **baby-sitter** **6** anyone, other than the medium, taking part in a seance **7** anything that is extremely easy, such as an easy catch in cricket

sitting (ˈsɪtɪŋ) *n* **1** a continuous period of being seated: *I read his novel at one sitting* **2** such a period in a restaurant, canteen, etc, where space and other facilities are limited: *dinner will be served in two sittings* **3** the act or period of posing for one's portrait to be painted, carved, etc **4** a meeting, esp of an official body, to conduct business **5** the

S

incubation period of a bird's eggs during which the mother sits on them to keep them warm ▷ *adj* **6** in office: *a sitting Member of Parliament* **7** (of a hen) brooding eggs **8** seated: *in a sitting position*

sitting room *n* a room in a private house or flat used for relaxation and entertainment of guests

sitting target *n* a person or thing in a defenceless or vulnerable position. Also called (informal): **sitting duck**

sitting tenant *n* a tenant occupying a house, flat, etc

sitting trot *n* a horse's trot during which the rider sits still in the saddle. Compare **rising trot**

situate ('sɪtjʊ,eɪt) *vb* **1** (*tr; often passive*) to allot a site to; place; locate ▷ *adj* **2** (now used esp in legal contexts) situated; located [c16 from Late Latin *situāre* to position, from Latin *situs* a SITE]

situation (,sɪtjʊ'eɪʃən) *n* **1** physical placement, esp with regard to the surroundings **2 a** state of affairs; combination of circumstances **b** a complex or critical state of affairs in a novel, play, etc **3** social or financial status, position, or circumstances **4** a position of employment; post ▷ ,situ'ational *adj*

USAGE *Situation* is often used in contexts in which it is redundant or imprecise. Typical examples are: *the company is in a crisis situation* or *people in a job situation*. In the first example, *situation* does not add to the meaning and should be omitted. In the second example, it would be clearer and more concise to substitute a phrase such as *people at work*

situation comedy *n* (on television or radio) a comedy series involving the same characters in various day-to-day situations which are developed as separate stories for each episode. Also called: **sitcom**

situla ('sɪtjʊlə) *n, pl* -**lae** (-liː) **1** a bucket-shaped container, usually of metal or pottery and often richly decorated: typical of the N Italian Iron Age ▷ *adj* **2** of or relating to the type of designs usually associated with these containers [from Latin]

sit under *vb* (*intr, preposition*) *cards* to be seated on the right of (the player)

sit up *vb* (*adverb*) **1** to raise (oneself or another) from a recumbent to an upright or alert sitting posture **2** (*intr*) to remain out of bed and awake, esp until a late hour **3** (*intr*) *informal* to become suddenly interested or alert: *devaluation of the dollar made the money market sit up* ▷ *n* **sit-up 4** Also: **trunk curl** a physical exercise in which the body is brought into a sitting position from one lying on the back

situs ('saɪtəs) *n, pl* -**tus** position or location, esp the usual or right position of an organ or part of the body [c18 from Latin: site, situation, position]

sitz bath (sɪts, zɪts) *n* a bath in which the buttocks and hips are immersed in hot water, esp for therapeutic effects, as after perineal or pelvic surgery [half translation of German *Sitzbad*, from *Sitz* SEAT + *Bad* BATH[1]]

sitzkrieg ('sɪts,kriːg, 'zɪts-) *n* a period during a war in which both sides change positions very slowly or not at all [c20 from German, from *sitzen* to sit + *Krieg* war]

sitzmark ('sɪts,mɑːk, 'zɪts-) *n skiing* a depression in the snow where a skier has fallen [German, literally: seat mark]

SI unit *n* any of the units adopted for international use under the Système International d'Unités, now employed for all scientific and most technical purposes. There are seven fundamental units: the metre, kilogram, second, ampere, kelvin, candela, and mole; and two supplementary units: the radian and the steradian. All other units are derived by multiplication or division of these units without the use of numerical factors

Siva ('siːvə, 'sɪvə) or **Shiva** *n Hinduism* the destroyer, one of the three chief divinities of the

later Hindu pantheon, the other two being Brahma and Vishnu. Siva is also the god presiding over personal destinies [from Sanskrit *Śiva*, literally: the auspicious (one)]

Sivaism ('siːvə,ɪzəm, 'sɪvə-) *n* the cult of Siva ▷ 'Sivaist *n* ,Siva'istic *adj*

Sivan (siː'vɑːn) *n* (in the Jewish calendar) the third month of the year according to biblical reckoning and the ninth month of the civil year, usually falling within May and June [from Hebrew]

Sivananda yoga (,sɪvə'nændə) *n* a gentle form of yoga which concentrates on breathing control, stretching, and silent meditation

Sivas (Turkish 'sɪvas) *n* a city in central Turkey, at an altitude of 1347 m (4420 ft): one of the chief cities in Asia Minor in ancient times; scene of the national congress (1919) leading to the revolution that established modern Turkey. Pop: 266 000 (2005 est)

siwash ('saɪwɒʃ) *n* **1** another name for **Cowichan sweater** ▷ *vb* **2** (*intr*) (in the Pacific Northwest) to camp out with only natural shelter [see SIWASH]

Siwash ('saɪwɒʃ) (*sometimes not capital*) *slang, derogatory* (in the Pacific Northwest) *n* **1** a North American Indian ▷ *adj* **2** of, characteristic of, or relating to Indians **3** worthless, stingy, or bad: *he's siwash* [c19 from Chinook Jargon, from French *sauvage* SAVAGE]

six (sɪks) *n* **1** the cardinal number that is the sum of five and one. See also **number** (sense 1) **2** a numeral, 6, VI, etc, representing this number **3** something representing, represented by, or consisting of six units, such as a playing card with six symbols on it **4** Also called: **six o'clock** six hours after noon or midnight **5** Also called: **sixer** *cricket* **a** a stroke in which the ball crosses the boundary without bouncing **b** the six runs scored for such a stroke **6** a division of a Brownie Guide or Cub Scout pack **7 at sixes and sevens a** in disagreement **b** in a state of confusion **8 knock (someone) for six** *informal* to upset or overwhelm (someone) completely; stun **9 six of one and half a dozen of the other** Also: **six and two threes** a situation in which the alternatives are considered equivalent ▷ *determiner* **10 a** amounting to six: *six nations* **b** (*as pronoun*): *set the table for six* ▷ Related prefixes: **hexa-, sex-** [Old English *siex*; related to Old Norse *sex*, Gothic *saihs*, Old High German *sehs*, Latin *sex*, Greek *hex*, Sanskrit *sastha*]

Six (French sis) *n* **Les** (le) a group of six young composers in France, who from about 1916 formed a temporary association as a result of interest in neoclassicism and in the music of Satie and the poetry of Cocteau. Its members were Darius Milhaud, Arthur Honegger, Francis Poulenc, Georges Auric, Louis Durey, and Germaine Tailleferre

sixain ('sɪkseɪn) *n* a stanza or poem of six lines [from French]

Six Counties *pl n* the historic counties of Northern Ireland, which no longer have a local government function

Six Day War *n* a war fought in the Middle East in June 1967, lasting six days. In it Israel defeated Egypt, Jordan, and Syria, occupying the Gaza Strip, the Sinai, Jerusalem, the West Bank of the Jordan, and the Golan Heights

six-eight time *n music* a form of compound duple time in which there are six quaver beats to the bar, indicated by the time signature ⁶⁄₈. Often shortened to: **six-eight**

sixer ('sɪksə) *n* a leader of a Brownie Guide or Cub Scout six

six-finger country *n Austral slang* an isolated area considered as being inhabited by people who practise inbreeding

sixfold ('sɪks,fəʊld) *adj* **1** equal to or having six times as many or as much **2** composed of six parts ▷ *adv* **3** by or up to six times as many or as much

six-footer *n* a person who is at least six feet tall

six-gun *n US informal* another word for **six-shooter**

sixmo ('sɪksməʊ) *n, pl* -**mos 1** Also called: **sexto** a book size resulting from folding a sheet of paper into six leaves or twelve pages, each one sixth the size of the sheet. Often written: **6mo, 6° 2** a book of this size

Six Nations *pl n* (in North America) the Indian confederacy of the Cayugas, Mohawks, Oneidas, Onondagas, Senecas, and Tuscaroras. Also called: **Iroquois**. See also **Five Nations**

Six Nations Championship *n rugby union* the annual competition involving national sides representing England, France, Ireland, Italy, Scotland, and Wales. Until the admission of Italy in 2000, it was known as the **Five Nations Championship**

six o'clock swill *n Austral and NZ informal* a period of heavy drinking, esp during the years when hotels had to close their bars at 6.00 pm

six-pack *n* **1** *informal* a package containing six units, esp six cans of beer **2** a set of highly developed abdominal muscles in a man **3** (*modifier*) *Austral* arranged in standard sets of six: *six-pack apartment blocks*

sixpence ('sɪkspəns) *n* a small British cupronickel coin with a face value of six pennies, worth 2½ (new) pence, not minted since 1970

sixpenny ('sɪkspənɪ) *adj* (*prenominal*) (of a nail) two inches in length

six-shooter *n US informal* a revolver with six chambers. Also called: **six-gun**

sixte (sɪkst) *n* the sixth of eight basic positions from which a parry or attack can be made in fencing [from French: (the) sixth (parrying position), from Latin *sextus* sixth]

sixteen ('sɪks'tiːn) *n* **1** the cardinal number that is the sum of ten and six. See also **number** (sense 1) **2** a numeral, 16, XVI, etc, representing this number **3** *music* the numeral 16 used as the lower figure of a time signature to indicate that the beat is measured in semiquavers **4** something represented by, representing, or consisting of 16 units ▷ *determiner* **5 a** amounting to sixteen: *sixteen tons* **b** (*as pronoun*): *sixteen are known to the police*

sixteenmo ('sɪks'tiːnməʊ) *n, pl* -**mos 1** Also called: **sextodecimo** a book size resulting from folding a sheet of paper into 16 leaves or 32 pages, each one sixteenth the size of the sheet. Often written: **16mo, 16° 2** a book of this size

sixteenth ('sɪks'tiːnθ) *adj* **1** (*usually prenominal*) **a** coming after the fifteenth in numbering or counting order, position, time, etc; being the ordinal number of *sixteen*: often written 16th **b** (*as noun*): *the sixteenth of the month* ▷ *n* **2 a** one of 16 equal or nearly equal parts of something **b** (*as modifier*): *a sixteenth part* **3** the fraction that is equal to one divided by 16 (1/16)

sixteenth note *n US and Canadian music* a note having the time value of one-sixteenth of a semibreve. also called (in certain other countries): **semiquaver**

sixth (sɪksθ) *adj* **1** (*usually prenominal*) **a** coming after the fifth and before the seventh in numbering or counting order, position, time, etc; being the ordinal number of *six*: often written 6th **b** (*as noun*): *the sixth to go* ▷ *n* **2 a** one of six equal or nearly equal parts of an object, quantity, measurement, etc **b** (*as modifier*): *a sixth part* **3** the fraction equal to one divided by six (1/6) **4** *music* **a** the interval between one note and another note six notes away from it counting inclusively along the diatonic scale **b** one of two notes constituting such an interval in relation to the other. See also **major** (sense 14), **minor** (sense 4), **interval** (sense 5) **c** short for **sixth chord** ▷ *adv* **5** Also: **sixthly** after the fifth person, position, etc ▷ *sentence connector* **6** Also: **sixthly** as the sixth point: linking what follows to the previous statements

sixth chord *n* (in classical harmony) the first

inversion of the triad, in which the note next above the root appears in the bass. See also **added sixth**

sixth form *n* (in England and Wales) the most senior class in a secondary school to which pupils, usually above the legal leaving age, may proceed to take A levels, retake GCSEs, etc ▷ 'sixth-ˌformer *n*

sixth-form college *n* (in England and Wales) a college offering A level and other courses to pupils over sixteen from local schools, esp from those that do not have sixth forms

sixth sense *n* any supposed sense or means of perception, such as intuition or clairvoyance, other than the five senses of sight, hearing, touch, taste, and smell

sixth year *n* (in Scotland) the most senior class in a secondary school to which pupils, usually above the legal leaving age, may proceed to take sixth-year studies, retake or take additional Highers, etc

sixtieth ('sɪkstɪɪθ) *adj* **1** (*usually prenominal*) **a** being the ordinal number of *sixty* in numbering or counting order, position, time, etc: often written 60th (**a** *as noun*): *the sixtieth in a row* ▷ *n* **2 a** one of 60 approximately equal parts of something **b** (*as modifier*): *a sixtieth part* **3** the fraction equal to one divided by 60 (1/60)

sixty ('sɪkstɪ) *n, pl* **-ties 1** the cardinal number that is the product of ten and six. See also **number** (sense 1) **2** a numeral, 60, LX, etc, representing sixty **3** something represented by, representing, or consisting of 60 units ▷ *determiner* **4 a** amounting to sixty: *sixty soldiers* **b** (*as pronoun*): *sixty are dead* [Old English *sixtig*]

sixty-fourmo (ˌsɪkstɪˈfɔːməʊ) *n, pl* **-mos 1** a book size resulting from folding a sheet of paper into 64 leaves or 128 pages, each one sixty-fourth the size of the sheet. Often written: 64mo, 64° **2** a book of this size

sixty-fourth note *n music, US and Canadian* a note having the time value of one sixty-fourth of a semibreve. Also called (in Britain and certain other countries): hemidemisemiquaver

sixty-four thousand dollar question *n* a crucial question or issue [C20 an elaboration of the earlier *sixty-four dollar question*, so called from the top prize on the US radio show *Take It or Leave It* (1941–48)]

sixty-nine *n* another term for **soixante-neuf**

six-yard line *n soccer* the line marking the limits of the goal area

sizable *or* **sizeable** ('saɪzəbəl) *adj* quite large ▷ 'sizableness *or* 'sizeableness *n* ▷ 'sizably *or* 'sizeably *adv*

sizar ('saɪzə) *n Brit* (at Peterhouse, Cambridge, and Trinity College, Dublin) an undergraduate receiving a maintenance grant from the college [C16 from earlier *sizer*, from SIZE¹ (meaning "an allowance of food, etc")] ▷ 'sizarˌship *n*

size¹ (saɪz) *n* **1** the dimensions, proportions, amount, or extent of something **2** large or great dimensions, etc **3** one of a series of graduated measurements, as of clothing: *she takes size 4 shoes* **4** *informal* state of affairs as summarized: *he's bankrupt, that's the size of it* ▷ *vb* **5** to sort according to size **6** (*tr*) to make or cut to a particular size or sizes [C13 from Old French *sise*, shortened from *assise* ASSIZE] ▷ 'sizer *n*

▌ **USAGE** The use of *-size* and *-sized* after *large* or *small* is redundant, except when describing something which is made in specific sizes: *a large* (not *large-size*) *organization*. Similarly, *in size* is redundant in the expressions *large in size* and *small in size*

size² (saɪz) *n* **1** Also called: **sizing** a thin gelatinous mixture, made from glue, clay, or wax, that is used as a sealer or filler on paper, cloth, or plaster surfaces ▷ *vb* **2** (*tr*) to treat or coat (a surface) with size [C15 perhaps from Old French *sise*; see SIZE¹] ▷ 'sizy *adj*

sized (saɪzd) *adj* of a specified size: *medium-sized*

▌ **USAGE** See at **size¹**

sizeism ('saɪzɪzəm) *n* discrimination on the basis of a person's size, esp against people considered to be overweight [C20 from SIZE¹ + -ISM, on the model of RACISM]

size up *vb* (*adverb*) **1** (*tr*) to make an assessment of (a person, problem, etc) **2** to conform to or make so as to conform to certain specifications of dimension

size-weight illusion *n* a standard sense illusion that a small object is heavier than a large object of the same weight

sizzle ('sɪzəl) *vb* (*intr*) **1** to make the hissing sound characteristic of frying fat **2** *informal* to be very hot **3** *informal* to be very angry ▷ *n* **4** a hissing sound [C17 of imitative origin. Compare *siss* (now dialect) to hiss, West Frisian *size*, *siizje*. See also FIZZ and FIZZLE]

sizzler ('sɪzlə) *n* **1** something that sizzles **2** *informal* a very hot day

sizzling ('sɪzlɪŋ) *adj* **1** extremely hot **2** very passionate or erotic: *a sizzling sex scene*

sj *the internet domain name for* Svalbard and Jan Mayen Islands

SJ *abbreviation for* Society of Jesus

SJA *abbreviation for* Saint John's Ambulance (Brigade or Association)

Sjælland (*Danish* 'sjɛlan) *n* the Danish name for Zealand

sjambok ('ʃæmbʌk, -bɒk) (in South Africa) *n* **1** a heavy whip of rhinoceros or hippopotamus hide **2** a stiff synthetic version of this, used in crowd control ▷ *vb* **-boks**, **-bokking**, **-bokked 3** (*tr*) to strike or beat with such a whip [C19 from Afrikaans, from Malay *samboq*, *chamboq*, from Urdu *chābuk*]

SJC (in the US) *abbreviation for* Supreme Judicial Court

SJD *abbreviation for* Doctor of Juridical Science [from Latin *Scientiae Juridicae Doctor*]

sjoe (ʃuː) *interj South African* an exclamation expressive of surprise, admiration, exhaustion, etc [from Afrikaans]

sk¹ *abbreviation for* sack

sk² *the internet domain name for* Slovak Republic

SK 1 *abbreviation for* (esp in postal addresses) Saskatchewan **2** *international car registration for* Slovakia

SK8 *text messaging abbreviation for* skate

ska (skɑː) *n* a type of West Indian pop music of the 1960s, accented on the second and fourth beats of a four-beat bar

skag (skæg) *n* a variant spelling of **scag¹**

Skagen ('skɑːgən) *n* **Cape** another name for the **Skaw**

Skagerrak ('skægəˌræk) *n* an arm of the North Sea between Denmark and Norway, merging with the Kattegat in the southeast

skald *or* **scald** (skɔːld) *n* (in ancient Scandinavia) a bard or minstrel [from Old Norse, of unknown origin] ▷ 'skaldic *or* 'scaldic *adj*

skanger ('skæŋə) *n Irish slang derogatory* a young working-class person who dresses in casual sports clothes

skank (skæŋk) *n* **1** a fast dance to reggae music **2** *slang* a promiscuous female ▷ *vb* (*intr*) **3** to perform this dance

skanky ('skæŋkɪ) *adj* **-kier**, **-kiest** *slang* **1** dirty, foul-smelling, or unattractive **2** promiscuous ▷ 'skankiness *n*

skanky-ho *n NZ slang* a promiscuous woman

Skara Brae ('skɑːrə) *n* a Neolithic village in NE Scotland, in the Orkney Islands: one of Europe's most perfectly preserved Stone Age villages, buried by a sand dune until uncovered by a storm in 1850

Skase ('skeɪs) *n* **do a Skase** *Austral informal* to skip the country while owing a large amount of money [C20 after the Australian businessman Christopher *Skase* (1948–2001), who fled Australia after the collapse of his business empire, owing millions of dollars]

skat (skæt) *n* a three-handed card game using 32 cards, popular in German-speaking communities [C19 from German, from Italian *scarto* played cards, from *scartare* to discard, from *s-* EX-¹ + *carta*, from Latin *charta* CARD¹]

skate¹ (skeɪt) *n* **1** See **roller skate, ice skate 2** the steel blade or runner of an ice skate **3** such a blade fitted with straps for fastening to a shoe **4** a current collector on an electric railway train that collects its current from a third rail. Compare **bow collector 5** get one's skates on to hurry ▷ *vb* (*intr*) **6** to glide swiftly on skates **7** to slide smoothly over a surface **8** skate on thin ice to place oneself in a dangerous or delicate situation [C17 via Dutch from Old French *éschasse* stilt, probably of Germanic origin]

skate² (skeɪt) *n, pl* **skate** *or* **skates** any large ray of the family *Rajidae*, of temperate and tropical seas, having flat pectoral fins continuous with the head, two dorsal fins, a short spineless tail, and a long snout [C14 from Old Norse *skata*]

skate³ (skeɪt) *n US slang* a person; fellow [from Scottish and northern English dialect *skate*, a derogatory term of uncertain origin]

skateboard ('skeɪtˌbɔːd) *n* **1** a narrow board mounted on roller-skate wheels, usually ridden while standing up ▷ *vb* **2** (*intr*) to ride on a skateboard ▷ 'skateˌboarder *n* ▷ 'skateˌboarding *n*

skate over *vb* (*intr, preposition*) **1** to cross on or as if on skates **2** to avoid dealing with (a matter) fully

skater ('skeɪtə) *n* **1** a person who skates **2** same as **skateboarder 3** *Brit informal* a young person who typically wears baggy clothes and spends a lot of time skateboarding **4** See **pond-skater**

skatole ('skætəʊl) *n* a white or brownish crystalline solid with a strong faecal odour, found in faeces, beetroot, and coal tar; B-methylindole. Formula: C_9H_9N [C19 from Greek *skat-*, stem of *skōr* excrement + -OLE¹]

Skaw (skɔː) *n* **the** a cape at the N tip of Denmark. Also called: (Cape) **Skagen**

skean (skiːn) *n* a kind of double-edged dagger formerly used in Ireland and Scotland [from Irish and Scottish Gaelic *scian*]

skean-dhu ('skiːənˈduː, 'skiːn-) *n Scot* a variant of **sgian-dhu**

skedaddle (skɪˈdædəl) *informal* ▷ *vb* **1** (*intr*) to run off hastily ▷ *n* **2** a hasty retreat [C19 of unknown origin]

skeef ('skiːəf) *adv, adj South African* **1** at an oblique angle; not straight **2** sideways; in a way likely to cause offence: *he was looking at me skeef* [from Afrikaans]

skeet (skiːt) *n* a form of clay-pigeon shooting in which targets are hurled from two traps at varying speeds and angles. Also called: **skeet shooting** [C20 changed from Old Norse *skeyti* a thrown object, from *skjóta* to shoot]

skeg (skɛg) *n nautical* **1** a reinforcing brace between the after end of a keel and the rudderpost **2** a support at the bottom of a rudder **3** a projection from the forefoot of a vessel for towing paravanes **4** any short keel-like projection at the stern of a boat **5** *Austral* a rear fin on the underside of a surfboard [C16 of Scandinavian origin; compare Icelandic *skegg* cutwater]

skein (skeɪn) *n* **1** a length of yarn, etc, wound in a long coil **2** something resembling this, such as a lock of hair **3** a flock of geese flying. Compare **gaggle** (sense 2) [C15 from Old French *escaigne*, of unknown origin]

skeleton ('skɛlɪtən) *n* **1** a hard framework consisting of inorganic material that supports and protects the soft parts of an animal's body and provides attachment for muscles: may be internal, as in vertebrates (see **endoskeleton**), or external, as in arthropods (see **exoskeleton**) **2** *informal* a very thin emaciated person or animal **3** the essential framework of any structure, such as a building or leaf, that supports or determines the shape of the rest of the structure **4** an outline consisting of bare essentials: *the skeleton of a novel*

S

5 (*modifier*) reduced to a minimum: *a skeleton staff* **6** **skeleton in the cupboard** *or* (*US and Canadian*) **closet** a scandalous fact or event in the past that is kept secret [C16 via New Latin from Greek: something desiccated, from *skellein* to dry up] > 'skeletal *adj* > 'skeletally *adv* > 'skeleton-,like *adj*

skeletonize *or* **skeletonise** ('skɛlɪtə,naɪz) *vb* (*tr*) **1** to reduce to a minimum framework, number, or outline **2** to create the essential framework of

skeleton key *n* a key with the serrated edge filed down so that it can open numerous locks. Also called: **passkey** [C19 so called because it has been reduced to its essential parts]

skelf (skɛlf) *n Scot and northern English dialect* **1** a splinter of wood, esp when embedded accidentally in the skin **2** a thin or diminutive person [from Scottish; see SHELF]

skellum ('skɛləm) *n archaic and dialect* a rogue [C17 via Dutch from Old High German *skelmo* devil]

skelly[1] ('skɛlɪ) *n, pl* **-lies** a whitefish, *Coregonus stigmaticus*, of certain lakes in the Lake District [C18 perhaps from dialect *skell* a shell or scale, and so called because of its large scales]

skelly[2] ('skɛlɪ) *Scot and northern English dialect* ▷ *vb* **-lies, -lying, -lied** (*intr*) **1** to look sideways or squint ▷ *n, pl* **-lies** **2** a quick look; glance ▷ *adj* **3** Also: **skelly-eyed** cross-eyed [probably from Old Norse, from *skjalgr* wry; related to Old English *sceolh* a squint]

skelm ('skɛlᵊm) *n South African informal* a villain or crook [Afrikaans]

Skelmersdale ('skɛlməz,deɪl) *n* a town in NW England, in Lancashire: designated a new town in 1962. Pop: 39 279 (2001)

skelp[1] (skɛlp) *dialect* ▷ *vb* **1** (*tr*) to slap ▷ *n* **2** a slap [C15 probably of imitative origin]

skelp[2] (skɛlp) *n* sheet or plate metal that has been curved and welded to form a tube [C19 perhaps from Scottish Gaelic *sgealb* thin strip of wood]

sken (skɛn) *vb* **skens, skenning, skenned** (*intr*) *Northern English dialect* to squint or stare [of obscure origin]

skep (skɛp) *n* **1** a beehive, esp one constructed of straw **2** *now chiefly dialect* a large basket of wickerwork or straw [Old English *sceppe*, from Old Norse *skeppa* bushel; related to Old High German *sceffil* bushel]

skeptic ('skɛptɪk) *n, adj* an archaic, and the usual US, spelling of **sceptic**. > 'skeptical *adj* > 'skeptically *adv* > 'skepticalness *n* > 'skepticism *n*

skerrick ('skɛrɪk) *n US, Austral, and NZ* a small fragment or amount (esp in the phrase **not a skerrick**) [C20 northern English dialect, probably of Scandinavian origin]

skerry ('skɛrɪ) *n, pl* **-ries** *chiefly Scot* **1** a small rocky island **2** a reef [C17 Orkney dialect, from Old Norse *sker* SCAR[2]]

sket (skɛt) *vb* **skets, sketting, sketted** (*tr*) *South Wales dialect* **1** to splash (water) **2** to splash (someone with water) [perhaps from Old Norse *skjóta* to shoot]

sketch (skɛtʃ) *n* **1** a rapid drawing or painting, often a study for subsequent elaboration **2** a brief usually descriptive and informal essay or other literary composition **3** a short play, often comic, forming part of a revue **4** a short evocative piece of instrumental music, esp for piano **5** any brief outline ▷ *vb* **6** to make a rough drawing (of) **7** (*tr; often foll by out*) to make a brief description of [C17 from Dutch *schets*, via Italian from Latin *schedius* hastily made, from Greek *skhedios* unprepared] > 'sketchable *adj* > 'sketcher *n*

sketchbook ('skɛtʃ,bʊk) *n* **1** a book of plain paper containing sketches or for making sketches in **2** a book of literary sketches

sketchy ('skɛtʃɪ) *adj* **sketchier, sketchiest** **1** characteristic of a sketch; existing only in outline **2** superficial or slight > 'sketchily *adv* > 'sketchiness *n*

skew (skjuː) *adj* **1** placed in or turning into an oblique position or course **2** *machinery* having a component that is at an angle to the main axis of an assembly or is in some other way asymmetrical: *a skew bevel gear* **3** *maths* **a** composed of or being elements that are neither parallel nor intersecting as, for example, two lines not lying in the same plane in a three-dimensional space **b** (of a curve) not lying in a plane **4** (of a statistical distribution) not having equal probabilities above and below the mean; non-normal **5** distorted or biased ▷ *n* **6** an oblique, slanting, or indirect course or position **7** *psychol* the system of relationships in a family in which one parent is extremely dominating while the other parent tends to be meekly compliant ▷ *vb* **8** to take or cause to take an oblique course or direction **9** (*intr*) to look sideways; squint **10** (*tr*) to place at an angle **11** (*tr*) to distort or bias [C14 from Old Norman French *escuer* to shun, of Germanic origin; compare Middle Dutch *schuwen* to avoid]

skew arch *n* an arch or vault, esp one used in a bridge or tunnel, that is set at an oblique angle to the span

skewback ('skjuː,bæk) *n* **1** the sloping surface on both sides of a segmental arch that takes the thrust **2** one or more stones that provide such a surface > 'skew,backed *adj*

skewbald ('skjuː,bɔːld) *adj* **1** marked or spotted in white and any colour except black ▷ *n* **2** a horse with this marking [C17 see SKEW, PIEBALD]

skewer ('skjʊə) *n* **1** a long pin for holding meat in position while being cooked, etc **2** a similar pin having some other function **3** *chess* a tactical manoeuvre in which an attacked man is made to move and expose another man to capture ▷ *vb* **4** (*tr*) to drive a skewer through or fasten with a skewer [C17 probably from dialect *skiver*]

skewness ('skjuːnɪs) *n* **1** the quality or condition of being skew **2** *statistics* a measure of the symmetry of a distribution around its mean, esp the statistic $B_1 = m_3/(m_2)^{3/2}$, where m_2 and m_3 are respectively the second and third moments of the distribution around the mean. In a normal distribution, $B_1 = 0$. Compare **kurtosis**

skew symmetry *n* symmetry of top left with bottom right, and top right with bottom left

skewwhiff ('skjuː'wɪf) *adj* (*postpositive*) *Brit informal* not straight; askew [C18 probably influenced by ASKEW]

ski (skiː) *n, pl* **skis** *or* **ski** **1** **a** one of a pair of wood, metal, or plastic runners that are used for gliding over snow. Skis are commonly attached to shoes for sport, but may also be used as landing gear for aircraft, etc **b** (*as modifier*): *a ski boot* **2** a water-ski ▷ *vb* **skis, skiing; skied** *or* **ski'd** **3** (*intr*) to travel on skis [C19 from Norwegian, from Old Norse *skith* snowshoes; related to Old English *scīd* piece of split wood] > 'skiable *adj* > 'skier *n* > 'skiing *n*

skiamachy (skaɪ'æməkɪ) *n, pl* **-chies** a variant of **sciamachy**

skiascope ('skaɪə,skəʊp) *n med* a medical instrument for examining the eye to detect errors of refraction. Also called: **retinoscope**. See also **retinoscopy** [C19 from Greek *skia* a shadow + -SCOPE]

skiascopy (skaɪ'æskəpɪ) *n med* another name for **retinoscopy**

skibob ('skiː,bɒb) *n* a vehicle made of two short skis, the forward one having a steering handle and the rear one supporting a low seat, for gliding down snow slopes [C20 from SKI + BOB[2]. See BOBSLEIGH] > 'skibobber *n* > 'skibobbing *n*

skid (skɪd) *vb* **skids, skidding, skidded** **1** to cause (a vehicle) to slide sideways or (of a vehicle) to slide sideways while in motion, esp out of control **2** (*intr*) to slide without revolving, as the wheel of a moving vehicle after sudden braking **3** (*tr*) *US and Canadian* to put or haul on a skid, esp along a special track **4** to cause (an aircraft) to slide sideways away from the centre of a turn when insufficiently banked or (of an aircraft) to slide in this manner ▷ *n* **5** an instance of sliding, esp sideways **6** *chiefly US and Canadian* one of the logs forming a skidway **7** a support on which heavy objects may be stored and moved short distances by sliding **8** a shoe or drag used to apply pressure to the metal rim of a wheel to act as a brake **9** **on the skids** in decline or about to fail [C17 perhaps of Scandinavian origin; compare SKI] > 'skiddy *adj*

skidlid ('skɪd,lɪd) *n* a slang word for **crash helmet**

Skidoo (skɪ'duː) *n trademark Canadian* another name for **snowmobile**

skidpan ('skɪd,pæn) *n chiefly Brit* an area made slippery so that vehicle drivers can practise controlling skids

skidproof ('skɪd,pruːf) *adj* (of a road surface, tyre, etc) preventing or resistant to skidding

skid road *n* (in the US and Canada) **1** a track made of a set of logs laid transversely on which freshly cut timber can be hauled **2** **a** (in the West) the part of a town frequented by loggers **b** another term for **skid row**

skid row (rəʊ) *or* **skid road** *n slang, chiefly US and Canadian* a dilapidated section of a city inhabited by vagrants, etc

skidway ('skɪd,weɪ) *n chiefly US and Canadian* **1** a platform on which logs ready for sawing are piled **2** a track made of logs for rolling objects along

skied[1] (skaɪd) *vb* the past tense and past participle of **sky**

skied[2] (skiːd) *vb* a past tense and past participle of **ski**

Skien (*Norwegian* 'ʃeːən) *n* a port in S Norway, on the **Skien River**: one of the oldest towns in Norway; timber industry. Pop: 50 507 (2004 est)

skiff (skɪf) *n* any of various small boats propelled by oars, sail, or motor [C18 from French *esquif*, from Old Italian *schifo* a boat, of Germanic origin; related to Old High German *schif* SHIP]

skiffle[1] ('skɪfᵊl) *n* a style of popular music of the 1950s, played chiefly on guitars and improvised percussion instruments [C20 of unknown origin]

skiffle[2] ('skɪfᵊl) *n Ulster dialect* a drizzle: *a skiffle of rain* [from Scottish *skiff*, from *skiff* to move lightly, probably changed from *skift*, from Old Norse *skipta* SHIFT]

skijoring (skiː'dʒɔːrɪŋ) *n* a sport in which a skier is pulled over snow or ice, usually by a horse [Norwegian *skikjöring*, literally: ski-driving] > ski'jorer *n*

ski jump *n* **1** a high ramp overhanging a slope from which skiers compete to make the longest jump ▷ *vb* **ski-jump** **2** (*intr*) to perform a ski jump > ski jumper *n*

Skikda ('skɪkdɑː) *n* a port in NE Algeria, on an inlet of the Mediterranean: founded by the French in 1838 on the site of a Roman city. Pop: 170 000 (2005 est). Former name: **Philippeville**

skilful *or US* **skillful** ('skɪlfʊl) *adj* **1** possessing or displaying accomplishment or skill **2** involving or requiring accomplishment or skill > 'skilfully *or US* 'skillfully *adv* > 'skilfulness *or US* 'skillfulness *n*

ski lift *n* any of various devices for carrying skiers up a slope, such as a chairlift

skill (skɪl) *n* **1** special ability in a task, sport, etc, esp ability acquired by training **2** something, esp a trade or technique, requiring special training or manual proficiency **3** *obsolete* understanding [C12 from Old Norse *skil* distinction; related to Middle Low German *schēle*, Middle Dutch *geschil* difference] > 'skill-less *or* 'skilless *adj*

Skillcentre ('skɪl,sɛntə) *n Brit* any of a number of agencies attached to the Manpower Services Commission and funded by the Government to provide vocational training or retraining for employed or unemployed people

skilled (skɪld) *adj* **1** possessing or demonstrating accomplishment, skill, or special training **2** (*prenominal*) involving skill or special training: *a skilled job*

skillet ('skɪlɪt) *n* **1** a small frying pan **2** *chiefly Brit* a saucepan [C15 probably from *skele* bucket, of Scandinavian origin; related to Old Norse *skjōla* bucket]

skilling ('skɪlɪŋ) *n* a former Scandinavian coin of

low denomination [c18 from Danish and Swedish; see SHILLING]

skillion ('skɪlɪən) *n Austral* **a** a part of a building having a lower, esp sloping, roof; lean-to **b** (*as modifier*): *a skillion roof* [c19 from English dialect *skilling* outhouse]

skilly ('skɪlɪ) *n chiefly Brit* a thin soup or gruel [c19 shortened from *skilligallee*, probably a fanciful formation]

Skil Saw (skɪl) *n trademark* a portable electric saw

skim (skɪm) *vb* **skims, skimming, skimmed** **1** (*tr*) to remove floating material from the surface of (a liquid), as with a spoon: *to skim milk* **2** to glide smoothly or lightly over (a surface) **3** (*tr*) to throw (something) in a path over a surface, so as to bounce or ricochet: *to skim stones over water* **4** (when *intr*, usually foll by *through*) to read (a book) in a superficial or cursory manner **5** to cover (a liquid) with a thin layer or (of liquid) to become coated in this way, as with ice, scum, etc ▷ *n* **6** the act or process of skimming **7** material skimmed off a liquid, esp off milk **8** the liquid left after skimming **9** any thin layer covering a surface ▷ See also **skim off** [c15 *skimmen*, probably from *scumen* to skim; see SCUM]

skimble-scamble ('skɪmbᵊl'skæmbᵊl) *archaic* ▷ *adj* **1** rambling; confused ▷ *n* **2** meaningless discourse [c16 whimsical formation based on dialect *scamble* to struggle]

skimboard ('skɪmbɔːd) *n* **1** a type of surfboard, shorter than standard and rounded at both ends ▷ *vb* **2** (*intr*) to surf on a skimboard > 'skim,board *n* > 'skim,boarder *n*

skimmed milk *n* milk from which the cream has been removed. Also called: **skim milk**. Compare **whole milk**

skimmer ('skɪmə) *n* **1** a person or thing that skims **2** any of several mainly tropical coastal aquatic birds of the genus *Rhynchops*, having long narrow wings and a bill with an elongated lower mandible for skimming food from the surface of the water: family *Rynchopidae*, order *Charadriiformes* **3** a flat perforated spoon used for skimming fat from liquids

skimmia ('skɪmɪə) *n* any rutaceous shrub of the S and SE Asian genus *Skimmia*, grown for their ornamental red berries and evergreen foliage [c18 New Latin from Japanese (*mijama-*)*shikimi*, a native name of the plant]

skimmings ('skɪmɪŋz) *pl n* **1** material that is skimmed off a liquid **2** the froth containing concentrated ore removed during a flotation process **3** slag, scum, or impurities removed from molten metals

skim off *vb* (*tr, adverb*) to take the best part of: *the teacher skimmed off the able pupils for his class*

skimp (skɪmp) *vb* **1** to be extremely sparing or supply (someone) sparingly; stint **2** to perform (work, etc) carelessly, hastily, or with inadequate materials [c17 perhaps a combination of SCANT and SCRIMP]

skimpy ('skɪmpɪ) *adj* **skimpier, skimpiest** **1** (of clothes, etc) made of too little material; scanty **2** excessively thrifty; mean; stingy > 'skimpily *adv* > 'skimpiness *n*

skim-read *vb* to read quickly and superficially, in order to pick up the important or significant details

skin (skɪn) *n* **1 a** the tissue forming the outer covering of the vertebrate body: it consists of two layers (see **dermis, epidermis**), the outermost of which may be covered with hair, scales, feathers, etc. It is mainly protective and sensory in function **b** (*as modifier*): *a skin disease*. Related adjs: **cutaneous, dermatoid** **2** a person's complexion: *a fair skin* **3** any similar covering in a plant or lower animal **4** any coating or film, such as one that forms on the surface of a liquid **5** unsplit leather made from the outer covering of various mammals, reptiles, etc. Compare **hide²** (sense 1) **6** the outer covering of a fur-bearing animal, dressed and finished with the hair on **7** a

container made from animal skin **8** the outer covering surface of a vessel, rocket, etc **9** a person's skin regarded as his life: *to save one's skin* **10** (*often plural*) *informal* (in jazz or pop use) a drum **11** *informal* short for **skinhead** **12** *slang* a cigarette paper used for rolling a cannabis cigarette **13** *Anglo-Irish slang* a person; sort: *he's a good old skin* **14** **by the skin of one's teeth** by a narrow margin; only just **15** **get under one's skin** *informal* to irritate one **16** **jump out of one's skin** to be very startled **17** **no skin off one's nose** *informal* not a matter that affects one adversely **18** **thick** (*or* **thin**) **skin** an insensitive (*or* sensitive) nature ▷ *vb* **skins, skinning, skinned** **19** (*tr*) to remove the outer covering from (fruit, etc) **20** (*tr*) to scrape a small piece of skin from (a part of oneself) in falling, etc: *he skinned his knee* **21** (often foll by *over*) to cover (something) with skin or a skinlike substance or (of something) to become covered in this way **22** (*tr*) *slang* to strip of money; swindle ▷ *adj* **23** relating to or for the skin: *skin cream* **24** *slang, chiefly US* involving or depicting nudity: *skin magazines* ▷ See also **skin up** [Old English *scinn*, from Old Norse *skinn*] > 'skinless *adj* > 'skin,like *adj*

skin-deep *adj* **1** superficial; shallow ▷ *adv* **2** superficially

skin diving *n* the sport or activity of diving and underwater swimming without wearing a diver's costume > 'skin-,diver *n*

skin effect *n* the tendency of alternating current to concentrate in the surface layer of a conductor, esp at high frequencies, thus increasing its effective resistance

skin flick *n slang* a film containing much nudity and explicit sex for sensational purposes

skinflint ('skɪn,flɪnt) *n* an ungenerous or niggardly person; miser [c18 referring to a person so avaricious that he would skin (swindle) a flint] > 'skin,flinty *adj*

skin food *n* a cosmetic cream for keeping the skin in good condition

skin friction *n* the friction acting on a solid body when it is moving through a fluid

skinful ('skɪn,fʊl) *n, pl* **-fuls** *slang* sufficient alcoholic drink to make one drunk (esp in the phrase **have a skinful**)

skin game *n slang* a swindling trick

skin graft *n* a piece of skin removed from one part of the body and surgically grafted at the site of a severe burn or similar injury

skinhead ('skɪn,hɛd) *n* **1** a member of a group of White youths, noted for their closely cropped hair, aggressive behaviour, and overt racism **2** a closely cropped hairstyle

skink (skɪŋk) *n* any lizard of the family *Scincidae*, commonest in tropical Africa and Asia, having reduced limbs and an elongated body covered with smooth scales. Related adj: **scincoid** [c16 from Latin *scincus* a lizard, from Greek *skinkos*]

skinned (skɪnd) *adj* **1** stripped of the skin **2 a** having a skin as specified **b** (*in combination*): *thick-skinned* **3** **keep one's eyes skinned** (*or* **peeled**) to watch carefully (for)

skinner ('skɪnə) *n* a person who prepares or deals in animal skins

Skinner box *n* a device for studying the learning behaviour of animals, esp rats and pigeons, consisting of a box in which the animal can move a lever to obtain a reward, such as a food pellet, or a punishment, such as an electric shock [c20 named after Burrhus Frederic *Skinner* (1904–90), US behavioural psychologist]

skinny ('skɪnɪ) *adj* **-nier, -niest** **1** lacking in flesh; thin **2** consisting of or resembling skin > 'skinniness *n*

skinny-dip *vb* **-dips, -dipping, -dipped** (*intr*) to swim in the nude > skinny dipping *n*

skin-pop *slang* ▷ *n* **1** the subcutaneous or intramuscular injection of a narcotic ▷ *vb* **-pops, -popping, -popped** **2** (*intr*) to take drugs in such a way

skint (skɪnt) *adj* (*usually postpositive*) *Brit slang*

without money [variant of *skinned*, past participle of SKIN]

skin test *n med* any test to determine immunity to a disease or hypersensitivity by introducing a small amount of the test substance beneath the skin or rubbing it into a fresh scratch. See **scratch test**

skintight ('skɪn'taɪt) *adj* (of garments) fitting tightly over the body; clinging

skin up *vb* (*adverb*) *slang* to roll (a cannabis cigarette)

skip¹ (skɪp) *vb* **skips, skipping, skipped** **1** (when *intr*, often foll by *over, along, into*, etc) to spring or move lightly, esp to move by hopping from one foot to the other **2** (*intr*) to jump over a skipping-rope **3** to cause (a stone, etc) to bounce or skim over a surface or (of a stone) to move in this way **4** to omit (intervening matter), as in passing from one part or subject to another: *he skipped a chapter of the book* **5** (*intr*; foll by *through*) *informal* to read or deal with quickly or superficially: *he skipped through the accounts before dinner* **6** **skip it!** *informal* it doesn't matter! **7** (*tr*) *informal* to miss deliberately: *to skip school* **8** (*tr*) *informal, chiefly US and Canadian* to leave (a place) in haste or secrecy: *to skip town* ▷ *n* **9** a skipping movement or gait **10** the act of passing over or omitting **11** *music, US and Canadian* another word for **leap** (sense 10) ▷ See also **skip off** [c13 probably of Scandinavian origin; related to Old Norse *skopa* to take a run, obsolete Swedish *skuppa* to skip]

skip² (skɪp) *n, vb* **skips, skipping, skipped** **1** *informal* short for **skipper¹** ▷ *n* **2** the captain of a curling or bowls team

skip³ (skɪp) *n* **1** a large open container for transporting building materials, etc **2** a cage used as a lift in mines, etc [c19 variant of SKEP]

skip⁴ (skɪp) *n* a college servant, esp of Trinity College, Dublin [c17 probably shortened from archaic *skip-kennel* a footman or lackey (from SKIP¹ + KENNEL²)]

ski pants *pl n* trousers usually of stretch material and kept taut by a strap under the foot, worn for skiing or as a fashion garment

skip distance *n* the shortest distance between a transmitter and a receiver that will permit reception of radio waves of a specified frequency by one reflection from the ionosphere

skipjack ('skɪp,dʒæk) *n, pl* **-jack** *or* **-jacks** **1** Also called: **skipjack tuna** an important food fish, *Katsuwonus pelamis*, that has a striped abdomen and occurs in all tropical seas: family *Scombridae* (mackerels and tunas) **2** **black skipjack** a small spotted tuna, *Euthynnus yaito*, of Indo-Pacific seas **3** any of several other unrelated fishes, such as the alewife and bonito **4** *nautical* an American sloop used for oystering and as a yacht **5** another name for a **click beetle** [c18 from SKIP¹ + JACK¹]

skiplane ('skiː,pleɪn) *n* an aircraft fitted with skis to enable it to land on and take off from snow

skip off *vb* (*intr, adverb*) *Brit informal* to leave work, school, etc, early or without authorization

skipper¹ ('skɪpə) *n* **1** the captain of any vessel **2** the captain of an aircraft **3** a manager or leader, as of a sporting team ▷ *vb* **4** to act as skipper (of) [c14 from Middle Low German, Middle Dutch *schipper* shipper]

skipper² ('skɪpə) *n* **1** a person or thing that skips **2** any small butterfly of the family *Hesperiidae*, having a hairy mothlike body and erratic darting flight **3** another name for the **saury** (a fish)

skippering ('skɪpərɪŋ) *n slang* the practice of sleeping rough [c20 of unknown origin]

skippet ('skɪpɪt) *n* a small round box for preserving a document or seal [c14 perhaps from *skeppe* SKEP]

skipping ('skɪpɪŋ) *n* the act of jumping over a rope that is held and swung either by the person jumping or by two other people, as a game or for exercise

skipping-rope *n Brit* a cord, usually having handles at each end, that is held in the hands and

S

swung round and down so that the holder or others can jump over it

Skipton ('skɪptən) *n* a market town in N England, in North Yorkshire: 11th-century castle. Pop: 14 313 (2001)

skip-tooth saw *n* a saw with alternate teeth absent

skip tracer *n* *US and Canadian* a person employed to search for missing debtors or defendants who have absconded whilst on bail

skip zone *n* a region surrounding a broadcasting station that cannot receive transmissions either directly or by reflection off the ionosphere

skirl (skɜːl; *Scot* skɪrl) *vb* (*intr*) 1 *Scot and northern English dialect* (esp of bagpipes) to emit a shrill sound 2 to play the bagpipes ▷ *n* 3 the sound of bagpipes 4 a shrill sound [c14 probably of Scandinavian origin; see SHRILL]

skirmish ('skɜːmɪʃ) *n* 1 a minor short-lived military engagement 2 any brisk clash or encounter, usually of a minor nature ▷ *vb* 3 (*intr*; often foll by *with*) to engage in a skirmish [c14 from Old French *eskirmir*, of Germanic origin; related to Old High German *skirmen* to defend] > 'skirmisher *n*

Skíros ('skɪrɒs) *n* transliteration of the Modern Greek name for **Skyros**

skirr (skɜː) *vb* 1 (*intr*; usually foll by *off, away,* etc) to move, run, or fly rapidly 2 (*tr*) *archaic or literary* to move rapidly over (an area, etc), esp in order to find or apprehend ▷ *n* 3 a whirring or grating sound, as of the wings of birds in flight [c16 variant of SCOUR²]

skirret ('skɪrɪt) *n* an umbelliferous Old World plant, *Sium sisarum,* cultivated in parts of Europe for its edible tuberous roots [C14 *skirwhite,* perhaps from obsolete *skir* bright (see SHEER¹) + WHITE]

skirt (skɜːt) *n* 1 a garment hanging from the waist, worn chiefly by women and girls 2 the part of a dress below the waist 3 Also called: **apron** a frieze or circular flap, as round the base of a hovercraft 4 the flaps on a saddle that protect a rider's legs 5 *Brit* a cut of beef from the flank 6 (*often plural*) a margin or outlying area 7 *NZ* the lower part of a sheep's fleece 8 **bit of skirt** *slang* a girl or woman ▷ *vb* 9 (*tr*) to form the edge of 10 (*tr*) to provide with a border 11 (when *intr,* foll by *around, along,* etc) to pass (by) or be situated (near) the outer edge of (an area, etc) 12 (*tr*) to avoid (a difficulty, etc): *he skirted the issue* 13 *chiefly Austral and NZ* to remove the trimmings or inferior wool from (a fleece) [c13 from Old Norse *skyrta* SHIRT] > 'skirted *adj*

skirter ('skɜːtə) *n* *Austral* a man who skirts fleeces. See **skirt** (sense 13)

skirting ('skɜːtɪŋ) *n* 1 a border, esp of wood or tiles, fixed round the base of an interior wall to protect it from kicks, dirt, etc 2 material used or suitable for skirts

skirting board *n* a skirting made of wood. US and Canadian name: **baseboard** US name: **mopboard**

skirtings ('skɜːtɪŋz) *pl n* ragged edges trimmed from the fleece of a sheep

ski run *n* a trail, slope, or course for skiing

ski stick or **pole** *n* a stick, usually with a metal point and a disc to prevent it from sinking into the snow, used by skiers to gain momentum and maintain balance

skit (skɪt) *n* 1 a brief satirical theatrical sketch 2 a short satirical piece of writing 3 a trick or hoax [c18 related to earlier verb *skit* to move rapidly, hence to score a satirical hit, probably of Scandinavian origin; related to Old Norse *skjóta* to shoot]

skitch (skɪtʃ) *vb* (*tr*) *NZ* (of a dog) to attack; catch

skite¹ (skaɪt) *Scot* ▷ *vb* 1 (*intr*) to slide or slip, as on ice 2 (*tr*) to strike with a sharp or glancing blow ▷ *n* 3 an instance of sliding or slipping 4 a sharp or glancing blow 5 **on the** (or **a**) **skite** *Scot, Irish* on a drinking spree [c18 of uncertain origin]

skite² (skaɪt) *Austral and NZ informal* ▷ *vb* (*intr*) 1 to boast ▷ *n* 2 boastful talk 3 a person who boasts

[c19 from Scottish and northern English dialect; see SKATE³]

ski touring *n* long-distance hiking on skis over open, mountainous country; noncompetitive cross-country skiing

ski tow *n* a device for pulling skiers uphill, usually a motor-driven rope grasped by the skier while riding on his skis

skitter ('skɪtə) *vb* 1 (*intr*; often foll by *off*) to move or run rapidly or lightly; scamper 2 to skim or cause to skim lightly and rapidly, as across the surface of water 3 (*intr*) *angling* to draw a bait lightly over the surface of water [c19 probably from dialect *skite* to dash about; related to Old Norse *skjóta* to SHOOT]

skittish ('skɪtɪʃ) *adj* 1 playful, lively, or frivolous 2 difficult to handle or predict 3 *now rare* coy [c15 probably of Scandinavian origin; compare Old Norse *skjóta* to SHOOT; see -ISH] > 'skittishly *adv* > 'skittishness *n*

skittle ('skɪtᵊl) *n* 1 a wooden or plastic pin, typically widest just above the base 2 (*plural; functioning as singular*) Also called (esp US): **ninepins** a bowling game in which players knock over as many skittles as possible by rolling a wooden ball at them 3 **beer and skittles** (*often used with a negative*) *informal* an easy time; amusement [c17 of obscure origin; perhaps related to Swedish, Danish *skyttel* shuttle]

skittle out *vb* (*tr, adverb*) *cricket* to dismiss (batsmen) quickly

skive¹ (skaɪv) *vb* (*tr*) to shave or remove the surface of (leather) [c19 from Old Norse *skifa;* related to English dialect *shive* a slice of bread]

skive² (skaɪv) *vb* (when *intr,* often foll by *off*) *Brit informal* to evade (work or responsibility) [c20 of unknown origin]

skiver¹ ('skaɪvə) *n* 1 the tanned outer layer split from a skin 2 a person, tool, or machine that skives

skiver² ('skaɪvə) *n* *Brit slang* a person who persistently avoids work or responsibility

skivvy¹ ('skɪvɪ) *n, pl* -vies 1 *chiefly Brit often contemptuous* a servant, esp a female, who does menial work of all kinds; drudge ▷ *vb* -vies, -vying, -vied 2 (*intr*) *Brit* to work as a skivvy [c20 of unknown origin]

skivvy² ('skɪvɪ) *n, pl* -vies 1 *slang, chiefly US* a man's T-shirt or vest 2 (*plural*) *slang, chiefly US* men's underwear 3 *Austral and NZ* a garment resembling a sweater with long sleeves and a polo neck, usually made of stretch cotton or cotton and polyester and worn by either sex [of unknown origin]

skokiaan ('skɔːkɪˌɑːn) *n* (in South Africa) a potent alcoholic beverage drunk by Black Africans in shebeens [c20 from Afrikaans, of unknown origin]

skol (skɒl) or **skoal** (skəʊl) *sentence substitute* 1 good health! (a drinking toast) ▷ *vb* **skols, skolling, skolled** (*tr*) 2 *Austral informal* to down (an alcoholic drink) in one go [c16 from Danish *skaal* bowl, from Old Norse *skal;* see SCALE²]

skolly or **skollie** ('skɒlɪ) *n, pl* -lies *South African* a Coloured hooligan, usually one of a gang [c20 of unknown origin]

skookum ('skuːkəm) *adj* *Canadian* strong or brave [c19 from Chinook Jargon]

skool (skuːl) *n* an ironically illiterate or childish spelling of **school**

skop, skiet en donder (skɒp skiːt ən 'dɒndə) *n South African informal* violent action and melodramatic adventure in a film [Afrikaans, literally: kick, shoot and thunder]

Skopje ('skɔːpjɛ) *n* the capital of (the Former Yugoslav Republic of) Macedonia, on the Vardar River: became capital of Serbia in 1346 and of Macedonia in 1945; suffered a severe earthquake in 1963; university (1949). Pop: 449 000 (2005 est). Serbo-Croat name: Skoplje ('skɔːpljɛ) Turkish name (1392–1913): Üsküb

skort (skɔːt) *n* a pair of shorts with a front panel

which gives the appearance of a skirt

skrike (skraɪk) *vb* (*intr*) *Northern English dialect* to cry

Skt or **Skr.** *abbreviation for* Sanskrit

skua ('skjuːə) *n* any predatory gull-like bird of the family *Stercorariidae,* such as the **great skua** or **bonxie** (*Stercorarius skua*) or **arctic skua** (*S. parasiticus*) both of which harass terns or gulls into dropping or disgorging fish they have caught [c17 from New Latin, from Faeroese *skúgvur,* from Old Norse *skúfr*]

skulduggery or *US* **skullduggery** (skʌl'dʌgərɪ) *n informal* underhand dealing; trickery [c19 altered from earlier Scot *sculduddery;* of obscure origin]

skulk (skʌlk) *vb* (*intr*) 1 to move stealthily so as to avoid notice 2 to lie in hiding; lurk 3 to shirk duty or evade responsibilities; malinger ▷ *n* 4 a person who skulks 5 *obsolete* a pack of foxes or other animals that creep about stealthily [c13 of Scandinavian origin; compare Norwegian *skulka* to lurk, Swedish *skolka,* Danish *skulke* to shirk] > 'skulker *n*

skull (skʌl) *n* 1 the bony skeleton of the head of vertebrates. See **cranium** Related adj: **cranial** 2 *often derogatory* the head regarded as the mind or intelligence: *to have a dense skull* 3 a picture of a skull used to represent death or danger [c13 of Scandinavian origin; compare Old Norse *skoltr,* Norwegian *skult,* Swedish dialect *skulle*]

skull and crossbones *n* a picture of the human skull above two crossed thighbones, formerly on the pirate flag, now used as a warning of danger or death

skullcap ('skʌlˌkæp) *n* 1 a rounded brimless hat fitting the crown of the head 2 the nontechnical name for **calvaria** 3 any of various perennial plants of the genus *Scutellaria,* esp *S. galericulata,* that typically have helmet-shaped flowers: family *Lamiaceae* (labiates)

skunk (skʌŋk) *n, pl* **skunks** or **skunk** 1 any of various American musteline mammals of the subfamily *Mephitinae,* esp *Mephitis mephitis* (**striped skunk**), typically having a black and white coat and bushy tail: they eject an unpleasant-smelling fluid from the anal gland when attacked 2 *informal* a despicable person 3 *slang* a strain of cannabis smoked for its exceptionally powerful psychoactive properties ▷ *vb* 4 (*tr*) *US and Canadian slang* to defeat overwhelmingly in a game [c17 from Algonquian; compare Abnaki *segákw* skunk]

skunk cabbage *n* 1 a low-growing fetid aroid swamp plant, *Symplocarpus foetidus* of E North America, having broad leaves and minute flowers enclosed in a mottled greenish or purple spathe 2 a similar aroid plant, *Lysichitum americanum,* of the W coast of North America and N Asia ▷ Also called: **skunkweed**

sky (skaɪ) *n, pl* **skies** 1 (*sometimes plural*) the apparently dome-shaped expanse extending upwards from the horizon that is characteristically blue or grey during the day, red in the evening, and black at night. Related adjs: **celestial, empyrean** 2 outer space, as seen from the earth 3 (*often plural*) weather, as described by the appearance of the upper air: *sunny skies* 4 the source of divine power; heaven 5 *informal* the highest level of attainment: *the sky's the limit* 6 **to the skies** highly; extravagantly ▷ *vb* **skies, skying, skied** 7 *rowing* to lift (the blade of an oar) too high before a stroke 8 (*tr*) *informal* to hit (a ball) high in the air [c13 from Old Norse *ský;* related to Old English *scio* cloud, Old Saxon *skio,* Old Norse *skjár* transparent skin] > 'sky,like *adj*

sky blue *n* a a light or pale blue colour b (*as adjective*): *a sky-blue jumper*

sky-blue pink *n, adj* a jocular name for a nonexistent, unknown, or unimportant colour

skyboard ('skaɪˌbɔːd) *n* a small board used in the sport of skysurfing

skybox ('skaɪˌbɒks) *n* *US* a luxurious suite high up in the stand of a sports stadium, which is rented out to groups of spectators, corporations, etc

skydive ('skaɪˌdaɪv) *vb* **-dives, -diving, -dived** or *US*

-dove; -dived (*intr*) to take part in skydiving
> ˈskyˌdiver *n*

skydiving (ˈskaɪˌdaɪvɪŋ) *n* the sport of parachute jumping, in which participants perform manoeuvres before opening the parachute and attempt to land accurately

Skye (skaɪ) *n* a mountainous island off the NW coast of Scotland, the largest island of the Inner Hebrides. tourist centre. Chief town: Portree. Pop: 9232 (2001). Area: 1735 sq km (670 sq miles)

Skye terrier *n* a short-legged long-bodied breed of terrier with long wiry hair and erect ears

skyf (skeɪf) *South African slang* ⊳ *n* **1** a cigarette or substance for smoking; a smoke ⊳ *vb* **2** to smoke (something, esp cannabis) [from Afrikaans]

sky-high *adj, adv* **1** at or to an unprecedented or excessive level: *prices rocketed sky-high* ⊳ *adv* **2** high into the air **3 blow sky-high** to destroy completely

skyhome (ˈskaɪˌhəʊm) *n Austral* a sub-penthouse flat in a tall residential building

skyjack (ˈskaɪˌdʒæk) *vb* (*tr*) to commandeer (an aircraft), usually at gunpoint during flight, forcing the pilot to fly somewhere other than to the scheduled destination [c20 from SKY + HIJACK] > ˈskyˌjacker *n*

Skylab (ˈskaɪˌlæb) *n* a US space station launched in May 1973 into an orbit inclined at 50° to the equatorial plane at a mean altitude of 430 kilometres (270 miles), the astronauts working there under conditions of zero gravity. It disintegrated, unmanned, in 1979, with some parts landing in the outback of Australia [c20 from SKY + LAB(ORATORY)]

skylark (ˈskaɪˌlɑːk) *n* **1** an Old World lark, *Alauda arvensis*, noted for singing while hovering at a great height **2** any of various Australian larks ⊳ *vb* **3** (*intr*) *informal* to romp or play jokes > ˈskyˌlarker *n*

skylight (ˈskaɪˌlaɪt) *n* a window placed in a roof or ceiling to admit daylight. Also called: **fanlight**

skylight filter *n photog* a very slightly pink filter that absorbs ultraviolet light and reduces haze and excessive blueness

skyline (ˈskaɪˌlaɪn) *n* **1** the line at which the earth and sky appear to meet; horizon **2** the outline of buildings, mountains, trees, etc, seen against the sky

sky marker *n* a parachute flare dropped to mark a target area

sky marshal *n* an armed security guard on a commercial aircraft

sky pilot *n slang* a chaplain in one of the military services

skyrocket (ˈskaɪˌrɒkɪt) *n* **1** another word for **rocket¹** (sense 1) ⊳ *vb* **2** (*intr*) *informal* to rise rapidly, as in price

Skyros or **Scyros** (ˈskiːrɒs) *n* a Greek island in the Aegean, the largest island in the N Sporades. Pop: 2602 (2001). Area: 199 sq km (77 sq miles). Modern Greek name: **Skíros**

skysail (ˈskaɪˌseɪl) *n nautical* **1** a square sail set above the royal on a square-rigger **2** a triangular sail set between the trucks of a racing schooner

skyscape (ˈskaɪˌskeɪp) *n* a painting, drawing, photograph, etc, representing or depicting the sky

skyscraper (ˈskaɪˌskreɪpə) *n* a very tall multistorey building

sky show *n Austral* a fireworks display

skysurfing (ˈskaɪˌsɜːfɪŋ) *n* the activity or sport of performing stunts while standing on a small board during the free-fall part of a parachute jump > ˈskyˌsurfer *n*

skyward (ˈskaɪwəd) *adj* **1** directed or moving towards the sky ⊳ *adv* **2** Also: **skywards** towards the sky

sky wave *n* a radio wave reflected back to the earth by the ionosphere (**ionospheric wave**), permitting transmission around the curved surface of the earth. Compare **ground wave**

skywriting (ˈskaɪˌraɪtɪŋ) *n* **1** the forming of words in the sky by the release of smoke or vapour from

an aircraft **2** the words so formed > ˈskyˌwriter *n*

sl¹ *bibliog abbreviation for* sine loco [Latin: without place (of publication)]

sl² *the internet domain name for* Sierra Leone

SL *abbreviation for* Solicitor at Law

S/L (in Canada) *abbreviation for* Squadron Leader

slab (slæb) *n* **1** a broad flat thick piece of wood, stone, or other material **2** a thick slice of cake, etc **3** any of the outside parts of a log that are sawn off while the log is being made into planks **4** *mountaineering* a flat sheet of rock lying at an angle of between 30° and 60° from the horizontal **5** a printer's ink table **6** (*modifier*) *Austral and NZ* made or constructed of coarse wooden planks: *a slab hut* **7** *informal, chiefly Brit* an operating or mortuary table **8** *chiefly Brit and Austral informal* a package containing 24 cans of beer ⊳ *vb* **slabs, slabbing, slabbed** (*tr*) **9** to cut or make into a slab or slabs **10** to cover or lay with slabs **11** to saw slabs from (a log) [c13 of unknown origin]

slabber (ˈslæbə) *vb, n* a dialect word for **slobber** [c16 variant of SLOBBER]

slack¹ (slæk) *adj* **1** not tight, tense, or taut **2** negligent or careless **3** (esp of water, etc) moving slowly **4** (of trade, etc) not busy **5** *phonetics* another term for **lax** (sense 4) ⊳ *adv* **6** in a slack manner ⊳ *n* **7** a part of a rope, etc, that is slack: *take in the slack* **8** a period of decreased activity **9 a** a patch of water without current **b** a slackening of a current **10** *prosody* (in sprung rhythm) the unstressed syllable or syllables ⊳ *vb* **11** to neglect (one's duty, etc) **12** (often foll by *off*) to loosen; to make slack **13** *chem* a less common word for **slake** (sense 3) ⊳ See also **slacks** [Old English *slæc, sleac;* related to Old High German *slah,* Old Norse *slākr* bad, Latin *laxus* LAX] > ˈslackly *adv* > ˈslackness *n*

slack² (slæk) *n* small pieces of coal with a high ash content [c15 probably from Middle Low German *slecke;* related to Dutch *slak,* German *Schlacke* dross]

slacken (ˈslækən) *vb* (often foll by *off*) **1** to make or become looser **2** to make or become slower, less intense, etc

slacker (ˈslækə) *n* **1** a person who evades work or duty; shirker **2** *informal* **a** an educated young adult characterized by cynicism and apathy **b** (*as modifier*): *slacker culture*

slacks (slæks) *pl n informal* trousers worn by both sexes

slack suit *n US* casual male dress consisting of slacks and a matching shirt or jacket

slack water *n* the period of still water around the turn of the tide, esp at low tide

slag (slæg) *n* **1** Also called: **cinder** the fused material formed during the smelting or refining of metals by combining the flux with gangue, impurities in the metal, etc. It usually consists of a mixture of silicates with calcium, phosphorus, sulphur, etc. See also **basic slag 2** a mass of rough fragments of pyroclastic rock and cinders derived from a volcanic eruption; scoria **3** a mixture of shale, clay, coal dust, and other mineral waste produced during coal mining **4** *Brit slang* a coarse or dissipated girl or woman ⊳ *vb* **slags, slagging, slagged 5** (*intr*) *Austral slang* to spit [c16 from Middle Low German *slagge,* perhaps from *slagen* to SLAY] > ˈslagging *n* > ˈslaggy *adj*

slag down *vb* (*tr, adverb*) *prison slang* to give a verbal lashing to

slag heap *n* a hillock of waste matter from coal mining, etc

slain (sleɪn) *vb* the past participle of **slay**

slàinte mhath (ˌslɑːndʒə ˈva), *Scot* **slàinte** or *Irish* **sláinte mhaith** (ˌslɑːntə ˈva) *interj* a drinking toast; cheers [Gaelic: good health]

slake (sleɪk) *vb* **1** (*tr*) *literary* to satisfy (thirst, desire, etc) **2** (*tr*) *poetic* to cool or refresh **3** Also: **slack** to undergo or cause to undergo the process in which lime reacts with water or moist air to produce calcium hydroxide **4** *archaic* to make or become less active or intense [Old English *slacian,* from *slæc* SLACK¹; related to Dutch *slaken* to

diminish, Icelandic *slaka*] > ˈslakable or ˈslakeable *adj* > ˈslaker *n*

slaked lime *n* another name for **calcium hydroxide,** esp when made by adding water to calcium oxide

slalom (ˈslɑːləm) *n* **1** *skiing* a race, esp one downhill, over a winding course marked by artificial obstacles **2** a similar type of obstacle race in canoes ⊳ *vb* **3** (*intr*) to take part in a slalom [Norwegian, from *slad* sloping + *lom* path]

slam¹ (slæm) *vb* **slams, slamming, slammed 1** to cause (a door or window) to close noisily and with force or (of a door, etc) to close in this way **2** (*tr*) to throw (something) down noisily and violently **3** (*tr*) *slang* to criticize harshly **4** (*intr;* usually foll by *into* or *out of*) *informal* to go (into or out of a room, etc) in violent haste or anger **5** (*tr*) to strike with violent force **6** (*tr*) *informal* to defeat easily ⊳ *n* **7** the act or noise of slamming **8** *slang* harsh criticism or abuse [c17 of Scandinavian origin; compare Old Norse *slamra,* Norwegian *slemma,* Swedish dialect *slämma*]

slam² (slæm) *n* **1 a** the winning of all (**grand slam**) or all but one (**little** or **small slam**) of the 13 tricks at bridge or whist **b** the bid to do so in bridge **2** an old card game [c17 of uncertain origin]

slam³ (slæm) *n* a poetry contest in which entrants compete with each other by reciting their work and are awarded points by the audience [c20 origin unknown]

slam-bang *adv* **1** another word for **slap-bang 2** *US informal* carelessly; recklessly

slam dance *vb* to hurl oneself repeatedly into or through a crowd at a rock-music concert

slam dunk *basketball* ⊳ *n* **1** a scoring shot in which a player jumps up and forces the ball down through the basket **2** *informal* a task so easy that success in it is deemed a certainty ⊳ *vb* **slam-dunk 3** to jump up and force (a ball) through a basket

slammer (ˈslæmə) *n* the *slang* prison

slander (ˈslɑːndə) *n* **1** *law* **a** defamation in some transient form, as by spoken words, gestures, etc **b** a slanderous statement, etc **2** any false or defamatory words spoken about a person; calumny ⊳ *vb* **3** to utter or circulate slander (about) [c13 via Anglo-French from Old French *escandle,* from Late Latin *scandalum* a cause of offence; see SCANDAL] > ˈslanderer *n* > ˈslanderous *adj* > ˈslanderously *adv* > ˈslanderousness *n*

slang (slæŋ) *n* **1 a** vocabulary, idiom, etc, that is not appropriate to the standard form of a language or to formal contexts, may be restricted as to social status or distribution, and is characteristically more metaphorical and transitory than standard language **b** (*as modifier*): *a slang word* **2** another word for **jargon** ⊳ *vb* **3** to abuse (someone) with vituperative language; insult [c18 of unknown origin] > ˈslangy *adj* > ˈslangily *adv* > ˈslanginess *n*

slanging match *n Brit* a dispute in which insults and accusations are made by each party against the other

slant (slɑːnt) *vb* **1** to incline or be inclined at an oblique or sloping angle **2** (*tr*) to write or present (news, etc) with a bias **3** (*intr;* foll by *towards*) (of a person's opinions) to be biased ⊳ *n* **4** an inclined or oblique line or direction; slope **5** a way of looking at something **6** a bias or opinion, as in an article **7** a less technical name for **solidus 8 on a** (or **the**) **slant** sloping ⊳ *adj* **9** oblique, sloping [c17 short for ASLANT, probably of Scandinavian origin] > ˈslanting *adj* > ˈslantingly or ˈslantly *adv*

slanter (ˈslæntə) *n Austral obsolete informal* a variant of **slinter**

slant rhyme *n prosody* another term for **half-rhyme**

slantwise (ˈslɑːntˌwaɪz) or **slantways** (ˈslɑːntˌweɪz) *adv, adj* (*prenominal*) in a slanting or oblique direction

slap (slæp) *n* **1** a sharp blow or smack, as with the

S

open hand, something flat, etc **2** the sound made by or as if by such a blow **3** a sharp rebuke; reprimand **4** (a bit of) slap and tickle *Brit informal* sexual play **5** **a slap in the face** an insult or rebuff **6** **a slap on the back** congratulation **7** **a slap on the wrist** a light punishment or reprimand ▷ *vb* **slaps, slapping, slapped** **8** (*tr*) to strike (a person or thing) sharply, as with the open hand or something flat **9** (*tr*) to bring down (the hand, something flat, etc) sharply **10** (when *intr,* usually foll by *against*) to strike (something) with or as if with a slap **11** (*tr*) *informal, chiefly Brit* to apply in large quantities, haphazardly, etc: *she slapped butter on the bread* **12** **slap on the back** to congratulate ▷ *adv informal* **13** exactly; directly: *slap on time* **14** forcibly or abruptly: *to fall slap on the floor* [C17 from Low German *slapp,* German *Schlappe,* of imitative origin] > **'slapper** *n*

slap-bang *adv informal, chiefly Brit* **1** in a violent, sudden, or noisy manner. US equivalent: **slam-bang** **2** directly or immediately

slap bass *n* a rock or jazz style of playing the electric or double bass in which the strings are plucked and released so as to vibrate sharply against the fretboard or fingerboard

slapdash ('slæp,dæʃ) *adv* **1** in a careless, hasty, or haphazard manner ▷ *adj* **2** careless, hasty, or haphazard ▷ *n* **3** slapdash activity or work **4** another name for **roughcast** (sense 1) [C17 from SLAP + DASH[1]]

slap down *vb* (*tr, adverb*) *informal* to rebuke sharply, as for impertinence

slap-happy *adj informal* **1** cheerfully irresponsible or careless **2** dazed or giddy from or as if from repeated blows; punch-drunk

slaphead ('slæp,hɛd) *n derogatory slang* a bald person [from SLAP + HEAD]

slapjack ('slæp,dʒæk) *n* **1** a simple card game **2** *US* another word for **pancake** [C19 from SLAP + JACK[1]]

slapped-cheek disease *n* another name for **fifth disease**

slapper ('slæpə) *n Brit slang* a promiscuous woman

slapshot ('slæp,ʃɒt) *n ice hockey* a hard, fast, often wild, shot executed with a powerful downward swing, and with the blade of the stick brushing firmly against the ice prior to striking the puck

slapstick ('slæp,stɪk) *n* **1 a** comedy characterized by horseplay and physical action **b** (*as modifier*): *slapstick humour* **2** a flexible pair of paddles bound together at one end, formerly used in pantomime to strike a blow to a person with a loud clapping sound but without injury

slap-up *adj* (*prenominal*) *Brit informal* (esp of meals) lavish; excellent; first-class

slart (slɑːt) *vb* (*tr*) *Northern English dialect* to spill (something): *to slart the salt*

slash (slæʃ) *vb* (*tr*) **1** to cut or lay about (a person or thing) with sharp sweeping strokes, as with a sword, knife, etc **2** to lash with a whip **3** to make large gashes in: *to slash tyres* **4** to reduce (prices, etc) drastically **5** *chiefly US* to criticize harshly **6** to slit (the outer fabric of a garment) so that the lining material is revealed **7** to clear (scrub or undergrowth) by cutting ▷ *n* **8** a sharp, sweeping stroke, as with a sword or whip **9** a cut or rent made by such a stroke **10** a decorative slit in a garment revealing the lining material **11** *US and Canadian* **a** littered wood chips and broken branches that remain after trees have been cut down **b** an area so littered **12** Also called: **diagonal, forward slash, separatrix, shilling mark, solidus, stroke, virgule** a short oblique stroke used in text to separate items of information, such as days, months, and years in dates (*18/7/80*), alternative words (*and/or*), numerator from denominator in fractions (*55/103*), etc **13** *Brit slang* the act of urinating (esp in the phrase **have a slash**) **14** an genre of erotic fiction written by women, to appeal to women [C14 *slaschen,* perhaps from Old French *esclachier* to break]

slash-and-burn *adj* denoting a short-term method of cultivation in which land is cleared by destroying and burning trees and other vegetation for temporary agricultural use

Slashdot effect ('slæʃ,dɒt) *n computing* a temporary surge in the numbers visiting a website and consequent service slowdown or even server crash that sometimes arises as a result of a new link being set up from a more popular website [C21 from the symbols SLASH + DOT, which are conventions of website addresses]

slasher ('slæʃə) *n* **1** a person or thing that slashes **2** *Austral and NZ* a wooden-handled cutting tool or tractor-drawn machine used for cutting scrub or undergrowth in the bush

slasher movie *n slang* a film in which victims, usually women, are slashed with knives, razors, etc

slashfest ('slæʃə,fɛst) *n slang* a film, animated film, or computer game in which victims are killed bloodily using blades [C21 from SLASH + FEST]

slashing ('slæʃɪŋ) *adj* aggressively or harshly critical (esp in the phrase **slashing attack**) > **'slashingly** *adv*

slash pocket *n* a pocket in which the opening is a slit in the seam of a garment

Śląsk (ʃlõsk) *n* the Polish name for **Silesia**

slat[1] (slæt) *n* **1** a narrow thin strip of wood or metal, as used in a Venetian blind, etc **2** a movable or fixed auxiliary aerofoil attached to the leading edge of an aircraft wing to increase lift, esp during landing and takeoff ▷ *vb* **slats, slatting, slatted** **3** (*tr*) to provide with slats [C14 from Old French *esclat* splinter, from *esclater* to shatter]

slat[2] (slæt) *dialect* ▷ *vb* **slats, slatting, slatted** **1** (*tr*) to throw violently; fling carelessly **2** (*intr*) to flap violently ▷ *n* **3** a sudden blow [C13 of Scandinavian origin; related to Old Norse, Icelandic *sletta* to slap]

slat[3] (slæt) *n Irish* a spent salmon [C19 of uncertain origin]

slate[1] (sleɪt) *n* **1 a** a compact fine-grained metamorphic rock formed by the effects of heat and pressure on shale. It can be split into thin layers along natural cleavage planes and is used as a roofing and paving material **b** (*as modifier*): *a slate tile* **2** a roofing tile of slate **3** (formerly) a writing tablet of slate **4** a dark grey colour, often with a purplish or bluish tinge **5** *chiefly US and Canadian* a list of candidates in an election **6** *films* **a** the reference information written on a clapperboard **b** *informal* the clapperboard itself **7 clean slate** a record without dishonour **8 have a slate loose** *Brit and Irish informal* to be eccentric or crazy **9 on the slate** *Brit informal* on credit **10 wipe the slate clean** *informal* to make a fresh start, esp by forgetting past differences ▷ *vb* (*tr*) **11** to cover (a roof) with slates **12** *chiefly US* to enter (a person's name) on a list, esp on a political slate **13 a** to choose or destine: *he was slated to go far* **b** to plan or schedule: *the trial is slated to begin in three weeks* ▷ *vb* **14** of the colour slate [C14 from Old French *esclate,* from *esclat* a fragment; see SLAT[1]]

slate[2] (sleɪt) *vb* (*tr*) *informal, chiefly Brit* **1** to criticize harshly; censure **2** to punish or defeat severely [C19 probably from SLATE[1]]

slater ('sleɪtə) *n* **1** a person trained in laying roof slates **2** *dialect, Austral and NZ* a woodlouse. See also **sea slater**

slatey ('sleɪtɪ) *adj* **slatier, slatiest** *Irish informal* slightly mad; crazy

slather ('slæðə) *n* **1** (*usually plural*) *informal* a large quantity **2 open slather** *Austral and NZ slang* a situation in which there are no restrictions; free-for-all ▷ *vb* (*tr*) *US and Canadian slang* **3** to squander or waste **4** to spread thickly or lavishly [C19 of unknown origin]

slating[1] ('sleɪtɪŋ) *n* **1** the act or process of laying slates **2** slates collectively, or material for making slates

slating[2] ('sleɪtɪŋ) *n informal, chiefly Brit* a severe reprimand or critical attack

slattern ('slætən) *n* a slovenly woman or girl; slut [C17 probably from *slattering,* from dialect *slatter* to slop; perhaps from Scandinavian; compare Old Norse *sletta* to slap] > **'slatternly** *adj* > **'slatternliness** *n*

slaty ('sleɪtɪ) *adj* **slatier, slatiest** **1** consisting of or resembling slate **2** having the colour of slate > **'slatiness** *n*

slaughter ('slɔːtə) *n* **1** the killing of animals, esp for food **2** the savage killing of a person **3** the indiscriminate or brutal killing of large numbers of people, as in war; massacre **4** *informal* a resounding defeat ▷ *vb* (*tr*) **5** to kill (animals), esp for food **6** to kill in a brutal manner **7** to kill in large numbers **8** *informal* to defeat resoundingly [Old English *sleaht;* related to Old Norse *slāttar* hammering, *slātr* butchered meat, Old High German *slahta,* Gothic *slauhts,* German *Schlacht* battle] > **'slaughterer** *n* > **'slaughterous** *adj*

slaughterhouse ('slɔːtə,haʊs) *n* a place where animals are butchered for food; abattoir

slaughterman ('slɔːtə,mæn) *n, pl* **-men** a person employed to kill animals in a slaughterhouse

Slav (slɑːv) *n* a member of any of the peoples of E Europe or NW Asia who speak a Slavonic language [C14 from Medieval Latin *Sclāvus* a captive Slav; see SLAVE]

slave (sleɪv) *n* **1** a person legally owned by another and having no freedom of action or right to property **2** a person who is forced to work for another against his will **3** a person under the domination of another person or some habit or influence: *a slave to television* **4** a person who works in harsh conditions for low pay **5 a** a device that is controlled by or that duplicates the action of another similar device (the master device) **b** (*as modifier*): *slave cylinder* ▷ *vb* **6** (*intr;* often foll by *away*) to work like a slave **7** (*tr*) an archaic word for **enslave** [C13 via Old French from Medieval Latin *Sclāvus* a Slav, one held in bondage (from the fact that the Slavonic races were frequently conquered in the Middle Ages), from Late Greek *Sklabos* a Slav]

slave ant *n* any of various ants, esp *Formica fusca,* captured and forced to do the work of a colony of ants of another species (**slave-making ants**). See also **amazon ant**

Slave Coast *n* the coast of W Africa between the Volta River and Mount Cameroon, chiefly along the Bight of Benin: the main source of African slaves (16th–19th centuries)

slave cylinder *n* a small cylinder containing a piston that operates the brake shoes or pads in hydraulic brakes or the working part in any other hydraulically operated system. Compare **master cylinder**

slave-driver *n* **1** (esp formerly) a person forcing slaves to work **2** an employer who demands excessively hard work from his employees

slaveholder ('sleɪv,həʊldə) *n* a person who owns slaves > **'slave,holding** *n*

slaver[1] ('sleɪvə) *n* **1** an owner of or dealer in slaves **2** another name for **slave ship**

slaver[2] ('slævə) *vb* (*intr*) **1** to dribble saliva **2** (often foll by *over*) **a** to fawn or drool (over someone) **b** to show great desire (for); lust (after) ▷ *n* **3** saliva dribbling from the mouth **4** *informal* drivel [C14 probably of Low Dutch origin; related to SLOBBER] > **'slaverer** *n*

Slave River *n* a river in W Canada, in the Northwest Territories and NE Alberta, flowing from Lake Athabaska northwest to Great Slave Lake. Length: about 420 km (260 miles). Also called: **Great Slave River**

slavery ('sleɪvərɪ) *n* **1** the state or condition of being a slave; a civil relationship whereby one person has absolute power over another and controls his life, liberty, and fortune **2** the subjection of a person to another person, esp in being forced into work **3** the condition of being subject to some influence or habit **4** work done in harsh conditions for low pay

slave ship *n* a ship used to transport slaves, esp formerly from Africa to the New World

Slave State *n US history* any of the 15 Southern states in which slavery was legal until the Civil War

slave trade *n* the business of trading in slaves, esp the transportation of Black Africans to America from the 16th to 19th centuries > 'slave-,trader *n* > 'slave-,trading *n*

slavey ('sleɪvɪ) *n Brit informal* a female general servant [c19 from SLAVE + -Y²]

Slavey ('sleɪvɪ) *n* a member of a Dene Native Canadian people of northern Canada [from Athapascan]

Slavic ('slɑ:vɪk) *n, adj* another word (esp US) for **Slavonic**

slavish ('sleɪvɪʃ) *adj* **1** of or befitting a slave **2** being or resembling a slave; servile **3** unoriginal; imitative **4** *archaic* ignoble > 'slavishly *adv* > 'slavishness *n*

Slavism ('slɑ:vɪzəm) *n* anything characteristic of, peculiar to, or associated with the Slavs or the Slavonic languages

Slavkov ('slafkɔf) *n* the Czech name for **Austerlitz**

slavocracy (slæ'vɒkrəsɪ) *n, pl -cies* (esp in the US before the Civil War) **1** slaveholders as a dominant class **2** domination by slaveholders

Slavonia (slə'vəʊnɪə) *n* a region in Croatia, mainly between the Drava and Sava Rivers

Slavonian (slə'vəʊnɪən) *adj* **1** of or relating to Slavonia, a region in Croatia, or its inhabitants ▷ *n* **2** a native or inhabitant of Slavonia

Slavonic (slə'vɒnɪk) *or esp US* **Slavic** *n* **1** a branch of the Indo-European family of languages, usually divided into three subbranches: **South Slavonic** (including Old Church Slavonic, Serbo-Croat, Bulgarian, etc), **East Slavonic** (including Ukrainian, Russian, etc), and **West Slavonic** (including Polish, Czech, Slovak, etc) **2** the unrecorded ancient language from which all of these languages developed ▷ *adj* **3** of, denoting, or relating to this group of languages **4** of, denoting, or relating to the people who speak these languages [c17 from Medieval Latin *Slavonicus, Sclavonicus,* from SLAVONIA]

Slavophile ('slɑ:vəʊfɪl, -,faɪl) *or* **Slavophil** *n* **1** a person who admires the Slavs or their cultures **2** (*sometimes not capital*) (in 19th-century Russia) a person who believed in the superiority and advocated the supremacy of the Slavs ▷ *adj* **3** admiring the Slavs and Slavonic culture, etc **4** (*sometimes not capital*) (in 19th-century Russia) of, characteristic of, or relating to the Slavophiles > Slavophilism (slə'vɒfɪ,lɪzəm, 'slɑ:vəʊfɪ,lɪzəm) *n*

slaw (slɔ:) *n chiefly US and Canadian* short for **coleslaw** [c19 from Danish *sla,* short for *salade* SALAD]

slay (sleɪ) *vb* **slays, slaying, slew, slain** (*tr*) **1** *archaic or literary* to kill, esp violently **2** *slang* to impress (someone of the opposite sex) **3** *obsolete* to strike [Old English *slēan;* related to Old Norse *slā,* Gothic, Old High German *slahan* to strike, Old Irish *slacaim* I beat] > 'slayer *n*

SLBM *abbreviation for* submarine-launched ballistic missile

SLCM *abbreviation for* sea-launched cruise missile: a type of cruise missile that can be launched from either a submarine or a surface ship

sld *abbreviation for* **1** sailed **2** sealed

SLD *abbreviation for* Social and Liberal Democratic Party (now the Liberal Democrats)

sleave (sli:v) *n* **1** a tangled thread **2** a thin filament unravelled from a thicker thread **3** *chiefly poetic* anything matted or complicated ▷ *vb* **4** to disentangle (twisted thread, etc) [Old English *slǣfan* to divide; related to Middle Low German *slēf,* Norwegian *sleiv* big spoon]

sleaze (sli:z) *n informal* **1** sleaziness **2** dishonest, disreputable, or immoral behaviour, especially of

public officials or employees: *political sleaze*

sleazeball ('sli:z,bɔ:l) *n slang* an odious and contemptible person

sleazy ('sli:zɪ) *adj* **-zier, -ziest** **1** sordid; disreputable: *a sleazy nightclub* **2** thin or flimsy, as cloth [c17 origin uncertain] > 'sleazily *adv* > 'sleaziness *n*

sled dog *n* any of various hardy thick-coated breeds of dog, such as the Eskimo dog, the husky, and the malamute, developed for hauling sledges in various parts of the highest northern latitudes

sledge¹ (slɛdʒ) *or esp US and Canadian* **sled** (slɛd) *n* **1** Also called: **sleigh** a vehicle mounted on runners, drawn by horses or dogs, for transporting people or goods, esp over snow **2** a light wooden frame used, esp by children, for sliding over snow; toboggan **3** *NZ* a farm vehicle mounted on runners, for use on rough or muddy ground ▷ *vb* **4** to convey, travel, or go by sledge [c17 from Middle Dutch *sleedse;* c14 *sled,* from Middle Low German, from Old Norse *slethi,* related to SLIDE] > 'sledger *n*

sledge² (slɛdʒ) *n* short for **sledgehammer**

sledge³ (slɛdʒ) *vb* **1** (*tr*) to bait (an opponent, esp a batsman in cricket) in order to upset his concentration ▷ *n* **2** an insult aimed at another player during a game of cricket [of uncertain origin; perhaps from SLEDGEHAMMER]

sledgehammer ('slɛdʒ,hæmə) *n* **1** a large heavy hammer with a long handle used with both hands for heavy work such as forging iron, breaking rocks, etc **2** (*modifier*) resembling the action of a sledgehammer in power, ruthlessness, etc: *a sledgehammer blow* ▷ *vb* **3** (*tr*) to strike (something) with or as if with a sledgehammer [c15 *sledge,* from Old English *slecg* a large hammer; related to Old Norse *sleggja,* Middle Dutch *slegge*]

sleek (sli:k) *adj* **1** smooth and shiny; polished **2** polished in speech or behaviour; unctuous **3** (of an animal or bird) having a shiny healthy coat or feathers **4** (of a person) having a prosperous appearance ▷ *vb* **5** to make smooth and glossy, as by grooming, etc **6** (usually foll by *over*) to cover (up), as by making more agreeable; gloss (over) [c16 variant of SLICK] > 'sleekly *adv* > 'sleekness *n* > 'sleeky *adj*

sleekit ('sli:kɪt) *adj Scot* **1** smooth; glossy **2** unctuous **3** deceitful; crafty; sly [Scottish, from past participle of SLEEK]

sleep (sli:p) *n* **1** a periodic state of physiological rest during which consciousness is suspended and metabolic rate is decreased. See also **paradoxical sleep** **2** *botany* the nontechnical name for **nyctitropism** **3** a period spent sleeping **4** a state of quiescence or dormancy **5** a poetic or euphemistic word for **death** **6** *informal* the dried mucoid particles often found in the corners of the eyes after sleeping ▷ *vb* **sleeps, sleeping, slept** **7** (*intr*) to be in or as in the state of sleep **8** (*intr*) (of plants) to show nyctitropism **9** (*intr*) to be inactive or quiescent **10** (*tr*) to have sleeping accommodation for (a certain number): *the boat could sleep six* **11** (*tr; foll by away*) to pass (time) sleeping **12** (*intr*) to fail to pay attention **13** (*intr*) *poetic or euphemistic* to be dead **14** sleep on it to give (something) extended consideration, esp overnight ▷ See also **sleep around, sleep in, sleep off, sleep out, sleep through, sleep with** [Old English *slǣpan;* related to Old Frisian *slēpa,* Old Saxon *slāpan,* Old High German *slāfan,* German *schlaff* limp]

sleep apnoea *n* the temporary cessation of breathing during sleep, which in some cases is due to obstruction of the upper airway by enlarged tonsils, uvula, etc, causing the sufferer to snore loudly and fight for breath

sleep around *vb* (*intr, adverb*) *informal* to be sexually promiscuous

sleeper ('sli:pə) *n* **1** a person, animal, or thing that sleeps **2** a railway sleeping car or compartment **3** *Brit* one of the blocks supporting the rails on a railway track. US and Canadian

equivalent: **tie 4** a heavy timber beam, esp one that is laid horizontally on the ground **5** *chiefly Brit* a small plain gold circle worn in a pierced ear lobe to prevent the hole from closing up **6** a wrestling hold in which a wrestler presses the sides of his opponent's neck, causing him to pass out **7** *US* an unbranded calf **8** Also called: **sleeper goby** any gobioid fish of the family *Eleotridae,* of brackish or fresh tropical waters, resembling the gobies but lacking a ventral sucker **9** *informal* a person or thing that achieves unexpected success after an initial period of obscurity **10** a spy planted in advance for future use, but not currently active

sleeper terrorist *n* a terrorist who is not currently active but assumes a guise in order to be in position, unsuspected, for future terrorist activities

sleep hygiene *n* the habits conducive to getting the right amount and quality of sleep

sleep in *vb* (*intr, adverb*) **1** *Brit* to sleep longer than usual **2** to sleep at the place of one's employment

sleeping bag *n* a large well-padded bag designed for sleeping in, esp outdoors

sleeping car *n* a railway car fitted with compartments containing bunks for people to sleep in

sleeping draught *n* any drink containing a drug or agent that induces sleep

sleeping partner *n* a partner in a business who does not play an active role, esp one who supplies capital

sleeping pill *n* a pill or tablet containing a sedative drug, such as a barbiturate, used to induce sleep

sleeping policeman *n* a bump built across roads, esp in housing estates, to deter motorists from speeding

sleeping sickness *n* **1** Also called: African sleeping sickness an African disease caused by infection with protozoans of the genus *Trypanosoma,* characterized by fever, wasting, and sluggishness **2** Also called (esp formerly): sleepy sickness an epidemic viral form of encephalitis characterized by extreme drowsiness. Technical name: encephalitis lethargica

sleepless ('sli:plɪs) *adj* **1** without sleep or rest: *a sleepless journey* **2** unable to sleep **3** always watchful or alert **4** *chiefly poetic* always active or moving: *the sleepless tides* > 'sleeplessly *adv* > 'sleeplessness *n*

sleep movement *n* the folding together of leaflets, petals, etc, that occurs at night in certain plants, such as the prayer plant (*Maranta leuconura*)

sleep off *vb* (*tr, adverb*) *informal* to lose by sleeping: *to sleep off a hangover*

sleep out *vb* (*intr, adverb*) **1** (esp of a tramp) to sleep in the open air **2** to sleep away from the place of work ▷ *n* **sleep-out 3** *Austral and NZ* an area of a veranda that has been glassed in or partitioned off so that it may be used as a bedroom

sleepover ('sli:p,əʊvə) *n informal, chiefly US* an instance of spending the night at someone else's home

sleep through *vb* (*intr, adverb*) *informal* (of a baby) to sleep all night without waking up

sleepwalk ('sli:p,wɔ:k) *vb* (*intr*) to walk while asleep. See also **somnambulism**. > 'sleep,walker *n* > 'sleep,walking *n, adj*

sleep with *vb* (*intr, preposition*) to have sexual intercourse and (usually) spend the night with. Also: sleep together

sleepy ('sli:pɪ) *adj* **sleepier, sleepiest** **1** inclined to or needing sleep; drowsy **2** characterized by or exhibiting drowsiness, sluggishness, etc **3** conducive to sleep; soporific **4** without activity or bustle: *a sleepy town* > 'sleepily *adv* > 'sleepiness *n*

sleepyhead ('sli:pɪ,hɛd) *n informal* a sleepy or lazy person > 'sleepy,headed *adj*

sleet (sli:t) *n* **1** partly melted falling snow or hail or (esp US) partly frozen rain **2** *chiefly US* the thin

S

coat of ice that forms when sleet or rain freezes on cold surfaces ▷ *vb* **3** (*intr*) to fall as sleet [C13 from Germanic; compare Middle Low German *slōten* hail, Middle High German *slōze*, German *Schlossen* hailstones] > ˈ**sleety** *adj*

sleeve (sliːv) *n* **1** the part of a garment covering the arm **2** a tubular piece that is forced or shrunk into a cylindrical bore to reduce the diameter of the bore or to line it with a different material; liner **3** a tube fitted externally over two cylindrical parts in order to join them; bush **4** a flat cardboard or plastic container to protect a gramophone record. US name: **jacket 5 (have a few tricks) up one's sleeve** (to have options, etc) secretly ready **6 roll up one's sleeves** to prepare oneself for work, a fight, etc ▷ *vb* **7** (*tr*) to provide with a sleeve or sleeves [Old English *slīf, slēf*; related to Dutch *sloof* apron] > ˈ**sleeveless** *adj* > ˈ**sleeve,like** *adj*

sleeve board *n* a small ironing board for pressing sleeves, fitted onto an ironing board or table

sleeveen (ˈsliːviːn) *n Irish* a sly obsequious smooth-tongued person [from Irish Gaelic *slíbhín*]

sleeve notes *pl n* the printed information on a record sleeve. US equivalent: **liner notes**

sleeve valve *n* (in an internal-combustion engine) a valve in the form of a thin steel sleeve fitted between the cylinder and piston and having a reciprocating and rotary oscillation movement

sleeving (ˈsliːvɪŋ) *n electronics, chiefly Brit* tubular flexible insulation into which bare wire can be inserted. US and Canadian name: **spaghetti**

sleigh (sleɪ) *n* **1** another name for **sledge**[1] (sense 1) ▷ *vb* **2** (*intr*) to travel by sleigh [C18 from Dutch *slee*, variant of *slede* SLEDGE[1]] > ˈ**sleigher** *n*

sleight (slaɪt) *n archaic* **1** skill; dexterity. See also **sleight of hand 2** a trick or stratagem **3** cunning; trickery [C14 from Old Norse *slægth*, from *slægr* SLY]

sleight of hand *n* **1** manual dexterity used in performing conjuring tricks **2** the performance of such tricks

slender (ˈslɛndə) *adj* **1** of small width relative to length or height **2** (esp of a person's figure) slim and well-formed **3** small or inadequate in amount, size, etc: *slender resources* **4** (of hopes, etc) having little foundation; feeble **5** very small: *a slender margin* **6** (of a sound) lacking volume **7** *phonetics* (now only in Irish phonology) relating to or denoting a close front vowel, such as *i* or *e* [C14 *slendre*, of unknown origin] > ˈ**slenderly** *adv* > ˈ**slenderness** *n*

slenderize *or* **slenderise** (ˈslɛndəˌraɪz) *vb chiefly US and Canadian* to make or become slender

slept (slɛpt) *vb* the past tense and past participle of **sleep**

Slesvig (ˈsleːsvi) *n* the Danish name for **Schleswig**

sleuth (sluːθ) *n* **1** an informal word for **detective 2** short for **sleuthhound** (sense 1) ▷ *vb* **3** (*tr*) to track or follow [C19 short for *sleuthhound*, from C12 *sleuth* trail, from Old Norse *sloth*; see SLOT[2]]

sleuthhound (ˈsluːθˌhaʊnd) *n* **1** a dog trained to track people, esp a bloodhound **2** an informal word for **detective**

S level *n Brit* a public examination in a subject taken for the General Certificate of Education: usually taken at the same time as A2 levels as an additional qualification

slew[1] (sluː) *vb* the past tense of **slay**

slew[2] *or esp US* **slue** (sluː) *vb* **1** to twist or be twisted sideways, esp awkwardly: *he slewed around in his chair* **2** *nautical* to cause (a mast) to rotate in its step or (of a mast) to rotate in its step ▷ *n* **3** the act of slewing [C18 of unknown origin]

slew[3] (sluː) *n* a variant spelling (esp US) of **slough**[1] (sense 2)

slew[4] *or* **slue** (sluː) *n informal, chiefly US and Canadian* a great number or amount; a lot [C20 from Irish Gaelic *sluagh*; related to Old Irish *slōg* army]

slewed (sluːd) *adj* (*postpositive*) *Brit slang* intoxicated; drunk [C19 from SLEW[2]]

slew rate *n electronics* the rate at which an electronic amplifier can respond to an abrupt change of input level

Slezsko (ˈslɛskɔ) *n* the Czech name for **Silesia**

slice (slaɪs) *n* **1** a thin flat piece cut from something having bulk: *a slice of pork* **2** a share or portion: *a slice of the company's revenue* **3** any of various utensils having a broad flat blade and resembling a spatula **4** (in golf, tennis, etc) **a** the flight of a ball that travels obliquely because it has been struck off centre **b** the action of hitting such a shot **c** the shot so hit ▷ *vb* **5** to divide or cut (something) into parts or slices **6** (when *intr*, usually foll by *through*) to cut in a clean and effortless manner **7** (when *intr*, foll by *through*) to move or go (through something) like a knife: *the ship sliced through the water* **8** (usually foll by *off, from, away*, etc) to cut or be cut (from) a larger piece **9** (*tr*) to remove by use of a slicing implement **10** to hit (a ball) with a slice **11** (*tr*) *rowing* to put the blade of the oar into (the water) slantwise [C14 from Old French *esclice* a piece split off, from *esclicier* to splinter] > ˈ**sliceable** *adj* > ˈ**slicer** *n*

slice bar *n* an iron bar used for raking out furnaces

slicer (ˈslaɪsə) *n* **1** a machine that slices bread, etc, usually with an electrically driven band knife or circular knife **2** *Electronics* a limiter having two boundary values, the portion of the signal between these values being passed on

slick (slɪk) *adj* **1** flattering and glib: *a slick salesman* **2** adroitly devised or executed: *a slick show* **3** *informal, chiefly US and Canadian* shrewd; sly **4** *informal* superficially attractive: *a slick publication* **5** *chiefly US and Canadian* smooth and glossy; slippery ▷ *n* **6** a slippery area, esp a patch of oil floating on water **7** a chisel or other tool used for smoothing or polishing a surface **8** the tyre of a racing car that has worn treads ▷ *vb* (*tr*) **9** *chiefly US and Canadian* to make smooth or sleek **10** *US and Canadian informal* (usually foll by *up*) to smarten or tidy (oneself) **11** (often foll by *up*) to make smooth or glossy [C14 probably of Scandinavian origin; compare Icelandic, Norwegian *slikja* to be or make smooth] > ˈ**slickly** *adv* > ˈ**slickness** *n*

slickenside (ˈslɪkənˌsaɪd) *n* a rock surface with a polished appearance and fine parallel scratches caused by abrasion during fault displacement [C18 from dialect *slicken*, variant of SLICK + SIDE]

slicker (ˈslɪkə) *n* **1** *informal* a sly or untrustworthy person (esp in the phrase **city slicker**) **2** *US and Canadian* a shiny raincoat, esp an oilskin **3** a small trowel used for smoothing the surfaces of a mould > ˈ**slickered** *adj*

slide (slaɪd) *vb* **slides, sliding, slid** (slɪd); **slid** *or* **slidden** (ˈslɪdᵊn) **1** to move or cause to move smoothly along a surface in continual contact with it: *doors that slide open; children sliding on the ice* **2** (*intr*) to lose grip or balance: *he slid on his back* **3** (*intr*; usually foll by *into, out of, away from*, etc) to pass or move gradually and unobtrusively: *she slid into the room* **4** (*intr*; usually foll by *into*) to go (into a specified condition) by degrees, unnoticeably, etc: *he slid into loose living* **5** (foll by *in, into*, etc) to move (an object) unobtrusively or (of an object) to move in this way: *he slid the gun into his pocket* **6** (*intr*) *music* to execute a portamento **7 let slide** to allow to follow a natural course, esp one leading to deterioration: *to let things slide* ▷ *n* **8** the act or an instance of sliding **9** a smooth surface, as of ice or mud, for sliding on **10** a construction incorporating an inclined smooth slope for sliding down in playgrounds, etc **11** *rowing* a sliding seat in a boat or its runners **12** a thin glass plate on which specimens are mounted for microscopic study **13** Also called: **transparency** a positive photograph on a transparent base, mounted in a cardboard or plastic frame or between glass plates, that can be viewed by means of a slide projector **14** Also called: **hair slide** *chiefly Brit* an ornamental clip to hold hair in place. US and Canadian name: **barrette 15** *machinery* **a** a sliding part or member **b** the track, guide, or channel on or in which such a part slides **16** *music* **a** the sliding curved tube of a trombone that is moved in or out to allow the production of different harmonic series and a wider range of notes **b** a portamento **17** *music* **a** a metal or glass tube placed over a finger held against the frets of a guitar to produce a portamento **b** the style of guitar playing using a slide. See also **bottleneck** (sense 3) **18** *geology* **a** the rapid downward movement of a large mass of earth, rocks, etc, caused by erosion, faulting, etc **b** the mass of material involved in this descent. See also **landslide** [Old English *slīdan*; related to *slidor* slippery, *sliderian* to SLITHER, Middle High German *slīten*] > ˈ**slidable** *adj* > ˈ**slider** *n*

slide-action *adj* (of a shoulder firearm) ejecting the empty case and reloading by means of a sliding lever

slide fastener *n chiefly US and Canadian* another name for **zip** (sense 1)

slide guitar *n* a technique of guitar playing derived from bottleneck, using a steel or glass tube on one finger across the frets

slide over *vb* (*intr, preposition*) **1** to cross by or as if by sliding **2** to avoid dealing with (a matter) fully

slide rest *n engineering* a stack of platforms that sits on a lathe saddle and carries a tool post, and is adjustable in rotation and at right angles by a lathe operator

slide rule *n obsolete* a mechanical calculating device consisting of two strips, one sliding along a central groove in the other, each strip graduated in two or more logarithmic scales of numbers, trigonometric functions, etc. It employs the same principles as logarithm tables

slide trombone *n* See **trombone**

slide valve *n* **1** a valve that slides across an aperture to expose the port or opening **2** (*modifier*) fitted with slide valves: *a slide-valve engine*

sliding (ˈslaɪdɪŋ) *adj* **1** rising or falling in accordance with given specifications: *fees were charged as a sliding percentage of income* **2** regulated or moved by sliding

sliding fit *n engineering* a fit that enables one part to be inserted into another by sliding or pushing, rather than by hammering. Also called: **push fit**

sliding friction *n engineering* frictional resistance to relative movement of surfaces on loaded contact. Compare **rolling friction**

sliding scale *n* a variable scale according to which specified wages, tariffs, prices, etc, fluctuate in response to changes in some other factor, standard, or conditions

sliding seat *n rowing* a seat that slides forwards and backwards with the oarsman, lengthening his stroke

slier (ˈslaɪə) *adj* a comparative of **sly**

sliest (ˈslaɪɪst) *adj* a superlative of **sly**

Slieve Donard (sliːv ˈdɒnɑːd) *n* a mountain in SE Northern Ireland, in the Mourne Mountains: highest peak in Northern Ireland. Height: 853 m (2798 ft)

slight (slaɪt) *adj* **1** small in quantity or extent **2** of small importance; trifling **3** slim and delicate **4** lacking in strength or substance **5** *Southwest English dialect* ill ▷ *vb* (*tr*) **6** to show indifference or disregard for (someone); snub **7** to treat as unimportant or trifling **8** *US* to devote inadequate attention to (work, duties, etc) ▷ *n* **9** an act or omission indicating supercilious neglect or indifference [C13 from Old Norse *slēttr* smooth; related to Old High German *slehtr*, Gothic *slaihts*, Middle Dutch *slecht* simple] > ˈ**slightness** *n*

slighting (ˈslaɪtɪŋ) *adj* characteristic of a slight; disparaging; disdainful: *in a slighting manner* > ˈ**slightingly** *adv*

slightly (ˈslaɪtlɪ) *adv* in small measure or degree

Sligo (ˈslaɪgəʊ) *n* **1** a county of NW Republic of Ireland, on the Atlantic: has a deeply indented low-lying coast; livestock and dairy farming. County town: Sligo. Pop: 58 200 (2002). Area: 1795 sq km (693 sq miles) **2** a port in NW Republic of

Ireland, county town of Co Sligo on **Sligo Bay**. Pop: 19 735 (2002)

slily ('slaɪlɪ) *adv* a variant spelling of **slyly**

slim (slɪm) *adj* **slimmer, slimmest 1** small in width relative to height or length **2** small in amount or quality: *slim chances of success* ▷ *vb* **slims, slimming, slimmed 3** to make or become slim, esp by diets and exercise **4** to reduce or decrease or cause to be reduced or decreased ▷ See also **slim down** [C17 from Dutch: crafty, from Middle Dutch *slimp* slanting; compare Old High German *slimbi* obliquity] > '**slimly** *adv* > '**slimmer** *n* > '**slimness** *n*

Slim (slɪm) *n* the E African name for **AIDS** [from its wasting effects]

slim down *vb* (*adverb*) **1** to make or become slim, esp intentionally **2** to make (an organization) more efficient or (of an organization) to become more efficient, esp by cutting staff ▷ *n* **slimdown 3** an instance of an organization slimming down

slime (slaɪm) *n* **1** soft thin runny mud or filth **2** any moist viscous fluid, esp when noxious or unpleasant **3** a mucous substance produced by various organisms, such as fish, slugs, and fungi ▷ *vb* (*tr*) **4** to cover with slime **5** to remove slime from (fish) before canning [Old English *slīm*; related to Old Norse *slīm*, Old High German *slīmen* to smooth, Russian *slimák* snail, Latin *līmax* snail]

slimeball ('slaɪm,bɔːl) *n slang* an odious and contemptible person

slime mould *n* any of various simple spore-producing organisms typically found as slimy masses on rotting vegetation, where they engulf food particles by amoeboid movements. Formerly regarded as fungi, they are now classified as protoctists of the phyla *Myxomycota* (true, or cellular slime moulds) or *Acrasiomycota* (plasmodial slime moulds)

slimline ('slɪm,laɪn) *adj* slim; giving the appearance of or conducive to slimness

slimming ('slɪmɪŋ) *n* **a** the process of or concern with becoming slim or slimmer as by losing weight **b** (*as modifier*): *slimming aids*

slimsy ('slɪmzɪ) *adj* **-sier, -siest** *US informal* frail [C19 from SLIM + FLIMSY]

slimy ('slaɪmɪ) *adj* **slimier, slimiest 1** characterized by, covered with, containing, secreting, or resembling slime **2** offensive or repulsive **3** *chiefly Brit* characterized by servility > '**slimily** *adv* > '**sliminess** *n*

sling¹ (slɪŋ) *n* **1** a simple weapon consisting of a loop of leather, etc, in which a stone is whirled and then let fly **2** a rope or strap by which something may be secured or lifted **3** a rope net swung from a crane, used for loading and unloading cargo **4** *nautical* **a** a halyard for a yard **b** (*often plural*) the part of a yard where the sling is attached **5** *med* a wide piece of cloth suspended from the neck for supporting an injured hand or arm across the front of the body **6** a loop or band attached to an object for carrying **7** *mountaineering* a loop of rope or tape used for support in belays, abseils, etc **8** the act of slinging ▷ *vb* **slings, slinging, slung 9** (*tr*) to hurl with or as if with a sling **10** to attach a sling or slings to (a load, etc) **11** (*tr*) to carry or hang loosely from or as if from a sling: *to sling washing from the line* **12** *informal* to throw **13** (*intr*) *Austral informal* to pay a part of one's wages or profits as a bribe or tip [C13 perhaps of Scandinavian origin; compare Old Norse *slyngva* to hurl, Old High German *slingan*] > '**slinger** *n*

sling² (slɪŋ) *n* a mixed drink with a spirit base, usually sweetened [C19 of uncertain origin]

slingback ('slɪŋ,bæk) *n* **a** a shoe with a strap instead of a full covering for the heel **b** (*as modifier*): *slingback shoes*

slinger ring *n* a tubular ring around the hub of an aircraft propeller through which antifreeze solution is spread over the propeller blades by centrifugal force

sling off *vb* (*intr, adverb*; often foll by *at*) *Austral and NZ informal* to laugh or jeer (at)

slingshot ('slɪŋʃɒt) *n* **1** *US and Canadian* a Y-shaped implement with a loop of elastic fastened to the ends of the two prongs, used mainly by children for shooting small stones, etc. Also called (in Britain and certain other countries): **catapult 2** another name for **sling¹** (sense 1)

slink (slɪŋk) *vb* **slinks, slinking, slunk 1** (*intr*) to move or act in a furtive or cringing manner from or as if from fear, guilt, etc **2** (*intr*) to move in a sinuous alluring manner **3** (*tr*) (of animals, esp cows) to give birth to prematurely ▷ *n* **4 a** an animal, esp a calf, born prematurely **b** (*as modifier*): *slink veal* [Old English *slincan*; related to Middle Low German *slinken* to shrink, Old Swedish *slinka* to creep, Danish *slunken* limp]

slinky ('slɪŋkɪ) *adj* **slinkier, slinkiest** *informal* **1** moving in a sinuously graceful or provocative way **2** (of clothes) figure-hugging; clinging **3** characterized by furtive movements > '**slinkily** *adv* > '**slinkiness** *n*

slinter ('slɪntə) *n Austral and NZ informal* a dodge, trick, or stratagem. Also (Austral obsolete): **slanter, slenter** [from Dutch *slenter*, perhaps via S African *schlenter*]

sliotar ('ʃlɪtər) *n* the ball used in hurling [Irish Gaelic]

slip¹ (slɪp) *vb* **slips, slipping, slipped 1** to move or cause to move smoothly and easily **2** (*tr*) to place, insert, or convey quickly or stealthily **3** (*tr*) to put on or take off easily or quickly: *to slip on a sweater* **4** (*intr*) to lose balance and slide unexpectedly: *he slipped on the ice* **5** to let loose or be let loose **6** to be released from (something); escape **7** (*tr*) to let go (mooring or anchor lines) over the side **8** (when *intr*, often foll by *from* or *out of*) to pass out of (the mind or memory) **9** (*tr*) to overlook, neglect, or miss: *to slip an opportunity* **10** (*intr*) to move or pass swiftly or unperceived: *to slip quietly out of the room* **11** (*intr*; sometimes foll by *up*) to make a mistake **12** Also: **sideslip** to cause (an aircraft) to slide sideways or (of an aircraft) to slide sideways **13** (*intr*) to decline in health, mental ability, etc **14** (*intr*) (of an intervertebral disc) to become displaced from the normal position **15** (*tr*) to dislocate (a bone) **16** (of animals) to give birth to (offspring) prematurely **17** (*tr*) to pass (a stitch) from one needle to another without knitting it **18 a** (*tr*) to operate (the clutch of a motor vehicle) so that it partially disengages **b** (*intr*) (of the clutch of a motor vehicle) to fail to engage, esp as a result of wear **19 let slip a** to allow to escape **b** to say unintentionally **20 slip one over on** *slang* to hoodwink or trick ▷ *n* **21** the act or an instance of slipping **22** a mistake or oversight: *a slip of the pen* **23** a moral lapse or failing **24** a woman's sleeveless undergarment, worn as a lining for and to give support to a dress **25** *US and Canadian* a narrow space between two piers in which vessels may dock **26** See **slipway 27** a kind of dog lead that allows for the quick release of the dog **28** a small block of hard steel of known thickness used for measurement, usually forming one of a set **29** the ratio between output speed and input speed of a transmission device when subtracted from unity, esp of a drive belt or clutch that is not transmitting full power **30** *cricket* **a** the position of the fielder who stands a little way behind and to the offside of the wicketkeeper **b** the fielder himself **31** the relative movement of rocks along a fault plane **32** a landslide, esp one blocking a road or railway line **33** *metallurgy, crystallog* the deformation of a metallic crystal caused when one part glides over another part along a plane **34** the deviation of a propeller from its helical path through a fluid, expressed as the difference between its actual forward motion and its theoretical forward motion in one revolution **35** another name for **sideslip** (sense 1) **36 give someone the slip** to elude or escape from someone ▷ See also **slip up** [C13 from Middle Low German or Dutch *slippen*] > '**slipless** *adj*

slip² (slɪp) *n* **1** a narrow piece; strip **2** a small piece of paper: *a receipt slip* **3** a part of a plant that, when detached from the parent, will grow into a new plant; cutting; scion **4** a young slender person: *a slip of a child* **5** *dialect* a young pig **6** *printing* **a** a long galley **b** a less common name for a **galley proof 7** *chiefly US* a pew or similar long narrow seat **8** a small piece of abrasive material of tapering section used in honing ▷ *vb* **slips, slipping, slipped 9** (*tr*) to detach (portions of stem, etc) from (a plant) for propagation [C15 probably from Middle Low German, Middle Dutch *slippe* to cut, strip]

slip³ (slɪp) *n* clay mixed with water to a creamy consistency, used for decorating or patching a ceramic piece [Old English *slyppe* slime; related to Norwegian *slipa* slime on fish; see SLOP¹]

slipcase ('slɪp,keɪs) *n* a protective case for a book or set of books that is open at one end so that only the spines of the books are visible

slipcover ('slɪp,kʌvə) *n* **1** *US and Canadian* a fitted but easily removable cloth cover for a chair, sofa, etc. Also called (in Britain and certain other countries): **loose cover 2** *US and Canadian* a book jacket; dust cover

slipe (slaɪp) *n NZ* **a** wool removed from the pelt of a slaughtered sheep by immersion in a chemical bath **b** (*as modifier*): *slipe wool* [from English dialect]

slip flow *n physics* gas flow occurring at hypersonic speeds in which molecular shearing occurs

slip gauge *n* a very accurately ground block of hardened steel used to measure a gap with close accuracy: used mainly in tool-making and inspection

slipknot ('slɪp,nɒt) *n* **1** Also called: **running knot** a nooselike knot tied so that it will slip along the rope round which it is made **2** a knot that can be easily untied by pulling one free end

slipnoose ('slɪp,nuːs) *n* a noose made with a slipknot, so that it tightens when pulled

slip-on *adj* **1** (of a garment or shoe) made so as to be easily and quickly put on or off ▷ *n* **2** a slip-on garment or shoe

slipover ('slɪp,əʊvə) *adj* **1** of or denoting a garment that can be put on easily over the head ▷ *n* **2** such a garment, esp a sleeveless pullover

slippage ('slɪpɪdʒ) *n* **1** the act or an instance of slipping **2** the amount of slipping or the extent to which slipping occurs **3 a** an instance of not reaching a norm, target, etc **b** the extent of this **4** the power lost in a mechanical device or system as a result of slipping

slipped disc *n pathol* a herniated intervertebral disc, often resulting in pain because of pressure on the spinal nerves

slipper ('slɪpə) *n* **1** a light shoe of some soft material, for wearing around the house **2** a woman's evening or dancing shoe ▷ *vb* **3** (*tr*) *informal* to hit or beat with a slipper > '**slippered** *adj* > '**slipper-,like** *adj*

slipper bath *n* **1** a bath in the shape of a slipper, with a covered end **2** *history* (*plural*) an establishment where members of the public paid to have a bath

slipper satin *n* a fine satin fabric with a mat finish

slipperwort ('slɪpə,wɜːt) *n* another name for **calceolaria** [C19 so called because of the slipper-like shape of the flower]

slippery ('slɪpərɪ, -prɪ) *adj* **1** causing or tending to cause objects to slip: *a slippery road* **2** liable to slip from the grasp, a position, etc **3** not to be relied upon; cunning and untrustworthy: *a slippery character* **4** (esp of a situation) liable to change; unstable **5 slippery slope** a course of action that will lead to disaster or failure [C16 probably coined by Coverdale to translate German *schlipfferig* in Luther's Bible (Psalm 35:6); related to Old English *slipor* slippery] > '**slipperily** *adv* > '**slipperiness** *n*

slippery dip *n Austral informal* a long slide at a playground or funfair

S

slippery elm *n* **1** a tree, *Ulmus fulva*, of E North America, having oblong serrated leaves, notched winged fruits, and a mucilaginous inner bark **2** the bark of this tree, used medicinally as a demulcent ▷ Also called: **red elm**

slippy ('slɪpɪ) *adj* **-pier, -piest 1** *informal or dialect* another word for **slippery** (senses 1, 2) **2** *Brit informal* alert; quick > 'slippiness *n*

slip rail *n Austral and NZ* a rail in a fence that can be slipped out of place to make an opening

slip ring *n electrical engineering* a metal ring, mounted on but insulated from a rotating shaft of a motor or generator, by means of which current can be led through stationary brushes into or out of a winding on the shaft

slip road *n Brit* a short road connecting a motorway, etc, to another road

slipsheet ('slɪp,ʃi:t) *n* **1** a sheet of paper that is interleaved between freshly printed sheets to prevent set-off ▷ *vb* **2** to interleave (printed sheets) with slipsheets

slipshod ('slɪp,ʃɒd) *adj* **1** (of an action) negligent; careless **2** (of a person's appearance) slovenly; down-at-heel [C16 from SLIP¹ + SHOD] > 'slip,shoddiness *or* 'slip,shodness *n*

slipslop ('slɪp,slɒp) *n* **1** *archaic* weak or unappetizing food or drink **2** *informal* maudlin or trivial talk or writing

slip-slop *n S African* a rubber-soled sandal attached to the foot by a thong between the big toe and the next toe

slip step *n* a dance step made by moving the left foot one step sideways and closing the right foot to the left foot: used when dancing in a circle during Scottish reels and jigs

slip stitch *n* **1** a sewing stitch for securing hems, etc, in which only two or three threads of the material are caught up by the needle each time, so that the stitches are nearly invisible from the right side ▷ *vb* **2** (*tr*) to join (two edges) using slip stitches [C19 from SLIP¹]

slipstream ('slɪp,stri:m) *n* **1** Also called: **airstream, race a** the stream of air forced backwards by an aircraft propeller **b** a stream of air behind any moving object ▷ *vb* **2** *motor racing* to follow (another car, etc) closely in order to take advantage of the decreased wind resistance immediately behind it

slip up *vb* (*intr, adverb*) **1** *informal* to make a blunder or mistake; err **2** to fall over ▷ *n* **slip-up 3** *informal* a mistake, blunder, or mishap

slipware ('slɪp,wɛə) *n* pottery that has been decorated with slip

slipway ('slɪp,weɪ) *n* **1** the sloping area in a shipyard, containing the ways **2** Also called: **marine railway** the ways on which a vessel is launched **3** the ramp of a whaling factory ship **4** a pillowcase; pillowslip

slit (slɪt) *vb* **slits, slitting, slit** (*tr*) **1** to make a straight long incision in; split open **2** to cut into strips lengthwise **3** to sever ▷ *n* **4** a long narrow cut **5** a long narrow opening [Old English *slītan* to slice; related to Old Norse *slita*, Old High German *slīzen*] > 'slitter *n*

slither ('slɪðə) *vb* **1** to move or slide or cause to move or slide unsteadily, as on a slippery surface **2** (*intr*) to travel with a sliding motion ▷ *n* **3** a slithering motion [Old English *slidrian*, from *slīdan* to SLIDE]

slithery ('slɪðərɪ) *adj* **-ier, -iest 1** moving with a slithering motion **2** suggestive of a slithering creature

slit pocket *n* a pocket on the underside of a garment, reached through a vertical opening

slit trench *n military* a narrow trench dug for the protection of a small number of people

sliver ('slɪvə) *n* **1** a thin piece that is cut or broken off lengthwise; splinter **2** a loose strand or fibre obtained by carding ▷ *vb* **3** to divide or be divided into splinters; split **4** (*tr*) to form (wool, etc) into slivers [C14 from *sliven* to split] > 'sliver-,like *adj*

slivovitz ('slɪvəvɪts, 'sli:və-) *n* a plum brandy from E Europe [from Serbo-Croat *šljivovica*, from *sljiva* plum]

SLO *international car registration for* Slovenia

Sloane Ranger (sləʊn) *n* (in Britain) *informal* a young upper-class or upper-middle-class person, esp a woman, having a home in London and in the country, characterized typically as wearing expensive informal country clothes. Also called: **Sloane** [C20 coined by Peter York, punning on *Sloane* Square, London SW1, and *Lone Ranger*, television cowboy character]

slob (slɒb) *n* **1** *informal* a slovenly, unattractive, and lazy person **2** *Irish* mire [C19 from Irish *slab* mud; compare SLAB] > 'slobbish *adj*

slobber ('slɒbə) *or* **slabber** *vb* **1** to dribble (saliva, food, etc) from the mouth **2** (*intr*) to speak or write mawkishly **3** (*tr*) to smear with matter dribbling from the mouth ▷ *n* **4** liquid or saliva spilt from the mouth **5** maudlin language or behaviour [C15 from Middle Low German, Middle Dutch *slubberen*; see SLAVER²] > 'slobberer *or* 'slabberer *n* > 'slobbery *or* 'slabbery *adj*

slob ice *n Canadian* sludgy masses of floating ice [see SLOB]

sloe (sləʊ) *n* **1** the small sour blue-black fruit of the blackthorn **2** another name for **blackthorn** [Old English *slāh*; related to Old High German *slēha*, Middle Dutch *sleuuwe*]

sloe-eyed *adj* having dark slanted or almond-shaped eyes

sloe gin *n* gin flavoured with sloe juice

slog (slɒg) *vb* **slogs, slogging, slogged 1** to hit with heavy blows, as in boxing **2** (*intr*) to work hard; toil **3** (*intr*; foll by *down, up, along,* etc) to move with difficulty; plod **4** *cricket* to score freely by taking large swipes at the ball ▷ *n* **5** a tiring hike or walk **6** long exhausting work **7** a heavy blow or swipe [C19 of unknown origin] > 'slogger *n*

slogan ('sləʊgən) *n* **1** a distinctive or topical phrase used in politics, advertising, etc **2** *Scot history* a Highland battle cry [C16 from Gaelic *sluagh-ghairm* war cry, from *sluagh* army + *gairm* cry]

sloganeer (,sləʊgə'nɪə) *n* **1** a person who coins or employs slogans frequently ▷ *vb* **2** (*intr*) to coin or employ slogans so as to sway opinion

slommock ('slɒmək) *vb* (*intr*) *Midland English dialect* to walk assertively with a hip-rolling gait

slo-mo ('sləʊ,məʊ) *n, adj informal* a variant spelling of **slow-mo**, see **slow motion**

sloop (slu:p) *n* a single-masted sailing vessel, rigged fore-and-aft, with the mast stepped about one third of the overall length aft of the bow. Compare **cutter** (sense 2) [C17 from Dutch *sloep*; related to French *chaloupe* launch, Old English *slūpan* to glide]

sloop of war *n* (formerly) a small fast sailing warship mounting some 10 to 30 small calibre guns on one deck

sloop-rigged *adj nautical* rigged as a sloop, typically with a jib and a mainsail

sloot (slu:t) *n South African* a ditch for irrigation or drainage [from Afrikaans, from Dutch *sluit, sluis* SLUICE]

slop¹ (slɒp) *vb* **slops, slopping, slopped 1** (when *intr*, often foll by *about*) to cause (liquid) to splash or spill or (of liquid) to splash or spill **2** (*tr*) to splash liquid upon **3** (*intr*; foll by *along, through,* etc) to tramp (through) mud or slush **4** (*tr*) to feed slop or swill to: *to slop the pigs* **5** (*tr*) to ladle or serve, esp clumsily **6** (*intr*; foll by *over*) *informal, chiefly US and Canadian* to be unpleasantly effusive ▷ *n* **7** a puddle of spilt liquid **8** (*plural*) wet feed, esp for pigs, made from kitchen waste, etc **9** (*plural*) waste food or liquid refuse **10** (*plural*) the beer, cider, etc, spilt from a barrel while being drawn **11** (*often plural*) the residue left after spirits have been distilled **12** (*often plural*) *informal* liquid or semiliquid food of low quality **13** soft mud, snow, etc **14** *informal* gushing speech or writing [C14 probably from Old English *-sloppe* in *cūsloppe* COWSLIP; see SLIP³]

slop² (slɒp) *n* **1** (*plural*) sailors' clothing and bedding issued from a ship's stores **2** any loose article of clothing, esp a smock **3** (*plural*) men's wide knee breeches worn in the 16th century **4** (*plural*) shoddy manufactured clothing [Old English *oferslop* surplice; related to Old Norse *slopps* gown, Middle Dutch *slop*]

slop around *vb* (*intr*) to move around in a casual and idle way: *he slops around the house in old slippers.* Also: **slop about**

slop basin *n* a bowl or basin into which the dregs from teacups are emptied at the table

slop chest *n* a stock of merchandise, such as clothing, tobacco, etc, maintained aboard merchant ships for sale to the crew. Compare **small stores**

slope (sləʊp) *vb* **1** to lie or cause to lie at a slanting or oblique angle **2** (*intr*) (esp of natural features) to follow an inclined course: *many paths sloped down the hillside* **3** (*intr*; foll by *off, away,* etc) to go furtively **4** (*tr*) *military* (formerly) to hold (a rifle) in the slope position (esp in the command **slope arms**) ▷ *n* **5** an inclined portion of ground **6** (*plural*) hills or foothills **7** any inclined surface or line **8** the degree or amount of such inclination **9** *maths* **a** (of a line) the tangent of the angle between the line and another line parallel to the x-axis **b** the first derivative of the equation of a curve at a given point **10** (formerly) the position adopted for British military drill when the rifle is rested on the shoulder **11** *US slang derogatory* a person from Southeast Asia, especially a Vietnamese [C15 short for *aslope*, perhaps from the past participle of Old English *āslūpan* to slip away, from *slūpan* to slip] > 'sloper *n* > 'sloping *adj* > 'slopingly *adv* > 'slopingness *n*

slop out *vb* (*intr, adverb*) (of prisoners) to empty chamber pots and collect water for washing

sloppy ('slɒpɪ) *adj* **-pier, -piest 1** (esp of ground conditions, etc) wet; slushy **2** *informal* careless; untidy **3** *informal* mawkishly sentimental **4** (of food or drink) watery and unappetizing **5** splashed with slops **6** (of clothes) loose; baggy > 'sloppily *adv* > 'sloppiness *n*

sloppy joe (dʒəʊ) *n informal* a long baggy thin sweater

slopwork ('slɒp,wɜːk) *n* **1** the manufacture of cheap shoddy clothing or the clothes so produced **2** any work of low quality > 'slop,worker *n*

slorm (slɔːm) *vb Midland English dialect* to wipe carelessly

slosh (slɒʃ) *n* **1** watery mud, snow, etc **2** *Brit slang* a heavy blow **3** the sound of splashing liquid **4** a popular dance with a traditional routine of steps, kicks, and turns performed in lines ▷ *vb* **5** (*tr*; foll by *around, on, in,* etc) *informal* to throw or pour (liquid) **6** (when *intr*, often foll by *about* or *around*) *informal* **a** to shake or stir (something) in a liquid **b** (of a person) to splash (around) in water, etc **7** (*tr*) *Brit slang* to deal a heavy blow to **8** (usually foll by *about* or *around*) *informal* to shake (a container of liquid) or (of liquid within a container) to be shaken [C19 variant of SLUSH, influenced by SLOP¹] > 'sloshy *adj*

sloshed (slɒʃt) *adj chiefly Brit* a slang word for **drunk**

slot¹ (slɒt) *n* **1** an elongated aperture or groove, such as one in a vending machine for inserting a coin **2** an air passage in an aerofoil to direct air from the lower to the upper surface, esp the gap formed behind a slat **3** a vertical opening between the leech of a foresail and a mast or the luff of another sail through which air spills from one against the other to impart forward motion **4** *informal* a place in a series or scheme ▷ *vb* **slots, slotting, slotted 5** (*tr*) to furnish with a slot or slots **6** (usually foll by *in* or *into*) to fit or adjust in a slot **7** *informal* to situate or be situated in a series or scheme [C13 from Old French *esclot* the depression of the breastbone, of unknown origin] > 'slotter *n*

slot² (slɒt) *n* the trail of an animal, esp a deer [C16 from Old French *esclot* horse's hoof-print, probably of Scandinavian origin; compare Old Norse *sloth* track; see SLEUTH]

slot aerial *or* **antenna** *n radio* a transmitting aerial in which the radiating elements are open slots in a surrounding metal sheet

sloth (sləʊθ) *n* **1** any of several shaggy-coated arboreal edentate mammals of the family *Bradypodidae,* esp *Bradypus tridactylus* (**three-toed sloth** or **ai**) or *Choloepus didactylus* (**two-toed sloth** or **unau**), of Central and South America. They are slow-moving, hanging upside down by their long arms and feeding on vegetation **2** reluctance to work or exert oneself [Old English *slǣwth;* from *slǣw,* variant of *slāw* SLOW]

sloth bear *n* a bear, *Melursus ursinus,* of forests of S India and Sri Lanka, having a shaggy coat and an elongated snout specialized for feeding on termites

slothful (ˈsləʊθfʊl) *adj* indolent > **ˈslothfully** *adv* > **ˈslothfulness** *n*

slot machine *n* a machine, esp one for selling small articles or for gambling, activated by placing a coin or metal disc in a slot

slouch (slaʊtʃ) *vb* **1** (*intr*) to sit or stand with a drooping bearing **2** (*intr*) to walk or move with an awkward slovenly gait **3** (*tr*) to cause (the shoulders) to droop > *n* **4** a drooping carriage **5** (*usually used in negative constructions*) *informal* an incompetent or slovenly person: *he's no slouch at football* [C16 of unknown origin] > **ˈsloucher** *n* > **ˈslouching** *adj* > **ˈslouchingly** *adv*

slouch hat *n* any soft hat with a brim that can be pulled down over the ears, esp an Australian army hat with the left side of the brim turned up

slouchy (ˈslaʊtʃɪ) *adj* **-ier, -iest** **1** slouching; lazy **2** (of clothes) casual, soft, and relatively unstructured > **ˈslouchily** *adv* > **ˈslouchiness** *n*

slough¹ (slaʊ) *n* **1** a hollow filled with mud; bog **2** (slu:) *US and Canadian* **a** (in the prairies) a large hole where water collects or the water in such a hole **b** (in the northwest) a sluggish side channel of a river **c** (on the Pacific coast) a marshy saltwater inlet **3** despair or degradation [Old English *slōh;* related to Middle High German *sluoche* ditch, Swedish *slaga* swamp] > **ˈsloughy** *adj*

slough² (slʌf) *n* **1** any outer covering that is shed, such as the dead outer layer of the skin of a snake, the cellular debris in a wound, etc **2** Also: **sluff** *bridge* a discarded card > *vb* **3** (often foll by *off*) to shed (a skin, etc) or (of a skin, etc) to be shed **4** Also: **sluff** *bridge* to discard (a card or cards) [C13 of Germanic origin; compare Middle Low German *slū* husk, German *Schlauch* hose, Norwegian *slō* fleshy part of a horn] > **ˈsloughy** *adj*

Slough (slaʊ) *n* **1** an industrial town in SE central England, in Slough unitary authority, Berkshire; food products, high-tech industries. Pop: 126 276 (2001) **2** a unitary authority in SE central England, in Berkshire. Pop: 118 800 (2003 est.). Area: 28 sq km (11 sq miles)

slough off (slʌf) *vb* (*tr, adverb*) to cast off (cares, etc)

Slovak (ˈsləʊvæk) *adj* **1** of, relating to, or characteristic of Slovakia, its people, or their language > *n* **2** the official language of Slovakia, belonging to the West Slavonic branch of the Indo-European family. Slovak is closely related to Czech, they are mutually intelligible **3** a native or inhabitant of Slovakia

Slovakia (sləʊˈvækɪə) *n* a country in central Europe: part of Hungary from the 11th century until 1918, when it united with Bohemia and Moravia to form Czechoslovakia; it became independent in 1993 and joined the EU in 2004. Official language: Slovak. Religion: Roman Catholic majority. Currency: koruna. Capital: Bratislava. Pop: 5 407 000 (2004 est.). Area: 49 036 sq km (18 940 sq miles)

Slovakian (sləʊˈvækɪən) *adj* **1** of, relating to, or characteristic of Slovakia, its people, or the Slovak language > *adj* **2** a native or inhabitant of Slovakia

sloven (ˈslʌvᵊn) *n* a person who is habitually negligent in appearance, hygiene, or work [C15 probably related to Flemish *sloef* dirty, Dutch *slof* negligent]

Slovene (sləʊˈviːn) *adj* also **Slovenian 1** of, relating to, or characteristic of Slovenia, its people, or their language > *n* **2** Also: **Slovenian** a South Slavonic language spoken in Slovenia, closely related to Serbo-Croat **3 a** a native or inhabitant of Slovenia **b** a speaker of Slovene

Slovenia (sləʊˈviːnɪə) *n* a republic in S central Europe: settled by the Slovenes in the 6th century; joined Yugoslavia in 1918 and became an autonomous republic in 1946; became fully independent in 1992 and joined the EU in 2004; rises over 2800 m (9000 ft) in the Julian Alps. Official language: Slovene. Religion: Roman Catholic majority. Currency: tolar. Capital: Ljubljana. Pop: 1 982 000 (2004 est.). Area: 20 251 sq km (7819 sq miles)

slovenly (ˈslʌvənlɪ) *adj* **1** frequently or habitually unclean or untidy **2** negligent and careless; slipshod: *slovenly manners* > *adv* **3** in a negligent or slovenly manner > **ˈslovenliness** *n*

slow (sləʊ) *adj* **1** performed or occurring during a comparatively long interval of time **2** lasting a comparatively long time: *a slow journey* **3** characterized by lack of speed: *a slow walker* **4** (*prenominal*) adapted to or productive of slow movement: *the slow lane of a motorway* **5** (of a clock, etc) indicating a time earlier than the correct time **6** given to or characterized by a leisurely or lazy existence: *a slow town* **7** not readily responsive to stimulation; intellectually unreceptive: *a slow mind* **8** dull or uninteresting: *the play was very slow* **9** not easily aroused: *a slow temperament* **10** lacking promptness or immediacy: *a slow answer* **11** unwilling to perform an action or enter into a state: *slow to anger* **12** behind the times **13** (of trade, etc) unproductive; slack **14** (of a fire) burning weakly **15** (of an oven) cool **16** *photog* requiring a relatively long time of exposure to produce a given density: *a slow lens* **17** *sport* (of a track, etc) tending to reduce the speed of the ball or the competitors **18** *cricket* (of a bowler, etc) delivering the ball slowly, usually with spin > *adv* **19** in a manner characterized by lack of speed; slowly > *vb* **20** (often foll by *up* or *down*) to decrease or cause to decrease in speed, efficiency, etc [Old English *slāw* sluggish; related to Old High German *slēo* dull, Old Norse *slǣr,* Dutch *sleeuw* slow] > **ˈslowly** *adv* > **ˈslowness** *n*

slow burn *n* a steadily penetrating show of anger or contempt

slowcoach (ˈsləʊˌkəʊtʃ) *n Brit informal* a person who moves, acts, or works slowly. US and Canadian equivalent: **slowpoke**

slowdown (ˈsləʊˌdaʊn) *n* **1** the usual US and Canadian word for **go-slow 2** any slackening of pace

slow food *n* food that has been prepared with care, using high-quality local and seasonal ingredients [C20 by analogy with FAST FOOD]

slow handclap *n Brit* slow rhythmic clapping, esp used by an audience to indicate dissatisfaction or impatience

slow march *n military* a march in slow time

slow match *n* a match or fuse that burns slowly without flame, esp a wick impregnated with potassium nitrate

slow-mo *or* **slo-mo** (ˈsləʊˌməʊ) *n, adj informal* short for **slow motion**

slow motion *n* **1** *films, television* action that is made to appear slower than normal by passing the film through the taking camera at a faster rate than normal or by replaying a video tape recording more slowly > *adj* **slow-motion 2** *films, television* of or relating to such action **3** moving or functioning at less than usual speed

slow neutron *n physics* a neutron having a kinetic energy of less than 100 electronvolts

slowpoke (ˈsləʊˌpəʊk) *n US and Canadian informal* a

person who moves, acts, or works slowly. also called (in Britain and certain other countries): **slowcoach**

slow time *n military* a slow marching pace, usually 65 or 75 paces to the minute: used esp in funeral ceremonies

slow virus *n* any of a class of virus-like disease-causing agents known as prions that are present in the body for a long time before becoming active or infectious and are very resistant to radiation and similar factors: believed to be the cause of BSE and scrapie

slow-witted *adj* slow in comprehension; unintelligent

slowworm (ˈsləʊˌwɜːm) *n* a Eurasian legless lizard, *Anguis fragilis,* with a brownish-grey snakelike body: family *Anguidae.* Also called: **blindworm**

SLR *abbreviation for* single-lens reflex. See **reflex camera**

SLSC (in Australia) *abbreviation for* Surf Life Saving Club

slub (slʌb) *n* **1** a lump in yarn or fabric, often made intentionally to give a knobbly effect **2** a loosely twisted roll of fibre prepared for spinning > *vb* **slubs, slubbing, slubbed 3** (*tr*) to draw out and twist (a sliver of fibre) preparatory to spinning > *adj* **4** (of material) having an irregular appearance [C18 of unknown origin]

slubberdegullion (ˌslʌbədɪˈgʌlɪən) *n archaic* a slovenly or worthless person [C17 from *slubber* (chiefly dialect variant of SLOBBER) + invented ending]

sludge (slʌdʒ) *n* **1** soft mud, snow, etc **2** any deposit or sediment **3** a surface layer of ice that has a slushy appearance **4** (in sewage disposal) the solid constituents of sewage that precipitate during treatment and are removed for subsequent purification [C17 probably related to SLUSH]

sludgy (ˈslʌdʒɪ) *adj* **-ier, -iest** consisting of, containing, or like sludge

slue¹ (slu:) *n, vb* a variant spelling (esp US) of **slew²**

slue² (slu:) *n* a variant spelling of **slough¹** (sense 2)

slue³ (slu:) *n US informal* a variant spelling of **slew⁴**

sluff (slʌf) *n, vb bridge* a variant spelling of **slough²**

slug¹ (slʌg) *n* **1** any of various terrestrial gastropod molluscs of the genera *Limax, Arion,* etc, in which the body is elongated and the shell is absent or very much reduced. Compare **sea slug** Related adj: **limacine 2** any of various other invertebrates having a soft slimy body, esp the larvae of certain sawflies **3** *informal, chiefly US and Canadian* a slow-moving or lazy person or animal [C15 (in the sense: a slow person or animal): probably of Scandinavian origin; compare Norwegian (dialect) *sluggje*]

slug² (slʌg) *n* **1** an fps unit of mass; the mass that will acquire an acceleration of 1 foot per second per second when acted upon by a force of 1 pound. 1 slug is approximately equal to 32.17 pounds **2** *metallurgy* a metal blank from which small forgings are worked **3** a bullet or pellet larger than a pellet of buckshot **4** *chiefly US and Canadian* a metal token for use in slot machines, etc **5** *printing* **a** a thick strip of type metal that is less than type-high and is used for spacing **b** a similar strip carrying a type-high letter, used as a temporary mark by compositors **c** a metal strip containing a line of characters as produced by a linecaster **6** a draught of a drink, esp an alcoholic one **7** a magnetic core that is screwed into or out of an inductance coil to adjust the tuning of a radio frequency amplifier [C17 (bullet), C19 (printing): perhaps from SLUG¹, with allusion to the shape of the animal]

slug³ (slʌg) *vb* **slugs, slugging, slugged 1** to hit very hard and solidly, as in boxing **2** (*intr*) *US and Canadian* to plod as if through snow **3** (*tr*) *Austral and NZ informal* to charge (someone) an exorbitant price **4** **slug it out** *informal* to fight, compete, or

S

struggle with fortitude ▷ *n* **5** an act of slugging; heavy blow **6** *Austral and NZ informal* an exorbitant charge or price [C19 perhaps from SLUG² (bullet)]

slugabed ('slʌgə,bɛd) *n* a person who remains in bed through laziness [C16 from SLUG(GARD) + ABED]

sluggard ('slʌgəd) *n* **1** a person who is habitually indolent ▷ *adj* **2** lazy [C14 *slogarde;* related to SLUG¹] > 'sluggardly *adj* > 'sluggardliness *n* > 'sluggardness *n*

slugger ('slʌgə) *n* (esp in boxing, baseball, etc) a person who strikes hard

sluggish ('slʌgɪʃ) *adj* **1** lacking energy; inactive; slow-moving **2** functioning at below normal rate or level **3** exhibiting poor response to stimulation > 'sluggishly *adv* > 'sluggishness *n*

sluice (sluːs) *n* **1** Also called: **sluiceway** a channel that carries a rapid current of water, esp one that has a sluicegate to control the flow **2** the body of water controlled by a sluicegate **3** See **sluicegate** **4** *mining* an inclined trough for washing ore, esp one having riffles on the bottom to trap particles **5** an artificial channel through which logs can be floated **6** *informal* a brief wash in running water ▷ *vb* **7** (*tr*) to draw out or drain (water, etc) from (a pond, etc) by means of a sluice **8** (*tr*) to wash or irrigate with a stream of water **9** (*tr*) *mining* to wash in a sluice **10** (*tr*) to send (logs, etc) down a sluice **11** (*intr;* often foll by *away* or *out*) (of water, etc) to run or flow from or as if from a sluice **12** (*tr*) to provide with a sluice [C14 from Old French *escluse,* from Late Latin *exclūsa aqua* water shut out, from Latin *exclūdere* to shut out, EXCLUDE] > 'sluice,like *adj*

sluicegate ('sluːs,geɪt) *n* a valve or gate fitted to a sluice to control the rate of flow of water. Sometimes shortened to: **sluice** See also **floodgate** (sense 1)

slum (slʌm) *n* **1** a squalid overcrowded house, etc **2** (*often plural*) a squalid section of a city, characterized by inferior living conditions and usually by overcrowding **3** (*modifier*) relating to, or characteristic of slums: *slum conditions* ▷ *vb* **slums, slumming, slummed** (*intr*) **4** to visit slums, esp for curiosity **5** Also: **slum it** to suffer conditions below those to which one is accustomed [C19 originally slang, of obscure origin] > 'slummer *n* > 'slummy *adj*

slumber ('slʌmbə) *vb* **1** (*intr*) to sleep, esp peacefully **2** (*intr*) to be quiescent or dormant **3** (*tr;* foll by *away*) to spend (time) sleeping ▷ *n* **4** (*sometimes plural*) sleep **5** a dormant or quiescent state [Old English *slūma* sleep (n); related to Middle High German *slummeren,* Dutch *sluimeren*] > 'slumberer *n* > 'slumberless *adj*

slumberous ('slʌmbərəs, -brəs) *adj chiefly poetic* **1** sleepy; drowsy **2** inducing sleep **3** characteristic of slumber > 'slumberously *adv* > 'slumberousness *n*

slumber party *n US and Canadian* a party attended by girls who dress in night clothes and pass the night eating and talking

slumgullion (slʌm'gʌljən, 'slʌm,gʌl-) *n US and Canadian* **1** *slang* an inexpensive stew **2** offal, esp the refuse from whale blubber **3** a reddish mud deposited in mine sluices [C19 from *slum* in US sense slime + *gullion,* perhaps variant of *cullion* testicles]

slumlord ('slʌm,lɔːd) *n informal, chiefly US and Canadian* an absentee landlord of slum property, esp one who profiteers

slump (slʌmp) *vb* (*intr*) **1** to sink or fall heavily and suddenly **2** to relax ungracefully **3** (of business activity, etc) to decline suddenly; collapse **4** (of health, interest, etc) to deteriorate or decline suddenly or markedly **5** (of soil or rock) to slip down a slope, esp a cliff, usually with a rotational movement ▷ *n* **6** a sudden or marked decline or failure, as in progress or achievement; collapse **7** a decline in commercial activity, prices, etc **8** *economics* another word for **depression** **9** the act of slumping **10** a slipping of

earth or rock; landslide [C17 probably of Scandinavian origin; compare Low German *slump* bog, Norwegian *slumpa* to fall]

Slump (slʌmp) *n* **the** another name for the Depression

slumpflation (slʌmp'fleɪʃən) *n* a situation in which economic depression is combined with increasing inflation [C20 blend of SLUMP + INFLATION]

slump test *n Brit* a test to determine the relative water content of concrete, depending on the loss in height (slump) of a sample obtained from a cone-shaped mould

slung (slʌŋ) *adj* the past tense and past participle of **sling¹**

slung shot *n* a weight attached to the end of a cord and used as a weapon

slunk (slʌŋk) *vb* the past tense and past participle of **slink**

slur (slɜː) *vb* **slurs, slurring, slurred** (*mainly tr*) **1** (often foll by *over*) to treat superficially, hastily, or without due deliberation; gloss **2** (*also intr*) to pronounce or utter (words, etc) indistinctly **3** to speak disparagingly of or cast aspersions on **4** *music* to execute (a melodic interval of two or more notes) smoothly, as in legato performance **5** (*also intr*) to blur or smear **6** *archaic* to stain or smear; sully ▷ *n* **7** an indistinct sound or utterance **8** a slighting remark; aspersion **9** a stain or disgrace, as upon one's reputation; stigma **10** *music* **a** a performance or execution of a melodic interval of two or more notes in a part **b** the curved line (⌢ or ⌣) indicating this **11** a blur or smear [C15 probably from Middle Low German; compare Middle Low German *slūren* to drag, trail, Middle Dutch *sloren,* Dutch *sleuren*]

slurp (slɜːp) *informal* ▷ *vb* **1** to eat or drink (something) noisily ▷ *n* **2** a sound produced in this way [C17 from Middle Dutch *slorpen* to sip; related to German *schlürfen*]

slurry ('slʌrɪ) *n, pl* **-ries** a suspension of solid particles in a liquid, as in a mixture of cement, clay, coal dust, manure, meat, etc with water [C15 *slory;* see SLUR]

slush (slʌʃ) *n* **1** any watery muddy substance, esp melting snow **2** *informal* sloppily sentimental language **3** *nautical* waste fat from the galley of a ship ▷ *vb* **4** (*intr;* often foll by *along*) to make one's way through or as if through slush **5** (*intr*) to make a slushing sound [C17 related to Danish *slus* sleet, Norwegian *slusk* slops; see SLUDGE, SLOSH]

slush fund *n* **1** a fund for financing political or commercial corruption **2** *US nautical* a fund accumulated from the sale of slush from the galley

slushy ('slʌʃɪ) *adj* **slushier, slushiest** **1** of, resembling, or consisting of slush ▷ *n, pl* **slushies** **2** an unskilled kitchen assistant > 'slushiness *n*

slut (slʌt) *n* **1** *derogatory* a dirty slatternly woman **2** *derogatory* an immoral woman **3** *archaic* a female dog [C14 of unknown origin] > 'sluttish *adj* > 'sluttishly *adv* > 'sluttishness *n*

slutch (slʌtʃ) *n Northern English dialect* mud > 'slutchy *adj*

sly (slaɪ) *adj* **slyer, slyest** *or* **slier, sliest** **1** crafty; artful: *a sly dodge* **2** insidious; furtive: *a sly manner* **3** playfully mischievous; roguish: *sly humour* ▷ *n* **4** **on the sly** in a secretive manner [C12 from Old Norse *slǣgr* clever, literally: able to strike, from *slā* to SLAY] > 'slyly *or* 'slily *adv* > 'slyness *n*

slyboots ('slaɪ,buːts) *pl n* (*functioning as singular*) a person who is sly

sly grog *n Austral and NZ old-fashioned* illicitly sold liquor

slype (slaɪp) *n* a covered passageway in a cathedral or church that connects the transept to the chapterhouse [C19 probably from Middle Flemish *slijpen* to slip]

sm *the internet domain name for* San Marino

Sm *the chemical symbol for* samarium

SM *abbreviation for* **1** sergeant major **2** sadomasochism

smaak (smɑːk) *vb South African slang* (*tr*) to like, love, or be keen on (someone or something) [from Afrikaans]

smack¹ (smæk) *n* **1** a smell or flavour that is distinctive though faint **2** a distinctive trace or touch: *the smack of corruption* **3** a small quantity, esp a mouthful or taste **4** a slang word for **heroin** ▷ *vb* (*intr;* foll by *of*) **5** to have the characteristic smell or flavour (of something): *to smack of the sea* **6** to have an element suggestive (of something): *his speeches smacked of bigotry* [Old English *smæc;* related to Old High German *smoc,* Icelandic *smekkr* a taste, Dutch *smaak*]

smack² (smæk) *vb* **1** (*tr*) to strike or slap smartly, with or as if with the open hand **2** to strike or send forcibly or loudly or to be struck or sent forcibly or loudly **3** to open and close (the lips) loudly, esp to show pleasure **4** (*tr*) to kiss noisily ▷ *n* **5** a sharp resounding slap or blow with something flat, or the sound of such a blow **6** a loud kiss **7** a sharp sound made by the lips, as in enjoyment **8** **have a smack at** *informal, chiefly Brit* to attempt **9** **smack in the eye** *informal, chiefly Brit* a snub or setback ▷ *adv informal* **10** directly; squarely **11** with a smack; sharply and unexpectedly [C16 from Middle Low German or Middle Dutch *smacken,* probably of imitative origin]

smack³ (smæk) *n* **1** a sailing vessel, usually sloop-rigged, used in coasting and fishing along the British coast **2** a fishing vessel equipped with a well for keeping the catch alive [C17 from Low German *smack* or Dutch *smak,* of unknown origin]

smacker ('smækə) *n slang* **1** a loud kiss; smack **2** a pound note or dollar bill

smackhead ('smæk,hɛd) *n Brit slang* a person who is addicted to heroin

smacking ('smækɪŋ) *adj* brisk; lively: *a smacking breeze*

small (smɔːl) *adj* **1** comparatively little; limited in size, number, importance, etc **2** of little importance or on a minor scale: *a small business* **3** lacking in moral or mental breadth or depth: *a small mind* **4** modest or humble: *small beginnings* **5** of low or inferior status, esp socially **6** (of a child or animal) young; not mature **7** unimportant, trivial: *a small matter* **8** not outstanding: *a small actor* **9** of, relating to, or designating the ordinary modern minuscule letter used in printing and cursive writing. Compare **capital¹** (sense 13) See also **lower case 10** lacking great strength or force: *a small effort* **11** in fine particles: *small gravel* **12** *obsolete* (of beer, etc) of low alcoholic strength ▷ *adv* **13** into small pieces: *you have to cut it small* **14** in a small or soft manner **15** **feel small** to be humiliated or inferior ▷ *n* **16** (often preceded by *the*) an object, person, or group considered to be small: *do you want the small or the large?* **17** a small slender part, esp of the back **18** (*plural*) *informal, chiefly Brit* items of personal laundry, such as underwear [Old English *smæl;* related to Old High German *smal,* Old Norse *smali* small cattle] > 'smallish *adj* > 'smallness *n*

small advertisement *or* **small ad** *n* a short, simply designed advertisement in a newspaper or magazine, usually set entirely in a small size of type. See **display advertisement**

smallage ('smɔːlɪdʒ) *n* an archaic name for **wild celery** [C13 from earlier *smalache,* from *smal* SMALL + *ache* wild celery, from Old French, from Latin *apium*]

small arms *pl n* portable firearms of relatively small calibre

small beer *n informal, chiefly Brit* people or things of no importance

small-bore *adj* (of a firearm) having a small bore, especially one of less than .22 calibre

smallboy ('smɔːl,bɔɪ) *n* the steward's assistant or deputy steward in European households in W Africa

small calorie *n* another name for **calorie**

small capital *n* a letter having the form of an

upper-case letter but the same height as a lower-case letter

small change n **1** coins, esp those of low value **2** a person or thing that is not outstanding or important

small chop pl n W African cocktail snacks

small circle n a circular section of a sphere that does not contain the centre of the sphere. Compare **great circle**

small claims court n Brit and Canadian a local court with jurisdiction to try civil actions involving small claims

smallclothes ('smɔːl,kləʊz, -,kləʊðz) pl n men's close-fitting knee breeches of the 18th and 19th centuries

small forward n basketball a versatile attacking player

small fry pl n **1** people or things regarded as unimportant **2** young children **3** young or small fishes

small game n Brit small animals that are hunted for sport

small goods pl n Austral and NZ meats bought from a delicatessen, such as sausages

smallholding ('smɔːl,həʊldɪŋ) n a holding of agricultural land smaller than a small farm > 'small,holder n

small hours pl n **the** the early hours of the morning, after midnight and before dawn

small intestine n the longest part of the alimentary canal, consisting of the duodenum, jejunum, and ileum, in which digestion is completed. Compare **large intestine**

small letter n a lower-case letter

small-minded adj narrow-minded; petty; intolerant; mean > ,small-'mindedly adv > ,small-'mindedness n

smallmouth bass ('smɔːl,maʊθ 'bæs) n a North American freshwater black bass, Micropterus dolomieu, that is a popular game fish

small pica n (formerly) a size of printer's type approximately equal to 11 point

small potatoes n (functioning as singular or plural) informal, chiefly US and Canadian someone or something of little significance or value, esp a small amount of money

smallpox ('smɔːl,pɒks) n an acute highly contagious viral disease characterized by high fever, severe prostration, and a pinkish rash changing in form from papules to pustules, which dry up and form scabs that are cast off, leaving pitted depressions. Technical name: variola Related adj: variolous [c16 from SMALL + POX. So called to distinguish it from the Great Pox, an archaic name for syphilis]

small print n matter in a contract, etc, printed in small type, esp when considered to be a trap for the unwary

small-scale adj **1** of limited size or scope **2** (of a map, model, etc) giving a relatively small representation of something, usually missing out details

small screen n an informal name for **television**

small slam n bridge another name for **little slam**

small stores pl n navy personal items, such as clothing, sold aboard ship or at a naval base. Compare **slop chest**

small stuff n nautical any light twine or yarn used aboard ship for serving lines, etc

smallsword ('smɔːl,sɔːd) n a light sword used in the 17th and 18th centuries: formerly a fencing weapon

small talk n light conversation for social occasions

small-time adj informal insignificant; minor: a small-time criminal > 'small-'timer n

small white n a small white butterfly, Artogeia rapae, with scanty black markings, the larvae of which feed on brassica leaves

smalt (smɔːlt) n **1** a type of silica glass coloured deep blue with cobalt oxide **2** a pigment made by crushing this glass, used in colouring enamels **3**

the blue colour of this pigment [c16 via French from Italian SMALTO, of Germanic origin; related to SMELT[1]]

smaltite ('smɔːltaɪt) n a silver-white to greyish mineral consisting chiefly of cobalt arsenide with nickel in cubic crystalline form. It occurs in veins associated with silver, nickel, and copper minerals, and is an important ore of cobalt and nickel. Formula: $(Co,Ni)As_{3-x}$ [c19 from SMALT + -ITE[1]]

smalto ('smaːltəʊ) n, pl -tos or -ti (-tiː) coloured glass, etc, used in mosaics [c18 from Italian; see SMALT]

smaragd ('smærægd) n archaic any green gemstone, such as the emerald [c13 via Latin from Greek smaragdos; see EMERALD] > smaragdine (smə'rægdɪn) adj

smaragdite (smə'rægdaɪt) n a green fibrous amphibole mineral

smarm (smaːm) Brit informal ▷ vb **1** (tr; often foll by down) to flatten (the hair, etc) with cream or grease **2** (when intr, foll by up to) to ingratiate oneself (with) ▷ n **3** obsequious flattery [c19 of unknown origin]

smarmy ('smaːmɪ) adj smarmier, smarmiest Brit informal obsequiously flattering or unpleasantly suave > 'smarmily adv > 'smarminess n

smart (smaːt) adj **1** astute, as in business; clever or bright **2** quick, witty, and often impertinent in speech: a smart talker **3** fashionable; chic: a smart hotel **4** well-kept; neat **5** causing a sharp stinging pain **6** vigorous or brisk **7** dialect considerable or numerous: a smart price **8** (of systems) operating as if by human intelligence by using automatic computer control **9** (of a projectile or bomb) containing a device that allows it to be guided to its target ▷ vb (mainly intr) **10** to feel, cause, or be the source of a sharp stinging physical pain or keen mental distress: a nettle sting smarts; he smarted under their abuse **11** (often foll by for) to suffer a harsh penalty ▷ n **12** a stinging pain or feeling ▷ adv **13** in a smart manner [Old English smeortan; related to Old High German smerzan, Latin mordēre to bite, Greek smerdnos terrible] > 'smartish adj > 'smartly adv > 'smartness n

smart aleck ('ælɪk) n, pl smart alecks informal an irritatingly oversmart person [c19 from Aleck, Alec, short for Alexander] > 'smart-,aleck or 'smart-,alecky adj

smartarse ('smaːt,aːs) n derogatory slang **a** a clever person, esp one who parades his knowledge offensively **b** (as modifier): smartarse guidebooks > 'smart,arsed adj

smart card n a plastic card with integrated circuits used for storing and processing computer data. Also called: laser card, intelligent card

smart dust n computing jargon same as **sensor network**

smarten ('smaːt[ə]n) vb (usually foll by up) **1** (intr) to make oneself neater **2** (tr) to make quicker or livelier

smart money n **1 a** money bet or invested by experienced gamblers or investors, esp with inside information **b** the gamblers or investors themselves **2** money paid in order to extricate oneself from an unpleasant situation or agreement, esp from military service **3** money paid by an employer to someone injured while working for him **4** US law damages awarded to a plaintiff where the wrong was aggravated by fraud, malice, etc

smartmouth ('smaːt,maʊθ) n informal **1** a witty or sarcastic person **2** witty or sarcastic comments

smartphone ('smaːt,fəʊn) n computing a mobile telephone with computer features that may enable it to interact with computerized systems, send e-mails, and access the web

smarts (smaːts) pl n slang, chiefly US know-how, intelligence, or wits: street smarts

smart sanction n (often plural) a sanction intended to affect only a particular area of a

country's activities or economy

smart set n (functioning as singular or plural) fashionable sophisticated people considered as a group

smart wool n chiefly Austral and NZ a textile produced by blending wool with a conductive fibre, which can be heated by means of a small battery

smarty or **smartie** ('smaːtɪ) n informal a would-be clever person

smarty-pants ('smaːtɪ,pænts) or **smarty-boots** ('smaːtɪ,buːts) n (functioning as singular) informal a would-be clever person

smash (smæʃ) vb **1** to break into pieces violently and usually noisily **2** (when intr, foll by against, through, into, etc) to throw or crash (against) vigorously, causing shattering: he smashed the equipment; it smashed against the wall **3** (tr) to hit forcefully and suddenly **4** (tr) tennis, squash, badminton to hit (the ball) fast and powerfully, esp with an overhead stroke **5** (tr) to defeat or wreck (persons, theories, etc) **6** (tr) to make bankrupt **7** (intr) to collide violently; crash **8** (intr; often foll by up) to go bankrupt **9** smash someone's face in informal to beat someone severely ▷ n **10** an act, instance, or sound of smashing or the state of being smashed **11** a violent collision, esp of vehicles **12** a total failure or collapse, as of a business **13** tennis, squash, badminton a fast and powerful overhead stroke **14** informal **a** something having popular success **b** (in combination): smash-hit **15** slang loose change; coins ▷ adv **16** with a smash [c18 probably from SM(ACK[2] + M)ASH] > 'smashable adj

smash-and-grab adj informal of or relating to a robbery in which a shop window is broken and the contents removed

smashed (smæʃt) adj slang **1** completely intoxicated with alcohol **2** noticeably under the influence of a drug

smasher ('smæʃə) n informal, chiefly Brit a person or thing that is very attractive or outstanding

smashing ('smæʃɪŋ) adj informal, chiefly Brit excellent or first-rate; wonderful: we had a smashing time

smash-up informal ▷ n **1** a bad collision, esp of cars ▷ vb smash up **2** (tr, adverb) to damage to the point of complete destruction: they smashed the place up

smatch (smætʃ) n a less common word for **smack[1]**

smatter ('smætə) vb **1** a smattering ▷ vb **2** (intr) rare to prattle **3** (tr) archaic to dabble in [c14 (in the sense: to prattle): of uncertain origin; compare Middle High German smetern to gossip] > 'smatterer n

smattering ('smætərɪŋ) n **1** a slight or superficial knowledge **2** a small amount > 'smatteringly adv

SMATV abbreviation for (originally) small master antenna television; now more commonly, satellite master antenna television: a system for relaying broadcast television signals, embodying a master receiving antenna with distribution by cable to a small group of dwellings, such as a block of flats

smaze (smeɪz) n US a smoky haze, less damp than fog [c20 from SM(OKE) + (H)AZE[1]]

SMD electronics abbreviation for surface-mounted device: a device such as resistor, capacitor, or integrated circuit on a printed circuit board

SME international car registration for Suriname

smear (smɪə) vb (mainly tr) **1** to bedaub or cover with oil, grease, etc **2** to rub over or apply thickly **3** to rub so as to produce a smudge **4** to slander **5** US slang to defeat completely **6** (intr) to be or become smeared or dirtied ▷ n **7** a dirty mark or smudge **8 a** a slanderous attack **b** (as modifier): smear tactics **9** a preparation of blood, secretions, etc, smeared onto a glass slide for examination under a microscope [Old English smeoru (11); related to Old Norse smjör fat, Old High German smero, Greek muron ointment] > 'smearer n

smear test n med another name for **Pap test**

smeary ('smɪərɪ) adj -rier, -riest smeared, dirty;

S

blurred by smearing > **'smearily** *adv*
> **'smeariness** *n*

smectic ('smɛktɪk) *adj chem* (of a substance) existing in or having a mesomorphic state in which the molecules are oriented in layers. Compare **nematic** See also **liquid crystal** [C17 via Latin from Greek *smēktikos*, from *smēkhein* to wash; from the soaplike consistency of a smectic substance]

smectite ('smɛktaɪt) *n* any of a group of clay minerals of which montmorillonite and saponite are members

smeddum ('smɛdəm) *n Scot* **1** any fine powder **2** spirit or mettle; vigour [Old English *smedema* fine flour]

smeech (smi:tʃ) *n, vb* a Southwest English dialect form of **smoke**

smegma ('smɛgmə) *n physiol* a whitish sebaceous secretion that accumulates beneath the prepuce [C19 via Latin from Greek *smēgma* detergent, from *smekhein* to wash]

smell (smɛl) *vb* **smells, smelling, smelt** or **smelled 1** (*tr*) to perceive the scent or odour of (a substance) by means of the olfactory nerves **2** (*copula*) to have a specified smell; appear to the sense of smell to be: *the beaches smell of seaweed; some tobacco smells very sweet* **3** (*intr*; often foll by *of*) to emit an odour (of): *the park smells of flowers* **4** (*intr*) to emit an unpleasant odour; stink **5** (*tr*; often foll by *out*) to detect through shrewdness or instinct **6** (*intr*) to have or use the sense of smell; sniff **7** (*intr*; foll by *of*) to give indications (of): *he smells of money* **8** (*intr*; foll by *around, about, etc*) to search, investigate, or pry **9** (*copula*) to be or seem to be untrustworthy or corrupt **10 smell a rat** to detect something suspicious ▷ *n* **11** that sense (olfaction) by which scents or odours are perceived. Related adj: **olfactory 12** anything detected by the sense of smell; odour; scent **13** a trace or indication **14** the act or an instance of smelling [C12 of uncertain origin; compare Middle Dutch *smöllen* to scorch] > **'smeller** *n*

smellies ('smɛlɪz) *pl n informal* pleasant-smelling products such as perfumes, body lotions, bath salts, etc

smelling salts *pl n* a pungent preparation containing crystals of ammonium carbonate that has a stimulant action when sniffed in cases of faintness, headache, etc

smelly ('smɛlɪ) *adj* **smellier, smelliest** having a strong or nasty smell > **'smelliness** *n*

smelt[1] (smɛlt) *vb* (*tr*) to extract (a metal) from (an ore) by heating [C15 from Middle Low German, Middle Dutch *smelten*; related to Old High German *smelzan* to melt]

smelt[2] (smɛlt) *n, pl* **smelt** or **smelts** any marine or freshwater salmonoid food fish of the family *Osmeridae*, such as *Osmerus eperlanus* of Europe, having a long silvery body and occurring in temperate and cold northern waters [Old English *smylt*; related to Dutch, Danish *smelt*, Norwegian *smelta*, German *Schmelz*]

smelt[3] (smɛlt) *vb* a past tense and past participle of **smell**

smelter ('smɛltə) *n* **1** a person engaged in smelting **2** Also called: **smeltery** ('smɛltərɪ) an industrial plant in which smelting is carried out

smew (smju:) *n* a merganser, *Mergus albellus*, of N Europe and Asia, having a male plumage of white with black markings [C17 of uncertain origin]

smidge (smɪdʒ) *n informal* a very small amount or part [C20 from SMIDGEN]

smidgen or **smidgin** ('smɪdʒən) *n informal* a very small amount or part [C20 of obscure origin]

smilacaceous (ˌsmaɪləˈkeɪʃəs) *adj* of, relating to, or belonging to the *Smilacaceae*, a temperate and tropical family of monocotyledonous flowering plants, most of which are climbing shrubs with prickly stems: includes smilax [C19 via New Latin from Latin SMILAX]

smilax ('smaɪlæks) *n* **1** any typically climbing shrub of the smilacaceous genus *Smilax*, of warm

and tropical regions, having slightly lobed leaves, small greenish or yellow flowers, and berry-like fruits: includes the sarsaparilla plant and greenbrier **2** a fragile, much branched liliaceous vine, *Asparagus asparagoides*, of southern Africa: cultivated by florists for its glossy bright green foliage [C17 via Latin from Greek: bindweed]

smile (smaɪl) *n* **1** a facial expression characterized by an upturning of the corners of the mouth, usually showing amusement, friendliness, etc, but sometimes scorn, etc **2** favour or blessing: *the smile of fortune* **3** an agreeable appearance ▷ *vb* **4** (*intr*) to wear or assume a smile **5** (*intr*; foll by *at*) **a** to look (at) with a kindly or amused expression **b** to look derisively (at) instead of being annoyed **c** to bear (troubles, etc) patiently **6** (*intr*; foll by *on* or *upon*) to show approval; bestow a blessing **7** (*tr*) to express by means of a smile: *she smiled a welcome* **8** (*tr*; often foll by *away*) to drive away or change by smiling: *smile away one's tears* **9 come up smiling** to recover cheerfully from misfortune [C13 probably of Scandinavian origin; compare Swedish *smila*, Danish *smile*; related to Middle High German *smielen*] > **'smiler** *n* > **'smiling** *adj* > **'smilingly** *adv* > **'smilingness** *n*

smiley ('smaɪlɪ) *adj* **1** given to smiling; cheerful **2** depicting a smile: *a smiley badge* ▷ *n* **3** any of a group of symbols depicting a smile, or other facial expression, used in electronic mail

smir, smirr (smɪr) or **smur** *Scot* ▷ *n* **1** drizzly rain ▷ *vb* **smirs** or **smirrs, smirring, smirred** (*intr*) **2** to drizzle lightly [C19 of uncertain origin; compare Dutch *smoor* mist]

smirch (smɜːtʃ) *vb* (*tr*) **1** to dirty; soil ▷ *n* **2** the act of smirching or state of being smirched **3** a smear or stain [C15 *smorchen*, of unknown origin] > **'smircher** *n*

smirk (smɜːk) *n* **1** a smile expressing scorn, smugness, etc, rather than pleasure ▷ *vb* **2** (*intr*) to give such a smile **3** (*tr*) to express with such a smile [Old English *smearcian*; related to *smer* derision, Old High German *bismer* contempt, *bismerōn* to scorn] > **'smirker** *n* > **'smirking** *adj* > **'smirkingly** *adv*

smirting ('smɜːtɪŋ) *n informal* the activity of flirting between smokers who are smoking cigarettes outside a no-smoking office, pub, etc [C21 a blend of *smoking + flirting*]

smit (smɪt) *n* the *Scot and northern English dialect* an infection: *he's got the smit* [Old English *smitte* a spot, and *smittian* to smear; related to Old High German *smiz*, whence Middle High German *smitz*]

smite (smaɪt) *vb* **smites, smiting, smote; smitten** or **smit** (*mainly tr*) *now archaic in most senses* **1** to strike with a heavy blow or blows **2** to damage with or as if with blows **3** to afflict or affect severely: *smitten with flu* **4** to afflict in order to punish **5** (*intr*; foll by *on*) to strike forcibly or abruptly: *the sun smote down on him* [Old English *smītan*; related to Old High German *smīzan* to smear, Gothic *bismeitan*, Old Swedish *smēta* to daub] > **'smiter** *n*

smith (smɪθ) *n* **1 a** a person who works in metal, esp one who shapes metal by hammering **b** (*in combination*): *a silversmith* **2** See **blacksmith** [Old English; related to Old Norse *smithr*, Old High German *smid*, Middle Low German *smide* jewellery, Greek *smilē* carving knife]

smithereens (ˌsmɪðəˈriːnz) *pl n* little shattered pieces or fragments [C19 from Irish Gaelic *smidirín*, from *smiodar*]

smithery ('smɪθərɪ) *n, pl* **-eries 1** the trade or craft of a blacksmith **2** a rare word for **smithy**

Smithsonian Institution (smɪθˈsəʊnɪən) *n* a national museum and institution in Washington, DC, founded in 1846 from a bequest by James Smithson, primarily concerned with ethnology, zoology, and astrophysics

smithsonite ('smɪθsəˌnaɪt) *n* a white mineral consisting of zinc carbonate in hexagonal crystalline form: occurs chiefly in dry limestone regions and is a source of zinc. Formula: $ZnCO_3$.

Also called (US): **calamine** [C19 named after James Smithson (1765–1829), English chemist and mineralogist]

smithy ('smɪðɪ) *n, pl* **smithies** a place in which metal, usually iron or steel, is worked by heating and hammering; forge [Old English *smiththe*; related to Old Norse *smithja*, Old High German *smidda*, Middle Dutch *smisse*]

smitten ('smɪt²n) *vb* a past participle of **smite**

smock (smɒk) *n* **1** any loose protective garment, worn by artists, laboratory technicians, etc **2** a woman's loose blouse-like garment, reaching to below the waist, worn over slacks, etc **3** Also called: **smock frock** a loose protective overgarment decorated with smocking, worn formerly esp by farm workers **4** *archaic* a woman's loose undergarment, worn from the 16th to the 18th centuries ▷ *vb* **5** to ornament (a garment) with smocking [Old English *smocc*; related to Old High German *smocco*, Old Norse *smokkr* blouse, Middle High German *gesmuc* decoration] > **'smock,like** *adj*

smocking ('smɒkɪŋ) *n* ornamental needlework used to gather and stitch material in a honeycomb pattern so that the part below the gathers hangs in even folds

smock mill *n* a type of windmill having a revolving top

smog (smɒg) *n* a mixture of smoke, fog, and chemical fumes [C20 from SM(OKE + F)OG[1]] > **'smoggy** *adj*

smoke (sməʊk) *n* **1** the product of combustion, consisting of fine particles of carbon carried by hot gases and air **2** any cloud of fine particles suspended in a gas **3 a** the act of smoking tobacco or other substances, esp in a pipe or as a cigarette or cigar **b** the duration of smoking such substances **4** *informal* **a** a cigarette or cigar **b** a substance for smoking, such as pipe tobacco or marijuana **5** something with no concrete or lasting substance: *everything turned to smoke* **6** a thing or condition that obscures **7** any of various colours similar to that of smoke, esp a dark grey with a bluish, yellowish, or greenish tinge **8 go or end up in smoke a** to come to nothing **b** to burn up vigorously **c** to flare up in anger ▷ *vb* **9** (*intr*) to emit smoke or the like, sometimes excessively or in the wrong place **10 a** to draw in on (a burning cigarette, etc) and exhale the smoke **b** to use tobacco for smoking **11** (*intr*) *slang* to use marijuana for smoking **12** (*tr*) to bring (oneself) into a specified state by smoking **13** (*tr*) to subject or expose to smoke **14** (*tr*) to cure (meat, fish, cheese, etc) by treating with smoke **15** (*tr*) to fumigate or purify the air of (rooms, etc) **16** (*tr*) to darken (glass, etc) by exposure to smoke **17** (*intr*) *slang* to move, drive, ride, etc, very fast **18** (*tr*) *obsolete* to tease or mock **19** (*tr*) *archaic* to suspect or detect ▷ See also **smoke out** [Old English *smoca* (*n*); related to Middle Dutch *smieken* to emit smoke] > **'smokable** or **'smokeable** *adj*

Smoke (sməʊk) *n* the short for **Big Smoke**

smoke and mirrors *n* irrelevant or misleading information serving to obscure the truth of a situation [C20 reference to the use of smoke and mirrors in conjuring illusions]

smoke bomb *n* a device that emits large quantities of smoke when ignited

smoke-dried *adj* (of fish, meat, etc) cured in smoke

smoked rubber *n* a type of crude natural rubber in the form of brown sheets obtained by coagulating latex with an acid, rolling it into sheets, and drying over open wood fires. It is the main raw material for natural rubber products. Also called: **ribbed and smoked sheet** Compare **crepe rubber**

smokeho ('sməʊkəʊ) *n* a variant spelling of **smoko**

smokehouse ('sməʊk,haʊs) *n* a building or special construction for curing meat, fish, etc, by smoking

smokejack ('sməʊkˌdʒæk) n a device formerly used for turning a roasting spit, operated by the movement of ascending gases in a chimney [c17 from SMOKE + JACK¹]

smokeless ('sməʊklɪs) adj having or producing little or no smoke: smokeless fuel

smokeless powder n any one of a number of explosives that burn with relatively little smoke. They consist mainly of nitrocellulose and are used as propellants

smokeless zone n an area designated by the local authority where only smokeless fuels are permitted

smoke out vb (tr, adverb) 1 to subject to smoke in order to drive out of hiding 2 to bring into the open; expose to the public: they smoked out the plot

smoker ('sməʊkə) n 1 a person who habitually smokes tobacco 2 Also called: smoking compartment a compartment of a train where smoking is permitted 3 an informal social gathering, as at a club 4 a vent on the ocean floor from which hot water and minerals erupt

Smokerlyzer ('sməʊkəˌlaɪzə) n trademark a device for estimating the amount of carbon monoxide in the breath: used in testing whether or not people, esp schoolchildren, have been smoking [c20 from SMOKER + (ANA)LYZER]

smoke screen n 1 military a cloud of smoke produced by artificial means to obscure movements or positions 2 something said or done in order to hide the truth

smokestack ('sməʊkˌstæk) n a tall chimney that conveys smoke into the air. Sometimes shortened to: stack

smokestack industry n informal any of the traditional British industries, esp heavy engineering or manufacturing, as opposed to such modern industries as electronics

smoke tree n 1 an anacardiaceous shrub, Cotinus coggygria, of S Europe and Asia, having clusters of yellowish feathery flowers 2 a related tree, Cotinus americanus, of the southern US [c19 so named because of the similarity between its flower clusters and a cloud of smoke]

smoking gun n a piece of irrefutable incriminating evidence

smoking jacket n a man's comfortable jacket of velvet, etc, closed by a tie belt or fastenings, worn at home [so called because it was formerly worn for smoking]

smoking room or esp Brit **smoke room** n a room, esp in a hotel or club, for those who wish to smoke

smoko or **smokeho** ('sməʊkəʊ) n, pl **-kos** or **-hos** Austral and NZ informal a short break from work for tea, a cigarette, etc [c19 from SMOKE + -O]

smoky ('sməʊkɪ) adj smokier, smokiest 1 emitting, containing, or resembling smoke 2 emitting smoke excessively or in the wrong place: a smoky fireplace 3 of or tinged with the colour smoke: a smoky cat 4 having the flavour of having been cured by smoking 5 made dark, dirty, or hazy by smoke > 'smokily adv > 'smokiness n

Smoky Mountains pl n See Great Smoky Mountains

smoky quartz n another name for cairngorm [so named because of its colour]

smolder ('sməʊldə) vb, n the US spelling of smoulder

Smolensk (Russian smaˈljɛnsk; English 'smɒlɛnsk) n a city in W Russia, on the Dnieper River: a major commercial centre in medieval times; scene of severe fighting (1941 and 1943) in World War II. Pop: 323 000 (2005 est)

smolt (sməʊlt) n a young salmon at the stage when it migrates from fresh water to the sea [c14 Scottish, of uncertain origin; perhaps related to SMELT²]

smooch (smuːtʃ) informal ▷ vb (intr) 1 Also (Austral and NZ): smoodge, smooge (of two people) to kiss and cuddle 2 Brit to dance very slowly and amorously with one's arms around another

person, or (of two people) to dance together in such a way ▷ n 3 the act of smooching 4 Brit a piece of music played for dancing to slowly and amorously [c20 variant of dialect smouch, of imitative origin]

smoodge or **smooge** (smuːdʒ) vb Austral and NZ variants of smooch (sense 1)

smooth (smuːð) adj 1 resting in the same plane; without bends or irregularities 2 silky to the touch: smooth velvet 3 lacking roughness of surface; flat 4 tranquil or unruffled: smooth temper 5 lacking obstructions or difficulties 6 a suave or persuasive, esp as suggestive of insincerity b (in combination): smooth-tongued 7 (of the skin) free from hair 8 of uniform consistency: smooth batter 9 not erratic; free from jolts: smooth driving 10 not harsh or astringent: a smooth wine 11 having all projections worn away: smooth tyres 12 maths (of a curve) differentiable at every point 13 phonetics without preliminary or simultaneous aspiration 14 gentle to the ear; flowing 15 physics (of a plane, surface, etc) regarded as being frictionless ▷ adv 16 in a calm or even manner; smoothly ▷ vb (mainly tr) 17 (also intr; often foll by down) to make or become flattened or without roughness or obstructions 18 (often foll by out or away) to take or rub (away) in order to make smooth: she smoothed out the creases in her dress 19 to make calm; soothe 20 to make easier: smooth his path 21 electrical engineering to remove alternating current ripple from the output of a direct current power supply 22 obsolete to make more polished or refined ▷ n 23 the smooth part of something 24 the act of smoothing 25 tennis, squash, badminton the side of a racket on which the binding strings form a continuous line. Compare rough (sense 27) ▷ See also smooth over [Old English smōth; related to Old Saxon māthmundi gentle-minded, smōthi smooth] > 'smoothable adj > 'smoother n > 'smoothly adv > 'smoothness n

smoothbore ('smuːðˌbɔː) n 1 (modifier) (of a firearm) having an unrifled bore: a smoothbore musket 2 such a firearm > 'smoothˌbored adj

smooth breathing n (in Greek) the sign (ʼ) placed over an initial vowel, indicating that (in ancient Greek) it was not pronounced with an h. Compare rough breathing

smoothen ('smuːðən) vb to make or become smooth

smooth hound n any of several small sharks of the genus Mustelus, esp M. mustelus, a species of North Atlantic coastal regions: family Triakidae. See also dogfish (sense 3) [c17 from HOUND(FISH); so called because it has no dorsal spines]

smoothie or **smoothy** ('smuːðɪ) n, pl smoothies 1 slang, usually derogatory a person, esp a man, who is suave or slick, esp in speech, dress, or manner 2 a smooth, thick drink made with puréed fresh fruit and yogurt, ice cream, or milk

smoothing circuit n electrical engineering a circuit used to remove ripple from the output of a direct current power supply

smoothing iron n a former name for iron (senses 2, 3)

smooth muscle n muscle that is capable of slow rhythmic involuntary contractions: occurs in the walls of the blood vessels, alimentary canal, etc. Compare striated muscle [so called because there is no cross-banding on the muscle]

smooth over vb (tr) to ease or gloss over: to smooth over a situation

smooth snake n any of several slender nonvenomous colubrid snakes of the European genus Coronella, esp C. austriaca, having very smooth scales and a reddish-brown coloration

smooth-spoken adj speaking or spoken in a gently persuasive or competent manner

smooth-tongued adj suave or persuasive in speech

smorgasbord ('smɔːgəsˌbɔːd, 'smɜː-) n a variety of cold or hot savoury dishes, such as pâté, smoked salmon, etc, served in Scandinavia as hors

d'oeuvres or as a buffet meal [Swedish, from smörgås sandwich + bord table]

smørrebrød (Danish 'smœrəˌbrœð) n small open savoury sandwiches, served esp in Denmark as hors d'oeuvres, etc [Danish, from smør butter + brød bread]

smote (sməʊt) vb the past tense of smite

smother ('smʌðə) vb 1 to suffocate or stifle by cutting off or being cut off from the air 2 (tr) to surround (with) or envelop (in): he smothered her with love 3 (tr) to extinguish (a fire) by covering so as to cut it off from the air 4 to be or cause to be suppressed or stifled: smother a giggle 5 (tr) to cook or serve (food) thickly covered with sauce, etc ▷ n 6 anything, such as a cloud of smoke, that stifles 7 a profusion or turmoil 8 archaic a state of smouldering or a smouldering fire [Old English smorian to suffocate; related to Middle Low German smōren] > 'smothery adj

smothered mate n chess checkmate given by a knight when the king is prevented from moving by surrounding men

smoulder or US **smolder** ('sməʊldə) vb (intr) 1 to burn slowly without flame, usually emitting smoke 2 (esp of anger, etc) to exist in a suppressed or half-suppressed state 3 to have strong repressed or half repressed feelings, esp anger ▷ n 4 dense smoke, as from a smouldering fire 5 a smouldering fire [c14 from smolder (n), of obscure origin]

smout or **smowt** (smaʊt) n Scot 1 a variant of smolt 2 a child or undersized person [c16 a variant of SMOLT]

SMP abbreviation for statutory maternity pay

smriti ('smrɪtɪ) n a class of Hindu sacred literature derived from the Vedas, containing social, domestic, and religious teaching [from Sanskrit smrti what is remembered, from samarati he remembers]

SMS abbreviation for short message service: a system used for sending text messages to and from mobile phones

SMTP abbreviation for simple mail transfer protocol: a protocol that enables e-mails to be sent between different servers

smudge (smʌdʒ) vb 1 to smear, blur, or soil or cause to do so 2 (tr) chiefly US and Canadian to fill (an area) with smoke in order to drive insects away or guard against frost ▷ n 3 a smear or dirty mark 4 a blurred form or area: that smudge in the distance is a quarry 5 chiefly US and Canadian a smoky fire for driving insects away or protecting fruit trees or plants from frost [c15 of uncertain origin] > 'smudgeless adj > 'smudgily or 'smudgedly adv

smudging ('smʌdʒɪŋ) n a traditional Native American method of using smoke from burning herbs to purify a space

smudgy (smʌdʒɪ) adj 1 smeared, blurred, or soiled, or likely to become so 2 made deliberately indistinct or cloudy: smudgy colours > 'smudginess n

smug (smʌg) adj smugger, smuggest 1 excessively self-satisfied or complacent 2 archaic trim or neat [c16 of Germanic origin; compare Low German smuck neat] > 'smugly adv > 'smugness n

smuggery ('smʌgərɪ) n the condition or an instance of being smug; smugness

smuggle ('smʌgəl) vb 1 to import or export (prohibited or dutiable goods) secretly 2 (tr; often foll by into or out of) to bring or take secretly, as against the law or rules 3 (tr; foll by away) to conceal; hide [c17 from Low German smukkelen and Dutch smokkelen, perhaps from Old English smūgen to creep; related to Old Norse smjūga] > 'smuggler n > 'smuggling n

smur (smʌr) n, vb Scot a variant of smir

smurfing ('smɜːfɪŋ) n 1 computing the activity of using a specially designed computer program to attack a computer network by flooding it with messages, thereby rendering it inoperable 2 the activity of laundering money by conducting a large number of small transactions through banks and bureaux de change [c20 (sense 1) from smurf, the name of the type of computer program used to carry out such attacks]

smut (smʌt) *n* **1** a small dark smudge or stain, esp one caused by soot **2** a speck of soot or dirt **3** something obscene or indecent **4 a** any of various fungal diseases of flowering plants, esp cereals, in which black sooty masses of spores cover the affected parts **b** any parasitic basidiomycetous fungus of the order *Ustilaginales* that causes such a disease **5** *angling* a minute midge or other insect relished by trout ▷ *vb* **smuts, smutting, smutted 6** to mark or become marked or smudged, as with soot **7** to affect (grain) or (of grain) to be affected with smut **8** (*tr*) to remove smut from (grain) **9** (*tr*) to make obscene **10** (*intr*) to emit soot or smut **11** (*intr*) *angling* (of trout) to feed voraciously on smuts [Old English *smitte*; related to Middle High German *smitze*; associated with SMUDGE, SMUTCH] > 'smutty *adj* > 'smuttily *adv* > 'smuttiness *n*

smutch (smʌtʃ) *vb* **1** (*tr*) to smudge; mark ▷ *n* **2** a mark; smudge **3** soot; dirt [C16 probably from Middle High German *smutzen* to soil; see SMUT] > 'smutchy *adj*

SMV (in Canada) *abbreviation for* Star of Military Valour

Smyrna ('smɜːnə) *n* an ancient city on the W coast of Asia Minor: a major trading centre in the ancient world; a centre of early Christianity. Modern name: Izmir

sn *the internet domain name for* Senegal

Sn *the chemical symbol for* tin [from New Latin *stannum*]

SN *international car registration for* Senegal

snack (snæk) *n* **1** a light quick meal eaten between or in place of main meals **2** a sip or bite **3** *rare* a share **4** *Austral informal* a very easy task ▷ *vb* **5** (*intr*) to eat a snack [C15 probably from Middle Dutch *snacken*, variant of *snappen* to SNAP]

snack bar *n* a place where light meals or snacks can be obtained, often with a self-service system

snackette ('snækɛt) *n* a Caribbean name for **snack bar**

snaffle ('snæf³l) *n* **1** Also called: **snaffle bit** a simple jointed bit for a horse ▷ *vb* (*tr*) **2** *Brit informal* to steal or take for oneself **3** to equip or control with a snaffle [C16 of uncertain origin; compare Old Frisian *snavel* mouth, Old High German *snabul* beak]

snafu (snæˈfuː) *slang chiefly military* ▷ *n* **1** confusion or chaos regarded as the normal state ▷ *adj* **2** (*postpositive*) confused or muddled up, as usual ▷ *vb* **-fues, -fuing, -fued 3** (*tr*) *US and Canadian* to throw into chaos [C20 from *s(ituation) n(ormal): a(ll) f(ucked or) ouled) u(p)*]

snag (snæg) *n* **1** a difficulty or disadvantage: *the snag is that I have nothing suitable to wear* **2** a sharp protuberance, such as a tree stump **3** a small loop or hole in a fabric caused by a sharp object **4** *engineering* a projection that brings to a stop a sliding or rotating component **5** *chiefly US and Canadian* a tree stump in a riverbed that is dangerous to navigation **6** *US and Canadian* a standing dead tree, esp one used as a perch by an eagle **7** (*plural*) *Austral slang* sausages ▷ *vb* **snags, snagging, snagged 8** (*tr*) to hinder or impede **9** (*tr*) to tear or catch (fabric) **10** (*intr*) to develop a snag **11** (*intr*) *chiefly US and Canadian* (of a boat) to strike or be damaged by a snag **12** (*tr*) *chiefly US and Canadian* to clear (a stretch of water) of snags **13** (*tr*) *US* to seize (an opportunity, benefit, etc) [C16 of Scandinavian origin; compare Old Norse *snaghyrndr* sharp-pointed, Norwegian *snage* spike, Icelandic *snagi* peg] > 'snag,like *adj*

snaggletooth ('snæg³l,tuːθ) *n, pl* **-teeth** a tooth that is broken or projecting > 'snaggle,toothed *adj*

snaggy ('snægɪ) *adj* **-gier, -giest** having sharp protuberances

snail (sneɪl) *n* **1** any of numerous terrestrial or freshwater gastropod molluscs with a spirally coiled shell, esp any of the family *Helicidae*, such as *Helix aspersa* (**garden snail**) **2** any other gastropod

with a spirally coiled shell, such as a whelk **3** a slow-moving or lazy person or animal [Old English *snægl*; related to Old Norse *snigill*, Old High German *snecko*] > 'snail-,like *adj*

snail cam *n mechanical engineering* a cam with spiral cross section used for progressive lifting of a lever as the cam revolves

snailfish ('sneɪl,fɪʃ) *n, pl* **-fish** *or* **-fishes** another name for **sea snail**

snail mail *informal* ▷ *n* **1** the conventional postal system, as opposed to electronic mail ▷ *vb* **snail-mail 2** (*tr*) to send by the conventional postal system, rather than by electronic mail [C20 so named because of the relative slowness of the conventional postal system]

snail's pace *n* a very slow or sluggish speed

snake (sneɪk) *n* **1** any reptile of the suborder *Ophidia* (or *Serpentes*), typically having a scaly cylindrical limbless body, fused eyelids, and a jaw modified for swallowing large prey: includes venomous forms such as cobras and rattlesnakes, large nonvenomous constrictors (boas and pythons), and small harmless types such as the grass snake. Related adjs: **colubrine, ophidian 2** Also called: **snake in the grass** a deceitful or treacherous person **3** anything resembling a snake in appearance or action **4** (in the European Union) a former system of managing a group of currencies by allowing the exchange rate of each of them only to fluctuate within narrow limits **5** a tool in the form of a long flexible wire for unblocking drains ▷ *vb* **6** (*intr*) to glide or move like a snake **7** (*tr*) *US* to haul (a heavy object, esp a log) by fastening a rope around one end of it **8** (*tr*) *US* (often foll by *out*) to pull jerkily **9** (*tr*) to move in or follow (a sinuous course) [Old English *snaca*; related to Old Norse *snākr* snake, Old High German *snahhan* to crawl, Norwegian *snōk* snail] > 'snake,like *adj*

snakebird ('sneɪk,bɜːd) *n* another name for **darter** (the bird)

snakebite ('sneɪk,baɪt) *n* **1** a bite inflicted by a snake, esp a venomous one **2** a drink of cider and lager

snake charmer *n* an entertainer, esp in Asia, who charms or appears to charm snakes by playing music and by rhythmic body movements

snake dance *n* **1** a ceremonial dance, performed by the priests of the American Hopi Indians, in which live snakes are held in the mouth **2 a** the swaying movements of snakes responding to a snake charmer **b** a Hindu dance in which performers imitate such snake movements

snake fly *n* any of various neuropterous insects of the family *Raphidiidae*, having an elongated thorax: order *Megaloptera*

snakehead ('sneɪk,hed) *n* a Chinese criminal involved in the illegal transport of Chinese citizens to other parts of the world [C20 origin uncertain]

snake juice *n Austral slang* any strong alcoholic drink, esp when home-made [C19 perhaps so called from its poisonous effects]

snakemouth ('sneɪk,maʊθ) *n* a terrestrial orchid, *Pogonia ophioglossoides*, of E North America, having solitary fragrant pinkish-purple flowers [so called because of the alleged similarity between the shape of the flower and a snake's mouth]

Snake River *n* a river in the northwestern US, rising in NW Wyoming and flowing west through Idaho, turning north as part of the border between Idaho and Oregon, and flowing west to the Columbia River near Pasco, Washington. Length: 1670 km (1038 miles)

snakeroot ('sneɪk,ruːt) *n* **1** any of various North American plants, such as *Aristolochia serpentaria* (**Virginia snakeroot**) and *Eupatorium urticaefolium* (**white snakeroot**), the roots or rhizomes of which have been used as a remedy for snakebite **2** the rhizome or root of any such plant **3** another name for **bistort** (senses 1, 2) ▷ Also called: **snakeweed**

snakes and ladders *n* (*functioning as singular*) a board game in which players move counters along a series of squares according to throws of a dice. A ladder provides a short cut to a square nearer the finish and a snake obliges a player to return to a square nearer the start

snake's head *n* a European fritillary plant, *Fritillaria meleagris*, of damp meadows, having purple-and-white chequered flowers [C19 so called because its buds are claimed to resemble a snake's head]

snakeskin ('sneɪk,skɪn) *n* the skin of a snake, esp when made into a leather valued for handbags, shoes, etc

snaky ('sneɪkɪ) *adj* **snakier, snakiest 1** of or like a snake; sinuous **2** treacherous or insidious **3** infested with snakes **4** *Austral and NZ informal* angry or bad-tempered > 'snakily *adv* > 'snakiness *n*

snap (snæp) *vb* **snaps, snapping, snapped 1** to break or cause to break suddenly, esp with a sharp sound **2** to make or cause to make a sudden sharp cracking sound **3** (*intr*) to give way or collapse suddenly, esp from strain **4** to move, close, etc, or cause to move, close, etc, with a sudden sharp sound **5** to move or cause to move in a sudden or abrupt way **6** (*intr*; often foll by *at* or *up*) to seize something suddenly or quickly **7** (when *intr*, often foll by *at*) to bite at (something) bringing the jaws rapidly together **8** to speak (words) sharply or abruptly **9** (*intr*) (of eyes) to flash or sparkle **10** to take a snapshot of (something) **11** (*intr*) *hunting* to fire a quick shot without taking deliberate aim **12** (*tr*) *American football* to put (the ball) into play by sending it back from the line of scrimmage to a teammate **13 snap one's fingers** *at informal* **a** to dismiss with contempt **b** to defy **14 snap out of it** *informal* to recover quickly, esp from depression, anger, or illness ▷ *n* **15** the act of breaking suddenly or the sound produced by a sudden breakage **16** a sudden sharp sound, esp of bursting, popping, or cracking **17** a catch, clasp, or fastener that operates with a snapping sound **18** a sudden grab or bite **19** the sudden release of something such as elastic thread **20** a brisk movement of the thumb against one or more fingers **21** a thin crisp biscuit: *ginger snaps* **22** *informal* See **snapshot 23** *informal* vigour, liveliness, or energy **24** *informal* a task or job that is easy or profitable to do **25** a short spell or period, esp of cold weather **26** *Brit dialect* food, esp a packed lunch taken to work **27** *Brit* a card game in which the word *snap* is called when two cards of equal value are turned up on the separate piles dealt by each player **28** *American football* the start of each play when the centre passes the ball back from the line of scrimmage to a teammate **29** (*modifier*) done on the spur of the moment, without consideration or warning: *a snap decision* **30** (*modifier*) closed or fastened with a snap ▷ *adv* **31** with a snap ▷ *interj* **32 a** *cards* the word called while playing snap **b** an exclamation used to draw attention to the similarity of two things ▷ See also **snap up** [C15 from Middle Low German or Middle Dutch *snappen* to seize; related to Old Norse *snapa* to snuffle] > 'snapless *adj* > 'snappable *adj*

snapback ('snæp,bæk) *n* a sudden rebound or change in direction

snap bean *n US and Canadian* **1** any of various bean plants that are cultivated in the US for their crisp edible unripe pods **2** the pod of such a plant ▷ See also **string bean** [C19 so called because the pods are broken into pieces for eating]

snapdragon ('snæp,drægən) *n* any of several scrophulariaceous chiefly Old World plants of the genus *Antirrhinum*, esp *A. majus*, of the Mediterranean region, having spikes of showy white, yellow, pink, red, or purplish flowers. Also called: **antirrhinum** [C16 so named because the flowers, which are claimed to look like a dragon's head, have a "mouth" which snaps shut if squeezed open and then released]

snap fastener *n* another name for **press stud**

snapper ('snæpə) *n, pl* **-per** *or* **-pers** **1** any large sharp-toothed percoid food fish of the family *Lutjanidae* of warm and tropical coastal regions. See also **red snapper** **2** a sparid food fish, *Chrysophrys auratus*, of Australia and New Zealand, that has a pinkish body covered with blue spots **3** another name for the **bluefish** or the **snapping turtle** **4** a person or thing that snaps **5** *informal* a person who take snapshots; photographer **6** *Irish informal* a baby ▷ Also called (for senses 1, 2): **schnapper**

snapper up *n* a person who snaps up bargains, etc

snapping beetle *n* another name for the **click beetle**

snapping turtle *n* any large aggressive North American river turtle of the family *Chelydridae*, esp *Chelydra serpentina* (**common snapping turtle**), having powerful hooked jaws and a rough shell. Also called: **snapper**

snappy ('snæpɪ) *adj* **-pier, -piest** **1** Also: **snappish** apt to speak sharply or irritably **2** Also: **snappish** apt to snap or bite **3** crackling in sound: *a snappy fire* **4** brisk, sharp, or chilly: *a snappy pace; snappy weather* **5** smart and fashionable: *a snappy dresser* **6** **make it snappy** *slang* be quick! hurry up! > '**snappily** *adv* > '**snappiness** *n*

snap ring *n mountaineering* another name for **karabiner**

snap roll *n* a manoeuvre in which an aircraft makes a fast roll

snapshot ('snæpˌʃɒt) *n* an informal photograph taken with a simple camera. Often shortened to: **snap**

snap shot *n sport* a sudden, fast shot at goal

snaptin ('snæptɪn) *n Northern English dialect* a container for food [from SNAP (sense 26) + TIN]

snap up *vb (tr, adverb)* **1** to avail oneself of eagerly and quickly: *she snapped up the bargains* **2** to interrupt abruptly

snare[1] (snɛə) *n* **1** a device for trapping birds or small animals, esp a flexible loop that is drawn tight around the prey **2** a surgical instrument for removing certain tumours, consisting of a wire loop that may be drawn tight around their base to sever or uproot them **3** anything that traps or entangles someone or something unawares ▷ *vb (tr)* **4** to catch (birds or small animals) with a snare **5** to catch or trap in or as if in a snare; capture by trickery [Old English *sneare*, from Old Norse *snara*; related to Old High German *snaraha*] > '**snareless** *adj* > '**snarer** *n*

snare[2] (snɛə) *n music* a set of gut strings wound with wire fitted against the lower drumhead of a snare drum. They produce a rattling sound when the drum is beaten. See **snare drum** [C17 from Middle Dutch *snaer* or Middle Low German *snare* string; related to Gothic *snōrjō* basket]

snare drum *n music* a cylindrical drum with two drumheads, the upper of which is struck and the lower fitted with a snare. See **snare**[2]

snarf (snɑːf) *vb informal* to eat or drink greedily

snarky ('snɒːkɪ) *adj informal* unpleasant and scornful [C20 from SARCASTIC + NASTY]

snarl[1] (snɑːl) *vb* **1** *(intr)* (of an animal) to growl viciously, baring the teeth **2** to speak or express (something) viciously or angrily ▷ *n* **3** a vicious growl, utterance, or facial expression **4** the act of snarling [C16 of Germanic origin; compare Middle Low German *snarren*, Middle Dutch *snarren* to drone] > '**snarling** *adj* > '**snarlingly** *adv* > '**snarly** *adj*

snarl[2] (snɑːl) *n* **1** a tangled mass of thread, hair, etc **2** a complicated or confused state or situation **3** a knot in wood ▷ *vb* **4** (often foll by *up*) to be, become, or make tangled or complicated **5** *(tr;* often foll by *up)* to confuse mentally **6** *(tr)* to flute or emboss (metal) by hammering on a tool held against the under surface [C14 of Scandinavian origin; compare Old Swedish *snarel* noose, Old Norse *snara* SNARE[1]] > '**snarler** *n* > '**snarly** *adj*

snarler ('snɑːlə) *n* **1** an animal or a person that snarls **2** *NZ informal* a sausage

snarl-up *n informal, chiefly Brit* a confusion, obstruction, or tangle, esp a traffic jam

snatch (snætʃ) *vb* **1** *(tr)* to seize or grasp (something) suddenly or peremptorily: *he snatched the chocolate out of my hand* **2** *(intr;* usually foll by *at)* to seize or attempt to seize suddenly **3** *(tr)* to take hurriedly: *to snatch some sleep* **4** *(tr)* to remove suddenly: *she snatched her hand away* **5** *(tr)* to gain, win, or rescue, esp narrowly: *they snatched victory in the closing seconds* **6** *(tr)* (in weightlifting) to lift (a weight) with a snatch **7** **snatch one's time** *Austral informal* to leave a job, taking whatever pay is due ▷ *n* **8** an act of snatching **9** a fragment or small incomplete part: *snatches of conversation* **10** a brief spell: *snatches of time off* **11** *weightlifting* a lift in which the weight is raised in one quick motion from the floor to an overhead position **12** *slang, chiefly US* an act of kidnapping **13** *Brit slang* a robbery: *a diamond snatch* [C13 *snacchen*; related to Middle Dutch *snakken* to gasp, Old Norse *snaka* to sniff around] > '**snatcher** *n*

snatch block *n nautical* a block that can be opened so that a rope can be inserted from the side, without threading it through from the end [C17 so called because the rope can be inserted quickly: figuratively, the block snatches it. See SNATCH]

snatch squad *n Brit* a squad of soldiers or police trained to deal with demonstrations by picking out and arresting the alleged ringleaders

snatchy ('snætʃɪ) *adj* **snatchier, snatchiest** disconnected or spasmodic > '**snatchily** *adv*

snath (snæθ) *or* **snathe** (sneɪð) *n* the handle of a scythe [C16 variant of earlier *snead*, from Old English *snǣd*, of obscure origin]

snazzy ('snæzɪ) *adj* **-zier, -ziest** *informal* (esp of clothes) stylishly and often flashily attractive [C20 perhaps from SN(APPY + J)AZZY] > '**snazzily** *adv* > '**snazziness** *n*

SNCC (snɪk) *n* (in the US) ▷ *acronym for* Student Nonviolent Coordinating Committee (1960–69) and Student National Coordinating Committee (from 1969); a civil-rights organization

SNCF *abbreviation for* Société Nationale des Chemins de Fer: the French national railway system

sneak (sniːk) *vb* **1** *(intr;* often foll by *along, off, in,* etc) to move furtively **2** *(intr)* to behave in a cowardly or underhand manner **3** *(tr)* to bring, take, or put stealthily **4** *(intr) informal, chiefly Brit* to tell tales (esp in schools) **5** *(tr) informal* to steal **6** *(intr;* foll by *off, out, away,* etc) *informal* to leave unobtrusively ▷ *n* **7** a person who acts in an underhand or cowardly manner, esp as an informer **8** **a** a stealthy act or movement **b** *(as modifier)*: *a sneak attack* **9** *Brit informal* an unobtrusive departure [Old English *snīcan* to creep; from Old Norse *snīkja* to hanker after] > '**sneaky** *adj* > '**sneakily** *adv* > '**sneakiness** *n*

sneakers ('sniːkəz) *pl n chiefly US and Canadian* canvas shoes with rubber soles worn for sports or informally

sneaking ('sniːkɪŋ) *adj* **1** acting in a furtive or cowardly way **2** secret: *a sneaking desire to marry a millionaire* **3** slight but nagging (esp in the phrase **a sneaking suspicion**) > '**sneakingly** *adv* > '**sneakingness** *n*

sneak preview *n* a screening of a film at an unexpected time to test audience reaction before its release

sneak thief *n* a person who steals paltry articles from premises, which he enters through open doors, windows, etc

sneck[1] (snɛk) *n* **1** a small squared stone used in a rubble wall to fill spaces between stones of different height **2** *dialect, chiefly Scot and northern English* the latch or catch of a door or gate ▷ *vb* **3** *dialect, chiefly Scot and northern English* to fasten (a latch) [C15 *snekk*, of uncertain origin]

sneck[2] (snɛk) *n, vb* a Scot word for **snick**

sneer (snɪə) *n* **1** a facial expression of scorn or contempt, typically with the upper lip curled **2** a scornful or contemptuous remark or utterance ▷ *vb* **3** *(intr)* to assume a facial expression of scorn or contempt **4** to say or utter (something) in a scornful or contemptuous manner [C16 perhaps from Low Dutch; compare North Frisian *sneere* contempt] > '**sneerer** *n* > '**sneerful** *adj* > '**sneering** *adj, n* > '**sneeringly** *adv*

sneery ('snɪərɪ) *adj* **sneerier, sneeriest** contemptuous or scornful; inclined to be dismissive

sneeze (sniːz) *vb* **1** *(intr)* to expel air and nasal secretions from the nose involuntarily, esp as the result of irritation of the nasal mucous membrane ▷ *n* **2** the act or sound of sneezing [Old English *fnēosan* (unattested); related to Old Norse *fnȳsa*, Middle High German *fnūsen*, Greek *pneuma* breath] > '**sneezeless** *adj* > '**sneezer** *n* > '**sneezy** *adj*

sneeze at *vb (intr, prep.;* usually with a negative) *informal* to dismiss lightly: *his offer is not to be sneezed at*

sneezewood ('sniːzˌwʊd) *n* **1** a tree, *Ptaeroxylon utile*, native to southern Africa: family *Ptaeroxylaceae* **2** the tough wood of this tree, which has a peppery smell and is used for bridges, piers, fencing posts, etc

sneezewort ('sniːzˌwɜːt) *n* a Eurasian plant, *Achillea ptarmica*, having daisy-like flowers and long grey-green leaves, which cause sneezing when powdered: family *Asteraceae* (composites). See also **yarrow**

snell (snɛl) *adj Scot* biting; bitter; sharp [Old English *snel* quick, active]

Snell's law (snɛlz) *n physics* the principle that the ratio of the sine of the angle of incidence to the sine of the angle of refraction is constant when a light ray passes from one medium to another [C17 named after Willebrord *Snell* (1591–1626), Dutch physicist]

S

SNG *abbreviation for* synthetic natural gas

snib (snɪb) *Scot* ▷ *n* **1** the bolt or fastening of a door, window, etc ▷ *vb* **snibs, snibbing, snibbed** *(tr)* **2** to bolt or fasten (a door) [C19 of uncertain origin; perhaps from Low German *snibbe* beak]

snick (snɪk) *n* **1** a small cut; notch **2** a knot in thread, etc **3** *cricket* **a** a glancing blow off the edge of the bat **b** the ball so hit ▷ *vb (tr)* **4** to cut a small corner or notch in (material, etc) **5** *cricket* to hit (the ball) with a snick [C18 probably of Scandinavian origin; compare Old Norse *snikka* to whittle, Swedish *snicka*]

snicker ('snɪkə) *n* **1** *chiefly US and Canadian* a sly or disrespectful laugh, esp one partly stifled ▷ *vb* **2** to utter such a laugh. equivalent term (in Britain and certain other countries): **snigger** **3** (of a horse) to whinny [C17 probably of imitative origin]

snickersnee ('snɪkəˌsniː) *n archaic* **1** a knife for cutting or thrusting **2** a fight with knives [C17 *stick or snee*, from Dutch *steken* to STICK[2] + *snijen* to cut]

snicket ('snɪkɪt) *n Northern English dialect* a passageway between walls or fences [of obscure origin]

Snickometer (snɪ'kɒmɪtə) *n trademark cricket* a device, which uses sound waves recorded by the stump microphone, employed by TV commentators to determine whether or not a batsman has made contact with the ball [C20 from SNICK (sense 5) + -METER]

snide[1] (snaɪd) *adj* **1** Also: **snidey** ('snaɪdɪ) (of a remark, etc) maliciously derogatory; supercilious **2** counterfeit; sham ▷ *n* **3** *slang* sham jewellery [C19 of unknown origin] > '**snidely** *adv* > '**snideness** *n*

snide[2] (snaɪd) *vb (tr; usually passive* and foll by *with*) *Northern English dialect* to fill or load

sniff (snɪf) *vb* **1** to inhale through the nose, usually in short rapid audible inspirations, as for the purpose of identifying a scent, for clearing a congested nasal passage, or for taking a drug or intoxicating fumes **2** (when *intr*, often foll by *at*) to perceive or attempt to perceive (a smell) by inhaling through the nose ▷ *n* **3** the act or sound of sniffing **4** a smell perceived by sniffing, esp a faint scent [C14 probably related to *snivelen* to SNIVEL] > ˈ**sniffing** *n, adj*

sniff at *vb* (*intr, preposition*) to express contempt or dislike for

sniffer (ˈsnɪfə) *n* **1** a device for detecting hidden substances such as drugs or explosives, esp by their odour **2** a computer program or device used to monitor, detect, and capture data on a network

sniffer dog *n* a police dog trained to detect drugs or explosives by smell

sniffle (ˈsnɪfᵊl) *vb* **1** (*intr*) to breathe audibly through the nose, as when the nasal passages are congested ▷ *n* **2** the act, sound, or an instance of sniffling > ˈ**sniffler** *n* > ˈ**sniffly** *adj*

sniffles (ˈsnɪfᵊlz) *or* **snuffles** *pl n informal* **1** the a cold in the head **2** the sniffling that sometimes accompanies weeping or prolonged crying

sniff out *vb* (*tr, adverb*) to detect through shrewdness or instinct

sniffy (ˈsnɪfɪ) *adj* **-fier, -fiest** *informal* contemptuous or disdainful > ˈ**sniffily** *adv* > ˈ**sniffiness** *n*

snifter (ˈsnɪftə) *n* **1** a pear-shaped glass with a short stem and a bowl that narrows towards the top so that the aroma of brandy or a liqueur is retained **2** *informal* a small quantity of alcoholic drink [C19 perhaps from dialect *snifter* to sniff, perhaps of Scandinavian origin; compare Danish *snifta* (obsolete) to sniff]

snig (snɪɡ) *vb* (*tr*) **snigs, snigging, snigged** *Austral and NZ* to drag (a log) along the ground by a chain fastened at one end [from English dialect]

snigger (ˈsnɪɡə) *or US and Canadian* **snicker** (ˈsnɪkə) *n* **1** a sly or disrespectful laugh, esp one partly stifled ▷ *vb* (*intr*) **2** to utter such a laugh [C18 variant of SNICKER]

snigging chain *n Austral and NZ* a chain attached to a log when being hauled out of the bush

sniggle (ˈsnɪɡᵊl) *vb* **1** (*intr*) to fish for eels by dangling or thrusting a baited hook into cavities **2** (*tr*) to catch (eels) by sniggling ▷ *n* **3** the baited hook used for sniggling eels [C17 from C15 *snig* young eel] > ˈ**sniggler** *n*

snip (snɪp) *vb* **snips, snipping, snipped** **1** to cut or clip with a small quick stroke or a succession of small quick strokes, esp with scissors or shears ▷ *n* **2** the act of snipping **3** the sound of scissors or shears closing **4** Also called: **snipping** a small piece of anything, esp one that has been snipped off **5** a small cut made by snipping **6** *chiefly Brit* an informal word for **bargain** **7** *informal* something easily done; cinch **8** *US and Canadian informal* a small or insignificant person or thing, esp an irritating or insolent one ▷ *interj* **9** (*often reiterated*) a representation of the sound of scissors or shears closing ▷ See also **snips** [C16 from Low German, Dutch *snippen*; related to Middle High German *snipfen* to snap the fingers]

snipe (snaɪp) *n, pl* **snipe** *or* **snipes** **1** any of various birds of the genus *Gallinago* (or *Capella*) and related genera, such as *G. gallinago* (**common** or **Wilson's snipe**), of marshes and river banks, having a long straight bill: family *Scolopacidae* (sandpipers, etc), order *Charadriiformes* **2** any of various similar related birds, such as certain sandpipers and curlews **3** a shot, esp a gunshot, fired from a place of concealment ▷ *vb* **4** (when *intr*, often foll by *at*) to attack (a person or persons) with a rifle from a place of concealment **5** (*intr*; often foll by *at*) to criticize adversely a person or persons from a position of security **6** (*intr*) to hunt or shoot snipe [C14 from Old Norse *snīpa*; related to Old High German *snepfa* Middle Dutch *snippe*] > ˈ**snipeˌlike** *adj*

snipefish (ˈsnaɪpˌfɪʃ) *n, pl* **-fish** *or* **-fishes** any teleost fish of the family *Macrorhamphosidae*, of tropical and temperate seas, having a deep body, long snout, and a single long dorsal fin: order *Solenichthyes* (sea horses, etc). Also called: **bellows fish** [C17 so called because of the resemblance between its snout and a snipe's bill]

snipe fly *n* any of various predatory dipterous flies of the family *Leptidae* (or *Rhagionidae*), such as *Rhagio scolopacea* of Europe, having an elongated body and long legs [named after the snipe because its flight resembles that of the bird]

sniper (ˈsnaɪpə) *n* a rifleman who fires from a concealed place, esp a military marksman who fires from cover usually at long ranges at individual enemy soldiers

sniperscope (ˈsnaɪpəˌskəʊp) *n* a telescope with crosshairs mounted on a sniper's rifle

snippet (ˈsnɪpɪt) *n* a small scrap or fragment [C17 from SNIP + -ET] > ˈ**snippetiness** *n* > ˈ**snippety** *adj*

snippy (ˈsnɪpɪ) *adj* **-pier, -piest** **1** scrappy; fragmentary **2** *informal* fault-finding **3** *dialect* mean; stingy > ˈ**snippily** *adv* > ˈ**snippiness** *n*

snips (snɪps) *pl n* a small pair of shears used for cutting sheet metal. Also called: **tin snips**

snit (snɪt) *n US and Austral* a fit of temper [C20 of unknown origin]

snitch (snɪtʃ) *slang* ▷ *vb* **1** (*tr*) to steal; take, esp in an underhand way **2** (*intr*) to act as an informer ▷ *n* **3** an informer; telltale **4** the nose [C17 of unknown origin] > ˈ**snitcher** *n*

snitch line *n Canadian* a direct telephone or other communications link set up to allow people to report neighbours, colleagues, etc suspected of wrongdoing

snitchy (ˈsnɪtʃɪ) *adj* **snitchier, snitchiest** *NZ informal* bad-tempered or irritable

snivel (ˈsnɪvᵊl) *vb* **-els, -elling, -elled** *or US* **-els, -eling, -eled** **1** (*intr*) to sniffle as a sign of distress, esp contemptibly **2** to utter (something) tearfully; whine **3** (*intr*) to have a runny nose ▷ *n* **4** an instance of snivelling [C14 *snivelen*; related to Old English *snyflung* mucus, Dutch *snuffelen* to smell out, Old Norse *snoppa* snout] > ˈ**sniveller** *n* > ˈ**snivelling** *adj, n* > ˈ**snivelly** *adj*

snob (snɒb) *n* **1** **a** a person who strives to associate with those of higher social status and who behaves condescendingly to others. Compare **inverted snob** **b** (*as modifier*): *snob appeal* **2** a person having similar pretensions with regard to his tastes, etc: *an intellectual snob* [C18 (in the sense: shoemaker; hence, C19 a person who flatters those of higher station, etc): of unknown origin] > ˈ**snobbery** *n* > ˈ**snobbish** *adj* > ˈ**snobbishly** *adv* > ˈ**snobbishness** *or* ˈ**snobbism** *n* > ˈ**snobby** *adj*

SNOBOL (ˈsnəʊbɒl) *n* String Oriented Symbolic Language: a computer-programming language for handling strings of symbols

Sno-Cat (ˈsnəʊˌkæt) *n trademark* a type of snowmobile

snoek (snʊk) *n* a South African edible marine fish, *Thyrsites atun* [Afrikaans, from Dutch *snoek* pike]

snoep (snʊp) *adj South African informal* mean or tight-fisted [Afrikaans *snoep* greedy]

snog (snɒɡ) *Brit slang* ▷ *vb* **snogs, snogging, snogged** **1** to kiss and cuddle (someone) ▷ *n* **2** the act of kissing and cuddling [of obscure origin]

snood (snuːd) *n* **1** a pouchlike hat, often of net, loosely holding a woman's hair at the back **2** a headband, esp one formerly worn by young unmarried women in Scotland **3** *vet science* a long fleshy appendage that hangs over the upper beak of turkeys ▷ *vb* **4** (*tr*) to hold (the hair) in a snood [Old English *snōd*; of obscure origin]

snook[1] (snuːk) *n, pl* **snook** *or* **snooks** **1** any of several large game fishes of the genus *Centropomus*, esp *C. undecimalis* of tropical American marine and fresh waters: family *Centropomidae* (robalos) **2** *Austral* the sea pike *Australuzza novaehollandiae* [C17 from Dutch *snoek* pike]

snook[2] (snuːk) *n Brit* **cock a snook** **a** to make a rude gesture by putting one thumb to the nose with the fingers of the hand outstretched **b** to show contempt by being insulting or offensive [C19 of obscure origin]

snooker (ˈsnuːkə) *n* **1** a game played on a billiard table with 15 red balls, six balls of other colours, and a white cue ball. The object is to pot the balls in a certain order **2** a shot in which the cue ball is left in a position such that another ball blocks the object ball. The opponent is then usually forced to play the cue ball off a cushion ▷ *vb* (*tr*) **3** to leave (an opponent) in an unfavourable position by playing a snooker **4** to place (someone) in a difficult situation **5** (*often passive*) to thwart; defeat [C19 of unknown origin]

snoop (snuːp) *informal* ▷ *vb* **1** (*intr*; often foll by *about* or *around*) to pry into the private business of others ▷ *n* **2** a person who pries into the business of others **3** an act or instance of snooping [C19 from Dutch *snoepen* to eat furtively] > ˈ**snoopy** *adj*

snooper (ˈsnuːpə) *n* **1** a person who snoops **2** *Brit informal* a person employed by the DSS to spy on claimants to make sure that they are not infringing the conditions of their eligibility for benefit

snooperscope (ˈsnuːpəˌskəʊp) *n military, US* an instrument that enables the user to see objects in the dark by illuminating the object with infrared radiation and converting the reflected radiation to a visual image

snoot (snuːt) *n* **1** *slang* the nose **2** *photog, films, television* a cone-shaped fitment on a studio light to control the scene area illuminated [C20 variant of SNOUT]

snooty (ˈsnuːtɪ) *adj* **snootier, snootiest** *informal* **1** aloof or supercilious **2** snobbish or exclusive: *a snooty restaurant* > ˈ**snootily** *adv* > ˈ**snootiness** *n*

snooze (snuːz) *informal* ▷ *vb* **1** (*intr*) to take a brief light sleep ▷ *n* **2** a nap [C18 of unknown origin] > ˈ**snoozer** *n* > ˈ**snoozy** *adj*

snore (snɔː) *vb* **1** (*intr*) to breathe through the mouth and nose while asleep with snorting sounds caused by vibrations of the soft palate ▷ *n* **2** the act or sound of snoring [C14 of imitative origin; related to Middle Low German, Middle Dutch *snorken*; see SNORT] > ˈ**snorer** *n*

snorkel (ˈsnɔːkᵊl) *n* **1** a device allowing a swimmer to breathe while face down on the surface of the water, consisting of a bent tube fitting into the mouth and projecting above the surface **2** (on a submarine) a retractable vertical device containing air-intake and exhaust pipes for the engines and general ventilation: its use permits extended periods of submergence at periscope depth **3** *military* a similar device on a tank, enabling it to cross shallow water obstacles **4** a type of parka or anorak with a hood that projects beyond the face ▷ *vb* **-kels, -kelling, -kelled** *or US* **-kels, -keling, -keled** **5** (*intr*) to swim with a snorkel [C20 from German *Schnorchel*; related to German *schnarchen* to SNORE]

snort (snɔːt) *vb* **1** (*intr*) to exhale forcibly through the nostrils, making a characteristic noise **2** (*intr*) (of a person) to express contempt or annoyance by such an exhalation **3** (*tr*) to utter in a contemptuous or annoyed manner **4** *slang* to inhale (a powdered drug) through the nostrils ▷ *n* **5** a forcible exhalation of air through the nostrils, esp (of persons) as a noise of contempt or annoyance **6** *slang* an instance of snorting a drug **7** Also called: **snorter** *slang* a short drink, esp an alcoholic one **8** *slang* the snorkel on a submarine [C14 *snorten*; probably related to *snoren* to SNORE] > ˈ**snorting** *n, adj* > ˈ**snortingly** *adv*

snorter (ˈsnɔːtə) *n* **1** a person or animal that snorts **2** *Brit slang* something outstandingly impressive or difficult **3** *Brit slang* something or someone ridiculous

snot (snɒt) *n* (*usually considered vulgar*) **1** nasal mucus or discharge **2** *slang* a contemptible person [Old English *gesnot*; related to Old High German *snuzza*, Norwegian, Danish *snot*, German *schneuzen* to blow one's nose]

snotter (ˈsnɒtər) *Scot* ▷ *n* **1** (*often plural*) another word for **snot** ▷ *vb* (*intr*) **2** to breathe through obstructed nostrils **3** to snivel or blubber

snotty (ˈsnɒtɪ) (*considered vulgar*) *adj* **-tier, -tiest** **1**

dirty with nasal discharge **2** slang contemptible; nasty **3** snobbish; conceited ▷ n, pl **-ties 4** a slang word for **midshipman**. > '**snottily** adv > '**snottiness** n

snout (snaʊt) n **1** the part of the head of a vertebrate, esp a mammal, consisting of the nose, jaws, and surrounding region, esp when elongated **2** the corresponding part of the head of such insects as weevils **3** anything projecting like a snout, such as a nozzle or the lower end of a glacier **4** slang a person's nose **5** Also called: **snout moth** a brownish noctuid moth, *Hypena proboscidalis*, that frequents nettles: named from the palps that project prominently from the head at rest **6** Brit slang a cigarette or tobacco **7** slang an informer [c13 of Germanic origin; compare Old Norse *snyta*, Middle Low German, Middle Dutch *snūte*] > '**snouted** adj > '**snoutless** adj > '**snout,like** adj

snout beetle n another name for **weevil** (sense 1) [c19 so named because of its long proboscis]

snow (snəʊ) n **1** precipitation from clouds in the form of flakes of ice crystals formed in the upper atmosphere. Related adj: **niveous 2** a layer of snowflakes on the ground **3** a fall of such precipitation **4** anything resembling snow in whiteness, softness, etc **5** the random pattern of white spots on a television or radar screen, produced by noise in the receiver and occurring when the signal is weak or absent **6** slang cocaine **7** See **carbon dioxide snow** ▷ vb **8** (intr; with *it* as subject) to be the case that snow is falling **9** (tr; usually passive, foll by *over, under, in*, or *up*) to cover or confine with a heavy fall of snow **10** (often with *it* as subject) to fall or cause to fall as or like snow **11** (tr) US and Canadian slang to deceive or overwhelm with elaborate often insincere talk. See **snow job 12 be snowed under** to be overwhelmed, esp with paperwork [Old English *snāw*; related to Old Norse *snjōr*, Gothic *snaiws*, Old High German *snēo*, Greek *nipha*] > '**snowless** adj > '**snow,like** adj

snow apple n a Canadian variety of eating apple

snowball ('snəʊ,bɔːl) n **1** snow pressed into a ball for throwing, as in play **2** a drink made of advocaat and lemonade **3** slang a mixture of heroin and cocaine **4** a dance started by one couple who separate and choose different partners. The process continues until all present are dancing ▷ vb **5** (intr) to increase rapidly in size, importance, etc: *their woes have snowballed since last year* **6** (tr) to throw snowballs at

snowball tree n any of several caprifoliaceous shrubs of the genus *Viburnum*, esp *V. opulus* var. *roseum*, a sterile cultivated variety with spherical clusters of white or pinkish flowers

snowberry ('snəʊbərɪ, -brɪ) n, pl **-ries 1** any of several caprifoliaceous shrubs of the genus *Symphoricarpos*, esp *S. albus*, cultivated for their small pink flowers and white berries **2** Also called: **waxberry** any of the berries of such a plant **3** any of various other white-berried plants

snowbird ('snəʊ,bɜːd) n **1** another name for the **snow bunting 2** US slang a person addicted to cocaine, or sometimes heroin

snowblading ('snəʊ,bleɪdɪŋ) n the activity or sport of skiing with short skis (**snowblades** and no poles > '**snow,blader** n

snow-blind adj temporarily unable to see or having impaired vision because of the intense reflection of sunlight from snow > **snow blindness** n

snowblink ('snəʊ,blɪŋk) n a whitish glare in the sky reflected from snow. Compare **iceblink**

snowblower ('snəʊ,bləʊə) n a snow-clearing machine that sucks in snow and blows it away to one side

snowboard ('snəʊ,bɔːd) n a shaped board, resembling a skateboard without wheels, on which a person can stand to slide across snow [c20 on the model of SURFBOARD]

snowboarding ('snəʊ,bɔːdɪŋ) n the sport of moving across snow on a snowboard

snowbound ('snəʊ,baʊnd) adj confined to one place by heavy falls or drifts of snow; snowed-in

snow bridge n mountaineering a mass of snow bridging a crevasse, sometimes affording a risky way across it

snow bunting n a bunting, *Plectrophenax nivalis*, of northern and arctic regions, having a white plumage with dark markings on the wings, back, and tail

snowcap ('snəʊ,kæp) n a cap of snow, as on the top of a mountain

snowcapped ('snəʊ,kæpt) adj (of a mountain, hill, etc) having a cap of snow on the top

snow cave n mountaineering another name for **snow hole**

snow day n US a day on which heavy snow makes it impossible for children to attend school

snow devil n Canadian a whirling column of snow

Snowdon ('snəʊdən) n a mountain in NW Wales, in Gwynedd: the highest peak in Wales. Height: 1085 m (3560 ft)

Snowdonia (snəʊ'dəʊnɪə) n **1** a massif in NW Wales, in Gwynedd, the highest peak being Snowdon **2** a national park in NW Wales, in Gwynedd and Conwy: includes the Snowdonia massif in the north. Area: 2189 sq km (845 sq miles)

snowdrift ('snəʊ,drɪft) n a bank of deep snow driven together by the wind

snowdrop ('snəʊ,drɒp) n any of several amaryllidaceous plants of the Eurasian genus *Galanthus*, esp *G. nivalis*, having drooping white bell-shaped flowers that bloom in early spring

snowdrop tree n another name for **silver bell**

snowed (snəʊd) adj slang under the influence of narcotic drugs

snowfall ('snəʊ,fɔːl) n **1** a fall of snow **2** meteorol the amount of snow received in a specified place and time

snow fence n a portable wire-and-paling fence erected to prevent snow from drifting across a road, drive, ski run, etc

snowfield ('snəʊ,fiːld) n a large area of permanent snow

snowflake ('snəʊ,fleɪk) n **1** one of the mass of small thin delicate arrangements of ice crystals that fall as snow **2** any of various European amaryllidaceous plants of the genus *Leucojum*, such as *L. vernum* (**spring snowflake**), that have white nodding bell-shaped flowers

snow goose n a North American goose, *Anser hyperboreus* (or *Chen hyperborea* or *A. caerulescens*), having a white plumage with black wing tips

snow grass n **1** Austral any of various grey-green grasses of the genus *Poa*, of SE Australian mountain regions **2** NZ any of various hill and high-country grasses of the genus *Danthonia*

snow gum n any of various eucalyptus trees that grow at high altitude, esp *Eucalyptus pauciflora* [so called because it grows at high altitude]

snow hole n mountaineering a shelter dug in deep usually drifted snow. Also called: **snow cave**

snow-in-summer n another name for **dusty miller** (sense 1) [c19 so called from the appearance of its flowers]

snow job n slang, chiefly US and Canadian an instance of deceiving or overwhelming someone with elaborate often insincere talk

snow leopard n a large feline mammal, *Panthera uncia*, of mountainous regions of central Asia, closely related to the leopard but having a long pale brown coat marked with black rosettes. Also called: **ounce**

snow line n the altitudinal or latitudinal limit of permanent snow

snowman ('snəʊ,mæn) n, pl **-men** a figure resembling a man, made of packed snow

snowmobile ('snəʊmə,biːl) n **a** a small open motor vehicle for travelling on snow, steered by two skis at the front and driven by a caterpillar track underneath **b** Also called: **bombardier** a larger closed motor vehicle with two skis at the front and a track at each side

snow-on-the-mountain n a North American euphorbiaceous plant, *Euphorbia marginata*, having white-edged leaves and showy white bracts surrounding small flowers

snow plant n a saprophytic plant, *Sarcodes sanguinea*, of mountain pine forests of W North America, having a fleshy scaly reddish stalk, no leaves, and pendulous scarlet flowers that are often produced before the snow melts: family *Monotropaceae*

snowplough ('snəʊ,plaʊ) n **1** an implement or vehicle for clearing away snow **2** skiing a technique of turning the points of the skis inwards to turn or stop

snowshed ('snəʊ,ʃed) n a shelter built over an exposed section of railway track to prevent its blockage by snow

snowshoe ('snəʊ,ʃuː) n **1** a device to facilitate walking on snow, esp a racket-shaped frame with a network of thongs stretched across it ▷ vb **-shoes, -shoeing, -shoed 2** (intr) to walk or go using snowshoes > '**snow,shoer** n

snowshoe cat n a breed of cat with soft short hair, blue eyes, an inverted V-shaped marking on the face, and white feet

snowshoe hare or **rabbit** n a N North American hare, *Lepus americanus*, having brown fur in summer, white fur in winter, and heavily furred feet

snowstorm ('snəʊ,stɔːm) n a storm with heavy snow

snowtubing ('snəʊ,tjuːɪŋ) n the sport of moving across snow on a large inflated inner tube

snow tyre n a motor vehicle tyre with deep treads and ridges to give improved grip on snow and ice

snow-white adj **1** white as snow **2** pure as white snow

snowy ('snəʊɪ) adj **snowier, snowiest 1** covered with or abounding in snow: *snowy hills* **2** characterized by snow: *snowy weather* **3** resembling snow in whiteness, purity, etc > '**snowily** adv > '**snowiness** n

S

snowy egret n a small American egret, *Egretta thula*, having a white plumage, yellow legs, and a black bill

Snowy Mountain adj of or relating to the Snowy Mountains of Australia or their inhabitants

Snowy Mountains pl n a mountain range in SE Australia, part of the Australian Alps: famous hydroelectric scheme. Also called (Austral informal): **the Snowy, the Snowies**

snowy owl n a large owl, *Nyctea scandiaca*, of tundra regions, having a white plumage flecked with brown

Snowy River n a river in SE Australia, rising in SE New South Wales: waters diverted through a system of dams and tunnels across the watershed into the Murray and Murrumbidgee Rivers for hydroelectric power and to provide water for irrigation. Length: 426 km (265 miles)

SNP abbreviation for **Scottish National Party**

Snr or **snr** abbreviation for senior

snub (snʌb) vb **snubs, snubbing, snubbed** (tr) **1** to insult (someone) deliberately **2** to stop or check the motion of (a boat, horse, etc) by taking turns of a rope or cable around a post or other fixed object ▷ n **3** a deliberately insulting act or remark **4** nautical **a** an elastic shock absorber attached to a mooring line **b** (as modifier): *a snub rope* ▷ adj **5** short and blunt. See also **snub-nosed** [c14 from Old Norse *snubba* to scold; related to Norwegian, Swedish dialect *snubba* to cut short, Danish *snubbe*] > '**snubber** n > '**snubby** adj

snub-nosed adj **1** having a short turned-up nose **2** (of a pistol) having an extremely short barrel

snuck (snʌk) vb chiefly US and Canadian not standard a past tense and past participle of **sneak**

snuff¹ (snʌf) vb **1** (tr) to inhale through the nose **2** (when intr, often foll by *at*) (esp of an animal) to examine by sniffing ▷ n **3** an act or the sound of snuffing [C16 probably from Middle Dutch *snuffen* to snuffle, ultimately of imitative origin] > 'snuffer *n*

snuff[2] (snʌf) *n* **1** finely powdered tobacco for sniffing up the nostrils or less commonly for chewing **2** a small amount of this **3** any powdered substance, esp one for sniffing up the nostrils **4 up to snuff** *informal* **a** in good health or in good condition **b** *chiefly Brit* not easily deceived ▷ *vb* **5** (*intr*) to use or inhale snuff [C17 from Dutch *snuf*, shortened from *snuftabale*, literally: tobacco for snuffing; see SNUFF[1]]

snuff[3] (snʌf) *vb* (*tr*) **1** (often foll by *out*) to extinguish (a light from a naked flame, esp a candle) **2** to cut off the charred part of (the wick of a candle, etc) **3** (usually foll by *out*) *informal* to suppress; put an end to **4 snuff it** *Brit informal* to die ▷ *n* **5** the burned portion of the wick of a candle [C14 *snoffe*, of obscure origin]

snuffbox ('snʌf,bɒks) *n* a container, often of elaborate ornamental design, for holding small quantities of snuff

snuff-dipping *n* the practice of absorbing nicotine by holding in one's mouth, between the cheek and the gum, a small amount of tobacco, either loose or enclosed in a sachet

snuffer ('snʌfə) *n* **1** a cone-shaped implement for extinguishing candles **2** (*plural*) an instrument resembling a pair of scissors for trimming the wick or extinguishing the flame of a candle **3** *rare* a person who takes snuff

snuffle ('snʌfᵊl) *vb* **1** (*intr*) to breathe noisily or with difficulty **2** to say or speak in a nasal tone **3** (*intr*) to snivel ▷ *n* **4** an act or the sound of snuffling **5** a nasal tone or voice **6 the snuffles** a condition characterized by snuffling [C16 from Low German or Dutch *snuffelen*; see SNUFF[1], SNIVEL] > 'snuffler *n* > 'snuffly *adj*

snuff movie *or* **film** *n slang* a pornographic film in which an unsuspecting actress or actor is murdered as the climax of the film

snuffy ('snʌfɪ) *adj* **snuffier, snuffiest** **1** of, relating to, or resembling snuff **2** covered with or smelling of snuff **3** unpleasant; disagreeable > 'snuffiness *n*

snug (snʌg) *adj* **snugger, snuggest** **1** comfortably warm and well-protected; cosy: *the children were snug in bed during the blizzard* **2** small but comfortable: *a snug cottage* **3** well-ordered; compact: *a snug boat* **4** sheltered and secure: *a snug anchorage* **5** fitting closely and comfortably **6** offering safe concealment ▷ *n* **7** (in Britain and Ireland) one of the bars in certain pubs, offering intimate seating for only a few persons **8** *engineering* a small peg under the head of a bolt engaging with a slot in the bolted component to prevent the bolt turning when the nut is tightened ▷ *vb* **snugs, snugging, snugged** **9** to make or become comfortable and warm **10** (*tr*) *nautical* to make (a vessel) ready for a storm by lashing down gear [C16 (in the sense: prepared for storms (used of a ship)): related to Old Icelandic *snöggr* short-haired, Swedish *snygg* tidy, Low German *snögger* smart] > 'snugly *adv* > 'snugness *n*

snuggery ('snʌgərɪ) *n, pl* **-geries** **1** a cosy and comfortable place or room **2** another name for **snug** (sense 7)

snuggle ('snʌgᵊl) *vb* **1** (*usually intr*; usually foll by *down, up,* or *together*) to nestle into or draw close to (somebody or something) for warmth or from affection ▷ *n* **2** the act of snuggling [C17 frequentative SNUG (vb)]

snye (snaɪ) *n Canadian* a side channel of a river [from Canadian French *chenail*, from French *chenal* CHANNEL[1]]

so[1] (səʊ) *adv* **1** (foll by an adjective or adverb and a correlative clause often introduced by *that*) to such an extent: *the river is so dirty that it smells* **2** (*used with a negative*; it replaces the first *as* in an equative comparison) to the same extent as: *she is not so old as you* **3** (intensifier): *it's so lovely; I love you so* **4** in the state or manner expressed or implied: *they're happy and will remain so* **5** (*not used with a negative*; foll by an auxiliary verb or *do, have,* or *be* used as main verbs) also; likewise: *I can speak Spanish and so can you* **6** *informal* indeed: used to contradict a negative statement: *You didn't tell the truth. I did so!* **7** *archaic* provided that **8 and so on** *or* **forth** and continuing similarly **9 just so** See **just** (sense 19) **10 or so** approximately: *fifty or so people came to see me* **11 quite so** I agree; exactly **12 so be it** used to express agreement or resignation **13 so much** **a** a certain degree or amount (of) **b** a lot (of): *it's just so much nonsense* **14 so much for** **a** no more can or need be said about **b** used to express contempt for something that has failed: *so much for your bright idea* ▷ *conj* (subordinating; often foll by *that*) **15** in order (that): *to die so that you might live* **16** with the consequence (that): *he was late home, so that there was trouble* **17 so as** (*takes an infinitive*) in order (to): *to slim so as to lose weight* ▷ *sentence connector* **18** in consequence; hence: *she wasn't needed, so she left* **19** used to introduce a sentence expressing resignation, amazement, or sarcasm: *so you're publishing a book!* **20** thereupon; and then: *and so we ended up in France* **21** used to introduce a sentence or clause to add emphasis: *he's crazy, so he is* **22 so what!** *informal* what importance does that have? ▷ *pron* **23** used to substitute for a clause or sentence, which may be understood: *you'll stop because I said so* ▷ *adj* **24** (used with *is, was,* etc) factual; true: *it can't be so* ▷ *interj* **25** an exclamation of agreement, surprise, etc [Old English *swā*; related to Old Norse *svā*, Old High German *sō*, Dutch *zoo*]

> USAGE In formal English, *so* is not used as a conjunction, to indicate either purpose (*he left by a back door so he could avoid photographers*) or result (*the project was abandoned so his services were no longer needed*). In the former case *to* or *in order to* should be used instead, and in the latter case *and so* or *and therefore* would be more acceptable. The expression *so therefore* should not be used

so[2] (səʊ) *n music* a variant spelling of **soh**

so[3] *the internet domain name for* Somalia

SO *international car registration for* Somalia

S.O. *baseball abbreviation for* strike out

soak (səʊk) *vb* **1** to make, become, or be thoroughly wet or saturated, esp by immersion in a liquid **2** (when *intr*, usually foll by *in* or *into*) (of a liquid) to penetrate or permeate **3** (*tr*; usually foll by *in* or *up*) (of a permeable solid) to take in (a liquid) by absorption: *the earth soaks up rainwater* **4** (*tr*; foll by *out* or *out of*) to remove by immersion in a liquid: *she soaked the stains out of the dress* **5** (*tr*) *metallurgy* to heat (a metal) prior to working **6** *informal* to drink excessively or make or become drunk **7** (*tr*) *US and Canadian slang* to overcharge **8** (*tr*) *Brit slang* to put in pawn ▷ *n* **9** the act of immersing in a liquid or the period of immersion **10** the liquid in which something may be soaked, esp a solution containing detergent **11** another name for **soakage** (sense 3) **12** *Brit informal* a heavy rainfall **13** *slang* a person who drinks to excess [Old English *sōcian* to cook; see SUCK] > 'soaker *n* > 'soaking *n, adj*

soakage ('səʊkɪdʒ) *n* **1** the process or a period in which a permeable substance is soaked in a liquid **2** liquid that has been soaked up or has seeped out **3** Also called: **soak** *Austral* a small pool of water or swampy patch

soakaway ('səʊkə,weɪ) *n* a pit filled with rubble, etc, into which rain or waste water drains

so-and-so *n, pl* **so-and-sos** *informal* **1** a person whose name is forgotten or ignored: *so-and-so came to see me* **2** *euphemistic* a person or thing regarded as unpleasant or difficult: *which so-and-so broke my razor?*

soap (səʊp) *n* **1** a cleaning or emulsifying agent made by reacting animal or vegetable fats or oils with potassium or sodium hydroxide. Soaps often contain colouring matter and perfume and act by emulsifying grease and lowering the surface tension of water, so that it more readily penetrates open materials such as textiles. See also **detergent** Related adj: **saponaceous** **2** any metallic salt of a fatty acid, such as palmitic or stearic acid. See also **metallic soap** **3** *slang* flattery or persuasive talk (esp in the phrase **soft soap**) **4** *informal* short for **soap opera** **5** *US and Canadian slang* money, esp for bribery **6 no soap** *US and Canadian slang* not possible or successful ▷ *vb* **7** (*tr*) to apply soap to **8** (*tr*; often foll by *up*) *slang* **a** to flatter or talk persuasively to **b** *US and Canadian* to bribe [Old English *sāpe*; related to Old High German *seipfa*, Old French *savon*, Latin *sāpō*] > 'soapless *adj* > 'soap,like *adj*

soapbark ('səʊp,bɑːk) *n* **1** Also called: **quillai** a W South American rosaceous tree, *Quillaja saponaria*, with undivided evergreen leaves and small white flowers **2** Also called: **quillai bark** the inner bark of this tree, formerly used as soap and as a source of saponin **3** any of several trees or shrubs that have a bark similar to this

soapberry ('səʊp,bɛrɪ) *n, pl* **-ries** **1** any of various chiefly tropical American sapindaceous trees of the genus *Sapindus*, esp *S. saponaria* (or *S. marginatus*), having pulpy fruit containing saponin **2** a related plant, *S. drummondii*, of the southwestern US **3** the fruit of any of these trees ▷ Also called: **chinaberry**

soap boiler *n* a manufacturer of soap > **soap boiling** *n*

soapbox ('səʊp,bɒks) *n* **1** a box or crate for packing soap **2** a crate used as a platform for speech-making **3** a child's homemade racing cart consisting of a wooden box set on a wooden frame with wheels and a steerable front axle

soap bubble *n* **1** a bubble formed from soapy water **2** something that is ephemeral but attractive

soapie *or* **soapy** ('səʊpɪ) *n Austral* an informal word for **soap opera**

soapolallie ('səʊpə,lælɪ) *n Canadian* a drink made by crushing soapberries [from SOAP(BERRY) + *lallie* (compare *-lolly* as in LOBLOLLY)]

soap opera *n* a serialized drama, usually dealing with domestic themes and characterized by sentimentality, broadcast on radio or television [C20 so called because manufacturers of soap were typical sponsors]

soapstone ('səʊp,stəʊn) *n* a massive compact soft variety of talc, used for making tabletops, hearths, ornaments, etc. Also called: **steatite** [C17 so called because it has a greasy feel and was sometimes used as soap]

soapsuds ('səʊp,sʌdz) *pl n* foam or lather made from soap > 'soap,sudsy *adj*

soapwort ('səʊp,wɜːt) *n* a Eurasian caryophyllaceous plant, *Saponaria officinalis*, having rounded clusters of fragrant pink or white flowers and leaves that were formerly used as a soap substitute. Also called: **bouncing Bet**

soapy ('səʊpɪ) *adj* **soapier, soapiest** **1** containing or covered with soap: *soapy water* **2** resembling or characteristic of soap **3** *slang* flattering or persuasive ▷ *n, pl* **-pies** **4** *Austral* a variant of **soapie**. > 'soapily *adv* > 'soapiness *n*

soar (sɔː) *vb* (*intr*) **1** to rise or fly upwards into the air **2** (of a bird, aircraft, etc) to glide while maintaining altitude by the use of ascending air currents **3** to rise or increase in volume, size, etc: *soaring prices* ▷ *n* **4** the act of soaring **5** the altitude attained by soaring [C14 from Old French *essorer*, from Vulgar Latin *exaurāre* (unattested) to expose to the breezes, from Latin EX-[1] + *aura* a breeze] > 'soarer *n*

soaraway ('sɔːrə,weɪ) *adj* exceedingly successful

Soave ('swɑːveɪ) *n* a dry white wine from the Veneto region of NE Italy [C20 named after a town near Verona where it is produced]

Soay ('səʊeɪ) *n* a breed of small horned sheep having long legs and dark brown wool that is plucked rather than shorn; found mainly on St

Kilda where they were probably introduced by the Vikings [named after *Soay*, an island in the St Kilda group, where they were first found]

sob (sɒb) *vb* **sobs, sobbing, sobbed** **1** (*intr*) to weep with convulsive gasps **2** (*tr*) to utter with sobs **3** to cause (oneself) to be in a specified state by sobbing: *to sob oneself to sleep* ▷ *n* **4** a convulsive gasp made in weeping [c12 probably from Low German; compare Dutch *sabben* to suck] > **'sobber** *n*

s.o.b. *slang, chiefly US and Canadian abbreviation for* son of a bitch

soba ('səʊbə) *n* (in Japanese cookery) noodles made from buckwheat flour [Japanese]

sobeit (səʊ'bi:ɪt) *conj archaic* provided that [c16 from so¹ + BE + IT: originally three words]

sober ('səʊbə) *adj* **1** not drunk **2** not given to excessive indulgence in drink or any other activity **3** sedate and rational: *a sober attitude to a problem* **4** (of colours) plain and dull or subdued **5** free from exaggeration or speculation: *he told us the sober truth* ▷ *vb* **6** (usually foll by *up*) to make or become less intoxicated, reckless, etc [c14 *sobre*, from Old French, from Latin *sōbrius*] > **'sobering** *adj* > **'soberingly** *adv* > **'soberly** *adv* > **'soberness** *n*

sobersides ('səʊbə,saɪdz) *n* (*functioning as singular*) a solemn and sedate person > **'sober,sided** *adj*

sobole ('səʊbəʊl) *n, pl* **soboles** (-li:z) a creeping underground stem that produces roots and buds; a sucker [back formation from *soboles* (originally a sing), from Latin *soboles* a shoot, from *subolescere* to grow]

Sobranje (səʊ'brɑ:njɪ) *n* the legislature of Bulgaria

sobriety (səʊ'braɪətɪ) *n* **1** the state or quality of being sober **2** the quality of refraining from excess **3** the quality of being serious or sedate

sobriquet *or* **soubriquet** ('səʊbrɪ,keɪ) *n* a humorous epithet, assumed name, or nickname [c17 from French *soubriquet*, of uncertain origin]

sob sister *n* a journalist, esp a woman, on a newspaper or magazine who writes articles of sentimental appeal

sob story *n* a tale of personal distress intended to arouse sympathy, esp one offered as an excuse or apology

sob stuff *n* material such as films, stories, etc, that play upon the emotions by the overuse of pathos and sentiment

Soc. *or* **soc.** *abbreviation for* **1** socialist **2** society

soca ('səʊkə) *n* a mixture of soul and calypso music typical of the E Caribbean [c20 a blend of *soul* and *calypso*]

SOCA ('səʊkə) *n acronym for* Serious Organized Crime Agency: a British government organization set up in 2004 specifically to combat organized crime

socage ('sɒkɪdʒ) *n* **1** *English legal history* the tenure of land by certain services, esp of an agricultural nature **2** *English law* the freehold tenure of land [c14 from Anglo-French, from *soc* SOKE] > **'socager** *n*

so-called *adj* **a** (*prenominal*) designated or styled by the name or word mentioned, esp (in the speaker's opinion) incorrectly: *a so-called genius* **b** (*also used parenthetically after a noun*): *these experts, so-called, are no help*

soccer ('sɒkə) *n* **a** a game in which two teams of eleven players try to kick or head a ball into their opponent's goal, only the goalkeeper on either side being allowed to touch the ball with his hands and arms except in the case of throw-ins **b** (*as modifier*): *a soccer player* ▷ Also called: **Association Football** [c19 from (*as*)*soc.* + *-er*]

soccer mom *n US* a woman who devotes much of her spare time to her children's activities, typically driving them to and from sports events in which they are involved

Socceroos (,sɒkə'ru:z) *pl n* the Australian men's national soccer team [from SOCCER + (KANGAR)OO]

Soche *or* **So-ch'e** ('səʊ'tʃe) *n* a variant transliteration of the Chinese name for **Shache**

Sochi (*Russian* 'sɔtʃi) *n* a city and resort in SW Russia, in the Krasnodar Territory on the Black Sea: hot mineral springs. Pop: 328 000 (2005 est)

sociable ('səʊʃəbəl) *adj* **1** friendly or companionable **2** (of an occasion) providing the opportunity for friendliness and conviviality ▷ *n* **3** *chiefly US* another name for **social** (sense 9) **4** a type of open carriage with two seats facing each other [c16 via French from Latin *sociābilis*, from *sociāre* to unite, from *socius* an associate] > ,socia'bility *or* 'sociableness *n* > 'sociably *adv*

social ('səʊʃəl) *adj* **1** living or preferring to live in a community rather than alone **2** denoting or relating to human society or any of its subdivisions **3** of, relating to, or characteristic of the experience, behaviour, and interaction of persons forming groups **4** relating to or having the purpose of promoting companionship, communal activities, etc: *a social club* **5** relating to or engaged in social services: *a social worker* **6** relating to or considered appropriate to a certain class of society, esp one thought superior **7** (esp of certain species of insects) living together in organized colonies: *social bees*. Compare **solitary** (sense 6) **8** (of plant species) growing in clumps, usually over a wide area ▷ *n* **9** an informal gathering, esp of an organized group, to promote companionship, communal activity, etc [c16 from Latin *sociālis* companionable, from *socius* a comrade] > **'socially** *adv* > **'socialness** *n*

social accounting *n* the analysis of the economy by sectors leading to the calculation and publication of economic statistics, such as gross national product and national income. Also called: **national accounting**

Social and Liberal Democratic Party *n* (in Britain) a centrist political party formed in 1988 by the merging of the Liberal Party and part of the Social Democratic Party. In 1989 it changed its name to the Liberal Democrats

social anthropology *n* the branch of anthropology that deals with cultural and social phenomena such as kinship systems or beliefs, esp of nonliterate peoples

social assistance *n* a former name for **social security**

social capital *n* the network of social connections that exist between people, and their shared values and norms of behaviour, which enable and encourage mutually advantageous social cooperation

Social Chapter *n* the section of the **Maastricht Treaty** concerning working conditions, consultation of workers, employment rights, and social security. The UK government negotiated an opt-out clause from this section of the treaty in 1993 but adopted it in 1997

Social Charter *n* a declaration of the rights, minimum wages, maximum hours, etc, of workers in the European Union, later adopted in the Social Chapter

social climber *n* a person who seeks advancement to a higher social class, esp by obsequious behaviour. Sometimes shortened to: **climber** > **social climbing** *n*

social contract *or* **compact** *n* (in the theories of Locke, Hobbes, Rousseau, and others) an agreement, entered into by individuals, that results in the formation of the state or of organized society, the prime motive being the desire for protection, which entails the surrender of some or all personal liberties

Social Credit *n* (esp in Canada) a right-wing Populist political party, movement, or doctrine based on the socioeconomic theories of Major C H Douglas > **Social Crediter** *n*

social democracy *n* (*sometimes capital*) the beliefs, principles, practices, or programme of a Social Democratic Party or of social democrats > **social democratic** *adj*

social democrat *n* **1** any socialist who believes in the gradual transformation of capitalism into democratic socialism **2** (*usually capital*) a member of a Social Democratic Party

Social Democratic and Labour Party *n* a Northern Irish political party, which advocates peaceful union with the Republic of Ireland

Social Democratic Party *n* **1** (in Britain 1981–90) a centre political party founded by ex-members of the Labour Party. It formed an alliance with the Liberal Party and continued in a reduced form after many members left to join the Social and Liberal Democratic Party in 1988 **2** one of the two major political parties in Germany (formerly in West Germany), favouring gradual reform **3** any of the parties in many other countries similar to that of Germany

social dumping *n* the practice of allowing employers to lower wages and reduce employees' benefits in order to attract and retain employment and investment

Social Education Centre *n* a daycentre, run by a local authority, for mentally handicapped people and sometimes also for physically handicapped or mentally ill adults

social engineering *n* the manipulation of the social position and function of individuals in order to manage change in a society

social evolution *n sociol* the process of social development from an early simple type of social organization to one that is complex and highly specialized

social exclusion *n sociol* the failure of society to provide certain individuals and groups with those rights and benefits normally available to its members, such as employment, adequate housing, health care, education and training, etc

social fund *n* (in Britain) a social security fund from which loans or payments may be made to people in cases of extreme need

social housing *n* accommodation provided by the state for renting

social inclusion *n sociol* the provision of certain rights to all individuals and groups in society, such as employment, adequate housing, health care, education and training, etc

social inquiry report *n* (in Britain) a report on a person and his or her circumstances, which may be required by a court before sentencing and is made by a probation officer or a social worker from a local authority social services department

social insurance *n* government insurance providing coverage for the unemployed, the injured, the old, etc: usually financed by contributions from employers and employees, as well as general government revenue. See also **social security, national insurance, social assistance**

Social Insurance Number *n Canadian* a nine-digit number used by the federal government to identify a citizen

socialism ('səʊʃə,lɪzəm) *n* **1** an economic theory or system in which the means of production, distribution, and exchange are owned by the community collectively, usually through the state. It is characterized by production for use rather than profit, by equality of individual wealth, by the absence of competitive economic activity, and, usually, by government determination of investment, prices, and production levels. Compare **capitalism** **2** any of various social or political theories or movements in which the common welfare is to be achieved through the establishment of a socialist economic system **3** (in Leninist theory) a transitional stage after the proletarian revolution in the development of a society from capitalism to communism: characterized by the distribution of income according to work rather than need

socialist ('səʊʃəlɪst) *n* **1** a supporter or advocate of socialism or any party promoting socialism (**socialist party**) ▷ *adj* **2** of, characteristic of, implementing, or relating to socialism **3** (*sometimes capital*) of, characteristic of, or relating to socialists or a socialist party

socialistic (ˌsəʊʃəˈlɪstɪk) *adj* resembling or sympathizing with socialism > ˌsocialˈistically *adv*

Socialist International *n* an international association of largely anti-Communist Social Democratic Parties founded in Frankfurt in 1951

Socialist Labor Party *n* (in the US) a minor Marxist party founded in 1876

socialist realism *n* (in Communist countries, esp formerly) the doctrine that art, literature, etc should present an idealized portrayal of reality, which glorifies the achievements of the Communist Party

socialite (ˈsəʊʃəˌlaɪt) *n* a person who is or seeks to be prominent in fashionable society

sociality (ˌsəʊʃɪˈælɪtɪ) *n, pl* **-ties** **1** the tendency of groups and persons to develop social links and live in communities **2** the quality or state of being social

socialization *or* **socialisation** (ˌsəʊʃəlaɪˈzeɪʃən) *n* **1** *psychol* the modification from infancy of an individual's behaviour to conform with the demands of social life **2** the act of socializing or the state of being socialized

socialize *or* **socialise** (ˈsəʊʃəˌlaɪz) *vb* **1** (*intr*) to behave in a friendly or sociable manner **2** (*tr*) to prepare for life in society **3** (*tr*) *chiefly US* to alter or create so as to be in accordance with socialist principles, as by nationalization > ˈsocialˌizable *or* ˈsocialˌisable *adj* > ˈsocialˌizer *or* ˈsocialˌiser *n*

socially excluded *adj* **a** suffering from social exclusion **b** (*as noun*): *the socially excluded*

socially included *adj* **a** benefiting from social inclusion **b** (*as noun*): *the socially included*

social market *n* **a** an economic system in which industry and commerce are run by private enterprise within limits set by the government to ensure equality of opportunity and social and environmental responsibility **b** (*as modifier*): *a social-market economy*

social organization *n* *sociol* the formation of a stable structure of relations inside a group, which provides a basis for order and patterns relationships for new members

social phobia *n* *psychol* a type of anxiety disorder characterized by shyness and heightened self-consciousness in particular social situations

social psychology *n* *psychol* the area of psychology concerned with the interaction between individuals and groups and the effect of society on behaviour

social realism *n* **1** the use of realist art, literature, etc as a medium for social or political comment **2** another name for **socialist realism**

social science *n* **1** the study of society and of the relationship of individual members within society, including economics, history, political science, psychology, anthropology, and sociology **2** any of these subjects studied individually > **social scientist** *n*

social secretary *n* **1** a member of an organization who arranges its social events **2** a personal secretary who deals with private correspondence, etc

social security *n* **1** public provision for the economic, and sometimes social, welfare of the aged, unemployed, etc, esp through pensions and other monetary assistance **2** (*often capitals*) a government programme designed to provide such assistance

social services *pl n* welfare activities organized by the state or a local authority and carried out by trained personnel

social stratification *n* *sociol* the hierarchical structures of class and status in any society

social studies *n* (*functioning as singular*) the study of how people live and organize themselves in society, embracing geography, history, economics, and other subjects

social welfare *n* **1** the various social services provided by a state for the benefit of its citizens **2** (*capitals*) (in New Zealand) a government department concerned with pensions and benefits for the elderly, the sick, etc

social work *n* any of various social services designed to alleviate the conditions of the poor and aged and to increase the welfare of children > **social worker** *n*

societal (səˈsaɪətəl) *adj* of or relating to society, esp human society or social relations > **soˈcietally** *adv*

societal marketing *n* **1** marketing that takes into account society's long-term welfare **2** the marketing of a social or charitable cause, such as an environmental campaign

society (səˈsaɪətɪ) *n, pl* **-ties** **1** the totality of social relationships among organized groups of human beings or animals **2** a system of human organizations generating distinctive cultural patterns and institutions and usually providing protection, security, continuity, and a national identity for its members **3** such a system with reference to its mode of social and economic organization or its dominant class: *middle-class society* **4** those with whom one has companionship **5** an organized group of people associated for some specific purpose or on account of some common interest: *a learned society* **6 a** the privileged class of people in a community, esp as considered superior or fashionable **b** (*as modifier*): *a society woman* **7** the social life and intercourse of such people: *to enter society as a debutante* **8** companionship; the fact or state of being together with someone else: *I enjoy her society* **9** *ecology* a small community of plants within a larger association [C16 via Old French *societé* from Latin *societās*, from *socius* a comrade]

Society Islands *pl n* a group of islands in the S Pacific: administratively part of French Polynesia; consists of the Windward Islands and the Leeward Islands; became a French protectorate in 1843 and a colony in 1880. Pop: 214 445 (2002). Area: 1595 sq km (616 sq miles)

Society of Jesus *n* the religious order of the Jesuits, founded by Ignatius Loyola

Socinian (səʊˈsɪnɪən) *n* **1** a supporter of the beliefs of Faustus and Laelius Socinus, who rejected such traditional Christian doctrines as the divinity of Christ, the Trinity, and original sin, and held that those who follow Christ's virtues will be granted salvation ▷ *adj* **2** of or relating to the Socinians or their beliefs > **Soˈcinianˌism** *n*

socio- *combining form* denoting social or society: *socioeconomic; sociopolitical; sociology*

sociobiology (ˌsəʊsɪəʊbaɪˈɒlədʒɪ) *n* the study of social behaviour in animals and humans, esp in relation to its survival value and evolutionary origins > ˌsociobiˈologist *n*

socioeconomic (ˌsəʊsɪəʊˌiːkəˈnɒmɪk, -ˌɛkə-) *adj* of, relating to, or involving both economic and social factors > ˌsocioˌecoˈnomically *adv*

sociol. *abbreviation for* sociology

sociolinguistics (ˌsəʊsɪəʊlɪŋˈɡwɪstɪks) *n* (*functioning as singular*) the study of language in relation to its social context > ˌsocioˈlinguist *n* > ˌsociolinˈguistic *adj*

sociology (ˌsəʊsɪˈɒlədʒɪ) *n* the study of the development, organization, functioning, and classification of human societies > **sociological** (ˌsəʊsɪəˈlɒdʒɪkəl) *adj* > ˌsocioˈlogically *adv* > ˌsociˈologist *n*

sociometry (ˌsəʊsɪˈɒmɪtrɪ) *n* the study of sociological relationships, esp of preferences, within social groups > **sociometric** (ˌsəʊsɪəˈmɛtrɪk) *adj* > ˌsociˈometrist *n*

sociopath (ˈsəʊsɪəˌpæθ) *n* *psychiatry* another name for **psychopath**. > ˌsocioˈpathic *adj* > **sociopathy** (ˌsəʊsɪˈɒpəθɪ) *n*

sociopolitical (ˌsəʊsɪəʊpəˈlɪtɪkəl) *adj* of, relating to, or involving both political and social factors

sock¹ (sɒk) *n* **1** a cloth covering for the foot, reaching to between the ankle and knee and worn inside a shoe **2** an insole put in a shoe, as to make it fit better **3** a light shoe worn by actors in ancient Greek and Roman comedy, sometimes taken to allude to comic drama in general (as in the phrase **sock and buskin**). See **buskin 4** another name for **windsock 5 pull one's socks up** *Brit informal* to make a determined effort, esp in order to regain control of a situation **6 put a sock in it** *Brit slang* be quiet! ▷ *vb* **7** (*tr*) to provide with socks **8 socked in** *US and Canadian slang* (of an airport) closed by adverse weather conditions [Old English *socc* a light shoe, from Latin *soccus*, from Greek *sukkhos*]

sock² (sɒk) *slang* ▷ *vb* **1** (*usually tr*) to hit with force **2 sock it to** to make a forceful impression on ▷ *n* **3** a forceful blow [C17 of obscure origin]

sock away *vb* (*tr*) *US, Canadian, and NZ informal* to save up

sockdologer *or* **sockdolager** (sɒkˈdɒlədʒə) *n* *slang, chiefly US* **1** a decisive blow or remark **2** an outstanding person or thing [C19 of uncertain origin; perhaps from SOCK² + DOXOLOGY (in the sense: the closing act of a church service) + -ER¹]

socket (ˈsɒkɪt) *n* **1** a device into which an electric plug can be inserted in order to make a connection in a circuit **2** *chiefly Brit* such a device mounted on a wall and connected to the electricity supply. Informal Brit names: **point**, **plug** US and Canadian name: **outlet 3** a part with an opening or hollow into which some other part, such as a pipe, probe, etc, can be fitted **4** a spanner head having a recess suitable to be fitted over the head of a bolt and a keyway into which a wrench can be fitted **5** *anatomy* **a** a bony hollow into which a part or structure fits: *a tooth socket; an eye socket* **b** the receptacle of a ball-and-socket joint ▷ *vb* **6** (*tr*) to furnish with or place into a socket [C13 from Anglo-Norman *soket* a little ploughshare, from *soc*, of Celtic origin; compare Cornish *soch* ploughshare]

socket wrench *n* a wrench having a handle onto which socketed heads of various sizes can be fitted

sockeye (ˈsɒkˌaɪ) *n* a Pacific salmon, *Oncorhynchus nerka*, having red flesh and valued as a food fish. Also called: **red salmon** [by folk etymology from Salishan *sukkegh*]

socle (ˈsəʊkəl) *n* another name for **plinth** (sense 1) [C18 via French from Italian *zoccolo*, from Latin *socculus* a little shoe, from *soccus* a SOCK¹]

socman (ˈsɒkmən, ˈsəʊk-) *or* **sokeman** (ˈsəʊkmən) *n, pl* **-men** *English history* a tenant holding land by socage [C16 from Anglo-Latin *socmannus*; see SOKE]

Socotra, Sokotra *or* **Suqutra** (səˈkəʊtrə) *n* an island in the Indian Ocean, about 240 km (150 miles) off Cape Guardafui, Somalia: administratively part of Yemen. Capital: Tamrida. Area: 3100 sq km (1200 sq miles)

Socratic (sɒˈkrætɪk) *adj* **1** of or relating to Socrates, the Athenian philosopher (?470–399 BC), his methods, etc ▷ *n* **2** a person who follows the teachings of Socrates > **Soˈcratically** *adv* > **Soˈcratiˌcism** *n* > **Socratist** (ˈsɒkrətɪst) *n*

Socratic irony *n* *philosophy* a means by which the pretended ignorance of a skilful questioner leads the person answering to expose his own ignorance

Socratic method *n* *philosophy* the method of instruction by question and answer used by Socrates in order to elicit from his pupils truths he considered to be implicitly known by all rational beings. Compare **maieutic**

Socred (ˈsəʊkrɛd) *Canadian* ▷ *n* **1** a supporter or member of a Social Credit movement or party ▷ *adj* **2** of or relating to Social Credit

sod¹ (sɒd) *n* **1** a piece of grass-covered surface soil held together by the roots of the grass; turf **2** *poetic* the ground ▷ *vb* **sods, sodding, sodded 3** (*tr*) to cover with sods [C15 from Low German; compare Middle Low German, Middle Dutch *sode*; related to Old Frisian *sātha*]

sod² (sɒd) *slang, chiefly Brit* ▷ *n* **1** a person considered to be obnoxious **2** a jocular word for a person: *the poor sod hasn't been out for weeks* **3 sod all**

slang nothing ▷ *interj* **4** **sod it** a strong exclamation of annoyance ▷ See also **sod off** [C19 shortened from SODOMITE] > **'sodding** *adj*

soda ('səʊdə) *n* **1** any of a number of simple inorganic compounds of sodium, such as sodium carbonate (**washing soda**), sodium bicarbonate (**baking soda**), and sodium hydroxide (**caustic soda**) **2** See **soda water 3** *US and Canadian* a fizzy drink **4** the top card of the pack in faro **5** a soda *Austral slang* something easily done; a pushover [C16 from Medieval Latin, from *sodanum* barilla, a plant that was burned to obtain a type of sodium carbonate, perhaps of Arabic origin]

soda ash *n* the anhydrous commercial form of sodium carbonate

soda biscuit *n* a biscuit leavened with sodium bicarbonate

soda bread *n* a type of bread leavened with sodium bicarbonate combined with milk and cream of tartar

soda fountain *n* *US and Canadian* **1** a counter that serves drinks, snacks, etc **2** an apparatus dispensing soda water

soda jerk *n* *US slang* a person who serves at a soda fountain

soda lake *n* a salt lake that has a high content of sodium salts, esp chlorides and sulphates

soda lime *n* a solid mixture of sodium and calcium hydroxides used to absorb carbon dioxide and to dry gases

sodalite ('səʊdə,laɪt) *n* a blue, grey, yellow, or colourless mineral consisting of sodium aluminium silicate and sodium chloride in cubic crystalline form. It occurs in basic igneous rocks. Formula: $Na_4Al_3Si_3O_{12}Cl$ [C19 from SODA + -LITE]

sodality (səʊ'dælɪtɪ) *n*, *pl* **-ties 1** *RC Church* a religious or charitable society **2** fraternity; fellowship [C16 from Latin *sodālitās* fellowship, from *sodālis* a comrade]

sodamide ('səʊdə,maɪd) *n* a white crystalline compound used as a dehydrating agent, as a chemical reagent, and in making sodium cyanide. Formula: $NaNH_2$. Also called: **sodium amide** [C19 from SOD(IUM) + AMIDE]

soda nitre *n* another name for **Chile saltpetre**

soda pop *n* *US informal* a fizzy drink

soda siphon *n* a sealed bottle containing and dispensing soda water. The water is forced up a tube reaching to the bottom of the bottle by the pressure of gas above the water. Also called (esp US): **siphon bottle**

soda water *n* an effervescent beverage made by charging water with carbon dioxide under pressure. Sometimes shortened to: **soda**

sodden ('sɒdᵊn) *adj* **1** completely saturated **2 a** dulled, esp by excessive drinking **b** (*in combination*): *a drink-sodden mind* **3** heavy or doughy, as bread is when improperly cooked ▷ *vb* **4** to make or become sodden [C13 *soden*, past participle of SEETHE] > **'soddenly** *adv* > **'soddenness** *n*

sod disease *n* *vet science* a disease of poultry characterized by blisters and scabs on the feet and legs [from prairie sods that the birds walked on in the US when the disease was first reported in 1920]

sodger ('sɒdʒər) *n*, *vb* a dialect variant of **soldier**

sodic ('səʊdɪk) *adj* **1** of or relating to sodium **2** containing sodium > **so'dicity** *n*

sodium ('səʊdɪəm) *n* **a** a very reactive soft silvery-white element of the alkali metal group occurring principally in common salt, Chile saltpetre, and cryolite. Sodium and potassium ions maintain the essential electrolyte balance in living cells. It is used in the production of chemicals, in metallurgy, and, alloyed with potassium, as a cooling medium in nuclear reactors. Symbol: Na; atomic no.: 11; atomic wt.: 22.989768; valency: 1; relative density: 0.971; melting pt.: 97.81±0.03°C; boiling pt.: 892.9°C **b** (*as modifier*): *sodium light* [C19 New Latin, from SODA + -IUM]

sodium amytal *n* another name for **Amytal**

sodium benzoate *n* a white crystalline soluble compound used as an antibacterial and antifungal agent in preserving food (**E211**), as an antiseptic, and in making dyes and pharmaceuticals. Formula: $(C_6H_5COO)Na$. Also called: **benzoate of soda**

sodium bicarbonate *n* a white crystalline soluble compound usually obtained by the Solvay process and used in effervescent drinks, baking powders, fire extinguishers, and in medicine as an antacid; sodium hydrogen carbonate. Formula: $NaHCO_3$. Also called: **bicarbonate of soda, baking soda**

sodium carbonate *n* a colourless or white odourless soluble crystalline compound existing in several hydrated forms and used in the manufacture of glass, ceramics, soap, and paper and as an industrial and domestic cleansing agent. It is made by the Solvay process and commonly obtained as the decahydrate (**washing soda** or **sal soda**) or a white anhydrous powder (**soda ash**). Formula: Na_2CO_3

sodium chlorate *n* a colourless crystalline soluble compound used as a bleaching agent, weak antiseptic, and weedkiller. Formula: $NaClO_3$

sodium chloride *n* common table salt; a soluble colourless crystalline compound occurring naturally as halite and in sea water; widely used as a seasoning and preservative for food and in the manufacture of chemicals, glass, and soap. Formula: $NaCl$. Also called: **salt**

sodium cyanide *n* a white odourless crystalline soluble poisonous compound with an odour of hydrogen cyanide when damp. It is used for extracting gold and silver from their ores and for case-hardening steel. Formula: $NaCN$

sodium dichromate *n* a soluble crystalline solid compound, usually obtained as red or orange crystals and used as an oxidizing agent, corrosion inhibitor, and mordant. Formula $Na_2Cr_2O_7$. Also called (not in technical usage): **sodium bichromate**

sodium fluoroacetate (,flʊərəʊ'æsɪ,teɪt) *n* a white crystalline odourless poisonous compound, used as a rodenticide. Formula: $(CH_2FCOO)Na$

sodium glutamate ('glu:tə,meɪt) *n* another name for **monosodium glutamate**

sodium hydroxide *n* a white deliquescent strongly alkaline solid used in the manufacture of rayon, paper, aluminium, soap, and sodium compounds. Formula: $NaOH$. Also called: **caustic soda** See also **lye**

sodium hyposulphite *n* another name (not in technical usage) for **sodium thiosulphate**

sodium lamp *n* another name for **sodium-vapour lamp**

sodium nitrate *n* a white crystalline soluble solid compound occurring naturally as Chile saltpetre and caliche and used in matches, explosives, and rocket propellants, as a fertilizer, and as a curing salt for preserving food such as bacon, ham, and cheese (**E251**). Formula: $NaNO_3$

Sodium Pentothal *n* *trademark* another name for **thiopental sodium**

sodium perborate *n* a white odourless crystalline compound used as an antiseptic and deodorant. Formula: $NaBO_3.4H_2O$

sodium peroxide *n* a yellowish-white odourless soluble powder formed when sodium reacts with an excess of oxygen: used as an oxidizing agent in chemical preparations, a bleaching agent, an antiseptic, and in removing carbon dioxide from air in submarines, etc Formula: Na_2O_2

sodium phosphate *n* any sodium salt of any phosphoric acid, esp one of three salts of orthophosphoric acid having formulas NaH_2PO_4 (**monosodium dihydrogen orthophosphate**), Na_2HPO_4 (**disodium monohydrogen orthophosphate**), and Na_3PO_4 (**trisodium orthophosphate**)

sodium propionate *n* a transparent crystalline soluble substance used as a medical fungicide and to prevent the growth of moulds, esp to retard spoilage in packed foods. Formula: $Na(C_2H_5COO)$

sodium silicate *n* **1** Also called: **soluble glass** a substance having the general formula, $Na_2O.xSiO_2$, where *x* varies between 3 and 5, existing as an amorphous powder or present in a usually viscous aqueous solution. See **water glass** (sense 1) **2** any sodium salt of orthosilicic acid or metasilicic acid

sodium sulphate *n* a solid white substance that occurs naturally as thenardite and is usually used as the white anhydrous compound (**salt cake**) or the white crystalline decahydrate (**Glauber's salt**) in making glass, detergents, and pulp. Formula: Na_2SO_4

sodium thiosulphate *n* a white soluble substance used, in the pentahydrate form, in photography as a fixer to dissolve unchanged silver halides and also to remove excess chlorine from chlorinated water. Formula: $Na_2S_2O_3$. Also called (not in technical usage): **sodium hyposulphite, hypo**

sodium-vapour lamp *n* a type of electric lamp consisting of a glass tube containing neon and sodium vapour at low pressure through which an electric current is passed to give an orange light. They are used in street lighting

sod off *vb* (*intr, adverb; usually imperative*) *slang*, *chiefly Brit* to go away; depart

USAGE This phrase was formerly considered to be taboo, and it was labelled as such in previous editions of *Collins English Dictionary*. However, it has now become acceptable in speech, although some older or more conservative people may object to its use

Sodom ('sɒdəm) *n* **1** *Old Testament* a city destroyed by God for its wickedness that, with Gomorrah, traditionally typifies depravity (Genesis 19:24) **2** this city as representing homosexuality **3** any place notorious for depravity

sodomite ('sɒdə,maɪt) *n* a person who practises sodomy

sodomize or **sodomise** ('sɒdə,maɪz) *vb* (*tr*) to be the active partner in anal intercourse

sodomy ('sɒdəmɪ) *n* anal intercourse committed by a man with another man or a woman. Compare **buggery** [C13 via Old French *sodomie* from Latin (Vulgate) *Sodoma* Sodom]

Sod's law (sɒdz) *n* *informal* a humorous or facetious precept stating that if something can go wrong or turn out inconveniently it will. Also called: **Murphy's Law**

SOE (in New Zealand) *abbreviation for* State Owned Enterprise

Soemba ('su:mbə) *n* a variant spelling of **Sumba**

Soembawa (su:m'bɑ:wə) *n* a variant spelling of **Sumbawa**

Soenda Islands ('su:ndə) *pl n* a variant spelling of **Sunda Islands**

Soenda Strait *n* a variant spelling of **Sunda Strait**

Soerabaja (,sʊərə'baɪə) *n* a variant spelling of **Surabaya**

soever (səʊ'ɛvə) *adv* in any way at all: used to emphasize or make less precise a word or phrase, usually in combination with *what, where, when, how*, etc, or else separated by intervening words. Compare **whatsoever**

sofa ('səʊfə) *n* an upholstered seat with back and arms for two or more people [C17 (in the sense: dais upholstered as a seat): from Arabic *suffah*]

sofa bed *n* a sofa that can be converted into a bed

sofar ('səʊfɑ:) *n* a system for determining a position at sea, esp that of survivors of a disaster, by exploding a charge underwater at that point. The times taken for the shock waves to travel through the water to three widely separated shore stations are used to calculate their position [C20 from so(und) f(ixing) a(nd) r(anging)]

soffit ('sɒfɪt) *n* **1** the underside of a part of a building or a structural component, such as an arch, beam, stair, etc **2** Also called: **crown, vertex**

S

the upper inner surface of a drain or sewer. Compare **invert** (sense 6) [c17 via French from Italian *soffitto*, from Latin *suffixus* something fixed underneath, from *suffigere*, from *sub-* under + *figere* to fasten]

Sofia ('səʊfɪə) *n* the capital of Bulgaria, in the west: colonized by the Romans in 29 AD; became capital of Bulgaria in 1879; university (1880). Pop: 1 045 000 (2005 est). Ancient name: **Serdica** Bulgarian name: **Sofiya** ('sɒfɪˌja)

S. of Sol. *Bible abbreviation for* Song of Solomon

soft (sɒft) *adj* **1** easy to dent, work, or cut without shattering; malleable **2** not hard; giving little or no resistance to pressure or weight **3** fine, light, smooth, or fluffy to the touch **4** gentle; tranquil **5** (of music, sounds, etc) low and pleasing **6** (of light, colour, etc) not excessively bright or harsh **7** (of a breeze, climate, etc) temperate, mild, or pleasant **8** *dialect* drizzly or rainy: *a soft day; the weather has turned soft* **9** slightly blurred; not sharply outlined: *soft focus* **10** (of a diet) consisting of easily digestible foods **11** kind or lenient, often excessively so **12** easy to influence or impose upon **13** prepared to compromise; not doctrinaire: *the soft left* **14** *informal* feeble or silly; simple (often in the phrase **soft in the head**) **15** unable to endure hardship, esp through too much pampering **16** physically out of condition; flabby: *soft muscles* **17** loving; tender: *soft words* **18** *informal* requiring little exertion; easy: *a soft job* **19** *chem* (of water) relatively free of mineral salts and therefore easily able to make soap lather **20** (of a drug such as cannabis) nonaddictive or only mildly addictive. Compare **hard** (sense 19) **21** (of news coverage) concentrating on trivial stories or those with human interest **22** *phonetics* **a** an older word for **lenis** **b** (not in technical usage) denoting the consonants *c* and *g* in English when they are pronounced as palatal or alveolar fricatives or affricates (s, dʒ, ʃ, ð, tʃ) before *e* and *i*, rather than as velar stops (k, g) **c** (in the Slavonic languages) palatalized before a front vowel or a special character (**soft sign**) written as ь **23 a** unprotected against attack: *a soft target* **b** *military* unarmoured, esp as applied to a truck by comparison with a tank **24** *finance, chiefly US* (of prices, a market, etc) unstable and tending to decline **25** (of a currency) in relatively little demand, esp because of a weak balance of payments situation **26** (of radiation, such as X-rays and ultraviolet radiation) having low energy and not capable of deep penetration of materials **27** *physics* (of valves or tubes) only partially evacuated **28** related to the performance of non-specific, undefinable tasks: *soft skills such as customer services and office support* **29 soft on** *or* **about a** gentle, sympathetic, or lenient towards **b** feeling affection or infatuation for ▷ *adv* **30** in a soft manner: *to speak soft* ▷ *n* **31** a soft object, part, or piece **32** *informal* See **softie** ▷ *interj archaic* **33** quiet! **34** wait! [Old English *sōfte*; related to Old Saxon *sāfti*, Old High German *semfti* gentle] ▷ '**softly** *adv*

softa ('sɒftə) *n* a Muslim student of divinity and jurisprudence, esp in Turkey [c17 from Turkish, from Persian *sōkhtah* aflame (with love of learning)]

softball ('sɒftˌbɔːl) *n* **1** a variation of baseball using a larger softer ball, pitched underhand **2** the ball used **3** *cookery* the stage in the boiling of a sugar syrup at which it may be rubbed into balls after dipping in cold water

soft-boiled *adj* **1** (of an egg) boiled for a short time so that the yolk is still soft **2** *informal* softhearted

soft-centred *adj* (of a chocolate or boiled sweet) having a centre consisting of cream, jelly, etc

soft chancre *n pathol* a venereal ulcer caused by an infection with the bacillus *Haemophilus ducreyi* that is not syphilitic. Also called: **chancroid**

soft clam *n* another name for the **soft-shell clam**

soft coal *n* another name for **bituminous coal**

soft-coated wheaten terrier *n* a strongly-built medium-sized variety of terrier with a soft, wavy or curly, wheat-coloured coat

soft commodities *pl n* nonmetal commodities such as cocoa, sugar, and grains, bought and sold on a futures market. Also called: **softs**

soft-core *adj* (of pornography) suggestive and titillating through not being totally explicit or detailed

soft-cover *adj* a less common word for **paperback**

soft drink *n* a nonalcoholic drink, usually cold

soften ('sɒfᵊn) *vb* **1** to make or become soft or softer **2** to make or become gentler **3** (*intr*) *commerce* **a** (of demand, a market, etc) to weaken **b** (of a price) to fall

softener ('sɒfᵊnə) *n* **1** a substance added to another substance to increase its softness, pliability, or plasticity **2** a substance, such as a zeolite, for softening water

softening of the brain *n* an abnormal softening of the tissues of the cerebrum characterized by various degrees of mental impairment

soften up *vb* (*adverb*) **1** to make or become soft **2** (*tr*) to weaken (an enemy's defences) by shelling, bombing, etc **3** (*tr*) to weaken the resistance of (a person) by persuasive talk, advances, etc

soft-finned *adj* (of certain teleost fishes) having fins that are supported by flexible cartilaginous rays. See also **malacopterygian** Compare **spiny-finned**

soft-focus lens *n photog* a lens designed to produce an image that is uniformly very slightly out of focus: typically used for portrait work

soft fruit *n Brit* any of various types of small edible stoneless fruit, such as strawberries, raspberries, and currants, borne mainly on low-growing plants or bushes

soft furnishings *pl n Brit* curtains, hangings, rugs, etc

soft goods *pl n* textile fabrics and related merchandise

soft-headed *adj informal* feeble-minded; stupid; simple ▷ ˌsoft-'**headedness** *n*

softhearted (ˌsɒft'hɑːtɪd) *adj* easily moved to pity ▷ ˌsoft'**heartedly** *adv* ▷ ˌsoft'**heartedness** *n*

soft hyphen *n* a hyphen, used in word processing to divide a word, which prints only when it appears at the end of a line. Also called: optional hyphen

softie *or* **softy** ('sɒftɪ) *n, pl* **softies** *informal* a person who is sentimental, weakly foolish, or lacking in physical endurance

soft iron *n* **a** iron that has a low carbon content and is easily magnetized and demagnetized with a small hysteresis loss **b** (as modifier): *a soft-iron core*

soft landing *n* **1** a landing by a spacecraft on the moon or a planet at a sufficiently low velocity for the equipment or occupants to remain unharmed **2** a decrease in demand that does not result in a country's economy falling into recession ▷ Compare **hard landing**

soft lens *n* a flexible hydrogel lens worn on the surface of the eye to correct defects of vision. Compare **hard lens, gas-permeable lens**

soft line *n* a moderate flexible attitude or policy ▷ ˌsoft-'**liner** *n*

soft loan *n* a loan on which interest is not charged, such as a loan made to an undeveloped country

softly-softly *adj* gradual, cautious, and discreet

soft money *n politics* (in the US) money that can be spent by a political party on grass-roots organization, recruitment, advertising, etc; it must be deposited in a party's non-federal (state-level) bank accounts, and must not be used in connection with presidential or congressional elections. Compare **hard money**

softness ('sɒftnɪs) *n* **1** the quality or an instance of being soft **2** *metallurgy* the tendency of a metal to distort easily. Compare **brittleness** (sense 2), **toughness** (sense 2)

soft option *n* in a number of choices, the one considered to be easy or the easiest to do, involving the least difficulty or exertion

soft palate *n* the posterior fleshy portion of the roof of the mouth. It forms a movable muscular flap that seals off the nasopharynx during swallowing and speech

soft paste *n* **a** artificial porcelain made from clay, bone ash, etc **b** (as modifier): *softpaste porcelain* [c19 from PASTE[1] (in the sense: the mixture from which porcelain is made); so called because of its consistency]

soft-pedal *vb* **-als, -alling, -alled** *or US* **-als, -aling, -aled** (*tr*) **1** to mute the tone of (a piano) by depressing the soft pedal **2** *informal* to make (something, esp something unpleasant) less obvious by deliberately failing to emphasize or allude to it ▷ *n* **soft pedal** **3** a foot-operated lever on a piano, the left one of two, that either moves the whole action closer to the strings so that the hammers strike with less force or causes fewer of the strings to sound. Compare **sustaining pedal** See **piano**[1]

soft porn *n informal* soft-core pornography

soft release *n* a means of gradually accustoming wild animals to a new environment before releasing them into it

soft rot *n* any of various bacterial or fungal plant diseases characterized by watery disintegration of fruits, roots, etc

softs (sɒfts) *pl n* another name for **soft commodities**

soft science *n* a science, such as sociology or anthropology, that deals with humans as its principle subject matter, and is therefore not generally considered to be based on rigorous experimentation

soft sell *n* a method of selling based on indirect suggestion or inducement. Compare **hard sell**

soft-shell clam *n* any of several marine clams of the genus *Mya*, esp *M. arenaria*, an edible species of coastal regions of the US and Europe, having a thin brittle shell. Sometimes shortened to: **soft-shell** Compare **quahog**

soft-shell crab *n* a crab, esp of the edible species *Cancer pagurus*, that has recently moulted and has not yet formed its new shell. Compare **hard-shell crab**

soft-shelled turtle *n* any freshwater turtle of the family *Trionychidae*, having a flattened soft shell consisting of bony plates covered by a leathery skin

soft-shoe *n* (*modifier*) relating to a type of tap dancing performed wearing soft-soled shoes: *the soft-shoe shuffle*

soft shoulder *or* **verge** *n* a soft edge along the side of a road that is unsuitable for vehicles to drive on

soft skills *pl n* desirable qualities for certain forms of employment that do not depend on acquired knowledge: they include common sense, the ability to deal with people, and a positive flexible attitude

soft soap *n* **1** *med* another name for **green soap** **2** *informal* flattering, persuasive, or cajoling talk ▷ *vb* **soft-soap** **3** *informal* to use such talk on (a person)

soft-spoken *adj* **1** speaking or said with a soft gentle voice **2** able to persuade or impress by glibness of tongue

soft spot *n* a sentimental fondness (esp in the phrase **have a soft spot for**)

soft tissue *n* the soft parts of the human body as distinct from bone and cartilage

soft top *n* a convertible car with a roof made of fabric rather than metal

soft touch *n informal* **a** person easily persuaded or imposed on, esp to lend money

soft tree fern *n* an Australian tree fern, *Dicksonia antarctica*, with a thick trunk and large spreading green fronds. Also called: Man fern

software ('sɒftˌwɛə) *n* **1** *computing* the programs that can be used with a particular computer system. Compare **hardware** (sense 2) **2** video cassettes and discs for use with a particular video system

software house *n* a commercial organization that specializes in the production of computer software packages

soft wheat *n* a type of wheat with soft kernels and a high starch content

softwood ('sɒft,wʊd) *n* **1** the open-grained wood of any of numerous coniferous trees, such as pine and cedar, as distinguished from that of a dicotyledonous tree **2** any tree yielding this wood ▷ Compare **hardwood**

SOGAT ('sɒʊɡæt) *n* (formerly, in Britain) *acronym for* Society of Graphical and Allied Trades

Sogdian ('sɒɡdɪən) *n* **1** a member of the people who lived in Sogdiana **2** the language of this people, now almost extinct, belonging to the East Iranian branch of the Indo-European family ▷ *adj* **3** of or relating to Sogdiana, its people, or their language

Sogdiana (,sɒɡdɪ'ɑːnə) *n* a region of ancient central Asia. Its chief city was Samarkand

soggy ('sɒɡɪ) *adj* -gier, -giest **1** soaked with liquid **2** (of bread, pastry, etc) moist and heavy **3** *informal* lacking in spirit or positiveness [c18 probably from dialect *sog* marsh, of obscure origin] > '**soggily** *adv* > '**sogginess** *n*

soh *or* **so** (sɒʊ) *n music* (in tonic sol-fa) the name used for the fifth note or dominant of any scale [c13 see GAMUT]

SOHF *text messaging abbreviation for* sense of humour failure

soho (sɒʊ'hɒʊ) *interj* **1** *hunting* an exclamation announcing the sighting of a hare **2** an exclamation announcing the discovery of something unexpected [an Anglo-French hunting call, probably of exclamatory origin]

Soho ('sɒʊhɒʊ) *n* a district of central London, in the City of Westminster: a foreign quarter since the late 17th century, now chiefly known for restaurants, nightclubs, striptease clubs, etc

soi-disant French (swadizɑ̃) *adj* so-called; self-styled [literally: calling oneself]

soigné *or feminine* **soignée** ('swɑ:njeɪ; *French* swaɲe) *adj* well-groomed; elegant [French, from *soigner* to take good care of, of Germanic origin; compare Old Saxon *sunnea* care]

soil¹ (sɒɪl) *n* **1** the top layer of the land surface of the earth that is composed of disintegrated rock particles, humus, water, and air. See **zonal soil, azonal soil, intrazonal soil, horizon** (senses 4, 5) Related adj: **telluric 2** a type of this material having specific characteristics: *loamy soil* **3** land, country, or region: *one's native soil* **4** the soil life and work on a farm; land: *he belonged to the soil, as his forefathers had* **5** any place or thing encouraging growth or development [c14 from Anglo-Norman, from Latin *solium* a seat, but confused with Latin *solum* the ground]

soil² (sɒɪl) *vb* **1** to make or become dirty or stained **2** (*tr*) to pollute with sin or disgrace; sully; defile: *he soiled the family honour by his cowardice* ▷ *n* **3** the state or result of soiling **4** refuse, manure, or excrement [c13 from Old French *soillier* to defile, from *soil* pigsty, probably from Latin *sūs* a swine]

soil³ (sɒɪl) *vb* (*tr*) to feed (livestock) freshly cut green fodder either to fatten or purge them [c17 perhaps from obsolete vb (c16) *soil* to manure, from SOIL² (n)]

soilage ('sɒɪlɪdʒ) *n* green fodder, esp when freshly cut and fed to livestock in a confined area

soil bank *n* (in the US) a federal programme by which farmers are paid to divert land to soil-enriching crops

soil conservation *n* the preservation of soil against deterioration or erosion, and the maintenance of the fertilizing elements for crop production

soil creep *n* the gradual downhill movement, under the force of gravity, of soil and loose rock material on a slope

soil mechanics *n* (functioning as singular) the study of the physical properties of soil, esp those properties that affect its ability to bear weight, such as water content, density, strength, etc

soil pipe *n* a pipe that conveys sewage or waste water from a toilet, etc, to a soil drain or sewer

soilure ('sɒɪljə) *n archaic* **1** the act of soiling or the state of being soiled **2** a stain or blot [c13 from Old French *soilleure*, from *soillier* to SOIL²]

soiree ('swɑːreɪ) *n* an evening party or other gathering given usually at a private house, esp where guests are invited to listen to, play, or dance to music [c19 from French, from Old French *soir* evening, from Latin *sērum* a late time, from *sērus* late]

Soissons (*French* swasɔ̃) *n* a city in N France, on the Aisne River: has Roman remains and an 11th-century abbey. Pop: 29 453 (1999)

soixante-neuf French (swasɑ̃tnœf) *n* a sexual activity in which two people simultaneously stimulate each other's genitalia with their mouths. Also called: **sixty-nine** [literally: sixty-nine, from the position adopted by the participants]

sojourn ('sɒdʒɜːn, 'sʌdʒ-) *n* **1** a temporary stay ▷ *vb* **2** (*intr*) to stay or reside temporarily [c13 from Old French *sojorner*, from Vulgar Latin *subdiurnāre* (unattested) to spend a day, from Latin *sub-* during + Late Latin *diurnum* day] > '**sojourner** *n*

soke (sɒʊk) *n English legal history* **1** the right to hold a local court **2** the territory under the jurisdiction of a particular court [c14 from Medieval Latin *sōca*, from Old English *sōcn* a seeking; see SEEK]

sokeman ('sɒʊkmən) *n, pl* -men (in the Danelaw) a freeman enjoying extensive rights, esp over his land

Sokoto ('sɒʊkə,tɒʊ) *n* **1** a state of NW Nigeria. Capital: Sokoto. Pop: 4 911 118 (1995 est). Area: 65 735 sq km (25 380 sq miles) **2** a town in NW Nigeria, capital of Sokoto state: capital of the Fulah Empire in the 19th century; Muslim place of pilgrimage. Pop: 444 000 (2005 est)

Sokotra (sə'kɒʊtrə) *n* a variant spelling of **Socotra**

sol¹ (sɒl) *n music* another name for **soh** [c14 see GAMUT]

sol² (sɒl) *n* **1** short for **new sol 2** a former French copper or silver coin, usually worth 12 deniers [c16 from Old French, from Late Latin SOLIDUS]

sol³ (sɒl) *n* a colloid that has a continuous liquid phase, esp one in which a solid is suspended in a liquid [c20 shortened from HYDROSOL]

sol⁴ (sɒl) *n astronomy* a solar day as measured on the planet Mars, equal to 24.65 hours [c20 from Latin *sōl* sun]

Sol (sɒl) *n* **1** the Roman god personifying the sun. Greek counterpart: **Helios 2** a poetic word for the **sun**

Sol. abbreviation for **1** Also: **Solr** solicitor **2** *Bible* Solomon

sola Latin ('sɒʊlə) *adj* the feminine form of **solus**

solace ('sɒlɪs) *n* **1** comfort in misery, disappointment, etc **2** something that gives comfort or consolation ▷ *vb* (*tr*) **3** to give comfort or cheer to (a person) in time of sorrow, distress, etc **4** to alleviate (sorrow, misery, etc) [c13 from Old French *solas*, from Latin *sōlātium* comfort, from *sōlārī* to console] > '**solacer** *n*

solan *or* **solan goose** ('sɒʊlən) *n* an archaic name for the **gannet** [c15 *soland*, of Scandinavian origin; compare Old Norse *sūla* gannet, *ŏnd* duck]

solanaceous (,sɒlə'neɪʃəs) *adj* of, relating to, or belonging to the *Solanaceae*, a family of plants having typically tubular flowers with reflexed petals, protruding anthers, and often poisonous or narcotic properties: includes the potato, tobacco, henbane, mandrake, and several nightshades [c19 from New Latin *Sōlānāceae*, from Latin *sōlānum* nightshade]

solander (sə'lændə) *n* a box for botanical specimens, maps, etc, made in the form of a book, the front cover being the lid [c18 named after D D *Solander* (1736–82), Swedish botanist]

solanine ('sɒʊlə,naɪn) *n* a poisonous alkaloid found in various solanaceous plants, including potatoes which have gone green through exposure to light [c19 from SOLAN(UM) + -INE²]

solanum (sɒʊ'leɪnəm) *n* any tree, shrub, or herbaceous plant of the mainly tropical solanaceous genus *Solanum*: includes the potato, aubergine, and certain nightshades [c16 from Latin: nightshade]

solar ('sɒʊlə) *adj* **1** of or relating to the sun: *solar eclipse* **2** operating by or utilizing the energy of the sun: *solar cell* **3** *astronomy* determined from the motion of the earth relative to the sun: *solar year* **4** *astrology* subject to the influence of the sun [c15 from Latin *sōlāris*, from *sōl* the sun]

solar apex *n* another name for **apex** (sense 4)

solar cell *n* a photovoltaic cell that produces electricity from the sun's rays, used esp in spacecraft

solar constant *n* the rate at which the sun's energy is received per unit area at the top of the earth's atmosphere when the sun is at its mean distance from the earth and atmospheric absorption has been corrected for. Its value is 1367 watts per square metre

solar day *n* See **day** (sense 6)

solar eclipse *n* See **eclipse** (sense 1)

solar energy *n* energy obtained from solar power

solar flare *n* a brief powerful eruption of particles and intense electromagnetic radiation from the sun's surface, associated with sunspots and causing disturbances to radio communication on earth. Sometimes shortened to: **flare** See also **solar wind**

solar furnace *n* a furnace utilizing the sun as a heat source, sunlight being concentrated at the focus of a system of concave mirrors

solar heating *n* heat radiation from the sun collected by heat-absorbing panels through which water is circulated: used for domestic hot water, central heating, and heating swimming pools

S

solarimeter (,sɒʊlə'rɪmɪtə) *n* any of various instruments for measuring solar radiation, as by use of a bolometer or thermopile. Also called: pyranometer

solarism ('sɒʊlə,rɪzəm) *n* the explanation of myths in terms of the movements and influence of the sun > '**solarist** *n*

solarium (sɒʊ'lɛərɪəm) *n, pl* -lariums *or* -laria (-'lɛərɪə) **1** a room built largely of glass to afford exposure to the sun **2** a bed equipped with ultraviolet lights used for acquiring an artificial suntan **3** an establishment offering such facilities [c19 from Latin: a terrace, from *sōl* sun]

solarize *or* **solarise** ('sɒʊlə,raɪz) *vb* (*tr*) **1** to treat by exposure to the sun's rays **2** *photog* to reverse some of the tones of (a negative or print) and introduce pronounced outlines of highlights, by exposing it briefly to light after developing and washing, and then redeveloping **3** to expose (a patient) to the therapeutic effects of solar or ultraviolet light > ,**solari'zation** *or* ,**solari'sation** *n*

solar mass *n* an astronomical unit of mass equal to the sun's mass, 1.981×10^{30} kilograms. Symbol: M☉

solar month *n* See **month** (sense 4)

solar myth *n* a myth explaining or allegorizing the origin or movement of the sun

solar panel *n* a panel exposed to radiation from the sun, used to heat water or, when mounted with solar cells, to produce electricity direct, esp for powering instruments in satellites

solar plexus *n* **1** *anatomy* the network of sympathetic nerves situated behind the stomach that supply the abdominal organs. Also called: **coeliac plexus 2** (*not in technical usage*) the part of the stomach beneath the diaphragm; pit of the stomach [c18 referring to resemblance between the radial network of nerves and ganglia and the rays of the sun]

solar power *n* heat radiation from the sun converted into electrical power

solar sail *n* a device that reflects light particles from the Sun, gaining momentum in the opposite direction to propel spacecraft forwards

solar system *n* the system containing the sun and the bodies held in its gravitational field, including the planets (Mercury, Venus, Earth, Mars, Jupiter, Saturn, Uranus, Neptune, Pluto), the asteroids, and comets

solar wind (wɪnd) *n* the constant stream of charged particles, esp protons and electrons, emitted by the sun at high velocities, its density and speed varying during periods of solar activity. It interacts with the earth's magnetic field, some of the particles being trapped by the magnetic lines of force, and causes auroral displays. See also Van Allen belt, magnetosphere

solar year *n* See year (sense 4)

solation (səʊˈleɪʃən) *n chem* the liquefaction of a gel

solatium (səʊˈleɪʃɪəm) *n, pl* **-tia** (-ʃɪə) *law, chiefly US and Scot* compensation awarded to a party for injury to the feelings as distinct from physical suffering and pecuniary loss [C19 from Latin: see SOLACE]

sold (səʊld) *vb* 1 the past tense and past participle of **sell** ▷ *adj* 2 **sold on** *slang* uncritically attached to or enthusiastic about

soldan ('səʊldən, 'sɒl-) *n* an archaic word for **sultan** [C13 via Old French from Arabic: SULTAN]

solder ('səʊldə; *US* 'sɒdər) *n* 1 an alloy for joining two metal surfaces by melting the alloy so that it forms a thin layer between the surfaces. **Soft solders** are alloys of lead and tin; **brazing solders** are alloys of copper and zinc 2 something that joins things together firmly; a bond ▷ *vb* 3 to join or mend or be joined or mended with or as if with solder [C14 via Old French from Latin *solidāre* to strengthen, from *solidus* SOLID] > **solderable** *adj* > **'solderer** *n*

soldering iron *n* a hand tool consisting of a handle fixed to a copper tip that is heated, electrically or in a flame, and used to melt and apply solder

soldier ('səʊldʒə) *n* 1 **a** a person who serves or has served in an army **b** Also called: **common soldier** a noncommissioned member of an army as opposed to a commissioned officer 2 a person who works diligently for a cause 3 a low-ranking member of the Mafia or other organized crime ring 4 *zoology* **a** an individual in a colony of social insects, esp ants, that has powerful jaws adapted for defending the colony, crushing large food particles, etc **b** (*as modifier*): *soldier ant* 5 *informal* a strip of bread or toast that is dipped into a soft-boiled egg ▷ *vb* 6 to serve as a soldier 7 *obsolete slang* to malinger or shirk [C13 from Old French *soudier*, from *soude* (army) pay, from Late Latin *solidus* a gold coin, from Latin: firm]

soldier beetle *n* a yellowish-red cantharid beetle, *Rhagonycha fulva*, having a somewhat elongated body

soldier bird *n* *Austral* another name for **noisy miner**

soldier crab *n* a small blue Australian estuarine crab of the *Mictyris* genus usually found in large numbers

soldierly ('səʊldʒəlɪ) *adj* of or befitting a good soldier > **'soldierliness** *n*

soldier of fortune *n* a man who seeks money or adventure as a soldier; mercenary

soldier on *vb* (*intr, adverb*) to persist in one's efforts in spite of difficulties, pressure, etc

soldier orchid *n* a European orchid, *Orchis militaris*, having pale purple flowers with a four-lobed lower lip. Also called: **military orchid** [from an imagined resemblance to a soldier]

soldier settlement *n* *Austral* the allocation of Crown land for farming to ex-servicemen > **soldier settler** *n*

soldiery ('səʊldʒərɪ) *n, pl* **-dieries** 1 soldiers collectively 2 a group of soldiers 3 the profession of being a soldier

soldo ('sɒldəʊ; *Italian* 'sɔldo) *n, pl* **-di** (-diː; *Italian* -di) a former Italian copper coin worth one twentieth of a lira [C16 from Italian, from Late Latin *solidum* a gold coin; see SOLDIER]

sole¹ (səʊl) *adj* 1 (*prenominal*) being the only one; only 2 (*prenominal*) of or relating to one individual or group and no other: *sole rights on a patent* 3 *law* having no wife or husband. See also **feme sole** 4 an archaic word for **solitary** [C14 from Old French *soule*, from Latin *sōlus* alone] > **'soleness** *n*

sole² (səʊl) *n* 1 the underside of the foot. Related adjs: **plantar, volar** 2 the underside of a shoe 3 **a** the bottom of a furrow **b** the bottom of a plough 4 the underside of a golf-club head 5 the bottom of an oven, furnace, etc ▷ *vb* 6 to provide (a shoe) with a sole 7 *golf* to rest (the club) on the ground, as when preparing to make a stroke [C14 via Old French from Latin *solea* sandal; probably related to *solum* the ground] > **'soleless** *adj*

sole³ (səʊl) *n, pl* **sole** or **soles** 1 any tongue-shaped flatfish of the family *Soleidae*, esp *Solea solea* (**European sole**): most common in warm seas and highly valued as food fishes 2 any of certain other similar fishes [C14 via Old French from Vulgar Latin *sola* (unattested), from Latin *solea* a sandal (from the fish's shape)]

sole-charge school *n* *NZ* a rural school with only one teacher

solecism ('sɒlɪˌsɪzəm) *n* 1 **a** the nonstandard use of a grammatical construction **b** any mistake, incongruity, or absurdity 2 a violation of good manners [C16 from Latin *soloecismus*, from Greek *soloikismos*, from *soloikos* speaking incorrectly, from *Soloi* an Athenian colony of Cilicia where the inhabitants spoke a corrupt form of Greek] > **'solecist** *n* > **sole'cistic** or **sole'cistical** *adj* > **sole'cistically** *adv*

solely ('səʊllɪ) *adv* 1 only; completely; entirely 2 without another or others; singly; alone 3 for one thing only

solemn ('sɒləm) *adj* 1 characterized or marked by seriousness or sincerity: *a solemn vow* 2 characterized by pomp, ceremony, or formality 3 serious, glum, or pompous 4 inspiring awe: *a solemn occasion* 5 performed with religious ceremony 6 gloomy or sombre: *solemn colours* [C14 from Old French *solempne*, from Latin *sōllemnis* appointed, perhaps from *sollus* whole] > **'solemnly** *adv* > **'solemnness** or **'solemness** *n*

solemnify (sə'lɛmnɪˌfaɪ) *vb* **-fies, -fying, -fied** (*tr*) to make serious or grave > **so,lemnifi'cation** *n*

solemnity (sə'lɛmnɪtɪ) *n, pl* **-ties** 1 the state or quality of being solemn 2 (*often plural*) solemn ceremony, observance, celebration, etc 3 *law* a formality necessary to validate a deed, act, contract, etc

solemnize or **solemnise** ('sɒləmˌnaɪz) *vb* (*tr*) 1 to celebrate or observe with rites or formal ceremonies, as a religious occasion 2 to celebrate or perform the ceremony of (marriage) 3 to make solemn or serious 4 to perform or hold (ceremonies, etc) in due manner > **,solemni'zation** or **,solemni'sation** *n* > **'solem,nizer** or **'solem,niser** *n*

Solemn League and Covenant *n* See **Covenant**

solenette ('səʊləˌnɛt, 'sɒlˌnɛt) *n* a small European sole, *Buglossidium luteum*, up to 13 cm (5 in.) in length; not caught commercially [SOLE³ + -ETTE]

solenodon (sə'lɛnədən) *n* either of two rare shrewlike nocturnal mammals of the Caribbean, *Atopogale cubana* (**Cuban solenodon**) or *Solenodon paradoxus* (**Haitian solenodon**), having a long hairless tail and an elongated snout: family *Solenodontidae*, order *Insectivora* (insectivores) [C19 from New Latin, from Latin *sōlēn* sea mussel, razor-shell (from Greek: pipe) + Greek *odōn* tooth]

solenoid ('səʊlɪˌnɔɪd) *n* 1 a coil of wire, usually cylindrical, in which a magnetic field is set up by passing a current through it 2 a coil of wire, partially surrounding an iron core, that is made to move inside the coil by the magnetic field set up by a current: used to convert electrical to mechanical energy, as in the operation of a switch 3 such a device used as a relay, as in a motor vehicle for connecting the battery directly to the starter motor when activated by the ignition switch [C19 from French *solénoïde*, from Greek *sōlēn* a pipe, tube] > **,sole'noidal** *adj* > **,sole'noidally** *adv*

Solent ('səʊlənt) *n* **the** the strait of the English Channel between the coast of Hampshire, on the English mainland, and the Isle of Wight. Width: up to 6 km (4 miles)

solera (sə'lɛərə) *n* **a** a system for aging sherry and other fortified wines, in which younger wines in upper rows of casks are used to top up casks of older wines stored below in order to produce a consistently aged blend **b** a blend of sherry produced by this system [Spanish, literally: bottom]

Soleure (sɔlœr) *n* the French name for **Solothurn**

sol-fa ('sɒl'faː) *n* 1 short for **tonic sol-fa** ▷ *vb* **-fas, -faing, -faed** 2 *US* to use tonic sol-fa syllables in singing (a tune) [C16 see GAMUT]

solfatara (ˌsɒlfə'taːrə) *n* a volcanic vent emitting only sulphurous gases and water vapour or sometimes hot mud [C18 from Italian: a sulphurous volcano near Naples, from *solfo* SULPHUR] > **,solfa'taric** *adj*

solfeggio (sɒl'fɛdʒɪəʊ) or **solfège** (sɒl'fɛʒ) *n, pl* **-feggi** (-'fɛdʒiː) **-feggios** or **-fèges** *music* 1 a voice exercise in which runs, scales, etc, are sung to the same syllable or syllables 2 solmization, esp the French or Italian system, in which the names correspond to the notes of the scale of C major [C18 from Italian *solfeggiare* to use the syllables sol-fa; see GAMUT]

solferino (ˌsɒlfə'riːnəʊ) *n* **a** a moderate purplish-red colour **b** (*as adjective*): *a solferino suit* [C19 from a dye discovered in 1859, the year a battle was fought at *Solferino*, a town in Italy]

soli ('səʊlɪ) *adj, adv music* (of a piece or passage) to be performed by or with soloists. Compare **tutti** [plural of SOLO]

solicit (sə'lɪsɪt) *vb* **-its, -iting, -ited** 1 (when *intr*, foll by *for*) to make a request, application, or entreaty to (a person for business, support, etc) 2 to accost (a person) with an offer of sexual relations in return for money 3 to provoke or incite (a person) to do something wrong or illegal [C15 from Old French *solliciter* to disturb, from Latin *sollicitāre* to harass, from *sollicitus* agitated, from *sollus* whole + *citus*, from *ciēre* to excite] > **so,lici'tation** *n*

solicitor (sə'lɪsɪtə) *n* 1 (in Britain) a lawyer who advises clients on matters of law, draws up legal documents, prepares cases for barristers, etc, and who may represent clients in certain courts. Compare **barrister** 2 (in the US) an officer responsible for the legal affairs of a town, city, etc 3 a person who solicits > **so'licitorship** *n*

Solicitor General *n, pl* **Solicitors General** 1 (in Britain) the law officer of the Crown ranking next to the Attorney General (in Scotland to the Lord Advocate) and acting as his assistant 2 (in New Zealand) the government's chief lawyer: head of the Crown Law Office and prosecutor for the Crown

solicitous (sə'lɪsɪtəs) *adj* 1 showing consideration, concern, attention, etc 2 keenly anxious or willing; eager [C16 from Latin *sollicitus* anxious; see SOLICIT] > **so'licitously** *adv* > **so'licitousness** *n*

solicitude (sə'lɪsɪˌtjuːd) *n* 1 the state or quality of being solicitous 2 (*often plural*) something that causes anxiety or concern 3 anxiety or concern

solid ('sɒlɪd) *adj* 1 of, concerned with, or being a substance in a physical state in which it resists changes in size and shape. Compare **liquid** (sense 1), **gas** (sense 1) 2 consisting of matter all through 3 of the same substance all through: *solid rock* 4 sound; proved or provable: *solid facts* 5 reliable or sensible; upstanding: *a solid citizen* 6 firm, strong, compact, or substantial: *a solid table; solid ground* 7 (of a meal or food) substantial 8 (*often postpositive*) without interruption or respite; continuous: *solid bombardment* **9** financially sound or solvent: *a solid institution* **10** strongly linked or consolidated: *a solid relationship* **11** *geometry* having or relating to three dimensions: *a solid figure; solid geometry* **12** (of a word composed of two or more other words or elements) written or printed as a single word without a hyphen **13** *printing* with no space or leads between lines of type **14** solid for unanimously in favour of **15** (of a writer, work, performance, etc) adequate; sensible **16** of or having a single uniform colour or tone **17** *NZ informal* excessive; unreasonably expensive ▷ *n* **18** *geometry* **a** a closed surface in three-dimensional space **b** such a surface together with the volume enclosed by it **19** a solid substance, such as wood, iron, or diamond [c14 from Old French *solide*, from Latin *solidus* firm; related to Latin *sollus* whole] > solidity (sə'lɪdɪtɪ) *n* > 'solidly *adv* > 'solidness *n*

solidago (ˌsɒlɪ'deɪɡəʊ) *n, pl* -gos any plant of the chiefly American genus *Solidago*, which includes the goldenrods: family *Asteraceae* (composites) [c18 via New Latin from Medieval Latin *soldago* a plant reputed to have healing properties, from *soldāre* to strengthen, from Latin *solidāre*, from *solidus* SOLID]

solid angle *n* a geometric surface consisting of lines originating from a common point (the vertex) and passing through a closed curve or polygon: measured in steradians

solidarity (ˌsɒlɪ'dærɪtɪ) *n, pl* -ties unity of interests, sympathies, etc, as among members of the same class

Solidarity (ˌsɒlɪ'dærɪtɪ) *n* the organization of free trade unions in Poland: recognized in 1980; outlawed in 1982; legalized and led the new noncommunist government in 1989 [c20 from Polish *solidarność*: solidarity]

solidary ('sɒlɪdərɪ, -drɪ) *adj* marked by unity of interests, responsibilities, etc [c19 from French *solidaire*, from *solide* SOLID]

solid fuel *n* **1** a domestic or industrial fuel, such as coal or coke, that is a solid rather than an oil or gas **2** Also called: solid propellant a rocket fuel that is a solid rather than a liquid or a gas

solid geometry *n* the branch of geometry concerned with the properties of three-dimensional geometric figures

solidify (sə'lɪdɪˌfaɪ) *vb* -fies, -fying, -fied **1** to make or become solid or hard **2** to make or become strong, united, determined, etc > so'lidiˌfiable *adj* > soˌlidifi'cation *n* > so'lidiˌfier *n*

solid injection *n* injection of fuel directly into the cylinder of an internal-combustion engine without the assistance of an air blast to atomize the fuel. Also called (in a petrol engine): direct injection Compare **blast injection**

solid solution *n* *chem* a crystalline material in which two or more elements or compounds share a common lattice

solid-state *n* **1** (*modifier*) (of an electronic device) activated by a semiconductor component in which current flow is through solid material rather than in a vacuum **2** (*modifier*) of, concerned with, characteristic of, or consisting of solid matter

solid-state physics *n* (*functioning as singular*) the branch of physics concerned with experimental and theoretical investigations of the properties of solids, such as superconductivity, photoconductivity, and ferromagnetism

solidus ('sɒlɪdəs) *n, pl* -di (-ˌdaɪ) **1** a technical name for **slash** (sense 12) **2** a gold coin of the Byzantine empire [c14 from Late Latin *solidus* (*nummus*) a gold coin (from *solidus* solid); in Medieval Latin, *solidus* referred to a shilling and was indicated by a long *s*, which ultimately became the virgule]

solifidian (ˌsɒlɪ'fɪdɪən) *n* *Christianity* a person who maintains that man is justified by faith alone [c16 from New Latin *sōlifidius*, from Latin *sōlus* sole + *fides* faith] > soli'fidianˌism *n*

solifluction *or* **solifluxion** ('sɒlɪˌflʌkʃən, ˈsəʊlɪ-) *n* slow downhill movement of soil, saturated with meltwater, over a permanently frozen subsoil in tundra regions [c20 from Latin *solum* soil + *fluctio* act of flowing]

Solihull (ˌsəʊlɪ'hʌl) *n* **1** a town in central England, in Solihull unitary authority in the S West Midlands near Birmingham: mainly residential. Pop: 94 753 (2001) **2** a unitary authority in central England, in the West Midlands. Pop: 200 300 (2003 est). Area: 180 sq km (70 sq miles)

soliloquize *or* **soliloquise** (sə'lɪləˌkwaɪz) *vb* (*intr*) to utter a soliloquy > soliloquist (sə'lɪləkwɪst), so'liloˌquizer *or* so'liloˌquiser *n*

soliloquy (sə'lɪləkwɪ) *n, pl* -quies **1** the act of speaking alone or to oneself, esp as a theatrical device **2** a speech in a play that is spoken in soliloquy: *Hamlet's first soliloquy* [c14 via Late Latin *sōliloquium*, from Latin *sōlus* sole + *loquī* to speak]

> **USAGE** *Soliloquy* is sometimes wrongly used where *monologue* is meant. Both words refer to a long speech by one person, but a *monologue* can be addressed to other people, whereas in a *soliloquy* the speaker is always talking to himself or herself

Solimões (suli'mõəʃ) *n* **the** the Brazilian name for the Amazon from the Peruvian border to the Rio Negro

Solingen (German 'zo:lɪŋən) *n* a city in W Germany, in North Rhine-Westphalia: a major European centre of the cutlery industry. Pop: 164 543 (2003 est)

solipsism ('sɒlɪpˌsɪzəm) *n* *philosophy* the extreme form of scepticism which denies the possibility of any knowledge other than of one's own existence [c19 from Latin *sōlus* alone + *ipse* self] > 'solipsist *n, adj* > ˌsolip'sistic *adj*

solitaire ('sɒlɪˌtɛə, ˌsɒlɪ'tɛə) *n* **1** Also called: pegboard a game played by one person, esp one involving moving and taking pegs in a pegboard or marbles on an indented circular board with the object of being left with only one **2** the US name for **patience** (the card game) **3** a gem, esp a diamond, set alone in a ring **4** any of several extinct birds of the genus *Pezophaps*, related to the dodo **5** any of several dull grey North American songbirds of the genus *Myadestes*: subfamily *Turdinae* (thrushes) [c18 from Old French: SOLITARY]

solitary ('sɒlɪtərɪ, -trɪ) *adj* **1** following or enjoying a life of solitude: *a solitary disposition* **2** experienced or performed alone: *a solitary walk* **3** (of a place) unfrequented **4** (*prenominal*) single; sole: *a solitary speck in the sky* **5** having few companions; lonely **6** (of animals) not living in organized colonies or large groups: *solitary bees; a solitary elephant.* Compare **social** (sense 7), **gregarious** (sense 2) **7** (of flowers) growing singly ▷ *n, pl* -taries **8** a person who lives in seclusion; hermit; recluse **9** *informal* short for **solitary confinement** [c14 from Latin *sōlitārius*, from *sōlus* SOLE] > 'solitarily *adv* > 'solitariness *n*

solitary confinement *n* isolation imposed on a prisoner, as by confinement in a special cell

soliton ('sɒlɪˌtɒn) *n* *physics* an isolated particle-like wave that is a solution of certain equations for propagation, occurring when two solitary waves do not change their form after collision and subsequently travelling for considerable distances [c20 from solit(ary) + -ON]

solitude ('sɒlɪˌtjuːd) *n* **1** the state of being solitary or secluded **2** *poetic* a solitary place [c14 from Latin *sōlitūdō*, from *sōlus* alone, SOLE] > ˌsoli'tudinous *adj*

solleret (ˌsɒlə'rɛt) *n* a protective covering for the foot consisting of riveted plates of armour [c19 from French, diminutive of Old French *soller* shoe, from Late Latin *subtēl* arch beneath the foot, from SUB- + *tālus* ankle]

sollicker ('sɒlɪkə) *n* *Austral slang* something very large [c19 from English dialect]

solmization *or* **solmisation** (ˌsɒlmɪ'zeɪʃən) *n* *music* a system of naming the notes of a scale by syllables instead of letters derived from the 11th-century hexachord system of Guido d'Arezzo, which assigns the names *ut* (or *do*), *re, mi, fa, sol, la, si* (or *ti*) to the degrees of the major scale of C (**fixed system**) or (excluding the syllables *ut* and *si*) to the major scale in any key (**movable system**). See also **tonic sol-fa** [c18 from French *solmisation*, from *solmiser* to use the sol-fa syllables, from SOL[1] + MI]

solo ('səʊləʊ) *n, pl* -los **1** *pl* -los *or* -li (-ˌliː) a musical composition for one performer with or without accompaniment **2** any of various card games in which each person plays on his own instead of in partnership with another, such as solo whist **3** a flight in which an aircraft pilot is unaccompanied **4** a any performance, mountain climb, or other undertaking carried out by an individual without assistance from others **b** (*as modifier*): *a solo attempt* ▷ *adj* **5** *music* unaccompanied ▷ *adv* **6** by oneself; alone: *to fly solo* ▷ *vb* **7** to undertake a venture alone, esp to operate an aircraft alone or climb alone [c17 via Italian from Latin *sōlus* alone, SOLE[1]]

soloist ('səʊləʊɪst) *n* a person who performs a solo

Solo man *n* a type of early man, *Homo soloensis*, of late Pleistocene times, having a skull resembling that of Neanderthal man but with a smaller cranial capacity [c20 after *Solo*, site in central Java where remains were found]

Solomon ('sɒləmən) *n* 10th century BC king of Israel, son of David and Bathsheba, credited with great wisdom > **Solomonic** (ˌsɒlə'mɒnɪk) *or* **Solomonian** (ˌsɒlə'məʊnɪən) *adj*

Solomon Gundy ('sɒləmən ˈɡʌndɪ) *n* *Canadian* a dish of salted marinated herring in vinegar and spices [from SALMAGUNDI]

Solomon Islands *pl n* an independent state in the SW Pacific comprising an archipelago extending for almost 1450 km (900 miles) in a northwest–southeast direction: the northernmost islands of the archipelago (Buka and Bougainville) form part of Papua New Guinea; the main islands are Guadalcanal, Malaita, San Cristobal, New Georgia, Santa Isabel, and Choiseul: a member of the Commonwealth. Official language: English. Religion: Christian majority. Currency: Solomon Islands dollar. Capital: Honiara. Pop: 491 000 (2004 est). Area: 29 785 sq km (11 500 sq miles)

Solomon Islands Pidgin *n* the variety of Neo-Melanesian spoken in the Solomon Islands and neighbouring islands

Solomon's seal *n* **1** another name for **Star of David 2** any of several liliaceous plants of the genus *Polygonatum* of N temperate regions, having greenish or yellow paired flowers, long narrow waxy leaves, and a thick underground stem with prominent leaf scars [c16 translation of Medieval Latin *sigillum Solomonis*, perhaps referring to the resemblance of the leaf scars to seals]

solo mother *n* *NZ* a mother with a dependent child or dependent children and no husband

solonchak (ˌsɒlən'tʃæk) *n* a type of intrazonal soil of arid regions with a greyish surface crust: contains large quantities of soluble salts [Russian, literally: salt marsh]

solonetz *or* **solonets** (ˌsɒlə'nɛts) *n* a type of intrazonal soil with a high saline content characterized by leaching [Russian *solonets* salt not obtained through decoction]

so long *sentence substitute* *informal* farewell; goodbye

solo parent *n* *NZ* the usual name for **single parent**

solo stop *n* any of various organ stops designed to imitate a solo performance on a particular musical instrument

Solothurn (German 'zo:loturn) *n* **1** a canton of NW Switzerland. Capital: Solothurn. Pop: 246 500 (2002 est). Area: 793 sq km (306 sq miles) **2** a town in NW Switzerland, capital of Solothurn canton, on the Aare River. Pop: 15 489 (2000) ▷ French name: Soleure

S

solo whist *n* a version of whist for four players acting independently, each of whom may bid to win or lose a fixed number of tricks before play starts, trumps having usually been decided by cutting

solstice ('splstɪs) *n* **1** either the shortest day of the year (**winter solstice**) or the longest day of the year (**summer solstice**) **2** either of the two points on the ecliptic at which the sun is overhead at the tropic of Cancer or Capricorn at the summer and winter solstices [c13 via Old French from Latin *sōlstitium*, literally: the (apparent) standing still of the sun, from *sōl* sun + *sistere* to stand still] > **solstitial** (spl'stɪʃəl) *adj*

solubility (ˌsɒljʊ'bɪlɪtɪ) *n, pl* **-ties 1** the ability of a substance to dissolve; the quality of being soluble **2** a measure of this ability for a particular substance in a particular solvent, equal to the quantity of substance dissolving in a fixed quantity of solvent to form a saturated solution under specified temperature and pressure. It is expressed in grams per cubic decametre, grams per hundred grams of solvent, moles per mole, etc

solubilize *or* **solubilise** ('sɒljʊbɪˌlaɪz) *vb* to make or become soluble, as in the addition of detergents to fats to make them dissolve in water

soluble ('sɒljʊbəl) *adj* **1** (of a substance) capable of being dissolved, esp easily dissolved in some solvent, usually water **2** capable of being solved or answered [c14 from Late Latin *solūbilis*, from Latin *solvere* to dissolve] > **solubleness** *n* > **'solubly** *adv*

soluble glass *n* another name for **sodium silicate** (sense 1)

soluble RNA *n* another name for **transfer RNA**

solum ('səʊləm) *n, pl* **-lums** *or* **-la** (-lə) the upper layers of the soil profile, affected by climate and vegetation [c19 New Latin from Latin: the ground]

solus ('səʊləs) *adj* **1** alone; separate **2** of or denoting the position of an advertising poster or press advertisement that is separated from competing advertisements: *a solus position* **3** of or denoting a retail outlet, such as a petrol station, that sells the products of one company exclusively: *a solus site* **4** (*fem* **sola**) alone; by oneself (formerly used in stage directions) [c17 from Latin *sōlus* alone]

solute (sɒ'lju:t) *n* **1** the component of a solution that changes its state in forming the solution or the component that is not present in excess; the substance that is dissolved in another substance. Compare **solvent** ▷ *adj* **2** botany, *now rare* loose or unattached; free [c16 from Latin *solūtus* free, unfettered, from *solvere* to release]

solution (sə'lu:ʃən) *n* **1** a homogeneous mixture of two or more substances in which the molecules or atoms of the substances are completely dispersed. The constituents can be solids, liquids, or gases **2** the act or process of forming a solution **3** the state of being dissolved (esp in the phrase **in solution**) **4** a mixture of two or more substances in which one or more components are present as small particles with colloidal dimension; colloid: *a colloidal solution* **5** a specific answer to or way of answering a problem **6** the act or process of solving a problem **7** maths **a** the unique set of values that yield a true statement when substituted for the variables in an equation **b** a member of a set of assignments of values to variables under which a given statement is satisfied; a member of a solution set **8** the stage of a disease, following a crisis, resulting in its termination **9** law the payment, discharge, or satisfaction of a claim, debt, etc [c14 from Latin *solūtiō* an unloosing, from *solūtus; see* SOLUTE]

solution set *n* another name for **truth set**

Solutrean (sə'lu:trɪən) *adj* of or relating to an Upper Palaeolithic culture of Europe that was characterized by leaf-shaped flint blades [c19 named after *Solutré*, village in central France where traces of this culture were originally found]

solvable ('sɒlvəbəl) *adj* another word for **soluble** (sense 2) > ˌsolva'bility *or* 'solvableness *n*

solvate ('sɒlveɪt) *vb chem* to undergo, cause to undergo, or partake in solvation [c20 from SOLVENT]

solvation (sɒl'veɪʃən) *n* the process in which there is some chemical association between the molecules of a solute and those of the solvent. An example is an aqueous solution of copper sulphate which contains complex ions of the type $[Cu(H_2O)_4]^{2+}$

Solvay process ('sɒlveɪ) *n* an industrial process for manufacturing sodium carbonate. Carbon dioxide is passed into a solution of sodium chloride saturated with ammonia. Sodium bicarbonate is precipitated and heated to form the carbonate [c19 named after Ernest Solvay (1838–1922), Belgian chemist who invented a process using salt, limestone, and ammonia]

solve (sɒlv) *vb* (*tr*) **1** to find the explanation for or solution to (a mystery, problem, etc) **2** maths **a** to work out the answer to (a problem) **b** to obtain the roots of (an equation) [c15 from Latin *solvere* to loosen, release, free from debt] > **'solver** *n*

solvency ('sɒlvənsɪ) *n* ability to pay all debts

solvent ('sɒlvənt) *adj* **1** capable of meeting financial obligations **2** (of a substance, esp a liquid) capable of dissolving another substance ▷ *n* **3** a liquid capable of dissolving another substance: *water is a solvent for salt* **4** the component of a solution that does not change its state in forming the solution or the component that is present in excess. Compare **solute 5** something that solves [c17 from Latin *solvēns* releasing, from *solvere* to free, SOLVE] > **'solvently** *adv*

solvent abuse *n* the deliberate inhaling of intoxicating fumes given off by certain solvents such as toluene. See also **glue-sniffing**

solvolysis (sɒl'vɒlɪsɪs) *n* a chemical reaction occurring between a dissolved substance and its solvent. See also **hydrolysis** [from SOLV(ENT) + -LYSIS]

Solway Firth ('sɒlweɪ) *n* an inlet of the Irish Sea between SW Scotland and NW England. Length: about 56 km (35 miles)

som (sɒm) *n, pl* **somy** ('sɒmɪ) the standard monetary unit of Kyrgyzstan, divided into 100 tyiyn

Som. *abbreviation for* Somerset

SOM1 *text messaging abbreviation for* someone

soma[1] ('səʊmə) *n, pl* **-mata** (-mətə) *or* **-mas** the body of an organism, esp an animal, as distinct from the germ cells [c19 via New Latin from Greek *sōma* the body]

soma[2] ('səʊmə) *n* an intoxicating plant juice drink used in Vedic rituals [from Sanskrit]

somaesthesia, *US* **somesthesia** (ˌsɒmɪs'θi:zɪə) *or* **somaesthesis**, *or US* **somesthesis** (ˌsɒmɪs'θi:sɪs) *n* sensory perception of bodily feelings like touch, pain, position of the limbs, etc [c20 from Greek *sōma* body + AESTHESIA] > **somaesthetic** *or US* **somesthetic** (ˌsɒmɪs'θɛtɪk) *adj*

Somali (səʊ'mɑ:lɪ) *n* **1** (*pl* **-lis** *or* **-li**) a member of a tall dark-skinned people inhabiting Somalia **2** the language of this people, belonging to the Cushitic subfamily of the Afro-Asiatic family of languages ▷ *adj* **3** of, relating to, or characteristic of Somalia, the Somalis, or their language

Somalia (səʊ'mɑ:lɪə) *n* a republic in NE Africa, on the Indian Ocean and the Gulf of Aden: the north became a British protectorate in 1884; the east and south were established as an Italian protectorate in 1889; gained independence and united as the Somali Republic in 1960. In 1991 the former British Somaliland region in the north unilaterally declared itself independent as the Republic of Somaliland, and other areas are also operating effectively as separate states, but this has not been recognized officially. Official languages: Arabic and Somali. Official religion: (Sunni) Muslim. Currency: Somali shilling.

Capital: Mogadishu. Pop: 10 312 000 (2004 est). Area: 637 541 sq km (246 154 sq miles)

Somalian (səʊ'mɑ:lɪən) *adj* **1** of or relating to Somalia or its inhabitants ▷ *n* **2** a native or inhabitant of Somalia

Somali cat *n* a breed of cat with medium-length silky hair, large ears, and a bushy tail

Somaliland (səʊ'mɑ:lɪˌlænd) *n* a former region of E Africa, between the equator and the Gulf of Aden: includes Somalia, Djibouti, and SE Ethiopia

soman ('səʊmən) *n* an organophosphorus compound developed as a nerve gas in Germany during World War II [c20 from German, of uncertain origin]

somatic (səʊ'mætɪk) *adj* **1** of or relating to the soma: *somatic cells* **2** of or relating to an animal body or body wall as distinct from the viscera, limbs, and head **3** of or relating to the human body as distinct from the mind: *a somatic disease* [c18 from Greek *sōmatikos* concerning the body, from *sōma* the body] > **so'matically** *adv*

somatic cell *n* any of the cells of a plant or animal except the reproductive cells. Compare **germ cell**

somatic cell nuclear transfer *n* another name for **therapeutic cloning**

somatic mutation *n* a mutation occurring in a somatic cell, resulting in a change in the morphology or some other aspect of one part of an organism (usually a plant). It may be maintained by vegetative propagation but not by sexual reproduction

somatic nervous system *n physiol* the section of the nervous system responsible for sensation and control of the skeletal muscles. Compare **autonomic nervous system**

somato- *or before a vowel* **somat-** *combining form* body: *somatoplasm* [from Greek *sōma, sōmat-* body]

somatogenic (ˌsəʊmætəʊ'dʒɛnɪk) *adj med* originating in the cells of the body: of organic, rather than mental, origin: *a somatogenic disorder*

somatology (ˌsəʊmə'tɒlədʒɪ) *n* **1** the branch of biology concerned with the structure and function of the body **2** the branch of anthropology dealing with the physical characteristics of man > **somatologic** (ˌsəʊmətə'lɒdʒɪk) *or* ˌsomato'logical *adj* > ˌsomato'logically *adv* > ˌsoma'tologist *n*

somatomedin (ˌsəʊmətə'mi:dɪn) *n* a protein hormone that promotes tissue growth under the influence of growth hormone [c20 from SOMATO- + Latin *medius* middle + -IN]

somatoplasm ('səʊmətəˌplæzəm) *n biology* **a** the protoplasm of a somatic cell **b** the somatic cells collectively. Compare **germ plasm**. > ˌsomato'plastic *adj*

somatopleure ('səʊmətəˌplʊə, -ˌplɜ:) *n* a mass of tissue in embryo vertebrates that is formed by fusion of the ectoderm with the outer layer of mesoderm: develops into the amnion, chorion, and part of the body wall [c19 from New Latin *somatopleura*, from SOMATO- + Greek *pleura* a side] > ˌsomato'pleural *or* ˌsomato'pleuric *adj*

somatostatin (ˌsəʊmətə'stætɪn) *n* a peptide hormone that prevents the release of growth hormone from the pituitary gland [c20 from SOMATO- + -STAT + -IN]

somatotonia (ˌsəʊmətəʊ'təʊnɪə) *n* a personality type characterized by assertiveness and energy: said to be correlated with a mesomorph body type. Compare **cerebrotonia, viscerotonia**

somatotrophin (ˌsəʊmətəʊ'trəʊfɪn) *or* **somatotropin** (ˌsəʊmətəʊ'trəʊpɪn) *n* other names for **growth hormone**. > ˌsomato'trophic *or* ˌsomato'tropic *adj*

somatotype ('səʊmətəˌtaɪp) *n* a type or classification of physique or body build. See **endomorph, mesomorph, ectomorph**

sombre *or US* **somber** ('sɒmbə) *adj* **1** dismal; melancholy: *a sombre mood* **2** dim, gloomy, or shadowy **3** (of colour, clothes, etc) sober, dull, or dark [c18 from French, from Vulgar Latin *subumbrāre* (unattested) to shade, from Latin *sub* beneath + *umbra* shade] ▷ 'sombrely or US 'somberly *adv* ▷ 'sombreness or US 'somberness *n* ▷ sombrous ('sɒmbrəs) *adj*

sombrero (sɒm'breərəʊ) *n, pl* -ros a felt or straw hat with a wide brim, as worn by men in Mexico [c16 from Spanish, from *sombrero de sol* shade from the sun]

some (sʌm; *unstressed* səm) *determiner* **1 a** (a) certain unknown or unspecified: *some lunatic drove into my car; some people never learn* **b** (*as pronoun; functioning as sing or plural*): *some can teach and others can't* **2 a** an unknown or unspecified quantity or amount of: *there's some rice on the table; he owns some horses* **b** (*as pronoun; functioning as sing or plural*): *we'll buy some* **3 a** a considerable number or amount of: *he lived some years afterwards* **b** a little: *show him some respect* **4** (*usually stressed*) *informal* an impressive or remarkable: *that was some game!* **5** a certain amount (more) (in the phrases **some more** and (*informal*) **and then some**) **6** about; approximately: *he owes me some thirty pounds* ▷ *adv* **7** US *not standard* to a certain degree or extent: *I guess I like him some* [Old English *sum*; related to Old Norse *sumr*, Gothic *sums*, Old High German *sum* some, Sanskrit *samá* any, Greek *hamē* somehow]

-some¹ *suffix forming adjectives* characterized by; tending to: *awesome; tiresome* [Old English *-sum*; related to Gothic *-sama*, German *-sam*]

-some² *suffix forming nouns* indicating a group of a specified number of members: *threesome* [Old English *sum*, special use of SOME (determiner)]

-some³ (-səum) *n combining form* a body: *chromosome* [from Greek *sōma* body]

somebody ('sʌmbədɪ) *pron* **1** some person; someone ▷ *n, pl* -bodies **2** a person of greater importance than others: *he seems to be somebody in this town*

　USAGE See at **everyone**

someday ('sʌm,deɪ) *adv* at some unspecified time in the (distant) future

somehow ('sʌm,haʊ) *adv* **1** in some unspecified way **2** Also: **somehow or other** by any means that are necessary

someone ('sʌm,wʌn, -wən) *pron* some person; somebody

　USAGE See at **everyone**

someplace ('sʌm,pleɪs) *adv* US *and Canadian informal* in, at, or to some unspecified place or region

somersault or **summersault** ('sʌmə,sɔːlt) *n* **1 a** a forward roll in which the head is placed on the ground and the trunk and legs are turned over it **b** a similar roll in a backward direction **2** an acrobatic feat in which either of these rolls are performed in midair, as in diving or gymnastics **3** a complete reversal of opinion, policy, etc ▷ *vb* **4** (*intr*) to perform a somersault [c16 from Old French *soubresault*, probably from Old Provençal *sobresaut*, from *sobre* over (from Latin *super*) + *saut* a jump, leap (from Latin *saltus*)]

Somerset ('sʌməsɪt, -,sɛt) *n* a county of SW England, on the Bristol Channel: the Mendip Hills lie in the north and Exmoor in the west: the geographical and ceremonial county includes the unitary authorities of North Somerset and Bath and North East Somerset (both part of Avon county from 1975 until 1996): mainly agricultural (esp dairying and fruit). Administrative centre: Taunton. Pop (excluding unitary authorities): 507 500 (2003 est). Area (excluding unitary authorities): 3452 sq km (1332 sq miles)

Somerset House *n* a building in London, in the Strand, built (1776–86) by Sir William Chambers; formerly housed the General Register Office of births, marriages, and deaths: contains (from 1990) the art collections of the Courtauld Institute

something ('sʌmθɪŋ) *pron* **1** an unspecified or unknown thing; some thing: *he knows something you don't; take something warm with you* **2 something or other** one unspecified thing or an alternative thing **3** an unspecified or unknown amount; bit: *something less than a hundred* **4** an impressive or important person, thing, or event: *isn't that something?* ▷ *adv* **5** to some degree; a little; somewhat: *to look something like me* **6** (foll by an *adjective*) *informal* (intensifier): *it hurts something awful*

-something *n combining form* **a** a person whose age can be approximately expressed by a specified decade **b** (*as modifier*): *the thirtysomething market* [c20 from the US television series *thirtysomething*]

sometime ('sʌm,taɪm) *adv* **1** at some unspecified point of time ▷ *adj* **2** (*prenominal*) having been at one time; former: *the sometime President* **3** (*prenominal*) US *occasional; infrequent*

　USAGE The form *sometime* should not be used to refer to a fairly long period of time: *he has been away for some time* (not *for sometime*)

sometimes ('sʌm,taɪmz) *adv* **1** now and then; from time to time; occasionally **2** *obsolete* formerly; sometime

someway ('sʌm,weɪ) *adv* in some unspecified manner

somewhat ('sʌm,wɒt) *adv* (not used with a negative) rather; a bit: *she found it somewhat less easy than he*

somewhere ('sʌm,wɛə) *adv* **1** in, to, or at some unknown or unspecified place or point: *somewhere in England; somewhere between 3 and 4 o'clock* **2 get somewhere** *informal* to make progress

somewise ('sʌm,waɪz) *adv* in some way or to some degree; somehow (archaic, except in the phrase **in somewise**) [c15 from SOME + -WISE]

somite ('səʊmaɪt) *n* **1** *embryol* any of a series of dorsal paired segments of mesoderm occurring along the notochord in vertebrate embryos. It develops into muscle and bone in the adult animal **2** *zoology* another name for **metamere** [c19 from Greek *sōma* a body] ▷ somital ('səʊmɪtᵊl) or somitic (səʊ'mɪtɪk) *adj*

Somme (French sɔm) *n* **1** a department of N France, in Picardy region. Capital: Amiens. Pop: 557 061 (2003 est). Area: 6277 sq km (2448 sq miles) **2** a river in N France, rising in Aisne department and flowing west to Amiens, then northwest to the English Channel: scene of heavy fighting in World War I. Length: 245 km (152 miles)

sommelier ('sʌməl,jeɪ) *n* a wine steward in a restaurant or hotel [French: butler, via Old French from Old Provençal *saumalier* pack-animal driver, from Late Latin *sagma* a packsaddle, from Greek]

somnambulate (sɒm'næmbjʊ,leɪt) *vb* (*intr*) to walk while asleep [c19 from Latin *somnus* sleep + *ambulāre* to walk] ▷ som'nambulant *adj, n* ▷ som,nambu'lation *n* ▷ som'nambu,lator *n*

somnambulism (sɒm'næmbjʊ,lɪzəm) *n* a condition that is characterized by walking while asleep or in a hypnotic trance. Also called: noctambulism ▷ som'nambulist *n* ▷ som,nambu'listic *adj*

somni- or before a vowel **somn-** *combining form* sleep: *somniferous* [from Latin *somnus*]

somniferous (sɒm'nɪfərəs) or **somnific** *adj rare* tending to induce sleep [c17 from Latin *somnifer* (from *somnus* sleep + *ferre* to do) + -OUS] ▷ som'niferously *adv*

somniloquy (sɒm'nɪləkwɪ) *n, pl* -quies *rare* the act of talking in one's sleep [c19 from Latin *somnus* sleep + *loqui* to speak; compare SOLILOQUY] ▷ som'niloquist *n* ▷ som'niloquous *adj*

somnolent ('sɒmnələnt) *adj* **1** drowsy; sleepy **2** causing drowsiness [c15 from Latin *somnus* sleep] ▷ 'somnolence or 'somnolency *n* ▷ 'somnolently *adv*

Somnus ('sɒmnəs) *n* the Roman god of sleep. Greek counterpart: **Hypnos**

Somoni ('sɒmɒnɪ) *n* the standard monetary unit of Tajikistan, consisting of 100 dirams

somy ('sɒmɪ) *n* the plural of **som**

son (sʌn) *n* **1** a male offspring; a boy or man in relation to his parents **2** a male descendant **3** (*often capital*) a familiar term of address for a boy or man **4** a male from a certain country, place, etc, or one closely connected with a certain environment: *a son of the circus; a son of the manse* ▷ Related adjective: **filial** [Old English *sunu*; related to Old Norse *sunr*, Gothic *sunus*, Old High German *sunu*, Lithuanian *sūnus*, Sanskrit *sūnu*] ▷ 'sonless *adj* ▷ 'son,like *adj*

Son (sʌn) *n Christianity* the second person of the Trinity, Jesus Christ

sonant ('səʊnɪnt) *adj* **1** *phonetics* denoting a voiced sound capable of forming a syllable or syllable nucleus **2** inherently possessing, exhibiting, or producing a sound ▷ *n* **3** *phonetics* a voiced sound belonging to the class of frictionless continuants or nasals (l, r, m, n, ŋ) considered from the point of view of being a vowel and, in this capacity, able to form a syllable or syllable nucleus [c19 from Latin *sonāns* sounding, from *sonāre* to make a noise, resound] ▷ 'sonance *n* ▷ sonantal (səʊ'næntᵊl) or so'nantic *adj*

sonar ('səʊnɑː) *n* a communication and position-finding device used in underwater navigation and target detection using echolocation [c20 from *so(und) na(vigation and) r(anging)*]

sonata (sə'nɑːtə) *n* **1** an instrumental composition, usually in three or more movements, for piano alone (**piano sonata**) or for any other instrument with or without piano accompaniment (**violin sonata**, **cello sonata**, etc). See also **sonata form, symphony** (sense 1), **concerto** (sense 1) **2** a one-movement keyboard composition of the baroque period [c17 from Italian, from *sonare* to sound, from Latin]

sonata form *n* a musical structure consisting of an expanded ternary form whose three sections (exposition, development, and recapitulation), followed by a coda, are characteristic of the first movement in a sonata, symphony, string quartet, concerto, etc

sonatina (,sɒnə'tiːnə) *n* a short sonata [c19 from Italian]

sondage (sɒn'dɑːʒ) *n, pl* -dages (-'dɑːʒɪz, -'dɑːʒ) *archaeol* a deep trial trench for inspecting stratigraphy [c20 from French: a sounding, from *sonder* to sound]

sonde (sɒnd) *n* a rocket, balloon, or probe used for observing in the upper atmosphere [c20 from French: plummet, plumb line; see SOUND³]

sone (səʊn) *n* a subjective unit of loudness equal to that experienced by a normal person hearing a 1 kHz tone at 40 dB [c20 from Latin *sonus* a sound]

son et lumière ('sɒn eɪ 'luːmɪ,ɛə; *French* sɔ̃n e lymjɛr) *n* an entertainment staged at night at a famous building, historical site, etc, whereby the history of the location is presented by means of lighting effects, sound effects, and narration [French, literally: sound and light]

song (sɒŋ) *n* **1 a** a piece of music, usually employing a verbal text, composed for the voice, esp one intended for performance by a soloist **b** the whole repertory of such pieces **c** (*as modifier*): *a song book* **2** poetical composition; poetry **3** the characteristic tuneful call or sound made by certain birds or insects **4** the act or process of singing: *they raised their voices in song* **5 for a song** at a bargain price **6 on song** *Brit informal* performing at peak efficiency or ability [Old English *sang*; related to Gothic *saggws*, Old High German *sang*; see SING] ▷ 'song,like *adj*

song and dance *n informal* **1** *Brit* a fuss, esp one that is unnecessary **2** US *and Canadian* a long or elaborate story or explanation, esp one that is evasive

songbird ('sɒŋ,bɜːd) *n* **1** any passerine bird of the suborder *Oscines*, having highly developed vocal organs and, in most, a musical call. Related adj: **oscine 2** any bird having a musical call

song cycle *n* any of several groups of songs written by composers during and after the Romantic period, each series employing texts, usually by one poet, relating a story or grouped around a central motif

song form *n* another name for **ternary form**

songful ('sɒŋfʊl) *adj* tuneful; melodious > 'songfully *adv* > 'songfulness *n*

Songhai (sɒŋ'gaɪ) *n* **1** (*pl* **-ghai** *or* **-ghais**) a member of a Nilotic people of W Africa, living chiefly in Mali and Niger in the central Niger valley **2** the language or group of dialects spoken by this people, now generally regarded as forming a branch of the Nilo-Saharan family

Songhua ('sʌŋ'wɑː) *n* a river in NE China, rising in SE Jilin province and flowing north and northeast to the Amur River near Tongjiang: the chief river of Manchuria and largest tributary of the Amur; frozen from November to April. Length: over 1300 km (800 miles). Also called: **Sungari**

Song Koi *or* **Song Coi** ('sɒŋ 'kɔɪ) *n* transliteration of the Vietnamese name for the **Red River** (sense 3)

songkok ('sɒŋkɒ) *n* (in Malaysia and Indonesia) a kind of oval brimless hat, resembling a skull [from Malay]

Song of Solomon *n* **the** a book of the Old Testament consisting of a collection of dramatic love poems traditionally ascribed to Solomon. Also called: **Song of Songs, Canticle of Canticles**

songololo (ˌsɒŋgə'ləʊləʊ) *or* **shongololo** (ˌʃɒŋgə'ləʊləʊ) *n*, *pl* **-los** a millipede, *Jurus terrestris*, having a hard shiny dark brown segmented exoskeleton [from Nguni *ukusonga* to roll up]

songsmith ('sɒŋˌsmɪθ) *n* a person who writes songs

song sparrow *n* a common North American finch, *Melospiza melodia*, having brown-and-white plumage and a melodious song

songster ('sɒŋstə) *n* **1** a singer or poet **2** a singing bird; songbird > 'songstress *fem n*

song thrush *n* a common Old World thrush, *Turdus philomelos*, that has a brown back and spotted breast and is noted for its song

songwriter ('sɒŋˌraɪtə) *n* a person who composes the words or music for songs in a popular idiom

sonic ('sɒnɪk) *adj* **1** of, involving, or producing sound **2** having a speed about equal to that of sound in air: 331 metres per second (741 miles per hour) at 0°C [c20 from Latin *sonus* sound]

sonic barrier *n* another name for **sound barrier**

sonic boom *n* a loud explosive sound caused by the shock wave of an aircraft, etc, travelling at supersonic speed

sonic depth finder *n* an instrument for detecting the depth of water or of a submerged object by means of sound waves; Fathometer. See also **sonar**

sonics ('sɒnɪks) *n* (*functioning as singular*) *physics* the study of mechanical vibrations in matter

soniferous (sɒ'nɪfərəs) *adj* carrying or producing sound

son-in-law *n*, *pl* **sons-in-law** the husband of one's daughter

sonnet ('sɒnɪt) *prosody* ▷ *n* **1** a verse form of Italian origin consisting of 14 lines in iambic pentameter with rhymes arranged according to a fixed scheme, usually divided either into octave and sestet or, in the English form, into three quatrains and a couplet ▷ *vb* **2** (*intr*) to compose sonnets **3** (*tr*) to celebrate in a sonnet [c16 via Italian from Old Provençal *sonet* a little poem, from *son* song, from Latin *sonus* a sound]

sonneteer (ˌsɒnɪ'tɪə) *n* a writer of sonnets

sonny ('sʌnɪ) *n*, *pl* **-nies** *often patronizing* a familiar term of address to a boy or man [c19 from SON + -Y²]

sonobuoy ('səʊnəˌbɔɪ) *n* a buoy equipped to detect underwater noises and transmit them by radio [from SONIC + BUOY]

son of a bitch *n*, *pl* **sons of bitches** *slang, chiefly US and Canadian* **1** a worthless or contemptible person: used as an insult **2** a humorous or affectionate term for a person, esp a man: *a lucky son of a bitch*

son of a gun *n*, *pl* **sons of guns** *slang, chiefly US and Canadian* a rogue or rascal: used as a jocular form of address

son of God *n* *Bible* **1** an angelic being **2** a Christian believer

Son of Man *n* *Bible* a title of Jesus Christ

sonogram ('səʊnəˌgræm) *n* *physics* a three-dimensional representation of a sound signal, using coordinates of frequency, time, and intensity

sonoluminescence (ˌsəʊnəʊˌluːmɪ'nɛsəns) *n* luminescence produced by ultrasound

Sonora (*Spanish* so'nora) *n* a state of NW Mexico, on the Gulf of California: consists of a narrow coastal plain rising inland to the Sierra Madre Occidental; an important mining area in colonial times. Capital: Hermosillo. Pop: 2 213 370 (2000). Area: 184 934 sq km (71 403 sq miles)

sonorant ('sɒnərənt) *n* *phonetics* **1** one of the frictionless continuants or nasals (l, r, m, n, ŋ) having consonantal or vocalic functions depending on its situation within the syllable **2** either of the two consonants represented in English orthography by *w* or *y* and regarded as either consonantal or vocalic articulations of the vowels (iː) and (uː) [from Latin *sonor* a noise + -ANT]

sonorous (sə'nɔːrəs, 'sɒnərəs) *adj* **1** producing or capable of producing sound **2** (of language, sound, etc) deep or resonant **3** (of speech) high-flown; grandiloquent [c17 from Latin *sonōrus* loud, from *sonor* a noise] > **sonority** (sə'nɒrɪtɪ) *n* > so'norously *adv* > so'norousness *n*

Sons of Freedom *pl n* a Doukhobor sect, located largely in British Columbia: notorious for its acts of terrorism in opposition to the government in the 1950s and 1960s. Also called: **Freedomites**

sonsy *or* **sonsie** ('sɒnsɪ) *adj* **-sier, -siest** *Scot, Irish, and English dialect* **1** plump; buxom; comely **2** cheerful; good-natured **3** lucky [c16 from Gaelic *sonas* good fortune]

Soo Canals (suː) *pl n* **the** the two ship canals linking Lakes Superior and Huron. There is a canal on the Canadian and on the US side of the rapids of the St Mary's River. See also **Sault Sainte Marie**

Soochow ('suː'tʃaʊ) *n* a variant transliteration of the Chinese name for **Suzhou**

sook¹ (sʊk) *n* **1** *Southwest English dialect* a baby **2** *derogatory* a coward **3** *NZ informal* a calf [perhaps from Old English *sūcan* to suck, influenced by Welsh *swci swead* tame]

sook² *or* **souk** (suːk) *Scot* ▷ *vb* **1** to suck ▷ *n* **2** the act or an instance of sucking **3** a sycophant; toady [Old English *sūcan*]

sool (suːl) *vb* (*tr*) to incite (a dog) to attack [c17 from English dialect *sowl* (esp of a dog) to pull or seize roughly]

soon (suːn) *adv* **1** in or after a short time; in a little while; before long: *the doctor will soon be here* **2** as soon as at the very moment that: *she burst into tears as soon as she saw him* **3** as soon...as used to indicate that the second alternative mentioned is not preferable to the first: *I'd just as soon go by train as drive* [Old English *sōna*; related to Old High German *sāno*, Gothic *suns*]

sooner ('suːnə) *adv* **1** the comparative of **soon** *he came sooner than I thought* **2** rather; in preference: *I'd sooner die than give up* **3** no sooner...than immediately after or when: *no sooner had he got home than the rain stopped; no sooner said than done* **4 sooner or later** eventually; inevitably

> USAGE When is sometimes used instead of *than* after *no sooner*, but this use is generally regarded as incorrect: *no sooner had he arrived than* (not *when*) *the telephone rang*

soonest ('suːnəst) *adv* **1** the superlative of **soon 2** as soon as possible; urgently; without delay: *send money soonest*

soot (sʊt) *n* **1** finely divided carbon deposited from flames during the incomplete combustion of organic substances such as coal ▷ *vb* **2** (*tr*) to cover with soot [Old English *sōt*; related to Old Norse, Middle Low German *sōt*, Lithuanian *sódis*, Old Slavonic *sažda*, Old Irish *sūide*]

sooth (suːθ) *archaic or poetic* ▷ *n* **1** truth or reality (esp in the phrase **in sooth**) ▷ *adj* **2** true or real **3** smooth [Old English *sōth*; related to Old Norse *sathr* true, Old High German *sand*, Gothic *sunja* truth, Latin *sōns* guilty, *sonticus* critical] > 'soothly *adv*

soothe (suːð) *vb* **1** (*tr*) to make calm or tranquil **2** (*tr*) to relieve or assuage (pain, longing, etc) **3** (*intr*) to bring tranquillity or relief [c16 (in the sense: to mollify): from Old English *sōthian* to prove; related to Old Norse *sanna* to assert; see SOOTH] > 'soother *n*

soothfast ('suːθˌfɑːst) *adj* *archaic* **1** truthful **2** loyal; true [from Old English *sōthfæst*; see SOOTH, FAST¹]

soothing ('suːðɪŋ) *adj* having a calming, assuaging, or relieving effect > 'soothingly *adv* > 'soothingness *n*

soothsay ('suːθˌseɪ) *vb* **-says, -saying, -said** (*intr*) to predict the future > 'sooth,saying *n*

soothsayer ('suːθˌseɪə) *n* a seer or prophet

sooty ('sʊtɪ) *adj* **sootier, sootiest 1** covered with soot **2** resembling or consisting of soot > 'sootily *adv* > 'sootiness *n*

sooty mould *n* **1** a fungal plant disease characterized by a blackish growth covering the surface of leaves, fruits, etc **2** any of various fungi, such as species of *Meliola* or *Capnodium*, that cause this disease

sop (sɒp) *n* **1** (*often plural*) food soaked in a liquid before being eaten **2** a concession, bribe, etc, given to placate or mollify: *a sop to one's feelings* **3** *informal* a stupid or weak person ▷ *vb* **sops, sopping, sopped 4** (*tr*) to dip or soak (food) in liquid **5** (*intr*, often foll by *in*) to soak or be soaked ▷ See also **sop up** [Old English *sopp*; related to Old Norse *soppa* soup, Old High German *sopfa* milk with bread; see SUP²]

SOP *abbreviation for* standard operating procedure

sop. *abbreviation for* soprano

sophism ('sɒfɪzəm) *n* an instance of sophistry. Compare **paralogism** [c14 from Latin *sophisma*, from Greek: ingenious trick, from *sophizesthai* to use clever deceit, from *sophos* wise, clever]

sophist ('sɒfɪst) *n* **1** (*often capital*) one of the pre-Socratic philosophers who were itinerant professional teachers of oratory and argument and who were prepared to enter into debate on any matter however specious **2** a person who uses clever or quibbling arguments that are fundamentally unsound [c16 from Latin *sophista*, from Greek *sophistēs* a wise man, from *sophizesthai* to act craftily]

sophister ('sɒfɪstə) *n* **1** (*esp formerly*) a second-year undergraduate at certain British universities **2** *rare* another word for **sophist**

sophistic (sə'fɪstɪk) *or* **sophistical** *adj* **1** of or relating to sophists or sophistry **2** consisting of sophisms or sophistry; specious > so'phistically *adv*

sophisticate *vb* (sə'fɪstɪˌkeɪt) **1** (*tr*) to make (someone) less natural or innocent, as by education **2** to pervert or corrupt (an argument, etc) by sophistry **3** (*tr*) to make more complex or refined **4** *rare* to falsify (a text, etc) by alterations ▷ *n* (sə'fɪstɪˌkeɪt, -kɪt) **5** a sophisticated person [c14 from Medieval Latin *sophisticāre*, from Latin *sophisticus* sophistic] > so,phisti'cation *n* > so'phisti,cator *n*

sophisticated (sə'fɪstɪˌkeɪtɪd) *adj* **1** having refined or cultured tastes and habits **2** appealing to sophisticates: *a sophisticated restaurant* **3** unduly refined or cultured **4** pretentiously or superficially wise **5** (of machines, methods, etc) complex and refined > so'phisti,catedly *adv*

sophistry ('sɒfɪstrɪ) *n*, *pl* **-ries 1 a** a method of argument that is seemingly plausible though actually invalid and misleading **b** the art of using such arguments **2** subtle but unsound or fallacious reasoning **3** an instance of this; sophism

Sophoclean (ˌsɒfə'kliːən) *adj* of or relating to

Sophocles, the Greek dramatist (?496–406 BC)

sophomore ('sɒfə,mɔː) *n chiefly US and Canadian* a second-year student at a secondary (high) school or college [C17 perhaps from earlier *sophumer*, from *sophum*, variant of SOPHISM + -ER[1]]

Sophy *or* **Sophi** ('səʊfɪ) *n, pl* **-phies** (formerly) a title of the Persian monarchs [C16 from Latin *sophī* wise men, from Greek *sophos* wise]

-sophy *n combining form* indicating knowledge or an intellectual system: *philosophy; theosophy* [from Greek *-sophia*, from *sophia* wisdom, from *sophos* wise] > **-sophic** *or* **-sophical** *adj combining form*

sopor ('səʊpə) *n* an abnormally deep sleep; stupor [C17 from Latin: a deep sleep, death; related to *somnus* sleep]

soporific (,sɒpə'rɪfɪk) *adj also or archaic* **soporiferous** **1** inducing sleep **2** drowsy; sleepy ▷ *n* **3** a drug or other agent that induces sleep > ,**sopo'rifically** *adv*

sopping ('sɒpɪŋ) *adj* completely soaked; wet through. Also: **sopping wet**

soppy ('sɒpɪ) *adj* **-pier, -piest** **1** wet or soggy **2** *Brit informal* silly or sentimental > '**soppily** *adv* > '**soppiness** *n*

sopranino (,sɒprə'niːnəʊ) *n, pl* **-nos** **a** the instrument with the highest possible pitch in a family of instruments **b** (*as modifier*): *a sopranino recorder* [Italian, diminutive of SOPRANO]

soprano (sə'prɑːnəʊ) *n, pl* **-pranos** *or* **-prani** (-'prɑːniː) **1** the highest adult female voice, having a range approximately from middle C to the A a thirteenth above it **2** the voice of a young boy before puberty **3** a singer with such a voice **4** the highest part of a piece of harmony **5** **a** the highest or second highest instrument in a family of instruments **b** (*as modifier*): *a soprano saxophone* ▷ See also **treble** [C18 from Italian, from *sopra* above, from Latin *suprā*]

soprano clef *n* the clef that establishes middle C as being on the bottom line of the staff. See also **C clef**

sop up *vb* (*tr, adverb*) to mop or take up (spilt water, etc) with or as if with a sponge

sora ('sɔːrə) *n* a North American rail, *Porzana carolina*, with a greyish-brown plumage and yellow bill [C18 of unknown origin]

Sorata (*Spanish* so'rata) *n* **Mount** a mountain in W Bolivia, in the Andes: the highest mountain in the Cordillera Real, with two peaks, Ancohuma, 6550 m (21 490 ft), and Illampu, 6485 m (21 276 ft)

sorb (sɔːb) *n* **1** another name for **service tree** (sense 1) **2** any of various related trees, esp the mountain ash **3** Also called: **sorb apple** the fruit of any of these trees [C16 from Latin *sorbus* the sorb, service tree] > '**sorbic** *adj*

Sorb (sɔːb) *n* a member of a Slavonic people living chiefly in the rural areas of E Germany between the upper reaches of the Oder and Elbe rivers (Lusatia). Also called: **Wend, Lusatian**

sorbefacient (,sɔːbɪ'feɪʃənt) *adj* **1** inducing absorption ▷ *n* **2** a sorbefacient drug [C19 from Latin *sorbē(re)* to absorb + -FACIENT]

sorbet ('sɔːbeɪ, -bɪt) *n* **1** a water ice made from fruit juice, egg whites, milk, etc **2** a US word for **sherbet** (sense 2) [C16 from French, from Old Italian *sorbetto*, from Turkish *şerbet*, from Arabic *sharbah* a drink]

Sorbian ('sɔːbɪən) *n* **1** a West Slavonic language spoken in the rural areas of E Germany between the upper reaches of the Oder and Elbe rivers; modern Wendish ▷ *adj* **2** of or relating to the Sorbs or their language

sorbic acid *n* a white crystalline unsaturated carboxylic acid found in berries of the mountain ash and used to inhibit the growth of moulds and as an additive for certain synthetic coatings, as of cheese (**E200**); 2,4-hexadienoic acid. It exists as *cis-* and *trans-* isomers, the latter being the one usually obtained. Formula: $CH_3CH{:}CHCH{:}CHCOOH$ [C19 from SORB (the tree), from its discovery in the berries of the mountain ash]

sorbitol ('sɔːbɪ,tɒl) *n* a white water-soluble crystalline alcohol with a sweet taste, found in certain fruits and berries and manufactured by the catalytic hydrogenation of sucrose: used as a sweetener (**E420**) and in the manufacture of ascorbic acid and synthetic resins. Formula: $C_6H_8(OH)_6$ [C19 from SORB + -ITOL]

Sorbonne (*French* sɔrbɔn) *n* **the** a part of the University of Paris containing the faculties of science and literature: founded in 1253 by Robert de Sorbon as a theological college; given to the university in 1808

sorbo rubber ('sɔːbəʊ) *n Brit* a spongy form of rubber [C20 from ABSORB]

sorbose ('sɔːbəʊs) *n biochem* a sweet-tasting hexose sugar derived from the berries of the mountain ash by bacterial action: used in the synthesis of ascorbic acid. Formula: $CH_2OH(CHOH)_3COCH_2OH$ [C19 from SORB + -OSE[2]]

sorcerer ('sɔːsərə) *or feminine* **sorceress** ('sɔːsərɪs) *n* a person who seeks to control and use magic powers; a wizard or magician [C16 from Old French *sorcier*, from Vulgar Latin *sortiārius* (unattested) caster of lots, from Latin *sors* lot]

sorcery ('sɔːsərɪ) *n, pl* **-ceries** the art, practices, or spells of magic, esp black magic, by which it is sought to harness occult forces or evil spirits in order to produce preternatural effects in the world [C13 from Old French *sorcerie*, from *sorcier* SORCERER] > '**sorcerous** *adj*

sordes ('sɔːdiːz) *pl n med* dark incrustations on the lips and teeth of patients with prolonged fever [C18 from Latin *sordēs* filth]

sordid ('sɔːdɪd) *adj* **1** dirty, foul, or squalid **2** degraded; vile; base: *a sordid affair* **3** selfish and grasping: *sordid avarice* [C16 from Latin *sordidus*, from *sordēre* to be dirty] > '**sordidly** *adv* > '**sordidness** *n*

sordino (sɔː'diːnəʊ) *n, pl* **-ni** (-niː) **1** a mute for a stringed or brass musical instrument **2** any of the dampers that arrest the vibrations of piano strings **3** **con sordino** *or* **sordini** a musical direction to play with a mute **4** **senza sordino** *or* **sordini** a musical direction to remove or play without the mute or (on the piano) with the sustaining pedal pressed down ▷ See also **sourdine** [Italian: from *sordo* deaf, from Latin *surdus*]

sore (sɔː) *adj* **1** (esp of a wound, injury, etc) painfully sensitive; tender **2** causing annoyance: *a sore point* **3** resentful; irked: *he was sore that nobody believed him* **4** urgent; pressing: *in sore need* **5** (*postpositive*) grieved; distressed **6** causing grief or sorrow ▷ *n* **7** a painful or sensitive wound, injury, etc **8** any cause of distress or vexation ▷ *adv* **9** *archaic* direly; sorely (now only in such phrases as **sore pressed, sore afraid**) [Old English *sār*; related to Old Norse *sārr*, Old High German *sēr*, Gothic *sair* sore, Latin *saevus* angry] > '**soreness** *n*

soredium (sɔː'riːdɪəm) *n* an organ of vegetative reproduction in lichens consisting of a cluster of algal cells enclosed in fungal hyphae: dispersed by wind, insects, or other means [C19 New Latin, from Greek *sōros* a heap]

sorehead ('sɔː,hɛd) *n informal, chiefly US and Canadian* a peevish or disgruntled person > ,**sore'headedly** *adv* > ,**sore'headedness** *n*

sorely ('sɔːlɪ) *adv* **1** painfully or grievously: *sorely wounded* **2** pressingly or greatly: *to be sorely taxed; he will be sorely missed*

sorghum ('sɔːɡəm) *n* any grass of the Old World genus *Sorghum*, having solid stems, large flower heads, and glossy seeds: cultivated for grain, hay, and as a source of syrup. See also **kaffir corn, durra** [C16 from New Latin, from Italian *sorgo*, probably from Vulgar Latin *Syricum grānum* (unattested) Syrian grain]

sorgo *or* **sorgho** ('sɔːɡəʊ) *n, pl* **-gos** *or* **-ghos** any of several varieties of sorghum that have watery sweet juice and are grown for fodder, silage, or syrup [Italian]

sori ('sɔːraɪ) *n* the plural of **sorus**

soricine ('sɒrɪ,saɪn) *adj* of, relating to, or resembling the shrews or the family (*Soricidae*) to which they belong [C18 from Latin *sōricīnus*, from *sōrex* a shrew]

sorites (sɒ'raɪtiːz) *n logic* **a** a polysyllogism in which the premises are arranged so that intermediate conclusions are omitted, being understood, and only the final conclusion is stated **b** a paradox of the form: *these few grains of sand do not constitute a heap, and the addition of a single grain never makes what is not yet a heap into a heap: so no matter how many single grains one adds it never becomes a heap* [C16 via Latin from Greek *sōreitēs*, literally: heaped, from *sōros* a heap] > **soritical** (sɒ'rɪtɪkəl) *or* **so'ritic** *adj*

sorn (sɔːn) *vb* (*intr*, often foll by *on* or *upon*) *Scot* to obtain food, lodging, etc, from another person by presuming on his generosity [C16 from earlier *sorren* a feudal obligation requiring vassals to offer free hospitality to their lord and his men, from obsolete Irish *sorthan* free quarters]

Sorocaba (*Portuguese* soro'kaba) *n* a city in S Brazil, in São Paulo state: industrial centre. Pop: 671 000 (2005 est)

Soroptimist (sə'rɒptɪmɪst) *n* a member of an organization of clubs (**Soroptimist International**) for professional and executive businesswomen [C20 from Latin *soror* sister + OPTIMIST]

sororate ('sɒrə,reɪt) *n* the custom in some societies of a widower marrying his deceased wife's younger sister [C20 from Latin *soror* a sister]

sororicide (sə'rɒrɪ,saɪd) *n* **1** the act of killing one's own sister **2** a person who kills his or her sister [C17 from Latin *sorōricīda* one who murders his sister, from *soror* sister + *caedere* to slay] > **so,rori'cidal** *adj*

sorority (sə'rɒrɪtɪ) *n, pl* **-ties** *chiefly US* a social club or society for university women [C16 from Medieval Latin *sorōritās*, from Latin *soror* sister]

sorosis (sə'rəʊsɪs) *n, pl* **-ses** (-siːz) a fleshy multiple fruit, such as that of the pineapple and mulberry, formed from flowers that are crowded together on a fleshy stem [C19 from New Latin, from Greek *sōros* a heap]

sorption ('sɔːpʃən) *n* the process in which one substance takes up or holds another; adsorption or absorption [C20 back formation from ABSORPTION, ADSORPTION]

sorrel[1] ('sɒrəl) *n* **1** **a** a light brown to brownish-orange colour **b** (*as adjective*): *a sorrel carpet* **2** a horse of this colour [C15 from Old French *sorel*, from *sor* a reddish brown, of Germanic origin; related to Middle Dutch *soor* desiccated]

sorrel[2] ('sɒrəl) *n* **1** any of several polygonaceous plants of the genus *Rumex*, esp *R. acetosa*, of Eurasia and North America, having acid-tasting leaves used in salads and sauces. See also **dock**[4], **sheep sorrel** **2** short for **wood sorrel** [C14 from Old French *surele*, from *sur* sour, of Germanic origin; related to Old High German *sūr* SOUR]

sorrel tree *n* a deciduous ericaceous tree, *Oxydendrum arboreum*, of E North America, having deeply fissured bark, sour-tasting leaves, and small white flowers. Also called: **sourwood** [C17 so called because the bitter flavour of the leaves is reminiscent of sorrel]

Sorrento (sə'rɛntəʊ; *Italian* sor'rɛnto) *n* a port in SW Italy, in Campania on a mountainous peninsula between the Bay of Naples and the Gulf of Salerno: a resort since Roman times. Pop: 16 536 (2001)

sorrow ('sɒrəʊ) *n* **1** the characteristic feeling of sadness, grief, or regret associated with loss, bereavement, sympathy for another's suffering, for an injury done, etc **2** a particular cause or source of regret, grief, etc **3** Also called: **sorrowing** the outward expression of grief or sadness ▷ *vb* **4** (*intr*) to mourn or grieve [Old English *sorg*; related to Old Norse *sorg*, Gothic *saurga*, Old High German *sworga*] > '**sorrower** *n* > '**sorrowful** *adj* > '**sorrowfully** *adv* > '**sorrowfulness** *n*

sorry ('sɒrɪ) *adj* **-rier, -riest** **1** (*usually postpositive*; often foll by *for*) feeling or expressing pity,

S

sympathy, remorse, grief, or regret: *I feel sorry for him* **2** pitiful, wretched, or deplorable: *a sorry sight* **3** poor; paltry: *a sorry excuse* **4** affected by sorrow; sad **5** causing sorrow or sadness ▷ *interj* **6** an exclamation expressing apology, used esp at the time of the misdemeanour, offence, etc [Old English *sārig;* related to Old High German *sērag;* see SORE] > **'sorrily** *adv* > **'sorriness** *n*

sort (sɔːt) *n* **1** a class, group, kind, etc, as distinguished by some common quality or characteristic **2** *informal* type of character, nature, etc: *he's a good sort* **3** a more or less definable or adequate example: *it's a sort of review* **4** *(often plural) printing* any of the individual characters making up a fount of type **5** *archaic* manner; way: *in this sort we struggled home* **6** **after a sort** to some extent **7** **of sorts** *or* **of a sort** **a** of an inferior kind **b** of an indefinite kind **8** **out of sorts** not in normal good health, temper, etc **9** **sort of** in some way or other; as it were; rather ▷ *vb* **10** *(tr)* to arrange according to class, type, etc **11** *(tr)* to put (something) into working order **12** *(tr)* to arrange (computer information) by machine in an order convenient to the computer user **13** *(tr; foll by with) informal* to supply, esp with drugs **14** *(intr; foll by with, together, etc) archaic or dialect* to associate, as on friendly terms **15** *(intr) archaic* to agree; accord [C14 from Old French, from Medieval Latin *sors* kind, from Latin: fate] > **'sortable** *adj* > **'sortably** *adv* > **'sorter** *n*

USAGE See at **kind²**

sortal ('sɔːtəl) *n logic, linguistics* **1** a concept grasp of which includes knowledge of criteria of individuation and reidentification, such as *dog* or *concerto,* but not *flesh* or *music* **2** a count noun representing such a concept

sortation (sɔː'teɪʃən) *n* the process of sorting items into groups sharing a distinguishing quality or characteristic

sort code *n* a sequence of numbers printed on a cheque or embossed on a bank or building-society card that identifies the branch holding the account

sorted ('sɔːtɪd) *slang* ▷ *interj* **1** an exclamation of satisfaction, approval, etc ▷ *adj* **2** possessing the desired recreational drugs

sortie ('sɔːtɪ) *n* **1** **a** (of troops, etc) the act of emerging from a contained or besieged position **b** the troops doing this **2** an operational flight made by one aircraft ▷ *vb* **-ties, -tieing, -tied** **3** *(intr)* to make a sortie [C17 from French: a going out, from *sortir* to go out]

sortilege ('sɔːtɪlɪdʒ) *n* **1** the act or practice of divination by drawing lots **2** magic or sorcery [C14 via Old French from Medieval Latin *sortilegium,* from Latin *sortilegus* a soothsayer, from *sors* fate + *legere* to select]

sortition (sɔː'tɪʃən) *n* the act of casting lots [C16 from Latin *sortitio,* from *sortiri* to cast lots]

sort out *vb (tr, adverb)* **1** to find a solution to (a problem, etc), esp to make clear or tidy: *it took a long time to sort out the mess* **2** to take or separate, as from a larger group: *he sorted out the most likely ones* **3** to organize into an orderly and disciplined group **4** *informal* to beat or punish

sorus ('sɔːrəs) *n, pl* **-ri** (-raɪ) **1** a cluster of sporangia on the undersurface of certain fern leaves **2** any of various similar spore-producing structures in some lichens and fungi [C19 via New Latin from Greek *sōros* a heap]

SOS *n* **1** an internationally recognized distress signal in which the letters SOS are repeatedly spelt out, as by radio-telegraphy: used esp by ships and aircraft **2** a message broadcast in an emergency for people otherwise unobtainable **3** *informal* a call for help [C20 letters chosen as the simplest to transmit and receive in Morse code; by folk etymology taken to be abbrev for *save our souls*]

sosatie (sə'sɑːtɪ) *n South African* a skewer of curried meat pieces [Afrikaans]

Sosnowiec *(Polish* sɔs'nɔvjɛts) *n* an industrial town in S Poland. Pop: 244 102 (1999 est)

so-so *informal* ▷ *adj* **1** *(postpositive)* neither good nor bad ▷ *adv* **2** in an average or indifferent manner

sostenuto (ˌsɒstə'nuːtəʊ) *adj, adv music* (preceded by a tempo marking) to be performed in a smooth sustained manner [C18 from Italian, from *sostenere* to sustain, from Latin *sustinēre* to uphold]

sostenuto pedal *n* another word for **sustaining pedal**

sot¹ (sɒt) *n* **1** a habitual or chronic drunkard **2** a person stupefied by or as if by drink [Old English, from Medieval Latin *sottus;* compare French *sot* a fool] > **'sottish** *adj*

sot² (sɒt) *adv Scot* indeed: used to contradict a negative statement: *I am not! — You are sot!* [a variant of so¹, altered to rhyme with *not*]

soteriology (sɒˌtɪərɪ'ɒlədʒɪ) *n theol* the doctrine of salvation [C19 from Greek *sōtēria* deliverance (from *sōtēr* a saviour) + -LOGY] > **soteriologic** (sɒˌtɪərɪə'lɒdʒɪk) *or* **soˌterio'logical** *adj*

Sothic ('səʊθɪk, 'sɒθ-) *adj* relating to the star Sirius or to the rising of this star [C19 from Greek *Sōthis,* from Egyptian, name of Sirius]

Sothic year *n* the fixed year of the ancient Egyptians, 365 days 6 hours long, beginning with the appearance of the star Sirius on the eastern horizon at dawn, which heralded the yearly flooding of the Nile. A **Sothic cycle** contained 1460 such years

Sothis ('səʊθɪs) *n* another name for **Sirius** [Greek; see SOTHIC]

Sotho ('suːtuː, 'səʊtəʊ) *n* **1** *(pl* **-tho** *or* **-thos)** a member of a large grouping of Negroid peoples of southern Africa, living chiefly in Botswana, South Africa, and Lesotho **2** the group of mutually intelligible languages of this people, including Lesotho, Tswana, and Pedi. It belongs to the Bantu group of the Niger-Congo family **3** *pl* **-tho** *or* **-thos** *South African* a member of the Basotho people; a Mosotho **4** *South African* the dialect of Sotho spoken by the Basotho; Sesotho. It is an official language of Lesotho along with English ▷ Former name (for senses 3, 4): **Basuto**

Soto (soto) *n* a Zen Buddhist school of Japan, characterized by the practice of sitting meditation leading to gradual enlightenment

sotto voce ('sɒtəʊ 'vəʊtʃɪ) *adv* in an undertone [C18 from Italian: under (one's) voice]

sou (suː) *n* **1** a former French coin of low denomination **2** a very small amount of money: *I haven't a sou to my name* [C19 from French, from Old French *sol,* from Latin: SOLIDUS]

soubise (suː'biːz) *n* a purée of onions mixed into a thick white sauce and served over eggs, fish, etc. Also called: **soubise sauce** [C18 named after Charles de Rohan *Soubise* (1715–87), marshal of France]

soubrette (suː'brɛt) *n* **1** a minor female role in comedy, often that of a pert lady's maid **2** any pert or flirtatious girl [C18 from French: maidservant, from Provençal *soubreto,* from *soubret* conceited, from *soubra* to exceed, from Latin *superāre* to surmount, from *super* above] > **sou'brettish** *adj*

soubriquet ('səʊbrɪˌkeɪ) *n* a variant spelling of **sobriquet**

souchong ('suː'ʃɒŋ, -'tʃɒŋ) *n* a black tea with large leaves [C18 from Chinese *hsiao-chung* small kind]

Soudan (sudɑ̃) *n* the French name for the **Sudan**

souffle ('suːfᵊl) *n med* a blowing sound or murmur heard in auscultation [C19 from French, from *souffler* to blow]

soufflé ('suːfleɪ) *n* **1** a very light fluffy dish made with egg yolks and stiffly beaten egg whites combined with cheese, fish, etc **2** a similar sweet or savoury cold dish, set with gelatine ▷ *adj also* **souffléed** **3** made light and puffy, as by beating and cooking [C19 from French, from *souffler* to blow, from Latin *sufflāre*]

Soufrière *(French* sufrjɛr) *n* **1** a volcano in the Caribbean, on N St Vincent: erupted in 1902, killing about 2000 people. Height: 1234 m (4048 ft) **2** a volcano in the Caribbean, on S Montserrat: the highest point on the island; erupted 1997, causing the effective destruction of the capital, Plymouth, and requiring the partial evacuation of the island. Height: 915 m (3002 ft) **3** a volcano in the Caribbean, on Guadeloupe. Height: 1484 m (4869 ft)

sough¹ (saʊ) *vb* **1** *(intr)* (esp of the wind) to make a characteristic sighing sound ▷ *n* **2** a soft continuous murmuring sound [Old English *swōgan* to resound; related to Gothic *gaswogjan* to groan, Lithuanian *svageti* to sound, Latin *vāgīre* to lament]

sough² (sʌf) *n Northern English dialect* a sewer or drain or an outlet channel [of obscure origin]

sought (sɔːt) *vb* the past tense and past participle of **seek**

sought-after *adj* in demand; wanted

souk¹ *or* **suq** (suːk) *n* (in Muslim countries, esp North Africa and the Middle East) an open-air marketplace [C20 from Arabic *sūq*]

souk² (suːk) *vb, n Scot* a variant spelling of **sook²**

soukous ('suːkʊs) *n* a style of African popular music that originated in Zaïre (now the Democratic Republic of Congo), characterized by syncopated rhythms and intricate contrasting guitar melodies [C20 perhaps from French *secouer* to shake]

soul (səʊl) *n* **1** the spirit or immaterial part of man, the seat of human personality, intellect, will, and emotions, regarded as an entity that survives the body after death. Related adj: **pneumatic** **2** *Christianity* the spiritual part of a person, capable of redemption from the power of sin through divine grace **3** the essential part or fundamental nature of anything **4** a person's feelings or moral nature as distinct from other faculties **5** **a** Also called: **soul music** a type of Black music resulting from the addition of jazz, gospel, and pop elements to the urban blues style **b** *(as modifier): a soul singer* **6** *(modifier)* of or relating to Black Americans and their culture: *soul brother; soul food* **7** nobility of spirit or temperament: *a man of great soul and courage* **8** an inspiring spirit or leading figure, as of a cause or movement **9** **the life and soul** See **life** (sense 28) **10** a person regarded as typifying some characteristic or quality: *the soul of discretion* **11** a person; individual: *an honest soul* **12** **upon my soul!** an exclamation of surprise [Old English *sāwol;* related to Old Frisian *sēle,* Old Saxon *sēola,* Old High German *sēula* soul] > **'soul-ˌlike** *adj*

Soul (səʊl) *n Christian Science* another word for **God**

soul-destroying *adj* (of an occupation, situation, etc) unremittingly monotonous

soul food *n informal* food, such as chitterlings or yams, traditionally eaten by Black people in the southern US

soulful ('səʊlfʊl) *adj sometimes ironic* expressing profound thoughts or feelings: *soulful music* > **'soulfully** *adv* > **'soulfulness** *n*

soulless ('səʊllɪs) *adj* **1** lacking any humanizing qualities or influences; dead; mechanical: *soulless work* **2** (of a person) lacking in sensitivity or nobility **3** heartless; cruel > **'soullessly** *adv* > **'soullessness** *n*

soul mate *n* a person for whom one has a deep affinity, esp a lover, wife, husband, etc

soul-searching *n* **1** deep or critical examination of one's motives, actions, beliefs, etc ▷ *adj* **2** displaying the characteristics of deep or painful self-analysis

sou marqué ('suː mɑː'keɪ; *French* su marke) *n, pl* **sous marqués** ('su mɑː'keɪz; *French* su marke) a French copper coin of the 18th century [French, literally: a marked sou]

sound¹ (saʊnd) *n* **1** **a** a periodic disturbance in the pressure or density of a fluid or in the elastic strain of a solid, produced by a vibrating object. It has a velocity in air at sea level at 0°C of 331 metres per second (741 miles per hour) and travels as longitudinal waves **b** *(as modifier): a sound wave* **2** *(modifier)* of or relating to radio as distinguished from television: *sound broadcasting; sound radio* **3** the sensation produced by such a periodic disturbance in the organs of hearing **4** anything that can be heard **5** a particular instance, quality, or type of sound: *the sound of running water* **6** volume or quality of sound: *a radio with poor sound* **7** the area or distance over which something can be heard: *to be born within the sound of Big Ben* **8** the impression or implication of something: *I don't like the sound of that* **9** *phonetics* the auditory effect produced by a specific articulation or set of related articulations **10** (*often plural*) *slang* music, esp rock, jazz, or pop ▷ *vb* **11** to cause (something, such as an instrument) to make a sound or (of an instrument, etc) to emit a sound **12** to announce or be announced by a sound: *to sound the alarm* **13** (*intr*) (of a sound) to be heard **14** (*intr*) to resonate with a certain quality or intensity: *to sound loud* **15** (*copula*) to give the impression of being as specified when read, heard, etc: *to sound reasonable* **16** (*tr*) to pronounce distinctly or audibly: *to sound one's consonants* **17** (*intr*; usually foll by *in*) *law* to have the essential quality or nature (of): *an action sounding in damages* ▷ See also **sound off** [C13 from Old French *soner* to make a sound, from Latin *sonāre*, from *sonus* a sound] > ˈ**soundable** *adj*

sound² (saʊnd) *adj* **1** free from damage, injury, decay, etc **2** firm; solid; substantial: *a sound basis* **3** financially safe or stable: *a sound investment* **4** showing good judgment or reasoning; sensible; wise: *sound advice* **5** valid, logical, or justifiable: *a sound argument* **6** holding approved beliefs; ethically correct; upright; honest **7** (of sleep) deep; peaceful; unbroken **8** thorough; complete: *a sound examination* **9** *Brit informal* excellent **10** *law* (of a title, etc) free from defect; legally valid **11** constituting a valid and justifiable application of correct principles; orthodox: *sound theology* **12** *logic* **a** (of a deductive argument) valid **b** (of an inductive argument) according with whatever principles ensure the high probability of the truth of the conclusion given the truth of the premises **c** another word for **consistent** (sense 5b) ▷ *adv* **13** soundly; deeply: now archaic except when applied to sleep [Old English *sund*; related to Old Saxon *gisund*, Old High German *gisunt*] > ˈ**soundly** *adv* > ˈ**soundness** *n*

sound³ (saʊnd) *vb* **1** to measure the depth of (a well, the sea, etc) by lowering a plumb line, by sonar, etc **2** to seek to discover (someone's views, etc), as by questioning **3** (*intr*) (of a whale, etc) to dive downwards swiftly and deeply **4** *med* **a** to probe or explore (a bodily cavity or passage) by means of a sound **b** to examine (a patient) by means of percussion and auscultation ▷ *n* **5** *med* an instrument for insertion into a bodily cavity or passage to dilate strictures, dislodge foreign material, etc ▷ See also **sound out** [C14 from Old French *sonder*, from *sonde* sounding line, probably of Germanic origin; related to Old English *sundgyrd* sounding pole, Old Norse *sund* strait, SOUND⁴; see SWIM]

sound⁴ (saʊnd) *n* **1** a relatively narrow channel between two larger areas of sea or between an island and the mainland **2** an inlet or deep bay of the sea **3** the air bladder of a fish [Old English *sund* swimming, narrow sea; related to Middle Low German *sunt* strait; see SOUND³]

Sound (saʊnd) *n* **the** a strait between SW Sweden and Zealand (Denmark), linking the Kattegat with the Baltic: busy shipping lane; spanned by a bridge in 2000. Length: 113 km (70 miles). Narrowest point: 5 km (3 miles). Danish name: **Øresund** Swedish name: **Öresund**

soundalike (ˈsaʊndəˌlaɪk) *n* **a** a person or thing that sounds like another, often well known, person or thing **b** (*as modifier*): *a soundalike band*

sound barrier *n* (*not in technical usage*) a hypothetical barrier to flight at or above the speed of sound, when a sudden large increase in drag occurs. Also called: **sonic barrier, transonic barrier**

sound bite *n* a short pithy sentence or phrase extracted from a longer speech for use on radio or television

sound bow (bəʊ) *n* the thick part of a bell against which the hammer strikes

soundbox (ˈsaʊndˌbɒks) *n* the resonating chamber of the hollow body of a violin, guitar, etc

soundcard (ˈsaʊndˌkɑːd) *n* a printed circuit board inserted into a computer, enabling the output and manipulation of sound

sound check *n* an on-the-spot rehearsal by a band before a gig to enable the sound engineer to set up the mixer

sound effect *n* any sound artificially produced, reproduced from a recording, etc, to create a theatrical effect, such as the bringing together of two halves of a hollow coconut shell to simulate a horse's gallop; used in plays, films, etc

sounder¹ (ˈsaʊndə) *n* an electromagnetic device formerly used in telegraphy to convert electric signals sent over wires into audible sounds

sounder² (ˈsaʊndə) *n* a person or device that measures the depth of water, etc

sound head *n* the part of a film projector that reproduces the sound in a film

sound hole *n* any of variously shaped apertures in the sounding board of certain stringed instruments, such as the '*f*' shaped holes of a violin

sounding¹ (ˈsaʊndɪŋ) *adj* **1** resounding; resonant **2** having an imposing sound and little content; pompous: *sounding phrases* > ˈ**soundingly** *adv*

sounding² (ˈsaʊndɪŋ) *n* **1** (*sometimes plural*) the act or process of measuring depth of water or examining the bottom of a river, lake, etc, as with a sounding line **2** an observation or measurement of atmospheric conditions, as made using a radiosonde or rocketsonde **3** (*often plural*) measurements taken by sounding **4** (*plural*) a place where a sounding line will reach the bottom, esp less than 100 fathoms in depth **5** on (*or* off) **soundings** in waters less than (or more than) 100 fathoms in depth

sounding board *n* **1** Also called: **soundboard** a thin wooden board in a piano or comprising the upper surface of a resonating chamber in a violin, cello, etc, serving to amplify the vibrations produced by the strings passing across it. See also **belly** (sense 6) **2** Also called: **soundboard** a thin screen suspended over a pulpit, stage, etc, to reflect sound towards an audience **3** a person, group, experiment, etc, used to test a new idea, policy, etc, for acceptance or applicability

sounding lead (lɛd) *n* a lead weight, usually conical and having a depression in the base for a dab of grease so that, when dropped to the bottom on a sounding line, a sample of sand, gravel, etc, can be retrieved

sounding line *n* a line marked off to indicate its length and having a sounding lead at one end. It is dropped over the side of a vessel to determine the depth of the water

soundless¹ (ˈsaʊndlɪs) *adj* extremely still or silent > ˈ**soundlessly** *adv* > ˈ**soundlessness** *n*

soundless² (ˈsaʊndlɪs) *adj chiefly poetic* extremely deep

sound mixer *n films, radio, television* **1** the person who mixes various sound sources into a composite programme **2** a piece of equipment designed for mixing sound

sound off *vb* (*intr, adverb*) **1** to proclaim loudly, as in venting one's opinions, grievances, etc **2** to speak angrily

sound out *vb* (*tr, adverb*) to question (someone) in order to discover (opinions, facts, etc)

soundpost (ˈsaʊndˌpəʊst) *n music* a small post, usually of pine, on guitars, violins, etc, that joins the front surface to the back, helps to support the bridge, and allows the whole body of the instrument to vibrate

soundproof (ˈsaʊndˌpruːf) *adj* **1** not penetrable by sound ▷ *vb* **2** (*tr*) to render soundproof

sound ranging *n* the determination of the location of a source of sound waves by measuring the time lapse between their transmission and their reception at microphones situated at three or more known positions

sound shift *n* a gradual alteration or series of alterations in the pronunciation of a set of sounds, esp of vowels. See also **Great Vowel Shift**

sound spectrograph *n* an electronic instrument that produces a record (**sound spectrogram**) of the way in which the frequencies and intensities of the components of a sound, such as a spoken word, vary with time

sound stage *n* a soundproof room or building in which cinematic films are shot

sound system *n* **1** any system of sounds, as in the speech of a language **2** integrated equipment for producing amplified sound, as in a hi-fi or as a public-address system on stage

soundtrack (ˈsaʊndˌtræk) *n* **1** the recorded sound accompaniment to a film. Compare **commentary** (sense 2) **2** a narrow strip along the side of a spool of film, which carries the sound accompaniment ▷ *vb* **3** (*tr*) to provide a continuous accompaniment of sounds, esp music

sound truck *n US and Canadian* a motor vehicle carrying a public address system. also called (in Britain and certain other countries): **loudspeaker van**

sound wave *n* a wave that propagates sound

soup (suːp) *n* **1** a liquid food made by boiling or simmering meat, fish, vegetables, etc, usually served hot at the beginning of a meal **2** *informal* a photographic developer **3** *informal* anything resembling soup in appearance or consistency, esp thick fog. See also **peasouper** **4** a slang name for **nitroglycerine** **5** **in the soup** *informal* in trouble or difficulties [C17 from Old French *soupe*, from Late Latin *suppa*, of Germanic origin; compare Middle High German *suppe*, Old Norse *soppa* soup]

soupçon *French* (supsɔ̃) *n* a slight amount; dash [C18 from French, ultimately from Latin *suspicio* SUSPICION]

S

soupfin *or* **soupfin shark** (ˈsuːpˌfɪn) *n* a Pacific requiem shark, *Galeorhinus zyopterus*, valued for its fins, which are used to make soup

soup kitchen *n* **1** a place or mobile stall where food and drink, esp soup, is served to destitute people **2** *military* a mobile kitchen

soup plate *n* a deep plate with a wide rim, used esp for drinking soup

soup up *informal* ▷ *vb* (*tr, adverb*) **1** to modify (a vehicle or vehicle engine) in order to increase its power **2** to make (something) more exciting or interesting. Also: **hot up**, (esp US and Canadian) **hop up** ▷ *adj* **souped-up** **3** (of a vehicle or vehicle engine) modified so as to be more powerful: *a souped-up scooter* **4** more exciting or interesting: *a souped-up version of their last single*

soupy (ˈsuːpɪ) *adj* **soupier, soupiest** **1** having the appearance or consistency of soup **2** *informal, chiefly US and Canadian* emotional or sentimental

sour (ˈsaʊə) *adj* **1** having or denoting a sharp biting taste like that of lemon juice or vinegar. Compare **bitter** (sense 1) **2** made acid or bad, as in the case of milk or alcohol, by the action of microorganisms **3** having a rancid or unwholesome smell **4** (of a person's temperament) sullen, morose, or disagreeable **5** (esp of the weather or climate) harsh and unpleasant **6** disagreeable; distasteful: *a sour experience* **7** (of land, etc) lacking in fertility, esp due to excessive acidity **8** (of oil, gas, or petrol) containing a relatively large amount of sulphur compounds **9** **go** *or* **turn sour** to become unfavourable or inharmonious: *his marriage went sour* ▷ *n* **10** something sour **11** *chiefly US* any of several iced drinks usually made with spirits, lemon juice, and ice: *a whiskey sour* **12** an acid used in laundering and bleaching clothes or in curing animal skins ▷ *vb* **13** to make or become sour [Old English *sūr*; related to Old Norse *sūrr*, Lithuanian *suras* salty, Old Slavonic *syrŭ* wet, raw, *surovu* green, raw, Sanskrit *surā* brandy] > '**sourish** *adj* > '**sourly** *adv* > '**sourness** *n*

Sour (suə) *n* a variant spelling of **Sur**

source (sɔːs) *n* **1** the point or place from which something originates **2 a** a spring that forms the starting point of a stream; headspring **b** the area where the headwaters of a river rise: *the source of the Nile* **3** a person, group, etc, that creates, issues, or originates something: *the source of a complaint* **4 a** any person, book, organization, etc, from which information, evidence, etc, is obtained **b** (*as modifier*): *source material* **5** anything, such as a story or work of art, that provides a model or inspiration for a later work **6** *electronics* the electrode region in a field-effect transistor from which majority carriers flow into the interelectrode conductivity channel **7 at source** at the point of origin ▷ *vb* **8** to determine the source of a news report or stor **9** (*tr; foll by from*) to originate from **10** (*tr*) to establish an originator or source of (a product, piece of information, etc) [c14 from Old French *sors*, from *sourdre* to spring forth, from Latin *surgere* to rise]

source code *n computing* the original form of a computer program before it is converted into a machine-readable code

source document *n* a document that has been or will be transcribed to a word processor or to the memory bank of a computer

source program *n* an original computer program written by a programmer that is converted into the equivalent object program, written in machine language, by the compiler or assembler

sour cherry *n* **1** a Eurasian rosaceous tree, *Prunus cerasus*, with white flowers: cultivated for its tart red fruits **2** the fruit of this tree. Compare **sweet cherry** See also **morello, amarelle**

sour cream *n* cream soured by lactic acid bacteria, used in making salads, dips, etc. Also called: **soured cream**

sourdine (suə'diːn) *n music* **1** a soft stop on an organ or harmonium **2** another word for **sordino** [C17 (meaning: a muted trumpet): from French: a mute, from Italian; see SORDINO]

sourdough ('sauə,dəu) *adj* **1** *dialect* (of bread) made with fermented dough used as a leaven ▷ *n* **2** (in Western US, Canada, and Alaska) an old-time prospector or pioneer

sour gourd *n* **1** a large bombacaceous tree, *Adansonia gregorii*, of N Australia, having gourdlike fruit **2** the acid-tasting fruit of this tree, which has a woody rind and large seeds **3** the fruit of the baobab tree

sour grapes *n* (*functioning as singular*) the attitude of affecting to despise something because one cannot or does not have it oneself [from a fable by Aesop]

sour gum *n* a cornaceous tree, *Nyssa sylvatica*, of the eastern US, having glossy leaves, soft wood, and sour purplish fruits. Also called: **black gum, pepperidge** See also **tupelo** Compare **sweet gum**

sour mash *n US* **1** a grain mash for use in distilling certain whiskeys, consisting of a mixture of new and old mash **2** any whiskey distilled from such a mash

sourpuss ('sauə,pus) *n informal* a person whose facial expression or nature is habitually gloomy or sullen [c20 from SOUR + PUSS²]

soursop ('sauə,sɒp) *n* **1** a small West Indian tree, *Annona muricata*, having large spiny fruit: family *Annonaceae* **2** the fruit of this tree, which has a tart edible pulp. Compare **sweetsop** [c19 so called because of the flavour and consistency of the pulp]

sourwood ('sauə,wud) *n* another name for **sorrel tree**

sousaphone ('suːzə,fəun) *n music* a large tuba that encircles the player's body and has a bell facing forwards [c20 named after John Philip *Sousa* (1854–1932), US bandmaster and composer of military marches] > '**sousa,phonist** *n*

souse¹ (saus) *vb* **1** to plunge (something, oneself, etc) into water or other liquid **2** to drench or be drenched **3** (*tr*) to pour or dash (liquid) over (a person or thing) **4** to steep or cook (food) in a marinade **5** (*tr; usually passive*) *slang* to make drunk ▷ *n* **6** the liquid or brine used in pickling **7** the act or process of sousing **8** *slang* a habitual drunkard [c14 from Old French *sous*, of Germanic origin; related to Old High German *sulza* brine]

souse² (saus) *falconry* (of hawks or falcons) *vb* (*intr*) **1** (often foll by *on* or *upon*) to swoop suddenly downwards (on a prey) ▷ *n* **2** a sudden downward swoop [c16 perhaps a variant of obsolete vb sense of SOURCE]

souslik ('suːslɪk) *n* a variant spelling of **suslik**

sou-sou *or* **susu** ('suːsuː) *n Caribbean* an arrangement made among friends whereby each person makes regular contributions to a fund, the money being drawn out periodically by each individual in turn [probably of W African origin, influenced by French *sou* small coin, via Creole]

Sousse (suːs), **Susa** *or* **Susah** *n* a port in E Tunisia, on the Mediterranean: founded by the Phoenicians in the 9th century BC. Pop: 191 000 (2005 est). Ancient name: **Hadrumetum** (,hædrə'miːtəm)

soutache (suː'tæʃ) *n* a narrow braid used as a decorative trimming [c19 from French, from Hungarian *sujtas*]

soutane (suː'tæn) *n RC Church* a priest's cassock [c19 from French, from Old Italian *sottana*, from Medieval Latin *subtanus* (adj) (worn) beneath, from Latin *subtus* below]

souter *or* **soutar** ('suːtər) *n Scot and northern English* a shoemaker or cobbler [Old English *sūtere*, from Latin *sutor*, from *suere* to sew]

souterrain ('suːtə,reɪn) *n archaeol* an underground chamber or passage [c18 from French]

south (sauθ) *n* **1** one of the four cardinal points of the compass, at 180° from north and 90° clockwise from east and anticlockwise from west **2** the direction along a meridian towards the South Pole **3 the south** (*often capital*) any area lying in or towards the south. Related adjs: **meridional, austral** **4** (*usually capital*) *cards* the player or position at the table corresponding to south on the compass ▷ *adj* **5** situated in, moving towards, or facing the south **6** (esp of the wind) from the south ▷ *adv* **7** in, to, or towards the south **8** *archaic* (of the wind) from the south ▷ Symbol: S [Old English *sūth;* related to Old Norse *suthr* southward, Old High German *sundan* from the south]

South (sauθ) *n* the **1** the southern part of England, generally regarded as lying to the south of an imaginary line between the Wash and the Severn **2** (in the US) **a** the area approximately south of Pennsylvania and the Ohio River, esp those states south of the Mason-Dixon line that formed the Confederacy during the Civil War **b** the Confederacy itself **3** the countries of the world that are not economically and technically advanced ▷ *adj* **4 a** of or denoting the southern part of a specified country, area, etc **b** (*capital as part of a name*): *the South Pacific*

South Africa *n* **Republic of** a republic occupying the southernmost part of the African continent: the Dutch Cape Colony (1652) was acquired by Britain in 1806 and British victory in the Boer War resulted in the formation of the Union of South Africa in 1910, which became a republic in 1961; implementation of the apartheid system began in 1948 and was abolished, following an intense civil rights campaign, in 1993, with multiracial elections held in 1994; a member of the Commonwealth, it withdrew in 1961 but was re-admitted in 1994. Mainly plateau with mountains in the south and east. Mineral production includes gold, diamonds, coal, and copper. Official languages: Afrikaans; English; Ndebele; Pedi; South Sotho; Swazi; Tsonga; Tswana; Venda; Xhosa; Zulu. Religion: Christian majority. Currency: rand. Capitals: Cape Town (legislative), Pretoria (administrative), Bloemfontein (judicial). Pop: 45 214 000 (2004 est). Area: 1 221 044 sq km (471 445 sq miles). Former name (1910–61): **Union of South Africa**

South African *adj* **1** of or relating to the Republic of South Africa, its inhabitants, or any of their languages ▷ *n* **2** a native or inhabitant of the Republic of South Africa

South African Dutch *n* (not used in South Africa) another name for **Afrikaans**

South America *n* the fourth largest of the continents, bordering on the Caribbean in the north, the Pacific in the west, and the Atlantic in the east and joined to Central America by the Isthmus of Panama. It is dominated by the Andes Mountains, which extend over 7250 km (4500 miles) and include many volcanoes; ranges from dense tropical jungle, desert, and temperate plains to the cold wet windswept region of Tierra del Fuego. Pop (Latin America and the Caribbean): 558 281 000 (2005 est). Area: 17 816 600 sq km (6 879 000 sq miles)

South American *adj* **1** of or relating to the continent of South America or its inhabitants ▷ *n* **2** a native or inhabitant of South America

South American trypanosomiasis *n pathol* another name for **Chagas' disease**

Southampton (sauθ'æmptən, -'hæmp-) *n* **1** a port in S England, in Southampton unitary authority, Hampshire on **Southampton Water** (an inlet of the English Channel): chief English passenger port; university (1952); shipyards and oil refinery. Pop: 234 224 (2001) **2** a unitary authority in S England, in Hampshire. Pop: 221 100 (2003 est). Area: 49 sq km (19 sq miles)

Southampton Island *n* an island in N Canada, in Nunavut at the entrance to Hudson Bay: inhabited chiefly by Inuit. Area: 49 470 sq km (19 100 sq miles)

South Arabia *n* **Federation of** the former name (1963–67) of **South Yemen** (excluding Aden)

South Arabian *adj* **1** of or relating to the former South Arabia (now South Yemen) or its inhabitants ▷ *n* **2** a native or inhabitant of South Arabia

South Australia *n* a state of S central Australia, on the Great Australian Bight: generally arid, with the Great Victoria Desert in the west central part, the Lake Eyre basin in the northeast, and the Flinders Ranges, Murray River basin, and salt lakes in the southeast. Capital: Adelaide. Pop: 1 531 375 (2003 est). Area: 984 395 sq km 380 070 sq miles)

South Australian *adj* **1** of or relating to the state of South Australia or its inhabitants ▷ *n* **2** a native or inhabitant of South Australia

South Ayrshire ('ɛəʃɪə, -ʃə) *n* a council area of SW Scotland, on the Firth of Clyde: comprises the S part of the historical county of Ayrshire; formerly part of Strathclyde Region (1975–96): chiefly agricultural, with fishing and tourism. Administrative centre: Ayr. Pop: 111 580 (2003 est). Area: 1202 sq km (464 sq miles)

South Bend *n* a city in the US, in N Indiana: university (1842). Pop: 105 540 (2003 est)

southbound ('sauθ,baund) *adj* going or leading towards the south

south by east *n* **1** one point on the compass east of south; 168° 45' clockwise from north ▷ *adj* ▷ *adv* **2** in, from, or towards this direction

south by west *n* **1** one point on the compass west of south; 191° 15' clockwise from north ▷ *adj* ▷ *adv* **2** in, from, or towards this direction

South Carolina *n* a state of the southeastern US, on the Atlantic: the first state to secede from the Union in 1860; consists largely of low-lying coastal plains, rising in the northwest to the Blue Ridge Mountains; the largest US textile producer. Capital: Columbia. Pop: 4 147 152 (2003 est). Area: 78 282 sq km (30 225 sq miles). Abbreviation and zip code: **SC**

South Carolinian (ˌkærəˈlɪnɪən) *adj* **1** of or relating to South Carolina or its inhabitants ▷ *n* **2** a native or inhabitant of South Carolina

South China Sea *n* part of the Pacific surrounded by SE China, Vietnam, the Malay Peninsula, Borneo, and the Philippines

South Dakota *n* a state of the western US: lies mostly in the Great Plains; the chief US producer of gold and beryl. Capital: Pierre. Pop: 764 309 (2003 est). Area: 196 723 sq km (75 955 sq miles). Abbreviations: **S. Dak**, (with zip code) **SD**

South Dakotan *adj* **1** of or relating to South Dakota or its inhabitants ▷ *n* **2** a native or inhabitant of South Dakota

South Devon *n* a breed of large red cattle originally from South Devon

Southdown (ˈsaʊˌdaʊn) *n* an English breed of sheep with short wool and a greyish-brown face and legs [c18 so called because it was originally bred on the SOUTH DOWNS]

South Downs *pl n* a range of low hills in S England, extending from E Hampshire to East Sussex

southeast (ˌsaʊθˈiːst; *Nautical* ˌsaʊˈiːst) *n* **1** the point of the compass or the direction midway between south and east, 135° clockwise from north ▷ *adj* *also* **southeastern 2** (*sometimes capital*) of or denoting the southeastern part of a specified country, area, etc **3** situated in, proceeding towards, or facing the southeast **4** (esp of the wind) from the southeast ▷ *adv* **5** in, to, towards, or (esp of the wind) from the southeast ▷ Symbol: **SE** > ˌsouth'easternmost *adj*

Southeast (ˌsaʊθˈiːst) *n* (usually preceded by *the*) the southeastern part of Britain, esp the London area

Southeast Asia *n* a region including Brunei, Cambodia, Indonesia, Laos, Malaysia, Myanmar, the Philippines, Thailand, and Vietnam

Southeast Asian *adj* **1** of or relating to Southeast Asia or its inhabitants ▷ *n* **2** a native or inhabitant of Southeast Asia

southeast by east *n* **1** one point on the compass north of southeast; 123° 45′ clockwise from north ▷ *adj* ▷ *adv* **2** in, from, or towards this direction

southeast by south *n* **1** one point on the compass south of southeast; 146° 15′ clockwise from north ▷ *adj* ▷ *adv* **2** in, from, or towards this direction

southeaster (ˌsaʊθˈiːstə; *Nautical* ˌsaʊˈiːstə) *n* a strong wind or storm from the southeast

southeasterly (ˌsaʊθˈiːstəlɪ; *Nautical* ˌsaʊˈiːstəlɪ) *adj*, *adv* **1** in, towards, or (esp of a wind) from the southeast ▷ *n*, *pl* **-lies 2** a strong wind or storm from the southeast

southeastward (ˌsaʊθˈiːstwəd; *Nautical* ˌsaʊˈiːstwəd) *adj* **1** towards or (esp of a wind) from the southeast ▷ *n* **2** a direction towards or area in the southeast ▷ *adv* **3** a variant of **southeastwards**

southeastwards (ˌsaʊθˈiːstwədz; *Nautical* ˌsaʊˈiːstwədz) *or* **southeastward** *adv* to the southeast

Southend-on-Sea (ˌsaʊθˈɛnd-) *n* **1** a town in SE England, in SE Essex on the Thames estuary: one of England's largest resorts, extending for about 11 km (7 miles) along the coast. Pop: 160 257 (2001) **2** a unitary authority in SE England, in Essex. Pop: 160 300 (2003 est). Area: 42 sq km (16 sq miles)

souther (ˈsaʊðə) *n* a strong wind or storm from the south

southerly (ˈsʌðəlɪ) *adj* **1** of, relating to, or situated in the south ▷ *adv*, *adj* **2** towards or in the direction of the south **3** from the south: *a southerly wind* ▷ *n*, *pl* **-lies 4** a wind from the south > ˈsoutherliness *n*

southerly buster *n* (*sometimes capitals*) a sudden violent cold wind on the SE coast of Australia causing a rapid drop in temperature. Sometimes shortened to: **southerly**

southern (ˈsʌðən) *adj* **1** situated in or towards the south **2** (of a wind, etc) coming from the south **3** native to, inhabiting, or growing in the south **4** (*sometimes capital*) *astronomy* south of the celestial equator

Southern (ˈsʌðən) *adj* of, relating to, or characteristic of the south of a particular region or country

Southern Alps *pl n* a mountain range in New Zealand, on South Island: the highest range in Australasia. Highest peak: Mount Cook (also known as Aorangi), 3754 m (12 316 ft)

Southern British English *n* the dialect of spoken English regarded as standard in England and considered as having high social status in comparison with other British English dialects. Historically, it is derived from the S East Midland dialect of Middle English. Abbreviation: **SBE** See also **Received Pronunciation**

Southern Cross *n* **1** a small conspicuous constellation in the S hemisphere lying in the Milky Way near Centaurus. The four brightest stars form a cross the longer arm of which points to the south celestial pole. Formal names: **Crux**, **Crux Australis 2** *Austral* the flag flown at the Eureka Stockade

Southerner (ˈsʌðənə) *n* (*sometimes not capital*) a native or inhabitant of the south of any specified region, esp the South of England or the Southern states of the US

southern fur seal *n* another name for **New Zealand fur seal**

southern hemisphere *n* (*often capitals*) **1** that half of the earth lying south of the equator **2** *astronomy* that half of the celestial sphere lying south of the celestial equator ▷ Abbreviation: **S hemisphere**

Southern Ireland *n* See **Ireland**¹ (sense 2)

southern lights *pl n* another name for **aurora australis**

southernly (ˈsʌðənlɪ) *adj*, *adv* a less common word for **southerly**

southernmost (ˈsʌðənˌməʊst) *adj* situated or occurring farthest south

Southern Ocean *n* another name for the **Antarctic Ocean**

Southern Rhodesia *n* the former name (until 1964) of **Zimbabwe**

Southern Rhodesian *adj* **1** of or relating to the former Southern Rhodesia (now Zimbabwe) or its inhabitants ▷ *n* **2** a native or inhabitant of Southern Rhodesia

Southern Sotho *n* another name for **Sesotho**

Southern Uplands *pl n* a hilly region extending across S Scotland: includes the Lowther, Moorfoot, and Lammermuir hills

southernwood (ˈsʌðənˌwʊd) *n* an aromatic shrubby wormwood, *Artemisia abrotanum*, of S Europe, having finely dissected leaves and small drooping heads of yellowish flowers. Also called: **old man, lad's love** [Old English. See SOUTHERN, WOOD]

South Georgia *n* an island in the S Atlantic, about 1300 km (800 miles) southeast of the Falkland Islands, part of the UK Overseas Territory of **South Georgia and the South Sandwich Islands**; no permanent population. Area: 3755 sq km (1450 sq miles)

South Georgian *adj* **1** of or relating to South Georgia or its inhabitants ▷ *n* **2** a native or inhabitant of South Georgia

South Glamorgan *n* a former county of S Wales, formed in 1974 from parts of Glamorgan and Monmouthshire plus the county borough of Cardiff: replaced in 1996 by the county boroughs of Cardiff and Vale of Glamorgan

South Gloucestershire *n* a unitary authority of SW England, in Gloucestershire: formerly (1975–96) part of the county of Avon. Pop: 246 800 (2003 est). Area: 510 sq km (197 sq miles)

South Holland *n* a province of the SW Netherlands, on the North Sea: lying mostly below sea level, it has a coastal strip of dunes and is drained chiefly by distributaries of the Rhine, with large areas of reclaimed land; the most densely populated province in the country, intensively cultivated and industrialized. Capital: The Hague. Pop: 3 440 000 (2003 est). Area: 3196 sq km (1234 sq miles). Dutch name: **Zuidholland**

southing (ˈsaʊðɪŋ) *n* **1** *navigation* movement, deviation, or distance covered in a southerly direction **2** *astronomy* a south or negative declination

South Island *n* **the** the largest island of New Zealand, separated from the North Island by the Cook Strait. Pop: 973 000 (2004 est). Area: 153 947 sq km (59 439 sq miles)

South Korea *n* a republic in NE Asia: established as a republic in 1948; invaded by North Korea and Chinese Communists in 1950 but division remained unchanged at the end of the war (1953); includes over 3000 islands; rapid industrialization. Language: Korean. Religions: Buddhist, Confucianist, Shamanist, and Chondokyo. Currency: won. Capital: Seoul. Pop: 47 950 000 (2004 est). Area: 98 477 sq km (38 022 sq miles). Korean name: **Hanguk**

South Korean *adj* **1** of or relating to South Korea or its inhabitants ▷ *n* **2** a native or inhabitant of South Korea

South Lanarkshire (ˈlænəkˌʃɪə, -ʃə) *n* a council area of S Scotland, comprising the S part of the historical county of Lanarkshire: included within Strathclyde Region from 1975 to 1996: has uplands in the S and part of the Glasgow conurbation in the N: mainly agricultural. Administrative centre: Hamilton. Pop: 303 010 (2003 est). Area: 1771 sq km (684 sq miles)

South Orkney Islands *pl n* an uninhabited group of islands in the S Atlantic, southeast of Cape Horn: formerly a dependency of the Falkland Islands; part of the British Antarctic Territory since 1962 (claims are suspended under the Antarctic Treaty). Area: 621 sq km (240 sq miles)

South Ossetia (əˈsiːʃə) *n* a region in Georgia on the S slopes of the Caucasus Mountains; in 1990 it voted to join Russia, leading to armed conflict with Georgian forces; it became an autonomous region in 1997. Capital: Tskhinvali. Pop: 99 800 (1990). Area: 3900 sq km (1500 sq miles). Georgian name: **Tskhinvali** Also called: **South Ossetian Autonomous Region**

southpaw (ˈsaʊθˌpɔː) *informal* ▷ *n* **1** a boxer who leads with his right hand and off his right foot as opposed to the orthodox style of leading with the left **2** any left-handed person ▷ *adj* **3** of or relating to a southpaw [c20 PAW (in the sense: hand): originally a term applied to a left-handed baseball player: perhaps so called because baseball pitchers traditionally face west, so that a left-handed pitcher would throw with the hand on the south side of his body]

South Pole *n* **1** the southernmost point on the earth's axis, at the latitude of 90°S **2** *astronomy* the point of intersection, in the constellation Octans, of the earth's extended axis and the southern half of the celestial sphere **3** (*usually not capitals*) the south-seeking pole of a freely suspended magnet

Southport (ˈsaʊθˌpɔːt) *n* a town and resort in NW England, in Sefton unitary authority, Merseyside on the Irish Sea. Pop: 91 404 (2001)

Southron (ˈsʌðrən) *n* **1** *chiefly Scot* a Southerner, esp an Englishman **2** *Scot* the English language as spoken in England **3** *dialect, chiefly Southern US* an inhabitant of the South, esp at the time of the Civil War ▷ *adj* **4** *chiefly Scot* of or relating to the South or to England [c15 Scottish variant of SOUTHERN]

South Saskatchewan *n* a river in S central Canada, rising in S Alberta and flowing east and northeast to join the North Saskatchewan River, forming the Saskatchewan River. Length: 1392 km (865 miles)

South Sea Bubble *n* *Brit history* the financial crash that occurred in 1720 after the **South Sea**

S

Company had taken over the national debt in return for a monopoly of trade with the South Seas, causing feverish speculation in their stocks [so named because the rapid expansion and sudden collapse of investment resembled the blowing up and bursting of a bubble]

South Sea Islands *pl n* the islands in the S Pacific that constitute Oceania

South Seas *pl n* the seas south of the equator

South Shetland Islands *pl n* a group of uninhabited islands in the S Atlantic, north of the Antarctic Peninsula: formerly a dependency of the Falkland Islands; part of British Antarctic Territory since 1962. (Claims are suspended under the Antarctic Treaty). Area: 4662 sq km (1800 sq miles)

South Shields *n* a port in NE England, in South Tyneside unitary authority, Tyne and Wear on the Tyne estuary opposite North Shields. Pop: 82 854 (2001)

south-southeast *n* **1** the point on the compass or the direction midway between southeast and south; 157° 30′ clockwise from north ▷ *adj* ▷ *adv* **2** in, from, or towards this direction ▷ Symbol: SSE

south-southwest *n* **1** the point on the compass or the direction midway between south and southwest; 202° 30′ clockwise from north ▷ *adj* ▷ *adv* **2** in, from, or towards this direction ▷ Symbol: SSW

South Tyneside ('taɪn,saɪd) *n* a unitary authority of NE England, in Tyne and Wear. Pop: 151 700 (2003 est). Area: 64 sq km (25 sq miles)

South Tyrol *or* **Tirol** *n* a former part of the Austrian state of Tyrol: ceded to Italy in 1919, becoming the Bolzano and Trento provinces of the Trentino-Alto Adige Autonomous Region. Area: 14 037 sq km (5420 sq miles)

South Vietnam *n* a former republic (1955–76) occupying the S of present-day Vietnam on the South China Sea and the Gulf of Siam

South Vietnamese *adj* **1** of or relating to the former South Vietnam (now part of Vietnam) or its inhabitants ▷ *n* **2** a native or inhabitant of South Vietnam

southward ('saʊθwəd; *Nautical* 'sʌðəd) *adj* **1** situated, directed, or moving towards the south ▷ *n* **2** the southward part, direction, etc; the south ▷ *adv* **3** a variant of **southwards** > **'southwardly** *adj, adv*

southwards ('saʊθwədz; *Nautical* 'sʌðədz) *or* **southward** *adv* towards the south

Southwark ('sʌðək) *n* a borough of S central Greater London, on the River Thames: site of the Globe Theatre, now reconstructed; the former docks and warehouses have been redeveloped. Pop: 253 800 (2003 est). Area: 29 sq km (11 sq miles)

southwest (,saʊθ'wɛst; *Nautical* ,saʊ'wɛst) *n* **1** the point of the compass or the direction midway between west and south, 225° clockwise from north ▷ *adj also* **southwestern 2** (*sometimes capital*) of or denoting the southwestern part of a specified country, area, etc: *southwest Italy* **3** situated in or towards the southwest **4** (*esp of the wind*) from the southwest ▷ *adv* **5** in, to, towards, or (*esp of the wind*) from the southwest ▷ Symbol: SW > ,**south'westernmost** *adj*

Southwest (,saʊθ'wɛst) *n* (*usually preceded by the*) the southwestern part of Britain, esp Cornwall, Devon, and Somerset

South West Africa *n* another name for **Namibia**

southwest by south *n* **1** one point on the compass south of southwest; 213° 45′ clockwise from north ▷ *adj* ▷ *adv* **2** in, from, or towards this direction

southwest by west *n* **1** one point on the compass north of southwest, 236° 15′ clockwise from north ▷ *adj* ▷ *adv* **2** in, from, or towards this direction

southwester (,saʊθ'wɛstə; *Nautical* ,saʊ'wɛstə) *n* a strong wind or storm from the southwest

southwesterly (,saʊθ'wɛstəlɪ; *Nautical* ,saʊ'wɛstəlɪ) *adj, adv* **1** in, towards, or (esp of a

wind) from the southwest ▷ *n, pl* -**lies 2** a wind or storm from the southwest

southwestward (,saʊθ'wɛstwəd; *Nautical* ,saʊ'wɛstwəd) *adj* **1** from or towards the southwest ▷ *adv* **2** a variant of **southwestwards** ▷ *n* **3** a direction towards or area in the southwest > ,**south'westwardly** *adj, adv*

southwestwards (,saʊθ'wɛstwədz; *Nautical* ,saʊ'wɛstwədz) *or* **southwestward** *adv* to the southwest

South Yemen *n* a former republic in SW Arabia, on the Gulf of Aden; now a part of Yemen: became a republic in 1967; merged with North Yemen in 1990. Official name (1967–90): **People's Democratic Republic of Yemen** Name from 1963 to 1967 (excluding Aden): (Federation of) **South Arabia** See also **Yemen, North Yemen**

South Yorkshire *n* a metropolitan county of N England, administered since 1986 by the unitary authorities of Barnsley, Doncaster, Sheffield, and Rotherham. Area: 1560 sq km (602 sq miles)

soutpiel ('saʊt,piːl) *or* **soutie** ('saʊtɪ) *n South African derogatory slang* an English-speaking South African [C20 Afrikaans, from *sout* salt + *piel* penis, implying that such a person has one foot in Africa and one in the UK, with the penis dangling in the Atlantic]

souvenir (,suːvə'nɪə, 'suːvə,nɪə) *n* **1** an object that recalls a certain place, occasion, or person; memento ▷ *vb* (*tr*) **2** *Austral and NZ euphemistic slang* to steal or keep (something, esp a small article) for one's own use; purloin [C18 from French, from (*se*) *souvenir* to remember, from Latin *subvenīre* to come to mind, from *sub*- up to + *venīre* to come]

souvlakia (suː'vlækɪə) *n* a Greek dish of kebabs, esp made with lamb [C20 from Modern Greek]

sou'wester (saʊ'wɛstə) *n* a waterproof hat having a very broad rim behind, worn esp by seamen [C19 a contraction of SOUTHWESTER]

sovereign ('sɒvrɪn) *n* **1** a person exercising supreme authority, esp a monarch **2** a former British gold coin worth one pound sterling ▷ *adj* **3** supreme in rank or authority: *a sovereign lord* **4** excellent or outstanding: *a sovereign remedy* **5** of, relating to, or characteristic of a sovereign **6** independent of outside authority: *a sovereign state* [C13 from Old French *soverain*, from Vulgar Latin *superānus* (unattested), from Latin *super* above; also influenced by REIGN] > **'sovereignly** *adv*

sovereigntist ('sɒvrəntɪst) *n* (in Canada) a supporter of sovereignty association

sovereignty ('sɒvrəntɪ) *n, pl* -**ties 1** supreme and unrestricted power, as of a state **2** the position, dominion, or authority of a sovereign **3** an independent state

sovereignty association *n* (in Canada) a proposed arrangement by which Quebec would become independent but would maintain a formal association with Canada

Sovetsk (*Russian* sa'vjɛtsk) *n* a town in W Russia, in the Kaliningrad Region on the Neman River: scene of the signing of the treaty (1807) between Napoleon I and Tsar Alexander I; passed from East Prussia to the Soviet Union in 1945. Former name (until 1945): **Tilsit**

soviet ('səʊvɪət, 'sɒv-) *n* **1** (in the former Soviet Union) an elected government council at the local, regional, and national levels, which culminated in the Supreme Soviet **2** (in prerevolutionary Russia) a local revolutionary council ▷ *adj* **3** of or relating to a soviet [C20 from Russian *sovyet* council, from Old Russian *sŭvĕtŭ*]

Soviet ('səʊvɪət, 'sɒv-) *adj* of, characteristic of, or relating to the former Soviet Union, its people, or its government

Soviet Central Asia *n* the region of the former Soviet Union now occupied by Kazakhstan, Kyrgyzstan, Tajikistan, Turkmenistan, and Uzbekistan. Also called: **Russian Turkestan, West Turkestan**

sovietism ('səʊvɪɪ,tɪzəm, 'sɒv-) *n* (*sometimes capital*) **1** the principle or practice of government through

soviets, esp as practised in the former Soviet Union **2** any characteristic deemed representative of Soviet ideology > **'sovietist** *n, adj* > ,**soviet'istic** *adj*

sovietize *or* **sovietise** ('səʊvɪɪ,taɪz, 'sɒv-) *vb* (*tr*; *often capital*) **1** to bring (a country, person, etc) under Soviet control or influence **2** to cause (a country) to conform to the Soviet model in its social, political, and economic structure > ,**sovieti'zation** *or* ,**sovieti'sation** *n*

Sovietologist (,səʊvɪə'tɒlədʒɪst, ,sɒv-) *n* a person who has studied the political policies and developments of the former Soviet government

Soviet Russia *n* (formerly) another name for the **Russian Soviet Federative Socialist Republic** or the **Soviet Union**

Soviets ('səʊvɪəts, 'sɒv-) *n* the people or government of the former Soviet Union

Soviet Union *n* a former federal republic in E Europe and central and N Asia: the revolution of 1917 achieved the overthrow of the Russian monarchy and the Soviet Union (the USSR) was established in 1922 as a Communist state. It was the largest country in the world, occupying a seventh of the total land surface. The collapse of Communist rule in 1991 was followed by declarations of independence by the constituent republics and the consequent break-up of the Soviet Union. Official name: **Union of Soviet Socialist Republics** Also called: **Russia, Soviet Russia** Abbreviation: USSR

Soviet Zone *n* that part of Germany occupied by Soviet forces in 1945–49: transformed into the German Democratic Republic in 1949–50. Also called: **Russian Zone**

sovkhoz (sɒf'kɒz; *Russian* saf'xɔs) *n pl*, **sovkhozy** (sɒf'kɒzɪ; *Russian* saf'xɔzi) (in the former Soviet Union) a large mechanized farm owned by the state [C20 Russian, from *sovetskoe khozyaistvo* soviet economy]

sovran ('sɒvrən) *n, adj* a literary word for **sovereign.** > **'sovranly** *adv* > **'sovranty** *n*

sow¹ (səʊ) *vb* **sows, sowing, sowed; sown** *or* **sowed 1** to scatter or place (seed, a crop, etc) in or on (a piece of ground, field, etc) so that it may grow: *to sow wheat; to sow a strip of land* **2** (*tr*) to implant or introduce: *to sow a doubt in someone's mind* [Old English *sāwan;* related to Old Norse *sā*, Old High German *sāen*, Old Slavonic *seja*, Latin *serere* to sow] > **'sowable** *adj* > **'sower** *n*

sow² (saʊ) *n* **1** a female adult pig **2** the female of certain other animals, such as the mink **3** *metallurgy* **a** the channels for leading molten metal to the moulds in casting pig iron **b** iron that has solidified in these channels [Old English *sugu;* related to Old Norse *sȳr*, Old High German *sū*, Latin *sūs*, Norwegian *sugga*, Dutch *zeug*: see SWINE]

sowback ('saʊ,bæk) *n* another name for **hogback** (sense 1)

sowbread ('saʊ,brɛd) *n* a S European primulaceous plant, *Cyclamen hederifolium*, with heart-shaped leaves and pink nodding flowers. See also **cyclamen** (sense 1) [C16 from sow² + BREAD, based on Medieval Latin *panis porcinus;* the tuberous roots are eaten by swine]

sow bug (saʊ) *n US and Canadian* any of various woodlice, esp any of the genera *Oniscus* and *Porcellio* [C18 from its resemblance to a pig in shape]

sowens ('səʊənz, 'suː-) *n Scot* a pudding made from oatmeal husks steeped and boiled [C16 from Scottish Gaelic *sùghan*, from *sùgh* sap; related to Old High German *sūgan* to SUCK]

Soweto (sə'wɛtəʊ, -'weɪtəʊ) *n* a contiguous group of Black African townships southwest of Johannesburg, South Africa: the largest purely Black African urban settlement in southern Africa: scene of riots (1976) following protests against the use of Afrikaans in schools for Black African children. Area: 62 sq km (24 sq miles). Pop: 858 649 (2001) [C20 from *so(uth) we(st) to(wnship)*]

sown (səʊn) *vb* a past participle of **sow¹**

sow thistle (saʊ) *n* any of various plants of the

Old World genus *Sonchus*, esp *S. oleraceus*, having milky juice, prickly leaves, and heads of yellow flowers: family *Asteraceae* (composites). Also called: **milk thistle**, (NZ) **puha**, (NZ) **rauriki** [C13 from *sugethistel*, perhaps variant of Old English *thugethistel*, *thuthistel* thowthistle, a dialect name of the sow thistle. See sow², THISTLE]

soya bean ('sɔɪə) *or US and Canadian* **soybean** ('sɔɪˌbiːn) *n* **1** an Asian bean plant, *Glycine max* (or *G. soja*), cultivated for its nutritious seeds, for forage, and to improve the soil **2** the seed of this plant, used as food, forage, and as the source of an oil [C17 *soya*, via Dutch *soya* from Japanese *shōyu*, from Chinese *chiang yu*, from *chiang* paste + *yu* sauce]

soy sauce (sɔɪ) *n* a salty dark brown sauce made from fermented soya beans, used esp in Japanese and Chinese cookery. Also called: **soya sauce**

Soyuz (sɔɪ'juz) *n* any of a series of Russian spacecraft used to ferry crew to and from space stations [C20 Russian: union]

sozzled ('sɒzəld) *adj* an informal word for **drunk** [C19 perhaps from obsolete *sozzle* stupor; related to SOUSE¹]

sp *abbreviation for* without issue [from Latin *sine prole*]

SP *abbreviation for* **1** standard play: the standard recording speed on a VCR **2** **starting price** ▷ *n* **3** *Brit slang* latest information

sp. *abbreviation for* **1** special **2** (*pl* **spp**) species **3** specific

Sp. *abbreviation for* **1** Spain **2** Spaniard **3** Spanish

spa (spɑː) *n* a mineral spring or a place or resort where such a spring is found [C17 named after SPA, Belgium]

Spa (spɑː) *n* a town in E Belgium, in Liège province: a resort with medicinal mineral springs (discovered in the 14th century). Pop: 10 491 (2004 est)

SpA *abbreviation for* Società per Azioni [Italian: limited company]

SPA *abbreviation for* Special Protection Area: an area designated by the European Union in order to protect endangered species, esp of birds

space (speɪs) *n* **1** the unlimited three-dimensional expanse in which all material objects are located. Related adj: **spatial** **2** an interval of distance or time between two points, objects, or events **3** a blank portion or area **4 a** an unoccupied area or room: *there is no space for a table* **b** (*in combination*): *space-saving*. Related adj: **spacious** **5** freedom to do what a person wishes to for his or her own personal development **6 a** the region beyond the earth's atmosphere containing the other planets of the solar system, stars, galaxies, etc; universe **b** (*as modifier*): *a space probe; space navigation* **7 a** the region beyond the earth's atmosphere occurring between the celestial bodies of the universe. The density is normally negligible although cosmic rays, meteorites, gas clouds, etc, can occur. It can be divided into **cislunar space** (between the earth and moon), **interplanetary space**, **interstellar space**, and **intergalactic space** **b** (*as modifier*): *a space station; a space simulator* **8** a seat or place, as on a train, aircraft, etc **9** *printing* **a** a piece of metal, less than type-high, used to separate letters or words in hot-metal printing **b** any of the gaps used to separate letters, words or lines in photocomposition, desktop publishing, etc **10** *music* any of the gaps between the lines that make up the staff **11** *maths* a collection of unspecified points having properties that obey a specified set of axioms: *Euclidean space* **12** Also called: **spacing telegraphy** the period of time that separates complete letters, digits, and other characters in Morse code ▷ *vb* (*tr*) **13** to place or arrange at intervals or with spaces between **14** to divide into or by spaces: *to space one's time evenly* **15** *printing* to separate (letters, words, or lines) by the insertion of spaces [C13 from Old French *espace*, from Latin *spatium*]

space age *n* **1** the period in which the exploration of space has become possible ▷ *adj* **space-age** **2** (*usually prenominal*) futuristic or ultramodern, esp when suggestive of space technology

spaceband ('speɪsˌbænd) *n* *printing* a device on a linecaster for evening up the spaces between words

space-bar *n* a horizontal bar on a typewriter that is depressed in order to leave a space between words, letters, etc

space blanket *n* a plastic insulating body wrapping coated on one or both sides with aluminium foil which reflects back most of the body heat lost by radiation: carried by climbers, mountaineers, etc, for use in cases of exposure or exhaustion [C20 material originally developed as part of the US space programme]

space cadet *n* *slang* a person who is eccentric or out of touch with reality, as if affected by drugs

space capsule *n* a vehicle, sometimes carrying people or animals, designed to obtain scientific information from space, planets, etc, and be recovered on returning to earth

space character *n* *computing* a keyed space in text or data

spacecraft ('speɪsˌkrɑːft) *n* a manned or unmanned vehicle designed to orbit the earth or travel to celestial objects for the purpose of research, exploration, etc

spaced out *adj* *slang* intoxicated through or as if through taking a drug. Often shortened to: **spaced**

space-filler *n* a short article of little or no importance written to fill space in a magazine or newspaper

space heater *n* a heater used to warm the air in an enclosed area, such as a room or office

Space Invaders *n* (*functioning as singular*) *trademark* a video or computer game, the object of which is to destroy attacking alien spacecraft

spacelab ('speɪsˌlæb) *n* a laboratory in space where scientific experiments are performed, esp one developed by the European Space Agency and carried on a space shuttle

space lattice *n* *crystallog* the more formal name for **lattice** (sense 4)

spaceless ('speɪslɪs) *adj* *chiefly literary* **1** having no limits in space; infinite or boundless **2** occupying no space

spaceman ('speɪsˌmæn) *or feminine* **spacewoman** *n, pl* **-men** *or feminine* **-women** a person who travels in outer space, esp one trained to participate in a space flight

space medicine *n* the branch of medicine concerned with the effects on man of flight outside the earth's atmosphere. Compare **aviation medicine**

space opera *n* a science fiction drama, such as a film or television programme, esp one dealing with interplanetary flight

space platform *n* another name for **space station**

spaceport ('speɪsˌpɔːt) *n* a base equipped to launch, maintain, and test spacecraft

space probe *n* a vehicle, such as a satellite, equipped to obtain scientific information, normally transmitted back to earth by radio, about the atmosphere, surface, and temperature of a planet, conditions in space, etc

spacer ('speɪsə) *n* **1** a piece of material used to create or maintain a space between two things **2** *computing* a keyed space in text or data; space character **3** a person who travels in outer space

spaceship ('speɪsˌʃɪp) *n* a manned spacecraft

space shuttle *n* any of a series of reusable US space vehicles (*Columbia* (exploded 2003), *Challenger* (exploded 1986), *Discovery*, *Atlantis*, *Endeavour*) that can be launched into earth orbit transporting astronauts and equipment for a period of observation, research, etc, before re-entry and an unpowered landing on a runway; the first

operational flight occurred in 1982

space sickness *n* the nausea that people can experience in the gravity-free environment of space

space station *n* any large manned artificial satellite designed to orbit the earth during a long period of time thus providing a base for scientific and medical research in space and a construction site, launch pad, and docking arrangements for spacecraft. Also called: **space platform**, **space laboratory**

spacesuit ('speɪsˌsuːt, -ˌsjuːt) *n* any of various types of sealed and pressurized suits worn by astronauts or cosmonauts that provide an artificial atmosphere, acceptable temperature, radiocommunication link, and protection from radiation for work outside a spacecraft

space-time *or* **space-time continuum** *n* *physics* the four-dimensional continuum having three spatial coordinates and one time coordinate that together completely specify the location of a particle or an event

spacewalk ('speɪsˌwɔːk) *n* **1** the act or an instance of floating and manoeuvring in space, outside but attached by a lifeline to a spacecraft. Technical name: **extravehicular activity** ▷ *vb* **2** (*intr*) to float and manoeuvre in space while outside but attached to a spacecraft

space writer *n* a writer paid by the area of his copy

spacey ('speɪsɪ) *adj* **spacier**, **spaciest** *slang* vague and dreamy, as if under the influence of drugs [C20 SPACE + -EY]

spacial ('speɪʃəl) *adj* a variant spelling of **spatial**

spacing ('speɪsɪŋ) *n* **1** the arrangement of letters, words, etc, on a page in order to achieve legibility or aesthetic appeal **2** the arrangement of objects in a space

spacious ('speɪʃəs) *adj* having a large capacity or area [C14 from Latin *spātiosus*, from *spatium* SPACE] > **'spaciously** *adv* > **'spaciousness** *n*

SPAD (spæd) *n* acronym for signal passed at danger: an incident in which a train goes through a red light

spade¹ (speɪd) *n* **1** a tool for digging, typically consisting of a flat rectangular steel blade attached to a long wooden handle **2 a** an object or part resembling a spade in shape **b** (*as modifier*): *a spade beard* **3** a heavy metallic projection attached to the trail of a gun carriage that embeds itself into the ground and so reduces recoil **4** a type of oar blade that is comparatively broad and short. Compare **spoon** (sense 7) **5** a cutting tool for stripping the blubber from a whale or skin from a carcass **6** **call a spade a spade** to speak plainly and frankly ▷ *vb* **7** (*tr*) to use a spade on [Old English *spadu*; related to Old Norse *spathi*, Old High German *spato*, Greek *spathē* blade] > **'spader** *n*

spade² (speɪd) *n* **1 a** the black symbol on a playing card resembling a heart-shaped leaf with a stem **b** a card with one or more of these symbols or (*when pl.*) the suit of cards so marked, usually the highest ranking of the four **2** a derogatory word for **Black** **3** **in spades** *informal* in an extreme or emphatic way [C16 from Italian *spada* sword, used as an emblem on playing cards, from Latin *spatha*, from Greek *spathē* blade, broadsword]

spadefish ('speɪdˌfɪʃ) *n, pl* **-fish** *or* **-fishes** any spiny-finned food fish of the family *Ephippidae*, esp *Chaetodipterus faber* of American Atlantic coastal waters, having a deeply compressed body

spade foot *n* a spadelike projection at the end of a chair leg

spade guinea *n* *Brit history* a guinea decorated with a spade-shaped shield, coined during the reign of George III

spadework ('speɪdˌwɜːk) *n* dull or routine preparatory work

spadger ('spædʒə) *n* *English dialect* a sparrow

spadiceous (speɪ'dɪʃəs) *adj* **1** *botany* producing or resembling a spadix **2** of a bright brown colour

[C17 from New Latin *spādīceus*, from Latin *spādix* palm branch; see SPADIX]

spadille (spəˈdɪl) *n cards* (in ombre and quadrille) the ace of spades [C18 from French, from Spanish *espadilla*, diminutive of *espada* sword; see SPADE²]

spadix (ˈspeɪdɪks) *n, pl* **spadices** (speɪˈdaɪsiːz) a racemose inflorescence having many small sessile flowers borne on a fleshy stem, the whole usually being surrounded by a spathe: typical of aroid plants [C18 from Latin: pulled-off branch of a palm, with its fruit, from Greek: torn-off frond; related to Greek *span* to pull off]

spae (speɪ) *vb Scot* to foretell (the future) [C14 from Old Norse]

spaewife (ˈspeɪˌwaɪf) *n, pl* -**wives** a woman who can supposedly foretell the future

spag¹ (spæg) *vb* **spags, spagging, spagged** (*tr*) *South Wales dialect* (of a cat) to scratch (a person) with the claws [of uncertain origin]

spag² (spæg) *n Austral offensive slang* an Italian [from SPAGHETTI]

spaghetti (spəˈgɛtɪ) *n* pasta in the form of long strings [C19 from Italian: little cords, from *spago* a cord]

spaghetti junction *n* an interchange, usually between motorways, in which there are a large number of underpasses and overpasses and intersecting roads used by a large volume of high-speed traffic [C20 from the nickname of the Gravelly Hill Interchange, Birmingham, where the M6, A38M, A38, and A5127 intersect]

spaghettini (ˌspægəˈtiːnɪ) *n* pasta in the form of long thin strings [Italian: small spaghetti]

spaghetti western *n* a cowboy film about the American West made, esp by an Italian director, in Europe

spagyric (spəˈdʒɪrɪk) *or* **spagyrical** *adj rare* of or relating to alchemy [C16 from New Latin *spagiricus*, probably coined by Paracelsus, of obscure origin] > spa'gyrically *adv*

spahi *or* **spahee** (ˈspɑːhiː, ˈspɑːiː) *n, pl* -**his** *or* -**hees** **1** (formerly) an irregular cavalryman in the Turkish armed forces **2** a member of a body of native Algerian cavalrymen in the French armed forces: disbanded after Algerian independence [C16 from Old French, from Turkish *sipahi*, from Persian *sipāhī* soldier; see SEPOY]

Spain (speɪn) *n* a kingdom of SW Europe, occupying the Iberian peninsula between the Mediterranean and the Atlantic: a leading European power in the 16th century, with many overseas possessions, esp in the New World; became a republic in 1931; under the fascist dictatorship of Franco following the Civil War (1936–39) until his death in 1975; a member of the European Union. It consists chiefly of a central plateau (the Meseta), with the Pyrenees and the Cantabrian Mountains in the north and the Sierra Nevada in the south. Official language: Castilian Spanish, with Catalan, Galician, and Basque official regional languages. Religion: Roman Catholic majority. Currency: euro. Capital: Madrid. Pop: 41 128 000 (2004 est). Area: 504 748 sq km (194 883 sq miles). Spanish name: España

spake (speɪk) *vb archaic or dialect* a past tense of speak

Spalato (ˈspɑːlato) *n* the Italian name for Split

Spalding (ˈspɔːldɪŋ) *n* a town in E England, in S Lincolnshire: noted for its bulbfields. Pop: 22 081 (2001)

spall (spɔːl) *n* **1** a splinter or chip of ore, rock, or stone ▷ *vb* **2** to split or cause to split into such fragments [C15 of unknown origin]

spallation (spəˈleɪʃən) *n physics* a type of nuclear reaction in which a photon or particle hits a nucleus and causes it to emit many other particles or photons [C20 from SPALL + -ATION]

spalpeen (ˈspælpiːn) *n Irish* **1** an itinerant seasonal labourer **2** a rascal or layabout [C18 from Irish Gaelic *spailpín* itinerant labourer]

spam (spæm) *computing slang* ▷ *vb* **spams, spamming, spammed 1** to send unsolicited electronic mail simultaneously to a number of newsgroups on the internet **2** to send unsolicited text messages simultaneously to a number of mobile phones ▷ *n* **3** unsolicited electronic mail or text messages sent in this way [C20 from the repeated use of the word Spam in a popular sketch from the British television show *Monty Python's Flying Circus*, first broadcast in 1969] > 'spammer *n*

Spam (spæm) *n trademark* a kind of tinned luncheon meat, made largely from pork

spammie (ˈspæmɪ) *n Northern English dialect* a love bite

spamming (ˈspæmɪŋ) *n* the sending of multiple unsolicited e-mails or text messages, usually for marketing purposes

span¹ (spæn) *n* **1** the interval, space, or distance between two points, such as the ends of a bridge or arch **2** the complete duration or extent: *the span of his life* **3** *psychol* the amount of material that can be processed in a single mental act: *apprehension span; span of attention* **4** short for **wingspan 5** a unit of length based on the width of an expanded hand, usually taken as nine inches ▷ *vb* **spans, spanning, spanned** (*tr*) **6** to stretch or extend across, over, or around **7** to provide with something that extends across or around: *to span a river with a bridge* **8** to measure or cover, esp with the extended hand [Old English *spann*; related to Old Norse *sponn*, Old High German *spanna*]

span² (spæn) *n* a team of horses or oxen, esp two matched animals [C16 (in the sense: yoke): from Middle Dutch: something stretched, from *spannen* to stretch; see SPAN¹]

span³ (spæn) *vb archaic or dialect* a past tense of spin

Span. *abbreviation for* Spanish

spancel (ˈspænsəl) *n* **1** a length of rope for hobbling an animal, esp a horse or cow ▷ *vb* -**cels, -celling, -celled** *or US* -**cels, -celing, -celed 2** (*tr*) to hobble (an animal) with a loose rope [C17 from Low German *spansel*, from *spannen* to stretch; see SPAN²]

spandex (ˈspændɛks) *n* a type of synthetic stretch fabric made from polyurethane fibre [C20 coined from an anagram of *expands*]

spandrel *or* **spandril** (ˈspændrəl) *n architect* **1** an approximately triangular surface bounded by the outer curve of an arch and the adjacent wall **2** the surface area between two adjacent arches and the horizontal cornice above them [C15 *spaundrell*, from Anglo-French *spaundre* spandrel, from Old French *spandre* to spread, EXPAND]

spang (spæŋ) *adv US and Canadian informal* exactly, firmly, or straight: *spang on target* [C19 of unknown origin]

spangle (ˈspæŋgəl) *n* **1** a small thin piece of metal or other shiny material used as a decoration, esp on clothes; sequin **2** any glittering or shiny spot or object ▷ *vb* **3** (*intr*) to glitter or shine with or like spangles **4** (*tr*) to decorate or cover with spangles [C15 diminutive of *spange*, perhaps from Middle Dutch: clasp; compare Old Norse *spöng*] > 'spangly *adj*

Spanglish (ˈspæŋglɪʃ) *chiefly US n* a variety of English heavily influenced by Spanish, commonly spoken in US Hispanic communities [C20 from a blend of SPANISH + ENGLISH]

Spaniard (ˈspænjəd) *n* **1** a native or inhabitant of Spain **2** *NZ* short for **wild Spaniard**

spaniel (ˈspænjəl) *n* **1** any of several breeds of gundog with long drooping ears, a silky coat, and formerly a docked tail. See **clumber spaniel, cocker spaniel, field spaniel, springer spaniel, Sussex spaniel, water spaniel 2** either of two toy breeds of spaniel: see **King Charles spaniel 3** an obsequiously devoted person [C14 from Old French *espaigneul* Spanish (dog), from Old Provençal *espanhol*, ultimately from Latin *Hispāniolus* Spanish]

Spanish (ˈspænɪʃ) *n* **1** the official language of Spain, Mexico, and most countries of South and Central America except Brazil: also spoken in Africa, the Far East, and elsewhere. It is the native language of approximately 200 million people throughout the world. Spanish is an Indo-European language belonging to the Romance group **2 the Spanish** (*functioning as plural*) Spaniards collectively ▷ *adj* **3** of or relating to the Spanish language or its speakers **4** of or relating to Spain or Spaniards

Spanish America *n* the parts of America colonized by Spaniards from the 16th century onwards and now chiefly Spanish-speaking: includes all of South America (except Brazil, Guyana, French Guiana, and Surinam), Central America (except Belize), Mexico, Cuba, Puerto Rico, the Dominican Republic, and a number of small Caribbean islands

Spanish-American *adj* **1** of or relating to any of the Spanish-speaking countries or peoples of the Americas ▷ *n* **2** a native or inhabitant of Spanish America **3** a Spanish-speaking person in the US

Spanish-American War *n* the war between the US and Spain (1898) resulting in Spain's withdrawal from Cuba and its cession of Guam, the Philippines, and Puerto Rico

Spanish Armada *n* the great fleet sent by Philip II of Spain against England in 1588: defeated in the Channel by the English fleets and almost completely destroyed by storms off the Hebrides. Also called: **the Armada**

Spanish bayonet *n* any of several American liliaceous plants of the genus *Yucca*, esp *Y. aloifolia*, that have a tall woody stem, stiff pointed leaves, and large clusters of white flowers: cultivated for ornament. See also **Adam's-needle**

Spanish cedar *n* a tall meliaceous tree, *Cedrela odorata*, of tropical America, the East Indies, and Australia, having smooth bark, pinnate leaves, yellow flowers, and light-coloured aromatic wood

Spanish Civil War *n* the civil war in Spain from 1936 to 1939 in which insurgent nationalists, led by General Franco, succeeded in overthrowing the republican government. During the war Spain became an ideological battleground for fascists and socialists from all countries

Spanish customs *or* **practices** *pl n informal* irregular practices among a group of workers to gain increased financial allowances, reduced working hours, etc. Also called: **old Spanish customs** *or* **practices**

Spanish fly *n* **1** a European blister beetle, *Lytta vesicatoria* (family *Meloidae*), the dried bodies of which yield the pharmaceutical product cantharides **2** another name for **cantharides**

Spanish Guinea *n* the former name (until 1964) of **Equatorial Guinea**

Spanish guitar *n* the classic form of the guitar; a six-stringed instrument with a waisted body and a central sound hole

Spanish Inquisition *n* the institution that guarded the orthodoxy of Catholicism in Spain, chiefly by the persecution of heretics, Jews, etc, esp from the 15th to 17th centuries. See also **Inquisition**

Spanish mackerel *n* **1** Also called: **kingfish** any scombroid food fish of the genus *Scomberomorus*, esp *S. maculatus*, of American coastal regions of the Atlantic: family *Scombridae* (mackerels, tunnies, etc) **2** a mackerel, *Scomber colias*, of European and E North American coasts that is similar to the common Atlantic mackerel **3** any of various related marine food fishes, esp *Scomberomerus Commerson*

Spanish Main *n* **1** the mainland of Spanish America, esp the N coast of South America from the Isthmus of Panama to the mouth of the Orinoco River, Venezuela **2** the Caribbean Sea, the S part of which in colonial times was the route of Spanish treasure galleons and the haunt of pirates

Spanish Moroccan *adj* **1** of or relating to the former Spanish colony of Spanish Morocco (now part of Morocco) or its inhabitants ▷ *n* **2** a native or inhabitant of Spanish Morocco

Spanish Morocco *n* a former Spanish colony on the N coast of Morocco: part of the kingdom of Morocco since 1956

Spanish moss *n* **1** an epiphytic bromeliaceous plant, *Tillandsia usneoides,* growing in tropical and subtropical regions as long bluish-grey strands suspended from the branches of trees **2** a tropical lichen, *Usnea longissima,* growing as long trailing green threads from the branches of trees. Also called: **long moss**

Spanish omelette *n* an omelette made by adding green peppers, onions, tomato, etc, to the eggs

Spanish onion *n* any of several varieties of large mild-flavoured onions

Spanish paprika *n* a mild seasoning made from a variety of red pepper grown in Spain

Spanish rice *n* rice cooked with tomatoes, onions, green peppers, etc, and often flavoured with saffron

Spanish Sahara *n* the former name (until 1975) of **Western Sahara**

Spanish topaz *n* an orange-brown form of quartz, used as a gemstone

Spanish West Africa *n* a former overseas territory of Spain in NW Africa: divided in 1958 into the overseas provinces of Ifni and Spanish Sahara

Spanish West African *adj* **1** of or relating to the former Spanish overseas territory of Spanish West Africa (now the overseas provinces of Ifni and Spanish Sahara) or its inhabitants ▷ *n* **2** a native or inhabitant of Spanish West Africa

Spanish windlass *n* a stick used as a device for twisting and tightening a rope or cable

spank¹ ('spæŋk) *vb* **1** (*tr*) to slap or smack with the open hand, esp on the buttocks ▷ *n* **2** a slap or series of slaps with the flat of the hand [c18 probably of imitative origin]

spank² ('spæŋk) *vb* (*intr*) to go at a quick and lively pace [c19 back formation from SPANKING²]

spanker ('spæŋkə) *n* **1** *nautical* a fore-and-aft sail or a mast that is aftermost in a sailing vessel **2** *informal* a person or animal that moves at a quick smart pace **3** *informal* something outstandingly fine or large

spanking¹ ('spæŋkɪŋ) *n* a series of spanks, esp on the buttocks, usually as a punishment for children

spanking² ('spæŋkɪŋ) *adj* (*prenominal*) **1** *informal* outstandingly fine, smart, large, etc **2** quick and energetic; lively **3** (esp of a breeze) fresh and brisk [c17 of uncertain origin. Compare Danish *spanke* to strut]

spanner ('spænə) *n* **1** a steel hand tool with a handle carrying jaws or a hole of particular shape designed to grip a nut or bolt head **2** *Brit informal* a source of impediment or annoyance (esp in the phrase **throw a spanner in the works**) [c17 from German, from *spannen* to stretch, SPAN¹]

span-new *adj archaic or dialect* absolutely new [c14 from Old Norse *spānnȳr,* from *spānn* chip + *nȳr* NEW]

span of apprehension *n psychol* the maximum number of objects that can be correctly assessed after a brief presentation

span roof *n* a roof consisting of two equal sloping sides

span saw *n building trades* another name for **frame saw**

spanspek ('span,spek) *n South African* a sweet rough-skinned melon; a cantaloupe: family *Cucurbitaceae* [c19 possibly from Afrikaans: literally, Spanish bacon]

spansule ('spænsjuːl) *n* a modified-release capsule of a drug

spar¹ (spɑː) *n* **1 a** any piece of nautical gear resembling a pole and used as a mast, boom, gaff, etc **b** (*as modifier*): *a spar buoy* **2** a principal supporting structural member of an aerofoil that runs from tip to tip or root to tip [c13 from Old Norse *sperra* beam; related to Old High German *sparro,* Old French *esparre*]

spar² (spɑː) *vb* spars, sparring, sparred (*intr*) **1**

boxing, martial arts to fight using light blows, as in training **2** to dispute or argue **3** (of gamecocks) to fight with the feet or spurs ▷ *n* **4** an unaggressive fight **5** an argument or wrangle **6** *informal* a close friend [Old English, perhaps from SPUR]

spar³ (spɑː) *n* any of various minerals, such as feldspar or calcite, that are light-coloured, microcrystalline, transparent to translucent, and easily cleavable. Related adj: **spathic** [c16 from Middle Low German *spar;* related to Old English *spærstān;* see FELDSPAR]

sparable ('spærəbᵊl) *n* a small nail with no head, used for fixing the soles and heels of shoes [c17 changed from *sparrow-bill,* referring to the nail's shape]

sparaxis (spəˈræksɪs) *n* any plant of the cormous S African genus *Sparaxis,* esp *S. grandiflora* and *S. tricolor,* grown for their dainty spikes of star-shaped purple, red, or orange flowers: family *Iridaceae* [New Latin, from Greek *sparassein* to tear (from the appearance of the spathes)]

spar buoy *n nautical* a buoy resembling a vertical log

spare (spɛə) *vb* **1** (*tr*) to refrain from killing, punishing, harming, or injuring **2** (*tr*) to release or relieve, as from pain, suffering, etc **3** (*tr*) to refrain from using: *spare the rod, spoil the child* **4** (*tr*) to be able to afford or give: *I can't spare the time* **5** (*usually passive*) (esp of Providence) to allow to survive: *I'll see you again next year if we are spared* **6** (*intr*) *now rare* to act or live frugally **7** (*intr*) *rare* to show mercy **8 not spare oneself** to exert oneself to the full **9 to spare** more than is required: *two minutes to spare* ▷ *adj* **10** (*used immediately postpositive*) in excess of what is needed; additional: *are there any seats spare?* **11** able to be used when needed: *a spare part* **12** (of a person) thin and lean **13** scanty or meagre **14** (*postpositive*) *Brit slang* upset, angry, or distracted (esp in the phrase **go spare**) ▷ *n* **15** a duplicate kept as a replacement in case of damage or loss **16** a spare tyre **17** *tenpin bowling* **a** the act of knocking down all the pins with the two bowls of a single frame **b** the score thus made. Compare **strike** (sense 40) [Old English *sparian* to refrain from injuring; related to Old Norse *spara,* Old High German *sparōn*] > 'sparely *adv* > 'spareness *n* > 'sparer *n*

spare part *n* a duplicate or replacement component for a machine or other equipment

spare-part surgery *n* surgical replacement of defective or damaged organs by transplant or insertion of artificial devices

sparerib (ˌspeəˈrɪb) *n* a cut of pork ribs with most of the meat trimmed off

spare tyre *n* **1** an additional tyre, usually mounted on a wheel, carried by a motor vehicle in case of puncture **2** *Brit slang jocular* a deposit of fat just above the waist

sparge (spɑːdʒ) *vb rare* to sprinkle or scatter (something) [c16 from Latin *spargere* to sprinkle] > 'sparger *n*

sparid ('spærɪd) *or* **sparoid** *n* **1** any marine percoid fish of the chiefly tropical and subtropical family *Sparidae,* having a deep compressed body and well-developed teeth: includes the sea breams and porgies **2** of, relating to, or belonging to the family *Sparidae* [c20 from New Latin *Sparidae,* from Latin *sparus* a sea bream, from Greek *sparos*]

sparing ('speərɪŋ) *adj* **1** (sometimes foll by *with* or *of*) economical or frugal (with) **2** scanty; meagre **3** merciful or lenient > 'sparingly *adv* > 'sparingness *n*

spark¹ (spɑːk) *n* **1** a fiery particle thrown out or left by burning material or caused by the friction of two hard surfaces **2 a** a momentary flash of light accompanied by a sharp crackling noise, produced by a sudden electrical discharge through the air or some other insulating medium between two points **b** the electrical discharge itself **c** (*as modifier*): *a spark gap* **3** anything that serves to animate, kindle, or excite **4** a trace or

hint: *she doesn't show a spark of interest* **5** vivacity, enthusiasm, or humour **6** a small piece of diamond, as used in the cutting of glass ▷ *vb* **7** (*intr*) to give off sparks **8** (*intr*) (of the sparking plug or ignition system of an internal-combustion engine) to produce a spark **9** (*tr; often foll by off*) to kindle, excite, or animate ▷ See also **spark off, sparks** [Old English *spearca;* related to Middle Low German *sparke,* Middle Dutch *spranke,* Lettish *spirgsti* cinders, Latin *spargere* to strew]

spark² (spɑːk) *rare* (except for sense 2) ▷ *n* **1** a fashionable or gallant young man **2 bright spark** *Brit usually ironic* a person who appears clever or witty: *some bright spark left the papers next to the open window* ▷ *vb* **3** to woo (a person) [c16 (in the sense: beautiful or witty woman): perhaps of Scandinavian origin; compare Old Norse *sparkr* vivacious] > 'sparkish *adj*

spark chamber *n physics* a device for detecting ionizing radiation, consisting of two oppositely charged metal plates in a chamber containing inert gas, so that a particle passing through the chamber ionizes the gas and causes a spark to jump between the electrodes

spark coil *n* an induction coil used to produce spark discharges

spark erosion *n engineering* a method of machining using a shaped electrode which erodes the workpiece by an electric spark discharge between itself and the workpiece

spark gap *n* the space between two electrodes across which a spark can jump. Sometimes shortened to: **gap**

sparkie ('spɑːkɪ) *n* an informal name for electrician

sparking plug *n* a device screwed into the cylinder head of an internal-combustion engine to ignite the explosive mixture by means of an electric spark which jumps across a gap between a point earthed to the body of the plug and the tip of a central insulated rod. Also called: **spark plug**

sparkle ('spɑːkᵊl) *vb* **1** to issue or reflect or cause to issue or reflect bright points of light **2** (*intr*) (of wine, mineral water, etc) to effervesce **3** (*intr*) to be vivacious or witty ▷ *n* **4** a point of light, spark, or gleam **5** vivacity or wit [c12 *sparklen,* frequentative of *sparken* to SPARK¹]

sparkler ('spɑːklə) *n* **1** a type of firework that throws out showers of sparks **2** *informal* a sparkling gem

sparkling wine *n* a wine made effervescent by carbon dioxide gas, introduced artificially or produced naturally by secondary fermentation

spark off *vb* (*tr, adverb*) to bring into being or action; activate or initiate: *to spark off an argument*

spark plug *n* another name for **sparking plug**

sparks (spɑːks) *n* (*functioning as singular*) *informal* **1** an electrician **2** a radio officer, esp on a ship

spark transmitter *n* an early type of radio transmitter in which power is generated by discharging a capacitor through an inductor in series with a spark gap

sparky ('spɑːkɪ) *adj* sparkier, sparkiest lively; vivacious; spirited

sparling ('spɑːlɪŋ) *n, pl* -lings *or* -ling **1** another name for the **European smelt** (see **smelt** (the fish)) **2** a young herring [c14 *sperlynge,* from Old French *esperling,* from Middle Dutch *spierlinc,* from *spier* young shoot]

sparoid ('spæroɪd) *adj, n* another word for **sparid** [c19 from New Latin *Sparoīdēs;* see SPARID]

sparring partner ('spɑːrɪŋ) *n* **1** a person who practises with a boxer during training **2** a person with whom one has friendly arguments

sparrow ('spærəʊ) *n* **1** any weaverbird of the genus *Passer* and related genera, esp the house sparrow, having a brown or grey plumage and feeding on seeds or insects **2** *US and Canadian* any of various North American finches, such as the chipping sparrow (*Spizella passerina*), that have a dullish streaked plumage ▷ See also **hedge**

S

sparrow, tree sparrow, song sparrow ▷ Related adjective: **passerine** [Old English *spearwa*; related to Old Norse *spörr*, Old High German *sparo*]
> 'sparrow-,like *adj*

sparrowfart ('spærəʊ,fɔːt) *n slang* the very early morning: *he woke up at sparrowfart*

sparrowgrass ('spærəʊ,grɑːs) *n* a dialect or popular name for **asparagus** [c17 variant of ASPARAGUS, associated by folk etymology with SPARROW and GRASS]

sparrowhawk ('spærəʊ,hɔːk) *n* any of several small hawks, esp *Accipiter nisus*, of Eurasia and N Africa that prey on smaller birds

sparrow hawk *n* a very small North American falcon, *Falco sparverius*, that is closely related to the kestrels

sparry ('spɑːrɪ) *adj geology* containing, relating to, or resembling spar: *sparry coal*

sparse (spɑːs) *adj* scattered or scanty; not dense [c18 from Latin *sparsus*, from *spargere* to scatter]
> 'sparsely *adv* > 'sparseness *or* 'sparsity *n*

Sparta ('spɑːtə) *n* an ancient Greek city in the S Peloponnese, famous for the discipline and military prowess of its citizens and for their austere way of life

Spartacist ('spɑːtəsɪst) *n* a member of a group of German radical socialists formed in 1916 and in 1919 becoming the German Communist Party, led by Karl Liebknecht and Rosa Luxemburg [c20 from the pen name Spartacus (after the Thracian slave (died 71 BC) who led a revolt of gladiators against Rome) adopted by Karl Liebknecht (1871–1919)]

Spartan ('spɑːtᵊn) *adj* 1 of or relating to Sparta or its citizens 2 (*sometimes not capital*) very strict or austere: *a Spartan upbringing* 3 (*sometimes not capital*) possessing courage and resolve ▷ *n* 4 a citizen of Sparta 5 (*sometimes not capital*) a disciplined or brave person 6 a Canadian variety of eating apple
> 'Spartanism *n*

sparteine ('spɑːtɪ,iːn, -ɪn) *n* a viscous oily alkaloid extracted from the broom plant and lupin seeds. It has been used in medicine to treat heart arrhythmias [c19 from New Latin *Spartium*, from Greek *spartos* broom]

spasm ('spæzəm) *n* 1 an involuntary muscular contraction, esp one resulting in cramp or convulsion 2 a sudden burst of activity, emotion, etc [c14 from Latin *spasmus*, from Greek *spasmos* a cramp, from *span* to tear]

spasmodic (spæz'mɒdɪk) *or rarely* **spasmodical** *adj* 1 taking place in sudden brief spells 2 of or characterized by spasms [c17 New Latin, from Greek *spasmos* SPASM] > spas'modically *adv*

spastic ('spæstɪk) *n* 1 a person who is affected by spasms or convulsions, esp one who has cerebral palsy 2 *offensive slang* a clumsy, incapable, or incompetent person ▷ *adj* 3 affected by or resembling spasms 4 *offensive slang* clumsy, incapable or incompetent [c18 from Latin *spasticus*, from Greek *spastikos*, from *spasmos* SPASM]
> 'spastically *adv* > spas'ticity (spæs'tɪsɪtɪ) *n*

spat¹ (spæt) *n* 1 *now rare* a slap or smack 2 a slight quarrel ▷ *vb* **spats, spatting, spatted** 3 *now rare* to slap (someone) 4 (*intr*) *US, Canadian, and (rarely) NZ* to have a slight quarrel [c19 probably imitative of the sound of quarrelling]

spat² (spæt) *vb* a past tense and past participle of **spit¹**

spat³ (spæt) *n* another name for **gaiter** (sense 2) [c19 short for SPATTERDASH]

spat⁴ (spæt) *n* 1 a larval oyster or similar bivalve mollusc, esp when it settles to the sea bottom and starts to develop a shell 2 such oysters or other molluscs collectively [c17 from Anglo-Norman *spat*; perhaps related to SPIT¹]

spatchcock ('spætʃ,kɒk) *n* 1 a chicken or game bird split down the back and grilled. Compare **spitchcock** ▷ *vb* (*tr*) 2 to interpolate (words, a story, etc) into a sentence, narrative, etc, esp inappropriately [c18 perhaps variant of *spitchcock* eel when prepared and cooked]

spate (speɪt) *n* 1 a fast flow, rush, or outpouring: *a spate of words* 2 *chiefly Brit* a sudden flood: *the rivers were in spate* 3 *chiefly Brit* a sudden heavy downpour [c15 (Northern and Scottish): of unknown origin]

spathe (speɪð) *n* a large bract, often coloured, that surrounds the inflorescence of aroid plants and palms [c18 from Latin *spatha*, from Greek *spathē* a blade] > spathaceous (spə'θeɪʃəs) *adj*
> spathed *adj*

spathic ('spæθɪk) *or* **spathose** ('spæθəʊs) *adj* (of minerals) resembling spar, esp in having good cleavage [c18 from German *Spat*, *Spath* SPAR³; related to Old High German *spān* chip; see SPOON]

spathulate ('spæθjʊlɪt) *adj* another word for **spatulate** (sense 2)

spatial *or* **spacial** ('speɪʃəl) *adj* 1 of or relating to space 2 existing or happening in space
> spatiality (,speɪʃɪ'ælɪtɪ) *n* > 'spatially *adv*

spatial frequency *n television* the measure of fine detail in an optical image in terms of cycles per millimetre

spatiotemporal (,speɪʃɪəʊ'tempərəl, -'temprəl) *adj* 1 of or existing in both space and time 2 of or concerned with space-time [c20 from Latin *spatium* space + *temporālis*, from *tempus* time]
> ,spatio'temporally *adv*

Spätlese ('ʃpɛt,leɪsə) *n* a wine, usually white, produced in Germany from grapes which have been allowed to ripen for longer than usual [c20 from German, from *spät* late + *Lese* harvest, vintage]

spatter ('spætə) *vb* 1 to scatter or splash (a substance, esp a liquid) or (of a substance) to splash (something) in scattered drops: *to spatter mud on the car; mud spattered in her face* 2 (*tr*) to sprinkle, cover, or spot (with a liquid) 3 (*tr*) to slander or defame 4 (*intr*) to shower or rain down: *bullets spattered around them* ▷ *n* 5 the sound of something spattering 6 something spattered, such as a spot or splash 7 the act or an instance of spattering [c16 of imitative origin; related to Low German, Dutch *spatten* to spout, Frisian *spatteren* to splash]

spatterdash ('spætə,dæʃ) *n* 1 *US* another name for **roughcast** 2 (*plural*) long leather leggings worn in the 18th century, as to protect from mud when riding [c17 see SPATTER, DASH¹]

spatula ('spætjʊlə) *n* a utensil with a broad flat, often flexible blade, used for lifting, spreading, or stirring foods, etc [c16 from Latin: a broad piece, from *spatha* a flat wooden implement; see SPATHE]
> 'spatular *adj*

spatulate ('spætjʊlɪt) *adj* 1 shaped like a spatula 2 Also: **spathulate** *botany* having a narrow base and a broad rounded apex: *a spatulate leaf*

spavin ('spævɪn) *n vet science* enlargement of the hock of a horse by a bony growth (**bony spavin**) or fluid accumulation in the joint (**bog spavin**), usually caused by inflammation or injury, and often resulting in lameness [c15 from Old French *espavin*, of unknown origin]

spavined ('spævɪnd) *adj* 1 *vet science* affected with spavin; lame 2 decrepit or worn out

spawn (spɔːn) *n* 1 the mass of eggs deposited by fish, amphibians, or molluscs 2 *often derogatory* offspring, product, or yield 3 *botany* the nontechnical name for **mycelium** ▷ *vb* 4 (of fish, amphibians, etc) to produce or deposit (eggs) 5 *often derogatory* (of people) to produce (offspring) 6 (*tr*) to produce or engender [c14 from Anglo-Norman *espaundre*, from Old French *spandre* to spread out, EXPAND] > 'spawner *n*

spay (speɪ) *vb* (*tr*) to remove the ovaries, and usually the uterus, from (a female animal) [c15 from Old French *espeer* to cut with the sword, from *espee* sword, from Latin *spatha*]

spaza shop ('spɑːzə) *n South African slang* a small informal shop in a township, often run from a private house [from township slang: dummy, camouflaged]

SPCK (in Britain) *abbreviation for* Society for Promoting Christian Knowledge

SPD *abbreviation for* Sozialdemokratische Partei Deutschlands [German: Social Democratic Party of Germany]

speak (spiːk) *vb* **speaks, speaking, spoke, spoken** 1 to make (verbal utterances); utter (words) 2 to communicate or express (something) in or as if in words: *I speak the truth* 3 (*intr*) to deliver a speech, discourse, etc 4 (*tr*) to know how to talk in (a language or dialect): *he does not speak German* 5 (*intr*) to make a characteristic sound: *the clock spoke* 6 (*intr*) (of dogs, esp hounds used in hunting) to give tongue; bark 7 (*tr*) *nautical* to hail and converse or communicate with (another vessel) at sea 8 (*intr*) (of a musical instrument) to produce a sound 9 (*intr*; foll by *for*) to be a representative or advocate (of): *he speaks for all the members* 10 **on speaking terms** on good terms; friendly 11 **so to speak** in a manner of speaking; as it were 12 **speak one's mind** to express one's opinions frankly and plainly 13 **to speak of** of a significant or worthwhile nature: *we have had no support to speak of* ▷ See also **speak for, speak out, speak to, speak up** [Old English *specan*; related to Old High German *spehhan*, Middle High German *spechten* to gossip, Middle Dutch *speken*; see SPEECH] > 'speakable *adj*

-speak *suffix forming nouns informal* the language or jargon of a specific group, organization, or field: *computerspeak* [c20 formed on the pattern of NEWSPEAK]

speakeasy ('spiːk,iːzɪ) *n*, *pl* **-easies** *US* a place where alcoholic drink was sold illicitly during Prohibition [c19 from SPEAK + EASY (in the sense: gently, quietly)]

speaker ('spiːkə) *n* 1 a person who speaks, esp at a formal occasion 2 See **loudspeaker**
> 'speakership *n*

Speaker ('spiːkə) *n* the presiding officer in any of numerous legislative bodies, including the House of Commons in Britain and Canada and the House of Representatives in the US, Australia, and New Zealand

speakerphone ('spiːkə,fəʊn) *n* a telephone incorporating an external microphone and loudspeaker, allowing several people to participate in a call at the same time

speak for *vb* (*intr, preposition*) 1 to speak as a representative of (other people) 2 **speak for itself** to be so evident that no further comment is necessary 3 **speak for yourself** *informal* (*used as an imperative*) do not presume that other people agree with you

speaking ('spiːkɪŋ) *adj* 1 (*prenominal*) eloquent, impressive, or striking 2 a able to speak b (*in combination*) able to speak a particular language: *French-speaking*

speaking clock *n Brit* a telephone service that gives a precise verbal statement of the correct time

speaking in tongues *n* another term for **gift of tongues**

speaking trumpet *n* a trumpet-shaped instrument used to carry the voice a great distance or held to the ear by a deaf person to aid his hearing

speaking tube *n* a tube or pipe for conveying a person's voice from one room, area, or building to another

speak out *vb* (*intr, adverb*) 1 to state one's beliefs, objections, etc, bravely and firmly 2 to speak more loudly and clearly

speak to *vb* (*intr, preposition*) 1 to address (a person) 2 to reprimand: *your father will speak to you later* 3 *formal* to give evidence of or comments on (a subject): *who will speak to this item?*

speak up *vb* (*intr, adverb*) 1 to speak more loudly 2 to state one's beliefs, etc, bravely and firmly

spear¹ (spɪə) *n* 1 a weapon consisting of a long shaft with a sharp pointed end of metal, stone, or wood that may be thrown or thrust 2 a similar implement used to catch fish 3 another name for **spearman** ▷ *vb* 4 to pierce (something) with or as if with a spear [Old English *spere*; related to Old

Norse *spjör* spears, Greek *sparos* gilthead]
> ꞏspearer *n*

spear² (spɪə) *n* a shoot, slender stalk or blade, as of grass, asparagus, or broccoli [c16 probably variant of SPIRE¹, influenced by SPEAR¹]

spearfish (ꞏspɪəˌfɪʃ) *n*, *pl* **-fish** or **-fishes** another name for **marlin** [so named because of its long pointed jaw]

spear grass *n* NZ **1** another name for **wild Spaniard 2** any of various native Australian grasses, esp of the genera *Stipa* or *Heteropogon*, with sharp-pointed seeds **3** any of various grasses with sharp stiff blades or seeds

spear gun *n* a device for shooting spears underwater

spearhead (ꞏspɪəˌhɛd) *n* **1** the pointed head of a spear **2** the leading force in a military attack **3** any person or thing that leads or initiates an attack, a campaign, etc ▷ *vb* **4** (*tr*) to lead or initiate (an attack, a campaign, etc)

spearman (ꞏspɪəmən) *n*, *pl* **-men** a soldier armed with a spear

Spearman's rank-order coefficient (ꞏspɪəmənz) *n* a statistic measuring the extent to which two sets of discrete data place the distinct items in the same order, given by $r_S = 1 − 6\Sigma d^2/n(n^2 − 1)$, where Σd^2 is the sum of the squares of the differences of ranks between the two orderings and *n* is the number of items in each. Also called: **Spearman's rank-order correlation coefficient** [named after Charles E *Spearman* (1863–1945), English mathematician and statistician]

spearmint (ꞏspɪəmɪnt) *n* a purple-flowered mint plant, *Mentha spicata*, of S and central Europe, cultivated for its leaves, which yield an oil used for flavouring [c16 so called because of its long narrow leaves]

spear side *n* the male side or branch of a family. Compare **distaff side**

spearwort (ꞏspɪəˌwɜːt) *n* any of several Eurasian ranunculaceous plants of the genus *Ranunculus*, such as R. *flammula* (**lesser spearwort**) and R. *lingua* (**great spearwort**), which grow in wet places and have long narrow leaves and yellow flowers. See also **buttercup**

spec (spɛk) *informal* ▷ *n* **1** **on spec** as a speculation or gamble: *all the tickets were sold so I went to the theatre on spec* ▷ *adj* **2** (*prenominal*) *Austral and NZ* speculative: *a spec developer* [c19 short for SPECULATION or SPECULATIVE]

spec. *abbreviation for* **1** specification **2** speculation

speccy (ꞏspɛkɪ) *adj slang* wearing spectacles

special (ꞏspɛʃəl) *adj* **1** distinguished, set apart from, or excelling others of its kind **2** (*prenominal*) designed or reserved for a particular purpose: *a special tool for working leather* **3** not usual or commonplace **4** (*prenominal*) particular or primary: *his special interest was music* **5** denoting or relating to the education of physically or mentally handicapped children: *a special school* ▷ *n* **6** a special person or thing, such as an extra edition of a newspaper or a train reserved for a particular purpose **7** a dish or meal given prominence, esp at a low price, in a café, etc **8** *Austral history slang* a convict given special treatment on account of his education, social class, etc **9** short for **special constable 10** *Austral, NZ, US and Canadian informal* an item in a store that is advertised at a reduced price; a loss leader ▷ *vb* **-cials, -cialling, -cialled** (*tr*) **11** *NZ informal* to advertise and sell (an item) at a reduced price: *we are specialling butter this week* [c13 from Old French *especial*, from Latin *speciālis* individual, special, from *speciēs* appearance, SPECIES] > ꞏspecially *adv* > ꞏspecialness *n*

▪ USAGE See at **especial**

Special Air Service *n* a regiment in the British Army specializing in clandestine operations

special assessment *n* (in the US) a special charge levied on property owners by a county or municipality to help pay the costs of a civic improvement that increases the value of their property

Special Boat Service *n* a unit of the Royal Marines specializing in reconnaissance and sabotage

Special Branch *n* (in Britain) the department of the police force that is concerned with political security

special case *n law* an agreed written statement of facts submitted by litigants to a court for a decision on a point of law

special clearing *n banking* (in Britain) the clearing of a cheque through a bank in less than the usual three days, for an additional charge

special constable *n* a person recruited for temporary or occasional police duties, esp in time of emergency

special delivery *n* the delivery of a piece of mail outside the time of a scheduled delivery

special drawing rights *pl n* (*sometimes capitals*) the reserve assets of the International Monetary Fund on which member nations may draw in proportion to their contribution to the Fund. Abbreviation: SDRs

special educational needs *pl n* another term for **special needs**

special effects *pl n films* techniques used in the production of scenes that cannot be achieved by normal techniques

special forces *pl n* élite, highly trained military forces, specially selected to work on difficult missions

specialism (ꞏspɛʃəˌlɪzəm) *n* the act or process of specializing in something, or the thing itself

specialist (ꞏspɛʃəlɪst) *n* **1 a** a person who specializes in or devotes himself to a particular area of activity, field of research, etc **b** (*as modifier*): *specialist knowledge* **2** an enlisted rank in the US Army denoting technical qualifications that entitle the holder to a noncommissioned officer's pay **3** *ecology* an organism that has special nutritional requirements and lives in a restricted habitat that provides these. Compare **generalist**. > ˌspecialꞏistic *adj*

specialist registrar *n* a hospital doctor senior to a house officer but junior to a consultant, specializing in medicine (**medical specialist registrar**), surgery (**surgical specialist registrar**), or some subspeciality of either

speciality (ˌspɛʃɪꞏælɪtɪ) *or chiefly US and Canadian* **specialty** *n*, *pl* **-ties 1** a special interest or skill **2 a** a service or product specialized in, as at a restaurant: *roast beef was a speciality of the house* **b** (*as modifier*): *a speciality dish* **3** a special or distinguishing feature or characteristic

specialize *or* **specialise** (ꞏspɛʃəˌlaɪz) *vb* **1** (*intr*) to train in or devote oneself to a particular area of study, occupation, or activity **2** (*usually passive*) to cause (organisms or their parts) to develop in a way most suited to a particular environment or way of life or (of organisms, etc) to develop in this way **3** (*tr*) to modify or make suitable for a special use or purpose **4** (*tr*) to mention specifically; specify **5** (*tr*) to endorse (a commercial paper) to a specific payee > ˌspecialiꞏzation *or* ˌspecialiꞏsation *n*

special jury *n* (*formerly*) a jury whose members were drawn from some profession or rank of society as well as possessing the usual qualifications for jury service

Special K *n slang* an animal anaesthetic, ketamine hydrochloride, sold illegally as a hallucinogenic drug [c20 named after a well-known brand of breakfast cereal]

special licence *n Brit* a licence permitting a marriage to take place by dispensing with the usual legal conditions

special needs *or* **special educational needs** *pl n* **a** the educational requirements of pupils or students suffering from any of a wide range of physical disabilities, medical conditions, intellectual difficulties, or emotional problems, including deafness, blindness, dyslexia, learning difficulties, and behavioural problems **b** (*as modifier*): *special-needs teachers*

special pleading *n law* **1** a pleading that alleges new facts that offset those put forward by the other side rather than directly admitting or denying those facts **2** a pleading that emphasizes the favourable aspects of a case while omitting the unfavourable

special privilege *n* a legally endorsed privilege granted exclusively to some individual or group

special school *n Brit* a school for children who are unable to benefit from ordinary schooling because they have learning difficulties, physical or mental handicaps, etc

special sort *n printing* a character, such as an accented letter, that is not a usual member of any fount. Also called: **peculiar, arbitrary**

special team *n American football* any of several predetermined permutations of the players within a team that play in situations, such as kickoffs and attempts at field goals, where the standard offensive and defensive formations are not appropriate

special theory of relativity *n* the theory proposed in 1905 by Einstein, which assumes that the laws of physics are equally valid in all nonaccelerated frames of reference and that the speed of electromagnetic radiation in free space has the same value for all inertial observers. It leads to the idea of a space-time continuum and the equivalence of mass and energy. In combination with quantum mechanics it forms the basis of the theory of elementary particles. Also called: **special relativity** See also **general theory of relativity**

specialty (ꞏspɛʃəltɪ) *n*, *pl* **-ties 1** *law* a formal contract or obligation expressed in a deed **2** *US and Canadian* a special interest or skill **3 a** a service or product specialized in, as at a restaurant: *roast beef was a specialty of the house* **b** (*as modifier*): *a specialty dish* **4** a special or distinguishing feature or characteristic. equivalent (in Britain and certain other countries): **speciality**

speciate (ꞏspiːsɪˌeɪt) *vb* to form or develop into a new biological species [c20 back formation from SPECIATION]

speciation (ˌspiːsɪꞏeɪʃən) *n* the evolutionary development of a biological species, as by geographical isolation of a group of individuals from the main stock [c20 from SPECIES + -ATION]

specie (ꞏspiːʃiː) *n* **1** coin money, as distinguished from bullion or paper money **2** **in specie a** (of money) in coin **b** in kind **c** *law* in the actual form specified [c16 from the Latin phrase *in speciē* in kind]

specie point *n* another name for **gold point**

species (ꞏspiːʃiːz; *Latin* ꞏspiːʃɪˌiːz) *n*, *pl* **-cies 1** *biology* **a** any of the taxonomic groups into which a genus is divided, the members of which are capable of interbreeding: often containing subspecies, varieties, or races. A species is designated in italics by the genus name followed by the specific name, for example *Felis domesticus* (the domestic cat). Abbreviation: **sp b** the animals of such a group **c** any group of related animals or plants not necessarily of this taxonomic rank **2** (*modifier*) denoting a plant that is a natural member of a species rather than a hybrid or cultivar: *a species clematis* **3** *logic* a group of objects or individuals, all sharing at least one common attribute, that forms a subdivision of a genus **4** a kind, sort, or variety: *a species of treachery* **5** *chiefly RC Church* the outward form of the bread and wine in the Eucharist **6** *obsolete* an outward appearance or form **7** *obsolete* specie [c16 from Latin: appearance, from *specere* to look]

speciesism (ꞏspiːʃiːzˌɪzəm) *n* a belief of humans that all other species of animals are inferior and may therefore be used for human benefit without regard to the suffering inflicted [c20 from SPECIES + -ISM] > ꞏspeciesist *adj*

specifiable (ꞏspɛsɪˌfaɪəbᵊl) *adj* able to be specified

specific (spɪꞏsɪfɪk) *adj* **1** explicit, particular, or

S

definite: *please be more specific* **2** relating to a specified or particular thing: *a specific treatment for arthritis* **3** of or relating to a biological species: *specific differences* **4** (of a disease) caused by a particular pathogenic agent **5** *physics* **a** characteristic of a property of a particular substance, esp in relation to the same property of a standard reference substance: *specific gravity* **b** characteristic of a property of a particular substance per unit mass, length, area, volume, etc: *specific heat* **c** (of an extensive physical quantity) divided by mass: *specific heat capacity; specific volume* **6** Also (rare): **specifical** *international trade* denoting a tariff levied at a fixed sum per unit of weight, quantity, volume, etc, irrespective of value ▷ *n* **7** (*sometimes plural*) a designated quality, thing, etc **8** *med* any drug used to treat a particular disease [C17 from Medieval Latin *specificus,* from Latin SPECIES] > **spe'cifically** *adv* > **specificity** (ˌspɛsɪˈfɪsɪtɪ) *n*

specification (ˌspɛsɪfɪˈkeɪʃən) *n* **1** the act or an instance of specifying **2** (in patent law) a written statement accompanying an application for a patent that describes the nature of an invention **3** a detailed description of the criteria for the constituents, construction, appearance, performance, etc, of a material, apparatus, etc, or of the standard of workmanship required in its manufacture **4** an item, detail, etc, specified

specific charge *n physics* the charge-to-mass ratio of an elementary particle

specific gravity *n* the ratio of the density of a substance to that of water. See **relative density**

specific heat capacity *n* the heat required to raise unit mass of a substance by unit temperature interval under specified conditions, such as constant pressure: usually measured in joules per kelvin per kilogram. Symbol: c_p (for constant pressure) Also called: **specific heat**

specific humidity *n* the mass of water vapour in a sample of moist air divided by the mass of the sample

specific impulse *n* the ratio of the thrust produced by a rocket engine to the rate of fuel consumption: it has units of time and is the length of time that unit weight of propellant would last if used to produce one unit of thrust continuously

specific performance *n law* a remedy awarded by a court requiring a person to fulfil obligations under a contract where damages are an insufficient remedy

specific resistance *n* the former name for **resistivity**

specific viscosity *n physics* a measure of the resistance to flow of a fluid, expressed as the ratio of the absolute viscosity of the fluid to that of a reference fluid (usually water in the case of liquids)

specific volume *n physics* the volume of matter per unit mass; the reciprocal of the density. Symbol: *v*

specify (ˈspɛsɪˌfaɪ) *vb* **-fies, -fying, -fied** (*tr; may take a clause as object*) **1** to refer to or state specifically **2** to state as a condition **3** to state or include in the specification of [C13 from Medieval Latin *specificāre* to describe] > **specificative** (ˈspɛsɪfɪˌkeɪtɪv) *adj* > **speci,fier** *n*

specimen (ˈspɛsɪmɪn) *n* **1 a** an individual, object, or part regarded as typical of the group or class to which it belongs **b** (*as modifier*): *a specimen signature; a specimen page* **2** *med* a sample of tissue, blood, urine, etc, taken for diagnostic examination or evaluation **3** the whole or a part of an organism, plant, rock, etc, collected and preserved as an example of its class, species, etc **4** *informal, often derogatory* a person [C17 from Latin: mark, evidence, proof, from *specere* to look at]

speciosity (ˌspiːʃɪˈɒsɪtɪ) *n, pl* **-ties 1** a thing or person that is deceptively attractive or plausible **2** the state of being specious **3** *obsolete* the state of being beautiful

specious (ˈspiːʃəs) *adj* **1** apparently correct or true, but actually wrong or false **2** deceptively attractive in appearance [C14 (originally: fair): from Latin *speciōsus* plausible, from *speciēs* outward appearance, from *specere* to look at] > **'speciously** *adv* > **'speciousness** *n*

speck (spɛk) *n* **1** a very small mark or spot **2** a small or tiny piece of something ▷ *vb* **3** (*tr*) to mark with specks or spots [Old English *specca;* related to Middle Dutch *spekelen* to sprinkle]

speckle (ˈspɛkəl) *n* **1** a small or slight mark usually of a contrasting colour, as on the skin, a bird's plumage, or eggs ▷ *vb* **2** (*tr*) to mark with or as if with speckles [C15 from Middle Dutch *spekkel;* see SPECK] > **'speckled** *adj*

speckled trout *n* another name for **brook trout**

speckled wood *n* a common woodland brown satyrid butterfly, *Pararge aegeria,* marked with pale orange or yellowish-white spots

speckle interferometry *n astronomy* a technique to increase the angular resolution of telescopes that are impaired by atmospheric turbulence, in which the information from a number of exposures of very short duration is combined

specs (spɛks) *pl n informal* **1** short for **spectacles 2** short for **specifications** (sense 3)

spec sheet *n* a list describing the specifications of a product or property that is for sale

spectacle (ˈspɛktəkəl) *n* **1** a public display or performance, esp a showy or ceremonial one **2** a thing or person seen, esp an unusual or ridiculous one: *he makes a spectacle of himself* **3** a strange or interesting object or phenomenon **4** (*modifier*) of or relating to spectacles: *a spectacle case* ▷ See also **spectacles** [C14 via Old French from Latin *spectaculum* a show, from *spectāre* to watch, from *specere* to look at]

spectacled (ˈspɛktəkəld) *adj* **1** wearing glasses **2** (of an animal) having markings around the eyes resembling a pair of glasses

spectacles (ˈspɛktəkəlz) *pl n* **1** a pair of glasses for correcting defective vision. Often (*informal*) shortened to: **specs 2** pair of spectacles *cricket* a score of 0 in each innings of a match

spectacular (spɛkˈtækjʊlə) *adj* **1** of or resembling a spectacle; impressive, grand, or dramatic **2** unusually marked or great: *a spectacular increase in spending* ▷ *n* **3** a lavishly produced performance > **spec'tacularly** *adv*

spectate (spɛkˈteɪt) *vb* (*intr*) to be a spectator, esp at a sporting event; watch [C20 back formation from SPECTATOR]

spectator (spɛkˈteɪtə) *n* a person viewing anything; onlooker; observer [C16 from Latin, from *spectāre* to watch; see SPECTACLE]

spectator sport *n* a sport that attracts more people as spectators than as participants

spectra (ˈspɛktrə) *n* the plural of **spectrum**

spectral (ˈspɛktrəl) *adj* **1** of or like a spectre **2** of or relating to a spectrum: *spectral colours* **3** *physics* (of a physical quantity) relating to a single wavelength of radiation: *spectral luminous efficiency* > **spectrality** (spɛkˈtrælɪtɪ) *or* **'spectralness** *n* > **'spectrally** *adv*

spectral luminous efficiency *n* a measure of the efficiency of radiation of a given wavelength in producing a visual sensation. It is equal to the ratio of the radiant flux at a standard wavelength to that at the given wavelength when the standard wavelength is chosen so that the maximum value of this ratio is unity. Symbol: $V(\lambda)$ (for photopic vision) or $V'(\lambda)$ (for scotopic vision)

spectral type *or* **class** *n* any of various groups into which stars are classified according to characteristic spectral lines and bands. The most important classification (**Harvard classification**) has a series of classes O, B, A, F, G, K, M, the series also being a scale of diminishing surface temperature

spectre *or US* **specter** (ˈspɛktə) *n* **1** a ghost; phantom; apparition **2** a mental image of something unpleasant or menacing: *the spectre of*

redundancy [C17 from Latin *spectrum,* from *specere* to look at]

spectrin (ˈspɛktrɪn) *n* any one of a class of fibrous proteins found in the membranes of red blood cells, the brain, the intestine, etc [C20 from SPECTR(E) + -IN, referring to the ghosts (isolated cell membranes) of red blood cells, the source of the first known member of the class]

spectro- *combining form* indicating a spectrum: *spectrogram*

spectrobolometer (ˌspɛktrəʊbəʊˈlɒmɪtə) *n* a combined spectroscope and bolometer for determining the wavelength distribution of radiant energy emitted by a source > **spectrobolometric** (ˌspɛktrəˌbəʊləˈmɛtrɪk) *adj*

spectrofluorimeter (ˌspɛktrəʊfluəˈrɪmɪtə) *or* **spectrofluorometer** *n* an instrument for recording fluorescence emission and absorption spectra

spectrograph (ˈspɛktrəʊˌɡrɑːf, -ˌɡræf) *n* a spectroscope or spectrometer that produces a photographic record (**spectrogram**) of a spectrum. See also **sound spectrograph**. > **ˌspectro'graphic** *adj* > **ˌspectro'graphically** *adv* > **spec'trography** *n*

spectroheliograph (ˌspɛktrəʊˈhiːlɪəˌɡrɑːf, -ˌɡræf) *n* an instrument used to obtain an image of the sun in light of a particular wavelength, such as calcium or hydrogen, to show the distribution of the element over the surface and in the solar atmosphere. The image obtained is a **spectroheliogram** [C19 from SPECTRO- + HELIO- + -GRAPH] > **ˌspectro,helio'graphic** *adj*

spectrohelioscope (ˌspɛktrəʊˈhiːlɪəʊˌskəʊp) *n* an instrument, similar to the spectroheliograph, used for observing solar radiation at one particular wavelength > **spectrohelioscopic** (ˌspɛktrəʊˌhiːlɪəʊˈskɒpɪk) *adj*

spectrometer (spɛkˈtrɒmɪtə) *n* any instrument for producing a spectrum, esp one in which wavelength, energy, intensity, etc, can be measured. See also **mass spectrometer** > **spectrometric** (ˌspɛktrəʊˈmɛtrɪk) *adj* > **spec'trometry** *n*

spectrophotometer (ˌspɛktrəʊfəʊˈtɒmɪtə) *n* an instrument for producing or recording a spectrum and measuring the photometric intensity of each wavelength present, esp such an instrument used for infrared, visible, and ultraviolet radiation. See also **spectrometer** [C19 from SPECTRO- + PHOTO- + -METER] > **spectrophotometric** (ˌspɛktrəʊˌfəʊtəˈmɛtrɪk) *adj* > **ˌspectropho'tometry** *n*

spectroscope (ˈspɛktrəˌskəʊp) *n* any of a number of instruments for dispersing electromagnetic radiation and thus forming or recording a spectrum. See also **spectrometer** [C19 from SPECTRO- + -SCOPE; from French, or on the model of German *Spektroskop*] > **spectroscopic** (ˌspɛktrəˈskɒpɪk) *or* **ˌspectro'scopical** *adj* > **ˌspectro'scopically** *adv*

spectroscopic analysis *n* the use of spectroscopy in determining the chemical or physical constitution of substances

spectroscopy (spɛkˈtrɒskəpɪ) *n* the science and practice of using spectrometers and spectroscopes and of analysing spectra, the methods employed depending on the radiation being examined. The techniques are widely used in chemical analysis and in studies of the properties of atoms, molecules, ions, etc > **spec'troscopist** *n*

spectrum (ˈspɛktrəm) *n, pl* **-tra** (-trə) **1** the distribution of colours produced when white light is dispersed by a prism or diffraction grating. There is a continuous change in wavelength from red, the longest wavelength, to violet, the shortest. Seven colours are usually distinguished: violet, indigo, blue, green, yellow, orange, and red **2** the whole range of electromagnetic radiation with respect to its wavelength or frequency **3** any particular distribution of electromagnetic radiation often showing lines or bands characteristic of the substance emitting the radiation or absorbing it. See also **absorption spectrum, emission spectrum** 4 any similar distribution or record of the energies, velocities, masses, etc, of atoms, ions, electrons, etc: *a mass spectrum* 5 any range or scale, as of capabilities, emotions, or moods 6 another name for an **afterimage** [C17 from Latin: appearance, image, from *spectāre* to observe, from *specere* to look at]

spectrum analyser *n* an instrument that splits an input waveform into its frequency components, which are then displayed

spectrum analysis *n* the analysis of a spectrum to determine the properties of its source, such as the analysis of the emission spectrum of a substance to determine the electron distribution in its molecules

specular ('spɛkjʊlə) *adj* 1 of, relating to, or having the properties of a mirror: *specular reflection* 2 of or relating to a speculum [C16 from Latin *speculāris*, from *speculum* a mirror, from *specere* to look at] > **'specularly** *adv*

speculate ('spɛkjʊ,leɪt) *vb* 1 (when *tr, takes a clause as object*) to conjecture without knowing the complete facts 2 (*intr*) to buy or sell securities, property, etc, in the hope of deriving capital gains 3 (*intr*) to risk loss for the possibility of considerable gain 4 (*intr*) NZ *rugby* to make an emergency forward kick of the ball without taking any particular aim [C16 from Latin *speculārī* to spy out, from *specula* a watchtower, from *specere* to look at]

speculation (,spɛkjʊ'leɪʃən) *n* 1 the act or an instance of speculating 2 a supposition, theory, or opinion arrived at through speculating 3 investment involving high risk but also the possibility of high profits

speculative ('spɛkjʊlətɪv) *adj* relating to or characterized by speculation, esp financial speculation > **'speculatively** *adv* > **'speculativeness** *n*

speculative fiction *n* a broad literary genre encompassing any fiction with supernatural, fantastical or futuristic elements [C20]

speculator ('spɛkjʊ,leɪtə) *n* 1 a person who speculates 2 NZ *rugby* an undirected kick of the ball

speculum ('spɛkjʊləm) *n, pl* **-la** (-lə) *or* **-lums** 1 a mirror, esp one made of polished metal for use in a telescope, etc 2 *med* an instrument for dilating a bodily cavity or passage to permit examination of its interior 3 a patch of distinctive colour on the wing of a bird, esp in certain ducks [C16 from Latin: mirror, from *specere* to look at]

speculum metal *n* a white hard brittle corrosion-resistant alloy of copper (55–70 per cent) and tin with smaller amounts of other metals. It takes a high polish and is used for mirrors, lamp reflectors, ornamental ware, etc

sped (spɛd) *vb* a past tense and past participle of **speed**

speech (spiːtʃ) *n* 1 a the act or faculty of speaking, esp as possessed by persons: *to have speech with somebody* b (*as modifier*): *speech therapy* 2 that which is spoken; utterance 3 a talk or address delivered to an audience 4 a person's characteristic manner of speaking 5 a national or regional language or dialect 6 *linguistics* another word for **parole** (sense 5) [Old English *spēc*; related to *specan* to SPEAK]

speech act *n philosophy* 1 an utterance that constitutes some act in addition to the mere act of uttering 2 an act or type of act capable of being so performed ▷ See also **performative**

speech community *n* a community consisting of all the speakers of a particular language or dialect

speech day *n Brit* (in schools) an annual day on which prizes are presented, speeches are made by guest speakers, etc

speech from the throne *n* (in Britain and the dominions of the Commonwealth) the speech at the opening of each session of Parliament in which the Government outlines its legislative programme. It is read by the sovereign or his or her representative. Also called (esp Brit): Queen's (*or* King's) speech

speechify ('spiːtʃɪ,faɪ) *vb* **-fies, -fying, -fied** (*intr*) 1 to make a speech or speeches 2 to talk pompously and boringly > ,speechifi'cation *n* > 'speechi,fier *n*

speechless ('spiːtʃlɪs) *adj* 1 not able to speak 2 temporarily deprived of speech 3 not expressed or able to be expressed in words: *speechless fear* > 'speechlessly *adv* > 'speechlessness *n*

speech-reading *n* another name for **lip-reading**

speech recognition *n* the understanding of continuous speech by a computer

speech therapy *n* treatment to improve the speech of children who have difficulty in learning to speak, for example because of partial deafness or brain damage, or to help restore the power of speech to adults who have lost it or partly lost it through accident or illness > **speech therapist** *n*

speed (spiːd) *n* 1 the act or quality of acting or moving fast; rapidity 2 the rate at which something moves, is done, or acts 3 *physics* a scalar measure of the rate of movement of a body expressed either as the distance travelled divided by the time taken (**average speed**) or the rate of change of position with respect to time at a particular point (**instantaneous speed**). It is measured in metres per second, miles per hour, etc 4 a rate of rotation, usually expressed in revolutions per unit time 5 a a gear ratio in a motor vehicle, bicycle, etc b (*in combination*): *a three-speed gear* 6 *photog* a numerical expression of the sensitivity to light of a particular type of film, paper, or plate. See also **ISO rating** 7 *photog* a measure of the ability of a lens to pass light from an object to the image position, determined by the aperture and also the transmitting power of the lens. It increases as the f-number is decreased and vice versa 8 a slang word for **amphetamine** 9 *archaic* prosperity or success 10 **at speed** quickly 11 **up to speed** a operating at an acceptable or competitive level b in possession of all the relevant or necessary information ▷ *vb* **speeds, speeding, sped** *or* **speeded** 12 to move or go or cause to move or go quickly 13 (*intr*) to drive (a motor vehicle) at a high speed, esp above legal limits 14 (*tr*) to help further the success or completion of 15 (*intr*) *slang* to take or be under the influence of amphetamines 16 (*intr*) to operate or run at a high speed 17 *archaic* a (*intr*) to prosper or succeed b (*tr*) to wish success to ▷ See also **speed up** [Old English *spēd* (originally in the sense: success); related to *spōwan* to succeed, Latin *spēs* hope, Old Slavonic *spěti* to be lucky] > 'speeder *n*

speedball ('spiːd,bɔːl) *n slang* a mixture of heroin with amphetamine or cocaine

speedboat ('spiːd,bəʊt) *n* a high-speed motorboat having either an inboard or outboard motor

speed camera *n* a fixed camera that photographs vehicles breaking the speed limit on a certain stretch of road

speed chess *n* a form of chess in which each player's game is limited to a total stipulated time, usually half an hour; the first player to exceed the time limit loses

speed dating *n* a method of meeting potential partners in which each participant has only a few minutes to talk to each of his or her dates before being moved on to the next one. At the end of the event, paticipants decide which dates they would like to see again > **speed dater** *n*

speedfreak ('spiːd,friːk) *n slang* an amphetamine addict

speed limit *n* the maximum permitted speed at which a vehicle may travel on certain roads

speed networking *n* the practice of trying to form business connections and contacts through meetings at which individuals are given the opportunity to have several conversations of limited duration with strangers

speedo ('spiːdəʊ) *n, pl* **speedos** an informal name for **speedometer** or (Austral) **odometer**

speedometer (spɪ'dɒmɪtə) *n* a device fitted to a vehicle to measure and display the speed of travel. See also **mileometer**

speed ramp *n Brit* a raised band across a road, designed to make motorists reduce their speed, esp in built-up areas

speed skating *n* a form of ice skating in which contestants race against each other or the clock over various distances

speedster ('spiːdstə) *n* a fast car, esp a sports model

speed trap *n* a section of road on which the police check the speed of vehicles, often using radar

speed up *vb* (*adverb*) 1 to increase or cause to increase in speed or rate; accelerate ▷ *n* **speed-up** 2 an instance of this; acceleration

> **USAGE** The past tense and past participle of *speed up* is *speeded up*, not *sped up*

speedway ('spiːd,weɪ) *n* 1 a the sport of racing on light powerful motorcycles round cinder tracks b (*as modifier*): *a speedway track* 2 the track or stadium where such races are held 3 *US and Canadian* a a racetrack for cars b a road on which fast driving is allowed

speedwell ('spiːd,wɛl) *n* any of various temperate scrophulariaceous plants of the genus *Veronica*, such as *V. officinalis* (**heath speedwell**) and *V. chamaedrys* (**germander speedwell**), having small blue or pinkish white flowers [C16 from SPEED + WELL[1]]

Speedwriting ('spiːd,raɪtɪŋ) *n* trademark a form of shorthand in which alphabetic combinations are used to represent groups of sounds or short common words

speedy ('spiːdɪ) *adj* **speedier, speediest** 1 characterized by speed of motion 2 done or decided without delay; quick > 'speedily *adv* > 'speediness *n*

speel (spiːl) *n Manchester dialect* a splinter of wood [probably from Old Norse; compare Norwegian *spela, spila*, Swedish *spjela, spjele* SPILL²]

speir *or* **speer** (spiːr) *vb Scot* to ask; inquire [Old English *spyrian* to seek after, search for]

speiss (spaɪs) *n* the arsenides and antimonides that form when ores containing arsenic or antimony are smelted [C18 from German *Speise* food]

spek (spɛk) *n South African* bacon, fat, or fatty pork used for larding venison or other game [Afrikaans]

spelaean *or* **spelean** (spɪ'liːən) *adj* of, found in, or inhabiting caves: *spelaean animals* [C19 via New Latin, from Latin *spēlaeum* a cave, from Greek *spēlaion*]

speleology *or* **spelaeology** (,spiːlɪ'ɒlədʒɪ) *n* 1 the scientific study of caves, esp in respect of their geological formation, flora and fauna, etc 2 the sport or pastime of exploring caves [C19 from Latin *spēlaeum* cave] > **speleological** *or* **spelaeological** (,spiːlɪə'lɒdʒɪkəl) *adj* > ,spele'ologist *or* ,spelae'ologist *n*

speleotherapy (,spiːlɪə'θɛrəpɪ) *n* a form of treatment for asthma sufferers that takes place in clinics in disused mines, in which the air is free of pollen, dust mites, and the other irritants that provoke an allergic reaction; used to reduce the risk of heart disease

spelk (spɛlk) *n Scot and northern English dialect* a splinter of wood [from Old English *spelc, spilc* surgical splint; related to Old Norse *spelkur* splints]

spell[1] (spɛl) *vb* **spells, spelling, spelt** *or* **spelled** 1 to write or name in correct order the letters that comprise the conventionally accepted form of (a word or part of a word) 2 (*tr*) (of letters) to go to make up the conventionally established form of (a word) when arranged correctly: *d-o-g spells dog* 3 (*tr*) to indicate or signify: *such actions spell disaster for our cause* ▷ See also **spell out** [C13 from Old French

S

espeller, of Germanic origin; related to Old Norse *spialla* to talk, Middle High German *spellen*]
> 'spellable *adj*

spell² (spɛl) *n* **1** a verbal formula considered as having magical force **2** any influence that can control the mind or character; fascination **3** a state induced by or as if by the pronouncing of a spell; trance: *to break the spell* **4** under a spell held in or as if in a spell ▷ *vb* **5** (*tr*) *rare* to place under a spell [Old English *spell* speech; related to Old Norse *spjall* tale, Gothic *spill,* Old High German *spel*]

spell³ (spɛl) *n* **1** an indeterminate, usually short, period of time: *a spell of cold weather* **2** a period or tour of duty after which one person or group relieves another **3** *Scot, Austral, and NZ* a period or interval of rest ▷ *vb* **4** (*tr*) to take over from (a person) for an interval of time; relieve temporarily **5** spell a paddock *NZ* to give a field a rest period by letting it lie fallow [Old English *spelian* to take the place of, of obscure origin]

spellbind ('spɛl,baɪnd) *vb* -binds, -binding, -bound (*tr*) to cause to be spellbound; entrance or enthral

spellbinder ('spɛl,baɪndə) *n* **1** a person capable of holding others spellbound, esp a political speaker **2** a novel, play, etc, that holds one enthralled

spellbound ('spɛl,baʊnd) *adj* having one's attention held as though one is bound by a spell

spellchecker ('spɛl,tʃɛkə) *n computing* a program that highlights any word in a word-processed document that is not recognized as being correctly spelt

speller ('spɛlə) *n* **1** a person who spells words in the manner specified: *a bad speller* **2** a book designed to teach or improve spelling

spellican ('spɛlɪkən) *n* a variant spelling of **spillikin**

spelling ('spɛlɪŋ) *n* **1** the act or process of writing words by using the letters conventionally accepted for their formation; orthography **2** the art or study of orthography **3** the actual way in which a word is spelt **4** the ability of a person to spell: *John's spelling is good*

spelling bee *n* a contest in which players are required to spell words according to orthographic conventions [c19 from BEE²]

spelling pronunciation *n* a pronunciation of a word that is influenced by the word's orthography and often comes about as the modification of an earlier or original rendering, such as the pronunciation of the British name *Mainwaring,* usually ('mænərɪŋ), as ('meɪn,wɛərɪŋ)

spell out *vb* (*tr, adverb*) **1** to make clear, distinct, or explicit; clarify in detail: *let me spell out the implications* **2** to read laboriously or with difficulty, working out each word letter by letter **3** to discern by study; puzzle out

spelt¹ (spɛlt) *vb* a past tense and past participle of **spell¹**

spelt² (spɛlt) *n* a species of wheat, *Triticum spelta,* that was formerly much cultivated and was used to develop present-day cultivated wheats [Old English; related to Old Saxon *spelta,* Old High German *spelza*]

spelter ('spɛltə) *n* impure zinc, usually containing about 3 per cent of lead and other impurities [c17 probably from Middle Dutch *speauter,* of obscure origin; compare Old French *peautre* pewter, Italian *peltro* PEWTER]

spelunker (spɪ'lʌŋkə) *n* a person whose hobby is the exploration and study of caves [c20 from Latin *spēlunca,* from Greek *spēlunx* a cave] > spe'lunking *n*

spence (spɛns) *n dialect* **a** a larder or pantry **b** any monetary allowance **c** a parlour, esp in a cottage [c14 from Old French *despense,* from Latin *dispendere* to distribute; see DISPENSE]

spencer¹ ('spɛnsə) *n* **1** a short fitted coat or jacket **2** a woman's knitted vest [c18 named after Earl *Spencer* (1758–1834)]

spencer² ('spɛnsə) *n nautical* a large loose-footed gaffsail on a square-rigger or barque [c19 perhaps after the surname *Spencer*]

Spencer Gulf *n* an inlet of the Indian Ocean in S Australia, between the Eyre and Yorke Peninsulas. Length: about 320 km (200 miles). Greatest width: about 145 km (90 miles)

spend (spɛnd) *vb* spends, spending, spent **1** to pay out (money, wealth, etc) **2** (*tr*) to concentrate (time, effort, thought, etc) upon an object, activity, etc **3** (*tr*) to pass (time) in a specific way, activity, place, etc **4** (*tr*) to use up completely: *the hurricane spent its force* **5** (*tr*) to give up (one's blood, life, etc) in a cause **6** (*intr*) *obsolete* to be used up or exhausted **7** spend a penny *Brit informal* to urinate ▷ *n* **8** an amount of money spent, esp regularly, or allocated to be spent ▷ See also **spends** [Old English *spendan,* from Latin *expendere;* influenced also by Old French *despendre* to spend, from Latin *dispendere;* see EXPEND, DISPENSE] > 'spendable *adj*

spender ('spɛndə) *n* a person who spends money in a manner specified: *a big spender*

spending money *n* an allowance for small personal expenses; pocket money

spends (spɛndz) *pl n Lancashire dialect* a child's pocket money

spendthrift ('spɛnd,θrɪft) *n* **1** a person who spends money in an extravagant manner ▷ *adj* **2** (*usually prenominal*) of or like a spendthrift: *spendthrift economies* [c17 from SPEND + THRIFT]

Spenserian (spɛn'sɪərɪən) *adj* **1** relating to, in the style of, or characteristic of Edmund Spenser, the English poet (??1552–99), or his poetry ▷ *n* **2** a student or imitator of Edmund Spenser

Spenserian sonnet *n prosody* a sonnet form used by the poet Spenser having the rhyme scheme a b a b b c b c c d c d e e

Spenserian stanza *n prosody* the stanza form used by the poet Spenser in his poem *The Faerie Queene,* consisting of eight lines in iambic pentameter and a concluding Alexandrine, rhyming a b a b b c b c c

spent (spɛnt) *vb* **1** the past tense and past participle of **spend** ▷ *adj* **2** used up or exhausted; consumed **3** (of a fish) exhausted by spawning

spent gnat *n* an angler's name for the spinner of various mayflies, esp *Ephemeris danica* and *E. vulgata,* particularly when lying spent on the water surface after mating and egg-laying

speos ('spiːɒs) *n* (esp in ancient Egypt) a temple or tomb cut into a rock face [c19 Greek, literally: a cave, grotto]

sperm¹ (spɜːm) *n, pl* sperms *or* sperm **1** another name for **semen 2** a male reproductive cell; male gamete [c14 from Late Latin *sperma,* from Greek; related to Greek *speirein* to sow]

sperm² (spɜːm) *n* short for **sperm whale, spermaceti** *or* **sperm oil**

-sperm *n combining form* (in botany) a seed: *gymnosperm* > -spermous *or* -spermal *adj combining form*

spermaceti (,spɜːmə'sɛtɪ, -'siːtɪ) *n* a white waxy substance obtained from oil from the head of the sperm whale: used in cosmetics, candles, ointments, etc [c15 from Medieval Latin *sperma cētī* whale's sperm, from *sperma* SPERM¹ + Latin *cētus* whale, from Greek *kētos*]

spermary ('spɜːmərɪ) *n, pl* -maries any organ in which spermatozoa are produced, esp a testis

spermatheca (,spɜːmə'θiːkə) *n* a sac or cavity within the body of many female invertebrates, esp insects, used for storing spermatozoa before fertilization takes place [c19 see SPERM¹, THECA] > ,sperma'thecal *adj*

spermatic (spɜː'mætɪk), **spermic** ('spɜːmɪk) *or* **spermous** ('spɜːməs) *adj* **1** of or relating to spermatozoa: *spermatic fluid* **2** of or relating to the testis: *the spermatic artery* **3** of or relating to a spermary [c16 from Late Latin *spermaticus,* from Greek *spermatikos* concerning seed, from *sperma* seed, SPERM¹] > sper'matically *adv*

spermatic cord *n* a cord in many male mammals that passes from each testis to the abdominal cavity and contains the spermatic artery and vein, vas deferens, and lymphatics

spermatic fluid *n* another name for **semen**

spermatid ('spɜːmətɪd) *n zoology* any of four immature male gametes that are formed from a spermatocyte, each of which develops into a spermatozoon

spermatium (spɜː'meɪtɪəm) *n, pl* -tia (-tɪə) a nonmotile male reproductive cell in red algae and some fungi [c19 New Latin, from Greek *spermation* a little seed; see SPERM¹]

spermato-, spermo- *or before a vowel* **spermat-, sperm-** *combining form* **1** indicating sperm: *spermatogenesis* **2** indicating seed: *spermatophyte* [from Greek *sperma, spermat-,* seed; see SPERM¹]

spermatocide ('spɜːmətəʊ,saɪd) *n* a less common word for **spermicide**. > ,spermato'cidal *adj*

spermatocyte ('spɜːmətəʊ,saɪt) *n* **1** *zoology* an immature male germ cell, developed from a spermatogonium, that gives rise, by meiosis, to four spermatids **2** *botany* a male germ cell that develops into an antherozoid

spermatogenesis (,spɜːmətəʊ'dʒɛnɪsɪs) *n* the formation and maturation of spermatozoa in the testis. See also **spermatocyte** (sense 1) > spermatogenetic (,spɜːmətəʊdʒə'nɛtɪk) *adj*

spermatogonium (,spɜːmətə'ɡəʊnɪəm) *n, pl* -nia (-nɪə) *zoology* an immature male germ cell that divides to form many spermatocytes [c19 from SPERMATO- + -GONIUM] > ,spermato'gonial *adj*

spermatophore ('spɜːmətəʊ,fɔː) *n* a capsule of spermatozoa extruded by some molluscs, crustaceans, annelids, and amphibians > ,spermato'phoral *adj*

spermatophyte ('spɜːmətəʊ,faɪt) *or* **spermophyte** *n* (in traditional classifications) any plant of the major division *Spermatophyta,* which includes all seed-bearing plants: an angiosperm or a gymnosperm. Former name: phanerogam > spermatophytic (,spɜːmətəʊ'fɪtɪk) *adj*

spermatorrhoea *or esp US* **spermatorrhea** (,spɜːmətəʊ'rɪə) *n* involuntary emission of semen without orgasm

spermatozoid (,spɜːmətəʊ'zəʊɪd) *n botany* another name for **antherozoid**

spermatozoon (,spɜːmətəʊ'zəʊɒn) *n, pl* -zoa (-'zəʊə) any of the male reproductive cells released in the semen during ejaculation, consisting of a flattened egg-shaped head, a long neck, and a whiplike tail by which it moves to fertilize the female ovum. Also called: sperm, zoosperm > ,spermato'zoal, ,spermato'zoan *or* ,spermato'zoic *adj*

sperm bank *n* a place in which semen is stored until it is required for artificial insemination

spermic ('spɜːmɪk) *adj* another word for **spermatic**

spermicide ('spɜːmɪ,saɪd) *n* any drug or other agent that kills spermatozoa > ,spermi'cidal *adj*

spermine ('spɜːmiːn, -mɪn) *n* a white or colourless basic water-soluble amine that is found in semen, sputum, and animal tissues; diaminopropyltetramethylenediamine. Formula: $C_{10}H_{26}N_4$

spermiogenesis (,spɜːmɪəʊ'dʒɛnɪsɪs) *n* the stage in spermatogenesis in which spermatozoa are formed from spermatids > spermiogenetic (,spɜːmɪəʊdʒə'nɛtɪk) *adj*

spermogonium (,spɜːmə'ɡəʊnɪəm) *n, pl* -nia (-nɪə) a reproductive body in some fungi and lichens, in which spermatia are formed

sperm oil *n* an oil obtained from the head of the sperm whale, used as a lubricant

spermophile ('spɜːməʊ,faɪl) *n* any of various North American ground squirrels of the genera *Citellus, Spermophilopsis,* etc, regarded as pests in many regions [c19 from SPERM(AT)O- + -PHILE, on the model of New Latin *spermophilus* a seed-lover]

spermophyte ('spɜːməʊ,faɪt) *n* a variant spelling of **spermatophyte**

spermous ('spɜːməs) *adj* **1** of or relating to the sperm whale or its products **2** another word for **spermatic**

sperm whale *n* a large toothed whale, *Physeter catodon*, having a square-shaped head and hunted for sperm oil, spermaceti, and ambergris: family *Physeteridae*. Also called: **cachalot** [c19 short for SPERMACETI *whale*]

Sperrin Mountains ('spɛrɪn) *n* a mountain range in NW Northern Ireland

sperrylite ('spɛrɪ,laɪt) *n* a white metallic mineral consisting of platinum arsenide in cubic crystalline form. Formula: PtAs₂ [c19 named after F L *Sperry*, Canadian chemist]

spessartite ('spɛsə,taɪt) *or* **spessartine** *n* a brownish red garnet that consists of manganese aluminium silicate and is used as a gemstone. Formula: Mn₃Al₂(SiO₄)₃ [c19 named after *Spessart*, mountain range in Germany]

speug (spjʌg) *n Scot* a sparrow [of unknown origin]

spew (spju:) *vb* **1** to eject (the contents of the stomach) involuntarily through the mouth; vomit **2** to spit (spittle, phlegm, etc) out of the mouth **3** (usually foll by *out*) to send or be sent out in a stream: *flames spewed out* ▷ *n* **4** something ejected from the mouth ▷ Also (archaic): **spue** [Old English *spīwan*; related to Old Norse *spýja*, Gothic *speiwan*, Old High German *spīwan*, Latin *spuere*, Lithuanian *spiauti*] > **'spewer** *n*

Spey (speɪ) *n* a river in E Scotland, flowing generally northeast through the Grampian Mountains to the Moray Firth: salmon fishing; parts of the surrounding area (**Speyside**) are famous for whisky distilleries. Length: 172 km (107 miles)

Speyer (*German* 'ʃpaɪər) *n* a port in SW Germany, in Rhineland-Palatinate on the Rhine: the scene of 50 imperial diets. Pop: 50 247 (2003 est). English name: **Spires**

SPF *abbreviation for* **1** sender policy framework: a mechanism designed to prevent an e-mail address being duplicated and used as a false address from which to send unsolicited e-mails **2** sun protection factor: an indicator of how effectively a sun cream, lotion, cosmetic, etc, protects the skin from the harmful rays of the sun: *SPF 25*

S.P.F. *abbreviation for vet science* specific pathogen free; denoting animals specially bred to ensure that they are free of specified diseases

sp. gr. *abbreviation for* specific gravity

sphagnum ('sfægnəm) *n* any moss of the genus *Sphagnum*, of temperate bogs, having leaves capable of holding much water: layers of these mosses decay to form peat. Also called: **peat moss**, **bog moss** [c18 from New Latin, from Greek *sphagnos* a variety of moss] > **'sphagnous** *adj*

sphairee (sfaɪ'ri:) *n Austral* a game resembling tennis played with wooden bats and a perforated plastic ball, devised by F A Beck in 1961 [from Greek *sphaira* a ball]

sphalerite ('sfælə,raɪt, 'sfeɪlə-) *n* a yellow to brownish-black mineral consisting of zinc sulphide in cubic crystalline form with varying amounts of iron, manganese, cadmium, gallium, and indium: the chief source of zinc. Formula: ZnS. Also called: **zinc blende** [c19 from Greek *sphaleros* deceitful, from *sphallein* to cause to stumble]

sphene (sfi:n) *n* a brown, yellow, green, or grey lustrous mineral consisting of calcium titanium silicate in monoclinic crystalline form. It occurs in metamorphic and acid igneous rocks and is used as a gemstone. Formula: CaTiSiO₅. Also called: **titanite** [c19 from French *sphène*, from Greek *sphēn* a wedge, alluding to its crystals]

sphenic ('sfi:nɪk) *adj* having the shape of a wedge [from Greek *sphēn* a wedge]

spheno- *or before a vowel* **sphen-** *combining form* having the shape of a wedge: *sphenogram* [from Greek *sphēn* wedge]

sphenodon ('sfi:nə,dɒn) *n* the technical name for the **tuatara** [c19 from Greek *sphēn* a wedge + *odōn* a tooth]

sphenogram ('sfi:nə,græm) *n* a character used in cuneiform script

sphenoid ('sfi:nɔɪd) *adj also* **sphenoidal 1** wedge-shaped **2** of or relating to the sphenoid bone ▷ *n* **3** See **sphenoid bone**

sphenoid bone *n* the large butterfly-shaped compound bone at the base of the skull, containing a protective depression for the pituitary gland

spheral ('sfɪərəl) *adj* **1** of or shaped like a sphere; spherical **2** perfectly rounded; symmetrical

sphere (sfɪə) *n* **1** *maths* **a** a three-dimensional closed surface such that every point on the surface is equidistant from a given point, the centre **b** the solid figure bounded by this surface or the space enclosed by it. Equation: $(x-a)^2 + (y-b)^2 + (z-c)^2 = r^2$, where *r* is the radius and (*a*, *b*, *c*) are the coordinates of the centre; surface area: $4\pi r^2$; volume: $4\pi r^3/3$ **2** any object having approximately this shape; globe **3** the night sky considered as a vaulted roof; firmament **4** any heavenly object such as a planet, natural satellite, or star **5** (in the Ptolemaic or Copernican systems of astronomy) one of a series of revolving hollow globes, arranged concentrically, on whose transparent surfaces the sun (or in the Copernican system the earth), the moon, the planets, and fixed stars were thought to be set, revolving around the earth (or in the Copernican system the sun) **6** particular field of activity; environment: *that's out of my sphere* **7** a social class or stratum of society ▷ *vb* (*tr*) *chiefly poetic* **8** to surround or encircle **9** to place aloft or in the heavens [c14 from Late Latin *sphēra*, from Latin *sphaera* globe, from Greek *sphaira*]

-sphere *n combining form* **1** having the shape or form of a sphere: *bathysphere* **2** indicating a spherelike enveloping mass: *atmosphere* > **-spheric** *adj combining form*

sphere of influence *n* a region of the world in which one state is dominant

spherical ('sfɛrɪkᵊl) *or* **spheric** *adj* **1** shaped like a sphere **2** of or relating to a sphere: *spherical geometry* **3** *geometry* formed on the surface of or inside a sphere: *a spherical triangle* **4 a** of or relating to heavenly bodies **b** of or relating to the spheres of the Ptolemaic or the Copernican system > **'spherically** *adv* > **'sphericalness** *n*

spherical aberration *n physics* a defect of optical systems that arises when light striking a mirror or lens near its edge is focused at different points on the axis to the light striking near the centre. The effect occurs when the mirror or lens has spherical surfaces. See also **aberration** (sense 4)

spherical angle *n* an angle formed at the intersection of two great circles of a sphere

spherical coordinates *pl n* three coordinates that define the location of a point in three-dimensional space in terms of the length *r* of its radius vector, the angle, θ, which this vector makes with one axis, and the angle, φ, made by a second axis, perpendicular to the first, with the plane containing the first axis and the point. Usually written (*r*, θ, φ)

spherical geometry *n* the branch of geometry concerned with the properties of figures formed on the surface of a sphere

spherical polygon *n* a closed geometric figure formed on the surface of a sphere that is bounded by three or more arcs of great circles

spherical triangle *n* a closed geometric figure formed on the surface of a sphere that is bounded by arcs of three great circles

spherical trigonometry *n* the branch of trigonometry concerned with the measurement of the angles and sides of spherical triangles

sphericity (sfɪ'rɪsɪtɪ) *n* the state or form of being spherical

spherics¹ ('sfɛrɪks) *n* (*functioning as singular*) the geometry and trigonometry of figures on the surface of a sphere

spherics² *or US* **sferics** ('sfɛrɪks, 'sfɪər-) *n* (*functioning as singular*) short for **atmospherics**

spheroid ('sfɪərɔɪd) *n maths* another name for **ellipsoid of revolution**

spheroidal (sfɪə'rɔɪdᵊl) *adj* **1** shaped like an ellipsoid of revolution; approximately spherical **2** of or relating to an ellipsoid of revolution > **sphe'roidally** *or* **sphe'roidically** *adv*

spheroidicity (,sfɪərɔɪ'dɪsɪtɪ) *n* the state or form of being spheroidal

spherometer (sfɪə'rɒmɪtə) *n* an instrument for measuring the curvature of a surface

spherule ('sfɛru:l) *n* a very small sphere or globule [c17 from Late Latin *spherula* a little SPHERE] > **'spherular** *adj*

spherulite ('sfɛru,laɪt) *n* any of several spherical masses of radiating needle-like crystals of one or more minerals occurring in rocks such as obsidian > **spherulitic** (,sfɛru'lɪtɪk) *adj*

sphery ('sfɪərɪ) *adj poetic* **1** resembling a sphere **2** resembling a celestial body or bodies; starlike

sphincter ('sfɪŋktə) *n anatomy* a ring of muscle surrounding the opening of a hollow organ or body and contracting to close it [c16 from Late Latin, from Greek *sphinkter*, from *sphingein* to grip tightly] > **'sphincteral** *adj*

sphingomyelin (,sfɪŋɡəʊ'maɪəlɪn) *n biochem* any of a group of phospholipids, derived from sphingosine, that occur in biological membranes, being especially abundant in the brain [from *sphingo-*, from Greek *sphingein* to bind + MYELIN]

sphingosine ('sfɪŋɡəsɪn, -,si:n) *n biochem* a long-chain compound occurring in sphingomyelins and cerebrosides, and from which it can be released by hydrolysis. Formula: $CH_3(CH_2)_{12}CH:CHCH(OH)CH(NH_2)CH_2OH$ [from *sphingos-*, from Greek *sphingein* to hold fast + -INE²]

sphinx (sfɪŋks) *n, pl* **sphinxes** *or* **sphinges** ('sfɪndʒi:z) **1** any of a number of huge stone statues built by the ancient Egyptians, having the body of a lion and the head of a man **2** an inscrutable person

Sphinx (sfɪŋks) *n the* **1** *Greek myth* a monster with a woman's head and a lion's body. She lay outside Thebes, asking travellers a riddle and killing them when they failed to answer it. Oedipus answered the riddle and the Sphinx then killed herself **2** the huge statue of a sphinx near the pyramids at El Gîza in Egypt, of which the head is a carved portrait of the fourth-dynasty Pharaoh, Chephrēn [c16 via Latin from Greek, apparently from *sphingein* to hold fast]

sphinxlike ('sfɪŋks,laɪk) *adj* like the Sphinx; enigmatic or inscrutable

sphinx moth *n US and Canadian* another name for the **hawk moth**

sphragistics (sfrə'dʒɪstɪks) *n* (*functioning as singular*) the study of seals and signet rings [c19 from Greek *sphragistikos*, from *sphragizein* to seal, from *sphragis* a seal] > **sphra'gistic** *adj*

sp. ht *abbreviation for* specific heat

sphygmic ('sfɪgmɪk) *adj physiol* of or relating to the pulse

sphygmo- *or before a vowel* **sphygm-** *combining form* indicating the pulse: *sphygmomanometer* [from Greek *sphugmos* pulsation, from *sphuzein* to throb]

sphygmograph ('sfɪgmə,grɑ:f, -,græf) *n med* an instrument for making a recording (**sphygmogram**) of variations in blood pressure and pulse > **sphygmographic** (,sfɪgməʊ'græfɪk) *adj* > **sphygmography** (sfɪg'mɒɡrəfɪ) *n*

sphygmoid ('sfɪgmɔɪd) *adj physiol* resembling the pulse

sphygmomanometer (,sfɪgməʊmə'nɒmɪtə) *n med* an instrument for measuring arterial blood pressure [c19 from SPHYGMO- + MANOMETER, on the model of French *sphygmomanomètre*]

Sphynx (sfɪŋks) *n* a breed of medium-sized hairless cat with large ears and a long whiplike tail

spic, spick *or* **spik** (spɪk) *n US slang* a derogatory word for a person from a Spanish-speaking country in South or Central America or a Spanish-speaking community in the US [C20 perhaps alluding to a foreigner's mispronunciation of *speak*]

spica ('spaɪkə) *n, pl* **-cae** (-siː) *or* **-cas** **1** *med* a spiral bandage formed by a series of overlapping figure-of-eight turns **2** *botany* another word for **spike**[2] (sense 1) [C15 from Latin: ear of corn]

Spica ('spiːkə) *n* the brightest star in the constellation Virgo. Distance: 260 light years

spicate ('spaɪkeɪt) *adj botany* having, arranged in, or relating to spikes: *a spicate inflorescence* [C17 from Latin *spīcātus* having spikes, from *spīca* a point]

spiccato (spɪ'kɑːtəʊ) *music* ▷ *n* **1** a style of playing a bowed stringed instrument in which the bow bounces lightly off the strings ▷ *adj, adv* **2** to be played in this manner [Italian: detached, from *spiccare* to make distinct]

spice (spaɪs) *n* **1 a** any of a variety of aromatic vegetable substances, such as ginger, cinnamon, nutmeg, used as flavourings **b** these substances collectively **2** something that represents or introduces zest, charm, or gusto **3** *rare* a small amount **4** *Yorkshire dialect* confectionery ▷ *vb (tr)* **5** to prepare or flavour (food) with spices **6** to introduce charm or zest into [C13 from Old French *espice*, from Late Latin *speciēs* (pl) spices, from Latin *speciēs* (sing) kind; also associated with Late Latin *spīcea* (unattested) fragrant herb, from Latin *spīceus* having spikes of foliage; see SPICA] > **'spicer** *n*

spiceberry ('spaɪsbərɪ, -brɪ) *n, pl* **-ries** **1** a myrtaceous tree, *Eugenia rhombea*, of the Caribbean and Florida, with orange or black edible fruits **2** the fruit of this tree **3** any of various other aromatic plants or shrubs having spicy edible berries, such as wintergreen

spicebush ('spaɪs,bʊʃ) *n* a North American lauraceous shrub, *Lindera benzoin*, having yellow flowers and aromatic leaves and bark

Spice Islands *pl n* the former name of the **Moluccas**

spicery ('spaɪsərɪ) *n, pl* **-eries** **1** spices collectively **2** the piquant or fragrant quality associated with spices **3** *obsolete* a place to store spices

spick-and-span *or* **spic-and-span** ('spɪkən'spæn) *adj* **1** extremely neat and clean **2** new and fresh [C17 shortened from *spick-and-span-new*, from obsolete *spick* spike, nail + SPAN-NEW]

spicule ('spɪkjuːl) *n* **1** Also called: **spiculum** a small slender pointed structure or crystal, esp any of the calcareous or siliceous elements of the skeleton of sponges, corals, etc **2** *astronomy* a spiked ejection of hot gas occurring over 5000 kilometres above the sun's surface (in its atmosphere) and having a diameter of about 1000 kilometres [C18 from Latin: SPICULUM] > **spiculate** ('spɪkjʊ,leɪt, -lɪt) *adj*

spiculum ('spɪkjʊləm) *n, pl* **-la** (-lə) another word for **spicule** (sense 1) [C18 from Latin: small sharp point, from SPICA]

spicy ('spaɪsɪ) *adj* **spicier, spiciest** **1** seasoned with or containing spice **2** highly flavoured; pungent **3** *informal* suggestive of scandal or sensation **4** producing or yielding spices > **'spicily** *adv* > **'spiciness** *n*

spide (spaɪd) *n Northern Irish informal derogatory* a young working-class man who dresses in casual sports clothes [C20 of unknown origin]

spider ('spaɪdə) *n* **1** any predatory silk-producing arachnid of the order *Araneae*, having four pairs of legs and a rounded unsegmented body consisting of abdomen and cephalothorax. See also **wolf spider, trap-door spider, tarantula, black widow** **2** any of various similar or related arachnids **3** a hub fitted with radiating spokes or arms that serve to transmit power or support a load **4** *agriculture* an instrument used with a cultivator to pulverize soil **5** any implement or tool having the shape of a spider **6** *nautical* a metal frame fitted at the base of a mast to which halyards are tied when not in use **7** any part of a machine having a number of radiating spokes, tines, or arms **8** Also called: **octopus** *Brit* a cluster of elastic straps fastened at a central point and used to hold a load on a car rack, motorcycle, etc **9** *billiards, snooker* a rest having long legs, used to raise the cue above the level of the height of the ball **10** *angling* an artificial fly tied with a hackle and no wings, perhaps originally thought to imitate a spider **11** *computing* a computer program that is capable of performing sophisticated recursive searches on the internet **12** short for **spider phaeton** [Old English *spīthra*; related to Danish *spinder*, German *Spinne*; see SPIN]

spider crab *n* any of various crabs of the genera *Macropodia, Libinia*, etc, having a small triangular body and very long legs

spider hole *n military* a foxhole with a camouflaged lid or cover in which a sniper hides

spider-hunting wasp *n* any solitary wasp of the superfamily *Pompiloidea*, having a slender elongated body: the fast-running female hunts spiders as a food store for her larvae

spiderman ('spaɪdə,mæn) *n, pl* **-men** *informal* **1** *chiefly Brit* a person who erects the steel structure of a building **2** another name for a **steeplejack**

spider mite *n* any of various plant-feeding mites of the family *Tetranychidae*, esp *Panonychus ulmi* (**red spider mite**), which is a serious orchard pest

spider monkey *n* **1** any of several arboreal New World monkeys of the genus *Ateles*, of Central and South America, having very long legs, a long prehensile tail, and a small head **2** **woolly spider monkey** a rare related monkey, *Brachyteles arachnoides*, of SE Brazil [C18 so called because its long limbs resemble the legs of a spider]

spider orchid *n* any of several European orchids of the genus *Ophrys*, esp *O. sphegodes*, having a flower with yellow, green, or pink sepals and a broad brown velvety lip

spider phaeton *n* (formerly) a light horse-drawn carriage with a high body and large slender wheels. Sometimes shortened to: **spider**

spider plant *n* any of various house plants, esp *Chlorophytum elatum*: see **chlorophytum**

spiderwood ('spaɪdə,wʊd) *n* another name for **neinei**

spiderwort ('spaɪdə,wɜːt) *n* **1** any of various plants of the American genus *Tradescantia*, esp *T. virginiana*, having blue, purplish, or pink flowers and widely grown as house plants: family *Commelinaceae*. See also **tradescantia** **2** any of various similar or related plants [C17 so called because of the spidery shape of its stamens]

spidery ('spaɪdərɪ) *adj* thin and angular like a spider's legs: *spidery handwriting*

spiegeleisen ('spiːgəl,aɪzən) *n* a type of pig iron that is rich in manganese and carbon [C19 German, from *Spiegel* mirror + *Eisen* IRON]

spiel (ʃpiːl) *n* **1** a glib plausible style of talk, associated esp with salesmen ▷ *vb* **2** *(intr)* to deliver a prepared spiel **3** *(tr; usually foll by off)* to recite (a prepared oration) [C19 from German *Spiel* play] > **'spieler** *n*

spif (spɪf) *n informal, chiefly Brit* a postage stamp perforated with the initials of a firm to avoid theft by employees. Former name: **perfin** [C20 from *s(tamp) p(erforated with) i(nitials of) f(irm)*]

spiffing ('spɪfɪŋ) *adj Brit slang old-fashioned* excellent; splendid [C19 probably from dialect *spiff* spruce, smartly dressed]

spiffy ('spɪfɪ) *adj* **-fier, -fiest** *US and Canadian slang* smart; stylish [C19 from dialect *spiff*] > **'spiffily** *adv* > **'spiffiness** *n*

spiflicate *or* **spifflicate** ('spɪflɪ,keɪt) *vb (tr) Brit school slang* to destroy; annihilate [C18 a humorous coinage]

spignel ('spɪgnəl) *n* a European umbelliferous plant, *Meum athamanticum*, of mountain regions, having white flowers and finely divided aromatic leaves. Also called: **baldmoney, meu** [C16 of uncertain origin]

spigot ('spɪgət) *n* **1** a stopper for the vent hole of a cask **2** a tap, usually of wood, fitted to a cask **3** a US name for **tap**[2] (sense 1) **4** a short cylindrical projection on one component designed to fit into a hole on another, esp the male part of a joint (**spigot and socket joint**) between two pipes [C14 probably from Old Provençal *espiga* a head of grain, from Latin *spīca* a point]

spik (spɪk) *n* a variant spelling of **spic**

spike[1] (spaɪk) *n* **1** a sharp point **2** any sharp-pointed object, esp one made of metal **3** a long metal nail **4** *physics* **a** a transient variation in voltage or current in an electric circuit **b** a graphical recording of this, such as one of the peaks on an electroencephalogram **5** *(plural)* shoes with metal projections on the sole and heel for greater traction, as used by athletes **6** the straight unbranched antler of a young deer **7** *Brit slang* another word for **dosshouse** ▷ *vb (tr)* **8** to secure or supply with or as with spikes **9** to render ineffective or block the intentions of; thwart **10** to impale on a spike **11** to add alcohol to (a drink) **12** *journalism* to reject (a news story) **13** *volleyball* to hit (a ball) sharply downwards with an overarm motion from the front of one's own court into the opposing court **14** (formerly) to render (a cannon) ineffective by blocking its vent with a spike **15** **spike (someone's) guns** to thwart (someone's) purpose [C13 *spyk*; related to Old English *spīcing* nail, Old Norse *spīk* splinter, Middle Low German *spīker* spike, Norwegian *spīk* SPOKE[2], Latin *spīca* sharp point; see SPIKE[2]]

spike[2] (spaɪk) *n botany* **1** an inflorescence consisting of a raceme of sessile flowers, as in the gladiolus and sedges **2** an ear of wheat, barley, or any other grass that has sessile spikelets [C14 from Latin *spīca* ear of corn]

spike heel *n* a very high heel on a woman's shoe, tapering to a very narrow tip. Often shortened to: **spike** Also called (esp Brit): **stiletto, stiletto heel**

spike lavender *n* a Mediterranean lavender plant, *Lavandula latifolia*, having pale purple flowers and yielding an oil used in paints [C17 from dialect *spick* lavender, via Old French and Old Provençal from Latin *spīca* SPIKE[2]]

spikelet ('spaɪklɪt) *n* **1** *botany* the unit of a grass inflorescence, typically consisting of two bracts (glumes) surrounding one or more florets, each of which is itself surrounded by two bracts ▷ See **lemma, palea** **2** the small inflorescence of plants of other families, esp the sedges

spikenard ('spaɪknɑːd, 'spaɪkə,nɑːd) *n* **1** an aromatic Indian valerianaceous plant, *Nardostachys jatamans*, having rose-purple flowers **2** an aromatic ointment obtained from this plant **3** any of various similar or related plants **4** a North American araliaceous plant, *Aralia racemosa*, having small green flowers and an aromatic root ▷ Also called (for senses 1, 2): **nard** [C14 from Medieval Latin *spīca nardī*; see SPIKE[2], NARD]

spike-rush *n* any perennial plant of the temperate cyperaceous genus *Eleocharis*, occurring esp by ponds, and having underground stems, narrow leaves, and small flowers

spiky ('spaɪkɪ) *adj* **spikier, spikiest** **1** resembling a spike **2** having a spike or spikes **3** *Brit informal* ill-tempered **4** characterized by violent or aggressive methods: *spiky protestors* > **'spikily** *adv* > **'spikiness** *n*

spile (spaɪl) *n* **1** a heavy timber stake or pile **2** *US and Canadian* a spout for tapping sap from the sugar maple tree **3** a plug or spigot ▷ *vb (tr)* **4** to provide or support with a spile **5** *US* to tap (a tree) with a spile **6** *Northern English dialect* a splinter [C16 probably from Middle Dutch *spile* peg; related to Icelandic *spila* skewer, Latin *spīna* thorn]

spill[1] (spɪl) *vb* **spills, spilling, spilt** *or* **spilled** *(mainly tr)* **1** (when *intr*, usually foll by *from, out of*, etc) to fall or cause to fall from or as from a container, esp unintentionally **2** to disgorge (contents, occupants, etc) or (of contents, occupants, etc) to be disgorged: *the car spilt its passengers onto the road; the crowd spilt out of the theatre* **3** to shed (blood) **4** Also: **spill the beans** *informal* to disclose something confidential **5** *nautical* to let (wind) escape from a sail or (of the wind) to escape from a sail ▷ *n* **6** *informal* a fall or tumble **7** short for **spillway 8** a spilling of liquid, etc, or the amount spilt **9** *Austral* the declaring of several political jobs vacant when one higher up becomes so: *the Prime Minister's resignation could mean a Cabinet spill* [Old English *spillan* to destroy; related to *spildan*, Old High German *spaltan* to split; see SPOIL] ▷ ˈspiller *n*

spill² (spɪl) *n* **1** a splinter of wood or strip of twisted paper with which pipes, fires, etc, are lit **2** a small peg or rod made of metal [c13 of Germanic origin; compare Old High German *spilla*, Middle Dutch *spile* stake]

spillage (ˈspɪlɪdʒ) *n* **1** an instance or the process of spilling **2** something spilt or the amount spilt

spillikin, spilikin (ˈspɪlɪkɪn) *or* **spellican** (ˈspɛlɪkən) *n* a thin strip of wood, cardboard, or plastic, esp one used in spillikins

spillikins (ˈspɪlɪkɪnz) *n* (*functioning as singular*) *Brit* a game in which players try to pick each spillikin from a heap without moving any of the others. Also called: **jackstraws** [c18 from SPILL² + diminutive ending. See -KIN]

spill over *vb* **1** (*intr, adverb*) to overflow or be forced out of an area, container, etc ▷ *n* **spillover 2** *chiefly US and Canadian* the act of spilling over **3** *chiefly US and Canadian* the excess part of something **4** *economics* any indirect effect of public expenditure **5** *astronomy* the part of the noise associated with a radio telescope using a dish antenna caused by pick-up by a secondary antenna from directions that do not intercept the dish

spillway (ˈspɪlˌweɪ) *n* a channel that carries away surplus water, as from a dam. Also called: **wasteweir, spill**

spilt (spɪlt) *vb* a past tense and past participle of **spill¹**

spim (spɪm) *n* unsolicited commercial communications received on a computer via an instant-messaging system [from *sp(am)* + *i(nstant) m(essaging)*]

spin (spɪn) *vb* **spins, spinning, spun 1** to rotate or cause to rotate rapidly, as on an axis **2 a** to draw out and twist (natural fibres, as of silk or cotton) into a long continuous thread **b** to make such a thread or filament from (synthetic resins, etc), usually by forcing through a nozzle **3** (of spiders, silkworms, etc) to form (webs, cocoons, etc) from a silky fibre exuded from the body **4** (*tr*) to shape (metal) into a rounded form on a lathe **5** (*tr*) *informal* to tell (a tale, story, etc) by drawing it out at great length (esp in the phrase **spin a yarn**) **6** to bowl, pitch, hit, or kick (a ball) so that it rotates in the air and changes direction or speed on bouncing, or (of a ball) to be projected in this way **7** (*intr*) (of wheels) to revolve rapidly without causing propulsion **8** to cause (an aircraft) to dive in a spiral descent or (of an aircraft) to dive in a spiral descent **9** (*intr*; foll by *along*) to drive or travel swiftly **10** (*tr*) Also: **spin-dry** to rotate (clothes) in a washing machine in order to extract surplus water **11** (*intr*) to reel or grow dizzy, as from turning around: *my head is spinning* **12** (*intr*) to fish by drawing a revolving lure through the water **13** (*intr*) *informal* to present news or information in a way that creates a favourable impression ▷ *n* **14** a swift rotating motion; instance of spinning **15** *physics* **a** the intrinsic angular momentum of an elementary particle or atomic nucleus, as distinguished from any angular momentum resulting from its motion **b** a quantum number determining values of this angular momentum in units of the Dirac constant, having integral or half-integral values. Symbol: *S* or *s* **16** a condition of loss of control of an aircraft or an intentional flight manoeuvre in which the aircraft performs a continuous spiral descent because the angle of maximum lift is less than the angle of incidence **17** a spinning motion imparted to a ball, etc **18** (in skating) any of

various movements involving spinning rapidly on the spot **19** *informal* a short or fast drive, ride, etc, esp in a car, for pleasure **20 flat spin** *informal, chiefly Brit* a state of agitation or confusion **21** *Austral and NZ informal* a period of time or an experience; chance or luck; fortune: *a bad spin* **22** *commerce informal* a sudden downward trend in prices, values, etc **23** *informal* the practice of presenting news or information in a way that creates a favourable impression **24 on the spin** *informal* one after another: *they have lost two finals on the spin* ▷ See also **spin off, spin out** [Old English *spinnan*; related to Old Norse *spinna*, Old High German *spinnan* to spin, Lithuanian *pinu* to braid]

spina bifida (ˈspaɪnə ˈbɪfɪdə) *n* a congenital condition in which the meninges of the spinal cord protrude through a gap in the backbone, sometimes causing enlargement of the skull (due to accumulation of cerebrospinal fluid) and paralysis [New Latin; see SPINE, BIFID]

spinach (ˈspɪnɪdʒ, -ɪtʃ) *n* **1** a chenopodiaceous annual plant, *Spinacia oleracea*, cultivated for its dark green edible leaves **2** the leaves of this plant, eaten as a vegetable [c16 from Old French *espinache*, from Old Spanish *espinaca*, from Arabic *isfānākh*, from Persian]

spinal (ˈspaɪnəl) *adj* **1** of or relating to the spine or the spinal cord **2** denoting a laboratory animal in which the spinal cord has been severed: *a spinal rat* ▷ *n* **3** short for **spinal anaesthesia**. ▷ ˈspinally *adv*

spinal anaesthesia *n* **1** *surgery* anaesthesia of the lower half of the body produced by injecting an anaesthetic beneath the arachnoid membrane surrounding the spinal cord. See also **epidural** (sense 2) **2** *pathol* loss of sensation in some part of the body as the result of injury of the spinal cord

spinal canal *n* the natural passage through the centre of the spinal column that contains the spinal cord

spinal column *n* a series of contiguous or interconnecting bony or cartilaginous segments that surround and protect the spinal cord. Also called: **spine, vertebral column, rachis** Nontechnical name: **backbone**

spinal cord *n* the thick cord of nerve tissue within the spinal canal, which in man gives rise to 31 pairs of spinal nerves, and together with the brain forms the central nervous system

spin bowler *n* *cricket* a bowler who specializes in bowling balls with a spinning motion

spindle (ˈspɪndəl) *n* **1** a rod or stick that has a notch in the top, used to draw out natural fibres for spinning into thread, and a long narrow body around which the thread is wound when spun **2** one of the thin rods or pins bearing bobbins upon which spun thread is wound in a spinning wheel or machine **3** any of various parts in the form of a rod, esp a rotating rod that acts as an axle, mandrel, or arbor **4** a piece of wood that has been turned, such as a baluster or table leg **5** a small square metal shaft that passes through the lock of a door and to which the door knobs or handles are fixed **6** a measure of length of yarn equal to 18 hanks (15 120 yards) for cotton or 14 400 yards for linen **7** *biology* a spindle-shaped structure formed by microtubules during mitosis or meiosis which draws the duplicated chromosomes apart as the cell divides **8** a less common name for a **hydrometer 9** a tall pole with a marker at the top, fixed to an underwater obstruction as an aid to navigation **10** a device consisting of a sharp upright spike on a pedestal on which bills, order forms, etc, are impaled ▷ *n* **11** short for: **spindle tree** ▷ *vb* **12** (*tr*) to form into a spindle or equip with spindles **13** (*intr*) *rare* (of a plant, stem, shoot, etc) to grow rapidly and become elongated and thin [Old English *spinel*; related to *spinnan* to SPIN, Old Saxon *spinnila* spindle, Old High German *spinnala*]

spindle-legged *or* **spindle-shanked** *adj* having long thin legs

spindlelegs (ˈspɪndəlˌlɛgz) *or* **spindleshanks** *pl n*

1 long thin legs **2** (*functioning as singular*) a person who has long thin legs

spindle tree *n* any of various shrubs or trees of the genus *Euonymus*, esp *E. europaeus*, of Europe and W Asia, typically having red fruits and yielding a hard wood formerly used in making spindles: family *Celastraceae*

spindling (ˈspɪndlɪŋ) *adj* **1** long and slender, esp disproportionately so **2** (of stalks, shoots, etc) becoming long and slender ▷ *n* **3** a spindling person or thing

spindly (ˈspɪndlɪ) *adj* **-dlier, -dliest** tall, slender, and frail; attenuated

spin doctor *n* *informal* a person who provides a favourable slant to an item of news, potentially unpopular policy, etc, esp on behalf of a political personality or party [c20 from the spin given to a ball in various sports to make it go in the desired direction]

spindrift (ˈspɪnˌdrɪft) *n* **1** spray blown up from the surface of the sea **2** powdery snow blown off a mountain ▷ Also called: **spoondrift** [c17 of Scottish origin, possibly from a variant of obsolete *spoon* to scud + DRIFT]

spin-dry *vb* **-dries, -drying, -dried** (*tr*) to dry (clothes, linen, etc) in a spin-dryer

spin-dryer *n* a device that extracts water from clothes, linen, etc, by spinning them in a perforated drum

spine (spaɪn) *n* **1** the spinal column **2** the sharply pointed tip or outgrowth of a leaf, stem, etc **3** *zoology* a hard pointed process or structure, such as the ray of a fin, the quill of a porcupine, or the ridge on a bone **4** the back of a book, record sleeve, etc **5** a ridge, esp of a hill **6** strength of endurance, will, etc **7** anything resembling the spinal column in function or importance; main support or feature [c14 from Old French *espine* spine, from Latin *spīna* thorn, backbone] ▷ **spined** *adj*

spine-bashing *n* *Austral informal* loafing or resting ▷ ˈspine-ˌbasher *n*

spine-chiller *n* a book, film, etc, that arouses terror

spine-chilling *adj* (of a book, film, etc) arousing terror

spinel (spɪˈnɛl) *n* **1** any of a group of hard glassy minerals of variable colour consisting of oxides of aluminium, magnesium, chromium, iron, zinc, or manganese and occurring in the form of octahedral crystals: used as gemstones **2** a hard, glassy mineral composed of magnesium-aluminium oxide found in metamorphosed limestones and many basic and ultrabasic igneous rocks. Formula: $MgAl_2O_4$ [c16 from French *spinelle*, from Italian *spinella*, diminutive of *spina* a thorn, from Latin; so called from the shape of the crystals]

spineless (ˈspaɪnlɪs) *adj* **1** lacking a backbone; invertebrate **2** having no spiny processes: *spineless stems* **3** lacking strength of character, resolution, or courage ▷ ˈspinelessly *adv* ▷ ˈspinelessness *n*

spinescent (spaɪˈnɛsᵊnt) *adj* *biology* **1** having or resembling a spine or spines **2** becoming spiny [c18 from Late Latin *spīnēscere* to become thorny, from Latin *spīna* a thorn] ▷ spiˈnescence *n*

spinet (spɪˈnɛt, ˈspɪnɪt) *n* a small type of harpsichord having one manual [c17 from Italian *spinetta*, perhaps from Giovanni *Spinetti*, 16th-century Italian maker of musical instruments and its supposed inventor]

spine-tingling *adj* causing a sensation of fear or excitement

spiniferous (spaɪˈnɪfərəs) *or* **spinigerous** (spaɪˈnɪdʒərəs) *adj* (esp of plants) bearing spines or thorns [c17 from Late Latin *spīnifer* having spines, from Latin *spīna* a thorn, spine + *ferre* to bear]

spinifex (ˈspɪnɪˌfɛks) *n* **1** Also called: **porcupine grass** *Austral* any of various coarse spiny-leaved inland grasses of the genus *Triodia* **2** any grass of the SE Asian genus *Spinifex*, having pointed leaves

S

and spiny seed heads: often planted to bind loose sand [C19 from New Latin, from Latin *spīna* a thorn + *-fex* maker, from *facere* to make]

spin machine *n* an organization or group of people acting together to present news or information in a way that creates a particular desired impression

spinmeister (ˈspɪnˌmaɪstə) *n* another name for **spin doctor** [C20 from SPIN (sense 23) + -MEISTER]

spinnaker (ˈspɪnəkə; *Nautical* ˈspæŋkə) *n* a large light triangular racing sail set from the foremast of a yacht when running or on a broad reach [C19 probably from SPIN + (MO)NIKER, but traditionally derived from *Sphinx*, the yacht that first adopted this type of sail]

spinner (ˈspɪnə) *n* **1** a person or thing that spins **2** *informal* a spin doctor **3** *cricket* **a** a ball that is bowled with a spinning motion **b** a bowler who specializes in bowling such balls **4** a streamlined fairing that fits over and revolves with the hub of an aircraft propeller **5** a fishing lure with a fin or wing that revolves when drawn through the water **6** an angler's name for the mature adult form (imago) of various flies, especially the mayflies. Compare **dun**[2] (sense 3)

spinneret (ˈspɪnəˌrɛt) *n* **1** any of several organs in spiders and certain insects through which silk threads are exuded **2** a finely perforated dispenser through which a viscous liquid is extruded in the production of synthetic fibres [C18 from SPINNER + -ET]

spinney (ˈspɪnɪ) *n* *chiefly Brit* a small wood or copse [C16 from Old French *espinei*, from *espine* thorn, from Latin *spīna*]

spinning (ˈspɪnɪŋ) *n* **1** **a** the act or process of spinning **b** (*as modifier*): *spinning yarn* **2** the act or technique of casting and drawing a revolving lure through the water so as to imitate the movement of a live fish, etc

spinning jenny *n* an early type of spinning frame with several spindles, invented by James Hargreaves in 1764 [C18 see JENNY; the reason for the adoption of the woman's name is unclear]

spinning mule *n* *textiles* See **mule**[1] (sense 3)

spinning top *n* another name for **top**[2] (the toy)

spinning wheel *n* a wheel-like machine for spinning at home, having one hand- or foot-operated spindle

spinode (ˈspaɪnəʊd) *n* *maths* another name for **cusp** (sense 4) [C19 from Latin *spīna* spine + NODE]

spin off *vb* **1** (*tr, preposition*) to turn (a part of a business enterprise) into a separate company ▷ *n* **spin-off** **2** any product or development derived incidentally from the application of existing knowledge or enterprise **3** a book, film, or television series derived from a similar successful book, film, or television series

spinose (ˈspaɪnəʊs, spaɪˈnəʊs) *adj* (esp of plants) bearing many spines [C17 from Latin *spīnōsus* prickly, from *spīna* a thorn] > ˈ**spinosely** *adv* > **spinosity** (spaɪˈnɒsɪtɪ) *n*

spinous (ˈspaɪnəs) *adj* *biology* **1** resembling a spine or thorn: *the spinous process of a bone* **2** having spines or spiny projections **3** another word for **spinose**

spin out *vb* (*tr, adverb*) **1** to extend or protract (a story, etc) by including superfluous detail; prolong **2** to spend or pass (time) **3** to contrive to cause (money, etc) to last as long as possible ▷ *n* **spinout** **4** a spinning skid in a car that causes it to run off the road

Spinozism (spɪˈnəʊzɪzəm) *n* the philosophical system of Baruch Spinoza, the Dutch philosopher (1632–77), esp the concept of God as the unique reality possessing an infinite number of attributes of which we can know at least thought and extension > **Spiˈnozist** *n*

spin stabilization *n* a technique by which a bullet, rocket, etc, is made to spin around its longitudinal axis to assist it in maintaining a steady flight path

spinster (ˈspɪnstə) *n* **1** an unmarried woman regarded as being beyond the age of marriage **2** *law* (in legal documents) a woman who has never married. Compare **feme sole** **3** (formerly) a woman who spins thread for her living [C14 (in the sense: a person, esp a woman, whose occupation is spinning; C17 a woman still unmarried): from SPIN + -STER] > ˈ**spinsterˌhood** *n* > ˈ**spinsterish** *adj*

spinthariscope (spɪnˈθærɪˌskəʊp) *n* a device for observing ionizing radiation, consisting of a tube with a magnifying lens at one end and a phosphorescent screen at the other. A particle hitting the screen produces a scintillation [C20 from Greek *spintharis* a little spark + -SCOPE]

spinule (ˈspaɪnjuːl) *n* *biology* a very small spine, thorn, or prickle [C18 from Late Latin *spīnula*] > **spinulose** (ˈspaɪnjʊˌləʊs) *adj*

spiny (ˈspaɪnɪ) *adj* **spinier, spiniest** **1** (of animals) having or covered with quills or spines **2** (of plants) covered with spines; thorny **3** troublesome to handle; puzzling **4** shaped like a spine > ˈ**spininess** *n*

spiny anteater *n* another name for **echidna**

spiny-finned *adj* (of certain fishes) having fins that are supported by stiff bony spines. See also **acanthopterygian** Compare **soft-finned**

spiny lobster *n* any of various large edible marine decapod crustaceans of the genus *Palinurus* and related genera, having a very tough spiny carapace. Also called: **rock lobster, crawfish, langouste**

spiracle (ˈspaɪərək[ə]l, ˈspaɪrə-) *n* **1** any of several paired apertures in the cuticle of an insect, by which air enters and leaves the trachea **2** a small paired rudimentary gill slit just behind the head in skates, rays, and related fishes **3** any similar respiratory aperture, such as the blowhole in whales **4** *geology* a protrusion of sediment into a lava flow, formed by the explosive transition of water into steam [C14 (originally: breath): from Latin *spīrāculum* vent, from *spīrāre* to breathe] > **spiracular** (spɪˈrækjʊlə) *adj* > **spiˈraculate** *adj*

spiraea *or esp US* **spirea** (spaɪˈrɪə) *n* any rosaceous plant of the genus *Spiraea*, having sprays of small white or pink flowers. See also **meadowsweet** (sense 2), **hardhack** [C17 via Latin from Greek *speiraia*, from *speira* SPIRE[2]]

spiral (ˈspaɪərəl) *n* **1** *geometry* one of several plane curves formed by a point winding about a fixed point at an ever-increasing distance from it. Polar equation of **Archimedes spiral:** $r = a\theta$; of **logarithmic spiral:** $\log r = a\theta$; of **hyperbolic spiral:** $r\theta = a$, (where a is a constant) **2** another name for **helix** (sense 1) **3** something that pursues a winding, usually upward, course or that displays a twisting form or shape **4** a flight manoeuvre in which an aircraft descends describing a helix of comparatively large radius with the angle of attack within the normal flight range. Compare **spin** (sense 16) **5** *economics* a continuous upward or downward movement in economic activity or prices, caused by interaction between prices, wages, demand, and production ▷ *adj* **6** having the shape of a spiral ▷ *vb* **-rals, -ralling, -ralled** *or US* **-rals, -raling, -raled** **7** to assume or cause to assume a spiral course or shape **8** (*intr*) to increase or decrease with steady acceleration: *wages and prices continue to spiral* [C16 via French from Medieval Latin *spīrālis*, from Latin *spīra* a coil; see SPIRE[2]] > ˈ**spirally** *adv*

spiral binding *n* *bookbinding* a method of securing the pages of a publication by passing a coil of wire through small holes punched at the back edge of the covers and individual pages

spiral galaxy *n* a galaxy consisting of an ellipsoidal nucleus of old stars from opposite sides of which arms, containing younger stars, spiral outwards around the nucleus. In a **barred spiral** the arms originate at the ends of a bar-shaped nucleus

spiral of Archimedes *n* *maths* a spiral having the equation $r = a\theta$, where a is a constant. It is the locus of a point moving to or from the origin at a constant speed along a line rotating around that origin at a constant speed

spiral staircase *n* a staircase constructed around a central axis

spirant (ˈspaɪrənt) *adj* **1** *phonetics* another word for **fricative** ▷ *n* **2** a fricative consonant [C19 from Latin *spīrāns* breathing, from *spīrāre* to breathe]

spire[1] (spaɪə) *n* **1** Also called: **steeple** a tall structure that tapers upwards to a point, esp one on a tower or roof or one that forms the upper part of a steeple **2** a slender tapering shoot or stem, such as a blade of grass **3** the apical part of any tapering formation; summit ▷ *vb* **4** (*intr*) to assume the shape of a spire; point up **5** (*tr*) to furnish with a spire or spires [Old English *spīr* blade; related to Old Norse *spīra* stalk, Middle Low German *spīr* shoot, Latin *spīna* thorn] > ˈ**spiry** *adj*

spire[2] (spaɪə) *n* **1** any of the coils or turns in a spiral structure **2** the apical part of a spiral shell [C16 from Latin *spīra* a coil, from Greek *speira*] > **spiriferous** (spaɪəˈrɪfərəs) *adj*

spirelet (ˈspaɪəlɪt) *n* another name for **flèche** (sense 1)

spireme (ˈspaɪriːm) *n* *cytology* the tangled mass of chromatin threads into which the nucleus of a cell is resolved at the start of mitosis [C19 from Greek *speirēma* a coil, from *speira* a coil, SPIRE[2]]

Spires (spaɪəz) *n* the English name for **Speyer**

spirillum (spaɪˈrɪləm) *n, pl* **-la** (-lə) **1** any bacterium having a curved or spirally twisted rodlike body. Compare **coccus** (sense 1), **bacillus** (sense 1) **2** any bacterium of the genus *Spirillum*, such as *S. minus*, which causes ratbite fever [C19 from New Latin, literally: a little coil, from *spīra* a coil] > **spiˈrillar** *adj*

spirit[1] (ˈspɪrɪt) *n* **1** the force or principle of life that animates the body of living things **2** temperament or disposition: *truculent in spirit* **3** liveliness; mettle: *they set to it with spirit* **4** the fundamental, emotional, and activating principle of a person; will: *the experience broke his spirit* **5** a sense of loyalty or dedication: *team spirit* **6** the prevailing element; feeling: *a spirit of joy pervaded the atmosphere* **7** state of mind or mood; attitude: *he did it in the wrong spirit* **8** (*plural*) an emotional state, esp with regard to exaltation or dejection: *in high spirits* **9** a person characterized by some activity, quality, or disposition: *a leading spirit of the movement* **10** the deeper more significant meaning as opposed to a pedantic interpretation: *the spirit of the law* **11** that which constitutes a person's intangible being as contrasted with his physical presence: *I shall be with you in spirit* **12** **a** an incorporeal being, esp the soul of a dead person **b** (*as modifier*): *spirit world* ▷ *vb* (*tr*) **13** (usually foll by *away* or *off*) to carry off mysteriously or secretly **14** (often foll by *up*) to impart animation or determination to [C13 from Old French *esperit*, from Latin *spīritus* breath, spirit; related to *spīrāre* to breathe]

spirit[2] (ˈspɪrɪt) *n* **1** (*often plural*) any distilled alcoholic liquor such as brandy, rum, whisky, or gin **2** *chem* **a** an aqueous solution of ethanol, esp one obtained by distillation **b** the active principle or essence of a substance, extracted as a liquid, esp by distillation **3** *pharmacol* **a** a solution of a volatile substance, esp a volatile oil, in alcohol **b** (*as modifier*): *a spirit burner* **4** *alchemy* any of the four substances sulphur, mercury, sal ammoniac, or arsenic [C14 special use of SPIRIT[1], name applied to alchemical substances (as in sense 4), hence extended to distilled liquids]

Spirit (ˈspɪrɪt) *n* **the** **1** **a** another name for the **Holy Spirt** **b** God, esp when regarded as transcending material limitations **2** the influence of God or divine things upon the soul **3** *Christian Science* God or divine substance

spirited (ˈspɪrɪtɪd) *adj* **1** displaying animation, vigour, or liveliness **2** (*in combination*) characterized by mood, temper, or disposition as specified: *high-spirited; public-spirited* > ˈ**spiritedly** *adv* > ˈ**spiritedness** *n*

spirit gum n a glue made from gum dissolved in ether used to stick a false beard, etc, onto the face

spiritism ('spɪrɪˌtɪzəm) n a less common word for **spiritualism**. > **'spiritist** n > **spirit'istic** adj

spirit lamp n a lamp that burns methylated or other spirits instead of oil

spiritless ('spɪrɪtlɪs) adj lacking courage or liveliness; melancholic > **'spiritlessly** adv > **'spiritlessness** n

spirit level n a device for setting horizontal surfaces, consisting of an accurate block of material in which a sealed slightly curved tube partially filled with liquid is set so that the air bubble rests between two marks on the tube when the block is horizontal

spirit of enterprise n the motivation to set up and succeed in business or commerce

spiritoso (ˌspɪrɪ'təʊsəʊ) adj, adv music (often preceded by a tempo marking) to be played in a spirited or animated manner: allegro spiritoso [Italian, from spirito spirit, from Latin spīritus breath; see SPIRIT[1]]

spiritous ('spɪrɪtəs) adj 1 a variant spelling of **spirituous** 2 archaic high-spirited 3 archaic ethereal; pure

spirits of ammonia n (functioning as singular or plural) another name for **sal volatile** (sense 2)

spirits of hartshorn n (functioning as singular or plural) another name for **aqueous ammonia** See **ammonium hydroxide**

spirits of salt n (functioning as singular or plural) a solution of hydrochloric acid in water

spirits of turpentine n (functioning as singular or plural) another name for **turpentine** (sense 3)

spirits of wine n (functioning as singular or plural) another name for **alcohol** (sense 1)

spiritual ('spɪrɪtjʊəl) adj 1 relating to the spirit or soul and not to physical nature or matter; intangible 2 of, relating to, or characteristic of sacred things, the Church, religion, etc 3 standing in a relationship based on communication between the souls or minds of the persons involved: a spiritual father 4 having a mind or emotions of a high and delicately refined quality ▷ n 5 See **Negro spiritual** 6 (often plural) the sphere of religious, spiritual, or ecclesiastical matters, or such matters in themselves 7 **the** the realm of spirits > **'spiritually** adv > **'spiritualness** n

spiritual bouquet n RC Church a collection of private devotional acts and prayers chosen and performed by one person for the benefit of another

spiritual incest n RC Church 1 marriage or a sexual relationship between persons related by spiritual affinity or with a person under a solemn vow of chastity 2 the holding of two benefices by the same priest or bishop

spiritualism ('spɪrɪtjʊəˌlɪzəm) n 1 the belief that the disembodied spirits of the dead, surviving in another world, can communicate with the living in this world, esp through mediums 2 the doctrines and practices associated with this belief 3 philosophy the belief that because reality is to some extent immaterial it is therefore spiritual 4 any doctrine (in philosophy, religion, etc) that prefers the spiritual to the material 5 the condition or quality of being spiritual > **'spiritualist** n > **spiritua'listic** adj

spirituality (ˌspɪrɪtjʊ'ælɪtɪ) n, pl **-ties** 1 the state or quality of being dedicated to God, religion, or spiritual things or values, esp as contrasted with material or temporal ones 2 the condition or quality of being spiritual 3 a distinctive approach to religion or prayer: the spirituality of the desert Fathers 4 (often plural) Church property or revenue or a Church benefice

spiritualize or **spiritualise** ('spɪrɪtjʊəˌlaɪz) vb (tr) to make spiritual or infuse with spiritual content > **spirituali'zation** or **spirituali'sation** n > **'spiritualˌizer** or **'spiritualˌiser** n

spiritualty ('spɪrɪtjʊəltɪ) n, pl **-ties** archaic 1 the clergy collectively 2 another word for **spirituality**

spirituel (ˌspɪrɪtjʊ'ɛl) adj having a refined and lively mind or wit. Also (feminine): **spirituelle** (ˌspɪrɪtjʊ'ɛl) [c17 from French]

spirituous ('spɪrɪtjʊəs) adj 1 characterized by or containing alcohol 2 (of a drink) being a spirit > **spirituosity** (ˌspɪrɪtjʊ'ɒsɪtɪ) or **'spirituousness** n

spiritus asper ('spɪrɪtəs 'æspə) n another term for **rough breathing** [Latin: rough breath]

spiritus lenis n another term for **smooth breathing** [Latin: gentle breath]

spirit varnish n a varnish consisting of a gum or resin, such as shellac or copal, dissolved in alcohol

spirketting ('spɜːkɪtɪŋ) n nautical 1 deck planking near the bulwarks 2 the interior lining between ports and the overhead interior surface of the cabin [c18 from obsolete spirket space between floor timbers in a ship]

spiro-[1] combining form indicating breath or respiration: spirograph [from Latin spīrāre to breathe]

spiro-[2] combining form spiral; coil: spirochaete [from Latin spīra, from Greek speira a coil]

spirochaete or US **spirochete** ('spaɪrəʊˌkiːt) n any of a group of spirally coiled rodlike bacteria that includes the causative agent of syphilis. See **treponema** [c19 from New Latin spīrochaeta; see SPIRO-[2], CHAETA]

spirochaetosis or US **spirochetosis** (ˌspaɪrəʊkɪ'təʊsɪs) n any disease caused by a spirochaete

spirograph ('spaɪrəˌgrɑːf, -ˌgræf) n med an instrument for recording the movements of breathing > **spiro'graphic** adj

spirogyra (ˌspaɪrə'dʒaɪərə) n any green freshwater multicellular alga of the genus Spirogyra, consisting of minute filaments containing spirally coiled chloroplasts [c20 from New Latin, from SPIRO-[2] + Greek guros a circle]

spiroid ('spaɪrɔɪd) adj resembling a spiral or displaying a spiral form [c19 from New Latin spīroīdēs, from Greek speiroeidēs, from speira a coil]

spirometer (spaɪ'rɒmɪtə) n an instrument for measuring the air capacity of the lungs. Compare **pneumatometer**. > **spirometric** (ˌspaɪrə'mɛtrɪk) adj > **spi'rometry** n

spironolactone (ˌspaɪrənəʊ'læktəʊn) n a diuretic that increases water loss from the kidneys and is much used to treat oedema in heart and kidney failure [c20 from SPIRO-[2] + linking syllable -no- + LACTONE]

spirt (spɜːt) n a variant spelling of **spurt**

spirula ('spaɪrʊlə) n a tropical cephalopod mollusc, Spirula peronii, having prominent eyes, short arms, and a small flattened spirally coiled internal shell: order Decapoda (cuttlefish and squids) [c19 via New Latin from Late Latin: a small twisted cake, from Latin spīra a coil]

spirulina (ˌspɪrʊ'laɪnə) n any filamentous cyanobacterium of the genus Spirulina: processed as a valuable source of proteins and other nutrients [from New Latin spirula small spiral]

spiry ('spaɪərɪ) adj poetic of spiral form; helical

spit[1] (spɪt) vb **spits, spitting, spat** or **spit** 1 (intr) to expel saliva from the mouth; expectorate 2 (intr) informal to show disdain or hatred by spitting 3 (of a fire, hot fat, etc) to eject (fragments of coal, sparks, etc) violently and with an explosive sound; splutter 4 (intr) to rain very lightly 5 (tr; often foll by out) to eject or discharge (something) from the mouth: he spat the food out; to spit blood 6 (tr; often foll by out) to utter (short sharp words or syllables), esp in a violent manner 7 **spit chips** Also (NZ): **spit tacks** Austral slang to be very angry 8 **spit it out!** Brit informal a command given to someone that he should speak forthwith ▷ n 9 another name for **spittle** 10 a light or brief fall of rain, snow, etc 11 the act or an instance of spitting 12 informal, chiefly Brit another word for **spitting image** [Old English spittan; related to sp$\overline{æ}$tan to spit, German dialect spitzen] > **'spitter** n

spit[2] (spɪt) n 1 a pointed rod on which meat is skewered and roasted before or over an open fire 2 Also called: **rotisserie, rotating spit** a similar

device rotated by electricity or clockwork, fitted onto a cooker 3 an elongated often hooked strip of sand or shingle projecting from the shore, deposited by longshore drift, and usually above water ▷ vb **spits, spitting, spitted** 4 (tr) to impale on or transfix with or as if with a spit [Old English spitu; related to Old High German spiz spit, Norwegian spit tip]

spit[3] (spɪt) n the depth of earth cut by a spade; a spade's depth [c16 from Middle Dutch and Middle Low German spit]

spital ('spɪtᵊl) n obsolete 1 a hospital, esp for the needy sick 2 a highway shelter [c13 spitel, changed from Medieval Latin hospitāle HOSPITAL]

spit and polish n informal punctilious attention to neatness, discipline, etc, esp in the armed forces

spitchcock ('spɪtʃˌkɒk) n an eel split and grilled or fried. Compare **spatchcock** [c16 of unknown origin; see SPATCHCOCK]

spit curl n US and Canadian a circular curl of hair pressed flat against the cheek or forehead. Also called (esp British): **kiss curl** [perhaps so called because it is sometimes plastered down with spittle]

spite (spaɪt) n 1 maliciousness involving the desire to harm another; venomous ill will 2 an instance of such malice; grudge 3 archaic something that induces vexation 4 **in spite of** (preposition) in defiance of; regardless of; notwithstanding ▷ vb (tr) 5 to annoy in order to vent spite 6 archaic to offend [c13 variant of DESPITE]

spiteful ('spaɪtfʊl) adj full of or motivated by spite; vindictive > **'spitefully** adv > **'spitefulness** n

spitfire ('spɪtˌfaɪə) n a person given to outbursts of spiteful temper and anger, esp a woman or girl

Spithead ('spɪtˌhɛd) n an extensive anchorage between the mainland of England and the Isle of Wight, off Portsmouth

Spitsbergen ('spɪtsˌbɜːgən) n another name for Svalbard

spitsticker ('spɪtˌstɪkə) n a wood-engraving tool with a fine prow-shaped point for cutting curved lines

spitting distance n a short space or distance

spitting image n informal a person who bears a strong physical resemblance to another, esp to a relative. Also called: **spit, spit and image** [c19 modification of spit and image, from SPIT[1] (as in the phrase the very spit of, the exact likeness of (someone))]

spitting snake n another name for the **rinkhals**

spittle ('spɪtᵊl) n 1 the fluid secreted in the mouth; saliva or spit 2 Also called: **cuckoo spit, frog spit** the frothy substance secreted on plants by the larvae of certain froghoppers [Old English spætl saliva; see SPIT[1]]

spittle insect or **spittlebug** ('spɪtᵊlˌbʌg) n other names for the **froghopper**

spittoon (spɪ'tuːn) n a receptacle for spit, usually in a public place [c19 from SPIT[1] + -oon: see SALOON, BALLOON, etc]

spitz (spɪts) n any of various breeds of dog characterized by very dense hair, a stocky build, a pointed muzzle, erect ears, and a tightly curled tail [c19 from German, from spitz pointed]

spiv (spɪv) n Brit slang a person who makes a living by underhand dealings or swindling; black marketeer [c20 back formation from dialect spiving smart; compare SPIFFY, SPIFFING] > **'spivvy** adj

splake (spleɪk) n a type of hybrid trout bred by Canadian zoologists [from sp(eckled) + lake (trout)]

splanchnic ('splæŋknɪk) adj of or relating to the viscera; visceral: a splanchnic nerve [c17 from New Latin splanchnicus, from Greek splankhnikos concerning the entrails, from splankhna the entrails]

splash (splæʃ) vb 1 to scatter (liquid) about in blobs; spatter 2 to descend or cause to descend upon in blobs: he splashed his jacket 3 to make (one's way) by or as if by splashing: he splashed through the

S

puddle **4** (*tr*) to print (a story or photograph) prominently in a newspaper ▷ *n* **5** an instance or sound of splashing **6** an amount splashed **7** a patch created by or as if by splashing: *a splash of colour* **8** *informal* an extravagant display, usually for effect (esp in the phrase **make a splash**) **9** a small amount of soda water, water, etc, added to an alcoholic drink [C18 alteration of PLASH[1]]

splashback (ˈsplæʃˌbæk) *n* a sheet of glass, plastic, etc, attached to a wall above a basin to protect the wall against splashing

splashboard (ˈsplæʃˌbɔːd) *n* **1** a guard on a vehicle to protect people from splashing water, mud, etc **2** *nautical* another word for **washboard** (sense 4b)

splashdown (ˈsplæʃˌdaʊn) *n* **1** the controlled landing of a spacecraft on water at the end of a space flight **2** the time scheduled for this event ▷ *vb* **splash down 3** (*intr, adverb*) (of a spacecraft) to make a splashdown

splasher (ˈsplæʃə) *n* anything used for protection against splashes

splash out *vb* (*adverb; often foll by on*) *informal, chiefly Brit* to spend (money) freely or extravagantly (on something)

splashy (ˈsplæʃɪ) *adj* **splashier, splashiest 1** having irregular marks **2** *informal* done to attract attention or make a sensation; showy **3** making a splash or splashes > ˈ**splashily** *adv* > ˈ**splashiness** *n*

splat[1] (splæt) *n* a wet slapping sound [C19 of imitative origin]

splat[2] (splæt) *n* a wide flat piece of wood, esp one that is the upright central part of a chair back [C19 perhaps related to Old English *splātan* to SPLIT]

splatter (ˈsplætə) *vb* **1** to splash with small blobs; spatter ▷ *n* **2** a splash of liquid, mud, etc

splatter movie *n slang* a film in which the main feature is the graphic and gory murder of numerous victims

splatterpunk (ˈsplætəˌpʌŋk) *n* a literary genre characterized by graphically described scenes of an extremely gory nature [C20 from SPLATTER + PUNK[1]]

splay (spleɪ) *adj* **1** spread out; broad and flat **2** turned outwards in an awkward manner ▷ *vb* **3** to spread out; turn out or expand **4** (*tr*) *vet science* to dislocate (a joint) ▷ *n* **5** a surface of a wall that forms an oblique angle to the main flat surfaces, esp at a doorway or window opening **6** enlargement [C14 short for DISPLAY]

Splayd (spleɪd) *n trademark Austral* an implement combining the functions of knife, fork, and spoon [from SP(OON) + (BL)ADE]

splayfoot (ˈspleɪˌfʊt) *n, pl* **-feet 1** *pathol* another word for **flatfoot** (sense 1) **2** a foot of which the toes are spread out, as in certain breeds of dog used in hunting waterfowl > ˈ**splayˌfooted** *adj* > ˈ**splayˌfootedly** *adv*

spleen (spliːn) *n* **1** a spongy highly vascular organ situated near the stomach in man. It forms lymphocytes, produces antibodies, aids in destroying worn-out red blood cells, and filters bacteria and foreign particles from the blood. Related adjs: **lienal, splenetic, splenic 2** the corresponding organ in other animals **3** spitefulness or ill humour; peevishness: *to vent one's spleen* **4** *archaic* the organ in the human body considered to be the seat of the emotions **5** *archaic* another word for **melancholy 6** *obsolete* whim; mood [C13 from Old French *esplen*, from Latin *splēn*, from Greek; related to Latin *lien* spleen] > ˈ**spleenish** *or* ˈ**spleeny** *adj*

spleenful (ˈspliːnfʊl) *adj* affected by spleen; bad-tempered or irritable > ˈ**spleenfully** *adv*

spleenwort (ˈspliːnˌwɜːt) *n* any of various ferns of the genus *Asplenium*, esp *A. trichomanes*, that often grows on walls, having linear or oblong sori on the undersurface of the fronds. See also **asplenium**

splendent (ˈsplɛndənt) *adj archaic* **1** shining brightly; lustrous: *a splendent sun* **2** famous; illustrious [C15 from Latin *splendēns* brilliant, from *splendēre* to shine]

splendid (ˈsplɛndɪd) *adj* **1** brilliant or fine, esp in appearance **2** characterized by magnificence; imposing **3** glorious or illustrious: *a splendid reputation* **4** brightly gleaming; radiant: *her splendid face; splendid colours* **5** very good or satisfactory: *a splendid time* [C17 from Latin *splendidus*, from *splendēre* to shine] > ˈ**splendidly** *adv* > ˈ**splendidness** *n*

splendiferous (splɛnˈdɪfərəs) *adj facetious* grand; splendid: *a really splendiferous meal* [C15 from Medieval Latin *splendiferus*, from Latin *splendor* radiance + *ferre* to bring] > **splenˈdiferously** *adv* > **splenˈdiferousness** *n*

splendour *or US* **splendor** (ˈsplɛndə) *n* **1** the state or quality of being splendid **2 sun in splendour** *heraldry* a representation of the sun with rays and a human face > ˈ**splendorous** *or* **splendrous** (ˈsplɛndrəs) *adj*

splenectomy (splɪˈnɛktəmɪ) *n, pl* **-mies** surgical removal of the spleen

splenetic (splɪˈnɛtɪk) *adj* **1** of or relating to the spleen **2** spiteful or irritable; peevish **3** *obsolete* full of melancholy ▷ *n* **4** a spiteful or irritable person [C16 from Late Latin *splēnēticus*, from Latin *splēn* SPLEEN] > **spleˈnetically** *adv*

splenic (ˈsplɛnɪk, ˈspliː-) *adj* **1** of, relating to, or in the spleen **2** having a disease or disorder of the spleen

splenitis (splɪˈnaɪtɪs) *n* inflammation of the spleen

splenius (ˈspliːnɪəs) *n, pl* **-nii** (-nɪˌaɪ) *anatomy* either of two flat muscles situated at the back of the neck that rotate, flex, and extend the head and neck [C18 via New Latin from Greek *splēnion* a plaster] > ˈ**splenial** *adj*

splenomegaly (ˌspliːnəʊˈmɛgəlɪ) *n pathol* abnormal enlargement of the spleen [C20 from Greek *splēno-*, from *splēn* SPLEEN + *megalo-*, from *megas* large + -Y[3]]

splice (splaɪs) *vb* (*tr*) **1** to join (two ropes) by intertwining the strands **2** to join up the trimmed ends of (two pieces of wire, film, magnetic tape, etc) with solder or an adhesive material **3** to join (timbers) by overlapping and binding or bolting the ends together **4** (*passive*) *informal* to enter into marriage: *the couple got spliced last Saturday* **5 splice the mainbrace** *nautical history* to issue and partake of an extra allocation of alcoholic spirits ▷ *n* **6** a join made by splicing **7** the place where such a join occurs **8** the wedge-shaped end of a cricket-bat handle or similar instrument that fits into the blade [C16 probably from Middle Dutch *splissen*; related to German *spleissen*, Swedish *splitsa*; see SPLIT] > ˈ**splicer** *n*

spliff (splɪf) *n slang* **1** cannabis, used as a drug **2** a cannabis cigarette

spline (splaɪn) *n* **1** any one of a series of narrow keys (**external splines**) formed longitudinally around the circumference of a shaft that fit into corresponding grooves (**internal splines**) in a mating part: used to prevent movement between two parts, esp in transmitting torque **2** a long narrow strip of wood, metal, etc; slat **3** a thin narrow strip made of wood, metal, or plastic fitted into a groove in the edge of a board, tile, etc, to connect it to another ▷ *vb* **4** (*tr*) to provide (a shaft, part, etc) with splines [C18 East Anglian dialect; perhaps related to Old English *splin* spindle; see SPLINT]

splint (splɪnt) *n* **1** a rigid support for restricting movement of an injured part, esp a broken bone **2** a thin sliver of wood, esp one that is used to light cigars, a fire, etc **3** a thin strip of wood woven with others to form a chair seat, basket, etc **4** *vet science* inflammation of the small metatarsal or metacarpal bones along the side of the cannon bone of a horse **5** one of the overlapping metal plates used in armour after about 1330 **6** another word for **splinter** ▷ *vb* **7** to apply a splint to (a broken arm, etc) [C13 from Middle Low German *splinte*; related to Middle Dutch *splinte* splint, Old High German *spaltan* to split] > ˈ**splintˌlike** *adj*

splint bone *n* one of the rudimentary metacarpal or metatarsal bones in horses and similar animals, occurring on each side of the cannon bone

splinter (ˈsplɪntə) *n* **1** a very small sharp piece of wood, glass, metal, etc, characteristically long and thin, broken off from a whole **2** a metal fragment, from the container of a shell, bomb, etc, thrown out during an explosion ▷ *vb* **3** to reduce or be reduced to sharp fragments; shatter **4** to break or be broken off in small sharp fragments [C14 from Middle Dutch *splinter*; see SPLINT]

splinter group *n* a number of members of an organization, political party, etc, who split from the main body and form an independent association, usually as the result of dissension

splintery (ˈsplɪntərɪ) *adj* liable to produce or break into splinters

split (splɪt) *vb* **splits, splitting, split 1** to break or cause to break, esp forcibly, by cleaving into separate pieces, often into two roughly equal pieces: *to split a brick* **2** to separate or be separated from a whole: *he split a piece of wood from the block* **3** to separate or be separated into factions, usually through discord **4** (often foll by *up*) to separate or cause to separate through a disagreement **5** (when *tr*, often foll by *up*) to divide or be divided among two or more persons: *split up the pie among the three of us* **6** *slang* to depart; leave: *let's split; we split the scene* **7** (*tr*) to separate (something) into its components by interposing something else: *to split a word with hyphens* **8** (*intr; usually foll by on*) *slang* to betray the trust, plans, etc (of); inform: *he split on me to the cops* **9** (*tr*) *US politics* to mark (a ballot, etc) so as to vote for the candidates of more than one party: *he split the ticket* **10** (*tr*) to separate (an animal hide or skin) into layers **11 split hairs** to make a fine but needless distinction **12 split one's sides** to laugh very heartily **13 split the difference a** to settle a dispute by effecting a compromise in which both sides give way to the same extent **b** to divide a remainder equally ▷ *n* **14** the act or process of splitting **15** a gap or rift caused or a piece removed by the process of splitting **16** a breach or schism in a group or the faction resulting from such a breach **17** a dessert of sliced fruit and ice cream, covered with whipped cream, nuts, etc: *banana split* **18** See **Devonshire split 19 a** a separated layer of an animal hide or skin other than the outer layer **b** leather made from such a layer **20** *tenpin bowling* a formation of the pins after the first bowl in which there is a large gap between two pins or groups of pins **21** *informal* an arrangement or process of dividing up loot or money ▷ *adj* **22** having been split; divided: *split logs* **23** having a split or splits: *hair with split ends* ▷ See also **splits, split up** [C16 from Middle Dutch *splitten* to cleave; related to Middle High German *splīzen*; see SPLICE] > ˈ**splitter** *n*

Split (*Serbo-Croat* split) *n* a port and resort in W Croatia on the Adriatic: remains of the palace of Diocletian (295–305). Pop: 188 000 (2005 est). Italian name: **Spalato**

split brain *n* a brain in which the tracts connecting the two halves of the cerebral cortex have been surgically split or are missing from birth

split cane *n angling* bamboo split into strips of triangular section, tapered, and glued to form a stiff but flexible hexagonal rod: used, esp formerly, for making fishing rods

split decision *n boxing* the award of a fight on a majority verdict of the judges as opposed to a unanimous decision

split infinitive *n* (in English grammar) an infinitive used with another word between *to* (the infinitive marker) and the verb itself, as in *I want to really finish it this time*

> **USAGE** The traditional rule against placing an adverb between *to* and its verb is gradually disappearing. Although it is true that a split

infinitive may result in a clumsy sentence (*he decided to firmly and definitively deal with the problem*), this is not enough to justify the absolute condemnation that this practice has attracted. Indeed, very often the most natural position of the adverb is between *to* and the verb (*he decided to really try next time*) and to change it would result in an artificial and awkward construction (*he decided really to try next time*). The current view is therefore that the split infinitive is not a grammatical error. Nevertheless, many writers prefer to avoid splitting infinitives in formal written English, since readers with a more traditional point of view are likely to interpret this type of construction as incorrect

split keyboarding *n computing* the act or practice of editing data from one terminal on another terminal

split-level *adj* (of a house, room, etc) having the floor level of one part about half a storey above or below the floor level of an adjoining part

split-new *adj Scot* brand-new

split pea *n* a pea dried and split and used in soups, pease pudding, or as a vegetable

split personality *n* **1** the tendency to change rapidly in mood or temperament **2** a nontechnical term for **multiple personality**

split pin *n* a metal pin made by bending double a wire, often of hemispherical section, so that it can be passed through a hole in a nut, shaft, etc, to secure another part by bending back the ends of the wire

split ring *n* a steel ring having two helical turns, often used as a key ring

split run *n Canadian* a divided print run of a periodical in which a number of copies contain advertisements not included in the rest, esp a Canadian edition of a US magazine which contains Canadian advertisements but no Canadian editorial content

splits (splɪts) *n* (*functioning as singular*) (in gymnastics, etc) the act of sinking to the floor to achieve a sitting position in which both legs are straight, pointing in opposite directions, and at right angles to the body

split-screen technique *n* a cinematic device by which two or more complete images are projected simultaneously onto separate parts of the screen. Also called: **split screen**

split second *n* **1** an extremely small period of time; instant ▷ *adj* **split-second** (*prenominal*) **2** made or arrived at in an infinitely short time: *a split-second decision* **3** depending upon minute precision: *split-second timing*

split shift *n* a work period divided into two parts that are separated by an interval longer than a normal rest period

split ticket *n* See **split** (sense 9) See also **straight ticket**

split tin *n Brit* a long loaf of bread split on top, giving a greater crust area

splitting ('splɪtɪŋ) *adj* **1** (of a headache) intolerably painful; acute **2** (of the head) assailed by an overpowering unbearable pain ▷ *n* **3** *psychoanal* the Freudian defence mechanism in which an object or idea (or, alternatively, the ego) is separated into two or more parts in order to remove its threatening meaning

split up *vb* (*adverb*) **1** (*tr*) to separate out into parts; divide **2** (*intr*) to become separated or parted through disagreement: *they split up after years of marriage* **3** to break down or be capable of being broken down into constituent parts: *I have split up the question into three parts* ▷ *n* **split-up** **4** the act or an instance of separating

split wings *pl n angling* **a** wings (of an artificial fly) that are dressed cocked up and separated into

a V shape **b** (*as modifier*): *a split-wing pattern*

splodge (splɒdʒ) *n* **1** a large irregular spot or blot ▷ *vb* **2** (*tr*) to mark (something) with such a blot or blots [c19 alteration of earlier SPLOTCH] ▷ **'splodgy** *adj*

sploosh (spluːʃ) *vb* **1** to splash or cause to splash about uncontrollably ▷ *n* **2** an instance or sound of splooshing

splore (splɔː(r)) *n Scot* a revel; binge; escapade [c18 of obscure origin]

splosh (splɒʃ) *vb* **1** to scatter (liquid) vigorously about in blobs: *visitors can splosh in the world's largest man-made waterfall* ▷ *n* **2** an instance or sound of sploshing

splotch (splɒtʃ) *n, vb* the usual US word for **splodge** [c17 perhaps a blend of SPOT + BLOTCH] ▷ **'splotchy** *adj*

splurge (splɜːdʒ) *n* **1** an ostentatious display, esp of wealth **2** a bout of unrestrained extravagance ▷ *vb* **3** (often foll by *on*) to spend (money) unrestrainedly or extravagantly [c19 of uncertain origin]

splutter ('splʌtə) *vb* **1** to spit out (saliva, food particles, etc) from the mouth in an explosive manner, as through choking or laughing **2** to utter (words) with spitting sounds, as through rage or choking **3** Also: **sputter** to eject or be ejected in an explosive manner: *sparks spluttered from the fire* **4** (*tr*) to bespatter (a person) with tiny particles explosively ejected: *he spluttered the boy next to him with ink* ▷ *n* **5** the process or noise of spluttering **6** spluttering incoherent speech, esp in argument **7** anything ejected through spluttering [c17 variant of SPUTTER, influenced by SPLASH] ▷ **'splutterer** *n*

spod (spɒd) *adj Brit informal* a person seen as being boring, unattractive, or excessively studious [c20 origin unknown] ▷ **'spoddy** *adj*

spode (spəʊd) *n* (*sometimes capital*) china or porcelain manufactured by Josiah Spode, English potter (1754–1827), or his company

spodumene ('spɒdjʊˌmiːn) *n* a greyish-white, green, or lilac pyroxene mineral consisting of lithium aluminium silicate in monoclinic crystalline form. It is an important ore of lithium and is used in the manufacture of glass and ceramics and as a gemstone. Formula: $LiAlSi_2O_6$ [c19 from French *spodumène*, from German *Spodumen*, from Greek *spodoumenos*, from *spodousthai* to be burnt to ashes, from *spodos* wood ash]

spoil (spɔɪl) *vb* **spoils, spoiling, spoilt** *or* **spoiled** **1** (*tr*) to cause damage to (something), in regard to its value, beauty, usefulness, etc **2** (*tr*) to weaken the character of (a child) by complying unrestrainedly with its desires **3** (*intr*) (of perishable substances) to become unfit for consumption or use: *the fruit must be eaten before it spoils* **4** (*intr*) *sport* to disrupt the play or style of an opponent, as to prevent him from settling into a rhythm **5** *archaic* to strip (a person or place) of (property or goods) by force or violence **6** **be spoiling for** to have an aggressive desire for (a fight, etc) ▷ *n* **7** waste material thrown up by an excavation **8** any treasure accumulated by a person: *this gold ring was part of the spoil* **9** *obsolete* **a** the act of plundering **b** a strategically placed building, city, etc, captured as plunder ▷ See also **spoils** [c13 from Old French *espoillier*, from Latin *spoliāre* to strip, from *spolium* booty]

spoilage ('spɔɪlɪdʒ) *n* **1** the act or an instance of spoiling or the state or condition of being spoilt **2** an amount of material that has been wasted by being spoilt: *the spoilage of corn was considerable*

spoiled priest *n Irish* a person who was a student for the priesthood but who has withdrawn or been dismissed

spoiler ('spɔɪlə) *n* **1** plunderer or robber **2** a person or thing that causes spoilage or corruption **3** a device fitted to an aircraft wing to increase drag and reduce lift. It is usually extended into the airflow to assist descent and banking. Compare **air brake** (sense 2) **4** a similar device

fitted to a car **5** *sport* a competitor who adopts spoiling tactics, as in boxing **6** a magazine, newspaper, etc produced specifically to coincide with the production of a rival magazine, newspaper, etc in order to divert public interest and reduce its sales

spoilfive ('spɔɪlˌfaɪv) *n* a card game for two or more players with five cards each

spoils (spɔɪlz) *pl n* (*sometimes singular*) valuables seized by violence, esp in war **2** *chiefly US* the rewards and benefits of public office regarded as plunder for the winning party or candidate. See also **spoils system**

spoilsman ('spɔɪlzmən) *n, pl* **-men** *US politics* a person who shares in the spoils of office or advocates the spoils system

spoilsport ('spɔɪlˌspɔːt) *n informal* a person who spoils the pleasure of other people by his actions or attitudes

spoils system *n chiefly US* the practice of filling appointive public offices with friends and supporters of the ruling political party. Compare **merit system**

spoilt (spɔɪlt) *vb* a past tense and past participle of **spoil**

Spokane (spəʊˈkæn) *n* a city in E Washington: commercial centre of an agricultural region. Pop: 196 624 (2003 est)

spoke¹ (spəʊk) *vb* **1** the past tense of **speak** **2** *archaic or dialect* a past participle of **speak**

spoke² (spəʊk) *n* **1** a radial member of a wheel, joining the hub to the rim **2** a radial projection from the rim of a wheel, as in a ship's wheel **3** a rung of a ladder **4** **put a spoke in someone's wheel** *Brit* to thwart someone's plans ▷ *vb* **5** (*tr*) to equip with or as if with spokes [Old English *spāca*]

spoken ('spəʊkən) *vb* **1** the past participle of **speak** ▷ *adj* **2** uttered through the medium of speech. Compare **written** **3** (*in combination*) having speech as specified: *soft-spoken* **4** spoken for engaged, reserved, or allocated

spokeshave ('spəʊkˌʃeɪv) *n* a small plane with two handles, one on each side of its blade, used for shaping or smoothing cylindrical wooden surfaces, such as spokes

spokesman ('spəʊksmən) *or* **spokesperson** ('spəʊksˌpɜːs⁽ə⁾n) *or feminine* **spokeswoman** ('spəʊksˌwʊmən) *n, pl* **-men, -persons** *or* **-people** *or* **-women** a person authorized to speak on behalf of another person, group of people, or organization

spoliate ('spəʊlɪˌeɪt) *vb* a less common word for **despoil**

spoliation (ˌspəʊlɪˈeɪʃən) *n* **1** the act or an instance of despoiling or plundering **2** the authorized seizure or plundering of neutral vessels on the seas by a belligerent state in time of war **3** *law* the material alteration of a document so as to render it invalid **4** *English ecclesiastical law* the taking of the fruits of a benefice by a person not entitled to them [c14 from Latin *spoliātiō*, from *spoliāre* to SPOIL] ▷ **'spoliatory** *adj*

spondaic (spɒnˈdeɪɪk) *adj prosody* of, relating to, or consisting of spondees

spondee ('spɒndiː) *n prosody* a metrical foot consisting of two long syllables (--) [c14 from Old French *spondée*, from Latin *spondēus*, from Greek *spondeios*, from *spondē* a ritual libation; from the use of spondee in the music that characteristically accompanied such ceremonies]

spondulix *or* **spondulicks** (spɒnˈdjuːlɪks) *n slang* money [c19 of obscure origin]

spondylitis (ˌspɒndɪˈlaɪtɪs) *n* inflammation of the vertebrae [c19 from New Latin, from Greek *spondulos* vertebra; see -ITIS]

sponge (spʌndʒ) *n* **1** any multicellular typically marine animal of the phylum *Porifera*, usually occurring in complex sessile colonies in which the porous body is supported by a fibrous, calcareous, or siliceous skeletal framework **2** a piece of the light porous highly absorbent elastic skeleton of certain sponges, used in bathing,

S

cleaning, etc. See also **spongin** **3** any of a number of light porous elastic materials resembling a sponge **4** another word for **sponger** (sense 1) **5** *informal* a person who indulges in heavy drinking **6** leavened dough, esp before kneading **7** See **sponge cake** **8** Also called: **sponge pudding** *Brit* a light steamed or baked pudding, spongy in texture, made with various flavourings or fruit **9** porous metal produced by electrolysis or by reducing a metal compound without fusion or sintering and capable of absorbing large quantities of gas: *platinum sponge* **10** a rub with a sponge **11** **throw in the sponge** See **throw in** (sense 4) ▷ *vb* **12** (*tr; often foll by off or down*) to clean (something) by wiping or rubbing with a damp or wet sponge **13** (*tr; usually foll by off, away, out, etc*) to remove (marks, etc) by rubbing with a damp or wet sponge or cloth **14** (when *tr*, often foll by *up*) to absorb (liquids, esp when spilt) in the manner of a sponge **15** (*tr; often foll by off*) to get (something) from (someone) by presuming on his generosity: *to sponge a meal off someone* **16** (*intr; often foll by off or on*) to obtain one's subsistence, welfare, etc, unjustifiably (from): *he sponges off his friends* **17** (*intr*) to go collecting sponges ▷ See also **sponge down** [Old English, from Latin *spongia*, from Greek] > **ˈsponge,like** *adj*

sponge bag *n* a small bag made of plastic, etc, that holds toilet articles, used esp when travelling

sponge bath *n* a washing of the body with a wet sponge or cloth, but without immersion in water

sponge cake *n* a light porous cake, made of eggs, sugar, flour, and flavourings traditionally without any fat

sponge cloth *n* any of various porous fabrics, usually made in a loose honeycomb weave

sponge down *vb* (*tr, adverb*) **1** to wipe clean with a damp sponge or cloth ▷ *n* **sponge-down** **2** the act or instance of sponging down

sponger (ˈspʌndʒə) *n* **1** *informal* a person who lives off other people by continually taking advantage of their generosity; parasite or scrounger **2** a person or ship employed in collecting sponges

spongiform (ˈspʌndʒɪˌfɔːm) *adj* **1** resembling a sponge in appearance, esp in having many holes **2** denoting diseases characterized by this appearance of affected tissues

spongin (ˈspʌndʒɪn) *n* a fibrous horny protein that forms the skeletal framework of the bath sponge and related sponges [c19 from German, from Latin *spongia* SPONGE + -IN]

spongioblast (ˈspʌndʒɪəʊˌblɑːst) *n* any of numerous columnar epithelial cells in the brain and spinal cord that develop into neuroglia [c20 from Greek *spongia* SPONGE + -BLAST]
> **spongioblastic** (ˌspʌndʒɪəʊˈblæstɪk) *adj*

spongy (ˈspʌndʒɪ) *adj* **-gier, -giest** **1** of or resembling a sponge, esp in texture, porosity, elasticity, or compressibility: *spongy bread; spongy bone* **2** of or like a sponge in respect of its capacity to absorb fluid and yield it when compressed
> **ˈspongily** *adv* > **ˈsponginess** *n*

sponsion (ˈspɒnʃən) *n* **1** the act or process of becoming surety; sponsorship **2** (*often plural*) *international law* an unauthorized agreement made by a public officer, esp an admiral or general in time of war, requiring ratification by the government of the state concerned **3** any act or promise, esp one made on behalf of someone else [c17 from Latin *sponsiō*, from *spondēre* to pledge]

sponson (ˈspɒnsən) *n* **1** *naval* an outboard support for a gun enabling it to fire fore and aft **2** a semicircular gun turret on the side of a tank **3** a float or flotation chamber along the gunwale of a boat or ship **4** a structural projection from the side of a paddle steamer for supporting a paddle wheel **5** a structural unit attached to a helicopter fuselage by fixed struts, housing the main landing gear and inflatable flotation bags [c19 perhaps from EXPANSION]

sponsor (ˈspɒnsə) *n* **1** a person or group that provides funds for an activity, esp **a** a commercial organization that pays all or part of the cost of putting on a concert, sporting event, etc **b** a person who donates money to a charity when the person requesting the donation has performed a specified activity as part of an organized fund-raising effort **2** *chiefly US and Canadian* a person or business firm that pays the costs of a radio or television programme in return for advertising time **3** a legislator who presents and supports a bill, motion, etc **4** Also called: **godparent** **a** an authorized witness who makes the required promises on behalf of a person to be baptized and thereafter assumes responsibility for his Christian upbringing **b** a person who presents a candidate for confirmation **5** *chiefly US* a person who undertakes responsibility for the actions, statements, obligations, etc, of another, as during a period of apprenticeship; guarantor ▷ *vb* **6** (*tr*) to act as a sponsor for [c17 from Latin, from *spondēre* to promise solemnly] > **sponsorial** (spɒnˈsɔːrɪəl) *adj* > **ˈsponsor,ship** *n*

sponsored (ˈspɒnsəd) *adj* denoting an activity organized to raise money for a charity in which sponsors agree to donate money on completion of the activity, or a specified period or amount of it, by participants: *a sponsored walk*

spontaneity (ˌspɒntəˈniːɪtɪ, -ˈneɪ-) *n, pl* **-ties** **1** the state or quality of being spontaneous **2** (*often plural*) the exhibiting of actions, impulses, or behaviour that are stimulated by internal processes

spontaneous (spɒnˈteɪnɪəs) *adj* **1** occurring, produced, or performed through natural processes without external influence: *spontaneous movement* **2** arising from an unforced personal impulse; voluntary; unpremeditated: *a spontaneous comment* **3** (of plants) growing naturally; indigenous [c17 from Late Latin *spontāneus*, from Latin *sponte* voluntarily] > **sponˈtaneously** *adv*
> **sponˈtaneousness** *n*

spontaneous combustion *n* the ignition of a substance or body as a result of internal oxidation processes, without the application of an external source of heat, occurring in finely powdered ores, coal, straw, etc

spontaneous generation *n* a theory, widely held in the 19th century and earlier but now discredited, stating that living organisms could arise directly and rapidly from nonliving material. Also called: **abiogenesis**

spontaneous recovery *n psychol* the reappearance of a response after its extinction has been followed by a period of rest

spontoon (spɒnˈtuːn) *n* a form of halberd carried by some junior infantry officers in the 18th and 19th centuries [c18 from French *esponton*, from Italian *spuntone*, from *punto* POINT]

spoof (spuːf) *informal* ▷ *n* **1** a mildly satirical mockery or parody; lampoon: *a spoof on party politics* **2** a good-humoured deception or trick; prank ▷ *vb* **3** to indulge in a spoof of (a person or thing) **4** to communicate electronically under a false identity [c19 coined by A. Roberts (1852–1933), English comedian, to designate a game of his own invention] > **ˈspoofer** *n*

spoofing *n* the act or an instance of impersonating another person on the internet or via email

spook (spuːk) *informal* ▷ *n* **1** a ghost or a person suggestive of this **2** *US and Canadian* a spy **3** *South African slang* any pale or colourless alcoholic spirit: *spook and diesel* ▷ *vb* (*tr*) *US and Canadian* **4** to frighten: *to spook horses; to spook a person* **5** (of a ghost) to haunt [c19 Dutch *spook*, from Middle Low German *spōk* ghost] > **ˈspookish** *adj*

spooky (ˈspuːkɪ) *adj* **spookier, spookiest** *informal* **1** ghostly or eerie: *a spooky house* **2** resembling or appropriate to a ghost **3** *US* easily frightened; highly strung > **ˈspookily** *adv* > **ˈspookiness** *n*

spool (spuːl) *n* **1** a device around which magnetic tape, film, cotton, etc, can be automatically wound, with plates at top and bottom to prevent it from slipping off **2** anything round which other materials, esp thread, are wound ▷ *vb* **3** (sometimes foll by *up*) to wind or be wound onto a spool or reel [c14 of Germanic origin; compare Old High German *spuolo*, Middle Dutch *spoele*]

spoon (spuːn) *n* **1** a metal, wooden, or plastic utensil having a shallow concave part, usually elliptical in shape, attached to a handle, used in eating or serving food, stirring, etc **2** Also called: **spoonbait** an angling lure for spinning or trolling, consisting of a bright piece of metal which swivels on a trace to which are attached a hook or hooks **3** *golf* a former name for a No. 3 wood **4** *informal* a foolish or useless person **5** **be born with a silver spoon in one's mouth** to inherit wealth or social standing **6** **wooden spoon** *Brit* another name for **booby prize** **7** *rowing* a type of oar blade that is curved at the edges and tip to gain a firm grip on the water. Compare **spade**[1] (sense 4) ▷ *vb* **8** (*tr*) to scoop up or transfer (food, liquid, etc) from one container to another with or as if with a spoon **9** (*intr*) *slang old-fashioned* to kiss and cuddle **10** to hollow out (a cavity or spoon-shaped bowl) (in something) **11** *sport* to hit (a ball) with a weak lifting motion, as in golf, cricket, etc [Old English *spōn* splinter; related to Old Norse *spōnn* spoon, chip, Old High German *spān*]

spoonbill (ˈspuːnˌbɪl) *n* any of several wading birds of warm regions, such as *Platalea leucorodia* (**common spoonbill**) and *Ajaia ajaja* (**roseate spoonbill**), having a long horizontally flattened bill: family *Threskiornithidae*, order *Ciconiiformes*

spoondrift (ˈspuːnˌdrɪft) *n* a less common spelling of **spindrift**

spoonerism (ˈspuːnəˌrɪzəm) *n* the transposition of the initial consonants or consonant clusters of a pair of words, often resulting in an amusing ambiguity of meaning, such as *hush my brat* for *brush my hat* [c20 named after W. A. Spooner (1844–1930), English clergyman renowned for slips of this kind]

spoon-feed *vb* **-feeds, -feeding, -fed** (*tr*) **1** to feed with a spoon **2** to overindulge or spoil **3** to provide (a person) with ready-made opinions, judgments, etc, depriving him of original thought or action

spoonful (ˈspuːnˌfʊl) *n, pl* **-fuls** **1** the amount that a spoon is able to hold **2** a small quantity

spoony *or* **spooney** (ˈspuːnɪ) *slang rare old-fashioned* ▷ *adj* **spoonier, spooniest** **1** foolishly or stupidly amorous ▷ *n, pl* **spoonies** **2** a fool or silly person, esp one in love

spoor (spʊə, spɔː) *n* **1** the trail of an animal or person, esp as discernible to the human eye ▷ *vb* **2** to track (an animal) by following its trail [c19 from Afrikaans, from Middle Dutch *spor*; related to Old English *spor* track, Old High German *spor*; see SPUR] > **ˈspoorer** *n*

Sporades (ˈspɒrəˌdiːz) *pl n* two groups of Greek islands in the Aegean: the **Northern Sporades**, lying northeast of Euboea, and the **Southern Sporades**, which include the Dodecanese and lie off the SW coast of Turkey

sporadic (spəˈrædɪk) *adj* **1** occurring at irregular points in time; intermittent: *sporadic firing* **2** scattered; isolated: *a sporadic disease* [c17 from Medieval Latin *sporadicus*, from Greek *sporadikos*, from *sporas* scattered; related to Greek *speirein* to sow; see SPORE] > **spoˈradically** *adv*
> **spoˈradicalness** *n*

sporangium (spəˈrændʒɪəm) *n, pl* **-gia** (-dʒɪə) any organ, esp in fungi, in which asexual spores are produced [c19 from New Latin, from SPORO- + Greek *angeion* receptacle] > **spoˈrangial** *adj*

spore (spɔː) *n* **1** a reproductive body, produced by bacteria, fungi, various plants and some protozoans, that develops into a new individual. A **sexual spore** is formed after the fusion of gametes and an **asexual spore** is the result of asexual reproduction **2** a germ cell, seed, dormant bacterium, or similar body ▷ *vb* **3** (*intr*) to produce, carry, or release spores [C19 from New Latin *spora*, from Greek: a sowing; related to Greek *speirein* to sow]

spore case *n* the nontechnical name for **sporangium**

spore print *n botany* the pattern produced by placing the cap of a mushroom on a piece of paper and allowing the spores to fall

sporo- *or before a vowel* **spor-** *combining form* (in botany) spore: *sporophyte* [from New Latin *spora*]

sporocarp (ˈspɔːrəʊˌkɑːp, ˈspɒ-) *n* **1** a specialized leaf branch in certain aquatic ferns that encloses the sori **2** the spore-producing structure in certain algae, lichens, and fungi

sporocyst (ˈspɔːrəʊˌsɪst, ˈspɒ-) *n* **1** a thick-walled rounded structure produced by sporozoan protozoans, in which sporozoites are formed **2** the saclike larva of a trematode worm that produces redia larvae by asexual reproduction **3** any similar structure containing spores

sporocyte (ˈspɔːrəʊˌsaɪt, ˈspɒ-) *n* a diploid cell that divides by meiosis to produce four haploid spores

sporogenesis (ˌspɔːrəʊˈdʒɛnɪsɪs, ˌspɒ-) *n* the process of spore formation in plants and animals > **sporogenous** (spɔːˈrɒdʒɪnəs, spɒ-) *adj*

sporogonium (ˌspɔːrəʊˈɡəʊnɪəm, ˌspɒ-) *n, pl* **-nia** (-nɪə) the sporophyte of mosses and liverworts, consisting of a spore-bearing capsule on a short stalk that arises from the parent plant (the gametophyte) > ˌ**sporoˈgonial** *adj*

sporogony (spɔːˈrɒɡənɪ, -ˈrɒdʒ-, spɒ-) *n* the process in sporozoans by which sporozoites are formed from an encysted zygote by multiple fission

sporophore (ˈspɔːrəʊˌfɔː, ˈspɒ-) *n* an organ in fungi that produces or carries spores, esp the massive spore-bearing body of mushrooms, etc

sporophyll *or* **sporophyl** (ˈspɔːrəʊfɪl, ˈspɒ-) *n* a leaf in ferns and other spore-bearing plants that bears the sporangia. See also **megasporophyll, microsporophyll**

sporophyte (ˈspɔːrəʊˌfaɪt, ˈspɒ-) *n* the diploid form of plants that have alternation of generations. It develops from a zygote and produces asexual spores. Compare **gametophyte** > **sporophytic** (ˌspɔːrəˈfɪtɪk, ˌspɒ-) *adj*

-sporous *adj combining form* (in botany) having a specified type or number of spores: *homosporous*

sporozoan (ˌspɔːrəˈzəʊən, ˌspɒ-) *n* **1** any parasitic protozoan of the phylum *Apicomplexa* (or *Sporozoa*), characterized by a complex life cycle, part of which is passed in the cells of the host, and the production of asexual spores: includes the malaria parasite. See **plasmodium** (sense 2) ▷ *adj* **2** of or relating to sporozoans

sporozoite (ˌspɔːrəˈzəʊaɪt, ˌspɒ-) *n* any of numerous small mobile usually infective individuals produced in sporozoans by sporogony

sporran (ˈspɒrən) *n* a large pouch, usually of fur, worn hanging from a belt in front of the kilt in men's Scottish Highland dress [C19 from Scottish Gaelic *sporan* purse; compare Irish Gaelic *sparán* purse, Late Latin *bursa* bag]

sport (spɔːt) *n* **1** an individual or group activity pursued for exercise or pleasure, often involving the testing of physical capabilities and taking the form of a competitive game such as football, tennis, etc **2** such activities considered collectively **3** any particular pastime indulged in for pleasure **4** the pleasure derived from a pastime, esp hunting, shooting, or fishing: *we had good sport today* **5** playful or good-humoured joking: *to say a thing in sport* **6** derisive mockery or the object of such mockery: *to make sport of someone* **7** someone or something that is controlled by external influences: *the sport of fate* **8** *informal* (sometimes qualified by *good, bad,* etc) a person who reacts cheerfully in the face of adversity, esp a good loser **9** *informal* a person noted for being scrupulously fair and abiding by the rules of a game **10** *informal* a person who leads a merry existence, esp a gambler: *he's a bit of a sport* **11** *Austral and NZ informal* a form of address used esp between males **12** *biology* **a** an animal or plant that differs conspicuously in one or more aspects from other organisms of the same species, usually because of a mutation **b** an anomalous characteristic of such an organism ▷ *vb* **13** (*tr*) *informal* to wear or display in an ostentatious or proud manner: *she was sporting a new hat* **14** (*intr*) to skip about or frolic happily **15** to amuse (oneself), esp in outdoor physical recreation **16** (*intr; often foll by with*) to dally or trifle (with) **17** (*tr; often foll by away*) *rare* to squander (time or money): *sporting one's life away* **18** (*intr; often foll by with*) *archaic* to make fun (of) **19** (*intr*) *biology* to produce or undergo a mutation ▷ See also **sports** [C15 *sporten*, variant of *disporten* to DISPORT] > ˈ**sporter** *n* > ˈ**sportful** *adj* > ˈ**sportfully** *adv* > ˈ**sportfulness** *n*

sporting (ˈspɔːtɪŋ) *adj* **1** (*prenominal*) of, relating to, or used or engaged in a sport or sports: *several sporting interests* **2** relating or conforming to sportsmanship; fair **3** of, relating to, or characterized by an interest in gambling **4** willing to take a risk > ˈ**sportingly** *adv*

sporting house *n* **1** *US rare* a euphemistic word for **brothel** **2** *archaic* a tavern or inn frequented by gamblers or other sportsmen

sportive (ˈspɔːtɪv) *adj* **1** playful or joyous **2** done in jest rather than seriously **3** of, relating to, or interested in sports **4** *obsolete* wanton or amorous: *a sportive wench* > ˈ**sportively** *adv* > ˈ**sportiveness** *n*

sports (spɔːts) *n* **1** (*modifier*) relating to, concerned with, or used in sports: *sports equipment* **2** (*modifier*) relating to or similar to a sports car: *sports seats* **3** Also called: **sports day** *Brit* a meeting held at a school or college for competitions in various athletic events

sports cap *n* **1** a hat designed for sports or to look sporty **2** a special top for a bottle, designed to aid drinking without spilling

sports car *n* a production car designed for speed, high acceleration, and manoeuvrability, having a low body and usually adequate seating for only two persons

sportscast (ˈspɔːtsˌkɑːst) *n* a radio or television broadcast consisting of sports news > ˈ**sportsˌcaster** *n*

sports coat *n US, Austral, and NZ* another name for **sports jacket**

sports jacket *n* a man's informal jacket, made esp of tweed: worn with trousers of different material. Also called (US, Austral, and NZ): **sports coat**

sportsman (ˈspɔːtsmən) *n, pl* **-men** **1** a man who takes part in sports, esp of the outdoor type **2** a person who exhibits qualities highly regarded in sport, such as fairness, generosity, observance of the rules, and good humour when losing > ˈ**sportsman-ˌlike** *or* ˈ**sportsmanly** *adj* > ˈ**sportsmanˌship** *n*

sports medicine *n* the branch of medicine concerned with injuries sustained through sport

sportsperson (ˈspɔːtsˌpɜːsən) *n* a person who takes part in sports, esp of the outdoor type

sports shirt *n* a man's informal shirt, sometimes of knitted wool or cotton, which may be worn outside the trousers

sportswear (ˈspɔːtsˌwɛə) *n* clothes worn for sport or outdoor leisure wear

sportswoman (ˈspɔːtsˌwʊmən) *n, pl* **-women** a woman who takes part in sports, esp of the outdoor type

sport utility vehicle *or* **sports utility vehicle** *n* a high-powered car with four-wheel drive, originally designed for off-road use. Sometimes shortened to: **sport utility, sports utility** Abbreviation: **SUV**

sporty (ˈspɔːtɪ) *adj* **sportier, sportiest** **1** (of a person) fond of sport or outdoor activities **2** (of clothes) having the appearance of sportswear **3** (of a car) having the performance or appearance of a sports car ▷ *n, pl* **-ies** **4** *Brit informal* a young person who typically wears sportswear, is competitive about sport , and takes an interest in his or her fitness > ˈ**sportily** *adv* > ˈ**sportiness** *n*

sporulate (ˈspɒrjʊˌleɪt) *vb* (*intr*) to produce spores, esp by multiple fission > ˌ**sporuˈlation** *n*

sporule (ˈspɒruːl) *n* a spore, esp a very small spore [C19 from New Latin *sporula* a little SPORE]

spot (spɒt) *n* **1** a small mark on a surface, such as a circular patch or stain, differing in colour or texture from its surroundings **2** a geographical area that is restricted in extent: *a beauty spot* **3** a location: *this is the exact spot on which he died* **4** a blemish of the skin, esp a pimple or one occurring through some disease **5** a blemish on the character of a person; moral flaw **6** *informal* a place of entertainment: *we hit all the night spots* **7** *informal, chiefly Brit* a small quantity or amount: *a spot of lunch* **8** *informal* an awkward situation: *that puts me in a bit of a spot* **9** a short period between regular television or radio programmes that is used for advertising **10** a position or length of time in a show assigned to a specific performer **11** short for **spotlight** **12** (in billiards) **a** Also called: **spot ball** the white ball that is distinguished from the plain by a mark or spot **b** the player using this ball **13** *billiards, snooker* one of several small black dots on a table that mark where a ball is to be placed **14** (*modifier*) **a** denoting or relating to goods, currencies, or securities available for immediate delivery and payment: *spot goods*. See also **spot market, spot price** **b** involving immediate cash payment: *spot sales* **15** **change one's spots** (*used mainly in negative constructions*) to reform one's character **16** **high spot** an outstanding event: *the high spot of the holiday was the visit to the winery* **17** **knock spots off** to outstrip or outdo with ease **18** **on the spot** **a** immediately **b** at the place in question **c** in the best possible position to deal with a situation **d** in an awkward predicament **e** without moving from the place of one's location, etc **f** (*as modifier*): *our on-the-spot reporter* **19** **soft spot** a special sympathetic affection or weakness for a person or thing **20** **tight spot** a serious, difficult, or dangerous situation **21** **weak spot** **a** some aspect of a character or situation that is susceptible to criticism **b** a flaw in a person's knowledge: *classics is my weak spot* ▷ *vb* **spots, spotting, spotted** **22** (*tr*) to observe or perceive suddenly, esp under difficult circumstances; discern **23** to put stains or spots upon (something) **24** (*intr*) (of some fabrics) to be susceptible to spotting by or as if by water: *silk spots easily* **25** (*tr*) to place here and there: *they spotted observers along the border* **26** to look out for and note (trains, talent, etc) **27** (*intr*) to rain slightly; spit **28** (*tr*) *billiards* to place (a ball) on one of the spots **29** *military* to adjust fire in order to correct deviations from (the target) by observation **30** (*tr*) *US informal* to yield (an advantage or concession) to (one's opponent): *to spot someone a piece in chess* [C12 (in the sense: moral blemish): of German origin; compare Middle Dutch *spotte*, Old Norse *spotti*] > ˈ**spottable** *adj*

spot check *n* **1** a quick random examination **2** a check made without prior warning ▷ *vb* **spot-check** **3** (*tr*) to perform a spot check on

spot height *n* a mark on a map indicating the height of a hill, mountain, etc

spotless (ˈspɒtlɪs) *adj* **1** free from stains; immaculate **2** free from moral impurity; unsullied: *a spotless character* > ˈ**spotlessly** *adv* > ˈ**spotlessness** *n*

spotlight (ˈspɒtˌlaɪt) *n* **1** a powerful light focused so as to illuminate a small area, usually mounted so that it can be directed at will **2** **the** the focus of attention ▷ *vb* **-lights, -lighting, -lit** *or* **-lighted** (*tr*) **3** to direct a spotlight on **4** to focus attention on

spot market *n commerce* a market in which commodities, currencies, or securities are traded for immediate delivery. Compare **forward market**

spot-on *adj informal* absolutely correct; very

S

accurate: *your prediction was spot-on*

spot price *n* the price of goods, currencies, or securities that are offered for immediate delivery and payment

spotted ('spɒtɪd) *adj* **1** characterized by spots or marks, esp in having a pattern of spots **2** stained or blemished; soiled or bespattered

spotted crake *n* a Eurasian rail, *Porzana porzana,* of swamps and marshes, having a buff speckled plumage and dark brown wings

spotted dick *n Brit* a steamed or boiled suet pudding containing dried fruit [c19 perhaps from the man's name *Dick* (short for *Richard*), or from dialect *dick* pudding. The dried fruit gives it a speckled appearance]

spotted dog *n* **1** an informal name for a **Dalmatian** **2** another name for **spotted dick**

spotted fever *n* any of various severe febrile diseases characterized by small irregular spots on the skin, as in Rocky Mountain spotted fever or tick fever

spotted flycatcher *n* a European woodland songbird, *Muscicapa striata,* with a greyish-brown streaked plumage: family *Muscicapidae* (Old World flycatchers)

spotted gum *n* **1** an Australian eucalyptus tree, *Eucalyptus maculata* **2** the wood of this tree, used for shipbuilding, sleepers, etc

spotted mackerel *n* a small mackerel, *Scomberomorus queenslandicus,* of northern Australian waters

Spotted Mist *n* the former name for **Australian Mist**

spotted orchid *n* **1** any of various common Eurasian orchids, esp the **heath** and **common spotted orchids** (*Dactylorhiza maculata* and *D. fuchsii*). The flowers are variable but usually have dark blotches **2** a tall orchid, *Dipodium punctatum,* with white pink-spotted flowers, found in Australia

spotted sandpiper *n* a North American sandpiper, *Actitis macularia,* having a spotted breast in its breeding plumage. Also called (US): **peetweet**

spotter ('spɒtə) *n* **1 a** a person or thing that watches or observes **b** (*as modifier*): *a spotter plane* **2** a person who makes a hobby of watching for and noting numbers or types of trains, buses, etc: *a train spotter* **3** *military* a person who orders or advises adjustment of fire on a target by observations **4** a person, esp one engaged in civil defence, who watches for enemy aircraft **5** *US informal* an employee assigned to spy on his colleagues in order to check on their honesty **6** *films* **a** a person who checks against irregularities and inconsistencies **b** a person who searches for new material, performers, etc

spottie ('spɒtɪ) *n NZ* a young deer of up to three months of age

spotty ('spɒtɪ) *adj* **-tier, -tiest** **1** abounding in or characterized by spots or marks, esp on the skin: *a spotty face* **2** not consistent or uniform; irregular or uneven, often in quality > '**spottily** *adv* > '**spottiness** *n*

spot-weld *vb* **1** (*tr*) to join (two pieces of metal, esp in the form of wire or sheet) by one or more small circular welds by means of heat, usually electrically generated, and pressure ▷ *n* **2** a weld so formed > '**spot-ˌwelder** *n*

spousal ('spaʊzᵊl) *n* **1** (*often plural*) **a** the marriage ceremony **b** a wedding ▷ *adj* **2** of or relating to marriage > '**spousally** *adv*

spouse *n* (spaʊs, spaʊz) **1** a person's partner in marriage. Related adj: **spousal** ▷ *vb* (spaʊz, spaʊs) **2** (*tr*) *obsolete* to marry [c12 from Old French *spus* (masculine), *spuse* (feminine), from Latin *sponsus, sponsa* betrothed man or woman, from *spondēre* to promise solemnly]

spout (spaʊt) *vb* **1** to discharge (a liquid) in a continuous jet or in spurts, esp through a narrow gap or under pressure, or (of a liquid) to gush thus **2** (of a whale, etc) to discharge air through the blowhole, so that it forms a spray at the surface of the water **3** *informal* to utter (a stream of words) on a subject, often at length ▷ *n* **4** a tube, pipe, chute, etc, allowing the passage or pouring of liquids, grain, etc **5** a continuous stream or jet of liquid **6** short for **waterspout** **7** **up the spout** *slang* **a** ruined or lost: *any hope of rescue is right up the spout* **b** pregnant [c14 perhaps from Middle Dutch *spouten,* from Old Norse *spyta* to spit] > '**spouter** *n*

spouting ('spaʊtɪŋ) *n NZ* **a** a rainwater downpipe on the exterior of a building **b** such pipes collectively

spp. *abbreviation for* species (plural)

SPQR *abbreviation for* Senatus Populusque Romanus [Latin: the Senate and People of Rome.]

SPR *abbreviation for* Society for Psychical Research

sprag (spræg) *n* **1** a chock or steel bar used to prevent a vehicle from running backwards on an incline **2** a support or post used in mining **3** *NZ mining* a steel bar inserted into the wheels of a box to act as a brake [c19 of uncertain origin]

sprain (spreɪn) *vb* **1** (*tr*) to injure (a joint) by a sudden twisting or wrenching of its ligaments ▷ *n* **2** the resulting injury to such a joint, characterized by swelling and temporary disability [c17 of uncertain origin]

spraint (spreɪnt) *n* (*often plural*) a piece of otter's dung [C15 *sprayntes* (pl), from Medieval French *espraintes* otter's dung, from *espreindre* to press out: compare EXPRESS]

sprang (spræŋ) *vb* the past tense of **spring**

sprat (spræt) *n* **1** a small marine food fish, *Clupea sprattus,* of the NE Atlantic Ocean and North Sea: family *Clupeidae* (herrings). See also **brisling** **2** any of various small or young herrings [c16 variant of Old English *sprott;* related to Middle Low German *sprott,* Norwegian *sprot* small rod]

Spratly Islands ('sprætlɪ) *n* a widely-scattered group of uninhabited islets and reefs in the S South China Sea, the subject of territorial claims wholly or in part by six neighbouring nations. Compare **Paracel Islands**

sprawl (sprɔːl) *vb* **1** (*intr*) to sit or lie in an ungainly manner with one's limbs spread out **2** to fall down or knock down with the limbs spread out in an ungainly way **3** to spread out or cause to spread out in a straggling fashion: *his handwriting sprawled all over the paper* ▷ *n* **4** the act or an instance of sprawling **5** a sprawling posture or arrangement of items **6 a** the urban area formed by the expansion of a town or city into surrounding countryside: *the urban sprawl* **b** the process by which this has happened [Old English *spreawlian;* related to Old English *spryttan* to sprout, SPURT, Greek *speirein* to scatter] > '**sprawler** *n* > '**sprawly** *adj*

spray[1] (spreɪ) *n* **1** fine particles of a liquid **2 a** a liquid, such as perfume, paint, etc, designed to be discharged from an aerosol or atomizer: *hair spray* **b** the aerosol or atomizer itself **3** a quantity of small objects flying through the air: *a spray of bullets* ▷ *vb* **4** to scatter (liquid) in the form of fine particles **5** to discharge (a liquid) from an aerosol or atomizer **6** (*tr*) to treat or bombard with a spray: *to spray the lawn* [c17 from Middle Dutch *sprāien;* related to Middle High German *spræjen*] > '**sprayer** *n*

spray[2] (spreɪ) *n* **1** a single slender shoot, twig, or branch that bears buds, leaves, flowers, or berries, either growing on or detached from a plant **2** a small decorative bouquet or corsage of flowers and foliage **3** a piece of jewellery designed to resemble a spray of flowers, leaves, etc [c13 of Germanic origin; compare Old English *sprǣc* young shoot, Old Norse *sprek* brittle wood, Old High German *spriuhhulu* splinter]

spray gun *n* a device that sprays a fluid in a finely divided form by atomizing the fluid in an air jet

spread (sprɛd) *vb* **spreads, spreading, spread** **1** to extend or unfold or be extended or unfolded to the fullest width: *she spread the map on the table* **2** to extend or cause to extend over a larger expanse of space or time: *the milk spread all over the floor; the political unrest spread over several years* **3** to apply or be applied in a coating: *butter does not spread very well when cold* **4** to distribute or be distributed over an area or region **5** to display or be displayed in its fullest extent: *the landscape spread before us* **6** (*tr*) to prepare (a table) for a meal **7** (*tr*) to lay out (a meal) on a table **8** to send or be sent out in all directions; disseminate or be disseminated: *someone has been spreading rumours; the disease spread quickly* **9** (of rails, wires, etc) to force or be forced apart **10** to increase the breadth of (a part), esp to flatten the head of a rivet by pressing, hammering, or forging **11** (*tr*) *agriculture* **a** to lay out (hay) in a relatively thin layer to dry **b** to scatter (seed, manure, etc) over a relatively wide area **12** (*tr; often foll by* around) *informal* to make (oneself) agreeable to a large number of people, often of the opposite sex **13** *phonetics* to narrow and lengthen the aperture of (the lips) as for the articulation of a front vowel, such as (iː) in English *see* (siː) ▷ *n* **14** the act or process of spreading; diffusion, dispersal, expansion, etc: *the spread of the Christian religion* **15** *informal* the wingspan of an aircraft **16** an extent of space or time; stretch: *a spread of 50 years* **17** *informal, chiefly US and Canadian* a ranch or relatively large tract of land **18** the limit of something fully extended: *the spread of a bird's wings* **19** a covering for a table or bed **20** *informal* a large meal or feast, esp when it is laid out on a table **21** a food which can be spread on bread, etc: *salmon spread* **22** two facing pages in a book or other publication **23** a widening of the hips and waist: *middle-age spread* **24** *stock exchange* **a** the difference between the bid and offer prices quoted by a market maker **b** the excess of the price at which stock is offered for public sale over the price paid for the same stock by an underwriter **c** *chiefly US* a double option. Compare **straddle** (sense 9) **25** *jewellery* the apparent size of a gemstone when viewed from above expressed in carats: *a diamond with a spread of four carats* ▷ *adj* **26** extended or stretched out, esp to the fullest extent **27** (of a gem) shallow and flat **28** *phonetics* **a** (of the lips) forming a long narrow aperture **b** (of speech sounds) articulated with spread lips: (iː) *in English "feel" is a spread vowel* [Old English *sprǣdan;* related to Old High German *spreiten* to spread, Old Lithuanian *sprainas* stiff] > ˌ**spreada'bility** *n* > '**spreadable** *adj*

spread betting *n* a form of gambling in which stakes are placed not on the results of contests but on the number of points scored, etc. Winnings and losses are calculated according to the accuracy or inaccuracy of the prediction

spread eagle *n* **1** the representation of an eagle with outstretched wings, used as an emblem of the US **2** an acrobatic skating figure

spread-eagle *adj also* **spread-eagled** **1** lying or standing with arms and legs outstretched ▷ *vb* **2** to assume or cause to assume the shape of a spread eagle **3** (*intr*) *skating* to execute a spread eagle

spreader ('sprɛdə) *n* **1** a machine or device used for scattering bulk materials, esp manure or fertilizer, over a relatively wide area **2** a device for keeping apart or spacing parallel objects, such as electric wires

spread sampling *n* the selection of a corpus for statistical analysis by selecting a number of short passages at random throughout the work and considering their aggregation. Compare **block sampling**

spreadsheet ('sprɛdˌʃiːt) *n* a computer program that allows easy entry and manipulation of figures, equations, and text, used esp for financial planning and budgeting

spreathed (spriːðd) *adj Southwestern English and south Wales dialect* sore; chapped [from *spreathe* to make sore: of obscure origin]

sprechgesang (*German* 'ʃprɛçɡəzaŋ) *n music* a type of vocalization between singing and recitation in which the voice sings the beginning of each note and then falls rapidly from the notated pitch. It was originated by Arnold Schoenberg, who used it in *Pierrot Lunaire* (1912) [c20 from German, literally: speaking-song]

sprechstimme (German ˈʃprɛçʃtɪmə) *n music* a vocal part employing sprechgesang [c20 from German: speaking voice]

spree (spriː) *n* **1** a session of considerable overindulgence, esp in drinking, squandering money, etc **2** a romp [c19 perhaps changed from Scottish *spreath* plundered cattle, ultimately from Latin *praeda* booty]

sprekelia (sprəˈkiːlɪə) *n* a bulbous plant, *Sprekelia formosissima*, from Mexico and Guatemala, related to hippeastrum and grown for its striking crimson or white pendent flowers, in the form of a cross: family *Amaryllidaceae* [named after J. H. von Sprekelsen (died 1764), German botanist]

sprig (sprɪg) *n* **1** a shoot, twig, or sprout of a tree, shrub, etc; spray **2** an ornamental device resembling a spray of leaves or flowers **3** a small wire nail without a head **4** *informal rare* a youth **5** *informal rare* a person considered as the descendant of an established family, social class, etc **6** *NZ* another name for **stud¹** (sense 7) ▷ *vb* **sprigs, sprigging, sprigged** (*tr*) **7** to fasten or secure with sprigs **8** to ornament (fabric, wallpaper, etc) with a design of sprigs **9** to make sprays from (twigs and branches) [c15 probably of Germanic origin; compare Low German *sprick*, Swedish *sprygg*] > **ˈsprigger** *n* > **ˈspriggy** *adj*

sprightly (ˈspraɪtlɪ) *adj* **-lier, -liest 1** full of vitality; lively ▷ *adv* **2** *obsolete* in a lively manner [c16 from *spright*, variant of SPRITE + -LY¹] > **ˈsprightliness** *n*

spring (sprɪŋ) *vb* **springs, springing, sprang** or **sprung, sprung 1** to move or cause to move suddenly upwards or forwards in a single motion **2** to release or be released from a forced position by elastic force: *the bolt sprang back* **3** (*tr*) to leap or jump over **4** (*intr*) to come, issue, or arise suddenly **5** (*intr*) (of a part of a mechanism, etc) to jump out of place **6** to make (wood, etc) warped or split or (of wood, etc) to become warped or split **7** to happen or cause to happen unexpectedly: *to spring a surprise; the boat sprung a leak* **8** (*intr*) to develop or originate: *the idea sprang from a chance meeting* **9** (*intr*; usually foll by *from*) to be descended: *he sprang from peasant stock* **10** (*intr*; often foll by *up*) to come into being or appear suddenly: *factories springing up* **11** (*tr*) (of a gun dog) to rouse (game) from cover **12** (*intr*) (of game or quarry) to start or rise suddenly from cover **13** (*intr*) to appear to have a strong upward movement: *the beam springs away from the pillar* **14** to explode (a mine) or (of a mine) to explode **15** (*tr*) to provide with a spring or springs **16** (*tr*) *informal* to arrange the escape of (someone) from prison **17** (*intr*) *archaic or poetic* (of daylight or dawn) to begin to appear ▷ *n* **18** the act or an instance of springing **19** a leap, jump, or bound **20 a** the quality of resilience; elasticity **b** (*as modifier*): *spring steel* **21** the act or an instance of moving rapidly back from a position of tension **22 a** a natural outflow of ground water, as forming the source of a stream **b** (*as modifier*): *spring water* **23 a** a device, such as a coil or strip of steel, that stores potential energy when it is compressed, stretched, or bent and releases it when the restraining force is removed **b** (*as modifier*): *a spring mattress* **24** a structural defect such as a warp or bend **25 a** (*sometimes capital*) the season of the year between winter and summer, astronomically from the March equinox to the June solstice in the N hemisphere and from the September equinox to the December solstice in the S hemisphere **b** (*as modifier*): *spring showers*. Related adj: **vernal 26** the earliest or freshest time of something **27** a source or origin **28** one of a set of strips of rubber, steel, etc, running down the inside of the handle of a cricket bat, hockey stick, etc **29** Also called:

spring line *nautical* a mooring line, usually one of a pair that cross amidships **30** a flock of teal **31** *architect* another name for **springing** [Old English *springan*; related to Old Norse *springa*, Old High German *springan*, Sanskrit *sprhayati* he desires, Old Slavonic *pragu* grasshopper] > **ˈspringless** *adj* > **ˈspringˌlike** *adj*

spring balance *or esp US* **spring scale** *n* a device in which an object to be weighed is attached to the end of a helical spring, the extension of which indicates the weight of the object on a calibrated scale

spring beauty *n* a pale green annual plant (*Claytonia perfoliata*) of the purslane family, originally North American, having small white flowers above fused leaves that encircle the stem

springboard (ˈsprɪŋˌbɔːd) *n* **1** a flexible board, usually projecting low over the water, used for diving **2** a similar board used for gaining height or momentum in gymnastics **3** *Austral and NZ* a board inserted into the trunk of a tree at some height above the ground on which a lumberjack stands to chop down the tree **4** anything that serves as a point of departure or initiation

springbok *or less commonly* **springbuck** (ˈsprɪŋˌbʌk) *n, pl* **-bok, -boks** or **-buck, -bucks** an antelope, *Antidorcas marsupialis*, of semidesert regions of southern Africa, which moves in leaps exposing a patch of white erectile hairs on the rump that are usually covered by a fold of skin [c18 from Afrikaans, from Dutch *springen* to SPRING + *bok* goat, BUCK¹]

Springbok (ˈsprɪŋˌbʌk, -ˌbɒk) *n* a person who has represented South Africa at rugby union

spring chicken *n* **1** Also called: **springer** *chiefly US and Canadian* a young chicken, tender for cooking, esp one from two to ten months old **2** he or she is no spring chicken *informal* he or she is no longer young

spring-clean *vb* **1** to clean (a house) thoroughly: traditionally at the end of the winter ▷ *n* **2** an instance of spring-cleaning > **ˌspring-ˈcleaning** *n*

springe (sprɪndʒ) *n* **1** a snare set to catch small wild animals or birds and consisting of a loop attached to a bent twig or branch under tension ▷ *vb* **2** (*intr*) to set such a snare **3** (*tr*) to catch (small wild animals or birds) with such a snare [c13 related to Old English *springan* to SPRING]

springer (ˈsprɪŋə) *n* **1** short for **springer spaniel 2** Also called: **springing cow** a cow about to give birth **3** a person or thing that springs **4** *architect* **a** the first and lowest stone of an arch **b** the impost of an arch

springer spaniel *n* either of two breeds of large quick-moving spaniels bred to spring game, having a slightly domed head and ears of medium length. The **English springer spaniel** is the larger and can be of various colours; the **Welsh springer spaniel** is always a rich red and white

spring fever *n* the feeling of restlessness experienced by many people at the onset of spring

Springfield (ˈsprɪŋˌfiːld) *n* **1** a city in S Massachusetts, on the Connecticut River: the site of the US arsenal and armoury (1794–1968), which developed the Springfield and Garand rifles. Pop: 152 157 (2003 est) **2** a city in SW Missouri. Pop: 150 867 (2003 est) **3** a city in central Illinois, capital of the state: the home and burial place of Abraham Lincoln. Pop: 113 586 (2003 est)

Springfield rifle *n* a magazine-fed bolt-action breech-loading .30 calibre rifle formerly used by the US Army [from SPRINGFIELD, Massachusetts]

springhaas (ˈsprɪŋˌhɑːs) *n, pl* **-haas** or **-hase** (-ˌhɑːzə) a S and E African nocturnal rodent, *Pedetes capensis*, resembling a small kangaroo: family *Pedetidae* [from Afrikaans: spring hare]

springhalt (ˈsprɪŋˌhɔːlt) *n vet science* another name for **stringhalt** [c17 probably an alteration, influenced by SPRING, of STRINGHALT]

springhead (ˈsprɪŋˌhɛd) *n* the source of a stream; spring

springhouse (ˈsprɪŋˌhaʊs) *n* a storehouse built

over a spring for keeping dairy products and meat cool and fresh

springing (ˈsprɪŋɪŋ) *n* the level where an arch or vault rises from a support. Also called: **spring, springing line, springing point**

springlet (ˈsprɪŋlɪt) *n* a small spring; brooklet or rill

spring lock *n* a type of lock having a spring-loaded bolt, a key being required only to unlock it

spring mattress *n* a mattress containing an arrangement of spiral springs

spring onion *n* an immature form of the onion (*Allium cepa*), widely cultivated for its tiny bulb and long green leaves which are eaten in salads, etc. Also called: **green onion, scallion**

spring roll *n* a Chinese dish consisting of a savoury mixture of vegetables and meat rolled up in a thin pancake and fried

Springs (sprɪŋz) *n* a city in E South Africa: developed around a coal mine established in 1885 and later became a major world gold-mining centre, now with uranium extraction. Pop: 80 776 (2001)

springtail (ˈsprɪŋˌteɪl) *n* any primitive wingless insect of the order *Collembola*, having a forked springing organ with which it projects itself forward

spring tide *n* **1** either of the two tides that occur at or just after new moon and full moon when the tide-generating force of the sun acts in the same direction as that of the moon, reinforcing it and causing the greatest rise and fall in tidal level. The highest spring tides (**equinoctial springs**) occur at the equinoxes. Compare **neap tide 2** any great rush or flood

springtime (ˈsprɪŋˌtaɪm) *n* **1** Also called: **springtide** (ˈsprɪŋˌtaɪd) the season of spring **2** the earliest, usually the most attractive, period of the existence of something

springwood (ˈsprɪŋˌwʊd) *n* the wood that is produced by a plant in the spring and early summer and consists of large thin-walled xylem cells. Compare **summerwood**

springy (ˈsprɪŋɪ) *adj* **springier, springiest 1** possessing or characterized by resilience or bounce **2** (of a place) having many wells or springs of water > **ˈspringily** *adv* > **ˈspringiness** *n*

sprinkle (ˈsprɪŋkᵊl) *vb* **1** to scatter (liquid, powder, etc) in tiny particles or droplets over (something) **2** (*tr*) to distribute over (something): *the field was sprinkled with flowers* **3** (*intr*) to drizzle slightly ▷ *n* **4** the act or an instance of sprinkling or a quantity that is sprinkled **5** a slight drizzle [c14 probably from Middle Dutch *sprenkelen*; related to Old English *spearca* SPARK¹]

sprinkler (ˈsprɪŋklə) *n* **1** a device perforated with small holes that is attached to a garden hose or watering can and used to spray plants, lawns, etc, with water **2** a person or thing that sprinkles **3** See **sprinkler system**

sprinkler system *n* a fire-extinguishing system that releases water from overhead pipes through nozzles (sprinklers) opened automatically by a rise in temperature

sprinkling (ˈsprɪŋklɪŋ) *n* a small quantity or amount: *a sprinkling of commonsense*

sprint (sprɪnt) *n* **1** *athletics* a short race run at top speed, such as the 100 metres **2** a fast finishing speed at the end of a longer race, as in running or cycling, etc **3** any quick run ▷ *vb* (*intr*) **4** to go at top speed, as in running, cycling, etc [c16 from Scandinavian; related to Old English *gesprintan* to emit, Old Norse *spretta* to jump up, Old High German *sprinzan* to jump up, Swedish *sprata* to kick] > **ˈsprinter** *n*

sprit (sprɪt) *n nautical* a light spar pivoted at the mast and crossing a fore-and-aft quadrilateral sail diagonally to the peak [Old English *spreot*; related to Old High German *spriuzen* to support, Dutch *spriet* sprit, Norwegian *spryta*]

sprite (spraɪt) *n* **1** (in folklore) a nimble elflike creature, esp one associated with water **2** a small

S

dainty person **3** an icon in a computer game which can be manoeuvred around the screen by means of a joystick, etc [c13 from Old French *esprit*, from Latin *spīritus* SPIRIT[1]]

spritsail ('sprɪt,seɪl; *Nautical* 'sprɪtsəl) *n nautical* **1** a rectangular sail mounted on a sprit in some 19th-century small vessels **2** (in medieval rigging) a square sail mounted on a yard on the bowsprit

spritzer ('sprɪtsə) *n* a drink, usually white wine, with soda water added [from German *spritzen* to splash]

spritzig *German* ('ʃprɪtsɪç; *English* 'sprɪtsɪg) *adj* (of wine) sparkling [German, from *spritzen* to splash]

sprocket ('sprɒkɪt) *n* **1** Also called: **sprocket wheel** a relatively thin wheel having teeth projecting radially from the rim, esp one that drives or is driven by a chain **2** an individual tooth on such a wheel **3** a cylindrical wheel with teeth on one or both rims for pulling film through a camera or projector **4** a small wedge-shaped piece of wood used to extend a roof over the eaves [c16 of unknown origin]

sprog (sprɒg) *n slang* **1** a child; baby **2** (esp in RAF) a recruit

sprout (spraʊt) *vb* **1** (of a plant, seed, etc) to produce (new leaves, shoots, etc) **2** (*intr*; often foll by *up*) to begin to grow or develop: *new office blocks are sprouting up all over the city* ▷ *n* **3** a newly grown shoot or bud **4** something that grows like a sprout **5** See **Brussels sprout** [Old English *sprūtan*; related to Middle High German *sprūzen* to sprout, Lettish *sprausties* to jostle]

spruce[1] (spruːs) *n* **1** any coniferous tree of the N temperate genus *Picea*, cultivated for timber and for ornament: family *Pinaceae*. They grow in a pyramidal shape and have needle-like leaves and light-coloured wood. See also **Norway spruce, blue spruce, white spruce, black spruce 2** the wood of any of these trees [c17 short for *Spruce fir*, from c14 *Spruce* Prussia, changed from *Pruce*, via Old French from Latin *Prussia*]

spruce[2] (spruːs) *adj* neat, smart, and trim [c16 perhaps from *Spruce leather* a fashionable leather imported from Prussia; see SPRUCE[1]] > **'sprucely** *adv* > **'spruceness** *n*

spruce beer *n* an alcoholic drink made of fermented molasses flavoured with spruce twigs and cones

spruce grouse *n* a game bird, *Dendragapus canadensis*, occurring in Canadian coniferous forests

spruce pine *n* **1** a large pine tree, *Pinus glabra*, of the southeastern US **2** any of several similar plants, such as certain pines, hemlocks, and spruces

spruce up *vb* (*adverb*) to make (oneself, a person, or thing) smart and neat

sprue[1] (spruː) *n* **1** a vertical channel in a mould through which plastic or molten metal is introduced or out of which it flows when the mould is filled **2** plastic or metal that solidifies in a sprue [c19 of unknown origin]

sprue[2] (spruː) *n* a chronic disease, esp of tropical climates, characterized by flatulence, diarrhoea, frothy foul-smelling stools, and emaciation [c19 from Dutch *spruw*; related to Middle Low German *sprüwe* tumour]

sprue[3] (spruː) *n London dialect* an inferior type of asparagus [c19 of unknown origin]

spruik ('spruːɪk) *vb* (*intr*) *Austral archaic slang* to speak in public (used esp of a showman or salesman) [c20 of unknown origin] > **'spruiker** *n*

spruit (spreɪt) *n South African* a small tributary stream or watercourse [Afrikaans *spruit* offshoot, tributary]

sprung (sprʌŋ) *vb* the past participle and a past tense of **spring**

sprung rhythm *n prosody* a type of poetic rhythm characterized by metrical feet of irregular composition, each having one strongly stressed syllable, often the first, and an indefinite number of unstressed syllables

spry (spraɪ) *adj* **spryer, spryest** or **sprier, spriest** active and brisk; nimble [c18 perhaps of Scandinavian origin; compare Swedish dialect *spragg* SPRIG] > **'spryly** *adv* > **'spryness** *n*

spt *abbreviation for* seaport

SPUC (spʌk) *n acronym for* Society for the Protection of the Unborn Child

spud (spʌd) *n* **1** an informal word for **potato** (sense 1) **2** a narrow-bladed spade for cutting roots, digging up weeds, etc **3** Also called: **spudder** a tool, resembling a chisel, for removing bark from trees ▷ *vb* **spuds, spudding, spudded 4** (*tr*) to remove (bark) or eradicate (weeds) with a spud **5** (*intr*) to drill the first foot of an oil-well [c15 *spudde* short knife, of unknown origin; applied later to a digging tool, and hence to a potato]

spud-bashing *n Brit slang chiefly military* the task of peeling potatoes, given as a punishment

spuddle ('spʌdəl) *n Southwest English dialect* a feeble movement

Spud Island *n* a slang name for **Prince Edward Island**

spue (spjuː) *vb* **spues, spuing, spued** an archaic spelling of **spew**. > **'spuer** *n*

spuggy ('spʊgɪ) or **spug** (spʊg) *n, pl* **spuggies** or **spugs** *Northeast English dialect* a house sparrow. Compare **speug** [variant of Scottish *sprug*, of obscure origin]

spume (spjuːm) *n* **1** foam or surf, esp on the sea; froth ▷ *vb* **2** (*intr*) to foam or froth [c14 from Old French *espume*, from Latin *spūma*; related to *spuere* to SPEW] > **'spumous** or **'spumy** *adj*

spumescent (spjuː'mɛsənt) *adj* producing or resembling foam or froth > **spu'mescence** *n*

spumone or **spumoni** (spuː'məʊnɪ; *Italian* spuˈmoːne) *n, pl* **-ni** (-nɪ) a creamy Italian ice cream, made in sections of different colouring, usually containing candied fruit and nuts [Italian, from *spuma* foam, SPUME]

spun (spʌn) *vb* **1** the past tense and past participle of **spin** ▷ *adj* **2** formed or manufactured by spinning: *spun gold; spun glass*

spunk (spʌŋk) *n* **1** *informal* courage or spirit **2** *Brit* a slang word for **semen 3** touchwood or tinder, esp originally made from various spongy types of fungus **4** *Austral and NZ informal* a person, esp male, who is attractive to the opposite sex [c16 (in the sense: a spark): from Scottish Gaelic *spong* tinder, sponge, from Latin *spongia* sponge] > **'spunky** *adj* > **'spunkily** *adv*

▌ **USAGE** The second sense of this word was formerly considered to be taboo, and it was labelled as such in previous editions of *Collins English Dictionary*. However, it has now become acceptable in speech, although some older or more conservative people may object to its use

spun silk *n* yarn or fabric made from silk waste

spun sugar *n US* another term for **candyfloss**

spun yarn *n nautical* small stuff made from rope yarns twisted together

spur (spɜː) *n* **1** a pointed device or sharp spiked wheel fixed to the heel of a rider's boot to enable him to urge his horse on **2** anything serving to urge or encourage: *the increase in salary was a spur to their production* **3** a sharp horny projection from the leg just above the claws in male birds, such as the domestic cock **4** a pointed process in any of various animals; calcar **5** a tubular extension at the base of the corolla in flowers such as larkspur **6** a short or stunted branch of a tree **7** a ridge projecting laterally from a mountain or mountain range **8** a wooden prop or a masonry reinforcing pier **9** another name for **groyne 10** Also called: **spur track** a railway branch line or siding **11** a short side road leading off from a main road: *a motorway spur* **12** a sharp cutting instrument attached to the leg of a gamecock **13 on the spur of the moment** on impulse **14 win one's spurs** *a history*

to earn knighthood **b** to prove one's ability; gain distinction ▷ *vb* **spurs, spurring, spurred 15** (*tr*) to goad or urge with or as if with spurs **16** (*intr*) to go or ride quickly; press on **17** (*tr*) to injure or strike with a spur **18** (*tr*) to provide with a spur or spurs [Old English *spura*; related to Old Norse *spori*, Old High German *sporo*]

spurge (spɜːdʒ) *n* any of various euphorbiaceous plants of the genus *Euphorbia* that have milky sap and small flowers typically surrounded by conspicuous bracts. Some species have purgative properties [c14 from Old French *espurge*, from *espurgier* to purge, from Latin *expurgāre* to cleanse, from EX-[1] + *purgāre* to PURGE]

spur gear or **wheel** *n* a gear having involuted teeth either straight or helically cut on a cylindrical surface. Two such gears are used to transmit power between parallel shafts

spurge laurel *n* See **laurel** (sense 4)

spurious ('spjʊərɪəs) *adj* **1** not genuine or real **2** (of a plant part or organ) having the appearance of another part but differing from it in origin, development, or function; false: *a spurious fruit* **3** (of radiation) produced at an undesired frequency by a transmitter, causing interference, etc **4** *rare* illegitimate [c17 from Latin *spurius* of illegitimate birth] > **'spuriously** *adv* > **'spuriousness** *n*

spurn (spɜːn) *vb* **1** to reject (a person or thing) with contempt **2** (when *intr*, often foll by *against*) *archaic* to kick (at) ▷ *n* **3** an instance of spurning **4** *archaic* a kick or thrust [Old English *spurnan*; related to Old Norse *sporna*, Old High German *spurnan*, Latin *spernere* to despise, Lithuanian *spiriu* to kick] > **'spurner** *n*

spurrey or **spurry** ('spʌrɪ) *n, pl* **-ries** any of several low-growing caryophyllaceous plants of the European genus *Spergula*, esp *S. arvensis*, having whorled leaves and small white flowers [c16 from Dutch *spurrie*, perhaps from Medieval Latin *spergula*; related to German *Spergel*]

spurrier ('spʌrɪə) *n* a maker of spurs

spurt or **spirt** (spɜːt) *vb* **1** to gush or cause to gush forth in a sudden stream or jet **2** to make a sudden effort ▷ *n* **3** a sudden forceful stream or jet **4** a short burst of activity, speed, or energy [c16 perhaps related to Middle High German *sprützen* to squirt]

spur veins *n vet science* the veins of a horse that can be damaged by a rider's spurs

Sputnik ('spʊtnɪk, 'spʌt-) *n* any of a series of unmanned Soviet satellites, **Sputnik 1** (launched in 1957) being the first man-made satellite to orbit the earth [c20 from Russian, literally: fellow traveller, from *s-* with + *put* path + *-nik* suffix indicating agent]

sputter ('spʌtə) *vb* **1** another word for **splutter** (senses 1–3) **2** *physics* **a** to undergo or cause to undergo a process in which atoms of a solid are removed from its surface by the impact of high-energy ions, as in a discharge tube **b** to coat (a film of a metal) onto (a solid surface) by using this process ▷ *n* **3** the process or noise of sputtering **4** incoherent stammering speech **5** something that is ejected while sputtering [c16 from Dutch *sputteren*, of imitative origin] > **'sputterer** *n*

sputum ('spjuːtəm) *n, pl* **-ta** (-tə) **1** a mass of salivary matter ejected from the mouth **2** saliva ejected from the mouth mixed with mucus or pus exuded from the respiratory passages, as in bronchitis or bronchiectasis [c17 from Latin: spittle, from *spuere* to spit out]

spy (spaɪ) *n, pl* **spies 1** a person employed by a state or institution to obtain secret information from rival countries, organizations, companies, etc **2** a person who keeps secret watch on others **3** *obsolete* a close view ▷ *vb* **spies, spying, spied 4** (*intr*; usually foll by *on*) to keep a secret or furtive watch (on) **5** (*intr*) to engage in espionage **6** (*tr*) to catch sight of; descry [c13 *spien*, from Old French *espier*, of Germanic origin; related to Old High German *spehōn*, Middle Dutch *spien*]

spyglass ('spaɪˌglɑːs) *n* a small telescope

spyhole ('spaɪˌhəʊl) *n* a small hole in a door, etc through which one may watch secretly; peephole

spy out *vb* (*tr, adverb*) **1** to discover by careful observation: *to spy out a route* **2** to make a close scrutiny of: *to spy out the land*

spyware ('spaɪˌwɛə) *n computing* software installed via the internet on a computer without the user's knowledge and used to send information about the user to another computer

Spy Wednesday *n* (in Ireland) the Wednesday before Easter, named for Judas' becoming a spy for the Sanhedrin

sq *abbreviation for* **1** sequence **2** square **3** (*pl* **sqq**) the following one [from Latin *sequens*]

Sq. *abbreviation for* **1** Squadron **2** (in place names) Square

SQA (in Britain) *abbreviation for* Scottish Qualifications Agency

SQL *abbreviation for* structured query language: a computer programming language used for database management

sqn *abbreviation for* squadron

Sqn Ldr *abbreviation for* squadron leader

sqq. *abbreviation for* the following ones [from Latin *sequentia*]

squab (skwɒb) *n, pl* **squabs** or **squab 1** a young unfledged bird, esp a pigeon **2** a short fat person **3 a** a well-stuffed bolster or cushion **b** a sofa ▷ *adj* **4** (of birds) recently hatched and still unfledged **5** short and fat [c17 probably of Germanic origin; compare Swedish dialect *sqvabb* flabby skin, *sqvabba* fat woman, German *Quabbe* soft mass, Norwegian *kvabb* mud] > **'squabby** *adj*

squabble ('skwɒbᵊl) *vb* **1** (*intr*) to quarrel over a small matter ▷ *n* **2** a petty quarrel [c17 probably of Scandinavian origin; related to Swedish dialect *sqvabbel* to quarrel] > **'squabbler** *n*

squacco ('skwækəʊ) *n, pl* **-cos** a S European heron, *Ardeola ralloides,* with a short thick neck and a buff-coloured plumage with white wings [c17 Italian dialect]

squad (skwɒd) *n* **1** the smallest military formation, typically comprising a dozen soldiers, used esp as a drill formation **2** any small group of people engaged in a common pursuit **3** *sport* a number of players from which a team is to be selected [c17 from Old French *esquade,* from Old Spanish *escuadra,* from *escuadrar* to square, from the square formations used]

squaddie or **squaddy** ('skwɒdɪ) *n, pl* **-dies** *Brit slang* a private soldier. Compare **swaddy** [c20 from SQUAD]

squadron ('skwɒdrən) *n* **1 a** a subdivision of a naval fleet detached for a particular task **b** a number of naval units usually of similar type and consisting of two or more divisions **2** a cavalry unit comprising two or more troops, headquarters, and supporting arms **3** the basic tactical and administrative air force unit comprising two or more flights ▷ Abbreviation: **sqn** [c16 from Italian *squadrone* soldiers drawn up in square formation, from *squadro* SQUARE]

squadron leader *n* an officer holding commissioned rank, between flight lieutenant and wing commander in the air forces of Britain and certain other countries

squalene ('skweɪˌliːn) *n biochem* a terpene first found in the liver of sharks but also present in the livers of most higher animals: an important precursor of cholesterol [c20 from New Latin *squalus* genus name of the shark]

squalid ('skwɒlɪd) *adj* **1** dirty and repulsive, esp as a result of neglect or poverty **2** sordid [c16 from Latin *squālidus,* from *squālēre* to be stiff with dirt] > **squalidity** (skwɒ'lɪdɪtɪ) or **'squalidness** *n* > **'squalidly** *adv*

squall¹ ('skwɔːl) *n* **1** a sudden strong wind or brief turbulent storm **2** any sudden commotion or show of temper ▷ *vb* **3** (*intr*) to blow in a squall [c18 perhaps a special use of SQUALL²] > **'squallish** *adj* > **'squally** *adj*

squall² (skwɔːl) *vb* **1** (*intr*) to cry noisily; yell ▷ *n* **2** a shrill or noisy yell or howl [c17 probably of Scandinavian origin; compare Icelandic *skvala* to shout; see SQUEAL] > **'squaller** *n*

squall line *n* a narrow zone along a cold front along which squalls occur. See also **line squall**

squalor ('skwɒlə) *n* the condition or quality of being squalid; disgusting dirt and filth [c17 from Latin]

squama ('skweɪmə) *n, pl* **-mae** (-miː) *biology* a scale or scalelike structure [c18 from Latin] > **squamate** ('skweɪmeɪt) *adj*

squamation (skweɪ'meɪʃən) *n* **1** the condition of having or forming scales or squamae **2** the arrangement of scales in fishes or reptiles

squamiform ('skweɪmɪˌfɔːm) *adj biology* resembling a scale: *squamiform cells*

squamosal (skwə'məʊsᵊl) *n* **1** a thin platelike paired bone in the skull of vertebrates: in mammals it forms part of the temporal bone ▷ *adj* **2** of or relating to this bone **3** a less common word for **squamous**

squamous ('skweɪməs) or **squamose** ('skweɪməʊs) *adj biology* **1** (of epithelium) consisting of one or more layers of flat platelike cells **2** covered with, formed of, or resembling scales [c16 from Latin *squāmōsus,* from *squāma* a scale] > **'squamosely** or **'squamosely** *adv* > **'squamousness** or **'squamoseness** *n*

squamulose ('skwæmjʊˌləʊs, -ˌləʊz, 'skweɪ-) *adj* (esp of plants or their parts) covered with minute scales [c19 from Latin *squāmula* diminutive of *squāma* a scale]

squander ('skwɒndə) *vb* (*tr*) **1** to spend wastefully or extravagantly; dissipate **2** an obsolete word for **scatter** ▷ *n* **3** *rare* extravagance or dissipation [c16 of unknown origin] > **'squanderer** *n*

square (skwɛə) *n* **1** a plane geometric figure having four equal sides and four right angles. Compare **rectangle, rhombus 2** any object, part, or arrangement having this or a similar shape: *a square of carpet; a square on a chess board* **3** (*capital when part of name*) an open area in a town, sometimes including the surrounding buildings, which may form a square **4** *maths* the product of two equal factors; the second power: *9 is the square of 3, written 3²* **5** an instrument having two strips of wood, metal, etc, set in the shape of a T or L, used for constructing or testing right angles **6** *cricket* the closely-cut area in the middle of a ground on which wickets are prepared **7** a body of soldiers drawn up in the form of a square **8** *rowing* the position of the blade of an oar perpendicular to the surface of the water just before and during a stroke **9** *informal* a person who is old-fashioned in views, customs, appearance, etc **10** *astrology* an aspect of about 90° between two planets, etc. Compare **conjunction** (sense 5), **opposition** (sense 9), **trine** (sense 1) **11** *obsolete* a standard, pattern, or rule **12** **back to square one** indicating a return to the starting-point of an investigation, experiment, etc, because of failure, lack of progress, etc **13** **on the square a** at right angles **b** on equal terms **c** *informal* honestly and openly **d** *slang* a phrase identifying someone as a Freemason: *he is on the square* **14** **out of square a** not at right angles or not having a right angle **b** not in order or agreement ▷ *adj* **15** being a square in shape **16** having or forming one or more right angles or being at right angles to something **17** square or rectangular in section: *a square bar* **18 a** (*prenominal*) denoting a measure of area of any shape: *a circle of four square feet* **b** (*immediately postpositive*) denoting a square having a specified length on each side: *a board four feet square contains 16 square feet* **19** fair and honest (esp in the phrase **a square deal**) **20** straight, even, or level: *a square surface* **21** *cricket* at right angles to the wicket: *square leg* **22** *sport* in a straight line across the pitch: *a square pass* **23** *nautical* (of the sails of a square-rigger) set at right angles to the keel **24** *informal* old-fashioned in views, customs, appearance, etc **25** stocky or sturdy: *square shoulders* **26** (*postpositive*) having no remaining debts or accounts to be settled **27** (of a horse's gait) sound, steady, or regular **28** (*prenominal*) unequivocal or straightforward: *a square contradiction* **29** (*postpositive*) neat and tidy **30** *maths* (of a matrix) having the same number of rows and columns **31** **all square** on equal terms; even in score **32** **square peg (in a round hole)** *informal* a person or thing that is a misfit, such as an employee in a job for which he is unsuited ▷ *vb* (*mainly tr*) **33** to make into a square or similar shape **34** *maths* to raise (a number or quantity) to the second power **35** to test or adjust for deviation with respect to a right angle, plane surface, etc **36** (sometimes foll by *off*) to divide into squares **37** to position so as to be rectangular, straight, or level: *square the shoulders* **38** (sometimes foll by *up*) to settle (debts, accounts, etc) **39** to level (the score) in a game, etc **40** (*also intr*; often foll by *with*) to agree or cause to agree: *your ideas don't square with mine* **41** *rowing* to turn (an oar) perpendicular to the surface of the water just before commencing a stroke **42** (in canoeing) to turn (a paddle) perpendicular to the direction of the canoe at the commencement of a stroke. Compare **feather** (sense 15) **43** to arrange (something), esp by a corrupt method or come to an arrangement with (someone), as by bribery **44** **square the circle** to attempt the impossible (in reference to the insoluble problem of constructing a square having exactly the same area as a given circle) ▷ *adv* **45** in order to be square **46** at right angles **47** *sport* in a straight line across the pitch: *pass the ball square* **48** *informal* squarely ▷ See also **square away, square off, square up** [c13 from Old French *esquare,* from Vulgar Latin *exquadra* (unattested), from Latin EX¹ + *quadrāre* to make square; see QUADRANT] > **'squareness** *n* > **'squarer** *n* > **'squarish** *adj*

square away *vb* (*adverb*) **1** to set the sails of (a square-rigger) at right angles to the keel **2** (*tr*) *US and Canadian* to make neat and tidy

square-bashing *n Brit military slang* drill on a barrack square

square bracket *n* **1** either of a pair of characters [ ], used to enclose a section of writing or printing to separate it from the main text **2** Also called: **bracket** either of these characters used as a sign of aggregation in mathematical or logical expressions indicating that the expression contained in the brackets is to be evaluated first and treated as a unit in the evaluation of the whole

square dance *n* **1** *chiefly US and Canadian* any of various formation dances, such as a quadrille, in which the couples form squares ▷ *vb* **square-dance 2** (*intr*) to perform such a dance > **'square-ˌdancer** *n*

square go *n Scot informal* a fair fight between two individuals

square knot *n* another name for **reef knot**

square leg *n cricket* **1** a fielding position on the on side approximately at right angles to the batsman **2** a person who fields in this position

squarely ('skwɛəlɪ) *adv* **1** in a direct way; straight: *he hit me squarely on the nose* **2** in an honest, frank, and just manner **3** at right angles

square matrix *n maths* a matrix in which the number of rows is equal to the number of columns

square meal *n* a substantial meal consisting of enough food to satisfy

square measure *n* a unit or system of units for measuring areas

square number *n* an integer, such as 1, 4, 9, or 16, that is the square of an integer

square off *vb* (*intr, adverb*) to assume a posture of offence or defence, as in boxing

square of opposition *n* See **opposition** (sense 10b)

S

square piano *n music* an obsolete form of piano, horizontally strung and with an oblong frame

square-rigged *adj nautical* rigged with square sails

square-rigger *n nautical* a square-rigged ship

square root *n* a number or quantity that when multiplied by itself gives a given number or quantity: *2 is a square root of 4, usually written* $\sqrt{4}$ *or* $4^{1/2}$

square sail *n nautical* a rectangular or square sail set on a horizontal yard rigged more or less athwartships

square shooter *n informal, chiefly US* an honest or frank person > **square shooting** *n*

square tin *n Brit* a medium-sized loaf having a crusty top, baked in a tin with a square base

square up *vb (adverb)* **1** to pay or settle (bills, debts, etc) **2** *informal* to arrange or be arranged satisfactorily **3** *(intr; foll by to)* to prepare to be confronted (with), esp courageously **4** *(tr; foll by to)* to adopt a position of readiness to fight (an opponent) **5** *(tr)* to transfer (a drawing) by aid of a network of squares

square wave *n* an oscillation, for example in voltage pulse, that alternates between two fixed values with a negligible transition time between the two, giving a rectangular waveform

squark (skwɑːk) *n* a hypothetical boson partner of a quark, the existence of which is implied by supersymmetry [C20 from S(UPER-) + QUARK[1]]

squarrose (ˈskwærəʊz, ˈskwɒ-) *adj* **1** *biology* having a rough surface, caused by the presence of projecting hairs, scales, etc **2** *botany* having or relating to parts that are recurved: *squarrose bracts* [C18 from Latin *squarrōsus* scabby]

squash[1] (skwɒʃ) *vb* **1** to press or squeeze or be pressed or squeezed in or down so as to crush, distort, or pulp **2** *(tr)* to suppress or overcome **3** *(tr)* to humiliate or crush (a person), esp with a disconcerting retort **4** *(intr)* to make a sucking, splashing, or squelching sound **5** *(often foll by in or into)* to enter or insert in a confined space ▷ *n* **6** *Brit* a still drink made from fruit juice or fruit syrup diluted with water **7** a crush, esp of people in a confined space **8** something that is squashed **9** the act or sound of squashing or the state of being squashed **10** Also called: **squash rackets, squash racquets** a game for two or four players played in an enclosed court with a small rubber ball and light long-handled rackets. The ball may be hit against any of the walls but must hit the facing wall at a point above a horizontal line. See also **rackets** **11** Also called: **squash tennis** a similar game played with larger rackets and a larger pneumatic ball [C16 from Old French *esquasser*, from Vulgar Latin *exquassāre* (unattested), from Latin EX-[1] + *quassāre* to shatter] > ˈ**squasher** *n*

squash[2] (skwɒʃ) *n, pl* **squashes** *or* **squash** *US and Canadian* **1** any of various marrow-like cucurbitaceous plants of the genus *Cucurbita*, esp *C. pepo* and *C. moschata*, the fruits of which have a hard rind surrounding edible flesh **2** the fruit of any of these plants, eaten as a vegetable [C17 from Narraganset *askutasquash*, literally: green vegetable eaten green]

squashable (ˈskwɒʃəbᵊl) *adj* **1** easily squashed; soft **2** easily subdued, disconcerted, or humiliated

squash bug *n* any of various heteropterous insects of the family *Coreidae*, esp a North American species, *Anasa tristis*, which is a pest of squash, pumpkin, and related plants

squash ladder *n* a list showing the relative order of merit of a set of squash players determined by the winning player in each match taking the higher of the two players' positions

squashy (ˈskwɒʃɪ) *adj* **squashier, squashiest** **1** easily squashed; pulpy: *a squashy peach* **2** soft and wet; marshy: *squashy ground* **3** having a squashed appearance: *a squashy face* > ˈ**squashily** *adv* > ˈ**squashiness** *n*

squat (skwɒt) *vb* **squats, squatting, squatted** *(intr)* **1** to rest in a crouching position with the knees bent and the weight on the feet **2** to crouch down, esp in order to hide **3** *law* to occupy land or property to which the occupant has no legal title *(tr)* **4** *weightlifting* to crouch down to one's knees and rise to a standing position while holding (a specified weight) behind one's neck ▷ *adj* **5** Also: **squatty** (ˈskwɒtɪ) short and broad: *a squat chair* ▷ *n* **6** a squatting position **7** *weightlifting* an exercise in which a person crouches down and rises up repeatedly while holding a barbell at shoulder height **8** a house occupied by squatters [C13 from Old French *esquater*, from *es-* EX-[1] + *catir* to press together, from Vulgar Latin *coactīre* (unattested), from Latin *cōgere* to compress, from CO- + *agere* to drive] > ˈ**squatly** *adv* > ˈ**squatness** *n*

squatter (ˈskwɒtə) *n* **1** a person who occupies property or land to which he has no legal title **2** (in Australia) **a** (formerly) a person who occupied a tract of land, esp pastoral land, as tenant of the Crown **b** a farmer of sheep or cattle on a large scale **3** (in New Zealand) a 19th-century settler who took up large acreage on a Crown lease

squatter sovereignty *n* a contemptuous term for **popular sovereignty**, used by its critics

squat thrust *n* an exercise in which the hands are kept on the floor with the arms held straight while the legs are straightened out behind and quickly drawn in towards the body again

squattocracy (skwɒˈtɒkrəsɪ) *n chiefly Austral* squatters collectively, regarded as rich and influential. See **squatter** (sense 2b) [C19 from SQUATTER + -CRACY]

squaw (skwɔː) *n* **1** *offensive* a North American Indian woman **2** *slang, usually facetious* a woman or wife [C17 of Algonquian origin; compare Natick *squa* female creature]

squawk (skwɔːk) *n* **1** a loud raucous cry; screech **2** *informal* a loud complaint or protest ▷ *vb* **3** to utter a squawk or with a squawk **4** *(intr) informal* to complain loudly [C19 of imitative origin] > ˈ**squawker** *n*

squaw man *n offensive* a White or other non-American-Indian man married to a North American Indian woman

squeak (skwiːk) *n* **1** a short shrill cry or high-pitched sound **2** *informal* an escape (esp in the phrases **narrow squeak, near squeak**) ▷ *vb* **3** to make or cause to make a squeak **4** *(intr; usually foll by through or by)* to pass with only a narrow margin: *to squeak through an examination* **5** *(intr) informal* to confess information about oneself or another **6** *(tr)* to utter with a squeak [C17 probably of Scandinavian origin; compare Swedish *skväka* to croak] > ˈ**squeaker** *n* > ˈ**squeaky** *adj* > ˈ**squeakily** *adv* > ˈ**squeakiness** *n*

squeaky-clean *adj* **1** (of hair) washed so clean that wet strands squeak when rubbed **2** completely clean **3** *informal, derogatory* (of a person) cultivating a virtuous and wholesome image

squeal (skwiːl) *n* **1** a high shrill yelp, as of pain **2** a screaming sound, as of tyres when a car brakes suddenly ▷ *vb* **3** to utter a squeal or with a squeal **4** *(intr) slang* to confess information about another **5** *(intr) informal, chiefly Brit* to complain or protest loudly [C13 *squelen*, of imitative origin] > ˈ**squealer** *n*

squeamish (ˈskwiːmɪʃ) *adj* **1** easily sickened or nauseated, as by the sight of blood **2** easily shocked; fastidious or prudish **3** easily frightened: *squeamish about spiders* [C15 from Anglo-French *escoymous*, of unknown origin] > ˈ**squeamishly** *adv* > ˈ**squeamishness** *n*

squeegee (ˈskwiːdʒiː) *or less commonly* **squilgee** *n* **1** an implement with a rubber blade used for wiping away surplus water from a surface, such as a windowpane **2** any of various similar devices used in photography for pressing the water out of wet prints or negatives or for squeezing prints onto a glazing surface ▷ *vb* **-gees, -geeing, -geed** **3** to remove (water or other liquid) from (something) by use of a squeegee **4** *(tr)* to press down (a photographic print, etc) with a squeegee [C19 probably of imitative origin, influenced by SQUEEZE]

squeeze (skwiːz) *vb (mainly tr)* **1** to grip or press firmly, esp so as to crush or distort; compress **2** to crush or press (something) so as to extract (a liquid): *to squeeze the juice from an orange; to squeeze an orange* **3** to apply gentle pressure to, as in affection or reassurance: *he squeezed her hand* **4** to push or force in a confined space: *to squeeze six lettuces into one box; to squeeze through a crowd* **5** to hug closely **6** to oppress with exacting demands, such as excessive taxes **7** to exert pressure on (someone) in order to extort (something): *to squeeze money out of a victim by blackmail* **8** *(intr)* to yield under pressure **9** to make an impression of (a coin, etc) in a soft substance **10** *bridge, whist* to lead a card that forces (opponents) to discard potentially winning cards ▷ *n* **11** the act or an instance of squeezing or of being squeezed **12** a hug or handclasp **13** a crush of people in a confined space **14** *chiefly Brit* a condition of restricted credit imposed by a government to counteract price inflation **15** an impression, esp of a coin, etc, made in a soft substance **16** an amount extracted by squeezing: *add a squeeze of lemon juice* **17** *commerce* any action taken by a trader or traders on a market that forces buyers to make purchases and prices to rise **18** *informal* pressure brought to bear in order to extort something (esp in the phrase **put the squeeze on**) **19** Also called: **squeeze play** *bridge, whist* a manoeuvre that forces opponents to discard potentially winning cards **20** *informal* a person with whom one is having a romantic relationship [C16 from Middle English *queysen* to press, from Old English *cwȳsan*] > ˈ**squeezable** *adj* > ˈ**squeezer** *n*

squeeze-box *n* an informal name for **concertina, accordion**

squeezy (ˈskwiːzɪ) *adj* (of bottles, tubes, mops, etc) designed to be squeezed, especially in order to extract something

squelch (skwɛltʃ) *vb* **1** *(intr)* to walk laboriously through soft wet material or with wet shoes, making a sucking noise **2** *(intr)* to make such a noise **3** *(tr)* to crush completely; squash **4** *(tr) informal* to silence, as by a crushing retort ▷ *n* **5** a squelching sound **6** something that has been squelched **7** *electronics* a circuit that cuts off the audio-frequency amplifier of a radio receiver in the absence of an input signal, in order to suppress background noise **8** *informal* a crushing remark [C17 of imitative origin] > ˈ**squelcher** *n* > ˈ**squelching** *adj* > ˈ**squelchy** *adj*

squeteague (skwɪˈtiːg) *n, pl* **-teague** *or* **-teagues** any of various sciaenid food fishes of the genus *Cynoscion*, esp *C. regalis*, of the North American coast of the Atlantic Ocean [C19 from Narraganset *pesukwiteag*, literally: they give glue; so called because glue is made from them]

squib (skwɪb) *n* **1** a firework, usually having a tube filled with gunpowder, that burns with a hissing noise and culminates in a small explosion **2** a firework that does not explode because of a fault; dud **3** a short witty attack; lampoon **4** an electric device for firing a rocket engine **5** *obsolete* an insignificant person **6** *Austral and NZ slang* a coward **7** **damp squib** something intended but failing to impress ▷ *vb* **squibs, squibbing, squibbed** **8** *(intr)* to sound, move, or explode like a squib **9** *(intr)* to let off or shoot a squib **10** to write a squib against (someone) **11** *(intr)* to move in a quick irregular fashion **12** *(intr) Austral slang* to behave in a cowardly fashion [C16 probably imitative of a quick light explosion]

squid[1] (skwɪd) *n, pl* **squid** *or* **squids** **1** any of various fast-moving pelagic cephalopod molluscs of the genera *Loligo, Ommastrephes*, etc, of most seas, having a torpedo-shaped body ranging from about 10 centimetres to 16.5 metres long and a pair of triangular tail fins: order *Decapoda* (decapods). See also **cuttlefish** ▷ *vb* **squids,**

squidding, squidded 2 (*intr*) (of a parachute) to assume an elongated squidlike shape owing to excess air pressure [c17 of unknown origin]

squid² (skwɪd) *n Brit slang* a pound sterling [c20 rhyming slang for QUID]

SQUID *abbreviation for* superconducting quantum interference device

squidgy ('skwɪdʒɪ) *adj* squidgier, squidgiest soft, moist, and squashy [of imitative origin]

squiffy ('skwɪfɪ) *adj* -fier, -fiest *Brit informal* slightly drunk. Also: **squiffed** [c19 of unknown origin]

squiggle ('skwɪgəl) *n* **1** a mark or movement in the form of a wavy line; curlicue **2** an illegible scrawl ▷ *vb* **3** (*intr*) to wriggle **4** (*intr*) to form or draw squiggles **5** (*tr*) to make into squiggles [c19 perhaps a blend of SQUIRM + WIGGLE] > **'squiggler** *n* > **'squiggly** *adj*

squilgee (skwɪl'dʒiː) *n* a variant of **squeegee** [c19 perhaps from SQUEEGEE, influenced by SQUELCH]

squill (skwɪl) *n* **1** See **sea squill 2** the bulb of the sea squill, formerly used medicinally as an expectorant after being sliced and dried **3** any Old World liliaceous plant of the genus *Scilla*, such as *S. verna* (**spring squill**) of Europe, having small blue or purple flowers [c14 from Latin *squilla* sea onion, from Greek *skilla*, of obscure origin]

squilla ('skwɪlə) *n, pl* -las *or* -lae (-liː) any mantis shrimp of the genus *Squilla* [c16 from Latin *squilla* shrimp, of obscure origin]

squillion ('skwɪljən) *informal* ▷ *n, pl* -lions *or* -lion **1** (*often plural*) an extremely large but unspecified number, quantity, or amount ▷ *determiner* **2 a** amounting to a squillion **b** (*as pronoun*): *there were squillions of them everywhere*

squinch (skwɪntʃ) *n* a small arch, corbelling, etc, across an internal corner of a tower, used to support a superstructure such as a spire. Also called: **squinch arch** [c15 from obsolete *scunch*, from Middle English *sconcheon*, from Old French *escoinson*, from *es-* EX-¹ + *coin* corner]

squint (skwɪnt) *vb* **1** (*usually intr*) to cross or partly close (the eyes) **2** (*intr*) to have a squint **3** (*intr*) to look or glance sideways or askance ▷ *n* **4** the nontechnical name for **strabismus 5** the act or an instance of squinting; glimpse **6** Also called: **hagioscope** a narrow oblique opening in a wall or pillar of a church to permit a view of the main altar from a side aisle or transept **7** *informal* a quick look; glance ▷ *adj* **8** having a squint **9** *informal* crooked; askew [c14 short for ASQUINT] > **'squinter** *n* > **'squinty** *adj*

squint-eyed *or* **squinty-eyed** *adj* **1** having a squint **2** looking sidelong

squire (skwaɪə) *n* **1** a country gentleman in England, esp the main landowner in a rural community **2** *feudal history* a young man of noble birth, who attended upon a knight **3** *rare* a man who courts or escorts a woman **4** *informal, chiefly Brit* a term of address used by one man to another, esp, unless ironic, to a member of a higher social class **5** *Austral* an immature snapper (see **snapper** (sense 2)) ▷ *vb* **6** (*tr*) (of a man) to escort (a woman) [c13 from Old French *esquier*; see ESQUIRE]

squirearchy *or* **squirarchy** ('skwaɪəˌrɑːkɪ) *n, pl* -chies **1** government by squires **2** squires collectively, esp as a political or social force [c19 from SQUIRE + -ARCHY, on the model of HIERARCHY, MONARCHY, etc] > **squire'archal, squire'archical** *or* **squir'archal, squir'archical** *adj*

squireen (skwaɪ'riːn) *or* **squireling** ('skwaɪəlɪŋ) *n rare* a petty squire [c19 from SQUIRE + -een, Anglo-Irish diminutive suffix, from Irish Gaelic *-ín*]

squirm (skwɜːm) *vb* (*intr*) **1** to move with a wriggling motion; writhe **2** to feel deep mental discomfort, guilt, embarrassment, etc ▷ *n* **3** a squirming movement [c17 of imitative origin (perhaps influenced by WORM)] > **'squirmer** *n* > **'squirming** *adj* > **'squirmingly** *adv*

squirmy ('skwɜːmɪ) *adj* **1** moving with a wriggling motion **2** making one squirm

squirrel ('skwɪrəl; *US* 'skwɜːrəl, 'skwʌr-) *n, pl* -rels

or -rel **1** any arboreal sciurine rodent of the genus *Sciurus*, such as *S. vulgaris* (**red squirrel**) *or S. carolinensis* (**grey squirrel**), having a bushy tail and feeding on nuts, seeds, etc. Related adj: **sciurine 2** any other rodent of the family *Sciuridae*, such as a ground squirrel or a marmot **3** the fur of such an animal **4** *informal* a person who hoards things ▷ *vb* -rels, -relling, -relled *or esp US* -rels, -reling, -reled **5** (*tr*; usually foll by *away*) *informal* to store for future use; hoard [c14 from Old French *esquireul*, from Late Latin *sciūrus*, from Greek *skiouros*, from *skia* shadow + *oura* tail] > **'squirrel-,like** *adj*

squirrel cage *n* **1** a cage consisting of a cylindrical framework that is made to rotate by a small animal running inside the framework **2** a repetitive purposeless task, way of life, etc **3** Also called: **squirrel-cage motor** *electrical engineering* the rotor of an induction motor with a cylindrical winding having copper bars around the periphery parallel to the axis **4** an electric fan with many long narrow blades arranged in parallel so as to form a cylinder about an axis around which they spin

squirrel corn *n* a North American plant, *Dicentra canadensis*, having yellow flowers and tubers resembling grains of corn: family *Fumariaceae*. Also called: **colicweed**

squirrelfish ('skwɪrəlˌfɪʃ) *n, pl* -fish *or* -fishes any tropical marine brightly coloured teleost fish of the family *Holocentridae* [c18 so called because it can make a squirrel-like noise]

squirrel monkey *n* **1** a small New World monkey, *Saimiri sciureus*, of N South American forests, having a yellowish-green coat and orange feet and limbs **2** **red-backed squirrel monkey** a related species, *Saimiri oerstedi*, of Central America, having a reddish coat and dark brown limbs [c18 so called because it is small and tree-dwelling]

squirrel-tail grass *n* an annual grass, *Hordeum marinum*, of salt marsh margins of Europe, having bushy awns

squirt (skwɜːt) *vb* **1** to force (a liquid) or (of a liquid) to be forced out of a narrow opening **2** (*tr*) to cover or spatter with liquid so ejected ▷ *n* **3** a jet or amount of liquid so ejected **4** the act or an instance of squirting **5** an instrument used for squirting **6** *informal* **a** a person regarded as insignificant or contemptible **b** a short person [c15 of imitative origin] > **'squirter** *n*

squirt gun *n US and Canadian* another name for **water pistol**

squirting cucumber *n* a hairy cucurbitaceous plant, *Ecballium elaterium*, of the Mediterranean region, having a fruit that discharges its seeds explosively when ripe

squish (skwɪʃ) *vb* **1** (*tr*) to crush, esp so as to make a soft splashing noise **2** (*intr*) (of mud, etc) to make a splashing noise ▷ *n* **3** a soft squashing sound [c17 of imitative origin]

squishy ('skwɪʃɪ) *adj* -ier, -iest soft and yielding to the touch

squit (skwɪt) *n Brit slang* **1** an insignificant person **2** nonsense; rubbish [c19 dialectal variant of SQUIRT]

squiz (skwɪz) *n, pl* squizzes *Austral and NZ slang* a look or glance, esp an inquisitive one [c20 perhaps a blend of SQUINT and QUIZ]

sr¹ *symbol for* steradian

sr² *the internet domain name for* Suriname

Sr *abbreviation for* **1** (after a name) senior **2** Señor **3** Sir **4** Sister (religious) **5** *the chemical symbol for* strontium

Sra *abbreviation for* Señora

SRA (in Britain) *abbreviation for* Strategic Rail Authority

Srbija ('sɜrbija) *n* a transliteration of the Serbian name for **Serbia**

S-R connection *n psychol* stimulus-response connection; the basic unit of learning according to behaviourist learning theory. See also **reflex arc**

Sri (ʃriː) *n Hinduism* **1** the consort of Vishnu **2** a title of honour used when addressing a

distinguished Hindu [literally: majesty, holiness]

Sri Lanka (ˌsriː 'læŋkə) *n* a republic in S Asia, occupying the island of Ceylon: settled by the Sinhalese from S India in about 550 BC; became a British colony 1802; gained independence in 1948, becoming a republic within the Commonwealth in 1972. Exports include tea, cocoa, cinnamon, and copra. Official languages: Sinhalese and Tamil; English is also widely spoken. Religion: Hinayana Buddhist majority. Currency: Sri Lanka rupee. Capital: Colombo (administrative), Sri Jayewardenepura Kotte (legislative). Parts of the coast suffered badly in the Indian Ocean tsunami of December 2004. Pop: 19 218 000 (2004 est). Area: 65 610 sq km (25 332 sq miles). Official name (since 1978): Democratic Socialist Republic of Sri Lanka Former name (until 1972): **Ceylon**

Sri Lankan (ˌsriː 'læŋkən) *adj* **1** of or relating to Sri Lanka or its inhabitants ▷ *n* **2** a native or inhabitant of Sri Lanka

Srinagar (sriː'nʌgə) *n* a city in N India, the summer capital of the state of Jammu and Kashmir, at an altitude of 1600 m (5250 ft) on the Jhelum River: seat of the University of Jammu and Kashmir (1948). Pop: 894 940 (2001)

SRN (formerly, in Britain) *abbreviation for* State Registered Nurse

SRO *abbreviation for* **1** standing room only **2** *Brit* Statutory Rules and Orders **3** self-regulatory organization

Srta *abbreviation for* Señorita

SS *abbreviation for* **1** a paramilitary organization within the Nazi party that provided Hitler's bodyguard, security forces including the Gestapo, concentration camp guards, and a corp of combat troops (the Waffen-SS) in World War II [German *Schutzstaffel* protection squad] **2** steamship **3** Sunday school

SS. *abbreviation for* Saints

SSB *abbreviation for* single sideband (transmission)

SSC *abbreviation for* **1** (in India) Secondary School Certificate **2** (in Scotland) solicitor to the Supreme Court

SSD (in Britain) *abbreviation for* Social Services Department

SSE *symbol for* south-southeast

SSHA *abbreviation for* Scottish Special Housing Association

SSL *abbreviation for* Secure Sockets Layer: a way of enabling the secure encrypted transmission of sensitive data via the internet

SSM *abbreviation for* surface-to-surface missile

SSN *abbreviation for* severely subnormal; used of a person of very limited intelligence who needs special schooling

SSP (in Britain) *abbreviation for* statutory sick pay

ssp. *pl* sspp. *biology abbreviation for* subspecies

SSR *abbreviation for* (formerly) Soviet Socialist Republic

SSRI *abbreviation for* selective serotonin reuptake inhibitor; any of a class of drugs, including fluvoxamine, paroxetine, fluoxetine (Prozac), and Lustral, that increase concentrations of serotonin in the brain: used in the treatment of depression

SSSI (in Britain) *abbreviation for* site of special scientific interest: an area identified by the Nature Conservancy Council or its successors as having flora, fauna, or geological features of special interest

SST *abbreviation for* supersonic transport

SSTA *abbreviation for* Scottish Secondary Teachers' Association

SSW *symbol for* south-southwest

st¹ *abbreviation for* short ton

st² *the internet domain name for* São Tomé and Principe

St *abbreviation for* **1** Saint (all entries that are usually preceded by *St* are in this dictionary listed alphabetically under **Saint**) **2** statute **3** strait **4** street

st. *abbreviation for* **1** stanza **2** statute **3** *cricket* stumped by

-st *suffix* a variant of **-est**[2]

Sta (in the names of places or churches) *abbreviation for* Saint (female) [Italian *Santa*]

stab (stæb) *vb* **stabs, stabbing, stabbed** **1** *(tr)* to pierce or injure with a sharp pointed instrument **2** *(tr)* (of a sharp pointed instrument) to pierce or wound: *the knife stabbed her hand* **3** (when *intr*, often foll by *at*) to make a thrust (at); jab: *he stabbed at the doorway* **4** *(tr)* to inflict with a sharp pain **5** **stab in the back** **a** *(verb)* to do damage to the reputation of (a person, esp a friend) in a surreptitious way **b** *(noun)* a treacherous action or remark that causes the downfall of or injury to a person ▷ *n* **6** the act or an instance of stabbing **7** an injury or rift made by stabbing **8** a sudden sensation, esp an unpleasant one: *a stab of pity* **9** *informal* an attempt (esp in the phrase **make a stab at**) [C14 from *stabbe* stab wound; probably related to Middle English *stob* stick] > **'stabber** *n*

Stabat Mater ('stɑːbæt 'mɑːtə) *n* **1** *RC Church* a Latin hymn, probably of the 13th century, commemorating the sorrows of the Virgin Mary at the crucifixion and used in the Mass and various other services **2** a musical setting of this hymn [from the opening words, literally: the mother was standing]

stabile ('steɪbaɪl) *n* **1** *arts* a stationary abstract construction, usually of wire, metal, wood, etc. Compare **mobile** (sense 6a) ▷ *adj* **2** fixed; stable **3** resistant to chemical change [C18 from Latin *stabilis*]

stability (stə'bɪlɪtɪ) *n, pl* **-ties** **1** the quality of being stable **2** the ability of an aircraft to resume its original flight path after inadvertent displacement **3** *meteorol* **a** the condition of an air or water mass characterized by no upward movement **b** the degree of susceptibility of an air mass to disturbance by convection currents **4** *ecology* the ability of an ecosystem to resist change **5** *electrical engineering* the ability of an electrical circuit to cope with changes in the operational conditions **6** a vow taken by every Benedictine monk attaching him perpetually to the monastery where he is professed

stability pact *or* **stability and growth pact** *n* an agreement between the member states of the EU which have joined the single currency, the aim of which is to secure the currency's stability by imposing fines on member states whose budget deficits exceed 3 per cent of their gross domestic product

stabilize *or* **stabilise** ('steɪbɪˌlaɪz) *vb* **1** to make or become stable or more stable **2** to keep or be kept stable **3** to put or keep (an aircraft, vessel, etc) in equilibrium by one or more special devices, or (of an aircraft, vessel, etc) to become stable > **ˌstabiliˈzation** *or* **ˌstabiliˈsation** *n*

stabilizer *or* **stabiliser** ('steɪbɪˌlaɪzə) *n* **1** any device for stabilizing an aircraft. See also **horizontal stabilizer, vertical stabilizer** **2** a substance added to something to maintain it in a stable or unchanging state, such as an additive to food to preserve its texture during distribution and storage **3** *nautical* **a** a system of one or more pairs of fins projecting from the hull of a ship and controllable to counteract roll **b** See **gyrostabilizer** **4** either of a pair of brackets supporting a small wheel that can be fitted to the back wheel of a bicycle to help an inexperienced cyclist to maintain balance **5** an electronic device for producing a direct current supply of constant voltage **6** *economics* a measure, such as progressive taxation, interest-rate control, or unemployment benefit, used to restrict swings in prices, employment, production, etc, in a free economy **7** a person or thing that stabilizes

stab kick *n Australian rules football* a rapid kick of the ball from one player to another member of his team. Also called: **stab pass**

stable[1] ('steɪbəl) *n* **1** a building, usually consisting of stalls, for the lodging of horses or other livestock **2** the animals lodged in such a building, collectively **3** **a** the racehorses belonging to a particular establishment or owner **b** the establishment itself **c** *(as modifier)*: *stable companion* **4** *informal* a source of training, such as a school, theatre, etc: *the two athletes were out of the same stable* **5** a number of people considered as a source of a particular talent: *a stable of writers* **6** *(modifier)* of, relating to, or suitable for a stable: *stable manners* ▷ *vb* **7** to put, keep, or be kept in a stable [C13 from Old French *estable* cowshed, from Latin *stabulum* shed, from *stāre* to stand]

stable[2] ('steɪbəl) *adj* **1** steady in position or balance; firm **2** lasting or permanent: *a stable relationship* **3** steadfast or firm of purpose **4** (of an elementary particle, atomic nucleus, etc) not undergoing decay; not radioactive: *a stable nuclide* **5** (of a chemical compound) not readily partaking in a chemical change **6** (of electronic equipment) with no tendency to self-oscillation [C13 from Old French *estable*, from Latin *stabilis* steady, from *stāre* to stand] > **'stableness** *n* > **'stably** *adv*

stableboy ('steɪbəlˌbɔɪ) *or* **stableman** ('steɪbəlˌmæn, -mən) *n, pl* **-boys** *or* **-men** a boy or man who works in a stable

stable door *n* a door with an upper and lower leaf that may be opened separately. US and Canadian equivalent: **Dutch door**

stable fly *n* a blood-sucking muscid fly, *Stomoxys calcitrans*, that attacks man and domestic animals

Stableford ('steɪbəlfəd) *n golf* **a** a scoring system in which points are awarded according to the number of strokes taken at each hole, whereby a hole completed in one stroke over par counts as one point, a hole completed in level par counts as two points, etc **b** *(as modifier)*: *a Stableford competition*. Compare **match play, stroke play** [C20 named after its inventor, Dr Frank *Stableford* (1870–1959), English amateur golfer]

stable lad *n* a person who looks after the horses in a racing stable

stabling ('steɪblɪŋ) *n* stable buildings or accommodation

stablish ('stæblɪʃ) *vb* an archaic variant of **establish**

Stabroek (*Dutch* 'staːbruːk) *n* the former name (until 1812) of **Georgetown** (sense 1)

stacc. *music abbreviation for* staccato

staccato (stə'kɑːtəʊ) *adj* **1** *music* (of notes) short, clipped, and separate **2** characterized by short abrupt sounds, as in speech: *a staccato command* ▷ *adv* **3** (esp used as a musical direction) in a staccato manner [C18 from Italian, from *staccare* to detach, shortened from *distaccare*]

stachys ('steɪkɪs) *n* any plant of the genus *Stachys*, esp *S. lanata* (lamb's ears) and *S. officinalis* (betony) [New Latin, from Greek *stachys* ear of corn, used as a plant name]

stack (stæk) *n* **1** an ordered pile or heap **2** a large orderly pile of hay, straw, etc, for storage in the open air **3** *(often plural) library science* compactly spaced bookshelves, used to house collections of books in an area usually prohibited to library users **4** a number of aircraft circling an airport at different altitudes, awaiting their signal to land **5** a large amount: *a stack of work* **6** *military* a pile of rifles or muskets in the shape of a cone **7** *Brit* a measure of coal or wood equal to 108 cubic feet **8** See **chimney stack, smokestack** **9** a vertical pipe, such as the funnel of a ship or the soil pipe attached to the side of a building **10** a high column of rock, esp one isolated from the mainland by the erosive action of the sea **11** an area in a computer memory for temporary storage ▷ *vb (tr)* **12** to place in a stack; pile: *to stack bricks on a lorry* **13** to load or fill up with piles of something: *to stack a lorry with bricks* **14** to control (a number of aircraft waiting to land at an airport) so that each flies at a different altitude **15** **stack the cards** to prearrange the order of a pack of cards secretly so that the deal will benefit someone [C13 from Old Norse *stakkr* haystack, of Germanic origin; related to Russian *stog*] > **'stackable** *adj* > **'stacker** *n*

stacked (stækt) *adj slang* a variant of **well-stacked**

stacking ('stækɪŋ) *n* the arrangement of aircraft traffic in busy flight lanes, esp while waiting to land at an airport, with a minimum vertical separation for safety of 1000 feet below 29 000 feet and 2000 feet above 29 000 feet

stacking truck *n* another name for **pallet truck**

stacte ('stæktiː) *n Old Testament* one of several sweet-smelling spices used in incense (Exodus 30:34) [C14 via Latin from Greek *staktē* oil of myrrh, from *staktos* distilling a drop at a time, from *stazein* to flow, drip]

staddle ('stædəl) *n* **1** a support or prop, esp a low flat-topped stone structure for supporting hay or corn stacks about two feet above ground level **2** a supporting frame for such a stack **3** the lower part of a hay or corn stack [Old English *stathol* base; related to Old Norse *stothull* cow pen, Old High German *stadal* barn]

staddlestone ('stædəlˌstəʊn) *n* (formerly) one of several supports for a hayrick, consisting of a truncated conical stone surmounted by a flat circular stone

stadholder *or* **stadtholder** ('stædˌhəʊldə) *n* **1** the chief magistrate of the former Dutch republic or of any of its provinces (from about 1580 to 1802) **2** a viceroy or governor of a province [C16 partial translation of Dutch *stad houder*, from *stad* city (see STEAD) + *houder* holder] > **'stadˌholderˌate, 'stadˌholdership, 'stadtˌholderˌate** *or* **'stadtˌholdership** *n*

stadia[1] ('steɪdɪə) *n* **1** **a** tacheometry that makes use of a telescopic surveying instrument and a graduated staff calibrated to correspond with the distance from the observer **b** *(as modifier)*: *stadia surveying* **2** the two parallel cross hairs or **stadia hairs** in the eyepiece of the instrument used **3** the staff used [C19 probably from STADIA[2]]

stadia[2] ('steɪdɪə) *n* a plural of **stadium**

stadiometer (ˌsteɪdɪ'ɒmɪtə) *n* an instrument that measures the length of curves, dashes, etc, by running a toothed wheel along them [C19 from *stadio-*, from STADIUM + -METER]

stadium ('steɪdɪəm) *n, pl* **-diums** *or* **-dia** (-dɪə) **1** a sports arena with tiered seats for spectators **2** (in ancient Greece) a course for races, usually located between two hills providing natural slopes for tiers of seats **3** an ancient Greek measure of length equivalent to about 607 feet or 184 metres **4** (in many arthropods) the interval between two consecutive moultings **5** *obsolete* a particular period or stage in the development of a disease [C16 via Latin from Greek *stadion*, changed from *spadion* a racecourse, from *spān* to pull; also influenced by Greek *stadios* steady]

staff[1] (stɑːf) *n, pl for senses 1, 3, 4* **staffs** *or for senses 5–9* **staffs** *or* **staves** (steɪvz) **1** a group of people employed by a company, individual, etc, for executive, clerical, sales work, etc **2** *(modifier)* attached to or provided for the staff of an establishment: *a staff doctor* **3** the body of teachers or lecturers of an educational institution, as distinct from the students **4** the officers appointed to assist a commander, service, or central headquarters organization in establishing policy, plans, etc **5** a stick with some special use, such as a walking stick or an emblem of authority **6** something that sustains or supports: *bread is the staff of life* **7** a pole on which a flag is hung **8** *chiefly Brit* a graduated rod used in surveying, esp for sighting to with a levelling instrument. Usual US name: **rod** **9** Also called: **stave** *music* **a** the system of horizontal lines grouped into sets of five (four in the case of plainsong) upon which music is written. The spaces between them are also used, being employed in conjunction with a clef in order to give a graphic indication of pitch **b** any set of five lines in this system together with its clef: *the treble staff* ▷ *vb* **10** *(tr)* to provide with a staff [Old English *stæf*; related to Old Frisian *stef*, Old Saxon *staf*, German *Stab*, Old Norse *stafr*, Gothic *Stafs*; see STAVE]

staff[2] (stɑːf) *n* *US* a mixture of plaster and hair used to cover the external surface of temporary structures and for decoration [c19 of unknown origin]

Staffa ('stæfə) *n* an island in W Scotland, in the Inner Hebrides west of Mull: site of Fingal's Cave

staff association *n* an association of employees that performs some of the functions of a trade union, such as representing its members in discussions with the management, and may also have other social and professional purposes

staff college *n* a training centre for executive military personnel

staff corporal *n* a noncommissioned rank in the British Army above that of staff sergeant and below that of warrant officer

staffer ('stɑːfə) *n* *informal* a member of staff, esp, in journalism, of editorial staff

staffman ('stɑːfˌmæn) *n, pl* -men *Brit* a person who holds the levelling staff when a survey is being made

staff nurse *n* (formerly, in Britain) a qualified nurse ranking immediately below a sister

staff of Aesculapius *n* an emblem consisting of a staff with a serpent entwined around it, used by the Royal Medical Corps and the American Medical Association. Compare **caduceus** (sense 2)

staff officer *n* a commissioned officer serving on the staff of a commander, service, or central headquarters

Stafford ('stæfəd) *n* a market town in central England, administrative centre of Staffordshire. Pop: 63 681 (2001)

Staffordshire ('stæfədˌʃɪə, -ʃə) *n* a county of central England: lowlands in the east and south rise to the Pennine uplands in the north; important in the history of industry, coal and iron having been worked at least as early as the 13th century. In 1974 the industrial area in the S passed to the new county of West Midlands; Stoke-on-Trent became an independent unitary authority in 1997. Administrative centre: Stafford. Pop (excluding Stoke-on-Trent): 811 000 (2003 est.). Area (excluding Stoke-on-Trent): 2624 sq km (1013 sq miles)

Staffordshire bull terrier *n* a breed of smooth-coated terrier with a stocky frame and generally a pied or brindled coat. See also **bull terrier**

Staffs (stæfs) *abbreviation for* Staffordshire

staff sergeant *n* *military* **1** *Brit* a noncommissioned officer holding a rank between sergeant and warrant officer and employed on administrative duties **2** *US* **a** (in the Army) a noncommissioned officer who ranks above sergeant and below sergeant first class **b** (in the Air Force) a noncommissioned officer who ranks above airman first class and below technical sergeant **c** (in the Marine Corps) a noncommissioned officer who ranks above sergeant and below gunnery sergeant

stag (stæg) *n* **1** the adult male of a deer, esp a red deer **2** a man unaccompanied by a woman at a social gathering **3** *stock exchange, Brit* **a** a speculator who applies for shares in a new issue in anticipation of a rise in price when trading commences in order to make a quick profit on resale **b** (*as modifier*): *stag operations* **4** (*modifier*) (of a social gathering) attended by men only **5** (*modifier*) pornographic in content: *a stag show* ▷ *adv* **6** without a female escort ▷ *vb* (*tr*) **7** *stock exchange* to apply for (shares in a new issue) with the intention of selling them for a quick profit when trading commences [Old English *stagga* (unattested); related to Old Norse *steggr* male bird]

stag beetle *n* any lamellicorn beetle of the family *Lucanidae*, the males of which have large branched mandibles

stage (steɪdʒ) *n* **1** a distinct step or period of development, growth, or progress: *a child at the toddling stage* **2** a raised area or platform **3** the platform in a theatre where actors perform **4** **the** the theatre as a profession **5** any scene regarded as a setting for an event or action **6** a portion of a journey or a stopping place after such a portion **7** short for **stagecoach** **8** *Brit* a division of a bus route for which there is a fixed fare **9** one of the separate propulsion units of a rocket that can be jettisoned when it has burnt out. See also **multistage** (sense 1) **10** any of the various distinct periods of growth or development in the life of an organism, esp an insect: *a larval stage; pupal stage* **11** the organism itself at such a period of growth **12** a small stratigraphical unit; a subdivision of a rock series or system **13** the platform on a microscope on which the specimen is mounted for examination **14** *electronics* a part of a complex circuit, esp one of a number of transistors with the associated elements required to amplify a signal in an amplifier **15** a university subject studied for one academic year: *Stage II French* **16** **by** or **in easy stages** not hurriedly: *he learned French by easy stages* ▷ *vb* **17** (*tr*) to perform (a play), esp on a stage: *we are going to stage "Hamlet"* **18** (*tr*) to set the action of (a play) in a particular time or place **19** (*tr*) to plan, organize, and carry out (an event) **20** (*intr*) *obsolete* to travel by stagecoach [c13 from Old French *estage* position, from Vulgar Latin *staticum* (unattested), from Latin *stāre* to stand]

stagecoach ('steɪdʒˌkəʊtʃ) *n* a large four-wheeled horse-drawn vehicle formerly used to carry passengers, mail, etc, on a regular route between towns and cities

stagecraft ('steɪdʒˌkrɑːft) *n* skill in or the art of writing or staging plays

stage direction *n* *theatre* an instruction to an actor or director, written into the script of a play

stage-dive *vb* -dives, -diving, -dived *or US* -dove (*intr*) to jump off the stage at a concert onto the crowd below > 'stage-ˌdiver *n*

stage door *n* a door at a theatre leading backstage

stage effect *n* a special effect created on the stage by lighting, sound, etc

stage fright *n* nervousness or panic that may beset a person about to appear in front of an audience

stagehand ('steɪdʒˌhænd) *n* a person who sets the stage, moves props, etc, in a theatrical production

stage left *n* the part of the stage to the left of a performer facing the audience

stage-manage *vb* **1** to work as stage manager for (a play, etc) **2** (*tr*) to arrange, present, or supervise from behind the scenes: *to stage-manage a campaign*

stage manager *n* a person who supervises the stage arrangements of a theatrical production

stager ('steɪdʒə) *n* **1** a person of experience; veteran (esp in the phrase **old stager**) **2** an archaic word for **actor**

stage right *n* the part of the stage to the right of a performer facing the audience

stage-struck *adj* infatuated with the glamour of theatrical life, esp with the desire to act

stage whisper *n* **1** a loud whisper from one actor to another onstage intended to be heard by the audience **2** any loud whisper that is intended to be overheard

stagey ('steɪdʒɪ) *adj* stagier, stagiest a variant spelling (in the US) of **stagy**. > 'stagily *adv* > 'staginess *n*

stagflation (stægˈfleɪʃən) *n* a situation in which inflation is combined with stagnant or falling output and employment [c20 blend of STAGNATION + INFLATION]

staggard ('stægəd) *n* a male red deer in the fourth year of life [c15 see STAG, -ARD]

stagger ('stægə) *vb* **1** (*usually intr*) to walk or cause to walk unsteadily as if about to fall **2** (*tr*) to astound or overwhelm, as with shock: *I am staggered by his ruthlessness* **3** (*tr*) to place or arrange in alternating or overlapping positions or time periods to prevent confusion or congestion: *a staggered junction; to stagger holidays* **4** (*intr*) to falter or hesitate: *his courage staggered in the face of the battle* **5** (*tr*) to set (the wings of a biplane) so that the leading edge of one extends beyond that of the other ▷ *n* **6** the act or an instance of staggering **7** a staggered arrangement on a biplane, etc ▷ See also **staggers** [c13 dialect *stacker*, from Old Norse *staka* to push] > 'staggerer *n*

staggerbush ('stægəˌbʊʃ) *n* an ericaceous deciduous shrub, *Lyonia mariana*, of E North America, having white or pinkish flowers: it is poisonous to livestock [c19 so named because it was believed to cause STAGGERS in sheep]

staggered directorships *pl n* *business* a defence against unwelcome takeover bids in which a company resolves that its directors should serve staggered terms of office and that no director can be removed from office without just cause, thus preventing a bidder from controlling the board for some years

staggered hours *pl n* a system of working in which the employees of an organization do not all arrive and leave at the same time, but have large periods of overlap

staggering ('stægərɪŋ) *adj* astounding or overwhelming; shocking: *a staggering increase in demand* > 'staggeringly *adv*

staggers ('stægəz) *n* (*functioning as singular or plural*) **1** a form of vertigo associated with decompression sickness **2** Also called: **blind staggers** a disease of horses and some other domestic animals characterized by a swaying unsteady gait, caused by infection, toxins, or lesions of the central nervous system

staghorn fern ('stægˌhɔːn) *n* any of various tropical and subtropical ferns of the genus *Platycerium* with fronds resembling antlers

staghound ('stægˌhaʊnd) *n* a breed of hound similar in appearance to the foxhound but larger. It is bred for stag hunting

staging ('steɪdʒɪŋ) *n* any temporary structure used in the process of building, esp the horizontal platforms supported by scaffolding [c14 from STAGE + -ING[1]]

staging area *n* a general locality used as a checkpoint or regrouping area for military formations in transit

staging post *n* a place where a journey is usually broken, esp a stopover on a flight

Stagira (stəˈdʒaɪrə) *n* an ancient city on the coast of Chalcidice in Macedonia: the birthplace of Aristotle

Stagirite ('stædʒɪˌraɪt) *n* **1** an inhabitant or native of Stagira **2** an epithet of Aristotle

stagnant ('stægnənt) *adj* **1** (of water, etc) standing still; without flow or current **2** brackish and foul from standing still **3** stale, sluggish, or dull from inaction **4** not growing or developing; static [c17 from Latin *stagnāns*, from *stagnāre* to be stagnant, from *stagnum* a pool] > 'stagnancy *or* 'stagnance *n* > 'stagnantly *adv*

stagnate (stægˈneɪt, 'stægˌneɪt) *vb* (*intr*) to be or to become stagnant > stagˈnation *n*

stag night *or* **party** *n* a party for men only, esp one held for a man before he is married. Compare **hen night, hen party**

stag's horn *or* **staghorn** ('stægˌhɔːn) *n* **1** the antlers of a stag used as a material for carved implements **2** a creeping variety of club moss, *Lycopodium clavatum*, growing on moors and mountains, having silvery hair points on its leaves

stagy *or US* **stagey** ('steɪdʒɪ) *adj* stagier, stagiest excessively theatrical or dramatic > 'stagily *adv* > 'staginess *n*

staid (steɪd) *adj* **1** of a settled, sedate, and steady character **2** *now rare* permanent [c16 obsolete past participle of STAY[1]] > 'staidly *adv* > 'staidness *n*

stain (steɪn) *vb* (*mainly tr*) **1** to mark or discolour with patches of something that dirties: *the dress was stained with coffee* **2** to dye with a penetrating dyestuff or pigment **3** to bring disgrace or shame on: *to stain someone's honour* **4** to colour (specimens) for microscopic study by treatment with a dye or

S

similar reagent **5** (*intr*) to produce indelible marks or discoloration: *does ink stain?* ▷ *n* **6** a spot, mark, or discoloration **7** a moral taint; blemish or slur **8** a dye or similar reagent, used to colour specimens for microscopic study **9** a solution or liquid used to penetrate the surface of a material, esp wood, and impart a rich colour without covering up the surface or grain **10** any dye that is made into a solution and used to colour textiles and hides [C14 *steynen* (vb), shortened from *disteynen* to remove colour from, from Old French *desteindre* to discolour, from *des-* DIS-[1] + *teindre*, from Latin *tingere* to TINGE] > **'stainable** *adj* > **,staina'bility** *n* > **'stainer** *n*

stained glass *n* **a** glass that has been coloured in any of various ways, as by fusing with a film of metallic oxide or burning pigment into the surface, used esp for church windows **b** (*as modifier*): *a stained-glass window*

stained glass ceiling *n* a situation in a church organization in which promotion for a female member of the clergy appears to be possible, but discrimination prevents it

Staines (steɪnz) *n* a town in SE England, in N Surrey on the River Thames. Pop: 50 538 (2001)

stainless ('steɪnlɪs) *adj* **1** resistant to discoloration, esp discoloration resulting from corrosion; rust-resistant: *stainless steel* **2** having no blemish: *a stainless reputation* ▷ *n* **3** stainless steel > **'stainlessly** *adv*

stainless steel *n* **a** a type of steel resistant to corrosion as a result of the presence of large amounts of chromium (12–15 per cent). The carbon content depends on the application, being 0.2–0.4 per cent for steel used in cutlery, etc, and about 1 per cent for use in scalpels and razor blades **b** (*as modifier*): *stainless-steel cutlery*

stair (stɛə) *n* **1** one of a flight of stairs **2** a series of steps: *a narrow stair* ▷ See also **stairs** [Old English *stæger*; related to *stīg* narrow path, *stīgan* to ascend, descend, Old Norse *steigurligr* upright, Middle Dutch *steiger* ladder]

staircase ('stɛə,keɪs) *n* a flight of stairs, its supporting framework, and, usually, a handrail or banisters

stairhead ('stɛə,hɛd) *n* the top of a flight of stairs

stairlift ('stɛə,lɪft) *n* a mechanical device with a seat for carrying an elderly or infirm person up a flight of stairs

stair rod *n* any of a series of rods placed in the angles between the steps of a carpeted staircase, used to hold the carpet in position

stairs (stɛəz) *pl n* **1** a flight of steps leading from one storey or level to another, esp indoors **2** **below stairs** *Brit* in the servants' quarters; in domestic service

stairway ('stɛə,weɪ) *n* a means of access consisting of stairs; staircase or flight of steps

stairwell ('stɛə,wɛl) *n* a vertical shaft or opening that contains a staircase

stake[1] (steɪk) *n* **1** a stick or metal bar driven into the ground as a marker, part of a fence, support for a plant, etc **2** one of a number of vertical posts that fit into sockets around a flat truck or railway wagon to hold the load in place **3** a method or the practice of executing a person by binding him to a stake in the centre of a pile of wood that is then set on fire **4** *Mormon Church* an administrative district consisting of a group of wards under the jurisdiction of a president **5** **pull up stakes** to leave one's home or temporary resting place and move on ▷ *vb* (*tr*) **6** to tie, fasten, or tether with or to a stake **7** (often foll by *out* or *off*) to fence or surround with stakes **8** (often foll by *out*) to lay (a claim) to land, rights, etc **9** to support with a stake [Old English *staca* pin; related to Old Frisian *staka*, Old High German *stehho*, Old Norse *stjaki*; see STICK[1]]

stake[2] (steɪk) *n* **1** the money or valuables that a player must hazard in order to buy into a gambling game or make a bet **2** an interest, often financial, held in something: *a stake in the company's future* **3** (*often plural*) the money that a player has available for gambling **4** (*often plural*) a prize in a race, etc, esp one made up of contributions from contestants or owners **5** (*plural*) *horse racing* a race in which all owners of competing horses contribute to the prize money **6** *US and Canadian informal* short for **grubstake** (sense 1) **7** **at stake** at risk: *two lives are at stake* **8** **raise the stakes** **a** to increase the amount of money or valuables hazarded in a gambling game **b** to increase the costs, risks, or considerations involved in taking an action or reaching a conclusion: *the Libyan allegations raised the stakes in the propaganda war between Libya and the United States* ▷ *vb* (*tr*) **9** to hazard (money, etc) on a result **10** to invest in or support by supplying with money, etc: *to stake a business enterprise* [C16 of uncertain origin]

Staked Plain *n* another name for the **Llano Estacado**

stakeholder ('steɪk,həʊldə) *n* **1** a person or group owning a significant percentage of a company's shares **2** a person or group not owning shares in an enterprise but affected by or having an interest in its operations, such as the employees, customers, local community, etc ▷ *adj* **3** of or relating to policies intended to allow people to participate in and benefit from decisions made by enterprises in which they have a stake: *a stakeholder economy*

stakeholder pension *n* (in Britain) a flexible pension scheme with low charges, in which contributors can stop and restart payments and switch funds to another scheme without paying a penalty

stakeout ('steɪkaʊt) *slang, chiefly US and Canadian* ▷ *n* **1** a police surveillance of an area, house, or criminal suspect **2** an area or house kept under such surveillance ▷ *vb* **stake out** **3** (*tr, adverb*) to keep under surveillance

Stakhanovism (stæ'kænə,vɪzəm) *n* (in the former Soviet Union) a system designed to raise production by offering incentives to efficient workers [C20 named after A. G. *Stakhanov* (1906–77), Soviet coal miner, the worker first awarded benefits under the system in 1935] > **Sta'khanov,ite** *n*

stalactite ('stælək,taɪt) *n* a cylindrical mass of calcium carbonate hanging from the roof of a limestone cave: formed by precipitation from continually dripping water. Compare **stalagmite** [C17 from New Latin *stalactites*, from Greek *stalaktos* dripping, from *stalassein* to drip] > **stalactiform** (stə'læktɪ,fɔːm) *adj* > **stalactitic** (,stælək'tɪtɪk) *or* **,stalac'titical** *adj*

stalag ('stælæg; *German* 'ʃtalak) *n* a German prisoner-of-war camp in World War II, esp for noncommissioned officers and other ranks [short for *Stammlager* base camp, from *Stamm* base (related to STEM[1]) + *Lager* camp]

stalagmite ('stæləg,maɪt) *n* a cylindrical mass of calcium carbonate projecting upwards from the floor of a limestone cave: formed by precipitation from continually dripping water. Compare **stalactite** [C17 from New Latin *stalagmites*, from Greek *stalagmos* dripping; related to Greek *stalassein* to drip; compare STALACTITE] > **stalagmitic** (,stæləg'mɪtɪk) *or* **,stalag'mitical** *adj*

stale[1] (steɪl) *adj* **1** (esp of food) hard, musty, or dry from being kept too long **2** (of beer, etc) flat and tasteless from being kept open too long **3** (of air) stagnant; foul **4** uninteresting from overuse; hackneyed: *stale clichés* **5** no longer new: *stale news* **6** lacking in energy or ideas through overwork or lack of variety **7** *banking* (of a cheque) not negotiable by a bank as a result of not having been presented within six months of being written **8** *law* (of a claim, etc) having lost its effectiveness or force, as by failure to act or by the lapse of time ▷ *vb* **9** to make or become stale [C13 (originally applied to liquor in the sense: well matured): probably via Norman French from Old French *estale* (unattested) motionless, of Frankish origin; related to STALL[1], INSTALL] > **'stalely** *adv* > **'staleness** *n*

stale[2] (steɪl) *vb* **1** (*intr*) (of livestock) to urinate ▷ *n* **2** the urine of horses or cattle [C15 perhaps from Old French *estaler* to stand in one position; see STALL[1]; compare Middle Low German *stallen* to urinate, Greek *stalassein* to drip]

stale bull *n* *business* a dealer or speculator who holds unsold commodities after a rise in market prices but who cannot trade because there are no buyers at the new levels and because his financial commitments prevent him from making further purchases

stalemate ('steɪl,meɪt) *n* **1** a chess position in which any of a player's possible moves would place his king in check: in this position the game ends in a draw **2** a situation in which two opposing forces find that further action is impossible or futile; deadlock ▷ *vb* **3** (*tr*) to subject to a stalemate [C18 from obsolete *stale*, from Old French *estal* STALL[1] + MATE[2]]

Stalin ('stɑːlɪn) *n* **1** Also called: Stalino a former name (from after the Revolution until 1961) of **Donetsk** **2** the former name (1950–61) of **Braşov** **3** the former name (1949–56) of **Varna**

Stalinabad (*Russian* stəlina'bat) *n* the former name (1929–61) of **Dushanbe**

Stalingrad ('stɑːlɪn,græd; *Russian* stəlin'grat) *n* the former name (1925–61) of **Volgograd**

Stalinism ('stɑːlɪ,nɪzəm) *n* the theory and form of government associated with the Soviet leader Joseph Stalin (original name *Iosif Vissarionovich Dzhugashvili*; 1879–1953): a variant of Marxism-Leninism characterized by totalitarianism, rigid bureaucracy, and loyalty to the state > **'Stalinist** *n, adj*

Stalinogrod (*Polish* stali'nɔgrɔt) *n* the former name (1953–56) for **Katowice**

Stalin Peak *n* a former name for **Kommunizma Peak**

Stalinsk (*Russian* 'stalinsk) *n* the former name (1932–61) of **Novokuznetsk**

stalk[1] (stɔːk) *n* **1** the main stem of a herbaceous plant **2** any of various subsidiary plant stems, such as a leafstalk (petiole) or flower stalk (peduncle) **3** a slender supporting structure in animals such as crinoids and certain protozoans, coelenterates, and barnacles **4** any long slender supporting shaft or column [C14 probably a diminutive formed from Old English *stalu* upright piece of wood; related to Old Frisian *staal* handle] > **stalked** *adj* > **'stalkless** *adj* > **'stalk,like** *adj*

stalk[2] (stɔːk) *vb* **1** to follow or approach (game, prey, etc) stealthily and quietly **2** to pursue persistently and, sometimes, attack (a person with whom one is obsessed, often a celebrity) **3** to spread over (a place) in a menacing or grim manner: *fever stalked the camp* **4** (*intr*) to walk in a haughty, stiff, or threatening way: *he stalked out in disgust* **5** to search or draw (a piece of land) for prey ▷ *n* **6** the act of stalking **7** a stiff or threatening stride [Old English *bestealcian* to walk stealthily; related to Middle Low German *stolkeren*, Danish *stalke*] > **'stalker** *n*

stalking-horse *n* **1** a horse or an imitation one used by a hunter to hide behind while stalking his quarry **2** something serving as a means of concealing plans; pretext **3** a candidate put forward by one group to divide the opposition or mask the candidacy of another person for whom the stalking-horse would then withdraw

stalky ('stɔːkɪ) *adj* **stalkier, stalkiest** **1** like a stalk; slender and tall **2** having or abounding in stalks > **'stalkily** *adv* > **'stalkiness** *n*

stall[1] (stɔːl) *n* **1** **a** a compartment in a stable or shed for confining or feeding a single animal **b** another name for **stable[1]** (sense 1) **2** a small often temporary stand or booth for the display and sale of goods **3** (in a church) **a** one of a row of seats, usually divided from the others by armrests or a small screen, for the use of the choir or clergy **b** a pen **4** an instance of an engine stalling **5** a condition of an aircraft in flight in which a reduction in speed or an increase in the aircraft's angle of attack causes a sudden loss of lift resulting in a downward plunge **6** any small room or compartment **7** *Brit* **a** a seat in a theatre or cinema that resembles a chair, usually fixed to the floor **b** (*plural*) the area of seats on the ground floor of a theatre or cinema nearest to the stage or screen **8** a tubelike covering for a finger, as in a glove **9** (*plural*) short for **starting stalls** **10** **set out one's stall** *Brit* to make the necessary arrangements for the achievement of something and show that one is determined to achieve it ▷ *vb* **11** to cause (a motor vehicle or its engine) to stop, usually by incorrect use of the clutch or incorrect adjustment of the fuel mixture, or (of an engine or motor vehicle) to stop, usually for these reasons **12** to cause (an aircraft) to go into a stall or (of an aircraft) to go into a stall **13** to stick or cause to stick fast, as in mud or snow **14** (*tr*) to confine (an animal) in a stall [Old English *steall* a place for standing; related to Old High German *stall*, and *stellen* to set]

stall² (stɔːl) *vb* **1** to employ delaying tactics towards (someone); be evasive **2** (*intr*) *sport, chiefly US* to play or fight below one's best in order to deceive ▷ *n* **3** an evasive move; pretext [c16 from Anglo-French *estale* bird used as a decoy, influenced by STALL¹]

stall-feed *vb* **-feeds, -feeding, -fed** (*tr*) to keep and feed (an animal) in a stall, esp as an intensive method of fattening it for slaughter

stallholder (ˈstɔːlˌhəʊldə) *n* a person who sells goods at a market stall

stalling angle *n* the angle between the chord line of an aerofoil and the undisturbed relative airflow at which stalling occurs. Also called: **stall angle, critical angle**

stallion (ˈstæljən) *n* an uncastrated male horse, esp one used for breeding [c14 *staloun*, from Old French *estalon* of Germanic origin; related to Old High German *stal* STALL¹]

stalwart (ˈstɔːlwət) *adj* **1** strong and sturdy; robust **2** solid, dependable, and courageous: *stalwart citizens* **3** resolute and firm ▷ *n* **4** a stalwart person, esp a supporter [Old English *stǣlwirthe* serviceable, from *stǣl*, shortened from *stathol* support + *wierthe* WORTH¹] > **ˈstalwartly** *adv* > **ˈstalwartness** *n*

Stambul *or* **Stamboul** (stæmˈbuːl) *n* the old part of Istanbul, Turkey, south of the Golden Horn: the site of ancient Byzantium; sometimes used as a name for the whole city

stamen (ˈsteɪmɛn) *n, pl* **stamens** *or* **stamina** (ˈstæmɪnə) the male reproductive organ of a flower, consisting of a stalk (filament) bearing an anther in which pollen is produced [c17 from Latin: the warp in an upright loom, from *stāre* to stand] > **staminal** (ˈstæmɪnᵊl) *adj* > **staminiferous** (ˌstæmɪˈnɪfərəs) *adj*

Stamford (ˈstæmfəd) *n* a city in SW Connecticut, on Long Island Sound: major chemical research laboratories. Pop: 120 107 (2003 est)

Stamford Bridge *n* a village in N England, east of York: site of a battle (1066) in which King Harold of England defeated his brother Tostig and King Harald Hardrada of Norway, three weeks before the Battle of Hastings

stamina¹ (ˈstæmɪnə) *n* enduring energy, strength, and resilience [c19 identical with STAMINA² from Latin *stāmen* thread, hence the threads of life spun out by the Fates, hence energy, etc] > **ˈstaminal** *adj*

stamina² (ˈstæmɪnə) *n* a plural of **stamen**

staminate (ˈstæmɪnɪt, -ˌneɪt) *adj* (of plants) having stamens, esp having stamens but no carpels; male [c19 from Latin *stāminātus* consisting of threads. See STAMEN, -ATE¹]

staminode (ˈstæmɪˌnəʊd) *or* **staminodium** (ˌstæmɪˈnəʊdɪəm) *n, pl* **-nodes** *or* **-nodia** (-ˈnəʊdɪə) a stamen that produces no pollen [c19 from STAMEN + -ODE¹]

staminody (ˈstæmɪˌnəʊdɪ) *n* the development of any of various plant organs, such as petals or sepals, into stamens

stammel (ˈstæməl) *n* **1** a coarse woollen cloth in former use for undergarments, etc, and usually dyed red **2** the bright red colour of this cloth [c16 from Old French *estamin*, from Latin *stāmineus* made of threads, from *stāmen* a thread; see STAMEN]

stammer (ˈstæmə) *vb* **1** to speak or say (something) in a hesitant way, esp as a result of a speech disorder or through fear, stress, etc ▷ *n* **2** a speech disorder characterized by involuntary repetitions and hesitations [Old English *stamerian*; related to Old Saxon *stamarōn*, Old High German *stamm*] > **ˈstammerer** *n* > **ˈstammering** *n, adj* > **ˈstammeringly** *adv*

stamp (stæmp) *vb* **1** (when *intr*, often foll by *on*) to bring (the foot) down heavily (on the ground, etc) **2** (*intr*) to walk with heavy or noisy footsteps **3** (*intr*; foll by *on*) to repress, extinguish, or eradicate: *he stamped on any criticism* **4** (*tr*) to impress or mark (a particular device or sign) on (something) **5** to mark (something) with an official impress, seal, or device: *to stamp a passport* **6** (*tr*) to fix or impress permanently: *the date was stamped on her memory* **7** (*tr*) to affix a postage stamp to **8** (*tr*) to distinguish or reveal: *that behaviour stamps him as a cheat* **9** to pound or crush (ores, etc) ▷ *n* **10** the act or an instance of stamping **11** **a** See **postage stamp** **b** a mark applied to postage stamps for cancellation purposes **12** a similar piece of gummed paper used for commercial or trading purposes **13** a block, die, etc, used for imprinting a design or device **14** a design, device, or mark that has been stamped **15** a characteristic feature or trait; hallmark: *the story had the stamp of authenticity* **16** a piece of gummed paper or other mark applied to official documents to indicate payment of a fee, validity, ownership, etc **17** *Brit informal* a national insurance contribution, formerly recorded by means of a stamp on an official card **18** type or class: *we want to employ men of his stamp* **19** an instrument or machine for crushing or pounding ores, etc, or the pestle in such a device ▷ See also **stamp out** [Old English *stampe*; related to Old High German *stampfōn* to stamp, Old Norse *stappa*] > **ˈstamper** *n*

Stamp Act *n* a law passed by the British Parliament requiring all publications and legal and commercial documents in the American colonies to bear a tax stamp (1765): a cause of unrest in the colonies

stamp collecting *n* another name for **philately** > **stamp collector** *n*

stamp duty *or* **tax** *n* a tax on legal documents, publications, etc, the payment of which is certified by the attaching or impressing of official stamps

stampede (stæmˈpiːd) *n* **1** an impulsive headlong rush of startled cattle or horses **2** headlong rush of a crowd: *a stampede of shoppers* **3** any sudden large-scale movement or other action, such as a rush of people to support a candidate **4** *Western US and Canadian* a rodeo event featuring fairground and social elements ▷ *vb* **5** to run away or cause to run away in a stampede [c19 from American Spanish *estampida*, from Spanish: a din, from *estampar* to stamp, of Germanic origin; see STAMP] > **stamˈpeder** *n*

stamping ground *n* a habitual or favourite meeting or gathering place

stamp mill *n metallurgy* a machine for crushing ore

stamp out *vb* (*tr, adverb*) **1** to put out or extinguish by stamping: *to stamp out a fire* **2** to crush or suppress by force: *to stamp out a rebellion*

stance (stæns, stɑːns) *n* **1** the manner and position in which a person or animal stands **2** *sport* the posture assumed when about to play the ball, as in golf, cricket, etc **3** general emotional or intellectual attitude: *a leftist stance* **4** *Scot* a place where buses or taxis wait **5** *mountaineering* a place at the top of a pitch where a climber can stand and belay [c16 via French from Italian *stanza* place for standing, from Latin *stāns*, from *stāre* to stand]

stanch (stɑːntʃ) *or* **staunch** (stɔːntʃ) *vb* **1** to stem the flow of (a liquid, esp blood) or (of a liquid) to stop flowing **2** to prevent the flow of a liquid, esp blood, from (a hole, wound, etc) **3** an archaic word for **assuage** ▷ *n* **4** a primitive form of lock in which boats are carried over shallow parts of a river in a rush of water released by the lock [c14 from Old French *estanchier*, from Vulgar Latin *stanticāre* (unattested) to cause to stand, from Latin *stāre* to stand, halt] > **ˈstanchable** *or* **ˈstaunchable** *adj* > **ˈstancher** *or* **ˈstauncher** *n*

stanchion (ˈstɑːnʃən) *n* **1** any vertical pole, rod, etc, used as a support ▷ *vb* **2** (*tr*) to provide or support with a stanchion or stanchions [c14 from Old French *estanchon*, from *estance*, from Vulgar Latin *stantia* (unattested) a standing, from Latin *stāre* to stand]

stand (stænd) *vb* **stands, standing, stood** (*mainly intr*) **1** (*also tr*) to be or cause to be in an erect or upright position **2** to rise to, assume, or maintain an upright position **3** (*copula*) to have a specified height when standing: *to stand six feet* **4** to be situated or located: *the house stands in the square* **5** to be or exist in a specified state or condition: *to stand in awe of someone* **6** to adopt or remain in a resolute position or attitude **7** (*may take an infinitive*) to be in a specified position: *I stand to lose money in this venture; he stands high in the president's favour* **8** to remain in force or continue in effect: *whatever the difficulties, my orders stand* **9** to come to a stop or halt, esp temporarily **10** (of water, etc) to collect and remain without flowing **11** (often foll by *at*) (of a score, account, etc) to indicate the specified position of the parties involved: *the score stands at 20 to 1* **12** (*also tr*; when *intr*, foll by *for*) to tolerate or bear: *I won't stand for your nonsense any longer; I can't stand spiders* **13** (*tr*) to resist; survive: *to stand the test of time* **14** (*tr*) to submit to: *to stand trial* **15** (often foll by *for*) *chiefly Brit* to be or become a candidate: *will he stand for Parliament?* **16** to navigate in a specified direction: *we were standing for Madeira when the storm broke* **17** (of a gun dog) to point at game **18** to halt, esp to give action, repel attack, or disrupt an enemy advance when retreating **19** (of a male domestic animal, esp a stallion) to be available as a stud **20** (*also tr*) *printing* to keep (type that has been set) or (of such type) to be kept, for possible use in future printings **21** (*tr*) *informal* to bear the cost of; pay for: *to stand someone a drink* **22** **stand a chance** to have a hope or likelihood of winning, succeeding, etc **23** **stand fast** to maintain one's position firmly **24** **stand one's ground** to maintain a stance or position in the face of opposition **25** **stand still** **a** to remain motionless **b** (foll by *for*) *US* to tolerate: *I won't stand still for your threats* **26** **stand to (someone)** *Irish informal* to be useful to (someone): *your knowledge of English will stand to you* ▷ *n* **27** the act or an instance of standing **28** an opinion, esp a resolutely held one: *he took a stand on capital punishment* **29** a halt or standstill **30** a place where a person or thing stands **31** *Austral and NZ* **a** a position on the floor of a shearing shed allocated to one shearer **b** the shearing equipment belonging to such a position **32** a structure, usually of wood, on which people can sit or stand **33** a frame or rack on which such articles as coats and hats may be hung **34** a small table or piece of furniture where articles may be placed or stored: *a music stand* **35** a supporting framework, esp for a tool or instrument **36** a stall, booth, or counter from which goods may be sold **37** an exhibition area in a trade fair **38** a halt to give action, etc, esp one taken during a retreat and having some duration or some success **39** *cricket* an extended period at the wicket by two batsmen **40** a growth of plants in a particular area, esp trees in a forest or a crop in a field **41** a stop made by a touring theatrical company, pop group, etc, to give a performance (esp in the phrase **one-night stand**) **42** *South African* a plot or site earmarked for the erection of a building **43** (of a gun dog) the act of pointing at game **44** a complete set, esp of arms or armour for one man **45** *military* the flags of a regiment ▷ See also **stand by, stand down, stand for, stand in, standoff, stand on, stand out, stand over, stand pat, stand to, stand up** [Old English *standan*; related to Old Norse *standa*, Old High German *stantan*, Latin *stāre* to stand; see STEAD] > **stander** *n*

stand-alone *adj computing* (of a device or system) capable of operating independently of any other device or system

standard ('stændəd) *n* **1** an accepted or approved example of something against which others are judged or measured **2** (*often plural*) a principle of propriety, honesty, and integrity: *she has no standards* **3** a level of excellence or quality: *a low standard of living* **4** any distinctive flag, device, etc, as of a nation, sovereign, or special cause **5 a** any of a variety of naval or military flags **b** the colours of a cavalry regiment **6** a flag or emblem formerly used to show the central or rallying point of an army in battle **7** a large tapering flag ending in two points, originally borne by a sovereign or high-ranking noble **8** the commodity or commodities in which is stated the value of a basic monetary unit: *the gold standard* **9** an authorized model of a unit of measure or weight **10** a unit of board measure equal to 1980 board feet **11** (in coinage) the prescribed proportion by weight of precious metal and base metal that each coin must contain **12** an upright pole or beam, esp one used as a support **13 a** a piece of furniture consisting of an upright pole or beam on a base or support **b** (*as modifier*): *a standard lamp* **14 a** a plant, esp a fruit tree, that is trained so that it has an upright stem free of branches **b** (*as modifier*): *a standard cherry* **15** a song or piece of music that has remained popular for many years **16** the largest petal of a leguminous flower, such as a sweetpea **17** (in New Zealand and, formerly, in England and Wales) a class or level of attainment in an elementary school ▷ *adj* **18** of the usual, regularized, medium, or accepted kind: *a standard size* **19** of recognized authority, competence, or excellence: *the standard work on Greece* **20** denoting or characterized by idiom, vocabulary, etc, that is regarded as correct and acceptable by educated native speakers. Compare **nonstandard, informal 21** *Brit* (formerly) (of eggs) of a size that is smaller than *large* and larger than *medium* [C12 from Old French *estandart* gathering place, flag to mark such a place, probably of Germanic origin; compare Old High German *stantan* to stand, Old High German *ort* place]

standard amenities *pl n* (in Britain) *social welfare* the sanitary facilities recommended for all dwellings by the housing law: a fixed bath or shower, wash-hand basin, and sink, all supplied with hot and cold water, and a flush toilet

standard assessment tasks, standard assessment tests *or* **standard attainment tests** *pl n Brit education* the former name for **National Tests** Abbreviation: **SATS** ('sæts)

standard-bearer *n* **1** an officer or man who carries a standard **2** a leader of a cause or party

standard-bred *n* a US and Canadian breed of trotting and pacing horse, used esp for harness-racing [C19 so called because they are bred to attain a prescribed standard of speed]

standard candle *n* another name for **candela**: not in scientific usage because of possible confusion with the former **international candle**

standard cell *n* a voltaic cell producing a constant and accurately known electromotive force that can be used to calibrate voltage-measuring instruments

standard cost *n accounting* the predetermined budgeted cost of a regular manufacturing process against which actual costs are compared

standard deviation *n statistics* a measure of dispersion obtained by extracting the square root of the mean of the squared deviations of the observed values from their mean in a frequency distribution

standard error *n statistics* the estimated standard deviation of a parameter, the value of which is not known exactly

standard function *n computing* a subprogram provided by a translator that carries out a task, for example the computation of a mathematical function, such as sine, square root, etc

standard gauge *n* **1** a railway track with a distance of 4 ft 8½ in. (1.435 m) between the lines; used on most railways. See also **narrow gauge, broad gauge** ▷ *adj* **standard-gauge** *or* **standard-gauged 2** of, relating to, or denoting a railway with a standard gauge

standard generalized mark-up language *n* See SGML

Standard Grade *n* (in Scotland) a type of examination designed to test skills and the application of knowledge, replaced O grade

standard housing benefit *n* (in Britain) *social welfare* a rebate of a proportion of a person's eligible housing costs paid by a local authority and calculated on the basis of level of income and family size

standardize *or* **standardise** ('stændə,daɪz) *vb* **1** to make or become standard **2** (*tr*) to test by or compare with a standard > ˌstandardiˈzation *or* ˌstandardiˈsation *n* > 'standard,izer *or* 'standard,iser *n*

standard model *n physics* a theory of fundamental interactions in which the electromagnetic, weak, and strong interactions are described in terms of the exchange of virtual particles

standard normal distribution *n statistics* a normal distribution with mean zero and variance 1, with probability density function $[\exp(-\frac{1}{2}x^2)]/\sqrt{2\pi}$

standard of living *n* a level of subsistence or material welfare of a community, class, or person

standard scratch score *n golf* the number of strokes a scratch player would need to go round a particular course, based on the length of each hole to the green and allowing 36 putts for the round

standard time *n* the official local time of a region or country determined by the distance from Greenwich of a line of longitude passing through the area

stand by *vb* **1** (*intr, adverb*) to be available and ready to act if needed or called upon **2** (*intr, adverb*) to be present as an onlooker or without taking any action: *he stood by at the accident* **3** (*intr, preposition*) to be faithful to: *to stand by one's principles* **4** (*tr, adverb*) *English law* (of the Crown) to challenge (a juror) without needing to show cause ▷ *n* **stand-by 5 a** a person or thing that is ready for use or can be relied on in an emergency **b** (*as modifier*): *stand-by provisions* **6** on stand-by in a state of readiness for action or use ▷ *adj* **7** (of an airline passenger, fare, or seat) not booked in advance but awaiting or subject to availability

stand down *vb* (*adverb*) **1** (*intr*) to resign or withdraw, esp in favour of another **2** (*intr*) to leave the witness box in a court of law after giving evidence **3** *chiefly Brit* to go or be taken off duty

standee (stæn'di:) *n* a person who stands, esp when there are no vacant seats

standfirst ('stænd,fɜːst) *n journalism* an introductory paragraph in an article, printed in larger or bolder type or in capitals, which summarizes the article

stand for *vb* (*intr, preposition*) **1** to represent or mean **2** *chiefly Brit* to be or become a candidate for **3** to support or recommend **4** *informal* to tolerate or bear: *he won't stand for any disobedience*

stand in *vb* **1** (*intr, adverb*; usually foll by *for*) to act as a substitute **2** stand (someone) in good stead

to be of benefit or advantage to (someone) ▷ *n* **stand-in 3 a** a person or thing that serves as a substitute **b** (*as modifier*): *a stand-in teacher* **4** a person who substitutes for an actor during intervals of waiting or in dangerous stunts

standing ('stændɪŋ) *n* **1** social or financial position, status, or reputation: *a man of some standing* **2** length of existence, experience, etc **3** (*modifier*) used to stand in or on: *standing room* > *adj* **4** *athletics* **a** (of the start of a race) begun from a standing position without the use of starting blocks **b** (of a jump, leap, etc) performed from a stationary position without a run-up **5** (*prenominal*) permanent, fixed, or lasting **6** (*prenominal*) still or stagnant: *a standing pond* **7** *printing* (of type) set and stored for future use. Compare **dead** (sense 17)

standing army *n* a permanent army of paid soldiers maintained by a nation

standing chop *n* NZ (in an axemen's competition) a chop with the log standing upright. Compare **underhand chop**

standing committee *n* a permanent committee appointed to deal with a specified subject

standing order *n* **1** Also called: banker's order an instruction to a bank by a depositor to pay a stated sum at regular intervals. Compare **direct debit 2** a rule or order governing the procedure, conduct, etc, of a legislative body **3** *military* one of a number of orders which have or are likely to have long-term validity

standing rigging *n* the stays, shrouds, and other more or less fixed, though adjustable, wires and ropes that support the masts of a sailing vessel. Compare **running rigging**

standing wave *n physics* the periodic disturbance in a medium resulting from the combination of two waves of equal frequency and intensity travelling in opposite directions. There are generally two kinds of displacement, and the maximum value of the amplitude of one of these occurs at the same points as the minimum value of the amplitude of the other. Thus in the case of electromagnetic radiation the amplitude of the oscillations of the electric field has its greatest value at the points at which the magnetic oscillation is zero, and vice versa. Also called: **stationary wave** Compare **node, antinode**

standish ('stændɪʃ) *n* a stand, usually of metal, for pens, ink bottles, etc [C15 of unknown origin]

standoff ('stænd,ɒf) *n* **1** *US and Canadian* the act or an instance of standing off or apart **2** a deadlock or stalemate **3** any situation or disposition of forces that counterbalances or neutralizes **4** *rugby* short for **stand-off half** ▷ *vb* **stand off** (*adverb*) **5** (*intr*) to navigate a vessel so as to avoid the shore, an obstruction, etc **6** (*tr*) to keep or cause to keep at a distance **7** (*intr*) to reach a deadlock or stalemate **8** (*tr*) to dismiss (workers), esp temporarily

stand-off half *n rugby* **1** a player who acts as a link between his scrum half and three-quarter backs **2** this position in a team ▷ Also called: **fly half**

standoffish (ˌstænd'ɒfɪʃ) *adj* reserved, haughty, or aloof > ˌstand'offishly *adv* > ˌstand'offishness *n*

standoff missile *n* a missile capable of striking a distant target after launch by an aircraft outside the range of missile defences

stand oil *n* a thick drying oil made by heating linseed, tung, or soya to over 300°C: used in oil enamel paints

stand on *vb* (*intr*) **1** (*adverb*) to continue to navigate a vessel on the same heading **2** (*preposition*) to insist on: *to stand on ceremony* **3** stand on one's own (two) feet *informal* to be independent or self-reliant

stand out *vb* (*intr, adverb*) **1** to be distinctive or conspicuous **2** to refuse to agree, consent, or comply: *they stood out for a better price* **3** to protrude or project **4** to navigate a vessel away from a port, harbour, anchorage, etc ▷ *n* **standout 5** *informal* **a**

a person or thing that is distinctive or outstanding **b** (*as modifier*): *the standout track from the album* **6** a person who refuses to agree or consent

stand over *vb* **1** (*intr, preposition*) to watch closely; keep tight control over **2** (*adverb*) to postpone or be postponed **3** (*intr, preposition*) *Austral and NZ informal* to threaten or intimidate (a person) ▷ *n* **standover 4** *Austral and NZ informal* a threatening or intimidating act

standover man ('stænd,əʊvə) *n Austral informal* a person who extorts money by intimidation

stand pat *vb* (*intr*) **1** *poker* to refuse the right to change any of one's cards; keep one's hand unchanged **2** to resist change or remain unchanged > 'stand,patter *n*

standpipe ('stænd,paɪp) *n* **1** a vertical pipe, open at the upper end, attached to a pipeline or tank serving to limit the pressure head to that of the height of the pipe **2** a temporary freshwater outlet installed in a street during a period when household water supplies are cut off

standpoint ('stænd,pɔɪnt) *n* a physical or mental position from which things are viewed

standstill ('stænd,stɪl) *n* a complete cessation of movement; stop; halt: *the car came to a standstill*

standstill agreement *n* an agreement that preserves the status quo, esp one between two countries when one country cannot pay its debts to the other that a certain fixed extension of time will be given to repay the debts

stand to *vb* **1** (*adverb*) *military* to assume positions or cause to assume positions to resist a possible attack **2 stand to reason** to conform with the dictates of reason: *it stands to reason that pigs can't fly*

stand up *vb* (*adverb*) **1** (*intr*) to rise to the feet **2** (*intr*) to resist or withstand wear, criticism, etc **3** (*tr*) *informal* to fail to keep an appointment with, esp intentionally **4 stand up for a** to support, side with, or defend **b** *US* to serve as best man for (the groom) at a wedding **5 stand up to a** to confront or resist courageously **b** to withstand or endure (wear, criticism, etc) ▷ *adj* **stand-up** (*prenominal*) **6** having or being in an erect position: *a stand-up collar* **7** done, performed, taken, etc, while standing: *a stand-up meal* **8** (of comedy or a comedian) performed or performing solo **9** *informal* (of a boxer) having an aggressive style without much leg movement: *a stand-up fighter* ▷ *n* **stand-up 10** a stand-up comedian **11** stand-up comedy

stane (steɪn) *n* a Scot word for **stone**

Stanford-Binet test ('stænfədbɪ'neɪ) *n psychol* a revision, esp for US use, of the Binet-Simon scale designed to measure mental ability by comparing the performance of an individual with the average performance for his age group. See also **Binet-Simon scale, intelligence test** [c20 named after *Stanford University*, California, and Alfred *Binet* (1857–1911), French psychologist]

stang (stæŋ) *vb archaic or dialect* a past tense of **sting**

stanhope ('stænəp) *n* a light one-seater carriage with two or four wheels [c18 named after Fitzroy *Stanhope* (1787–1864), English clergyman for whom it was first built]

stank¹ (stæŋk) *vb* a past tense of **stink**

stank² (stæŋk) *n* **1** a small cofferdam, esp one of timber made watertight with clay **2** *Scot and northern English dialect* a pond or pool ▷ *vb* **3** (*tr*) to make (a stream, cofferdam, etc) watertight, esp with clay [c13 from Old French *estanc*, probably from *estancher* to stanch]

stank³ (stæŋk) *n dialect* **1** a drain, as in a roadway **2** a draining board adjacent to a sink unit [special use of STANK² (in the sense: pool, pond)]

Stanley ('stænlɪ) *n* **1** the capital of the Falkland Islands, in NE East Falkland Island: scene of fighting in the Falklands War of 1982. Pop: 1989 (2001) **2** a town in NE England, in N Durham. Pop: 19 072 (2001) **3** Mount. a mountain in central Africa, between Uganda and the Democratic

Republic of Congo (formerly Zaïre): the highest peak of the Ruwenzori range. Height: 5109 m (16 763 ft). Congolese name: **Ngaliema Mountain**

Stanley Falls *pl n* the former name of **Boyoma Falls**

Stanley knife *n trademark* a type of knife used for carpet fitting, etc, consisting of a thick hollow metal handle with a short, very sharp, replaceable blade inserted at one end [c19 named after F.T. *Stanley*, US businessman and founder of the Stanley Rule and Level Company]

Stanley Pool *n* a lake between the Democratic Republic of Congo (formerly Zaïre) and Congo-Brazzaville, formed by a widening of the River Congo. Area: 829 sq km (320 sq miles). Congolese name: **Pool Malebo**

Stanleyville ('stænlɪ,vɪl) *n* the former name (until 1966) of **Kisangani**

stann- *combining form* denoting tin: *stannite* [from Late Latin *stannum* tin]

Stannaries ('stænərɪz) *n* **the.** a tin-mining district of Devon and Cornwall, formerly under the jurisdiction of special courts

stannary ('stænərɪ) *n, pl* **-ries** a place or region where tin is mined or worked [c15 from Medieval Latin *stannāria*, from Late Latin: STANNUM, TIN]

stannic ('stænɪk) *adj* of or containing tin, esp in the tetravalent state [c18 from Late Latin *stannum* tin]

stannic sulphide *n* an insoluble solid compound of tin usually existing as golden crystals or as a yellowish-brown powder: used as a pigment. Formula: SnS_2. See also **mosaic gold**

stanniferous (stə'nɪfərəs) *adj* containing tin; tin-bearing [c18 from Late Latin *stannum* tin + -FEROUS]

stannite ('stænaɪt) *n* a grey metallic mineral that consists of a sulphide of tin, copper, and iron and is a source of tin. Formula: Cu_2FeSnS_4 [c19 from STANNUM + -ITE¹]

stannous ('stænəs) *adj* of or containing tin, esp in the divalent state

stannum ('stænəm) *n* an obsolete name for **tin** (the metal) [c18 from Late Latin: tin, from Latin: alloy of silver and lead, perhaps of Celtic origin; compare Welsh *ystaen* tin]

Stanovoi Range *or* **Stanovoy Range** (*Russian* stəna'vɔj) *n* a mountain range in SE Russia; forms part of the watershed between rivers flowing to the Arctic and the Pacific. Highest peak: Mount Skalisty, 2482 m (8143 ft)

Stans (*German* ʃtans) *n* a town in central Switzerland, capital of Nidwalden demicanton, 11 km (7 miles) southeast of Lucerne: tourist centre. Pop: 6983 (2000)

stanza ('stænzə) *n* **1** *prosody* a fixed number of verse lines arranged in a definite metrical pattern, forming a unit of a poem **2** *US and Austral* a half or a quarter in a football match [c16 from Italian: halting place, from Vulgar Latin *stantia* (unattested) station, from Latin *stāre* to stand] > 'stanzaed *adj* > stanzaic (stæn'zeɪɪk) *adj*

stapelia (stə'piːlɪə) *n* any fleshy cactus-like leafless African plant of the asclepiadaceous genus *Stapelia*, having thick four-angled stems and large typically fetid mottled flowers [c18 from New Latin, named after J. B. van *Stapel*, (died 1636), Dutch botanist]

stapes ('steɪpiːz) *n, pl* **stapes** *or* **stapedes** (stæ'piːdiːz) the stirrup-shaped bone that is the innermost of three small bones in the middle ear of mammals. Nontechnical name: **stirrup bone** Compare **incus, malleus** [c17 via New Latin from Medieval Latin, perhaps a variant of *staffa, stapeda* stirrup, influenced in form by Latin *stāre* to stand + *pēs* a foot] > stapedial (stæ'piːdɪəl) *adj*

staphylo- *combining form* **1** uvula: *staphyloplasty* **2** resembling a bunch of grapes: *staphylococcus* [from Greek *staphulē* bunch of grapes, uvula]

staphylococcus (,stæfɪləʊ'kɒkəs) *n, pl* **-cocci** (-'kɒkaɪ; *US* -'kɒksaɪ) any spherical Gram-positive bacterium of the genus *Staphylococcus*, typically occurring in clusters and including many

pathogenic species, causing boils, infection in wounds, and septicaemia: family *Micrococcaceae*. Often shortened to: **staph** [c19 from STAPHYLO- (in the sense: like a bunch of grapes) + COCCUS so called because of their shape] > **staphylococcal** (,stæfɪləʊ'kɒk³l) *or* **staphylococcic** (,stæfɪləʊ'kɒksɪk; *US* -'kɒksɪk) *adj*

staphyloplasty ('stæfɪləʊ,plæstɪ) *n* plastic surgery or surgical repair involving the soft palate or the uvula [c19 from STAPHYLO- + -PLASTY] > ,staphylo'plastic *adj*

staphylorrhaphy (,stæfɪ'lɒrəfɪ) *n* repair of a cleft palate by means of staphyloplasty and suturing [c19 from STAPHYLO- (in the sense: uvula) + Greek *raphē* a sewing or suture] > staphylorrhaphic (,stæfɪlɒ'ræfɪk) *adj*

staple¹ ('steɪp³l) *n* **1** a short length of thin wire bent into a square U-shape, used to fasten papers, cloth, etc **2** a short length of stiff wire formed into a U-shape with pointed ends, used for holding a hasp to a post, securing electric cables, etc ▷ *vb* **3** (*tr*) to secure (papers, wire, etc) with a staple or staples [Old English *stapol* prop, of Germanic origin; related to Middle Dutch *stapel* step, Old High German *staffal*]

staple² ('steɪp³l) *adj* **1** of prime importance; principal: *staple foods* **2** (of a commodity) forming a predominant element in the product, consumption, or trade of a nation, region, etc ▷ *n* **3** a staple commodity **4** a main constituent; integral part **5** *chiefly US and Canadian* a principal raw material produced or grown in a region **6** the fibre of wool, cotton, etc, graded as to length and fineness **7** (in medieval Europe) a town appointed to be the exclusive market for one or more major exports of the land ▷ *vb* **8** (*tr*) to arrange or sort (wool, cotton, etc) according to length and fineness [c15 from Middle Dutch *stapel* warehouse; see STAPLE¹]

staple gun *n* a mechanism that fixes staples to a surface

stapler ('steɪplə) *n* a machine that inserts staples into sheets of paper, etc, to hold them together

star (stɑː) *n* **1** any of a vast number of celestial objects that are visible in the clear night sky as points of light **2 a** a hot gaseous mass, such as the sun, that radiates energy, esp as light and infrared radiation, usually derived from thermonuclear reactions in the interior, and in some cases as ultraviolet, radio waves, and X-rays. The surface temperature can range from about 2100 to 40 000°C. See also **Hertzsprung-Russell diagram, giant star, white dwarf, neutron star, black hole b** (*as modifier*): *a star catalogue*. Related adjs: **astral, sidereal, stellar 3 a** astrology a celestial body, esp a planet, supposed to influence events, personalities, etc **b** (*plural*) another name for **horoscope** (sense 1) **4** an emblem shaped like a conventionalized star, usually with five or more points, often used as a symbol of rank, an award, etc **5** a small white blaze on the forehead of an animal, esp a horse **6** Also called: **star facet** any of the eight triangular facets cut in the crown of a brilliant **7 a** a distinguished or glamorous celebrity, often from the entertainment world **b** (*as modifier*): *star quality* **8** another word for **asterisk 9** *prison slang* a convict serving his first prison sentence **10 see stars** to see or seem to see bright moving pinpoints of light, as from a blow on the head, increased blood pressure, etc ▷ *vb* **stars, starring, starred 11** (*tr*) to mark or decorate with a star or stars **12** to feature or be featured as a star: *"Greed" starred Erich von Stroheim; Olivier starred in "Hamlet"* [Old English *steorra*; related to Old Frisian *stēra*, Old Norse *stjarna*, German *Stern*, Latin *stella*] > 'starless *adj* > 'star,like *adj*

star-apple *n* **1** a West Indian sapotaceous tree, *Chrysophyllum cainito*, with smooth skinned edible greenish-purple fruit **2** the fruit of this tree which, when cut across, reveals a star-shaped arrangement of seeds

Stara Zagora (*Bulgarian* 'stara za'gɔra) *n* a city in

S

central Bulgaria: ceded to Bulgaria by Turkey in 1877. Pop: 163 000 (2005 est)

starboard ('stɑːbəd, -ˌbɔːd) *n* **1** the right side of an aeroplane or vessel when facing the nose or bow. Compare **port²** ▷ *adj* **2** relating to or on the starboard ▷ *vb* **3** to turn or be turned towards the starboard [Old English *stēorbord*, literally: steering side, from *stēor* steering paddle + *bord* side; see STEER¹, board; from the fact that boats were formerly steered by a paddle held over the right-hand side]

starburst ('stɑːbɜːst) *n* **1** a pattern of rays or lines radiating from a light source **2** *photog* a lens attachment which produces a starburst effect

starch (stɑːtʃ) *n* **1** a polysaccharide composed of glucose units that occurs widely in plant tissues in the form of storage granules, consisting of amylose and amylopectin. Related adj: **amylaceous 2** Also called: **amylum** a starch obtained from potatoes and some grain: it is fine white powder that forms a translucent viscous solution on boiling with water and is used to stiffen fabric and in many industrial processes **3** any food containing a large amount of starch, such as rice and potatoes **4** stiff or pompous formality of manner or conduct ▷ *vb* **5** (*tr*) to stiffen with or soak in starch ▷ *adj* **6** (of a person) formal; stiff [Old English *stercan* (unattested except by the past participle *sterced*) to stiffen; related to Old Saxon *sterkian*, Old High German *sterken* to strengthen, Dutch *sterken*; see STARK] > 'starcher *n* > 'starchˌlike *adj*

Star Chamber *n* **1** *English history* the Privy Council sitting as a court of equity, esp powerful under the Tudor monarchs; abolished 1641 **2** (*sometimes not capitals*) any arbitrary tribunal dispensing summary justice **3** (*sometimes not capitals*) (in Britain, in a Conservative government) a group of senior ministers who make the final decision on the public spending of each government department

starch-reduced *adj* (of food, esp bread) having the starch content reduced, as in proprietary slimming products

starchy ('stɑːtʃɪ) *adj* **starchier, starchiest 1** of, relating to, or containing starch: *starchy foods* **2** extremely formal, stiff, or conventional: *a starchy manner* **3** stiffened with starch > 'starchily *adv* > 'starchiness *n*

star connection *n* a connection used in a polyphase electrical device or system of devices in which the windings each have one end connected to a common junction, the **star point**, and the other end to a separate terminal. See also **Y connection** Compare **delta connection**

star-crossed *adj* dogged by ill luck; destined to misfortune [C16 from CROSS (in the sense: thwart): so called because of the astrological belief that the stars affect people's destinies]

stardom ('stɑːdəm) *n* **1** the fame and prestige of being a star in films, sport, etc **2** the world of celebrities

stardust ('stɑːˌdʌst) *n* **1** dusty material found between the stars **2** a large number of distant stars appearing to the observer as a cloud of dust **3** a dreamy romantic or sentimental quality or feeling

stare¹ (steə) *vb* **1** (*intr*; often foll by *at*) to look or gaze fixedly, often with hostility or rudeness **2** (*intr*) (of an animal's fur, bird's feathers, etc) to stand on end because of fear, ill health, etc **3** (*intr*) to stand out as obvious; glare **4 stare one in the face** to be glaringly obvious or imminent ▷ *n* **5** the act or an instance of staring [Old English *starian*; related to Old Norse *stara*, Old High German *starēn* to stare, Greek *stereos* stiff, Latin *consternāre* to confuse] > 'starer *n*

stare² (steə) *n dialect* a starling [Old English *stær*]

stare out or **down** *vb* (*tr, adverb*) to look at (a person or animal) fixedly until his gaze is turned away

starfish ('stɑːˌfɪʃ) *n, pl* **-fish** or **-fishes** any

echinoderm of the class *Asteroidea*, such as *Asterias rubens*, typically having a flattened body covered with a flexible test and five arms radiating from a central disc

starfished ('stɑːˌfɪʃd) *adj informal* lying with arms and legs outstretched; spread-eagled

starflower ('stɑːˌflaʊə) *n* any of several plants with starlike flowers, esp the star-of-Bethlehem

star fruit *n* another name for **carambola**

starfucker ('stɑːˌfʌkə) *offensive taboo slang n* **1** a person who seeks to have sexual relations with celebrities; groupie **2** a person who seeks to associate with famous or powerful people > 'starˌfucking *n*

stargaze ('stɑːˌgeɪz) *vb* (*intr*) **1** to observe the stars **2** to daydream > 'starˌgazer *n* > 'starˌgazing *n, adj*

star grass *n* any of various temperate and tropical plants of the amaryllidaceous genus *Hypoxis*, having long grasslike leaves and yellow star-shaped flowers

stark (stɑːk) *adj* **1** (*usually prenominal*) devoid of any elaboration; blunt: *the stark facts* **2** grim; desolate: *a stark landscape* **3** (*usually prenominal*) utter; absolute: *stark folly* **4** *archaic* severe; violent **5** *archaic or poetic* rigid, as in death (esp in the phrases **stiff and stark, stark dead**) **6** short for **stark-naked 7** *adv* completely: *stark mad* [Old English *stearc* stiff; related to Old Norse *sterkr*, Gothic *gastaurknan* to stiffen] > 'starkly *adv* > 'starkness *n*

Stark effect (*German* ʃtark) *n* the splitting of the lines of a spectrum when the source of light is subjected to a strong electrostatic field, discovered by Johannes Stark (1874–1957) in 1913

stark-naked *adj* completely naked. Informal word (postpositive): **starkers** [C13 *stert naket*, literally: tail naked; *stert*, from Old English *steort* tail; related to Old Norse *stertr* tail + NAKED]

starlet ('stɑːlɪt) *n* **1** a young and inexperienced actress who is projected as a potential star **2** a small star

starlight ('stɑːˌlaɪt) *n* **1** the light emanating from the stars ▷ *adj also* **starlighted 2** of or like starlight **3** Also: **starlit** ('stɑːˌlɪt) illuminated by starlight

starling¹ ('stɑːlɪŋ) *n* any gregarious passerine songbird of the Old World family *Sturnidae*, esp *Sturnus vulgaris*, which has a blackish plumage and a short tail [Old English *stærlinc*, from *stær* starling (related to Icelandic *stari*) + -LING¹]

starling² ('stɑːlɪŋ) *n* an arrangement of piles that surround a pier of a bridge to protect it from debris, etc [C17 probably changed from *staddling*, from STADDLE]

star-nosed mole *n* an E North American amphibious mole, *Condylura cristata*, having a ring of pink fleshy tentacles around the nose

star-of-Bethlehem *n* **1** Also called: **starflower** a Eurasian liliaceous plant, *Ornithogalum umbellatum*, naturalized in the eastern US, having narrow leaves and starlike white flowers **2** any of several similar and related plants

Star of Bethlehem *n* the star that is supposed to have appeared above Bethlehem at the birth of Christ

Star of Courage *n* a Canadian award for bravery

Star of David *n* an emblem symbolizing Judaism and consisting of a six-pointed star formed by superimposing one inverted equilateral triangle upon another of equal size. Also called: **Magen David**

starred (stɑːd) *adj* **a** having luck or fortune as specified **b** (*in combination*): *ill-starred*

star ruby *n* a ruby that resembles a starlike figure in reflected light because of its crystalline structure

starry ('stɑːrɪ) *adj* **-rier, -riest 1** filled, covered with, or illuminated by stars **2** of, like, or relating to a star or stars > 'starrily *adv* > 'starriness *n*

starry-eyed *adj* given to naive wishes, judgments, etc; full of unsophisticated optimism; gullible

Stars and Bars *n* (*functioning as singular*) **the** the flag of the Confederate States of America

Stars and Stripes *n* (*functioning as singular*) **the** the national flag of the United States of America, consisting of 50 white stars representing the present states on a blue field and seven red and six white horizontal stripes representing the original states. Also called: **the Star-Spangled Banner**

star sapphire *n* a sapphire showing a starlike figure in reflected light because of its crystalline structure

star shell *n* an artillery shell containing a flare or other illuminant: often containing a parachute to prolong the descent of the illuminating material

star-spangled *adj* marked or decorated with stars

Star-Spangled Banner *n* **the 1** the national anthem of the United States of America **2** another term for the **Stars and Stripes**

star stream *n* one of two main streams of stars that, because of the rotation of the Milky Way, appear to move in opposite directions, one towards Orion, the other towards Ara

starstruck ('stɑːstrʌk) *adj* completely overawed by someone's celebrity status

star-studded *adj* featuring a large proportion of well-known actors or other performers: *a star-studded cast*

star system *n* **1** *astronomy* a group of celestial bodies that are associated as a result of natural laws **2** the practice of casting one or two famous actors or actresses in a film, play, etc, so that their popularity ensures its success **3** a design for laying cables for cable television in which each house is fed by an individual cable from a local central distribution point

start (stɑːt) *vb* **1** to begin or cause to begin (something or to do something); come or cause to come into being, operation, etc: *he started a quarrel; they started to work* **2** (when *intr*, sometimes foll by *on*) to make or cause to make a beginning of (a process, series of actions, etc): *they started on the project* **3** (sometimes foll by *up*) to set or be set in motion: *he started up the machine* **4** (*intr*) to make a sudden involuntary movement of one's body, from or as if from fright; jump **5** (*intr*; sometimes foll by *up, away*, etc) to spring or jump suddenly from a position or place **6** to establish or be established; set up: *to start a business* **7** (*tr*) to support (someone) in the first part of a venture, career, etc **8** to work or cause to work loose **9** to enter or be entered in a race **10** (*intr*) to flow violently from a source: *wine started from a hole in the cask* **11** (*tr*) to rouse (game) from a hiding place, lair, etc **12** (*intr*) (esp of eyes) to bulge; pop **13** an archaic word for **startle 14** (*intr*) *Brit informal* to commence quarrelling or causing a disturbance **15 to start with** in the first place ▷ *n* **16** the first or first part of a series of actions or operations, a journey, etc **17** the place or time of starting, as of a race or performance **18** a signal to proceed, as in a race **19** a lead or advantage, either in time or distance and usually of specified extent, in a competitive activity **20** a slight involuntary movement of the body, as through fright, surprise, etc: *she gave a start as I entered* **21** an opportunity to enter a career, undertake a project, etc **22** *informal* a surprising incident **23** a part that has come loose or been disengaged **24 by fits and starts** spasmodically; without concerted effort **25 for a start** in the first place ▷ See also **start in, start off, start on, start out, start up** [Old English *styrtan*; related to Old Norse *sterta* to crease, Old High German *sturzen* to rush]

START (stɑːt) *n acronym for* Strategic Arms Reduction Talks

starter ('stɑːtə) *n* **1** a device for starting an internal-combustion engine, usually consisting of a powerful electric motor that engages with the flywheel. formerly called: **self-starter 2** *US* a person who organizes the timely departure of buses, trains, etc **3** a person who supervises and signals the start of a race **4** a competitor who starts in a race or contest **5** *informal, chiefly Austral and NZ* an acceptable or practicable proposition, plan, idea, etc **6** *Austral and NZ informal* a person who is willing to engage in a particular activity **7** a culture of bacteria used to start fermentation, as in making cheese or yogurt **8** *chiefly Brit* the first course of a meal **9** (*modifier*) designed to be used by a novice: *a starter kit* **10** **for starters** *slang* in the first place **11** **under starter's orders** **a** (of horses in a race) awaiting the start signal **b** (of a person) eager or ready to begin

starter home *n* a compact flat or house marketed by price and size specifications to suit the requirements of first-time home buyers

star thistle *n* any of several plants of the genus *Centaurea*, esp *C. calcitrapa*, of Eurasia, which has spiny purplish flower heads: family *Asteraceae* (composites). See also **centaury** (sense 2) [C16 so called because it has a thistle-shaped flower surrounded by radiating spines]

start in *vb* (*adverb*) to undertake (something or doing something); commence or begin

starting block *n* one of a pair of adjustable devices with pads or blocks against which a sprinter braces his feet in crouch starts

starting gate *n* **1** a movable barrier so placed on the starting line of a racecourse that the raising of it releases all the contestants simultaneously **2** the US name for **starting stalls**

starting grid *n* *motor racing* a marked section of the track at the start where the cars line up according to their times in practice, the fastest occupying the front position

starting price *n* (esp in horse racing) the latest odds offered by bookmakers at the start of a race

starting rate *n* (in Britain) a rate of income tax below the basic rate

starting stalls *pl n* *Brit* a line of stalls in which horses are enclosed at the start of a race and from which they are released by the simultaneous springing open of retaining barriers at the front of each stall

startle (ˈstɑːtəl) *vb* to be or cause to be surprised or frightened, esp so as to start involuntarily [Old English *steartlian* to stumble; related to Middle High German *starzen* to strut, Norwegian *sterta* to strain oneself] > ˈ**startler** *n*

startle colour *n* *zoology* a bright region of an animal's coloration, normally hidden from view and often part of a design resembling birds' eyes, etc, exposed when the animal is disturbed by a predator

startling (ˈstɑːtlɪŋ) *adj* causing surprise or fear; striking; astonishing > ˈ**startlingly** *adv*

start off *vb* (*adverb*) **1** (*intr*) to set out on a journey **2** to be or make the first step in an activity; initiate: *he started the show off with a lively song* **3** (*tr*) to cause (a person) to act or do something, such as to laugh, to tell stories, etc

start on *vb* (*intr, preposition*) *Brit informal* to pick a quarrel with (someone)

start out *vb* (*intr, adverb*) **1** to set out on a journey **2** to take the first steps, as in life, one's career, etc: *he started out as a salesman* **3** to take the first actions in an activity in a particular way or specified aim: *they started out wanting a house, but eventually bought a flat*

start up *vb* (*adverb*) **1** to come or cause to come into being for the first time; originate **2** (*intr*) to spring or jump suddenly from a position or place **3** to set in or go into motion, activity, etc: *he started up the engine; the orchestra started up* ▷ *adj* **start-up** **4** of or relating to input, usually financial, made to establish a new project or business: *a start-up mortgage* ▷ *n* **start-up** **5** a business enterprise that has been launched recently

starvation (stɑːˈveɪʃən) *n* **a** the act or an instance of starving or state of being starved **b** (*as modifier*): *a starvation diet; starvation wages*

starve (stɑːv) *vb* **1** to die or cause to die from lack of food **2** to deprive (a person or animal) or (of a person, etc) to be deprived of food **3** (*intr*) *informal* to be very hungry **4** (foll by *of* or *for*) to deprive or be deprived (of something necessary), esp so as to cause suffering or malfunctioning: *the engine was starved of fuel* **5** (*tr*; foll by *into*) to bring (to) a specified condition by starving: *to starve someone into submission* **6** *archaic* to be or cause to be extremely cold [Old English *steorfan* to die; related to Old Frisian *sterva* to die, Old High German *sterban* to die] > ˈ**starver** *n*

starveling (ˈstɑːvlɪŋ) *archaic* ▷ *n* **1** **a** a starving or poorly fed person, animal, etc **b** (*as modifier*): *a starveling child* ▷ *adj* **2** insufficient; meagre; scant [C16 from STARVE + -LING[1]]

Star Wars *n* (*functioning as singular*) **1** (in the US) a proposed system of artificial satellites armed with lasers to destroy enemy missiles in space. Formal name: **Strategic Defense Initiative** Abbreviation: **SDI** **2** (*modifier; sometimes not capitals*) of, relating to, or denoting this system: *Star Wars defence; star wars policy* [C20 popularly named after the science fiction film *Star Wars* (1977) by George Lucas]

starwort (ˈstɑːˌwɜːt) *n* **1** any of several plants with star-shaped flowers, esp the stitchwort **2** **water starwort** any of several aquatic plants of the genus *Callitriche*, having a star-shaped rosette of floating leaves: family *Callitrichaceae*

stash (stæʃ) *vb* **1** (*tr*; often foll by *away*) *informal* to put or store (money, valuables, etc) in a secret place, as for safekeeping ▷ *n* **2** *informal* a secret store or the place where this is hidden **3** *slang* drugs kept for personal consumption [C20 origin unknown]

stashie (ˈstæʃɪ) *n* *Scot* a variant of **stushie**

Stasi (ˈstɑːzɪ) *n* formerly, the secret police in East Germany [from German *Sta(ats)si(cherheitsdienst)*, literally: state security service]

stasis (ˈsteɪsɪs) *n* **1** *pathol* a stagnation in the normal flow of bodily fluids, such as the blood or urine **2** *literature* a state or condition in which there is no action or progress; static situation: *dramatic stasis* [C18 via New Latin from Greek: a standing, from *histanai* to cause to stand; related to Latin *stāre* to stand]

stat. *abbreviation for* **1** (in prescriptions) immediately [from Latin *statim*] **2** stationary **3** statute

-stat *n combining form* indicating a device that causes something to remain stationary or constant: *thermostat* [from Greek *-statēs*, from *histanai* to cause to stand]

statant (ˈsteɪtənt) *adj* *heraldry* (of an animal) in profile with all four feet on the ground [C15 from Latin, apparently from irregularly formed present participle of *stāre* to stand]

state (steɪt) *n* **1** the condition of a person, thing, etc, with regard to main attributes **2** the structure, form, or constitution of something: *a solid state* **3** any mode of existence **4** position in life or society; estate **5** ceremonious style, as befitting wealth or dignity: *to live in state* **6** a sovereign political power or community **7** the territory occupied by such a community **8** the sphere of power in such a community: *affairs of state* **9** (*often capital*) one of a number of areas or communities having their own governments and forming a federation under a sovereign government, as in the US **10** (*often capital*) the body politic of a particular sovereign power, esp as contrasted with a rival authority such as the Church **11** *obsolete* a class or order; estate **12** *informal* a nervous, upset, or excited condition (esp in the phrase **in a state**) **13** **lie in state** (of a body) to be placed on public view before burial **14** **state of affairs** a situation; present circumstances or condition **15** **state of play** the current situation ▷ *modifier* **16** controlled or financed by a state: *state university* **17** of, relating to, or concerning the State: *State trial* **18** involving ceremony or concerned with a ceremonious occasion: *state visit* ▷ *vb* (*tr; may take a clause as object*) **19** to articulate in words; utter **20** to declare formally or publicly: *to state one's innocence* **21** to resolve [C13 from Old French *estat*, from Latin *status* a standing, from *stāre* to stand] > ˈ**statable** or ˈ**stateable** *adj* > ˈ**statehood** *n*

state bank *n* (in the US) a commercial bank incorporated under a State charter and not required to be a member of the Federal Reserve System. Compare **national bank**

state capitalism *n* a form of capitalism in which the state owns or controls most of the means of production and other capital: often very similar to state socialism

statecraft (ˈsteɪtˌkrɑːft) *n* the art of conducting public affairs; statesmanship

stated (ˈsteɪtɪd) *adj* **1** (esp of a sum) determined by agreement; fixed **2** explicitly formulated or narrated: *a stated argument*

stated case *n* another term for **case stated**

State Department *n* the US government department in charge of foreign affairs

State Duma *n* another name for **duma** (sense 3)

State Enrolled Nurse *n* (formerly, in Britain) a nurse with training and examinations enabling him or her to perform many nursing services. Abbreviation: **SEN**

state function *n* *physics* a thermodynamic quantity that has definite values for given states of a system, such as entropy, enthalpy, free energy, etc

state house *n* *NZ* a house built by the government for renting

Statehouse (ˈsteɪtˌhaʊs) *n* **1** (in the US) the building which houses a state legislature; State capitol **2** a building in which public affairs or state ceremonies are conducted

stateless (ˈsteɪtlɪs) *adj* **1** without nationality: *stateless persons* **2** without a state or states **3** *chiefly Brit* without ceremonial dignity > ˈ**statelessness** *n*

statelet (ˈsteɪtlɪt) *n* a small state: *the Gaza Strip statelet*

stately (ˈsteɪtlɪ) *adj* **-lier, -liest** **1** characterized by a graceful, dignified, and imposing appearance or manner ▷ *adv* **2** in a stately manner > ˈ**stateliness** *n*

stately home *n* *Brit* a large mansion, esp one open to the public

statement (ˈsteɪtmənt) *n* **1** the act of stating **2** something that is stated, esp a formal prepared announcement or reply **3** *law* a declaration of matters of fact, esp in a pleading **4** an account containing a summary of bills or invoices and displaying the total amount due **5** an account prepared by a bank for each of its clients, usually at regular intervals, to show all credits and debits since the last account and the balance at the end of the period **6** *music* the presentation of a musical theme or idea, such as the subject of a fugue or sonata **7** a computer instruction written in a source language, such as FORTRAN, which is converted into one or more machine code instructions by a compiler **8** *logic* the content of a sentence that affirms or denies something and may be true or false; what is thereby affirmed or denied abstracted from the act of uttering it. Thus *I am warm* said by me and *you are warm* said to me make the same statement. Compare **proposition** (sense 2b) **9** *Brit education* a legally binding account of the needs of a pupil with special educational needs and the provisions that will be made to meet them ▷ *vb* (*tr; usually passive*) **10** to assess (a pupil) with regard to his or her special educational needs

statement of claim *n* *law* (in England) the first pleading made by the claimant in a civil court action showing the facts upon which he or she relies in support of the claim and the relief asked for

statements of case *plural n* *law* the formal written statements presented alternately by the plaintiff and defendent in a lawsuit setting out the respective matters relied upon. Former name: **pleadings**

S

Staten Island ('stætᵊn) *n* an island in SE New York State, in New York Harbor: a borough of New York city; heavy industry. Pop: 443 728 (2000). Area: 155 sq km (60 sq miles)

state of the art *n* **1** the level of knowledge and development achieved in a technique, science, etc, esp at present ▷ *adj* (*prenominal*) **state-of-the-art 2** the most recent and therefore considered the best; up-to-the-minute: *a state-of-the-art amplifier*

state of war *n* **1** a period of armed conflict between states, regardless of whether or not war has been officially declared **2** a legal condition begun by a declaration of war and ended formally, during which the rules of international law applicable to warfare may be invoked

state prayers *pl n Church of England* prayers for the Sovereign, the royal family, the clergy, and Parliament said at matins and evensong

State prison *n* (in the US) a prison where persons convicted of serious crimes are confined

stater ('steɪtə) *n* any of various usually silver coins of ancient Greece [c14 via Late Latin from Greek *statēr* a standard of weight, from *histanai* to stand]

State Registered Nurse *n* (formerly in Britain) a nurse who had extensive training and passed examinations enabling him or her to perform all nursing services. Abbreviation: **SRN** See **Registered General Nurse**

stateroom ('steɪt,ruːm, -,rʊm) *n* **1** a private cabin or room on a ship, train, etc **2** *chiefly Brit* a large room in a palace or other building for use on state occasions

States (steɪts) *n* (*functioning as singular or plural*) **the** an informal name for the **United States of America**

state school *n* any school maintained by the state, in which education is free

state services *pl n Church of England* services appointed to commemorate days of national celebration or deliverance such as the accession of a sovereign

State Services Commission *n* (in New Zealand) a government-appointed body in charge of the public service

state's evidence *n* (in the US) **1** the evidence for the prosecution given on behalf of a state in a criminal prosecution **2** evidence given for the state by an accomplice against his former associates in crime (esp in the phrase **turn state's evidence**). Brit equivalent: **queen's** (or **king's**) **evidence**

States General *pl n* **1** the bicameral legislature of the Netherlands **2** *history* **a** an assembly of the estates of an entire country in contrast to those of a single province **b** Also called: **Estates General** the assembly of the estates of all France, last meeting in 1789 **c** the sovereign body of the Dutch republic from the 16th to 18th century

stateside ('steɪt,saɪd) *adj, adv US* of, in, to, or towards the US

statesman ('steɪtsmən) *n, pl* **-men 1** a political leader whose wisdom, integrity, etc, win great respect **2** a person active and influential in the formulation of high government policy, such as a cabinet member **3** a politician > **'statesman-,like** or **'statesmanly** *adj* > **'statesmanship** *n* > **'states,woman** *fem n*

state socialism *n* a variant of socialism in which the power of the state is employed for the purpose of creating an egalitarian society by means of public control of major industries, banks, etc, coupled with economic planning and a social security system > **state socialist** *n*

States of the Church *pl n* another name for the **Papal States**

states' rights *pl n* (*often capitals*) (in the US) **1** the rights and powers generally conceded to the states, or all those powers claimed for the states under some interpretations of the Constitution **2** a doctrine advocating the severe curtailment of

Federal powers by such an interpretation of the Constitution > **states' righter** *n*

state trooper *n US* a state policeman

static ('stætɪk) *adj also* **statical 1** not active or moving; stationary **2** (of a weight, force, or pressure) acting but causing no movement **3** of or concerned with forces that do not produce movement. Compare **dynamic** (sense 1) **4** relating to or causing stationary electric charges; electrostatic **5** of or relating to interference in the reception of radio or television transmissions **6** of or concerned with statics **7** *sociol* characteristic of or relating to a society that has reached a state of equilibrium so that no changes are taking place **8** *computing* (of a memory) not needing its contents refreshed periodically. Compare **dynamic** (sense 5) ▷ *n* **9** random hissing or crackling or a speckled picture caused by the interference of electrical disturbances in the reception of radio or television transmissions **10** electric sparks or crackling produced by friction ▷ See also **statics** [c16 from New Latin *staticus*, from Greek *statikos* causing to stand, from *histanai* to stand, put on the scales] > **'statically** *adv*

statice ('stætɪsɪ) *n* a plant name formerly held to include both *Armeria* (see **thrift**) and *Limonium* (see **sea lavender**). The gardener's statice comprises various species of the latter, esp those whose flowers can be dried and kept: family *Plumbaginaceae* [Latin: thrift, from Greek *statikē*, from *statikos* astringent (from a medicinal use of thrift)]

static line *n* a line attaching the pack of a parachute to an aircraft, so that the parachute is opened when it has fallen clear of the aircraft

statics ('stætɪks) *n* (*functioning as singular*) the branch of mechanics concerned with the forces that produce a state of equilibrium in a system of bodies. Compare **dynamics** (sense 1)

static tube *n* an open-ended tube used to measure the static pressure at a point in a moving fluid and positioned in such a way that it is unaffected by the fluid's motion

statin ('stætɪn) *n* any of a class of drugs, including atorvastatin and simvastatin, that lower the levels of low-density lipoproteins in the blood by inhibiting the activity of an enzyme involved in the production of cholesterol in the liver

station ('steɪʃən) *n* **1** the place or position at which a thing or person stands or is supposed to stand **2** **a** a place along a route or line at which a bus, train, etc, stops for fuel or to pick up or let off passengers or goods, esp one with ancillary buildings and services: *railway station* **b** (*as modifier*): *a station buffet* **3** **a** the headquarters or local offices of an official organization such as the police or fire services **b** (*as modifier*): *a station sergeant*. See **police station**, **fire station** **4** **a** building, depot, etc, with special equipment for some particular purpose: *power station; petrol station; television station* **5** *military* a place of duty: *an action station* **6** *navy* **a** a location to which a ship or fleet is assigned for duty **b** an assigned location for a member of a ship's crew **7** a radio or television channel **8** a position or standing, as in a particular society or organization **9** the type of one's occupation; calling **10** (in British India) a place where the British district officials or garrison officers resided **11** *biology* the type of habitat occupied by a particular animal or plant **12** *Austral and NZ* a large sheep or cattle farm **13** *surveying* a point at which a reading is made or which is used as a point of reference **14** (*often capital*) *RC Church* **a** one of the Stations of the Cross **b** any of the churches (**station churches**) in Rome that have been used from ancient times as points of assembly for religious processions and ceremonies on particular days (**station days**) **15** (*plural*) (in rural Ireland) mass, preceded by confessions, held annually in a parishioner's dwelling and attended by other parishioners ▷ *vb*

16 (*tr*) to place in or assign to a station [c14 via Old French from Latin *statiō* a standing still, from *stāre* to stand]

stationary ('steɪʃənərɪ) *adj* **1** not moving; standing still **2** not able to be moved **3** showing no change: *the doctors said his condition was stationary* **4** tending to remain in one place [c15 from Latin *statiōnārius*, from *statiō* STATION] > **'stationarily** *adv* > **'stationariness** *n*

◗ **USAGE** Avoid confusion with **stationery**

stationary engine *n* an engine that remains in a fixed position, esp one in a building that drives generators or other machinery > **stationary engineer** *n*

stationary orbit *n astronautics* an orbit lying in, or approximately in, the plane of the equator for which the orbital period is equal to the spin period of the central body

stationary point *n* **1** a point on a curve at which the tangent is either horizontal or vertical, such as a maximum, a minimum, or a point of inflection **2** *astronomy* a point in the apparent path of a planet when it reverses direction

stationary wave *n* another name for **standing wave**

stationer ('steɪʃənə) *n* **1** a person who sells stationery or a shop where stationery is sold **2** *obsolete* a publisher or bookseller [c14 from Medieval Latin *stationarius* a person having a regular station, hence a shopkeeper (esp a bookseller) as distinguished from an itinerant tradesman; see STATION]

Stationers' Company *n* a guild, established by Royal Charter from Queen Mary in 1557, composed of booksellers, printers, etc

stationery ('steɪʃənərɪ) *n* any writing materials, such as paper, envelopes, pens, ink, rulers, etc

◗ **USAGE** Avoid confusion with **stationary**

Stationery Office *n* **the** (in the UK) the company that supplies the civil service with all its office supplies, machinery, printing and binding, etc

station house *n chiefly US* a house that is situated by or serves as a station, esp as a police or fire station

stationmaster ('steɪʃən,mɑːstə) or **station manager** *n* the senior official in charge of a railway station

Stations of the Cross *pl n RC Church* **1** a series of 14 crosses, often accompanied by 14 pictures or carvings, arranged in order around the walls of a church, to commemorate 14 supposed stages in Christ's journey to Calvary **2** a devotion consisting of 14 prayers relating to each of these stages

station wagon *n US, Canadian, Austral, NZ, and South African* a car with a comparatively long body containing a large carrying space, reached through a rear door: usually the back seats can be folded forward to increase the carrying space. British term: **estate car**

statism ('steɪtɪzəm) *n* the theory or practice of concentrating economic and political power in the state, resulting in a weak position for the individual or community with respect to the government

statist ('steɪtɪst) *n* **1** an advocate of statism **2** a less common name for a **statistician** **3** *archaic* a politician or statesman ▷ *adj* **4** of, characteristic of, advocating, or relating to statism

statistic (stə'tɪstɪk) *n* any function of a number of random variables, usually identically distributed, that may be used to estimate a population parameter. See also **sampling statistic**, **estimator** (sense 2), **parameter** (sense 3)

statistical (stə'tɪstɪkᵊl) *adj* of or relating to statistics

statistical dependence *n* a condition in which two random variables are not independent. X and Y are **positively dependent** if the conditional probability, $P(X|Y)$, of X given Y is greater than the probability, P(X), of X, or equivalently if P(X&Y) > P(X).P(Y). They are **negatively dependent** if the inequalities are reversed

statistical inference *n* the theory, methods, and practice of forming judgments about the parameters of a population, usually on the basis of random sampling. Also called: **inferential statistics** Compare **hypothesis testing**

statistically (stə'tɪstɪkəlɪ, -klɪ) *adv* in terms of or according to statistics

statistical mechanics *n* (*functioning as singular*) the study of the properties of physical systems as predicted by the statistical behaviour of their constituent particles

statistical tables *pl n* tables showing the values of the cumulative distribution functions, probability functions, or probability density functions of certain common distributions for different values of their parameters, and used esp to determine whether or not a particular statistical result exceeds the required significance level. See **hypothesis testing**

statistician (ˌstætɪ'stɪʃən) *n* **1** a person who specializes in or is skilled at statistics **2** a person who compiles statistics

statistics (stə'tɪstɪks) *n* **1** (*functioning as plural*) quantitative data on any subject, esp data comparing the distribution of some quantity for different subclasses of the population: *statistics for earnings by different age groups* **2** (*functioning as singular*) **a** the classification and interpretation of such data in accordance with probability theory and the application of methods such as hypothesis testing to them **b** the mathematical study of the theoretical nature of such distributions and tests. See also **descriptive statistics, statistical inference** [C18 (originally "science dealing with facts of a state"): via German *Statistik*, from New Latin *statisticus* concerning state affairs, from Latin *status* STATE]

stative ('steɪtɪv) *grammar* ▷ *adj* **1** denoting a verb describing a state rather than an activity, act, or event, such as *know* and *want* as opposed to *leave* and *throw*. Compare **nonstative** ▷ *n* **2** a stative verb [C19 from New Latin *stativus*, from Latin *stāre* to stand]

stato- *combining form* static; standing; fixed: *statolith* [from Greek *statos* standing, set]

statoblast ('stætəʊˌblɑːst) *n zoology* an encapsulated bud produced asexually by certain bryozoans that can survive adverse conditions and that gives rise to a new colony

statocyst ('stætəʊsɪst) *n* an organ of balance in some invertebrates, such as crustaceans, that consists of a sensory vesicle containing small granules (see **statolith**)

statolatry (steɪ'tɒlətrɪ) *n rare* the act or practice of idolizing the state [C19 from STATE + -LATRY]

statolith ('stætəˌlɪθ) *n* **1** Also called: **otolith** any of the granules of calcium carbonate occurring in a statocyst: movement of statoliths, caused by a change in position of the animal, stimulates hair cells, which convey the information to the brain by nerve fibres **2** any of various movable inclusions, such as starch grains, that occur in plant cells and are thought to function in geotropic responses > ˌstato'lithic *adj*

stator ('steɪtə) *n* **1** the stationary part of a rotary machine or device, esp of a motor or generator **2** a system of nonrotating radially arranged parts within a rotating assembly, esp the fixed blades of an axial flow compressor in a gas turbine ▷ Compare **rotor** (sense 1) [C20 from Latin: one who stands (by), from *stāre* to stand]

statoscope ('stætəˌskəʊp) *n* a very sensitive form of aneroid barometer used to detect and measure small variations in atmospheric pressure, such as one used in an aircraft to indicate small changes in altitude

statuary ('stætjʊərɪ) *n* **1** statues collectively **2** the art of making statues ▷ *adj* **3** of, relating to, or suitable for statues [C16 from Latin *statuārius*]

statue ('stætjuː) *n* a wooden, stone, metal, plaster, or other kind of sculpture of a human or animal figure, usually life-size or larger [C14 via Old French from Latin *statua*, from *statuere* to set up; compare STATUTE]

statued ('stætjuːd) *adj* decorated with or portrayed in a statue or statues

Statue of Liberty *n* a monumental statue personifying liberty, in New York Harbor, on Liberty Island: a gift from France, erected in 1885. Official name: **Liberty Enlightening the World**

statuesque (ˌstætjʊ'ɛsk) *adj* like a statue, esp in possessing great formal beauty or dignity [C19 from STATUE + -ESQUE, on the model of PICTURESQUE] > ˌstatu'esquely *adv* > ˌstatu'esqueness *n*

statuette (ˌstætjʊ'ɛt) *n* a small statue

stature ('stætʃə) *n* **1** the height of something, esp a person or animal when standing **2** the degree of development of a person: *the stature of a champion* **3** intellectual or moral greatness: *a man of stature* [C13 via Old French from Latin *statūra*, from *stāre* to stand]

status ('steɪtəs) *n*, *pl* **-tuses 1** a social or professional position, condition, or standing to which varying degrees of responsibility, privilege, and esteem are attached **2** the relative position or standing of a person or thing **3** a high position or standing; prestige: *he has acquired a new status since he has been in that job* **4** the legal standing or condition of a person **5** a state of affairs [C17 from Latin: posture, from *stāre* to stand]

status asthmaticus (æs'mætɪkəs) *n* a severe attack of asthma in which the patient may die from respiratory failure if not treated with inhaled oxygen or other appropriate measures

status bar *n* a narrow horizontal area at the foot of a computer screen or window in which details are displayed about the program that is running or the document that is being edited

status epilepticus (ˌɛpɪ'lɛptɪkəs) *n* a condition in which repeated epileptic seizures occur without the patient gaining consciousness between them. If untreated for a prolonged period it can lead to long-term disability or death

status Indian *n Canadian* a member of a native Canadian people who is registered as an Indian under the federal Indian Act

status quo (kwəʊ) *n* (usually preceded by *the*) the existing state of affairs [literally: the state in which]

status symbol *n* a possession which is regarded as proof of the owner's social position, wealth, prestige, etc

status zero *n* the condition of young people who are out of school but not in further education or training, permanently or regularly out of work, and dropping out of the mainstream of society

statutable ('stætjʊtəbəl) *adj* a variant of **statutory** (senses 2, 3) > ˌstatutably *adv*

statute ('stætjuːt) *n* **1 a** an enactment of a legislative body expressed in a formal document **b** this document **2** a permanent rule made by a body or institution for the government of its internal affairs [C13 from Old French *estatut*, from Late Latin *statūtum*, from Latin *statuere* to set up, decree, ultimately from *stāre* to stand]

statute book *n chiefly Brit* a register of enactments passed by the legislative body of a state, usually made up of a series of volumes that form a complete official record: *not on the statute book*

statute law *n* **1** a law enacted by a legislative body **2** a particular example of this ▷ Compare **common law, equity**

statute mile *n* a legal or formal name for **mile** (sense 1)

statute of limitations *n* a legislative enactment prescribing the period of time within which proceedings must be instituted to enforce a right or bring an action at law. See also **laches**

Statute of Westminster *n* the act of Parliament

(1931) that formally recognized the independence of the dominions within the Empire

statutory ('stætjʊtərɪ, -trɪ) *adj* **1** of, relating to, or having the nature of a statute **2** prescribed or authorized by statute **3** (of an offence) **a** recognized by statute **b** subject to a punishment or penalty prescribed by statute > 'statutorily *adv*

statutory declaration *n law* a declaration made under statutory authority before a justice of the peace or commissioner for oaths which may in certain cases be substituted for a statement on oath

statutory order *n* a statute that applies further legislation to an existing act

statutory rape *n* (in the US) the criminal offence of having sexual intercourse with a girl who has not reached the age of consent

staun (stɔːn) *vb, n* a Scot word for **stand**

staunch¹ (stɔːntʃ) *adj* **1** loyal, firm, and dependable: *a staunch supporter* **2** solid or substantial in construction **3** *rare* (of a ship, etc) watertight; seaworthy [C15 (originally: watertight): from Old French *estanche*, from *estanchier* to STANCH] > 'staunchly *adv* > 'staunchness *n*

staunch² (stɔːntʃ) *vb, n* a variant spelling of **stanch**

staurolite ('stɔːrəˌlaɪt) *n* a brown glassy mineral consisting of iron aluminium silicate in the form of prismatic crystals: used as a gemstone. Formula: $Fe_2Al_9Si_4O_{11}(OH)$ [C19 from Greek *stauros* a cross + -LITE] > **staurolitic** (ˌstɔːrə'lɪtɪk) *adj*

stauroscope ('stɔːrəˌskəʊp) *n obsolete* an optical instrument for studying the crystal structure of minerals under polarized light [C19 from Greek *stauros* a cross + -SCOPE] > **stauroscopic** (ˌstɔːrə'skɒpɪk) *adj* > ˌstauro'scopically *adv*

Stavanger (*Norwegian* sta'vaŋər) *n* a port in SW Norway: canning and shipbuilding industries. Pop: 112 405 (2004 est)

stave (steɪv) *n* **1** any one of a number of long strips of wood joined together to form a barrel, bucket, boat hull, etc **2** any of various bars, slats, or rods, usually of wood, such as a rung of a ladder or a crosspiece bracing the legs of a chair **3** any stick, staff, etc **4** a stanza or verse of a poem **5** *music* **a** *Brit* an individual group of five lines and four spaces used in staff notation **b** another word for **staff¹** (sense 9) ▷ *vb* **staves**, **staving**, **staved** or **stove 6** (often foll by *in*) to break or crush (the staves of a boat, barrel, etc) or (of the staves of a boat) to be broken or crushed **7** (*tr*; usually foll by *in*) to burst or force (a hole in something) **8** (*tr*) to provide (a ladder, chair, etc) with a stave or staves **9** (*tr*) *Scot* to sprain (a finger, toe, etc) [C14 back formation from *staves*, plural of STAFF¹]

stave off *vb* (*tr, adverb*) to avert or hold off (something undesirable or harmful), esp temporarily: *to stave off hunger*

staves (steɪvz) *n* a plural of **staff¹** or **stave**

stavesacre ('steɪvzˌeɪkə) *n* **1** a Eurasian ranunculaceous plant, *Delphinium staphisagria*, having purple flowers and poisonous seeds **2** the seeds of this plant, which have strong emetic and cathartic properties [C14 *staphisagre*, from Latin *staphis agria*, from Greek, from *staphis* raisin + *agria* wild]

Stavropol (*Russian* 'stavrəpəlj) *n* **1** a city in SW Russia: founded as a fortress in 1777. Pop: 362 000 (2005 est). Former name (1940–44): **Voroshilovsk 2** the former name (until 1964) of **Togliatti**

stay¹ (steɪ) *vb* **1** (*intr*) to continue or remain in a certain place, position, etc: *to stay outside* **2** (*copula*) to continue to be; remain: *to stay awake* **3** (*intr*; often foll by *at*) to reside temporarily, esp as a guest: *to stay at a hotel* **4** (*tr*) to remain for a specified period: *to stay the weekend* **5** (*intr*) *Scot and South African* to reside permanently or habitually; live **6** *archaic* to stop or cause to stop **7** (*intr*) to wait, pause, or tarry **8** (*tr*) to delay or hinder **9** (*tr*) **a** to discontinue or suspend (a judicial proceeding) **b** to hold in abeyance or restrain

S

from enforcing (an order, decree, etc) **10** to endure (something testing or difficult, such as a race): *a horse that stays the course* **11** (*intr*; usually foll by *with*) to keep pace (with a competitor in a race, etc) **12** (*intr*) *poker* to raise one's stakes enough to stay in a round **13** (*tr*) to hold back or restrain: *to stay one's anger* **14** (*tr*) to satisfy or appease (an appetite, etc) temporarily **15** (*tr*) *archaic* to quell or suppress **16** (*intr*) *archaic* to stand firm **17** **stay put** See **put** (sense 18) ▷ *n* **18** the act of staying or sojourning in a place or the period during which one stays **19** the act of stopping or restraining or state of being stopped, etc **20** the suspension of a judicial proceeding, etc: *stay of execution* ▷ See also **stay out** [C15 *staien*, from Anglo-French *estaier*, to stay, from Old French *ester* to stay, from Latin *stāre* to stand]

stay² (steɪ) *n* **1** anything that supports or steadies, such as a prop or buttress **2** a thin strip of metal, plastic, bone, etc, used to stiffen corsets, etc ▷ *vb* (*tr*) *archaic* **3** (often foll by *up*) to prop or hold **4** (often foll by *up*) to comfort or sustain **5** (foll by *on* or *upon*) to cause to rely or depend ▷ See also **stays** (sense 1) [C16 from Old French *estaye*, of Germanic origin; compare STAY³]

stay³ (steɪ) *n* a rope, cable, or chain, usually one of a set, used for bracing uprights, such as masts, funnels, flagpoles, chimneys, etc; guy ▷ See also **stays** (senses 2, 3) [Old English *stæg*; related to Old Norse *stag*, Middle Low German *stach*, Norwegian *stagle* wooden post]

stay-at-home *adj* **1** (of a person) enjoying a quiet, settled, and unadventurous use of leisure ▷ *n* **2** a stay-at-home person **3** a person who does not bother to vote in a political election

stayer (ˈsteɪə) *n* **1** a person or thing that stays **2** *informal* **a** a persistent or tenacious person **b** *horse racing* a persistent horse

staying power *n* endurance; stamina

Stayman (ˈsteɪmən) *n* (in contract bridge) a conventional response in clubs to a partner's opening no-trump bid, as a request for the partner to show any four-card major [C20 named after Samuel M. *Stayman* (1909–94), US bridge expert]

stay out *vb* (*adverb*) **1** (*intr*) to remain away from home: *the cat stayed out all night* **2** (*tr*) to remain beyond the end of: *to stay out a welcome* **3** (*tr*) to remain throughout: *to stay the night out*

stays (steɪz) *pl n* **1** *now rare* corsets with bones in them **2** a position of a sailing vessel relative to the wind so that the sails are luffing or aback. Compare **irons** (sense 2) **3** **miss stays** Also: **refuse stays** (of a sailing vessel) to fail to come about

staysail (ˈsteɪˌseɪl) *nautical* (ˈsteɪsᵊl) *n* an auxiliary sail, often triangular, set to catch the wind, as between the masts of a yawl (**mizzen staysail**), aft of a spinnaker (**spinnaker staysail**), etc

stay stitching *n* a line of stitches made in the seam allowance to prevent the edges from stretching

stbd *abbreviation for* starboard

STC (in India) *abbreviation for* State Trading Corporation

std *abbreviation for* standard

STD *abbreviation for* **1** **subscriber trunk dialling** **2** NZ subscriber toll dialling **3** sexually transmitted disease **4** Doctor of Sacred Theology

STD code *n* *Brit* a code of four or more digits, other than those comprising a subscriber's local telephone number, that determines the routing of a call [C20 *s(ubscriber) t(runk) d(ialling)*]

Ste *abbreviation for* Saint (female) [French *Sainte*]

stead (stɛd) *n* **1** (preceded by *in*) *rare* the place, function, or position that should be taken by another: *to come in someone's stead* **2** **stand (someone) in good stead** to be useful or of good service to (someone) ▷ *vb* **3** (*tr*) *archaic* to help or benefit [Old English *stede*; related to Old Norse *stathr* place, Old High German *stat* place, Latin *statiō* a standing, *statim* immediately]

steadfast *or* **stedfast** (ˈstɛdfəst, -ˌfɑːst) *adj* **1** (esp of a person's gaze) fixed in intensity or direction; steady **2** unwavering or determined in purpose, loyalty, etc: *steadfast resolve* > ˈ**steadfastly** *or* ˈ**stedfastly** *adv* > ˈ**steadfastness** *or* ˈ**stedfastness** *n*

Steadicam *n* (ˈstɛdɪˌkæm) *n* *trademark* a mechanism for steadying a hand-held camera, consisting of a shock-absorbing arm to which the camera is attached and a harness worn by the camera operator

steading (ˈstɛdɪŋ) *n* *Brit* **1** a farmstead **2** the outbuildings of a farm [C15 from STEAD + -ING¹]

steady (ˈstɛdɪ) *adj* **steadier, steadiest** **1** not able to be moved or disturbed easily; stable **2** free from fluctuation: *the level stayed steady* **3** not easily excited; imperturbable **4** staid; sober **5** regular; habitual: *a steady drinker* **6** continuous: *a steady flow* **7** *nautical* (of a vessel) keeping upright, as in heavy seas ▷ *vb* **steadies, steadying, steadied** **8** to make or become steady ▷ *adv* **9** in a steady manner **10** **go steady** *informal* to date one person regularly ▷ *n, pl* **steadies** **11** *informal* one's regular boyfriend or girlfriend ▷ *interj* **12** *nautical* an order to the helmsman to stay on a steady course **13** a warning to keep calm, be careful, etc **14** *Brit* a command to get set to start, as in a race: *ready, steady, go!* [C16 from STEAD + -Y¹; related to Old High German *stātīg*, Middle Dutch *stēdig*] > ˈ**steadier** *n* > ˈ**steadily** *adv* > ˈ**steadiness** *n*

steady state *n* *physics* the condition of a system when some or all of the quantities describing it are independent of time but not necessarily in thermodynamic or chemical equilibrium. See also **equilibrium** (sense 6)

steady-state theory *n* a cosmological theory postulating that the universe exists throughout time in a steady state such that the average density of matter does not vary with distance or time. Matter is continuously created in the space left by the receding stars and galaxies of the expanding universe. Compare **big-bang theory**

steak (steɪk) *n* **1** See **beefsteak** **2** any of various cuts of beef of varying quality, used for braising, stewing, etc **3** a thick slice of pork, veal, etc, or of a large fish, esp cod or salmon **4** minced meat prepared in the same way as steak: *hamburger steak* [C15 from Old Norse *steik* roast; related to *steikja* to roast on a spit; see STICK¹]

steakhouse (ˈsteɪkˌhaʊs) *n* a restaurant that has steaks as its speciality

steak tartare *or* **tartar** *n* raw minced steak, mixed with onion, seasonings, and raw egg. Also called: **tartare steak, tartar steak**

steal (stiːl) *vb* **steals, stealing, stole, stolen** **1** to take (something) from someone, etc without permission or unlawfully, esp in a secret manner **2** (*tr*) to obtain surreptitiously **3** (*tr*) to appropriate (ideas, etc) without acknowledgment, as in plagiarism **4** to move or convey stealthily: *they stole along the corridor* **5** (*intr*) to pass unnoticed: *the hours stole by* **6** (*tr*) to win or gain by strategy or luck, as in various sports: *to steal a few yards* **7** **steal a march on** to obtain an advantage over, esp by a secret or underhand measure **8** **steal someone's thunder** to detract from the attention due to another by forestalling him **9** **steal the show** to be looked upon as the most interesting, popular, etc, esp unexpectedly ▷ *n* *informal* **10** the act of stealing **11** something stolen or acquired easily or at little cost [Old English *stelan*; related to Old Frisian, Old Norse *stela* Gothic *stilan*, German *stehlen*]

stealer (ˈstiːlə) *n* **a** a person who steals something **b** (*in combination*) *scene-stealer*

stealth (stɛlθ) *n* **1** the act or characteristic of moving with extreme care and quietness, esp so as to avoid detection: *the stealth of a cat* **2** cunning or underhand procedure or dealing **3** *archaic* the act of stealing [C13 *stelthe*; see STEAL, -TH¹] > ˈ**stealthful** *adj*

Stealth (stɛlθ) *n* (*modifier*) *informal* denoting or referring to technology that aims to reduce the radar, thermal, and acoustic recognizability of aircraft and missiles

Stealth bomber *or* **plane** *n* a type of US military aircraft using advanced technology to render it virtually undetectable to sight, radar, or infrared sensors. Also called: **B-2**

stealth tax *n* *Brit informal* an indirect tax, such as that on fuel or pension funds, esp one of which people are unaware or that is felt to be unfair

stealthy (ˈstɛlθɪ) *adj* **stealthier, stealthiest** characterized by great caution, secrecy, etc; furtive > ˈ**stealthily** *adv* > ˈ**stealthiness** *n*

steam (stiːm) *n* **1** the gas or vapour into which water is changed when boiled **2** the mist formed when such gas or vapour condenses in the atmosphere **3** any vaporous exhalation **4** *informal* power, energy, or speed **5** **get up steam** **a** (of a ship, etc) to work up a sufficient head of steam in a boiler to drive an engine **b** *informal* to go quickly **6** **let off steam** *informal* to release pent-up energy or emotions **7** **under one's own steam** without the assistance of others **8** *Austral slang* cheap wine **9** (*modifier*) driven, operated, heated, powered, etc, by steam: *a steam radiator* **10** (*modifier*) treated by steam: *steam ironed; steam cleaning* **11** (*modifier*) *humorous* old-fashioned; outmoded: *steam radio* ▷ *vb* **12** to emit or be emitted as steam **13** (*intr*) to generate steam, as a boiler, etc **14** (*intr*) to move or travel by steam power, as a ship, etc **15** (*intr*) *informal* to proceed quickly and sometimes forcefully **16** to cook or be cooked in steam **17** (*tr*) to treat with steam or apply steam to, as in cleaning, pressing clothes, etc ▷ See also **steam up** [Old English; related to Dutch *stoom* steam, perhaps to Old High German *stioban* to raise dust, Gothic *stubjus* dust]

steam bath *n* **1** a room or enclosure that can be filled with steam in which people bathe to induce sweating and refresh or cleanse themselves **2** an act of taking such a bath **3** an enclosure through which steam can be passed continuously, used in laboratories for sterilizing equipment, maintaining a constant temperature, etc

steamboat (ˈstiːmˌbəʊt) *n* a boat powered by a steam engine

steam-boiler *n* a vessel in which water is boiled to generate steam. An industrial boiler usually consists of a system of parallel tubes through which water passes, suspended above a furnace

steam-chest *n* a chamber that encloses the slide valve of a steam engine and forms a manifold for the steam supply to the valve

steam coal *n* coal suitable for use in producing steam, as in a steam-boiler

steam-engine *n* an engine that uses the thermal energy of steam to produce mechanical work, esp one in which steam from a boiler is expanded in a cylinder to drive a reciprocating piston

steamer (ˈstiːmə) *n* **1** a boat or ship driven by steam engines **2** Also called: **steam box** an apparatus for steaming wooden beams and planks to make them pliable for shipbuilding **3** a vessel used to cook food by steam **4** *Austral slang* a clash of sporting teams characterized by rough play

steamer chair *n* a type of reclinable chair with a wooden or wicker frame, sometimes upholstered, designed for relaxing in

steam-generating heavy-water reactor *n* a nuclear reactor using heavy water as the moderator, light water (H_2O) as the coolant, and uranium oxide cased in zirconium alloy as the fuel. Abbreviation: **SGHWR**

steamie (ˈstiːmɪ) *n* *Scot urban dialect* a public wash house

steaming (ˈstiːmɪŋ) *adj* **1** very hot **2** *informal* angry **3** *slang* drunk ▷ *n* **4** *informal* robbery, esp of passengers in a railway carriage or bus, by a large gang of armed youths

steam iron *n* an electric iron that emits steam from channels in the iron face to facilitate the pressing and ironing of clothes, etc, the steam being produced from water contained within the iron

steam jacket *n engineering* a jacket containing steam that surrounds and heats a cylinder

steam organ *n* a type of organ powered by steam, once common at fairgrounds, in which the pipes are sounded either by a keyboard or in a sequence determined by a moving punched card. US name: calliope

steam point *n* the temperature at which the maximum vapour pressure of water is equal to one atmosphere (1.01325×10^5 N/m^2). It has the value of 100° on the Celsius scale. Compare **ice point**

steam reforming *n chem* a process in which methane from natural gas is heated, with steam, usually with a catalyst, to produce a mixture of carbon monoxide and hydrogen used in organic synthesis and as a fuel

steam roller ('sti:m,rəʊlə) *n* **1 a** a steam-powered vehicle with heavy rollers at the front and rear used for compressing road surfaces during road-making **b** another word for **roadroller 2 a** an overpowering force or a person with such force that overcomes all opposition **b** (*as modifier*): *steamroller tactics* ▷ *vb* **3** (*tr*) to crush (opposition, etc) by overpowering force

steam room *n* a room that can be filled with steam for use as a steam bath

steamship ('sti:m,ʃɪp) *n* a ship powered by one or more steam engines

steam-shovel *n* a steam-driven mechanical excavator, esp one having a large bucket or grab on a beam slung from a revolving jib

steamtight ('sti:m,taɪt) *adj* (of joints, cylinders, etc) being sealed in such a way that steam cannot leak out > 'steam,tightness *n*

steam trap *n* a device in a steam pipe that collects and discharges condensed water

steam turbine *n* a turbine driven by steam

steam up *vb* (*adverb*) **1** to cover (windows, etc) or (of windows, etc) to become covered with a film of condensed steam **2** (*tr; usually passive*) *slang* to excite or make angry: *he's all steamed up about the delay*

steam whistle *n* a type of whistle sounded by a blast of steam, as used formerly in factories, on locomotives, etc

steamy ('sti:mɪ) *adj* steamier, steamiest **1** of, resembling, full of, or covered with steam **2** *informal* lustful or erotic: *steamy nightlife* > 'steamily *adv* > 'steaminess *n*

steapsin (stɪ'æpsɪn) *n biochem* a pancreatic lipase [C19 from Greek *stear* fat + PEPSIN]

stearate ('stɪə,reɪt) *n* any salt or ester of stearic acid

stearic (stɪ'ærɪk) *adj* **1** of or relating to suet or fat **2** of, consisting of, containing, or derived from stearic acid [C19 from French *stéarique*, from Greek *stear* fat, tallow]

stearic acid *n* a colourless odourless insoluble waxy carboxylic acid used for making candles and suppositories; octadecanoic acid. Formula: $CH_3(CH_2)_{16}COOH$. See also **stearin** (sense 2)

stearin *or* **stearine** ('stɪərɪn) *n* **1** Also called: tristearin a colourless crystalline ester of glycerol and stearic acid, present in fats and used in soap and candles; glycerol tristearate; glycerol trioctadecanoate. Formula: $(C_{17}H_{35}COO)_3C_3H_5$ **2** another name for **stearic acid**, esp a commercial grade containing other fatty acids **3** fat in its solid form [C19 from French *stéarine*, from Greek *stear* fat, tallow + -IN]

stearoptene (,stɪə'rɒpti:n) *n* the part of an essential oil that separates out as a solid on cooling or standing [C19 from New Latin *stearoptenum*, from Greek *stear* fat + -*ptenum*, from *ptēnos* winged (volatile)]

steatite ('stɪə,taɪt) *n* another name for **soapstone** [C18 from Latin *steatitēs*, from Greek *stear* fat + -ITE[1]] > steatitic (,stɪə'tɪtɪk) *adj*

steato- *combining form* denoting fat [from Greek *stear, steat-* fat, tallow]

steatolysis (,stɪə'tɒlɪsɪs) *n physiol* **1** the digestive

process whereby fats are emulsified and then hydrolysed to fatty acids and glycerine **2** the breaking down of fat

steatopygia (,stɪətəʊ'pɪdʒɪə, -'paɪ-) *or* **steatopyga** (,stɪətəʊ'paɪɡə) *n* excessive fatness of the buttocks [C19 from New Latin, from STEATO- + Greek *pugē* the buttocks] > steatopygic (,stɪətə'pɪdʒɪk) *or* steatopygous (,stɪə'tɒpɪɡəs) *adj*

steatorrhoea *or esp US* **steatorrhea** (,stɪətə'rɪə) *n pathol* a condition in which the stools are abnormally fatty

Stębark ('stɛmbark) *n* the Polish name for Tannenberg

stedfast ('stɛdfəst, -,fɑ:st) *adj* a less common spelling of **steadfast**

steed (sti:d) *n archaic or literary* a horse, esp one that is spirited or swift [Old English *stēda* stallion; related to German *Stute* female horse; see STUD[2]]

steel (sti:l) *n* **1 a** any of various alloys based on iron containing carbon (usually 0.1–1.7 per cent) and often small quantities of other elements such as phosphorus, sulphur, manganese, chromium, and nickel. Steels exhibit a variety of properties, such as strength, machinability, malleability, etc, depending on their composition and the way they have been treated **b** (*as modifier*): *steel girders*. See also **stainless steel 2** something that is made of steel **3** a steel stiffener in a corset, etc **4** a ridged steel rod with a handle used for sharpening knives **5** the quality of hardness, esp with regard to a person's character or attitudes **6** *stock exchange* the quotation for steel shares. See also **steels 7** (*modifier*) resembling steel: *steel determination* ▷ *vb* (*tr*) **8** to fit, plate, edge, or point with steel **9** to make hard and unfeeling: *he steeled his heart against her sorrow; he steeled himself for the blow* [Old English *stēli*; related to Old High German *stehli*, Middle Dutch *stael*] > 'steely *adj* > 'steeliness *n*

steel band *n music* a type of instrumental band, popular in the Caribbean Islands, consisting mainly of tuned percussion instruments made chiefly from the heads of oil drums, hammered or embossed to obtain different notes

steel blue *n* **a** a dark bluish-grey colour **b** (*as adjective*): *steel-blue eyes*

steel engraving *n* **a** a method or art of engraving (letters, etc) on a steel plate **b** a print made from such a plate

steel grey *n* **a** a dark grey colour, usually slightly purple **b** (*as adjective*): *a steel-grey suit*

steel guitar *n* See **Hawaiian guitar, pedal steel guitar**

steelhead ('sti:l,hɛd) *n, pl* -heads *or* -head a silvery North Pacific variety of the rainbow trout (*Salmo gairdneri*)

steels (sti:lz) *pl n stock exchange* shares and bonds of steel companies

steel wool *n* a tangled or woven mass of fine steel fibres, used for cleaning or polishing

steelwork ('sti:l,wɜ:k) *n* a frame, foundation, or building, made of steel > 'steel,working *n*

steelworks ('sti:l,wɜ:ks) *n* (*functioning as singular or plural*) a plant in which steel is made from iron ore and rolled or forged into blooms, billets, bars, or sheets > 'steel,worker *n*

steelyard ('sti:l,jɑ:d) *n* a portable balance consisting of a pivoted bar with two unequal arms. The load is suspended from the shorter one and the bar is returned to the horizontal by adding weights to the longer one [C17 from STEEL + YARD[1] (in the archaic sense: a rod or pole)]

Steen (sti:n) *n South African* **1** (in South Africa) the white grape variety known elsewhere as Chenin Blanc **2** any of the white wines made from this grape [Afrikaans]

steenbok ('sti:n,bɒk) *n, pl* -boks *or* -bok a small antelope, *Raphicerus campestris*, of central and southern Africa, having a reddish-brown coat and straight smooth horns. Also called: steinbok [C18 from Afrikaans, from Dutch *steen* stone + *bok* BUCK[1]; Compare STEINBOCK]

steenbras ('sti:n,bræs) *n South African* a variety of

sea bream, *Lithognathos lithognathos*, valued as a food fish in South Africa [C17 from Afrikaans, from Dutch *steen* stone + *brasen* bream]

steep[1] (sti:p) *adj* **1 a** having or being a slope or gradient approaching the perpendicular **b** (*as noun*): *the steep* **2** *informal* (of a fee, price, demand, etc) unduly high; unreasonable (esp in the phrase **that's a bit steep**) **3** *informal* excessively demanding or ambitious: *a steep task* **4** *Brit informal* (of a statement) extreme or far-fetched **5** *obsolete* elevated [Old English *steap*; related to Old Frisian *stāp*, Old High German *stouf* cliff, Old Norse *staup*] > 'steeply *adv* > 'steepness *n*

steep[2] (sti:p) *vb* **1** to soak or be soaked in a liquid in order to soften, cleanse, extract an element, etc **2** (*tr; usually passive*) to saturate; imbue: *steeped in ideology* ▷ *n* **3** an instance or the process of steeping or the condition of being steeped **4** a liquid or solution used for the purpose of steeping something [Old English *stēpan*; related to *steap* vessel, cup, Old High German *stouf*, Old Norse *staup*, Middle Dutch *stōp*] > 'steeper *n*

steepen ('sti:pən) *vb* to become or cause to become steep or steeper

steeple ('sti:pəl) *n* **1** a tall ornamental tower that forms the superstructure of a church, temple, etc **2** such a tower with the spire above it **3** any spire or pointed structure [Old English *stēpel*; see STEEP[1]] > 'steepled *adj*

steeplebush ('sti:pəl,bʊʃ) *n* another name for **hardhack** [C19 so called because of the shape of its flower clusters]

steeplechase ('sti:pəl,tʃeɪs) *n* **1** a horse race over a course equipped with obstacles to be jumped, esp artificial hedges, ditches, water jumps, etc **2** a track race, usually of 3000 metres, in which the runners have to leap hurdles, a water jump, etc **3** *archaic* **a** a horse race across a stretch of open countryside including obstacles to be jumped **b** a rare word for **point-to-point** ▷ *vb* **4** (*intr*) to take part in a steeplechase [C19 so called because it originally took place cross-country, with a church tower serving as a landmark to guide the riders] > 'steeple,chasing *n*

steeplechaser ('sti:pəl,tʃeɪsə) *n* a horse or an athlete that takes part in steeplechases

steeplejack ('sti:pəl,dʒæk) *n* a person trained and skilled in the construction and repair of steeples, chimneys, etc [C19 from STEEPLE + JACK[1] (in the sense: a man or fellow)]

steer[1] (stɪə) *vb* **1** to direct the course of (a vehicle or vessel) with a steering wheel, rudder, etc **2** (*tr*) to guide with tuition: *his teachers steered him through his exams* **3** (*tr*) to direct the movements or course of (a person, conversation, etc) **4** to pursue (a specified course) **5** (*intr*) (of a vessel, vehicle, etc) to admit of being guided in a specified fashion: *this boat does not steer properly* **6** steer clear of to keep away from; shun ▷ *n* **7** *chiefly US* information; guidance (esp in the phrase **a bum steer**) [Old English *stīeran*; related to Old Frisian *stiūra*, Old Norse *stýra*, German *stevern*; see STARBOARD, STERN[2]] > 'steerable *adj* > 'steerer *n*

steer[2] (stɪə) *n* a castrated male ox or bull; bullock [Old English *stēor*; related to Old Norse *stjōrr*, Gothic *stiur*, Old High German *stior*, Middle Dutch *stēr*]

steerage ('stɪərɪdʒ) *n* **1** the cheapest accommodation on a passenger ship, originally the compartments containing the steering apparatus **2** an instance or the practice of steering and the effect of this on a vessel or vehicle

steerageway ('stɪərɪdʒ,weɪ) *n nautical* enough forward movement to allow a vessel to be steered

steering column *n* (in a motor vehicle) the shaft on which a steering wheel is mounted and by which it is connected with the steering gear

steering committee *n* a committee set up to prepare and arrange topics to be discussed, the order of business, etc, for a legislative assembly or other body

S

steering gear *n* any mechanism used for steering a vehicle, ship, aircraft, etc

steering wheel *n* a wheel turned by the driver of a motor vehicle, ship, etc, when he wishes to change direction. It is connected to the front wheels, rudder, etc

steersman ('stɪəzmən) *n, pl* -men the helmsman of a vessel

steeve¹ (stiːv) *n* **1** a spar having a pulley block at one end, used for stowing cargo on a ship ▷ *vb* **2** (*tr*) to stow (cargo) securely in the hold of a ship [C15 *steven*, probably from Spanish *estibar* to pack tightly, from Latin *stīpāre* to cram full]

steeve² (stiːv) *nautical* ▷ *vb* **1** to incline (a bowsprit or other spar) upwards or (of a bowsprit) to incline upwards at an angle from the horizontal ▷ *n* **2** such an angle [C17 of uncertain origin]

Stefan's law ('stɛfənz) *n* the principle that the energy radiated per second by unit area of a black body at thermodynamic temperature T is directly proportional to T^4. The constant of proportionality is the **Stefan constant**, equal to 5.670400×10^{-8} $Wm^{-2} K^{-4}$. Also called: Stefan-Boltzmann law [C19 named after Josef *Stefan* (1835–93), Austrian physicist]

stegodon ('stɛgəˌdɒn) *or* **stegodont** ('stɛgəˌdɒnt) *n* any proboscidean mammal of the genus *Stegodon*, of Pliocene to Pleistocene times, similar to the mastodons [C19 New Latin (literally: ridge-toothed), from Greek *stegos* roof, from *stegein* to cover + *odōn* tooth]

stegomyia (ˌstɛgəˈmaɪə) *n* a former name for **aedes** [C19 from Greek *stegos* roof + *-myia*, from *muia* a fly]

stegosaur ('stɛgəˌsɔː) *or* **stegosaurus** (ˌstɛgəˈsɔːrəs) *n* any quadrupedal herbivorous ornithischian dinosaur of the suborder *Stegosauria*, esp any of the genus *Stegosaurus*, of Jurassic and early Cretaceous times, having an armour of bony plates [C19 from Greek *stegos* roof + -SAUR]

Steier (*German* 'ʃtaɪər) *n* a variant spelling of **Steyr**

Steiermark ('ʃtaɪərˌmark) *n* the German name for **Styria**

stein (staɪn) *n* **1** an earthenware beer mug, esp of a German design **2** the quantity contained in such a mug [German, literally: STONE]

steinbock ('staɪnˌbɒk) *n* another name for **ibex** [C17 from German *Steinbock*; compare STEENBOK]

steinbok ('staɪnˌbɒk) *n, pl* -boks *or* -bok a variant spelling of **steenbok**

stele ('stiːlɪ, stiːl) *n, pl* stelae ('stiːliː) *or* steles ('stiːlɪz, stiːlz) **1** an upright stone slab or column decorated with figures or inscriptions, common in prehistoric times **2** a prepared vertical surface that has a commemorative inscription or design, esp one on the face of a building **3** the conducting tissue of the stems and roots of plants, which is in the form of a cylinder, principally containing xylem, phloem, and pericycle. See also **protostele, siphonostele** ▷ Also called (for senses 1, 2): **stela** ('stiːlə) [C19 from Greek *stēlē*; related to Greek *histanai* to stand, Latin *stāre*] > **stelar** ('stiːlə) *adj*

stell (stɛl) *n* a shelter for cattle or sheep built on moorland or hillsides [C19]

stellar ('stɛlə) *adj* **1** of, relating to, involving, or resembling a star or stars **2** of or relating to star entertainers **3** *informal* outstanding or immense: *companies are registering stellar profits* [C17 from Late Latin *stellāris*, from Latin *stella* star]

stellarator ('stɛləˌreɪtə) *n physics* an apparatus used in research into thermonuclear reactions, consisting of a toroidal vessel designed so that a plasma may be contained within it by a helical magnetic field. The magnetic field is produced by current carrying coils [C20 from STELLAR + (GENER)ATOR]

stellar evolution *n astronomy* the sequence of changes that occurs in a star as it ages

stellate ('stɛlɪt, -eɪt) *or* **stellated** *adj* resembling a star in shape; radiating from the centre: *a stellate arrangement of petals* [C16 from Latin *stellātus* starry,

from *stellāre* to stud with stars, from *stella* a star] > **'stellately** *adv*

stelliferous (stɛˈlɪfərəs) *adj* full of stars [C16 from Latin *stellifer* star-bearing, from *stella* star; see -FEROUS]

stelliform ('stɛlɪˌfɔːm) *adj* star-shaped [C18 from New Latin *stelliformis*, from Latin *stella* star + *forma* shape]

stellify ('stɛlɪˌfaɪ) *vb* -fies, -fying, -fied to change or be changed into a star [C14 from Latin *stella* a star]

Stellite ('stɛlaɪt) *n trademark* any of various alloys containing cobalt, chromium, carbon, tungsten, and molybdenum: characteristically very hard and wear-resistant, they are used as castings or hard surface-coatings

stellular ('stɛljʊlə) *adj* **1** displaying or abounding in small stars: *a stellular pattern* **2** resembling a little star or little stars [C18 from Late Latin *stellula*, diminutive of Latin *stella* star] > **'stellularly** *adv*

stem¹ (stɛm) *n* **1** the main axis of a plant, which bears the leaves, axillary buds, and flowers and contains a hollow cylinder of vascular tissue **2** any similar subsidiary structure in such plants that bears a flower, fruit, or leaf **3** a corresponding structure in algae and fungi **4** any long slender part, such as the hollow part of a tobacco pipe that lies between the bit and the bowl, or the support between the base and the bowl of a wineglass, goblet, etc **5** a banana stalk with several bunches attached **6** the main line of descent or branch of a family **7** a round pin in some locks on which a socket in the end of a key fits and about which it rotates **8** any projecting feature of a component: a shank or cylindrical pin or rod, such as the pin that carries the winding knob on a watch **9** *linguistics* the form of a word that remains after removal of all inflectional affixes; the root of a word, esp as occurring together with a thematic element. Compare **root¹** (sense 9) **10** the main, usually vertical, stroke of a letter or of a musical note such as a minim **11** *electronics* the tubular glass section projecting from the base of a light bulb or electronic valve, on which the filament or electrodes are mounted **12 a** the main upright timber or structure at the bow of a vessel **b** the very forward end of a vessel (esp in the phrase **from stem to stern**) ▷ *vb* stems, stemming, stemmed **13** (*intr*; usually foll by *from*) to be derived; originate: *the instability stems from the war* **14** (*tr*) to make headway against (a tide, wind, etc) **15** (*tr*) to remove or disengage the stem or stems from **16** (*tr*) to supply (something) with a stem or stems [Old English *stemn*; related to Old Norse *stafn* stem of a ship, German *Stamm* tribe, Gothic *stōma* basis, Latin *stāmen* thread] > **'stem,like** *adj* > **'stemmer** *n*

stem² (stɛm) *vb* stems, stemming, stemmed **1** (*tr*) to restrain or stop (the flow of something) by or as if by damming up **2** (*tr*) to pack tightly or stop up **3** *skiing* to manoeuvre (a ski or skis), as in performing a stem ▷ *n* **4** *skiing* a technique in which the heel of one ski or both skis is forced outwards from the direction of movement in order to slow down or turn [C15 *stemmen*, from Old Norse *stemma*; related to Old Norse *stamr* blocked, stammering, German *stemmen* to prop; see STAMMER] > **'stemmer** *n*

Stem (stɛm) *n* **die** (di) the South African national anthem until 1991, when part of it was incorporated into the current anthem, **Nkosi sikelel' iAfrika** [C19 from Afrikaans, the call]

stem-and-leaf diagram *n statistics* a histogram in which the data points falling within each class interval are listed in order

stem cell *n histology* an undifferentiated cell that gives rise to specialized cells, such as blood cells

stem ginger *n* the choice pieces of the underground stem of the ginger plant, which are crystallized or preserved in syrup and eaten as a sweetmeat

stemhead ('stɛmˌhɛd) *n nautical* the head of the

stem of a vessel

stemma ('stɛmə) *n* a family tree; pedigree [C19 via Latin from Greek *stemma* garland, wreath, from *stephein* to crown, wreathe]

stemmed (stɛmd) *adj* **1 a** having a stem **b** (*in combination*): *a thin-stemmed plant; a long-stemmed glass* **2** having had the stem or stems removed

stemson ('stɛmsən) *n nautical* a curved timber scarfed into or bolted to the stem and keelson at the bow of a wooden vessel. Compare **sternson** [C18 from STEM¹ + (KEEL)SON]

stem turn *n skiing* a turn in which the heel of one ski is stemmed and the other ski is brought parallel. Also called: **stem**

stemware ('stɛmˌwɛə) *n* a collective term for glasses, goblets, etc, with stems

stem-winder *n* a watch wound by an expanded crown on the bar projecting outside the case, as opposed to one wound by a separate key. Also called: **stem-winding watch**

stench (stɛntʃ) *n* a strong and extremely offensive odour; stink [Old English *stenc*; related to Old Saxon, Old High German *stank*; see STINK]

stench trap *n* a trap in a sewer that by means of a water seal prevents the upward passage of foul-smelling gases. Also called: **stink trap**

stencil ('stɛnsəl) *n* **1** a device for applying a design, characters, etc, to a surface, consisting of a thin sheet of plastic, metal, cardboard, etc in which the design or characters have been cut so that ink or paint can be applied through the incisions onto the surface **2** a decoration, design, or characters produced in this way ▷ *vb* -cils, -cilling, -cilled *or US* -cils, -ciling, -ciled (*tr*) **3** to mark (a surface) with a stencil **4** to produce (characters or a design) with a stencil [C14 *stanselen* to decorate with bright colours, from Old French *estenceler*, from *estencele* a spark, from Latin *scintilla*] > **'stenciller** *n*

stengah ('stɛŋə) *n* another name for **stinger** (sense 3) [from Malay *sa tengah* one half]

Sten gun (stɛn) *n* a light 9 mm sub-machine-gun formerly used in the British Army and Commonwealth forces, developed during World War II [C20 from *s* and *t* (initials of Shepherd and Turpin, the inventors) + *-en*, as in BREN GUN]

steno ('stɛnəʊ) *n, pl* stenos *US and Canadian informal* short for **stenographer**

steno- *or before a vowel* **sten-** *combining form* indicating narrowness or contraction: *stenography; stenosis* [from Greek *stenos* narrow]

stenograph ('stɛnəˌgræf, -ˌgrɑːf) *n* **1** any of various keyboard machines for writing in shorthand **2** any character used in shorthand ▷ *vb* **3** (*tr*) to record (speeches, minutes, letters, etc) in shorthand

stenographer (stəˈnɒgrəfə) *n* a *Chiefly US and Canadian* Brit equivalent: **shorthand typist** a person skilled in the use of shorthand and in typing **b** a peson with these skills whose job it is to record verbatim everything that is said during a court case

stenography (stəˈnɒgrəfɪ) *n* **1** the act or process of writing in shorthand by hand or machine **2** matter written in shorthand > **stenographic** (ˌstɛnəˈgræfɪk) *or* **steno'graphical** *adj* > **,steno'graphically** *adv*

stenohaline (ˌstɛnəʊˈheɪliːn, -laɪn) *adj* (of certain aquatic animals) able to exist only within a narrow range of salinity. Compare **euryhaline** [C20 from STENO- + *haline*, from Greek *hals* salt + -INE¹]

stenopetalous (ˌstɛnəʊˈpɛtələs) *adj* (of flowers) having narrow petals

stenophagous (stəˈnɒfəgəs) *adj* (of animals) feeding on a single type or limited variety of food [C17 from STENO- + *-phagous* (via Latin from Greek *phagos* eating)]

stenophyllous (ˌstɛnəʊˈfɪləs) *adj* (of plants) having narrow leaves

stenosis (stɪˈnəʊsɪs) *n, pl* -ses (-siːz) *pathol* an abnormal narrowing of a bodily canal or passage [C19 via New Latin from Greek *stenōsis*, from *stenoun* to constrict, from *stenos* narrow] **> stenotic** (stɪˈnɒtɪk) *adj*

stenothermal (ˌstɛnəˈθɜːməl) *adj* (of animals or plants) able to exist only within a narrow range of temperature. Compare **eurythermal**

stenotopic (ˌstɛnəʊˈtɒpɪk) *adj ecology* (of a species, group, etc) able to tolerate only a narrow range of environmental changes. Also (sometimes influenced by -TROPIC): **stenotropic** Compare **eurytopic** [from STENO- + *top* from Greek *topos* place + -IC]

Stenotype (ˈstɛnəˌtaɪp) *n* **1** *trademark* a machine with a keyboard for recording speeches, etc, in a phonetic shorthand **2** any machine resembling this **3** the phonetic symbol typed in one stroke of such a machine

stenotypy (ˈstɛnəˌtaɪpɪ) *n* a form of shorthand in which alphabetic combinations are used to represent groups of sounds or short common words [C19 from STENO- + TYPE + -Y³, on the model of STENOGRAPHY] **> stenotypic** (ˌstɛnəˈtɪpɪk) *adj* **> ˈstenoˌtypist** *n*

stent (stɛnt) *n medicine* a tube of plastic or sprung metal mesh placed inside a hollow tube to reopen it or keep it open; uses in surgery include preventing a blood vessel from closing, esp after angioplasty, and assisting healing after an anastomosis

stentor (ˈstɛntɔː) *n* **1** a person with an unusually loud voice **2** any trumpet-shaped protozoan of the genus *Stentor*, having a ciliated spiral feeding funnel at the wider end: phylum *Ciliophora* (ciliates) [C19 after STENTOR]

Stentor (ˈstɛntɔː) *n Greek myth* a Greek herald with a powerful voice who died after he lost a shouting contest with Hermes, herald of the gods

stentorian (stɛnˈtɔːrɪən) *adj* (of the voice, etc) uncommonly loud: *stentorian tones*

step (stɛp) *n* **1** the act of motion brought about by raising the foot and setting it down again in coordination with the transference of the weight of the body **2** the distance or space covered by such a motion **3** the sound made by such a movement **4** the impression made by such movement of the foot; footprint **5** the manner of walking or moving the feet; gait: *he received his prize with a proud step* **6** a sequence of foot movements that make up a particular dance or part of a dance: *I have mastered the steps of the waltz* **7** any of several paces or rhythmic movements in marching, dancing, etc: *the goose step* **8** (*plural*) a course followed by a person in walking or as walking: *they followed in their leader's steps* **9** one of a sequence of separate consecutive stages in the progression towards some goal: *another step towards socialism* **10** a rank or grade in a series or scale: *he was always a step behind* **11** an object or device that offers support for the foot when ascending or descending **12** (*plural*) a flight of stairs, esp out of doors **13** (*plural*) another name for **stepladder 14** a very short easily walked distance: *it is only a step to my place* **15** *music* a melodic interval of a second. See **whole tone, half-step 16** an offset or change in the level of a surface similar to the step of a stair **17** a strong block or frame bolted onto the keel of a vessel and fitted to receive the base of a mast **18** a ledge cut in mining or quarrying excavations **19** **break step** to cease to march in step **20** **keep step** to remain walking, marching, dancing, etc, in unison or in a specified rhythm **21** **in step a** marching, dancing, etc, in conformity with a specified pace or moving in unison with others **b** *informal* in agreement or harmony **22** **out of step a** not moving in conformity with a specified pace or in accordance with others **b** *informal* not in agreement; out of harmony **23** **step by step** with care and deliberation; gradually **24** **take steps** to undertake measures (to do something) with a view to the attainment of some end **25** **watch one's step a** *informal* to conduct oneself with caution and good behaviour **b** to walk or move

carefully ▷ *vb* **steps, stepping, stepped 26** (*intr*) to move by raising the foot and then setting it down in a different position, transferring the weight of the body to this foot and repeating the process with the other foot **27** (*intr*; often foll by *in, out,* etc) to move or go on foot, esp for a short distance: *step this way, ladies* **28** (*intr*) *informal, chiefly US* to move, often in an attractive graceful manner, as in dancing: *he can really step around* **29** (*intr*; usually foll by *on* or *upon*) to place or press the foot; tread: *to step on the accelerator* **30** (*intr*; usually foll by *into*) to enter (into a situation) apparently with ease: *she stepped into a life of luxury* **31** (*tr*) to walk or take (a number of paces, etc): *to step ten paces* **32** (*tr*) to perform the steps of: *they step the tango well* **33** (*tr*) to set or place (the foot) **34** (*tr*; usually foll by *off* or *out*) to measure (some distance of ground) by stepping **35** (*tr*) to arrange in or supply with a series of steps so as to avoid coincidence or symmetry **36** (*tr*) to raise (a mast) and fit it into its step ▷ See also **step down, step in, step on, step out, step up** [Old English *stepe, stæpe*; related to Old Frisian *stap, stepe*, Old High German *stapfo* (German *Stapfe* footprint), Old Norse *stapi* high rock] **> ˈstepˌlike** *adj*

Step (stɛp) *n* **a** a set of aerobic exercises designed to improve the cardiovascular system, which consists of stepping on and off a special box of adjustable height **b** (*as modifier*): *Step aerobics*

STEP (stɛp) *n acronym for* Special Temporary Employment Programme

step- *combining form* indicating relationship through the previous marriage of a spouse or parent rather than by blood: *stepson; stepfather* [Old English *stēop-*; compare *āstȳpan* to bereave]

stepbrother (ˈstɛpˌbrʌðə) *n* a son of one's stepmother or stepfather by a union with someone other than one's father or mother respectively

step change *n* a significant change, esp an improvement

stepchild (ˈstɛpˌtʃaɪld) *n, pl* **-children** a stepson or stepdaughter

stepdame (ˈstɛpˌdeɪm) *n* an archaic word for **stepmother** [C14 from STEP- + DAME (in the archaic sense: mother; see DAM²)]

step dance *n* a dance in which a display of steps is more important than gesture or posture, esp a solo dance

stepdaughter (ˈstɛpˌdɔːtə) *n* a daughter of one's husband or wife by a former union

step down *vb* (*adverb*) **1** (*tr*) to reduce gradually **2** (*intr*) *informal* to resign or abdicate (from a position) **3** (*intr*) *informal* to assume an inferior or less senior position ▷ *adj* **step-down** (*prenominal*) **4** (of a transformer) reducing a high voltage applied to the primary winding to a lower voltage on the secondary winding. Compare **step-up** (sense 3) **5** decreasing or falling by stages ▷ *n* **step-down 6** *informal* a decrease in quantity or size

stepfather (ˈstɛpˌfɑːðə) *n* a man who has married one's mother after the death or divorce of one's father

Stepford (ˈstɛpˌfəd) *adj informal derogatory* **1** blandly conformist and submissive: *a Stepford employee* ▷ *n* **2** **Stepford wife** a married woman who submits to her husband's will and is preoccupied by domestic concerns and her own personal appearance [C20 from *The Stepford Wives* (1972), a book by US writer Ira Levin which depicted a neighbourhood in which men turn their wives into placid and obedient robots]

step function *n* an electrical waveform that rises or falls instantly from one level to another

stephanotis (ˌstɛfəˈnəʊtɪs) *n* any climbing asclepiadaceous shrub of the genus *Stephanotis*, esp *S. floribunda*, of Madagascar and Malaya: cultivated for their fragrant white waxy flowers [C19 via New Latin from Greek: fit for a crown, from *stephanos* a crown]

step in *vb* **1** (*intr, adverb*) *informal* to intervene or

involve oneself, esp dramatically or at a senior level ▷ *adj* **step-in 2** (*prenominal*) (of garments, etc) put on by being stepped into; without fastenings **3** (of a ski binding) engaging automatically when the boot is positioned on the ski ▷ *n* **step-in 4** (*often plural*) a step-in garment, esp underwear

stepladder (ˈstɛpˌlædə) *n* a folding portable ladder that is made of broad flat steps fixed to a supporting frame hinged at the top to another supporting frame

stepmother (ˈstɛpˌmʌðə) *n* a woman who has married one's father after the death or divorce of one's mother

stepney (ˈstɛpnɪ) *n Indian* a spare tyre [C20 from *Stepney Street*, Llanelli, the address of a tyre manufacturer]

step on *vb* (*intr, preposition*) **1** to place or press the foot on **2** *informal* to behave harshly or contemptuously towards **3** *slang* to adulterate drugs **4** **step on it** *informal* to go more quickly, hurry up

step out *vb* (*intr, adverb*) **1** to go outside or leave a room, building, etc, esp briefly **2** to begin to walk more quickly and take longer strides **3** *US and Canadian informal* to withdraw from involvement; bow out **4** **step out with** *informal* to be a boyfriend or girlfriend (of someone), esp publicly

step-parent (ˈstɛpˌpɛərənt) *n* a stepfather or stepmother **> ˈstep-ˌparenting** *n*

steppe (stɛp) *n* (*often plural*) an extensive grassy plain usually without trees. Compare **prairie, pampas** [C17 from Old Russian *step* lowland]

stepper (ˈstɛpə) *n* a person who or animal that steps, esp a horse or a dancer

Steppes (stɛps) *pl n* **the 1** the huge grasslands of Eurasia, chiefly in Ukraine and Russia **2** another name for **Kyrgyz Steppe**

stepping stone *n* **1** one of a series of stones acting as footrests for crossing streams, marshes, etc **2** a circumstance that assists progress towards some goal

stepsister (ˈstɛpˌsɪstə) *n* a daughter of one's stepmother or stepfather by a union with someone other than one's father or mother respectively

stepson (ˈstɛpˌsʌn) *n* a son of one's husband or wife by a former union

step up *vb* (*adverb*) *informal* **1** (*tr*) to increase or raise by stages; accelerate **2** (*intr*) to make progress or effect an advancement; be promoted ▷ *adj* **step-up** (*prenominal*) **3** (of a transformer) increasing a low voltage applied to the primary winding to a higher voltage on the secondary winding. Compare **step-down** (sense 4) **4** *informal* involving a rise by stages ▷ *n* **step-up 5** *informal* an increment in quantity, size, etc

stepwise (ˈstɛpˌwaɪz) *adj* **1** arranged in the manner of or resembling steps **2** *music, US* proceeding by melodic intervals of a second ▷ *adv* **3** with the form or appearance of steps; step by step **4** *music, US* in a stepwise motion

-ster *suffix forming nouns* **1** indicating a person who is engaged in a certain activity: *prankster; songster*. Compare **-stress 2** indicating a person associated with or being something specified: *mobster; youngster* [Old English *-estre*]

steradian (stəˈreɪdɪən) *n* an SI unit of solid angle; the angle that, having its vertex in the centre of a sphere, cuts off an area of the surface of the sphere equal to the square of the length of the radius. Symbol: **sr** [C19 from STEREO- + RADIAN]

stercoraceous (ˌstɜːkəˈreɪʃəs) *adj* of, relating to, or consisting of dung or excrement [C18 from Latin *stercus* dung + -ACEOUS]

stercoricolous (ˌstɜːkəˈrɪkələs) *adj* (of organisms) living in dung [C19 from Latin *stercus* dung + *colere* to live]

sterculia (stɜːˈkjuːlɪə) *n* a dietary fibre used as a food stabilizer and denture adhesive. It is the dried gum tapped from the trunk and stems of the tree *Sterculia urens*, native to Central India and Pakistan

S

sterculiaceous (stɜːˌkjuːlɪˈeɪʃəs) *adj* of, relating to, or belonging to the *Sterculiaceae*, a chiefly tropical family of plants that includes cacao and cola [C18 via New Latin from Latin *Sterculius* god of manuring, from *stercus* dung, alluding to the odour of some species]

stere (stɪə) *n* a unit used to measure volumes of stacked timber equal to one cubic metre (35.315 cubic feet) [C18 from French *stère*, from Greek *stereos* solid]

stereo ('stɛrɪəʊ, 'stɪər-) *adj* **1** short for **stereophonic** or **stereoscopic** ▷ *n*, *pl* **stereos 2** stereophonic sound: *to broadcast in stereo* **3** a stereophonic record player, tape recorder, etc **4** *photog* **a** stereoscopic photography **b** a stereoscopic photograph **5** *printing* short for **stereotype** [C20 shortened form]

stereo- or sometimes before a vowel **stere-** *combining form* indicating three-dimensional quality or solidity: *stereoscope* [from Greek *stereos* solid]

stereobate ('stɛrɪəʊˌbeɪt, 'stɪər-) *n* **1** another name for **stylobate 2** a foundation of a building in the form of a platform of masonry [C19 via Latin, from Greek *stereobatēs* from *stereos* solid + *-batēs* base, from *bainein* to walk]

stereochemistry (ˌstɛrɪəʊˈkɛmɪstrɪ, ˌstɪər-) *n* the study of the spatial arrangement of atoms in molecules and the effect of spatial arrangement on chemical properties

stereochrome ('stɛrɪəʊˌkrəʊm, 'stɪər-) *n* **1** a picture made by stereochromy ▷ *vb* **2** (*tr*) to produce (a picture) by the process of stereochromy

stereochromy ('stɛrɪəˌkrəʊmɪ, 'stɪər-) *n* a method of wall painting in which water glass is used either as a painting medium or as a final fixative coat [C19 via German *Stereochromie*, from STEREO- + Greek *khrōma* colour]

stereognosis (ˌstɛrɪɒɡˈnəʊsɪs, ˌstɪər-) *n* the perception of depth or three-dimensionality through any of the senses [C20 STEREO- + GNOSIS]

stereogram ('stɛrɪəˌɡræm, 'stɪər-) *n* **1** *Brit* a stereo radiogram **2** another name for **stereograph**

stereograph ('stɛrɪəˌɡræf, -ˌɡrɑːf, 'stɪər-) *n* two almost identical pictures, or one special picture, that when viewed through special glasses or a stereoscope form a single three-dimensional image. Also called: **stereogram**

stereography (ˌstɛrɪˈɒɡrəfɪ, ˌstɪər-) *n* **1** the study and construction of geometrical solids **2** the art of drawing a solid figure on a flat surface ▷ **stereographic** (ˌstɛrɪəˈɡræfɪk, ˌstɪər-) or **ˌstereoˈgraphical** *adj* ▷ **ˌstereoˈgraphically** *adv*

stereoisomer (ˌstɛrɪəʊˈaɪsəmə, ˌstɪər-) *n chem* one of the isomers of a compound that exhibits stereoisomerism

stereoisomerism (ˌstɛrɪəʊaɪˈsɒməˌrɪzəm, ˌstɪər-) *n chem* isomerism caused by differences in the spatial arrangement of atoms in molecules ▷ **stereoisometric** (ˌstɛrɪəʊˌaɪsəˈmɛtrɪk, ˌstɪər-) *adj*

stereome ('stɛrɪˌəʊm) *n botany, now rare* the tissue of a plant that provides mechanical support

stereometry (ˌstɛrɪˈɒmɪtrɪ, ˌstɪər-) *n* the measurement of volume ▷ **stereometric** (ˌstɛrɪəʊˈmɛtrɪk, ˌstɪər-) or **ˌstereoˈmetrical** *adj*

stereophonic (ˌstɛrɪəˈfɒnɪk, ˌstɪər-) *adj* (of a system for recording, reproducing, or broadcasting sound) using two or more separate microphones to feed two or more loudspeakers through separate channels in order to give a spatial effect to the sound. Often shortened to: **stereo** Compare **monophonic, quadraphonics** ▷ **ˌstereoˈphonically** *adv* ▷ **stereophony** (ˌstɛrɪˈɒfənɪ, ˌstɪər-) *n*

stereopsis (ˌstɛrɪˈɒpsɪs, ˌstɪər-) *n* stereoscopic vision [from STEREO- + Greek *opsis* vision]

stereopticon (ˌstɛrɪˈɒptɪkᵊn, ˌstɪər-) *n* a type of projector with two complete units arranged so that one picture dissolves as the next is forming [C19 from STEREO- + Greek *optikon*, neuter form of *optikos* OPTIC]

stereoscope ('stɛrɪəˌskəʊp, 'stɪər-) *n* an optical instrument for viewing two-dimensional pictures and giving them an illusion of depth and relief. It has a binocular eyepiece through which two slightly different pictures of the same object are viewed, one with each eye

stereoscopic (ˌstɛrɪəˈskɒpɪk, ˌstɪər-) *adj* **1** of, concerned with, or relating to seeing space three-dimensionally as a result of binocular disparity: *stereoscopic vision* **2** of, relating to, or formed by a stereoscope ▷ **ˌstereoˈscopically** *adv*

stereoscopy (ˌstɛrɪˈɒskəpɪ, ˌstɪər-) *n* **1** the viewing or appearance of objects in or as if in three dimensions **2** the study and use of the stereoscope ▷ **ˌstereoˈoscopist** *n*

stereospecific (ˌstɛrɪəʊspɪˈsɪfɪk, ˌstɪər-) *adj chem* relating to or having fixed position in space, as in the spatial arrangements of atoms in certain polymers

stereospecific catalyst *n chem* a catalyst for stereospecific chemical reactions. See also **Ziegler catalyst**

stereospecific polymer *n* an organic polymer in which the steric arrangements of groups on assymetric carbon atoms occur in a regular sequence. Many natural and synthetic rubbers are stereospecific polymers

stereotactic (ˌstɛrɪəˈtæktɪk, ˌstɪər-) *adj* **1** of or relating to stereotaxis **2** *med* of or relating to precise localization of a tissue, esp in the brain: *stereotactic surgery* ▷ **ˌstereoˈtactically** *adv*

stereotaxis (ˌstɛrɪəˈtæksɪs, ˌstɪər-) *n* the movement of an organism in response to the stimulus of contact with a solid object [C20 from STEREO- + -TAXIS]

stereotomy (ˌstɛrɪˈɒtəmɪ, ˌstɪər-) *n* the art of cutting three-dimensional solids into particular shapes [C18 from French *stéréotomie*. See STEREO-, -TOMY]

stereotropism (ˌstɛrɪˈɒtrəˌpɪzəm, ˌstɪər-) *n* another name for **thigmotropism**. ▷ **stereotropic** (ˌstɛrɪəˈtrɒpɪk, ˌstɪər-) *adj*

stereotype ('stɛrɪəˌtaɪp, 'stɪər-) *n* **1 a** a method of producing cast-metal printing plates from a mould made from a forme of type matter in papier-mâché or some other material **b** the plate so made **2** another word for **stereotypy 3** an idea, trait, convention, etc, that has grown stale through fixed usage **4** *sociol* a set of inaccurate, simplistic generalizations about a group that allows others to categorize them and treat them accordingly ▷ *vb* (*tr*) **5 a** to make a stereotype of **b** to print from a stereotype **6** to impart a fixed usage or convention to ▷ **ˈstereoˌtyper** or **ˈstereoˈtypist** *n* ▷ **stereotypic** (ˌstɛrɪəˈtɪpɪk, ˌstɪər-) or **ˌstereoˈtypical** *adj*

stereotyped ('stɛrɪəˌtaɪpt, 'stɪər-) *adj* **1** lacking originality or individuality; conventional; trite **2** reproduced from or on a stereotype printing plate

stereotypy ('stɛrɪəˌtaɪpɪ, 'stɪər-) *n* **1** the act or process of making stereotype printing plates **2** a tendency to think or act in rigid, repetitive, and often meaningless patterns

stereovision ('stɛrɪəʊˌvɪʒən, 'stɪər-) *n* the perception or exhibition of three-dimensional objects in three dimensions

steric ('stɛrɪk, 'stɪər-) or **sterical** *adj chem* concerned with, or caused by the spatial arrangement of atoms in a molecule [C19 from STEREO- + -IC] ▷ **ˈsterically** *adv*

sterigma (stəˈrɪɡmə) *n biology* a minute stalk bearing a spore or chain of spores in certain fungi [C19 New Latin from Greek *stērigma* support, from *stērizein* to sustain]

sterilant ('stɛrɪlənt) *n* any substance or agent used in sterilization

sterile ('stɛraɪl) *adj* **1** unable to produce offspring; infertile **2** free from living, esp pathogenic, microorganisms; aseptic **3** (of plants or their parts) not producing or bearing seeds, fruit, spores, stamens, or pistils **4** lacking inspiration or vitality; fruitless **5** *economics, US* (of gold) not being used to support credit creation or an increased money supply [C16 from Latin *sterilis*]

▷ **ˈsterilely** *adv* ▷ **sterility** (stɛˈrɪlɪtɪ) *n*

sterilization or **sterilisation** (ˌstɛrɪlaɪˈzeɪʃən) *n* **1** the act or procedure of sterilizing or making sterile **2** the state of being sterile

sterilize or **sterilise** ('stɛrɪˌlaɪz) *vb* (*tr*) to render sterile; make infertile or barren ▷ **ˈsteriˌlizable** or **ˈsteriˌlisable** *adj*

sterilizer or **steriliser** ('stɛrɪˌlaɪzə) *n* a person, substance, or device that sterilizes

sterlet ('stɜːlɪt) *n* a small sturgeon, *Acipenser ruthenus*, of seas and rivers in N Asia and E Europe: used as a food fish and a source of caviar [C16 from Russian *sterlyad*, of Germanic origin; compare Old High German *sturio* sturgeon]

sterling ('stɜːlɪŋ) *n* **1 a** British money: *pound sterling* **b** (*as modifier*): *sterling reserves* **2** the official standard of fineness of British coins: for gold 0.91666 and for silver 0.925 **3 a** short for **sterling silver b** (*as modifier*): *a sterling bracelet* **4** an article or articles manufactured from sterling silver **5** a former British silver penny ▷ *adj* **6** (*prenominal*) genuine and reliable; first-class: *sterling quality* [C13 probably from Old English STAR + -LING¹; referring to a small star on early Norman pennies; related to Old French *esterlin*]

sterling area *n* a group of countries that use sterling as a medium of international payments and sometimes informally as a currency against which to peg their own currencies. For these purposes they deposit sterling balances and hold gold and dollar reserves in the Bank of England. Also called: **sterling bloc, scheduled territories**

sterling silver *n* **1** an alloy containing not less than 92.5 per cent of silver, the remainder usually being copper **2** sterling-silver articles collectively

Sterlitamak (*Russian* stjerlita'mak) *n* an industrial city in W Russia, in the Bashkir Republic. Pop: 268 000 (2005 est)

stern¹ (stɜːn) *adj* **1** showing uncompromising or inflexible resolve; firm, strict, or authoritarian **2** lacking leniency or clemency; harsh or severe **3** relentless; unyielding: *the stern demands of parenthood* **4** having an austere or forbidding appearance or nature [Old English *styrne*; related to Old High German *stornēn* to alarm, Latin *sternāx* stubborn, Greek *stereos* hard] ▷ **ˈsternly** *adv* ▷ **ˈsternness** *n*

stern² (stɜːn) *n* **1** the rear or after part of a vessel, opposite the bow or stem **2** the rear part of any object **3** the tail of certain breeds of dog, such as the foxhound or beagle ▷ *adj* **4** relating to or located at the stern [C13 from Old Norse *stjörn* steering; see STEER¹]

stern-chaser *n* a gun mounted at the stern of a vessel for firing aft at a pursuing vessel

sternforemost ('stɜːnˈfɔːˌməʊst) *adv nautical* backwards

sternmost ('stɜːnˌməʊst) *adj nautical* **1** farthest to the stern; aftmost **2** nearest the stern

sternpost ('stɜːnˌpəʊst) *n nautical* the main upright timber or structure at the stern of a vessel

stern sheets *pl n nautical* the part of an open boat near the stern

sternson ('stɜːnsᵊn) *n nautical* a timber scarfed into or bolted to the sternpost and keelson at the stern of a wooden vessel. Compare **stemson** [C19 from STERN² + -son, on the model of KEELSON]

sternum ('stɜːnəm) *n, pl* **-na** (-nə) or **-nums 1** (in man) a long flat vertical bone, situated in front of the thorax, to which are attached the collarbone and the first seven pairs of ribs. Nontechnical name: **breastbone 2** the corresponding part in many other vertebrates **3** a cuticular plate covering the ventral surface of a body segment of an arthropod. Compare **tergum** [C17 via New Latin from Greek *sternon* breastbone] ▷ **ˈsternal** *adj*

sternutation (ˌstɜːnjʊˈteɪʃən) *n* a sneeze or the act of sneezing [C16 from Late Latin *sternūtāre* to sneeze, from *sternuere* to sputter (of a light)]

sternutator ('stɜːnjʊˌteɪtə) *n* a substance that causes sneezing, coughing, and tears; used in chemical warfare

sternutatory (stɜːˈnjuːtətərɪ, -trɪ) *adj also* **sternutative** **1** causing or having the effect of sneezing ▷ *n, pl* **-tories** **2** an agent or substance that causes sneezing

sternwards (ˈstɜːnwədz) *or* **sternward** *adv nautical* towards the stern; astern

sternway (ˈstɜːnˌweɪ) *n nautical* movement of a vessel sternforemost

stern-wheeler *n* a vessel, esp a riverboat, propelled by a large paddle wheel at the stern. Compare **sidewheeler**

steroid (ˈstɪərɔɪd, ˈstɛr-) *n biochem* any of a large group of fat-soluble organic compounds containing a characteristic chemical ring system. The majority, including the sterols, bile acids, many hormones, and the D vitamins, have important physiological action [C20 from STEROL + -OID] > steˈroidal *adj*

sterol (ˈstɛrɒl) *n biochem* any of a group of natural steroid alcohols, such as cholesterol and ergosterol, that are waxy insoluble substances [C20 shortened from CHOLESTEROL, ERGOSTEROL, etc]

stertor (ˈstɜːtə) *n* laborious or noisy breathing caused by obstructed air passages [C17 from New Latin, from Latin *stertere* to snore]

stertorous (ˈstɜːtərəs) *adj* **1** marked or accompanied by heavy snoring **2** breathing in this way > ˈ**stertorously** *adv* > ˈ**stertorousness** *n*

stet (stɛt) *n* **1** a word or mark indicating that certain deleted typeset or written matter is to be retained. Compare **dele** ▷ *vb* **stets, stetting, stetted** **2** (*tr*) to mark (matter to be retained) with a stet [Latin, literally: let it stand]

stethoscope (ˈstɛθəˌskəʊp) *n* **1** *med* an instrument for listening to the sounds made within the body, typically consisting of a hollow disc that transmits the sound through hollow tubes to earpieces **2** a narrow cylinder expanded at both ends to recieve and transmit fetal sounds. Also called: **obstetric stethoscope** [C19 from French, from Greek *stēthos* breast + -SCOPE] > **stethoscopic** (ˌstɛθəˈskɒpɪk) *adj* > **stethoscopy** (stɛˈθɒskəpɪ) *n*

Stetson (ˈstɛtsᵊn) *n trademark* a type of felt hat with a broad brim and high crown, worn mainly by cowboys [C20 named after John *Stetson* (1830–1906), American hatmaker who designed it]

Stettin (ʃtɛˈtiːn) *n* the German name for **Szczecin**

stevedore (ˈstiːvɪˌdɔː) *n* **1** a person employed to load or unload ships ▷ *vb* **2** to load or unload (a ship, ship's cargo, etc) [C18 from Spanish *estibador* a packer, from *estibar* to load (a ship), from Latin *stīpāre* to pack full]

stevedore's knot *n* a knot forming a lump in a line, used by stevedores to secure ropes passing through holes

Stevenage (ˈstiːvənɪdʒ) *n* a town in SE England, in N Hertfordshire on the Great North Road: developed chiefly as the first of the new towns (1946). Pop: 81 482 (2001)

Stevengraph (ˈstiːvᵊnˌgrɑːf) *or* **Stevensgraph** *n* a picture, usually small, woven in silk [named after Thomas *Stevens* (1828–88), English weaver]

stew[1] (stjuː) *n* **1 a** a dish of meat, fish, or other food, cooked by stewing **b** (*as modifier*): *stew pot* **2** *informal* a difficult or worrying situation or a troubled state (esp in the phrase **in a stew**) **3** a heterogeneous mixture: *a stew of people of every race* **4** (*usually plural*) *archaic* a brothel **5** *obsolete* a public room for hot steam baths ▷ *vb* **6** to cook or cause to cook by long slow simmering **7** (*intr*) *informal* to be troubled or agitated **8** (*intr*) *informal* to be oppressed with heat or crowding **9** to cause (tea) to become bitter or (of tea) to become bitter through infusing for too long **10** **stew in one's own juice** to suffer unaided the consequences of one's actions [C14 *stuen* to take a very hot bath, from Old French *estuver*, from Vulgar Latin *extūfāre* (unattested), from EX-[1] + (unattested) *tūfus* vapour, from Greek *tuphos*]

stew[2] (stjuː) *n Brit* **1** a fishpond or fishtank **2** an artificial oyster bed [C14 from Old French *estui*, from *estoier* to shut up, confine, ultimately from Latin *studium* STUDY]

steward (ˈstjʊəd) *n* **1** a person who administers the property, house, finances, etc, of another **2** a person who manages the eating arrangements, staff, or service at a club, hotel, etc **3** a waiter on a ship or aircraft **4** a mess attendant in a naval mess afloat or ashore **5** a person who helps to supervise some event or proceedings in an official capacity **6** short for **shop steward** ▷ *vb* **7** to act or serve as a steward (of something) [Old English *stigweard*, from *stig* hall (see STY) + *weard* WARD] > ˈ**steward,ship** *n*

stewardess (ˈstjʊədɪs, ˌstjʊəˈdɛs) *n* a woman who performs a steward's job on an aircraft or ship

Stewart Island *n* the third largest island of New Zealand, in the SW Pacific off the S tip of South Island. Pop: 387 (2001). Area: 1735 sq km (670 sq miles)

stewed (stjuːd) *adj* **1** (of meat, fruit, etc) cooked by stewing **2** *Brit* (of tea) having a bitter taste through having been left to infuse for too long **3** a slang word for **drunk** (sense 1)

Steyr *or* **Steier** (*German* ˈʃtaiər) *n* an industrial city in N central Austria, in Upper Austria. Pop: 39 340 (2001)

stg *abbreviation for* sterling

stge *abbreviation for* storage

Sth *abbreviation for* South

sthenic (ˈsθɛnɪk) *adj* abounding in energy or bodily strength; active or strong [C18 from New Latin *sthenicus*, from Greek *sthenos* force, on the model of *asthenic*]

Stheno (ˈsθiːnəʊ, ˈsθɛnəʊ) *n Greek myth* one of the three Gorgons

stibine (ˈstɪbaɪn) *n* **1** a colourless slightly soluble poisonous gas with an offensive odour: made by the action of hydrochloric acid on an alloy of antimony and zinc. Formula: SbH_3 **2** any one of a class of stibine derivatives in which one or more hydrogen atoms have been replaced by organic groups [C19 from Latin STIBIUM + -INE[2]]

stibium (ˈstɪbɪəm) *n* an obsolete name for **antimony** [C14 from Latin: antimony (used as a cosmetic in ancient Rome), via Greek from Egyptian *stm*] > ˈ**stibial** *adj*

stibnite (ˈstɪbnaɪt) *n* a soft greyish mineral consisting of antimony sulphide in orthorhombic crystalline form. It occurs in quartz veins and is the chief ore of antimony. Formula: Sb_2S_3 [C19 from obsolete *stibine* stibnite + -ITE[1]]

stich (stɪk) *n* a line of poetry; verse [C18 from Greek *stikhos* row, verse; related to *steikhein* to walk] > ˈ**stichic** *adj* > ˈ**stichically** *adv*

stichometry (stɪˈkɒmɪtrɪ) *n prosody* the practice of writing out a prose text in lines that correspond to the sense units and indicate the phrasal rhythms [C18 from Late Greek *stikhometria*. See STICH, -METRY] > **stichometric** (ˌstɪkəʊˈmɛtrɪk) *or* ˌ**sticho**ˈ**metrical** *adj*

stichomythia (ˌstɪkəʊˈmɪθɪə) *or* **stichomythy** (stɪˈkɒmɪθɪ) *n* a form of dialogue originating in Greek drama in which single lines are uttered by alternate speakers [C19 from Greek *stikhomuthein* to speak alternate lines, from *stikhos* line + *muthos* speech; see MYTH] > ˌ**sticho**ˈ**mythic** *adj*

-stichous *adj combining form* having a certain number of rows: *distichous* [from Late Latin *-stichus*, from Greek *-stikhos*, from *stikhos* line, row; see STICH]

stick[1] (stɪk) *n* **1** a small thin branch of a tree **2 a** any long thin piece of wood **b** such a piece of wood having a characteristic shape for a special purpose: *a walking stick; a hockey stick* **c** a baton, wand, staff, or rod **3** an object or piece shaped like a stick: *a stick of celery; a stick of dynamite* **4** See **control stick** **5** *informal* the lever used to change gear in a motor vehicle **6** *nautical* a mast or yard **7** *printing* See **composing stick** **8 a** a group of bombs arranged to fall at intervals across a target **b** a number of paratroops jumping in sequence **9** *slang* **a** verbal abuse, criticism: *I got some stick for that blunder* **b** physical power, force (esp in the phrase **give it some stick**) **10** (*usually plural*) a piece of furniture: *these few sticks are all I have* **11** (*plural*) *informal* a rural area considered remote or backward (esp in the phrase **in the sticks**) **12** (*plural*) *W and NW Canadian informal* the wooded interior part of the country **13** (*plural*) *hockey* a declaration made by the umpire if a player's stick is above the shoulders **14** (*plural*) goalposts **15** *US obsolete* a cannabis cigarette **16** a means of coercion **17** *informal* a dull boring person **18** (usually preceded by *old*) *informal* a familiar name for a person: *not a bad old stick* **19** **in a cleft stick** in a difficult position **20** **wrong end of the stick** a complete misunderstanding of a situation, explanation, etc ▷ *vb* **sticks, sticking, sticked** **21** to support (a plant) with sticks; stake [Old English *sticca*; related to Old Norse *stikka*, Old High German *stecca*]

stick[2] (stɪk) *vb* **sticks, sticking, stuck** **1** (*tr*) to pierce or stab with or as if with something pointed **2** to thrust or push (a sharp or pointed object) or (of a sharp or pointed object) to be pushed into or through another object **3** (*tr*) to fasten in position by pushing or forcing a point into something: *to stick a peg in a hole* **4** (*tr*) to fasten in position by or as if by pins, nails, etc: *to stick a picture on the wall* **5** (*tr*) to transfix or impale on a pointed object **6** (*tr*) to cover with objects piercing or set in the surface **7** (when *intr*, foll by *out, up, through*, etc) to put forward or be put forward; protrude or cause to protrude: *to stick one's head out of the window* **8** (*tr*) *informal* to place or put in a specified position: *stick your coat on this chair* **9** to fasten or be fastened by or as if by an adhesive substance: *stick the pages together; they won't stick* **10** (*tr*) *informal* to cause to become sticky **11** (when *tr*, *usually passive*) to come or cause to come to a standstill: *we were stuck for hours in a traffic jam; the wheels stuck* **12** (*intr*) to remain for a long time: *the memory sticks in my mind* **13** (*tr*) *slang, chiefly Brit* to tolerate; abide: *I can't stick that man* **14** (*intr*) to be reluctant **15** (*tr; usually passive*) *informal* to cause to be at a loss; baffle, puzzle, or confuse: *I was totally stuck for an answer* **16** (*tr*) *slang* to force or impose something unpleasant on: *they stuck me with the bill for lunch* **17** (*tr*) to kill by piercing or stabbing **18** **stick in one's throat** (*or* **craw**) *informal* to be difficult, or against one's conscience, for one to accept, utter, or believe **19** **stick one's nose into** See **nose** (sense 17) **20** **stick to the ribs** *informal* (of food) to be hearty and satisfying ▷ *n* **21** the state or condition of adhering **22** *informal* a substance causing adhesion **23** *obsolete* something that causes delay or stoppage ▷ See also **stick around, stick at, stick by, stick down, stick out, stick to, stick together, stick-up, stick with, stuck** [Old English *stician*; related to Old High German *stehhan* to sting, Old Norse *steikja* to roast on a spit]

stick around *or* **about** *vb* (*intr, adverb*) *informal* to remain in a place, esp awaiting something

stick at *vb* (*intr, preposition*) **1** to continue constantly at: *to stick at one's work* **2** **stick at nothing** to be prepared to do anything; be unscrupulous or ruthless

stick by *vb* (*intr, preposition*) to remain faithful to; adhere to

stick down *vb* (*tr, adverb*) *informal* to write: *stick your name down here*

sticker (ˈstɪkə) *n* **1** an adhesive label, poster, or paper **2** a person or thing that sticks **3** a persevering or industrious person **4** something prickly, such as a thorn, that clings to one's clothing, etc **5** *informal* something that perplexes **6** *informal* a knife used for stabbing or piercing

stick float *n angling* a float attached at the top and bottom to the line

stickhandle (ˈstɪkˌhændᵊl) *vb ice hockey* to manoeuvre (the puck) deftly > ˈ**stick,handler** *n*

sticking plaster *n* a thin cloth with an adhesive substance on one side, used for covering slight or

S

superficial wounds. Usual US term: **adhesive tape**
sticking point *n* a problem or point on which agreement cannot be reached, preventing progress from being made
stick insect *n* any of various mostly tropical insects of the family *Phasmidae* that have an elongated cylindrical body and long legs and resemble twigs: order *Phasmida*. Also called (US and Canadian): **walking stick** See also **leaf insect**
stick-in-the-mud *n informal* a staid or predictably conservative person who lacks initiative or imagination
stickle ('stɪkᵊl) *vb (intr)* **1** to dispute stubbornly, esp about minor points **2** to refuse to agree or concur, esp by making petty stipulations [C16 *stightle* (in the sense: to arbitrate): frequentative of Old English *stihtan* to arrange; related to Old Norse *stētta* to support]
stickleback ('stɪkᵊl,bæk) *n* any small teleost fish of the family *Gasterosteidae*, such as *Gasterosteus aculeatus* (**three-spined stickleback**) of rivers and coastal regions and *G. pungitius* (**ten-spined stickleback**) confined to rivers. They have a series of spines along the back and occur in cold and temperate northern regions [C15 from Old English *stickel* prick, sting + BACK[1]]
stickler ('stɪklə) *n* **1** (usually foll by *for*) a person who makes insistent demands: *a stickler for accuracy* **2** a problem or puzzle: *the investigation proved to be a stickler*
stick-on ('stɪkɒn) *n informal* an event with a certain outcome
stick out *vb (adverb)* **1** to project or cause to project **2** *(tr) informal* to endure (something disagreeable) (esp in the phrase **stick it out**) **3** **stick out a mile** *or* **like a sore thumb** *informal* to be extremely obvious **4** **stick out for** *(intr)* to insist on (a demand), refusing to yield until it is met: *the unions stuck out for a ten per cent wage rise*
stick pin *n* the US name for **tiepin**
stickseed ('stɪk,si:d) *n* any of various Eurasian and North American plants of the boraginaceous genus *Lappula*, having red-and-blue flowers and small prickly fruits. Also called: **beggar's-lice** [C19 from STICK[2]; so called because its seeds have adhesive hooks on them]
stick shift *n US and Canadian* **1** **a** a manually operated transmission system in a motor vehicle **b** a motor vehicle having manual transmission **2** a gear lever
sticktight ('stɪk,taɪt) *n* any of various plants, esp the bur marigold, that have barbed clinging fruits
stick to *vb (preposition, mainly intr)* **1** *(also tr)* to adhere or cause to adhere to **2** to continue constantly at **3** to remain faithful to **4** not to move or digress from: *the speaker stuck closely to his subject* **5** **stick to someone's fingers** *informal* to be stolen by someone
stick together *vb (intr, adverb) informal* to remain loyal or friendly to one another
stick-up *n* **1** *slang, chiefly US* a robbery at gunpoint; hold-up ▷ *vb* **stick up** *(adverb)* **2** *(tr) slang, chiefly US* to rob, esp at gunpoint **3** *(intr; foll by for) informal* to support or defend: *stick up for oneself*
stickweed ('stɪk,wi:d) *n* any of several plants that have clinging fruits or seeds, esp the ragweed
stick with *vb (intr, preposition) informal* to persevere with; remain faithful to
sticky ('stɪkɪ) *adj* **stickier, stickiest** **1** covered or daubed with an adhesive or viscous substance: *sticky fingers* **2** having the property of sticking to a surface **3** (of weather or atmosphere) warm and humid; muggy **4** (of prices) tending not to fall in deflationary conditions **5** *informal* difficult, awkward, or painful: *a sticky business* **6** *US informal* sentimental **7** (of a website) encouraging users to visit repeatedly ▷ *vb* **stickies, stickying, stickied** **8** *(tr) informal* to make sticky ▷ *n, pl* **stickies** *Austral informal* **9** short for **stickybeak** **10** an inquisitive look or stare (esp in the phrase **have a sticky at**) > '**stickily** *adv* > '**stickiness** *n*
stickybeak ('stɪkɪ,bi:k) *Austral and NZ informal* ▷ *n* **1** an inquisitive person ▷ *vb* **2** *(intr)* to pry [from STICKY + BEAK[1] (in the slang sense: a human nose)]
sticky blood *n* a condition of the blood, particularly associated with Hughes syndrome, in which antibodies tend to adhere to platelets and glue them together, leading to an increased likelihood of clotting
sticky end *n informal* an unpleasant finish or death (esp in the phrase **come to** *or* **meet a sticky end**)
sticky-fingered *adj informal* given to thieving
sticky wicket *n* **1** a cricket pitch that is rapidly being dried by the sun after rain and is particularly conducive to spin **2** *informal* a difficult or awkward situation (esp in the phrase **on a sticky wicket**)
sticky willie *n* another name for **cleavers**
stiction ('stɪkʃən) *n* the frictional force to be overcome to set one object in motion when it is in contact with another [C20 blend of STATIC + FRICTION]
stiff (stɪf) *adj* **1** not easily bent; rigid; inflexible **2** not working or moving easily or smoothly: *a stiff handle* **3** difficult to accept in its severity or harshness: *a stiff punishment* **4** moving with pain or difficulty; not supple: *a stiff neck* **5** difficult; arduous: *a stiff climb* **6** unrelaxed or awkward; formal **7** firmer than liquid in consistency; thick or viscous **8** powerful; strong: *a stiff breeze; a stiff drink* **9** excessively high: *a stiff price* **10** *nautical* (of a sailing vessel) relatively resistant to heeling or rolling. Compare **tender**[1] (sense 11) **11** lacking grace or attractiveness **12** stubborn or stubbornly maintained: *a stiff fight* **13** *obsolete* tightly stretched; taut **14** *slang, chiefly Austral* unlucky **15** *slang* intoxicated **16** **stiff upper lip** See **lip** (sense 9) **17** **stiff with** *informal* amply provided with ▷ *n* **18** *slang* a corpse **19** *slang* anything thought to be a loser or a failure; flop ▷ *adv* **20** completely or utterly: *bored stiff; frozen stiff* ▷ *vb* **21** *(intr) slang* to fail: *the film stiffed* **22** *(tr) slang, chiefly US* to cheat or swindle **23** *(tr) slang* to kill [Old English *stīf*; related to Old Norse *stīfla* to dam up, Middle Low German *stīf* stiff, Latin *stīpēs* wooden post, *stīpāre* to press] > '**stiffish** *adj* > '**stiffly** *adv* > '**stiffness** *n*
stiffen ('stɪfᵊn) *vb* **1** to make or become stiff or stiffer **2** *(intr)* to become suddenly tense or unyielding > '**stiffener** *n*
stiff-necked *adj* haughtily stubborn or obstinate
stiffy ('sɪfɪ) *n, pl* **-fies** *slang* an erection of the penis
stifle[1] ('staɪfᵊl) *vb* **1** *(tr)* to smother or suppress: *stifle a cough* **2** to feel or cause to feel discomfort and difficulty in breathing **3** to prevent or be prevented from breathing so as to cause death **4** *(tr)* to crush or stamp out [C14 variant of *stuflen*, probably from Old French *estouffer* to smother] > '**stifler** *n*
stifle[2] ('staɪfᵊl) *n* the joint in the hind leg of a horse, dog, etc, between the femur and tibia [C14 of unknown origin]
stifling ('staɪflɪŋ) *adj* oppressively hot or stuffy: *a stifling atmosphere* > '**stiflingly** *adv*
stigma ('stɪgmə) *n, pl* **stigmas** *or for sense 7* **stigmata** ('stɪgmətə, stɪg'mɑ:tə) **1** a distinguishing mark of social disgrace: *the stigma of having been in prison* **2** a small scar or mark such as a birthmark **3** *pathol* **a** any mark on the skin, such as one characteristic of a specific disease **b** any sign of a mental deficiency or emotional upset **4** *botany* the receptive surface of a carpel, where deposited pollen germinates **5** *zoology* **a** a pigmented eyespot in some protozoans and other invertebrates **b** the spiracle of an insect **6** *archaic* a mark branded on the skin **7** *(plural) Christianity* marks resembling the wounds of the crucified Christ, believed to appear on the bodies of certain individuals [C16 via Latin from Greek: brand, from *stizein* to tattoo]
stigmasterol (stɪg'mæstə,rɒl) *n biochem* a sterol obtained from Calabar beans and soya beans and used in the manufacture of progesterone. Formula: $C_{29}H_{47}OH$ [C20 from New Latin *(physo)stigma* genus name of the Calabar bean + STEROL; see PHYSOSTIGMINE]
stigmatic (stɪg'mætɪk) *adj* **1** relating to or having a stigma or stigmata **2** another word for **anastigmatic** ▷ *n also* **stigmatist** ('stɪgmətɪst) **3** *chiefly RC Church* a person marked with the stigmata
stigmatism ('stɪgmə,tɪzəm) *n* **1** *physics* the state or condition of being anastigmatic **2** *pathol* the condition resulting from or characterized by stigmata
stigmatize *or* **stigmatise** ('stɪgmə,taɪz) *vb (tr)* **1** to mark out or describe (as something bad) **2** to mark with a stigma or stigmata > ,**stigmati'zation** *or* ,**stigmati'sation** *n* > '**stigma,tizer** *or* '**stigma,tiser** *n*
Stijl (staɪl) *n* **De** See **De Stijl**
stilb (stɪlb) *n physics* a unit of luminance equal to 1 candela per square centimetre. Symbol: **sb** [C20 from Greek *stilbē* lamp]
stilbene ('stɪlbi:n) *n* a colourless or slightly yellow crystalline water-insoluble unsaturated hydrocarbon used in the manufacture of dyes; *trans*-1,2-diphenylethene. Formula: $C_6H_5CH{:}CHC_6H_5$ [C19 from Greek *stilbos* glittering + -ENE]
stilbestrol *or* **stilboestrol** (stɪl'bi:strəl) *n* another name for **diethylstilbestrol** [C20 from STILBENE + OESTRUS + -OL[1]]
stilbite ('stɪlbaɪt) *n* a white or yellow zeolite mineral consisting of hydrated calcium sodium aluminium silicate, often in the form of sheaves of monoclinic crystals. Formula: $(Na_2Ca)Al_2Si_7O_{18}.7H_2O$ [C19 from Greek *stilbos* glittering (from *stilbein* to shine) + -ITE[1]]
stile[1] (staɪl) *n* **1** a set of steps or rungs in a wall or fence to allow people, but not animals, to pass over **2** short for **turnstile** [Old English *stigel*; related to *stīgan* to climb, Old High German *stigilla*; see STAIR]
stile[2] (staɪl) *n* a vertical framing member in a door, window frame, or piece of panelling. Compare **rail**[1] (sense 3) [C17 probably from Dutch *stijl* pillar, ultimately from Latin *stilus* writing instrument; see STYLE]
stiletto (stɪ'lɛtəʊ) *n, pl* **-tos** **1** a small dagger with a slender tapered blade **2** a sharply pointed tool used to make holes in leather, cloth, etc **3** Also called: **spike heel, stiletto heel** a very high heel on a woman's shoe, tapering to a very narrow tip ▷ *vb* **-toes, -toeing, -toed** **4** *(tr)* to stab with a stiletto [C17 from Italian, from *stilo* a dagger, from Latin *stilus* a stake, pen; see STYLUS]
still[1] (stɪl) *adj* **1** *(usually predicative)* motionless; stationary **2** undisturbed or tranquil; silent and calm **3** not sparkling or effervescent: *a still wine* **4** gentle or quiet; subdued **5** *obsolete* (of a child) dead at birth ▷ *adv* **6** continuing now or in the future as in the past: *do you still love me?* **7** up to this or that time; yet: *I still don't know your name* **8** *(often used with a comparative)* even or yet: *still more insults* **9** quiet or without movement: *sit still* **10** *poetic and dialect* always ▷ *n* **11** *poetic* silence or tranquillity: *the still of the night* **12** **a** a still photograph, esp of a scene from a motion-picture film **b** *(as modifier)*: *a still camera* ▷ *vb* **13** to make or become still, quiet, or calm **14** *(tr)* to allay or relieve: *her fears were stilled* ▷ *sentence connector* **15** even then; nevertheless: *the child has some new toys and still cries* [Old English *stille*; related to Old Saxon, Old High German *stilli*, Dutch *stollen* to curdle, Sanskrit *sthānús* immobile] > '**stillness** *n*
still[2] (stɪl) *n* **1** an apparatus for carrying out distillation, consisting of a vessel in which a mixture is heated, a condenser to turn the vapour back to liquid, and a receiver to hold the distilled liquid, used esp in the manufacture of spirits **2** a place where spirits are made; distillery [C16 from Old French *stiller* to drip, from Latin *stillāre*, from *stilla* a drip; see DISTIL]
stillage ('stɪlɪdʒ) *n* **1** a frame or stand for keeping

things off the ground, such as casks in a brewery **2** a container in which goods, machinery, etc, are transported [C16 probably from Dutch *stillagie* frame, scaffold, from *stellen* to stand; see -AGE]

stillbirth (ˈstɪlˌbɜːθ) *n* **1** birth of a dead fetus or baby **2** a stillborn fetus or baby

stillborn (ˈstɪlˌbɔːn) *adj* **1** (of a fetus) dead at birth **2** (of an idea, plan, etc) fruitless; abortive; unsuccessful ▷ *n* **3** a stillborn fetus or baby

still frame *n* continuous display of a single frame of a film or of a single picture from a television signal

still hunt *n* **1** the hunting of game by stalking or ambushing ▷ *vb* **still-hunt** **2** to hunt (quarry) in this way

stillicide (ˈstɪlɪˌsaɪd) *n* *law* a right or duty relating to the drainage of water from the eaves of a roof onto adjacent land [C17 from Latin *stillicidium*, from *stilla* drop + *-cidium*, from *cadere* to fall]

stilliform (ˈstɪlɪˌfɔːm) *adj* *rare* having the shape of a drop or globule [C20 from Latin *stilla* a drop + -FORM]

still life *n, pl* **still lifes** **1 a** a painting or drawing of inanimate objects, such as fruit, flowers, etc **b** (*as modifier*): *a still-life painting* **2** the genre of such paintings

still room *n* *Brit* **1** a room in which distilling is carried out **2** a pantry or storeroom, as in a large house

Stillson wrench (ˈstɪlsᵊn) *n* *trademark* a large wrench having adjustable jaws that tighten as the pressure on the handle is increased

stilly *adv* (ˈstɪllɪ) **1** *archaic or literary* quietly or calmly ▷ *adj* (ˈstɪlɪ) **2** *poetic* still, quiet, or calm

stilt (stɪlt) *n* **1** either of a pair of two long poles with footrests on which a person stands and walks, as used by circus clowns **2** a long post or column that is used with others to support a building above ground level **3** any of several shore birds of the genera *Himantopus* and *Cladorhynchus*, similar to the avocets but having a straight bill ▷ *vb* **4** (*tr*) to raise or place on or as if on stilts [C14 (in the sense: crutch, handle of a plough): related to Low German *stilte* pole, Norwegian *stilta*]

stilted (ˈstɪltɪd) *adj* **1** (of speech, writing, etc) formal, pompous, or bombastic **2** not flowing continuously or naturally: *stilted conversation* **3** *architect* (of an arch) having vertical piers between the impost and the springing > ˈ**stiltedly** *adv* > ˈ**stiltedness** *n*

Stilton (ˈstɪltən) *n* *trademark* either of two rich cheeses made from whole milk, blue-veined (**blue Stilton**) or white (**white Stilton**), both very strong in flavour [C18 named after *Stilton*, Cambridgeshire, where it was originally sold]

stilt root *n* a large prop root

stim (stɪm) *n* *Irish* (*used with a negative*) a very small amount: *I couldn't see a stim; she hasn't a stim of sense* [of uncertain origin]

stimulant (ˈstɪmjʊlənt) *n* **1** a drug or similar substance that increases physiological activity, esp of a particular organ **2** any stimulating agent or thing ▷ *adj* **3** increasing physiological activity; stimulating [C18 from Latin *stimulāns* goading, from *stimulāre* to urge on; see STIMULUS]

stimulate (ˈstɪmjʊˌleɪt) *vb* **1** (*tr; usually passive*) to fill (a person) with ideas or enthusiasm: *he was stimulated by the challenge* **2** (*tr*) *physiol* to excite (a nerve, organ, etc) with a stimulus **3** to encourage (something) to start or progress further: *a cut in interest rates should help stimulate economic recovery* [C16 from Latin *stimulāre*; see STIMULANT] > ˈ**stimulable** *adj* > ˌ**stimuˈlation** *n* > ˈ**stimulative** *adj, n* > ˈ**stimuˌlator** *or* ˈ**stimuˌlater** *n*

stimulating (ˈstɪmjʊˌleɪtɪŋ) *adj* **1** inspiring new ideas or enthusiasm **2** (of a physical activity) making one feel refreshed and energetic > ˈ**stimuˌlatingly** *adv*

stimulus (ˈstɪmjʊləs) *n, pl* **-li** (-ˌlaɪ, -ˌliː) **1** something that stimulates or acts as an incentive **2** any drug, agent, electrical impulse, or other factor able to cause a response in an organism **3** an object or event that is apprehended by the senses **4** *med* a former name for **stimulant** [C17 from Latin: a cattle goad]

sting (stɪŋ) *vb* **stings, stinging, stung** **1** (of certain animals and plants) to inflict a wound on (an organism) by the injection of poison **2** to feel or cause to feel a sharp mental or physical pain **3** (*tr*) to goad or incite (esp in the phrase **sting into action**) **4** (*tr*) *informal* to cheat, esp by overcharging ▷ *n* **5** a skin wound caused by the poison injected by certain insects or plants **6** pain caused by or as if by the sting of a plant or animal **7** a mental pain or pang: *a sting of conscience* **8** a sharp pointed organ, such as the ovipositor of a wasp, by which poison can be injected into the prey **9** the ability to sting: *a sharp sting in his criticism* **10** something as painful or swift of action as a sting: *the sting of death* **11** a sharp stimulus or incitement **12** *botany* another name for **stinging hair** **13** *slang* a swindle or fraud **14** *slang* a trap set up by the police to entice a person to commit a crime and thereby produce evidence **15** **sting in the tail** an unexpected and unpleasant ending [Old English *stingan*; related to Old Norse *stinga* to pierce, Gothic *usstangan* to pluck out, Greek *stakhus* ear of corn] > ˈ**stinging** *adj* > ˈ**stingingly** *adv* > ˈ**stingingness** *n*

stingaree (ˈstɪŋəˌriː, ˌstɪŋəˈriː) *n* *US, Canadian, and Austral* a popular name for the **stingray** [C19 variant of STINGRAY]

stinger (ˈstɪŋə) *n* **1** a person, plant, animal, etc, that stings or hurts **2** *Austral* any marine creature that stings its victims, esp the box jellyfish **3** Also called: **stengah** a whisky and soda with crushed ice

Stinger (ˈstɪŋə) *n* *trademark* a device, consisting of a long track of raised spikes, laid across a road by police to puncture the tyres of escaping vehicles

stinging hair *n* a multicellular hair in plants, such as the stinging nettle, that injects an irritant fluid when in contact with an animal

stinging nettle *n* See **nettle** (sense 1)

stinging tree *n* any of various Australian trees and shrubs of the genus *Dendrocnide* with rigid stinging hairs

stingray (ˈstɪŋˌreɪ) *n* any ray of the family *Dasyatidae*, having a whiplike tail bearing a serrated venomous spine capable of inflicting painful weals on man

stingy[1] (ˈstɪndʒɪ) *adj* **-gier, -giest** **1** unwilling to spend or give **2** insufficient or scanty [C17 (perhaps in the sense: ill-tempered): perhaps from *stinge*, dialect variant of STING] > ˈ**stingily** *adv* > ˈ**stinginess** *n*

stingy[2] (ˈstɪŋɪ) *adj* **stingier, stingiest** **1** *informal* stinging or capable of stinging ▷ *n, pl* **stingies** **2** *South Wales dialect* a stinging nettle: *I put my hand on a stingy*

stink (stɪŋk) *n* **1** a strong foul smell; stench **2** *slang* a great deal of trouble (esp in the phrase **to make** *or* **raise a stink**) **3** **like stink** intensely; furiously ▷ *vb* **stinks, stinking, stank** *or* **stunk, stunk** (*mainly intr*) **4** to emit a foul smell **5** *slang* to be thoroughly bad or abhorrent: *this town stinks* **6** *informal* to have a very bad reputation: *his name stinks* **7** to be of poor quality **8** (foll by *of* or *with*) *slang* to have or appear to have an excessive amount (of money) **9** (*tr*; usually foll by *up*) *informal* to cause to stink ▷ See also **stink out** [Old English *stincan*; related to Old Saxon *stinkan*, German *stinken*, Old Norse *stökkva* to burst; see STENCH]

stink ball *n* another name for **stinkpot** (sense 4)

stink bomb *n* a small glass globe, used by practical jokers: it releases a liquid with an offensive smell when broken

stinker (ˈstɪŋkə) *n* **1** a person or thing that stinks **2** *slang* a difficult or very unpleasant person or thing **3** *slang* something of very poor quality **4** *informal* any of several fulmars or related birds that feed on carrion

stinkhorn (ˈstɪŋkˌhɔːn) *n* any of various basidiomycetous saprotrophic fungi of the genus *Phallus*, such as *P. impudicus*, having an offensive odour

stinking (ˈstɪŋkɪŋ) *adj* **1** having a foul smell **2** *informal* unpleasant or disgusting **3** (*postpositive*) *slang* very drunk ▷ *adv* **4** *informal* (intensifier, expressing contempt for the person referred to): *stinking rich* > ˈ**stinkingly** *adv* > ˈ**stinkingness** *n*

stinking badger *n* another name for **teledu**

stinking iris *n* an iris plant, *Iris foetidissima*, of W Europe and N Africa, having purplish flowers and a strong unpleasant smell when bruised. Also called: **gladdon**

stinking smut *n* a smut that affects wheat and is caused by the fungus *Tilletia caries*. Also called: **bunt**

stinko (ˈstɪŋkəʊ) *adj* (*postpositive*) a slang word for **drunk**

stink out *vb* (*tr, adverb*) **1** to drive out or away by a foul smell **2** *Brit* to cause to stink: *the smell of orange peel stinks out the room*

stinkpot (ˈstɪŋkˌpɒt) *n* **1** *slang* a person or thing that stinks **2** *slang* a person considered to be unpleasant **3** another name for **musk turtle** **4** Also called: **stink ball** *military* (formerly) a container filled with material that gives off noxious or suffocating vapours

stinkstone (ˈstɪŋkˌstəʊn) *n* any of various rocks producing a fetid odour when struck, esp certain limestones

stink trap *n* another name for **stench trap**

stinkweed (ˈstɪŋkˌwiːd) *n* **1** Also called: **wall mustard** a plant, *Diplotaxis muralis*, naturalized in Britain and S and central Europe, having pale yellow flowers, cylindrical seed pods, and a disagreeable smell when bruised: family *Brassicaceae* (crucifers) **2** any of various other ill-smelling plants, such as mayweed

stinkwood (ˈstɪŋkˌwʊd) *n* **1** any of various trees having offensive-smelling wood, esp *Ocotea bullata*, a southern African lauraceous tree yielding a hard wood used for furniture **2** the heavy durable wood of any of these trees **3** Also called (NZ): **hupiro** a New Zealand shrub or small tree, *Coprosma foetidissima*, whose leaves give off an unpleasant smell when they are crushed

stinky (ˈstɪŋkɪ) *adj* **-ier, -iest** **1** having a foul smell **2** *informal* unpleasant or disgusting **3** *informal* of poor quality; contemptible

stint[1] (stɪnt) *vb* **1** to be frugal or miserly towards (someone) with (something) **2** *archaic* to stop or check (something) ▷ *n* **3** an allotted or fixed amount of work **4** a limitation or check **5** *obsolete* a pause or stoppage [Old English *styntan* to blunt; related to Old Norse *stytta* to cut short; see STUNT[1]] > ˈ**stinter** *n*

stint[2] (stɪnt) *n* any of various small sandpipers of the chiefly northern genus *Calidris* (or *Erolia*), such as *C. minuta* (**little stint**) [Old English; related to Middle High German *stinz* small salmon, Swedish dialect *stinta* teenager; see STUNT[1]]

stipe (staɪp) *n* **1** a stalk in plants that bears reproductive structures, esp the stalk bearing the cap of a mushroom **2** the stalk that bears the leaflets of a fern or the thallus of a seaweed **3** *zoology* any stalklike part; stipes [C18 via French from Latin *stīpes* tree trunk; related to Latin *stīpāre* to pack closely; see STIFF]

stipel (ˈstaɪpᵊl) *n* a small paired leaflike structure at the base of certain leaflets; secondary stipule [C19 via New Latin from Latin *stipula*, diminutive of *stīpes* a log] > **stipellate** (staɪˈpɛlɪt, -eɪt) *adj*

stipend (ˈstaɪpɛnd) *n* a fixed or regular amount of money paid as a salary or allowance, as to a clergyman [C15 from Old French *stipende*, from Latin *stīpendium* tax, from *stips* a contribution + *pendere* to pay out]

stipendiary (staɪˈpɛndɪərɪ) *adj* **1** receiving or working for regular pay: *a stipendiary magistrate* **2** paid for by a stipend ▷ *n, pl* **-aries** **3** a person who receives regular payment [C16 from Latin

S

stīpendiārius concerning tribute, from *stīpendium* STIPEND]

stipes ('staɪpiːz) *n, pl* **stipites** ('stɪpɪˌtiːz) *zoology* **1** the second maxillary segment in insects and crustaceans **2** the eyestalk of a crab or similar crustacean **3** any similar stemlike structure [C18 from Latin; see STIPE] > **stipiform** ('staɪpɪˌfɔːm) *or* **stipitiform** ('stɪpɪtɪˌfɔːm) *adj*

stipitate ('stɪpɪˌteɪt) *adj botany* possessing or borne on the end of a stipe [C18 from New Latin *stīpitātus* having a stalk, from Latin *stīpes*; see STIPE]

stipple ('stɪpəl) *vb* (*tr*) **1** to draw, engrave, or paint using dots or flecks **2** to apply paint, powder, etc, to (something) with many light dabs **3** to give (wet paint, cement, etc) a granular effect ▷ *n also* **stippling 4** the technique of stippling or a picture produced by or using stippling [C18 from Dutch *stippelen*, from *stippen* to prick, from *stip* point] > 'stippler *n*

stipulate¹ ('stɪpjʊˌleɪt) *vb* **1** (*tr; may take a clause as object*) to specify, often as a condition of an agreement **2** (*intr*; foll by *for*) to insist (on) as a term of an agreement **3** *Roman law* to make (an oral contract) in the form of question and answer necessary to render it legally valid **4** (*tr; may take a clause as object*) to guarantee or promise [C17 from Latin *stipulārī*, probably from Old Latin *stipulus* firm, but perhaps from *stipula* a stalk, from the convention of breaking a straw to ratify a promise] > **stipulable** ('stɪpjʊləbəl) *adj* > ˌstipu'lation *n* > 'stipuˌlator *n* > **stipulatory** ('stɪpjʊlətərɪ, -trɪ) *adj*

stipulate² ('stɪpjʊlɪt, -ˌleɪt) *adj* (of a plant) having stipules

stipule ('stɪpjuːl) *n* a small paired usually leaflike outgrowth occurring at the base of a leaf or its stalk [C18 from Latin; see STIPE, STIPES] > **stipular** ('stɪpjʊlə) *adj*

stir¹ (stɜː) *vb* **stirs, stirring, stirred 1** to move an implement such as a spoon around in (a liquid) so as to mix up the constituents: *she stirred the porridge* **2** to change or cause to change position; disturb or be disturbed: *he stirred in his sleep* **3** (*intr*; often foll by *from*) to venture or depart (from one's usual or preferred place): *he won't stir from the fireside* **4** (*intr*) to be active after a rest; be up and about **5** (*tr*) to excite or stimulate, esp emotionally **6** to move (oneself) briskly or vigorously; exert (oneself) **7** (*tr*) to rouse or awaken: *to stir someone from sleep; to stir memories* **8** *informal* (when *tr*, foll by *up*) to cause or incite others to cause (trouble, arguments, etc) **9 stir one's stumps** *informal* to move or become active ▷ *n* **10** the act or an instance of stirring or the state of being stirred **11** a strong reaction, esp of excitement: *his publication caused a stir* **12** a slight movement **13** *NZ informal* a noisy party ▷ See also **stir up** [Old English *styrian*; related to Middle High German *stürn* to poke, stir, Norwegian *styrja* to cause a commotion; see STORM, STURGEON] > 'stirrable *adj*

stir² (stɜː) *n* a slang word for **prison** in **stir** [C19 perhaps from Romany *stariben* prison]

Stir. *abbreviation for* Stirlingshire

stirabout ('stɜːrəˌbaʊt) *n* **1** a kind of porridge orginally made in Ireland **2** a bustling person

stir-crazy *adj slang* mentally disturbed as a result of being in prison or otherwise confined

stir-fry ('stɜːˈfraɪ) *vb* **-fries, -frying, -fried 1** to cook (small pieces of meat, vegetables, etc) rapidly by stirring them in a wok or frying pan over a high heat: used esp for Chinese food ▷ *n, pl* **-fries 2** a dish cooked in this way

stirk (stɜːk) *n* **1** a heifer of 6 to 12 months old **2** a yearling heifer or bullock [Old English *stierc*; related to Middle Low German *sterke*, Old High German *stero* ram, Latin *sterilis* sterile, Greek *steira*; see STEER²]

Stirling ('stɜːlɪŋ) *n* **1** a city in central Scotland, in Stirling council area on the River Forth: its castle was a regular residence of many Scottish monarchs between the 12th century and 1603. Pop: 32 673 (2001) **2** a council area of central

Scotland, created from part of Central Region in 1996; includes most of the historical county of Stirlingshire: the Forth valley rises to the Grampian Mountains in the N. Administrative centre: Stirling. Pop: 86 370 (2003 est). Area: 2173 sq km (839 sq miles)

Stirling engine *n* an external-combustion engine that uses air or an inert gas as the working fluid operating on a highly efficient thermodynamic cycle (the **Stirling cycle**) [named after Robert *Stirling* (1790–1878), Scottish minister who invented it]

Stirling's formula *n* a formula giving the approximate value of the factorial of a large number *n*, as $n! \cong (n/e)^n \sqrt{(2\pi n)}$ [named after James *Stirling* (1692–1770), Scottish mathematician]

Stirlingshire ('stɜːlɪŋˌʃɪə, -ʃə) *n* a former county of central Scotland: mostly became part of Central Region in 1975: now covered by the council areas of Stirling, Falkirk, and East Dunbartonshire

stirps (stɜːps) *n, pl* **stirpes** ('stɜːpiːz) **1** *genealogy* a line of descendants from an ancestor; stock or strain **2** *botany* a race or variety, esp one in which the characters are maintained by cultivation [C17 from Latin: root, family origin]

stirrer ('stɜːrə) *n* **1** a person or thing that stirs **2** *informal* a person who deliberately causes trouble **3** *Austral and NZ informal* a political activist or agitator

stirring ('stɜːrɪŋ) *adj* **1** exciting the emotions; stimulating **2** active, lively, or busy > 'stirringly *adv*

stirrup ('stɪrəp) *n* **1** Also called: **stirrup iron** either of two metal loops on a riding saddle, with a flat footpiece through which a rider puts his foot for support. They are attached to the saddle by **stirrup leathers 2** a U-shaped support or clamp made of metal, wood, leather, etc **3** *nautical* one of a set of ropes fastened to a yard at one end and having a thimble at the other through which a footrope is rove for support **4** the usual US name for **étrier** [Old English *stigrāp*, from *stig* path, step (related to Old High German *stīgan* to move up) + *rāp* ROPE; related to Old Norse *stigreip*, Old High German *stegareif*]

stirrup bone *n* the nontechnical name for **stapes** [C17 so called because of its stirrup-like shape]

stirrup cup *n* a cup containing an alcoholic drink offered to a horseman ready to ride away

stirrup pump *n* a hand-operated vertical reciprocating pump, such as one used in fire-fighting, etc, in which the base of the cylinder is placed in a bucket of water

stir up *vb* (*tr, adverb*) to set in motion; instigate: *he stirred up trouble*

stishie ('stɪʃɪ) *n Scot* a variant of **stushie**

stitch (stɪtʃ) *n* **1** a link made by drawing a thread through material by means of a needle **2** a loop of yarn formed around an implement used in knitting, crocheting, etc **3** a particular method of stitching or shape of stitch **4** a sharp spasmodic pain in the side resulting from running or exercising **5** (*usually used with a negative*) *informal* the least fragment of clothing: *he wasn't wearing a stitch* **6** *agriculture* the ridge between two furrows **7 in stitches** *informal* laughing uncontrollably **8 drop a stitch** to allow a loop of wool to fall off a knitting needle accidentally while knitting ▷ *vb* **9** (*tr*) to sew, fasten, etc, with stitches **10** (*intr*) to be engaged in sewing **11** (*tr*) to bind together (the leaves of a book, pamphlet, etc) with wire staples or thread ▷ *n* ▷ *vb* **12** an informal word for **suture** (senses 1b, 6) ▷ See also **stitch up** [Old English *stice* sting; related to Old Frisian *steke*, Old High German *stih*, Gothic *stiks*, Old Norse *tikta* sharp] > 'stitcher *n*

stitchery ('stɪtʃərɪ) *n* needlework, esp modern embroidery

stitch up *vb* (*tr, adverb*) **1** to join or mend by means of stitches or sutures **2** *slang* **a** to incriminate (someone) on a false charge by manufacturing evidence **b** to betray, cheat, or defraud **3** *slang* to

prearrange (something) in a clandestine manner ▷ *n* **stitch-up 4** *slang* a matter that has been prearranged clandestinely

stitch wheel *n* a notched wheel used by a harness maker to mark out the spacing for stitching

stitchwort ('stɪtʃˌwɜːt) *n* any of several low-growing N temperate herbaceous plants of the caryophyllaceous genus *Stellaria*, having small white star-shaped flowers [C13 so named because it was once thought to be a remedy for stitches in the side]

stithy ('stɪðɪ) *n, pl* **stithies 1** *archaic or dialect* a forge or anvil ▷ *vb* **stithies, stithying, stithied 2** (*tr*) *obsolete* to forge on an anvil [C13 from Old Norse *stedhi*]

stiver ('staɪvə) *n* **1** a former Dutch coin worth one twentieth of a guilder **2** a small amount, esp of money [C16 from Dutch *stuiver*; related to Middle Low German *stüver*, Danish *styver*]

stk *abbreviation for* stock

stoa ('stəʊə) *n, pl* **stoae** ('stəʊiː) *or* **stoas** a covered walk that has a colonnade on one or both sides, esp as used in ancient Greece [C17 from Greek]

stoat (stəʊt) *n* a small Eurasian musteline mammal, *Mustela erminea*, closely related to the weasels, having a brown coat and a black-tipped tail: in the northern parts of its range it has a white winter coat and is then known as an ermine [C15 of unknown origin]

stob (stɒb) *n Scot, northern English, and US dialect* a post or stump [C14 variant of STUB]

stochastic (stɒˈkæstɪk) *adj* **1** *statistics* **a** (of a random variable) having a probability distribution, usually with finite variance **b** (of a process) involving a random variable the successive values of which are not independent **c** (of a matrix) square with non-negative elements that add to unity in each row **2** *rare* involving conjecture [C17 from Greek *stokhastikos* capable of guessing, from *stokhazesthai* to aim at, conjecture, from *stokhos* a target] > stoˈchastically *adv*

stock (stɒk) *n* **1 a** (*sometimes plural*) the total goods or raw material kept on the premises of a shop or business **b** (*as modifier*): *a stock clerk; stock book* **2** a supply of something stored for future use: *he keeps a good stock of whisky* **3** *finance* **a** the capital raised by a company through the issue and subscription of shares entitling their holders to dividends, partial ownership, and usually voting rights **b** the proportion of such capital held by an individual shareholder **c** the shares of a specified company or industry **d** (formerly) the part of an account or tally given to a creditor **e** the debt represented by this **4** standing or status **5 a** farm animals, such as cattle and sheep, bred and kept for their meat, skins, etc **b** (*as modifier*): *stock farming* **6** the trunk or main stem of a tree or other plant **7** *horticulture* **a** a rooted plant into which a scion is inserted during grafting **b** a plant or stem from which cuttings are taken. See also **rootstock 8** the original type from which a particular race, family, group, etc, is derived **9** a race, breed, or variety of animals or plants **10** (*often plural*) a small pen in which a single animal can be confined **11** a line of descent **12** any of the major subdivisions of the human species; race or ethnic group **13** the part of a rifle, sub-machine-gun, etc, into which the barrel and firing mechanism is set: held by the firer against the shoulder **14** the handle of something, such as a whip or fishing rod **15** the main body of a tool, such as the block of a plane **16** short for **diestock, gunstock** *or* **rolling stock 17** (formerly) the part of a plough to which the irons and handles were attached **18** the main upright part of a supporting structure **19** a liquid or broth in which meat, fish, bones, or vegetables have been simmered for a long time **20** film material before exposure and processing **21** *metallurgy* **a** a portion of metal cut from a bar upon which a specific process, such as forging, is to be carried out **b** the material that is smelted in a blast furnace **22** Also called: **gillyflower** any of several plants of the genus *Matthiola*, such as *M. incana* and *M. bicornis* (**evening** or **night-scented stock**), of the Mediterranean region, cultivated for their brightly coloured flowers: *Brassicaceae* (crucifers) **23** **Virginian stock** a similar and related North American plant, *Malcolmia maritima* **24** a long usually white neckcloth wrapped around the neck, worn in the 18th century and as part of modern riding dress **25** *cards* a pile of cards left after the deal in certain games, from which players draw **26** a the repertoire of plays available to a repertory company **b** (*as modifier*): *a stock play* **27** (on some types of anchors) a crosspiece at the top of the shank under the ring **28** the centre of a wheel **29** an exposed igneous intrusion that is smaller in area than a batholith **30** a log or block of wood **31** See **laughing stock 32** an archaic word for **stocking 33** **in stock a** stored on the premises or available for sale or use **b** supplied with goods of a specified kind **34** **out of stock a** not immediately available for sale or use **b** not having goods of a specified kind immediately available **35** **take stock a** to make an inventory **b** to make a general appraisal, esp of prospects, resources, etc **36** **take stock in** to attach importance to **37** **lock, stock, and barrel** See **lock¹** (sense 7) ▷ *adj* **38** staple, standard: *stock sizes in clothes* **39** (*prenominal*) being a cliché; hackneyed: *a stock phrase* ▷ *vb* **40** (*tr*) to keep (goods) for sale **41** (*intr*; usually foll by *up* or *up on*) to obtain a store of (something) for future use or sale: *to stock up on beer* **42** (*tr*) to supply with live animals, fish, etc: *to stock a farm* **43** (*intr*) (of a plant) to put forth new shoots **44** (*tr*) *obsolete* to punish by putting in the stocks ▷ See also **stocks** [Old English *stocc* trunk (of a tree), stem, stick (the various senses developed from these meanings, as trunk of a tree, hence line of descent; structures made of timber; a store of timber or other goods for future use, hence an aggregate of goods, animals, etc); related to Old Saxon, Old High German *stock* stick, stump] ▷ '**stocker** *n*

stockade (stɒ'keɪd) *n* **1** an enclosure or barrier of stakes and timbers **2** *US* a military prison or detention area ▷ *vb* **3** (*tr*) to surround with a stockade [C17 from Spanish *estacada*, from *estaca* a stake, post, of Germanic origin; see STAKE¹]

stock and station agent *n Austral and NZ* a firm dealing in and financing farm activities

stockbreeder ('stɒk,briːdə) *n* a person who breeds or rears livestock as an occupation ▷ '**stock,breeding** *n*

stockbroker ('stɒk,brəʊkə) *n* a person who buys and sells securities on a commission basis for customers. Often shortened to: **broker** ▷ **stockbrokerage** ('stɒk,brəʊkərɪdʒ) *or* '**stock,broking** *n*

stockbroker belt *n Brit informal* the area outside a city, esp London, in which rich commuters live. Compare **exurbia**

stock car *n* **1 a** a car, usually a production saloon, strengthened and modified for a form of racing in which the cars often collide **b** (*as modifier*): *stock-car racing* **2** *US and Canadian* a railway wagon designed for carrying livestock. also called (in Britain and certain other countries): **cattle truck**

stock certificate *n* the US equivalent of **share certificate**

stock company *n* **1** *US* a business enterprise the capital of which is divided into transferable shares **2** a US term for **repertory company**

stock dove *n* a European dove, *Columba oenas*, smaller than the wood pigeon and having a uniformly grey plumage [C14 so called because it lives in tree trunks. See STOCK]

stock exchange *n* (*often capitals*) **1** Also called: **stock market a** a highly organized market facilitating the purchase and sale of securities and operated by professional stockbrokers and market makers according to fixed rules **b** a place

where securities are regularly traded **c** (*as modifier*): *a stock-exchange operator; stock-exchange prices* **2** the prices or trading activity of a stock exchange: *the stock exchange fell heavily today*

stock farm *n* a farm on which livestock is bred ▷ **stock farmer** *n* ▷ **stock farming** *n*

stockfish ('stɒk,fɪʃ) *n, pl* -**fish** *or* -**fishes** fish, such as cod or haddock, cured by splitting and drying in the air [C13 of uncertain origin. Perhaps from STOCK (in the sense: stem, tree trunk) because it was dried on wooden racks. Compare Middle Dutch *stocvisch*]

stockholder ('stɒk,həʊldə) *n* **1** an owner of corporate capital stock **2** *Austral* a person who keeps livestock ▷ '**stock,holding** *n*

Stockholm ('stɒkhəʊm; *Swedish* 'stɔkholm) *n* the capital of Sweden, a port in the E central part at the outflow of Lake Mälar into the Baltic: situated partly on the mainland and partly on islands; traditionally founded about 1250; university (1877). Pop: 765 582 (2004 est)

Stockholm syndrome *n* a psychological condition in which hostages or kidnap victims become sympathetic towards their captors [C20 after a group of hostages in Stockholm in 1973]

stockhorse ('stɒk,hɔːs) *n Austral* a horse trained in the handling of stock

stockinet (,stɒkɪ'nɛt) *n* a machine-knitted elastic fabric used, esp formerly, for stockings, undergarments, etc [C19 perhaps changed from earlier *stocking-net*]

stocking ('stɒkɪŋ) *n* **1** one of a pair of close-fitting garments made of knitted yarn to cover the foot and part or all of the leg **2** something resembling this in position, function, appearance, etc **3** **in (one's) stocking** *or* **stockinged feet** wearing stockings or socks but no shoes [C16 from dialect *stock* stocking + -ING¹]

stocking cap *n* a conical knitted cap, often with a tassel

stockinged ('stɒkɪŋd) *adj* wearing stockings or socks

stockinger ('stɒkɪŋə) *n* a person who knits on a stocking frame

stocking filler *n Brit* a present, esp a toy, of a size suitable for inclusion in a child's Christmas stocking

stocking frame *n* a type of knitting machine. Also called: **stocking loom, stocking machine**

stocking mask *n* a nylon stocking worn over the face by a criminal to disguise the features

stocking stitch *n* a pattern of stitches in knitting consisting of alternate rows of plain and purl stitch [C19 so named because of its use in hosiery]

stock in trade *n* **1** goods in stock necessary for carrying on a business **2** anything constantly used by someone as a part of his profession, occupation, or trade: *friendliness is the salesman's stock in trade*

stockish ('stɒkɪʃ) *adj* stupid or dull ▷ '**stockishly** *adv* ▷ '**stockishness** *n*

stockist ('stɒkɪst) *n commerce, Brit* a dealer who undertakes to maintain stocks of a specified product at or above a certain minimum in return for favourable buying terms granted by the manufacturer of the product

stockjobber ('stɒk,dʒɒbə) *n* **1** *Brit* (formerly) a wholesale dealer on a stock exchange who sold securities to brokers without transacting directly with the public. Often shortened to: **jobber**. See also **market maker 2** *US disparaging* a stockbroker, esp one dealing in worthless securities ▷ '**stock,jobbery** *or* '**stock,jobbing** *n*

stock lock *n* a lock that is enclosed in a wooden case

stockman ('stɒkmən, -,mæn) *n, pl* -**men 1 a** a man engaged in the rearing or care of farm livestock, esp cattle **b** an owner of cattle or other livestock **2** *US and Canadian* a man employed in a warehouse or stockroom

stock market *n* **1** another name for **stock**

exchange (sense 1) **2** the usual US name for **stock exchange** (sense 2)

stockpile ('stɒk,paɪl) *vb* **1** to acquire and store a large quantity of (something) ▷ *n* **2** a large store or supply accumulated for future use ▷ '**stock,piler** *n*

Stockport ('stɒk,pɔːt) *n* **1** a town in NW England, in Stockport unitary authority, Greater Manchester: an early textile centre and scene of several labour disturbances in the early 19th century; engineering, electronics. Pop: 136 082 (2001) **2** a unitary authority in NW England, in Greater Manchester. Pop: 282 500 (2003 est). Area: 126 sq km (49 sq miles)

stockpot ('stɒk,pɒt) *n chiefly Brit* a pot in which stock for soup, etc, is made or kept

stockroom ('stɒk,ruːm, -,rʊm) *n* a room in which a stock of goods is kept, as in a shop or factory

stockroute ('stɒk,ruːt) *n Austral and NZ* a route designated for droving sheep or cattle

stocks (stɒks) *pl n* **1** *history* an instrument of punishment consisting of a heavy wooden frame with holes in which the feet, hands, or head of an offender were locked **2** a frame in which an animal is held while receiving veterinary attention or while being shod **3** a frame used to support a boat while under construction **4** *nautical* a vertical post or shaft at the forward edge of a rudder, extended upwards for attachment to the steering controls **5** **on the stocks** in preparation or under construction

stock saddle *n chiefly US* a cowboy's saddle, esp an ornamental one

stock-still *adv* absolutely still; motionless

stocktaking ('stɒk,teɪkɪŋ) *n* **1** the examination, counting, and valuing of goods on hand in a shop or business **2** a reassessment of one's current situation, progress, prospects, etc

Stockton ('stɒktən) *n* an inland port in central California, on the San Joaquin River: seat of the University of the Pacific (1851). Pop: 271 466 (2003 est)

Stockton-on-Tees *n* **1** a former port and industrial centre in NE England, in Stockton-on-Tees unitary authority, Co Durham, on the River Tees: famous for the **Stockton-Darlington Railway** (1825), the first passenger-carrying railway in the world; now mainly residential. Pop: 80 060 (2001) **2** a unitary authority in NE England, in Co Durham and North Yorkshire: created in 1996 from part of Cleveland county. Pop: 186 300 (2003 est). Area: 195 sq km (75 sq miles)

stock unit *n NZ* **a** the tax basis for evaluating farmers' stock. Cattle, sheep, and deer are each given differing stock-unit values, the basic measure being the ewe equivalent **b** (*as modifier*): *stock-unit values*

stock watering *n business* the creation of more new shares in a company than is justified by its assets

stock whip *n* a whip with a long lash and a short handle, as used to herd cattle

stocky ('stɒkɪ) *adj* **stockier, stockiest** (usually of a person) thickset; sturdy ▷ '**stockily** *adv* ▷ '**stockiness** *n*

stockyard ('stɒk,jɑːd) *n* a large yard with pens or covered buildings where farm animals are assembled, sold, etc

stodge (stɒdʒ) *informal* ▷ *n* **1** heavy filling starchy food **2** *dialect, chiefly Southern English* baked or steamed pudding **3** a dull person or subject ▷ *vb* **4** to stuff (oneself or another) with food [C17 perhaps a blend of STUFF + PODGE]

stodgy ('stɒdʒɪ) *adj* **stodgier, stodgiest 1** (of food) heavy or uninteresting **2** excessively formal and conventional [C19 from STODGE] ▷ '**stodgily** *adv* ▷ '**stodginess** *n*

stoep (stʊp) *n South African* a veranda [Afrikaans from Dutch]

stogy *or* **stogey** ('stəʊgɪ) *n, pl* -**gies** *US* any long cylindrical inexpensive cigar [C19 from *stoga*, short for *Conestoga*, a town in Pennsylvania]

S

stoic ('stəʊɪk) *n* **1** a person who maintains stoical qualities ▷ *adj* **2** a variant of **stoical**

Stoic ('stəʊɪk) *n* **1** a member of the ancient Greek school of philosophy founded by Zeno of Citium, the Greek philosopher (?336–?264 BC), holding that virtue and happiness can be attained only by submission to destiny and the natural law ▷ *adj* **2** of or relating to the doctrines of the Stoics [C16 via Latin from Greek *stōikos*, from *stoa* the porch in Athens where Zeno taught]

stoical ('stəʊɪkᵊl) *adj* characterized by impassivity or resignation > 'stoically *adv* > 'stoicalness *n*

stoichiology, stoicheiology *or* **stoechiology** (ˌstɔɪkɪ'ɒlədʒɪ) *n* the branch of biology concerned with the study of the cellular components of animal tissues [C19 from Greek *stoikheion* element + -LOGY] > stoichiological, stoicheiological *or* stoechiological (ˌstɔɪkɪə'lɒdʒɪkᵊl) *adj*

stoichiometric, stoicheiometric *or* **stoechiometric** (ˌstɔɪkɪə'mɛtrɪk) *adj chem* **1** concerned with, involving, or having the exact proportions for a particular chemical reaction: *a stoichiometric mixture* **2** (of a compound) having its component elements present in the exact proportions indicated by its formula **3** of or concerned with stoichiometry [C19 see STOICHIOMETRY]

stoichiometry, stoicheiometry *or* **stoechiometry** (ˌstɔɪkɪ'ɒmɪtrɪ) *n* the branch of chemistry concerned with the proportions in which elements are combined in compounds and the quantitative relationships between reactants and products in chemical reactions [C19 from Greek *stoikheion* element + -METRY]

stoicism ('stəʊɪˌsɪzəm) *n* **1** indifference to pleasure and pain **2** (*capital*) the philosophy of the Stoics

stoke (stəʊk) *vb* **1** to feed, stir, and tend (a fire, furnace, etc) **2** (*tr*) to tend the furnace of; act as a stoker for ▷ See also **stoke up** [C17 back formation from STOKER]

stoked (stəʊkt) *adj NZ informal* very pleased; elated: *really stoked to have got the job*

stokehold ('stəʊkˌhəʊld) *n nautical* **1** a coal bunker for a ship's furnace **2** the hold for a ship's boilers; fire room

stokehole ('stəʊkˌhəʊl) *n* **1** another word for **stokehold** **2** a hole in a furnace through which it is stoked

Stoke-on-Trent *n* **1** a city in central England, in Stoke-on-Trent unitary authority, Staffordshire on the River Trent: a centre of the pottery industry; university (1992). Pop: 259 252 (2001) **2** a unitary authority in central England, in N Staffordshire. Pop: 238 000 (2003 est). Area: 93 sq km (36 sq miles)

stoker ('stəʊkə) *n* a person employed to tend a furnace, as on a steamship [C17 from Dutch, from *stoken* to STOKE]

stokes (stəʊks) *or* **stoke** *n* the cgs unit of kinematic viscosity, equal to the viscosity of a fluid in poise divided by its density in grams per cubic centimetre. 1 stokes is equivalent to 10⁻⁴ square metre per second. Symbol: St [C20 named after Sir George *Stokes* (1819–1903), British physicist]

Stokesay Castle ('stəʊksɪ) *n* a fortified manor house near Craven Arms in Shropshire: built in the 12th century, with a 16th-century gatehouse

stoke up *vb* (*adverb*) **1** to feed and tend (a fire, etc) with fuel **2** (*intr*) to fill oneself with food

stokvel ('stɒkˌfɛl) *n South African* an informal savings pool or syndicate, usually among Black people, in which funds are contributed in rotation, allowing participants lump sums for family needs (esp funerals) [C20 of uncertain origin]

STOL (stɒl) *n* **1** a system in which an aircraft can take off and land in a short distance **2** an aircraft using this system. Compare VTOL [C20 *s(hort) t(ake) o(ff and) l(anding)*]

stole¹ (stəʊl) *vb* the past tense of **steal**

stole² (stəʊl) *n* **1** a long scarf or shawl, worn by women **2** a long narrow scarf worn by various officiating clergymen [Old English *stole*, from Latin *stola*, Greek *stolē* clothing; related to *stellein* to array]

stolen ('stəʊlən) *vb* the past participle of **steal**

stolid ('stɒlɪd) *adj* showing little or no emotion or interest [C17 from Latin *stolidus* dull; compare Latin *stultus* stupid; see STILL¹] > stolidity (stɒ'lɪdɪtɪ) *or* 'stolidness *n* > 'stolidly *adv*

stollen ('stɒlən; *German* 'ʃtɔlən) *n* a rich sweet bread containing nuts, raisins, etc [German, from *Stollen* wooden post, prop; so called from its shape; see STALL¹]

stolon ('stəʊlən) *n* **1** a long horizontal stem, as of the currants, that grows along the surface of the soil and propagates by producing roots and shoots at the nodes or tip **2** a branching structure in lower animals, esp the anchoring rootlike part of colonial organisms, such as hydroids, on which the polyps are borne [C17 from Latin *stolō* shoot] > stoloniferous (ˌstəʊlə'nɪfərəs) *adj*

stoma ('stəʊmə) *n, pl* stomata ('stəʊmətə, 'stɒm-, stəʊ'mɑːtə) **1** *botany* an epidermal pore, present in large numbers in plant leaves, that controls the passage of gases into and out of a plant **2** *zoology, anatomy* a mouth or mouthlike part **3** *surgery* an artificial opening made in a tubular organ, esp the colon or ileum. See **colostomy, ileostomy** [C17 via New Latin from Greek: mouth]

stomach ('stʌmək) *n* **1** (in vertebrates) the enlarged muscular saclike part of the alimentary canal in which food is stored until it has been partially digested and rendered into chyme. Related adj: **gastric** **2** the corresponding digestive organ in invertebrates **3** the abdominal region **4** desire, appetite, or inclination **5** an archaic word for **temper** **6** an obsolete word for **pride** ▷ *vb* (*tr; used mainly in negative constructions*) **7** to tolerate; bear: *I can't stomach his bragging* **8** to eat or digest: *he cannot stomach oysters* [C14 from Old French *stomaque*, from Latin *stomachus* (believed to be the seat of the emotions), from Greek *stomakhos*, from *stoma* mouth]

stomachache ('stʌmək,eɪk) *n* pain in the stomach or abdominal region, as from acute indigestion. Technical name: **gastralgia** Also called: **stomach upset, upset stomach**

stomacher ('stʌməkə) *n* a decorative V-shaped panel of stiff material worn over the chest and stomach by men and women in the 16th century, later only by women

stomachic (stə'mækɪk) *adj also* **stomachical** **1** stimulating gastric activity **2** of or relating to the stomach ▷ *n* **3** a stomachic medicine

stomach pump *n med* a suction device for removing stomach contents by a tube inserted through the mouth

stomach worm *n* any of various nematode worms that are parasitic in the stomach of mammals, esp *Haemonchus contortus*, which infests sheep: family *Trichostrongylidae*

stomachy ('stʌmækɪ) *adj* **1** having a large belly; paunchy **2** *dialect* easily angered; irritable

stomack ('stʌmək) *n* have a stomack *E African informal* to be pregnant

stomata ('stəʊmətə, 'stɒm-, stəʊ'mɑːtə) *n* the plural of **stoma**

stomatal ('stəʊmətᵊl, 'stɒm-) *or* **stomatous** ('stɒmətəs, 'stəʊ-) *adj* of, relating to, or possessing stomata or a stoma

stomatic (stəʊ'mætɪk) *adj* of or relating to a mouth or mouthlike part

stomatitis (ˌstəʊmə'taɪtɪs, ˌstɒm-) *n* inflammation of the mouth > stomatitic (ˌstəʊmə'tɪtɪk, ˌstɒm-) *adj*

stomato- *or before a vowel* **stomat-** *combining form* indicating the mouth or a mouthlike part: *stomatology* [from Greek *stoma, stomat-*]

stomatology (ˌstəʊmə'tɒlədʒɪ) *n* the branch of medicine or dentistry concerned with the structures, functions, and diseases of the mouth

> stomatological (ˌstəʊmətə'lɒdʒɪkᵊl) *adj*

stomatoplasty ('stɒmətə,plæstɪ, 'stəʊ-) *n* plastic surgery or surgical repair involving the mouth

stomatopod ('stɒmətə,pɒd, 'stəʊ-) *n* any marine crustacean of the order *Stomatopoda*, having abdominal gills: subclass *Malacostraca*. The group includes the mantis shrimp [C19 via New Latin from Greek *stoma* mouth + *-podos, pous* foot]

-stome *n combining form* indicating a mouth or opening resembling a mouth: *peristome* [from Greek *stoma* mouth, and *stomion* little mouth]

stomium ('stəʊmɪəm) *n* the part of the sporangium of ferns that ruptures to release the spores [C20 via New Latin from Greek *stomion*, diminutive of *stoma* mouth]

stomodaeum *or* **stomodeum** (ˌstəʊmə'diːəm, ˌstɒm-) *n, pl* **-daea** *or* **-dea** (-'diːə) the oral cavity of a vertebrate embryo, which is formed from an invagination of the ectoderm and develops into the part of the alimentary canal between the mouth and stomach [C19 from New Latin, from Greek *stoma* mouth + *hodaios* on the way, from *hodos* way] > ˌstomo'daeal *or* ˌstomo'deal *adj*

-stomous *adj combining form* having a specified type of mouth: *monostomous*

stomp (stɒmp) *vb* (*intr*) **1** *informal* to tread or stamp heavily ▷ *n* **2** a rhythmic stamping jazz dance [variant of STAMP]

stomper ('stɒmpə) *n* **1** a rock or jazz song with a particularly strong and danceable beat **2** a person or animal that stomps

stompie ('stɒmpɪ) *n South African slang* **1** a cigarette butt **2** a short man **3** pick up stompies to come late to a conversation and so misunderstand what is being discussed [from Afrikaans *stomp* stump]

-stomy *n combining form* indicating a surgical operation performed to make an artificial opening into or for a specified part: *cytostomy* [from Greek *-stomia*, from *stoma* mouth]

stone (stəʊn) *n* **1** the hard compact nonmetallic material of which rocks are made. Related adj: **lithic** **2** a small lump of rock; pebble **3** *jewellery* short for **gemstone** **4 a** a piece of rock designed or shaped for some particular purpose **b** (*in combination*): *gravestone; millstone* **5 a** something that resembles a stone **b** (*in combination*): *hailstone* **6** the woody central part of such fruits as the peach and plum, that contains the seed; endocarp **7** any similar hard part of a fruit, such as the stony seed of a date **8** *pl* stone *Brit* a unit of weight, used esp to express human body weight, equal to 14 pounds or 6.350 kilograms **9** Also called: **granite** the rounded heavy mass of granite or iron used in the game of curling **10** *pathol* a nontechnical name for **calculus** **11** *printing* a table with a very flat iron or stone surface upon which hot-metal pages are composed into formes; imposition table **12** *rare* (in certain games) a piece or man **13 a** any of various dull grey colours **b** (*as adjective*): *stone paint* **14** (*modifier*) relating to or made of stone: *a stone house* **15** (*modifier*) made of stoneware: *a stone jar* **16** cast a stone (at) cast aspersions (upon) **17** heart of stone an obdurate or unemotional nature **18** leave no stone unturned to do everything possible to achieve an end ▷ *adv* **19** (*in combination*) completely: *stone-cold; stone-deaf* ▷ *vb* (*tr*) **20** to throw stones at, esp to kill **21** to remove the stones from **22** to furnish or provide with stones **23** stone the crows *Brit and Austral slang* an expression of surprise, dismay, etc [Old English *stān*; related to Old Saxon *stēn*, German *Stein*, Old Norse *steinn*, Gothic *stains*, Greek *stion* pebble] > 'stonable *or* 'stoneable *adj* > 'stoneless *adj* > 'stonelessness *n* > 'stone,like *adj*

Stone Age *n* **1** a period in human culture identified by the use of stone implements and usually divided into the Palaeolithic, Mesolithic, and Neolithic stages ▷ *modifier* **Stone-Age** **2** (*sometimes not capitals*) of or relating to this period: *stone-age man*

stone axe *n* **1** a primitive axe made of chipped

stone **2** a blunt axe used for cutting stone

stone bass (bæs) *n* a large sea perch, *Polyprion americanus*, of the Atlantic and Mediterranean. Also called: **wreckfish**

stone-blind *adj* completely blind. Compare **sand-blind**

stoneboat ('stəʊnˌbəʊt) *n US and Canadian* a type of sleigh used for moving rocks from fields, for hauling milk cans, etc

stone boiling *n* a primitive method of boiling liquid with heated stones

stone bramble *n* a herbaceous Eurasian rosaceous plant, *Rubus saxatilis*, of stony places, having white flowers and berry-like scarlet fruits (drupelets). See also **bramble** (sense 1) [C18 so called because it grows in stony places]

stonecast ('stəʊnˌkɑːst) *n* a less common name for **stone's throw**

stonechat ('stəʊnˌtʃæt) *n* an Old World songbird, *Saxicola torquata*, having a black plumage with a reddish-brown breast: subfamily *Turdinae* (thrushes) [C18 so called from its cry, which sounds like clattering pebbles]

stone-cold *adj* **1** completely cold ▷ *adv* **2** (intensifier): *stone-cold sober*

stonecrop ('stəʊnˌkrɒp) *n* **1** any of various N temperate crassulaceous plants of the genus *Sedum*, having fleshy leaves and typically red, yellow, or white flowers **2** any of various similar or related plants [Old English: so named because it grows on rocks and walls]

stone curlew *n* any of several brownish shore birds of the family *Burhinidae*, esp *Burhinus oedicnemus*, having a large head and eyes: order *Charadriiformes*. Also called: **thick-knee** [C17 so called because it nests in stony habitats and resembles a curlew]

stonecutter ('stəʊnˌkʌtə) *n* **1** a person who is skilled in cutting and carving stone **2** a machine used to dress stone > **stone-cutting** *n*

stoned (stəʊnd) *adj slang* under the influence of drugs or alcohol

stone-dead *adj* completely lifeless

stone-deaf *adj* completely deaf

stonefish ('stəʊnˌfɪʃ) *n*, *pl* **-fish** *or* **-fishes** a venomous tropical marine scorpaenid fish, *Synanceja verrucosa*, that resembles a piece of rock on the seabed

stonefly ('stəʊnˌflaɪ) *n*, *pl* **-flies** any insect of the order *Plecoptera*, in which the larvae are aquatic, living beneath stones, and the adults have long antennae and two pairs of large wings and occur near water [C15 so called because its larvae live under stones in rivers]

stone fruit *n* the nontechnical name for **drupe**

stoneground ('stəʊnˌgraʊnd) *adj* (of flour) ground with millstones

Stonehenge (ˌstəʊn'hendʒ) *n* a prehistoric ruin in S England, in Wiltshire on Salisbury Plain: constructed over the period of roughly 3000–1600 BC; one of the most important megalithic monuments in Europe; believed to have had religious and astronomical purposes

stone-lily *n* the fossil of any of several species of sea lily or crinoid

stone marten *n* **1** a marten, *Martes foina*, of Eurasian woods and forests, having a brown coat with a pale underfur **2** the highly valued fur of this animal

stonemason ('stəʊnˌmeɪsᵊn) *n* a person who is skilled in preparing stone for building > **stone-masonry** *n*

stone massage *n* a form of massage using heated smooth stones

stone parsley *n* a roadside umbelliferous plant, *Sison amomum*, of W Europe and the Mediterranean region, having clusters of small white flowers and aromatic seeds

stone pine *n* a Mediterranean pine tree, *Pinus pinea*, having a short bole and radiating branches forming an umbrella shape. Also called: **umbrella pine**

stone pit *n* a less common name for **quarry¹**

stoner ('stəʊnə) *n* **1** a device for removing stones from fruit **2** *slang* a person who is habitually under the influence of drugs or alcohol

stone roller *n* a small silvery freshwater cyprinid fish, *Campostoma anomalum*, of the eastern US, having a narrow black stripe on the dorsal and anal fins [C19 so called because it pushes stones about in building its nest]

stone saw *n* an untoothed iron saw used to cut stone

Stone sheep *or* **Stone's sheep** *n* a wild sheep found in the Yukon and the northern Rocky Mountains [C19 after the US naturalist Andrew Jackson Stone, who first discovered the breed in 1896]

stone shoot *n mountaineering* a long steeply sloping line of loose boulder-strewn scree

stone's throw *n* a short distance. Also called: stonecast

stonewall (ˌstəʊn'wɔːl) *vb* **1** (*intr*) *cricket* (of a batsman) to play defensively **2** (*tr*) to obstruct or hinder (parliamentary business) > **stone'waller** *n*

stoneware ('stəʊnˌwɛə) *n* **1** a hard opaque pottery, fired at a very high temperature ▷ *adj* **2** made of stoneware

stonewashed ('stəʊnˌwɒʃt) *adj* (of new clothes or fabric, esp denim jeans) given a worn faded look by being subjected to the abrasive action of many small pieces of pumice

stonework ('stəʊnˌwɜːk) *n* **1** any structure or part of a building made of stone **2** the process of dressing or setting stones > **stone-worker** *n*

stonewort ('stəʊnˌwɜːt) *n* any of various green algae of the genus *Chara*, which grow in brackish or fresh water and have jointed fronds encrusted with lime

Stoney ('stəʊnɪ) *n* a member of a Native Canadian people of Alberta [from Siouan]

stonk (stɒŋk) *vb* (*tr*) **1** to bombard (soldiers, buildings, etc) with artillery ▷ *n* **2** a concentrated bombardment by artillery [C20 from st(*andard*) (*linear*) (*c*)*onc*(*entration*)]

stonkered ('stɒŋkəd) *adj slang* completely exhausted or beaten; whacked [C20 from *stonker* to beat, of unknown origin]

stony *or* **stoney** ('stəʊnɪ) *adj* **stonier**, **stoniest** **1** of or resembling stone **2** abounding in stone or stones **3** unfeeling, heartless, or obdurate **4** short for **stony-broke**. > **stonily** *adv* > **stoniness** *n*

stony-broke *adj Brit slang* completely without money; penniless. US and Canadian term: **stone-broke**

stony coral *n* any coral of the order *Madreporaria*, having a calcareous skeleton, aggregations of which form reefs and islands

stony-hearted *adj* unfeeling; hardhearted > **stony-heartedness** *n*

stony meteorite *n* a meteorite composed mainly of silicates

stood (stʊd) *vb* the past tense and past participle of **stand**

stooge (stuːdʒ) *n* **1** an actor who feeds lines to a comedian or acts as his foil or butt **2** *slang* someone who is taken advantage of by another ▷ *vb* (*intr*) **3** *slang* to act as a stooge **4** (foll by *about* or *around*) *slang* (esp in the RAF) to fly or move about aimlessly [C20 of unknown origin]

stook (stuːk) *n* **1** a number of sheaves set upright in a field to dry with their heads together ▷ *vb* **2** (*tr*) to set up (sheaves) in stooks [C15 variant of *stouk*, of Germanic origin; compare Middle Low German *stūke*, Old High German *stūhha* sleeve] > **stooker** *n*

stookie ('stʊkɪ) *n Scot* **1** stucco **2** plaster; plaster of Paris **3** a statue: *he stood there like a stookie*

stool (stuːl) *n* **1** a backless seat or footrest consisting of a small flat piece of wood, etc, resting on three or four legs, a pedestal, etc **2** a rootstock or base of a plant, usually a woody plant, from which shoots, etc, are produced **3** a cluster of shoots growing from such a base **4**

chiefly US a decoy used in hunting **5** waste matter evacuated from the bowels **6** a lavatory seat **7** (in W Africa, esp Ghana) a chief's throne **8** **fall between two stools a** to fail through vacillation between two alternatives **b** to be in an unsatisfactory situation through not belonging to either of two categories or groups ▷ *vb* (*intr*) **9** (of a plant) to send up shoots from the base of the stem, rootstock, etc **10** to lure wildfowl with a decoy [Old English *stōl*; related to Old Norse *stōll*, Gothic *stōls*, Old High German *stuol* chair, Greek *stulos* pillar]

stool ball *n* a game resembling cricket, still played by girls and women in Sussex, England

stool pigeon *n* **1** a living or dummy pigeon used to decoy others **2** an informer for the police; nark **3** *US slang* a person acting as a decoy

stoop¹ (stuːp) *vb* (*mainly intr*) **1** (*also tr*) to bend (the body or the top half of the body) forward and downward **2** to carry oneself with head and shoulders habitually bent forward **3** (often foll by *to*) to abase or degrade oneself **4** (often foll by *to*) to condescend; deign **5** (of a bird of prey) to swoop down **6** *archaic* to give in ▷ *n* **7** the act, position, or characteristic of stooping **8** a lowering from a position of dignity or superiority **9** a downward swoop, esp of a bird of prey [Old English *stūpan*; related to Middle Dutch *stupen* to bow, Old Norse *stūpa*, Norwegian *stupa* to fall; see STEEP¹] > **stooper** *n* > **stooping** *adj* > **stoopingly** *adv*

stoop² (stuːp) *n US and Canadian* a small platform with steps up to it at the entrance to a building [C18 from Dutch *stoep*, of Germanic origin; compare Old High German *stuofa* stair, Old English *stōpel* footprint; see STEP]

stoop³ (stuːp) *n archaic* a pillar or post [C15 variant of dialect *stulpe*, probably from Old Norse *stolpe*; see STELE]

stoop⁴ (stuːp) *n* a less common spelling of **stoup**

stoor (stuːr) *n Scot* a variant of **stour**

stop (stɒp) *vb* **stops**, **stopping**, **stopped** **1** to cease from doing or being (something); discontinue: *stop talking* **2** to cause (something moving) to halt or (of something moving) to come to a halt: *to stop a car; the car stopped* **3** (*tr*) to prevent the continuance or completion of: *to stop a show* **4** (*tr*; often foll by *from*) to prevent or restrain: *to stop George from fighting* **5** (*tr*) to keep back: *to stop supplies to the navy* **6** (*tr*) to intercept or hinder in transit: *to stop a letter* **7** (*tr*; often foll by *up*) to block or plug, esp so as to close: *to stop up a pipe* **8** (*tr*; often foll by *up*) to fill a hole or opening in: *to stop up a wall* **9** (*tr*) to staunch or stem: *to stop a wound* **10** (*tr*) to instruct a bank not to honour (a cheque) **11** (*tr*) to deduct (money) from pay **12** (*tr*) *Brit* to provide with punctuation **13** (*tr*) *boxing* to beat (an opponent) either by a knockout or a technical knockout **14** (*tr*) *informal* to receive (a blow, hit, etc) **15** (*intr*) to stay or rest: *we stopped at the Robinsons' for three nights* **16** (*tr*) *rare* to defeat, beat, or kill **17** (*tr*) *music* **a** to alter the vibrating length of (a string on a violin, guitar, etc) by pressing down on it at some point with the finger **b** to alter the vibrating length of an air column in a wind instrument by closing (a finger hole, etc) **c** to produce (a note) in this manner **18** (*tr*) to place a hand inside (the bell of a French horn) to alter the tone colour and pitch or play (a note) on a French horn in such a manner **19** *bridge* to have a protecting card or winner in (a suit in which one's opponents are strong) **20** **stop at nothing** to be prepared to do anything; be unscrupulous or ruthless ▷ *n* **21** an arrest of movement or progress **22** the act of stopping or the state of being stopped **23** a place where something halts or pauses: *a bus stop* **24** a stay in or as if in the course of a journey **25** the act or an instance of blocking or obstructing **26** a plug or stopper **27** a block, screw, or other device or object that prevents, limits, or terminates the motion of a mechanism or moving part **28** *Brit* a punctuation mark, esp a

S

full stop **29** Also called: **stop thrust** *fencing* a counterthrust made without a parry in the hope that one's blade will touch before one's opponent's blade will touch **30** short for **stop payment** or **stop order** **31** *music* **a** the act of stopping the string, finger hole, etc, of an instrument **b** a set of organ pipes or harpsichord strings that may be allowed to sound as a group by muffling or silencing all other such sets **c** a knob, lever, or handle on an organ, etc, that is operated to allow sets of pipes to sound **d** an analogous device on a harpsichord or other instrument with variable registers, such as an electrophonic instrument **32** **pull out all the stops a** to play at full volume **b** to spare no effort **33** *Austral* a stud on a football boot **34** the angle between the forehead and muzzle of a dog or cat, regarded as a point in breeding **35** *nautical* a short length of line or small stuff used as a tie, esp for a furled sail **36** Also called: **stop consonant** *phonetics* any of a class of consonants articulated by first making a complete closure at some point of the vocal tract and then releasing it abruptly with audible plosion. Stops include the labials (p, b), the alveolars or dentals (t, d), the velars (k, g). Compare **continuant** **37** Also called: **f-stop** *photog* **a** a setting of the aperture of a camera lens, calibrated to the corresponding f-number **b** another name for **diaphragm** (sense 4) **38** a block or carving used to complete the end of a moulding **39** Also called: **stopper** *bridge* a protecting card or winner in a suit in which one's opponents are strong ▷ See also **stop down, stop off, stop out, stopover, stops** [C14 from Old English *stoppian* (unattested), as in *forstoppian* to plug the ear, ultimately from Late Latin *stuppāre* to stop with a tow, from Latin *stuppa* tow, from Greek *stuppē*] > '**stoppable** *adj*

stopbank ('stɒp,bæŋk) *n* NZ an embankment to prevent flooding

stop bath *n* a weakly acidic solution used in photographic processing to stop the action of a developer on a film, plate, or paper before the material is immersed in fixer

stop chorus *n* *jazz* a solo during which the rhythm section plays only the first beat of each phrase of music

stopcock ('stɒp,kɒk) *n* a valve used to control or stop the flow of a fluid in a pipe

stop down *vb* (*adverb*) to reduce the size of the aperture of (a camera lens)

stope (stəʊp) *n* **1** a steplike excavation made in a mine to extract ore ▷ *vb* **2** to mine (ore, etc) by cutting stopes [C18 probably from Low German *stope*; see STOOP²]

stop-frame *adj* *films* of or relating to animated films involving models, puppets, etc, in which each frame is photographed individually

stopgap ('stɒp,gæp) *n* **a** a temporary substitute for something else **b** (*as modifier*): *a stopgap programme*

stop-go *adj* *Brit* (of economic policy) characterized by deliberate alternate expansion and contraction of aggregate demand in an effort to curb inflation and eliminate balance of payments deficits, and yet maintain full employment

stoping ('stəʊpɪŋ) *n* *geology* the process by which country rock is broken up and engulfed by the upward movement of magma. Also called: **magmatic stoping** See also **stope**

stoplight ('stɒp,laɪt) *n* **1** a red light on a traffic signal indicating that vehicles or pedestrians coming towards it should stop **2** another word for **brake light**

stop-loss *adj* *business* of or relating to an order to a broker in a commodity or security market to close an open position at a specified price in order to limit any loss

stop-motion *n* **a** a technique used in animation and photography in which a subject is filmed then adjusted a frame at a time **b** (*as modifier*): *stop-motion animation*

stop off, stop in *or esp US* **stop by** *vb* **1** (*intr, adverb; often foll by at*) to halt and call somewhere, as on a visit or errand, esp en route to another place ▷ *n* **stopoff** **2 a** a break in a journey **b** (*as modifier*): *stopoff point*

stop order *n* *stock exchange* an instruction to a broker to sell one or more shares when the price offered for them falls below a stipulated level. Also called: **stop-loss order**

stop out *vb* (*tr, adverb*) to cover (part of the area) of a piece of cloth, printing plate, etc, to prevent it from being dyed, etched, etc

stopover ('stɒp,əʊvə) *n* **1** a stopping place on a journey ▷ *vb* **stop over** **2** (*intr, adverb*) to make a stopover

stoppage ('stɒpɪdʒ) *n* **1** the act of stopping or the state of being stopped **2** something that stops or blocks **3** a deduction of money, as from pay **4** an organized cessation of work, as during a strike

stoppage time *n* *sport* another name for **injury time**

stop payment *n* an instruction to a bank by the drawer of a cheque to refuse payment on it

stopped (stɒpt) *adj* (of a pipe or tube, esp an organ pipe) closed at one end and thus sounding an octave lower than an open pipe of the same length

stopper ('stɒpə) *n* **1** Also called: **stopple** ('stɒpᵊl) a plug or bung for closing a bottle, pipe, duct, etc **2** a person or thing that stops or puts an end to something **3** *bridge* another name for **stop** (sense 39) ▷ *vb* **4** (*tr*) Also: **stopple** to close or fit with a stopper

stopping ('stɒpɪŋ) *n* **1** *Brit informal* a dental filling **2** a solid barrier in a mine tunnel to seal off harmful gases, fire, fresh air from used air, etc ▷ *adj* **3** *chiefly Brit* making many stops in a journey: *a stopping train*

stopping power *n* *physics* a measure of the effect a substance has on the kinetic energy of a particle passing through it

stop press *n* *Brit* **1** news items inserted into a newspaper after the printing has been started **2** the space regularly left blank for this

stops (stɒps) *n* (*functioning as singular*) any one of several card games in which players must play their cards in certain sequences

stop thrust *n* *fencing* another name for **stop** (sense 29)

stop time *n* *jazz* a passage where the beat stops temporarily

stopwatch ('stɒp,wɒtʃ) *n* a type of watch used for timing events, such as sporting events, accurately, having a device for stopping the hand or hands instantly

storage ('stɔːrɪdʒ) *n* **1** the act of storing or the state of being stored **2** space or area reserved for storing **3** a charge made for storing **4** *computing* **a** the act or process of storing information in a computer memory or on a magnetic tape, disk, etc **b** (*as modifier*): *a storage device; storage capacity*

storage battery *n* another name (esp US) for **accumulator** (sense 1)

storage capacity *n* the maximum number of bits, bytes, words, or items that can be held in a memory system such as that of a computer or of the brain

storage device *n* a piece of computer equipment, such as a magnetic tape, disk, etc, in or on which data and instructions can be stored, usually in binary form

storage heater *n* an electric device capable of accumulating and radiating heat generated by off-peak electricity

storage tube *n* *electronics* an electron tube in which information is stored as charges for a predetermined time

storax ('stɔːræks) *n* **1** any of numerous styracaceous trees or shrubs of the genus *Styrax*, of tropical and subtropical regions, having drooping showy white flowers **2** a vanilla-scented solid resin obtained from one of these trees, *Styrax*

officinalis of the Mediterranean region and SW Asia, formerly used as incense and in perfumery and medicine **3** a liquid aromatic balsam obtained from liquidambar trees, esp *Liquidambar orientalis* of SW Asia, and used in perfumery and medicine [C14 via Late Latin from Greek, variant of STYRAX]

store (stɔː) *vb* **1** (*tr*) to keep, set aside, or accumulate for future use **2** (*tr*) to place in a warehouse, depository, etc, for safekeeping **3** (*tr*) to supply, provide, or stock **4** (*intr*) to be put into storage **5** *computing* to enter or retain (information) in a storage device ▷ *n* **6 a** an establishment for the retail sale of goods and services **b** (*in combination*): *storefront* **7 a** a large supply or stock kept for future use **b** (*as modifier*): *store ship* **8** short for **department store** **9 a** a storage place such as a warehouse or depository **b** (*in combination*): *storeman* **10** the state of being stored (esp in the phrase **in store**) **11** a large amount or quantity **12** *computing, chiefly Brit* another name for **memory** (sense 7) **13** Also called: **store pig** a pig that has not yet been weaned and weighs less than 40 kg **14 a** an animal bought lean to be fattened up for market **b** (*as modifier*): *store cattle* **15** **in store** forthcoming or imminent **16** **lay, put,** *or* **set store by** to value or reckon as important ▷ See also **stores** [C13 from Old French *estor*, from *estorer* to restore, from Latin *instaurāre* to refresh; related to Greek *stauros* stake] > '**storable** *adj*

store and forward *vb* to store (information) in a computer for later forward transmission through a telecommunication network

Store Bælt ('sdoːrə 'bɛld) *n* the Danish name for the **Great Belt**

store card *n* another name for **charge card**

storehouse ('stɔː,haʊs) *n* a place where things are stored

storekeeper ('stɔː,kiːpə) *n* a manager, owner, or keeper of a store > '**store,keeping** *n*

store of value *n* *economics* the function of money that enables goods and services to be paid for a considerable time after they have been acquired

storeroom ('stɔː,ruːm, -,rʊm) *n* **1** a room in which things are stored **2** room for storage

stores (stɔːz) *pl n* **1** a supply or stock of something, esp essentials, for a specific purpose: *the ship's stores* **2** specifically, munitions slung externally on a military aircraft airframe

storey *or US* **story** ('stɔːrɪ) *n*, *pl* **-reys** *or* **-ries** **1** a floor or level of a building **2** a set of rooms on one level [C14 from Anglo-Latin *historia*, picture, from Latin: narrative, probably arising from the pictures on medieval windows]

storeyed *or US* **storied** ('stɔːrɪd) *adj* **a** having a storey or storeys **b** (*in combination*): *a two-storeyed house*

storey house *n* (in W Africa) a house having more than one storey

storiated ('stɔːrɪ,eɪtɪd) *adj* another word for **historiated** *or* **storied** (sense 2)

storied ('stɔːrɪd) *adj* **1** recorded in history or in a story; fabled **2** decorated with narrative scenes or pictures

stork (stɔːk) *n* **1** any large wading bird of the family *Ciconiidae*, chiefly of warm regions of the Old World, having very long legs and a long stout pointed bill, and typically having a white-and-black plumage: order *Ciconiiformes* **2** (*sometimes capital*) a variety of domestic fancy pigeon resembling the fairy swallow [Old English *storc*; related to Old High German *storah*, Old Norse *storkr*, Old English *stearc* stiff; from the stiff appearance of its legs; see STARK]

storksbill ('stɔːks,bɪl) *n* any of various geraniaceous plants of the genus *Erodium*, esp *E. cicutarium* (**common storksbill**), having pink or reddish-purple flowers and fruits with a beaklike process

storm (stɔːm) *n* **1 a** a violent weather condition of strong winds, rain, hail, thunder, lightning, blowing sand, snow, etc **b** (*as modifier*): *storm signal; storm sail* **c** (*in combination*): *stormproof* **2** *meteorol* a violent gale of force 10 on the Beaufort scale reaching speeds of 55 to 63 mph **3** a strong or violent reaction: *a storm of protest* **4** a direct assault on a stronghold **5** a heavy discharge or rain, as of bullets or missiles **6** short for **storm window** (sense 1) **7 storm in a teacup** *Brit* a violent fuss or disturbance over a trivial matter. US equivalent: **tempest in a teapot 8 take by storm a** to capture or overrun by a violent assault **b** to overwhelm and enthral ▷ *vb* **9** to attack or capture (something) suddenly and violently **10** (*intr*) to be vociferously angry **11** (*intr*) to move or rush violently or angrily **12** (*intr; with it* as subject) to rain, hail, or snow hard and be very windy, often with thunder or lightning [Old English, related to Old Norse *stormr*, German *Sturm; see* STIR¹] > 'storm,like *adj*

storm belt *n* an area of the earth's surface in which storms are frequent

stormbound ('stɔːm,baʊnd) *adj* detained or harassed by storms

storm centre *n* **1** the centre of a cyclonic storm, etc, where pressure is lowest **2** the centre of any disturbance or trouble

storm cloud *n* **1** a heavy dark cloud presaging rain or a storm **2** a herald of disturbance, anger, or violence: *the storm clouds of war*

storm-cock *n* another name for **mistle thrush** [C18 so called because it was believed to give forewarning of bad weather]

storm collar *n* a high collar on a coat

storm cone *n Brit* a canvas cone hoisted as a warning of high winds

storm door *n* an extra outer door for protection in bad weather

stormer ('stɔːmə) *n informal* an outstanding example of its kind: *that film was a real stormer*

storm glass *n* a sealed tube containing a solution supposed to change in appearance according to the weather

storming ('stɔːmɪŋ) *adj informal* characterized by or displaying dynamism, speed, and energy: *a storming performance*

storm lantern *n* another name for **hurricane lamp**

Stormont ('stɔːmənt) *n* a suburb of Belfast: site of Parliament House (1928–30), formerly the seat of the parliament of Northern Ireland (1922–72) and since 1998 of the Northern Ireland assembly, and Stormont Castle, formerly the residence of the prime minister of Northern Ireland and since 1998 the office of the province's first minister

storm petrel *n* any small petrel, such as the northern *Hydrobates pelagicus,* of the family *Hydrobatidae,* typically having a dark plumage with paler underparts. Also called: **Mother Carey's chicken, stormy petrel** [C19 so named because it was thought to be a harbinger of rough weather]

stormproof ('stɔːm,pruːf) *adj* withstanding or giving protection against storms

storm trooper *n* **1** a member of the Nazi SA **2** a member of a force of shock troops

storm warning *n* **1** a pattern of lights, flags, etc, displayed at certain ports as a warning to shipping of an approaching storm **2** an announcement on radio or television of an approaching storm **3** any warning of approaching danger or trouble

storm window *n* **1** an additional window fitted to the outside of an ordinary window to provide insulation against wind, cold, rain, etc **2** a type of dormer window

stormy ('stɔːmɪ) *adj* stormier, stormiest **1** characterized by storms **2** subject to, involving, or characterized by violent disturbance or emotional outburst > 'stormily *adv* > 'storminess *n*

stormy petrel *n* **1** another name for **storm petrel 2** a person who brings or portends trouble

Stornoway ('stɔːnə,weɪ) *n* a port in NW Scotland, on the E coast of Lewis in the Outer Hebrides,

administrative centre of the Western Isles. Pop: 5602 (2001)

Storting or **Storthing** ('stɔːtɪŋ) *n* the parliament of Norway. See also **Lagting, Odelsting** [C19 Norwegian, from *stor* great + *thing* assembly]

story¹ ('stɔːrɪ) *n, pl* -ries **1** a narration of a chain of events told or written in prose or verse **2** Also called: **short story** a piece of fiction, briefer and usually less detailed than a novel **3** Also called: **story line** the plot of a book, film, etc **4** an event that could be the subject of a narrative **5** a report or statement on a matter or event **6** the event or material for such a report **7** *informal* a lie, fib, or untruth **8 cut** (*or* **make**) **a long story short** to leave out details in a narration **9** *informal* **the same old story** the familiar or regular course of events **10 the story goes** it is commonly said or believed ▷ *vb* -ries, -rying, -ried (*tr*) **11** to decorate (a pot, wall, etc) with scenes from history or legends [C13 from Anglo-French *estorie,* from Latin *historia; see* HISTORY]

story² ('stɔːrɪ) *n, pl* -ries another spelling (esp US) of **storey**

story arc *n* a continuing storyline in a television series that gradually unfolds over several episodes

storyboard ('stɔːrɪ,bɔːd) *n* (in films, television, advertising, etc) a series of sketches or photographs showing the sequence of shots or images planned for a film

storybook ('stɔːrɪ,bʊk) *n* **1** a book containing stories, esp for children ▷ *adj* **2** unreal or fantastic: *a storybook world*

story line *n* the plot of a book, film, play, etc

storyteller ('stɔːrɪ,tɛlə) *n* **1** a person who tells stories **2** *informal* a liar > 'story,telling *n, adj*

stoss (stɒs; *German* ʃtoːs) *adj* (of the side of a hill, crag, etc) facing the onward flow of a glacier or the direction in which a former glacier flowed [German, from *stossen* to thrust]

stot¹ (stɒt) *n dialect* **1** a bullock **2** a castrated male ox [Old English]

stot² (stɒt, stot) *vb* stots, stotting, stotted *Scot and northern English dialect* **1** to bounce or cause to bounce **2** (*intr*) Also: **stotter** to stagger [of obscure origin]

stotin (stɒ'tɪn) *n, pl* stotin a monetary unit of Slovenia, worth one hundredth of a tolar

stotinka (stɒ'tɪŋkə) *n, pl* -ki (-kɪ) a monetary unit of Bulgaria, worth one hundredth of a lev [from Bulgarian; related to *suto* hundred]

stotious ('stəʊʃəs) *adj Now chiefly Irish dialect* drunk; inebriated [of obscure origin; perhaps from STOT²]

stotter ('stɒtə; *Scot* 'stɒtər) *Scot dialect, chiefly Glasgow* ▷ *vb* (*intr*) **1** to stagger ▷ *n* **2** anything outstanding, esp a good-looking person [from STOT²]

stottie ('stɒtɪ) *n Northeast English dialect* a wedge of bread cut from a flat round loaf (**stottie cake**) that has been split and filled with meat, cheese, etc [origin unknown]

stound (staʊnd) *n Brit dialect* **1** a short while; instant **2** a pang or pain [Old English *stund;* related to Old High German *stunta* period of time, hour]

stoup or **stoop** (stuːp) *n* **1** a small basin for holy water **2** *Scot and northern English dialect* Also: **stowp** a bucket or drinking vessel [C14 (in the sense: bucket): of Scandinavian origin; compare Old Norse *staup* beaker, Old English *stēap* flagon; see STEEP¹]

stour (staʊə) or *Scot* **stoor** (stuːr) *n Scot and northern English dialect* **1** turmoil or conflict **2** dust; a cloud of dust [C14 from Old French *estour* armed combat, of Germanic origin; related to Old High German *sturm* STORM]

Stour (staʊə) *n* **1** Also called: **Great Stour** a river in S England, in Kent, rising in the Weald and flowing N to the North Sea: separates the Isle of Thanet from the mainland **2** any of several smaller rivers in England

Stourbridge ('staʊə,brɪdʒ) *n* an industrial town

in W central England, in Dudley unitary authority, West Midlands. Pop: 55 480 (2001)

Stourhead ('staʊə,hed) *n* a Palladian mansion near Mere in Wiltshire: built (1722) for Henry Hoare; famous for its landscaped gardens laid out (1741) by Flitcroft

stoush (staʊʃ) *Austral and NZ slang* ▷ *vb* **1** (*tr*) to hit or punch ▷ *n* **2** fighting, violence, or a fight [C19 of uncertain origin]

stout (staʊt) *adj* **1** solidly built or corpulent **2** (*prenominal*) resolute or valiant: *stout fellow* **3** strong, substantial, and robust **4 a stout heart** courage; resolution ▷ *n* **5** strong porter highly flavoured with malt [C14 from Old French *estout* bold, of Germanic origin; related to Middle High German *stolz* proud, Middle Dutch *stolt* brave] > 'stoutish *adj* > 'stoutly *adv* > 'stoutness *n*

stouthearted (,staʊt'hɑːtɪd) *adj* valiant; brave > ,stout'heartedly *adv* > ,stout'heartedness *n*

stove¹ (stəʊv) *n* **1** another word for **cooker** (sense 1) **2** any heating apparatus, such as a kiln ▷ *vb* (*tr*) **3** to process (ceramics, metalwork, etc) by heating in a stove **4** *Scot* to stew (meat, vegetables, etc) [Old English *stofa* bathroom; related to Old High German *stuba* steam room, Greek *tuphos* smoke]

stove² (stəʊv) *vb* a past tense and past participle of **stave**

stove enamel *n* a type of enamel made heatproof by treatment in a stove

stovepipe ('stəʊv,paɪp) *n* **1** a pipe that serves as a flue to a stove **2** Also called: **stovepipe hat** a man's tall silk hat

stovepipes ('stəʊv,paɪps) *pl n informal* tight trousers with narrow legs

stover ('stəʊvə) *n* **1** *chiefly Brit* fodder **2** *US* cornstalks used as fodder [C14 shortened from ESTOVERS]

stovetop ('stəʊv,tɒp) *n* the US word for **hob¹** (sense 1)

stovies ('stəʊvɪz, 'stəʊ-) *pl n Scot* potatoes stewed with onions [from STOVE¹]

stow (stəʊ) *vb* (*tr*) **1** (often foll by *away*) to pack or store **2** to fill by packing **3** *nautical* to pack or put away (cargo, sails and other gear, etc) **4** to have enough room for **5** (*usually imperative*) *Brit slang* to cease from: *stow your noise!; stow it!* [Old English *stōwian* to keep, hold back, from *stōw* a place; related to Old High German *stouwen* to accuse, Gothic *stōjan* to judge, Old Slavonic *staviti* to place]

stowage ('stəʊɪdʒ) *n* **1** space, room, or a charge for stowing goods **2** the act or an instance of stowing or the state of being stowed **3** something that is stowed

stowaway ('stəʊə,weɪ) *n* **1** a person who hides aboard a vehicle, ship, or aircraft in order to gain free passage ▷ *vb* **stow away 2** (*intr, adverb*) to travel in such a way

Stowe (stəʊ) *n* a mansion near Buckingham in N Buckinghamshire: built and decorated in the 17th and 18th centuries by Vanbrugh, Robert Adam, Grinling Gibbons, and William Kent; formerly the seat of the Dukes of Buckingham; fine landscaped gardens: now occupied by a public school

stowp (staʊp) *n Scot* a variant of **stoup** (sense 2)

STP *abbreviation for* **1** *trademark* scientifically treated petroleum: an oil substitute promising renewed power for an internal-combustion engine **2** Also: **NTP** standard temperature and pressure: standard conditions of 0°C temperature and 101.325 kPa (760 mmHg) pressure **3** Professor of Sacred Theology [from Latin: *Sanctae Theologiae Professor*] ▷ *n* **4** a synthetic hallucinogenic drug related to mescaline [Sense 4 from humorous reference to the extra power resulting from scientifically treated petroleum]

str *abbreviation for* steamer

Strabane (strə'bæn) *n* a district of W Northern Ireland, in Co Tyrone. Pop: 38 565 (2003 est) Area: 862 sq km (333 sq miles)

strabismus (strə'bɪzməs) *n* abnormal alignment of one or both eyes, characterized by a turning inwards or outwards from the nose thus

S

preventing parallel vision: caused by paralysis of an eye muscle, etc. Also called: **squint** [c17 via New Latin from Greek *strabismos,* from *strabizein* to squint, from *strabos* cross-eyed] > stra'**bismal,** stra'**bismic** or stra'**bismical** *adj*

strabotomy (strə'bɒtəmɪ) *n, pl* -**mies** a former method of treating strabismus by surgical division of one or more muscles of the eye [c19 from French *strabotomie,* from Greek *strabos* squinting + -TOMY]

straddle ('stræd³l) *vb* 1 (*tr*) to have one leg, part, or support on each side of 2 (*tr*) *US and Canadian informal* to be in favour of both sides of (something) 3 (*intr*) to stand, walk, or sit with the legs apart 4 (*tr*) to spread (the legs) apart 5 *military* to fire a number of shots slightly beyond and slightly short of (a target) to determine the correct range 6 (*intr*) (in poker, of the second player after the dealer) to double the ante before looking at one's cards > *n* 7 the act or position of straddling 8 a noncommittal attitude or stand 9 *business* a contract or option permitting its purchaser to either sell or buy securities or commodities within a specified period of time at specified prices. It is a combination of a put and a call option. Compare **spread** (sense 24c) 10 *athletics* a high-jumping technique in which the body is parallel with the bar and the legs straddle it at the highest point of the jump 11 (in poker) the stake put up after the ante in poker by the second player after the dealer 12 *Irish* a wooden frame placed on a horse's back to which panniers are attached [c16 frequentative formed from obsolete *strad-* (Old English *strode*), past stem of STRIDE] > '**straddler** *n*

Stradivarius (ˌstrædɪ'vɛərɪəs) *n* any of a number of violins manufactured by Antonio Stradivari (?1644–1737), Italian violin, viola, and cello maker, or his family. Often (*informal*) shortened to: **Strad**

strafe (streɪf, strɑːf) *vb* (*tr*) 1 to machine-gun (troops, etc) from the air 2 *slang* to punish harshly > *n* 3 an act or instance of strafing [c20 from German *strafen* to punish] > '**strafer** *n*

straggle ('stræg³l) *vb* (*intr*) 1 to go, come, or spread in a rambling or irregular way; stray 2 to linger behind or wander from a main line or part [c14 of uncertain origin; perhaps related to STRAKE and STRETCH] > '**straggler** *n* > '**straggling** *adj* > '**stragglingly** *adv* > '**straggly** *adj*

straight (streɪt) *adj* 1 not curved or crooked; continuing in the same direction without deviating 2 straightforward, outright, or candid: *a straight rejection* 3 even, level, or upright in shape or position 4 in keeping with the facts; accurate 5 honest, respectable, or reliable 6 accurate or logical: *straight reasoning* 7 continuous; uninterrupted 8 (esp of an alcoholic drink) undiluted; neat 9 not crisp, kinked, or curly: *straight hair* 10 correctly arranged; orderly 11 (of a play, acting style, etc) straightforward or serious 12 *journalism* (of a story, article, etc) giving the facts without unnecessary embellishment 13 *US* sold at a fixed unit price irrespective of the quantity sold 14 *boxing* (of a blow) delivered with an unbent arm: *a straight left* 15 (of the cylinders of an internal-combustion engine) in line, rather than in a V-formation or in some other arrangement: *a straight eight* 16 a slang word for **heterosexual** 17 *informal* no longer owing or being owed something: *if you buy the next round we'll be straight* 18 *slang* conventional in views, customs, appearance, etc 19 *slang* not using narcotics; not addicted > *adv* 20 in a straight line or direct course 21 immediately; at once: *he came straight back* 22 in an even, level, or upright position 23 without cheating, lying, or unreliability: *tell it to me straight* 24 continuously; uninterruptedly 25 *US* without discount regardless of the quantity sold 26 (often foll by *out*) frankly; candidly: *he told me straight out* 27 **go straight** *informal* to reform after having been dishonest or a criminal > *n* 28 the state of being straight 29 a straight line, form, part, or position 30 *Brit* a straight part of a

racetrack. US name: **straightaway** 31 *poker* **a** five cards that are in sequence irrespective of suit **b** a hand containing such a sequence **c** (*as modifier*): *a straight flush* 32 *slang* a conventional person 33 *slang* a heterosexual person 34 *slang* a cigarette containing only tobacco, without marijuana, etc [c14 from the past participle of Old English *streccan* to STRETCH] > '**straightly** *adv* > '**straightness** *n*

straight and narrow *n informal* the proper, honest, and moral path of behaviour [perhaps an alteration of *strait and narrow,* an allusion to Matthew 7:14: "strait is the gate, and narrow is the way, which leadeth unto life"]

straight angle *n* an angle of 180°

straight-arm *adj* 1 *rugby* (of a tackle) performed with the arm fully extended > *vb* 2 (*tr*) to ward off (an opponent) with the arm outstretched

straight arm lift *n* a wrestling attack, in which a wrestler twists his opponent's arm against the joint and lifts him by it, often using his shoulder as a fulcrum

straight arrow *n informal, chiefly US* **a** a clean-living and honest person **b** (*as modifier*): *a straight-arrow cop*

straightaway (ˌstreɪtə'weɪ) *adv* also **straight away** 1 at once > *n* 2 the US word for **straight** (sense 30)

straight bat *n* 1 *cricket* a bat held vertically 2 *Brit informal* honest or honourable behaviour

straight chain *n* **a** an open chain of atoms in a molecule with no attached side chains **b** (*as modifier*): *a straight-chain hydrocarbon* > Compare **branched chain**

straight chair *n* a straight-backed side chair

straightedge ('streɪtˌɛdʒ) *n* a stiff strip of wood or metal that has one edge straight and true and is used for ruling and testing straight lines > '**straight,edged** *adj*

straight-edge *adj informal* not indulging in any kind of drug-taking or sexual activities

straighten ('streɪt³n) *vb* (sometimes foll by *up* or *out*) 1 to make or become straight 2 (*tr*) to make neat or tidy: *straighten your desk* > '**straightener** *n*

straighten out *vb* (*adverb*) 1 to make or become less complicated or confused 2 *US and Canadian* to reform or become reformed

straighten up *vb* (*adverb*) 1 to become or cause to become erect 2 *chiefly US* to reform or become reformed

straight face *n* a serious facial expression, esp one that conceals the impulse to laugh > '**straight-'faced** *adj*

straight fight *n* a contest between two candidates only

straight flush *n* (in poker) five consecutive cards of the same suit

straightforward (ˌstreɪt'fɔːwəd) *adj* 1 (of a person) honest, frank, or simple 2 *chiefly Brit* (of a task, etc) simple; easy > *adj* 3 in a straight course > ˌstraight'**forwardly** *adv* > ˌstraight'**forwardness** *n*

straightjacket ('streɪtˌdʒækɪt) *n* a less common spelling of **straitjacket**

straight joint *n* a vertical joint in brickwork that is directly above a vertical joint in the course below

straight-laced *adj* a variant spelling of **strait-laced**

straight-line *n* (*modifier*) 1 (of a machine) having components that are arranged in a row or that move in a straight line when in operation 2 of or relating to a method of depreciation whereby equal charges are made against gross profit for each year of an asset's expected life

straight man *n* a subsidiary actor who acts as stooge to a comedian

straight off *adv informal* without deliberation or hesitation: *tell me the answer straight off*

straight-out *adj informal* 1 complete; thoroughgoing 2 frank or honest

straight razor *n* another name for **cut-throat** (sense 2)

straight ticket *n US* a ballot for all the candidates of one and only one political party. Compare **split ticket**

straight up *sentence substitute Brit slang* honestly; truly; exactly

straightway ('streɪtˌweɪ) *adv archaic* at once

strain[1] (streɪn) *vb* 1 to draw or be drawn taut; stretch tight 2 to exert, tax, or use (resources) to the utmost extent 3 to injure or damage or be injured or damaged by overexertion: *he strained himself* 4 to deform or be deformed as a result of a stress 5 (*intr*) to make intense or violent efforts; strive 6 to subject or be subjected to mental tension or stress 7 to pour or pass (a substance) or (of a substance) to be poured or passed through a sieve, filter, or strainer 8 (*tr*) to draw off or remove (one part of a substance or mixture from another) by or as if by filtering 9 (*tr*) to clasp tightly; hug 10 (*tr*) *obsolete* to force or constrain 11 (*intr;* foll by *at*) **a** to push, pull, or work with violent exertion (upon) **b** to strive (for) **c** to balk or scruple (from) > *n* 12 the act or an instance of straining 13 the damage resulting from excessive exertion 14 an intense physical or mental effort 15 *music* (often *plural*) a theme, melody, or tune 16 a great demand on the emotions, resources, etc 17 a feeling of tension and tiredness resulting from overwork, worry, etc; stress 18 a particular style or recurring theme in speech or writing 19 *physics* the change in dimension of a body under load expressed as the ratio of the total deflection or change in dimension to the original unloaded dimension. It may be a ratio of lengths, areas, or volumes [c13 from Old French *estreindre* to press together, from Latin *stringere* to bind tightly]

strain[2] (streɪn) *n* 1 the main body of descendants from one ancestor 2 a group of organisms within a species or variety, distinguished by one or more minor characteristics 3 a variety of bacterium or fungus, esp one used for a culture 4 a streak; trace 5 *archaic* a kind, type, or sort [Old English *strēon;* related to Old High German *gistriuni* gain, Latin *struere* to CONSTRUCT]

strained (streɪnd) *adj* 1 (of an action, performance, etc) not natural or spontaneous 2 (of an atmosphere, relationship, etc) not relaxed; tense

strainer ('streɪnə) *n* 1 a sieve used for straining sauces, vegetables, tea, etc 2 a gauze or simple filter used to strain liquids 3 *Austral and NZ* a self-locking device or a tool for tightening fencing wire 4 *Austral and NZ* the main post in a wire fence, often diagonally braced

strain gauge *n* a device for measuring strain in a machine or other structure, usually consisting of a metal filament that is attached to it and receives the same strain. The strain can be measured by the change in the electrical properties of the filament

strain hardening *n* a process in which a metal is permanently deformed in order to increase its resistance to further deformation

straining piece or **beam** *n* a horizontal tie beam that connects the top of two queen posts of a roof truss

strait (streɪt) *n* 1 (often *plural*) **a** a narrow channel of the sea linking two larger areas of sea **b** (*capital as part of a name*): *the Strait of Gibraltar* 2 (often *plural*) a position of acute difficulty (often in the phrase **in dire** or **desperate straits**) 3 *archaic* a narrow place or passage > *adj archaic* 4 (of spaces, etc) affording little room 5 (of circumstances, etc) limiting or difficult 6 severe, strict, or scrupulous [c13 from Old French *estreit* narrow, from Latin *strictus* constricted, from *stringere* to bind tightly] > '**straitly** *adv* > '**straitness** *n*

straiten ('streɪt³n) *vb* 1 (*tr; usually passive*) to embarrass or distress, esp financially 2 (*tr*) to limit, confine, or restrict 3 *archaic* to make or become narrow

straitjacket ('streɪtˌdʒækɪt) *n* 1 Also called: **straightjacket** a jacket made of strong canvas material with long sleeves for binding the arms of violent prisoners or mental patients **2** a severe restriction or limitation ▷ *vb* **3** (*tr*) to confine in or as if in a straitjacket

strait-laced *or* **straight-laced** *adj* prudish or puritanical

Straits Settlements (streɪts) *n* (formerly) a British crown colony of SE Asia that included Singapore, Penang, Malacca, Labuan, and some smaller islands

strake (streɪk) *n* **1 a** a curved metal plate forming part of the metal rim on a wooden wheel **b** any metal plate let into a rubber tyre **2** Also called: **streak** *nautical* one of a continuous range of planks or plates forming the side of a vessel **3** a profiled piece of wood carried on an arm that rotates round a fixed post: used to sweep the internal shape of a mould, as for a bell or a ship's propeller blade, in sand or loam [c14 related to Old English *streccan* to STRETCH]

Stralsund (*German* ˈʃtraːlzʊnt) *n* a port in NE Germany, in Mecklenburg-West Pomerania on a strait of the Baltic: one of the leading towns of the Hanseatic League. Pop: 59 140 (2003 est)

stramash (strəˈmæʃ) *Scot* ▷ *n* **1** an uproar; tumult; brawl ▷ *vb* (*tr*) **2** to destroy; smash [c18 perhaps expanded from SMASH]

stramonium (strəˈməʊnɪəm) *n* **1** a preparation of the dried leaves and flowers of the thorn apple, containing hyoscyamine and formerly used as a drug to treat asthma **2** another name for **thorn apple** (sense 1) [c17 from New Latin, of uncertain origin]

strand¹ (strænd) *vb* **1** to leave or drive (ships, fish, etc) aground or ashore or (of ships, fish, etc) to be left or driven ashore **2** (*tr; usually passive*) to leave helpless, as without transport or money, etc ▷ *n* **3** *chiefly poetic* a shore or beach **4** a foreign country [Old English; related to Old Norse *strönd* side, Middle High German *strant* beach, Latin *sternere* to spread]

strand² (strænd) *n* **1** a set of or one of the individual fibres or threads of string, wire, etc, that form a rope, cable, etc **2** a single length of string, hair, wool, wire, etc **3** a string of pearls or beads **4** a constituent element in a complex whole: *one strand of her argument* ▷ *vb* **5** (*tr*) to form (a rope, cable, etc) by winding strands together [c15 of uncertain origin]

Strand (strænd) *n* **the** a street in W central London, parallel to the Thames: famous for its hotels and theatres

Strandloper (ˈstrantˌlʊəpə) *n* a member of an extinct tribe of Khoikhoi or Bushmen who lived on sea food gathered on the beaches of southern Africa [c17 from Afrikaans *strand* beach + *loper* walker]

strandwolf (ˈstrændˌwʊlf; *Afrikaans* ˈstrantˌvɔlf) *n, pl* -wolves a species of hyena (*Hyaena brunnea*) that scavenges on shores of southern Africa. Also called: **brown hyena** [c19 Afrikaans, from Dutch *strand* beach + Afrikaans *wolf* hyena]

strange (streɪndʒ) *adj* **1** odd, unusual, or extraordinary in appearance, effect, manner, etc; peculiar **2** not known, seen, or experienced before; unfamiliar: *a strange land* **3** not easily explained: *a strange phenomenon* **4** (*usually foll by to*) inexperienced (in) or unaccustomed (to): *strange to a task* **5** not of one's own kind, locality, etc; alien; foreign **6** shy; distant; reserved **7 strange to say** it is unusual or surprising that **8** *physics* **a** denoting a particular flavour of quark **b** denoting or relating to a hypothetical form of matter composed of such quarks: *strange matter; a strange star* ▷ *adv* **9** *not standard* in a strange manner [c13 from Old French *estrange*, from Latin *extrāneus* foreign; see EXTRANEOUS] ▷ ˈstrangely *adv*

strange attractor *n maths* a type of chaotic dynamical system

strangeness (ˈstreɪndʒnɪs) *n* **1** the state or quality of being strange **2** *physics* a property of certain elementary particles, characterized by a

quantum number (**strangeness number**) conserved in strong and electromagnetic but not in weak interactions. It is associated with the presence of strange quarks

stranger (ˈstreɪndʒə) *n* **1** any person whom one does not know **2** a person who is new to a particular locality, from another region, town, etc **3** a guest or visitor **4** (foll by *to*) a person who is unfamiliar (with) or new (to) something: *he is no stranger to computers* **5** *law* a person who is neither party nor privy to a transaction

stranger's gallery *n* another name for **public gallery**

strangle (ˈstræŋɡ°l) *vb* **1** (*tr*) to kill by compressing the windpipe; throttle **2** (*tr*) to prevent or inhibit the growth or development of: *to strangle originality* **3** (*tr*) to suppress (an utterance) by or as if by swallowing suddenly: *to strangle a cry* ▷ See also **strangles** [c13 via Old French, ultimately from Greek *strangalē* a halter]

stranglehold (ˈstræŋɡ°lˌhəʊld) *n* **1** a wrestling hold in which a wrestler's arms are pressed against his opponent's windpipe. See also **Japanese stranglehold 2** complete power or control over a person or situation

strangler (ˈstræŋɡlə) *n* **1** a person or thing that strangles **2** a plant, esp a fig in tropical rain forests, that starts as an epiphyte but sends roots to the ground and eventually forms a tree with many aerial roots, usually killing the host

strangles (ˈstræŋɡ°lz) *n* (*functioning as singular*) an acute bacterial disease of horses caused by infection with *Streptococcus equi*, characterized by inflammation of the mucous membranes of the respiratory tract, resulting in abscesses and a nasal discharge. Also called: **equine distemper** [c18 from STRANGLE]

strangulate (ˈstræŋɡjʊˌleɪt) *vb* (*tr*) **1** to constrict (a hollow organ, vessel, etc) so as to stop the natural flow of air, blood, etc, through it **2** another word for **strangle** [c18 from Latin *strangulāt-*, past participle stem of *strangulāre* to STRANGLE] ▷ ˌstranguˈlation *n*

strangury (ˈstræŋɡjʊrɪ) *n pathol* painful excretion of urine, drop by drop, caused by muscular spasms of the urinary tract [c14 from Latin *strangūria*, from Greek, from *stranx* a drop squeezed out + *ouron* urine]

Stranraer (strænˈrɑː) *n* a market town in SW Scotland, in W Dumfries and Galloway: fishing port with a ferry service to Northern Ireland. Pop: 10 851 (2001)

strap (stræp) *n* **1** a long strip of leather or similar material, for binding trunks, baggage, or other objects **2** a strip of leather or similar material used for carrying, lifting, or holding **3** a loop of leather, rubber, etc, suspended from the roof in a bus or train for standing passengers to hold on to **4** a razor strop **5** *business* a triple option on a security or commodity consisting of one put option and two call options at the same price and for the same period. Compare **strip²** (sense 5) **6** *Irish derogatory slang* a shameless or promiscuous woman **7 the strap** a beating with a strap as a punishment **8** short for **shoulder strap** ▷ *vb* **straps, strapping, strapped** (*tr*) **9** to tie or bind with a strap **10** to beat with a strap **11** to sharpen with a strap or strop [c16 variant of STROP]

straphanger (ˈstræpˌhæŋə) *n informal* a passenger in a bus, train, etc, who has to travel standing, esp by holding on to a strap ▷ ˈstrapˌhanging *n*

strap hinge *n* a hinge with a long leaf or flap attached to the face of a door, gate, etc

strapless (ˈstræplɪs) *adj* (of a woman's formal dress, brassiere, etc) without straps over the shoulders

strapline (ˈstræpˌlaɪn) *n* a subheading in a newspaper or magazine article or in any advertisement

strap-oil *n slang* a beating

strappado (strəˈpeɪdəʊ, -ˈpɑː-) *n, pl* -does a system of torture in which a victim was hoisted by a rope

tied to his wrists and then allowed to drop until his fall was suddenly checked by the rope [c16 from French *strapade*, from Italian *strappare* to tug sharply, probably of Germanic origin; related to German (dialect) *strapfen* to make taut]

strapped (stræpt) *adj* (*postpositive*; often foll by *for*) *slang* badly in need (of money, manpower, etc); short of

strapper (ˈstræpə) *n informal* a strapping person

strapping (ˈstræpɪŋ) *adj* (*prenominal*) tall and sturdy [c17 from STRAP (in the archaic sense: to work vigorously)]

strap work *n architect* decorative work resembling interlacing straps

Strasbourg (*French* strasbur; *English* ˈstræzbɜːɡ) *n* a city in NE France, on the Rhine: the chief French inland port; under German rule (1870–1918); university (1567); seat of the Council of Europe and of the European Parliament. Pop: 264 115 (1999). German name: Strassburg (ˈʃtraːsbʊrk)

strass (stræs) *n jewellery* another word for **paste¹** (sense 6) [c19 German, named after J. *Strasser*, 18th-century German jeweller who invented it]

strata (ˈstrɑːtə) *n* a plural of **stratum**

> USAGE *Strata* is sometimes wrongly used as a singular noun: *this stratum* (not *strata*) *of society is often disregarded*

stratagem (ˈstrætɪdʒəm) *n* a plan or trick, esp one to deceive an enemy [c15 ultimately from Greek *stratēgos* a general, from *stratos* an army + *agein* to lead]

strata title *n Austral* a system of registered ownership of space in multistorey buildings, to be equivalent to the ownership of the land of a single-storey building. NZ equivalent: stratum title

strategic (strəˈtiːdʒɪk) *or* **strategical** *adj* **1** of, relating to, or characteristic of strategy **2** important to a strategy or to strategy in general **3** (of weapons, attacks, etc) directed against an enemy's homeland rather than used on a battlefield: *a strategic missile; strategic bombing* ▷ straˈtegically *adv*

strategics (strəˈtiːdʒɪks) *n* (*functioning as singular*) strategy, esp in a military sense

strategist (ˈstrætɪdʒɪst) *n* a specialist or expert in strategy

strategy (ˈstrætɪdʒɪ) *n, pl* -gies **1** the art or science of the planning and conduct of a war; generalship **2** a particular long-term plan for success, esp in business or politics. Compare **tactics** (sense 2) **3** a plan or stratagem [c17 from French *stratégie*, from Greek *stratēgia* function of a general; see STRATAGEM]

Stratford-on-Avon *or* **Stratford-upon-Avon** (ˈstrætfəd) *n* a market town in central England, in SW Warwickshire on the River Avon: the birthplace and burial place of William Shakespeare and home of the Royal Shakespeare Company; tourist centre. Pop: 22 187 (2001)

strath (stræθ) *n Scot* a broad flat river valley [c16 from Scot and Irish Gaelic *srath*, Welsh *ystrad*]

Strathclyde Region (ˌstræθˈklaɪd) *n* a former local government region in W Scotland: formed in 1975 from Glasgow, Renfrewshire, Lanarkshire, Buteshire, Dunbartonshire, and parts of Argyllshire, Ayrshire, and Stirlingshire; replaced in 1996 by the council areas of Glasgow, Renfrewshire, East Renfrewshire, Inverclyde, North Lanarkshire, South Lanarkshire, Argyll and Bute, East Dunbartonshire, West Dunbartonshire, North Ayrshire, South Ayrshire, and East Ayrshire

strathspey (ˌstræθˈspeɪ) *n* **1** a Scottish dance with gliding steps, slower than a reel **2** a piece of music in four-four time composed for this dance

strati- *combining form* indicating stratum or strata: *stratiform; stratigraphy*

straticulate (strəˈtɪkjʊlɪt, -ˌleɪt) *adj* (of a rock formation) composed of very thin even strata [c19 from New Latin *strāticulum* (unattested), diminutive of Latin *strātum* something strewn; see STRATUS] ▷ straˌticuˈlation *n*

S

stratification (ˌstrætɪfɪˈkeɪʃən) *n* **1** the arrangement of sedimentary rocks in distinct layers (strata), each layer representing the sediment deposited over a specific period **2** the act of stratifying or state of being stratified **3** *sociol* See **social stratification** [C17 (in the obsolete sense: the act of depositing in layers) and C18 (in the current senses): from New Latin *strātificātiōnem*, from *stratificāre* to STRATIFY] > ˌ**stratifiˈcational** *adj*

stratificational grammar *n linguistics* a theory of grammar analysing language in terms of several structural strata or layers with different syntactic rules

stratified sample *n statistics* a sample that is not drawn at random from the whole population, but separately from a number of disjoint strata of the population in order to ensure a more representative sample. See also **frame** (sense 13)

stratiform (ˈstrætɪˌfɔːm) *adj* **1** (of rocks) occurring as or arranged in strata **2** *meteorol* resembling a stratus cloud

stratify (ˈstrætɪˌfaɪ) *vb* **-fies, -fying, -fied 1** to form or be formed in layers or strata **2** (*tr*) to preserve or render fertile (seeds) by storing between layers of sand or earth **3** *sociol* to divide (a society) into horizontal status groups or (of a society) to develop such groups [C17 from French *stratifier*, from New Latin *stratificāre*, from Latin STRATUM]

stratigraphy (strəˈtɪɡrəfɪ) *n* **1** the study of the composition, relative positions, etc, of rock strata in order to determine their geological history. Abbreviation: **stratig 2** *archaeol* a vertical section through the earth showing the relative positions of the human artefacts and therefore the chronology of successive levels of occupation > **stratigrapher** (strəˈtɪɡrəfə) *or* **stratigraphist** (strəˈtɪɡrəfɪst) *n* > **stratigraphic** (ˌstrætɪˈɡræfɪk) *or* ˌ**stratiˈgraphical** *adj*

strato- *combining form* **1** denoting stratus: *stratocumulus* **2** denoting the stratosphere: *stratopause*

stratocracy (strəˈtɒkrəsɪ) *n, pl* **-cies** military rule [C17 from Greek *stratos* an army + -CRACY] > **stratocrat** (ˈstrætəˌkræt) *n* > **stratocratic** (ˌstrætəˈkrætɪk) *adj*

stratocumulus (ˌstrætəʊˈkjuːmjʊləs, ˌstreɪtəʊ-) *n, pl* **-li** (-ˌlaɪ) *meteorol* a uniform stretch of cloud containing dark grey globular masses

stratopause (ˈstrætəˌpɔːz) *n meteorol* the transitional zone of maximum temperature between the stratosphere and the mesosphere

stratosphere (ˈstrætəˌsfɪə) *n* the atmospheric layer lying between the troposphere and the mesosphere, in which temperature generally increases with height > **stratospheric** (ˌstrætəˈsfɛrɪk) *or* ˌ**stratoˈspherical** *adj*

stratum (ˈstrɑːtəm) *n, pl* **-ta** (-tə) *or* **-tums 1** (*usually plural*) any of the distinct layers into which sedimentary rocks are divided **2** *biology* a single layer of tissue or cells **3** a layer of any material, esp one of several parallel layers **4** a layer of ocean or atmosphere either naturally or arbitrarily demarcated **5** a level of a social hierarchy that is distinguished according to such criteria as educational achievement or caste status [C16 via New Latin from Latin: something strewn, from *sternere* to scatter] > ˈ**stratal** *adj*

stratum title *n NZ* a system of registered ownership of space in multistorey buildings, to be equivalent to the ownership of the land of a single-storey building. Austral equivalent: **strata title**

stratus (ˈstreɪtəs) *n, pl* **-ti** (-taɪ) a grey layer cloud. Compare **cirrus** (sense 1), **cumulus** [C19 via New Latin from Latin: strewn, from *sternere* to extend]

stravaig (strəˈveɪɡ) *vb* (*intr*) *Scot and northern English dialect* to wander aimlessly [C19 perhaps a variant of obsolete *extravage*, from Medieval Latin *extrāvagārī*, from *vagārī* to wander]

straw[1] (strɔː) *n* **1 a** stalks of threshed grain, esp of wheat, rye, oats, or barley, used in plaiting hats, baskets, etc, or as fodder **b** (*as modifier*): *a straw hat* **2** a single dry or ripened stalk, esp of a grass **3** a long thin hollow paper or plastic tube or stem of a plant, used for sucking up liquids into the mouth **4** (*usually used with a negative*) anything of little value or importance: *I wouldn't give a straw for our chances* **5** a measure or remedy that one turns to in desperation (esp in the phrases **clutch** *or* **grasp at a straw** *or* **straws**) **6 a** a pale yellow colour **b** (*as adjective*): *straw hair* **7 the last straw** a small incident, setback, etc that, coming after others, proves intolerable **8 straw in the wind** a hint or indication ▷ *adj* **9** *chiefly US* having little value or substance ▷ See also **man of straw** [Old English *streaw*; related to Old Norse *strā*, Old Frisian *strē*, Old High German *strō*; see STREW] > ˈ**strawˌlike** *adj*

straw[2] (strɔː) *vb archaic* another word for **strew**

strawberry (ˈstrɔːbərɪ, -brɪ) *n, pl* **-ries 1 a** any of various low-growing rosaceous plants of the genus *Fragaria*, such as *F. vesca* (**wild strawberry**) and *F. ananassa* (**garden strawberry**), which have white flowers and red edible fruits and spread by runners **b** (*as modifier*): *a strawberry patch* **2 a** the fruit of any of these plants, consisting of a sweet fleshy receptacle bearing small seedlike parts (the true fruits) **b** (*as modifier*): *strawberry ice cream* **3 barren strawberry** a related Eurasian plant, *Potentilla sterilis*, that does not produce edible fruit **4 a** a purplish-red colour **b** (*as adjective*): *strawberry shoes* **5** another name for **strawberry mark** [Old English *streawberige*; perhaps from the strawlike appearance of the runners]

strawberry blonde *adj* **1** (of hair) reddish blonde ▷ *n* **2** a woman with such hair

strawberry bush *n* **1** an E North American shrub or small tree, *Euonymus americanus*, having pendulous capsules that split when ripe to reveal scarlet seeds: family *Celastraceae* **2** any of various similar or related plants

strawberry mark *n* a soft vascular red birthmark. Technical name: **haemangioma simplex** Also called: **strawberry**

strawberry tomato *n* **1** a tropical solanaceous annual plant, *Physalis peruviana*, having bell-shaped whitish-yellow flowers and small edible round yellow berries **2** a similar and related plant, *Physalis pubescens* **3** the fruit of either of these plants, eaten fresh or made into preserves and pickles ▷ Also called: **Cape gooseberry**

strawberry tree *n* a S European evergreen tree, *Arbutus unedo*, having white or pink flowers and red strawberry-like berries. See also **arbutus**

strawboard (ˈstrɔːˌbɔːd) *n* a board made of compressed straw and adhesive, used esp in book covers

strawflower (ˈstrɔːˌflaʊə) *n* an Australian plant, *Helichrysum bracteatum*, in which the coloured bracts retain their colour when the plant is dried: family *Asteraceae* (composites). See also **immortelle**

straw man *n chiefly US* **1** a figure of a man made from straw **2** another term for **man of straw**

straw poll *or chiefly US, Canadian, and NZ* **vote** *n* an unofficial poll or vote taken to determine the opinion of a group or the public on some issue

strawweight (ˈstrɔːˌweɪt) *n* **a** a professional boxer weighing not more than 47.6 kg (105 pounds) **b** (*as modifier*): *the strawweight title* ▷ Also called: **mini-flyweight**

straw wine *n* any of several wines made from grapes dried on straw mats to increase their sugar strength

strawworm (ˈstrɔːˌwɜːm) *n* another name for a **caddis worm**

strawy (ˈstrɔːɪ) *adj* **strawier, strawiest** containing straw, or like straw in colour or texture

stray (streɪ) *vb* (*intr*) **1** to wander away, as from the correct path or from a given area **2** to wander haphazardly **3** to digress from the point, lose concentration, etc **4** to deviate from certain moral standards ▷ *n* **5 a** a domestic animal, fowl, etc, that has wandered away from its place of keeping and is lost **b** (*as modifier*): *stray dogs* **6** a lost or homeless person, esp a child: *waifs and strays* **7** an isolated or random occurrence, specimen, etc, that is out of place or outside the usual pattern ▷ *adj* **8** scattered, random, or haphazard: *a stray bullet grazed his thigh* [C14 from Old French *estraier*, from Vulgar Latin *estragāre* (unattested), from Latin *extrā-* outside + *vagārī* to roam; see ASTRAY, EXTRAVAGANT, STRAVAIG] > ˈ**strayer** *n*

strays (streɪz) *pl n* **1** Also called: **stray capacitance** *electronics* undesired capacitance in equipment, occurring between the wiring, between the wiring and the chassis, or between components and the chassis **2** *telecomm* another word for **static** (sense 9)

strayve (streɪv) *vb* (*intr*) **strayves, strayving, strayved** *Midland English dialect* to wander aimlessly

streak[1] (striːk) *n* **1** a long thin mark, stripe, or trace of some contrasting colour **2 a** (of lightning) a sudden flash **b** (*as modifier*): *streak lightning* **3** an element or trace, as of some quality or characteristic **4** a strip, vein, or layer: *fatty streaks* **5** a short stretch or run, esp of good or bad luck **6** *mineralogy* the powdery mark made by a mineral when rubbed on a hard or rough surface: its colour is an important distinguishing characteristic **7** *bacteriol* the inoculation of a solid culture medium by drawing a wire contaminated with the microorganisms across it **8** *informal* an act or the practice of running naked through a public place ▷ *vb* **9** (*tr*) to mark or daub with a streak or streaks **10** (*intr*) to form streaks or become streaked **11** (*intr*) to move rapidly in a straight line **12** (*intr*) *informal* to run naked through a crowd of people in a public place in order to shock or amuse them [Old English *strica*, related to Old Frisian *strike*, Old High German *strih*, Norwegian, Swedish *strika*] > **streaked** *adj* > ˈ**streaker** *n* > ˈ**streakˌlike** *adj*

streak[2] (striːk) *n* a variant spelling of **strake** (sense 2)

streaking (ˈstriːkɪŋ) *n* **1** an act or instance of running naked through a public place **2** *television* light or dark streaks to the right of a bright object in a television picture, caused by distortion in the transmission chain

streaky (ˈstriːkɪ) *adj* **streakier, streakiest 1** marked with streaks **2** occurring in streaks **3** (of bacon) having alternate layers of meat and fat **4** of varying or uneven quality > ˈ**streakily** *adv* > ˈ**streakiness** *n*

stream (striːm) *n* **1** a small river; brook **2** any steady flow of water or other fluid **3** something that resembles a stream in moving continuously in a line or particular direction **4** a rapid or unbroken flow of speech, etc: *a stream of abuse* **5** a flow of money into a business: *a revenue stream* **6** *Brit* any of several parallel classes of schoolchildren, or divisions of children within a class, grouped together because of similar ability **7 go** (*or* **drift**) **with the stream** to conform to the accepted standards **8 off stream** (of an industrial plant, manufacturing process, etc) shut down or not in production **9 on stream a** (of an industrial plant, manufacturing process, etc) in or about to go into operation or production **b** available or in existence ▷ *vb* **10** to emit or be emitted in a continuous flow: *his nose streamed blood* **11** (*intr*) to move in unbroken succession, as a crowd of people, vehicles, etc **12** (*intr*) to float freely or with a waving motion: *bunting streamed in the wind* **13** (*tr*) to unfurl (a flag, etc) **14** (*intr*) to move causing a trail of light, condensed gas, etc, as a jet aircraft **15** (when *intr*, often foll by *for*) *mining* to wash (earth, gravel, etc) in running water in prospecting (for gold, etc), to expose the particles of ore or metal **16** *Brit education* to group or divide (children) in streams [Old English; related to Old Frisian *strām*, Old Norse *straumr*, Old High German *stroum*, Greek *rheuma*] > ˈ**streamlet** *n* > ˈ**streamˌlike** *adj*

streamer ('striːmə) *n* **1** a long narrow flag or part of a flag **2** a long narrow coiled ribbon of coloured paper that becomes unrolled when tossed **3** a stream of light, esp one appearing in some forms of the aurora **4** *journalism* a large heavy headline printed across the width of a page of a newspaper **5** *computing* another word for **tape streamer**

streamline ('striːmˌlaɪn) *n* **1** a contour on a body that offers the minimum resistance to a gas or liquid flowing around it **2** an imaginary line in a fluid such that the tangent at any point indicates the direction of the velocity of a particle of the fluid at that point ▷ *vb* (*tr*) **3** to make streamlined

streamlined ('striːmˌlaɪnd) *adj* **1** offering or designed to offer the minimum resistance to the flow of a gas or liquid **2** made more efficient, esp by simplifying

streamline flow *n* flow of a fluid in which its velocity at any point is constant or varies in a regular manner. It can be represented by streamlines. Also called: **viscous flow.** Compare **turbulent flow.** See also **laminar flow**

stream of consciousness *n* **1** *psychol* the continuous flow of ideas, thoughts, and feelings forming the content of an individual's consciousness. The term was originated by William James **2 a** a literary technique that reveals the flow of thoughts and feelings of characters through long passages of soliloquy **b** (*as modifier*): *a stream-of-consciousness novel*

streamy ('striːmɪ) *adj* **streamier, streamiest** *chiefly poetic* **1** (of an area, land, etc) having many streams **2** flowing or streaming > '**streaminess** *n*

streel (striːl) *n* *Irish* a slovenly woman [from Irish Gaelic *straoill*]

street (striːt) *n* **1 a** (*capital when part of a name*) a public road that is usually lined with buildings, esp in a town: *Oxford Street* **b** (*as modifier*): *a street directory* **2** the buildings lining a street **3** the part of the road between the pavements, used by vehicles **4** the people living, working, etc, in a particular street **5** (*modifier*) of or relating to the urban counterculture: *street style; street drug* **6 man in the street** an ordinary or average citizen **7 on the streets a** earning a living as a prostitute **b** homeless **8 (right) up one's street** *informal* (just) what one knows or likes best **9 streets ahead of** *informal* superior to, more advanced than, etc **10 streets apart** *informal* markedly different ▷ *vb* (*tr*) **11** *Austral* to outdistance [Old English *strǣt*, from Latin *via strāta* paved way (*strāta*, from *strātus*, past participle of *sternere* to stretch out); compare Old Frisian *strēte*, Old High German *strāza*; see STRATUS]

street Arab *n* *literary and old-fashioned* a homeless child, esp one who survives by begging and stealing; urchin

streetcar ('striːtˌkɑː) *n* *US and Canadian* an electrically driven public transport vehicle that runs on rails let into the surface of the road, power usually being taken from an overhead wire. also called: **trolley car,** (esp Brit) **tram, tramcar**

street credibility *n* a convincing command or display of the style, fashions, knowledge, etc, associated with urban counterculture. Often shortened to: **street cred** > ˌ**street-'credible** *adj*

street cry *n* (*often plural*) the cry of a street hawker

street door *n* the door of a house that opens onto the street

street furniture *n* pieces of equipment, such as streetlights and pillar boxes, placed in the street for the benefit of the public

street justice *n* the punishment given by members of the public to people regarded as criminals or wrongdoers

streetlight ('striːtˌlaɪt) *or* **streetlamp** *n* a light, esp one carried on a lamppost, that illuminates a road, etc

street luge *n* the sport of descending a steep road or track on a large type of skateboard on which riders lie on their backs, descending feet first

street piano *n* another name for **barrel organ**

street theatre *n* dramatic entertainments performed esp in shopping precincts

street value *n* the monetary worth of a commodity, usually an illicit commodity such as a drug, considered as the price it would fetch when sold to the ultimate user

streetwalker ('striːtˌwɔːkə) *n* a prostitute who solicits on the streets > '**streetˌwalking** *n, adj*

streetwear ('striːtˌwɛə) *n* fashionable casual clothes

streetwise ('striːtˌwaɪz) *adj* attuned to and adept at surviving in an urban, poor and often criminal environment. Also: **street-smart** > **street wisdom** *n*

strelitzia (strɛ'lɪtsɪə) *n* any southern African perennial herbaceous plant of the genus *Strelitzia*, cultivated for its showy flowers: includes the bird-of-paradise flower: family *Strelitziaceae* [C18 named after Charlotte of Mecklenburg-*Strelitz* (1744–1818), queen of George III of Great Britain and Ireland]

strength (strɛŋθ) *n* **1** the state or quality of being physically or mentally strong **2** the ability to withstand or exert great force, stress, or pressure **3** something that is regarded as being beneficial or a source of power **4** potency, as of a drink, drug, etc **5** power to convince: *the strength of an argument* **6** degree of intensity or concentration of colour, light, sound, flavour, etc **7** the full or part of the full complement as specified: *at full strength* **8** *finance* firmness of or a rising tendency in prices, esp security prices **9** *archaic or poetic* a stronghold or fortress **10** *Austral and NZ informal* the general idea, the main purpose: *to get the strength of something* **11 from strength to strength** with ever-increasing success **12 in strength** in large numbers **13 on the strength of** on the basis of or relying upon [Old English *strengthu*; related to Old High German *strengida*; see STRONG]

strengthen ('strɛŋθən) *vb* to make or become stronger > '**strengthener** *n*

strenuous ('strɛnjʊəs) *adj* **1** requiring or involving the use of great energy or effort **2** characterized by great activity, effort, or endeavour [C16 from Latin *strēnuus* brisk, vigorous] > **strenuosity** (ˌstrɛnjʊ'ɒsɪtɪ) *or* '**strenuousness** *n* > '**strenuously** *adv*

strep (strɛp) *n* *informal* short for **streptococcus**

strepitoso ('strɛpɪ'təʊsəʊ) *adj, adv* *music* (to be performed) boisterously [Italian, literally; noisily]

strepitous ('strɛpɪtəs) *or* **strepitant** *adj* *rare* noisy; boisterous [C17 from Latin *strepitus* a din]

strepto- *combining form* **1** indicating a shape resembling a twisted chain: *streptococcus* **2** indicating streptococcus: *streptolysin* [from Greek *streptos* twisted, from *strephein* to twist]

streptocarpus (ˌstrɛptə'kɑːpəs) *n* any plant of the typically stemless subtropical perennial genus *Streptocarpus*, some species of which are grown as greenhouse plants for their tubular flowers in a range of bright colours: family *Gesneriaceae* [New Latin, from Greek *streptos* twisted + *karpos* fruit (from the shape of the capsule)]

streptococcus (ˌstrɛptəʊ'kɒkəs) *n, pl* **-cocci** (-'kɒkaɪ; US -'kɒksaɪ) any Gram-positive spherical bacterium of the genus *Streptococcus*, typically occurring in chains and including many pathogenic species, such as *S. pyogenes*, which causes scarlet fever, sore throat, etc: family *Lactobacillaceae*. Often shortened to: **strep** > **streptococcal** (ˌstrɛptəʊ'kɒkᵊl) *or less commonly* **streptococcic** (ˌstrɛptəʊ'kɒkɪk; US -'kɒksɪk) *adj*

streptokinase (ˌstrɛptəʊ'kaɪneɪs) *n* an enzyme produced by streptococci that causes the fibrin of certain animal species to undergo lysis

streptomycin (ˌstrɛptəʊ'maɪsɪn) *n* an antibiotic obtained from the bacterium *Streptomyces griseus*: used in the treatment of tuberculosis and Gram-negative bacterial infections. Formula: $C_{21}H_{39}N_7O_{12}$ [from *Streptomyces*, genus name of bacteria (from STREPTO- + Greek *mukēs* fungus + -IN)]

streptothricin (ˌstrɛptəʊ'θraɪsɪn) *n* an antibiotic active against bacteria and some fungi, produced by the bacterium *Streptomyces lavendulae* [from *Streptothrix*, genus name of bacteria (from STREPTO- + Greek *thrix* hair + -IN)]

stress (strɛs) *n* **1** special emphasis or significance attached to something **2** mental, emotional, or physical strain or tension **3** emphasis placed upon a syllable by pronouncing it more loudly than those that surround it **4** such emphasis as part of a regular rhythmic beat in music or poetry **5** a syllable so emphasized **6** *physics* **a** force or a system of forces producing deformation or strain **b** the force acting per unit area ▷ *vb* **7** (*tr*) to give emphasis or prominence to **8** (*tr*) to pronounce (a word or syllable) more loudly than those that surround it **9** (*tr*) to subject to stress or strain **10** *informal* (*intr*) to become stressed or anxious [C14 *stresse*, shortened from DISTRESS] > '**stressful** *adj* > '**stressfully** *adv* > '**stressfulness** *n*

-stress *suffix forming nouns* indicating a woman who performs or is engaged in a certain activity: *songstress; seamstress*. Compare **-ster** (sense 1) [from -ST(E)R + -ESS]

stress ball *n* a small rubber ball squeezed in the hand as a means of relieving stress

stressbuster ('strɛsˌbʌstə) *n* a product, practice, system, etc that is designed to alleviate stress > '**stressˌbusting** *adj*

stressor ('strɛsə) *n* an event, experience, etc, that causes stress

stretch (strɛtʃ) *vb* **1** to draw out or extend or be drawn out or extended in length, area, etc **2** to extend or be extended to an undue degree, esp so as to distort or lengthen permanently **3** to extend (the limbs, body, etc) **4** (*tr*) to reach or suspend (a rope, etc) from one place to another **5** (*tr*) to draw tight; tighten **6** (often foll by *out, forward*, etc) to reach or hold (out); extend **7** (*intr*; usually foll by *over*) to extend in time: *the course stretched over three months* **8** (*intr*; foll by *for, over*, etc) (of a region, etc) to extend in length or area **9** (*intr*) (esp of a garment) to be capable of expanding, as to a larger size: *socks that will stretch* **10** (*tr*) to put a great strain upon or extend to the limit **11** to injure (a muscle, tendon, ligament, etc) by means of a strain or sprain **12** (*tr*; often foll by *out*) to make do with (limited resources): *to stretch one's budget* **13** (*tr*) *informal* to expand or elaborate (a story, etc) beyond what is credible or acceptable: *that's stretching it a bit* **14** (*tr; often passive*) to extend, as to the limit of one's abilities or talents **15** *archaic or slang* to hang or be hanged by the neck **16 stretch a point a** to make a concession or exception not usually made **b** to exaggerate **17 stretch one's legs** to take a walk, esp after a period of inactivity ▷ *n* **18** the act of stretching or state of being stretched **19** a large or continuous expanse or distance: *a stretch of water* **20** extent in time, length, area, etc **21 a** capacity for being stretched, as in some garments **b** (*as modifier*): *stretch pants* **22** *horse racing* the section or sections of a racecourse that are straight, esp the final straight section leading to the finishing line **23** *slang* a term of imprisonment **24 at a stretch** *chiefly Brit* **a** with some difficulty; by making a special effort **b** if really necessary or in extreme circumstances [Old English *streccan*; related to Old Frisian *strekka*, Old High German *strecken*; see STRAIGHT, STRAKE] > '**stretchable** *adj* > ˌ**stretcha'bility** *n*

stretcher ('strɛtʃə) *n* **1** a device for transporting the ill, wounded, or dead, consisting of a frame covered by canvas or other material **2** a strengthening often decorative member joining the legs of a chair, table, etc **3** the wooden frame on which canvas is stretched and fixed for oil painting **4** a tie beam or brace used in a structural framework **5** a brick or stone laid horizontally with its length parallel to the length of a wall. Compare **header** (sense 4) **6** *rowing* a fixed board across a boat on which an oarsman

S

braces his feet **7** *Austral and NZ* a camp bed **8** *slang* an exaggeration or lie ▷ *vb (tr)* **9** to transport (a sick or injured person) on a stretcher

stretcher-bearer *n* a person who helps to carry a stretcher, esp in wartime

stretch limo *n informal* a limousine that has been lengthened to provide extra seating accommodation and more legroom. In full: **stretch limousine**

stretchmarks (ˈstrɛtʃˌmɑːks) *pl n* marks that remain visible on the abdomen after its distension, esp in pregnancy

stretchy (ˈstrɛtʃɪ) *adj* **stretchier, stretchiest** characterized by elasticity > ˈ**stretchiness** *n*

Stretford (ˈstrɛtfəd) *n* an industrial town in NW England, in Trafford unitary authority, Greater Manchester. Pop: 42 103 (2001)

stretto (ˈstrɛtəʊ) *n, pl* **-tos** *or* **-ti** (-tiː) **1** (in a fugue) the close overlapping of two parts or voices, the second one entering before the first has completed its statement of the subject **2** Also called: **stretta** (ˈstrɛtə) a concluding passage in a composition, played at a faster speed than the earlier material [C17 from Italian, from Latin *strictus* tightly bound; see STRICT]

streusel (ˈstruːsᵊl, ˈstrɔɪ-; *German* ˈʃtrɔyzəl) *n chiefly US* a crumbly topping for rich pastries [German, from *streuen* to STREW]

strew (struː) *vb* **strews, strewing, strewed, strewn** *or* **strewed** to spread or scatter or be spread or scattered, as over a surface or area [Old English *streowian;* related to Old Norse *strā*, Old High German *streuwen*, Latin *struere* to spread] > ˈ**strewer** *n*

strewth (struːθ) *interj* an expression of surprise or dismay [C19 alteration of *God's truth*]

stria (ˈstraɪə) *n, pl* **striae** (ˈstraɪiː) *(often plural)* **1** Also called: **striation** *geology* any of the parallel scratches or grooves on the surface of a rock caused by abrasion resulting from the passage of a glacier, motion on a fault surface, etc **2** fine ridges and grooves on the surface of a crystal caused by irregular growth **3** *biology, anatomy* a narrow band of colour or a ridge, groove, or similar linear mark, usually occurring in a parallel series **4** *architect* a narrow channel, such as a flute on the shaft of a column [C16 from Latin: a groove]

striate *adj* (ˈstraɪɪt) *also* **striated 1** marked with striae; striped ▷ *vb* (ˈstraɪeɪt) **2** *(tr)* to mark with striae [C17 from Latin *striāre* to make grooves, from STRIA]

striation (straɪˈeɪʃən) *n* **1** an arrangement or pattern of striae **2** the condition of being striate **3** another word for **stria** (sense 1)

strick (strɪk) *n textiles* any bast fibres preparatory to being made into slivers [C15 *stric*, perhaps of Low German origin; compare Middle Dutch *stric*, Middle Low German *strik* rope]

stricken (ˈstrɪkən) *adj* **1** laid low, as by disease or sickness **2** deeply affected, as by grief, love, etc **3** *archaic* wounded or injured [C14 past participle of STRIKE] > ˈ**strickenly** *adv*

strickle (ˈstrɪkᵊl) *n* **1** Also called: **strike** a board used for sweeping off excess material in a container **2** a template used for shaping a mould **3** a bar of abrasive material for sharpening a scythe ▷ *vb* **4** *(tr)* to level, form, or sharpen with a strickle [Old English *stricel;* related to Latin *strigilis* scraper, German *Striegel;* see STRIKE]

strict (strɪkt) *adj* **1** adhering closely to specified rules, ordinances, etc: *a strict faith* **2** complied with or enforced stringently; rigorous: *a strict code of conduct* **3** severely correct in attention to rules of conduct or morality: *a strict teacher* **4** (of a punishment, etc) harsh; severe **5** *(prenominal)* complete; absolute: *in strict secrecy* **6** *logic, maths* (of a relation) **a** applying more narrowly than some other relation often given the same name, as *strict inclusion*, which holds only between pairs of sets that are distinct, while *simple inclusion* permits the case in which they are identical. See also **proper** (sense 9), **ordering b** distinguished from a relation of the same name that is not the subject of formal study **7** *botany rare* very straight, narrow, and upright: *strict panicles* [C16 from Latin *strictus*, from *stringere* to draw tight] > ˈ**strictly** *adv* > ˈ**strictness** *n*

stricture (ˈstrɪktʃə) *n* **1** a severe criticism; censure **2** *pathol* an abnormal constriction of a tubular organ, structure, or part **3** *obsolete* severity [C14 from Latin *strictūra* contraction; see STRICT] > ˈ**strictured** *adj*

stride (straɪd) *n* **1** a long step or pace **2** the space measured by such a step **3** a striding gait **4** an act of forward movement by an animal, completed when the legs have returned to their initial relative positions **5** progress or development (esp in the phrase **make rapid strides**) **6** a regular pace or rate of progress: *to get into one's stride; to be put off one's stride* **7** *rowing* the distance covered between strokes **8** Also called: **stride piano** *jazz* a piano style characterized by single bass notes on the first and third beats and chords on the second and fourth **9** *(plural) informal, chiefly Austral* men's trousers **10 take (something) in one's stride** to do (something) without difficulty or effort ▷ *vb* **strides, striding, strode, stridden 11** *(intr)* to walk with long regular or measured paces, as in haste, etc **12** *(tr)* to cover or traverse by striding: *he strode thirty miles* **13** (often foll by *over, across*, etc) to cross (over a space, obstacle, etc) with a stride **14** *(intr) rowing* to achieve the desired rhythm in a racing shell [Old English *strīdan;* related to Old High German *strītan* to quarrel; see STRADDLE] > ˈ**strider** *n*

strident (ˈstraɪdᵊnt) *adj* **1** (of a shout, voice, etc) having or making a loud or harsh sound **2** urgent, clamorous, or vociferous: *strident demands* [C17 from Latin *strīdēns*, from *strīdēre* to make a grating sound] > ˈ**stridence** *or* ˈ**stridency** *n* > ˈ**stridently** *adv*

stridor (ˈstraɪdɔː) *n* **1** *pathol* a high-pitched whistling sound made during respiration, caused by obstruction of the air passages **2** *chiefly literary* a harsh or shrill sound [C17 from Latin; see STRIDENT]

stridulate (ˈstrɪdjʊˌleɪt) *vb (intr)* (of insects such as the cricket) to produce sounds by rubbing one part of the body against another [C19 back formation from *stridulation*, from Latin *strīdulus* creaking, hissing, from *strīdēre* to make a harsh noise] > ˌ**striduˈlation** *n* > ˈ**striduˌlator** *n* > **stridulatory** (ˈstrɪdjʊˌleɪtərɪ) *adj*

stridulous (ˈstrɪdjʊləs) *or* **stridulant** *adj* **1** making a harsh, shrill, or grating noise **2** *pathol* of, relating to, or characterized by stridor [C17 from Latin *strīdulus*, from *strīdēre* to make a harsh noise. See STRIDENT] > ˈ**stridulously** *or* ˈ**stridulantly** *adv* > ˈ**stridulousness** *or* ˈ**stridulance** *n*

strife (straɪf) *n* **1** angry or violent struggle; conflict **2** rivalry or contention, esp of a bitter kind **3** *Austral and NZ* trouble or discord of any kind: *to get into strife* **4** *archaic* striving [C13 from Old French *estrif*, probably from *estriver* to STRIVE]

strigiform (ˈstrɪdʒɪˌfɔːm) *adj* of, relating to, or belonging to the *Strigiformes*, an order of birds comprising the owls [via New Latin from Latin *strix* a screech owl]

strigil (ˈstrɪdʒɪl) *n* **1** a curved blade used by the ancient Romans and Greeks to scrape the body after bathing **2** *architect* a decorative fluting, esp one in the shape of the letter *S* as used in Roman architecture [C16 from Latin *strigilis*, from *stringere* to graze]

strigose (ˈstraɪgəʊs) *adj* **1** *botany* bearing stiff hairs or bristles: *strigose leaves* **2** *zoology* marked with fine closely set grooves or ridges [C18 via New Latin *strigōsus*, from *striga* a bristle, from Latin: grain cut down]

strike (straɪk) *vb* **strikes, striking, struck 1** to deliver (a blow or stroke) to (a person) **2** to come or cause to come into sudden or violent contact (with) **3** *(tr)* to make an attack on **4** to produce (fire, sparks, etc) or (of fire, sparks, etc) to be produced by ignition **5** to cause (a match) to light by friction or (of a match) to be lighted **6** to press (the key of a piano, organ, etc) or to sound (a specific note) in this or a similar way **7** to indicate (a specific time) by the sound of a hammer striking a bell or by any other percussive sound **8** (of a venomous snake) to cause injury by biting **9** *(tr)* to affect or cause to affect deeply, suddenly, or radically, as if by dealing a blow: *her appearance struck him as strange* **10** *(past part* **struck** *or* **stricken** *(tr; passive;* usually foll by *with)* to render incapable or nearly so: *she was stricken with grief* **11** *(tr)* to enter the mind of: *it struck me that he had become very quiet* **12** *past part* **struck** *or* **stricken**) to render: *I was struck dumb* **13** *(tr)* to be perceived by: *the glint of metal struck his eye* **14** to arrive at or come upon (something), esp suddenly or unexpectedly: *to strike the path for home; to strike upon a solution* **15** *(intr;* sometimes foll by *out)* to set (out) or proceed, esp upon a new course: *to strike for the coast* **16** *(tr; usually passive)* to afflict with a disease, esp unexpectedly: *he was struck with polio when he was six* **17** *(tr)* to discover or come upon a source of (ore, petroleum, etc) **18** *(tr)* (of a plant) to produce or send down (a root or roots) **19** *(tr)* to take apart or pack up; break (esp in the phrase **strike camp**) **20** *(tr)* to take down or dismantle (a stage set, formwork, etc) **21** *(tr) nautical* **a** to lower or remove (a specified piece of gear) **b** to haul down or dip (a flag, sail, etc) in salute or in surrender **c** to lower (cargo, etc) into the hold of a ship **22** to attack (an objective) with the intention of causing damage to, seizing, or destroying it **23** to impale the hook in the mouth of (a fish) by suddenly tightening or jerking the line after the bait or fly has been taken **24** *(tr)* to form or impress (a coin, metal, etc) by or as if by stamping **25** to level (a surface) by use of a flat board **26** *(tr)* to assume or take up (an attitude, posture, etc) **27** *(intr)* (of workers in a factory, etc) to cease work collectively as a protest against working conditions, low pay, etc **28** *(tr)* to reach by agreement: *to strike a bargain* **29** *(tr)* to form (a jury, esp a special jury) by cancelling certain names among those nominated for jury service until only the requisite number remains. See also **special jury 30** *(tr) rowing* to make (a certain number of strokes) per minute: *Oxford were striking 38* **31** to make a stroke or kick in swimming **32** *(tr)* (in Malaysia) to win (a lottery or raffle) **33 strike home a** to deliver an effective blow **b** to achieve the intended effect **34 strike (it) lucky** to have some good luck **35 strike it rich** *informal* **a** to discover an extensive deposit of a mineral, petroleum, etc **b** to have an unexpected financial success ▷ *n* **36** an act or instance of striking **37** a cessation of work by workers in a factory, industry, etc, as a protest against working conditions or low pay: *the workers are on strike again* **38** a military attack, esp an air attack on a surface target **39** *baseball* a pitched ball judged good but missed or not swung at, three of which cause a batter to be out **40** Also called: **ten-strike** *tenpin bowling* **a** the act or an instance of knocking down all the pins with the first bowl of a single frame **b** the score thus made. Compare **spare** (sense 17) **41** a sound made by striking **42** the mechanism that makes a clock strike **43** the discovery of a source of ore, petroleum, etc **44** the horizontal direction of a fault, rock stratum, etc, which is perpendicular to the direction of the dip **45** *angling* the act or an instance of striking **46** the number of coins or medals made at one time **47** another name for **strickle** (sense 1) **48** *informal* an unexpected or complete success, esp one that brings financial gain **49 take strike** *cricket* (of a batsman) to prepare to play a ball delivered by the bowler ▷ See also **strike down, strike off, strike out, strike through, strike up** [Old English *strīcan;* related to Old Frisian *strīka* to stroke, Old High German *strīhhan* to smooth, Latin *stria* furrow] > ˈ**strikeless** *adj*

strikebound (ˈstraɪkˌbaʊnd) *adj* (of a factory, etc) closed or made inoperative by a strike

strikebreaker (ˈstraɪkˌbreɪkə) *n* a person who tries to make a strike ineffectual by working or by taking the place of those on strike > ˈ**strike**ˌ**breaking** *n, adj*

strike down *vb (tr, adverb)* to cause to die, esp suddenly: *he was struck down in his prime*

strike fault *n* a fault that runs parallel to the strike of the affected rocks

strike note *or esp US* **strike tone** *n* the note produced by a bell when struck, defining its musical pitch

strike off *vb (tr)* **1** to remove or erase from (a list, record, etc) by or as if by a stroke of the pen **2** *(adverb)* to cut off or separate by or as if by a blow: *she was struck off from the inheritance*

strike out *vb (adverb)* **1** *(tr)* to remove or erase **2** *(intr)* to start out or begin: *to strike out on one's own* **3** *baseball* to put out or be put out on strikes **4** *(intr) US and Canadian informal* to fail utterly

strike pay *n* money paid to strikers from the funds of a trade union

striker (ˈstraɪkə) *n* **1** a person who is on strike **2** the hammer in a timepiece that rings a bell or alarm **3** any part in a mechanical device that strikes something, such as the firing pin of a gun **4** *soccer informal* an attacking player, esp one who generally positions himself near his opponent's goal in the hope of scoring **5** *cricket* the batsman who is about to play a ball **6 a** a person who harpoons whales or fish **b** the harpoon itself

strike-slip fault *n* a geological fault on which the movement is along the strike of the fault

strike through *vb (tr)* to draw (a line) through (something) to delete it

strike up *vb (adverb)* **1** (of a band, orchestra, etc) to begin to play or sing **2** *(tr)* to bring about; cause to begin: *to strike up a friendship* **3** *(tr)* to emboss (patterns, etc) on (metal)

striking (ˈstraɪkɪŋ) *adj* **1** attracting attention; fine; impressive: *a striking beauty* **2** conspicuous; noticeable: *a striking difference* > ˈ**strikingly** *adv* > ˈ**strikingness** *n*

striking circle *n hockey* the semicircular area in front of each goal, which an attacking player must have entered before scoring a goal

Strimmer (ˈstrɪmə) *n trademark* an electrical tool for trimming the edges of lawns

Strimon (ˈstrimɔn) *n* a transliteration of the Greek name for the **Struma**

Strine (straɪn) *n* a humorous transliteration of Australian pronunciation, as in *Gloria Soame* for *glorious home* [C20 a jocular rendering, coined by Alastair Morrison, of the Australian pronunciation of *Australian*]

string (strɪŋ) *n* **1** a thin length of cord, twine, fibre, or similar material used for tying, hanging, binding, etc **2** a group of objects threaded on a single strand: *a string of beads* **3** a series or succession of things, events, acts, utterances, etc: *a string of oaths* **4** a number, chain, or group of similar things, animals, etc, owned by or associated with one person or body: *a string of girlfriends* **5** a tough fibre or cord in a plant: *the string of an orange; the string of a bean* **6** *music* a tightly stretched wire, cord, etc, found on stringed instruments, such as the violin, guitar, and piano **7** short for **bowstring** **8** *architect* short for **string course** *or* **stringer** (sense 1) **9** *maths, linguistics* a sequence of symbols or words **10** *linguistics* a linear sequence, such as a sentence as it is spoken **11** *physics* a one-dimensional entity postulated to be a fundamental component of matter in some theories of particle physics. See also **cosmic string** **12** *billiards* another word for **lag¹** (sense 6) **13** a group of characters that can be treated as a unit by a computer program **14** *(plural; usually preceded by the)* **a** violins, violas, cellos, and double basses collectively **b** the section of a symphony orchestra constituted by such instruments **15** *(plural)* complications or conditions (esp in the phrase **no strings attached**) **16** *(modifier)* composed of stringlike strands woven in a large mesh: *a string bag; string vest* **17 first (second, etc) string** a person or thing regarded as a primary (secondary, etc) source of strength **18 keep on a string** to have control or a hold over (a person), esp emotionally **19 pull strings** *informal* to exert personal influence, esp secretly or unofficially **20 pull the strings** to have real or ultimate control of something ▷ *vb* **strings, stringing, strung** (strʌŋ) **21** *(tr)* to provide with a string or strings **22** *(tr)* to suspend or stretch from one point to another **23** *(tr)* to thread on a string **24** *(tr)* to form or extend in a line or series **25** (foll by *out*) to space or spread out at intervals **26** *(tr; usually foll by up) informal* to kill (a person) by hanging **27** *(tr)* to remove the stringy parts from (vegetables, esp beans) **28** *(intr)* (esp of viscous liquids) to become stringy or ropey **29** *(tr; often foll by up)* to cause to be tense or nervous **30** *billiards* another word for **lag¹** (sense 3) [Old English *streng;* related to Old High German *strang,* Old Norse *strengr;* see STRONG] > ˈ**string**ˌ**like** *adj*

string along *vb (adverb) informal* **1** *(intr; often foll by with)* to agree or appear to be in agreement (with) **2** *(tr)* Also: **string on** to deceive, fool, or hoax, esp in order to gain time

string band *n* **1** a band consisting of stringed instruments **2** an informal name for **string orchestra**

string bass (beɪs) *n* another name for **double bass**

string bean *n* **1** any of several bean plants, such as the scarlet runner, cultivated for their edible unripe pods. See also **green bean, wax bean** **2** *informal* a tall thin person

stringboard (ˈstrɪŋˌbɔːd) *n* a skirting that covers the ends of the steps in a staircase. Also called: **stringer**

string course *n* another name for **cordon** (sense 4)

stringed (strɪŋd) *adj* (of musical instruments) having or provided with strings

stringed instrument *n* any musical instrument in which sound is produced by the vibration of a string across a soundboard or soundbox. Also called: **chordophone**

stringendo (strɪnˈdʒɛndəʊ) *adj, adv music* to be performed with increasing speed [Italian, from *stringere* to compress, from Latin: to draw tight; see STRINGENT]

stringent (ˈstrɪndʒənt) *adj* **1** requiring strict attention to rules, procedure, detail, etc **2** *finance* characterized by or causing a shortage of credit, loan capital, etc [C17 from Latin *stringere* to bind] > ˈ**stringency** *n* > ˈ**stringently** *adv*

stringer (ˈstrɪŋə) *n* **1** *architect* **a** a long horizontal beam that is used for structural purposes **b** another name for **stringboard** **2** *nautical* a longitudinal structural brace for strengthening the hull of a vessel **3** a journalist retained by a newspaper or news service on a part-time basis to cover a particular town or area

stringhalt (ˈstrɪŋˌhɔːlt) *n vet science* a sudden spasmodic lifting of the hind leg of a horse, resulting from abnormal contraction of the flexor muscles of the hock. Also called: **springhalt** [C16 probably STRING + HALT²]

string line *n billiards* another name for **baulk line** (sense 1)

string orchestra *n* an orchestra consisting only of violins, violas, cellos, and double basses

stringpiece (ˈstrɪŋˌpiːs) *n* a long horizontal timber beam used to strengthen or support a framework

string quartet *n music* **1** an instrumental ensemble consisting of two violins, one viola, and one cello **2** a piece of music written for such a group, usually having the form and commonest features of a sonata

string tie *n* a very narrow tie, usually tied in a bow

string variable *n computing* data on which arithmetical operations will not be performed

stringy (ˈstrɪŋɪ) *adj* **stringier, stringiest** **1** made of strings or resembling strings **2** (of meat, etc) fibrous **3** (of a person's build) wiry; sinewy **4** (of liquids) forming in strings > ˈ**stringily** *adv* > ˈ**stringiness** *n*

stringy-bark *n Austral* any of several eucalyptus trees having a fibrous bark

strip¹ (strɪp) *vb* **strips, stripping, stripped** **1** to take or pull (the covering, clothes, etc) off (oneself, another person, or thing): *to strip a wall; to strip a bed* **2** *(intr)* **a** to remove all one's clothes **b** to perform a striptease **3** *(tr)* to denude or empty completely **4** *(tr)* to deprive: *he was stripped of his pride* **5** *(tr)* to rob or plunder **6** *(tr)* to remove (paint, varnish, etc) from (a surface, furniture, etc) by sanding, with a solvent, etc: *stripped pine* **7** *(tr)* Also: **pluck** to pull out the old coat of hair from (dogs of certain long- and wire-haired breeds) **8 a** to remove the leaves from the stalks of (tobacco, etc) **b** to separate the two sides of a leaf from the stem of (tobacco, etc) **9** *(tr) agriculture* to draw the last milk from each of the teats of (a cow) **10** to dismantle (an engine, mechanism, etc) **11** to tear off or break (the thread) from (a screw, bolt, etc) or (the teeth) from (a gear) **12** (often foll by *down*) to remove the accessories from (a motor vehicle): *his car was stripped down* **13** to remove (the most volatile constituent) from (a mixture of liquids) by boiling, evaporation, or distillation **14** *printing* (usually foll by *in*) to combine (pieces of film or paper) to form a composite sheet from which a plate can be made **15** *(tr)* (in freight transport) to unpack (a container). See also **stuffing and stripping** ▷ *n* **16** the act or an instance of undressing or of performing a striptease ▷ See also **strip out** [Old English *bestriepan* to plunder; related to Old High German *stroufen* to plunder, strip]

strip² (strɪp) *n* **1** a relatively long, flat, narrow piece of something **2** short for **airstrip** **3** *philately* a horizontal or vertical row of three or more unseparated postage stamps **4** the clothes worn by the members of a team, esp a football team **5** *business* a triple option on a security or commodity consisting of one call option and two put options at the same price and for the same period. Compare **strap** (sense 5) **6** *NZ* short for **dosing strip** **7 tear (someone) off a strip** *informal* to rebuke (someone) angrily ▷ *vb* **strips, stripping, stripped** **8** to cut or divide into strips [C15 from Middle Dutch *strīpe* STRIPE¹]

S

strip cartoon *n* another term for **comic strip**

strip club *n* a small club in which striptease performances take place

strip cropping *n* a method of growing crops in strips or bands arranged to serve as barriers against erosion

stripe¹ (straɪp) *n* **1** a relatively long band of distinctive colour or texture that differs from the surrounding material or background **2** a fabric having such bands **3** a strip, band, or chevron of fabric worn on a military uniform, etc, esp one that indicates rank **4** *chiefly US and Canadian* kind; sort; type: *a man of a certain stripe* ▷ *vb* **5** *(tr)* to mark with a stripe or stripes [C17 probably from Middle Dutch *strīpe;* related to Middle High German *strīfe,* of obscure origin]

stripe² (straɪp) *n* a stroke from a whip, rod, cane, etc [C15 perhaps from Middle Low German *strippe;* related to STRIPE¹]

striped (straɪpt) *adj* marked or decorated with stripes

striped muscle *or* **striated muscle** *n* a type of contractile tissue that is marked by transverse striations; it is concerned with moving skeletal parts to which it is usually attached. Also called: **skeletal muscle** Compare **smooth muscle**

striper (ˈstraɪpə) *n military slang* an officer who has a stripe or stripes on his uniform, esp in the navy: *a two-striper* (lieutenant)

strip lighting *n* electric lighting by means of long glass tubes that are fluorescent lamps or that contain long filaments

stripling ('strɪplɪŋ) *n* a lad [c13 from STRIP² + -LING¹]

strip mill *n* a mill in which steel slabs are rolled into strips

strip mining *n* another term (esp US) for opencast mining

strip out *vb* 1 (*tr*) to remove the working parts of (a machine) 2 to remove (a chemical or component) from a mixture

stripped-down *adj* reduced to the bare essentials; spare

stripper ('strɪpə) *n* 1 a striptease artist 2 a person or thing that strips 3 a device or substance for removing paint, varnish, etc

strip poker *n* a card game in which a player's losses are paid by removing an article of clothing

strip-search *vb* 1 (*tr*) (of police, customs officials, etc) to strip (a prisoner or suspect) naked to search him or her for contraband, narcotics, etc ▷ *n* 2 a search that involves stripping a person naked > 'strip-,searching *n*

striptease ('strɪp,tiːz) *n* a a form of erotic entertainment in which a person gradually undresses to music b (*as modifier*): *a striptease club* [from STRIP¹ + TEASE] > 'strip,teaser *n*

stripy or **stripey** ('straɪpɪ) *adj* **stripier, stripiest** marked by or with stripes; striped

strive (straɪv) *vb* **strives, striving, strove, striven** ('strɪvᵊn) 1 (*may take a clause as object or an infinitive*) to make a great and tenacious effort: *to strive to get promotion* 2 (*intr*) to fight; contend [c13 from Old French *estriver*, of Germanic origin; related to Middle High German *streben* to strive, Old Norse *strītha* to fight] > 'striver *n*

strobe (strəʊb) *n* 1 short for **strobe lighting** or **stroboscope** ▷ *vb* 2 to give the appearance of arrested or slow motion by using intermittent illumination

strobe lighting *n* 1 a high-intensity flashing beam of light produced by rapid electrical discharges in a tube or by a perforated disc rotating in front of an intense light source: used in discotheques, etc 2 the use of or the apparatus for producing such light. Sometimes shortened to: **strobe**

strobe tuner *n* an electronic instrument tuner that uses stroboscopic light

strobic ('strəʊbɪk) *adj* spinning or appearing to spin [c19 from Greek *strobos* act of spinning]

strobila ('strəʊbɪlə) *n, pl* **-bilae** (-bɪliː) 1 the body of a tapeworm, consisting of a string of similar segments (proglottides) 2 a less common name for **scyphistoma** [c19 from New Latin, from Greek *strobilē* plug of lint twisted into a cone shape, from *strobilos* a fir cone]

strobilaceous (ˌstrəʊbɪˈleɪʃəs) *adj botany* relating to or resembling a cone or cones

strobilation (ˌstrəʊbɪˈleɪʃən) *n* asexual reproduction by division into segments, as in tapeworms and jellyfishes

strobilus ('strəʊbɪləs) or **strobile** ('strəʊbaɪl) *n, pl* **-biluses, -bili** (-bɪlaɪ) or **-biles** *botany* the technical name for **cone** (sense 3) [c18 via Late Latin from Greek *strobilos* a fir cone; see STROBILA]

stroboscope ('strəʊbə,skəʊp) *n* 1 an instrument producing a flashing light, the frequency of which can be synchronized with some multiple of the frequency of rotation, vibration, or operation of an object, etc, making it appear stationary. It is used to determine speeds of rotation or vibration, or to adjust objects or parts. Sometimes shortened to: **strobe** 2 a similar device synchronized with the opening of the shutter of a camera so that a series of still photographs can be taken of a moving object [c19 from *strobo-*, from Greek *strobos* a twisting, whirling + -SCOPE] > **stroboscopic** (ˌstrəʊbəˈskɒpɪk) or ˌstroboˈscopical *adj* > ˌstroboˈscopically *adv*

strode (strəʊd) *vb* the past tense of **stride**

stroganoff ('strɒgə,nɒf) *n* short for **beef stroganoff**

stroke (strəʊk) *n* 1 the act or an instance of striking; a blow, knock, or hit 2 a sudden action, movement, or occurrence: *a stroke of luck* 3 a brilliant or inspired act or feat: *a stroke of genius* 4 *pathol* apoplexy; rupture of a blood vessel in the brain resulting in loss of consciousness, often followed by paralysis, or embolism or thrombosis affecting a cerebral vessel 5 a the striking of a clock b the hour registered by the striking of a clock: *on the stroke of three* 6 a mark, flourish, or line made by a writing implement 7 another name for **solidus**, used esp when dictating or reading aloud 8 a light touch or caress, as with the fingers 9 a pulsation, esp of the heart 10 a single complete movement or one of a series of complete movements 11 *sport* the act or manner of striking the ball with a racket, club, bat, etc 12 any one of the repeated movements used by a swimmer to propel himself through the water 13 a manner of swimming, esp one of several named styles such as the crawl or butterfly 14 a any one of a series of linear movements of a reciprocating part, such as a piston b the distance travelled by such a part from one end of its movement to the other 15 a single pull on an oar or oars in rowing 16 manner or style of rowing 17 the oarsman who sits nearest the stern of a shell, facing the cox, and sets the rate of striking for the rest of the crew 18 *US informal* a compliment or comment that enhances a persons self-esteem 19 (*modifier*) *slang, chiefly US* pornographic; masturbatory: *stroke magazines* 20 a stroke (of work) (*usually used with a negative*) a small amount of work 21 off one's stroke performing or working less well than usual 22 on the stroke (of) punctually (at) ▷ *vb* 23 (*tr*) to touch, brush, or caress lightly or gently 24 (*tr*) to mark a line or a stroke on or through 25 to act as the stroke of (a racing shell) 26 (*tr*) *sport* to strike (a ball) with a smooth swinging blow 27 (*tr*) *US and Canadian informal* to handle or influence (someone) with care, using persuasion, flattery, etc [Old English *strācian*; related to Middle Low German *strēken*; see STRIKE]

stroke play *n golf* a scoring by counting the number of strokes taken b (*as modifier*): *a strokeplay tournament* ▷ Also called: **medal play** Compare **match play, Stableford**

stroll (strəʊl) *vb* 1 to walk about in a leisurely manner 2 (*intr*) to wander from place to place ▷ *n* 3 a leisurely walk [c17 probably from dialect German *strollen*, of obscure origin; compare German *Strolch* tramp]

stroller ('strəʊlə) *n US, Canadian, and Austral* a usually collapsible chair-shaped carriage in which a small child may be wheeled. also called (in Britain and certain other countries): **buggy, pushchair**

stroma ('strəʊmə) *n, pl* **-mata** (-mətə) *biology* 1 the gel-like matrix of chloroplasts and certain cells 2 the fibrous connective tissue forming the matrix of the mammalian ovary and testis 3 a dense mass of hyphae that is produced by certain fungi and gives rise to spore-producing bodies [c19 via New Latin from Late Latin: a mattress, from Greek; related to Latin *sternere* to strew] > stromatic (strəʊˈmætɪk) or **stromatous** *adj*

stromatolite (strəʊˈmætə,laɪt) *n* a rocky mass consisting of layers of calcareous material and sediment formed by the prolific growth of cyanobacteria: such structures date back to Precambrian times [c20 from Greek, from *strōma* covering + -LITE] > stromatolitic (ˌstrəʊˌmætəˈlɪtɪk) *adj*

Stromboli ('strɒmbəlɪ) *n* an island in the Tyrrhenian Sea, in the Lipari Islands off the N coast of Sicily: famous for its active volcano, 927 m (3040 ft) high

Strombolian (strɒmˈbəʊlɪən) *adj* relating to or denoting a type of volcanic eruption characterized by repeated fountaining or jetting of fluid lava

into the air

strong (strɒŋ) *adj* **stronger** ('strɒŋɡə) **strongest** ('strɒŋɡɪst) 1 involving or possessing physical or mental strength 2 solid or robust in construction; not easily broken or injured 3 having a resolute will or morally firm and incorruptible character 4 intense in quality; not faint or feeble: *a strong voice; a strong smell* 5 easily defensible; incontestable or formidable 6 concentrated; not weak or diluted 7 a (*postpositive*) containing or having a specified number: *a navy 40 000 strong* b (*in combination*): *a 40 000-strong navy* 8 having an unpleasantly powerful taste or smell 9 having an extreme or drastic effect: *strong discipline* 10 emphatic or immoderate: *strong language* 11 convincing, effective, or cogent 12 (of a colour) having a high degree of saturation or purity; being less saturated than a vivid colour but more so than a moderate colour; produced by a concentrated quantity of colouring agent 13 *grammar* a denoting or belonging to a class of verbs, in certain languages including the Germanic languages, whose conjugation shows vowel gradation, as *sing, sang, sung* b belonging to any part-of-speech class, in any of various languages, whose inflections follow the less regular of two possible patterns. Compare **weak** (sense 10) 14 (of a wind, current, etc) moving fast 15 (of a syllable) accented or stressed 16 (of an industry, market, currency, securities, etc) firm in price or characterized by firm or increasing prices 17 (of certain acids and bases) producing high concentrations of hydrogen or hydroxide ions in aqueous solution 18 *Irish* prosperous; well-to-do (esp in the phrase **a strong farmer**) 19 have a strong stomach not to be prone to nausea ▷ *adv* 20 *informal* in a strong way; effectively: *going strong* 21 come on strong to make a forceful or exaggerated impression [Old English *strang*; related to Old Norse *strangr*, Middle High German *strange*, Lettish *strans* courageous] > **strongish** *adj* > 'strongly *adv* > 'strongness *n*

strong-arm *informal* ▷ *n* 1 (*modifier*) relating to or involving physical force or violence: *strong-arm tactics* ▷ *vb* 2 (*tr*) to show violence towards

strongbox ('strɒŋ,bɒks) *n* a specially designed box or safe in which valuables are locked for safety

strong breeze *n meteorol* a considerable wind of force six on the Beaufort scale, reaching speeds of 25–31 mph

strong drink *n* alcoholic drink

strong-eye dog *n NZ* a dog trained to control sheep by its gaze

strong gale *n meteorol* a strong wind of force nine on the Beaufort scale, reaching speeds of 47–54 mph: capable of causing minor structural damage to buildings

stronghold ('strɒŋ,həʊld) *n* 1 a defensible place; fortress 2 a major centre or area of predominance [c15 from STRONG + HOLD¹ (in the archaic sense: a fortified place)]

strong interaction or **force** *n physics* an interaction between elementary particles responsible for the forces between nucleons in the nucleus. It operates at distances less than about 10^{-15} metres, and is about a hundred times more powerful than the electromagnetic interaction. Also called: **strong nuclear interaction** or **force**. See **interaction** (sense 2)

strongman ('strɒŋ,mæn) *n, pl* **-men** 1 a performer, esp one in a circus, who performs feats of strength 2 any person regarded as a source of power, capability, initiative, etc

strong meat *n* anything arousing fear, anger, repulsion, etc, except among a tolerant or receptive minority: *some scenes in the film were strong meat*

strong-minded *adj* having strength of mind; firm, resolute, and determined > ˌstrong-'mindedly *adv* > ˌstrong-'mindedness *n*

strong point *n* something at which one excels;

forte: *tactfulness was never his strong point*

strongpoint ('strɒŋ,pɔɪnt) *n military* **1** a location that is by its site and nature easily defended **2** a spot in a defensive position that is heavily defended

strongroom ('strɒŋ,ruːm, -,rʊm) *n* a specially designed room in which valuables are locked for safety

strong waters *pl n* an archaic name for alcoholic drink

strong-willed *adj* having strength of will

strongyle ('strɒndʒɪl) *or* **strongyl** ('strɒndʒəl) *n* any parasitic nematode worm of the family *Strongylidae*, chiefly occurring in the intestines of horses [C19 via New Latin *Strongylus*, from Greek *strongulos* round]

strongyloidiasis (,strɒndʒɪlɔɪˈdaɪəsɪs) *or* **strongyloidosis** (-ˈdəʊsɪs) *n* an intestinal disease caused by infection with the nematode worm *Strongyloides stercoralis*

strontia ('strɒntɪə) *n* another name for **strontium monoxide** [C19 changed from STRONTIAN]

strontian ('strɒntɪən) *n* **1** another name for **strontianite** **2** another name for **strontium** *or* **strontium monoxide** [C18 named after a parish in Argyll, where it was discovered]

strontianite ('strɒntɪəˌnaɪt) *n* a white, lightly coloured, or colourless mineral consisting of strontium carbonate in orthorhombic crystalline form: it is a source of strontium compounds. Formula: $SrCO_3$

strontium ('strɒntɪəm) *n* a soft silvery-white element of the alkaline earth group of metals, occurring chiefly in celestite and strontianite. Its compounds burn with a crimson flame and are used in fireworks. The radioisotope **strontium-90**, with a half-life of 28.1 years, is used in nuclear power sources and is a hazardous nuclear fall-out product. Symbol: Sr; atomic no.: 38; atomic wt.: 87.62; valency: 2; relative density: 2.54; melting pt.: 769°C; boiling pt.: 1384°C [C19 from New Latin, from STRONTIAN]

strontium monoxide *n* a white insoluble solid substance used in making strontium salts and purifying sugar. Formula: SrO. Also called: **strontium oxide, strontia**

strontium unit *n* a unit expressing the concentration of strontium-90 in an organic medium, such as soil, milk, bone, etc, relative to the concentration of calcium in the same medium. Abbreviation: SU

strop (strɒp) *n* **1** a leather strap or an abrasive strip for sharpening razors **2** a rope or metal band around a block or deadeye for support **3** *informal* a temper tantrum: *he threw a strop and stormed off* ▷ *vb* **strops, stropping, stropped** **4** (*tr*) to sharpen (a razor, etc) on a strop [C14 (in nautical use: a strip of rope): via Middle Low German or Middle Dutch *strop*, ultimately from Latin *stroppus*, from Greek *strophos* cord; see STROPHE]

strophanthin (strəʊˈfænθɪn) *n* a toxic glycoside or mixture of glycosides obtained from the ripe seeds of certain species of strophanthus: used as a cardiac stimulant

strophanthus (strəʊˈfænθəs) *n* **1** any small tree or shrub of the apocynaceous genus *Strophanthus*, of tropical Africa and Asia, having strap-shaped twisted petals. The seeds of certain species yield the drug strophanthin **2** the seeds of any of these plants [C19 New Latin, from Greek *strophos* twisted cord + *anthos* flower]

strophe ('strəʊfɪ) *n prosody* **1** (in ancient Greek drama) **a** the first of two movements made by a chorus during the performance of a choral ode **b** the first part of a choral ode sung during this movement **2** (in classical verse) the first division of the threefold structure of a Pindaric ode **3** the first of two metrical systems used alternately within a poem ▷ See also **antistrophe, epode** [C17 from Greek: a verse, literally: a turning, from *strephein* to twist]

strophic ('strɒfɪk, 'strəʊ-) *or less commonly*

strophical *adj* **1** of, relating to, or employing a strophe or strophes **2** (of a song) having identical or related music in each verse. Compare **through-composed**

stroppy ('strɒpɪ) *adj* **-pier, -piest** *Brit informal* angry or awkward [C20 changed and shortened from OBSTREPEROUS] > **'stroppily** *adv* > **'stroppiness** *n*

stroud (straʊd) *n* a coarse woollen fabric [C17 perhaps named after *Stroud*, textile centre in Gloucestershire]

strove (strəʊv) *vb* the past tense of **strive**

strow (strəʊ) *vb* **strows, strowing, strowed; strown** *or* **strowed** an archaic variant of **strew**

stroy (strɔɪ) *vb* an archaic variant of **destroy** > **'stroyer** *n*

struck (strʌk) *vb* **1** the past tense and past participle of **strike** ▷ *adj* **2** *chiefly US and Canadian* (of an industry, factory, etc) shut down or otherwise affected by a labour strike

struck measure *n* a measure of grain, etc, in which the contents are made level with the top of the container rather than being heaped up

structural ('strʌktʃərəl) *adj* **1** of, relating to, or having structure or a structure **2** of, relating to, or forming part of the structure of a building **3** of or relating to the structure and deformation of rocks and other features of the earth's crust **4** of or relating to the structure of organisms; morphological **5** *chem* of, concerned with, caused by, or involving the arrangement of atoms in molecules > **'structurally** *adv*

structural formula *n* a chemical formula showing the composition and structure of a molecule. The atoms are represented by symbols and the structure is indicated by showing the relative positions of the atoms in space and the bonds between them: $H-C\equiv C-H$ *is the structural formula of acetylene.* See also **empirical formula, molecular formula**

structuralism ('strʌktʃərəˌlɪzəm) *n* **1** an approach to anthropology and other social sciences and to literature that interprets and analyses its material in terms of oppositions, contrasts, and hierarchical structures, esp as they might reflect universal mental characteristics or organizing principles. Compare **functionalism** **2** an approach to linguistics that analyses and describes the structure of language, as distinguished from its comparative and historical aspects > **'structuralist** *n, adj*

structural linguistics *n* (*functioning as singular*) a descriptive approach to a synchronic or diachronic analysis of language on the basis of its structure as reflected by irreducible units of phonological, morphological, and semantic features

structural psychology *n* (formerly) a school of psychology using introspection to analyse experience into basic units

structural steel *n* a strong mild steel used in construction work

structural unemployment *n economics* unemployment resulting from changes in the structure of an industry as a result of changes in either technology or taste

structure ('strʌktʃə) *n* **1** a complex construction or entity **2** the arrangement and interrelationship of parts in a construction, such as a building **3** the manner of construction or organization: *the structure of society* **4** *biology* morphology; form **5** *chem* the arrangement of atoms in a molecule of a chemical compound: *the structure of benzene* **6** *geology* the way in which a mineral, rock, rock mass or stratum, etc, is made up of its component parts **7** *now rare* the act of constructing ▷ *vb* **8** (*tr*) to impart a structure to [C15 from Latin *structūra*, from *struere* to build]

structured ('strʌktʃəd) *adj* **1** having a distinct physical shape or form, often provided by an internal structure **2** planned in broad outline; organized: *structured play for preschoolers* **3** having a

definite predetermined pattern; rigid

strudel ('struːdᵊl; German 'ʃtruːdəl) *n* a thin sheet of filled dough rolled up and baked: *apple strudel* [German, from Middle High German *strodel* eddy, whirlpool, so called from the way the pastry is rolled]

struggle ('strʌgᵊl) *vb* **1** (*intr*; usually foll by *for* or *against*; may take an infinitive) to exert strength, energy, and force; work or strive: *to struggle to obtain freedom* **2** (*intr*) to move about strenuously so as to escape from something confining **3** (*intr*) to contend, battle, or fight **4** (*intr*) to go or progress with difficulty ▷ *n* **5** a laboured or strenuous exertion or effort **6** a fight or battle **7** the act of struggling **8** **the struggle** *S African* the radical and armed opposition to apartheid, especially by the military wings of the ANC and the PAC [C14 of obscure origin] > **'struggler** *n* > **'struggling** *adj* > **'strugglingly** *adv*

struggle for existence *n* (*not in technical usage*) competition between organisms of a population, esp as a factor in the evolution of plants and animals. See also **natural selection**

strum (strʌm) *vb* **strums, strumming, strummed** **1** to sound (the strings of a guitar, banjo, etc) with a downward or upward sweep of the thumb or of a plectrum **2** to play (chords, a tune, etc) in this way [C18 probably of imitative origin; see THRUM¹] > **'strummer** *n*

struma ('struːmə) *n, pl* **-mae** (-miː) **1** *pathol* an abnormal enlargement of the thyroid gland; goitre **2** *botany* a swelling, esp one at the base of a moss capsule **3** another word for **scrofula** [C16 from Latin: a scrofulous tumour, from *struere* to heap up] > **strumatic** (struːˈmætɪk), **strumous** ('struːməs) *or* **strumose** ('struːməʊs) *adj*

Struma ('struːmə) *n* a river in S Europe, rising in SW Bulgaria near Sofia and flowing generally southeast through Greece to the Aegean. Length: 362 km (225 miles). Greek names: **Strimon, Strymon**

strumpet ('strʌmpɪt) *n archaic* a prostitute or promiscuous woman [C14 of unknown origin]

strung (strʌŋ) *vb* **1** a past tense and past participle of **string** ▷ *adj* **2 a** (of a piano, etc) provided with strings, esp of a specified kind or in a specified manner **b** (in combination): *gut-strung* **3** **highly strung** very nervous or volatile in character. Usual US and Canadian phrase: **high-strung**

strung out *adj slang* **1** addicted to a drug **2** (of a drug addict) suffering or distressed because of the lack of a drug

strung up *adj* (*postpositive*) *informal* tense or nervous

strut (strʌt) *vb* **struts, strutting, strutted** **1** (*intr*) to walk in a pompous manner; swagger **2** (*tr*) to support or provide with struts **3** **strut one's stuff** *informal* to behave or perform in a proud and confident manner; show off ▷ *n* **4** a structural member used mainly in compression, esp as part of a framework **5** an affected, proud, or stiff walk [C14 *strouten* (in the sense: swell, stand out; C16 to walk stiffly), from Old English *strūtian* to stand stiffly; related to Low German *strutt* stiff] > **'strutter** *n* > **'strutting** *adj* > **'struttingly** *adv*

struthious ('struːθɪəs) *adj* **1** (of birds) related to or resembling the ostrich **2** of, relating to, or designating all flightless (ratite) birds [C18 from Late Latin *strūthiō*, from Greek *strouthiōn*, from *strouthos* an ostrich]

strychnic ('strɪknɪk) *adj* of, relating to, or derived from strychnine

strychnine ('strɪkniːn) *n* a white crystalline very poisonous alkaloid, obtained from the plant nux vomica: formerly used in small quantities as a stimulant of the central nervous system and the appetite. Formula: $C_{21}H_{22}O_2N_2$ [C19 via French from New Latin *Strychnos*, from Greek *strukhnos* nightshade]

strychninism ('strɪknɪˌnɪzəm) *n pathol* poisoning caused by the excessive or prolonged use of

S

strychnine
Strymon ('straɪmən) *n* transliteration of the Greek name for the **Struma**
stub (stʌb) *n* **1** a short piece remaining after something has been cut, removed, etc: *a cigar stub* **2** the residual piece or section of a receipt, ticket, cheque, etc **3** *US and Canadian* the part of a cheque, postal order, receipt, etc, detached and retained as a record of the transaction. also called (in Britain): **counterfoil** **4** any short projection or blunted end **5** the stump of a tree or plant ▷ *vb* **stubs, stubbing, stubbed** (*tr*) **6** to strike (one's toe, foot, etc) painfully against a hard surface **7** (usually foll by *out*) to put (out a cigarette or cigar) by pressing the end against a surface **8** to clear (land) of stubs **9** to dig up (the roots) of (a tree or bush) [Old English *stubb;* related to Old Norse *stubbi*, Middle Dutch *stubbe*, Greek *stupos* stem, stump]
stub axle *n* a short axle that carries one of the front steered wheels of a motor vehicle and is capable of limited angular movement about a kingpin
Stubbies ('stʌbɪz) *pl n trademark Austral* a type of shorts
stubble ('stʌbᵊl) *n* **1** **a** the stubs of stalks left in a field where a crop has been cut and harvested **b** (*as modifier*): *a stubble field* **2** any bristly growth or surface [C13 from Old French *estuble*, from Latin *stupula*, variant of *stipula* stalk, stem, stubble] > '**stubbly** *adj*
stubbled ('stʌbᵊld) *adj* **1** **a** having the stubs of stalks left after a crop has been cut and harvested **2** having a bristly growth or surface
stubble-jumper *n Canadian slang* a prairie grain farmer
stubborn ('stʌbᵊn) *adj* **1** refusing to comply, agree, or give in; obstinate **2** difficult to handle, treat, or overcome **3** persistent and dogged: *a stubborn crusade* [C14 *stoborne*, of obscure origin] > '**stubbornly** *adv* > '**stubbornness** *n*
stubby ('stʌbɪ) *adj* **-bier, -biest** **1** short and broad; stumpy or thickset **2** bristling and stiff ▷ *n* **3** Also called: **stubbie** *Austral slang* a small bottle of beer > '**stubbily** *adv* > '**stubbiness** *n*
stub nail *n* **1** a short thick nail **2** a worn nail in a horseshoe
STUC *abbreviation for* Scottish Trades Union Congress
stucco ('stʌkəʊ) *n, pl* **-coes** *or* **-cos** **1** a weather-resistant mixture of dehydrated lime, powdered marble, and glue, used in decorative mouldings on buildings **2** any of various types of cement or plaster used for coating outside walls **3** Also called: **stuccowork** decorative work moulded in stucco ▷ *vb* **-coes** *or* **-cos, -coing, -coed** **4** (*tr*) to apply stucco to [C16 from Italian, of Germanic origin; compare Old High German *stukki* a fragment, crust, Old English *stycce*] > '**stuccoer** *n*
stuck (stʌk) *vb* **1** the past tense and past participle of **stick²** ▷ *adj* **2** *informal* baffled or nonplussed **3** (foll by *on*) *slang* keen (on) or infatuated (with) **4** **get stuck in** *or* **into** *informal* **a** to perform (a task) with determination **b** to attack (a person) verbally or physically
stuck-up *adj informal* conceited, arrogant, or snobbish > '**stuck-'upness** *n*
stud¹ (stʌd) *n* **1** a large-headed nail or other projection protruding from a surface, usually as decoration **2** a type of fastener consisting of two discs at either end of a short shank, used to fasten shirtfronts, collars, etc **3** *building trades* a vertical member made of timber, steel, etc, that is used with others to construct the framework of a wall **4** a headless bolt that is threaded at both ends, the centre portion being unthreaded **5** any short projection on a machine, such as the metal cylinder that forms a journal for the gears on a screw-cutting lathe **6** the crossbar in the centre of a link of a heavy chain **7** one of a number of rounded projections on the sole of a boot or shoe to give better grip, as on a football boot ▷ *vb* **studs, studding, studded** (*tr*) **8** to provide, ornament, or make with studs **9** to dot or cover (with): *the park was studded with daisies* **10** *building trades* to provide or support (a wall, partition, etc) with studs [Old English *studu;* related to Old Norse *stoth* post, Middle High German *stud* post]
stud² (stʌd) *n* **1** a group of pedigree animals, esp horses, kept for breeding purposes **2** any male animal kept principally for breeding purposes, esp a stallion **3** a farm or stable where a stud is kept **4** the state or condition of being kept for breeding purposes: *at stud; put to stud* **5** (*modifier*) of or relating to such animals or the place where they are kept: *a stud farm; a stud horse* **6** *slang* a virile or sexually active man **7** short for **stud poker** [Old English *stōd;* related to Old Norse *stōth*, Old High German *stuot*]
studbook ('stʌd,bʊk) *n* a written record of the pedigree of a purebred stock, esp of racehorses
studding ('stʌdɪŋ) *n* **1** building studs collectively, esp as used to form a wall or partition. See also **stud¹** (sense 3) **2** material that is used to form studs or serve as studs
studdingsail ('stʌdɪŋ,seɪl; *Nautical* 'stʌnsᵊl) *n nautical* a light auxiliary sail set outboard on spars on either side of a square sail. Also called: **stunsail, stuns'l** [C16 *studding*, perhaps from Middle Low German, Middle Dutch *stōtinge*, from *stōten* to thrust; related to German *stossen*]
student ('stju:dᵊnt) *n* **1** **a** a person following a course of study, as in a school, college, university, etc **b** (*as modifier*): *student teacher* **2** a person who makes a thorough study of a subject [C15 from Latin *studēns* diligent, from *studēre* to be zealous; see STUDY]
student adviser *n* another word for **counsellor** (sense 6)
studentification (stju:,dɛntɪfɪ'keɪʃən) *n* the renting of particular accommodation exclusively to students
studentship ('stju:dᵊntʃɪp) *n* **1** the role or position of a student **2** another word for **scholarship** (sense 3)
Student's t *n* a statistic often used to test the hypothesis that a random sample of normally distributed observations has a given mean, μ; given by $t = (\bar{x}-\mu)\sqrt{n/s}$ where $\bar{x}$ is the mean of the sample, *s* is its standard deviation, and *n* is the size of the sample [after *Student*, the pen name of W. S. Gosset (1876–1937), English statistician and research scientist]
student teacher *n* a person who is teaching in a school for a limited period under supervision as part of a course to qualify as a teacher
studenty ('stju:dəntɪ) *adj informal, sometimes derogatory* denoting or exhibiting the characteristics believed typical of an undergraduate student
studhorse ('stʌd,hɔ:s) *n* another word for **stallion**
studied ('stʌdɪd) *adj* **1** carefully practised, designed, or premeditated: *a studied reply* **2** an archaic word for **learned.** > '**studiedly** *adv* > '**studiedness** *n*
studio ('stju:dɪ,əʊ) *n, pl* **-dios** **1** a room in which an artist, photographer, or musician works **2** a room used to record television or radio programmes, make films, etc **3** (*plural*) the premises of a radio, television, or film company [C19 from Italian, literally: study, from Latin *studium* diligence]
studio couch *n* an upholstered couch, usually backless, convertible into a double bed
studio flat *n* a flat with one main room
studious ('stju:dɪəs) *adj* **1** given to study **2** of a serious, thoughtful, and hard-working character **3** showing deliberation, care, or precision [C14 from Latin *studiōsus* devoted to, from *studium* assiduity] > '**studiously** *adv* > '**studiousness** *n*
stud poker *n* a variety of poker in which the first card is dealt face down before each player and the next four are dealt face up (**five-card stud**) or in which the first two cards and the last card are dealt face down and the intervening four cards are dealt face up (**seven-card stud**), with bets made after each round. Often shortened to: **stud** [C19 from STUD² + POKER²]
stud welding *n* the semiautomatic welding of a stud or similar piece of metal to a flat part, usually by means of an electric arc
studwork ('stʌd,wɜ:k) *n* **1** work decorated with studs **2** the supporting framework of a wall or partition
study ('stʌdɪ) *vb* **studies, studying, studied** **1** to apply the mind to the learning or understanding of (a subject), esp by reading: *to study languages; to study all night* **2** (*tr*) to investigate or examine, as by observation, research, etc: *to study the effects of heat on metal* **3** (*tr*) to look at minutely; scrutinize **4** (*tr*) to give much careful or critical thought to **5** to take a course in (a subject), as at a college **6** (*tr*) to try to memorize: *to study a part for a play* **7** (*intr*) to meditate or contemplate; reflect ▷ *n, pl* **studies** **8** **a** the act or process of studying **b** (*as modifier*): *study group* **9** a room used for studying, reading, writing, etc **10** (*often plural*) work relating to a particular discipline: *environmental studies* **11** an investigation and analysis of a subject, situation, etc: *a study of transport provision in rural districts* **12** a product of studying, such as a written paper or book **13** a drawing, sculpture, etc, executed for practice or in preparation for another work **14** a musical composition intended to develop one aspect of performing technique: *a study in spiccato bowing* **15** *theatre* a person who memorizes a part in the manner specified: *a quick study* **16** **in a brown study** in a reverie or daydream [C13 from Old French *estudie*, from Latin *studium* zeal, inclination, from *studēre* to be diligent]
stuff (stʌf) *vb* (*mainly tr*) **1** to pack or fill completely; cram **2** (*intr*) to eat large quantities **3** to force, shove, or squeeze: *to stuff money into a pocket* **4** to fill (food such as poultry or tomatoes) with a stuffing **5** to fill (an animal's skin) with material so as to restore the shape of the live animal **6** *slang* to have sexual intercourse with (a woman) **7** *tanning* to treat (an animal skin or hide) with grease **8** *US and Canadian* to fill (a ballot box) with a large number of fraudulent votes **9** (in marine transport) to pack (a container). See also **stuffing and stripping** **10** *slang* to ruin, frustrate, or defeat ▷ *n* **11** the raw material or fabric of something **12** woollen cloth or fabric **13** any general or unspecified substance or accumulation of objects **14** stupid or worthless actions, speech, ideas, etc **15** subject matter, skill, etc: *he knows his stuff* **16** a slang word for **money** **17** *slang* a drug, esp cannabis **18** *informal* **do one's stuff** to do what is expected of one **19** **that's the stuff** that is what is needed **20** *Brit slang* a girl or woman considered sexually (esp in the phrase **bit of stuff**) [C14 from Old French *estoffe*, from *estoffer* to furnish, provide, of Germanic origin; related to Middle High German *stopfen* to cram full] > '**stuffer** *n*

> USAGE Sense 6 of this word was formerly considered to be taboo, and it was labelled as such in previous editions of *Collins English Dictionary*. However, it has now become acceptable in speech, although some older or more conservative people may object to its use

stuffed (stʌft) *adj* **1** filled with something, esp (of poultry and other food) filled with stuffing **2** (foll by *up*) (of the nasal passages) blocked with mucus **3** **get stuffed!** *Brit slang* an exclamation of contemptuous anger or annoyance, esp against another person
stuffed shirt *n informal* a pompous or formal person
stuff gown *n Brit* a woollen gown worn by a barrister who has not taken silk
stuffing ('stʌfɪŋ) *n* **1** the material with which something is stuffed **2** a mixture of chopped and seasoned ingredients with which poultry, meat,

etc, is stuffed before cooking **3** **knock the stuffing out of (someone)** to upset or dishearten (someone) completely

stuffing and stripping *n* (in marine transport) the packing and unpacking of containers

stuffing box *n* a small chamber in which an annular packing is compressed around a reciprocating or rotating rod or shaft to form a seal. Also called: **packing box**

stuffing nut *n* a large nut that is tightened to compress the packing in a stuffing box

stuffy (ˈstʌfɪ) *adj* **stuffier, stuffiest 1** lacking fresh air **2** excessively dull, staid, or conventional **3** (of the nasal passages) blocked with mucus > ˈ**stuffily** *adv* > ˈ**stuffiness** *n*

stukkend (ˈstʌkɪnt) *South African slang* ▷ *adj* **1** broken; wrecked **2** drunk ▷ *adv* **3** very much; extremely [from Afrikaans]

stull (stʌl) *n mining* a timber prop or platform in a stope [C18 perhaps from German *Stollen*, from Old High German *stollo*]

stultify (ˈstʌltɪˌfaɪ) *vb* **-fies, -fying, -fied** (*tr*) **1** to make useless, futile, or ineffectual, esp by routine **2** to cause to appear absurd or inconsistent **3** to prove (someone) to be of unsound mind and thus not legally responsible [C18 from Latin *stultus* stupid + *facere* to make] > ˌ**stultifiˈcation** *n* > ˈ**stultiˌfier** *n*

stum (stʌm) (in wine-making) *n* **1** a less common word for **must[2]** **2** partly fermented wine added to fermented wine as a preservative ▷ *vb* **stums, stumming, stummed 3** to preserve (wine) by adding stum [C17 from Dutch *stom* dumb; related to German *stumm*]

stumble (ˈstʌmbᵊl) *vb* (*intr*) **1** to trip or fall while walking or running **2** to walk in an awkward, unsteady, or unsure way **3** to make mistakes or hesitate in speech or actions **4** (foll by *across* or *upon*) to come (across) by accident **5** to commit a grave mistake or sin ▷ *n* **6** a false step, trip, or blunder **7** the act of stumbling [C14 related to Norwegian *stumla*, Danish dialect *stumle*; see STAMMER] > ˈ**stumbler** *n* > ˈ**stumbling** *adj* > ˈ**stumblingly** *adv*

stumbling block *n* any impediment or obstacle

stumer (ˈstjuːmə) *n* **1** *slang* a forgery or cheat **2** *Irish dialect* a poor bargain **3** *Scot* a stupid person **4** **come a stumer** *Austral slang* to crash financially [of unknown origin]

stump (stʌmp) *n* **1** the base part of a tree trunk left standing after the tree has been felled or has fallen **2** the part of something, such as a tooth, limb, or blade, that remains after a larger part has been removed **3** *informal, facetious* **a** (*often plural*) a leg **b** **stir one's stumps** to move or become active **4** *cricket* any of three upright wooden sticks that, with two bails laid across them, form a wicket (the **stumps**) **5** Also called: **tortillon** a short sharply-pointed stick of cork or rolled paper or leather, used in drawing and shading **6** a heavy tread or the sound of heavy footsteps **7** a platform used by an orator when addressing a meeting **8** **on the stump** *chiefly US and Canadian* engaged in campaigning, esp by political speech-making **9** (*often plural*) *Austral* a pile used to support a house ▷ *vb* **10** (*tr*) to stop, confuse, or puzzle **11** (*intr*) to plod or trudge heavily **12** (*tr*) *cricket* (of a fielder, esp a wicketkeeper) to dismiss (a batsman) by breaking his wicket with the ball or with the ball in the hand while he is out of his crease **13** *chiefly US and Canadian* to campaign or canvass (an area), esp by political speech-making **14** (*tr*) to reduce to a stump; lop **15** (*tr*) to clear (land) of stumps [C14 from Middle Low German *stump*; related to Dutch *stomp*, German *Stumpf*; see STAMP] > ˈ**stumper** *n*

stumpage (ˈstʌmpɪdʒ) *n* **1** *US and Canadian* standing timber or its value **2** *US and Canadian* the right to fell timber on another person's land **3** *Canadian* a tax or royalty payable on each tree felled, esp on crown land

stump-jump plough *n Austral* a plough designed for use on land not cleared of stumps

stump ranch *or* **farm** *n Canadian informal* (in British Columbia) an undeveloped ranch in the bush where animals graze among the stumps of felled trees

stump up *vb* (*adverb*) *Brit informal* to give (the money required)

stumpwork (ˈstʌmpˌwɜːk) *n* a type of embroidery of the 15th to 17th centuries featuring raised or embossed figures, padded with cotton wool or hair

stumpy (ˈstʌmpɪ) *adj* **stumpier, stumpiest 1** short and thickset like a stump; stubby **2** abounding in or full of stumps > ˈ**stumpiness** *n*

stun (stʌn) *vb* **stuns, stunning, stunned** (*tr*) **1** to render unconscious, as by a heavy blow or fall **2** to shock or overwhelm **3** to surprise or astound ▷ *n* **4** the state or effect of being stunned [C13 *stunen*, from Old French *estoner* to daze, stupefy, from Vulgar Latin *extonāre* (unattested), from Latin EX-[1] + *tonāre* to thunder]

stung (stʌŋ) *vb* **1** the past tense and past participle of **sting** ▷ *adj* **2** *Austral slang* drunk; intoxicated

stun gun *n* a device designed to immobilize an animal or person temporarily without inflicting serious injury

stunk (stʌŋk) *vb* a past tense and past participle of **stink**

stunner (ˈstʌnə) *n informal* a person or thing of great beauty, quality, size, etc

stunning (ˈstʌnɪŋ) *adj informal* very attractive, impressive, astonishing, etc > ˈ**stunningly** *adv*

stunsail *or* **stuns'l** (ˈstʌnsᵊl) *n* another word for **studdingsail**

stunt[1] (stʌnt) *vb* **1** (*tr*) to prevent or impede (the growth or development) of (a plant, animal, etc) ▷ *n* **2** the act or an instance of stunting **3** a person, animal, or plant that has been stunted [C17 (as vb: to check the growth of): perhaps from C15 *stont* of short duration, from Old English *stunt* simple, foolish; sense probably influenced by Old Norse *stuttr* short in stature, dwarfed] > ˈ**stunted** *adj* > ˈ**stuntedness** *n*

stunt[2] (stʌnt) *n* **1** an acrobatic, dangerous, or spectacular action **2** an acrobatic or dangerous piece of action in a film or television programme **3** anything spectacular or unusual done to gain publicity ▷ *vb* **4** (*intr*) to perform a stunt or stunts [C19 US student slang, of unknown origin]

stuntman (ˈstʌntmən) *or feminine* **stuntwoman** *n, pl* **-men** *or* **-women** a person who performs dangerous acts in a film, television programme, etc in place of an actor

stupa (ˈstuːpə) *n* a domed edifice housing Buddhist or Jain relics. Also called: **tope** [C19 from Sanskrit: dome]

stupe[1] (stjuːp) *n med* a hot damp cloth, usually sprinkled with an irritant, applied to the body to relieve pain by counterirritation [C14 from Latin *stuppa* flax, from Greek *stuppē*]

stupe[2] (stjuːp) *n US slang* a stupid person; clot

stupefacient (ˌstjuːpɪˈfeɪʃɪənt) *n* **1** a drug that causes stupor ▷ *adj* **2** of, relating to, or designating this type of drug [C17 from Latin *stupefacere* to make senseless, from *stupēre* to be stunned + *facere* to make]

stupefaction (ˌstjuːpɪˈfækʃən) *n* **1** astonishment **2** the act of stupefying or the state of being stupefied

stupefy (ˈstjuːpɪˌfaɪ) *vb* **-fies, -fying, -fied** (*tr*) **1** to render insensitive or lethargic **2** to confuse or astound [C16 from Old French *stupefier*, from Latin *stupefacere*; see STUPEFACIENT] > ˈ**stupeˌfier** *n* > ˈ**stupeˌfying** *adj* > ˈ**stupeˌfyingly** *adv*

stupendous (stjuːˈpɛndəs) *adj* astounding, wonderful, huge, etc [C17 from Latin *stupēre* to be amazed] > **stuˈpendously** *adv* > **stuˈpendousness** *n*

stupid (ˈstjuːpɪd) *adj* **1** lacking in common sense, perception, or normal intelligence **2** (*usually postpositive*) stunned, dazed, or stupefied: *stupid from lack of sleep* **3** having dull mental responses; slow-witted **4** trivial, silly, or frivolous ▷ *n* **5** *informal* a stupid person [C16 from French *stupide*, from Latin *stupidus* silly, from *stupēre* to be amazed] > ˈ**stupidly** *adv* > ˈ**stupidness** *n*

stupidity (stjuːˈpɪdɪtɪ) *n, pl* **-ties 1** the quality or state of being stupid **2** a stupid act, remark, etc

stupor (ˈstjuːpə) *n* **1** a state of unconsciousness **2** mental dullness; torpor [C17 from Latin, from *stupēre* to be aghast] > ˈ**stuporous** *adj*

sturdy[1] (ˈstɜːdɪ) *adj* **-dier, -diest 1** healthy, strong, and vigorous **2** strongly built; stalwart [C13 (in the sense: rash, harsh): from Old French *estordi* dazed, from *estordir* to stun, perhaps ultimately related to Latin *turdus* a thrush (taken as representing drunkenness)] > ˈ**sturdily** *adv* > ˈ**sturdiness** *n*

sturdy[2] (ˈstɜːdɪ) *n vet science* another name for **staggers** (sense 2) or **gid** (in sheep) [C17 from STURDY[1] (in the obsolete sense: giddy)] > ˈ**sturdied** *adj*

sturgeon (ˈstɜːdʒən) *n* any primitive bony fish of the family *Acipenseridae*, of temperate waters of the N hemisphere, having an elongated snout and rows of spines along the body: valued as a source of caviar and isinglass [C13 from Old French *estourgeon*, of Germanic origin; related to Old English *styria*, Old High German *sturio*]

Sturmabteilung *German* (ˈʃtʊrmˈaptailʊŋ) *n* the full name of the Nazi **SA** [literally: storm division]

Sturmer (ˈstɜːmə) *n* a variety of eating apple having a pale green skin and crisp tart flesh [C19 named after *Sturmer*, Suffolk]

Sturm und Drang *German* (ˈʃtʊrm ʊnt ˈdraŋ) *n* a German literary movement of the latter half of the 18th century, characterized by a reaction against rationalism [literally: storm and stress, from the title of a play by F. M. von Klinger (1752–1831), German dramatist]

Sturt's desert pea *n Austral* the desert pea [named after Charles *Sturt* (1795–1869), English explorer of the Australian interior]

stushie (ˈstʊʃɪ), **stishie** *or* **stashie** *n Scot* **1** a commotion, rumpus, or row **2** a state of excitement or anxiety; a tizzy ▷ Also called: **stooshie, stoushie** [C19 perhaps shortened from *ecstasy*]

stutter (ˈstʌtə) *vb* **1** to speak (a word, phrase, etc) with recurring repetition of consonants, esp initial ones **2** to make (an abrupt sound) repeatedly: *the gun stuttered* ▷ *n* **3** the act or habit of stuttering **4** a stuttering sound [C16 related to Middle Low German *stötern*, Old High German *stōzan* to push against, Latin *tundere* to beat] > ˈ**stutterer** *n* > ˈ**stuttering** *n, adj* > ˈ**stutteringly** *adv*

Stuttgart (*German* ˈʃtʊtgart) *n* an industrial city in W Germany, capital of Baden-Württemberg state, on the River Neckar: developed around a stud farm (*Stuotgarten*) of the Counts of Württemberg. Pop: 589 161 (2003 est)

STV *abbreviation for* **1** Scottish Television **2** **Single Transferable Vote**

sty (staɪ) *n, pl* **sties 1** a pen in which pigs are housed and fed **2** any filthy or corrupt place ▷ *vb* **sties, stying, stied 3** to enclose or be enclosed in a sty [Old English *stig*; related to Old Norse *stīa* pen, fold, Old High German *stīga*, Middle Dutch *stije*]

stye *or* **sty** (staɪ) *n, pl* **styes** *or* **sties** inflammation of a sebaceous gland of the eyelid, usually caused by bacteria technical name: **hordeolum** [C15 *styanye* (mistakenly taken as *sty on eye*), from Old English *stīgend* rising, hence swelling, stye + *ye* eye]

Stygian (ˈstɪdʒɪən) *adj* **1** of or relating to the river Styx **2** *chiefly literary* **a** dark, gloomy, or hellish **b** completely inviolable, as a vow sworn by the river Styx [C16 from Latin *Stygius*, from Greek *Stugios*, from *Stux* STYX; related to *stugein* to hate]

style (staɪl) *n* **1** a form of appearance, design, or production; type or make: *a new style of house* **2** the way in which something is done: *good or bad style* **3** the manner in which something is expressed or performed, considered as separate from its intrinsic content, meaning, etc **4** a distinctive,

S

formal, or characteristic manner of expression in words, music, painting, etc **5** elegance or refinement of manners, dress, etc **6** prevailing fashion in dress, looks, etc **7** a fashionable or ostentatious mode of existence: *to live in style* **8** the particular mode of orthography, punctuation, design, etc, followed in a book, journal, etc, or in a printing or publishing house **9** *chiefly Brit* the distinguishing title or form of address of a person or firm **10** *botany* the stalk of a carpel, bearing the stigma **11** *zoology* a slender pointed structure, such as the piercing mouthparts of certain insects **12** a method of expressing or calculating dates. See **Old Style, New Style** **13** another word for **stylus** (sense 1) **14** the arm of a sundial ▷ *vb (mainly tr)* **15** to design, shape, or tailor: *to style hair* **16** to adapt or make suitable (for) **17** to make consistent or correct according to a printing or publishing style **18** to name or call; designate: *to style a man a fool* **19** *(intr)* to decorate objects using a style or stylus [C13 from Latin *stylus, stilus* writing implement, hence characteristics of the writing, style] > **'stylar** *adj* > **'styler** *n*

stylebook ('staɪlˌbʊk) *n* a book containing rules and examples of punctuation, typography, etc, for the use of writers, editors, and printers

stylet ('staɪlɪt) *n* **1** *surgery* **a** a wire for insertion into a flexible cannula or catheter to maintain its rigidity or patency during passage **b** a slender probe **2** *zoology* any small pointed bristle-like part [C17 from French *stilet*, from Old Italian STILETTO; influenced in spelling by Latin *stylus* STYLE]

stylie ('staɪlɪ) *adj NZ informal* fashion-conscious

styliform ('staɪlɪˌfɔːm) *adj zoology* shaped like a stylus or bristle: *a styliform antenna* [C16 from New Latin *stiliformis*, from Latin STYLUS]

styling mousse *n hairdressing* a light foamy substance applied to the hair before styling in order to retain the shape of the style

stylish ('staɪlɪʃ) *adj* having style; smart; fashionable > **'stylishly** *adv* > **'stylishness** *n*

stylist ('staɪlɪst) *n* **1** a person who performs, writes, or acts with attention to style **2** a designer of clothes, décor, etc **3** a hairdresser who styles hair **4** a designer whose job is to coordinate the style of products, advertising material, etc

stylistic (staɪ'lɪstɪk) *adj* of or relating to style, esp artistic or literary style > **sty'listically** *adv*

stylistics (staɪ'lɪstɪks) *n (functioning as singular or plural)* a branch of linguistics concerned with the study of characteristic choices in use of language, esp literary language, as regards sound, form, or vocabulary, made by different individuals or social groups in different situations of use

stylite ('staɪlaɪt) *n Christianity* one of a class of recluses who in ancient times lived on the top of high pillars [C17 from Late Greek *stulitēs*, from Greek *stulos* a pillar] > **stylitic** (staɪ'lɪtɪk) *adj*

stylize *or* **stylise** ('staɪlaɪz) *vb (tr)* to give a conventional or established stylistic form to > **ˌstyli'zation** *or* **ˌstyli'sation** *n* > **'stylizer** *or* **'styliser** *n*

stylo- *or before a vowel* **styl-** *combining form* **1** (in biology) a style: *stylopodium* **2** indicating a column or point: *stylobate; stylograph* [from Greek *stulos* column]

stylobate ('staɪləˌbeɪt) *n* a continuous horizontal course of masonry that supports a colonnade [C17 from Latin *stylobatēs*, from Greek *stulos* pillar + *-batēs*, from *bainein* to tread, walk]

stylograph ('staɪləˌgræf, -ˌgrɑːf) *n* a fountain pen having a fine hollow tube as the writing point instead of a nib [C19 from STYL(US) + -GRAPH]

stylographic (ˌstaɪlə'græfɪk) *or* **stylographical** *adj* of or relating to a stylograph or stylography > **ˌstylo'graphically** *adv*

stylography (staɪ'lɒgrəfɪ) *n* the art or method of writing, drawing, or engraving with a stylus or style

styloid ('staɪlɔɪd) *adj* **1** resembling a stylus **2** *anatomy* of or relating to a projecting process of the temporal bone [C18 from New Latin *styloides*, from Greek *stuloeidēs* like a STYLUS; influenced also by Greek *stulos* pillar]

stylolite ('staɪləˌlaɪt) *n* any of the small striated columnar or irregular structures within the strata of some limestones [C19 from Greek *stulos* pillar + -LITE] > **stylolitic** (ˌstaɪlə'lɪtɪk) *adj*

stylophone ('staɪləˌfəʊn) *n* a type of battery-powered electronic instrument played with a steel-tipped penlike stylus [C20 from STYL(US) + -PHONE]

stylopize *or* **stylopise** ('staɪləˌpaɪz) *vb (tr)* (of a stylops) to parasitize (a host): *the bee was stylopized*

stylopodium (ˌstaɪlə'pəʊdɪəm) *n, pl* **-dia** (-dɪə) *botany* a swelling at the base of the style in umbelliferous plants [C19 New Latin, from Greek *stulos* pillar + -PODIUM]

stylops ('staɪlɒps) *n, pl* **-lopes** (-ləˌpiːz) any insect of the order *Strepsiptera*, including the genus *Stylops*, living as a parasite in other insects, esp bees and wasps: the females remain in the body of the host but the males move between hosts [C19 New Latin, from Greek, from *stulos* a pillar + *ōps* an eye, from the fact that the male insect has stalked compound eyes]

stylostixis (ˌstaɪləʊ'stɪksɪs) *n med* another name for **acupuncture** [C20 New Latin, from Greek *stulos* style (pointed instrument) + *stixis* mark, spot]

stylus ('staɪləs) *n, pl* **-li** (-laɪ) *or* **-luses** **1** Also called: **style** a pointed instrument for engraving, drawing, or writing **2** a tool used in ancient times for writing on wax tablets, which was pointed at one end and blunt at the other for erasing mistakes **3** a device attached to the cartridge in the pick-up arm of a record player that rests in the groove in the record, transmitting the vibrations to the sensing device in the cartridge. It consists of or is tipped with a hard material, such as diamond or sapphire [C18 from Latin, variant of *stilus* writing implement; see STYLE] > **'stylar** *adj*

stymie *or* **stymy** ('staɪmɪ) *vb* **-mies, -mieing, -mied** *or* **-mies, -mying, -mied** *(tr; often passive)* **1** to hinder or thwart **2** *golf* to impede with a stymie ▷ *n, pl* **-mies** **3** *golf* (formerly) a situation on the green in which an opponent's ball is blocking the line between the hole and the ball about to be played: an obstructing ball may now be lifted and replaced by a marker **4** a situation of obstruction [C19 of uncertain origin]

stypsis ('stɪpsɪs) *n* the action, application, or use of a styptic [C19 via New Latin from Late Latin: astringency, from Greek *stupsis*, from *stuphein* to contract]

styptic ('stɪptɪk) *adj* **1** contracting the blood vessels or tissues ▷ *n* **2** a styptic drug [C14 via Late Latin, from Greek *stuptikos* capable of contracting; see STYPSIS] > **stypticity** (stɪp'tɪsɪtɪ) *n*

styptic pencil *n* a styptic agent in the form of a small stick, for application to razor nicks, etc

styracaceous (ˌstaɪrə'keɪʃəs) *adj* of, relating to, or belonging to the *Styracaceae*, a family of Asian and American trees and shrubs having leathery leaves: includes storax and silver bell [C19 *styrac-*, from STYRAX]

styrax ('staɪræks) *n* any tropical or subtropical tree of the genus *Styrax*, which includes the storaxes [C16 via Latin from Greek *sturax*]

styrene ('staɪriːn) *n* a colourless oily volatile flammable water-insoluble liquid made from ethylene and benzene. It is an unsaturated compound and readily polymerizes: used in making synthetic plastics and rubbers. Formula: $C_6H_5CH{:}CH_2$. See also **polystyrene** [C20 from STYR(AX) + -ENE]

Styria ('stɪərɪə) *n* a mountainous state of SE Austria: rich mineral resources. Capital: Graz. Pop: 1 190 574 (2003 est). Area: 16 384 sq km (6326 sq miles). German name: **Steiermark**

Styrofoam ('staɪrəˌfəʊm) *n trademark (sometimes not capital)* a light, expanded polystyrene plastic [C20 from POLYSTYRENE + FOAM]

Styx (stɪks) *n Greek myth* a river in Hades across which Charon ferried the souls of the dead [from Greek *Stux*; related to *stugein* to hate]

SU *abbreviation for* **1** **strontium unit** **2** ▷ *international car registration for* Belarus [from Soviet Union]

suable ('sjuːəbᵊl) *adj* liable to be sued in a court [C17 from SUE + -ABLE] > **ˌsua'bility** *n*

Suakin ('suːɑːkɪn) *n* a port in the NE Sudan, on the Red Sea: formerly the chief port of the African Red Sea; now obstructed by a coral reef. Pop: 5511 (latest est)

suasion ('sweɪʒən) *n* a rare word for **persuasion** [C14 from Latin *suāsiō*, from *suādēre* to PERSUADE] > **'suasive** *adj*

suave (swɑːv) *adj* (esp of a man) displaying smoothness and sophistication in manner or attitude; urbane [C16 from Latin *suāvis* sweet] > **'suavely** *adv* > **suavity** ('swɑːvɪtɪ) *or* **'suaveness** *n*

sub (sʌb) *n* **1** short for several words beginning with *sub-*, such as **subaltern, subeditor, submarine, subordinate, subscription, substandard, substitute**, and **substratum** (in photography) **2** *Brit informal* an advance payment of wages or salary. Formal term: **subsistence allowance** ▷ *vb* **subs, subbing, subbed** **3** *(intr)* to serve as a substitute **4** *(intr) informal* to act as a substitute (for) **5** *Brit informal* to grant or receive (an advance payment of wages or salary) **6** *(tr) informal* short for **subedit** **7** *(tr) photog* to apply a substratum to (a film or plate base)

sub. *abbreviation for* **1** subeditor **2** subito (in music) **3** subscription **4** substitute

sub- *prefix* **1** situated under or beneath: *subterranean* **2** secondary in rank; subordinate: *subeditor* **3** falling short of; less than or imperfectly: *subarctic; subhuman* **4** forming a subdivision or subordinate part of a whole: *subcommittee* **5** (in chemistry) **a** indicating that a compound contains a relatively small proportion of a specified element: *suboxide* **b** indicating that a salt is basic salt: *subacetate* [from Latin *sub*]

subacetate (sʌb'æsɪˌteɪt) *n* any one of certain crystalline basic acetates containing hydroxide ions in addition to acetate ions. For example, the subacetate of aluminium is probably $Al_3(OH)_2(CH_3COO)$

subacid (sʌb'æsɪd) *adj* (esp of some fruits) moderately acid or sour > **subacidity** (ˌsʌbə'sɪdɪtɪ) *or* **sub'acidness** *n* > **sub'acidly** *adv*

subacute (ˌsʌbə'kjuːt) *adj* intermediate between acute and chronic

subadar *or* **subahdar** ('suːbəˌdɑː) *n* (formerly) the chief native officer of a company of Indian soldiers in the British service. Also called: **subah** [C17 via Urdu from Persian, from *sūba* province + *-dār* holding]

subah ('suːbɑː) *n* (in India) **1** a province in the Mogul empire **2** another word for **subadar** [C18 via Urdu and Persian from Arabic *sūba* province]

subalpine (sʌb'ælpaɪn) *adj* **1** situated in or relating to the regions at the foot of mountains **2** (of plants) growing below the treeline in mountainous regions

subaltern ('sʌbᵊltən) *n* **1** a commissioned officer below the rank of captain in certain armies, esp the British **2** a person of inferior rank or position **3** *logic* **a** the relation of one proposition to another when the first is implied by the second, esp the relation of a particular to a universal proposition **b** *(as modifier)*: *a subaltern relation* ▷ *adj* **4** of inferior position or rank [C16 from Late Latin *subalternus*, from Latin SUB- + *alternus* alternate, from *alter* the other]

subalternate (sʌb'ɔːltənɪt) *adj* **1** (of leaves) having an arrangement intermediate between alternate and opposite **2** following in turn **3** of lesser quality or status > **subalternation** (sʌbˌɔːltə'neɪʃən) *n*

subantarctic (ˌsʌbænt'ɑːktɪk) *adj* of or relating to latitudes immediately north of the Antarctic Circle

subapostolic (ˌsʌbæpə'stɒlɪk) *adj Christianity* of or

relating to the era after that of the Apostles

subaqua (ˌsʌbˈækwə) *adj* of or relating to underwater sport: *subaqua swimming; a subaqua club* [from SUB- + Latin *aqua* water]

subaquatic (ˌsʌbəˈkwætɪk, -ˈkwɒt-) *adj* **1** living or growing partly in water and partly on land **2** of or relating to conditions, existence, or activities under water

subaqueous (sʌbˈeɪkwɪəs, -ˈækwɪ-) *adj* occurring, appearing, formed, or used under water

subarctic (sʌbˈɑːktɪk) *adj* of or relating to latitudes immediately south of the Arctic Circle

subarid (sʌbˈærɪd) *adj* receiving slightly more rainfall than arid regions; moderately dry

subassembly (ˌsʌbəˈsɛmblɪ) *n, pl* **-blies** a number of machine components integrated into a unit forming part of a larger assembly

subastral (sʌbˈæstrəl) *adj* a rare word for **terrestrial**

subatomic (ˌsʌbəˈtɒmɪk) *adj* **1** of, relating to, or being a particle making up an atom or a process occurring within atoms: *the electron is a subatomic particle* **2** having dimensions smaller than atomic dimensions

subaudition (ˌsʌbɔːˈdɪʃən) *n* **1** something that is not directly stated but implied **2** the ability or act of understanding that which is only implied [C18 from Late Latin *subaudīre*, from SUB- + Latin *audīre* to hear]

subauricular (ˌsʌbɔːˈrɪkjʊlə) *adj anatomy* situated below the auricle of the ear

subaxillary (ˌsʌbˈæksɪlərɪ) *adj* **1** situated or growing beneath the axil of a plant: *subaxillary bracts* **2** situated beneath the armpit

subbase (ˈsʌbˌbeɪs) *n* the lowest part of a pedestal, base, or skirting. Compare **surbase**

subbasement (ˈsʌbˌbeɪsmənt) *n* an underground storey of a building beneath the main basement

subbass *or* **subbase** (ˈsʌbˌbeɪs) *n* another name for **bourdon**

Subbuteo (səˈbjuːtɪəʊ) *n trademark* a football game played on a table, with toy players affixed to rounded bases which are flicked with the fingers [C20 arbitrarily named, from Latin *subbuteo,* the specific name of the hobby hawk *Falco subbuteo*]

subcalibre *or US* **subcaliber** (sʌbˈkælɪbə) *adj* **1** (of a projectile) having a calibre less than that of the firearm from which it is discharged and therefore either fitted with a disc or fired through a tube inserted into the barrel **2** of, relating to, or firing subcalibre projectiles

subcarrier (ˈsʌbˌkærɪə) *n* a subsidiary carrier wave that is modulated with information and applied as modulation to a main carrier wave that is already modulated with other information

subcartilaginous (sʌbˌkɑːtɪˈlædʒɪnəs) *adj* **1** composed partly of cartilage: *a subcartilaginous skeleton* **2** situated beneath a cartilage or a cartilaginous structure

subcelestial (ˌsʌbsɪˈlɛstɪəl) *adj* **1** beneath the heavens; terrestrial ▷ *n* **2** a subcelestial object

subception (səbˈsɛpʃən) *n psychol* another word for **subliminal perception**

subchloride (sʌbˈklɔːraɪd) *n* a chloride of an element that contains less chlorine than its common chloride

subclass (ˈsʌbˌklɑːs) *n* **1** a principal subdivision of a class **2** *biology* a taxonomic group that is a subdivision of a class **3** *maths* another name for **subset** (sense 1) ▷ *vb* **4** (*tr*) to assign to a subclass

sub-clause *n* a subordinate section of a larger clause in a document, contract, etc

subclavian (sʌbˈkleɪvɪən) *adj anatomy* (of an artery, vein, area, etc) situated below the clavicle [C17 from New Latin *subclāvius,* from Latin SUB- + *clavis* key]

subclimax (sʌbˈklaɪmæks) *n ecology* a community in which development has been arrested before climax has been attained > **subclimactic** (ˌsʌbklaɪˈmæktɪk) *adj*

subclinical (sʌbˈklɪnɪkˀl) *adj med* of or relating to the stage in the course of a disease before the symptoms are first noted > **sub'clinically** *adv*

subcommission (ˈsʌbkəˌmɪʃən) *n* a committee of people answering to a larger commission

subcommittee (ˈsʌbkəˌmɪtɪ) *n* a distinct and often subordinate division of a committee

subconscious (sʌbˈkɒnʃəs) *adj* **1** acting or existing without one's awareness: *subconscious motive* ▷ *n* **2** *psychoanal* that part of the mind which is on the fringe of consciousness and contains material of which it is possible to become aware by redirecting attention. Compare **preconscious** (sense 2), **unconscious** (sense 5) > **sub'consciously** *adv* > **sub'consciousness** *n*

subcontinent (sʌbˈkɒntɪnənt) *n* a large land mass that is a distinct part of a continent, such as India is of Asia > **subcontinental** (ˌsʌbkɒntɪˈnɛntˀl) *adj*

subcontract *n* (sʌbˈkɒntrækt) **1** a subordinate contract under which the supply of materials, services, or labour is let out to someone other than a party to the main contract ▷ *vb* (ˌsʌbkənˈtrækt) **2** (*intr;* often foll by *for*) to enter into or make a subcontract **3** (*tr*) to let out (work) on a subcontract

subcontractor (ˌsʌbkənˈtræktə) *n* a person, company, etc, that enters into a subcontract, esp a firm that undertakes to complete part of another's contract

subcontrary (sʌbˈkɒntrərɪ) *logic* ▷ *adj* **1** (of a pair of propositions) related such that they cannot both be false at once, although they may be true together. Compare **contrary** (sense 5), **contradictory** (sense 3) ▷ *n, pl* **-ries** **2** a statement that cannot be false when a given statement is false

subcortex (sʌbˈkɔːtɛks) *n, pl* **-tices** (-tɪˌsiːz) *anatomy* the matter of the brain situated beneath the cerebral cortex > **subcortical** (sʌbˈkɔːtɪkˀl) *adj*

subcritical (sʌbˈkrɪtɪkˀl) *adj physics* (of a nuclear reaction, power station, etc) having or involving a chain reaction that is not self-sustaining; not yet critical

subculture *n* (ˈsʌbˌkʌltʃə) **1** a subdivision of a national culture or an enclave within it with a distinct integrated network of behaviour, beliefs, and attitudes **2** a culture of microorganisms derived from another culture ▷ *vb* (sʌbˈkʌltʃə) **3** (*tr*) to inoculate (bacteria from one culture medium) onto another medium > **sub'cultural** *adj*

subcutaneous (ˌsʌbkjuːˈteɪnɪəs) *adj med* situated, used, or introduced beneath the skin: *a subcutaneous injection* [C17 from Late Latin *subcutāneus,* from SUB- + Latin *cutis* skin + -EOUS] > **ˌsubcu'taneously** *adv*

subdeacon (sʌbˈdiːkən) *n chiefly RC Church* **1** a cleric who assists at High Mass **2** (formerly) a person ordained to the lowest of the major orders > **subdeaconate** (sʌbˈdiːkənɪt) *n*

subdelirium (ˌsʌbdəˈlɪrɪəm) *n, pl* **-liriums** *or* **-liria** (-ˈlɪrɪə) mild or intermittent delirium

subdiaconate (ˌsʌbdaɪˈækənɪt, -ˌneɪt) *n* the rank or office of a subdeacon [C18 from Medieval Latin *subdiaconus* subdeacon + -ATE²; see DEACON] > ˌsubdi'aconal *adj*

subdistrict (ˈsʌbˌdɪstrɪkt) *n* **a** a smaller part of a larger area marked off for administrative or other purposes **b** (*as modifier*): *subdistrict regional police*

subdivide (ˌsʌbdɪˈvaɪd, ˈsʌbdɪˌvaɪd) *vb* **1** to divide (something) resulting from an earlier division **2** (*tr*) *US and Canadian* to divide (land) into lots for sale > ˌsubdi'vider *n*

subdivision (ˈsʌbdɪˌvɪʒən) *n* **1** the process, instance, or state of being divided again following upon an earlier division **2** a portion that is the result of subdividing **3** *US and Canadian* a tract of land for building resulting from subdividing land **4** *Canadian* a housing development built on such a tract > ˌsubdi'visional *adj*

subdominant (sʌbˈdɒmɪnənt) *music* ▷ *n* **1** the fourth degree of a major or minor scale **2** a key or chord based on this ▷ *adj* **3** of or relating to the subdominant

subduct (səbˈdʌkt) *vb* (*tr*) **1** *physiol* to draw or turn (the eye, etc) downwards **2** *rare* to take away; deduct [C17 from Latin *subdūcere,* from SUB- + *dūcere* to lead, bring]

subduction (səbˈdʌkʃən) *n* **1** the act of subducting, esp of turning the eye downwards **2** *geology* the process of one tectonic plate sliding under another, resulting in tensions and faulting in the earth's crust, with earthquakes and volcanic eruptions

subduction zone *n geology* a long narrow, often arcuate, zone along which subduction takes place

subdue (səbˈdjuː) *vb* **-dues, -duing, -dued** (*tr*) **1** to establish ascendancy over by force **2** to overcome and bring under control, as by intimidation or persuasion **3** to hold in check or repress (feelings, emotions, etc) **4** to render less intense or less conspicuous [C14 *sobdue,* from Old French *soduire* to mislead, from Latin *subdūcere* to remove; English sense influenced by Latin *subdere* to subject] > **sub'duable** *adj* > **sub'duably** *adv* > **sub'dual** *n*

subdued (səbˈdjuːd) *adj* **1** cowed, passive, or shy **2** gentle or quiet: *a subdued whisper* **3** (of colours, etc) not harsh or bright: *subdued lighting* > **sub'duedly** *adv* > **sub'duedness** *n*

subdural (sʌbˈdjʊərəl) *adj anatomy* between the dura mater and the arachnoid: *subdural haematoma*

subedit (sʌbˈɛdɪt) *vb* to edit and correct (written or printed material)

subeditor (sʌbˈɛdɪtə) *n* a person who checks and edits copy, esp on a newspaper

subequatorial (ˌsʌbˌɛkwəˈtɔːrɪəl) *adj* situated in or characteristic of regions immediately north or south of equatorial regions

suberic acid (sjuːˈbɛrɪk) *n* another name for **octanedioic acid** [C18 from French *subérique,* from Latin *sūber* cork (from which the acid is obtained)]

suberin (ˈsjuːbərɪn) *n* a fatty or waxy substance that is present in the walls of cork cells, making them impermeable to water and resistant to decay [C19 from Latin *sūber* cork + -IN]

suberize *or* **suberise** (ˈsjuːbəˌraɪz) *vb* (*tr*) *botany* to impregnate (cell walls) with suberin during the formation of corky tissue > ˌsuberi'zation *or* ˌsuberi'sation *n*

suberose (ˈsjuːbəˌrəʊs), **subereous** (sjuːˈbɛrɪəs) *or* **suberic** (sjuːˈbɛrɪk) *adj botany* relating to, resembling, or consisting of cork; corky

subfamily (ˈsʌbˌfæmɪlɪ) *n, pl* **-lies** **1** *biology* a taxonomic group that is a subdivision of a family **2** any analogous subdivision, as of a family of languages

subfloor (ˈsʌbˌflɔː) *n* a rough floor that forms a base for a finished floor

subfusc (ˈsʌbfʌsk) *adj* **1** devoid of brightness or appeal; drab, dull, or dark ▷ *n* **2** (at Oxford University) formal academic dress [C18 from Latin *subfuscus* dusky, from *fuscus* dark]

subgenus (sʌbˈdʒiːnəs, -ˈdʒɛn-, ˈsʌbˌdʒiːnəs, -ˌdʒɛn-) *n, pl* **-genera** (-ˈdʒɛnərə) *or* **-genuses** *biology* a taxonomic group that is a subdivision of a genus but of higher rank than a species > **subgeneric** (ˌsʌbdʒəˈnɛrɪk) *adj*

subglacial (sʌbˈgleɪsɪəl) *adj* formed or occurring at the bottom of a glacier > **sub'glacially** *adv*

subgrade (ˈsʌbˌgreɪd) *n* the ground beneath a roadway or pavement

subgroup (ˈsʌbˌgruːp) *n* **1** a distinct and often subordinate division of a group **2** a mathematical group whose members are members of another group, both groups being subject to the same rule of combination

subha (ˈsuːbɑː) *n Islam* a string of beads used in praying and meditating [from Arabic]

subharmonic (ˌsʌbhɑːˈmɒnɪk) *n* a fraction of a frequency

subheading (ˈsʌbˌhɛdɪŋ) *or* **subhead** *n* **1** the heading or title of a subdivision or subsection of a printed work **2** a division subordinate to a main heading or title

subhuman (sʌbˈhjuːmən) *adj* **1** of, relating to, or designating animals that are below man (*Homo*

S

sapiens) in evolutionary development **2** less than human

subimago (ˌsʌbɪ'meɪɡəʊ) *n, pl* **-imagoes** or **-imagines** (-ɪ'mædʒəˌniːz) the first winged stage of the mayfly, with dull opaque wings, known to anglers as a **dun**, before it metamorphoses into the shiny gauzy imago or **spinner**

subindex (sʌb'ɪndɛks) *n, pl* **-dices** (-dɪˌsiːz) or **-dexes 1** another word for **subscript** (sense 2) **2** *US* an index to a subcategory

subinfeudate (ˌsʌbɪn'fjuːdeɪt) *vb* to grant (lands) by subinfeudation

subinfeudation (ˌsʌbɪnfjʊ'deɪʃən) *n* **1** (in feudal society) the granting of land by a vassal to another man who became his vassal **2** the tenure or relationship so established

subinfeudatory (ˌsʌbɪn'fjuːdətərɪ, -trɪ) (in feudal society) *n, pl* **-ries 1** a man who held his fief by a subinfeudation ▷ *adj* **2** of or relating to subinfeudation

subirrigate (sʌb'ɪrɪˌɡeɪt) *vb* to irrigate (land) by means of an underground system of pipe lines or by natural moisture in the subsoil > ˌsubirri'gation *n*

subitize or **subitise** ('sʌbɪˌtaɪz) *vb psychol* to perceive the number of (a group of items) at a glance and without counting: *the maximum number of items that can be subitized is about five* [c20 from Latin *subitus* sudden + -IZE]

subito ('suːbɪˌtəʊ) *adv music* (preceding or following a dynamic marking, etc) suddenly; immediately. Abbreviation: **sub** [c18 via Italian from Latin: suddenly, from *subitus* sudden, from *subīre* to approach, from SUB- (indicating stealth) + *īre* to go]

subj. *abbreviation for* **1** subject **2** subjective(ly) **3** subjunctive

subjacent (sʌb'dʒeɪsᵊnt) *adj* **1** forming a foundation; underlying **2** lower than though not directly below: *tall peaks and their subjacent valley* [c16 from Latin *subjacēre* to lie close, adjoin, be under, from SUB- + *jacēre* to lie] > sub'jacency *n* > sub'jacently *adv*

subject *n* ('sʌbdʒɪkt) **1 a** the predominant theme or topic, as of a book, discussion, etc **b** (*in combination*): *subject-heading* **2** any branch of learning considered as a course of study **3** *grammar, logic* a word, phrase, or formal expression about which something is predicated or stated in a sentence; for example, *the cat* in the sentence *The cat catches mice* **4** a person or thing that undergoes experiment, analysis, treatment, etc **5** a person who lives under the rule of a monarch, government, etc **6** an object, figure, scene, etc, as selected by an artist or photographer for representation **7** *philosophy* **a** that which thinks or feels as opposed to the object of thinking and feeling; the self or the mind **b** a substance as opposed to its attributes **8** *Also* called: **theme** *music* a melodic or thematic phrase used as the principal motif of a fugue, the basis from which the musical material is derived in a sonata-form movement, or the recurrent figure in a rondo **9** *logic* **a** the term of a categorial statement of which something is predicated **b** the reference or denotation of the subject term of a statement. The subject of *John is tall* is not the name *John*, but John himself **10** an originating motive **11 change the subject** to select a new topic of conversation ▷ *adj* ('sʌbdʒɪkt) (*usually postpositive* and *foll by to*) **12** being under the power or sovereignty of a ruler, government, etc: *subject peoples* **13** showing a tendency (towards): *a child subject to indiscipline* **14** exposed or vulnerable: *subject to ribaldry* **15** conditional upon: *the results are subject to correction* ▷ *adv* **16 subject to** (*preposition*) under the condition that: *we accept, subject to her agreement* ▷ *vb* (səb'dʒɛkt) (*tr*) **17** (*foll by to*) to cause to undergo the application (of): *they subjected him to torture* **18** (*often passive; foll by to*) to expose or render vulnerable or liable (to some experience): *he was subjected to great danger* **19** (*foll by to*) to bring

under the control or authority (of): *to subject a soldier to discipline* **20** *now rare* to subdue or subjugate **21** *rare* to present for consideration; submit **22** *obsolete* to place below ▷ Abbreviation: **subj** [c14 from Latin *subjectus* brought under, from *subicere* to place under, from SUB- + *jacere* to throw] > sub'jectable *adj* > subjecta'bility *n* > 'subjectless *adj* > 'subject-ˌlike *adj*

subject catalogue *n library science* a catalogue with entries arranged by subject in a classified sequence

subjectify (səb'dʒɛktɪˌfaɪ) *vb* **-fies, -fying, -fied** (*tr*) to make subjective or interpret subjectively > subjectifi'cation *n*

subjection (səb'dʒɛkʃən) *n* the act or process of subjecting or the state of being subjected

subjective (səb'dʒɛktɪv) *adj* **1** belonging to, proceeding from, or relating to the mind of the thinking subject and not the nature of the object being considered **2** of, relating to, or emanating from a person's emotions, prejudices, etc: *subjective views* **3** relating to the inherent nature of a person or thing; essential **4** existing only as perceived and not as a thing in itself **5** *med* (of a symptom, condition, etc) experienced only by the patient and incapable of being recognized or studied by anyone else **6** *grammar* denoting a case of nouns and pronouns, esp in languages having only two cases, that identifies the subject of a finite verb and (in formal use in English) is selected for predicate complements, as in *It is I*. See also **nominative** (sense 1) ▷ *n* **7** *grammar* **a** the subjective case **b** a subjective word or speech element ▷ Abbreviation: **subj** Compare **objective** > sub'jectively *adv* > ˌsubjec'tivity or sub'jectiveness *n*

subjective idealism *n philosophy* the theory that all experience is of ideas in the mind

subjective intension *n logic* the associations that an expression has for an individual; the intension he believes it to have

subjectivism (səb'dʒɛktɪˌvɪzəm) *n* **1** the meta-ethical doctrine that there are no absolute moral values but that these are variable in the same way as taste is **2** any similar philosophical theory, for example, about truth or perception **3** any theological theory that attaches primary importance to religious experience **4** the quality or condition of being subjective > sub'jectivist *n* > subjecti'vistic *adj* > subjecti'vistically *adv*

subject matter *n* the substance or main theme of a book, discussion, debate, etc

subject-raising *n transformational grammar* a rule that moves the subject of a complement clause into the clause in which it is embedded, as in the derivation of *He is likely to be late* from *It is likely that he will be late*

subjoin (sʌb'dʒɔɪn) *vb* (*tr*) to add or attach at the end of something spoken, written, etc [c16 from French *subjoindre*, from Latin *subjungere* to add to, from *sub-* in addition + *jungere* to JOIN] > sub'joinder *n* > subjunction (sʌb'dʒʌŋkʃən) *n*

sub judice ('dʒuːdɪsɪ) *adj* (*usually postpositive*) before a court of law or a judge; under judicial consideration [Latin]

subjugate ('sʌbdʒʊˌɡeɪt) *vb* (*tr*) **1** to bring into subjection **2** to make subservient or submissive [c15 from Late Latin *subjugāre* to subdue, from Latin SUB- + *jugum* yoke] > subjugable ('sʌbdʒəɡəbᵊl) *adj* > ˌsubju'gation *n* > 'subjuˌgator *n*

subjunctive (səb'dʒʌŋktɪv) *adj* **1** *grammar* denoting a mood of verbs used when the content of the clause is being doubted, supposed, feared true, etc, rather than being asserted. The rules for its use and the range of meanings it may possess vary considerably from language to language. In the following sentence, *were* is in the subjunctive: *I'd think very seriously about that if I were you*. Compare **indicative** ▷ *n* **2** *grammar* **a** the subjunctive mood **b** a verb in this mood ▷ Abbreviation: **subj** [c16 via Late Latin *subjunctīvus*, from Latin *subjungere* to SUBJOIN] > sub'junctively *adv*

subkingdom (sʌb'kɪŋdəm) *n biology* a taxonomic group that is a subdivision of a kingdom

sublapsarianism (ˌsʌblæp'sɛərɪəˌnɪzəm) *n* another word for **infralapsarianism** [C17 *sublapsarian*, via New Latin, from Latin SUB- + *lāpsus* a fall] > sublap'sarian *n, adj*

sublease *n* ('sʌbˌliːs) **1** a lease of property made by a person who is himself a lessee or tenant of that property ▷ *vb* (sʌb'liːs) **2** to grant a sublease of (property); sublet **3** (*tr*) to take, obtain, or hold by sublease > sublessee (ˌsʌbleˈsiː) *n* > sublessor (ˌsʌbleˈsɔː) *n*

sublet *vb* (sʌb'lɛt) **-lets, -letting, -let 1** to grant a sublease of (property) **2** to let out (work, etc) under a subcontract ▷ *n* ('sʌbˌlɛt) **3** *informal, chiefly US* a sublease

sublieutenant (ˌsʌbləˈtɛnənt) *n* the most junior commissioned officer in the Royal Navy and certain other navies > ˌsublieu'tenancy *n*

sublimate ('sʌblɪˌmeɪt) *vb* **1** *psychol* to direct the energy of (a primitive impulse, esp a sexual one) into activities that are considered to be socially more acceptable **2** (*tr*) to make purer; refine ▷ *n* **3** *chem* the material obtained when a substance is sublimed ▷ *adj* **4** exalted or purified [c16 from Latin *sublimāre* to elevate, from *sublimis* lofty; see SUBLIME] > sublimable ('sʌbləməbᵊl) *adj*

sublimation (ˌsʌblɪ'meɪʃən) *n* **1** (in Freudian psychology) the diversion of psychic energy derived from sexual impulses into nonsexual activity, esp of a creative nature **2** the process or an instance of sublimating **3** something sublimated **4** *chem* the process or instance or subliming

sublime (sə'blaɪm) *adj* **1** of high moral, aesthetic, intellectual, or spiritual value; noble; exalted **2** inspiring deep veneration, awe, or uplifting emotion because of its beauty, nobility, grandeur, or immensity **3** unparalleled; supreme: *a sublime compliment* **4** *poetic* of proud bearing or aspect **5** *archaic* raised up ▷ *n* **the sublime 6** something that is sublime **7** the ultimate degree or perfect example: *the sublime of folly* ▷ *vb* **8** (*tr*) to make higher or purer **9** to change or cause to change directly from a solid to a vapour or gas without first melting: *to sublime iodine; many mercury salts sublime when heated* **10** to undergo or cause to undergo this process followed by a reverse change directly from a vapour to a solid: *to sublime iodine onto glass* [c14 from Latin *sublīmis* lofty, perhaps from *sub-* up to + *līmen* lintel] > sub'limely *adv* > sublimity (sə'blɪmɪtɪ) *n*

Sublime Porte *n* the full name of the **Porte**

subliminal (sʌb'lɪmɪnᵊl) *adj* **1** resulting from processes of which the individual is not aware **2** (of stimuli) less than the minimum intensity or duration required to elicit a response [c19 from Latin SUB- below + *līmen* threshold] > sub'liminally *adv*

subliminal advertising *n* a form of advertising on film or television that employs subliminal images to influence the viewer unconsciously

subliminal perception *n psychol* perception of or reaction to a stimulus that occurs without awareness or consciousness. Also called: subception

sublingual (sʌb'lɪŋɡwəl) *adj anatomy* situated beneath the tongue

sublittoral (sʌb'lɪtərəl) *adj* **1** (of marine organisms) growing, living, or situated close to the seashore: *a sublittoral plant* **2** of or relating to the zone between the low tide mark and 100 m depth

sublunary (sʌb'luːnərɪ) *adj* **1** situated between the moon and the earth **2** of or relating to the earth or world [c16 via Late Latin, from Latin SUB- + *lūna* moon]

subluxate (sʌb'lʌkseɪt) *vb* (*tr*) *pathol* to partially dislocate > sublux'ation *n*

sub-machine-gun *n* a portable automatic or semiautomatic light gun with a short barrel, firing pistol ammunition: designed to be fired from the hip or shoulder

submarginal (sʌbˈmɑːdʒɪnəl) *adj* **1** below the minimum requirements **2** situated close to the margin of an organ or part **3** (of land) infertile and unprofitable for cultivation > subˈmarginally *adv*

submarine (ˈsʌbməˌriːn, ˌsʌbməˈriːn) *n* **1** a vessel, esp one designed for warfare, capable of operating for protracted periods below the surface of the sea. Often shortened to: **sub 2** (*modifier*) **a** of or relating to a submarine: *a submarine captain* **b** occurring or situated below the surface of the sea: *a submarine cable*

submariner (sʌbˈmærɪnə) *n* a crewman in a submarine

submaxillary (ˌsʌbmækˈsɪləɪ) *adj* of, relating to, or situated close to the lower jaw

submaxillary gland *n* (in mammals) either of a pair of salivary glands situated on each side behind the lower jaw

submediant (sʌbˈmiːdɪənt) *music* ▷ *n* **1** the sixth degree of a major or minor scale **2** a key or chord based on this ▷ *adj* **3** of or relating to the submediant ▷ Also (US and Canadian): **superdominant**

submental (sʌbˈmɛntəl) *adj anatomy* situated beneath the chin [from SUB- + Latin *mentum* chin]

submerge (səbˈmɜːdʒ) or **submerse** (səbˈmɜːs) **1** to plunge, sink, or dive or cause to plunge, sink, or dive below the surface of water, etc **2** (*tr*) to cover with water or some other liquid **3** (*tr*) to hide; suppress **4** (*tr*) to overwhelm, as with work, difficulties, etc [c17 from Latin *submergere*, from SUB- + *mergere* to immerse] > subˈmergence or submersion (səbˈmɜːʃən) *n*

submerged (səbˈmɜːdʒd) or **submersed** (səbˈmɜːst) *adj* **1** (of plants or plant parts) growing beneath the surface of the water **2** hidden; obscured **3** overwhelmed or overburdened

submerged arc welding *n* a type of heavy electric-arc welding using mechanically fed bare wire with the arc submerged in powdered flux to keep out oxygen

submersible (səbˈmɜːsəbəl) or **submergible** (səbˈmɜːdʒɪbəl) *adj* **1** able to be submerged **2** capable of operating under water, etc ▷ *n* **3** a vessel designed to operate under water for short periods **4** a submarine taking one or more men that is designed and equipped to carry out work in deep water below the levels at which divers can work > subˈmersiˈbility or subˈmergiˈbility *n*

submicroscopic (ˌsʌbmaɪkrəˈskɒpɪk) *adj* too small to be seen through an optical microscope > ˌsubmicroˈscopically *adv*

subminiature (sʌbˈmɪnɪətʃə) *adj* smaller than miniature

subminiature camera *n* a pocket-sized camera, usually using 16 millimetre film with a very fine grain so that negatives can produce considerably enlarged prints

subminiaturize or **subminiaturise** (sʌbˈmɪnɪətʃəˌraɪz) *vb* (*tr*) to make subminiature, as in the manufacture of electronic equipment, etc > subˌminiaturiˈzation or subˌminiaturiˈsation *n*

submiss (səbˈmɪs) *adj* archaic or poetic **1** docile; submissive **2** soft in tone [c16 from Latin *submissus* lowered, gentle, from *submittere* to reduce, from SUB- + *mittere* to send]

submission (səbˈmɪʃən) *n* **1** an act or instance of submitting **2** something submitted; a proposal, argument, etc **3** the quality or condition of being submissive to another **4** the act of referring a document, etc, for the consideration of someone else **5** *law* **a** an agreement by the parties to a dispute to refer the matter to arbitration **b** the instrument referring a disputed matter to arbitration **6** (in wrestling) the act of causing such pain to one's opponent that he submits. Compare **fall** (sense 48) **7** *archaic* a confession of error

submissive (səbˈmɪsɪv) *adj* of, tending towards, or indicating submission, humility, or servility

> subˈmissively *adv* > subˈmissiveness *n*

submit (səbˈmɪt) *vb* **-mits, -mitting, -mitted 1** (often foll by *to*) to yield (oneself), as to the will of another person, a superior force, etc **2** (foll by *to*) to subject or be voluntarily subjected (to analysis, treatment, etc) **3** (*tr;* often foll by *to*) to refer (something to someone) for judgment or consideration: *to submit a claim* **4** (*tr;* may take a *clause as object*) to state, contend, or propose deferentially **5** (*intr;* often foll by *to*) to defer or accede (to the decision, opinion, etc, of another) [c14 from Latin *submittere* to place under, from SUB- + *mittere* to send] > subˈmittable or subˈmissible *adj* > subˈmittal *n* > subˈmitter *n*

submontane (sʌbˈmɒnteɪn) *adj* **1** situated on or characteristic of the lower slopes of a mountain **2** beneath a mountain or mountain range [c19 from Latin SUB- + *mōns* mountain] > subˈmontanely *adv*

submucosa (ˌsʌbmjuːˈkəʊsə) *n, pl* -cosae (-ˈkəʊsiː) *anatomy* the connective tissue beneath a mucous membrane

submultiple (sʌbˈmʌltɪpəl) *n* **1** a number that can be divided into another number an integral number of times without a remainder ▷ *adj* **2** being a submultiple of a quantity or number

subnormal (sʌbˈnɔːməl) *adj* **1** less than the normal **2** having a low intelligence, esp having an IQ of less than 70 ▷ *n* **3** a subnormal person > subnormality (ˌsʌbnɔːˈmælɪtɪ) *n* > subˈnormally *adv*

subnuclear (sʌbˈnjuːklɪə) *adj* **1** of or relating to particles within the nucleus of an atom **2** of a lesser level of organization than the nucleus of an atom

suboceanic (ˌsʌbˌəʊʃɪˈænɪk) *adj* formed or situated beneath the ocean or ocean floor

subofficer (sʌbˈɒfɪsə) *n* a subordinate officer

suborbital (sʌbˈɔːbɪtəl) *adj* **1** (of a rocket, missile, etc) having a flight path that is less than one complete orbit of the earth or other celestial body **2** *anatomy* situated beneath the orbit of the eye

suborder (ˈsʌbˌɔːdə) *n biology* a taxonomic group that is a subdivision of an order > subˈordinal *adj*

subordinary (sʌbˈɔːdɪnərɪ, -dɪnrɪ) *n, pl* -naries any of several heraldic bearings of secondary importance to the ordinary, such as the lozenge, the orle, and the fret

subordinate *adj* (səˈbɔːdɪnɪt) **1** of lesser order or importance **2** under the authority or control of another: *a subordinate functionary* ▷ *n* (səˈbɔːdɪnɪt) **3** a person or thing that is subordinate ▷ *vb* (səˈbɔːdɪˌneɪt) (*tr;* usually foll by *to*) **4** to put in a lower rank or position (than) **5** to make subservient: *to subordinate mind to heart* [c15 from Medieval Latin *subordināre*, from Latin SUB- + *ordō* rank] > subˈordinately *adv* > subˌordiˈnation or subˈordinateness *n* > subˈordinative *adj*

subordinate clause *n grammar* a clause with an adjectival, adverbial, or nominal function, rather than one that functions as a separate sentence in its own right. Compare **coordinate clause, main clause**

subordinated debt *n commerce* a debt that an unsecured creditor can only claim, in the event of a liquidation, after the claims of secured creditors have been paid

subordinating conjunction *n* a conjunction that introduces subordinate clauses, such as *if, because, although,* and *until.* Compare **coordinating conjunction**

subordinationism (səˌbɔːdɪˈneɪʃəˌnɪzəm) *n* either of two interpretations of the doctrine of the Trinity, often regarded as heretical, according to which the Son is subordinate to the Father or the Holy Ghost is subordinate to both > subˌordiˈnationist *n*

suborn (səˈbɔːn) *vb* (*tr*) **1** to bribe, incite, or instigate (a person) to commit a wrongful act **2** *criminal law* to induce (a witness) to commit perjury [c16 from Latin *subornāre*, from *sub-* secretly + *ornāre* to furnish] > subornation (ˌsʌbɔːˈneɪʃən) *n* > subˈornative (sʌˈbɔːnətɪv) *adj* > subˈorner *n*

Subotica (*Serbo-Croat* ˈsubɔtitsa) *n* a town in NE Serbia and Montenegro, in Serbia near the border with Hungary: agricultural and industrial centre. Pop: 107 139 (2002). Hungarian name: **Szabadka**

suboxide (sʌbˈɒksaɪd) *n* an oxide of an element containing less oxygen than the common oxide formed by the element: *carbon suboxide,* C_2O_3

subphylum (sʌbˈfaɪləm) *n, pl* -la (-lə) *biology* a taxonomic group that is a subdivision of a phylum > subˈphylar *adj*

subplot (ˈsʌbˌplɒt) *n* a subordinate or auxiliary plot in a novel, play, film, etc

subpoena (səbˈpiːnə) *n* **1** a writ issued by a court of justice requiring a person to appear before the court at a specified time ▷ *vb* -nas, -naing, -naed **2** (*tr*) to serve with a subpoena [c15 from Latin: under penalty]

subpopulation (ˌsʌbpɒpjʊˈleɪʃən) *n statistics* a subgroup of a statistical population

sub-post office *n* (in Britain) a post office run by a **sub-postmaster** or **sub-postmistress** as a self-employed agent for the Post Office

subprincipal (sʌbˈprɪnsɪpəl) *n* a vice-principal in a college, etc

subprogram (ˈsʌbˌprəʊgræm) *n computing* a part of a program that can be designed and tested independently

subregion (sʌbˈriːdʒən) *n* a subdivision of a region, esp a zoogeographical or ecological region > subˈregional *adj*

subreption (səbˈrɛpʃən) *n* **1** *now rare* the concealment of facts in order to obtain a benefit, esp an ecclesiastical benefit or, in Scots Law, a grant from the Crown. Compare **obreption 2** any deceitful misrepresentation or concealment of facts [c17 from Latin *subreptiō* theft, from *subripere,* from *sub-* secretly + *rapere* to seize] > subreptitious (ˌsʌbrɛpˈtɪʃəs) *adj*

subrogate (ˈsʌbrəˌgeɪt) *vb* (*tr*) *law* to put (one person or thing) in the place of another in respect of a right or claim [c16 from Latin *subrogāre,* from *sub-* in place of + *rogāre* to ask]

subrogation (ˌsʌbrəˈgeɪʃən) *n law* the substitution of one person or thing for another, esp the placing of a surety who has paid the debt in the place of the creditor, entitling him to payment from the original debtor

sub rosa (ˈrəʊzə) *adv* in secret [Latin, literally: under the rose; from the rose that, in ancient times, was hung over the council table, as a token of secrecy]

subroutine (ˈsʌbruːˌtiːn) *n* a section of a computer program that is stored only once but can be used when required at several different points in the program, thus saving space. Also called: **procedure**

sub-Saharan *adj* in, of, or relating to Africa south of the Sahara desert

subscapular (sʌbˈskæpjʊlə) *adj* **1** (of a muscle or artery) situated beneath the scapula ▷ *n* **2** any subscapular muscle or artery

subscribe (səbˈskraɪb) *vb* **1** (usually foll by *to*) to pay or promise to pay (a sum of money) as a contribution (to a fund or charity, for a magazine, etc), esp at regular intervals **2** to inscribe or sign (one's name, etc) at the end of a contract, will, or other document **3** (*intr;* foll by *to*) to give support or approval: *to subscribe to the theory of transubstantiation* [c15 from Latin *subscrībere* to write underneath, from SUB- + *scrībere* to write] > subˈscriber *n*

subscriber trunk dialling *n Brit* a service by which telephone subscribers can obtain trunk calls by dialling direct without the aid of an operator. Abbreviation: **STD**. US and Canadian equivalent: **direct distance dialing**

subscript (ˈsʌbskrɪpt) *adj* **1** *printing* (of a character) written or printed below the line. Compare **superscript** ▷ *n* **2** Also called: **subindex** a subscript character

subscription (səbˈskrɪpʃən) *n* **1** a payment or promise of payment for consecutive issues of a

S

magazine, newspaper, book, etc, over a specified period of time **2 a** the advance purchase of tickets for a series of concerts, operas, etc **b** (*as modifier*): *a subscription concert* **3** an amount of money paid or promised, as to a charity, or the fund raised in this way **4** an offer to buy shares or bonds issued by a company **5** the act of signing one's name to a document, etc **6** a signature or other appendage attached to the bottom of a document, etc **7** agreement, consent, or acceptance expressed by or as if by signing one's name **8** a signed document, statement, etc **9** *chiefly Brit* the membership dues or fees paid to a society or club **10** acceptance of a fixed body of articles of faith, doctrines, or principles laid down as universally binding upon all the members of a Church **11** *med* that part of a written prescription directing the pharmacist how to mix and prepare the ingredients: rarely seen today as modern drugs are mostly prepackaged by the manufacturers **12** an advance order for a new product **13 a** the sale of books, etc, prior to printing **b** (*as modifier*): *a subscription edition* **14** *archaic* allegiance; submission ▷ Abbreviation: **sub** > sub'scriptive *adj*

subscription library *n* a commercial lending library

subscription television *n* another name for **pay television**

subsection (ˈsʌbˌsɛkʃən) *n* a section of a section; subdivision

subsellium (sʌbˈsɛlɪəm) *n* a rare word for **misericord** (sense 1) [c19 from Latin, from sub- + *sella* seat]

subsequence (ˈsʌbsɪkwəns) *n* **1** the fact or state of being subsequent **2** a subsequent incident or occurrence **3** (ˌsʌbˈsiːkwəns) *maths* a sequence derived from a given sequence by selecting certain of its terms and retaining their order. Thus, <a₂, a₃> is a subsequence of <a₁, a₂, a₃>, while <a₃, a₂> is not

subsequent (ˈsʌbsɪkwənt) *adj* occurring after; succeeding [c15 from Latin *subsequēns* following on, from *subsequī*, from sub- near + *sequī* to follow] > 'subsequently *adv* > 'subsequentness *n*

subsere (ˈsʌbˌsɪə) *n* a secondary sere arising when the progress of a sere is towards its climax has been interrupted [c20 sub- + sere²]

subserve (səbˈsɜːv) *vb* (*tr*) **1** to be helpful or useful to **2** *obsolete* to be subordinate to [c17 from Latin *subservīre* to be subject to, from sub- + *servīre* to serve]

subservient (səbˈsɜːvɪənt) *adj* **1** obsequious in behaviour or attitude **2** serving as a means to an end **3** a less common word for **subordinate** (sense 2) [c17 from Latin *subserviēns* complying with, from *subservīre* to SUBSERVE] > sub'serviently *adv* > sub'servience or sub'serviency *n*

subset (ˈsʌbˌsɛt) *n* **1** *maths* **a** a set the members of which are all members of some given class: *A is a subset of B* is usually written A⊆B **b** **proper subset** one that is strictly contained within a larger class and excludes some of its members. Symbol: A⊂B **2** a set within a larger set

subshrub (ˈsʌbˌʃrʌb) *n* a small bushy plant that is woody except for the tips of the branches > 'sub,shrubby *adj*

subside (səbˈsaɪd) *vb* (*intr*) **1** to become less loud, excited, violent, etc; abate **2** to sink or fall to a lower level **3** (of the surface of the earth, etc) to cave in; collapse **4** (of sediment, etc) to sink or descend to the bottom; settle [c17 from Latin *subsīdere* to settle down, from sub- down + *sīdere* to settle] > sub'sider *n*

subsidence (səbˈsaɪdᵊns, ˈsʌbsɪdᵊns) *n* **1** the act or process of subsiding or the condition of having subsided **2** *geology* the gradual sinking of landforms to a lower level as a result of earth movements, mining operations, etc

subsidiarity (səbˌsɪdɪˈærɪtɪ) *n* **1** (in the Roman Catholic Church) a principle of social doctrine that all social bodies exist for the sake of the

individual so that what individuals are able to do, society should not take over, and what small societies can do, larger societies should not take over **2** (in political systems) the principle of devolving decisions to the lowest practical level

subsidiary (səbˈsɪdɪərɪ) *adj* **1** serving to aid or supplement; auxiliary **2** of lesser importance; subordinate in function ▷ *n, pl* **-aries 3** a person who or thing that is subsidiary **4** short for **subsidiary company** [c16 from Latin *subsidiārius* supporting, from *subsidium* SUBSIDY] > sub'sidiarily *adv* > sub'sidiariness *n*

subsidiary coin *n* a coin of denomination smaller than that of the standard monetary unit

subsidiary company *n* a company with at least half of its capital stock owned by another company

subsidize or **subsidise** (ˈsʌbsɪˌdaɪz) *vb* (*tr*) **1** to aid or support with a subsidy **2** to obtain the aid of by means of a subsidy > ˌsubsi'dizable or ˌsubsi'disable *adj* > ˌsubsidi'zation or ˌsubsidi'sation *n* > 'subsiˌdizer or 'subsiˌdiser *n*

subsidy (ˈsʌbsɪdɪ) *n, pl* **-dies 1** a financial aid supplied by a government, as to industry, for reasons of public welfare, the balance of payments, etc **2** *English history* a financial grant made originally for special purposes by Parliament to the Crown **3** any monetary contribution, grant, or aid [c14 from Anglo-Norman *subsidie*, from Latin *subsidium* assistance, from *subsidēre* to remain, from sub- down + *sedēre* to sit]

subsist (səbˈsɪst) *vb* (*mainly intr*) **1** (often foll by *on*) to be sustained; manage to live: *to subsist on milk* **2** to continue in existence **3** (foll by *in*) to lie or reside by virtue (of); consist **4** *philosophy* **a** to exist as a concept or relation rather than a fact **b** to be conceivable **5** (*tr*) *obsolete* to provide with support [c16 from Latin *subsistere* to stand firm, from sub- up + *sistere* to make a stand] > sub'sistent *adj* > sub'sister *n*

subsistence (səbˈsɪstəns) *n* **1** the means by which one maintains life **2** the act or condition of subsisting **3** a thing that has real existence **4** the state of being inherent **5** *philosophy* an inferior mode of being ascribed to the references of general terms which do not in fact exist. See also **nonbeing**

subsistence allowance *n chiefly Brit* **1** an advance paid to an employee before his pay begins **2** a payment to an employee to reimburse expenses, as while on assignments

subsistence farming *n* a type of farming in which most of the produce (**subsistence crop**) is consumed by the farmer and his family, leaving little or nothing to be marketed

subsistence level *n* a standard of living barely adequate to support life

subsistence wage *n* the lowest wage upon which a worker and his family can survive

subsocial (sʌbˈsəʊʃəl) *adj* lacking a complex or definite social structure > sub'socially *adv*

subsoil (ˈsʌbˌsɔɪl) *n* **1 a** Also called: **undersoil** the layer of soil beneath the surface soil and overlying the bedrock **b** (*as modifier*): *a subsoil plough* ▷ *vb* **2** (*tr*) to plough (land) to a depth below the normal ploughing level and so break up the subsoil > 'subˌsoiler *n*

subsolar (sʌbˈsəʊlə) *adj* **1** (of a point on the earth) directly below the sun **2** situated between the tropics; equatorial

subsong (ˈsʌbˌsɒŋ) *n* a subdued form of birdsong modified from the full territorial song and used by some birds esp in courtship

subsonic (sʌbˈsɒnɪk) *adj* being, having, or travelling at a velocity below that of sound: *a subsonic aircraft*

subspecies (ˈsʌbˌspiːʃiːz) *n, pl* **-cies** *biology* a taxonomic group that is a subdivision of a species: usually occurs because of isolation within a species. Abbreviation: **ssp** > **subspecific** (ˌsʌbspɪˈsɪfɪk) *adj* > ˌsubspe'cifically *adv*

subspontaneous (ˌsʌbspɒnˈteɪnɪəs) *adj* (of a plant species, such as rhododendron) spreading naturally after having originally been introduced

subst. *abbreviation for* **1** substantive **2** substitute

substage (ˈsʌbˌsteɪdʒ) *n* the part of a microscope below the stage, usually consisting of an adjustable assembly holding a condenser lens for illuminating the specimen

substance (ˈsʌbstəns) *n* **1** the tangible matter of which a thing consists **2** a specific type of matter, esp a homogeneous material with a definite composition **3** the essence, meaning, etc, of a written or spoken thought **4** solid or meaningful quality **5** material density: *a vacuum has no substance* **6** material possessions or wealth: *a man of substance* **7** *philosophy* **a** the supposed immaterial substratum that can receive modifications and in which attributes and accidents inhere **b** a thing considered as a continuing whole that survives the changeability of its properties **8** *Christian Science* that which is eternal **9** a euphemistic term for any illegal drug **10 in substance** with regard to the salient points [c13 via Old French from Latin *substantia*, from *substāre*, from sub- + *stāre* to stand] > 'substanceless *adj*

substandard (sʌbˈstændəd) *adj* **1** below an established or required standard **2** another word for **nonstandard**

substantial (səbˈstænʃəl) *adj* **1** of a considerable size or value: *substantial funds* **2** worthwhile; important: *a substantial reform* **3** having wealth or importance **4** (of food or a meal) sufficient and nourishing **5** solid or strong in construction, quality, or character: *a substantial door* **6** real; actual; true: *the evidence is substantial* **7** of or relating to the basic or fundamental substance or aspects of a thing **8** *philosophy* of or relating to substance rather than to attributes, accidents, or modifications > **substantiality** (səbˌstænʃɪˈælɪtɪ) or sub'stantialness *n* > sub'stantially *adv*

substantialism (səbˈstænʃəˌlɪzəm) *n philosophy* **1** the doctrine that a substantial reality underlies phenomena **2** the doctrine that matter is a real substance > sub'stantialist *n*

substantialize or **substantialise** (səbˈstænʃəˌlaɪz) *vb* to make or become substantial or actual

substantia nigra (səbˈstænʃə ˈnaɪgrə) *n* a layer of grey matter in the brain that produces dopamine and contains pigmented nerve cells, loss of which has been associated with Parkinson's disease [c20 from Latin, literally: dark material]

substantiate (səbˈstænʃɪˌeɪt) *vb* (*tr*) **1** to establish as valid or genuine **2** to give form or real existence to [c17 from New Latin *substantiāre*, from Latin *substantia* SUBSTANCE] > subˌstanti'ation *n* > sub'stantiative *adj* > sub'stantiˌator *n*

substantive (ˈsʌbstəntɪv) *n* **1** *grammar* a noun or pronoun used in place of a noun ▷ *adj* **2** of, relating to, containing, or being the essential element of a thing **3** having independent function, resources, or existence **4** of substantial quantity **5** solid in foundation or basis **6** *grammar* denoting, relating to, or standing in place of a noun **7** (səbˈstæntɪv) relating to the essential legal principles administered by the courts, as opposed to practice and procedure. Compare **adjective** (sense 3) **8** (səbˈstæntɪv) (of a dye or colour) staining the material directly without use of a mordant ▷ Abbreviations: **s, sb, subst** [c15 from Late Latin *substantīvus*, from Latin *substāre* to stand beneath; see SUBSTANCE] > **substantival** (ˌsʌbstənˈtaɪvᵊl) *adj* > ˌsubstan'tivally *adv* > 'substantively *adv* > 'substantiveness *n*

substantive agreements (səbˈstæntɪv) *pl n* collective agreements that regulate jobs, pay, and conditions

substantive rank (səbˈstæntɪv) *n* a permanent rank in the armed services obtained by length of service, selection, etc

substantivize or **substantivise** (ˈsʌbstəntɪˌvaɪz)

vb (*tr*) to make (a word other than a noun) play the grammatical role of a noun in a sentence > ˌsubstantiviˈzation *or* ˌsubstantiviˈsation *n*

substation (ˈsʌbˌsteɪʃən) *n* **1** a subsidiary station **2** an installation at which electricity is received from one or more power stations for conversion from alternating to direct current, reducing the voltage, or switching before distribution by a low-tension network

substituent (sʌbˈstɪtjʊənt) *n* **1** *chem* an atom or group that replaces another atom or group in a molecule or can be regarded as replacing an atom in a parent compound ▷ *adj* **2** substituted or substitutable [C19 from Latin *substituere* to SUBSTITUTE]

substitute (ˈsʌbstɪˌtjuːt) *vb* **1** (often foll by *for*) to serve or cause to serve in place of another person or thing **2** *chem* to replace (an atom or group in a molecule) with (another atom or group) **3** *logic, maths* to replace (one expression) by (another) in the context of a third, as replacing *x* + *y* for *x* in 3*x* = *k* gives 3*x* + 3*y* = *k* ▷ *n* **4 a** a person or thing that serves in place of another, such as a player in a game who takes the place of an injured colleague **b** (*as modifier*): *a substitute goalkeeper.* Often shortened to: **sub 5** *grammar* another name for **pro-form 6** *Canadian* another name for **supply teacher 7** *nautical* another word for **repeater** (sense 5) **8** (formerly) a person paid to replace another due for military service [C16 from Latin *substituere*, from *sub-* in place of + *statuere* to set up] > ˌsubstiˈtutable *adj* > ˌsubstiˈtutaˈbility *n*

USAGE *Substitute* is sometimes wrongly used where *replace* is meant: *he replaced* (not *substituted*) *the worn tyre with a new one*

substitution (ˌsʌbstɪˈtjuːʃən) *n* **1** the act of substituting or state of being substituted **2** something or someone substituted **3** *maths* the replacement of a term of an equation by another that is known to have the same value in order to simplify the equation **4** *maths, logic* **a** the uniform replacement of one expression by another **b** substitution instance an expression so derived from another

substitutive (ˈsʌbstɪˌtjuːtɪv) *adj* **1** acting or able to act as a substitute **2** of or involving substitution > ˈsubstiˌtutively *adv*

substitutivity (ˌsʌbstɪtjuːˈtɪvɪtɪ) *n* *logic, philosophy* the principle that expressions with the same reference can be substituted for one another without affecting the truth-value of any context in which they occur. See also **transparent context, opaque context**

substrate (ˈsʌbstreɪt) *n* **1** *biochem* the substance upon which an enzyme acts **2** another word for **substratum 3** *electronics* the semiconductor base on which other material is deposited, esp in the construction of integrated circuits

substratum (sʌbˈstrɑːtəm, -ˈstreɪ-) *n, pl* **-strata** (-ˈstrɑːtə, -ˈstreɪtə) **1** any layer or stratum lying underneath another **2** a basis or foundation; groundwork **3** the nonliving material on which an animal or plant grows or lives **4** *geology* **a** the solid rock underlying soils, gravels, etc; bedrock **b** the surface to which a fixed organism is attached **5** *sociol* any of several subdivisions or grades within a stratum **6** *photog* a binding layer by which an emulsion is made to adhere to a glass or film base. Sometimes shortened to: **sub 7** *philosophy* substance considered as that in which attributes and accidents inhere **8** *linguistics* the language of an indigenous population when replaced by the language of a conquering or colonizing population, esp as it influences the form of the dominant language or of any mixed languages arising from their contact. Compare **superstratum** (sense 2) [C17 from New Latin, from Latin *substrātus* strewn beneath, from *substernere* to spread under, from *sub-* + *sternere* to spread] > subˈstrative *or* subˈstratal *adj*

substructure (ˈsʌbˌstrʌktʃə) *n* **1** a structure, pattern, etc, that forms the basis of anything **2** a structure forming a foundation or framework for a building or other construction > subˈstructural *adj*

subsume (səbˈsjuːm) *vb* (*tr*) **1** to incorporate (an idea, proposition, case, etc) under a comprehensive or inclusive classification or heading **2** to consider (an instance of something) as part of a general rule or principle [C16 from New Latin *subsumere*, from Latin *sub-* + *sumere* to take] > subˈsumable *adj*

subsumption (səbˈsʌmpʃən) *n* the act of subsuming or the state of being subsumed > subˈsumptive *adj*

sub-surface *n* the layer just below the surface of water, the earth, etc

subtangent (sʌbˈtændʒənt) *n geometry* a segment of the *x*-axis lying between the *x*-coordinate of the point at which a tangent is drawn to a curve and the intercept of the tangent with the axis

subteen (ˌsʌbˈtiːn) *n US and Canadian rare* a young person who has not yet become a teenager

subtemperate (sʌbˈtɛmpərɪt) *adj* of or relating to the colder temperate regions

subtenant (sʌbˈtɛnənt) *n* a person who rents or leases property from a tenant > subˈtenancy *n*

subtend (səbˈtɛnd) *vb* (*tr*) **1** *geometry* to be opposite to and delimit (an angle or side) **2** (of a bract, stem, etc) to have (a bud or similar part) growing in its axil **3** to mark off **4** to underlie; be inherent in [C16 from Latin *subtendere* to extend beneath, from *sub-* + *tendere* to stretch out]

subterfuge (ˈsʌbtəˌfjuːdʒ) *n* a stratagem employed to conceal something, evade an argument, etc [C16 from Late Latin *subterfugium*, from Latin *subterfugere* to escape by stealth, from *subter* secretly + *fugere* to flee]

subterminal (sʌbˈtɜːmɪnəl) *adj* almost at an end

subternatural (ˌsʌbtəˈnætʃərəl, -ˈnætʃrəl) *adj rare* falling below what is accepted as natural; less than natural [C19 from Latin *subter-* below + NATURAL]

subterranean (ˌsʌbtəˈreɪnɪən) *adj* **1** Also: **subterraneous, subterrestrial** situated, living, or operating below the surface of the earth **2** existing or operating in concealment [C17 from Latin *subterrāneus*, from *sub-* + *terra* earth] > ˌsubterˈraneanly *or* ˌsubterˈraneously *adv*

subtext (ˈsʌbˌtɛkst) *n* **1** an underlying theme in a piece of writing **2** a message which is not stated directly but can be inferred

subtile (ˈsʌtˀl) *adj* a rare spelling of **subtle** > ˈsubtilely *adv* > subtility (sʌbˈtɪlɪtɪ) *or* ˈsubtileness *n* > ˈsubtilty *n*

subtilize *or* **subtilise** (ˈsʌtɪˌlaɪz) *vb* **1** (*tr*) to bring to a purer state; refine **2** to debate subtly **3** (*tr*) to make (the mind, etc) keener > ˌsubtiliˈzation *or* ˌsubtiliˈsation *n* > ˈsubtilˌizer *or* ˈsubtilˌiser *n*

subtitle (ˈsʌbˌtaɪtˀl) *n* **1** an additional subordinate title given to a literary or other work **2** (*often plural*) Also called: **caption** *films* **a** a written translation superimposed on a film that has foreign dialogue **b** explanatory text on a silent film ▷ *vb* **3** (*tr; usually passive*) to provide a subtitle for > **subtitular** (sʌbˈtɪtjʊlə, -ˈtɪtʃə-) *adj*

subtle (ˈsʌtˀl) *adj* **1** not immediately obvious or comprehensible **2** difficult to detect or analyse, often through being delicate or highly refined: *a subtle scent* **3** showing or making or capable of showing or making fine distinctions of meaning **4** marked by or requiring mental acuteness or ingenuity; discriminating **5** delicate or faint: *a subtle shade* **6** cunning or wily: *a subtle rogue* **7** operating or executed in secret: *a subtle intrigue* [C14 from Old French *soutil*, from Latin *subtīlis* finely woven] > ˈsubtleness *n* > ˈsubtly *adv*

subtlety (ˈsʌtˀltɪ) *n, pl* **-ties 1** the state or quality of being subtle; delicacy **2** a fine distinction or the ability to make such a distinction **3** something subtle

subtonic (sʌbˈtɒnɪk) *n music* the seventh degree of a major or minor scale. Also called: **leading note**

subtopia (sʌbˈtəʊpɪə) *n Brit* suburban development that encroaches on rural areas yet appears to offer the attractions of country life to suburban dwellers [C20 blend of SUBURB + UTOPIA] > subˈtopian *adj*

subtorrid (sʌbˈtɒrɪd) *adj* an obsolete word for **subtropical**

subtotal (sʌbˈtəʊtˀl, ˈsʌbˌtəʊtˀl) *n* **1** the total made up by a column of figures, etc, forming part of the total made up by a larger column or group ▷ *vb* **-tals, -talling, -talled** *or US* **-tals, -taling, -taled 2** to establish or work out a subtotal for (a column, group, etc)

subtract (səbˈtrækt) *vb* **1** to calculate the difference between (two numbers or quantities) by subtraction **2** to remove (a part of a thing, quantity, etc) from the whole [C16 from Latin *subtractus* withdrawn, from *subtrahere* to draw away from beneath, from *sub-* + *trahere* to draw] > subˈtracter *n*

subtraction (səbˈtrækʃən) *n* **1** the act or process of subtracting **2** a mathematical operation in which the difference between two numbers or quantities is calculated. Usually indicated by the symbol (−)

subtractive (səbˈtræktɪv) *adj* **1** able or tending to remove or subtract **2** indicating or requiring subtraction; having a minus sign: −*x is a subtractive quantity*

subtractive process *n* a photographic process in which all but the desired colours are removed by passing the illuminating light through subtractive filters. Compare **additive process**

subtrahend (ˈsʌbtrəˌhɛnd) *n* the number to be subtracted from another number (the **minuend**) [C17 from Latin *subtrahendus*, from *subtrahere* to SUBTRACT]

subtreasury (sʌbˈtrɛʒərɪ) *n, pl* **-uries** *US* a branch treasury > subˈtreasurer *n* > subˈtreasurership *n*

subtropical (sʌbˈtrɒpɪkˀl) *adj* situated in, used in, characteristic of, or relating to the subtropics

subtropics (sʌbˈtrɒpɪks) *pl n* the region lying between the tropics and temperate lands

subtype (ˈsʌbˌtaɪp) *n* a secondary or subordinate type or genre, esp a specific one considered as falling under a general classification > **subtypical** (sʌbˈtɪpɪkˀl) *adj*

subulate (ˈsuːbjəlɪt, -ˌleɪt) *adj* (esp of plant parts) tapering to a point; awl-shaped [C18 from New Latin *subulatus* like an awl, from Latin *sūbula* awl]

subunit (sʌbˈjuːnɪt) *n* a distinct part or component of something larger

suburb (ˈsʌbɜːb) *n* a residential district situated on the outskirts of a city or town [C14 from Latin *suburbium*, from *sub-* close to + *urbs* a city] > ˈsuburbed *adj*

suburban (səˈbɜːbˀn) *adj* **1** of, relating to, situated in, or inhabiting a suburb or the suburbs **2** characteristic of or typifying a suburb or the suburbs **3** *mildly derogatory* narrow or unadventurous in outlook ▷ *n* **4** another word for **suburbanite**

suburbanite (səˈbɜːbəˌnaɪt) *n* a person who lives in a suburb

suburbanize *or* **suburbanise** (sʌˈbɜːbəˌnaɪz) *vb* (*tr*) to make suburban

suburbia (səˈbɜːbɪə) *n* **1** suburbs or the people living in them considered as an identifiable community or class in society **2** the life, customs, etc, of suburbanites

suburbicarian (səˌbɜːbɪˈkɛərɪən) *adj RC Church* situated near the city of Rome: used esp of the dioceses surrounding Rome [C17 from Late Latin *suburbicārius*, from *suburbium* SUBURB]

subvene (səbˈviːn) *vb* (*intr*) *rare* to happen in such a way as to be of assistance, esp in preventing something [C18 from Latin *subvenire*, from *venīre* to come]

subvention (səbˈvɛnʃən) *n* **1** a grant, aid, or subsidy, as from a government to an educational institution **2** the act or process of providing aid or help of any sort **3** *sport* a fee paid indirectly to a supposedly amateur athlete for appearing at a meeting [C15 from Late Latin *subventiō* assistance, from Latin *subvenīre* to SUBVENE] > **sub'ventionary** *adj*

subversion (səb'vɜːʃən) *n* **1** the act or an instance of subverting or overthrowing a legally constituted government, institution, etc **2** the state of being subverted; destruction or ruin **3** something that brings about an overthrow [C14 from Late Latin *subversiō* destruction, from Latin *subvertere* to SUBVERT]

subversive (səb'vɜːsɪv) *adj* **1** liable to subvert or overthrow a government, legally constituted institution, etc ▷ *n* **2** a person engaged in subversive activities, etc > **sub'versively** *adv* > **sub'versiveness** *n*

subvert (səb'vɜːt) *vb* (*tr*) **1** to bring about the complete downfall or ruin of (something existing or established by a system of law, etc) **2** to undermine the moral principles of (a person, etc); corrupt [C14 from Latin *subvertere* to overturn, from *sub-* from below + *vertere* to turn] > **sub'verter** *n*

subviral (sʌb'vaɪrəl) *adj* of, caused by, or denoting a part of the structure of a virus

subway ('sʌbˌweɪ) *n* **1** *Brit* an underground passage or tunnel enabling pedestrians to cross a road, railway, etc **2** an underground passage or tunnel for traffic, electric power supplies, etc **3** *chiefly US and Canadian* an underground railway

subzero (sʌb'zɪərəʊ) *adj* (esp of temperature) lower or less than zero

succah (su'kɑ, 'sukɔ, 'sukə) *n Judaism* a variant spelling of **sukkah**

succedaneum (ˌsʌksɪ'deɪnɪəm) *n, pl* **-nea** (-nɪə) *obsolete* something that is used as a substitute, esp any medical drug or agent that may be taken or prescribed in place of another [C17 from Latin *succēdāneus* following after, from *succēdere* to SUCCEED] > **ˌsucce'daneous** *adj*

succeed (sək'siːd) *vb* **1** (*intr*) to accomplish an aim, esp in the manner desired: *he succeeded in winning* **2** (*intr*) to happen in the manner desired: *the plan succeeded* **3** (*intr*) to acquit oneself satisfactorily or do well, as in a specified field: *to succeed in publishing* **4** (when *intr*, often foll by *to*) to come next in order (after someone or something) **5** (when *intr*, often foll by *to*) to take over an office, post, etc (from a person): *he succeeded to the vice presidency* **6** (*intr*; usually foll by *to*) to come into possession (of property, etc); inherit **7** (*intr*) to have a result according to a specified manner: *the plan succeeded badly* **8** (*intr*) to devolve upon: *the estate succeeded to his son* [C15 from Latin *succēdere* to follow after, from *sub-* after + *cēdere* to go] > **suc'ceedable** *adj* > **suc'ceeder** *n* > **suc'ceeding** *adj* > **suc'ceedingly** *adv*

succentor (sək'sɛntə) *n* the deputy of the precentor of a cathedral that has retained its statutes from pre-Reformation days [C17 from Late Latin: one who accompanies singing, from *succinere* to accompany, from Latin *canere* to sing] > **suc'centorship** *n*

succès de scandale *French* (syksɛ də skɑ̃dal) *n, pl* ***succès de scandale*** success of a play, book, etc, because of notoriety or its scandalous character [literally: success of scandal]

succès d'estime *French* (syksɛ dɛstim) *n, pl* ***succès d'estime*** success, as of a book, play, etc, based on the appreciation of the critics rather than popular acclaim [literally: success of esteem]

succès fou *French* (syksɛ fu) *n, pl* ***succès fous*** (syksɛ fu) a fantastic success [literally: mad success]

success (sək'sɛs) *n* **1** the favourable outcome of something attempted **2** the attainment of wealth, fame, etc **3** an action, performance, etc, that is characterized by success **4** a person or thing that is successful **5** *obsolete* any outcome [C16 from Latin *successus* an outcome, from *succēdere* to SUCCEED] > **suc'cessless** *adj*

successful (sək'sɛsfʊl) *adj* **1** having succeeded in one's endeavours **2** marked by a favourable outcome **3** having obtained fame, wealth, etc > **suc'cessfully** *adv* > **suc'cessfulness** *n*

succession (sək'sɛʃən) *n* **1** the act or an instance of one person or thing following another **2** a number of people or things following one another in order **3** the act, process, or right by which one person succeeds to the office, etc, of another **4** the order that determines how one person or thing follows another **5** a line of descent to a title, etc **6** *ecology* the sum of the changes in the composition of a community that occur during its development towards a stable climax community **7** **in succession** in a manner such that one thing is followed uninterruptedly by another [C14 from Latin *successio*, from *succēdere* to SUCCEED] > **suc'cessional** *adj* > **suc'cessionally** *adv*

succession state *n* any of a number of usually new states that are established in or expand over the territory formerly ruled by one large state: *Czechoslovakia was a succession state of the Austro-Hungarian monarchy*

successive (sək'sɛsɪv) *adj* **1** following another without interruption **2** of or involving succession: *a successive process* > **suc'cessively** *adv* > **suc'cessiveness** *n*

successor (sək'sɛsə) *n* **1** a person or thing that follows, esp a person who succeeds another in an office **2** *logic* the element related to a given element by a serial ordering, esp the natural number next larger to a given one. The successor of *n* is *n* + 1, usually written *Sn* or *n′* > **suc'cessoral** *adj*

succinate ('sʌksɪˌneɪt) *n* any salt or ester of succinic acid [C18 from SUCCIN(IC) + -ATE²]

succinct (sək'sɪŋkt) *adj* **1** marked by brevity and clarity; concise **2** compressed into a small area **3** *archaic* **a** encircled by or as if by a girdle **b** drawn up tightly; closely fitting [C15 from Latin *succinctus* girt about, from *succingere* to gird from below, from *sub-* from below + *cingere* to gird] > **suc'cinctly** *adv* > **suc'cinctness** *n*

succinic (sʌk'sɪnɪk) *adj* **1** of, relating to, or obtained from amber **2** of, consisting of, containing, or derived from succinic acid [C18 from French *succinique*, from Latin *succinum* amber]

succinic acid *n* a colourless odourless water-soluble dicarboxylic acid found in plant and animal tissues: used in making lacquers, dyes, perfumes, etc; 1,4-butanedioic acid. Formula: $HOOCCH_2{:}CH_2COOH$

succise (sək'saɪz) *adj botany* ending abruptly, as if cut off: *succise roots* [from Latin *succisus* cut below]

succory ('sʌkərɪ) *n, pl* **-cories** another name for **chicory** [C16 variant of *cicoree* CHICORY; related to Middle Low German *suckerie*, Dutch *suikerei*]

succotash ('sʌkəˌtæʃ) *n US and Canadian* a mixture of cooked sweet corn kernels and lima beans, served as a vegetable [C18 from Narraganset *msiquatash*, literally: broken pieces]

Succoth ('sʊkəʊt, -kəʊθ; *Hebrew* suː'kɔt) *n* a variant spelling of **Sukkoth**

succour *or US* **succor** ('sʌkə) *n* **1** help or assistance, esp in time of difficulty **2** a person or thing that provides help ▷ *vb* **3** (*tr*) to give aid to [C13 from Old French *sucurir*, from Latin *succurrere* to hurry to help, from *sub-* under + *currere* to run] > **'succourable** *or US* **'succorable** *adj* > **'succourer** *or US* **'succorer** *n* > **'succourless** *or US* **'succorless** *adj*

succubous ('sʌkjʊbəs) *adj* (of a liverwort) having the leaves arranged so that the upper margin of each leaf is covered by the lower margin of the next leaf along ▷ Compare **incubous** [C19 from Late Latin *succubare*: see SUCCUBUS]

succubus ('sʌkjʊbəs) *n, pl* **-bi** (-ˌbaɪ) **1** Also called: **succuba** a female demon fabled to have sexual intercourse with sleeping men. Compare **incubus** **2** any evil demon [C16 from Medieval Latin, from Late Latin *succuba* harlot, from Latin *succubāre* to lie beneath, from SUB- + *cubāre* to lie]

succulent ('sʌkjʊlənt) *adj* **1** abundant in juices; juicy **2** (of plants) having thick fleshy leaves or stems **3** *informal* stimulating interest, desire, etc ▷ *n* **4** a plant that is able to exist in arid or salty conditions by using water stored in its fleshy tissues [C17 from Latin *succulentus*, from *sūcus* juice] > **'succulence** *or* **'succulency** *n* > **'succulently** *adv*

succumb (sə'kʌm) *vb* (*intr*; often foll by *to*) **1** to give way in face of the overwhelming force (of) or desire (for) **2** to be fatally overwhelmed (by disease, old age, etc); die (of) [C15 from Latin *succumbere* to be overcome, from SUB- + *-cumbere* from *cubāre* to lie down] > **suc'cumber** *n*

succursal (sʌ'kɜːsᵊl) *adj* **1** (esp of a religious establishment) subsidiary ▷ *n* **2** a subsidiary establishment [C19 from French, from Medieval Latin *succursus*, from Latin *succurrere* to SUCCOUR]

succuss (sʌ'kʌs) *vb* **1** *med* to shake (a patient) to detect the sound of fluid in the thoracic or another bodily cavity **2** *rare* to shake, esp with sudden force [C17 from Latin *succussus* flung aloft, from *succutere* to toss up, from *sub-* from below + *quatere* to shake] > **succussion** (sʌ'kʌʃən) *n* > **suc'cussive** *adj*

such (sʌtʃ) (often foll by a corresponding subordinate clause introduced by *that* or *as*) *determiner* **1** **a** of the sort specified or understood: *such books shouldn't be sold here* **b** (*as pronoun*): *such is life; robbers, rapists, and such* **2** so great; so much: *such a help; I've never seen such weeping* **3** **as such** **a** in the capacity previously specified or understood: *a judge as such hasn't so much power* **b** in itself or themselves: *intelligence as such can't guarantee success* **4** **such and such** specific, but not known or named: *at such and such a time* **5** **such as** **a** for example: *animals, such as elephants and tigers* **b** of a similar kind as; like: *people such as your friend John make me angry* **c** of the (usually small) amount, etc: *the food, such as there was, was excellent* **6** **such that** so that: used to express purpose or result: *power such that it was effortless* ▷ *adv* **7** (intensifier): *such nice people; such a nice person that I gave him a present* [Old English *swilc*; related to Old Frisian *sālik*, Old Norse *slīkr*, Gothic *swaleiks*, Old High German *sulih*]

suchlike ('sʌtʃˌlaɪk) *adj* **1** (*prenominal*) of such a kind; similar: *John, Ken, and other suchlike idiots* ▷ *n* **2** such or similar persons or things: *hyenas, jackals, and suchlike*

Su-chou ('suː'tʃaʊ) *n* a variant transliteration of the Chinese name for **Suzhou**

Süchow ('ʃuː'tʃaʊ) *n* a variant transliteration of the Chinese name for **Xuzhou**

suck (sʌk) *vb* **1** to draw (a liquid or other substance) into the mouth by creating a partial vacuum in the mouth **2** to draw in (fluid, etc) by or as if by a similar action: *plants suck moisture from the soil* **3** to drink milk from (a mother's breast); suckle **4** (*tr*) to extract fluid content from (a solid food): *to suck a lemon* **5** (*tr*) to take into the mouth and moisten, dissolve, or roll around with the tongue: *to suck one's thumb* **6** (*tr*; often foll by *down*, *in*, etc) to draw by using irresistible force: *the whirlpool sucked him down* **7** (*intr*) (of a pump) to draw in air because of a low supply level or leaking valves, pipes, etc **8** (*tr*) to assimilate or acquire (knowledge, comfort, etc) **9** (*intr*) *slang* to be contemptible or disgusting **10** **sucking diesel** *informal* doing very well; successful **11** **suck it and see** *informal* to try something to find out what it is, what it is like, or how it works ▷ *n* **12** the act or an instance of sucking **13** something that is sucked, esp milk from the mother's breast **14** **give suck to** to give (a baby or young animal) milk from the breast or udder **15** an attracting or sucking force: *the suck of the whirlpool was very strong* **16** a sound caused by sucking ▷ See also **suck in**, **suck off**, **sucks**, **suck up to** [Old English *sūcan*; related to Old Norse *súga*, Middle Dutch *sūgen*, Latin *sūgere* to suck, exhaust; see SOAK] > **'suckless** *adj*

sucker ('sʌkə) *n* **1** a person or thing that sucks **2** *slang* a person who is easily deceived or swindled **3** *slang* a person who cannot resist the attractions of a particular type of person or thing: *he's a sucker* for blondes **4** a young animal that is not yet weaned, esp a suckling pig **5** zoology an organ that is specialized for sucking or adhering **6** a cup-shaped device, generally made of rubber, that may be attached to articles allowing them to adhere to a surface by suction **7** botany **a** a strong shoot that arises in a mature plant from a root, rhizome, or the base of the main stem **b** a short branch of a parasitic plant that absorbs nutrients from the host **8** a pipe or tube through which a fluid is drawn by suction **9** any small mainly North American cyprinoid fish of the family Catostomidae, having toothless jaws and a large sucking mouth **10** any of certain fishes that have sucking discs, esp the clingfish or sea snail **11** a piston in a suction pump or the valve in such a piston ▷ vb **12** (tr) to strip off the suckers from (a plant) **13** (intr) (of a plant) to produce suckers

suckerfish ('sʌkəˌfɪʃ) or **suckfish** n, pl -fish or -fishes other names for **remora** [c18 so called because of the suction disc on its head]

sucker punch n **1** a sudden surprise punch, esp from behind **2** a sudden unexpected defeat or setback

suck in vb (adverb) **1** (tr) to attract by using an inexorable force, inducement, etc: the current sucked him in **2** to draw in (one's breath) sharply **3** (tr) slang to deceive or defraud

sucking ('sʌkɪŋ) adj **1** not yet weaned: sucking pig **2** not yet fledged: sucking dove

sucking louse n any insect of the order Anoplura. See **louse** (sense 1) [so named because it has a mouth adapted for sucking the body fluids of its host]

suckle ('sʌkəl) vb **1** to give (a baby or young animal) milk from the breast or (of a baby, etc) to suck milk from the breast **2** (tr) to bring up; nurture [c15 probably back formation from SUCKLING] > 'suckler n

suckling ('sʌklɪŋ) n **1** an infant or young animal that is still taking milk from the mother **2** a very young child [c15 see SUCK, -LING¹; related to Middle Dutch sūgeling, Middle High German sōgelinc]

suck off vb (tr, adverb) slang to perform the act of fellatio or cunnilingus on

sucks (sʌks) interj slang **1** an expression of disappointment **2** an exclamation of defiance or derision (esp in the phrase **yah boo sucks to you**)

suck up to vb (intr, adverb + preposition) informal to flatter for one's own profit; toady

sucrase ('sjuːkreɪz) n another name for **invertase** [c19 from French sucre sugar + -ASE]

sucre (Spanish 'sukre) n the former standard monetary unit of Ecuador (until the US dollar was adopted in 2000), divided into 100 centavos [c19 after Antonio José de Sucre (1795–1830), South American liberator]

Sucre (Spanish 'sukre) n the legal capital of Bolivia, in the south central part of the country in the E Andes: university (1624). Pop: 231 000 (2005 est). Former name (until 1839): **Chuquisaca**

sucrose ('sjuːkrəʊz, -krəʊs) n the technical name for **sugar** (sense 1) [c19 from French sucre sugar + -OSE²]

suction ('sʌkʃən) n **1** the act or process of sucking **2** the force or condition produced by a pressure difference, as the force holding a suction cap onto a surface **3** the act or process of producing such a force or condition [c17 from Late Latin suctiō a sucking, from Latin sūgere to suck] > 'suctional adj

suction pump n a pump for raising water or other fluid by suction. It usually consists of a cylinder containing a piston fitted with a flap valve

suction stop n phonetics another word for **click** (sense 3)

suction valve n a nonreturn valve in a pump suction to prevent the pump draining or depriming when not in service. Also called: **foot valve**

suctorial (sʌk'tɔːrɪəl) adj **1** specialized for sucking or adhering: the suctorial mouthparts of certain insects **2**

relating to or possessing suckers or suction [c19 from New Latin suctōrius, from Latin sūgere to suck]

SUD international car registration for Sudan

Sudan (suːˈdɑːn, -ˈdæn) n **1** a republic in NE Africa, on the Red Sea: the largest country in Africa; conquered by Mehemet Ali of Egypt (1820–22) and made an Anglo-Egyptian condominium in 1899 after joint forces defeated the Mahdist revolt; became a republic in 1956; civil war has been waged between separatists, in the mainly Christian south, and the government since independence, apart from a period of peace (1972–83). It consists mainly of a plateau, with the Nubian Desert in the north. Official language: Arabic. Official religion: Muslim; there are large Christian and animist minorities. Currency: Sudanese dinar. Capital: Khartoum. Pop: 34 333 000 (2004 est). Area: 2 505 805 sq km (967 491 sq miles). Former name (1899–1956): Anglo-Egyptian Sudan French name: Soudan **2 the** a region stretching across Africa south of the Sahara and north of the tropical zone: inhabited chiefly by Negroid tribes rather than Arabs

Sudanese (ˌsuːdəˈniːz) adj **1** of or relating to the republic of Sudan or its inhabitants ▷ adj **2** of or relating to the African region of the Sudan or its inhabitants ▷ n **3** a native or inhabitant of the republic of Sudan **4** a native or inhabitant of the African region of the Sudan

Sudanic (suːˈdænɪk) n **1** a group of languages spoken in scattered areas of the Sudan, most of which are now generally assigned to the Chari-Nile branch of the Nilo-Saharan family ▷ adj **2** relating to or belonging to this group of languages **3** of or relating to the Sudan

sudarium (sjuːˈdɛərɪəm) n, pl -daria (-ˈdɛərɪə) another word for **sudatorium** or **veronica²** [c17 from Latin, from sūdāre to sweat]

sudatorium (ˌsjuːdəˈtɔːrɪəm) or **sudatory** n, pl -toria (-ˈtɔːrɪə) or -tories a room, esp in a Roman bathhouse, where sweating is induced by heat [c18 from Latin, from sūdāre to sweat]

sudatory ('sjuːdətərɪ, -trɪ) adj **1** relating to or producing sweating; sudorific ▷ n, pl -ries **2** med a sudatory agent **3** another word for **sudatorium**

Sudbury ('sʌdbərɪ, -brɪ) n a city in central Canada, in Ontario: a major nickel-mining centre. Pop: 103 879 (2001)

sudd (sʌd) n floating masses of reeds and weeds that occur on the White Nile and obstruct navigation [c19 from Arabic, literally: obstruction]

sudden ('sʌdən) adj **1** occurring or performed quickly and without warning **2** marked by haste; abrupt **3** rare rash; precipitate ▷ n **4** archaic an abrupt occurrence or the occasion of such an occurrence (in the phrase **on a sudden**) **5** all of a sudden without warning; unexpectedly ▷ adv **6** chiefly poetic without warning; suddenly [c13 via French from Late Latin subitāneus, from Latin subitus unexpected, from subīre to happen unexpectedly, from sub- secretly + īre to go] > 'suddenness n

sudden adult death syndrome n the unexpected death of a young adult, usually due to undetected inherited heart disease. Also called: **sudden death syndrome, sudden cardiac death** Abbrevs: SADS, SDS, SCD

sudden death n **1** (in sports, etc) an extra game or contest to decide the winner of a tied competition **2** an unexpected or quick death

sudden infant death syndrome n a technical term for **cot death**. Abbreviation: SIDS

suddenly ('sʌdənlɪ) adv quickly and without warning; unexpectedly

Sudetenland (suːˈdeɪtənˌlænd) n a mountainous region of the N Czech Republic: part of Czechoslovakia (1919–38; 1945–93); occupied by Germany (1938–45). Also called: **the Sudeten**

Sudetes (suːˈdiːtiːz) or **Sudeten Mountains** pl n a mountain range in E central Europe, along the N border of the Czech Republic, extending into Germany and Poland: rich in minerals, esp coal.

Highest peak: Schneekoppe, 1603 m (5259 ft)

sudor ('sjuːdɔː) n a technical name for **sweat** [Latin] > sudoral ('sjuːdərəl) adj

sudoriferous (ˌsjuːdəˈrɪfərəs) adj producing or conveying sweat. Also: sudoriparous (ˌsjuːdəˈrɪpərəs) [c16 via New Latin from SUDOR + Latin ferre to bear] > ˌsudor'iferousness n

sudorific (ˌsjuːdəˈrɪfɪk) adj **1** producing or causing sweating; sudatory ▷ n **2** a sudorific agent [c17 from New Latin sūdōrificus, from SUDOR + Latin facere to make]

Sudra ('sjuːdrə) n the lowest of the four main Hindu castes, the workers [c17 from Sanskrit]

suds (sʌdz) pl n **1** the bubbles on the surface of water in which soap, detergents, etc, have been dissolved; lather **2** soapy water **3** slang, chiefly US and Canadian beer or the bubbles floating on it [c16 probably from Middle Dutch sudse marsh; related to Middle Low German sudde swamp; see SEETHE] > 'sudsy adj

sue (sjuː, suː) vb sues, suing, sued **1** to institute legal proceedings (against) **2** to make suppliant requests of (someone for something) **3** archaic to pay court (to) [c13 via Anglo-Norman from Old French sivre, from Latin sequī to follow] > 'suer n

suede (sweɪd) n **a** a leather finished with a fine velvet-like nap, usually on the flesh side of the skin or hide, produced by abrasive action **b** (as modifier): a suede coat [c19 from French gants de Suède, literally: gloves from Sweden]

suent ('sjuːənt) adj Southwest English dialect smooth

suet ('suːɪt, 'sjuːɪt) n a hard waxy fat around the kidneys and loins in sheep, cattle, etc, used in cooking and making tallow [c14 from Old French seu, from Latin sēbum] > 'suety adj

suet pudding n Brit any of a variety of sweet or savoury puddings made with suet and steamed or boiled

Suez ('suːɪz) n **1** a port in NE Egypt, at the head of the Gulf of Suez at the S end of the Suez Canal: an ancient trading site and a major naval station under the Ottoman Empire; port of departure for pilgrims to Mecca; oil-refining centre. It suffered severely in the Arab-Israeli conflicts of 1967 and 1973. Pop: 513 000 (2005 est) **2 Isthmus of** a strip of land in NE Egypt, between the Mediterranean and the Red Sea: links Africa and Asia and is crossed by the Suez Canal **3 Gulf of** the NW arm of the Red Sea: linked with the Mediterranean by the Suez Canal

Suez Canal n a sea-level canal in NE Egypt, crossing the Isthmus of Suez and linking the Mediterranean with the Red Sea: built (1854–69) by de Lesseps with French and Egyptian capital; nationalized in 1956 by the Egyptians. Length: 163 km (101 miles)

suf. abbreviation for suffix

Suff. abbreviation for **1** Suffolk **2** Suffragan

suffer ('sʌfə) vb **1** to undergo or be subjected to (pain, punishment, etc) **2** (tr) to undergo or experience (anything): to suffer a change of management **3** (intr) to be set at a disadvantage: this author suffers in translation **4** to be prepared to endure (pain, death, etc): he suffers for the cause of freedom **5** (tr) archaic to permit (someone to do something): suffer the little children to come unto me **6** suffer from **a** to be ill with, esp recurrently **b** to be given to: he suffers from a tendency to exaggerate [c13 from Old French soffrir, from Latin sufferre, from SUB- + ferre to bear] > 'sufferer n

sufferable ('sʌfərəbəl, 'sʌfrə-) adj able to be tolerated or suffered; endurable > 'sufferably adv

sufferance ('sʌfərəns, 'sʌfrəns) n **1** tolerance arising from failure to prohibit; tacit permission **2** capacity to endure pain, injury, etc **3** the state or condition of suffering **4** archaic patient endurance **5** on sufferance with reluctance [c13 via Old French from Late Latin sufferentia endurance, from Latin sufferre to SUFFER]

suffering ('sʌfərɪŋ, 'sʌfrɪŋ) n **1** the pain, misery, or loss experienced by a person who suffers **2** the state or an instance of enduring pain, etc

> 'sufferingly adv

suffice (sə'faɪs) vb **1** to be adequate or satisfactory for (something) **2 suffice it to say that** (takes a clause as object) let us say no more than that; I shall just say that [c14 from Old French suffire, from Latin sufficere from sub- below + facere to make]
> suf'ficer n

sufficiency (sə'fɪʃənsɪ) n, pl -cies **1** the quality or condition of being sufficient **2** an adequate amount or quantity, as of income **3** archaic efficiency

sufficient (sə'fɪʃənt) adj **1** enough to meet a need or purpose; adequate **2** logic (of a condition) assuring the truth of a statement; requiring but not necessarily required by some other state of affairs. Compare **necessary** (sense 3e) **3** archaic competent; capable ▷ n **4** a sufficient quantity [c14 from Latin sufficiens supplying the needs of, from sufficere to SUFFICE] > suf'ficiently adv

sufficient reason n philosophy **1** the principle that nothing happens by pure chance, but that an explanation must always be available **2** the view that such an explanation is a reason for God to have chosen one alternative rather than another

suffix n ('sʌfɪks) **1** grammar an affix that follows the stem to which it is attached, as for example -s and -ness in dogs and softness. Compare **prefix** (sense 1) **2** anything that is added at the end of something else ▷ vb ('sʌfɪks, sə'fɪks) **3** (tr) grammar to add (a morpheme) as a suffix to the end of a word **4** (tr) to add (something) at the end of a sentence, comment, or piece of writing [c18 from New Latin suffixum, from Latin suffixus fastened below, from suffigere, from sub- + figere to fasten] > suffixal ('sʌfɪksəl) adj > suffixion (sʌ'fɪkʃən) n

sufflate (sʌ'fleɪt) vb an archaic word for **inflate** [c17 from Latin sufflāre from sub- + flāre blow] > suf'flation n

suffocate ('sʌfə,keɪt) vb **1** to kill or be killed by the deprivation of oxygen, as by obstruction of the air passage or inhalation of noxious gases **2** to block the air passages or have the air passages blocked **3** to feel or cause to feel discomfort from heat and lack of air [c16 from Latin suffōcāre, from sub- + faucēs throat] > 'suffo,cating adj
> 'suffo,catingly adv > ,suffo'cation n
> 'suffo,cative adj

Suffolk¹ ('sʌfək) n a county of SE England, on the North Sea: its coast is flat and marshy, indented by broad tidal estuaries. Administrative centre: Ipswich. Pop: 678 100 (2003 est). Area: 3800 sq km (1467 sq miles)

Suffolk² ('sʌfək) n a black-faced breed of sheep

Suffolk punch n a breed of draught horse with a chestnut coat and short legs [c18 from dialect punch squat, short and thick]

Suffr. abbreviation for Suffragan

suffragan ('sʌfrəgən) adj **1 a** (of any bishop of a diocese) subordinate to and assisting his superior archbishop or metropolitan **b** (of any assistant bishop) having the duty of assisting the bishop of the diocese to which he is appointed but having no ordinary jurisdiction in that diocese ▷ n **2** a suffragan bishop [c14 from Medieval Latin suffrāgāneus, from suffrāgium assistance, from Latin: SUFFRAGE] > 'suffraganship n

suffrage ('sʌfrɪdʒ) n **1** the right to vote, esp in public elections; franchise **2** the exercise of such a right; casting a vote **3** a supporting vote **4** a prayer, esp a short intercessory prayer [c14 from Latin suffrāgium]

suffragette (,sʌfrə'dʒɛt) n a female advocate of the extension of the franchise to women, esp a militant one, as in Britain at the beginning of the 20th century [c20 from SUFFRAG(E) + -ETTE] > ,suffra'gettism n

suffragist ('sʌfrədʒɪst) n an advocate of the extension of the franchise, esp to women > 'suffragism n

suffruticose (sə'fruːtɪ,kəʊz) adj (of a plant) having a permanent woody base and herbaceous branches [c18 from New Latin suffruticōsus, from Latin SUB- + frutex a shrub]

suffumigate (sə'fjuːmɪ,geɪt) vb (tr) to fumigate from or as if from beneath [c16 from Latin suffūmigāre, from sub- + fūmigāre to FUMIGATE] > suf,fumi'gation n

suffuse (sə'fjuːz) vb (tr; usually passive) to spread or flood through or over (something): the evening sky was suffused with red [c16 from Latin suffūsus overspread with, from suffundere, from sub- + fundere to pour] > suffusion (sə'fjuːʒən) n > suf'fusive adj

Sufi ('suːfɪ) n, pl -fis an adherent of any of various Muslim mystical orders or teachings, which emphasize the direct personal experience of God [c17 from Arabic sūfiy, literally: (man) of wool, from sūf wool; probably from the ascetic's woollen garments] > 'Sufic adj

Sufism ('suːfɪzəm) n the mystical doctrines of the Sufis > Sufistic (suː'fɪstɪk) adj

Sufu ('fuː'fuː) n a variant spelling of **Shufu**

súgán ('suːgaːn) n Irish **1** a straw rope **2** súgán chair a chair with a seat made from woven súgáns [Irish Gaelic]

sugar ('ʃʊgə) n **1** Also called: **sucrose, saccharose** a white crystalline sweet carbohydrate, a disaccharide, found in many plants and extracted from sugar cane and sugar beet: it is used esp as a sweetening agent in food and drinks. Formula: $C_{12}H_{22}O_{11}$. Related adj: **saccharine 2** any of a class of simple water-soluble carbohydrates, such as sucrose, lactose, and fructose **3** informal, chiefly US and Canadian a term of affection, esp for one's sweetheart **4** rare a slang word for **money 5** a slang name for **LSD** ▷ vb **6** (tr) to add sugar to; make sweet **7** (tr) to cover or sprinkle with sugar **8** (intr) to produce sugar **9 sugar the pill** or **medicine** to make something unpleasant more agreeable by adding something pleasant: the government stopped wage increases but sugared the pill by reducing taxes [c13 suker, from Old French çucre, from Medieval Latin zuccārum, from Italian zucchero, from Arabic sukkar, from Persian shakar, from Sanskrit śarkarā] > 'sugarless adj > 'sugar-,like adj

sugarallie ('ʃʊgər,ælɪ) n Scot liquorice [c19 from earlier sugar alicreesh]

sugar apple n another name for **sweetsop**

sugar bag n Austral and NZ a small hessian bag occasionally still used, esp in rural areas, as a rough-and-ready measure for dry goods

sugar beet n a variety of the plant Beta vulgaris that is cultivated for its white roots from which sugar is obtained. Compare **sugar cane**

sugar bird n a South African nectar-eating bird, Promerops cafer, with a long curved bill and long tail: family Meliphagidae (honey-eaters)

sugar bush n an anacardiaceous evergreen shrub, Rhus ovata, of S California and Arizona, having pale oval leaves, spikes of yellow-tinged red flowers, and deep red fruits

sugar candy n **1** Also called: **rock candy** large crystals of sugar formed by suspending strings in a strong sugar solution that hardens on the strings, used chiefly for sweetening coffee **2** chiefly US confectionery; sweets

sugar cane n a coarse perennial grass, Saccharum officinarum, of Old World tropical regions, having tall stout canes that yield sugar: widely cultivated in tropical regions. Compare **sugar beet**

sugar-coat vb (tr) **1** to coat or cover with sugar **2** to cause to appear more attractive; make agreeable

sugar corn n another name for **sweet corn** (sense 1)

sugar daddy n slang a rich usually middle-aged or old man who bestows expensive gifts on a young person in return for companionship or sexual favours

sugar diabetes n an informal name for **diabetes mellitus**

sugared ('ʃʊgəd) adj made sweeter or more appealing with or as with sugar

sugar glider n a common Australian phalanger,

Petaurus breviceps, that glides from tree to tree feeding on insects and nectar

sugar gum n Austral a small eucalyptus tree, Eucalyptus cladocalyx, having smooth bark and barrel-shaped fruits and grown for timber and ornament. It has sweet-tasting leaves which are often eaten by livestock

sugaring ('ʃʊgərɪŋ) n a method of removing unwanted body hair, whereby a thick viscous paste of sugar and water is applied to the hair, allowed to thicken, and then removed sharply, pulling the hairs out by their roots

sugar loaf n **1** a large conical mass of hard refined sugar. See also **loaf sugar 2** something resembling this in shape

Sugar Loaf Mountain n a mountain in SE Brazil, in Rio de Janeiro on Guanabara Bay. Height: 390 m (1280 ft). Portuguese name: Pão de Açúcar

sugar maple n a North American maple tree, Acer saccharum, that is grown as a source of sugar, which is extracted from the sap, and for its hard wood

sugar of lead (lɛd) n another name for **lead acetate**

sugar of milk n another name for **lactose**

sugar pea n another name for **mangetout**

sugar pie n Canadian an open pie with a brown sugar filling

sugar pine n a pine tree, Pinus lambertiana, of California and Oregon, having spreading pendulous branches, light brown cones, and sugary resin

sugarplum ('ʃʊgə,plʌm) n a crystallized plum

sugar soap n an alkaline compound used for cleaning or stripping paint

sugary ('ʃʊgərɪ) adj **1** of, like, or containing sugar **2** containing too much sugar; excessively sweet **3** deceptively pleasant; insincere > 'sugariness n

suggest (sə'dʒɛst; US səg'dʒɛst) vb (tr; may take a clause as object) **1** to put forward (a plan, idea, etc) for consideration: I suggest Smith for the post; a plan suggested itself **2** to evoke (a person, thing, etc) in the mind of someone by the association of ideas: that painting suggests home to me **3** to give an indirect or vague hint of: his face always suggests his peace of mind [c16 from Latin suggerere to bring up, from sub- + gerere to bring] > sug'gester n

suggestibility (sə,dʒɛstɪ'bɪlɪtɪ) n psychol a state, esp under hypnosis, in which a person will accept the suggestions of another person and act accordingly

suggestible (sə'dʒɛstɪbˀl) adj **1** easily influenced by ideas provided by other persons **2** characteristic of something that can be suggested > sug'gestibleness n > sug'gestibly adv

suggestion (sə'dʒɛstʃən) n **1** something that is suggested **2** a hint or indication: a suggestion of the odour of violets **3** psychol the process whereby the mere presentation of an idea to a receptive individual leads to the acceptance of that idea. See also **autosuggestion**

suggestive (sə'dʒɛstɪv) adj **1** (postpositive; foll by of) conveying a hint (of something): this painting is suggestive of a hot summer day **2** tending to suggest something improper or indecent **3** able or liable to suggest an idea, plan, etc > sug'gestively adv > sug'gestiveness n

suicidal (,suːɪ'saɪdˀl, ,sjuː-) adj **1** involving, indicating, or tending towards suicide **2** liable to result in suicide: a suicidal attempt **3** liable to destroy one's own interests or prospects; dangerously rash > ,sui'cidally adv

suicide ('suːɪ,saɪd, 'sjuː-) n **1** the act or an instance of killing oneself intentionally **2** the self-inflicted ruin of one's own prospects or interests: a merger would be financial suicide **3** a person who kills himself intentionally **4** (modifier) reckless; extremely dangerous: a suicide mission **5** (modifier) (of an action) undertaken or (of a person) undertaking an action in the knowledge that it will result in the death of the person performing it in order that maximum damage may be inflicted on an enemy: *a suicide attack; suicide bomber* [C17 from New Latin *suīcīdium,* from Latin *suī* of oneself + *-cīdium,* from *caedere* to kill]

suicide bomber *n* a terrorist who carries out a bomb attack, knowing that he or she will be killed in the explosion. Also called: **homicide bomber**

suicide watch *n* a round-the-clock watch by warders on a prisoner considered to be in danger of harming him- or herself

sui generis (ˌsuːaɪ ˈdʒɛnərɪs) *adj* unique [Latin, literally: of its own kind]

sui juris (ˈsuːaɪ ˈdʒʊərɪs) *adj (usually postpositive) law* of full age and not under disability; legally competent to manage one's own affairs; independent [C17 from Latin, literally: of one's own right]

suint (ˈsuːɪnt, swɪnt) *n* a water-soluble substance found in the fleece of sheep, consisting of peptides, organic acids, metal ions, and inorganic cations and formed from dried perspiration [C18 from French *suer* to sweat, from Latin *sūdāre*]

suiplap (ˈseɪpˌlap) *n South African slang* a drunkard [from Afrikaans]

Suisse (sɥis) *n* the French name for **Switzerland**

suit (suːt, sjuːt) *n* **1** any set of clothes of the same or similar material designed to be worn together, now usually (for men) a jacket with matching trousers or (for women) a jacket with matching or contrasting skirt or trousers **2** (*in combination*) any outfit worn for a specific purpose: *a spacesuit* **3** any set of items, such as the full complement of sails of a vessel or parts of personal armour **4** any of the four sets of 13 cards in a pack of playing cards, being spades, hearts, diamonds, and clubs. The cards in each suit are two to ten, jack, queen, and king in the usual order of ascending value, with ace counting as either the highest or lowest according to the game **5** a civil proceeding; lawsuit **6** the act or process of suing in a court of law **7** a petition or appeal made to a person of superior rank or status or the act of making such a petition **8** *slang* a business executive or white-collar manager **9** a man's courting of a woman **10** **follow suit a** to play a card of the same suit as the card played immediately before it **b** to act in the same way as someone else **11** **strong** *or* **strongest suit** something that one excels in ▷ *vb* **12** to make or be fit or appropriate for: *that dress suits you* **13** to meet the requirements or standards (of) **14** to be agreeable or acceptable to (someone) **15** **suit oneself** to pursue one's own intentions without reference to others [C13 from Old French *sieute* set of things, from *sivre* to follow; compare SUE] ▷ 'suitˌlike *adj*

suitable (ˈsuːtəbᵊl, 'sjuː-) *adj* appropriate; proper; fit ▷ ˌsuitaˈbility *or* 'suitableness *n* ▷ 'suitably *adv*

suitcase (ˈsuːtˌkeɪs, 'sjuː-) *n* a portable rectangular travelling case, usually stiffened, for carrying clothing, etc

suite (swiːt) *n* **1** a series of items intended to be used together; set **2** a number of connected rooms in a hotel forming one living unit: *the presidential suite* **3** a matching set of furniture, esp of two armchairs and a settee **4** a number of attendants or followers **5** *music* **a** an instrumental composition consisting of several movements in the same key based on or derived from dance rhythms, esp in the baroque period **b** an instrumental composition in several movements less closely connected than a sonata **c** a piece of music containing movements based on or extracted from music already used in an opera, ballet, play, etc [C17 from French, from Old French *sieute;* see SUIT]

suiter (ˈsuːtə, 'sjuː-) *n* a piece of luggage for carrying suits and dresses

suiting (ˈsuːtɪŋ, 'sjuː-) *n* a fabric used for suits

suitor (ˈsuːtə, 'sjuː-) *n* **1** a man who courts a woman; wooer **2** *law* a person who brings a suit in a court of law; plaintiff **3** *rare* a person who makes a request or appeal for anything [C13 from Anglo-Norman *suter,* from Latin *secūtor* follower,

from *sequī* to follow]

Suiyüan (ˈswiːˈjɑːn) *n* a former province in N China: now part of the Inner Mongolian Autonomous Region

Sukarnapura (sʊˌkɑːnəˈpʊərə) *n* a former name of **Jayapura**

Sukarno Peak *n* a former name of (Mount) **Jaya**

suka wena (ˈsuːkə ˈwɛnə) *interj South African informal offensive* an expression of dismissal or rejection; go away [from Zulu]

Sukhumi (*Russian* suˈxumi) *n* a port and resort in W Georgia, on the Black Sea: site of an ancient Greek colony. Pop: 134 000 (2005 est)

sukiyaki (ˌsuːkɪˈjɑːkɪ) *n* a Japanese dish consisting of very thinly sliced beef or other meat, vegetables, and seasonings cooked together quickly, usually at the table [from Japanese]

sukkah *or* **succah** (suˈkɑ, ˈsukɔ, 'sukə) *n* a temporary structure with a roof of branches in which orthodox Jews eat and, if possible, sleep during the festival of Sukkoth. Also called: **tabernacle** [from Hebrew, literally: tabernacle]

Sukkoth *or* **Succoth** (ˈsukəʊt, -kəʊθ; *Hebrew* suːˈkɔt) *n* an eight-day Jewish harvest festival beginning on Tishri 15, which commemorates the period when the Israelites lived in the wilderness. Also called: **Feast of Tabernacles** [from Hebrew, literally: tabernacles]

Sulawesi (ˌsuːləˈweɪsɪ) *n* an island in E Indonesia: mountainous and forested, with volcanoes and hot springs. Pop: 14 768 400 (1999 est). Area (including adjacent islands): 229 108 sq km (88 440 sq miles). Also called: **Celebes**

sulcate (ˈsʌlkeɪt) *adj biology* marked with longitudinal parallel grooves: *sulcate stems* [C18 via Latin *sulcātus* from *sulcāre* to plough, from *sulcus* a furrow] ▷ ˈsulˈcation *n*

sulcus (ˈsʌlkəs) *n, pl* **-ci** (-saɪ) **1** a linear groove, furrow, or slight depression **2** any of the narrow grooves on the surface of the brain that mark the cerebral convolutions. Compare **fissure** [C17 from Latin]

sulf- *combining form* a US variant of **sulph-**
▅▅▅▅ USAGE See at **sulph-**

sulfadiazine (ˌsʌlfəˈdaɪəˌziːn) *n* an important sulfa drug used chiefly in combination with an antibiotic. Formula: $C_{10}H_{10}N_4O_2S$

sulfadimidine (ˌsʌlfəˈdaɪmɪˌdiːn) *n* an antibacterial sulfa drug used in human and veterinary medicine. It is effective against chlamydia, toxoplasma, and cocidia. US name: sulfamethazine

sulfa drug (ˈsʌlfə) *n* any of a group of sulfonamide compounds that inhibit the activity of bacteria and are used in medicine to treat bacterial infections

sulfamethazine (ˌsʌlfəˈmɛθəˌziːn) *n* US name for **sulfadimidine**

sulfathiazole (ˌsʌlfəˈθaɪəˌzəʊl) *n* an antimicrobial sulfa drug used in veterinary medicine and formerly in clinical medicine. Formula: $C_9H_9N_3O_2S_2$

sulfur (ˈsʌlfə) *n* the US preferred spelling of **sulphur**

sulk (sʌlk) *vb* **1** (*intr*) to be silent and resentful because of a wrong done to one, esp in order to gain sympathy; brood sullenly: *the child sulked in a corner after being slapped* ▷ *n* **2** (*often plural*) a state or mood of feeling resentful or sullen: *he's got the sulks* **3** Also: **sulker** a person who sulks [C18 perhaps a back formation from SULKY¹]

sulky¹ (ˈsʌlkɪ) *adj* **sulkier, sulkiest 1** sullen, withdrawn, or moody, through or as if through resentment **2** dull or dismal: *sulky weather* [C18 perhaps from obsolete *sulke* sluggish, probably related to Old English *āseolcan* to be lazy] ▷ 'sulkily *adv* ▷ 'sulkiness *n*

sulky² (ˈsʌlkɪ) *n, pl* **sulkies** a light two-wheeled vehicle for one person, usually drawn by one horse [C18 from SULKY¹, because it can carry only one person]

sullage (ˈsʌlɪdʒ) *n* **1** filth or waste, esp sewage **2**

sediment deposited by running water [C16 perhaps from French *souiller* to sully; compare Old English *sol* mud]

sullen (ˈsʌlən) *adj* **1** unwilling to talk or be sociable; sulky; morose **2** sombre; gloomy: *a sullen day* **3** *literary* sluggish; slow: *a sullen stream* **4** *obsolete* threatening ▷ *n* **5** (*plural*) *archaic* a sullen mood [C16 perhaps from Anglo-French *solain* (unattested), ultimately related to Latin *sōlus* alone] ▷ 'sullenly *adv* ▷ 'sullenness *n*

Sullom Voe (ˈsʌləm vəʊ) *n* a deep coastal inlet in the Shetland Islands, on the N coast of Mainland. It is used for the storage and transshipment of oil

sully (ˈsʌlɪ) *vb* **-lies, -lying, -lied 1** to stain or tarnish (a reputation, etc) or (of a reputation) to become stained or tarnished ▷ *n, pl* **-lies 2** a stain **3** the act of sullying [C16 probably from French *souiller* to soil] ▷ 'sulliable *adj*

sulph- *or US* **sulf-** *combining form* containing sulphur: *sulphate; sulphonic acid*

▐ USAGE The "ph" spelling of *sulphur* and related words is used in British English. In the US the spelling is *sulfur.* However, the recommended spelling in chemistry is *sulfur* and this is found in technical writing. Also the *sulf-* spelling is used in the names of generic drugs

sulphanilamide (ˌsʌlfəˈnɪləˌmaɪd) *n* a white odourless crystalline compound formerly used in medicine in the treatment of bacterial infections. Formula: $NH_2C_6H_4SO_2NH_2$. See also **sulfa drug**

sulphate (ˈsʌlfeɪt) *n* **1** any salt or ester of sulphuric acid, such as sodium sulphate, Na_2SO_4, sodium hydrogen sulphate, or diethyl sulphate, $(C_2H_5)_2SO_4$ **2** *slang* amphetamine sulphate. Often shortened to: **sulph** ▷ *vb* **3** (*tr*) to treat with a sulphate or convert into a sulphate **4** to undergo or cause to undergo the formation of a layer of lead sulphate on the plates of an accumulator [C18 from New Latin *sulfātum;* see SULPHUR] ▷ sulˈphation *n*

sulphate-resisting cement *n* a type of Portland cement that resists normal concentrations of sulphates: used in concrete for flues and underwater work

sulphide (ˈsʌlfaɪd) *n* **1** a compound of sulphur with a more electropositive element **2** another name for **thio-ether**

sulphinyl (ˈsʌlfənɪl) *n* (*modifier*) another term (no longer in technical usage) for **thionyl** [C20 from SULF- + -IN + -YL]

sulphite (ˈsʌlfaɪt) *n* any salt or ester of sulphurous acid, containing the ions $SO_3{}^{2-}$ or $HSO_3{}^-$ (**hydrogen sulphite**) or the groups $-SO_3$ or $-HSO_3$. The salts are usually soluble crystalline compounds ▷ **sulphitic** (sʌlˈfɪtɪk) *adj*

sulphonamide (sʌlˈfɒnəˌmaɪd) *n* any of a class of organic compounds that are amides of sulphonic acids containing the group $-SO_2NH_2$ or a group derived from this. An important class of sulphonamides are the sulfa drugs

sulphonate (ˈsʌlfəˌneɪt) *chem* ▷ *n* **1** a salt or ester of any sulphonic acid containing the ion RSO_2O^- or the group RSO_2O-, R being an organic group ▷ *vb* **2** (*tr*) to introduce a sulphonic acid group, $-SO_2OH$, into (a molecule)

sulphone (ˈsʌlfəʊn) *n* any of a class of organic compounds containing the divalent group $-SO_2$ linked to two other organic groups. Certain sulphones are used in the treatment of leprosy and tuberculosis

sulphonic acid (sʌlˈfɒnɪk) *n* any of a large group of strong organic acids that contain the group $-SO_2OH$ and are used in the manufacture of dyes and drugs

sulphonium compound *or* **salt** (sʌlˈfəʊnɪəm) *n* any one of a class of salts derived by the addition of a proton to the sulphur atom of a thiol or thio-ether thus producing a positive ion (**sulphonium ion**)

sulphonmethane (ˌsʌlfɒnˈmiːˌθeɪn) *n* a colourless

S

crystalline compound used medicinally as a hypnotic. Formula: $C_7H_{16}O_4S_2$

sulphonyl ('sʌlfənɪl) n (modifier) another term for **sulphuryl**

sulphur or US **sulfur** ('sʌlfə) n **a** an allotropic nonmetallic element, occurring free in volcanic regions and in combined state in gypsum, pyrite, and galena. The stable yellow rhombic form converts on heating to monoclinic needles. It is used in the production of sulphuric acid, in the vulcanization of rubber, and in fungicides. Symbol: S; atomic no.: 16; atomic wt.: 32.066; valency: 2, 4, or 6; relative density: 2.07 (rhombic), 1.957 (monoclinic); melting pt.: 115.22°C (rhombic), 119.0°C (monoclinic); boiling pt.: 444.674°C. Related adj: **thionic b** (as modifier): sulphur springs [C14 soufre, from Old French, from Latin sulfur] > **sulphuric** or US **sulfuric** (sʌl'fjʊərɪk) adj

sulphurate ('sʌlfjʊ,reɪt) vb (tr) to combine or treat with sulphur or a sulphur compound > ,sulphu'ration n

sulphur-bottom n another name for **blue whale**

sulphur-crested cockatoo n a large Australian white parrot, Kakatoe galerita, with a yellow erectile crest. Also called: **white cockatoo**

sulphur dioxide n a colourless soluble pungent gas produced by burning sulphur. It is both an oxidizing and a reducing agent and is used in the manufacture of sulphuric acid, the preservation of a wide range of foodstuffs (**E220**), bleaching, and disinfecting. Formula: SO_2. Systematic name: sulphur(IV) oxide

sulphureous (sʌl'fjʊərɪəs) adj **1** another word for **sulphurous** (sense 1) **2** of the yellow colour of sulphur > sul'phureously adv > sul'phureousness n

sulphuret ('sʌlfjʊ,rɛt) vb **-rets**, **-retting**, **-retted** or US **-rets**, **-reting**, **-reted** (tr) to treat or combine with sulphur

sulphuretted hydrogen n another name for **hydrogen sulphide**

sulphuric acid n a colourless dense oily corrosive liquid produced by the reaction of sulphur trioxide with water and used in accumulators and in the manufacture of fertilizers, dyes, and explosives. Formula: H_2SO_4. Systematic name: sulphuric(VI) acid

sulphurize or **sulphurise** ('sʌlfjʊ,raɪz) vb (tr) to combine or treat with sulphur or a sulphur compound > ,sulphuri'zation or ,sulphuri'sation n

sulphurous ('sʌlfərəs) adj **1** Also: **sulphureous** of, relating to, or resembling sulphur: a sulphurous colour **2** of or containing sulphur with an oxidation state of 4: sulphurous acid **3** of or relating to hellfire **4** hot-tempered > 'sulphurously adv > 'sulphurousness n

sulphurous acid n an unstable acid produced when sulphur dioxide dissolves in water: used as a preservative for food and a bleaching agent. Formula: H_2SO_3. Systematic name: sulphuric(IV) acid

sulphur trioxide n a white corrosive substance existing in three crystalline forms of which the stable (alpha-) form is usually obtained as silky needles. It is produced by the oxidation of sulphur dioxide, and is used in the sulphonation of organic compounds. Formula: SO_3. Systematic name: sulphur(VI) oxide

sulphur tuft n a poisonous basidiomycetous fungus, Hypholoma fasciculare, having a sulphurous yellow cap and found in clumps on and around broad-leaved trees

sulphuryl ('sʌlfjʊrɪl, -fərɪl) n (modifier) of, consisting of, or containing the divalent group, –SO₂: sulphuryl chloride. Also: **sulphonyl** ('sʌlfə,nɪl)

sultan ('sʌltən) n **1** the sovereign of a Muslim country, esp of the former Ottoman Empire **2** an arbitrary ruler; despot **3** a small domestic fowl with a white crest and heavily feathered legs and feet: originated in Turkey [C16 from Medieval Latin sultānus, from Arabic sultān rule, from Aramaic salita to rule] > **sultanic** (sʌl'tænɪk) adj

> 'sultan-,like adj > 'sultanship n

sultana (sʌl'tɑːnə) n **1 a** the dried fruit of a small white seedless grape, originally produced in SW Asia: used in cakes, curries, etc; seedless raisin **b** the grape itself **2** Also called: **sultaness** a wife, concubine, or female relative of a sultan **3** a mistress; concubine [C16 from Italian, feminine of sultano SULTAN]

sultanate ('sʌltə,neɪt) n **1** the territory or a country ruled by a sultan **2** the office, rank, or jurisdiction of a sultan

sultry ('sʌltrɪ) adj **-trier**, **-triest 1** (of weather or climate) oppressively hot and humid **2** characterized by or emitting oppressive heat **3** displaying or suggesting passion; sensual: sultry eyes [C16 from obsolete sulter to SWELTER + -Y¹] > 'sultrily adv > 'sultriness n

Sulu Archipelago ('suːluː) n a chain of over 500 islands in the SW Philippines, separating the Sulu Sea from the Celebes Sea: formerly a sultanate, ceded to the Philippines in 1940. Capital: Jolo. Pop: 619 668 (2000). Area: 2686 sq km (1037 sq miles)

Sulu Sea n part of the W Pacific between Borneo and the central Philippines

sum¹ (sʌm) n **1 a** the result of the addition of numbers, quantities, objects, etc **b** the cardinality of the union of disjoint sets whose cardinalities are the given numbers **2** one or more columns or rows of numbers to be added, subtracted, multiplied, or divided **3** maths the limit of a series of sums of the first n terms of a converging infinite series as n tends to infinity **4** (plural) another name for **number work 5** a quantity, esp of money: he borrows enormous sums **6** the essence or gist of a matter (esp in the phrases **in sum, in sum and substance**) **7** a less common word for **summary 8** archaic the summit or maximum **9** (modifier) complete or final (esp in the phrase **sum total**) ▷ vb **sums**, **summing**, **summed 10** (often foll by up) to add or form a total of (something) **11** (tr) to calculate the sum of (the terms in a sequence) ▷ See also **sum up** [C13 summe, from Old French, from Latin summa the top, sum, from summus highest, from superus in a higher position; see SUPER]

sum² (sʊm) n, pl **sumy** (sʊmɪ) the standard monetary unit of Uzbekistan, divided into 100 tiyin

sumach or US **sumac** ('suːmæk, 'ʃuː-) n **1** any temperate or subtropical shrub or small tree of the anacardiaceous genus Rhus, having compound leaves, clusters of green flowers, and red hairy fruits. See also **poison sumach 2** a preparation of powdered leaves of certain species of Rhus, esp R. coriaria, used in dyeing and tanning **3** the wood of any of these plants [C14 via Old French from Arabic summāq]

Sumatra (sʊ'mɑːtrə) n a mountainous island in W Indonesia, in the Greater Sunda Islands, separated from the Malay Peninsula by the Strait of Malacca: Dutch control began in the 16th century; joined Indonesia in 1945. Northern coastal areas, esp Aceh province, suffered devastation as a result of the Indian Ocean tsunami of December 2004. Pop: 24 284 400 (1999 est). Area: 473 606 sq km (182 821 sq miles)

Sumatran (sʊ'mɑːtrən) adj **1** of or relating to Sumatra or its inhabitants ▷ n **2** a native or inhabitant of Sumatra

Sumba or **Soemba** ('suːmbə) n an island in Indonesia, in the Lesser Sunda Islands, separated from Flores by the Sumba Strait: formerly important for sandalwood exports. Pop: 355 073 (1990). Area: 11 153 sq km (4306 sq miles). Former name: **Sandalwood Island**

Sumbawa or **Soembawa** (suːm'bɑːwə) n a mountainous island in Indonesia, in the Lesser Sunda Islands, between Lombok and Flores Islands. Pop: 373 000 (1990 est). Area: 14 750 sq km (5695 sq miles)

Sumer ('suːmə) n the S region of Babylonia; seat of a civilization of city-states that reached its height in the 3rd millennium BC

Sumerian (suː'mɪərɪən, -'mɛər-) n **1** a member of a people who established a civilization in Sumer during the 4th millennium BC **2** the extinct language of this people, of no known relationship to any other language ▷ adj **3** of or relating to ancient Sumer, its inhabitants, or their language or civilization

summa ('sʊmɑː) n, pl **-mae** (-miː) **1** medieval Christianity theol a compendium of theology, philosophy, or canon law, or sometimes of all three together. The **Summa Theologica** of St Thomas Aquinas, written between 1265 and 1274, was the most famous of all such compendia **2** rare a comprehensive work or survey [C15 from Latin: SUM¹]

summa cum laude ('sʊmɑː kʊm 'laʊdeɪ) adv, adj chiefly US with the utmost praise: the highest of three designations for above-average achievement in examinations. In Britain it is sometimes used to designate a first-class honours degree. Compare **cum laude, magna cum laude** [from Latin]

summand ('sʌmænd, sʌ'mænd) n a number or quantity forming part of a sum [C19 from Medieval Latin summandus, from Latin summa SUM¹]

summarize or **summarise** ('sʌmə,raɪz) vb (tr) to make or be a summary of; express concisely
> 'summa,rizable or 'summa,risable adj
> ,summari'zation or ,summari'sation n
> 'summa,rizer, 'summa,riser or 'summarist n

summary ('sʌmərɪ) n, pl **-maries 1** a brief account giving the main points of something ▷ adj (usually prenominal) **2** performed arbitrarily and quickly, without formality: a summary execution **3** (of legal proceedings) short and free from the complexities and delays of a full trial **4** **summary jurisdiction** the right a court has to adjudicate immediately upon some matter arising during its proceedings **5** giving the gist or essence [C15 from Latin summārium, from summa SUM¹] > 'summarily adv > 'summariness n

summary offence n an offence that is triable in a magistrates' court

summat ('sʌmət) pron Brit not standard something: you gonna do summat about it or what?

summation (sʌ'meɪʃən) n **1** the act or process of determining a sum; addition **2** the result of such an act or process **3** a summary **4** US law the concluding statements made by opposing counsel in a case before a court [C18 from Medieval Latin summātiō, from summāre to total, from Latin summa SUM¹] > sum'mational adj > 'summative adj

summative assessment ('sʌmətɪv) n Brit education general assessment of a pupil's achievements over a range of subjects by means of a combined appraisal of formative assessments

summer¹ ('sʌmə) n **1** (sometimes capital) **a** the warmest season of the year, between spring and autumn, astronomically from the June solstice to the September equinox in the N hemisphere and at the opposite time of year in the S hemisphere **b** (as modifier): summer flowers; a summer dress. Related adj: **aestival 2** the period of hot weather associated with the summer **3** a time of blossoming, greatest happiness, etc **4** chiefly poetic a year represented by this season: a child of nine summers ▷ vb **5** (intr) to spend the summer (at a place) **6** (tr) to keep or feed (farm animals) during the summer: they summered their cattle on the mountain slopes [Old English sumor; related to Old Frisian sumur, Old Norse sumar, Old High German sumar, Sanskrit samā season] > 'summerless adj
> 'summer-,like adj > 'summerly adj, adv
> 'summery adj > 'summeriness n

summer² ('sʌmə) n **1** Also called: **summer tree** a large horizontal beam or girder, esp one that supports floor joists **2** another name for **lintel 3** a stone on the top of a column, pier, or wall that supports an arch or lintel [C14 from Anglo-Norman somer, from Old French somier beam, packhorse, from Late Latin *sagmārius* (*equus*) pack(horse), from *sagma* a packsaddle, from Greek]

summer cypress *n* another name for **kochia**

summerhouse ('sʌmə,haʊs) *n* a small building in a garden or park, used for shade or recreation in the summer

summer pudding *n Brit* a pudding made by filling a bread lined basin with a purée of fruit, leaving it to soak, and then turning it out

summersault ('sʌmə,sɔ:lt) *n, vb* a variant spelling of **somersault**

summer school *n* a school, academic course, etc, held during the summer

summer solstice *n* **1** the time at which the sun is at its northernmost point in the sky (southernmost point in the S hemisphere), appearing at noon at its highest altitude above the horizon. It occurs about June 21 (December 22 in the S hemisphere) **2** *astronomy* the point on the celestial sphere, opposite the **winter solstice**, at which the ecliptic is furthest north from the celestial equator. Right ascension: 6 hours; declination: 23.5°

summer sores *n vet science* a condition of horses in which itchy lesions are caused by infestation of wounds with *Habronema* larvae from flies

summertime ('sʌmə,taɪm) *n* the period or season of summer

summer time *n Brit* any daylight-saving time, esp British Summer Time

summerweight ('sʌmə,weɪt) *adj* (of clothes) suitable in weight for wear in the summer; relatively light

summerwood ('sʌmə,wʊd) *n* the wood that is produced by a plant near the end of the growing season: consists of small thick-walled xylem cells. Compare **springwood**

summing-up *n* **1** a review or summary of the main points of an argument, speech, etc **2** a direction regarding the law and a summary of the evidence, given by a judge in his address to the jury before they retire to consider their verdict

summit ('sʌmɪt) *n* **1** the highest point or part, esp of a mountain or line of communication; top **2** the highest possible degree or state; peak or climax: *the summit of ambition* **3** the highest level, importance, or rank: *a meeting at the summit* **4 a** a meeting of chiefs of governments or other high officials **b** (*as modifier*): *a summit conference* [c15 from Old French *somet*, diminutive of *som*, from Latin *summum*; see SUM¹] > **'summital** *adj*
> **'summitless** *adj*

summiteer (,sʌmɪ'tɪə) *n* a person who participates in a summit conference

summitry ('sʌmɪtrɪ) *n chiefly US* the practice of conducting international negotiations by summit conferences

summon ('sʌmən) *vb* (*tr*) **1** to order to come; send for, esp to attend court, by issuing a summons **2** to order or instruct (to do something) or call (to something): *the bell summoned them to their work* **3** to call upon to meet or convene **4** (often foll by *up*) to muster or gather (one's strength, courage, etc) [c13 from Latin *summonēre* to give a discreet reminder, from *monēre* to advise]
> **'summonable** *adj*

summons ('sʌmənz) *n, pl* **-monses 1** a call, signal, or order to do something, esp to appear in person or attend at a specified place or time **2 a** an official order requiring a person to attend court, either to answer a charge or to give evidence **b** the writ making such an order. Compare **warrant 3** a call or command given to the members of an assembly to convene a meeting ▷ *vb* **4** to take out a summons against (a person) [c13 from Old French *somonse*, from *somondre* to SUMMON]

summum bonum *Latin* ('sʊmʊm 'bɒnʊm) *n* the principle of goodness in which all moral values are included or from which they are derived; highest or supreme good

sumo ('su:məʊ) *n* the national style of wrestling of Japan, the object of which is to force one's opponent to touch the ground with any part of his body except the soles of his feet or to step out of the ring [from Japanese *sumō*]

sump (sʌmp) *n* **1** a receptacle, such as the lower part of the crankcase of an internal-combustion engine, into which liquids, esp lubricants, can drain to form a reservoir **2** another name for **cesspool 3** *mining* **a** a depression at the bottom of a shaft where water collects before it is pumped away **b** the front portion of a shaft or tunnel, ahead of the main bore **4** *Brit dialect* a muddy pool or swamp [c17 from Middle Dutch *somp* marsh; see SWAMP]

sumph (sʌmf) *n Scot* a stupid person; simpleton [c18 of uncertain origin]

sumpter ('sʌmptə) *n archaic* a packhorse, mule, or other beast of burden [c14 from Old French *sometier* driver of a baggage horse, from Vulgar Latin *sagmatārius* (unattested), from Late Latin *sagma* packsaddle]

sumptuary ('sʌmptjʊərɪ) *adj* relating to or controlling expenditure or extravagance [c17 from Latin *sumptuārius* concerning expense, from *sumptus* expense, from *sūmere* to spend]

sumptuary law *n* (formerly) a law imposing restraint on luxury, esp by limiting personal expenditure or by regulating personal conduct in religious and moral spheres

sumptuous ('sʌmptjʊəs) *adj* **1** expensive or extravagant: *sumptuous costumes* **2** magnificent; splendid: *a sumptuous scene* [c16 from Old French *somptueux*, from Latin *sumptuōsus* costly, from *sumptus*; see SUMPTUARY] > **'sumptuously** *adv*
> **'sumptuousness** or **sumptuosity** (,sʌmptjʊ'ɒsɪtɪ) *n*

Sumter ('sʌmtə) *n* See **Fort Sumter**

sum up *vb* (*adverb*) **1** to summarize (feelings, the main points of an argument, etc): *the judge began to sum up* **2** (*tr*) to form a quick opinion of: *I summed him up in five minutes*

Sumy (*Russian* 'sumɪ) *n* a city in Ukraine, on the River Pysol: site of early Slav settlements. Pop: 294 000 (2005 est)

sun (sʌn) *n* **1** the star at the centre of our solar system. It is a gaseous body having a highly compressed core, in which energy is generated by thermonuclear reactions (at about 15 million kelvins), surrounded by less dense radiative and convective zones serving to transport the energy to the surface (the **photosphere**). The atmospheric layers (the **chromosphere** and **corona**) are normally invisible except during a total eclipse. Mass and diameter: 333 000 and 109 times that of earth respectively; mean distance from earth: 149.6 million km (1 astronomical unit). Related adj: **solar 2** any star around which a planetary system revolves **3** the sun as it appears at a particular time or place: *the winter sun* **4** the radiant energy, esp heat and light, received from the sun; sunshine **5** a person or thing considered as a source of radiant warmth, glory, etc **6** a pictorial representation of the sun, often depicted with a human face **7** *poetic* a year or a day **8** *poetic* a climate **9** *archaic* sunrise or sunset (esp in the phrase **from sun to sun**) **10 catch the sun** to become slightly sunburnt **11 place in the sun** a prominent or favourable position **12 take** or **shoot the sun** *nautical* to measure the altitude of the sun in order to determine latitude **13 touch of the sun** slight sunstroke **14 under** or **beneath the sun** on earth; at all: *nobody under the sun eats more than you do* ▷ *vb* **suns, sunning, sunned 15** to expose (oneself) to the sunshine **16** (*tr*) to expose to the sunshine in order to warm, tan, etc [Old English *sunne*; related to Old High German *sunna*, Old Frisian *senne*, Gothic *sunno*] > **'sun,like** *adj*

Sun. *abbreviation for* Sunday

sunbake ('sʌn,beɪk) *Austral informal* ▷ *vb* (*intr*) **1** to sunbathe, esp in order to become tanned ▷ *n* **2** a period of sunbaking

sunbaked ('sʌn,beɪkt) *adj* **1** (esp of roads, etc) dried or cracked by the sun's heat **2** baked hard by the heat of the sun: *sunbaked bricks*

sun bath *n* the exposure of the body to the rays of the sun or a sun lamp, esp in order to get a suntan

sunbathe ('sʌn,beɪð) *vb* (*intr*) to bask in the sunshine, esp in order to get a suntan
> **'sun,bather** *n*

sunbeam ('sʌn,bi:m) *n* **1** a beam, ray, or stream of sunlight **2** *Austral slang* a piece of crockery or cutlery laid for a meal but remaining unused
> **'sun,beamed** or **'sun,beamy** *adj*

sun bear *n* a small bear, *Helarctos malayanus*, of tropical forests in S and SE Asia, having a black coat and a yellowish snout and feeding mostly on honey and insects. Also called: **honey bear**

sunbed ('sʌn,bed) *n Brit* **1** a piece of equipment, usu consisting of rows of lights, which surrounds a person with ultraviolet rays in order to induce an artificial suntan **2** a bed or couch for lying on in the sun

Sunbelt ('sʌn,belt) *n* the southern states of the USA

sunbird ('sʌn,bɜ:d) *n* any small songbird of the family *Nectariniidae*, of tropical regions of the Old World, esp Africa, having a long slender curved bill and a bright plumage in the males

sun bittern *n* a cranelike bird, *Eurypyga helias*, of tropical American forests, having a greyish plumage with orange and brown wings: family *Eurypygidae*, order *Gruiformes* (cranes, rails, etc)

sun blind *n chiefly Brit* a blind, such as a Venetian blind, that shades a room from the sun's glare

sun block *n* a chemical, usually in the form of a cream, applied to exposed skin to block out all or almost all of the ultraviolet rays of the sun

sunbonnet ('sʌn,bɒnɪt) *n* a hat that shades the face and neck from the sun, esp one made of cotton with a projecting brim now worn esp by babies > **'sun,bonneted** *adj*

sunbow ('sʌn,bəʊ) *n* a bow of prismatic colours similar to a rainbow, produced when sunlight shines through spray

sunburn ('sʌn,bɜ:n) *n* **1** inflammation of the skin caused by overexposure to the sun. Technical name: **erythema solare 2** another word for **suntan.** > **'sun,burnt** or **'sun,burned** *adj*

sunburst ('sʌn,bɜ:st) *n* **1** a burst of sunshine, as through a break in the clouds **2** a pattern or design resembling that of the sun **3** a jewelled brooch with this pattern

sunburst pleats *pl n* the US term for **sunray pleats**

Sunbury-on-Thames ('sʌnbərɪ, -brɪ) *n* a town in SE England, in N Surrey. Pop: 27 415 (2001)

sun-cured *adj* cured or preserved by exposure to the sun

sundae ('sʌndɪ, -deɪ) *n* ice cream topped with a sweet sauce, nuts, whipped cream, etc [c20 of uncertain origin]

Sunda Islands ('sʌndə) or **Soenda Islands** *pl n* a chain of islands in the Malay Archipelago, consisting of the **Greater Sunda Islands** (chiefly Sumatra, Java, Borneo, and Sulawesi) and **Nusa Tenggara** (the Lesser Sunda Islands)

sun dance *n* a North American Indian ceremony associated with the sun, performed at the summer solstice

Sunda Strait or **Soenda Strait** *n* a strait between Sumatra and Java, linking the Java Sea with the Indian Ocean. Narrowest point: about 26 km (16 miles)

Sunday ('sʌndɪ) *n* the first day of the week and the Christian day of worship [Old English *sunnandæg*, translation of Latin *diēs sōlis* day of the sun, translation of Greek *hēmera hēliou*; related to Old Norse *sunnu dagr*, German *Sonntag*]

Sunday best *n* one's best clothes, esp regarded as those most suitable for churchgoing

Sunday driver *n informal* a person who drives slowly, timorously, or unskilfully, as if used to driving only on Sundays when the roads are relatively quiet

Sunday painter *n* a person who paints pictures

S

as a hobby

Sunday punch *n informal, chiefly US* **1** *boxing* a heavy blow intended to knock out one's opponent **2** any manoeuvre or action intended to crush an opponent

Sunday school *n* **1 a** a school for the religious instruction of children on Sundays, usually held in a church hall and formerly also providing secular education **b** (*as modifier*): *a Sunday-school outing* **2** the members of such a school

sun deck *n* **1** an upper open deck on a passenger ship **2** *US, Austral, and NZ* a balcony or deck attached to a house, originally used for sunbathing

sunder ('sʌndə) *archaic or literary ▷ vb* **1** to break or cause to break apart or in pieces ▷ *n* **2 in sunder** into pieces; apart [Old English *sundrian*; related to Old Norse *sundr* asunder, Gothic *sundrō* apart, Old High German *suntar*, Latin *sine* without] > '**sunderable** *adj* > '**sunderance** *n* > '**sunderer** *n*

Sunderland ('sʌndələnd) *n* **1** a city and port in NE England, in Sunderland unitary authority, Tyne and Wear: at the mouth of the River Wear: formerly known for shipbuilding now has car manufacturing, chemicals; university (1992). Pop: 177 739 (2001) **2** a unitary authority in NE England, in Tyne and Wear. Pop: 283 100 (2003 est). Area: 138 sq km (53 sq miles)

sundew ('sʌn,dju:) *n* any of several bog plants of the genus *Drosera*, having leaves covered with sticky hairs that trap and digest insects: family *Droseraceae* [c16 translation of Latin *ros solis*]

sundial ('sʌn,daɪəl) *n* a device indicating the time during the hours of sunlight by means of a stationary arm (the **gnomon**) that casts a shadow onto a plate or surface marked in hours

sun disc *n* a disc symbolizing the sun, esp one flanked by two serpents and the extended wings of a vulture, used as a religious figure in ancient Egypt

sundog ('sʌn,dɒg) *n* **1** another word for **parhelion** **2** a small rainbow or halo near the horizon

sundown ('sʌn,daʊn) *n* another name for **sunset**

sundowner ('sʌn,daʊnə) *n* **1** *Austral and NZ obsolete slang* a tramp, esp one who seeks food and lodging at sundown when it is too late to work **2** *nautical* a strict ship's officer **3** *informal, chiefly Brit* an alcoholic drink taken at sunset **4** *NZ slang* a lazy sheepdog

sundress ('sʌn,drɛs) *n* a dress for hot weather that exposes the shoulders, arms, and back, esp one with straps over the shoulders

sun-dried *adj* dried or preserved by exposure to the sun

sundry ('sʌndrɪ) *determiner* **1** several or various; miscellaneous ▷ *pron* **2 all and sundry** all the various people, individually and collectively ▷ *n, pl* -**dries 3** (*plural*) miscellaneous unspecified items **4** *Austral cricket* a run not scored from the bat, such as a wide, no-ball, bye, or leg bye. also called: **extra** [Old English *syndrig* separate; related to Old High German *suntarig*; see SUNDER, -Y¹]

sundry shop *n* (in Malaysia) a shop, similar to a delicatessen, that sells predominantly Chinese foodstuffs

Sundsvall (*Swedish* 'sʊndsval) *n* a port in E Sweden, on the Gulf of Bothnia: icebound in winter; cellulose industries. Pop: 93 623 (2004 est)

sunfast ('sʌn,fɑ:st) *adj chiefly US and Canadian* not fading in sunlight

sunfish ('sʌn,fɪʃ) *n, pl* -**fish** *or* -**fishes 1** any large plectognath fish of the family *Molidae*, of temperate and tropical seas, esp *Mola mola*, which has a large rounded compressed body, long pointed dorsal and anal fins, and a fringelike tail fin **2** any of various small predatory North American freshwater percoid fishes of the family *Centrarchidae*, typically having a compressed brightly coloured body

sunflower ('sʌn,flaʊə) *n* **1** any of several American plants of the genus *Helianthus*, esp *H. annuus*, having very tall thick stems, large flower heads with yellow rays, and seeds used as food, esp for poultry: family *Asteraceae* (composites). See also **Jerusalem artichoke 2 sunflower seed oil** the oil extracted from sunflower seeds, used as a salad oil, in the manufacture of margarine, etc

sung (sʌŋ) *vb* **1** the past participle of **sing** ▷ *adj* **2** produced by singing: *a sung syllable*

🔲 USAGE See at **ring²**

Sungari ('sʊŋgərɪ) *n* another name for the Songhua

Sungkiang ('sʊŋ'kjæŋ, -kaɪ'æŋ) *n* a former province of NE China: now part of the Inner Mongolian AR

sunglass ('sʌn,glɑ:s) *n* a convex lens used to focus the sun's rays and thus produce heat or ignition; burning glass

sunglasses ('sʌn,glɑ:sɪz) *pl n* glasses with darkened or polarizing lenses that protect the eyes from the sun's glare

sunglow ('sʌn,gləʊ) *n* a pinkish glow often seen in the sky before sunrise or after sunset. It is caused by scattering or diffraction of sunlight by particles in the atmosphere

sun-god *n* **1** the sun considered as a personal deity **2** a deity associated with the sun or controlling its movements

sungrebe ('sʌn,gri:b) *n* another name for **finfoot**

sunhat ('sʌn,hæt) *n* a hat that shades the face and neck from the sun

sunk (sʌŋk) *vb* **1** a past participle of **sink** ▷ *adj* **2** *informal* with all hopes dashed; ruined: *if the police come while we're opening the safe, we'll be sunk*

sunken ('sʌŋkən) *vb* **1** a past participle of **sink** ▷ *adj* **2** unhealthily hollow: *sunken cheeks* **3** situated at a lower level than the surrounding or usual one **4** situated under water; submerged **5** depressed; low: *sunken spirits*

sunk fence *n* a ditch, one side of which is made into a retaining wall so as to enclose an area of land while remaining hidden in the total landscape. Also called: **ha-ha**

sun lamp *n* a lamp that generates ultraviolet rays, used for obtaining an artificial suntan, for muscular therapy, etc **2** a lamp used in film studios, etc, to give an intense beam of light by means of parabolic mirrors

sunless ('sʌnlɪs) *adj* **1** without sun or sunshine **2** gloomy; depressing > '**sunlessly** *adv* > '**sunlessness** *n*

sunlight ('sʌnlaɪt) *n* **1** the light emanating from the sun **2** an area or the time characterized by sunshine > '**sunlit** *adj*

sun lounge *or US* **sun parlor** *n* a room with large windows positioned to receive as much sunlight as possible

sunn (sʌn) *n* **1** a leguminous plant, *Crotalaria juncea*, of the East Indies, having yellow flowers **2** the hemplike fibre obtained from the inner bark of this plant, used in making rope, sacking, etc [c18 from Hindi *san*, from Sanskrit *śáná* hempen]

Sunna ('sʌnə) *n* the body of traditional Islamic law accepted by most orthodox Muslims as based on the words and acts of Mohammed [c18 from Arabic *sunnah* rule]

Sunni ('sʌnɪ) *n* **1** one of the two main branches of orthodox Islam (the other being the Shiah), consisting of those who acknowledge the authority of the Sunna **2** *pl* -**nis** *or* -**ni** another term for **Sunnite**

sunnies ('sʌnɪz) *pl n NZ informal* a pair of sunglasses

Sunnite ('sʌnaɪt) *n Islam* an adherent of the Sunni

sunny ('sʌnɪ) *adj* -**nier**, -**niest 1** full of or exposed to sunlight **2** radiating good humour **3** of or resembling the sun > '**sunnily** *adv* > '**sunniness** *n*

sunny side *n* **1** the cheerful aspect or point of view: *look on the sunny side of things* **2 on the sunny side of** *informal* younger than (a specified age)

sunny-side up *adj* (of eggs) fried on one side only

sunray pleats ('sʌn,reɪ) *pl n Brit* bias-cut knife pleats that are narrower at the top than at the bottom, producing a flared effect, used esp for skirts. US term: **sunburst pleats**

sunrise ('sʌn,raɪz) *n* **1** the daily appearance of the sun above the horizon **2** the atmospheric phenomena accompanying this appearance **3** Also called (esp US): **sunup** the time at which the sun rises at a particular locality **4** (*modifier*) of or relating to sunrise industry: *sunrise technology; sunrise sector*

sunrise industry *n* any of the high-technology industries, such as electronics, that hold promise of future development

sunroof ('sʌn,ru:f) *or* **sunshine roof** *n* a panel, often translucent, that may be opened in the roof of a car

sunroom ('sʌn,ru:m, 'sʌn,rʊm) *n* a room or glass-enclosed porch designed to display beautiful views, to admit and retain the sun's heat in cool countries, and reflect it away in warm countries

sunscreen ('sʌn,skri:n) *n* a cream or lotion applied to exposed skin to protect it from the ultraviolet rays of the sun

sunset ('sʌn,sɛt) *n* **1** the daily disappearance of the sun below the horizon **2** the atmospheric phenomena accompanying this disappearance **3** Also called: **sundown** the time at which the sun sets at a particular locality **4** the final stage or closing period, as of a person's life

sunshade ('sʌn,ʃeɪd) *n* a device, esp a parasol or awning, serving to shade from the sun

sunshine ('sʌn,ʃaɪn) *n* **1** the light received directly from the sun **2** the warmth from the sun **3** a sunny area **4** a light-hearted or ironic term of address > '**sun,shiny** *adj*

sunspot ('sʌn,spɒt) *n* **1** any of the dark cool patches, with a diameter of up to several thousand kilometres, that appear on the surface of the sun and last about a week. They occur in approximately 11-year cycles and possess a strong magnetic field **2** *informal* a sunny holiday resort **3** *Austral* a small cancerous spot produced by overexposure to the sun > '**sun,spotted** *adj*

sunstar ('sʌn,stɑ:) *n* any starfish of the genus *Solaster*, having up to 13 arms radiating from a central disc

sunstone ('sʌn,stəʊn) *n* another name for **aventurine** (sense 2) [c17 so called because it contains red and gold flecks which reflect the light]

sunstroke ('sʌn,strəʊk) *n* heatstroke caused by prolonged exposure to intensely hot sunlight

sunsuit ('sʌn,su:t, -,sju:t) *n* a child's outfit consisting of a brief top and shorts or a short skirt

suntan ('sʌn,tæn) *n* **a** a brownish colouring of the skin caused by the formation of the pigment melanin within the skin on exposure to the ultraviolet rays of the sun or a sunlamp. Often shortened to: **tan b** (*as modifier*): *suntan oil* > '**sun,tanned** *adj*

suntrap ('sʌn,træp) *n* a very sunny sheltered place

sunup ('sʌn,ʌp) *n* another name (esp US) for **sunrise** (sense 3)

sunward ('sʌnwəd) *adj* **1** directed or moving towards the sun ▷ *adv* **2** a variant of **sunwards**

sunwards ('sʌnwədz) *or* **sunward** *adv* towards the sun

sunwise ('sʌn,waɪz) *adv* moving in the same direction as the sun; clockwise

suo jure ('su:əʊ 'dʒʊərɪ) *adv chiefly law* in one's own right [Latin]

suo loco ('su:əʊ 'lɒkəʊ) *adv chiefly law* in a person or thing's own or rightful place [Latin]

Suomi ('sʊɒmɪ) *n* the Finnish name for **Finland**

sup¹ (sʌp) *vb* **sups, supping, supped 1** (*intr*) *archaic* to have supper **2** (*tr*) *obsolete* to provide with supper [c13 from Old French *soper*; see SUP²]

sup² (sʌp) *vb* **sups, supping, supped 1** to partake of (liquid) by swallowing a little at a time **2** *Scot and northern English dialect* to drink ▷ *n* **3** a sip [Old English *sūpan*; related to Old High German *sūfan*, German *saufen*; see also SUP¹]

sup. *abbreviation for* **1** above [from Latin *supra*] **2** superior **3** *grammar* superlative

super ('su:pə) *adj* **1** *informal* outstanding; exceptionally fine ▷ *n* **2** petrol with a high octane rating **3** *informal* a superintendent or supervisor **4** *Austral and NZ informal* superannuation benefits **5** *Austral and NZ informal* superphosphate ▷ *interj* **6** *Brit informal* an enthusiastic expression of approval or assent [from Latin: above]

super- *prefix* **1** placed above or over: *superscript* **2** of greater size, extent, quality, etc: *supermarket* **3** surpassing others; outstanding: *superstar* **4** beyond a standard or norm; exceeding or exceedingly: *supersonic* **5** indicating that a chemical compound contains a specified element in a higher proportion than usual: *superoxide* [from Latin *super* above]

superable ('su:pərəbəl, -prəbəl) *adj* able to be surmounted or overcome [c17 from Latin *superābilis*, from *superāre* to overcome] > ,supera'bility or 'superableness *n* > 'superably *adv*

superabound (,su:pərə'baʊnd) *vb* **1** (*intr*) to abound abnormally; be in surplus **2** *rare* to be more abundant than (something else) > superabundance (,su:pərə'bʌndəns) *n* > ,supera'bundant *adj*

superadd (,su:pər'æd) *vb* (*tr*) to add (something) to something that has already been added; add as extra > ,superad'dition *n* > ,superad'ditional *adj*

superaerodynamics (,su:pə,ɛərəʊdaɪ'næmɪks) *n* (*functioning as singular*) the study of aerodynamics at very high altitudes, where the air density is very low

superaltar ('su:pər,ɔ:ltə) *n Christianity* a consecrated portable stone slab for use on an unconsecrated altar

superannuate (,su:pər'ænjʊ,eɪt) *vb* (*tr*) **1** to pension off **2** to discard as obsolete or old-fashioned

superannuated (,su:pər'ænjʊ,eɪtɪd) *adj* **1** discharged, esp with a pension, owing to age or illness **2** too old to serve usefully **3** *obsolete* [c17 from Medieval Latin *superannnātus* aged more than one year, from Latin SUPER- + *annus* a year]

superannuation (,su:pər,ænjʊ'eɪʃən) *n* **1 a** the amount deducted regularly from employees' incomes in a contributory pension scheme **b** the pension finally paid to such employees **2** the act or process of superannuating or the condition of being superannuated

superb (sʊ'pɜ:b, sjʊ-) *adj* **1** surpassingly good; excellent: *a superb actor* **2** majestic or imposing: *a superb mansion* **3** magnificently rich; luxurious: *the jubilee was celebrated with a superb banquet* [c16 from Old French *superbe*, from Latin *superbus* distinguished, from *super* above] > su'perbly *adv* > su'perbness *n*

superbazaar or **superbazar** ('su:pəbə'zɑ:) *n* (in India) a large department store or supermarket, esp one set up as a cooperative store by the government

superb blue wren *n* a small Australian bird, *Malurus cyaneus*, the adult male of which has bright blue plumage

superbike ('su:pə,baɪk) *n* a high-performance motorcycle

Super Bowl *n American football* the main championship game of the sport, held annually in January between the champions of the American Football Conference and the National Football Conference

superbug ('su:pə,bʌg) *n informal* an infective microorganism that has become resistant to antibiotics

supercalender (,su:pə'kæləndə) *n* **1** a calender with a number of rollers that gives a high gloss to paper ▷ *vb* **2** (*tr*) to produce a glossy finish on (paper) by pressing in a supercalender > ,super'calendered *adj*

supercar ('su:pə,kɑ:) *n* a very expensive fast or powerful car with a centrally located engine

supercargo (,su:pə'kɑ:gəʊ) *n, pl* -goes an officer on a merchant ship who supervises commercial matters and is in charge of the cargo [c17 changed from Spanish *sobrecargo*, from *sobre* over (from Latin SUPER) + *cargo* CARGO]

supercharge ('su:pə,tʃɑ:dʒ) *vb* (*tr*) **1** to increase the air intake pressure of (an internal-combustion engine) with a supercharger; boost **2** to charge (the atmosphere, a remark, etc) with an excess amount of (tension, emotion, etc) **3** to apply pressure to (a fluid); pressurize

supercharger ('su:pə,tʃɑ:dʒə) *n* a device, usually a fan or compressor driven by the engine, that increases the mass of air drawn into an internal-combustion engine by raising the intake pressure. Also called: blower, booster

superciliary (,su:pə'sɪliəri) *adj* relating to or situated over the eyebrow or a corresponding region in lower animals [c18 from New Latin *superciliaris*, from Latin *supercilium*, from SUPER- + *cilium* eyelid]

supercilious (,su:pə'sɪliəs) *adj* displaying arrogant pride, scorn, or indifference [c16 from Latin *superciliōsus*, from *supercilium* eyebrow; see SUPERCILIARY] > ,super'ciliously *adv* > ,super'ciliousness *n*

superclass ('su:pə,klɑ:s) *n* a taxonomic group that is a subdivision of a subphylum

supercolumnar (,su:pəkə'lʌmnə) *adj architect* **1** having one colonnade above another **2** placed above a colonnade or a column > ,supercol,umni'ation *n*

supercomputer (,su:pəkəm'pju:tə) *n* a powerful computer that can process large quantities of data of a similar type very quickly > ,supercom'puting *n*

superconductivity (,su:pə,kɒndʌk'tɪvɪti) *n physics* the property of certain substances that have no electrical resistance. In metals it occurs at very low temperatures, but higher temperature superconductivity occurs in some ceramic materials > superconduction (,su:pəkən'dʌkʃən) *n* > ,supercon'ductive or ,supercon'ducting *adj* > ,supercon'ductor *n*

supercontinent ('su:pə,kɒntɪnənt) *n* a great landmass thought to have existed in the geological past and to have split into smaller landmasses, which drifted and formed the present continents

supercool (,su:pə'ku:l) *vb chem* to cool or be cooled without freezing or crystallization to a temperature below that at which freezing or crystallization should occur. Supercooled liquids are not in equilibrium

supercow ('su:pə,kaʊ) *n* a dairy cow that produces a very high milk yield as a result of selective breeding or genetic modification [c20]

supercritical (,su:pə'krɪtɪkəl) *adj* **1** *physics* (of a fluid) brought to a temperature and pressure higher than its critical temperature and pressure, so that its physical and chemical properties change **2** *nuclear physics* of or containing more than the critical mass

superdense ('su:pə,dɛns) *adj astronomy* of or relating to an extreme condition in which matter is forced into nonclassical states, as when electrons are forced into protons, leaving only neutrons: *superdense matter*

superdense theory (,su:pə'dɛns) *n astronomy* a former name for the big-bang theory

superdominant (,su:pə'dɒmɪnənt) *n US and Canadian* another word for submediant

super-duper (,su:pə'du:pə) *adj informal* extremely pleasing, impressive, etc: often used as an exclamation

superego (,su:pər'i:gəʊ, -'ɛgəʊ) *n, pl* -gos *psychoanal* that part of the unconscious mind that acts as a conscience for the ego, developing mainly from the relationship between a child and his parents. See also id, ego

superelastic (,su:pərɪ'læstɪk) *adj physics* (of collisions) involving an overall increase in translational kinetic energy

superelevation (,su:pər,ɛlɪ'veɪʃən) *n* **1** another name for bank² (sense 7) **2** the difference between the heights of the sides of a road or railway track on a bend

supereminent (,su:pər'ɛmɪnənt) *adj* of distinction, dignity, or rank superior to that of others; pre-eminent > ,super'eminence *n*

supererogate (,su:pər'ɛrə,geɪt) *vb* (*intr*) *obsolete* to do or perform more than is required [c16 from Late Latin *superērogāre* to spend over and above, from Latin SUPER- + *ērogāre* to pay out] > ,super'ero,gator *n*

supererogation (,su:pər,ɛrə'geɪʃən) *n* **1** the performance of work in excess of that required **2** *RC Church* supererogatory prayers, devotions, etc

supererogatory (,su:pərɛ'rɒgətəri, -tri) *adj* **1** performed to an extent exceeding that required or expected **2** exceeding what is needed; superfluous **3** *RC Church* of, characterizing, or relating to prayers, good works, etc, performed over and above those prescribed as obligatory [c16 from Medieval Latin *superērogātōrius*; see SUPEREROGATE] > ,super'erogatorily *adv*

superette (,su:pə'rɛt) *n NZ informal* a small store or dairy laid out along the lines of a supermarket

superfamily ('su:pə,fæmɪli) *n, pl* -lies **1** *biology* a taxonomic group that is a subdivision of a suborder **2** any analogous group, such as a group of related languages

superfecundation (,su:pə,fi:kən'deɪʃən) *n physiol* the fertilization of two or more ova, produced during the same menstrual cycle, by sperm ejaculated during two or more acts of sexual intercourse

superfemale ('su:pə,fi:meɪl) *n* a former name for **metafemale**

superfetation (,su:pəfi:'teɪʃən) *n physiol* the presence in the uterus of two fetuses developing from ova fertilized at different times [C17 *superfetate*, from Latin *superfētāre* to fertilize when already pregnant, from SUPER- + *fētāre* to impregnate, from *fētus* offspring] > superfetate (,su:pə'fi:teɪt) *adj*

superficial (,su:pə'fɪʃəl) *adj* **1** of, relating to, being near, or forming the surface: *superficial bruising* **2** displaying a lack of thoroughness or care: *a superficial inspection* **3** only outwardly apparent rather than genuine or actual: *the similarity was merely superficial* **4** of little substance or significance; trivial: *superficial differences* **5** lacking originality or profundity: *the film's plot was quite superficial* **6** (of measurements) involving only the surface area [c14 from Late Latin *superficiālis* of the surface, from Latin SUPERFICIES] > superficiality (,su:pə,fɪʃɪ'ælɪti) or less commonly ,super'ficialness *n* > ,super'ficially *adv*

superficies (,su:pə'fɪʃi:z) *n, pl* -cies *rare* **1** a surface or outer face **2** the outward form of a thing [c16 from Latin: upper side, from SUPER- + *faciēs* face]

superfine (,su:pə'faɪn) *adj* **1** of exceptional fineness or quality **2** excessively refined > ,super'fineness *n*

superfix ('su:pə,fɪks) *n linguistics* a suprasegmental feature distinguishing the meaning or grammatical function of one word or phrase from that of another, as stress does for example between the noun *conduct* and the verb *conduct* [from SUPER- + -*fix*, on the model of PREFIX, SUFFIX]

superfluid (,su:pə'flu:ɪd) *n* **1** *physics* a fluid in a state characterized by a very low viscosity, high thermal conductivity, high capillarity, etc The only known example is that of liquid helium at temperatures close to absolute zero ▷ *adj* **2** being or relating to a superfluid

superfluidity (,su:pəflu:'ɪdɪti) *n physics* the state of being or property of becoming a superfluid

superfluity (,su:pə'flu:ɪti) *n* **1** the condition of being superfluous **2** a quantity or thing that is in excess of what is needed **3** a thing that is not needed [c14 from Old French *superfluité*, via Late Latin from Latin *superfluus* SUPERFLUOUS]

S

superfluous (suːˈpɜːfluəs) *adj* **1** exceeding what is sufficient or required **2** not necessary or relevant; uncalled-for **3** *obsolete* extravagant in expenditure or oversupplied with possessions [c15 from Latin *superfluus* overflowing, from SUPER- + *fluere* to flow] > su'**perfluously** *adv* > su'**perfluousness** *n*

superfuse (ˌsuːpəˈfjuːz) *vb obsolete* to pour or be poured so as to cover something [c17 from Latin *superfūsus* poured over, from *superfundere,* from SUPER- + *fundere* to pour] > ˌsuper'**fusion** *n*

Super-G *n skiing* a type of slalom in which the course is shorter than in a standard slalom and the obstacles are farther apart than in a giant slalom [c20 from SUPER- + G(IANT)]

supergiant (ˈsuːpəˌdʒaɪənt) *n* any of a class of extremely large and luminous stars, such as Betelgeuse, which have expanded to a large diameter and are eventually likely to explode as supernovae. Compare **giant star, white dwarf**

superglacial (ˌsuːpəˈɡleɪsɪəl) *adj* on or originating from the surface of a glacier

superglue (ˈsuːpəˌɡluː) *n* any of various impact adhesives that quickly make an exceptionally strong bond

supergrass (ˈsuːpəˌɡrɑːs) *n* an informer whose information implicates a large number of people in terrorist activities or other major crimes

supergravity (ˌsuːpəˈɡrævɪtɪ) *n physics* any of various theories in which supersymmetry is applied to the theory of gravitation

supergroup (ˈsuːpəˌɡruːp) *n* a rock band whose members are individually famous from previous groups

superheat (ˌsuːpəˈhiːt) *vb* (*tr*) **1** to heat (a vapour, esp steam) to a temperature above its saturation point for a given pressure **2** to heat (a liquid) to a temperature above its boiling point without boiling occurring **3** to heat excessively; overheat > ˌsuper'**heater** *n*

superheavy (ˌsuːpəˈhɛvɪ) *n physics* denoting or relating to elements of high atomic number (above 109) postulated to exist with special stability as a consequence of the shell model of the nucleus

superheavyweight (ˌsuːpəˈhɛvɪweɪt) *n* **a** an amateur boxer weighing more than 91 kg **b** (*as modifier*): *a superheavyweight bout*

superhero (ˈsuːpəˌhɪərəʊ) *n, pl* -**roes** any of various comic-strip characters with superhuman abilities or magical powers, wearing a distinctive costume, and fighting against evil

super-heroine *n* a fictional woman character with superhuman abilities or magical powers, wearing a distinctive costume, and fighting against evil

superhet (ˈsuːpəˌhɛt) *n* See **superheterodyne receiver**

superheterodyne receiver (ˌsuːpəˈhɛtərəˌdaɪn) *n* a radio receiver that combines two radio-frequency signals by heterodyne action, to produce a signal above the audible frequency limit. This signal is amplified and demodulated to give the desired audio-frequency signal. Sometimes shortened to: **superhet** [c20 from SUPER(SONIC) + HETERODYNE]

superhigh frequency (ˈsuːpəˌhaɪ) *n* a radio-frequency band or radio frequency lying between 30 000 and 3000 megahertz. Abbreviation: **SHF**

superhighway (ˈsuːpəˌhaɪweɪ) *n chiefly US* a fast dual-carriageway road

superhuman (ˌsuːpəˈhjuːmən) *adj* **1** having powers above and beyond those of mankind **2** exceeding normal human ability or experience > ˌsuperhu'**manity** *or* ˌsuper'**humanness** *n* > ˌsuper'**humanly** *adv*

superhumeral (ˌsuːpəˈhjuːmərəl) *n* an ecclesiastical vestment worn over the shoulders [c17 from Late Latin *superhumerāle;* see SUPER-, HUMERAL]

superimpose (ˌsuːpərɪmˈpəʊz) *vb* (*tr*) **1** to set or place on or over something else **2** (usually foll by

on or *upon*) to add (to) > ˌsuper,impoˈsition *n*

superincumbent (ˌsuːpərɪnˈkʌmbənt) *adj* **1** lying or being on top of something else **2** situated or suspended above; overhanging > ˌsuperinˈcumbence *or* ˌsuperinˈcumbency *n* > ˌsuperinˈcumbently *adv*

superinduce (ˌsuːpərɪnˈdjuːs) *vb* (*tr*) to introduce as an additional feature, factor, etc > ˌsuperinˈducement *n* > **superinduction** (ˌsuːpərɪnˈdʌkʃən) *n*

superintend (ˌsuːpərɪnˈtɛnd, ˌsuːprɪn-) *vb* to undertake the direction or supervision (of); manage [c17 from Church Latin *superintendere,* from Latin SUPER- + *intendere* to give attention to] > ˌsuperinˈtendence *n*

superintendency (ˌsuːpərɪnˈtɛndənsɪ, ˌsuːprɪn-) *n, pl* -**cies** **1** the office or jurisdiction of a superintendent **2** a district under the jurisdiction of a superintendent

superintendent (ˌsuːpərɪnˈtɛndənt, ˌsuːprɪn-) *n* **1** a person who directs and manages an organization, office, etc **2** (in Britain) a senior police officer higher in rank than an inspector but lower than a chief superintendent **3** (in the US) the head of a police department **4** *chiefly US and Canadian* a caretaker, esp of a block of apartments ▷ *adj* **5** of or relating to supervision; superintending [c16 from Church Latin *superintendens* overseeing]

superior (suːˈpɪərɪə) *adj* **1** greater in quality, quantity, etc **2** of high or extraordinary worth, merit, etc **3** higher in rank or status: *a superior tribunal* **4** displaying a conscious sense of being above or better than others; supercilious **5** (*often postpositive;* foll by *to*) not susceptible (to) or influenced (by) **6** placed higher up; situated further from the base **7** *astronomy* **a** (of a planet) having an orbit further from the sun than the orbit of the earth **b** (of a conjunction) occurring when the sun lies between the earth and an inferior planet **8** (of a plant ovary) situated above the calyx and other floral parts **9** *anatomy* (of one part in relation to another) situated above or higher **10** *printing* (of a character) written or printed above the line; superscript ▷ *n* **11** a person or thing of greater rank or quality **12** *printing* a character set in a superior position **13** (*often capital*) the head of a community in a religious order [c14 from Latin, from *superus* placed above, from *super* above] > su'**perioress** *fem n* > **superiority** (suːˌpɪərɪˈɒrɪtɪ) *n* > su'**periorly** *adv*

USAGE *Superior* should not be used with *than: he is a better* (not *a superior*) *poet than his brother; his poetry is superior to* (not *superior than*) *his brother's*

Superior (suːˈpɪərɪə, sjuː-) *n* **Lake** a lake in the N central US and S Canada: one of the largest freshwater lakes in the world and westernmost of the Great Lakes. Area: 82 362 sq km (31 800 sq miles)

superior court *n* **1** (in England) a higher court not subject to control by any other court except by way of appeal. See also **Supreme Court of Judicature 2** *US* (in several states) a court of general jurisdiction ranking above the inferior courts and below courts of last resort

superiority complex *n informal* an inflated estimate of one's own merit, usually manifested in arrogance

superior planet *n* any of the six planets (Mars, Jupiter, Saturn, Uranus, Neptune, and Pluto) whose orbit lies outside that of the earth

superjacent (ˌsuːpəˈdʒeɪsənt) *adj* lying immediately above or upon [c17 from Late Latin *superjacēre,* from Latin SUPER- + *jacēre* to lie]

superkingdom (ˈsuːpəˌkɪŋdəm) *n* another name for **domain** (sense 12)

superlative (suːˈpɜːlətɪv) *adj* **1** of outstanding quality, degree, etc; supreme **2** *grammar* denoting the form of an adjective or adverb that expresses the highest or a very high degree of quality. In English the superlative degree is usually marked

by the suffix *-est* or the word *most,* as in *loudest* or *most loudly.* Compare **positive** (sense 10), **comparative** (sense 3) **3** (of language or style) excessive; exaggerated ▷ *n* **4** a thing that excels all others or is of the highest quality **5** *grammar* the superlative form of an adjective **6** the highest degree; peak [c14 from Old French *superlatif,* via Late Latin from Latin *superlātus* extravagant, from *superferre* to carry beyond, from SUPER- + *ferre* to bear] > su'**perlatively** *adv* > su'**perlativeness** *n*

superload (ˈsuːpəˌləʊd) *n* another name for **live load**

superloo (ˈsuːpəˌluː) *n informal* an automated public toilet

superluminal (ˌsuːpəˈluːmɪnəl) *adj physics* of or relating to a speed or velocity exceeding the speed of light

superlunar (ˌsuːpəˈluːnə) *adj* situated beyond the moon; celestial > ˌsuper'**lunary** *adj*

supermale (ˈsuːpəˌmeɪl) *n* a former name for **metamale**

superman (ˈsuːpəˌmæn) *n, pl* -**men 1** (in the philosophy of Nietzsche) an ideal man who through integrity and creativity would rise above good and evil and who represents the goal of human evolution **2** any man of apparently superhuman powers

supermarket (ˈsuːpəˌmɑːkɪt) *n* a large self-service store retailing food and household supplies

supermassive (ˌsuːpəˈmæsɪv) *adj* (of a black hole or star) having a mass in the range of millions or billions of times that of the sun

supermax (ˈsuːpəˌmæks) *n* (*modifier*) having or relating to the very highest levels of security: *a supermax jail*

supermembrane (ˌsuːpəˈmɛmbreɪn) *n physics* a type of two-dimensional entity postulated in certain theories of elementary particles that involve supersymmetry

supermini (ˈsuːpəˌmɪnɪ) *n* (*pl* -**nis**) a small car, usually a hatchback, that is economical to run but has a high level of performance

supermodel (ˈsuːpəˌmɒdəl) *n* a very successful and well-known photographic or catwalk model

supermoto (ˌsuːpəˈməʊtə) *n* a form of motorcycle racing in which powerful motorbikes are raced over a circuit that is part tarmac and part dirt [c20 from SUPERBIKE + MOTOCROSS]

supermundane (ˌsuːpəˈmʌndeɪn) *adj* of or relating to what is elevated above earthly things

supernal (suːˈpɜːnəl, sjuː-) *adj literary* **1** of or from the world of the divine; celestial **2** of or emanating from above or from the sky [c15 from Medieval Latin *supernālis,* from Latin *supernus* that is on high, from *super* above] > su'**pernally** *adv*

supernatant (ˌsuːpəˈneɪtənt) *adj* **1** floating on the surface or over something **2** *chem* (of a liquid) lying above a sediment or settled precipitate [c17 from Latin *supernatāre* to float, from SUPER- + *natāre* to swim] > ˌsuperna'**tation** *n*

supernational (ˌsuːpəˈnæʃnəl) *adj* a less common word for **supranational**. > ˌsuper'**nationalism** *n* > ˌsuper'**nationalist** *n* > ˌsuper'**nationally** *adv*

supernatural (ˌsuːpəˈnætʃrəl, -ˈnætʃərəl) *adj* **1** of or relating to things that cannot be explained according to natural laws **2** characteristic of or caused by or as if by a god; miraculous **3** of, involving, or ascribed to occult beings **4** exceeding the ordinary; abnormal ▷ *n* **5** **the supernatural** supernatural forces, occurrences, and beings collectively or their realm > ˌsuper'**naturally** *adv* > ˌsuper'**naturalness** *n*

supernaturalism (ˌsuːpəˈnætʃrəlɪzəm, -ˈnætʃərə-) *n* **1** the quality or condition of being supernatural **2** a supernatural agency, the effects of which are felt to be apparent in this world **3** belief in supernatural forces or agencies as producing effects in this world > ˌsuper'**naturalist** *n, adj* > ˌsuper,natural'**istic** *adj*

supernormal (ˌsuːpəˈnɔːməl) *adj* greatly exceeding the normal > **supernormality** (ˌsuːpənɔːˈmælɪtɪ) *n* > ˌsuper'**normally** *adv*

supernova (ˌsuːpəˈnəʊvə) *n, pl* **-vae** (-viː) *or* **-vas** a star that explodes catastrophically owing to either instabilities following the exhaustion of its nuclear fuel or gravitational collapse following the accretion of matter from an orbiting companion star, becoming for a few days up to one hundred million times brighter than the sun. The expanding shell of debris (the **supernova remnant**) creates a nebula that radiates radio waves, X-rays, and light, for hundreds or thousands of years. Compare **nova**

supernumerary (ˌsuːpəˈnjuːmərərɪ, -ˈnjuːmrərɪ) *adj* **1** exceeding a regular or proper number; extra **2** functioning as a substitute or assistant with regard to a regular body or staff ▷ *n, pl* **-aries 3** a person or thing that exceeds the normal, required, or regular number **4** a person who functions as a substitute or assistant **5** an actor who has no lines, esp a nonprofessional one [c17 from Late Latin *supernumerārius,* from Latin SUPER- + *numerus* number]

supernurse (ˈsuːpəˌnɜːs) *n* (in Britain) an experienced senior nurse on an elevated salary who is responsible for running clinics and managing nursing teams

supernutrient (ˌsuːpəˈnjuːtrɪənt) *n* any of various dietary supplements containing strong concentrations of vitamins and other substances designed to remedy nutrient deficiencies in the body

superorder (ˈsuːpərˌɔːdə) *n biology* a taxonomic group that is a subdivision of a subclass

superordinate *adj* (ˌsuːpərˈɔːdɪnɪt) **1** of higher status or condition ▷ *n* (ˌsuːpərˈɔːdɪnɪt) **2** a person or thing that is superordinate **3** a word the meaning of which includes the meaning of another word or words: *"red" is a superordinate of "scarlet", "vermilion", and "crimson".* Compare **hyponym, synonym, antonym** ▷ *vb* (ˌsuːpərˈɔːdɪˌneɪt) **4** (*tr*) *rare* to make superordinate

superorganic (ˌsuːpərɔːˈgænɪk) *adj sociol* (no longer widely used) relating to those aspects of a culture that are conceived as being superior to the individual members of the society > ˌsuperorˈganicism *n* > ˌsuperorˈganicist *n*

superoxide (ˌsuːpərˈɒksaɪd) *n* any of certain metal oxides that contain the O₂⁻ ion: *potassium superoxide,* KO_2

superparticle (ˈsuːpərˌpaːtɪkᵊl) *n physics* (in supersymmetry theory) a theoretical particle that is a partner to an observed particle, having the same mass but a different spin

superphosphate (ˌsuːpəˈfɒsfeɪt) *n* **1** a mixture of the diacid calcium salt of orthophosphoric acid $Ca(H_2PO_4)_2$ with calcium sulphate and small quantities of other phosphates: used as a fertilizer **2** a salt of phosphoric acid formed by incompletely replacing its acidic hydrogen atoms; acid phosphate; hydrogen phosphate

superphysical (ˌsuːpəˈfɪzɪkᵊl) *adj* not explained by the known physical laws and phenomena; supernatural

superplastic (ˌsuːpəˈplæstɪk) *adj* **1** (of a metal, alloy, etc) very easily moulded at high temperatures without fracturing ▷ *n* **2** such a metal, alloy, etc > ˌsuperplasˈticity *n*

superpose (ˌsuːpəˈpəʊz) *vb* (*tr*) **1** *geometry* to transpose (the coordinates of one geometric figure) to coincide with those of another **2** a rare word for **superimpose** (sense 1) [c19 from French *superposer,* from Latin *superpōnere,* from SUPER- + *pōnere* to place] > ˌsuperˈposable *adj*

superposition (ˌsuːpəpəˈzɪʃən) *n* **1** the act of superposing or state of being superposed **2** *geology* the principle that in any sequence of sedimentary rocks which has not been disturbed, the oldest strata lie at the bottom and the youngest at the top

superpower (ˈsuːpəˌpaʊə) *n* **1** an extremely powerful state, such as the US **2** extremely high power, esp electrical or mechanical > ˈsuperˌpowered *adj*

superrealism (ˌsuːpəˈrɪəˌlɪzəm) *n* another name for **surrealism.** > ˌsuperˈrealist *n, adj*

supersaturated (ˌsuːpəˈsætʃəˌreɪtɪd) *adj* **1** (of a solution) containing more solute than a saturated solution and therefore not in equilibrium **2** (of a vapour) containing more material than a saturated vapour and therefore not in equilibrium > ˌsuperˌsatuˈration *n*

superscribe (ˌsuːpəˈskraɪb) *vb* (*tr*) to write (an inscription, name, etc) above, on top of, or outside [c16 from Latin *superscrībere,* from SUPER- + *scrībere* to write]

superscript (ˈsuːpəˌskrɪpt) *adj* **1** *printing* (of a character) written or printed above the line; superior. Compare **subscript** ▷ *n* **2** a superscript or superior character **3** *obsolete* a superscription on a document, letter, etc [c16 from Latin *superscriptus;* see SUPERSCRIBE]

superscription (ˌsuːpəˈskrɪpʃən) *n* **1** the act of superscribing **2** a superscribed title, address, etc **3** the symbol (℞) at the head of a medical prescription, which stands for the Latin word *recipe* (take)

supersede (ˌsuːpəˈsiːd) *vb* (*tr*) **1** to take the place of (something old-fashioned or less appropriate); supplant **2** to replace in function, office, etc; succeed **3** to discard or set aside or cause to be set aside as obsolete or inferior [c15 via Old French from Latin *supersedēre* to sit above, from SUPER- + *sedēre* to sit] > ˌsuperˈsedable *adj* > ˌsuperˈsedence *n* > ˌsuperˈseder *n* > **supersedure** (ˌsuːpəˈsiːdʒə) *n* > **supersession** (ˌsuːpəˈseʃən) *n*

supersensible (ˌsuːpəˈsɛnsɪbᵊl) *or* **supersensory** (ˌsuːpəˈsɛnsərɪ) *adj* imperceptible to or beyond reach of the senses > ˌsuperˈsensibly *adv*

supersex (ˈsuːpəˌsɛks) *n genetics* a sterile organism in which the ratio between the sex chromosomes is disturbed. See **metafemale, metamale**

supersize (ˈsuːpəˌsaɪz) *adj also* **supersized 1** larger than standard size: *supersize fries* ▷ *vb* (*tr*) **-sizes, -sizing, -sized 2** to increase the size of (something, such as a standard portion of food)

super-slick *adj* very well-executed or presented

supersonic (ˌsuːpəˈsɒnɪk) *adj* being, having, or capable of reaching a speed in excess of the speed of sound: *supersonic aircraft* > ˌsuperˈsonically *adv*

supersonics (ˌsuːpəˈsɒnɪks) *n* (*functioning as singular*) **1** the study of supersonic motion **2** a less common name for **ultrasonics**

superstar (ˈsuːpəˌstaː) *n* a popular singer, film star, etc, who is idolized by fans and elevated to a position of importance in the entertainment industry > ˈsuperˌstardom *n*

superstate (ˈsuːpəˌsteɪt) *n* a large state, esp created from a federation of states

superstition (ˌsuːpəˈstɪʃən) *n* **1** irrational belief usually founded on ignorance or fear and characterized by obsessive reverence for omens, charms, etc **2** a notion, act or ritual that derives from such belief **3** any irrational belief, esp with regard to the unknown [c15 from Latin *superstitiō* dread of the supernatural, from *superstāre* to stand still by something (as in amazement)]

superstitious (ˌsuːpəˈstɪʃəs) *adj* **1** disposed to believe in superstition **2** of or relating to superstition > ˌsuperˈstitiously *adv* > ˌsuperˈstitiousness *n*

superstore (ˈsuːpəˌstɔː) *n* a very large supermarket, often selling household goods, clothes, etc, as well as food

superstratum (ˌsuːpəˈstraːtəm, -ˈstreɪ-) *n, pl* **-ta** (-tə) *or* **-tums 1** *geology* a layer or stratum overlying another layer or similar structure **2** *linguistics* the language of a conquering or colonizing population as it supplants that of an indigenous population, as for example French and English in the Caribbean. Compare **substratum** (sense 8)

superstring (ˈsuːpəˌstrɪŋ) *n physics* a type of one-dimensional entity postulated in certain theories of elementary particles that involve

supersymmetry

superstruct (ˌsuːpəˈstrʌkt) *vb* (*tr*) to erect upon a foundation or on top of another building or part

superstructure (ˈsuːpəˌstrʌktʃə) *n* **1** the part of a building above its foundation **2** any structure or concept erected on something else **3** *nautical* any structure above the main deck of a ship with sides flush with the sides of the hull **4** the part of a bridge supported by the piers and abutments **5** (in Marxist theory) an edifice of interdependent agencies of the state, including legal and political institutions and ideologies, each possessing some autonomy but remaining products of the dominant mode of economic production > ˈsuperˌstructural *adj*

supersymmetry (ˌsuːpəˈsɪmɪtrɪ) *n physics* a symmetry of elementary particles having a higher order than that in the standard model, postulated to encompass the behaviour of both bosons and fermions

supertanker (ˈsuːpəˌtæŋkə) *n* a large fast tanker of more than 275 000 tons capacity

supertax (ˈsuːpəˌtæks) *n* a tax levied in addition to the basic tax, esp a graduated surtax on incomes above a certain level

superteacher (ˈsuːpəˌtiːtʃə) *n Brit education* an informal name for an **advanced skills teacher**

supertitles (ˈsuːpəˌtaɪtᵊlz) *pl n* another word for **surtitles**

supertonic (ˌsuːpəˈtɒnɪk) *n music* **1** the second degree of a major or minor scale **2** a key or chord based on this

supertruck (ˈsuːpəˌtrʌk) *n* **1** a fast powerful truck used in truck racing **2** a very large truck used for transporting heavy loads in quarries and other heavy engineering sites, but which is too large for use on public roads

Super Tuesday *n US politics* the Tuesday, typically in March, on which party members in over 20 states vote in primary elections to select their party's presidential candidate

Super Twelve *n* an annual international southern hemisphere Rugby Union tournament between teams from South Africa, Australia, and New Zealand

supervene (ˌsuːpəˈviːn) *vb* (*intr*) **1** to follow closely; ensue **2** to occur as an unexpected or extraneous development [c17 from Latin *supervenīre* to come upon, from SUPER- + *venīre* to come] > ˌsuperˈvenience *or* ˌsuperˈvention (ˌsuːpəˈvɛnʃən) *n*

supervenient (ˌsuːpəˈviːnɪənt) *adj* **1** supervening **2** *philosophy* (of a property) inseparable from the other properties of something. Two objects may be identical except that one is red and the other not, but they cannot be identical except that one is beautiful and the other not; beauty is thus a supervenient property

supervise (ˈsuːpəˌvaɪz) *vb* (*tr*) **1** to direct or oversee the performance or operation of **2** to watch over so as to maintain order, etc [c16 from Medieval Latin *supervidēre,* from Latin SUPER- + *vidēre* to see] > **supervision** (ˌsuːpəˈvɪʒən) *n*

supervision order *n* (in Britain) *social welfare* an order by a juvenile court requiring a named probation officer or local-authority social worker to advise, assist, and befriend a child or young person who is the subject of care proceedings, over a period of up to three years

supervisor (ˈsuːpəˌvaɪzə) *n* **1** a person who manages or supervises **2** a foreman or forewoman **3** (in some British universities) a tutor supervising the work, esp research work, of a student **4** (in some US schools) an administrator running a department of teachers **5** (in some US states) the elected chief official of a township or other subdivision of a county **6** *obsolete* a spectator > ˈsuperˌvisorship *n*

supervisory (ˈsuːpəˌvaɪzərɪ) *adj* of, involving, or limited to supervision: *a supervisory capacity*

supervisory board *n* a board of management of which nonmanagerial workers are members, having supervisory powers over some aspects of

S

management decision-making

superwaif ('suːpəˌweɪf) *n informal* a very young and very thin supermodel

superweed ('suːpəˌwiːd) *n* a hybrid plant that contains genes for herbicide resistance: produced by accidental crossing of genetically engineered crop plants with wild plants

superwoman ('suːpəˌwʊmən) *n, pl* **-women** a woman who fulfils her many roles with apparently superhuman efficiency

supinate ('suːpɪˌneɪt, 'sjuː-) *vb* to turn (the hand and forearm) so that the palm faces up or forwards [C19 from Latin *supīnāre* to lay on the back, from *supīnus* SUPINE] > ˌ**supi'nation** *n*

supinator ('suːpɪˌneɪtə, 'sjuː-) *n anatomy* the muscle of the forearm that can produce the motion of supination

supine *adj* (suː'paɪn, sjuː-, 'suːpaɪn, 'sjuː-) **1** lying or resting on the back with the face, palm, etc, upwards **2** displaying no interest or animation; lethargic ▷ *n* ('suːpaɪn, 'sjuː-) **3** *grammar* a noun form derived from a verb in Latin, often used to express purpose with verbs of motion. Abbreviation: **sup** [C15 from Latin *supīnus* related to *sub* under, up; (in grammatical sense) from Latin *verbum supīnum* supine word (the reason for this use is unknown)] > **su'pinely** *adv* > **su'pineness** *n*

suplex ('suːplɛks) *n* a wrestling hold in which a wrestler grasps his opponent round the waist from behind and carries him backwards [C20 of uncertain origin]

supper ('sʌpə) *n* **1** an evening meal, esp a light one **2** an evening social event featuring a supper **3** **sing for one's supper** to obtain something by performing a service ▷ *vb* **4** *(tr) rare* to give supper to **5** *(intr) rare* to eat supper [C13 from Old French *soper*; see SUP[1]] > **'supperless** *adj*

supper club *n US and Canadian* (formerly) a small expensive nightclub

supplant (sə'plɑːnt) *vb (tr)* to take the place of, often by trickery or force: *he easily supplanted his rival* [C13 via Old French from Latin *supplantāre* to trip up, from *sub-* from below + *planta* sole of the foot] > **supplantation** (ˌsʌplɑːn'teɪʃən) *n* > **sup'planter** *n*

supple ('sʌpᵊl) *adj* **1** bending easily without damage **2** capable of or showing easy or graceful movement; lithe **3** mentally flexible; responding readily **4** disposed to agree, sometimes to the point of servility ▷ *vb* **5** *rare* to make or become supple [C13 from Old French *souple*, from Latin *supplex* bowed] > **'suppleness** *n*

supplejack ('sʌpᵊlˌdʒæk) *n* **1** a North American twining rhamnaceous woody vine, *Berchemia scandens*, that has greenish-white flowers and purple fruits **2** a liliaceous plant of New Zealand, *Ripogonum scandens*, having tough climbing vines **3** a tropical American woody sapindaceous vine, *Paullinia curassavica*, having strong supple wood **4** any of various other vines with strong supple stems **5** *US* a walking stick made from the wood of *Paullinia curassavica* [C18 from SUPPLE + JACK[1]]

supplement *n* ('sʌplɪmənt) **1** an addition designed to complete, make up for a deficiency, etc **2** a section appended to a publication to supply further information, correct errors, etc **3** a magazine or section inserted into a newspaper or periodical, such as one with colour photographs issued every week **4** *geometry* **a** either of a pair of angles whose sum is 180° **b** an arc of a circle that when added to another arc forms a semicircle ▷ Abbreviations: **sup, supp** ▷ *vb* ('sʌplɪˌmɛnt) **5** *(tr)* to provide a supplement to, esp in order to remedy a deficiency [C14 from Latin *supplēmentum*, from *supplēre* to SUPPLY[1]] > ˌ**supplemen'tation** *n* > **'suppleˌmenter** *n*

supplementary (ˌsʌplɪ'mɛntərɪ, -trɪ) *adj* **1** Also (less commonly): **supplemental** (ˌsʌplɪ'mɛntᵊl) forming or acting as a supplement ▷ *n, pl* **-ries** **2** a person or thing that is a supplement > ˌ**supple'mentarily** *or less commonly* ˌ**supple'mentally** *adv*

supplementary angle *n* either of two angles whose sum is 180°. Compare **complementary angle**

suppletion (sə'pliːʃən) *n* the use of an unrelated word to complete the otherwise defective paradigm of a given word, as for example the use of *went* for the past tense of *go* [C14 from Medieval Latin *supplētiō* a completing, from Latin *supplēre* to SUPPLY[1]] > **sup'pletive** *n, adj*

suppletory ('sʌplɪtərɪ, -trɪ) *adj archaic* remedying deficiencies; supplementary > **'suppletorily** *adv*

Supplex ('sʌplɛks) *n trademark* a type of synthetic fabric which is breathable, stretchable, and fast-drying, used esp for sportswear

suppliant ('sʌplɪənt) *adj* **1** expressing entreaty or supplication ▷ *n* ▷ *adj* **2** another word for **supplicant** [C15 from French *supplier* to beseech, from Latin *supplicāre* to kneel in entreaty; see SUPPLE] > **'suppliantly** *adv* > **'suppliance** *n*

supplicant ('sʌplɪkənt) *or* **suppliant** *n* **1** a person who supplicates ▷ *adj* **2** entreating humbly; supplicating [C16 from Latin *supplicāns* beseeching; see SUPPLE]

supplicate ('sʌplɪˌkeɪt) *vb* **1** to make a humble request to (someone); plead **2** *(tr)* to ask for or seek humbly [C15 from Latin *supplicāre* to beg on one's knees; see SUPPLE] > **'suppliˌcatory** *adj*

supplication (ˌsʌplɪ'keɪʃən) *n* **1** the act of supplicating **2** a humble entreaty or petition; prayer

supply[1] (sə'plaɪ) *vb* **-plies, -plying, -plied** **1** *(tr; often foll by with)* to furnish with something that is required: *to supply the community with good government* **2** *(tr; often foll by to or for)* to make available or provide (something that is desired or lacking): *to supply books to the library* **3** *(tr)* to provide for adequately; make good; satisfy: *who will supply their needs?* **4** to serve as a substitute, usually temporary, in (another's position, etc): *there are no clergymen to supply the pulpit* **5** *(tr) Brit* to fill (a vacancy, position, etc) ▷ *n, pl* **-plies** **6** **a** the act of providing or something that is provided **b** *(as modifier)*: *a supply dump* **7** *(often plural)* an amount available for use; stock **8** *(plural)* food, equipment, etc, needed for a campaign or trip **9** *economics* **a** willingness and ability to offer goods and services for sale **b** the amount of a commodity that producers are willing and able to offer for sale at a specified price. Compare **demand** (sense 9) **10** *military* **a** the management and disposal of food and equipment **b** *(as modifier)*: *supply routes* **11** *(often plural)* a grant of money voted by a legislature for government expenses, esp those not covered by other revenues **12** (in Parliament and similar legislatures) the money voted annually for the expenses of the civil service and armed forces **13** **a** a person who acts as a temporary substitute **b** *(as modifier)*: *a supply vicar* **14** a source of electrical energy, gas, etc **15** *obsolete* aid or assistance [C14 from Old French *souppleier*, from Latin *supplēre* to complete, from *sub-* up + *plēre* to fill] > **sup'pliable** *adj* > **sup'plier** *n*

supply[2] ('sʌplɪ), **supplely** ('sʌpᵊlɪ) *adv* in a supple manner

supply chain *n marketing* a channel of distribution beginning with the supplier of materials or components, extending through a manufacturing process to the distributor and retailer, and ultimately to the consumer

supply-side economics *n (functioning as singular)* a school of economic thought that emphasizes the importance to a strong economy of policies that remove impediments to supply

supply teacher *n* a teacher employed to replace other teachers when they are absent

support (sə'pɔːt) *vb (tr)* **1** to carry the weight of **2** to bear or withstand (pressure, weight, etc) **3** to provide the necessities of life for (a family, person, etc) **4** to tend to establish (a theory, statement, etc) by providing new facts; substantiate **5** to speak in favour of (a motion) **6** to give aid or courage to **7** to give approval to (a cause, principle, etc); subscribe to: *to support a political candidature* **8** to endure with forbearance: *I will no longer support bad behaviour* **9** to give strength to; maintain: *to support a business* **10** *(tr)* (in a concert) to perform earlier than (the main attraction) **11** *films, theatre* **a** to play a subordinate role to **b** to accompany (the feature) in a film programme **12** to act or perform (a role or character) ▷ *n* **13** the act of supporting or the condition of being supported **14** a thing that bears the weight or part of the weight of a construction **15** a person who or thing that furnishes aid **16** the means of maintenance of a family, person, etc **17** a band or entertainer not topping the bill **18** (often preceded by *the*) an actor or group of actors playing subordinate roles **19** *med* an appliance worn to ease the strain on an injured bodily structure or part **20** the solid material on which a painting is executed, such as canvas **21** See **athletic support** [C14 from Old French *supporter*, from Latin *supportāre* to bring, from *sub-* up + *portāre* to carry] > **sup'portless** *adj*

supportable (sə'pɔːtəbᵊl) *adj* able to be supported or endured; bearable > **supˌporta'bility** *or* **sup'portableness** *n* > **sup'portably** *adv*

support area *n military* an area containing concentrations of personnel and materiel ready to support a force in the field

supporter (sə'pɔːtə) *n* **1** a person who or thing that acts as a support **2** a person who backs a sports team, politician, etc **3** a garment or device worn to ease the strain on or restrict the movement of a bodily structure or part **4** *heraldry* a figure or beast in a coat of arms depicted as holding up the shield

supporting (sə'pɔːtɪŋ) *adj* **1** (of a role) being a fairly important but not leading part, esp in a play or film **2** (of an actor or actress) playing a supporting role

supportive (sə'pɔːtɪv) *adj* providing support, esp moral or emotional support > **sup'portively** *adv* > **sup'portiveness** *n*

supportive therapy *n* **1** *med* any treatment, such as the intravenous administration of certain fluids, designed to reinforce or sustain the physiological well-being of a patient **2** *psychol* a form of therapy for mental disturbances employing guidance and encouragement to develop the patient's own resources

suppose (sə'pəʊz) *vb (tr; may take a clause as object)* **1** to presume (something) to be true without certain knowledge: *I suppose he meant to kill her* **2** to consider as a possible suggestion for the sake of discussion, elucidation, etc; postulate: *suppose that he wins the election* **3** (of theories, propositions, etc) to imply the inference or assumption (of): *your policy supposes full employment* [C14 from Old French *supposer*, from Medieval Latin *suppōnere*, from Latin: to substitute, from SUB- + *pōnere* to put] > **sup'posable** *adj* > **sup'poser** *n*

supposed (sə'pəʊzd, -'pəʊzɪd) *adj* **1** *(prenominal)* presumed to be true without certain knowledge: *his supposed date of birth* **2** *(prenominal)* believed to be true on slight grounds; highly doubtful: *the supposed existence of ghosts* **3** (sə'pəʊzd) *(postpositive; foll by to)* expected or obliged (to): *I'm supposed to be there at nine* **4** *(postpositive; used in negative; foll by to)* expected or obliged not (to): *you're not supposed to walk on the grass* > **supposedly** (sə'pəʊzɪdlɪ) *adv*

supposition (ˌsʌpə'zɪʃən) *n* **1** the act of supposing **2** a fact, theory, etc, that is supposed > ˌ**suppo'sitional** *adj* > ˌ**suppo'sitionally** *adv* > ˌ**suppo'sitionless** *adj*

suppositious (ˌsʌpə'zɪʃəs) *adj* deduced from supposition; hypothetical > ˌ**suppo'sitiously** *adv* > ˌ**suppo'sitiousness** *n*

supposititious (səˌpɒzɪ'tɪʃəs) *adj* substituted with intent to mislead or deceive > **supˌposi'titiously** *adv* > **supˌposi'titiousness** *n*

suppositive (sə'pɒzɪtɪv) *adj* **1** of, involving, or arising out of supposition **2** *grammar* denoting a conjunction introducing a clause expressing a supposition, as for example *if, supposing,* or *provided* *that* ▷ *n* **3** *grammar* a suppositive conjunction > sup'positively *adv*

suppository (sə'pɒzɪtərɪ, -trɪ) *n, pl* -ries *med* an encapsulated or solid medication for insertion into the vagina, rectum, or urethra, where it melts and releases the active substance [c14 from Medieval Latin *suppositōrium*, from Latin *suppositus* placed beneath, from *suppōnere; see* SUPPOSE]

suppress (sə'prɛs) *vb* (*tr*) **1** to put an end to; prohibit **2** to hold in check; restrain: *I was obliged to suppress a smile* **3** to withhold from circulation or publication: *to suppress seditious pamphlets* **4** to stop the activities of; crush: *to suppress a rebellion* **5** *electronics* **a** to reduce or eliminate (unwanted oscillations) in a circuit **b** to eliminate (a particular frequency or group of frequencies) in a signal **6** *psychiatry* **a** to resist consciously (an idea or a desire entering one's mind) **b** to exercise self-control by preventing the expression of (certain desires). Compare **repress** (sense 3) [c14 from Latin *suppressus* held down, from *supprimere* to restrain, from *sub-* down + *premere* to press] > sup'presser *n* > sup'pressible *adj*

suppressant (sə'prɛsənt) *adj* **1** tending to suppress or restrain an action or condition ▷ *n* **2** a suppressant drug or agent: *a cough suppressant*

suppressed carrier modulation *n radio* an amplitude-modulated wave in which only the sidebands are transmitted, the carrier being removed

suppression (sə'prɛʃən) *n* **1** the act or process of suppressing or the condition of being suppressed **2** *psychoanal* the conscious avoidance of unpleasant thoughts. Compare **repression** (sense 2) **3** *electronics* the act or process of suppressing a frequency, oscillation, etc **4** *biology* the failure of an organ or part to develop **5** *med* the cessation of any physiological process

suppressive (sə'prɛsɪv) *adj* **1** tending or acting to suppress; involving suppression **2** *psychiatry* tending to prevent the expression of certain of one's desires or to resist the emergence of mental symptoms

suppressor (sə'prɛsə) *n* **1** a person or thing that suppresses **2** a device fitted to an electrical appliance to suppress unwanted electrical interference to audiovisual signals

suppressor grid *n* an electrode placed between the screen grid and anode of a valve. Its negative potential, relative to both screen and anode, prevents secondary electrons from the anode reaching the screen

suppurate ('sʌpjʊˌreɪt) *vb* (*intr*) *pathol* (of a wound, sore, etc) to discharge pus; fester [c16 from Latin *suppūrāre*, from SUB- + *pūs* PUS]

suppuration (ˌsʌpjʊ'reɪʃən) *n* **1** the discharging of pus from a wound, sore, etc **2** the discharge itself

suppurative ('sʌpjʊrətɪv) *adj* **1** causing suppuration ▷ *n* **2** any suppurative drug

supra ('suːprə) *adv* above, esp referring to earlier parts of a book etc [c15 from Latin; related to SUPER-]

supra- *prefix* over, above, beyond, or greater than: *supranational; supramolecular* [from Latin *suprā* above]

supraglottal (ˌsuːprə'glɒtəl, ˌsjuː-) *adj anatomy* situated above the glottis: *supraglottal obstruction*

supralapsarian (ˌsuːprəlæp'sɛərɪən, ˌsjuː-) *n christian theol, chiefly Calvinist* a person who believes that God decreed the election or nonelection of individuals to salvation even before the Fall. Compare **infralapsarian** [c17 from New Latin *suprālapsārius*, from Latin SUPRA- + *lapsus* a fall] > ˌsupralap'sarianism *n*

supraliminal (ˌsuːprə'lɪmɪnəl, ˌsjuː-) *adj* of or relating to any stimulus that is above the threshold of sensory awareness. Compare **subliminal**. > ˌsupra'liminally *adv*

supramaxillary (ˌsuːprə'mæksɪlərɪ) *adj* of or relating to the upper jaw

supramolecular (ˌsuːprəmə'lɛkjʊlə, ˌsjuː-) *adj* **1** more complex than a molecule **2** consisting of more than one molecule

supranational (ˌsuːprə'næʃnəl, ˌsjuː-) *adj* beyond the authority or jurisdiction of one national government: *the supranational institutions of the EU* > ˌsupra'nationalism *n* > ˌsupra'nationally *adv*

supraorbital (ˌsuːprə'ɔːbɪtəl, ˌsjuː-) *adj anatomy* situated above the orbit

suprarenal (ˌsuːprə'riːnəl, ˌsjuː-) *adj anatomy* situated above a kidney [c19 from New Latin *suprārēnālis*. See SUPRA-, RENAL]

suprarenal gland *n* another name for **adrenal gland**

suprasegmental (ˌsuːprəsɛg'mɛntəl, ˌsjuː-) *adj linguistics* denoting those features of a sound or sequence of sounds that accompany rather than form part of the consecutive segments of a word or sentence, as for example stress and pitch in English > ˌsupraseg'mentally *adv*

supremacist (sʊ'prɛməsɪst, sjʊ-) *n* **1** a person who promotes or advocates the supremacy of any particular group ▷ *adj* **2** characterized by belief in the supremacy of any particular group > su'premacism *or* su'prematism *n*

supremacy (sʊ'prɛməsɪ, sjʊ-) *n* **1** supreme power; authority **2** the quality or condition of being supreme

Suprematism (sʊ'prɛməˌtɪzəm, sjʊ-) *n* a form of pure cubist art, launched in Russia in 1913, and based on the principle that paintings should be composed only of rectangles, circles, triangles, or crosses [c20 from *suprematist* a supporter of this theory, from French *suprémacie* SUPREMACY] > Su'prematist *n, adj*

supreme (sʊ'priːm, sjʊ-) *adj* **1** of highest status or power: *a supreme tribunal* **2** (*usually prenominal*) of highest quality, importance, etc: *supreme endeavour* **3** greatest in degree; extreme: *supreme folly* **4** (*prenominal*) final or last, esp being last in one's life or progress; ultimate: *the supreme judgment* [c16 from Latin *suprēmus* highest, from *superus* that is above, from *super* above] > su'premely *adv* > su'premeness *n*

suprême (sʊ'priːm, -'prɛm, sjʊ-) *n* **1** Also called: **suprême sauce** a rich velouté sauce made with a base of veal or chicken stock, with cream or egg yolks added **2** the best or most delicate part of meat, esp the breast and wing of chicken, cooked in suprême sauce [French: SUPREME]

Supreme Being *n* the most exalted being; God

supreme commander *n* the military officer in overall command of all forces in one theatre of operations

Supreme Court *n* **1** (in the US) **1** the highest Federal court, possessing final appellate jurisdiction and exercising supervisory jurisdiction over the lower courts **2** (in many states) the highest state court

Supreme Court of Judicature *n* (in England) a court formed in 1873 by the amalgamation of several superior courts into two divisions, the High Court of Justice and the Court of Appeal

supreme sacrifice *n* **the** the sacrifice of one's life

Supreme Soviet *n* (in the former Soviet Union) **1** the bicameral legislature, comprising the **Soviet of the Union** and the **Soviet of the Nationalities**; officially the highest organ of state power **2** a similar legislature in each former Soviet republic

Supreme Truth Cult *n* another name for **Aum Shinrikyo**

supremo (sʊ'priːməʊ, sjʊ-) *n, pl* -mos *Brit informal* a person in overall authority [c20 from SUPREME]

Supt *or* **supt** *abbreviation for* superintendent

suq (suːk) *n* a variant spelling of **souk¹**

Suqutra (sə'kəʊtrə) *n* a variant spelling of **Socotra**

Sur *or* **Sour** (sʊə) *n* transliteration of the Arabic name for **Tyre**

sur-¹ *prefix* over; above; beyond: *surcharge; surrealism*. Compare **super-** [from Old French, from Latin SUPER-]

sur-² *prefix* a variant of **sub-** before r: *surrogate*

sura ('sʊərə) *n* any of the 114 chapters of the Koran [c17 from Arabic *sūrah* section]

Surabaya, Surabaja *or* **Soerabaja** (ˌsʊərə'baɪə) *n* a port in Indonesia, on E Java on the **Surabaya Strait**: the country's second port and chief naval base; university (1954); fishing and ship-building industries; oil refinery. Pop: 2 599 796 (2000)

surah ('sʊərə) *n* a twill-weave fabric of silk or rayon, used for dresses, blouses, etc [c19 from the French pronunciation of SURAT]

Surakarta (ˌsʊərə'kaːtə) *n* a town in Indonesia, on central Java: textile manufacturing. Pop: 516 500 (1995 est)

sural ('sjʊərəl) *adj anatomy* of or relating to the calf of the leg [c17 via New Latin from Latin *sūra* calf]

surat (sjuː'ræt) *n* (formerly) a cotton fabric from the Surat area of India

Surat (sʊ'ræt, 'sʊərət) *n* a port in W India, in W Gujarat: a major port in the 17th century; textile manufacturing. Pop: 2 433 787 (2001)

surbase ('sɜːˌbeɪs) *n* the uppermost part, such as a moulding, of a pedestal, base, or skirting. Compare **subbase**. > sur'basement *n*

surbased ('sɜːˌbeɪst) *adj architect* **1** having a surbase **2** (of an arch) having a rise of less than half the span [c18 from French *surbaisser* to depress, from *sur-* (intensive) + *baisser* to lower, from *bas* low; see BASE¹]

surcease (sɜː'siːs) *archaic* ▷ *n* **1** cessation or intermission ▷ *vb* **2** to desist from (some action) **3** to cease or cause to cease [c16 from earlier *sursesen*, from Old French *surseoir*, from Latin *supersedēre; see* SUPERSEDE]

surcharge *n* ('sɜːˌtʃɑːdʒ) **1** a charge in addition to the usual payment, tax, etc **2** an excessive sum charged, esp when unlawful **3** an extra and usually excessive burden or supply **4** *law* the act or an instance of surcharging **5** an overprint that alters the face value of a postage stamp ▷ *vb* (sɜː'tʃɑːdʒ, 'sɜːˌtʃɑːdʒ) (*tr*) **6** to charge an additional sum, tax, etc **7** to overcharge (a person) for something **8** to put an extra physical burden upon; overload **9** to fill to excess; overwhelm **10** *law* to insert credits that have been omitted in (an account) **11** to overprint a surcharge on (a stamp) > sur'charger *n*

surcingle ('sɜːˌsɪŋgəl) *n* **1** a girth for a horse which goes around the body, used esp with a racing saddle **2** the belt worn with a cassock ▷ *vb* **3** to put a surcingle on or over (a horse) [c14 from Old French *surcengle*, from *sur-* over + *cengle* a belt, from Latin *cingulum*]

surcoat ('sɜːˌkəʊt) *n* **1** a tunic, often embroidered with heraldic arms, worn by a knight over his armour during the Middle Ages **2** an outer coat or other garment

surculose ('sɜːkjʊˌləʊs) *adj* (of a plant) bearing suckers [c19 from Latin *surculōsus* woody, from *surculus* twig, from *sūrus* a branch]

surd (sɜːd) *n* **1** *maths* an expression containing one or more irrational roots of numbers, such as $2\sqrt{3} + 3\sqrt{2} + 6$ **2** *phonetics* a voiceless consonant, such as (t) ▷ *adj* **3** of or relating to a surd [c16 from Latin *surdus* muffled]

sure (ʃʊə, ʃɔː) *adj* **1** (sometimes foll by *of*) free from hesitancy or uncertainty (with regard to a belief, conviction, etc): *we are sure of the accuracy of the data; I am sure that he is lying* **2** (foll by *of*) having no doubt, as of the occurrence of a future state or event: *sure of success* **3** always effective; unfailing: *a sure remedy* **4** reliable in indication or accuracy: *a sure criterion* **5** (of persons) worthy of trust or confidence: *a sure friend* **6** not open to doubt: *sure proof* **7** admitting of no vacillation or doubt: *he is very sure in his beliefs* **8** bound to be or occur; inevitable: *victory is sure* **9** (*postpositive*) bound inevitably (to be or do something); certain: *she is sure to be there tonight* **10** physically secure or dependable: *a sure footing* **11** *obsolete* free from exposure to harm or danger **12** **be sure** (*usually imperative or dependent imperative; takes a clause as object or an infinitive, sometimes with *to* replaced by *and*)* to be careful or certain: *be sure and shut the door; I told him to be sure to shut the door* **13** *for* sure without a doubt; surely **14 make sure a** (*takes a clause as object*) to make certain; ensure **b** (foll by *of*) to establish or confirm power or possession (over) **15 sure enough** *informal* as might have been confidently expected; definitely: often used as a sentence substitute **16 to be sure a** without doubt; certainly **b** it has to be acknowledged; admittedly ▷ *adv* **17** (*sentence substitute*) *informal* willingly; yes **18** (*sentence modifier*) *informal, chiefly US and Canadian* without question; certainly [C14 from Old French *seur*, from Latin *sēcūrus* SECURE] > ˈ**sureness** *n*

sure-fire *adj* (*usually prenominal*) *informal* certain to succeed or meet expectations; assured

sure-footed *adj* **1** unlikely to fall, slip, or stumble **2** not likely to err or fail, as in judgment > ˌ**sure-ˈfootedly** *adv* > ˌ**sure-ˈfootedness** *n*

surely (ˈʃʊəlɪ, ˈʃɔː-) *adv* **1** without doubt; assuredly: *things could surely not have been worse* **2** without fail; inexorably (esp in the phrase **slowly but surely**) **3** (*sentence modifier*) am I not right in thinking that?; I am sure that: *surely you don't mean it?* **4** *rare* in a sure manner **5** *archaic* safely; securely **6** (*sentence substitute*) *chiefly US and Canadian* willingly; of course; yes

sure thing *informal* ▷ *adv* **1** (*sentence substitute*) *chiefly US* all right! yes indeed! used to express enthusiastic assent ▷ *n* **2** something guaranteed to be successful

surety (ˈʃʊətɪ, ˈʃʊərɪtɪ) *n, pl* **-ties 1** a person who assumes legal responsibility for the fulfilment of another's debt or obligation and himself becomes liable if the other defaults **2** security given against loss or damage or as a guarantee that an obligation will be met **3** *obsolete* the quality or condition of being sure **4** *obsolete* a means of assurance or safety **5 stand surety** to act as a surety [C14 from Old French *seurte*, from Latin *sēcūritās* SECURITY] > ˈ**suretyˌship** *n*

surf (sɜːf) *n* **1** waves breaking on the shore or on a reef **2** foam caused by the breaking of waves ▷ *vb* **3** (*intr*) to take part in surfing **4 a** *computing* (on the internet) to move freely from website to website (esp in the phrase **surf the net**) **b** to move freely between (TV channels or radio stations) **5 a** *informal* to be carried on top of something: *that guy's surfing the audience* **b** (*in combination*): *trainsurfing* [C17 probably variant of SOUGH[1]] > ˈ**surfable** *adj* > ˈ**surfˌlike** *adj*

surface (ˈsɜːfɪs) *n* **1 a** the exterior face of an object or one such face **b** (*as modifier*): *surface gloss* **2 a** the area or size of such a face **b** (*as modifier*): *surface measurements* **3** material resembling such a face, with length and width but without depth **4 a** the superficial appearance as opposed to the real nature **b** (*as modifier*): *a surface resemblance* **5** *geometry* **a** the complete boundary of a solid figure **b** a continuous two-dimensional configuration **6 a** the uppermost level of the land or sea **b** (*as modifier*): *surface transportation* **7 come to the surface** to emerge; become apparent **8 on the surface** to all appearances ▷ *vb* **9** to rise or cause to rise to or as if to the surface (of water, etc) **10** (*tr*) to treat the surface of, as by polishing, smoothing, etc **11** (*tr*) to furnish with a surface **12** (*intr*) *mining* **a** to work at or near the ground surface **b** to wash surface ore deposits **13** (*intr*) to become apparent; emerge **14** (*intr*) *informal* **a** to wake up **b** to get up [C17 from French, from *sur* on + *face* FACE, probably on the model of Latin SUPERFICIES] > ˈ**surfaceless** *adj* > ˈ**surfacer** *n*

surface acoustic wave *n* an acoustic wave generated on the surface of a piezoelectric substrate: used as a filter in electronic circuits

surface-active *adj* (of a substance, esp a detergent) capable of lowering the surface tension of a liquid, usually water. See also **surfactant**

surface condenser *n* a steam condenser usually associated with a steam turbine in which the steam is condensed on the surface of tubes through which water is passed. Compare **jet condenser**

surface friction drag *n* the part of the drag on a body moving through a fluid that is dependent on the nature of the surface of the body. Also called: **skin friction**

surface mail *n* mail transported by land or sea. Compare **airmail**

surface noise *n* noise produced by the friction of the needle or stylus of a record player with the rotating record, caused by a static charge, dust, or irregularities on the surface of a record

surface plate *n* another name for **faceplate** (sense 2)

surface structure *n generative grammar* a representation of a string of words or morphemes as they occur in a sentence, together with labels and brackets that represent syntactic structure. Compare **deep structure**

surface tension *n* **1** a property of liquids caused by intermolecular forces near the surface leading to the apparent presence of a surface film and to capillarity, etc **2** a measure of this property expressed as the force acting normal to one side of a line of unit length on the surface: measured in newtons per metre. Symbol: **T**, γ *or* σ

surface-to-air *adj* of or relating to a missile launched from the surface of the earth against airborne targets

surface-to-surface *adj* of or relating to a missile launched from the surface of the earth against surface targets

surfactant (sɜːˈfæktənt) *n* **1** Also called: **surface-active agent** a substance, such as a detergent, that can reduce the surface tension of a liquid and thus allow it to foam or penetrate solids; a wetting agent ▷ *adj* **2** having the properties of a surfactant [C20 *surf(ace)-act(ive) a(ge)nt*]

surfbird (ˈsɜːfˌbɜːd) *n* an American shore bird, *Aphriza virgata*, having a spotted plumage, with a black and white tail: family *Scolopacidae* (sandpipers, etc), order *Charadriiformes*

surfboard (ˈsɜːfˌbɔːd) *n* a long narrow board used in surfing

surfboat (ˈsɜːfˌbəʊt) *n* a boat with a high bow and stern and flotation chambers, equipped for use in rough surf

surfcasting (ˈsɜːfˌkɑːstɪŋ) *n* fishing from the shore by casting into the surf > ˈ**surfˌcaster** *n*

surfeit (ˈsɜːfɪt) *n* **1** (*usually foll by of*) an excessive or immoderate amount **2** overindulgence, esp in eating or drinking **3** disgust, nausea, etc, caused by such overindulgence ▷ *vb* **4** (*tr*) to supply or feed excessively; satiate **5** (*intr*) *archaic* to eat, drink, or be supplied to excess **6** (*intr*) *obsolete* to feel uncomfortable as a consequence of overindulgence [C13 from French *sourfait*, from *sourfaire* to overdo, from SUR-[1] + *faire*, from Latin *facere* to do] > ˈ**surfeiter** *n*

surfie (ˈsɜːfɪ) *n Austral and NZ slang* a young person whose main interest is in surfing, esp when considered as a cult figure

surfing (ˈsɜːfɪŋ) *n* the sport of riding towards shore on the crest of a wave by standing or lying on a surfboard > ˈ**surfer** *or* ˈ**surfˌrider** *n*

surf mat *n Austral informal* a small inflatable rubber mattress used to ride on waves

surf music *n* a US West Coast style of pop music of the early 1960s, characterized by high harmony vocals and strong trebly guitar riffs

surf 'n' turf *n* a dish consisting of meat served with seafood

surfperch (ˈsɜːfˌpɜːtʃ) *n* any viviparous marine percoid fish of the family *Embiotocidae*, of North American Pacific coastal waters. Also called: **sea perch**

surf scoter *or* **duck** *n* a North American scoter, *Melanitta perspicillata*, having white patches on the head

surg. *abbreviation for* **1** surgeon **2** surgery **3** surgical

surge (sɜːdʒ) *n* **1** a strong rush or sweep; sudden increase: *a surge of anger* **2** the rolling swell of the sea, esp after the passage of a large wave **3** a heavy rolling motion or sound: *the surge of the trumpets* **4** an undulating rolling surface, as of hills **5** a billowing cloud or volume **6** *nautical* a temporary release or slackening of a rope or cable **7** a large momentary increase in the voltage or current in an electric circuit **8** an upward instability or unevenness in the power output of an engine **9** *astronomy* a short-lived disturbance, occurring during the eruption of a solar flare ▷ *vb* **10** (*intr*) (of waves, the sea, etc) to rise or roll with a heavy swelling motion **11** (*intr*) to move like a heavy sea **12** *nautical* to slacken or temporarily release (a rope or cable) from a capstan or (of a rope, etc) to be slackened or released and slip back **13** (*intr*) (of an electric current or voltage) to undergo a large momentary increase **14** (*tr*) *rare* to cause to move in or as if in a wave or waves [C15 from Latin *surgere* to rise, from *sub-* up + *regere* to lead] > ˈ**surgeless** *adj* > ˈ**surger** *n*

surgeon (ˈsɜːdʒən) *n* **1** a medical practioner who specializes in surgery **2** a medical officer in the Royal Navy [C14 from Anglo-Norman *surgien*, from Old French *cirurgien*; see SURGERY]

surgeoncy (ˈsɜːdʒənsɪ) *n, pl* **-cies** *chiefly Brit* the office, duties, or position of a surgeon, esp in the army or navy

surgeonfish (ˈsɜːdʒənˌfɪʃ) *n, pl* **-fish** *or* **-fishes** any tropical marine spiny-finned fish of the family *Acanthuridae*, having a compressed brightly coloured body with one or more knifelike spines at the base of the tail

surgeon general *n, pl* **surgeons general 1** (in the British, US, and certain other armies and navies) the senior officer of the medical service **2** the head of the public health service in the US

surgeon's knot *n* a knot used by surgeons in tying ligatures, etc

surgery (ˈsɜːdʒərɪ) *n, pl* **-geries 1** the branch of medicine concerned with treating disease, injuries, etc, by means of manual or operative procedures, esp by incision into the body **2** the performance of such procedures by a surgeon **3** *Brit* a place where a doctor, dentist, etc, can be consulted **4** *Brit* an occasion when an MP, lawyer, etc, is available for consultation **5** *US and Canadian* an operating theatre where surgical operations are performed [C14 via Old French from Latin *chirurgia*, from Greek *kheirurgia*, from *kheir* hand + *ergon* work]

surge tank *n engineering* a tank used to absorb surges in flow

surge tide *n* a powerful and often destructive tide that may occur when an abnormally high tide (eg at the autumn equinox) coincides with high wind and low atmospheric pressure

surgical (ˈsɜːdʒɪkᵊl) *adj* of, relating to, involving, or used in surgery > ˈ**surgically** *adv*

surgical boot *n* a specially designed boot or shoe that compensates for deformities of the foot or leg

surgical spirit *n* methylated spirit containing small amounts of oil of wintergreen and castor oil: used medically for sterilizing

Suribachi (ˌsʊərɪˈbɑːtʃɪ) *n* **Mount** a volcanic hill in the Volcano Islands, on Iwo Jima: site of a US victory (1945) over the Japanese in World War II

suricate (ˈsjʊərɪˌkeɪt) *n* another name for **slender-tailed meerkat** (see **meerkat**) [C18 from French *surikate*, probably from a native South African word]

surimi (ˌsuːˈriːmɪ) *n* a blended seafood product made from precooked fish, restructured into stick shapes

Surinam (ˌsʊərɪˈnæm) *or* **Suriname** *n* a republic in NE South America, on the Atlantic: became a self-governing part of the Netherlands in 1954 and fully independent in 1975. Official languages: Dutch; English is also widely spoken. Religion: Hindu, Christian, and Muslim. Currency: guilder. Capital: Paramaribo. Pop: 439 000 (2004 est). Area: 163 820 sq km (63 251 sq miles). Former names: **Dutch Guiana, Netherlands Guiana**

Surinam toad *n* another name for **pipa**

surjection (sɜːˈdʒɛkʃən) *n* a mathematical function or mapping for which every element of the image space is a value for some members of the domain. See also **injection** (sense 5), **bijection** [C20 from SUR-¹ + *-jection*, on the model of PROJECTION] > **surˈjective** *adj*

surly (ˈsɜːlɪ) *adj* **-lier, -liest** **1** sullenly ill-tempered or rude **2** (of an animal) ill-tempered or refractory **3** dismal **4** *obsolete* arrogant [C16 from obsolete *sirly* haughty; see SIR] > **ˈsurlily** *adv* > **ˈsurliness** *n*

surmise *vb* (sɜːˈmaɪz) **1** (when *tr, may take a clause as object*) to infer (something) from incomplete or uncertain evidence ▷ *n* (sɜːˈmaɪz, ˈsɜːmaɪz) **2** an idea inferred from inconclusive evidence [C15 from Old French, from *surmettre* to accuse, from Latin *supermittere* to throw over, from SUPER- + *mittere* to send] > **surˈmisable** *adj* > **surˈmiser** *n*

surmount (sɜːˈmaʊnt) *vb* (*tr*) **1** to prevail over; overcome: *to surmount tremendous difficulties* **2** to ascend and cross to the opposite side of **3** to lie on top of or rise above **4** to put something on top of or above **5** *obsolete* to surpass or exceed [C14 from Old French *surmonter*, from SUR-¹ + *monter* to MOUNT¹] > **surˈmountable** *adj* > **surˈmountableness** *n* > **surˈmounter** *n*

surmullet (sɜːˈmʌlɪt) *n* a US name for the **red mullet** [C17 from French *sormulet*, from *sor* brown + MULLET]

surname (ˈsɜːˌneɪm) *n* **1** Also called: **last name, second name** a family name as opposed to a first or Christian name **2** (formerly) a descriptive epithet attached to a person's name to denote a personal characteristic, profession, etc; nickname ▷ *vb* **3** (*tr*) to furnish with or call by a surname [C14 via Anglo-French from Old French *surnom*. See SUR-¹, NAME] > **ˈsurˌnamer** *n*

surpass (sɜːˈpɑːs) *vb* (*tr*) **1** to be greater than in degree, extent, etc **2** to be superior to in achievement or excellence **3** to overstep the limit or range of: *the theory surpasses my comprehension* [C16 from French *surpasser*, from SUR-¹ + *passer* to PASS] > **surˈpassable** *adj*

surpassing (sɜːˈpɑːsɪŋ) *adj* **1** exceptional; extraordinary ▷ *adv* **2** *obsolete or poetic* (intensifier): *surpassing fair* > **surˈpassingly** *adv*

surplice (ˈsɜːplɪs) *n* a loose wide-sleeved liturgical vestment of linen, reaching to the knees, worn over the cassock by clergymen, choristers, and acolytes [C13 via Anglo-French from Old French *sourpelis*, from Medieval Latin *superpellīcium*, from SUPER- + *pellīcium* coat made of skins, from Latin *pellis* a skin] > **ˈsurpliced** *adj*

surplus (ˈsɜːpləs) *n, pl* **-pluses** **1** a quantity or amount in excess of what is required **2** *accounting* **a** an excess of total assets over total liabilities **b** an excess of actual net assets over the nominal value of capital stock **c** an excess of revenues over expenditures during a certain period of time **3** *economics* **a** an excess of government revenues over expenditures during a certain financial year **b** an excess of receipts over payments on the balance of payments ▷ *adj* **4** being in excess; extra [C14 from Old French, from Medieval Latin *superplūs*, from Latin SUPER- + *plūs* more]

surplusage (ˈsɜːpləsɪdʒ) *n* **1** *law* (in pleading, etc) irrelevant matter, such as a superfluous allegation **2** an excess of words **3** a less common word for **surplus**

surprint (ˈsɜːˌprɪnt) *vb* **1** (*tr*) to print (additional matter) over something already printed; overprint ▷ *n* **2** marks, printed matter, etc, that have been surprinted

surprise (səˈpraɪz) *vb* (*tr*) **1** to cause to feel amazement or wonder **2** to encounter or discover unexpectedly or suddenly **3** to capture or assault suddenly and without warning **4** to present with something unexpected, such as a gift **5** (foll by *into*) to provoke (someone) to unintended action by a trick, etc: *to surprise a person into an indiscretion* **6** (often foll by *from*) to elicit by unexpected behaviour or by a trick: *to surprise information from a prisoner* ▷ *n* **7** the act or an instance of surprising; the act of taking unawares **8** a sudden or unexpected event, gift, etc **9** the feeling or condition of being surprised; astonishment **10** (*modifier*) causing, characterized by, or relying upon surprise: *a surprise move* **11 take by surprise** **a** to come upon suddenly and without warning **b** to capture unexpectedly or catch unprepared **c** to astonish; amaze [C15 from Old French, from *surprendre* to overtake, from SUR-¹ + *prendre* from Latin *prehendere* to grasp; see PREHENSILE] > **surˈprisal** *n* > **surˈprised** *adj* > **surprisedly** (səˈpraɪzɪdlɪ) *adv* > **surˈpriser** *n*

surprising (səˈpraɪzɪŋ) *adj* causing surprise; unexpected or amazing > **surˈprisingly** *adv* > **surˈprisingness** *n*

surra (ˈsʊərə) *n* a tropical febrile disease of cattle, horses, camels, and dogs, characterized by severe emaciation: caused by the protozoan *Trypanosoma evansi* and transmitted by fleas [from Marathi]

surreal (səˈrɪəl) *adj* **1** suggestive of surrealism; dreamlike ▷ *n* **2** **the** the atmosphere or qualities evoked by surrealism

surrealism (səˈrɪəˌlɪzəm) *n* (*sometimes capital*) a movement in art and literature in the 1920s, which developed esp from dada, characterized by the evocative juxtaposition of incongruous images in order to include unconscious and dream elements [C20 from French *surréalisme*, from SUR-¹ + *réalisme* REALISM] > **surˈrealist** *n, adj* > **surˌrealˈistic** *adj* > **surˌrealˈistically** *adv*

surrebuttal (ˌsɜːrɪˈbʌtᵊl) *n* *law* (in pleading) the giving of evidence in support of a surrebutter

surrebutter (ˌsɜːrɪˈbʌtə) *n* *law* (in pleading) the claimant's reply to the defendant's rebutter

surrejoinder (ˌsɜːrɪˈdʒɔɪndə) *n* *law* (in pleading) the claimant's reply to the defendant's rejoinder

surrender (səˈrɛndə) *vb* **1** (*tr*) to relinquish to the control or possession of another under duress or on demand: *to surrender a city* **2** (*tr*) to relinquish or forego (an office, position, etc), esp as a voluntary concession to another: *he surrendered his place to a lady* **3** to give (oneself) up physically, as or as if to an enemy **4** to allow (oneself) to yield, as to a temptation, influence, etc **5** (*tr*) to give up (hope, etc) **6** (*tr*) *law* to give up or restore (an estate), esp to give up a lease before expiration of the term **7** (*tr*) *obsolete* to return or render (thanks, etc) **8** **surrender to bail** to present oneself at court at the appointed time after having been on bail ▷ *n* **9** the act or instance of surrendering **10** *insurance* the voluntary discontinuation of a life policy by its holder in return for a consideration (the **surrender value**) **11** *law* **a** the yielding up or restoring of an estate, esp the giving up of a lease before its term has expired **b** the giving up to the appropriate authority of a fugitive from justice **c** the act of surrendering or being surrendered to bail **d** the deed by which a legal surrender is effected [C15 from Old French *surrendre* to yield, from SUR-¹ + *rendre* to RENDER] > **surˈrenderer** *n*

surreptitious (ˌsʌrəpˈtɪʃəs) *adj* **1** done, acquired, etc, in secret or by improper means **2** operating by stealth **3** characterized by fraud or misrepresentation of the truth [C15 from Latin *surreptīcius* furtive, from *surripere* to steal, from *sub-* secretly + *rapere* to snatch] > **ˌsurrepˈtitiously** *adv* > **ˌsurrepˈtitiousness** *n*

surrey (ˈsʌrɪ) *n* a light four-wheeled horse-drawn carriage having two or four seats [C19 shortened from *Surrey cart*, after SURREY, where it was originally made]

Surrey (ˈsʌrɪ) *n* a county of SE England, on the River Thames: urban in the northeast; crossed from east to west by the North Downs and drained by tributaries of the Thames. Administrative centre: Kingston upon Thames. Pop: 1 064 600 (2003 est). Area: 1679 sq km (648 sq miles)

surrogate *n* (ˈsʌrəgɪt) **1** a person or thing acting as a substitute **2** *chiefly Brit* a deputy, such as a clergyman appointed to deputize for a bishop in granting marriage licences **3** *psychiatry* a person who is a substitute for someone else, esp in childhood when different persons, such as a brother or teacher, can act as substitutes for the parents **4** (in some US states) a judge with jurisdiction over the probate of wills, etc **5** (*modifier*) of, relating to, or acting as a surrogate: *a surrogate pleasure* ▷ *vb* (ˈsʌrəˌgeɪt) (*tr*) **6** to put in another's position as a deputy, substitute, etc **7** to appoint as a successor to oneself [C17 from Latin *surrogāre* to substitute; see SUBROGATE] > **ˈsurrogateship** *n* > **ˌsurroˈgation** *n*

surrogate mother *n* a woman who bears a child on behalf of a couple unable to have a child, either by artificial insemination from the man or implantation of an embryo from the woman > **surrogacy** (ˈsʌrəgəsɪ) *n*

surround (səˈraʊnd) *vb* (*tr*) **1** to encircle or enclose or cause to be encircled or enclosed **2** to deploy forces on all sides of (a place or military formation), so preventing access or retreat **3** to exist around: *I dislike the people who surround her* ▷ *n* **4** *chiefly Brit* a border, esp the area of uncovered floor between the walls of a room and the carpet or around an opening or panel **5** *chiefly US* **a** a method of capturing wild beasts by encircling the area in which they are believed to be **b** the area so encircled [C15 *surrounden* to overflow, from Old French *suronder*, from Late Latin *superundāre*, from Latin SUPER- + *undāre* to abound, from *unda* a wave] > **surˈrounding** *adj*

surroundings (səˈraʊndɪŋz) *pl n* the conditions, scenery, etc, around a person, place, or thing; environment

surround sound *n* a system of sound recording and reproduction that uses three or more independent recording channels and loudspeakers in order to give the impression that the listener is surrounded by the sound sources. Compare **quadraphonics** See also **ambisonics**

sursum corda (ˈsɜːsəm ˈkɔːdə) *n* **1** *RC Church* a Latin versicle meaning *Lift up your hearts*, said by the priest at Mass **2** a cry of exhortation, hope, etc [C16 Latin, literally: up hearts]

surtax (ˈsɜːˌtæks) *n* **1** a tax, usually highly progressive, levied on the amount by which a person's income exceeds a specific level **2** an additional tax on something that has already been taxed ▷ *vb* **3** (*tr*) to assess for liability to surtax; charge with an extra tax

surtitles (ˈsɜːˌtaɪtᵊlz) *pl n* brief translations of the text of an opera or play that is being sung or spoken in a foreign language, projected above the stage

surtout (ˈsɜːtuː; *French* syrtu) *n* a man's overcoat resembling a frock coat, popular in the late 19th century [C17 from French, from *sur* over + *tout* all]

surv. *abbreviation for* **1** Also: **survey** surveying **2** surveyor

surveil (sɜːˈveɪl) *vb* (*tr*) to observe closely the activities of (a person or group) [C20 back formation from SURVEILLANCE]

surveillance (sɜːˈveɪləns) *n* close observation or supervision maintained over a person, group, etc, esp one in custody or under suspicion [C19 from French, from *surveiller* to watch over, from SUR-¹ + *veiller* to keep watch (from Latin *vigilāre*; see VIGIL)] > **surˈveillant** *adj, n*

surveillance society *n* a society where surveillance technology is widely used to monitor people's everyday activities

survey *vb* (sɜːˈveɪ, ˈsɜːveɪ) **1** (*tr*) to view or consider in a comprehensive or general way: *to survey the situation* **2** (*tr*) to examine carefully, as or as if to appraise value: *to survey oneself in a mirror* **3** to plot a detailed map of (an area of land) by measuring or calculating distances and height **4** *Brit* to inspect a building to determine its condition and value **5** to examine a vessel thoroughly in order to determine its seaworthiness **6** (*tr*) to run a statistical survey on (incomes, opinions, etc) ▷ *n* (ˈsɜːveɪ) **7** a comprehensive or general view: *a*

S

survey of English literature **8** a critical, detailed, and formal inspection: *a survey of the nation's hospitals* **9** *Brit* an inspection of a building to determine its condition and value **10** a report incorporating the results of such an inspection **11 a** a body of surveyors **b** an area surveyed **12** *statistics* a random sample [c15 from French *surveoir*, from SUR-¹ + *veoir* to see, from Latin *vidēre*] > sur'veyable *adj*

surveying (sɜːˈveɪɪŋ) *n* **1** the study or practice of measuring altitudes, angles, and distances on the land surface so that they can be accurately plotted on a map **2** the setting out on the ground of the positions of proposed construction or engineering works

surveyor (sɜːˈveɪə) *n* **1** a person whose occupation is to survey land or buildings. See also **quantity surveyor 2** *chiefly Brit* a person concerned with the official inspection of something for purposes of measurement and valuation **3** a person who carries out surveys, esp of ships (**marine surveyor**) to determine seaworthiness, etc **4** a customs official **5** *archaic* a supervisor > sur'veyor,ship *n*

surveyor's chain *n* a measuring chain 22 yards in length; Gunter's chain. See **chain** (sense 7)

surveyor's level *n* another term for **level** (sense 19)

surveyor's measure *n* the system of measurement based on the chain (66 feet) as a unit

survival (səˈvaɪvəl) *n* **1** a person or thing that survives, such as a custom **2 a** the act or fact of surviving or condition of having survived **b** (*as modifier*): *survival kit*

survival bag *n* a large plastic bag carried by climbers for use in an emergency as protection against exposure

survivalist (səˈvaɪvəlɪst) *n US* **a** a person who believes in ensuring his personal survival of a catastrophic event by arming himself and often by living in the wild **b** (*as modifier*): *survivalist weapons* > sur'vival,ism *n*

survival of the fittest *n* a popular term for **natural selection**

survive (səˈvaɪv) *vb* **1** (*tr*) to live after the death of (another): *he survived his wife by 12 years* **2** to continue in existence or use after (a passage of time, an adversity, etc) **3** *informal* to endure (something): *I don't know how I survive such an awful job* [c15 from Old French *sourvivre*, from Latin *supervīvere*, from SUPER- + *vīvere* to live] > sur'vivable *adj* > sur,viva'bility *n*

survivor (səˈvaɪvə) *n* **1** a person or thing that survives **2** *property law* one of two or more specified persons having joint interests in property who lives longer than the other or others and thereby becomes entitled to the whole property > sur'vivor,ship *n*

sus (sʌs) *Brit slang* ▷ *n* **1** suspicion **2** a suspect ▷ *adj* **3** suspicious ▷ *vb* **4** a variant spelling of **suss** (sense 2) ▷ See also **sus laws** [c20 shortened from SUSPICION]

Susa (ˈsuːsə) *n* an ancient city north of the Persian Gulf: capital of Elam and of the Persian Empire; flourished as a Greek polis under the Seleucids and Parthians. Biblical name: Shushan

Susah or **Susa** (ˈsuːzə) *n* other names for **Sousse**

Susanna (suːˈzænə) *n* the book of the Apocrypha containing the story of Susanna, who was condemned to death for adultery because of a false accusation but saved by Daniel's sagacity

susceptance (səˈsɛptəns) *n physics* the imaginary component of the admittance [c19 from SUSCEPT(IBILITY) + -ANCE]

susceptibility (sə,sɛptəˈbɪlɪtɪ) *n*, *pl* -ties **1** the quality or condition of being susceptible **2** the ability or tendency to be impressed by emotional feelings; sensitivity **3** (*plural*) emotional sensibilities; feelings **4** *physics* **a** Also called: **electric susceptibility** (of a dielectric) the amount by which the relative permittivity differs from unity. Symbol: X **b** Also called: **magnetic**

susceptibility (of a magnetic medium) the amount by which the relative permeability differs from unity. Symbol: K

susceptible (səˈsɛptəbəl) *adj* **1** (*postpositive; foll by of* or *to*) yielding readily to; capable (of): *hypotheses susceptible of refutation; susceptible to control* **2** (*postpositive; foll by to*) liable to be afflicted (by): *susceptible to colds* **3** easily impressed emotionally [c17 from Late Latin *susceptibilis*, from Latin *suscipere* to take up, from SUB- + *capere* to take] > sus'ceptibleness *n* > sus'ceptibly *adv*

susceptive (səˈsɛptɪv) *adj* **1** another word for **receptive 2** a variant of **susceptible**. > sus'ceptivity (,sʌsɛpˈtɪvɪtɪ) or sus'ceptiveness *n*

sushi (ˈsuːʃɪ) *n* a Japanese dish consisting of small cakes of cold rice with a topping esp raw fish [from Japanese]

Susian (ˈsuːzɪən) *n, adj* another word for **Elamite** [c16 from *Susiana*, a province of the ancient Persian Empire with its capital at SUSA]

sus laws or **suss laws** *pl n Brit slang* laws authorizing the arrest and punishment of suspected persons frequenting, or loitering in, public places with criminal intent. In England, the sus law formed part of the Vagrancy Act of 1824, repealed in 1981

suslik (ˈsʌslɪk) or **souslik** *n* a central Eurasian ground squirrel, *Citellus citellus*, of dry open areas, having large eyes and small ears [from Russian]

suspect *vb* (səˈspɛkt) **1** (*tr*) to believe guilty of a specified offence without proof **2** (*tr*) to think false, questionable, etc: *she suspected his sincerity* **3** (*tr; may take a clause as object*) to surmise to be the case; think probable: *to suspect fraud* **4** (*intr*) to have suspicion ▷ *n* (ˈsʌspɛkt) **5** a person who is under suspicion ▷ *adj* (ˈsʌspɛkt) **6** causing or open to suspicion [c14 from Latin *suspicere* to mistrust, from SUB- + *specere* to look] > sus'pecter *n* > 'suspectless *adj*

suspend (səˈspɛnd) *vb* **1** (*tr*) to hang from above so as to permit free movement **2** (*tr; passive*) to cause to remain floating or hanging: *a cloud of smoke was suspended over the town* **3** (*tr*) to render inoperative or cause to cease, esp temporarily: *to suspend interest payments* **4** (*tr*) to hold in abeyance; postpone action on: *to suspend a decision* **5** (*tr*) to debar temporarily from privilege, office, etc, as a punishment **6** (*tr*) *chem* to cause (particles) to be held in suspension in a fluid **7** (*tr*) *music* to continue (a note) until the next chord is sounded, with which it usually forms a dissonance. See **suspension** (sense 11) **8** (*intr*) to cease payment, as from incapacity to meet financial obligations **9** (*tr*) *obsolete* to put or keep in a state of anxiety or wonder **10** (*intr*) *obsolete* to be attached from above [c13 from Latin *suspendere* from SUB- + *pendere* to hang] > sus'pendible or sus'pensible *adj* > sus,pendi'bility *n*

suspended animation *n* a temporary cessation of the vital functions, as by freezing an organism

suspended sentence *n* a sentence of imprisonment that is not served by an offender unless he commits a further offence during its currency. Compare **deferred sentence**

suspender (səˈspɛndə) *n* **1** (*often plural*) *Brit* **a** an elastic strap attached to a belt or corset having a fastener at the end, for holding up women's stockings **b** a similar fastener attached to a garter worn by men in order to support socks. US and Canadian equivalent: **garter 2** (*plural*) *US and Canadian* a pair of straps worn over the shoulders by men for holding up the trousers. also called (in Britain and certain other countries): **braces 3** a person or thing that suspends, such as one of the vertical cables that carries the deck in a suspension bridge

suspender belt *n* a belt with suspenders hanging from it to hold up women's stockings. US and Canadian name: **garter belt**

suspense (səˈspɛns) *n* **1** the condition of being insecure or uncertain: *the matter of the succession remained in suspense for many years* **2** mental

uncertainty; anxiety: *their father's illness kept them in a state of suspense* **3** excitement felt at the approach of the climax: *a play of terrifying suspense* **4** the condition of being suspended [c15 from Medieval Latin *suspensum* delay, from Latin *suspendere* to hang up; see SUSPEND] > sus'penseful *adj*

suspense account *n* book-keeping an account in which entries are made until determination of their proper disposition

suspenser (səˈspɛnsə) *n* a film that creates a feeling of suspense

suspension (səˈspɛnʃən) *n* **1** an interruption or temporary revocation: *the suspension of a law* **2** a temporary debarment, as from position, privilege, etc **3** a deferment, esp of a decision, judgment, etc **4** *law* **a** a postponement of execution of a sentence or the deferring of a judgment, etc **b** a temporary extinguishment of a right or title **5** cessation of payment of business debts, esp as a result of insolvency **6** the act of suspending or the state of being suspended **7** a system of springs, shock absorbers, etc, that supports the body of a wheeled or tracked vehicle and insulates it and its occupants from shocks transmitted by the wheels. See also **hydraulic suspension 8** a device or structure, usually a wire or spring, that serves to suspend or support something, such as the pendulum of a clock **9** *chem* a dispersion of fine solid or liquid particles in a fluid, the particles being supported by buoyancy. See also **colloid 10** the process by which eroded particles of rock are transported in a river **11** *music* one or more notes of a chord that are prolonged until a subsequent chord is sounded, usually to form a dissonance

suspension bridge *n* a bridge that has a deck suspended by cables or rods from other cables or chains that hang between two towers and are anchored at both ends

suspension point *n chiefly US* one of a group of dots, usually three, used in written material to indicate the omission of a word or words. Compare **ellipsis** (sense 2)

suspensive (səˈspɛnsɪv) *adj* **1** having the power of deferment; effecting suspension **2** causing, characterized by, or relating to suspense **3** inclined to defer judgment; undecided > sus'pensively *adv* > sus'pensiveness *n*

suspensoid (səˈspɛnsɔɪd) *n chem* a system consisting of a suspension of solid particles in a liquid

suspensor (səˈspɛnsə) *n* **1** another name for **suspensory** (sense 1) **2** *botany* (in a seed) a row of cells attached to the embryo plant, by means of which it is pushed into the endosperm

suspensory (səˈspɛnsərɪ) *n, pl* -ries **1** Also called: **suspensor** *anatomy* a ligament or muscle that holds a structure or part in position **2** *med* a bandage, sling, etc, for supporting a dependent part **3** another name (esp US) for **jockstrap** ▷ *adj* **4** suspending or supporting **5** *anatomy* (of a ligament or muscle) supporting or holding a structure or part in position

suspicion (səˈspɪʃən) *n* **1** the act or an instance of suspecting; belief without sure proof, esp that something is wrong **2** the feeling of mistrust of a person who suspects **3** the state of being suspected: *to be shielded from suspicion* **4** a slight trace **5** above suspicion in such a position that no guilt may be thought or implied, esp through having an unblemished reputation **6** on suspicion as a suspect **7** under suspicion regarded with distrust [c14 from Old French *sospeçon*, from Latin *suspiciō* distrust, from *suspicere* to mistrust; see SUSPECT] > sus'picional *adj* > sus'picionless *adj*

suspicious (səˈspɪʃəs) *adj* **1** exciting or liable to excite suspicion; questionable **2** disposed to suspect something wrong **3** indicative or expressive of suspicion > sus'piciously *adv* > sus'piciousness *n*

suspire (səˈspaɪə) *vb archaic or poetic* **1** to sigh or utter with a sigh; yearn **2** (*intr*) to breathe; respire [c15 from Latin *suspīrāre* to take a deep breath, from SUB- + *spīrāre* to breathe] > **suspiration** (ˌsʌspɪˈreɪʃən) *n*

Susquehanna (ˌsʌskwɪˈhænə) *n* a river in the eastern US, rising in Otsego Lake and flowing generally south to Chesapeake Bay at Havre de Grace: the longest river in the eastern US Length: 714 km (444 miles)

suss (sʌs) *vb* (*tr*) *slang* **1** (often foll by *out*) to attempt to work out (a situation, person's character, etc), esp using one's intuition **2** Also: **sus** to become aware of; suspect (esp in the phrase **suss it**) ▷ *n* **3** sharpness of mind; social astuteness ▷ See also **sus laws** [c20 shortened from SUSPECT]

sussed (sʌst) *adj Brit informal* well-informed; aware

Sussex (ˈsʌsɪks) *n* **1** (until 1974) a county of SE England, now divided into the separate counties of East Sussex and West Sussex **2** (in Anglo-Saxon England) the kingdom of the South Saxons, which became a shire of the kingdom of Wessex in the early 9th century AD **3** a breed of red beef cattle originally from Sussex **4** a heavy and long-established breed of domestic fowl used principally as a table bird

Sussex spaniel *n* a short-legged breed of spaniel with a golden-liver coloured coat [so named because it was bred in Sussex, in the late 18th century]

sustain (səˈsteɪn) *vb* (*tr*) **1** to hold up under; withstand: *to sustain great provocation* **2** to undergo (an injury, loss, etc); suffer: *to sustain a broken arm* **3** to maintain or prolong: *to sustain a discussion* **4** to support physically from below **5** to provide for or give support to, esp by supplying necessities: *to sustain one's family; to sustain a charity* **6** to keep up the vitality or courage of **7** to uphold or affirm the justice or validity of: *to sustain a decision* **8** to establish the truth of; confirm ▷ *n* **9** *music* the prolongation of a note, by playing technique or electronics [c13 via Old French from Latin *sustinēre* to hold up, from SUB- + *tenēre* to hold] > **sus'tained** *adj* > **sustainedly** (səˈsteɪnɪdlɪ) *adv* > **sus'taining** *adj* > **sus'tainingly** *adv* > **sus'tainment** *n*

sustainable (səˈsteɪnəbəl) *adj* **1** capable of being sustained **2** (of economic development, energy sources, etc) capable of being maintained at a steady level without exhausting natural resources or causing severe ecological damage: *sustainable development* **3** (of economic growth) non-inflationary

sustainer (səˈsteɪnə) *n* a rocket engine that maintains the velocity of a space vehicle after the booster has been jettisoned

sustaining pedal *n music* a foot-operated lever on a piano, usually the right one of two, that keeps the dampers raised from the strings when keys are released, allowing them to continue to vibrate. Compare **soft pedal** (sense 3)

sustaining program *n US and Canadian* a television or radio programme promoted by the broadcasting network or station itself and not by a commercial sponsor

sustenance (ˈsʌstɪnəns) *n* **1** means of sustaining health or life; nourishment **2** means of maintenance; livelihood **3** Also: **sustention** (səˈstɛnʃən) the act or process of sustaining or the quality of being sustained [c13 from Old French *sostenance,* from *sustenir* to SUSTAIN]

sustentacular (ˌsʌstɛnˈtækjʊlə) *adj anatomy* (of fibres, cells, etc) supporting or forming a support [c19 from Latin *sustentāculum* a stay, from *sustentāre* to support, from *sustinēre* to SUSTAIN]

sustentation (ˌsʌstɛnˈteɪʃən) *n* a less common word for **sustenance** [c14 from Latin *sustentātio,* from *sustentāre,* frequentative of *sustinēre* to SUSTAIN]

sustentation fund *n* a fund, esp in the Church of Scotland, to augment the support of ministers

susu (ˈsuːsuː) *n* a variant form of **sou-sou**

Susu (ˈsuːsuː) *n* **1** (*pl* **-su** *or* **-sus**) a member of a Negroid people of W Africa, living chiefly in Guinea, the Sudan, and Sierra Leone **2** the language of this people, belonging to the Mande branch of the Niger-Congo family

susurrate (ˈsjuːsəˌreɪt) *vb* (*intr*) *literary* to make a soft rustling sound; whisper; murmur [c17 from Latin *susurrāre* to whisper] > **susurrant** (sjuːˈsʌrənt) *adj* > ˌ**susur'ration** *or* ˈ**susurrus** *n*

Suth. *abbreviation for* Sutherland

Sutherland (ˈsʌðələnd) *n* (until 1975) a county of N Scotland, now part of Highland

Sutherland Falls *n* a waterfall in New Zealand, on SW South Island. Height: 580 m (1904 ft)

Sutlej (ˈsʌtlɪdʒ) *n* a river in S Asia, rising in SW Tibet and flowing west through the Himalayas: crosses Himachal Pradesh and the Punjab (India), enters Pakistan, and joins the Chenab west of Bahawalpur: the longest of the five rivers of the Punjab. Length: 1368 km (850 miles)

sutler (ˈsʌtlə) *n* (formerly) a merchant who accompanied an army in order to sell provisions to the soldiers [c16 from obsolete Dutch *soeteler,* from Middle Low German *suteler,* from Middle High German *sudelen* to do dirty work; related to SOOT, SEETHE] > ˈ**sutler,ship** *n*

sutra (ˈsuːtrə) *n* **1** *Hinduism* Sanskrit sayings or collections of sayings on Vedic doctrine dating from about 200 AD onwards **2** (*modifier*) *Hinduism* **a** of or relating to the last of the Vedic literary periods, from about 500 to 100 BC: *the sutra period* **b** of or relating to the sutras or compilations of sutras of about 200 AD onwards **3** *Buddhism* collections of dialogues and discourses of classic Mahayana Buddhism dating from the 2nd to the 6th centuries A.D [c19 from Sanskrit: list of rules]

suttee (sʌˈtiː, ˈsʌtiː) *n* **1** the former Hindu custom whereby a widow burnt herself to death on her husband's funeral pyre **2** a Hindu widow who immolated herself in this way [c18 from Sanskrit *satī* virtuous woman, from *sat* good] > **sut'teeism** *n*

Sutton (ˈsʌtən) *n* a borough of S Greater London. Pop: 178 500 (2003 est). Area: 43 sq km (17 sq miles)

Sutton Coldfield (-ˈkəʊld,fiːld) *n* a town in central England, in Birmingham unitary authority, West Midlands; a residential suburb of Birmingham. Pop: 105 452 (2001)

Sutton Hoo (huː) *n* an archaeological site in Suffolk where a Saxon long boat containing rich grave goods, probably for a 7th century East Anglian king, was found in 1939

Sutton-in-Ashfield (-ˈæʃ,fiːld) *n* a market town in N central England, in W Nottinghamshire. Pop: 41 951 (2001)

suture (ˈsuːtʃə) *n* **1** *surgery* **a** catgut, silk thread, or wire used to stitch together two bodily surfaces **b** the surgical seam formed after joining two surfaces, also called: **seam 2** *anatomy* a type of immovable joint, esp between the bones of the skull (**cranial suture**) **3** a seam or joining, as in sewing **4** *zoology* a line of junction in a mollusc shell, esp the line between adjacent chambers of a nautiloid shell **5** *botany* a line marking the point of dehiscence in a seed pod or capsule ▷ *vb* **6** (*tr*) *surgery* to join (the edges of a wound, etc) by means of sutures [c16 from Latin *sūtūra,* from *suere* to SEW] > ˈ**sutural** *adj* > ˈ**suturally** *adv*

SUV *abbreviation for* **sport** *or* **sports utility vehicle**

Suva (ˈsuːvə) *n* the capital and chief port of Fiji, on the SE coast of Viti Levu; popular tourist resort; University of the South Pacific (1968). Pop: 219 000 (2005 est)

Suwannee (sʊˈwɒnɪ) *or* **Swanee** *n* a river in the southeastern US, rising in SE Georgia and flowing across Florida to the Gulf of Mexico at **Suwannee Sound**. Length: about 400 km (250 miles)

suzerain (ˈsuːzəˌreɪn) *n* **1 a** a state or sovereign exercising some degree of dominion over a dependent state, usually controlling its foreign affairs **b** (*as modifier*): *a suzerain power* **2 a** a feudal overlord **b** (*as modifier*): *suzerain lord* [c19 from French, from *sus* above (from Latin *sursum* turned

upwards, from *sub-* up + *vertere* to turn) + *-erain,* as in *souverain* SOVEREIGN]

suzerainty (ˈsuːzərəntɪ) *n, pl* **-ties 1** the position, power, or dignity of a suzerain **2** the relationship between suzerain and dependent state

Suzhou (ˈsuːˈdʒəʊ), **Su-chou** *or* **Soochow** *n* a city in E China, in S Jiangsu on the Grand Canal: noted for its gardens; produces chiefly silk. Pop: 1 201 000 (2005 est). Also called: **Wuhsien**

sv¹ *abbreviation for* **1** sailing vessel **2** side valve **3** sub verbo *or* voce [sense 3 from Latin: under the word *or* voice]

sv² *the internet domain name for* El Salvador

SV *abbreviation for* **1** Sancta Virgo [Latin: Holy Virgin] **2** Sanctitas Vestra [Latin: Your Holiness]

Svalbard (*Norwegian* ˈsvɑːlbɑr) *n* a Norwegian archipelago in the Arctic Ocean, about 650 km (400 miles) north of Norway: consists of the main group (Spitsbergen, North East Land, Edge Island, Barents Island, and Prince Charles Foreland) and a number of outlying islands; sovereignty long disputed but granted to Norway in 1920; coal mining. Administrative centre: Longyearbyen. Area: 62 050 sq km (23 958 sq miles). Also called: **Spitsbergen**

svelte (svɛlt, sfɛlt) *adj* **1** attractively or gracefully slim; slender **2** urbane or sophisticated [c19 from French, from Italian *svelto,* from *svellere* to pull out, from Latin *ēvellere,* from EX-¹ + *vellere* to pull]

Svengali (svɛnˈɡɑːlɪ) *n* a person who controls another's mind, usually with sinister intentions [after a character in George Du Maurier's novel *Trilby* (1894)]

Sverdlovsk (*Russian* svɪrˈdlɒfsk) *n* the former name (1924–91) of **Yekaterinburg**

Sverige (ˈsværjə) *n* the Swedish name for **Sweden**

SVGA *abbreviation for* super video graphics array. See **VGA**

Svizzera (ˈzvittsera) *n* the Italian name for **Switzerland**

SVQ *abbreviation for* Scottish Vocational Qualification

SW 1 *symbol for* southwest(ern) **2** ▷ *abbreviation for* short wave

Sw. *abbreviation for* **1** Sweden **2** Swedish

swab (swɒb) *n* **1** *med* **a** a small piece of cotton, gauze, etc, for use in applying medication, cleansing a wound, or obtaining a specimen of a secretion, etc **b** the specimen so obtained **2** a mop for cleaning floors, decks, etc **3** a brush used to clean a firearm's bore **4** *slang* an uncouth or worthless fellow ▷ *vb* **swabs, swabbing, swabbed 5** (*tr*) to clean or medicate with or as if with a swab **6** (*tr;* foll by *up*) to take up with a swab [c16 probably from Middle Dutch *swabbe* mop; related to Norwegian *svabba* to splash, Dutch *zwabberen* to mop, German *schwappen* to slop over]

swabber (ˈswɒbə) *n* **1** a person who uses a swab **2** a device designed for swabbing **3** *slang* an uncouth fellow

Swabia (ˈsweɪbɪə) *n* a region and former duchy (from the 10th century to 1313) of S Germany, now part of Baden-Württemberg and Bavaria: part of West Germany until 1990. German name: **Schwaben** (ˈʃvaːbən)

Swabian (ˈsweɪbɪən) *adj* **1** of or relating to the German region of Swabia or its inhabitants ▷ *n* **2** a native or inhabitant of Swabia

swacked (swækt) *adj slang* in a state of intoxication, stupor, or euphoria induced by drugs or alcohol [c20 perhaps from Scottish *swack* a heavy blow, of imitative origin]

swaddle (ˈswɒdəl) *vb* (*tr*) **1** to wind a bandage round **2** to wrap (a baby) in swaddling clothes **3** to restrain as if by wrapping with bandages; smother ▷ *n* **4** *chiefly US* swaddling clothes [c15 from Old English *swæthel* swaddling clothes; related to *swathian* to SWATHE]

swaddling clothes *pl n* **1** long strips of linen or other cloth formerly wrapped round a newly born baby **2** restrictions or supervision imposed on the immature

S

swaddy or **swaddie** ('swɒdɪ) *n, pl* -dies *Brit slang* a private soldier. Compare **squaddie** [c19 from dialect *swad* a country bumpkin]

Swadeshi (swə'deɪʃɪ) *adj* **1** (in present-day India) produced within the country; not imported ▷ *n* **2** (in British India) the encouragement of domestic production and boycott of foreign goods as part of the campaign for independence [c20 from Bengali *svadeśī*, from Sanskrit *svadeśin*, from *sva* one's own + *deśa* country]

swag (swæg) *n* **1** *slang* property obtained by theft or other illicit means **2** *slang* goods; valuables **3** an ornamental festoon of fruit, flowers, or drapery or a representation of this **4** a swaying movement; lurch **5** *Midland English dialect* a depression filled with water, resulting from mining subsidence **6** *Austral and NZ informal* (formerly) a swagman's pack containing personal belongings **7** **go on the swag** *Austral and NZ informal* to become a tramp **8** **swags of** *Austral and NZ informal* lots of ▷ *vb* **swags, swagging, swagged** **9** *chiefly Brit* to lurch or sag or cause to lurch or sag **10** (*tr*) to adorn or arrange with swags **11** (*intr*) *Austral informal* to tramp about carrying a pack of personal belongings [c17 perhaps of Scandinavian origin; compare Norwegian *svagga* to **SWAY**]

swage (sweɪdʒ) *n* **1** a shaped tool or die used in forming cold metal by hammering, pressing, etc **2** a decorative moulding ▷ *vb* **3** (*tr*) to form (metal) with a swage [c19 from French *souage*, of unknown origin] > **'swager** *n*

swage block *n* an iron block cut with holes, recesses, and grooves to assist in the cold-working of metal

swagger[1] ('swægə) *vb* **1** (*intr*) to walk or behave in an arrogant manner **2** (*often foll by about*) to brag loudly **3** (*tr*) *rare* to force, influence, etc, by blustering ▷ *n* **4** arrogant gait, conduct, or manner ▷ *adj* **5** *Brit informal, rare* elegantly fashionable [c16 probably from **SWAG**] > **'swaggerer** *n* > **'swaggering** *adj* > **'swaggeringly** *adv*

swagger[2] ('swægə), **swaggie** ('swægɪ) *n* other names for **swagman**

swagger stick or *esp Brit* **swagger cane** *n* a short cane or stick carried on occasion mainly by army officers

swaggie ('swægɪ) *n Austral and NZ slang* short for **swagman**

swagman ('swæg,mæn, -mən) *n, pl* -men *Austral and NZ informal* a labourer who carries his personal possessions in a pack or swag while travelling about in search of work; vagrant worker. Also called: **swagger, swaggie**

Swahili (swɑː'hiːlɪ) *n* **1** Also called: **Kiswahili** a language of E Africa that is an official language of Kenya and Tanzania and is widely used as a lingua franca throughout E and central Africa. It is a member of the Bantu group of the Niger-Congo family, originally spoken in Zanzibar, and has a large number of loan words taken from Arabic and other languages **2** (*pl* -lis or -li Also called: **Mswahili** *pl* **Waswahili**) a member of a people speaking this language, living chiefly in Zanzibar ▷ *adj* **3** of or relating to the Swahilis or their language [c19 from Arabic *sawāhil* coasts] > **Swaˈhilian** *adj*

swain (sweɪn) *n archaic or poetic* **1** a male lover or admirer **2** a country youth [Old English *swān* swineherd; related to Old High German *swein*, Old Norse *sveinn* boy; see **SWINE**] > **'swainish** *adj*

swale (sweɪl) *n chiefly US* **a** a moist depression in a tract of land, usually with rank vegetation **b** (*as modifier*): *swell and swale topography* [c16 probably of Scandinavian origin; compare Old Norse *svala* to chill]

Swaledale ('sweɪl,deɪl) *n* a breed of small hardy sheep kept esp in northern England for its coarse wool which is used for making tweeds and carpets [from *Swaledale*, Yorkshire]

SWALK (swɔːlk) *acronym for* sealed with a loving kiss: sometimes written on the back of envelopes

swallow[1] ('swɒləʊ) *vb* (*mainly tr*) **1** to pass (food, drink, etc) through the mouth to the stomach by means of the muscular action of the oesophagus **2** (*often foll by up*) to engulf or destroy as if by ingestion: *Nazi Germany swallowed up several small countries* **3** *informal* to believe gullibly: *he will never swallow such an excuse* **4** to refrain from uttering or manifesting: *to swallow one's disappointment* **5** to endure without retaliation **6** to enunciate (words, etc) indistinctly; mutter **7** (*often foll by down*) to eat or drink reluctantly **8** (*intr*) to perform or simulate the act of swallowing, as in gulping **9** **swallow one's words** to retract a statement, argument, etc, often in humiliating circumstances ▷ *n* **10** the act of swallowing **11** the amount swallowed at any single time; mouthful **12** Also called: **crown, throat** *nautical* the opening between the shell and the groove of the sheave of a block, through which the rope is passed **13** *rare* another word for **throat** or **gullet 14** *rare* a capacity for swallowing; appetite [Old English *swelgan*; related to Old Norse *svelga*, Old High German *swelgan* to swallow, Swedish *svalg* gullet] > **'swallowable** *adj* > **'swallower** *n*

swallow[2] ('swɒləʊ) *n* **1** any passerine songbird of the family *Hirundinidae*, esp *Hirundo rustica* (**common** or **barn swallow**), having long pointed wings, a forked tail, short legs, and a rapid flight. Related *adj*: **hirundine 2** See **fairy swallow** [Old English *swealwe*; related to Old Frisian *swale*, Old Norse *svala*, Old High German *swalwa*] > **'swallow-,like** *adj*

swallow dive *n* a type of dive in which the diver arches back while in the air, keeping his legs straight and together and his arms outstretched, finally entering the water headfirst. US and Canadian equivalent: **swan dive**

swallow hole *n chiefly Brit* another word for **sinkhole** (sense 1)

swallowtail ('swɒləʊ,teɪl) *n* **1** any of various butterflies of the genus *Papilio* and related genera, esp *P. machaon* of Europe, having a tail-like extension of each hind wing: family *Papilionidae* **2** the forked tail of a swallow or similar bird **3** short for **swallow-tailed coat**

swallow-tailed *adj* **1** (of a bird) having a deeply forked tail **2** having a part resembling a swallow's tail

swallow-tailed coat *n* another name for **tail coat**

swallowwort ('swɒləʊ,wɜːt) *n* **1** any of several Eurasian vines of the genus *Cynanchum*, esp *C. nigrum*, having small brownish-purple flowers: family *Asclepiadaceae* **2** a related European herbaceous plant, *Vincetoxicum officinale* (or *Cynanchum vincetoxicum*), having an emetic root **3** another name for **greater celandine** [c16 so called because the shape of its pod is reminiscent of a flying swallow]

swam (swæm) *vb* the past tense of **swim**

swami ('swɑːmɪ) *n, pl* -mies or -mis (in India) a title of respect for a Hindu saint or religious teacher [c18 from Hindi *svāmī*, from Sanskrit *svāmin* master, from *sva* one's own]

swamp (swɒmp) *n* **1 a** permanently waterlogged ground that is usually overgrown and sometimes partly forested. Compare **marsh b** (*as modifier*): *swamp fever* ▷ *vb* **2** to drench or submerge or be drenched or submerged **3** *nautical* to cause (a boat) to sink or fill with water or (of a boat) to sink or fill with water **4** to overburden or overwhelm or be overburdened or overwhelmed, as by excess work or great numbers: *we have been swamped with applications* **5** to sink or stick or cause to sink or stick in or as if in a swamp **6** (*tr*) to render helpless [c17 probably from Middle Dutch *somp*; compare Middle High German *sumpf*, Old Norse *svöppr* sponge, Greek *somphos* spongy] > **'swampish** *adj* > **'swampless** *adj* > **'swampy** *adj*

swamp boat *n* a shallow-draught boat powered by an æroplane engine mounted on a raised structure for use in swamps. Also called: **airboat**

swamp buggy *n* (esp in the US and Canada) a light aerofoil conveyance for use in regions with swamps, lakes, etc

swamp cypress *n* a North American deciduous coniferous tree, *Taxodium distichum*, that grows in swamps and sends up aerial roots from its base. Also called: **bald cypress**

swamper ('swɒmpə) *n US* **a** a person who lives or works in a swampy region, esp in the southern US **b** a person who clears a swamp of trees and undergrowth or who clears a path in a forest for transporting logs

swamp fever *n* **1** Also called: **equine infectious anaemia** a viral disease of horses characterized by recurring fever, staggering gait, and general debility **2** *US* another name for **malaria**

swampland ('swɒmp,lænd) *n* a permanently waterlogged area; marshland

swan (swɒn) *n* **1** any large aquatic bird of the genera *Cygnus* and *Coscoroba*, having a long neck and usually a white plumage: family *Anatidae*, order *Anseriformes* **2** *rare, literary* **a** a poet **b** (*capital when part of a title or epithet*): *the Swan of Avon* (Shakespeare) ▷ *vb* **swans, swanning, swanned 3** (*intr; usually foll by around or about*) *informal* to wander idly [Old English; related to Old Norse *svanr*, Middle Low German *swōn*] > **'swan,like** *adj*

Swan (swɒn) *n* a river in SW Western Australia, rising as the Avon northeast of Narrogin and flowing northwest and west to the Indian Ocean below Perth. Length: about 240 km (150 miles)

swan dive *n US and Canadian* a type of dive in which the diver arches back while in the air, keeping his legs straight and together and his arms outstretched, finally entering the water headfirst. Also called (in Britain and certain other countries): **swallow dive**

Swanee ('swɒnɪ) *n* a variant spelling of Suwannee

swanherd ('swɒn,hɜːd) *n* a person who herds swans

swank (swæŋk) *informal* ▷ *vb* **1** (*intr*) to show off or swagger ▷ *n* **2** Also called: **swankpot** *Brit* a swaggering or conceited person **3** *chiefly US* elegance or style, esp of a showy kind **4** swagger; ostentation ▷ *adj* **5** another word (esp US) for **swanky** [c19 perhaps from Middle High German *swanken* to sway; see **SWAG**]

swanky ('swæŋkɪ) *adj* **swankier, swankiest** *informal* **1** expensive and showy; stylish: *a swanky hotel* **2** boastful or conceited > **'swankily** *adv* > **'swankiness** *n*

swan maiden *n* any of a group of maidens in folklore who by magic are transformed into swans

Swanndri or **Swandri** ('swɒn,draɪ) *n, pl* -dris *trademark NZ* an all-weather heavy woollen shirt. Also called: **swannie** ('swɒnɪ)

swan neck *n* a tube, rail, etc, curved like a swan's neck

swannery ('swɒnərɪ) *n, pl* -neries a place where swans are kept and bred

swan's-down *n* **1** the fine soft down feathers of a swan, used to trim powder puffs, clothes, etc **2** a thick soft fabric of wool with silk, cotton, or rayon, used for infants' clothing, etc **3** a cotton fabric with a heavy nap

Swansea ('swɒnzɪ) *n* **1** a port in S Wales, in Swansea county on an inlet of the Bristol Channel (**Swansea Bay**); a metallurgical and oil-refining centre; university (1920). Pop: 169 880 (2001) **2** a county of S Wales on the Bristol Channel, created in 1996 from part of West Glamorgan: includes the Swansea conurbation and the Gower peninsula. Administrative centre: Swansea. Pop: 224 600 (2003 est). Area: 378 sq km (146 sq miles)

swanskin ('swɒn,skɪn) *n* **1** the skin of a swan with the feathers attached **2** a fine twill-weave flannel fabric

swan song *n* **1** the last act, appearance, publication, or utterance of a person before retirement or death **2** the song that a dying swan is said to sing

swan-upping *n Brit* **1** the practice or action of marking nicks in swans' beaks as a sign of ownership **2** the annual swan-upping of royal cygnets on the River Thames [C16 from UP (in the archaic sense: to catch and mark a swan)]

Swanz (swɒnz) *pl n* **the** the women's international soccer team of New Zealand

swap *or* **swop** (swɒp) *vb* **swaps, swapping, swapped** *or* **swops, swopping, swopped 1** to trade or exchange (something or someone) for another ▷ *n* **2** an exchange **3** something that is exchanged **4** *finance* Also called: **swap option, swaption** a contract in which the parties to it exchange liabilities on outstanding debts, often exchanging fixed interest-rate for floating-rate debts (**debt swap**), either as a means of managing debt or in trading (**swap trading**) [C14 (in the sense: to shake hands on a bargain, strike): probably of imitative origin] > **'swapper** *or* **'swopper** *n*

SWAPO *or* **Swapo** ('swɑːpəʊ) *n acronym for* South-West Africa People's Organization

swap shop *n* a place or occasion at which articles no longer wanted may be exchanged for other articles

swaption ('swɒpʃən) *n* another name for **swap** (sense 4)

swaraj (swəˈrɑːdʒ) *n* (in British India) self-government; independence [C20 from Sanskrit *svarāj*, from *sva* self + *rājya* rule] > **swaˈrajism** *n* > **swaˈrajist** *n, adj*

sward (swɔːd) *n* **1** turf or grass or a stretch of turf or grass ▷ *vb* **2** to cover or become covered with grass [Old English *sweard* skin; related to Old Frisian *swarde* scalp, Middle High German *swart* hide]

swarf (swɔːf, swɑːf) *n* **1** material removed by cutting or grinding tools in the machining of metals, stone, etc **2** radioactive metal waste from a nuclear power station **3** small fragments of disintegrating spacecraft, orbiting the earth [C16 of Scandinavian origin; related to Old Norse *svarf* metallic dust]

swarm[1] (swɔːm) *n* **1** a group of social insects, esp bees led by a queen, that has left the parent hive in order to start a new colony **2** a large mass of small animals, esp insects **3** a throng or mass, esp when moving or in turmoil ▷ *vb* **4** (*intr*) (of small animals, esp bees) to move in or form a swarm **5** (*intr*) to congregate, move about or proceed in large numbers **6** (when *intr*, often foll by *with*) to overrun or be overrun (with): *the house swarmed with rats* **7** (*tr*) to cause to swarm [Old English *swearm*; related to Old Norse *svarmr* uproar, Old High German *swaram* swarm]

swarm[2] (swɔːm) *vb* (when *intr*, usually foll by *up*) to climb (a ladder, etc) by gripping with the hands and feet: *the boys swarmed up the rigging* [C16 of unknown origin]

swarm cell *or* **spore** *n* another name for **zoospore**

swart (swɔːt) *or* **swarth** (swɔːθ) *adj archaic or dialect* swarthy [Old English *sweart*; related to Old Frisian *swart*, Old Norse *svartr*, Old High German *swarz* black, Latin *sordēs* dirt; see SORDID] > **'swartness** *or* **'swarthness** *n*

swarthy ('swɔːðɪ) *adj* **swarthier, swarthiest** dark-hued or dark-complexioned [C16 from obsolete *swarty*, from SWART + -Y[1]] > **'swarthily** *adv* > **'swarthiness** *n*

swash (swɒʃ) *vb* **1** (*intr*) (esp of water or things in water) to wash or move with noisy splashing **2** (*tr*) to dash (a liquid, esp water) against or upon **3** (*intr*) *archaic* to swagger or bluster ▷ *n* **4** Also called: **send** the dashing movement or sound of water, such as that of waves on a beach. Compare **backwash 5** any other swashing movement or sound **6** a sandbar washed by the waves **7** Also called: **swash channel** a channel of moving water cutting through or running behind a sandbank **8** *archaic* **a** swagger or bluster **b** a swashbuckler [C16 probably of imitative origin]

swashbuckler ('swɒʃˌbʌklə) *n* a swaggering or flamboyant adventurer [C16 from SWASH (in the archaic sense: to make the noise of a sword striking a shield) + BUCKLER]

swashbuckling ('swɒʃˌbʌklɪŋ) *adj* (usually *prenominal*) **1** of or characteristic of a swashbuckler **2** (esp of films in period costume) full of adventure and excitement

swash letter *n printing* a decorative letter, esp an ornamental italic capital [C17 *swash* (n, in the sense: the decorative flourish of an ornamental letter) from *aswash* aslant]

swash plate *n engineering* a collar or face plate on a shaft that is inclined at an oblique angle to the axis of rotation and either imparts reciprocating motion to push rods parallel to the shaft axis as in a **swash plate pump** or, conversely, converts reciprocating motion to rotation as in a **swash plate motor**. Also called: **wobble plate** [from *swash* (obsolete n) an oblique figure or ornament, from *aswash*: see SWASH LETTER]

swastika ('swɒstɪkə) *n* **1** a primitive religious symbol or ornament in the shape of a Greek cross, usually having the ends of the arms bent at right angles in either a clockwise or anticlockwise direction **2** this symbol with clockwise arms, officially adopted in 1935 as the emblem of Nazi Germany [C19 from Sanskrit *svastika*, from *svasti* prosperity; from the belief that it brings good luck]

swat[1] (swɒt) *vb* **swats, swatting, swatted** (*tr*) **1** to strike or hit sharply: *to swat a fly* ▷ *n* **2** another word (esp Brit) for **swatter** (sense 1) **3** a sharp or violent blow ▷ Also: **swot** [C17 northern English dialect and US variant of SQUAT]

swat[2] (swɒt) *vb* **swats, swatting, swatted**, *n* a variant of **swot**[1]

Swat (swɒt) *n* **1** a former princely state of NW India: passed to Pakistan in 1947 **2** a river in Pakistan, rising in the north and flowing south to the Kabul River north of Peshawar. Length: about 640 km (400 miles)

SWAT (swɒt) *n acronym for* Special Weapons and Tactics: a military-like unit within the US police force, trained to deal with specially dangerous situations, such as hostage-taking and riots

swatch (swɒtʃ) *n* **1** a sample of cloth **2** a number of such samples, usually fastened together in book form **3** *printing* **a** a small sample of colour supplied to the printer for matching during printing **b** a sample of ink spread on paper by a printer to check the accuracy of a required colour [C16 Scottish and northern English, of uncertain origin]

swath (swɔːθ) *or* **swathe** (sweɪð) *n, pl* **swaths** (swɔːðz) *or* **swathes 1** the width of one sweep of a scythe or of the blade of a mowing machine **2** the strip cut by either of these in one course **3** the quantity of cut grass, hay, or similar crop left in one course of such mowing **4** a long narrow strip or belt [Old English *swæth*; related to Old Norse *svath* smooth patch]

swathe (sweɪð) *vb* (*tr*) **1** to bandage (a wound, limb, etc), esp completely **2** to wrap a band, garment, etc, around, esp so as to cover completely; swaddle **3** to envelop ▷ *n* **4** a bandage or wrapping **5** a variant spelling of **swath** [Old English *swathian*; related to Old English *swæthel* swaddling clothes, Old High German *swedil*, Dutch *zwadel*; see SWADDLE] > **'swathable** *or* **'swatheable** *adj*

Swatow ('swɒˈtaʊ) *n* a variant transliteration of the Chinese name for **Shantou**

swatter ('swɒtə) *n* **1** a device for killing insects, esp a meshed flat attached to a handle **2** a person who swats

sway (sweɪ) *vb* **1** (usually *intr*) to swing or cause to swing to and fro **2** (usually *intr*) to lean or incline or cause to lean or incline to one side or in different directions in turn **3** (usually *intr*) to vacillate or cause to vacillate between two or more opinions **4** to be influenced or swerve or influence or cause to swerve to or from a purpose or opinion **5** (*tr*) *nautical* to hoist (a yard, mast, or other spar) **6** *archaic or poetic* to rule or wield power (over) **7** (*tr*) *archaic* to wield (a weapon) ▷ *n* **8** control; power **9** a swinging or leaning movement **10** *archaic* dominion; governing authority **11 hold sway** to be master; reign [C16 probably from Old Norse *sveigja* to bend; related to Dutch *zwaaien*, Low German *swājen*] > **'swayable** *adj* > **'swayer** *n* > **'swayful** *adj*

sway-back *n* **1** *vet science* an abnormal sagging or concavity of the spine in older horses **2** a paralytic disease of new-born and young lambs caused by demyelination of the central nervous system due to copper deficiency > **'sway-ˌbacked** *adj*

Swazi ('swɑːzɪ) *n* **1** (*pl* **-zis** *or* **-zi**) a member of a racially mixed people of southern Africa living chiefly in Swaziland, who first formed into a strong political group in the late 19th century **2** the language of this people: an official language of Swaziland along with English. It belongs to the Niger-Congo family and is closely related to Xhosa and Zulu

Swaziland ('swɑːzɪˌlænd) *n* a kingdom in southern Africa: made a protectorate of the Transvaal by Britain in 1894; gained independence in 1968; a member of the Commonwealth. Official languages: Swazi and English. Religion: Christian majority, traditional beliefs. Currency: lilangeni (plural emalangeni) and South African rand. Capital: Mbabane (administrative), Lobamba (legislative). Pop: 1 083 000 (2004 est). Area: 17 363 sq km (6704 sq miles)

Swazi Territory *n* the former name of **KaNgwane**

swazzle *or* **swozzle** ('swɒzəl) *n* a small metal instrument held in the mouth of a Punch and Judy puppeteer, used to produce the characteristic shrill voice of Mr Punch [C19 imitative of the sound produced]

swear (sweə) *vb* **swears, swearing, swore, sworn 1** to declare or affirm (a statement) as true, esp by invoking a deity, etc, as witness **2** (foll by *by*) **a** to invoke (a deity, etc) by name as a witness or guarantee to an oath **b** to trust implicitly; have complete confidence (in) **3** (*intr*; often foll by *at*) to curse, blaspheme, or use swearwords **4** (when *tr*, *may take a clause as object or an infinitive*) to promise solemnly on oath; vow **5** (*tr*) to assert or affirm with great emphasis or earnestness **6** (*intr*) to give evidence or make any statement or solemn declaration on oath **7** to take an oath in order to add force or solemnity to (a statement or declaration) **8 swear blind** *informal* to assert emphatically ▷ *n* **9** a period of swearing [Old English *swerian*; related to Old Norse *sverja*, Gothic *swaran*, Old Frisian *swera*, German *schwören*] > **'swearer** *n*

swear in *vb* (*tr, adverb*) to administer an oath to (a person) on his assuming office, entering the witness box to give evidence, etc

swear off *vb* (*intr, preposition*) to promise to abstain from something: *to swear off drink*

swear out *vb* (*tr, adverb*) US to secure the issue of (a warrant for an arrest) by making a charge under oath

swearword ('sweəˌwɜːd) *n* a socially taboo word or phrase of a profane, obscene, or insulting character

sweat (swɛt) *n* **1** the secretion from the sweat glands, esp when profuse and visible, as during strenuous activity, from excessive heat, etc; commonly also called perspiration. Related adjs: **sudatory, sudorific 2** the act or process of secreting this fluid **3** the act of inducing the exudation of moisture **4** drops of moisture given forth or gathered on the surface of something **5** *informal* a state or condition of worry or eagerness (esp in the phrase **in a sweat**) **6** *slang* drudgery or hard labour: *mowing lawns is a real sweat!* **7** *chiefly US* an exercise gallop given to a horse, esp on the day of a race **8** *slang, chiefly Brit* a soldier, esp one who

S

is old and experienced **9 no sweat!** (*interjection*) *slang* an expression suggesting that something can be done without problems or difficulty ▷ *vb* **sweats, sweating; sweat** *or* **sweated 10** to secrete (sweat) through the pores of the skin, esp profusely **11** (*tr*) to make wet or stain with sweat **12** to give forth or cause to give forth (moisture) in droplets: *a sweating cheese; the maple sweats sap* **13** (*intr*) to collect and condense moisture on an outer surface: *a glass of beer sweating in the sun* **14** (*intr*) (of a liquid) to pass through a porous surface in droplets **15** (of tobacco leaves, cut and dried hay, etc) to exude moisture and, sometimes, begin to ferment or to cause (tobacco leaves, etc) to exude moisture **16** (*tr*) to heat (food, esp vegetables) slowly in butter in a tightly closed saucepan **17** (*tr*) to join (pieces of metal) by pressing together and heating **18** (*tr*) to heat (solder) until it melts **19** (*tr*) to heat (a partially fused metal) to extract an easily fusible constituent **20** to shake together (coins, esp gold coins) so as to remove particles for illegal use **21** *informal* to suffer anxiety, impatience, or distress **22** *informal* to overwork or be overworked **23** (*tr*) *informal* to employ at very low wages and under bad conditions **24** (*tr*) *informal* to extort, esp by torture: *to sweat information out of a captive* **25** (*intr*) *informal* to suffer punishment: *you'll sweat for this!* **26 sweat blood** *informal* **a** to work very hard **b** to be filled with anxiety or impatience ▷ See also **sweat off, sweat out** See also **hidrosis** [Old English *swætan* to sweat, from *swāt* sweat; related to Old Saxon *swēt*, Old Norse *sveiti*, Old High German *sweiz*, Latin *sūdor*, Sanskrit *svedas*] > **'sweatless** *adj*

sweatband ('swɛtˌbænd) *n* **1** a band of material set in a hat or cap to protect it from sweat **2** a piece of cloth tied around the forehead to keep sweat out of the eyes or around the wrist to keep the hands dry, as in sports

sweatbox ('swɛtˌbɒks) *n* **1** a device for causing tobacco leaves, fruit, or hides to sweat **2** a very small pen or cubicle where a pig is fattened intensively **3** *informal, chiefly US* a narrow room or cell for a prisoner **4** *informal* any place where a person sweats on account of confinement, heat, etc

sweated ('swɛtɪd) *adj* **1** made by exploited labour: *sweated goods* **2** (of workers, etc) forced to work in poor conditions for low pay

sweater ('swɛtə) *n* **1 a** a garment made of knitted or crocheted material covering the upper part of the body, esp a heavy one worn for warmth **b** (*as modifier*): *a sweater dress* **2** a person or thing that sweats **3** an employer who overworks and underpays his employees

sweater girl *n slang, now rare* a young woman or girl with large breasts who wears tight sweaters

sweat gland *n* any of the coiled tubular subcutaneous glands that secrete sweat by means of a duct that opens on to the skin

sweating sickness *n* **1** the nontechnical name for **miliary fever 2** an acute infectious febrile disease that was widespread in Europe during the late 15th century, characterized by profuse sweating **3** a disease of cattle, esp calves, prevalent in southern Africa. Transmitted by ticks, it is characterized by sweating, hair loss, and inflammation of the mouth and eyes

sweat lodge *n* (among native North American peoples) a structure in which water is poured onto hot stones to make the occupants sweat for religious or medicinal purposes

sweat off *or* **away** *vb* (*tr, adverb*) *informal* to get rid of (weight) by strenuous exercise or sweating

sweat out *vb* (*tr, adverb*) **1** to cure or lessen the effects of (a cold, respiratory infection, etc) by sweating **2** *informal* to endure (hardships) for a time (often in the phrase **sweat it out**) **3 sweat one's guts out** *informal* to work extremely hard

sweat pants *pl n* loose thick cotton trousers with elasticated cuffs and an elasticated or drawstring waist, worn esp by athletes warming up or training

sweats (swɛts) *pl n* sweatshirts and sweat-suit trousers: *jeans and sweats*

sweatshirt ('swɛtˌʃɜːt) *n* a long-sleeved knitted cotton sweater worn by athletes, etc

sweatshop ('swɛtˌʃɒp) *n* a workshop where employees work long hours under bad conditions for low wages

sweat suit *n* a suit worn by athletes for training comprising knitted cotton trousers fitting closely at the ankle and a light cotton sweater

sweaty ('swɛtɪ) *adj* **sweatier, sweatiest 1** covered with sweat; sweating **2** smelling of or like sweat **3** causing sweat > **'sweatily** *adv* > **'sweatiness** *n*

swede (swiːd) *n* **1** a Eurasian plant, *Brassica napus* (or *B. napobrassica*), cultivated for its bulbous edible root, which is used as a vegetable and as cattle fodder: family *Brassicaceae* (crucifers) **2** the root of this plant **3** *NZ* a slang word for **head** (sense 1) ▷ Also called (for senses 1, 2): **Swedish turnip** *US* and Canadian name: **rutabaga** [C19 so called after being introduced into Scotland from Sweden in the 18th century]

Swede (swiːd) *n* a native, citizen, or inhabitant of Sweden

Sweden ('swiːdᵊn) *n* a kingdom in NW Europe, occupying the E part of the Scandinavian Peninsula, on the Gulf of Bothnia and the Baltic: first united during the Viking period (8th–11th centuries); a member of the European Union. About 50 per cent of the total area is forest and 9 per cent lakes. Exports include timber, pulp, paper, iron ore, and steel. Official language: Swedish. Official religion: Church of Sweden (Lutheran). Currency: krona. Capital: Stockholm. Pop: 8 886 000 (2004 est). Area: 449 793 sq km (173 665 sq miles). Swedish name: **Sverige**

Swedenborgianism (ˌswiːdᵊnˈbɔːdʒɪəˌnɪzəm, -gɪ-) *or* **Swedenborgism** ('swiːdᵊnˌbɔːdʒɪzəm, -gɪz-) *n* the system of philosophical and religious doctrines of Emanuel Swedenborg, the Swedish scientist and theologian (1688–1772), emphasizing the spiritual structure of the universe, the possibility of direct contact with spirits, and the divinity of Christ. This provided the basis for the **New Jerusalem Church** (or **New Church**) founded by Swedenborg's followers > ˌ**Sweden'borgian** *n, adj*

swedger ('swɛdʒə) *n* (*often plural*) *Scot dialect* a sweet [C20]

Swedish ('swiːdɪʃ) *adj* **1** of, relating to, or characteristic of Sweden, its people, or their language ▷ *n* **2** the official language of Sweden, belonging to the North Germanic branch of the Indo-European family: one of the two official languages of Finland **3 the Swedish** (*functioning as plural*) the people of Sweden collectively

Swedish massage *n* massage combined with a system (**Swedish movements** or **gymnastics**) of passive and active exercising of muscles and joints

Swedish mile *n* a unit of length used in Sweden, equal to 10 kilometres

Swedish vallhund ('vælˌhʊnd) *n* a small sturdy dog of a Swedish breed with a long body and pricked pointed ears [from Swedish *vall* + *hund* dog]

sweeny ('swiːnɪ) *n vet science* a wasting of the shoulder muscles of a horse, esp as the result of a nerve injury [C19 probably from German dialect *Schweine* emaciation, atrophy]

sweep (swiːp) *vb* **sweeps, sweeping, swept 1** to clean or clear (a space, chimney, etc) with a brush, broom, etc **2** (often foll by *up*) to remove or collect (dirt, rubbish, etc) with a brush, broom, etc **3** to move in a smooth or continuous manner, esp quickly or forcibly: *cars swept along the road* **4** to move in a proud or dignified fashion: *she swept past* **5** to spread or pass rapidly across, through, or along (a region, area, etc): *the news swept through the town* **6** (*tr*) to direct (the gaze, line of fire, etc) over; survey **7** (*tr*; foll by *away* or *off*) to overwhelm emotionally: *she was swept away by his charm* **8** (*tr*) to brush or lightly touch (a surface, etc): *the dress swept along the ground* **9** (*tr*; often foll by *away*) to convey, clear, or abolish, esp with strong or continuous movements: *the sea swept the sandcastle away; secondary modern schools were swept away* **10** (*intr*) to extend gracefully or majestically, esp in a wide circle: *the plains sweep down to the sea* **11** to search (a body of water) for mines, etc, by dragging **12** to search (a room, area, etc) electronically to detect spying devices **13** (*tr*) to win overwhelmingly, esp in an election: *Labour swept the country* **14** *cricket* to play (a ball) with a sweep **15** (*tr*) to propel (a boat) with sweeps **16 sweep the board a** (in gambling) to win all the cards or money **b** to win every event or prize in a contest **17 sweep (something) under the carpet** to conceal (something, esp a problem) in the hope that it will be overlooked by others ▷ *n* **18** the act or an instance of sweeping; removal by or as if by a brush or broom **19** a swift or steady movement, esp in an arc: *with a sweep of his arms* **20** the distance, arc, etc, through which something, such as a pendulum, moves **21** a wide expanse or scope: *the sweep of the plains* **22** any curving line or contour **23** *cards* **a** the winning of every trick in a hand of whist **b** the taking, by pairing, of all exposed cards in cassino **24** short for **sweepstake 25** *cricket* a shot in which the ball is hit more or less square on the leg side from a half-kneeling position with the bat held nearly horizontal **26 a** a long oar used on an open boat **b** *Austral* a person steering a surf boat with such an oar **27** any of the sails of a windmill **28** *electronics* a steady horizontal or circular movement of an electron beam across or around the fluorescent screen of a cathode-ray tube **29** *agriculture* **a** a rakelike attachment for the front of a motor vehicle for pushing hay into piles **b** a triangular blade on a cultivator used to cut through roots below the surface of the soil **30** a curving driveway **31** *chiefly Brit* See **chimney sweep 32** another name for **swipe** (sense 6) **33 clean sweep a** an overwhelming victory or success **b** a complete change; purge: *to make a clean sweep* [C13 *swepen*; related to Old English *swāpan*, Old Norse *sveipa*; see SWIPE, SWOOP] > **'sweepy** *adj*

sweepback ('swiːpˌbæk) *n* the rearward inclination of a component or surface, such as an aircraft wing, fin, etc

sweeper ('swiːpə) *n* **1** a person employed to sweep, such as a roadsweeper **2** any device for sweeping: *a carpet sweeper* **3** *informal soccer* a player who supports the main defenders, as by intercepting loose balls, etc

sweep hand *n horology* a long hand that registers seconds or fractions of seconds on the perimeter of the dial

sweeping ('swiːpɪŋ) *adj* **1** comprehensive and wide-ranging: *sweeping reforms* **2** indiscriminate or without reservations: *sweeping statements* **3** decisive or overwhelming: *a sweeping victory* **4** taking in a wide area: *a sweeping glance* **5** driving steadily onwards, esp over a large area: *a sweeping attack* > **'sweepingly** *adv* > **'sweepingness** *n*

sweepings ('swiːpɪŋz) *pl n* debris, litter, or refuse

sweep-saw *n* a saw with a thin blade that can be used for cutting curved shapes

sweepstake ('swiːpˌsteɪk) *or esp US* **sweepstakes** *n* **1 a** a lottery in which the stakes of the participants constitute the prize **b** the prize itself **2** any event involving a lottery, esp a horse race in which the prize is the competitors' stakes ▷ Often shortened to: **sweep** [C15 originally referring to someone who *sweeps* or takes all the stakes in a game]

sweer (swiːr) *vb Scot* a variant spelling of **sweir**[1] and **sweir**[2]

sweet (swiːt) *adj* **1** having or denoting a pleasant taste like that of sugar **2** agreeable to the senses or the mind: *sweet music* **3** having pleasant manners; gentle: *a sweet child* **4** (of wine, etc) having a relatively high sugar content; not dry **5** (of foods) not decaying or rancid: *sweet milk* **6** not salty: *sweet water* **7** free from unpleasant odours: *sweet air* **8** containing no corrosive substances: *sweet soil* **9** (of petrol) containing no sulphur compounds **10** sentimental or unrealistic **11** individual; particular: *the electorate went its own sweet way* **12** *jazz* performed with a regular beat, with the emphasis on clearly outlined melody and little improvisation **13** *Austral slang* satisfactory or in order; all right **14** *archaic* respected; dear (used in polite forms of address): *sweet sir* **15** smooth and precise; perfectly executed: *a sweet shot* **16** **sweet on** fond of or infatuated with **17** **keep (someone) sweet** to ingratiate oneself in order to ensure cooperation ▷ *adv* **18** *informal* in a sweet manner ▷ *n* **19** a sweet taste or smell; sweetness in general **20** (*often plural*) *Brit* any of numerous kinds of confectionery consisting wholly or partly of sugar, esp of sugar boiled and crystallized (**boiled sweets**) **21** *Brit* a pudding, fruit, or any sweet dish served as a dessert **22** dear; sweetheart (used as a form of address) **23** anything that is sweet **24** (*often plural*) a pleasurable experience, state, etc: *the sweets of success* **25** *US* See **sweet potato** [Old English *swēte*; related to Old Saxon *swōti*, Old High German *suozi*, Old Norse *sætr*, Latin *suādus* persuasive, *suāvis* sweet, Greek *hēdus*, Sanskrit *svādu*; see PERSUADE, SUAVE] ▷ '**sweetish** *adj* ▷ '**sweetly** *adv* ▷ '**sweetness** *n*

sweet alyssum *n* a Mediterranean plant, *Lobularia maritima*, having clusters of small fragrant white or violet flowers, that is widely grown in gardens: family *Brassicaceae* (crucifers). See also **alyssum**

sweet-and-sour *adj* (of food) cooked in a sauce made from sugar and vinegar and other ingredients

sweet basil *n* See **basil** (sense 1)

sweet bay *n* a small tree, *Magnolia virginiana*, of SE North America, having large fragrant white flowers: family *Magnoliaceae* (magnolias). Sometimes shortened to: **bay**

sweetbread ('swiːtˌbrɛd) *n* the pancreas (**stomach sweetbread**) or the thymus gland (**neck** or **throat sweetbread**) of an animal, used for food [C16 SWEET + BREAD, perhaps from Old English *brǣd* meat; related to Old Saxon *brādo* ham, Old High German *brāt*, Old Norse *brāth*]

sweetbrier ('swiːtˌbraɪə) *n* a Eurasian rose, *Rosa rubiginosa*, having a tall bristly stem, fragrant leaves, and single pink flowers. Also called: **eglantine**

sweet cherry *n* **1** either of two types of cherry tree that are cultivated for their red edible sweet fruit, the gean having tender-fleshed fruit, the bigarreau having firm-fleshed fruit **2** the fruit of any of these trees. See also **heart cherry** ▷ Also called: **dessert cherry**. Compare **sour cherry**

sweet chestnut *n* See **chestnut** (sense 1)

sweet cicely *n* **1** Also called: **myrrh** an aromatic umbelliferous European plant, *Myrrhis odorata*, having compound leaves and clusters of small white flowers **2** the leaves of this plant, formerly used in cookery for their flavour of aniseed **3** any of various plants of the umbelliferous genus *Osmorhiza*, of Asia and America, having aromatic roots and clusters of small white flowers

sweet cider *n* **1** *Brit* cider having a high sugar content **2** *US and Canadian* unfermented apple juice. Compare **hard cider**

sweet clover *n* another name for **melilot**

sweet corn *n* **1** Also called: **sugar corn, green corn** a variety of maize, *Zea mays saccharata*, whose kernels are rich in sugar and eaten as a vegetable when young **2** the unripe ears of maize, esp the sweet kernels removed from the cob, cooked as a vegetable

sweeten ('swiːtᵊn) *vb* (*mainly tr*) **1** (*also intr*) to make or become sweet or sweeter **2** to mollify or soften (a person) **3** to make more agreeable **4** (*also intr*) *chem* to free or be freed from unpleasant odours, acidic or corrosive substances, or the like

5 *finance, chiefly US* to raise the value of (loan collateral) by adding more securities **6** *informal poker* to enlarge (the pot) by adding chips

sweetener ('swiːtᵊnə) *n* **1** a sweetening agent, esp one that does not contain sugar **2** *informal* a bribe **3** *informal* a financial inducement

sweetening ('swiːtᵊnɪŋ) *n* something that sweetens

sweet fern *n* a North American shrub, *Comptonia* (or *Myrica*) *asplenifolia*, having scented fernlike leaves and heads of brownish flowers: family *Myricaceae*

sweet flag *n* an aroid marsh plant, *Acorus calamus*, having swordlike leaves, small greenish flowers, and aromatic roots. Also called: **calamus** [C18 see FLAG²]

sweet gale *n* a shrub, *Myrica gale*, of northern swamp regions, having yellow catkin-like flowers and aromatic leaves: family *Myricaceae*. Also called: **bog myrtle**. Often shortened to: **gale** [C17 see GALE²]

sweet gum *n* **1** a North American liquidambar tree, *Liquidambar styraciflua*, having prickly spherical fruit clusters and fragrant sap: the wood (called **satin walnut**) is used to make furniture. Compare **sour gum 2** the sap of this tree ▷ Also called: **red gum**

sweetheart ('swiːtˌhɑːt) *n* **1** a person loved by another **2** *informal* a lovable, generous, or obliging person **3** a term of endearment for a beloved or lovable person ▷ *adj* **4** of or relating to a garment with a sweetheart neckline: *sweetheart cardigan*

sweetheart agreement *n* **1** an industrial agreement made at a local level between an employer and employees, often with clauses advantageous to the employer, such as no strikes, but without the recognition of the national union representing the employees **2** *Austral* an industrial agreement negotiated directly between employers and employees, without resort to arbitration

sweetheart neckline *n* a neckline on a woman's dress that is low at the front and shaped like the top of a heart

sweetie ('swiːtɪ) *n informal* **1** sweetheart; darling: used as a term of endearment **2** *Brit* another word for **sweet** (sense 20) **3** *chiefly Brit* an endearing person **4** a large seedless variety of grapefruit which has a green to yellow rind and juicy sweet pulp

sweetiewife ('swiːtɪˌwaɪf) *n, pl* -wives *Scot dialect* **1** a garrulous person **2** (*formerly*) a woman selling sweets

sweeting ('swiːtɪŋ) *n* **1** a variety of sweet apple **2** an archaic word for **sweetheart**

sweetman ('swiːtˌmæn) *n, pl* -men (in the Caribbean) a man kept by a woman

sweet marjoram *n* another name for **marjoram** (sense 1)

sweet marten *n* a name for the pine marten, referring to the fact that its scent glands produce a less offensive scent marker than that of the polecat (the foul marten or foumart)

sweetmeal ('swiːtˌmiːl) *adj* (of biscuits) sweet and wholemeal

sweetmeat ('swiːtˌmiːt) *n* a sweetened delicacy, such as a preserve, sweet, or, formerly, a cake or pastry

sweetness and light *n* an apparently affable reasonableness [C19 adopted by Matthew Arnold from Swift's *Battle of the Books* (1704)]

sweet oil *n* another name for **olive oil**

sweet pea *n* a climbing leguminous plant, *Lathyrus odoratus*, of S Europe, widely cultivated for its butterfly-shaped fragrant flowers of delicate pastel colours

sweet pepper *n* **1** a pepper plant, *Capsicum frutescens grossum*, with large bell-shaped fruits that are eaten unripe (**green pepper**) or ripe (**red pepper**) **2** the fruit of this plant

sweet potato *n* **1** a convolvulaceous twining

plant, *Ipomoea batatas*, of tropical America, cultivated in the tropics for its edible fleshy yellow root **2** the root of this plant ▷ Also called (*NZ*): **kumara**

sweet shop *n chiefly Brit* a shop solely or largely selling sweets, esp boiled sweets

sweetsop ('swiːtˌsɒp) *n* **1** a small West Indian tree, *Annona squamosa*, having yellowish-green fruit: family *Annonaceae* **2** the fruit of this tree, which has a sweet edible pulp ▷ Also called: **sugar apple, custard apple** Compare **soursop** [C19 so called because of the flavour and consistency of its pulp]

sweet spot *n sport* the centre area of a racquet, golf club, etc, from which the cleanest shots are made

sweet-talk *informal* ▷ *vb* **1** to coax, flatter, or cajole (someone) ▷ *n* **sweet talk 2** cajolery; coaxing

sweet tooth *n* a strong liking for sweet foods

sweet william *n* a widely cultivated Eurasian caryophyllaceous plant, *Dianthus barbatus*, with flat clusters of white, pink, red, or purple flowers

sweet woodruff *n* a Eurasian and North African rubiaceous plant, *Galium odoratum* (or *Asperula odorata*), having whorls of leaves and clusters of fragrant white flowers

sweir¹ (swiːr) *vb, n* a Scot word for **swear**

sweir² (swiːr) *adj Scot* **1** lazy **2** loath; disinclined [Old English]

swell (swɛl) *vb* swells, swelling, swelled, swollen or swelled **1** to grow or cause to grow in size, esp as a result of internal pressure. Compare **contract** (senses 1, 3) **2** to expand or cause to expand at a particular point or above the surrounding level; protrude **3** to grow or cause to grow in size, amount, intensity, or degree: *the party is swelling with new recruits* **4** to puff or be puffed up with pride or another emotion **5** (*intr*) (of seas or lakes) to rise in waves **6** (*intr*) to well up or overflow **7** (*tr*) to make (a musical phrase) increase gradually in volume and then diminish ▷ *n* **8 a** the undulating movement of the surface of the open sea **b** a succession of waves or a single large wave **9** a swelling or being swollen; expansion **10** an increase in quantity or degree; inflation **11** a bulge; protuberance **12** a gentle hill **13** *informal* a person very fashionably dressed **14** *informal* a man of high social or political standing **15** *music* a crescendo followed by an immediate diminuendo **16** Also called: **swell organ** *music* **a** a set of pipes on an organ housed in a box (**swell box**) fitted with a shutter operated by a pedal, which can be opened or closed to control the volume **b** the manual on an organ controlling this. Compare **choir** (sense 4), **great** (sense 21) ▷ *adj* **17** *informal* stylish or grand **18** *slang* excellent; first-class [Old English *swellan*; related to Old Norse *svella*, Old Frisian *swella*, German *schwellen*]

swelled head or **swollen head** *n informal* an inflated view of one's own worth, often caused by sudden success

swelled-headed, swell-headed or **swollen-headed** *adj informal* conceited

swellfish ('swɛlˌfɪʃ) *n, pl* -fish or -fishes a popular name for **puffer** (sense 2)

swelling ('swɛlɪŋ) *n* **1** the act of expansion or inflation **2** the state of being or becoming swollen **3** a swollen or inflated part or area **4** an abnormal enlargement of a bodily structure or part, esp as the result of injury. Related adj: **tumescent**

swelter ('swɛltə) *vb* **1** (*intr*) to suffer under oppressive heat, esp to sweat and feel faint **2** (*tr*) *archaic* to exude (venom) **3** (*tr*) *rare* to cause to suffer under oppressive heat ▷ *n* **4** a sweltering condition (esp in the phrase **in a swelter**) **5** oppressive humid heat [C15 *swelten*, from Old English *sweltan* to die; related to Old Norse *svelta* to starve, Old High German *swelzan* to burn with passion; see SULTRY]

S

sweltering ('swɛltərɪŋ) *adj* oppressively hot and humid: *a sweltering day* > **'swelteringly** *adv*

swept (swɛpt) *vb* the past tense of **sweep**

sweptback ('swɛpt,bæk) *adj* (of an aircraft wing) having leading edge and trailing edges inclined backwards towards the rear of the fuselage

swept volume *n* another term for **volumetric displacement**

sweptwing ('swɛpt,wɪŋ) *adj* (of an aircraft, winged missile, etc) having wings swept (usually) backwards

swerve (swɜːv) *vb* **1** to turn or cause to turn aside, usually sharply or suddenly, from a course **2** (*tr*) to avoid (a person or event) ▷ *n* **3** the act, instance, or degree of swerving [Old English *sweorfan* to scour; related to Old High German *swerban* to wipe off, Gothic *afswairban* to wipe off, Old Norse *sverfa* to file] > **'swervable** *adj* > **'swerver** *n*

sweven ('swɛvᵊn) *n archaic* a vision or dream [Old English *swefn*; related to Old Norse *svefn* dream, sleep, Lithuanian *sãpnas*, Old Slavonic *sunu*, Latin *somnus*]

SWFF *Austral* ▷ *abbreviation for* saltwater fly-fishing

SWG *n* Standard Wire Gauge; a notation for the diameters of metal rods or thickness of metal sheet ranging from 16 mm to 0.02 mm or from 0.5 inch to 0.001 inch

swidden ('swɪdᵊn) *n* **a** an area of land where slash-and-burn techniques have been used to prepare it for cultivation **b** (*as modifier*): *small-scale swidden agriculture* [c18 Northern English dialect variant of *swithen* to burn]

swift (swɪft) *adj* **1** moving or able to move quickly; fast **2** occurring or performed quickly or suddenly; instant: *a swift response* **3** (*postpositive; foll by to*) prompt to act or respond: *swift to take revenge* ▷ *adv* **4 a** swiftly or quickly **b** (*in combination*): *swift-moving* ▷ *n* **5** any bird of the families *Apodidae* and *Hemiprocnidae*, such as *Apus apus* (**common swift**) of the Old World: order *Apodiformes*. They have long narrow wings and spend most of the time on the wing **6** (*sometimes capital*) a variety of domestic fancy pigeon originating in Egypt and Syria and having an appearance somewhat similar to a swift **7** short for **swift moth 8** any of certain North American lizards of the genera *Sceloporus* and *Uta* that can run very rapidly: family *Iguanidae* (iguanas) **9** the main cylinder in a carding machine **10** an expanding circular frame used to hold skeins of silk, wool, etc [Old English, from *swīfan* to turn; related to Old Norse *svifa* to rove, Old Frisian *swīvia* to waver, Old High German *sweib* a reversal; see SWIVEL] > **'swiftly** *adv* > **'swiftness** *n*

swifter ('swɪftə) *n nautical* a line run around the ends of capstan bars to prevent their falling out of their sockets [c17 related to the nautical term *swift* to fasten with tight-drawn ropes; probably Scandinavian in origin: compare Old Norse *svipta* to reef]

swift fox *n* a small fox, *Vulpes velox*, of the plains of W North America. Also called: **kit fox**

Swiftian ('swɪftɪən) *adj* of, relating to, or reminiscent of Jonathan Swift, the Anglo-Irish satirist and churchman (1667–1745)

swiftie *or* **swifty** ('swɪftɪ) *n, pl* **-ties** *slang, chiefly Austral* a trick, ruse, or deception

swiftlet ('swɪftlɪt) *n* any of various small swifts of the Asian genus *Collocalia* that often live in caves and use echolocation: the nests, which are made of hardened saliva, are used in oriental cookery to make birds' nest soup

swift moth *n* any of five species of fast-flying moths of the family Hepialidae, regarded as primitive in development, having forewings and hind wings similar in size and shape: the best known is the **ghost swift**, *Hepialus humili*. Often shortened to: **swift**

swig (swɪg) *informal* ▷ *n* **1** a large swallow or deep drink, esp from a bottle ▷ *vb* **swigs, swigging, swigged 2** to drink (some liquid) deeply, esp from

a bottle [c16 of unknown origin] > **'swigger** *n*

swiler ('swaɪlə) *n Canadian* (in Newfoundland) a seal hunter [variant of SEALER²]

swill (swɪl) *vb* **1** to drink large quantities of (liquid, esp alcoholic drink); guzzle **2** (*tr; often foll by out*) *chiefly Brit* to drench or rinse in large amounts of water **3** (*tr*) to feed swill to (pigs, etc) ▷ *n* **4** wet feed, esp for pigs, consisting of kitchen waste, skimmed milk, etc **5** garbage or refuse, esp from a kitchen **6** a deep draught of drink, esp beer **7** any liquid mess **8** the act of swilling [Old English *swilian* to wash out] > **'swiller** *n*

swim (swɪm) *vb* **swims, swimming, swam, swum 1** (*intr*) to move along in water, etc, by means of movements of the body or parts of the body, esp the arms and legs, or (in the case of fish) tail and fins **2** (*tr*) to cover (a distance or stretch of water) in this way **3** (*tr*) to compete in (a race) in this way **4** (*intr*) to be supported by and on a liquid; float **5** (*tr*) to use (a particular stroke) in swimming **6** (*intr*) to move smoothly, usually through air or over a surface **7** (*intr*) to reel or seem to reel: *my head swam; the room swam around me* **8** (*intr; often foll by in or with*) to be covered or flooded with water or other liquid **9** (*intr; often foll by in*) to be liberally supplied (with): *he's swimming in money* **10** (*tr*) to cause to float or swim **11** (*tr*) to provide (something) with water deep enough to float in **12 swim with** (*or* **against**) **the stream** *or* **tide** to conform to (or resist) prevailing opinion ▷ *n* **13** the act, an instance, or period of swimming **14** any graceful gliding motion **15** a condition of dizziness; swoon **16** a pool in a river good for fishing **17 in the swim** *informal* fashionable or active in social or political activities [Old English *swimman*; related to Old Norse *svima*, German *schwimmen*, Gothic *swumsl* pond, Norwegian *svamla* to paddle] > **'swimmable** *adj* > **'swimmer** *n* > **'swimming** *n, adj*

swim bladder *n ichthyol* another name for **air bladder** (sense 1)

swimfeeder ('swɪm,fiːdə) *n angling* a device containing bait, attached to the line to ensure the gradual baiting of the swim from under the surface

swimmeret ('swɪmə,rɛt) *n* any of the small paired appendages on the abdomen of crustaceans, used chiefly in locomotion and reproduction. Also called: **pleopod** [c19 from SWIM + -ER¹ + -ET]

swimmers ('swɪməz) *pl n Austral* a swimming costume

swimming bath *n* (*often plural*) an indoor swimming pool

swimming costume *or* **bathing costume** *n chiefly Brit* any apparel worn for swimming or sunbathing, such as a woman's one-piece garment covering most of the torso but not the limbs

swimmingly ('swɪmɪŋlɪ) *adv* successfully, effortlessly, or well (esp in the phrase **go swimmingly**)

swimming pool *n* an artificial pool for swimming

swimsuit ('swɪm,suːt, -,sjuːt) *n* a woman's one-piece swimming garment that leaves the arms and legs bare

swindle ('swɪndᵊl) *vb* **1** to cheat (someone) of money, etc; defraud **2** (*tr*) to obtain (money, etc) by fraud ▷ *n* **3** a fraudulent scheme or transaction [c18 back formation from German *Schwindler*, from *schwindeln*, from Old High German *swintilōn*, frequentative of *swintan* to disappear] > **'swindler** *n*

swindle sheet *n* a slang term for **expense account**

Swindon ('swɪndən) *n* **1** a town in S England, in NE Wiltshire: railway workshops, high technology. Pop: 155 432 (2001) **2** a unitary authority in S England, in Wiltshire. Pop: 181 200 (2003 est). Area: 230 sq km (89 sq miles)

swine (swaɪn) *n* **1** (*pl* **swines**) a coarse or

contemptible person **2** *pl* **swine** another name for a **pig** [Old English *swīn*; related to Old Norse *svīn*, Gothic *swein*, Latin *suīnus* relating to swine] > **'swine,like** *adj* > **'swinish** *adj* > **'swinishly** *adv* > **'swinishness** *n*

swine fever *n* an infectious viral disease of pigs, characterized by fever, refusal to eat, weight loss, and diarrhoea. US term: **hog cholera**

swineherd ('swaɪn,hɜːd) *n archaic* a person who looks after pigs

swinepox ('swaɪn,pɒks) *n* **1** Also called: **variola porcina** (pɔː'saɪnə) an acute infectious viral disease of pigs characterized by skin eruptions **2** a form of chickenpox in which the skin eruptions are not pitted

swine's cress *n* another name for **wart cress**

swine vesicular disease *n* a viral disease of swine characterized by vesicular lesions on the feet, legs, snout, and tongue

swing (swɪŋ) *vb* **swings, swinging, swung 1** to move or cause to move rhythmically to and fro, as a free-hanging object; sway **2** (*intr*) to move, walk, etc, with a relaxed and swaying motion **3** to pivot or cause to pivot, as on a hinge **4** to move or cause to move in a curve: *the car swung around the bend* **5** to move or cause to move by suspending or being suspended **6** to hang or be hung so as to be able to turn freely **7** (*intr*) *slang* to be hanged: *he'll swing for it* **8** to alter or cause to alter habits, a course, etc **9** (*tr*) *informal* to influence or manipulate successfully: *I hope he can swing the deal* **10** (*tr; foll by up*) to raise or hoist, esp in a sweeping motion **11** (*intr; often foll by at*) to hit out or strike (at), esp with a sweeping motion **12** (*tr*) to wave (a weapon, etc) in a sweeping motion; flourish **13** to arrange or play (music) with the rhythmically flexible and compulsive quality associated with jazz **14** (*intr*) (of popular music, esp jazz, or of the musicians who play it) to have this quality **15** *slang* to be lively and modern **16** (*intr*) *slang* to swap sexual partners in a group, esp habitually **17** (*intr*) *cricket* to bowl (a ball) with swing or (of a ball) to move with a swing **18** to turn (a ship or aircraft) in order to test compass error **19 swing both ways** *slang* to enjoy sexual partners of both sexes **20 swing the lead** *informal* to malinger or make up excuses ▷ *n* **21** the act or manner of swinging or the distance covered while swinging: *a wide swing* **22** a sweeping stroke or blow **23** *boxing* a wide punch from the side similar to but longer than a hook **24** *cricket* the lateral movement of a bowled ball through the air **25** any free-swaying motion **26** any curving movement; sweep **27** something that swings or is swung, esp a suspended seat on which a person may sit and swing back and forth **28 a** a kind of popular dance music influenced by jazz, usually played by big bands and originating in the 1930s **b** (*as modifier*): *swing music* **29** See **swingbeat 30** *prosody* a steady distinct rhythm or cadence in prose or verse **31** *informal* the normal round or pace: *get into the swing of things* **32 a** a fluctuation, as in some business activity, voting pattern etc **b** (*as modifier*) able to bring about a swing in a voting pattern: *swing party* **c** (*as modifier*) having a mixed voting history, and thus becoming a target for political election campaigners: *a swing state* **33** *US informal* free scope; freedom of activity **34** *chiefly US* a circular tour **35** *Canadian* a tour of a particular area or region **36 go with a swing** to go well; be successful **37 in full swing** at the height of activity **38 swings and roundabouts** equal advantages and disadvantages [Old English *swingan*; related to Old Frisian *swinga*, Old High German *swingan*]

swingbeat ('swɪŋ,biːt) *n* a type of modern dance music that combines soul, rhythm and blues, and hip-hop

swingboat ('swɪŋ,bəʊt) *n* a piece of fairground equipment consisting of a boat-shaped carriage for swinging in

swing bridge *n* **1** Also called: **pivot bridge, turn**

bridge a low bridge that can be rotated about a vertical axis, esp to permit the passage of ships. Compare **drawbridge 2** NZ a pedestrian bridge over a river, suspended by heavy wire cables

swing by vb (prep) informal to go somewhere to pay a visit

swing door or **swinging door** n a door pivoted or hung on double-sided hinges so that it can open either way

swinge (swɪndʒ) vb swinges, swingeing or swinging, swinged (tr) archaic to beat, flog, or punish [Old English swengan; related to Old Frisian swenga to drench, Gothic afswaggwjan to cause to sway; see SWING]

swingeing ('swɪndʒɪŋ) adj chiefly Brit punishing; severe

swinger ('swɪŋə) slang ▷ n 1 a person regarded as being modern and lively 2 a person who swaps sexual partners in a group, esp habitually

swinging ('swɪŋɪŋ) adj 1 moving rhythmically to and fro 2 slang modern and lively ▷ n 3 slang the practice of swapping sexual partners in a group, esp habitually > 'swingingly adv

swinging voter n Austral and NZ informal a person who does not vote consistently for any single political party. also called (esp in Britain): **floating voters**

swingle ('swɪŋɡəl) n 1 a flat-bladed wooden instrument used for beating and scraping flax or hemp to remove coarse matter from it ▷ vb 2 (tr) to use a swingle on [Old English swingel stroke; related to Middle High German swüngel, Middle Dutch swinghel]

swingletree ('swɪŋɡəlˌtriː) n a crossbar in a horse's harness to which the ends of the traces are attached. Also called: **whippletree**, (esp US) **whiffletree** [C15 from SWINGLE + TREE (in the sense: a post or bar)]

swingometer (swɪŋ'ɒmɪtə) n a device used in television broadcasting during a general election to indicate the swing of votes from one political party to another

swing shift n US and Canadian 1 a group of workers who work a shift from late afternoon to midnight in an industry or occupation where a day shift or a night shift is also worked 2 the period worked. also called (in Britain and certain other countries): **back shift**

swing-wing adj 1 of or relating to a variable-geometry aircraft ▷ n 2 a such an aircraft b either wing of such an aircraft

swink (swɪŋk) archaic ▷ vb 1 (intr) to toil or drudge ▷ n 2 toil or drudgery [Old English swinc, from swincan] > 'swinker n

swipe (swaɪp) vb 1 (when intr, usually foll by at) informal to hit hard with a sweeping blow 2 (tr) slang to steal 3 (tr) to pass a machine-readable card, such as a credit card, debit card, etc, through a machine that electronically interprets the information encoded, usu. in a magnetic strip, on the card ▷ n 4 informal a hard blow 5 an unexpected criticism of someone or something while discussing another subject 6 Also called: **sweep** a type of lever for raising and lowering a weight, such as a bucket in a well [C19 perhaps related to SWEEP]

swipe card n a credit card, identity card, etc, with a magnetic strip that holds encoded information that can be electronically interpreted as it is passed through the slot of a machine designed to read it

swipes (swaɪps) pl n Brit slang beer, esp when poor or weak [C18 probably related to SWEEP]

swipple or **swiple** ('swɪpəl) n the part of a flail that strikes the grain [C15 swipyl, variant of swepyl, from swep(en) to SWEEP + -yl, suffix denoting an instrument]

swirl (swɜːl) vb 1 to turn or cause to turn in a twisting spinning fashion 2 (intr) to be dizzy; swim: my head was swirling ▷ n 3 a whirling or spinning motion, esp in water 4 a whorl; curl 5 the act of swirling or stirring 6 dizzy confusion

[C15 probably from Dutch zwirrelen; related to Norwegian svirla, German schwirren] > 'swirling adj > 'swirlingly adv > 'swirly adj

swish (swɪʃ) vb 1 to move with or make or cause to move with or make a whistling or hissing sound 2 (intr) (esp of fabrics) to rustle 3 (tr) slang, now rare to whip; flog 4 (tr; foll by off) to cut with a swishing blow ▷ n 5 a hissing or rustling sound or movement 6 a rod for flogging or a blow from such a rod 7 US slang an effeminate male homosexual 8 a W African building material composed of mortar and mud or laterite, or more recently of cement and earth ▷ adj 9 informal, chiefly Brit fashionable; smart 10 US slang effeminate and homosexual [C18 of imitative origin] > 'swisher n > 'swishing adj > 'swishingly adv

swishy ('swɪʃɪ) adj -shier, -shiest 1 moving with a swishing sound 2 US slang effeminate and homosexual

Swiss (swɪs) adj 1 of, relating to, or characteristic of Switzerland, its inhabitants, or their dialects of German, French, and Italian ▷ n 2 a native, inhabitant, or citizen of Switzerland

Swiss chard n another name for **chard**

Swiss cheese n a hard white or pale yellow cheese with holes, such as Gruyère or Emmenthal

Swiss cheese plant n See **monstera**

Swiss Guard n 1 the bodyguard of the pope, recruited from Swiss nationals 2 a member of this bodyguard 3 one of a group of Swiss mercenaries who acted as bodyguards to the French kings: destroyed in the Revolution

swiss muslin n a fine muslin dress fabric, usually having a raised or woven pattern of dolls or figures [C19 so called because it was formerly imported from Switzerland]

Swiss Re Tower (riː) n a bluish cigar-shaped office block, London's first environmental skyscraper, located at 30 St Mary Axe, in the City of London: headquarters of the financial services group Swiss Re. Standing 180 m (585 ft) high and having 40 storeys, the building was completed in 2004

swiss roll n a sponge cake spread with jam, cream, or some other filling, and rolled up

Swiss tournament n (in certain games and sports) a tournament system in which players are paired in each round according to the scores they then have, playing a new opponent each time. More players can take part than in an all-play-all tournament of the same duration [named from a chess tournament held in Zürich in 1895]

switch (swɪtʃ) n 1 a mechanical, electrical, electronic, or optical device for opening or closing a circuit or for diverting energy from one part of a circuit to another 2 a swift and usually sudden shift or change 3 an exchange or swap 4 a flexible rod or twig, used esp for punishment 5 the sharp movement or blow of such an instrument 6 a tress of false hair used to give added length or bulk to a woman's own hairstyle 7 the tassel-like tip of the tail of cattle and certain other animals 8 any of various card games in which the suit is changed during play 9 US and Canadian a railway siding 10 US and Canadian a railway point 11 Austral informal See **switchboard** ▷ vb 12 to shift, change, turn aside, or change the direction of (something) 13 to exchange (places); replace (something by something else): the battalions switched fronts 14 chiefly US and Canadian to transfer (rolling stock) from one railway track to another 15 (tr) to cause (an electric current) to start or stop flowing or to change its path by operating a switch 16 to swing or cause to swing, esp back and forth 17 (tr) to lash or whip with or as if with a switch ▷ See also **switch off, switch on** [C16 perhaps from Middle Dutch swijch branch, twig] > 'switcher n > 'switch,like adj

switchback ('swɪtʃˌbæk) n 1 a mountain road, railway, or track which rises and falls sharply many times or a sharp rise and fall on such a

road, railway, or track 2 another word (esp Brit) for **big dipper**

switchblade or **switchblade knife** ('swɪtʃˌbleɪd) n US and Canadian a knife with a retractable blade that springs out when a button is pressed. also called (in Britain and certain other countries): **flick knife**

switchboard ('swɪtʃˌbɔːd) n 1 an installation in a telephone exchange, office, hotel, etc, at which the interconnection of telephone lines is manually controlled 2 an assembly of switchgear for the control of power supplies in an installation or building

switched-on adj informal well-informed or aware of what is up to date

switched-star adj denoting or relating to a cable television system in which only one or two programme channels are fed to each subscriber, who can select other channels by remote control of a central switching point: a switched-star network. Compare **tree-and-branch**

switcheroo (ˌswɪtʃə'ruː) n US slang a surprising or unexpected change or variation [C20 from SWITCH]

switchgear ('swɪtʃˌɡɪə) n electrical engineering any of several devices used for opening and closing electric circuits, esp those that pass high currents

switchgirl ('swɪtʃˌɡɜːl) n informal, chiefly Austral a woman who operates a telephone switchboard

switch-hitter n US and Canadian 1 baseball a batsman who can hit either right- or left-handed 2 slang a bisexual person

switchman ('swɪtʃmən) n, pl -men US and Canadian a person who operates railway points. Also called (in Britain and certain other countries): **pointsman**

switch off vb (adverb) 1 to cause (a device) to stop operating by or as if by moving a switch, knob, or lever; turn off 2 informal to cease to interest or be interested; make or become bored, alienated, etc

switch on vb (adverb) 1 to cause (a device) to operate by or as if by moving a switch, knob, or lever; turn on 2 (tr) informal to produce (charm, tears, etc) suddenly or automatically 3 (tr) informal (now slightly dated) to make up-to-date, esp regarding outlook, dress, etc 4 (tr) slang to arouse emotionally or sexually 5 (intr) slang to take or become intoxicated by drugs 6 (tr) slang to introduce (someone) to drugs

switchover ('swɪtʃˌəʊvə) n the act or an instance of changing from one method, policy, or technology to another: the switchover to digital television

switch selling n a system of selling, now illegal in Britain, whereby potential customers are attracted by a special offer on some goods but the salesman's real aim is to sell other more expensive goods instead

switch yard n US and Canadian an area in a railway system where rolling stock is shunted, as in forming trains

swither ('swɪðər) Scot ▷ vb (intr) 1 to hesitate; vacillate; be perplexed ▷ n 2 hesitation; perplexity; agitation [C16 of unknown origin]

Switz. or **Swit.** abbreviation for Switzerland

Switzer ('swɪtsə) n 1 a less common word for Swiss 2 a member of the Swiss Guard [C16 from Middle High German, from Swīz Switzerland]

Switzerland ('swɪtsələnd) n a federal republic in W central Europe: the cantons of Schwyz, Uri, and Unterwalden formed a defensive league against the Hapsburgs in 1291, later joined by other cantons; gained independence in 1499; adopted a policy of permanent neutrality from 1516; a leading centre of the Reformation in the 16th century. It lies in the Jura Mountains and the Alps, with a plateau between the two ranges. Official languages: German, French, and Italian; Romansch minority. Religion: mostly Protestant and Roman Catholic. Currency: Swiss franc. Capital: Bern. Pop: 7 163 000 (2004 est). Area: 41 288 sq km (15 941 sq miles). German name: **Schweiz** French name: **Suisse** Italian name: **Svizzera** Latin

S

name: **Helvetia** (hɛl'viːʃə)

swive (swaɪv) *vb archaic* to have sexual intercourse with (a person) [Old English *swīfan* to revolve, SWIVEL]

swivel ('swɪv³l) *n* **1** a coupling device which allows an attached object to turn freely **2** such a device made of two parts which turn independently, such as a compound link of a chain **3 a** a pivot on which is mounted a gun that may be swung from side to side in a horizontal plane **b** Also called: **swivel gun** the gun itself ⊳ *vb* **-els, -elling, -elled** *or US* **-els, -eling, -eled 4** to turn or swing on or as if on a pivot **5** (*tr*) to provide with, secure by, or support with a swivel [C14 from Old English *swīfan* to turn; see SWIFT] > 'swivel-like *adj*

swivel chair *n* a chair, the seat of which is joined to the legs by a swivel and which thus may be spun round

swivel pin *n* another name for **kingpin** (sense 3)

swivet ('swɪvɪt) *n US informal* a state of anxiety, confusion, or excitement: *don't get yourself in a swivet* [C19 origin unknown]

swiz *or* **swizz** (swɪz) *n Brit informal* a swindle or disappointment; swizzle

swizzle ('swɪz³l) *n* **1** *US* an unshaken cocktail **2** a Caribbean drink of milk and rum **3** *Brit informal* a swiz ⊳ *vb* **4** (*tr*) to stir a swizzle stick in (a drink) **5** *Brit informal* to swindle; cheat [C19 of unknown origin]

swizzle stick *n* a small rod used to agitate an effervescent drink to facilitate the escape of carbon dioxide

swob (swɒb) *n, vb* **swobs, swobbing, swobbed** a less common word for **swab**

swoffing ('swɒfɪŋ) *n Austral* the sport of saltwater fly-fishing > 'swoffer *n* [C20 formed from *s(alt) w(ater) f(ly) f(ish)ing*]

swollen ('swəʊlən) *vb* **1** a past participle of **swell** ⊳ *adj* **2** tumid or enlarged by or as if by swelling **3** turgid or bombastic > 'swollenly *adv* > 'swollenness *n*

swollen head *n* another term for **swelled head**

swollen-headed *adj informal* conceited

swoon (swuːn) *vb* (*intr*) **1** a literary word for **faint 2** to become ecstatic ⊳ *n* **3** an instance of fainting ⊳ Also (archaic or dialect): **swound** [Old English *geswōgen* insensible, past participle of *swōgan* (unattested except in compounds) to suffocate] > 'swooning *adj* > 'swooningly *adv*

swoop (swuːp) *vb* **1** (*intr*; usually foll by *down, on,* or *upon*) to sweep or pounce suddenly **2** (*tr*; often foll by *up, away,* or *off*) to seize or scoop suddenly ⊳ *n* **3** the act of swooping **4** a swift descent [Old English *swāpan* to sweep; related to Old High German *sweifan* to swing around, Old Norse *sveipa* to throw]

swoosh (swuːʃ) *vb* **1** to make or cause to make a rustling or swirling sound, esp when moving or pouring out ⊳ *n* **2** a swirling or rustling sound or movement [C20 of imitative origin (probably influenced by SWISH and SWOOP)]

swop (swɒp) *n, vb* **swops, swopping, swopped** a variant spelling of **swap**

sword (sɔːd) *n* **1** a thrusting, striking, or cutting weapon with a long blade having one or two cutting edges, a hilt, and usually a crosspiece or guard **2** such a weapon worn on ceremonial occasions as a symbol of authority **3** something resembling a sword, such as the snout of a swordfish **4 cross swords** to argue or fight **5 the sword a** violence or power, esp military power **b** death; destruction: *to put to the sword* [Old English *sweord*; related to Old Saxon *swerd*, Old Norse *sverth*, Old High German *swert*] > 'swordless *adj* > 'sword,like *adj*

sword bayonet *n* a bayonet with a swordlike blade and hilt, capable of use as a sword

swordbearer ('sɔːd,bɛərə) *n* an official who carries a ceremonial sword

sword belt *n* a belt with a sling or strap for a sword

swordbill ('sɔːd,bɪl) *n* a South American hummingbird, *Ensifera ensifera*, having a bill as long as its body

sword cane *n* another name for **swordstick**

swordcraft ('sɔːd,krɑːft) *n* the art of using a sword

sword dance *n* a dance in which the performers dance nimbly over swords on the ground or brandish them in the air > **sword dancer** *n* > **sword dancing** *n*

sword fern *n* any of numerous ferns having sword-shaped fronds

swordfish ('sɔːd,fɪʃ) *n, pl* **-fish** *or* **-fishes** a large scombroid fish, *Xiphias gladius*, with a very long upper jaw: valued as a food and game fish: family *Xiphiidae*

sword grass *n* any of various grasses and other plants having sword-shaped sharp leaves

sword knot *n* a loop on the hilt of a sword by which it was attached to the wrist, now purely decorative

sword lily *n* another name for **gladiolus** (sense 1) [C18 so called because of its sword-shaped leaves]

Sword of Damocles *n* a closely impending disaster [see DAMOCLES]

swordplay ('sɔːd,pleɪ) *n* **1** the action or art of fighting with a sword **2** verbal sparring > 'sword,player *n*

swordsman ('sɔːdzmən) *n, pl* **-men** one who uses or is skilled in the use of a sword > 'swordsman,ship *n*

swordstick ('sɔːd,stɪk) *n* a hollow walking stick containing a short sword or dagger

sword-swallower *n* a performer who simulates the swallowing of swords

swordtail ('sɔːd,teɪl) *n* any of several small freshwater cyprinodont fishes of the genus *Xiphophorus*, esp *X. helleri*, of Central America, having a long swordlike tail

swore (swɔː) *vb* the past tense of **swear**

sworn (swɔːn) *vb* **1** the past participle of **swear** ⊳ *adj* **2** bound, pledged, or made inveterate, by or as if by an oath: *a sworn statement; he was sworn to God*

swot[1] (swɒt) *Brit informal* ⊳ *vb* **swots, swotting, swotted 1** (often foll by *up*) to study (a subject) intensively, as for an examination; cram ⊳ *n* **2** Also called: **swotter** ('swɒtə) a person who works or studies hard **3** hard work or grind ⊳ Also: **swat** [C19 dialect variant of SWEAT (n)]

swot[2] (swɒt) *vb* **swots, swotting, swotted,** *n* a variant of **swat**[1]

SWOT *abbreviation for* strengths, weaknesses, opportunities, and threats: an analysis of a product made before it is marketed

swotty ('swɒtɪ) *adj* **-tier, -tiest** *Brit informal* given to studying hard, esp to the exclusion of other activities

swound (swaʊnd) *n, vb* an archaic or dialect word for **swoon**

swounds *or* '**swounds** (zwaʊndz, zaʊndz) *interj archaic* less common spellings of **zounds**

swozzle ('swɒzəl) *n* a variant spelling of **swazzle**

swum (swʌm) *vb* the past participle of **swim**

swung (swʌŋ) *vb* the past tense and past participle of **swing**

swung dash *n* a mark, ~, traditionally used in text to indicate the omission of a word or part of a word

swy (swaɪ) *n Austral* another name for **two-up** [C20 from German *zwei* two]

sy *the internet domain name for* Syrian Arab Republic

SY *international car registration for* Seychelles

Sybaris ('sɪbərɪs) *n* a Greek colony in S Italy, on the Gulf of Taranto: notorious for its luxurious living, founded about 720 BC and sacked in 510

sybarite ('sɪbə,raɪt) *n* **1** (*sometimes capital*) a devotee of luxury and the sensual vices ⊳ *adj* **2** luxurious; sensuous [C16 from Latin *Sybarīta*, from Greek *Subarītēs* inhabitant of SYBARIS] > sybaritic (,sɪbə'rɪtɪk) *or less commonly* ,syba'ritical *adj* > ,syba'ritically *adv* > 'sybaritism *n*

Sybarite ('sɪbə,raɪt) *n* a native or inhabitant of the ancient Greek colony of Sybaris

Sybaritic (,sɪbə'rɪtɪk) *adj* of or relating to the ancient Greek colony of Sybaris or its inhabitants

sybo, syboe *or* **sybow** ('saɪbɪ, 'saɪ-, -bəʊ) *n, pl* **syboes** *or* **sybows** *Scot* a spring onion [C16 from *cibol*, from French *ciboule*, from Latin *cepulla* onion bed, from *cepa* onion]

sycamine ('sɪkə,maɪn) *n* a mulberry tree mentioned in the Bible, thought to be the black mulberry, *Morus nigra* [C16 from Greek *sukaminon*, from Hebrew *shiqmāh*]

sycamore ('sɪkə,mɔː) *n* **1** a Eurasian maple tree, *Acer pseudoplatanus*, naturalized in Britain and North America, having five-lobed leaves, yellow flowers, and two-winged fruits **2** *US and Canadian* an American plane tree, *Platanus occidentalis*. See **plane tree 3** Also: **sycomore** a moraceous tree, *Ficus sycomorus*, of N Africa and W Asia, having an edible figlike fruit [C14 from Old French *sicamor*, from Latin *sȳcomorus*, from Greek *sukomoros*, from *sukon* fig + *moron* mulberry]

syce, sice *or* **saice** (saɪs) *n* **1** (formerly, in India) a servant employed to look after horses, drive carriages, etc **2** (in Malaysia) a driver or chauffeur [C17 from Urdu *sā'is*, from Arabic, from *sāsa* to administer]

sycee *or* **sycee silver** (saɪ'siː) *n* silver ingots formerly used as a medium of exchange in China [C18 from Chinese *sai sz* fine silk; so called because the silver can be made into threads as fine as silk]

syconium (saɪ'kəʊnɪəm) *n, pl* **-nia** (-nɪə) *botany* the fleshy fruit of the fig, consisting of a greatly enlarged receptacle completely surrounding the inflorescence [C19 from New Latin, from Greek *sukon* fig]

sycophant ('sɪkəfənt) *n* a person who uses flattery to win favour from individuals wielding influence; toady [C16 from Latin *sȳcophanta*, from Greek *sukophantēs*, literally: the person showing a fig, apparently referring to the fig sign used in making an accusation, from *sukon* fig + *phainein* to show; sense probably developed from "accuser" to "informer, flatterer"] > 'sycophancy *n*

sycophantic (,sɪkə'fæntɪk) *adj* using flattery to win favour from individuals wielding influence; toadyish; obsequious > ,syco'phantically *adv*

sycosis (saɪ'kəʊsɪs) *n* chronic inflammation of the hair follicles, esp those of the beard, caused by a staphylococcal infection [C16 via New Latin from Greek *sukōsis*, from *sukon* fig]

Sydenham's chorea ('sɪdᵊnəmz) *n* a form of chorea affecting children, often associated with rheumatic fever. Nontechnical name: **Saint Vitus's dance** [named after T. *Sydenham* (1624–89), English physician]

Sydney ('sɪdnɪ) *n* **1** a port in SE Australia, capital of New South Wales, on an inlet of the S Pacific: the largest city in Australia and the first British settlement, established as a penal colony in 1788; developed rapidly after 1820 with the discovery of gold in its hinterland; large wool market; three universities. Pop: 3 502 301 (2001) **2** a port in SE Canada, in Nova Scotia on NE Cape Breton Island: capital of Cape Breton Island until 1820, when the island united administratively with Nova Scotia. Pop: 26 063 (1991)

Sydneysider ('sɪdnɪ,saɪdə) *n chiefly Austral* a resident of Sydney

Sydney silky *n, pl* **-kies** a small silky-coated breed of terrier, originally from Australia. Also called: **silky terrier**

Syene (saɪ'iːnɪ) *n* transliteration of the Ancient Greek name for **Aswan**

syenite ('saɪə,naɪt) *n* a light-coloured coarse-grained plutonic igneous rock consisting of feldspars with hornblende or biotite [C18 from French *syénite*, from Latin *syēnītēs lapis* stone from *Syene* (Aswan), where it was originally quarried] > syenitic (,saɪə'nɪtɪk) *adj*

SYHA *abbreviation for* Scottish Youth Hostels Association

Syktyvkar (*Russian* siktif'kar) *n* a city in NW

Russia, capital of the Komi Republic: timber industry. Pop: 230 000 (2005 est)

syllabary ('sɪləbərɪ) *n, pl* **-baries** 1 a table or list of syllables 2 a set of symbols used in certain writing systems, such as one used for Japanese, in which each symbol represents a spoken syllable [c16 from New Latin *syllabārium*, from Latin *syllaba* SYLLABLE]

syllabi ('sɪləˌbaɪ) *n* a plural of **syllabus**

syllabic (sɪ'læbɪk) *adj* 1 of or relating to syllables or the division of a word into syllables 2 denoting a kind of verse line based on a specific number of syllables rather than being regulated by stresses or quantities 3 (of a consonant) constituting a syllable 4 (of plainsong and similar chanting) having each syllable sung to a different note ▷ *n* 5 a syllabic consonant > **syl'labically** *adv*

syllabify (sɪ'læbɪˌfaɪ) *or* **syllabicate** *vb* **-fies, -fying, -fied** *or* **-cates, -cating, -cated** (*tr*) to divide (a word) into its constituent syllables > **sylˌlabifi'cation** *or* **sylˌlabi'cation** *n*

syllabism ('sɪləˌbɪzəm) *n* use of a writing system consisting of characters for syllables rather than for individual sounds or whole words. Also called: **syllabography**

syllable ('sɪləbᵊl) *n* 1 a combination or set of one or more units of sound in a language that must consist of a sonorous element (a sonant or vowel) and may or may not contain less sonorous elements (consonants or semivowels) flanking it on either or both sides: for example "paper" has two syllables. See also **open** (sense 34b), **closed** (sense 6a) 2 (in the writing systems of certain languages, esp ancient ones) a symbol or set of symbols standing for a syllable 3 the least mention in speech or print: *don't breathe a syllable of it* 4 **in words of one syllable** simply; bluntly ▷ *vb* 5 to pronounce syllables of (a text); articulate 6 (*tr*) to write down in syllables [c14 via Old French from Latin *syllaba*, from Greek *sullabē*, from *sullambanein* to collect together, from *sul-* SYN- + *lambanein* to take]

syllabogram (sɪ'læbəʊˌgræm) *n* a written symbol representing a single syllable

syllabography (ˌsɪlə'bɒgrəfɪ) *n* another word for **syllabism**. Compare **logography, phonography**

syllabub *or* **sillabub** ('sɪləˌbʌb) *n* 1 a spiced drink made of milk with rum, port, brandy, or wine, often hot 2 *Brit* a cold dessert made from milk or cream beaten with sugar, wine, and lemon juice [c16 of unknown origin]

syllabus ('sɪləbəs) *n, pl* **-buses** *or* **-bi** (-ˌbaɪ) 1 an outline of a course of studies, text, etc 2 *Brit* **a** the subjects studied for a particular course **b** a document which lists these subjects and states how the course will be assessed [c17 from Late Latin, erroneously from Latin *sittybus* parchment strip giving title and author, from Greek *sittuba*]

Syllabus ('sɪləbəs) *n* *RC Church* 1 Also called: **Syllabus of Errors** a list of 80 doctrinal theses condemned as erroneous by Pius IX in 1864 2 a list of 65 Modernist propositions condemned as erroneous by Pius X in 1907

syllepsis (sɪ'lɛpsɪs) *n, pl* **-ses** (-siːz) 1 (in grammar or rhetoric) the use of a single sentence construction in which a verb, adjective, etc is made to cover two syntactical functions, as the verb form *have* in *she and they have promised to come* 2 another word for **zeugma** [c16 from Late Latin, from Greek *sullēpsis*, from *sul-* SYN- + *lēpsis* a taking, from *lambanein* to take] > **syl'leptic** *adj* > **syl'leptically** *adv*

syllogism ('sɪləˌdʒɪzəm) *n* 1 a deductive inference consisting of two premises and a conclusion, all of which are categorial propositions. The subject of the conclusion is the **minor term** and its predicate the **major term;** the **middle term** occurs in both premises but not the conclusion. There are 256 such arguments but only 24 are valid. *Some men are mortal; some men are angelic; so some mortals are angelic* is invalid, while *some temples are in ruins; all ruins are fascinating; so some temples are fascinating* is valid. Here *fascinating, in ruins,* and *temples* are respectively major, middle, and minor terms 2 a deductive inference of certain other forms with two premises, such as the **hypothetical syllogism,** *if P then Q; if Q then R; so if P then R* 3 a piece of deductive reasoning from the general to the particular 4 a subtle or deceptive piece of reasoning [c14 via Latin from Greek *sullogismos*, from *sullogizesthai* to reckon together, from *sul-* SYN- + *logizesthai* to calculate, from *logos* a discourse]

syllogistic (ˌsɪlə'dʒɪstɪk) *adj also* **syllogistical** 1 of, relating to or consisting of syllogisms ▷ *n* (*often plural*) 2 the branch of logic concerned with syllogisms 3 reasoning by means of syllogisms > **ˌsyllo'gistically** *adv*

syllogize *or* **syllogise** ('sɪləˌdʒaɪz) *vb* to reason or infer by using syllogisms [c15 via Old French from Late Latin *syllogizāre*, from Greek *sullogizesthai;* see SYLLOGISM] > **ˌsyllogi'zation** *or* **ˌsyllogi'sation** *n* > **'sylloˌgizer** *or* **'sylloˌgiser** *n*

sylph (sɪlf) *n* 1 a slender graceful girl or young woman 2 any of a class of imaginary beings assumed to inhabit the air [c17 from New Latin *sylphus*, probably coined from Latin *silva* wood + Greek *numphē* NYMPH] > **'sylphˌlike** *or less commonly* **'sylphic, 'sylphish** *or* **'sylphy** *adj*

sylva *or* **silva** ('sɪlvə) *n, pl* **-vas** *or* **-vae** (-viː) the trees growing in a particular region [c17 Latin *silva* a wood]

sylvan *or* **silvan** ('sɪlvən) *chiefly poetic* ▷ *adj* 1 of, characteristic of, or consisting of woods or forests 2 living or located in woods or forests 3 idyllically rural or rustic ▷ *n* 4 an inhabitant of the woods, esp a spirit [c16 from Latin *silvānus*, from *silva* forest]

sylvanite ('sɪlvəˌnaɪt) *n* a silver-white mineral consisting of a telluride of gold and silver in the form of elongated striated crystals: a source of gold in Australia and North America. Formula: $(Au,Ag)Te_2$ [c18 from (TRAN)SYLVAN(IA) + -ITE[1], with reference to the region where it was first found]

Sylvanus (sɪl'veɪnəs) *n* a variant spelling of **Silvanus**

sylvatic (sɪl'vætɪk) *adj* growing, living, or occurring in a wood or beneath a tree. Also: **sylvestral** (sɪl'vɛstrəl)

sylviculture ('sɪlvɪˌkʌltʃə) *n* a variant spelling of **silviculture**

sylvite ('sɪlvaɪt) *or* **sylvine** ('sɪlviːn) *n* a soluble colourless, white, or coloured mineral consisting of potassium chloride in cubic crystalline form with sodium impurities: it occurs chiefly in sedimentary beds and is an important ore of potassium. Formula: KCl [c19 *sylvite*, alteration of *sylvine*, from New Latin *sal digestiva Sylvii* digestive salt of Sylvius, after Franciscus *Sylvius* (died 1672), German anatomist. See -ITE[1], -INE[2]]

sym- *prefix* a variant of **syn-** before *b, p,* and *m*

symbiont ('sɪmbɪˌɒnt) *n* an organism living in a state of symbiosis [c19 from Greek *sumbioun* to live together, from *bioun* to live] > **ˌsymbi'ontic** *adj* > **ˌsymbi'ontically** *adv*

symbiosis (ˌsɪmbɪ'əʊsɪs, ˌsɪmbaɪ'əʊsɪs) *n* 1 a close and usually obligatory association of two organisms of different species that live together, often to their mutual benefit 2 a similar relationship between interdependent persons or groups [c19 via New Latin from Greek: a living together; see SYMBIONT] > **ˌsymbi'otic** *or less commonly* **ˌsymbi'otical** *adj*

symbol ('sɪmbᵊl) *n* 1 something that represents or stands for something else, usually by convention or association, esp a material object used to represent something abstract 2 an object, person, idea, etc, used in a literary work, film, etc, to stand for or suggest something else with which it is associated either explicitly or in some more subtle way 3 a letter, figure, or sign used in mathematics, science, music, etc to represent a quantity, phenomenon, operation, function, etc 4 *psychoanal* the end product, in the form of an object or act, of a conflict in the unconscious between repression processes and the actions and thoughts being repressed: *the symbols of dreams* 5 *psychol* any mental process that represents some feature of external reality ▷ *vb* **-bols, -bolling, -bolled** *or US* **-bols, -boling, -boled** 6 (*tr*) another word for **symbolize** [c15 from Church Latin *symbolum*, from Greek *sumbolon* sign, from *sumballein* to throw together, from SYN- + *ballein* to throw]

symbolic (sɪm'bɒlɪk) *or* **symbolical** *adj* 1 of or relating to a symbol or symbols 2 serving as a symbol 3 characterized by the use of symbols or symbolism > **sym'bolically** *adv* > **sym'bolicalness** *n*

symbolical books *pl n* *Christianity* the books containing the creeds, beliefs, or doctrine of religious groups that have emerged since the Reformation

symbolic logic *n* another term for **formal logic**

symbolism ('sɪmbəˌlɪzəm) *n* 1 the representation of something in symbolic form or the attribution of symbolic meaning or character to something 2 a system of symbols or symbolic representation 3 a symbolic significance or quality 4 (*often capital*) a late 19th-century movement in art that sought to express mystical or abstract ideas through the symbolic use of images. See also **synthetism** 5 *theol* any symbolist interpretation of the Eucharist

symbolist ('sɪmbəlɪst) *n* 1 a person who uses or can interpret symbols, esp as a means to revealing aspects of truth and reality 2 an artist or writer who practises symbolism in his work 3 (*usually capital*) a writer associated with the symbolist movement 4 (*often capital*) an artist associated with the movement of symbolism 5 *christian theol* a person who rejects any interpretation of the Eucharist that suggests that Christ is really present in it, and who maintains that the bread and wine are only symbols of his body and blood ▷ *adj* 6 of, relating to, or characterizing symbolism or symbolists > **ˌsymbol'istic** *adj* > **ˌsymbol'istically** *adv*

symbolist movement *n* (*usually capital*) a movement beginning in French and Belgian poetry towards the end of the 19th century with the verse of Mallarmé, Valéry, Verlaine, Rimbaud, Maeterlinck, and others, and seeking to express states of mind rather than objective reality by making use of the power of words and images to suggest as well as denote

symbolize *or* **symbolise** ('sɪmbəˌlaɪz) *vb* 1 (*tr*) to serve as or be a symbol of 2 (*tr;* usually foll by *by*) to represent by a symbol or symbols 3 (*intr*) to use symbols 4 (*tr*) to treat or regard as symbolic or figurative > **ˌsymboli'zation** *or* **ˌsymboli'sation** *n*

symbology (sɪm'bɒlədʒɪ) *n* the use, study, or interpretation of symbols > **symbological** (ˌsɪmbə'lɒdʒɪkᵊl) *adj* > **sym'bologist** *n*

symbol retailer *n* any member of a voluntary group of independent retailers, often using a common name or symbol, formed to obtain better prices from wholesalers or manufacturers in competition with supermarket chains. Also called: **voluntary retailer**

symmetallism *or US* **symmetalism** (sɪ'mɛtəˌlɪzəm) *n* 1 the use of an alloy of two or more metals in fixed relative value as the standard of value and currency 2 the economic policies and doctrine supporting a symmetallic standard [c19 from SYM- + *-metallism*, on the model of BIMETALLISM] > **ˌsymme'tallic** *adj*

symmetric (sɪ'mɛtrɪk) *adj* 1 *logic, maths* (of a relation) holding between a pair of arguments *x* and *y* when and only when it holds between *y* and *x*, as *... is a sibling of ...* but not *... is a brother of ....* Compare **asymmetric** (sense 5), **antisymmetric, nonsymmetric** 2 another word for **symmetrical** (sense 5)

symmetrical (sɪ'mɛtrɪkᵊl) *adj* 1 possessing or displaying symmetry. Compare **asymmetric** 2 *maths* **a** (of two points) capable of being joined by a line that is bisected by a given point or bisected

S

perpendicularly by a given line or plane: *the points (x, y) and (−x, −y) are symmetrical about the origin* **b** (of a configuration) having pairs of points that are symmetrical about a given point, line, or plane: *a circle is symmetrical about a diameter* **c** (of an equation or function of two or more variables) remaining unchanged in form after an interchange of two variables: *x + y = z is a symmetrical equation* **3** *chem* (of a compound) having a molecular structure in which substituents are symmetrical about the molecule **4** *botany* another word for **isomerous 5** Also: **symmetric** (of a disease, infection, etc) affecting both sides of the body or corresponding parts, such as both legs > **sym'metrically** *adv* > **sym'metricalness** *n*

symmetric matrix *n maths* a square matrix that is equal to its transpose, being symmetrical about its main diagonal. A **skew symmetric matrix** is equal to the negation of its transpose. Compare **orthogonal matrix**

symmetrize *or* **symmetrise** ('sɪmɪˌtraɪz) *vb* (tr) to render symmetrical or perfectly balanced > ˌsymmetri'zation *or* ˌsymmetri'sation *n*

symmetry ('sɪmɪtrɪ) *n, pl* -**tries 1** similarity, correspondence, or balance among systems or parts of a system **2** *maths* an exact correspondence in position or form about a given point, line, or plane. See **symmetrical** (sense 2) **3** beauty or harmony of form based on a proportionate arrangement of parts **4** *physics* the independence of a property with respect to direction; isotropy [C16 from Latin *symmetria*, from Greek *summetria* proportion, from SYN- + *metron* measure]

sympathectomy (ˌsɪmpə'θɛktəmɪ) *n, pl* -**mies** the surgical excision or chemical destruction (**chemical sympathectomy**) of one or more parts of the sympathetic nervous system [C20 from SYMPATHETIC + -ECTOMY]

sympathetic (ˌsɪmpə'θɛtɪk) *adj* **1** characterized by, feeling, or showing sympathy; understanding **2** in accord with the subject's personality or mood; congenial: *a sympathetic atmosphere* **3** (when postpositive, often foll by *to* or *towards*) showing agreement (with) or favour (towards): *sympathetic to the proposals* **4** *anatomy, physiol* of or relating to the division of the autonomic nervous system that acts in opposition to the parasympathetic system accelerating the heartbeat, dilating the bronchi, inhibiting the smooth muscles of the digestive tract, etc. Compare **parasympathetic 5** relating to vibrations occurring as a result of similar vibrations in a neighbouring body: *sympathetic strings on a sitar* > ˌsympa'thetically *adv*

sympathetic ink *n* another term for **invisible ink**

sympathetic magic *n* a type of magic in which it is sought to produce a large-scale effect, often at a distance, by performing some small-scale ceremony resembling it, such as the pouring of water on an altar to induce rainfall

sympathin ('sɪmpəθɪn) *n* a substance released at certain sympathetic nerve endings: thought to be identical with adrenaline [C20 from SYMPATH(ETIC) + -IN]

sympathize *or* **sympathise** ('sɪmpəˌθaɪz) *vb* (intr; often foll by *with*) **1** to feel or express compassion or sympathy (for); commiserate: *he sympathized with my troubles* **2** to share or understand the sentiments or ideas (of); be in sympathy (with) > 'sympaˌthizer *or* 'sympaˌthiser *n*

sympatholytic (ˌsɪmpəθəʊ'lɪtɪk) *med* ▷ *adj* **1 a** inhibiting or antagonistic to nerve impulses of the sympathetic nervous system **b** of or relating to such inhibition ▷ *n* **2** a sympatholytic drug. Compare **sympathomimetic** [C20 from SYMPATH(ETIC) + -LYTIC]

sympathomimetic (ˌsɪmpəθəʊmɪ'mɛtɪk) *med* ▷ *adj* **1** causing a physiological effect similar to that produced by stimulation of the sympathetic nervous system ▷ *n* **2** a sympathomimetic drug. Compare **sympatholytic** [C20 from SYMPATH(ETIC) + MIMETIC]

sympathy ('sɪmpəθɪ) *n, pl* -**thies 1** the sharing of another's emotions, esp of sorrow or anguish; pity; compassion **2** an affinity or harmony, usually of feelings or interests, between persons or things: *to be in sympathy with someone* **3** mutual affection or understanding arising from such a relationship; congeniality **4** the condition of a physical system or body when its behaviour is similar or corresponds to that of a different system that influences it, such as the vibration of sympathetic strings **5** (*sometimes plural*) a feeling of loyalty, support, or accord, as for an idea, cause, etc **6** *physiol* the mutual relationship between two organs or parts whereby a change in one has an effect on the other [C16 from Latin *sympathīa*, from Greek *sumpatheia*, from *sumpathēs*, from SYN- + *pathos* suffering]

sympathy strike *n* a strike organized in support of another section of workers or a cause and not because of direct grievances. Also called: **sympathetic strike**

sympatric (sɪm'pætrɪk) *adj* (of biological speciation or species) taking place or existing in the same or overlapping geographical areas. Compare **allopatric** [C20 from SYN- + -*patric*, from Greek *patra* native land, from *patēr* father] > sym'patrically *adv*

sympetalous (sɪm'pɛtələs) *adj botany* another word for **gamopetalous**

symphile ('sɪmfaɪl) *n* an insect or other organism that lives in the nests of social insects, esp ants and termites, and is fed and reared by the inmates. Compare **synoekete** [C20 from Greek *sumphilein* to love mutually; see SYN-, -PHILE]

symphonic poem *n music* an extended orchestral composition, originated by Liszt, based on nonmusical material, such as a work of literature or folk tale. Also called: **tone poem**

symphonious (sɪm'fəʊnɪəs) *adj literary* harmonious or concordant > sym'phoniously *adv*

symphonist ('sɪmfənɪst) *n* a person who composes symphonies

symphony ('sɪmfənɪ) *n, pl* -**nies 1** an extended large-scale orchestral composition, usually with several movements, at least one of which is in sonata form. The classical form of the symphony was fixed by Haydn and Mozart, but the innovations of subsequent composers have freed it entirely from classical constraints. It continues to be a vehicle for serious, large-scale orchestral music **2** a piece of instrumental music in up to three very short movements, used as an overture to or interlude in a baroque opera **3** any purely orchestral movement in a vocal work, such as a cantata or oratorio **4** short for **symphony orchestra 5** (in musical theory, esp of classical Greece) **a** another word for **consonance** (sense 3) Compare **diaphony** (sense 2) **b** the interval of unison **6** anything distinguished by a harmonious composition: *the picture was a symphony of green* **7** *archaic* harmony in general; concord [C13 from Old French *symphonie*, from Latin *symphōnia* concord, concert, from Greek *sumphōnia*, from SYN- + *phōnē* sound] > **symphonic** (sɪm'fɒnɪk) *adj* > sym'phonically *adv*

symphony orchestra *n music* an orchestra capable of performing symphonies, esp the large orchestra comprising strings, brass, woodwind, harp and percussion

symphysis ('sɪmfɪsɪs) *n, pl* -**ses** (-ˌsiːz) **1** *anatomy, botany* a growing together of parts or structures, such as two bony surfaces joined by an intermediate layer of fibrous cartilage **2** a line marking this growing together **3** *pathol* an abnormal adhesion of two or more parts or structures [C16 via New Latin from Greek *sumphusis*, from *sumphuein*, from SYN- + *phuein* to grow] > **symphysial** *or* **symphyseal** (sɪm'fɪzɪəl) *adj*

symplast ('sɪmplæst) *n botany* the continuous system of protoplasts, linked by plasmodesmata and bounded by the cell wall > sym'plastic *adj*

sympodium (sɪm'pəʊdɪəm) *n, pl* -**dia** (-dɪə) the main axis of growth in the grapevine and similar plants: a lateral branch that arises from just behind the apex of the main stem, which ceases to grow, and continues growing in the same direction as the main stem. Compare **monopodium** [C19 from New Latin, from SYN- + Greek *podion* a little foot, from *pous* foot] > sym'podial *adj* > sym'podially *adv*

symposiac (sɪm'pəʊzɪˌæk) *adj* **1** of, suitable for, or occurring at a symposium ▷ *n* **2** an archaic word for **symposium** [C17 from Latin *symposiacus*; see SYMPOSIUM]

symposiarch (sɪm'pəʊzɪˌɑːk) *n* **1** the president of a symposium, esp in classical Greece **2** a rare word for **toastmaster** [C17 from Greek; see SYMPOSIUM, -ARCH]

symposiast (sɪm'pəʊzɪˌæst) *n* a person who takes part in a symposium

symposium (sɪm'pəʊzɪəm) *n, pl* -**siums** *or* -**sia** (-zɪə) **1** a conference or meeting for the discussion of some subject, esp an academic topic or social problem **2** a collection of scholarly contributions, usually published together, on a given subject **3** (in classical Greece) a drinking party with intellectual conversation, music, etc [C16 via Latin from Greek *sumposion*, from *sumpinein* to drink together, from *sum*- SYN- + *pinein* to drink]

symptom ('sɪmptəm) *n* **1** *med* any sensation or change in bodily function experienced by a patient that is associated with a particular disease. Compare **sign** (sense 9) **2** any phenomenon or circumstance accompanying something and regarded as evidence of its existence; indication [C16 from Late Latin *symptōma*, from Greek *sumptōma* chance, from *sumpiptein* to occur, from SYN- + *piptein* to fall] > 'symptomless *adj*

symptomatic (ˌsɪmptə'mætɪk) *adj* **1** (often foll by *of*) being a symptom; indicative: *symptomatic of insanity* **2** of or relating to a symptom or symptoms **3** according to symptoms: *a symptomatic analysis of a case* > ˌsympto'matically *adv*

symptomatology (ˌsɪmptəmə'tɒlədʒɪ) *or* **symptomology** *n* the branch of medicine concerned with the study and classification of the symptoms of disease

syn (saɪn, sɪn) *adv, prep, conj* a variant of **syne¹**

syn. *abbreviation for* synonym(ous)

syn- *prefix* **1** with or together: *synecology* **2** fusion: *syngamy* [from Greek *sun* together, with]

synaeresis (sɪ'nɪərɪsɪs) *n* a variant spelling of **syneresis**

synaesthesia *or US* **synesthesia** (ˌsɪniːs'θiːzɪə) *n* **1** *physiol* a sensation experienced in a part of the body other than the part stimulated **2** *psychol* the subjective sensation of a sense other than the one being stimulated. For example, a sound may evoke sensations of colour [from New Latin, from SYN- + -*esthesia*, from Greek *aisthēsis* sensation] > **synaesthetic** *or US* **synesthetic** (ˌsɪniːs'θɛtɪk) *adj*

synagogue ('sɪnəˌgɒg) *n* **1 a** a building for Jewish religious services and usually also for religious instruction **b** (*as modifier*): *synagogue services* **2** a congregation of Jews who assemble for worship or religious study **3** the religion of Judaism as organized in such congregations [C12 from Old French *sinagoge*, from Late Latin *synagōga*, from Greek *sunagōgē* a gathering, from *sunagein* to bring together, from SYN- + *agein* to lead] > **synagogical** (ˌsɪnə'gɒdʒɪkᵊl) *or* **synagogal** ('sɪnəˌgɒgᵊl) *adj*

synalepha *or* **synaloepha** (ˌsɪnə'liːfə) *n linguistics* vowel elision, esp as it arises when one word ends in a vowel and the following word begins with one [C16 from Late Latin *synaloepha*, from Greek *sunaliphō*, from SYN- + *aleiphein* to melt, smear]

synapse ('saɪnæps) *n* the point at which a nerve impulse is relayed from the terminal portion of an axon to the dendrites of an adjacent neuron

synapsis (sɪ'næpsɪs) *n, pl* -**ses** (-siːz) **1** *cytology* the association in pairs of homologous chromosomes at the start of meiosis **2** another word for

synapse [c19 from New Latin, from Greek *sunapsis* junction, from *sunaptein* to join together, from SYN- + *haptein* to connect]

synaptic (sɪˈnæptɪk) or **synaptical** *adj* of or relating to a synapse > syn**apticaly** *adv*

synarchy (ˈsɪnəkɪ) *n, pl* -**chies** joint rule [c18 from Greek *sunarchia*, from *sunarchein* to rule jointly]

synarthrosis (ˌsɪnɑːˈθrəʊsɪs) *n, pl* -**ses**(-siːz) *anatomy* any of various joints which lack a synovial cavity and are virtually immovable; a fixed joint [via New Latin from Greek *sunarthrōsis*, from *sunarthrousthai* to be connected by joints, from *sun-* SYN- + *arthron* a joint] > ˌsynar'throdial *adj* > ˌsynar'throdially *adv*

sync or **synch** (sɪŋk) *films, television, computing* ▷ *vb* **1** an informal word for **synchronize** ▷ *n* **2** an informal word for **synchronization** (esp in the phrases **in** or **out of sync**)

syncarp (ˈsɪnkɑːp) *n botany* a fleshy multiple fruit, formed from two or more carpels of one flower or the aggregated fruits of several flowers [c19 from New Latin *syncarpium*, from SYN- + Greek *karpos* fruit]

syncarpous (sɪnˈkɑːpəs) *adj* **1** (of the ovaries of certain flowering plants) consisting of united carpels. Compare **apocarpous 2** of or relating to a syncarp > syn'carpy (ˈsɪnkɑːpɪ) *n*

syncategorematic (sɪnˌkætəˌɡɔːrəˈmætɪk) *adj philosophy* applying to expressions that are not in any of Aristotle's categories, but form meaningful expressions together with them, such as conjunctions and adverbs

synchro (ˈsɪŋkrəʊ) *n, pl* -**chros 1** any of a number of electrical devices in which the angular position of a rotating part is transformed into a voltage, or vice versa. Also called: **selsyn 2** short for **synchronized swimming**

synchro- *combining form* indicating synchronization: *synchroflash*

synchrocyclotron (ˌsɪŋkrəʊˈsaɪkləˌtrɒn) *n* a type of cyclotron in which the frequency of the electric field is modulated to allow for relativistic effects at high velocities and thus produce higher energies

synchroflash (ˈsɪŋkrəʊˌflæʃ) *n* a mechanism in a camera that enables the shutter to be fully open while the light from a flashbulb or electronic flash is at its brightest

synchromesh (ˈsɪŋkrəʊˌmɛʃ) *adj* **1** (of a gearbox, etc) having a system of clutches that synchronizes the speeds of the driving and driven members before engagement to avoid shock in gear changing and to reduce noise and wear ▷ *n* **2** a gear system having these features [c20 shortened from *synchronized mesh*]

synchronic (sɪnˈkrɒnɪk) *adj* **1** concerned with the events or phenomena at a particular period without considering historical antecedents: *synchronic linguistics*. Compare **diachronic 2** synchronous > syn'chronically *adv*

synchronicity (ˌsɪŋkrəˈnɪsɪtɪ) *n* an apparently meaningful coincidence in time of two or more similar or identical events that are causally unrelated [c20 coined by Carl Jung from SYNCHRONIC + -ITY]

synchronism (ˈsɪŋkrəˌnɪzəm) *n* **1** the quality or condition of being synchronous **2** a chronological usually tabular list of historical persons and events, arranged to show parallel or synchronous occurrence **3** the representation in a work of art of one or more incidents that occurred at separate times [c16 from Greek *sunkhronismos*; see SYNCHRONOUS, -ISM]

synchronistic (ˌsɪŋkrəˈnɪstɪk) *adj* of, relating to, or exhibiting synchronism > ˌsynchro'nistically *adv*

synchronize or **synchronise** (ˈsɪŋkrəˌnaɪz) *vb* **1** (when *intr*, usually foll by *with*) to occur or recur or cause to occur or recur at the same time or in unison **2** to indicate or cause to indicate the same time **3** (*tr*) *films* to establish (the picture and soundtrack records) in their correct relative position **4** (*tr*) to designate (events) as

simultaneous > ˌsynchroni'zation or ˌsynchroni'sation *n* > 'synchro,nizer or 'synchro,niser *n*

synchronized skating *n* the art or sport of teams of up to twenty skaters holding onto each other and moving in patterns in time to music

synchronized swimming *n* the art or sport of one or more swimmers moving in patterns in the water in time to music. Sometimes shortened to: synchro or synchro swimming

synchronous (ˈsɪŋkrənəs) *adj* **1** occurring at the same time; contemporaneous **2** *physics* (of periodic phenomena, such as voltages) having the same frequency and phase **3** occurring or recurring exactly together and at the same rate [c17 from Late Latin *synchronus*, from Greek *sunkhronos*, from SYN- + *khronos* time] > 'synchronously *adv* > 'synchronousness *n*

synchronous converter *n* a synchronous machine that converts alternating current to direct current, or vice versa

synchronous machine *n* an electrical machine, whose rotating speed is proportional to the frequency of the alternating-current supply and independent of the load

synchronous motor *n* an alternating-current motor that runs at a speed that is equal to or is a multiple of the frequency of the supply

synchronous orbit *n astronautics* an orbit in which the orbital period of a satellite is identical to the spin period of the central body

synchrony (ˈsɪŋkrənɪ) *n* the state of being synchronous; simultaneity

synchroscope (ˈsɪŋkrəˌskəʊp) or synchronoscope (sɪnˈkrɒnəˌskəʊp) *n* an instrument used to indicate whether two periodic quantities or motions are synchronous

synchrotron (ˈsɪŋkrəˌtrɒn) *n* a type of particle accelerator similar to a betatron but having an electric field of fixed frequency with electrons but not with protons as well as a changing magnetic field. It is capable of producing very high energies in the GeV range [c20 from SYNCHRO- + (ELEC)TRON]

synchrotron radiation *n* electromagnetic radiation emitted in narrow beams tangential to the orbit of very high energy charged particles, such as electrons, spiralling along the lines of force in a strong magnetic field. It occurs in synchrotron accelerators and in many cosmic environments, such as radio galaxies and supernova remnants

synclastic (sɪnˈklæstɪk) *adj maths* (of a surface) having a curvature at a given point and in a particular direction that is of the same sign as the curvature at that point in perpendicular direction. Compare **anticlastic** [c19 from SYN- (alike) + Greek *klastos* bent, from *klan* to bend]

syncline (ˈsɪnklaɪn) *n* a downward fold of stratified rock in which the strata slope towards a vertical axis. Compare **anticline** [c19 from SYN- + Greek *klīnein* to lean] > syn'clinal *adj*

synclinorium (ˌsɪŋklɪˈnɔːrɪəm) *n, pl* -**ria**(-rɪə) a vast elongated syncline with its strata further folded into anticlines and synclines [c19 New Latin, from SYNCLINE + -*orium*, suffix indicating a place]

Syncom (ˈsɪnˌkɒm) *n* a communications satellite in stationary orbit [c20 from *syn*(*chronous*) *com*(*munication*)]

syncopate (ˈsɪŋkəˌpeɪt) *vb* (*tr*) **1** *music* to modify or treat (a beat, rhythm, note, etc) by syncopation **2** to shorten (a word) by omitting sounds or letters from the middle [c17 from Medieval Latin *syncopāre* to omit a letter or syllable, from Late Latin *syncopa* SYNCOPE] > 'synco,pator *n*

syncopation (ˌsɪŋkəˈpeɪʃən) *n* **1** *music* **a** the displacement of the usual rhythmic accent away from a strong beat onto a weak beat **b** a note, beat, rhythm, etc, produced by syncopation **2** another word for **syncope** (sense 2)

syncope (ˈsɪŋkəpɪ) *n* **1** *pathol* a technical word for

a faint **2** the omission of one or more sounds or letters from the middle of a word [c16 from Late Latin *syncopa*, from Greek *sunkopē* a cutting off, from SYN- + *koptein* to cut] > **syncopic** (sɪnˈkɒpɪk) or 'syncopal *adj*

syncretism (ˈsɪŋkrɪˌtɪzəm) *n* **1** the tendency to syncretize **2** the historical tendency of languages to reduce their use of inflection, as in the development of Old English with all its case endings into Modern English [c17 from New Latin *syncrētismus*, from Greek *sunkrētismos* alliance of Cretans, from *sunkrētizein* to join forces (in the manner of the Cretan towns), from SYN- + *Krēs* a Cretan] > **syncretic** (sɪŋˈkrɛtɪk) or ˌsyncre'tistic *adj* > 'syncretist *n*

syncretize or **syncretise** (ˈsɪŋkrɪˌtaɪz) *vb* to combine or attempt to combine the characteristic teachings, beliefs, or practices of (differing systems of religion or philosophy) > ˌsyncreti'zation or ˌsyncreti'sation *n*

syncytium (sɪnˈsɪtɪəm) *n, pl* -**cytia**(-ˈsɪtɪə) *zoology* a mass of cytoplasm containing many nuclei and enclosed in a cell membrane [c19 New Latin; see SYN-, CYTO-, -IUM] > syn'cytial *adj*

synd (saɪnd) *vb, n Scot* a variant of **syne²**

syndactyl (sɪnˈdæktɪl) *adj* **1** (of certain animals) having two or more digits growing fused together ▷ *n* **2** an animal with this arrangement of digits > syn'dactylism *n*

syndesis (sɪnˈdiːsɪs) *n grammar* **1** the use of syndetic constructions **2** another name for **polysyndeton** (sense 2) [c20 from Greek, from *sundein* to bind together, from SYN- + *dein* to bind]

syndesmosis (ˌsɪndɛsˈməʊsɪs) *n, pl* -**ses**(-siːz) *anatomy* a type of joint in which the articulating bones are held together by a ligament of connective tissue [New Latin, from Greek *sundein* to bind together; see SYNDESIS] > **syndesmotic** (ˌsɪndɛsˈmɒtɪk) *adj*

syndetic (sɪnˈdɛtɪk) *adj* denoting a grammatical construction in which two clauses are connected by a conjunction. Compare **asyndetic** (sense 2) [c17 from Greek *sundetikos*, from *sundetos* bound together; see SYNDESIS] > syn'detically *adv*

syndeton (sɪnˈdiːtᵊn) *n grammar* a syndetic construction. Compare **asyndeton** (sense 2) [c20 from Greek *sundeton* a bond, from *sundein* to bind together; see SYNDESIS]

syndic (ˈsɪndɪk) *n* **1** *Brit* a business agent of some universities or other bodies **2** (in several countries) a government administrator or magistrate with varying powers [c17 via Old French from Late Latin *syndicus*, from Greek *sundikos* defendant's advocate, from SYN- + *dikē* justice] > 'syndic,ship *n* > 'syndical *adj*

syndicalism (ˈsɪndɪkəˌlɪzəm) *n* **1** a revolutionary movement and theory advocating the seizure of the means of production and distribution by syndicates of workers through direct action, esp a general strike **2** an economic system resulting from such action > 'syndical *adj* > 'syndicalist *adj, n* > ˌsyndical'istic *adj*

syndicate *n* (ˈsɪndɪkɪt) **1** an association of business enterprises or individuals organized to undertake a joint project requiring considerable capital **2** a news agency that sells articles, photographs, etc, to a number of newspapers for simultaneous publication **3** any association formed to carry out an enterprise or enterprises of common interest to its members **4** a board of syndics or the office of syndic **5** (in Italy under the Fascists) a local organization of employers or employees ▷ *vb* (ˈsɪndɪˌkeɪt) **6** (*tr*) to sell (articles, photographs, etc) to several newspapers for simultaneous publication **7** (*tr*) *US* to sell (a programme or programmes) to several local commercial television or radio stations **8** to form a syndicate of (people) [c17 from Old French *syndicat* office of a SYNDIC] > ˌsyndi'cation *n*

syndiotactic (ˌsɪndɪəʊˈtæktɪk) *adj chem* (of a stereospecific polymer) having alternating stereochemical configurations of the groups on

1633

successive carbon atoms in the chain. Compare **isotactic** [C20 from *syndyo,* from Greek *sunduo* two together + -TACTIC]

syndrome ('sɪndrəʊm) *n* **1** *med* any combination of signs and symptoms that are indicative of a particular disease or disorder **2** a symptom, characteristic, or set of symptoms or characteristics indicating the existence of a condition, problem, etc [C16 via New Latin from Greek *sundromē,* literally: a running together, from SYN- + *dramein* to run] > **syndromic** (sɪn'drɒmɪk) *adj*

syndrome X *n* another name for IRS (sense 2)

syne¹ or **syn** (saɪn) *adv, prep, conj* a Scot word for **since** [C14 probably related to Old English *sīth* since]

syne² (saɪn) or **synd** *Scot* ▷ *vb* **1** (*tr*) to rinse; wash out ▷ *n* **2** a rinse [C14 of uncertain origin]

synecdoche (sɪn'ɛkdəkɪ) *n* a figure of speech in which a part is substituted for a whole or a whole for a part, as in *50 head of cattle* for *50 cows,* or *the army* for *a soldier* [C14 via Latin from Greek *sunekdokhē,* from SYN- + *ekdokhē* interpretation, from *dekhesthai* to accept] > **synecdochic** (,sɪnɛk'dɒkɪk) or ,**synec'dochical** *adj* > ,**synec'dochically** *adv*

synecious (sɪ'niːʃəs) *adj* a variant spelling of **synoecious**

synecology (,sɪnɪ'kɒlədʒɪ) *n* the ecological study of communities of plants and animals. Compare **autecology.** > **synecologic** (sɪn,ɛkə'lɒdʒɪk) or syn,eco'logical *adj* > syn,eco'logically *adv*

synectics (sɪ'nɛktɪks) *n* (*functioning as singular*) a method of identifying and solving problems that depends on creative thinking, the use of analogy, and informal conversation among a small group of individuals with diverse experience and expertise [C20 from SYN- + ECTO- + -ICS, in the sense: working together from outside]

syneresis or **synaeresis** (sɪ'nɪərɪsɪs) *n* **1** *chem* the process in which a gel contracts on standing and exudes liquid, as in the separation of whey in cheese-making **2** the contraction of two vowels into a diphthong **3** another word for **synizesis** [C16 via Late Latin from Greek *sunairesis* a shortening, from *sunairein* to draw together, from SYN- + *hairein* to take]

synergetic (,sɪnə'dʒɛtɪk) or **synergistic** *adj* another word for **synergistic** [C17 from Greek *sunergētikos,* from SYN- + -*gētikos,* from *ergon* work; see ENERGY]

synergism ('sɪnə,dʒɪzəm, sɪ'nɜː-) *n* **1** Also called: **synergy** the working together of two or more drugs, muscles, etc, to produce an effect greater than the sum of their individual effects **2** another name for **synergy** (sense 1) **3** *Christian theol* the doctrine or belief that the human will cooperates with the Holy Spirit and with divine grace, esp in the act of conversion or regeneration [C18 from New Latin *synergismus,* from Greek *sunergos,* from SYN- + *ergon* work]

synergist ('sɪnədʒɪst, sɪ'nɜː-) *n* **1** a drug, muscle, etc, that increases the action of another **2** *Christian theol* an upholder of synergism ▷ *adj* **3** of or relating to synergism

synergistic (,sɪnə'dʒɪstɪk) or **synergetic** (,sɪnə'dʒɛtɪk) *adj* **1** acting together **2** (of people, groups, or companies) working together in a creative, innovative, and productive manner [C17 from Greek *sunergētikos,* from SYN- + -*ergētikos,* from *ergon* work; see ENERGY] > ,**syner'gistically** or ,**syner'getically** *adv*

synergy ('sɪnədʒɪ) *n, pl* -gies **1** Also called: **synergism** the potential ability of individual organizations or groups to be more successful or productive as a result of a merger **2** another name for **synergism** (sense 1) [C19 from New Latin *synergia,* from Greek *sunergos;* see SYNERGISM] > **synergic** (sɪ'nɜːdʒɪk) *adj*

synesis ('sɪnɪsɪs) *n* a grammatical construction in which the inflection or form of a word is conditioned by the meaning rather than the syntax, as for example the plural form *have* with

the singular noun *group* in the sentence *the group have already assembled* [via New Latin from Greek *sunesis* union, from *sunienai* to bring together, from SYN- + *hienai* to send]

synesthesia (,sɪniːs'θiːzɪə) *n* the usual US spelling of **synaesthesia.** > **synesthetic** (,sɪniːs'θɛtɪk) *adj*

syngamy ('sɪŋgəmɪ) or **syngenesis** (sɪn'dʒɛnɪsɪs) *n* other names for **sexual reproduction.** > **syngamic** (sɪŋ'gæmɪk) or **syngamous** ('sɪŋgəməs) *adj*

synizesis (,sɪnɪ'ziːsɪs) *n* **1** *phonetics* the contraction of two vowels originally belonging to separate syllables into a single syllable, without diphthongization. Compare **syneresis 2** *cytology* the contraction of chromatin towards one side of the nucleus during the prophase of meiosis [C19 via Late Latin from Greek *sunizēsis* a collapse, from *sunizanein* to sink down, from SYN- + *hizein* to sit]

synkaryon (sɪn'kærɪˌɒn) *n* *biology* the nucleus of a fertilized egg [C20 New Latin, from SYN- + Greek *karuon* a nut] > syn,kary'onic *adj*

synod ('sɪnəd, 'sɪnɒd) *n* a local or special ecclesiastical council, esp of a diocese, formally convened to discuss ecclesiastical affairs [C14 from Late Latin *synodus,* from Greek *sunodos,* from SYN- + *hodos* a way] > '**synodal** or less commonly syn'odical *adj*

synodic (sɪ'nɒdɪk) *adj* relating to or involving a conjunction or two successive conjunctions of the same star, planet, or satellite: *the synodic month*

synodic month *n* See **month** (sense 6)

Synod of Whitby *n* the synod held in 664 at Whitby at which the Roman date for Easter was accepted and the Church in England became aligned with Rome

synoecious, synecious (sɪ'niːʃəs) or **synoicous** (sɪ'nɔɪkəs) *adj* (of a bryophyte) having male and female organs together on a branch, usually mixed at the tip [C19 SYN- + -*oecious,* from Greek *oikion* diminutive of *oikos* house]

synoekete (sɪ'niːkiːt) or **synoecete** (sɪ'niːsiːt) *n* an insect that lives in the nests of social insects, esp ants, without receiving any attentions from the inmates. Compare **symphile** [C20 from Greek *sunoiketēs* house-fellow, from *sunoikia* community]

synonym ('sɪnənɪm) *n* **1** a word that means the same or nearly the same as another word, such as *bucket* and *pail* **2** a word or phrase used as another name for something, such as *Hellene* for a *Greek* **3** *biology* a taxonomic name that has been superseded or rejected [C16 via Late Latin from Greek *sunōnumon,* from SYN- + *onoma* name] > ,**syno'nymic** or ,**syno'nymical** *adj* > ,**syno'nymity** *n*

synonymize or **synonymise** (sɪ'nɒnɪˌmaɪz) *vb* (*tr*) to analyse the synonyms of or provide with synonyms

synonymous (sɪ'nɒnɪməs) *adj* **1** (often foll by *with*) being a synonym (of) **2** (*postpositive;* foll by *with*) closely associated (with) or suggestive (of): *his name was synonymous with greed* > syn'onymously *adv* > syn'onymousness *n*

synonymy (sɪ'nɒnɪmɪ) *n, pl* -mies **1** the study of synonyms **2** the character of being synonymous; equivalence **3** a list or collection of synonyms, esp one in which their meanings are discriminated **4** *biology* a collection of the synonyms of a species or group

synop. *abbreviation for* synopsis

synopsis (sɪ'nɒpsɪs) *n, pl* -ses (-siːz) a condensation or brief review of a subject; summary [C17 via Late Latin from Greek *sunopsis,* from SYN- + *opsis* view]

synopsize or **synopsise** (sɪ'nɒpsaɪz) *vb* (*tr*) **1** to make a synopsis of **2** *US* variants of **epitomize**

synoptic (sɪ'nɒptɪk) *adj* **1** of or relating to a synopsis **2** (*often capital*) *Bible* **a** (of the Gospels of Matthew, Mark, and Luke) presenting the narrative of Christ's life, ministry, etc from a point of view held in common by all three, and with close similarities in content, order, etc **b** of, relating to, or characterizing these three Gospels **3** *meteorol* showing or concerned with the

distribution of meteorological conditions over a wide area at a given time: *a synoptic chart* ▷ *n* **4** (*often capital*) *Bible* **a** any of the three synoptic Gospels **b** any of the authors of these three Gospels [C18 from Greek *sunoptikos,* from SYNOPSIS] > syn'optically *adv* > syn'optist *n*

synovia (saɪ'nəʊvɪə, sɪ-) *n* a transparent viscid lubricating fluid, secreted by the membrane lining joints, tendon sheaths, etc [C17 from New Latin, probably from SYN- + Latin *ōvum* egg]

synovial (saɪ'nəʊvɪəl, sɪ-) *adj* of or relating to the synovia; (of a joint) surrounded by a synovia-secreting membrane > syn'ovially *adv*

synovitis (,saɪnəʊ'vaɪtɪs, ,sɪn-) *n* inflammation of the membrane surrounding a joint > **synovitic** (,saɪnəʊ'vɪtɪk, ,sɪn-) *adj*

synroc ('sɪn,rɒk) *n* a titanium-ceramic substance that can incorporate nuclear waste in its crystals [from syn(thetic) + roc(k)]

synsepalous (sɪn'sɛpələs) *adj* another word for **gamosepalous**

syntactic (sɪn'tæktɪk) *adj* **1** Also: syntactical relating to or determined by syntax **2** *logic, linguistics* describable wholly with respect to the grammatical structure of an expression or the rules of well-formedness of a formal system > syn'tactically *adv*

syntactics (sɪn'tæktɪks) *n* (*functioning as singular*) the branch of semiotics that deals with the formal properties of symbol systems; proof theory

syntagma (sɪn'tægmə) or **syntagm** ('sɪn,tæm) *n, pl* -tagmata (-'tægmətə) or -tagms **1** a syntactic unit or a word or phrase forming a syntactic unit **2** a systematic collection of statements or propositions [C17 from Late Latin, from Greek, from *suntassein* to put in order]

syntagmatic (,sɪntæg'mætɪk) *adj* **1** of or denoting a syntagma **2** Also: syntagmic (sɪn'tægmɪk) *linguistics* denoting or concerning the relationship between a word and other members of a syntactic unit containing it

syntax ('sɪntæks) *n* **1** the branch of linguistics that deals with the grammatical arrangement of words and morphemes in the sentences of a language or of languages in general **2** the totality of facts about the grammatical arrangement of words in a language **3** a systematic statement of the rules governing the grammatical arrangement of words and morphemes in a language **4** *logic* a systematic statement of the rules governing the properly formed formulas of a logical system **5** any orderly arrangement or system [C17 from Late Latin *syntaxis,* from Greek *suntaxis,* from *suntassein* to put in order, from SYN- + *tassein* to arrange]

synteny (sɪn'tɛnɪ) *n* the presence of two or more genes on the same chromosome [C20 SYN- + Greek *tainia* ribbon] > syn'tenic *adj*

synth (sɪnθ) *n* short for **synthesizer**

synthesis ('sɪnθɪsɪs) *n, pl* -ses (-,siːz) **1** the process of combining objects or ideas into a complex whole. Compare **analysis 2** the combination or whole produced by such a process **3** the process of producing a compound by a chemical reaction or series of reactions, usually from simpler or commonly available starting materials **4** *linguistics* the use of inflections rather than word order and function words to express the syntactic relations in a language. Compare **analysis** (sense 5) **5** *philosophy archaic* synthetic reasoning **6** *philosophy* **a** (in the writings of Kant) the unification of one concept with another not contained in it. Compare **analysis** (sense 7) **b** the final stage in the Hegelian dialectic, that resolves the contradiction between thesis and antithesis [C17 via Latin from Greek *sunthesis,* from *suntithenai* to put together, from SYN- + *tithenai* to place] > 'synthesist *n*

synthesis gas *n* *chem* **1** a mixture of carbon dioxide, carbon monoxide, and hydrogen formerly made by using water gas and reacting it with steam to enrich the proportion of hydrogen for use in the synthesis of ammonia **2** a similar mixture of gases made by steam reforming natural gas, used for synthesizing organic chemicals and as a fuel

synthesize ('sɪnθɪˌsaɪz), **synthetize, synthesise** or **synthetise** vb **1** to combine or cause to combine into a whole **2** (tr) to produce by synthesis > ˌsynthesiˈzation, ˌsynthetiˈzation, ˌsynthesiˈsation or ˌsynthetiˈsation n

synthesizer ('sɪnθɪˌsaɪzə) n **1** an electrophonic instrument, usually operated by means of a keyboard and pedals, in which sounds are produced by voltage-controlled oscillators, filters, and amplifiers, with an envelope generator module that controls attack, decay, sustain, and release **2** a person or thing that synthesizes

synthespian (ˌsɪnˈθɛspɪən) n a computer-generated image of a film actor, esp used in place of the real actor when shooting special effects or stunts [c20 from SYN(THETIC) + THESPIAN]

synthetic (sɪnˈθɛtɪk) adj also **synthetical 1** (of a substance or material) made artificially by chemical reaction **2** not genuine; insincere: synthetic compassion **3** denoting languages, such as Latin, whose morphology is characterized by synthesis. Compare **polysynthetic, agglutinative** (sense 2), **analytic** (sense 3) **4** philosophy **a** (of a proposition) having a truth-value that is not determined solely by virtue of the meanings of the words, as in all men are arrogant **b** contingent. Compare **a posteriori, empirical** ⊳ n **5** a synthetic substance or material [c17 from New Latin syntheticus, from Greek sunthetikos expert in putting together, from suntithenai to put together; see SYNTHESIS] > synˈthetically adv

synthetic resin n See **resin** (sense 2)

synthetic rubber n any of various synthetic materials, similar to natural rubber, made by polymerizing unsaturated hydrocarbons, such as isoprene and butadiene

synthetism ('sɪnθɪˌtɪzəm) n (often capital) the symbolism of Paul Gauguin, the French postimpressionist painter (1848–1903) and the Nabis, a group of French painters much influenced by him, who reacted against the impressionists and realists by seeking to produce brightly coloured abstractions of their inner experience [c19 from Greek sunthetos composite; see SYNTHETIC] > ˈsynthetist n

synth-pop n a type of pop music in which synthesizers are used to create the dominant sound

syntonic (sɪnˈtɒnɪk) adj psychol emotionally in harmony with one's environment [c20 from Greek suntonos in harmony with; see SYN-, TONE] > synˈtonically adv

Syon House ('saɪən) n a mansion near Brentford in London: originally a monastery, rebuilt in the 16th century, altered by Inigo Jones in the 17th century, and by Robert Adam in the 18th century; seat of the Dukes of Northumberland; gardens laid out by Capability Brown

sypher ('saɪfə) vb (tr) to lap (a chamfered edge of one plank over that of another) in order to form a flush surface [c19 variant of CIPHER] > ˈsyphering n

syphilis ('sɪfɪlɪs) n a venereal disease caused by infection with the microorganism Treponema pallidum: characterized by an ulcerating chancre, usually on the genitals and progressing through the lymphatic system to nearly all tissues of the body, producing serious clinical manifestations [c18 from New Latin Syphilis (sive Morbus Gallicus) "Syphilis (or the French disease)", title of a poem (1530) by G. Fracastoro, Italian physician and poet, in which a shepherd Syphilus is portrayed as the first victim of the disease] > syphilitic (ˌsɪfɪˈlɪtɪk) adj , ˌsyphiˈlitically adv > ˈsyphiˌloid adj

syphilology (ˌsɪfɪˈlɒlədʒɪ) n the branch of medicine concerned with the study and treatment of syphilis > ˌsyphiˈlologist n

syphiloma (ˌsɪfɪˈləʊmə) n, pl -mas or -mata (-mətə) pathol a tumour or gumma caused by

infection with syphilis [c19 from SYPHILIS + -oma, as in sarcoma]

syphon ('saɪfᵊn) n a variant spelling of **siphon**

SYR international car registration for Syria

Syr. abbreviation for **1** Syria **2** Syriac **3** Syrian

Syracuse n **1** ('saɪrəˌkjuːz) a port in SW Italy, in SE Sicily on the Ionian Sea: founded in 734 BC by Greeks from Corinth and taken by the Romans in 212 BC, after a siege of three years. Pop. 123 657 (2001). Italian name: Siracusa **2** ('sɪrəˌkjuːs) a city in central New York State, on Lake Onondaga: site of the capital of the Iroquois Indian federation. Pop: 144 001 (2003 est)

Syrah ('saɪrə) n **1** a red grape grown in France and Australia, used, often in a blend, for making wine **2** any of various wines made from this grape. Australian name: Shiraz [from SHIRAZ¹, the city in Iran where the wine supposedly originated]

Syr Darya (Russian sir darj'ja) n a river in central Asia, formed from two headstreams rising in the Tian Shan: flows generally west to the Aral Sea: the longest river in central Asia. Length: (from the source of the Naryn) 2900 km (1800 miles). Ancient name: Jaxartes

Syria ('sɪrɪə) n **1** a republic in W Asia, on the Mediterranean: ruled by the Ottoman Turks (1516–1918); made a French mandate in 1920; became independent in 1944; joined Egypt in the United Arab Republic (1958–61). Official language: Arabic. Religion: Muslim majority. Currency: Syrian pound. Capital: Damascus. Pop: 18 223 000 (2004 est). Area: 185 180 sq km (71 498 sq miles) **2** (formerly) the region between the Mediterranean, the Euphrates, the Taurus, and the Arabian Desert

Syriac ('sɪrɪˌæk) n a dialect of Aramaic spoken in Syria until about the 13th century AD and still in use as a liturgical language of certain Eastern churches

Syrian ('sɪrɪən) adj **1** of, relating to, or characteristic of Syria, its people, or their dialect of Arabic **2** Eastern Church of or relating to Christians who belong to churches with Syriac liturgies ⊳ n **3** a native or inhabitant of Syria **4** Eastern Church a Syrian Christian

syringa (sɪˈrɪŋɡə) n another name for **mock orange** and **lilac** (sense 1) [c17 from New Latin, from Greek surinx tube, alluding to the use of its hollow stems for pipes]

syringe ('sɪrɪndʒ, sɪˈrɪndʒ) n **1** med an instrument, such as a hypodermic syringe or a rubber ball with a slender nozzle, for use in withdrawing or injecting fluids, cleaning wounds, etc **2** any similar device for injecting, spraying, or extracting liquids by means of pressure or suction ⊳ vb **3** (tr) to cleanse, inject, or spray with a syringe [c15 from Late Latin, from Latin: SYRINX]

syringomyelia (səˌrɪŋɡəʊmaɪˈiːlɪə) n a chronic progressive disease of the spinal cord in which cavities form in the grey matter: characterized by loss of the sense of pain and temperature [c19 syringo-, from Greek: SYRINX + -myelia from Greek muelos marrow] > syringomyelic (səˌrɪŋɡəʊmaɪˈɛlɪk) adj

syrinx ('sɪrɪŋks) n, pl **syringes** (sɪˈrɪndʒiːz) or **syrinxes** **1** the vocal organ of a bird, which is situated in the lower part of the trachea **2** (in classical Greek music) a panpipe or set of panpipes **3** anatomy another name for the **Eustachian tube** [c17 via Latin from Greek surinx pipe] > syringeal (sɪˈrɪndʒɪəl) adj

Syrinx ('sɪrɪŋks) n Greek myth a nymph who was changed into a reed to save her from the amorous pursuit of Pan. From this reed Pan then fashioned his musical pipes

Syro- ('saɪrəʊ-) combining form **1** indicating Syrian and: Syro-Lebanese **2** indicating Syriac and: Syro-Aramaic [from Greek Suro-, from Suros a Syrian]

syrphid ('sɜːfɪd) n any dipterous fly of the family Syrphidae, typically having a coloration mimicking that of certain bees and wasps: includes the hover flies [c19 from Greek surphos gnat]

Syrtis Major ('sɜːtɪs) n a conspicuous dark region

visible in the N hemisphere of Mars

syrup ('sɪrəp) n **1** a solution of sugar dissolved in water and often flavoured with fruit juice: used for sweetening fruit, etc **2** any of various thick sweet liquids prepared for cooking or table use from molasses, sugars, etc **3** a liquid medicine containing a sugar solution for flavouring or preservation **4** Brit slang a wig ⊳ vb (tr) **5** to bring to the consistency of syrup **6** to cover, fill, or sweeten with syrup ⊳ Also: sirup [c15 from Medieval Latin syrupus, from Arabic sharāb a drink, from shariba to drink: sense 4 from rhyming slang syrup of fig] > ˈsyrup-ˌlike adj

syrupy ('sɪrəpɪ) adj **1** (of a liquid) thick or sweet **2** cloyingly sentimental: a syrupy version of the Blue Danube

sysop or **SYSOP** ('sɪsˌɒp) n computing a person who runs a system or network [c20 SYS(TEM) + OP(ERATOR)]

syssarcosis (ˌsɪsɑːˈkəʊsɪs) n, pl -ses (-siːz) anatomy the union or articulation of bones by muscle [c17 from New Latin, from Greek sussarkōsis, from sussarkousthai, from sus- SYN- + sarkoun to become fleshy, from sarx flesh] > syssarcotic (ˌsɪsɑːˈkɒtɪk) adj

systaltic (sɪˈstæltɪk) adj (esp of the action of the heart) of, relating to, or characterized by alternate contractions and dilations; pulsating [c17 from Late Latin systalticus, from Greek sustaltikos, from sustellein to contract, from SYN- + stellein to place]

system ('sɪstəm) n **1** a group or combination of interrelated, interdependent, or interacting elements forming a collective entity; a methodical or coordinated assemblage of parts, facts, concepts, etc: a system of currency; the Copernican system **2** any scheme of classification or arrangement: a chronological system **3** a network of communications, transportation, or distribution **4** a method or complex of methods: he has a perfect system at roulette **5** orderliness; an ordered manner **6** the system (often capital) society seen as an environment exploiting, restricting, and repressing individuals **7** an organism considered as a functioning entity **8** any of various bodily parts or structures that are anatomically or physiologically related: the digestive system **9** one's physiological or psychological constitution: get it out of your system **10** any assembly of electronic, electrical, or mechanical components with interdependent functions, usually forming a self-contained unit: a brake system **11** a group of celestial bodies that are associated as a result of natural laws, esp gravitational attraction: the solar system **12** chem a sample of matter in which there are one or more substances in one or more phases. See also **phase rule 13** a point of view or doctrine used to interpret a branch of knowledge **14** mineralogy one of a group of divisions into which crystals may be placed on the basis of the lengths and inclinations of their axes. also called **crystal system 15** geology a stratigraphical unit for the rock strata formed during a period of geological time. It can be subdivided into series [c17 from French système, from Late Latin systēma, from Greek sustēma, from SYN- + histanai to cause to stand] > ˈsystemless adj

systematic (ˌsɪstɪˈmætɪk) adj **1** characterized by the use of order and planning; methodical: a systematic administrator **2** comprising or resembling a system: systematic theology **3** Also: **systematical** (sɪstəˈmætɪkᵊl) biology of or relating to the taxonomic classification of organisms > ˌsystemˈatically adv

systematic desensitization n psychol a treatment of phobias in which the patient while relaxed is exposed, often only in imagination, to progressively more frightening aspects of the phobia

systematics (ˌsɪstɪˈmætɪks) n (functioning as singular) the study of systems and the principles of classification and nomenclature

systematism ('sɪstɪməˌtɪzəm) n **1** the practice of

S

classifying or systematizing **2** adherence to a system **3** a systematic classification; systematized arrangement

systematist ('sɪstɪmətɪst) *n* **1** a person who constructs systems **2** an adherent of a system **3** a taxonomist

systematize ('sɪstɪmə,taɪz), **systemize, systematise** *or* **systemise** *vb* (*tr*) to arrange in a system > ,systemati'zation, ,systemati'sation, ,systemi'zation *or* ,systemi'sation *n* > 'systema,tizer, 'systema,tiser, 'system,izer *or* 'system,iser *n*

systematology (,sɪstɪmə'tɒlədʒɪ) *n* the study of the nature and formation of systems

system building *n* a method of building in which prefabricated components are used to speed the construction of buildings > **system built** *adj*

Système International d'Unités (*French* sistɛm ɛ̃tɛrnasjɔnal dynite) *n* the International System of units. See **SI unit**

systemic (sɪ'stɛmɪk, -'stiː-) *adj* **1** another word for **systematic** (senses 1, 2) **2** *physiol* (of a poison, disease, etc) affecting the entire body **3** (of a pesticide, fungicide, etc) spreading through all the parts of a plant and making it toxic to pests or parasites without destroying it ▷ *n* **4** a systemic pesticide, fungicide, etc > **sys'temically** *adv*

systemic availability *n* another name for **bioavailability**

systemic grammar *n* a grammar in which description is founded on the relationships among the various units at different ranks of a language, and in which language is viewed as a system of meaning-creating choices. Compare **transformational grammar, case grammar**

systems analysis *n* the analysis of the requirements of a task and the expression of those requirements in a form that permits the assembly of computer hardware and software to perform the task > **systems analyst** *n*

systems disk *n* a disk used to store computer programs, esp the basic operating programs of a computer

systems engineering *n* the branch of engineering, based on systems analysis and information theory, concerned with the design of integrated systems

systems theory *n* an approach to industrial relations which likens the enterprise to an organism with interdependent parts, each with its own specific function and interrelated responsibilities

systole ('sɪstəlɪ) *n* contraction of the heart, during which blood is pumped into the aorta and the arteries that lead to the lungs. Compare **diastole** [c16 via Late Latin from Greek *sustolē*, from *sustellein* to contract; see SYSTALTIC] > **systolic** (sɪ'stɒlɪk) *adj*

syver *or* **siver** ('saɪvər) *n Scot* **1** a street drain or the grating over it **2** a street gutter [c17 of uncertain origin]

Syzran (*Russian* 'sizrənj) *n* a port in W central Russia, on the Volga River: oil refining. Pop: 191 000 (2005 est)

syzygy ('sɪzɪdʒɪ) *n, pl* **-gies 1** either of the two positions (conjunction or opposition) of a celestial body when sun, earth, and the body lie in a straight line: *the moon is at syzygy when full* **2** (in classical prosody) a metrical unit of two feet **3** *rare* any pair, usually of opposites **4** *biology* the aggregation in a mass of certain protozoans, esp when occurring before sexual reproduction [c17 from Late Latin *syzygia*, from Greek *suzugia*, from *suzugos* yoked together, from SYN- + *zugon* a yoke] > **syzygial** (sɪ'zɪdʒɪəl), **syzygetic** (,sɪzɪ'dʒɛtɪk) *or* **syzygal** ('sɪzɪgəl) *adj* > ,syzy'getically *adv*

sz *the internet domain name for* Swaziland

Szabadka ('sɔbɔtkɔ) *n* the Hungarian name for **Subotica**

Szczecin (*Polish* 'ʃtʃetsin) *n* a port in NW Poland, on the River Oder: the busiest Polish port and leading coal exporter; shipbuilding. Pop: 435 000 (2005 est). German name: **Stettin**

Szechuan *or* **Szechwan** ('sɪtʃwɑːn) *n* a variant transliteration of the Chinese name for **Sichuan**

Szeged (*Hungarian* 'sɛgɛd) *n* an industrial city in S Hungary, on the Tisza River. Pop: 162 860 (2003 est)

Szombathely (*Hungarian* 'sombɔthɛj) *n* a city in W Hungary: site of the Roman capital of Pannonia. Pop: 81 113 (2003 est)

Tt

t or **T** (tiː) *n, pl* **t's, T's** or **Ts** **1** the 20th letter and 16th consonant of the modern English alphabet **2** a speech sound represented by this letter, usually a voiceless alveolar stop, as in *tame* **3 a** something shaped like a T **b** (*in combination*): *a T-junction* **4 to a T** in every detail; perfectly: *the work suited her to a T*

t *symbol for* **1** tonne(s) **2** troy (weight) **3** *statistics* distribution **4** *statistics* See **Student's t**

T *symbol for* **1** absolute temperature **2** tera- **3** *chem* tritium **4** *biochem* thymine **5** tesla **6** surface tension **7** *international car registration for* Thailand

t. *abbreviation for* **1** *commerce* tare **2** teaspoon(ful) **3** temperature **4** *music* tempo [Latin: in the time of] **5** tenor **6** *grammar* tense **7** ton(s) **8** transitive

't *contraction of* it

T- *abbreviation for* trainer (aircraft): *T-37*

ta (taː) *interj Brit informal* thank you [c18 imitative of baby talk]

Ta *the chemical symbol for* tantalum

TA (*in Britain*) *abbreviation for* Territorial Army (now superseded by **TAVR**)

taal (taːl) *n* **the South African** language: usually, by implication, Afrikaans [Afrikaans from Dutch]

Taal (taːˈaːl) *n* an active volcano in the Philippines, on S Luzon on an island in the centre of **Lake Taal**. Height: 300 m (984 ft). Area of lake: 243 sq km (94 sq miles)

taata ('tata) *n E African* a child's word for **father**

tab¹ (tæb) *n* **1** a small flap of material, esp one on a garment for decoration or for fastening to a button **2** any similar flap, such as a piece of paper attached to a file for identification **3** a small auxiliary aerofoil on the trailing edge of a rudder, aileron, or elevator, etc, to assist in the control of the aircraft in flight. See also **trim tab 4** *Brit military* the insignia on the collar of a staff officer **5** *chiefly US and Canadian* a bill, esp one for a meal or drinks **6** *Scot and northern English dialect* a cigarette **7 keep tabs on** *informal* to keep a watchful eye on ▷ *vb* **tabs, tabbing, tabbed 8** (*tr*) to supply (files, clothing, etc) with a tab or tabs [c17 of unknown origin]

tab² (tæb) *n* **1** short for **tabulator** or **tablet 2** *slang* a portion of a drug, esp LSD or ecstasy

TAB *abbreviation for* **1** typhoid-paratyphoid A and B (vaccine) **2** *Austral and NZ* Totalizator Agency Board

tab. *abbreviation for* table (list or chart)

tabanid ('tæbənɪd) *n* any stout-bodied fly of the dipterous family *Tabanidae,* the females of which have mouthparts specialized for sucking blood: includes the horseflies [c19 from Latin *tabānus* horsefly]

tabard ('tæbəd) *n* a sleeveless or short-sleeved jacket, esp one worn by a herald, bearing a coat of arms, or by a knight over his armour [c13 from Old French *tabart,* of uncertain origin]

tabaret ('tæbərɪt) *n* a hard-wearing fabric of silk or similar cloth with stripes of satin or moire, used esp for upholstery [c19 perhaps from TABBY¹]

Tabasco¹ (təˈbæskəʊ) *n trademark* a very hot red sauce made from matured capsicums

Tabasco² (*Spanish* taˈβasko) *n* a state in SE Mexico, on the Gulf of Campeche: mostly flat and marshy with extensive jungles; hot and humid climate. Capital: Villahermosa. Pop: 1 889 367 (2000). Area: 24 661 sq km (9520 sq miles)

tabbouleh or **tabbouli** (təˈbuːlɪ) *n* a kind of Middle Eastern salad made with cracked wheat, mint, parsley, and usually cucumber [c20 from Arabic *tabbūla*]

tabby¹ ('tæbɪ) *n* a fabric with a watered pattern, esp silk or taffeta [c17 from Old French *tabis* silk cloth, from Arabic *al-'attabiya,* literally: the quarter of (Prince) 'Attab, the part of Baghdad where the fabric was first made]

tabby² ('tæbɪ) *adj* **1** (esp of cats) brindled with dark stripes or wavy markings on a lighter background **2** having a wavy or striped pattern, particularly in colours of grey and brown ▷ *n, pl* -bies **3** a tabby cat **4** any female domestic cat **5** *Brit informal* a gossiping old woman **6** *Austral slang* any girl or woman [c17 from *Tabby,* pet form of the girl's name *Tabitha,* probably influenced by TABBY¹]

tabernacle ('tæbə,nækᵊl) *n* **1** (*often capital*) *Old Testament* **a** the portable sanctuary in the form of a tent in which the ancient Israelites carried the Ark of the Covenant (Exodus 25–27) **b** the Jewish Temple regarded as the shrine of the divine presence **2** *Judaism* an English word for **sukkah 3** a meeting place for worship used by Mormons or Nonconformists **4** a small ornamented cupboard or box used for the reserved sacrament of the Eucharist **5** the human body regarded as the temporary dwelling of the soul **6** *chiefly RC Church* a canopied niche or recess forming the shrine of a statue **7** *nautical* a strong framework for holding the foot of a mast stepped on deck, allowing it to be swung down horizontally to pass under low bridges, etc [c13 from Latin *tabernāculum* a tent, from *taberna* a hut; see TAVERN] ▷ ,taber'nacular *adj*

Tabernacles ('tæbə,nækᵊlz) *pl n Judaism* an English name for **Sukkoth**

tabes ('teɪbiːz) *n, pl* **tabes 1** a wasting of a bodily organ or part **2** short for **tabes dorsalis** [c17 from Latin: a wasting away] > **tabetic** (təˈbɛtɪk) *adj*

tabescent (təˈbɛsᵊnt) *adj* **1** progressively emaciating; wasting away **2** of, relating to, or having tabes [c19 from Latin *tabēscere,* from TABES] > ta'bescence *n*

tabes dorsalis (dɔːˈsɑːlɪs) *n* a form of late syphilis that attacks the spinal cord causing degeneration of the nerve fibres, pains in the legs, paralysis of the leg muscles, acute abdominal pain, etc. Also called: **locomotor ataxia** [New Latin, literally: tabes of the back; see TABES, DORSAL]

tab-hang *vb Midland English dialect* to eavesdrop

tabla ('tʌblə, 'taːblaː) *n* a musical instrument of India consisting of a pair of drums whose pitches can be varied [Hindu, from Arabic *tabla* drum]

tablature ('tæblətʃə) *n* **1** *music* any of a number of forms of musical notation, esp for playing the lute, consisting of letters and signs indicating rhythm and fingering **2** an engraved or painted tablet or other flat surface [c16 from French, ultimately from Latin *tabulātum* wooden floor, from *tabula* a plank]

table ('teɪbᵊl) *n* **1** a flat horizontal slab or board, usually supported by one or more legs, on which objects may be placed. Related adj: **mensal 2 a** such a slab or board on which food is served: *we were six at table* **b** (*as modifier*): *table linen* **c** (*in combination*): *a tablecloth* **3** food as served in a particular household or restaurant: *a good table* **4** such a piece of furniture specially designed for any of various purposes: *a backgammon table; bird table* **5 a** a company of persons assembled for a meal, game, etc **b** (*as modifier*): *table talk* **6** any flat or level area, such as a plateau **7** a rectangular panel set below or above the face of a wall **8** *architect* another name for **cordon** (sense 4) **9** an upper horizontal facet of a cut gem **10** *music* the sounding board of a violin, guitar, or similar stringed instrument **11 a** an arrangement of words, numbers, or signs, usually in parallel columns, to display data or relations: *a table of contents* **b** See **multiplication table 12** a tablet on which laws were inscribed by the ancient Romans, the Hebrews, etc **13** *palmistry* an area of the palm's surface bounded by four lines **14** *printing* a slab of smooth metal on which ink is rolled to its proper consistency **15 a** either of the two bony plates that form the inner and outer parts of the flat bones of the cranium **b** any thin flat plate, esp of bone **16 on the table** put forward for discussion and acceptance: *we currently have our final offer on the table* **17 turn the tables on (someone)** to cause a complete reversal of circumstances, esp to defeat or get the better of (someone) who was previously in a stronger position ▷ *vb* (*tr*) **18** to place on a table **19** *Brit* to submit (a bill, etc) for consideration by a legislative body **20** *US* to suspend discussion of (a bill, etc) indefinitely or for some time **21** to enter in or form into a list; tabulate [c12 via Old French from Latin *tabula* a writing tablet] > 'tableful *n* > 'tableless *adj*

tableau ('tæbləʊ) *n, pl* **-leaux** (-ləʊ, -ləʊz) or **-leaus 1** See **tableau vivant 2** a pause during or at the end of a scene on stage when all the performers briefly freeze in position **3** any dramatic group or scene **4** *logic* short for **semantic tableau** [c17 from French, from Old French *tablel* a picture, diminutive of TABLE]

tableau vivant *French* (tablo vivã) *n, pl* **tableaux vivants** (tablo vivã) a representation of a scene, painting, sculpture, etc, by a person or group posed silent and motionless [c19 literally: living picture]

Table Bay *n* the large bay on which Cape Town is situated, on the SW coast of South Africa

tablecloth ('teɪbᵊl,klɒθ) *n* a cloth for covering the

top of a table, esp during meals

table dancing *n* a form of entertainment in which naked or scantily dressed women dance erotically at the tables of individual members of the audience, who must remain seated > **table dancer** *n*

table d'hôte ('tɑːbᵊl 'dəʊt; *French* tablə dot) *adj* **1** (of a meal) consisting of a set number of courses with limited choice of dishes offered at a fixed price. Compare **à la carte**, **prix fixe** ▷ *n, pl* **tables d'hôte** ('tɑːblz 'dəʊt; *French* tablə dot) **2** a table d'hôte meal or menu [C17 from French, literally: the host's table]

table football *n* a game based on soccer, played on a table with sets of miniature human figures mounted on rods allowing them to be tilted or spun to strike the ball. US name: **foosball**

tableland ('teɪbᵊlˌlænd) *n* flat elevated land; a plateau

table licence *n* a licence authorizing the sale of alcoholic drinks with meals only

table money *n* an allowance for official entertaining of visitors, etc, esp in the army

Table Mountain *n* a mountain in SW South Africa, overlooking Cape Town and Table Bay: flat-topped and steep-sided. Height: 1087 m (3567 ft)

table napkin *n* See **napkin** (sense 1)

table-rapping *n* the sounds of knocking or tapping made without any apparent physical agency while a group of people sit round a table, and attributed by spiritualists to the spirit of a dead person using this as a means of communication with the living

table salt *n* salt that is used at table rather than for cooking

tablespoon ('teɪbᵊlˌspuːn) *n* **1** a spoon, larger than a dessertspoon, used for serving food, etc **2** Also called: **tablespoonful** the amount contained in such a spoon **3** a unit of capacity used in cooking, medicine, etc, equal to half a fluid ounce or three teaspoons

tablet ('tæblɪt) *n* **1** a medicinal formulation made of a compressed powdered substance containing an active drug and excipients **2** a flattish cake of some substance, such as soap **3** *Scot* a sweet made of butter, sugar, and condensed milk, usually shaped in a flat oblong block **4** a slab of stone, wood, etc, esp one formerly used for inscriptions **5 a** a thinner rigid sheet, as of bark, ivory, etc, used for similar purposes **b** (*often plural*) a set or pair of these fastened together, as in a book **6** a pad of writing paper **7** *NZ* a token giving right of way to the driver of a train on a single line section [C14 from Old French *tablete* a little table, from Latin *tabula* a board]

table talk *n* informal conversation on a range of topics, as that at table during and after a meal

table tennis *n* a miniature form of tennis played on a table with small bats and a light hollow ball

table-turning *n* **1** the movement of a table attributed by spiritualists to the power of spirits working through a group of persons placing their hands or fingers on the table top **2** *often derogatory* spiritualism in general

tableware ('teɪbᵊlˌwɛə) *n* articles such as dishes, plates, knives, forks, etc, used at meals

table wine *n* a wine considered suitable for drinking with a meal

tabloid ('tæblɔɪd) *n* **1** a newspaper with pages about 30 cm (12 inches) by 40 cm (16 inches), usually characterized by an emphasis on photographs and a concise and often sensational style. Compare **broadsheet 2** (*modifier*) designed to appeal to a mass audience or readership; sensationalist: *the tabloid press; tabloid television* [C20 from earlier *Tabloid*, a trademark for a medicine in tablet form]

taboo *or* **tabu** (tə'buː) *adj* **1** forbidden or disapproved of; placed under a social prohibition or ban: *taboo words* **2** (in Polynesia and other islands of the South Pacific) marked off as simultaneously sacred and forbidden ▷ *n, pl* -**boos**

or -**bus 3** any prohibition resulting from social or other conventions **4** ritual restriction or prohibition, esp of something that is considered holy or unclean ▷ *vb* **5** (*tr*) to place under a taboo [C18 from Tongan *tapu*]

tabor *or* **tabour** ('teɪbə) *n music* a small drum used esp in the Middle Ages, struck with one hand while the other held a three-holed pipe. See **pipe¹** (sense 7) [C13 from Old French *tabour*, perhaps from Persian *tabīr*] > **taborer** *or* **tabourer** *n*

Tabor ('teɪbə) *n* **Mount** a mountain in N Israel, near Nazareth: traditionally regarded as the mountain where the Transfiguration took place. Height: 588 m (1929 ft)

taboret *or* **tabouret** ('tæbərɪt) *n* **1** a low stool, originally in the shape of a drum **2** a frame, usually round, for stretching out cloth while it is being embroidered **3** Also called: **taborin**, **tabourin** ('tæbərɪn) a small tabor [C17 from French *tabouret*, diminutive of TABOR]

Tabriz (tæ'briːz) *n* a city in NW Iran: an ancient city, situated in a volcanic region of hot springs; university (1947); carpet manufacturing. Pop: 1 396 000 (2005 est.). Ancient name: **Tauris** ('tɔːrɪs)

tabular ('tæbjʊlə) *adj* **1** arranged in systematic or table form **2** calculated from or by means of a table **3** like a table in form; flat [C17 from Latin *tabulāris* concerning boards, from *tabula* a board] > **tabularly** *adv*

tabula rasa ('tæbjʊlə 'rɑːsə) *n, pl* **tabulae rasae** ('tæbjʊliː 'rɑːsiː) **1** (esp in the philosophy of Locke) the mind in its uninformed original state **2** an opportunity for a fresh start; clean slate [Latin: a scraped tablet (one from which the writing has been erased)]

tabulate *vb* ('tæbjʊˌleɪt) (*tr*) **1** Also: **tabularize** ('tæbjʊləˌraɪz) to set out, arrange, or write in tabular form **2** to form or cut with a flat surface ▷ *adj* ('tæbjʊlɪt, -ˌleɪt) **3** having a flat surface **4** (of certain corals) having transverse skeletal plates [C18 from Latin *tabula* a board] > **tabulable** *adj* > **tabu'lation** *n*

tabulator ('tæbjʊˌleɪtə) *n* **1** a device for setting the automatic stops that locate the column margins on a typewriter **2** *computing* a machine that reads data from one medium, such as punched cards, producing lists, tabulations, or totals, usually on a continuous sheet of paper **3** any machine that tabulates data

tabun (tɑː'buːn) *n* an organic compound used in chemical warfare as a lethal nerve gas. Formula: $C_2H_5OP(O)(CN)N(CH_3)_2$ [C20 from German, of uncertain origin]

TAC (in South Africa) *abbreviation for* Treatment Action Campaign, a pressure group that campaigns for the medical rights of pregnant women with HIV or AIDS

tacamahac ('tækəməˌhæk) *or* **tacmahack** *n* **1** any of several strong-smelling resinous gums obtained from certain trees, used in making ointments, incense, etc **2** any tree yielding this resin, esp the balsam poplar [C16 from Spanish *tacamahaca*, from Nahuatl *tecomahca* aromatic resin]

Tacan ('tækən) *n* an electronic ultrahigh-frequency navigation system for aircraft which gives a continuous indication of bearing and distance from a transmitting station [C20 *tac(tical) a(ir) n(avigation)*]

tace (tæs, teɪs) *n* a less common word for **tasset**

tacet ('teɪsɛt, 'tæs-) *vb* (*intr*) (on a musical score) a direction indicating that a particular instrument or singer does not take part in a movement or part of a movement [C18 from Latin: it is silent, from *tacēre* to be quiet]

tache¹ (tæʃ, tɑːʃ) *n archaic* a buckle, clasp, or hook [C17 from Old French, of Germanic origin; compare TACK¹]

tache² (tæʃ) *n informal* short for **moustache**

tacheo- *combining form* a variant of **tachy-**

tacheometer (ˌtækɪ'ɒmɪtə) *or* **tachymeter** *n surveying* a type of theodolite designed for the

rapid measurement of distances, elevations, and directions

tacheometry (ˌtækɪ'ɒmɪtrɪ) *or* **tachymetry** *n surveying* the measurement of distance, etc, using a tacheometer > **tacheometric** (ˌtækɪə'mɛtrɪk), ˌtacheo'metrical, ˌtachy'metric *or* ˌtachy'metrical *adj* > ˌtacheo'metrically *or* ˌtachy'metrically *adv*

tachina fly ('tækɪnə) *n* any bristly fly of the dipterous family *Tachinidae*, the larvae of which live parasitically in caterpillars, beetles, hymenopterans, and other insects [C19 via New Latin *Tachina*, from Greek *takhinos* swift, from *takhos* fleetness]

tachisme ('tɑːʃɪzəm; *French* taʃism) *n* a type of action painting evolved in France in which haphazard dabs and blots of colour are treated as a means of instinctive or unconscious expression [C20 French, from *tache* stain]

tachistoscope (tə'kɪstəˌskəʊp) *n* an instrument, used mainly in experiments on perception and memory, for displaying visual images for very brief intervals, usually a fraction of a second [C20 from Greek *takhistos* swiftest (see TACHY-) + -SCOPE] > **tachistoscopic** (təˌkɪstə'skɒpɪk) *adj* > taˌchisto'scopically *adv*

tacho- *combining form* speed: *tachograph; tachometer* [from Greek *takhos*]

tachograph ('tækəˌɡrɑːf, -ˌɡræf) *n* a tachometer that produces a graphical record (**tachogram**) of its readings, esp a device for recording the speed of and distance covered by a heavy goods vehicle. Often shortened to: **tacho**

tachometer (tæ'kɒmɪtə) *n* any device for measuring speed, esp the rate of revolution of a shaft. Tachometers (rev counters) are often fitted to cars to indicate the number of revolutions per minute of the engine > **tachometric** (ˌtækə'mɛtrɪk) *or* ˌtacho'metrical *adj* > ˌtacho'metrically *adv* > ta'chometry *n*

tachy- *or* **tacheo-** *combining form* swift or accelerated: *tachycardia; tachygraphy; tachylyte; tachyon; tachyphylaxis* [from Greek *takhus* swift]

tachycardia (ˌtækɪ'kɑːdɪə) *n pathol* abnormally rapid beating of the heart, esp over 100 beats per minute. Compare **bradycardia**. > **tachycardiac** (ˌtækɪ'kɑːdɪˌæk) *adj*

tachygraphy (tæ'kɪɡrəfɪ) *n* shorthand, esp as used in ancient Rome or Greece > **ta'chygrapher** *or* **ta'chygraphist** *n* > **tachygraphic** (ˌtækɪ'ɡræfɪk) *adj* > ˌtachy'graphically *adv*

tachylyte *or* **tachylite** ('tækɪˌlaɪt) *n* a black basaltic glass often found on the edges of intrusions of basalt [C19 from German *Tachylit*, from TACHY- + Greek *lutos* soluble, melting, from *luein* to release; so called because it fuses easily when heated. The form *tachylite* is influenced by -LITE stone] > **tachylytic** (ˌtækɪ'lɪtɪk) *or* ˌtachy'litic *adj*

tachymeter (tæ'kɪmɪtə) *n* another name for **tacheometer**

tachymetry (tæ'kɪmɪtrɪ) *n* another name for **tacheometry**

tachyon ('tækɪˌɒn) *n physics* a hypothetical elementary particle capable of travelling faster than the velocity of light [C20 from TACHY- + -ON]

tachyphylaxis (ˌtækɪfɪ'læksɪs) *n* very rapid development of tolerance or immunity to the effects of a drug [New Latin, from TACHY- + *phylaxis* on the model of *prophylaxis*. See PROPHYLACTIC]

tachypnoea *or* US **tachypnea** (ˌtækɪp'nɪə) *n pathol* abnormally rapid breathing

tacit ('tæsɪt) *adj* **1** implied or inferred without direct expression; understood: *a tacit agreement* **2** created or having effect by operation of law, rather than by being directly expressed [C17 from Latin *tacitus*, past participle of *tacēre* to be silent] > 'tacitly *adv* > 'tacitness *n*

taciturn ('tæsɪˌtɜːn) *adj* habitually silent, reserved, or uncommunicative; not inclined to conversation [C18 from Latin *taciturnus*, from *tacitus* silent, from *tacēre* to be silent] > ˌtaci'turnity *n* > 'taciˌturnly *adv*

tack[1] (tæk) *n* **1** a short sharp-pointed nail, usually with a flat and comparatively large head **2** *Brit* a long loose temporary stitch used in dressmaking, etc **3** See **tailor's-tack** **4** a temporary fastening **5** stickiness, as of newly applied paint, varnish, etc **6** *nautical* the heading of a vessel sailing to windward, stated in terms of the side of the sail against which the wind is pressing **7** *nautical* **a** a course sailed by a sailing vessel with the wind blowing from forward of the beam **b** one such course or a zigzag pattern of such courses **8** *nautical* **a** a sheet for controlling the weather clew of a course **b** the weather clew itself **9** *nautical* the forward lower clew of a fore-and-aft sail **10** a course of action differing from some previous course: *he went off on a fresh tack* **11 on the wrong tack** under a false impression ▷ *vb* **12** (*tr*) to secure by a tack or series of tacks **13** *Brit* to sew (something) with long loose temporary stitches **14** (*tr*) to attach or append: *tack this letter onto the other papers* **15** *nautical* to change the heading of (a sailing vessel) to the opposite tack **16** *nautical* to steer (a sailing vessel) on alternate tacks **17** (*intr*) *nautical* (of a sailing vessel) to proceed on a different tack or to alternate tacks **18** (*intr*) to follow a zigzag route; keep changing one's course of action [C14 *tak* fastening, nail; related to Middle Low German *tacke* pointed instrument] > **'tacker** *n* > **'tackless** *adj*

tack[2] (tæk) *n informal* food, esp when regarded as inferior or distasteful. See also **hardtack** [C19 of unknown origin]

tack[3] (tæk) *n* **a** a riding harness for horses, such as saddles, bridles, etc **b** (*as modifier*): *the tack room* [C20 shortened from TACKLE]

tack[4] (tæk) *n Scot* **1** a lease **2** an area of land held on a lease [C15 from *tak* a Scots word for *take*]

tacker ('tækə) *n Austral slang* a young person; child

tacket ('tækɪt) *n Scot and northern English dialect* a nail, esp a hobnail [C14 from TACK[1]] > **'tackety** *adj*

tack hammer *n* a light hammer for driving tacks

tackies or **takkies** ('tækɪz) *pl n, sing* **tacky** *South African informal* tennis shoes or plimsolls [C20 probably from TACKY[1], with reference to their nonslip rubber soles]

tackle ('tækᵊl; *Nautical often* 'teɪkᵊl) *n* **1** any mechanical system for lifting or pulling, esp an arrangement of ropes and pulleys designed to lift heavy weights **2** the equipment required for a particular occupation, etc: *fishing tackle* **3** *nautical* the halyards and other running rigging aboard a vessel **4** *slang* a man's genitals **5** *sport* a physical challenge to an opponent, as to prevent his progress with the ball **6** *American football* a defensive lineman ▷ *vb* **7** (*tr*) to undertake (a task, problem, etc) **8** (*tr*) to confront (a person, esp an opponent) with a difficult proposition **9** *sport* (esp in football games) to challenge (an opponent) with a tackle [C13 related to Middle Low German *takel* ship's rigging, Middle Dutch *taken* to TAKE] > **'tackler** *n*

tack rag *n building trades* a cotton cloth impregnated with an oil, used to remove dust from a surface prior to painting

tack room *n* a room in a stable building in which bridles, saddles, etc are kept

tacksman ('tæksmən) *n, pl* **-men** a leaseholder, esp a tenant in the Highlands who sublets [C16 from TACK[4]]

tack welding *n engineering* short intermittent welds made to hold components in place before full welding is begun

tacky[1] or **tackey** ('tækɪ) *adj* **tackier, tackiest** slightly sticky or adhesive: *the varnish was still tacky* [C18 from TACK[1] (in the sense: stickiness)] > **'tackily** *adv* > **'tackiness** *n*

tacky[2] ('tækɪ) *adj* **tackier, tackiest** *informal* **1** shabby or shoddy **2** ostentatious and vulgar **3** *US* (of a person) dowdy; seedy [C19 from dialect *tacky* an inferior horse, of unknown origin] > **'tackiness** *n*

tacmahack ('tækmə,hæk) *n* a variant of **tacamahac**

Tacna-Arica (*Spanish* 'taknaa'rika) *n* a coastal desert region of W South America, long disputed by Chile and Peru: divided in 1929 into the Peruvian department of Tacna and the Chilean department of Arica

tacnode ('tæk,nəʊd) *n* another name for **osculation** (sense 1) [C19 from Latin *tactus* touch (from *tangere* to touch) + NODE]

taco ('tɑːkəʊ) *n, pl* **-cos** *Mexican cookery* a tortilla folded into a roll with a filling and usually fried [from Mexican Spanish, from Spanish: literally, a snack, a bite to eat]

Tacoma (tə'kəʊmə) *n* a port in W Washington, on Puget Sound: industrial centre. Pop: 196 790 (2003 est)

taconite ('tækə,naɪt) *n* a fine-grained sedimentary rock containing magnetite, haematite, and silica, which occurs in the Lake Superior region: a low-grade iron ore [C20 named after the *Taconic* Mountains in New England]

tact (tækt) *n* **1** a sense of what is fitting and considerate in dealing with others, so as to avoid giving offence or to win good will; discretion **2** skill or judgment in handling difficult or delicate situations; diplomacy [C17 from Latin *tactus* a touching, from *tangere* to touch] > **'tactful** *adj* > **'tactfully** *adv* > **'tactfulness** *n* > **'tactless** *adj* > **'tactlessly** *adv* > **'tactlessness** *n*

tactic ('tæktɪk) *n* a piece of tactics; tactical move. See also **tactics**

-tactic *adj combining form* having a specified kind of pattern or arrangement or having an orientation determined by a specified force: *syndiotactic; phototactic* [from Greek *taktikos* relating to order or arrangement; see TACTICS]

tactical ('tæktɪkᵊl) *adj* **1** of, relating to, or employing tactics: *a tactical error* **2** (of weapons, attacks, etc) used in or supporting limited military operations: *a tactical missile* **3** skilful or diplomatic > **'tactically** *adv*

tactical voting *n* (in an election) the practice of casting one's vote not for the party of one's choice but for the second strongest contender in order to defeat the likeliest winner

tactics ('tæktɪks) *pl n* **1** (*functioning as singular*) *military* the art and science of the detailed direction and control of movement or manoeuvre of forces in battle to achieve an aim or task **2** the manoeuvres used or plans followed to achieve a particular short-term aim [C17 from New Latin *tactica*, from Greek *ta taktika* the matters of arrangement, neuter plural of *taktikos* concerning arrangement or order, from *taktos* arranged (for battle), from *tassein* to arrange] > **tac'tician** *n*

tactile ('tæktaɪl) *adj* **1** of, relating to, affecting, or having a sense of touch: *a tactile organ; tactile stimuli* **2** *now rare* capable of being touched; tangible [C17 from Latin *tactilis*, from *tangere* to touch] > **tactility** (tæk'tɪlɪtɪ) *n*

taction ('tækʃən) *n obsolete* the act of touching; contact [C17 from Latin *tactiō* a touching, from *tangere* to touch]

tactual ('tæktjʊəl) *adj* **1** caused by touch; causing a tactile sensation **2** of or relating to the tactile sense or the organs of touch [C17 from Latin *tactus* a touching; see TACT] > **'tactually** *adv*

tad (tæd) *n informal* **1** *US and Canadian* a small boy; lad **2** *US and Canadian* a small bit or piece **3 a tad** a little; rather: *she may be a tad short but she got a top modelling job* [C20 short for TADPOLE]

Tadmor ('tædmɔː) *n* the biblical name for **Palmyra**

tadpole ('tæd,pəʊl) *n* the aquatic larva of frogs, toads, etc, which develops from a limbless tailed form with external gills into a form with internal gills, limbs, and a reduced tail [C15 *taddepol*, from *tadde* TOAD + *pol* head, POLL]

Tadzhik or **Tadjik** ('tɑːdʒɪk, tɑː'dʒiːk) *n, pl* **-dzhik** or **-djik** variant spellings of **Tajik**

Tadzhikistan or **Tadjikistan** (tɑː,dʒɪkɪ'stɑːn, -stæn) *n* variant spellings of **Tajikistan**

tae[1] (te) *prep, adv* a Scot word for **to**

tae[2] (te) *adv* a Scot word for **too**

tae[3] (te) *n* a Scot word for **toe**

Tae Bo ('taɪ 'bəʊ) *n* a form of exercise based on martial arts movements [C20 from TAE (KWON DO) + BO(XING)]

taedium vitae ('tiːdɪəm 'viːtaɪ, 'vaɪtiː) *n* the feeling that life is boring and dull [Latin, literally: weariness of life]

Taegu (tɛ'guː) *n* a city in SE South Korea: textile and agricultural trading centre. Pop: 2 510 000 (2005 est)

Taejon (tɛ'dʒɒn) *n* a city in W South Korea: market centre of an agricultural region. Pop: 1 464 000 (2005 est)

tae kwon do ('taɪ 'kwɒn 'dəʊ, 'teɪ) *n* a Korean martial art that resembles karate [C20 Korean *tae* kick + *kwon* fist + *do* way, method]

tael (teɪl) *n* **1** a unit of weight, used in the Far East, having various values between one to two and a half ounces **2** (formerly) a Chinese monetary unit equivalent in value to a tael weight of standard silver [C16 from Portuguese, from Malay *tahil* weight, perhaps from Hindi *tolā* weight of a new rupee, from Sanskrit *tulā* weight]

ta'en (teɪn) *vb* a poetic contraction of **taken**

taenia or *US* **tenia** ('tiːnɪə) *n, pl* **-niae** (-nɪ,iː) **1** (in ancient Greece) a narrow fillet or headband for the hair **2** *architect* the fillet between the architrave and frieze of a Doric entablature **3** *anatomy* any bandlike structure or part **4** any tapeworm of the genus *Taenia*, such as *T. soleum*, a parasite of man that uses the pig as its intermediate host [C16 via Latin from Greek *tainia* narrow strip; related to Greek *teinein* to stretch]

taeniacide or *US* **teniacide** ('tiːnɪə,saɪd) *n* a substance, esp a drug, that kills tapeworms

taeniafuge or *US* **teniafuge** ('tiːnɪə,fjuːdʒ) *n* a substance, esp a drug, that expels tapeworms from the body of their host

taeniasis or *US* **teniasis** (tiː'naɪəsɪs) *n pathol* infestation with tapeworms of the genus *Taenia*

TAFE ('tæfɪ) *n* (in Australia) ▷ *acronym for* Technical and Further Education

Tafelwein ('tɑːfəl,vaɪn) *n* German table wine [C20 from German *Tafel* table + *Wein* wine]

taffeta ('tæfɪtə) *n* **1 a** a crisp lustrous plain-weave silk, rayon, etc, used esp for women's clothes **b** (*as modifier*): *a taffeta petticoat* **2** any of various similar fabrics [C14 from Medieval Latin *taffata*, from Persian *tāftah* spun, from *tāftan* to spin]

taffrail ('tæf,reɪl) *n nautical* **1** a rail at the stern or above the transom of a vessel **2** the upper part of the transom of a vessel, esp a sailing vessel, often ornately decorated [C19 changed (through influence of RAIL[1]) from earlier *tafferel*, from Dutch *taffereel* panel (hence applied to the part of a vessel decorated with carved panels), variant of *tafeleel* (unattested), from *tafel* TABLE]

taffy ('tæfɪ) *n, pl* **-fies** **1** *US and Canadian* a chewy sweet made of brown sugar or molasses and butter, boiled and then pulled so that it becomes glossy **2** *chiefly US and Canadian* a less common term for **toffee** [C19 perhaps from TAFIA]

Taffy ('tæfɪ) *n, pl* **-fies** a slang word or nickname for a Welshman [C17 from the supposed Welsh pronunciation of *Davy* (from *David*, Welsh *Dafydd*), a common Welsh Christian name]

tafia or **taffia** ('tæfɪə) *n* a type of rum, esp from Guyana or the Caribbean [C18 from French, from West Indian Creole, probably from RATAFIA]

Tafilelt (tæ'fiːlɛlt) or **Tafilalet** (,tæfɪ'lɑːlɛt) *n* an oasis in SE Morocco, the largest in the Sahara. Area: about 1300 sq km (500 sq miles)

tag[1] (tæg) *n* **1** a piece or strip of paper, plastic, leather, etc, for attaching to something by one end as a mark or label: *a price tag* **2** an electronic device worn, usually on the wrist or ankle, by an offender serving a noncustodial sentence, which monitors the offender's whereabouts by means of a link to a central computer through the telephone system. Also called: **electronic tag 3** a small piece of material hanging from or loosely attached to a part or piece **4** a point of metal or other hard substance at the end of a cord, lace, etc, to prevent it from fraying and to facilitate threading **5** an epithet or verbal appendage, the refrain of a song, the moral of a fable, etc **6** a brief quotation, esp one in a foreign language: *his speech was interlarded with Horatian tags* **7** *grammar* **a** Also called: **tag question** a clause added on to another clause to invite the hearer's agreement or conversational cooperation. Tags are usually in the form of a question with a pronoun as subject, the antecedent of which is the subject of the main clause; as *isn't it in the bread is on the table, isn't it?* **b** a linguistic item added on to a sentence but not forming part of it, as *John in are you there, John?* **8** an ornamental flourish as at the end of a signature **9** the contrastingly coloured tip to an animal's tail **10** a matted lock of wool or hair **11** *angling* a strand of tinsel, wire, etc, tied to the body of an artificial fly **12** *slang* a graffito consisting of a nickname or personal symbol ▷ *vb* **tags, tagging, tagged** (*mainly tr*) **13** to mark with a tag **14** to monitor the whereabouts of (an offender) by means of an electronic tag **15** to add or append as a tag **16** to supply (prose or blank verse) with rhymes **17** (*intr*; usually foll by *on* or *along*) to trail (behind): *many small boys tagged on behind the procession* **18** to name or call (someone something): *they tagged him Lanky* **19** to cut the tags of wool or hair from (an animal) **20** *slang* to paint one's tag on (a building, wall, etc) [c15 of uncertain origin; related to Swedish *tagg* point, perhaps also to TACK[1]]

tag[2] (tæg) *n* **1** Also called: **tig** a children's game in which one player chases the others in an attempt to catch one of them who will then become the chaser **2** the act of tagging one's partner in tag wrestling **3** (*modifier*) denoting or relating to a wrestling contest between two teams of two wrestlers, in which only one from each team may be in the ring at one time. The contestant outside the ring may change places with his team-mate inside the ring after touching his hand ▷ *vb* **tags, tagging, tagged** (*tr*) **4** to catch (another child) in the game of tag **5** (in tag wrestling) to touch the hand of (one's partner) [c18 perhaps from TAG[1]]

Tagalog (təˈgɑːlɒg) *n* **1** (*pl* **-logs** *or* **-log**) a member of a people of the Philippines, living chiefly in the region around Manila **2** the language of this people, belonging to the Malayo-Polynesian family: the official language of the Philippines ▷ *adj* **3** of or relating to this people or their language

Taganrog (*Russian* təgan'rɔk) *n* a port in SW Russia, on the **Gulf of Taganrog** (an inlet of the Sea of Azov): founded in 1698 as a naval base and fortress by Peter the Great: industrial centre. Pop: 281 000 (2005 est)

tagareen (təgaːˈriːn) *n* *English dialect* a junk shop
tag end *n* **1** the last part of something: *the tag end of the day* **2** a loose end of cloth, thread, etc
tagetes (tæˈdʒiːtiːz) *n* See **marigold** (sense 1)
taggers (ˈtægəz) *pl n* very thin iron or steel sheet coated with tin [c19 perhaps so called because it was used to make tags for laces]
tagine *or* **tajine** (tæˈʒiːn) *n* **1** a large, heavy N African cooking pot with a conical lid **2** a N African stew with vegetables, olives, lemon, garlic and spices, cooked in a tagine [from Moroccan Arabic *tažin*, from Arabic *tājun* frying pan]
tagliatelle (ˌtæljəˈtɛlɪ) *n* a form of pasta made in narrow strips [Italian, from *tagliare* to cut]
tag line *n* **1** an amusing or memorable phrase designed to catch attention in an advertisement **2** another name for **punch line**
tagma (ˈtægmə) *n*, *pl* **-mata** (-mətə) *zoology* a distinct region of the body of an arthropod, such as the head, thorax, or abdomen of an insect [c19

from Greek: something arranged, from *tassein* to put in order]
tagmeme (ˈtægmiːm) *n* *linguistics* a class of speech elements all of which may fulfil the same grammatical role in a sentence; the minimum unit of analysis in tagmemics [c20 from Greek *tagma* order, from *tassein* to put in order + -EME] ▷ **tag'memic** *adj*
tagmemics (tægˈmiːmɪks) *pl n* (*functioning as singular*) *linguistics* a type of grammatical analysis based on the concept of function in sentence slots and the determination of classes of words that can fill each slot
taguan (ˈtægˌwæn) *n* a large nocturnal flying squirrel, *Petaurista petaurista*, of high forests in the East Indies that uses its long tail as a rudder [c19 its Filipino name]
Tagus (ˈteɪgəs) *n* a river in SW Europe, rising in E central Spain and flowing west to the border with Portugal, then southwest to the Atlantic at Lisbon: the longest river of the Iberian Peninsula. Length: 1007 km (626 miles). Portuguese name: **Tejo** Spanish name: **Tajo**
taha Māori (ˈtɑːhə) *n* NZ a Māori perspective or dimension of a subject [Māori]
tahini (təˈhiːnɪ) *or* **tahina** (təˈhiːnə) *n* a paste made from sesame seeds originating in the Middle East, often used as an ingredient of hummus and other dips [from Arabic]
Tahiti (təˈhiːtɪ) *n* an island in the S Pacific, in the Windward group of the Society Islands: the largest and most important island in French Polynesia; became a French protectorate in 1842 and a colony in 1880. Capital: Papeete. Pop: 169 674 (2002). Area: 1005 sq km (388 sq miles)
Tahitian (təˈhiːtɪən, təˈhiːʃɪən) *adj* **1** of or relating to Tahiti or its inhabitants ▷ *n* **2** a native or inhabitant of Tahiti
Tahltan (ˈtæltən) *n* **1** a member of a North American Indian people inhabiting NW British Columbia **2** the language of this people, belonging to the Athapascan group of the Na-Dene phylum
Tahoe (ˈtɑːhəʊ, ˈteɪ-) *n* **Lake** a lake between E California and W Nevada, in the Sierra Nevada Mountains at an altitude of 1899 m (6229 ft). Area: about 520 sq km (200 sq miles)
tahou (tɑːuːˈhəʊuː) *n* NZ another name for **white-eye** [Māori]
tahr *or* **thar** (tɑː) *n* any of several goatlike bovid mammals of the genus *Hemitragus*, such as *H. jemlahicus* (**Himalayan tahr**), of mountainous regions of S and SW Asia, having a shaggy coat and curved horns [from Nepali *thār*]
tahsil (təˈsiːl) *n* an administrative division of a zila in certain states in India [Urdu, from Arabic: collection]
tahsildar (təˈsiːldɑː) *n* the officer in charge of the collection of revenues, etc, in a tahsil [c18 via Hindi from Persian, from TAHSIL + Persian *-dār* having]
Tai (taɪ) *adj, n* a variant spelling of **Thai**
TAI *abbreviation for* **International Atomic Time**
taiaha (ˈtaɪəˌhɑː) *n* NZ a carved weapon in the form of a staff, now used in Māori ceremonial oratory [Māori]
t'ai chi ch'uan (ˈtaɪ dʒiː ˈtʃwɑːn) *n* a Chinese system of callisthenics characterized by coordinated and rhythmic movements. Often shortened to: **t'ai chi** (ˈtaɪ ˈdʒiː) [Chinese, literally: great art of boxing]
Taichung *or* **T'ai-chung** (ˈtaɪˈtʃʊŋ) *n* a city in W Taiwan: commercial centre of an agricultural region. Pop: 1 066 000 (2005 est)
taig (teɪg) *n* Ulster dialect often derogatory **a** Roman Catholic [variant of the Irish name *Tadhg*, originally signifying any Irishman]
taiga (ˈtaɪgə) *n* the coniferous forests extending across much of subarctic North America and Eurasia, bordered by tundra to the north and steppe to the south [from Russian, of Turkic origin; compare Turkish *dağ* mountain]

taihoa (ˈtaɪhəʊə) *interj* NZ hold on! no hurry! [Māori]
taikonaut (ˈtaɪkəʊˌnɔːt) *n* an astronaut from the People's Republic of China [c20 from Cantonese *taikon(g)* cosmos + -NAUT]
tail[1] (teɪl) *n* **1** the region of the vertebrate body that is posterior to or above the anus and contains an elongation of the vertebral column, esp forming a flexible movable appendage. Related adj: **caudal 2** anything resembling such an appendage in form or position; the bottom, lowest, or rear part: *the tail of a shirt* **3** the last part or parts: *the tail of the storm* **4** the rear part of an aircraft including the fin, tail plane, and control surfaces; empennage **5** *astronomy* the luminous stream of gas and dust particles, up to 200 million kilometres long, driven from the head of a comet, when close to the sun, under the effect of the solar wind and light pressure **6** the rear portion of a bomb, rocket, missile, etc, usually fitted with guiding or stabilizing vanes **7** a line of people or things **8** a long braid or tress of hair: *a ponytail; a pigtail* **9** *angling* **tailfly** the lowest fly on a wet-fly cast **10** a final short line in a stanza **11** *informal* a person employed to follow and spy upon another or others **12** an informal word for **buttocks 13** *taboo slang* **a** the female genitals **b** a woman considered sexually (esp in the phrases **piece of tail, bit of tail**) **14** *printing* **a** the margin at the foot of a page **b** the bottom edge of a book **15** the lower end of a pool or part of a stream **16** *informal* the course or track of a fleeing person or animal: *the police are on my tail* **17** (*modifier*) coming from or situated in the rear: *a tail wind* **18** **turn tail** to run away; escape **19** **with one's tail between one's legs** in a state of utter defeat or cowardice ▷ *vb* **20** to form or cause to form the tail **21** to remove the tail of (an animal); dock **22** (*tr*) to remove the stalk of: *to top and tail the gooseberries* **23** (*tr*) to connect (objects, ideas, etc) together by or as if by the tail **24** (*tr*) *informal* to follow stealthily **25** (*tr*) *Austral* to tend (cattle) on foot **26** (*intr*) (of a vessel) to assume a specified position, as when at a mooring **27** to build the end of (a brick, joist, etc) into a wall or (of a brick, etc) to have one end built into a wall ▷ See also **tail off, tail out, tails** [Old English *tægel*; related to Old Norse *tagl* horse's tail, Gothic *tagl* hair, Old High German *zagal* tail] ▷ **'tailless** *adj* ▷ **'taillessly** *adv* ▷ **'taillessness** *n* ▷ **'tail-like** *adj*
tail[2] (teɪl) *property law* ▷ *n* **1** the limitation of an estate or interest to a person and the heirs of his body. See also **entail** ▷ *adj* **2** (*immediately postpositive*) (of an estate or interest) limited in this way [c15 from Old French *taille* a division; see TAILOR, TALLY] ▷ **'tailless** *adj*
tailback (ˈteɪlˌbæk) *n* a queue of traffic stretching back from an obstruction
tailboard (ˈteɪlˌbɔːd) *n* a board at the rear of a lorry, wagon, etc, that can be removed or let down on a hinge
tail coat *n* **1** Also called: **tails** a man's black coat having a horizontal cut over the hips and a tapering tail with a vertical slit up to the waist: worn as part of full evening dress **2** Also called: **swallow-tailed coat** another name for **morning coat**
tail covert *n* any of the covert feathers of a bird covering the bases of the tail feathers
tail end *n* the last, endmost, or final part
tail fan *n* the fanned structure at the hind end of a lobster or related crustacean, formed from the telson and uropods
tailgate (ˈteɪlˌgeɪt) *n* **1** another name for **tailboard 2** a door at the rear of a hatchback vehicle ▷ *vb* **3** to drive very close behind (a vehicle) ▷ **'tailˌgater** *n*
tail gate *n* a gate that is used to control the flow of water at the lower end of a lock. Compare **head gate**
tail-heavy *adj* (of an aircraft) having too much weight at the rear because of overloading or poor design

tailing ('teɪlɪŋ) *n* the part of a beam, rafter, projecting brick or stone, etc, embedded in a wall

tailings ('teɪlɪŋz) *pl n* waste left over after certain processes, such as from an ore-crushing plant or in milling grain

taille (taɪ; *French* tɑj) *n, pl* **tailles** (taɪ, taɪz; *French* tɑj) (in France before 1789) a tax levied by a king or overlord on his subjects [c17 from French, from Old French *taillier* to shape; see TAILOR]

tail-light *or* **tail lamp** *n* other names for **rear light**

tail off *or* **away** *vb* (*adverb, usually intr*) to decrease or cause to decrease in quantity, degree, etc, esp gradually: *his interest in collecting stamps tailed off over the years*

tailor ('teɪlə) *n* **1** a person who makes, repairs, or alters outer garments, esp menswear. Related adj: **sartorial 2** a voracious and active marine food fish, *Pomatomus saltator*, of Australia with scissor-like teeth ▷ *vb* **3** to cut or style (material, clothes, etc) to satisfy certain requirements **4** (*tr*) to adapt so as to make suitable for something specific: *he tailored his speech to suit a younger audience* **5** (*intr*) to follow the occupation of a tailor [c13 from Anglo-Norman *taillour*, from Old French *taillier* to cut, from Latin *tālea* a cutting; related to Greek *talis* girl of marriageable age]

tailorbird ('teɪlə,bɜːd) *n* any of several tropical Asian warblers of the genus *Orthotomus*, which build nests by sewing together large leaves using plant fibres

tailor-made *adj* **1** made by a tailor to fit exactly: *a tailor-made suit* **2** perfectly meeting a particular purpose: *a girl tailor-made for him* ▷ *n* **3** a tailor-made garment **4** *slang* a cigarette made in a factory rather than rolled by hand

tailor's chalk *n* pipeclay used by tailors and dressmakers to mark seams, darts, etc, on material

tailor's-tack *n* one of a series of loose looped stitches used to transfer markings for seams, darts, etc, from a paper pattern to material

tail out *vb* (*tr, adverb*) to guide (timber) as it emerges from a power saw

tailpiece ('teɪl,piːs) *n* **1** an extension or appendage that lengthens or completes something **2** *printing* a decorative design at the foot of a page or end of a chapter **3** *music* a piece of wood to which the strings of a violin, etc, are attached at their lower end. It is suspended between the taut strings and the bottom of the violin by a piece of gut or metal **4** Also called: **tail beam** *architect* a short beam or rafter that has one end embedded in a wall

tailpipe ('teɪl,paɪp) *n* a pipe from which the exhaust gases from an internal-combustion engine are discharged, esp the terminal pipe of the exhaust system of a motor vehicle

tailplane ('teɪl,pleɪn) *n* a small horizontal wing at the tail of an aircraft to provide longitudinal stability. Also called (esp US): **horizontal stabilizer**

tailrace ('teɪl,reɪs) *n* **1** a channel that carries water away from a water wheel, turbine, etc. Compare **headrace 2** *mining* the channel for removing tailings in water

tail rotor *n* a small propeller fitted to the rear of a helicopter to counteract the torque reaction of the main rotor and thus prevent the body of the helicopter from rotating in an opposite direction

tails (teɪlz) *pl n* **1** an informal name for **tail coat** ▷ *interj* ▷ *adv* **2** with the reverse side of a coin uppermost: used as a call before tossing a coin. Compare **heads**

tailskid ('teɪl,skɪd) *n* **1** a runner under the tail of an aircraft **2** a rear-wheel skid of a motor vehicle

tailspin ('teɪl,spɪn) *n* **1** *aeronautics* another name for **spin** (sense 16) **2** *informal* a state of confusion or panic

tailstock ('teɪl,stɒk) *n* a casting that slides on the bed of a lathe in alignment with the headstock and is locked in position to support the free end of a workpiece

tail wheel *n* a wheel fitted to the rear of a vehicle, esp the landing wheel under the tail of an aircraft

tailwind ('teɪl,wɪnd) *n* a wind blowing in the same direction as the course of an aircraft or ship. Compare **headwind**

Taimyr Peninsula (*Russian* taj'mir) *n* a large peninsula of N central Russia, between the Kara Sea and the Laptev Sea. Also called: **Taymyr Peninsula**

tain (teɪn) *n* tinfoil used in backing mirrors [from French, from *étain* tin, from Old French *estain*, from Latin *stagnum* alloy of silver and lead; see STANNUM]

Tainan *or* **T'ai-nan** ('taɪ'næn) *n* a city in the SW Taiwan: an early centre of Chinese emigration from the mainland; largest city and capital of the island (1638–1885); Chengkung University. Pop: 754 000 (2005 est)

Taínaron ('tɛnarɔn) *n* transliteration of the Modern Greek name for (Cape) **Matapan**

Taino ('taɪnəʊ) *n* **1** (*pl* **-nos** *or* **-no**) a member of an American Indian people of the Greater Antilles and the Bahamas **2** the language of this people, belonging to the Arawakan family

taint (teɪnt) *vb* **1** to affect or be affected by pollution or contamination: *oil has tainted the water* **2** to tarnish (someone's reputation, etc) ▷ *n* **3** a defect or flaw: *a taint on someone's reputation* **4** a trace of contamination or infection [c14 (influenced by *attaint* infected, from ATTAIN) from Old French *teindre* to dye, from Latin *tingere* to dye] > '**taintless** *adj*

taipan[1] ('taɪ,pæn) *n* a large highly venomous elapid snake, *Oxyuranus scutellatus*, of NE Australia [c20 from a native Australian language]

taipan[2] ('taɪ,pæn) *n* the foreign head of a business in China [c19 from dialectal form of Chinese *tai* great + *ban* company, class]

Taipei *or* **T'ai-pei** ('taɪ'peɪ) *n* the capital of Taiwan (the Republic of China), at the N tip of the island: became capital in 1885; industrial centre; two universities. Pop: 2 473 000 (2005 est)

Taiping ('taɪ'pɪŋ) *n history* a person who supported or took part in the movement of religious mysticism and agrarian unrest in China between 1850 and 1864 (**Taiping rebellion**), which weakened the Manchu dynasty but was eventually suppressed with foreign aid [c19 from Chinese, from *tai* great + *ping* peace]

Taisho (taɪ'ʃəʊ) *n* the period of Japanese history and artistic style associated with the reign of Yoshihito (1879–1926), emperor of Japan (1912–26)

Taiwan ('taɪ'wɑːn) *n* an island in SE Asia between the East China Sea and the South China Sea, off the SE coast of the People's Republic of China: the principal territory of the Republic of China; claimed by the People's Republic of China since its political separation from mainland China in the late 1940s. Pop: 22 610 000 (2003 est). Former name: **Formosa**

Taiwanese (,taɪwɑː'niːz) *adj* **1** of or relating to Taiwan or its inhabitants ▷ *n* **2** a native or inhabitant of Taiwan

Taiwan Strait *n* another name for **Formosa Strait**

Taiyuan *or* **T'ai-yüan** ('taɪjuː'ɑːn) *n* a city in N China, capital of Shanxi: founded before 450 AD; an industrial centre, surrounded by China's largest reserves of high-grade bituminous coal. Pop: 2 516 000 (2005 est)

Ta'izz (tæ'ɪz, teɪ'iːz) *n* a town in SW Yemen, in the former North Yemen until 1990: agricultural trading centre. Pop: 541 000 (2005 est)

taj (tɑːdʒ) *n* a tall conical cap worn as a mark of distinction by Muslims [via Arabic from Persian: crown, crest]

Tajik ('tɑːdʒɪk, tɑː'dʒiːk) *n, pl* **-jik** a member of a Persian-speaking Muslim people inhabiting Tajikistan and parts of Sinkiang in W China

Tajiki, Tadzhiki (tɑː'dʒɪkiː, -'dʒiː-) *or* **Tajik, Tadzhik** *n* **1** the language of the Tajik, belonging to the West Iranian subbranch of the Indo-European family ▷ *adj* **2** of or relating to the Tajik or their language

Tajikistan, Tadzhikistan *or* **Tadjikistan** (tɑː,dʒɪkɪ'stɑːn, -stæn) *n* a republic in central Asia: under Uzbek rule from the 15th century until taken over by Russia in the 1860s, it became an autonomous Soviet republic in 1929 and gained full independence from the Soviet Union in 1991; it is mainly mountainous. Official language: Tajik or Tajiki. Religion: believers are mainly Muslim. Currency: somoni. Capital: Dushanbe. Pop: 6 297 000 (2004 est). Area: 143 100 sq km (55 240 sq miles)

tajine (tæ'ʒiːn) *n* a variant spelling of **tagine**

Taj Mahal ('tɑːdʒ mə'hɑːl) *n* a white marble mausoleum in central India, in Agra on the Jumna River: built (1632–43) by the emperor Shah Jahan in memory of his beloved wife, Mumtaz Mahal; regarded as the finest example of Mogul architecture [Urdu, literally: crown of buildings]

Tajo ('taxo) *n* the Spanish name for the **Tagus**

taka ('tɑːkɑː) *n* the standard monetary unit of Bangladesh, divided into 100 paise [from Bengali]

takahe ('tɑːkə,hiː) *n* a very rare flightless New Zealand rail, *Notornis mantelli* [from Māori, of imitative origin]

Takamatsu (,tækə'mætsuː) *n* a port in SW Japan, on NE Shikoku on the Inland Sea. Pop: 333 387 (2002 est)

Takao (tæ'kaʊ) *n* the Japanese name for **Kaohsiung**

take[1] (teɪk) *vb* **takes, taking, took, taken** (*mainly tr*) **1** (*also intr*) to gain possession of (something) by force or effort **2** to appropriate or steal: *to take other people's belongings* **3** to receive or accept into a relationship with oneself: *to take a wife* **4** to pay for or buy **5** to rent or lease: *to take a flat in town* **6** to receive or obtain by regular payment: *we take a newspaper every day* **7** to obtain by competing for; win: *to take first prize* **8** to obtain or derive from a source: *he took his good manners from his older brother* **9** to assume the obligations of: *to take office* **10** to endure, esp with fortitude: *to take punishment* **11** to adopt as a symbol of duty, obligation, etc: *to take the veil* **12** to receive or react to in a specified way: *she took the news very well* **13** to adopt as one's own: *to take someone's part in a quarrel* **14** to receive and make use of: *to take advice* **15** to receive into the body, as by eating, inhaling, etc: *to take a breath* **16** to eat, drink, etc, esp habitually: *to take sugar in one's tea* **17** to have or be engaged in for one's benefit or use: *to take a rest* **18** to work at or study: *to take economics at college* **19** to make, do, or perform (an action): *to take a leap* **20** to make use of: *to take an opportunity* **21** to put into effect; adopt: *to take measures* **22** (*also intr*) to make a photograph of or admit of being photographed **23** to act or perform: *she takes the part of the Queen* **24** to write down or copy: *to take notes* **25** to experience or feel: *to take pride in one's appearance; to take offence* **26** to consider, believe, or regard: *I take him to be honest* **27** to consider or accept as valid: *I take your point* **28** to hold or maintain in the mind: *his father took a dim view of his career* **29** to deal or contend with: *the tennis champion took her opponent's best strokes without difficulty* **30** to use as a particular case: *take hotels for example* **31** (*intr; often foll by* from) to diminish or detract: *the actor's bad performance took from the effect of the play* **32** to confront successfully: *the horse took the jump at the third attempt* **33** (*intr*) to have or produce the intended effect; succeed: *her vaccination took; the glue is taking well* **34** (*intr*) (of seeds, plants, etc) to start growing successfully **35** to aim or direct: *he took a swipe at his opponent* **36** to deal a blow to in a specified place **37** *archaic* to have sexual intercourse with **38** to carry off or remove from a place **39** to carry along or have in one's possession: *don't forget to take your umbrella* **40** to convey or transport: *the train will take us out of the city* **41** to use as a means of transport: *I shall take the bus* **42** to conduct or lead: *this road takes you to the station* **43** to escort or accompany: *may I take you out tonight?* **44** to bring or deliver to a state, position,

t

etc: *his ability took him to the forefront in his field* **45** to go to look for; seek: *to take cover* **46** to ascertain or determine by measuring, computing, etc: *to take a pulse; take a reading from a dial* **47** (*intr*) (of a mechanism) to catch or engage (a part) **48** to put an end to; destroy: *she took her own life* **49** to come upon unexpectedly; discover **50** to contract: *he took a chill* **51** to affect or attack: *the fever took him one night* **52** (*copula*) to become suddenly or be rendered (ill): *he took sick; he was taken sick* **53** (*also intr*) to absorb or become absorbed by something: *to take a polish* **54** (*usually passive*) to charm or captivate: *she was very taken with the puppy* **55** (*intr*) to be or become popular; win favour **56** to require or need: *this job will take a lot of attention; that task will take all your time* **57** to subtract or deduct: *to take six from ten leaves four* **58** to hold or contain: *the suitcase won't take all your clothes* **59** to quote or copy: *he has taken several paragraphs from the book for his essay* **60** to proceed to occupy: *to take a seat* **61** (often foll by *to*) to use or employ: *to take steps to ascertain the answer* **62** to win or capture (a trick, counter, piece, etc) **63** (*also intr*) to catch as prey or catch prey **64** *slang* to cheat, deceive, or victimize **65** **take amiss** to be annoyed or offended by **66** **take at one's word** See **word** (sense 17) **67** **take care** to pay attention; be heedful **68** **take care of** to assume responsibility for; look after **69** **take chances** *or* **a chance** to behave in a risky manner **70** **take five** (*or* **ten**) *informal, chiefly US and Canadian* to take a break of five (or ten) minutes **71** **take heart** to become encouraged **72** **take it** **a** to assume; believe: *I take it you'll be back later* **b** *informal* to stand up to or endure criticism, abuse, harsh treatment, etc **73** **take one's time** to use as much time as is needed; not rush **74** **take place** to happen or occur **75** **take (someone's) name in vain** **a** to use a name, esp of God, disrespectfully or irreverently **b** *jocular* to say (someone's) name **76** **take (something) upon oneself** to assume the right to do or responsibility for (something) ▷ *n* **77** the act of taking **78** the number of quarry killed or captured on one occasion **79** *informal, chiefly US* the amount of anything taken, esp money **80** *films, music* **a** one of a series of recordings from which the best will be selected for release **b** the process of taking one such recording **c** a scene or part of a scene photographed without interruption **81** *informal* **a** any objective indication of a successful vaccination, such as a local skin reaction **b** a successful skin graft **82** *printing* a part of an article, story, etc, given to a compositor or keyboard operator for setting in type **83** *informal* a try or attempt **84** *informal, chiefly US* a version or interpretation: *Cronenberg's harsh take on the sci-fi story* ▷ See also **take aback, take after, take against, take apart, take away, take back, take down, take for, take in, take off, take on, take out, take over, take to, take up** [Old English *tacan*, from Old Norse *taka*; related to Gothic *tekan* to touch] > ˈ**takable** *or* ˈ**takeable** *adj*

take² (ˈtɑːkɪ) *n* NZ a topic or cause [Māori]

take aback *vb* (*tr, adverb*) to astonish or disconcert

take after *vb* (*intr, preposition*) **1** to resemble in appearance, character, behaviour, etc **2** to follow as an example

take against *vb* (*intr, preposition*) to start to dislike, esp without good reason

take apart *vb* (*tr, adverb*) **1** to separate (something) into component parts **2** to criticize or punish severely: *the reviewers took the new play apart*

take away *vb* (*tr, adverb*) **1** to deduct; subtract: *take away four from nine to leave five* ▷ *prep* **2** minus: *nine take away four is five* ▷ *adj* **takeaway** *Brit, Austral, and NZ* **3** sold for consumption away from the premises on which it is prepared: *a takeaway meal* **4** preparing and selling food for consumption away from the premises: *a takeaway Indian restaurant* ▷ *n* **takeaway** *Brit, Austral, and NZ* **5** a shop or restaurant that sells such food: *let's go to the Chinese takeaway* **6** a meal bought at such a shop or restaurant: *we'll have a Chinese takeaway tonight to save cooking* ▷ Scot word (for senses 3–6): **carry-out** US and Canadian word (for senses 3–6): **takeout**

take back *vb* (*adverb, mainly tr*) **1** to retract or withdraw (something said, written, promised, etc) **2** to regain possession of **3** to return for exchange: *to take back a substandard garment* **4** to accept (someone) back (into one's home, affections, etc) **5** to remind one of the past; cause one to reminisce: *that tune really takes me back* **6** (*also intr*) *printing* to move (copy) to the previous line

take down *vb* (*tr, adverb*) **1** to record in writing **2** to dismantle or tear down: *to take down an old shed* **3** to lower or reduce in power, arrogance, etc (esp in the phrase **to take down a peg**) ▷ *adj* **take-down** **4** made or intended to be disassembled

take for *vb* (*tr, preposition*) *informal* to consider or suppose to be, esp mistakenly: *the fake coins were taken for genuine; who do you take me for?*

take-home pay *n* the remainder of one's pay after all income tax and other compulsory deductions have been made

take in *vb* (*tr, adverb*) **1** to comprehend or understand **2** to include or comprise: *his thesis takes in that point* **3** to receive into one's house in exchange for payment: *to take in washing; take in lodgers* **4** to make (an article of clothing, etc) smaller by altering seams **5** to include: *the tour takes in the islands as well as the mainland* **6** *informal* to cheat or deceive **7** to go to; visit: *let's take in a movie tonight* ▷ *n* **take-in** **8** *informal* the act or an instance of cheating or deceiving

taken (ˈteɪkən) *vb* **1** the past participle of **take** ▷ *adj* **2** (*postpositive; foll by with*) enthusiastically impressed (by); infatuated (with)

take off *vb* (*adverb*) **1** (*tr*) to remove or discard (a garment) **2** (*intr*) (of an aircraft) to become airborne **3** *informal* to set out or cause to set out on a journey: *they took off for Spain* **4** (*tr*) (of a disease) to prove fatal to; kill **5** (*tr*) *informal* to mimic or imitate, esp in an amusing or satirical manner **6** (*intr*) *informal* to become successful or popular, esp suddenly ▷ *n* **takeoff** **7** the act or process of making an aircraft airborne **8** the stage of a country's economic development when rapid and sustained economic growth is first achieved **9** *informal* an act of mimicry; imitation

take on *vb* (*adverb, mainly tr*) **1** to employ or hire: *to take on new workmen* **2** to assume or acquire: *his voice took on a plaintive note* **3** to agree to do; undertake: *I'll take on that job for you* **4** to compete against, oppose, or fight: *I will take him on at tennis; I'll take him on any time* **5** (*intr*) *informal* to exhibit great emotion, esp grief

take out *vb* (*tr, adverb*) **1** to extract or remove **2** to obtain or secure (a licence, patent, etc) from an authority **3** to go out with; escort: *George is taking Susan out next week* **4** *bridge* to bid a different suit from (one's partner) in order to rescue him from a difficult contract **5** *slang* to kill or destroy **6** *Austral informal* to win, esp in sport: *he took out the tennis championship* **7** **take it** *or* **a lot out of** *informal* to sap the energy or vitality of **8** **take out on** *informal* to vent (anger, frustration, etc) on (esp an innocent person) **9** **take someone out of himself** *informal* to make someone forget his anxieties, problems, etc ▷ *adj* **takeout** **10** *bridge* of or designating a conventional informatory bid, asking one's partner to bid another suit ▷ *adj* **11** **takeout** *US and Canadian* sold for consumption away from the premises on which it is prepared: *a takeout meal* **12** preparing and selling food for consumption away from the premises: *a takeout Indian restaurant* ▷ *n* **takeout** *US and Canadian* **13** a shop or restaurant that sells such food: *let's go to the Chinese takeout* **14** a meal bought at such a shop or restaurant: *we'll have a takeout tonight to save cooking*

take over *vb* (*adverb*) **1** to assume the control or management of **2** *printing* to move (copy) to the next line ▷ *n* **takeover** **3** **a** the act of seizing or assuming power, control, etc **b** (*as modifier*): *takeover bid* **4** *sport* another word for **changeover** (sense 3)

taker (ˈteɪkə) *n* a person who takes something, esp a bet, wager, or offer of purchase

take to *vb* (*intr, preposition*) **1** to make for; flee to: *to take to the hills* **2** to form a liking for, esp after a short acquaintance: *I took to him straightaway* **3** to have recourse to: *to take to the bottle* **4** **take to heart** to regard seriously

take up *vb* (*adverb, mainly tr*) **1** to adopt the study, practice, or activity of: *to take up gardening* **2** *Austral and NZ* to occupy and break in (uncultivated land): *he took up some hundreds of acres in the back country* **3** to shorten (a garment or part of a garment): *she took all her skirts up three inches* **4** to pay off (a note, mortgage, etc) **5** to agree to or accept (an invitation, etc) **6** to pursue further or resume (something): *he took up French where he left off* **7** to absorb (a liquid) **8** to adopt as a protégé; act as a patron to **9** to occupy or fill (space or time) **10** to interrupt, esp in order to contradict or criticize **11** **take up on** **a** to argue or dispute with (someone): *can I take you up on two points in your talk?* **b** to accept what is offered by (someone): *let me take you up on your invitation* **12** **take up with** **a** to discuss with (someone); refer to: *to take up a fault with the manufacturers* **b** (*intr*) to begin to keep company or associate with ▷ *n* **take-up** **13** **a** the claiming or acceptance of something, esp a state benefit, that is due or available **b** (*as modifier*): *take-up rate* **14** *machinery* the distance through which a part must move to absorb the free play in a system **15** (*modifier*) denoting the part of a mechanism on which film, tape, or wire is wound up: *a take-up spool on a tape recorder*

takin (ˈtɑːkiːn) *n* a massive bovid mammal, *Budorcas taxicolor*, of mountainous regions of S Asia, having a shaggy coat, short legs, and horns that point backwards and upwards [C19 from Mishmi]

taking (ˈteɪkɪŋ) *adj* **1** charming, fascinating, or intriguing **2** *informal* infectious; catching ▷ *n* **3** something taken **4** (*plural*) receipts; earnings > ˈ**takingly** *adv* > ˈ**takingness** *n*

takkies (ˈtækɪz) *pl n* *South African informal* a variant spelling of **tackies**

Takoradi (ˌtɑːkəˈrɑːdɪ) *n* the chief port of Ghana, in the southwest on the Gulf of Guinea: modern harbour opened in 1928. Pop (with Sekondi): 335 000 (2005 est)

tala (ˈtɑːlə) *n* the standard monetary unit of Samoa, divided into 100 sene

Talaing (tɑːˈlaɪŋ) *n* another name for **Mon**

talapoin (ˈtæləˌpɔɪn) *n* **1** the smallest of the guenon monkeys, *Cercopithecus talapoin*, of swampy central W African forests, having olive-green fur and slightly webbed digits **2** (in Myanmar and Thailand) **a** a Buddhist monk **b** a title of respect used in addressing such a monk [C16 from French, literally: Buddhist monk, from Portuguese *talapão*, from Mon *tala pōi* our lord; originally jocular, from the appearance of the monkey]

talaq *or* **talak** (t[ae]ˈlɑːk) *n* a form of divorce under Islamic law in which the husband repudiates the marriage by saying 'talaq' three times [C21 from Arabic *ṭalaķ* divorce, from *ṭalaķas* to repudiate]

talaria (təˈlɛərɪə) *pl n* *Greek myth* winged sandals, such as those worn by Hermes [C16 from Latin, from *tālāris* belonging to the ankle, from *tālus* ankle]

Talavera de la Reina (*Spanish* talaˈβera ðe la ˈrɛina) *n* a walled town in central Spain, on the Tagus River: scene of the defeat of the French by British and Spanish forces (1809) during the Peninsular War; agricultural processing centre. Pop: 79 916 (2003 est)

talbot (ˈtɔːlbət) *n* (formerly) an ancient breed of large hound, usually white or light-coloured, having pendulous ears and strong powers of scent [C16 supposed to have been brought to England by the *Talbot* family]

talc (tælk) *n also* **talcum** **1** See **talcum powder** **2** a white, grey, brown, or pale green mineral, found in metamorphic rocks. It is used in the manufacture of talcum powder and electrical insulators. Composition: hydrated magnesium silicate. Formula: $Mg_3Si_4O_{10}(OH)_2$. Crystal structure: monoclinic ▷ *vb* **talcs, talcking, talcked** *or* **talcs, talcing, talced** **3** (*tr*) to apply talc to [C16 from Medieval Latin *talcum*, from Arabic *ṭalq* mica, from Persian *talk*] > ˈ**talcose** *or* ˈ**talcous** *adj*

Talca (*Spanish* ˈtalka) *n* a city in central Chile: scene of the declaration of Chilean independence (1818). Pop: 206 000 (2005 est)

Talcahuano (*Spanish* talkaˈwano) *n* a port in S central Chile, near Concepción on an inlet of the Pacific: oil refinery. Pop: 251 000 (2005 est)

talcum powder (ˈtælkəm) *n* a powder made of purified talc, usually scented, used for perfuming the body and for absorbing excess moisture. Often shortened to: **talc**

tale (teɪl) *n* **1** a report, narrative, or story **2** one of a group of short stories connected by an overall narrative framework **3** **a** a malicious or meddlesome rumour or piece of gossip: *to bear tales against someone* **b** (*in combination*): *talebearer; taleteller* **4** a fictitious or false statement **5** **tell tales** **a** to tell fanciful lies **b** to report malicious stories, trivial complaints, etc, esp to someone in authority **6** **tell a tale** to reveal something important **7** **tell its own tale** to be self-evident **8** *archaic* **a** a number; amount **b** computation or enumeration **9** an obsolete word for **talk** [Old English *talu* list; related to Old Frisian *tele* talk, Old Saxon, Old Norse *tala* talk, number, Old High German *zala* number]

Taleb (ˈtælɪb) *n* (in Afghanistan) a member of the Taliban

talent (ˈtælənt) *n* **1** innate ability, aptitude, or faculty, esp when unspecified; above average ability: *a talent for cooking; a child with talent* **2** a person or persons possessing such ability **3** any of various ancient units of weight and money **4** *informal* members of the opposite sex collectively, esp those living in a particular place: *the local talent* **5** an obsolete word for **inclination** [Old English *talente*, from Latin *talenta*, pl of *talentum* sum of money, from Greek *talanton* unit of money or weight; in Medieval Latin the sense was extended to ability through the influence of the parable of the talents (Matthew 25:14–30)] > ˈ**talented** *adj*

talent scout *n* a person whose occupation is the search for talented artists, sportsmen, performers, etc, for engagements as professionals

taler (ˈtɑːlə) *n, pl* **-ler** *or* **-lers** a variant spelling of **thaler**

tales (ˈteɪliːz) *n law* **1** (*functioning as plural*) a group of persons summoned from among those present in court or from bystanders to fill vacancies on a jury panel **2** (*functioning as singular*) the writ summoning such jurors [C15 from Medieval Latin phrase *tālēs dē circumstantibus* such men from among the bystanders, from Latin *tālis* such] > ˈ**talesman** *n*

Taliban, Taleban *or* **Talibaan** (ˈtælɪbæn) *n* (in Afghanistan) a fundamentalist Islamic army: in 1996 it defeated the ruling mujaheddin factions and seized control of the country; overthrown in 2001 by US-led forces [C20 from Arabic *tālibān* seekers]

taligrade (ˈtælɪˌgreɪd) *adj* (of mammals) walking on the outer side of the foot [C20 from New Latin, from Latin *tālus* ankle, heel + -GRADE]

talion (ˈtælɪən) *n* the system or legal principle of making the punishment correspond to the crime; retaliation [C15 via Old French from Latin *tāliō*, from *tālis* such]

taliped (ˈtælɪˌpɛd) *adj* **1** *pathol* having a club foot ▷ *n* **2** a club-footed person [C19 see TALIPES]

talipes (ˈtælɪˌpiːz) *n* **1** a congenital deformity of the foot by which it is twisted in any of various positions **2** a technical name for **club foot** [C19 New Latin, from Latin *tālus* ankle + *pēs* foot]

talipot *or* **talipot palm** (ˈtælɪˌpɒt) *n* a palm tree, *Corypha umbraculifera*, of the East Indies, having large leaves that are used for fans, thatching houses, etc [C17 from Bengali: palm leaf, from Sanskrit *tālī* fan palm + *pattra* leaf]

talisman (ˈtælɪzmən) *n, pl* **-mans** **1** a stone or other small object, usually inscribed or carved, believed to protect the wearer from evil influences **2** anything thought to have magical or protective powers [C17 via French or Spanish from Arabic *tilsam*, from Medieval Greek *telesma* ritual, from Greek: consecration, from *telein* to perform a rite, complete, from *telos* end, result] > **talismanic** (ˌtælɪzˈmænɪk) *adj*

talk (tɔːk) *vb* **1** (*intr; often foll by to or with*) to express one's thoughts, feelings, or desires by means of words (to); speak (to) **2** (*intr*) to communicate or exchange thoughts by other means: *lovers talk with their eyes* **3** (*intr; usually foll by about*) to exchange ideas, pleasantries, or opinions (about): *to talk about the weather* **4** (*intr*) to articulate words; verbalize: *his baby can talk* **5** (*tr*) to give voice to; utter: *to talk rubbish* **6** (*tr*) to hold a conversation about; discuss: *to talk business* **7** (*intr*) to reveal information: *the prisoner talked after torture* **8** (*tr*) to know how to communicate in (a language or idiom): *he talks English* **9** (*intr*) to spread rumours or gossip: *we don't want the neighbours to talk* **10** (*intr*) to make sounds suggestive of talking **11** (*intr*) to be effective or persuasive: *money talks* **12** **now you're talking** *informal* at last you're saying something agreeable **13** **talk big** to boast or brag **14** **talk shop** to speak about one's work, esp when meeting socially, sometimes with the effect of excluding those not similarly employed **15** **talk the talk** to speak convincingly on a particular subject, showing apparent mastery of its jargon and themes; often used in combination with the expression *walk the walk*. See also **walk** (sense 18) **16** **you can talk** *informal* you don't have to worry about doing a particular thing yourself **17** **you can** *or* **can't talk** *informal* you yourself are guilty of offending in the very matter you are upholding or decrying ▷ *n* **18** a speech or lecture: *a talk on ancient Rome* **19** an exchange of ideas or thoughts: *a business talk with a colleague* **20** idle chatter, gossip, or rumour: *there has been a lot of talk about you two* **21** a subject of conversation; theme: *our talk was of war* **22** (*often plural*) a conference, discussion, or negotiation: *talks about a settlement* **23** a specific manner of speaking: *children's talk* ▷ See also **talk about, talk at, talk back, talk down, talk into, talk out, talk round, talk through, talk up** [C13 *talkien* to talk; related to Old English *talu* TALE, Frisian *talken* to talk] > ˈ**talkable** *adj* > ˌ**talkaˈbility** *n* > ˈ**talker** *n*

talk about *vb* (*intr, preposition*) **1** to discuss **2** used informally and often ironically to add emphasis to a statement: *all his plays have such ridiculous plots — talk about good drama!* **3** **know what one is talking about** to have thorough or specialized knowledge

talk at *vb* (*intr, preposition*) to speak to (a person) in a way that indicates a response is not really wanted: *I wish he'd talk to me rather than at me*

talkative (ˈtɔːkətɪv) *adj* given to talking a great deal > ˈ**talkatively** *adv* > ˈ**talkativeness** *n*

talk back *vb* (*intr, adverb*) **1** to answer boldly or impudently **2** NZ to conduct a telephone dialogue for immediate transmission over the air ▷ *n* **talkback** **3** *television, radio* a system of telephone links enabling spoken directions to be given during the production of a programme **4** NZ **a** a broadcast telephone dialogue **b** (*as modifier*): *a talkback show*

talkbox (ˈtɔːkˌbɒks) *n* another name for **voice box** (sense 2)

talk down *vb* (*adverb*) **1** (*intr; often foll by to*) to behave (towards) in a superior or haughty manner **2** (*tr*) to override (a person or argument) by continuous or loud talking **3** (*tr*) to give instructions to (an aircraft) by radio to enable it to land

talkie (ˈtɔːkɪ) *n informal* an early film with a soundtrack. Full name: **talking picture**

Talking Book *n trademark* a recording of a book, designed to be used by blind people

talking head *n* (on television) a person, such as a newscaster, who is shown only from the shoulders up, and speaks without the use of any illustrative material

talking shop *n informal* a group or committee that has discussions that never result in action

talking-to *n informal* a session of criticism, as of the work or attitude of a subordinate by a person in authority

talk into *vb* (*tr, preposition*) to persuade to by talking: *I talked him into buying the house*

talk out *vb* (*adverb*) **1** (*tr*) to resolve or eliminate by talking: *they talked out their differences* **2** (*tr*) *Brit* to block (a bill, etc) in a legislative body by lengthy discussion **3** **talk out of** to dissuade from by talking: *she was talked out of marriage*

talk round *vb* **1** (*tr, adverb*) Also: **talk over** to persuade to one's opinion: *I talked him round to buying a car* **2** (*intr, preposition*) to discuss the arguments relating to (a subject), esp without coming to a conclusion: *to talk round the problem of the human condition* **3** (*intr, preposition*) to discuss (a subject) vaguely without considering basic facts: *they talked round the idea of moving house quite forgetting they hadn't enough money*

talk show *n* **1** a television or radio show in which guests discuss controversial topics or personal issues **2** US name for **chat show**

talk through *vb* (*tr*) **1** (*adverb*) to discuss (a problem or situation) in detail **2** (*preposition*) to explain to (a person) all the stages of a process: *ask a friend to talk you through the exercise*

talk up *vb* (*tr, adverb*) to speak of or discuss favourably in order to arouse interest or support

talky (ˈtɔːkɪ) *adj* **talkier, talkiest** containing too much dialogue or inconsequential talk: *a talky novel*

tall (tɔːl) *adj* **1** of more than average height **2** **a** (*postpositive*) having a specified height: *a woman five feet tall* **b** (*in combination*): *a twenty-foot-tall partition* **3** *informal* exaggerated or incredible: *a tall story* **4** *informal* difficult to accomplish: *a tall order* **5** an archaic word for **excellent** [C14 (in the sense: big, comely, valiant); related to Old English *getæl* prompt, Old High German *gizal* quick, Gothic *untals* foolish] > ˈ**tallness** *n*

tallage (ˈtælɪdʒ) *English history* ▷ *n* **1** **a** a tax levied by the Norman and early Angevin kings on their Crown lands and royal towns **b** a toll levied by a lord upon his tenants or by a feudal lord upon his vassals ▷ *vb* **2** (*tr*) to levy a tax (upon); impose a tax (upon) [C13 from Old French *taillage*, from *taillier* to cut; see TAILOR]

Tallahassee (ˌtæləˈhæsɪ) *n* a city in N Florida, capital of the state: two universities. Pop: 153 938 (2003 est)

Tall Blacks *pl n* **the** the international basketball team of New Zealand

tallboy (ˈtɔːlˌbɔɪ) *n* **1** a high chest of drawers made in two sections and placed one on top of the other; chest-on-chest **2** a fitting on the top of a chimney to prevent downdraughts [C18 from TALL + BOY]

tallet (ˈtælət) *n Western English dialect* a loft [Welsh *taflod*, from Late Latin *tābulata* flooring]

Tallinn *or* **Tallin** (ˈtælɪn) *n* the capital of Estonia, on the Gulf of Finland: founded by the Danes in 1219; a port and naval base. Pop: 384 000 (2005 est). German name: **Reval**

tallis (ˈtɑlɪs) *or* **tallith** (tɑˈlit) *n Judaism* a fringed shawl worn by Jewish men during morning prayers [from Hebrew, literally: a cover]

tallit (ˈtælɪθ; *Hebrew* taˈliːt) *n, pl* **tallaisim** (tæˈleɪsɪm) **tallites** *or* **tallitot** (*Hebrew* -liːˈtɔt) **1** a white shawl with fringed corners worn over the head and shoulders by Jewish males during religious services **2** a smaller form of this worn under the outer garment during waking hours by

t

some Jewish males [c17 from Hebrew *tallīt*]

tall oil *n* any of various oily liquid mixtures obtained by acidifying the liquor resulting from the treatment of wood pulp with sodium hydroxide: it contains chiefly rosin acids and fatty acids and is used in making soaps and lubricants [c20 partial translation of German *Tallöl*, from Swedish *tallolja*, from *tall* pine + *olja* OIL]

tallow ('tæləʊ) *n* 1 a fatty substance consisting of a mixture of glycerides, including stearic, palmitic, and oleic acids and extracted chiefly from the suet of sheep and cattle: used for making soap, candles, food, etc ▷ *vb* 2 (*tr*) to cover or smear with tallow [Old English *tælg*, a dye; related to Middle Low German *talch* tallow, Dutch *talk*, Icelandic *tólg*] > **'tallowy** *adj*

tallow wood *n Austral* a tall eucalyptus tree, *Eucalyptus microcorys*, of coastal regions, having soft fibrous bark and conical fruits and yielding a greasy timber

tall poppy *n Austral informal* a person who has a high salary or is otherwise prominent [perhaps from Tarquin's decapitation of the tallest poppies in his garden, to indicate the fate of the most prominent citizens of Gabii]

tall poppy syndrome *n Austral informal* a tendency to disparage any person who has achieved great prominence or wealth

tall ship *n* any square-rigged sailing ship

tally ('tælɪ) *vb* -lies, -lying, -lied 1 (*intr*) to correspond one with the other: *the two stories don't tally* 2 (*tr*) to supply with an identifying tag 3 (*intr*) to keep score 4 (*tr*) *obsolete* to record or mark ▷ *n, pl* -lies 5 any record of debit, credit, the score in a game, etc 6 a ticket, label, or mark, used as a means of identification, classification, etc 7 a counterpart or duplicate of something, such as the counterfoil of a cheque 8 a stick used (esp formerly) as a record of the amount of a debt according to the notches cut in it 9 a notch or mark cut in or made on such a stick 10 a mark or number of marks used to represent a certain number in counting 11 *Austral and NZ* the total number of sheep shorn by one shearer in a specified period of time [c15 from Medieval Latin *tālea*, from Latin: a stick; related to Latin *tālus* heel] > **'tallier** *n*

tally clerk *n* a person, esp on a wharf or dock or in an airport, who checks the count of goods being loaded or unloaded

tally-ho (,tælɪ'həʊ) *interj* 1 the cry of a participant at a hunt to encourage the hounds when the quarry is sighted ▷ *n, pl* -hos 2 an instance of crying tally-ho 3 another name for **four-in-hand** (sense 1) ▷ *vb* -hos, -hoing, -hoed *or* -ho'd 4 (*intr*) to make the cry of tally-ho [c18 perhaps from French *taïaut* cry used in hunting]

tallyman ('tælɪmən) *n, pl* -men 1 a scorekeeper or recorder 2 *dialect* a travelling salesman for a firm specializing in hire-purchase > **'tally,woman** *fem n*

tally-woman *n Northern English dialect* a mistress

Talmud ('tælmʊd) *n Judaism* 1 the primary source of Jewish religious law, consisting of the Mishnah and the Gemara 2 either of two recensions of this compilation, the Palestinian Talmud of about 375 AD, or the longer and more important Babylonian Talmud of about 500 AD [c16 from Hebrew *talmūdh*, literally: instruction, from *lāmadh* to learn] > Tal'mudic *or* Tal'mudical *adj* > 'Talmudism *n*

Talmudist ('tælmʊdɪst) *n* 1 a scholar specializing in the study of the Talmud 2 any of the writers of or contributors to the Talmud

talon ('tælən) *n* 1 a sharply hooked claw, esp of a bird of prey 2 anything resembling a bird's claw 3 the part of a lock that the key presses on when it is turned 4 *cards* the pile of cards left after the deal 5 *architect* another name for **ogee** 6 *stock exchange* a printed slip attached to some bearer bonds to enable the holder to apply for a new sheet of coupons [c14 from Old French: heel, from Latin *tālus* heel] > **'taloned** *adj*

Talos ('teɪlɒs) *n Greek myth* the nephew and

apprentice of Daedalus, who surpassed his uncle as an inventor and was killed by him out of jealousy

taluk ('tɑːlʊk, tɑːˈlʊk) *or* **taluka, talooka** (tɑːˈluːkə) *n* (in India) 1 a subdivision of a district; a group of several villages organized for revenue purposes 2 a hereditary estate [c18 from Urdu *ta' alluk* estate, ultimately from Arabic]

talus[1] ('teɪləs) *n, pl* -li (-laɪ) the bone of the ankle that articulates with the leg bones to form the ankle joint. Nontechnical name: **anklebone** [c18 from Latin: ankle]

talus[2] ('teɪləs) *n, pl* -luses 1 *geology* another name for **scree** 2 *fortifications* the sloping side of a wall [c17 from French, from Latin *talūtium* slope, perhaps of Iberian origin]

talweg ('tɑːlvɛg) *n* a variant spelling of **thalweg**

tam (tæm) *n* short for **tam-o'-shanter**

tamale (təˈmɑːlɪ) *n* a Mexican dish made of minced meat mixed with crushed maize and seasonings, wrapped in maize husks and steamed [c19 erroneously for *tamal*, from Mexican Spanish, from Nahuatl *tamalli*]

tamandua (,tæmənˈdʊə) *or* **tamandu** ('tæmən,du:) *n* a small arboreal edentate mammal, *Tamandua tetradactyla*, of Central and South America, having a prehensile tail and tubular mouth specialized for feeding on termites: family *Myrmecophagidae*. Also called: **lesser anteater** [c17 via Portuguese from Tupi: ant trapper, from *taixi* ant + *mondê* to catch]

tamarack ('tæmə,ræk) *n* 1 any of several North American larches, esp *Larix laricina*, which has reddish-brown bark, bluish-green needle-like leaves, and shiny oval cones 2 the wood of any of these trees [c19 from Algonquian]

tamarau *or* **tamarao** ('tæmə,raʊ) *n* a small rare member of the cattle tribe, *Anoa mindorensis*, of lowland areas of Mindoro in the Philippines. Compare **anoa** [from Tagalog *tamaráw*]

tamari (təˈmɒːrɪ) *n* a Japanese variety of soy sauce [Japanese]

tamarillo (,tæməˈrɪləʊ) *n, pl* -los another name for **tree tomato**

tamarin ('tæmərɪn) *n* any of numerous small monkeys of the genera *Saguinus* (or *Leontocebus*) and *Leontideus*, of South and Central American forests; similar to the marmosets: family *Callithricidae* [c18 via French from Galibi]

tamarind ('tæmərɪnd) *n* 1 a leguminous tropical evergreen tree, *Tamarindus indica*, having pale yellow red-streaked flowers and brown pulpy pods, each surrounded by a brittle shell 2 the acid fruit of this tree, used as a food and to make beverages and medicines 3 the wood of this tree [c16 from Medieval Latin *tamarindus*, ultimately from Arabic *tamr hindī* Indian date, from *tamr* date + *hindī* Indian, from *Hind* India]

tamarisk ('tæmərɪsk) *n* any of various ornamental trees and shrubs of the genus *Tamarix*, of the Mediterranean region and S and SE Asia, having scalelike leaves, slender branches, and feathery clusters of pink or whitish flowers: family *Tamaricaceae* [c15 from Late Latin *tamariscus*, from Latin *tamarix*]

tamasha (təˈmɑːʃə) *n* (in India) a show; entertainment [c17 via Urdu from Arabic: a stroll, saunter]

Tamatave (*French* tamatav) *n* the former name (until 1979) of **Toamasina**

Tamaulipas (*Spanish* tamauˈlipas) *n* a state of NE Mexico, on the Gulf of Mexico. Capital: Ciudad Victoria. Pop: 2 747 114 (2000). Area: 79 829 sq km (30 822 sq miles)

tambac ('tæmbæk) *n* a variant spelling of **tombac**

Tambora ('tæmbə,rɑː) *n* a volcano in Indonesia, on N Sumbawa: violent eruption of 1815 reduced its height from about 4000 m (13 000 ft) to 2850 m (9400 ft)

tambour ('tæmbʊə) *n* 1 *real Tennis* the sloping buttress on one side of the receiver's end of the court 2 a small round embroidery frame,

consisting of two concentric hoops over which the fabric is stretched while being worked 3 embroidered work done on such a frame 4 a sliding door on desks, cabinets, etc, made of thin strips of wood glued side by side onto a canvas backing 5 *architect* a wall that is circular in plan, esp one that supports a dome or one that is surrounded by a colonnade 6 a drum ▷ *vb* 7 to embroider (fabric or a design) on a tambour [c15 from French, from *tabour* TABOR]

tamboura (tæmˈbʊərə) *n* an instrument with a long neck, four strings, and no frets, used in Indian music to provide a drone [from Persian *tanbūr*, from Arabic *tunbūr*]

tambourin ('tæmbʊrɪn) *n* 1 an 18th-century Provençal folk dance 2 a piece of music composed for or in the rhythm of this dance 3 a small drum [c18 from French: a little drum, from TAMBOUR]

tambourine (,tæmbəˈriːn) *n music* a percussion instrument consisting of a single drumhead of skin stretched over a circular wooden frame hung with pairs of metal discs that jingle when it is struck or shaken [c16 from Middle Flemish *tamborijn* a little drum, from Old French: TAMBOURIN] > ,tambou'rinist *n*

Tambov (*Russian* tamˈbɔf) *n* an industrial city in W Russia: founded in 1636 as a Muscovite fort; a major engineering centre. Pop: 293 000 (2005 est)

tame (teɪm) *adj* 1 changed by man from a naturally wild state into a tractable, domesticated, or cultivated condition 2 (of animals) not fearful of human contact 3 lacking in spirit or initiative; meek or submissive: *a tame personality* 4 flat, insipid, or uninspiring: *a tame ending to a book* 5 slow-moving: *a tame current* ▷ *vb* (*tr*) 6 to make tame; domesticate 7 to break the spirit of, subdue, or curb 8 to tone down, soften, or mitigate [Old English *tam*; related to Old Norse *tamr*, Old High German *zam*] > **'tamable** *or* **'tameable** *adj* > ,tama'bility, ,tame'ability, **'tamableness** *or* **tameableness** *n* > **'tameless** *adj* > **'tamely** *adv* > **'tameness** *n* > **'tamer** *n*

Tameside ('teɪm,saɪd) *n* a unitary authority of NW England, in Greater Manchester. Pop: 213 400 (2003 est). Area: 103 sq km (40 sq miles)

Tamil ('tæmɪl) *n* 1 (*pl* -ils *or* -il) a member of a mixed Dravidian and Caucasoid people of S India and Sri Lanka 2 the language of this people: the state language of Tamil Nadu, also spoken in Sri Lanka and elsewhere, belonging to the Dravidian family of languages ▷ *adj* 3 of or relating to this people or their language

Tamil Eelam ('tæmɪl 'iːləm) *n* the separate Tamil state that the **Tamil Tigers** have sought to establish in northern Sri Lanka [from Tamil *eelam* homeland]

Tamil Nadu ('tæmɪl nɑːˈduː) *n* a state of SE India, on the Coromandel Coast: reorganized in 1956 and 1960 and made smaller; consists of a coastal plain backed by hills, including the Nilgiri Hills in the west. Capital: Madras. Pop: 62 110 839 (2001). Area: 130 058 sq km (50 216 sq miles). Former name (until 1968): **Madras**

Tamil Tigers *pl n* (usually preceded by *the*) a Sri Lankan Tamil separatist movement founded in the early 1970s that seeks to establish an independent Tamil homeland (Tamil Eelam) in northern Sri Lanka

tamis ('tæmɪ, -ɪs) *n, pl* -ises (-ɪz, -ɪsɪz) a less common word for **tammy**[3] (sense 1)

Tammany Hall ('tæmənɪ) *n US politics* the central organization of the Democratic Party in New York county. Originally founded as a benevolent society (**Tammany Society**) in 1789, Tammany Hall was notorious for the corruption in city and state politics that it fostered in the 19th and early 20th centuries. Also called: **Tammany** > 'Tammanyism *n* > 'Tammanyite *n*

tammar ('tæmə) *n* a small scrub wallaby, *Macropus eugenii*, of Australia, having a thick dark-coloured coat [c19 from a native Australian language]

Tammerfors (ˈtamərˈfɔrs) *n* the Swedish name for **Tampere**

Tammuz (ˈtæmuːz, -ʊz) *n* (in the Jewish calendar) the fourth month of the year according to biblical reckoning and the tenth month of the civil year, usually falling within June and July [from Hebrew]

tammy[1] (ˈtæmɪ) *n, pl* **-mies** a glazed woollen or mixed fabric, used for linings, undergarments, etc [c17 of unknown origin]

tammy[2] (ˈtæmɪ) *n, pl* **-mies** another word for **tam-o'-shanter**

tammy[3] (ˈtæmɪ) *n, pl* **-mies 1** Also called: **tammy cloth, tamis** (esp formerly) a rough-textured woollen cloth used for straining sauces, soups, etc ▷ *vb* **-mies, -mying, -mied 2** (*tr*) (esp formerly) to strain (sauce, soup, etc) through a tammy [c18 changed (through influence of TAMMY¹) from French *tamis*, perhaps of Celtic origin; compare Breton *tamouez* strainer]

tam-o'-shanter (ˌtæməˈʃæntə) *n* a Scottish brimless wool cap with a bobble in the centre, usually worn pulled down at one side. Also called: **tam, tammy** [c19 named after the hero of Burns' poem *Tam o' Shanter* (1790)]

tamoxifen (təˈmɒksɪfɛn) *n* a drug that antagonizes the action of oestrogen and is used to treat breast cancer and some types of infertility in women [c20 altered from T(RANS-) + AM(INE) + OXY-² + PHEN(OL)]

tamp[1] (tæmp) *vb* (*tr*) **1** to force or pack down firmly by repeated blows **2** to pack sand, earth, etc into (a drill hole) over an explosive [c17 probably a back formation from *tampin* (obsolete variant of TAMPION), which was taken as being a present participle *tamping*]

tamp[2] (tæmp) *vb South Wales dialect* **1** (*tr*) to bounce (a ball) **2** (*intr; usually foll by down*) to pour with rain [probably special use of TAMP¹]

Tampa (ˈtæmpə) *n* a port and resort in W Florida, on **Tampa Bay** (an arm of the Gulf of Mexico): two universities. Pop: 317 647 (2003 est)

tamper[1] (ˈtæmpə) *vb* (*intr*) **1** (usually foll by *with*) to interfere or meddle **2** to use corrupt practices such as bribery or blackmail **3** (usually foll by *with*) to attempt to influence or corrupt, esp by bribery: *to tamper with the jury* [c16 alteration of TEMPER (verb)] ▷ **'tamperer** *n*

tamper[2] (ˈtæmpə) *n* **1** a person or thing that tamps, esp an instrument for packing down tobacco in a pipe **2** a casing around the core of a nuclear weapon to increase its efficiency by reflecting neutrons and delaying the expansion

Tampere (*Finnish* ˈtɑmpɛrɛ) *n* a city in SW Finland: the second largest town in Finland; textile manufacturing. Pop: 200 966 (2003 est). Swedish name: **Tammerfors**

Tampico (*Spanish* tamˈpiko) *n* a port and resort in E Mexico, in Tamaulipas on the Pánuco River: oil refining. Pop: 702 000 (2005 est)

tamping *or* **tamping mad** (ˈtæmpɪŋ) *adj* (*postpositive*) *South Wales dialect* very angry [see TAMP¹]

tampion (ˈtæmpɪən) *or* **tompion** *n* a plug placed in a gun's muzzle when the gun is not in use to keep out moisture and dust [c15 from French: TAMPON]

tampon (ˈtæmpɒn) *n* **1** a plug of lint, cotton wool, cotton, etc, inserted into an open wound or body cavity to stop the flow of blood, absorb secretions, etc, esp one inserted into the vagina to absorb menstrual blood ▷ *vb* **2** (*tr*) to plug (a wound, etc) with a tampon [c19 via French from Old French *tapon* a little plug, from *tape* a plug, of Germanic origin] ▷ **'tamponage** *n*

tam-tam *n* another name for **gong** (sense 1) [from Hindi: see TOM-TOM]

Tamworth (ˈtæmwəθ) *n* (*often capital*) any of a hardy rare breed of long-bodied reddish pigs [named after TAMWORTH, England, where it was developed]

Tamworth (ˈtæmwəθ) *n* **1** a market town in W

central England, in SE Staffordshire. Pop: 71 650 (2001) **2** a city in SE Australia, in E central New South Wales: industrial centre of an agricultural region. Pop: 32 543 (2001)

tan[1] (tæn) *n* **1** the brown colour produced by the skin after intensive exposure to ultraviolet rays, esp those of the sun **2** a light or moderate yellowish-brown colour **3** short for **tanbark** ▷ *vb* **tans, tanning, tanned 4** to go brown or cause to go brown after exposure to ultraviolet rays: *she tans easily* **5** to convert (a skin or hide) into leather by treating it with a tanning agent, such as vegetable tannins, chromium salts, fish oils, or formaldehyde **6** (*tr*) *slang* to beat or flog ▷ *adj* **tanner, tannest 7** of the colour tan: *tan gloves* **8** used in or relating to tanning [Old English *tannian* (unattested as infinitive, attested as *getanned*, past participle), from Medieval Latin *tannāre*, from *tannum* tanbark, perhaps of Celtic origin; compare Irish *tana* thin] ▷ **'tannable** *adj* ▷ **'tannish** *adj*

tan[2] (tæn) *abbreviation for* tangent (sense 2)

tana (ˈtɑːnə) *n* **1** a small Madagascan lemur, *Phaner furcifer* **2** a large tree shrew, *Tupaia tana*, of Sumatra and Borneo [c19 from Malay *tūpai tana* ground squirrel]

Tana (ˈtɑːnə) *n* **1** Lake Also called: (Lake) **Tsana**. a lake in NW Ethiopia, on a plateau 1800 m (6000 ft) high: the largest lake of Ethiopia; source of the Blue Nile. Area: 3673 sq km (1418 sq miles) **2** a river in E Kenya, rising in the Aberdare Range and flowing in a wide curve east to the Indian Ocean: the longest river in Kenya. Length: 708 km (440 miles) **3** a river in NE Norway, flowing generally northeast as part of the border between Norway and Finland to the Arctic Ocean by Tana Fjord. Length: about 320 km (200 miles). Finnish name: **Teno**

Tanach *Hebrew* (taˈnax) *n* the Hebrew Bible as used by Jews, divided into the Torah, Prophets, and Hagiographa [from Hebrew, acronym formed from *tōrāh* (the Pentateuch), *nebī'īm* (the prophets), and *ketūbīm* (the Hagiographa)]

tanager (ˈtænədʒə) *n* any American songbird of the family *Thraupidae*, having a short thick bill and a brilliantly coloured male plumage [c19 from New Latin *tanagra*, based on Tupi *tangara*]

Tanagra (ˈtænəgrə) *n* a town in ancient Boeotia, famous for terracotta figurines of the same name, first discovered in its necropolis

Tanana (ˈtænənɑː) *n* a river in central Alaska, rising in the Wrangell Mountains and flowing northwest to the Yukon River. Length: about 765 km (475 miles)

Tananarive (*French* tananariv) *n* the former name of **Antananarivo**

tanbark (ˈtænˌbɑːk) *n* the bark of certain trees, esp the oak and hemlock, used as a source of tannin. Often shortened to: **tan**

tandem (ˈtændəm) *n* **1** a bicycle with two sets of pedals and two saddles, arranged one behind the other for two riders **2** a two-wheeled carriage drawn by two horses harnessed one behind the other **3** a team of two horses so harnessed **4** any arrangement of two things in which one is placed behind the other **5 in tandem** together or in conjunction ▷ *adj* **6** *Brit* used as, used in, or routed through an intermediate automatic telephone exchange: *a tandem exchange* ▷ *adv* **7** one behind the other: *to ride tandem* [c18 whimsical use of Latin *tandem* at length, to indicate a vehicle of elongated appearance]

tandem roller *n* a type of road roller in which the front and back wheels consist of rollers of about the same diameter

T & G *abbreviation for* Transport and General Workers' Union

Tandjungpriok *or* **Tanjungpriok** (ˌtændʒʊŋˈpriːɒk) *n* a port in Indonesia, on the NW coast of Java adjoining the capital, Jakarta: a major shipping and distributing centre for the whole archipelago

tandoori (tænˈdʊərɪ) *n* **a** an Indian method of

cooking meat or vegetables on a spit in a clay oven **b** (*as modifier*): *tandoori chicken* [from Urdu, from *tandoor* an oven]

tang (tæŋ) *n* **1** a strong taste or flavour: *the tang of the sea* **2** a pungent or characteristic smell: *the tang of peat fires* **3** a trace, touch, or hint of something: *a tang of cloves in the apple pie* **4** the pointed end of a tool, such as a chisel, file, knife, etc, which is fitted into a handle, shaft, or stock [c14 from Old Norse *tangi* point; related to Danish *tange* point, spit]

Tang (tæŋ) *n* the imperial dynasty of China from 618–907 AD

tanga (ˈtæŋgə) *n* **1** a triangular loincloth worn by indigenous peoples in tropical America **2** a type of very brief bikini [from Portuguese, ultimately of Banth origin]

Tanga (ˈtæŋgə) *n* a port in N Tanzania, on the Indian Ocean: Tanzania's second port. Pop: 190 000 (2005 est)

Tanganyika (ˌtæŋgəˈnjiːkə) *n* **1** a former state in E Africa: became part of German East Africa in 1884; ceded to Britain as a League of Nations mandate in 1919 and as a UN trust territory in 1946; gained independence in 1961 and united with Zanzibar in 1964 as the United Republic of Tanzania **2** Lake a lake in central Africa between Tanzania and the Democratic Republic of Congo (formerly Zaïre), bordering also on Burundi and Zambia, in the Great Rift Valley: the longest freshwater lake in the world. Area: 32 893 sq km (12 700 sq miles). Length: 676 km (420 miles)

Tanganyikan (ˌtæŋgəˈnjiːkən) *adj* **1** of or relating to the former state of Tanganyika (now part of Tanzania) or its inhabitants ▷ *n* **2** a native of inhabitant of Tanganyika

tangata māori (ˈtɑːŋgɑːtə ˈmaʊrɪ) *n, pl* tangata māori *NZ* someone of Māori origin [Māori]

tangata tiriti (ˈtɑːŋgɑːtə ˈtiːriːtɪ) *n NZ* a Māori term for non-Māori people [Māori, literally: people of the Treaty (of Waitangi)]

tangata whenua (ˈtɑːŋgɑːtə ˈfɛnuːə) *n NZ* the indigenous Māori people of a particular area of New Zealand or of the country as a whole [Māori, literally: people of the land]

tangelo (ˈtændʒəˌləʊ) *n, pl* **-los 1** a hybrid produced by crossing a tangerine tree with a grapefruit tree **2** the fruit of this hybrid, having orange acid-tasting flesh [c20 from TANG(ERINE) + (POM)ELO]

tangent (ˈtændʒənt) *n* **1** a geometric line, curve, plane, or curved surface that touches another curve or surface at one point but does not intersect it **2** (of an angle) a trigonometric function that in a right-angled triangle is the ratio of the length of the opposite side to that of the adjacent side; the ratio of sine to cosine. Abbreviation: tan **3** the straight part on a survey line between curves **4** *music* a part of the action of a clavichord consisting of a small piece of metal that strikes the string to produce a note **5 on** *or* **at a tangent** on a completely different or divergent course, esp of thought: *to go off at a tangent* ▷ *adj* **6 a** of or involving a tangent **b** touching at a single point **7** touching **8** almost irrelevant [c16 from Latin phrase *līnea tangēns* the touching line, from *tangere* to touch] ▷ **'tangency** *n*

tangent galvanometer *n* a type of galvanometer having a vertical coil of wire with a horizontal magnetic needle at its centre. The current to be measured is passed through the coil and produces a proportional magnetic field which deflects the needle

tangential (tænˈdʒɛnʃəl) *adj* **1** of, being, relating to, or in the direction of a tangent **2** Also: transverse *astronomy* (of velocity) in a direction perpendicular to the line of sight of a celestial object. Compare **radial** (sense 6) **3** of superficial relevance only; digressive ▷ **tanˈgentiˈality** *n* ▷ **tanˈgentially** *or* **tanˈgentally** *adv*

tangerine (ˌtændʒəˈriːn) *n* **1** an Asian citrus tree, *Citrus reticulata*, cultivated for its small edible orange-like fruits **2** the fruit of this tree, having a loose rind and sweet spicy flesh **3 a** a reddish-orange colour **b** (as adjective): a tangerine door [C19 from TANGIER]

Tangerine (ˌtændʒəˈriːn) n **1** a native of inhabitant of Tangier ▷ adj **2** of or relating to Tangier or its inhabitants

tangi (ˈtʌŋiː) n, pl -gis NZ a Māori funeral ceremony **2** informal a lamentation [Māori]

tangible (ˈtændʒəbəl) adj **1** capable of being touched or felt; having real substance: a tangible object **2** capable of being clearly grasped by the mind; substantial rather than imaginary: tangible evidence **3** having a physical existence; corporeal: tangible assets ▷ n **4** (often plural) a tangible thing or asset [C16 from Late Latin tangibilis, from Latin tangere to touch] > ˌtangiˈbility or ˈtangibleness n > ˈtangibly adv

Tangier (tænˈdʒɪə) n a port in N Morocco, on the Strait of Gibraltar: a Phoenician trading post in the 15th century BC; a neutral international zone (1923–56); made the summer capital of Morocco and a free port in 1962; commercial and financial centre. Pop: 526 000 (2003)

tangle¹ (ˈtæŋɡəl) n **1** a confused or complicated mass of hairs, lines, fibres, etc, knotted or coiled together **2** a complicated problem, condition, or situation ▷ vb **3** to become or cause to become twisted together in a confused mass **4** (intr; often foll by with) to come into conflict; contend: to tangle with the police **5** (tr) to involve in matters which hinder or confuse: to tangle someone in a shady deal **6** (tr) to ensnare or trap, as in a net [C14 tangilen, variant of tagilen, probably of Scandinavian origin; related to Swedish dialect taggla to entangle] > ˈtanglement n > ˈtangler n > ˈtangly adj

tangle² or **tangle weed** (ˈtæŋɡəl) n alternative names (esp Scot) for oarweed [C16 of Scandinavian origin: compare Danish tang seaweed]

tango (ˈtæŋɡəʊ) n, pl -gos **1** a Latin American dance in duple time, characterized by long gliding steps and sudden pauses **2** a piece of music composed for or in the rhythm of this dance ▷ vb -goes, -going, -goed (intr) to perform this dance [C20 from American Spanish, probably of Niger-Congo origin; compare Ibibio tamgu to dance] > ˈtangoist n

Tango (ˈtæŋɡəʊ) n communications a code word for the letter t

tangram (ˈtæŋɡræm) n a Chinese puzzle in which a square, cut into a parallelogram, a square, and five triangles, is formed into figures [C19 perhaps from Chinese t'ang Chinese + -GRAM]

Tangshan (ˈtæŋˈʃæn) n an industrial city in NE China, in Hebei province. Pop 1 773 000 (2005 est)

tangy (ˈtæŋɪ) adj tangier, tangiest having a pungent, fresh, or briny flavour or aroma: a tangy sea breeze

tanh (θæn, tænʃ) n hyperbolic tangent; a hyperbolic function that is the ratio of sinh to cosh [C20 from TAN(GENT) + H(YPERBOLIC)]

Tanis (ˈteɪnɪs) n an ancient city located in the E part of the Nile delta: abandoned after the 6th century BC; at one time the capital of Egypt. Biblical name: **Zoan**

tanist (ˈtænɪst) n history the heir apparent of a Celtic chieftain chosen by election during the chief's lifetime: usually the worthiest of his kin [C16 from Irish Gaelic tánaiste, literally: the second person] > ˈtanistry n

taniwha (ˈtʌniːfɑː, ˈtʌniːwɑː) n NZ a legendary Māori monster [Māori]

Tanjore (tænˈdʒɔː) n the former name of Thanjavur

Tanjungpriok (ˌtændʒʊŋˈpriːɒk) n a variant spelling of Tandjungpriok

tank (tæŋk) n **1** a large container or reservoir for the storage of liquids or gases: tanks for storing oil **2 a** an armoured combat vehicle moving on tracks and armed with guns, etc, originally developed in World War I **b** (as modifier): a tank commander; a tank

brigade **3** Brit and US dialect a reservoir, lake, or pond **4** photog **a** a light-tight container inside which a film can be processed in daylight, the solutions and rinsing waters being poured in and out without light entering **b** any large dish or container used for processing a number of strips or sheets of film **5** slang, chiefly US **a** a jail **b** a jail cell **6** Also called: **tankful** the quantity contained in a tank **7** Austral a dam formed by excavation ▷ vb **8** (tr) to put or keep in a tank **9** (intr) to move like a tank, esp heavily and rapidly **10** slang to defeat heavily **11** (intr) informal to fail, esp commercially ▷ See also **tank up** [C17 from Gujarati tānkh artificial lake, but influenced also by Portuguese tanque, from estanque pond, from estancar to dam up, from Vulgar Latin stanticāre (unattested) to block, STANCH] > **tankless** adj > ˈtankˌlike adj

tanka (ˈtɑːŋkə) n, pl -kas or -ka a Japanese verse form consisting of five lines, the first and third having five syllables, the others seven [C19 from Japanese, from tan short + ka verse]

tankage (ˈtæŋkɪdʒ) n **1** the capacity or contents of a tank or tanks **2** the act of storing in a tank or tanks, or a fee charged for such storage **3** agriculture **a** fertilizer consisting of the dried and ground residues of animal carcasses **b** a protein supplement feed for livestock

tankard (ˈtæŋkəd) n **a** a large one-handled drinking vessel, commonly made of silver, pewter, or glass, sometimes fitted with a hinged lid **b** the quantity contained in a tankard [C14 related to Middle Dutch tankaert, French tanquart]

tank engine or **locomotive** n a steam locomotive that carries its water supply in tanks mounted around its boiler

tanker (ˈtæŋkə) n a ship, lorry, or aeroplane designed to carry liquid in bulk, such as oil

tank farming n another name for **hydroponics** > tank farmer n

tankini (ˌtæŋˈkiːnɪ) n a woman's two-piece swimming costume consisting of a vest or camisole top and bikini briefs [C20 a blend of TANK (TOP) and (BIK)INI]

tank top n a sleeveless upper garment with wide shoulder straps and a low neck, usually worn over a shirt, blouse, or jumper [C20 named after tank suits, one-piece bathing costumes of the 1920s worn in tanks or swimming pools]

tank trap n any obstacle, such as a number of concrete stumps set in the ground, designed to stop a military tank

tank up vb (adverb) chiefly Brit **1** to fill the tank of (a vehicle) with petrol **2** slang to imbibe or cause to imbibe a large quantity of alcoholic drink

tank wagon or esp US and Canadian **tank car** n a form of railway wagon carrying a tank for the transport of liquids

tannage (ˈtænɪdʒ) n **1** the act or process of tanning **2** a skin or hide that has been tanned

tannate (ˈtæneɪt) n any salt or ester of tannic acid

Tannenberg (German ˈtanənberk) n a village in N Poland, formerly in East Prussia: site of a decisive defeat of the Teutonic Knights by the Poles in 1410 and of a decisive German victory over the Russians in 1914. Polish name: **Stębark**

tanner¹ (ˈtænə) n a person who tans skins and hides

tanner² (ˈtænə) n Brit (formerly) an informal word for sixpence [C19 of unknown origin]

tannery (ˈtænərɪ) n, pl -neries a place or building where skins and hides are tanned

tannic (ˈtænɪk) adj of, relating to, containing, or produced from tan, tannin, or tannic acid

tannie (ˈtænɪ) n South African a title of respect used to refer to an elderly woman [Afrikaans; literally: aunt]

tannin (ˈtænɪn) n any of a class of yellowish or brownish solid compounds found in many plants and used as tanning agents, mordants, medical astringents, etc Tannins are derivatives of gallic

acid with the approximate formula $C_{76}H_{52}O_{46}$. Also called: **tannic acid** [C19 from French tanin, from TAN¹]

Tannoy (ˈtænɔɪ) n trademark a sound-amplifying apparatus used as a public-address system esp in a large building, such as a university

Tans (tænz) pl n the Irish informal short for the Black and Tans

tansy (ˈtænzɪ) n, pl -sies **1** any of numerous plants of the genus Tanacetum, esp T. vulgare, having yellow flowers in flat-topped clusters and formerly used in medicine and for seasoning: family Asteraceae (composites) **2** any of various similar plants [C15 from Old French tanesie, from Medieval Latin athanasia tansy (with reference to its alleged power to prolong life), from Greek: immortality]

Tanta (ˈtæntə) n a city in N Egypt, on the Nile delta: noted for its Muslim festivals. Pop: 413 000 (2005 est)

tantalate (ˈtæntəleɪt) n any of various salts of tantalic acid formed when the pentoxide of tantalum dissolves in an alkali

tantalic (tænˈtælɪk) adj of or containing tantalum, esp in the pentavalent state

tantalic acid n a white gelatinous substance produced by hydrolysis of tantalic halides. It dissolves in strong bases to give tantalates

tantalite (ˈtæntəlaɪt) n a heavy brownish mineral consisting of a tantalum oxide of iron and manganese in orthorhombic crystalline form: it occurs in coarse granite, often with columbite, and is an ore of tantalum. Formula: $(Fe,Mn)(Ta,N6)_2O_6$ [C19 from TANTALUM + -ITE¹]

tantalize or **tantalise** (ˈtæntəˌlaɪz) vb (tr) to tease or make frustrated, as by tormenting with the sight of something greatly desired but inaccessible [C16 from the punishment of TANTALUS] > ˌtantaliˈzation or ˌtantaliˈsation n > ˈtantaˌlizer or ˈtantaˌliser n > ˈtantaˌlizing or ˈtantaˌlising adj > ˈtantaˌlizingly or ˈtantaˌlisingly adv

tantalous (ˈtæntələs) adj of or containing tantalum in the trivalent state [C19 from TANTAL(UM) + -OUS]

tantalum (ˈtæntələm) n a hard greyish-white metallic element that occurs with niobium in tantalite and columbite: used in electrical capacitors in most circuit boards and in alloys to increase hardness and chemical resistance, esp in surgical instruments. Symbol: Ta; atomic no: 73; atomic wt: 180.9479; valency: 2, 3, 4, or 5; relative density: 16.654; melting pt: 3020°C; boiling pt: 5458±100°C [C19 named after TANTALUS, with reference to the metal's incapacity to absorb acids]

tantalus (ˈtæntələs) n Brit a case in which bottles may be locked with their contents tantalizingly visible

Tantalus (ˈtæntələs) n Greek myth a king, the father of Pelops, punished in Hades for his misdeeds by having to stand in water that recedes when he tries to drink it and under fruit that moves away as he reaches for it

tantamount (ˈtæntəˌmaʊnt) adj (postpositive; foll by to) as good (as); equivalent in effect (to): his statement was tantamount to an admission of guilt [C17 basically from Anglo-French tant amunter to amount to as much, from tant so much + amunter to AMOUNT]

tantara (ˈtæntərə, tænˈtɑːrə) n a blast, as on a trumpet or horn [C16 from Latin taratantara, imitative of the sound of the tuba]

tantivy (tænˈtɪvɪ) adv **1** at full speed; rapidly ▷ n, pl -tivies interj **2** a hunting cry, esp at full gallop [C17 perhaps imitative of galloping hooves]

tant mieux French (tɑ̃ mjø) so much the better

tanto (French; Italian ˈtanto) adv too much: allegro ma non tanto. See **non troppo** [C19 from Italian, from Latin tantum so much]

tant pis French (tɑ̃ pi) so much the worse

Tantra (ˈtæntrə, ˈtʌn-) n Hinduism, Buddhism the

sacred books of Tantrism, written between the 7th and 17th centuries AD, mainly in the form of a dialogue between Siva and his wife [c18 from Sanskrit: warp, hence underlying principle, from *tanoti* he weaves]

Tantric ('tæntrɪk) *adj Hinduism, Buddhism* of or relating to Tantrism

Tantrism ('tæntrɪzəm) *n* **1** a movement within Hinduism combining magical and mystical elements and with sacred writings of its own **2** a similar movement within Buddhism [c18 from Sanskrit *tantra*, literally: warp, hence, doctrine] > 'Tantrist *n*

tantrum ('tæntrəm) *n* (often plural) a childish fit of rage; outburst of bad temper [c18 of unknown origin]

Tan-tung ('tæn'tʊŋ) *n* a variant transliteration of Dandong, the alternative name for **Andong**

Tanzania (ˌtænzə'nɪə) *n* a republic in E Africa, on the Indian Ocean: formed by the union of the independent states of Tanganyika and Zanzibar in 1964; a member of the Commonwealth. Exports include coffee, tea, sisal, and cotton. Official languages: Swahili and English. Religions: Christian, Muslim, and animist. Currency: Tanzanian shilling. Capital: Dodoma. Pop: 37 671 000 (2004 est). Area: 945 203 sq km (364 943 sq miles)

Tanzanian (ˌtænzə'nɪən) *adj* **1** of or relating to Tanzania or its inhabitants ▷ *n* **2** a native or inhabitant of Tanzania

Tanzim ('tæn,zɪm) *n* a Palestinian militia belonging to a militant faction of Al Fatah

Tao (taʊ) *n* (in the philosophy of Taoism) **1** that in virtue of which all things happen or exist **2** the rational basis of human conduct **3** the course of life and its relation to eternal truth [Chinese, literally: path, way]

Taoiseach ('tiːʃæx) *n* the prime minister of the Republic of Ireland [from Irish Gaelic, literally: leader]

Taoism ('taʊɪzəm) *n* **1** the philosophy of Lao Zi, the Chinese philosopher (?604–?531 BC), that advocates a simple honest life and noninterference with the course of natural events **2** a popular Chinese system of religion and philosophy claiming to be teachings of Lao Zi but also incorporating pantheism and sorcery > 'Taoist *n, adj* > Tao'istic *adj*

taonga (ta'ɒŋə) *n* NZ treasure; anything highly prized [Māori]

tap¹ (tæp) *vb* taps, tapping, tapped **1** to strike (something) lightly and usually repeatedly: *to tap the table; to tap on the table* **2** (tr) to produce by striking in this way: *to tap a rhythm* **3** (tr) to strike lightly with (something): *to tap one's finger on the desk* **4** (intr) to walk with a tapping sound: *she tapped across the floor* **5** (tr) to attach metal or leather reinforcing pieces to (the toe or heel of a shoe) ▷ *n* **6** a light blow or knock, or the sound made by it **7** the metal piece attached to the toe or heel of a shoe used for tap-dancing **8** short for **tap-dancing** **9** *phonetics* the contact made between the tip of the tongue and the alveolar ridge as the tongue is flicked upwards in the execution of a flap or vibrates rapidly in the execution of a trill or roll ▷ See also **taps** [c13 *tappen*, probably from Old French *taper*, of Germanic origin; related to Middle Low German *tappen* to pluck, Swedish dialect *täpa* to tap] > 'tappable *adj*

tap² (tæp) *n* **1** a valve by which a fluid flow from a pipe can be controlled by opening and closing an orifice. US and Canadian name: **faucet 2** a stopper to plug a cask or barrel and enable the contents to be drawn out in a controlled flow **3** a particular quality of alcoholic drink, esp when contained in casks: *an excellent tap* **4** *Brit* short for **taproom 5** the surgical withdrawal of fluid from a bodily cavity: *a spinal tap* **6** Also called: **screw tap** a tool for cutting female screw threads, consisting of a threaded steel cylinder with longitudinal

grooves forming cutting edges. Compare **die²** (sense 2) **7** *electronics, chiefly US and Canadian* a connection made at some point between the end terminals of an inductor, resistor, or some other component. Usual Brit name: **tapping 8** *stock exchange* **a** an issue of a government security released slowly onto the market when its market price reaches a predetermined level **b** (as modifier): *tap stock; tap issue* **9** a concealed listening or recording device connected to a telephone or telegraph wire for the purpose of obtaining information secretly **10** on tap *informal* ready for immediate use **b** (of drinks) on draught ▷ *vb* taps, tapping, tapped (tr) **11** to furnish with a tap **12** to draw off with or as if with a tap **13** to cut into (a tree) and draw off sap from it **14** *Brit informal* to ask or beg (someone) for money: *he tapped me for a fiver* **15 a** to connect a tap to (a telephone or telegraph wire) **b** to listen in secret to (a telephone message, etc) by means of a tap **16** to make a connection to (a pipe, drain, etc) **17** to cut a female screw thread in (an object or material) by use of a tap **18** to withdraw (fluid) from (a bodily cavity) **19** *informal* (of a sports team or an employer) to make an illicit attempt to recruit (a player or employee bound by an existing contract) [Old English *tæppa*; related to Old Norse *tappi* tap, Old High German *zapfo*] > 'tappable *adj*

tap³ (tæp) *n, vb* a Scot word for **top¹**

tapa ('tɑːpə) *n* **1** the inner bark of the paper mulberry **2** a paper-like cloth made from this in the Pacific islands [c19 from Marquesan and Tahitian]

tapadera (ˌtæpə'dɛərə) *n* the leather covering for the stirrup on an American saddle [via American Spanish from Spanish: cover, from *tapar* to cover, of Germanic origin; compare TAMPON, TAP²]

Tapajós (Portuguese tapa'ʒɒs) *n* a river in N Brazil, rising in N central Mato Grosso and flowing northeast to the Amazon. Length: about 800 km (500 miles)

tapas ('tæpəs) *pl n* **a** light snacks or appetizers, usually eaten with drinks **b** (as modifier): *a tapas bar* [from Spanish *tapa* cover, lid]

tap dance *n* **1** a step dance in which the performer wears shoes with taps that make a rhythmic sound on the stage as he dances ▷ *vb* **tap-dance** (intr) **2** to perform a tap dance > 'tap-,dancer *n* > 'tap-,dancing *n*

tape (teɪp) *n* **1** a long thin strip, made of cotton, linen, etc, used for binding, fastening, etc **2** any long narrow strip of cellulose, paper, metal, etc, having similar uses **3** a string stretched across the track at the end of a race course **4** *military slang*, chiefly Brit another word for **stripe¹** (sense 3) **5** See **magnetic tape, ticker tape, paper tape, tape recording** ▷ *vb* (mainly tr) **6** (also intr) Also: **tape-record** to record (speech, music, etc) **7** to furnish with tapes **8** to bind, measure, secure, or wrap with tape **9** (usually passive) Brit informal to take stock of (a person or situation); sum up: *he's got the job taped* [Old English *tæppe*; related to Old Frisian *tapia* to pull, Middle Dutch *tapen* to tear] > 'tape,like *adj* > 'tapen *n*

tape deck *n* **1** a tape recording unit in a hi-fi system **2** the platform supporting the spools, cassettes, or cartridges of a tape recorder, incorporating the motor or motors that drive them and the playback, recording, and erasing heads ▷ Sometimes shortened to: **deck**

tape drive *n computing* a device for reading from or writing to magnetic tape

tape echo *n* a means of delaying the repeat of a sound by adjusting the time lapse between the recording and playback heads of a tape recorder. Also called: **tape slap**

tape grass *n* any of several submerged freshwater plants of the genus *Vallisneria*, esp *V. spiralis*, of warm temperate regions, having ribbon-like leaves: family *Hydrocharitaceae*

tape machine *n* **1** another word for **tape recorder 2** a telegraphic receiving device that records

messages electronically or on ticker tape. US equivalent: **ticker**

tape measure *n* a tape or length of metal marked off in inches, centimetres, etc, used principally for measuring and fitting garments. Also called (esp US): **tapeline**

tapenade ('tæpənɑːd) *n* a savoury paste made from capers, olives, and anchovies, with olive oil and lemon juice [c20 French, from Provençal *tapéo* capers]

taper ('teɪpə) *vb* **1** to become or cause to become narrower towards one end: *the spire tapers to a point* **2** (often foll by off) to become or cause to become smaller or less significant ▷ *n* **3** a thin candle **4** a thin wooden or waxed strip for transferring a flame; spill **5** a narrowing **6** *engineering* (in conical parts) the amount of variation in the diameter per unit of length **7** any feeble source of light [Old English *tapor*, probably from Latin *papȳrus* PAPYRUS (from its use as a wick)] > 'taperer *n* > 'tapering *adj* > 'taperingly *adv*

tape-record *vb* to make a tape recording (of)

tape recorder *n* an electrical device used for recording sounds on magnetic tape and usually also for reproducing them, consisting of a tape deck and one or more amplifiers and loudspeakers

tape recording *n* **1** the act or process of recording on magnetic tape **2** the speech, music, etc, so recorded

tapered roller bearing *n engineering* a rolling bearing that uses tapered rollers running in coned races and is able to accept axial thrust as well as providing shaft location. Compare **thrust bearing**

taper pin *n* a short round metal rod having a small amount of taper so that when driven into a hole it tightens on the taper so that it can act as a stop or wedge

taper relief *n* (in Britain) a system of relief from capital gains tax under which the percentage of a chargeable gain considered taxable is reduced for each whole year (from April 1998) that the asset was held by the vendor

tape slap *n* another term for **tape echo**

tape streamer *n computing* an electromechanical device that enables data to be copied byte by byte from a hard disk onto magnetic tape for security or storage

tapestry ('tæpɪstrɪ) *n, pl* -tries **1** a heavy ornamental fabric, often in the form of a picture, used for wall hangings, furnishings, etc, and made by weaving coloured threads into a fixed warp **2** another word for **needlepoint 3** a colourful and complicated situation: *the rich tapestry of London life* [c15 from Old French *tapisserie* carpeting, from Old French *tapiz* carpet; see TAPIS] > 'tapestried *adj* > 'tapestry-,like *adj*

tapestry moth *n* one of the larger tineid moths, *Trichophaga tapetzella*, the larvae of which devour animal fibres. It is brown, with white-tipped forewings, and prefers damp environments

tape transport *n* the motorized mechanism that moves tape evenly across the recording and playback heads of a tape recorder or cassette player

tapetum (tə'piːtəm) *n, pl* -ta (-tə) **1** a layer of nutritive cells in the sporangia of ferns and anthers of flowering plants that surrounds developing spore cells **2 a** a membranous reflecting layer of cells in the choroid of the eye of nocturnal vertebrates **b** a similar structure in the eyes of certain nocturnal insects **3** *anatomy* a covering layer of cells behind the retina of the eye [c18 from New Latin, from Medieval Latin: covering, from Latin *tapēte* carpet, from Greek *tapēs* carpet] > ta'petal *adj*

tapeworm ('teɪp,wɜːm) *n* any parasitic ribbon-like flatworm of the class *Cestoda*, having a body divided into many egg-producing segments and lacking a mouth and gut. The adults inhabit the intestines of vertebrates. See also **echinococcus, taenia**

taphephobia (ˌtæfɪ'fəʊbɪə) *n med* a pathological

t

fear of being buried alive [from Greek *taphos* grave + -PHOBIA] > ˌtaphe'phobic *adj*

taphole ('tæpˌhəʊl) *n* a hole in a furnace for running off molten metal or slag

taphonomy (tə'fɒnəmɪ) *n* the study of the processes affecting an organism after death that result in its fossilization [C20 from Greek *taphos* grave + -NOMY] > **taphonomic** (ˌtæfə'nɒmɪk) *or* ˌtapho'nomical *adj*

taphouse ('tæpˌhaʊs) *n now rare* an inn or bar

taphrogenesis (ˌtæfrəʊ'dʒɛnɪsɪs) *n geology* the process of forming rifts, resulting in regional faulting and subsidence [C20 from German *Tafrogenese*, from Greek *taphros* pit + -GENESIS]

tap-in *n soccer* a goal scored without great effort by simply knocking the ball into the goal from close range

tapioca (ˌtæpɪ'əʊkə) *n* a beadlike starch obtained from cassava root, used in cooking as a thickening agent, esp in puddings [C18 via Portuguese from Tupi *tipioca* pressed-out juice, from *tipi* residue + *ok* to squeeze out]

tapir ('teɪpə) *n, pl* **-pirs** *or* **-pir** any perissodactyl mammal of the genus *Tapirus*, such as *T. indicus* (**Malayan tapir**), of South and Central America and SE Asia, having an elongated snout, three-toed hind legs, and four-toed forelegs: family *Tapiridae* [C18 from Tupi *tapiíra*]

tapis ('tæpɪ:, 'tæpɪ; *French* tapi) *n, pl* **tapis** tapestry or carpeting, esp as formerly used to cover a table in a council chamber [C17 from French, from Old French *tapiz*, from Greek *tapētion* rug, from *tapēs* carpet]

tapper ('tæpə) *n* **1** a person who taps **2** a tool or instrument that taps **3** *Northern English dialect* an unstable and violent person

tappet ('tæpɪt) *n* a mechanical part that reciprocates to receive or transmit intermittent motion, esp the part of an internal-combustion engine that transmits motion from the camshaft to the push rods or valves [C18 from TAP[1] + -ET]

tapping up *n Brit informal* (esp of a professional soccer club) the illicit practice of attempting to recruit a player while he is still bound by contract to another team

tappit-hen ('tæpɪt'hɛn) *n Scot* **1** a hen with a crest **2** a pewter tankard, usually with a distinctive knob on the lid [C18 from Scottish *tappit* topped, crested + HEN]

taproom ('tæpˌru:m, -ˌrʊm) *n* a bar, as in a hotel or pub

taproot ('tæpˌru:t) *n* the large single root of plants such as the dandelion, which grows vertically downwards and bears smaller lateral roots [C17 from TAP[2] + ROOT[1]] > 'tapˌrooted *adj*

taps (tæps) *n (functioning as singular)* **1** *chiefly US* **a** (in army camps, etc) a signal given on a bugle, drum, etc, indicating that lights are to be put out **b** any similar signal, as at a military funeral **2** (in the Guide movement) a closing song sung at an evening camp fire or at the end of a meeting [C19 from TAP[1]]

tapsalteerie ('tæpsəl'ti:rɪ) *adj, adv, n Scot* topsy-turvy [C17 of uncertain origin]

tapster ('tæpstə) *n* **1** *rare* a barman **2** (in W Africa) a man who taps palm trees to collect and sell palm wine [Old English *tæppestre*, feminine of *tæppere*, from *tappian* to TAP[2]] > 'tapstress *fem n*

tapu ('ta:pu:) NZ ▷ *adj* **1** sacred; forbidden ▷ *n* **2** a Māori religious or superstitious restriction on something [Māori, from Tongan]

tap water *n* water drawn off through taps from pipes in a house, as distinguished from distilled water, mineral water, etc

tar[1] (ta:) *n* **1** any of various dark viscid substances obtained by the destructive distillation of organic matter such as coal, wood, or peat **2** another name for **coal tar** ▷ *vb* **tars, tarring, tarred** (*tr*) **3** to coat with tar **4** **tar and feather** to punish by smearing tar and feathers over (someone) **5** **tarred with the same brush** regarded as having the same faults [Old English *teoru*; related to Old

Frisian *tera*, Old Norse *tjara*, Middle Low German *tere* tar, Gothic *triu* tree] > 'tarry *adj* > 'tarriness *n*

tar[2] (ta:) *n* an informal word for **seaman** [C17 short for TARPAULIN]

tara (ta:) *n, pl* **tara** another name for **white-fronted tern** [Māori]

Tara ('ta:rə, 'ta:rə) *n* a village in Co Meath near Dublin, by the **Hill of Tara**, the historic seat of the ancient Irish kings

ta-ra (tæ'ra:) *sentence substitute informal, chiefly Northern English* goodbye; farewell [C20 variant of TA-TA]

Tarabulus el Gharb (tə'ra:bələs ɛl 'ga:b) *n* transliteration of the Arabic name for **Tripoli** (Libya)

Tarabulus esh Sham (tə'ra:bələs ɛʃ 'ʃæm) *n* transliteration of the Arabic name for **Tripoli** (Lebanon)

taradiddle ('tærəˌdɪdᵊl) *n* another spelling of **tarradiddle**

taraire (ta:ra:i:rə) *n, pl* **taraire** a large New Zealand forest tree, *Beilschmiedia taraire*, with broad green leaves and purple fruit [Māori]

tarakihi ('tærəˌki:hi:) *or* **terakihi** *n, pl* **-kihis** a common edible sea fish of New Zealand waters

taramasalata (ˌtærəməsə'la:tə) *n* a creamy pale pink pâté, made from the roe of grey mullet or smoked cod and served as an hors d'oeuvre [C20 from Modern Greek, from *tarama* cod's roe]

taramea (ta:ra:'mi:a:) *n* a New Zealand speargrass, *Aciphylla aurea*. Also called: **golden Spaniard, golden speargrass** [Māori]

Taranaki gate (ˌtærə'næki:) *n NZ* a rough-and-ready gate in a fence made from wire and battens [first used on dairy farms in *Taranaki*, province of NZ]

Taranaki wind *n NZ informal* natural gas from Taranaki

tarantass (ˌta:rən'tæs) *n* a large horse-drawn four-wheeled Russian carriage without springs [C19 from Russian *tarantas*, from Kazan Tatar *taryntas*]

tarantella (ˌtærən'tɛlə) *n* **1** a peasant dance from S Italy **2** a piece of music composed for or in the rhythm of this dance, in fast six-eight time [C18 from Italian, from *Taranto* TARANTO; associated with TARANTISM]

Tarantinoesque (ˌtærənˌti:nəʊ'ɛsk) *adj* referring to or reminiscent of the work of the American film-maker and actor Quentin Tarantino (born 1963), known for the violence, style, and wit of his films

tarantism ('tærənˌtɪzəm) *n* a nervous disorder marked by uncontrollable bodily movement, widespread in S Italy during the 15th to 17th centuries: popularly thought to be caused by the bite of a tarantula [C17 from New Latin *tarantismus*, from TARANTO; see TARANTULA]

Taranto (tə'ræntəʊ; *Italian* 'ta:ranto) *n* a port in SE Italy, in Apulia on the **Gulf of Taranto** (an inlet of the Ionian Sea): the chief city of Magna Graecia; taken by the Romans in 272 BC Pop: 202 033 (2001). Latin name: **Tarentum**

tarantula (tə'ræntjʊlə) *n, pl* **-las** *or* **-lae** (-ˌli:) **1** any of various large hairy mostly tropical spiders of the American family *Theraphosidae* **2** a large hairy spider, *Lycosa tarentula* of S Europe, the bite of which was formerly thought to cause tarantism [C16 from Medieval Latin, from Old Italian *tarantola*, from TARANTO]

Tarantula nebula *n* a huge bright emission nebula located in the S hemisphere in the Large Magellanic Cloud

Tararua biscuit ('ta:ra:ˌru:ə) *n NZ informal* a tramper's home-made biscuit with a high calorie content

Tarawa (tə'ra:wə) *n* an atoll in Kiribati, occupying a chain of islets surrounding a lagoon in the W central Pacific: the capital of Kiribati, Bairiki, is on this atoll. Pop: 32 354 (1995)

taraxacum (tə'ræksəkəm) *n* **1** any perennial plant of the genus *Taraxacum*, such as the

dandelion, having dense heads of small yellow flowers and seeds with a feathery attachment: family *Asteraceae* (composites) **2** the dried root of the dandelion, used as a laxative, diuretic, and tonic [C18 from Medieval Latin, from Arabic *tarakhshaqūn* wild chicory, perhaps of Persian origin]

Taraz (tə'rats) *n* a city in S Kazakhstan: chemical manufacturing. Pop: 339 000 (2005 est). Former names: Dzhambul (1938–91), Auliye-Ata (1991–97)

Tarbes (*French* tarb) *n* a town in SW France: noted for the breeding of Anglo-Arab horses. Pop: 46 275 (1999)

tarboosh, tarbush *or* **tarbouche** (ta:'bu:ʃ) *n* a felt or cloth brimless cap resembling the fez, usually red and often with a silk tassel, worn alone or as part of a turban by Muslim men [C18 from Arabic *tarbūsh*]

tar boy *n Austral and NZ informal* a boy who applies tar to the skin of sheep cut during shearing

Tardenoisian (ˌta:də'nɔɪzɪən) *adj* of or referring to a Mesolithic culture characterized by small flint instruments [C20 after *Tardenois*, France, where implements were found]

tardigrade ('ta:dɪˌgreɪd) *n* **1** any minute aquatic segmented eight-legged invertebrate of the phylum *Tardigrada*, related to the arthropods, occurring in soil, ditches, etc. Popular name: **water bear** ▷ *adj* **2** of, relating to, or belonging to the *Tardigrada* [C17 via Latin *tardigradus*, from *tardus* sluggish + *gradī* to walk]

tardy ('ta:dɪ) *adj* **-dier, -diest 1** occurring later than expected: *tardy retribution* **2** slow in progress, growth, etc: *a tardy reader* [C15 from Old French *tardif*, from Latin *tardus* slow] > 'tardily *adv* > 'tardiness *n*

tare[1] (tɛə) *n* **1** any of various vetch plants, such as *Vicia hirsuta* (**hairy tare**) of Eurasia and N Africa **2** the seed of any of these plants **3** *Bible* a troublesome weed, thought to be the darnel [C14 of unknown origin]

tare[2] (tɛə) *n* **1** the weight of the wrapping or container in which goods are packed **2** a deduction from gross weight to compensate for this **3** the weight of a vehicle without its cargo, passengers, etc **4** an empty container used as a counterbalance in determining net weight ▷ *vb* **5** (*tr*) to weigh (a package, etc) in order to calculate the amount of tare [C15 from Old French: waste, from Medieval Latin *tara*, from Arabic *tarhah* something discarded, from *taraha* to reject]

Tarentum (tə'rɛntəm) *n* the Latin name of **Taranto**

targe (ta:dʒ) *n* an archaic word for **shield** [C13 from Old French, of Germanic origin; related to Old High German *zarga* rim, frame, Old Norse *targa* shield]

target ('ta:gɪt) *n* **1 a** an object or area at which an archer or marksman aims, usually a round flat surface marked with concentric rings **b** (*as modifier*): *target practice* **2 a** any point or area aimed at; the object of an attack or a takeover bid **b** (*as modifier*): *target area; target company* **3** a fixed goal or objective: *the target for the appeal is £10 000* **4** a person or thing at which an action or remark is directed or the object of a person's feelings: *a target for the teacher's sarcasm* **5** a joint of lamb consisting of the breast and neck **6** *surveying* a marker on which sights are taken, such as the sliding marker on a levelling staff **7** (formerly) a small round shield **8** *physics, electronics* **a** a substance, object, or system subjected to bombardment by electrons or other particles, or to irradiation **b** an electrode in a television camera tube whose surface, on which image information is stored, is scanned by the electron beam **9** *electronics* an object to be detected by the reflection of a radar or sonar signal, etc **10 on target** on the correct course to meet a target or objective ▷ *vb* **-gets, -geting, -geted** (*tr*) **11** to make a target of **12** to direct or aim: *to target benefits at those most in need* [C14 from Old French *targette* a little shield, from Old French

TARGE] > 'targetless adj

targetitis (ˌtɑːgɪt'aɪtɪs) n jocular the setting of more targets than is strictly necessary for the effective functioning of an organization, esp when it leads to an increase in bureaucracy [c20 TARGET + -ITIS (sense 2)]

target language n 1 the language into which a text, document, etc, is translated 2 a language that is being or is to be learnt

target man n soccer an attacking player to whom high crosses and centres are played, esp a tall forward

Targum ('tɑːgəm; Hebrew tar'gum) n an Aramaic translation, usually in the form of an expanded paraphrase, of various books or sections of the Old Testament [c16 from Aramaic: interpretation] > **Targumic** (tɑː'guːmɪk) or **Tar'gumical** adj > **'Targumist** n

tariff ('tærɪf) n 1 a a tax levied by a government on imports or occasionally exports for purposes of protection, support of the balance of payments, or the raising of revenue b a system or list of such taxes 2 any schedule of prices, fees, fares, etc 3 chiefly Brit a a method of charging for the supply of services, esp public services, such as gas and electricity: block tariff b a schedule of such charges 4 chiefly Brit a bill of fare with prices listed; menu ▷ vb (tr) 5 Brit the level of punishment imposed for a criminal offence 6 to set a tariff on 7 to set a price on according to a schedule of tariffs [c16 from Italian tariffa, from Arabic ta'rīfa to inform] > **'tariffless** adj

tariff office n insurance a company whose premiums are based on a tariff agreed with other insurance companies

Tarim ('tɑː'riːm) n a river in NW China, in Xinjiang Uygur AR: flows east along the N edge of the Taklimakan Shama desert, dividing repeatedly and forming lakes among the dunes, finally disappearing in the Lop Nor depression; the chief river of Xinjiang Uygur AR; drains the great **Tarim Basin** between the Tian Shan and Kunlun mountain systems of central Asia, an area of about 906 500 sq km (350 000 sq miles). Length: 2190 km (1360 miles)

tarlatan ('tɑːlətən) n an open-weave cotton fabric, used for stiffening garments [c18 from French tarlatane, variant of tarnatane type of muslin, perhaps of Indian origin]

tarmac ('tɑːmæk) n 1 a paving material that consists of crushed stone rolled and bound with a mixture of tar and bitumen, esp as formerly used for a road, airport runway, etc. Full name: tarmacadam (ˌtɑːmə'kædəm) See also **macadam** 2 the tarmac a runway at an airport: on the tarmac at Nairobi airport ▷ vb -macs, -macking, -macked (tr) 3 (usually not capital) to apply tarmac to

tarn (tɑːn) n a small mountain lake or pool [c14 of Scandinavian origin; related to Old Norse tjörn pool]

Tarn (French tarn) n 1 a department of S France, in Midi-Pyrénées region. Capital: Albi. Pop: 350 477 (2003 est). Area: 5780 sq km (2254 sq miles) 2 a river in SW France, rising in the Massif Central and flowing generally west to the Garonne River. Length: 375 km (233 miles)

tarnal ('tɑːnᵊl) US dialect ▷ adj 1 (prenominal) damned ▷ adv 2 (intensifier): tarnal lucky! [c18 aphetic dialect pronunciation of ETERNAL] > **'tarnally** adv

tarnation (tɑː'neɪʃən) n a euphemism for **damnation**

Tarn-et-Garonne (French tarnegarɔn) n a department of SW France, in Midi-Pyrénées region. Capital: Montauban. Pop: 214 488 (2003 est). Area: 3731 sq km (1455 sq miles)

tarnish ('tɑːnɪʃ) vb 1 to lose or cause to lose the shine, esp by exposure to air or moisture resulting in surface oxidation; discolour: silver tarnishes quickly 2 to stain or become stained; taint or spoil: a fraud that tarnished his reputation ▷ n 3 a tarnished condition, surface, or film [c16 from Old French

ternir to make dull, from terne lustreless, of Germanic origin; related to Old High German tarnen to conceal, Old English dierne hidden] > **'tarnishable** adj > **'tarnisher** n

Tarnopol (tar'nɔpɔl) n the Polish name for **Ternopol**

Tarnów (Polish 'tarnuf) n an industrial city in SE Poland. Pop: 119 000 (2005 est)

taro ('tɑːrəʊ) n, pl -ros 1 an aroid plant, Colocasia esculenta, cultivated in the tropics for its large edible rootstock 2 the rootstock of this plant ▷ Also called: **elephant's-ear, dasheen, eddo, Chinese eddo** [c18 from Tahitian and Māori]

tarot ('tærəʊ) n 1 one of a special pack of cards, now used mainly for fortune-telling, consisting of 78 cards (4 suits of 14 cards each (the minor arcana), and 22 other cards (the major arcana)) 2 a card in a tarot pack with distinctive symbolic design, such as the Wheel of Fortune ▷ adj 3 relating to tarot cards [c16 from French, from Old Italian tarocco, of unknown origin]

tarp (tɑːp) n US, Austral, and NZ an informal word for **tarpaulin**

tarpan ('tɑːpæn) n a European wild horse, Equus caballus gomelini, common in prehistoric times but now extinct [from Kirghiz Tatar]

tarpaulin (tɑː'pɔːlɪn) n 1 a heavy hard-wearing waterproof fabric made of canvas or similar material coated with tar, wax, or paint, for outdoor use as a protective covering against moisture 2 a sheet of this fabric 3 a hat of or covered with this fabric, esp a sailor's hat 4 a rare word for **seaman** [c17 probably from TAR¹ + PALL¹ + -ING¹]

Tarpeia (tɑː'piːə) n (in Roman legend) a vestal virgin, who betrayed Rome to the Sabines and was killed by them when she requested a reward

Tarpeian Rock (tɑː'piːən) n (in ancient Rome) a cliff on the Capitoline hill from which traitors were hurled

tarpon ('tɑːpən) n, pl -pons or -pon 1 a large silvery clupeoid game fish, Tarpon atlanticus, of warm Atlantic waters, having a compressed body covered with large scales: family Elopidae 2 Austral another name for **ox-eye herring** 3 any similar related fish [c17 perhaps from Dutch tarpoen, of unknown origin]

Tarquin ('tɑːkwɪn) n 1 Latin name Lucius Tarquinius Priscus, fifth legendary king of Rome (616–578 BC) 2 Latin name Lucius Tarquinius Superbus, seventh and last legendary king of Rome (534–510 BC)

tarradiddle ('tærəˌdɪdᵊl) n 1 a trifling lie 2 nonsense; twaddle [of unknown origin]

tarragon ('tærəgən) n 1 an aromatic perennial plant, Artemisia dracunculus, of the Old World, having whitish flowers and small toothed leaves, which are used as seasoning: family Asteraceae (composites) 2 the leaves of this plant ▷ Also called: **estragon** [c16 from Medieval Latin targon, from Medieval Latin tarcon, from Arabic tarkhūn, perhaps from Greek drakontion adderwort]

Tarragona (Spanish tarra'yona) n a port in NE Spain, on the Mediterranean: one of the richest seaports of the Roman Empire; destroyed by the Moors (714). Pop: 121 076 (2003 est). Latin name: Tarraco (tə'rɑːkəʊ)

Tarrasa (Spanish ta'rrasa) n a city in NE Spain: textile centre. Pop: 184 829 (2003 est). Also called: **Terrassa**

tarriance ('tærɪəns) n an archaic word for **delay**

tarry ('tærɪ) vb -ries, -rying, -ried 1 (intr) to delay in coming or going; linger 2 (intr) to remain temporarily or briefly 3 (intr) to wait or stay 4 (tr) archaic or poetic to await ▷ n, pl -ries 5 rare a stay [c14 tarien, of uncertain origin] > **'tarrier** n

tarsal ('tɑːsᵊl) adj 1 of, relating to, or constituting the tarsus or tarsi ▷ n 2 a tarsal bone

tar sand n a sandstone in which hydrocarbons have been trapped; the lighter compounds evaporate, leaving a residue of asphalt in the rock pores

tarseal ('tɑːˌsiːl) n NZ 1 the bitumen surface of a

road 2 **the** the main highway

Tarshish ('tɑːʃɪʃ) n Old Testament an ancient port, mentioned in I Kings 10:22, situated in Spain or in one of the Phoenician colonies in Sardinia

tarsia ('tɑːsɪə) n another term for **intarsia** [c17 from Italian, from Arabic tarsi; see INTARSIA]

tarsier ('tɑːsɪə) n any of several nocturnal arboreal prosimian primates of the genus Tarsius, of Indonesia and the Philippines, having huge eyes, long hind legs, and digits ending in pads to facilitate climbing: family Tarsiidae [c18 from French, from tarse the flat of the foot; see TARSUS]

tarsometatarsus (ˌtɑːsəʊˌmɛtə'tɑːsəs) n, pl -si (-saɪ) a bone in the lower part of a bird's leg consisting of the metatarsal bones and some of the tarsal bones fused together [c19 tarso-, from TARSUS + METATARSUS] > ˌtarsoˌmeta'tarsal adj

tarsus ('tɑːsəs) n, pl -si (-saɪ) 1 the bones of the ankle and heel, collectively 2 a the corresponding part in other mammals and in amphibians and reptiles b another name for **tarsometatarsus** 3 the dense connective tissue supporting the free edge of each eyelid 4 the part of an insect's leg that lies distal to the tibia [c17 from New Latin, from Greek tarsos flat surface, instep]

Tarsus ('tɑːsəs) n 1 a city in SE Turkey, on the Tarsus River: site of ruins of ancient Tarsus, capital of Cilicia, and birthplace of St Paul. Pop: 231 000 (2005 est) 2 a river in SE Turkey, in Cilicia, rising in the Taurus Mountains and flowing south past Tarsus to the Mediterranean. Length: 153 km (95 miles). Ancient name: **Cydnus**

tart¹ (tɑːt) n a pastry case often having no top crust, with a sweet filling of fruit, jam, custard, etc [c14 from Old French tarte, of uncertain origin; compare Medieval Latin tarte]

tart² (tɑːt) adj 1 (of a flavour, food, etc) sour, acid, or astringent 2 cutting, sharp, or caustic: a tart remark [Old English teart rough; related to Dutch tarten to defy, Middle High German traz defiance] > **'tartish** adj > **'tartishly** adv > **'tartly** adv > **'tartness** n

tart³ (tɑːt) n informal a promiscuous woman, esp a prostitute: often a term of abuse. See also **tart up** [c19 shortened from SWEETHEART] > **'tarty** adj

tartan¹ ('tɑːtᵊn) n 1 a a design of straight lines, crossing at right angles to give a chequered appearance, esp the distinctive design or designs associated with each Scottish clan: the Buchanan tartan b (as modifier): a tartan kilt 2 a woollen fabric or garment with this design 3 **the tartan** Highland dress [c16 perhaps from Old French tertaine linsey-woolsey, from Old Spanish tiritaña a fine silk fabric, from tiritar to rustle] > **'tartaned** adj

tartan² ('tɑːtᵊn) n a single-masted vessel used in the Mediterranean, usually with a lateen sail [c17 from French, perhaps from Provençal tartana falcon, buzzard, since a ship was frequently given the name of a bird]

tartanry ('tɑːtᵊnrɪ) n derogatory the excessive use of tartan and other Scottish imagery to produce a distorted sentimental view of Scotland and its history [c20 TARTAN¹ + -RY]

tartar¹ ('tɑːtə) n 1 dentistry a hard crusty deposit on the teeth, consisting of food, cellular debris, and mineral salts 2 Also called: **argol** a brownish-red substance consisting mainly of potassium hydrogen tartrate, present in grape juice and deposited during the fermentation of wine [c14 from Medieval Latin tartarum, from Medieval Greek tartaron]

tartar² ('tɑːtə) n (sometimes capital) a fearsome or formidable person [c16 special use of TARTAR]

Tartar ('tɑːtə) n, adj a variant spelling of **Tatar**

tartare or **tartar sauce** n a mayonnaise sauce mixed with hard-boiled egg yolks, chopped herbs, capers, and gherkins [from French sauce tartare, from TARTAR]

Tartarean (tɑː'tɛərɪən, -'tɑːrɪ-) adj literary of or relating to Tartarus; infernal

tartar emetic n another name for **antimony**

potassium tartrate

Tartarian (tɑːˈtɛərɪən) *adj* a variant spelling of **Tatarian**

tartaric (tɑːˈtærɪk) *adj* of, concerned with, containing, or derived from tartar or tartaric acid. Systematic name: **2,3-dihydroxybutanedioic acid**

Tartaric (tɑːˈtærɪk) *adj* a variant spelling of **Tataric**

tartaric acid *n* a colourless or white odourless crystalline water-soluble dicarboxylic acid existing in four stereoisomeric forms, the commonest being the dextrorotatory (*d*-) compound which is found in many fruits: used as a food additive (**E334**) in soft drinks, confectionery, and baking powders and in tanning and photography. Formula: HOOCCH(OH)CH(OH)COOH

tartarize *or* **tartarise** (ˈtɑːtəˌraɪz) *vb* (*tr*) to impregnate or treat with tartar or tartar emetic > ˌtartariˈzation *or* ˌtartariˈsation *n*

tartarous (ˈtɑːtərəs) *adj* consisting of, containing, or resembling tartar

tartar steak *n* a variant term for **steak tartare**

Tartarus (ˈtɑːtərəs) *n Greek myth* **1** an abyss under Hades where the Titans were imprisoned **2** a part of Hades reserved for evildoers **3** the underworld; Hades **4** a primordial god who became the father of the monster Typhon [c16 from Latin, from Greek *Tartaros*, of obscure origin]

Tartary (ˈtɑːtərɪ) *n* a variant spelling of **Tatary**

tartine (tɑːˈtiːn) *n* an open sandwich, esp one with a rich or elaborate topping [c21 from French, diminutive of *tarte* TART[1]]

tartlet (ˈtɑːtlɪt) *n Brit* an individual pastry case with a filling of fruit or other sweet or savoury mixture

tartrate (ˈtɑːtreɪt) *n* any salt or ester of tartaric acid

tartrated (ˈtɑːtreɪtɪd) *adj* being in the form of a tartrate

tartrazine (ˈtɑːtrəˌziːn, -zɪn) *n* an azo dye that produces a yellow colour: widely used as a food additive (**E102**) in convenience foods, soft drinks, sweets, etc, and in drugs, and also to dye textiles

Tartu (*Russian* ˈtartu) *n* a city in SE Estonia: successively under Polish, Swedish, and Russian rule; university (1632). Pop: 95 000 (2005 est). Former name (11th century until 1918): **Yurev** German name: **Dorpat**

Tartuffe *or* **Tartufe** (tɑːˈtʊf, -ˈtuːf) *n* a person who hypocritically pretends to be deeply pious [from the character in the comedy *Tartuffe* (1664) by the French dramatist Molière (1622–73)] > **Tarˈtuffian** *or* **Tarˈtufian** *adj*

tart up *vb* (*tr, adverb*) *Brit informal* **1** to dress and make (oneself) up in a provocative way **2** to decorate or improve the appearance of: *to tart up a bar*

tarwhine (ˈtɑːˌwaɪn) *n* a bream, *Rhabdosargus sarba*, of E Australia, silver in colour with gold streaks [from a native Australian language]

Tarzan (ˈtɑːzən) *n* (*sometimes not capital*) *informal often ironic* a man with great physical strength, agility, and virility [c20 after the hero of a series of stories by Edgar Rice Burroughs (1875–1950), US novelist]

Taser (ˈteɪzə) (*sometimes not capital*) *n* **1** *trademark* a weapon that fires electrical probes that give an electric shock, causing temporary paralysis ▷ *vb* **2** (*tr*) to stun (someone) with a taser

Tashi Lama (ˈtɑːʃɪ ˈlɑːmə) *n* another name for the **Panchen Lama** [from *Tashi* (*Lumpo*), the name of the Tibetan monastery over which this Lama presides]

Tashkent (*Russian* tɑʃˈkjɛnt) *n* the capital of Uzbekistan: one of the oldest and largest cities in central Asia; cotton textile manufacturing. Pop: 2 160 000 (2005 est). Uzbek name: **Toshkent**

tasimeter (təˈsɪmɪtə) *n* a device for measuring small temperature changes. It depends on the changes of pressure resulting from expanding or contracting solids [c19 *tasi*-, from Greek *tasis*

tension + -METER] > **tasimetric** (ˌtæsɪˈmɛtrɪk) *adj* > taˈsimetry *n*

task (tɑːsk) *n* **1** a specific piece of work required to be done as a duty or chore **2** an unpleasant or difficult job or duty **3** any piece of work **4** **take to task** to criticize or reprove ▷ *vb* (*tr*) **5** to assign a task to **6** to subject to severe strain; tax [c13 from Old French *tasche*, from Medieval Latin *tasca*, from *taxa* tax, from Latin *taxāre* to TAX] > 'tasker *n* > 'taskless *adj*

taskbar (ˈtɑːskˌbɑː) *n* a row of selectable buttons and icons typically running along the bottom of a computer screen, displaying information such as the names of running programs

task force *n* **1** a temporary grouping of military units formed to undertake a specific mission **2** any semipermanent organization set up to carry out a continuing task

taskmaster (ˈtɑːskˌmɑːstə) *n* a person, discipline, etc, that enforces work, esp hard or continuous work: *his teacher is a hard taskmaster* > 'task,mistress *fem n*

task-oriented *adj* focusing on the completion of particular tasks as a measure of success

taskwork (ˈtɑːskˌwɜːk) *n* **1** hard or unpleasant work **2** a rare word for **piecework**

Tasmania (tæzˈmeɪnɪə) *n* an island in the S Pacific, south of mainland Australia: forms, with offshore islands, the smallest state of Australia; discovered by the Dutch explorer Tasman in 1642; used as a penal colony by the British (1803–53); mostly forested and mountainous. Capital: Hobart. Pop: 479 958 (2003 est). Area: 68 332 sq km (26 383 sq miles). Former name (1642–1855): **Van Diemen's Land**

Tasmanian (tæzˈmeɪnɪən) *adj* **1** of or relating to Tasmania or its inhabitants ▷ *n* **2** a native or inhabitant of Tasmania

Tasmanian devil *n* a small ferocious carnivorous marsupial, *Sarcophilus harrisi*, of Tasmania, having black fur with pale markings, strong jaws, and short legs: family *Dasyuridae*. Also called: **ursine dasyure**

Tasmanian wolf *or* **tiger** *n* other names for **thylacine**

Tasman Sea *n* the part of the Pacific between SE Australia and NW New Zealand

tass (tæs) *or* **tassie** (ˈtæsɪ) *n Scot and northern English dialect* **1** a cup, goblet, or glass **2** the contents of such a vessel [c15 from Old French *tasse* cup, from Arabic *tassah* basin, from Persian *tast*]

Tass (tæs) *n* (formerly) the principal news agency of the Soviet Union: replaced in 1992 by **Itar Tass** [T(*elegrafnoye*) A(*genstvo*) S(*ovetskovo*) S(*oyuza*) Telegraphic Agency of the Soviet Union]

tassel (ˈtæsəl) *n* **1** a tuft of loose threads secured by a knot or ornamental knob, used to decorate soft furnishings, clothes, etc **2** anything resembling this tuft, esp the tuft of stamens at the tip of a maize inflorescence ▷ *vb* -sels, -selling, -selled *or US* -sels, -seling, -seled **3** (*tr*) to adorn with a tassel or tassels **4** (*intr*) (of maize) to produce stamens in a tuft **5** (*tr*) to remove the tassels from [c13 from Old French, from Vulgar Latin *tassellus* (unattested), changed from Latin *taxillus* a small die, from *tālus* gaming die] > 'tasselly *adj*

tasset (ˈtæsɪt), **tasse** (tæs) *or less commonly* **tace** *n* a piece of armour consisting of one or more plates fastened on to the bottom of a cuirass to protect the thigh [c19 from French *tassette* small pouch, from Old French *tasse* purse]

Tassie *or* **Tassy** (ˈtæzɪ) *n, pl* -sies *Austral informal* **1** Tasmania **2** a native or inhabitant of Tasmania

taste (teɪst) *n* **1** the sense by which the qualities and flavour of a substance are distinguished by the taste buds **2** the sensation experienced by means of the taste buds **3** the act of tasting **4** a small amount eaten, drunk, or tried on the tongue **5** a brief experience of something: *a taste of the whip* **6** a preference or liking for something;

inclination: *to have a taste for danger* **7** the ability to make discerning judgments about aesthetic, artistic, and intellectual matters; discrimination: *to have taste* **8** judgment of aesthetic or social matters according to a generally accepted standard: *bad taste* **9** discretion; delicacy: *that remark lacks taste* **10** *obsolete* the act of testing ▷ *vb* **11** to distinguish the taste of (a substance) by means of the taste buds **12** (*usually tr*) to take a small amount of (a food, liquid, etc) into the mouth, esp in order to test the quality: *to taste the wine* **13** (often foll by *of*) to have a specific flavour or taste: *the tea tastes of soap; this apple tastes sour* **14** (when *intr*, usually foll by *of*) to have an experience of (something): *to taste success* **15** (*tr*) an archaic word for **enjoy** **16** (*tr*) *obsolete* to test by touching [c13 from Old French *taster*, ultimately from Latin *taxāre* to appraise] > 'tastable *adj*

taste bud *n* any of the elevated oval-shaped sensory end organs on the surface of the tongue, by means of which the sensation of taste is experienced

tasteful (ˈteɪstfʊl) *adj* **1** indicating good taste: *a tasteful design* **2** a rare word for **tasty**. > 'tastefully *adv* > 'tastefulness *n*

tasteless (ˈteɪstlɪs) *adj* **1** lacking in flavour; insipid **2** lacking social or aesthetic taste **3** *rare* unable to taste > 'tastelessly *adv* > 'tastelessness *n*

tastemaker (ˈteɪstˌmeɪkə) *n* a person or group that sets a new fashion

taster (ˈteɪstə) *n* **1** a person who samples food or drink for quality **2** any device used in tasting or sampling **3** a person employed, esp formerly, to taste food and drink prepared for a king, etc, to test for poison **4** a sample or preview of a product, experience, etc, intended to stimulate interest in the product, experience, etc, itself: *the single serves as a taster for the band's new album*

-tastic *adj combining form jocular* denoting excellence in a specified area: *the fun-tastic theme park; their poptastic new single* [c20 from (FAN)TASTIC]

tasty (ˈteɪstɪ) *adj* tastier, tastiest **1** having a pleasant flavour **2** *Brit informal* attractive: used chiefly by men when talking of women **3** *Brit informal* skilful or impressive: *she was a bit tasty with a cutlass* **4** *NZ* (of cheddar cheese) having a strong flavour > 'tastily *adv* > 'tastiness *n*

tat[1] (tæt) *vb* tats, tatting, tatted to make (something) by tatting [c19 of unknown origin]

tat[2] (tæt) *n* **1** tatty articles or a tatty condition **2** tasteless articles **3** a tangled mass [c20 back formation from TATTY]

tat[3] (tæt) *n* short for **tattoo**[2] (sense 2)

tat[4] (tæt) *n* See **tit for tat**

ta-ta (tæˈtɑː) *sentence substitute Brit informal* goodbye; farewell [c19 of unknown origin]

tatahash (ˈteɪtəhæʃ) *n Northern English dialect* a stew containing potatoes and cheap cuts of meat

tatami (təˈtɑːmɪ, tæˈtæmɪ) *n, pl* -mi *or* -mis a thick rectangular mat of woven straw, used as a standard to measure a Japanese room [Japanese]

Tatar *or* **Tartar** (ˈtɑːtə) *n* **1 a** a member of a Mongoloid people who under Genghis Khan established a vast and powerful state in central Asia from the 13th century until conquered by Russia in 1552 **b** a descendant of this people, now scattered throughout Russia but living chiefly in the Tatar Republic **2** any of the languages spoken by the present-day Tatars, belonging to various branches of the Turkic family of languages, esp Kazan Tatar ▷ *adj* **3** of, relating to, or characteristic of the Tatars [c14 from Old French *Tartare*, from Medieval Latin *Tartarus* (associated with Latin *Tartarus* the underworld), from Persian *Tātār*] > **Tatarian** (tɑːˈtɛərɪən), **Tarˈtarian**, **Tataric** (tɑːˈtærɪk) *or* **Tarˈtaric** *adj*

Tatar Republic *n* a constituent republic of W Russia, around the confluence of the Volga and Kama Rivers. Capital: Kazan. Pop: 3 779 800 (2002). Area: 68 000 sq km (26 250 sq miles)

Tatar Strait *n* an arm of the Pacific between the mainland of SE Russia and Sakhalin Island, linking the Sea of Japan with the Sea of Okhotsk. Length: about 560 km (350 miles). Also called: **Gulf of Tatary**

Tatary or **Tartary** ('tɑːtərɪ) n **1** a historical region (with indefinite boundaries) in E Europe and Asia, inhabited by Bulgars until overrun by the Tatars in the mid-13th century: extended as far east as the Pacific under Genghis Khan **2** *Gulf of* another name for the **Tatar Strait**

Tate Galleries *pl n* two art galleries in London, the original Tate Gallery (1897), now **Tate Britain**, and **Tate Modern**, created in the former Bankside power station in 2000

tater ('teɪtə) *n* a dialect word for **potato**

tatouay ('tætʊˌeɪ, ˌtætʊ'aɪ) *n* a large armadillo, *Cabassous tatouay*, of South America [c16 from Spanish *tatuay*, from Guarani *tatu ai*, from *tatu* armadillo + *ai* worthless (because inedible)]

Tatra Mountains ('tɑːtrə, 'tæt-) *pl n* a mountain range along the border between Slovakia and Poland, extending for about 64 km (40 miles): the highest range of the central Carpathians. Highest peak: Gerlachovka, 2663 m (8737 ft). Also called: **High Tatra**

TATT *abbreviation for* tired all the time: a term used to describe a set of symptoms often related to doctors by patients

tatter ('tætə) *vb* **1** to make or become ragged or worn to shreds ▷ *n* **2** (*plural*) torn or ragged pieces, esp of material **3 in tatters a** torn to pieces; in shreds **b** destroyed or ruined [c14 of Scandinavian origin; compare Icelandic *töturr* rag, Old English *tættec*, Old High German *zæter* rag]

tatterdemalion (ˌtætədɪ'meɪljən, -'mæl-) *n rare* **a** a person dressed in ragged clothes **b** (*as modifier*): *a tatterdemalion dress* [c17 from TATTER + *-demalion*, of uncertain origin]

tattered ('tætəd) *adj* **1** ragged or worn: *a tattered old book* **2** wearing ragged or torn clothing: *tattered refugees* **3** damaged, defeated, or in disarray: *he believes he can bring the tattered party together*

tattersall ('tætəˌsɔːl) *n* **a** a fabric, sometimes brightly coloured, having stripes or bars in a checked or squared pattern **b** (*as modifier*): *a tattersall coat* [c19 after TATTERSALL'S; the horse blankets at the market originally had this pattern]

Tattersall's ('tætəˌsɔːlz) *n* **1** a large horse market in London founded in the eighteenth century **2** *Austral* a large-scale lottery based in Melbourne. Also (informal): Tatt's **3** a name used for sportsmen's clubs in Australia [named after Richard *Tattersall* (died 1795), English horseman, who founded the market]

tattie or **tatty** ('tætɪ) *n, pl* -ties a Scot or dialect word for **potato**

tattie-bogle (ˌtætɪ'bog°l) *n Scot* a scarecrow [TATTIE + BOGLE¹]

tattie-peelin ('tætɪ'piːlɪn) *adj Central Scot dialect* (esp of speech) highfalutin, affected, or pretentious [from *potato-peeling*; sense development obscure]

tatting ('tætɪŋ) *n* **1** an intricate type of lace made by looping a thread of cotton or linen by means of a hand shuttle **2** the act or work of producing this [c19 of unknown origin]

tattle ('tæt°l) *vb* **1** (*intr*) to gossip about another's personal matters or secrets **2** (*tr*) to reveal by gossiping: *to tattle a person's secrets* **3** (*intr*) to talk idly; chat ▷ *n* **4** the act or an instance of tattling **5** a scandalmonger or gossip [c15 (in the sense: to stammer, hesitate): from Middle Dutch *tatelen* to prate, of imitative origin]

tattler ('tætlə) *n* **1** a person who tattles; gossip **2** any of several sandpipers of the genus *Heteroscelus*, such as *H. incanus* (**Polynesian tattler**), of Pacific coastal regions

tattletale ('tæt°lˌteɪl) *chiefly US and Canadian* ▷ *n* **1** a scandalmonger or gossip **2** another word for **telltale** (sense 1)

tattoo¹ (tæ'tuː) *n, pl* -toos **1** (formerly) a signal by drum or bugle ordering the military to return to

their quarters **2** a military display or pageant, usually at night **3** any similar beating on a drum, etc [c17 from Dutch *taptoe*, from the command *tap toe!* turn off the taps! from *tap* tap of a barrel + *toe* to shut]

tattoo² (tæ'tuː) *vb* -toos, -tooing, -tooed **1** to make (pictures or designs) on (the skin) by pricking and staining with indelible colours ▷ *n, pl* -toos **2** a design made by this process **3** the practice of tattooing [c18 from Tahitian *tatau*] > **tat'tooer** or **tat'tooist** *n*

tatty ('tætɪ) *adj* -tier, -tiest *chiefly Brit* worn out, shabby, tawdry, or unkempt [c16 of Scottish origin, probably related to Old English *tættec* a tatter] > **'tattily** *adv* > **'tattiness** *n*

tau (tɔː, taʊ) *n* the 19th letter in the Greek alphabet (T or τ), a consonant, transliterated as *t* [c13 via Latin from Greek, of Semitic origin; see TAV]

tau cross *n* a cross shaped like the Greek letter tau. Also called: **Saint Anthony's cross**

taught (tɔːt) *vb* the past tense and past participle of **teach**

tauhinu (tɑːuːhiːnuː) *n NZ* another name for **cottonwood** (sense 2) [Māori]

tauiwi (taʊ'iːwɪ) *n NZ* a Māori term for the non-Māori people of New Zealand [Māori, literally: foreign race]

tau neutrino *n physics* a type of neutrino associated with tau particles

taunt¹ (tɔːnt) *vb* (*tr*) **1** to provoke or deride with mockery, contempt, or criticism **2** to tease; tantalize ▷ *n* **3** a jeering remark **4** *archaic* the object of mockery [c16 from French phrase *tant pour tant* like for like, rejoinder] > **'taunter** *n* > **'taunting** *adj* > **'tauntingly** *adv*

taunt² (tɔːnt) *adj nautical* (of the mast or masts of a sailing vessel) unusually tall [c15 of uncertain origin]

Taunton ('tɔːntən) *n* a market town in SW England, administrative centre of Somerset: scene of Judge Jeffreys' "Bloody Assize" (1685) after the Battle of Sedgemoor. Pop: 58 241 (2001)

tauon ('taʊɒn) *n physics* a negatively charged elementary particle of mass 3477.48 × electron mass classed as a lepton, with an associated antiparticle and neutrino [c20 from Greek letter TAU + -ON]

tau particle *n physics* another name for **tauon**

taupata (tɑːuːpɑːtɑː) *n, pl* taupata a New Zealand shrub or tree of the genus *Coprosma*, esp *C. repens*, with shiny dark green leaves [Māori]

taupe (təʊp) *n* **a** a brownish-grey colour **b** (*as adjective*): *a taupe coat* [c20 from French, literally: mole, from Latin *talpa*]

Taupo ('taʊpəʊ) *n* **Lake** a lake in New Zealand, on central North Island: the largest lake of New Zealand. Area: 616 sq km (238 sq miles)

Tauranga (taʊ'rænə) *n* a port in New Zealand, on NE North Island on the Bay of Plenty: exports dairy produce, meat, and timber. Pop: 101 300 (2004 est)

taurine¹ ('tɔːraɪn) *adj* of, relating to, or resembling a bull [c17 from Latin *taurīnus*, from *taurus* a bull]

taurine² ('tɔːriːn, -rɪn) *n* a derivative of the amino acid, cysteine, obtained from the bile of animals; 2-aminoethanesulphonic acid. Formula: $NH_2CH_2CH_2SO_3H$ [c19 from TAURO- (as in *taurocholic acid*, so called because discovered in ox bile) + -INE²]

tauro- or before a vowel **taur-** *combining form* denoting a bull: *tauromachy* [from Latin *taurus* bull, Greek *tauros*]

tauromachy (tɔː'rɒməkɪ) *n* the art or act of bullfighting [c19 Greek *tauromakhia*, from TAURO- + *makhē* fight] > **tauromachian** (ˌtɔːrə'meɪkɪən) *adj*

Taurus ('tɔːrəs) *n, Latin genitive* Tauri ('tɔːraɪ) **1** *astronomy* a zodiacal constellation in the N hemisphere lying close to Orion and between Aries and Gemini. It contains the star Aldebaran, the star clusters Hyades and Pleiades, and the

Crab Nebula **2** *astrology* **a** Also called: **the Bull** the second sign of the zodiac, symbol ♉, having a fixed earth classification and ruled by the planet Venus. The sun is in this sign between about April 20 and May 20 **b** a person born when the sun is in this sign ▷ *adj* **3** born under or characteristic of Taurus ▷ Also (for senses 2b, 3): **Taurean** ('tɔːrɪən, tɔː'rɪən) [c14 from Latin: bull]

Taurus Mountains *pl n* a mountain range in S Turkey, parallel to the Mediterranean coast: crossed by the Cilician Gates; continued in the northeast by the Anti-Taurus range. Highest peak: Kaldi Dağ, 3734 m (12 251 ft)

taut (tɔːt) *adj* **1** tightly stretched; tense **2** showing nervous strain; stressed **3** *chiefly nautical* in good order; neat [c14 *tought*; probably related to Old English *togian* to TOW¹] > **'tautly** *adv* > **'tautness** *n*

tauten ('tɔːt°n) *vb* to make or become taut or tense

tauto- or before a vowel **taut-** *combining form* identical or same: *tautology; tautonym* [from Greek *tauto*, from *to auto*]

tautog (tɔː'tɒg) *n* a large dark-coloured wrasse, *Tautoga onitis*, of the North American coast of the Atlantic Ocean: used as a food fish. Also called: **blackfish** [c17 from Narraganset *tautauog*, plural of *tautau* sheepshead]

tautologize or **tautologise** (tɔː'tɒləˌdʒaɪz) *vb* (*intr*) to express oneself tautologically > **tau'tologist** *n*

tautology (tɔː'tɒlədʒɪ) *n, pl* -gies **1** the use of words that merely repeat elements of the meaning already conveyed, as in the sentence *Will these supplies be adequate enough?* in place of *Will these supplies be adequate?* **2** *logic* a statement that is always true, esp a truth-functional expression that takes the value true for all combinations of values of its components, as in *either the sun is out or the sun is not out*. Compare **inconsistency** (sense 3), **contingency** (sense 5) [c16 from Late Latin *tautologia*, from Greek, from *tautologos*] > **tautological** (ˌtɔːtə'lɒdʒɪk°l), ˌtauto'logic or tau'tologous *adj* > ˌtauto'logically or tau'tologously *adv*

tautomer ('tɔːtəmə) *n* either of the two forms of a chemical compound that exhibits tautomerism

tautomerism (tɔː'tɒməˌrɪzəm) *n* the ability of certain chemical compounds to exist as a mixture of two interconvertible isomers in equilibrium. See also **keto-enol tautomerism** [c19 from TAUTO- + ISOMERISM] > **tautomeric** (ˌtɔːtə'mɛrɪk) *adj*

tautonym ('tɔːtənɪm) *n biology* a taxonomic name in which the generic and specific components are the same, as in *Rattus rattus* (black rat) [c20 from Greek *tautonymos*. See TAUTO-, -ONYM] > ˌtauto'nymic or tautonymous (tɔː'tɒnɪməs) *adj* > tau'tonymy *n*

tav or **taw** (tɑːv, tɑːf; *Hebrew* tav, taf) *n* the 22nd and last letter in the Hebrew alphabet (ת), transliterated as *t* or when final *th* [from Hebrew: cross, mark]

Tavel (tɑː'vɛl) *n* a fine rosé wine produced in the Rhône valley near the small town of Tavel in S France

tavern ('tævən) *n* **1** a less common word for **pub 2** *US, Eastern Canadian, and NZ* a place licensed for the sale and consumption of alcoholic drink [c13 from Old French *taverne*, from Latin *taberna* hut]

taverna (tə'vɜːnə) *n* **1** (in Greece) a guesthouse that has its own bar **2** a Greek restaurant [c20 Modern Greek, from Latin *taberna*]

taverner ('tævənə) *n* **1** *archaic* a keeper of a tavern **2** *obsolete* a constant frequenter of taverns

TAVR *abbreviation for* Territorial and Army Volunteer Reserve

taw¹ (tɔː) *n* **1** the line from which the players shoot in marbles **2 back to taws** *Austral informal* back to the beginning **3** a large marble used for shooting **4** a game of marbles [c18 of unknown origin]

taw² (tɔː) *vb* (*tr*) **1** to convert (skins) into white

t

leather by treatment with mineral salts, such as alum and salt, rather than by normal tanning processes **2** *archaic or dialect* to flog; beat [Old English *tawian;* compare Old High German *zouwen* to prepare, Gothic *taujan* to make] > **'tawer** *n*

tawa ('tɑːwə) *n* a tall timber tree, *Beilschmiedia tawa,* of New Zealand, having edible purple berries [Māori]

tawai ('tɑːˌwaɪ) *or* **tawhai** ('tɑːˌhwaɪ) *n* any of various species of beech of the genus *Nothofagus* of New Zealand, originally called "birches" by the settlers [Māori]

tawdry ('tɔːdrɪ) *adj* **-drier, -driest** cheap, showy, and of poor quality: *tawdry jewellery* [C16 *tawdry lace,* shortened and altered from *Seynt Audries lace,* finery sold at the fair of St *Audrey* (Etheldrida), 7th-century queen of Northumbria and patron saint of Ely, Cambridgeshire] > **'tawdrily** *adv* > **'tawdriness** *n*

tawheowheo ('tɑːfɛəʊfɛəʊ) *n* a broadleaved evergreen, *Quintinia serrata,* of New Zealand's North Island [Māori]

tawhiri ('tɑːfiːriː) *n, pl* **tawhiri** a small New Zealand tree, *Pittosporum tenuifolium,* with wavy green glossy leaves. Also called: **black matipo** [Māori 'wave to', from the Māori practice of waving tawhiri branches to welcome approaching visitors]

tawny *or* **tawney** ('tɔːnɪ) *n* **a** a light brown to brownish-orange colour **b** (*as adjective*): *tawny port* [C14 from Old French *tané,* from *taner* to TAN[1]] > **'tawniness** *n*

tawny owl *n* a European owl, *Strix aluco,* having a reddish-brown or grey plumage, black eyes, and a round head. Also called: **brown owl, wood owl**

Tawny Owl *n* a name (no longer in official use) for an assistant Brownie Guider

tawny pipit *n* a small sandy-brown European bird, *Anthus campestris,* of the wagtail family; an irregular migrant to some parts of Britain

tawse *or* **taws** (tɔːz) *chiefly Scot* ▷ *n* **1** a leather strap having one end cut into thongs, formerly used as an instrument of punishment by a schoolteacher ▷ *vb* **2** to punish (someone) with or as if with a tawse; whip [C16 probably plural of obsolete *taw* strip of leather; see TAW[2]]

tax (tæks) *n* **1** a compulsory financial contribution imposed by a government to raise revenue, levied on the income or property of persons or organizations, on the production costs or sales prices of goods and services, etc **2** a heavy demand on something; strain: *a tax on our resources* ▷ *vb* (*tr*) **3** to levy a tax on (persons, companies, etc, or their incomes, etc) **4** to make heavy demands on; strain: *to tax one's intellect* **5** to accuse, charge, or blame: *he was taxed with the crime* **6** to determine (the amount legally chargeable or allowable to a party to a legal action), as by examining the solicitor's bill of costs: *to tax costs* **7** *Brit informal* to steal [C13 from Old French *taxer,* from Latin *taxāre* to appraise, from *tangere* to touch] > **'taxer** *n* > **'taxless** *adj*

taxable ('tæksəb°l) *adj* **1** capable of being taxed; able to bear tax **2** subject to tax ▷ *n* **3** (*often plural*) *US* a person, income, property, etc, that is subject to tax > **ˌtaxa'bility** *or* **'taxableness** *n* > **'taxably** *adv*

taxaceous (tæk'seɪʃəs) *adj* of, relating to, or belonging to the *Taxaceae,* a family of coniferous trees that includes the yews [C19 from New Latin *taxāceus,* from Latin *taxus* a yew]

taxation (tæk'seɪʃən) *n* **1** the act or principle of levying taxes or the condition of being taxed **2 a** an amount assessed as tax **b** a tax rate **3** revenue from taxes > **tax'ational** *adj*

tax avoidance *n* reduction or minimization of tax liability by lawful methods. Compare **tax evasion**

tax credit *n* (in Britain) a social security benefit paid in the form of an additional income tax allowance

tax-deductible *adj* (of an expense, loss, etc) legally deductible from income or wealth before

tax assessment

tax disc *n* a paper disc displayed on the windscreen of a motor vehicle showing that the tax due on it has been paid

taxeme ('tæksiːm) *n linguistics* any element of speech that may differentiate one utterance from another with a different meaning, such as the occurrence of a particular phoneme, the presence of a certain intonation, or a distinctive word order [C20 from Greek *taxis* order, arrangement + -EME] > **tax'emic** *adj*

tax evasion *n* reduction or minimization of tax liability by illegal methods. Compare **tax avoidance**

tax-exempt *adj* **1** (of an income or property) exempt from taxation **2** (of an asset) earning income that is not subject to taxation

tax exile *n* a person having a high income who chooses to live abroad so as to avoid paying high taxes

tax-free *adj* not needing to have tax paid on it: *tax-free savings schemes*

tax haven *n* a country or state having a lower rate of taxation than elsewhere

tax holiday *n* a period during which tax concessions are made for some reason; examples include an export incentive or an incentive to start a new business given by some governments, in which a company is excused all or part of its tax liability

taxi ('tæksɪ) *n, pl* **taxis** *or* **taxies 1** Also called: **cab, taxicab** a car, usually fitted with a taximeter, that may be hired, along with its driver, to carry passengers to any specified destination ▷ *vb* **taxies, taxiing** *or* **taxying, taxied 2** to cause (an aircraft) to move along the ground under its own power, esp before takeoff and after landing, or (of an aircraft) to move along the ground in this way **3** (*intr*) to travel in a taxi [C20 shortened from *taximeter cab*]

taxi dancing *n* a system, as in a dance hall or hotel, whereby a person pays for a partner (**taxi dancer**) for a dance, payment being required for each individual dance during an evening

taxidermy ('tæksɪˌdɜːmɪ) *n* the art or process of preparing, stuffing, and mounting animal skins so that they have a lifelike appearance [C19 from Greek *taxis* arrangement + *-dermy,* from Greek *derma* skin] > **ˌtaxi'dermal** *or* **ˌtaxi'dermic** *adj* > **'taxiˌdermist** *n*

taximeter ('tæksɪˌmiːtə) *n* a meter fitted to a taxi to register the fare, based on the length of the journey [C19 from French *taximètre;* see TAX, -METER]

taxing ('tæksɪŋ) *adj* demanding, onerous, and wearing > **'taxingly** *adv*

taxiplane ('tæksɪˌpleɪn) *n US* an aircraft that is available for hire

taxi rank *n* a place where taxis wait to be hired

taxis ('tæksɪs) *n* **1** the movement of a cell or organism in a particular direction in response to an external stimulus **2** *surgery* the repositioning of a displaced organ or part by manual manipulation only [C18 via New Latin from Greek: arrangement, from *tassein* to place in order]

-taxis *or* **-taxy** *n combining form* **1** indicating movement towards or away from a specified stimulus: *thermotaxis* **2** order or arrangement: *phyllotaxis* [from New Latin, from Greek *taxis* order] > **-tactic** *or* **-taxic** *adj combining form*

taxi truck *n Austral* a truck with a driver that can be hired

taxiway ('tæksɪˌweɪ) *n* a marked path along which aircraft taxi to or from a runway, parking area, etc. Also called: **taxi strip, peritrack**

tax loss *n* a loss sustained by a company that can be set against future profits for tax purposes

taxman ('tæksˌmæn) *n, pl* **-men 1** a collector of taxes **2** *informal* a tax-collecting body personified: *he was convicted of conspiring to cheat the taxman of five million pounds*

taxon ('tæksɒn) *n, pl* **taxa** ('tæksə) *biology* any

taxonomic group or rank [C20 back formation from TAXONOMY]

taxonomy (tæk'sɒnəmɪ) *n* **1 a** the branch of biology concerned with the classification of organisms into groups based on similarities of structure, origin, etc **b** the practice of arranging organisms in this way **2** the science or practice of classification [C19 from French *taxonomie,* from Greek *taxis* order + -NOMY] > **taxonomic** (ˌtæksə'nɒmɪk) *or* **ˌtaxo'nomical** *adj* > **ˌtaxo'nomically** *adv* > **tax'onomist** *or* **tax'onomer** *n*

taxpayer ('tæksˌpeɪə) *n* a person or organization that pays taxes or is liable to taxation > **'taxˌpaying** *adj*

tax rate *n* the percentage of income, wealth, etc, assessed as payable in taxation

tax relief *n* a reduction in the amount of tax a person or company has to pay

tax return *n* a declaration of personal income made annually to the tax authorities and used as a basis for assessing an individual's liability for taxation

tax shelter *n commerce* a form into which business or financial activities may be organized to minimize taxation

-taxy *n combining form* a variant of -taxis

tax year *n* a period of twelve months used by a government as a basis for calculating taxes

tay (teɪ) *n* an Irish dialect word for **tea**

Tay (teɪ) *n* **1 Firth of** the estuary of the River Tay on the North Sea coast of Scotland. Length: 40 km (25 miles) **2** a river in central Scotland, flowing northeast through Loch Tay, then southeast to the Firth of Tay: the longest river in Scotland; noted for salmon fishing. Length: 193 km (120 miles) **3 Loch** a lake in central Scotland, in Stirling council area. Length: 23 km (14 miles)

tayberry ('teɪbərɪ) *n, pl* **-ries 1** a hybrid shrub produced by crossing a blackberry, raspberry, and loganberry **2** the large sweet red fruit of this plant [C20 so named because first grown at Blairgowrie on *Tayside,* Scotland]

Taylor's Gold *n* a variety of pear from New Zealand

Taylor's series *n maths* an infinite sum giving the value of a function f(z) in the neighbourhood of a point *a* in terms of the derivatives of the function evaluated at *a*. Under certain conditions, the series has the form $f(z) = f(a) + [f'(a)(z - a)]/1! + [f''(a)(z - a)^2]/2! + ...$ See also **Maclaurin's series** [C18 named after Brook *Taylor* (1685–1731), English mathematician]

Taymyr Peninsula (taɪ'mɪə) *n* a variant spelling of **Taimyr Peninsula**

tayra ('taɪrə) *n* a large arboreal musteline mammal, *Eira barbara,* of Central and South America, having a dark brown body and paler head [C19 from Tupi *taira*]

Tay-Sachs disease (ˌteɪ'sæks) *n* an inherited disorder, caused by a faulty recessive gene, in which lipids accumulate in the brain, leading to mental retardation and blindness. It occurs mostly in Ashkenazi Jews [C20 named after W *Tay* (1843–1927), British physician, and B *Sachs* (1858–1944), US neurologist]

Tayside Region ('teɪˌsaɪd) *n* a former local government region in E Scotland: formed in 1975 from Angus, Kinross-shire, and most of Perthshire; replaced in 1996 by the council areas of Angus, City of Dundee, and Perth and Kinross

tazza ('tætsə) *n* a wine cup with a shallow bowl and a circular foot [C19 from Italian, probably from Arabic *tassah* bowl]

tb *abbreviation for* **1** trial balance **2** Also: **TB** tuberculosis

Tb *the chemical symbol for* terbium

TB *abbreviation for* **1** torpedo boat **2** Also: **tb** tuberculosis

tba *or* **TBA** *abbreviation for* to be arranged

T-bar *n* **1** a T-shaped wrench for use with a socket **2** a metal bar having a T-shaped cross section **3** a

T-shaped bar on a ski tow which skiers hold on to while being pulled up slopes **4** (*modifier*) another term for **T-strap**

tbc *or* **TBC** *abbreviation for* to be confirmed

Tbilisi (təbɪˈliːsɪ) *n* the capital of Georgia, on the Kura River: founded in 458; taken by the Russians in 1801; university (1918); a major industrial centre. Pop: 1 042 000 (2005 est). Russian name: **Tiflis**

T-bone steak *n* a large choice steak cut from the sirloin of beef, containing a T-shaped bone

tbs. *or* **tbsp.** *abbreviation for* tablespoon(ful)

TBT *abbreviation for* tri-*n*-butyl tin: a biocide used in marine paints to prevent fouling

tc *the internet domain name for* Turks and Caicos Islands

Tc *the chemical symbol for* technetium

TC (on cars, etc) *abbreviation for* twin carburettors

TCA cycle *abbreviation for* tricarboxylic acid cycle: another name for **Krebs cycle**

TCAS *abbreviation for* traffic collision avoidance system: a safety system in aircraft that is designed to prevent mid-air collisions

T-cell *n* another name for **T-lymphocyte**

TCH *or* **TD** *international car registration for* Chad [from TCHAD]

Tchad (tʃad) *n* the French name for **Chad**

Tchebychev's inequality (ˌtʃɛbɪˈʃɒfs) *n* See **Chebyshev's inequality**

TCM *abbreviation for* traditional Chinese medicine: Chinese-based alternative therapies, including acupuncture, certain forms of massage, and some herbal remedies

TCO *abbreviation for* total cost of ownership: the real cost of owning and using a piece of equipment such as a computer, taking into account the price of the hardware, software, maintenance, training, and technical support that may be needed

TCP *n trademark* a mild disinfectant used for cleansing minor wounds, gargling, etc [abbrev for *t(ri)c(hloro)p(henylmethyliodisalicyl)*]

td *the internet domain name for* Chad

TD *abbreviation for* **1** (in Ireland) Teachta Dála [Irish Gaelic: member of the Dáil.] **2** technical drawing **3** (in Britain) Territorial Decoration **4** Also: **td** touchdown

t.d.c. *abbreviation for* top dead-centre

t distribution *n* See **Student's t**

tdm *abbreviation for* time-division multiplex. See **multiplex** (sense 1)

te *or* **ti** (tiː) *n music* (in tonic sol-fa) the syllable used for the seventh note or subtonic of any scale [see GAMUT]

Te *the chemical symbol for* tellurium

tea (tiː) *n* **1** an evergreen shrub or small tree, *Camellia sinensis*, of tropical and subtropical Asia, having toothed leathery leaves and white fragrant flowers: family *Theaceae* **2 a** the dried shredded leaves of this shrub, used to make a beverage by infusion in boiling water **b** such a beverage, served hot or iced **c** (*as modifier*): *tea caddy; tea urn* **3 a** any of various plants that are similar to *Camellia sinensis* or are used to make a tealike beverage **b** any such beverage **4** *chiefly Brit* **a** Also called: **afternoon tea** a light meal eaten in mid-afternoon, usually consisting of tea and cakes, biscuits, or sandwiches **b** (*as modifier*): *a tea party* **c** Also called: **high tea** afternoon tea that also includes a light cooked dish **5** *Brit, Austral, and NZ* the main evening meal **6** *US and Canadian dated slang* marijuana **7 tea and sympathy** *informal* a caring attitude, esp to someone in trouble [C17 from Chinese (Amoy) *t'e*, from Ancient Chinese *d'a*]

tea bag *n* a small bag of paper or cloth containing tea leaves, infused in boiling water to make tea

tea ball *n chiefly US* a perforated metal ball filled with tea leaves and put in boiling water to make tea

teaberry (ˈtiːbərɪ, -brɪ) *n, pl* -**ries 1** the berry of the wintergreen (*Gaultheria procumbens*) **2** another

name for **wintergreen** (sense 1) [C19 so called because its dried leaves have been used as a substitute for tea]

tea biscuit *n Brit* any of various semisweet biscuits

teabread (ˈtiːˌbrɛd) *n* **1** a loaf-shaped cake that contains dried fruit which has been steeped in cold tea before baking: served sliced and buttered **2** any of a variety of loaf-shaped, usually light, cakes: *banana teabread*

tea break *n Brit* a short rest period during working hours during which tea, coffee, etc is drunk

TEAC (tiːˈæk) (in New Zealand) *n acronym for* Tertiary Education Advisory Committee

teacake (ˈtiːˌkeɪk) *n Brit* a flat cake made from a yeast dough with raisins in it, usually eaten toasted and buttered

teacart (ˈtiːˌkɑːt) *n US and Canadian* a trolley from which tea is served. Also called (in eg Britain): **tea trolley**

teach (tiːtʃ) *vb* **teaches, teaching, taught 1** (*tr; may take a clause as object or an infinitive; often foll by how*) to help to learn; tell or show (how): *to teach someone to paint; to teach someone how to paint* **2** to give instruction or lessons in (a subject) to (a person or animal): *to teach French; to teach children; she teaches* **3** (*tr; may take a clause as object or an infinitive*) to cause to learn or understand: *experience taught him that he could not be a journalist* **4** Also: **teach (someone) a lesson** *informal* to cause (someone) to suffer the unpleasant consequences of some action or behaviour [Old English *tǣcan*; related to *tácen* TOKEN, Old Frisian *tēken*, Old Saxon *tēkan*, Old High German *zeihhan*, Old Norse *teikn* sign] > **'teachable** *adj*

teacher (ˈtiːtʃə) *n* **1** a person whose occupation is teaching others, esp children **2** a personified concept that teaches: *nature is a good teacher* > **'teacherless** *adj*

teachers' centre *n* (in Britain) a place that provides a central store of educational aids, such as films and display material, and also in-service training, and is available for use to all the teachers within a particular area

teach-in *n* an informal conference, esp on a topical subject, usually held at a university or college and involving a panel of visiting speakers, lecturers, students, etc

teaching (ˈtiːtʃɪŋ) *n* **1** the art or profession of a teacher **2** (*sometimes plural*) something taught; precept **3** (*modifier*) denoting a person or institution that teaches: *a teaching hospital* **4** (*modifier*) used in teaching: *teaching aids*

teaching aid *n* any device, object, or machine used by a teacher to clarify or enliven a subject

teaching assistant *n* another name for **classroom assistant**

teaching fellow *n* a postgraduate student who is given tuition, accommodation, expenses, etc, in return for some teaching duties > **teaching fellowship** *n*

teaching hospital *n* a hospital that is affiliated to a medical school and provides the students with teaching and supervised practical experience

teaching machine *n* a machine that presents information and questions to the user, registers the answers, and indicates whether these are correct or acceptable

teaching practice *n* a temporary period of teaching in a school undertaken under supervision by a person who is training to become a teacher

tea cloth *n* another name for **tea towel**

tea cosy *n* a covering for a teapot to keep the contents hot, often having holes for the handle and spout

teacup (ˈtiːˌkʌp) *n* **1** a cup out of which tea may be drunk, larger than a coffee cup **2** Also called: **teacupful** the amount a teacup will hold, about four fluid ounces

tea dance *n* a dance held in the afternoon at which tea is served

tea garden *n* **1** an open-air restaurant that serves tea and light refreshments **2** a tea plantation

tea gown *n* (formerly) a long loose decorative dress worn esp when entertaining guests to afternoon tea

teahouse (ˈtiːˌhaʊs) *n* a restaurant, esp in Japan or China, where tea and light refreshments are served

teak (tiːk) *n* **1** a large verbenaceous tree, *Tectona grandis*, of the East Indies, having white flowers and yielding a valuable dense wood **2** the hard resinous yellowish-brown wood of this tree, used for furniture making, etc **3** any of various similar trees or their wood **4** a brown or yellowish-brown colour [C17 from Portuguese *teca*, from Malayalam *tēkka*]

teakettle (ˈtiːˌkɛtᵊl) *n* a kettle for boiling water to make tea

teal (tiːl) *n, pl* **teals** *or* **teal 1** any of various small ducks, such as the Eurasian *Anas crecca* (**common teal**) that are related to the mallard and frequent ponds, lakes, and marshes **2** a greenish-blue colour [C14 related to Middle Low German *tēlink*, Middle Dutch *tēling*]

tea lady *n* a woman employed in a factory, office, etc to make tea during a tea break

tea leaf *n* **1** the dried leaf of the tea shrub, used to make tea **2** (*usually plural*) shredded parts of these leaves, esp after infusion **3** *Brit and Austral slang* a thief [sense 3 rhyming slang]

tea light *n* a small round candle in a disposable metal container

team (tiːm) *n* (*sometimes functioning as plural*) **1** a group of people organized to work together **2** a group of players forming one of the sides in a sporting contest **3** two or more animals working together to pull a vehicle or agricultural implement **4** such animals and the vehicle: *the coachman riding his team* **5** *dialect* a flock, herd, or brood **6** *obsolete* ancestry ▷ *vb* **7** (when *intr*, often foll by *up*) to make or cause to make a team: *he teamed George with Robert* **8** (*tr*) *US and Canadian* to drag or transport in or by a team **9** (*intr*) *US and Canadian* to drive a team [Old English *team* offspring; related to Old Frisian *tām* bridle, Old Norse *taumr* chain yoking animals together, Old High German *zoum* bridle]

tea-maker *n* a device with perforations used to infuse tea in a cup of boiling water. Also called (esp Brit): **infuser, tea egg**

team-mate *n* a fellow member of a team

team spirit *n* willingness to cooperate as part of a team

teamster (ˈtiːmstə) *n* **1** a driver of a team of horses used for haulage **2** *US and Canadian* the driver of a lorry

team teaching *n* a system whereby two or more teachers pool their skills, knowledge, etc, to teach combined classes

teamwork (ˈtiːmˌwɜːk) *n* **1** the cooperative work done by a team **2** the ability to work efficiently as a team

tea party *n* a social gathering in the afternoon at which tea is served

teapot (ˈtiːˌpɒt) *n* a container with a lid, spout, and handle, in which tea is made and from which it is served

teapoy (ˈtiːpɔɪ) *n* **1** a small table or stand with a tripod base **2** a tea caddy on such a table or stand [C19 from Hindi *tipāī*, from Sanskrit *tri* three + *pāda* foot; compare Persian *sipae* three-legged stand]

tear¹ (tɪə) *n* **1** a drop of the secretion of the lacrimal glands. See **tears 2** something shaped like a hanging drop: *a tear of amber* ▷ Also called: **teardrop** [Old English *tēar*, related to Old Frisian, Old Norse *tār*, Old High German *zahar*, Greek *dakri*] > **'tearless** *adj*

tear² (tɛə) *vb* **tears, tearing, tore, torn 1** to cause (material, paper, etc) to come apart or (of material, etc) to come apart; rip **2** (*tr*) to make (a hole or split) in (something): *to tear a hole in a dress* **3** (*intr; often foll by along*) to hurry or rush: *to tear along the street* **4** (*tr; usually foll by away or from*) to remove or take by force **5** (when *intr, often foll by at*) to cause pain, distress, or anguish (to): *it tore at my heartstrings to see the starving child* **6** **tear one's hair** *informal* to be angry, frustrated, very worried, etc ▷ *n* **7** a hole, cut, or split **8** the act of tearing **9** a great hurry; rush **10** **on a tear** *slang* a sudden burst of energy ▷ See also **tear away, tear down, tear into, tear off, torn** [Old English *teran*; related to Old Saxon *terian*, Gothic *gatairan* to destroy, Old High German *zeran* to destroy] > **'tearable** *adj* > **'tearer** *n*

tear away (tɛə) *vb* **1** (*tr, adverb*) to persuade (oneself or someone else) to leave: *I couldn't tear myself away from the television* ▷ *n* **tearaway 2** *Brit* **a** a reckless impetuous unruly person **b** (*as modifier*): *a tearaway young man*

tear down (tɛə) *vb* (*tr, adverb*) to destroy or demolish: *to tear a wall down; to tear down an argument*

tear duct (tɪə) *n* the nontechnical name for **lacrimal duct**

tearful ('tɪəfʊl) *adj* **1** about to cry **2** accompanying or indicative of weeping: *a tearful expression* **3** tending to produce tears; sad > **'tearfully** *adv* > **'tearfulness** *n*

tear gas (tɪə) *n* any one of a number of gases or vapours that make the eyes smart and water, causing temporary blindness; usually dispersed from grenades and used in warfare and to control riots. Also called: **lacrimator**

tearing ('tɛərɪŋ) *adj* violent or furious (esp in the phrase **tearing hurry** or **rush**)

tear into (tɛə) *vb* (*intr, preposition*) *informal* to attack vigorously and damagingly

tear-jerker ('tɪəˌdʒɜːkə) *n* *informal* an excessively sentimental film, play, book, etc

tear off (tɛə) *vb* **1** (*tr*) to separate by tearing **2** (*intr, adverb*) to rush away; hurry **3** (*tr, adverb*) to produce in a hurry; do quickly and carelessly: *to tear off a letter* **4** **tear (someone) off a strip** *Brit informal* to reprimand or rebuke (someone) forcibly ▷ *adj* **tear-off 5** (of paper, etc) produced in a roll or block and marked with perforations so that one section at a time can be torn off

tearoom ('tiːˌruːm, -ˌrʊm) *n* **1** another name for **teashop 2** *NZ* a room in a school or university where hot drinks are served

tea rose *n* **1** any of several varieties of hybrid rose that are derived from *Rosa odorata* and have pink or yellow flowers with a scent resembling that of tea **2 a** a yellowish-pink colour **b** (*as adjective*): *tea-rose walls*

tears (tɪəz) *pl n* **1** the clear salty solution secreted by the lacrimal glands that lubricates and cleanses the surface of the eyeball and inner surface of the eyelids. Related adj: **lachrymal 2** a state of intense frustration (esp in the phrase **bored to tears**) **3 in tears** weeping **4 without tears** presented so as to be easily assimilated: *reading without tears*

tear sheet (tɛə) *n* a page in a newspaper or periodical that is cut or perforated so that it can be easily torn out

teary ('tɪərɪ) *adj* **tearier, teariest 1** characterized by, covered with, or secreting tears **2** given to weeping; tearful > **'tearily** *adv* > **'teariness** *n*

tease (tiːz) *vb* **1** to annoy (someone) by deliberately offering something with the intention of delaying or withdrawing the offer **2** to arouse sexual desire in (someone) with no intention of satisfying it **3** to vex (someone) maliciously or playfully, esp by ridicule **4** (*tr*) to separate the fibres of; comb; card **5** (*tr*) to raise the nap of (a fabric) with a teasel **6** *US and Canadian* to comb the under layers of (the hair) towards the roots to give more bulk to a hairstyle. Also: **backcomb 7** (*tr*) to loosen or pull apart (biological tissues, etc) by delicate agitation or prodding with an instrument ▷ *n* **8** a person or thing that teases **9** the act of teasing ▷ See also

tease out [Old English *tǣsan*; related to Old High German *zeisan* to pick] > **'teasing** *adj* > **'teasingly** *adv*

teasel, teazel or **teazle** ('tiːzəl) *n* **1** any of various stout biennial plants of the genus *Dipsacus*, of Eurasia and N Africa, having prickly leaves and prickly heads of yellow or purple flowers: family *Dipsacaceae*. See also **fuller's teasel 2 a** the prickly dried flower head of the fuller's teasel, used for teasing **b** any manufactured implement used for the same purpose ▷ *vb* **-sels, -selling, -selled** or *US* **-sels, -seling, -seled 3** (*tr*) to tease (a fabric) [Old English *tǣsel*; related to Old High German *zeisala* teasel, Norwegian *tīsl* undergrowth, *tīsla* to tear to bits; see TEASE] > **'teaseller** *n*

tease out *vb* (*tr, adverb*) to extract (information) with difficulty

teaser ('tiːzə) *n* **1** a person who teases **2** a preliminary advertisement in a campaign that attracts attention by making people curious to know what product is being advertised **3** a difficult question **4** *vet science* a vasectomized male animal, such as an ox, used to detect oestrus in females

tea service or **set** *n* the china or pottery articles used in serving tea, including a teapot, cups, saucers, etc

teashop ('tiːˌʃɒp) *n* *Brit* a restaurant where tea and light refreshments are served. Also called: **tearoom**

teaspoon ('tiːˌspuːn) *n* **1** a small spoon used for stirring tea, eating certain desserts, etc **2** Also called: **teaspoonful** ('tiːˌspuːnfʊl) the amount contained in such a spoon **3** a unit of capacity used in cooking, medicine, etc, equal to about one fluid dram

teat (tiːt) *n* **1 a** the nipple of a mammary gland **b** (in cows, etc) any of the projections from the udder through which milk is discharged. See **nipple 2** something resembling a teat in shape or function, such as the rubber mouthpiece of a feeding bottle [c13 from Old French *tete*, of Germanic origin; compare Old English *titt*, Middle High German *zitze*]

tea towel or **cloth** *n* a towel for drying dishes and kitchen utensils. US name: **dishtowel**

tea tree *n* any of various myrtaceous trees of the genus *Leptospermum*, of Australia and New Zealand, that yield an oil used as an antiseptic

tea trolley *n* *chiefly Brit* a trolley from which tea is served

tea wagon *n* a US and Canadian variant for **tea trolley**

Tebet (te'vet) *n* a variant spelling of **Tevet**

tebi- ('tɛbɪ) *prefix computing* denoting 2⁴⁰: *tebibyte*. Symbol: Ti [c20 from TE(RA-) + BI(NARY)]

tec or **'tec** (tɛk) *n* *informal* short for **detective**

TEC (tɛk) (in Britain) *n acronym for* Training and Enterprise Council. See **Training Agency**

tech (tɛk) *n* *informal* short for **technical college**

tech. *abbreviation for* **1** technical **2** technology

techie or **techy** ('tɛkɪ) *informal* ▷ *n, pl* **techies 1** a person who is skilled in the use of technological devices, such as computers ▷ *adj* **2** of, relating to, or skilled in the use of technological devices, such as computers

technetium (tɛk'niːʃɪəm) *n* a silvery-grey metallic element, artificially produced by bombardment of molybdenum by deuterons: used to inhibit corrosion in steel. The radioisotope **technetium-99m**, with a half-life of six hours, is used in radiotherapy. Symbol: Tc; atomic no: 43; half-life of most stable isotope, ⁹⁷Tc: 2.6 × 10⁶ years; valency: 0, 2, 4, 5, 6, or 7; relative density: 11.50 (calculated), melting pt. 2204°C, boiling pt. 4265°C [c20 New Latin, from Greek *tekhnētos* manmade, from *tekhnasthai* to devise artificially, from *tekhnē* skill]

technic *n* **1** (tɛk'niːk) another word for **technique 2** ('tɛknɪk) another word for **technics** [c17 from Latin *technicus*, from Greek *tekhnikos*, from *tekhnē* art, skill]

technical ('tɛknɪkᵊl) *adj* **1** of, relating to, or specializing in industrial, practical, or mechanical arts and applied sciences: *a technical institute* **2** skilled in practical and mechanical arts rather than theoretical or abstract thinking **3** relating to or characteristic of a particular field of activity: *the technical jargon of linguistics* **4** existing by virtue of a strict application of the rules or a strict interpretation of the wording: *a technical loophole in the law; a technical victory* **5** of, derived from, or showing technique: *technical brilliance* **6** (of a financial market) having prices determined by internal speculative or manipulative factors rather than by general or economic conditions: *a technical rally* > **'technically** *adv* > **'technicalness** *n*

technical area *n* *soccer* the area at the side of the pitch to which managers, trainers, coaches, etc are restricted during play

technical college *n* *Brit* an institution for further education that provides courses in technology, art, secretarial skills, agriculture, etc. Sometimes (informal) shortened to: **tech**

technical drawing *n* the study and practice, esp as a subject taught in school, of the basic techniques of draughtsmanship, as employed in mechanical drawing, architecture, etc. Abbreviation: **TD**

technical institute *n* *NZ* a higher-education institution. Sometimes (informal) shortened to: **tech**

technicality (ˌtɛknɪ'kælɪtɪ) *n, pl* **-ties 1** a petty formal point arising from a strict interpretation of rules, etc: *the case was dismissed on a technicality* **2** the state or quality of being technical **3** technical methods and vocabulary

technical knockout *n* *boxing* a judgment of a knockout given when a boxer is in the referee's opinion too badly beaten to continue without risk of serious injury

technical sergeant *n* a noncommissioned officer in the US Marine Corps or Air Force ranking immediately subordinate to a master sergeant

technician (tɛk'nɪʃən) *n* **1** a person skilled in mechanical or industrial techniques or in a particular technical field **2** a person employed in a laboratory, technical college, or scientific establishment to do practical work **3** a person having specific artistic or mechanical skill, esp if lacking original flair or genius

Technicolor ('tɛknɪˌkʌlə) *n* *trademark* the process of producing colour film by means of superimposing synchronized films of the same scene, each of which has a different colour filter, to obtain the desired mix of colour

technicolour ('tɛknɪˌkʌlə) or **technicoloured** ('tɛknɪˌkʌləd) *adj* brightly, showily, or garishly coloured; vividly noticeable

technics ('tɛknɪks) *n* (*functioning as singular*) the study or theory of industry and industrial arts

technikon ('tɛknɪˌkɒn) *n* *South African* a technical college

technique or **technic** (tɛk'niːk) *n* **1** a practical method, skill, or art applied to a particular task **2** proficiency in a practical or mechanical skill **3** special facility; knack: *he had the technique of turning everything to his advantage* [c19 from French, from *technique* (adj) TECHNIC]

techno ('tɛknəʊ) *n* a type of very fast dance music, using electronic sounds and fast heavy beats

techno- *combining form* **1** craft or art: *technology; technography* **2** technological or technical: *technocracy* **3** relating to or using technology: *technophobia* [from Greek *tekhnē* skill]

technocracy (tɛk'nɒkrəsɪ) *n, pl* **-cies 1** a theory or system of society according to which government is controlled by scientists, engineers, and other experts **2** a body of such experts **3** a state considered to be governed or organized according to these principles > **technocrat** ('tɛknəˌkræt) *n* > ˌtechno'cratic *adj*

technofear (ˈtɛknəˌfɪə) *n* fear of using technological devices, such as computers; technophobia

technography (tɛkˈnɒɡrəfɪ) *n* the study and description of the historical development of the arts and sciences in the context of their ethnic and geographical background

technol. *abbreviation for* **1** technological **2** technology

technology (tɛkˈnɒlədʒɪ) *n, pl* **-gies 1** the application of practical sciences to industry or commerce **2** the methods, theory, and practices governing such application: *a highly developed technology* **3** the total knowledge and skills available to any human society for industry, art, science, etc [C17 from Greek *tekhnologia* systematic treatment, from *tekhnē* art, skill] > **technological** (ˌtɛknəˈlɒdʒɪkəl) *adj* > ˌtechnoˈlogically *adv* > **techˈnologist** *n*

technology agreement *n* a framework designed by trade unions for negotiating changes in employment caused by the introduction of new technology

technophile (ˈtɛknəʊˌfaɪl) *n* **1** a person who is enthusiastic about technology ▷ *adj* **2** enthusiastic about technology

technophobe (ˈtɛknəʊˌfəʊb) *n* **1** someone who fears the effects of technological development on society and the environment **2** someone who is afraid of using technological devices, such as computers

technophobia (ˌtɛknəʊˈfəʊbɪə) *n* **1** fear of the effects of technological developments on society or the environment **2** fear of using technological devices, such as computers

technostructure (ˈtɛknəʊˌstrʌktʃə) *n* the people who control the technology of a society, such as professional administrators, experts in business management, etc

techy¹ (ˈtɛkɪ) *n, pl* **techies**, *adj informal* a variant spelling of **techie**

techy² (ˈtɛtʃɪ) *adj* **techier**, **techiest** a variant spelling of **tetchy**. > ˈtechily *adv* > ˈtechiness *n*

tectibranch (ˈtɛktɪˌbræŋk) *n* a mollusc of the suborder *Tectibranchia* (or *Tectibranchiata*) (order: *Opisthobranchia*) which includes the sea slugs and sea hares [C19 New Latin, from *tectus* covered, from *tegere* to cover + *branchia*: see -BRANCH]

tectonic (tɛkˈtɒnɪk) *adj* **1** denoting or relating to construction or building **2** *geology* **a** (of landforms, rock masses, etc) resulting from distortion of the earth's crust due to forces within it **b** (of processes, movements, etc) occurring within the earth's crust and causing structural deformation [C17 from Late Latin *tectonicus*, from Greek *tektonikos* belonging to carpentry, from *tektōn* a builder] > **tecˈtonically** *adv*

tectonics (tɛkˈtɒnɪks) *n* (*functioning as singular*) **1** the art and science of construction or building **2** the study of the processes by which the earth's crust has attained its present structure. See also **plate tectonics**

tectorial membrane (tɛkˈtɔːrɪəl) *n* the membrane in the inner ear that covers the organ of Corti [C19 *tectorial*, from Latin *tectōrium* a covering, from *tegere* to cover]

tectrix (ˈtɛktrɪks) *n, pl* **tectrices** (ˈtɛktrɪˌsiːz, tɛkˈtraɪsiːz) (*usually plural*) *ornithol* another name for **covert** (sense 6) [C19 New Latin, from Latin *tector* plasterer, from *tegere* to cover] > **tectricial** (tɛkˈtrɪʃəl) *adj*

ted¹ (tɛd) *vb* **teds, tedding, tedded** to shake out and loosen (hay), so as to dry it [C15 from Old Norse *tethja*; related to *tad* dung, Old High German *zetten* to spread]

ted² (tɛd) *n informal* short for **teddy boy**

tedder (ˈtɛdə) *n* **1** a machine equipped with a series of small rotating forks for tedding hay **2** a person who teds

teddy (ˈtɛdɪ) *n, pl* **-dies** a woman's one-piece undergarment, incorporating a chemise top and panties

teddy bear *n* a stuffed toy bear made from soft or fluffy material. Often shortened to: **teddy** [C20 from *Teddy*, from *Theodore*, after Theodore Roosevelt (1858–1919), 26th president of the US (1901–09), who was well known as a hunter of bears]

teddy boy *n* **1** (in Britain, esp in the mid-1950s) one of a cult of youths who wore mock Edwardian fashions, such as tight narrow trousers, pointed shoes, and long sideboards. Often shortened to: **ted 2** any tough or delinquent youth [C20 from *Teddy*, from *Edward*, referring to the Edwardian dress]

teddy girl *n* a girl companion to a teddy boy

Te Deum (ˌtiː ˈdɪəm) *n* **1** an ancient Latin hymn in rhythmic prose, sung or recited at matins in the Roman Catholic Church and in English translation at morning prayer in the Church of England and used by both Churches as an expression of thanksgiving on special occasions **2** a musical setting of this hymn **3** a service of thanksgiving in which the recital of this hymn forms a central part [from the Latin canticle beginning *Tē Deum laudāmus*, literally: Thee, God, we praise]

tedious (ˈtiːdɪəs) *adj* **1** causing fatigue or tedium; monotonous **2** *obsolete* progressing very slowly > ˈtediously *adv* > ˈtediousness *n*

tedium (ˈtiːdɪəm) *n* the state of being bored or the quality of being boring; monotony [C17 from Latin *taedium*, from *taedēre* to weary]

tee¹ (tiː) *n* **1** a pipe fitting in the form of a letter T, used to join three pipes **2** a metal section with a cross section in the form of a letter T, such as a rolled-steel joist **3** any part or component shaped like a T

tee² (tiː) *golf* ▷ *n* **1** Also called: **teeing ground** an area, often slightly elevated, from which the first stroke of a hole is made **2** a support for a golf ball, usually a small wooden or plastic peg, used when teeing off or in long grass, etc ▷ *vb* **tees, teeing, teed 3** (when *intr*, often foll by *up*) to position (the ball) ready for striking, on or as if on a tee ▷ See also **tee off** [C17 *teaz*, of unknown origin]

tee³ (tiː) *n* a mark used as a target in certain games such as curling and quoits [C18 perhaps from T-shaped marks, which may have originally been used in curling]

tee-hee *or* **te-hee** (ˈtiːˈhiː) *interj* **1** an exclamation of laughter, esp when mocking ▷ *n* **2** a chuckle ▷ *vb* **-hees, -heeing, -heed 3** (*intr*) to snigger or laugh, esp derisively [C14 of imitative origin]

tee-joint *n* a variant spelling of **T-joint**

teek (tiːk) *adj Hinglish* well; in good health [C21 Punjabi]

teem¹ (tiːm) *vb* **1** (*intr*; usually foll by *with*) to be prolific or abundant (in); abound (in) **2** *obsolete* to bring forth (young) [Old English *tēman* to produce offspring; related to West Saxon *tīeman*; see TEAM]

teem² (tiːm) *vb* **1** (*intr*; often foll by *down* or *with rain*) to pour in torrents: *it's teeming down* **2** (*tr*) to pour or empty out [C15 *temen* to empty, from Old Norse *tœma*; related to Old English *tōm*, Old High German *zuomīg* empty] > ˈteemer *n*

teen¹ (tiːn) *adj informal* another word for **teenage**

teen² (tiːn) *n obsolete* affliction or woe [Old English *tēona*; related to Old Saxon *tiono*, Old Frisian *tiona* injury]

-teen *n combining form* ten: added to modified forms of the numbers 3 to 9 to form the numbers 13 to 19 [Old English *-tēne, -tȳne*] > **-teenth** *adj combining form*

teenage (ˈtiːnˌeɪdʒ) *adj also* **teenaged 1** (*prenominal*) of or relating to the time in a person's life between the ages of 13 and 19 inclusive ▷ *n* **2** this period of time

teenager (ˈtiːnˌeɪdʒə) *n* a person between the ages of 13 and 19 inclusive

teens (tiːnz) *pl n* **1** the years of a person's life between the ages of 13 and 19 inclusive **2** all the numbers that end in *-teen*

teeny (ˈtiːnɪ) *adj* **-nier, -niest** *informal* extremely small; tiny. Also: **teeny-weeny** (ˈtiːnɪˈwiːnɪ) *or*

teensy-weensy (ˈtiːnzɪˈwiːnzɪ) [C19 variant of TINY]

teenybopper (ˈtiːnɪˌbɒpə) *n slang* a young teenager, usually a girl, who avidly follows fashions in clothes and pop music [C20 *teeny*, from TEENAGE + -*bopper* see BOP¹] > ˈteenyˌbop *adj*

tee off *vb* (*adverb*) **1** *golf* to strike (the ball) from a tee, as when starting a hole **2** *informal* to begin; start

teepee (ˈtiːpiː) *n* a variant spelling of **tepee**

tee-piece *n* a variant spelling of **T-piece**

tee-plate *n* a variant spelling of **T-plate**

Tees (tiːz) *n* a river in N England, rising in the N Pennines and flowing southeast and east to the North Sea at Middlesbrough. Length: 113 km (70 miles)

tee shirt *n* a variant of **T-shirt**

tee-square *n* a variant spelling of **T-square**

Teesside (ˈtiːzˌsaɪd) *n* the industrial region around the lower Tees valley and estuary: a county borough, containing Middlesbrough, from 1968 to 1974

teeter (ˈtiːtə) *vb* **1** to move or cause to move unsteadily; wobble ▷ *n* **2** *another word for* **seesaw** [C19 from Middle English *titeren*, related to Old Norse *titra* to tremble, Old High German *zittarōn* to shiver]

teeth (tiːθ) *n* **1** the plural of **tooth 2** the most violent part: *the teeth of the gale* **3** the power to produce a desired effect: *that law has no teeth* **4 by the skin of one's teeth** See **skin** (sense 14) **5 get one's teeth into** to become engrossed in **6 in the teeth of** in direct opposition to; against: *in the teeth of violent criticism he went ahead with his plan* **7 to the teeth** to the greatest possible degree: *armed to the teeth* **8 show one's teeth** to threaten, esp in a defensive manner

teethe (tiːð) *vb* (*intr*) to cut one's baby (deciduous) teeth

teething ring *n* a plastic, hard rubber, or bone ring on which babies may bite while teething

teething troubles *pl n* the difficulties or problems that arise during the initial stages of a project, enterprise, etc

teetotal (tiːˈtəʊtəl) *adj* **1** of, relating to, or practising abstinence from alcoholic drink **2** *dialect* complete [C19 allegedly coined in 1833 by Richard Turner, English advocate of total abstinence from alcoholic liquors; probably from TOTAL, with emphatic reduplication] > **teeˈtotaller** *n* > **teeˈtotally** *adv* > **teeˈtotalism** *n*

teetotum (tiːˈtəʊtəm) *n archaic* **1** a spinning top bearing letters of the alphabet on its four sides **2** such a top used as a die in gambling games [C18 from T *totum*, from T initial inscribed on one of the faces + *totum* the name of the toy, from Latin *tōtum* the whole]

tef *or* **teff** (tɛf) *n* an annual grass, *Eragrostis abyssinica*, of NE Africa, grown for its grain [C18 from Amharic *tēf*]

tefillah *or* **tephillah** (təˈfiːlə) *n, pl* **-lin** (-lɪn) *Judaism* another name for **phylactery** (sense 1) [from Hebrew]

TEFL (ˈtɛfəl) *acronym for* Teaching (of) English as a Foreign Language

Teflon (ˈtɛflɒn) *n* **1** a trademark for **polytetrafluoroethylene** when used in nonstick cooking vessels ▷ *adj* **2** *facetious* denoting the ability to evade blame: *the Teflon president*

teg (tɛg) *n* **1** a two-year-old sheep **2** the fleece of a two-year-old sheep [C16 of unknown origin]

tegmen (ˈtɛɡmən) *n, pl* **-mina** (-mɪnə) either of the leathery forewings of the cockroach and related insects **3** any similar covering or layer [C19 from Latin: a cover, variant of *tegimen*, from *tegere* to cover] > **ˈtegminal** *adj*

Tegucigalpa (*Spanish* teɣuθiˈɣalpa) *n* the capital of Honduras, in the south on the Choluteca River: founded about 1579; university (1847). Pop: 1 061 000 (2005 est)

tegular (ˈtɛɡjʊlə) *adj* **1** of, relating to, or resembling a tile or tiles **2** *biology* overlapping like a series of tiles: *tegular scales* [C18 from Latin *tēgula* a tile, from *tegere* to cover] > **'tegularly** *adv*

tegument ('tɛgjʊmənt) *n* a less common word for **integument** [c15 from Latin *tegumentum* a covering, from *tegere* to cover] > **tegumental** (ˌtɛgjʊ'mɛntªl) *or* ˌtegu'mentary *adj*

te-hee ('tiː'hiː) *interj, n, vb* a variant spelling of **tee-hee**

Tehran *or* **Teheran** (tɛə'rɑːn, -'ræn) *n* the capital of Iran, at the foot of the Elburz Mountains: built on the site of the ancient city Ray, destroyed by Mongols in 1220; became capital in the 1790s; three universities. Pop: 7 352 000 (2005 est)

Tehuantepec (tə'wɑːntəˌpɛk) *n* **Isthmus of** the narrowest part of S Mexico, with the Bay of Campeche on the north coast and the **Gulf of Tehuantepec** (an inlet of the Pacific) on the south coast

Teide *or* **Teyde** (Spanish 'tɛiðe) *n* **Pico de** ('piko de). a volcanic mountain in the Canary Islands, on Tenerife. Height: 3718 m (12 198 ft)

te igitur (Latin tei 'igiˌtʊə; English tei 'idʒiˌtʊə) *n* RC Church the first prayer of the canon of the Mass, which begins *Te igitur clementissime Pater* (*Thee, therefore, most merciful Father*)

teind (tiːnd) *n, vb* a Scot and northern English word for **tithe**

Tejo ('təʒu) *n* the Portuguese name for the **Tagus**

tektite ('tɛktaɪt) *n* a small dark glassy object found in several areas around the world, thought to be a product of meteorite impact. See also **moldavite** [c20 from Greek *tēktos* molten]

tel- *combining form* a variant of **tele-** and **telo-** before a vowel

tela ('tiːlə) *n, pl* **-lae** (-liː) *anatomy* any delicate tissue or weblike structure [from New Latin, from Latin: a web]

telaesthesia *or US* **telesthesia** (ˌtɛlɪs'θiːzɪə) *n* the alleged perception of events that are beyond the normal range of perceptual processes. Compare **telegnosis, clairvoyance**. > **telaesthetic** *or US* **telesthetic** (ˌtɛlɪs'θɛtɪk) *adj*

telamon ('tɛləmən) *n, pl* **telamones** (ˌtɛlə'məʊniːz) *or* **-mons** a column in the form of a male figure, used to support an entablature. Also called: **atlas** Compare **caryatid** [c18 via Latin from Greek, from *tlēnai* to bear]

Telamon ('tɛləmən, -ˌmɒn) *n* Greek myth a king of Salamis; brother of Peleus and father of Teucer and Ajax

Telanaipura (ˌtɛlənaɪ'pʊərə) *n* another name for **Jambi**

telangiectasis (tɪˌlændʒɪ'ɛktəsɪs) *or* **telangiectasia** (tɪˌlændʒɪɛk'teɪzɪə) *n, pl* **-ses** (-ˌsiːz) *pathol* an abnormal dilation of the capillaries or terminal arteries producing blotched red spots, esp on the face or thighs [c19 New Latin, from Greek *telos* end + *angeion* vessel + *ektasis* dilation] > **telangiectatic** (tɪˌlændʒɪɛk'tætɪk) *adj*

Telautograph (tɛl'ɔːtəˌgræf, -ˌgrɑːf) *n* trademark a telegraphic device for reproducing handwriting, drawings, etc, the movements of an electromagnetically controlled pen at one end being transmitted along a line to a similar pen at the receiving end > **telˌauto'graphic** *adj* > **telautography** (ˌtɛlɔː'tɒgrəfɪ) *n*

Tel Aviv ('tɛl ə'viːv) *n* a city in W Israel, on the Mediterranean: the largest city and chief financial centre in Israel; incorporated the city of Jaffa in 1950; university (1953): the capital of Israel according to the UN and international law. Pop: 363 400 (2003 est). Official name: **Tel Aviv-Jaffa** ('tɛl ə'viːv'dʒæfə)

telco ('tɛlˌkəʊ) *n* (pl **-cos**) a telecommunications company [c20 from TEL(ECOMMUNICATIONS) + CO(MPANY)]

tele- *or before a vowel* **tel-** *combining form* **1** at or over a distance; distant: *telescope; telegony; telekinesis; telemeter* **2** television: *telecast* **3** by means of or via telephone or television [from Greek *tele* far]

telecast ('tɛlɪˌkɑːst) *vb* **-casts, -casting, -cast** *or* **-casted 1** to broadcast (a programme) by

television ▷ *n* **2** a television broadcast > **'teleˌcaster** *n*

telecine ('tɛlɪˌsɪnɪ) *n* apparatus for producing a television signal from cinematograph film

telecom ('tɛlɪˌkɒm) *or* **telecoms** ('tɛlɪˌkɒmz) *n* (functioning as singular) short for **telecommunications**

telecommunication (ˌtɛlɪkəˌmjuːnɪ'keɪʃən) *n* the telegraphic or telephonic communication of audio, video, or digital information over a distance by means of radio waves, optical signals, etc, or along a transmission line

telecommunications (ˌtɛlɪkəˌmjuːnɪ'keɪʃənz) *n* (functioning as singular) the science and technology of communications by telephony, radio, television, etc

telecommuting ('tɛlɪkəˌmjuːtɪŋ) *n* another name for **teleworking**. > **'telecomˌmuter** *n*

teleconference ('tɛlɪˌkɒnfərəns) *n* a conference in which the participants communicate from different places via a telephone or video network

teleconnection ('tɛlɪkəˌnɛkʃən) *n* **1** connection via telephone or television **2** long-distance relationship between weather patterns, as when evaporation from the Amazon basin falls as rain in S Africa, etc

telecottage ('tɛlɪˌkɒtɪdʒ) *n* a communal workplace, situated in a rural area, which contains computers and other facilities linked into a communications network, thereby enabling people to work from remote locations

teledu ('tɛlɪˌduː) *n* a badger, *Mydaus javanensis*, of SE Asia and Indonesia, having dark brown hair with a white stripe along the back and producing a fetid secretion from the anal glands when attacked [c19 from Malay]

téléférique (teɪleɪfeɪ'riːk) *n* a variant spelling of **téléphérique**

telega (tɛ'leɪgə) *n* a rough four-wheeled cart used in Russia [c16 from Russian]

telegenic (ˌtɛlɪ'dʒɛnɪk) *adj* having or showing a pleasant television image [c20 from TELE(VISION) + (PHOTO)GENIC] > **ˌtele'genically** *adv*

telegnosis (ˌtɛlə'nəʊsɪs, ˌtɛləg-) *n* knowledge about distant events alleged to have been obtained without the use of any normal sensory mechanism. Compare **clairvoyance** [c20 from TELE- + -*gnosis*, from Greek *gnōsis* knowledge] > **telegnostic** (ˌtɛlə'nɒstɪk, ˌtɛləg-) *adj*

Telegonus (tɪ'lɛgənəs) *n* Greek myth a son of Odysseus and Circe, who sought his father and mistakenly killed him, later marrying Odysseus' widow Penelope

telegony (tɪ'lɛgənɪ) *n* genetics the supposed influence of a previous sire on offspring borne by a female to other sires [c19 from TELE- + -GONY. Compare Greek *tēlegonos* "born far from one's homeland"] > **telegonic** (ˌtɛlɪ'gɒnɪk) *or* **te'legonous** *adj*

telegram ('tɛlɪˌgræm) *n* a communication transmitted by telegraph. See also **cable** (sense 5), **Telemessage**. > **telegrammatic** (ˌtɛlɪgrə'mætɪk) *or* ˌtele'grammic *adj*

telegraph ('tɛlɪˌgræf, -ˌgrɑːf) *n* **1 a** a device, system, or process by which information can be transmitted over a distance, esp using radio signals or coded electrical signals sent along a transmission line connected to a transmitting and a receiving instrument **b** (as modifier): *telegraph pole* **2** a message transmitted by such a device, system, or process; telegram ▷ *vb* **3** to send a telegram to (a person or place); wire **4** (tr) to transmit or send by telegraph **5** (tr) boxing informal to prepare to deliver (a punch) so obviously that one's opponent has ample time to avoid it **6** (tr) to give advance notice of (anything), esp unintentionally **7** (tr) Canadian informal to cast (votes) illegally by impersonating registered voters > **telegraphist** (tɪ'lɛgrəfɪst) *or* **te'legrapher** *n*

telegraphic (ˌtɛlɪ'græfɪk) *adj* **1** used in or transmitted by telegraphy **2** of or relating to a telegraph **3** having a concise style; clipped:

telegraphic speech > **teleˈgraphically** *adv*

telegraph plant *n* a small tropical Asian leguminous shrub, *Desmodium gyrans*, having small leaflets that turn in various directions during the day and droop at night

telegraphy (tɪ'lɛgrəfɪ) *n* **1** a system of telecommunications involving any process providing reproduction at a distance of written, printed, or pictorial matter. See also **facsimile** (sense 2) **2** the skill or process of operating a telegraph

Telegu ('tɛləˌguː) *n, adj* a variant spelling of **Telugu**

telehealth ('tɛlɪˌhɛlθ) *n* US and Canadian health care based on consultation by telephone and telemedicine

telekinesis (ˌtɛlɪkɪ'niːsɪs, -kaɪ-) *n* **1** the movement of a body caused by thought or willpower without the application of a physical force **2** the ability to cause such movement > **telekinetic** (ˌtɛlɪkɪ'nɛtɪk, -kaɪ-) *adj*

Telemachus (tɪ'lɛməkəs) *n* Greek myth the son of Odysseus and Penelope, who helped his father slay his mother's suitors

telemark ('tɛlɪˌmɑːk) *n* **1** skiing a turn in which one ski is placed far forward of the other and turned gradually inwards **2** a step in ballroom dancing involving a heel pivot [c20 named after *Telemark*, county in Norway]

telemarketing ('tɛlɪˌmɑːkɪtɪŋ) *n* another name for **telesales** [c20 short for TELE(PHONE) MARKETING] > **'teleˌmarketer** *n*

telematics (ˌtɛlɪ'mætɪks) *n* (functioning as singular) the branch of science concerned with the use of technological devices to transmit information over long distances [c20 from TELE- + (INFOR)MATICS] > **ˌtele'matic** *adj*

telemedicine ('tɛlɪˌmɛdɪsɪn, -ˌmɛdsɪn) *n* the treatment of disease or injury by consultation with a specialist in a distant place, esp by means of a computer or satellite link

Telemessage ('tɛlɪˌmɛsɪdʒ) *n* trademark a message sent by telephone or telex and delivered in printed form; in Britain, it has replaced the telegram

telemeter (tɪ'lɛmɪtə) *n* **1** any device for recording or measuring a distant event and transmitting the data to a receiver or observer **2** any device or apparatus used to measure a distance without directly comparing it with a measuring rod, etc, esp one that depends on the measurement of angles ▷ *vb* **3** (tr) to obtain and transmit (data) from a distant source, esp from a spacecraft > **telemetric** (ˌtɛlɪ'mɛtrɪk) *or* **ˌtele'metrical** *adj* > **ˌtele'metrically** *adv*

telemetry (tɪ'lɛmɪtrɪ) *n* **1** the use of radio waves, telephone lines, etc, to transmit the readings of measuring instruments to a device on which the readings can be indicated or recorded. See also **radiotelemetry 2** the measurement of linear distance using a tellurometer

telencephalon (ˌtɛlɛn'sɛfəˌlɒn) *n* the cerebrum together with related parts of the hypothalamus and the third ventricle > **telencephalic** (ˌtɛlɛnsɪ'fælɪk) *adj*

teleological argument *n* philosophy the argument purporting to prove the existence of God from empirical facts, the premise being that the universe shows evidence of order and hence design. Also called: **argument from design** Compare **ontological argument, cosmological argument**

teleology (ˌtɛlɪ'ɒlədʒɪ, ˌtiːlɪ-) *n* **1** philosophy **a** the doctrine that there is evidence of purpose or design in the universe, and esp that this provides proof of the existence of a Designer **b** the belief that certain phenomena are best explained in terms of purpose rather than cause **c** the systematic study of such phenomena ▷ See also **final cause 2** biology the belief that natural phenomena have a predetermined purpose and are not determined by mechanical laws [c18 from New Latin *teleologia*, from Greek *telos* end + -LOGY] > **teleological** (ˌtɛlɪə'lɒdʒɪkªl, ˌtiːlɪ-) *or* ˌteleo'logic *adj*

teleost ('tɛlɪˌɒst, 'tiːlɪ-) n **1** any bony fish of the subclass *Teleostei*, having rayed fins and a swim bladder: the group contains most of the bony fishes, including the herrings, carps, eels, cod, perches, etc ▷ adj **2** of, relating to, or belonging to the *Teleostei* [C19 from New Latin *teleosteī* (pl) creatures having complete skeletons, from Greek *teleos* complete + *osteon* bone]

telepath ('tɛlɪˌpæθ) n **1** a person who is telepathic ▷ vb (intr) **2** to practise telepathy

telepathize or **telepathise** (tɪ'lɛpəˌθaɪz) vb (intr) to practise telepathy

telepathy (tɪ'lɛpəθɪ) n *psychol* the communication between people of thoughts, feelings, desires, etc, involving mechanisms that cannot be understood in terms of known scientific laws. Also called: thought transference Compare **telegnosis**, **clairvoyance** [C19 from TELE- + Greek *patheia* feeling, perception: see -PATHY] > telepathic (ˌtɛlɪ'pæθɪk) adj > ˌtele'pathically adv > te'lepathist n

téléphérique or **téléférique** (teɪleɪfeɪ'riːk) n **1** a mountain cable car **2** a cableway [C20 from French]

telephone ('tɛlɪˌfəʊn) n **1 a** Also called: **telephone set** an electrical device for transmitting speech, consisting of a microphone and receiver mounted on a handset **b** (as modifier): *a telephone receiver* **2 a** a worldwide system of communications using telephones. The microphone in one telephone converts sound waves into electrical signals that are transmitted along a telephone wire or by radio to one or more distant sets, the receivers of which reconvert the incoming signal into the original sound **b** (as modifier): *a telephone exchange; a telephone call* **3** See **telephone box** ▷ vb **4** to call or talk to (a person) by telephone **5** to transmit (a recorded message, radio or television programme, or other information) by telephone, using special transmitting and receiving equipment ▷ Often shortened to: **phone** > 'teleˌphoner n > telephonic (ˌtɛlɪ'fɒnɪk) adj > ˌtele'phonically adv

telephone answering machine n the full name for **answering machine**

telephone banking n a facility enabling customers to make use of banking services, such as oral payment instructions, account movements, raising loans, etc, over the telephone rather than by personal visit

telephone box n an enclosure from which a paid telephone call can be made. Also called: **telephone kiosk**, **telephone booth**

telephone directory n a book listing the names, addresses, and telephone numbers of subscribers in a particular area

telephone number n **1** a set of figures identifying the telephone of a particular subscriber, and used in making connections to that telephone **2** (plural) extremely large numbers, esp in reference to salaries or prices

telephone selling n another name for **telesales**

telephonist (tɪ'lɛfənɪst) n *Brit* a person who operates a telephone switchboard. Also called (esp US): **telephone operator**

telephony (tɪ'lɛfənɪ) n a system of telecommunications for the transmission of speech or other sounds

telephotography (ˌtɛlɪfə'tɒgrəfɪ) n the process or technique of photographing distant objects using a telephoto lens > **telephotographic** (ˌtɛlɪˌfəʊtə'græfɪk) adj

telephoto lens ('tɛlɪˌfəʊtəʊ) n a compound camera lens in which the focal length is greater than that of a simple lens of the same dimensions and thus produces a magnified image of a distant object. See also **zoom lens**

telepoint ('tɛlɪˌpɔɪnt) n **a** a system providing a place where a cordless telephone can be connected to a telephone network **b** a place

where a cordless telephone can be connected to a telephone network

teleport ('tɛlɪˌpɔːt) vb (tr) (in science fiction) to transport (a person or object) across a distance instantaneously [C20 from TELE- + PORT⁵] > ˌtelepor'tation n

telepresence ('tɛlɪˌprɛzəns) n the use of virtual reality technology to operate machinery by remote control or to create the effect of being at a different or imaginary location

teleprinter ('tɛlɪˌprɪntə) n **1** a telegraph apparatus consisting of a keyboard transmitter, which converts a typed message into coded pulses for transmission along a wire or cable, and a printing receiver, which converts incoming signals and prints out the message. US name: teletypewriter See also **telex**, **radioteletype 2** a network of such devices, formerly used for communicating information, etc **3** a similar device used for direct input/output of data into a computer at a distant location

teleprocessing (ˌtɛlɪ'prəʊsɛsɪŋ) n the use of remote computer terminals connected to a central computer to process data

Teleprompter ('tɛlɪˌprɒmptə) n *trademark US and Canadian* an electronic television prompting device whereby a prepared script, unseen by the audience, is enlarged line by line for the speaker. equivalent in Britain (and certain other countries): **Autocue**

Teleran ('tɛləˌræn) n *trademark* an electronic navigational aid in which the image of a ground-based radar system is televised to aircraft in flight so that a pilot can see the position of his aircraft in relation to others [C20 from *Tele*(*vision*) R(*adar*) A(*ir*) N(*avigation*)]

telerecording (ˌtɛlɪrɪ'kɔːdɪŋ) n the recording of television signals on tape or, more usually, on film

telesales ('tɛlɪˌseɪlz) n (functioning as singular) the selling or attempted selling of a particular commodity or service by a salesman who makes his initial approach by telephone. Also called: telemarketing, telephone selling

telescience ('tɛlɪˌsaɪəns) n *astronautics* the investigation of remotely controlled scientific experiments

telescope ('tɛlɪˌskəʊp) n **1** an optical instrument for making distant objects appear larger and brighter by use of a combination of lenses (**refracting telescope**) or lenses and curved mirrors (**reflecting telescope**). See also **terrestrial telescope**, **astronomical telescope**, **Cassegrain telescope**, **Galilean telescope**, **Newtonian telescope 2** any instrument, such as a radio telescope, for collecting, focusing, and detecting electromagnetic radiation from space ▷ vb **3** to crush together or be crushed together, as in a collision: *the front of the car was telescoped by the impact* **4** to fit together like a set of cylinders that slide into one another, thus allowing extension and shortening **5** to make or become smaller or shorter: *the novel was telescoped into a short play* [C17 from Italian *telescopio* or New Latin *telescopium*, literally: far-seeing instrument; see TELE-, -SCOPE]

telescopic (ˌtɛlɪ'skɒpɪk) adj **1** of or relating to a telescope **2** seen through or obtained by means of a telescope **3** visible only with the aid of a telescope **4** able to see far **5** having or consisting of parts that telescope: *a telescopic umbrella* > ˌtele'scopically adv

telescopic sight n a telescope mounted on a rifle, etc, used for sighting

Telescopium (ˌtɛlɪ'skəʊpɪəm) n, *Latin genitive* Telescopii (ˌtɛlɪ'skəʊpɪˌaɪ) an inconspicuous constellation in the S hemisphere, close to Sagittarius and Ara [New Latin; see TELESCOPE]

telescopy (tɪ'lɛskəpɪ) n the branch of astronomy concerned with the use and design of telescopes

teleshopping ('tɛlɪˌʃɒpɪŋ) n the purchase of goods by telephone or via the internet

telesis ('tɛlɪsɪs) n the purposeful use of natural

and social processes to obtain specific social goals [C19 from Greek: event, from *telein* to fulfil, from *telos* end]

telesoftware (ˌtɛlɪ'sɒftweə) n the transmission of computer programs on a teletext system

telespectroscope (ˌtɛlɪ'spɛktrəˌskəʊp) n a combination of a telescope and a spectroscope, used for spectroscopic analysis of radiation from stars and other celestial bodies

telestereoscope (ˌtɛlɪ'stɪərɪəˌskəʊp, -'stɛrɪə-) n an optical instrument for obtaining stereoscopic images of distant objects

telesthesia (ˌtɛlɪs'θiːzɪə) n the usual US spelling of **telaesthesia**. > **telesthetic** (ˌtɛlɪs'θɛtɪk) adj

telestich (tɪ'lɛstɪk, 'tɛlɪˌstɪk) n a short poem in which the last letters of each successive line form a word [C17 from Greek *telos* end + STICH]

telesurgery (ˌtɛlɪ'sɜːdʒərɪ) n surgical operations carried out by a surgeon in a distant place by means of a computer or satellite link and robotic instruments

teletex ('tɛlɪˌtɛks) n an international means of communicating text between a variety of terminals

teletext ('tɛlɪˌtɛkst) n a form of videotex in which information is broadcast by a television station and received on an adapted television set

Teletext ('tɛlɪˌtɛkst) n *trademark* (in Britain) the ITV teletext service. See **Ceefax**

telethon ('tɛləˌθɒn) n a lengthy television programme to raise charity funds, etc [C20 from TELE- + MARATHON]

Teletype ('tɛlɪˌtaɪp) n **1** *trademark* a type of teleprinter **2** (sometimes not capital) a network of such devices, used for communicating messages, information, etc ▷ vb **3** (sometimes not capital) to transmit (a message) by Teletype

Teletypesetter (ˌtɛlɪ'taɪpˌsɛtə, 'tɛlɪˌtaɪp-) n *trademark printing* a keyboard device whose output can either be punched tape, which can be used directly to operate a line-casting machine, or be transmitted by cable or wire to operate such a machine indirectly > ˌtele'typeˌsetting n

teletypewriter (ˌtɛlɪ'taɪpˌraɪtə, 'tɛlɪˌtaɪp-) n a US name for **teleprinter**

teleutospore (tɪ'luːtəˌspɔː) n another name for **teliospore** [C19 from Greek *teleutē*, from *telos* end + SPORE] > teˌleuto'sporic adj

televangelist (ˌtɛlɪ'vændʒəlɪst) n *US* an evangelical preacher who appears regularly on television, preaching the gospel and appealing for donations from viewers [C20 from TELE(VISION + E)VANGELIST]

televise ('tɛlɪˌvaɪz) vb **1** to put (a programme) on television **2** (tr) to transmit (a programme, signal, etc) by television

television ('tɛlɪˌvɪʒən) n **1** the system or process of producing on a distant screen a series of transient visible images, usually with an accompanying sound signal. Electrical signals, converted from optical images by a camera tube, are transmitted by UHF or VHF radio waves or by cable and reconverted into optical images by means of a television tube inside a television set **2** Also called: **television set** a device designed to receive and convert incoming electrical signals into a series of visible images on a screen together with accompanying sound **3** the content, etc, of television programmes **4** the occupation or profession concerned with any aspect of the broadcasting of television programmes: *he's in television* **5** (modifier) of, relating to, or used in the transmission or reception of video and audio UHF or VHF radio signals: *a television transmitter* ▷ Abbreviation: TV [C20 from TELE- + VISION] > ˌtele'visional adj > ˌtele'visionally adv > ˌtele'visionary adj

television tube n a cathode-ray tube designed for the reproduction of television pictures. Sometimes shortened to: **tube** Also called: **picture tube**

televisual (ˌtɛlɪ'vɪʒʊəl, -zjʊ-) adj relating to,

shown on, or suitable for production on television > ˌteleˈvisually *adv*

teleworking (ˈtɛlɪˌwɜːkɪŋ) *n* the use of home computers, telephones, etc, to enable a person to work from home while maintaining contact with colleagues, customers, or a central office. Also called: **telecommuting** > ˈteleˌworker *n*

telewriter (ˈtɛlɪˌraɪtə) *n* a telegraphic device for reproducing handwriting by converting the manually controlled movements of a pen into signals that, after transmission, control the movements of a similar pen

telex (ˈtɛlɛks) *n* 1 an international telegraph service in which teleprinters are rented out to subscribers for the purpose of direct communication 2 a teleprinter used in such a service 3 a message transmitted or received by telex ▷ *vb* 4 to transmit (a message) to (a person, office, etc) by telex [c20 from *tel(eprinter) ex(change)*]

telfer (ˈtɛlfə) *n* a variant spelling of **telpher**

telferage (ˈtɛlfərɪdʒ) *n* a variant spelling of **telpherage**

Telford (ˈtɛlfəd) *n* a town in W central England, in Telford and Wrekin unitary authority, Shropshire: designated a new town in 1963. Pop: 138 241 (2001)

Telford and Wrekin *n* a unitary authority in W Central England, in Shropshire. Pop: 160 300 (2003 est). Area: 289 sq km (112 sq miles)

telic (ˈtɛlɪk) *adj* 1 directed or moving towards some goal; purposeful 2 (of a clause or phrase) expressing purpose [c19 from Greek *telikos* final, from *telos* end]

Telidon (ˈtɛlɪˌdɒn) *n* *trademark* a Canadian interactive viewdata service

teliospore (ˈtiːlɪəˌspɔː) *n* any of the dark noninfective spores that are produced in each telium of the rust fungi and remain dormant during the winter. Also called: **teleutospore** [c20 from TELIUM + SPORE]

telium (ˈtiːlɪəm, ˈtɛl-) *n, pl* **telia** (ˈtiːlɪə, ˈtɛlɪə) the spore-producing body of some rust fungi in which the teliospores are formed [c20 New Latin, from Greek *teleion*, from *teleios* complete, from *telos* end] > ˈtelial *adj*

Telkom (ˈtɛlˌkɒm) *n* the official telephone service in South Africa

tell¹ (tɛl) *vb* **tells, telling, told** 1 (when *tr*, may take a clause as object) to let know or notify: *he told me that he would go* 2 (*tr*) to order or instruct (someone to do something): *I told her to send the letter airmail* 3 (when *intr*, usually foll by *of*) to give an account or narration (of something): *she told me her troubles* 4 (*tr*) to communicate by words; utter: *to tell the truth* 5 (*tr*) to make known; disclose: *to tell fortunes* 6 (*intr*; often foll by *of*) to serve as an indication: *her blush told of her embarrassment* 7 (*tr*; used with *can*, etc; may take a clause as object) to comprehend, discover, or discern: *I can tell what is wrong* 8 (*tr*; used with *can*, etc) to distinguish or discriminate: *he couldn't tell chalk from cheese* 9 (*intr*) to have or produce an impact, effect, or strain: *every step told on his bruised feet* 10 (*intr*; sometimes foll by *on*) *informal* to reveal secrets or gossip (about): *don't tell!; she told on him* 11 (*tr*) to assure: *I tell you, I've had enough!* 12 (*tr*) to count (votes) 13 (*intr*) *dialect* to talk or chatter 14 *informal, chiefly US* to tell the truth no matter how unpleasant it is 15 **tell the time** to read the time from a clock 16 **you're telling me** *slang* I know that very well ▷ See also **tell apart, tell off** [Old English *tellan*; related to Old Saxon *tellian*, Old High German *zellen* to tell, count, Old Norse *telja*] > ˈtellable *adj*

tell² (tɛl) *n* a large mound resulting from the accumulation of rubbish on a long-settled site, esp one with mudbrick buildings, particularly in the Middle East [c19 from Arabic *tall*]

tell apart *vb* (*tr, adverb*) to distinguish between; discern: *can you tell the twins apart?*

Tell el Amarna (ˈtɛl ɛl əˈmɑːnə) *n* a group of ruins and rock tombs in Upper Egypt, on the Nile below Asyut: site of the capital of Amenhotep IV, built about 1375 BC; excavated from 1891 onwards

teller (ˈtɛlə) *n* 1 another name for **cashier¹** (sense 2) 2 a person appointed to count votes in a legislative body, assembly, etc 3 a person who tells; narrator > ˈtellerˌship *n*

tellin (ˈtɛlɪn) *n* any of various slim marine bivalve molluscs of the genus *Tellina* (or *Macoma*) that live in intertidal sand, esp the smooth oval delicately tinted *T. tenuis* [from New Latin *tellina*, from Greek *tellinē* a shellfish]

telling (ˈtɛlɪŋ) *adj* 1 having a marked effect or impact: *a telling blow* 2 revealing: *a telling smile* > ˈtellingly *adv*

tell off *vb* (*tr, adverb*) 1 *informal* to reprimand; scold 2 to count and dismiss: *he told off four more soldiers* > telling off *or* telling-off *n*

telltale (ˈtɛlˌteɪl) *n* 1 a person who tells tales about others 2 a an outward indication of something concealed b (*as modifier*): *a telltale paw mark* 3 any of various indicators or recording devices used to monitor a process, machine, etc 4 *nautical* a another word for **dogvane** b one of a pair of light vanes mounted on the main shrouds of a sailing boat to indicate the apparent direction of the wind

tellurate (ˈtɛljʊˌreɪt) *n* any salt or ester of telluric acid

tellurian (tɛˈlʊərɪən) *adj* 1 of or relating to the earth ▷ *n* 2 (esp in science fiction) an inhabitant of the earth [c19 from Latin *tellūs* the earth]

telluric¹ (tɛˈlʊərɪk) *adj* 1 of, relating to, or originating on or in the earth or soil; terrestrial, esp in reference to natural electrical or magnetic fields 2 *astronomy* (of spectral lines or bands) observed in the spectra of celestial objects and caused by oxygen, water vapour, and carbon dioxide in the earth's atmosphere [c19 from Latin *tellūs* the earth]

telluric² (tɛˈlʊərɪk) *adj* of or containing tellurium, esp in a high valence state [c20 from TELLUR(IUM) + -IC]

telluric acid *n* a white crystalline dibasic acid produced by the oxidation of tellurium by hydrogen peroxide. Formula: H_6TeO_6

telluride (ˈtɛljʊˌraɪd) *n* any compound of tellurium, esp one formed between tellurium and a more electropositive element or group

tellurion *or* **tellurian** (tɛˈlʊərɪən) *n* an instrument that shows how day and night and the seasons result from the tilt of the earth, its rotation on its axis, and its revolution around the sun [c19 from Latin *tellūs* the earth]

tellurite (ˈtɛljʊˌraɪt) *n* any salt or ester of tellurous acid

tellurium (tɛˈlʊərɪəm) *n* a brittle silvery-white nonmetallic element occurring both uncombined and in combination with metals: used in alloys of lead and copper and as a semiconductor. Symbol: Te; atomic no: 52; atomic wt: 127.60; valency: 2, 4, or 6; relative density: 6.24; melting pt: 449.57±0.3°C; boiling pt: 988°C [c19 New Latin, from Latin *tellūs* the earth, formed by analogy with URANIUM]

tellurize *or* **tellurise** (ˈtɛljʊˌraɪz) *vb* (*tr*) to mix or combine with tellurium

tellurometer (ˌtɛljʊˈrɒmɪtə) *n* *surveying* an electronic instrument for measuring distances of up to about 30 miles that consists of two units, one at each end of the distance to be measured, between which radio waves are transmitted [c20 from Latin *tellūs* the earth + -METER]

tellurous (ˈtɛljʊrəs, tɛˈlʊərəs) *adj* of or containing tellurium, esp in a low valence state

Tellus (ˈtɛləs) *n* the Roman goddess of the earth; protectress of marriage, fertility, and the dead

telly (ˈtɛlɪ) *n, pl* **-lies** *informal, chiefly Brit* short for **television**

telo- *or before a vowel* **tel-** *combining form* 1 complete; final; perfect: *telophase* 2 end; at the end: *telencephalon* [from Greek *telos* end]

telocentric (ˌtɛləˈsɛntrɪk) *adj* *genetics* (of a chromosome) having the centromere at or close to the end

telomerase (tɛˈlɒməˌreɪz) *n* an enzyme that is involved in the formation and repair of telomeres, so that chromosomes are not shortened during cell division

telomere (ˈtɛləˌmɪə) *n* *genetics* either of the ends of a chromosome [c20 from Greek *telos* end + *meros* part]

telomerization *or* **telomerisation** (tɛˌlɒməraɪˈzeɪʃən) *n* *chem* polymerization in the presence of a chain transfer agent to yield a series of products of low molecular weight [c20 from TELO- + -MER]

telophase (ˈtɛləˌfeɪz) *n* 1 the final stage of mitosis, during which a set of chromosomes is present at each end of the cell and a nuclear membrane forms around each, producing two new nuclei. See also **prophase, metaphase, anaphase** 2 the corresponding stage of the first division of meiosis > ˌteloˈphasic *adj*

telpher *or* **telfer** (ˈtɛlfə) *n* 1 a load-carrying car in a telpherage 2 a another word for **telpherage** b (*as modifier*): *a telpher line; a telpher system* ▷ *vb* 3 (*tr*) to transport (a load) by means of a telpherage [c19 changed from *telephore*, from TELE- + -PHORE] > ˈtelpheric *or* ˈtelferic *adj*

telpherage *or* **telferage** (ˈtɛlfərɪdʒ) *n* an overhead transport system in which an electrically driven truck runs along a single rail or cable, the load being suspended in a separate car beneath. Also called: **telpher line, telpher**

telson (ˈtɛlsən) *n* the last segment or an appendage on the last segment of the body of crustaceans and arachnids [c19 from Greek: a boundary; probably related to *telos* end] > **telsonic** (tɛlˈsɒnɪk) *adj*

Telstar (ˈtɛlˌstɑː) *n* either of two low-altitude active communications satellites launched in 1962 and 1963 by the US and used in the transmission of television programmes, telephone messages, etc

Telugu *or* **Telegu** (ˈtɛləˌguː) *n* 1 a language of SE India, belonging to the Dravidian family of languages: the state language of Andhra Pradesh 2 (*pl* **-gus** *or* **-gu**) a member of the people who speak this language ▷ *adj* 3 of or relating to this people or their language

Telukbetung *or* **Teloekbetoeng** (təˌlʊkbəˈtʊŋ) *n* a port in Indonesia, in S Sumatra on the Sunda Strait. Pop: 742 749 (2000)

Tema (ˈtiːmə) *n* a port in SE Ghana on the Atlantic: new harbour opened in 1962; oil-refining. Pop: 160 000 (2005 est)

temazepam (təˈmæzəˌpæm) *n* a benzodiazepine sedative; the gel-like capsule formulation is properly taken orally but has also been melted and injected by drug users

Témbi (ˈtɛmbiː) *n* transliteration of the Modern Greek name for **Tempe**

temblor (ˈtɛmblə, -blɔː) *n, pl* **temblors** *or* **temblores** (tɛmˈblɔːreɪz) *chiefly US* an earthquake or earth tremor [c19 American Spanish, from Spanish *temblar* to shake, tremble]

temerity (tɪˈmɛrɪtɪ) *n* rashness or boldness [c15 from Latin *temeritās* accident, from *temere* at random] > **temerarious** (ˌtɛməˈrɛərɪəs) *adj*

Temesvár (ˈtɛmɛʃvaːr) *n* the Hungarian name for **Timişoara**

Temne (ˈtɛmnɪ, ˈtɪm-) *n* 1 (*pl* **-nes** *or* **-ne**) a member of a Negroid people of N Sierra Leone 2 the language of this people, closely related to Bantu

temp (tɛmp) *informal* ▷ *n* 1 a person, esp a typist or other office worker, employed on a temporary basis ▷ *vb* (*intr*) 2 to work as a temp

temp. *abbreviation for* 1 temperate 2 temperature 3 temporary 4 tempore [(for sense 4) Latin: in the time of]

Tempe (ˈtɛmpɪ) *n* **Vale of** a wooded valley in E Greece, in Thessaly between the mountains Olympus and Ossa. Modern Greek name: **Témbi**

tempeh (ˈtɛmpeɪ) *n* fermented soya beans [c20 from Indonesian *tempe*]

temper ('tɛmpə) *n* **1** a frame of mind; mood or humour: *a good temper* **2** a sudden outburst of anger; tantrum **3** a tendency to exhibit uncontrolled anger; irritability **4** a mental condition of moderation and calm (esp in the phrases **keep one's temper, lose one's temper, out of temper**) **5** the degree of hardness, elasticity, or a similar property of a metal or metal object ▷ *vb* (*tr*) **6** to make more temperate, acceptable, or suitable by adding something else; moderate: *he tempered his criticism with kindly sympathy* **7** to strengthen or toughen (a metal or metal article) by heat treatment, as by heating and quenching **8** *music* **a** to adjust the frequency differences between the notes of a scale on (a keyboard instrument) in order to allow modulation into other keys **b** to make such an adjustment to the pitches of notes in (a scale) **9** a rare word for **adapt 10** an archaic word for **mix** [Old English *temprian* to mingle, (influenced by Old French *temprer*), from Latin *temperāre* to mix, probably from *tempus* time] ▷ 'temperable *adj* ▷ ˌtempera'bility *n* ▷ 'temperer *n*

tempera ('tɛmpərə) *n* **1** a painting medium for powdered pigments, consisting usually of egg yolk and water **2 a** any emulsion used as a painting medium, with casein, glue, wax, etc, as a base **b** the paint made from mixing this with pigment **3** the technique of painting with tempera [c19 from Italian phrase *pingere a tempera* painting in tempera, from *temperare* to mingle; see TEMPER]

temperament ('tɛmpərəmənt, -prəmənt) *n* **1** an individual's character, disposition, and tendencies as revealed in his reactions **2** excitability, moodiness, or anger, esp when displayed openly: *an actress with temperament* **3** the characteristic way an individual behaves, esp towards other people. See also **character, personality 4 a** an adjustment made to the frequency differences between notes on a keyboard instrument to allow modulation to other keys **b** any of several systems of such adjustment, such as **just temperament**, a system not practically possible on keyboard instruments (see **just intonation**), **mean-tone temperament**, a system giving an approximation to natural tuning, and **equal temperament**, the system commonly used in keyboard instruments, giving a scale based on an octave divided into twelve exactly equal semitones **5** *obsolete* the characteristic way an individual behaves, viewed as the result of the influence of the four humours (blood, phlegm, yellow bile, and black bile) **6** *archaic* compromise or adjustment **7** an obsolete word for **temperature** [c15 from Latin *temperāmentum* a mixing in proportion, from *temperāre* to TEMPER]

temperamental (ˌtɛmpərə'mɛntəl, -prə'mɛntəl) *adj* **1** easily upset or irritated; excitable; volatile **2** of, relating to, or caused by temperament **3** *informal* working erratically and inconsistently; unreliable: *a temperamental sewing machine* ▷ ˌtempera'mentally *adv*

temperance ('tɛmpərəns) *n* **1** restraint or moderation, esp in yielding to one's appetites or desires **2** abstinence from alcoholic drink [c14 from Latin *temperantia*, from *temperāre* to regulate]

temperate ('tɛmpərɪt, 'tɛmprɪt) *adj* **1** having a climate intermediate between tropical and polar; moderate or mild in temperature **2** mild in quality or character; exhibiting temperance [c14 from Latin *temperātus*] ▷ 'temperately *adv* ▷ 'temperateness *n*

Temperate Zone *n* those parts of the earth's surface lying between the Arctic Circle and the tropic of Cancer and between the Antarctic Circle and the tropic of Capricorn

temperature ('tɛmprɪtʃə) *n* **1** the degree of hotness of a body, substance, or medium; a physical property related to the average kinetic energy of the atoms or molecules of a substance **2** a measure of this degree of hotness, indicated on a scale that has one or more fixed reference points **3** *informal* a body temperature in excess of the normal **4** *archaic* **a** compromise **b** temperament **c** temperance [c16 (originally: a mingling): from Latin *temperātūra* proportion, from *temperāre* to TEMPER]

temperature gradient *n* the rate of change in temperature in a given direction, esp in altitude

temperature-humidity index *n* an index of the effect on human comfort of temperature and humidity levels, 65 being the highest comfortable level

temperature inversion *n meteorol* an abnormal increase in temperature with height in the troposphere

tempered ('tɛmpəd) *adj* **1** *music* **a** (of a scale) having the frequency differences between notes adjusted in accordance with the system of equal temperament. See **temperament b** (of an interval) expanded or contracted from the state of being pure **2** (*in combination*) having a temper or temperament as specified: *ill-tempered*

tempest ('tɛmpɪst) *n* **1** *chiefly literary* a violent wind or storm **2** a violent commotion, uproar, or disturbance ▷ *vb* **3** (*tr*) *poetic* to agitate or disturb violently [c13 from Old French *tempeste*, from Latin *tempestās* storm, from *tempus* time]

tempestuous (tɛm'pɛstjʊəs) *adj* **1** of or relating to a tempest **2** violent or stormy: *a tempestuous love affair* ▷ tem'pestuously *adv* ▷ tem'pestuousness *n*

tempi ('tɛmpiː) *n* (in musical senses) the plural of **tempo**

Templar ('tɛmplə) *n* **1** a member of a military religious order (**Knights of the Temple of Solomon**) founded by Crusaders in Jerusalem around 1118 to defend the Holy Sepulchre and Christian pilgrims; suppressed in 1312 **2** (*sometimes not capital*) *Brit* a lawyer, esp a barrister, who lives or has chambers in the Inner or Middle Temple in London [c13 from Medieval Latin *templārius* of the temple, from Latin *templum* TEMPLE[1]; first applied to the knightly order because their house was near the site of the Temple of Solomon]

template *or* **templet** ('tɛmplɪt) *n* **1** a gauge or pattern, cut out in wood or metal, used in woodwork, etc, to help shape something accurately **2** a pattern cut out in card or plastic, used in various crafts to reproduce shapes **3** a short beam, made of metal, wood, or stone, that is used to spread a load, as over a doorway **4** *biochem* the molecular structure of a compound that serves as a pattern for the production of the molecular structure of another specific compound in a reaction [c17 *templet* (later spelling influenced by PLATE), probably from French, diminutive of TEMPLE[3]]

temple[1] ('tɛmpəl) *n* **1** a building or place dedicated to the worship of a deity or deities **2** a Mormon church **3** *US* another name for a **synagogue 4** any Christian church, esp a large or imposing one **5** any place or object regarded as a shrine where God makes himself present, esp the body of a person who has been sanctified or saved by grace **6** a building regarded as the focus of an activity, interest, or practice: *a temple of the arts* [Old English *tempel*, from Latin *templum*; probably related to Latin *tempus* TIME, Greek *temenos* sacred enclosure, literally: a place cut off, from *temnein* to cut] ▷ 'templed *adj* ▷ 'temple-ˌlike *adj*

temple[2] ('tɛmpəl) *n* the region on each side of the head in front of the ear and above the cheek bone. Related adj: **temporal** [c14 from Old French *temple*, from Latin *tempora* the temples, from *tempus* temple of the head]

temple[3] ('tɛmpəl) *n* the part of a loom that keeps the cloth being woven stretched to the correct width [c15 from French, from Latin *templum* a small timber]

Temple ('tɛmpəl) *n* **1** either of two buildings in London and Paris that belonged to the Templars. The one in London now houses two of the chief law societies **2** any of three buildings or groups of buildings erected by the Jews in ancient Jerusalem for the worship of Jehovah

Temple of Artemis *n* the large temple at Ephesus, on the W coast of Asia Minor: one of the Seven Wonders of the World

tempo ('tɛmpəʊ) *n, pl* **-pos** *or* **-pi** (-piː) **1** the speed at which a piece or passage of music is meant to be played, usually indicated by a musical direction (**tempo marking**) or metronome marking **2** rate or pace [c18 from Italian, from Latin *tempus* time]

tempolabile (ˌtɛmpəʊ'leɪbaɪl) *adj chem* changing irregularly with time

temporal[1] ('tɛmpərəl, 'tɛmprəl) *adj* **1** of or relating to time **2** of or relating to secular as opposed to spiritual or religious affairs: *the lords spiritual and temporal* **3** lasting for a relatively short time **4** *grammar* of or relating to tense or the linguistic expression of time in general: *a temporal adverb* [c14 from Latin *temporālis*, from *tempus* time] ▷ 'temporally *adv* ▷ 'temporalness *n*

temporal[2] ('tɛmpərəl, 'tɛmprəl) *adj anatomy* of, relating to, or near the temple or temples [c16 from Late Latin *temporālis* belonging to the temples; see TEMPLE[2]]

temporal bone *n* either of two compound bones forming part of the sides and base of the skull: they surround the organs of hearing

temporality (ˌtɛmpə'rælɪtɪ) *n, pl* **-ties 1** the state or quality of being temporal **2** something temporal **3** (*often plural*) a secular possession or revenue belonging to a Church, a group within the Church, or the clergy

temporal lobe *n* the laterally protruding portion of each cerebral hemisphere, situated below the parietal lobe and associated with sound perception and interpretation: it is thought to be the centre for memory recall

temporary ('tɛmpərərɪ, 'tɛmprərɪ) *adj* **1** not permanent; provisional: *temporary accommodation* **2** lasting only a short time; transitory: *temporary relief from pain* ▷ *n, pl* **-raries 3** a person, esp a secretary or other office worker, employed on a temporary basis. Often shortened to: **temp** [c16 from Latin *temporārius*, from *tempus* time] ▷ 'temporarily *adv* ▷ 'temporariness *n*

temporary hardness *n chem* hardness of water due to the presence of magnesium and calcium hydrogencarbonates, which can be precipitated as carbonates by boiling

temporize *or* **temporise** ('tɛmpəˌraɪz) *vb* (*intr*) **1** to delay, act evasively, or protract a discussion, negotiation, etc, esp in order to gain time or effect a compromise **2** to adapt oneself to the circumstances or occasion, as by temporary or apparent agreement [c16 from French *temporiser*, from Medieval Latin *temporizāre*, from Latin *tempus* time] ▷ ˌtempori'zation *or* ˌtempori'sation *n* ▷ 'tempoˌrizer *or* 'tempoˌriser *n*

tempt (tɛmpt) *vb* (*tr*) **1** to attempt to persuade or entice to do something, esp something morally wrong or unwise **2** to allure, invite, or attract **3** to give rise to a desire in (someone) to do something; dispose: *their unfriendliness tempted me to leave the party* **4** to risk provoking (esp in the phrase **tempt fate**) [c13 from Old French *tempter*, from Latin *temptāre* to test] ▷ 'temptable *adj* ▷ 'tempter *n*

temptation (tɛmp'teɪʃən) *n* **1** the act of tempting or the state of being tempted **2** a person or thing that tempts

Tempter ('tɛmptə) *n* **the** Satan regarded as trying to lead men into sin

tempting ('tɛmptɪŋ) *adj* attractive or inviting: *a tempting meal* ▷ 'temptingly *adv* ▷ 'temptingness *n*

temptress ('tɛmptrɪs) *n* a woman who sets out to allure or seduce a man or men; seductress

tempura ('tɛmpərə) *n* a Japanese dish of seafood or vegetables dipped in batter and deep-fried, often at the table [from Japanese: fried food]

tempus fugit (*Latin* 'tɛmpəs 'fjuːdʒɪt, -gɪt) time flies

t

Temuco (*Spanish* te'muko) *n* a city in S Chile: agricultural trading centre. Pop: 287 000 (2005 est)

ten (tɛn) *n* **1** the cardinal number that is the sum of nine and one. It is the base of the decimal number system and the base of the common logarithm. See also **number** (sense 1) **2** a numeral, 10, X, etc, representing this number **3** something representing, represented by, or consisting of ten units, such as a playing card with ten symbols on it **4** Also called: **ten o'clock** ten hours after noon or midnight ▷ *determiner* **5 a** amounting to ten: *ten tigers* **b** (*as pronoun*): *to sell only ten* ▷ Related adjective: **decimal** Related prefixes: **deca-, deci-** [Old English *tēn*; related to Old Saxon *tehan*, Old High German *zehan*, Gothic *taihun*, Latin *decem*, Greek *deka*, Sanskrit *dasa*]

ten- *combining form* a variant of **teno-** before a vowel

tenable ('tɛnəb(ə)l) *adj* able to be upheld, believed, maintained, or defended [C16 from Old French, from *tenir* to hold, from Latin *tenēre*] > ˌ**tena'bility** *or* '**tenableness** *n* > '**tenably** *adv*

tenace ('tɛneɪs) *n bridge, whist* a holding of two nonconsecutive high cards of a suit, such as the ace and queen [C17 from French, from Spanish *tenaza* forceps, ultimately from Latin *tenāx* holding fast, from *tenēre* to hold]

tenacious (tɪ'neɪʃəs) *adj* **1** holding or grasping firmly; forceful: *a tenacious grip* **2** retentive: *a tenacious memory* **3** stubborn or persistent: *a tenacious character* **4** holding together firmly; tough or cohesive: *tenacious cement* **5** tending to stick or adhere: *tenacious mud* [C16 from Latin *tenāx*, from *tenēre* to hold] > **te'naciously** *adv* > **te'naciousness** *or* **tenacity** (tɪ'næsɪtɪ) *n*

ten-acre block *n NZ* a block of subdivided farming land, usually within commuting distance of a city, that provides a semirural way of life

tenaculum (tɪ'nækjʊləm) *n, pl* **-la** (-lə) a surgical or dissecting instrument for grasping and holding parts, consisting of a slender hook mounted in a handle [C17 from Late Latin, from Latin *tenēre* to hold]

tenaille (tɛ'neɪl) *n fortifications* a low outwork in the main ditch between two bastions [C16 from French, literally: tongs, from Late Latin *tenācula*, pl of TENACULUM]

tena koe (tə'nɑː 'kwɔɪ) *interj NZ* a Māori greeting to one person

tena korua ('tənɑː 'kɒruːɑː) *interj NZ* a Māori greeting to two people [Māori]

tena koutou ('tənɑː 'kɒuːtɒuː) *interj NZ* a Māori greeting to two or more people [Māori]

tenancy ('tɛnənsɪ) *n, pl* **-cies 1** the temporary possession or holding by a tenant of lands or property owned by another **2** the period of holding or occupying such property **3** the period of holding office, a position, etc **4** property held or occupied by a tenant

tenant ('tɛnənt) *n* **1** a person who holds, occupies, or possesses land or property by any kind of right or title, esp from a landlord under a lease **2** a person who has the use of a house, flat, etc, subject to the payment of rent **3** any holder or occupant ▷ *vb* **4** (*tr*) to hold (land or property) as a tenant **5** (*intr*; foll by *in*) *rare* to dwell [C14 from Old French, literally: (one who is) holding, from *tenir* to hold, from Latin *tenēre*] > '**tenantable** *adj* > '**tenantless** *adj* > '**tenant-**ˌ**like** *adj*

tenant farmer *n* a person who farms land rented from another, the rent usually taking the form of part of the crops grown or livestock reared

tenant-in-chief *n* (in feudal society) a tenant who held some or all of his lands directly from the king

tenantry ('tɛnəntrɪ) *n* **1** tenants collectively, esp those with the same landlord **2** the status or condition of being a tenant

tenants association *n* an organization of tenants, usually with a written constitution and charitable status, whose aim is to improve the housing conditions, amenities, community life, and contractual positions of its members. See also **community association, residents association**

tenants' charter *n* (in Britain) a package of legal rights to which tenants of local authorities, new towns, and housing associations are entitled, including security of tenure, and the rights to buy the dwelling cheaply, to take in lodgers, and to sublet

Tencel ('tɛnˌsɛl) *n trademark* a fabric made from wood pulp cellulose, having a silky texture

tench (tɛntʃ) *n* a European freshwater cyprinid game fish, *Tinca tinca*, having a thickset dark greenish body with a barbel at each side of the mouth [C14 from Old French *tenche*, from Late Latin *tinca*]

Ten Commandments *pl n* **the** *Old Testament* the commandments summarizing the basic obligations of man towards God and his fellow men, delivered to Moses on Mount Sinai engraved on two tables of stone (Exodus 20:1–17). Also called: **the Decalogue**

tend[1] (tɛnd) *vb* (when *intr*, usually foll by *to* or *towards*) **1** (when *tr*, *takes an infinitive*) to have a general disposition (to do something); be inclined: *children tend to prefer sweets to meat* **2** (*intr*) to have or be an influence (towards a specific result); be conducive: *the party atmosphere tends to hilarity* **3** (*intr*) to go or move (in a particular direction): *to tend to the south* [C14 from Old French *tendre*, from Latin *tendere* to stretch]

tend[2] (tɛnd) *vb* **1** (*tr*) to care for: *to tend wounded soldiers* **2** (when *intr*, often foll by *to*) to attend (to): *to tend to someone's needs* **3** (*tr*) to handle or control: *to tend a fire* **4** (*intr*; often foll by *to*) *informal, chiefly US and Canadian* to pay attention [C14 variant of ATTEND]

tendance ('tɛndəns) *n* **1** *rare* care and attention; ministration **2** *obsolete* attendants collectively

tendency ('tɛndənsɪ) *n, pl* **-cies 1** (often foll by *to*) an inclination, predisposition, propensity, or leaning: *she has a tendency to be frivolous; a tendency to frivolity* **2** the general course, purport, or drift of something, esp a written work **3** a faction, esp one within a political party: *the militant tendency* [C17 from Medieval Latin *tendentia*, from Latin *tendere* to TEND[1]]

tendentious *or* **tendencious** (tɛn'dɛnʃəs) *adj* having or showing an intentional tendency or bias, esp a controversial one [C20 from TENDENCY] > **ten'dentiously, ten'denciously, ten'dentially** *or* **ten'dencially** *adv* > **ten'dentiousness** *or* **ten'denciousness** *n*

tender[1] ('tɛndə) *adj* **1** easily broken, cut, or crushed; soft; not tough: *a tender steak* **2** easily damaged; vulnerable or sensitive: *a tender youth; at a tender age* **3** having or expressing warm and affectionate feelings: *a tender smile* **4** kind, merciful, or sympathetic: *a tender heart* **5** arousing warm feelings; touching: *a tender memory* **6** gentle and delicate: *a tender breeze* **7** requiring care in handling; ticklish: *a tender question* **8** painful or sore: *a tender wound* **9** sensitive to moral or spiritual feelings: *a tender conscience* **10** (*postpositive*; foll by *of*) careful or protective: *tender of one's emotions* **11** (of a sailing vessel) easily keeled over by a wind; crank. Compare **stiff** (sense 10) ▷ *vb* **12** (*tr*) *rare* **a** to make tender **b** to treat tenderly [C13 from Old French *tendre*, from Latin *tener* delicate] > '**tenderly** *adv* > '**tenderness** *n*

tender[2] ('tɛndə) *vb* **1** (*tr*) to give, present, or offer: *to tender one's resignation; tender a bid* **2** (*intr*; foll by *for*) to make a formal offer or estimate for (a job or contract) **3** (*tr*) *law* to offer (money or goods) in settlement of a debt or claim ▷ *n* **4** the act of an instance of tendering; offer **5** *commerce* a formal offer to supply specified goods or services at a stated cost or rate **6** something, esp money, used as an official medium of payment: *legal tender* [C16 from Anglo-French *tendre*, from Latin *tendere* to extend; see TEND[1]] > '**tenderable** *adj* > '**tenderer** *n*

tender[3] ('tɛndə) *n* **1** a small boat, such as a dinghy, towed or carried by a yacht or ship **2** a vehicle drawn behind a steam locomotive to carry the fuel and water **3** an ancillary vehicle used to carry supplies, spare parts, etc, for a mobile operation, such as an outside broadcast **4** a person who tends [C15 variant of *attender*]

tenderfoot ('tɛndəˌfʊt) *n, pl* **-foots** *or* **-feet 1** a newcomer, esp to the mines or ranches of the southwestern US **2** (formerly) a beginner in the Scouts or Guides

tenderhearted (ˌtɛndə'hɑːtɪd) *adj* having a compassionate, kindly, or sensitive disposition > ˌ**tender'heartedly** *adv* > ˌ**tender'heartedness** *n*

tenderize *or* **tenderise** ('tɛndəˌraɪz) *vb* (*tr*) to make (meat) tender by pounding it to break down the fibres, by steeping it in a marinade, or by treating it with a tenderizer > ˌ**tenderi'zation** *or* ˌ**tenderi'sation** *n*

tenderizer *or* **tenderiser** ('tɛndəˌraɪzə) *n* a substance, such as the plant enzyme papain, rubbed onto meat to soften the fibres and make it more tender

tenderloin ('tɛndəˌlɔɪn) *n* **1** a tender cut of pork or other meat from between the sirloin and ribs **2** *US* a district of a city that is particularly noted for vice and corruption [sense 2 from *Tenderloin*, former district of New York City, regarded as an easy source of bribes for a corrupt policeman]

tendinous ('tɛndɪnəs) *adj* of, relating to, possessing, or resembling tendons; sinewy [C17 from New Latin *tendinōsus*, from Medieval Latin *tendō* TENDON]

tendon ('tɛndən) *n* a cord or band of white inelastic collagenous tissue that attaches a muscle to a bone or some other part; sinew [C16 from Medieval Latin *tendō*, from Latin *tendere* to stretch; related to Greek *tenōn* sinew]

tendril ('tɛndrɪl) *n* **1** a specialized threadlike part of a leaf or stem that attaches climbing plants to a support by twining or adhering **2** something resembling a tendril, such as a wisp of hair [C16 perhaps from Old French *tendron* tendril (confused with Old French *tendron* bud), from Medieval Latin *tendō* TENDON] > '**tendrillar** *or* '**tendrilous** *adj*

Tenebrae ('tɛnəˌbreɪ) *n* (*functioning as singular or plural*) *RC Church* (formerly) the matins and lauds for Thursday, Friday, and Saturday of Holy Week, usually sung in the evenings or at night [C17 from Latin: darkness]

tenebrism ('tɛnəˌbrɪzəm) *n* (*sometimes capital*) a school, style, or method of painting, adopted chiefly by 17th-century Spanish and Neapolitan painters, esp Caravaggio, characterized by large areas of dark colours, usually relieved with a shaft of light > '**tenebrist** *n, adj*

tenebrous ('tɛnəbrəs) *or* **tenebrious** (tə'nɛbrɪəs) *adj* gloomy, shadowy, or dark [C15 from Latin *tenebrōsus* from *tenebrae* darkness] > **tenebrosity** (ˌtɛnə'brɒsɪtɪ), '**tenebrousness** *or* **te'nebriousness** *n*

Tenedos ('tɛnɪˌdɒs) *n* an island in the NE Aegean, near the entrance to the Dardanelles: in Greek legend the base of the Greek fleet during the siege of Troy. Modern Turkish name: **Bozcaada**

tenement ('tɛnəmənt) *n* **1** Also called: **tenement building** (now esp in Scotland) a large building divided into separate flats **2** a dwelling place or residence, esp one intended for rent **3** *chiefly Brit* a room or flat for rent **4** *property law* any form of permanent property, such as land, dwellings, offices, etc [C14 from Medieval Latin *tenementum*, from Latin *tenēre* to hold] > **tenemental** (ˌtɛnə'mɛnt(ə)l) *or* ˌ**tene'mentary** *adj* > '**tene**ˌ**mented** *adj*

Tenerife (ˌtɛnə'riːf; *Spanish* tene'rife) *n* a Spanish island in the Atlantic, off the NW coast of Africa: the largest of the Canary Islands; volcanic and mountainous; tourism and agriculture. Capital: Santa Cruz. Pop: 778 071 (2002 est). Area: 2058 sq km (795 sq miles)

tenesmus (tɪ'nɛzməs, -'nɛs-) *n pathol* an ineffective painful straining to empty the bowels in response to the sensation of a desire to defecate, without producing a significant quantity of faeces [C16 from Medieval Latin, from Latin *tēnesmos,* from Greek *teinesmos,* from *teinein* to strain] > te'nesmic *adj*

tenet ('tɛnɪt, 'tiːnɪt) *n* a belief, opinion, or dogma [C17 from Latin, literally: he (it) holds, from *tenēre* to hold]

tenfold ('tɛnˌfəʊld) *adj* **1** equal to or having 10 times as many or as much: *a tenfold increase in population* **2** composed of 10 parts ▷ *adv* **3** by or up to 10 times as many or as much: *the population increased tenfold*

ten-gallon hat *n* (in the US and Canada) a cowboy's broad-brimmed felt hat with a very high crown [C20 so called because of its large size]

tenge (tɛnˈɡeɪ) *n* the standard monetary unit of Kazakhstan, divided into 100 tiyn

Tengri Khan ('tɛngrɪ 'kɑːn) *n* a mountain in central Asia, on the border between Kyrgyzstan and the Xinjiang Uygur Autonomous Region of W China. Height: 6995 m (22 951 ft)

Tengri Nor ('tɛngrɪ 'nɔː) *n* another name for **Nam Co**

Ten Gurus *pl n* the ten leaders of the Sikh religion from the founder of Sikhism Guru Nanak (1469–1538) to Guru Govind Singh (1666–1708), who ended the line of gurus by calling on Sikhs to rely on the holy text of the Granth to guide them

tenia ('tiːnɪə) *n, pl* **-niae** (-nɪˌiː) the US spelling of **taenia**

teniacide ('tiːnɪəˌsaɪd) *n* the US spelling of **taeniacide**

teniafuge ('tiːnɪəˌfjuːdʒ) *n* the US spelling of **taeniafuge**

teniasis (tiːˈnaɪəsɪs) *n* the US spelling of **taeniasis**

Tenn. *abbreviation for* Tennessee

tenner ('tɛnə) *n informal* **1** *Brit* **a** a ten-pound note **b** the sum of ten pounds **2** *US* a ten-dollar bill

Tennessean (ˌtɛnɪˈsiːən) *n* **1** a native or inhabitant of Tennessee ▷ *adj* **2** of or relating to Tennessee or its inhabitants

Tennessee (ˌtɛnɪˈsiː) *n* **1** a state of the E central US: consists of a plain in the west, rising to the Appalachians and the Cumberland Plateau in the east. Capital: Nashville. Pop: 5 841 748 (2003 est). Area: 109 412 sq km (42 244 sq miles). Abbreviations: **Tenn,** (with zip code) **TN 2** a river in the E central US, flowing southwest from E Tennessee into N Alabama, then west and north to the Ohio River at Paducah: the longest tributary of the Ohio; includes a series of dams and reservoirs under the Tennessee Valley Authority. Length: 1049 km (652 miles)

Tennessee Walking Horse *n* an American breed of horse, marked by its stamina and trained to move at a fast running walk. Often shortened to: **Walking Horse**

tennis ('tɛnɪs) *n* **a** a racket game played between two players or pairs of players who hit a ball to and fro over a net on a rectangular court of grass, asphalt, clay, etc. See also **lawn tennis, real tennis, court tennis, table tennis b** (*as modifier*): *tennis court; tennis racket* [C14 probably from Anglo-French *tenetz* hold (imperative), from Old French *tenir* to hold, from Latin *tenēre*]

tennis ball *n* a hollow rubber ball covered with felt, used in tennis

tennis elbow *n* a painful inflammation of the elbow caused by exertion in playing tennis and similar games

tennis shoe *n* a rubber-soled canvas shoe tied with laces

tenno ('tɛnəʊ) *n, pl* **-no** or **-nos** the formal title of the Japanese emperor, esp when regarded as a divine religious leader [from Japanese *tennō*]

Tennysonian (ˌtɛnɪˈsəʊnɪən) *adj* **1** of, relating to, or reminiscent of Alfred, Lord Tennyson, the English poet (1809 92) ▷ *n* **2** a follower or admirer of Tennyson

Teno ('tɛnɔ) *n* the Finnish name for **Tana** (sense 3)

teno- or before a vowel **ten-** *combining form* tendon: *tenosynovitis* [from Greek *tenōn*]

Tenochtitlán (tɛˌnɔːtʃtiːˈtlɑːn) *n* an ancient city and capital of the Aztec empire on the present site of Mexico City; razed by Cortés in 1521

tenon ('tɛnən) *n* **1** the projecting end of a piece of wood formed to fit into a corresponding mortise in another piece ▷ *vb* (*tr*) **2** to form a tenon on (a piece of wood) **3** to join with a tenon and mortise [C15 from Old French, from *tenir* to hold, from Latin *tenēre*] > 'tenoner *n*

tenon saw *n* a small fine-toothed saw with a strong back, used esp for cutting tenons

tenor ('tɛnə) *n* **1** *music* **a** the male voice intermediate between alto and baritone, having a range approximately from the B a ninth below middle C to the G a fifth above it **b** a singer with such a voice **c** a saxophone, horn, recorder, etc, intermediate in compass and size between the alto and baritone or bass **d** (*as modifier*): *a tenor sax* **2** general drift of thought; purpose: *to follow the tenor of an argument* **3 a** (in early polyphonic music) the part singing the melody or the cantus firmus **b** (in four-part harmony) the second lowest part lying directly above the bass **4** *bell-ringing* **a** the heaviest and lowest-pitched bell in a ring **b** (*as modifier*): *a tenor bell* **5** a settled course of progress **6** *archaic* general tendency **7** *finance* the time required for a bill of exchange or promissory note to become due for payment **8** *law* **a** the exact words of a deed, etc, as distinct from their effect **b** an exact copy or transcript [C13 (originally: general meaning or sense): from Old French *tenour,* from Latin *tenor* a continuous holding to a course, from *tenēre* to hold; musical sense via Italian *tenore,* referring to the voice part that was continuous, that is, to which the melody was assigned] > 'tenorless *adj*

tenor clef *n* the clef that establishes middle C as being on the fourth line of the staff, used for the writing of music for the bassoon, cello, or tenor trombone. See also **C clef**

tenorite ('tɛnəˌraɪt) *n* a black mineral found in copper deposits and consisting of copper oxide in the form of either metallic scales or earthy masses. Formula: CuO [C19 named after G. *Tenore* (died 1861), Italian botanist]

tenorrhaphy (tɪˈnɒrəfɪ) *n, pl* **-phies** *surgery* the union of torn or divided tendons by means of sutures [C19 from TENO- + Greek *raphē* a sewing or suture]

tenosynovitis ('tɛnəʊˌsaɪnəʊˈvaɪtɪs) *n* painful swelling and inflammation of tendons, usually of the wrist, often the result of repetitive movements such as typing

tenotomy (təˈnɒtəmɪ) *n, pl* **-mies** surgical division of a tendon > te'notomist *n*

tenpenny ('tɛnpənɪ) *adj* (*prenominal*) *US and Canadian* (of a nail) three inches in length

tenpin ('tɛnˌpɪn) *n* one of the pins used in tenpin bowling. See also **tenpins**

tenpin bowling *n* a bowling game in which heavy bowls are rolled down a long lane to knock over the ten target pins at the other end. Also called (esp US and Canadian): **tenpins**

tenpins ('tɛnˌpɪnz) *n* (*functioning as singular*) a US and Canadian name for **tenpin bowling**

tenrec ('tɛnrɛk) *n* any small mammal, such as *Tenrec ecaudatus* (**tailless tenrec**), of the Madagascan family *Tenrecidae,* resembling hedgehogs or shrews: order *Insectivora* (insectivores) [C18 via French from Malagasy *trăndraka*]

TENS (tɛnz) *n acronym for* transcutaneous electrical nerve stimulation: the application of low-voltage electric impulses to the skin to relieve rheumatic pain and provide some pain relief in labour. The pulses are said to stimulate the release of pain-killing endorphins

tense¹ (tɛns) *adj* **1** stretched or stressed tightly; taut or rigid **2** under mental or emotional strain **3** producing mental or emotional strain: *a tense day* **4** (of a speech sound) pronounced with considerable muscular effort and having

relatively precise accuracy of articulation and considerable duration: *in English the vowel* (iː) *in "beam" is tense.* Compare **lax** (sense 4) ▷ *vb* **5** (often foll by *up*) to make or become tense [C17 from Latin *tensus* taut, from *tendere* to stretch] > 'tensely *adv* > 'tenseness *n*

tense² (tɛns) *n grammar* a category of the verb or verbal inflections, such as present, past, and future, that expresses the temporal relations between what is reported in a sentence and the time of its utterance [C14 from Old French *tens* time, from Latin *tempus*] > 'tenseless *adj*

tense logic *n logic* the study of the logical properties of tense operators, and of the logical relations between sentences having tense, by means of consideration of appropriate formal systems

tensible ('tɛnsəbᵊl) *adj* capable of being stretched; tensile > ˌtensi'bility or 'tensibleness *n* > 'tensibly *adv*

tensile ('tɛnsaɪl) *adj* **1** of or relating to tension **2** sufficiently ductile to be stretched or drawn out [C17 from New Latin *tensilis,* from Latin *tendere* to stretch] > 'tensilely *adv* > tensility (tɛnˈsɪlɪtɪ) or 'tensileness *n*

tensile strength *n* a measure of the ability of a material to withstand a longitudinal stress, expressed as the greatest stress that the material can stand without breaking

tensimeter (tɛnˈsɪmɪtə) *n* an instrument used to compare the vapour pressures of two liquids, usually consisting of two sealed bulbs containing the liquids, each being connected to one limb of a manometer [C20 from TENSI(ON) + -METER]

tensiometer (ˌtɛnsɪˈɒmɪtə) *n* **1** an instrument for measuring the tensile strength of a wire, beam, etc **2** a device that measures differences in vapour pressures. It is used to determine transition points by observing changes of vapour pressure with temperature **3** an instrument for measuring the surface tension of a liquid, usually consisting of a sensitive balance for measuring the force needed to pull a wire ring from the surface of the liquid **4** an instrument for measuring the moisture content of soil

tension ('tɛnʃən) *n* **1** the act of stretching or the state or degree of being stretched **2** mental or emotional strain; stress **3** a situation or condition of hostility, suspense, or uneasiness **4** *physics* a force that tends to produce an elongation of a body or structure **5** *physics* **a** voltage, electromotive force, or potential difference **b** (*in combination*): *high-tension; low-tension* **6** a device for regulating the tension in a part, string, thread, etc, as in a sewing machine **7** *knitting* the degree of tightness or looseness with which a person knits [C16 from Latin *tensiō,* from *tendere* to strain] > 'tensional *adj* > 'tensionless *adj*

tensity ('tɛnsɪtɪ) *n* a rare word for **tension** (senses 1–3)

tensive ('tɛnsɪv) *adj* of or causing tension or strain

tensor ('tɛnsə, -sɔː) *n* **1** *anatomy* any muscle that can cause a part to become firm or tense **2** *maths* a set of components, functions of the coordinates of any point in space, that transform linearly between coordinate systems. For three-dimensional space there are 3^r components, where *r* is the rank. A tensor of zero rank is a scalar, of rank one, a vector [C18 from New Latin, literally: a stretcher] > tensorial (tɛnˈsɔːrɪəl) *adj*

ten-strike *n tenpin bowling* another word for **strike** (sense 40)

tent¹ (tɛnt) *n* **1 a** a portable shelter of canvas, plastic, or other waterproof material supported on poles and fastened to the ground by pegs and ropes **b** (*as modifier*): *tent peg* **2** something resembling this in function or shape ▷ *vb* **3** (*intr*) to camp in a tent **4** (*tr*) to cover with or as if with a tent or tents **5** (*tr*) to provide with a tent as shelter [C13 from Old French *tente,* from Latin *tentōrium* something stretched out, from *tendere* to

t

stretch] ▷ ˈtented *adj* ▷ ˈtentless *adj* ▷ ˈtentˌlike *adj*

tent² (tɛnt) *med* ▷ *n* **1** a plug of soft material for insertion into a bodily canal, etc, to dilate it or maintain its patency ▷ *vb* **2** (*tr*) to insert such a plug into (a bodily canal, etc) [C14 (in the sense: a probe): from Old French *tente* (noun), ultimately from Latin *temptāre* to try; see TEMPT]

tent³ (tɛnt) *n obsolete* a red table wine from Alicante, Spain [C16 from Spanish *tinto* dark-coloured; see TINT]

tent⁴ (tɛnt) *Scot* ▷ *n* **1** heed; attention ▷ *vb* (*tr*) **2** to pay attention to; take notice of **3** to attend to [C14 from *attent* ATTEND and INTENT] ▷ ˈtenter *n*

tentacle (ˈtɛntəkᵊl) *n* **1** any of various elongated flexible organs that occur near the mouth in many invertebrates and are used for feeding, grasping, etc **2** any of the hairs on the leaf of an insectivorous plant that are used to capture prey **3** something resembling a tentacle, esp in its ability to reach out or grasp [C18 from New Latin *tentāculum*, from Latin *tentāre*, variant of *temptāre* to feel] ▷ ˈtentacled *adj* ▷ ˈtentacle-ˌlike *or* tentaculoid (tɛnˈtækjʊˌlɔɪd) *adj* ▷ tentacular (tɛnˈtækjʊlə) *adj*

tentage (ˈtɛntɪdʒ) *n* **1** tents collectively **2** a supply of tents or tenting equipment

tentation (tɛnˈteɪʃən) *n* a method of achieving the correct adjustment of a mechanical device by a series of trials [C14 from Latin *tentātiō*, variant of *temptātiō* TEMPTATION]

tentative (ˈtɛntətɪv) *adj* **1** provisional or experimental; conjectural **2** hesitant, uncertain, or cautious [C16 from Medieval Latin *tentātīvus*, from Latin *tentāre* to test] ▷ ˈtentatively *adv* ▷ ˈtentativeness *n*

tent caterpillar *n* the larva of various moths of the family *Lasiocampidae*, esp *Malacosoma americana* of North America, which build communal webs in trees

tent dress *n* a very full tent-shaped dress, having no darts, waistline, etc

tenter (ˈtɛntə) *n* **1** a frame on which cloth is stretched during the manufacturing process in order that it may retain its shape while drying **2** a person who stretches cloth on a tenter ▷ *vb* **3** (*tr*) to stretch (cloth) on a tenter [C14 from Medieval Latin *tentōrium*, from Latin *tentus* stretched, from *tendere* to stretch]

tenterhook (ˈtɛntəˌhʊk) *n* **1** one of a series of hooks or bent nails used to hold cloth stretched on a tenter **2 on tenterhooks** in a state of tension or suspense

tenth (tɛnθ) *adj* **1** (*usually prenominal*) **a** coming after the ninth in numbering or counting order, position, time, etc; being the ordinal number of *ten*: often written 10th **b** (*as noun*): *see you on the tenth; tenth in line* ▷ *n* **2 a** one of 10 approximately equal parts of something **b** (*as modifier*): *a tenth part* **3** one of 10 equal divisions of a particular measurement, etc. Related prefix: **deci-** *decibel* **4** the fraction equal to one divided by ten (1/10) **5** *music* **a** an interval of one octave plus a third **b** one of two notes constituting such an interval in relation to the other ▷ *adv* **6** Also: **tenthly** after the ninth person, position, event, etc ▷ *sentence connector* **7** Also: **tenthly** as the 10th point: linking what follows with the previous statements, as in a speech or argument [C12 *tenthe*, from Old English *tēotha*; see TEN, -TH²]

tent stitch *n* another term for **petit point** (sense 1) [C17 of uncertain origin]

tenuis (ˈtɛnjʊɪs) *n, pl* **tenues** (ˈtɛnjʊˌiːz) (in the grammar of classical Greek) any of the voiceless stops as represented by kappa, pi, or tau (k, p, t) [C17 from Latin: thin]

tenuous (ˈtɛnjʊəs) *adj* **1** insignificant or flimsy: *a tenuous argument* **2** slim, fine, or delicate: *a tenuous thread* **3** diluted or rarefied in consistency or density: *a tenuous fluid* [C16 from Latin *tenuis*] ▷ **tenuity** (tɛˈnjuːɪtɪ) *or* ˈtenuousness *n* ▷ ˈtenuously *adv*

tenure (ˈtɛnjʊə, ˈtɛnjə) *n* **1** the possession or holding of an office or position **2** the length of

---

time an office, position, etc, lasts; term **3** *chiefly US and Canadian* the improved security status of a person after having been in the employ of the same company or institution for a specified period **4** the right to permanent employment until retirement, esp for teachers, lecturers, etc **5** *property law* **a** the holding or occupying of property, esp realty, in return for services rendered, etc **b** the duration of such holding or occupation [C15 from Old French, from Medieval Latin *tenitūra*, ultimately from Latin *tenēre* to hold] ▷ tenˈurial *adj* ▷ tenˈurially *adv*

tenured (ˈtɛnjʊəd, ˈtɛnjəd) *adj chiefly US and Canadian* **a** having tenure of office: *a tenured professor* **b** guaranteeing tenure of office: *a tenured post*

tenuto (tɪˈnjuːtəʊ) *adj, adv music* (of a note) to be held for or beyond its full time value. Symbol: - (written above a note) [from Italian, literally: held, from *tenere* to hold, from Latin *tenēre*]

ten-yard rule *n rugby* the rule allowing a referee, when a player disputes the award of a penalty or free kick, to penalize the offending side further by moving the place from which the kick is to be taken ten yards further forward

teocalli (ˌtiːəʊˈkælɪ) *n, pl* -lis any of various truncated pyramids built by the Aztecs as bases for their temples [C17 from Nahuatl, from *teotl* god + *calli* house]

teosinte (ˌtiːəʊˈsɪntɪ) *n* a tall Central American annual grass, *Euchlaena mexicana,* related to maize and grown for forage in the southern US [C19 from Nahuatl *teocentli*, from *teotl* god + *centli* dry ear of corn]

tepal (ˈtiːpᵊl, ˈtɛpᵊl) *n* any of the subdivisions of a perianth that is not clearly differentiated into calyx and corolla [C20 from French *tépale* changed (on analogy with *sépale* sepal) from *pétale* PETAL]

tepee *or* **teepee** (ˈtiːpiː) *n* a cone-shaped tent of animal skins used by certain North American Indians [C19 from Siouan *tīpī*, from *ti* to dwell + *pi* used for]

tepefy (ˈtɛpɪˌfaɪ) *vb* **-fies, -fying, -fied** to make or become tepid [C17 from Latin *tepēre*] ▷ **tepefaction** (ˌtɛpɪˈfækʃən) *n*

tephra (ˈtɛfrə) *n chiefly US* solid matter ejected during a volcanic eruption [C20 Greek, literally: ashes]

tephrite (ˈtɛfraɪt) *n* a variety of basalt containing plagioclase, augite, and a feldspathoid, commonly nepheline, or leucite [C17 from Greek *tephros*, from *tephra* ashes; see -ITE¹] ▷ **tephritic** (tɪˈfrɪtɪk) *adj*

Tepic (Spanish teˈpik) *n* a city in W central Mexico, capital of Nayarit state: agricultural, trading and processing centre. Pop: 341 000 (2005 est)

tepid (ˈtɛpɪd) *adj* **1** slightly warm; lukewarm **2** relatively unenthusiastic or apathetic: *the play had a tepid reception* [C14 from Latin *tepidus*, from *tepēre* to be lukewarm] ▷ teˈpidity *or* ˈtepidness *n* ▷ ˈtepidly *adv*

teppan-yaki (ˌtɛpænˈjækɪ) *n* a Japanese dish of meat and vegetables stir-fried on, and eaten from, a hot steel plate that forms the centre of a table [C21 Japanese, from *teppan* a steel plate + *yaki* to fry]

tequila (tɪˈkiːlə) *n* **1** a spirit that is distilled in Mexico from an agave plant and forms the basis of many mixed drinks **2** the plant, *Agave tequilana,* from which this drink is made [C19 from Mexican Spanish, from *Tequila*, region of Mexico]

ter- *combining form* three, third, or three times: *tercentenary* [from Latin *ter* thrice; related to *trēs* THREE]

tera- *prefix* denoting 10^{12}: *terameter.* Symbol: T [from Greek *teras* monster]

terabyte (ˈtɛrəˌbaɪt) *n computing* 10^{12} or 2^{40} bytes

teraflop (ˈtɛrəˌflɒp) *n computing* a measure of processing speed, consisting of a thousand billion floating-point operations a second [C20 from TERA- + flo(ating) p(oint)]

teraglin (təˈræɡlən) *n* an edible marine fish, *Zeluco atelodus,* of Australia which has fine scales

---

and is blue in colour [from a native Australian language]

Terai (təˈraɪ) *n* **1** (in India) a belt of marshy land at the foot of mountains, esp at the foot of the Himalayas in N India **2** a felt hat with a wide brim worn in subtropical regions

terakihi (ˌtɛrəˈkiːhiː) *n, pl* -kihis See tarakihi

teraph (ˈtɛrəf) *n, pl* -aphim (-əfɪm) *Old Testament* any of various small household gods or images venerated by ancient Semitic peoples. (Genesis 31:19–21; I Samuel 19:13–16) [C14 from Hebrew, of uncertain origin]

terat- *or* **terato-** *combining form* indicating a monster or something abnormal: *teratism; teratoid* [from Greek *terat-, teras* monster, prodigy]

teratism (ˈtɛrəˌtɪzəm) *n* a malformed animal or human, esp in the fetal stage; monster

teratogen (ˈtɛrətədʒən, tɪˈrætə-) *n* any substance, organism, or process that causes malformations in a fetus. Teratogens include certain drugs (such as thalidomide), infections (such as German measles), and ionizing radiation ▷ ˌteratoˈgenic *adj* ▷ ˌteratoˈgenicist *n* ▷ ˌteratogeˈnicity *n*

teratoid (ˈtɛrəˌtɔɪd) *adj biology* resembling a monster

teratology (ˌtɛrəˈtɒlədʒɪ) *n* **1** the branch of medical science concerned with the development of physical abnormalities during the fetal or early embryonic stage **2** the branch of biology that is concerned with the structure, development, etc, of monsters **3** a collection of tales about mythical or fantastic creatures, monsters, etc ▷ **teratologic** (ˌtɛrətəˈlɒdʒɪk) *or* ˌteratoˈlogical *adj* ▷ ˌteraˈtologist *n*

teratoma (ˌtɛrəˈtəʊmə) *n, pl* -mata (-mətə) *or* -mas a tumour or group of tumours composed of tissue foreign to the site of growth

teratophobia (ˌtɛrətəʊˈfəʊbɪə) *n psychiatry* fear of giving birth to a monster

terbia (ˈtɜːbɪə) *n* another name (not in technical usage) for **terbium oxide**

terbium (ˈtɜːbɪəm) *n* a soft malleable silvery-grey element of the lanthanide series of metals, occurring in gadolinite and monazite and used in lasers and for doping solid-state devices. Symbol: Tb; atomic no: 65; atomic wt: 158.92534; valency: 3 or 4; relative density: 8.230; melting pt: 1356°C; boiling pt: 3230°C [C19 from New Latin, named after *Ytterby*, Sweden, village where it was discovered] ▷ ˈterbic *adj*

terbium metal *n chem* any of a group of related lanthanides, including terbium, europium, and gadolinium

terbium oxide *n* an amorphous white insoluble powder. Formula: Tb_2O_3. Also called: **terbia**

terce (tɜːs) *or* **tierce** *n chiefly RC Church* the third of the seven canonical hours of the divine office, originally fixed at the third hour of the day, about 9 a.m. [a variant of TIERCE]

Terceira (Portuguese tərˈsəirə) *n* an island in the N Atlantic in the Azores: NATO military air base. Pop: 55 833 (2001). Area: 397 sq km (153 sq miles)

tercel (ˈtɜːsᵊl) *or* **tiercel** *n* a male falcon or hawk, esp as used in falconry [C14 from Old French, from Vulgar Latin *tertiolus* (unattested), from Latin *tertius* third, referring to the tradition that only one egg in three hatched a male chick]

tercentenary (ˌtɜːsɛnˈtiːnərɪ) *or* **tercentennial** *adj* **1** of or relating to a period of 300 years **2** of or relating to a 300th anniversary or its celebration ▷ *n, pl* -tenaries *or* -tennials **3** an anniversary of 300 years or its celebration ▷ Also: **tricentennial**

tercet (ˈtɜːsɪt, ˈtɜːˈsɛt) *n* a group of three lines of verse that rhyme together or are connected by rhyme with adjacent groups of three lines [C16 from French, from Italian *terzetto*, diminutive of *terzo* third, from Latin *tertius*]

terebene (ˈtɛrəˌbiːn) *n* a mixture of hydrocarbons prepared from oil of turpentine and sulphuric acid, used to make paints and varnishes and medicinally as an expectorant and antiseptic [C19 from TEREB(INTH) + -ENE]

terebic acid (tɛˈrɛbɪk) *n* a white crystalline carboxylic acid produced by the action of nitric acid on turpentine. Formula: $C_7H_{10}O_4$ [c19 from TEREB(INTH) + -IC]

terebinth (ˈtɛrɪbɪnθ) *n* a small anacardiaceous tree, *Pistacia terebinthus*, of the Mediterranean region, having winged leafstalks and clusters of small flowers, and yielding a turpentine [c14 from Latin *terebinthus*, from Greek *terebinthos* turpentine tree]

terebinthine (ˌtɛrɪˈbɪnθaɪn) *adj* 1 of or relating to terebinth or related plants 2 of, consisting of, or resembling turpentine

terebrate (ˈtɛrɪˌbreɪt) *adj* (of animals, esp insects) having a boring or penetrating organ, such as a sting [c20 from Latin *terebra* borer + -ATE¹]

teredo (tɛˈriːdəʊ) *n*, *pl* **-dos** *or* **-dines** (-dɪˌniːz) any marine bivalve mollusc of the genus *Teredo*. See shipworm [c17 via Latin from Greek *terēdōn* wood-boring worm; related to Greek *tetrainein* to pierce]

Terengganu (tɛrɛŋˈɡɑːnuː) *n* a variant spelling of Trengganu

te reo (teɪ ˈreɪəʊ) *n* NZ the Māori language [Māori, literally: the language]

terephthalic acid (ˌtɛrɛfˈθælɪk) *n* a white crystalline water-insoluble carboxylic acid used in making polyester resins such as Terylene; 1,4-benzenedicarboxylic acid. Formula: $C_6H_4(COOH)_2$ [c20 from TEREBENE + PHTHALIC ACID]

Teresina (Portuguese tereˈzina) *n* an inland port in NE Brazil, capital of Piauí state, on the Parnaíba River: chief commercial centre of the Parnaíba valley. Pop: 895 000 (2005 est). Former name: Therezina

terete (ˈtɛriːt) *adj* (esp of plant parts) smooth and usually cylindrical and tapering [c17 from Latin *teres* smooth, from *terere* to rub]

Tereus (ˈtɪərɪəs) *n* Greek myth a prince of Thrace, who raped Philomela, sister of his wife Procne, and was punished by being turned into a hoopoe

tergiversate (ˈtɜːdʒɪvəˌseɪt) *vb* (intr) 1 to change sides or loyalties; apostatize 2 to be evasive or ambiguous; equivocate [c17 from Latin *tergiversārī* to turn one's back, from *tergum* back + *vertere* to turn] > ˌtergiverˈsation *n* > ˈtergiverˌsator *n* tergiversant (ˈtɜːdʒɪˌvɜːsᵊnt) *n* > ˌtergiˈversatory *adj*

tergum (ˈtɜːɡəm) *n*, *pl* **-ga** (-ɡə) a cuticular plate covering the dorsal surface of a body segment of an arthropod. Compare sternum (sense 3) [c19 from Latin: the back] > ˈtergal *adj*

teriyaki (ˌtɛrɪˈjækɪ) *adj* 1 Japanese cookery basted with soy sauce and rice wine and broiled over an open fire ▷ *n* 2 a dish prepared in this way [from Japanese, from *teri* glaze + *yaki* to broil]

term (tɜːm) *n* 1 a name, expression, or word used for some particular thing, esp in a specialized field of knowledge: *a medical term* 2 any word or expression 3 a limited period of time: *his second term of office; a prison term* 4 any of the divisions of the academic year during which a school, college, etc, is in session 5 a point in time determined for an event or for the end of a period 6 Also called: full term the period at which childbirth is imminent 7 *law* **a** an estate or interest in land limited to run for a specified period: *a term of years* **b** the duration of an estate, etc **c** (formerly) a period of time during which sessions of courts of law were held **d** time allowed to a debtor to settle 8 *maths* either of the expressions the ratio of which is a fraction or proportion, any of the separate elements of a sequence, or any of the individual addends of a polynomial or series 9 *logic* **a** the word or phrase that forms either the subject or predicate of a proposition **b** a name or variable, as opposed to a predicate **c** one of the relata of a relation **d** any of the three subjects or predicates occurring in a syllogism 10 Also called: terminal, terminus, terminal figure architect a sculptured post, esp one in the form of an armless bust or an animal on the top of a square pillar 11 *Australian rules football* the usual word for **quarter**

(sense 10) 12 *archaic* a boundary or limit ▷ *vb* 13 (tr) to designate; call: *he was termed a thief* ▷ See also terms [c13 from Old French *terme*, from Latin *terminus* end] > ˈtermly *adv*

termagant (ˈtɜːməɡənt) *n* **a** a shrewish woman; scold **b** (*as modifier*): *a termagant woman* [c13 from earlier *Tervagaunt*, from Old French *Tervagan*, from Italian *Trivigante*; after an arrogant character in medieval mystery plays who was supposed to be a Muslim deity] > ˈtermagancy *n* > ˈtermagantly *adv*

termer (ˈtɜːmə) *n* a variant spelling of **termor** **-termer** *n* (in combination) a person serving a specified length of time in prison: *a short-termer*

terminable (ˈtɜːmɪnəbᵊl, ˈtɜːmnəbᵊl) *adj* 1 able to be terminated 2 terminating after a specific period or event: *a terminable annuity* > ˌterminaˈbility or ˈterminableness *n* ˈterminably *adv*

terminal (ˈtɜːmɪnᵊl) *adj* 1 of, being, or situated at an end, terminus, or boundary: *a terminal station; terminal buds* 2 of, relating to, or occurring after or in a term: *terminal leave* 3 (of a disease) terminating in death: *terminal cancer* 4 *informal* extreme: *terminal boredom* 5 of or relating to the storage or delivery of freight at a warehouse: *a terminal service* ▷ *n* 6 a terminating point, part, or place 7 **a** a point at which current enters or leaves an electrical device, such as a battery or a circuit **b** a conductor by which current enters or leaves at such a point 8 *computing* a device having input/output links with a computer but situated at a distance from the computer 9 *architect* **a** an ornamental carving at the end of a structure **b** another name for **term** (sense 10) 10 **a** a point or station usually at the end of the line of a railway, serving as an important access point for passengers or freight **b** a less common name for **terminus** 11 a purpose-built reception and departure structure at the terminus of a bus, sea, or air transport route 12 a site where raw material is unloaded, stored, in some cases reprocessed, and reloaded for further transportation, esp an onshore installation designed to receive offshore oil or gas from tankers or a pipeline 13 *physiol* **a** the smallest arteriole before its division into capillaries **b** either of two veins that collect blood from the thalamus and surrounding structures and empty it into the internal cerebral vein **c** the portion of a bronchiole just before it subdivides into the air sacs of the lungs [c15 from Latin *terminālis*, from *terminus* end] > ˈterminally *adv*

terminal market *n* a commodity market in a trading centre rather than at a producing centre

terminal platform *n* (in the oil industry) an offshore platform from which oil or gas is pumped ashore through a pipeline

terminal velocity *n* 1 the constant maximum velocity reached by a body falling under gravity through a fluid, esp the atmosphere 2 the velocity of a missile or projectile when it reaches its target 3 the maximum velocity attained by a rocket, missile, or shell flying in a parabolic flight path 4 the maximum velocity that an aircraft can attain, as determined by its total drag

terminate (ˈtɜːmɪˌneɪt) *vb* 1 (when intr, often foll by in or with) to form, be, or put an end (to); conclude: *to terminate a pregnancy; their relationship terminated amicably* 2 (tr) to connect (suitable circuitry) to the end of an electrical transmission line to absorb the energy and avoid reflections 3 (intr) *maths* (of a decimal expansion) to have only a finite number of digits 4 (tr) *slang* to kill (someone) [c16 from Latin *terminātus* limited, from *termināre* to set boundaries, from *terminus* end; (sense 4) c20 probably influenced by the 1979 film *Apocalypse Now* and its phrase 'terminate with extreme prejudice', meaning 'assassinate'] > ˈterminative *adj* > ˈterminatory *adj*

termination (ˌtɜːmɪˈneɪʃən) *n* 1 the act of terminating or the state of being terminated 2 something that terminates 3 a final result > ˌtermiˈnational *adj*

terminator (ˈtɜːmɪˌneɪtə) *n* the line dividing the illuminated and dark part of the moon or a planet

terminator seed *n* a seed that produces sterile plants, used in some genetically modified crops so that a new supply of seeds has to be bought every year

terminology (ˌtɜːmɪˈnɒlədʒɪ) *n*, *pl* **-gies** 1 the body of specialized words relating to a particular subject 2 the study of terms [c19 from Medieval Latin *terminus* term, from Latin: end] > terminological (ˌtɜːmɪnəˈlɒdʒɪkᵊl) *adj* > ˌterminoˈlogically *adv* > ˌtermiˈnologist *n*

term insurance *n* life assurance, usually low in cost and offering no cash value, that provides for the payment of a specified sum of money only if the insured dies within a stipulated period of time

terminus (ˈtɜːmɪnəs) *n*, *pl* **-ni** (-naɪ) *or* **-nuses** 1 the last or final part or point 2 either end of a railway, bus route, etc, or a station or town at such a point 3 a goal aimed for 4 a boundary or boundary marker 5 architect another name for **term** (sense 10) [c16 from Latin: end; related to Greek *termōn* boundary]

Terminus (ˈtɜːmɪnəs) *n* the Roman god of boundaries

terminus ad quem (Latin ˈtɜːmɪˌnʊs æd ˈkwɛm) *n* the aim or terminal point [literally: the end to which]

terminus a quo (Latin ˈtɜːmɪˌnʊs ɑː ˈkwəʊ) *n* the starting point; beginning [literally: the end from which]

termitarium (ˌtɜːmɪˈtɛərɪəm) *n*, *pl* **-ia** (-ɪə) the nest of a termite colony [c20 from TERMITE + -ARIUM]

termite (ˈtɜːmaɪt) *n* any whitish ant-like social insect of the order *Isoptera*, of warm and tropical regions. Some species feed on wood, causing damage to furniture, buildings, trees, etc. Also called: white ant [c18 from New Latin *termitēs* white ants, pl of *termes*, from Latin: a woodworm; related to Greek *tetrainein* to bore through] > termitic (tɜːˈmɪtɪk) *adj*

termless (ˈtɜːmlɪs) *adj* 1 without limit or boundary 2 unconditional 3 an archaic word for **indescribable**

termor *or* **termer** (ˈtɜːmə) *n* property law a person who holds an estate for a term of years or until he dies [c14 from Anglo-French *termer*, from *terme* TERM]

terms (tɜːmz) *pl n* 1 (usually specified prenominally) the actual language or mode of presentation used: *he described the project in loose terms* 2 conditions of an agreement: *you work here on our terms* 3 a sum of money paid for a service or credit; charges 4 (usually preceded by on) mutual relationship or standing: *they are on affectionate terms* 5 **in terms of** as expressed by; regarding: *in terms of money he was no better off* 6 **come to terms** to reach acceptance or agreement: *to come to terms with one's failings*

terms of trade *pl n* economics, Brit the ratio of export prices to import prices. It measures a nation's trading position, which improves when export prices rise faster or fall slower than import prices

tern¹ (tɜːn) *n* any aquatic bird of the subfamily *Sterninae*, having a forked tail, long narrow wings, a pointed bill, and a typically black-and-white plumage: family *Laridae* (gulls, etc), order *Charadriiformes* [c18 from Old Norse *therna*; related to Norwegian *terna*, Swedish *tärna*]

tern² (tɜːn) *n* 1 a three-masted schooner 2 rare a group of three [c14 from Old French *terne*, from Italian *terno*, from Latin *ternī* three each; related to Latin *ter* thrice, *trēs* three]

ternary (ˈtɜːnərɪ) *adj* 1 consisting of three or groups of three 2 *maths* **a** (of a number system) to the base three **b** involving or containing three variables 3 (of an alloy, mixture, or chemical compound) having three different components or composed of three different elements ▷ *n*, *pl* **-ries**

t

4 a group of three [C14 from Latin *ternārius*, from *ternī* three each]

ternary form *n* a musical structure consisting of two contrasting sections followed by a repetition of the first; the form *aba*. Also called: **song form**

ternate ('tɜːnɪt, -neɪt) *adj* **1** (esp of a leaf) consisting of three leaflets or other parts **2** (esp of plants) having groups of three members [C18 from New Latin *ternātus*, from Medieval Latin *ternāre* to increase threefold] > '**ternately** *adv*

terne (tɜːn) *n* **1** Also called: **terne metal** an alloy of lead containing tin (10–20 per cent) and antimony (1.5–2 per cent) **2** Also called: **terne plate** steel plate coated with this alloy [C16 perhaps from French *terne* dull, from Old French *ternir* to TARNISH]

Terni (*Italian* 'tɛrni) *n* an industrial city in central Italy, in Umbria: site of waterfalls created in Roman times. Pop: 105 018 (2001)

ternion ('tɜːnɪən) *n rare* a group of three [C16 from Latin *terniō* triad, from *ternī* three each; related to *ter* thrice]

Ternopol (*Russian* tɪr'nɔpəlj) *n* a town in W Ukraine, on the River Seret: formerly under Polish rule. Pop: 235 000 (2005 est.). Polish name: **Tarnopol**

terotechnology (,tɪərəʊtɛk'nɒlədʒɪ, ,tɛr-) *n* a branch of technology that utilizes management, financial, and engineering expertise in the installation and efficient operation and maintenance of equipment and machinery [C20 from Greek *tērein* to care for + TECHNOLOGY]

terpene ('tɜːpiːn) *n* any one of a class of unsaturated hydrocarbons, such as the carotenes, that are found in the essential oils of many plants. Their molecules contain isoprene units and have the general formula $(C_5H_8)_n$ [C19 *terp-* from obsolete *terpentine* TURPENTINE + -ENE] > **ter'penic** *adj*

terpineol (tɜː'pɪnɪˌɒl) *n* a terpene alcohol with an odour of lilac, present in several essential oils. A mixture of the isomers is used as a solvent and in flavourings and perfumes. Formula: $C_{10}H_{17}OH$ [C20 from TERPENE + -INE² + -OL¹]

Terpsichore (tɜːp'sɪkərɪ) *n* the Muse of the dance and of choral song [C18 via Latin from Greek, from *terpsikhoros* delighting in the dance, from *terpein* to delight + *khoros* dance; see CHORUS]

Terpsichorean (,tɜːpsɪkə'rɪən, -'kɔːrɪən) *often used facetiously* ▷ *adj also* **Terpsichoreal 1** of or relating to dancing or the art of dancing **2** a dancer

terr. *abbreviation for* **1** terrace **2** territory

terra ('tɛrə) *n* (in legal contexts) earth or land [from Latin]

terra alba ('ælbə) *n* **1** a white finely powdered form of gypsum, used to make paints, paper, etc **2** any of various other white earthy substances, such as kaolin, pipeclay, and magnesia [from Latin, literally: white earth]

terrace ('tɛrəs) *n* **1** a horizontal flat area of ground, often one of a series in a slope **2 a** a row of houses, usually identical and having common dividing walls, or the street onto which they face **b** (*cap when part of a street name*): *Grosvenor Terrace* **3** a paved area alongside a building, serving partly as a garden **4** a balcony or patio **5** the flat roof of a house built in a Spanish or Oriental style **6** a flat area bounded by a short steep slope formed by the down-cutting of a river or by erosion **7** (*usually plural*) **a** unroofed tiers around a football pitch on which the spectators stand **b** the spectators themselves ▷ *vb* **8** (*tr*) to make into or provide with a terrace or terraces [C16 from Old French *terrasse*, from Old Provençal *terrassa* pile of earth, from *terra* earth, from Latin] > **terraceless** *adj*

terraced house *n Brit* a house that is part of a terrace. US and Canadian names: **row house, town house** > **terraced housing** *n*

terracing ('tɛrəsɪŋ) *n* **1** a series of terraces, esp one dividing a slope into a steplike system of flat narrow fields **2** the act of making a terrace or terraces **3** another name for **terrace** (sense 7a)

terracotta (,tɛrə'kɒtə) *n* **1** a hard unglazed brownish-red earthenware, or the clay from which it is made **2** something made of terracotta, such as a sculpture **3** a strong reddish-brown to brownish-orange colour ▷ *adj* **4** made of terracotta: *a terracotta urn* **5** of the colour terracotta: *a terracotta carpet* [C18 from Italian, literally: baked earth]

terra firma ('fɜːmə) *n* the solid earth; firm ground [C17 from Latin]

terraforming ('tɛrəˌfɔːmɪŋ) *n* planetary engineering designed to enhance the capacity of an extraterrestrial planetary environment to sustain life [C20 from Latin *terra* earth + *forming*]

terrain (tə'reɪn, 'tɛreɪn) *n* **1** ground or a piece of ground, esp with reference to its physical character or military potential: *radio reception can be difficult in mountainous terrain; a rocky terrain* **2** a variant spelling of **terrane** [C18 from French, ultimately from Latin *terrēnum* ground, from *terra* earth]

terra incognita (*Latin* 'tɛrə ɪn'kɒɡnɪtə) *n* an unexplored or unknown land, region, or area for study

Terramycin (,tɛrə'maɪsɪn) *n trademark* a broad-spectrum antibiotic, oxytetracycline, used in treating various infections

terrane *or* **terrain** ('tɛreɪn) *n* **1** a series of rock formations, esp one having a prevalent type of rock **2** an allocthonous, fault-bounded section of the earth's crust [C19 see TERRAIN]

terrapin ('tɛrəpɪn) *n* any of various web-footed chelonian reptiles that live on land and in fresh water and feed on small aquatic animals: family *Emydidae*. Also called: **water tortoise** [C17 of Algonquian origin; compare Delaware *torope* turtle]

terrarium (tɛ'rɛərɪəm) *n, pl* **-rariums** *or* **-raria** (-'rɛərɪə) **1** an enclosure for keeping small land animals **2** a glass container, often a globe, in which plants are grown [C19 New Latin, from Latin *terra* earth]

terra sigillata ('tɛrə ,sɪdʒɪ'lɑːtə) *n* **1** *rare* a reddish-brown clayey earth found on the Aegean island of Lemnos: formerly used as an astringent and in the making of earthenware pottery **2** any similar earth resembling this **3** earthenware pottery made from this or a similar earth, esp Samian ware [from Latin: sealed earth]

terrazzo (tɛ'rætsəʊ) *n* a floor or wall finish made by setting marble or other stone chips into a layer of mortar and polishing the surface [C20 from Italian: TERRACE]

Terre Adélie (*French* tɛr adeli) *n* the French name for Adélie Land

terrene (tɛ'riːn) *adj* **1** of or relating to the earth; worldly; mundane **2** *rare* of earth; earthy ▷ *n* **3** a land **4** a rare word for **earth** [C14 from Anglo-Norman, from Latin *terrēnus*, from *terra* earth] > **ter'renely** *adv*

terreplein ('tɛəˌpleɪn) *n* **1** the top of a rampart where guns are placed behind the parapet **2** an embankment with a level top surface [C16 from French, from Medieval Latin phrase *terrā plēnus* filled with earth]

terrestrial (tə'rɛstrɪəl) *adj* **1** of or relating to the earth **2** of or belonging to the land as opposed to the sea or air **3** (of animals and plants) living or growing on the land **4** earthly, worldly, or mundane **5** (of television signals) sent over the earth's surface from a transmitter on land, rather than by satellite ▷ *n* **6** an inhabitant of the earth [C15 from Latin *terrestris*, from *terra* earth] > **ter'restrially** *adv* > **ter'restrialness** *n*

terrestrial guidance *n* a method of missile or rocket guidance in which the flight path is controlled by reference to the strength and direction of the earth's gravitational or magnetic field. Compare **inertial guidance**

terrestrial telescope *n* a telescope for use on earth rather than for making astronomical observations. Such telescopes contain an additional lens or prism system to produce an erect image. Compare **astronomical telescope**

terret ('tɛrɪt) *n* **1** either of the two metal rings on a harness saddle through which the reins are passed **2** the ring on a dog's collar for attaching the lead [C15 variant of *toret*, from Old French, diminutive of *tor* loop; see TOUR]

terre-verte ('tɛəˌvɜːt) *n* **1** a greyish-green pigment used in paints, consisting of powdered glauconite ▷ *adj* **2** of a greyish-green colour [C17 from French, literally: green earth]

terrible ('tɛrəbəl) *adj* **1** very serious or extreme: *a terrible cough* **2** *informal* of poor quality; unpleasant or bad: *a terrible meal; a terrible play* **3** causing terror **4** causing awe: *the terrible nature of God* [C15 from Latin *terribilis*, from *terrēre* to terrify] > **'terribleness** *n*

terribly ('tɛrəblɪ) *adv* **1** in a terrible manner **2** (intensifier): *you're terribly kind*

terricolous (tɛ'rɪkələs) *adj* living on or in the soil [C19 from Latin *terricola*, from *terra* earth + *colere* to inhabit]

terrier¹ ('tɛrɪə) *n* any of several usually small, active, and short-bodied breeds of dog, originally trained to hunt animals living underground [C15 from Old French *chien terrier* earth dog, from Medieval Latin *terrārius* belonging to the earth, from Latin *terra* earth]

terrier² ('tɛrɪə) *n English legal history* a register or survey of land [C15 from Old French, from Medieval Latin *terrārius* of the land, from Latin *terra* land]

Terrier ('tɛrɪə) *n informal* a member of the British Army's Territorial and Volunteer Reserve

terrific (tə'rɪfɪk) *adj* **1** very great or intense: *a terrific noise* **2** *informal* very good; excellent: *a terrific singer* **3** very frightening [C17 from Latin *terrificus*, from *terrēre* to frighten; see -FIC] > **ter'rifically** *adv*

terrify ('tɛrɪˌfaɪ) *vb* **-fies, -fying, -fied** (*tr*) to inspire fear or dread in; frighten greatly [C16 from Latin *terrificāre*, from *terrēre* to alarm + *facere* to cause] > **'terriˌfier** *n*

terrifying ('tɛrɪˌfaɪɪŋ) *adj* causing great fear or dread; extremely frightening > **'terriˌfyingly** *adv*

terrigenous (tɛ'rɪdʒɪnəs) *adj* **1** of or produced by the earth **2** (of geological deposits) formed in the sea from material derived from the land by erosion [C17 from Latin *terrigenus*, from *terra* earth + *gignere* to beget]

terrine (tɛ'riːn) *n* **1** an oval earthenware cooking dish with a tightly fitting lid used for pâtés, etc **2** the food cooked or served in such a dish, esp pâté **3** another word for **tureen** [C18 earlier form of TUREEN]

territorial (,tɛrɪ'tɔːrɪəl) *adj* **1** of or relating to a territory or territories **2** restricted to or owned by a particular territory: *the Indian territorial waters* **3** local or regional **4** pertaining to a territorial army, providing a reserve of trained men for use in emergency > **ˌterri'torially** *adv*

Territorial (,tɛrɪ'tɔːrɪəl) *n* a member of a territorial army, esp the British Army's Territorial and Volunteer Reserve

Territorial Army *n* (in Britain) a standing reserve army originally organized between 1907 and 1908. Full name: **Territorial and Volunteer Reserve**

territorialism (,tɛrɪ'tɔːrɪəlɪzəm) *n* **1** a social system under which the predominant force in the state is the landed class **2** a former Protestant theory that the civil government has the right to determine the religious beliefs of the subjects of a state > **ˌterri'torialist** *n*

territoriality (,tɛrɪˌtɔːrɪ'ælɪtɪ) *n* **1** the state or rank of being a territory **2** the behaviour shown by an animal when establishing and defending its territory

territorialize *or* **territorialise** (,tɛrɪ'tɔːrɪəˌlaɪz) *vb* (*tr*) **1** to make a territory of **2** to place on a territorial basis: *the militia was territorialized* **3** to enlarge (a country) by acquiring more territory **4** to make territorial > **ˌterriˌtoriali'zation** *or* **ˌterriˌtoriali'sation** *n*

territorial waters *pl n* the waters over which a nation exercises jurisdiction and control
Territorian (ˌtɛrɪˈtɔːrɪən) *n Austral* an inhabitant of the Northern Territory
territory (ˈtɛrɪtərɪ, -trɪ) *n, pl* **-ries** **1** any tract of land; district **2** the geographical domain under the jurisdiction of a political unit, esp of a sovereign state **3** the district for which an agent, etc, is responsible: *a salesman's territory* **4** an area inhabited and defended by an individual animal or a breeding group of animals **5** an area of knowledge: *science isn't my territory* **6** (in football, hockey, etc) the area defended by a team **7** (*often capital*) a region of a country, esp of a federal state, that enjoys less autonomy and a lower status than most constituent parts of the state **8** (*often capital*) a protectorate or other dependency of a country [C15 from Latin *territōrium* land surrounding a town, from *terra* land]
Territory (ˈtɛrɪtərɪ, -trɪ) *n* **the** *Austral* See **Northern Territory**
terroir *French* (tɛrwar) *n winemaking* the combination of factors, including soil, climate, and environment, that gives a wine its distinctive character [literally: soil]
terror (ˈtɛrə) *n* **1** great fear, panic, or dread **2** a person or thing that inspires great dread **3** *informal* a troublesome person or thing, esp a child **4** terrorism [C14 from Old French *terreur*, from Latin *terror*, from *terrēre* to frighten; related to Greek *trein* to run away in terror] > ˈ**terrorful** *adj* > ˈ**terrorless** *adj*
terrorism (ˈtɛrəˌrɪzəm) *n* **1** systematic use of violence and intimidation to achieve some goal **2** the act of terrorizing **3** the state of being terrorized
terrorist (ˈtɛrərɪst) *n* **a** a person who employs terror or terrorism, esp as a political weapon **b** (*as modifier*): *terrorist tactics* > ˌ**terrorˈistic** *adj*
terrorize *or* **terrorise** (ˈtɛrəˌraɪz) *vb* (*tr*) **1** to coerce or control by violence, fear, threats, etc **2** to inspire with dread; terrify > ˌ**terroriˈzation** *or* ˌ**terroriˈsation** *n* > ˈ**terrorˌizer** *or* ˈ**terrorˌiser** *n*
terror-stricken *or* **terror-struck** *adj* in a state of terror
terry (ˈtɛrɪ) *n, pl* **-ries** **1** an uncut loop in the pile of towelling or a similar fabric **2** **a** a fabric with such a pile on both sides **b** (*as modifier*): *a terry towel* [C18 perhaps variant of TERRET]
terse (tɜːs) *adj* **1** neatly brief and concise **2** curt; abrupt [C17 from Latin *tersus* precise, from *tergēre* to polish] > ˈ**tersely** *adv* > ˈ**terseness** *n*
tertial (ˈtɜːʃəl) *adj, n* another word for **tertiary** (senses 5, 6) [C19 from Latin *tertius* third, from *ter* thrice, from *trēs* three]
tertian (ˈtɜːʃən) *adj* **1** (of a fever or the symptoms of a disease, esp malaria) occurring every other day ▷ *n* **2** a tertian fever or symptoms [C14 from Latin *febris tertiāna* fever occurring every third day, reckoned inclusively, from *tertius* third]
tertiary (ˈtɜːʃərɪ) *adj* **1** third in degree, order, etc **2** (of education) taking place after secondary school, such as at university, college, etc **3** (of an industry) involving services as opposed to extraction or manufacture, such as transport, finance, etc. Compare **primary** (sense 8b), **secondary** (sense 7) **4** *RC Church* of or relating to a Third Order **5** *chem* **a** (of an organic compound) having a functional group attached to a carbon atom that is attached to three other groups **b** (of an amine) having three organic groups attached to a nitrogen atom **c** (of a salt) derived from a tribasic acid by replacement of all its acidic hydrogen atoms with metal atoms or electropositive groups **6** Also: **tertial** *ornithol rare* of, relating to, or designating any of the small flight feathers attached to the part of the humerus nearest to the body ▷ *n, pl* **-tiaries** **7** Also called: **tertial** *ornithol rare* any of the tertiary feathers **8** *RC Church* a member of a Third Order [C16 from Latin *tertiārius* containing one third, from *tertius* third]
Tertiary (ˈtɜːʃərɪ) *adj* **1** of, denoting, or formed in the first period of the Cenozoic era, which lasted for 63 million years, during which mammals became dominant ▷ *n* **2** **the** the Tertiary period or rock system, divided into Palaeocene, Eocene, Oligocene, Miocene, and Pliocene epochs or series
tertiary bursary *n NZ* a noncompetitive award granted to all pupils who have passed a university entrance examination
tertiary college *n Brit* a college system incorporating the secondary school sixth form and vocational courses
tertiary colour *n* a colour formed by mixing two secondary colours
tertium quid (ˈtɜːtɪəm ˈkwɪd) *n* an unknown or indefinite thing related in some way to two known or definite things, but distinct from both: *there is either right or wrong, with no tertium quid* [C18 from Late Latin, rendering Greek *triton ti* some third thing]
Teruel (*Spanish* teˈrwɛl) *n* a city in E central Spain: 15th-century cathedral; scene of fierce fighting during the Spanish Civil War. Pop: 32 304 (2003 est)
tervalent (tɜːˈveɪlənt) *adj chem* another word for **trivalent**. > **terˈvalency** *n*
Terylene (ˈtɛrɪˌliːn) *n trademark* a synthetic polyester fibre or fabric based on terephthalic acid, characterized by lightness and crease resistance and used for clothing, sheets, ropes, sails, etc. US name (trademark): **Dacron**
terza rima (ˈtɛətsə ˈriːmə) *n, pl* **terze rime** (ˈtɛətseɪ ˈriːmeɪ) a verse form of Italian origin consisting of a series of tercets in which the middle line of one tercet rhymes with the first and third lines of the next [C19 from Italian, literally: third rhyme]
terzetto (tɜːˈtsɛtəʊ) *n, pl* **-tos** *or* **-ti** (-tɪ) *music* a trio, esp a vocal one [C18 Italian: trio; see TERCET]
TES *abbreviation for* Times Educational Supplement
TE score (in Australia) *abbreviation for* Tertiary Entrance score: a score based on a pupil's performance in secondary school that determines his or her prospects of gaining entrance to tertiary educational institutions
TESL (ˈtɛsᵊl) *acronym for* Teaching (of) English as a Second Language
tesla (ˈtɛslə) *n* the derived SI unit of magnetic flux density equal to a flux of 1 weber in an area of 1 square metre. Symbol: T [C20 named after Nikola *Tesla* (1857–1943), Croatian-born US electrical engineer and inventor]
tesla coil *n* a step-up transformer with an air core, used for producing high voltages at high frequencies. The secondary circuit is tuned to resonate with the primary winding [C20 named after Nikola *Tesla* (1857–1943), Croatian-born US electrical engineer and inventor]
TESSA (ˈtɛsə) *n* (in Britain) ▷ *acronym for* Tax Exempt Special Savings Account; a former (available 1991–99) tax-free savings scheme
tessellate (ˈtɛsɪˌleɪt) *vb* **1** (*tr*) to construct, pave, or inlay with a mosaic of small tiles **2** (*intr*) (of identical shapes) to fit together exactly: *triangles will tessellate but octagons will not* [C18 from Latin *tessellātus* checked, from *tessella* small stone cube, from TESSERA]
tessellation (ˌtɛsɪˈleɪʃən) *n* **1** the act of tessellating **2** the form or a specimen of tessellated work
tessera (ˈtɛsərə) *n, pl* **-serae** (-səˌriː) **1** a small square tile of stone, glass, etc, used in mosaics **2** a die, tally, etc, used in classical times, made of bone or wood [C17 from Latin, from Ionic Greek *tesseres* four] > ˈ**tesseral** *adj*
Tessin (tɛˈsiːn) *n* the German name for **Ticino**
tessitura (ˌtɛsɪˈtʊərə) *n music* **1** the general pitch level of a piece of vocal music: *an uncomfortably high tessitura* **2** the compass or range of a voice [Italian: texture, from Latin *textura*; see TEXTURE]
test[1] (tɛst) *vb* **1** to ascertain (the worth, capability, or endurance) of (a person or thing) by subjection to certain examinations; try **2** (often foll by *for*) to carry out an examination on (a substance, material, or system) by applying some chemical or physical procedure designed to indicate the presence of a substance or the possession of a property: *to test food for arsenic; to test for magnetization* **3** (*intr*) to achieve a specified result in a test: *a quarter of the patients at the clinic tested positive for the AIDS virus* **4** (*tr*) to put under severe strain: *the long delay tested my patience* **5** **test the water** to make an exploratory or initial approach; sound out ▷ *n* **6** a method, practice, or examination designed to test a person or thing **7** a series of questions or problems designed to test a specific skill or knowledge: *an intelligence test* **8** a standard of judgment; criterion **9** **a** a chemical reaction or physical procedure for testing a substance, material, etc **b** a chemical reagent used in such a procedure: *litmus is a test for acids* **c** the result of the procedure or the evidence gained from it: *the test for alcohol was positive* **10** *sport* See **test match** **11** *archaic* a declaration or confirmation of truth, loyalty, etc; oath **12** (*modifier*) performed as a test: *test drive; test flight* [C14 (in the sense: vessel used in treating metals): from Latin *testum* earthen vessel] > ˈ**testable** *adj* > ˌ**testaˈbility** *n* > ˈ**testing** *adj*
test[2] (tɛst) *n* **1** the hard or tough outer covering of certain invertebrates and tunicates **2** a variant of **testa** [C19 from Latin *testa* shell]
testa (ˈtɛstə) *n, pl* **-tae** (-tiː) a hard protective outer layer of the seeds of flowering plants; seed coat [C18 from Latin: shell; see TEST[2]]
testaceous (tɛˈsteɪʃəs) *adj biology* **1** of, relating to, or possessing a test or testa **2** of the reddish-brown colour of terra cotta [C17 from Latin *testācens*, from TESTA]
Test Act *n* a law passed in 1673 in England to exclude Catholics from public life by requiring all persons holding offices under the Crown, such as army officers, to take the Anglican Communion and perform other acts forbidden to a Catholic: repealed in 1828
testament (ˈtɛstəmənt) *n* **1** *law* a will setting out the disposition of personal property (esp in the phrase **last will and testament**) **2** a proof, attestation, or tribute: *his success was a testament to his skills* **3** **a** a covenant instituted between God and man, esp the covenant of Moses or that instituted by Christ **b** a copy of either the Old or the New Testament, or of the complete Bible [C14 from Latin: a will, from *testārī* to bear witness, from *testis* a witness] > ˌ**testaˈmental** *adj*
Testament (ˈtɛstəmənt) *n* **1** either of the two main parts of the Bible; the Old Testament or the New Testament **2** the New Testament as distinct from the Old
testamentary (ˌtɛstəˈmɛntərɪ) *adj* **1** of or relating to a will or testament **2** derived from, bequeathed, or appointed by a will **3** contained or set forth in a will
testate (ˈtɛsteɪt, ˈtɛstɪt) *adj* **1** having left a legally valid will at death ▷ *n* **2** a person who dies testate ▷ Compare **intestate** [C15 from Latin *testārī* to make a will; see TESTAMENT] > **testacy** (ˈtɛstəsɪ) *n*
testator (tɛˈsteɪtə) *or feminine* **testatrix** (tɛˈsteɪtrɪks) *n* a person who makes a will, esp one who dies testate [C15 from Anglo-French *testatour*, from Late Latin *testātor*, from Latin *testārī* to make a will; see TESTAMENT]
test ban *n* an agreement among nations to forgo tests of some or all types of nuclear weapons
test-bed *n engineering* an area equipped with instruments, etc, used for testing machinery, engines, etc, under working conditions
test card *or* **pattern** *n* a complex pattern used to test the characteristics of a television transmission system
test case *n* a legal action that serves as a precedent in deciding similar succeeding cases
test-drive *vb* (*tr*) **-drives, -driving, -drove, -driven** to drive (a car or other motor vehicle) for a limited period in order to assess its capabilities and limitations

t

tester¹ ('tɛstə) *n* a person or thing that tests or is used for testing

tester² ('tɛstə) *n* (in furniture) a canopy, esp the canopy over a four-poster bed [c14 from Medieval Latin *testerium*, from Late Latin *testa* a skull, from Latin: shell]

tester³ ('tɛstə) *n* another name for **teston** (sense 2)

testes ('tɛsti:z) *n* the plural of **testis**

testicle ('tɛstɪkªl) *n* either of the two male reproductive glands, in most mammals enclosed within the scrotum, that produce spermatozoa and the hormone testosterone. Also called: **testis** [c15 from Latin *testiculus*, diminutive of *testis* testicle] > **testicular** (tɛˈstɪkjʊlə) *adj*

testiculate (tɛˈstɪkjʊlɪt) *adj botany* shaped like testicles: *the testiculate tubers of certain orchids* [c18 from Late Latin *testiculātus*; see TESTICLE]

testify ('tɛstɪˌfaɪ) *vb* **-fies**, **-fying**, **-fied** **1** (when *tr*, *may take a clause as object*) to state (something) formally as a declaration of fact: *I testify that I know nothing about him* **2** *law* to declare or give (evidence) under oath, esp in court **3** (when *intr*, often foll by *to*) to be evidence (of); serve as witness (to): *the money testified to his good faith* **4** (*tr*) to declare or acknowledge openly [c14 from Latin *testificārī*, from *testis* witness] > **testifiˈcation** *n* > **testiˌfier** *n*

testimonial (ˌtɛstɪˈməʊnɪəl) *n* **1 a** a recommendation of the character, ability, etc, of a person or of the quality of a consumer product or service, esp by a person whose opinion is valued **b** (*as modifier*): *testimonial advertising* **2** a formal statement of truth or fact **3** a tribute given for services or achievements **4** a sports match to raise money for a particular player ▷ *adj* **5** of or relating to a testimony or testimonial

> **USAGE** *Testimonial* is sometimes wrongly used where *testimony* is meant: *his re-election is a testimony (not a testimonial) to his popularity with his constituents*

testimony ('tɛstɪmənɪ) *n*, *pl* **-nies** **1** a declaration of truth or fact **2** *law* evidence given by a witness, esp orally in court under oath or affirmation **3** evidence testifying to something **4** *Old Testament* **a** the Ten Commandments, as inscribed on the two stone tables **b** the Ark of the Covenant as the receptacle of these (Exodus 25:16; 16:34) [c15 from Latin *testimōnium*, from *testis* witness]

testing station *n* NZ an establishment licensed to issue warrants of fitness for motor vehicles

testis ('tɛstɪs) *n*, *pl* **-tes** (-ti:z) another word for **testicle** [c17 from Latin, literally: witness (to masculinity)]

test marketing *n* the use of a representative segment of a total market for experimental purposes, as to test a new product about to be launched or a price change

test match *n* (in various sports, esp cricket) an international match, esp one of a series

teston ('tɛstən) *or* **testoon** (tɛˈstu:n) *n* **1** a French silver coin of the 16th century **2** Also called: **tester** an English silver coin of the 16th century, originally worth one shilling, bearing the head of Henry VIII [c16 from Italian *testone*, from *testa* head, from Late Latin: skull, from Latin: shell]

testosterone (tɛˈstɒstəˌrəʊn) *n* a potent steroid hormone secreted mainly by the testes. It can be extracted from the testes of animals or synthesized and used to treat androgen deficiency or promote anabolism. Formula: $C_{19}H_{28}O_2$ [c20 from TESTIS + STEROL + -ONE]

test paper *n* **1** *chem* paper impregnated with an indicator for use in chemical tests. See also **litmus** **2** *Brit education* **a** the question sheet of a test **b** the paper completed by a test candidate

test pilot *n* a pilot who flies aircraft of new design to test their performance in the air

test tube *n* **1** a cylindrical round-bottomed glass tube open at one end: used in scientific experiments **2** (*modifier*) made synthetically in, or as if in, a test tube: *a test-tube product*

test-tube baby *n* **1** a fetus that has developed from an ovum fertilized in an artificial womb **2** a baby conceived by artificial insemination

testudinal (tɛˈstju:dɪnªl) *or* **testudinary** *adj* of, relating to, or resembling a tortoise or turtle or the shell of either of these animals [c19 from Latin TESTUDO]

testudo (tɛˈstju:dəʊ) *n*, *pl* **-dines** (-dɪˌni:z) a form of shelter used by the ancient Roman Army for protection against attack from above, consisting either of a mobile arched structure or of overlapping shields held by the soldiers over their heads [c17 from Latin: a tortoise, from *testa* a shell]

testy ('tɛstɪ) *adj* **-tier**, **-tiest** irritable or touchy [c14 from Anglo-Norman *testif* headstrong, from Old French *teste* head, from Late Latin *testa* skull, from Latin: shell] > **testily** *adv* > **testiness** *n*

Tet (tɛt) *n* the New Year as celebrated in Vietnam during the first seven days of the first lunar month of the year [Vietnamese]

tetanic (təˈtænɪk) *adj* **1** of, relating to, or producing tetanus or the spasms of tetanus ▷ *n* **2** a tetanic drug or agent > **teˈtanically** *adv*

tetanize *or* **tetanise** ('tɛtəˌnaɪz) *vb* (*tr*) to induce tetanus in (a muscle); affect (a muscle) with tetanic spasms > ˌtetaniˈzation *or* ˌtetaniˈsation *n*

tetanus ('tɛtənəs) *n* **1** Also called: **lockjaw** an acute infectious disease in which sustained muscular spasm, contraction, and convulsion are caused by the release of exotoxins from the bacterium, *Clostridium tetani*: infection usually occurs through a contaminated wound **2** *physiol* any tense contraction of a muscle, esp when produced by electric shocks [c16 via Latin from Greek *tetanos*, from *tetanos* taut, from *teinein* to stretch] > 'tetanal *adj* > 'tetaˌnoid *adj*

tetany ('tɛtənɪ) *n pathol* an abnormal increase in the excitability of nerves and muscles resulting in spasm of the arms and legs, caused by a deficiency of parathyroid secretion [c19 from French *tétanie*. See TETANUS]

tetartohedral (tɪˌtɑ:təʊˈhi:drəl) *adj* (of a crystal) having one quarter of the number of faces necessary for the full symmetry of its crystal system [c19 from Greek *tetartos* one fourth + -HEDRAL] > teˌtartoˈhedrally *adv* > teˌtartoˈhedralism *or* teˌtartoˈhedrism *n*

tetchy ('tɛtʃɪ) *adj* **tetchier**, **tetchiest** being or inclined to be cross, irritable, or touchy [c16 probably from obsolete *tetch* defect, from Old French *tache* spot, of Germanic origin] > 'tetchily *adv* > 'tetchiness *n*

tête-à-tête (ˌteɪtɑːˈteɪt) *n*, *pl* **-têtes** *or* **-tête** **1 a** a private conversation between two people **b** (*as modifier*): *a tête-à-tête conversation* **2** a small sofa for two people, esp one that is S-shaped in plan so that the sitters are almost face to face ▷ *adv* **3** intimately; in private [c17 from French, literally: head to head]

tête-bêche (tɛtˈbɛʃ) *adj philately* (of an unseparated pair of stamps) printed so that one is inverted in relation to the other [c19 from French, from *tête* head + *bêche*, from obsolete *béchevet* double-headed (originally of a bed)]

teth (tɛs; *Hebrew* tɛt) *n* the ninth letter of the Hebrew alphabet (ט) transliterated as *t* and pronounced more or less like English *t* with pharyngeal articulation

tether ('tɛðə) *n* **1** a restricting rope, chain, etc, by which an animal is tied to a particular spot **2** the range of one's endurance, etc **3** **at the end of one's tether** distressed or exasperated to the limit of one's endurance ▷ *vb* (*tr*) **4** to tie or limit with or as if with a tether [c14 from Old Norse *tjothr*; related to Middle Dutch *tūder* tether, Old High German *zeotar* pole of a wagon]

Tethys¹ ('ti:θɪs, 'tɛθ-) *n Greek myth* a Titaness and sea goddess, wife of Oceanus

Tethys² ('ti:θɪs, 'tɛθ-) *n* a large satellite of the planet Saturn

Tethys³ ('ti:θɪs, 'tɛθ-) *n* the sea that lay between Laurasia and Gondwanaland, the two supercontinents formed by the first split of the larger supercontinent Pangaea. The Tethys Sea can be regarded as the predecessor of today's smaller Mediterranean. See also **Pangaea**

Teton Range ('ti:tªn) *n* a mountain range in the N central US, mainly in NW Wyoming. Highest peak: Grand Teton, 4196 m (13 766 ft)

tetra ('tɛtrə) *n*, *pl* **-ra** *or* **-ras** any of various brightly coloured tropical freshwater fishes of the genus *Hemigrammus* and related genera: family Characidae (characins) [c20 short for New Latin *tetragonopterus* (former genus name), from TETRAGON + -O- + -pterous, from Greek *pteron* wing]

tetra- *or before a vowel* **tetr-** *combining form* four: *tetrameter* [from Greek]

tetrabasic (ˌtɛtrəˈbeɪsɪk) *adj* (of an acid) containing four replaceable hydrogen atoms > tetrabasicity (ˌtɛtrəbeɪˈsɪsɪtɪ) *n*

tetrabrach ('tɛtrəˌbræk) *n* (in classical prosody) a word or metrical foot composed of four short syllables (⏑⏑⏑⏑) [c19 from Greek *tetrabrakhus*, from TETRA- + *brakhus* short]

tetrabranchiate *adj* (ˌtɛtrəˈbræŋkɪɪt, -ˌeɪt) **1** of, relating to, or belonging to the Tetrabranchiata, a former order of cephalopod molluscs having four gills and including the pearly nautilus ▷ *n* (ˌtɛtrəˈbræŋkɪˌeɪt) **2** any mollusc belonging to the Tetrabranchiata

tetrachloride (ˌtɛtrəˈklɔːraɪd) *n* any compound that contains four chlorine atoms per molecule: *carbon tetrachloride*, CCl_4

tetrachloromethane (ˈtɛtrəˌklɔːrəʊˌmiːˈθeɪn) *n* the systematic name for **carbon tetrachloride**

tetrachord ('tɛtrəˌkɔːd) *n* (in musical theory, esp of classical Greece) any of several groups of four notes in descending order, in which the first and last notes form a perfect fourth [c17 from Greek *tetrakhordos* four-stringed, from TETRA- + *khordē* a string] > ˌtetraˈchordal *adj*

tetracid (tɛˈtræsɪd) *adj* (of a base) capable of reacting with four molecules of a monobasic acid

tetracyclic (ˌtɛtrəˈsaɪklɪk) *adj chem* (of a compound) containing four rings in its molecular structure

tetracycline (ˌtɛtrəˈsaɪklaɪn, -klɪn) *n* an antibiotic synthesized from chlortetracycline or derived from the bacterium *Streptomyces viridifaciens*: used in treating rickettsial infections and various bacterial infections. Formula: $C_{22}H_{24}N_2O_8$ [c20 from TETRA- + CYCL(IC) + -INE²]

tetrad ('tɛtræd) *n* **1** a group or series of four **2** the number four **3** *botany* a group of four cells formed by meiosis from one diploid cell **4** *genetics* a four-stranded structure, formed during the pachytene stage of meiosis, consisting of paired homologous chromosomes that have each divided into two chromatids **5** *chem* an element, atom, group, or ion with a valency of four **6** *ecology* a square of 2×2 km used in distribution mapping [c17 from Greek *tetras*, from *tettares* four]

tetradactyl (ˌtɛtrəˈdæktɪl) *n* **1** a four-toed animal ▷ *adj also* **tetraˈdactylous** **2** having four toes or fingers [c19 from Greek *tetradaktulos*, from TETRA- + *dactulos* finger]

tetradymite (tɛˈtrædɪˌmaɪt) *n* a grey metallic mineral consisting of a telluride and sulphide of bismuth. Formula: Bi_2Te_2S [c19 from Late Greek *tetradumos* fourfold, from Greek TETRA- + *didumos* double]

tetradynamous (ˌtɛtrəˈdaɪnəməs, -ˈdɪn-) *adj* (of plants) having six stamens, two of which are shorter than the others [c19 from TETRA- + Greek *dunamis* power]

tetraethyl lead (ˌtɛtrəˈiːθaɪl lɛd) *n* a colourless oily insoluble liquid used in petrol to prevent knocking. Formula: $Pb(C_2H_5)_4$. Systematic name: **lead tetraethyl**

tetrafluoroethene ('tɛtrəˌflʊərəʊˈɛθiːn) *n chem* a dense colourless gas that is polymerized to make polytetrafluorethene (PTFE). Formula: $F_2C:CF_2$. Also called: **tetrafluoroethylene** [c20 from TETRA- + FLUORO- + ETHENE]

tetragon ('tɛtrə,gɒn) *n* a less common name for **quadrilateral** (sense 2) [c17 from Greek *tetragōnon*; see TETRA-, -GON]

tetragonal (tɛ'trægən³l) *adj* **1** Also: **dimetric** *crystallog* relating or belonging to the crystal system characterized by three mutually perpendicular axes of which only two are equal **2** of, relating to, or shaped like a quadrilateral ▷ te'tragonally *adv* ▷ te'tragonalness *n*

tetragram ('tɛtrə,græm) *n* any word of four letters

Tetragrammaton (,tɛtrə'græmət³n) *n Bible* the Hebrew name for God revealed to Moses on Mount Sinai (Exodus 3), consisting of the four consonants Y H V H (or Y H W H) and regarded by Jews as too sacred to be pronounced. It is usually transliterated as *Jehovah* or *Yahweh*. Sometimes shortened to: **Tetragram** [c14 from Greek, from *tetragrammatos* having four letters, from TETRA- + *gramma* letter]

tetrahedrite (,tɛtrə'hi:draɪt) *n* a grey metallic mineral consisting of a sulphide of copper, iron, and antimony, often in the form of tetrahedral crystals: it is a source of copper. Formula: $(Cu,Fe)_{12}Sb_4S_{13}$

tetrahedron (,tɛtrə'hi:drən) *n, pl* **-drons** or **-dra** (-drə) **1** a solid figure having four plane faces. A **regular tetrahedron** has faces that are equilateral triangles. See also **polyhedron 2** any object shaped like a tetrahedron [c16 from New Latin, from Late Greek *tetraedron*; see TETRA-, -HEDRON] ▷ ,tetra'hedral *adj* ▷ ,tetra'hedrally *adv*

tetrahydrocannabidinol (,tɛtrə'haɪdrəʊ,kænə'bɪdɪnɒl) *n* the full name for THC

tetrahydrogestrinone ('tɛtrə'haɪdrəʊ'dʒɛstrɪnəʊn) *n* a synthetic anabolic steroid. Formula: $C_{21}H_{28}O_2$. Abbreviation: THG

tetralogy (tɛ'trælədʒɪ) *n, pl* **-gies 1** a series of four related works, as in drama or opera **2** (in ancient Greece) a group of four dramas, the first three tragic and the last satiric **3** *pathol* a group of four symptoms present in one disorder, esp Fallot's tetralogy [c17 from Greek *tetralogia*; see TETRA-, -LOGY]

tetramerous (tɛ'træmərəs) *adj* **1** (esp of animals or plants) having or consisting of four parts **2** (of certain flowers) having parts arranged in whorls of four members [c19 from New Latin *tetramerus*, from Greek *tetramerēs*] ▷ te'tramerism *n*

tetrameter (tɛ'træmɪtə) *n prosody* **1** a line of verse consisting of four metrical feet **2** a verse composed of such lines **3** (in classical prosody) a line of verse composed of four dipodies

tetramethyldiarsine (,tɛtrə,mi:θaɪldɑː'si:n) *n* an oily slightly water-soluble poisonous liquid with garlic-like odour. Its derivatives are used as accelerators for rubber. Also called (not in technical usage): **cacodyl, dicacodyl**

tetraplegia (,tɛtrə'pli:dʒɪə) *n* another name for **quadriplegia** [from TETRA- + Greek *plegē* a blow, from *plēssein* to strike] ▷ ,tetra'plegic *adj*

tetraploid ('tɛtrə,plɔɪd) *genetics* ▷ *adj* **1** having four times the haploid number of chromosomes in the nucleus ▷ *n* **2** a tetraploid organism, nucleus, or cell

tetrapod ('tɛtrə,pɒd) *n* **1** any vertebrate that has four limbs **2** Also called: **caltrop** a device consisting of four arms radiating from a central point, each at about 109° to the others, so that regardless of its position on a surface, three arms form a supporting tripod and the fourth is vertical **3** *engineering* a very large cast concrete structure of a similar shape piled in large numbers round breakwaters and sea defence systems to dissipate the energy of the waves

tetrapody (tɛ'træpədɪ) *n, pl* **-dies** *prosody* a metrical unit consisting of four feet ▷ **tetrapodic** (,tɛtrə'pɒdɪk) *adj*

tetrapterous (tɛ'træptərəs) *adj* **1** (of certain insects) having four wings **2** *biology* having four winglike extensions or parts [c19 from New Latin *tetrapterus*, from Greek *tetrapteros*, from TETRA- + *pteron* wing]

tetrarch ('tɛtrɑːk) *n* **1** the ruler of one fourth of a country **2** a subordinate ruler, esp of Syria under the Roman Empire **3** the commander of one of the smaller subdivisions of a Macedonian phalanx **4** any of four joint rulers [c14 from Greek *tetrarkhēs*, see TETRA-, -ARCH] ▷ **tetrarchate** (tɛ'trɑː,keɪt, -kɪt) *n* ▷ te'trarchic or te'trarchical *adj* ▷ 'tetrarchy *n*

tetraspore ('tɛtrə,spɔː) *n* any of the asexual spores that are produced in groups of four in the sporangium (**tetrasporangium**) of any of the red algae ▷ **tetrasporic** (,tɛtrə'spɒrɪk) or **tetrasporous** (,tɛtrə'spɔːrəs, tɪ'træspərəs) *adj*

tetrastich ('tɛtrə,stɪk) *n* a poem, stanza, or strophe that consists of four lines [c16 via Latin from Greek *tetrastikhon*, from TETRA- + *stikhos* row] ▷ **tetrastichic** (,tɛtrə'stɪkɪk) or **tetrastichal** (tɛ'træstɪk³l) *adj*

tetrastichous (tɛ'træstɪkəs) *adj* (of flowers or leaves on a stalk) arranged in four vertical rows

tetrasyllable (,tɛtrə'sɪləb³l) *n* a word of four syllables ▷ **tetrasyllabic** (,tɛtrəsɪ'læbɪk) or ,tetrasyl'labical *adj*

tetratomic (,tɛtrə'tɒmɪk) *adj* composed of four atoms or having four atoms per molecule

tetravalent (,tɛtrə'veɪlənt) *adj chem* **1** having a valency of four **2** Also: **quadrivalent** having four valencies ▷ ,tetra'valency *n*

tetrode ('tɛtrəʊd) *n* **1** an electronic valve having four electrodes, namely a cathode, control grid, screen grid, and anode **2** (*modifier*) (of a transistor) having two terminals on the base or gate to improve the performance at high frequencies

tetrodotoxin (,tɛtrəʊdəʊ'tɒksɪn) *n* a highly lethal neurotoxin found in certain puffer fish and in newts of the genus *Taricha*. Formula: $C_{11}H_{17}N_3O_3$ [c20 from New Latin *Tetrodon* (puffer fish genus name, from Greek *tetra-* fourfold + *odont-* tooth) + TOXIN]

tetroxide (tɛ'trɒksaɪd) or **tetroxid** (tɛ'trɒksɪd) *n* any oxide that contains four oxygen atoms per molecule: *osmium tetroxide, OsO_4*

tetryl ('tɛtrɪl) *n* a yellow crystalline explosive solid used in detonators; trinitrophenylmethylnitramine. Formula: $(NO_2)_3C_6H_2N(NO_2)CH_3$. Also called: **nitramine**

tetter ('tɛtə) *n* **1** a blister or pimple **2** *informal* any of various skin eruptions, such as eczema [Old English *teter*; related to Old High German *zitaroh*, Sanskrit *dadru*, Late Latin *derbita*]

Tetuán (tɛ'twɑːn) *n* a city in N Morocco: capital of Spanish Morocco (1912–56). Pop: 499 000 (2003)

Teucer ('tju:sə) *n Greek myth* **1** a Cretan leader, who founded Troy **2** a son of Telamon and Hesione, who distinguished himself by his archery on the side of the Greeks in the Trojan War

teuchter ('tju:xtər) *n Scot* (*sometimes capital*) **a** a derogatory word used by Lowlanders for a Highlander **b** (*as modifier*): *teuchter music* [c20 of uncertain origin]

Teucrian ('tju:krɪən) *n, adj* another word for **Trojan**

Teutoburger Wald (*German* 'tɔytobʊrgər valt) *n* a low wooded mountain range in N Germany: possible site of the annihilation of three Roman legions by Germans under Arminius in 9 AD

Teuton ('tju:tən) *n* **1** a member of an ancient Germanic people from Jutland who migrated to S Gaul in the 2nd century BC: annihilated by a Roman army in 102 BC **2** a member of any people speaking a Germanic language, esp a German ▷ *adj* **3** Teutonic [c18 from Latin *Teutonī* the Teutons, of Germanic origin]

Teutonic (tju:'tɒnɪk) *adj* **1** characteristic of or relating to the German people: *Teutonic thoroughness* **2** of or relating to the ancient Teutons **3** (not used in linguistics) of or relating to the Germanic languages ▷ *n* **4** an obsolete name for **Germanic** ▷ Teu'tonically *adv*

Teutonic order *n* a military and religious order of German knights, priests, and serving brothers founded about 1190 during the Third Crusade, later conquering large parts of the Baltic provinces and Russia. Also called: **Teutonic Knights**

Teutonism ('tju:tə,nɪzəm) *n* **1** a German idiom, custom, or characteristic **2** German society or civilization

Teutonize or **Teutonise** ('tju:tə,naɪz) *vb* to make or become German or Germanic; Germanize ▷ ,Teutoni'zation or ,Teutoni'sation *n*

Tevere ('te:vere) *n* the Italian name for the **Tiber**

Tevet or **Tebet** (te'vet) *n* (in the Jewish calendar) the tenth month of the year according to biblical reckoning and the fourth month of the civil year, usually falling within December and January [from Hebrew]

Te Waipounamu (tə hwaɪ'pɒːnɑːmu:) *n* a Māori name for New Zealand's South Island [Māori 'water and greenstone', from the presence of this stone on the South Island]

Tewkesbury ('tju:ksbərɪ, -brɪ) *n* a town in W England, in N Gloucestershire at the confluence of the Rivers Severn and Avon: scene of a decisive battle (1471) of the Wars of the Roses in which the Yorkists defeated the Lancastrians; 12th-century abbey. Pop: 9978 (2001)

tex *n* a unit of weight used to measure the density of yarns. It is equal to 1 gram per 1000 metres [c20 from French, from *textile* TEXTILE]

Tex. *abbreviation for* **1** Texan **2** Texas

Texan ('tɛksən) *n* **1** a native or inhabitant of Texas ▷ *adj* **2** of or relating to Texas or its inhabitants

Texas ('tɛksəs) *n* a state of the southwestern US, on the Gulf of Mexico: the second largest state; part of Mexico from 1821 to 1836, when it was declared an independent republic; joined the US in 1845; consists chiefly of a plain, with a wide flat coastal belt rising up to the semiarid Sacramento and Davis Mountains of the southwest; a major producer of cotton, rice, and livestock; the chief US producer of oil and gas; a leading world supplier of sulphur. Capital: Austin. Pop: 22 118 509 (2003 est.). Area: 678 927 sq km (262 134 sq miles). Abbreviations: **Tex**, (with zip code) **TX**

Texas fever *n vet science* another name for **blackwater fever**

Texas hedge *n finance* the opposite of a normal hedging operation, in which risk is increased by buying more than one financial instrument of the same kind

Texas Rangers *pl n* the state police of Texas, originally formed in the 19th century to defend outlying regions against Indians and Mexicans and to fight lawlessness

Texel ('tɛks³l) *n* a breed of sheep originating from the Netherlands having a heavy white fleece: kept for the production of lean lambs [c20 named after *Texel*, one of the West Frisian Islands off the Netherlands]

Tex-Mex ('tɛks,mɛks) *adj* of, relating to, or denoting the Texan version of something Mexican, such as music, food, or language

text (tɛkst) *n* **1** the main body of a printed or written work as distinct from commentary, notes, illustrations, etc **2** the words of something printed or written **3** (*often plural*) a book prescribed as part of a course of study **4** *computing* the words printed, written, or displayed on a visual display unit **5** the original exact wording of a work, esp the Bible, as distinct from a revision or translation **6** a short passage of the Bible used as a starting point for a sermon or adduced as proof of a doctrine **7** the topic or subject of a discussion or work **8** *printing* any one of several styles of letters or types **9** short for **textbook** ▷ *vb* **10** to send a text message from a mobile phone [c14 from Medieval Latin *textus* version, from Latin *textus* texture, from *texere* to compose] ▷ 'textless *adj*

textbook ('tɛkst,bʊk) *n* **a** a book used as a

t

standard source of information on a particular subject **b** (*as modifier*): *a textbook example* > '**text,bookish** *adj*

texter ('tɛkstə) *n* a person who communicates by text messaging

textile ('tɛkstaɪl) *n* **1** any fabric or cloth, esp woven **2** raw material suitable to be made into cloth; fibre or yarn **3** a non-nudist, as described by nudists; one who wears clothes ▷ *adj* **4** of or relating to fabrics or the making of fabrics [C17 from Latin *textilis* woven, from *texere* to weave]

text message *n* a message sent by means of a mobile phone

text messaging *n* communication by means of text messages sent from mobile phones

text processing *n* the handling of alphabetic characters by a computer

textual ('tɛkstjʊəl) *adj* **1** of or relating to a text or texts **2** based on or conforming to a text > '**textually** *adv*

textual criticism *n* **1** the scholarly study of manuscripts, esp of the Bible, in an effort to establish the original text **2** literary criticism emphasizing a close analysis of the text > **textual critic** *n*

textualism ('tɛkstjʊə,lɪzəm) *n* **1** doctrinaire adherence to a text, esp of the Bible **2** textual criticism, esp of the Bible > '**textualist** *n*, *adj*

textuary ('tɛkstjʊərɪ) *adj* **1** of, relating to, or contained in a text ▷ *n*, *pl* -**aries** **2** a textual critic

texture ('tɛkstʃə) *n* **1** the surface of a material, esp as perceived by the sense of touch: *a wall with a rough texture* **2** the structure, appearance, and feel of a woven fabric **3** the general structure and disposition of the constituent parts of something: *the texture of a cake* **4** the distinctive character or quality of something: *the texture of life in America* **5** the nature of a surface other than smooth: *woollen cloth has plenty of texture* **6** *art* the representation of the nature of a surface: *the painter caught the grainy texture of the sand* **7 a** *music* considered as the interrelationship between the horizontally presented aspects of melody and rhythm and the vertically represented aspect of harmony: *a contrapuntal texture* **b** the nature and quality of the instrumentation of a passage, piece, etc ▷ *vb* **8** (*tr*) to give a distinctive usually rough or grainy texture to [C15 from Latin *textūra* web, from *texere* to weave] > '**textural** *adj* '**texturally** *adv* > '**textureless** *adj*

Teyde (*Spanish* 'tɛiðe) *n* a variant spelling of **Teide**

tf *the internet domain name for* French Southern Territories

tg[1] *abbreviation for biology* type genus

tg[2] *the internet domain name for* Togo

TG 1 *abbreviation for* **transformational grammar 2** *international car registration for* Togo

T-group *n psychol* a group that meets for educational or therapeutic purposes to study its own communication [C20 from (*Sensitivity*) *T*(*raining*) *Group*]

TGV (*French* teʒeve) (in France) *abbreviation for* train à grande vitesse: a high-speed passenger train

TGWU (in Britain) *abbreviation for* Transport and General Workers' Union

th *the internet domain name for* Thailand

Th *the chemical symbol for* thorium

-th[1] *suffix forming nouns* **1** (*from verbs*) indicating an action or its consequence: *growth* **2** (*from adjectives*) indicating a quality: *width* [from Old English -*thu*, -*tho*]

-th[2] *or* **-eth** *suffix* forming ordinal numbers: *fourth; thousandth* [from Old English -(*o*)*tha*, -(*o*)*the*]

Thabana-Ntlenyana (tɑːˈbɑːnəˈn'tleɪnjənə) *n* a mountain in Lesotho: the highest peak of the Drakensberg Mountains. Height: 3482 m (11 425 ft). Also called: **Thadentsonyane**, **Thabantshonyana**

Thaddeus *or* **Thadeus** ('θædɪəs) *n New Testament* one of the 12 apostles (Matthew 10:3; Mark 3:18), traditionally identified with Jude

Thadentsonyane (,tɑːdənˈtsɒnjənə) *n* another

name for **Thabana-Ntlenyana**

Thai (taɪ) *adj* **1** of, relating to, or characteristic of Thailand, its people, or their language ▷ *n* **2** (*pl* **Thais** *or* **Thai**) a native or inhabitant of Thailand **3** the language of Thailand, sometimes classified as belonging to the Sino-Tibetan family ▷ Also called: **Siamese**

Thailand ('taɪ,lænd) *n* a kingdom in SE Asia, on the Andaman Sea and the Gulf of Siam: united as a kingdom in 1350 and became a major SE Asian power; consists chiefly of a central plain around the Chao Phraya river system, mountains rising over 2400 m (8000 ft) in the northwest, and rainforest the length of the S peninsula. Parts of the SW coast suffered badly in the Indian Ocean tsunami of December 2004. Official language: Thai. Official religion: (Hinayana) Buddhist. Currency: baht. Capital: Bangkok. Pop: 63 465 000 (2004 est). Area: 513 998 sq km (198 455 sq miles). Former name (until 1939 and 1945–49): **Siam**

thalamencephalon (,θæləmɛnˈsɛfəˌlɒn) *n*, *pl* -**lons** *or* -**la** (-lə) *anatomy* **1** the part of the diencephalon of the brain that includes the thalamus, pineal gland, and adjacent structures **2** another name for **diencephalon** > **thalamencephalic** (,θæləˌmɛnsəˈfælɪk) *adj*

thalamus ('θæləməs) *n*, *pl* -**mi** (-,maɪ) **1** either of the two contiguous egg-shaped masses of grey matter at the base of the brain **2** both of these masses considered as a functional unit **3** the receptacle or torus of a flower [C18 from Latin, Greek *thalamos* inner room; probably related to Greek *tholos* vault] > **thalamic** (θəˈlæmɪk) *adj* > thaˈlamically *adv*

thalassaemia *or US* **thalassemia** (,θæləˈsiːmɪə) *n* a hereditary disease, common in many parts of the world, resulting from defects in the synthesis of the red blood pigment haemoglobin. Also called: **Cooley's anaemia** ('kuːlɪz) [New Latin, from Greek *thalassa* sea + -AEMIA, from it being esp prevalent round the eastern Mediterranean Sea]

thalassic (θəˈlæsɪk) *adj* **1** of or relating to the sea **2** of or relating to small or inland seas, as opposed to open waters **3** inhabiting or growing in the sea; marine: *thalassic fauna* [C19 from French *thalassique*, from Greek *thalassa* sea]

thalassocracy (,θæləˈsɒkrəsɪ) *or* **thalattocracy** *n* the government of a nation having dominion over large expanses of the seas [C19 from Attic Greek *thalassocratia*, from *thalassa* sea + -CRACY]

thalassotherapy (,θæləsəʊˈθɛrəpɪ) *n* the use of sea water and marine products as a therapeutic treatment [C20 from Greek *thalassa* sea + THERAPY]

thaler *or* **taler** ('taːlə) *n*, *pl* -**ler** *or* -**lers** a former German, Austrian, or Swiss silver coin [from German; see DOLLAR]

thali ('taːlɪ) *n Indian cookery* a meal consisting of several small meat or vegetable dishes accompanied by rice, bread, etc, and sometimes by a starter or a sweet [C20 from Hindi *thālī* a plate or tray on which food is served]

Thalia (θəˈlaɪə) *n Greek myth* **1** the Muse of comedy and pastoral poetry **2** one of the three Graces [C17 via Latin from Greek, from *thaleia* blooming]

thalidomide (θəˈlɪdəˌmaɪd) *n* **a** a synthetic drug formerly used as a sedative and hypnotic but withdrawn from the market when found to cause abnormalities in developing fetuses. Formula: $C_{13}H_{10}N_2O_4$ **b** (*as modifier*): *a thalidomide baby* [C20 from THALLIC + -*id*- (from IMIDE) + IMIDE]

thallic ('θælɪk) *adj* of or containing thallium, esp in the trivalent state

thallium ('θælɪəm) *n* a soft malleable highly toxic white metallic element used as a rodent and insect poison and in low-melting glass. Its compounds are used as infrared detectors and in photoelectric cells. Symbol: Tl; atomic no: 81; atomic wt: 204.3833; valency: 1 or 3; relative density: 11.85; melting pt: 304°C; boiling pt: 1473±10°C [C19 from New Latin, from Greek *thallos* a green shoot; referring to the green line in its spectrum]

thallophyte ('θæləˌfaɪt) *n obsolete* any organism of the former division *Thallophyta*, lacking true stems, leaves, and roots: includes the algae, fungi, lichens, and bacteria, all now regarded as separate phyla [C19 from New Latin *thallophyta*, from Greek *thallos* a young shoot + *phuton* a plant] > **thallophytic** (,θæləˈfɪtɪk) *adj*

thallous ('θæləs) *adj* of or containing thallium, esp in the monovalent state

thallus ('θæləs) *n*, *pl* **thalli** ('θælaɪ) *or* **thalluses** the undifferentiated vegetative body of algae, fungi, and lichens [C19 from Latin, from Greek *thallos* green shoot, from *thallein* to bloom] > '**thalloid** *adj*

thalweg *or* **talweg** ('taːlvɛg) *n geography rare* **1** the longitudinal outline of a riverbed from source to mouth **2** the line of steepest descent from any point on the land surface [C19 from German, from *Thal* valley + *Weg* way, path]

Thames *n* **1** (tɛmz) a river in S England, rising in the Cotswolds in several headstreams and flowing generally east through London to the North Sea by a large estuary. Length: 346 km (215 miles). Ancient name: **Tamesis** (ˈtæməsɪs) **2** (teɪmz, θeɪmz) a river in SE Canada, in Ontario, flowing south to London, then southwest to Lake St Clair. Length: 217 km (135 miles)

Thammuz ('tæmuːz, -ʊz) *n* a variant spelling of **Tammuz**

than (ðæn; *unstressed* ðən) *conj* (*coordinating*) ▷ *prep* **1** used to introduce the second element of a comparison, the first element of which expresses difference: *shorter than you; couldn't do otherwise than love him; he swims faster than I run* **2** used after adverbs such as *rather* or *sooner* to introduce a rejected alternative in an expression of preference: *rather than be imprisoned, I shall die* **3** other than: besides; in addition to [Old English *thanne; related to Old Saxon, Old High German thanna; see THEN]

> **USAGE** In formal English, *than* is usually regarded as a conjunction governing an unexpressed verb: *he does it far better than I (do)*. The case of any pronoun therefore depends on whether it is the subject or object of the unexpressed verb: *she likes him more than I (like him); she likes him more than (she likes) me*. However in ordinary speech and writing *than* is usually treated as a preposition and is followed by the object form of a pronoun: *my brother is younger than me*

thanatology (,θænəˈtɒlədʒɪ) *n* the scientific study of death and the phenomena and practices relating to it [C19 from Greek *thanatos* death + -LOGY]

thanatopsis (,θænəˈtɒpsɪs) *n* a meditation on death, as in a poem [C19 from Greek *thanatos* death + *opsis* a view]

Thanatos ('θænəˌtɒs) *n* the Greek personification of death: son of Nyx, goddess of night. Roman counterpart: **Mors**. Thanatos was the name chosen by Freud to represent a universal death instinct. Compare **Eros**[1] > **Thanatotic** (,θænəˈtɒtɪk) *adj*

thane *or commonly* **thegn** (θeɪn) *n* **1** (in Anglo-Saxon England) a member of an aristocratic class, ranking below an ealdorman, whose status was hereditary and who held land from the king or from another nobleman in return for certain services **2** (in medieval Scotland) **a** a person of rank, often the chief of a clan, holding land from the king **b** a lesser noble who was a Crown official holding authority over an area of land [Old English *thegn; related to Old Saxon, Old High German *thegan* thane] > **thanage** ('θeɪnɪdʒ) *n*

Thanet ('θænɪt) *n* **Isle of** an island in SE England, in NE Kent, separated from the mainland by two branches of the River Stour: scene of many Norse invasions. Area: 109 sq km (42 sq miles)

thangka ('θæŋkə) *n* (in Tibetan Buddhism) a religious painting on a scroll [from Tibetan]

Thanjavur (ˌtʌndʒəˈvʊə) *n* a city in SE India, in E Tamil Nadu: headquarters of the earliest Protestant missions in India. Pop: 215 725 (2001). Former name: **Tanjore**

thank (θæŋk) *vb (tr)* **1** to convey feelings of gratitude to **2** to hold responsible: *he has his creditors to thank for his bankruptcy* **3** used in exclamations of relief: *thank goodness; thank God* **4** I'll thank you to used ironically to intensify a command, request, etc: *I'll thank you to mind your own business* [Old English *thancian*; related to Old Frisian *thankia*, Old Norse *thakka*, Old Saxon, Old High German *thancōn*]

thankful (ˈθæŋkfʊl) *adj* grateful and appreciative > ˈ**thankfulness** *n*

thankfully (ˈθæŋkfʊlɪ) *adv* **1** showing gratitude or appreciation **2** *informal* fortunately: *thankfully she was not injured*

> USAGE The use of *thankfully* to mean *fortunately* was formerly considered incorrect by many people, but has now become acceptable in informal contexts

thankless (ˈθæŋklɪs) *adj* **1** receiving no thanks or appreciation: *a thankless job* **2** ungrateful: *a thankless pupil* > ˈ**thanklessly** *adv* > ˈ**thanklessness** *n*

thanks (θæŋks) *pl n* **1** an expression of appreciation or gratitude or an acknowledgment of services or favours given **2** **thanks to** because of: *thanks to him we lost the match* ▷ *interj* **3** *informal* an exclamation expressing acknowledgment, gratitude, or appreciation

thanksgiving (ˈθæŋksˌɡɪvɪŋ; US θæŋksˈɡɪvɪŋ) *n* **1** the act of giving thanks **2** **a** an expression of thanks to God **b** a public act of religious observance or a celebration in acknowledgment of divine favours

Thanksgiving Day *n* an annual day of holiday celebrated in thanksgiving to God on the fourth Thursday of November in the United States, and on the second Monday of October in Canada. Often shortened to: **Thanksgiving**

thank you *interj* ▷ *n* a conventional expression of gratitude

Thapsus (ˈθæpsəs) *n* an ancient town near Carthage in North Africa: site of Caesar's victory over Pompey in 46 BC

thar (tɑː) *n* a variant spelling of **tahr**

Thar Desert (tɑː) *n* a desert in NW India, mainly in NW Rajasthan state and extending into Pakistan. Area: over 260 000 sq km (100 000 sq miles). Also called: **Indian Desert, Great Indian Desert**

Thásos (ˈθæsɒs) *n* a Greek island in the N Aegean: colonized by Greeks from Paros in the 7th century BC as a gold-mining centre; under Turkish rule (1455–1912). Pop: 13 761 (2001). Area: 379 sq km (146 sq miles)

that (ðæt; *unstressed* ðət) *determiner (used before a singular noun)* **1** **a** used preceding a noun that has been mentioned at some time or is understood: *that idea of yours* **b** *(as pronoun)*: *don't eat that; that's what I mean* **2** **a** used preceding a noun that denotes something more remote or removed: *that dress is cheaper than this one; that building over there is for sale* **b** *(as pronoun)*: *that is John and this is his wife; give me that*. Compare **this** **3** used to refer to something that is familiar: *that old chap from across the street* **4** **and (all) that** *informal* everything connected with the subject mentioned: *he knows a lot about building and that* **5** **at that** *(completive-intensive)* additionally, all things considered, or nevertheless: *he's a pleasant fellow at that; I might decide to go at that* **6** **like that** **a** with ease; effortlessly: *he gave me the answer just like that* **b** of such a nature, character, etc: *he paid for all our tickets — he's like that* **7** **that is** **a** to be precise **b** in other words **c** for example **8** **that's more like it** that is better, an improvement, etc **9** **that's that** there is no more to be done, discussed, etc **10** **with** (*or* **at**) **that** thereupon; having said or done that ▷ *conj (subordinating)* **11** used to introduce a noun clause: *I believe that you'll come* **12** Also: **so that, in order that** used to introduce a clause of purpose: *they fought that others might have peace* **13** used to introduce a clause of result: *he laughed so hard that he cried* **14** used to introduce a clause after an understood sentence expressing desire, indignation, or amazement: *oh, that I had never lived!* ▷ *adv* **15** used with adjectives or adverbs to reinforce the specification of a precise degree already mentioned: *go just that fast and you should be safe* **16** Also: **all that** *(usually used with a negative) informal* (intensifier): *he wasn't that upset at the news* **17** *dialect* (intensifier): *the cat was that weak after the fight* ▷ *pron* **18** used to introduce a restrictive relative clause: *the book that we want* **19** used to introduce a clause with the verb *to be* to emphasize the extent to which the preceding noun is applicable: *genius that she is, she outwitted the computer* [Old English *thæt*; related to Old Frisian *thet*, Old Norse, Old Saxon *that*, Old High German *daz*, Greek *to*, Latin *istud*, Sanskrit *tad*]

> USAGE Precise stylists maintain a distinction between *that* and *which*: *that* is used as a relative pronoun in restrictive clauses and *which* in nonrestrictive clauses. In *the book that is on the table is mine*, the clause *that is on the table* is used to distinguish one particular book (the one on the table) from another or others (which may be anywhere, but not on the table). In *the book, which is on the table, is mine*, the *which* clause is merely descriptive or incidental. The more formal the level of language, the more important it is to preserve the distinction between the two relative pronouns; but in informal or colloquial usage, the words are often used interchangeably

thatch (θætʃ) *n* **1** **a** Also called: **thatching** a roofing material that consists of straw, reed, etc **b** a roof made of such a material **2** anything resembling this, such as the hair of the head **3** Also called: **thatch palm** any of various palms with leaves suitable for thatching ▷ *vb* **4** to cover (a roof) with thatch [Old English *theccan* to cover; related to *thæc* roof, Old Saxon *thekkian* to thatch, Old High German *decchen*, Old Norse *thekja*] > ˈ**thatcher** *n* > ˈ**thatchless** *adj* > ˈ**thatchy** *adj*

Thatcherism (ˈθætʃəˌrɪzəm) *n* the policies of monetarism, privatization, and self-help promoted by the British Conservative stateswoman and prime minister (1979–90) Margaret, Baroness Thatcher (born Margaret Hilda Roberts, 1925) > **Thatcherite** (ˈθætʃəˌraɪt) *n, adj*

thaumato- *or before a vowel* **thaumat-** *combining form* miracle; marvel: *thaumaturge* [from Greek *thauma, thaumat-* a marvel]

thaumatology (ˌθɔːməˈtɒlədʒɪ) *n* the study of or a treatise on miracles

thaumatrope (ˈθɔːməˌtrəʊp) *n* a toy in which partial pictures on the two sides of a card appear to merge when the card is twirled rapidly [C19 from THAUMATO- + -TROPE] > **thaumatropical** (ˌθɔːməˈtrɒpɪkᵊl) *adj*

thaumaturge (ˈθɔːməˌtɜːdʒ) *n* *rare* a performer of miracles; magician [C18 from Medieval Latin *thaumaturgus*, from Greek *thaumatourgos* miracle-working, from THAUMATO- + *-ourgos* working, from *ergon* work] > ˈ**thaumaˌturgy** *n* > ˌ**thaumaˈturgic** *adj*

thaw (θɔː) *vb* **1** to melt or cause to melt from a solid frozen state: *the snow thawed* **2** to become or cause to become unfrozen; defrost **3** *(intr)* to be the case that the ice or snow is melting: *it's thawing fast* **4** *(intr)* to become more sociable, relaxed, or friendly ▷ *n* **5** the act or process of thawing **6** a spell of relatively warm weather, causing snow or ice to melt **7** an increase in relaxation or friendliness [Old English *thawian*; related to Old High German *douwen* to thaw, Old Norse *theyja* to thaw, Latin *tabēre* to waste away] > ˈ**thawer** *n* > ˈ**thawless** *adj*

ThB *abbreviation for* Bachelor of Theology

THC *abbreviation for* tetrahydrocannabidinol: the active ingredient in cannabis, giving it its narcotic and psychoactive effects

ThD *abbreviation for* Doctor of Theology

the[1] (*stressed or emphatic* ðiː; *unstressed before a consonant* ðə; *unstressed before a vowel* ðɪ) *determiner (article)* **1** used preceding a noun that has been previously specified: *the pain should disappear soon; the man then opened the door*. Compare **a**[1] **2** used with a qualifying word or phrase to indicate a particular person, object, etc, as distinct from others: *ask the man standing outside; give me the blue one*. Compare **a**[1] **3** used preceding certain nouns associated with one's culture, society, or community: *to go to the doctor; listen to the news; watch the television* **4** used preceding present participles and adjectives when they function as nouns: *the singing is awful; the dead salute you* **5** used preceding titles and certain uniquely specific or proper nouns, such as place names: *the United States; the Honourable Edward Brown; the Chairman; the moon* **6** used preceding a qualifying adjective or noun in certain names or titles: *William the Conqueror; Edward the First* **7** used preceding a noun to make it refer to its class generically: *the white seal is hunted for its fur; this is good for the throat; to play the piano* **8** used instead of *my, your, her*, etc, with parts of the body: *take me by the hand* **9** *(usually stressed)* the best, only, or most remarkable: *Harry's is the club in this town* **10** used with proper nouns when qualified: *written by the young Hardy* **11** another word for **per**, esp with nouns or noun phrases of cost *fifty pence the pound* **12** *often facetious or derogatory* my; our: *the wife goes out on Thursdays* **13** used preceding a unit of time in phrases or titles indicating an outstanding person, event, etc: *match of the day; housewife of the year* [Middle English, from Old English *thē*, a demonstrative adjective that later superseded *sē* (masculine singular) and *sēo, sio* (feminine singular); related to Old Frisian *thi, thiu*, Old High German *der, diu*]

the[2] (ðə, ðɪ) *adv* **1** *(often foll by for)* used before comparative adjectives or adverbs for emphasis: *she looks the happier for her trip* **2** used correlatively before each of two comparative adjectives or adverbs to indicate equality: *the sooner you come, the better; the more I see you, the more I love you* [Old English *thī, thȳ*, instrumental case of THE[1] and THAT; related to Old Norse *thī*, Gothic *thei*]

the- *combining form* a variant of **theo-** before a vowel

theaceous (θiːˈeɪʃəs) *adj* of, relating to, or belonging to the *Theaceae*, a family of evergreen trees and shrubs of tropical and warm regions: includes the tea plant

theanthropism (θiːˈænθrəˌpɪzəm) *n* **1** the ascription of human traits or characteristics to a god or gods **2** *christian theol* the doctrine of the hypostatic union of the divine and human natures in the single person of Christ [C19 from Ecclesiastical Greek *theanthrōpos* (from *theos* god + *anthrōpos* man) + -ISM] > ˌ**theanˈthropic** *adj* > **theˈanthropist** *n*

thearchy (ˈθiːɑːkɪ) *n, pl* **-chies** rule or government by God or gods; theocracy [C17 from Church Greek *thearkhia*; see THEO-, -ARCHY] > **theˈarchic** *adj*

theatre *or US* **theater** (ˈθɪətə) *n* **1** **a** a building designed for the performance of plays, operas, etc **b** *(as modifier)*: *a theatre ticket* **c** *(in combination)*: *a theatregoer* **2** a large room or hall, usually with a raised platform and tiered seats for an audience, used for lectures, film shows, etc **3** Also called: **operating theatre** a room in a hospital or other medical centre equipped for surgical operations **4** plays regarded collectively as a form of art **5** **the theatre** the world of actors, theatrical companies, etc: *the glamour of the theatre* **6** a setting for dramatic or important events **7** writing that is suitable for dramatic presentation: *a good piece of theatre* **8** *US, Austral, NZ* the usual word for **cinema** (sense 1) **9** a major area of military activity: *the*

t

theatre of operations **10** a circular or semicircular open-air building with tiers of seats [c14 from Latin *theātrum*, from Greek *theatron* place for viewing, from *theasthai* to look at; related to Greek *thauma* miracle]

theatre-in-the-round *n, pl* **theatres-in-the-round 1** a theatre with seats arranged around a central acting area **2** drama written or designed for performance in such a theatre ▷ Also called: **arena theatre**

theatre of cruelty *n* a type of theatre advocated by Antonin Artaud in *Le Théâtre et son double* that seeks to communicate to its audience a sense of pain, suffering, and evil, using gesture, movement, sound, and symbolism rather than language

theatre of the absurd *n* drama in which normal conventions and dramatic structure are ignored or modified in order to present life as irrational or meaningless

theatrical (θɪˈætrɪkˀl) *adj* **1** of or relating to the theatre or dramatic performances **2** exaggerated and affected in manner or behaviour; histrionic > theˌatriˈcality *or* theˈatricalness *n* > theˈatrically *adv*

theatricals (θɪˈætrɪkˀlz) *pl n* dramatic performances and entertainments, esp as given by amateurs

theatrics (θɪˈætrɪks) *n (functioning as singular)* **1** the art of staging plays **2** exaggerated mannerisms or displays of emotions

Thebaic (θɪˈbeɪɪk) *adj* **1** of or relating to the ancient Greek city of Thebes or its inhabitants **2** of or relating to the ancient Egyptian city of Thebes or its inhabitants

Thebaid (ˈθiːbeɪɪd, -bɪ-) *n* the territory around ancient Thebes in Egypt, or sometimes around Thebes in Greece

thebaine (ˈθiːbəˌiːn, θɪˈbeɪɪn, -aɪn) *n* a poisonous white crystalline alkaloid, found in opium but without opioid actions. Formula: $C_{19}H_{21}NO_3$. Also called: **paramorphine** [c19 from New Latin *thebaia* opium of Thebes (with reference to Egypt as a chief source of opium) + -INE²]

Theban (ˈθiːbən) *adj* **1** of or relating to the ancient Greek city of Thebes or its inhabitants **2** of or relating to the ancient Egyptian city of Thebes or its inhabitants ▷ *n* **3** a native or inhabitant of Thebes

Thebe (ˈθiːbɪ) *n astronomy* an inner satellite of Jupiter discovered in 1979 [c20 named after *Thebe*, mythical queen of THEBES]

Thebes (θiːbz) *n* **1** (in ancient Greece) the chief city of Boeotia, destroyed by Alexander the Great (336 BC) **2** (in ancient Egypt) a city on the Nile: at various times capital of Upper Egypt or of the entire country

theca (ˈθiːkə) *n, pl* **-cae** (-siː) **1** *botany* an enclosing organ, cell, or spore case, esp the capsule of a moss **2** *zoology* a hard outer covering, such as the cup-shaped container of a coral polyp [c17 from Latin *thēca*, from Greek *thēkē* case; related to Greek *tithenai* to place] > ˈthecal *or* ˈthecate *adj*

thecodont (ˈθiːkəˌdɒnt) *adj* **1** (of mammals and certain reptiles) having teeth that grow in sockets **2** of or relating to teeth of this type ▷ *n* **3** any extinct reptile of the order *Thecodontia*, of Triassic times, having teeth set in sockets: they gave rise to the dinosaurs, crocodiles, pterodactyls, and birds [c20 New Latin *Thecondontia*, from Greek *thēkē* case + -ODONT]

thé dansant *French* (te dãsã) *n, pl* **thés dansant** (te dãsã) a dance held while afternoon tea is served, popular in the 1920s and 1930s [literally: dancing tea]

thee (ðiː) *pron* **1** the objective form of **thou¹ 2** *(subjective) rare* refers to the person addressed: used mainly by members of the Society of Friends [Old English *thē*; see THOU¹]

theft (θɛft) *n* **1** *criminal law* the dishonest taking of property belonging to another person with the intention of depriving the owner permanently of

its possession **2** *rare* something stolen [Old English *thēofth*; related to Old Norse *thyfth*, Old Frisian *thiūvethe*, Middle Dutch *düfte*; see THIEF] > ˈtheftless *adj*

thegn (θeɪn) *n* a variant spelling of **thane**

theine (ˈθiːiːn, -ɪn) *n* another name for **caffeine**, esp when present in tea [c19 from New Latin *thea* tea + -INE²]

their (ðeə) *determiner* **1** of, belonging to, or associated in some way with them: *their finest hour; their own clothes; she tried to combat their mocking her* **2** belonging to or associated in some way with people in general not including the speaker or people addressed: *in many countries they wash their clothes in the river* **3** belonging to or associated in some way with an indefinite antecedent such as *one, whoever,* or *anybody: everyone should bring their own lunch* [c12 from Old Norse *theira* (genitive plural); see THEY, THEM]

▪ USAGE See at **they**

theirs (ðeəz) *pron* **1** something or someone belonging to or associated in some way with them: *theirs is difficult* **2** *not standard* something or someone belonging to or associated in some way with an indefinite antecedent such as *one, whoever,* or *anybody: everyone thinks theirs is best* **3** *of theirs* belonging to or associated with them

theism (ˈθiːɪzəm) *n* **1** the form of the belief in one God as the transcendent creator and ruler of the universe that does not necessarily entail further belief in divine revelation. Compare **deism 2** the belief in the existence of a God or gods. Compare **atheism** [c17 from Greek *theos* god + -ISM] > ˈtheist *n, adj* > theˈistic *or* theˈistical *adj* > theˈistically *adv*

them (ðem; *unstressed* ðəm) *pron* **1** *(objective)* refers to things or people other than the speaker or people addressed: *I'll kill them; what happened to them?* **2** *chiefly US* a dialect word for **themselves** when used as an indirect object: *they got them a new vice president* ▷ *determiner* **3** a nonstandard word for **those** *three of them oranges* [Old English *thǣm*, influenced by Old Norse *theim*; related to Old Frisian *thām*, Old Saxon, Old High German *thēm*, Old Norse *theimr*, Gothic *thaim*]

▪ USAGE See at **me¹, they**

thematic (θɪˈmætɪk) *adj* **1** of, relating to, or consisting of a theme or themes **2** *linguistics* denoting a word that is the theme of a sentence **3** *grammar* **a** denoting a vowel or other sound or sequence of sounds that occurs between the root of a word and any inflectional or derivational suffixes **b** of or relating to the stem or root of a word ▷ *n* **4** *grammar* a thematic vowel: *"-o-" is a thematic in the combining form "psycho-"* > theˈmatically *adv*

thematic apperception test *n psychol* a projective test in which drawings of interacting people are shown and the person being tested is asked to make up a story about them

thematization *or* **thematisation** (ˌθiːmətaɪˈzeɪʃən) *n linguistics* the mental act or process of selecting particular topics as themes in discourse or words as themes in sentences

theme (θiːm) *n* **1** an idea or topic expanded in a discourse, discussion, etc **2** (in literature, music, art, etc) a unifying idea, image, or motif, repeated or developed throughout a work **3** *music* a group of notes forming a recognizable melodic unit, often used as the basis of the musical material in a composition **4** a short essay, esp one set as an exercise for a student **5** *linguistics* the first major constituent of a sentence, usually but not necessarily the subject. In the sentence *history I do like*, "history" is the theme of the sentence, even though it is the object of the verb **6** *grammar* another word for **root¹** (sense 9) or **stem¹** (sense 9) **7** (in the Byzantine Empire) a territorial unit consisting of several provinces under a military commander **8** *(modifier)* planned or designed round one unifying subject, image, etc: *a theme holiday* ▷ *vb* (tr) **9** to design, decorate, arrange, etc, in accordance with a theme [c13 from Latin

thema, from Greek: deposit, from *tithenai* to lay down] > ˈthemeless *adj*

theme park *n* an area planned as a leisure attraction, in which all the displays, buildings, activities, etc, are based on or relate to one particular subject

theme song *n* **1** a melody used, esp in a film score, to set a mood, introduce a character, etc **2** another term for **signature tune**

Themis (ˈθiːmɪs) *n Greek myth* a goddess of order and justice

themselves (ðəmˈsɛlvz) *pron* **1 a** the reflexive form of **they** or **them b** (intensifier): *the team themselves voted on it* **2** (preceded by a copula) their normal or usual selves: *they don't seem themselves any more* **3** Also: **themself** *not standard* a reflexive form of an indefinite antecedent such as *one, whoever,* or *anybody: everyone has to look after themselves*

then (ðen) *adv* **1** at that time; over that period of time **2** (sentence modifier) in that case; that being so: *then why don't you ask her?; if he comes, then you'll have to leave; go on then, take it* **3** **then and there** a variant of **there and then**: see **there** (sense 6) ▷ *sentence connector* **4** after that; with that: *then John left the room and didn't return* ▷ *n* **5** that time: *before then; from then on* ▷ *adj* **6** (prenominal) existing, functioning, etc, at that time: *the then prime minister* [Old English *thenne*; related to Old Saxon, Old High German *thanna*; see THAN]

thenar (ˈθiːnɑː) *anatomy* ▷ *n* **1** the palm of the hand **2** the fleshy area of the palm at the base of the thumb ▷ *adj* **3** of or relating to the palm or the region at the base of the thumb [c17 via New Latin from Greek; related to Old High German *tenar* palm of the hand]

thenardite (θɪˈnɑːdaɪt, tɪ-) *n* a whitish vitreous mineral that consists of anhydrous sodium sulphate and occurs in saline residues. Formula: Na_2SO_4 [c19 named after Baron L J Thénard (1777–1857), French chemist; see -ITE¹]

Thénard's blue (ˈteɪnɑːz, -nɑːdz) *n* another name for **cobalt blue** [c19 named after Baron L J Thénard; see THENARDITE]

thence (ðens) *adv* **1** from that place **2** Also: **thenceforth** (ˈðensˈfɔːθ) from that time or event; thereafter **3** therefore [c13 *thannes*, from *thanne*, from Old English *thanon*; related to Gothic *thanana*, Old Norse *thanan*]

thenceforward (ˈðensˈfɔːwəd) *or* **thenceforwards** *adv* from that time or place on; thence

theo- *or before a vowel* **the-** *combining form* indicating God or gods: *theology* [from Greek *theos* god]

theobromine (ˌθiːəʊˈbrəʊmiːn, -mɪn) *n* a white crystalline slightly water-soluble alkaloid that occurs in many plants, such as tea and cacao: formerly used to treat asthma. Formula: $C_7H_8N_4O_2$. See also **xanthine** (sense 2) [c18 from New Latin *theobroma* genus of trees, literally: food of the gods, from THEO- + Greek *brōma* food + -INE²]

theocentric (ˌθiːəˈsɛntrɪk) *adj theol* having God as the focal point of attention > ˌtheoˈcentricity *n* > ˌtheoˈcentrism *or* theocentricism (ˌθiːəʊˈsɛntrɪˌsɪzəm) *n*

theocracy (θɪˈɒkrəsɪ) *n, pl* **-cies 1** government by a deity or by a priesthood **2** a community or political unit under such government > ˈtheoˌcrat *n* > ˌtheoˈcratic *or* ˌtheoˈcratical *adj* > ˌtheoˈcratically *adv*

theocrasy (θɪˈɒkrəsɪ) *n* **1** a mingling into one of deities or divine attributes previously regarded as distinct **2** the union of the soul with God in mysticism [c19 from Greek *theokrasia*, from THEO- + *krasia* from *krasis* a blending]

theodicy (θɪˈɒdɪsɪ) *n, pl* **-cies** the branch of theology concerned with defending the attributes of God against objections resulting from physical and moral evil [c18 coined by Leibnitz in French as *théodicée*, from THEO- + Greek *dikē* justice] > theˌodiˈcean *adj*

theodolite (θɪˈɒdəˌlaɪt) *n* a surveying instrument

for measuring horizontal and vertical angles, consisting of a small tripod-mounted telescope that is free to move in both the horizontal and vertical planes. Also called (in the US and Canada): **transit** [c16 from New Latin *theodolitus*, of uncertain origin] > **theodolitic** (ˌθɪəˈdɒlɪtɪk) *adj*

theogony (θɪˈɒɡənɪ) *n, pl* **-nies 1** the origin and descent of the gods **2** an account of this, often recited in epic poetry [c17 from Greek *theogonia*, see THEO-, -GONY] > **theogonic** (ˌθɪəˈɡɒnɪk) *adj* > **theˈogonist** *n*

theol. *abbreviation for* **1** theologian **2** theological **3** theology

theologian (ˌθɪəˈləʊdʒɪən) *n* a person versed in or engaged in the study of theology, esp Christian theology

theological (ˌθɪəˈlɒdʒɪkəl) *adj* **1** of, relating to, or based on theology **2** based on God's revelation to man of his nature, his designs, and his will **3** *informal* difficult to understand; esoteric > ˌtheoˈlogically *adv*

theological virtues *pl n* (esp among the scholastics) those virtues that are infused into man by a special grace of God, specifically faith, hope, and charity. Compare **natural virtues**

theologize *or* **theologise** (θɪˈɒlədʒaɪz) *vb* **1** (*intr*) to speculate upon theological subjects, engage in theological study or discussion, or formulate theological arguments **2** (*tr*) to render theological or treat from a theological point of view > the ˌologiˈzation *or* the ˌologiˈsation *n* > the ˈolo ˌgizer *or* the ˈolo ˌgiser *n*

theology (θɪˈɒlədʒɪ) *n, pl* **-gies 1** the systematic study of the existence and nature of the divine and its relationship to and influence upon other beings **2** a specific branch of this study, undertaken from the perspective of a particular group: *feminist theology* **3** the systematic study of Christian revelation concerning God's nature and purpose, esp through the teaching of the Church **4** a specific system, form, or branch of this study, esp for those preparing for the ministry or priesthood [c14 from Late Latin *theologia*, from Latin; see THEO-, -LOGY] > theˈologist *n*

theomachy (θɪˈɒməkɪ) *n, pl* **-chies** a battle among the gods or against them [c16 from Greek *theomakhia*, from THEO- + *makhē* battle]

theomancy (ˈθɪ ːəʊmænsɪ) *n* divination or prophecy by an oracle or by people directly inspired by a god [c17 from THEO- + -MANCY]

theomania (ˌθɪəˈmeɪnɪə) *n* religious madness, esp when it takes the form of believing oneself to be a god > ˌtheoˈmani ˌac *n*

theomorphic (ˌθɪəˈmɔːfɪk) *adj* of or relating to the conception or representation of man as having the form of God or a deity [c19 from Greek *theomorphos*, from THEO- + *morphē* form] > ˌtheoˈmorphism *n*

theonomy (θɪˈɒnəmɪ) *n* the state of being governed by God

theopathy (θɪˈɒpəθɪ) *n* religious emotion engendered by the contemplation of or meditation upon God [c18 from THEO- + -*pathy*, from SYMPATHY] > **theopathic** (ˌθɪəpəˈθɛtɪk) *or* **theopathic** (ˌθɪəˈpæθɪk) *adj*

theophagy (θɪˈɒfədʒɪ) *n, pl* **-gies** the sacramental eating of a god

theophany (θɪˈɒfənɪ) *n, pl* **-nies** *theol* a manifestation of a deity to man in a form that, though visible, is not necessarily material [c17 from Late Latin *theophania*, from Late Greek *theophaneia*, from THEO- + *phainein* to show] > **theophanic** (θɪəˈfænɪk) *or* **theˈophanous** *adj*

Theophilus (θɪˈɒfɪləs) *n* a conspicuous crater in the SE quadrant of the moon, 100 kilometres in diameter [after *Theophilus* (died 842 AD), Byzantine emperor and patron of learning]

theophobia (ˌθɪəˈfəʊbɪə) *n* morbid fear or hatred of God > ˌtheoˈphobi ˌac *n*

theophylline (ˌθɪəˈfɪliːn, -ɪn, θɪˈɒfɪlɪn) *n* a white crystalline slightly water-soluble alkaloid that is an isomer of theobromine: it occurs in plants,

such as tea, and is used to treat asthma. Formula: $C_7H_8N_4O_2$. See also **xanthine** (sense 2) [c19 from THEO(BROMINE) + PHYLLO- + -INE²]

theorbo (θɪˈɔːbəʊ) *n, pl* **-bos** *music* an obsolete form of the lute, having two necks, one above the other, the second neck carrying a set of unstopped sympathetic bass strings [c17 from Italian *teorba*, probably from Venetian, variant of *tuorba* travelling bag, ultimately from Turkish *torba* bag] > theˈorbist *n*

theorem (ˈθɪərəm) *n maths, logic* a statement or formula that can be deduced from the axioms of a formal system by means of its rules of inference [c16 from Late Latin *theōrēma*, from Greek: something to be viewed, from *theōrein* to view] > **theorematic** (ˌθɪərəˈmætɪk) *or* **theoremic** (ˌθɪəˈrɛmɪk) *adj* > ˌtheoreˈmatically *adv*

theoretic (ˌθɪəˈrɛtɪk) *adj* **1** another word for **theoretical** ▷ *n* **2** another word for **theoretics**

theoretical (ˌθɪəˈrɛtɪkəl) *or* **theoretic** *adj* **1** of or based on theory **2** lacking practical application or actual existence; hypothetical **3** using or dealing in theory; impractical > ˌtheoˈretically *adv*

theoretician (ˌθɪərɪˈtɪʃən) *n* a student or user of the theory rather than the practical aspects of a subject

theoretics (ˌθɪəˈrɛtɪks) *n* (*functioning as singular or plural*) the theory of a particular subject. Also called (less commonly): **theoretic**

theorist (ˈθɪərɪst) *n* the originator of a theory; a person who is concerned with theory; a theoretician

theorize *or* **theorise** (ˈθɪəraɪz) *vb* (*intr*) to produce or use theories; speculate > ˌtheoriˈzation *or* ˌtheoriˈsation *n* > ˈtheoˌrizer *or* ˈtheoˌriser *n*

theory (ˈθɪərɪ) *n, pl* **-ries 1** a system of rules, procedures, and assumptions used to produce a result **2** abstract knowledge or reasoning **3** a speculative or conjectural view or idea: *I have a theory about that* **4** an ideal or hypothetical situation (esp in the phrase **in theory**) **5** a set of hypotheses related by logical or mathematical arguments to explain and predict a wide variety of connected phenomena in general terms: *the theory of relativity* **6** a nontechnical name for **hypothesis** (sense 1) [c16 from Late Latin *theōria*, from Greek: a sight, from *theōrein* to gaze upon]

theory-laden *adj* (of an expression) capable of being understood only within the context of a specific theory, as for example *superego*, which requires the apparatus of Freudian theory in explanation

theory of games *n* another name for **game theory**

theos. *abbreviation for* **1** theosophical **2** theosophy

theosophy (θɪˈɒsəfɪ) *n* **1** any of various religious or philosophical systems claiming to be based on or to express an intuitive insight into the divine nature **2** the system of beliefs of the Theosophical Society founded in 1875, claiming to be derived from the sacred writings of Brahmanism and Buddhism, but denying the existence of any personal God [c17 from Medieval Latin *theosophia*, from Late Greek; see THEO-, -SOPHY] > **theosophical** (ˌθɪəˈsɒfɪkəl) *adj* > ˌtheoˈsophically *adv* > theˈosophism *n* > theˈosophist *n*

Thera (ˈθɪərə) *n* a Greek island in the Aegean Sea, in the Cyclades: site of a Minoan settlement and of the volcano that ended Minoan civilization on Crete. Pop: 13 402 (2001). Also called: **Santoríni** Modern Greek name: **Thíra**

therapeutic (ˌθɛrəˈpjuːtɪk) *adj* **1** of or relating to the treatment of disease; curative **2** serving or performed to maintain health: *therapeutic abortion* [c17 from New Latin *therapeuticus*, from Greek *therapeutikos*, from *therapeuein* to minister to, from *theraps* an attendant] > ˌtheraˈpeutically *adv*

therapeutic cloning *n* the permitted creation of cloned human tissues for surgical transplant

therapeutics (ˌθɛrəˈpjuːtɪks) *n* (*functioning as singular*) the branch of medicine concerned with

the treatment of disease

therapist (ˈθɛrəpɪst) *n* a person skilled in a particular type of therapy: *a physical therapist*

therapsid (θəˈræpsɪd) *n* any extinct reptile of the order *Therapsida*, of Permian to Triassic times: considered to be the ancestors of mammals [c20 from New Latin *Therapsida*, from Greek *theraps* attendant]

therapy (ˈθɛrəpɪ) *n, pl* **-pies a** the treatment of physical, mental, or social disorders or disease **b** (*in combination*): *physiotherapy; electrotherapy* [c19 from New Latin *therapia*, from Greek *therapeia* attendance; see THERAPEUTIC]

Theravada (ˌθɛrəˈvɑːdə) *n* the southern school of Buddhism, the name preferred by Hinayana Buddhists for their doctrines [from Pali: doctrine of the elders]

there (ðɛə) *adv* **1** in, at, or to that place, point, case, or respect: *we never go there; I'm afraid I disagree with you there* ▷ *pron* **2** used as a grammatical subject with some verbs, esp *be*, when the true subject is an indefinite or mass noun phrase following the verb as complement: *there is a girl in that office; there doesn't seem to be any water left* ▷ *adj* **3** (*postpositive*) who or which is in that place or position: *that boy there did it* **4** **all there** (*predicative*) having his wits about him; of normal intelligence **5** **so there** an exclamation that usually follows a declaration of refusal or defiance: *you can't have any more, so there!* **6** **there and then** on the spot; immediately; instantly **7** **there it is** that is the state of affairs **8** **there you are a** an expression used when handing a person something requested or desired **b** an exclamation of triumph: *there you are, I knew that would happen!* ▷ *n* **9** that place: *near there; from there* ▷ *interj* **10** an expression of sympathy, as in consoling a child [Old English *thǣr*; related to Old Frisian *thēr*, Old Saxon *thār*, Old High German *thār*, Old Norse, Gothic *thar*]

t

> USAGE In correct usage, the verb should agree with the number of the subject in such constructions as *there is a man waiting* and *there are several people waiting*. However, where the subject is compound, it is common in speech to use the singular as in *there's a police car and an ambulance outside*

thereabouts (ˈðɛərəˌbaʊts) *or* US **thereabout** *adv* near that place, time, amount, etc: *fifty or thereabouts*

thereafter (ˌðɛərˈɑːftə) *adv* from that time on or after that time: *thereafter, he ceased to pay attention*

thereat (ˌðɛərˈæt) *adv rare* **1** at that point or time **2** for that reason

thereby (ˌðɛəˈbaɪ, ˈðɛəˌbaɪ) *adv* **1** by that means; because of that **2** *archaic* by or near that place; thereabouts

therefor (ˌðɛəˈfɔː) *adv archaic* for this, that, or it: *he will be richer therefor*

therefore (ˈðɛəˌfɔː) *sentence connector* **1** thus; hence: used to mark an inference on the speaker's part: *those people have their umbrellas up: therefore, it must be raining* **2** consequently; as a result: *they heard the warning on the radio and therefore took another route*

therefrom (ˌðɛəˈfrɒm) *adv archaic* from that or there: *the roads that lead therefrom*

therein (ˌðɛərˈɪn) *adv formal* in or into that place, thing, etc

thereinafter (ˌðɛərɪnˈɑːftə) *adv formal* from this point on in that document, statement, etc

thereinto (ˌðɛərˈɪntuː) *adv formal* into that place, circumstance, etc

theremin (ˈθɛrəmɪn) *n* an electronic musical instrument, played by moving the hands through electromagnetic fields created by two metal rods [c20 named after Leon *Theremin* (1896-1993), Russian scientist who invented it]

thereof (ˌðɛərˈɒv) *adv formal* **1** of or concerning that or it **2** from or because of that

thereon (ˌðɛərˈɒn) *adv* an archaic word for **thereupon**

thereto (ˌðɛəˈtuː) adv 1 formal to that or it: the form attached thereto 2 obsolete in addition to that

theretofore (ˌðɛətʊˈfɔː) adv formal before that time; previous to that

thereunder (ˌðɛərˈʌndə) adv formal 1 (in documents, etc) below that or it; subsequently in that 2 under the terms or authority of that

thereupon (ˌðɛərəˈpɒn) adv 1 immediately after that; at that point: thereupon, the whole class applauded 2 formal upon that thing, point, subject, etc

therewith (ˌðɛəˈwɪθ, -ˈwɪð) or **therewithal** adv 1 formal with or in addition to that 2 a less common word for **thereupon** (sense 1) 3 archaic by means of or on account of that

Therezina (Portuguese tereˈzina) n the former name of Teresina

theriac (ˈθɪərɪæk) n archaic an ointment or potion of varying composition, used as an antidote to a poison [c14 from Latin thēriaca antidote to poison]

therianthropic (ˌθɪərɪənˈθrɒpɪk) adj 1 (of certain mythical creatures or deities) having a partly animal, partly human form 2 of or relating to such creatures or deities [c19 from Greek thērion wild animal + anthrōpos man] > therianthropism (ˌθɪərɪˈænθrəˌpɪzəm) n

theriomorphic (ˌθɪərɪəʊˈmɔːfɪk) or **theriomorphous** adj (esp of a deity) possessing or depicted in the form of a beast [c19 from Greek thēriomorphos, from thērion wild animal + morphē shape] > ˈtherioˌmorph n

therm (θɜːm) n Brit a unit of heat equal to 100 000 British thermal units. One therm is equal to 1.055 056 × 10⁸ joules [c19 from Greek thermē heat]

thermae (ˈθɜːmiː) pl n public baths or hot springs, esp in ancient Greece or Rome [c17 from Latin, from Greek thermai, pl of thermē heat]

thermaesthesia or US **thermesthesia** (ˌθɜːmɪsˈθiːzɪə) n sensitivity to various degrees of heat and cold [c19 from New Latin, from THERM- + Greek aisthēsis feeling]

thermal (ˈθɜːməl) adj 1 Also: thermic (ˈθɜːmɪk) of, relating to, caused by, or generating heat or increased temperature 2 hot or warm: thermal baths; thermal spring 3 (of garments or fabrics) specially designed so as to have exceptional heat-retaining properties ▷ n 4 meteorol a column of rising air caused by local unequal heating of the land surface, and used by gliders and birds to gain height 5 (plural) thermal garments, esp underclothes > ˈthermally adv

thermal barrier n an obstacle to flight at very high speeds as a result of the heating effect of air friction. Also called: **heat barrier**

thermal conductivity n a measure of the ability of a substance to conduct heat, determined by the rate of heat flow normally through an area in the substance divided by the area and by minus the component of the temperature gradient in the direction of flow: measured in watts per metre per kelvin. Symbol: λ or k Sometimes shortened to: conductivity

thermal efficiency n the ratio of the work done by a heat engine to the energy supplied to it. Compare **efficiency**

thermal equator n an imaginary line round the earth running through the point on each meridian with the highest average temperature. It lies mainly to the north because of the larger landmasses and therefore greater summer heating

thermal imaging n the use of heat-sensitive equipment to detect or provide images of people or things

thermalize or **thermalise** (ˈθɜːməˌlaɪz) vb physics to undergo or cause to undergo a process in which neutrons lose energy in a moderator and become thermal neutrons > ˌthermaliˈzation or ˌthermaliˈsation n

thermal neutrons pl n slow neutrons that are approximately in thermal equilibrium with a

moderator. They have a distribution of speeds similar to that of the molecules of a gas at the temperature of the moderator. Data concerning nuclear interactions are often given for standard thermal neutrons of speed 2200 metres per second, which is approximately the most probable speed at normal laboratory temperatures

thermal noise n electrical noise caused by thermal agitation of conducting electrons

thermal printer n computing another name for **electrothermal printer**

thermal reactor n a nuclear reactor in which most of the fission is caused by thermal neutrons

thermal shock n a fluctuation in temperature causing stress in a material. It often results in fracture, esp in brittle materials such as ceramics

thermette (θɜːˈmɛt) n NZ a device, used outdoors, for boiling water rapidly

Thermidor French (tɛrmidɔr) n the month of heat: the eleventh month of the French revolutionary calendar, extending from July 20 to Aug 18. Also called: **Fervidor** [c19 from French, from Greek thermē heat + dōron gift]

thermion (ˈθɜːmɪən) n physics an electron or ion emitted by a body at high temperature

thermionic (ˌθɜːmɪˈɒnɪk) adj of, relating to, or operated by electrons emitted from materials at high temperatures: a thermionic valve

thermionic current n an electric current produced between two electrodes as a result of electrons emitted by thermionic emission

thermionic emission n the emission of electrons from very hot solids or liquids: used for producing electrons in valves, electron microscopes, X-ray tubes, etc

thermionics (ˌθɜːmɪˈɒnɪks) n (functioning as singular) the branch of electronics concerned with the emission of electrons by hot bodies and with devices based on this effect, esp the study and design of thermionic valves

thermionic valve or esp US and Canadian **tube** n an electronic valve in which electrons are emitted from a heated rather than a cold cathode

thermistor (θɜːˈmɪstə) n a semiconductor device having a resistance that decreases rapidly with an increase in temperature. It is used for temperature measurement, to compensate for temperature variations in a circuit, etc [c20 from THERMO- + (RES)ISTOR]

Thermit (ˈθɜːmɪt) or **Thermite** (ˈθɜːmaɪt) n trademark a mixture of aluminium powder and a metal oxide, such as iron oxide, which when ignited reacts with the evolution of heat to yield aluminium oxide and molten metal: used for welding and in some types of incendiary bombs

thermite process n another name for **aluminothermy**

thermo- or before a vowel **therm-** combining form related to, caused by, or measuring heat: thermodynamics; thermophile [from Greek thermos hot, thermē heat]

thermobaric (ˌθɜːməʊˈbærɪk) adj (of an explosive device or explosion) detonated by means of an explosive substance reacting spontaneously with air

thermobarograph (ˌθɜːməʊˈbærəˌɡrɑːf, -ˌɡræf) n a device that simultaneously records the temperature and pressure of the atmosphere

thermobarometer (ˌθɜːməʊbəˈrɒmɪtə) n an apparatus that provides an accurate measurement of pressure by observation of the change in the boiling point of a fluid

thermochemistry (ˌθɜːməʊˈkɛmɪstrɪ) n the branch of chemistry concerned with the study and measurement of the heat evolved or absorbed during chemical reactions > ˌthermoˈchemical adj > ˌthermoˈchemically adv > ˌthermoˈchemist n

thermochromism (ˌθɜːməʊˈkrəʊmɪzəm) n a phenomenon in which certain dyes made from liquid crystals change colour reversibly when their temperature is changed > ˈthermoˈchromy n > ˌthermoˈchromic adj

thermocline (ˈθɜːməʊˌklaɪn) n a temperature gradient in a thermally stratified body of water, such as a lake

thermocouple (ˈθɜːməʊˌkʌpəl) n 1 a device for measuring temperature consisting of a pair of wires of different metals or semiconductors joined at both ends. One junction is at the temperature to be measured, the second at a fixed temperature. The electromotive force generated depends upon the temperature difference 2 a similar device with only one junction between two dissimilar metals or semiconductors [c19 from THERMO- + COUPLE]

thermodynamic (ˌθɜːməʊdaɪˈnæmɪk) or **thermodynamical** adj 1 of or concerned with thermodynamics 2 determined by or obeying the laws of thermodynamics > ˌthermodyˈnamically adv

thermodynamic equilibrium n the condition of an isolated system in which the quantities that specify its properties, such as pressure, temperature, etc, all remain unchanged. Sometimes shortened to: **equilibrium**

thermodynamics (ˌθɜːməʊdaɪˈnæmɪks) n (functioning as singular) the branch of physical science concerned with the interrelationship and interconversion of different forms of energy and the behaviour of macroscopic systems in terms of certain basic quantities, such as pressure, temperature, etc. See also **law of thermodynamics**

thermodynamic temperature n temperature defined in terms of the laws of thermodynamics and not in terms of the properties of any real material. It is usually expressed on the Kelvin scale. Also called: **absolute temperature**

thermoelectric (ˌθɜːməʊɪˈlɛktrɪk) or **thermoelectrical** adj 1 of, relating to, used in, or operated by the generation of an electromotive force by the Seebeck effect or the Thomson effect: a thermoelectric thermometer 2 of, relating to, used in, or operated by the production or absorption of heat by the Peltier effect: a thermoelectric cooler > ˌthermoeˈlectrically adv

thermoelectric effect n another name for the **Seebeck effect** or **Peltier effect**

thermoelectricity (ˌθɜːməʊɪlɛkˈtrɪsɪtɪ) n 1 electricity generated by a thermocouple 2 the study of the relationship between heat and electrical energy. See also **Seebeck effect, Peltier effect**

thermoelectron (ˌθɜːməʊɪˈlɛktrɒn) n an electron emitted at high temperature, such as one produced in a thermionic valve

thermogenesis (ˌθɜːməʊˈdʒɛnɪsɪs) n the production of heat by metabolic processes > thermogenous (θɜːˈmɒdʒɪnəs), thermogenetic (ˌθɜːməʊdʒɪˈnɛtɪk) or ˌthermoˈgenic adj

thermogram (ˈθɜːməʊˌɡræm) n 1 med a picture produced by thermography, using photographic film sensitive to infrared radiation 2 the record produced by a thermograph

thermograph (ˈθɜːməʊˌɡrɑːf, -ˌɡræf) n a type of thermometer that produces a continuous record of a fluctuating temperature

thermography (θɜːˈmɒɡrəfɪ) n 1 any writing, printing, or recording process involving the use of heat 2 a printing process which produces raised characters by heating special powder or ink placed on the paper 3 med the measurement and recording of heat produced by a part of the body: used in the diagnosis of tumours, esp of the breast (**mammothermography**), which have an increased blood supply and therefore generate more heat than normal tissue. See also thermogram. > therˈmographer n > thermographic (ˌθɜːməʊˈɡræfɪk) adj

thermojunction (ˌθɜːməʊˈdʒʌŋkʃən) n a point of electrical contact between two dissimilar metals across which a voltage appears, the magnitude of which depends on the temperature of the contact and the nature of the metals. See also **Seebeck effect**

thermolabile (ˌθɜːməʊˈleɪbɪl) *adj* (of certain biochemical and chemical compounds) easily decomposed or subject to a loss of characteristic properties by the action of heat: *a thermolabile enzyme*. Compare **thermostable** (sense 1) [C20 from THERMO- + LABILE]

thermoluminescence (ˌθɜːməʊˌluːmɪˈnɛsəns) *n* phosphorescence of certain materials or objects as a result of heating. It is caused by pre-irradiation of the material inducing defects which are removed by the heat, the energy released appearing as light: used in archaeological dating > ˌthermoˌlumiˈnescent *adj*

thermolysis (θɜːˈmɒlɪsɪs) *n* **1** *physiol* loss of heat from the body **2** the dissociation of a substance as a result of heating > **thermolytic** (ˌθɜːməʊˈlɪtɪ) *adj*

thermomagnetic (ˌθɜːməʊmægˈnɛtɪk) *adj* of or concerned with the relationship between heat and magnetism, esp the change in temperature of a body when it is magnetized or demagnetized. Former term: **pyromagnetic**

thermometer (θəˈmɒmɪtə) *n* an instrument used to measure temperature, esp one in which a thin column of liquid, such as mercury, expands and contracts within a graduated sealed tube. See also **clinical thermometer, gas thermometer, resistance thermometer, thermocouple, pyrometer**

thermometry (θəˈmɒmɪtrɪ) *n* the branch of physics concerned with the measurement of temperature and the design and use of thermometers and pyrometers > **thermometric** (ˌθɜːməˈmɛtrɪk) *or* ˌthermoˈmetrical *adj* > ˌthermoˈmetrically *adv*

thermomotor (ˌθɜːməʊˈməʊtə) *n* an engine that produces force from the expansion of a heated fluid

thermonasty (ˈθɜːməʊˌnæstɪ) *n* *botany* a nastic movement in response to a temperature change, as occurs in the opening of certain flowers

thermonuclear (ˌθɜːməʊˈnjuːklɪə) *adj* **1** involving nuclear fusion: *a thermonuclear reaction* **2** involving thermonuclear weapons: *a thermonuclear war*

thermonuclear bomb *n* another name for **fusion bomb**

thermonuclear reaction *n* a nuclear fusion reaction occurring at a very high temperature: responsible for the energy produced in the sun, nuclear weapons, and fusion reactors. See **nuclear fusion, hydrogen bomb**

thermoperiodism (ˌθɜːməʊˈpɪərɪədɪzəm) *or* **thermoperiodicity** (ˌθɜːməʊˌpɪərɪəˈdɪsɪtɪ) *n* *botany* the response of a plant to cycles of temperature fluctuation > ˌthermoˌperiˈodic *adj*

thermophile (ˈθɜːməʊˌfaɪl) *or* **thermophil** (ˈθɜːməʊˌfɪl) *n* **1** an organism, esp a bacterium or plant, that thrives under warm conditions ▷ *adj* **2** thriving under warm conditions > ˌthermoˈphilic *or* thermophilous (θɜːˈmɒfɪləs) *adj*

thermopile (ˈθɜːməʊˌpaɪl) *n* an instrument for detecting and measuring heat radiation or for generating a thermoelectric current. It consists of a number of thermocouple junctions, usually joined together in series [C19 from THERMO- + PILE[1] (in the sense: voltaic pile)]

thermoplastic (ˌθɜːməʊˈplæstɪk) *adj* **1** (of a material, esp a synthetic plastic or resin) becoming soft when heated and rehardening on cooling without appreciable change of properties. Compare **thermosetting** ▷ *n* **2** a synthetic plastic or resin, such as polystyrene, with these properties > **thermoplasticity** (ˌθɜːməʊplæˈstɪsɪtɪ) *n*

Thermopylae (θəˈmɒpɪˌliː) *n* (in ancient Greece) a narrow pass between the mountains and the sea linking Locris and Thessaly: a defensible position on a traditional invasion route from N Greece; scene of a famous battle (480 BC) in which a greatly outnumbered Greek army under Leonidas fought to the death to delay the advance of the Persians during their attempted conquest of Greece

Thermos *or* **Thermos flask** (ˈθɜːməs) *n* *trademark* a type of stoppered vacuum flask used to preserve the temperature of its contents. See also **Dewar flask**

thermoscope (ˈθɜːməˌskəʊp) *n* a device that indicates a change in temperature, esp one that does not measure the actual temperature > **thermoscopic** (ˌθɜːməˈskɒpɪk) *or* ˌthermoˈscopical *adj* > ˌthermoˈscopically *adv*

thermosetting (ˌθɜːməʊˈsɛtɪŋ) *adj* (of a material, esp a synthetic plastic or resin) hardening permanently after one application of heat and pressure. Thermosetting plastics, such as phenol-formaldehyde, cannot be remoulded. Compare **thermoplastic**

thermosiphon (ˌθɜːməʊˈsaɪfən) *n* a system in which a coolant is circulated by convection caused by a difference in density between the hot and cold portions of the liquid

thermosphere (ˈθɜːməˌsfɪə) *n* an atmospheric layer lying between the mesosphere and the exosphere, reaching an altitude of about 400 kilometres where the temperature is over 1000°C

thermostable (ˌθɜːməʊˈsteɪbªl) *adj* **1** (of certain chemical and biochemical compounds) capable of withstanding moderate heat without loss of characteristic properties: *a thermostable plastic*. Compare **thermolabile 2** not affected by high temperatures > **thermostability** (ˌθɜːməʊstəˈbɪlɪtɪ) *n*

thermostat (ˈθɜːməˌstæt) *n* **1** a device that maintains a system at a constant temperature. It often consists of a bimetallic strip that bends as it expands and contracts with temperature, thus breaking and making contact with an electrical power supply **2** a similar device that actuates equipment, such as a sprinkler, when a certain temperature is reached > ˌthermoˈstatic *adj* > ˌthermoˈstatically *adv*

thermostatics (ˌθɜːməˈstætɪks) *n* (*functioning as singular*) the branch of science concerned with thermal equilibrium

thermotaxis (ˌθɜːməʊˈtæksɪs) *n* the directional movement of an organism in response to the stimulus of a source of heat > ˌthermoˈtaxic *adj*

thermotensile (ˌθɜːməʊˈtɛnsaɪl) *adj* of or relating to tensile strength in so far as it is affected by temperature

thermotherapy (ˌθɜːməʊˈθɛrəpɪ) *n* *med* treatment of a bodily structure or part by the application of heat

thermotolerant (ˌθɜːməʊˈtɒlərənt) *adj* (of plants) able to tolerate, but not thriving in, high temperatures

thermotropism (ˌθɜːməʊˈtrəʊpɪzəm) *n* the directional growth of a plant in response to the stimulus of heat > ˌthermoˈtropic *adj*

-thermy *n combining form* indicating heat: *diathermy* [from New Latin -*thermia*, from Greek *thermē*] > -**thermic** *or* -**thermal** *adj combining form*

theroid (ˈθɪərɔɪd) *adj* of, relating to, or resembling a beast [C19 from Greek *thēroeidēs*, from *thēr* wild animal; see -OID]

therophyte (ˈθɪərəˌfaɪt) *n* a plant that overwinters as a seed [from Greek *theros* summer + -PHYTE]

theropod (ˈθɪərəˌpɒd) *n* any bipedal carnivorous saurischian dinosaur of the suborder *Theropoda*, having strong hind legs and grasping hands. They lived in Triassic to Cretaceous times and included tyrannosaurs and megalosaurs [C19 from New Latin *theropoda*, from Greek *thēr* beast + *pous* foot] > **theropodan** (θɪˈrɒpədªn) *n, adj*

Thersites (θəˈsaɪtiːz) *n* the ugliest and most evil-tongued fighter on the Greek side in the Trojan War, killed by Achilles when he mocked him

thersitical (θəˈsɪtɪkªl) *adj rare* abusive and loud [C17 from THERSITES]

thesaurus (θɪˈsɔːrəs) *n, pl* -ruses *or* -ri (-raɪ) **1** a book containing systematized lists of synonyms and related words **2** a dictionary of selected words or topics **3** *rare* a treasury [C18 from Latin,

Greek: TREASURE]

these (ðiːz) *determiner* **a** the form of **this** used before a plural noun: *these men* **b** (*as pronoun*): *I don't much care for these*

Theseus (ˈθiːsɪəs) *n* *Greek myth* a hero of Attica, noted for his many great deeds, among them the slaying of the Minotaur, the conquest of the Amazons, whose queen he married, and participation in the Calydonian hunt > **Thesean** (θɪˈsiːən) *adj*

thesis (ˈθiːsɪs) *n, pl* -ses (-siːz) **1** a dissertation resulting from original research, esp when submitted by a candidate for a degree or diploma **2** a doctrine maintained or promoted in argument **3** a subject for a discussion or essay **4** an unproved statement, esp one put forward as a premise in an argument **5** *music* the downbeat of a bar, as indicated in conducting **6** (in classical prosody) the syllable or part of a metrical foot not receiving the ictus. Compare **arsis 7** *philosophy* the first stage in the Hegelian dialectic, that is challenged by the antithesis [C16 via Late Latin from Greek: a placing, from *tithenai* to place]

thespian (ˈθɛspɪən) *adj* **1** of or relating to drama and the theatre; dramatic ▷ *n* **2** *often facetious* an actor or actress [C19 from Thespis, the 6th century BC Greek poet, regarded as the founder of tragic drama]

Thess. *Bible abbreviation for* Thessalonians

Thessalian (θɛˈseɪlɪən) *adj* **1** of or relating to the Greek region of Thessaly or its inhabitants ▷ *n* **2** a native or inhabitant of Thessaly

Thessalonian (ˌθɛsəˈləʊnɪən) *adj* **1** of or relating to ancient Thessalonica (modern Salonika) ▷ *n* **2** an inhabitant of ancient Thessalonica

Thessalonians (ˌθɛsəˈləʊnɪənz) *n* (*functioning as singular*) either of two books of the New Testament (in full **The First and Second Epistles of Paul the Apostle to the Thessalonians**)

Thessaloníki (*Greek* θɛsalɔˈniki) *n* a port in NE Greece, in central Macedonia at the head of the **Gulf of Salonika** (an inlet of the Aegean): capital of the Roman province of Macedonia; university (1926). Pop: 824 000 (2005 est). Latin name: Thessalonica (ˌθɛsəˈlɒnɪkə) English name: **Salonika** *or* **Salonica**

Thessaly (ˈθɛsəlɪ) *n* a region of E Central Greece, on the Aegean: an extensive fertile plain, edged with mountains. Pop: 609 100 (2001). Area: 14 037 sq km (5418 sq miles). Modern Greek name: Thessalía (ˌθɛsaˈljia)

theta (ˈθiːtə) *n* **1** the eighth letter of the Greek alphabet (Θ, θ), a consonant, transliterated as *th* **2** the lower-case form of this letter used in phonetic transcription to represent the voiceless dental fricative *th* as in *thick, both*. Compare **edh** [C17 from Greek, of Semitic origin; compare Hebrew *tēth*]

Thetford Mines (ˈθɛtfəd) *n* a city in SE Canada, in S Quebec: asbestos industry. Pop: 21 651 (2001)

thetic (ˈθɛtɪk) *adj* **1** (in classical prosody) of, bearing, or relating to a metrical stress **2** positive and arbitrary; prescriptive [C17 from Greek *thetikos*, from *thetos* laid down, from *tithenai* to place] > ˈthetically *adv*

Thetis (ˈθiːtɪs) *n* one of the Nereids and mother of Achilles by Peleus

theurgy (ˈθiːˌɜːdʒɪ) *n, pl* -gies **1 a** the intervention of a divine or supernatural agency in the affairs of man **b** the working of miracles by such intervention **2** beneficent magic as taught and performed by Egyptian Neoplatonists and others [C16 from Late Latin *theūrgia*, from Late Greek *theourgia* the practice of magic, from *theo-* THEO- + -*urgia*, from *ergon* work] > theˈurgic *or* theˈurgical *adj* > theˈurgically *adv* > ˈtheurgist *n*

thew (θjuː) *n* **1** muscle, esp if strong or well-developed **2** (*plural*) muscular strength [Old English *thēaw*; related to Old Saxon, Old High German *thau* discipline, Latin *tuērī* to observe, *tūtus* secure] > ˈthewy *adj* > ˈthewless *adj*

they (ðeɪ) *pron* (*subjective*) **1** refers to people or things other than the speaker or people

t

addressed: *they fight among themselves* **2** refers to unspecified people or people in general not including the speaker or people addressed: *in Australia they have Christmas in the summer* **3** *not standard* refers to an indefinite antecedent such as *one, whoever,* or *anybody*: *if anyone objects, they can go* **4** an archaic word for **those** *blessed are they that mourn* [C12 *thei* from Old Norse *their*, masculine nominative plural, equivalent to Old English *thā*]

USAGE It was formerly considered correct to use *he, him,* or *his* after pronouns such as *everyone, no-one, anyone,* or *someone* as in *everyone did his best*, but it is now more common to use *they, them,* or *their*, and this use has become acceptable in all but the most formal contexts: *everyone did their best*

they'd (ðeɪd) *contraction of* they would *or* they had
they'll (ðeɪl) *contraction of* they will *or* they shall
they're (ðɛə, ˈðeɪə) *contraction of* they are
they've (ðeɪv) *contraction of* they have
THG *abbreviation for* tetrahydrogestrinone
THI *abbreviation for* **temperature-humidity index**
thi- *combining form* a variant of **thio-**
thiamine (ˈθaɪəˌmiːn, -mɪn) *or* **thiamin** (ˈθaɪəmɪn) *n biochem* a soluble white crystalline vitamin that occurs in the outer coat of rice and other grains. It forms part of the vitamin B complex and is essential for carbohydrate metabolism: deficiency leads to nervous disorders and to the disease beriberi. Formula: $C_{12}H_{17}ON_4SCl.H_2O$. Also called: **vitamin B₁, aneurin** [C20 THIO- + (VIT)AMIN]
thiazine (ˈθaɪəˌziːn, -ˌzaɪn) *n* any of a group of organic compounds containing a ring system composed of four carbon atoms, a sulphur atom, and a nitrogen atom
thiazole (ˈθaɪəˌzəʊl) *or* **thiazol** (ˈθaɪəˌzɒl) *n* **1** a colourless liquid with a pungent smell that contains a ring system composed of three carbon atoms, a sulphur atom, and a nitrogen atom. It is used in dyes and fungicides. Formula: C_3H_3NS **2** any of a group of compounds derived from this substance that are used in dyes
thick (θɪk) *adj* **1** of relatively great extent from one surface to the other; fat, broad, or deep: *a thick slice of bread* **2 a** (*postpositive*) of specific fatness: *ten centimetres thick* **b** (*in combination*): *a six-inch-thick wall* **3** having a relatively dense consistency; not transparent: *thick soup* **4** abundantly covered or filled: *a piano thick with dust* **5** impenetrable; dense: *a thick fog* **6** stupid, slow, or insensitive: *a thick person* **7** throaty or badly articulated: *a voice thick with emotion* **8** (of accents, etc) pronounced **9** *informal* very friendly (esp in the phrase **thick as thieves**) **10 a bit thick** *Brit* unfair or excessive **11 a thick ear** *informal* a blow on the ear delivered as punishment, in anger, etc ▷ *adv* **12** in order to produce something thick: *to slice bread thick* **13** profusely; in quick succession (esp in the phrase **thick and fast**) **14 lay it on thick** *informal* **a** to exaggerate a story, statement, etc **b** to flatter excessively ▷ *n* **15** a thick piece or part **16 the thick** the busiest or most intense part **17 through thick and thin** in good times and bad [Old English *thicce*; related to Old Saxon, Old High German *thikki*, Old Norse *thykkr*] > ˈ**thickish** *adj* > ˈ**thickly** *adv*
thick client *n computing* a computer having its own hard drive, as opposed to one on a network where most functions are carried out on a central server. See **thin client**
thicken (ˈθɪkən) *vb* **1** to make or become thick or thicker: *thicken the soup by adding flour* **2** (*intr*) to become more involved: *the plot thickened* > ˈ**thickener** *n*
thickening (ˈθɪkənɪŋ) *n* **1** something added to a liquid to thicken it **2** a thickened part or piece
thicket (ˈθɪkɪt) *n* a dense growth of small trees, shrubs, and similar plants [Old English *thiccet*; see THICK]
thickhead (ˈθɪkˌhɛd) *n* **1** a stupid or ignorant person; fool **2** Also called: **whistler** any of various Australian and SE Asian songbirds of the family *Muscicapidae* (flycatchers, etc) > ˌ**thick**ˈ**headed** *adj* > ˌ**thick**ˈ**headedness** *n*
thickie *or* **thicky** (ˈθɪkɪ) *n, pl* **-ies** *Brit slang* a variant of **thicko**
thick-knee *n* another name for **stone curlew** [C19 so called because it has thick knee joints]
thickleaf (ˈθɪkˌliːf) *n, pl* **-leaves** any of various succulent plants of the crassulaceous genus *Crassula*, having sessile or short-stalked fleshy leaves
thickness (ˈθɪknɪs) *n* **1** the state or quality of being thick **2** the dimension through an object, as opposed to length or width **3** a layer of something **4** a thick part
thicko (ˈθɪkəʊ) *n, pl* **thickos** *or* **thickoes** *Brit slang* a slow-witted unintelligent person. Also: **thickie, thicky**
thickset (ˌθɪkˈsɛt) *adj* **1** stocky in build; sturdy **2** densely planted or placed ▷ *n* **3** a rare word for **thicket**
thick-skinned *adj* insensitive to criticism or hints; not easily upset or affected
thick-witted *or* **thick-skulled** *adj* stupid, dull, foolish, or slow to learn > ˌ**thick-**ˈ**wittedly** *adv* > ˌ**thick-**ˈ**wittedness** *n*
thief (θiːf) *n, pl* **thieves** (θiːvz) **1** a person who steals something from another **2** *criminal law* a person who commits theft [Old English *thēof*; related to Old Frisian *thiāf*, Old Saxon *thiof*, Old High German *diob*, Old Norse *thjōfr*, Gothic *thiufs*] > ˈ**thievish** *adj* > ˈ**thievishly** *adv* > ˈ**thievishness** *n*
thieve (θiːv) *vb* to steal (someone's possessions) [Old English *thēofian*, from *thēof* THIEF] > ˈ**thievery** *n*
thieving (ˈθiːvɪŋ) *adj* given to stealing other people's possessions
thigh (θaɪ) *n* **1** the part of the leg between the hip and the knee in man **2** the corresponding part in other vertebrates and insects ▷ Related adjectives: **crural, femoral** [Old English *thēh*; related to Old Frisian *thiāch*, Old High German *dioh* thigh, Old Norse *thjō* buttock, Old Slavonic *tyku* fat]
thighbone (ˈθaɪˌbəʊn) *n* a nontechnical name for the **femur**
thigmotaxis (ˌθɪgməˈtæksɪs) *n* another name for **stereotaxis** [C19 from Greek *thigma* touch + -TAXIS] > ˌ**thigmo**ˈ**tactic** *adj* > ˌ**thigmo**ˈ**tactically** *adv*
thigmotropism (ˌθɪgməʊˈtrəʊpɪzəm) *n* the directional growth of a plant, in response to the stimulus of direct contact. Also called: **haptotropism, stereotropism** [C19 from Greek *thigma* touch + -TROPISM] > ˌ**thigmo**ˈ**tropic** *adj*
thill (θɪl) *n archaic* another word for **shaft** (sense 6) [C14 perhaps related to Old English *thille* board, planking, Old High German *dilla* plank, Old Norse *thili*]
thimble (ˈθɪmbᵊl) *n* **1** a cap of metal, plastic, etc, used to protect the end of the finger when sewing **2** any small metal cap resembling this **3** *nautical* a loop of metal having a groove at its outer edge for a rope or cable, for lining the inside of an eye **4** short for **thimbleful** [Old English *thȳmel* thumbstall, from *thūma* THUMB]
thimbleful (ˈθɪmbᵊlˌfʊl) *n* a very small amount, esp of a liquid
thimblerig (ˈθɪmbᵊlˌrɪg) *n* **1** a game in which the operator rapidly moves about three inverted thimbles, often with sleight of hand, one of which conceals a token, the other player betting on which thimble the token is under ▷ *vb* **-rigs, -rigging, -rigged** (*tr*) **2** to cheat or swindle, as in this game [C19 from THIMBLE + *rig* (in obsolete sense: a trick, scheme)] > ˈ**thimble**ˌ**rigger** *n*
thimbleweed (ˈθɪmbᵊlˌwiːd) *n US* any of various plants having a thimble-shaped fruit, esp an American anemone, *Anemone virginiana*, and a rudbeckia, *Rudbeckia laciniata*
thimblewit (ˈθɪmbᵊlˌwɪt) *n chiefly US* a silly or dimwitted person; dunce > ˈ**thimble**ˌ**witted** *adj*
Thimbu (ˈθɪmbuː) *or* **Thimphu** (ˈθɪmfuː) *n* the capital of Bhutan, in the west in the foothills of the E Himalayas: became the official capital in 1962. Pop: 40 000 (2005 est)
thimerosal (θaɪˈmɛrəˌsæl) *n* a creamy white crystalline compound of mercury, used in solution as an antiseptic. Formula: $C_9H_9HgNaO_2S$ [C20 from THIO- + MER(CURY) + SAL(ICYLATE)]
thin (θɪn) *adj* **thinner, thinnest 1** of relatively small extent from one side or surface to the other; fine or narrow **2** slim or lean **3** sparsely placed; meagre: *thin hair* **4** of relatively low density or viscosity: *a thin liquid* **5** weak; poor; insufficient: *a thin disguise* **6** (of a photographic negative) having low density, usually insufficient to produce a satisfactory positive **7** *mountaineering* a climb or pitch on which the holds are few and small **8 thin on the ground** few in number; scarce ▷ *adv* **9** in order to produce something thin: *to cut bread thin* ▷ *vb* **thins, thinning, thinned 10** to make or become thin or sparse [Old English *thynne*; related to Old Frisian *thenne*, Old Saxon, Old High German *thunni*, Old Norse *thunnr*, Latin *tenuis* thin, Greek *teinein* to stretch] > ˈ**thinly** *adv* > ˈ**thinness** *n*
thin client *n computing* a computer on a network where most functions are carried out on a central server. See **thick client**
thine (ðaɪn) *determiner archaic* **a** (*preceding a vowel*) of, belonging to, or associated in some way with you (thou): *thine eyes* **b** (*as pronoun*): *thine is the greatest burden* ▷ Compare **thy** [Old English *thīn*; related to Old High German *dīn*, Gothic *theina*]
thin-film *adj* (of an electronic component, device, or circuit) composed of one or more extremely thin layers of metal, semiconductor, etc, deposited on a ceramic or glass substrate: *thin-film capacitor*
thing¹ (θɪŋ) *n* **1** an object, fact, affair, circumstance, or concept considered as being a separate entity **2** any inanimate object **3** an object or entity that cannot or need not be precisely named **4** *informal* a person or animal regarded as the object of pity, contempt, etc: *you poor thing* **5** an event or act **6** a thought or statement **7** *law* any object or right that may be the subject of property (as distinguished from a person) **8** a device, means, or instrument **9** (*often plural*) a possession, article of clothing, etc **10** *informal* the normal pattern of behaviour in a particular context: *not interested in the marriage thing* **11** *informal* a mental attitude, preoccupation or obsession (esp in the phrase **have a thing about**) **12** an activity or mode of behaviour satisfying to one's personality (esp in the phrase **do one's (own) thing**) **13 the done thing** acceptable or normal behaviour **14 the thing** the latest fashion **15 be on to a good thing** to be in a profitable situation or position **16 make a thing of** to make a fuss about; exaggerate the importance of [Old English *thing* assembly; related to Old Norse *thing* assembly, Old High German *ding* assembly]
thing² (θɪŋ, tɪŋ) *n* (*often capital*) a law court or public assembly in the Scandinavian countries. Also: **ting** [C19 from Old Norse *thing* assembly (the same word as THING¹)]
thing-in-itself *n* (in the philosophy of Kant) an element of the noumenal rather than the phenomenal world, of which the senses give no knowledge but whose bare existence can be inferred from the nature of experience
thingumabob *or* **thingamabob** (ˈθɪŋəməˌbɒb) *n informal* a person or thing the name of which is unknown, temporarily forgotten, or deliberately overlooked. Also: **thingumajig, thingamajig** (ˈθɪŋəməˌdʒɪg) *or* **thingummy** (ˈθɪŋəmɪ) [C18 from THING¹, with humorous suffix]
think (θɪŋk) *vb* **thinks, thinking, thought 1** (*tr; may take a clause as object*) to consider, judge, or believe: *he thinks my ideas impractical* **2** (*intr*; often foll by *about*) to exercise the mind as in order to make a decision; ponder **3** (*intr*) to be capable of conscious thought: *man is the only animal that thinks* **4** to remember; recollect: *I can't think what his name is* **5** (*intr*; foll by *of*) to make the mental choice (of): *think of a number* **6** (*may take a clause as object or an infinitive*) **a** to expect; suppose: *I didn't think to see you*

here **b** to be considerate or aware enough (to do something): *he did not think to thank them* **7** (*intr*; foll by *of*) to consider; regard: *she thinks of herself as a poet* **8** (*intr*) to focus the attention on being: *think thin; think big* **9** (*tr*) to bring into or out of a specified condition by thinking: *to think away one's fears* **10** **I don't think** *slang* a phrase added to an ironical statement: *you're the paragon of virtue, I don't think* **11** **think again** to reconsider one's decision, opinion, etc **12** **think better of a** to change one's mind about (a course of action, decision, etc) **b** to have a more favourable opinion of (a person) **13** **think much of** (*usually negative*) to have a high opinion of **14** **think nothing of a** to regard as routine, easy, or natural **b** to have no compunction or hesitation about **c** to have a very low opinion of **15** **think twice** to consider carefully before deciding (about something) ▷ *n* **16** *informal* a careful, open-minded assessment: *let's have a fresh think about this problem* **17** (*modifier*) *informal* characterized by or involving thinkers, thinking, or thought: *a think session* **18** **you've** (he's, she's, etc) **got another think coming** *slang* you (etc) are mistaken and will soon have to alter your opinion ▷ See also **think out, think over, think up** [Old English *thencan*; related to Old Frisian *thenza*, Old Saxon *thenkian*, Old High German *denken*, Old Norse *thekkja*, Gothic *thagkjan*] > **'thinker** *n*

thinkable ('θɪŋkəbəl) *adj* able to be conceived or considered; possible; feasible

thinking ('θɪŋkɪŋ) *n* **1** opinion or judgment **2** the process of thought ▷ *adj* **3** (*prenominal*) using or capable of using intelligent thought: *thinking people* **4** **put on one's thinking cap** to ponder a matter or problem

think out *or* **through** *vb* (*tr, adverb*) to consider carefully and rationally in order to reach a conclusion

think over *vb* (*tr, adverb*) to ponder or consider: *to think over a problem*

thinkpiece ('θɪŋk,piːs) *n* a newspaper or magazine article expressing the writer's thoughts or opinions about a particular matter

think-tank *n* *informal* a group of specialists organized by a business enterprise, governmental body, etc, and commissioned to undertake intensive study and research into specified problems

think up *vb* (*tr, adverb*) to invent or devise: *to think up a plan*

thin-layer chromatography *n* a form of chromatography in which components of a liquid mixture are separated by means of a thin layer of adsorbent material coated on a glass, plastic, or foil sheet. Abbreviation: **TLC**

thinner ('θɪnə) *n* (*often plural, functioning as singular*) a solvent, such as turpentine, added to paint or varnish to dilute it, reduce its opacity or viscosity, or increase its penetration into the ground

thin-skinned *adj* sensitive to criticism or hints; easily upset or affected

thio- *or before a vowel* **thi-** *combining form* indicating that a chemical compound contains sulphur, esp denoting that a compound is derived from a specified compound by the replacement of an oxygen atom with a sulphur atom: *thiol; thiosulphate* [from Greek *theion* sulphur]

thioalcohol (,θaɪəʊˈælkəˌhɒl) *n* another name for a **thiol**

thiocarbamide (,θaɪəʊˈkɑːbəˌmaɪd) *n* another name for **thiourea**

thiocyanate (,θaɪəʊˈsaɪəˌneɪt) *n* any salt or ester of thiocyanic acid

thiocyanic acid (,θaɪəʊsaɪˈænɪk) *n* an unstable acid known in the form of thiocyanate salts. Formula: HSCN

thio-ether (,θaɪəʊˈiːθə) *n* any of a class of organic compounds in which a sulphur atom is bound to two hydrocarbon groups

thiofuran (,θaɪəʊˈfjʊəræn) *n* another name for **thiophen** [C20 from THIO- + FURAN]

thiol ('θaɪɒl) *n* any of a class of sulphur-

containing organic compounds with the formula RSH, where R is an organic group. Also called (not in technical usage): **mercaptan**

thionate ('θaɪəˌneɪt) *n* any salt or ester of thionic acid

thionic (θaɪˈɒnɪk) *adj* of, relating to, or containing sulphur

thionine ('θaɪəʊˌniːn, -ˌnaɪn) *or* **thionin** ('θaɪənɪn) *n* **1** a crystalline derivative of thiazine used as a violet dye to stain microscope specimens **2** any of a class of related dyes [C19 by shortening, from *ergothioneine*, a crystalline betaine found in ergot and blood]

thionyl ('θaɪənɪl) *n* (*modifier*) of, consisting of, or containing the divalent group SO: *a thionyl group or radical; thionyl chloride.* Also: **sulphinyl** [C19 *thion-*, from Greek *theion* sulphur + -YL]

thiopental sodium (,θaɪəʊˈpɛntæl) *n* a barbiturate drug used in medicine as an intravenous general anaesthetic. Formula: $C_{11}H_{17}NaN_2O_2S$. Also called: **Sodium Pentothal.** See also **truth drug**

thiophen ('θaɪəʊˌfɛn) *or* **thiophene** ('θaɪəʊˌfiːn) *n* a colourless liquid heterocyclic compound found in the benzene fraction of coal tar and manufactured from butane and sulphur. It has an odour resembling that of benzene and is used as a solvent and in the manufacture of dyes, pharmaceuticals, and resins. Formula: C_4H_4S. Also called: **thiofuran**

thiosinamine (,θaɪəʊˈsɪnəˌmiːn, -sɪˈnæmɪn) *n* a white crystalline bitter-tasting compound with a slight garlic-like odour, occurring in mustard oil and used in organic synthesis; 1-allyl-2-thiourea. Formula: $CH_2:CHCH_2NHCSNH_2$ [C19 from THIO- + *sin-* (from Latin *sināpis* mustard) + AMINE]

thiosulphate (,θaɪəʊˈsʌlfeɪt) *n* any salt of thiosulphuric acid

thiosulphuric acid (,θaɪəʊsʌlˈfjʊərɪk) *n* an unstable acid known only in solutions and in the form of its salts. Formula: $H_2S_2O_3$

thiouracil (,θaɪəʊˈjʊərəsɪl) *n* a white crystalline water-insoluble substance with an intensely bitter taste, used in medicine to treat hyperthyroidism; 2-thio-4-oxypyrimidine. Formula: $C_4H_4N_2OS$ [from THIO- + *uracil* (URO-¹ + AC(ETIC) + -il -ILE)]

thiourea (,θaɪəʊˈjʊərɪə) *n* a white water-soluble crystalline substance with a bitter taste that forms addition compounds with metal ions and is used in photographic fixing, rubber vulcanization, and the manufacture of synthetic resins. Formula: H_2NCSNH_2

third (θɜːd) *adj* (*usually prenominal*) **1 a** coming after the second and preceding the fourth in numbering or counting order, position, time, etc; being the ordinal number of *three*: often written 3rd **b** (*as noun*): *he arrives on the third; the third got a prize* **2** rated, graded, or ranked below the second level **3** denoting the third from lowest forward ratio of a gearbox in a motor vehicle ▷ *n* **4 a** one of three equal or nearly equal parts of an object, quantity, etc **b** (*as modifier*): *a third part* **5** the fraction equal to one divided by three (1/3) **6** the forward ratio above second of a gearbox in a motor vehicle. In some vehicles it is the top gear **7 a** the interval between one note and another three notes away from it counting inclusively along the diatonic scale **b** one of two notes constituting such an interval in relation to the other. See also **interval** (sense 5), **major** (sense 14a), **minor** (sense 4d) **8** *Brit* an honours degree of the third and usually the lowest class. Full term: **third class honours degree 9** (*plural*) goods of a standard lower than that of seconds ▷ *adv* **10** Also: **thirdly** in the third place ▷ *sentence connector* **11** Also: **thirdly** as the third point: linking what follows with the previous statements as in a speech or argument [Old English *thirda*, variant of *thridda*; related to Old Frisian *thredda*, Old Saxon *thriddio*, Old High German *dritto*, Old Norse *thrithi*, Latin *tertius*] > **'thirdly** *adv*

Third Age *n* the old age, esp when viewed as an opportunity for travel, further education, etc

third class *n* **1** the class or grade next in value, quality, etc, to the second ▷ *adj* (**third-class** *when prenominal*) **2** of the class or grade next in value, quality, etc, to the second **3** of or denoting the class of accommodation in a hotel, on a ship, etc, next in quality and price to the second: usually the cheapest **4** (in the US and Canada) of or relating to a class of mail consisting largely of unsealed printed matter **5** *Brit* See **third** (sense 8) ▷ *adv* **6** by third-class mail, transport, etc

third degree *n* *informal* torture or bullying, esp used to extort confessions or information

third-degree burn *n* *pathol* See **burn**¹ (sense 22)

third dimension *n* the additional dimension by which a solid object may be distinguished from a two-dimensional drawing or picture of it or from any planar object

third estate *n* the third order or class in a country or society divided into estates, esp for representation in a parliament; the commons, townsmen, or middle class

third eye *n* the pineal gland, believed by some people to be the source of spiritual insight

third eyelid *n* another name for **nictitating membrane**

third house *n* *US* a political lobby for a special interest

Third International *n* another name for **Comintern**

third man *n* *cricket* **a** a fielding position on the off side near the boundary behind the batsman's wicket **b** a fielder in this position

third man argument *n* (in the philosophy of Aristotle) the argument against the existence of Platonic Forms that since the Form of Man is itself a perfect man, a further form (the "third" man) would be required to explain this, and so ad infinitum

Third Market *n* a market established by the London Stock Exchange in 1987 to trade in shares in companies required to provide less detailed information than that required by the main market or the unlisted securities market

Third Order *n* *RC Church* a religious society of laymen affiliated to one of the religious orders and following a mitigated form of religious rule

third party *n* **1** a person who is involved by chance or only incidentally in a legal proceeding, agreement, or other transaction, esp one against whom a defendant claims indemnity ▷ *adj* **2** *insurance* providing protection against liability caused by accidental injury or death of other persons or damage to their property: *third-party insurance*

third person *n* a grammatical category of pronouns and verbs used when referring to objects or individuals other than the speaker or his addressee(s)

third rail *n* an extra rail from which an electric train picks up current by means of a sliding collector to feed power to its motors

third-rate *adj* not of high quality; mediocre or inferior > **'third-'rater** *n*

third reading *n* (in a legislative assembly) **1** *Brit* the process of discussing the committee's report on a bill **2** *US* the final consideration of a bill

Third Reich *n* See **Reich**¹ (sense 4)

Third Republic *n* in France **1** the governmental system established after the fall of Napoleon III in the Franco-Prussian War and lasting until the German occupation of 1940 **2** the period during which this governmental system functioned (1870–1940)

third space *n* *informal* the coffee shop considered as an alternative to a bar or restaurant as a place to socialize outside the home

thirdstream ('θɜːd,striːm) *adj* **1** (of music) combining jazz and classical elements ▷ *n* **2** such music

Third Way *n* **a** a political ideology that seeks to

combine egalitarian and individualist policies, and elements of socialism and capitalism **b** (*as modifier*): *Third Way government*

Third World *n* the less economically advanced countries of Africa, Asia, and Latin America collectively, esp when viewed as underdeveloped and as neutral in the East-West alignment. Also called: **developing world**

thirl[1] (θɜːl) *vb* (*tr*) *dialect* **a** to bore or drill **b** to thrill [Old English *thyrelian*, from *thyrel* hole; see NOSTRIL]

thirl[2] (θɪrl, θɜːl) *vb* (*tr*) *chiefly Scot* to enslave; bind [C16 variant of earlier *thrill* THRALL]

thirlage (ˈθɜːlɪdʒ) *n* *Scots law* (formerly) **1** an obligation imposed upon tenants of certain lands requiring them to have their grain ground at a specified mill **2** the fee paid for grinding the grain [C16 variant of earlier *thrillage*, from *thrill*, Scottish variant of THRALL]

Thirlmere (ˈθɜːlmɪə) *n* a lake in NW England, in Cumbria in the Lake District: provides part of Manchester's water supply. Length: 6 km (4 miles)

thirst (θɜːst) *n* **1** a craving to drink, accompanied by a feeling of dryness in the mouth and throat **2** an eager longing, craving, or yearning: *a thirst for knowledge* ▷ *vb* (*intr*) **3** to feel a thirst: *to thirst for a drink; to thirst after righteousness* [Old English *thyrstan*, from *thurst* thirst; related to Old Norse *thyrsta* to thirst, Old High German *dursten* to thirst, Latin *torrēre* to parch]

thirsty (ˈθɜːstɪ) *adj* **thirstier, thirstiest** **1** feeling a desire to drink **2** dry; arid: *the thirsty soil* **3** (foll by *for*) feeling an eager desire: *thirsty for information* **4** causing thirst: *thirsty work* > ˈ**thirstily** *adv* > ˈ**thirstiness** *n*

thirteen (ˈθɜːˈtiːn) *n* **1** the cardinal number that is the sum of ten and three and is a prime number. See also **number** (sense 1) **2** a numeral, 13, XIII, etc, representing this number **3** the amount or quantity that is three more than ten; baker's dozen **4** something represented by, representing, or consisting of 13 units ▷ *determiner* **5** **a** amounting to thirteen: *thirteen buses* **b** (*as pronoun*): *thirteen of them fell* [Old English *threotēne*; see THREE, -TEEN]

thirteenth (ˈθɜːˈtiːnθ) *adj* **1** (*usually prenominal*) **a** coming after the twelfth in numbering or counting order, position, time, etc; being the ordinal number of *thirteen*: often written 13th **b** (*as noun*): *Friday the thirteenth* ▷ *n* **2** **a** one of 13 equal or nearly equal parts of something **b** (*as modifier*): *a thirteenth part* **3** the fraction equal to one divided by 13 (1/13) **4** *music* **a** an interval of one octave plus a sixth. See also **interval** (sense 5) **b** short for **thirteenth chord**

thirteenth chord *n* a chord much used in jazz and pop, consisting of a major or minor triad upon which are superimposed the seventh, ninth, eleventh, and thirteenth above the root. Often shortened to: **thirteenth**

thirtieth (ˈθɜːtɪɪθ) *adj* **1** (*usually prenominal*) **a** being the ordinal number of *thirty* in counting order, position, time, etc: often written 30th **b** (*as noun*): *the thirtieth of the month* ▷ *n* **2** **a** one of 30 approximately equal parts of something **b** (*as modifier*): *a thirtieth part* **3** the fraction equal to one divided by 30 (1/30)

thirty (ˈθɜːtɪ) *n, pl* **-ties** **1** the cardinal number that is the product of ten and three. See also **number** (sense 1) **2** a numeral, 30, XXX, etc, representing this number **3** (*plural*) the numbers 30–39, esp the 30th to the 39th year of a person's life or of a century **4** the amount or quantity that is three times as big as ten **5** something representing, represented by, or consisting of 30 units ▷ *determiner* **6** **a** amounting to thirty: *thirty trees* **b** (*as pronoun*): *thirty are broken* [Old English *thrītig*; see THREE, -TY[1]]

Thirty-nine Articles *pl n* a set of formulas defining the doctrinal position of the Church of England, drawn up in the 16th century, to which the clergy are required to give general consent

thirty-second note *n* *music, US and Canadian* a note having the time value of one thirty-second of a semibreve. Also called (in Britain and certain other countries): **demisemiquaver**

thirty-three *n* a former name for **LP[1]** [C20 so called because it is played at thirty-three and a third revolutions per minute]

thirty-twomo (ˌθɜːtɪˈtuːməʊ) *n, pl* **-mos** a book size resulting from folding a sheet of paper into 32 leaves or 64 pages. Often written: **32mo, 32°**

Thirty Years' War *n* a major conflict involving principally Austria, Denmark, France, Holland, the German states, Spain, and Sweden, that devastated central Europe, esp large areas of Germany (1618–48). It began as a war between Protestants and Catholics but was gradually transformed into a struggle to determine whether the German emperor could assert more than nominal authority over his princely vassals. The Peace of Westphalia gave the German states their sovereignty and the right of religious toleration and confirmed French ascendancy

Thiruvananthapuram (ˌθɪruːvəˈnæntæˌpuːrɑːm) *n* the official name of **Trivandrum**

this (ðɪs) *determiner* (*used before a singular noun*) **1** **a** used preceding a noun referring to something or someone that is closer: distinct from **that**: *this dress is cheaper than that one; look at this picture* **b** (*as pronoun*): *this is Mary and that is her boyfriend; take this* **2** **a** used preceding a noun that has just been mentioned or is understood: *this plan of yours won't work* **b** (*as pronoun*): *I first saw this on Sunday* **3** **a** used to refer to something about to be said, read, etc: *consider this argument* **b** (*as pronoun*): *listen to this* **4** **a** the present or immediate: *this time you'll know better* **b** (*as pronoun*): *before this, I was mistaken* **5** *informal* an emphatic form of **a[1]** or **the[1]**: used esp on relating a story: *I saw this big brown bear* **6** **this and that** various unspecified and trivial actions, matters, objects, etc **7** **this here** *US not standard* an emphatic form of **this** (senses 1–3) **8** **with** (*or* **at**) **this** after this; thereupon ▷ *adv* **9** used with adjectives and adverbs to specify a precise degree that is about to be mentioned: *go just this fast and you'll be safe* [Old English *thēs, thēos, this* (masculine, feminine, neuter singular); related to Old Saxon *thit*, Old High German *diz*, Old Norse *thessi*]

Thisbe (ˈθɪzbɪ) *n* See **Pyramus and Thisbe**

thistle (ˈθɪsᵊl) *n* **1** any of numerous plants of the genera *Cirsium*, *Carduus*, and related genera, having prickly-edged leaves, pink, purple, yellow, or white dense flower heads, and feathery hairs on the seeds: family *Asteraceae* (composites) **2** a thistle, or a representation of one, as the national emblem of Scotland [Old English *thīstel*, related to Old Saxon, Old High German *thīstil*, Old Norse *thīstill*] > ˈ**thistly** *adj*

Thistle (ˈθɪsᵊl) *n* **the** **1** See **Order of the Thistle** **2** (*sometimes not capital*) **a** the emblem of this Order **b** membership of this Order

thistledown (ˈθɪsᵊlˌdaʊn) *n* **1** the mass of feathery plumed seeds produced by a thistle **2** anything resembling this

thither (ˈðɪðə) *or* **thitherward** *adv* *obsolete or formal* to or towards that place; in that direction: *the flowers and music which attract people thither* [Old English *thider*, variant of *thæder*, influenced by *hider* HITHER; related to Old Norse *thathra* there]

thitherto (ˌðɪðəˈtuː, ˈðɪðəˌtuː) *adv* *obsolete or formal* until that time

thixotropic (ˌθɪksəˈtrɒpɪk) *adj* (of fluids and gels) having a viscosity that decreases when a stress is applied, as when stirred: *thixotropic paints* [C20 from Greek *thixis* the act of touching + -TROPIC] > **thixotropy** (θɪkˈsɒtrəpɪ) *n* > **thixotrope** (ˈθɪksəˌtrəʊp) *n*

tho' *or* **tho** (ðəʊ) *conj, adv* *informal* a variant spelling of **though**

thole[1] (θəʊl), **tholepin** (ˈθəʊlˌpɪn) *n* a wooden pin or one of a pair, set upright in the gunwales of a rowing boat to serve as a fulcrum in rowing [Old English *tholl*, related to Middle Low German *dolle*, Norwegian *toll*, Icelandic *thollr*]

thole[2] (θəʊl) *vb* **1** (*tr*) *Scot and northern English dialect* to put up with; bear **2** an archaic word for **suffer** [Old English *tholian*; related to Old Saxon, Old High German *tholōn*, Old Norse *thola* to endure: compare Latin *tollere* to bear up]

tholos (ˈθəʊlɒs) *n, pl* **-loi** (-lɔɪ) a dry-stone beehive-shaped tomb associated with the Mycenaean culture of Greece in the 16th to the 12th century BC [C17 from Greek]

Thomism (ˈtəʊmɪzəm) *n* the comprehensive system of philosophy and theology developed by the Italian theologian, scholastic philosopher, and Dominican friar Saint Thomas Aquinas (1225–74), and since taught and maintained by his followers, esp in the Dominican order > ˈ**Thomist** *n, adj* > **Thoˈmistic** *or* **Thoˈmistical** *adj*

Thompson sub-machine-gun *n* *trademark* a .45 calibre sub-machine-gun. Also called: **Tommy gun** [C20 after John T *Thompson* (1860–1940), US Army Officer, its coinventor]

Thomson effect *n* *physics* the phenomenon in which a temperature gradient along a metallic (or semiconductor) wire or strip causes an electric potential gradient to form along its length [named after Sir William *Thomson*, 1st Baron Kelvin (1824–1907), British physicist]

thon (ðɒn) *determiner* a Scot word for **yon** [C19 of uncertain origin]

-thon *suffix forming nouns* indicating a large-scale event or operation of a specified kind: *telethon* [C20 on the pattern of MARATHON]

Thonburi (ˌtɒnbʊˈriː) *n* a city in central Thailand, part of Bankok Metropolis on the Chao Phraya River; the national capital (1767–82)

thonder (ˈðɒndər) *adv, determiner* a Scot word for **yonder** [C19 of uncertain origin]

thong (θɒŋ) *n* **1** a thin strip of leather or other material, such as one used for lashing things together **2** a whip or whiplash, esp one made of leather **3** *US, Canadian, Austral, and NZ* the usual name for **flip-flop** (sense 5) **4** **a** a skimpy article of beachwear, worn by men or women, consisting of thin strips of leather or cloth attached to a piece of material that covers the genitals while leaving the buttocks bare **b** a similar item of underwear [Old English *thwang*; related to Old High German *dwang* reins, Old Norse *thvengr* strap]

Thor (θɔː) *n* *Norse myth* the god of thunder, depicted as wielding a hammer, emblematic of the thunderbolt [Old English *Thōr*, from Old Norse *thōrr* THUNDER]

thoracentesis (ˌθɔːrəsɛnˈtiːsɪs) *or* **thoracocentesis** (ˌθɔːrəkəʊsɛnˈtiːsɪs) *n* *med* the surgical puncture of the pleural cavity using a hollow needle, in order to withdraw fluid, drain blood, etc. Also called: **pleurocentesis**

thoracic (θɔːˈræsɪk) *adj* of, near, or relating to the thorax

thoracic duct *n* the major duct of the lymphatic system, beginning below the diaphragm and ascending in front of the spinal column to the base of the neck

thoraco- *or before a vowel* **thorac-** *combining form* thorax: *thoracotomy*

thoracoplasty (ˈθɔːrəkəʊˌplæstɪ) *n, pl* **-ties** **1** plastic surgery of the thorax **2** surgical removal of several ribs or a part of them to permit the collapse of a diseased lung, used in cases of pulmonary tuberculosis and bronchiectasis

thoracoscope (ˈθɔːrəkəʊˌskəʊp) *n* *med* an instrument used for examining the pleural cavity

thoracotomy (ˌθɔːrəˈkɒtəmɪ) *n, pl* **-mies** surgical incision into the chest wall

thorax (ˈθɔːræks) *n, pl* **thoraxes** *or* **thoraces** (ˈθɔːrəˌsiːz, θɔːˈreɪsiːz) **1** the part of the human body enclosed by the ribs **2** the corresponding part in other vertebrates **3** the part of an insect's body between the head and abdomen, which bears the wings and legs [C16 via Latin from Greek *thōrax* breastplate, chest]

thoria (ˈθɔːrɪə) *n* another name for **thorium**

dioxide [C19 THORIUM + -a, on the model of *magnesia*]

thorianite ('θɔːrɪəˌnaɪt) *n* a rare black mineral consisting of thorium and uranium oxides. Formula: $ThO_2.U_3O_8$

thorite ('θɔːraɪt) *n* a yellow, brownish, or black radioactive mineral consisting of tetragonal thorium silicate. It occurs in coarse granite and is a source of thorium. Formula: $ThSiO_4$

thorium ('θɔːrɪəm) *n* a soft ductile silvery-white metallic element. It is radioactive and occurs in thorite and monazite: used in gas mantles, magnesium alloys, electronic equipment, and as a nuclear power source. Symbol: Th; atomic no: 90; atomic wt: 232.0381; half-life of most stable isotope, ^{232}Th: 1.41×10^{10} years; valency: 4; relative density: 11.72; melting pt: 1755°C; boiling pt: 4788°C [C19 New Latin, from THOR + -IUM] > '**thoric** *adj*

thorium dioxide *n* a heavy insoluble white powder used in incandescent mantles. Formula: ThO_2. Also called: **thoria**

thorium series *n* a radioactive series that starts with thorium-232 and ends with lead-208

thorn (θɔːn) *n* **1** a sharp pointed woody extension of a stem or leaf. Compare **prickle** (sense 1) **2 a** any of various trees or shrubs having thorns, esp the hawthorn **b** the wood of any of these plants **3** short for **thorn moth 4** a Germanic character of runic origin Þ used in Old and Modern Icelandic to represent the voiceless dental fricative sound of *th*, as in *thin*, *bath*. Its use in phonetics for the same purpose is now obsolete. See **theta 5** this same character as used in Old and Middle English as an alternative to *edh*, but indistinguishable from it in function or sound. Compare **edh 6** *zoology* any of various sharp spiny parts **7** a source of irritation (esp in the phrases **a thorn in one's side** or **flesh**) [Old English; related to Old High German *dorn*, Old Norse *thorn*] > '**thornless** *adj*

Thorn (tɔːrn) *n* the German name for **Toruń**

thorn apple *n* **1** a poisonous solanaceous plant, *Datura stramonium*, of the N hemisphere, having white funnel-shaped flowers and spiny capsule fruits. US and Canadian name: **jimson weed** See also **stramonium 2** any other plant of the genus *Datura* **3** the fruit of certain types of hawthorn

thornback ('θɔːnˌbæk) *n* **1** a European ray, *Raja clavata*, having a row of spines along the back and tail **2** a similar fish, *Platyrhinoidis triseriata*, of the Pacific Ocean

thornbill ('θɔːnˌbɪl) *n* **1** any of various South American hummingbirds of the genera *Chalcostigma*, *Ramphomicron*, etc, having a thornlike bill **2** Also called: **thornbill warbler** any of various Australasian wrens of the genus *Acanthiza* and related genera: family *Muscicapidae* **3** any of various other birds with thornlike bills

Thorndike's law or **Thorndike's law of effect** ('θɔːnˌdaɪk) *n* the principle that all learnt behaviour is regulated by rewards and punishments, proposed by Edward Lee Thorndike (1874–1949), US psychologist

thorn moth *n* any of various woodland geometrid moths, typified by the **large thorn** (*Ennomos autumnaria*), having wings set somewhat at an angle and held up when at rest. Often shortened to: **thorn**

thorny ('θɔːnɪ) *adj* thornier, thorniest **1** bearing or covered with thorns **2** difficult or unpleasant: *a thorny problem* **3** sharp > '**thornily** *adv* > '**thorniness** *n*

thoron ('θɔːrɒn) *n* a radioisotope of radon that is a decay product of thorium. Symbol: Tn or ^{220}Rn; atomic no: 86; half-life: 54.5s [C20 from THORIUM + -ON]

thorough ('θʌrə) *adj* **1** carried out completely and carefully: *a thorough search* **2** (*prenominal*) utter: *a thorough bore* **3** painstakingly careful: *my work is thorough* [Old English *thurh*; related to Old Frisian *thruch*, Old Saxon *thuru*, Old High German *duruh*; see THROUGH] > '**thoroughly** *adv* '**thoroughness** *n*

Thorough ('θʌrə) *n* thoroughgoing policy, as adopted in England by Strafford and Laud during the reign of Charles I

thorough bass (beɪs) *n* **a** Also called: **basso continuo, continuo** (esp during the baroque period) a bass part underlying a piece of concerted music. It is played on a keyboard instrument, usually supported by a cello, viola da gamba, etc. See also **figured bass b** (*us modifier*) *a thorough-bass part*

thorough brace *n chiefly US* either of two strong leather straps upon which the body of certain types of carriage is supported > '**thorough-ˌbraced** *adj*

thoroughbred ('θʌrəˌbred) *adj* **1** purebred ▷ *n* **2 a** pedigree animal; purebred **3** a person regarded as being of good breeding

Thoroughbred ('θʌrəˌbred) *n* a British breed of horse the ancestry of which can be traced to English mares and Arab sires; most often used as a racehorse

thoroughfare ('θʌrəˌfɛə) *n* **1** a road from one place to another, esp a main road **2** way through or access: *no thoroughfare*

thoroughgoing ('θʌrəˌɡəʊɪŋ) *adj* **1** extremely thorough **2** (*usually prenominal*) absolute; complete: *thoroughgoing incompetence* > '**thoroughˌgoingly** *adv* > '**thoroughˌgoingness** *n*

thoroughpaced ('θʌrəˌpeɪst) *adj* **1** (of a horse) showing performing ability in all paces **2** thoroughgoing

thoroughpin ('θʌrəˌpɪn) *n* an inflammation and swelling on both sides of the hock joint of a horse affecting the sheath of the deep flexor tendon [C18 so called because it makes the leg look as if it has a pin stuck through it]

thorp or **thorpe** (θɔːp) *n obsolete except in place names* a small village [Old English; related to Old Norse *thorp* village, Old High German *dorf*, Gothic *thaurp*]

Thorshavn (*Danish* 'tɔːrshaun) or **Tórshavn** (*Faeroese*) *n* the capital of the Faeroes, a port on the northernmost island. Pop: 17 549 (2004 est)

those (ðəʊz) *determiner* the form of **that** used before a plural noun [Old English *thās*, plural of THIS]

Thoth (θəʊθ, təʊt) *n* (in Egyptian mythology) a moon deity, scribe of the gods and protector of learning and the arts

thou[1] (ðaʊ) *pron* (*subjective*) **1** *archaic dialect* refers to the person addressed: used mainly in familiar address or to a younger person or inferior **2** (*usually capital*) refers to God when addressed in prayer, etc [Old English *thū*; related to Old Saxon *thū*, Old High German *du*, Old Norse *thū*, Latin *tū*, Doric Greek *tu*]

thou[2] (ðaʊ) *n*, *pl* **thous** or **thou 1** one thousandth of an inch. 1 thou is equal to 0.0254 millimetre **2** *informal* short for **thousand**

though (ðəʊ) *conj* (*subordinating*) **1** (sometimes preceded by *even*) despite the fact that: *though he tries hard, he always fails; poor though she is, her life is happy* **2 as though** as if: *he looked as though he'd seen a ghost* ▷ *adv* **3** nevertheless; however: *he can't dance: he sings well, though* [Old English *theah*; related to Old Frisian *thāch*, Old Saxon, Old High German *thōh*, Old Norse *thō*]

thought (θɔːt) *vb* **1** the past tense and past participle of **think** ▷ *n* **2** the act or process of thinking; deliberation, meditation, or reflection **3** a concept, opinion, or idea **4** philosophical or intellectual ideas typical of a particular time or place: *German thought in the 19th century* **5** application of mental attention; consideration: *he gave the matter some thought* **6** purpose or intention: *I have no thought of giving up* **7** expectation: *no thought of reward* **8** a small amount; trifle: *you could be a thought more enthusiastic* **9** kindness or regard: *he has no thought for his widowed mother* [Old English *thōht*; related to Old Frisian *thochta*, Old Saxon, Old High German *githācht*]

thought disorder *n psychiatry* a cognitive disorder in which the patient's thoughts or conversations are characterized by irrationality or sudden changes of subject

thoughtful ('θɔːtfʊl) *adj* **1** considerate in the treatment of other people **2** showing careful thought **3** pensive; reflective > '**thoughtfully** *adv* > '**thoughtfulness** *n*

thoughtless ('θɔːtlɪs) *adj* **1** inconsiderate: *a thoughtless remark* **2** having or showing lack of thought: *a thoughtless essay* **3** unable to think; not having the power of thought > '**thoughtlessly** *adv* > '**thoughtlessness** *n*

thought-out *adj* conceived and developed by careful thought: *a well thought-out scheme*

thought police *n* a group of people with totalitarian views on a given subject, who constantly monitor others for any deviation from prescribed thinking [C20 from the *Thought Police* described by George Orwell in his novel *Nineteen Eighty-Four* (1949)]

thought transference *n psychol* another name for **telepathy**

thousand ('θaʊzənd) *n* **1** the cardinal number that is the product of 10 and 100. See also **number** (sense 1) **2** a numeral, 1000, 10^3, M, etc, representing this number **3** (*often plural*) a very large but unspecified number, amount, or quantity: *they are thousands of miles away* **4** (*plural*) the numbers 2000–9999: *the price of the picture was in the thousands* **5** the amount or quantity that is one hundred times greater than ten **6** something represented by, representing, or consisting of 1000 units **7** *maths* the position containing a digit representing that number followed by three zeros: *in 4760, 4 is in the thousand's place* ▷ *determiner* **8 a** amounting to a thousand: *a thousand ships* **b** (*as pronoun*): *a thousand is hardly enough* **9** amounting to 1000 times a particular scientific unit. Related prefix: **kilo-** ▷ Related adjective: **millenary** [Old English *thūsend*; related to Old Saxon *thūsind*, Old High German *thūsunt*, Old Norse *thūsund*]

Thousand and One Nights *n* See **Arabian Nights' Entertainments**

Thousand Guineas *n* **the** (*functioning as singular*) *usually written* **1000 Guineas** an annual horse race, restricted to fillies, run at Newmarket since 1814. Also called: **the One Thousand Guineas**

Thousand Island *adj* of or relating to the Thousand Islands or their inhabitants

Thousand Island dressing *n* a salad dressing made from mayonnaise with ketchup, chopped gherkins, etc [probably from the THOUSAND ISLANDS]

Thousand Islands *pl n* a group of about 1500 islands between the US and Canada, in the upper St Lawrence River: administratively divided between the two countries

thousand-jacket *n* another name for **ribbonwood**

thousandth ('θaʊzənθ) *adj* **1** (*usually prenominal*) **a** being the ordinal number of 1000 in numbering or counting order, position, time, etc **b** (*as noun*): *the thousandth in succession* ▷ *n* **2 a** one of 1000 approximately equal parts of something **b** (*as modifier*): *a thousandth part* **3** one of 1000 equal divisions of a particular scientific quantity. Related prefix: **milli-** *millivolt* **4** the fraction equal to one divided by 1000 (1/1000)

Thrace (θreɪs) *n* **1** an ancient country in the E Balkan Peninsula: successively under the Persians, Macedonians, and Romans **2** a region of SE Europe, corresponding to the S part of the ancient country: divided by the Maritsa River into **Western Thrace** (Greece) and **Eastern Thrace** (Turkey)

Thracian ('θreɪʃɪən) *n* **1** a member of an ancient Indo-European people who lived in the SE corner of the Balkan Peninsula **2** the ancient language spoken by this people, belonging to the Thraco-Phrygian branch of the Indo-European family: extinct by the early Middle Ages ▷ *adj* **3** of or relating to Thrace, its inhabitants, or the extinct

Thracian language

Thraco-Phrygian (ˌθreɪkəʊˈfrɪdʒɪən) *n* **1** a branch of the Indo-European family of languages, all members of which are extinct except for Armenian ▷ *adj* **2** relating to or belonging to this group of languages [from *Thraco-*, from Greek *Thraikē* Thrace; see PHRYGIAN]

thraiping (ˈθreɪpɪŋ) *n* **1** *Northern English dialect* a thrashing **2** an utter defeat in a game or contest: *we gave their team a good thraiping*

thrall (θrɔːl) *n* **1** Also called: **thraldom,** (US) **thralldom** (ˈθrɔːldəm) the state or condition of being in the power of another person **2** a person who is in such a state **3** a person totally subject to some need, desire, appetite, etc ▷ *vb* **4** (*tr*) to enslave or dominate [Old English *thrǣl* slave, from Old Norse *thrǣll*]

thrang (θræŋ) *Scot* ▷ *n* **1** a throng; crowd ▷ *vb* **2** to throng; crowd ▷ *adj* **3** crowded; busy **4** engaged or occupied; busy [Scot variant of THRONG]

thrapple (ˈθræpəl) *Scot* ▷ *n* **1** the throat or windpipe ▷ *vb* **2** to throttle [c18 a variant of earlier *thropple*, of uncertain origin]

thrash (θræʃ) *vb* **1** (*tr*) to beat soundly, as with a whip or stick **2** (*tr*) to defeat totally; overwhelm **3** (*intr*) to beat or plunge about in a wild manner **4** (*intr*) to move the legs up and down in the water, as in certain swimming strokes **5** to sail (a boat) against the wind or tide or (of a boat) to sail in this way **6** another word for **thresh** ▷ *n* **7** the act of thrashing; blow; beating **8** *informal* a party or similar social gathering ▷ See also **thrash out** [Old English *threscan*; related to Old High German *dreskan*, Old Norse *thriskja*]

thrasher[1] (ˈθræʃə) *n* another name for **thresher** (the shark)

thrasher[2] (ˈθræʃə) *n* any of various brown thrushlike American songbirds of the genus *Toxostoma* and related genera, having a long downward-curving bill and long tail: family *Mimidae* (mockingbirds) [c19 perhaps from English dialect *thresher, thrusher* a thrush]

thrashing (ˈθræʃɪŋ) *n* **1** a physical assault; flogging **2** a convincing defeat: *a 5–1 thrashing*

thrash metal *n* a type of very fast, very loud rock music that combines elements of heavy metal and punk rock. Often shortened to: **thrash**

thrash out *vb* (*tr, adverb*) to discuss fully or vehemently, esp in order to come to a solution or agreement

thrasonical (θrəˈsɒnɪkəl) *adj rare* bragging; boastful [c16 from Latin *Thrasō* name of boastful soldier in *Eunuchus*, a play by Terence, from Greek *Thrasōn*, from *thrasus* forceful] > **thra'sonically** *adv*

thrave (θreɪv) *n Scot and northern English dialect* twenty-four sheaves of corn [Old English *threfe*, of Scandinavian origin]

thrawn (θrɔːn) *adj Scot and northern English dialect* **1** crooked or twisted **2** stubborn; perverse [Northern English dialect, variant of THROWN, from Old English *thrāwan* to twist about, THROW]

thread (θrɛd) *n* **1** a fine strand, filament or fibre of some material **2** a fine cord of twisted filaments, esp of cotton, used in sewing, weaving, etc **3** any of the filaments of which a spider's web is made **4** any fine line, stream, mark, or piece: *from the air, the path was a thread of white* **5** a helical groove in a cylindrical hole (**female thread**), formed by a tap or lathe tool, or a helical ridge on a cylindrical bar, rod, shank, etc (**male thread**), formed by a die or lathe tool **6** a very thin seam of coal or vein of ore **7** something acting as the continuous link or theme of a whole: *the thread of the story* **8** the course of an individual's life believed in Greek mythology to be spun, measured, and cut by the Fates ▷ *vb* **9** (*tr*) to pass (thread, film, magnetic tape, etc) through (something): *to thread a needle; to thread cotton through a needle* **10** (*tr*) to string on a thread: *she threaded the beads* **11** to make (one's way) through or over (something) **12** (*tr*) to produce a screw thread by

cutting, rolling, tapping, or grinding **13** (*tr*) to pervade: *hysteria threaded his account* **14** (*intr*) (of boiling syrup) to form a fine thread when poured from a spoon ▷ See also **threads** [Old English *thrǣd*; related to Old Frisian *thrēd*, Old High German *drāt*, Old Norse *thrāthr* thread] > **'threader** *n* > **'threadless** *adj* > **'thread,like** *adj*

threadbare (ˈθrɛdˌbɛə) *adj* **1** (of cloth, clothing, etc) having the nap worn off so that the threads are exposed **2** meagre or poor: *a threadbare existence* **3** hackneyed: *a threadbare argument* **4** wearing threadbare clothes; shabby > **'thread,bareness** *n*

threadfin (ˈθrɛdˌfɪn) *n, pl* **-fin** *or* **-fins** any spiny-finned tropical marine fish of the family *Polynemidae*, having pectoral fins consisting partly of long threadlike rays

thread mark *n* a mark put into paper money to prevent counterfeiting, consisting of a pattern of silk fibres

Threadneedle Street (ˌθrɛdˈniːdəl, ˈθrɛdˌniːdəl) *n* a street in the City of London famous for its banks, including the Bank of England, known as **The Old Lady of Threadneedle Street**

thread rolling *n engineering* the production of a screw thread by a rolling swaging process using hardened profiled rollers. Rolled threads are stronger than threads machined by a cutting tool

threads (θrɛdz) *pl n* a slang word for **clothes**

thread vein *n* a small red or purple capillary near to the surface of the skin

threadworm (ˈθrɛdˌwɜːm) *n* any of various nematodes, esp the pinworm

thready (ˈθrɛdɪ) *adj* **threadier, threadiest** **1** of, relating to, or resembling a thread or threads **2** *med* (of the pulse) barely perceptible; weak; fine **3** sounding thin, weak, or reedy: *a thready tenor* > **'threadiness** *n*

threap *or* **threep** (θriːp) *vb* (*tr*) *Scot and northern English dialect* **1** to scold **2** to contradict [Old English *thrēapian* to blame; related to Old Frisian *thrūwa*, Old High German *threwen*, Old Norse *threa*] > **'threaper** *or* **'threeper** *n*

threat (θrɛt) *n* **1** a declaration of the intention to inflict harm, pain, or misery **2** an indication of imminent harm, danger, or pain **3** a person or thing that is regarded as dangerous or likely to inflict pain or misery ▷ *vb* **4** an archaic word for **threaten** [Old English; related to Old Norse *thraut*, Middle Low German *drōt*]

threaten (ˈθrɛtən) *vb* **1** (*tr*) to be a threat to **2** to be a menacing indication of (something); portend: *dark clouds threatened rain* **3** (when *tr*, may take a clause as object) to express a threat to (a person or people) > **'threatener** *n* > **'threatening** *adj* > **'threateningly** *adv*

three (θriː) *n* **1** the cardinal number that is the sum of two and one and is a prime number. See also **number** (sense 1) **2** a numeral, 3, III, (iii), representing this number **3** the amount or quantity that is one greater than two **4** something representing, represented by, or consisting of three units such as a playing card with three symbols on it **5** Also called: **three o'clock** three hours after noon or midnight ▷ *determiner* **6 a** amounting to three: *three ships* **b** (*as pronoun*): *three were killed* ▷ Related adjectives: **ternary, tertiary, treble, triple** ▷ Related prefixes: **tri-, ter-** [Old English *thrēo*; related to Old Norse *thrīr*, Old High German *drī*, Latin *trēs*, Greek *treis*]

three-card trick *n* a game in which players bet on which of three inverted playing cards is the queen

three-colour *adj* of, relating to, or comprising a colour print or a photomechanical process in which a picture is reproduced by superimposing three prints from half-tone plates in inks corresponding to the three primary colours

three-D *or* **3-D** *n* a three-dimensional effect

three-day event *n* See **eventing**

three-day measles *n pathol* an informal name for **rubella**

three-decker *n* **1 a** anything having three levels

or layers **b** (*as modifier*): *a three-decker sandwich* **2** a warship with guns on three decks

three-dimensional, three-D *or* **3-D** *adj* **1** of, having, or relating to three dimensions: *three-dimensional space* **2** (of a film, transparency, etc) simulating the effect of depth by presenting slightly different views of a scene to each eye **3** having volume **4** lifelike or real

threefold (ˈθriːˌfəʊld) *adj* **1** equal to or having three times as many or as much; triple: *a threefold decrease* **2** composed of three parts: *a threefold purpose* ▷ *adv* **3** by or up to three times as many or as much

three-four time *n music* a form of simple triple time in which there are three crotchet beats to the bar, indicated by the time signature ¾. Often shortened to: **three-four.** Also called (esp US and Canadian): **three-quarter time**

three-gaited *adj chiefly US* (of a horse) having the three usual paces, the walk, trot, and canter

three-legged race *n* a race in which pairs of competitors run with their adjacent legs tied together

three-line whip *n* See **whip** (sense 20c)

three-mile limit *n international law* the range of a nation's territorial waters, extending to three nautical miles from shore

threep (θriːp) *vb* a variant spelling of **threap**

threepenny bit *or* **thrupenny bit** (ˈθrʌpnɪ, -ənɪ, ˈθrɛp-) *n* a twelve-sided British coin of nickel-brass, valued at three old pence, obsolete since 1971

three-phase *adj* (of an electrical system, circuit, or device) having, generating, or using three alternating voltages of the same frequency, displaced in phase by 120°

three-piece *adj* **1** having three pieces, esp (of a suit, suite, etc) consisting of three matching parts ▷ *n* **2** a three-piece suite, suit, etc

three-ply *adj* **1** having three layers or thicknesses **2 a** (of knitting wool, etc) three-stranded **b** (*as noun*): *the sweater was knitted in three-ply*

three-point landing *n* **1** an aircraft landing in which the two main wheels and the nose or tail wheel all touch the ground simultaneously **2** a successful conclusion

three-point turn *n* a turn reversing the direction of motion of a motor vehicle using forward and reverse gears alternately, and completed after only three movements

three-quarter *adj* **1** being three quarters of something: *a three-quarter turn* **2** being of three quarters the normal length ▷ *n* **3** *rugby* **a** any of the four players between the fullback and the halfbacks **b** this position **c** (*as modifier*): *three-quarter play*

three-quarter binding *n* a bookbinding style in which the spine and much of the sides are in a different material (esp leather) from the rest of the covers

three-ring circus *n US and Canadian* **1** a circus with three rings in which separate performances are carried on simultaneously **2** a situation of confusion, characterized by a bewildering variety of events or activities

Three Rivers *n* the English name for **Trois-Rivières**

three Rs *pl n* **the** the three skills regarded as the fundamentals of education; reading, writing, and arithmetic [from the humorous spelling *reading, 'riting,* and *'rithmetic*]

threescore (ˈθriːˈskɔː) *determiner* an archaic word for **sixty**

threesome (ˈθriːsəm) *n* **1** a group of three **2** *golf* a match in which a single player playing his own ball competes against two others playing alternate strokes on the same ball **3** any game, etc, for three people **4** (*modifier*) performed by three: *a threesome game*

three-square *adj* having a cross section that is an equilateral triangle: *a three-square file*

three-way *adj* **1** providing connections to three

routes from a central point **2** involving three things or people

three-wheeler *n* a light car that has three wheels

thremmatology (ˌθrɛməˈtɒlədʒɪ) *n* the science of breeding domesticated animals and plants [c19 from Greek *thremma* nursling + -LOGY]

threnody (ˈθrɛnədɪ, ˈθriː-) *or* **threnode** (ˈθriːnəʊd, ˈθrɛn-) *n, pl* **threnodies** *or* **threnodes** an ode, song, or speech of lamentation, esp for the dead [c17 from Greek *thrēnōidia*, from *thrēnos* dirge + *ōidē* song] ▷ **threnodial** (θrɪˈnəʊdɪəl) *or* **threnodic** (θrɪˈnɒdɪk) *adj* ▷ **threnodist** (ˈθrɛnədɪst, ˈθriː-) *n*

threonine (ˈθriːəˌniːn, -nɪn) *n* an essential amino acid that occurs in certain proteins [c20 *threon-*, probably from Greek *eruthron*, from *eruthros* red (see ERYTHRO-) + -INE²]

thresh (θrɛʃ) *vb* **1** to beat or rub stalks of ripe corn or a similar crop either with a hand implement or a machine to separate the grain from the husks and straw **2** (*tr*) to beat or strike **3** (*intr*; often foll by *about*) to toss and turn; thrash ▷ *n* **4** the act of threshing [Old English *threscan*; related to Gothic *thriskan*, Old Norse *thriskja*; see THRASH]

thresher (ˈθrɛʃə) *n* **1** a person who threshes **2** short for **threshing machine 3** Also called: **thrasher, thresher shark** any of various large sharks of the genus *Alopias*, esp *A. vulpinus*, occurring in tropical and temperate seas: family *Alopiidae*. They have a very long whiplike tail with which they are thought to round up the small fish on which they feed

threshing machine *n* a machine for threshing crops

threshold (ˈθrɛʃəʊld, ˈθrɛʃˌhəʊld) *n* **1** Also called: **doorsill** a sill, esp one made of stone or hardwood, placed at a doorway **2** any doorway or entrance **3** the starting point of an experience, event, or venture: *on the threshold of manhood* **4** *psychol* the strength at which a stimulus is just perceived: *the threshold of consciousness*. Compare **absolute threshold, difference threshold 5** a level or point at which something would happen, would cease to happen, or would take effect, become true, etc **b** (*as modifier*): *threshold price; threshold effect* **6 a** the minimum intensity or value of a signal, etc, that will produce a response or specified effect: *a frequency threshold* **b** (*as modifier*): *a threshold current* **7** (*modifier*) designating or relating to a pay agreement, clause, etc, that raises wages to compensate for increases in the cost of living ▷ Related adjective: **liminal** [Old English *therscold*; related to Old Norse *threskoldr*, Old High German *driscubli*, Old Swedish *thriskuldi*]

threshold agreement *n* an agreement between an employer and employees or their union to increase wages by a specified sum if inflation exceeds a specified level in a specified time

thresh out *vb* another term for **thrash out**

threw (θruː) *vb* the past tense of **throw**

thrice (θraɪs) *adv* **1** three times **2** in threefold degree **3** *archaic* greatly [Old English *thrīwa, thrīga*; see THREE]

thrift (θrɪft) *n* **1** wisdom and caution in the management of money **2** Also called: **sea pink** any of numerous perennial plumbaginaceous low-growing plants of the genus *Armeria*, esp *A. maritima*, of Europe, W Asia, and North America, having narrow leaves and round heads of pink or white flowers **3** *rare* vigorous thriving or growth, as of a plant **4** *US* a building society, savings bank, or credit union **5** an obsolete word for **prosperity** [c13 from Old Norse: success; see THRIVE] ▷ **thriftless** *adj* ▷ **thriftlessly** *adv* ▷ **thriftlessness** *n*

thrifty (ˈθrɪftɪ) *adj* **thriftier, thriftiest 1** showing thrift; economical or frugal **2** *rare* thriving or prospering ▷ **thriftily** *adv* ▷ **thriftiness** *n*

thrill (θrɪl) *n* **1** a sudden sensation of excitement and pleasure: *seeing his book for sale gave him a thrill* **2** a situation producing such a sensation: *it was a thrill to see Rome for the first time* **3** a trembling

sensation caused by fear or emotional shock **4** *pathol* an abnormal slight tremor associated with a heart or vascular murmur, felt on palpation ▷ *vb* **5** to feel or cause to feel a thrill **6** to tremble or cause to tremble; vibrate or quiver [Old English *thȳrlian* to pierce, from *thyrel* hole; see NOSTRIL, THROUGH]

thriller (ˈθrɪlə) *n* **1** a book, film, play, etc, depicting crime, mystery, or espionage in an atmosphere of excitement and suspense **2** a person or thing that thrills

thrilling (ˈθrɪlɪŋ) *adj* **1** very exciting or stimulating **2** vibrating or trembling ▷ **thrillingly** *adv*

thrill-seeker *n* a person who enjoys taking part in extreme sports and other activities involving physical risk

thrips (θrɪps) *n, pl* **thrips** any of various small slender-bodied insects of the order *Thysanoptera*, typically having piercing mouthparts and narrow feathery wings and feeding on plant sap. Some species are serious plant pests [c18 via New Latin from Greek: woodworm]

thrive (θraɪv) *vb* **thrives, thriving; thrived** *or* **throve; thrived** *or* **thriven** (ˈθrɪvˈn) (*intr*) **1** to grow strongly and vigorously **2** to do well; prosper [c13 from Old Norse *thrīfask* to grasp for oneself, reflexive of *thrīfa* to grasp, of obscure origin] ▷ **thriver** *n* ▷ **thriving** *adj* ▷ **thrivingly** *adv*

thro' *or* **thro** (θruː) *prep, adv informal* *or* *poetic* variant spellings of **through**

throat (θrəʊt) *n* **1 a** that part of the alimentary and respiratory tracts extending from the back of the mouth (nasopharynx) to just below the larynx **b** the front part of the neck **2** something resembling a throat, esp in shape or function: *the throat of a chimney* **3** *botany* the gaping part of a tubular corolla or perianth **4** *informal* a sore throat **5 cut one's (own) throat** to bring about one's own ruin **6 have by the throat** to have compete control over (a person or thing) **7 jump down someone's throat** See **jump** (sense 24) **8 ram or force (something) down someone's throat** to insist that someone listen to or accept (something): *he rammed his own opinions down my throat* **9 stick in one's throat** (*or* **craw**) *informal* to be difficult, or against one's conscience, for one to accept, utter, or believe ▷ Related adjectives: **gular, guttural, jugular, laryngeal** [Old English *throtu*; related to Old High German *drozza* throat, Old Norse *throti* swelling]

throatlash (ˈθrəʊtˌlæʃ) *or* **throatlatch** *n* the strap that holds a bridle in place, fastening under the horse's jaw

throat microphone *n* a type of microphone that is held against the throat to pick up voice vibrations. Also called: **throat mike**

throaty (ˈθrəʊtɪ) *adj* **throatier, throatiest 1** indicating a sore throat; hoarse: *a throaty cough* **2** of, relating to, or produced in or by the throat **3** deep, husky, or guttural ▷ **throatily** *adv* ▷ **throatiness** *n*

throb (θrɒb) *vb* **throbs, throbbing, throbbed** (*intr*) **1** to pulsate or beat repeatedly, esp with increased force: *to throb with pain* **2** (of engines, drums, etc) to have a strong rhythmic vibration or beat ▷ *n* **3** the act or an instance of throbbing, esp a rapid pulsation of the heart: *a throb of pleasure* [c14 perhaps of imitative origin] ▷ **throbbing** *adj* ▷ **throbbingly** *adv*

throe (θrəʊ) *n rare* a pang or pain [Old English *thrāwu* threat; related to Old High German *drawa* threat, Old Norse *thrā* desire, *thrauka* to endure]

throes (θrəʊz) *pl n* **1** a condition of violent pangs, pain, or convulsions: *death throes* **2** struggling with great effort with: *a country in the throes of revolution*

thrombin (ˈθrɒmbɪn) *n biochem* an enzyme that acts on fibrinogen in blood causing it to clot

thrombo- *or sometimes before a vowel* **thromb-** *combining form* indicating a blood clot: *thromboembolism* [from Greek *thrombos* lump, clot]

thrombocyte (ˈθrɒmbəˌsaɪt) *n* another name for **platelet**. ▷ **thrombocytic** (ˌθrɒmbəˈsɪtɪk) *adj*

thrombocytopenia (ˌθrɒmbəʊˌsaɪtəʊˈpiːnɪə) *n pathol* an abnormal decrease in the number of platelets in the blood [c20 from German *thrombocytopenie* from THROMBOCYTE + Greek *penia* poverty]

thromboembolism (ˌθrɒmbəʊˈɛmbəˌlɪzəm) *n pathol* the obstruction of a blood vessel by a thrombus that has become detached from its original site

thrombogen (ˈθrɒmbəˌdʒɛn) *n* a protein present in blood that is essential for the formation of thrombin

thrombokinase (ˌθrɒmbəʊˈkaɪneɪs) *n* another name for **thromboplastin**

thrombolysis (ˌθrɒmˈbɒlɪsɪs) *n* the breaking up of a blood clot

thrombolytic (ˌθrɒmbəˈlɪtɪk) *adj* **1** causing the break-up of a blood clot ▷ *n* **2** a thrombolytic drug

thrombophlebitis (ˌθrɒmbəʊflɪˈbaɪtɪs) *n* inflammation of a vein associated with the formation of a thrombus

thromboplastic (ˌθrɒmbəʊˈplæstɪk) *adj* causing or enhancing the formation of a blood clot

thromboplastin (ˌθrɒmbəʊˈplæstɪn) *n* any of a group of substances that are liberated from damaged blood platelets and other tissues and convert prothrombin to thrombin. Also called: **thrombokinase**

thrombose (ˈθrɒmbəʊz) *vb* to become or affect with a thrombus [c19 back formation from THROMBOSIS]

thrombosis (θrɒmˈbəʊsɪs) *n, pl* **-ses** (siːz) **1** the formation or presence of a thrombus **2** *informal* short for **coronary thrombosis** [c18 from New Latin, from Greek: curdling, from *thrombousthai* to clot, from *thrombos* THROMBUS] ▷ **thrombotic** (θrɒmˈbɒtɪk) *adj*

thrombus (ˈθrɒmbəs) *n, pl* **-bi** (-baɪ) a clot of coagulated blood that forms within a blood vessel or inside the heart and remains at the site of its formation, often impeding the flow of blood. Compare **embolus** [c17 from New Latin, from Greek *thrombos* lump, of obscure origin]

throne (θrəʊn) *n* **1** the ceremonial seat occupied by a monarch, bishop, etc on occasions of state **2** the power, duties, or rank ascribed to a royal person **3** a person holding royal rank **4** (*plural*; *often capital*) the third of the nine orders into which the angels are traditionally divided in medieval angelology ▷ *vb* **5** to place or be placed on a throne [c13 from Old French *trone*, from Latin *thronus*, from Greek *thronos* throne] ▷ **throneless** *adj*

throng (θrɒŋ) *n* **1** a great number of people or things crowded together ▷ *vb* **2** to gather in or fill (a place) in large numbers; crowd **3** (*tr*) to hem in (a person); jostle ▷ *adj* **4** *Yorkshire dialect* (*postpositive*) busy [Old English *gethrang*; related to Old Norse *throng*, Old High German *drangōd*]

thronner (ˈθrɒnə) *n Northern English dialect* a person who is good at doing odd jobs

throstle (ˈθrɒsˈl) *n* **1** a poetic name for **thrush¹**, esp the song thrush **2** a spinning machine for wool or cotton in which the fibres are twisted and wound continuously [Old English; related to Old Saxon *throsla*, Old Norse *thröstr*, Middle High German *drostel*]

throttle (ˈθrɒtˈl) *n* **1** Also called: **throttle valve** any device that controls the quantity of fuel or fuel and air mixture entering an engine **2** an informal or dialect word for **throat** ▷ *vb* (*tr*) **3** to kill or injure by squeezing the throat **4** to suppress: *to throttle the press* **5** to control or restrict (a flow of fluid) by means of a throttle valve [c14 *throtelen*, from *throte* THROAT] ▷ **throttler** *n*

through (θruː) *prep* **1** going in or starting at one side and coming out or stopping at the other side of: *a path through the wood* **2** occupying or visiting several points scattered around in (an area) **3** as a result of; by means of: *the thieves were captured* *through his vigilance* **4** *chiefly US* up to and including: *Monday through Friday* **5** during: *through the night* **6** at the end of; having (esp successfully) completed **7** **through with** having finished with (esp when dissatisfied with) ▷ *adj* **8** (*postpositive*) having successfully completed some specified activity **9** (on a telephone line) connected **10** (*postpositive*) no longer able to function successfully in some specified capacity: *as a journalist, you're through* **11** (*prenominal*) (of a route, journey, etc) continuous or unbroken: *a through train* ▷ *adv* **12** through some specified thing, place, or period of time **13** thoroughly; completely ▷ Also (informal or poetic) **thro'**, (informal or poetic) **thro** (chiefly US) **thru** [Old English *thurh;* related to Old Frisian *thruch,* Old Saxon *thuru,* Old High German *duruh*]

through bridge *n civil engineering* a bridge in which the track is carried by the lower horizontal members

through-composed *adj music* of or relating to a song in stanzaic form, in which different music is provided for each stanza. Compare **strophic** (sense 2)

throughly ('θru:lɪ) *adv archaic* thoroughly; completely

through-other *adj Scot* **1** untidy or dishevelled **2** mixed up; in disorder

throughout (θru:'aʊt) *prep* **1** right through; through the whole of (a place or a period of time): *throughout the day* ▷ *adv* **2** through the whole of some specified period or area

throughput ('θru:ˌpʊt) *n* the quantity of raw material or information processed or communicated in a given period, esp by a computer

throughway ('θru:ˌweɪ) *n US* a thoroughfare, esp a motorway

throve (θrəʊv) *vb* a past tense of **thrive**

throw (θrəʊ) *vb* **throws, throwing, threw, thrown** (*mainly tr*) **1** (*also intr*) to project or cast (something) through the air, esp with a rapid motion of the arm and wrist **2** (foll by *in, on, onto,* etc) to put or move suddenly, carelessly, or violently: *she threw her clothes onto the bed* **3** to bring to or cause to be in a specified state or condition, esp suddenly or unexpectedly: *the news threw the family into a panic* **4** to direct or cast (a shadow, light, etc) **5** to project (the voice) so as to make it appear to come from other than its source **6** to give or hold (a party) **7** to cause to fall or be upset; dislodge: *the horse soon threw his rider* **8 a** to tip (dice) out onto a flat surface **b** to obtain (a specified number) in this way **9** to shape (clay) on a potter's wheel **10** to move (a switch or lever) to engage or disengage a mechanism **11** to be subjected to (a fit) **12** to turn (wood, etc) on a lathe **13** *informal* to baffle or astonish; confuse: *the last question on the test paper threw me* **14** *boxing* to deliver (a punch) **15** *wrestling* to hurl (an opponent) to the ground **16** *informal* to lose (a contest, fight, etc) deliberately, esp in boxing **17 a** to play (a card) **b** to discard (a card) **18** (of a female animal, esp a cow) to give birth to (young) **19** to twist or spin (filaments) into thread **20** **throw cold water on (something)** *informal* to be unenthusiastic about or discourage (something) **21** **throw oneself at** to strive actively to attract the attention or affection of **22** **throw oneself into** to involve oneself enthusiastically in **23** **throw oneself on** to rely entirely upon: *he threw himself on the mercy of the police* ▷ *n* **24** the act or an instance of throwing **25** the distance or extent over which anything may be thrown: *a stone's throw* **26** *informal* a chance, venture, or try **27** an act or result of throwing dice **28 a** the eccentricity of a cam **b** the radial distance between the central axis of a crankshaft and the axis of a crankpin forming part of the shaft **29 a** decorative light blanket or cover, as thrown over a chair **30** a sheet of fabric used for draping over an easel or unfinished painting, etc, to keep the dust off **31** *geology* the vertical displacement of rock strata at a fault **32** *physics* the deflection of a measuring instrument as a result of a sudden fluctuation ▷ See also **throw about, throwaway, throwback, throw in, throw off, throw out, throw over, throw together, throw up** [Old English *thrāwan* to turn, torment; related to Old High German *drāen* to twist, Latin *terere* to rub]
> '**thrower** *n*

throw about *vb* (*tr, adverb*) **1** to spend (one's money) in a reckless and flaunting manner **2** **throw one's weight about** *informal* to act in an authoritarian or aggressive manner

throwaway ('θrəʊəˌweɪ) *adj* (*prenominal*) **1** said or done incidentally, esp for rhetorical effect; casual: *a throwaway remark* **2 a** anything designed to be discarded after use rather than reused, refilled, etc; disposable **b** (*as modifier*): *a throwaway carton* ▷ *n* **3** *chiefly US and Canadian* a handbill or advertisement distributed in a public place ▷ *vb* **throw away** (*tr, adverb*) **4** to get rid of; discard **5** to fail to make good use of; waste: *to throw away all one's money on horses*

throwback ('θrəʊˌbæk) *n* **1 a** a person, animal, or plant that has the characteristics of an earlier or more primitive type **b** a reversion to such an organism ▷ *vb* **throw back** (*adverb*) **2** (*intr*) to revert to an earlier or more primitive type **3** (*tr;* foll by *on*) to force to depend (on): *the crisis threw her back on her faith in God*

throw in *vb* (*tr, adverb*) **1** to add (something extra) at no additional cost **2** to contribute or interpose (a remark, argument, etc), esp in a discussion **3** **throw in one's hand a** (in cards) to concede defeat by putting one's cards down **b** to give in and accept defeat; discontinue a venture **4** **throw in the towel** (*or* **sponge**) **a** (in boxing) to concede defeat by the throwing of a towel (or sponge) into the ring by a second **b** to give in and accept defeat; discontinue a venture ▷ *n* **throw-in** **5** *soccer* the method of putting the ball into play after it has gone into touch by throwing it two-handed from behind the head to a teammate, both feet being kept on the ground

throwing stick *n* a primitive device for hurling a spear with greater leverage, consisting of a rod with a groove in it and a hook or projection at the back end to hold the weapon until its release

thrown (θrəʊn) *vb* the past participle of **throw**

throw off *vb* (*mainly tr, adverb*) **1** to free oneself of; discard **2** to produce or utter in a casual manner: *to throw off a witty remark* **3** to escape from or elude: *the fox rapidly threw off his pursuers* **4** to confuse or disconcert: *the interruption threw the young pianist off* **5** (*intr, often foll by at*) *Austral and NZ informal* to deride or ridicule

throw out *vb* (*tr, adverb*) **1** to discard or reject **2** to expel or dismiss, esp forcibly **3** to construct (something projecting or prominent, such as a wing of a building) **4** to put forward or offer: *the chairman threw out a new proposal* **5** to utter in a casual or indirect manner: *to throw out a hint* **6** to confuse or disconcert: *the noise threw his concentration out* **7** to give off or emit **8** *cricket* (of a fielder) to put (the batsman) out by throwing the ball to hit the wicket **9** *baseball* to make a throw to a teammate who in turn puts out (a base runner)

throw over *vb* (*tr, adverb*) to forsake or abandon; jilt

throwster ('θrəʊstə) *n* a person who twists silk or other fibres into yarn [C15 *throwestre,* from THROW + -STER]

throw together *vb* (*tr, adverb*) **1** to assemble hurriedly **2** to cause to become casually acquainted

throw up *vb* (*adverb, mainly tr*) **1** to give up; abandon, relinquish **2** to build or construct hastily **3** to reveal; produce: *every generation throws up its own leaders* **4** (*also intr*) *informal* to vomit

throw weight *n* the maximum weight of supplementary mechanisms that can be lifted by the boost stages of a particular missile

thru (θru:) *prep* (*adverb, adjective*) *chiefly US* a variant spelling of **through**

thrum[1] (θrʌm) *vb* **thrums, thrumming, thrummed** **1** to strum rhythmically but without expression on (a musical instrument) **2** (*intr*) to drum incessantly: *rain thrummed on the roof* **3** to repeat (something) monotonously ▷ *n* **4** a repetitive strumming or recitation [C16 of imitative origin]
> '**thrummer** *n*

thrum[2] (θrʌm) *textiles* ▷ *n* **1 a** any of the unwoven ends of warp thread remaining on the loom when the web has been removed **b** such ends of thread collectively **2** a fringe or tassel of short unwoven threads ▷ *vb* **thrums, thrumming, thrummed** **3** (*tr*) to trim with thrums [C14 from Old English; related to Old High German *drum* remnant, Dutch *dreum*]

thrum-eyed *adj* (of flowers, esp primulas) having the stigma on a short style below the anthers, which lie in the mouth of the corolla on big stamens. Compare **pin-eyed** [C19 from THRUM[2], because of the ring of anthers visible at the neck of the corolla]

thrupenny bit ('θrʌpnɪ, -ənɪ, 'θrɛp-) *n* a variant spelling of **threepenny bit**

thrush[1] (θrʌʃ) *n* any songbird of the subfamily *Turdinae,* esp those having a brown plumage with a spotted breast, such as the mistle thrush and song thrush: family *Muscicapidae*. Compare **water thrush.** Related adj: **turdine** [Old English *thrȳsce;* related to Old High German *drōsca;* see THROSTLE, THROAT]

thrush[2] (θrʌʃ) *n* **1 a** a fungal disease of the mouth, esp of infants, and the genitals, characterized by the formation of whitish spots and caused by infection with the fungus *Candida albicans* **b** another word for **sprue** **2** a softening of the frog of a horse's hoof characterized by degeneration and a thick foul discharge [C17 related to Old Danish *törsk,* Danish *troske*]

thrust (θrʌst) *vb* **thrusts, thrusting, thrust** **1** (*tr*) to push (someone or something) with force or sudden strength: *she thrust him away; she thrust it into the fire* **2** (*tr*) to force or impose upon (someone) or into (some condition or situation): *they thrust extra responsibilities upon her; she was thrust into the limelight* **3** (*tr;* foll by *through*) to pierce; stab **4** (*intr;* usually foll by *through* or *into*) to force a passage or entrance **5** (*intr*) to push forwards, upwards, or outwards **6** (*intr;* foll by *at*) to make a stab or lunge at (a person or thing) ▷ *n* **7** a forceful drive, push, stab, or lunge **8** a force, esp one that produces motion **9 a** a propulsive force produced by the fluid pressure or the change of momentum of the fluid in a jet engine, rocket engine, etc **b** a similar force produced by a propeller **10** a pressure that is exerted continuously by one part of an object, structure, etc, against another, esp the axial force by or on a shaft **11** *geology* **a** the compressive force in the earth's crust that produces recumbent folds and thrust or reverse faults **b** See **thrust fault** **12** *civil engineering* a force exerted in a downwards and outwards direction, as by an arch or rafter, or the horizontal force exerted by retained earth **13** force, impetus, or drive: *a man with thrust and energy* **14** the essential or most forceful part: *the thrust of the argument* [C12 from Old Norse *thrysta;* related to Latin *trūdere;* see INTRUDE]

thrust bearing *n engineering* a low-friction bearing on a rotating shaft that resists axial thrust in the shaft. Usually it consists of a collar which bears against a ring of well lubricated stationary and sometimes tilting pads. Compare **tapered roller bearing**

thruster ('θrʌstə) *n* **1** a person or thing that thrusts **2** Also called: **vernier rocket** a small rocket engine, esp one used to correct the altitude or course of a spacecraft **3** an auxiliary propeller on a ship, capable of acting athwartships

thrust fault *n* a fault in which the rocks on the upper side of an inclined fault plane have been displaced upwards, usually by compression; a reverse fault

thrusting ('θrʌstɪŋ) *adj* ambitious and having

great drive: *a thrusting young executive*

thrutch (θrʌtʃ) *n Northern English dialect* a narrow, fast-moving stream

thud (θʌd) *n* **1** a dull heavy sound: *the book fell to the ground with a thud* **2** a blow or fall that causes such a sound ▷ *vb* **thuds, thudding, thudded 3** to make or cause to make such a sound [Old English *thyddan* to strike; related to *thoddettan* to beat, perhaps of imitative origin]

thug (θʌg) *n* **1** a tough and violent man, esp a criminal **2** (*sometimes capital*) (formerly) a member of an organization of robbers and assassins in India who typically strangled their victims [c19 from Hindi *thag* thief, from Sanskrit *sthaga* scoundrel, from *sthagati* to conceal] > **'thuggery** *n* > **'thuggish** *adj*

thuggee (θʌ'giː) *n history* the methods and practices of the thugs of India [c19 from Hindi *thagī*; see THUG]

thuja *or* **thuya** (ˈθuːjə) *n* any of various coniferous trees of the genus *Thuja*, of North America and East Asia, having scalelike leaves, small cones, and an aromatic wood: family *Cupressaceae*. See also **arbor vitae** [c18 from New Latin, from Medieval Latin *thuia*, ultimately from Greek *thua* name of an African tree]

Thule (ˈθjuːliː) *n* Also called: **ultima Thule** a region believed by ancient geographers to be the northernmost land in the inhabited world: sometimes thought to have been Iceland, Norway, or one of the Shetland Islands **2** an Inuit settlement in NW Greenland: a Danish trading post, founded in 1910, and US air force base

thulium (ˈθjuːlɪəm) *n* a malleable ductile silvery-grey element occurring principally in monazite. The radioisotope **thulium-170** is used as an electron source in portable X-ray units. Symbol: Tm; atomic no: 69; atomic wt: 168.93421; valency: 3; relative density: 9.321; melting pt: 1545°C; boiling pt: 1950°C [c19 New Latin, from THULE + -IUM]

thumb (θʌm) *n* **1** the first and usually shortest and thickest of the digits of the hand, composed of two short bones. Technical name: **pollex** Related adj: **pollical 2** the corresponding digit in other vertebrates **3** the part of a glove shaped to fit the thumb **4** *architect* another name for **ovolo 5 all thumbs** clumsy **6 thumbs down** an indication of refusal, disapproval, or negation: *he gave the thumbs down on our proposal* **7 thumbs up** an indication of encouragement, approval, or acceptance **8 under someone's thumb** at someone's mercy or command ▷ *vb* **9** (*tr*) to touch, mark, or move with the thumb **10** to attempt to obtain (a lift or ride) by signalling with the thumb **11** (when *intr*, often foll by *through*) to flip the pages of (a book, magazine, etc) perfunctorily in order to glance at the contents **12 thumb one's nose at** to deride or mock, esp by placing the thumb on the nose with fingers extended [Old English *thūma*; related to Old Saxon *thūma*, Old High German *thūmo*, Old Norse *thumall* thumb of a glove, Latin *tumēre* to swell] > **'thumbless** *adj* > **'thumb,like** *adj*

thumb drive *n* a thumb-sized portable computer hard drive and data storage device

thumb index *n* **1** a series of indentations cut into the fore edge of a book to facilitate quick reference ▷ *vb* **thumb-index 2** (*tr*) to furnish with a thumb index

thumb knot *n* another name for **overhand knot**

thumbnail (ˈθʌmˌneɪl) *n* **1** the nail of the thumb **2** (*modifier*) concise and brief: *a thumbnail sketch* **3** *computing* a small image which can be expanded

thumbnut (ˈθʌmˌnʌt) *n* a nut with projections enabling it to be turned by the thumb and forefinger; wing nut

thumb piano *n* another name for **mbira**

thumbprint (ˈθʌmˌprɪnt) *n* an impression of the upper part of the thumb, used esp for identification purposes. See **fingerprint**

thumbscrew (ˈθʌmˌskruː) *n* **1** an instrument of

torture that pinches or crushes the thumbs **2** a screw with projections on its head enabling it to be turned by the thumb and forefinger

thumbstall (ˈθʌmˌstɔːl) *n* a protective sheathlike cover for the thumb

thumbtack (ˈθʌmˌtæk) *n chiefly US and Canadian* a short tack with a broad smooth head for fastening papers to a drawing board, etc. Also called (esp in Britain): **drawing pin**

Thummim (ˈθʌmɪm) *n Old Testament* See **Urim and Thummim**

thump (θʌmp) *n* **1** the sound of a heavy solid body hitting or pounding a comparatively soft surface **2** a heavy blow with the hand: *he gave me a thump on the back* ▷ *vb* **3** (*tr*) to strike or beat heavily; pound **4** (*intr*) to throb, beat, or pound violently: *his heart thumped with excitement* [c16 related to Icelandic, Swedish dialect *dumpa* to thump; see THUD, BUMP] > **'thumper** *n*

thumping (ˈθʌmpɪŋ) *adj* (*prenominal*) *slang* huge or excessive: *a thumping loss* > **'thumpingly** *adv*

Thun (German tuːn) *n* **1** a town in central Switzerland, in Bern canton on Lake Thun. Pop: 40 377 (2000) **2** a lake in central Switzerland, formed by a widening of the Aar River. Length: about 17 km (11 miles). Width: 3 km (2 miles). German name: **Thuner See**

thunbergia (θʌnˈbɜːdʒɪə) *n* any plant of the typically climbing tropical genus *Thunbergia* such as black-eyed Susan: family *Acanthaceae* [named after K P *Thunberg* (1743–1822), Swedish traveller and botanist]

thunder (ˈθʌndə) *n* **1** a loud cracking or deep rumbling noise caused by the rapid expansion of atmospheric gases which are suddenly heated by lightning **2** any loud booming sound **3** *rare* a violent threat or denunciation **4 steal someone's thunder** to detract from the attention due to another by forestalling him ▷ *vb* **5** to make (a loud sound) or utter (words) in a manner suggesting thunder **6** (*intr; with it* as subject) to be the case that thunder is being heard **7** (*intr*) to move fast and heavily: *the bus thundered downhill* **8** (*intr*) to utter vehement threats or denunciation; rail [Old English *thunor*; related to Old Saxon *thunar*, Old High German *donar*, Old Norse *thōrr*; see THOR, THURSDAY] > **'thunderer** *n* > **'thundery** *adj*

Thunder Bay *n* a port in central Canada, in Ontario on Lake Superior: formed in 1970 by the amalgamation of Fort William and Port Arthur; the head of the St Lawrence Seaway for Canada. Pop: 103 215 (2001)

thunderbird (ˈθʌndəˌbɜːd) *n* a legendary bird that produces thunder, lightning, and rain according to the folk belief of several North American Indian peoples

thunderbolt (ˈθʌndəˌbəʊlt) *n* **1** a flash of lightning accompanying thunder **2** the imagined agency of destruction produced by a flash of lightning **3** (in mythology) the destructive weapon wielded by several gods, esp the Greek god Zeus. See also **Thor 4** something very startling

thunderbox (ˈθʌndəˌbɒks) *n slang* **1** a portable boxlike lavatory seat that can be placed over a hole in the ground **2** any portable lavatory

thunderclap (ˈθʌndəˌklæp) *n* **1** a loud outburst of thunder **2** something as violent or unexpected as a clap of thunder

thundercloud (ˈθʌndəˌklaʊd) *n* **1** a towering electrically charged cumulonimbus cloud associated with thunderstorms **2** anything that is threatening

thunderhead (ˈθʌndəˌhɛd) *n chiefly US and Canadian* the anvil-shaped top of a cumulonimbus cloud

thundering (ˈθʌndərɪŋ) *adj* (*prenominal*) *slang* very great or excessive: *a thundering idiot* > **'thunderingly** *adv*

thunderous (ˈθʌndərəs) *adj* **1** resembling thunder, esp in loudness: *thunderous clapping* **2** threatening and extremely angry: *she gave him a*

thunderous look > **'thunderously** *adv*

thunder sheet *n* a large sheet of metal that can be shaken to produce a noise resembling thunder as a sound effect for a theatrical production

thundershower (ˈθʌndəˌʃaʊə) *n* a heavy shower during a thunderstorm

thunderstone (ˈθʌndəˌstəʊn) *n* **1** a long tapering stone, fossil, or similar object, formerly thought to be a thunderbolt **2** an archaic word for **thunderbolt**

thunderstorm (ˈθʌndəˌstɔːm) *n* a storm caused by strong rising air currents and characterized by thunder and lightning and usually heavy rain or hail

thunderstruck (ˈθʌndəˌstrʌk) *or* **thunderstricken** (ˈθʌndəˌstrɪkən) *adj* **1** completely taken aback; amazed or shocked **2** *rare* struck by lightning

thunk (θʌŋk) *n* ▷ *vb informal* another word for **thud**

Thurgau (German ˈtuːrgau) *n* a canton of NE Switzerland, on Lake Constance: annexed by the confederated Swiss states in 1460. Capital: Frauenfeld. Pop: 229 800 (2002 est). Area: 1007 sq km (389 sq miles). French name: **Thurgovie** (tyrgɔvi)

thurible (ˈθjʊərɪbəl) *n* another word for **censer** [c15 from Latin *tūribulum* censer, from *tūs* incense]

thurifer (ˈθjʊərɪfə) *n* a person appointed to carry the censer at religious ceremonies [c19 from Latin, from *tūs* incense + *ferre* to carry]

Thuringia (θjʊˈrɪndʒɪə) *n* a state of central Germany, formerly in East Germany. Pop: 2 373 000 (2003 est). German name: **Thüringen** (ˈtyːrɪŋən)

Thuringian (θjʊˈrɪndʒɪən) *adj* **1** of or relating to the German state of Thuringia or its inhabitants ▷ *n* **2** a native or inhabitant of Thuringia

Thuringian Forest *n* a forested mountainous region in E central Germany, rising over 900 m (3000 ft). German name: **Thüringer Wald** (ˈtyːrɪŋər ˈvalt)

Thurrock (ˈθʌrək) *n* a unitary authority in SE England, in Essex. Pop: 145 300 (2003 est). Area: 163 sq km (63 sq miles)

Thurs. *abbreviation for* Thursday

Thursday (ˈθɜːzdɪ) *n* the fifth day of the week; fourth day of the working week [Old English *Thursdæg*, literally: Thor's day; related to Old High German *Donares tag*; see THOR, THUNDER, DAY]

Thursday Island *n* an island in Torres Strait, between NE Australia and New Guinea: administratively part of Queensland, Australia. Area: 4 sq km (1.5 sq miles)

thus (ðʌs) *adv* **1** in this manner: *do it thus* **2** to such a degree: *thus far and no further* ▷ *sentence connector* **3** therefore: *We have failed. Thus we have to take the consequences* [Old English; related to Old Frisian, Old Saxon *thus*]

thuya (ˈθuːjə) *n* a variant spelling of **thuja**

thwack (θwæk) *vb* **1** to beat, hit, or flog, esp with something flat ▷ *n* **2 a** a blow with something flat **b** the sound made by it ▷ *interj* **3** an exclamation imitative of this sound [c16 of imitative origin] > **'thwacker** *n*

thwaite (θweɪt) *n* obsolete except in place names a piece of land cleared from forest or reclaimed from wasteland [from Old Norse *thveit* paddock]

thwart (θwɔːt) *vb* **1** to oppose successfully or prevent; frustrate: *they thwarted the plan* **2** obsolete to be or move across ▷ *n* **3** *nautical* **a** a seat lying across a boat and occupied by an oarsman **b** ▷ *adj* **4** passing or being situated across **5** archaic perverse or stubborn ▷ *prep* ▷ *adv* **6** obsolete across [c13 from Old Norse *thvert*, from *thverr* transverse; related to Old English *thweorh* crooked, Old High German *twerh* transverse] > **'thwartedly** *adv* > **'thwarter** *n*

THX *text messaging abbreviation for* thanks

thy (ðaɪ) *determiner* (usually preceding a consonant) archaic belonging to or associated in some way with you (thou): *thy goodness and mercy*. Compare **thine** [c12 variant of THINE]

t

Thyestes (θaɪˈɛstiːz) *n Greek myth* son of Pelops and brother of Atreus, with whose wife he committed adultery. In revenge, Atreus killed Thyestes' sons and served them to their father at a banquet ▷ **Thyestean** or **Thyestian** (θaɪˈɛstɪən, ˌθaɪɛˈstiːən) *adj*

thylacine (ˈθaɪləˌsaɪn) *n* an extinct or very rare doglike carnivorous marsupial, *Thylacinus cynocephalus*, of Tasmania, having greyish-brown fur with dark vertical stripes on the back: family *Dasyuridae*. Also called: **Tasmanian tiger, Tasmanian wolf** [c19 from New Latin *thȳlacīnus*, from Greek *thulakos* pouch, sack]

thyme (taɪm) *n* any of various small shrubs of the temperate genus *Thymus*, having a strong mintlike odour, small leaves, and white, pink, or red flowers: family *Lamiaceae* (labiates) [c14 from Old French *thym*, from Latin *thymum*, from Greek *thumon*, from *thuein* to make a burnt offering] ▷ ˈ**thymy** *adj*

thymectomy (θaɪˈmɛktəmɪ) *n, pl* **-mies** surgical removal of the thymus

thymelaeaceous (ˌθɪmɪlɪˈeɪʃəs) *adj* of, relating to, or belonging to the *Thymelaeaceae*, a family of trees and shrubs having tough acrid bark and simple leaves: includes spurge laurel, leatherwood, and mezereon [c19 via New Latin, from Greek *thumelaia*, from *thumon* THYME + *elaia* olive]

-thymia *n combining form* indicating a certain emotional condition, mood, or state of mind: *cyclothymia* [New Latin, from Greek *thumos* temper]

thymic (ˈθaɪmɪk) *adj* of or relating to the thymus

thymidine (ˈθaɪmɪˌdiːn) *n* the crystalline nucleoside of thymine, found in DNA. Formula: $C_{10}H_{14}N_2O_5$ [c20 from THYM(INE) + -IDE + -INE²]

thymidylic acid (ˌθaɪmɪˈdɪlɪk) *n* a nucleotide consisting of thymine, deoxyribose, and a phosphate group. It is a constituent of DNA. Also called: **thymidine monophosphate**

thymine (ˈθaɪmiːn) *n* a white crystalline pyrimidine base found in DNA. Formula: $C_5H_6N_2O_2$ [c19 from THYMIC (see THYMUS) + -INE²]

thymocyte (ˈθaɪməsaɪt) *n* a lymphocyte found in the thymus

thymol (ˈθaɪmɒl) *n* a white crystalline substance with an aromatic odour, obtained from the oil of thyme and used as a fungicide, antiseptic, and anthelmintic and in perfumery and embalming; 2-isopropylphenol. Formula: $(CH_3)_2CHC_6H_3(CH_3)OH$ [c19 from THYME + -OL²]

thymus (ˈθaɪməs) *n, pl* **-muses** or **-mi** (-maɪ) a glandular organ of vertebrates, consisting in man of two lobes situated below the thyroid. In early life it produces lymphocytes and is thought to influence certain immunological responses. It atrophies with age and is almost nonexistent in the adult [c17 from New Latin, from Greek *thumos* sweetbread]

thyratron (ˈθaɪrəˌtrɒn) *n electronics* a gas-filled tube that has three electrodes and can be switched between an 'off' state and an 'on' state. It has been superseded, except for application involving high-power switching, by the thyristor [c20 originally a trademark, from Greek *thura* door, valve + -TRON]

thyristor (θaɪˈrɪstə) *n* any of a group of semiconductor devices, such as the silicon-controlled rectifier, that can be switched between two states [c20 from THYR(ATRON) + (TRANS)ISTOR]

thyro- or before a vowel **thyr-** combining form thyroid: *thyrotoxicosis; thyrotropin*

thyrocalcitonin (ˌθaɪrəʊˌkælsɪˈtəʊnɪn) *n* another name for **calcitonin** [c20 from THYRO- + CALCITONIN]

thyroid (ˈθaɪrɔɪd) *adj* 1 of or relating to the thyroid gland 2 of or relating to the largest cartilage of the larynx ▷ *n* 3 See **thyroid gland** 4 Also: **thyroid extract** the powdered preparation made from the thyroid gland of certain animals, used to treat hypothyroidism [c18 from New Latin *thyroīdēs*, from Greek *thureoeidēs*, from *thureos* oblong (literally: door-shaped) shield, from *thura* door]

thyroidectomy (ˌθaɪrɔɪˈdɛktəmɪ) *n, pl* **-mies** surgical removal of all or part of the thyroid gland

thyroid gland *n* an endocrine gland of vertebrates, consisting in man of two lobes near the base of the neck. It secretes hormones that control metabolism and body growth

thyroiditis (ˌθaɪrɔɪˈdaɪtɪs) *n* inflammation of the thyroid gland

thyroid-stimulating hormone *n* another name for **thyrotropin** Abbreviation: **TSH**

thyrotoxicosis (ˌθaɪrəʊˌtɒksɪˈkəʊsɪs) *n* another name for **hyperthyroidism**

thyrotropin (ˌθaɪrəʊˈtrəʊpɪn) or **thyrotrophin** *n* a glycoprotein hormone secreted by the anterior lobe of the pituitary gland: it stimulates the activity of the thyroid gland. Also called: **thyroid-stimulating hormone** [c20 from THYRO- + -TROPE + -IN]

thyroxine (θaɪˈrɒksiːn, -sɪn) or **thyroxin** (θaɪˈrɒksɪn) *n* the principal hormone produced by the thyroid gland: it increases the metabolic rate of tissues and also controls growth, as in amphibian metamorphosis. It can be synthesized or extracted from the thyroid glands of animals and used to treat hypothyroidism. Chemical name: tetra-iodothyronine; formula: $C_{15}H_{11}I_4NO_4$ [c19 from THYRO- + OXY-² + -INE²]

thyrse (θɜːs) or **thyrsus** (ˈθɜːsəs) *n, pl* **thyrses** or **thyrsi** (ˈθɜːsaɪ) *botany* a type of inflorescence, occurring in the lilac and grape, in which the main branch is racemose and the lateral branches cymose [c17 from French: THYRSUS] ▷ ˈ**thyrsoid** *adj*

thyrsus (ˈθɜːsəs) *n, pl* **-si** (-saɪ) 1 *Greek myth* a staff, usually one tipped with a pine cone, borne by Dionysus (Bacchus) and his followers 2 a variant spelling of **thyrse** [c18 from Latin, from Greek *thursos* stalk]

thysanuran (ˌθɪsəˈnjʊərən) *n* 1 any primitive wingless insect of the order *Thysanura*, which comprises the bristletails ▷ *adj* 2 of, relating to, or belonging to the order *Thysanura* [c19 from New Latin, from Greek *thusanos* fringe + *oura* tail] ▷ ˌ**thysaˈnurous** *adj*

thyself (ðaɪˈsɛlf) *pron archaic* **a** the reflexive form of **thou** or **thee** **b** (intensifier): *thou, thyself, wouldst know*

ti¹ (tiː) *n music* a variant spelling of **te**

ti² (tiː) *n, pl* **tis** 1 a woody palmlike agave plant, *Cordyline terminalis*, of the East Indies, having white, mauve, or reddish flowers. The sword-shaped leaves are used for garments, fodder, thatch, etc, and the root for food and liquor 2 a similar and related plant, *Cordyline australis*, of New Zealand [of Polynesian origin]

Ti the chemical symbol for titanium

TIA *med abbreviation for* transient ischaemic attack; a stroke causing minor and temporary symptoms

Tia Juana (ˈtɪə ˈwɑːnə; *Spanish* ˈtia ˈxwana) *n* a variant spelling of **Tijuana**

Tia Maria (ˈtɪə məˈrɪə) *n trademark* a coffee-flavoured liqueur from the Caribbean

Tianjin (ˈtjɛnˈdʒɪn), **Tientsin** or **T'ien-ching** *n* an industrial city in NE China, in Hebei province, on the Grand Canal, 51 km (32 miles) from the Yellow Sea: the third largest city in China; seat of Nankai University (1919). Pop: 9 346 000 (2005 est)

Tian Shan or **Tien Shan** (ˈtjɛnˈʃɑːn) *n* a great mountain system of central Asia, in Kyrgyzstan and the Xinjiang Uygur Autonomous Region of W China, extending for about 2500 km (1500 miles). Highest peak: Pobeda Peak, 7439 m (24 406 ft). Russian name: **Tyan-Shan**

tiara (tɪˈɑːrə) *n* 1 a woman's semicircular jewelled headdress for formal occasions 2 a high headdress worn by Persian kings in ancient times 3 *RC Church* **a** a headdress worn by the pope, consisting of a beehive-shaped diadem surrounded by three coronets **b** the office or rank of pope [c16 via Latin from Greek, of Oriental origin] ▷ **tiˈaraed** *adj*

Tiber (ˈtaɪbə) *n* a river in central Italy, rising in the Tuscan Apennines and flowing south through Rome to the Tyrrhenian Sea. Length: 405 km (252 miles). Ancient name: **Tiberis** (ˈtiːbərɪs) Italian name: **Tevere**

Tiberias (taɪˈbɪərɪˌæs) *n* 1 a resort in N Israel, on the Sea of Galilee: an important Jewish centre after the destruction of Jerusalem by the Romans. Pop: 40 100 (2003 est) 2 **Lake** another name for the (Sea of) **Galilee**

Tibesti or **Tibesti Massif** (tɪˈbɛstɪ) *n* a mountain range of volcanic origin in NW Chad, in the central Sahara extending for about 480 km (300 miles). Highest peak: Emi Koussi, 3415 m (11 204 ft)

Tibet (tɪˈbɛt) *n* an autonomous region of SW China: Europeans strictly excluded in the 19th century; invaded by China in 1950; rebellion (1959) against Chinese rule suppressed and the Dalai Lama fled to India; military rule imposed (1989–90) after continued demands for independence; consists largely of a vast high plateau between the Himalayas and Kunlun Mountains; formerly a theocracy and the centre of Lamaism. Capital: Lhasa. Pop: 2 700 000 (2003 est). Area: 1 221 601 sq km (471 660 sq miles). Chinese names: **Xizang Autonomous Region, Sitsang**

Tibetan (tɪˈbɛtᵊn) *adj* 1 of, relating to, or characteristic of Tibet, its people, or their language ▷ *n* 2 a native or inhabitant of Tibet 3 the language of Tibet, belonging to the Sino-Tibetan family

Tibetan mastiff *n* a heavy well-built dog of a Tibetan breed with a long thick coat and a bushy tail carried curled over its back, often used as a guard dog

Tibetan spaniel *n* a small long-bodied variety of spaniel with a long silky coat and a well-feathered tail carried curled over its back

Tibetan terrier *n* a breed of dog with a long dense shaggy coat: it resembles a small Old English sheepdog

Tibeto-Burman (tɪˈbɛtəʊˈbɜːmən) *n* 1 a branch of the Sino-Tibetan family of languages, sometimes regarded as a family in its own right. Compare **Sinitic** ▷ *adj* 2 belonging or relating to this group of languages

tibia (ˈtɪbɪə) *n, pl* **tibiae** (ˈtɪbɪˌiː) or **tibias** 1 Also called: **shinbone** the inner and thicker of the two bones of the human leg between the knee and ankle. Compare **fibula** 2 the corresponding bone in other vertebrates 3 the fourth segment of an insect's leg, lying between the femur and the tarsus [c16 from Latin: leg, pipe] ▷ ˈ**tibial** *adj*

tibiotarsus (ˌtɪbɪəʊˈtɑːsəs) *n* the bone in the leg of a bird formed by fusion of the tibia and some of the tarsal bones [c19 from *tibio-* (combining form of TIBIA) + TARSUS]

Tibur (ˈtaɪbə) *n* the ancient name for **Tivoli**

tic (tɪk) *n pathol* 1 spasmodic twitching of a particular group of muscles 2 See **tic douloureux** [c19 from French, of uncertain origin; compare Italian *ticche*]

tical (tɪˈkɑːl, -ˈkɔːl, ˈtiːkᵊl) *n, pl* **-cals** or **-cal** 1 the former standard monetary unit of Thailand, replaced by the baht in 1928 2 a unit of weight, formerly used in Thailand, equal to about half an ounce or 14 grams [c17 via Siamese and Portuguese from Malay *tikal* monetary unit]

tic douloureux (ˈtɪk ˌduːləˈruː) *n* a condition of momentary stabbing pain along the trigeminal nerve. Also called: **trigeminal neuralgia** [c19 from French, literally: painful tic]

tichy (ˈtɪtʃɪ) *adj* **tichier, tichiest** a variant spelling of **titchy**

Ticino (Italian tiˈtʃiːno) *n* 1 a canton in S Switzerland: predominantly Italian speaking and Roman Catholic; mountainous. Capital: Bellinzona. Pop: 314 600 (2002 est). Area: 2810 sq km (1085 sq miles). German name: **Tessin** 2 a river in S central Europe, rising in S central Switzerland and flowing southeast and west to Lake Maggiore, then southeast to the River Po.

Length: 248 km (154 miles)

tick[1] (tɪk) *n* **1** a recurrent metallic tapping or clicking sound, such as that made by a clock or watch **2** *Brit informal* a moment or instant **3** a mark (✓) or dash used to check off or indicate the correctness of something **4** *commerce* the smallest increment of a price fluctuation in a commodity exchange. Tick size is usually 0.01% of the nominal value of the trading unit ▷ *vb* **5** to produce a recurrent tapping sound or indicate by such a sound: *the clock ticked the minutes away* **6** (when *tr*, often foll by *off*) to mark or check (something, such as a list) with a tick **7** **what makes someone tick** *informal* the basic drive or motivation of a person ▷ See also **tick off, tick over** [c13 from Low German *tikk* touch; related to Old High German *zekōn* to pluck, Norwegian *tikke* to touch]

tick[2] (tɪk) *n* **1** any of various small parasitic arachnids of the families *Ixodidae* (**hard ticks**) and *Argasidae*, (**soft ticks**), typically living on the skin of warm-blooded animals and feeding on the blood and tissues of their hosts: order *Acarina* (mites and ticks). See also **sheep tick** (sense 1) Related adj: **acaroid** **2** any of certain other arachnids of the order *Acarina* **3** any of certain insects of the dipterous family *Hippoboscidae* that are ectoparasitic on horses, cattle, sheep, etc, esp the sheep ked [Old English *ticca*; related to Middle High German *zeche* tick, Middle Irish *dega* stag beetle]

tick[3] (tɪk) *n* **1** the strong covering of a pillow, mattress, etc **2** *informal* short for **ticking** [c15 probably from Middle Dutch *tīke*; related to Old High German *ziecha* pillow cover, Latin *tēca* case, Greek *thēkē*]

tick[4] (tɪk) *n Brit informal* account or credit (esp in the phrase **on tick**) [c17 shortened from TICKET]

tick-bird *n* another name for **oxpecker** [c19 so called because it eats insects off animals' backs]

tick-borne typhus *n* another name for **Rocky Mountain spotted fever**

tick box *n* (on a form, questionnaire, or test) a square in which one places a tick to show agreement with the accompanying statement

ticker ('tɪkə) *n* **1** *slang* **a** the heart **b** a watch **2** a person or thing that ticks **3** *stock exchange* the US word for **tape machine** (sense 2)

ticker tape *n* **1** *stock exchange* a continuous paper ribbon on which a tape machine automatically prints current stock quotations **2** **ticker-tape reception** (*or* **parade**) (mainly in New York) the showering of the motorcade of a distinguished politician, visiting head of state, etc, with ticker tape as a sign of welcome

ticket ('tɪkɪt) *n* **1** **a** a piece of paper, cardboard, etc, showing that the holder is entitled to certain rights, such as travel on a train or bus, entry to a place of public entertainment, etc **b** (*modifier*) concerned with or relating to the issue, sale, or checking of tickets: *a ticket office; ticket collector* **2** a piece of card, cloth, etc, attached to an article showing information such as its price, size, or washing instructions **3** a summons served for a parking offence or violation of traffic regulations **4** *informal* the certificate of competence issued to a ship's captain or an aircraft pilot **5** *chiefly US and NZ* the group of candidates nominated by one party in an election; slate **6** *chiefly US* the declared policy of a political party at an election **7** *Brit informal* a certificate of discharge from the armed forces **8** *informal* the right or appropriate thing: *that's the ticket* **9** **have (got) tickets on oneself** *Austral informal* to be conceited ▷ *vb* **-ets, -eting, -eted** (*tr*) **10** to issue or attach a ticket or tickets to **11** *informal* to earmark for a particular purpose [c17 from Old French *etiquet*, from *estiquier* to stick on, from Middle Dutch *steken* to STICK[2]] > **'ticketing** *n*

ticket day *n* (on the London Stock Exchange) the day on which selling brokers receive from buying brokers the names of investors who have made purchases during the previous account. Also called: **name day** Compare **account day**

ticket of leave *n* (formerly in Britain) a permit allowing a convict (**ticket-of-leave man**) to leave prison, after serving only part of his sentence, with certain restrictions placed on him

tickets ('tɪkɪts) *pl n South African informal* the end; that was it [of unknown origin]

ticket tout *n* See **tout** (sense 6)

tickety-boo (ˌtɪkɪtɪ'buː) *adj Brit old-fashioned informal* as it should be; correct; satisfactory [c20 of obscure origin]

tickey ('tɪkɪ) *n* a South African threepenny piece, which was replaced by the five-cent coin in 1961 [of uncertain origin]

tick fever *n* **1** any acute infectious febrile disease caused by the bite of an infected tick **2** another name for **Rocky Mountain spotted fever**

ticking ('tɪkɪŋ) *n* a strong cotton fabric, often striped, used esp for mattress and pillow covers [c17 from TICK[3]]

ticklace ('tɪkəˌlæs) *n Canadian* (in Newfoundland) a kittiwake [imitative of the bird's cry]

tickle ('tɪkᵊl) *vb* **1** to touch, stroke, or poke (a person, part of the body, etc) so as to produce pleasure, laughter, or a twitching sensation **2** (*tr*) to excite pleasurably; gratify **3** (*tr*) to delight or entertain (often in the phrase **tickle one's fancy**) **4** (*intr*) to itch or tingle **5** (*tr*) to catch (a fish, esp a trout) by grasping it with the hands and gently moving the fingers into its gills **6** **tickle pink** *or* **to death** *informal* to please greatly: *he was tickled pink to be elected president* ▷ *n* **7** a sensation of light stroking or itching **8** the act of tickling [c14 related to Old English *tinclian*, Old High German *kizziton*, Old Norse *kitla*, Latin *titillāre* to TITILLATE] > **'tickly** *adj*

tickler ('tɪklə) *n* **1** *informal, chiefly Brit* a difficult or delicate problem **2** Also called: **tickler file** *US* a memorandum book or file **3** *accounting, US* a single-entry business journal **4** a person or thing that tickles

tickler coil *n* a small inductance coil connected in series in the anode circuit of a valve and magnetically coupled to a coil in the grid circuit to provide feedback

ticklish ('tɪklɪʃ) *adj* **1** susceptible and sensitive to being tickled **2** delicate or difficult: *a ticklish situation* **3** easily upset or offended > **'ticklishly** *adv* > **'ticklishness** *n*

tick off *vb* (*tr, adverb*) **1** to mark with a tick **2** *informal, chiefly Brit* to scold; reprimand > **ticking off** *or* **ticking-off** *n*

tick over *vb* (*intr, adverb*) **1** Also: **idle** *Brit* (of an engine) to run at low speed with the throttle control closed and the transmission disengaged **2** to run smoothly without any major changes: *keep the firm ticking over until I get back* ▷ *n* **tick-over** **3** *Brit* **a** the speed of an engine when it is ticking over **b** (*as modifier*): *tick-over speed*

ticktack ('tɪkˌtæk) *n* **1** *Brit* a system of sign language, mainly using the hands, by which bookmakers transmit their odds to each other at racecourses **2** *US* a ticking sound, as made by a clock [from TICK[1]]

tick-tack-toe (ˌtɪktæk'təʊ) *or* **tick-tack-too** (ˌtɪktæk'tuː) *n US and Canadian* a game in which two players, one using a nought, "O", the other a cross, "X", alternately mark one square out of nine formed by two pairs of crossed lines, the winner being the first to get three of his symbols in a row. Also called (in Britain and certain other countries): **noughts and crosses** [c19 from TICKTACK (meaning: an obsolete variety of backgammon)]

ticktock ('tɪkˌtɒk) *n* **1** a ticking sound as made by a clock ▷ *vb* **2** (*intr*) to make a ticking sound

tick trefoil *n* any of various tropical and subtropical leguminous plants of the genus *Desmodium*, having trifoliate leaves, clusters of small purplish or white flowers, and sticky jointed seed pods, which separate into segments that cling to animals. Also called: **beggar-ticks**

Ticonderoga (ˌtaɪkɒndə'rəʊgə) *n* a village in NE New York State, on Lake George: site of Fort Ticonderoga, scene of battles between the British and French (1758–59) and a strategic point in the War of American Independence

t.i.d. (in prescriptions) *abbreviation for* ter in die [Latin: three times a day]

tidal ('taɪdᵊl) *adj* **1** relating to, characterized by, or affected by tides: *a tidal estuary* **2** dependent on the state of the tide: *a tidal ferry* **3** (of a glacier) reaching the sea and discharging floes or icebergs > **'tidally** *adv*

tidal basin *n* a basin for vessels that is filled at high tide

tidal energy *n* energy obtained by harnessing tidal power

tidal power *n* the use of the rise and fall of tides involving very large volumes of water at low heads to generate electric power

tidal volume *n* **1** the volume of water associated with a rising tide **2** *physiol* the amount of air passing into and out of the lungs during normal breathing

tidal wave *n* **1** a name (not accepted in technical usage) for **tsunami** **2** an unusually large incoming wave, often caused by high winds and spring tides **3** a forceful and widespread movement in public opinion, action, etc

tidbit ('tɪdˌbɪt) *n* the usual US spelling of **titbit**

tiddler ('tɪdlə) *n Brit informal* **1** a very small fish or aquatic creature, esp a stickleback, minnow, or tadpole **2** a small child, esp one undersized for its age [c19 from dialectal *tittlebat*, childish variant of STICKLEBACK, influenced by TIDDLY[1]]

tiddly[1] ('tɪdlɪ) *adj* **-dlier, -dliest** *Brit* small; tiny [c19 childish variant of LITTLE]

tiddly[2] ('tɪdlɪ) *adj* **-dlier, -dliest** *slang, chiefly Brit* slightly drunk [C19 (meaning: a drink): of unknown origin]

tiddlywink ('tɪdlɪˌwɪŋk) *n* any of the discs used in the game of tiddlywinks

tiddlywinks ('tɪdlɪˌwɪŋks) *n* (*functioning as singular*) a game in which players try to flick discs of plastic into a cup by pressing them sharply on the side with other larger discs [c19 probably from TIDDLY[1] + dialect *wink*, variant of WINCH[1]]

tide[1] (taɪd) *n* **1** the cyclic rise and fall of sea level caused by the gravitational pull of the sun and moon. There are usually two high tides and two low tides in each lunar day. See also **tide-generating force, neap tide, spring tide** **2** the current, ebb, or flow of water at a specified place resulting from these changes in level: *the tide is coming in* **3** See **ebb** (sense 3) and **flood** (sense 3) **4** a widespread tendency or movement: *the tide of resentment against the government* **5** a critical point in time; turning point: *the tide of his fortunes* **6** *Northern English dialect* a fair or holiday **7** *archaic except in combination* a season or time: *Christmastide* **8** *rare* any body of mobile water, such as a stream **9** *archaic* a favourable opportunity ▷ *vb* **10** to carry or be carried with or as if with the tide **11** (*intr*) to ebb and flow like the tide [Old English *tīd* time; related to Old High German *zīt*, Old Norse *tīthr* time] > **'tideless** *adj* > **'tideˌlike** *adj*

tide[2] (taɪd) *vb* (*intr*) *archaic* to happen [Old English *tīdan*; related to Old Frisian *tīdia* to proceed to, Middle Low German *tīden* to hurry, Old Norse *tītha* to desire]

tide-gauge *n* a gauge used to measure extremes or the present level of tidal movement

tide-generating force *n* the difference between the force of gravity exerted by the moon or the sun on a particle of water in the ocean and that exerted on an equal mass of matter at the centre of the earth. The lunar tide-generating forces are about 2.2 times greater than are the solar ones. See also **neap tide, spring tide, tide**[1]

tideland ('taɪdˌlænd) *n US* land between high-water and low-water marks

tidemark ('taɪdˌmɑːk) *n* **1** a mark left by the

t

highest or lowest point of a tide **2** a marker indicating the highest or lowest point reached by a tide **3** *chiefly Brit* a mark showing a level reached by a liquid: *a tidemark on the bath* **4** *informal, chiefly Brit* a dirty mark on the skin, indicating the extent to which someone has washed

tide over *vb* (*tr*) to help to get through (a period of difficulty, distress, etc): *the money tided him over until he got a job*

tide race *n* a fast-running tidal current

tide-rip *n* another word for **riptide** (sense 1)

tide table *n* a table showing the height of the tide at different times of day over a period at a particular place

tidewaiter ('taɪdˌweɪtə) *n* (formerly) a customs officer who boarded and inspected incoming ships

tidewater ('taɪdˌwɔːtə) *n* **1** water that advances and recedes with the tide **2** water that covers land that is dry at low tide **3** *US* **a** coastal land drained by tidal streams **b** (*as modifier*): *tidewater regions*

tideway ('taɪdˌweɪ) *n* a strong tidal current or its channel, esp the tidal part of a river

tidings ('taɪdɪŋz) *pl n* information or news [Old English *tīdung*; related to Middle Low German *tīdinge* information, Old Norse *tidhendi* events; see TIDE[2]]

tidy ('taɪdɪ) *adj* **-dier, -diest 1** characterized by or indicating neatness and order **2** *informal* considerable: *a tidy sum of money* ▷ *vb* **-dies, -dying, -died 3** (when *intr*, usually foll by *up*) to put (things) in order; neaten ▷ *n, pl* **-dies 4 a** a small container in which odds and ends are kept **b sink tidy** a container with holes in the bottom, kept in the sink to retain rubbish that might clog the plug hole **5** *chiefly US and Canadian* an ornamental protective covering for the back or arms of a chair [C13 (in the sense: timely, seasonable, excellent): from TIDE[1] + -Y[1]; related to Dutch *tijdig* timely]
> **'tidily** *adv* > **'tidiness** *n*

tie (taɪ) *vb* **ties, tying, tied 1** (when *tr*, often foll by *up*) to fasten or be fastened with string, thread, etc **2** to make (a knot or bow) in (something): *to tie a knot; tie a ribbon* **3** (*tr*) to restrict or secure **4** to equal the score of a competitor or fellow candidate **5** (*tr*) *informal* to unite in marriage **6** *music* **a** to execute (two successive notes of the same pitch) as though they formed one note of composite time value **b** to connect (two printed notes) with a tie **7 fit to be tied** *slang* very angry or upset ▷ *n* **8** a bond, link, or fastening **9** a restriction or restraint **10** a string, wire, ribbon, etc, with which something is tied **11** a long narrow piece of material worn, esp by men, under the collar of a shirt, tied in a knot close to the throat with the ends hanging down the front. US name: **necktie 12 a** an equality in score, attainment, etc, in a contest **b** the match or competition in which such a result is attained **13** a structural member carrying tension, such as a tie beam or tie rod **14** *sport, Brit* a match or game in an eliminating competition: *a cup tie* **15** (*usually plural*) a shoe fastened by means of laces **16** the US and Canadian name for **sleeper** (on a railway track) **17** *music* a slur connecting two notes of the same pitch indicating that the sound is to be prolonged for their joint time value **18** *surveying* one of two measurements running from two points on a survey line to a point of detail to fix its position **19** *lacemaking* another name for **bride**[2] ▷ See also **tie in, tie up** [Old English *tīgan* to tie; related to Old Norse *teygja* to draw, stretch out, Old English *tēon* to pull; see TUG, TOW[1], TIGHT]

tieback ('taɪˌbæk) *n* **a** a length of cord, ribbon, or other fabric used for tying a curtain to one side **b** a curtain having such a device

tie beam *n* a horizontal beam that serves to prevent two other structural members from separating, esp one that connects two corresponding rafters in a roof or roof truss

tie-break *or* **tie-breaker** ('taɪˌbreɪkə) *n* **1** *tennis* a method of deciding quickly the result of a set drawn at six-all, usually involving the playing of one deciding game for the best of twelve points in which the service changes after every two points **2** any contest or game played to decide a winner when contestants have tied scores

tie clasp *n* a clip, often ornamental, which holds a tie in place against a shirt. Also called: **tie clip**

tied (taɪd) *adj Brit* **1** (of a public house, retail shop, etc) obliged to sell only the beer, products, etc of a particular producer: *a tied house; tied outlet* **2** (of a house or cottage) rented out to the tenant for as long as he is employed by the owner **3** (of a loan) made by one nation to another on condition that the money is spent on goods or services provided by the lending nation

tie-dyed *adj* (of textiles) given a pattern by tie-dyeing

tie-dyeing *n* a method of dyeing textiles to produce patterns by tying sections of the cloth together so that they will not absorb the dye. Also called: **tie-and-dye**

tie in *vb* (*adverb*) **1** to come or bring into a certain relationship; coordinate ▷ *n* **tie-in 2** a link, relationship, or coordination **3** publicity material, a book, tape, etc, linked to a film or broadcast programme or series **4** *US* **a** a sale or advertisement offering products of which a purchaser must buy one or more in addition to his purchase **b** an item sold or advertised in this way, esp the extra item **c** (*as modifier*): *a tie-in sale*

tie line *n* a telephone line between two private branch exchanges or private exchanges that may or may not pass through a main exchange

tiemannite ('tiːməˌnaɪt) *n* a grey mineral consisting of mercury selenide. Formula: HgSe [C19 named after J C W F *Tiemann* (1848–99), German scientist]

Tien Shan ('tjɛn'ʃɑːn) *n* a variant transliteration of the Chinese name for the **Tian Shan**

Tientsin ('tjɛn'tsɪn) *n* a variant transliteration of the Chinese name for **Tianjin**

tiepin ('taɪˌpɪn) *n* an ornamental pin of various shapes used to pin the two ends of a tie to a shirt

tier[1] (tɪə) *n* **1** one of a set of rows placed one above and behind the other, such as theatre seats **2 a** a layer or level **b** (*in combination*): *a three-tier cake* **3** a rank, order, or row ▷ *vb* **4** to be or arrange in tiers [C16 from Old French *tire* rank, of Germanic origin; compare Old English *tīr* embellishment]

tier[2] ('taɪə) *n* a person or thing that ties

tierce (tɪəs) *n* **1** a variant of **terce 2** the third of eight basic positions from which a parry or attack can be made in fencing **3** (tɜːs) *cards* a sequence of three cards in the same suit **4** an obsolete measure of capacity equal to 42 wine gallons [C15 from Old French, feminine of *tiers* third, from Latin *tertius*]

tierce de Picardie (*French* tjɛrs də pikardi) *n* another term for **Picardy third**

tiercel ('tɪəsᵊl) *n* a variant of **tercel**

tie rod *n* any rod- or bar-shaped structural member designed to prevent the separation of two parts, as in a vehicle

Tierra del Fuego (*Spanish* 'tjɛrra ðɛl 'fweɣo) *n* an archipelago at the S extremity of South America, separated from the mainland by the Strait of Magellan: the west and south belong to Chile, the east to Argentina. Area: 73 643 sq km (28 434 sq miles)

tie up *vb* (*adverb*) **1** (*tr*) to attach or bind securely with or as if with string, rope, etc **2** to moor (a vessel) **3** (*tr; often passive*) to engage the attentions of: *he's tied up at the moment and can't see you* **4** (*tr; often passive*) to conclude (the organization of something): *the plans for the trip were tied up well in advance* **5** to come or bring to a complete standstill **6** (*tr*) to invest or commit (funds, etc) and so make unavailable for other uses **7** (*tr*) to subject (property) to conditions that prevent sale, alienation, or other action ▷ *n* **tie-up 8** a link or connection **9** *chiefly US and Canadian* a standstill **10** *chiefly US and Canadian* an informal term for **traffic jam**

tiff[1] (tɪf) *n* **1** a petty quarrel **2** a fit of ill humour ▷ *vb* **3** (*intr*) to have or be in a tiff [C18 of unknown origin]

tiff[2] (tɪf) *n archaic* a small draught of alcoholic drink; dram [C18 see TIFFIN]

Tiffanie ('tɪfənɪ) *n* a breed of cat with semi-long hair, having a white undercoat with the ends coloured. Also called: **Australian Tiffanie, Asian semi-longhair**

tiffany ('tɪfənɪ) *n, pl* **-nies** a sheer fine gauzy fabric [C17 (in the sense: a fine dress worn on Twelfth Night): from Old French *tifanie*, from ecclesiastical Latin *theophania* Epiphany; see THEOPHANY]

Tiffany[2] *n, pl* **-nies** another name for **Chantilly** (sense 2)

Tiffany glass *n* another term for **Favrile glass**

tiffin ('tɪfɪn) *n* (in India) a light meal, esp one taken at midday [C18 probably from obsolete *tiffing*, from *tiff* to sip]

Tiflis (tɪf'liːs) *n* transliteration of the Russian name for **Tbilisi**

tig (tɪg) *n, vb* **tigs, tigging, tigged** another name for **tag**[1] (senses 1, 4)

tiger ('taɪgə) *n* **1** a large feline mammal, *Panthera tigris*, of forests in most of Asia, having a tawny yellow coat with black stripes **2** (*not in technical use*) any of various other animals, such as the jaguar, leopard, and thylacine **3** a dynamic, forceful, or cruel person **4 a** a country, esp in E Asia, that is achieving rapid economic growth **b** (*as modifier*): *a tiger economy* **5** *archaic* a servant in livery, esp a page or groom **6** short for **tiger moth 7** *South African slang* a ten-rand note **8 have a tiger by the tail** *informal* to find oneself in a situation that has turned out to be much more difficult to control than one had expected [C13 from Old French *tigre*, from Latin *tigris*, from Greek, of Iranian origin]
> **'tigerish** *or* **'tigrish** *adj* > **'tigerishly** *adv*
> **'tigerishness** *n* > **'tiger-like** *adj*

Tiger ('taɪgə) *n* See **TIGR**

Tiger balm *n trademark* a mentholated ointment widely used as a panacea

tiger beetle *n* any active predatory beetle of the family *Cicindelidae*, chiefly of warm dry regions, having powerful mandibles and long legs [C19 so called because it has patterned, sometimes striped, wing covers]

tiger cat *n* **1** a medium-sized feline mammal, *Felis tigrina*, of Central and South America, having a dark-striped coat **2** any similar feline with tiger-like markings, such as the margay

tiger lily *n* **1** a lily plant, *Lilium tigrinum*, of China and Japan, cultivated for its flowers, which have black-spotted orange reflexed petals **2** any of various similar lilies

tiger market *n informal* any of the four most important markets on the Pacific rim after Japan: Hong Kong, South Korea, Singapore, and Taiwan. Compare **dragon market**

tiger moth *n* any of a group of arctiid moths, mostly boldly marked, often in black, orange, and yellow, of the genera *Arctia, Parasemia, Euplagia*, etc, producing woolly bear larvae and typified by the **garden tiger** (*Arctia caja*). Often shortened to: **tiger**

tiger prawn *n* a large edible prawn of the genus *Penaeus* with dark bands across the body, fished commercially in the Indian and Pacific oceans

tiger's-eye ('taɪgəzˌaɪ) *or* **tigereye** ('taɪgərˌaɪ) *n* **1** a golden brown silicified variety of crocidolite, used as an ornamental stone **2** a glaze resembling this, used on pottery

tiger shark *n* **1** a voracious omnivorous requiem shark, *Galeocerdo cuvieri*, chiefly of tropical waters, having a striped or spotted body **2** any of certain other spotted sharks, such as *Stegostoma tigrinum*, of the Indian Ocean

tiger snake *n* a highly venomous brown-and-yellow elapid snake, *Notechis scutatus*, of Australia

Tiggerish ('tɪgərɪʃ) *adj* irrepressibly bouncy and cheerful [C20 after *Tigger*, a character in the

Winnie the Pooh children's stories by the English writer A A Milne (1882–1956)]

tight (taɪt) *adj* **1** stretched or drawn so as not to be loose; taut: *a tight cord* **2** fitting or covering in a close manner: *a tight dress* **3** held, made, fixed, or closed firmly and securely: *a tight knot* **4 a** of close and compact construction or organization, esp so as to be impervious to water, air, etc **b** (*in combination*): *watertight*; *airtight* **5** unyielding or stringent: *to keep a tight hold on resources* **6** cramped or constricted: *a tight fit* **7** mean or miserly **8** difficult and problematic: *a tight situation* **9** hardly profitable: *a tight bargain* **10** *economics* **a** (of a commodity) difficult to obtain; in excess demand **b** (of funds, money, etc) difficult and expensive to borrow because of high demand or restrictive monetary policy **c** (of markets) characterized by excess demand or scarcity with prices tending to rise. Compare **easy** (sense 8) **11** (of a match or game) very close or even **12** (of a team or group, esp of a pop group) playing well together, in a disciplined coordinated way **13** *informal* drunk **14** *informal* (of a person) showing tension **15** *archaic or dialect* neat ▷ *adv* **16** in a close, firm, or secure way: *pull it tight* **17 sit tight a** to wait patiently; bide one's time **b** to maintain one's position, stand, or opinion firmly **18 sleep tight** to sleep soundly [C14 probably variant of *thight*, from Old Norse *thēttr* close; related to Middle High German *dīhte* thick] > **'tightly** *adv* > **'tightness** *n*

tightass ('taɪt,æs) *n slang, chiefly US* an inhibited or excessively self-controlled person > **'tight,assed** *adj*

tighten ('taɪtᵊn) *vb* **1** to make or become tight or tighter **2 tighten one's belt** to economize > **'tightener** *n*

tightfisted (,taɪt'fɪstɪd) *adj* mean; miserly

tight forward *n rugby* one of a number of forwards who are bound wholly into the scrum. Compare **loose forward**

tight head *n rugby* the prop on the hooker's right in the front row of a scrum. Compare **loose head**

tightknit (,taɪt'nɪt) *adj* **1** closely integrated: *a tightknit community* **2** organized carefully and concisely

tight-lipped *adj* **1** reticent, secretive, or taciturn **2** with the lips pressed tightly together, as through anger

tightrope ('taɪt,rəʊp) *n* **1** a rope or cable stretched taut above the ground on which acrobats walk or perform balancing feats **2** to be in a difficult situation that demands careful and considered behaviour

tightrope walker *n* an acrobat who performs on a tightrope > **tightrope walking** *n*

tights (taɪts) *pl n* **1 a** Also called (US, Canadian, Austral, and NZ): **pantyhose** a one-piece clinging garment covering the body from the waist to the feet, worn by women in place of stockings **b** *US and Canadian* Also called: **leotards** a similar, tight-fitting garment worn instead of trousers by either sex **2** a similar garment formerly worn by men, as in the 16th century with a doublet

tightwad ('taɪt,wɒd) *n slang, chiefly US and Canadian* a stingy person; miser

tiglic acid ('tɪglɪk) *n* a syrupy liquid or crystalline colourless unsaturated carboxylic acid, with the *trans*-configuration, found in croton oil and used in perfumery; *trans*-2-methyl-2-butenoic acid. Formula: $CH_3CH{:}C(CH_3)COOH$ [C19 *tiglic*, from New Latin phrase *Croton tiglium* (name of the croton plant), of uncertain origin]

Ti2GO *text messaging abbreviation for* time to go

tigon ('taɪgən) *or* **tiglon** ('tɪglɒn) *n* the hybrid offspring of a male tiger and a female lion

TIGR *abbreviation for* Treasury Investment Growth Receipts: a bond denominated in dollars and linked to US treasury bonds, the yield on which is taxed in the UK as income when it is cashed or redeemed. Also called: **Tiger**

Tigré *or* **Tigray** ('ti:greɪ) *n* **1** an autonomous region of N Ethiopia, bordering on Eritrea: formerly a separate kingdom. Capital: Mekele. Pop: 3 136 267 (1994). Area: 53 498 sq km (20 656 sq miles) **2** a language of NE Ethiopia, belonging to the SE Semitic subfamily of the Afro-Asiatic family

tigress ('taɪgrɪs) *n* **1** a female tiger **2** a fierce, cruel, or wildly passionate woman

tigridia (taɪ'grɪdɪə) *n* any plant of the bulbous genus *Tigridia*, native to subtropical and tropical America, esp *T. pavonia*, the tiger flower or peacock tiger flower, grown for its large strikingly marked red, white, or yellow concave flowers: family *Iridaceae* [New Latin, from Greek *tigris*, *tigridis* tiger]

Tigrinya (tɪ'gri:njə) *n* a language of Eritrea and N Ethiopia, belonging to the SE Semitic subfamily of the Afro-Asiatic family

Tigris ('taɪgrɪs) *n* a river in SW Asia, rising in E Turkey and flowing southeast through Baghdad to the Euphrates in SE Iraq, forming the delta of the Shatt-al-Arab, which flows into the Persian Gulf: part of a canal and irrigation system as early as 2400 BC, with many ancient cities (including Nineveh) on its banks. Length: 1900 km (1180 miles)

TIG welding (tɪg) *n* tungsten-electrode inert gas welding: a method of welding in which the arc is maintained by a tungsten electrode and shielded from the access of air by an inert gas. Compare **MIG welding**

Tihwa *or* **Tihua** ('ti:'hwa:) *n* a former name for **Urumchi**

Tijuana (ti:'wa:nə; *Spanish* ti'xwana) *or* **Tia Juana** *n* a city in NW Mexico, in Baja California (Norte). Pop: 1 570 000 (2005 est)

tika ('ti:kə) *n* a variant of **tikka²**

tikanga (tə'kæŋə) *n NZ* Māori ways or customs [Māori]

tike (taɪk) *n* a variant spelling of **tyke**

tiki ('ti:kɪ) *n* **1** an amulet or figurine in the form of a carved representation of an ancestor, worn in some Māori cultures ▷ *vb* **2** (*intr*) *NZ* to take a scenic tour around an area [from Māori]

tiki tour *n NZ* a scenic tour of an area

tikka¹ ('ti:kə) *adj* (*immediately postpositive*) *Indian cookery* (of meat, esp chicken or lamb) marinated in spices then dry-roasted, usu. in a clay oven

tikka² *or* **tika** ('ti:kə) *n* **1** another word for **tilak 2** the act of marking a tikka on the forehead [from Hindi *tika*, Punjabi *tikka* spot, mark]

tikoloshe (,tɪkɒ'lɒʃ, -'lɒʃɪ) *n* a variant of **tokoloshe**

Tikrit (tɪ'kri:t) *n* a town in N central Iraq on the River Tigris; birthplace of Saladin and Saddam Hussein. Pop: 28 900 (2002 est)

tik-tik ('tɪk'tɪk) *n South African slang* a crystal form of methamphetamine used as a stimulant

til (tɪl, ti:l) *n* another name for **sesame**, esp a variety grown in India [C19 from Hindi, from Sanskrit *tilá* sesame]

tilak ('tɪlək) *n, pl* **-ak** *or* **-aks** a coloured spot or mark worn by Hindus, esp on the forehead, often indicating membership of a religious sect, caste, etc, or (in the case of a woman) marital status [from Sanskrit *tilaka*]

tilapia (tɪ'læpɪə, -'leɪ-) *n* any mouthbrooding cichlid fish of the African freshwater genus *Tilapia*: used as food fishes [C18 from New Latin]

Tilburg ('tɪlbɜ:g; *Dutch* 'tɪlbyrx) *n* a city in the S Netherlands, in North Brabant: textile industries. Pop: 198 000 (2003 est)

tilbury ('tɪlbərɪ, -brɪ) *n, pl* **-buries** a light two-wheeled horse-drawn open carriage, seating two people [C19 probably named after the inventor]

Tilbury ('tɪlbərɪ, -brɪ) *n* an area in Essex, on the River Thames: extensive docks; principal container port of the Port of London

tilde ('tɪldə) *n* the diacritical mark (~) placed over a letter to indicate a palatal nasal consonant, as in Spanish *señor*. This symbol is also used in the International Phonetic Alphabet to represent any nasalized vowel [C19 from Spanish, from Latin *titulus* title, superscription]

tile (taɪl) *n* **1** a flat thin slab of fired clay, rubber, linoleum, etc, usually square or rectangular and sometimes ornamental, used with others to cover a roof, floor, wall, etc. Related adj: **tegular 2** a short pipe made of earthenware, concrete, or plastic, used with others to form a drain **3** tiles collectively **4** a rectangular block used as a playing piece in mah jong and other games **5** *Brit old-fashioned slang* a hat **6 on the tiles** *informal* on a spree, esp of drinking or debauchery ▷ *vb* **7** (*tr*) to cover with tiles [Old English *tīgele*, from Latin *tēgula*; related to German *Ziegel*] > **'tiler** *n*

tilefish ('taɪl,fɪʃ) *n, pl* **-fish** *or* **-fishes** a large brightly coloured deep-sea percoid food fish, *Lopholatilus chamaeleonticeps*, of warm and tropical seas, esp the North American coast of the Atlantic: family *Branchiostegidae* [C19 from New Latin *-tilus*, ending of genus name *Lopholatilus*; perhaps also from a resemblance between its colours and patterning and ornamental tiles]

tiliaceous (,tɪlɪ'eɪʃəs) *adj* of, relating to, or belonging to the *Tiliaceae*, a family of flowering plants, mostly trees and shrubs of warm and tropical regions: includes linden and jute [C19 from Late Latin *tiliāceus*, from Latin *tilia* linden]

tiling ('taɪlɪŋ) *n* **1** tiles collectively **2** something made of or surfaced with tiles

till¹ (tɪl) *conj, prep* **1** short for **until** Also (not standard): **'til 2** *Scot* to; towards **3** *dialect* in order that: *come here till I tell you* [Old English *til*; related to Old Norse *til* to, Old High German *zil* goal, aim]

> **USAGE** *Till* is a variant of *until* that is acceptable at all levels of language. *Until* is, however, often preferred at the beginning of a sentence in formal writing: *until his behaviour improves, he cannot become a member*

till² (tɪl) *vb* (*tr*) **1** to cultivate and work (land) for the raising of crops **2** another word for **plough** [Old English *tilian* to try, obtain; related to Old Frisian *tilia* to obtain, Old Saxon *tilōn* to obtain, Old High German *zilōn* to hasten towards] > **'tillable** *adj* > **'tiller** *n*

till³ (tɪl) *n* a box, case, or drawer into which the money taken from customers is put, now usually part of a cash register [C15 *tylle*, of obscure origin]

till⁴ (tɪl) *n* an unstratified glacial deposit consisting of rock fragments of various sizes. The most common is boulder clay [C17 of unknown origin]

tillage ('tɪlɪdʒ) *n* **1** the act, process, or art of tilling **2** tilled land

tillandsia (tɪ'lændzɪə) *n* any bromeliaceous epiphytic plant of the genus *Tillandsia*, such as Spanish moss, of tropical and subtropical America [C18 New Latin, named after Elias *Tillands* (died 1693), Finno-Swedish botanist]

tiller¹ ('tɪlə) *n nautical* a handle fixed to the top of a rudderpost to serve as a lever in steering it [C14 from Anglo-French *teiler* beam of a loom, from Medieval Latin *tēlārium*, from Latin *tēla* web] > **'tillerless** *adj*

tiller² ('tɪlə) *n* **1** a shoot that arises from the base of the stem in grasses **2** a less common name for **sapling** ▷ *vb* **3** (*intr*) (of a plant) to produce tillers [Old English *telgor* twig; related to Icelandic *tjalga* branch]

Till Eulenspiegel ('tɪl 'ɔɪlən,ʃpi:gᵊl) *n* ?14th century, legendary German peasant, whose pranks became the subject of many tales

tillicum ('tɪlɪkəm) *n US and Canadian informal* (in the Pacific Northwest) a friend [from Chinook Jargon, from Chinook *tlxam* kin, esp as distinguished from chiefs]

Tilsit ('tɪlzɪt) *n* the former name (until 1945) of **Sovetsk**

tilt¹ (tɪlt) *vb* **1** to incline or cause to incline at an angle **2** (*usually intr*) to attack or overthrow (a person or people) in a tilt or joust **3** (*when intr*, often foll by *at*) to aim or thrust: *to tilt a lance* **4** (*tr*) to work or forge with a tilt hammer ▷ *n* **5** a slope or angle: *at a tilt* **6** the act of tilting **7** (esp in medieval Europe) **a** a jousting contest **b** a thrust

t

with a lance or pole delivered during a tournament **8** an attempt to win a contest **9** See **tilt hammer 10** (*at*) **full tilt** at full speed or force [Old English *tealtian*; related to Dutch *touteren* to totter, Norwegian *tylta* to tiptoe, *tylten* unsteady] ▷ **'tilter** *n*

tilt² (tɪlt) *n* **1** an awning or canopy, usually of canvas, for a boat, booth, etc ▷ *vb* **2** (*tr*) to cover or provide with a tilt [Old English *teld*; related to Old High German *zelt* tent, Old Norse *tjald* tent]

tilth (tɪlθ) *n* **1** the act or process of tilling land **2** the condition of soil or land that has been tilled, esp with respect to suitability for promoting plant growth [Old English *tilthe*; see TILL²]

tilt hammer *n* a drop hammer consisting of a heavy head moving at the end of a pivoted arm; used in forging

tiltyard ('tɪlt,jɑːd) *n* (formerly) an enclosed area for tilting

Tim. *Bible abbreviation for* Timothy

Timaru ('tɪmə,ruː) *n* a port and resort in S New Zealand, on E South Island. Pop: 43 100 (2004 est)

timbal *or* **tymbal** ('tɪmb°l) *n music* a type of kettledrum [C17 from French *timbale*, from Old French *tamballe*, (associated also with *cymbale* cymbal), from Old Spanish *atabal*, from Arabic *at-tabl* the drum]

timbale (tæm'bɑːl; *French* tɛ̃bal) *n* **1** a mixture of meat, fish, etc, in a rich sauce, cooked in a mould lined with potato or pastry **2** a plain straight-sided mould in which such a dish is prepared [C19 from French: kettledrum]

timber ('tɪmbə) *n* **1 a** wood, esp when regarded as a construction material. Usual US and Canadian word: **lumber b** (*as modifier*): *a timber cottage* **2 a** trees collectively **b** *chiefly US* woodland **3** a piece of wood used in a structure **4** *nautical* a frame in a wooden vessel **5** potential material, for a post, rank, etc: *he is managerial timber* ▷ *vb* **6** (*tr*) to provide with timbers ▷ *interj* **7** a lumberjack's shouted warning when a tree is about to fall [Old English; related to Old High German *zimbar* wood, Old Norse *timbr* timber, Latin *domus* house]

timbered ('tɪmbəd) *adj* **1** made of or containing timber or timbers **2** covered with trees; wooded

timberhead ('tɪmbə,hɛd) *n nautical* a timber, the top of which rises above deck level and is used as a bollard

timber hitch *n* a knot used for tying a rope round a spar, log, etc, for haulage

timbering ('tɪmbərɪŋ) *n* **1** timbers collectively **2** work made of timber

timberland ('tɪmbə,lænd) *n US and Canadian* land covered with trees grown for their timber

timberline ('tɪmbə,laɪn) *n* the altitudinal or latitudinal limit of normal tree growth. See also **tree line**

timberman ('tɪmbəmən) *n, pl* **-men** any of various longicorn beetles that have destructive wood-eating larvae. Also called: **timberman beetle**

timber wolf *n* a variety of the wolf, *Canis lupus,* having a grey brindled coat and occurring in forested northern regions, esp of North America. Also called: **grey wolf**

timberwork ('tɪmbə,wɜːk) *n* a structure made of timber

timberyard ('tɪmbə,jɑːd) *n Brit* an establishment where timber and sometimes other building materials are stored or sold. US and Canadian word: **lumberyard**

timbre ('tɪmbə, 'tæmbə; *French* tɛ̃brə) *n* **1** *phonetics* the distinctive tone quality differentiating one vowel or sonant from another **2** *music* tone colour or quality of sound, esp a specific type of tone colour [C19 from French: note of a bell, from Old French: drum, from Medieval Greek *timbanon,* from Greek *tumpanon* drum]

timbrel ('tɪmbrəl) *n chiefly biblical* another word for **tambourine** [C16 from Old French; see TIMBRE]

Timbuktu (,tɪmbʌk'tuː) *n* **1** a town in central Mali, on the River Niger: terminus of a trans-Saharan caravan route; a great Muslim centre

(14th–16th centuries). Pop: 31 925 (latest est). French name: **Tombouctou 2** any distant or outlandish place: *from here to Timbuktu*

time (taɪm) *n* **1 a** the continuous passage of existence in which events pass from a state of potentiality in the future, through the present, to a state of finality in the past **b** (*as modifier*): *time travel.* Related adj: **temporal 2** *physics* a quantity measuring duration, usually with reference to a periodic process such as the rotation of the earth or the vibration of electromagnetic radiation emitted from certain atoms (see **caesium clock,** **second²** (sense 1)). In classical mechanics, time is absolute in the sense that the time of an event is independent of the observer. According to the theory of relativity it depends on the observer's frame of reference. Time is considered as a fourth coordinate required, along with three spatial coordinates, to specify an event. See **space-time continuum 3** a specific point on this continuum expressed in terms of hours and minutes: *the time is four o'clock* **4** a system of reckoning for expressing time: *Greenwich mean time* **5 a** a definite and measurable portion of this continuum **b** (*as modifier*): *time limit* **6 a** an accepted period such as a day, season, etc **b** (*in combination*): *springtime* **7** an unspecified interval; a while: *I was there for a time* **8** (*often plural*) a period or point marked by specific attributes or events: *the Victorian times; time for breakfast* **9** a sufficient interval or period: *have you got time to help me?* **10** an instance or occasion: *I called you three times* **11** an occasion or period of specified quality: *have a good time; a miserable time* **12** the duration of human existence **13** the heyday of human life: *in her time she was a great star* **14** a suitable period or moment: *it's time I told you* **15** the expected interval in which something is done: *the flying time from New York to London was seven hours* **16** a particularly important moment, esp childbirth or death: *her time had come* **17** (*plural*) indicating a degree or amount calculated by multiplication with the number specified: *ten times three is thirty; he earns four times as much as me* **18** (*often plural*) the fashions, thought, etc, of the present age (esp in the phrases **ahead of one's time, behind the times**) **19** *Brit* (in bars, pubs, etc) short for **closing time 20** *informal* a term in jail (esp in the phrase **do time**) **21 a** a customary or full period of work **b** the rate of pay for this period **22** Also (esp US): **metre a** the system of combining beats or pulses in music into successive groupings by which the rhythm of the music is established **b** a specific system having a specific number of beats in each grouping or bar: *duple time* **23** *music* short for **time value 24** *prosody* a unit of duration used in the measurement of poetic metre; mora **25 against time** in an effort to complete something in a limited period **26 ahead of time** before the deadline **27 all in good time** in due course **28 all the time** continuously **29 at one time a** once; formerly **b** simultaneously **30 at the same time a** simultaneously **b** nevertheless; however **31 at times** sometimes **32 beat time** (of a conductor, etc) to indicate the tempo or pulse of a piece of music by waving a baton or a hand, tapping out the beats, etc **33 before one's time** prematurely **34 for the time being** for the moment; temporarily **35 from time to time** at intervals; occasionally **36 gain time** See **gain¹** (sense 9) **37 have no time for** to have no patience with; not tolerate **38 in good time a** early **b** quickly **39 in no time** very quickly; almost instantaneously **40 in one's own time a** outside paid working hours **b at one's own rate 41 in time a** early or at the appointed time **b** eventually **c** *music* at a correct metrical or rhythmic pulse **42 keep time** to observe correctly the accent or rhythmic pulse of a piece of music in relation to tempo **43 lose time** (of a timepiece) to operate too slowly **44 lose no time** to do something without delay **45 make time a** to find an opportunity **b** (often foll by

with) *US informal* to succeed in seducing **46** See **mark** (sense 35) **47 in the nick of time** at the last possible moment; at the critical moment **48 on time a** at the expected or scheduled time **b** *US* payable in instalments **49 pass the time of day** to exchange casual greetings (with an acquaintance) **50 time about** *Scot* alternately; turn and turn about **51 time and again** frequently **52 time off** a period when one is absent from work for a holiday, through sickness, etc **53 time on** *Austral* an additional period played at the end of a match, to compensate for time lost through injury or (in certain circumstances) to allow the teams to achieve a conclusive result. Also called: (in Britain and certain other countries): **extra time 54 time out of mind** from time immemorial **55 time of one's life** a memorably enjoyable time **56** (*modifier*) operating automatically at or for a set time, for security or convenience: *time lock; time switch* ▷ *vb* (*tr*) **57** to ascertain or calculate the duration or speed of **58** to set a time for **59** to adjust to keep accurate time **60** to pick a suitable time for **61** *sport* to control the execution or speed of (an action, esp a shot or stroke) so that it has its full effect at the right moment ▷ *interj* **62** the word called out by a publican signalling that it is closing time [Old English *tīma*; related to Old English *tīd* time, Old Norse *tími*, Alemannic *zīme*; see TIDE¹]

time and a half *n* the rate of pay equalling one and a half times the normal rate, often offered for overtime work

time and motion study *n* the analysis of industrial or work procedures to determine the most efficient methods of operation. Also: **time and motion, time study, motion study**

time bomb *n* **1** a bomb containing a timing mechanism that determines the time at which it will detonate **2** a situation which, if allowed to continue, will develop into a serious problem

time capsule *n* a container holding articles, documents, etc, representative of the current age, buried in the earth or in the foundations of a new building for discovery in the future

timecard ('taɪm,kɑːd) *n* a card used with a time clock

time charter *n* the hire of a ship or aircraft for a specified period. Compare **voyage charter**

time clock *n* a clock which records, by punching or stamping cards inserted into it, the time of arrival or departure of people, such as employees in a factory

time code *n* (on video or audio tape) a separate track on which time references are continually recorded in digital form as an aid to editing

time constant *n electronics* the time required for the current or voltage in a circuit to rise or fall exponentially through approximately 63 per cent of its amplitude

time-consuming *adj* taking up or involving a great deal of time

time deposit *n* a bank deposit from which withdrawals may be made only after advance notice or at a specified future date. Compare **demand deposit**

time dilation *or* **dilatation** *n* the principle predicted by relativity that time intervals between events in a system have larger values measured by an observer moving with respect to the system than those measured by an observer at rest with respect to it

time-division multiplex *n* See **multiplex** (sense 1)

time exposure *n* **1** an exposure of a photographic film for a relatively long period, usually a few seconds **2** a photograph produced by such an exposure

time frame *n* the period of time within which certain events are scheduled to occur

time-honoured *adj* having been observed for a long time and sanctioned by custom

time immemorial *n* **1** the distant past beyond memory or record **2** *law* time beyond legal memory, fixed by English statute as before the reign of Richard I (1189)

timekeeper ('taɪmˌkiːpə) *n* **1** a person or thing that keeps or records time **2** an employee who maintains a record of the hours worked by the other employees **3** a device for indicating time; timepiece **4** an employee with respect to his record of punctuality: *a good timekeeper* > 'time,keeping *n*

time-lag *n* an interval between two connected events

time-lapse photography *n* the technique of recording a very slow process, such as the withering of a flower, by taking a large number of photographs on a strip of film at regular intervals. The film is then projected at normal speed

timeless ('taɪmlɪs) *adj* **1** unaffected or unchanged by time; ageless **2** eternal **3** an archaic word for **untimely.** > 'timelessly *adv* > 'timelessness *n*

timeline ('taɪmˌlaɪn) *n* **1** a graphic representation showing the passage of time as a line **timeline 2** a time frame during which something is scheduled to happen

time loan *n* a loan repayable before or at a specified future date. Compare **call loan**

timely ('taɪmlɪ) *adj* **-lier, -liest** ▷ *adv* **1** at the right or an opportune or appropriate time **2** an archaic word for **early.** > 'timeliness *n*

time machine *n* (in science fiction) a machine in which people or objects can be transported into the past or the future

time management *n* the analysis of how working hours are spent and the prioritization of tasks in order to maximize personal efficiency in the workplace

timeous ('taɪməs) *adj Scot* in good time; sufficiently early: *a timeous warning* [c15 Scottish; see TIME, -OUS] > 'timeously *adv*

time-out *n* **1** *sport* an interruption in play during which players rest, discuss tactics, or make substitutions **2** a break taken during working hours **3** *computing* a condition occurring when the amount of time a computer has been instructed to wait for another device to perform a task has expired, usually indicated by an error message ▷ *vb* (*intr*) **time out 4** (of a computer) to stop operating because of a time-out

timepass ('taɪmˌpɑːs) *n* **1** a way of passing the time ▷ *vb* **2** (*intr*) to pass the time ▷ *adj* **3** moderately entertaining: *a timepass movie*

timepiece ('taɪmˌpiːs) *n* **1** any of various devices, such as a clock, watch, or chronometer, which measure and indicate time **2** a device which indicates the time but does not strike or otherwise audibly mark the hours

time-poor *adj* **1** lacking spare time or leisure time **2** under pressure to complete activities quickly

timer ('taɪmə) *n* **1** a device for measuring, recording, or indicating time **2** a switch or regulator that causes a mechanism to operate at a specific time or at predetermined intervals **3** a person or thing that times

time-saving ('taɪmˌseɪvɪŋ) *adj* shortening the length of time required for an operation, activity, etc > 'time-ˌsaver *n*

timescale ('taɪmˌskeɪl) *n* the span of time within which certain events occur or are scheduled to occur considered in relation to any broader period of time

time-sensitive *adj* **1** physically changing as time passes **2** only relevant or applicable for a short period of time

time series *n statistics* a series of values of a variable taken in successive periods of time

time-served *adj* (of a craftsman or tradesman) having completed an apprenticeship; fully trained and competent: *a time-served mechanic*

timeserver ('taɪmˌsɜːvə) *n* a person who compromises and changes his opinions, way of

life, etc, to suit the current fashions > 'time,serving *adj, n*

time-share *adj* denoting, relating to, or forming part of time sharing of property: *time-share villas*

time sharing *n* **1 a** a system of part ownership of a property, such as a flat or villa, for use as a holiday home, whereby each participant buys the right to use the property for the same fixed period annually **b** (*as modifier*): *a time-sharing system* **2 a** a system by which users at different terminals of a computer can, because of its high speed, apparently communicate with it at the same time. Compare **batch processing b** (*as modifier*): *a time-sharing computer*

time sheet *n* a card on which are recorded the hours spent working by an employee or employees

time signal *n* an announcement of the correct time, esp on radio or television

time signature *n music* a sign usually consisting of two figures, one above the other, the upper figure representing the number of beats per bar and the lower one the time value of each beat. This sign is placed after the key signature at the outset of a piece or section of a piece

time sovereignty *n* control by an employee of the use of his or her time, involving flexibility of working hours

Times Square *n* a square formed by the intersection of Broadway and Seventh Avenue in New York City, extending from 42nd to 45th Street

time-stamp *vb* (*tr*) to assign an accurate time to (a message, transaction, etc)

time study *n* short for **time and motion study**

time switch *n* an electric switch that can be set to operate an appliance, such as a light or an oven, at a particular time

timetable ('taɪmˌteɪbᵊl) *n* **1** a list or table of events arranged according to the time when they take place; schedule ▷ *vb* **2** (*tr*) to include in or arrange according to a timetable **3** (*intr*) to draw up a timetable

time trial *n* (esp in cycling) a race in which the competitors compete against the clock over a specified course > 'time-ˌtrialling *n*

time value *n music* the duration of a given printed note relative to other notes in a composition or section and considered in relation to the basic tempo. Often shortened to: **time** Also called: **note value, time**

time warp *n* **1** any distortion of space-time **2** a hypothetical distortion of time in which people and events from one age can be imagined to exist in another age **3** *informal* an illusion in which time appears to stand still: *he is living in a time warp*

timework ('taɪmˌwɜːk) *n* work paid for by the length of time taken, esp by the hour or the day. Compare **piecework.** > 'time,worker *n*

timeworn ('taɪmˌwɔːn) *adj* **1** showing the adverse effects of overlong use or of old age **2** hackneyed; trite

time zone *n* a region throughout which the same standard time is used. There are 24 time zones in the world, demarcated approximately by meridians at 15° intervals, an hour apart. See also **zonetime**

timid ('tɪmɪd) *adj* **1** easily frightened or upset, esp by human contact; shy **2** indicating shyness or fear [c16 from Latin *timidus*, from *timēre* to fear] > ti'midity *or* 'timidness *n* > 'timidly *adv*

timing ('taɪmɪŋ) *n* the process or art of regulating actions or remarks in relation to others to produce the best effect, as in music, the theatre, sport, etc

timing gear *n* (in an internal-combustion engine) the drive between the crankshaft and the camshaft, usually giving a ratio of 2 : 1

Timişoara (*Romanian* timiˈʃwara) *n* a city in W Romania: formerly under Turkish and then Hapsburg rule, being allotted to Romania in 1920; scene of violence during the revolution of 1989. Pop: 296 000 (2005 est). Hungarian name: **Temesvár**

timocracy (taɪˈmɒkrəsɪ) *n, pl* **-cies 1** a political unit or system in which possession of property serves as the first requirement for participation in government **2** a political unit or system in which love of honour is deemed the guiding principle of government [c16 from Old French *tymocracie*, ultimately from Greek *timokratia*, from *timē* worth, honour, price + -CRACY] > **timocratic** (ˌtaɪmə'krætɪk) *or* ˌtimo'cratical *adj*

Timor ('tiːmɔː, ˌtaɪ-) *n* an island in the Malay Archipelago, the largest and easternmost of the Lesser Sunda Islands: the west was a Dutch possession (part of the Dutch East Indies) until 1949, when it became part of Indonesia: the east was held by Portugal until 1975, when it declared independence but was immediately invaded by Indonesia; East Timor finally became an independent state in 2002. Area: 30 775 sq km (11 883 sq miles)

Timor-Leste ('tiːmɔːˈlɛsteɪ) *n* the official name of **East Timor**

timorous ('tɪmərəs) *adj* **1** fearful or timid **2** indicating fear or timidity [c15 from Old French *temoros*, from Medieval Latin *timōrōsus*, from Latin *timor* fear, from *timēre* to be afraid] > 'timorously *adv* > 'timorousness *n*

Timor pony *n* a small stocky breed of pony originally bred in Timor, used on Australian ranches

Timor Sea *n* an arm of the Indian Ocean between Australia and Timor. Width: about 480 km (300 miles)

Timothy ('tɪməθɪ) either of the two books addressed to St Timothy, a disciple of Paul, who became leader of the Christian community at Ephesus (in full **The First and Second Epistles of Paul the Apostle to Timothy**), containing advice on pastoral matters

timothy grass *or* **timothy** ('tɪməθɪ) *n* a perennial grass, *Phleum pratense*, of temperate regions, having erect stiff stems and cylindrical flower spikes: grown for hay and pasture [c18 apparently named after a *Timothy* Hanson, who brought it to colonial Carolina]

timpani *or* **tympani** ('tɪmpənɪ) *pl n* (*sometimes functioning as singular*) a set of kettledrums, two or more in number. Often (*informal*) shortened to: **timps** [from Italian, pl of *timpano* kettledrum, from Latin: TYMPANUM] > 'timpanist *or* 'tympanist *n*

tin (tɪn) *n* **1** a metallic element, occurring in cassiterite, that has several allotropes; the ordinary malleable silvery-white metal slowly changes below 13.2°C to a grey powder. It is used extensively in alloys, esp bronze and pewter, and as a noncorroding coating for steel. Symbol: Sn; atomic no: 50; atomic wt: 118.710; valency: 2 or 4; relative density: 5.75 (grey), 7.31 (white); melting pt: 231.9°C; boiling pt: 2603°C. Related adjs: **stannic, stannous 2** Also called (esp US and Canadian): **can** an airtight sealed container of thin sheet metal coated with tin, used for preserving and storing food or drink **3** any container made of metallic tin **4** *fill her tins NZ* to complete a home baking of cakes, biscuits, etc **5** Also called: **tinful** the contents of a tin or the amount a tin will hold **6** *Brit, Austral, and NZ* corrugated or galvanized iron: *a tin roof* **7** any metal regarded as cheap or flimsy **8** *Brit* a loaf of bread with a rectangular shape, baked in a tin **9** *slang* money **10** *it does exactly what it says on the tin* it lives up to expectations ▷ *vb* **tins, tinning, tinned** (*tr*) **11** to put (food, etc) into a tin or tins; preserve in a tin **12** to plate or coat with tin **13** to prepare (a metal) for soldering or brazing by applying a thin layer of solder to the surface [Old English; related to Old Norse *tin*, Old High German *zin*] > 'tin,like *adj*

tinamou ('tɪnəˌmuː) *n* any bird of the order *Tinamiformes* of Central and South America, having small wings, a heavy body, and an inconspicuous plumage [c18 via French from Carib (Galibi) *tinamu*]

t

tincal (ˈtɪŋkᵊl) *n* another name for **borax** (sense 1) [C17 from Malay *tingkal*, from Sanskrit *tankana*]
tin can *n* a metal food container, esp when empty
tinct (tɪŋkt) *n, vb* **1** an obsolete word for **tint** ▷ *adj* **2** *poetic* tinted or coloured [C15 from Latin *tinctus*, from *tingere* to colour]
tinctorial (tɪŋkˈtɔːrɪəl) *adj* **1** of or relating to colouring, staining, or dyeing **2** imbuing with colour [C17 from Latin *tinctōrius*, from *tingere* to tinge] > **tincˈtorially** *adv*
tincture (ˈtɪŋktʃə) *n* **1** *pharmacol* a medicinal extract in a solution of alcohol **2** a tint, colour, or tinge **3** a slight flavour, aroma, or trace **4** any one of the colours or either of the metals used on heraldic arms **5** *obsolete* a dye or pigment ▷ *vb* **6** (*tr*) to give a tint or colour to [C14 from Latin *tinctūra* a dyeing, from *tingere* to dye]
tinder (ˈtɪndə) *n* **1** dry wood or other easily combustible material used for lighting a fire **2** anything inflammatory or dangerous: *his speech was tinder to the demonstrators' unrest* [Old English *tynder*; related to Old Norse *tundr*, Old High German *zuntara*] > **ˈtindery** *adj*
tinderbox (ˈtɪndəˌbɒks) *n* **1** a box used formerly for holding tinder, esp one fitted with a flint and steel **2** a person or thing that is particularly touchy or explosive
tine (taɪn) *n* **1** a slender prong, esp of a fork **2** any of the sharp terminal branches of a deer's antler [Old English *tind*; related to Old Norse *tindr*, Old High German *zint*] > **tined** *adj*
tinea (ˈtɪnɪə) *n* any fungal skin disease, esp ringworm [C17 from Latin: worm] > **ˈtineal** *adj*
tineid (ˈtɪnɪɪd) *n* **1** any moth of the family *Tineidae*, which includes the clothes moths ▷ *adj* **2** of, relating to, or belonging to the family *Tineidae* [C19 from New Latin *Tineidae*, from Latin: TINEA]
tinfoil (ˈtɪnˌfɔɪl) *n* **1** thin foil made of tin or an alloy of tin and lead **2** thin foil made of aluminium; used for wrapping foodstuffs
ting[1] (tɪŋ) *n* **1** a high metallic sound such as that made by a small bell ▷ *vb* **2** to make or cause to make such a sound [C15 of imitative origin]
ting[2] (tɪŋ) *n* (*often capital*) a variant spelling of **thing**[2]
ting-a-ling (ˈtɪŋəˈlɪŋ) *n* the sound of a small bell
tinge (tɪndʒ) *n* **1** a slight tint or colouring: *her hair had a tinge of grey* **2** any slight addition ▷ *vb* **tinges, tingeing** *or* **tinging, tinged** (*tr*) **3** to colour or tint faintly **4** to impart a slight trace to: *her thoughts were tinged with nostalgia* [C15 from Latin *tingere* to colour]
tingle (ˈtɪŋgᵊl) *vb* **1** (*usually intr*) to feel or cause to feel a prickling, itching, or stinging sensation of the flesh, as from a cold plunge or electric shock ▷ *n* **2** a sensation of tingling [C14 perhaps a variant of TINKLE] > **ˈtingler** *n* > **ˈtingling** *adj* > **ˈtinglingly** *adv* > **ˈtingly** *adj*
tin god *n* **1** a self-important dictatorial person **2** a person erroneously regarded as holy or venerable
tin hat *n* *obsolete informal* a steel helmet worn by military personnel for protection against small metal fragments
tinhorn (ˈtɪnˌhɔːn) *US slang* ▷ *n* **1** a cheap pretentious person, esp a gambler with extravagant claims ▷ *adj* **2** cheap and showy
tinker (ˈtɪŋkə) *n* **1** (esp formerly) a travelling mender of pots and pans **2** a clumsy worker **3** the act of tinkering **4** *Scot and Irish* another name for a **Gypsy** **5** *Brit informal* a mischievous child **6** any of several small mackerels that occur off the North American coast of the Atlantic ▷ *vb* **7** (*intr*; foll by *with*) to play, fiddle, or meddle (with machinery, etc), esp while undertaking repairs **8** to mend (pots and pans) as a tinker [C13 *tinkere*, perhaps from *tink* tinkle, of imitative origin] > **ˈtinkerer** *n*
tinker's damn *or* **cuss** *n* *slang* the slightest heed (esp in the phrase **not give a tinker's damn** *or* **cuss**)
tinkle (ˈtɪŋkᵊl) *vb* **1** to ring or cause to ring with a series of high tinny sounds, like a small bell **2** (*tr*) to announce or summon by such a ringing **3** (*intr*) *Brit informal* to urinate ▷ *n* **4** a high clear ringing sound **5** the act of tinkling **6** *Brit informal* a telephone call [C14 of imitative origin] > **ˈtinkling** *adj, n* > **ˈtinkly** *adj*
tin lizzie (ˈlɪzɪ) *n* *informal* an old or decrepit car; jalopy [originally a nickname for the Model T Ford]
tinned (tɪnd) *adj* **1** plated, coated, or treated with tin **2** *chiefly Brit* preserved or stored in airtight tins: *tinned soup* **3** coated with a layer of solder
tinner (ˈtɪnə) *n* **1** a tin miner **2** a worker in tin; tinsmith **3** a person or organization that puts food, etc, into tins; canner
tinnitus (ˈtɪnɪtəs, tɪˈnaɪtəs) *n* *pathol* a ringing, hissing, or booming sensation in one or both ears, caused by infection of the middle or inner ear, a side effect of certain drugs, etc [C19 from Latin, from *tinnīre* to ring]
tinny (ˈtɪnɪ) *adj* **-nier, -niest** **1** of, relating to, or resembling tin **2** cheap, badly made, or shoddy **3** (of a sound) high, thin, and metallic **4** (of food or drink) flavoured with metal, as from a container **5** *Austral informal* lucky ▷ *n, pl* **-nies** **6** *Austral slang* a can of beer **7** *Austral informal* Also: **tinnie** a small fishing or pleasure boat with an aluminium hull > **ˈtinnily** *adv* > **ˈtinniness** *n*
tin-opener *n* a small tool for opening tins
Tin Pan Alley *n* **1** a district in a city concerned with the production of popular music, originally a small district in New York **2** *derogatory* the strictly commercial side of show business and pop music
tin plate *n* **1** thin steel sheet coated with a layer of tin that protects the steel from corrosion ▷ *vb* **tin-plate** **2** (*tr*) to coat (a metal or object) with a layer of tin, usually either by electroplating or by dipping in a bath of molten tin > **ˈtin-ˌplater** *n*
tinpot (ˈtɪnˌpɒt) *adj* (*prenominal*) *Brit informal* **1** inferior, cheap, or worthless **2** paltry; unimportant
tinsel (ˈtɪnsəl) *n* **1** a decoration consisting of a piece of string with thin strips of metal foil attached along its length **2** a yarn or fabric interwoven with strands of glittering thread **3** anything cheap, showy, and gaudy ▷ *vb* **-sels, -selling, -selled** *or US* **-sels, -seling, -seled** (*tr*) **4** to decorate with or as if with tinsel: *snow tinsels the trees* **5** to give a gaudy appearance to ▷ *adj* **6** made of or decorated with tinsel **7** showily but cheaply attractive; gaudy [C16 from Old French *estincele* a spark, from Latin *scintilla*; compare STENCIL] > **ˈtinsel-ˌlike** *adj* > **ˈtinselly** *adj*
Tinseltown (ˈtɪnsəlˌtaʊn) *n* an informal name for **Hollywood** [C20 from the insubstantial glitter of the film world]
tinsmith (ˈtɪnˌsmɪθ) *n* a person who works with tin or tin plate
tin soldier *n* **1** a miniature toy soldier, usually made of lead **2** a person who enjoys playing at being a soldier
tinstone (ˈtɪnˌstəʊn) *n* another name for **cassiterite**
tint (tɪnt) *n* **1** a shade of a colour, esp a pale one **2** a colour that is softened or desaturated by the addition of white **3** a tinge **4** a semipermanent dye for the hair **5** a trace or hint: *a tint of jealousy in his voice* **6** *engraving* uniform shading, produced esp by hatching **7** *printing* a panel of colour serving as a background to letters or other matter ▷ *vb* **8** (*tr*) to colour or tinge **9** (*tr*) to change or influence slightly: *his answer was tinted by his prior knowledge* **10** (*intr*) to acquire a tint [C18 from earlier TINCT] > **ˈtinter** *n*
Tintagel Head (tɪnˈtædʒəl) *n* a promontory in SW England, on the W coast of Cornwall: ruins of **Tintagel Castle**, legendary birthplace of King Arthur
tintinnabulation (ˌtɪntɪˌnæbjʊˈleɪʃən) *n* the act or an instance of the ringing or pealing of bells > **ˌtintinˈnabular, ˌtintinˈnabulary** *or* **ˌtintinˈnabulous** *adj*
tintinnabulum (ˌtɪntɪˈnæbjʊləm) *n, pl* **-la** (-lə) a small high-pitched bell [C16 from Latin, from *tintinnāre* to tinkle, from *tinnīre* to ring; see TINNITUS]
tintometer (tɪnˈtɒmɪtə) *n* another name for **colorimeter** (sense 1)
tintookie (ˌtɪnˈtʊkɪ) *n* *Austral informal* a fawning or servile person [C20 from *Tintookies*, marionettes that appeared on Australian television in the 1960s]
tint tool *n* a kind of burin used in wood engraving for carving lines of even thickness, as in hatching
tintype (ˈtɪnˌtaɪp) *n* another name for **ferrotype** (senses 1, 2)
tinware (ˈtɪnˌwɛə) *n* objects made of tin plate
tin whistle *n* another name for **penny whistle**
tinwork (ˈtɪnˌwɜːk) *n* objects made of tin
tinworks (ˈtɪnˌwɜːks) *n* (*functioning as singular or plural*) a place where tin is mined, smelted, or rolled
tiny (ˈtaɪnɪ) *adj* **tinier, tiniest** very small; minute [C16 *tine*, of uncertain origin] > **ˈtinily** *adv* > **ˈtininess** *n*
-tion *suffix forming nouns* indicating state, condition, action, process, or result: *election*; *prohibition*. Compare **-ation, -ion** [from Old French, from Latin *-tiō, -tiōn-*]
tip[1] (tɪp) *n* **1** the extreme end of something, esp a narrow or pointed end **2** the top or summit **3** a small piece forming an extremity or end: *a metal tip on a cane* ▷ *vb* **tips, tipping, tipped** (*tr*) **4** to adorn or mark the tip of **5** to cause to form a tip [C15 from Old Norse *typpa*; related to Middle Low German, Middle Dutch *tip*] > **ˈtipless** *adj*
tip[2] (tɪp) *vb* **tips, tipping, tipped** **1** to tilt or cause to tilt **2** (usually foll by *over* or *up*) to tilt or cause to tilt, so as to overturn or fall **3** *Brit* to dump (rubbish, etc) **4** **tip one's hat** to take off, raise, or touch one's hat in salutation ▷ *n* **5** the act of tipping or the state of being tipped **6** *Brit* a dump for refuse, etc [C14 of uncertain origin; related to TOP[1], TOPPLE] > **ˈtippable** *adj*
tip[3] (tɪp) *n* **1** a payment given for services in excess of the standard charge; gratuity **2** a helpful hint, warning, or other piece of information **3** a piece of inside information, esp in betting or investing ▷ *vb* **tips, tipping, tipped** **4** to give a tip to (a person) [C18 perhaps from TIP[4]]
tip[4] (tɪp) *vb* **tips, tipping, tipped** (*tr.*) **1** to hit or strike lightly **2** to hit (a ball) indirectly so that it glances off the bat in cricket ▷ *n* **3** a light blow **4** a glancing hit in cricket [C13 perhaps from Low German *tippen*]
tip and run *n* **1** a form of cricket in which the batsman must run if his bat touches the ball ▷ *adj* **tip-and-run** **2** (*prenominal*) characterized by a rapid departure immediately after striking: *a tip-and-run raid*
tipcat (ˈtɪpˌkæt) *n* a game in which a short sharp-ended piece of wood (the cat) is tipped in the air with a stick
tipi (ˈtiːpɪ) *n, pl* **-pis** a variant spelling of **tepee**
tip-off *n* **1** a warning or hint, esp given confidentially and based on inside information **2** *basketball* the act or an instance of putting the ball in play by a jump ball ▷ *vb* **tip off** **3** (*tr, adverb*) to give a hint or warning to
tippee (tɪˈpiː) *n* a person who receives a tip, esp regarding share prices
tipper (ˈtɪpə) *n* **1** a person who gives or leaves a tip: *he is a generous tipper* **2** short for **tipper truck**
Tipperary (ˌtɪpəˈrɛərɪ) *n* a county of S Republic of Ireland, in Munster province; divided into the North Riding and South Riding: mountainous. County town: Clonmel; Nenagh serves as administrative capital of the North Riding. Pop: 140 131 (2002). Area: 4255 sq km (1643 sq miles)
tipper truck *or* **lorry** *n* a truck or lorry the rear platform of which can be raised at the front end to enable the load to be discharged by gravity. Also called: **tip truck**

tippet ('tɪpɪt) *n* **1** a woman's fur cape for the shoulders, often consisting of the whole fur of a fox, marten, etc **2** the long stole of Anglican clergy worn during a service **3** a long streamer-like part to a sleeve, hood, etc, esp in the 16th century **4** the ruff of a bird **5** a tippet feather or something similar used in dressing some artificial angling flies [c14 perhaps from TIP¹]

tipping point ('tɪpɪŋ) *n* the crisis stage in a process, when a significant change takes place

tipple¹ ('tɪpªl) *vb* **1** to make a habit of taking (alcoholic drink), esp in small quantities ▷ *n* **2** alcoholic drink [c15 back formation from obsolete *tippler* tapster, of unknown origin] > **'tippler** *n*

tipple² ('tɪpªl) *n* **1** a device for overturning ore trucks, mine cars, etc, so that they discharge their load **2** a place at which such trucks are tipped and unloaded ▷ *vb* **3** *Northern English dialect* to fall or cause to fall [c19 from *tipple* to overturn, from TIP²]

tippler ('tɪplə) *n* (*sometimes capital*) **1** a variety of domestic pigeon bred mainly for flying. Also called: **high-flying tippler 2** a domestic fancy pigeon of a smaller rounder type kept mainly for exhibition. Usual name: **show tippler** [c19 from TIPPLE¹ + -ER¹]

tipstaff ('tɪp,stɑːf) *n* **1** a court official having miscellaneous duties, mostly concerned with the maintenance of order in court **2** a metal-tipped staff formerly used as a symbol of office [c16 *tipped staff*; see TIP¹, STAFF¹]

tipster ('tɪpstə) *n* a person who sells tips on horse racing, the stock market, etc

tipsy ('tɪpsɪ) *adj* **-sier, -siest 1** slightly drunk **2** slightly tilted or tipped; askew [c16 from TIP²] > **'tipsily** *adv* > **'tipsiness** *n*

tipsy cake *n Brit* a kind of trifle made from a sponge cake soaked with white wine or sherry and decorated with almonds and crystallized fruit

tip-tilted *adj* (of a nose) slightly turned up

tiptoe ('tɪp,təʊ) *vb* **-toes, -toeing, -toed** (*intr*) **1** to walk with the heels off the ground and the weight supported by the ball of the foot and the toes **2** to walk silently or stealthily ▷ *n* **3** on tiptoe **a** on the tips of the toes or on the ball of the foot and the toes **b** eagerly anticipating something **c** stealthily or silently ▷ *adv* **4** on tiptoe ▷ *adj* **5** walking or standing on tiptoe **6** stealthy or silent

tiptop (,tɪp'tɒp) *adj, adv* **1** at the highest point of health, excellence, etc **2** at the topmost point ▷ *n* **3** the best in quality **4** the topmost point

Tiptronic or **tiptronic** (tɪp'trɒnɪk) *n trademark* a type of gearbox that has both automatic and manual options

tip truck *n* another name for **tipper truck**

tipuna or **tupuna** (tə'puːnə) *n NZ* an ancestor [Māori]

tip-up *adj* (*prenominal*) able to be turned upwards around a hinge or pivot: *a tip-up seat*

TIR (on continental lorries) *abbreviation for* Transports Internationaux Routiers [French: International Road Transport]

tirade (taɪ'reɪd) *n* **1** a long angry speech or denunciation **2** *prosody rare* a speech or passage dealing with a single theme [c19 from French, literally: a pulling, from Italian *tirata*, from *tirare* to pull, of uncertain origin]

tirage (tɪ'rɑːʒ) *n* **1** the drawing of wine from a barrel prior to bottling **2** the process in the making of a sparkling wine in which fermentable sugar and yeast is added to induce secondary fermentation [from French: drawing, pulling]

tiramisu (,tiːrəmɪ'suː) *n* an Italian dessert made with sponge soaked in coffee and Marsala, topped with soft cheese and powdered chocolate [c20 from Italian *tira! mi* me + *su* up]

Tiran (tɪ'rɑːn) *n* **Strait of** a strait between the Gulf of Aqaba and the Red Sea. Length: 16 km (10 miles). Width: 8 km (5 miles)

Tirana (tɪ'rɑːnə) or **Tiranë** (*Albanian* tiˈranə) *n* the capital of Albania, in the central part 32 km (20

miles) from the Adriatic: founded in the early 17th century by Turks; became capital in 1920; the country's largest city and industrial centre. Pop: 390 000 (2005 est)

tire¹ ('taɪə) *vb* **1** (*tr*) to reduce the energy of, esp by exertion; weary **2** (*tr; often passive*) to reduce the tolerance of; bore or irritate: *I'm tired of the children's chatter* **3** (*intr*) to become wearied or bored; flag [Old English *tēorian*, of unknown origin] > **'tiring** *adj*

tire² ('taɪə) *n, vb* the US spelling of **tyre**

tire³ ('taɪə) *vb, n* an archaic word for **attire**

tired ('taɪəd) *adj* **1** weary; fatigued **2** (foll by *of*) **a** having lost interest in; bored: *I'm tired of playing cards* **b** having lost patience with; exasperated by: *I'm tired of his eternal excuses* **3** hackneyed; stale: *the same tired old jokes* **4** **tired and emotional** a euphemism for slightly drunk > **'tiredly** *adv* > **'tiredness** *n*

Tiree (taɪˈriː) *n* an island off the W coast of Scotland, in the Inner Hebrides. Pop: 770 (2001). Area: 78 sq km (30 sq miles)

tireless ('taɪəlɪs) *adj* unable to be tired; indefatigable > **'tirelessly** *adv* > **'tirelessness** *n*

Tiresias (taɪˈriːsɪ,æs) *n Greek myth* a blind soothsayer of Thebes, who revealed to Oedipus that the latter had murdered his father and married his mother

tiresome ('taɪəsəm) *adj* boring and irritating; irksome > **'tiresomely** *adv* > **'tiresomeness** *n*

tirewoman ('taɪə,wʊmən) *n, pl* **-women** an obsolete term for **lady's maid** [c17 see TIRE³]

Tîrgu Mureş (*Romanian* 'tirgu 'mureʃ) *n* a city in central Romania: manufacturing and cultural centre. Pop: 127 000 (2005 est)

Tirich Mir ('tɪərɪtʃ 'mɪə) *n* a mountain in N Pakistan: highest peak of the Hindu Kush. Height: 7690 m (25 230 ft)

tiring room *n archaic* a dressing room in a theatre

tiriti ('tiːriːtiː) *n* another name for the **Treaty of Waitangi**. see **Waitangi Day** [Māori]

tiro ('taɪrəʊ) *n, pl* **-ros** a variant spelling of **tyro**

Tirol (tɪ'rəʊl, 'tɪrəʊl; *German* tiˈroːl) *n* a variant spelling of **Tyrol**

Tirolean (,tɪrəʊ'liən) *adj, n* a variant spelling of **Tyrolean**

Tirolese (,tɪrə'liːz) *adj, n* a variant spelling of **Tyrolese**

Tiros ('taɪrɒs) *n* one of a series of US weather satellites carrying infrared and television camera equipment for transmitting meteorological data to the earth [c20 from *T(elevision and) I(nfra-)R(ed) O(bservation) S(atellite)*]

Tiruchirapalli (,tɪrətʃɪrə'pʌlɪ, tɪ,ruːtʃɪ'rɑːpəlɪ) or **Trichinopoly** *n* an industrial city in S India, in central Tamil Nadu on the Cauvery River: dominated by a rock fortress 83 m (273 ft) high. Pop: 746 062 (2001)

Tirunelveli (,tɪruˈnɛlvɛlɪ) *n* a city in S India, in Tamil Nadu: site of St Francis Xavier's first preaching in India; textile manufacturing. Pop: 411 298 (2001)

'tis (tɪz) *poetic or dialect* ▷ *contraction of* it is

Tisa ('tɪsɑ) *n* the Slavonic and Romanian name for the **Tisza**

tisane (tɪ'zæn) *n* an infusion of dried or fresh leaves or flowers, as camomile [c19 from French, from Latin *ptisana* barley water; see PTISAN]

Tishah b'Av (tiˈʃɑ bə'av) *n Judaism* the ninth day of the month of Av observed as a fast day in memory of the destruction of the First and Second Temples

Tishri (tɪʃ'riː) *n* (in the Jewish calendar) the seventh month of the year according to biblical reckoning and the first month of the civil year, usually falling within September and October [from Hebrew]

Tisiphone (tɪ'sɪfənɪ) *n Greek myth* one of the three Furies; the others are Alecto and Megaera

tissue ('tɪsjuː, 'tɪʃuː) *n* **1** a part of an organism consisting of a large number of cells having a similar structure and function: *connective tissue;*

nerve tissue **2** a thin piece of soft absorbent paper, usually of two or more layers, used as a disposable handkerchief, towel, etc **3** See **tissue paper 4** an interwoven series: *a tissue of lies* **5** a woven cloth, esp of a light gauzy nature, originally interwoven with threads of gold or silver ▷ *vb* (*tr*) **6** *rare* to weave into tissue **7** to decorate or clothe with tissue or tissue paper [c14 from Old French *tissu* woven cloth, from *tistre* to weave, from Latin *texere*]

tissue culture *n* **1** the growth of small pieces of animal or plant tissue in a sterile controlled medium **2** the tissue produced as a result of this process

tissue paper *n* very thin soft delicate paper used to wrap breakable goods, as decoration, etc

tissue type *n* the inherited chemical characteristics of the bodily tissue of an individual that are recognized and, when grafted, are accepted or rejected by the immune system of another individual. The tissue type is determined by the histocompatibility antigens

Tisza (*Hungarian* 'tisɔ) *n* a river in S central Europe, rising in W Ukraine and flowing west, forming part of the border between Ukraine and Romania, then southwest across Hungary into Serbia to join the Danube north of Belgrade. Slavonic and Romanian name: **Tisa**

tit¹ (tɪt) *n* **1** any of numerous small active Old World songbirds of the family *Paridae* (titmice), esp those of the genus *Parus* (bluetit, great tit, etc). They have a short bill and feed on insects and seeds **2** any of various similar small birds **3** *archaic or dialect* a worthless or worn-out horse; nag [c16 perhaps of imitative origin, applied to small animate or inanimate objects; compare Icelandic *tittr* pin]

tit² (tɪt) *n* **1** *slang* a female breast **2** a teat or nipple **3** *derogatory* a girl or young woman **4** *slang* a despicable or unpleasant person: often used as a term of address [Old English *titt*; related to Middle Low German *title*, Norwegian *titta*]

Tit. *Bible abbreviation for* Titus

titan ('taɪtªn) *n* a person of great strength or size [c17 from TITAN¹]

Titan¹ ('taɪtªn) or *feminine* **Titaness** *n Greek myth* **1** any of a family of primordial gods, the sons and daughters of Uranus (sky) and Gaea (earth) **2** any of the offspring of the children of Uranus and Gaea

Titan² ('taɪtªn) *n* the largest satellite of the planet Saturn, having a thick atmosphere consisting mainly of nitrogen. Diameter: 5150 km

titanate ('taɪtə,neɪt) *n* any salt or ester of titanic acid

Titanesque (,taɪtə'nɛsk) *adj* resembling a Titan; gigantic

titania (taɪ'teɪnɪə) *n* another name for **titanium dioxide**

Titania¹ (tɪ'tɑːnɪə) *n* **1** (in medieval folklore) the queen of the fairies and wife of Oberon **2** (in classical antiquity) a poetic epithet used variously to characterize Circe, Diana, Latona, or Pyrrha

Titania² (tɪ'tɑːnɪə) *n* the largest of the satellites of Uranus and the second furthest from the planet

titanic¹ (taɪ'tænɪk) *adj* of or containing titanium, esp in the tetravalent state

titanic² (taɪ'tænɪk) *adj* possessing or requiring colossal strength: *a titanic battle* > **ti'tanically** *adv*

Titanic (taɪ'tænɪk) *n* **the** a luxury British liner that struck an iceberg near Newfoundland on its maiden voyage on the night of April 14–15, 1912, with the loss of 1513 lives

titanic acid *n* any of various white substances regarded as hydrated forms of titanium dioxide, typical formulas being H_4TiO_4 and H_2TiO_3

titanic oxide *n* another name for **titanium dioxide**

titaniferous (,taɪtə'nɪfərəs) *adj* of or containing titanium; bearing titanium: *a titaniferous ore*

Titanism ('taɪtə,nɪzəm) *n* a spirit of defiance of and rebellion against authority, social convention, etc

t

titanite ('taɪtəˌnaɪt) n another name for **sphene** [c19 from German *Titanit*, so named because it contained TITANIUM]

titanium (taɪ'teɪnɪəm) n a strong malleable white metallic element, which is very corrosion-resistant and occurs in rutile and ilmenite. It is used in the manufacture of strong lightweight alloys, esp aircraft parts. Symbol: Ti; atomic no: 22; atomic wt: 47.88; valency: 2, 3, or 4; relative density: 4.54; melting pt: 1670±10°C; boiling pt: 3289°C [c18 New Latin; see TITAN, -IUM]

titanium dioxide n a white insoluble powder occurring naturally as rutile and used chiefly as a pigment of high covering power and durability. Formula: TiO₂. Also called: **titanium oxide, titanic oxide, titania**

Titanomachy (ˌtaɪtə'nɒməkɪ) n *Greek myth* the unsuccessful revolt of the family of the Titan Iapetus against Zeus [c19 from Greek *titanomakhia*, from TITAN¹ + *makhē* a battle]

titanosaur (taɪ'tænəˌsɔː) n any of various herbivorous quadrupedal dinosaurs of the family *Titanosauridae*, of Jurassic and Cretaceous times: suborder *Sauropoda* (sauropods) [c19 from New Latin *Tītānosaurus*, from Greek TITAN + -SAUR]

titanothere (taɪ'tænəˌθɪə) n any of various very large horse-like perissodactyl mammals of the genera *Menodus, Brontotherium*, etc, that lived in Eocene and Oligocene times in North America. See also **chalicothere** [c19 from New Latin *Tītānotherium* giant animal, from Greek TITAN + *thēr* wild beast]

titanous ('taɪtənəs) adj of or containing titanium, esp in the trivalent state

titarakura ('tɪtɑːrəˌkuːrə) n NZ another name for **bully²**

titbit ('tɪtˌbɪt) or esp US **tidbit** n 1 a tasty small piece of food; dainty 2 a pleasing scrap of anything, such as scandal [c17 perhaps from dialect *tid* tender, of obscure origin]

titchy or **tichy** ('tɪtʃɪ) adj titchier, titchiest or tichier, tichiest Brit slang very small; tiny [c20 from *tich* or *titch* a small person, from *Little Tich*, the stage name of Harry Relph (1867–1928), English actor noted for his small stature]

titer ('taɪtə, 'tiː-) n the usual US spelling of **titre**

titfer ('tɪtfə) n Brit slang a hat [from rhyming slang *tit for tat* hat]

tit for tat n an equivalent given in return or retaliation; blow for blow [c16 from earlier *tip for tap*]

tithable ('taɪðəb³l) adj 1 (until 1936) liable to pay tithes 2 (of property, etc) subject to the payment of tithes

tithe (taɪð) n 1 (often plural) Christianity a tenth part of agricultural or other produce, personal income, or profits, contributed either voluntarily or as a tax for the support of the church or clergy or for charitable purposes 2 any levy, esp of one tenth 3 a tenth or very small part of anything ▷ vb 4 (tr) a to exact or demand a tithe or tithes from (an individual or group) b to levy a tithe upon (a crop or amount of produce, etc) 5 (intr) to pay a tithe or tithes [Old English *teogoth*; related to Old Frisian *tegotha*, Old Saxon *tegotho*, Old High German *zehando*, Old Norse *tīundi*, Gothic *taihunda*] > 'tither n

tithe barn n a large barn where, formerly, the agricultural tithe of a parish was stored

tithing ('taɪðɪŋ) n English history 1 a a tithe; tenth b the exacting or paying of tithes 2 a company of ten householders in the system of frankpledge 3 a rural division, originally regarded as a tenth of a hundred

Tithonus (tɪ'θəʊnəs) n Greek myth the son of Laomedon of Troy who was loved by the goddess Eos. She asked that he be made immortal but forgot to ask that he be made eternally young. When he aged she turned him into a grasshopper

titi¹ ('tiːtiː) n, pl -tis any of several small omnivorous New World monkeys of the genus *Callicebus*, of South America, having long beautifully coloured fur and a long nonprehensile tail [via Spanish from Aymaran, literally: little cat]

titi² ('tiːtiː) n, pl -tis any of various evergreen shrubs or small trees of the family *Cyrillaceae* of the southern US, esp the leatherwood and *Cliftonia monophylla*, which has white or pinkish fragrant flowers [c19 of American Indian origin]

titi³ ('tiːtiː) n, pl titi NZ the sooty shearwater, *Puffinus griseus*. See **mutton bird** (sense 1) [Māori, of imitative origin]

Titian ('tɪʃən) adj (sometimes not capital) reddish-gold, like the hair colour used in many of the works of Titian (original name *Tiziano Vecellio*), the Italian painter of the Venetian school (?1490–1576). Also called: **Titian red**

Titicaca (Spanish titi'kaka) n **Lake** a lake between S Peru and W Bolivia, in the Andes: the highest large lake in the world; drained by the Desaguadero River flowing into Lake Poopó. Area: 8135 sq km (3141 sq miles). Altitude: 3809 m (12 497 ft). Depth: 370 m (1214 ft)

titillate ('tɪtɪˌleɪt) vb (tr) 1 to arouse, tease, interest, or excite pleasurably and often superficially 2 to cause a tickling or tingling sensation in, esp by touching [c17 from Latin *tītillāre*] > 'titilˌlating adj > 'titilˌlatingly adv > ˌtitil'lation n > 'titilˌlative adj

titipounamu (ˌtiːtiːˌpɒuˈnaːmuː) n, pl titipounamu NZ another name for **rifleman** (sense 2) [Māori]

titivate or **tittivate** ('tɪtɪˌveɪt) vb 1 to smarten up (oneself or another), as by making up, doing the hair, etc 2 (tr) to smarten up (a thing): to titivate a restaurant [c19 earlier *tidivate*, perhaps based on TIDY and CULTIVATE] > ˌtiti'vation or ˌtitti'vation n > 'titiˌvator or 'tittiˌvator n

titlark ('tɪtˌlɑːk) n another name for **pipit**, esp the meadow pipit (*Anthus pratensis*) [c17 from TIT¹ + LARK¹]

title ('taɪt³l) n 1 the distinctive name of a work of art, musical or literary composition, etc 2 a descriptive name, caption, or heading of a section of a book, speech, etc 3 See **title page** 4 a name or epithet signifying rank, office, or function 5 a formal designation, such as *Mr, Mrs*, or *Miss* 6 an appellation designating nobility 7 films a short for **subtitle** (sense 2) b written material giving credits in a film or television programme 8 sport a championship 9 property law a the legal right to possession of property, esp real property b the basis of such right c the documentary evidence of such right: *title deeds* 10 law a the heading or a division of a statute, book of law, etc b the heading of a suit or action at law 11 a any customary or established right b a claim based on such a right 12 a definite spiritual charge or office in the church, without appointment to which a candidate for holy orders cannot lawfully be ordained 13 RC Church a titular church ▷ vb 14 (tr) to give a title to [c13 from Old French, from Latin *titulus*]

titled ('taɪt³ld) adj having a title: *the titled classes*

title deed n a deed or document evidencing a person's legal right or title to property, esp real property

titleholder ('taɪt³lˌhəʊldə) n a person who holds a title, esp a sporting championship > 'titleˌholding adj

title page n the page in a book that bears the title, author's name, publisher's imprint, etc

title role n the role of the character after whom a play, etc, is named

titman ('tɪtmən) n, pl -men (of pigs) the runt of a litter [tit- (as in TITMOUSE) + MAN]

titmouse ('tɪtˌmaʊs) n, pl -mice (usually plural) any small active songbird of the family *Paridae*, esp those of the genus *Parus* (see **tit¹**) [c14 *titemous*, from *tite* (see TIT¹) + MOUSE]

Titograd (Serbo-Croat 'titograːd) n the former name (1946–92) of **Podgorica**

Titoism ('tiːtəʊˌɪzəm) n 1 the variant of Communism practised by the Yugoslav statesman Marshal Tito (original name *Josip Broz*; 1892–1980) in the former Yugoslavia, characterized by independence from the Soviet bloc and neutrality in East-West controversies, a considerable amount of decentralization, and a large degree of worker control of industries 2 any variant of Communism resembling Titoism > **'Titoist** n, adj

titoki (tɪ'təʊkiː) n, pl titoki a New Zealand evergreen tree, *Alectryon excelsus*, with a spreading crown and glossy green leaves. Also called: **New Zealand ash** [Māori]

titrant ('taɪtrənt) n the solution in a titration that is added from a burette to a measured quantity of another solution

titrate ('taɪtreɪt) vb (tr) to measure the volume or concentration of (a solution) by titration [c19 from French *titrer*; see TITRE] > **'titratable** adj

titration (taɪ'treɪʃən) n an operation, used in volumetric analysis, in which a measured amount of one solution is added to a known quantity of another solution until the reaction between the two is complete. If the concentration of one solution is known, that of the other can be calculated

titre or US **titer** ('taɪtə, 'tiː-) n 1 a the concentration of a solution as determined by titration b the minimum quantity of a solution required to complete a reaction in a titration 2 the quantity of antibody present in an organism [c19 from French *titre* proportion of gold or silver in an alloy, from Old French *title* TITLE]

titter ('tɪtə) vb 1 (intr) to snigger, esp derisively or in a suppressed way 2 (tr) to express by tittering ▷ n 3 a suppressed laugh, chuckle, or snigger [c17 of imitative origin] > **'titterer** n > **'tittering** adj > **'titteringly** adv

tittivate ('tɪtɪˌveɪt) vb a less common spelling of **titivate**

tittle ('tɪt³l) n 1 a small mark in printing or writing, esp a diacritic 2 a jot; particle [c14 from Medieval Latin *titulus* label, from Latin: TITLE]

tittle-tattle n 1 idle chat or gossip ▷ vb 2 (intr) to chatter or gossip > **'tittle-ˌtattler** n

tittup ('tɪtəp) vb -tups, -tupping, -tupped or US -tups, -tuping, -tuped 1 (intr) to prance or frolic ▷ n 2 a caper 3 the sound made by high-heeled shoes [c18 (in the sense: a horse's gallop): probably imitative]

titubation (ˌtɪtjʊ'beɪʃən) n pathol 1 a disordered gait characterized by stumbling or staggering, often caused by a lesion of the cerebellum 2 Also called: **lingual titubation** stuttering or stammering [c17 from Latin *titubātiō*, from *titubāre* to reel]

titular ('tɪtjʊlə) or **titulary** ('tɪtjʊlərɪ) adj 1 of, relating to, or of the nature of a title 2 in name only 3 bearing a title 4 giving a title 5 RC Church designating any of certain churches in Rome to whom cardinals or bishops are attached as their nominal incumbents ▷ n, pl -lars or -laries 6 the bearer of a title 7 the bearer of a nominal office [c18 from French *titulaire*, from Latin *titulus* TITLE] > **'titularly** adv

titulus ('tɪtjʊləs) n, pl -li (-laɪ) (in crucifixion) a sign attached to the top of the cross on which were written the condemned man's name and crime [from Latin, literally: inscription, label, title]

Titus ('taɪtəs) n New Testament the epistle written by Saint Paul to Titus, his Greek disciple and helper (in full **The Epistle of Paul the Apostle to Titus**), containing advice on pastoral matters

Tiu ('tiːuː) n (in Anglo-Saxon mythology) the god of war and the sky. Norse counterpart: **Tyr**

Tiv (tɪv) n 1 (pl Tivs or Tiv) a member of a Negroid people of W Africa, living chiefly in the savanna of the Benue area of S Nigeria and noted by anthropologists for having no chiefs 2 the language of this people, belonging to the Benue-Congo branch of the Niger-Congo family

Tivoli ('tɪvəlɪ; Italian 'tiːvoli) n a town in central Italy, east of Rome: a summer resort in Roman times; contains the Renaissance Villa d'Este and the remains of Hadrian's Villa. Pop: 49 342 (2001). Ancient name: **Tibur**

tix (tɪks) *pl n informal* tickets [C20 from *tics*, shortened from *tickets*]

tizzy ('tɪzɪ) *n, pl* -zies *informal* a state of confusion, anxiety, or excitement. Also called: **tizz, tiz-woz** ('tɪz,wɒz) [C19 of unknown origin]

tj *the internet domain name for* Tajikistan

TJ *international car registration for* Tajikistan

Tjirebon *or* **Cheribon** ('tʃɪərə,bɒn) *n* a port in S central Indonesia, on N Java on the Java Sea: scene of the signing of the **Tjirebon Agreement** of Indonesian independence (1946) by the Netherlands. Pop: 272 263 (2000)

T-joint *n* a right-angled joint, esp one in wood, making the shape of the letter T

T-junction *n* a road junction in which one road joins another at right angles but does not cross it

tk *the internet domain name for* Tokelau

TKO *boxing abbreviation for* **technical knockout**

Tl *the chemical symbol for* thallium

TLA *abbreviation for* **1** three-letter abbreviation **2** three-letter acronym

Tlaxcala (*Spanish* tlas'kala) *n* **1** a state of S central Mexico: the smallest Mexican state; formerly an Indian principality, the chief Indian ally of Cortés in the conquest of Mexico. Capital: Tlaxcala. Pop: 961 912 (2000 est). Area: 3914 sq km (1511 sq miles) **2** a city in E central Mexico, on the central plateau, capital of Tlaxcala state: the church of San Francisco (founded 1521 by Cortés) is the oldest in the Americas. Pop: 25 000 (1990 est). Official name: **Tlaxcala de Xicohténcatl**

TLC *abbreviation for informal* **1** tender loving care **2** thin-layer chromatography

Tlemcen (*French* tlɛmsɛn) *n* a city in NW Algeria: capital of an Arab kingdom from the 12th to the late 14th century. Pop: 177 000 (2005 est)

Tlingit ('tlɪŋɡɪt) *n* **1** (*pl* -gits *or* -git) a member of a seafaring group of North American Indian peoples inhabiting S Alaska and N British Columbia **2** the language of these peoples, belonging to the Na-Dene phylum

TLS *abbreviation for* Times Literary Supplement

T-lymphocyte *n* a type of lymphocyte that matures in the thymus gland and has an important role in the immune response. There are several subclasses: **killer T-cells** are responsible for killing cells that are infected by a virus; **helper T-cells** induce other cells (**B-lymphocytes**) to produce antibodies. Also called: **T-cell**

tm *the internet domain name for* Turkmenistan

Tm *the chemical symbol for* thulium

TM **1** *abbreviation for* **transcendental meditation 2** *international car registration for* Turkmenistan

T-man *n, pl* -men *US* a law-enforcement agent of the US Treasury

tmesis (tə'miːsɪs, 'miːsɪs) *n* interpolation of a word or group of words between the parts of a compound word [C16 via Latin from Greek, literally: a cutting, from *temnein* to cut]

TMI *abbreviation for* too much information: an expression of distaste or boredom at the information being offered

TMS *abbreviation for* **transcranial magnetic stimulation**

TMT *abbreviation for* telecommunications, media, and technology

TMV *abbreviation for* **tobacco mosaic virus**

tn *the internet domain name for* Tunisia

TN **1** *abbreviation for* Tennessee **2** *international car registration for* Tunisia

tng *abbreviation for* training

TNT *n* 2,4,6-trinitrotoluene; a yellow solid: used chiefly as a high explosive and is also an intermediate in the manufacture of dyestuffs. Formula: CH$_3$C$_6$H$_2$(NO$_2$)$_3$

T-number *or* **T number** *n photog* a function of the f-number of a camera lens that takes into account the amount of light actually transmitted by the lens [from T(*otal Light Transmission*) Number]

to[1] (tuː; *unstressed before a vowel* tʊ; *unstressed before a consonant* tə) *prep* **1** used to indicate the destination of the subject or object of an action: *he climbed to the top* **2** used to mark the indirect object of a verb in a sentence: *telling stories to children* **3** used to mark the infinitive of a verb: *he wanted to go* **4** as far as; until: *working from Monday to Friday* **5** used to indicate equality: *16 ounces to the pound* **6** against; upon; onto: *put your ear to the wall* **7** before the hour of: *five minutes to four* **8** accompanied by: *dancing to loud music* **9** as compared with, as against: *the score was eight to three* **10** used to indicate a resulting condition: *he tore her dress to shreds; they starved to death* **11** a dialect word for **at**[1]: *he's to town; where's it to?* ▷ *adv* **12** towards a fixed position, esp (of a door) closed [Old English *tō*; related to Old Frisian, Old Saxon *to*, Old High German *zuo*, Latin *do-* as in *dōnec* until]

to[2] *the internet domain name for* Tonga

toad (təʊd) *n* **1** any anuran amphibian of the class *Bufonidae*, such as *Bufo bufo* (**common toad**) of Europe. They are similar to frogs but are more terrestrial, having a drier warty skin. Related adj: **batrachian 2** any of various similar amphibians of different families **3** a loathsome person [Old English *tādige*, of unknown origin; see TADPOLE] ▷ '**toadish** *or* '**toad,like** *adj*

toadeater ('təʊd,iːtə) *n* a rare word for **toady** (sense 1) [C17 originally a mountebank's assistant who would pretend to eat toads (believed to be poisonous), hence a servile flatterer, toady]

toadfish ('təʊd,fɪʃ) *n, pl* -fish *or* -fishes any spiny-finned bottom-dwelling marine fish of the family *Batrachoididae*, of tropical and temperate seas, having a flattened tapering body and a wide mouth

toadflax ('təʊd,flæks) *n* any of various scrophulariaceous plants of the genus *Linaria*, esp *L. vulgaris*, having narrow leaves and spurred two-lipped yellow-orange flowers. Also called: **butter-and-eggs**

toad-in-the-hole *n Brit and Austral* a dish made of sausages baked in a batter

toad spit *or* **spittle** *n* another name for **cuckoo spit**

toadstone ('təʊd,stəʊn) *n rare* an amygdaloidal basalt occurring in the limestone regions of Derbyshire [C18 perhaps from a supposed resemblance to a toad's spotted skin]

toadstool ('təʊd,stuːl) *n* (*not in technical use*) any basidiomycetous fungus with a capped spore-producing body that is not edible. Compare **mushroom** (sense 1a) [C14 from TOAD + STOOL]

toady ('təʊdɪ) *n, pl* toadies a person who flatters and ingratiates himself in a servile way; sycophant ▷ *vb* toadies, toadying, toadied **2** to fawn on and flatter (someone) [C19 shortened from TOADEATER] ▷ '**toadyish** *adj* ▷ '**toadyism** *n*

Toamasina (*Portuguese* tōʊma'sinɐ) *n* a port in E Madagascar, on the Indian Ocean: the country's chief commercial centre. Pop: 198 000 (2005 est). Former name (until 1979): **Tamatave**

to and fro *adj, adv* to-and-fro **1** back and forth **2** here and there ▷ **toing and froing** *n*

toast[1] (təʊst) *n* **1** sliced bread browned by exposure to heat, usually under a grill, over a fire, or in a toaster **2** be **toast** *informal* to face certain destruction or defeat ▷ *vb* **3** (*tr*) to brown under a grill or over a fire: *to toast cheese* **4** to warm or be warmed in a similar manner: *to toast one's hands by the fire* [C14 from Old French *toster*, from Latin *tōstus* parched, baked from *torrēre* to dry with heat; see THIRST, TORRID]

toast[2] (təʊst) *n* **1** a tribute or proposal of health, success, etc, given to a person or thing by a company of people and marked by raising glasses and drinking together **2** a person or thing honoured by such a tribute or proposal **3** (*esp formerly*) an attractive woman to whom such tributes are frequently made: *she was the toast of the town* ▷ *vb* **4** to propose or drink a toast to (a person or thing) **5** (*intr*) to add vocal effects to a

prerecorded track: a disc-jockey technique. See also **rap**[1] (sense 6) [C17 (in the sense: a lady to whom the company is asked to drink): from TOAST[1],from the idea that the name of the lady would flavour the drink like a piece of spiced toast] ▷ '**toaster** *n*

toaster ('təʊstə) *n* a device for toasting bread, usually electric, and often equipped with an automatic timer

toastmaster ('təʊst,mɑːstə) *n* a person who introduces after-dinner speakers, proposes or announces toasts, etc, at public or formal dinners ▷ '**toast,mistress** *fem n*

toast rack *n* a small stand consisting of a usually oblong base with a number of open-sided partitions between which pieces of toast may be stood upright

toasty[1] *or* **toastie** ('təʊstɪ) *n, pl* toasties a toasted sandwich

toasty[2] ('təʊstɪ) *adj* -tier, -tiest tasting or smelling like toast

Tob. *abbreviation for* Tobit

tobacco (tə'bækəʊ) *n, pl* -cos *or* -coes **1** any of numerous solanaceous plants of the genus *Nicotiana*, having mildly narcotic properties, tapering hairy leaves, and tubular or funnel-shaped fragrant flowers. The species *N. tabacum* is cultivated as the chief source of commercial tobacco **2** the leaves of certain of these plants dried and prepared for snuff, chewing, or smoking [C16 from Spanish *tabaco*, perhaps from Taino: leaves rolled for smoking, assumed by the Spaniards to be the name of the plant] ▷ to'**baccoless** *adj*

tobacco mosaic virus *n* the virus that causes mosaic disease in tobacco and related plants: its discovery in 1892 provided the first evidence of the existence of viruses. Abbreviation: **TMV**

tobacconist (tə'bækənɪst) *n chiefly Brit* a person or shop that sells tobacco, cigarettes, pipes, etc

Tobago (tə'beɪɡəʊ) *n* an island in the SE Caribbean, northeast of Trinidad: ceded to Britain in 1814; joined with Trinidad in 1888 as a British colony; part of the independent republic of Trinidad and Tobago. Pop: 54 084 (2000)

Tobagonian (,təʊbə'ɡəʊnɪən) *adj* **1** of or relating to Tobago or its inhabitants ▷ *n* **2** a native or inhabitant of Tobago

-to-be *adj* (*in combination*) about to be; future: *a mother-to-be; the bride-to-be*

Tobin tax ('təʊbɪn) *n* a proposed tax on foreign-exchange transactions intended to discourage destabilizing speculation while also raising large revenues that could be channelled to the developing world [late C20 after James Tobin (1918–2002), US economist who proposed it]

Tobit ('təʊbɪt) *n Old Testament* **1** a pious Jew who was released from blindness through the help of the archangel Raphael **2** a book of the Apocrypha relating this story

toboggan (tə'bɒɡən) *n* **1** a light wooden frame on runners for sliding over snow and ice **2** a long narrow sledge made of a thin board curved upwards and backwards at the front ▷ *vb* -gans, -ganing, -ganed (*intr*) **3** to ride on a toboggan [C19 from Canadian French, from Algonquian; related to Abnaki *udābāgan*] ▷ to'**bogganer** *or* to'**bogganist** *n*

Tobol (*Russian* ta'bɔl) *n* a river in central Asia, rising in N Kazakhstan and flowing northeast into Russia to join the Irtysh River. Length: about 1300 km (800 miles)

Tobolsk (*Russian* ta'bɔljsk) *n* a town in central Russia, at the confluence of the Irtysh and Tobol Rivers: the chief centre for the early Russian colonization of Siberia. Pop: 100 000 (2000 est)

Tobruk (tə'brʊk, təʊ-) *n* a small port in NE Libya, in E Cyrenaica on the Mediterranean coast road: scene of severe fighting in World War II: taken from the Italians by the British in Jan 1941, from the British by the Germans in June 1942, and finally taken by the British in Nov 1942

toby ('təʊbɪ) *n, pl* -bies a water stopcock at the

t

boundary of a street and house section

toby jug *n* a beer mug or jug typically in the form of a stout seated man wearing a three-cornered hat and smoking a pipe. Also called: **toby** [C19 from the familiar form of the Christian name *Tobias*]

TOC or **toc** (tɒk) *n acronym for* train operating company

Tocantins (Portuguese tokã'tĩs) *n* 1 a state of N Brazil, created from the northern part of Goiás state in 1988. Capital: Palmas. Pop: 1 207 014 (2002). Area: 278 421 sq km (107 499 sq miles) 2 a river in E Brazil, rising in S central Goiás state and flowing generally north to the Pará River. Length: about 2700 km (1700 miles)

toccata (tə'kɑːtə) *n* a rapid keyboard composition for organ, harpsichord, etc, dating from the baroque period, usually in a rhythmically free style [C18 from Italian, literally: touched, from *toccare* to play (an instrument), TOUCH]

Toc H (tɒk 'eɪtʃ) *n* a society formed in England after World War I to fight loneliness and hate and to encourage Christian comradeship [C20 from the obsolete telegraphic code for TH, initials of *Talbot House*, Poperinge, Belgium, the original headquarters of the society]

Tocharian or **Tokharian** (tɒ'kɑːrɪən) *n* 1 a member of an Asian people with a complex material culture, sometimes thought to be of European origin, who lived in the Tarim Basin until overcome by the Uighurs around 800 AD 2 the language of this people, known from records in a N Indian script of the 7th and 8th centuries AD. It belongs to the Indo-European family, is regarded as forming an independent branch, and shows closer affinities with the W or European group than with the E or Indo-Iranian group. The language is recorded in two dialects, known as **Tocharian A** and **Tocharian B** [C20 ultimately from Greek *Tokharoi*, name of uncertain origin]

tocher ('tɒxər) *Scot* ▷ *n* 1 a dowry ▷ *vb* 2 (tr) to give a dowry to [C15 from Scottish Gaelic *tochradh*]

tockley ('tɒklɪ) *n Austral* a slang word for **penis**

tocky ('tɒkɪ) *adj* **tockier**, **tockiest** *Midland English dialect* muddy

tocology or **tokology** (tɒ'kɒlədʒɪ) *n* the branch of medicine concerned with childbirth; obstetrics [C19 from Greek *tokos* childbirth, from *tiktein* to bear]

tocopherol (tɒ'kɒfəˌrɒl) *n biochem* any of a group of fat-soluble alcohols that occur in wheat-germ oil, watercress, lettuce, egg yolk, etc They are thought to be necessary for healthy human reproduction. Also called: **vitamin E** [C20 from *toco-*, from Greek *tokos* offspring (see TOCOLOGY) + *-pher-*, from *pherein* to bear + -OL¹]

tocsin ('tɒksɪn) *n* 1 an alarm or warning signal, esp one sounded on a bell 2 an alarm bell [C16 from French, from Old French *toquassen*, from Old Provençal *tocasenh*, from *tocar* to TOUCH + *senh* bell, from Latin *signum*]

tod¹ (tɒd) *n Brit* a unit of weight, used for wool, etc, usually equal to 28 pounds [C15 probably related to Frisian *todde* rag, Old High German *zotta* tuft of hair]

tod² (tɒd) *n* **on one's tod** *Brit slang* on one's own [C19 rhyming slang *Tod Sloan/alone*, after *Tod Sloan*, a jockey]

tod³ (tɒd) *n* a Scot and northern English dialect word for a **fox** [C12 of unknown origin]

today (tə'deɪ) *n* 1 this day, as distinct from yesterday or tomorrow 2 the present age: *children of today* ▷ *adv* 3 during or on this day 4 nowadays [Old English *tō dæge*, literally: on this day, from TO + *dæge*, dative of *dæg* DAY]

toddle ('tɒdˀl) *vb* (intr) 1 to walk with short unsteady steps, as a child does when learning to walk 2 (foll by *off*) *jocular* to depart 3 (foll by *round*, *over*, etc) *jocular* to stroll; amble ▷ *n* 4 the act or an instance of toddling [C16 (Scottish and northern English): of obscure origin]

toddler ('tɒdlə) *n* 1 a young child, usually one

between the ages of one and two and a half 2 (modifier) designed or suitable for a toddler: *toddler suits* > '**toddler**ˌ**hood** *n*

toddy ('tɒdɪ) *n, pl* **-dies** 1 a drink made from spirits, esp whisky, with hot water, sugar, and usually lemon juice 2 **a** the sap of various palm trees (**toddy** or **wine palms**), used as a beverage **b** the liquor prepared from this sap 3 (in Malaysia) a milky-white sour alcoholic drink made from fermented coconut milk, drunk chiefly by Indians [C17 from Hindi *tāṛī* juice of the palmyra palm, from *tāṛ* palmyra palm, from Sanskrit *tāra*, probably of Dravidian origin]

to-do (tə'duː) *n, pl* **-dos** a commotion, fuss, or quarrel

tody ('təʊdɪ) *n, pl* **-dies** any small bird of the family *Todidae* of the Caribbean, having a red-and-green plumage and long straight bill: order *Coraciiformes* (kingfishers, etc) [C18 from French *todier*, from Latin *todus* small bird]

toe (təʊ) *n* 1 any one of the digits of the foot 2 the corresponding part in other vertebrates 3 the part of a shoe, sock, etc, covering the toes 4 anything resembling a toe in shape or position 5 the front part of the head of a golf club, hockey stick, etc 6 the lower bearing of a vertical shaft assembly 7 the tip of a cam follower that engages the cam profile 8 **dip one's toe** (or **toes**) **in** *informal* to begin doing or try something new or unfamiliar 9 **on one's toes** alert 10 **tread on someone's toes** to offend or insult a person, esp by trespassing on his field of responsibility 11 **turn up one's toes** *informal* to die 12 *Austral slang* speed: *a player with plenty of toe* ▷ *vb* **toes**, **toeing**, **toed** 13 (tr) to touch, kick, or mark with the toe 14 (tr) *golf* to strike (the ball) with the toe of the club 15 (tr) to drive (a nail, spike, etc) obliquely 16 (intr) to walk with the toes pointing in a specified direction: *to toe inwards* 17 to conform to expected standards, attitudes, etc [Old English *tā*; related to Old Frisian *tāne*, Old Norse *tā*, Old High German *zēha*, Latin *digitus* finger] > '**toe**ˌ**like** *adj*

toea ('təʊɑː) *n, pl* **toea** a monetary unit of Papua New Guinea, worth one-hundredth of a kina [from a Papuan language]

toe and heel *n* a technique used by racing drivers while changing gear on sharp bends, in which the brake is operated by the toe (or heel) of the right foot while the heel (or toe) simultaneously operates the accelerator

toebie ('tuːbiː) *n South African slang* a sandwich [from Afrikaans *toebroodjie* sandwich]

toecap ('təʊˌkæp) *n* a reinforced covering for the toe of a boot or shoe

toe crack *n vet science* a sand crack occurring on the forepart of the hind foot of a horse

toe-curling *adj informal* causing feelings of acute embarrassment > '**toe-**ˌ**curlingly** *adv*

toed (təʊd) *adj* 1 having a part resembling a toe 2 (of a vertical or oblique member of a timber frame) fixed by nails driven in at the foot 3 (in combination) having a toe or toes as specified: *five-toed*

toe dance *n* 1 a dance performed on tiptoe ▷ *vb* **toe-dance** 2 (intr) *ballet* to dance on pointes > **toe dancer** *n*

toehold ('təʊˌhəʊld) *n* 1 a small foothold to facilitate climbing 2 any means of gaining access, support, etc: *the socialist party gained a toehold in the local elections* 3 a wrestling hold in which the opponent's toe is held and his leg twisted against the joints

toe-in *n* a slight forward convergence given to the wheels of motor vehicles to improve steering and equalize tyre wear

toenail ('təʊˌneɪl) *n* 1 a thin horny translucent plate covering part of the dorsal surface of the end joint of each toe. Related adjs: **ungual, ungular** 2 *carpentry* a nail driven obliquely, as in joining one beam at right angles to another 3 *printing slang* a parenthesis ▷ *vb* 4 (tr) *carpentry* to join (beams) by driving nails obliquely

toerag ('təʊˌræg) *n Brit slang* a contemptible or despicable person [C20 originally, a beggar, tramp: from the pieces of rag they wrapped round their feet]

toetoe ('tɔɪtɔɪ, 'təʊɪːˌtəʊɪː, ˌtəʊɪːˈtəʊɪː) *N* See **toitoi**

toe-to-toe *informal* ▷ *adv* 1 in one-to-one combat or in direct competition: *there aren't many fighters willing to go toe-to-toe with him* ▷ *adj* 2 (of battles, confrontations, or contests) involving two people or groups fighting with or competing against each other: *a toe-to-toe battle* ▷ *n* 3 a fight, confrontation, or contest between two people or groups

toey ('təʊɪ) *adj Austral slang* 1 (of a person) nervous or anxious 2 *rare* (of a horse) eager to race 3 **toey as a Roman sandal** very anxious

toff (tɒf) *n Brit slang* a rich, well-dressed, or upper-class person, esp a man [C19 perhaps variant of TUFT, nickname for a titled student at Oxford University, wearing a cap with a gold tassel]

toffee or **toffy** ('tɒfɪ) *n, pl* **-fees** or **-fies** 1 a sweet made from sugar or treacle boiled with butter, nuts, etc 2 **for toffee** (preceded by *can't*) *informal* to be incompetent at a specified activity: *he can't sing for toffee* [C19 variant of earlier TAFFY]

toffee-apple *n* an apple fixed on a stick and coated with a thin layer of toffee

toffee-nosed *adj slang, chiefly Brit* pretentious or supercilious; used esp of snobbish people [C20 perhaps coined as a pun on *toffy* stylish, grand: see TOFF]

toffish ('tɒfɪʃ) *adj Brit informal* belonging to or characteristic of the upper class

toft (tɒft) *n Brit history* 1 a homestead 2 an entire holding, consisting of a homestead and the attached arable land [Old English, from Old Norse *topt*]

tofu ('təʊˌfuː) *n* unfermented soya-bean curd, a food with a soft cheeselike consistency made from soya-bean milk [from Japanese]

tog¹ (tɒg) *informal* ▷ *vb* **togs**, **togging**, **togged** 1 (often foll by *up* or *out*) to dress oneself, esp in smart clothes ▷ *n* 2 See **togs** [C18 probably short for obsolete cant *togemans* coat, from Latin *toga* TOGA + *-mans*, of uncertain origin]

tog² (tɒg) *n* **a** a unit of thermal resistance used to measure the power of insulation of a fabric, garment, quilt, etc. The tog-value of an article is equal to ten times the temperature difference between its two faces, in degrees Celsius, when the flow of heat across it is equal to one watt per m² **b** (*as modifier*): *tog-rating* [C20 arbitrary coinage from TOG¹ (noun)]

toga ('təʊgə) *n* 1 a garment worn by citizens of ancient Rome, consisting of a piece of cloth draped around the body 2 the official vestment of certain offices [C16 from Latin, related to *tegere* to cover] > **togaed** ('təʊgəd) *adj*

toga praetexta (priːˈtɛkstə) *n* (in ancient Rome) a toga with a broad purple border worn by certain magistrates and priests and by boys until they assumed the toga virilis [Latin, literally: bordered toga]

toga virilis (vɪˈraɪlɪs) *n* (in ancient Rome) the toga assumed by a youth at the age of 14 as a symbol of manhood and citizenship [Latin, literally: manly (ie, man's) toga]

together (tə'gɛðə) *adv* 1 with cooperation and interchange between constituent elements, members, etc: *we worked together* 2 in or into contact or union with each other: *to stick papers together* 3 in or into one place or assembly; with each other: *the people are gathered together* 4 at the same time: *we left school together* 5 considered collectively or jointly: *all our wages put together couldn't buy that car* 6 continuously: *working for eight hours together* 7 closely, cohesively, or compactly united or held: *water will hold the dough together* 8 mutually or reciprocally: *to multiply 7 and 8 together* 9 *informal* organized: *to get things together* 10 **together with** in addition to ▷ *adj* 11 *slang* self-possessed and well-organized; mentally and emotionally stable: *she's a very together lady* [Old English *tōgædre*; related to Old Frisian *togadera*, Middle High German *gater*; see GATHER]

⬛ **USAGE** See at **plus**

togetherness (tə'ɡɛðənɪs) *n* a feeling of closeness or affection from being united with other people

togger ('tɒɡə) *vb* (*intr*) *Northern English dialect* to play football

toggery ('tɒɡərɪ) *n informal* clothes; togs

toggle ('tɒɡ³l) *n* **1** a wooden peg or metal rod fixed crosswise through an eye at the end of a rope, chain, or cable, for fastening temporarily by insertion through an eye in another rope, chain, etc **2** a wooden or plastic bar-shaped button inserted through a loop for fastening **3** a pin inserted into a nautical knot to keep it secure **4** *machinery* a toggle joint or a device having such a joint ▷ *vb* **5** (*tr*) to supply or fasten with a toggle or toggles **6** *computing* (*intr*, often foll by *between*) to switch to a different option, view, application, etc [c18 of unknown origin] > 'toggler *n*

toggle iron *n* a whaling harpoon with a pivoting barb near its head to prevent a harpooned whale pulling free. Also called: **toggle harpoon**

toggle joint *n* a device consisting of two arms pivoted at a common joint and at their outer ends and used to apply pressure by straightening the angle between the two arms

toggle switch *n* **1** an electric switch having a projecting lever that is manipulated in a particular way to open or close a circuit **2** a computer device that is used to turn a feature on or off

Togliatti (ˌtɒlɪ'ætɪ) *n* a city in W central Russia, on the Volga River: automobile industry: renamed in honour of Palmiro Togliatti, an Italian communist. Pop: 718 000 (2005 est). Former name (until 1964): **Stavropol** Russian name: **Tolyatti**

Togo ('təʊɡəʊ) *n* a republic in West Africa, on the Gulf of Guinea: became French Togoland (a League of Nations mandate) after the division of German Togoland in 1922; independent since 1960. Official language: French. Religion: animist majority. Currency: franc. Capital: Lomé. Pop: 5 017 000 (2004 est). Area: 56 700 sq km (20 900 sq miles)

Togoland ('təʊɡəʊˌlænd) *n* a former German protectorate in West Africa on the Gulf of Guinea: divided in 1922 into the League of Nations mandates of British Togoland (west) and French Togoland (east); the former joined Ghana in 1957; the latter became independent as Togo in 1960

Togolander ('təʊɡəʊˌlændə) *n* a native or inhabitant of the former British Togoland (now part of Ghana) or French Togoland (now Togo)

Togolese (ˌtəʊɡə'liːz) *adj* **1** of or relating to Togo or its inhabitants *n*, *pl* **-lese 2** a native or inhabitant of Togo

togs (tɒɡz) *pl n informal* **1** clothes **2** *Austral, NZ, and Irish* a swimming costume [from TOG¹]

toheroa (ˌtəʊə'rəʊə) *n* **1** a bivalve mollusc, *Amphidesma* (or *Semele*) *ventricosum*, of New Zealand **2** a greenish soup made of this [from Māori]

tohunga ('tɒhʊŋə, tɒ'hʊŋə) *n NZ* a Māori priest, the repository of traditional lore

toil¹ (tɔɪl) *n* **1** hard or exhausting work **2** an obsolete word for **strife** ▷ *vb* **3** (*intr*) to labour **4** (*intr*) to progress with slow painful movements: *to toil up a hill* **5** (*tr*) *archaic* to achieve by toil [c13 from Anglo-French *toiler* to struggle, from Old French *toeillier* to confuse, from Latin *tudiculāre* to stir, from *tudicula* machine for bruising olives, from *tudes* a hammer, from *tundere* to beat] > 'toiler *n*

toil² (tɔɪl) *n* **1** (*often plural*) a net or snare: *the toils of fortune had ensnared him* **2** *archaic* a trap for wild beasts [c16 from Old French *toile*, from Latin *tēla* loom]

toile (twɑːl) *n* **1** a transparent linen or cotton fabric **2** a garment of exclusive design made up in cheap cloth so that alterations and

experiments can be made [c19 from French, from Latin *tēla* a loom]

toilet ('tɔɪlɪt) *n* **1** another word for **lavatory 2** *old-fashioned* the act of dressing and preparing oneself: *to make one's toilet* **3** *old-fashioned* a dressing table or the articles used when making one's toilet **4** *rare* costume **5** the cleansing of a wound, etc, after an operation or childbirth [c16 from French *toilette* dress, from TOILE]

toilet paper *or* **tissue** *n* thin absorbent paper, often wound in a roll round a cardboard cylinder (**toilet roll**), used for cleaning oneself after defecation or urination

toiletry ('tɔɪlɪtrɪ) *n*, *pl* **-ries** an object or cosmetic used in making up, dressing, etc

toilet set *n* a matching set consisting of a hairbrush, comb, mirror, and clothes brush

toilet soap *n* a mild soap, often coloured and scented, used for washing oneself

toilette (twɑː'lɛt; *French* twalɛt) *n usually literary or affected* another word for **toilet** (sense 2) [c16 from French; see TOILET]

toilet training *n* the process of teaching young children to control the timing of bladder and bowel movements and to use the lavatory

toilet water *n* a form of liquid perfume lighter than cologne. Compare **cologne** Also called: **eau de toilette**

toilsome ('tɔɪlsəm) *or* **toilful** *adj* laborious > 'toilsomely *or* 'toilfully *adv* > 'toilsomeness *or* 'toilfulness *n*

toitoi¹ ('tɔɪtɔɪ) *or* **toetoe** *n*, *pl* **-tois** *or* **-toes** any of various tall grasses of the genus *Cortaderia* of New Zealand, with feathery fronds [Māori]

toitoi² ('tɔɪtɔɪ) *n NZ* another name for **bully²**

tokamak ('tɒkəˌmæk) *n physics* a toroidal reactor used in thermonuclear experiments, in which a strong helical magnetic field keeps the plasma from contacting the external walls. The magnetic field is produced partly by current-carrying coils and partly by a large inductively driven current through the plasma [c20 from Russian *to(roidál'naya) kám(era s) ak(siál'nym magnitnym pólem)*, toroidal chamber with magnetic field]

tokay ('təʊkeɪ) *n* a small gecko, *Gekko gecko*, of S and SE Asia, having a retractile claw at the tip of each digit [from Malay *toke*, of imitative origin]

Tokay (təʊ'keɪ) *n* **1** a fine sweet wine made near Tokaj, Hungary **2** a variety of large sweet grape used to make this wine **3** a similar wine made elsewhere

toke (təʊk) *slang* ▷ *n* **1** a draw on a cannabis cigarette ▷ *vb* **2** (*intr*) to take a draw on a cannabis cigarette > 'toker *n*

Tokelau ('təʊkəˌlaʊ) *or* **Tokelau Islands** *pl n* an island group in the South Pacific composed of three atolls, Nukunono, Atafu, and Fakaofo, which in 1948 was included within the territorial boundaries of New Zealand. Pop: 2000 (2003 est). Area: about 11 sq km (4 sq miles)

token ('təʊkən) *n* **1** an indication, warning, or sign of something **2** a symbol or visible representation of something **3** something that indicates authority, proof, or authenticity **4** a metal or plastic disc, such as a substitute for currency for use in slot machines **5** a memento **6** a gift voucher that can be used as payment for goods of a specified value **7** (*modifier*) as a matter of form only; nominal: *a token increase in salary* **8** *linguistics* a symbol regarded as an individual concrete mark, not as a class of identical symbols. Compare **type** (sense 11) **9** *philosophy* an individual instance: if the same sentence has different truth-values on different occasions of utterance the truth-value may be said to attach to the sentence-token. Compare **type** (sense 13) **10** **by the same token** moreover and for the same or a similar reason ▷ *vb* **11** (*tr*) to act or serve as a warning or symbol of; betoken [Old English *tācen*; related to Old Frisian *tēken*, Old Saxon *tēkan*, Old High German *zeihhan*, Old Norse *teikn*; see TEACH]

token economy *n* a type of psychotherapy in

which the inmates of an institution are rewarded for good behaviour with tokens that can be exchanged for privileges

tokenism ('təʊkəˌnɪzəm) *n* the practice of making only a token effort or doing no more than the minimum, esp in order to comply with a law > ˌtoken'istic *adj*

token money *n* coins of the regular issue having greater face value than the value of their metal content

token payment *n* a small payment made in acknowledgment of the existence of debt

token strike *n* a brief strike intended to convey strength of feeling on a disputed issue

token vote *n* a Parliamentary vote of money in which the amount quoted to aid discussion is not intended to be binding

Tokharian (tɒ'kɑːrɪən) *n* a variant spelling of **Tocharian**

tokology (tɒ'kɒlədʒɪ) *n* a variant spelling of **tocology**

tokoloshe (ˌtɒkʊ'lɒʃ, -'lɒʃɪ) *or* **tokoloshi** *n* (in Bantu folklore) a malevolent mythical manlike animal of short stature. Also called: **tikoloshe** [from Xhosa *uthikoloshe*]

tokotoko (ˌtɒkʊ'tɒkʊ) *n NZ* a ceremonial carved Māori walking stick [Māori]

toktokkie (tɒk'tɒkɪ) *n* a large South African beetle, *Dichtha cubica* [from Afrikaans, from Dutch *tokken* to tap]

Tokyo ('təʊkjəʊ, -kɪˌəʊ) *n* the capital of Japan, a port on SE Honshu on **Tokyo Bay** (an inlet of the Pacific): part of the largest conurbation in the world (the Tokyo-Yokohama metropolitan area) of over 35 million people; major industrial centre and the chief cultural centre of Japan. Pop (city proper): 8 025 538 (2002 est)

tola ('təʊlə) *n* a unit of weight, used in India, equal to 180 ser or 180 grains [c17 from Hindi *tolā*, from Sanskrit *tulā* scale, from *tul* to weigh]

tolan ('təʊlæn) *or* **tolane** ('təʊleɪn) *n* a white crystalline derivative of acetylene; diphenylacetylene; diphenylethyne. Formula: $C_6H_5C{:}CC_6H_5$ [c19 from TOL(UENE) + *-an* (see *-ANE*)]

tolar ('təʊlɑː) *n*, *pl* **tolarji** ('təʊlɑːjɪ) the standard monetary unit of Slovenia, divided into 100 stotin [c20 Slovene, from German *Taler* DOLLAR]

tolbooth ('təʊlˌbuːθ, -ˌbuːð, 'tɒl-) *n* **1** *chiefly Scot* a town hall **2** a variant spelling of **tollbooth**

tolbutamide (tɒl'bjuːtəˌmaɪd) *n* a synthetic crystalline compound administered orally in the treatment of diabetes to lower blood glucose concentrations. Formula: $C_{12}H_{18}N_2O_3S$ [c20 from TOL(UYL) + BUT(YRIC ACID) + AMIDE]

told (təʊld) *vb* **1** the past tense and past participle of **tell¹** ▷ *adj* **2** See **all told**

tole (təʊl) *n* enamelled or lacquered metal ware, usually gilded, popular in the 18th century [from French *tôle* sheet metal, from French (dialect): table, from Latin *tabula* table]

Toledo *n* **1** (tɒ'leɪdəʊ; *Spanish* to'leðo) a city in central Spain, on the River Tagus: capital of Visigothic Spain, and of Castile from 1087 to 1560; famous for steel and swords since the first century. Pop: 72 549 (2003 est). Ancient name: Toletum (tə'liːtəm) **2** (tə'liːdəʊ) an inland port in NW Ohio, on Lake Erie: one of the largest coal-shipping ports in the world; transportation and industrial centre; university (1872). Pop: 308 973 (2003 est) **3** a fine-tapered sword or sword blade

tolerable ('tɒlərəb³l) *adj* **1** able to be tolerated; endurable **2** permissible **3** *informal* fairly good > 'tolerableness *or* ˌtolera'bility *n* > 'tolerably *adv*

tolerance ('tɒlərəns) *n* **1** the state or quality of being tolerant **2** capacity to endure something, esp pain or hardship **3** the permitted variation in some measurement or other characteristic of an object or workpiece **4** *physiol* the capacity of an organism to endure the effects of a poison or other substance, esp after it has been taken over a prolonged period

tolerance zone *n* an designated area where

t

prostitutes can work without being arrested

tolerant (ˈtɒlərənt) *adj* **1** able to tolerate the beliefs, actions, opinions, etc, of others **2** permissive **3** able to withstand extremes, as of heat and cold **4** *med* (of a patient) exhibiting tolerance to a drug > ˈtolerantly *adv*

tolerate (ˈtɒləˌreɪt) *vb* (*tr*) **1** to treat with indulgence, liberality, or forbearance **2** to permit **3** to be able to bear; put up with **4** to have tolerance for (a drug, poison, etc) [C16 from Latin *tolerāre* sustain; related to THOLE²] > ˈtolerative *adj* > ˈtolerˌator *n*

toleration (ˌtɒləˈreɪʃən) *n* **1** the act or practice of tolerating **2** freedom to hold religious opinions that differ from the established or prescribed religion of a country > ˌtolerˈationism *n* > ˌtolerˈationist *n*

tolidine (ˈtɒlɪˌdiːn) *n* any of several isomeric compounds, esp the *ortho*- isomer, which is a white or reddish crystalline substance used in the manufacture of dyes and resins. Formula: $(C_6H_3NH_2CH_3)_2$ [C19 from TOL(UENE) + -ID³ + -INE²]

Tolima (*Spanish* toˈlima) *n* a volcano in W Colombia, in the Andes. Height: 5215 m (17 110 ft)

Tolkienesque (ˌtɒlkiːnˈɛsk) *adj* referring to or reminiscent of the work of the British novelist and critic J.R.R. Tolkien (1892–1973), who is best known for his fantasy novels *The Hobbit* and *The Lord of the Rings*

toll¹ (təʊl) *vb* **1** to ring or cause to ring slowly and recurrently **2** (*tr*) to summon, warn, or announce by tolling **3** *US and Canadian* to decoy (game, esp ducks) ▷ *n* **4** the act or sound of tolling [C15 perhaps related to Old English *-tyllan*, as in *fortyllan* to attract]

toll² (təʊl, tɒl) *n* **1 a** an amount of money levied, esp for the use of certain roads, bridges, etc, to cover the cost of maintenance **b** (*as modifier*): *toll road; toll bridge* **2** loss or damage incurred through an accident, disaster, etc: *the war took its toll of the inhabitants* **3** Also called: **tollage** (formerly) the right to levy a toll **4** Also called: **toll charge** NZ a charge for a telephone call beyond a free-dialling area [Old English *toln*; related to Old Frisian *tolene*, Old High German *zol* toll, from Late Latin *telōnium* customs house, from Greek *telónion*, ultimately from *telos* tax]

tollbooth or **tolbooth** (ˈtəʊlˌbuːθ, -ˌbuːð, ˈtɒl-) *n* a booth or kiosk at which a toll is collected

toll call *n* **1** *Brit obsolete* a short-distance trunk call **2** *US* a long-distance telephone call at a rate higher than that for a local call **3** *NZ* a telephone call beyond a free-dialling area for which a charge is made

tollgate (ˈtəʊlˌgeɪt, ˈtɒl-) *n* a gate across a toll road or bridge at which travellers must stop and pay

tollhouse (ˈtəʊlˌhaʊs, ˈtɒl-) *n* a small house at a tollgate occupied by a toll collector

tolly or **tollie** (ˈtɒlɪ) *n, pl* **-lies** *South African* a castrated calf [C19 from Xhosa *ithole* calf on which the horns have begun to appear]

Tolpuddle Martyrs (ˈtɒlˌpʌdᵊl) *n* six farm workers sentenced to transportation for seven years in 1834 for administering an unlawful oath to form a trade union in the village of Tolpuddle, Dorset

Toltec (ˈtɒltɛk) *n, pl* **-tecs** or **-tec 1** a member of a Central American Indian people who dominated the valley of Mexico from their capital Tula from about 950 to 1160 AD, when the valley was overrun by the Aztecs ▷ *adj also* **Toltecan 2** of or relating to this people [C19 from Spanish *tolteca*, of American Indian origin]

tolu (tɒˈluː) *n* an aromatic balsam obtained from a South American tree, *Myroxylon balsamum*. See **balsam** (sense 1) [C17 after *Santiago de Tolu*, Colombia, from which it was exported]

toluate (ˈtɒljuˌeɪt) *n* any salt or ester of any of the three isomeric forms of toluic acid [C19 from TOLU(IC ACID) + -ATE¹]

Toluca (*Spanish* toˈluka) *n* **1** a city in S central Mexico, capital of Mexico state, at an altitude of 2640 m (8660 ft). Pop: 1 987 000 (2005 est). Official name: **Toluca de Lerdo** (deˈlɛrðo) **2 Nevado de** (neˈβaðo de) a volcano in central Mexico, in Mexico state near Toluca: crater partly filled by a lake. Height: 4577 m (15 017 ft)

toluene (ˈtɒljuˌiːn) *n* a colourless volatile flammable liquid with an odour resembling that of benzene, obtained from petroleum and coal tar and used as a solvent and in the manufacture of many organic chemicals. Formula: $C_6H_5CH_3$ [C19 from TOLU + -ENE, since it was previously obtained from tolu]

toluic acid (tɒˈluːɪk) *n* a white crystalline derivative of toluene existing in three isomeric forms; methylbenzoic acid. The *ortho*- and *para*-isomers are used in synthetic resins and the *meta*-isomer is used as an insect repellent. Formula: $C_6H_4CH_3COOH$ [C19 from TOLU(ENE) + -IC]

toluidine (tɒˈljuːɪˌdiːn) *n* an amine derived from toluene existing in three isomeric forms; aminotoluene. The *ortho*- and *meta*- isomers are liquids and the *para*- isomer is a crystalline solid. All three are used in making dyes. Formula: $C_6H_4CH_3NH_2$ [C19 from TOLU(ENE) + -IDE + -INE²]

toluol (ˈtɒljuˌɒl) *n* another name for **toluene**

toluyl (ˈtɒljuɪl) *n* (*modifier*) of, consisting of, or containing any of three isomeric groups $CH_3C_6H_4CO-$, derived from a toluic acid by removal of the hydroxyl group: *toluyl group or radical* [C19 from TOLU(ENE) + -YL]

tolyl (ˈtɒlɪl) *n* **1** (*modifier*) of, consisting of, or containing any of three isomeric groups, $CH_3C_6H_4-$, derived from toluene: *tolyl group or radical* **2** (*modifier*) another word for **benzyl**. Also called: α-**tolyl** [C19 from TOLU (see TOLUENE) + -YL]

tom¹ (tɒm) *n* **a** the male of various animals, esp the cat **b** (*as modifier*): *a tom turkey* **c** (*in combination*): *a tomcat* [C16 special use of the shortened form of *Thomas*, applied to any male, often implying a common or ordinary type of person, etc]

tom² (tɒm) *n* *Austral and NZ* a temporary supporting post [from a specialized use of TOM¹]

tomahawk (ˈtɒməˌhɔːk) *n* **1** a fighting axe, with a stone or later an iron head, used by the North American Indians **2** *chiefly Austral* the usual word for **hatchet** [C17 from Virginia Algonquian *tamahaac*]

tomalley (ˈtɒmælɪ) *n* fat from a lobster, called "liver", and eaten as a delicacy [C17 of Caribbean origin; compare Galibi *tumali* sauce of crab or lobster liver]

toman (təˈmɑːn) *n* a gold coin formerly issued in Persia [C16 from Persian, of Mongolian origin]

Tom and Jerry *n* *US* a hot mixed drink containing rum, brandy, egg, nutmeg, and sometimes milk

tomato (təˈmɑːtəʊ) *n, pl* **-toes 1** a solanaceous plant, *Lycopersicon* (or *Lycopersicum*) *esculentum*, of South America, widely cultivated for its red fleshy many-seeded edible fruits **2** the fruit of this plant, which has slightly acid-tasting flesh and is eaten in salads, as a vegetable, etc **3** *US and Canadian slang* a girl or woman [C17 *tomate*, from Spanish, from Nahuatl *tomatl*]

tomb (tuːm) *n* **1** a place, esp a vault beneath the ground, for the burial of a corpse **2** a stone or other monument to the dead **3 the tomb** a poetic term for **death 4** anything serving as a burial place: *the sea was his tomb* ▷ *vb* **5** (*tr*) *rare* to place in a tomb; entomb [C13 from Old French *tombe*, from Late Latin *tumba* burial mound, from Greek *tumbos*; related to Latin *tumēre* to swell, Middle Irish *tomm* hill] > ˈtombˌlike *adj*

tombac (ˈtɒmbæk) or **tambac** (ˈtæmbæk) *n* any of various brittle alloys containing copper and zinc and sometimes tin and arsenic: used for making cheap jewellery, etc [C17 from French, from Dutch *tombak*, from Malay *tambâga* copper, apparently from Sanskrit *tāmraka*, from *tāmra* dark coppery red]

tombola (tɒmˈbəʊlə) *n* *Brit* a type of lottery, esp at a fête, in which tickets are drawn from a revolving drum [C19 from Italian, from *tombolare* to somersault; see TUMBLE]

tombolo (ˈtɒmbəˌləʊ) *n, pl* **-los** a narrow sand or shingle bar linking a small island with another island or the mainland [C20 from Italian, from Latin *tumulus* mound; see TUMULUS]

Tombouctou (tɔ̃buktu) *n* the French name for **Timbuktu**

tomboy (ˈtɒmˌbɔɪ) *n* a girl who acts or dresses in a boyish way, liking rough outdoor activities > ˈtomˌboyish *adj* > ˈtomˌboyishly *adv* > ˈtomˌboyishness *n*

tombstone (ˈtuːmˌstəʊn) *n* another word for **gravestone**

Tombstone (ˈtuːmˌstəʊn) *n* a town in the US, in Arizona: scene of the gunfight at the OK Corral in 1881. Pop: 1547 (2003 est)

Tom Collins *n* a long drink consisting of gin, lime or lemon juice, sugar or syrup, and soda water

Tom, Dick, and (or) Harry *n* an ordinary, undistinguished, or common person (esp in the phrases **every Tom, Dick, and Harry; any Tom, Dick, or Harry**)

tome (təʊm) *n* **1** a large weighty book **2** one of the several volumes of a work [C16 from French, from Latin *tomus* section of larger work, from Greek *tomos* a slice, from *temnein* to cut; related to Latin *tondēre* to shear]

-tome *n combining form* indicating an instrument for cutting: *osteotome* [from Greek *tomē* a cutting, *tomos* a slice, from *temnein* to cut]

tomentum (təˈmɛntəm) *n, pl* **-ta** (-tə) **1** a feltlike covering of downy hairs on leaves and other plant parts **2** a network of minute blood vessels occurring in the human brain between the pia mater and cerebral cortex [C17 New Latin, from Latin: stuffing for cushions; related to Latin *tumēre* to swell] > **tomentose** (təˈmɛntəʊs) *adj*

tomfool (ˌtɒmˈfuːl) *n* **a** a fool **b** (*as modifier*): *tomfool ideas* [C14 from TOM¹ + FOOL¹] > ˈtomˈfoolish *adj* > ˌtomˈfoolishness *n*

tomfoolery (ˌtɒmˈfuːlərɪ) *n, pl* **-eries 1** foolish behaviour **2** utter nonsense; rubbish

tommy (ˈtɒmɪ) *n, pl* **-mies** (*often capital*) *Brit informal* a private in the British Army. Also called: **Tommy Atkins** (ˈætkɪnz) [C19 originally *Thomas Atkins*, a name representing a typical private in specimen forms; compare TOM¹]

tommy bar *n* a short bar used as a lever to provide torque for tightening a box spanner or key

Tommy gun *n* an informal name for **Thompson sub-machine-gun**

tommyrot (ˈtɒmɪˌrɒt) *n* utter nonsense; tomfoolery

tommy rough *n* *Austral* another name for **roughie¹**

tomo (ˈtɒmɒ) *n* *NZ* a shaft formed by the action of water on limestone or volcanic rock [Māori]

tomography (təˈmɒɡrəfɪ) *n* any of a number of techniques used to obtain an X-ray photograph of a selected plane section of the human body or some other solid object [C20 from Greek *tomē* a cutting + -GRAPHY]

tomorrow (təˈmɒrəʊ) *n* **1** the day after today **2** the future ▷ *adv* **3** on the day after today **4** at some time in the future [Old English *tō morgenne*, from TO¹ (at, on) + *morgenne*, dative of *morgen* MORNING; see MORROW]

tompion (ˈtɒmpɪən) *n* a variant of **tampion**

Tomsk (*Russian* tɔmsk) *n* a city in central Russia: formerly an important gold-mining town and administrative centre for a large area of Siberia; university (1888); engineering industries. Pop: 486 000 (2005 est)

Tom Thumb *n* a dwarf, midget [after *Tom Thumb*, the tiny hero of several English folk tales]

tomtit (ˈtɒmˌtɪt) *n* *Brit* any of various tits, esp the bluetit

tom-tom *n* **1** a drum associated either with the American Indians or with Eastern cultures, usually beaten with the hands as a signalling instrument **2** a standard cylindrical drum, normally with one drumhead **3** a monotonous drumming or beating sound ▷ *vb* **-toms, -tomming, tommed 4** (*tr*) *informal* to pass (information, esp gossip) around a community very quickly [c17 from Hindi *tamtam*, of imitative origin]

-tomy *n combining form* indicating a surgical cutting of a specified part or tissue: *lobotomy* [from Greek *-tomia*; see -TOME]

ton[1] (tʌn) *n* **1** Also called: **long ton** *Brit* a unit of weight equal to 2240 pounds or 1016.046909 kilograms **2** Also called: **short ton, net ton** *US* a unit of weight equal to 2000 pounds or 907.184 kilograms **3** Also called: **metric ton, tonne** a unit of weight equal to 1000 kilograms **4** Also called: **freight ton** a unit of volume or weight used for charging or measuring freight in shipping. It depends on the type of material being shipped but is often taken as 40 cubic feet, 1 cubic metre, or 1000 kilograms: *freight is charged at £40 per ton of 1 cubic metre* **5** Also called: **measurement ton, shipping ton** a unit of volume used in shipping freight, equal to 40 cubic feet, irrespective of the commodity shipped **6** Also called: **displacement ton** a unit used for measuring the displacement of a ship, equal to 35 cubic feet of sea water or 2240 pounds **7** Also called: **register ton** a unit of internal capacity of ships equal to 100 cubic feet ▷ See also **tons** [c14 variant of TUN]

ton[2] *French* (tɔ̃) *n* style, fashion, or distinction [c18 from French, from Latin *tonus* TONE]

ton[3] (tʌn) *n slang, chiefly Brit* a score or achievement of a hundred, esp a hundred miles per hour, as on a motorcycle [c20 special use of TON[1] applied to quantities of one hundred]

tonal (ˈtəʊnᵊl) *adj* **1** of or relating to tone **2** of, relating to, or utilizing the diatonic system; having an established key. Compare **atonal 3 a** (of an answer in a fugue) not having the same melodic intervals as the subject, so as to remain in the original key **b** denoting a fugue as having such an answer. Compare **real[1]** (sense 11) > ˈ**tonally** *adv*

tonality (təʊˈnælɪtɪ) *n, pl* **-ties 1** *music* **a** the actual or implied presence of a musical key in a composition **b** the system of major and minor keys prevalent in Western music since the decline of modes. Compare **atonality 2** the overall scheme of colours and tones in a painting

to-name *n Scot* a nickname used to distinguish one person from others of the same name

Tonbridge (ˈtʌnˌbrɪdʒ) *n* a market town in SE England, in SW Kent on the River Medway. Pop: 35 833 (2001)

tondo (ˈtɒndəʊ) *n, pl* **-di** (-diː) a circular easel painting or relief carving [c19 from Italian: a circle, shortened from *rotondo* round]

tone (təʊn) *n* **1** sound with reference to quality, pitch, or volume **2** short for **tone colour 3** *US and Canadian* another word for **note** (sense 10) **4** (in acoustic analysis) a sound resulting from periodic or regular vibrations, composed either of a simple sinusoidal waveform (**pure tone**) or of several such waveforms superimposed upon one main one (**compound tone**) **5** an interval of a major second; whole tone **6** Also called: **Gregorian tone** any of several plainsong melodies or other chants used in the singing of psalms **7** *linguistics* any of the pitch levels or pitch contours at which a syllable may be pronounced, such as high tone, falling tone, etc **8** the quality or character of a sound: *a nervous tone of voice* **9** general aspect, quality, or style: *I didn't like the tone of his speech* **10** high quality or style: *to lower the tone of a place* **11** the quality of a given colour, as modified by mixture with white or black; shade; tint: *a tone of red* **12** *physiol* **a** the normal tension of a muscle at rest **b** the natural firmness of the tissues and normal functioning of bodily organs in health **13** the overall effect of the colour values and gradations of light and dark in a picture **14** *photog* a colour or shade of colour, including black or grey, of a particular area on a negative or positive that can be distinguished from surrounding lighter or darker areas ▷ *vb* **15** (*intr*; often foll by *with*) to be of a matching or similar tone (to): *the curtains tone with the carpet* **16** (*tr*) to give a tone to or correct the tone of **17** (*tr*) *photog* to soften or change the colour of the tones of (a photographic image) by chemical means (*tr*) **18** to give greater firmness or strength to (the body or a part of the body) **19** an archaic word for **intone** ▷ See also **tone down, tone up** [c14 from Latin *tonus*, from Greek *tonos* tension, tone, from *teinein* to stretch]

tone arm *n* another name for **pick-up** (sense 1)

tone cluster *n music* a group of adjacent notes played simultaneously, either in an orchestral score or, on the piano, by depressing a whole set of adjacent keys

tone colour *n* the quality of a musical sound that is conditioned or distinguished by the upper partials or overtones present in it. Often shortened to: **tone** See also **timbre** (sense 2)

tone control *n* a device in a radio, etc, by which the relative intensities of high and low frequencies may be varied

tone-deaf *adj* unable to distinguish subtle differences in musical pitch > **tone deafness** *n*

tone down *vb* (*adverb*) to moderate or become moderated in tone: *to tone down an argument; to tone down a bright colour*

tone language *n* a language, such as Chinese or certain African languages, in which differences in tone may make differences in meaning

toneless (ˈtəʊnlɪs) *adj* **1** having no tone **2** lacking colour or vitality > ˈ**tonelessly** *adv* > ˈ**tonelessness** *n*

toneme (ˈtəʊniːm) *n linguistics* a phoneme that is distinguished from another phoneme only by its tone [c20 from TONE + -EME] > toˈ**nemic** *adj*

tone poem *n* another term for **symphonic poem**

toner (ˈtəʊnə) *n* **1** a person or thing that tones or produces tones, esp a concentrated pure organic pigment **2** a cosmetic preparation that is applied to produce a required effect, such as one that softens or alters hair colour or one that reduces the oiliness of the skin **3** *photog* a chemical solution that softens or alters the colour of the tones of a photographic image **4** a powdered chemical used in photocopying machines and laser printers, which is transferred onto paper to form the printed image

tone row *or* **series** *n music* a group of notes having a characteristic pattern or order that forms the basis of the musical material in a serial composition, esp one consisting of the twelve notes of the chromatic scale. Also called: **note row** See also **serialism, twelve-tone**

tone-setter *n* a person or thing that establishes the quality or character that is to be followed subsequently

tonetic (təʊˈnɛtɪk) *adj* (of a language) distinguishing words semantically by distinction of tone as well as by other sounds. See **tone language** [c20 from TONE + -*etic*, as in PHONETIC] > toˈ**netically** *adv*

tone up *vb* (*adverb*) to make or become more vigorous, healthy, etc: *exercise tones up the muscles*

tong[1] (tɒŋ) *vb* (*tr*) **1** to gather or seize with tongs **2** to curl or style (hair) with curling tongs

tong[2] (tɒŋ) *n* (formerly) a Chinese secret society or association, esp one popularly assumed to engage in criminal activities [c20 from Chinese (Cantonese) *t'ong* meeting place]

tonga (ˈtɒŋgə) *n* a light two-wheeled vehicle used in rural areas of India [c19 from Hindi *tāṅgā*]

Tonga[1] (ˈtɒŋgə, ˈtɒŋə) *n* **1** (*pl* **-gas** *or* **-ga**) a member of a Negroid people of S central Africa, living chiefly in Zambia and Zimbabwe **2** the language of this people, belonging to the Bantu group of the Niger-Congo family

Tonga[2] (ˈtɒŋə, ˈtɒŋgə) *n* a kingdom occupying an archipelago of more than 150 volcanic and coral islands in the SW Pacific, east of Fiji: inhabited by Polynesians; became a British protectorate in 1900 and gained independence in 1970; a member of the Commonwealth. Official languages: Tongan and English. Religion: Christian majority. Currency: pa'anga. Capital: Nuku'alofa. Pop: 104 000 (2004 est). Area: 750 sq km (290 sq miles). Also called: **Friendly Islands**

Tongan (ˈtɒŋən, ˈtɒŋgən) *adj* **1** of or relating to the kingdom of Tonga, its inhabitants, or their language ▷ *n* **2** a member of the people that inhabits Tonga **3** the language of this people, belonging to the Polynesian family

tongs (tɒŋz) *pl n* a tool for grasping or lifting, consisting of a hinged, sprung, or pivoted pair of arms or levers, joined at one end. Also called: **pair of tongs** [plural of Old English *tange*; related to Old Saxon *tanga*, Old High German *zanga*, Old Norse *tong*]

tongue (tʌŋ) *n* **1** a movable mass of muscular tissue attached to the floor of the mouth in most vertebrates. It is the organ of taste and aids the mastication and swallowing of food. In man it plays an important part in the articulation of speech sounds. Related adjs: **glottic, lingual 2** an analogous organ in invertebrates **3** the tongue of certain animals used as food **4** a language, dialect, or idiom: *the English tongue* **5** the ability to speak: *to lose one's tongue* **6** a manner of speaking: *a glib tongue* **7** utterance or voice (esp in the phrase **give tongue**) **8** (*plural*) See **gift of tongues 9** anything which resembles a tongue in shape or function: *a tongue of flame; a tongue of the sea* **10** a promontory or spit of land **11** a flap of leather on a shoe, either for decoration or under the laces or buckles to protect the instep **12** *music* the reed of an oboe or similar instrument **13** the clapper of a bell **14** the harnessing pole of a horse-drawn vehicle **15** a long and narrow projection on a machine or structural part that serves as a guide for assembly or as a securing device **16** a projecting strip along an edge of a board that is made to fit a corresponding groove in the edge of another board **17 hold one's tongue** to keep quiet **18 on the tip of one's tongue** about to come to mind: *her name was on the tip of his tongue* **19 with (one's) tongue in (one's) cheek** Also: **tongue in cheek** with insincere or ironical intent ▷ *vb* **tongues, tonguing, tongued 20** to articulate (notes played on a wind instrument) by the process of tonguing **21** (*tr*) to lick, feel, or touch with the tongue **22** (*tr*) *carpentry* to provide (a board) with a tongue **23** (*intr*) (of a piece of land) to project into a body of water **24** (*tr*) *obsolete* to reproach; scold [Old English *tunge*; related to Old Saxon, Old Norse *tunga*, Old High German *zunga*, Latin *lingua*] > ˈ**tongueless** *adj* > ˈ**tongue,like** *adj*

tongue-and-groove joint *n* a joint made between two boards by means of a tongue along the edge of one board that fits into a groove along the edge of the other board

tongued (tʌŋd) *adj* **1 a** having a tongue or tongues **b** (*in combination*): *long-tongued* **2** (*in combination*) having a manner of speech as specified: *sharp-tongued*

tongue-lash *vb* (*tr*) to reprimand severely; scold > ˈ**tongue-,lashing** *n, adj*

tongue-tie *n* a congenital condition in which the tongue has restricted mobility as the result of an abnormally short frenulum

tongue-tied *adj* **1** speechless, esp with embarrassment or shyness **2** having a condition of tongue-tie

tongue twister *n* a sentence or phrase that is difficult to articulate clearly and quickly, such as *Peter Piper picked a peck of pickled pepper*

tongue worm *n vet science* a parasitic worm, *Linguatula serrata*, found in the nose of dogs, so called because of the shape of the worm

tonguing (ˈtʌŋɪŋ) *n* a technique of articulating notes on a wind instrument. See **single-tongue, double-tongue, triple-tongue**

tonic (ˈtɒnɪk) *n* **1** a medicinal preparation intended to improve and strengthen the functioning of the body or increase the feeling of wellbeing **2** anything that enlivens or strengthens: *his speech was a tonic to the audience* **3** Also called: **tonic water** a mineral water, usually carbonated and containing quinine and often mixed with gin or other alcoholic drinks **4** *music* **a** the first degree of a major or minor scale and the tonal centre of a piece composed in a particular key **b** a key or chord based on this **5** a stressed syllable in a word ▷ *adj* **6** serving to enliven and invigorate: *a tonic wine* **7** of or relating to a tone or tones **8** *music* of or relating to the first degree of a major or minor scale **9** of or denoting the general effect of colour and light and shade in a picture **10** *physiol* of, relating to, characterized by, or affecting normal muscular or bodily tone: *a tonic spasm* **11** of or relating to stress or the main stress in a word **12** denoting a tone language [c17 from New Latin *tonicus*, from Greek *tonikos* concerning tone, from *tonos* TONE] > **'tonically** *adv*

tonic accent *n* **1** emphasis imparted to a note by virtue of its having a higher pitch, rather than greater stress or long duration relative to other notes **2** another term for **pitch accent**

tonicity (təʊˈnɪsɪtɪ) *n* **1** the state, condition, or quality of being tonic **2** *physiol* another name for **tonus**

tonic sol-fa *n* a method of teaching music, esp singing, used mainly in Britain, by which the syllables of a movable system of solmization are used as names for the notes of the major scale in any key. In this system *sol* is usually replaced by *so* as the name of the fifth degree. See **solmization**

tonight (təˈnaɪt) *n* **1** the night or evening of this present day ▷ *adv* **2** in or during the night or evening of this day **3** *archaic* last night [Old English *tōniht*, from TO¹ (at) + NIGHT]

2NITE *text messaging abbreviation for* tonight

tonk¹ (tɒŋk) *vb informal* to strike with a heavy blow [c20 of imitative origin]

tonk² (tɒŋk) *n Austral slang* an effete or effeminate man [c20 origin unknown]

tonka bean ('tɒŋkə) *n* **1** a tall leguminous tree, *Coumarouna odorata,* of tropical America, having fragrant black almond-shaped seeds **2** the seeds of this tree, used in the manufacture of perfumes, snuff, etc [c18 probably from Tupi *tonka*]

Tonkin ('tɒnˈkɪn) *or* **Tongking** ('tɒŋˈkɪŋ) *n* **1** a former state of N French Indochina (1883–1946), on the Gulf of Tonkin: forms the largest part of N Vietnam **2 Gulf of** an arm of the South China Sea, bordered by N Vietnam, the Leizhou Peninsula of SW China, and Hainan Island. Length: about 500 km (300 miles)

Tonkinese (ˌtɒŋkɪnˈiːz) *or* **Tongkingese** (ˌtɒŋkɪŋˈiːz) *n, pl* **-ese** a breed of medium-sized cat with almond-shaped aqua-coloured eyes and a soft silky coat

Tonle Sap ('tɒnlɪ 'sæp) *n* a lake in W central Cambodia, linked with the Mekong River by the **Tonle Sap River.** Area: (dry season) about 2600 sq km (1000 sq miles); (rainy season) about 10 000 sq km (3860 sq miles)

tonnage *or* **tunnage** ('tʌnɪdʒ) *n* **1** the capacity of a merchant ship expressed in tons, for which purpose a ton is considered as 40 cubic feet of freight or 100 cubic feet of bulk cargo, unless such an amount would weigh more than 2000 pounds in which case the actual weight is used **2** the weight of the cargo of a merchant ship **3** the total amount of shipping of a port or nation, estimated by the capacity of its ships **4** a duty on ships based either on their capacity or their register tonnage [c15 from Old French, from *tonne* barrel]

tonne (tʌn) *n* a unit of mass equal to 1000 kg or 2204.6 pounds. Also called (not in technical use): **metric ton** [from French]

tonneau ('tɒnəʊ) *n, pl* **-neaus** *or* **-neaux** (-nəʊ, -nəʊz) **1** Also called: **tonneau cover a** a detachable cover to protect the rear part of an open car when it is not carrying passengers **b** a similar cover that fits over all the passenger seats, but not the driver's, in an open vehicle **2** *rare* the part of an open car in which the rear passengers sit [c20 from French: special type of vehicle body, from Old French *tonnel* cask, from *tonne* tun]

tonometer (təʊˈnɒmɪtə) *n* **1** an instrument for measuring the pitch of a sound, esp one consisting of a set of tuning forks **2** any of various types of instrument for measuring pressure or tension, such as the blood pressure, vapour pressure, etc [c18 from Greek *tonos* TONE + -METER] > **tonometric** (ˌtəʊnəˈmɛtrɪk, ˌtəʊ-) *adj* > **to'nometry** *n*

tonoplast ('təʊnəˌplæst) *n botany* the membrane enclosing a vacuole in a plant cell [c20 from Greek *tonos* tone + -PLAST]

tons (tʌnz) *informal* ▷ *pl n* **1** a large amount or number: *tons of money; I have tons of shoes* ▷ *adv* **2** (intensifier): *I looked and felt tons better*

tonsil ('tɒnsəl) *n* **1** Also called: **palatine tonsil** either of two small masses of lymphatic tissue situated one on each side of the back of the mouth. Related adj: **amygdaline 2** *anatomy* any small rounded mass of tissue, esp lymphatic tissue [c17 from Latin *tōnsillae* (pl) tonsils, of uncertain origin] > **'tonsillar** *or* **'tonsillary** *adj*

tonsillectomy (ˌtɒnsɪˈlɛktəmɪ) *n, pl* **-mies** surgical removal of the palatine tonsils

tonsillitis (ˌtɒnsɪˈlaɪtɪs) *n* inflammation of the palatine tonsils, causing enlargement, occasionally to the extent that they nearly touch one another > **tonsillitic** (ˌtɒnsɪˈlɪtɪk) *adj*

tonsillotomy (ˌtɒnsɪˈlɒtəmɪ) *n, pl* **-mies** surgical incision into one or both of the palatine tonsils, usually followed by removal (tonsillectomy)

tonsorial (tɒnˈsɔːrɪəl) *adj* often facetious of or relating to barbering or hairdressing [c19 from Latin *tōnsōrius* concerning shaving, from *tondēre* to shave]

tonsure ('tɒnʃə) *n* **1** (in certain religions and monastic orders) **a** the shaving of the head or the crown of the head only **b** the part of the head left bare by shaving **c** the state of being shaven thus ▷ *vb* **2** (*tr*) to shave the head of [c14 from Latin *tōnsūra* a clipping, from *tondēre* to shave] > **'tonsured** *adj*

tontine ('tɒntiːn, tɒnˈtiːn) *n* **1 a** an annuity scheme by which several subscribers accumulate and invest a common fund out of which they receive an annuity that increases as subscribers die until the last survivor takes the whole **b** the subscribers to such a scheme collectively **c** the share of each subscriber **d** the common fund accumulated **e** (*as modifier*): *a tontine fund* **2** a system of mutual life assurance by which benefits are received by those participants who survive and maintain their policies throughout a stipulated period (the **tontine period**) [c18 from French, named after Lorenzo *Tonti,* Neapolitan banker who devised the scheme]

ton-up *Brit informal* ▷ *adj* (*prenominal*) **1** (esp of a motorcycle) capable of speeds of a hundred miles per hour or more **2** liking to travel at such speeds: *a ton-up boy* ▷ *n* **3** a person who habitually rides at such speeds

tonus ('təʊnəs) *n physiol* the normal tension of a muscle at rest; tone [c19 from Latin, from Greek *tonos* TONE]

tony ('təʊnɪ) *adj* **tonier, toniest** *US and Canadian informal* stylish or distinctive; classy [c20 from TONE]

Tony ('təʊnɪ) *n, pl* **Tonies** *or* **Tonys** any of several medallions awarded annually in the United States by a professional school for the performing arts for outstanding achievement in the theatre [from *Tony,* the nickname of Antoinette Perry (died 1946), US actress and producer]

too (tuː) *adv* **1** as well; in addition; also: *can I come too?* **2** in or to an excessive degree; more than a fitting or desirable amount: *I have too many things to do* **3** extremely: *you're too kind* **4** *US and Canadian informal* indeed: used to reinforce a command: *you will too do it!* **5 too right!** *Brit, Austral, and NZ* certainly; indeed [Old English *tō;* related to Old Frisian, Old Saxon *to,* Old High German *zou;* see TO¹]

▪ USAGE See at **very**

toodle-oo (ˌtuːdˈlˈuː) *or* **toodle-pip** *sentence substitute Brit informal rare* goodbye [c20 perhaps imitative of the horn of a car]

took (tʊk) *vb* the past tense of **take**

tool (tuːl) *n* **1 a** an implement, such as a hammer, saw, or spade, that is used by hand **b** a power-driven instrument; machine tool **c** (*in combination*): a toolkit **2** the cutting part of such an instrument **3 a** any of the instruments used by a bookbinder to impress a design on a book cover **b** a design so impressed **4** anything used as a means of performing an operation or achieving an end: *he used his boss's absence as a tool for gaining influence* **5** a person used to perform dishonourable or unpleasant tasks for another **6** a necessary medium for or adjunct to one's profession: *numbers are the tools of the mathematician's trade* **7** *slang* another word for **penis 8** *Brit* an underworld slang word for **gun** ▷ *vb* **9** to work, cut, shape, or form (something) with a tool or tools **10** (*tr*) to decorate (a book cover) with a bookbinder's tool **11** (*tr,* often foll by *up*) to furnish with tools **12** (when *intr,* often foll by *along*) to drive (a vehicle) or (of a vehicle) to be driven, esp in a leisurely or casual style [Old English *tōl;* related to Old Norse *tōl* weapon, Old English *tawian* to prepare; see TAW²] > **'tooler** *n* > **'toolless** *adj*

toolbar ('tuːlˌbɑː) *n* a horizontal row or vertical column of selectable buttons displayed on a computer screen, allowing the user to select a variety of functions

tooled up *adj slang* equipped with a weapon, esp a gun

tooling ('tuːlɪŋ) *n* **1** any decorative work done with a tool, esp a design stamped onto a book cover, piece of leatherwork, etc **2** the selection, provision, and setting up of tools, esp for a machining operation

toolkit ('tuːlˌkɪt) *n* **1** a set of tools designed to be used together or for a particular purpose **2** software designed to perform a specific function, esp to solve a problem: *your on-line printer toolkit*

tool-maker ('tuːlˌmeɪkə) *n* a person who specializes in the production or reconditioning of precision tools, cutters, etc > **'tool-ˌmaking** *n*

tool post *n* the rigid holding device which holds the cutting tool on a lathe and some other machine tools

tool pusher *n* a foreman who supervises drilling operations on an oil rig

toolroom ('tuːlruːm, -rʊm) *n* a room, as in a machine shop, where tools are made or stored

toolset ('tuːlˌsɛt) *n computing* a set of predefined tools (for opening files, cutting and pasting, etc) that is associated with a particular computer application

tool shed *n* a small shed in the garden or yard of a house used for storing tools, esp those for gardening

tool steel *n* any of various steels whose hardness and ability to retain a cutting edge make them suitable for use in tools for cutting wood and metal

toon¹ (tuːn) *n* **1** a large meliaceous tree, *Cedrela toona,* of the East Indies and Australia, having clusters of flowers from which a dye is obtained **2** the close-grained red wood of this tree, used for furniture, carvings, etc [from Hindi *tūn,* from Sanskrit *tunna*]

toon² (tuːn) *n* a cartoon character

toonie *or* **twonie** ('tuːnɪ) *n Canadian informal* a Canadian two-dollar coin

toorie *or* **tourie** ('tʊrɪ) *n Scot* **1** a tassel or bobble on a bonnet **2** Also: **toorie bonnet** a bonnet with a toorie [c19 from Scot *toor* tower]

tooshie (ˈtʊʃɪ) *adj Austral slang* angry; upset [from TUSH buttocks, by analogy with ARSEY]

toot[1] (tu:t) *vb* **1** to give or cause to give (a short blast, hoot, or whistle): *to toot a horn; to toot a blast; the train tooted* ▷ *n* **2** the sound made by or as if by a horn, whistle, etc **3** *slang* any drug for snorting, esp cocaine **4** *US and Canadian slang* a drinking spree **5** (tʊt) *Austral slang* a lavatory [C16 from Middle Low German *tuten*, of imitative origin] > ˈ**tooter** *n*

toot[2] (tu:t) *n NZ* an informal name for **tutu**[2]

tooth (tu:θ) *n, pl* **teeth** (ti:θ) **1** any of various bonelike structures set in the jaws of most vertebrates and modified, according to the species, for biting, tearing, or chewing. Related adj: **dental** **2** any of various similar structures in invertebrates, occurring in the mouth or alimentary canal **3** anything resembling a tooth in shape, prominence, or function: *the tooth of a comb* **4** any of the various small indentations occurring on the margin of a leaf, petal, etc **5** any one of a number of uniform projections on a gear, sprocket, rack, etc, by which drive is transmitted **6** taste or appetite (esp in the phrase **sweet tooth**) **7** **long in the tooth** old or ageing: used originally of horses, because their gums recede with age **8** **tooth and nail** with ferocity and force: *we fought tooth and nail* ▷ *vb* (tu:ð, tu:θ) **9** (*tr*) to provide with a tooth or teeth **10** (*intr*) (of two gearwheels) to engage [Old English *tōth*; related to Old Saxon *tand*, Old High German *zand*, Old Norse *tonn*, Gothic *tunthus*, Latin *dens*] > ˈ**toothless** *adj* > ˈ**toothˌlike** *adj*

toothache (ˈtu:θˌeɪk) *n* a pain in or about a tooth. Technical name: **odontalgia**

toothache tree *n* another name for **prickly ash**

toothbrush (ˈtu:θˌbrʌʃ) *n* a small brush, usually with a long handle, for cleaning the teeth

toothed (tu:θt) *adj* **a** having a tooth or teeth **b** (*in combination*): *sabre-toothed; six-toothed*

toothed whale *n* any whale belonging to the cetacean suborder *Odontoceti*, having a single blowhole and numerous simple teeth and feeding on fish, smaller mammals, molluscs, etc: includes dolphins and porpoises. Compare **whalebone whale**

toothing (ˈtu:θɪŋ) *n slang* the practice of attempting to intitiate sex with strangers through text messages sent using Bluetooth telephone technology

toothpaste (ˈtu:θˌpeɪst) *n* a paste used for cleaning the teeth, applied with a toothbrush

toothpick (ˈtu:θˌpɪk) *n* **1** a small sharp sliver of wood, plastic, etc, used for extracting pieces of food from between the teeth **2** a slang word for **bowie knife**

tooth powder *n* a powder used for cleaning the teeth, applied with a toothbrush

tooth shell *n* another name for the **tusk shell**

toothsome (ˈtu:θsəm) *adj* **1** of delicious or appetizing appearance, flavour, or smell **2** attractive; alluring > ˈ**toothsomely** *adv* > ˈ**toothsomeness** *n*

toothwort (ˈtu:θˌwɜ:t) *n* **1** a parasitic European scrophulariaceous plant, *Lathraea squamaria*, having no green parts, scaly cream or pink stems, pinkish flowers, and a rhizome covered with toothlike scales **2** any North American or Eurasian plant of the genus *Dentaria*, having creeping rhizomes covered with toothlike projections: family *Brassicaceae* (crucifers). See also **crinkleroot**

toothy (ˈtu:θɪ) *adj* **toothier, toothiest** having or showing numerous, large, or projecting teeth: *a toothy grin* > ˈ**toothily** *adv* > ˈ**toothiness** *n*

tootle[1] (ˈtu:tᵊl) *vb* **1** to toot or hoot softly or repeatedly: *the flute tootled quietly* ▷ *n* **2** a soft hoot or series of hoots [C19 from TOOT[1]] > ˈ**tootler** *n*

tootle[2] (ˈtu:tᵊl) *Brit informal* ▷ *vb* **1** (*intr*) to go, esp by car ▷ *n* **2** a drive, esp a short pleasure trip [C19 from TOOTLE[1], imitative of the horn of a car]

toots (tʊts) *or* **tootsy** *n, pl* **tootses** *or* **tootsies** *informal, chiefly US* darling; sweetheart [C20 perhaps related to earlier dialect *toot* worthless person, of obscure origin]

tootsy *or* **tootsie** (ˈtʊtsɪ) *n, pl* **-sies** a child's word for **toe**

Toowoomba (təˈwʊmbə) *n* a city in E Australia, in SE Queensland: agricultural and industrial centre. Pop: 89 338 (2001)

top[1] (tɒp) *n* **1** the highest or uppermost part of anything: *the top of a hill* **2** the most important or successful position: *to be at the top of the class; the top of the table* **3** the part of a plant that is above ground: *carrot tops* **4** a thing that forms or covers the uppermost part of anything, esp a lid or cap: *put the top on the saucepan* **5** the highest degree or point: *at the top of his career* **6** the most important person: *he's the top of this organization* **7** the best or finest part of anything: *we've got the top of this year's graduates* **8** the loudest or highest pitch (esp in the phrase **top of one's voice**) **9** short for **top gear** **10** *cards* the highest card of a suit in a player's hand **11** *sport* **a** a stroke that hits the ball above its centre **b** short for **topspin** **12** a platform around the head of a lower mast of a sailing vessel, the edges of which serve to extend the topmast shrouds **13** *chem* the part of a volatile liquid mixture that distils first **14** a garment, esp for a woman, that extends from the shoulders to the waist or hips **15** **a** the high-frequency content of an audio signal **b** (*as modifier*): *this amplifier has a good top response* **16** **blow one's top** *informal* to lose one's temper **17** **on top of** **a** in addition to: *on top of his accident, he caught pneumonia* **b** *informal* in complete control of (a difficult situation, job, etc) **18** **off the top of one's head** with no previous preparation; extempore **19** **over the top** **a** over the parapet or leading edge of a trench **b** over the limit; excessive(ly); lacking restraint or a sense of proportion **20** **the top of the morning** a morning greeting regarded as characteristic of Irishmen ▷ *adj* **21** of, relating to, serving as, or situated on the top: *the top book in a pile* **22** *Brit informal* excellent: *a top night out* ▷ *vb* **tops, topping, topped** (*mainly tr*) **23** to form a top on (something): *to top a cake with whipped cream* **24** to remove the top of or from: *to top carrots* **25** to reach or pass the top of: *we topped the mountain* **26** to be at the top of: *he tops the team* **27** to exceed or surpass **28** *slang* to kill **29** (*also intr*) *sport* **a** to hit (a ball) above the centre **b** to make (a stroke) by hitting the ball in this way **30** *chem* to distil off (the most volatile part) from a liquid mixture **31** to add other colorants to (a dye) in order to modify the shade produced **32** **top and tail** **a** to trim off the ends of (fruit or vegetables) before cooking them **b** to wash a baby's face and bottom without immersion in a bath ▷ See also **top off, top out, tops, top up** [Old English *topp*; related to Old High German *zopf* plait, Old Norse *toppr* tuft]

top[2] (tɒp) *n* **1** a toy that is spun on its pointed base by a flick of the fingers, by pushing a handle at the top up and down, etc **2** anything that spins or whirls around **3** **sleep like a top** to sleep very soundly [Old English, of unknown origin]

top- *combining form* a variant of **topo-** before a vowel

topagnosia (ˌtɒpægˈnəʊzɪə) *or* **topagnosis** (ˌtɒpægˈnəʊsɪs) *n* a symptom of disease of or damage to the brain in which a person cannot identify a part of the body that has been touched

topalgia (tɒˈpældʒɪə) *n* pain restricted to a particular spot: a neurotic or hysterical symptom

toparch (ˈtɒpɑ:k) *n* the ruler of a small state or realm [C17 from Greek *toparchēs*, from *topos* a place + -ARCH] > ˈ**toparchy** *n*

topaz (ˈtəʊpæz) *n* **1** a white or colourless mineral often tinted by impurities, found in cavities in igneous rocks and in quartz veins. It is used as a gemstone. Composition: hydrated aluminium silicate. Formula: $Al_2SiO_4(F,OH)_2$. Crystal structure: orthorhombic **2** **oriental topaz** a yellowish-brown variety of sapphire **3** **false topaz** another name for **citrine** **4** **a** a yellowish-brown colour, as in some varieties of topaz **b** (*as adjective*): *topaz eyes* **5** either of two South American hummingbirds, *Topaza pyra* and *T. pella* [C13 from Old French *topaze*, from Latin *topazus*, from Greek *topazos*]

topazolite (təʊˈpæzəˌlaɪt) *n* a yellowish-green variety of andradite garnet [C19 from TOPAZ + -LITE; so called because it is the same colour as some topaz]

top banana *n slang, chiefly US* **1** the leading comedian in vaudeville, burlesque, etc **2** the leader; boss

top boot *n* a high boot, often with a decorative or contrasting upper section

top brass *n* (*functioning as plural*) *informal* the most important or high-ranking officials or leaders, as in politics, industry, etc. See also **brass** (sense 5)

top cat *n informal* **a** the most powerful or important person **b** (*as modifier*): *the top-cat jobs*

topcoat (ˈtɒpˌkəʊt) *n* an outdoor coat worn over a suit, etc

top dead-centre *n engineering* the position of the crank of a reciprocating engine or pump when the piston is at the top of its stroke. Abbreviation: t.d.c.

top dog *n informal* the leader or chief of a group

top dollar *n informal* the highest level of payment

top-down *adj* controlled, directed, or organized from the top

top drawer *n* people of the highest standing, esp socially (esp in the phrase **out of the top drawer**)

top-dress *vb* (*tr*) to spread manure or fertilizer on the surface of (land) without working it into the soil

top dressing *n* **1** a surface application of manure or fertilizer to land **2** a thin layer of loose gravel that covers the top of a road surface

tope[1] (təʊp) *vb* to consume (alcoholic drink) as a regular habit, usually in large quantities [C17 from French *toper* to keep an agreement, from Spanish *topar* to take a bet; probably because a wager was generally followed by a drink] > ˈ**toper** *n*

tope[2] (təʊp) *n* **1** a small grey requiem shark, *Galeorhinus galeus*, of European coastal waters **2** any of various other small sharks [C17 of uncertain origin; compare Norfolk dialect *toper* dogfish]

tope[3] (təʊp) *n* another name for a **stupa** [C19 from Hindi *tōp*; compare Sanskrit *stūpa* STUPA]

topee *or* **topi** (ˈtəʊpi:, -pɪ) *n, pl* **-pees** *or* **-pis** another name for **pith helmet** [C19 from Hindi *topī* hat]

Topeka (təˈpi:kə) *n* a city in E central Kansas, capital of the state, on the Kansas River: university (1865). Pop: 122 008 (2003 est)

top end *n* (in vertical engines) another name for **little end** (sense 1)

Top End *n* **the** *Austral* the northern part of the Northern Territory

top-end *adj* of or relating to the best or most expensive products of their kind: *a range of top-end vehicles*

top-flight *adj* of superior or excellent quality; outstanding

topfull (ˈtɒpˌfʊl) *adj rare* full to the top

topgallant (ˌtɒpˈgælənt; *Nautical* təˈgælənt) *n* **1** Also called: **topgallant mast** a mast on a square-rigger above a topmast or an extension of a topmast **2** Also called: **topgallant sail** a sail set on a yard of a topgallant mast **3** (*modifier*) of or relating to a topgallant [C16 from TOP[1] + GALLANT]

top gear *n* the highest gear in a motor vehicle, often shortened to **top**

top hat *n* a man's hat with a tall cylindrical crown and narrow brim, often made of silk, now worn for some formal occasions. Also called: **high hat**

top-hat scheme *n informal* a pension scheme for the senior executives of an organization

top-heavy *adj* **1** unstable or unbalanced through being overloaded at the top **2** *finance* (of an enterprise or its capital structure) characterized by or containing too much debt capital in relation to revenue or profit so that too little is left over for dividend distributions; overcapitalized **3** (of a business enterprise) having too many executives > ˌtop-ˈheavily *adv* > ˈtop-ˈheaviness *n*

Tophet or **Topheth** (ˈtəʊfɛt) *n Old Testament* a place in the valley immediately to the southwest of Jerusalem; the Shrine of Moloch, where human sacrifices were offered [from Hebrew *Tōpheth*]

top-hole *interj, adj Brit informal* excellent; splendid

tophus (ˈtəʊfəs) *n, pl* **-phi** (-faɪ) *pathol* a deposit of sodium urate in the helix of the ear or surrounding a joint: a diagnostic of advanced or chronic gout. Also called: **chalkstone** [c16 from Latin, variant of *tōfus* TUFA, TUFF] > **tophaceous** (təʊˈfeɪʃəs) *adj*

topi[1] (ˈtəʊpɪ) *n, pl* **-pis 1** an antelope, *Damaliscus korrigum*, of grasslands and semideserts of Africa, having angular curved horns and an elongated muzzle [c19 from an African language]

topi[2] (ˈtəʊpiː, -pɪ) *n, pl* **-pis 1** another name for **pith helmet** [c19 from Hindi: hat]

topiary (ˈtəʊpɪərɪ) *adj* **1** of, relating to, or characterized by the trimming or training of trees or bushes into artificial decorative animal, geometric, or other shapes ▷ *n* **2** *pl* **-aries a** a topiary work **b** a topiary garden **3** the art of topiary [c16 from French *topiaire*, from Latin *topia* decorative garden work, from Greek *topion* little place, from *topos* place] > **topiarian** (ˌtəʊpɪˈɛərɪən) *adj* > **topiarist** *n*

topic (ˈtɒpɪk) *n* **1** a subject or theme of a speech, essay, book, etc **2** a subject of conversation; item of discussion **3** (in rhetoric, logic, etc) a category or class of arguments or ideas which may be drawn on to furnish proofs [c16 from Latin *topica* translating Greek *ta topika*, literally: matters relating to commonplaces, title of a treatise by Aristotle, from *topoi*, pl of *topos* place, commonplace]

topical (ˈtɒpɪk³l) *adj* **1** of, relating to, or constituting current affairs **2** relating to a particular place; local **3** of or relating to a topic or topics **4** (of a drug, ointment, etc) for application to the body surface; local > **topicality** (ˌtɒpɪˈkælɪtɪ) *n* > **topically** *adv*

topic sentence *n* a sentence in a paragraph that expresses the main idea or point of the whole paragraph

topknot (ˈtɒpˌnɒt) *n* **1** a crest, tuft, decorative bow, chignon, etc, on the top of the head **2** any of several European flatfishes of the genus *Zeugopterus* and related genera, esp *Z. punctatus*, which has an oval dark brown body marked with darker blotches: family *Bothidae* (turbot, etc)

topless (ˈtɒplɪs) *adj* **1** having no top **2 a** denoting a costume which has no covering for the breasts **b** wearing such a costume **3** *archaic* immeasurably high > **toplessness** *n*

top-level *n* (*modifier*) of, involving, or by those on the highest level of influence or authority: *top-level talks*

toplofty (ˈtɒpˌlɒftɪ) *adj informal* haughty or pretentious > ˈtopˌloftily *adv* > ˈtopˌloftiness *n*

top management or **senior management** *n* the most senior staff of an organization or business, including the heads of various divisions or departments led by the chief executive. Compare **middle management**

topmast (ˈtɒpˌmɑːst; *Nautical* ˈtɒpməst) *n* the mast next above a lower mast on a sailing vessel

topminnow (ˈtɒpˌmɪnəʊ) *n, pl* **-now** or **-nows** any of various small American freshwater cyprinodont fishes that are either viviparous (genera *Heterandria, Gambusia*, etc) or egg-laying (genus *Fundulus*) [from TOP[1] + MINNOW; so called because they are small and swim near the surface of the water]

topmost (ˈtɒpˌməʊst) *adj* highest; at or nearest the top

top-notch (ˈtɒpˈnɒtʃ) *adj informal* excellent; superb > ˈtop-ˈnotcher *n*

topo (ˈtɒpəʊ) *n, pl* **topos** *mountaineering* a picture of a mountain with details of climbing routes superimposed on it [c20 shortened from *topographical picture*]

topo- or before a vowel **top-** *combining form* indicating place or region: *topography; topology; toponym; topotype* [from Greek *topos* a place, commonplace]

topochemistry (ˌtɒpəˈkɛmɪstrɪ) *n chem* the study of reactions that only occur at specific regions in a system

top off *vb* (*tr, adverb*) to finish or complete, esp with some decisive action: *he topped off the affair by committing suicide*

topog. *abbreviation for* **1** topographical **2** topography

topography (təˈpɒɡrəfɪ) *n, pl* **-phies 1** the study or detailed description of the surface features of a region **2** the detailed mapping of the configuration of a region **3** the land forms or surface configuration of a region **4** the surveying of a region's surface features **5** the study or description of the configuration of any object > **topographer** *n* > **topographic** (ˌtɒpəˈɡræfɪk) or ˌtopoˈgraphical *adj* > ˌtopoˈgraphically *adv*

topological group *n maths* a group, such as the set of all real numbers, that constitutes a topological space and in which multiplication and inversion are continuous

topological space *n maths* a set *S* with an associated family of subsets τ that is closed under set union and finite intersection. *S* and the empty set are members of τ

topology (təˈpɒlədʒɪ) *n* **1** the branch of mathematics concerned with generalization of the concepts of continuity, limit, etc **2** a branch of geometry describing the properties of a figure that are unaffected by continuous distortion, such as stretching or knotting. Former name: **analysis situs 3** *maths* a family of subsets of a given set *S*, such that *S* is a topological space **4** the arrangement and interlinking of computers in a computer network **5** the study of the topography of a given place, esp as far as it reflects its history **6** the anatomy of any specific bodily area, structure, or part > **topologic** (ˌtɒpəˈlɒdʒɪk) or ˌtopoˈlogical *adj* > ˌtopoˈlogically *adv* > toˈpologist *n*

toponym (ˈtɒpənɪm) *n* **1** the name of a place **2** any name derived from a place name

toponymy (təˈpɒnɪmɪ) *n* **1** the study of place names **2** *rare* the anatomical nomenclature of bodily regions, as distinguished from that of specific organs or structures > **toponymic** (ˌtɒpəˈnɪmɪk) or ˌtopoˈnymical *adj*

topos (ˈtɒpɒs) *n, pl* **-oi** (-ɔɪ) a basic theme or concept, esp a stock topic in rhetoric [c20 Greek, literally: place]

topotype (ˈtɒpəˌtaɪp) *n* a specimen plant or animal taken from an area regarded as the typical habitat

top out *vb* (*adverb*) to place the highest stone on (a building) or perform a ceremony on this occasion

topper (ˈtɒpə) *n* **1** an informal name for **top hat 2** a person or thing that tops **3** *informal* a remark that caps the one before

topping (ˈtɒpɪŋ) *n* **1** something that tops something else, esp a sauce or garnish for food **2** *angling* part of a brightly-coloured feather, usually from a golden pheasant crest, used to top some artificial flies ▷ *adj* **3** high or superior in rank, degree, etc **4** *Brit slang* excellent; splendid

topping lift *n nautical* a line or cable for raising the end of a boom that is away from the mast

topple (ˈtɒp³l) *vb* **1** to tip over or cause to tip over, esp from a height **2** (*intr*) to lean precariously or totter **3** (*tr*) to overthrow; oust [c16 frequentative of TOP[1] (verb)]

tops (tɒps) *slang* ▷ *n* **1** a person or thing of top quality ▷ *adj* **2** (*postpositive*) excellent; superb

topsail (ˈtɒpˌseɪl; *Nautical* ˈtɒps³l) *n* a square sail carried on a yard set on a topmast

top-secret *adj* containing information whose disclosure would cause exceedingly grave damage to the nation and therefore classified as needing the highest level of secrecy and security

top-shell *n* any marine gastropod mollusc of the mainly tropical Old World family *Trochidae*, having a typically brightly coloured top-shaped or conical shell

topside (ˈtɒpˌsaɪd) *n* **1** the uppermost side of anything **2** *Brit and NZ* a lean cut of beef from the thigh containing no bone **3** (*often plural*) **a** the part of a ship's sides above the waterline **b** the parts of a ship above decks

top slicing *n* the act or process of using a specific part of a sum of money for a special purpose, such as assessing a taxable gain

topsoil (ˈtɒpˌsɔɪl) *n* **1** the surface layer of soil ▷ *vb* (*tr*) **2** to spread topsoil on (land) **3** to remove the topsoil from (land)

topspin (ˈtɒpˌspɪn) *n sport* spin imparted to make a ball bounce or travel exceptionally far, high, or quickly, as by hitting it with a sharp forward and upward stroke. Compare **backspin**

topsy-turvy (ˈtɒpsɪˈtɜːvɪ) *adj* **1** upside down **2** in a state of confusion ▷ *adv* **3** in a topsy-turvy manner ▷ *n* **4** a topsy-turvy state [c16 probably from *tops*, plural of TOP[1] + obsolete *tervy* to turn upside down; perhaps related to Old English *tearflian* to roll over]

top up *vb* (*tr, adverb*) *Brit* **1** to raise the level of (a liquid, powder, etc) in (a container), usually bringing it to the brim of the container: *top up the sugar in those bowls* **2 a** to increase the benefits from (an insurance scheme), esp to increase a pension when a salary rise enables higher premiums to be paid **b** to add money to (a loan, bank account, etc) in order to keep it at a constant or acceptable level ▷ *n* **top-up 3 a** an amount added to something in order to raise it to or maintain it at a desired level **b** (*as modifier*): *a top-up loan; a top-up policy*

top-up card *n* a card bought by a mobile phone user entitling him or her to a stipulated amount of credit for future calls

top whack *n informal* the maximum price: *paying top whack for your child's education*

toque (təʊk) *n* **1** a woman's small round brimless hat, popular esp in Edwardian times **2** a hat with a small brim and a pouched crown, popular in the 16th century **3** *Canadian* same as **tuque** (sense 2) **4** a chef's tall white hat [c16 from French, from Old Spanish *toca* headdress, probably from Basque *tauka* hat]

tor (tɔː) *n* **1** a high hill, esp a bare rocky one **2** *chiefly Southwestern Brit* a prominent rock or heap of rocks, esp on a hill [Old English *torr*, probably of Celtic origin; compare Scottish Gaelic *torr* pile, Welsh *twr*]

Torah (ˈtɔːrə; *Hebrew* tɔˈra) *n* **1 a** the Pentateuch **b** the scroll on which this is written, used in synagogue services **2** the whole body of traditional Jewish teaching, including the Oral Law **3** (*modifier*) promoting or according with traditional Jewish Law [c16 from Hebrew: precept, from *yārāh* to instruct]

Torbay (ˌtɔːˈbeɪ) *n* **1** a unitary authority in SW England, in Devon, consisting of Torquay and two neighbouring coastal resorts. Pop: 131 300 (2003 est). Area: 63 sq km (24 sq miles) **2** Also: **Tor Bay** an inlet of the English Channel on the coast of SW England, near Torquay

torbernite (ˈtɔːbəˌnaɪt) *n* a green secondary mineral consisting of hydrated copper uranium phosphate in the form of square platelike crystals. Formula: $Cu(UO_2)_2(PO_4)_2.12H_2O$ [c19 named after *Torbern O. Bergman* (1735–84), Swedish chemist; see -ITE[1]]

torc (tɔːk) *n* another spelling of **torque** (sense 1)

torch (tɔːtʃ) *n* **1** a small portable electric lamp powered by one or more dry batteries. US and Canadian word: **flashlight 2** a wooden or tow shaft dipped in wax or tallow and set alight **3** anything regarded as a source of enlightenment, guidance, etc: *the torch of evangelism* **4** any apparatus that burns with a hot flame for welding, brazing, or soldering **5 carry a torch for** to be in love with, esp unrequitedly **6 put to the torch** to set fire to; burn down: *the looted monastery was put to the torch* ⊳ *vb* **7** (*tr*) *slang* to set fire to, esp deliberately as an act of arson [c13 from Old French *torche* handful of twisted straw, from Vulgar Latin *torca* (unattested), from Latin *torquēre* to twist] > **'torch,like** *adj*

torchbearer ('tɔːtʃ,bɛərə) *n* **1** a person or thing that carries a torch **2** a person who leads or inspires

torchère (tɔː'ʃɛə) *n* a tall narrow stand for holding a candelabrum [c20 from French, from *torche* TORCH]

torchier *or* **torchiere** ('tɔːtʃɪə) *n* a standing lamp with a bowl for casting light upwards and so giving all-round indirect illumination [c20 from TORCHÈRE]

torchon lace ('tɔːʃən; *French* tɔrʃɔ̃) *n* a coarse linen or cotton lace with a simple openwork pattern [c19 *torchon,* from French: a cleaning cloth, from *torcher* to wipe, from Old French *torche* bundle of straw; see TORCH]

torch song *n* a sentimental or romantic popular song, usually sung by a woman [c20 from the phrase *to carry a torch for (someone)*] > **torch singer** *n*

torchwood ('tɔːtʃ,wʊd) *n* **1** any of various rutaceous trees or shrubs of the genus *Amyris,* esp *A. balsamifera,* of Florida and the Caribbean, having hard resinous wood used for torches **2** any of various similar trees the wood of which is used for torches **3** the wood of any of these trees

tore[1] (tɔː) *vb* the past tense of **tear**

tore[2] (tɔː) *n* *architect* another name for **torus** (sense 1) [c17 from French, from Latin: TORUS]

toreador ('tɒrɪə,dɔː) *n* a bullfighter [c17 from Spanish, from *torear* to take part in bullfighting, from *toro* a bull, from Latin *taurus;* compare STEER[2]]

toreador pants *pl n* tight-fitting women's trousers reaching to midcalf or above the ankle

torero (tɒ'rɛərəʊ) *n, pl* -**ros** a bullfighter, esp one who fights on foot [c18 from Spanish, from Late Latin *taurārius,* from Latin *taurus* a bull]

toreutics (tə'ruːtɪks) *n* (*functioning as singular or plural*) the art of making detailed ornamental reliefs, esp in metal, by embossing and chasing [c19 from Greek *toreutikos* concerning work in relief, from *toreuein* to bore through, from *toreus* tool for boring] > **to'reutic** *adj*

Torfaen ('tɔː,væn) *n* a county borough of SE Wales, created in 1996 from part of Gwent. Administrative centre: Pontypool. Pop: 90 700 (2003 est). Area: 290 sq km (112 sq miles)

tori ('tɔːraɪ) *n* the plural of **torus**

toric ('tɒrɪk) *adj* of, relating to, or having the form of a torus

toric lens *n* a lens used to correct astigmatism, having one of its surfaces shaped like part of a torus so that its focal lengths are different in different meridians

torii ('tɔːrɪ,iː) *n, pl* -**rii** a gateway, esp one at the entrance to a Japanese Shinto temple [c19 from Japanese, literally: a perch for birds]

Torino (tɔ'riːno) *n* the Italian name for **Turin**

torment *vb* (tɔː'mɛnt) (*tr*) **1** to afflict with great pain, suffering, or anguish; torture **2** to tease or pester in an annoying way ⊳ *n* ('tɔːmɛnt) **3** physical or mental pain **4** a source of pain, worry, annoyance, etc **5** *archaic* an instrument of torture **6** *archaic* the infliction of torture [c13 from Old French, from Latin *tormentum,* from *torquēre*] > **tor'mented** *adj* > **tor'mentedly** *adv* > **tor'menting** *adj* > **tor'mentingly** *adv*

tormentil ('tɔːməntɪl) *n* a rosaceous downy perennial plant, *Potentilla erecta,* of Europe and W Asia, having serrated leaves, four-petalled yellow flowers, and an astringent root used in medicine, tanning, and dyeing. Also called: **bloodroot** [c15

from Old French *tormentille,* from Medieval Latin *tormentilla,* from Latin *tormentum* agony; referring to its use in relieving pain; see TORMENT]

tormentor *or* **tormenter** (tɔː'mɛntə) *n* **1** a person or thing that torments **2** a curtain or movable piece of stage scenery at either side of the proscenium arch, used to mask lights or exits and entrances **3** *films* a panel of sound-insulating material placed outside the field of the camera to control the acoustics on the sound stage

torn (tɔːn) *vb* **1** the past participle of **tear** (sense 2) **2 that's torn it** *Brit slang* an unexpected event or circumstance has upset one's plans ⊳ *adj* **3** split or cut **4** divided or undecided, as in preference

tornado (tɔː'neɪdəʊ) *n, pl* -**does** *or* -**dos 1** Also called: **cyclone,** (US and Canadian informal) **twister** a violent storm with winds whirling around a small area of extremely low pressure, usually characterized by a dark funnel-shaped cloud causing damage along its path **2** a small but violent squall or whirlwind, such as those occurring on the West African coast **3** any violently active or destructive person or thing [c16 probably alteration of Spanish *tronada* thunderstorm (from *tronar* to thunder, from Latin *tonāre*), through influence of *tornar* to turn, from Latin *tornāre* to turn in a lathe] > **tornadic** (tɔː'nædɪk) *adj* > **tor'nado-,like** *adj*

toroid ('tɔːrɔɪd) *n* **1** *geometry* a surface generated by rotating a closed plane curve about a coplanar line that does not intersect the curve **2** the solid enclosed by such a surface. See also **torus** > **to'roidal** *adj*

Toronto (tə'rɒntəʊ) *n* a city in S central Canada, capital of Ontario, on Lake Ontario: the major industrial centre of Canada; two universities. Pop: 2 481 494 (2001)

Toronto Blessing *n* **the** a variety of emotional reactions such as laughing, weeping, and fainting, experienced by participants in a form of charismatic Christian worship [c20 from TORONTO, where it originated]

Torontonian (tɒrən'təʊnɪən) *adj* **1** of or relating to Toronto or its inhabitants ⊳ *n* **2** a native or inhabitant of Toronto

torose ('tɔːrəʊz, tɔː'rəʊz) *or* **torous** ('tɔːrəs) *adj* *biology* (of a cylindrical part) having irregular swellings; knotted [c18 from Latin *torōsus* muscular, from *torus* a swelling] > **torosity** (tɔː'rɒsɪtɪ) *n*

torpedo (tɔː'piːdəʊ) *n, pl* -**does 1** a cylindrical self-propelled weapon carrying explosives that is launched from aircraft, ships, or submarines and follows an underwater path to hit its target **2** *obsolete* a submarine mine **3** *US and Canadian* a firework containing gravel and a percussion cap that explodes when dashed against a hard surface **4** *US and Canadian* a detonator placed on a railway line as a danger signal **5** any of various electric rays of the genus *Torpedo* ⊳ *vb* -**does,** -**doing,** -**doed** (*tr*) **6** to hit (a ship, etc) with one or a number of torpedoes **7** to render ineffective; destroy or wreck: *to torpedo the administration's plan* [c16 from Latin: crampfish (whose electric discharges can cause numbness), from *torpēre* to be inactive; see TORPID] > **tor'pedo-,like** *adj*

torpedo boat *n* (formerly) a small high-speed warship designed to carry out torpedo attacks in coastal waters

torpedo-boat destroyer *n* (formerly) a large powerful high-speed torpedo boat designed to destroy enemy torpedo boats: a forerunner of the modern destroyer, from which the name is derived

torpedo tube *n* the tube from which a torpedo is discharged from submarines or surface ships

torpid ('tɔːpɪd) *adj* **1** apathetic, sluggish, or lethargic **2** (of a hibernating animal) dormant; having greatly reduced metabolic activity **3** unable to move or feel [c17 from Latin *torpidus,* from *torpēre* to be numb, motionless] > **tor'pidity** *n* > **'torpidly** *adv*

torpor ('tɔːpə) *n* a state of torpidity [c17 from Latin: inactivity, from *torpēre* to be motionless] > **,torpor'ific** *adj*

Torquay (,tɔː'kiː) *n* a town and resort in SW England, in Torbay unitary authority, S Devon. Pop: 62 968 (2001)

torque (tɔːk) *n* **1** Also: **torc** a necklace or armband made of twisted metal, worn esp by the ancient Britons and Gauls **2** any force or system of forces that causes or tends to cause rotation **3** the ability of a shaft to cause rotation [c19 from Latin *torquēs* necklace, and *torquēre* to twist]

torque converter *n* a hydraulic device for the smooth transmission of power in which an engine-driven impeller transmits its momentum to a fluid held in a sealed container, which in turn drives a rotor. Also called: **hydraulic coupling**

torque meter *n* *engineering* a device designed to determine the torque or torsion in a shaft, usually by measuring the twist in a calibrated length of shafting. Also called: **torsion meter**

torques ('tɔːkwiːz) *n* a distinctive band of hair, feathers, skin, or colour around the neck of an animal; a collar [c17 from Latin: necklace, from *torquēre* to twist] > **torquate** ('tɔːkwɪt, -kweɪt) *adj*

torque spanner *n* a spanner having a torque-limiting mechanism which can be set to a predetermined value

torque wrench *n* a type of wrench with a gauge attached to indicate the torque applied to the workpiece

torr (tɔː) *n, pl* **torr** a unit of pressure equal to one millimetre of mercury (133.322 newtons per square metre) [c20 named after Evangelista Torricelli (1608–47), Italian physicist and mathematician]

Torrance ('tɒrəns) *n* a city in SW California, southwest of Los Angeles: developed rapidly with the discovery of oil. Pop: 142 621 (2003 est)

Torre del Greco (*Italian* 'torre del 'grɛːko) *n* a city in SW Italy, in Campania near Vesuvius on the Bay of Naples: damaged several times by eruptions. Pop: 90 607 (2001)

torrefy ('tɒrɪ,faɪ) *vb* -**fies,** -**fying,** -**fied** (*tr*) to dry (drugs, ores, etc) by subjection to intense heat; roast [c17 from French *torréfier,* from Latin *torrefacere,* from *torrēre* to parch + *facere* to make] > **torrefaction** (,tɒrɪ'fækʃən) *n*

Torrens ('tɒrənz) *n* **Lake** a shallow salt lake in E central South Australia, about 8 m (25 ft) below sea level. Area: 5776 sq km (2230 sq miles)

Torrens title *n* *Austral* legal title to land based on record of registration rather than on title deeds [from Sir Robert Richard *Torrens* (1814–84), who introduced the system as premier of South Australia in 1857]

torrent ('tɒrənt) *n* **1** a fast, voluminous, or violent stream of water or other liquid **2** an overwhelming flow of thoughts, words, sound, etc ⊳ *adj* **3** *rare* like or relating to a torrent [c17 from French, from Latin *torrēns* (noun), from *torrēns* (adjective) burning, from *torrēre* to burn]

torrential (tɒ'rɛnʃəl, tə-) *adj* **1** of or relating to a torrent **2** pouring or flowing fast, violently, or heavily: *torrential rain* **3** abundant, overwhelming, or irrepressible: *torrential abuse* > **tor'rentially** *adv*

Torreón (*Spanish* tɔrre'ɔn) *n* an industrial city in N Mexico, in Coahuila state. Pop: 1 057 000 (2005 est)

Torres Strait ('tɒːrɪz, 'tɒr-) *n* a strait between NE Australia and S New Guinea, linking the Arafura Sea with the Coral Sea. Width: about 145 km (90 miles)

Torricellian tube (,tɒrɪ'sɛlɪən) *n* a vertical glass tube partly evacuated and partly filled with mercury, the height of which is used as a measure of atmospheric pressure [c17 named after Evangelista *Torricelli* (1608–47), Italian physicist and mathematician]

Torricellian vacuum *n* the vacuum at the top of a Torricellian tube [c17 named after Evangelista *Torricelli* (1608–47), Italian physicist and mathematician]

torrid ('tɒrɪd) *adj* **1** so hot and dry as to parch or

t

scorch **2** arid or parched **3** highly charged emotionally: *a torrid love scene* [C16 from Latin *torridus*, from *torrēre* to scorch] > **tor'ridity** *or* **'torridness** *n* > **'torridly** *adv*

Torrid Zone *n rare* that part of the earth's surface lying between the tropics of Cancer and Capricorn

torsade (tɔːˈseɪd) *n* an ornamental twist or twisted cord, as on hats [C19 from French, from obsolete *tors* twisted, from Late Latin *torsus*, from Latin *torquēre* to twist]

Tórshavn (ˈtɔːrʃhaʊn) *n* the Faeroese name for **Thorshavn**

torsi (ˈtɔːsɪ) *n rare* a plural of **torso**

torsibility (ˌtɔːsəˈbɪlɪtɪ) *n* **1** the ability to be twisted **2** the degree of resistance to or the capacity of recovering from being twisted

torsion (ˈtɔːʃən) *n* **1 a** the twisting of a part by application of equal and opposite torques at either end **b** the condition of twist and shear stress produced by a torque on a part or component **2** the act of twisting or the state of being twisted [C15 from Old French, from medical Latin *torsiō* griping pains, from Latin *torquēre* to twist, torture] > **'torsional** *adj* > **'torsionally** *adv*

torsion balance *n* an instrument used to measure small forces, esp electric or magnetic forces, by the torsion they produce in a thin wire, thread, or rod

torsion bar *n* a metal bar acting as a torsional spring, esp as used in the suspensions of some motor vehicles

torsion meter *n* another name for **torque meter**

torsk (tɔːsk) *n, pl* **torsks** *or* **torsk** a gadoid food fish, *Brosmius brosme*, of northern coastal waters, having a single long dorsal fin. Usual US and Canadian name: **cusk** [C17 of Scandinavian origin; related to Old Norse *thorskr* codfish, Danish *torsk*]

torso (ˈtɔːsəʊ) *n, pl* **-sos** *or* **-si** (-sɪ) **1** the trunk of the human body **2** a statue of a nude human trunk, esp without the head or limbs **3** something regarded as incomplete or truncated [C18 from Italian: stalk, stump, from Latin: THYRSUS]

tort (tɔːt) *n law* a civil wrong arising from an act or failure to act, independently of any contract, for which an action for personal injury or property damages may be brought [C14 from Old French, from Medieval Latin *tortum*, literally: something twisted, from Latin *torquēre* to twist]

torte (tɔːt; *German* ˈtɔrtə) *n* a rich cake, originating in Austria, usually decorated or filled with cream, fruit, nuts, and jam [C16 ultimately perhaps from Late Latin *tōrta* a round loaf, of uncertain origin]

tortellini (ˌtɔːtəˈliːnɪ) *n* pasta cut into small rounds, folded about a filling, and boiled [from Italian, diminutive of *tortelli* a type of pie, ultimately from Late Latin *tōrta* a round loaf or cake; see TORTE]

tort-feasor (ˈtɔːtˈfiːzə) *n law* a person guilty of tort [C17 from Old French, literally: wrongdoer, from TORT + *faiseur*, from *faire* to do]

torticollis (ˌtɔːtɪˈkɒlɪs) *n pathol* an abnormal position of the head, usually with the neck bent to one side, caused congenitally by contracture of muscles, muscular spasm, etc [C19 New Latin, from Latin *tortus* twisted (from *torquēre* to twist) + *collum* neck] > **ˌtortiˈcollar** *adj*

tortile (ˈtɔːtaɪl) *adj rare* twisted or coiled [C17 from Latin *tortilis* winding, from *tortus* twisted, from *torquēre* to twist] > **tortility** (tɔːˈtɪlɪtɪ) *n*

tortilla (tɔːˈtiːə) *n Mexican cookery* a kind of thin pancake made from corn meal and cooked on a hot griddle until dry [C17 from Spanish: a little cake, from *torta* a round cake, from Late Latin; see TORTE]

tortillon (ˌtɔːtiːˈɒn, -ˈəʊn; *French* tɔrtijɔ̃) *n* another word for **stump** (sense 5) [from French: something twisted, from Old French *tortiller* to twist]

tortious (ˈtɔːʃəs) *adj law* having the nature of or involving a tort; wrongful [C14 from Anglo-French *torcious*, from *torcion*, literally: a twisting, from Late Latin *tortiō* torment, from Latin *torquēre* to twist; influenced in meaning by TORT] > **'tortiously** *adv*

tortoise (ˈtɔːtəs) *n* **1** any herbivorous terrestrial chelonian reptile of the family *Testudinidae*, of most warm regions, having a heavy dome-shaped shell and clawed limbs. Related adjs: **chelonian, testudinal** **2** **water tortoise** another name for **terrapin** **3** a slow-moving person **4** another word for **testudo**. See also **giant tortoise** [C15 probably from Old French *tortue* (influenced by Latin *tortus* twisted), from Medieval Latin *tortūca*, from Late Latin *tartarūcha* coming from Tartarus, from Greek *tartaroukhos*; referring to the belief that the tortoise originated in the underworld]

tortoise beetle *n* a metallic-coloured leaf beetle of the genus *Cassida*, in which the elytra and terga cover the body like a shell

tortoiseshell (ˈtɔːtəsˌʃɛl) *n* **1** a horny translucent yellow-and-brown mottled substance obtained from the outer layer of the shell of the hawksbill turtle: used for making ornaments, jewellery, etc **2** a similar synthetic substance, esp plastic or celluloid, now more widely used than the natural product **3** a breed of domestic cat, usually female, having black, cream, and brownish markings **4** any of several nymphalid butterflies of the genus *Nymphalis*, and related genera, having orange-brown wings with black markings **5** **tortoiseshell turtle** another name for **hawksbill turtle** **6 a** a yellowish-brown mottled colour **b** (*as adjective*): *a tortoiseshell décor* **7** (*modifier*) made of tortoiseshell: *a tortoiseshell comb*

Tortola (tɔːˈtəʊlə) *n* an island in the NE Caribbean, in the Leeward Islands group: chief island of the British Virgin Islands. Pop: 13 568 (1991). Area: 62 sq km (24 sq miles)

tortoni (tɔːˈtəʊnɪ) *n* a rich ice cream often flavoured with sherry [from Italian: probably from the name of a 19th-century Italian caterer in Paris]

tortricid (ˈtɔːtrɪsɪd) *n* **1** any small moth of the chiefly temperate family *Tortricidae*, the larvae of which live concealed in leaves, which they roll or tie together, and are pests of fruit and forest trees: includes the codling moth ▷ *adj* **2** of, relating to, or belonging to the family *Tortricidae* [C19 from New Latin *Tortrīcidae*, from *tortrix*, feminine of *tortor*, literally: twister, referring to the leaf-rolling of the larvae, from *torquēre* to twist]

Tortuga (tɔːˈtuːgə) *n* an island in the Caribbean, off the NW coast of Haiti: haunt of pirates in the 17th century. Area: 180 sq km (70 sq miles). French name: **La Tortue** (la tɔrty)

tortuosity (ˌtɔːtjʊˈɒsɪtɪ) *n, pl* **-ties** **1** the state or quality of being tortuous **2** a twist, turn, or coil

tortuous (ˈtɔːtjʊəs) *adj* **1** twisted or winding: *a tortuous road* **2** devious or cunning: *a tortuous mind* **3** intricate > **'tortuously** *adv* > **'tortuousness** *n*

torture (ˈtɔːtʃə) *vb (tr)* **1** to cause extreme physical pain to, esp in order to extract information, break resistance, etc: *to torture prisoners* **2** to give mental anguish to **3** to twist into a grotesque form ▷ *n* **4** physical or mental anguish **5** the practice of torturing a person **6** a cause of mental agony or worry [C16 from Late Latin *tortūra* a twisting, from *torquēre* to twist] > **'tortured** *adj* > **'torturedly** *adv* > **'torturer** *n* > **'torturesome** *or* **'torturous** *adj* > **'torturing** *adj* > **'torturingly** *adv* > **'torturously** *adv*

> USAGE The adjective *torturous* is sometimes confused with *tortuous*. One speaks of a *torturous* experience, ie one that involves pain or suffering, but of a *tortuous* road, ie one that winds or twists

Toruń (*Polish* ˈtɔrunj) *n* an industrial city in N Poland, on the River Vistula: developed around a castle that was founded by the Teutonic Knights in 1230; under Prussian rule (1793–1919). Pop: 214 000 (2005 est). German name: **Thorn**

torus (ˈtɔːrəs) *n, pl* **-ri** (-raɪ) **1** Also called: **tore** a large convex moulding approximately semicircular in cross section, esp one used on the base of a classical column **2** *geometry* a ring-shaped surface generated by rotating a circle about a coplanar line that does not intersect the circle. Area: $4\pi^2Rr$; volume: $2\pi^2Rr^2$, where r is the radius of the circle and R is the distance from the line to the centre of the circle **3** *botany* another name for **receptacle** (sense 2) **4** *anatomy* a ridge, fold, or similar linear elevation **5** *astronomy* a dense ring of gas and dust which surrounds a dying star, containing most of the star's ejected gas [C16 from Latin: a swelling, of obscure origin]

Tory (ˈtɔːrɪ) *n, pl* **-ries** **1** a member or supporter of the Conservative Party in Great Britain or Canada **2** a member of the English political party that opposed the exclusion of James, Duke of York from the royal succession (1679–80). Tory remained the label for subsequent major conservative interests until they gave birth to the Conservative Party in the 1830s **3** an American supporter of the British cause; loyalist. Compare **Whig** **4** (*sometimes not capital*) an ultraconservative or reactionary **5** (in the 17th century) an Irish Roman Catholic, esp an outlaw who preyed upon English settlers ▷ *adj* **6** of, characteristic of, or relating to Tories **7** (*sometimes not capital*) ultraconservative or reactionary [C17 from Irish *tōraidhe* outlaw, from Middle Irish *tōir* pursuit] > **'Toryish** *adj* > **'Toryism** *n*

tosa (ˈtəʊsə) *n* a large dog, usually red in colour, which is a cross between a mastiff and a Great Dane: originally developed for dog-fighting; it is not recognized as a breed by kennel clubs outside Japan [C20 from the name of a province of the island of Shikoku, Japan]

Toscana (tosˈkaːna) *n* the Italian name for **Tuscany**

tosh (tɒʃ) *n slang, chiefly Brit* nonsense; rubbish [C19 of unknown origin]

toss (tɒs) *vb* **1** *(tr)* to throw lightly or with a flourish, esp with the palm of the hand upwards **2** to fling or be flung about, esp constantly or regularly in an agitated or violent way: *a ship tosses in a storm* **3** to discuss or put forward for discussion in an informal way **4** *(tr)* (of an animal such as a horse) to throw (its rider) **5** *(tr)* (of an animal) to butt with the head or the horns and throw into the air: *the bull tossed the matador* **6** *(tr)* to shake, agitate, or disturb **7** to toss up a coin with (someone) in order to decide or allot something: *I'll toss you for it; let's toss for it* **8** *(intr)* to move away angrily or impatiently: *she tossed out of the room* ▷ *n* **9** an abrupt movement **10** a rolling or pitching motion **11** the act or an instance of tossing **12** the act of tossing up a coin. See **toss-up** **13** **argue the toss** to wrangle or dispute at length **14** a fall from a horse or other animal **15** **give a toss** *slang* to be concerned or interested (esp in the phrase **not give a toss**) [C16 of Scandinavian origin; related to Norwegian, Swedish *tossa* to strew]

tosser (ˈtɒsə) *n Brit slang* a stupid or despicable person [C20 probably from TOSS OFF (to masturbate)]

toss off *vb (adverb)* **1** *(tr)* to perform, write, consume, etc, quickly and easily: *he tossed off a letter to Jim* **2** *(tr)* to drink quickly at one draught **3** *(intr) Brit slang* to masturbate

tosspot (ˈtɒsˌpɒt) *n* **1** *archaic or literary* a habitual drinker **2** *Brit slang* a stupid or contemptible person

toss up *vb (adverb)* **1** to spin (a coin) in the air in order to decide between alternatives by guessing which side will fall uppermost **2** *(tr)* to prepare (food) quickly ▷ *n* **toss-up** **3** an instance of tossing up a coin **4** *informal* an even chance or risk; gamble

tostada (tɒˈstɑːdə) *or* **tostado** (tɒˈstɑːdəʊ) *n, pl* **-das** *or* **-dos** a crispy deep-fried tortilla topped with meat, cheese, and refried beans [Spanish, literally: toasted, past participle of *tostar*]

tot[1] (tɒt) *n* **1** a young child; toddler **2** *chiefly Brit* a small amount of anything **3** a small measure of spirits [C18 perhaps short for *totterer*; see TOTTER]

tot[2] (tɒt) *vb* **tots, totting, totted** (usually foll by *up*) *chiefly Brit* to total; add [C17 shortened from TOTAL or from Latin *totum* all]

total (ˈtəʊtᵊl) *n* **1** the whole, esp regarded as the complete sum of a number of parts ▷ *adj* **2** complete; absolute: *the evening was a total failure; a total eclipse* **3** (*prenominal*) being or related to a total: *the total number of passengers* ▷ *vb* **-tals, -talling, -talled** *or US* **-tals, -taling, -taled** **4** (when *intr*, sometimes foll by *to*) to amount: *to total six pounds* **5** (*tr*) to add up: *to total a list of prices* **6** (*tr*) *slang* to kill or badly injure (someone) **7** (*tr*) *chiefly US* to damage (a vehicle) beyond repair [C14 from Old French, from Medieval Latin *tōtālis*, from Latin *tōtus* all] > ˈ**totally** *adv*

total allergy syndrome *n* a condition in which a person suffers from a large number of symptoms that are claimed to be caused by allergies to various substances used or encountered in modern life

total depravity *n chiefly Calvinist theol* the doctrine that man's nature is totally corrupt as a result of the Fall

total eclipse *n* an eclipse as seen from a particular area of the earth's surface where the eclipsed body is completely hidden. Compare **annular eclipse, partial eclipse**

total fighting *n* a combat sport in which very few restrictions are placed on the type of blows or tactics that may be used

total football *n* an attacking style of play, popularized by the Dutch national team of the 1970s, in which there are no fixed positions and every outfield player can join in the attack

total heat *n* another term for **enthalpy**

total internal reflection *n physics* the complete reflection of a light ray at the boundary of two media, when the ray is in the medium with greater refractive index

totalitarian (təʊˌtælɪˈtɛərɪən) *adj* **1** of, denoting, relating to, or characteristic of a dictatorial one-party state that regulates every realm of life ▷ *n* **2** a person who advocates or practises totalitarian policies [from TOTALITY + -ARIAN] > **toˌtaliˈtarianism** *n*

totality (təʊˈtælɪtɪ) *n, pl* **-ties** **1** the whole amount **2** the state of being total **3** the state or period of an eclipse when light from the eclipsed body is totally obscured

totalizator (ˈtəʊtᵊlaɪˌzeɪtə), **totalizer, totalisator** *or* **totaliser** *n* **1** a system of betting on horse races in which the aggregate stake, less an administration charge and tax, is paid out to winners in proportion to their stake **2** the machine that records bets in this system and works out odds, pays out winnings, etc **3** an apparatus for registering totals, as of a particular function or measurement ▷ US and Canadian term (for senses 1, 2): **pari-mutuel**

totalize *or* **totalise** (ˈtəʊtᵊˌlaɪz) *vb* to combine or make into a total > ˌ**totaliˈzation** *or* ˌ**totaliˈsation** *n*

totalizer *or* **totaliser** (ˈtəʊtᵊˌlaɪzə) *n* **1** a variant of **totalizator** **2** *chiefly US* an adding machine

total quality management *n* an approach to the management of an organization that integrates the needs of customers with a deep understanding of the technical details, costs, and human-resource relationships of the organization. Abbreviation: **TQM**

total recall *n psychol* the faculty or an instance of complete and clear recall of every detail of something

total serialism *or* **serialization** *n* (in some music after 1945) the use of serial techniques applied to such elements as rhythm, dynamics, and tone colour, as found in the early works of Karlheinz Stockhausen (born 1928), the German composer Pierre Boulez, (born 1925) the French composer and conductor, etc

totaquine (ˈtəʊtəˌkwiːn, -kwɪn) *n* a mixture of quinine and other alkaloids derived from cinchona bark, used as a substitute for quinine in treating malaria [C20 from New Latin *tōtaquīna*, from TOTA(L) + Spanish *quina* cinchona bark; see QUININE]

totara (ˈtəʊtərə) *n* a tall coniferous forest tree, *Podocarpus totara*, of New Zealand, having a hard durable wood [Māori]

tote (təʊt) *informal* ▷ *vb* **1** (*tr*) to carry, convey, or drag ▷ *n* **2** the act of or an instance of toting **3** something toted [C17 of obscure origin] > ˈ**toter** *n*

Tote (təʊt) *n* (usually preceded by *the*) (*sometimes not cap*) *trademark* short for **totalizator** (senses 1, 2)

tote bag *n* a large roomy handbag or shopping bag

totem (ˈtəʊtəm) *n* **1** (in some societies, esp among North American Indians) an object, species of animal or plant, or natural phenomenon symbolizing a clan, family, etc, often having ritual associations **2** a representation of such an object [C18 from Ojibwa *nintōtēm* mark of my family] > **totemic** (təʊˈtɛmɪk) *adj* > **toˈtemically** *adv*

totemism (ˈtəʊtəˌmɪzəm) *n* **1** the belief in kinship of groups or individuals having a common totem **2** the rituals, taboos, and other practices associated with such a belief > ˈ**totemist** *n* > ˌ**totemˈistic** *adj*

totem pole *n* a pole carved or painted with totemic figures set up by certain North American Indians, esp those of the NW Pacific coast, within a village as a tribal symbol or, sometimes, in memory of a dead person

tother *or* **t'other** (ˈtʌðə) *adj, n archaic or dialect* the other [C13 *the tother*, by mistaken division from *thet other* (*thet*, from Old English *thæt*, neuter of THE[1])]

totipalmate (ˌtəʊtɪˈpælmɪt, -ˌmeɪt) *adj* (of certain birds) having all four toes webbed [C19 from Latin *tōtus* entire + *palmate*, from Latin *palmātus* shaped like a hand, from *palma* PALM[1]] > ˌ**totipalˈmation** *n*

totipotent (təʊˈtɪpətənt) *adj* (of an animal cell) capable of differentiation and so forming a new individual, tissue, organ, etc [C20 from Latin *tōtus* entire + POTENT[1]] > **toˈtipotency** *n*

totter (ˈtɒtə) *vb* (*intr*) **1** to walk or move in an unsteady manner, as from old age **2** to sway or shake as if about to fall **3** to be failing, unstable, or precarious ▷ *n* **4** the act or an instance of tottering [C12 perhaps from Old English *tealtrian* to waver, and Middle Dutch *touteren* to stagger] > ˈ**totterer** *n* > ˈ**tottering** *adj* > ˈ**totteringly** *adv* > ˈ**tottery** *adj*

tottie *or* **totty** (ˈtɒtɪ) *adj chiefly Scot* very small; tiny [from TOT[1]]

totting (ˈtɒtɪŋ) *n Brit* the practice of searching through rubbish for usable or saleable items [C19 of unknown origin]

totty (ˈtɒtɪ) *n Brit informal* people, esp women, collectively considered as sexual objects [C19 diminutive of TOT[1]]

toucan (ˈtuːkən) *n* any tropical American arboreal fruit-eating bird of the family *Ramphastidae*, having a large brightly coloured bill with serrated edges and a bright plumage [C16 from French, from Portuguese *tucano*, from Tupi *tucana*, probably imitative of its cry]

touch (tʌtʃ) *n* **1** the sense by which the texture and other qualities of objects can be experienced when they come in contact with a part of the body surface, esp the tips of the fingers. Related adjs: **haptic, tactile, tactual** **2** the quality of an object as perceived by this sense; feel; feeling **3** the act or an instance of something coming into contact with the body **4** a gentle push, tap, or caress **5** a small amount; hint: *a touch of sarcasm* **6** a noticeable effect; influence: *the house needed a woman's touch* **7** any slight stroke or mark: *with a touch of his brush he captured the scene* **8** characteristic manner or style: *the artist had a distinctive touch* **9** a detail of some work, esp a literary or artistic work: *she added a few finishing touches to the book* **10** a slight attack, as of a disease: *a touch of bronchitis* **11** a specific ability or facility: *the champion appeared to have lost his touch* **12** the state of being aware of a situation or in contact with someone: *to get in touch with someone* **13** the state of being in physical contact **14** a trial or test (esp in the phrase **put to the touch**) **15** *rugby, soccer* the area outside the touchlines, beyond which the ball is out of play (esp in the phrase **in touch**) **16** *archaic* **a** an official stamp on metal indicating standard purity **b** the die stamp used to apply this mark. Now usually called: **hallmark** **17** a scoring hit in competitive fencing **18** an estimate of the amount of gold in an alloy as obtained by use of a touchstone **19** the technique of fingering a keyboard instrument **20** the quality of the action of a keyboard instrument with regard to the relative ease with which the keys may be depressed: *this piano has a nice touch* **21** *bell-ringing* any series of changes where the permutations are fewer in number than for a peal **22** *slang* **a** the act of asking for money as a loan or gift, often by devious means **b** the money received in this way **c** a person asked for money in this way: *he was an easy touch* ▷ *vb* **23** (*tr*) to cause or permit a part of the body to come into contact with **24** (*tr*) to tap, feel, or strike, esp with the hand: *don't touch the cake!* **25** to come or cause (something) to come into contact with (something else): *their hands touched briefly; he touched the match to the fuse* **26** (*intr*) to be in contact **27** (*tr; usually used with a negative*) to take hold of (a person or thing), esp in violence: *don't touch the baby!* **28** to be adjacent to (each other): *the two properties touch* **29** (*tr*) to move or disturb by handling: *someone's touched my desk* **30** (*tr*) to have an effect on: *the war scarcely touched our town* **31** (*tr*) to produce an emotional response in: *his sad story touched her* **32** (*tr*) to affect; concern **33** (*tr; usually used with a negative*) to partake of, eat, or drink **34** (*tr; usually used with a negative*) to handle or deal with: *I wouldn't touch that business* **35** (when *intr*, often foll by *on*) to allude (to) briefly or in passing: *the speech touched on several subjects* **36** (*tr*) to tinge or tint slightly: *brown hair touched with gold* **37** (*tr*) to spoil or injure slightly: *blackfly touched the flowers* **38** (*tr*) to mark, as with a brush or pen **39** (*tr*) to compare to in quality or attainment; equal or match: *there's no-one to touch him* **40** (*tr*) to reach or attain: *he touched the high point in his career* **41** (*intr*) to dock or stop briefly: *the ship touches at Tenerife* **42** (*tr*) *slang* to ask for a loan or gift of money from **43** *rare* **a** to finger (the keys or strings of an instrument) **b** to play (a tune, piece of music, etc) in this way **44** **touch base** See **base**[1] (sense 26) ▷ See also **touchdown, touch off, touch up** [C13 from Old French *tochier*, from Vulgar Latin *toccāre* (unattested) to strike, ring (a bell), probably imitative of a tapping sound] > ˈ**touchable** *adj* > ˈ**touchableness** *n* > ˈ**toucher** *n* > ˈ**touchless** *adj*

touch and go *adj* (**touch-and-go** *when prenominal*) risky or critical: *a touch-and-go situation*

touchback (ˈtʌtʃˌbæk) *n American football* a play in which the ball is put down by a player behind his own goal line when the ball has been put across the goal line by an opponent. Compare **safety** (sense 4b)

touchdown (ˈtʌtʃˌdaʊn) *n* **1** the moment at which a landing aircraft or spacecraft comes into contact with the landing surface **2** *rugby* the act of placing or touching the ball on the ground behind the goal line, as in scoring a try **3** *American football* a scoring play worth six points, achieved by being in possession of the ball in the opposing team's end zone. Abbreviation: **TD** See also **field goal** ▷ *vb* **touch down** (*intr, adverb*) **4** (of a space vehicle, aircraft, etc) to land **5** *rugby* to place the ball behind the goal line, as when scoring a try **6** *informal* to pause during a busy schedule in order to catch up, reorganize, or rest

touché (tuːˈʃeɪ) *interj* **1** an acknowledgment that a scoring hit has been made in a fencing competition **2** an acknowledgment of the striking home of a remark or the capping of a witticism [from French, literally: touched]

touched (tʌtʃt) *adj* (*postpositive*) **1** moved to

sympathy or emotion; affected **2** showing slight insanity

touch football *n* an informal version of American football chiefly characterized by players being touched rather than tackled

touchhole ('tʌtʃˌhəʊl) *n* a hole in the breech of early cannon and firearms through which the charge was ignited

touching ('tʌtʃɪŋ) *adj* **1** evoking or eliciting tender feelings: *your sympathy is touching* ▷ *prep* **2** on the subject of; relating to > '**touchingly** *adv* > '**touchingness** *n*

touch-in-goal *n* *rugby* the area at each end of a pitch between the goal line and the dead-ball line

touch judge *n* either of the two linesmen in rugby

touchline ('tʌtʃˌlaɪn) *n* either of the lines marking the side of the playing area in certain games, such as rugby

touchmark ('tʌtʃˌmɑːk) *n* a maker's mark stamped on pewter objects

touch-me-not *n* any of several balsaminaceous plants of the genus *Impatiens*, esp *I. noli-me-tangere*, having yellow spurred flowers and seed pods that burst open at a touch when ripe. Also called: **noli-me-tangere**

touch off *vb* (*tr, adverb*) **1** to cause to explode, as by touching with a match **2** to cause (a disturbance, violence, etc) to begin: *the marchers' action touched off riots*

touchpaper ('tʌtʃˌpeɪpə) *n* **1** paper soaked in saltpetre and used for firing gunpowder **2 light the (blue) touchpaper** to do something that will cause much anger or excitement

touch rugby *n* a limited-contact version of rugby in which players seek to evade being touched (rather than tackled) while in possession of the ball

touch screen *n* **a** a visual display unit screen that allows the user to give commands to the computer by touching parts of the screen instead of using the keyboard **b** (*as modifier*): *a touch-screen computer*

touch-sensitive *adj* (of a computer input device) activated by the user touching parts of it, esp a screen

touchstone ('tʌtʃˌstəʊn) *n* **1** a criterion or standard by which judgment is made **2** a hard dark siliceous stone, such as basalt or jasper, that is used to test the quality of gold and silver from the colour of the streak they produce on it

touch system *n* a typing system in which the fingers are trained to find the correct keys, permitting the typist to read and type copy without looking at the keyboard

touch-tone *adj* of or relating to a telephone dialling system in which each of the buttons pressed generates a tone of a different pitch, which is transmitted to the exchange

touch-type *vb* (*intr*) to type without having to look at the keys of the typewriter > '**touch-ˌtypist** *n*

touch up *vb* (*tr, adverb*) **1** to put extra or finishing touches to **2** to enhance, renovate, or falsify by putting extra touches to: *to touch up a photograph* **3** to stimulate or rouse as by a tap or light blow **4** *Brit slang* to touch or caress (someone), esp to arouse sexual feelings ▷ *n* **touch-up 5** a renovation or retouching, as of a painting

touchwood ('tʌtʃˌwʊd) *n* something, esp dry wood or fungus material such as amadou, used as tinder [c16 TOUCH (in the sense: to kindle) + WOOD[1]]

touchy ('tʌtʃɪ) *adj* **touchier, touchiest 1** easily upset or irritated; oversensitive **2** extremely risky **3** easily ignited > '**touchily** *adv* > '**touchiness** *n*

touchy-feely ('tʌtʃɪ'fiːlɪ) *adj* *informal, sometimes derogatory* openly displaying one's emotions and affections > ˌtouchy-'**feeliness** *n*

tough (tʌf) *adj* **1** strong or resilient; durable: *a tough material* **2** not tender: *he could not eat the tough steak* **3** having a great capacity for endurance; hardy and fit: *a tough mountaineer* **4** rough or pugnacious: *a tough gangster* **5** resolute or

intractable: *a tough employer* **6** difficult or troublesome to do or deal with: *a tough problem* **7** *informal* unfortunate or unlucky: *it's tough on him* ▷ *n* **8** a rough, vicious, or pugnacious person ▷ *adv* **9** *informal* violently, aggressively, or intractably: *to treat someone tough* **10 hang tough** *informal* to be or appear to be strong or determined ▷ *vb* **11** (*tr*) *slang* to stand firm, hold out against (a difficulty or difficult situation) (esp in **tough it out**) [Old English *tōh*; related to Old High German *zāhi* tough, Old Norse *tā* trodden ground in front of a house] > '**toughish** *adj* > '**toughly** *adv*

toughen ('tʌfən) *vb* to make or become tough or tougher

tough love *n* the practice of taking a stern attitude towards a relative or friend suffering from an addiction, etc, to help the addict overcome the problem

tough-minded *adj* practical, unsentimental, stern or intractable > ˌtough-'**mindedly** *adv* > ˌtough-'**mindedness** *n*

toughness ('tʌfnɪs) *n* **1** the quality or an instance of being tough **2** *metallurgy* the ability of a metal to withstand repeated twisting and bending, measured by the energy in kilojoules needed to break it. Compare **brittleness** (sense 2), **softness** (sense 2)

Toul (tuːl) *n* a town in NE France: a leading episcopal see in the Middle Ages. Pop: 16 945 (1999)

Toulon (*French* tulɔ̃) *n* a fortified port and naval base in SE France, on the Mediterranean: naval arsenal developed by Henry IV and Richelieu, later fortified by Vauban. Pop: 160 639 (1999)

Toulouse (tuːˈluːz) *n* a city in S France, on the Garonne River: scene of severe religious strife in the early 13th and mid-16th centuries; university (1229). Pop: 390 350 (1999). Ancient name: **Tolosa** (təˈləʊsə)

toun (tuːn) *n* *Scot* **1** a town **2** a farmstead

toupee ('tuːpeɪ) *n* **1** a wig or hairpiece worn, esp by men, to cover a bald or balding place **2** (formerly) a prominent lock on a periwig, esp in the 18th century [c18 apparently from French *toupet* forelock, from Old French *toup* top, of Germanic origin; see TOP[1]]

tour (tʊə) *n* **1** an extended journey, usually taken for pleasure, visiting places of interest along the route **2** *military* a period of service, esp in one place of duty **3** a short trip, as for inspection **4** a trip made by a theatre company, orchestra, etc, to perform in several different places: *a concert tour* **5** an overseas trip made by a cricket or rugby team, etc, to play in several places ▷ *vb* **6** to make a tour of (a place) **7** to perform (a show) or promote (a product) in several different places [c14 from Old French: a turn, from Latin *tornus* a lathe, from Greek *tornos*; compare TURN]

touraco or **turaco** ('tʊərəˌkəʊ) *n, pl* **-cos** any brightly coloured crested arboreal African bird of the family *Musophagidae*: order *Cuculiformes* (cuckoos, etc) [c18 of West African origin]

Touraine (*French* tyʀɛn) *n* a former province of NW central France: at its height in the 16th century as an area of royal residences, esp along the Loire. Chief town: **Tours**

Tourane (tuːˈraːn) *n* the former name of **Da Nang**

tourbillion (tʊəˈbɪljən) *n* a rare word for **whirlwind** [c15 from French *tourbillon*, ultimately from Latin *turbō* something that spins, from *turbāre* to confuse]

Tourcoing (*French* tuʀkwɛ̃) *n* a town in NE France: textile manufacturing. Pop: 93 540 (1999)

tour de force *French* (tur də fɔrs; *English* 'tʊə də 'fɔːs) *n, pl* **tours de force** (tur; *English* 'tʊə) a masterly or brilliant stroke, creation, effect, or accomplishment [literally: feat of skill or strength]

tourer ('tʊərə) *n* a large open car with a folding top, usually seating a driver and four passengers. Also called (esp US): **touring car**

Tourette syndrome (tʊəˈrɛt) *n* a brain disorder characterized by involuntary outbursts of

swearing, spitting, barking, etc, and sudden involuntary movements. Also called: **Gilles de la Tourette syndrome, Tourette's syndrome, Tourette's** [c20 named after Georges Gilles de la *Tourette* (1857–1904), French neurologist]

tourie ('tʊərɪ) *n* *Scot* a variant spelling of **toorie**

tourism ('tʊərɪzəm) *n* tourist travel and the services connected with it, esp when regarded as an industry

tourist ('tʊərɪst) *n* **1 a** a person who travels for pleasure, usually sightseeing and staying in hotels **b** (*as modifier*): *tourist attractions* **2** a person on an excursion or sightseeing tour **3** a person travelling abroad as a member of a sports team that is playing a series of usually international matches **4** Also called: **tourist class** the lowest class of accommodation on a passenger ship ▷ *adj* **5** of or relating to tourist accommodation > **tour'istic** *adj*

touristy ('tʊərɪstɪ) *adj* *informal, often derogatory* abounding in or designed for tourists

tourmaline ('tʊəməˌliːn) *n* any of a group of hard glassy minerals of variable colour consisting of complex borosilicates of aluminium with quantities of lithium, sodium, calcium, potassium, iron, and magnesium in hexagonal crystalline form: used in optical and electrical equipment and in jewellery [c18 from German *Turmalin*, from Sinhalese *toramalli* carnelian] > **tourmalinic** (ˌtʊəməˈlɪnɪk) *adj*

Tournai (*French* turnɛ) *n* a city in W Belgium, in Hainaut province on the River Scheldt: under several different European rulers until 1814. Pop: 67 341 (2004 est). Flemish name: **Doornik**

tournament ('tʊənəmənt, 'tɔː-, 'tɜː-) *n* **1** a sporting competition in which contestants play a series of games to determine an overall winner **2** a meeting for athletic or other sporting contestants: *an archery tournament* **3** *medieval history* **a** (originally) a martial sport or contest in which mounted combatants fought for a prize **b** (later) a meeting for knightly sports and exercises [c13 from Old French *torneiement*, from *torneier* to fight on horseback, literally: to turn, from the constant wheeling round of the combatants; see TOURNEY]

tournedos ('tʊənəˌdəʊ) *n, pl* **-dos** (-ˌdəʊz) a thick round steak of beef cut from the fillet or undercut of sirloin [from French, from *tourner* to TURN + *dos* back]

tourney ('tʊənɪ, 'tɔː-) *medieval history* ▷ *n* **1** a knightly tournament ▷ *vb* **2** (*intr*) to engage in a tourney [c13 from Old French *torneier*, from Vulgar Latin *tornidiāre* (unattested) to turn constantly, from Latin *tornāre* to TURN (in a lathe); see TOURNAMENT] > '**tourneyer** *n*

tourniquet ('tʊənɪˌkeɪ, 'tɔː-) *n* *med* any instrument or device for temporarily constricting an artery of the arm or leg to control bleeding [c17 from French: device that operates by turning, from *tourner* to TURN]

tour operator *n* a person or company that provides package holidays

Tours (*French* tur) *n* a town in W central France, on the River Loire: nearby is the scene of the defeat of the Arabs in 732, which ended the advance of Islam in W Europe. Pop: 132 820 (1999)

tourtière (ˌtuːrtɪˈɛə; *French* turtjɛr) *n* *Canadian* a type of meat pie [from French]

tousle ('taʊzəl) *vb* (*tr*) **1** to tangle, ruffle, or disarrange **2** to treat roughly ▷ *n* **3** a disorderly, tangled, or rumpled state **4** a dishevelled or disordered mass, esp of hair [c15 from Low German *tūsen* to shake; related to Old High German *zirzūsōn* to tear to pieces]

tous-les-mois (ˌtuːleɪˈmwaː) *n* **1** a large widely cultivated plant, *Canna edulis*, of the Caribbean and South America, having purplish stems and leaves, bright red flowers and edible tubers: family *Cannaceae* **2** Also called: **Queensland arrowroot** the tuber of this plant, used as a source of starch [c19 from French, literally: all the months, probably an attempt to give phonetic reproduction of *tolomane*, from native West Indian name]

tout (taʊt) *vb* **1** to solicit (business, customers, etc) or hawk (merchandise), esp in a brazen way **2** (*intr*) **a** to spy on racehorses being trained in order to obtain information for betting purposes **b** to sell, or attempt to sell, such information or to take bets, esp in public places **3** (*tr*) *informal* to recommend flatteringly or excessively ▷ *n* **4 a** a person who spies on racehorses so as to obtain betting information to sell **b** a person who sells information obtained by such spying **5** a person who solicits business in a brazen way **6** Also called: **ticket tout** a person who sells tickets unofficially for a heavily booked sporting event, concert, etc, at greatly inflated prices **7** *Northern Ireland* a police informer [C14 (in the sense: to peer, look out): related to Old English *tȳtan* to peep out] > ˈ**touter** *n*

tout à fait *French* (tut a fɛ) *adv* completely; absolutely

tout court *French* (tu kur) *adv* simply; briefly

tout de suite *French* (tud sɥit) *adv* at once; immediately

tout ensemble *French* (tut āsāblə) *adv* **1** everything considered; all in all ▷ *n* **2** the total impression or effect

tout le monde *French* (tu lə mɔ̃d) *n* all the world; everyone

touzle (ˈtaʊzᵊl) *vb, n* a rare spelling of **tousle**

tovarisch, tovarich *or* **tovarish** (təˈvɑːrɪʃ; *Russian* ta'varistʃ) *n* comrade: a term of address [from Russian]

tow¹ (təʊ) *vb* **1** (*tr*) to pull or drag (a vehicle, boat, etc), esp by means of a rope or cable ▷ *n* **2** the act or an instance of towing **3** the state of being towed (esp in the phrases **in tow, under tow, on tow**) **4** something used for towing **6 in tow** in one's charge or under one's influence **7** *informal* (in motor racing, etc) the act of taking advantage of the slipstream of another car (esp in the phrase **get a tow**) **8** short for **ski tow** [Old English *togian*; related to Old Frisian *togia*, Old Norse *toga*, Old High German *zogōn*] > ˈ**towable** *adj*

tow² (təʊ) *n* **1** the fibres of hemp, flax, jute, etc, in the scutched state **2** synthetic fibres preparatory to spinning **3** the coarser fibres discarded after combing [Old English *tōw*; related to Old Saxon *tou*, Old Norse *tō* tuft of wool, Dutch *touwen* to spin] > ˈ**towy** *adj*

towage (ˈtəʊɪdʒ) *n* **1** a charge made for towing **2** the act of towing or the state of being towed

toward *adj* (ˈtəʊəd) **1** *now rare* in progress; afoot **2** *obsolete* about to happen; imminent **3** *obsolete* promising or favourable ▷ *prep* (təˈwɔːd, tɔːd) **4** a variant of **towards** [Old English *tōweard*; see TO, -WARD] > ˈ**towardness** *n*

towardly (ˈtəʊədlɪ) *adj archaic* **1** compliant **2** propitious or suitable > ˈ**towardliness** *n*

towards (təˈwɔːdz, tɔːdz) *prep* **1** in the direction or vicinity of: *towards London* **2** with regard to: *her feelings towards me* **3** as a contribution or help to: *money towards a new car* **4** just before: *towards one o'clock* **5** *Irish* in comparison with: *it's no work towards having to do it by hand* ▷ Also: **toward**

towbar (ˈtəʊˌbɑː) *n* a rigid metal bar or frame used for towing vehicles. Compare **towrope, towline**

towboat (ˈtəʊˌbəʊt) *n* another word for **tug** (the boat)

tow-coloured *adj* pale yellow; flaxen

towel (ˈtaʊəl) *n* **1** a square or rectangular piece of absorbent cloth or paper used for drying the body **2** a similar piece of cloth used for drying plates, cutlery, etc **3 throw in the towel** See **throw in** (sense 4) ▷ *vb* **-els, -elling, -elled** *or US* **-els, -eling, -eled 4** (*tr*) to dry or wipe with a towel **5** (*tr*; often foll by *up*) *Austral slang* to assault or beat (a person) [C13 from Old French *toaille*, of Germanic origin; related to Old High German *dwahal* bath, Old Saxon *twahila* towel, Gothic *thwahan* to wash]

towelling (ˈtaʊəlɪŋ) *n* an absorbent fabric, esp with a nap, used for making towels, bathrobes, etc

towel rail *n* a rail or frame in a bathroom, etc, for hanging towels on

tower (ˈtaʊə) *n* **1** a tall, usually square or circular structure, sometimes part of a larger building and usually built for a specific purpose: *a church tower; a control tower* **2** a place of defence or retreat **3** a mobile structure used in medieval warfare to attack a castle, etc **4 tower of strength** a person who gives support, comfort, etc ▷ *vb* **5** (*intr*) to be or rise like a tower; loom [C12 from Old French *tur*, from Latin *turris*, from Greek]

tower crane *n* a rotatable cantilever jib on top of a steelwork tower used on building sites where the operator needs to command a good view of the site

towered (ˈtaʊəd) *adj* **a** having a tower or towers **b** (*in combination*): *four-towered; high-towered*

Tower Hamlets *n* a borough of E Greater London, on the River Thames: contains the main part of the East End. Pop: 206 600 (2003 est). Area: 20 sq km (8 sq miles)

towering (ˈtaʊərɪŋ) *adj* **1** very tall; lofty **2** outstanding, as in importance or stature **3** (*prenominal*) very intense: *a towering rage* > ˈ**toweringly** *adv*

Tower of London *n* a fortress in the City of London, on the River Thames: begun 1078; later extended and used as a palace, the main state prison, and now as a museum containing the crown jewels

tow-haired (ˌtəʊˈhɛəd) *adj* having blond and sometimes tousled hair

towhead (ˈtəʊˌhɛd) *n often disparaging* **1** a person with blond or yellowish hair **2** a head of such hair [from TOW² (flax)]

towheaded (ˌtəʊˈhɛdɪd) *adj often disparaging* (of a person) having blond or yellowish hair

towhee (ˈtaʊhiː, ˈtəʊ-) *n* any of various North American brownish-coloured sparrows of the genera *Pipilo* and *Chlorura* [C18 imitative of its note]

towie (ˈtəʊɪ) *n Austral informal* a truck used for towing

towing path *n* another name for **towpath**

towkay (taʊˈkeɪ) *n sir*; master: used as a form of address [of Chinese origin]

towline (ˈtəʊˌlaɪn) *n* another name for **towrope**

town (taʊn) *n* **1 a** a densely populated urban area, typically smaller than a city and larger than a village, having some local powers of government and a fixed boundary **b** (*as modifier*): *town life*. Related adj: **urban 2** a city, borough, or other urban area **3** (in the US) a territorial unit of local government that is smaller than a county; township **4** the nearest town or commercial district **5** London or the chief city of an area **6** the inhabitants of a town **7** the permanent residents of a university town as opposed to the university staff and students. Compare **gown** (sense 3) **8 go to town a** to make a supreme or unrestricted effort; go all out **b** *Austral and NZ informal* to lose one's temper **9 on the town** seeking out entertainments and amusements [Old English *tūn* village; related to Old Saxon, Old Norse *tūn*, Old High German *zūn* fence, Old Irish *dūn*] > ˈ**townish** *adj* > ˈ**townless** *adj*

town clerk *n* **1** (in Britain until 1974) the secretary and chief administrative officer of a town or city **2** (in the US) the official who keeps the records of a town

town crier *n* (formerly) a person employed by a town to make public announcements in the streets

town gas *n* coal gas manufactured for domestic and industrial use

town hall *n* the chief building in which municipal business is transacted, often with a hall for public meetings

townhall clock (ˈtaʊnˌhɔːl) *n Brit* another name for **moschatel**

town house *n* **1** a terraced house in an urban area, esp a fashionable one, often having the main living room on the first floor with an integral garage on the ground floor **2** a person's town residence as distinct from his country residence **3** another name (now chiefly Scot) for **town hall 4** *US and Canadian* a house that is part of a terrace. Also called: **row house**, (chiefly Brit) **terraced house**

townie (ˈtaʊnɪ) *or* **townee** (taʊˈniː) *n chiefly Brit informal, often disparaging* **1** a permanent resident in a town, esp as distinct from country dwellers or students **2** a young working-class person who dresses in casual sports clothes

townland (ˈtaʊnlænd) *n Irish* a division of land of various sizes

town meeting *n US* **1** an assembly of the inhabitants of a town **2** (esp in New England) an assembly of the qualified voters of a town. Such a meeting may exercise all the powers of local government

town milk *n NZ* milk treated by pasteurization for direct consumption, as opposed to dairy factory milk for the production of butter, cheese, etc

town planning *n* the comprehensive planning of the physical and social development of a town, including the construction of facilities. US term: **city planning** > **town planner** *n*

townscape (ˈtaʊnskeɪp) *n* a view of an urban scene

township (ˈtaʊnʃɪp) *n* **1** a small town **2** (in the Scottish Highlands and islands) a small crofting community **3** (in the US and Canada) a territorial area, esp a subdivision of a county: often organized as a unit of local government **4** (formerly, in South Africa) a planned urban settlement of Black Africans or Coloured people. Compare **location** (sense 4) **5** *English history* **a** any of the local districts of a large parish, each division containing a village or small town **b** the particular manor or parish itself as a territorial division **c** the inhabitants of a township collectively

townsman (ˈtaʊnzmən) *n, pl* **-men 1** an inhabitant of a town **2** a person from the same town as oneself > ˈ**towns,woman** *fem n*

townspeople (ˈtaʊnz,piːᵖl) *or* **townsfolk** *n* the inhabitants of a town; citizens

Townsville (ˈtaʊnzvɪl) *n* a port in E Australia, in NE Queensland on the Coral Sea: centre of a vast agricultural and mining hinterland. Pop: 119 504 (2001)

towpath (ˈtəʊ,pɑːθ) *n* a path beside a canal or river, used by people or animals towing boats. Also called: **towing path**

towrope (ˈtəʊ,rəʊp) *n* a rope or cable used for towing a vehicle or vessel. Also called: **towline**

tow truck *n* a motor vehicle equipped for towing away wrecked or disabled cars. Also called: **breakdown van**, (US and Canadian) **wrecker**

tox. *or* **toxicol.** *abbreviation for* toxicology

tox-, toxic- *or before a consonant* **toxo-, toxico-** *combining form.* indicating poison: *toxalbumin* [from Latin *toxicum*]

toxaemia *or US* **toxemia** (tɒkˈsiːmɪə) *n* **1** a condition characterized by the presence of bacterial toxins in the blood **2** the condition in pregnancy of pre-eclampsia or eclampsia [C19 from TOX- + -AEMIA] > tox'aemic *or US* tox'emic *adj*

toxalbumin (ˌtɒksælˈbjuːmɪn) *n biochem* any of a group of toxic albumins that occur in certain plants, such as toadstools, and in snake venom

toxaphene (ˈtɒksə,fiːn) *n* an amber waxy solid with a pleasant pine odour, consisting of chlorinated terpenes, esp chlorinated camphene: used as an insecticide

toxic (ˈtɒksɪk) *adj* **1** of, relating to, or caused by a toxin or poison; poisonous **2** harmful or deadly [C17 from medical Latin *toxicus*, from Latin *toxicum* poison, from Greek *toxikon (pharmakon)* (poison) used on arrows, from *toxon* arrow] > ˈ**toxically** *adv*

t

toxicant ('tɒksɪkənt) *n* **1** a toxic substance; poison **2** a rare word for **intoxicant** ▷ *adj* **3** poisonous; toxic [C19 from Medieval Latin *toxicāre* to poison; see TOXIC]

toxic effect *n* an adverse effect of a drug produced by an exaggeration of the effect that produces the theraputic response

toxicity (tɒk'sɪsɪtɪ) *n* **1** the degree of strength of a poison **2** the state or quality of being poisonous

toxicogenic (,tɒksɪkəʊ'dʒɛnɪk) *adj* **1** producing toxic substances or effects **2** caused or produced by a toxin

toxicology (,tɒksɪ'kɒlədʒɪ) *n* the branch of science concerned with poisons, their nature, effects, and antidotes > **toxicological** (,tɒksɪkə'lɒdʒɪkəl) *or* **toxico'logic** *adj* > ,toxico'logically *adv* > ,toxi'cologist *n*

toxicosis (,tɒksɪ'kəʊsɪs) *n* any disease or condition caused by poisoning [C19 from New Latin, from TOXIC + -OSIS]

toxic shock syndrome *n* a potentially fatal condition in women, characterized by fever, stomachache, a painful rash, and a drop in blood pressure, that is caused by staphylococcal blood poisoning, most commonly from a retained tampon during menstruation

toxin ('tɒksɪn) *n* **1** any of various poisonous substances produced by microorganisms that stimulate the production of neutralizing substances (antitoxins) in the body. See also **endotoxin, exotoxin 2** any other poisonous substance of plant or animal origin

toxin-antitoxin *n* a mixture of a specific toxin and antitoxin. The diphtheria toxin-antitoxin was formerly used in the US for active immunization

toxocariasis (,tɒksəkə'raɪəsɪs) *n* the infection of humans with the larvae of a genus of roundworms, *Toxocara*, of dogs and cats. It can cause swelling of the liver and, sometimes, damage to the eyes

toxoid ('tɒksɔɪd) *n* a toxin that has been treated to reduce its toxicity and is used in immunization to stimulate production of antitoxins

toxophilite (tɒk'sɒfɪ,laɪt) *formal* ▷ *n* **1** an archer ▷ *adj* **2** of or relating to archery [C18 from *Toxophilus*, the title of a book (1545) by Ascham, designed to mean: a lover of the bow, from Greek *toxon* bow + *philos* loving] > **tox'ophily** *n*

toxoplasmosis (,tɒksəʊplæz'məʊsɪs) *n* a protozoal disease characterized by jaundice, enlarged liver and spleen, and convulsions, caused by infection with *Toxoplasma gondii* > ,toxo'plasmic *adj*

toy (tɔɪ) *n* **1** an object designed to be played with **2 a** something that is a nonfunctioning replica of something else, esp a miniature one **b** (*as modifier*): *a toy guitar* **3** any small thing of little value; trifle **4 a** something small or miniature, esp a miniature variety of a breed of dog **b** (*as modifier*): *a toy poodle* ▷ *vb* **5** (*intr*; usually foll by *with*) to play, fiddle, or flirt [C16 (in the sense: amorous dalliance): of uncertain origin] > **'toyer** *n* > **'toyless** *adj* > **'toy,like** *adj*

Toyama ('təʊja:,ma:) *n* a city in central Japan, on W Honshu on **Toyama Bay** (an inlet of the Sea of Japan): chemical and textile centre. Pop: 321 049 (2002 est)

toy boy *n* the much younger male lover of an older woman

toytown ('tɔɪ,taʊn) *adj* **1** having an unreal and picturesque appearance: *toytown chalets* **2** not deserving to be taken seriously: *toytown revolutionaries* [C20 from *Toy Town*, the fictional setting of children's stories by Enid Blyton]

toy-toy ('tɔɪ'tɔɪ) *or* **toyi-toyi** *South African* ▷ *n* **1** a dance expressing defiance and protest ▷ *vb* **2** (*intr*) to dance in this way [of uncertain origin]

tp *the internet domain name for* East Timor

TPI *abbreviation for* tax and price index: a measure of the increase in taxable income needed to compensate for an increase in retail prices

T-piece *n* a strut or part shaped like a T

T-plate *n* a metal plate shaped like a T used to strengthen or effect a right-angled joint between two beams, etc

TPN *n biochem* triphosphopyridine nucleotide; a former name for NADP

Tpr *abbreviation for* Trooper

TPWS *abbreviation for* train protection warning system: a rail safety system fitted to track signals

TQM *abbreviation for* total quality management

tr¹ *abbreviation for* treasurer

tr² *the internet domain name for* Turkey

TR *international car registration for* Turkey

tr. *abbreviation for* **1** transitive **2** translated **3** *music* trill

trabeated ('treɪbɪ,eɪtɪd) *or* **trabeate** ('treɪbɪɪt, -eɪt) ▷ *adj architect* constructed with horizontal beams as opposed to arches. Compare **arcuate** [C19 back formation from *trabeation*, from Latin *trabs* a beam] > ,trabe'ation *n*

trabecula (trə'bɛkjʊlə) *n, pl* **-lae** (-,li:) *anatomy, botany* **1** any of various rod-shaped structures that divide organs into separate chambers **2** any of various rod-shaped cells or structures that bridge a cavity, as within the capsule of a moss or across the lumen of a cell [C19 via New Latin from Latin: a little beam, from *trabs* a beam] > tra'becular *or* tra'beculate *adj*

trabs (træbz) *pl n Northern English dialect* training shoes

Trabzon ('tra:bzɒn) *or* **Trebizond** *n* a port in NE Turkey, on the Black Sea: founded as a Greek colony in the 8th century BC at the terminus of an important trade route from central Europe to Asia. Pop: 246 000 (2005 est)

tracasserie (trə'kæsərɪ) *n* a turmoil; annoyance [from French, from *tracasser* to fuss about]

trace¹ (treɪs) *n* **1** a mark or other sign that something has been in a place; vestige **2** a tiny or scarcely detectable amount or characteristic **3** a footprint or other indication of the passage of an animal or person **4** any line drawn by a recording instrument or a record consisting of a number of such lines **5** something drawn, such as a tracing **6** *chiefly US* a beaten track or path **7** the postulated alteration in the cells of the nervous system that occurs as the result of any experience or learning. See also **memory trace, engram 8** *geometry* the intersection of a surface with a coordinate plane **9** *maths* the sum of the diagonal entries of a square matrix **10** *linguistics* a symbol inserted in the constituent structure of a sentence to mark the position from which a constituent has been moved in a generative process **11** *meteorol* an amount of precipitation that is too small to be measured **12** *archaic* a way taken; route ▷ *vb* **13** (*tr*) to follow, discover, or ascertain the course or development of (something): *to trace the history of China* **14** (*tr*) to track down and find, as by following a trail **15** to copy (a design, map, etc) by drawing over the lines visible through a superimposed sheet of transparent paper or other material **16** (*tr*; often foll by *out*) **a** to draw or delineate a plan or diagram of: *she spent hours tracing the models one at a time* **b** to outline or sketch (an idea, policy, etc): *he traced out his scheme for the robbery* **17** (*tr*) to decorate with tracery **18** (*tr*) to imprint (a design) on cloth, etc **19** (usually foll by *back*) to follow or be followed to source; date back: *his ancestors trace back to the 16th century* **20** *archaic* to make one's way over, through, or along (something) [C13 from French *tracier*, from Vulgar Latin *tractiāre* (unattested) to drag, from Latin *tractus*, from *trahere* to drag] > **'traceable** *adj* > ,tracea'bility *or* 'traceableness *n* > 'traceably *adv* > 'traceless *adj* > 'tracelessly *adv*

trace² (treɪs) *n* **1** either of the two side straps that connect a horse's harness to the swingletree **2** *angling* a length of nylon or, formerly, gut attaching a hook or fly to a line **3** **kick over the traces** to escape or defy control [C14 *trais*, from Old French *trait*, ultimately from Latin *trahere* to drag]

trace element *n* any of various chemical elements, such as iron, manganese, zinc, copper, and iodine, that occur in very small amounts in organisms and are essential for many physiological and biochemical processes

trace fossil *n* the fossilized remains of a track, trail, footprint, burrow, etc, of an organism

tracer ('treɪsə) *n* **1** a person or thing that traces **2 a** a projectile that can be observed when in flight by the burning of chemical substances in its base **b** ammunition consisting of such projectiles **c** (*as modifier*): *tracer fire* **3** *med* any radioactive isotope introduced into the body to study metabolic processes, absorption, etc, by following its progress through the body with a gamma camera or other detector **4** an investigation to trace missing cargo, mail, etc

tracer bullet *n* a round of small arms ammunition containing a tracer

tracery ('treɪsərɪ) *n, pl* **-eries 1** a pattern of interlacing ribs, esp as used in the upper part of a Gothic window, etc **2** any fine pattern resembling this > 'traceried *adj*

traceur (træ'sɜ:) *n* a participant in the sport or activity of parkour [C20 French, literally: one who traces]

trachea (trə'ki:ə) *n, pl* **-cheae** (-'ki:i:) **1** *anatomy, zoology* the membranous tube with cartilaginous rings that conveys inhaled air from the larynx to the bronchi. Nontechnical name: **windpipe 2** any of the tubes in insects and related animals that convey air from the spiracles to the tissues **3** *botany* another name for **vessel** (sense 5) or **tracheid** [C16 from Medieval Latin, from Greek *trakheia*, shortened from (*artēria*) *trakheia* rough (artery), from *trakhus* rough] > tra'cheal *or* tra'cheate *adj*

tracheid ('treɪkiɪd) *or* **tracheide** *n botany* an element of xylem tissue consisting of an elongated lignified cell with tapering ends and large pits [C19 from TRACHEA (in the sense: a vessel in a plant) + -ID²] > tracheidal (trə'ki:ɪdəl, ,treɪki'aɪdəl) *adj*

tracheitis (,treɪkɪ'aɪtɪs) *n* inflammation of the trachea

tracheo- *or before a vowel* **trache-** *combining form* denoting the trachea: *tracheotomy*

tracheophyte ('treɪkɪəʊ,faɪt) *n* any plant that has a conducting system of xylem and phloem elements; a vascular plant

tracheostomy (,treɪkɪ'ɒstəmɪ) *n, pl* **-mies** the surgical formation of a temporary or permanent opening into the trachea following tracheotomy

tracheotomy (,treɪkɪ'ɒtəmɪ) *n, pl* **-mies** surgical incision into the trachea, usually performed when the upper air passage has been blocked

trachoma (trə'kəʊmə) *n* a chronic contagious disease of the eye characterized by inflammation of the conjunctiva and cornea and the formation of scar tissue, caused by infection with the virus-like bacterium *Chlamydia trachomatis* [C17 from New Latin, from Greek *trakhōma* roughness, from *trakhus* rough] > **trachomatous** (trə'kɒmətəs, -'kəʊ-) *adj*

trachyte ('treɪkaɪt, 'træ-) *n* a light-coloured fine-grained volcanic rock of rough texture consisting of feldspars with small amounts of pyroxene or amphibole [C19 from French, from Greek *trakhutēs*, from *trakhus* rough] > **trachytoid** ('trækɪ,tɔɪd, 'treɪ-) *adj*

trachytic (trə'kɪtɪk) *adj* (of the texture of certain igneous rocks) characterized by a parallel arrangement of crystals, which mark the flow of the lava when still molten

tracing ('treɪsɪŋ) *n* **1** a copy made by tracing **2** the act of making a trace **3** a record made by an instrument

tracing paper *n* strong transparent paper used for tracing

track (træk) *n* **1** the mark or trail left by something that has passed by: *the track of an animal* **2** any road or path affording passage, esp a rough one **3** a rail or pair of parallel rails on which a vehicle, such as a locomotive, runs, esp the rails together with the sleepers, ballast, etc, on a railway **4** a course of action, thought, etc: *don't start on that track again!* **5** a line of motion or travel, such as flight **6** an endless jointed metal band driven by the wheels of a vehicle such as a tank or tractor to enable it to move across rough or muddy ground **7** *physics* the path of a particle of ionizing radiation as observed in a cloud chamber, bubble chamber, or photographic emulsion **8 a** a course for running or racing **b** (*as modifier*): *track events* **9** *US and Canadian* **a** sports performed on a track **b** track and field events as a whole **10** a path on a magnetic recording medium, esp magnetic tape, on which information, such as music or speech, from a single input channel is recorded **11** any of a number of separate sections in the recording on a record, CD, or cassette **12** a metal path that makes the interconnections on an integrated circuit **13** the distance between the points of contact with the ground of a pair of wheels, such as the front wheels of a motor vehicle or the paired wheels of an aircraft undercarriage **14** a hypothetical trace made on the surface of the earth by a point directly below an aircraft in flight **15** keep (*or* lose) track of to follow (or fail to follow) the passage, course, or progress of **16** off the beaten track See **beaten** (sense 4) **17** off the track away from what is correct or true **18** on the track of on the scent or trail of; pursuing **19** the right (*or* wrong) track pursuing the correct (or incorrect) line of investigation, inquiry, etc ▷ *vb* **20** to follow the trail of (a person, animal, etc) **21** to follow the flight path of (a satellite, spacecraft, etc) by picking up radio or radar signals transmitted or reflected by it **22** *US railways* **a** to provide with a track **b** to run on a track of (a certain width) **23** (of a camera or camera operator) to follow (a moving object) in any direction while operating **24** to move (a camera) towards the scene (**track in**) or away from the scene (**track out**) **25** to follow a track through (a place): *to track the jungles* **26** (*intr*) (of the pick-up, stylus, etc, of a record player) to follow the groove of a record: *the pick-up tracks badly* ▷ See also **tracks** [C15 from Old French *trac*, probably of Germanic origin; related to Middle Dutch *tracken* to pull, Middle Low German *trecken*; compare Norwegian *trakke* to trample] ▷ **'trackable** *adj* ▷ **'tracker** *n*

trackball ('træk,bɔːl) *or* **trackerball** ('trækə,bɔːl) *n* *computing* a device consisting of a small ball, mounted in a cup, which can be rotated to move the cursor around the screen

track down *vb* (*tr, adverb*) to find by tracking or pursuing

tracker dog *n* a dog specially trained to hunt fugitives or to search for missing people

tracker fund *n* *finance* an investment fund that is administered so that its value changes in line with the average value of shares in a market

track event *n* a competition in athletics, such as relay running or sprinting, that takes place on a running track

tracking ('trækɪŋ) *n* **1** the act or process of following something or someone **2** *electrical engineering* a leakage of electric current between two points separated by an insulating material caused by dirt, carbon particles, moisture, etc **3** the way wheels on a vehicle are aligned **4** a function of a video cassette recorder, which adjusts the alignment of the heads in order to achieve the best possible audio and video reproduction from each recording

tracking radar *n* a radar system emitting a narrow beam which oscillates about the target, thus compensating for abrupt changes of direction

tracking shot *n* a camera shot in which the cameraman follows a specific person or event in the action

tracking station *n* a station that can use a radio

or radar beam to determine and follow the path of an object, esp a spacecraft or satellite, in space or in the atmosphere

tracklaying ('træk,leɪɪŋ) *adj* (of a vehicle) having an endless jointed metal band around the wheels

trackless ('træklɪs) *adj* **1** having or leaving no trace or trail **2** (of a vehicle) using or having no tracks ▷ **'tracklessly** *adv* ▷ **'tracklessness** *n*

trackman ('trækmən) *n, pl* -men *US and Canadian* a workman who lays and maintains railway track. Also called (in Britain and certain other countries): platelayer

track meet *n* *US and Canadian* an athletics meeting

track record *n* *informal* the past record of the accomplishments and failures of a person, business, etc

track rod *n* the rod connecting the two front wheels of a motor vehicle ensuring that they turn at the same angle

tracks (træks) *pl n* **1** (*sometimes singular*) marks, such as footprints, tyre impressions, etc, left by someone or something that has passed **2** in one's tracks on the very spot where one is standing (esp in the phrase **stop in one's tracks**) **3** make tracks to leave or depart **4** make tracks for to go or head towards **5** the wrong side of the tracks the unfashionable or poor district or stratum of a community

track shoe *n* either of a pair of light running shoes fitted with steel spikes for better grip. Also called: **spike**

tracksuit ('træk,suːt, -,sjuːt) *n* a warm suit worn by athletes, etc usually over the clothes, esp during training

tract[1] (trækt) *n* **1** an extended area, as of land **2** *anatomy* a system of organs, glands, or other tissues that has a particular function: *the digestive tract* **3** a bundle of nerve fibres having the same function, origin, and termination: *the optic tract* **4** *archaic* an extended period of time [C15 from Latin *tractus* a stretching out, from *trahere* to drag]

tract[2] (trækt) *n* a treatise or pamphlet, esp a religious or moralistic one [C15 from Latin *tractātus* TRACTATE]

tract[3] (trækt) *n* *RC Church* an anthem in some Masses [C14 from Medieval Latin *tractus cantus* extended song; see TRACT[1]]

tractable ('træktəb³l) *adj* **1** easily controlled or persuaded **2** readily worked; malleable [C16 from Latin *tractābilis*, from *tractāre* to manage, from *trahere* to draw] ▷ **,tracta'bility** *or* **'tractableness** *n* ▷ **'tractably** *adv*

Tractarianism (træk'tɛərɪə,nɪzəm) *n* another name for the **Oxford Movement.** ▷ **Trac'tarian** *n, adj*

tractate ('trækteɪt) *n* **1** a short tract; treatise **2** *Judaism* one of the volumes of the Talmud [C15 from Latin *tractātus*, from *tractāre* to handle; see TRACTABLE]

tractile ('træktaɪl) *adj* capable of being drawn out; ductile [C17 from Latin *trahere* to drag] ▷ **tractility** (træk'tɪlɪtɪ) *n*

traction ('trækʃən) *n* **1** the act of drawing or pulling, esp by motive power **2** the state of being drawn or pulled **3** *med* the application of a steady pull on a part during healing of a fractured or dislocated bone, using a system of weights and pulleys or splints **4** the adhesive friction between a wheel and a surface, as between a driving wheel of a motor vehicle and the road [C17 from Medieval Latin *tractiō*, from Latin *tractus* dragged; see TRACTILE] ▷ **'tractional** *adj* ▷ **tractive** ('træktɪv) *adj*

traction control *n* (in motor racing cars) a method of preventing wheels from spinning when traction is applied by limiting the amount of power supplied to the wheel

traction engine *n* a steam-powered locomotive used, esp formerly, for drawing heavy loads along roads or over rough ground. It usually has two large rear wheels and a rope drum for haulage purposes

traction load *n* *geology* the solid material that is carried along the bed of a river

tractive force *n* the force measured in the drawbar of a locomotive or tractor

tractor ('træktə) *n* **1** a motor vehicle used to pull heavy loads, esp farm machinery such as a plough or harvester. It usually has two large rear wheels with deeply treaded tyres **2** a short motor vehicle with a powerful engine and a driver's cab, used to pull a trailer, as in an articulated lorry **3** an aircraft with its propeller or propellers mounted in front of the engine [C18 from Late Latin: one who pulls, from *trahere* to drag]

tractorfeed ('træktə,fiːd) *n* *computing* the automatic movement of a continuous roll of edge-perforated paper through the platen of the printer

trad (træd) *n* **1** *chiefly Brit* traditional jazz, as revived in the 1950s ▷ *adj* **2** short for **traditional**

trade (treɪd) *n* **1** the act or an instance of buying and selling goods and services either on the domestic (wholesale and retail) markets or on the international (import, export, and entrepôt) markets. Related adj: **mercantile 2** a personal occupation, esp a craft requiring skill **3** the people and practices of an industry, craft, or business **4** exchange of one thing for something else **5** the regular clientele of a firm or industry **6** amount of custom or commercial dealings; business **7** a specified market or business: *the tailoring trade* **8** an occupation in commerce, as opposed to a profession **9** commercial customers, as opposed to the general public: *trade only; trade advertising* **10** *homosexual slang* a sexual partner or sexual partners collectively **11** *archaic* a custom or habit ▷ *vb* **12** (*tr*) to buy and sell (commercial merchandise) **13** to exchange (one thing) for another **14** (*intr*) to engage in trade **15** (*intr*) to deal or do business (with): *we trade with them regularly* ▷ *adj* **16** intended for or available only to people in industry or business: *trade prices* ▷ See also **trade down, trade-in, trade on, trade up** [C14 (in the sense: track, hence, a regular business): related to Old Saxon *trada*, Old High German *trata* track; see TREAD] ▷ **'tradable** *or* **'tradeable** *adj* ▷ **'tradeless** *adj*

trade agreement *n* a commercial treaty between two or more nations

trade association *n* an association of organizations in the same trade formed to further their collective interests, esp in negotiating with governments, trade unions, etc

trade bill *n* a bill of exchange drawn on and accepted (**trade acceptance**) by a trader in payment for goods

trade book *or* **edition** *n* an ordinary edition of a book sold in the normal way in shops, as opposed to a de luxe or mail-order edition

trade cycle *n* the recurrent fluctuation between boom and depression in the economic activity of a capitalist country. Also called (esp US and Canadian): business cycle

trade discount *n* a sum or percentage deducted from the list price of a commodity allowed by a manufacturer, distributor, or wholesaler to a retailer or by one enterprise to another in the same trade

traded option *n* *stock exchange* an option that can itself be bought and sold on a stock exchange. Compare traditional option

trade down *vb* (*intr, adverb*) to sell a large or relatively expensive house, car, etc, and replace it with a smaller or less expensive one

trade gap *n* the amount by which the value of a country's visible imports exceeds that of visible exports; an unfavourable balance of trade

trade-in *n* **1 a** a used article given in part payment for the purchase of a new article **b** a transaction involving such part payment **c** the valuation put on the article traded in **d** (*as modifier*): *a trade-in dealer* ▷ *vb* **trade in 2** (*tr, adverb*) to give (a used article) as part payment for the purchase of a new article

t

trade journal *n* a periodical containing new developments, discussions, etc, concerning a trade or profession

trade-last *n US informal* a compliment that one has heard about someone, which one offers to tell to that person in exchange for a compliment heard about oneself

trademark ('treɪd,mɑːk) *n* **1** the name or other symbol used to identify the goods produced by a particular manufacturer or distributed by a particular dealer and to distinguish them from products associated with competing manufacturers or dealers. A trademark that has been officially registered and is therefore legally protected is known as a **Registered Trademark 2** any distinctive sign or mark of the presence of a person or animal ▷ *vb (tr)* **3** to label with a trademark **4** to register as a trademark

trade name *n* **1** the name used by a trade to refer to a commodity, service, etc **2** the name under which a commercial enterprise operates in business

trade-off *n* an exchange, esp as a compromise

trade on *vb (intr, preposition)* to exploit or take advantage of: *he traded on her endless patience*

trade plate *n* a numberplate attached temporarily to a vehicle by a dealer, etc, before the vehicle has been registered

trader ('treɪdə) *n* **1** a person who engages in trade; dealer; merchant **2** a vessel regularly employed in foreign or coastal trade **3** *stock exchange, US* a member who operates mainly on his own account rather than for customers' accounts > 'trader,ship *n*

trade reference *n* a reference in which one trader gives his opinion as to the creditworthiness of another trader in the same trade, esp to a supplier

tradescantia (,trædes'kænʃɪə) *n* any plant of the American genus *Tradescantia*, widely cultivated for their striped variegated leaves: family *Commelinaceae*. See also **wandering Jew, spiderwort** [c18 New Latin, named after John *Tradescant* (1570–1638), English botanist and gardener]

trade school *n* a school or teaching unit organized by an industry or large company to provide trade training, apprentice education, and similar courses

Trades Council *n* (in Britain) an association of the different trade unions in one town or area

trade secret *n* a secret formula, technique, process, etc, known and used to advantage by only one manufacturer

tradesman ('treɪdzmən) *n, pl* **-men 1** a man engaged in trade, esp a retail dealer **2** a skilled worker > 'trades,woman *fem n*

tradespeople ('treɪdz,piːpˀl) *or* **tradesfolk** ('treɪdz,fəʊk) *pl n chiefly Brit* people engaged in trade, esp shopkeepers

Trades Union Congress *n* the major association of British trade unions, which includes all the larger unions. Abbreviation: **TUC**

trade union *or* **trades union** *n* an association of employees formed to improve their incomes and working conditions by collective bargaining with the employer or employer organizations > **trade unionism** *or* **trades unionism** *n* > **trade unionist** *or* **trades unionist** *n*

trade up *vb (intr, adverb)* to sell a small or relatively inexpensive house, car, etc, and replace it with a larger or more expensive one

trade-weighted *adj* (of exchange rates) weighted according to the volume of trade between the various countries involved

trade wind (wɪnd) *n* a wind blowing obliquely towards the equator either from the northeast in the N hemisphere or the southeast in the S hemisphere, approximately between latitudes 30° N and S, forming part of the planetary wind system [c17 from *to blow trade* to blow steadily in one direction, from TRADE in the obsolete sense: a track]

trading card *n* any of a set of cards printed with images or information relating to a specific subject, intended to be traded between collectors seeking to acquire a full set

trading estate *n chiefly Brit* a large area in which a number of commercial or industrial firms are situated. Also called: **industrial estate**

trading floor *n* the area in a bank or stock exchange where securities are traded

trading post *n* **1** a general store established by a trader in an unsettled or thinly populated region **2** *stock exchange* a booth or location on an exchange floor at which a particular security is traded

trading stamp *n* (esp formerly) a stamp of stated value given by some retail organizations to customers, according to the value of their purchases and redeemable for articles offered on a premium list

tradition (trə'dɪʃən) *n* **1** the handing down from generation to generation of the same customs, beliefs, etc, esp by word of mouth **2** the body of customs, thought, practices, etc, belonging to a particular country, people, family, or institution over a relatively long period **3** a specific custom or practice of long standing **4** *Christianity* a doctrine or body of doctrines regarded as having been established by Christ or the apostles though not contained in Scripture **5** *(often capital) Judaism* a body of laws regarded as having been handed down from Moses orally and only committed to writing in the 2nd century AD **6** the beliefs and customs of Islam supplementing the Koran, esp as embodied in the Sunna **7** *law, chiefly Roman and Scots* the act of formally transferring ownership of movable property; delivery [c14 from Latin *trāditiō* a handing down, surrender, from *trādere* to give up, transmit, from TRANS- + *dāre* to give] > tra'ditionless *adj* > tra'ditionist *n*

traditional (trə'dɪʃənˀl) *adj* **1** of, relating to, or being a tradition **2** of or relating to the style of jazz originating in New Orleans, characterized by collective improvisation by a front line of trumpet, trombone, and clarinet accompanied by various rhythm instruments > **traditionality** (trə,dɪʃə'nælɪtɪ) *n* > tra'ditionally *adv*

traditionalism (trə'dɪʃənˀ,lɪzəm) *n* **1** the doctrine that all knowledge originates in divine revelation and is perpetuated by tradition **2** adherence to tradition, esp in religion > tra'ditionalist *n, adj* > tra,ditional'istic *adj*

traditional option *n stock exchange* an option that once purchased cannot be resold. Compare **traded option**

traditional policy *n* a life assurance policy in which the policyholder's premiums are paid into a general fund and his investment benefits are calculated according to actuarial formulae. Compare **unit-linked policy**

traditional weapon *n South African* a weapon having ceremonial tribal significance, such as an assegai or knobkerrie

traditor ('trædɪtə) *n, pl* **traditores** (,trædɪ'tɔːriːz) *or* **traditors** *Early Church* a Christian who betrayed his fellow Christians at the time of the Roman persecutions [c15 from Latin: traitor, from *trādere* to hand over]

traduce (trə'djuːs) *vb (tr)* to speak badly of [c16 from Latin *trādūcere* to lead over, transmit, disgrace, from TRANS- + *dūcere* to lead] > tra'ducement *n* > tra'ducer *n* > tra'ducible *adj*

traducianism (trə'djuːʃə,nɪzəm) *n* the theory that the soul is transmitted to a child in the act of generation or concomitantly with its body. Compare **creationism** [c18 from Church Latin *trādūciānus*, from *trādux* transmission; see TRADUCE] > tra'ducianist *or* tra'ducian *n, adj* > tra,ducian'istic *adj*

Trafalgar (trə'fælgə; *Spanish* trafal'ɣar) *n* **Cape.** a cape on the SW coast of Spain, south of Cádiz: scene of the decisive naval battle (1805) in which the French and Spanish fleets were defeated by

the British under Nelson, who was mortally wounded

traffic ('træfɪk) *n* **1 a** the vehicles coming and going in a street, town, etc **b** *(as modifier)*: *traffic lights* **2** the movement of vehicles, people, etc, in a particular place or for a particular purpose: *sea traffic* **3 a** the business of commercial transportation by land, sea, or air **b** the freight, passengers, etc, transported **4** (usually foll by *with*) dealings or business: *have no traffic with that man* **5** trade, esp of an illicit or improper kind: *drug traffic* **6** the aggregate volume of messages transmitted through a communications system in a given period **7** *chiefly US* the number of customers patronizing a commercial establishment in a given time period ▷ *vb* **-fics, -ficking, -ficked** *(intr)* **8** (often foll by *in*) to carry on trade or business, esp of an illicit kind **9** (usually foll by *with*) to have dealings [c16 from Old French *trafique*, from Old Italian *traffico*, from *trafficare* to engage in trade] > 'trafficker *n* > 'trafficless *adj*

trafficator ('træfɪ,keɪtə) *n* (formerly) an illuminated arm on a motor vehicle that was raised to indicate a left or right turn. Compare **indicator** (sense 5)

traffic calming *n* the use of a series of devices, such as bends and humps in the road, to slow down traffic, esp in residential areas

traffic circle *n US and Canadian* a road junction in which traffic streams circulate around a central island. Also called (in Britain and certain other countries): **roundabout**

traffic cop *n informal* a policeman who supervises road traffic

traffic court *n law* a magistrates' court dealing with traffic offences

traffic engineering *n* a discipline which includes the design of highways and pedestrian ways, the study and application of traffic statistics, and the environmental aspects of the transportation of goods and people

traffic island *n* a raised area in the middle of a road, designed as a guide for traffic and to provide a stopping place for pedestrians

traffic jam *n* a number of vehicles so obstructed that they can scarcely move > 'traffic-jammed *adj*

trafficky ('træfɪkɪ) *adj informal* (of a street, area, town, etc) busy with motor vehicles

traffic light *or* **signal** *n* one of a set of coloured lights placed at crossroads, junctions, etc, to control the flow of traffic. A red light indicates that traffic must stop and a green light that it may go: usually an amber warning light is added between the red and the green

traffic pattern *n* a pattern of permitted lanes in the air around an airport to which an aircraft is restricted

traffic warden *n Brit* a person who is appointed to supervise road traffic and report traffic offences

Trafford ('træfəd) *n* a unitary authority in NW England, in Greater Manchester. Pop: 211 800 (2003 est). Area: 106 sq km (41 sq miles)

tragacanth ('trægə,kænθ) *n* **1** any of various spiny leguminous plants of the genus *Astragalus*, esp *A. gummifer*, of Asia, having clusters of white, yellow, or purple flowers, and yielding a substance that is made into a gum **2** the gum obtained from any of these plants, used in the manufacture of pills and lozenges, etc [c16 from French *tragacante*, from Latin *tragacantha* goat's thorn, from Greek *tragakantha*, from *tragos* goat + *akantha* thorn]

tragedian (trə'dʒiːdɪən) *or feminine* **tragedienne** (trə,dʒiːdɪ'ɛn) *n* **1** an actor who specializes in tragic roles **2** a writer of tragedy

tragedy ('trædʒɪdɪ) *n, pl* **-dies 1** (esp in classical and Renaissance drama) a play in which the protagonist, usually a man of importance and outstanding personal qualities, falls to disaster through the combination of a personal failing and circumstances with which he cannot deal **2**

(in later drama, such as that of Ibsen) a play in which the protagonist is overcome by a combination of social and psychological circumstances **3** any dramatic or literary composition dealing with serious or sombre themes and ending with disaster **4** (in medieval literature) a literary work in which a great person falls from prosperity to disaster, often through no fault of his own **5** the branch of drama dealing with such themes **6** the unfortunate aspect of something **7** a shocking or sad event; disaster ▷ Compare **comedy** [C14 from Old French *tragédie*, from Latin *tragoedia*, from Greek *tragōidia*, from *tragos* goat + *ōidē* song; perhaps a reference to the goat-satyrs of Peloponnesian plays]

tragic (ˈtrædʒɪk) *or less commonly* **tragical** *adj* **1** of, relating to, or characteristic of tragedy **2** mournful or pitiable: *a tragic face* > ˈ**tragically** *adv*

tragic flaw *n* a failing of character in the hero of a tragedy that brings about his downfall

tragic irony *n* the use of dramatic irony in a tragedy (originally, in Greek tragedy), so that the audience is aware that a character's words or actions will bring about a tragic or fatal result, while the character himself is not

tragicomedy (ˌtrædʒɪˈkɒmɪdɪ) *n, pl* **-dies 1 a** a drama in which aspects of both tragedy and comedy are found **b** the dramatic genre of works of this kind **2** an event or incident having both comic and tragic aspects [C16 from French, ultimately from Late Latin *tragicōmoedia*; see TRAGEDY, COMEDY] > ˌ**tragiˈcomic** *or* ˌ**tragiˈcomical** *adj* > ˌ**tragiˈcomically** *adv*

tragopan (ˈtræɡəˌpæn) *n* any pheasant of the genus *Tragopan*, of S and SE Asia, having a brilliant plumage and brightly coloured fleshy processes on the head [C19 via Latin from Greek, from *tragos* goat + PAN]

tragus (ˈtreɪɡəs) *n, pl* **-gi** (-dʒaɪ) **1** the cartilaginous fleshy projection that partially covers the entrance to the external ear **2** any of the hairs that grow just inside this entrance [C17 from Late Latin, from Greek *tragos* hairy projection of the ear, literally: goat] > ˈ**tragal** *adj*

trail (treɪl) *vb* **1** to drag or stream, or permit to drag or stream along a surface, esp the ground: *her skirt trailed; she trailed her skipping rope* **2** to make (a track or path) through (a place): *to trail a way; to trail a jungle* **3** to chase, follow, or hunt (an animal or person) by following marks or tracks **4** (when *intr*, often foll by *behind*) to lag or linger behind (a person or thing) **5** (*intr*) to be falling behind in a race or competition: *the favourite is trailing at the last fence* **6** (*tr*) to tow (a boat, caravan, etc) behind a motor vehicle **7** (*tr*) to carry (a rifle) at the full length of the right arm in a horizontal position, with the muzzle to the fore **8** (*intr*) to move wearily or slowly: *we trailed through the city* **9** (*tr*) (on television or radio) to advertise (a future programme) with short extracts **10 trail one's coat** to invite a quarrel by deliberately provocative behaviour ▷ *n* **11** a print, mark, or marks made by a person, animal, or object **12** the act or an instance of trailing **13** the scent left by a moving person or animal that is followed by a hunting animal **14** a path, track, or road, esp one roughly blazed **15** something that trails behind or trails in loops or strands **16** the part of a towed gun carriage and limber that connects the two when in movement and rests on the ground as a partial support when unlimbered **17** *engineering* the distance between the point of contact of a steerable wheel and a line drawn from the swivel pin axis to the ground **18** (on television or radio) an advertisement for a future programme [C14 from Old French *trailler* to draw, tow, from Vulgar Latin *tragulāre* (unattested), from Latin *trāgula* dragnet, from *trahere* to drag; compare Middle Dutch *traghelen* to drag] > ˈ**trail-less** *adj*

trail away *or* **off** *vb* (*intr, adverb*) to become fainter, quieter, or weaker: *his voice trailed off*

trail bike *n* a motorcycle adapted for riding on rough tracks

trailblazer (ˈtreɪlˌbleɪzə) *n* **1** a leader or pioneer in a particular field **2** a person who blazes a trail > ˈ**trailˌblazing** *adj, n*

trailer (ˈtreɪlə) *n* **1** a road vehicle, usually two-wheeled, towed by a motor vehicle: used for transporting boats, etc **2** the part of an articulated lorry that is drawn by the cab **3** a series of short extracts from a film, used to advertise it in a cinema or on television **4** a person or thing that trails **5** *US and Canadian* a large enclosed vehicle capable of being pulled by a car or lorry and equipped to be lived in. Also called (in Britain and certain other countries): **caravan**

trailer park *n US* a mobile home site

trailer trash *n disparaging* **a** poor people living in trailer parks in the US **b** (*as modifier*): *trailer-trash culture*

trailing (ˈtreɪlɪŋ) *adj* (of a plant) having a long stem which spreads over the ground or hangs loosely: *trailing ivy*

trailing arbutus *n* a creeping evergreen ericaceous plant, *Epigaea repens*, of E North America, having clusters of fragrant pink or white flowers. Also called: **mayflower**

trailing edge *n* **1** the rear edge of a propeller blade or aerofoil. Compare **leading edge 2** *physics* the edge of a pulse signal as its amplitude falls

trailing vortex drag *n* drag arising from vortices that occur behind a body moving through a gas or liquid. Often shortened to: **vortex drag** Former name: **induced drag**

trail rope *n* **1** another name for **dragrope** (sense 2) **2** a long rope formerly used for various military purposes, esp to allow a vehicle, horses, or men to pull a gun carriage

train (treɪn) *vb* **1** (*tr*) to guide or teach (to do something), as by subjecting to various exercises or experiences: *to train a man to fight* **2** (*tr*) to control or guide towards a specific goal: *to train a plant up a wall* **3** (*intr*) to do exercises and prepare for a specific purpose: *the athlete trained for the Olympics* **4** (*tr*) to improve or curb by subjecting to discipline: *to train the mind* **5** (*tr*) to focus or bring to bear (on something): *to train a telescope on the moon* ▷ *n* **6 a** a line of coaches or wagons coupled together and drawn by a railway locomotive **b** (*as modifier*): *a train ferry* **7** a sequence or series, as of events, thoughts, etc: *a train of disasters* **8** a procession of people, vehicles, etc, travelling together, such as one carrying supplies of ammunition or equipment in support of a military operation **9** a series of interacting parts through which motion is transmitted: *a train of gears* **10** a fuse or line of gunpowder to an explosive charge, etc **11** something drawn along, such as the long back section of a dress that trails along the floor behind the wearer **12** a retinue or suite **13** proper order or course [C14 from Old French *trahiner*, from Vulgar Latin *tragīnāre* (unattested) to draw; related to Latin *trahere* to drag] > ˈ**trainable** *adj* > ˈ**trainless** *adj*

trainband (ˈtreɪnˌbænd) *n* a company of English militia from the 16th to the 18th century [C17 altered from *trained band*]

trainbearer (ˈtreɪnˌbɛərə) *n* an attendant in a procession who holds up the train of a dignitary's robe

trainee (treɪˈniː) *n* **a** a person undergoing training **b** (*as modifier*): *a trainee journalist*

trainer (ˈtreɪnə) *n* **1** a person who trains athletes in a sport **2** a piece of equipment employed in training, such as a simulated aircraft cockpit **3** *horse racing* a person who schools racehorses and prepares them for racing **4** (*plural*) an informal name for **training shoes**

trainer sock *n* a sock designed to be worn with a training shoe, often cut low at the ankle so that very little shows above the shoe

training (ˈtreɪnɪŋ) *n* **1 a** the process of bringing a person, etc, to an agreed standard of proficiency, etc, by practice and instruction: *training for the priesthood; physical training* **b** (*as modifier*): *training college* **2 in training a** undergoing physical training **b** physically fit **3 out of training** physically unfit

Training Agency *n* (in Britain) an organization established in 1989 to replace the Training Commission, which itself replaced the Manpower Services Commission; it provides training and retraining for adult workers and operates the Youth Training Scheme, in England and Wales working through the local **Training and Enterprise Councils** (TECs) and in Scotland through the Local Enterprise Companies (LECs) set up in 1990

training shoes *pl n* **1** running shoes for sports training, esp in contrast to studded or spiked shoes worn for the sport itself **2** shoes in the style of those used for sports training ▷ Also called: **trainers**

train oil *n* oil obtained from the blubber of various marine animals, esp the whale [C16 from earlier *train* or *trane*, from Middle Low German *trān* or Middle Dutch *traen* tear, exudation]

train smash *n South African informal* a disaster or serious setback (esp in the phrase **it's not a train smash**)

train spotter *n* **1** a person who collects the numbers of railway locomotives **2** *informal* a person who is obsessed with trivial details, esp of a subject generally considered uninteresting

trainspotterish (ˈtreɪnˌspɒtərɪʃ) *adj informal* obsessed with trivial details, esp of a subject generally considered uninteresting

traipse *or* **trapes** (treɪps) *informal* ▷ *vb* **1** (*intr*) to walk heavily or tiredly ▷ *n* **2** a long or tiring walk; trudge [C16 of unknown origin]

trait (treɪt, treɪ) *n* **1** a characteristic feature or quality distinguishing a particular person or thing **2** *rare* a touch or stroke [C16 from French, from Old French: a pulling, from Latin *tractus*, from *trahere* to drag]

traitor (ˈtreɪtə) *n* a person who is guilty of treason or treachery, in betraying friends, country, a cause or trust, etc [C13 from Old French *traitour*, from Latin *trāditor* TRADITOR] > ˈ**traitorous** *adj* > ˈ**traitorously** *adv* > ˈ**traitorˌship** *n* > ˈ**traitress** *fem n*

traject (trəˈdʒɛkt) *vb* (*tr*) *archaic* to transport or transmit [C17 from Latin *trājectus* cast over, from *trāicere* to throw across, from TRANS- + *iacere* to throw] > traˈ**jection** *n*

trajectory (trəˈdʒɛktərɪ, -trɪ) *n, pl* **-ries 1** the path described by an object moving in air or space under the influence of such forces as thrust, wind resistance, and gravity, esp the curved path of a projectile **2** *geometry* a curve that cuts a family of curves or surfaces at a constant angle > **trajectile** (trəˈdʒɛktaɪl) *adj*

tra-la (ˌtrɑːˈlɑː) *or* **tra-la-la** (ˌtrɑːlɑːˈlɑː) *n* a set of nonsensical syllables used in humming music, esp for a melody or refrain

Tralee (trəˈliː) *n* a market town in SW Republic of Ireland, county town of Kerry, near **Tralee Bay** (an inlet of the Atlantic). Pop: 21 987 (2002)

TRALI *abbreviation for* transfusion-related acute lung injury: a potentially fatal condition that can affect a female blood donor who has been pregnant

tram¹ (træm) *n* **1** Also called: **tramcar** an electrically driven public transport vehicle that runs on rails let into the surface of the road, power usually being taken from an overhead wire. US and Canadian names: **streetcar, trolley car 2** a small vehicle on rails for carrying loads in a mine; tub [C16 (in the sense: shaft of a cart): probably from Low German *traam* beam; compare Old Norse *thrömr*, Middle Dutch *traem* beam, tooth of a rake] > ˈ**tramless** *adj*

tram² (træm) *n* **1** *machinery* a fine adjustment that ensures correct function or alignment ▷ *vb* **trams, tramming, trammed 2** (*tr*) to adjust (a mechanism) to a fine degree of accuracy [C19 short for TRAMMEL]

tram³ (træm) *n* (in weaving) a weft yarn of two or

t

more twisted strands of silk [c17 from French *trame*, from Latin *trāma*; related to Latin *trāns* across, *trāmes* footpath]

TRAM flap (træm) *n acronym for* transverse rectus abdominis myocutaneous flap: a piece of tissue, consisting of skin, muscle, and fat, taken from the abdomen of a woman and used in the reconstruction of her breast after mastectomy

tramline ('træm,laɪn) *n* **1** (*often plural*) Also called: **tramway** the tracks on which a tram runs **2** the route taken by a tram **3** (*often plural*) the outer markings along the sides of a tennis or badminton court **4** (*plural*) a set of guiding principles

trammel ('træməl) *n* **1** (*often plural*) a hindrance to free action or movement **2** Also called: **trammel net** a fishing net in three sections, the two outer nets having a large mesh and the middle one a fine mesh **3** *rare* a fowling net **4** *US* a fetter or shackle, esp one used in teaching a horse to amble **5** a device for drawing ellipses consisting of a flat sheet of metal, plastic, or wood having a cruciform slot in which run two pegs attached to a beam. The free end of the beam describes an ellipse **6** (*sometimes plural*) another name for **beam compass 7** Also called: **tram** a gauge for setting up machines correctly **8** a device set in a fireplace to support cooking pots ▷ *vb* **-els, -elling, -elled** *or US* **-els, -eling, -eled** (*tr*) **9** to hinder or restrain **10** to catch or ensnare **11** to produce an accurate setting of (a machine adjustment), as with a trammel [c14 from Old French *tramail* three-mesh net, from Late Latin *trēmaculum*, from Latin *trēs* three + *macula* hole, mesh in a net] > '**trammeller** *or US* '**trammeler** *n*

trammie ('træmɪ) *n Austral informal* the conductor or driver of a tram

tramontane (trə'mɒnteɪn) *adj also* **transmontane 1** being or coming from the far side of the mountains, esp from the other side of the Alps as seen from Italy **2** foreign or barbarous **3** (of a wind) blowing down from the mountains ▷ *n* **4** an inhabitant of a tramontane country **5** Also called: **tramontana** a cold dry wind blowing south or southwest from the mountains in Italy and the W Mediterranean **6** *rare* a foreigner or barbarian [c16 from Italian *tramontano*, from Latin *trānsmontānus*, from TRANS- + *montānus*, from *mōns* mountain]

tramp (træmp) *vb* **1** (*intr*) to walk long and far; hike **2** to walk heavily or firmly across or through (a place); march or trudge **3** (*intr*) to wander about as a vagabond or tramp **4** (*tr*) to make (a journey) or traverse (a place) on foot, esp laboriously or wearily: *to tramp the streets in search of work* **5** (*tr*) to tread or trample **6** (*intr*) *NZ* to walk for sport or recreation, esp in the bush ▷ *n* **7** a person who travels about on foot, usually with no permanent home, living by begging or doing casual work **8** a long hard walk; hike **9** a heavy or rhythmic step or tread **10** the sound of heavy treading **11** Also called: **tramp steamer** a merchant ship that does not run between ports on a regular schedule but carries cargo wherever the shippers desire **12** *slang, chiefly US and Canadian* a prostitute or promiscuous girl or woman **13** an iron plate on the sole of a boot [c14 probably from Middle Low German *trampen*; compare Gothic *ana-trimpan* to press heavily upon, German *trampen* to hitchhike] > '**tramping** *n* > '**trampish** *adj*

tramper ('træmpə) *n* **1** a person who tramps **2** a person who walks long distances, often over rough terrain, for recreation

tramping club *n NZ* an organization of people who walk for recreation, esp in the bush

tramping hut *n NZ* a hut in the bush for the use of trampers

trample ('træmpəl) *vb* (*when intr, usually foll by* *on, upon*, or *over*) **1** to stamp or walk roughly (on): *to trample the flowers* **2** to encroach (upon) so as to violate or hurt: *to trample on someone's feelings* ▷ *n* **3** the action or sound of trampling [c14

frequentative of TRAMP; compare Middle High German *trampeln*] > '**trampler** *n*

trampoline ('træmpəlɪn, -,li:n) *n* **1** a tough canvas sheet suspended by springs or elasticated cords from a frame, used by acrobats, gymnasts, etc ▷ *vb* **2** (*intr*) to exercise on a trampoline [c18 via Spanish from Italian *trampolino*, from *trampoli* stilts, of Germanic origin; compare TRAMPLE] > '**trampoliner** *or* '**trampolinist** *n*

tramway ('træm,weɪ) *n* **1** another name for **tramline** (sense 1) **2** *Brit* **a** a public transportation system using trams **b** the company owning or running such a system ▷ Also called (esp *US*): **tramroad** a small or temporary railway for moving freight along tracks, as in a quarry

trance (trɑːns) *n* **1** a hypnotic state resembling sleep **2** any mental state in which a person is unaware or apparently unaware of the environment, characterized by loss of voluntary movement, rigidity, and lack of sensitivity to external stimuli **3** a dazed or stunned state **4** a state of ecstasy or mystic absorption so intense as to cause a temporary loss of consciousness at the earthly level **5** *spiritualism* a state in which a medium, having temporarily lost consciousness, can supposedly be controlled by an intelligence from without as a means of communication with the dead **6** a type of electronic dance music with repetitive rhythms, aiming at a hypnotic effect ▷ *vb* **7** (*tr*) to put into or as into a trance [c14 from Old French *transe*, from *transir* to faint, pass away, from Latin *trānsīre* to go over, from TRANS- + *īre* to go] > '**trance,like** *adj*

trance out *vb* (*intr, adverb*) *slang* to go into a trancelike or ecstatic state, esp through the effects of drugs or music

tranche (trɑːnʃ) *n* a portion or instalment, esp of a loan or share issue [from French, literally: a slice]

trannie *or* **tranny** ('trænɪ) *n, pl* **-nies 1** a transistor radio **2** a transvestite

tranquil ('træŋkwɪl) *adj* calm, peaceful or quiet [c17 from Latin *tranquillus*] > '**tranquilly** *adv* > '**tranquilness** *n*

tranquillity *or sometimes US* **tranquility** (træŋ'kwɪlɪtɪ) *n* a state of calm or quietude

tranquillize, tranquillise *or US* **tranquilize** ('træŋkwɪ,laɪz) *vb* to make or become calm or calmer > ,**tranquilli'zation**, ,**tranquilli'sation** *or US* ,**tranquili'zation** *n*

tranquillizer, tranquilliser *or US* **tranquilizer** ('træŋkwɪ,laɪzə) *n* **1** a drug that calms a person without affecting clarity of consciousness **2** anything that tranquillizes

trans. *abbreviation for* **1** transaction **2** transferred **3** transitive **4** translated **5** translator

trans- *or sometimes before s-* **tran-** *prefix* **1** across, beyond, crossing, on the other side: *transoceanic; trans-Siberian; transatlantic* **2** changing thoroughly: *transliterate* **3** transcending: *transubstantiation* **4** transversely: *transect* **5** (*often in italics*) indicating that a chemical compound has a molecular structure in which two groups or atoms are on opposite sides of a double bond: *trans-butadiene*. Compare **cis-** (sense 2) [from Latin *trāns* across, through, beyond]

transact (træn'zækt) *vb* to do, conduct, or negotiate (business, a deal, etc) [c16 from Latin *trānsactus*, from *trānsigere*, literally: to drive through, from TRANS- + *agere* to drive] > trans'**actor** *n*

transactinide (,træns'æktɪ,naɪd) *n* any artificially produced element with an atomic number greater than 103 [c20 from TRANS- + ACTINIDE]

transaction (træn'zækʃən) *n* **1** something that is transacted, esp a business deal or negotiation **2** the act of transacting or the state of being transacted **3** (*plural*) the published records of the proceedings of a society, conference, etc **4** (in business computing) the act of obtaining and paying for an item or service **5** (in general

computing) the transmission and processing of an item of data > trans'**actional** *adj* > trans'**actionally** *adv*

transactional analysis *n psychol* a form of psychotherapy that attributes neuroses to lack of balance in the personality between the conflicting ego-states of child, adult, and parent

transalpine (trænz'ælpaɪn) *adj* (*prenominal*) **1** situated in or relating to places beyond the Alps, esp from Italy **2** passing over the Alps ▷ *n* **3** a transalpine person

Transalpine Gaul *n* (in the ancient world) that part of Gaul northwest of the Alps

transaminase (trænz'æmɪ,neɪz, -,neɪs) *n biochem* an enzyme that catalyses the transfer of an amino group from one molecule, esp an amino acid, to another, esp a keto acid, in the process of transamination

transatlantic (,trænzət'læntɪk) *adj* **1** on or from the other side of the Atlantic **2** crossing the Atlantic

transaxle (trænz'æksəl) *n* a unit in a motor vehicle engine that combines the differential, transmission, and drive axle

transcalent (træns'keɪlənt) *adj rare* permitting the passage of heat [c19 TRANS- + *-calent*, from Latin *calēre* to be hot] > trans'**calency** *n*

Transcaucasia (,trænskɔː'keɪzjə) *n* a region in central Asia, south of the Caucasus Mountains between the Black and Caspian Seas in Georgia, Armenia, and Azerbaijan: a constituent republic of the Soviet Union from 1918 until 1936

Transcaucasian (,trænskɔː'keɪzjən) *adj* **1** of or relating to the central Asian region of Transcaucasia or its inhabitants ▷ *n* **2** a native or inhabitant of Transcaucasia

transceiver (træn'si:və) *n* a device which transmits and receives radio or electronic signals [c20 from TRANS(MITTER) + (RE)CEIVER]

transcend (træn'send) *vb* **1** to go above or beyond (a limit, expectation, etc), as in degree or excellence **2** (*tr*) to be superior to **3** *philosophy, theol* (esp of the Deity) to exist beyond (the material world) [c14 from Latin *trānscendere* to climb over, from TRANS- + *scandere* to climb] > trans'**cendingly** *adv*

transcendent (træn'sendənt) *adj* **1** exceeding or surpassing in degree or excellence **2 a** (in the philosophy of Kant) beyond or before experience; a priori **b** (of a concept) falling outside a given set of categories **c** beyond consciousness or direct apprehension **3** *theol* (of God) having continuous existence outside the created world **4** free from the limitations inherent in matter ▷ *n* **5** *philosophy* a transcendent thing > tran'**scendence** *or* tran'**scendency** *n* > tran'**scendently** *adv* > tran'**scendentness** *n*

transcendental (,trænsen'dentəl) *adj* **1** transcendent, superior, or surpassing **2** (in the philosophy of Kant) **a** (of a judgment or logical deduction) being both synthetic and a priori **b** of or relating to knowledge of the presuppositions of thought **3** *philosophy* beyond our experience of phenomena, although not beyond potential knowledge **4** *theol* surpassing the natural plane of reality or knowledge; supernatural or mystical > ,**transcenden'tality** *n* > ,**transcen'dentally** *adv*

transcendental argument *n philosophy* an argument designed to make explicit the conditions under which a certain kind of knowledge is possible, esp those of Kant

transcendental function *n maths* a function that is not capable of expression in terms of a finite number of arithmetical operations, such as sin *x*

transcendental idealism *n philosophy* the Kantian doctrine that reality consists not of appearances, but of some other order of being whose existence can be inferred from the nature of human reason

transcendentalism (,trænsen'dentə,lɪzəm) *n* **1 a** any system of philosophy, esp that of Immanuel

Kant, the German philosopher (1724–1804), holding that the key to knowledge of the nature of reality lies in the critical examination of the processes of reason on which depends the nature of experience **b** any system of philosophy, esp that of Emerson, that emphasizes intuition as a means to knowledge or the importance of the search for the divine **2** vague philosophical speculation **3** the state of being transcendental **4** something, such as thought or language, that is transcendental > ˌtranscen'dentalist *n, adj*

Transcendental Meditation *n Trademark in the US* a technique, based on Hindu traditions, for relaxing and refreshing the mind and body through the silent repetition of a mantra. Disseminated by an international organization founded by Maharishi Mahesh Yogi (born 1917), an Indian-born guru. Abbreviation: **TM**

transcendental number *n maths* a number or quantity that is real but nonalgebraic, that is, one that is not a root of any polynomial with rational coefficients such as π or *e*

transcontinental (ˌtrænzkɒntɪ'nɛntᵊl) *adj* **1** crossing a continent **2** on or from the far side of a continent > ˌtranscontiˈnentally *adv*

transcranial (trænz'kreɪnɪəl) *adj* across or through the skull

transcranial magnetic stimulation *n* the electromagnetic stimulation of areas of the brain, used in studying or treating the effects of strokes. Abbreviation: **TMS**

transcribe (træn'skraɪb) *vb (tr)* **1** to write, type, or print out fully from speech, notes, etc **2** to make a phonetic transcription of **3** to transliterate or translate **4** to make an electrical recording of (a programme or speech) for a later broadcast **5** *music* to rewrite (a piece of music) for an instrument or medium other than that originally intended; arrange **6** *computing* **a** to transfer (information) from one storage device, such as punched cards, to another, such as magnetic tape **b** to transfer (information) from a computer to an external storage device **7** *(usually passive) biochem* to convert the genetic information in (a strand of DNA) into a strand of RNA, esp messenger RNA. See also **genetic code, translate** (sense 6) [c16 from Latin *transcrībere*, from TRANS- + *scrībere* to write] > tran'scribable *adj* > tran'scriber *n*

transcript ('trænskrɪpt) *n* **1** a written, typed, or printed copy or manuscript made by transcribing **2** *education, chiefly US and Canadian* an official record of a student's school progress and achievements **3** any reproduction or copy [c13 from Latin *transcriptum*, from *transcrībere* to TRANSCRIBE]

transcriptase (træn'skrɪpteɪz) *n* See **reverse transcriptase**

transcription (træn'skrɪpʃən) *n* **1** the act or an instance of transcribing or the state of being transcribed **2** something transcribed **3** a representation in writing of the actual pronunciation of a speech sound, word, or piece of continuous text, using not a conventional orthography but a symbol or set of symbols specially designated as standing for corresponding phonetic values > tran'scriptional *or* tran'scriptive *adj* > tran'scriptionally *or* tran'scriptively *adv*

transculturation (ˌtrænzkʌltʃʊ'reɪʃən) *n* the introduction of foreign elements into an established culture

transcurrent (trænz'kʌrənt) *adj* running across; transverse

transdermal (trænz'dɜːməl) *adj* (of a medicine) entering the bloodstream by absorption through the skin [c20 from TRANS- + DERMAL]

Transdniestria ('trænzdnɪˌɛstrɪə) *n* a region of E Moldova: unilaterally declared itself independent and was the scene of fighting between government troops and separatists in 1992

transducer (trænz'djuːsə) *n* any device, such as a microphone or electric motor, that converts one

form of energy into another [c20 from Latin *transducere* to lead across, from TRANS- + *ducere* to lead]

transduction (trænz'dʌkʃən) *n genetics* the transfer by a bacteriophage of genetic material from one bacterium to another [c17 from Latin *transductiō*, variant of *trāductiō* a leading along, from *trādūcere* to lead over; see TRADUCE]

transect *vb* (træn'sɛkt) *(tr)* **1** to cut or divide crossways ▷ *n* ('trænsɛkt) **2** a sample strip of land used to monitor plant distribution, animal populations, etc, within a given area [c17 from Latin TRANS- + *secāre* to cut] > tran'section *n*

transept ('trænsɛpt) *n* either of the two wings of a cruciform church at right angles to the nave [c16 from Anglo-Latin *transeptum*, from Latin TRANS- + *saeptum* enclosure] > tran'septal *adj*

transeunt ('trænsɪənt) *or* **transient** *adj philosophy* (of a mental act) causing effects outside the mind. Compare **immanent** (sense 2) [c17 from Latin *transiēns* going over, from *transīre* to pass over; see TRANCE]

trans-fatty acid *or* **trans fat** *n* a polyunsaturated fatty acid that has been converted from the cis-form by hydrogenation: used in the manufacture of margarine

transfect (træns'fɛkt) *vb (tr)* to bring about transfection in [from TRANS- + (IN)FECT]

transfection (træns'fɛkʃən) *n* the transfer into another cell of genetic material isolated from a cell or virus

transfer *vb* (træns'fɜː) -fers, -ferring, -ferred **1** to change or go or cause to change or go from one thing, person, or point to another: *they transferred from the Park Hotel to the Imperial; she transferred her affections to her dog* **2** to change (buses, trains, etc) **3** *law* to make over (property, etc) to another; convey **4** to displace (a drawing, design, etc) from one surface to another **5** (of a football player, esp a professional) to change clubs or (of a club, manager, etc) to sell or release (a player) to another club **6** to leave one school, college, etc, and enrol at another **7** to change (the meaning of a word, etc), esp by metaphorical extension ▷ *n* ('trænsfɜː) **8** the act, process, or system of transferring, or the state of being transferred **9** **a** a person or thing that transfers or is transferred **b** *(as modifier): a transfer student* **10** a design or drawing that is transferred from one surface to another, as by ironing a printed design onto cloth **11** *law* the passing of title to property or other right from one person to another by act of the parties or by operation of law; conveyance **12** *finance* **a** the act of transferring the title of ownership to shares or registered bonds in the books of the issuing enterprise **b** *(as modifier): transfer deed; transfer form* **13** any document or form effecting or regulating a transfer **14** *chiefly US and Canadian* a ticket that allows a passenger to change routes [c14 from Latin *transferre*, from TRANS- + *ferre* to carry] > trans'ferable *or* trans'ferrable *adj* > ˌtransfera'bility *n*

transferable vote *n* a vote that is transferred to a second candidate indicated by the voter if the first is eliminated from the ballot

transferase ('trænsfəˌreɪs) *n* any enzyme that catalyses the transfer of a chemical group from one substance to another

transfer characteristic *n electronics* the relationship between output and input of an electronic or electromechanical system, esp as depicted graphically

transferee (ˌtrænsfə'riː) *n* **1** *property law* a person to whom property is transferred **2** a person who is transferred

transference ('trænsfərəns, -frəns) *n* **1** the act or an instance of transferring or the state of being transferred **2** *psychoanal* the redirection of attitudes and emotions towards a substitute, such as towards the analyst during therapy > transferential (ˌtrænsfə'rɛnʃəl) *adj*

transfer fee *n* a sum of money paid by one

football club to another for a transferred player

transfer list *n* a list of football players available for transfer

transferor *or* **transferrer** (træns'fɜːrə) *n property law* a person who makes a transfer, as of property

transfer payment *n (usually plural)* money received by an individual or family from the state or other body, often a pension or unemployment benefit. It is not reckoned when calculating the national income as it is money transferred rather than paid for merchandise or a service rendered

transfer pricing *n* the setting of a price for the transfer of raw materials, components, products, or services between the trading units of a large organization

transferral *or* **transferal** (ˌtræns'fɜrəl) *n* the act or an instance of transferring or being transferred

transferrin (træns'fɜːrɪn) *n biochem* any of a group of blood glycoproteins that transport iron. Also called: beta globulin, siderophilin [c20 from TRANS- + FERRO- + -IN]

transfer RNA *n biochem* any of several soluble forms of RNA of low molecular weight, each of which transports a specific amino acid to a ribosome during protein synthesis. Sometimes shortened to: **t-RNA** Also called: **soluble RNA** See also **messenger RNA, genetic code**

transfer station *n NZ* a municipal depot where rubbish is sorted for recycling or relocation to a landfill site

transfiguration (ˌtrænsfɪgjʊ'reɪʃən) *n* the act or an instance of transfiguring or the state of being transfigured

Transfiguration (ˌtrænsfɪgjʊ'reɪʃən) *n* **1** *New Testament* the change in the appearance of Christ that took place before three disciples (Matthew 17:1–9) **2** the Church festival held in commemoration of this on Aug 6

transfigure (træns'fɪgə) *vb (usually tr)* **1** to change or cause to change in appearance **2** to become or cause to become more exalted [c13 from Latin *transfigūrāre*, from TRANS- + *figūra* appearance] > trans'figurement *n*

transfinite (træns'faɪnaɪt) *adj* extending beyond the finite

transfinite number *n* a cardinal or ordinal number used in the comparison of infinite sets for which several types of infinity can be classified: *the set of integers and the set of real numbers have different transfinite numbers*

transfix (træns'fɪks) *vb* -fixes, -fixing, -fixed *or* -fixt *(tr)* **1** to render motionless, esp with horror or shock **2** to impale or fix with a sharp weapon or other device **3** *med* to cut through (a limb or other organ), as in amputation [c16 from Latin *transfīgere* to pierce through, from TRANS- + *figere* to thrust in] > transfixion (træns'fɪkʃən) *n*

transform *vb* (træns'fɔːm) **1** to alter or be altered radically in form, function, etc **2** *(tr)* to convert (one form of energy) to another form **3** *(tr) maths* to change the form of (an equation, expression, etc) by a mathematical transformation **4** *(tr)* to increase or decrease (an alternating current or voltage) using a transformer ▷ *n* ('trænsˌfɔːm) **5** *maths* the result of a mathematical transformation, esp (of a matrix or an element of a group) another related to the given one by $B = X^{-1}AX$ for some appropriate X [c14 from Latin *transformāre*, from TRANS- + *formāre* to FORM] > trans'formable *adj* > trans'formative *adj*

transformation (ˌtrænsfə'meɪʃən) *n* **1** a change or alteration, esp a radical one **2** the act of transforming or the state of being transformed **3** *maths* **a** a change in position or direction of the reference axes in a coordinate system without an alteration in their relative angle **b** an equivalent change in an expression or equation resulting from the substitution of one set of variables by another **4** *physics* a change in an atomic nucleus to a different nuclide as the result of the emission of either an alpha-particle or a beta-particle. Compare **transition** (sense 5) **5** *linguistics* another

t

word for **transformational rule 6** an apparently miraculous change in the appearance of a stage set **7** (in South Africa) a national strategy aimed at attaining national unity, promoting reconciliation through negotiated settlement and non-racism > ˌtransforˈmational *adj*

transformational grammar *n* a grammatical description of a language making essential use of transformational rules. Such grammars are usually but not necessarily generative grammars. Compare **systemic grammar, case grammar**

transformational rule *n* **1** *generative grammar* a rule that converts one phrase marker into another. Taken together, these rules, which form the **transformational component** of the grammar, convert the deep structures of sentences into their surface structures **2** (*plural*) *logic* a rule that specifies in purely syntactic terms a method by which theorems may be derived from the axioms of a formal system

transformer (træns'fɔ:mə) *n* **1** a device that transfers an alternating current from one circuit to one or more other circuits, usually with an increase (**step-up transformer**) or decrease (**step-down transformer**) of voltage. The input current is fed to a primary winding, the output being taken from a secondary winding or windings inductively linked to the primary **2** a person or thing that transforms

transformism (træns'fɔ:mɪzəm) *n* a less common word for **evolution,** esp the theory of evolution > **trans'formist** *n*

transfuse (træns'fju:z) *vb* (*tr*) **1** to permeate or infuse: *a blush transfused her face* **2 a** to inject (blood, etc) into a blood vessel **b** to give a transfusion to (a patient) **3** *rare* to transfer from one vessel to another, esp by pouring [c15 from Latin *transfundere* to pour out, from TRANS- + *fundere* to pour] > **trans'fuser** *n* > **trans'fusible** or **trans'fusable** *adj* > **trans'fusive** *adj*

transfusion (træns'fju:ʒən) *n* **1** the act or an instance of transfusing **2** the injection of blood, blood plasma, etc, into the blood vessels of a patient

transgender (ˌtrænz'dʒɛndə) *adj* of or relating to a person who wants to belong to the opposite sex > ˌtrans'gendered *adj*

transgene ('trænz,dʒi:n) *n* a gene that is transferred from an organism of one species to an organism of another species by genetic engineering

transgenic (trænz'dʒɛnɪk) *adj* (of an animal or plant) containing genetic material artificially transferred from another species

transgenics (ˌtrænz'dʒɛnɪks) *n* (*functioning as singular*) the branch of biology concerned with the transfer of genetic material from one species to another

transgress (trænz'grɛs) *vb* **1** to break (a law, rule, etc) **2** to go beyond or overstep (a limit) [c16 from Latin *transgredī*, from TRANS- + *gradī* to step] > **trans'gressor** *n*

transgression (trænz'grɛʃən) *n* **1** a breach of a law, etc; sin or crime **2** the act or an instance of transgressing

transgressive (ˌtrænz'grɛsɪv) *adj* going beyond accept boundaries of taste, convention, or the law: *transgressive art; transgressive pursuits* > **trans'gressively** *adv*

tranship (træn'ʃɪp) *vb* -ships, -shipping, -shipped a variant spelling of **transship.** > **tran'shipment** *n*

transhumance (træns'hju:məns) *n* the seasonal migration of livestock to suitable grazing grounds [c20 from French, from *transhumer* to change one's pastures, from Spanish *trashumar,* from Latin TRANS- + *humus* ground] > **trans'humant** *adj*

transient ('trænzɪənt) *adj* **1** for a short time only; temporary or transitory **2** *philosophy* a variant of **transeunt** ⊳ *n* **3** a transient person or thing **4** *physics* a brief change in the state of a system, such as a sudden short-lived oscillation in the current flowing through a circuit [c17 from Latin

transiēns going over, from *transīre* to pass over, from TRANS- + *īre* to go] > 'transiently *adv* > 'transience or 'transiency *n*

transilient (træn'sɪlɪənt) *adj* passing quickly from one thing to another [c19 from Latin *transilīre* to jump over, from TRANS- + *salīre* to leap] > tran'silience *n*

transilluminate (ˌtrænzɪ'lu:mɪˌneɪt) *vb* (*tr*) *med* to pass a light through the wall of (a bodily cavity, membrane, etc) in order to detect fluid, lesions, etc > ˌtransilˌlumi'nation *n* > ˌtransil'lumiˌnator *n*

transistor (træn'zɪstə) *n* **1** a semiconductor device, having three or more terminals attached to electrode regions, in which current flowing between two electrodes is controlled by a voltage or current applied to one or more specified electrodes. The device is capable of amplification, etc, and has replaced the valve in most circuits since it is much smaller, more robust, and works at a much lower voltage. See also **junction transistor, field-effect transistor 2** *informal* a transistor radio [c20 originally a trademark, from TRANSFER + RESISTOR, referring to the transfer of electric signals across a resistor]

transistorize or **transistorise** (træn'zɪstəˌraɪz) *vb* **1** to convert (a system, device, industry, etc) to the use or manufacture of or operation by transistors and other solid-state components **2** to equip (a device or circuit) with transistors and other solid-state components

transit ('trænzɪt, 'trænz-) *n* **1 a** the passage or conveyance of goods or people **b** (*as modifier*): *a transit visa* **2** a change or transition **3** a route **4** *astronomy* **a** the passage of a celestial body or satellite across the face of a relatively larger body as seen from the earth **b** the apparent passage of a celestial body across the meridian, caused by the earth's diurnal rotation **5** *astrology* the passage of a planet across some special point on the zodiac **6 in transit** while being conveyed; during passage ⊳ *vb* **7** to make a transit through or over (something) **8** *astronomy* to make a transit across (a celestial body or the meridian) **9** to cause (the telescope of a surveying instrument) to turn over or (of such a telescope) to be turned over in a vertical plane so that it points in the opposite direction [c15 from Latin *transitus* a going over, from *transīre* to pass over; see TRANSIENT] > 'transitable *adj*

transit camp *n* a camp in which refugees, soldiers, etc, live temporarily before moving to another destination

transit instrument *n* an astronomical instrument, mounted on an E-W axis, in which the reticle of a telescope is always in the plane of the meridian. It is used to time the transit of a star, etc, across the meridian

transition (træn'zɪʃən) *n* **1** change or passage from one state or stage to another **2** the period of time during which something changes from one state or stage to another **3** *music* **a** a movement from one key to another; modulation **b** a linking passage between two divisions in a composition; bridge **4** Also called: **transitional** a style of architecture that was used in western Europe in the late 11th and early 12th century, characterized by late Romanesque forms combined with early Gothic details **5** *physics* **a** any change that results in a change of physical properties of a substance or system, such as a change of phase or molecular structure **b** a change in the configuration of an atomic nucleus, involving either a change in energy level resulting from the emission of a gamma-ray photon or a transformation to another element or isotope **6** a sentence, passage, etc, that connects a topic to one that follows or that links sections of a written work [c16 from Latin *transitio*; see TRANSIENT] > tran'sitional or *rarely* tran'sitionary *adj* > tran'sitionally *adv*

transition element or **metal** *n* *chem* any element belonging to one of three series of

elements with atomic numbers between 21 and 30, 39 and 48, and 57 and 80. They have an incomplete penultimate electron shell and tend to exhibit more than one valency and to form complexes

transition point *n* **1** the point at which a transition of physical properties takes place, such as the point at which laminar flow changes to turbulent flow **2** See **transition temperature**

transition temperature *n* the temperature at which a sudden change of physical properties occurs, such as a change of phase or crystalline structure, or at which a substance becomes superconducting

transitive ('trænsɪtɪv) *adj* **1** *grammar* **a** denoting an occurrence of a verb when it requires a direct object or denoting a verb that customarily requires a direct object: *"to find" is a transitive verb* **b** (*as noun*): *these verbs are transitives* **2** *grammar* denoting an adjective, such as *fond,* or a noun, such as *husband,* that requires a noun phrase and cannot be used without some implicit or explicit reference to such a noun phrase **3** *logic, maths* having the property that if one object bears a relationship to a second object that also bears the same relationship to a third object, then the first object bears this relationship to the third object: *mathematical equality is transitive, since if x = y and y = z then x = z* ⊳ Compare **intransitive** [c16 from Late Latin *transitīvus* from Latin *transitus* a going over; see TRANSIENT] > 'transitively *adv* > ˌtransi'tivity or 'transitiveness *n*

transitory ('trænsɪtərɪ, -trɪ) *adj* of short duration; transient or ephemeral [c14 from Church Latin *transitōrius* passing, from Latin *transitus* a crossing over; see TRANSIENT] > 'transitorily *adv* > 'transitoriness *n*

transitory action *n* *law* an action that can be brought in any country regardless of where it originated

transit theodolite *n* a theodolite the telescope of which can be rotated completely about its horizontal axis

Trans-Jordan *n* the former name (1922–49) of Jordan

Trans-Jordanian *adj* **1** of or relating to the former Trans-Jordan (now Jordan) or its inhabitants ⊳ *n* **2** a native or inhabitant of Trans-Jordan

Transkei (træn'skaɪ) *n* the largest of South Africa's former Bantu homelands and the first Bantu self-governing territory (1963); declared an independent state in 1976 but this status was not recognized outside South Africa; abolished in 1993 when South African citizenship was restored to its inhabitants. Capital: Umtata

Transkeian (træns'kaɪən) *adj* **1** of or relating to the former Bantu homeland of Transkei (now part of South Africa) or its inhabitants ⊳ *n* **2** a native or inhabitant of Transkei

translate (træns'leɪt, trænz-) *vb* **1** to express or be capable of being expressed in another language or dialect: *he translated Shakespeare into Afrikaans; his books translate well* **2** (*intr*) to act as translator **3** (*tr*) to express or explain in simple or less technical language **4** (*tr*) to interpret or infer the significance of (gestures, symbols, etc) **5** (*tr*) to transform or convert: *to translate hope into reality* **6** (*tr; usually passive*) *biochem* to transform the molecular structure of (messenger RNA) into a polypeptide chain by means of the information stored in the genetic code. See also **transcribe** (sense 7) **7** to move or carry from one place or position to another **8** (*tr*) **a** to transfer (a cleric) from one ecclesiastical office to another **b** to transfer (a see) from one place to another **9** (*tr*) *RC Church* to transfer (the body or the relics of a saint) from one resting place to another **10** (*tr*) *theol* to transfer (a person) from one place or plane of existence to another, as from earth to heaven **11** *maths, physics* to move (a figure or body) laterally, without rotation, dilation, or angular displacement **12** (*intr*) (of an aircraft, missile, etc)

to fly or move from one position to another **13** *(tr)* *archaic* to bring to a state of spiritual or emotional ecstasy [c13 from Latin *translātus* transferred, carried over, from *transferre* to TRANSFER]
> **trans'latable** *adj* > ˌtransla'tability *n*

translation (trænsˈleɪʃən, trænz-) *n* **1** something that is or has been translated, esp a written text **2** the act of translating or the state of being translated **3** *maths* a transformation in which the origin of a coordinate system is moved to another position so that each axis retains the same direction or, equivalently, a figure or curve is moved so that it retains the same orientation to the axes > **trans'lational** *adj*

translator (trænsˈleɪtə, trænz-) *n* **1** a person or machine that translates speech or writing **2** *radio* a relay transmitter that retransmits a signal on a carrier frequency different from that on which it was received **3** *computing* a computer program that converts a program from one language to another > ˌtransla'torial *adj*

transliterate (trænzˈlɪtəˌreɪt) *vb (tr)* to transcribe (a word, etc, in one alphabet) into corresponding letters of another alphabet: *the Greek word λογος can be transliterated as "logos"* [c19 TRANS- + -literate, from Latin *lǐttera* LETTER] > ˌtransliter'ation *n* > **trans'literˌator** *n*

translocate (ˌtrænzləʊˈkeɪt) *vb (tr)* to move; displace

translocation (ˌtrænzləʊˈkeɪʃən) *n* **1** *genetics* the transfer of one part of a chromosome to another part of the same or a different chromosome, resulting in rearrangement of the genes **2** *botany* the transport of minerals, sugars, etc, in solution within a plant **3** a movement from one position or place to another

translucent (trænzˈluːsᵊnt) *adj* allowing light to pass through partially or diffusely; semitransparent [c16 from Latin *translūcēre* to shine through, from TRANS- + *lūcēre* to shine] > **trans'lucence** *or* **trans'lucency** *n* > **trans'lucently** *adv*

translunar (trænzˈluːnə) *or* **translunary** (trænzˈluːnərɪ) *adj* **1** lying beyond the moon. Compare **cislunar 2** unworldly or ethereal

transmarine (ˌtrænzməˈriːn) *adj* a less common word for **overseas** [c16 from Latin *transmarīnus*, from TRANS- + *marīnus*, from *mare* sea]

transmigrant (trænzˈmaɪɡrənt, ˈtrænzmɪɡrənt) *n* **1** an emigrant on the way to the country of immigration ▷ *adj* **2** passing through from one place or stage to another

transmigrate (ˌtrænzmaɪˈɡreɪt) *vb (intr)* **1** to move from one place, state, or stage to another **2** (of souls) to pass from one body into another at death > ˌtransmi'gration *n* > ˌtransmi'grational *adj* > **trans'migrative** *adj* > ˌtransmi'grator *n* > **trans'migratory** *adj*

transmissible spongiform encephalopathy *n* the full name for **TSE**

transmission (trænzˈmɪʃən) *n* **1** the act or process of transmitting **2** something that is transmitted **3** the extent to which a body or medium transmits light, sound, or some other form of energy **4** the transference of motive force or power **5** a system of shafts, gears, torque converters, etc, that transmits power, esp the arrangement of such parts that transmits the power of the engine to the driving wheels of a motor vehicle **6** the act or process of sending a message, picture, or other information from one location to one or more other locations by means of radio waves, electrical signals, light signals, etc **7** a radio or television broadcast [c17 from Latin *transmissiō* a sending across; see TRANSMIT] > **trans'missible** *adj* > **trans'missi'bility** *n* > **trans'missive** *adj* > **trans'missively** *adv* > **trans'missiveness** *n*

transmission density *n physics* a measure of the extent to which a substance transmits light or other electromagnetic radiation, equal to the logarithm to base ten of the reciprocal of the

transmittance. Symbol: τ Former name: **optical density**

transmission line *n* a coaxial cable, waveguide, or other system of conductors that transfers electrical signals from one location to another. Sometimes shortened to: **line**

transmissivity (ˌtrænzmɪˈsɪvɪtɪ) *n physics* a measure of the ability of a material to transmit radiation, equal to the internal transmittance of the material under conditions in which the path of the radiation has unit length

transmit (trænzˈmɪt) *vb* -mits, -mitting, -mitted **1** *(tr)* to pass or cause to go from one place or person to another **2** *(tr)* to pass on or impart (a disease, infection, etc) **3** *(tr)* to hand down to posterity **4** *(tr; usually passive)* to pass (an inheritable characteristic) from parent to offspring **5** to allow the passage of (particles, energy, etc): *radio waves are transmitted* **6 a** to send out (signals) by means of radio waves or along a transmission line **b** to broadcast (a radio or television programme) **7** *(tr)* to transfer (a force, motion, power, etc) from one part of a mechanical system to another [c14 from Latin *transmittere* to send across, from TRANS- + *mittere* to send] > **trans'mittable** *or* **trans'mittible** *adj* > **trans'mittal** *n*

transmittance (trænzˈmɪtᵊns) *n* **1** the act of transmitting **2** Also called: **transmission factor** *physics* a measure of the ability of anything to transmit radiation, equal to the ratio of the transmitted flux to the incident flux; the reciprocal of the opacity. For a plate of material the ratio of the flux leaving the entry surface to that reaching the exit surface is the internal transmittance. Symbol: τ Compare **reflectance, absorptance**

transmittancy (trænzˈmɪtᵊnsɪ) *n physics* a measure of the extent to which a solution transmits radiation. It is equal to the ratio of the transmittance of the solution to the transmittance of a pure solvent of the same dimensions

transmitter (trænzˈmɪtə) *n* **1** a person or thing that transmits **2** the equipment used for generating and amplifying a radio-frequency carrier, modulating the carrier with information, and feeding it to an aerial for transmission **3** the microphone in a telephone that converts sound waves into audio-frequency electrical signals **4** a device that converts mechanical movements into coded electrical signals transmitted along a telegraph circuit **5** *physiol* short for **neurotransmitter**

transmittivity (ˌtrænzmɪˈtɪvɪtɪ) *n physics* the transmittance of unit thickness of a substance, neglecting any scattering effects

transmogrify (trænzˈmɒɡrɪˌfaɪ) *vb* -fies, -fying, -fied *(tr)* *jocular* to change or transform into a different shape, esp a grotesque or bizarre one [c17 of unknown origin] > ˌtransˌmogrifi'cation *n*

transmontane (trænzˈmɒnteɪn) *adj, n* another word for **tramontane**

transmundane (trænzˈmʌndeɪn) *adj* beyond this world or worldly considerations

transmutation (ˌtrænzmjuːˈteɪʃən) *n* **1** the act or an instance of transmuting **2** the change of one chemical element into another by a nuclear reaction **3** the attempted conversion, by alchemists, of base metals into gold or silver > ˌtransmu'tational *or* **trans'mutative** *adj* > ˌtransmu'tationist *n, adj*

transmute (trænzˈmjuːt) *vb (tr)* **1** to change the form, character, or substance of **2** to alter (an element, metal, etc) by alchemy [c15 via Old French from Latin *transmūtāre* to shift, from TRANS- + *mūtāre* to change] > ˌtrans'muta'bility *n* > **trans'mutable** *adj* > **trans'mutably** *adv* > **trans'muter** *n*

transnational (trænzˈnæʃənəl) *adj* extending beyond the boundaries, interests, etc, of a single nation

Transnet (ˈtrænzˌnɛt) *n South African* the official

rail and transport service in South Africa

Trans-New Guinea phylum *n* the largest grouping of the non-Austronesian languages of Papua and New Guinea and the surrounding regions. Older term: **New Guinea Macrophylum**

transoceanic (ˈtrænzˌəʊʃɪˈænɪk) *adj* **1** on or from the other side of an ocean **2** crossing an ocean

transom (ˈtrænsəm) *n* **1** Also called: **traverse** a horizontal member across a window. Compare **mullion 2** a horizontal member that separates a door from a window over it **3** the usual US name for **fanlight 4** *nautical* **a** a surface forming the stern of a vessel, either vertical or canted either forwards (**reverse transom**) or aft at the upper side **b** any of several transverse beams used for strengthening the stern of a vessel [c14 earlier *traversayn*, from Old French *traversin*, from TRAVERSE] > **'transomed** *adj*

transonic (trænˈsɒnɪk) *adj* of or relating to conditions when travelling at or near the speed of sound

transonic barrier *n* another name for **sound barrier**

transpacific (ˌtrænzpəˈsɪfɪk) *adj* **1** crossing the Pacific **2** on or from the other side of the Pacific

transpadane (ˈtrænzpəˌdeɪn, trænsˈpeɪdeɪn) *adj* (*prenominal*) on or from the far (or north) side of the River Po, as viewed from Rome. Compare **cispadane** [c17 from Latin *Transpadānus*, from TRANS- + *Padus* the River Po]

transparency (trænsˈpærənsɪ, -ˈpɛər-) *n, pl* -cies **1** Also called: **transparence** the state of being transparent **2** Also called: **slide** a positive photograph on a transparent base, usually mounted in a frame or between glass plates. It can be viewed by means of a slide projector

transparent (trænsˈpærᵊnt, -ˈpɛər-) *adj* **1** permitting the uninterrupted passage of light; clear: *a window is transparent* **2** easy to see through, understand, or recognize; obvious **3** (of a substance or object) permitting the free passage of electromagnetic radiation: *a substance that is transparent to X-rays* **4** candid, open, or frank [c15 from Medieval Latin *transpārēre* to show through, from Latin TRANS- + *pārēre* to appear] > **trans'parently** *adv* > **trans'parentness** *n*

transparent context *n philosophy, logic* an expression in which any term may be replaced by another with the same reference without changing its truth-value. Compare **opaque context**

transpicuous (trænˈspɪkjʊəs) *adj* a less common word for **transparent** [c17 from Medieval Latin *transpicuus*, from Latin *transpicere* to look through, from TRANS- + *specere* to look] > **tran'spicuously** *adv*

transpierce (trænsˈpɪəs) *vb (tr)* to pierce through

transpire (trænˈspaɪə) *vb* **1** *(intr)* to come to light; be known **2** *(intr)* *informal* to happen or occur **3** *physiol* to give off or exhale (water or vapour) through the skin, a mucous membrane, etc **4** (of plants) to lose (water in the form of water vapour), esp through the stomata of the leaves [c16 from Medieval Latin *transpīrāre*, from Latin TRANS- + *spīrāre* to breathe] > **tran'spirable** *adj* > **transpiration** (ˌtrænspəˈreɪʃən) *n* > **tran'spiratory** *adj*

USAGE It is often maintained that *transpire* should not be used to mean happen or occur, as in *the event transpired late in the evening*, and that the word is properly used to mean become known, as in *it transpired later that the thief had been caught*. The word is, however, widely used in the former sense, esp in spoken English

transplant *vb* (trænsˈplɑːnt) **1** *(tr)* to remove or transfer (esp a plant) from one place to another **2** *(intr)* to be capable of being transplanted **3** *surgery* to transfer (an organ or tissue) from one part of the body to another or from one person or animal to another during a grafting or transplant operation ▷ *n* (ˈtrænsˌplɑːnt) **4** *surgery* **a** the procedure involved in such a transfer **b** the organ or tissue transplanted > **trans'plantable** *adj* > **,transplan'tation** *n* > **trans'planter** *n*

transpolar (trænz'pəʊlə) *adj* crossing a polar region

transponder *or* **transpondor** (træn'spɒndə) *n* **1** a type of radio or radar transmitter-receiver that transmits signals automatically when it receives predetermined signals **2** the receiver and transmitter in a communications or broadcast satellite, relaying received signals back to earth [C20 from TRANSMITTER + RESPONDER]

transpontine (trænz'pɒntaɪn) *adj* **1** on or from the far side of a bridge **2** *archaic* on or from the south side of the Thames in London [C19 TRANS- + -pontine, from Latin *pōns* bridge]

transport *vb* (træns'pɔːt) (*tr*) **1** to carry or cause to go from one place to another, esp over some distance **2** to deport or exile to a penal colony **3** (*usually passive*) to have a strong emotional effect on ▷ *n* ('træns,pɔːt) **4 a** the business or system of transporting goods or people **b** (*as modifier*): *a modernized transport system* **5** *Brit* freight vehicles generally **6 a** a vehicle used to transport goods or people, esp lorries or ships used to convey troops **b** (*as modifier*): *a transport plane* **7** the act of transporting or the state of being transported **8** ecstasy, rapture, or any powerful emotion **9** a convict sentenced to be transported [C14 from Latin *transportāre*, from TRANS- + *portāre* to carry] > **trans'portable** *adj* > **,transporta'bility** *n* > **trans'porter** *n* > **trans'portive** *adj*

transportation (,trænspɔː'teɪʃən) *n* **1** a means or system of transporting **2** the act of transporting or the state of being transported **3** (*esp formerly*) deportation to a penal colony **4** *chiefly US* a ticket or fare

transport café *n Brit* an inexpensive eating place on a main route, used mainly by long-distance lorry drivers

transporter bridge *n* a bridge consisting of a movable platform suspended from cables, for transporting vehicles, etc, across a body of water

transpose (træns'pəʊz) *vb* **1** (*tr*) to alter the positions of; interchange, as words in a sentence; put into a different order **2** *music* **a** to play (notes, music, etc) in a different key from that originally intended **b** to move (a note or series of notes) upwards or downwards in pitch **3** (*tr*) *maths* to move (a term) from one side of an equation to the other with a corresponding reversal in sign ▷ *n* **4** *maths* the matrix resulting from interchanging the rows and columns of a given matrix [C14 from Old French *transposer*, from Latin *transpōnere* to remove, from TRANS- + *pōnere* to place] > **trans'posable** *adj* > **,transpoṣa'bility** *n* > **trans'posal** *n* > **trans'poser** *n*

transposing instrument *n* a musical instrument, esp a horn or clarinet, pitched in a key other than C major, but whose music is written down as if its basic scale were C major. A piece of music in the key of F intended to be played on a horn pitched in F is therefore written down a fourth lower than an ordinary part in that key and has the same key signature as a part written in C

transposition (,trænspə'zɪʃən) *n* **1** the act of transposing or the state of being transposed **2** something transposed > **,transpo'sitional** *or* **transpositive** (træns'pɒzɪtɪv) *adj*

transposon (træns'pəʊzɒn) *n genetics* a genetic element that can move from one site in a chromosome to another in the same or a different chromosome and thus alter the genetic constitution of the organism [C20 TRANSPOS(E) + -ON]

transputer (trænz'pjuːtə) *n computing* a type of fast powerful microchip that is the equivalent of a 32-bit microprocessor with its own RAM facility [C20 from TRANS(ISTOR) + (COM)PUTER]

transsexual *or* **transexual** (trænz'sɛksjʊəl) *n* **1** a person who permanently acts the part of and completely identifies with the opposite sex **2** a person who has undergone medical and surgical procedures to alter external sexual characteristics to those of the opposite sex

transsexualism *or* **transexualism** (trænz'sɛksjʊə,lɪzəm) *n* a strong desire to change sex

transship (træns'ʃɪp) *or* **tranship** *vb* -ships, -shipping, -shipped to transfer or be transferred from one vessel or vehicle to another > **trans'shipment** *or* **tran'shipment** *n*

Trans-Siberian Railway *n* a railway in S Russia, extending from Moscow to Vladivostok on the Pacific: constructed between 1891 and 1916, making possible the settlement and industrialization of sparsely inhabited regions. Length: 9335 km (5800 miles)

transubstantiate (,trænsəb'stænʃɪ,eɪt) *vb* **1** (*intr*) *RC theol* (of the Eucharistic bread and wine) to undergo transubstantiation **2** (*tr*) to change (one substance) into another; transmute [C16 from Medieval Latin *transsubstantiāre*, from Latin TRANS- + *substantia* SUBSTANCE] > **,transub'stantial** *adj* > **,transub'stantially** *adv*

transubstantiation (,trænsəb,stænʃɪ'eɪʃən) *n* **1** (*esp in Roman Catholic theology*) **a** the doctrine that the whole substance of the bread and wine changes into the substance of the body and blood of Christ when consecrated in the Eucharist **b** the mystical process by which this is believed to take place during consecration. Compare **consubstantiation 2** a substantial change; transmutation > **,transub'stanti'ationist** *n*

transudate ('trænsʊ,deɪt) *n physiol* any fluid without a high protein content that passes through a membrane, esp through the wall of a capillary. Compare **exudate** (sense 2) **2** anything that has been transuded

transude (træn'sjuːd) *vb* (of a fluid) to ooze or pass through interstices, pores, or small holes [C17 from New Latin *transūdāre*, from Latin TRANS- + *sūdāre* to sweat] > **transudation** (,trænsjʊ'deɪʃən) *n* > **tran'sudatory** *adj*

transuranic (,trænzjʊ'rænɪk), **transuranian** (,trænzjʊ'reɪnɪən) *or* **transuranium** (trænzjʊ'reɪnɪəm) *adj* **1** (of an element) having an atomic number greater than that of uranium **2** of, relating to, or having the behaviour of transuranic elements [C20 from TRANS- + *uranic*, from URANIUM]

Transvaal (trænz'vɑːl) *n* former province of NE South Africa: colonized by the Boers after the Great Trek (1836); became a British colony in 1902; joined South Africa in 1910; replaced in 1994 for administrative purposes by a new system of provinces (Eastern Transvaal (later Mpumalanga), Northern Transvaal (later Limpopo), Gauteng, and North West province. Capital: Pretoria

Transvaalian (trænz'vɑːlɪən) *adj* of or relating to the former South African province of Transvaal or its inhabitants

transvaginal (,trænzvə'dʒaɪnəl, ,trænz'vædʒɪnəl) *adj* through or via the vagina: *transvaginal ultrasound*

transvalue (trænz'væljuː) *vb* -ues, -uing, -ued (*tr*) to evaluate by a principle that varies from the accepted standards > **trans,valu'ation** *n* > **trans'valuer** *n*

transversal (trænz'vɜːsəl) *n* **1** *geometry* a line intersecting two or more other lines ▷ *adj* **2** a less common word for **transverse** > **trans'versally** *adv*

transverse (trænz'vɜːs) *adj* **1** crossing from side to side; athwart; crossways **2** *geometry* denoting the axis that passes through the foci of a hyperbola **3** (of a flute, etc) held almost at right angles to the player's mouth, so that the breath passes over a hole in the side to create a vibrating air column within the tube of the instrument **4** *astronomy* another word for **tangential** (sense 2) ▷ *n* **5** a transverse piece or object [C16 from Latin *transversus*, from *transvertere* to turn across, from TRANS- + *vertere* to turn] > **trans'versely** *adv* > **trans'verseness** *n*

transverse colon *n anatomy* the part of the large intestine passing transversely in front of the liver and stomach

transverse flute *n* the normal orchestral flute, as opposed to the recorder (or **fipple flute**)

transverse process *n anatomy* either of the projections that arise from either side of a vertebra and provide articulation for the ribs

transverse wave *n* a wave, such as an electromagnetic wave, that is propagated in a direction perpendicular to the direction of displacement of the transmitting field or medium. Compare **longitudinal wave**

transverter (trænz'vɜːtə) *n* a piece of equipment attached to a radio transceiver to enable it to transmit and receive on additional frequencies

transvestite (trænz'vestaɪt) *n* a person who seeks sexual pleasure from wearing clothes that are normally associated with the opposite sex [C19 from German *Transvestit*, from TRANS- + Latin *vestītus* clothed, from *vestīre* to clothe] > **trans'vestism** *or* **trans'vestitism** *n*

Transylvania (,trænsɪl'veɪnɪə) *n* a region of central and NW Romania: belonged to Hungary from the 11th century until 1918; restored to Romania in 1947

Transylvanian Alps (,trænsɪl'veɪnɪən) *pl n* a mountain range in S Romania; a SW extension of the Carpathian Mountains. Highest peak: Mount Negoiu, 2548 m (8360 ft)

trap¹ (træp) *n* **1** a mechanical device or enclosed place or pit in which something, esp an animal, is caught or penned **2** any device or plan for tricking a person or thing into being caught unawares **3** anything resembling a trap or prison **4** a fitting for a pipe in the form of a U-shaped or S-shaped bend that contains standing water to prevent the passage of gases **5** any similar device **6** a device that hurls clay pigeons into the air to be fired at by trapshooters **7** any one of a line of boxlike stalls in which greyhounds are enclosed before the start of a race **8** See **trap door 9** a light two-wheeled carriage **10** a slang word for **mouth 11** *golf* an obstacle or hazard, esp a bunker **12** (*plural*) *jazz slang* percussion instruments **13** (*usually plural*) *Austral obsolete slang* a policeman ▷ *vb* **traps, trapping, trapped 14** (*tr*) to take, catch, or pen in or as if in a trap; entrap **15** (*tr*) to ensnare by trickery; trick **16** (*tr*) to provide (a pipe) with a trap **17** to set traps in (a place), esp for animals [Old English *træppe*; related to Middle Low German *trappe*, Medieval Latin *trappa*] > **'trap,like** *adj*

trap² (træp) *n* **1** an obsolete word for **trappings** (sense 2) ▷ *vb* **traps, trapping, trapped 2** (*tr*; often foll by *out*) to dress or adorn. ▷ See also **traps** [C11 probably from Old French *drap* cloth]

trap³ (træp) *or* **traprock** *n* **1** any fine-grained often columnar dark igneous rock, esp basalt **2** any rock in which oil or gas has accumulated [C18 from Swedish *trappa* stair (from its steplike formation); see TRAP¹]

trapan (trə'pæn) *vb* -pans, -panning, -panned, *n* a variant spelling of **trepan** (sense 2) > **tra'panner** *n*

Trapani (Italian 'traːpani) *n* a port in S Italy, in NW Sicily: Carthaginian naval base, ceded to the Romans after the First Punic War. Pop: 68 346 (2001)

trap door *n* **1** a door or flap flush with and covering an opening, esp in a ceiling **2** the opening so covered

trap-door spider *n* any of various spiders of the family *Ctenizidae* that construct a silk-lined hole in the ground closed by a hinged door of earth and silk

trapes (treɪps) *vb, n* a less common spelling of **traipse**

trapeze (trə'piːz) *n* **1** a free-swinging bar attached to two ropes, used by circus acrobats, etc **2** a sling like a bosun's chair at one end of a line attached to the masthead of a light racing sailing boat, used in sitting out [C19 from French *trapèze*, from New Latin; see TRAPEZIUM]

trapeziform (trə'piːzɪˌfɔːm) *adj rare* shaped like a trapezium: *a trapeziform part*

trapezium (trə'piːzɪəm) *n, pl* **-ziums** *or* **-zia** (-zɪə) **1** *chiefly Brit* a quadrilateral having two parallel sides of unequal length. Usual US and Canadian name: **trapezoid** **2** *Now chiefly US and Canadian* a quadrilateral having neither pair of sides parallel **3** a small bone of the wrist near the base of the thumb [C16 via Late Latin from Greek *trapezion*, from *trapeza* table] > **tra'pezial** *adj*

trapezius (trə'piːzɪəs) *n, pl* **-uses** either of two flat triangular muscles, one covering each side of the back and shoulders, that rotate the shoulder blades [C18 from New Latin *trapezius (musculus)* trapezium-shaped (muscle)]

trapezohedron (trəˌpiːzəʊ'hiːdrən) *n, pl* **-drons** *or* **-dra** (-drə) *crystallog* a crystal form in which all the crystal's faces are trapeziums [C19 from *trapezo-* combining form of TRAPEZIUM + -HEDRON, on the model of TETRAHEDRON] > **traˌpezo'hedral** *adj*

trapezoid ('træpɪˌzɔɪd) *n* **1** a quadrilateral having neither pair of sides parallel **2** *US and Canadian* a quadrilateral having two parallel sides of unequal length. Also called (Brit, Austral, NZ, and South African): **trapezium** **3** a small bone of the wrist near the base of the index finger [C18 from New Latin *trapezoidēs*, from Late Greek *trapezoeidēs* trapezium-shaped, from *trapeza* table]

trapezoid rule *n* a rule for estimating the area of an irregular figure, by dividing it into parallel strips of equal width, each strip being a trapezium. It can also be adapted to obtaining an approximate value of a definite integral

trappean ('træpɪən, trə'piən) *adj rare* of, relating to, or consisting of igneous rock, esp a basalt [C19 from TRAP[3]]

trapper ('træpə) *n* a person who traps animals, esp for their furs or skins

trappings ('træpɪŋz) *pl n* **1** the accessories and adornments that characterize or symbolize a condition, office, etc: *the visible trappings of success* **2** ceremonial harness for a horse or other animal, including bridles, saddles, etc [C16 from TRAP[2]]

Trappist ('træpɪst) *n* **a** a member of a branch of the Cistercian order of Christian monks, the Reformed Cistercians of the Strict Observance which originated at La Trappe in France in 1664. They are noted for their rule of silence **b** (*as modifier*): *a Trappist monk*

traprock ('træpˌrɒk) *n* another name for **trap[3]**

traps (træps) *pl n* belongings; luggage [C19 probably shortened from TRAPPINGS]

trapshooting ('træpʃuːtɪŋ) *n* the sport of shooting at clay pigeons thrown up by a trap > **'trapˌshooter** *n*

trapunto (trə'pʊntəʊ) *n, pl* **-tos** a type of quilting that is only partly padded in a design [Italian, from *trapungere* to embroider, from *pungere* to prick (from Latin)]

trash[1] (træʃ) *n* **1** foolish ideas or talk; nonsense **2** *chiefly US and Canadian* useless or unwanted matter or objects **3** a literary or artistic production of poor quality **4** *chiefly US and Canadian* a poor or worthless person or a group of such people **5** bits that are broken or lopped off, esp the trimmings from trees or plants **6** the dry remains of sugar cane after the juice has been extracted ▷ *vb* **7** to remove the outer leaves and branches from (growing plants, esp sugar cane) **8** *slang* to attack or destroy (someone or something) wilfully or maliciously [C16 of obscure origin; perhaps related to Norwegian *trask*] > **'trashery** *n*

trash[2] (træʃ) *archaic* ▷ *vb* **1** (*tr*) to restrain with or as if with a lead ▷ *n* **2** a lead for a dog [C17 perhaps from obsolete French *tracier* to track, TRACE[1]]

trash can *n* a US name for **dustbin**. Also called: **ash can, garbage can**

trashed (træʃt) *adj informal* drunk

trash farming *n US* cultivation by leaving stubble, etc, on the surface of the soil to serve as a mulch

trashy ('træʃɪ) *adj* **trashier, trashiest** cheap, worthless, or badly made > **'trashily** *adv* > **'trashiness** *n*

Trasimene ('træzɪˌmiːn) *n* **Lake.** a lake in central Italy, in Umbria: the largest lake in central Italy; scene of Hannibal's victory over the Romans in 217 BC. Area: 128 sq km (49 sq miles). Italian name: **Trasimeno** Also called: **Perugia**

trass (træs) *n* a variety of the volcanic rock tuff, used to make a hydraulic cement [from Dutch *tras*, *tarasse*, from Italian *terrazza* worthless earth; see TERRACE]

trattoria (ˌtrætə'rɪə) *n* an Italian restaurant [C19 from Italian, from *trattore* innkeeper, from French *traiteur*, from Old French *tretier* to TREAT]

trauchle ('trɒxᵊl) *Scot* ▷ *n* **1** work or a task that is tiring, monotonous, and lengthy ▷ *vb* **2** (*intr*) to walk or work slowly and wearily [C19 of uncertain origin]

trauchled ('trɒxᵊld) *adj Scot* exhausted by long hard work or concern

trauma ('trɔːmə) *n, pl* **-mata** (-mətə) *or* **-mas** **1** *psychol* a powerful shock that may have long-lasting effects **2** *pathol* any bodily injury or wound [C18 from Greek: a wound] > **traumatic** (trɔː'mætɪk) *adj* > **trau'matically** *adv*

traumatism ('trɔːməˌtɪzəm) *n* **1** any abnormal bodily condition caused by injury, wound, or shock **2** (not in technical usage) another name for **trauma** (sense 2)

traumatize *or* **traumatise** ('trɔːməˌtaɪz) *vb* **1** (*tr*) to wound or injure (the body) **2** to subject or be subjected to mental trauma > **ˌtraumati'zation** *or* **ˌtraumati'sation** *n*

travail ('træveɪl) *literary* ▷ *n* **1** painful or excessive labour or exertion **2** the pangs of childbirth; labour ▷ *vb* **3** (*intr*) to suffer or labour painfully, esp in childbirth [C13 from Old French *travaillier*, from Vulgar Latin *tripaliāre* (unattested) to torture, from Late Latin *trepālium* instrument of torture, from Latin *tripālis* having three stakes, from *trēs* three + *pālus* stake]

Travancore (ˌtrævən'kɔː) *n* a former princely state of S India which joined with Cochin in 1949 to form **Travancore-Cochin**: part of Kerala state since 1956

trave (treɪv) *n* **1** a stout wooden cage in which difficult horses are shod **2** another name for **crossbeam** **3** a bay formed by crossbeams [C15 from Old French *trave* beam, from Latin *trabs*]

travel ('trævᵊl) *vb* **-els, -elling, -elled** *or US* **-els, -eling, -eled** (*mainly intr*) **1** to go, move, or journey from one place to another: *he travels to improve his mind; she travelled across France* **2** (*tr*) to go, move, or journey through or across (an area, region, etc): *he travelled the country* **3** to go, move, or cover a specified or unspecified distance **4** to go from place to place as a salesman: *to travel in textiles* **5** (esp of perishable goods) to withstand a journey **6** (of light, sound, etc) to be transmitted or move: *the sound travelled for miles* **7** to progress or advance **8** *basketball* to take an excessive number of steps while holding the ball **9** (of part of a mechanism) to move in a fixed predetermined path **10** *informal* to move rapidly: *that car certainly travels* **11** (often foll by *with*) *informal* to be in the company (of); associate ▷ *n* **12** **a** the act of travelling **b** (*as modifier*): *a travel brochure.* Related adj: **itinerant** **13** (*usually plural*) a tour or journey **14** the distance moved by a mechanical part, such as the stroke of a piston **15** movement or passage [C14 *travaillen* to make a journey, from Old French *travaillier* to TRAVAIL]

travel agency *or* **bureau** *n* an agency that arranges and negotiates flights, holidays, etc, for travellers > **travel agent** *n*

travelator ('trævəˌleɪtə) *n* a variant spelling of **travolator**

travelled *or US* **traveled** ('trævəld) *adj* having experienced or undergone much travelling: *a travelled urbane epicure*

traveller *or US* **traveler** ('trævələ, 'trævlə) *n* **1** a person who travels, esp habitually **2** See **travelling salesman** **3** (*sometimes capital*) a member of the travelling people **4** a part of a mechanism that moves in a fixed course **5** *nautical* **a** a thimble fitted to slide freely on a rope, spar, or rod **b** the fixed rod on which such a thimble slides **6** *Austral* a swagman

traveller's cheque *n* a cheque in any of various denominations sold for use abroad by a bank, etc, to the bearer, who signs it on purchase and can cash it by signing it again

traveller's joy *n* a ranunculaceous Old World climbing plant, *Clematis vitalba*, having white flowers and heads of feathery plumed fruits. Also called: **old man's beard**

travelling people *or* **folk** *pl n* (*sometimes capitals*) *Brit* Gypsies or other itinerant people: a term used esp by such people of themselves

travelling salesman *n* a salesman who travels within an assigned territory in order to sell merchandise or to solicit orders for the commercial enterprise he represents by direct personal contact with customers and potential customers. Also called: **commercial traveller, traveller**

travelling wave *n* **a** a wave carrying energy away from its source **b** (*as modifier*): *a travelling-wave aerial*

travelling-wave tube *n* an electronic tube in which an electron beam interacts with a distributed high-frequency magnetic field so that energy is transferred from the beam to the field

travelogue *or sometimes US* **travelog** ('trævᵊlɒg) *n* a film, lecture, or brochure on travels and travelling [C20 from TRAVEL + -LOGUE]

travel-sick *adj* nauseated from riding in a moving vehicle > **'travel-ˌsickness** *n*

traverse ('trævɜːs, trə'vɜːs) *vb* **1** to pass or go over or back and forth over (something); cross **2** (*tr*) to go against; oppose; obstruct **3** to move or cause to move sideways or crosswise **4** (*tr*) to extend or reach across **5** to turn (an artillery gun) laterally on its pivot or mount or (of an artillery gun) to turn laterally **6** (*tr*) to look over or examine carefully **7** (*tr*) *law* to deny (an allegation of fact), as in pleading **8** (*intr*) *fencing* to slide one's blade towards an opponent's hilt while applying pressure against his blade **9** *mountaineering* to move across (a face) horizontally **10** (*tr*) *nautical* to brace (a yard) fore and aft ▷ *n* **11** something being or lying across, such as a transom **12** a gallery or loft inside a building that crosses it **13** *maths* another name for **transversal** (sense 1) **14** an obstruction or hindrance **15** *fortifications* a protective bank or other barrier across a trench or rampart **16** a railing, screen, or curtain **17** the act or an instance of traversing or crossing **18** a path or road across **19** *nautical* the zigzag course of a vessel tacking frequently **20** *law* the formal denial of a fact alleged in the opposite party's pleading **21** *surveying* a survey consisting of a series of straight lines, the length of each and the angle between them being measured **22** *mountaineering* a horizontal move across a face ▷ *adj* **23** being or lying across; transverse ▷ *adv* **24** an archaic word for **across** [C14 from Old French *traverser*, from Late Latin *trānsversāre*, from Latin *trānsversus* TRANSVERSE] > **'traversable** *adj* > **tra'versal** *n* > **'traverser** *n*

travertine *or* **travertin** ('trævətɪn) *n* a porous rock consisting of calcium carbonate, used for building. Also called: **calc-sinter** [C18 from Italian *travertino* (influenced by *tra-* TRANS-), from Latin *lapis Tīburtīnus* Tiburtine stone, from *Tībur*s the district around Tibur (now Tivoli)]

travesty ('trævɪstɪ) *n, pl* **-ties** **1** a farcical or grotesque imitation; mockery; parody ▷ *vb* **-ties, -tying, -tied** (*tr*) **2** to make or be a travesty of [C17 from French *travesti* disguised, from *travestir* to disguise, from Italian *travestire*, from *tra-* TRANS- + *vestire* to clothe]

travois (trə'vɔɪ) *n, pl* **-vois** (-'vɔɪz) a sled formerly

t

used by the Plains Indians of North America, consisting of two poles joined by a frame and dragged by an animal [from Canadian French, from French *travail* TRAVE]

travolator *or* **travelator** ('trævə,leɪtə) *n* a moving pavement for transporting pedestrians, as in a shopping precinct or an airport [c20 coined on the model of ESCALATOR]

trawl (trɔ:l) *n* *sea fishing* **1** Also called: **trawl net** a large net, usually in the shape of a sock or bag, drawn at deep levels behind special boats (trawlers) **2** Also called: **trawl line** a long line to which numerous shorter hooked lines are attached, suspended between buoys. See also **setline, trotline** **3** the act of trawling ▷ *vb* **4** *sea fishing* to catch or try to catch (fish) with a trawl net or trawl line **5** *sea fishing* (*tr*) to drag (a trawl net) or suspend (a trawl line) **6** (*intr*; foll by *for*) to seek or gather (something, such as information, or someone, such as a likely appointee) from a wide variety of sources ▷ *n*, *vb* **7** *angling* another word for **troll¹** [c17 from Middle Dutch *traghelen* to drag, from Latin *trāgula* dragnet; see TRAIL]

trawler ('trɔ:lə) *n* **1** a vessel used for trawling **2** a person who trawls

tray (treɪ) *n* **1** a thin flat board or plate of metal, plastic, etc, usually with a raised edge, on which things can be carried **2** a shallow receptacle for papers, etc, sometimes forming a drawer in a cabinet or box [Old English *trieg*; related to Old Swedish *trö* corn measure, Old Norse *treyja* carrier, Greek *driti* tub, German *Trog* TROUGH]

traymobile ('treɪmə,bi:l) *n* *Austral informal* a small table on casters used for conveying food, drink, etc

TRC (in South Africa) *abbreviation for* Truth and Reconciliation Commission, a body established in 1996 to investigate political crimes committed under the apartheid system

treacherous ('trɛtʃərəs) *adj* **1** betraying or likely to betray faith or confidence **2** unstable, unreliable, or dangerous: *treacherous weather; treacherous ground* > '**treacherously** *adv* > '**treacherousness** *n*

treachery ('trɛtʃərɪ) *n*, *pl* **-eries** **1** the act or an instance of wilful betrayal **2** the disposition to betray [c13 from Old French *trecherie*, from *trechier* to cheat; compare TRICK]

treacle ('tri:kᵊl) *n* **1** Also called: **black treacle** *Brit* a dark viscous syrup obtained during the refining of sugar **2** *Brit* another name for **golden syrup** **3** anything sweet and cloying **4** *obsolete* any of various preparations used as an antidote to poisoning [c14 from Old French *triacle*, from Latin *thēriaca* antidote to poison] > '**treacly** *adj* > '**treacliness** *n*

treacle mustard *n* a N temperate cruciferous annual plant, *Erysimum cheiranthoides*, having small yellow flowers. It is a common weed in cultivated ground [c16 so called because of its alleged medicinal properties. See TREACLE]

tread (trɛd) *vb* **treads, treading, trod, trodden** *or* **trod** **1** to walk or trample in, on, over, or across (something) **2** (when *intr*, foll by *on*) to crush or squash by or as if by treading: *to tread grapes; to tread on a spider* **3** (*intr*; sometimes foll by *on*) to subdue or repress, as by doing injury (to): *to tread on one's inferiors* **4** (*tr*) to do by walking or dancing: *to tread a measure* **5** (*tr*) (of a male bird) to copulate with (a female bird) **6** **tread lightly** to proceed with delicacy or tact **7** **tread on (someone's) toes** to offend or insult (someone), esp by infringing on his sphere of action, etc **8** **tread water** to stay afloat in an upright position by moving the legs in a walking motion ▷ *n* **9** a manner or style of walking, dancing, etc: *a light tread* **10** the act of treading **11** the top surface of a step in a staircase **12** the outer part of a tyre or wheel that makes contact with the road, esp the grooved surface of a pneumatic tyre **13** the part of a rail that wheels touch **14** the part of a shoe that is generally in contact with the ground **15** *vet science* an injury to a horse's foot caused by the opposite foot, or the foot of another horse **16** a rare word for **footprint** [Old English *tredan*; related to Old Norse *trotha* , Old High German *tretan*, Swedish *träda*] > '**treader** *n*

treadle ('trɛdᵊl) *n* **1** **a** a rocking lever operated by the foot to drive a machine **b** (*as modifier*): *a treadle sewing machine* ▷ *vb* **2** to work (a machine) with a treadle [Old English *tredel*, from *trǣde* something firm, from *tredan* to TREAD] > '**treadler** *n*

treadmill ('trɛd,mɪl) *n* **1** Also called: **treadwheel** (formerly) an apparatus used to produce rotation, in which the weight of men or animals climbing steps on or around the periphery of a cylinder or wheel caused it to turn **2** a dreary round or routine **3** an exercise machine that consists of a continuous moving belt on which to walk or jog

treas. *abbreviation for* **1** treasurer **2** treasury

treason ('tri:zᵊn) *n* **1** violation or betrayal of the allegiance that a person owes his sovereign or his country, esp by attempting to overthrow the government; high treason **2** any treachery or betrayal [c13 from Old French *traïson*, from Latin *trāditiō* a handing over; see TRADITION, TRADITOR] > '**treasonable** *or* '**treasonous** *adj* > '**treasonableness** *n* > '**treasonably** *adv*

treasure ('trɛʒə) *n* **1** wealth and riches, usually hoarded, esp in the form of money, precious metals, or gems **2** a thing or person that is highly prized or valued ▷ *vb* (*tr*) **3** to prize highly as valuable, rare, or costly **4** to store up and save; hoard [c12 from Old French *tresor*, from Latin *thēsaurus* anything hoarded, from Greek *thēsauros*] > '**treasurable** *adj* > '**treasureless** *adj*

treasure flower *n* another name for **gazania**

treasure hunt *n* a game in which players act upon successive clues and are eventually directed to a prize

treasurer ('trɛʒərə) *n* a person appointed to look after the funds of a society, company, city, or other governing body > '**treasurership** *n*

Treasurer ('trɛʒərə) *n* (in the Commonwealth of Australia and each of the Australian states) the minister of finance

treasure-trove *n* (in Britain) **1** *law* valuable articles, such as coins, bullion, etc, found hidden in the earth or elsewhere and of unknown ownership. Such articles become the property of the Crown, which compensates the finder if the treasure is declared. In 1996 treasure was defined as any item over 300 years old and containing more than 5% precious metal **2** anything similarly discovered that is of value [c16 from Anglo-French *tresor trové* treasure found, from Old French *tresor* TREASURE + *trover* to find]

treasury ('trɛʒərɪ) *n*, *pl* **-uries** **1** a storage place for treasure **2** the revenues or funds of a government, private organization, or individual **3** a place where funds are kept and disbursed **4** Also: **treasure house** a collection or source of valuable items: *a treasury of information* [c13 from Old French *tresorie*, from *tresor* TREASURE]

Treasury ('trɛʒərɪ) *n* (in various countries) the government department in charge of finance. In Britain the Treasury is also responsible for economic strategy

Treasury Bench *n* (in Britain) the front bench to the right of the Speaker in the House of Commons, traditionally reserved for members of the Government

Treasury bill *n* a short-term noninterest-bearing obligation issued by the Treasury, payable to bearer and maturing usually in three months, within which it is tradable on a discount basis on the open market

treasury bond *n* a long-term interest-bearing bond issued by the US Treasury

treasury certificate *n* a short-term obligation issued by the US Treasury, maturing in 12 months with interest payable by coupon redemption

treasury note *n* a note issued by a government treasury and generally receivable as legal tender for any debt, esp **a** a medium-term interest-bearing obligation issued by the US Treasury, maturing in from one to five years **b** Also called: **currency note** a note issued by the British Treasury in 1914 to the value of £1 or ten shillings: amalgamated with banknotes in 1928

treasury tag *n* a short piece of cord having metal ends one of which can be slotted inside the other: used for holding papers together or fastening them into a file

treat (tri:t) *n* **1** a celebration, entertainment, gift, or feast given for or to someone and paid for by another **2** any delightful surprise or specially pleasant occasion **3** the act of treating ▷ *vb* **4** (*tr*) to deal with or regard in a certain manner: *she treats school as a joke* **5** (*tr*) to apply treatment to: *to treat a patient for malaria* **6** (*tr*) to subject to a process or to the application of a substance: *to treat photographic film with developer* **7** (often foll by *to*) to provide (someone) (with) as a treat: *he treated the children to a trip to the zoo* **8** (*intr*; usually foll by *of*) *formal* to deal (with), as in writing or speaking **9** (*intr*) *formal* to discuss settlement; negotiate [c13 from Old French *tretier*, from Latin *tractāre* to manage, from *trahere* to drag] > '**treatable** *adj* > '**treater** *n*

treatise ('tri:tɪz) *n* **1** a formal work on a subject, esp one that deals systematically with its principles and conclusions **2** an obsolete word for **narrative** [c14 from Anglo-French *tretiz*, from Old French *tretier* to TREAT]

treatment ('tri:tmənt) *n* **1** the application of medicines, surgery, psychotherapy, etc, to a patient or to a disease or symptom **2** the manner of handling or dealing with a person or thing, as in a literary or artistic work **3** the act, practice, or manner of treating **4** *films* an expansion of a script into sequence form, indicating camera angles, dialogue, etc **5** **the treatment** *slang* the usual manner of dealing with a particular type of person (esp in the phrase **give someone the** (**full**) **treatment**)

treaty ('tri:tɪ) *n*, *pl* **-ties** **1** **a** a formal agreement or contract between two or more states, such as an alliance or trade arrangement **b** the document in which such a contract is written **2** any international agreement **3** any pact or agreement **4** an agreement between two parties concerning the purchase of property at a price privately agreed between them **5** *archaic* negotiation towards an agreement **6** (in Canada) **a** any of the formal agreements between Indian bands and the federal government by which the Indians surrender their land rights in return for various forms of aid **b** (*as modifier*): *treaty Indians; treaty money* **7** an obsolete word for **entreaty** [c14 from Old French *traité*, from Medieval Latin *tractātus* treaty, from Latin: discussion, from *tractāre* to manage; see TREAT] > '**treatyless** *adj*

treaty port *n* (in China, Japan, and Korea during the second half of the 19th and first half of the 20th century) a city, esp a port, in which foreigners, esp Westerners, were allowed by treaty to conduct trade

Trebizond ('trɛbɪ,zɒnd) *n* a variant of **Trabzon**

treble ('trɛbᵊl) *adj* **1** threefold; triple **2** of, relating to, or denoting a soprano voice or part or a high-pitched instrument ▷ *n* **3** treble the amount, size, etc **4** a soprano voice or part or a high-pitched instrument **5** the highest register of a musical instrument **6** **a** the high-frequency response of an audio amplifier, esp in a record player or tape recorder **b** a control knob on such an instrument by means of which the high-frequency gain can be increased or decreased **7** *bell-ringing* the lightest and highest bell in a ring **8** **a** the narrow inner ring on a dartboard **b** a hit on this ring ▷ *vb* **9** to make or become three times as much [c14 from Old French, from Latin *triplus* threefold, TRIPLE] > '**trebleness** *n* > '**trebly** *adv, adj*

treble chance *n* a method of betting in football pools in which the chances of winning are related to the number of draws and the number of home and away wins forecast by the competitor

treble clef *n music* the clef that establishes G a fifth above middle C as being on the second line of the staff. Symbol: 𝄞

Treblinka (trɛˈblɪŋkə) *n* a Nazi concentration camp in central Poland, on the Bug River northeast of Warsaw: chiefly remembered as the place where the Jews of the Warsaw ghetto were put to death

trebuchet (ˈtrɛbjʊˌʃɛt) *or* **trebucket** (ˈtriːbʌkɪt) *n* a large medieval siege engine for hurling missiles consisting of a sling on a pivoted wooden arm set in motion by the fall of a weight [C13 from Old French, from *trebuchier* to stumble, from *tre-* TRANS- + *-buchier*, from *buc* trunk of the body, of Germanic origin; compare Old High German *būh* belly, Old English *buc*]

trecento (treɪˈtʃɛntəʊ) *n* the 14th century, esp with reference to Italian art and literature [C19 shortened from Italian *mille trecento* one thousand three hundred] > **treˈcentist** *n*

tree (triː) *n* **1** any large woody perennial plant with a distinct trunk giving rise to branches or leaves at some distance from the ground. Related adj: **arboreal** **2** any plant that resembles this but has a trunk not made of wood, such as a palm tree **3** a wooden post, bar, etc **4** See **family tree, shoetree, saddletree** **5** *chem* a treelike crystal growth; dendrite **6** **a** a branching diagrammatic representation of something, such as the grammatical structure of a sentence **b** (*as modifier*): *a tree diagram* **7** an archaic word for **gallows** **8** *archaic* the cross on which Christ was crucified **9** **at the top of the tree** in the highest position of a profession, etc **10** **up a tree** *US and Canadian informal* in a difficult situation; trapped or stumped ▷ *vb* **trees, treeing, treed** (*tr*) **11** to drive or force up a tree **12** to shape or stretch (a shoe) on a shoetree [Old English *trēo*; related to Old Frisian, Old Norse *trē*, Old Saxon *trio*, Gothic *triu*, Greek *doru* wood, *drus* tree] > **ˈtreeless** *adj* > **ˈtreelessness** *n* > **ˈtreeˌlike** *adj*

tree-and-branch *adj* denoting a cable television system in which all available programme channels are fed to each subscriber. Compare **switched-star**

tree creeper *n* any small songbird of the family *Certhiidae* of the N hemisphere, having a brown-and-white plumage and slender downward-curving bill. They creep up trees to feed on insects

tree farm *n* an area of forest in which the growth of the trees is managed on a commercial basis

tree fern *n* any of numerous large tropical ferns, mainly of the family *Cyatheaceae*, having a trunklike stem bearing fronds at the top

tree frog *n* **1** any arboreal frog of the family *Hylidae*, chiefly of SE Asia, Australia, and America. They are strong jumpers and have long toes ending in adhesive discs, which assist in climbing **2** any of various other arboreal frogs of different families

tree fuchsia *n* another name for **kohutuhutu**

tree heath *n* another name for **briar**[1] (sense 1)

treehopper (ˈtriːˌhɒpə) *n* any homopterous insect of the family *Membracidae*, which live among trees and other plants and typically have a large hoodlike thoracic process curving backwards over the body

tree-hugger (ˈtriːˌhʌgə) *n informal, derogatory* an environmental campaigner [C20 from the tactic of embracing trees to prevent their being felled]

tree kangaroo *n* any of several arboreal kangaroos of the genus *Dendrolagus*, of New Guinea and N Australia, having hind and forelegs of a similar length and a long tail

tree layer *n* See **layer** (sense 2)

tree line *n* the zone, at high altitudes or high latitudes, beyond which no trees grow. Trees growing between the timberline and the tree line are typically stunted

tree mallow *n* a malvaceous treelike plant, *Lavatera arborea*, of rocky coastal areas of Europe and N Africa, having a woody stem, rounded leaves, and red-purple flowers

treen (ˈtriːən) *adj* **1** made of wood; wooden ▷ *n* **2** another name for **treenware** **3** the art of making treenware [Old English *trēowen*, from *trēow* TREE]

treenail, trenail (ˈtriːneɪl, ˈtrɛnᵊl) *or* **trunnel** (ˈtrʌnᵊl) *n* a dowel used for pinning planks or timbers together

treenware (ˈtriːənˌwɛə) *n* dishes and other household utensils made of wood, as by pioneers in North America [from TREEN + WARE[1]]

tree of heaven *n* another name for **ailanthus**

tree of knowledge of good and evil *n Old Testament* the tree in the Garden of Eden bearing the forbidden fruit that Adam and Eve ate, thus incurring loss of primal innocence (Genesis 2:9; 3:2–7)

tree of life *n* **1** *Old Testament* a tree in the Garden of Eden, the fruit of which had the power of conferring eternal life (Genesis 2:9; 3:22) **2** *New Testament* a tree in the heavenly Jerusalem, for the healing of the nations (Revelation 22:2)

tree ring *n* another name for **annual ring**

tree runner *n Austral* another name for **sitella**

tree shrew *n* any of numerous small arboreal mammals of the family *Tupaiidae* and order *Scandentia*, of SE Asia, having large eyes and resembling squirrels

tree snake *n* any of various slender arboreal colubrid snakes of the genera *Chlorophis* (**green tree snakes**), *Chrysopelea* (**golden tree snakes**), etc

tree sparrow *n* **1** a small European weaverbird, *Passer montanus*, similar to the house sparrow but having a brown head **2** a small North American finch, *Spizella arborea*, having a reddish-brown head, grey underparts, and brown striped back and wings

tree surgery *n* the treatment of damaged trees by filling cavities, applying braces, etc > **tree surgeon** *n*

tree toad *n* a less common name for **tree frog**

tree tomato *n* **1** an arborescent shrub, *Cyphomandra betacea* or *C. crassifolia*, native to South America but widely cultivated, bearing red egg-shaped edible fruit: family *Solanaceae* **2** the fruit of this plant. Also called: **tamarillo**

treeware (ˈtriːˌwɛə) *n* books, magazines, or other reading materials that are printed on paper made from wood pulp as opposed to texts in the form of computer software, CD-ROM, audio books, etc

tref, treif (treɪf) *or* **treifa** (ˈtreɪfə) *adj Judaism* ritually unfit to be eaten; not kosher [Yiddish, from Hebrew *terēphāh*, literally: torn (ie, animal meat torn by beasts), from *tāraf* to tear]

trefoil (ˈtrɛfɔɪl) *n* **1** any of numerous leguminous plants of the temperate genus *Trifolium*, having leaves divided into three leaflets and dense heads of small white, yellow, red, or purple flowers **2** any of various related plants having leaves divided into three leaflets, such as bird's-foot trefoil **3** a leaf having three leaflets **4** *architect* an ornament in the form of three arcs arranged in a circle [C14 from Anglo-French *trifoil*, from Latin *trifolium* three-leaved herb, from TRI- + *folium* leaf] > **ˈtrefoiled** *adj*

trehala (trɪˈhɑːlə) *n* an edible sugary substance obtained from the pupal cocoon of an Asian weevil, *Larinus maculatus* [C19 from Turkish *tīgāla*, from Persian *tighāl*]

trehalose (ˈtriːhəˌləʊs, -ˌləʊz) *n* a white crystalline disaccharide that occurs in yeast and certain fungi. Formula: $C_{12}H_{22}O_{11}$ [C19 from TREHALA]

treillage (ˈtreɪlɪdʒ) *n* latticework; trellis [C17 from French, from Old French *treille* bower, from Latin *trichila*; see -AGE]

trek (trɛk) *n* **1** a long and often difficult journey **2** *South African* a journey or stage of a journey, esp a migration by ox wagon ▷ *vb* **treks, trekking, trekked** **3** (*intr*) to make a trek **4** (*tr*) *South African* (of an ox, etc) to draw (a load) [C19 from Afrikaans, from Middle Dutch *trekken* to travel; related to Old Frisian *trekka*] > **ˈtrekker** *n*

trellis (ˈtrɛlɪs) *n* **1** a structure or pattern of latticework, esp one used to support climbing plants **2** an arch made of latticework ▷ *vb* (*tr*) **3** to interweave (strips of wood, etc) to make a trellis **4** to provide or support with a trellis [C14 from Old French *treliz* fabric of open texture, from Late Latin *trilīcius* woven with three threads, from Latin TRI- + *līcium* thread] > **ˈtrellis-ˌlike** *adj*

trelliswork (ˈtrɛlɪsˌwɜːk) *n* **a** work or patterns of trellis; latticework **b** (*as modifier*): *a trelliswork fence*

trematode (ˈtrɛməˌtəʊd, ˈtriː-) *n* any parasitic flatworm of the class *Trematoda*, which includes the flukes [C19 from New Latin *Trematoda*, from Greek *trēmatōdēs* full of holes, from *trēma* a hole]

tremble (ˈtrɛmbᵊl) *vb* (*intr*) **1** to vibrate with short slight movements; quiver **2** to shake involuntarily, as with cold or fear; shiver **3** to experience fear or anxiety ▷ *n* **4** the act or an instance of trembling [C14 from Old French *trembler*, from Medieval Latin *tremulāre*, from Latin *tremulus* quivering, from *tremere* to quake] > **ˈtrembling** *adj* > **ˈtremblingly** *adv* > **ˈtrembly** *adj*

trembler (ˈtrɛmblə) *n electrical engineering* a device that vibrates to make or break an electrical circuit

trembles (ˈtrɛmbᵊlz) *n* (*functioning as singular*) **1** Also called: **milk sickness** a disease of cattle and sheep characterized by muscular incoordination and tremor, caused by ingestion of white snakeroot or rayless goldenrod **2** a nontechnical name for **Parkinson's disease**

trembling poplar *n* another name for **aspen**

tremendous (trɪˈmɛndəs) *adj* **1** vast; huge **2** *informal* very exciting or unusual **3** *informal* (intensifier): *a tremendous help* **4** *archaic* terrible or dreadful [C17 from Latin *tremendus* terrible, literally: that is to be trembled at, from *tremere* to quake] > **treˈmendously** *adv* > **treˈmendousness** *n*

tremie (ˈtrɛmɪ) *n civil engineering* a large metal hopper and pipe used to distribute freshly mixed concrete over an underwater site. The foot of the pipe is kept below the concrete level, while the upper level of the concrete in the pipe is kept above the water level to prevent the water diluting the concrete [C20 from French, from Italian *tramoggia*, from Latin *trimodia* a three-peck measure]

tremolite (ˈtrɛməˌlaɪt) *n* a white or pale green mineral of the amphibole group consisting of calcium magnesium silicate. When occurring in fibrous habit, it is used as a form of asbestos Formula: $Ca_2(Mg,Fe)_5Si_8O_{22}(OH)_2$ [C18 from *Tremola*, name of Swiss valley where it was found + -ITE]

tremolo (ˈtrɛməˌləʊ) *n, pl* **-los** *music* **1** **a** (in playing the violin, cello, etc) the rapid repetition of a single note produced by a quick back-and-forth movement of the bow **b** the rapid reiteration of two notes usually a third or greater interval apart (**fingered tremolo**). Compare **trill**[1] (sense 1) **2** (in singing) a fluctuation in pitch. Compare **vibrato** **3** a vocal ornament of late renaissance music consisting of the increasingly rapid reiteration of a single note **4** another word for **tremulant** [C19 from Italian: quavering, from Medieval Latin *tremulāre* to TREMBLE]

tremolo arm *n* a metal lever attached to the bridge of an electric guitar, used to vary the pitch of a played note

tremor (ˈtrɛmə) *n* **1** an involuntary shudder or vibration, as from illness, fear, shock, etc **2** any trembling or quivering movement **3** a vibrating or trembling effect, as of sound or light **4** Also called: **earth tremor** a minor earthquake ▷ *vb* (*intr*) **5** to tremble [C14 from Latin: a shaking, from *tremere* to tremble, quake] > **ˈtremorless** *adj* > **ˈtremorous** *adj*

tremulant (ˈtrɛmjʊlənt) *n music* **a** a device on an organ by which the wind stream is made to fluctuate in intensity producing a tremolo effect **b** a device on an electrophonic instrument designed to produce a similar effect [C19 from Medieval Latin *tremulāre* to TREMBLE]

tremulous ('trɛmjʊləs) *adj* **1** vibrating slightly; quavering; trembling: *a tremulous voice* **2** showing or characterized by fear, anxiety, excitement, etc [C17 from Latin *tremulus* quivering, from *tremere* to shake] > 'tremulously *adv* > 'tremulousness *n*

trenail ('triːneɪl, 'trɛn³l) *n* a variant spelling of **treenail**

trench (trɛntʃ) *n* **1** a deep ditch or furrow **2** a ditch dug as a fortification, having a parapet of the excavated earth ▷ *vb* **3** to make a trench in (a place) **4** (*tr*) to fortify with a trench or trenches **5** to slash or be slashed **6** (*intr*; foll by on or *upon*) to encroach or verge ▷ See also **trenches** [C14 from Old French *trenche* something cut, from *trenchier* to cut, from Latin *truncāre* to cut off]

trenchant ('trɛntʃənt) *adj* **1** keen or incisive: *trenchant criticism* **2** vigorous and effective: *a trenchant foreign policy* **3** distinctly defined: *a trenchant outline* **4** *archaic or poetic* sharp: *a trenchant sword* [C14 from Old French *trenchant* cutting, from *trenchier* to cut; see TRENCH] > 'trenchancy *n* > 'trenchantly *adv*

trench coat *n* a belted double-breasted waterproof coat of gabardine, etc, resembling a military officer's coat

trencher[1] ('trɛntʃə) *n* **1** (esp formerly) a wooden board on which food was served or cut **2** Also called: **trencher cap** another name for **mortarboard** (sense 1) [C14 *trenchour* knife, plate for carving on, from Old French *trencheoir*, from *trenchier* to cut; see TRENCH]

trencher[2] ('trɛntʃə) *n* a person or thing that digs trenches

trencherman ('trɛntʃəmən) *n, pl* -men **1** a person who enjoys food; hearty eater **2** *archaic* a person who sponges on others; parasite [C16 from TRENCHER[1] + MAN]

trenches ('trɛntʃɪz) *pl n* a system of excavations used for the protection of troops, esp those (**the Trenches**) used at the front line in World War I

trench fever *n* an acute infectious disease characterized by fever and muscular aches and pains, caused by the microorganism *Rickettsia quintana* and transmitted by the bite of a body louse

trench foot *n* a form of frostbite affecting the feet of persons standing for long periods in cold water

trench knife *n* a double-edged steel knife, often with a guard in the form of a knuckle-duster, designed for close combat [C20 so called because such knives were carried by patrols in the Trenches during World War I]

trench mortar *n* a portable mortar used in trench warfare to shoot projectiles at a high trajectory over a short range

trench mouth *n* a bacterial ulcerative disease characterized by inflammation of the tonsils, gums, etc [C20 so called because it was prevalent in soldiers in the Trenches during World War I]

trench warfare *n* a type of warfare in which opposing armies face each other in entrenched positions

trend (trɛnd) *n* **1** general tendency or direction **2** fashion; mode ▷ *vb* **3** (*intr*) to take a certain trend [Old English *trendan* to turn; related to Middle Low German *trenden*]

trendify ('trɛndɪˌfaɪ) *vb* -fies, -fying, -fied (*tr*) to render fashionable; remodel in line with current trends

trendsetter ('trɛndˌsɛtə) *n* a person or thing that creates, or may create, a new fashion > 'trendˌsetting *adj*

trendy ('trɛndɪ) *Brit informal often derogatory* ▷ *adj* trendier, trendiest **1** consciously fashionable ▷ *n, pl* trendies **2** a trendy person > 'trendily *adv* > 'trendiness *n*

Trengganu *or* **Terengganu** (trɛŋˈɡɑːnuː, tɛrɛŋ-) *n* a state of E Peninsular Malaysia, on the South China Sea: under Thai suzerainty until becoming a British protectorate in 1909; joined the Federation of Malaya in 1948; an isolated forested region; mainly agricultural. Capital: Kuala Trengganu. Pop: 898 825 (2000). Area: 13 020 sq km (5027 sq miles)

Trent (trɛnt) *n* **1** a river in central England, rising in Staffordshire and flowing generally northeast into the Humber: the chief river of the Midlands. Length: 270 km (170 miles) **2** Also: **Trient** the German name for **Trento**

trente et quarante (*French* trɑ̃t e karɑ̃t) *n* another name for **rouge et noir** [C17 French, literally: thirty and forty; referring to the rule that forty is the maximum number that may be dealt and the winning colour is the one closest to thirty-one]

Trentino-Alto Adige (trɛnˈtiːnəʊˈɑːltəʊ, ˈɑːdɪˌdʒeɪ) *n* a region of N Italy: consists of the part of the Tyrol south of the Brenner Pass, ceded by Austria after World War I. Pop: 950 495 (2003 est). Area: 13 613 sq km (5256 sq miles). Former name (until 1947): Venezia Tridentina

Trento (*Italian* 'trɛnto) *n* a city in N Italy, in Trentino-Alto Adige region on the Adige River: Roman military base; seat of the Council of Trent (1545-1563). Pop: 104 946 (2001). Latin name: Tridentum German name: Trent

Trenton ('trɛntən) *n* a city in W New Jersey, capital of the state, on the Delaware River: settled by English Quakers in 1679; scene of the defeat of the British by Washington (1776) during the War of American Independence. Pop: 85 314 (2003 est)

trepan[1] (trɪˈpæn) *n* **1** *surgery* an instrument resembling a carpenter's brace and bit formerly used to remove circular sections of bone (esp from the skull). Compare **trephine 2** a tool for cutting out circular blanks or for making grooves around a fixed centre **3** *a* the operation of cutting a hole with such a tool **b** the hole so produced ▷ *vb* -pans, -panning, -panned (*tr*) **4** to cut (a hole or groove) with a trepan **5** *surgery* another word for **trephine** [C14 from Medieval Latin *trepanum* rotary saw, from Greek *trupanon* auger, from *trupan* to bore, from *trupa* a hole] > trepanation (ˌtrɛpəˈneɪʃən) *n* > treˈpanner *n*

trepan[2] (trɪˈpæn), **trapan** (trəˈpæn) *archaic* ▷ *vb* -pans, -panning, -panned (*tr*) **1** to entice, ensnare, or entrap **2** to swindle or cheat ▷ *n* **3** a person or thing that traps [C17 of uncertain origin]

trepang (trɪˈpæŋ) *n* any of various large sea cucumbers of tropical Oriental seas, the body walls of which are used as food by the Japanese and Chinese. Also called: **bêche-de-mer** [C18 from Malay *tĕripang*]

trephine (trɪˈfiːn) *n* **1** a surgical sawlike instrument for removing circular sections of bone, esp from the skull ▷ *vb* **2** (*tr*) to remove a circular section of bone from (esp the skull) ▷ Also called: **trepan** [C17 from French *tréphine*, from obsolete English *trefine* TREPAN[1], allegedly from Latin *trēs fīnēs* literally: three ends; influenced also by English *trepane* TREPAN[1]] > trephination (ˌtrɛfɪˈneɪʃən) *n*

trepidation (ˌtrɛpɪˈdeɪʃən) *n* **1** a state of fear or anxiety **2** a condition of quaking or palpitation, esp one caused by anxiety [C17 from Latin *trepidātiō*, from *trepidāre* to be in a state of alarm; compare INTREPID]

treponema (ˌtrɛpəˈniːmə) *or* **treponeme** ('trɛpəniːm) *n, pl* -nemas, -nemata (-ˈniːmətə) *or* -nemes any anaerobic spirochaete bacterium of the genus *Treponema*, such as *T. pallidum* which causes syphilis [C19 from New Latin, from Greek *trepein* to turn + *nēma* thread] > treponematous (ˌtrɛpəˈnɛmətəs) *adj*

trespass ('trɛspəs) *vb* (*intr*) **1** (often foll by on or upon) to go or intrude (on the property, privacy, or preserves of another) with no right or permission **2** *law* to commit trespass, esp to enter wrongfully upon land belonging to another **3** *archaic* (often foll by against) to sin or transgress ▷ *n* **4** *law* **a** any unlawful act committed with force or violence, actual or implied, which causes injury to another person, his property, or his rights **b** a wrongful entry upon another's land **c** an action to recover damages for such injury or wrongful entry **5** an intrusion on another's privacy or preserves **6** a sin or offence [C13 from Old French *trespas* a passage, from *trespasser* to pass through, from *tres-* TRANS- + *passer*, ultimately from Latin *passus* a PACE[1]] > 'trespasser *n*

tress (trɛs) *n* **1** (*often plural*) a lock of hair, esp a long lock of woman's hair **2** a plait or braid of hair ▷ *vb* (*tr*) **3** to arrange in tresses [C13 from Old French *trece*, of uncertain origin] > 'tressy *adj*

tressed (trɛst) *adj* (*in combination*) having a tress or tresses as specified: *gold-tressed; long-tressed*

tressure ('trɛʃə, 'trɛsjʊə) *n* *heraldry* a narrow inner border on a shield, usually decorated with fleurs-de-lys [C14 from Old French *tressour*, from *trecier* to plait, from *trece* TRESS] > 'tressured *adj*

trestle ('trɛs³l) *n* **1** a framework in the form of a horizontal member supported at each end by a pair of splayed legs, used to carry scaffold boards, a table top, etc **2 a** a braced structural tower-like framework of timber, metal, or reinforced concrete that is used to support a bridge or ropeway **b** a bridge constructed of such frameworks [C14 from Old French *trestel*, ultimately from Latin *trānstrum* TRANSOM]

trestletree ('trɛs³lˌtriː) *n* *nautical* either of a pair of fore-and-aft timbers fixed horizontally on opposite sides of a lower masthead to support an upper mast

trestlework ('trɛs³lˌwɜːk) *n* an arrangement of trestles, esp one that supports or makes a bridge

tret (trɛt) *n* *commerce* (formerly) an allowance according to weight granted to purchasers for waste due to transportation. It was calculated after deduction for tare [C15 from Old French *trait* pull, tilt of the scale; see TRAIT]

trevally (trɪˈvælɪ) *n, pl* -lies any of various marine food and game fishes of the genus *Caranx*: family Carangidae. Also called (NZ): araara [C19 probably alteration of *cavally*; see CAVALLA]

Trèves (trɛv) *n* the French name for **Trier**

Treviso (*Italian* treˈviːzo) *n* a city in N Italy, in Veneto region: agricultural market centre. Pop: 80 144 (2001)

Trevor Nunn (ˌtrɛvəˈnʌn) *n* *Brit informal* a university degree graded 2:1 (second class upper bracket). Often shortened to: Trevor [C20 from rhyming slang, after *Trevor Nunn* (born 1940), British theatre director]

trews (truːz) *pl n* *chiefly Brit* close-fitting trousers, esp of tartan cloth and worn by certain Scottish soldiers [C16 from Scottish Gaelic *triubhas*, from Old French *trebus*; see TROUSERS]

trey (treɪ) *n* any card or dice throw with three spots [C14 from Old French *treis* three, from Latin *trēs*]

TRH *abbreviation for* Their Royal Highnesses

tri- *prefix* **1** three or thrice: *triaxial; trigon; trisect* **2** occurring every three: *trimonthly* [from Latin *trēs*, Greek *treis*]

triable ('traɪəb³l) *adj* **1 a** liable to be tried judicially **b** subject to examination or determination by a court of law **2** *rare* able to be tested > 'triableness *n*

triacid (traɪˈæsɪd) *adj* (of a base) capable of reacting with three molecules of a monobasic acid

triad ('traɪæd) *n* **1** a group of three; trio **2** *chem* an atom, element, group, or ion that has a valency of three **3** *music* a three-note chord consisting of a note and the third and fifth above it **4** an aphoristic literary form used in medieval Welsh and Irish literature **5** the US strategic nuclear force, consisting of intercontinental ballistic missiles, submarine-launched ballistic missiles, and bombers [C16 from Late Latin *trias*, from Greek; related to Greek *treis* three] > tri'adic *adj* > 'triadism *n*

Triad ('traɪæd) *n* any of several Chinese secret societies, esp one involved in criminal activities, such as drug trafficking

triage (ˈtriːˌɑːʒ, ˌtriːˈɑːʒ, ˈtraɪ-) *n* **1** (in a hospital) the principle or practice of sorting emergency patients into categories of priority for treatment **2** the principle or practice of sorting casualties in battle or disaster into categories of priority for treatment **3** the principle or practice of allocating limited resources, as of food or foreign aid, on a basis of expediency rather than according to moral principles or the needs of the recipients [C18 (in the sense: sorting (goods) according to quality): from French; see TRY, -AGE]

trial[1] (ˈtraɪəl, traɪl) *n* **1** **a** the act or an instance of trying or proving; test or experiment **b** (*as modifier*): *a trial run* **2** *law* **a** the judicial examination of the issues in a civil or criminal cause by a competent tribunal and the determination of these issues in accordance with the law of the land **b** the determination of an accused person's guilt or innocence after hearing evidence for the prosecution and for the accused and the judicial examination of the issues involved **c** (*as modifier*): *trial proceedings* **3** an effort or attempt to do something: *we had three trials at the climb* **4** trouble or grief **5** an annoying or frustrating person or thing **6** (*often plural*) a competition for individuals: *sheepdog trials* **7** a motorcycling competition in which the skills of the riders are tested over rough ground **8** *ceramics* a piece of sample material used for testing the heat of a kiln and its effects **9** **on trial** **a** undergoing trial, esp before a court of law **b** being tested, as before a commitment to purchase ▷ *vb* **trials, trialling, trialled** (*tr*) **10** to test or make experimental use of (something): *the idea has been trialled in several schools* [C16 from Anglo-French, from *trier* to TRY] > ˈ**trialling** *n*

trial[2] (ˈtraɪəl) *n grammar* **1** a grammatical number occurring in some languages for words in contexts where exactly three of their referents are described or referred to **2** (*modifier*) relating to or inflected for this number [C19 from TRI- + -AL[1]]

trial and error *n* a method of discovery, solving problems, etc, based on practical experiment and experience rather than on theory

trial balance *n book-keeping* a statement of all the debit and credit balances in the ledger of a double-entry system, drawn up to test their equality

trial balloon *n* a tentative action or statement designed to test public opinion on a controversial matter. Compare **ballon d'essai**

trial by battle *or* **trial by combat** *n history* a method of trying an accused person or of settling a dispute by a personal fight between the two parties involved or, in some circumstances, their permitted champions, in the presence of a judge. It was introduced to England after the Norman Conquest and abolished in 1819

trial court *n law* the first court before which the facts of a case are decided

triallist *or* **trialist** (ˈtraɪəlɪst, ˈtraɪlɪst) *n* **1** a person who takes part in a competition, esp a motorcycle trial **2** *sport* a person who takes part in a preliminary match or heat held to determine selection for an event, a team, etc

trial run *n* **1** a test drive in a vehicle to assess its performance **2** a test or rehearsal of something new or untried to assess its effectiveness

trialware (ˈtraɪəlˌwɛə) *n* computer software that can be used free of charge for a limited evaluation period

triangle (ˈtraɪˌæŋɡᵊl) *n* **1** *geometry* a three-sided polygon that can be classified by angle, as in an acute triangle, or by side, as in an equilateral triangle. Sum of interior angles: 180°; area: ½ base × height **2** any object shaped like a triangle **3** any situation involving three parties or points of view. See also **eternal triangle** **4** *music* a percussion instrument consisting of a sonorous metal bar bent into a triangular shape, beaten with a metal stick **5** a group of three [C14 from Latin *triangulum* (noun), from *triangulus* (adjective), from TRI- + *angulus* corner] > ˈ**triˌangled** *adj*

triangle of forces *n physics* a triangle whose sides represent the magnitudes and directions of three forces in equilibrium whose resultant is zero and which are therefore in equilibrium

triangular (traɪˈæŋɡjʊlə) *adj* **1** Also: **trigonal** of, shaped like, or relating to a triangle; having three corners or sides **2** of or involving three participants, pieces, or units **3** *maths* having a base shaped like a triangle > **triangularity** (traɪˌæŋɡjʊˈlærɪtɪ) *n* > **triˈangularly** *adv*

triangulate *vb* (traɪˈæŋɡjʊˌleɪt) (*tr*) **1** **a** to survey by the method of triangulation **b** to calculate trigonometrically **2** to divide into triangles **3** to make triangular ▷ *adj* (traɪˈæŋɡjʊlɪt, -ˌleɪt) **4** marked with or composed of triangles > **triˈangulately** *adv*

triangulation (traɪˌæŋɡjʊˈleɪʃən) *n* **1** a method of surveying in which an area is divided into triangles, one side (the base line) and all angles of which are measured and the lengths of the other lines calculated trigonometrically **2** the network of triangles so formed **3** the fixing of an unknown point, as in navigation, by making it one vertex of a triangle, the other two being known **4** *chess* a key manoeuvre in the endgame in which the king moves thrice in a triangular path to leave the opposing king with the move and at a disadvantage

triangulation station *n* a point used in triangulation as a basis for making maps. Triangulation stations are marked in a number of ways, such as by a tapering stone pillar on a hilltop. Also called (informal): **trig point**, (Austral and NZ) **trig**

Triangulum (traɪˈæŋɡjʊləm) *n, Latin genitive* **Trianguli** (traɪˈæŋɡjʊˌlaɪ) a small triangular constellation in the N hemisphere, close to Perseus and Aries

Triangulum Australe (ɒˈstreɪlɪ) *n, Latin genitive* **Trianguli Australis** (ɒˈstreɪlɪs) a small bright triangular constellation in the S hemisphere, lying between Ara and the Southern Cross, that contains an open star cluster [New Latin: southern triangle]

triarchy (ˈtraɪɑːkɪ) *n, pl* **-chies** **1** government by three people; a triumvirate **2** a country ruled by three people **3** an association of three territories each governed by its own ruler **4** any of the three such territories

Triassic (traɪˈæsɪk) *adj* **1** of, denoting, or formed in the first period of the Mesozoic era that lasted for 42 million years and during which reptiles flourished ▷ *n* **2** **the** Also called: **Trias** the Triassic period or rock system [C19 from Latin *trias* triad, with reference to the three subdivisions]

triathlon (traɪˈæθlɒn) *n* an athletic contest in which each athlete competes in three different events, swimming, cycling, and running [C20 from TRI- + Greek *athlon* contest] > ˌ**triˈathlete** *n*

triatomic (ˌtraɪəˈtɒmɪk) *adj chem* having three atoms in the molecule > ˌ**triaˈtomically** *adv*

triaxial (traɪˈæksɪəl) *adj* having three axes

triazine (ˈtraɪəˌziːn, -zɪn, traɪˈæziːn, -zɪn) *or* **triazin** (ˈtraɪəzɪn, traɪˈæzɪn) *n* **1** any of three azines that contain three nitrogen atoms in their molecules. Formula: $C_3H_3N_3$ **2** any substituted derivative of any of these compounds

triazole (ˈtraɪəˌzɒl, -ˌzəʊl, traɪˈæzɒl, -zəʊl) *n* **1** any of four heterocyclic compounds having a five-membered ring with the formula $C_2H_3N_3$ **2** any substituted derivative of any of these compounds [C19 from TRI- + AZOLE] > **triazolic** (ˌtraɪəˈzɒlɪk) *adj*

tribade (ˈtrɪbəd) *n* a lesbian, esp one who practises tribadism [C17 from Latin *tribas*, from Greek *tribein* to rub] > **tribadic** (trɪˈbædɪk) *adj*

tribadism (ˈtrɪbəˌdɪzəm) *n* a lesbian practice in which one partner lies on top of the other and simulates the male role in heterosexual intercourse

tribal (ˈtraɪbᵊl) *adj* **1** of or denoting a tribe or tribes: *tribal chiefs* **2** displaying loyalty to a tribe, group, or tribal values > ˈ**tribally** *adv*

tribalism (ˈtraɪbəˌlɪzəm) *n* **1** the state of existing as a separate tribe or tribes **2** the customs and beliefs of a tribal society **3** loyalty to a tribe or tribal values > ˈ**tribalist** *n, adj* > ˌ**tribalˈistic** *adj*

tribasic (traɪˈbeɪsɪk) *adj* **1** (of an acid) containing three replaceable hydrogen atoms in the molecule **2** (of a molecule) containing three monovalent basic atoms or groups in the molecule

tribe (traɪb) *n* **1** a social division of a people, esp of a preliterate people, defined in terms of common descent, territory, culture, etc **2** an ethnic or ancestral division of ancient cultures, esp of one of the following **a** any of the three divisions of the ancient Romans, the Latins, Sabines, and Etruscans **b** one of the later political divisions of the Roman people **c** any of the 12 divisions of ancient Israel, each of which was named after and believed to be descended from one of the 12 patriarchs **d** a phyle of ancient Greece **3** *informal often jocular* **a** a large number of persons, animals, etc **b** a specific class or group of persons **c** a family, esp a large one **4** *biology* a taxonomic group that is a subdivision of a subfamily **5** *stockbreeding* a strain of animals descended from a common female ancestor through the female line [C13 from Latin *tribus*; probably related to Latin *trēs* three] > ˈ**tribeless** *adj*

tribesman (ˈtraɪbzmən) *n, pl* **-men** a member of a tribe

triblet (ˈtrɪblɪt) *n* a spindle or mandrel used in making rings, tubes, etc [C17 from French *triboulet*, of unknown origin]

tribo- *combining form* indicating friction: *triboelectricity* [from Greek *tribein* to rub]

triboelectricity (ˌtraɪbəʊɪlɛkˈtrɪsɪtɪ, -ˌiːlɛk-) *n* static electricity generated by friction. Also called: **frictional electricity** > ˌ**triboeˈlectric** *adj*

tribology (traɪˈbɒlədʒɪ) *n* the study of friction, lubrication, and wear between moving surfaces

triboluminescence (ˌtraɪbəʊˌluːmɪˈnɛsəns) *n* luminescence produced by friction, such as the emission of light when certain crystals are crushed > ˌ**triboˌlumiˈnescent** *adj*

tribrach[1] (ˈtraɪbræk, ˈtrɪb-) *n prosody* a metrical foot of three short syllables (⏑⏑⏑) [C16 from Latin *tribrachys*, from Greek *tribrakhus*, from TRI- + *brakhus* short] > **triˈbrachic** *or* **triˈbrachial** *adj*

tribrach[2] (ˈtrɪbræk) *n archaeol* a three-armed object, esp a flint implement [C19 from TRI- + Greek *brakhiōn* arm]

tribromoethanol (traɪˌbrəʊməʊˈɛθəˌnɒl) *n* a soluble white crystalline compound with a slight aromatic odour, used as a general anaesthetic; 2,2,2-tribromoethanol. Formula: CBr_3CH_2OH

tribulation (ˌtrɪbjʊˈleɪʃən) *n* **1** a cause of distress **2** a state of suffering or distress [C13 from Old French, from Church Latin *trībulātiō*, from Latin *trībulāre* to afflict, from *trībulum* a threshing board, from *terere* to rub]

tribunal (traɪˈbjuːnᵊl, trɪ-) *n* **1** a court of justice or any place where justice is administered **2** (in Britain) a special court, convened by the government to inquire into a specific matter **3** a raised platform containing the seat of a judge or magistrate, originally that in a Roman basilica [C16 from Latin *tribūnus* TRIBUNE[1]]

tribunate (ˈtrɪbjʊnɪt) *or* **tribuneship** *n* the office or rank of a tribune

tribune[1] (ˈtrɪbjuːn) *n* **1** (in ancient Rome) **a** an officer elected by the plebs to protect their interests. Originally there were two of these officers but finally there were ten **b** a senior military officer **2** a person or institution that upholds public rights; champion [C14 from Latin *tribunus*, probably from *tribus* TRIBE] > ˈ**tribunary** *adj*

tribune[2] (ˈtrɪbjuːn) *n* **1** **a** the apse of a Christian basilica that contains the bishop's throne **b** the throne itself **2** a gallery or raised area in a church **3** *rare* a raised platform from which a speaker may address an audience; dais [C17 via French from Italian *tribuna*, from Medieval Latin *tribūna*,

t

variant of Latin *tribūnal* TRIBUNAL]

Tribune Group *n* (in Britain) a group made up of left-wing Labour Members of Parliament: founded 1966 [named after the *Tribune* newspaper, with which it is associated] > 'Tribun,ite *n*, *adj*

tributary ('trɪbjʊtərɪ, -trɪ) *n*, *pl* **-taries 1** a stream, river, or glacier that feeds another larger one **2** a person, nation, or people that pays tribute ▷ *adj* **3** (of a stream, etc) feeding a larger stream **4** given or owed as a tribute **5** paying tribute > 'tributarily *adv*

tribute ('trɪbjuːt) *n* **1** a gift or statement made in acknowledgment, gratitude, or admiration **2 a** a payment by one ruler or state to another, used as an acknowledgment of submission **b** any tax levied for such a payment **3** (in feudal society) homage or a payment rendered by a vassal to his lord **4** the obligation to pay tribute [c14 from Latin *tribūtum*, from *tribuere* to grant (originally: to distribute among the tribes), from *tribus* TRIBE]

tribute band *n* a group that plays the songs of a band they admire, often dressing in the style of the original band members

tricarboxylic acid cycle (traɪ,kɑːbɒk'sɪlɪk) *n* *biochem* another name for **Krebs cycle**. Abbreviation: **TCA cycle**

trice¹ (traɪs) *n* moment; instant (esp in the phrase **in a trice**) [c15 (in the phrase *at* or *in a trice*, in the sense: at one tug): apparent substantive use of TRICE²]

trice² (traɪs) *vb* (*tr*; often foll by *up*) *nautical* to haul up or secure [c15 from Middle Dutch *trīsen*, from *trīse* pulley]

tricentenary (,traɪsɛn'tiːnərɪ) or **tricentennial** (,traɪsɛn'tɛnɪəl) *adj* **1** of or relating to a period of 300 years **2** of or relating to a 300th anniversary or its celebration ▷ *n* **3** an anniversary of 300 years or its celebration ▷ Also: **tercentenary**, **tercentennial**

triceps ('traɪsɛps) *n*, *pl* **-cepses** (-sɛpsɪz) or **-ceps** any muscle having three heads, esp the one (*triceps brachii*) that extends the forearm [c16 from Latin, from TRI- + *caput* head]

triceratops (traɪ'sɛrə,tɒps) *n* any rhinoceros-like herbivorous dinosaur of the ornithischian genus *Triceratops*, of Cretaceous times, having a heavily armoured neck and three horns on the skull [c19 from New Latin, from TRI- + Greek *kerat-*, *keras* horn + *ōps* eye]

trich- *combining form* a variant of **tricho-** before a vowel

trichiasis (trɪ'kaɪəsɪs) *n* *pathol* **1** an abnormal position of the eyelashes that causes irritation when they rub against the eyeball **2** the presence of hairlike filaments in the urine [c17 via Late Latin from Greek *trikhiasis*, from *thrix* a hair + -IASIS]

trichina (trɪ'kaɪnə) *n*, *pl* **-nae** (-niː) a parasitic nematode worm, *Trichinella spiralis*, occurring in the intestines of pigs, rats, and man and producing larvae that form cysts in skeletal muscle [c19 from New Latin, from Greek *trikhinos* relating to hair, from *thrix* a hair]

trichinize or **trichinise** ('trɪkɪ,naɪz) *vb* (*tr*) to infest (an organism) with trichinae > ,trichini'zation or ,trichini'sation *n*

Trichinopoly (,trɪkɪ'nɒpəlɪ) *n* another name for **Tiruchirapalli**

trichinosis (,trɪkɪ'nəʊsɪs) *n* a disease characterized by nausea, fever, diarrhoea, and swelling of the muscles, caused by ingestion of pork infected with trichina larvae. Also called: **trichiniasis** (,trɪkɪ'naɪəsɪs) [c19 from New Latin TRICHINA]

trichinous ('trɪkɪnəs) *adj* **1** of, relating to, or having trichinosis **2** infested with trichinae

trichite ('trɪkaɪt) *n* **1** any of various needle-shaped crystals that occur in some glassy volcanic rocks **2** *biology* any of various hairlike structures > trichitic (trɪ'kɪtɪk) *adj*

trichloride (traɪ'klɔːraɪd) *n* any compound that contains three chlorine atoms per molecule

trichloroacetic acid (traɪ,klɔːrəʊə'siːtɪk, -'sɛtɪk) *n* a corrosive deliquescent crystalline acid with a characteristic odour, used as a veterinary astringent and antiseptic. Formula: CCl_3COOH

trichloroethane (traɪ,klɔːrəʊ'iːθeɪn) *n* a volatile nonflammable colourless liquid with low toxicity used for cleaning electrical apparatus and as a solvent; 1,2,3-trichloroethane. Formula: CH_3CCl_3. Also called: **methyl chloroform**

trichloroethylene (traɪ,klɔːrəʊ'ɛθɪ,liːn) or **trichlorethylene** *n* a volatile nonflammable mobile colourless liquid with an odour resembling that of chloroform. It is a good solvent for certain organic materials and is also an inhalation anaesthetic. Formula $CHCl:CCl_2$

trichlorophenoxyacetic acid (traɪ'klɔːrəʊfə,nɒksɪə'siːtɪk) *n* an insoluble crystalline solid; 2,4,5-trichlorophenoxyacetic acid. It is a plant hormone and is used as a weedkiller. Formula: $C_8H_5Cl_3O_3$. Also called: **2,4,5-T**

tricho- or before a vowel **trich-** *combining form* indicating hair or a part resembling hair: *trichocyst* [from Greek *thrix* (genitive *trikhos*) hair]

trichocyst ('trɪkə,sɪst) *n* any of various cavities on the surface of some ciliate protozoans, each containing a sensory thread that can be ejected > ,tricho'cystic *adj*

trichogyne ('trɪkə,dʒaɪn, -dʒɪn) *n* a hairlike projection of the female reproductive organs of certain algae, fungi, and lichens, which receives the male gametes before fertilization takes place [c19 from TRICHO- + Greek *gunē* woman] > ,tricho'gynial or ,tricho'gynic *adj*

trichoid ('trɪkɔɪd) *adj* *zoology* resembling a hair; hairlike

trichology (trɪ'kɒlədʒɪ) *n* the branch of medicine concerned with the hair and its diseases > trichological (,trɪkə'lɒdʒɪkªl) *adj* > tri'chologist *n*

trichome ('traɪkəʊm, 'trɪk-) *n* **1** any hairlike outgrowth from the surface of a plant **2** any of the threadlike structures that make up the filaments of blue-green algae [c19 from Greek *trikhōma*, from *trikhoun* to cover with hair, from *thrix* a hair] > trichomic (trɪ'kɒmɪk) *adj*

trichomonad (,trɪkə'mɒnæd) *n* any parasitic flagellate protozoan of the genus *Trichomonas*, occurring in the digestive and reproductive systems of man and animals > ,tricho'monadal or trichomonal (,trɪkə'mɒnªl, -'məʊ-, trɪ'kɒmənªl) *adj*

trichomoniasis (,trɪkəʊmə'naɪəsɪs) *n* **1** inflammation of the vagina characterized by a frothy discharge, caused by infection with parasitic protozoa (*Trichomonas vaginalis*) **2** any infection caused by parasitic protozoa of the genus *Trichomonas* [c19 New Latin; see TRICHOMONAD, -IASIS]

trichopteran (traɪ'kɒptərən) *n* **1** any insect of the order *Trichoptera*, which comprises the caddis flies ▷ *adj* **2** Also: **trichopterous** (trɪ'kɒptərəs) of, relating to, or belonging to the order *Trichoptera* [c19 from New Latin *Trichoptera*, literally: having hairy wings, from Greek *thrix* a hair + *pteron* wing]

trichosis (trɪ'kəʊsɪs) *n* any abnormal condition or disease of the hair [c19 via New Latin from Greek *trikhōsis* growth of hair]

trichotomy (traɪ'kɒtəmɪ) *n*, *pl* **-mies 1** division into three categories **2** *theol* the division of man into body, spirit, and soul [c17 probably from New Latin *trichotomia*, from Greek *trikhotomein* to divide into three, from *trikha* triple + *temnein* to cut] > trichotomic (,trɪkə'tɒmɪk) or tri'chotomous *adj* > tri'chotomously *adv*

trichroism ('traɪkrəʊ,ɪzəm) *n* a property of biaxial crystals as a result of which they show a perceptible difference in colour when viewed along three different axes. See **pleochroism** [c19 from Greek *trikhroos* three-coloured, from TRI- + *khrōma* colour] > tri'chroic *adj*

trichromat ('traɪkrəʊ,mæt) *n* any person with normal colour vision, who can therefore see the three primary colours

trichromatic (,traɪkrəʊ'mætɪk) or **trichromic** (traɪ'krəʊmɪk) *adj* **1** *photog*, *printing* involving the combination of three primary colours in the production of any colour **2** of, relating to, or having normal colour vision **3** having or involving three colours

trichromatism (traɪ'krəʊmə,tɪzəm) *n* **1** the use or combination of three primary colours for colour reproduction in photography, printing, television, etc **2** *rare* the state of being trichromatic

trichuriasis (,trɪkjʊə'raɪəsɪs) *n* infection of the large intestine with the whipworm *Trichuris trichiura*, resulting in anaemia, weakness, etc

trick (trɪk) *n* **1** a deceitful, cunning, or underhand action or plan **2 a** a mischievous, malicious, or humorous action or plan; joke: *the boys are up to their tricks again* **b** (as modifier): *a trick spider* **3** an illusory or magical feat or device **4** a simple feat learned by an animal or person **5** an adroit or ingenious device; knack: *a trick of the trade* **6** a behavioural trait, habit, or mannerism **7** a turn or round of duty or work **8** *cards* **a** a batch of cards containing one from each player, usually played in turn and won by the player or side that plays the card with the highest value **b** a card that can potentially win a trick **9 can't take a trick** *Austral slang* to be consistently unsuccessful or unlucky **10 do the trick** *informal* to produce the right or desired result **11 how's tricks?** *slang* how are you? **12 turn a trick** *slang* (of a prostitute) to gain a customer ▷ *vb* **13** to defraud, deceive, or cheat (someone), esp by means of a trick [c15 from Old Northern French *trique*, from *trikier* to deceive, from Old French *trichier*, ultimately from Latin *trīcārī* to play tricks] > 'tricker *n* > 'trickless *adj*

trick cyclist *n* a slang term for **psychiatrist**

trickery ('trɪkərɪ) *n*, *pl* **-eries** the practice or an instance of using tricks

trickle ('trɪkªl) *vb* **1** to run or cause to run in thin or slow streams: *she trickled the sand through her fingers* **2** (*intr*) to move, go, or pass gradually: *the crowd trickled away* ▷ *n* **3** a thin, irregular, or slow flow of something **4** the act of trickling [c14 perhaps of imitative origin] > 'trickling *adj* > 'tricklingly *adv* > 'trickly *adj*

trickle charger *n* a small mains-operated battery charger, esp one that delivers less than 5 amperes and is used by car owners

trickle-down *adj* of or concerning the theory that granting concessions such as tax cuts to the rich will benefit all levels of society by stimulating the economy

trick or treat *sentence substitute chiefly US and Canadian* the cry by children at Halloween when they call at houses, indicating that they want a present or money or else they will play a trick on the householder

trick out or **up** *vb* (*tr*, *adverb*) to dress up; deck out

trickster ('trɪkstə) *n* a person who deceives or plays tricks

tricksy ('trɪksɪ) *adj* **-sier**, **-siest 1** playing tricks habitually; mischievous **2** crafty or difficult to deal with **3** *archaic* well-dressed; spruce; smart > 'tricksiness *n*

tricktrack ('trɪk,træk) *n* a variant spelling of **trictrac**

tricky ('trɪkɪ) *adj* **trickier**, **trickiest 1** involving difficulties: *a tricky job* **2** needing careful and tactful handling: *a tricky situation* **3** characterized by tricks; sly > 'trickily *adv* > 'trickiness *n*

triclinic (traɪ'klɪnɪk) *adj* relating to or belonging to the crystal system characterized by three unequal axes, no pair of which are perpendicular. Also: **anorthic**

triclinium (traɪ'klɪnɪəm) *n*, *pl* **-ia** (-ɪə) (in ancient Rome) **1** an arrangement of three couches around a table for reclining upon while dining **2** a dining room, esp one containing such an arrangement of couches [c17 from Latin, from Greek *triklinion*, from TRI- + *klinē* a couch]

tricolour or US **tricolor** ('trɪkələ, 'traɪ,kʌlə) *adj* also **tricoloured** or US **tricolored** ('traɪ,kʌləd) **1** having or involving three colours ▷ *n* **2** (*often capital*) the French national flag, having three equal vertical stripes in blue, white, and red **3** any flag, badge, ribbon, etc, with three colours

tricorn ('traɪˌkɔːn) *n also* **tricorne 1** a cocked hat with opposing brims turned back and caught in three places **2** an imaginary animal having three horns ▷ *adj also* **tricornered 3** having three horns or corners [c18 from Latin *tricornis*, from TRI- + *cornu* HORN]

tricostate (traɪˈkɒsteɪt) *adj biology* having three ribs or riblike parts: *tricostate leaves* [c19 from TRI- + COSTATE]

tricot ('trɪkəʊ, 'triː-) *n* **1** a thin rayon or nylon fabric knitted or resembling knitting, used for dresses, etc **2** a type of ribbed dress fabric [c19 from French, from *tricoter* to knit, of unknown origin]

tricotine (ˌtrɪkəˈtiːn, ˌtriː-) *n* a twill-weave woollen fabric resembling gabardine [c20 from French; see TRICOT]

tricrotic (traɪˈkrɒtɪk) *adj physiol* (of the pulse) having a tracing characterized by three elevations with each beat [c19 from Greek *trikrotos* having three beats, from TRI- + *krotos* a beat] > **tricrotism** ('traɪkrəˌtɪzəm, 'trɪk-) *n*

trictrac *or* **tricktrack** ('trɪkˌtræk) *n* a game similar to backgammon [c17 from French, imitative]

tricuspid (traɪˈkʌspɪd) *anatomy* ▷ *adj also* **tricuspidal 1 a** having three points, cusps, or segments: *a tricuspid tooth; a tricuspid valve* **b** ▷ *n* **2** a tooth having three cusps

tricycle ('traɪsɪkəl) *n* **1** a three-wheeled cycle, esp one driven by pedals **2** a three-wheeler for invalids ▷ *vb* **3** (*intr*) to ride a tricycle > '**tricyclist** *n*

tricyclic (traɪˈsaɪklɪk) *adj* **1** (of a chemical compound) containing three rings in the molecular structure ▷ *n* **2** an antidepressant drug having a tricyclic molecular structure

tridactyl (traɪˈdæktəl) *or* **tridactylous** *adj* having three digits on the hand or foot

trident ('traɪdənt) *n* **1** a three-pronged spear, originally from the East **2** (in Greek and Roman mythology) the three-pronged spear that the sea god Poseidon (Neptune) is represented as carrying **3** a three-pronged instrument, weapon, or symbol ▷ *adj* **4** having three prongs [c16 from Latin *tridēns* three-pronged, from TRI- + *dēns* tooth]

Trident ('traɪdənt) *n* a type of US submarine-launched ballistic missile with independently targetable warheads

tridentate (traɪˈdenteɪt) *or* **tridental** *adj anatomy, botany* having three prongs, teeth, or points

Tridentine (traɪˈdentaɪn) *adj* **1** *history* **a** of or relating to the Council of Trent **b** in accord with Tridentine doctrine ▷ *n* **2** an orthodox Roman Catholic [c16 from Medieval Latin *Tridentīnus*, from *Tridentum* TRENT]

Tridentum (traɪˈdentəm) *n* the Latin name for Trento

tridimensional (ˌtraɪdɪˈmenʃənəl, -daɪ-) *adj* a less common word for **three-dimensional** > ˌtridiˈmensionˈality *n* > ˌtridiˈmensionally *adv*

triduum ('trɪdjʊəm, 'traɪ-) *n RC Church* a period of three days for prayer before a feast [c19 Latin, perhaps from *triduum spatium* a space of three days]

triecious (traɪˈiːʃəs) *adj* a variant spelling of **trioecious**

tried (traɪd) *vb* the past tense and past participle of **try**

triella (trɪˈelə) *n Austral* three nominated horse races in which the punter bets on selecting the three winners

triene ('traɪˌiːn) *n* a chemical compound containing three double bonds

triennial (traɪˈenɪəl) *adj* **1** relating to, lasting for, or occurring every three years ▷ *n* **2** a third anniversary **3** a triennial period, thing, or occurrence [c17 from Latin TRIENNIUM] > triˈennially *adv*

triennium (traɪˈenɪəm) *n, pl* -niums *or* -nia (-nɪə) a

period or cycle of three years [c19 from Latin, from TRI- + *annus* a year]

Trient (triˈent) *n* the German name for **Trento** Also: **Trent**

trier ('traɪə) *n* a person or thing that tries

Trier (*German* triːr) *n* a city in W Germany, in the Rhineland-Palatinate on the Moselle River: one of the oldest towns of central Europe, ancient capital of a Celto-Germanic tribe (the *Treveri*); an early centre of Christianity, ruled by powerful archbishops until the 18th century; wine trade; important Roman remains. Pop: 100 180 (2003 est). Latin name: **Augusta Treverorum** (aʊˈguːstə ˌtrevəˈrɔːrəm) French name: **Trèves**

trierarch ('traɪəˌrɑːk) *n Greek history* **1** a citizen responsible for fitting out a state trireme, esp in Athens **2** the captain of a trireme [c17 from Latin, from Greek *triērarkhos*, from *triērēs* equipped with three banks of oars + *arkhein* to command]

trierarchy ('traɪəˌrɑːkɪ) *n, pl* -chies *Greek history* **1** the responsibility for fitting out a state trireme, esp in Athens **2** the office of a trierarch **3** trierarchs collectively

Trieste (triːˈest; *Italian* triˈeste) *n* **1** a port in NE Italy, capital of Friuli-Venezia Giulia region, on the **Gulf of Trieste** at the head of the Adriatic Sea: under Austrian rule (1382–1918); capital of the Free Territory of Trieste (1947–54); important transit port for central Europe. Pop: 211 184 (2001). Slovene and Serbo-Croat name: **Trst 2 Free Territory of.** a former territory on the N Adriatic: established by the UN in 1947; most of the N part passed to Italy and the remainder to Yugoslavia in 1954

trifacial (traɪˈfeɪʃəl) *adj* another word for **trigeminal**

trifecta (traɪˈfektə) *n* a form of betting in which the punter selects the first three place-winners in a horse race in the correct order [from TRI- + (per)*fecta*, a US system of betting]

triffid ('trɪfɪd) *n* any of a species of fictional plants that supposedly grew to a gigantic size, were capable of moving about, and could kill humans [from the science fiction novel *The Day of the Triffids* (1951) by John Wyndham]

trifid ('traɪfɪd) *adj* divided or split into three parts or lobes [c18 from Latin *trifidus* from TRI- + *findere* to split]

trifle ('traɪfəl) *n* **1** a thing of little or no value or significance **2** a small amount; bit: *a trifle more enthusiasm* **3** *Brit* a cold dessert made with sponge cake spread with jam or fruit, soaked in wine or sherry, covered with a custard sauce and cream, and decorated **4** a type of pewter of medium hardness **5** articles made from this pewter ▷ *vb* **6** (*intr; usually foll by with*) to deal (with) as if worthless; dally: *to trifle with a person's affections* **7** to waste (time) frivolously [c13 from Old French *trufle* mockery, from *trufler* to cheat] > '**trifler** *n*

trifling ('traɪflɪŋ) *adj* **1** insignificant or petty **2** frivolous or idle > '**triflingly** *adv* > '**triflingness** *n*

trifocal *adj* (traɪˈfəʊkəl) **1** having three focuses **2** having three focal lengths ▷ *n* (traɪˈfəʊkəl, 'traɪˌfəʊkəl) **3** (*plural*) glasses with trifocal lenses

trifold ('traɪˌfəʊld) *adj* a less common word for **triple**

trifoliate (traɪˈfəʊlɪɪt, -ˌeɪt) *or* **trifoliated** *adj* having three leaves, leaflike parts, or (of a compound leaf) leaflets

trifolium (traɪˈfəʊlɪəm) *n* any leguminous plant of the temperate genus *Trifolium*, having leaves divided into three leaflets and dense heads of small white, yellow, red, or purple flowers: includes the clovers and trefoils [c17 from Latin, from TRI- + *folium* leaf]

triforium (traɪˈfɔːrɪəm) *n, pl* -ria (-rɪə) an arcade above the arches of the nave, choir, or transept of a church [c18 from Anglo-Latin, apparently from Latin TRI- + *foris* a doorway; referring to the fact that each bay characteristically had three openings] > triˈforial *adj*

trifurcate ('traɪfɜːkɪt, -ˌkeɪt) *or* **trifurcated** *adj* having three branches or forks [from Latin

trifurcus, from TRI- + *furca* a fork] > ˌtrifurˈcation *n*

trig[1] (trɪg) *archaic or dialect* ▷ *adj* **1** neat or spruce ▷ *vb* **trigs, trigging, trigged 2** to make or become trim or spruce [c12 (originally: trusty): of Scandinavian origin; related to Old Norse *tryggr* true] > '**trigly** *adv* > '**trigness** *n*

trig[2] (trɪg) *chiefly dialect* ▷ *n* **1** a wedge or prop ▷ *vb* **trigs, trigging, trigged** (*tr*) **2** to block or stop **3** to prop or support [c16 probably of Scandinavian origin; compare Old Norse *tryggja* to make secure; see TRIG[1]]

trig. *abbreviation for* **1** trigonometry **2** trigonometrical

trigeminal (traɪˈdʒemɪnəl) *adj anatomy* of or relating to the trigeminal nerve [c19 from Latin *trigeminus* triplet, from TRI- + *geminus* twin]

trigeminal nerve *n* either one of the fifth pair of cranial nerves, which supply the muscles of the mandible and maxilla. Their ophthalmic branches supply the area around the orbit of the eye, the nasal cavity, and the forehead

trigeminal neuralgia *n pathol* another name for **tic douloureux**

trigger ('trɪgə) *n* **1** a small projecting lever that activates the firing mechanism of a firearm **2** *machinery* a device that releases a spring-loaded mechanism or a similar arrangement **3** any event that sets a course of action in motion ▷ *vb* (*tr*) **4** (*usually foll by off*) to give rise (to); set off **5** to fire or set in motion by or as by pulling a trigger [c17 *tricker*, from Dutch *trekker*, from *trekken* to pull; see TREK] > '**triggered** *adj* > '**triggerless** *adj*

triggerfish ('trɪgəˌfɪʃ) *n, pl* -fish *or* -fishes any plectognath fish of the family *Balistidae*, of tropical and temperate seas. They have a compressed body with erectile spines in the first dorsal fin

trigger-happy *adj informal* **1** tending to resort to the use of firearms or violence irresponsibly **2** tending to act rashly or without consideration

triggerman ('trɪgəˌmæn) *n, pl* -men a person, esp a criminal, who shoots another person

trigger plant *n Austral* any of several small grasslike plants of the genus *Stylidium*, having sensitive stamens that are erected when disturbed: family *Stylidiaceae*

trigger word *n* a word that initiates a process or course of action

triglyceride (traɪˈglɪsəˌraɪd) *n* any ester of glycerol and one or more carboxylic acids, in which each glycerol molecule has combined with three carboxylic acid molecules. Most natural fats and oils are triglycerides

triglyph ('traɪglɪf) *n architect* a stone block in a Doric frieze, having three vertical channels [c16 via Latin from Greek *trigluphos* three-grooved, from *tri-* three + *gluphē* carving. See GLYPH] > triˈglyphic *adj*

trigon ('traɪgɒn) *n* **1** (in classical Greece or Rome) a triangular harp or lyre **2** an archaic word for **triangle** [c17 via Latin from Greek *trigōnon* triangle. See TRI-, -GON]

trigonal ('trɪgənəl) *adj* **1** another word for **triangular** (sense 1) **2** Also: **rhombohedral** relating or belonging to the crystal system characterized by three equal axes that are equally inclined and not perpendicular to each other

trigonometric function *n* **1** Also called: **circular function** any of a group of functions of an angle expressed as a ratio of two of the sides of a right-angled triangle containing the angle. The group includes sine, cosine, tangent, secant, cosecant, and cotangent **2** any function containing only sines, cosines, etc, and constants

trigonometry (ˌtrɪgəˈnɒmɪtrɪ) *n* the branch of mathematics concerned with the properties of trigonometric functions and their application to the determination of the angles and sides of triangles. Used in surveying, navigation, etc. Abbreviation: **trig** [c17 from New Latin *trigōnometria* from Greek *trigōnon* triangle] > **trigonometric** (ˌtrɪgənəˈmetrɪk) *or* ˌtrigonoˈmetrical *adj* > ˌtrigonoˈmetrically *adv*

trigonous ('trɪgənəs) *adj* (of stems, seeds, and

t

similar parts) having a triangular cross section

trig point *n* an informal name for **triangulation station**. Also called (Austral and NZ): **trig**

trigraph ('traɪ,grɑːf, -,græf) *n* a combination of three letters used to represent a single speech sound or phoneme, such as *eau* in French *beau* > **trigraphic** (traɪ'græfɪk) *adj*

trihalomethane (traɪ,heɪləʊ'miːθeɪn) *n* a type of chemical compound in which three of the hydrogen atoms in a methane molecule have been replaced by halogen atoms, esp by chlorine in drinking water. Trihalomethanes are thought to be carcinogenic

trihedral (traɪ'hiːdrəl) *adj* **1** having or formed by three plane faces meeting at a point ▷ *n* **2** a figure formed by the intersection of three lines in different planes [c18 from TRI- + Greek *hedra* base, seat + -AL[1]]

trihedron (traɪ'hiːdrən) *n, pl* **-drons** or **-dra** (-drə) a figure determined by the intersection of three planes

trihydrate (traɪ'haɪdreɪt) *n chem* a substance that contains three molecules of water > **tri'hydrated** *adj*

trihydric (traɪ'haɪdrɪk) *or* **trihydroxy** (,traɪhaɪ'drɒksɪ) *adj* (of an alcohol or similar compound) containing three hydroxyl groups

triiodomethane (,traɪaɪ,əʊdəʊ'miːθeɪn) *n* another name for **iodoform**

triiodothyronine (,traɪaɪ,əʊdəʊ'θaɪrə,niːn) *n* an amino acid hormone that contains iodine and is secreted by the thyroid gland with thyroxine, to which it has a similar action. Formula: $C_{15}H_{12}I_3NO_4$ [c20 from TRI- + IODO- + THYRO- + -INE2]

trike (traɪk) *n* **1** short for **tricycle 2** short for **trichloroethylene 3** a microlight aircraft with three fixed wheels for landing and take-off

trilateral (traɪ'lætərəl) *adj* having three sides > **tri'laterally** *adv*

trilateration (,traɪlætə'reɪʃən) *n* a method of surveying in which a whole area is divided into triangles, the sides of which are measured, usually by electromagnetic distance measuring for geodetic control or by chain survey for a detailed survey

trilby ('trɪlbɪ) *n, pl* **-bies 1** *chiefly Brit* a man's soft felt hat with an indented crown **2** (*plural*) *slang* feet [c19 named after *Trilby*, the heroine of a dramatized novel (1893) of that title by George du Maurier]

trilemma (traɪ'lɛmə) *n* **1** a quandary posed by three alternative courses of action **2** an argument one of the premises of which is the disjunction of three statements from each of which the same conclusion is derived [c17 formed on the model of DILEMMA, from TRI- + Greek *lēmma* assumption]

trilinear (traɪ'lɪnɪə) *adj* consisting of, bounded by, or relating to three lines

trilingual (traɪ'lɪŋgwəl) *adj* **1** able to speak three languages fluently **2** expressed or written in three languages > **tri'lingualism** *n* > **tri'lingually** *adv*

triliteral (traɪ'lɪtərəl) *adj* **1** having three letters **2** (of a word root in Semitic languages) consisting of three consonants ▷ *n* **3** a word root of three consonants

trilithon (traɪ'lɪθɒn, 'traɪlɪ,θɒn) *or* **trilith** ('traɪlɪθ) *n* a structure consisting of two upright stones with a third placed across the top, such as those of Stonehenge [c18 from Greek; see TRI-, -LITH] > **trilithic** (traɪ'lɪθɪk) *adj*

trill[1] (trɪl) *n* **1** *music* a melodic ornament consisting of a rapid alternation between a principal note and the note a whole tone or semitone above it. Usual symbol: *tr.* or *tr* (written above a note) **2** a shrill warbling sound, esp as made by some birds **3** *phonetics* **a** the articulation of an (r) sound produced by holding the tip of the tongue close to the alveolar ridge, allowing the tongue to make a succession of taps against the ridge **b** the production of a similar effect using

the uvula against the back of the tongue ▷ *vb* **4** to sound, sing, or play (a trill or with a trill) **5** (*tr*) to pronounce (an (r) sound) by the production of a trill [c17 from Italian *trillo*, from *trillare*, apparently from Middle Dutch *trillen* to vibrate]

trill[2] (trɪl) *vb, n* an archaic or poetic word for **trickle** [c14 probably of Scandinavian origin; related to Norwegian *trilla* to roll; see TRILL[1]]

trillion ('trɪljən) *n* **1** the number represented as one followed by twelve zeros (10^{12}); a million million **2** (formerly, in Britain) the number represented as one followed by eighteen zeros (10^{18}); a million million million **3** (*often plural*) an exceptionally large but unspecified number ▷ *determiner* **4** (preceded by *a* or a numeral) **a** amounting to a trillion: *a trillion stars* **b** (*as pronoun*): *there are three trillion* [c17 from French, on the model of *million*] > **trillionth** *n, adj*

trillionaire (,trɪljə'nɛə) *n* a person whose assets are worth over a trillion of the monetary units of his or her country

trillium ('trɪljəm) *n* any herbaceous plant of the genus *Trillium*, of Asia and North America, having a whorl of three leaves at the top of the stem with a single central white, pink, or purple three-petalled flower: family *Trilliaceae* [c18 from New Latin, modification by Linnaeus of Swedish *trilling* triplet]

trilobate (traɪ'ləʊbeɪt, 'traɪlə,beɪt) *adj* (esp of a leaf) consisting of or having three lobes or parts

trilobite ('traɪlə,baɪt) *n* any extinct marine arthropod of the group *Trilobita*, abundant in Palaeozoic times, having a segmented exoskeleton divided into three parts [c19 from New Latin *Trilobītēs*, from Greek *trilobos* having three lobes; see TRI-, LOBE] > **trilobitic** (,traɪlə'bɪtɪk) *adj*

trilocular (traɪ'lɒkjʊlə) *adj* (esp of a plant ovary or anther) having or consisting of three chambers or cavities [c18 from TRI- + Latin *loculus* compartment (from *locus* place) + -AR]

trilogy ('trɪlədʒɪ) *n, pl* **-gies 1** a series of three related works, esp in literature, etc **2** (in ancient Greece) a series of three tragedies performed together at the Dionysian festivals [c19 from Greek *trilogia*; see TRI-, -LOGY]

trim (trɪm) *adj* **trimmer, trimmest 1** neat and spruce in appearance **2** slim; slender **3** in good condition ▷ *vb* **trims, trimming, trimmed** (*mainly tr*) **4** to put in good order, esp by cutting or pruning **5** to shape and finish (timber) **6** to adorn or decorate **7** (sometimes foll by *off* or *away*) to cut so as to remove: *to trim off a branch* **8** to cut down to the desired size or shape: *to trim material to a pattern* **9** *dialect* to decorate: *to trim a Christmas tree* **10** *nautical* **a** (*also intr*) to adjust the balance of (a vessel) or (of a vessel) to maintain an even balance, by distribution of ballast, cargo, etc **b** (*also intr*) to adjust (a vessel's sails) to take advantage of the wind **c** to stow (cargo) **11** to balance (an aircraft) before flight by adjusting the position of the load or in flight by the use of trim tabs, fuel transfer, etc **12** (*also intr*) to modify (one's opinions, etc) to suit opposing factions or for expediency **13** *informal* to thrash or beat **14** *informal* to rebuke **15** *obsolete* to furnish or equip ▷ *n* **16** a decoration or adornment **17** the upholstery and decorative facings, as on the door panels, of a car's interior **18** proper order or fitness; good shape: *in trim* **19** a haircut that neatens but does not alter the existing hairstyle **20** *nautical* **a** the general set and appearance of a vessel **b** the difference between the draught of a vessel at the bow and at the stern **c** the fitness of a vessel **d** the position of a vessel's sails relative to the wind **e** the relative buoyancy of a submarine **21** dress or equipment **22** *US* window-dressing **23** the attitude of an aircraft in flight when the pilot allows the main control surfaces to take up their own positions **24** *films* a section of shot cut out during editing **25** material that is trimmed off **26** decorative mouldings,

such as architraves, picture rails, etc [Old English *tryman* to strengthen; related to *trum* strong, Old Irish *druma* tree, Russian *drom* thicket] > **trimly** *adv* > **'trimness** *n*

Trim (trɪm) *n* the county town of Meath, Republic of Ireland; 12th-century castle, medieval cathedral Pop: 5894 (2002)

trimaran ('traɪmə,ræn) *n* a vessel, usually of shallow draught, with two hulls flanking the main hull [c20 from TRI- + (CATA)MARAN]

trimer ('traɪmə) *n* a polymer or a molecule of a polymer consisting of three identical monomers > **trimeric** (traɪ'mɛrɪk) *adj*

trimerous ('trɪmərəs) *adj* **1** (of plants) having parts arranged in groups of three **2** consisting of or having three parts

trimester (traɪ'mɛstə) *n* **1** a period of three months **2** (in some US and Canadian universities or schools) any of the three academic sessions [c19 from French *trimestre*, from Latin *trimēstris* of three months, from TRI- + *mēnsis* month] > **tri'mestral** *or* **tri'mestrial** *adj*

trimeter ('trɪmɪtə) *prosody* ▷ *n* **1** a verse line consisting of three metrical feet ▷ *adj* **2** designating such a line

trimethadione (,traɪmɛθə'daɪəʊn) *n* a crystalline compound with a bitter taste and camphor-like odour, used in the treatment of epilepsy. Formula: $C_6H_9NO_3$ [from TRI- + METH(YL) + DI-[1] + -ONE]

trimetric (traɪ'mɛtrɪk) *or* **trimetrical** *adj* **1** *prosody* of, relating to, or consisting of a trimeter or trimeters **2** *crystallog* another word for **orthorhombic**

trimetric projection *n* a geometric projection, used in mechanical drawing, in which the three axes are at arbitrary angles, often using different linear scales

trimetrogon (traɪ'mɛtrə,gɒn) *n* **a** a method of aerial photography for rapid topographic mapping, in which one vertical and two oblique photographs are taken simultaneously **b** (*as modifier*): *trimetrogon photography* [from TRI- + *metro*-, from Greek *metron* measure + -GON]

trimmer ('trɪmə) *n* **1** Also called: **trimmer joist** a beam in a floor or roof structure attached to truncated joists in order to leave an opening for a staircase, chimney, etc **2** a machine for trimming timber **3** Also called: **trimming capacitor** *electronics* a variable capacitor of small capacitance used for making fine adjustments, etc **4** a person who alters his or her opinions on the grounds of expediency **5** a person who fits out motor vehicles

trimming ('trɪmɪŋ) *n* **1** an extra piece used to decorate or complete **2** (*plural*) usual or traditional accompaniments: *roast turkey with all the trimmings* **3** (*plural*) parts that are cut off **4** (*plural*) *dialect* ornaments; decorations: *Christmas trimmings* **5** *informal* a reproof, beating, or defeat

trimolecular (,traɪmə'lɛkjʊlə) *adj chem* of, concerned with, formed from, or involving three molecules

trimonthly (traɪ'mʌnθlɪ) *adj, adv* every three months

trimorph ('traɪmɔːf) *n* **1** a substance, esp a mineral, that exists in three distinct forms **2** any of the forms in which such a structure exists

trimorphism (traɪ'mɔːfɪzəm) *n* **1** *biology* the property exhibited by certain species of having or occurring in three different forms **2** the property of certain minerals of existing in three crystalline forms [c19 from Greek *trimorphos* (from TRI- + *morphē* form) + -ISM] > **tri'morphic** *or* **tri'morphous** *adj*

trim size *n* the size of a book or a page of a book after all excess material has been trimmed off

trim tab *n* a small control surface attached to the trailing edge of a main control surface to enable the pilot to trim an aircraft

Trimurti (trɪ'mʊətɪ) *n* the triad of the three chief gods of later Hinduism, consisting of Brahma the Creator, Vishnu the Sustainer, and Siva the

Destroyer [from Sanskrit, from *tri* three + *mūrti* form]

Trinacria (trɪˈneɪkrɪə, traɪ-) *n* the Latin name for Sicily

Trinacrian (trɪˈneɪkrɪən, traɪ-) *adj* of or relating to Trinacria (the Latin name for Sicily) or its inhabitants

trinary (ˈtraɪnərɪ) *adj* **1** made up of three parts; ternary **2** going in threes [c15 from Late Latin *trīnārius* of three sorts, from Latin *trīnī* three each, from *trēs* three]

Tri-Nations Championship *n rugby union* the annual tournament in which the national sides representing Australia, New Zealand, and South Africa compete

Trincomalee (ˌtrɪŋkəʊməˈliː) *n* a port in NE Sri Lanka, on the **Bay of Trincomalee** (an inlet of the Bay of Bengal); British naval base until 1957. Pop: 51 000 (latest est)

trine (traɪn) *n* **1** *astrology* an aspect of 120° between two planets, an orb of 8° being allowed. Compare **conjunction** (sense 5), **opposition** (sense 9), **square** (sense 10) **2** anything comprising three parts ▷ *adj* **3** of or relating to a trine **4** threefold; triple [c14 from Old French *trin*, from Latin *trīnus* triple, from *trēs* three] > ˈ**trinal** *adj*

Trini (ˈtrɪnɪ) *n*, *pl* **Trinis** *Caribbean informal* a native or inhabitant of Trinidad; Trinidadian [c20 a shortened form of *Trinidadian*]

Trinidad (ˈtrɪnɪˌdæd) *n* an island in the West Indies, off the NE coast of Venezuela: colonized by the Spanish in the 17th century and ceded to Britain in 1802; joined with Tobago in 1888 as a British colony; now part of the independent republic of Trinidad and Tobago. Pop: 1 208 282 (2000)

Trinidad and Tobago *n* an independent republic in the Caribbean, occupying the two southernmost islands of the Lesser Antilles: became a British colony in 1888 and gained independence in 1962; became a republic in 1976; a member of the Commonwealth. Official language: English. Religion: Christian majority, with a large Hindu minority. Currency: Trinidad and Tobago dollar. Capital: Port of Spain. Pop: 1 307 000 (2004 est). Area: 5128 sq km (1980 sq miles)

Trinidadian (ˌtrɪnɪˈdædɪən) *adj* **1** of or relating to Trinidad or its inhabitants ▷ *n* **2** a native or inhabitant of Trinidad

Trinil man (ˈtriːnɪl) *n* another name for **Java man** [c20 named after the village in Java where remains were found]

Trinitarian (ˌtrɪnɪˈtɛərɪən) *n* **1** a person who believes in the doctrine of the Trinity **2** a member of the Holy Trinity. See **Trinity** (sense 3) ▷ *adj* **3** of or relating to the doctrine of the Trinity or those who uphold it **4** of or relating to the Holy Trinity > ˌTriniˈtarianˌism *n*

trinitrobenzene (traɪˌnaɪtrəʊˈbɛnziːn, -bɛnˈziːn) *n* any of three explosive crystalline isomeric compounds with the formula $C_6H_3(NO_2)_3$. They are less sensitive to impact than TNT but more powerful in their explosive force

trinitrocresol (traɪˌnaɪtrəʊˈkriːsɒl) *n* a yellow crystalline highly explosive compound. Formula: $CH_3C_6H(OH)(NO_2)_3$

trinitroglycerine (traɪˌnaɪtrəʊˈɡlɪsəˌriːn) *n* the full name for **nitroglycerine**

trinitrophenol (traɪˌnaɪtrəʊˈfiːnɒl) *n* another name for **picric acid**

trinitrotoluene (traɪˌnaɪtrəʊˈtɒljuˌiːn) *or* **trinitrotoluol** (traɪˌnaɪtrəʊˈtɒljuˌɒl) *n* the full name for **TNT**

trinity (ˈtrɪnɪtɪ) *n*, *pl* **-ties 1** a group of three **2** the state of being threefold [c13 from Old French *trinite*, from Late Latin *trīnitās*, from Latin *trīnus* triple]

Trinity (ˈtrɪnɪtɪ) *n* **1** Also called: **Holy Trinity**, **Blessed Trinity** *Christian theol* the union of three persons, the Father, Son, and Holy Spirit, in one Godhead **2** See **Trinity Sunday 3** Holy Trinity a religious order founded in 1198

Trinity Brethren *pl n* the members of Trinity House

Trinity House *n* an association that provides lighthouses, buoys, etc, around the British coast

Trinity Sunday *n* the Sunday after Whit Sunday

Trinity term *n* the summer term at the Inns of Court and some educational establishments

trinket (ˈtrɪŋkɪt) *n* **1** a small or worthless ornament or piece of jewellery **2** a trivial object; trifle [c16 perhaps from earlier *trenket* little knife, via Old Northern French, from Latin *truncāre* to lop] > ˈ**trinketry** *n*

trinocular (traɪˈnɒkjʊlə) *adj* of or relating to a binocular microscope having a lens for photographic recording while direct visual observation is taking place [c20 from TRI- + (BI)NOCULAR]

trinomial (traɪˈnəʊmɪəl) *adj* **1** *maths* consisting of or relating to three terms **2** *biology* denoting or relating to the three-part name of an organism that incorporates its genus, species, and subspecies ▷ *n* **3** *maths* a polynomial consisting of three terms, such as $ax^2 + bx + c$ **4** *biology* the third word in the trinomial name of an organism, which distinguishes between subspecies [c18 TRI- + *-nomial* on the model of *binomial*] > triˈnomially *adv*

trio (ˈtriːəʊ) *n*, *pl* **trios 1** a group of three people or things **2** *music* **a** a group of three singers or instrumentalists or a piece of music composed for such a group **b** a subordinate section in a scherzo, minuet, etc, that is contrastive in style and often in a related key **3** *piquet* three cards of the same rank [c18 from Italian, ultimately from Latin *trēs* three; compare DUO]

triode (ˈtraɪəʊd) *n* **1** an electronic valve having three electrodes, a cathode, an anode, and a grid, the potential of the grid controlling the flow of electrons between the cathode and anode. It has been replaced by the transistor **2** any electronic device, such as a thyratron, having three electrodes [c20 TRI- + ELECTRODE]

trioecious *or* **triecious** (traɪˈiːʃəs) *adj* (of a plant species) having male, female, and hermaphrodite flowers in three different plants [c18 from New Latin *trioecia*, from Greek *oikos* house]

triol (ˈtraɪɒl) *n* any of a class of alcohols that have three hydroxyl groups per molecule. Also called: **trihydric alcohol** [from TRI- + -OL¹]

triolein (traɪˈəʊlɪɪn) *n* a naturally occurring glyceride of oleic acid, found in fats and oils. Formula: $(C_{17}H_{33}COO)_3C_3H_5$. Also called: **olein**

triolet (ˈtriːəʊˌlɛt) *n* a verse form of eight lines, having the first line repeated as the fourth and seventh and the second line as the eighth, rhyming a b a a a b a b [c17 from French: a little TRIO]

triose (ˈtraɪəʊz, -əʊs) *n* a simple monosaccharide produced by the oxidation of glycerol. Formula: $CH_2OHCHOHCHO$

trio sonata *n* **1** a type of baroque composition in several movements scored for two upper parts and a bass part **2** a similar type of composition played on a keyboard instrument, esp an organ

trioxide (traɪˈɒksaɪd) *n* any oxide that contains three oxygen atoms per molecule: *sulphur trioxide*, SO_3

trip (trɪp) *n* **1** an outward and return journey, often for a specific purpose **2** any tour, journey, or voyage **3** a false step; stumble **4** any slip or blunder **5** a light step or tread **6** a manoeuvre or device to cause someone to trip **7** Also called: **tripper a** any catch on a mechanism that acts as a switch **b** (*as modifier*): *trip button* **8** a surge in the conditions of a chemical or other automatic process resulting in an instability **9** *informal* a hallucinogenic drug experience **10** *informal* any stimulating, profound, etc, experience ▷ *vb* **trips**, **tripping**, **tripped 11** (*often foll by up*, or when *intr*, by *on* or *over*) to stumble or cause to stumble **12** to make or cause to make a mistake or blunder **13** (*tr; often foll by up*) to trap or catch in a mistake **14** (*intr*) to go on a short tour or journey **15** (*intr*) to move or tread lightly **16** (*intr*) *informal* to experience the effects of LSD or any other hallucinogenic drug **17** (*tr*) **a** to activate (a mechanical trip) **b** **trip a switch** to switch electric power off by moving the switch armature to disconnect the supply ▷ See also **trip out** [c14 from Old French *triper* to tread, of Germanic origin; related to Low German *trippen* to stamp, Middle Dutch *trippen* to walk trippingly, *trepelen* to trample] > ˈ**trippingly** *adv*

tripalmitin (traɪˈpælmɪtɪn) *n* another name for **palmitin**

tripartite (traɪˈpɑːtaɪt) *adj* **1** divided into or composed of three parts **2** involving three participants **3** (*esp of leaves*) consisting of three parts formed by divisions extending almost to the base > triˈpartitely *adv*

tripartition (ˌtraɪpɑːˈtɪʃən) *n* division into or among three

tripe (traɪp) *n* **1** the stomach lining of an ox, cow, or other ruminant, prepared for cooking **2** *informal* something silly; rubbish **3** (*plural*) *archaic informal* intestines; belly [c13 from Old French, of unknown origin]

tripersonal (traɪˈpɜːsənˀl) *adj Christian theol* (of God) existing as the Trinity. Compare **unipersonal** > ˌtriperˈsonality *n*

triphammer (ˈtrɪpˌhæmə) *n* a power hammer that is raised or tilted by a cam and allowed to fall under gravity

triphenylmethane (traɪˌfiːnaɪlˈmiːθeɪn, -ˌfɛn-) *n* a colourless crystalline solid used for the preparation of many dyes. Formula: $(C_6H_5)_3CH$

triphibious (traɪˈfɪbɪəs) *adj* (*esp of military operations*) occurring on land, at sea, and in the air [c20 from TRI- + (AM)PHIBIOUS]

trip-hop (ˈtrɪpˌhɒp) *n* a type of British electronic dance music of the 1990s, influenced by drug culture [c20 TRIP (in the sense: drug experience) + HIP-HOP]

triphthong (ˈtrɪfθɒŋ, ˈtrɪp-) *n* **1** a composite vowel sound during the articulation of which the vocal organs move from one position through a second, ending in a third **2** a trigraph representing a composite vowel sound such as this [c16 via New Latin from Medieval Greek *triphthongos*, from TRI- + *phthongos* sound; compare DIPHTHONG] > triphˈthongal *adj*

triphylite (ˈtrɪfɪˌlaɪt) *n* a bluish-grey rare mineral that consists of lithium iron phosphate in orthorhombic crystalline form and occurs in pegmatites. Formula: $LiFePO_4$ [c19 from TRI- + *phyl-*, from Greek *phulon* family + -ITE1, referring to its three bases]

tripinnate (traɪˈpɪnɪt, -eɪt) *adj* (of a bipinnate leaf) having the pinnules themselves pinnate > triˈpinnately *adv*

Tripitaka (trɪˈpɪtəkə) *n Buddhism* the three collections of books making up the Buddhist canon of scriptures [from Pali *tri* three + *pitaka* basket]

triplane (ˈtraɪˌpleɪn) *n* an aeroplane having three wings one above the other

triple (ˈtrɪpˀl) *adj* **1** consisting of three parts; threefold **2** (of musical time or rhythm) having three beats in each bar **3** three times as great or as much ▷ *n* **4** a threefold amount **5** a group of three ▷ *vb* **6** to increase or become increased threefold; treble [c16 from Latin *triplus*] > ˈ**triply** *adv*

triple A *n military* anti-aircraft artillery: written as AAA

Triple Alliance *n* **1** the secret alliance between Germany, Austria-Hungary, and Italy formed in 1882 and lasting until 1914 **2** the alliance of France, the Netherlands, and Britain against Spain in 1717 **3** the alliance of England, Sweden, and the Netherlands against France in 1668

triple bond *n* a type of chemical bond consisting of three distinct covalent bonds linking two atoms in a molecule

triple crown *n* **1** *RC Church* the Pope's tiara **2** *horse* *racing* the winning of three important races in one season **3** (*often capital*) *rugby union* a victory by Scotland, England, Wales, or Ireland in all three games against the others in the annual Six (formerly, Five) Nations Championship. Compare **grand slam** (sense 3)

Triple Entente *n* the understanding between Britain, France, and Russia that developed between 1894 and 1907 and counterbalanced the Triple Alliance of 1882. The Entente became a formal alliance on the outbreak of World War I and was ended by the Russian Revolution in 1917

triple expansion engine *n* (formerly) a steam engine in which the steam is expanded in three stages in cylinders of increasing diameter to accommodate the increasing volume of the steam

triple jump *n* an athletic event in which the competitor has to perform successively a hop, a step, and a jump in continuous movement. Also called: **hop, step, and jump**

triple-nerved *adj* (of a leaf) having three main veins

triple play *n* the supply to a customer by one provider of telephone, internet, and television services

triple point *n chem* the temperature and pressure at which the three phases of a substance are in equilibrium. The triple point of water, 273.16 K at a pressure of 611.2 Pa, is the basis of the definition of the kelvin

triplet ('trɪplɪt) *n* **1** a group or set of three similar things **2** one of three offspring born at one birth **3** *music* a group of three notes played in a time value of two, four, etc **4** *chem* a state of a molecule or free radical in which there are two unpaired electrons [c17 from TRIPLE, on the model of *doublet*]

tripletail ('trɪpə̩l̩,teɪl) *n*, *pl* -**tail** *or* -**tails** any percoid fish of the family *Lobotidae*, esp *Lobotes surinamensis*, of brackish waters of SE Asia, having tail-like dorsal and anal fins

triple time *n* musical time with three beats in each bar

triple-tongue *vb music* to play (very quick staccato passages of notes grouped in threes) on a wind instrument by a combination of single- and double-tonguing. Compare **single-tongue, double-tongue**. > triple tonguing *n*

triplex ('trɪplɛks) *adj* a less common word for **triple** [c17 from Latin: threefold, from TRI- + *-plex* -FOLD]

Triplex ('trɪplɛks) *n trademark Brit* a laminated safety glass, as used in car windows

triplicate *adj* ('trɪplɪkɪt) **1** triple ▷ *vb* ('trɪplɪ̩keɪt) **2** to multiply or be multiplied by three ▷ *n* ('trɪplɪkɪt) **3 a** a group of three things **b** one of such a group **4** in triplicate written out three times [c15 from Latin *triplicāre* to triple, from TRIPLEX] > ,tripli'cation *n*

triplicity (trɪ'plɪsɪtɪ) *n*, *pl* -**ties** **1** a group of three things **2** the state of being three **3** *astrology* any of four groups, earth, air, fire, and water, each consisting of three signs of the zodiac that are thought to have something in common in their nature [c14 from Late Latin *triplicitās*, from Latin *triplex* threefold; see TRIPLEX]

triploblastic (,trɪpləʊ'blæstɪk) *adj* (of all multicellular animals except coelenterates) having a body developed from all three germ layers. Compare **diploblastic** [c19 from *triplo-* threefold (from Greek *triploos*) + -BLAST]

triploid ('trɪplɔɪd) *adj* **1** having or relating to three times the haploid number of chromosomes: *a triploid organism* ▷ *n* **2** a triploid organism [c19 from Greek *triploos* triple + (HAPL)OID]

tripod ('traɪpɒd) *n* **1** an adjustable and usually collapsible three-legged stand to which a camera, etc, can be attached to hold it steady **2** a stand or table having three legs [c17 via Latin from Greek *tripod-, tripous* three-footed, from TRI- + *pous* foot] > tripodal ('trɪpəd°l) *adj*

tripody ('trɪpədɪ) *n*, *pl* -**dies** *prosody* a metrical unit consisting of three feet

tripoli ('trɪpəlɪ) *n* a lightweight porous siliceous rock derived by weathering and used in a powdered form as a polish, filter, etc [c17 named after TRIPOLI, in Libya or in Lebanon]

Tripoli ('trɪpəlɪ) *n* **1** the capital and chief port of Libya, in the northwest on the Mediterranean: founded by Phoenicians in about the 7th century BC; the only city that has survived of the three (Oea, Leptis Magna, and Sabratha) that formed the African Tripolis ("three cities"); fishing and manufacturing centre. Pop: 1 223 300 (2002 est). Ancient name: **Oea** ('iːə) Arabic name: **Tarabulus el Gharb 2** a port in N Lebanon, on the Mediterranean: the second largest town in Lebanon; taken by the Crusaders in 1109 after a siege of five years; oil-refining and manufacturing centre. Pop: 212 000 (2005 est). Ancient name: Tripolis Arabic name: Tarabulus esh Sham

Tripolitania (,trɪpəlɪ'teɪnɪə) *n* the NW part of Libya: established as a Phoenician colony in the 7th century BC; taken by the Turks in 1551 and became one of the Barbary states; under Italian rule from 1912 until World War II

Tripolitanian (,trɪpəlɪ'teɪnɪən) *adj* **1** of or relating to Tripolitania (now part of Libya) or its inhabitants ▷ *n* **2** a native or inhabitant of Tripolitania

tripos ('traɪpɒs) *n Brit* the final honours degree examinations in all subjects at Cambridge University [c16 from Latin *tripūs*, influenced by Greek noun ending *-os*]

trip out *vb* (*adverb*) (of an electrical circuit) to disconnect or be disconnected or (of a machine) to stop or be stopped by means of a trip switch or trip button

tripper ('trɪpə) *n* **1** a person who goes on a trip **2** *chiefly Brit* a tourist; excursionist **3** another word for **trip** (sense 7) **4 a** any device that generates a signal causing a trip to operate **b** the signal so generated

trippet ('trɪpɪt) *n* any mechanism that strikes or is struck at regular intervals, as by a cam [c15 (in the sense: a piece of wood used in a game): from *trippen* to TRIP]

trippy ('trɪpɪ) *adj* -**pier**, -**piest** *informal* suggestive of or resembling the effect produced by a hallucinogenic drug

trip switch *n* an electric switch arranged to interrupt a circuit suddenly and disconnect power from a running machine so that the machine is stopped

triptane ('trɪpteɪn) *n* a colourless highly flammable liquid alkane hydrocarbon, isomeric with heptane, used in aviation fuel; 2,2,3-trimethylbutane. Formula: $CH_3C(CH_3)_2CH(CH_3)CH_3$ [c20 shortened and altered from *trimethylbutane*; see TRI-, METHYL, BUTANE]

tripterous ('trɪptərəs) *adj* (of fruits, seeds, etc) having three winglike extensions or parts [c19 from TRI- + Greek *-pteros*, from *pteron* wing]

Triptolemus (trɪp'tɒlɪməs) *n Greek myth* a favourite of Demeter, sent by her to teach mankind agriculture

triptych ('trɪptɪk) *n* **1** a set of three pictures or panels, usually hinged so that the two wing panels fold over the larger central one: often used as an altarpiece **2** a set of three hinged writing tablets [c18 from Greek *triptukhos*, from TRI- + *ptux* plate; compare DIPTYCH]

triptyque (trɪp'tiːk) *n* a customs permit for the temporary importation of a motor vehicle [from French: TRIPTYCH (referring to its three sections)]

Tripura ('trɪpʊrə) *n* a state of NE India: formerly a princely state, ruled by the Maharajahs for over 1300 years; became a union territory in 1956 and a state in 1972; extensive jungles. Capital: Agartala. Pop: 3 191 168 (2001). Area: 10 486 sq km (4051 sq miles)

tripwire ('trɪp̩,waɪə) *n* a wire that activates a trap, mine, etc, when tripped over

triquetrous (traɪ'kwiːtrəs, -'kwɛt-) *adj* triangular, esp in cross section: *a triquetrous stem* [c17 from Latin *triquetrus* having three corners]

triradiate (traɪ'reɪdɪɪt, -,eɪt) *adj biology* having or consisting of three rays or radiating branches > tri'radiately *adv*

trireme ('traɪriːm) *n* a galley, developed by the ancient Greeks as a warship, with three banks of oars on each side [c17 from Latin *trirēmis*, from TRI- + *rēmus* oar]

trisaccharide (traɪ'sækə̩,raɪd) *n* an oligosaccharide whose molecules have three linked monosaccharide molecules

trisect (traɪ'sɛkt) *vb* (*tr*) to divide into three parts, esp three equal parts [c17 TRI- + *-sect* from Latin *secāre* to cut] > trisection *n* > tri'sector *n*

triserial (traɪ'sɪərɪəl) *adj* arranged in three rows or series

trishaw ('traɪ̩,ʃɔː) *n* another name for **rickshaw** (sense 2) [c20 from TRI- + RICKSHAW]

triskaidekaphobia (,trɪskaɪ̩,dɛkə'fəʊbɪə) *n* an abnormal fear of the number thirteen [c20 from Greek *triskaideka* thirteen + -PHOBIA] > ,triskai,deka'phobic *adj, n*

triskelion (trɪ'skɛlɪ̩,ɒn, -ən) *or* **triskele** ('trɪski:l) *n*, *pl* triskelia (trɪ'skɛlɪə) *or* triskeles a symbol consisting of three bent limbs or lines radiating from a centre [c19 from Greek *triskelēs* three-legged, from TRI- + *skelos* leg]

Trismegistus (,trɪsmɪ'dʒɪstəs) *n* See **Hermes Trismegistus**

trismus ('trɪzməs) *n pathol* the state or condition of being unable to open the mouth because of sustained contractions of the jaw muscles, caused by a form of tetanus. Nontechnical name: lockjaw [c17 from New Latin, from Greek *trismos* a grinding] > 'trismic *adj*

trisoctahedron (trɪs̩,ɒktə'hiːdrən) *n*, *pl* -**drons** *or* -**dra** (-drə) a solid figure having 24 identical triangular faces, groups of three faces being formed on an underlying octahedron [c19 from Greek *tris* three times + OCTAHEDRON] > tris,octa'hedral *adj*

trisomy ('traɪsəʊmɪ) *n* the condition of having one chromosome of the set represented three times in an otherwise diploid organism, cell, etc Trisomy of chromosome 21 results in Down's syndrome [c20 from TRI- + (CHROMO)SOM(E) + -Y³] > trisomic (traɪ'səʊmɪk) *adj*

Tristan ('trɪstən) *or* **Tristram** ('trɪstrəm) *n* (in medieval romance) the nephew of King Mark of Cornwall who fell in love with his uncle's bride, Iseult, after they mistakenly drank a love potion

Tristan da Cunha (də 'kuːnjə) *n* a group of four small volcanic islands in the S Atlantic, about halfway between South Africa and South America: comprises the main island of Tristan and the uninhabited islands of Gough, Inaccessible, and Nightingale; discovered in 1506 by the Portuguese admiral Tristão da Cunha; annexed to Britain in 1816; whole population of Tristan evacuated for two years after the volcanic eruption of 1961. Pop: 284 (2003 est). Area: about 100 sq km (40 sq miles)

tristate ('traɪ̩,steɪt) *adj* (of a digital computer chip) having high, low, and floating output states

triste (triːst) *or* **tristful** ('trɪstfʊl) *adj archaic* words for **sad** [from French] > 'tristfully *adv* > 'tristfulness *n*

tristearin (traɪ'stɪərɪn) *n* another name for **stearin**

tristich ('trɪstɪk) *n prosody* a poem, stanza, or strophe that consists of three lines [c19 from Greek, from TRI- + *stikhos* STICH, on the model of DISTICH] > tris'tichic *adj*

tristichous ('trɪstɪkəs) *adj* arranged in three rows, esp (of plants) having three vertical rows of leaves

tristimulus values (traɪ'stɪmjʊləs) *pl n* three values that together are used to describe a colour and are the amounts of three reference colours that can be mixed to give the same visual sensation as the colour considered. Symbol: X, Y, Z

See also **chromaticity coordinates**

trisulphide (traɪˈsʌlfaɪd) *n* any sulphide containing three sulphur atoms per molecule

trisyllable (ˌtraɪˈsɪləbªl) *n* a word of three syllables > trisyllabic (ˌtraɪsɪˈlæbɪk) *adj* > ˌtrisylˈlabically *adv*

tritanopia (ˌtraɪtəˈnəʊpɪə, ˌtrɪt-) *n* a form of colour blindness in which there is a tendency to confuse blues and greens and in which sensitivity to blue is reduced [C19/20: from New Latin, from Greek *tritos* third + New Latin *anopia* blindness; signifying that only two thirds of the spectrum can be distinguished] > tritanopic (ˌtraɪtəˈnɒpɪk, ˌtrɪt-) *adj*

trite (traɪt) *adj* **1** hackneyed; dull: *a trite comment* **2** *archaic* frayed or worn out [C16 from Latin *trītus* worn down, from *terere* to rub] > ˈtritely *adv* > ˈtriteness *n*

tritheism (ˈtraɪθɪˌɪzəm) *n theol* belief in three gods, esp in the Trinity as consisting of three distinct gods > ˈtritheist *n, adj* > ˌtritheˈistic or ˌtritheˈistical *adj*

tritiate (ˈtrɪtɪˌeɪt) *vb* (*tr*) to replace normal hydrogen atoms in (a compound) by those of tritium [C20 from TRITI(UM) + -ATE[1]] > ˌtritiˈation *n*

triticale (ˌtrɪtɪˈkɑːlɪ) *n* a fertile hybrid cereal, a cross between wheat (*Triticum*) and rye (*Secale*), produced by polyploidy [C20 from *Tritic(um)* + (*Sec*)*ale*]

triticum (ˈtrɪtɪkəm) *n* any annual cereal grass of the genus *Triticum*, which includes the wheats [C19 Latin, literally: wheat, probably from *tritum*, supine of *terere* to grind]

tritium (ˈtrɪtɪəm) *n* a radioactive isotope of hydrogen, occurring in trace amounts in natural hydrogen and produced in a nuclear reactor. Tritiated compounds are used as tracers. Symbol: T or ³H; half-life: 12.5 years [C20 New Latin, from Greek *tritos* third]

triton[1] (ˈtraɪtªn) *n* any of various chiefly tropical marine gastropod molluscs of the genera *Charonia, Cymatium*, etc, having large beautifully-coloured spiral shells [C16 via Latin from Greek *tritōn*]

triton[2] (ˈtraɪtɒn) *n physics* a nucleus of an atom of tritium, containing two neutrons and one proton [C20 from TRIT(IUM) + -ON]

Triton[1] (ˈtraɪtªn) *n Greek myth* **1** a sea god, son of Poseidon and Amphitrite, depicted as having the upper parts of a man with a fish's tail and holding a trumpet made from a conch shell **2** one of a class of minor sea deities

Triton[2] (ˈtraɪtªn) *n* the largest satellite of the planet Neptune. Diameter: 2700 km

tritone (ˈtraɪˌtəʊn) *n* a musical interval consisting of three whole tones; augmented fourth

tritonia (traɪˈtəʊnɪə) *n* any plant of the perennial cormous S African genus *Tritonia*, with typically scarlet or orange flowers: family *Iridaceae* [New Latin, from Greek *Tritōn* TRITON[1]]

triturate (ˈtrɪtjʊˌreɪt) *vb* **1** (*tr*) to grind or rub into a fine powder or pulp; masticate ▷ *n* **2** the powder or pulp resulting from this grinding [C17 from Late Latin *trītūrāre* to thresh, from Latin *trītūra* a threshing, from *terere* to grind] > ˈtriturable *adj* > ˈtrituˌrator *n*

trituration (ˌtrɪtjʊˈreɪʃən) *n* **1** the act of triturating or the state of being triturated **2** *pharmacol* a mixture of one or more finely ground powdered drugs

triumph (ˈtraɪəmf) *n* **1** the feeling of exultation and happiness derived from a victory or major achievement **2** the act or condition of being victorious; victory **3** (in ancient Rome) a ritual procession to the Capitoline Hill held in honour of a victorious general **4** *obsolete* a public display or celebration **5** *cards* an obsolete word for **trump**[1] ▷ *vb* (*intr*) **6** (often foll by *over*) to win a victory or control: *to triumph over one's weaknesses* **7** to rejoice over a victory **8** to celebrate a Roman triumph [C14 from Old French *triumphe*, from Latin *triumphus*, from Old Latin *triumpus*; probably related to Greek *thriambos* Bacchic hymn] > ˈtriumpher *n*

triumphal (traɪˈʌmfəl) *adj* **1** celebrating a triumph: *a triumphal procession* **2** resembling triumph

triumphal arch *n* an arch built to commemorate a victory

triumphalism (traɪˈʌmfəlɪzəm) *n* excessive celebration of the defeat of one's enemies or opponents > triˈumphalist *adj*

triumphant (traɪˈʌmfənt) *adj* **1** experiencing or displaying triumph **2** exultant through triumph **3** *obsolete* **a** magnificent **b** triumphal > triˈumphantly *adv*

triumvir (traɪˈʌmvə) *n, pl* -virs or -viri (-vɪˌriː) (esp in ancient Rome) a member of a triumvirate [C16 from Latin: one of three administrators, from *triumvirōrum* of three men, from *trēs* three + *vir* man] > triˈumviral *adj*

triumvirate (traɪˈʌmvɪrɪt) *n* **1** (in ancient Rome) **a** a board of three officials jointly responsible for some task **b** the political alliance of Caesar, Crassus, and Pompey, formed in 60 BC (**First Triumvirate**) **c** the coalition and joint rule of the Roman Empire by Antony, Lepidus, and Octavian, begun in 43 BC (**Second Triumvirate**) **2** any joint rule by three men **3** any group of three men associated in some way **4** the office of a triumvir

triune (ˈtraɪjuːn) *adj* **1** constituting three in one, esp the three persons in one God of the Trinity ▷ *n* **2** a group of three **3** (*often capital*) another word for **Trinity** [C17 TRI- + -*une*, from Latin *ūnus* one] > triˈunity *n*

Triunitarian (traɪˌjuːnɪˈtɛərɪən) *n, adj* a less common word for **Trinitarian**

trivalent (traɪˈveɪlənt, ˈtrɪvələnt) *adj chem* **1** having a valency of three **2** having three valencies Also: tervalent > triˈvalency *n*

Trivandrum (trɪˈvændrəm) *n* a city in S India, capital of Kerala, on the Malabar Coast: made capital of the kingdom of Travancore in 1745; University of Kerala (1937). Pop: 744 739 (2001). Official name: Thiruvananthapuram

trivet (ˈtrɪvɪt) *n* **1** a stand, usually three-legged and metal, on which cooking vessels are placed over a fire **2** a short metal stand on which hot dishes are placed on a table **3** as right as a trivet *old-fashioned* in perfect health [Old English *trefet* (influenced by Old English *thrifēte* having three feet), from Latin *tripēs* having three feet]

trivia (ˈtrɪvɪə) *n* (*functioning as singular or plural*) petty details or considerations; trifles; trivialities [from New Latin, plural of Latin *trivium* junction of three roads; for meaning, see TRIVIAL]

trivial (ˈtrɪvɪəl) *adj* **1** of little importance; petty or frivolous: *trivial complaints* **2** ordinary or commonplace; trite: *trivial conversation* **3** *maths* (of the solutions of a set of homogeneous equations) having zero values for all the variables **4** *biology* denoting the specific name of an organism in binomial nomenclature **5** *biology, chem* denoting the popular name of an organism or substance, as opposed to the scientific one **6** of or relating to the trivium [C15 from Latin *triviālis* belonging to the public streets, common, from *trivium* crossroads, junction of three roads, from TRI- + *via* road] > ˈtrivially *adv* > ˈtrivialness *n*

triviality (ˌtrɪvɪˈælɪtɪ) *n, pl* -ties **1** the state or quality of being trivial **2** something, such as a remark, that is trivial ▷ Also called: trivialism (ˈtrɪvɪəˌlɪzəm)

trivialize (ˈtrɪvɪəˌlaɪz) or **trivialise** *vb* (*tr*) to cause to seem trivial or more trivial; minimize > ˌtrivialiˈzation or ˌtrivialiˈsation *n*

trivium (ˈtrɪvɪəm) *n, pl* -ia (-ɪə) (in medieval learning) the lower division of the seven liberal arts, consisting of grammar, rhetoric, and logic. Compare **quadrivium** [C19 from Medieval Latin, from Latin: crossroads; see TRIVIAL]

triweekly (traɪˈwiːklɪ) *adj, adv* **1** every three weeks **2** three times a week ▷ *n, pl* -lies **3** a triweekly publication

-trix *suffix forming nouns* indicating a feminine agent, corresponding to nouns ending in *-tor*: *executrix* [from Latin]

t-RNA *abbreviation for* transfer RNA

Troas (ˈtrəʊæs) *n* the region of NW Asia Minor surrounding the ancient city of Troy. Also called: the Troad (ˈtrəʊæd)

troat (trəʊt) *vb* (*intr*) (of a rutting buck) to call or bellow [C17 probably related to Old French *trout, trut*, a cry used by hunters to urge on the dogs]

Trobriand Islander (ˈtrəʊbrɪˌænd) *n* a native or inhabitant of the Trobriand Islands of Papua New Guinea

Trobriand Islands *pl n* a group of coral islands in the Solomon Sea, north of the E part of New Guinea: part of Papua New Guinea. Area: about 440 sq km (170 sq miles)

trocar (ˈtrəʊkɑː) *n* a surgical instrument for removing fluid from bodily cavities, consisting of a puncturing device situated inside a tube [C18 from French *trocart* literally: with three sides, from *trois* three + *carre* side]

trochaic (trəʊˈkeɪɪk) *prosody* ▷ *adj* **1** of, relating to, or consisting of trochees ▷ *n* **2** another word for **trochee 3** a verse composed of trochees > troˈchaically *adv*

trochal (ˈtrəʊkªl) *adj zoology* shaped like a wheel: *the trochal disc of a rotifer* [C19 from Greek *trokhos* wheel]

trochanter (trəʊˈkæntə) *n* **1** any of several processes on the upper part of the vertebrate femur, to which muscles are attached **2** the third segment of an insect's leg [C17 via French from Greek *trokhantēr*, from *trekhein* to run]

troche (trəʊʃ) *n med* another name for **lozenge** (sense 1) [C16 from French *trochisque*, from Late Latin *trochiscus*, from Greek *trokhiskos* little wheel, from *trokhos* wheel]

trochee (ˈtrəʊkiː) *n prosody* a metrical foot of two syllables, the first long and the second short (--). Compare **iamb** [C16 via Latin from Greek *trokhaios pous*, literally: a running foot, from *trekhein* to run]

trochelminth (ˈtrɒkªlˌmɪnθ) *n* any invertebrate of the former taxonomic group *Trochelminthes*, which included the rotifers and gastrotrichs, now classed as separate phyla [C19 from New Latin *trochelminthes*, from Greek *trokhos* wheel, from *trekhein* to run + HELMINTH]

trochilus (ˈtrɒkɪləs) *n, pl* -li (-ˌlaɪ) **1** another name for **hummingbird 2** any of several Old World warblers, esp *Phylloscopus trochilus* (willow warbler) [C16 via Latin from Greek *trokhilos* name of a small Egyptian bird said by ancient writers to pick the teeth of crocodiles, from *trekhein* to run]

trochlea (ˈtrɒklɪə) *n, pl* -leae (-lɪˌiː) any bony or cartilaginous part with a grooved surface over which a bone, tendon, etc, may slide or articulate [C17 from Latin, from Greek *trokhileia* a sheaf of pulleys; related to *trokhos* wheel, *trekhein* to run]

trochlear nerve (ˈtrɒklɪə) *n* either one of the fourth pair of cranial nerves, which supply the superior oblique muscle of the eye

trochoid (ˈtrəʊkɔɪd) *n* **1** the curve described by a fixed point on the radius or extended radius of a circle as the circle rolls along a straight line ▷ *adj also* trochoidal **2** rotating or capable of rotating about a central axis **3** *anatomy* (of a structure or part) resembling or functioning as a pivot or pulley [C18 from Greek *trokhoeidēs* circular, from *trokhos* wheel] > troˈchoidally *adv*

trochophore (ˈtrɒkəˌfɔː) or **trochosphere** (ˈtrɒkəsˌfɪə) *n* the ciliated planktonic larva of many invertebrates, including polychaete worms, molluscs, and rotifers [C19 from Greek *trokhos* wheel + -PHORE]

trod (trɒd) *vb* the past tense and a past participle of **tread**

trodden (ˈtrɒdªn) *vb* a past participle of **tread**

trode (trəʊd) *vb archaic* a past tense of **tread**

trog (trɒg) *vb* trogs, trogging, trogged (*intr*; often foll by *along*) *Brit informal* to walk, esp aimlessly or heavily; stroll [C20 perhaps a blend of TRUDGE and SLOG]

troglodyte (ˈtrɒgləˌdaɪt) *n* **1** a cave dweller, esp one of the prehistoric peoples thought to have

t

lived in caves **2** *informal* a person who lives alone and appears eccentric [c16 via Latin from Greek *trōglodutēs* one who enters caves, from *trōglē* hole + *duein* to enter] ⊳ **troglodytic** (ˌtrɒgləˈdɪtɪk) *or* ˌtrogloˈdytical *adj*

trogon (ˈtrəʊgɒn) *n* any bird of the order *Trogoniformes* of tropical and subtropical regions of America, Africa, and Asia. They have a brilliant plumage, short hooked bill, and long tail. See also **quetzal** [c18 from New Latin, from Greek *trōgōn*, from *trōgein* to gnaw]

troika (ˈtrɔɪkə) *n* **1** a Russian vehicle drawn by three horses abreast **2** three horses harnessed abreast **3** a triumvirate [c19 from Russian, from *troe* three]

troilism (ˈtrɔɪlɪzəm) *n* sexual activity involving three people [c20 perhaps from French *trois* three (compare MÉNAGE À TROIS) + -l-, as in DUALISM] ⊳ **troilist** *adj*

Troilus (ˈtrɔɪləs, ˈtrəʊɪləs) *n Greek myth* the youngest son of King Priam and Queen Hecuba, slain at Troy. In medieval romance he is portrayed as the lover of Cressida

Trois-Rivières (*French* trwa rivjɛr) *n* a port in central Canada, in Quebec on the St Lawrence River: one of the world's largest centres of newsprint production. Pop: 46 264 (2001). English name: Three Rivers

Trojan (ˈtrəʊdʒən) *n* **1** a native or inhabitant of ancient Troy **2** a person who is hard-working and determined ⊳ *adj* **3** of or relating to ancient Troy or its inhabitants

Trojan asteroid *n* one of a number of asteroids that have the same mean motion and orbit as Jupiter, preceding or following the planet by a longitude of 60º

Trojan Horse *n* **1** Also called: **the Wooden Horse** *Greek myth* the huge wooden hollow figure of a horse left outside Troy by the Greeks when they feigned retreat and dragged inside by the Trojans. The men concealed inside it opened the city to the final Greek assault **2** a trap intended to undermine an enemy **3** *computing* a bug inserted into a program or system designed to be activated after a certain time or a certain number of operations

Trojan War *n Greek myth* a war fought by the Greeks against the Trojans to avenge the abduction of Helen from her Greek husband Menelaus by Paris, son of the Trojan king. It lasted ten years and ended in the sack of Troy

troll¹ (trəʊl) *vb* **1** *angling* **a** to draw (a baited line, etc) through the water, often from a boat **b** to fish (a stretch of water) by trolling **c** to fish (for) by trolling **2** to roll or cause to roll **3** *archaic* to sing (a refrain, chorus, etc) or (of a refrain, etc) to be sung in a loud hearty voice **4** (*intr*) *Brit informal* to walk or stroll **5** (*intr*) *homosexual slang* to stroll around looking for sexual partners; cruise **6** (*intr*) *computing slang* to post deliberately inflammatory articles on an internet discussion board ⊳ *n* **7** *computing slang* a person who submits deliberately inflammatory articles to an internet discussion the act or an instance of trolling **8** *angling* a bait or lure used in trolling, such as a spinner [c14 from Old French *troller* to run about; related to Middle High German *trollen* to run with short steps] ⊳ **ˈtroller** *n*

troll² (trəʊl) *n* (in Scandinavian folklore) one of a class of supernatural creatures that dwell in caves or mountains and are depicted either as dwarfs or as giants [c19 from Old Norse: demon; related to Danish *trold*]

trolley (ˈtrɒlɪ) *n* **1** *Brit* a small table on casters used for conveying food, drink, etc **2** *Brit* a wheeled cart or stand pushed by hand and used for moving heavy items, such as shopping in a supermarket or luggage at a railway station **3** *Brit* (in a hospital) a bed mounted on casters and used for moving patients who are unconscious, immobilized, etc **4** *Brit* See **trolley-bus 5** *US and Canadian* See **trolley car 6** a device that collects

the current from an overhead wire (**trolley wire**), third rail, etc, to drive the motor of an electric vehicle **7** a pulley or truck that travels along an overhead wire in order to support a suspended load **8** *chiefly Brit* a low truck running on rails, used in factories, mines, etc, and on railways **9** a truck, cage, or basket suspended from an overhead track or cable for carrying loads in a mine, quarry, etc **10** **off one's trolley** *slang* **a** mentally confused or disorganized **b** insane ⊳ *vb* **11** (*tr*) to transport (a person or object) on a trolley ⊳ See also **trolleys** [c19 probably from TROLL¹]

trolleybus (ˈtrɒlɪˌbʌs) *n* an electrically driven public-transport vehicle that does not run on rails but takes its power from an overhead wire through a trolley

trolley car *n US and Canadian* another word for **streetcar**

trolley dolly *n informal* a female flight attendant

trolleys (ˈtrɒlɪz) *pl n slang* men's underpants

trollius (ˈtrɒlɪəs) *n* See **globeflower** [New Latin, from German *Trollblume* globeflower]

trollop (ˈtrɒləp) *n* **1** a promiscuous woman, esp a prostitute **2** an untidy woman; slattern [c17 perhaps from German dialect *Trolle* prostitute; perhaps related to TRULL] ⊳ **trollopy** *adj*

tromba marina (ˈtrɒmbə məˈriːnə) *n* an obsolete viol with a long thin body and a single string. It resembled the natural trumpet in its range of notes (limited to harmonics) and its tone [from Italian, literally: marine trumpet]

trombidiasis (ˌtrɒmbɪˈdaɪəsɪs) *n pathol* infestation with mites of the family *Trombiculidae* [c20 New Latin, from *Trombid(ium)* genus name + -IASIS]

trombone (trɒmˈbəʊn) *n* **1** a brass instrument, low-pitched counterpart of the trumpet, consisting of a tube the effective length of which is varied by means of a U-shaped slide The usual forms of this instrument are the **tenor trombone** (range: about two and a half octaves upwards from E) and the **bass trombone** (pitched a fourth lower) **2** a person who plays this instrument in an orchestra [c18 from Italian, from *tromba* a trumpet, from Old High German *trumba*] ⊳ **tromˈbonist** *n*

trommel (ˈtrɒməl) *n* a revolving cylindrical sieve used to screen crushed ore [c19 from German: a drum]

trompe (trɒmp) *n* an apparatus for supplying the blast of air in a forge, consisting of a thin column down which water falls, drawing in air through side openings [c19 from French, literally: trumpet]

trompe l'oeil (*French* trɔ̃p lœj) *n, pl* **trompe l'oeils** (trɔ̃p lœj) **1** a painting or decoration giving a convincing illusion of reality **2** an effect of this kind [from French, literally: deception of the eye]

Tromsø (ˈtrɒmsəʊ; *Norwegian* ˈtrumsø) *n* a port in N Norway, on a small island between Kvaløy and the mainland: fishing and sealing centre. Pop: 61 897 (2004 est)

tron (trɒn) *n* **1** a public weighing machine **2** the place where a tron is set up; marketplace [c15 from Old French *trone*, from Latin *trutina*, from Greek *trutanē* balance, set of scales]

-tron *suffix forming nouns* **1** indicating a vacuum tube: *magnetron* **2** indicating an instrument for accelerating atomic or subatomic particles: *synchrotron* [from Greek, suffix indicating instrument]

trona (ˈtrəʊnə) *n* a greyish mineral that consists of hydrated sodium carbonate and occurs in salt deposits. Formula: $Na_2CO_3NaHCO_3.2H_2O$ [c18 from Swedish, probably from Arabic *natrūn* NATRON]

tronc (trɒŋk) *n* a pool into which waiters, waitresses, hotel workers, etc, pay their tips and into which some managements pay service charges for later distribution to staff by a **tronc master**, according to agreed percentages [c20 from French: collecting box]

Trondheim (ˈtrɒndˌhaɪm; *Norwegian* ˈtrɒnhɛim) *n* a

port in central Norway, on Trondheim Fjord (an inlet of the Norwegian Sea): national capital until 1380; seat of the Technical University of Norway. Pop: 154 351 (2004 est). Former name (until the 16th century and from 1930 to 1931): Nidaros

tronk (trɒŋk) *n South African informal* a jail [Afrikaans]

troop (truːp) *n* **1** a large group or assembly; flock: *a troop of children* **2** a subdivision of a cavalry squadron or artillery battery of about platoon size **3** (*plural*) armed forces; soldiers **4** a large group of Scouts comprising several patrols **5** an archaic spelling of **troupe** ⊳ *vb* **6** (*intr*) to gather, move, or march in or as if in a crowd **7** (*tr*) *military, chiefly Brit* to parade (the colour or flag) ceremonially: *trooping the colour* **8** (*tr*) *Brit military slang* (formerly) to report (a serviceman) for a breach of discipline **9** (*intr*) an archaic word for **consort** (sense 1) [c16 from French *troupe*, from *troupeau* flock, of Germanic origin]

troop carrier *n* a vehicle, aircraft, or ship designed for the carriage of troops

trooper (ˈtruːpə) *n* **1** a soldier in a cavalry regiment **2** *US and Austral* a mounted policeman **3** *US* a state policeman **4** a cavalry horse **5** *informal, chiefly Brit* a troopship

troopship (ˈtruːpˌʃɪp) *n* a ship, usually a converted merchant ship, used to transport military personnel

troostite (ˈtruːstaɪt) *n* a reddish or greyish mineral that is a variety of willemite in which some of the zinc is replaced by manganese [c19 named after Gerard *Troost* (died 1850), US geologist]

tropaeolin (trəʊˈpiːəlɪn) *n* any of certain yellow and orange azo dyes of complex structure [c19 see TROPAEOLUM]

tropaeolum (trəʊˈpiːələm) *n, pl* **-lums** *or* **-la** (-lə) any garden plant of the genus *Tropaeolum* esp the nasturtium [c18 from New Latin, from Latin *tropaeum* TROPHY; referring to the shield-shaped leaves and helmet-shaped flowers]

trope (trəʊp) *n* **1** *rhetoric* a word or expression used in a figurative sense **2** an interpolation of words or music into the plainsong settings of the Roman Catholic liturgy [c16 from Latin *tropus* figurative use of a word, from Greek *tropos* style, turn; related to *trepein* to turn]

-trope *n combining form* indicating a turning towards, development in the direction of, or affinity to: *heliotrope* [from Greek *tropos* a turn]

trophallaxis (ˌtrɒfəˈlæksɪs) *n* the exchange of regurgitated food that occurs between adults and larvae in colonies of social insects [C19/20: from New Latin, from TROPHO- + Greek *allaxis* exchange, from *allassein* to change, from *allos* other] ⊳ ˌtrophalˈlactic *adj*

trophic (ˈtrɒfɪk) *adj* of or relating to nutrition: *the trophic levels of a food chain* [c19 from Greek *trophikos*, from *trophē* food, from *trephein* to feed] ⊳ ˈtrophically *adv*

tropho- *or before a vowel* **troph-** *combining form* indicating nourishment or nutrition: *trophozoite* [from Greek *trophē* food, from *trephein* to feed]

trophoblast (ˈtrɒfəˌblæst) *n* the outer layer of cells of the embryo of placental mammals, which is attached to the uterus wall and absorbs nourishment from the uterine fluids [c19 from TROPHO- + -BLAST] ⊳ ˌtrophoˈblastic *adj*

trophoplasm (ˈtrɒfəˌplæzəm) *n biology* the cytoplasm that is involved in the nutritive processes of a cell

trophozoite (ˌtrɒfəˈzəʊaɪt) *n* the form of a sporozoan protozoan in the feeding stage. In the malaria parasite this stage occurs in the human red blood cell. Compare **merozoite**

trophy (ˈtrəʊfɪ) *n, pl* **-phies 1** an object such as a silver or gold cup that is symbolic of victory in a contest, esp a sporting contest; prize **2** a memento of success, esp one taken in war or hunting **3** (in ancient Greece and Rome) **a** a memorial to a victory, usually consisting of captured arms raised on the battlefield or in a public place **b** a representation of such a memorial **4** an ornamental carving that represents a group of weapons, etc **5** (*modifier*) *informal* highly desirable and regarded as a symbol of wealth or success: *a trophy wife* [c16 from French *trophée*, from Latin *tropaeum*, from Greek *tropaion*, from *tropē* a turning, defeat of the enemy; related to Greek *trepein* to turn]

-trophy *n combining form* indicating a certain type of nourishment or growth: *dystrophy* [from Greek *-trophia*, from *trophē* nourishment] > **-trophic** *adj combining form*

tropic ('trɒpɪk) *n* **1** (*sometimes capital*) either of the parallel lines of latitude at about 23½°N (**tropic of Cancer**) and 23½°S (**tropic of Capricorn**) of the equator **2** the tropics (*often capital*) that part of the earth's surface between the tropics of Cancer and Capricorn; the Torrid Zone *astronomy* either of the two parallel circles on the celestial sphere having the same latitudes and names as the corresponding lines on the earth ▷ *adj* **4** a less common word for **tropical** [c14 from Late Latin *tropicus* belonging to a turn, from Greek *tropikos*, from *tropos* a turn; from the ancient belief that the sun turned back at the solstices]

-tropic *adj combining form* turning or developing in response to a certain stimulus: *heliotropic* [from Greek *tropos* a turn; see TROPE]

tropical ('trɒpɪk³l) *adj* **1** situated in, used in, characteristic of, or relating to the tropics **2** (of weather) very hot, esp when humid **3** *rhetoric* of or relating to a trope > ˌtropi'cality *n*
> 'tropically *adv*

tropicalize or **tropicalise** ('trɒpɪkᵊˌlaɪz) *vb* (*tr*) to adapt to tropical use, temperatures, etc
> ˌtropicali'zation or ˌtropicali'sation *n*

tropical year *n* another name for **solar year** See **year** (sense 4)

tropicbird ('trɒpɪkˌbɜːd) *n* any aquatic bird of the tropical family *Phaethontidae*, having long slender tail feathers and a white plumage with black markings: order *Pelecaniformes* (pelicans, cormorants, etc) [c17 so called because it is found in the tropical regions]

tropine ('trəʊpiːn, -pɪn) *n* a white crystalline poisonous hygroscopic alkaloid obtained by heating atropine or hyoscyamine with barium hydroxide. Formula: $C_8H_{15}NO$ [c19 shortened from ATROPINE]

tropism ('trəʊpɪzəm) *n* the response of an organism, esp a plant, to an external stimulus by growth in a direction determined by the stimulus [from Greek *tropos* a turn] > ˌtropis'matic *adj*
> tropistic (trəʊ'pɪstɪk) *adj*

-tropism or **-tropy** *n combining form* indicating a tendency to turn or develop in response to a certain stimulus: *phototropism* [from Greek *tropos* a turn]

tropo- *combining form* indicating change or a turning: *tropophyte* [from Greek *tropos* a turn]

tropology (trɒ'pɒlədʒɪ) *n, pl* **-gies 1** *rhetoric* the use of figurative language in speech or writing **2** *christian theol* the educing of moral or figurative meanings from the Scriptures **3** a treatise on tropes or figures of speech [c16 via Late Latin from Greek *tropalogia*; see TROPE, -LOGY] > ˌtropo'logic or ˌtropo'logical *adj*

tropopause ('trɒpəˌpɔːz) *n meteorol* the plane of discontinuity between the troposphere and the stratosphere, characterized by a sharp change in the lapse rate and varying in altitude from about 18 km (11 miles) above the equator to 6 km (4 miles) at the Poles

tropophyte ('trɒpəˌfaɪt) *n* a plant living in a seasonal climate that can become dormant in unfavourable conditions > **tropophytic** (ˌtrɒpə'fɪtɪk) *adj*

troposphere ('trɒpəˌsfɪə) *n* the lowest atmospheric layer, about 18 kilometres (11 miles) thick at the equator to about 6 km (4 miles) at the Poles, in which air temperature decreases

normally with height at about 6.5°C per km
> ˌtropo'spheric (ˌtrɒpə'sfɛrɪk) *adj*

-tropous *adj combining form* indicating a turning away: *anatropous* [from Greek *-tropos* concerning a turn]

troppo¹ ('trɒpəʊ) *adv music* too much; excessively. See **non troppo** [Italian]

troppo² ('trɒpəʊ) *adj Austral slang* mentally affected by a tropical climate

Trossachs ('trɒsəks) *n* (*functioning as plural or singular*) the **1** a narrow wooded valley in central Scotland, between Loch Achray and Loch Katrine: made famous by Sir Walter Scott's descriptions **2** (*popularly*) the area extending northwards from Loch Ard and Aberfoyle to Lochs Katrine, Achray, and Venachar

trot (trɒt) *vb* **trots, trotting, trotted 1** to move or cause to move at a trot **2** *angling* to fish (a fast-moving stream or river) by using a float and weighted line that carries the baited hook just above the bottom ▷ *n* **3** a gait of a horse or other quadruped, faster than a walk, in which diagonally opposite legs come down together. See also **jog trot, rising trot, sitting trot 4** a steady brisk pace **5** (in harness racing) a race for horses that have been trained to trot fast **6** *angling* **a** one of the short lines attached to a trotline **b** the trotline **7** *Austral and NZ informal* a run of luck: *a good trot* **8** *chiefly Brit* a small child; tot **9** *US slang* a student's crib **10** on the trot *informal* **a** one after the other: *to read two books on the trot* **b** busy, esp on one's feet **11** the trots *informal* **a** diarrhoea **b** NZ trotting races [c13 from Old French *trot*, from *troter* to trot, of Germanic origin; related to Middle High German *trotten* to run]

Trot (trɒt) *n informal* a follower of Trotsky

troth (trəʊθ) *n archaic* **1** a pledge or oath of fidelity, esp a betrothal **2** truth (esp in the phrase **in troth**) **3** loyalty; fidelity [Old English *trēowth*; related to Old High German *gitriuwida* loyalty; see TRUTH]

trothplight ('trəʊθˌplaɪt) *archaic* ▷ *n* **1** a betrothal ▷ *vb* **2** (*tr*) to betroth ▷ *adj* **3** betrothed; engaged [c14 from TROTH + PLIGHT²]

trotline ('trɒtˌlaɪn) *n angling* a long line suspended across a stream, river, etc, to which shorter hooked and baited lines are attached. Compare **trawl** (sense 2) See also **setline**

trot out *vb* (*tr, adverb*) *informal* to bring forward, as for approbation or admiration, esp repeatedly: *he trots out the same excuses every time*

Trotskyism ('trɒtskɪˌɪzəm) *n* the theory of Communism developed by the Russian revolutionary Leon Trotsky (original name *Lev Davidovich Bronstein*; 1879–1940), in which he called for immediate worldwide revolution by the proletariat > 'Trotskyist or 'Trotskyite *n, adj*

Trotskyist International *n* any of several international Trotskyist organizations that have developed from the international federation of anti-Stalinist Communists founded by Trotsky in 1936

trotter ('trɒtə) *n* **1** a person or animal that trots, esp a horse that is specially trained to trot fast **2** (*usually plural*) the foot of certain animals, esp of pigs

trotting race *n NZ* a race for standard-bred horses driven in sulkies and harnessed in a special way to cause them to use the correct gait. Also called (in Britain and certain other countries): **harness race**

trotyl ('trəʊtɪl, -tiːl) *n* another name for **TNT** [c20 from (TRINI)TROT(OLUENE) + -YL]

troubadour ('truːbəˌdʊə) *n* **1** any of a class of lyric poets who flourished principally in Provence and N Italy from the 11th to the 13th centuries, writing chiefly on courtly love in complex metric form **2** a singer [c18 from French, from Old Provençal *trobador*, from *trobar* to write verses, perhaps ultimately from Latin *tropus* TROPE]

trouble ('trʌb³l) *n* **1** a state or condition of mental distress or anxiety **2** a state or condition of

disorder or unrest: *industrial trouble* **3** a condition of disease, pain, or malfunctioning: *she has liver trouble* **4** a cause of distress, disturbance, or pain; problem: *what is the trouble?* **5** effort or exertion taken to do something: *he took a lot of trouble over this design* **6** liability to suffer punishment or misfortune (esp in the phrase **be in trouble**): *he's in trouble with the police* **7** a personal quality that is regarded as a weakness, handicap, or cause of annoyance: *his trouble is that he's too soft* **8** (*plural*) **a** political unrest or public disturbances **b** the **Troubles** political violence in Ireland during the 1920s or in Northern Ireland since the late 1960s **9** the condition of an unmarried girl who becomes pregnant (esp in the phrase **in trouble**) ▷ *vb* **10** (*tr*) to cause trouble to; upset, pain, or worry **11** (*intr; usually with a negative and foll by about*) to put oneself to inconvenience; be concerned: *don't trouble about me* **12** (*intr; usually with a negative*) to take pains; exert oneself: *please don't trouble to write everything down* **13** (*tr*) to cause inconvenience or discomfort to: *does this noise trouble you?* **14** (*tr; usually passive*) to agitate or make rough: *the seas were troubled* **15** (*tr*) *Caribbean* to interfere with: *he wouldn't like anyone to trouble his new bicycle* [c13 from Old French *troubler*, from Vulgar Latin *turbulāre* (unattested), from Late Latin *turbidāre*, from *turbidus* confused, from *turba* commotion]
> 'troubled *adj* > 'troubler *n*

troublemaker ('trʌb³lˌmeɪkə) *n* a person who makes trouble, esp between people
> 'trouble,making *adj, n*

troubleshooter ('trʌb³lˌʃuːtə) *n* a person who locates the cause of trouble and removes or treats it > 'trouble,shooting *n, adj*

troublesome ('trʌb³lsəm) *adj* **1** causing a great deal of trouble; worrying, upsetting, or annoying **2** characterized by violence; turbulent
> 'troublesomely *adv* > 'troublesomeness *n*

trouble spot *n* a place of recurring trouble, esp of political unrest

troublous ('trʌbləs) *adj archaic or literary* unsettled; agitated > 'troublously *adv* 'troublousness *n*

trouch (trautʃ) *n Southwestern English dialect* rubbish; junk

trough (trɒf) *n* **1** a narrow open container, esp one in which food or water for animals is put **2** a narrow channel, gutter, or gulley **3** a narrow depression either in the land surface, ocean bed, or between two successive waves **4** *meteorol* an elongated area of low pressure, usually an extension of a depression. Compare **ridge** (sense 6) **5** a single or temporary low point; depression **6** *physics* the portion of a wave, such as a light wave, in which the amplitude lies below its average value **7** *economics* the lowest point or most depressed stage of the trade cycle ▷ *vb* **8** (*intr*) *informal* to eat, consume, or take greedily [Old English *trōh*; related to Old Saxon, Old Norse *trog* trough, Dutch *trügge* ladle] > 'trough,like *adj*

trounce (trauns) *vb* (*tr*) to beat or defeat utterly; thrash [c16 of unknown origin]

troupe (truːp) *n* **1** a company of actors or other performers, esp one that travels ▷ *vb* **2** (*intr*) (esp of actors) to move or travel in a group [c19 from French; see TROOP]

trouper ('truːpə) *n* **1** a member of a troupe **2** an experienced or dependable worker or associate

troupial ('truːpɪəl) *n* any of various American orioles of the genus *Icterus*, esp *I. icterus*, a bright orange-and-black South American bird [c19 from French *troupiale*, from *troupe* flock; referring to its gregarious habits]

trous-de-loup (ˌtruːd³'luː) *n, pl* **trous-de-loup** (ˌtruːd³'luː) *military* any of a series of conical-shaped pits with a stake fixed in the centre, formerly used as protection against enemy cavalry [c18 from French, literally: wolf's holes]

trouse (trauz) *pl n Brit* close-fitting breeches worn in Ireland [from Irish and Scot Gaelic *triubhas*: compare TREWS]

trouser ('trauzə) *n* **1** (*modifier*) of or relating to

t

trousers: *trouser buttons* ▷ *vb* **2** *(tr) slang* to take (something, esp money), often surreptitiously or unlawfully

trousers (ˈtraʊzəz) *pl n* **1** a garment shaped to cover the body from the waist to the ankles or knees with separate tube-shaped sections for both legs **2** **wear the trousers** *Brit informal* to have control, esp in a marriage. US equivalent: **wear the pants** [C17 from earlier *trouse*, a variant of TREWS, influenced by DRAWERS] > ˈ**trousered** *adj* > ˈ**trouserless** *adj*

trouser suit *n chiefly Brit* a woman's suit of a jacket or top and trousers. Also called (esp US and Canadian): **pant suit**

trousseau (ˈtruːsəʊ) *n, pl* **-seaux** *or* **-seaus** (-səʊz) the clothes, linen, etc, collected by a bride for her marriage [C19 from Old French, literally: a little bundle, from *trusse* a bundle; see TRUSS]

trout (traʊt) *n, pl* **trout** *or* **trouts** **1** any of various game fishes, esp *Salmo trutta* and related species, mostly of fresh water in northern regions: family *Salmonidae* (salmon). They resemble salmon but are smaller and spotted **2** any of various similar or related fishes, such as a sea trout **3** *Austral* any of various fishes of the *Salmo* or *Oncorhynchus* genera smaller than the salmon, esp European and American varieties naturalized in Australia **4** *Brit informal* an irritating or grumpy person, esp a woman [Old English *trūht*, from Late Latin *tructa*, from Greek *troktēs* sharp-toothed fish]

trouvère (truːˈvɛə; *French* truvɛr) *or* **trouveur** (*French* truvœr) *n* any of a group of poets of N France during the 12th and 13th centuries who composed chiefly narrative works [C19 from French, from Old French *troveor*, from *trover* to compose; related to TROUBADOUR]

trove (trəʊv) *n* See **treasure-trove**

trover (ˈtrəʊvə) *n law* (formerly) the act of wrongfully assuming proprietary rights over personal goods or property belonging to another [C16 from Old French, from *trover* to find; see TROUVÈRE, TROUBADOUR]

trow (trəʊ) *vb archaic* to think, believe, or trust [Old English *treow*; related to Old Frisian *triūwe*, Old Saxon *treuwa*, Old High German *triuwa*; see TROTH, TRUE]

Trowbridge (ˈtrəʊˌbrɪdʒ) *n* a market town in SW England, administrative centre of Wiltshire: woollen manufacturing. Pop: 34 401 (2001)

trowel (ˈtraʊəl) *n* **1** any of various small hand tools having a flat metal blade attached to a handle, used for scooping or spreading plaster or similar materials **2** a similar tool with a curved blade used by gardeners for lifting plants, etc ▷ *vb* **-els, -elling, -elled** *or US* **-els, -eling, -eled** **3** *(tr)* to use a trowel on (plaster, soil, etc) [C14 from Old French *truele*, from Latin *trulla* a scoop, from *trua* a stirring spoon] > ˈ**troweller** *or US* ˈ**troweler** *n*

Troy (trɔɪ) *n* any of nine ancient cities in NW Asia Minor, each of which was built on the ruins of its predecessor. The seventh was the site of the Trojan War (mid-13th century BC). Greek name: **Ilion** Latin name: **Ilium** Related adj: **Trojan**

Troyes (*French* trwa) *n* an industrial city in NE France: became prosperous through its great fairs in the early Middle Ages. Pop: 60 958 (1999)

troy weight *or* **troy** (trɔɪ) *n* a system of weights used for precious metals and gemstones, based on the grain, which is identical to the avoirdupois grain. 24 grains = 1 pennyweight; 20 pennyweights = 1 (troy) ounce; 12 ounces = 1 (troy) pound [C14 named after the city of *Troyes*, France, where it was first used]

trs *printing abbreviation for* transpose

Trst (trst) *n* the Slovene and Serbo-Croat name for **Trieste**

truant (ˈtruːənt) *n* **1** a person who is absent without leave, esp from school ▷ *adj* **2** being or relating to a truant ▷ *vb* **3** *(intr)* to play truant [C13 from Old French: vagabond, probably of Celtic origin; compare Welsh *truan* miserable, Old Irish *trōg* wretched] > ˈ**truancy** *n*

truce (truːs) *n* **1** an agreement to stop fighting, esp temporarily **2** temporary cessation of something unpleasant [C13 from the plural of Old English *treow* TROW; see TRUE, TRUST]

Trucial States (ˈtruːʃəl) *pl n* a former name (until 1971) of the **United Arab Emirates.** Also called: **Trucial Sheikhdoms, Trucial Oman, Trucial Coast**

truck[1] (trʌk) *n* **1** *Brit* a vehicle for carrying freight on a railway; wagon **2** *US, Canadian, and Austral* a large motor vehicle designed to carry heavy loads, esp one with a flat platform. Also called (esp in Britain): **lorry** **3** a frame carrying two or more pairs of wheels and usually springs and brakes, attached under an end of a railway coach, etc **4** *nautical* **a** a disc-shaped block fixed to the head of a mast having sheave holes for receiving signal halyards **b** the head of a mast itself **5** any wheeled vehicle used to move goods ▷ *vb* **6** to convey (goods) in a truck **7** *(intr) chiefly US and Canadian* to drive a truck [C17 perhaps shortened from TRUCKLE[2]]

truck[2] (trʌk) *n* **1** commercial goods **2** dealings (esp in the phrase **have no truck with**) **3** commercial exchange **4** *archaic* payment of wages in kind **5** miscellaneous articles **6** *informal* rubbish **7** *US and Canadian* vegetables grown for market ▷ *vb* **8** *archaic* to exchange (goods); barter **9** *(intr)* to traffic or negotiate [C13 from Old French *troquer* (unattested) to barter, equivalent to Medieval Latin *trocare*, of unknown origin]

truckage (ˈtrʌkɪdʒ) *n US* **1** conveyance of cargo by truck **2** the charge for this

trucker[1] (ˈtrʌkə) *n chiefly US and Canadian* **1** a lorry driver **2** a person who arranges for the transport of goods by lorry

trucker[2] (ˈtrʌkə) *n US and Canadian* **1** a market gardener **2** another word for **hawker**

truck farm *n US and Canadian* a market garden > **truck farmer** *n* > **truck farming** *n*

truckie (ˈtrʌkɪ) *n Austral informal* a truck driver

trucking[1] (ˈtrʌkɪŋ) *n chiefly US and Canadian* the transportation of goods by lorry

trucking[2] (ˈtrʌkɪŋ) *n* **1** *US and Canadian* the business of growing fruit and vegetables on a commercial scale. Also called: **truck farming**, (Brit, Austral, NZ, and South African) **market gardening** **2** commercial exchange; barter

truckle[1] (ˈtrʌkᵊl) *vb (intr; usually foll by* to) to yield weakly; give in [C17 from obsolete *truckle* to sleep in a truckle bed; see TRUCKLE[2]] > ˈ**truckler** *n*

truckle[2] (ˈtrʌkᵊl) *n* **1** a small wheel; caster **2** a small barrel-shaped cheese ▷ *vb* **3** *(intr)* to roll on truckles **4** *(tr)* to push (a piece of furniture) along on truckles [C15 *trokel*, from Anglo-Norman *trocle*, from Latin *trochlea* sheaf of a pulley; see TROCHLEA]

truckle bed *n* a low bed on wheels, stored under a larger bed, used esp formerly by a servant

truckload (ˈtrʌkˌləʊd) *n* the amount carried by a truck

truck racing *n* a motor sport in which powerful trucks, without their containers, are raced around a circuit

truckstop (ˈtrʌkˌstɒp) *n chiefly US and Canadian* a place that supplies fuel, oil, etc for lorries and trucks, and often provides facilities such as a restaurant for drivers

truck system *n* a system during the early years of the Industrial Revolution of forcing workers to accept payment of wages in kind, usually to the employer's advantage [C19 from TRUCK[2]]

truculent (ˈtrʌkjʊlənt) *adj* **1** defiantly aggressive, sullen, or obstreperous **2** *archaic* savage, fierce, or harsh [C16 from Latin *truculentus*, from *trux* fierce] > ˈ**truculence** *or* ˈ**truculency** *n* > ˈ**truculently** *adv*

Trudeaumania (ˌtruːdəʊˈmeɪnɪə) *n* the obsessional enthusiasm in Canada for former prime minister Pierre Trudeau (1919–2000)

trudge (trʌdʒ) *vb* **1** *(intr)* to walk or plod heavily or wearily **2** *(tr)* to pass through or over by trudging ▷ *n* **3** a long tiring walk [C16 of obscure origin] > ˈ**trudger** *n*

trudgen (ˈtrʌdʒən) *n* a type of swimming stroke that uses overarm action, as in the crawl, and a scissors kick [C19 named after John *Trudgen*, English swimmer, who introduced it]

true (truː) *adj* **truer, truest** **1** not false, fictional, or illusory; factual or factually accurate; conforming with reality **2** *(prenominal)* being of real or natural origin; genuine; not synthetic: *true leather* **3** **a** unswervingly faithful and loyal to friends, a cause, etc: *a true follower* **b** *(as collective noun*; preceded by *the)*: *the loyal and the true* **4** faithful to a particular concept of truth, esp of religious truth: *a true believer* **5** conforming to a required standard, law, or pattern: *a true aim; a true fit* **6** exactly in tune: *a true note* **7** (of a compass bearing) according to the earth's geographical rather than magnetic poles: *true north* **8** *biology* conforming to the typical structure of a designated type: *sphagnum moss is a true moss, Spanish moss is not* **9** *physics* not apparent or relative; taking into account all complicating factors: *the true expansion of a liquid takes into account the expansion of the container.* Compare **apparent** (sense 3) **10** **not true** *informal* unbelievable; remarkable: *she's got so much money it's not true* **11** **true to life** exactly comparable with reality ▷ *n* **12** correct alignment (esp in the phrases **in true, out of true**) ▷ *adv* **13** truthfully; rightly **14** precisely or unswervingly: *he shot true* **15** *biology* without variation from the ancestral type: *to breed true* ▷ *vb* **trues, truing, trued** **16** *(tr)* to adjust so as to make true [Old English *triewe*; related to Old Frisian *triūwe*, Old Saxon, Old High German *triuwi* loyal, Old Norse *tryggr*; see TROW, TRUST] > ˈ**trueness** *n*

true bill *n criminal law* (formerly in Britain; now only US) the endorsement made on a bill of indictment by a grand jury certifying it to be supported by sufficient evidence to warrant committing the accused to trial

true-blue *adj* **1** unwaveringly or staunchly loyal, esp to a person, a cause, etc ▷ *n* **true blue** **2** *chiefly Brit* a staunch royalist or Conservative

true-born *adj* being such by birth: *a true-born Scot*

true level *n* a hypothetical surface that is perpendicular at every point to the plumb line, such as the mean sea level or geoid

true-life *adj* directly comparable to reality: *a true-life romance*

truelove (ˈtruːˌlʌv) *n* **1** someone truly loved; sweetheart **2** another name for **herb Paris**

truelove knot *or* **true-lovers' knot** *n* a complicated bowknot that is hard to untie, symbolizing ties of love

true north *n* the direction from any point along a meridian towards the North Pole. Also called: **geographic north** Compare **magnetic north**

true rib *n* any of the upper seven pairs of ribs in man

true time *n* the time shown by a sundial; solar time. When the sun is at the highest point in its daily path, the true time is exactly noon. Compare **mean time**

truffle (ˈtrʌfᵊl) *n* **1** Also called: **earthnut** any of various edible saprotrophic ascomycetous subterranean fungi of the European genus *Tuber*. They have a tuberous appearance and are regarded as a delicacy **2** Also called: **rum truffle** *chiefly Brit* a sweet resembling this fungus in shape, flavoured with chocolate or rum [C16 from French *truffe*, from Old Provençal *trufa*, ultimately from Latin *tūber*]

trug (trʌg) *n Brit* a long shallow basket made of curved strips of wood and used for carrying flowers, fruit, etc [C16 perhaps dialect variant of TROUGH]

trugo (ˈtruːgəʊ) *n Austral* a game similar to croquet, originally improvised in Victoria from the rubber discs used as buffers on railway carriages [from *true go*, when the wheel is hit between the goalposts]

truism (ˈtruːɪzəm) *n* an obvious truth; platitude [C18 from TRUE + -ISM] > truˈ**istic** *adj*

Trujillo (*Spanish* truˈxijo) *n* a city in NW Peru:

founded 1535; university (1824); centre of a district producing rice and sugar cane. Pop: 686 000 (2005 est)

Truk Islands (trʌk) *pl n* a group of islands in the W Pacific, in the E Caroline Islands: administratively part of the US Trust Territory of the Pacific Islands from 1947; became self-governing in 1979 as part of the Federated States of Micronesia; consists of 11 chief islands; a major Japanese naval base during World War II. Pop: 52 870 (1994). Area: 130 sq km (50 sq miles)

trull (trʌl) *n archaic* a prostitute; harlot [C16 from German *Trulle*; see TROLLOP]

truly ('tru:lɪ) *adv* **1** in a true, just, or faithful manner **2** (intensifier): *a truly great man* **3** indeed; really ▷ See also **yours truly**

trumeau (trʊ'məʊ) *n, pl* **-meaux** (-'məʊz) *architect* a section of a wall or pillar between two openings [from French]

trump[1] (trʌmp) *n* **1** Also called: **trump card** **a** any card from the suit chosen as trumps **b** this suit itself; trumps **2** Also called: **trump card** a decisive or advantageous move, resource, action, etc **3** *informal* a fine or reliable person ▷ *vb* **4** to play a trump card on (a suit, or a particular card of a suit, that is not trumps) **5** (*tr*) to outdo or surpass ▷ See also **trumps, trump up** [C16 variant of TRIUMPH] > **'trumpless** *adj*

trump[2] (trʌmp) *archaic or literary* ▷ *n* **1** a trumpet or the sound produced by one **2** **the last trump** the final trumpet call that according to the belief of some will awaken and raise the dead on the Day of Judgment ▷ *vb* **3** (*intr*) to produce a sound upon or as if upon the trumpet **4** (*tr*) to proclaim or announce with or as if with a fanfare **5** (*intr*) *Brit slang* to expel intestinal gas through the anus [C13 from Old French *trompe*, from Old High German *trumpa* trumpet; compare TROMBONE]

trumpery ('trʌmpərɪ) *n, pl* **-eries** **1** foolish talk or actions **2** a useless or worthless article; trinket ▷ *adj* **3** useless or worthless [C15 from Old French *tromperie* deceit, from *tromper* to cheat]

trumpet ('trʌmpɪt) *n* **1** a valved brass instrument of brilliant tone consisting of a narrow tube of cylindrical bore ending in a flared bell, normally pitched in B flat. Range: two and a half octaves upwards from F sharp on the fourth line of the bass staff **2** any instrument consisting of a valveless tube ending in a bell, esp a straight instrument used for fanfares, signals, etc **3** a person who plays a trumpet in an orchestra **4** a loud sound such as that of a trumpet, esp when made by an animal: *the trumpet of the elephants* **5** an eight-foot reed stop on an organ **6** something resembling a trumpet in shape, esp in having a flared bell **7** short for **ear trumpet** **8** **blow one's own trumpet** to boast about oneself; brag ▷ *vb* **-pets, -peting, -peted** **9** to proclaim or sound loudly [C13 from Old French *trompette* a little TRUMP[2]] > **'trumpet-ˌlike** *adj*

trumpeter ('trʌmpɪtə) *n* **1** a person who plays the trumpet, esp one whose duty it is to play fanfares, signals, etc **2** any of three birds of the genus *Psophia* of the forests of South America, having a rounded body, long legs, and a glossy blackish plumage: family *Psophiidae*, order *Gruiformes* (cranes, rails, etc) **3** (*sometimes capital*) a breed of domestic fancy pigeon with a long ruff

trumpeter swan *n* a large swan, *Cygnus buccinator*, of W North America, having a white plumage and black bill

trumpet flower *n* **1** any of various plants having trumpet-shaped flowers **2** the flower of any of these plants

trumpet honeysuckle *n* a North American honeysuckle shrub, *Lonicera sempervirens*, having orange, scarlet, or yellow trumpet-shaped flowers

trumpet vine *n* either of two bignoniaceous vines, *Campsis radicans* of the eastern US or *C. grandiflora* of E Asia, with clumps of trumpet-shaped flowers: grown as ornamentals. Also called: **trumpet climber, trumpet flower**

trumpetweed ('trʌmpɪtˌwi:d) *n US* any of various eupatorium plants, esp joe-pye weed [C19 so called because it has a hollow stem which children sometimes use as imitation trumpets]

trumps (trʌmps) *pl n* **1** (*sometimes singular*) *cards* any one of the four suits, decided by cutting or bidding, that outranks all the other suits for the duration of a deal or game **2** **turn up trumps** (of a person) to bring about a happy or successful conclusion (to an event, problem, etc), esp unexpectedly

trump up *vb* (*tr, adverb*) to concoct or invent (a charge, accusation, etc) so as to deceive or implicate someone

truncate *vb* (trʌŋ'keɪt, 'trʌŋkeɪt) **1** (*tr*) to shorten by cutting off a part, end, or top ▷ *adj* ('trʌŋkeɪt) **2** cut short; truncated **3** *biology* having a blunt end, as though cut off at the tip: *a truncate leaf* [C15 from Latin *truncāre* to lop] > **trun'cately** *adv* > **trun'cation** *n*

truncated (trʌŋ'keɪtɪd) *adj* **1** *maths* (of a cone, pyramid, prism, etc) having an apex or end removed by a plane intersection that is usually nonparallel to the base **2** (of a crystal) having edges or corners cut off **3** shortened by or as if by cutting off; truncate

truncheon ('trʌntʃən) *n* **1** *chiefly Brit* a short thick club or cudgel carried by a policeman **2** a baton of office: *a marshal's truncheon* **3** *archaic* a short club or cudgel **4** the shaft of a spear ▷ *vb* **5** (*tr*) to beat with a truncheon [C16 from Old French *tronchon* stump, from Latin *truncus* trunk; see TRUNCATE]

trundle ('trʌndᵊl) *vb* **1** to move heavily on or as if on wheels: *the bus trundled by* **2** (*tr*) *archaic* to rotate or spin ▷ *n* **3** the act or an instance of trundling **4** a small wheel or roller **5** **a** the pinion of a lantern **b** any of the bars in a lantern pinion **6** a small truck with low wheels [Old English *tryndel*; related to Middle High German *trendel* disc]

trundle bed *n* a less common word for **truckle bed**

trundler ('trʌndlə) *n NZ* **1** a golf bag or shopping trolley **2** a child's pushchair

trunk (trʌŋk) *n* **1** the main stem of a tree, usually thick and upright, covered with bark and having branches at some distance from the ground **2** a large strong case or box used to contain clothes and other personal effects when travelling and for storage **3** *anatomy* the body excluding the head, neck, and limbs; torso **4** the elongated prehensile nasal part of an elephant; proboscis **5** *US and Canadian* an enclosed compartment of a car for holding luggage, etc, usually at the rear. Also called (Brit, Austral, NZ, and South African): **boot** **6** *anatomy* the main stem of a nerve, blood vessel, etc **7** *nautical* a watertight boxlike cover within a vessel with its top above the waterline, such as one used to enclose a centreboard **8** an enclosed duct or passageway for ventilation, etc **9** (*modifier*) of or relating to a main road, railway, etc, in a network: *a trunk line* ▷ See also **trunks** [C15 from Old French *tronc*, from Latin *truncus*, from *truncus* (adj) lopped] > **'trunkˌful** *n* > **'trunkless** *adj*

trunk cabin *n nautical* a long relatively low cabin above the deck of a yacht

trunk call *n chiefly Brit* a long-distance telephone call

trunk curl *n* another name for **sit-up**

trunkfish ('trʌŋkˌfɪʃ) *n, pl* **-fish** *or* **-fishes** any tropical plectognath fish of the family *Ostraciidae*, having the body encased in bony plates with openings for the fins, eyes, mouth, etc. Also called: **boxfish, cowfish**

trunk hose *n* a man's puffed-out breeches reaching to the thighs and worn with tights in the 16th century [C17 of uncertain origin; perhaps from the obsolete *trunk* to truncate]

trunking ('trʌŋkɪŋ) *n* **1** *telecomm* the cables that take a common route through an exchange building linking ranks of selectors **2** plastic housing used to conceal wires, etc; casing **3** the delivery of goods over long distances, esp by road vehicles to local distribution centres, from which deliveries and collections are made

trunk line *n* **1** a direct link between two telephone exchanges or switchboards that are a considerable distance apart **2** the main route or routes on a railway

trunk road *n Brit* a main road, esp one that is suitable for heavy vehicles

trunks (trʌŋks) *pl n* **1** Also called: **swimming trunks** a man's garment worn for swimming, either fairly loose and extending from the waist to the thigh or briefer and close-fitting **2** shorts worn for some sports **3** *chiefly Brit* men's underpants with legs that reach midthigh

trunnel ('trʌnᵊl) *n* a variant spelling of **treenail**

trunnion ('trʌnjən) *n* **1** one of a pair of coaxial projections attached to opposite sides of a container, cannon, etc, to provide a support about which it can turn in a vertical **2** the structure supporting such a projection [C17 from Old French *trognon* trunk] > **'trunnioned** *adj*

Truro ('trʊərəʊ) *n* a market town in SW England, administrative centre of Cornwall. Pop: 20 920 (2001)

truss (trʌs) *vb* (*tr*) **1** (sometimes foll by *up*) to tie, bind, or bundle: *to truss up a prisoner* **2** to fasten or bind the wings and legs of (a fowl) before cooking to keep them in place **3** to support or stiffen (a roof, bridge, etc) with structural members **4** *informal* to confine (the body or a part of it) in tight clothes **5** *falconry* (of falcons) to hold (the quarry) in the stoop without letting go **6** *med* to supply or support with a truss ▷ *n* **7** a structural framework of wood or metal, esp one arranged in triangles, used to support a roof, bridge, etc **8** *med* a device for holding a hernia in place, typically consisting of a pad held in position by a belt **9** *horticulture* a cluster of flowers or fruit growing at the end of a single stalk **10** *nautical* a metal fitting fixed to a yard at its centre for holding it to a mast while allowing movement **11** *architect* another name for **corbel** **12** a bundle or pack **13** *chiefly Brit* a bundle of hay or straw, esp one having a fixed weight of 36, 56, or 60 pounds [C13 from Old French *trousse*, from *trousser*, apparently from Vulgar Latin *torciāre* (unattested), from *torca* (unattested) a bundle, TORCH] > **'trusser** *n*

truss bridge *n* a bridge that is constructed of trusses

trussing ('trʌsɪŋ) *n engineering* **1** a system of trusses, esp for strengthening or reinforcing a structure **2** the parts that form a truss

trust (trʌst) *n* **1** reliance on and confidence in the truth, worth, reliability, etc, of a person or thing; faith. Related adj: **fiducial** **2** a group of commercial enterprises combined to monopolize and control the market for any commodity: illegal in the US **3** the obligation of someone in a responsible position: *a position of trust* **4** custody, charge, or care: *a child placed in my trust* **5** a person or thing in which confidence or faith is placed **6** commercial credit **7** **a** an arrangement whereby a person to whom the legal title to property is conveyed (the trustee) holds such property for the benefit of those entitled to the beneficial interest **b** property that is the subject of such an arrangement **c** the confidence put in the trustee. Related adj: **fiduciary** **8** (in the British National Health Service) a self-governing hospital, group of hospitals, or other body providing health-care services, which operates as an independent commercial unit within the NHS **9** See **trust company, trust account** (sense 2) **10** (*modifier*) of or relating to a trust or trusts: *trust property* ▷ *vb* **11** (*tr; may take a clause as object*) to expect, hope, or suppose: *I trust that you are well* **12** (when *tr, may take an infinitive;* when *intr,* often foll by *in* or *to*) to place confidence in (someone to do something); have faith (in); rely (upon): *I trust him to tell her* **13** (*tr*) to consign for care: *the child was trusted to my care* **14** (*tr*) to allow (someone to do something) with confidence in his or her good sense or honesty: I

t

trust my daughter to go **15** (*tr*) to extend business credit to [C13 from Old Norse *traust*; related to Old High German *trost* solace] > ˈtrustable *adj* > ˌtrustaˈbility *n* > ˈtruster *n*

trust account *n* **1** Also called: **trustee account** a savings account deposited in the name of a trustee who controls it during his lifetime, after which the balance is payable to a prenominated beneficiary **2** property under the control of a trustee or trustees

trustafarian (ˌtrʌstəˈfɛərɪən) *n* (*sometimes capital*) *Brit informal* a young person from a wealthy background whose trust fund enables him or her to eschew conventional attitudes to work, dress, etc [C20 from TRUST (FUND) + (RAST)AFARIAN]

trustbuster (ˈtrʌstˌbʌstə) *n US informal* a person who seeks the dissolution of corporate trusts, esp a federal official who prosecutes trusts under the antitrust laws > ˈtrustˌbusting *n*

trust company *n* a commercial bank or other enterprise organized to perform trustee functions. Also called: **trust corporation**

trust deed *n* a document that transfers the legal title to property to a trustee

trustee (trʌˈstiː) *n* **1** a person to whom the legal title to property is entrusted to hold or use for another's benefit **2** a member of a board that manages the affairs and administers the funds of an institution or organization

trustee in bankruptcy *n* a person entrusted with the administration of a bankrupt's affairs and with realizing his assets for the benefit of the creditors

trustee investment *n stock exchange* an investment in which trustees are authorized to invest money belonging to a trust fund

trusteeship (trʌˈstiːʃɪp) *n* **1** the office or function of a trustee **2 a** the administration or government of a territory by a foreign country under the supervision of the **Trusteeship Council** of the United Nations **b** (*often capital*) any such dependent territory; trust territory

trustful (ˈtrʌstfʊl) *or* **trusting** *adj* characterized by a tendency or readiness to trust others > ˈtrustfully *or* ˈtrustingly *adv* > ˈtrustfulness *or* ˈtrustingness *n*

trust fund *n* money, securities, etc, held in trust

trust hotel *or* **tavern** *n NZ* a licensed hotel or a bar owned by a publicly elected committee as trustees, the profits of which go to public amenities

trustless (ˈtrʌstlɪs) *adj archaic or literary* **1** untrustworthy; deceitful **2** distrusting; wary; suspicious > ˈtrustlessly *adv* > ˈtrustlessness *n*

trust territory *n* (*sometimes capital*) another name for a **trusteeship** (sense 2)

trustworthy (ˈtrʌstˌwɜːðɪ) *adj* worthy of being trusted; honest, reliable, or dependable > ˈtrustˌworthily *adv* > ˈtrustˌworthiness *n*

trusty (ˈtrʌstɪ) *adj* **trustier, trustiest 1** faithful or reliable **2** *archaic* trusting > *n, pl* **trusties 3** someone who is trusted, esp a convict to whom special privileges are granted > ˈtrustily *adv* > ˈtrustiness *n*

truth (truːθ) *n* **1** the quality of being true, genuine, actual, or factual: *the truth of his statement was attested* **2** something that is true as opposed to false: *you did not tell me the truth* **3** a proven or verified principle or statement; fact: *the truths of astronomy* **4** (*usually plural*) a system of concepts purporting to represent some aspect of the world: *the truths of ancient religions* **5** fidelity to a required standard or law **6** faithful reproduction or portrayal: *the truth of a portrait* **7** an obvious fact; truism; platitude **8** honesty, reliability, or veracity: *the truth of her nature* **9** accuracy, as in the setting, adjustment, or position of something, such as a mechanical instrument **10** the state or quality of being faithful; allegiance ▷ Related adj: **veritable, veracious** [Old English *trīewth*; related to Old High German *gitriuwida* fidelity, Old Norse *tryggr* true] > ˈtruthless *adj*

truth-condition *n logic, philosophy* **1** the circumstances under which a statement is true **2** a statement of these circumstances: sometimes identified with the meaning of the statement

truth drug *or* **serum** *n informal* any of various drugs supposed to have the property of making people tell the truth, as by relaxing them

truthful (ˈtruːθfʊl) *adj* **1** telling or expressing the truth; honest or candid **2** realistic: *a truthful portrayal of the king* > ˈtruthfully *adv* > ˈtruthfulness *n*

truth-function *n logic* **1** a function that determines the truth-value of a complex sentence solely in terms of the truth-values of the component sentences without reference to their meaning **2** a complex sentence whose truth-value is so determined, such as a negation or conjunction

truth set *n* **1** *logic, maths* Also called: **solution set** the set of values that satisfy an open sentence, equation, inequality, etc, having no unique solution **2** *logic* the set of possible worlds in which a statement is true

truth table *n* **1** a table, used in logic, indicating the truth-value of a compound statement for every truth-value of its component propositions **2** a similar table, used in transistor technology, to indicate the value of the output signal of a logic circuit for every value of input signal

truth-value *n logic* **a** either of the values, true or false, that may be taken by a statement **b** by analogy, any of the values that a semantic theory may accord to a statement

truth-value gap *n logic* the possibility in certain semantic systems of a statement being neither true nor false while also not being determinately of any third truth-value, as *all my children are asleep* uttered by a childless person

try (traɪ) *vb* **tries, trying, tried 1** (when *tr*, may take an infinitive, sometimes with *to* replaced by *and*) to make an effort or attempt: *he tried to climb a cliff* **2** (*tr*; often foll by *out*) to sample, test, or give experimental use to (something) in order to determine its quality, worth, etc: *try her cheese flan* **3** (*tr*) to put strain or stress on: *he tries my patience* **4** (*tr*; *often passive*) to give pain, affliction, or vexation to: *I have been sorely tried by those children* **5 a** to examine and determine the issues involved in (a cause) in a court of law **b** to hear evidence in order to determine the guilt or innocence of (an accused) **c** to sit as judge at the trial of (an issue or person) **6** (*tr*) to melt (fat, lard, etc) in order to separate out impurities **7** (*tr*; usually foll by *out*) *obsolete* to extract (a material) from an ore, mixture, etc, usually by heat; refine ▷ *n, pl* **tries 8** an experiment or trial **9** an attempt or effort **10** *rugby* the act of an attacking player touching the ball down behind the opposing team's goal line, scoring five or, in Rugby League, four points **11** Also called: **try for a point** *American football* an attempt made after a touchdown to score an extra point by kicking a goal or, for two extra points, by running the ball or completing a pass across the opponents' goal line ▷ See also **try on, try out** [C13 from Old French *trier* to sort, sift, of uncertain origin]

> **USAGE** The use of *and* instead of *to* after *try* is very common, but should be avoided in formal writing: *we must try to prevent* (not *try and prevent*) *this happening*

trying (ˈtraɪɪŋ) *adj* upsetting, difficult, or annoying: *a trying day at the office* > ˈtryingly *adv* > ˈtryingness *n*

trying plane *n* a plane with a long body for planing the edges of long boards

tryke (traɪk) *n* a variant spelling of **trike** (sense 3)

try line *n* the line behind which the ball must be placed to score a try in a rugby match

tryma (ˈtraɪmə) *n, pl* **-mata** (-mətə) *botany* a drupe produced by the walnut and similar plants, in which the endocarp is a hard shell and the epicarp is dehiscent [C19 from New Latin, from

Greek *truma* a hole (referring to the hollow drupe), from *truein* to wear away]

try on *vb* (*tr, adverb*) **1** to put on (an article of clothing) to find out whether it fits or is suitable **2 try it on** *informal* to attempt to deceive or fool someone ▷ *n* **try-on 3** *Brit informal* an action or statement made to test out a person's gullibility, tolerance, etc

try out *vb* (*adverb*) **1** (*tr*) to test or put to experimental use: *I'm going to try the new car out* **2** (when *intr*, usually foll by *for*) *US and Canadian* (of an athlete, actor, etc) to undergo a test or to submit (an athlete, actor, etc) to a test to determine suitability for a place in a team, an acting role, etc ▷ *n* **tryout 3** *chiefly US and Canadian* a trial or test, as of an athlete or actor

trypan blue (ˈtrɪpən, ˈtraɪpæn, trɪˈpæn) *n* a dye obtained from tolidine that is absorbed by the macrophages of the reticuloendothelial system and is therefore used for staining cells in biological research [so called because it is *trypanocidal*: see TRYPANOSOME, -CIDE]

trypanosome (ˈtrɪpənəˌsəʊm) *n* any parasitic flagellate protozoan of the genus *Trypanosoma*, which lives in the blood of vertebrates, is transmitted by certain insects, and causes sleeping sickness and certain other diseases [C19 from New Latin *Trypanosoma*, from Greek *trupanon* borer + *sōma* body] > ˌtrypanoˈsomal *or* trypanosomic (ˌtrɪpənəˈsɒmɪk) *adj*

trypanosomiasis (ˌtrɪpənəsəˈmaɪəsɪs) *n* any infection of an animal or human with a trypanosome. See also **sleeping sickness, Chagas' disease**

tryparsamide (trɪˈpɑːsəmaɪd) *n* a synthetic crystalline compound of arsenic used in the treatment of trypanosomal and other protozoan infections. Formula: $C_8H_{10}AsN_2O_4Na \cdot \frac{1}{2}H_2O$ [C20 from a trademark]

trypsin (ˈtrɪpsɪn) *n* an enzyme occurring in pancreatic juice: it catalyses the hydrolysis of proteins to peptides and is secreted from the pancreas in the form of trypsinogen. See also **chymotrypsin** [C19 *tryp-*, from Greek *tripsis* a rubbing, from *tribein* to rub + -IN; referring to the fact that it was originally produced by rubbing the pancreas with glycerine] > **tryptic** (ˈtrɪptɪk) *adj*

trypsinogen (trɪpˈsɪnədʒən) *n* the inactive precursor of trypsin that is converted to trypsin by the enzyme enterokinase

tryptophan (ˈtrɪptəˌfæn) *n* an essential amino acid; a component of proteins necessary for growth [C20 from TRYPT(IC) + -O + -*phan* variant of -PHANE]

trysail (ˈtraɪˌseɪl; *Nautical* ˈtraɪsᵊl) *n* a small fore-and-aft sail, triangular or square, set on the mainmast of a sailing vessel in foul weather to help keep her head to the wind. Also called: **storm trysail**

try square *n* a device for testing or laying out right angles, usually consisting of a metal blade fixed at right angles to a wooden handle

tryst (trɪst, traɪst) *archaic or literary* ▷ *n* **1** an appointment to meet, esp secretly **2** the place of such a meeting or the meeting itself ▷ *vb* **3** (*intr*) to meet at or arrange a tryst [C14 from Old French *triste* lookout post, apparently of Scandinavian origin; compare Old Norse *traust* trust] > ˈtryster *n*

tsade (ˈtsɑːdiː, ˈsɑː-; *Hebrew* ˈtsadi) *n* a variant spelling of **sadhe**

Tsana (ˈtsɑːnə) *n* **Lake.** another name for (Lake) **Tana**

tsantsa (ˈtsæntsə) *n* (among the Shuar subgroup of the Jivaro people of Ecuador) the shrunken head of an enemy kept as a trophy [from Shuar]

tsar *or* **czar** (zɑː, tsɑː) *n* **1** (until 1917) the emperor of Russia **2** a tyrant; autocrat **3** *informal* a public official charged with responsibility for dealing with a certain problem or issue: *a drugs tsar* **4** *informal* a person in authority; leader **5** (formerly) any of several S Slavonic rulers, such as any of the princes of Serbia in the 14th century. Also (less commonly): **tzar** [from Russian *tsar*, via Gothic *kaisar* from Latin: from *Caesar* emperor, from the cognomen of Gaius Julius Caesar (100–44 BC), Roman general, statesman, and historian] > **'tsardom** or **'czardom** *n*

tsarevitch or **czarevitch** ('zɑːrəvɪtʃ) *n* a son of a Russian tsar, esp the eldest son [from Russian *tsarevich*, from TSAR + -*evich*, masculine patronymic suffix]

tsarevna or **czarevna** (zɑːˈrɛvnə) *n* **1** a daughter of a Russian tsar **2** the wife of a Russian tsarevitch [from Russian, from TSAR + -*evna*, feminine patronymic suffix]

tsarina, czarina (zɑːˈriːnə) or **tsaritsa, czaritza** (zɑːˈrɪtsə) *n* the wife of a Russian tsar; Russian empress [from Italian, Spanish *czarina*, from German *Czarin*]

tsarism or **czarism** ('zɑːrɪzəm) *n* **1** a system of government by a tsar, esp in Russia until 1917 **2** absolute rule; dictatorship > **'tsarist** or **'czarist** *n, adj*

Tsaritsyn (*Russian* tsaˈritsin) *n* a former name (until 1925) of **Volgograd**

TSB *abbreviation for* (the former) Trustee Savings Bank, now incorporated in Lloyds TSB

TSE *abbreviation for* **1** transmissible spongiform encephalopathy: any of a group of degenerative brain diseases, including BSE in cattle, that can be transmitted from one individual or species to another **2** Toronto Stock Exchange

Tselinograd (*Russian* tsəlinəˈgrat) *n* a former name (1961–94) for **Akmola**

tsetse fly or **tzetze fly** ('tsɛtsɪ) *n* any of various bloodsucking African dipterous flies of the genus *Glossina*, which transmit the pathogens of various diseases: family *Muscidae* [C19 via Afrikaans from Tswana]

TSH *abbreviation for* thyroid-stimulating hormone; another name for **thyrotropin**

Tshiluba (tʃɪˈluːbə) *n* the language of the Luba people, used as a trade language in the Democratic Republic of Congo (formerly Zaïre). See **Luba**

T-shirt or **tee shirt** *n* a lightweight simple garment for the upper body, usually short-sleeved [so called because of its shape]

Tshwane ('tʃwɒnɪ) *n* another name for **Pretoria**

Tsimshian ('tʃɪmʃɪən) *n* **1** a member of a Native Canadian people of northern British Columbia **2** the Penutian language of this people [C19 from Tsimshian, inside the Skeena River]

Tsinan ('tsiːˈnæn) *n* a variant transliteration of the Chinese name for **Jinan**

Tsinghai ('tsɪŋˈhaɪ) *n* **1** a variant transliteration of the Chinese name for **Qinghai** **2** a variant transliteration of the Chinese name for **Koko Nor**

Tsingtao ('tsɪŋˈtaʊ) *n* a variant transliteration of the Chinese name for **Qingdao**

Tsingyuan ('tsɪŋˈjwɑːn) or **Ch'ing-yüan** *n* the former name of **Baoding**

Tsitsihar ('tsɪtsɪˌhɑː) *n* a variant transliteration of the Chinese name for **Qiqihar**

tsitsith ('tsɪtsɪs, tsiˈtsiːt) *n* (*functioning as singular or plural*) *Judaism* the tassels or fringes of thread attached to the four corners of the tallith [from Hebrew *sīsīth*]

Tskhinvali ('tskɪnˌvɑːlɪ) *n* the Georgian name for **South Ossetia**

TSO *abbreviation for* The Stationery Office, formerly His (or Her) Majesty's Stationery Office

Tsonga ('tsɒŋgə) *n* **1** (*pl* **-ga** or **-gas**) a member of a Negroid people of S Mozambique, Swaziland, and South Africa **2** the language of this people, of the Bantu group of the Niger-Congo family

tsotsi ('tsɒtsɪ, 'tsɔ:-) *n, pl* **-tsis** a Black street thug or gang member; wide boy [C20 perhaps from Nguni *tsotsa* to dress flashily]

tsotsitaal ('tsɔ:tsɪˌtɑ:l) *n South African* a type of street slang used by tsotsis [C20 from Nguni *tsotsi* thug + Afrikaans *taal* language]

tsp. *abbreviation for* teaspoon

T-square *n* a T-shaped ruler used in mechanical drawing, consisting of a short crosspiece, which slides along the edge of the drawing board, and a long horizontal piece: used for drawing horizontal lines and to support set squares when drawing vertical and inclined lines

T-stop *n* a setting of the lens aperture on a camera calibrated photometrically and assigned a T-number

T-strap *n* (*modifier*) denoting a type of woman's shoe fastened with a T-shaped strap having one part passing across the ankle and the other attached to it in the middle and lying along the length of the foot. Also called: **T-bar**

Tsugaru Strait ('tsuɡaˌru) *n* a channel between N Honshu and S Hokkaido islands, Japan. Width: about 30 km (20 miles)

tsunami (tsʊˈnæmɪ) *n, pl* **-mis** or **-mi** **1** a large, often destructive, sea wave produced by a submarine earthquake, subsidence, or volcanic eruption. Sometimes incorrectly called a tidal wave **2** a sudden increase in or overwhelming number or volume of: *the tsunami of Olympic visitors* [from Japanese, from *tsu* port + *nami* wave]

Tsushima ('tsuːʃiːˌmɑ:) *n* a group of five rocky islands between Japan and South Korea, in the Korea Strait: administratively part of Japan; scene of a naval defeat for the Russians (1905) during the Russo-Japanese war. Pop: 41 230 (2000). Area: 698 sq km (269 sq miles)

tsutsugamushi disease (ˌtsʊtsʊɡəˈmʊʃɪ) *n* **1** one of the five major groups of acute infectious rickettsial diseases affecting man, common in Asia and including scrub typhus. It is caused by the microorganism *Rickettsia tsutsugamushi*, transmitted by the bite of mites **2** another name for **scrub typhus** [from Japanese, from *tsutsuga* disease + *mushi* insect]

Tswana ('tswɑːnə) *n* **1** (*pl* **-na, -nas**) a member of a mixed Negroid and Bushman people of the Sotho group of southern Africa, living chiefly in Botswana **2** the language of this people, belonging to the Bantu group of the Niger-Congo family: the principal language of Botswana

tt *the internet domain name for* Trinidad and Tobago

TT *abbreviation for* **1** teetotal **2** teetotaller **3** telegraphic transfer: a method of sending money abroad by cabled transfer between banks **4** Tourist Trophy (annual motorcycle races held in the Isle of Man) **5** tuberculin-tested **6** *international car registration for* Trinidad and Tobago

TTA (*in Britain*) *abbreviation for* Teacher Training Agency

TTFN *abbreviation for* ta-ta for now

TTL *abbreviation for* **1** transistor transistor logic: a method of constructing electronic logic circuits **2** through-the-lens: denoting a system of light metering in cameras

TTS *computing abbreviation for* text-to-speech: a technology that allows written text to be output as speech

TTYL *text messaging abbreviation for* talk to you later

TU *abbreviation for* trade union

Tuamotu Archipelago (ˌtuːəˈməʊtuː) *n* a group of about 80 coral islands in the S Pacific, in French Polynesia. Pop: 15 973 (2002). Area: 860 sq km (332 sq miles). Also called: **Low Archipelago, Paumotu Archipelago**

tuan[1] ('tuːɑːn) *n* (in Malay-speaking countries) sir; lord: a form of address used as a mark of respect [Malay]

tuan[2] ('tuːən, 'tjuː-) *n* a flying phalanger, *Phascogale tapoatafa*, of Australia. It is about the size of a rat, bluish grey in colour, brush-tailed, arboreal, and nocturnal. Also called: **wambenger, brush-tailed phascogale, phascogale** [C19 from a native Australian language]

Tuareg ('twɑːrɛɡ) *n* **1** (*plural* **-reg** or **-regs**) a member of a nomadic Berber people of the Sahara **2** the dialect of Berber spoken by this people

tuart ('tuːɑːt) *n* a eucalyptus tree, *Eucalyptus gomphocephala*, of Australia, yielding a very durable light-coloured timber [from a native Australian language]

tuatara (ˌtuːəˈtɑːrə) *n* a greenish-grey lizard-like rhynchocephalian reptile, *Sphenodon punctatus*, occurring only on certain small islands near New Zealand: it is the sole surviving member of a group common in Mesozoic times [C19 from Māori, from *tua* back + *tara* spine]

tuatua ('tuːɑːˌtuːɑː) *n, pl* **tuatua** an edible marine bivalve, *Paphies subtriangulata*, of New Zealand waters [Māori]

tub (tʌb) *n* **1** a low wide open container, typically round, originally one made of wood and used esp for washing: now made of wood, plastic, metal, etc, and used in a variety of domestic and industrial situations **2** a small plastic or cardboard container of similar shape for ice cream, margarine, etc **3** Also called: **bathtub** another word (esp US and Canadian) for **bath**[1] (sense 1) **4** Also called: **tubful** the amount a tub will hold **5** a clumsy slow boat or ship **6** *informal* (in rowing) a heavy wide boat used for training novice oarsmen **7** Also called: **tram, hutch a** a small vehicle on rails for carrying loads in a mine **b** a container for lifting coal or ore up a mine shaft; skip ▷ *vb* **tubs, tubbing, tubbed 8** *Brit informal* to wash (oneself or another) in a tub **9** (*tr*) to keep or put in a tub [C14 from Middle Dutch *tubbe*] > **'tubbable** *adj* > **'tubber** *n*

tuba ('tjuːbə) *n, pl* **-bas** or **-bae** (-biː) **1** a valved brass instrument of bass pitch, in which the bell points upwards and the mouthpiece projects at right angles. The tube is of conical bore and the mouthpiece cup-shaped **2** any other bass brass instrument such as the euphonium, helicon, etc **3** a powerful reed stop on an organ **4** a form of trumpet of ancient Rome [Latin]

tubal ('tjuːbəl) *adj* **1** of or relating to a tube **2** of, relating to, or developing in a Fallopian tube: *a tubal pregnancy*

Tubal-cain ('tjuːbəlˌkeɪn) *n Old Testament* a son of Lamech, said in Genesis 4:22 to be the first artificer of metals

tubal ligation *n* the tying of the Fallopian tubes as a method of sterilization

tubate ('tjuːbeɪt) *adj* a less common word for **tubular**

tubby ('tʌbɪ) *adj* **-bier, -biest 1** plump **2** shaped like a tub **3** *rare* having little resonance > **'tubbiness** *n*

tube (tjuːb) *n* **1** a long hollow and typically cylindrical object, used for the passage of fluids or as a container **2** a collapsible cylindrical container of soft metal or plastic closed with a cap, used to hold viscous liquids or pastes **3** *anatomy* short for **Eustachian tube** or **Fallopian tube b** any hollow cylindrical structure **4** *botany* **a** the lower part of a gamopetalous corolla or gamosepalous calyx, below the lobes **b** any other hollow structure in a plant **5** *Brit* **the tube a** Also called: **the underground** an underground railway system. US and Canadian equivalent: **subway b** the tunnels through which the railway runs **c** the train itself **d** (*capital*) *trademark* the London underground railway system **6** *electronics* another name for **valve** (sense 2) **b** See **electron tube, cathode-ray tube, television tube 7** (*preceded by the*) *slang* a television set **8** *Brit slang* a stupid or despicable person **9** *Austral slang* a bottle or can of beer **10** *surfing* the cylindrical passage formed when a wave breaks and the crest tips forward **11** an archaic word for **telescope** ▷ *vb* (*tr*) **12** to fit or supply with a tube or tubes **13** to carry or convey in a tube **14** to shape like a tube [C17 from Latin *tubus*] > **'tube-like** *adj*

tube fly *n angling* an artificial fly with the body tied on a hollow tube that can slide up the leader when a fish takes

tube foot *n* any of numerous tubular outgrowths of the body wall of most echinoderms that are used as organs of locomotion and respiration and to aid ingestion of food

tubeless tyre ('tjuːblɪs) *n* a pneumatic tyre in which the outer casing makes an airtight seal

t

with the rim of the wheel so that an inner tube is unnecessary

tuber ('tju:bə) *n* **1** a fleshy underground stem (as in the potato) or root (as in the dahlia) that is an organ of vegetative reproduction and food storage **2** *anatomy* a raised area; swelling [c17 from Latin *tūber* hump]

tubercle ('tju:bək°l) *n* **1** any small rounded nodule or elevation, esp on the skin, on a bone, or on a plant **2** any small rounded pathological lesion of the tissues, esp one characteristic of tuberculosis [c16 from Latin *tūberculum* a little swelling, diminutive of TUBER]

tubercle bacillus *n* a rodlike Gram-positive bacterium, *Mycobacterium tuberculosis*, that causes tuberculosis: family *Mycobacteriaceae*

tubercular (tjʊˈbɜːkjʊlə) *adj* **1** of, relating to, or symptomatic of tuberculosis **2** of or relating to a tubercle or tubercles **3** characterized by the presence of tubercles ▷ *n* **4** a person with tuberculosis > tu'**bercularly** *adv*

tuberculate (tjʊˈbɜːkjʊlɪt) *adj* covered with tubercles > tu'**berculately** *adv* > tu,**bercu'lation** *n*

tuberculin (tjʊˈbɜːkjʊlɪn) *n* a sterile liquid prepared from cultures of attenuated tubercle bacillus and used in the diagnosis of tuberculosis

tuberculin-tested *adj* (of milk) produced by cows that have been certified as free of tuberculosis

tuberculosis (tjʊˌbɜːkjʊˈləʊsɪs) *n* a communicable disease caused by infection with the tubercle bacillus, most frequently affecting the lungs (**pulmonary tuberculosis**). Also called: **consumption, phthisis** Abbreviation: TB [c19 from New Latin; see TUBERCLE, -OSIS]

tuberculous (tjʊˈbɜːkjʊləs) *adj* of or relating to tuberculosis or tubercles; tubercular > tu'**berculously** *adv*

tuberose *n* ('tju:bəˌrəʊz) **1** a perennial Mexican agave plant, *Polianthes tuberosa*, having a tuberous root and spikes of white fragrant lily-like flowers ▷ *adj* ('tju:bəˌrəʊs) **2** a variant of **tuberous** [c17 from Latin *tūberōsus* full of lumps; referring to its root]

tuberosity (ˌtju:bəˈrɒsɪtɪ) *n, pl* -ties any protuberance on a bone, esp for the attachment of a muscle or ligament

tuberous ('tju:bərəs) *or* **tuberose** ('tju:bəˌrəʊs) *adj* **1** (of plants or their parts) forming, bearing, or resembling a tuber or tubers: *a tuberous root* **2** *anatomy* of, relating to, or having warty protuberances or tubers [c17 from Latin *tūberōsus* full of knobs; see TUBER]

tube worm *n* any of various polychaete worms that construct and live in a tube made of sand, lime, etc

tubicolous (tju:ˈbɪkələs) *adj* (of certain invertebrate animals) living in a self-constructed tube

tubifex ('tju:bɪˌfɛks) *n, pl* -fex *or* -fexes any small reddish freshwater oligochaete worm of the genus *Tubifex*; it characteristically lives in a tube in sand and is used as food for aquarium fish [c19 from New Latin, from Latin *tubus* tube + *facere* to make, do]

tubing ('tju:bɪŋ) *n* **1** tubes collectively **2** a length of tube **3** a system of tubes **4** fabric in the form of a tube, used for pillowcases and some cushions

Tübingen ('tju:bɪŋən) *n* a town in SW Germany, in Baden-Württemberg: university (1477). Pop: 83 137 (2003 est)

tub-thumper *n* a noisy, violent, or ranting public speaker

tub-thumping *adj* **1** (of a speech or speaker) noisy, violent, or ranting ▷ *n* **2** noisy, violent, or ranting public speaking

Tubuai Islands (ˌtu:buˈaɪ) *pl n* a chain of small islands extending about 1400 km (850 miles) in the S Pacific, in French Polynesia; discovered by Captain Cook in 1777; annexed by France in 1880. Pop: 1979 (2002). Area: 173 sq km (67 sq miles). Also called: **Austral Islands**

tubular ('tju:bjʊlə) *adj* **1** Also: tubiform

('tju:bɪˌfɔ:m) having the form of a tube or tubes **2** of or relating to a tube or tubing > ˌtubu'**larity** *n* > '**tubularly** *adv*

tubular bells *pl n* *music* an orchestral percussion instrument of 18 chromatically tuned metal tubes suspended vertically and struck near the top

tubulate *vb* ('tju:bjʊˌleɪt) (*tr*) **1** to form or shape into a tube **2** to fit or furnish with a tube ▷ *adj* ('tju:bjʊlɪt, -ˌleɪt) **3** a less common word for **tubular** [c18 from Latin *tubulātus*, from *tubulus* a little pipe, from *tubus* pipe] > ˌtubu'**lation** *n* > '**tubuˌlator** *n*

tubule ('tju:bju:l) *n* any small tubular structure, esp one in an animal, as in the kidney, testis, etc [c17 from Latin *tubulus* a little TUBE]

tubuliflorous (ˌtju:bjʊlɪˈflɔ:rəs) *adj* (of plants) having flowers or florets with tubular corollas [c19 from TUBULE + -FLOROUS]

tubulous ('tju:bjʊləs) *adj* **1** tube-shaped; tubular **2** characterized by or consisting of small tubes [c17 from New Latin *tubulōsus*] > '**tubulously** *adv*

TUC (in Britain) *abbreviation for* **Trades Union Congress**

Tucana (tu:ˈkɑːnə) *n, Latin genitive* **Tucanae** (tu:ˈkɑːni:) a faint extensive constellation in the S hemisphere close to Hydrus and Eridanus, containing most of the Small Magellanic Cloud [probably from Tupi: toucan]

tuchun (tu:ˈtʃu:n) *n* (formerly) a Chinese military governor or warlord [from Chinese, from *tu* to superintend + *chün* troops]

tuck¹ (tʌk) *vb* **1** (*tr*) to push or fold into a small confined space or concealed place or between two surfaces: *to tuck a letter into an envelope* **2** (*tr*) to thrust the loose ends or sides of (something) into a confining space, so as to make neat and secure: *to tuck the sheets under the mattress* **3** to make a tuck or tucks in (a garment) **4** (*usually tr*) to draw together, contract, or pucker ▷ *n* **5** a tucked object or part **6** a pleat or fold in a part of a garment, usually stitched down so as to make it a better fit or as decoration **7** the part of a vessel where the after ends of the planking or plating meet at the sternpost **8** *Brit* **a** an informal or schoolchild's word for **food**, esp cakes and sweets **b** (*as modifier*): *a tuck box* **9** a position of the body in certain dives in which the legs are bent with the knees drawn up against the chest and tightly clasped ▷ See also **tuck away, tuck in** [c14 from Old English *tūcian* to torment; related to Middle Dutch *tucken* to tug, Old High German *zucchen* to twitch]

tuck² (tʌk) *n archaic* a rapier [c16 from French *estoc* sword, from Old French: tree trunk, sword, of Germanic origin]

tuck³ (tʌk) *dialect* ▷ *n* **1** a touch, blow, or stroke ▷ *vb* **2** (*tr*) to touch or strike **3** (*intr*) to throb or bump [c16 from Middle English *tukken* to beat a drum, from Old Northern French *toquer* to TOUCH; compare TUCKET]

Tuck (tʌk) *n* Friar See **Friar Tuck**

tuck away *vb* (*tr, adverb*) *informal* **1** to eat (a large amount of food) **2** to store, esp in a place difficult to find

tucker¹ ('tʌkə) *n* **1** a person or thing that tucks **2** a detachable yoke of lace, linen, etc, often white, worn over the breast, as of a low-cut dress **3** an attachment on a sewing machine used for making tucks at regular intervals **4** *Austral and NZ old-fashioned* an informal word for **food**

tucker² ('tʌkə) *vb* (*tr; often passive; usually foll by out*) *informal, chiefly US and Canadian* to weary or tire completely

tucker-bag *or* **tuckerbox** ('tʌkəˌbɒks) *n Austral informal old-fashioned* a bag or box used for carrying food

tucket ('tʌkɪt) *n archaic* a flourish on a trumpet [c16 from Old Northern French *toquer* to sound (on a drum)]

tuck in *vb* (*adverb*) **1** (*tr*) Also: **tuck into** to put to bed and make snug **2** (*tr*) to thrust the loose ends or sides of (something) into a confining space **3** (*intr*) Also: tuck into *informal* to eat, esp heartily

▷ *n* **tuck-in 4** *Brit informal* a meal, esp a large one

tuck shop *n chiefly Brit* a shop, esp one in or near a school, where cakes and sweets are sold

tucotuco (ˌtu:kəʊˈtu:kəʊ) *or* **tucutucu** (ˌtu:ku:ˈtu:ku:) *n* any of various colonial burrowing South American hystricomorph rodents of the genus *Ctenomys*, having long-clawed feet and a stocky body: family *Ctenomyidae* [c19 of South American Indian origin]

Tucson ('tu:sɒn) *n* a city in SE Arizona, at an altitude of 700m (2400 ft): resort and seat of the University of Arizona (1891). Pop: 507 658 (2003 est)

Tucumán (Spanish tuku'man) *n* a city in NW Argentina: scene of the declaration (1816) of Argentinian independence from Spain; university (1914). Pop: 837 000 (2005 est)

'**tude** (tju:d, tu:d) *n slang* a hostile or defiant manner [c20 from ATTITUDE]

-tude *suffix forming nouns* indicating state or condition: *plenitude* [from Latin *-tūdō*]

Tudor ('tju:də) *adj* denoting a style of architecture of the late perpendicular period and characterized by half-timbered houses [from the Tudor royal house of England, ruling from 1485 to 1603]

Tudorbethan (ˌtju:dəˈbi:θən) *adj disparaging* (of a contemporary building) imitative of Tudor and Elizabethan architecture

Tues. *abbreviation for* Tuesday

Tuesday ('tju:zdɪ) *n* the third day of the week; second day of the working week [Old English *tīwesdæg*, literally: day of Tiw, representing Latin *diēs Martis* day of Mars; compare Old Norse *tȳsdagr*, Old High German *zīostag*; see TIU, DAY]

TUF (in New Zealand) *abbreviation for* Trade Union Federation

tufa ('tju:fə) *n* a soft porous rock consisting of calcium carbonate deposited from springs rich in lime. Also called: **calc-tufa** [c18 from Italian *tufo*, from Late Latin *tōfus*] > **tufaceous** (tju:ˈfeɪʃəs) *adj*

tuff (tʌf) *n* a rock formed by the fusing together on the ground of small rock fragments (less than 2 mm across) ejected from a volcano [c16 from Old French *tuf*, from Italian *tufo*; see TUFA] > **tuffaceous** (tʌˈfeɪʃəs) *adj*

tuffet ('tʌfɪt) *n* a small mound or low seat [c16 alteration of TUFT]

tuft (tʌft) *n* **1** a bunch of feathers, grass, hair, etc, held together at the base **2** a cluster of threads drawn tightly through upholstery, a mattress, a quilt, etc, to secure and strengthen the padding **3** a small clump of trees or bushes **4** (formerly) a gold tassel on the cap worn by titled undergraduates at English universities **5** a person entitled to wear such a tassel ▷ *vb* **6** (*tr*) to provide or decorate with a tuft or tufts **7** to form or be formed into tufts **8** to secure and strengthen (a mattress, quilt, etc) with tufts [c14 perhaps from Old French *tufe*, of Germanic origin; compare TOP¹] > '**tufter** *n* > '**tufty** *adj*

tufted ('tʌftɪd) *adj* **1** having a tuft or tufts **2** (of plants or plant parts) having or consisting of one or more groups of short branches all arising at the same level

tufted duck *n* a European lake-dwelling duck, *Aythya fuligula*, the male of which has a black plumage with white underparts and a long black drooping crest

tug (tʌg) *vb* **tugs, tugging, tugged 1** (when *intr*, sometimes foll by *at*) to pull or drag with sharp or powerful movements: *the boy tugged at the door handle* **2** (*tr*) to tow (a vessel) by means of a tug **3** (*intr*) to work; toil ▷ *n* **4** a strong pull or jerk: *he gave the rope a tug* **5** Also called: **tugboat** a boat with a powerful engine, used for towing barges, ships, etc **6** a hard struggle or fight **7** a less common word for **trace²** (sense 1) [c13 related to Old English *tēon* to TOW; see TOW¹] > '**tugger** *n*

Tugela (tu:ˈgeɪlə) *n* a river in E South Africa, rising in the Drakensberg where it forms the **Tugela Falls**, 856 m (2810 ft) high (highest waterfall in Africa), before flowing east to the Indian Ocean: scene of battles during the Zulu

War (1879) and the Boer War (1899–1902). Length: about 500 km (312 miles)

tug-of-love *n* a conflict over custody of a child between divorced parents or between natural parents and foster or adoptive parents

tug-of-war *n* **1** a contest in which two people or teams pull opposite ends of a rope in an attempt to drag the opposition over a central line **2** any hard struggle, esp between two equally matched factions

tugrik *or* **tughrik** ('tuːˌɡriːk) *n* the standard monetary unit of Mongolia, divided into 100 möngös [from Mongolian]

tui ('tuːiː) *n, pl* tuis a New Zealand honeyeater, *Prosthemadera novaeseelandiae*, having a glossy bluish-green plumage with white feathers at the throat: it mimics human speech and the songs of other birds [from Māori]

Tuileries ('twiːlərɪ; *French* tɥilri) *n* a former royal residence in Paris: begun in 1564 by Catherine de' Medici and burned in 1871 by the Commune; site of the **Tuileries Gardens** (a park near the Louvre)

tuition (tjuːˈɪʃən) *n* **1** instruction, esp that received in a small group or individually **2** the payment for instruction, esp in colleges or universities [c15 from Old French *tuicion*, from Latin *tuitiō* a guarding, from *tuērī* to watch over] > tuˈitional *adj*

Tukkie ('tʌkɪ) *n South African informal* a student at the University of Pretoria, esp one representing the University in a sport [from the initials of *Transvaalse Universiteits Kollege*]

tuktu *or* **tuktoo** ('tʌkˌtuː) *n* (in Canada) another name for **caribou** [from Inuktitut]

tuk-tuk ('tʌkˌtʌk) *n* (in Thailand) a three-wheeled motor vehicle used as a taxi [c20 of imitative origin]

Tula (*Russian* 'tulə) *n* an industrial city in W central Russia. Pop: 460 000 (2005 est)

tularaemia *or US* **tularemia** (ˌtuːləˈriːmɪə) *n* an acute infectious bacterial disease of rodents, transmitted to man by infected ticks or flies or by handling contaminated flesh. It is characterized by fever, chills, and inflammation of the lymph glands. Also called: **rabbit fever** [c19/20: from New Latin, from *Tulare*, county in California where it was first observed; see -AEMIA] > ˌtulaˈraemic *or US* > ˌtulaˈremic *adj*

tulip ('tjuːlɪp) *n* **1** any spring-blooming liliaceous plant of the temperate Eurasian genus *Tulipa*, having tapering bulbs, long broad pointed leaves, and single showy bell-shaped flowers **2** the flower or bulb of any of these plants [c17 from New Latin *tulipa*, from Turkish *tülbend* turban, which the opened bloom was thought to resemble] > 'tulip-ˌlike *adj*

tulip tree *n* **1** Also called: **tulip poplar, yellow poplar** a North American magnoliaceous forest tree, *Liriodendron tulipifera*, having tulip-shaped greenish-yellow flowers and long conelike fruits **2** a similar and related Chinese tree, *L. chinense* **3** any of various other trees with tulip-shaped flowers, such as the magnolia

tulipwood ('tjuːlɪpˌwʊd) *n* **1** Also called: **white poplar, yellow poplar** the light soft wood of the tulip tree, used in making furniture and veneer **2** any of several woods having stripes or streaks of colour, esp that of *Dalbergia variabilis*, a tree of tropical South America

Tullamore (ˌtʌləˈmɔː) *n* the county town of Offaly, Republic of Ireland; food processing and brewing. Pop: 11 098 (2002)

tulle (tjuːl) *n* a fine net fabric of silk, rayon, etc, used for evening dresses, as a trimming for hats, etc [c19 from French, from *Tulle*, city in S central France, where it was first manufactured]

tullibee ('tʌlɪˌbiː) *n* a cisco of the Great Lakes of Canada, *Coregonus artedii tullibee* [c19 from French *toulibi*, from Ojibwa]

tulpa ('tʊlpə) *n* a being or object that is created in the imagination by visualization techniques such as in Tibetan mysticism [from Tibetan]

Tulsa ('tʌlsə) *n* a city in NE Oklahoma, on the Arkansas River: a major oil centre; two universities. Pop: 387 807 (2003 est)

tum (tʌm) *n* an informal or childish word for **stomach**

tumatakuru ('tuːmɑːˌtɑːˌkuːruː) *n, pl* tumatakuru another name for **matagouri** [Māori]

tumble ('tʌmbᵊl) *vb* **1** to fall or cause to fall, esp awkwardly, precipitately, or violently **2** (*intr*; usually foll by *about*) to roll or twist, esp in playing: *the kittens tumbled about on the floor* **3** (*intr*) to perform leaps, somersaults, etc **4** to go or move in a heedless or hasty way **5** (*tr*) to polish (gemstones) in a tumbler **6** (*tr*) to disturb, rumple, or toss around: *to tumble the bedclothes* ▷ *n* **7** the act or an instance of tumbling **8** a fall or toss **9** an acrobatic feat, esp a somersault **10** a decrease in value, number, etc: *stock markets have taken a tumble* **11** a state of confusion **12** a confused heap or pile: *a tumble of clothes* ▷ See also **tumble to** [Old English *tumbian*, from Old French *tomber*; related to Old High German *tūmōn* to turn]

tumbledown ('tʌmbᵊlˌdaʊn) *adj* falling to pieces; dilapidated; crumbling

tumble-dry *vb* -dries, -drying, -dried (*tr*) to dry (laundry) in a tumble dryer

tumble dryer *or* **tumble drier** *n* a machine that dries wet laundry by rotating it in warmed air inside a metal drum. Also called: **tumbler dryer, tumbler**

tumblehome ('tʌmbᵊlˌhəʊm) *n* the inward curvature of the upper parts of the sides of a vessel at or near the stern

tumbler ('tʌmblə) *n* **1 a** a flat-bottomed drinking glass with no handle or stem. Originally, a tumbler had a round or pointed base and so could not stand upright **b** Also called: **tumblerful** the contents or quantity such a glass holds **2** a person, esp a professional entertainer, who performs somersaults and other acrobatic feats **3** another name for **tumble dryer** **4** Also called: **tumbling box** a pivoted box or drum rotated so that the contents (usually inferior gemstones) tumble about and become smooth and polished **5** the part of a lock that retains or releases the bolt and is moved by the action of a key **6** a lever in a gunlock that receives the action of the mainspring when the trigger is pressed and thus forces the hammer forwards **7 a** a part that moves a gear in a train of gears into and out of engagement **b** a single cog or cam that transmits motion to the part with which it engages **8** a toy, often a doll, that is so weighted that it rocks when touched **9** (*often capital*) a breed of domestic pigeon kept for exhibition or flying. The performing varieties execute backward somersaults in flight

tumbler gear *n* a train of gears in which the gear-selection mechanism is operated by tumblers

tumbler switch *n* a switch that is turned over to connect or disconnect an electric current

tumble to *vb* (*intr, preposition*) *informal* to understand; become aware of

tumbleweed ('tʌmbᵊlˌwiːd) *n* any densely branched plant that breaks off near the ground on withering and is rolled about by the wind, esp one of several amaranths of the western US and Australia

tumbrel *or* **tumbril** ('tʌmbrəl) *n* **1** a farm cart for carrying dung, esp one that tilts backwards to deposit its load. A cart of this type was used to take condemned prisoners to the guillotine during the French Revolution **2** (formerly) a covered cart that accompanied artillery in order to carry ammunition, tools, etc **3** an obsolete word for a **ducking stool** [c14 *tumberell* ducking stool, from Medieval Latin *tumbrellum* from Old French *tumberel* dump cart, from *tomber* to tumble, of Germanic origin]

tumefacient (ˌtjuːmɪˈfeɪʃɪənt) *adj* producing or capable of producing swelling: *a tumefacient drug*

[c16 from Latin *tumefacere* to cause to swell, from *tumēre* to swell + *facere* to cause]

tumefaction (ˌtjuːmɪˈfækʃən) *n* **1** the act or process of swelling **2** a puffy or swollen part

tumefy ('tjuːmɪˌfaɪ) *vb* -fies, -fying, -fied to make or become tumid; swell or puff up [c16 from French *tuméfier*, from Latin *tumefacere*; see TUMEFACIENT]

tumescent (tjuːˈmɛsənt) *adj* swollen or becoming swollen [c19 from Latin *tumescere* to begin to swell, from *tumēre*] > tuˈmescence *n*

tumid ('tjuːmɪd) *adj* **1** (of an organ or part) enlarged or swollen **2** bulging or protuberant **3** pompous or fulsome in style: *tumid prose* [c16 from Latin *tumidus*, from *tumēre* to swell] > tuˈmidity *or* 'tumidness *n* > 'tumidly *adv*

tummler ('tʌmlə) *n* a comedian or other entertainer employed to encourage audience participation or to encourage guests at a resort to take part in communal activities [c20 Yiddish, from *tumlen* to stir, bustle]

tummy ('tʌmɪ) *n, pl* -mies an informal or childish word for **stomach**

tummy tuck *n* an informal name for **abdominoplasty**

tumour *or US* **tumor** ('tjuːmə) *n* **1** *pathol* **a** any abnormal swelling **b** a mass of tissue formed by a new growth of cells, normally independent of the surrounding structures **2** *obsolete* pompous style or language [c16 from Latin, from *tumēre* to swell] > 'tumorous *or* 'tumoral *adj*

tump (tʌmp) *n Western English dialect* a small mound or clump [c16 of unknown origin]

tumpline ('tʌmpˌlaɪn) *n* (in the US and Canada, esp formerly) a leather or cloth band strung across the forehead or chest and attached to a pack or load in order to support it. Also called: **tump** [c19 from *tump*, of Algonquian origin + LINE¹; compare Abnaki *mádǔmbi* pack strap]

tumular ('tjuːmjʊlə) *adj* of, relating to, or like a mound

tumulose ('tjuːmjʊləʊs) *or* **tumulous** ('tjuːmjʊləs) *adj* **1** abounding in small hills or mounds **2** being or resembling a mound [c18 from Latin *tumulōsus*, from *tumulus* a hillock] > tumulosity (ˌtjuːmjʊˈlɒsɪtɪ) *n*

tumult ('tjuːmʌlt) *n* **1** a loud confused noise, as of a crowd **2** violent agitation or disturbance **3** great emotional or mental agitation [c15 from Latin *tumultus*, from *tumēre* to swell up]

tumultuous (tjuːˈmʌltjʊəs) *adj* **1** uproarious, riotous, or turbulent: *a tumultuous welcome* **2** greatly agitated, confused, or disturbed: *a tumultuous dream* **3** making a loud or unruly disturbance: *tumultuous insurgents* > tuˈmultuously *adv* > tuˈmultuousness *n*

tumulus ('tjuːmjʊləs) *n, pl* -li (-laɪ) *archaeol* (no longer in technical usage) another word for **barrow²** [c17 from Latin: a hillock, from *tumēre* to swell up]

tun (tʌn) *n* **1** a large beer cask **2** a measure of capacity, usually equal to 252 wine gallons **3** a cask used during the manufacture of beer ▷ *vb* tuns, tunning, tunned **4** (*tr*) to put into or keep in tuns [Old English *tunne*; related to Old High German, Old Norse *tunna*, Medieval Latin *tunna*]

tuna¹ ('tjuːnə) *n, pl* -na *or* -nas **1** Also called: **tunny** any of various large marine spiny-finned fishes of the genus *Thunnus*, esp *T. thynnus*, chiefly of warm waters: family *Scombridae*. They have a spindle-shaped body and widely forked tail, and are important food fishes **2** any of various similar and related fishes [c20 from American Spanish, from Spanish *atún*, from Arabic *tūn*, from Latin *thunnus* tunny, from Greek]

tuna² ('tjuːnə) *n* **1** any of various tropical American prickly pear cacti, esp *Opuntia tuna*, that are cultivated for their sweet edible fruits **2** the fruit of any of these cacti [c16 via Spanish from Taino]

tunable *or* **tuneable** ('tjuːnəbᵊl) *adj* **1** able to be tuned **2** *archaic or poetic* melodious or tuneful

Tunbridge Wells ('tʌnˌbrɪdʒ) *n* a town and resort in SE England, in SW Kent: chalybeate spring discovered in 1606; an important social centre in the 17th and 18th centuries. Pop: 60 095 (2001). Official name: Royal Tunbridge Wells

tundra ('tʌndrə) *n* **a** a vast treeless zone lying between the ice cap and the timberline of North America and Eurasia and having a permanently frozen subsoil **b** (*as modifier*): *tundra vegetation* [c19 from Russian, from Lapp *tundar* hill; related to Finnish *tunturi* treeless hill]

tune (tjuːn) *n* **1** a melody, esp one for which harmony is not essential **2** the most important part in a musical texture: *the cello has the tune at that point* **3** the condition of producing accurately pitched notes, intervals, etc (esp in the phrases **in tune, out of tune**): *he can't sing in tune* **4** accurate correspondence of pitch and intonation between instruments (esp in the phrases **in tune, out of tune**): *the violin is not in tune with the piano* **5** the correct adjustment of a radio, television, or some other electronic circuit with respect to the required frequency (esp in the phrases **in tune, out of tune**) **6** a frame of mind; disposition or mood **7** *obsolete* a musical sound; note **8** **call the tune** to be in control of the proceedings **9** **change one's tune** *or* **sing another** (*or* a different) **tune** to alter one's attitude or tone of speech **10** **to the tune of** *informal* to the amount or extent of: *costs to the tune of a hundred pounds* ▷ *vb* **11** to adjust (a musical instrument or a changeable part of one) to a certain pitch **12** to adjust (a note, etc) so as to bring it into harmony or concord **13** (*tr*) to adapt or adjust (oneself); attune **14** (*tr*; often foll by *up*) to make fine adjustments to (an engine, machine, etc) to obtain optimum performance **15** *electronics* to adjust (one or more circuits) for resonance at a desired frequency **16** *obsolete* to utter (something) musically or in the form of a melody; sing **17** **tune someone grief** *South African slang* to annoy or harass someone ▷ See also **tune in, tune out, tune up** [c14 variant of TONE]

tuneful ('tjuːnfʊl) *adj* **1** having a pleasant or catchy tune; melodious **2** producing a melody or music > 'tunefully *adv* > 'tunefulness *n*

tune in *vb* (*adverb*; often foll by *to*) **1** to adjust (a radio or television) to receive (a station or programme) **2** *slang* to make or become more aware, knowledgeable, etc (about)

tuneless ('tjuːnlɪs) *adj* **1** having no melody or tune **2** *chiefly poetic* not producing or able to produce music; silent > 'tunelessly *adv* > 'tunelessness *n*

tune out *vb* (*intr, adverb*; often foll by *of*) *informal* to cease to take an interest (in) or pay attention (to)

tuner ('tjuːnə) *n* **1** a person who tunes instruments, esp pianos **2** the part of a radio or television receiver for selecting only those signals having a particular frequency

tunesmith ('tjuːnˌsmɪθ) *n* *informal* a composer of light or popular music and songs

tune up *vb* (*adverb*) **1** to adjust (a musical instrument) to a particular pitch, esp a standard one **2** (esp of an orchestra or other instrumental ensemble) to tune (instruments) to a common pitch **3** (*tr*) to adjust (an engine) in (a car, etc) to improve performance ▷ *n* **tune-up** **4** adjustments made to an engine to improve its performance

tung oil (tʌŋ) *n* a fast-drying oil obtained from the seeds of a central Asian euphorbiaceous tree, *Aleurites fordii*, used in paints, varnishes, etc, as a drying agent and to give a water-resistant finish. Also called: Chinese wood oil [partial translation of Chinese *yu t'ung tung* tree oil, from *yu* oil + *t'ung* tung tree]

tungstate ('tʌŋsteɪt) *n* a salt of tungstic acid [c20 from TUNGST(EN) + -ATE[1]]

tungsten ('tʌŋstən) *n* a hard malleable ductile greyish-white element. It occurs principally in wolframite and scheelite and is used in lamp filaments, electrical contact points, X-ray targets, and, alloyed with steel, in high-speed cutting tools. Symbol: W; atomic no: 74; atomic wt: 183.85; valency: 2–6; relative density: 19.3; melting pt: 3422±20°C; boiling pt: 5555°C. Also called: wolfram [c18 from Swedish *tung* heavy + *sten* STONE]

tungsten carbide *n* a fine very hard crystalline grey powder produced by heating tungsten and carbon to a very high temperature: used in the manufacture of drill bits, dies, etc. Symbol: WC; melting pt: 2870°C

tungsten lamp *n* a lamp in which light is produced by a tungsten filament heated to incandescence by an electric current. The glass bulb enclosing the filament contains a low pressure of inert gas, usually argon. Sometimes small amounts of a halogen, such as iodine, are added to improve the intensity (**tungsten-halogen lamp**)

tungsten steel *n* any of various hard steels containing tungsten (1–20 per cent) and traces of carbon. They are resistant to wear at high temperatures and are used in tools

tungstic ('tʌŋstɪk) *adj* of or containing tungsten, esp in a high valence state [c18 from TUNGST(EN) + -IC]

tungstic acid *n* any of various oxyacids of tungsten obtained by neutralizing alkaline solutions of tungstates. They are often polymeric substances, typical examples being H_2WO_4 (**orthotungstic acid**), $H_2W_4O_{13}$ (**metatungstic acid**), and $H_{10}W_{12}O_{14}$ (**paratungstic acid**)

tungstite ('tʌŋstaɪt) *n* a yellow earthy rare secondary mineral that consists of tungsten oxide and occurs with tungsten ores. Formula: WO_3 [c20 from TUNGST(EN) + -ITE[1]]

tungstous ('tʌŋstəs) *adj* of or containing tungsten in a low valence state

Tungting *or* **Tung-t'ing** (ˌtʊŋ'tɪŋ) *n* a variant transliteration of the Chinese name for the **Dongting**

Tungus ('tʊŋɡʊs) *n* **1** (*pl* -guses *or* -gus) a member of a formerly nomadic Mongoloid people of E Siberia **2** Also called: Evenki the language of this people, belonging to the Tungusic branch of the Altaic family

Tungusic (tʊŋ'ɡʊsɪk) *n* **1** a branch or subfamily of the Altaic family of languages, including Tungus and Manchu ▷ *adj also* Tungusian (tʊŋ'ɡuːzɪən) **2** of or relating to these languages or their speakers

Tunguska (*Russian* tun'ɡuskə) *n* any of three rivers in Russia, in central Siberia, all tributaries of the Yenisei: the **Lower** (Nizhnyaya) **Tunguska** 2690 km (1670 miles) long; the **Stony** (Podkamennaya) **Tunguska** 1550 km (960 miles) long; the **Upper** (Verkhnyaya) **Tunguska** which is the lower course of the Angara

tunic ('tjuːnɪk) *n* **1** any of various hip-length or knee-length garments, such as the loose sleeveless garb worn in ancient Greece or Rome, the jacket of some soldiers, or a woman's hip-length garment, worn with a skirt or trousers **2** *anatomy, botany, zoology* a covering, lining, or enveloping membrane of an organ or part. See also **tunica 3** *chiefly RC Church* another word for **tunicle** [Old English *tunice* (unattested except in the accusative case), from Latin *tunica*]

tunica ('tjuːnɪkə) *n* **1** *anatomy* tissue forming a layer or covering of an organ or part, such as any of the tissue layers of a blood vessel wall **2** *botany* the outer layer or layers of cells of the meristem at a shoot tip, which produces the epidermis and cells beneath it ▷ Compare **corpus** (sense 4) [c17 from Latin *tunica* TUNIC]

tunicate ('tjuːnɪkɪt, -ˌkeɪt) *n* **1** any minute primitive marine chordate animal of the subphylum Tunicata (or Urochordata, Urochorda). The adults have a saclike unsegmented body enclosed in a cellulose-like outer covering (tunic) and only the larval forms have a notochord: includes the sea squirts. See also **ascidian** ▷ *adj also* **tunicated 2** of, relating to, or belonging to the subphylum Tunicata **3** (esp of a bulb) having or consisting of concentric layers of tissue [c18 from Latin *tunicātus* clad in a TUNIC]

tunicle ('tjuːnɪkᵊl) *n* *chiefly RC Church* the liturgical vestment worn by the subdeacon and bishops at High Mass and other religious ceremonies [c14 from Latin *tunicula* a little TUNIC]

tuning ('tjuːnɪŋ) *n* *music* **1** a set of pitches to which the open strings of a guitar, violin, etc, are tuned: *the normal tuning on a violin is G, D, A, E* **2** the accurate pitching of notes and intervals by a choir, orchestra, etc; intonation

tuning fork *n* a two-pronged metal fork that when struck produces a pure note of constant specified pitch. It is used to tune musical instruments and in acoustics

tuning key *n* a device that may be placed over a wrest pin on a piano, etc, and turned to alter the tension and pitch of a string

Tunis ('tjuːnɪs) *n* the capital and chief port of Tunisia, in the northeast on the **Gulf of Tunis** (an inlet of the Mediterranean): dates from Carthaginian times, the ruins of ancient Carthage lying to the northeast; university (1960). Pop: 2 063 000 (2005 est)

Tunisia (tjuː'nɪzɪə, -'nɪsɪə) *n* a republic in N Africa, on the Mediterranean: settled by the Phoenicians in the 12th century BC; made a French protectorate in 1881 and gained independence in 1955. It consists chiefly of the Sahara in the south, a central plateau, and the Atlas Mountains in the north. Exports include textiles, petroleum, and phosphates. Official language: Arabic; French is also widely spoken. Official religion: Muslim. Currency: dinar. Capital: Tunis. Pop: 9 937 000 (2004 est). Area: 164 150 sq km (63 380 sq miles)

Tunisian (tjuː'nɪzɪən, -'nɪsɪən) *adj* **1** of or relating to Tunisia or its inhabitants ▷ *n* **2** a native or inhabitant of Tunisia

tunnage ('tʌnɪdʒ) *n* a variant spelling of **tonnage**

tunnel ('tʌnᵊl) *n* **1** an underground passageway, esp one for trains or cars that passes under a mountain, river, or a congested urban area **2** any passage or channel through or under something **3** a dialect word for **funnel 4** *obsolete* the flue of a chimney ▷ *vb* -nels, -nelling, -nelled *or US* -nels, -neling, -neled **5** (*tr*) to make or force (a way) through or under (something): *to tunnel a hole in the wall* **6** (*intr*; foll by *through, under,* etc) to make or force a way (through or under something) [c15 from Old French *tonel* cask, from *tonne* tun, from Medieval Latin *tonna* barrel, of Celtic origin] > 'tunneller *or US* 'tunneler *n*

tunnel diode *n* an extremely stable semiconductor diode, having a very narrow highly doped p-n junction, in which electrons travel across the junction by means of the tunnel effect. Also called: Esaki diode

tunnel disease *n* another name (esp formerly) for **decompression sickness** [so called because it used to be common among people who were digging tunnels]

tunnel effect *n* *physics* the phenomenon in which an object, usually an elementary particle, tunnels through a potential barrier even though it does not have sufficient energy to surmount the barrier. It is explained by wave mechanics and is the cause of alpha decay, field emission, and certain conduction processes in semiconductors

tunnel vault *n* another name for **barrel vault**

tunnel vision *n* **1** a condition in which peripheral vision is greatly restricted **2** narrowness of viewpoint resulting from concentration on a single idea, opinion, etc, to the exclusion of others

tunny ('tʌnɪ) *n, pl* -nies *or* -ny another name for **tuna** [c16 from Old French *thon*, from Old Provençal *ton*, from Latin *thunnus*, from Greek]

tup (tʌp) *n* **1** *chiefly Brit* an uncastrated male sheep; ram **2** the head of a pile-driver or steam hammer ▷ *vb* tups, tupping, tupped (*tr*) **3** to cause (a ram) to mate with a ewe, or (of a ram) to mate with (a ewe) **4** *Lancashire dialect* to butt

Tupamaro (ˌtuːpəˈmɑːrəʊ) n, pl -ros any of a group of Marxist urban guerrillas in Uruguay [c20 after *Tupac Amaru*, 18th-century Peruvian Indian who led a rebellion against the Spaniards]

tupelo (ˈtjuːpɪˌləʊ) n, pl -los **1** any of several cornaceous trees of the genus *Nyssa*, esp *N. aquatica*, a large tree of deep swamps and rivers of the southern US **2** the light strong wood of any of these trees [c18 from Creek *ito opilwa*, from *ito* tree + *opilwa* swamp]

Tupi (tuːˈpiː) n **1** (pl -pis or -pi) a member of a South American Indian people of Brazil and Paraguay **2** the language of this people, belonging to the Tupi-Guarani family > Tuˈpian adj

Tupi-Guarani n a family of South American Indian languages spoken in Brazil, Paraguay, and certain adjacent regions: possibly distantly related to Quechua > ˈTupiˌ-Guaraˈnian adj

tupik or **tupek** (ˈtuːpək) n Canadian (esp in the Arctic) a tent of animal skins, a traditional type of Inuit summer dwelling [from Inuktitut *tupiq*]

tuple (ˈtjʊpəl, ˈtʌpəl) n computing a row of values in a relational database

-tuple n and adj combining form indicating a set of the number specified

tuppence (ˈtʌpəns) n Brit a variant spelling of **twopence**

tuppenny (ˈtʌpənɪ) adj a variant spelling of **twopenny**

Tupperware (ˈtʌpəweə) n trademark a range of plastic containers used for storing food [c20 *Tupper*, US manufacturing company + WARE[1]]

tupuna (təˈpuːnə) n a variant spelling of **tipuna**

Tupungato (Spanish tupunˈgato) n a mountain on the border between Argentina and Chile, in the Andes. Height: 6550 m (21 484 ft)

tuque (tuːk) n Canadian **1** a knitted cap with a long tapering end **2** Also called: **toque** a close-fitting knitted hat often with a tassel or pompom [c19 from Canadian French, from French: TOQUE]

tu quoque (Latin tjuː ˈkwəʊkwɪ) interj you likewise: a retort made by a person accused of a crime implying that the accuser is also guilty of the same crime

turaco (ˈtʊərəˌkəʊ) n, pl -cos a variant spelling of **touraco**

turangawaewae (təˌrʌŋəˈweɪweɪ) n NZ the area that is a person's home [Māori, literally: standing on one's feet]

Turanian (tjʊˈreɪnɪən) n **1** a member of any of the peoples inhabiting ancient Turkestan, or their descendants **2** another name for **Ural-Altaic** ▷ adj **3** of or relating to the Ural-Altaic languages or any of the peoples who speak them **4** of or relating to Turkestan or its people

turban (ˈtɜːbən) n **1** a man's headdress, worn esp by Muslims, Hindus, and Sikhs, made by swathing a length of linen, silk, etc, around the head or around a caplike base **2** a woman's brimless hat resembling this **3** any headdress resembling this [c16 from Turkish *tülbend*, from Persian *dulband*] > ˈturbaned adj > ˈturban-ˌlike adj

turbary (ˈtɜːbərɪ) n, pl -ries **1** land where peat or turf is cut or has been cut **2** Also called: **common of turbary** (in England) the legal right to cut peat for fuel on a common [c14 from Old French *turbarie*, from Medieval Latin *turbāria*, from *turba* peat, TURF]

turbellarian (ˌtɜːbɪˈlɛərɪən) n **1** any typically aquatic free-living flatworm of the class *Turbellaria*, having a ciliated epidermis and a simple life cycle: includes the planarians ▷ adj **2** of, relating to, or belonging to the class *Turbellaria* [c19 from New Latin *Turbellāria*, from Latin *turbellae* (pl) bustle, from *turba* brawl, referring to the swirling motion created in the water]

turbid (ˈtɜːbɪd) adj **1** muddy or opaque, as a liquid clouded with a suspension of particles **2** dense, thick, or cloudy: *turbid fog* **3** in turmoil or confusion [c17 from Latin *turbidus*, from *turbāre* to agitate, from *turba* crowd] > turˈbidity or

ˈturbidness n > ˈturbidly adv

turbidimeter (ˌtɜːbɪˈdɪmɪtə) n a device that measures the turbidity of a liquid

turbidite (ˈtɜːbɪˌdaɪt) n a sediment deposited by a turbidity current [c20 from TURBID + -ITE[1]]

turbidity current n a swirling mass of water and suspended material stirred up by a tsunami, a storm, a river in flood, etc

turbinate (ˈtɜːbɪnɪt, -ˌneɪt) or **turbinal** (ˈtɜːbɪn²l) adj also **turbinated 1** anatomy of or relating to any of the thin scroll-shaped bones situated on the walls of the nasal passages **2** shaped like a spiral or scroll **3** (esp of the shells of certain molluscs) shaped like an inverted cone ▷ n **4** Also called: **nasal concha** a turbinate bone **5** a turbinate shell [c17 from Latin *turbō* spinning top] > ˌturbiˈnation n

turbine (ˈtɜːbɪn, -baɪn) n any of various types of machine in which the kinetic energy of a moving fluid is converted into mechanical energy by causing a bladed rotor to rotate. The moving fluid may be water, steam, air, or combustion products of a fuel. See also **reaction turbine, impulse turbine, gas turbine** [c19 from French, from Latin *turbō* whirlwind, from *turbāre* to throw into confusion]

turbine blade n any of a number of bladelike vanes assembled around the periphery of a turbine rotor to guide the steam or gas flow

turbit (ˈtɜːbɪt) n a crested breed of domestic pigeon [c17 from Latin *turbō* spinning top, with reference to the bird's shape; compare TURBOT]

turbo- combining form of, relating to, or driven by a turbine: *turbofan*

turbocar (ˈtɜːbəʊˌkɑː) n a car driven by a gas turbine

turbo-charge vb (tr) **1** to supply (an internal-combustion engine or a motor vehicle) with a turbocharger **2** to inject extra force and energy into (an activity, undertaking, etc)

turbocharger (ˈtɜːbəʊˌtʃɑːdʒə) n a centrifugal compressor which boosts the intake pressure of an internal-combustion engine, driven by an exhaust-gas turbine fitted to the engine's exhaust manifold

turbo-electric (ˌtɜːbəʊɪˈlɛktrɪk) adj of, relating to, or using an electric generator driven by a turbine

turbofan (ˈtɜːbəʊˌfæn) n **1** Also called: **high bypass ratio engine** a type of by-pass engine in which a large fan driven by a turbine and housed in a short duct forces air rearwards around the exhaust gases in order to increase the propulsive thrust **2** an aircraft driven by one or more turbofans **3** the ducted fan in such an engine Also called (for senses 1, 2): **fanjet**

turbogenerator (ˌtɜːbəʊˈdʒɛnəˌreɪtə) n a large electrical generator driven by a steam turbine

turbojet (ˈtɜːbəʊˌdʒɛt) n **1** short for **turbojet engine 2** an aircraft powered by one or more turbojet engines

turbojet engine n a gas turbine in which the exhaust gases provide the propulsive thrust to drive an aircraft

turboprop (ˌtɜːbəʊˈprɒp) n **1** an aircraft propulsion unit where a propeller is driven by a gas turbine **2** an aircraft powered by turboprops

turbosupercharger (ˌtɜːbəʊˈsuːpəˌtʃɑːdʒə) n obsolete a supercharging device for an internal-combustion engine, consisting of a turbine driven by the exhaust gases

turbot (ˈtɜːbət) n, pl -bot or -bots **1** a European flatfish, *Scophthalmus maximus*, having a pale brown speckled scaleless body covered with tubercles: family *Bothidae*. It is highly valued as a food fish **2** any of various similar or related fishes [c13 from Old French *tourbot*, from Medieval Latin *turbō*, from Latin: spinning top, from a fancied similarity in shape; see TURBIT, TURBINE]

turbulence (ˈtɜːbjʊləns) or rarely **turbulency** n **1** a state or condition of confusion, movement, or agitation; disorder **2** meteorol local instability in the atmosphere, oceans, or rivers **3** turbulent flow in a liquid or gas

turbulent (ˈtɜːbjʊlənt) adj **1** being in a state of turbulence **2** wild or insubordinate; unruly [c16 from Latin *turbulentus*, from *turba* confusion] > ˈturbulently adv

turbulent flow n flow of a fluid in which its velocity at any point varies rapidly in an irregular manner. Compare **laminar flow** See also **streamline flow**

Turco (ˈtɜːkəʊ) n, pl -cos (formerly) an Algerian serving in the light infantry of the French army [c19 via French from Italian: a Turk]

Turco- or **Turko-** combining form indicating Turkey or Turkish: *Turco-Greek*

turd (tɜːd) n slang **1** a lump of dung; piece of excrement **2** an unpleasant or contemptible person or thing [Old English *tord*; related to Old Norse *tordýfill* dung beetle, Dutch *tort* dung]

▎ USAGE This word was formerly considered to be taboo, and it was labelled as such in previous editions of *Collins English Dictionary*. However, it has now become acceptable in speech, although some older or more conservative people may object to its use

turdine (ˈtɜːdaɪn, -dɪn) adj of, relating to, or characteristic of thrushes [c19 from Latin *turdus* thrush]

tureen (təˈriːn) n a large deep rounded dish with a cover, used for serving soups, stews, etc [c18 from French *terrine* earthenware vessel, from *terrin* made of earthenware, from Vulgar Latin *terrīnus* (unattested) earthen, from Latin *terra* earth]

turf (tɜːf) n, pl turfs or turves (tɜːvz) **1** the surface layer of fields and pastures, consisting of earth containing a dense growth of grasses with their roots; sod **2** a piece cut from this layer, used to form lawns, verges, etc **3 a** a track, usually of grass or dirt, where horse races are run **b** horse racing as a sport or industry **4** US slang the territory or area of activity over which a person or group claims exclusive rights **5** an area of knowledge or influence **6** another term for **peat 7** go with the turf informal to be an unavoidable part of a particular situation or process ▷ vb **8** (tr) to cover with pieces of turf [Old English; related to Old Norse *torfa*, Old High German *zurba*, Sanskrit *darbha* tuft of grass]

turf accountant n Brit a formal name for a **bookmaker**

turfman (ˈtɜːfmən) n, pl -men chiefly US a person devoted to horse racing. Also called: **turfite**

turf out vb (tr, adverb) Brit informal to throw out or dismiss; eject: *we were turfed out of the club*

turf war n informal **1** a dispute between criminals or gangs over the right to operate within a particular area **2** any dispute in which one party seeks to obtain increased rights or influence

turfy (ˈtɜːfɪ) adj turfier, turfiest **1** of, covered with, or resembling turf **2** relating to or characteristic of horse racing or persons connected with it > ˈturfiness n

turgent (ˈtɜːdʒənt) adj an obsolete word for **turgid** [c15 from Latin *turgēre* to swell] > ˈturgently adv

turgescent (tɜːˈdʒɛsənt) adj becoming or being swollen > turˈgescence or turˈgescency n

turgid (ˈtɜːdʒɪd) adj **1** swollen and distended; congested **2** (of style or language) pompous and high-flown; bombastic [c17 from Latin *turgidus*, from *turgēre* to swell] > turˈgidity or ˈturgidness n > ˈturgidly adv

turgite (ˈtɜːdʒaɪt) n a red or black mineral consisting of hydrated ferric oxide. Formula: $Fe_2O_3.nH_2O$

turgor (ˈtɜːgə) n the normal rigid state of a cell, caused by pressure of the cell contents against the cell wall or membrane. See also **turgor pressure** [c19 from Late Latin: a swelling, from Latin *turgēre* to swell]

turgor pressure n the pressure exerted on a plant cell wall by water passing into the cell by osmosis. Also called: **hydrostatic pressure**

Turin (tjʊəˈrɪn) *n* a city in NW Italy, capital of Piedmont region, on the River Po: became capital of the Kingdom of Sardinia in 1720; first capital (1861–65) of united Italy; university (1405); a major industrial centre, producing most of Italy's cars. Pop: 865 263 (2001). Italian name: **Torino**

Turing machine (ˈtʊərɪŋ) *n* a hypothetical universal computing machine able to modify its original instructions by reading, erasing, or writing a new symbol on a moving tape of fixed length that acts as its program. The concept was instrumental in the early development of computer systems [C20 after Alan *Turing* (1912–54), English mathematician]

Turing test *n* a proposed test of a computer's ability to think, requiring that the covert substitution of the computer for one of the participants in a keyboard and screen dialogue should be undetectable by the remaining human participant [C20 after Alan *Turing* (1912–54), English mathematician]

turion (ˈtʊərɪən) *n* a perennating bud produced by many aquatic plants: it detaches from the parent plant and remains dormant until the following spring [C17 from French *turion*, from Latin *turio* shoot]

Turk (tɜːk) *n* **1** a native, inhabitant, or citizen of Turkey **2** a native speaker of any Turkic language, such as an inhabitant of Turkmenistan or Kyrgyzstan **3** *obsolete derogatory* a violent, brutal, or domineering person

Turk. *abbreviation for* **1** Turkey **2** Turkish

Turkana (tɜːˈkɑːnə) *n* **Lake.** a long narrow lake in E Africa, in the Great Rift Valley. Area: 7104 sq km (2743 sq miles). Former name: (Lake) Rudolf

Turkestan *or* **Turkistan** (ˌtɜːkɪˈstɑːn) *n* an extensive region of central Asia between Siberia in the north and Tibet, India, Afghanistan, and Iran in the south: formerly divided into **West** (**Russian**) **Turkestan** (also called Soviet Central Asia), comprising present-day Turkmenistan, Uzbekistan, Tajikistan, and Kyrgyzstan and the S part of Kazakhstan, and **East** (**Chinese**) **Turkestan** consisting of the Xinjiang Uygur Autonomous Region

Turkestani (ˌtɜːkɪˈstɑːnɪ) *adj* **1** of or relating to the central Asian region of Turkestan or its inhabitants ▷ *n* **2** a native or inhabitant of Turkestan

turkey (ˈtɜːkɪ) *n, pl* **-keys** *or* **-key** **1** a large gallinaceous bird, *Meleagris gallopavo*, of North America, having a bare wattled head and neck and a brownish iridescent plumage. The male is brighter and has a fan-shaped tail. A domestic variety is widely bred for its flesh **2** the flesh of the turkey used as food **3** a similar and related bird, *Agriocharis ocellata* (**ocellated turkey**), of Central and N South America **4** any of various Australian birds considered to resemble the turkey, such as the bush turkey **5** *slang, chiefly US and Canadian* **a** a dramatic production that fails; flop **b** a thing or person that fails; dud **6** *slang, chiefly US and Canadian* a stupid, incompetent, or unappealing person **7** *slang* (in tenpin bowling) three strikes in a row **8** See **cold turkey** **9** **talk turkey** *informal, chiefly US and Canadian* to discuss frankly and practically [C16 shortened from *Turkey cock* (hen), used at first to designate the African guinea fowl (apparently because the bird was brought through Turkish territory), later applied by mistake to the American bird]

Turkey (ˈtɜːkɪ) *n* a republic in W Asia and SE Europe, between the Black Sea, the Mediterranean, and the Aegean: the centre of the Ottoman Empire; became a republic in 1923. The major Asian part, consisting mainly of an arid plateau, is separated from European Turkey by the Bosporus, Sea of Marmara, and Dardanelles. Official languages: Turkish; Kurdish and Arabic minority languages. Religion: Muslim majority. Currency: lira. Capital: Ankara. Pop: 72 320 000 (2004 est). Area: 780 576 sq km (301 380 sq miles)

turkey brown *n* an angler's name for a species of mayfly, *Paraleptophlebia submarginata*

turkey buzzard *or* **vulture** *n* a New World vulture, *Cathartes aura*, having a dark plumage and naked red head

Turkey carpet *n* a wool carpet made in one piece and having a deep velvety pile and rich colours

turkey cock *n* **1** a male turkey **2** an arrogant person

turkey nest *n Austral* a small earth dam adjacent to, and higher than, a larger earth dam, to feed water by gravity to a cattle trough, etc

Turkey oak *n* an oak tree, *Quercus cerris*, of W and S Europe, with deeply lobed hairy leaves [C18 so called because its acorns are often eaten by turkeys]

Turkey red *n* **1 a** a moderate or bright red colour **b** (*as adjective*): *a Turkey-red fabric* **2** a cotton fabric of a bright red colour

turkey trot *n* an early ragtime one-step, popular in the period of World War I

Turki (ˈtɜːkɪ) *adj* **1** of or relating to the Turkic languages, esp those of central Asia **2** of or relating to speakers of these languages ▷ *n* **3** these languages collectively; esp Eastern Turkic

Turkic (ˈtɜːkɪk) *n* a branch or subfamily of the Altaic family of languages, including Turkish, Turkmen, Kirghiz, Tatar, etc, members of which are found from Turkey to NE China, esp in central Asia

Turkish (ˈtɜːkɪʃ) *adj* **1** of, relating to, or characteristic of Turkey, its people, or their language ▷ *n* **2** the official language of Turkey, belonging to the Turkic branch of the Altaic family. See also **Osmanli**. ▷ **'Turkishness** *n*

Turkish Angora (ænˈɡɒrə) *n* a long-haired breed of cat, similar to the Persian

Turkish bath *n* **1** a type of bath in which the bather sweats freely in hot dry air, is then washed, often massaged, and has a cold plunge or shower **2** (*sometimes plural*) an establishment where such a bath is obtainable

Turkish coffee *n* very strong black coffee made with finely ground coffee beans

Turkish delight *n* a jelly-like sweet flavoured with flower essences, usually cut into cubes and covered in icing sugar

Turkish Empire *n* another name for the **Ottoman Empire**

Turkish tobacco *n* a fragrant dark tobacco cultivated in E Europe, esp Turkey and Greece

Turkish towel *n* a rough loose-piled towel; terry towel

Turkish Van *n* a breed of cat with soft white semi-long hair and coloured markings on the head and tail [C20 named after *Van*, town in Turkey]

Turkism (ˈtɜːkɪzəm) *n rare* **1** the culture, beliefs, and customs of the Turks **2** a Turkish word, fashion, etc

Turkmen (ˈtɜːkmɛn) *n* the language of the Turkomans, belonging to the Turkic branch of the Altaic family

Turkmenistan (ˌtɜːkmɛnɪˈstɑːn) *n* a republic in central Asia: the area has been occupied by a succession of empires; a Turkmen state was established in the 15th century but suffered almost continual civil strife and was gradually conquered by Russia; in 1918 it became a Soviet republic and gained independence from the Soviet Union in 1991: deserts including the **Kara Kum** cover most of the region; agricultural communities are concentrated around oases; there are rich mineral deposits. Official language: Turkmen. Religion: believers are mainly Muslim. Currency: manat. Capital: Ashkhabad. Pop: 4 940 000 (2004 est). Area: 488 100 sq km (186 400 sq miles)

Turko- *combining form* a variant spelling of **Turco-**

Turkoman (ˈtɜːkəmən) *or* **Turkman** *n* **1** (*pl* **-mans** *or* **-men**) a member of a formerly nomadic people of central Asia, now living chiefly in Turkmenistan and in NE Iran **2** the Turkmen language ▷ *adj* **3** of or relating to this people or their language [C16 from Medieval Latin *Turcomannus*, from Persian *turkumān* resembling a Turk, from *turk* Turk + *māndan* to be like]

Turks and Caicos Islands *pl n* a UK Overseas Territory in the Caribbean, southeast of the Bahamas: consists of the eight **Turks Islands**, separated by the Turks Island Passage from the Caicos group, which has six main islands. Capital: Grand Turk. Pop: 21 000 (2003 est). Area: 430 sq km (166 sq miles)

Turk's-cap lily *n* any of several cultivated lilies, such as *Lilium martagon* and *L. superbum*, that have brightly coloured flowers with reflexed petals. See also **martagon** [C17 so called because of a resemblance between its flowers and a turban]

Turk's-head *n* an ornamental turban-like knot made by weaving small cord around a larger rope

Turku (*Finnish* ˈturku) *n* a city and port in SW Finland, on the Gulf of Bothnia: capital of Finland until 1812. Pop: 175 059 (2003 est). Swedish name: **Åbo**

turlough (ˈtɜːlɒx) *n* a seasonal lake or pond: a low-lying area on limestone, esp in Ireland, that becomes flooded in wet weather by the upsurge of underlying ground water [C17 from Irish *tur* dry + LOUGH]

turmeric (ˈtɜːmərɪk) *n* **1** a tropical Asian zingiberaceous plant, *Curcuma longa*, having yellow flowers and an aromatic underground stem **2** the powdered stem of this plant, used as a condiment and as a yellow dye **3** any of several other plants with similar roots [C16 from Old French *terre merite*, from Medieval Latin *terra merita*, literally: meritorious earth, name applied for obscure reasons to curcuma]

turmeric paper *n chem* paper impregnated with turmeric used as a test for alkalis, which turn it brown, and for boric acid, which turns it reddish brown

turmoil (ˈtɜːmɔɪl) *n* **1** violent or confused movement; agitation; tumult ▷ *vb* **2** *archaic* to make or become turbulent [C16 perhaps from TURN + MOIL]

turn (tɜːn) *vb* **1** to move or cause to move around an axis: *a wheel turning* **2** (sometimes foll by *round*) to change or cause to change positions by moving through an arc of a circle: *he turned the chair to face the light* **3** to change or cause to change in course, direction, etc: *he turned left at the main road* **4** (of soldiers, ships, etc) to alter the direction of advance by changing direction simultaneously or (of a commander) to cause the direction of advance to be altered simultaneously **5** to go or pass to the other side (a corner, etc) **6** to assume or cause to assume a rounded, curved, or folded form: *the road turns here* **7** to reverse or cause to reverse position **8** (*tr*) to pass round (an enemy or enemy position) so as to attack it from the flank or rear: *the Germans turned the Maginot line* **9** (*tr*) to perform or do by a rotating movement: *to turn a somersault* **10** (*tr*) to shape or cut a thread in (a workpiece, esp one of metal, wood, or plastic) by rotating it on a lathe against a fixed cutting tool **11** (when *intr*, foll by *into* or *to*) to change or convert or be changed or converted: *the alchemists tried to turn base metals into gold* **12** (foll by *into*) to change or cause to change in nature, character, etc: *the frog turned into a prince* **13** (*copula*) to change so as to become: *he turned nasty when he heard the price* **14** to cause (foliage, etc) to change colour or (of foliage, etc) to change colour: *frost turned the trees a vivid orange* **15** to cause (milk, etc) to become rancid or sour or (of milk, etc) to become rancid or sour **16** to change or cause to change in subject, trend, etc: *the conversation turned to fishing* **17** to direct or apply or be directed or applied: *he turned his attention to the problem* **18** (*intr*; usually foll by *to*) to appeal or apply (to) for help, advice, etc: *she was very frightened and didn't know where to turn* **19** to reach, pass, or progress beyond in age, time, etc: *she has just turned* *twenty* **20** (*tr*) to cause or allow to go: *to turn an animal loose* **21** to affect or be affected with nausea: *the sight of the dead body turned his stomach* **22** to affect or be affected with giddiness: *my head is turning* **23** (*tr*) to affect the mental or emotional stability of (esp in the phrase **turn (someone's) head**) **24** (*tr*) to release from a container: *she turned the fruit into a basin* **25** (*tr*) to render into another language **26** (usually foll by *against* or *from*) to transfer or reverse or cause to transfer or reverse (one's loyalties, affections, etc) **27** (*tr*) to cause (an enemy agent) to become a double agent working for one's own side: *the bureau turned some of the spies it had caught* **28** (*tr*) to bring (soil) from lower layers to the surface **29** to blunt (an edge) or (of an edge) to become blunted **30** (*tr*) to give a graceful form to: *to turn a compliment* **31** (*tr*) to reverse (a cuff, collar, etc) in order to hide the outer worn side **32** (*intr*) *US* to be merchandised as specified: *shirts are turning well this week* **33** *cricket* to spin (the ball) or (of the ball) to spin **34** **turn one's hand to** to undertake (something, esp something practical) **35** **turn tail** to run away; flee **36** **turn the tables (on someone)** See **table** (sense 17) **37** **turn the tide** to reverse the general course of events ▷ *n* **38** an act or instance of turning or the state of being turned or the material turned: *a turn of a rope around a bollard* **39** a movement of complete or partial rotation **40** a change or reversal of direction or position **41** direction or drift: *his thoughts took a new turn* **42** a deviation or departure from a course or tendency **43** the place, point, or time at which a deviation or change occurs **44** another word for **turning** (sense 1) **45** the right or opportunity to do something in an agreed order or succession: *we'll take turns to play* **46** a change in nature, condition, etc: *his illness took a turn for the worse* **47** a period of action, work, etc **48** a short walk, ride, or excursion: *to take a turn in the park* **49** natural inclination: *he is of a speculative turn of mind; she has a turn for needlework* **50** distinctive form or style: *a neat turn of phrase* **51** requirement, need, or advantage: *to serve someone's turn* **52** a deed performed that helps or hinders someone: *to do an old lady a good turn* **53** a twist, bend, or distortion in shape **54** *music* a melodic ornament that makes a turn around a note, beginning with the note above, in a variety of sequences **55** *theatre, chiefly Brit* a short theatrical act, esp in music hall, cabaret, etc **56** *stock exchange* **a** *Brit* the difference between a market maker's bid and offer prices, representing the market maker's profit **b** a transaction including both a purchase and a sale **57** a military manoeuvre in which men or ships alter their direction of advance together **58** *Austral slang* a party **59** *informal* a shock or surprise **60** **at every turn** on all sides or occasions **61** **by turns** one after another; alternately **62** **on the turn** *informal* **a** at the point of change **b** about to go rancid **63** **out of turn** **a** not in the correct or agreed order of succession **b** improperly, inappropriately, or inopportunely **64** **turn and turn about** one after another; alternately **65** **to a turn** to the proper amount; perfectly: *cooked to a turn* ▷ See also **turn against, turn away, turn down, turn in, turn off, turn on, turn out, turn over, turn to, turn up** [Old English *tyrnian*, from Old French *torner*, from Latin *tornāre* to turn in a lathe, from *tornus* lathe, from Greek *tornos* dividers] > ˈ**turnable** *adj*

turnabout (ˈtɜːnəˌbaʊt) *n* **1** the act of turning so as to face a different direction **2** a change or reversal of opinion, attitude, etc

turn against *vb* (*preposition*) to change or cause to change one's attitude so as to become hostile or to retaliate

turnaround (ˈtɜːnəˌraʊnd) *n* **1** **a** the act or process in which a ship, aircraft, etc, unloads passengers and freight at the end of a trip and reloads for the next trip **b** the time taken for this **2** the total time taken by a ship, aircraft, or other vehicle in a round trip **3** a complete reversal of a situation or set of circumstances. Also called: turnround

turnaround time *n* *computing* the total time taken between the submission of a program for execution and the return of the complete output to the customer

turn away *vb* (*adverb*) **1** to move or cause to move in a different direction so as not to face something: *one child turned away while the others hid* **2** (*tr*) to refuse admittance or assistance to

turn bridge *n* another name for **swing bridge**

turnbuckle (ˈtɜːnˌbʌkᵊl) *n* an open mechanical sleeve usually having a swivel at one end and a thread at the other to enable a threaded wire or rope to be tightened [C19 from TURN + BUCKLE]

turncoat (ˈtɜːnˌkəʊt) *n* a person who deserts one cause or party for the opposite faction; renegade

turncock (ˈtɜːnˌkɒk) *n* (formerly) an official employed to turn on the water for the mains supply

turn down *vb* (*tr, adverb*) **1** to reduce (the volume or brightness) of (something) **2** to reject or refuse **3** to fold down (a collar, sheets on a bed, etc) ▷ *adj* **turndown** **4** (*prenominal*) capable of being or designed to be folded or doubled down

turner (ˈtɜːnə) *n* **1** a person or thing that turns, esp a person who operates a lathe **2** (*US*) a member of a society of gymnasts

turnery (ˈtɜːnərɪ) *n, pl* **-eries** **1** objects made on a lathe **2** Also called: **turning** the process or skill of turning objects on a lathe **3** the workshop of a lathe operator

turn in *vb* (*adverb*) *informal* **1** (*intr*) to go to bed for the night **2** (*tr*) to hand in; deliver: *to turn in an essay* **3** (*tr*) to deliver (someone accused of a crime) into police custody **4** to give up or conclude (something): *we turned in the game when it began to rain* **5** (*tr*) to record (a score, etc) **6** **turn in on oneself** to withdraw or cause to withdraw from contact with others and become preoccupied with one's own problems

turning (ˈtɜːnɪŋ) *n* **1** Also called: **turn** a road, river, or path that turns off the main way: *the fourth turning on the right* **2** the point where such a way turns off **3** a bend in a straight course **4** an object made on a lathe **5** another name for **turnery** (sense 2) **6** (*plural*) the waste produced in turning on a lathe

turning circle *n* the smallest circle in which a vehicle can turn

turning point *n* **1** a moment when the course of events is changed: *the turning point of his career* **2** a point at which there is a change in direction or motion **3** *maths* a stationary point at which the first derivative of a function changes sign, so that typically its graph does not cross a horizontal tangent **4** *surveying* a point to which a foresight and a backsight are taken in levelling; change point

turnip (ˈtɜːnɪp) *n* **1** a widely cultivated plant, *Brassica rapa*, of the Mediterranean region, with a large yellow or white edible root: family *Brassicaceae* (crucifers) **2** the root of this plant, which is eaten as a vegetable **3** any of several similar or related plants **4** another name for **kohlrabi** ▷ Also called (for senses 1, 2): **navew** [C16 from earlier *turnepe*, perhaps from TURN (indicating its rounded shape) + *nepe*, from Latin *nāpus* turnip; see NEEP]

turnip moth *n* a common noctuid moth, *Agrotis segetum*, drab grey-brown in colour, the larvae of which feed on root crops and brassica stems

turnkey (ˈtɜːnˌkiː) *n* **1** *archaic* a keeper of the keys, esp in a prison; warder or jailer ▷ *adj* **2** denoting a project, as in civil engineering, in which a single contractor has responsibility for the complete job from the start to the time of installation or occupancy

turnkey project *n* *engineering* a complete project usually including many major units of plant completed under one overall contract, such as a chemical works or power station complex [C20 from use of *turnkey* in the construction industry to describe the day a job will be completed and the owner able to turn the key in the door]

turnkey system *n* a computer or computer system supplied to a customer in such a complete form that it can be put to immediate use

turn off *vb* **1** to leave (a road, pathway, etc) **2** (of a road, pathway, etc) to deviate from (another road, etc) **3** (*tr, adverb*) to cause (something) to cease operating by turning a knob, pushing a button, etc: *to turn off the radio* **4** (*tr*) *informal* to cause (a person, etc) to feel dislike or distaste for (something): *this music turns me off* **5** (*tr, adverb*) *Brit informal* to dismiss from employment ▷ *n* **turn-off** **6** a road or other way branching off from the main thoroughfare **7** *informal* a person or thing that elicits dislike or distaste

turn on *vb* **1** (*tr, adverb*) to cause (something) to operate by turning a knob, etc: *to turn on the light* **2** (*intr, preposition*) to depend or hinge on: *the success of the party turns on you* **3** (*preposition*) to change or cause to change one's attitude so as to become hostile or to retaliate: *the dog turned on the children* **4** (*tr, adverb*) *informal* to produce (charm, tears, etc) suddenly or automatically **5** (*tr, preposition*, foll by *to*) *informal* to interest (someone) in something: *how to turn kids on to drama* **6** (*tr, adverb*) *slang* to arouse emotionally or sexually **7** (*intr, adverb*) *slang* to take or become intoxicated by drugs **8** (*tr, adverb*) *slang* to introduce (someone) to drugs ▷ *n* **turn-on** **9** *slang* a person or thing that causes emotional or sexual arousal

turn out *vb* (*adverb*) **1** (*tr*) to cause (something, esp a light) to cease operating by or as if by turning a knob, etc **2** (*tr*) to produce by an effort or process: *she turned out 50 units per hour* **3** (*tr*) to dismiss, discharge, or expel: *the family had been turned out of their home* **4** (*tr*) to empty the contents of, esp in order to clean, tidy, or rearrange: *to turn out one's pockets* **5** (*copula*) **a** to prove to be: *her work turned out to be badly done* **b** to end up; result: *it all turned out well* **6** (*tr*) to fit as with clothes **7** (*intr*) to assemble or gather **8** (of a soldier) to parade or to call (a soldier) to parade **9** (*intr*) *informal* to get out of bed **10** (*intr*; foll by *for*) *informal* to make an appearance, esp in a sporting competition: *he was asked to turn out for Liverpool* ▷ *n* **turnout** **11** the body of people appearing together at a gathering **12** the quantity or amount produced **13** an array of clothing or equipment **14** the manner in which a person or thing is arrayed or equipped

turn over *vb* (*adverb*) **1** to change or cause to change position, esp so as to reverse top and bottom **2** to start (an engine), esp with a starting handle, or (of an engine) to start or function correctly **3** to shift or cause to shift position, as by rolling from side to side **4** (*tr*) to deliver; transfer **5** (*tr*) to consider carefully: *he turned over the problem for hours* **6** (*tr*) **a** to sell and replenish (stock in trade) **b** to transact business and so generate gross revenue of (a specified sum) **7** (*tr*) to invest and recover (capital) **8** (*tr*) *slang* to rob **9** (*tr*) *slang* to defeat utterly **10** **turn over a new leaf** to reform; resolve to improve one's behaviour ▷ *n* **turnover** **11** **a** the amount of business, usually expressed in terms of gross revenue, transacted during a specified period **b** (*as modifier*): *a turnover tax* **12** the rate at which stock in trade is sold and replenished **13** a change or reversal of position **14** a small semicircular or triangular pastry case filled with fruit, jam, etc **15** **a** the number of workers employed by a firm in a given period to replace those who have left **b** the ratio between this number and the average number of employees during the same period **16** *banking* the amount of capital funds loaned on call during a specified period ▷ *adj* **17** (*prenominal*) able or designed to be turned or folded over

turnpike (ˈtɜːnˌpaɪk) *n* **1** (between the mid-16th and late 19th centuries) **a** gates or some other barrier set across a road to prevent passage until a toll had been paid **b** a road on which a turnpike

t

was operated **2** an obsolete word for **turnstile** (sense 1) **3** *US* a motorway for use of which a toll is charged [C15 from TURN + PIKE[2]]
turnround ('tɜːnˌraʊnd) *n* another word for **turnaround**
turnsole ('tɜːnˌsəʊl) *n* **1** any of various plants having flowers that are said to turn towards the sun **2** a euphorbiaceous plant, *Croton tinctoria*, of the Mediterranean region that yields a purple dye **3** the dye extracted from this plant [C14 from Old French *tournesole*, from Old Italian *tornasole*, from *tornare* to TURN + *sole* sun, from Latin *sōl* sun]
turnspit ('tɜːnˌspɪt) *n* **1** (formerly) a servant or small dog whose job was to turn the spit on which meat, poultry, etc, was roasting **2** a spit that can be so turned
turnstile ('tɜːnˌstaɪl) *n* **1** a mechanical gate or barrier with metal arms that are turned to admit one person at a time, usually in one direction only **2** any similar device that admits foot passengers but no large animals or vehicles **3** Also called: **gatepost** *logic* a symbol of the form ⊢, ⊨, or ⊢, used to represent logical consequence when inserted between expressions to form a sequent, or when prefixed to a single expression to indicate its status as a theorem
turnstone ('tɜːnˌstəʊn) *n* either of two shore birds of the genus *Arenaria*, esp *A. interpres* (**ruddy turnstone**). They are related and similar to plovers and sandpipers [C17 so called because it turns over stones in search of food]
turntable ('tɜːnˌteɪbᵊl) *n* **1** the circular horizontal platform that rotates a gramophone record while it is being played **2** a flat circular platform that can be rotated about its centre, used for turning locomotives and cars **3** the revolvable platform on a microscope on which specimens are examined
turntable ladder *n Brit* a power-operated extending ladder mounted on a fire engine. US and Canadian name: **aerial ladder**
turn to *vb* (*intr, adverb*) to set about a task
turn up *vb* (*adverb*) **1** (*intr*) to arrive or appear: *he turned up late at the party* **2** to find or be found, esp by accident: *his book turned up in the cupboard* **3** (*tr*) to increase the flow, volume, etc, of: *to turn up the radio* **4** (*tr*) *informal* to cause to vomit ▷ *n* **turn-up 5** (*often plural*) *Brit* the turned-up fold at the bottom of some trouser legs. US and Canadian name: **cuff 6** *informal* an unexpected or chance occurrence
turpentine ('tɜːpᵊnˌtaɪn) *n* **1** Also called: **gum turpentine** any of various viscous oleoresins obtained from various coniferous trees, esp from the longleaf pine, and used as the main source of commercial turpentine **2** a brownish-yellow sticky viscous oleoresin that exudes from the terebinth tree **3** Also called: **oil of turpentine, spirits of turpentine** a colourless flammable volatile liquid with a pungent odour, distilled from turpentine oleoresin. It is an essential oil containing a mixture of terpenes and is used as a solvent for paints and in medicine as a rubefacient and expectorant. Sometimes (esp Brit) shortened to: **turps 4** Also called: **turpentine substitute, white spirit** (*not in technical usage*) any one of a number of thinners for paints and varnishes, consisting of fractions of petroleum. Related adj: **terebinthine** ▷ *vb* (*tr*) **5** to treat or saturate with turpentine **6** to extract crude turpentine from (trees) [C14 *terebentyne*, from Medieval Latin *terbentīna*, from Latin *terebinthīna* turpentine, from *terebinthus* the turpentine tree, TEREBINTH]
turpentine tree *n* **1** a tropical African leguminous tree, *Copaifera mopane*, yielding a hard dark wood and a useful resin **2** either of two Australian evergreen myrtaceous trees, *Syncarpia laurifolia* or *S. glomulifera*, that have durable wood and are sometimes planted as shade trees
turpeth ('tɜːpɪθ) *n* **1** a convolvulaceous plant, *Operculina turpethum*, of the East Indies, having roots with purgative properties **2** the root of this plant or the drug obtained from it [C14 from Medieval Latin *turbithum*, ultimately from Arabic *turbid*]
turpitude ('tɜːpɪˌtjuːd) *n* base character or action; depravity [C15 from Latin *turpitūdō* ugliness, from *turpis* base]
turps (tɜːps) *n* (*functioning as singular*) **1** *Brit* short for **turpentine** (sense 3) **2** *Austral and NZ slang* alcoholic drink, esp beer (esp in the phrase **on the turps**)
turquoise ('tɜːkwɔɪz, -kwɑːz) *n* **1** a greenish-blue fine-grained secondary mineral consisting of hydrated copper aluminium phosphate. It occurs in igneous rocks rich in aluminium and is used as a gemstone. Formula: $CuAl_6(PO_4)_4(OH)_8.4H_2O$ **2 a** the colour of turquoise **b** (*as adjective*): *a turquoise dress* [C14 from Old French *turqueise* Turkish (stone)]
turret ('tʌrɪt) *n* **1** a small tower that projects from the wall of a building, esp a medieval castle **2 a** a self-contained structure, capable of rotation, in which weapons are mounted, esp in tanks and warships **b** a similar structure on an aircraft that houses one or more guns and sometimes a gunner **3** a tall wooden tower on wheels used formerly by besiegers to scale the walls of a fortress **4** (on a machine tool) a turret-like steel structure with tools projecting radially that can be indexed round to select or to bring each tool to bear on the work [C14 from Old French *torete*, from *tor* tower, from Latin *turris*]
turreted ('tʌrɪtɪd), **turriculate** (tʌ'rɪkjʊlɪt, -ˌleɪt) *or* **turriculated** *adj* **1** having or resembling a turret or turrets **2** (of a gastropod shell) having the shape of a long spiral
turret lathe *n* another name for **capstan lathe**
turtle[1] ('tɜːtᵊl) *n* **1** any of various aquatic chelonian reptiles, esp those of the marine family *Chelonidae*, having a flattened shell enclosing the body and flipper-like limbs adapted for swimming. Related adjs: **chelonian, testudinal 2** *US and Canadian* any of the chelonian reptiles, including the tortoises and terrapins **3** *nautical* a zip bag made as part of a spinnaker for holding the sail so that it can be set rapidly **4 turn turtle** to capsize ▷ *vb* **5** (*intr*) to catch or hunt turtles [C17 from French *tortue* TORTOISE (influenced by TURTLE[2])] > '**turtler** *n*
turtle[2] ('tɜːtᵊl) *n* an archaic name for **turtledove** [Old English *turtla*, from Latin *turtur*, of imitative origin; related to German *Turteltaube*]
turtleback ('tɜːtᵊlˌbæk) *n* **1** an arched projection over the upper deck of a ship at the bow and sometimes at the stern for protection in heavy seas **2** (*now obsolete in archaeological usage*) a crude convex stone axe
turtledove ('tɜːtᵊlˌdʌv) *n* **1** any of several Old World doves of the genus *Streptopelia*, having a brown plumage with speckled wings and a long dark tail **2** a gentle or loving person [see TURTLE[2]]
turtleneck ('tɜːtᵊlˌnɛk) *n* **a** a round high close-fitting neck on a sweater or the sweater itself **b** (*as modifier*): *a turtleneck sweater*
turves (tɜːvz) *n* a plural of **turf**
Tuscan ('tʌskən) *adj* **1** of or relating to Tuscany, its inhabitants, or their dialect of Italian **2** of, denoting, or relating to one of the five classical orders of architecture: characterized by a column with an unfluted shaft and a capital and base with mouldings but no decoration. See also **Ionic, Composite, Doric, Corinthian** ▷ *n* **3** a native or inhabitant of Tuscany **4** any of the dialects of Italian spoken in Tuscany, esp the dialect of Florence: the standard form of Italian
Tuscany ('tʌskənɪ) *n* a region of central Italy, on the Ligurian and Tyrrhenian Seas: corresponds roughly to ancient Etruria; a region of numerous small states in medieval times; united in the 15th and 16th centuries under Florence; united with the rest of Italy in 1861. Capital: Florence. Pop: 3 516 296 (2003 est). Area: 22 990 sq km (8876 sq miles). Italian name: **Toscana**
Tuscarora (ˌtʌskə'rɔːrə) *n* **1** (*pl* **-ras** *or* **-ra**) a member of a North American Indian people formerly living in North Carolina, who later moved to New York State and joined the Iroquois **2** the language of this people, belonging to the Iroquoian family
tusche (tʊʃ) *n* a substance used in lithography for drawing the design and as a resist in silk-screen printing and lithography [from German, from *tuschen* to touch up with colour or ink, from French *toucher* to TOUCH]
Tusculan ('tʌskjʊlən) *adj* of or relating to the ancient Italian city of Tusculum or its inhabitants
Tusculum ('tʌskjʊləm) *n* an ancient city in Latium near Rome
tush[1] (tʌʃ) *interj archaic* an exclamation of disapproval or contempt [C15 Middle English, of imitative origin]
tush[2] (tʌʃ) *n rare* a small tusk [Old English *tūsc*; see TUSK]
tush[3] (tʊʃ) *n US slang* the buttocks [C20 from Yiddish *tokhes*, from Hebrew *tahath* beneath]
tushery ('tʌʃərɪ) *n literary* the use of affectedly archaic language in novels, etc [coined by Robert Louis Stevenson (1850–94), Scottish writer, from TUSH[1] + -ERY]
tusk (tʌsk) *n* **1** a pointed elongated usually paired tooth in the elephant, walrus, and certain other mammals that is often used for fighting **2** the canine tooth of certain animals, esp horses **3** a sharp pointed projection **4** Also called: **tusk tenon** *building trades* a tenon shaped with an additional oblique shoulder to make a stronger joint ▷ *vb* **5** to stab, tear, or gore with the tusks [Old English *tūsc*; related to Old Frisian *tosk*; see TOOTH] > **tusked** *adj* > '**tuskˌlike** *adj*
tusker ('tʌskə) *n* any animal with prominent tusks, esp a wild boar or elephant
tusk shell *n* any of various burrowing seashore molluscs of the genus *Dentalium* and related genera that have a long narrow tubular shell open at both ends: class *Scaphopoda*. Also called: **tooth shell**
tussis ('tʌsɪs) *n* the technical name for a **cough**. See **pertussis** [Latin: cough] > '**tussal** *adj* > '**tussive** *adj*
tussle ('tʌsᵊl) *vb* **1** (*intr*) to fight or wrestle in a vigorous way; struggle ▷ *n* **2** a vigorous fight; scuffle; struggle [C15 related to Old High German *zūsen*; see TOUSLE]
tussock ('tʌsək) *n* **1** a dense tuft of vegetation, esp of grass **2** *Austral and NZ* **a** short for **tussock grass b the**. country where tussock grass grows [C16 perhaps related to TUSK] > '**tussocky** *adj*
tussock grass *n Austral and NZ* any of several pasture grasses of the genus *Poa*
tussock moth *n* any of various pale or dull-coloured moths of the family *Lymantriidae* (or *Laparidae*), the hairy caterpillars of which are pests of many trees. See also **gipsy moth, brown-tail moth, goldtail moth** [C19 so named because of the tufts of hair on the caterpillars]
tussore (tʊ'sɔː, 'tʌsə), **tusser** ('tʌsə) *or chiefly US* **tussah** ('tʌsə) *n* **1** a strong coarse brownish Indian silk obtained from the cocoons of an Oriental saturniid silkworm, *Antheraea paphia* **2** a fabric woven from this silk **3** the silkworm producing this silk [C17 from Hindi *tasar* shuttle, from Sanskrit *tasara* a wild silkworm]
tut (*pronounced as an alveolar click*) (*spelling pron.* tʌt) *interj, n, vb* **tuts, tutting, tutted** short for **tut-tut**
tutee (tjuː'tiː) *n* one who is tutored, esp in a university
tutelage ('tjuːtɪlɪdʒ) *n* **1** the act or office of a guardian or tutor **2** instruction or guidance, esp by a tutor **3** the condition of being under the supervision of a guardian or tutor [C17 from Latin *tūtēla* a caring for, from *tuērī* to watch over; compare TUITION]
tutelary ('tjuːtɪlərɪ) *or* **tutelar** ('tjuːtɪlə) *adj* **1** invested with the role of guardian or protector **2** of or relating to a guardian or guardianship ▷ *n*, *pl* **-laries** *or* **-lars 3** a tutelary person, deity, or saint
tutiorism ('tjuːtɪəˌrɪzəm) *n* (in Roman Catholic

moral theology) the doctrine that in cases of moral doubt it is best to follow the safer course or that in agreement with the law [c19 from Latin *tutior* safer, comparative of *tutus* safe] > **'tutiorist** *n*

tutor ('tju:tə) *n* **1** a teacher, usually instructing individual pupils and often engaged privately **2** (at universities, colleges, etc) a member of staff responsible for the teaching and supervision of a certain number of students **3** *Scots law* the guardian of a pupil. See **pupil¹** (sense 2) ▷ *vb* **4** to act as a tutor to (someone); instruct **5** (*tr*) to act as guardian to; have care of **6** (*intr*) *chiefly US* to study under a tutor **7** (*tr*) *rare* to admonish, discipline, or reprimand [c14 from Latin: a watcher, from *tuērī* to watch over] > **'tutorage** *or* **'tutor,ship** *n*

tutorial (tju:'tɔ:rɪəl) *n* **1** a period of intensive tuition given by a tutor to an individual student or to a small group of students ▷ *adj* **2** of or relating to a tutor

tutorial system *n* a system, mainly in universities, in which students receive guidance in academic or personal matters from tutors

tutsan ('tʌtsən) *n* a woodland shrub, *Hypericum androsaemum*, of Europe and W Asia, having yellow flowers and reddish-purple fruits: family *Hypericaceae*. See also **Saint John's wort** [c15 from Old French *toute-saine* (unattested), literally: all healthy]

Tutsi ('tu:tsɪ) *n*, *pl* -si *or* -sis a member of a people of Rwanda and Burundi, probably a Nilotic people

tutti ('tʊtɪ) *adj, adv music* to be performed by the whole orchestra, choir, etc. Compare **soli** [c18 from Italian, pl of *tutto* all, from Latin *tōtus*]

tutti-frutti ('tu:tɪ'fru:tɪ) *n* **1** (*pl* -fruttis) an ice cream containing small pieces of candied or fresh fruits **2** a preserve of chopped mixed fruits, often with brandy syrup **3** a flavour like that of many fruits combined ▷ *adj* **4** having such a flavour [from Italian, literally: all the fruits]

tut-tut (*pronounced as alveolar clicks*) (*spelling pron.* 'tʌt'tʌt) *interj* **1** an exclamation of mild reprimand, disapproval, or surprise ▷ *vb* -tuts, -tutting, -tutted **2** (*intr*) to express disapproval by the exclamation of "tut-tut." ▷ *n* **3** the act of tut-tutting ▷ Often shortened to: **tut**

tutty ('tʌtɪ) *n* finely powdered impure zinc oxide obtained from the flues of zinc-smelting furnaces and used as a polishing powder [c14 from Old French *tutie*, from Arabic *tūtiyā*, probably from Persian, from Sanskrit *tuttha*]

tutu¹ ('tu:tu:) *n* a very short skirt worn by ballerinas, made of projecting layers of stiffened sheer material [from French, changed from the nursery word *cucu* backside, from *cul*, from Latin *cūlus* the buttocks]

tutu² ('tu:tu:) *n* a shrub, *Coriaria arborea*, of New Zealand, having seeds that are poisonous to farm animals [Māori]

Tutuila (,tu:tu:'i:lə) *n* the largest island of American Samoa, in the SW Pacific. Chief town and port: Pago Pago. Pop: 55 876 (2000). Area: 135 sq km (52 sq miles)

Tuvalu (,tu:və'lu:) *n* a country in the SW Pacific, comprising a group of nine coral islands: established as a British protectorate in 1892. From 1915 until 1975 the islands formed part of the British colony of the Gilbert and Ellice Islands; achieved full independence in 1978; a member of the Commonwealth (formerly a special member not represented at all meetings, until 2000). Languages: English and Tuvaluan. Religion: Christian majority. Currency: Australian dollar; Tuvalu dollars are also used. Capital: Funafuti. Pop: 11 000 (2003 est). Area: 26 sq km (10 sq miles). Former names: **Lagoon Islands, Ellice Islands**

Tuvaluan (,tu:və'lu:ən) *adj* **1** relating to, denoting, or characteristic of Tuvalu, its inhabitants, or their language ▷ *n* **2** a native or inhabitant of Tuvalu **3** the Austronesian language of Tuvalu

Tuva Republic ('tu:və) *n* a constituent republic of S Russia: mountainous. Capital: Kizyl. Pop: 305 500 (2002). Area: 170 500 sq km (65 800 sq miles). Also called: **Tuvinian Autonomous Republic** (tʊ'vɪnɪən)

tu-whit tu-whoo (tə'wɪt tə'wu:) *interj* an imitation of the sound made by an owl

tuxedo (tʌk'si:dəʊ) *n*, *pl* -dos the usual US and Canadian name for **dinner jacket**, often shortened to **tux** [c19 named after a country club in *Tuxedo Park*, New York]

Tuxtla Gutiérrez (*Spanish* 'tustla gu'tjɛrrɛθ) *n* a city in SE Mexico, capital of Chiapas state: agricultural centre. Pop: 723 000 (2005 est)

tuyère ('twi:ɛə, 'twaɪə; *French* tɥijɛr) *or* **twyer** ('twaɪə) *n* a water-cooled nozzle through which air is blown into a cupola, blast furnace, or forge [c18 from French, from *tuyau* pipe, from Old French *tuel*, probably of Germanic origin]

tv *the internet domain name for* Tuvalu

TV *abbreviation for* **1** television **2** transvestite

TVEI (in Britain) *abbreviation for* technical and vocational educational initiative: a national educational scheme in which pupils gain practical experience in technology and industry often through work placement

Tver (*Russian* tvjerj) *n* a city in central Russia, at the confluence of the Volga and Tversta Rivers: chief port of the upper Volga, linked by canal with Moscow. Pop: 402 000 (2005 est). Former name (1932–91): **Kalinin**

TVM *abbreviation for* television movie: a film made specifically for television, and not intended for release in cinemas

TVNZ *abbreviation for* Television New Zealand

TVP *abbreviation for* textured vegetable protein: a protein obtained from soya beans or other vegetables that have been spun into fibres and flavoured: used esp as a substitute for meat

TVR *abbreviation for* television rating: a measurement of the popularity of a television programme based on a survey

TVRO *abbreviation for* television receive only: an antenna and associated apparatus for reception from a broadcasting satellite

tw *the internet domain name for* Taiwan

twa (two:) *or* **twae** (twe) *n, determiner* a Scot word for **two**

twaddle ('twɒdəl) *n* **1** silly, trivial, or pretentious talk or writing; nonsense ▷ *vb* **2** to talk or write (something) in a silly or pretentious way [c16 *twattle*, variant of *twittle* or *tittle*; see TITTLE-TATTLE] > **'twaddler** *n*

twain (tweɪn) *determiner, n* an archaic word for **two** [Old English *twēgen*; related to Old Saxon *twēne*, Old High German *zwēne*, Old Norse *tveir*, Gothic *twai*]

twang (twæŋ) *n* **1** a sharp ringing sound produced by or as if by the plucking of a taut string: *the twang of a guitar* **2** the act of plucking a string to produce such a sound **3** a strongly nasal quality in a person's speech, esp in certain dialects ▷ *vb* **4** to make or cause to make a twang: *to twang a guitar* **5** to strum (music, a tune, etc): *to twang on a guitar* **6** to speak or utter with a sharp nasal voice **7** (*intr*) to be released or move with a twang [c16 of imitative origin] > **'twangy** *adj*

'twas (twɒz; *unstressed* twəz) *poetic or dialect* contraction of *it was*

twat (twæt, twɒt) *n taboo slang* **1** the female genitals **2** a girl or woman considered sexually **3** a foolish or despicable person [of unknown origin]

twattle ('twɒtəl) *n* a rare word for **twaddle**

twayblade ('tweɪ,bleɪd) *n* **1** any terrestrial orchid of the genus *Listera*, having a basal pair of oval unstalked leaves arranged opposite each other **2** any of various other orchids with paired basal leaves [c16 translation of Medieval Latin *bifolium* having two leaves, from obsolete *tway* TWO + BLADE]

tweak (twi:k) *vb* (*tr*) **1** to twist, jerk, or pinch with a sharp or sudden movement **2** *motor racing slang* to tune (a car or engine) for peak performance **3** *informal* to make a minor alteration ▷ *n* **4** an instance of tweaking **5** *informal* a minor alteration [Old English *twiccian*; related to Old High German *zwecchōn*; see TWITCH] > **'tweaky** *adj*

tweaker ('twi:kə) *n slang* an engineer's small screwdriver, used for fine adjustments

twee (twi:) *adj Brit* excessively sentimental, sweet, or pretty [c19 from *tweet*, mincing or affected pronunciation of SWEET] > **'tweely** *adv* > **'tweeness** *n*

tweed (twi:d) *n* **1 a** a thick woollen often knobbly cloth produced originally in Scotland **b** (*as modifier*): *a tweed coat* **2** (*plural*) clothes made of this cloth, esp a man's or woman's suit **3** (*plural*) *Austral informal* trousers [c19 probably from *tweel*, a Scottish variant of TWILL, influenced by TWEED]

Tweed (twi:d) *n* a river in SE Scotland and NE England, flowing east and forming part of the border between Scotland and England, then crossing into England to enter the North Sea at Berwick. Length: 156 km (97 miles)

Tweeddale ('twi:d,deɪl) *n* another name for **Peeblesshire**

Tweedledum and Tweedledee (,twi:dəl'dʌm, ,twi:dəl'di:) *n* any two persons or things that differ only slightly from each other; two of a kind [c19 from the proverbial names of George Frederick Handel (1685–1759), German composer, and the musician Buononcini, who were supported by rival factions though it was thought by some that there was nothing to choose between them. The names were popularized by Lewis Carroll's use of them in *Through the Looking Glass* (1872)]

tweedy ('twi:dɪ) *adj* tweedier, tweediest **1** of, made of, or resembling tweed **2** showing a fondness for a hearty outdoor life, usually associated with wearers of tweeds > **'tweediness** *n*

'tween (twi:n) *poetic or dialect* contraction of between

tweenager ('twi:n,eɪdʒə) *n informal* a child of approximately eight to fourteen years of age [from (BE)TWEEN + (TEEN)AGER]

'tween deck *or* **decks** *n nautical* a space between two continuous decks of a vessel

tweeny ('twi:nɪ) *n*, *pl* tweenies **1** *Brit informal obsolete* a maid who assists both cook and housemaid **2** Also: **tweenie** *informal* **a** a child of approximately eight to fourteen years of age **b** (*as modifier*): *tweeny magazines* [c19 shortened from BETWEEN (for sense 1, that is, a maid between cook and housemaid)]

tweet (twi:t) *interj* **1** (*often reiterated*) an imitation or representation of the thin chirping sound made by small or young birds ▷ *vb* **2** (*intr*) to make this sound [c19 of imitative origin]

tweeter ('twi:tə) *n* a loudspeaker used in high-fidelity systems for the reproduction of high audio frequencies. It is usually employed in conjunction with a woofer and a crossover network [c20 from TWEET]

tweeze (twi:z) *vb chiefly US* to take hold of or pluck (hair, small objects, etc) with or as if with tweezers [c17 back formation from TWEEZERS]

tweezers ('twi:zəz) *pl n* a small pincer-like instrument for handling small objects, plucking out hairs, etc. Also called: **pair of tweezers**, (*esp US*) **tweezer** [c17 plural of *tweezer* (on the model of *scissors*, etc), from *tweeze* case of instruments, from French *étuis* cases (of instruments), from Old French *estuier* to preserve, from Vulgar Latin *studiāre* (unattested) to keep, from Latin *studēre* to care about]

twelfth (twɛlfθ) *adj* **1** (*usually prenominal*) **a** coming after the eleventh in number or counting order, position, time, etc; being the ordinal number of twelve: often written 12th **b** (*as noun*): *the twelfth of the month* ▷ *n* **2 a** one of 12 equal or nearly equal parts of an object, quantity, measurement, etc **b** (*as modifier*): *a twelfth part* **3** the fraction equal to one divided by 12 (1/12) **4** *music* **a** an interval of one octave plus a fifth **b** one of two notes constituting such an interval in

t

relation to the other **c** an organ stop sounding a note one octave and a fifth higher than that normally produced by the key depressed [from Old English *twelfta*]

Twelfth Day *n* **a** Jan 6, the twelfth day after Christmas and the feast of the Epiphany, formerly observed as the final day of the Christmas celebrations **b** (*as modifier*): *Twelfth-Day celebrations*

twelfth man *n* a reserve player in a cricket team

Twelfth Night *n* **a** the evening of Jan 5, the eve of Twelfth Day, formerly observed with various festal celebrations **b** the evening of Twelfth Day itself **c** (*as modifier*): *Twelfth-Night customs*

Twelfthtide (ˈtwɛlfθˌtaɪd) *n* **a** the season of Epiphany **b** (*as modifier*): *the Twelfthtide celebrations*

twelve (twɛlv) *n* **1** the cardinal number that is the sum of ten and two. See also **number** (sense 1) **2** a numeral, 12, XII, etc, representing this number **3** something represented by, representing, or consisting of 12 units **4** Also called: **twelve o'clock** noon or midnight ▷ *determiner* **5 a** amounting to twelve: *twelve loaves* **b** (*as pronoun*): *twelve have arrived* ▷ Related adjective: **duodecimal** Related prefix: **dodeca-** See also **dozen** [Old English *twelf*; related to Old Frisian *twelif*, Old High German *zwelif*, Old Norse *tolf*, Gothic *twalif*]

twelve-inch *n* a gramophone record 12 inches in diameter and played at 45 revolutions per minute, usually containing an extended remix of a single

twelve-mile limit *n* the offshore boundary 12 miles from the coast claimed by some states as marking the extent of their territorial jurisdiction

twelvemo (ˈtwɛlvməʊ) *n, pl* **-mos** *bookbinding* another word for **duodecimo**

twelvemonth (ˈtwɛlvˌmʌnθ) *n chiefly Brit* an archaic or dialect word for a **year**

twelve pitch *n* another name for **elite** (sense 2)

twelve-step *adj chiefly US* of or relating to a method of treatment for addiction which consists of twelve stages and stresses the need for patients to acknowledge their problem and to take personal responsibility for it

Twelve Tables *pl n* **the**. the earliest code of Roman civil, criminal, and religious law, promulgated in 451–450 BC

twelve-tone *adj* of, relating to, or denoting the type of serial music invented and developed by Arnold Schoenberg, which uses as musical material a tone row formed by the 12 semitones of the chromatic scale, together with its inverted and retrograde versions. The technique has been applied in various ways by different composers and usually results in music in which there are few, if any, tonal centres. See **serialism**

twentieth (ˈtwɛntɪɪθ) *adj* **1** (*usually prenominal*) **a** coming after the nineteenth in numbering or counting order, position, time, etc; being the ordinal number of *twenty*: often written 20th **b** (*as noun*): *he left on the twentieth* ▷ *n* **2 a** one of 20 approximately equal parts of something **b** (*as modifier*): *a twentieth part* **3** the fraction that is equal to one divided by 20 (1/20) [from Old English *twentigotha*]

twenty (ˈtwɛntɪ) *n, pl* **-ties 1** the cardinal number that is the product of ten and two; a score. See also **number** (sense 1) **2** a numeral, 20, XX, etc, representing this number **3** something representing, represented by, or consisting of 20 units ▷ *determiner* **4 a** amounting to twenty: *twenty questions* **b** (*as pronoun*): *to order twenty* ▷ Related adjs: **vicenary, vigesimal** Related prefix: **icosa-** [Old English *twēntig*; related to Old High German *zweinzug*, German *zwanzig*]

twenty-four seven *or* **24/7** *adv informal* twenty-four hours a day, seven days a week; constantly; all the time: *consultants would not be available 24/7*

twenty-one *n* another name (esp US) for **pontoon²** (sense 1)

twenty-six counties *pl n* the counties of the Republic of Ireland

twenty-sixer *n Canadian informal* a liquor bottle of around 26 ounces (0.750 litre) capacity

twenty-twenty *adj med* (of vision) being of normal acuity: usually written 20/20

'twere (twɜː; *unstressed* twə) *poetic or dialect contraction of* it were

twerp *or* **twirp** (twɜːp) *n informal* a silly, weak-minded, or contemptible person [c20 of unknown origin] > ˈ**twerpy** *or* ˈ**twirpy** *adj*

Twi (twiː) *n* **1** a language of S Ghana: one of the two chief dialects of Akan. Formerly called: **Ashanti** Compare **Fanti 2** (*pl* **Twi** *or* **Twis**) a member of the Negroid people who speak this language

twibill *or* **twibil** (ˈtwaɪˌbɪl) *n* **1** a mattock with a blade shaped like an adze at one end and like an axe at the other **2** *archaic* a double-bladed battle-axe [Old English, from *twi-* two, double + *bill* sword, BILL³]

twice (twaɪs) *adv* **1** two times; on two occasions or in two cases: *he coughed twice* **2** double in degree or quantity: *twice as long* [Old English *twiwa*; related to Old Norse *tvisvar*, Middle Low German *twiges*]

twice-laid *adj* **1** made from strands of used rope **2** made from old or used material or retwisted yarn [c16 from LAY¹ (in the sense: to twist together)]

twice-told *adj* hackneyed through repeated use

Twickenham (ˈtwɪkənəm) *n* a former town in SE England, on the River Thames: part of the Greater London borough of Richmond-upon-Thames since 1965; contains the English Rugby Football Union ground

twiddle (ˈtwɪdᵊl) *vb* **1** (when *intr*, often foll by *with*) to twirl or fiddle (with), often in an idle way **2** to do nothing; be unoccupied **3** (*intr*) to turn, twirl, or rotate **4** (*intr*) *rare* to be occupied with trifles ▷ *n* **5** an act or instance of twiddling [c16 probably a blend of TWIRL + FIDDLE] > ˈ**twiddler** *n*

twig¹ (twɪɡ) *n* **1** any small branch or shoot of a tree or other woody plant **2** something resembling this, esp a minute branch of a blood vessel [Old English *twigge*; related to Old Norse *dvika* consisting of two, Old High German *zwīg* twig, Old Danish *tvige* fork] > ˈ**twigˌlike** *adj*

twig² (twɪɡ) *vb* **twigs, twigging, twigged** *Brit informal* **1** to understand (something) **2** to find out or suddenly comprehend (something) **3** (*tr*) *rare* to perceive (something) [c18 perhaps from Scottish Gaelic *tuig* I understand]

twiggy (ˈtwɪɡɪ) *adj* **-gier, -giest 1** of or relating to a twig or twigs **2** covered with twigs **3** slender or fragile

twilight (ˈtwaɪˌlaɪt) *n* **1** the soft diffused light occurring when the sun is just below the horizon, esp following sunset. Related adj: **crepuscular 2** the period in which this light occurs **3** the period of time during which the sun is a specified angular distance below the horizon (6°, 12°, and 18° for **civil twilight, nautical twilight**, and **astronomical twilight**, respectively) **4** any faint light **5** a period in which strength, importance, etc, are waning: *the twilight of his life* **6** (*modifier*) **a** of or relating to the period towards the end of the day: *the twilight shift* **b** of or relating to the final phase of a particular era: *the twilight days of the Bush presidency* **c** denoting irregularity and obscurity: *a twilight existence* [c15 literally: half-light (between day and night), from Old English *twi-* half + LIGHT¹] > **twilit** (ˈtwaɪˌlɪt) *adj*

Twilight of the Gods *n* another term for **Götterdämmerung** *or* **Ragnarök**

twilight sleep *n med* a state of partial anaesthesia in which the patient retains a slight degree of consciousness

twilight zone *n* **1** any indefinite or transitional condition or area **2** an area of a city or town where houses have become dilapidated **3** the lowest level of the ocean to which light can penetrate

twill (twɪl) *adj* **1** (in textiles) of or designating a weave in which the weft yarns are worked around two or more warp yarns to produce an effect of parallel diagonal lines or ribs ▷ *n* **2** any fabric so woven ▷ *vb* **3** (*tr*) to weave in this fashion [Old English *twilic* having a double thread; related to Old High German *zwilīth* twill, Latin *bilīx* two-threaded]

'twill (twɪl) *poetic or dialect contraction of* it will

twin (twɪn) *n* **1 a** either of two persons or animals conceived at the same time **b** (*as modifier*): *a twin brother*. See also **identical** (sense 3), **fraternal** (sense 3) **2 a** either of two persons or things that are identical or very similar; counterpart **b** (*as modifier*): *twin carburettors* **3** Also called: **macle** a crystal consisting of two parts each of which has a definite orientation to the other ▷ *vb* **twins, twinning, twinned 4** to pair or be paired together; couple **5** (*intr*) to bear twins **6** (*intr*) (of a crystal) to form into a twin **7** (*intr*) *archaic* to be born as a twin **8** (*tr*) **a** to create a reciprocal relation between (two towns in different countries); pair (a town) with another in a different country **b** (*intr*) (of a town) to be paired with a town in a different country [Old English *twinn*; related to Old High German *zwiniling* twin, Old Norse *tvinnr* double] > ˈ**twinning** *n*

twin bed *n* one of a pair of matching single beds

twinberry (ˈtwɪnbərɪ, -brɪ) *n, pl* **-ries** another name for **partridgeberry** (sense 1)

twin bill *n US* an informal name for **double feature** *or* **double-header** (sense 2)

twine (twaɪn) *n* **1** string made by twisting together fibres of hemp, cotton, etc **2** the act or an instance of twining **3** something produced or characterized by twining **4** a twist, coil, or convolution **5** a knot, tangle, or snarl ▷ *vb* **6** (*tr*) to twist together; interweave: *she twined the wicker to make a basket* **7** (*tr*) to form by or as if by twining: *to twine a garland* **8** (when *intr*, often foll by *around*) to wind or cause to wind, esp in spirals: *the creeper twines around the tree* [Old English *twīn*; related to Old Frisian *twīne*, Dutch *twijn* twine, Lithuanian *dvynu* twins; see TWIN] > ˈ**twiner** *n*

twinflower (ˈtwɪnˌflaʊə) *n* an evergreen caprifoliaceous trailing shrub, *Linnaea borealis*, of circumpolar distribution, having round leaves, white or pink fragrant bell-shaped flowers arranged in pairs, and yellow fruits

twinge (twɪndʒ) *n* **1** a sudden brief darting or stabbing pain **2** a sharp emotional pang: *a twinge of guilt* ▷ *vb* **3** to have or cause to have a twinge **4** (*tr*) *obsolete* to pinch; tweak [Old English *twengan* to pinch; related to Old High German *zwengen*]

twink (twɪŋk) *n NZ* white correction fluid for deleting written text

twinkle (ˈtwɪŋkᵊl) *vb* (*mainly intr*) **1** to emit or reflect light in a flickering manner; shine brightly and intermittently; sparkle: *twinkling stars* **2** (of the eyes) to sparkle, esp with amusement or delight **3** *rare* to move about quickly **4** (*also tr*) *rare* to wink (the eyes); blink ▷ *n* **5** an intermittent gleam of light; flickering brightness; sparkle or glimmer **6** an instant **7** a rare word for **wink¹** [Old English *twinclian*; related to Middle High German *zwinken* to blink] > ˈ**twinkler** *n*

twinkling (ˈtwɪŋklɪŋ) *or* **twink** (twɪŋk) *n* a very short time; instant; moment. Also called: **twinkling of an eye**

twink out *vb* (*tr, adverb*) *NZ* to delete (written text) with white correction fluid

twin-lens reflex *n* See **reflex camera**

twin paradox *n* a phenomenon predicted by relativity. One of a pair of identical twins is supposed to live normally in an inertial system whilst the other is accelerated to a high speed in a spaceship, travels for a long time, and finally returns to rest beside his twin. The travelled twin will be found to be younger than his brother

Twins (twɪnz) *pl n* **the**. the constellation Gemini, the third sign of the zodiac

twin-screw *adj* (of a vessel) having two propellers

twinset (ˈtwɪnˌsɛt) *n Brit* a matching jumper and cardigan

twin town *n Brit* a town that has civic associations, such as reciprocal visits and cultural exchanges, with a foreign town, usually of similar size and sometimes with other similarities, as in commercial activities

twin-tub *n* a type of washing machine that has two revolving drums, one for washing and the other for spin-drying

twirl (twɜːl) *vb* **1** to move or cause to move around rapidly and repeatedly in a circle **2** (*tr*) to twist, wind, or twiddle, often idly: *she twirled her hair around her finger* **3** (*intr; often foll by* around *or* about) to turn suddenly to face another way: *she twirled around angrily to face him* ▷ *n* **4** an act of rotating or being rotated; whirl or twist **5** something wound around or twirled; coil **6** a written flourish or squiggle [c16 perhaps a blend of TWIST + WHIRL] > ˈtwirler *n*

twirp (twɜːp) *n* a variant spelling of **twerp**

twist (twɪst) *vb* **1** to cause (one end or part) to turn or (of one end or part) to turn in the opposite direction from another; coil or spin **2** to distort or be distorted; change in shape **3** to wind or cause to wind; twine, coil, or intertwine: *to twist flowers into a wreath* **4** to force or be forced out of the natural form or position: *to twist one's ankle* **5** (*usually passive*) to change or cause to change for the worse in character, meaning, etc; pervert: *his ideas are twisted*; *she twisted the statement* **6** to revolve or cause to revolve; rotate **7** (*tr*) to wrench with a turning action: *to twist something from someone's grasp* **8** (*intr*) to follow a winding course **9** (*intr*) to squirm, as with pain **10** (*intr*) to dance the twist **11** (*tr*) *Brit informal* to cheat; swindle **12** twist someone's arm to persuade or coerce someone ▷ *n* **13** the act or an instance of twisting **14** something formed by or as if by twisting: *a twist of hair* **15** a decisive change of direction, aim, meaning, or character **16** (in a novel, play, etc) an unexpected event, revelation, or other development **17** a bend: *a twist in the road* **18** a distortion of the original or natural shape or form **19** a jerky pull, wrench, or turn **20** a strange personal characteristic, esp a bad one **21** a confused mess, tangle, or knot made by twisting **22** a twisted thread used in sewing where extra strength is needed **23** (in weaving) a specified direction of twisting the yarn **24** the twist a modern dance popular in the 1960s, in which couples vigorously twist the hips in time to rhythmic music **25** a bread loaf or roll made of one or more pieces of twisted dough **26** a thin sliver of peel from a lemon, lime, etc, twisted and added to a drink **27 a** a cigar made by twisting three cigars around one another **b** chewing tobacco made in the form of a roll by twisting the leaves together **28** *physics* torsional deformation or shear stress or strain **29** *sport, chiefly US and Canadian* spin given to a ball in various games, esp baseball **30** the extent to which the grooves in the bore of a rifled firearm are spiralled **31** round the twist *Brit slang* mad; eccentric [Old English; related to German dialect *Zwist* a quarrel, Dutch *twisten* to quarrel] > ˈtwistable *adj* > ˌtwistaˈbility *n* > ˈtwisted *adj* > ˈtwisting *adj* > ˈtwisty *adj*

twist drill *n* a drill bit having two helical grooves running from the point along the shank to clear swarf and cuttings

twister (ˈtwɪstə) *n* **1** *Brit* a swindling or dishonest person **2** a person or thing that twists, such as a device used in making ropes **3** *US and Canadian* an informal name for **tornado** **4** a ball moving with a twisting motion

twist grip *n* a handlebar control in the form of a ratchet-controlled rotating grip, used on some bicycles and motorcycles as a gear-change control and on motorcycles as an accelerator

twit[1] (twɪt) *vb* twits, twitting, twitted **1** (*tr*) to tease, taunt, or reproach, often in jest ▷ *n* **2** *US and Canadian informal* a nervous or excitable state **3** *rare* a reproach; taunt [Old English *ætwitan*, from *æt* against + *wītan* to accuse; related to Old High German *wīzan* to punish]

twit[2] (twɪt) *n* informal, chiefly Brit a foolish or

stupid person; idiot [c19 from TWIT[1] (originally in the sense: a person given to twitting)]

twitch (twɪtʃ) *vb* **1** to move or cause to move in a jerky spasmodic way **2** (*tr*) to pull or draw (something) with a quick jerky movement **3** (*intr*) to hurt with a sharp spasmodic pain **4** (*tr*) *rare* to nip ▷ *n* **5** a sharp jerking movement **6** a mental or physical twinge **7** a sudden muscular spasm, esp one caused by a nervous condition. Compare **tic** **8** a loop of cord used to control a horse by drawing it tight about its upper lip [Old English *twiccian* to pluck; related to Old High German *zwecchōn* to pinch, Dutch *twicken*] > ˈtwitching *adj, n*

twitcher (ˈtwɪtʃə) *n* **1** a person or thing that twitches **2** *informal* a bird-watcher who tries to spot as many rare varieties as possible

twitch grass *n* another name for **couch grass** Sometimes shortened to: **twitch** [c16 a variant of QUITCH GRASS]

twitchy (ˈtwɪtʃɪ) *adj* nervous, worried, and ill-at-ease: *he was twitchy with anticipation*

twite (twaɪt) *n* a N European finch, *Acanthis flavirostris*, with a brown streaked plumage [c16 imitative of its cry]

twitten (ˈtwɪtᵊn) *n* Southeast English dialect a narrow alleyway

twitter (ˈtwɪtə) *vb* **1** (*intr*) (esp of a bird) to utter a succession of chirping sounds **2** (*intr*) to talk or move rapidly and tremulously **3** (*intr*) to giggle: *her schoolmates twittered behind their desks* **4** (*tr*) to utter in a chirping way ▷ *n* **5** a twittering sound, esp of a bird **6** the act of twittering **7** a state of nervous excitement (esp in the phrase **in a twitter**) [c14 of imitative origin] > ˈtwitterer *n* > ˈtwittery *adj*

ˈtwixt or **twixt** (twɪkst) *poetic contraction of* betwixt

two (tuː) *n* **1** the cardinal number that is the sum of one and one. It is a prime number. See also **number** (sense 1) **2** a numeral, 2, II, (ii), etc, representing this number **3** *music* the numeral 2 used as the lower figure in a time signature, indicating that the beat is measured in minims **4** something representing, represented by, or consisting of two units, such as a playing card with two symbols on it **5** Also called: two o'clock two hours after noon or midnight **6** in two in or into two parts: *break the bread in two* **7** put two and two together to make an inference from available evidence, esp an obvious inference **8** that makes two of us the same applies to me ▷ *determiner* **9 a** amounting to two: *two nails* **b** (*as pronoun*): *he bought two* ▷ Related adjs: **binary, double, dual** Related prefixes: **di-, bi-** [Old English *twā* (feminine); related to Old High German *zwā*, Old Norse *tvau*, Latin, Greek *duo*]

Two-and-a-half International *n* another name for the **Vienna Union**

two-bit *adj* (*prenominal*) *slang, chiefly US and Canadian* worth next to nothing; cheap [c20 from the phrase *two bits* a small sum]

two-by-four *n* **1** a length of untrimmed timber with a cross section that measures 2 inches by 4 inches **2** a trimmed timber joist with a cross section that measures 1½ inches by 3½ inches

twoccing or **twocking** (ˈtwɒkɪŋ) *n Brit slang* the act of breaking into a motor vehicle and driving it away [c20 from T(*aking*) W(*ithout*) O(*wner's*) C(*onsent*), the legal offence with which car thieves may be charged] > ˈtwoccer or ˈtwocker *n*

two-cycle *adj* US and Canadian relating to or designating an internal-combustion engine whose piston makes two strokes for every explosion. Also called (in Britain and certain other countries): two-stroke compare **four-stroke**

two-dimensional *adj* **1** of, having, or relating to two dimensions, usually describable in terms of length and breadth or length and height **2** lying on a plane; having an area but not enclosing any volume **3** lacking in depth, as characters in a literary work **4** (of painting or drawing) lacking the characteristics of form or depth > ˈtwo-

diˌmensionˈality *n* > ˌtwo-diˈmensionally *adv*

two-edged *adj* **1** having two cutting edges **2** (esp of a remark) having two interpretations, such as *she looks nice when she smiles*

two-faced *adj* deceitful; insincere; hypocritical > **two-facedly** (ˌtuːˈfeɪsɪdlɪ, -ˈfeɪst-) *adv* > ˌtwo-ˈfacedness *n*

two-fisted *adj* US strong, tough, and vigorous

twofold (ˈtuːˌfəʊld) *adj* **1** equal to twice as many or twice as much; double: *a twofold increase* **2** made of two parts; dual: *a twofold reason* ▷ *adv* **3** doubly

two-four *n Canadian informal* a box containing 24 bottles of beer

two-four time *n music* a form of simple duple time in which there are two crotchet beats in each bar

two-handed *adj* **1** requiring the use of both hands **2** ambidextrous **3** requiring the participation or cooperation of two people > ˌtwo-ˈhandedly *adv*

two-hander (ˌtuːˈhændə) *n* a play for two actors

two-line *n* (*modifier*) (formerly) denoting double the normal size of printer's type: *two-line pica*

two-name paper *n US finance* a commercial paper signed by two persons both of whom accept full liability

twonie (ˈtuːnɪ) *n* variant spelling of **toonie**

Two Oceans *n* (*functioning as singular*) an annual road marathon run in Cape Town, South Africa

two-pack *adj* (of a paint, filler, etc) supplied as two separate components, for example a base and a catalyst, that are mixed together immediately before use

two-party system *n* a condition or system in which two major parties dominate a political unit

twopence or **tuppence** (ˈtʌpəns) *n Brit* **1** the sum of two pennies **2** (*used with a negative*) something of little value (in the phrase **not care** or **give twopence**) **3** a former British silver coin, now only coined as Maundy money

twopenny or **tuppenny** (ˈtʌpənɪ) *adj chiefly Brit* **1** Also: **twopenny-halfpenny**. cheap or tawdry **2** (*intensifier*): *a twopenny damn* **3** worth two pence

two-phase *adj* (of an electrical circuit, device, etc) generating or using two alternating voltages of the same frequency, displaced in phase by 90°. Also: quarter-phase

two-piece *adj* **1** consisting of two separate parts, usually matching, as of a garment ▷ *n* **2** such an outfit

two-ply *adj* **1** made of two thicknesses, layers, or strands ▷ *n, pl* -plies **2** a two-ply wood, knitting yarn, etc

two-pot screamer *n Austral slang* a person easily influenced by alcohol

two-seater *n* a vehicle providing seats for two people

Two Sicilies *pl n* the a former kingdom of S Italy, consisting of the kingdoms of Sicily and Naples (1061–1860)

two-sided *adj* **1** having two sides or aspects **2** controversial; debatable: *a two-sided argument*

twosome (ˈtuːsəm) *n* **1** two together, esp two people **2** a match between two people **3** (*modifier*) consisting of or played by two: *a twosome song*

two-spot *n* a card with two pips; two; deuce

two-step *n* **1** an old-time dance in duple time **2** a piece of music composed for or in the rhythm of such a dance

two-stroke *adj* relating to or designating an internal-combustion engine whose piston makes two strokes for every explosion. US and Canadian word: two-cycle Compare **four-stroke**

two-tailed *adj statistics* (of a significance test) concerned with the hypothesis that an observed value of a sampling statistic differs significantly from a given value, where an error in either direction is relevant: for instance, in testing the fairness of scales, an inspector will seek to exclude both overweight and underweight goods. Compare **one-tailed**

two-tailed pasha *n* a distinctive vanessid

t

butterfly of S Europe, *Charaxes jasius,* having mottled brown wings with a yellow-orange margin and frilled hind edges

Two Thousand Guineas *n (functioning as singular) usually written* **2000 Guineas** an annual horse race run at Newmarket since 1809

two-tier *adj* involving or comprising two levels of structure, policy, etc

two-time *vb informal* to deceive (someone, esp a lover) by carrying on a relationship with another > ˌtwo-ˈtimer *n*

two-tone *adj* **1** of two colours or two shades of the same colour **2** (esp of sirens, car horns, etc) producing or consisting of two notes

two-tooth *n, pl* **-tooths** *Austral and NZ* a sheep between one and two years old with two permanent incisor teeth

'twould (twʊd) *poetic or dialect contraction of* it would

two-up *n chiefly Austral* a gambling game in which two coins are tossed or spun. Bets are made on both coins landing with the same face uppermost

two-way *adj* **1** moving, permitting movement, or operating in either of two opposite directions: *two-way traffic; a two-way valve* **2** involving two participants: *a two-way agreement* **3** involving reciprocal obligation or mutual action: *a two-way process* **4** (of a radio, telephone, etc) allowing communications in two directions using both transmitting and receiving equipment

two-way mirror *n* a half-silvered sheet of glass that functions as a mirror when viewed from one side but is translucent from the other

two-way street *n* an arrangement or a situation involving reciprocal obligation or mutual action

twp (tʊp) *adj (predicative) South Wales dialect* stupid; daft [Welsh]

twyer ('twaɪə) *n* a variant of **tuyère**

TX *text messaging abbreviation for* **1** Texas **2** thanks

TXT *text messaging abbreviation for* text

-ty¹ *suffix of numerals* denoting a multiple of ten: *sixty; seventy* [from Old English *-tig* TEN]

-ty² *suffix forming nouns* indicating state, condition, or quality: *cruelty* [from Old French *-te, -tet,* from Latin *-tās, -tāt-;* related to Greek *-tēs*]

Tyan-Shan ('tjanˈʃan) *n* transliteration of the Russian name for the **Tian Shan**

Tyburn ('taɪbɜːn) *n* (formerly) a place of execution in London, on the **River Tyburn** (a tributary of the Thames, now entirely below ground)

Tyche ('taɪkɪ) *n Greek myth* the goddess of fortune. Roman counterpart: **Fortuna**

tychism ('taɪkɪzəm) *n philosophy* the theory that chance is an objective reality at work in the universe, esp in evolutionary adaptations [from Greek *tukhē* chance]

Tycho ('taɪkəʊ) *n* a relatively young crater in the SW quadrant of the moon, 4 km deep and 84 km in diameter, with a central peak. It is the centre of a conspicuous system of rays [named after *Tycho* Brahe (1546–1601), Danish astronomer]

tycoon (taɪˈkuːn) *n* **1** a business man of great wealth and power **2** an archaic name for a **shogun** [c19 from Japanese *taikun,* from Chinese *ta* great + *chün* ruler]

tyke *or* **tike** (taɪk) *n* **1** a dog, esp a mongrel **2** *informal* a small or cheeky child: used esp in affectionate reproof **3** *Brit dialect* a rough ill-mannered person **4** Also called: **Yorkshire tyke** *Brit slang often offensive* a person from Yorkshire **5** *Austral slang offensive* a Roman Catholic [c14 from Old Norse *tík* bitch]

tylopod ('taɪləʊˌpɒd) *n* any artiodactyl mammal of the suborder *Tylopoda,* having padded, rather than hoofed, digits: includes the camels and llamas [c19 from New Latin, from Greek *tulos* knob or *tulē* cushion + -POD]

tylosis (taɪˈləʊsɪs) *n botany* a bladder-like outgrowth from certain cells in woody tissue that extends into and blocks adjacent conducting xylem cells [c19 from Greek *tulōsis,* from *tulos* knob or *tulē* callus + -OSIS]

tymbal ('tɪmbəl) *n* a variant spelling of **timbal**

tympan ('tɪmpən) *n* **1** a membrane stretched over a frame or resonating cylinder, bowl, etc **2** *printing* packing interposed on a hand-operated text between the platen and the paper to be printed in order to provide an even impression **3** *architect* another name for **tympanum** (sense 3) [Old English *timpana,* from Latin; see TYMPANUM]

tympani ('tɪmpənɪ) *pl n* a variant spelling of **timpani**

tympanic (tɪmˈpænɪk) *adj* **1** *anatomy, architect* of, relating to, or having a tympanum **2** of, relating to, or resembling a drumhead

tympanic bone *n* the part of the temporal bone in the mammalian skull that surrounds the auditory canal

tympanic membrane *n* the thin translucent oval membrane separating the external ear from the middle ear. It transmits vibrations produced by sound waves, via the ossicles, to the cochlea. Also called: **tympanum** Nontechnical name: **eardrum**

tympanist ('tɪmpənɪst) *n* a person who plays a drum, now specifically the kettledrum

tympanites (ˌtɪmpəˈnaɪtiːz) *n* distension of the abdomen caused by an abnormal accumulation of gas in the intestinal or peritoneal cavity, as in peritonitis. Also called: **meteorism, tympany** [c14 from Late Latin, from Greek *tumpanitēs* concerning a drum, from *tumpanon* drum] > **tympanitic** (ˌtɪmpəˈnɪtɪk) *adj*

tympanitis (ˌtɪmpəˈnaɪtɪs) *n* inflammation of the eardrum. Also called: **otitis media**

tympanum ('tɪmpənəm) *n, pl* **-nums** *or* **-na** (-nə) **1 a** the cavity of the middle ear **b** another name for **tympanic membrane 2** any diaphragm resembling that in the middle ear in function **3** Also called: **tympan** *architect* **a** the recessed space bounded by the cornices of a pediment, esp one that is triangular in shape and ornamented **b** the recessed space bounded by an arch and the lintel of a doorway or window below it **4** *music* a tympan or drum **5** a scoop wheel for raising water [c17 from Latin, from Greek *tumpanon* drum; related to Greek *tuptein* to beat]

tympany ('tɪmpənɪ) *n, pl* **-nies 1** another name for **tympanites 2** *obsolete* excessive pride or arrogance

Tyndall effect ('tɪndəl) *n* the phenomenon in which light is scattered by particles of matter in its path. It enables a beam of light to become visible by illuminating dust particles, etc [c19 named after John *Tyndall* (1820–93), Irish physicist]

tyndallimetry (ˌtɪndəˈlɪmətrɪ) *n chem* the determination of the concentration of suspended material in a liquid by measuring the amount of light scattered [c20 from TYNDALL EFFECT + -METRY]

Tyndareus (tɪnˈdærɪəs) *n Greek myth* a Spartan king; the husband of Leda

Tyne (taɪn) *n* a river in N England, flowing east to the North Sea. Length: 48 km (30 miles)

Tyne and Wear *n* a metropolitan county of NE England, administered since 1986 by the unitary authorities of Newcastle upon Tyne, North Tyneside, Gateshead, South Tyneside, and Sunderland. Area: 540 sq km (208 sq miles)

Tynemouth ('taɪnˌmaʊθ) *n* a port in NE England, in North Tyneside unitary authority, Tyne and Wear, at the mouth of the River Tyne: includes the port and industrial centre of North Shields; fishing, ship-repairing, and marine engineering. Pop: 17 056 (2001)

Tyneside ('taɪnˌsaɪd) *n* the conurbation on the banks of the Tyne from Newcastle to the coast. Related word: **Geordie**

Tynwald ('tɪnwəld, 'taɪn-) *n* **the** the Parliament of the Isle of Man, consisting of the crown, lieutenant governor, House of Keys, and legislative council. Full name: **Tynwald Court** [c15 from Old Norse *thingvollr,* from *thing* assembly + *vollr* field]

typ., typo. *or* **typog.** *abbreviation for* **1**

typographer **2** typographic(al) **3** typography

typal ('taɪpəl) *adj* a rare word for **typical**

type (taɪp) *n* **1** a kind, class, or category, the constituents of which share similar characteristics **2** a subdivision of a particular class of things or people; sort: *what type of shampoo do you use?* **3** the general form, plan, or design distinguishing a particular group **4** *informal* a person who typifies a particular quality: *he's the administrative type* **5** *informal* a person, esp of a specified kind: *he's a strange type* **6 a** a small block of metal or more rarely wood bearing a letter or character in relief for use in printing **b** such pieces collectively **7** characters printed from type; print **8** *biology* **a** the taxonomic group the characteristics of which are used for defining the next highest group, for example *Rattus norvegicus* (brown rat) is the type species of the rat genus *Rattus* **b** (*as modifier*): *a type genus; a type species* **9** See **type specimen 10** the characteristic device on a coin **11** *linguistics* a symbol regarded as standing for the class of all symbols identical to it. Compare **token** (sense 8) **12** *logic* a class of expressions or of the entities they represent that can all enter into the same syntactic relations. The **theory of types** was advanced by Bertrand Russell to avoid the liar paradox, Russell's paradox, etc **13** *philosophy* a universal. If a sentence always has the same meaning whenever it is used, the meaning is said to be a property of the sentence-type. Compare **token** (sense 9) **14** *chiefly Christian theol* a figure, episode, or symbolic factor resembling some future reality in such a way as to foreshadow or prefigure it **15** *rare* a distinctive sign or mark ▷ *vb* **16** to write (copy) on a typewriter **17** (*tr*) to be a symbol of; typify **18** (*tr*) to decide the type of; clarify into a type **19** (*tr*) *med* to determine the blood group of (a blood sample) **20** (*tr*) *chiefly Christian theol* to foreshadow or serve as a symbol of (some future reality) [c15 from Latin *typus* figure, from Greek *tupos* image, from *tuptein* to strike]

-type *n combining form* **1** type or form: *archetype* **2** printing type or photographic process: *collotype* [from Latin *-typus,* from Greek *-typos,* from *tupos* TYPE]

typebar ('taɪpˌbɑː) *n* one of the bars in a typewriter that carry the type and are operated by keys

typecase ('taɪpˌkeɪs) *n* a compartmental tray for storing printer's type

typecast ('taɪpˌkɑːst) *vb* **-casts, -casting, -cast** (*tr*) to cast (an actor) in the same kind of role continually, esp because of his physical appearance or previous success in such roles > 'type,caster *n*

type I error *n statistics* the error of rejecting the null hypothesis when it is true, the probability of which is the significance level of a result

type II error *n statistics* the error of not rejecting the null hypothesis when it is false. The probability of avoiding such an error is the power of the test and is a function of the alternative hypothesis

typeface ('taɪpˌfeɪs) *n* another name for **face** (sense 17)

type founder *n* a person who casts metallic printer's type > **type founding** *n* > **type foundry** *n*

type-high *adj* having the height of a piece of type, standardized as 0.918 inches

type metal *n printing* an alloy of tin, lead, and antimony, from which type is cast

typescript ('taɪpˌskrɪpt) *n* **1** a typed copy of a document, literary script, etc **2** any typewritten material

typeset ('taɪpˌsɛt) *vb* **-sets, -setting, -set** (*tr*) *printing* to set (textual matter) in type

typesetter ('taɪpˌsɛtə) *n* **1** a person who sets type; compositor **2** a typesetting machine

type specimen *n biology* the original specimen from which a description of a new species is made. Also called: **holotype**

typewrite ('taɪpˌraɪt) *vb* -writes, -writing, -wrote, -written to write by means of a typewriter; type

typewriter ('taɪpˌraɪtə) *n* **1** a keyboard machine for writing mechanically in characters resembling print. It may be operated entirely by hand (**manual typewriter**) or be powered by electricity (**electric typewriter**) **2** *printing* a style of type resembling typescript

typewriting ('taɪpˌraɪtɪŋ) *n* **1** the act or skill of using a typewriter **2** copy produced by a typewriter; typescript

typhlitis (tɪf'laɪtɪs) *n* **1** inflammation of the caecum **2** an obsolete name for **appendicitis** [C19 from New Latin, from Greek *typhlon* the caecum, from *tuphlos* blind] > **typhlitic** (tɪf'lɪtɪk) *adj*

typhlology (tɪf'lɒlədʒɪ) *n* the branch of science concerned with blindness and the care of the blind [C19 from Greek *tuphlos* blind]

Typhoeus (taɪ'fiːəs) *n Greek myth* the son of Gaea and Tartarus who had a hundred dragon heads, which spurted fire, and a bellowing many-tongued voice. He created the whirlwinds and fought with Zeus before the god hurled him beneath Mount Etna > **Ty'phoean** *adj*

typhogenic (ˌtaɪfəʊ'dʒɛnɪk) *adj* causing typhus or typhoid fever

typhoid ('taɪfɔɪd) *pathol* ▷ *adj also* **typhoidal 1** resembling typhus ▷ *n* **2** short for **typhoid fever**

typhoid fever *n* an acute infectious disease characterized by high fever, rose-coloured spots on the chest or abdomen, abdominal pain, and occasionally intestinal bleeding. It is caused by the bacillus *Salmonella typhosa* ingested with food or water. Also called: **enteric fever** [C19 from TYPHUS + -OID; so called because the symptoms resemble those of typhus]

typhoidin (taɪ'fɔɪdɪn) *n med* a culture of dead typhoid bacillus for injection into the skin to test for typhoid fever

Typhon ('taɪfɒn) *n Greek myth* a monster and one of the whirlwinds: later confused with his father Typhoeus

typhoon (taɪ'fuːn) *n* **1** a violent tropical storm or cyclone, esp in the China seas and W Pacific **2** a violent storm of India [C16 from Chinese *tai fung* great wind, from *tai* great + *fung* wind; influenced by Greek *tuphōn* whirlwind] > **typhonic** (taɪ'fɒnɪk) *adj*

typhus ('taɪfəs) *n* any one of a group of acute infectious rickettsial diseases characterized by high fever, skin rash, and severe headache. Also called: **typhus fever** [C18 from New Latin *tȳphus*, from Greek *tuphos* fever; related to *tuphein* to smoke] > **typhous** *adj*

typical ('tɪpɪkəl) *adj* **1** being or serving as a representative example of a particular type; characteristic: *the painting is a typical Rembrandt* **2** considered to be an example of some undesirable trait: *that is typical of you!* **3** of or relating to a representative specimen or type **4** conforming to a type **5** *biology* having most of the characteristics of a particular taxonomic group: *a typical species of a genus* ▷ Also (poetic): **typic** [C17 from Medieval Latin *typicālis*, from Late Latin *typicus* figurative, from Greek *tupikos*, from *tupos* TYPE] > **'typically** *adv* > **'typicalness** *or* **ˌtypi'cality** *n*

typify ('tɪpɪˌfaɪ) *vb* -fies, -fying, -fied (*tr*) **1** to be typical of; characterize **2** to symbolize or represent completely, by or as if by a type [C17 from Latin *typus* TYPE + -IFY] > **ˌtypifi'cation** *n* > **'typiˌfier** *n*

typing ('taɪpɪŋ) *n* **1** the work or activity of using a typewriter or word processor **2** the skill of using a typewriter quickly and accurately

typist ('taɪpɪst) *n* a person who types, for a living

typo ('taɪpəʊ) *n, pl* -pos *informal* a typographical error. Also called (Brit): **literal**

typo. *or* **typog.** *abbrev* variants of **typ.**

typographer (taɪ'pɒɡrəfə) *n* **1** a person skilled in typography **2** another name for **compositor**

typography (taɪ'pɒɡrəfɪ) *n* **1** the art, craft, or process of composing type and printing from it **2** the selection and planning of type for printed publications > **typographical** (ˌtaɪpə'ɡræfɪkəl) *or* **ˌtypo'graphic** *adj* > **ˌtypo'graphically** *adv*

typology (taɪ'pɒlədʒɪ) *n chiefly Christian theol* the doctrine or study of types or of the correspondence between them and the realities which they typify > **typological** (ˌtaɪpə'lɒdʒɪkəl) *or* **ˌtypo'logic** *adj* > **ˌtypo'logically** *adv* > **ty'pologist** *n*

typothetae (taɪ'pɒθɪˌtiː, ˌtaɪpə'θiːtiː) *pl n US* printers collectively; used in the names of organized associations, as of master printers [C19 New Latin: typesetters, from Greek *tupos* TYPE + *thetēs* one who places, from *tithenai* to place]

Tyr *or* **Tyrr** (tjʊə, tɪə) *n Norse myth* the god of war, son of Odin. Anglo-Saxon counterpart: Tiu

tyramine ('taɪrəˌmiːn, 'tɪ-) *n* a colourless crystalline amine derived from phenol and found in ripe cheese, ergot, decayed animal tissue, and mistletoe and used for its sympathomimetic action; 4-hydroxyphenethylamine. Formula: $(C_2H_4NH_2)C_6H_4OH$ [C20 from TYR(OSINE) + AMINE]

tyrannical (tɪ'rænɪkəl) *or* **tyrannic** *adj* characteristic of or relating to a tyrant or to tyranny; oppressive > **ty'rannically** *adv* > **ty'rannicalness** *n*

tyrannicide (tɪ'rænɪˌsaɪd) *n* **1** the killing of a tyrant **2** a person who kills a tyrant > **tyrˌranni'cidal** *adj*

tyrannize *or* **tyrannise** ('tɪrəˌnaɪz) *vb* (when *intr*, often foll by *over*) to rule or exercise power (over) in a cruel or oppressive manner > **'tyranˌnizer** *or* **'tyranˌniser** *n*

tyrannosaurus (tɪˌrænə'sɔːrəs) *or* **tyrannosaur** (tɪ'rænəˌsɔː) *n* any large carnivorous bipedal dinosaur of the genus *Tyrannosaurus*, common in North America in upper Jurassic and Cretaceous times: suborder *Theropoda* (theropods) [C19 from New Latin, from Greek *turannos* TYRANT + *sauros* lizard]

tyranny ('tɪrənɪ) *n, pl* -nies **1 a** government by a tyrant or tyrants; despotism **b** similarly oppressive and unjust government by more than one person **2** arbitrary, unreasonable, or despotic behaviour or use of authority **3** any harsh discipline or oppression: *the tyranny of the clock* **4** a political unit ruled by a tyrant **5** (esp in ancient Greece) government by a usurper **6** a tyrannical act [C14 from Old French *tyrannie*, from Medieval Latin *tyrannia*, from Latin *tyrannus* TYRANT] > **'tyrannous** *adj* > **'tyrannously** *adv* > **'tyrannousness** *n*

tyrant ('taɪrənt) *n* **1** a person who governs oppressively, unjustly, and arbitrarily; despot **2** any person who exercises authority in a tyrannical manner **3** anything that exercises tyrannical influence **4** (esp in ancient Greece) a ruler whose authority lacked the sanction of law or custom; usurper [C13 from Old French *tyrant*, from Latin *tyrannus*, from Greek *turannos*]

tyrant flycatcher *n* any passerine bird of the American family *Tyrannidae*. Often shortened to: **flycatcher**

tyre *or US* **tire** ('taɪə) *n* **1** a rubber ring placed over the rim of a wheel of a road vehicle to provide traction and reduce road shocks, esp a hollow inflated ring (**pneumatic tyre**) consisting of a reinforced outer casing enclosing an inner tube. See also **tubeless tyre, cross-ply, radial-ply 2** a ring of wear-resisting steel shrunk thermally onto a cast-iron railway wheel **3** a metal band or hoop attached to the rim of a wooden cartwheel ▷ *vb* **4** (*tr*) to fit a tyre or tyres to (a wheel, vehicle, etc) [C18 variant of C15 *tire*, probably from TIRE³]

Tyre *or* **Tyr** ('taɪə) *n* a port in S Lebanon, on the Mediterranean: founded about the 15th century BC; for centuries a major Phoenician seaport, famous for silks and its Tyrian-purple dye; now a small market town. Pop: 141 000 (2005 est.). Arabic name: Sur

Tyrian ('tɪrɪən) *n* **1** a native or inhabitant of ancient Tyre **2** short for **Tyrian purple** (sense 2) ▷ *adj* **3** of or relating to ancient Tyre

Tyrian purple *n* **1** a deep purple dye obtained from molluscs of the genus *Murex* and highly prized in antiquity **2 a** a vivid purplish-red colour **b** (*as adjective*): *a Tyrian-purple robe*. Sometimes shortened to: **Tyrian**

tyro *or* **tiro** ('taɪrəʊ) *n, pl* -ros a novice or beginner [C17 from Latin *tīrō* recruit] > **tyronic** *or* **tironic** (taɪ'rɒnɪk) *adj*

tyrocidine (ˌtaɪrəʊ'saɪdiːn) *n* an antibiotic that is the main constituent of tyrothricin [C20 from TYRO(SINE) + -CID(E) + -INE¹]

Tyrol *or* **Tirol** (tɪ'rəʊl, 'tɪrəʊl; *German* tiˈroːl) *n* a mountainous state of W Austria: passed to the Hapsburgs in 1363; S part transferred to Italy in 1919. Capital: Innsbruck. Pop: 683 317 (2003 est.). Area: 12 648 sq km (4883 sq miles)

Tyrolese (ˌtɪrə'liːz) *or* **Tyrolean** (ˌtɪrəʊ'lɪən) *adj* **1** of or relating to the Austrian state of Tyrol or its inhabitants ▷ *n* **2** a native or inhabitant of Tyrol

Tyrolienne (tɪˌrəʊlɪ'ɛn) *n* **1** a lively peasant dance from the Tyrol **2** a song composed for or in the style of this dance, characterized by the yodel [French: of the TYROL]

Tyrone (tɪ'rəʊn) *n* a historical county of W Northern Ireland, occupying almost a quarter of the total area of Northern Ireland; in 1973 its administrative functions were devolved to several district councils

tyropitta (tɪ'rɒpɪtə) *n* a Greek cheese pie [C20 from Modern Greek]

tyrosinase (ˌtaɪrəʊsɪ'neɪz, ˌtɪrəʊ-) *n* an enzyme occurring in many organisms that is a catalyst in the conversion of tyrosine to the pigment melanin; inactivity of this enzyme results in albinism

tyrosine ('taɪrəˌsiːn, -sɪn, 'tɪrə-) *n* an aromatic nonessential amino acid; a component of proteins. It is a metabolic precursor of thyroxine, the pigment melanin, and other biologically important compounds [C19 from Greek *turos* cheese + -INE²]

tyrothricin (ˌtaɪrəʊ'θraɪsɪn) *n* an antibiotic, obtained from the soil bacterium *Bacillus brevis*, consisting of tyrocidine and gramicidin and active against Gram-positive bacteria such as staphylococci and streptococci: applied locally for the treatment of ulcers and abscesses [C20 from New Latin *Tyrothrix* (genus name), from Greek *turos* cheese + *thrix* hair]

Tyrr (tjʊə, tɪə) *n* a variant spelling of **Tyr**

Tyrrhenian Sea (tɪ'riːnɪən) *n* an arm of the Mediterranean between Italy and the islands of Corsica, Sardinia, and Sicily

Tyumen (*Russian* tju'mjenj) *n* a port in S central Russia, on the Tura River: one of the oldest Russian towns in Siberia; industrial centre with nearby oil and natural gas reserves. Pop: 518 000 (2005 est)

tz *the internet domain name for* Tanzania

tzar (zɑː) *n* a less common spelling of **tsar** > **'tzarism** *n*

tzatziki (tsæt'sɪkɪ) *n* a Greek dip made from yogurt, chopped cucumber, and mint [C20 from Modern Greek]

Tzekung ('tsɛ'kʊŋ) *or* **Tzu-kung** ('tsuː'kʊŋ) *n* a variant transliteration of the Chinese name for Zigong

tzetze fly ('tsɛtsɪ) *n* a variant spelling of **tsetse fly**

Tzigane (tsɪ'ɡɑːn, sɪ-) *n* **a** a Gypsy, esp a Hungarian one **b** (*as modifier*): *Tzigane music* [C19 via French from Hungarian *czigány* Gypsy, of uncertain origin]

tzitzit ('tsɪtsɪt; *Hebrew* tsitˈsiːt) *pl n* the fringes or tassels on the corners of the tallit [from Hebrew, literally: tassel]

T-zone *n* the T-shaped area of a person's face that includes the forehead, nose, and chin

Tzu-po ('tsuː'pəʊ) *or* **Tzepo** ('tsɛ'pəʊ) *n* a variant transliteration of the Chinese name for **Zibo**

t

1741

Uu

u or **U** (ju:) *n, pl* **u's, U's** or **Us** **1** the 21st letter and fifth vowel of the modern English alphabet **2** any of several speech sounds represented by this letter, in English as in *mute, cut, hurt, sure, pull,* or *minus* **3 a** something shaped like a U **b** (*in combination*): *a U-bolt; a U-turn*

U¹ *symbol for* **1** united **2** unionist **3** university **4** (in Britain) **a** universal (used to describe a category of film certified as suitable for viewing by anyone) **b** (*as modifier*): *a U film* **5** *chem* uranium **6** *biochem* uracil **7** *text messaging abbreviation for* you ▷ *adj* **8** *Brit dated informal* (esp of language habits) characteristic of or appropriate to the upper class. Compare **non-U**

U² (u:) *n* a Burmese title of respect for men, equivalent to *Mr*

U. *abbreviation for* **1** *maths* union **2** unit **3** united **4** university **5** upper

U2 *text messaging abbreviation for* you too

ua *the internet domain name for* Ukraine

UA 1 *abbreviation for* (in Britain) **unitary authority** **2** *international car registration for* Ukraine

UAE *abbreviation for* United Arab Emirates

UAM *abbreviation for* underwater-to-air missile

UAR *abbreviation for* United Arab Republic

UART ('juːˌɑːt) *n electronics acronym for* Universal Asynchronous Receiver Transmitter

UAV *abbreviation for* unmanned aerial vehicle

UB40 *n* (in Britain) **1** a registration card issued by the Department of Employment to a person registering as unemployed **2** *informal* a person registered as unemployed

Ubangi (juːˈbæŋɡɪ) *n* a river in central Africa, flowing west and south, forming the border between the Democratic Republic of Congo (formerly Zaïre) and the Central African Republic and Congo-Brazzaville, into the River Congo. Length (with the Uele): 2250 km (1400 miles). French name: Oubangui

Ubangi-Shari *n* a former name (until 1958) of the **Central African Republic**

UBE *abbreviation for computing* unsolicited bulk e-mail

U-bend *n* a U-shaped bend in a pipe or drain that traps water in the lower part of the U and prevents the escape of noxious fumes or vapours

uber- or **über-** ('uːbə) *combining form* indicating the highest, greatest, or most extreme example of something: *America's ubernerd, Bill Gates; the uber-hip young Bohemians* [c20 from German *über* over, above]

Übermensch *German* ('yːbərˌmɛnʃ) *n, pl* **-menschen** (-mɛnʃən) (esp in the writings of Nietzsche) the German word for **superman** [literally: over-man]

uberrima fides ('juːbəˌrɪːmə 'faɪdiːz, juːˈbɛrɪmə) *n* another name for **utmost good faith** [Latin: utmost good faith]

ubiety (juːˈbaɪɪtɪ) *n* the condition of being in a particular place [c17 from Latin *ubī* where + *-ety*, on the model of *society*]

ubiquinone (juːˈbɪkwɪˌnəʊn) *n* another name for **coenzyme Q**

ubiquitarian (juːˌbɪkwɪˈtɛərɪən) *n* **1** a member of the Lutheran church who holds that Christ is no more present in the elements of the Eucharist than elsewhere, as he is present in all places at all times ▷ *adj* **2** denoting, relating to, or holding this belief [c17 from Latin *ubīque* everywhere; see UBIQUITOUS] > uˌbiquiˈtarianˌism *n*

ubiquitin (juːˈbɪkwɪtɪn) *n biochemistry* a small polypeptide, found in most eukaryotic cells, that combines with other proteins to make them susceptible to degradation [c20 from UBIQUITOUS + -IN] > uˌbiquitiˈnation *n*

ubiquitous (juːˈbɪkwɪtəs) *adj* having or seeming to have the ability to be everywhere at once; omnipresent [c14 from Latin *ubīque* everywhere, from *ubī* where] > u'biquitously *adv* > u'biquity or u'biquitousness *n*

ubi supra *Latin* ('uːbɪ 'suːprɑː) where (mentioned or cited) above

U-boat *n* a German submarine, esp in World Wars I and II [from German *U-Boot,* abbreviation for *Unterseeboot,* literally: undersea boat]

U bolt *n* a metal bar bent into the shape of a U and threaded at both ends to receive securing nuts: used to secure leaf springs, ring bolts, shackles, etc

UBR *abbreviation for* **Uniform Business Rate**

Ubuntu (ʊˈbuːntʊ) *n South African* humanity or fellow feeling; kindness [Nguni]

UC *abbreviation for* University College

u.c. *printing abbreviation for* upper case

UCAS ('juːkæs) *n* (in Britain) *acronym for* Universities and Colleges Admissions Service

UCATT ('ʌkət) *n acronym for* Union of Construction, Allied Trades and Technicians

Ucayali (*Spanish* ukaˈjali) *n* a river in E Peru, flowing north into the Marañón above Iquitos. Length: 1600 km (1000 miles)

UCCA ('ʌkə) *n* (formerly, in Britain) *acronym for* Universities Central Council on Admissions

UCE *computing abbreviation for* unsolicited commercial e-mail

UCL *abbreviation for* University College London

UCT *abbreviation for* University of Cape Town

UDA *abbreviation for* **Ulster Defence Association**

Udaipur (uːˈdaɪpʊə, ˈuːdaɪˌpʊə) *n* **1** Also called: **Mewar.** A former state of NW India: became part of Rajasthan in 1947 **2** a city in NW India, in S Rajasthan. Pop: 389 317 (2001)

udal ('juːdᵊl) *n law* a form of freehold possession of land existing in northern Europe before the introduction of the feudal system and still used in Orkney and Shetland [c16 Orkney and Shetland dialect, from Old Norse *othal;* related to Old English *ēthel, ōethel,* Old High German *wodal*]

UDC (formerly, in Britain) *abbreviation for* Urban District Council

udder ('ʌdə) *n* the large baglike mammary gland of cows, sheep, etc, having two or more teats [Old English *ūder;* related to Old High German *ūtar,* Old Norse *jūr,* Latin *über,* Sanskrit *ūdhar*]

UDI *abbreviation for* **Unilateral Declaration of Independence**

Udine (*Italian* 'uːdine) *n* a city in NE Italy, in Friuli-Venezia Giulia region: partially damaged in an earthquake in 1976. Pop: 95 030 (2001)

Udmurt Republic ('ʊdmʊət) *n* a constituent republic of W central Russia, in the basin of the middle Kama. Capital: Izhevsk. Pop: 1 570 500 (2002). Area: 42 100 sq km (16 250 sq miles)

udo ('uːdəʊ) *n, pl* **udos** a stout araliaceous perennial plant, *Aralia cordata,* of Japan and China, having berry-like black fruits and young shoots that are edible when blanched [from Japanese]

udometer (juːˈdɒmɪtə) *n* an archaic term for **rain gauge** [c19 from French, from Latin *ūdus* damp]

udon ('uːdɒn) *n* (in Japanese cookery) large noodles made of wheat flour [Japanese]

UDR *abbreviation for* Ulster Defence Regiment

U4E *text messaging abbreviation for* yours for ever

UEFA (juːˈeɪfə) *n acronym for* Union of European Football Associations

Uele ('weɪlə) *n* a river in central Africa, rising near the border between the Democratic Republic of Congo (formerly Zaïre) and Uganda and flowing west to join the Bomu River and form the Ubangi River. Length: about 1100 km (700 miles)

Ufa (*Russian* uˈfa) *n* a city in W central Russia, capital of the Bashkir Republic: university (1957). Pop: 1 035 000 (2005 est)

Uffizi (juːˈfiːtsɪ) *n* an art gallery in Florence; built by Giorgio Vasari in the 16th century and opened as a museum in 1765: contains chiefly Italian Renaissance paintings

UFO (*sometimes* 'juːfəʊ) *abbreviation for* unidentified flying object

ufology (ˌjuːˈfɒlədʒɪ) *n* the study of UFOs > u'fologist *n*

ug *the internet domain name for* Uganda

ugali (uːˈɡali) *n E African* a type of stiff porridge made by mixing corn meal with boiling water: the basic starch constituent of a meal [from Swahili]

Uganda (juːˈɡændə) *n* a republic in E Africa: British protectorate established in 1894–96; gained independence in 1962 and became a republic in 1963; a member of the Commonwealth. It consists mostly of a savanna plateau with part of Lake Victoria in the southeast and mountains in the southwest, reaching 5109 m (16 763 ft) in the Ruwenzori Range. Official language: English; Swahili, Luganda, and Luo are also widely spoken. Religion: Christian majority. Currency: Ugandan shilling. Capital: Kampala. Pop: 26 699 000 (2004 est). Area: 235 886 sq km (91 076 sq miles)

Ugandan (juːˈɡændən) *adj* **1** of or relating to Uganda or its inhabitants ▷ *n* **2** a native or inhabitant of Uganda

Ugaritic (ˌuːɡəˈrɪtɪk) *n* **1** an extinct Semitic language of N Syria ▷ *adj* **2** of or relating to this language [c19 after *Ugarit* (modern name: Ras

Shamra), an ancient Syrian city-state]

UGC (in Britain) abbreviation for University Grants Committee

ugh (ʊx, ʊh, ʌh) interj an exclamation of disgust, annoyance, or dislike

UGLI (ˈʌɡlɪ) n, pl UGLIS or UGLIES trademark a large juicy yellow-skinned citrus fruit of the Caribbean: a cross between a tangerine, grapefruit, and orange. Also called: UGLI fruit [c20 probably an alteration of UGLY, referring to its wrinkled skin]

uglify (ˈʌɡlɪˌfaɪ) vb -fies, -fying, -fied to make or become ugly or more ugly ▷ ˌuglifiˈcation n ▷ ˈugliˌfier n

ugly (ˈʌɡlɪ) adj -lier, -liest **1** of unpleasant or unsightly appearance **2** repulsive, objectionable, or displeasing in any way: war is ugly **3** ominous or menacing: an ugly situation **4** bad-tempered, angry, or sullen: an ugly mood [c13 from Old Norse uggligr dreadful, from ugga fear] ▷ ˈuglily adv ▷ ˈugliness n

ugly duckling n a person or thing, initially ugly or unpromising, that changes into something beautiful or admirable [an allusion to The Ugly Duckling, a story by Hans Christian Andersen]

Ugrian (ˈuːɡrɪən, ˈjuː-) adj **1** of or relating to a light-haired subdivision of the Turanian people, who include the Samoyeds, Voguls, Ostyaks, and Magyars ▷ n **2** a member of this group of peoples **3** another word for **Ugric** [c19 from Old Russian Ugre Hungarians]

Ugric (ˈuːɡrɪk, ˈjuː-) n **1** one of the two branches of the Finno-Ugric family of languages, including Hungarian and some languages of NW Siberia. Compare **Finnic** ▷ adj **2** of or relating to this group of languages or their speakers

UHF radio abbreviation for **ultrahigh frequency**

uh-huh (əˈhə) sentence substitute informal a less emphatic variant of **yes**

uhlan or **ulan** (ˈuːlɑːn, ˈjuːlən) n history a member of a body of lancers first employed in the Polish army and later in W European armies [c18 via German from Polish ulan, from Turkish ōlan young man]

UHT abbreviation for ultra heat treated

uh-uh (ˈʌˈʌ) sentence substitute informal, chiefly US a less emphatic variant of **no¹**

uhuru (uːˈhuːruː) n (esp in E Africa) **1** national independence **2** freedom [c20 from Swahili]

Uigur or **Uighur** (ˈwiːɡʊə) n **1** (pl -gur or -gurs) a member of a Mongoloid people of NW China, Uzbekistan, Kyrgyzstan, and Kazakhstan **2** the language of this people, belonging to the Turkic branch of the Altaic family ▷ Uiˈgurian, Uiˈghurian, Uiˈguric or Uiˈghuric adj

uillean pipes (ˈɪlɪn, ˈɪlən) pl n bagpipes developed in Ireland and operated by squeezing bellows under the arm. Also called: Irish pipes, union pipes [c19 Irish píob uilleann, from píob pipe + uilleann genitive sing of uille elbow]

Uinta Mountains (jʊˈɪntə) pl n a mountain range in NE Utah: part of the Rocky Mountains. Highest peak: Kings Peak, 4123 m (13 528 ft)

uintathere (juːˈɪntəˌθɪə) n any of various extinct Tertiary rhinoceros-like mammals of North America, having six horny processes on the head. Also called: dinoceras [from Uinta, a county in Wyoming + Greek thērion wild animal]

uitlander (ˈeɪtˌlandə, -ˌlæn-, ˈɔɪt-) n (sometimes capital) South African a foreigner; alien [c19 Afrikaans: outlander]

ujamaa village (uːˈdʒɑːˈmɑː) n (sometimes capitals) a communally organized village in Tanzania [c20 ujamaa socialism, from Swahili: brotherhood]

Ujiji (uːˈdʒiːdʒɪ) n a town in W Tanzania, on Lake Tanganyika: a former slave and ivory centre; the place where Stanley found Livingstone in 1871. It merged with the neighbouring town of Kigoma to form Kigoma-Ujiji in the 1960s

Ujjain (uːˈdʒeɪn) n a city in W central India, in Madhya Pradesh: one of the seven sacred cities of the Hindus; a major agricultural trade centre. Pop: 429 933 (2001)

Ujung Pandang (ˈuːdʒʊŋ pænˈdæŋ) n a port in central Indonesia, on SW Sulawesi: an important native port before Portuguese (16th century) and Dutch (17th century) control; capital of the Dutch East Indies (1946–49); a major Indonesian distribution and transshipment port. Pop: 1 100 019 (2000). Also called: Makasar, Makassar, Macassar

uk the internet domain name for United Kingdom

UK abbreviation for United Kingdom

UKAEA abbreviation for United Kingdom Atomic Energy Authority

ukase (juːˈkeɪz) n **1** (in imperial Russia) an edict of the tsar **2** a rare word for **edict** [c18 from Russian ukaz, from ukazat to command]

UKCC abbreviation for United Kingdom Central Council for Nursing, Midwifery, and Health Visiting

UKIP (ˈjuːˌkɪp) n acronym for United Kingdom Independence Party: a political party founded in 1993 to seek Britain's withdrawal from the European Union

ukiyo-e (ˌuːkiːjəʊˈjeɪ) n a school of Japanese painting depicting subjects from everyday life [Japanese: pictures of the floating world]

UK Overseas Territory n any of the territories that are governed by the UK but lie outside the British Isles; many were formerly British **crown colonies**: includes Bermuda, Falkland Islands, and Montserrat

Ukr. abbreviation for Ukraine

Ukraine (juːˈkreɪn) n a republic in SE Europe, on the Black Sea and the Sea of Azov: ruled by the Khazars (7th–9th centuries), by Ruik princes with the Mongol conquest in the 13th century, then by Lithuania, by Poland, and by Russia; one of the four original republics that formed the Soviet Union in 1922; unilaterally declared independence in 1990, which was recognized in 1991. Consists chiefly of lowlands; economy based on rich agriculture and mineral resources and on the major heavy industries of the Donets Basin. Official language: Ukrainian; Russian is also widely spoken. Religion: believers are mainly Christian. Currency: hryvna. Capital: Kiev. Pop: 48 151 000 (2004 est). Area: 603 700 sq km (231 990 sq miles)

Ukrainian (juːˈkreɪnɪən) adj **1** of or relating to Ukraine, its people, or their language ▷ n **2** the official language of Ukraine: an East Slavonic language closely related to Russian **3** a native or inhabitant of Ukraine ▷ Formerly called: Little Russian

ukulele or **ukelele** (ˌjuːkəˈleɪlɪ) n a small four-stringed guitar, esp of Hawaii [c19 from Hawaiian, literally: jumping flea, from 'uku flea + lele jumping]

ulama¹ or **ulema** (ˈuːlɪmə) n **1** a body of Muslim scholars or religious leaders **2** a member of this body [c17 from Arabic 'ulamā scholars, from 'alama to know]

ulama² (ˌuːˈlɑːmə) n a Meso-American team ball game, with a history dating back to as early as 1500 BC, played with a solid rubber ball on a long narrow court [from Nahuatl Ullamalitztli ball game]

ulan (ˈuːlɑːn, ˈjuːlən) n a less common variant of **uhlan**

Ulan Bator (ʊˈlɑːn ˈbɑːtɔː) n the capital of Mongolia, in the N central part: developed in the mid-17th century around the Da Khure monastery, residence until 1924 of successive "living Buddhas" (third in rank of Buddhist-Lamaist leaders), and main junction of caravan routes across Mongolia; university (1942); industrial and commercial centre. Pop: 842 000 (2005 est). Former name (until 1924): Urga. Chinese name: Kulun

Ulan-Ude (ʊˈlɑːnʊˈdɛ) n an industrial city in SE Russia, capital of the Buryat Republic: an important rail junction. Pop: 361 000 (2005 est). Former name (until 1934): Verkhne-Udinsk

ULCC abbreviation for **ultralarge crude carrier**

ulcer (ˈʌlsə) n **1** a disintegration of the surface of the skin or a mucous membrane resulting in an open sore that heals very slowly. See also **peptic ulcer 2** a source or element of corruption or evil [c14 from Latin ulcus; related to Greek helkos a sore]

ulcerate (ˈʌlsəˌreɪt) vb to make or become ulcerous

ulceration (ˌʌlsəˈreɪʃən) n **1** the development or formation of an ulcer **2** an ulcer or an ulcerous condition

ulcerative (ˈʌlsərətɪv) adj of, relating to, or characterized by ulceration: ulcerative colitis

ulcerous (ˈʌlsərəs) adj **1** relating to, characteristic of, or characterized by an ulcer or ulcers **2** being or having a corrupting influence ▷ **ulcerously** adv ▷ **ulcerousness** n

-ule suffix forming nouns indicating smallness: globule [from Latin -ulus, diminutive suffix]

Uleåborg (ˈuːliɔˌbɔrjə) n the Swedish name for **Oulu**

ulema (ˈuːlɪmə) n a variant of **ulama¹**

-ulent suffix forming adjectives abundant or full of: fraudulent [from Latin -ulentus]

ullage (ˈʌlɪdʒ) n **1** the volume by which a liquid container falls short of being full **2 a** the quantity of liquid lost from a container due to leakage or evaporation **b** (in customs terminology) the amount of liquid remaining in a container after such loss ▷ vb (tr) **3** to create ullage in **4** to determine the amount of ullage in **5** to fill up ullage in [c15 from Old French ouillage filling of a cask, from ouiller to fill a cask, from ouil eye, from Latin oculus eye] ▷ **ullaged** adj

ullage rocket n a small hydrogen peroxide rocket engine that produces sufficient acceleration to keep propellants in their places when the main rocket is shut off

Ullswater (ˈʌlzˌwɔːtə) n a lake in NW England, in Cumbria in the Lake District. Length: 12 km (7.5 miles)

Ulm (German ʊlm) n an industrial city in S Germany, in Baden-Württemberg on the Danube: a free imperial city (1155–1802). Pop: 119 807 (2003 est)

ulmaceous (ʌlˈmeɪʃəs) adj of, relating to, or belonging to the Ulmaceae, a temperate and tropical family of deciduous trees and shrubs having scaly buds, simple serrated leaves, and typically winged fruits: includes the elms [c19 via New Latin Ulmāceae, from Latin ulmus elm tree]

ulna (ˈʌlnə) n, pl -nae (-niː) or -nas **1** the inner and longer of the two bones of the human forearm **2** the corresponding bone in other vertebrates [c16 from Latin: elbow, ELL¹] ▷ **ulnar** adj

ulnar nerve n a nerve situated along the inner side of the arm and passing below to the surface of the skin near the elbow. See **funny bone**

ulotrichous (juːˈlɒtrɪkəs) adj having woolly or curly hair [c19 from New Latin Ulotrichī (classification applied to humans having this type of hair), from Greek oulothrix, from oulos curly + thrix hair] ▷ uˈlotrichy n

ulster (ˈʌlstə) n a man's heavy double-breasted overcoat with a belt or half-belt at the back [c19 so called because it was first produced in Northern Ireland]

Ulster (ˈʌlstə) n **1** a province and former kingdom of N Ireland: passed to the English Crown in 1461; confiscated land given to English and Scottish Protestant settlers in the 17th century, giving rise to serious long-term conflict; partitioned in 1921, six counties forming Northern Ireland and three counties joining the Republic of Ireland. Pop (three Ulster counties of the Republic of Ireland): 46 714 (2002); (six Ulster counties of Northern Ireland): 1 702 628 (2003 est). Area (Republic of Ireland): 8013 sq km (3094 sq miles); (Northern Ireland): 14 121 sq km (5452 sq miles) **2** an informal name for **Northern Ireland**

Ulster Defence Association n (in Northern Ireland) a Loyalist paramilitary organization. Abbreviation: UDA

u

Ulster Democratic Unionist Party *n* a Northern Irish political party advocating the maintenance of union with the UK

Ulsterman ('ʌlstəmən) *n, pl* -men a native or inhabitant of Ulster ▷ 'Ulster,woman *fem n*

Ulster Unionist Council *n* a Northern Irish political party advocating the maintenance of union with the UK

ult. *abbreviation for* **1** ultimate(ly) **2** Also: ulto ultimo

ulterior (ʌl'tɪərɪə) *adj* **1** lying beneath or beyond what is revealed, evident, or supposed: *ulterior motives* **2** succeeding, subsequent, or later **3** lying beyond a certain line or point [c17 from Latin: further, from *ulter* beyond] ▷ ul'teriorly *adv*

ultima ('ʌltɪmə) *n* the final syllable of a word [from Latin: the last, feminine of *ultimus* last; see ULTIMATE]

ultimate ('ʌltɪmɪt) *adj* **1** conclusive in a series or process; last; final: *an ultimate question* **2** the highest or most significant: *the ultimate goal* **3** elemental, fundamental, basic, or essential **4** most extreme: *genocide is the ultimate abuse of human rights* **5** final or total: *an ultimate cost of twenty million pounds* ▷ *n* **6** the most significant, highest, furthest, or greatest thing [c17 from Late Latin *ultimāre* to come to an end, from Latin *ultimus* last, from *ulter* distant] ▷ 'ultimateness *n*

ultimate constituent *n* a constituent of something, such as a linguistic construction, that cannot be further subdivided in the terms of the analysis being undertaken. Compare **immediate constituent**

ultimately ('ʌltɪmɪtlɪ) *adv* in the end; at last; finally

ultimate strength *n* the maximum tensile stress that a material can withstand before rupture

ultima Thule ('θjuːlɪ) *n* **1** another name for **Thule 2** any distant or unknown region **3** a remote goal or aim [Latin: the most distant Thule]

ultimatum (ʌltɪ'meɪtəm) *n, pl* -tums *or* -ta (-tə) **1** a final communication by a party, esp a government, setting forth conditions on which it insists, as during negotiations on some topic **2** any final or peremptory demand, offer, or proposal [c18 from New Latin, neuter of *ultimatus* ULTIMATE]

ultimo ('ʌltɪ,məʊ) *adv* now rare except when abbreviated in formal correspondence in or during the previous month: *a letter of the 7th ultimo*. Abbreviation: **ult.** Compare **instant, proximo** [c16 from Latin *ultimō* on the last]

ultimogeniture (ʌltɪməʊ'dʒɛnɪtʃə) *n law* **1** a principle of inheritance whereby the youngest son succeeds to the estate of his ancestor. Compare **primogeniture 2** another name for **borough-English** [c19 *ultimo-* from Latin *ultimus* last + Late Latin *genitura* a birth]

ultra ('ʌltrə) *adj* **1** extreme or immoderate, esp in beliefs or opinions ▷ *n* **2** an extremist [c19 from Latin: beyond, from *ulter* distant]

ultra- *prefix* **1** beyond or surpassing a specified extent, range, or limit: *ultramicroscopic* **2** extreme or extremely: *ultramodern* [from Latin *ultrā* beyond; see ULTRA]

ultrabasic (ʌltrə'beɪsɪk) *adj* (of such igneous rocks as peridotite) containing less than 45 per cent silica

ultracentrifuge (ʌltrə'sɛntrɪ,fjuːdʒ) *chem* ▷ *n* **1** a high-speed centrifuge used to separate colloidal solutions ▷ *vb* **2** (*tr*) to subject to the action of an ultracentrifuge ▷ **ultracentrifugal** (ʌltrəsɛn'trɪfjʊɡ°l, -,sɛntrɪ'fjuːɡ°l) *adj* ▷ ,ultracen'trifugally *adv* ▷ **ultracentrifugation** (ʌltrə,sɛntrɪfjʊ'ɡeɪʃən) *n*

ultraconservative (ʌltrəkən'sɜːvətɪv) *adj* **1** highly reactionary ▷ *n* **2** a reactionary person

ultra-distance *n* (*modifier*) athletics covering a distance in excess of 30 miles, often as part of a longer race or competition: *an ultra-distance runner*

ultrafast ('ʌltrə,fɑːst) *adj* extremely fast: *an*

ultrafast internet connection

ultrafiche ('ʌltrə,fiːʃ) *n* a sheet of film, usually the size of a filing card, that is similar to a microfiche but has a much larger number of microcopies [c20 from ULTRA- + French *fiche* small card. See MICROFICHE]

ultrafilter (ʌltrə'fɪltə) *n* a filter with small pores used to separate very small particles from a suspension or colloidal solution ▷ ultrafiltration (ʌltrəfɪl'treɪʃən) *n*

ultra filtration *n engineering* filtration that removes particles less than 10 microns (10^{-6}m) in diameter

ultrahigh frequency ('ʌltrə,haɪ) *n* a radio-frequency band or radio frequency lying between 3000 and 300 megahertz. Abbreviation: UHF

ultraism ('ʌltrə,ɪzəm) *n* extreme philosophy, belief, or action ▷ 'ultraist *n, adj* ▷ ,ultra'istic *adj*

ultralarge crude carrier (ʌltrə'lɑːdʒ) *n* an oil tanker with a capacity of over 400 000 tons

ultramarine (ʌltrəmə'riːn) *n* **1** a blue pigment consisting of sodium and aluminium silicates and some sodium sulphide, obtained by powdering natural lapis lazuli or made synthetically: used in paints, printing ink, plastics, etc **2** a vivid blue colour ▷ *adj* **3** of the colour ultramarine **4** from across the seas [c17 from Medieval Latin *ultramarinus*, from *ultrā* beyond (see ULTRA-) + *mare* sea; so called because the lapis lazuli from which the pigment was made was imported from Asia]

ultramicrometer (ʌltrəmaɪ'krɒmɪtə) *n* a micrometer for measuring extremely small distances

ultramicroscope (ʌltrə'maɪkrə,skəʊp) *n* a microscope used for studying colloids, in which the sample is strongly illuminated from the side and colloidal particles are seen as bright points on a dark background. Also called: dark-field microscope

ultramicroscopic (ʌltrə,maɪkrə'skɒpɪk) *adj* **1** too small to be seen with an optical microscope **2** of or relating to an ultramicroscope ▷ ultramicroscopy (ʌltrəmaɪ'krɒskəpɪ) *n*

ultramodern (ʌltrə'mɒdən) *adj* extremely modern ▷ ,ultra'modernism *n* ▷ ,ultra'modernist *n* ▷ ,ultra,modern'istic *adj*

ultramontane (ʌltrəmɒn'teɪn) *adj* **1** on the other side of the mountains, esp the Alps, from the speaker or writer. Compare **cismontane 2** of or relating to a movement in the Roman Catholic Church which favours the centralized authority and influence of the pope as opposed to local independence. Compare **cisalpine** (sense 2) ▷ *n* **3** a resident or native from beyond the mountains, esp the Alps **4** a member of the ultramontane party of the Roman Catholic Church

ultramontanism (ʌltrə'mɒntɪ,nɪzəm) *n RC Church* the doctrine of central papal supremacy. Compare **Gallicanism**. ▷ ,ultra'montanist *n*

ultramundane (ʌltrə'mʌndeɪn) *adj* extending beyond the world, this life, or the universe

ultranationalism (ʌltrə'næʃnə,lɪzəm) *n* extreme devotion to one's own nation ▷ ,ultra'national *adj* ▷ ,ultra'nationalist *adj, n* ▷ ,ultra,national'istic *adj*

ultrared (ʌltrə'rɛd) *adj* an obsolete word for **infrared**

ultrashort (ʌltrə'ʃɔːt) *adj* (of a radio wave) having a wavelength shorter than 10 metres

ultrasonic (ʌltrə'sɒnɪk) *adj* of, concerned with, or producing waves with the same nature as sound waves but frequencies above audio frequencies. See also **ultrasound**. ▷ ,ultra'sonically *adv*

ultrasonic cleaning *n* the use of ultrasound to vibrate a piece to be cleaned while the piece is immersed in a cleaning fluid. The process produces a very high degree of cleanliness, and is used for jewellery and ornately shaped items

ultrasonics (ʌltrə'sɒnɪks) *n* (*functioning as singular*) the branch of physics concerned with ultrasonic waves. Also called: **supersonics**

ultrasonic testing *n engineering* the scanning of

material with an ultrasonic beam, during which reflections from faults in the material can be detected: a powerful nondestructive test method

ultrasonic welding *n* the use of high-energy vibration of ultrasonic frequency to produce a weld between two components which are held in close contact

ultrasonography (,ʌltrəsə'nɒɡrəfɪ) *n* the technique of using ultrasound to produce pictures of structures within the body, as for example of a fetus

ultrasound ('ʌltrə,saʊnd) *n* ultrasonic waves at frequencies above the audible range (above about 20 kHz), used in cleaning metallic parts, echo sounding, medical diagnosis and therapy, etc

ultrasound scanner *n* a device used to examine an internal bodily structure by the use of ultrasonic waves, esp for the diagnosis of abnormality in a fetus

ultrastructure ('ʌltrə,strʌktʃə) *n* the minute structure of a tissue or cell, as revealed by microscopy, esp electron microscopy ▷ ,ultra'structural *adj*

ultraviolet (,ʌltrə'vaɪəlɪt) *n* **1** the part of the electromagnetic spectrum with wavelengths shorter than light but longer than X-rays; in the range 0.4×10^{-6} and 1×10^{-8} metres ▷ *adj* **2** of, relating to, or consisting of radiation lying in the ultraviolet: *ultraviolet radiation*. Abbreviation: UV

ultraviolet astronomy *n* the study of radiation from celestial sources in the wavelength range 91.2 to 320 nanometres, 12 to 91.2 nanometres being the extreme ultraviolet range

ultra vires ('vaɪriːz) *adv, adj* (*predicative*) *law* beyond the legal power or authority of a person, corporation, agent, etc [Latin, literally: beyond strength]

ultravirus (ʌltrə'vaɪrəs) *n* a virus small enough to pass through the finest filter

ultrawideband (,ʌltrə'waɪd,bænd) *n* a transmission technique using a very wide spectrum of frequencies that enables high-speed transfer of data. Abbreviation: UWB

ululate ('juːljʊ,leɪt) *vb* (*intr*) to howl or wail, as with grief [c17 from Latin *ululāre* to howl, from *ulula* screech owl] ▷ 'ululant *adj* ▷ ,ulu'lation *n*

Ulundi ('juː,lʊndɪ) *n* a town in South Africa: the traditional Zulu capital of KwaZulu/Natal

Uluru (,uː'ləˈruː) *n* a large isolated desert rock, sometimes described as the world's largest monolith, in the Northern Territory of Australia: sacred to local Aboriginal people. Height: 330m (1100 ft). Base circumference: 9 km (5.6 miles). Former name: Ayers Rock

Ulyanovsk (*Russian* ulj'janəfsk) *n* the former name (1924–91) of **Simbirsk**

Ulysses ('juːlɪ,siːz, juː'lɪsiːz) *n* the Latin name of **Odysseus**

um¹ (ʌm, ˀm) *interj* a representation of a common sound made when hesitating in speech

um² *the internet domain name for* US Minor Outlying Islands

umbel ('ʌmbˀl) *n* an inflorescence, characteristic of umbelliferous plants, in which the flowers arise from the same point in the main stem and have stalks of the same length, to give a cluster with the youngest flowers at the centre [c16 from Latin *umbella* a sunshade, from *umbra* shade] ▷ **umbellate** ('ʌmbɪlɪt, -,leɪt), umbellar (ʌm'bɛlə) *or* 'umbel,lated *adj* ▷ 'umbellately *adv*

umbelliferous (,ʌmbɪ'lɪfərəs) *adj* **1** of, relating to, or belonging to the *Umbelliferae*, a family of herbaceous plants and shrubs, typically having hollow stems, divided or compound leaves, and flowers in umbels: includes fennel, dill, parsley, carrot, celery, and parsnip **2** designating any other plant bearing umbels [c17 from New Latin *umbellifer*, from Latin *umbella* sunshade + *ferre* to bear] ▷ um'bellifer *n*

umbellule (ʌm'bɛljuːl, 'ʌmbɪljuːl) *n* any of the small secondary umbels that make up a compound umbel [c18 from New Latin *umbellula*,

diminutive of Latin *umbella*; see UMBEL]
> **umbellulate** (ʌmˈbɛljʊlɪt, -ˌleɪt) *adj*

umber (ˈʌmbə) *n* **1** any of various natural brown earths containing ferric oxide together with lime and oxides of aluminium, manganese, and silicon. See also **burnt umber 2** any of the dark brown to greenish-brown colours produced by this pigment **3** short for **umber moth 4** *obsolete* **a** shade or shadow **b** any dark, dusky, or indefinite colour ▷ *adj* **5** of, relating to, or stained with umber [c16 from French (*terre d'*)*ombre* or Italian (*terra di*) *ombra* shadow (earth), from Latin *umbra* shade]

umber moth *n* any of various brownish geometrid moths, esp the **waved umber** (*Menophra abruptaria*) and **small waved umber** (*Horisme vitalbata*), that are cryptically marked to merge with tree bark, and the **mottled umber** (*Erannis defoliaria*) whose looper larvae can strip branches and even trees. Often shortened to: umber

umbilical (ʌmˈbɪlɪkəl, ˌʌmbɪˈlaɪkəl) *adj* **1** of, relating to, or resembling the umbilicus or the umbilical cord **2** in the region of the umbilicus: *an umbilical hernia* ▷ *n* **3** short for **umbilical cord**
> **um'bilically** *adv*

umbilical cord *n* **1** the long flexible tubelike structure connecting a fetus with the placenta: it provides a means of metabolic interchange with the mother **2** any flexible cord, tube, or cable used to transfer information, power, oxygen, etc, as between an astronaut walking in space and his spacecraft or a deep-sea diver and his boat

umbilicate (ʌmˈbɪlɪkɪt, -ˌkeɪt) *adj* **1** having an umbilicus or navel **2** having a central depression: *an umbilicate leaf* **3** shaped like a navel, as some bacterial colonies

umbilication (ʌmˌbɪlɪˈkeɪʃən) *n* **1** *biology, anatomy* a navel-like notch or depression, as in the centre of a vesicle **2** the condition of being umbilicated

umbilicus (ʌmˈbɪlɪkəs, ˌʌmbɪˈlaɪkəs) *n, pl* -bilici (-ˈbɪlɪˌsaɪ, -bɪˈlaɪsaɪ) **1** *biology* a hollow or navel-like structure, such as the cavity at the base of a gastropod shell **2** *anatomy* a technical name for the **navel** [c18 from Latin: navel, centre; compare Latin *umbō* shield boss, Greek *omphalos* navel]
> **umbiliform** (ʌmˈbɪlɪˌfɔːm) *adj*

umble pie (ˈʌmbəl) *n* See **humble pie** (sense 1)

umbles (ˈʌmbəlz) *pl n* another term for **numbles**

umbo (ˈʌmbəʊ) *n, pl* **umbones** (ʌmˈbəʊniːz) or **umbos 1** a small hump projecting from the centre of the cap in certain mushrooms **2** a hooked prominence occurring at the apex of each half of the shell of a bivalve mollusc **3** *anatomy* the slightly convex area at the centre of the outer surface of the eardrum, where the malleus is attached on the internal surface **4** a large projecting central boss on a shield, esp on a Saxon shield [c18 from Latin: boss of a shield, projecting piece] > **umbonate** (ˈʌmbənɪt, -ˌneɪt), **umbonal** (ˈʌmbənəl) or **umbonic** (ʌmˈbɒnɪk) *adj*

umbra (ˈʌmbrə) *n, pl* **-brae** (-briː) or **-bras 1** a region of complete shadow resulting from the total obstruction of light by an opaque object, esp the shadow cast by the moon onto the earth during a solar eclipse **2** the darker inner region of a sunspot ▷ Compare **penumbra** [c16 from Latin: shade, shadow] > **umbral** *adj*

umbrage (ˈʌmbrɪdʒ) *n* **1** displeasure or resentment; offence (in the phrase **give** or **take umbrage**) **2** the foliage of trees, considered as providing shade **3** *rare* shadow or shade **4** *archaic* a shadow or semblance [c15 from Old French *umbrage*, from Latin *umbrāticus* relating to shade, from *umbra* shade, shadow]

umbrageous (ʌmˈbreɪdʒəs) *adj* shady or shading > **um'brageously** *adv* > **um'brageousness** *n*

umbrella (ʌmˈbrɛlə) *n* **1** a portable device used for protection against rain, snow, etc, and consisting of a light canopy supported on a collapsible metal frame mounted on a central rod **2** the flattened cone-shaped contractile body of a jellyfish or other medusa **3** a protective shield or screen, esp

of aircraft or gunfire **4** anything that has the effect of a protective screen or cover **5 a** any system or agency that provides centralized organization or general cover for a group of related companies, organizations, etc: *dance umbrella* **b** (*as modifier*): *an umbrella fund; umbrella group* [c17 from Italian *ombrella*, diminutive of *ombra* shade; see UMBRA] > **um'brella-ˌlike** *adj*

umbrella bird *n* a black tropical American passerine bird, *Cephalopterus ornatus*, having a large overhanging crest and a long feathered wattle: family *Cotingidae* (cotingas)

umbrella pine *n* another name for **stone pine**

umbrella plant *n* an African sedge, *Cyperus alternifolius*, having large umbrella-like whorls of slender leaves: widely grown as an ornamental water plant

umbrella stand *n* an upright rack or stand for umbrellas

umbrella tree *n* **1** a North American magnolia, *Magnolia tripetala*, having long leaves clustered into an umbrella formation at the ends of the branches and unpleasant-smelling white flowers **2** Also called: umbrella bush. Any of various other trees or shrubs having leaves shaped like an umbrella or growing in an umbrella-like cluster

Umbria (ˈʌmbrɪə; *Italian* ˈumbrja) *n* a mountainous region of central Italy, in the valley of the Tiber. Pop: 834 210 (2003 est). Area: 8456 sq km (3265 sq miles)

Umbrian (ˈʌmbrɪən) *adj* **1** of or relating to Umbria, its inhabitants, their dialect of Italian, or the ancient language once spoken there **2** of or relating to a Renaissance school of painting that included Raphael ▷ *n* **3** a native or inhabitant of Umbria **4** an extinct language of ancient S Italy, belonging to the Italic branch of the Indo-European family. See also **Osco-Umbrian**

Umbriel (ˈʌmbrɪəl) *n* one of the main satellites of Uranus

umfazi (ʊmˈfɑːzɪ) *n South African* an African married woman [Nguni]

umiak or **oomiak** (ˈuːmɪˌæk) *n* a large open boat made of stretched skins, used by Inuit. Compare **kayak** [c18 from Greenland Inuktitut: boat for the use of women]

UMIST (ˈjuːmɪst) *n acronym for* University of Manchester Institute of Science and Technology

UML *computing trademark abbreviation for* unified modeling language: a standardized language for describing and visualizing the different parts of software systems; used for designing software

umlaut (ˈʊmlaʊt) *n* **1** the mark (¨) placed over a vowel in some languages, such as German, indicating modification in the quality of the vowel. Compare **diaeresis 2** (esp in Germanic languages) the change of a vowel within a word brought about by the assimilating influence of a vowel or semivowel in a preceding or following syllable [c19 German, from *um* around (in the sense of changing places) + *Laut* sound]

umlungu (ʊmˈlʊŋɡʊ) *n South African* a white man [Nguni: a white man]

Ummah (ˈʊmə) *n* the Muslim community throughout the world [from Arabic: community]

umpie or **umpy** (ˈʌmpɪ) *n, pl* **umpies** *Austral* an informal word for **umpire**

umpire (ˈʌmpaɪə) *n* **1** an official who rules on the playing of a game, as in cricket or baseball **2** a person who rules on or judges disputes between contesting parties ▷ *vb* **3** to act as umpire in (a game, dispute, or controversy) [c15 by mistaken division from *a noumpere*, from Old French *nomper* not one of a pair, from *nom-, non-* not + *per* equal, PEER¹] > **'umpireship** or **'umpirage** *n*

umpteen (ˌʌmpˈtiːn) *determiner informal* **a** very many: *umpteen things to do* **b** (*as pronoun*): *umpteen of them came* [c20 from *umpty* a great deal (perhaps from *-enty* as in *twenty*) + *-teen* ten] > **ˌump'teenth** *n, adj*

Umtali (ʊmˈtɑːlɪ) *n* the former name (until 1982) of **Mutare**

Umtata (ʌmˈtɑːtə) *n* a city in South Africa, in Eastern Cape province; the capital of the former Transkei Bantu homeland. Pop: 94 778 (2001)

umu (ˈuːmuː) *n, pl* **umu** *NZ* another name for **hangi** (sense 1) [Māori]

umwelt (ˈʊmvɛlt) *n biology, psychol* the environmental factors, collectively, that are capable of affecting the behaviour of an animal or individual [c20 from German *Umwelt* environment]

UN *abbreviation for* United Nations

un-¹ *prefix* (*freely used with adjectives, participles, and their derivative adverbs and nouns: less frequently used with certain other nouns*) not; contrary to; opposite of: *uncertain; uncomplaining; unemotionally; untidiness; unbelief; unrest; untruth* [from Old English *on-, un-*; related to Gothic *on-*, German *un-*, Latin *in-*]

un-² *prefix forming verbs* **1** denoting reversal of an action or state: *uncover; untangle* **2** denoting removal from, release, or deprivation: *unharness; unman; unthrone* **3** (*intensifier*): *unloose* [from Old English *un-, on-*; related to Gothic *and-*, German *ent-*, Latin *ante*]

'un or **un** (ən) *pron* a spelling of **one** intended to reflect a dialectal or informal pronunciation: *that's a big 'un*

UNA (in Britain) *abbreviation for* United Nations Association

unabashed (ˌʌnəˈbæʃt) *adj* not ashamed, embarrassed, or ill at ease

unabated (ˌʌnəˈbeɪtɪd) *adj* without losing any original force or violence; undiminished > **ˌuna'batedly** *adv*

unable (ʌnˈeɪbəl) *adj* **1** (*postpositive; foll by* **to**) lacking the necessary power, ability, or authority (to do something); not able **2** *archaic* incompetent

unabridged (ˌʌnəˈbrɪdʒd) *adj* (of a book, speech, etc) not reduced in length by condensing

unacceptable (ˌʌnəkˈsɛptəbəl) *adj* **1** not satisfactory; inadequate: *the standard was wholly unacceptable* **2** intolerable: *hitting children is unacceptable*

unaccommodated (ˌʌnəˈkɒməˌdeɪtɪd) *adj* **1** not suitable or apt; not adapted **2** unprovided for

unaccompanied (ˌʌnəˈkʌmpənɪd) *adj* **1** not accompanied **2** *music* **a** (of an instrument) playing alone **b** (of music for a group of singers) without instrumental accompaniment

unaccomplished (ˌʌnəˈkɒmplɪʃt) *adj* **1** not accomplished or finished **2** lacking accomplishments

unaccountable (ˌʌnəˈkaʊntəbəl) *adj* **1** allowing of no explanation; inexplicable **2** puzzling; extraordinary: *an unaccountable fear of hamburgers* **3** not accountable or answerable to > **ˌunac'countableness** or **ˌunacˌcounta'bility** *n* > **ˌunac'countably** *adv*

unaccounted (ˌʌnəˈkaʊntɪd) *adj* (usually foll by **for**) **1** missing: *as many as 100 people are unaccounted for* **2** not included in an account: *70 million dollars of unaccounted money* **3** not explained adequately: *unaccounted friendliness*

unaccustomed (ˌʌnəˈkʌstəmd) *adj* **1** (foll by **to**) not used (to): *unaccustomed to pain* **2** not familiar; strange or unusual > **ˌunac'customedness** *n*

unacknowledged (ˌʌnəkˈnɒlɪdʒd) *adj* not having been acknowledged or recognized: *unacknowledged legislators of the world*

una corda (ˈuːnə ˈkɔːdə) *adj, adv music* (of the piano) to be played with the soft pedal depressed [Italian, literally: one string; the pedal moves the mechanism so that only one string of the three tuned to each note is struck by the hammer]

unacquainted (ˌʌnəˈkweɪntɪd) *adj* **1** not familiar or conversant with (someone or something) **2** (of people) not having met or been introduced

unaddressed (ˌʌnəˈdrɛst) *adj* (of a letter, package, etc) not having an address

unadopted (ˌʌnəˈdɒptɪd) *adj* **1** (of a child) not adopted **2** *Brit* (of a road, etc) not maintained by a local authority

unadorned (ˌʌnəˈdɔːnd) *adj* not decorated; plain:

u

a bare unadorned style

unadulterated (ˌʌnəˈdʌltəreɪtɪd) *adj* not debased or made impure

unadventurous (ˌʌnədˈvɛntʃərəs) *adj* not daring or enterprising

unadvised (ˌʌnədˈvaɪzd) *adj* **1** rash or unwise **2** not having received advice > **unadvisedly** (ˌʌnədˈvaɪzɪdlɪ) *adv* > **unadˈvisedness** *n*

unaffected[1] (ˌʌnəˈfɛktɪd) *adj* unpretentious, natural, or sincere > **unafˈfectedly** *adv* > **unafˈfectedness** *n*

unaffected[2] (ˌʌnəˈfɛktɪd) *adj* not affected

unaffiliated (ˌʌnəˈfɪlɪˌeɪtɪd) *adj* not officially connected or associated with an organization

unafraid (ˌʌnəˈfreɪd) *adj* (*postpositive*; often foll by *of*) not frightened: *unafraid to break new ground*

unaided (ʌnˈeɪdɪd) *adj* without having received any help

Unalaska Island (ˌuːnəˈlæskə) *n* a large volcanic island in SW Alaska, in the Aleutian Islands. Length: 120 km (75 miles). Greatest width: about 40 km (25 miles)

unalienable (ʌnˈeɪljənəbʰl) *adj law* a variant of **inalienable**

unalloyed (ˌʌnəˈlɔɪd) *adj* not mixed or intermingled with any other thing; pure: *unalloyed metal; unalloyed pleasure*

unalterable (ʌnˈɔːltərəbʰl, -ˈɔːltrəbʰl) *adj* (of a condition, truth, etc) unable to be changed or altered

unaltered (ʌnˈɔːltəd) *adj* not altered; unchanged

unambiguous (ˌʌnæmˈbɪɡjʊəs) *adj* not ambiguous; clear: *an unambiguous message*

unambitious (ˌʌnæmˈbɪʃəs) *adj* lacking in ambition: *they were unambitious for their daughters*

un-American *adj* **1** not in accordance with the aims, ideals, customs, etc, of the US **2** against the interests of the US > **un-Aˈmericanˌism** *n*

unamused (ˌʌnəˈmjuːzd) *adj* not entertained, diverted, or laughing: *they looked on, unamused*

unaneled (ˌʌnəˈniːld) *adj archaic* not having received extreme unction [c17 from UN-[1] + ANELE]

unanimous (juːˈnænɪməs) *adj* **1** in complete or absolute agreement **2** characterized by complete agreement: *a unanimous decision* [c17 from Latin *ūnanimus* from *ūnus* one + *animus* mind] > **uˈnanimously** *adv* > **unanimity** (ˌjuːnəˈnɪmɪtɪ) *or* **uˈnanimousness** *n*

unannounced (ˌʌnəˈnaʊnst) *adj* not made known publicly or declared in advance: *an unannounced visit*

unanswerable (ʌnˈɑːnsərəbʰl) *adj* **1** incapable of being refuted **2** (of a question) not admitting of any answer > **unˈanswerableness** *n* > **unˈanswerably** *adv*

unanswered (ʌnˈɑːnsəd) *adj* not answered or replied to: *many unanswered questions*

unanticipated (ˌʌnænˈtɪsɪˌpeɪtɪd) *adj* not anticipated; unforeseen

unappealable (ˌʌnəˈpiːləbʰl) *adj law* (of a judgment, etc) not capable of being appealed against > **ˌunapˈpealableness** *n* > **ˌunapˈpealably** *adv*

unappealing (ˌʌnəˈpiːlɪŋ) *adj* not attractive or pleasing

unappetizing *or* **unappetising** (ʌnˈæpɪˌtaɪzɪŋ) *adj* **1** (of food) not pleasing or stimulating to the appetite **2** (of a prospect, person, etc) not appealing or attractive: *unappetizing to investors*

unappreciated (ˌʌnəˈpriːʃɪˌeɪtɪd, -sɪ-) *adj* not given or shown thanks or gratitude > **ˌunapˈpreciative** *adj*

unapproachable (ˌʌnəˈprəʊtʃəbʰl) *adj* **1** discouraging intimacy, friendliness, etc; aloof **2** inaccessible **3** not to be rivalled > **ˌunapˈproachableness** *n* > **ˌunapˈproachably** *adv*

unappropriated (ˌʌnəˈprəʊprɪˌeɪtɪd) *adj* **1** not set aside for specific use **2** *accounting* designating that portion of the profits of a business enterprise that is retained in the business and not withdrawn by the proprietor **3** (of property) not having been taken into any person's possession or control

unapproved (ˌʌnəˈpruːvd) *adj* not having been given approval or sanction

unapt (ʌnˈæpt) *adj* **1** (*usually postpositive*; often foll by *for*) not suitable or qualified; unfitted **2** mentally slow **3** (*postpositive; may take an infinitive*) not disposed or likely (to) > **unˈaptly** *adv* > **unˈaptness** *n*

unarguable (ʌnˈɑːɡjʊəbʰl) *adj* **1** incapable of being argued **2** incontestable; indisputable > **unˈarguably** *adv*

unarm (ʌnˈɑːm) *vb* a less common word for **disarm**

unarmed (ʌnˈɑːmd) *adj* **1** without weapons **2** (of animals and plants) having no claws, prickles, spines, thorns, or similar structures **3** of or relating to a projectile that does not use a detonator to initiate explosive action

unary (ˈjuːnərɪ) *adj* consisting of, or affecting, a single element or component; monadic [c16 (in the obsolete sense: a unit): from Latin *unus* one + -ARY]

unashamed (ˌʌnəˈʃeɪmd) *adj* **1** lacking moral restraints **2** not embarrassed, contrite, or apologetic > **unashamedly** (ˌʌnəˈʃeɪmɪdlɪ) *adv* > **ˌunaˈshamedness** *n*

unasked (ʌnˈɑːskt) *adj* **1** not requested or demanded **2** not invited

unassailable (ˌʌnəˈseɪləbʰl) *adj* **1** not able to be attacked **2** undeniable or irrefutable > **ˌunasˈsailableness** *n* > **ˌunasˈsailably** *adv*

unassisted (ˌʌnəˈsɪstɪd) *adj* without aid or help; alone

unassuming (ˌʌnəˈsjuːmɪŋ) *adj* modest or unpretentious > **ˌunasˈsumingly** *adv* > **ˌunasˈsumingness** *n*

unattached (ˌʌnəˈtætʃt) *adj* **1** not connected with any specific thing, body, group, etc; independent **2** not engaged or married **3** (of property) not seized or held as security or in satisfaction of a judgment

unattainable (ˌʌnəˈteɪnəbʰl) *adj* not achievable or accomplishable: *an unattainable goal*

unattended (ˌʌnəˈtɛndɪd) *adj* **1** not looked after or cared for **2** unaccompanied or alone **3** not listened to

unattractive (ˌʌnəˈtræktɪv) *adj* **1** not appealing to the senses or mind through beauty, form, character, etc **2** not arousing interest: *an unattractive proposition*

unattributed (ˌʌnəˈtrɪbjuːtɪd) *adj* not having been ascribed or attributed (to someone) > **ˌunatˈtributable** *adj*

unau (ˈjuːnaʊ) *n* another name for the **two-toed sloth** (see **sloth** (sense 1)) [c18 via French from Tupi]

unauthorized *or* **unauthorised** (ʌnˈɔːθəˌraɪzd) *adj* not having official permission

unavailable (ˌʌnəˈveɪləbʰl) *adj* not obtainable or accessible: *unavailable for comment*

unavailing (ˌʌnəˈveɪlɪŋ) *adj* useless or futile > **ˌunaˈvailingly** *adv*

unavoidable (ˌʌnəˈvɔɪdəbʰl) *adj* **1** unable to be avoided; inevitable **2** *law* not capable of being declared null and void > **ˌunaˌvoidaˈbility** *or* **ˌunaˈvoidableness** *n* > **ˌunaˈvoidably** *adv*

unaware (ˌʌnəˈwɛə) *adj* **1** (*postpositive*) not aware or conscious (of): *unaware of the danger, he ran across the road* **2** not fully cognizant of what is going on in the world: *he's the most unaware person I've ever met* ▷ *adv* **3** a variant of **unawares**. > **ˌunaˈwarely** *adv* > **ˌunaˈwareness** *n*

unawares (ˌʌnəˈwɛəz) *adv* **1** without prior warning or plan; unexpectedly: *she caught him unawares* **2** without being aware of or knowing: *he lost it unawares*

unbacked (ʌnˈbækt) *adj* **1** (of a book, chair, etc) not having a back **2** bereft of support, esp on a financial basis **3** (of a horse) **a** not supported by bets **b** never having been ridden

unbalance (ʌnˈbæləns) *vb* (*tr*) **1** to upset the equilibrium or balance of **2** to disturb the mental stability of (a person or his mind) ▷ *n* **3** imbalance or instability

unbalanced (ʌnˈbælənst) *adj* **1** lacking balance **2** irrational or unsound; erratic **3** mentally disordered or deranged **4** biased; one-sided: *unbalanced reporting* **5** (in double-entry bookkeeping) not having total debit balances equal to total credit balances **6** *electronics* (of signals or circuitry) not symmetrically disposed about earth or zero reference potential

unbar (ʌnˈbɑː) *vb* -bars, -barring, -barred (*tr*) **1** to take away a bar or bars from **2** to unfasten bars, locks, etc, from (a door); open

unbated (ʌnˈbeɪtɪd) *adj* **1** a less common spelling of **unabated 2** *archaic* (of a sword, lance, etc) not covered with a protective button

unbearable (ʌnˈbɛərəbʰl) *adj* not able to be borne or endured > **unˈbearableness** *n* > **unˈbearably** *adv*

unbeatable (ʌnˈbiːtəbʰl) *adj* unable to be defeated or outclassed; surpassingly excellent

unbeaten (ʌnˈbiːtʰn) *adj* **1** having suffered no defeat **2** not worn down; untrodden **3** not mixed or stirred by beating: *unbeaten eggs* **4** not beaten or struck

unbecoming (ˌʌnbɪˈkʌmɪŋ) *adj* **1** unsuitable or inappropriate, esp through being unattractive: *an unbecoming hat* **2** (when *postpositive*, usually foll by *of* or an object) not proper or seemly (for): *manners unbecoming a lady* > **ˌunbeˈcomingly** *adv* > **ˌunbeˈcomingness** *n*

unbeknown (ˌʌnbɪˈnəʊn) *adv* **1** (*sentence modifier*; foll by *to*) Also (esp Brit): **unbeknownst** without the knowledge (of a person): *unbeknown to him she had left the country* ▷ *adj* **2** (*postpositive*; usually foll by *to*) *rare* not known (to) [c17 from the archaic *beknown* known; see BE-, KNOW]

unbelief (ˌʌnbɪˈliːf) *n* disbelief or rejection of belief

unbelievable (ˌʌnbɪˈliːvəbʰl) *adj* unable to be believed; incredible or astonishing > **ˌunbeˌlievaˈbility** *or* **ˌunbeˈlievableness** *n*

unbelievably (ˌʌnbɪˈliːvəblɪ) *adv* **1** in a manner that is hard to believe; astonishingly: *it gets unbelievably hot* **2** (*sentence modifier*) it is hard to believe that; incredibly: *unbelievably, he remained utterly cheerful*

unbeliever (ˌʌnbɪˈliːvə) *n* a person who does not believe or withholds belief, esp in religious matters

unbelieving (ˌʌnbɪˈliːvɪŋ) *adj* **1** not believing; sceptical **2** proceeding from or characterized by scepticism > **ˌunbeˈlievingly** *adv* > **ˌunbeˈlievingness** *n*

unbelt (ʌnˈbɛlt) *vb* (*tr*) **1** to unbuckle the belt of (a garment) **2** to remove (something) from a belt

unbend (ʌnˈbɛnd) *vb* -bends, -bending, -bent **1** to release or be released from the restraints of formality and ceremony **2** *informal* to relax (the mind) or (of the mind) to become relaxed **3** to become or be made straightened out from an originally bent shape or position **4** (*tr*) *nautical* **a** to remove (a sail) from a stay, mast, yard, etc **b** to untie (a rope, etc) or cast (a cable) loose > **unˈbendable** *adj*

unbending (ʌnˈbɛndɪŋ) *adj* **1** rigid or inflexible **2** characterized by sternness or severity: *an unbending rule* > **unˈbendingly** *adv* > **unˈbendingness** *n*

unbent (ʌnˈbɛnt) *vb* **1** the past tense and past participle of **unbend** ▷ *adj* **2** not bent or bowed **3** not compelled to yield or give way by force

unbiased *or* **unbiassed** (ʌnˈbaɪəst) *adj* **1** having no bias or prejudice; fair or impartial **2** *statistics* **a** (of a sample) not affected by any extraneous factors, conflated variables, or selectivity which influence its distribution; random **b** (of an estimator) having an expected value equal to the parameter being estimated; having zero bias **c** Also called: **discriminatory** (of a significance test). Having a power greater than the predetermined significance level > **unˈbiasedly** *or* **unˈbiassedly** *adv* > **unˈbiasedness** *or* **unˈbiassedness** *n*

unbidden (ʌnˈbɪdʰn) *adj* **1** not ordered or

commanded; voluntary or spontaneous **2** not invited or asked

unbind (ʌnˈbaɪnd) *vb* -binds, -binding, -bound (*tr*) **1** to set free from restraining bonds or chains; release **2** to unfasten or make loose (a bond, tie, etc)

unbirthday (ˌʌnˈbɜːθdeɪ) *n Brit jocular* **a** any day other than one's birthday **b** (*as modifier*): *an unbirthday present* [C19 coined by Lewis Carroll in *Through the Looking-Glass*]

unbleached (ʌnˈbliːtʃt) *adj* not having been made or become white or lighter through exposure to sunlight or by the action of chemical agents, etc

unblemished (ʌnˈblɛmɪʃt) *adj* not blemished or tarnished in any way

unblenched (ʌnˈblɛntʃt) *adj obsolete* undismayed [C17 from UN-¹ + BLENCH¹]

unblessed (ʌnˈblɛst) *adj* **1** deprived of blessing **2** unhallowed, cursed, or evil **3** unhappy or wretched > **unblessedness** (ʌnˈblɛsɪdnɪs) *n*

unblinking (ʌnˈblɪŋkɪŋ) *adj* **1** without blinking **2** showing no visible response or emotion **3** not wavering through trepidation or fear > **un'blinkingly** *adv*

unblock (ʌnˈblɒk) *vb* (*tr*) to remove a blockage from (a pipe, etc)

unblown (ʌnˈbləʊn) *adj* **1** *archaic* (of a flower) still in the bud **2** not blown

unblushing (ʌnˈblʌʃɪŋ) *adj* immodest or shameless > **un'blushingly** *adv* > **un'blushingness** *n*

unbolt (ʌnˈbəʊlt) *vb* (*tr*) **1** to unfasten a bolt of (a door) **2** to undo (the nut) on a bolt

unbolted (ʌnˈbəʊltɪd) *adj* (of grain, meal, or flour) not sifted

unboned (ʌnˈbəʊnd) *adj* **1** (of meat, fish, etc) not having had the bones removed **2** (of animals) having no bones

unborn (ʌnˈbɔːn) *adj* **1** not yet born or brought to birth **2** still to come in the future: *the unborn world*

unbosom (ʌnˈbʊzəm) *vb* (*tr*) to relieve (oneself) of (secrets, etc) by telling someone [C16 from UN-² + BOSOM (in the sense: seat of the emotions); compare Dutch *ontboezemen*] > **un'bosomer** *n*

unbound (ʌnˈbaʊnd) *vb* **1** the past tense and past participle of **unbind** ▷ *adj* **2** (of a book) not bound within a cover **3** not restrained or tied down by bonds **4** (of a morpheme) able to form a word by itself; free

unbounded (ʌnˈbaʊndɪd) *adj* having no boundaries or limits > **un'boundedly** *adv* > **un'boundedness** *n*

unbowed (ʌnˈbaʊd) *adj* **1** not bowed or bent **2** free or unconquered

unbrace (ʌnˈbreɪs) *vb* (*tr*) **1** to remove tension or strain from; relax **2** to remove a brace or braces from

unbreakable (ʌnˈbreɪkəbəl) *adj* not able to be broken

unbred (ʌnˈbrɛd) *adj* **1** a less common word for **ill-bred 2** not taught or instructed **3** *obsolete* not born

unbridle (ʌnˈbraɪdəl) *vb* (*tr*) **1** to remove the bridle from (a horse) **2** to remove all controls or restraints from

unbridled (ʌnˈbraɪdəld) *adj* **1** with all restraints removed **2** (of a horse, etc) wearing no bridle > **un'bridledly** *adv* > **un'bridledness** *n*

unbroken (ʌnˈbrəʊkən) *adj* **1** complete or whole **2** continuous or incessant **3** undaunted in spirit **4** (of animals, esp horses) not tamed; wild **5** not disturbed or upset: *the unbroken silence of the afternoon* **6** (of a record, esp at sport) not improved upon **7** (of a contract, law, etc) not broken or infringed > **un'brokenly** *adv* > **un'brokenness** *n*

unbundle (ʌnˈbʌndəl) *vb* (*tr*) *computing* to separate (hardware from software) for sales purposes

unbundling (ʌnˈbʌndlɪŋ) *n commerce* the takeover of a large conglomerate with a view to retaining the core business and selling off some of the subsidiaries to help finance the takeover

unburden (ʌnˈbɜːdən) *vb* (*tr*) **1** to remove a load or

burden from **2** to relieve or make free (one's mind, oneself, etc) of a worry, trouble, etc, by revelation or confession. ▷ Archaic spelling: **unburthen** (ʌnˈbɜːðən)

unbutton (ʌnˈbʌtən) *vb* **1** to undo by unfastening (the buttons) of (a garment) **2** *informal* to release or relax (oneself, tension, etc)

unbuttoned (ʌnˈbʌtənd) *adj* **1** with buttons not fastened **2** *informal* uninhibited; unrestrained: *hours of unbuttoned self-revelation*

uncaged (ʌnˈkeɪdʒd) *adj* at liberty

uncalled-for (ʌnˈkɔːldfɔː) *adj* unnecessary or unwarranted

uncanny (ʌnˈkænɪ) *adj* **1** characterized by apparently supernatural wonder, horror, etc **2** beyond what is normal or expected: *an uncanny accuracy* > **un'cannily** *adv* > **un'canniness** *n*

uncap (ʌnˈkæp) *vb* -caps, -capping, -capped **1** (*tr*) to remove a cap or top from (a container): *to uncap a bottle* **2** to remove a cap from (the head)

uncared-for (ʌnˈkɛədfɔː) *adj* not cared for; neglected

uncaused (ʌnˈkɔːzd) *adj now rare* not brought into existence by any cause; spontaneous or natural

unceasing (ʌnˈsiːsɪŋ) *adj* not ceasing or ending > **un'ceasingly** *adv* > **un'ceasingness** *n*

uncensored (ʌnˈsɛnsəd) *adj* (of a publication, film, letter, etc) not having been banned or edited

unceremonious (ˌʌnsɛrɪˈməʊnɪəs) *adj* without ceremony; informal, abrupt, rude, or undignified > ˌunceri'moniously *adv* > ˌunceri'moniousness *n*

uncertain (ʌnˈsɜːtən) *adj* **1** not able to be accurately known or predicted: *the issue is uncertain* **2** (when *postpositive*, often foll by *of*) not sure or confident (about): *a man of uncertain opinion* **3** not precisely determined, established, or decided: *uncertain plans* **4** not to be depended upon; unreliable: *an uncertain vote* **5** liable to variation; changeable: *the weather is uncertain* **6** in no uncertain terms **a** unambiguously **b** forcefully > **un'certainly** *adv* > **un'certainness** *n*

uncertainty (ʌnˈsɜːtəntɪ) *n*, *pl* -ties **1** Also called: **uncertainness**. The state or condition of being uncertain **2** an uncertain matter, contingency, etc

uncertainty principle *n* **the** the principle that energy and time or position and momentum of a quantum mechanical system, cannot both be accurately measured simultaneously. The product of their uncertainties is always greater than or of the order of *h*, where *h* is the Planck constant. Also called: Heisenberg uncertainty principle, indeterminacy principle

unchain (ʌnˈtʃeɪn) *vb* (*tr*) **1** to remove a chain or chains from **2** to set at liberty; make free

unchallenged (ʌnˈtʃælɪndʒd) *adj* not having been challenged or questioned: *thirty years of unchallenged power* > **un'challengeable** *adj*

unchancy (ʌnˈtʃɑːnsɪ) *adj Scot* unlucky, ill-omened, or dangerous. Compare **wanchancy**

unchangeable (ʌnˈtʃeɪndʒəbəl) *adj* not capable of being changed or altered

unchanged (ʌnˈtʃeɪndʒd) *adj* not altered or different in any way

unchanging (ʌnˈtʃeɪndʒɪŋ) *adj* remaining the same; constant: *an unchanging nature*

uncharacteristic (ˌʌnkærɪktəˈrɪstɪk) *adj* not typical or usual

uncharged (ʌnˈtʃɑːdʒd) *adj* **1** (of land or other property) not subject to a charge **2** having no electric charge; neutral **3** *archaic* (of a firearm) not loaded

uncharitable (ʌnˈtʃærɪtəbəl) *adj* (of a person, remark, etc) unkind or lacking in generosity: *an uncharitable criticism*

uncharted (ʌnˈtʃɑːtɪd) *adj* (of a physical or nonphysical region or area) not yet mapped, surveyed, or investigated: *uncharted waters; the uncharted depths of the mind*

unchartered (ʌnˈtʃɑːtəd) *adj* **1** not authorized by charter; unregulated **2** unauthorized, lawless, or irregular

USAGE Care should be taken not to use *unchartered* where *uncharted* is meant: *uncharted* (not *unchartered*) *territory*

unchecked (ʌnˈtʃɛkt) *adj* **1** not prevented from continuing or growing: *unchecked population growth* **2** not examined or inspected ▷ *adv* **3** without being stopped or hindered: *the virus could spread unchecked* **4** without being examined or inspected: *our luggage passed unchecked through customs*

unchristian (ʌnˈkrɪstʃən) *adj* **1** not in accordance with the principles or ethics of Christianity **2** non-Christian or pagan > **un'christianly** *adv*

unchurch (ʌnˈtʃɜːtʃ) *vb* (*tr*) **1** to excommunicate **2** to remove church status from (a building)

uncial (ˈʌnsɪəl) *adj* **1** of, relating to, or written in majuscule letters, as used in Greek and Latin manuscripts of the third to ninth centuries, that resemble modern capitals, but are characterized by much greater curvature and inclination and general inequality of height **2** pertaining to an inch or an ounce **3** pertaining to the duodecimal system ▷ *n* **4** an uncial letter or manuscript [C17 from Late Latin *unciāles litterae* letters an inch long, from Latin *unciālis*, from *uncia* one twelfth, inch, OUNCE¹] > **'uncially** *adv*

unciform (ˈʌnsɪˌfɔːm) *adj* **1** *anatomy*, *zoology* having the shape of a hook ▷ *n* **2** Also called: **hamate bone** *anatomy* any hook-shaped structure or part, esp a small bone of the wrist (**unciform bone**) [C18 from New Latin *unciformis*, from Latin *uncus* a hook]

uncinariasis (ˌʌnsɪnəˈraɪəsɪs) *n* the condition of being infested with hookworms; hookworm disease [C20 via New Latin *Uncināria*, from Late Latin *uncīnus* a hook, from Latin *uncus*]

uncinate (ˈʌnsɪnɪt, -ˌneɪt) *adj biology* **1** shaped like a hook: *the uncinate process of the ribs of certain vertebrates* **2** of, relating to, or possessing uncini [C18 from Latin *uncīnātus*, from *uncīnus* a hook, from *uncus*]

uncinus (ʌnˈsaɪnəs) *n*, *pl* -cini (-ˈsaɪnaɪ) *zoology* a small hooked structure, such as any of the hooked chaetae of certain polychaete worms [C19 from Late Latin: hook, from Latin *uncus*]

uncircumcised (ʌnˈsɜːkəmˌsaɪzd) *adj* **1** not circumcised **2** not Jewish; gentile **3** *theol* not purified

uncircumcision (ˌʌnsɜːkəmˈsɪʒən) *n chiefly New Testament* the state of being uncircumcised

uncivil (ʌnˈsɪvəl) *adj* **1** lacking civility or good manners **2** an obsolete word for **uncivilized** > **uncivility** (ˌʌnsɪˈvɪlɪtɪ) *or* **un'civilness** *n* > **un'civilly** *adv*

uncivilized *or* **uncivilised** (ʌnˈsɪvɪˌlaɪzd) *adj* **1** (of a tribe or people) not yet civilized, esp preliterate **2** lacking culture or sophistication > **uncivilizedly** *or* **uncivilisedly** (ʌnˈsɪvɪˌlaɪzɪdlɪ) *adv* > **un'civi,lizedness** *or* **un'civi,lisedness** *n*

unclad (ʌnˈklæd) *adj* having no clothes on; naked

unclaimed (ʌnˈkleɪmd) *adj* not having been claimed: *£7 million in unclaimed prizes*

unclasp (ʌnˈklɑːsp) *vb* **1** (*tr*) to unfasten the clasp of (something) **2** to release one's grip (upon an object)

unclassified (ʌnˈklæsɪˌfaɪd) *adj* **1** not arranged in any specific order or grouping **2** (of information) not possessing a security classification **3** (of football results) not arranged in any special order or in divisions

uncle (ˈʌŋkəl) *n* **1** a brother of one's father or mother **2** the husband of one's aunt **3** a term of address sometimes used by children for a male friend of their parents **4** *slang* a pawnbroker ▷ Related adjective: **avuncular** [C13 from Old French *oncle*, from Latin *avunculus*; related to Latin *avus* grandfather]

unclean (ʌnˈkliːn) *adj* lacking moral, spiritual, ritual, or physical cleanliness > **un'cleanness** *n*

uncleanly¹ (ʌnˈkliːnlɪ) *adv* in an unclean manner

uncleanly² (ʌnˈklɛnlɪ) *adj* characterized by an absence of cleanliness; unclean > **un'cleanliness** *n*

unclear (ʌnˈklɪə) *adj* not clear or definite; ambiguous ▷ un'**clearly** *adv* ▷ un'**clearness** *n*

uncle-ji *n Hinglish informal* a name given to a man from the generation older than oneself [C20 from UNCLE + -JI]

Uncle Sam *n* a personification of the government of the United States [C19 apparently a humorous interpretation of the letters stamped on army supply boxes during the War of 1812: US]

Uncle Tom *n informal derogatory* a Black whose behaviour towards Whites is regarded as obsequious and servile [C20 after the slave who is the main character of HB Stowe's novel *Uncle Tom's Cabin* (1852)] ▷ **Uncle Tomism** *n*

unclog (ʌnˈklɒɡ) *vb* -clogs, -clogging, -clogged (*tr*) to remove an obstruction from (a drain, etc)

unclose (ʌnˈkləʊz) *vb* **1** to open or cause to open **2** to come or bring to light; reveal or be revealed

unclothe (ʌnˈkləʊð) *vb* -clothes, -clothing, -clothed *or* -clad (*tr*) **1** to take off garments from; strip **2** to uncover or lay bare

uncluttered (ʌnˈklʌtəd) *adj* not having too many objects, details, etc

unco¹ (ˈʌŋkəʊ) *Scot* ▷ *adj* **uncoer, uncoest** **1** unfamiliar, strange, or odd **2** remarkable or striking ▷ *adv* **3** very; extremely **4 the unco guid** narrow-minded, excessively religious, or self-righteous people ▷ *n, pl* **uncos** *or* **uncoes 5** a novel or remarkable person or thing **6** *obsolete* a stranger **7** (*plural*) news [C15 variant of UNCOUTH]

unco² (ˈʌŋkəʊ) *Austral informal* ▷ *adj* **1** awkward; clumsy ▷ *n, pl* **uncos 2** an awkward or clumsy person [C20 shortened form of UNCOORDINATED]

uncoil (ʌnˈkɔɪl) *vb* to unwind or become unwound; untwist

uncoined (ʌnˈkɔɪnd) *adj* (of a metal) not made into coin

uncollected (ˌʌnkəˈlɛktɪd) *adj* not having been called for, gathered, or collected

uncomfortable (ʌnˈkʌmftəbᵊl) *adj* **1** not comfortable **2** feeling or causing discomfort or unease; disquieting ▷ un'**comfortableness** *n* ▷ un'**comfortably** *adv*

uncommercial (ˌʌnkəˈmɜːʃəl) *adj* **1** not concerned with commerce or trade **2** not in accordance with the aims or principles of business or trade

uncommitted (ˌʌnkəˈmɪtɪd) *adj* not bound or pledged to a specific opinion, course of action, or cause

uncommon (ʌnˈkɒmən) *adj* **1** outside or beyond normal experience, conditions, etc; unusual **2** in excess of what is normal: *an uncommon liking for honey* ▷ *adv* **3** an archaic word for **uncommonly** (sense 2) ▷ un'**commonness** *n*

uncommonly (ʌnˈkɒmənlɪ) *adv* **1** in an uncommon or unusual manner or degree; rarely **2** (intensifier): *you're uncommonly friendly*

uncommunicative (ˌʌnkəˈmjuːnɪkətɪv) *adj* disinclined to talk or give information or opinions ▷ ˌuncom'**municatively** *adv* ▷ ˌuncom'**municativeness** *n*

uncompetitive (ˌʌnkəmˈpɛtɪtɪv) *adj* not able or willing to compete

uncomplaining (ˌʌnkəmˈpleɪnɪŋ) *adj* not complaining or resentful; resigned

uncomplicated (ʌnˈkɒmplɪˌkeɪtɪd) *adj* not complicated; simple

uncomplimentary (ˌʌnkɒmplɪˈmɛntərɪ, -trɪ) *adj* not conveying, containing, or resembling a compliment

uncomprehending (ˌʌnkɒmprɪˈhɛndɪŋ) *adj* not able to understand; puzzled: *a long, uncomprehending look*

uncompromising (ʌnˈkɒmprəˌmaɪzɪŋ) *adj* not prepared to give ground or to compromise ▷ un'**compro,misingly** *adv* ▷ un'**compro,misingness** *n*

unconcealed (ˌʌnkənˈsiːld) *adj* (of feelings, attitudes, etc) not hidden or concealed; open

unconcern (ˌʌnkənˈsɜːn) *n* apathy or indifference

unconcerned (ˌʌnkənˈsɜːnd) *adj* **1** lacking in concern or involvement **2** not worried;

untroubled ▷ ˌuncon'**cernedly** (ˌʌnkənˈsɜːnɪdlɪ) *adv* ▷ ˌuncon'**cernedness** *n*

unconditional (ˌʌnkənˈdɪʃənᵊl) *adj* **1** without conditions or limitations; total: *unconditional surrender* **2** *maths* (of an equality) true for all values of the variable: *(x+1)>x is an unconditional equality* ▷ ˌuncon'**ditionally** *adv* ▷ ˌuncon'**ditionalness** *or* ˌuncon,dition'**ality** *n*

unconditioned (ˌʌnkənˈdɪʃənd) *adj* **1** *psychol* characterizing an innate reflex and the stimulus and response that form parts of it. Compare **conditioned** (sense 2) **2** *metaphysics* unrestricted by conditions; infinite; absolute **3** without limitations; unconditional ▷ ˌuncon'**ditionedness** *n*

unconditioned response *n* a reflex action innately elicited by a stimulus without the intervention of any learning process. Also called (esp formerly): **unconditioned reflex.** Compare **conditioned response**

unconditioned stimulus *n psychol* any stimulus evoking an unlearnt response, esp in the context of classical conditioning, in which the conditioned stimulus is followed by the unconditioned one

unconfined (ˌʌnkənˈfaɪnd) *adj* **1** not enclosed or restricted; free **2** (of an emotion) not restricted or disguised: *unconfined joy*

unconfirmed (ˌʌnkənˈfɜːmd) *adj* not confirmed; uncorroborated: *unconfirmed reports*

unconformable (ˌʌnkənˈfɔːməbᵊl) *adj* **1** not conformable to or conforming **2** (of rock strata) consisting of a series of younger strata that do not succeed the underlying older rocks in age or in parallel position, as a result of a long period of erosion or nondeposition ▷ ˌuncon,forma'**bility** *or* ˌuncon'**formableness** *n* ▷ ˌuncon'**formably** *adv*

unconformity (ˌʌnkənˈfɔːmɪtɪ) *n, pl* -ties **1** lack of conformity **2** the contact surface between younger and older rocks representing a discontinuity in the geological record. Most commonly it represents an erosional surface

uncongenial (ˌʌnkənˈdʒiːnjəl, -nɪəl) *adj* not friendly, pleasant, or agreeable

unconnected (ˌʌnkəˈnɛktɪd) *adj* **1** not linked; separate or independent **2** disconnected or incoherent ▷ ˌuncon'**nectedly** *adv* ▷ ˌuncon'**nectedness** *n*

unconscionable (ʌnˈkɒnʃənəbᵊl) *adj* **1** unscrupulous or unprincipled: *an unconscionable liar* **2** immoderate or excessive: *unconscionable demands* ▷ un'**conscionableness** *n* ▷ un'**conscionably** *adv*

unconscious (ʌnˈkɒnʃəs) *adj* **1** lacking normal sensory awareness of the environment; insensible **2** not aware of one's actions, behaviour, etc: *unconscious of his bad manners* **3** characterized by lack of awareness or intention: *an unconscious blunder* **4** coming from or produced by the unconscious: *unconscious resentment* ▷ *n* **5** *psychoanal* the part of the mind containing instincts, impulses, images, and ideas that are not available for direct examination. See also **collective unconscious.** Compare **subconscious, preconscious** ▷ un'**consciously** *adv*

unconsciousness (ʌnˈkɒnʃəsnɪs) *n* the state of being without normal sensory awareness; insensibility

unconsecrated (ʌnˈkɒnsɪˌkreɪtɪd) *adj* not having been made or declared sacred or holy

unconsidered (ˌʌnkənˈsɪdəd) *adj* **1** not considered; disregarded **2** done without consideration

unconstitutional (ˌʌnkɒnstɪˈtjuːʃᵊnᵊl) *adj* at variance with or not permitted by a constitution ▷ ˌunconsti,tution'**ality** *n*

unconstitutional strike *n* a stoppage of work which violates the dispute procedure agreed between the employer and the trade union or trade unions concerned

unconstrained (ˌʌnkənˈstreɪnd) *adj* not having any constraints

unconsummated (ʌnˈkɒnsəˌmeɪtɪd) *adj* (of a

marriage, relationship, etc) not having been consummated

uncontaminated (ˌʌnkənˈtæmɪˌneɪtɪd) *adj* not having been polluted, infected, or made impure

uncontested (ˌʌnkənˈtɛstɪd) *adj* not having been challenged, called into question, or disputed

uncontrollable (ˌʌnkənˈtrəʊləbᵊl) *adj* incapable of being controlled or managed ▷ ˌuncon,trolla'**bility** *or* ˌuncon'**trollableness** *n* ▷ ˌuncon'**trollably** *adv*

uncontrolled (ˌʌnkənˈtrəʊld) *adj* not controlled or regulated; uncurbed

uncontroversial (ˌʌnkɒntrəˈvɜːʃᵊl) *adj* not inspiring or causing controversy

unconventional (ˌʌnkənˈvɛnʃᵊnᵊl) *adj* not conforming to accepted rules or standards ▷ ˌuncon,vention'**ality** *n* ▷ ˌuncon'**ventionally** *adv*

unconverted (ˌʌnkənˈvɜːtɪd) *adj* **1** not having been changed or adapted: *an unconverted barn* **2 a** not having changed one's beliefs, opinions, etc **b** (*as collective noun; preceded by the*): *he'll be preaching to the unconverted*

unconvinced (ˌʌnkənˈvɪnst) *adj* not convinced or persuaded: *I remain unconvinced*

unconvincing (ˌʌnkənˈvɪnsɪŋ) *adj* not credible or plausible

uncooked (ʌnˈkʊkt) *adj* not cooked; raw: *uncooked meat or fish*

uncool (ʌnˈkuːl) *adj slang* **1** unsophisticated; unfashionable **2** excitable; tense; not cool

uncoordinated (ˌʌnkəʊˈɔːdɪˌneɪtɪd) *adj* **1** lacking order, system, or organization **2** (of a person, action, etc) lacking muscular or emotional coordination

uncork (ʌnˈkɔːk) *vb* (*tr*) **1** to draw the cork from (a bottle, etc) **2** to release or unleash (emotions, etc)

uncorrected (ˌʌnkəˈrɛktɪd) *adj* (of proofs, a transcript, etc) not having been corrected or amended

uncorroborated (ˌʌnkəˈrɒbəˌreɪtɪd) *adj* (of evidence, a statement, etc) lacking confirmation or evidence

uncorrupted (ˌʌnkəˈrʌptɪd) *adj* **1** not having been corrupted: *you're touchingly uncorrupted by power* **2** not contaminated: *food that is uncorrupted by chemicals*

uncountable (ʌnˈkaʊntəbᵊl) *adj* **1** too many to be counted; innumerable **2** *linguistics* denoting a noun that does not refer to an isolable object. See **mass noun**

uncounted (ʌnˈkaʊntɪd) *adj* **1** unable to be counted; innumerable **2** not counted

uncouple (ʌnˈkʌpᵊl) *vb* **1** to disconnect or unfasten or become disconnected or unfastened **2** (*tr*) to set loose; release

uncouth (ʌnˈkuːθ) *adj* lacking in good manners, refinement, or grace [Old English *uncūth*, from UN-¹ + *cūth* familiar; related to Old High German *kund* known, Old Norse *kunnr*] ▷ un'**couthly** *adv* ▷ un'**couthness** *n*

uncovenanted (ʌnˈkʌvənəntɪd) *adj law* **1** not guaranteed or promised by a covenant **2** not in accordance with or sanctioned by a covenant

uncover (ʌnˈkʌvə) *vb* **1** (*tr*) to remove the cover, cap, top, etc, from **2** (*tr*) to reveal or disclose: *to uncover a plot* **3** to take off (one's head covering), esp as a mark of respect

uncovered (ʌnˈkʌvəd) *adj* **1** not covered; revealed or bare **2** not protected by insurance, security, etc **3** with hat removed as a mark of respect

uncritical (ʌnˈkrɪtɪkᵊl) *adj* not containing or making severe or negative judgments

uncrowded (ʌnˈkraʊdɪd) *adj* (of a confined space, area, etc) not containing too many people or things

uncrowned (ʌnˈkraʊnd) *adj* **1** having the power of royalty without the title **2** not having yet assumed the crown **3 uncrowned king** *or* **queen** a man or woman of high status among a certain group

UNCTAD *abbreviation for* United Nations Conference on Trade and Development

unction (ˈʌŋkʃən) *n* **1** *chiefly RC and Eastern Churches* the act of anointing with oil in sacramental ceremonies, in the conferring of holy orders **2** excessive suavity or affected charm **3** an ointment or unguent **4** anything soothing or comforting [c14 from Latin *unctiō* an anointing, from *ungere* to anoint; see UNGUENT] > 'unctionless *adj*

unctuous ('ʌŋktjʊəs) *adj* **1** slippery or greasy **2** affecting an oily charm [c14 from Medieval Latin *unctuōsus*, from Latin *unctum* ointment, from *ungere* to anoint] > **unctuosity** (,ʌŋktjʊ'ɒsɪtɪ) *or* 'unctuousness *n* > 'unctuously *adv*

uncultivated (ʌn'kʌltɪ,veɪtɪd) *adj* **1** (of a garden, fields, the earth, etc) not having been tilled and prepared or planted **2** (of a mind, person, etc) not improved by education

uncultured (ʌn'kʌltʃəd) *adj* lacking good taste, manners, upbringing, and education

uncurl (ʌn'kɜːl) *vb* to move or cause to move out of a curled or rolled up position

uncus ('ʌŋkəs) *n, pl* **unci** ('ʌnsaɪ) *zoology, anatomy* a hooked part or process, as in the human cerebrum [c19 from Latin: hook]

uncustomary (ʌn'kʌstəmərɪ, -təmrɪ) *adj* not in accordance with custom or habitual practice

uncut (ʌn'kʌt) *adj* **1** (of a book) not having the edges of its pages trimmed or slit **2** (of a gemstone) not cut and faceted **3** not abridged or shortened

undamaged (ʌn'dæmɪdʒd) *adj* not damaged

undamped (ʌn'dæmpt) *adj* **1** (of an oscillating system) having unrestricted motion; not damped **2** not repressed, discouraged, or subdued; undiminished

undated (ʌn'deɪtɪd) *adj* (of a manuscript, letter, etc) not having an identifying date

undaunted (ʌn'dɔːntɪd) *adj* not put off, discouraged, or beaten > un'dauntedly *adv* > un'dauntedness *n*

undead (ʌn'dɛd) *adj* **a** (of a fictional being, such as a vampire) technically dead but reanimated **b** (*as collective noun; preceded by the*): *the undead*

undecagon (ʌn'dɛkə,gɒn) *n* a polygon having eleven sides [c18 from Latin *undecim* eleven (from *unus* one + *decem* ten) + -GON]

undeceive (,ʌndɪ'siːv) *vb* (*tr*) to reveal the truth to (someone previously misled or deceived); enlighten > ,unde'ceivable *adj* > ,unde'ceiver *n*

undecided (,ʌndɪ'saɪdɪd) *adj* **1** not having made up one's mind **2** (of an issue, problem, etc) not agreed or decided upon > ,unde'cidedly *adv* > ,unde'cidedness *n*

undeclared (,ʌndɪ'klɛəd) *adj* not announced or acknowledged publicly

undefeated (,ʌndɪ'fiːtɪd) *adj* not having been defeated

undefended (,ʌndɪ'fɛndɪd) *adj* not having people to provide resistance against danger, attack, or harm

undefined (,ʌndɪ'faɪnd) *adj* not defined or made clear > ,unde'finable *adj*

undemanding (,ʌndɪ'mɑːndɪŋ) *adj* not requiring great patience, skill, attention, etc

undemocratic (,ʌndɛmə'krætɪk) *adj* not characterized by, derived from, or relating to the principles of democracy

undemonstrative (,ʌndɪ'mɒnstrətɪv) *adj* tending not to show the feelings; of a reserved nature > ,unde'monstratively *adv* > ,unde'monstrativeness *n*

undeniable (,ʌndɪ'naɪəbᵊl) *adj* **1** unquestionably true **2** of unquestionable excellence **3** unable to be resisted or denied > ,unde'niableness *n*

undeniably (,ʌndɪ'naɪəblɪ) *adv* in an unquestionable or obvious manner; irrefutably

under ('ʌndə) *prep* **1** directly below; on, to, or beneath the underside or base of: *under one's feet* **2** less than: *under forty years* **3** lower in rank than: *under a corporal* **4** subject to the supervision, jurisdiction, control, or influence of **5** subject to (conditions); in (certain circumstances) **6** within a classification of: *a book under theology* **7** known by: *under an assumed name* **8** planted with: *a field*

under corn **9** powered by: *under sail* **10** *astrology* during the period that the sun is in (a sign of the zodiac): *born under Aries* ▷ *adv* **11** below; to a position underneath something [Old English; related to Old Saxon, Gothic *undar*, Old High German *untar*, Old Norse *undir*, Latin *infra*]

under- *prefix* **1** below or beneath: *underarm; underground* **2** of lesser importance or lower rank: *undersecretary* **3** to a lesser degree than is proper; insufficient or insufficiently: *undercharge; underemployed* **4** indicating secrecy or deception: *underhand*

underachieve (,ʌndərə'tʃiːv) *vb* (*intr*) to fail to achieve a performance appropriate to one's age or talents > ,undera'chiever *n* > ,undera'chievement *n*

underact (,ʌndər'ækt) *vb theatre* to play (a role) without adequate emphasis. Compare **overact**

underactive (,ʌndər'æktɪv) *adj* (of the thyroid or adrenal glands) not functioning at full capacity

underage (,ʌndər'eɪdʒ) *adj* below the required or standard age, esp below the legal age for voting

underarm ('ʌndər,ɑːm) *adj* **1** (of a measurement) extending along the arm from wrist to armpit **2** *sport* of or denoting a style of throwing, bowling, or serving in which the hand is swung below shoulder level **3** below the arm ▷ *adv* **4** in an underarm style

underbelly ('ʌndə,bɛlɪ) *n, pl* **-lies** **1** the part of an animal's belly nearest to the ground **2** a vulnerable or unprotected part, aspect, or region

underbid (,ʌndə'bɪd) *vb* **-bids, -bidding, -bid** (*tr*) **1** to submit a bid lower than that of (others): *Irena underbid the other dealers* **2** to submit an excessively low bid for **3** *bridge* to make a bid that will win fewer tricks than is justified by the strength of the hand: *he underbid his hand* > 'under,bidder *n*

underbody ('ʌndə,bɒdɪ) *n, pl* **-bodies** the underpart of a body, as of an animal or motor vehicle

underbred (,ʌndə'brɛd) *adj* **1** of impure stock; not thoroughbred **2** a less common word for **ill-bred** > ,under'breeding *n*

underbrush ('ʌndə,brʌʃ) *or* **underbush** *n chiefly US and Canadian* undergrowth

underbuy (,ʌndə'baɪ) *vb* **-buys, -buying, -bought** **1** to buy (stock in trade) in amounts lower than required **2** (*tr*) to buy at a price below that paid by (others) **3** (*tr*) to pay a price less than the true value for

undercapitalize *or* **undercapitalise** (,ʌndə'kæpɪtə,laɪz) *vb* to provide or issue capital for (a commercial enterprise) in an amount insufficient for efficient operation

undercarriage ('ʌndə,kærɪdʒ) *n* **1** Also called: **landing gear** the assembly of wheels, shock absorbers, struts, etc, that supports an aircraft on the ground and enables it to take off and land **2** the framework that supports the body of a vehicle, carriage, etc

undercart (,ʌndə,kɑːt) *n Brit informal* another name for **undercarriage** (sense 1)

undercharge (,ʌndə'tʃɑːdʒ) *vb* **1** to charge too little (for) **2** (*tr*) to load (a gun, cannon, etc,) with an inadequate charge ▷ *n* **3** an insufficient charge

underclass ('ʌndə,klɑːs) *n* a class beneath the usual social scale consisting of the most disadvantaged people, such as the unemployed in inner cities

underclay ('ʌndə,kleɪ) *n* a grey or whitish clay rock containing fossilized plant roots and occurring beneath coal seams. When used as a refractory, it is known as fireclay

underclothes ('ʌndə,kləʊðz) *pl n* a variant of **underwear**. Also called: **underclothing**

undercoat ('ʌndə,kəʊt) *n* **1** a coat of paint or other substance applied before the top coat **2** a coat worn under an overcoat **3** *zoology* another name for **underfur** **4** the US name for **underseal** ▷ *vb* **5** (*tr*) to apply an undercoat to (a surface)

undercool (,ʌndə'kuːl) *vb* a less common word for **supercool**

undercover (,ʌndə'kʌvə) *adj* done or acting in secret: *undercover operations*

undercroft ('ʌndə,krɒft) *n* an underground chamber, such as a church crypt, often with a vaulted ceiling [c14 from *croft* a vault, cavern, from earlier *crofte*, ultimately from Latin *crypta* CRYPT]

undercurrent ('ʌndə,kʌrənt) *n* **1** a current that is not apparent at the surface or lies beneath another current **2** an opinion, emotion, etc, lying beneath apparent feeling or meaning ▷ Also called: **underflow**

undercut *vb* (,ʌndə'kʌt, 'ʌndə,kʌt) **-cuts, -cutting, -cut** **1** to charge less than (a competitor) in order to obtain trade **2** to cut away the under part of (something) **3** *sport* to hit (a ball) in such a way as to impart backspin to the ball ▷ *n* ('ʌndə,kʌt) **4** the act or an instance of cutting underneath **5** a part that is cut away underneath **6** a tenderloin of beef, including the fillet **7** *forestry, chiefly US and Canadian* a notch cut in a tree trunk, to ensure a clean break in felling **8** *sport* a stroke that imparts backspin to the ball

underdaks ('ʌndə,dæks) *pl n Austral* an informal word for **underpants**

underdevelop (,ʌndədɪ'vɛləp) *vb* (*tr*) *photog* to process (a film, plate, or paper) in developer for less than the required time, or at too low a temperature, or in an exhausted solution > ,underde'velopment *n*

underdeveloped (,ʌndədɪ'vɛləpt) *adj* **1** immature or undersized **2** relating to societies in which both the surplus capital and the social organization necessary to advance are lacking **3** *photog* (of a film, plate, or print) processed in developer for less than the required time, thus lacking in contrast

underdog ('ʌndə,dɒg) *n* **1** the competitor least likely to win a fight or contest **2** a person in adversity or in a position of inferiority

underdone (,ʌndə'dʌn) *adj* insufficiently or lightly cooked

underdrain *n* (,ʌndə,dreɪn) **1** a drain buried below agricultural land ▷ *vb* (,ʌndə'dreɪn) **2** to bury such drains below (agricultural land) > 'under,drainage *n*

underdressed (,ʌndə'drɛst) *adj* wearing clothes that are not elaborate or formal enough for a particular occasion

underemployed (,ʌndərɪm'plɔɪd) *adj* not fully or adequately employed > ,underem'ployment *n*

underestimate *vb* (,ʌndər'ɛstɪ,meɪt) (*tr*) **1** to make too low an estimate of: *he underestimated the cost* **2** to think insufficiently highly of: *to underestimate a person* ▷ *n* (,ʌndər'ɛstɪmɪt) **3** too low an estimate > ,under,esti'mation *n*

USAGE *Underestimate* is sometimes wrongly used where *overestimate* is meant: *the importance of his work cannot be overestimated* (not *cannot be underestimated*)

underexpose (,ʌndərɪk'spəʊz) *vb* (*tr*) **1** *photog* to expose (a film, plate, or paper) for too short a period or with insufficient light so as not to produce the required effect **2** (*often passive*) to fail to subject to appropriate or expected publicity

underexposure (,ʌndərɪk'spəʊʒə) *n* **1** *photog* **a** inadequate exposure to light **b** an underexposed negative, print, or transparency **2** insufficient attention or publicity

underfeed *vb* (,ʌndə'fiːd) **-feeds, -feeding, -fed** (*tr*) **1** to give too little food to **2** to supply (a furnace, engine, etc) with fuel from beneath ▷ *n* ('ʌndə,fiːd) **3** an apparatus by which fuel, etc, is supplied from below

underfelt ('ʌndə,fɛlt) *n* thick felt laid between floorboards and carpet to increase insulation and resilience

underfloor ('ʌndə,flɔː) *adj* situated beneath the floor: *underfloor heating*

underflow ('ʌndə,fləʊ) *n* **1** another word for **undercurrent** **2** *computing* a condition that occurs when arithmetic operations produce results too small to store in the available register

underfoot (ˌʌndəˈfʊt) *adv* **1** underneath the feet; on the ground **2** in a position of subjugation or subservience **3** in the way

underfunded (ˌʌndəˈfʌndɪd) *adj* having or provided with insufficient funding

underfur (ˈʌndəˌfɜː) *n* the layer of dense soft fur occurring beneath the outer coarser fur in certain mammals, such as the otter and seal. Also called: **undercoat** (sense 3)

undergarment (ˈʌndəˌɡɑːmənt) *n* any garment worn under the visible outer clothes, usually next to the skin

undergird (ˌʌndəˈɡɜːd) *vb* -girds, -girding, -girded or -girt (*tr*) to strengthen or reinforce by passing a rope, cable, or chain around the underside of (an object, load, etc) [C16 from UNDER- + GIRD¹]

underglaze (ˈʌndəˌɡleɪz) *adj* **1** *ceramics* applied to pottery or porcelain before the application of glaze ▷ *n* **2** a pigment, etc, applied in this way

undergo (ˌʌndəˈɡəʊ) *vb* -goes, -going, -went, -gone (*tr*) to experience, endure, or sustain: *to undergo a dramatic change of feelings* [Old English: earlier meanings were more closely linked with the senses of *under* and *go*] ▷ ˈunderˌgoer *n*

undergraduate (ˌʌndəˈɡrædjʊɪt) *n* a person studying in a university for a first degree. Sometimes shortened to: **undergrad** ▷ ˌunderˈgraduateship *n*

underground *adj* (ˈʌndəˌɡraʊnd) ▷ *adv* (ˌʌndəˈɡraʊnd) **1** occurring, situated, used, or going below ground level: *an underground tunnel; an underground explosion* ▷ *n* (ˈʌndəˌɡraʊnd) **3** a space or region below ground level **4 a** a movement dedicated to overthrowing a government or occupation forces, as in the European countries occupied by the German army in World War II **b** (*as modifier*): *an underground group* **5** (*often preceded by the*) an electric passenger railway operated in underground tunnels. US and Canadian equivalent: **subway 6** (*usually preceded by the*) **a** any avant-garde, experimental, or subversive movement in popular art, films, music, etc **b** (*as modifier*): *the underground press; underground music*

underground railroad *n* (*often capitals*) (in the pre-Civil War US) the system established by abolitionists to aid escaping slaves

undergrown (ˈʌndəˌɡrəʊn, ˌʌndəˈɡrəʊn) *adj* **1** not having the expected height **2** having undergrowth

undergrowth (ˈʌndəˌɡrəʊθ) *n* **1** small trees, bushes, ferns, etc, growing beneath taller trees in a wood or forest **2** the condition of being undergrown **3** a growth of short fine hairs beneath longer ones; underfur

underhand (ˈʌndəˌhænd) *adj also* **underhanded 1** clandestine, deceptive, or secretive **2** *sport* another word for **underarm** ▷ *adv* **3** in an underhand manner or style

underhand chop *n* NZ (in an axemen's competition) a chop where the axeman stands on the log, which is placed on the ground. Compare **standing chop**

underhanded (ˌʌndəˈhændɪd) *adj* another word for **underhand** or **short-handed** ▷ ˌunderˈhandedly *adv* ▷ ˌunderˈhandedness *n*

underhung (ˌʌndəˈhʌŋ) *adj* **1** (of the lower jaw) projecting beyond the upper jaw; undershot **2** (of a sliding door, etc) supported at its lower edge by a track or rail

underinsured (ˌʌndərɪnˈʃʊəd) *adj* not having enough insurance to cover the cost of a loss

underlaid (ˌʌndəˈleɪd) *adj* **1** laid underneath **2** having an underlay or supporting layer underneath ▷ *vb* **3** the past tense and past participle of **underlay**

underlay *vb* (ˌʌndəˈleɪ) -lays, -laying, -laid (*tr*) **1** to place (something) under or beneath **2** to support by something laid beneath **3** to achieve the correct printing pressure all over (a forme block) or to bring (a block) up to type height by adding

material, such as paper, to the appropriate areas beneath it ▷ *n* (ˈʌndəˌleɪ) **4** a layer, lining, support, etc, laid underneath something else **5** *printing* material, such as paper, used to underlay a forme or block **6** felt, rubber, etc, laid beneath a carpet to increase insulation and resilience

underleaf (ˈʌndəˌliːf) *n* (in liverworts) any of the leaves forming a row on the underside of the stem: usually smaller than the two rows of lateral leaves and sometimes absent

underlet (ˌʌndəˈlɛt) *vb* -lets, -letting, -let (*tr*) **1** to let for a price lower than expected or justified **2** a less common word for **sublet.** ▷ ˈunderˌletter *n*

underlie (ˌʌndəˈlaɪ) *vb* -lies, -lying, -lay, -lain (*tr*) **1** to lie or be placed under or beneath **2** to be the foundation, cause, or basis of: *careful planning underlies all our decisions* **3** *finance* to take priority over (another claim, liability, mortgage, etc): *a first mortgage underlies a second* **4** to be the root or stem from which (a word) is derived: *"happy" underlies "happiest"* ▷ ˈunderˌlier *n*

underline *vb* (ˌʌndəˈlaɪn) (*tr*) **1** to put a line under **2** to state forcibly; emphasize or reinforce ▷ *n* (ˈʌndəˌlaɪn) **3** a line underneath, esp under written matter

underlinen (ˈʌndəˌlɪnən) *n* underclothes, esp when made of linen

underling (ˈʌndəlɪŋ) *n* a subordinate or lackey

underlying (ˌʌndəˈlaɪɪŋ) *adj* **1** concealed but detectable: *underlying guilt* **2** fundamental; basic **3** lying under **4** *finance* (of a claim, liability, etc) taking precedence; prior

undermentioned (ˈʌndəˌmɛnʃənd) *adj* mentioned below or subsequently

undermine (ˌʌndəˈmaɪn) *vb* (*tr*) **1** (of the sea, wind, etc) to wear away the bottom or base of (land, cliffs, etc) **2** to weaken gradually or insidiously: *their insults undermined her confidence* **3** to tunnel or dig beneath ▷ ˌunderˈminer *n*

undermost (ˈʌndəˌməʊst) *adj* **1** being the furthest under; lowest ▷ *adv* **2** in the lowest place

underneath (ˌʌndəˈniːθ) *prep, adv* **1** under; beneath ▷ *adj* **2** lower ▷ *n* **3** a lower part, surface, etc [Old English *underneothan,* from UNDER + *neothan* below; related to Old Danish *underneden;* see BENEATH]

undernourish (ˌʌndəˈnʌrɪʃ) *vb* (*tr; usually passive*) to deprive of or fail to provide with nutrients essential for health and growth ▷ ˌunderˈnourishment *n*

underpaid (ˌʌndəˈpeɪd) *adj* not paid enough: *underpaid and overworked*

underpainting (ˈʌndəˌpeɪntɪŋ) *n* the first layer in a painting, indicating the design and main areas of light and shade

underpants (ˈʌndəˌpænts) *pl n* a man's undergarment covering the body from the waist or hips to the top of the thighs or knees. Often shortened to: **pants**

underpass (ˈʌndəˌpɑːs) *n* **1** a section of a road that passes under another road, railway line, etc **2** another word for **subway** (sense 1)

underpay (ˌʌndəˈpeɪ) *vb* -pays, -paying, -paid to pay (someone) insufficiently ▷ ˌunderˈpayment *n*

underpin (ˌʌndəˈpɪn) *vb* -pins, -pinning, -pinned (*tr*) **1** to support from beneath, esp by a prop, while avoiding damaging or weakening the superstructure: *to underpin a wall* **2** to give corroboration, strength, or support to

underpinning (ˈʌndəˌpɪnɪŋ) *n* a structure of masonry, concrete, etc, placed beneath a wall to provide support

underpinnings (ˈʌndəˌpɪnɪŋz) *pl n* any supporting structure or system

underpitch vault (ˈʌndəˌpɪtʃ) *n architect* a vault that is intersected by one or more vaults of lower pitch

underplant (ˌʌndəˈplɑːnt) *vb* (*tr*) to plant smaller plants around (a larger plant)

underplay (ˌʌndəˈpleɪ) *vb* **1** to play (a role) with restraint or subtlety **2** to achieve (an effect) by deliberate lack of emphasis **3** (*intr*) *cards* to lead

or follow suit with a lower card when holding a higher one

underplot (ˈʌndəˌplɒt) *n* **1** a subsidiary plot in a literary or dramatic work **2** an undercover plot

underpopulated (ˌʌndəˈpɒpjʊˌleɪtɪd) *adj* having a low population rate

underpowered (ˌʌndəˈpaʊəd) *adj* lacking or low in power: *two-litre cars are underpowered*

underprice (ˌʌndəˈpraɪs) *vb* (*tr*) to price (an article for sale) at too low a level or amount

underprivileged (ˌʌndəˈprɪvɪlɪdʒd) *adj* lacking the rights and advantages of other members of society; deprived

underproduction (ˌʌndəprəˈdʌkʃən) *n commerce* production below full capacity or below demand

underproof (ˌʌndəˈpruːf) *adj* (of a spirit) containing less than 57.1 per cent alcohol by volume

underprop (ˌʌndəˈprɒp) *vb* -props, -propping, -propped (*tr*) to prop up from beneath ▷ ˈunderˌpropper *n*

underquote (ˌʌndəˈkwəʊt) *vb* **1** to offer for sale (securities, goods, or services) at a price lower than the market price **2** (*tr*) to quote a price lower than that quoted by (another)

underrate (ˌʌndəˈreɪt) *vb* (*tr*) to underestimate

undersaturated (ˌʌndəˈsætʃəˌreɪtɪd) *adj* (of an igneous rock) having a low silica content

underscore *vb* (ˌʌndəˈskɔː) (*tr*) **1** to draw or score a line or mark under **2** to stress or reinforce ▷ *n* (ˈʌndəˌskɔː) **3** a line drawn under written matter

undersea (ˈʌndəˌsiː) *adj, adv also* **underseas** (ˌʌndəˈsiːz) below the surface of the sea

underseal (ˈʌndəˌsiːl) *Brit* ▷ *n* **1** a coating of a tar or rubber-based material applied to the underside of a motor vehicle to retard corrosion. US name: **undercoat** ▷ *vb* **2** (*tr*) to apply a coating of underseal to (a motor vehicle)

undersecretary (ˌʌndəˈsɛkrətrɪ) *n, pl* -taries **1** (in Britain) **a** any of various senior civil servants in certain government departments **b** short for **undersecretary of state**: any of various high officials subordinate only to the minister in charge of a department **2** (in the US) a high government official subordinate only to the secretary in charge of a department ▷ ˌunderˈsecretaryˌship *n*

undersell (ˌʌndəˈsɛl) *vb* -sells, -selling, -sold **1** to sell for less than the usual or expected price **2** (*tr*) to sell at a price lower than that of (another seller) **3** (*tr*) to advertise (merchandise) with moderation or restraint ▷ ˈunderˌseller *n*

underset (ˈʌndəˌsɛt) *n* **1** an ocean undercurrent **2** an underlying vein of ore ▷ *vb* -sets, -setting, -set **3** (*tr*) to support from underneath

undersexed (ˌʌndəˈsɛkst) *adj* having weaker sex urges or responses than is considered normal

undersheriff (ˈʌndəˌʃɛrɪf) *n* a deputy sheriff

undershirt (ˈʌndəˌʃɜːt) *n chiefly US and Canadian* an undergarment worn under a blouse or shirt. Brit name: **vest**

undershoot (ˌʌndəˈʃuːt) *vb* -shoots, -shooting, -shot **1** (of a pilot) to cause (an aircraft) to land short of (a runway) or (of an aircraft) to land in this way **2** to shoot a projectile so that it falls short of (a target)

undershorts (ˈʌndəˌʃɔːts) *pl n* another word for **shorts** (sense 2)

undershot (ˈʌndəˌʃɒt) *adj* **1** (of the lower jaw) projecting beyond the upper jaw; underhung **2** (of a water wheel) driven by a flow of water that passes under the wheel rather than over it. Compare **overshot**

undershrub (ˈʌndəˌʃrʌb) *n* another name for **subshrub**

underside (ˈʌndəˌsaɪd) *n* the bottom or lower surface

undersigned (ˈʌndəˌsaɪnd) *n* **1** **the** the person or persons who have signed at the foot of a document, statement, etc ▷ *adj* **2** having signed one's name at the foot of a document, statement, etc **3** (of a document) signed at the foot **4** signed at the foot of a document

undersized (ˌʌndəˈsaɪzd) *adj* of less than usual size

underskirt (ˈʌndəˌskɜːt) *n* any skirtlike garment worn under a skirt

underslung (ˌʌndəˈslʌŋ) *adj* 1 suspended below a supporting member, esp (of a motor vehicle chassis) suspended below the axles 2 having a low centre of gravity

undersoil (ˈʌndəˌsɔɪl) *n* another word for **subsoil** (sense 1a)

underspend (ˌʌndəˈspɛnd) *vb* -spends, -spending, -spent 1 to spend less than (one can afford or is allocated) ▷ *n* (ˈʌndəˌspɛnd) 2 the amount by which someone or something is underspend

understaffed (ˌʌndəˈstɑːft) *adj* not having enough staff: *her department is understaffed*

understand (ˌʌndəˈstænd) *vb* -stands, -standing, -stood 1 (*may take a clause as object*) to know and comprehend the nature or meaning of: *I understand you* 2 (*may take a clause as object*) to realize or grasp (something) 3 (*tr; may take a clause as object*) to assume, infer, or believe 4 (*tr*) to know how to translate or read: *can you understand Spanish?* 5 (*tr; may take a clause as object; often passive*) to accept as a condition or proviso 6 (*tr*) to be sympathetic to or compatible with: *we understand each other* [Old English *understandan*; related to Old Frisian *understonda*, Middle High German *understān* step under; see UNDER, STAND] ▷ ˌunderˈstandable *adj* ▷ ˌunderˈstandably *adv*

understanding (ˌʌndəˈstændɪŋ) *n* 1 the ability to learn, judge, make decisions, etc; intelligence or sense 2 personal opinion or interpretation of a subject: *my understanding of your predicament* 3 a mutual agreement or compact, esp an informal or private one 4 *chiefly Brit* an unofficial engagement to be married 5 *philosophy archaic* the mind, esp the faculty of reason 6 **on the understanding that** with the condition that; providing ▷ *adj* 7 sympathetic, tolerant, or wise towards people 8 possessing judgment and intelligence ▷ ˌunderˈstandingly *adv*

understate (ˌʌndəˈsteɪt) *vb* 1 to state (something) in restrained terms, often to obtain an ironic effect 2 to state that (something, such as a number) is less than it is

understatement (ˌʌndəˈsteɪtmənt) *n* the act or an instance of stating something in restrained terms, or as less than it is

understeer (ˌʌndəˈstɪə) *vb* (*intr*) (of a vehicle) to turn less sharply, for a particular movement of the steering wheel, than anticipated

understood (ˌʌndəˈstʊd) *vb* 1 the past tense and past participle of **understand** ▷ *adj* 2 implied or inferred 3 taken for granted; assumed

understorey (ˌʌndəˈstɔːrɪ) *n* a lower tier of shrubs and small trees under the main canopy of forest trees

understrapper (ˈʌndəˌstræpə) *n* a less common word for **underling** [c18 from STRAP (in the archaic sense: to work hard)]

understudy (ˈʌndəˌstʌdɪ) *vb* -studies, -studying, -studied 1 (*tr*) to study (a role or part) so as to be able to replace the usual actor or actress if necessary 2 to act as understudy to (an actor or actress) ▷ *n, pl* -studies 3 an actor or actress who studies a part so as to be able to replace the usual actor or actress if necessary 4 anyone who is trained to take the place of another in case of need

undertake (ˌʌndəˈteɪk) *vb* -takes, -taking, -took, -taken 1 (*tr*) to contract to or commit oneself to (something) or (to do something): *to undertake a job; to undertake to deliver the goods* 2 (*tr*) to attempt to; agree to start 3 (*tr*) to take (someone) in charge 4 (*intr; foll by for*) *archaic* to make oneself responsible (for) 5 (*tr*) to promise

undertaker (ˈʌndəˌteɪkə) *n* a person whose profession is the preparation of the dead for burial or cremation and the management of funerals; funeral director

undertaking (ˈʌndəˌteɪkɪŋ) *n* 1 something undertaken; task, venture, or enterprise 2 an agreement to do something 3 the business of an undertaker 4 *informal* the practice of overtaking on an inner lane a vehicle which is travelling in an outer lane

under the table *adj* 1 (**under-the-table** when prenominal) done illicitly and secretly 2 *slang* drunk

underthings (ˈʌndəˌθɪŋz) *pl n* girls' or women's underwear

underthrust (ˈʌndəˌθrʌst) *n* *geology* a reverse fault in which the rocks on the lower surface of a fault plane have moved under the relatively static rocks on the upper surface. Compare **overthrust**

undertime (ˈʌndəˌtaɪm) *n* *informal* the time spent by an employee at work in non-work-related activities like socializing, surfing the internet, making personal telephone calls, etc

undertint (ˈʌndəˌtɪnt) *n* a slight, subdued, or delicate tint

undertone (ˈʌndəˌtəʊn) *n* 1 a quiet or hushed tone of voice 2 an underlying tone or suggestion in words or actions: *his offer has undertones of dishonesty* 3 a pale or subdued colour

undertook (ˌʌndəˈtʊk) *vb* the past tense of **undertake**

undertow (ˈʌndəˌtəʊ) *n* 1 the seaward undercurrent following the breaking of a wave on the beach 2 any strong undercurrent flowing in a different direction from the surface current

undertrick (ˈʌndəˌtrɪk) *n* *bridge* a trick by which a declarer falls short of making his contract

undertrump (ˌʌndəˈtrʌmp) *vb* (*intr*) *cards* to play a lower trump on a trick to which a higher trump has already been played

undervalue (ˌʌndəˈvæljuː) *vb* -values, -valuing, -valued (*tr*) to value at too low a level or price ▷ ˌunderˌvaluˈation *n* ▷ ˌunderˈvaluer *n*

undervest (ˈʌndəˌvɛst) *n* *Brit* another name for **vest** (sense 1)

underwater (ˈʌndəˈwɔːtə) *adj* 1 being, occurring, or going under the surface of the water, esp the sea: *underwater exploration* 2 *nautical* below the water line of a vessel 3 (of a stock option or other asset) having a market value below its purchase value ▷ *adv* 4 beneath the surface of the water

under way *adj* (*postpositive*) 1 in progress; in operation: *the show was under way* 2 *nautical* in motion

underwear (ˈʌndəˌwɛə) *n* clothing worn under the outer garments, usually next to the skin. Also called: **underclothes**

underweight (ˌʌndəˈweɪt) *adj* 1 weighing less than is average, expected, or healthy 2 *finance* **a** having a lower proportion of one's investments in a particular sector of the market than the size of that sector relative to the total market would suggest **b** (of a fund etc) disproportionately invested in this way

underwent (ˌʌndəˈwɛnt) *vb* the past tense of **undergo**

underwhelm (ˌʌndəˈwɛlm) *vb* (*tr*) to make no positive impact or impression on; disappoint [c20 originally a humorous coinage based on *overwhelm*]

underwhelming (ˌʌndəˈwɛlmɪŋ) *adj* failing to make a positive impact or impression; disappointing

underwing (ˈʌndəˌwɪŋ) *n* 1 the hind wing of an insect, esp when covered by the forewing 2 See **red underwing, yellow underwing**

underwood (ˈʌndəˌwʊd) *n* a less common word for **undergrowth**

underworld (ˈʌndəˌwɜːld) *n* 1 **a** criminals and their associates considered collectively **b** (*as modifier*): *underworld connections* 2 *Greek and Roman myth* the regions below the earth's surface regarded as the abode of the dead; Hades. Related adjs: **chthonian, chthonic**

underwrite (ˈʌndəˌraɪt, ˌʌndəˈraɪt) *vb* -writes, -writing, -wrote, -written (*tr*) 1 *finance* to undertake to purchase at an agreed price any

unsold portion of (a public issue of shares, etc) 2 to accept financial responsibility for (a commercial project or enterprise) 3 *insurance* **a** to sign and issue (an insurance policy) thus accepting liability if specified losses occur **b** to insure (a property or risk) **c** to accept liability up to (a specified amount) in an insurance policy 4 to write (words, a signature, etc) beneath (other written matter); subscribe 5 to support or concur with (a decision, statement, etc) by or as if by signature

underwriter (ˈʌndəˌraɪtə) *n* 1 a person or enterprise that underwrites public issues of shares, bonds, etc 2 **a** a person or enterprise that underwrites insurance policies **b** an employee or agent of an insurance company who assesses risks and determines the premiums payable

undescended (ˌʌndɪˈsɛndɪd) *adj* (of the testes) remaining in the abdominal cavity rather than descending to lie in the scrotum

undeserved (ˌʌndɪˈzɜːvd) *adj* not earned or merited; unwarranted: *an undeserved reputation*

undesigned (ˌʌndɪˈzaɪnd) *adj* 1 (of an action) unintentional 2 not yet designed

undesigning (ˌʌndɪˈzaɪnɪŋ) *adj* (of a person) frank; straightforward

undesirable (ˌʌndɪˈzaɪərəbəl) *adj* 1 not desirable or pleasant; objectionable ▷ *n* 2 a person or thing that is considered undesirable ▷ ˌundeˌsiraˈbility *or* ˌundeˈsirableness *n* ▷ ˌundeˈsirably *adv*

undetected (ˌʌndɪˈtɛktɪd) *adj* not perceived, noticed, or discovered: *the fake bomb passed undetected*

undetermined (ˌʌndɪˈtɜːmɪnd) *adj* 1 not yet resolved; undecided 2 not known or discovered

undeterred (ˌʌndɪˈtɜːd) *adj* not discouraged or dissuaded

undeveloped (ˌʌndɪˈvɛləpt) *adj* not having developed or been developed

undiagnosed (ˌʌndaɪəgˈnəʊzd) *adj* (of a medical condition, a problem, etc) not having been identified

undid (ʌnˈdɪd) *vb* the past tense of **undo**

undies (ˈʌndɪz) *pl n* *informal* women's underwear

undifferentiated (ˌʌndɪfəˈrɛnʃɪˌeɪtɪd) *adj* not having any distinguishing features

undignified (ʌnˈdɪgnɪˌfaɪd) *adj* lacking in dignity

undiluted (ˌʌndaɪˈluːtɪd) *adj* 1 not diluted with water or any other liquid: *undiluted fruit juice* 2 not moderated or qualified in any way

undiminished (ˌʌndɪˈmɪnɪʃt) *adj* not reduced or lessened

undimmed (ʌnˈdɪmd) *adj* 1 (of eyes, light, etc) still bright or shining 2 (of enthusiasm, admiration, etc) not diminished or lessened

undine (ˈʌndiːn) *n* any of various female water spirits [c17 from New Latin *undina*, from Latin *unda* a wave]

undiplomatic (ˌʌndɪpləˈmætɪk) *adj* lacking in diplomacy

undirected (ˌʌndɪˈrɛktɪd, -daɪ-) *adj* 1 lacking a clear purpose or objective 2 (of a letter, parcel, etc) having no address

undisciplined (ʌnˈdɪsɪˌplɪnd) *adj* not exhibiting self-control or good behaviour

undisclosed (ˌʌndɪsˈkləʊzd) *adj* not made known or revealed: *an undisclosed sum*

undiscovered (ˌʌndɪˈskʌvəd) *adj* not discovered or encountered

undisguised (ˌʌndɪsˈgaɪzd) *adj* not disguised or concealed: *with undisguised glee*

undisputed (ˌʌndɪˈspjuːtɪd) *adj* not challenged or questioned; accepted: *of undisputed importance*

undisputed world champion *n* *boxing* a boxer who holds the World Boxing Association, the World Boxing Council, the World Boxing Organization, and the International Boxing Federation world championship titles simultaneously

undistinguished (ˌʌndɪˈstɪŋgwɪʃt) *adj* 1 not particularly good or bad 2 without distinction

undistributed (ˌʌndɪsˈtrɪbjʊtɪd) *adj* 1 *logic* (of a

u

term) referring only to some members of the class designated by the term, as *doctors* in *some doctors are overworked* **2** *business* (of a profit) not paid in dividends to the shareholders of a company but retained to help finance its trading

undisturbed (ˌʌndɪˈstɜːbd) *adj* not disturbed; uninterrupted: *lots of undisturbed sleep*

undivided (ˌʌndɪˈvaɪdɪd) *adj* **1** not divided into parts or groups **2** concentrated on one object, idea, etc: *undivided attention*

undo (ʌnˈduː) *vb* -does, -doing, -did, -done (*mainly tr*) **1** (*also intr*) to untie, unwrap, or open or become untied, unwrapped, etc **2** to reverse the effects of **3** to cause the downfall of **4** *obsolete* to explain or solve > un'doer *n*

undoing (ʌnˈduːɪŋ) *n* **1** ruin; downfall **2** the cause of downfall: *drink was his undoing*

undone¹ (ʌnˈdʌn) *adj* not done or completed; unfinished

undone² (ʌnˈdʌn) *adj* **1** ruined; destroyed **2** unfastened; untied

undoubted (ʌnˈdaʊtɪd) *adj* beyond doubt; certain or indisputable

undoubtedly (ʌnˈdaʊtɪdlɪ) *adv* **1** certainly or definitely; unquestionably: *he is undoubtedly talented* **2** (*sentence modifier*) without doubt; certainly or indisputably: *undoubtedly there will be changes*

undreamed (ʌnˈdriːmd) *or* **undreamt** (ʌnˈdrɛmt) *adj* (often foll by *of*) not thought of, conceived, or imagined

undress *vb* (ʌnˈdrɛs) **1** to take off clothes from (oneself or another) **2** (*tr*) to strip of ornamentation **3** (*tr*) to remove the dressing from (a wound) ⊳ *n* (ʌnˈdrɛs) **4** partial or complete nakedness **5** informal or normal working clothes or uniform ⊳ *adj* (ˈʌndrɛs) **6** characterized by or requiring informal or normal working dress or uniform

undressed (ʌnˈdrɛst) *adj* **1** partially or completely naked **2** (of an animal hide) not fully processed **3** (of food, esp salad) not prepared with sauce or dressing

undrinkable (ʌnˈdrɪŋkəbəl) *adj* not pleasant or safe enough to be drunk

UNDRO (ˈʌnˌdrəʊ) *n acronym for* United Nations Disaster Relief Organization

undue (ʌnˈdjuː) *adj* **1** excessive or unwarranted **2** unjust, improper, or illegal **3** (of a debt, bond, etc) not yet payable

USAGE The use of *undue* in sentences such as *there is no cause for undue alarm* is redundant and should be avoided

undulant (ˈʌndjʊlənt) *adj rare* resembling waves; undulating > 'undulance *n*

undulant fever *n* another name for **brucellosis** [c19 so called because the fever symptoms are intermittent]

undulate (ˈʌndjʊˌleɪt) *vb* **1** to move or cause to move in waves or as if in waves **2** to have or provide with a wavy form or appearance ⊳ *adj* (ˈʌndjʊlɪt, -ˌleɪt) *also* **undulated 3** having a wavy or rippled appearance, margin, or form: *an undulate leaf* [c17 from Latin *undulātus*, from *unda* a wave] > 'undu,lator *n*

undulation (ˌʌndjʊˈleɪʃən) *n* **1** the act or an instance of undulating **2** any wave or wavelike form, line, etc

undulatory (ˈʌndjʊlətərɪ, -trɪ) *adj* **1** caused by or characterized by waves or undulations **2** having a wavelike motion or form

unduly (ʌnˈdjuːlɪ) *adv* **1** immoderately; excessively **2** in contradiction of moral or legal standards

undying (ʌnˈdaɪɪŋ) *adj* unending; eternal > un'dyingly *adv*

unearned (ʌnˈɜːnd) *adj* **1** not deserved **2** not yet earned

unearned income *n* income from property, investment, etc, comprising rent, interest, and dividends

unearned increment *n* a rise in the market value of landed property resulting from general economic factors

unearth (ʌnˈɜːθ) *vb* (*tr*) **1** to dig up out of the earth **2** to reveal or discover, esp by exhaustive searching

unearthly (ʌnˈɜːθlɪ) *adj* **1** ghostly; eerie; weird: *unearthly screams* **2** heavenly; sublime: *unearthly music* **3** ridiculous or unreasonable (esp in the phrase **unearthly hour**) > un'earthliness *n*

uneasy (ʌnˈiːzɪ) *adj* **1** (of a person) anxious; apprehensive **2** (of a condition) precarious; uncomfortable: *an uneasy truce* **3** (of a thought, etc) disturbing; disquieting > un'ease *n* > un'easily *adv* > un'easiness *n*

uneatable (ʌnˈiːtəbəl) *adj* not pleasant or safe enough to be eaten

uneaten (ʌnˈiːtən) *adj* (of food) not having been consumed; leftover

uneconomic (ˌʌniːkəˈnɒmɪk, ˌʌnɛkə-) *adj* not economic; not profitable

uneconomical (ˌʌniːkəˈnɒmɪkəl, ˌʌnɛkə-) *adj* not economical; wasteful

unedifying (ʌnˈɛdɪˌfaɪɪŋ) *adj* not having the result of improving morality, intellect, etc

uneducated (ʌnˈɛdjʊˌkeɪtɪd) *adj* not having been educated to a good standard: *poor uneducated people*

UNEF (ˈjuːnɛf) *n acronym for* United Nations Emergency Force

unelectable (ˌʌnɪˈlɛktəbəl) *adj* (of a political party, candidate, etc) not likely to be elected

unembarrassed (ˌʌnɪmˈbærəst) *adj* not embarrassed, disconcerted, or flustered

unemotional (ˌʌnɪˈməʊʃənəl) *adj* lacking in strong feeling

unemployable (ˌʌnɪmˈplɔɪəbəl) *adj* unable or unfit to keep a job > ˌunemˌploya'bility *n*

unemployed (ˌʌnɪmˈplɔɪd) *adj* **1 a** without remunerative employment; out of work **b** (*as collective noun; preceded by the*): *the unemployed* **2** not being used; idle

unemployment (ˌʌnɪmˈplɔɪmənt) *n* **1** the condition of being unemployed **2** the number of unemployed workers, often as a percentage of the total labour force

unemployment benefit *n* **1** (in Britain, formerly) a regular payment to a person who is out of work: replaced by jobseeker's allowance in 1996. Informal term: **dole 2** (in New Zealand) a means-tested monetary benefit paid weekly by the Social Security Department to the unemployed

unemployment compensation *n* (in the US) payment by a governmental agency to unemployed people

unencumbered (ˌʌnɪnˈkʌmbəd) *adj* not burdened, impeded, or hampered

unending (ʌnˈɛndɪŋ) *adj* having or seeming to have no end; interminable

unendurable (ˌʌnɪnˈdjʊərəbəl) *adj* not able to be undergone or tolerated; insufferable

unenforced (ˌʌnɪnˈfɔːst) *adj* (of a law, decision, etc) not having been imposed or enforced

unenlightened (ˌʌnɪnˈlaɪtənd) *adj* not well-informed, tolerant, or rational

unentered (ʌnˈɛntəd) *adj* **1** not having been entered previously **2** (of hounds) not having been put into a pack yet

unenthusiastic (ˌʌnɪnθjuːzɪˈæstɪk) *adj* lacking in enthusiasm

unenviable (ʌnˈɛnvɪəbəl) *adj* not to be envied

unequal (ʌnˈiːkwəl) *adj* **1** not equal in quantity, size, rank, value, etc **2** (foll by *to*) inadequate; insufficient **3** not evenly balanced **4** (of character, quality, etc) irregular; varying; inconsistent **5** (of a contest, etc) having competitors of different ability **6** *obsolete* unjust > un'equally *adv*

unequalled *or US* **unequaled** (ʌnˈiːkwəld) *adj* not equalled; unparalleled or unrivalled; supreme

unequipped (ˌʌnɪˈkwɪpt) *adj* not furnished with the necessary supplies, abilities, etc

unequivocal (ˌʌnɪˈkwɪvəkəl) *adj* not ambiguous; plain > ˌune'quivocally *adv* > ˌune'quivocalness *n*

unerring (ʌnˈɜːrɪŋ) *adj* **1** not missing the mark or target **2** consistently accurate; certain > un'erringly *adv* > un'erringness *n*

UNESCO (juːˈnɛskəʊ) *n acronym for* United Nations Educational, Scientific, and Cultural Organization: an agency of the United Nations that sponsors programmes to promote education, communication, the arts, etc

unescorted (ˌʌnɪsˈkɔːtɪd) *adj* not accompanied by an escort

unessential (ˌʌnɪˈsɛnʃəl) *adj* **1** a less common word for **inessential** ⊳ *n* **2** something that is not essential > ˌunes'sentially *adv*

unethical (ʌnˈɛθɪkəl) *adj* not ethical; improper

uneven (ʌnˈiːvən) *adj* **1** (of a surface, etc) not level or flat **2** spasmodic or variable **3** not parallel, straight, or horizontal **4** not fairly matched: *an uneven race* **5** *archaic* not equal **6** *obsolete* unjust > un'evenly *adv* > un'evenness *n*

uneventful (ˌʌnɪˈvɛntfʊl) *adj* ordinary, routine, or quiet > ˌune'ventfully *adv* > ˌune'ventfulness *n*

unexampled (ˌʌnɪɡˈzɑːmpəld) *adj* without precedent or parallel

unexceptionable (ˌʌnɪkˈsɛpʃənəbəl) *adj* beyond criticism or objection > ˌunex'ceptionableness *or* ˌunex,ceptiona'bility *n* > ˌunex'ceptionably *adv*

unexceptional (ˌʌnɪkˈsɛpʃənəl) *adj* **1** usual, ordinary, or normal **2** subject to or allowing no exceptions **3** *not standard* another word for **unexceptionable.** > ˌunex'ceptionally *adv*

unexcited (ˌʌnɪkˈsaɪtɪd) *adj* **1** not aroused to pleasure, interest, agitation, etc **2** (of an atom, molecule, etc) remaining in its ground state

unexciting (ˌʌnɪkˈsaɪtɪŋ) *adj* not interesting, stirring, or stimulating: *unexciting but likable*

unexpected (ˌʌnɪkˈspɛktɪd) *adj* surprising or unforeseen > ˌunex'pectedly *adv* > ˌunex'pectedness *n*

unexperienced (ˌʌnɪkˈspɪərɪənst) *adj* **1** (of a situation, sensation, fact, etc) not having been undergone or known by experience **2** inexperienced

unexplained (ˌʌnɪkˈspleɪnd) *adj* not explained or understood > ˌunex'plainable *adj*

unexploited (ˌʌnɪksˈplɔɪtɪd) *adj* (of resources) not being used effectively: *rich with unexploited minerals*

unexplored (ˌʌnɪkˈsplɔːd) *adj* not having been explored

unexposed (ˌʌnɪkˈspəʊzd) *adj* **1** not having been exhibited or brought to public notice **2** (of a slide, photograph, etc) not having been subjected to the exposure process

unexpressed (ˌʌnɪkˈsprɛst) *adj* **1** not expressed or said **2** understood without being expressed

unexpurgated (ʌnˈɛkspəˌɡeɪtɪd) *adj* (of a book, text, etc) not amended or censored by removing potentially offensive material

unfailing (ʌnˈfeɪlɪŋ) *adj* **1** not failing; unflagging **2** continuous or unceasing **3** sure; certain > un'failingly *adv* > un'failingness *n*

unfair (ʌnˈfɛə) *adj* **1** characterized by inequality or injustice **2** dishonest or unethical > un'fairly *adv* > un'fairness *n*

unfaithful (ʌnˈfeɪθfʊl) *adj* **1** not true to a promise, vow, etc **2** not true to a wife, husband, lover, etc, esp in having sexual intercourse with someone else **3** inaccurate; inexact; unreliable **4** *obsolete* not having religious faith; infidel **5** *obsolete* not upright; dishonest > un'faithfully *adv* > un'faithfulness *n*

unfamiliar (ˌʌnfəˈmɪljə) *adj* **1** not known or experienced; strange **2** (*postpositive*; foll by *with*) not familiar > unfamiliarity (ˌʌnfəˌmɪlɪˈærɪtɪ) *n* > ˌunfa'miliarly *adv*

unfashionable (ʌnˈfæʃənəbəl) *adj* not fashionable

unfasten (ʌnˈfɑːsən) *vb* to undo, untie, or open or become undone, untied, or opened

unfathered (ʌnˈfɑːðəd) *adj* **1** having no known father **2** of unknown or uncertain origin **3** *archaic* fatherless

unfathomable (ʌnˈfæðəməbəl) *adj* **1** incapable of being fathomed; immeasurable **2**

incomprehensible > un'fathomableness *n*
> un'fathomably *adv*

unfavourable *or US* **unfavorable** (ʌnˈfeɪvərəbᵊl, -ˈfeɪvrə-) *adj* not favourable; adverse or inauspicious > unˈfavourableness *or US* unˈfavorableness *n* > unˈfavourably *or US* unˈfavorably *adv*

unfavoured *or US* **unfavored** (ʌnˈfeɪvəd) *adj* **1** not regarded with especial kindness or approval **2** not regarded with partiality or favouritism

unfazed (ʌnˈfeɪzd) *adj informal* not disconcerted; unperturbed

unfeasible (ʌnˈfiːzəbᵊl) *adj* not able to be done or put into effect; impossible

Unfederated Malay States (ʌnˈfedəˌreɪtɪd) *pl n* a former group of native states in the Malay Peninsula that became British protectorates between 1885 and 1909. All except Brunei joined the Malayan Union (later Federation of Malaya) in 1946. Brunei joined the Federation of Malaysia in 1963 but later became an independent nation

unfeeling (ʌnˈfiːlɪŋ) *adj* **1** without sympathy; callous **2** without physical feeling or sensation > unˈfeelingly *adv* > unˈfeelingness *n*

unfertilized *or* **unfertilised** (ʌnˈfɜːtɪˌlaɪzd) *adj* (of an animal, plant, or egg cell) not fertilized

unfetter (ʌnˈfetə) *vb* (*tr*) **1** to release from fetters, bonds, etc **2** to release from restraint or inhibition

unfettered (ʌnˈfetəd) *adj* released from physical or mental bonds; unrestrained

unfilled (ʌnˈfɪld) *adj* **1** (of a container, receptacle, etc) not having become or been made full: *unfilled stomachs* **2** (of a job, role, etc) not occupied **3** (of a cake, doughnut, etc) with no filling

unfiltered (ʌnˈfɪltəd) *adj* **1** (of oil, coffee, smoke, etc) not having been passed through a filter **2** not having been toned down, censored, or edited **3** (of a cigarette) not having a filter tip

unfinished (ʌnˈfɪnɪʃt) *adj* **1** incomplete or imperfect **2** (of paint, polish, varnish, etc) without an applied finish; rough **3** (of fabric) unbleached or not processed **4** (of fabric) with a short nap

unfit (ʌnˈfɪt) *adj* **1** (*postpositive; often foll by for*) unqualified, incapable, or incompetent **2** (*postpositive; often foll by for*) unsuitable or inappropriate **3** in poor physical condition > unˈfitness *n*

unfitted (ʌnˈfɪtɪd) *adj* unsuitable: *unused to and unfitted for any form of manual labour*

unfix (ʌnˈfɪks) *vb* (*tr*) **1** to unfasten, detach, or loosen **2** to unsettle or disturb

unflagging (ʌnˈflægɪŋ) *adj* not declining in strength or vigour; tireless

unflappable (ʌnˈflæpəbᵊl) *adj informal* hard to upset; imperturbable; calm; composed > unˌflappaˈbility *or* unˈflappableness *n* > unˈflappably *adv*

unflattering (ʌnˈflætərɪŋ) *adj* not flattering

unfledged (ʌnˈfledʒd) *adj* **1** (of a young bird) not having developed adult feathers **2** immature and undeveloped

unflinching (ʌnˈflɪntʃɪŋ) *adj* not shrinking from danger, difficulty, etc > unˈflinchingly *adv*

unfold (ʌnˈfəʊld) *vb* **1** to open or spread out or be opened or spread out from a folded state **2** to reveal or be revealed: *the truth unfolds* **3** to develop or expand or be developed or expanded > unˈfolder *n*

unforced (ʌnˈfɔːst) *adj* not forced or having been forced: *unforced errors*

unforeseeable (ˌʌnfɔːˈsiːəbᵊl) *adj* not able to be foreseen or known beforehand

unforeseen (ˌʌnfɔːˈsiːn) *adj* not seen or known beforehand; unanticipated

unforgettable (ˌʌnfəˈgetəbᵊl) *adj* impossible to forget; highly memorable > ˌunforˈgettably *adv*

unforgivable (ˌʌnfəˈgɪvəbᵊl) *adj* so bad as to be unable to be excused or pardoned

unforgiving (ˌʌnfəˈgɪvɪŋ) *adj* **1** not willing to forgive; unmerciful **2** (of a machine, system, etc)

allowing little or no opportunity for mistakes to be corrected **3** harsh and unremitting

unformed (ʌnˈfɔːmd) *adj* **1** shapeless **2** immature

unforthcoming (ˌʌnfɔːˈθkʌmɪŋ) *adj* not inclined to talk about something: *she was unforthcoming about her past*

unfortunate (ʌnˈfɔːtʃənɪt) *adj* **1** causing or attended by misfortune **2** unlucky, unsuccessful, or unhappy **3** regrettable or unsuitable ▷ *n* **4** an unlucky person > unˈfortunateness *n*

unfortunately (ʌnˈfɔːtʃənɪtlɪ) *adv* (*sentence modifier*) it is regrettable that; unluckily

unfounded (ʌnˈfaʊndɪd) *adj* **1** (of ideas, allegations, etc) baseless; groundless **2** not yet founded or established > unˈfoundedly *adv* > unˈfoundedness *n*

unfranked income (ʌnˈfræŋkt) *n* any income from an investment that does not qualify as franked investment income

unfreeze (ʌnˈfriːz) *vb* -freezes, -freezing, -froze, -frozen **1** to thaw or cause to thaw **2** (*tr*) to relax governmental restrictions on (wages, prices, credit, etc) or on the manufacture or sale of (goods, etc)

unfriended (ʌnˈfrendɪd) *adj now rare* without a friend or friends; friendless

unfriendly (ʌnˈfrendlɪ) *adj* -lier, -liest **1** not friendly; hostile **2** unfavourable or disagreeable ▷ *adv* **3** *rare* in an unfriendly manner > unˈfriendliness *n*

unfrock (ʌnˈfrɒk) *vb* (*tr*) to deprive (a person in holy orders) of ecclesiastical status

unfruitful (ʌnˈfruːtfʊl) *adj* **1** barren, unproductive, or unprofitable **2** failing to produce or develop into fruit > unˈfruitfully *adv* > unˈfruitfulness *n*

unfulfilled (ˌʌnfʊlˈfɪld) *adj* **1** not completed or achieved: *unfulfilled ambitions* **2** not having achieved one's potential or desires

unfunded debt (ʌnˈfʌndɪd) *n* a short-term floating debt not represented by bonds

unfunny (ʌnˈfʌnɪ) *adj* -nier, -niest not funny

unfurl (ʌnˈfɜːl) *vb* to unroll, unfold, or spread out or be unrolled, unfolded, or spread out from a furled state

unfurnished (ʌnˈfɜːnɪʃt) *adj* (of a room, property, etc) not having any furniture

unfussy (ʌnˈfʌsɪ) *adj* unfussier, unfussiest **1** not characterized by overelaborate detail **2** not particular

ungainly (ʌnˈgeɪnlɪ) *adj* -lier, -liest **1** lacking grace when moving **2** difficult to move or use; unwieldy **3** *rare* crude or coarse ▷ *adv* **4** *rare* clumsily [c17 from UN-¹ + obsolete or dialect GAINLY graceful] > unˈgainliness *n*

Ungava (ʊŋˈgeɪvə, -ˈgɑː-) *n* a sparsely inhabited region of NE Canada, in N Quebec east of Hudson Bay, part of the Labrador peninsula: rich mineral resources. Area: 911 110 sq km (351 780 sq miles)

ungenerous (ʌnˈdʒenərəs, -ˈdʒenrəs) *adj* not willing and liberal in giving away one's money, time, etc

unglamorous (ʌnˈglæmərəs) *adj* lacking in glamour, allure, or fascination: *the unglamorous side of the music business*

ungodly (ʌnˈgɒdlɪ) *adj* -lier, -liest **1 a** wicked; sinful **b** (*as collective noun; preceded by the*): *the ungodly* **2** *informal* unseemly; outrageous (esp in the phrase **an ungodly hour**) > unˈgodliness *n*

ungotten (ʌnˈgɒtᵊn) *adj archaic* not obtained or won

ungovernable (ʌnˈgʌvənəbᵊl) *adj* not able to be disciplined, restrained, etc: *an ungovernable temper* > unˈgovernableness *n* > unˈgovernably *adv*

ungracious (ʌnˈgreɪʃəs) *adj* not characterized by or showing kindness and courtesy

ungrammatical (ˌʌngrəˈmætɪkᵊl) *adj* (of a sentence) not regarded as correct by native speakers of the language

ungrateful (ʌnˈgreɪtfʊl) *adj* **1** not grateful or thankful **2** unrewarding or unpleasant;

thankless **3** (of land) failing to increase fertility in response to cultivation > unˈgratefully *adv* > unˈgratefulness *n*

ungrudging (ʌnˈgrʌdʒɪŋ) *adj* liberal; unstinted; willing: *ungrudging support* > unˈgrudgingly *adv*

ungual (ˈʌŋgwəl) *or* **ungular** (ˈʌŋgjʊlə) *adj* **1** of, relating to, or affecting the fingernails or toenails **2** of or relating to an unguis [c19 from Latin *unguis* nail, claw]

unguarded (ʌnˈgɑːdɪd) *adj* **1** unprotected; vulnerable **2** guileless; open; frank **3** incautious or careless > unˈguardedly *adv* > unˈguardedness *n*

unguent (ˈʌŋgwənt) *n* a less common name for an **ointment** [c15 from Latin *unguentum,* from *unguere* to anoint] > ˈunguentary *adj*

unguiculate (ʌŋˈgwɪkjʊlɪt, -ˌleɪt) *adj* **1** (of mammals) having claws or nails **2** (of petals) having a clawlike base ▷ *n* **3** an unguiculate mammal [c19 from New Latin *unguiculātus,* from Latin *unguiculus,* diminutive of *unguis* nail, claw]

unguided (ʌnˈgaɪdɪd) *adj* **1** (of a missile, bomb, etc) not having a flight path controlled either by radio signals or internal preset or self-actuating homing devices **2** without a guide: *guided and unguided hikes*

unguinous (ˈʌŋgwɪnəs) *adj obsolete* fatty; greasy; oily [c17 from Latin *unguinōsus* oily, from *unguin-, unguen* a fatty substance, from *unguere* to anoint, besmear]

unguis (ˈʌŋgwɪs) *n, pl* -gues (-gwiːz) **1** a nail, claw, or hoof, or the part of the digit giving rise to it **2** the clawlike base of certain petals [c18 from Latin]

ungula (ˈʌŋgjʊlə) *n, pl* -lae (-ˌliː) **1** *maths* a truncated cone, cylinder, etc **2** a rare word for **hoof** [c18 from Latin: hoof, from *unguis* nail] > ˈungular *adj*

ungulate (ˈʌŋgjʊlɪt, -ˌleɪt) *n* any of a large group of mammals all of which have hooves: divided into odd-toed ungulates (see **perissodactyl**) and even-toed ungulates (see **artiodactyl**) [c19 from Late Latin *ungulātus* having hooves, from UNGULA]

unguligrade (ˈʌŋgjʊlɪˌgreɪd) *adj* (of horses, etc) walking on hooves [c19 from Latin *ungula* hoof + -GRADE]

unhair (ʌnˈheə) *vb* to remove the hair from (a hide)

unhallow (ʌnˈhæləʊ) *vb* (*tr*) *archaic* to desecrate

unhallowed (ʌnˈhæləʊd) *adj* **1** not consecrated or holy: *unhallowed ground* **2** sinful or profane

unhampered (ʌnˈhæmpəd) *adj* allowed to move or progress freely

unhand (ʌnˈhænd) *vb* (*tr*) *archaic or literary* to release from the grasp

unhandy (ʌnˈhændɪ) *adj* **1** not skilful with one's hands; clumsy; awkward **2** inconvenient

unhappy (ʌnˈhæpɪ) *adj* -pier, -piest **1** not joyful; sad or depressed **2** unfortunate or wretched **3** tactless or inappropriate **4** *archaic* unfavourable > unˈhappily *adv* > unˈhappiness *n*

unharmed (ʌnˈhɑːmd) *adj* not having sustained physical, moral, or mental injury

unharness (ʌnˈhɑːnɪs) *vb* (*tr*) **1** to remove the harness from (a horse, etc) **2** *archaic* to remove the armour from

unhatched (ʌnˈhætʃt) *adj* **1** (of an egg) not having broken to release the fully developed young **2** (of a bird, snake, etc) not having emerged from the egg **3** (of a plan, mission, etc) not having been fully developed or carried out

UNHCR *abbreviation for* United Nations High Commissioner for Refugees

unhealed (ʌnˈhiːld) *adj* not having healed physically, mentally, or emotionally

unhealthy (ʌnˈhelθɪ) *adj* -healthier, -healthiest **1** characterized by ill-health; sick; unwell **2** characteristic of, conducive to, or resulting from ill-health: *an unhealthy complexion; an unhealthy atmosphere* **3** morbid or unwholesome **4** *informal* dangerous; risky > unˈhealthily *adv* > unˈhealthiness *n*

unheard (ʌnˈhɜːd) *adj* **1** not heard; not perceived by the ear **2** not listened to or granted a hearing:

u

his warning went unheard **3** *archaic* unheard-of

unheard-of *adj* **1** previously unknown: *an unheard-of actress* **2** without precedent: *an unheard-of treatment* **3** highly offensive: *unheard-of behaviour*

unheated (ʌn'hiːtɪd) *adj* not having been warmed up

unheeded (ʌn'hiːdɪd) *adj* noticed or heard but disregarded

unhelm (ʌn'hɛlm) *vb* to remove the helmet of (oneself or another) [C15 from UN-² + HELM²]

unhelpful (ʌn'hɛlpfʊl) *adj* not serving a useful function

unheralded (ʌn'hɛrəldɪd) *adj* not previously announced, notified, or expected

unhesitating (ʌn'hɛzɪˌteɪtɪŋ) *adj* **1** steadfast; unwavering: *unhesitating loyalty* **2** without hesitation; prompt > **un'hesiˌtatingly** *adv*

unhindered (ʌn'hɪndəd) *adj* without hindrance: *he could proceed unhindered*

unhinge (ʌn'hɪndʒ) *vb (tr)* **1** to remove (a door, gate, etc) from its hinges **2** to derange or unbalance (a person, his mind, etc) **3** to disrupt or unsettle (a process or state of affairs) **4** (usually foll by *from*) to detach or dislodge

unhip (ʌn'hɪp) *adj* **unhipper, unhippest** *slang* not at all fashionable or up to date

unholy (ʌn'həʊlɪ) *adj* **-lier, -liest 1** not holy or sacred **2** immoral or depraved **3** *informal* outrageous or unnatural: *an unholy alliance* > **un'holiness** *n*

unhook (ʌn'hʊk) *vb* **1** *(tr)* to remove (something) from a hook **2** *(tr)* to unfasten the hook of (a dress, etc) **3** *(intr)* to become unfastened or be capable of unfastening: *the dress wouldn't unhook*

unhoped-for (ˌʌn'həʊptfɔː) *adj* (esp of something pleasant) not anticipated; unexpected

unhorse (ʌn'hɔːs) *vb (tr)* **1** *(usually passive)* to knock or throw from a horse **2** to overthrow or dislodge, as from a powerful position **3** *now rare* to unharness horses from (a carriage, etc)

unhouseled (ʌn'haʊzəld) *adj archaic* not having received the Eucharist [C16 from *un-* + obsolete *housel* to administer the sacrament, from Old English *hūsl* (n), *hūslian* (vb), of unknown origin]

unhurried (ʌn'hʌrɪd) *adj* leisurely or deliberate: *an unhurried walk* > **un'hurriedly** *adv*

unhurt (ʌn'hɜːt) *adj* not having sustained any injury

unhygienic (ˌʌnhaɪ'dʒiːnɪk) *adj* not promoting health or cleanliness; unsanitary

uni ('juːnɪ) *n informal* short for **university**

uni- *combining form* consisting of, relating to, or having only one: *unilateral; unisexual* [from Latin *ūnus* one]

Uniat ('juːnɪˌæt) *or* **Uniate** ('juːnɪɪt, -ˌeɪt) *adj* **1** designating any of the Eastern Churches that retain their own liturgy but submit to papal authority ▷ *n* **2** a member of one of these Churches [C19 from Russian *uniyat*, from Polish *unja* union, from Late Latin *ūniō*; see UNION] > **'UniˌatisM** *n*

uniaxial (ˌjuːnɪ'æksɪəl) *adj* **1** (esp of plants) having an unbranched main axis **2** (of a crystal) having only one direction along which double refraction of light does not occur > **ˌuni'axially** *adv*

unibrow ('juːnɪˌbraʊ) *n informal* a single eyebrow created when the two eyebrows meet in the middle above the bridge of the nose

unicameral (ˌjuːnɪ'kæmərəl) *adj* of or characterized by a single legislative chamber > **ˌuni'cameralism** *n* > **ˌuni'cameralist** *n* > **ˌuni'camerally** *adv*

UNICEF ('juːnɪˌsɛf) *n acronym for* United Nations Children's Fund (formerly, United Nations International Children's Emergency Fund): an agency of the United Nations that administers programmes to aid education and child and maternal health in developing countries

unicellular (ˌjuːnɪ'sɛljʊlə) *adj* (of organisms, such as protozoans and certain algae) consisting of a single cell > **ˌuniˌcellu'larity** *n*

Unicode ('juːnɪˌkəʊd) *n computing* a character set for all languages

unicolour *or US* **unicolor** ('juːnɪˌkʌlə) *adj* of one colour; monochromatic

unicorn ('juːnɪˌkɔːn) *n* **1** an imaginary creature usually depicted as a white horse with one long spiralled horn growing from its forehead **2** *Old Testament* a two-horned animal, thought to be either the rhinoceros or the aurochs (Deuteronomy 33:17): mistranslation in the Authorized Version of the original Hebrew [C13 from Old French *unicorne*, from Latin *ūnicornis* one-horned, from *ūnus* one + *cornu* a horn]

unicostate (ˌjuːnɪ'kɒsteɪt) *adj biology* having only one rib or riblike part: *unicostate leaves*

unicycle ('juːnɪˌsaɪkᵊl) *n* a one-wheeled vehicle driven by pedals, esp one used in a circus, etc. Also called: **monocycle** [from UNI- + CYCLE, on the model of TRICYCLE] > **'uniˌcyclist** *n*

unidentified (ˌʌnaɪ'dɛntɪˌfaɪd) *adj* not identified or recognized: *an unidentified man* > **ˌuni'dentiˌfiable** *adj*

unidirectional (ˌjuːnɪdɪ'rɛkʃənᵊl, -daɪ-) *adj* having, moving in, or operating in only one direction

UNIDO (juː'niːdəʊ) *n acronym for* United Nations Industrial Development Organization

UniFi *or* **UNiFI** ('juːnɪˌfaɪ) *n acronym for* Union Finance, a finance sector union [C20 from UNI(ON) + FI(NANCE)]

unific (juː'nɪfɪk) *adj rare* unifying; uniting

unification (ˌjuːnɪfɪ'keɪʃən) *n* **1** an act, instance, or process of uniting **2** the state of being united

Unification Church *n* a religious sect founded in 1954 by Sun Myung Moon (born 1920), S Korean industrialist and religious leader. See also **Moonie**

unified atomic mass unit *n* another name for **atomic mass unit**

unified field theory *n* any theory capable of describing in one set of equations the properties of gravitational fields, electromagnetic fields, and strong and weak nuclear interactions. No satisfactory theory has yet been found

Unified Modeling Language *n trademark* See **UML**

unified screw thread *n* a screw thread system introduced for defence equipment (1939–44), in which the thread form and pitch were a compromise between British Standard Whitworth and American Standard Sellers: adopted by the International Standards Organization

unifilar (ˌjuːnɪ'faɪlə) *adj rare* composed of, having, or using only one wire, thread, filament, etc [from UNI- + Latin *fīlum* thread; see FILAMENT, FILAR]

unifoliate (ˌjuːnɪ'fəʊlɪɪt, -ˌeɪt) *adj* having a single leaf or leaflike part

unifoliolate (ˌjuːnɪ'fəʊlɪəˌleɪt) *adj* (of a compound leaf) having only one leaflet

uniform ('juːnɪˌfɔːm) *n* **1** a prescribed identifying set of clothes for the members of an organization, such as soldiers or schoolchildren **2** a single set of such clothes **3** a characteristic feature or fashion of some class or group **4** *informal* a police officer who wears a uniform ▷ *adj* **5** unchanging in form, quality, quantity, etc; regular **6** identical; alike or like ▷ *vb (tr)* **7** to fit out (a body of soldiers, etc) with uniforms **8** to make uniform [C16 from Latin *ūniformis*, from *ūnus* one + *forma* shape] > **'uniˌformly** *adv* > **'uniˌformness** *n*

Uniform ('juːnɪˌfɔːm) *n communications* a code word for the letter *u*

Uniform Business Rate *n* a local tax in the UK paid by businesses, based on a local valuation of their premises and a rate fixed by central government that applies throughout the country. Abbreviation: **UBR**

uniformitarian (ˌjuːnɪˌfɔːmɪ'tɛərɪən) *adj* **1** of or relating to uniformitarianism **2** of, characterized by, or conforming to uniformity ▷ *n* **3** a supporter of a theory of uniformity or of uniformitarianism

uniformitarianism (ˌjuːnɪˌfɔːmɪ'tɛərɪəˌnɪzəm) *n* the concept that the earth's surface was shaped in the past by gradual processes, such as erosion, and by small sudden changes, such as earthquakes, of the type acting today rather than by the sudden divine acts, such as the flood survived by Noah (Genesis 6–8), demanded by the doctrine of catastrophism

uniformity (ˌjuːnɪ'fɔːmɪtɪ) *n, pl* **-ties 1** a state or condition in which everything is regular, homogeneous, or unvarying **2** lack of diversity or variation, esp to the point of boredom or monotony; sameness

unify ('juːnɪˌfaɪ) *vb* **-fies, -fying, -fied** to make or become one; unite [C16 from Medieval Latin *ūnificāre*, from Latin *ūnus* one + *facere* to make] > **'uniˌfiable** *adj* > **'uniˌfier** *n*

unijugate (ˌjuːnɪ'dʒuːgɪt, -ˌgeɪt) *adj* (of a compound leaf) having only one pair of leaflets

unilateral (ˌjuːnɪ'lætərəl) *adj* **1** of, having, affecting, or occurring on only one side **2** involving or performed by only one party of several **3** *law* (of contracts, obligations, etc) made by, affecting, or binding one party only and not involving the other party in reciprocal obligations **4** *botany* having or designating parts situated or turned to one side of an axis **5** *sociol* relating to or tracing the line of descent through ancestors of one sex only. Compare **bilateral** (sense 5) **6** *phonetics* denoting an (l) sound produced on one side of the tongue only > **ˌuni'lateralism** *or* **ˌuniˌlater'ality** *n* > **ˌuni'laterally** *adv*

Unilateral Declaration of Independence *n* a declaration of independence made by a dependent state without the assent of the protecting state. Abbreviation: **UDI**

unilateral neglect *n* a symptom of brain damage in which a person is unaware of one side of his body and of anything in the external world on the same side

unilingual (ˌjuːnɪ'lɪŋgwəl) *adj* **1** of or relating to only one language **2** *chiefly Canadian* knowing only one language ▷ *n* **3** *chiefly Canadian* a person who knows only one language > **ˌuni'lingualˌism** *n*

uniliteral (ˌjuːnɪ'lɪtərəl) *adj* consisting of one letter

unilocular (ˌjuːnɪ'lɒkjʊlə) *adj* (esp of a plant ovary or anther) having or consisting of a single chamber or cavity

unimaginable (ˌʌnɪ'mædʒɪnəbᵊl) *adj* difficult or impossible to believe; inconceivable > **ˌunim'aginably** *adv*

unimaginative (ˌʌnɪ'mædʒɪnətɪv) *adj* lacking in imagination or imaginative thought; dull > **ˌunim'aginatively** *adv*

unimagined (ˌʌnɪ'mædʒɪnd) *adj* not having been conceived of: *a hitherto unimagined scale*

Unimak Island ('juːnɪˌmæk) *n* an island in SW Alaska, in the Aleutian Islands. Length: 113 km (70 miles)

unimpaired (ˌʌnɪm'pɛəd) *adj* not reduced or weakened in strength, quality, etc

unimpeachable (ˌʌnɪm'piːtʃəbᵊl) *adj* unquestionable as to honesty, truth, etc > **ˌunimˌpeacha'bility** *or* **ˌunim'peachableness** *n* > **ˌunim'peachably** *adv*

unimpeded (ˌʌnɪm'piːdɪd) *adj* not impeded; unhindered

unimportant (ˌʌnɪm'pɔːtᵊnt) *adj* lacking in significance or value: *unimportant matters*

unimpressed (ˌʌnɪm'prɛst) *adj* not having a favourable opinion: *unimpressed by his arguments*

unimpressive (ˌʌnɪm'prɛsɪv) *adj* not capable of impressing, esp by size, magnificence, etc: *an unimpressive performance*

unimproved (ˌʌnɪm'pruːvd) *adj* **1** not improved or made better **2** (of land) not cleared, drained, cultivated, etc **3** neglected; unused

unimproved value *n NZ* the valuation of land for rating purposes, disregarding the value of buildings or other development

unincorporated (ˌʌnɪn'kɔːpəˌreɪtɪd) *adj* **1** *law* lacking corporate status **2** not unified or included

unincorporated business *n* a privately owned

business, often owned by one person who has unlimited liability as the business is not legally registered as a company

uninfected (ˌʌnɪnˈfɛktɪd) *adj* (of a person, wound, etc) not having been contaminated with pathogenic microorganisms

uninformed (ˌʌnɪnˈfɔːmd) *adj* not having knowledge or information about a situation, subject, etc

uninhabitable (ˌʌnɪnˈhæbɪtəbᵊl) *adj* not capable of being lived in

uninhabited (ˌʌnɪnˈhæbɪtɪd) *adj* (of a place) not having inhabitants: *an uninhabited island*

uninhibited (ˌʌnɪnˈhɪbɪtɪd) *adj* lacking in inhibitions or restraint

uninitiated (ˌʌnɪˈnɪʃɪeɪtɪd) *adj* **a** not having gained knowledge or experience of a particular subject or activity **b** (*as collective noun*; preceded by *the*): *the uninitiated*

uninjured (ʌnˈɪndʒəd) *adj* not having sustained any injury; unhurt

uninspired (ˌʌnɪnˈspaɪəd) *adj* dull or ordinary; unimaginative: *an uninspired painting*

uninspiring (ˌʌnɪnˈspaɪᵊrɪŋ) *adj* not stimulating or invigorating: *an uninspiring performance*

uninstall (ˈʌnɪnˌstɔːl) *vb* (*tr*) *computing* to remove (a program)

uninsurable (ˌʌnɪnˈʃʊərəbᵊl, -ˈʃɔː) *adj* not eligible for insurance

uninsured (ˌʌnɪnˈʃʊəd, -ˈʃɔːd) *adj* not covered by insurance: *uninsured motorists*

unintellectual (ˌʌnɪntɪˈlɛktʃʊəl) *adj* **1** not expressing or enjoying mental activity **2** not appealing to people with a developed intellect

unintelligent (ˌʌnɪnˈtɛlɪdʒənt) *adj* **1** lacking intelligence; stupid; foolish **2** not endowed with a mind or intelligence ▷ ˌunin'telligence *n* ▷ ˌunin'telligently *adv*

unintelligible (ˌʌnɪnˈtɛlɪdʒɪbᵊl) *adj* not able to be understood; incomprehensible

unintended (ˌʌnɪnˈtɛndɪd) *adj* not intended; unplanned

unintentional (ˌʌnɪnˈtɛnʃənᵊl) *adj* not deliberate; accidental: *the killing had been unintentional* ▷ ˌunin'tentionally *adv*

uninterested (ʌnˈɪntrɪstɪd, -tərɪs-) *adj* indifferent; unconcerned ▷ un'interestedly *adv* ▷ un'interestedness *n*

■ USAGE See at **disinterested**

uninteresting (ʌnˈɪntrɪstɪŋ, -ˈɪntərɪs-) *adj* not interesting; boring: *lifeless and uninteresting*

uninterrupted (ˌʌnɪntəˈrʌptɪd) *adj* not broken, discontinued, or hindered: *an uninterrupted view*

uninvited (ˌʌnɪnˈvaɪtɪd) *adj* not having been invited: *uninvited guests*

uninviting (ˌʌnɪnˈvaɪtɪŋ) *adj* not tempting, alluring, or attractive

uninvolved (ˌʌnɪnˈvɒlvd) *adj* not included or involved: *uninvolved bystanders*

union (ˈjuːnjən) *n* **1** the condition of being united, the act of uniting, or a conjunction formed by such an act **2** an association, alliance, or confederation of individuals or groups for a common purpose, esp political **3** agreement or harmony **4** short for **trade union 5** the act or state of marriage or sexual intercourse **6** a device on a flag representing union, such as another flag depicted in the top left corner **7** a device for coupling or linking parts, such as pipes **8** (*often capital*) **a** an association of students at a university or college formed to look after the students' interests, provide facilities for recreation, etc **b** the building or buildings housing the facilities of such an organization **9** Also called: join. *maths* a set containing all members of two given sets. Symbol: ∪, as in A∪B **10** (in 19th-century England) **a** a number of parishes united for the administration of poor relief **b** a workhouse supported by such a combination **11** *textiles* a piece of cloth or fabric consisting of two different kinds of yarn **12** (*modifier*) of or related to a union, esp a trade union

[c15 from Church Latin *ūniō* oneness, from Latin *ūnus* one]

Union (ˈjuːnjən) *n* **the 1** *Brit* **a** the union of England and Wales from 1543 **b** the union of the English and Scottish crowns (1603–1707) **c** the union of England and Scotland from 1707 **d** the political union of Great Britain and Ireland (1801–1920) **e** the union of Great Britain and Northern Ireland from 1920 **2** *US* **a** the United States of America **b** the northern states of the US during the Civil War **c** (*as modifier*): *Union supporters* **3** short for the **Union of South Africa**

union card *n* a membership card for a trade union

union catalogue *n* a catalogue listing every publication held at cooperating libraries

Union flag *n* the national flag of the United Kingdom, being a composite design composed of St George's Cross (England), Saint Andrew's Cross (Scotland), and Saint Patrick's Cross (Ireland). Often called: Union Jack

unionism (ˈjuːnjəˌnɪzəm) *n* **1** the principles of trade unions **2** adherence to the principles of trade unions **3** the principle or theory of any union

Unionism (ˈjuːnjəˌnɪzəm) *n* (*sometimes not capital*) the principles or adherence to the principles of Unionists

unionist (ˈjuːnjənɪst) *n* **1** a supporter or advocate of unionism or union **2** a member of a trade union ▷ *adj* **3** *chiefly Brit* of or relating to union or unionism, esp trade unionism ▷ ˌunion'istic *adj*

Unionist (ˈjuːnjənɪst) *n* **1** (*sometimes not capital*) **a** (before 1920) a supporter of the union of all Ireland and Great Britain **b** (since 1920) a supporter of union between Britain and Northern Ireland **2** a supporter of the US federal Union, esp during the Civil War ▷ *adj* **3** of, resembling, or relating to Unionists

Unionist Party *n* (formerly, in Northern Ireland) the major Protestant political party, closely identified with union with Britain. It formed the Northern Ireland Government from 1920 to 1972. See also **Ulster Democratic Unionist Party, Ulster Unionist Council**

unionize *or* **unionise** (ˈjuːnjəˌnaɪz) *vb* **1** to organize (workers) into a trade union **2** to join or cause to join a trade union **3** (*tr*) to subject to the rules or codes of a trade union **4** to join or become joined in marriage or civil partnership ▷ ˌunioni'zation *or* ˌunioni'sation *n*

Union Jack *n* **1** a common name for **Union flag 2** (*often not capitals*) a national flag flown at the jackstaff of a vessel

Union of South Africa *n* the former name (1910–61) of (the Republic of) **South Africa**

Union of Soviet Socialist Republics *n* the official name of the former **Soviet Union**

union pipes *pl n* another name for **uillean pipes**

union shop *n* (formerly) an establishment whose employment policy is governed by a contract between employer and a trade union permitting the employment of nonunion labour only on the condition that such labour joins the union within a specified time period. Compare **open shop, closed shop**

union territory *n* one of the 6 administrative territories that, with 28 states, make up the Republic of India

uniparous (juːˈnɪpərəs) *adj* **1** (of certain animals) producing a single offspring at each birth **2** (of a woman) having borne only one child **3** *botany* (of a cyme) giving rise to only one branch from each flowering stem

unipersonal (ˌjuːnɪˈpɜːsᵊnᵊl) *adj* **1** existing in the form of only one person or being. Compare **tripersonal 2** (of a verb) existing or used in only one person; for example, *rain* is used only in the third person ▷ ˌuni,person'ality *n*

uniplanar (ˌjuːnɪˈpleɪnə) *adj* situated in one plane

unipod (ˈjuːnɪˌpɒd) *n* a one-legged support, as for a camera

unipolar (ˌjuːnɪˈpəʊlə) *adj* **1** of, concerned with, or having a single magnetic or electric pole **2** (of a nerve cell) having a single process **3** (of a transistor) utilizing charge carriers of one polarity only, as in a field-effect transistor **4** (of nervous depression) occurring without accompanying bouts of mania **5** dominated by one superpower, esp the United States. Compare **bipolar** ▷ **unipolarity** (ˌjuːnɪpəʊˈlærɪtɪ) *n*

unique (juːˈniːk) *adj* **1** being the only one of a particular type; single; sole **2** without equal or like; unparalleled **3** *informal* very remarkable or unusual **4** *maths* **a** leading to only one result: *the sum of two integers is unique* **b** having precisely one value: *the unique positive square root of 4 is 2* [c17 via French from Latin *ūnicus* unparalleled, from *ūnus* one] ▷ u'niquely *adv* ▷ u'niqueness *n*

■ USAGE *Unique* is normally taken to describe an absolute state, i.e. one that cannot be qualified. Thus something is either *unique* or *not unique*; it cannot be *rather unique* or *very unique*. However, *unique* is sometimes used informally to mean very remarkable or unusual and this makes it possible to use comparatives or intensifiers with it, although many people object to this use

uniramous (ˌjuːnɪˈreɪməs) *adj* (esp of the appendages of crustaceans) consisting of a single branch; undivided. Also: uniramose (ˌjuːnɪˈreɪməʊs, -ˈræˈməʊs)

UNISA (juːˈniːsə) *n acronym for* **1** University of South Africa **2** University of South Australia

uniseptate (ˌjuːnɪˈsɛpteɪt) *adj* *biology* having only one partition or septum: *a uniseptate fruit*

uniserial (ˌjuːnɪˈsɪərɪəl) *adj* in or relating to a single series

uniseriate (ˌjuːnɪˈsɪərɪˌeɪt) *adj* *botany* (of parts, cells, etc) arranged in a single row, layer, or series

unisex (ˈjuːnɪˌsɛks) *adj* of or relating to clothing, a hairstyle, etc, that can be worn by either sex [c20 from UNI- + SEX]

unisexual (ˌjuːnɪˈsɛksjʊəl) *adj* **1** of or relating to one sex only **2** (of some organisms) having either male or female reproductive organs but not both ▷ ˌuni,sexu'ality *n* ▷ ˌuni'sexually *adv*

unison (ˈjuːnɪsᵊn, -zᵊn) *n* **1** *music* **a** the interval between two sounds of identical pitch **b** (*modifier*) played or sung at the same pitch: *unison singing* **2** complete agreement; harmony (esp in the phrase **in unison**) [c16 from Late Latin *ūnisonus,* from UNI- + *sonus* sound] ▷ u'nisonous, u'nisonal *or* u'nisonant *adj*

UNISON (ˈjuːnɪsᵊn) *n* (in Britain) a trade union representing local government, health care, and other workers: formed in 1993 by the amalgamation of COHSE, NALGO, and NUPE

unit (ˈjuːnɪt) *n* **1** a single undivided entity or whole **2** any group or individual, esp when regarded as a basic element of a larger whole **3** a mechanical part or integrated assembly of parts that performs a subsidiary function **4** a complete system, apparatus, or establishment that performs a specific function **5** a subdivision of a larger military formation **6** Also called: unit of measurement. A standard amount of a physical quantity, such as length, mass, energy, etc, specified multiples of which are used to express magnitudes of that physical quantity **7** the amount of a drug, vaccine, etc, needed to produce a particular effect **8** a standard measure used in calculating alcohol intake and its effect **9** *maths* **a** (*usually plural*) the first position in a place-value counting system, representing a single-digit number **b** (*modifier*) having a value defined as one for the system: *unit vector* **10** Also called: unit set. *maths, logic* a set having a single member **11** short for **home unit 12** short for **stock unit 13** *NZ* a self-propelled railcar [c16 back formation from UNITY, perhaps on the model of *digit*]

Unit. *abbreviation for* Unitarian

UNITA (juːˈniːtə) *n acronym for* União Nacional para a Independencia Total de Angola [Portuguese: National Union for the Total Independence of Angola]

unitarian (ˌjuːnɪˈtɛərɪən) *n* **1** a supporter of unity or centralization ▷ *adj* **2** of or relating to unity or centralization **3** another word for **unitary**

Unitarian (ˌjuːnɪˈtɛərɪən) *n* **1** *theol* a person who believes that God is one being and rejects the doctrine of the Trinity **2** *ecclesiast* an upholder of Unitarianism, esp a member of the Church (**Unitarian Church**) that embodies this system of belief ▷ *adj* **3** of or relating to Unitarians or Unitarianism

unitarianism (ˌjuːnɪˈtɛərɪəˌnɪzəm) *n* any unitary system, esp of government

Unitarianism (ˌjuːnɪˈtɛərɪəˌnɪzəm) *n* a system of Christian belief that maintains the unipersonality of God, rejects the Trinity and the divinity of Christ, and takes reason, conscience, and character as the criteria of belief and practice

unitary (ˈjuːnɪtərɪ, -trɪ) *adj* **1** of a unit or units **2** based on or characterized by unity **3** individual; whole **4** of or relating to a system of government in which all governing authority is held by the central government. Compare **federal**

unitary authority *n* (in the United Kingdom) a district administered by a single tier of local government, esp those districts of England that became administratively independent of the county councils in 1996–98

unitary matrix *n maths* a square matrix that is the inverse of its Hermitian conjugate

unit cell *n crystallog* the smallest group of atoms, ions, or molecules that is characteristic of a particular crystal lattice

unit character *n genetics* a character inherited as a single unit and dependent on a single gene

unit cost *n* the actual cost of producing one article

unite¹ (juːˈnaɪt) *vb* **1** to make or become an integrated whole or a unity; combine **2** to join, unify or be unified in purpose, action, beliefs, etc **3** to enter or cause to enter into an association or alliance **4** to adhere or cause to adhere; fuse **5** (*tr*) to possess or display (qualities) in combination or at the same time: *he united charm with severity* **6** *archaic* to join or become joined in marriage [c15 from Late Latin *ūnīre*, from *ūnus* one] ▷ **uˈniter** *n*

unite² (ˈjuːnaɪt, juːˈnaɪt) *n* an English gold coin minted in the Stuart period, originally worth 20 shillings [c17 from obsolete *unite* joined, alluding to the union of England and Scotland (1603)]

united (juːˈnaɪtɪd) *adj* **1** produced by two or more persons or things in combination or from their union or amalgamation: *a united effort* **2** in agreement **3** in association or alliance ▷ **uˈnitedly** *adv* ▷ **uˈnitedness** *n*

United Arab Emirates *pl n* a group of seven emirates in SW Asia, on the Persian Gulf: consists of Abu Dhabi, Dubai, Sharjah, Ajman, Umm al Qaiwain, Ras el Khaimah, and Fujairah; a former British protectorate; became fully independent in 1971; consists mostly of flat desert, with mountains in the east; rich petroleum resources. Official language: Arabic. Official religion: Muslim. Currency: dirham. Capital: Abu Dhabi. Pop: 3 051 000 (2004 est). Area: 83 600 sq km (32 300 sq miles). Former name (until 1971): **Trucial States**. Abbreviation: **UAE**

United Arab Republic *n* the official name (1958–71) of **Egypt**

United Arab States *pl n* a federation (1958–61) between the United Arab Republic and Yemen

United Church of Canada *n* the largest Protestant denomination in Canada, formed in the 1920s by incorporating some Presbyterians and most Methodists

United Church of Christ *n* a US Protestant denomination formed in 1957 from the Evangelical and Reformed Church and the Congregational Christian Church

United Empire Loyalist *n Canadian history* any of the American colonists who settled in Canada during or after the War of American Independence because of loyalty to the British Crown

United Kingdom *n* a kingdom of NW Europe, consisting chiefly of the island of Great Britain together with Northern Ireland: became the world's leading colonial power in the 18th century; the first country to undergo the Industrial Revolution. It became the **United Kingdom of Great Britain and Northern Ireland** in 1921, after the rest of Ireland became autonomous as the Irish Free State. Primarily it is a trading nation, the chief exports being manufactured goods; joined the Common Market (now the European Union) in January 1973. Official language: English; Gaelic, Welsh, and other minority languages. Religion: Christian majority. Currency: pound sterling. Capital: London. Pop: 59 428 000 (2004 est). Area: 244 110 sq km (94 251 sq miles). Abbreviation: **UK**. See also **Great Britain**

United Kingdom Overseas Territory *n* See **UK Overseas Territory**

United Kingdom Unionists *n* (in Britain) a political party, based in Northern Ireland: non-sectarian but opposed to a united Ireland

United Nations *n* (*functioning as singular or plural*) **1** an international organization of independent states, with its headquarters in New York City, that was formed in 1945 to promote peace and international cooperation and security. Abbreviation: **UN 2** (in World War II) a coalition of 26 nations that signed a joint declaration in Jan 1942, pledging their full resources to defeating the Axis powers

United Party *n* (formerly, in South Africa) the major opposition party, founded by General Smuts in 1934: the official Opposition in Parliament from 1948, the party was disbanded in 1977. See also **National Party, Progressive Federal Party**

United Provinces *pl n* **1** a Dutch republic (1581–1795) formed by the union of the seven northern provinces of the Netherlands, which were in revolt against their suzerain, Philip II of Spain **2** short for **United Provinces of Agra and Oudh**: the former name of **Uttar Pradesh**

United Reformed Church *n* (in England and Wales) a Protestant denomination formed from the union of the Presbyterian and Congregational churches in 1972

United States of America *n* (*functioning as singular or plural*) a federal republic mainly in North America consisting of 50 states and the District of Columbia: colonized principally by the English and French in the 17th century, the native Indians being gradually defeated and displaced; 13 colonies under British rule made the Declaration of Independence in 1776 and became the United States after the War of American Independence. The northern states defeated the South in the Civil War (1861–65). It is the world's most productive industrial nation and also exports agricultural products. It participated in World Wars I and II but since the establishment of the United Nations in 1945 has played a major role in international affairs. It consists generally of the Rocky Mountains in the west, the Great Plains in the centre, the Appalachians in the east, deserts in the southwest, and coastal lowlands and swamps in the southeast. Language: predominantly English; Spanish is also widely spoken. Religion: Christian majority. Currency: dollar. Capital: Washington, DC. Pop: 297 043 000 (2004 est). Area: 9 518 323 sq km (3 675 031 sq miles). Often shortened to: **United States**. Abbreviations: **US, USA**

unit factor *n genetics* the gene responsible for the inheritance of a unit character

unit holder *n* an investor in a unit trust fund

unitive (ˈjuːnɪtɪv) *adj* **1** tending to unite or capable of uniting **2** characterized by unity

▷ **ˈunitively** *adv*

unitize *or* **unitise** (ˈjuːnɪˌtaɪz) *vb* (*tr*) *finance* to convert (an investment trust) into a unit trust ▷ ˌuniti'zation *or* ˌuniti'sation *n*

unit-linked policy *n* a life-assurance policy, the investment benefits of which are directly in proportion to the number of units in a unit trust purchased on the policyholder's behalf. Compare **traditional policy**

unit magnetic pole *n* the strength of a magnetic pole that will repel a similar pole 1 centimetre distant from it, in a vacuum, with a force of 1 dyne

unit of account *n* **1** *economics* the function of money that enables the user to keep accounts, value transactions, etc **2** a monetary denomination used for accounting purposes, etc, but not necessarily corresponding to any real currency. Also called (esp US and Canadian): **money of account 3** the unit of currency of a country

unit price *n* a price for foodstuffs, etc, stated or shown as the cost per unit, as per pound, per kilogram, per dozen, etc

unit pricing *n* a system of pricing foodstuffs, etc, in which the cost of a single unit is shown to enable shoppers to see the advantage of buying multipacks

unit process *n chemical engineering* any of a number of standard operations, such as filtration or distillation, that are widely used in various chemical and process industries

unit trust *n Brit* an investment trust that issues units for public sale, the holders of which are creditors and not shareholders with their interests represented by a trust company independent of the issuing agency

unity (ˈjuːnɪtɪ) *n, pl* **-ties 1** the state or quality of being one; oneness **2** the act, state, or quality of forming a whole from separate parts **3** something whole or complete that is composed of separate parts **4** mutual agreement; harmony or concord **5** uniformity or constancy **6** *maths* **a** the number or numeral one **b** a quantity assuming the value of one **c** the element of a set producing no change in a number following multiplication **7** the arrangement of the elements in a work of art in accordance with a single overall design or purpose **8** any one of the three principles of dramatic structure deriving from Aristotle's *Poetics* by which the action of a play should be limited to a single plot (unity of action), a single location (unity of place), and the events of a single day (unity of time) [c13 from Old French *unité*, from Latin *ūnitās*, from *ūnus* one]

unity of interest *n property law* the equal interest in property held by joint tenants

unity ticket *n Austral* a how-to-vote card in a union election associating Labor and Communist candidates

Univ. *abbreviation for* University

univalent (ˌjuːnɪˈveɪlənt, juːˈnɪvələnt) *adj* **1** (of a chromosome during meiosis) not paired with its homologue **2** *chem* another word for **monovalent** ▷ ˌuni'valency *n*

univalve (ˈjuːnɪˌvælv) *zoology* ▷ *adj* **1** relating to, designating, or possessing a mollusc shell that consists of a single piece (valve) ▷ *n* **2** a gastropod mollusc or its shell

universal (ˌjuːnɪˈvɜːsəl) *adj* **1** of, relating to, or typical of the whole of mankind or of nature **2** common to, involving, or proceeding from all in a particular group **3** applicable to or affecting many individuals, conditions, or cases; general **4** existing or prevailing everywhere **5** applicable or occurring throughout or relating to the universe; cosmic **6** (esp of a language) capable of being used and understood by all **7** embracing or versed in many fields of knowledge, activity, interest, etc **8** *machinery* designed or adapted for a range of sizes, fittings, or uses **9** *linguistics* (of a constraint in a formal grammar) common to the grammatical description of all human languages, actual or possible **10** *logic* (of a statement or proposition) affirming or denying something about every member of a class, as in *all men are wicked*. Compare **particular** (sense 6) ▷ *n* **11** *philosophy* **a** a general term or concept or the type such a term signifies **b** a metaphysical entity taken to be the reference of a general term, as distinct from the class of individuals it describes. See also **realism** (sense 5) **c** a Platonic Idea or Aristotelian form **12** *logic* **a** a universal proposition, statement, or formula **b** a universal quantifier **13** a characteristic common to every member of a particular culture or to every human being **14** short for **universal joint** ▷ ˌuni'versalness *n*

USAGE The use of *more universal* as in *his writings have long been admired by fellow scientists, but his latest book should have more universal appeal* is acceptable in modern English usage

universal beam *n* a broad-flanged rolled steel joist suitable for a stanchion (axial load) or beam (bending load)

universal class *or* **set** *n* (in Boolean algebra) the class containing all points and including all other classes

universal donor *n* a person who has blood of group O and whose blood may be safely transfused to persons with most other blood types

universal gas constant *n* another name for **gas constant**

universal grammar *n* *linguistics* (in Chomskyan transformation linguistics) the abstract limitations on the formal grammatical description of all human languages, actual or possible, that make them human languages

universalism (ˌjuːnɪˈvɜːsəˌlɪzəm) *n* **1** a universal feature or characteristic **2** another word for **universality 3** *social welfare* the principle that welfare services should be available to all by right, according to need, and not restricted by individual ability to pay, but funded by general contributions through taxes, rates, or national insurance payments

Universalism (ˌjuːnɪˈvɜːsəˌlɪzəm) *n* a system of religious beliefs maintaining that all men are predestined for salvation ▷ ˌUni'versalist *n, adj*

universalist (ˌjuːnɪˈvɜːsəlɪst) *n* **1** a person who has a wide range of interests, knowledge, activities, etc ▷ *adj* **2** characterized by universality ▷ ˌuniˈversalˈistic *adj*

universality (ˌjuːnɪvɜːˈsælɪtɪ) *n* the state or quality of being universal

universalizability *or* **universalisability** (ˌjuːnɪˌvɜːsəlaɪzəˈbɪlɪtɪ) *n ethics* **1** the thesis that any moral judgment must be equally applicable to every relevantly identical situation **2** the Kantian principle that if a course of action cannot be universally adopted it must be morally impermissible

universalize *or* **universalise** (ˌjuːnɪˈvɜːsəˌlaɪz) *vb* (*tr*) to make universal ▷ ˌuniˌversaliˈzation *or* ˌuniˌversaliˈsation *n*

universal joint *or* **coupling** *n* a form of coupling between two rotating shafts allowing freedom of angular movement in all directions

universally (ˌjuːnɪˈvɜːsəlɪ) *adv* everywhere or in every case; without exception: *this principle applies universally*

universal motor *n* an electric motor capable of working on either direct current or single-phase alternating current at approximately the same speed and output

universal quantifier *n logic* a formal device indicating that the open sentence that follows is true of every member of the relevant universe of interpretation, as (∀x)(Fx→Gx) or (x)(Fx→Gx): literally, for everything, if it is an F it is a G; that is, all Fs are Gs. Usual symbol: ∀

Universal Soul *or* **Spirit** *n Hinduism* Brahman in its aspect as the sacred syllable Om, the eternal and spiritual principle that permeates the universe

universal time *n* **1** (from 1928) name adopted internationally for Greenwich Mean Time (measured from Greenwich midnight), now split into several slightly different scales, one of which (UT1) is used by astronomers. Abbreviation: **UT 2** Also called: **universal coordinated time**. An internationally agreed system for civil timekeeping introduced in 1960 and redefined in 1972 as an atomic timescale. Available from broadcast signals, it has a second equal to the International Atomic Time (TAI) second, the difference between UTC and TAI being an integral number of seconds with leap seconds inserted when necessary to keep it within 0.9 seconds of UT1. Abbreviation: **UTC**

universe (ˈjuːnɪˌvɜːs) *n* **1** *astronomy* the aggregate of all existing matter, energy, and space **2** human beings collectively **3** a province or sphere of thought or activity **4** *statistics* another word for **population** (sense 7) [C16 from French *univers*, from Latin *ūniversum* the whole world, from *ūniversus* all together, from UNI- + *vertere* to turn]

universe of discourse *n logic* the complete range of objects, events, attributes, relations, ideas, etc, that are expressed, assumed, or implied in a discussion

university (ˌjuːnɪˈvɜːsɪtɪ) *n, pl* **-ties 1** an institution of higher education having authority to award bachelors' and higher degrees, usually having research facilities **2** the buildings, members, staff, or campus of a university [C14 from Old French *universite*, from Medieval Latin *universitās* group of scholars, from Late Latin: guild, society, body of men, from Latin: whole, totality, universe]

university entrance *n* (in New Zealand) **a** an examination taken by pupils of postprimary schools **b** the certificate issued to a successful candidate. Abbreviation **UE**

univocal (ˌjuːnɪˈvəʊkᵊl) *adj* **1** unambiguous or unmistakable ▷ *n* **2** a word or term that has only one meaning ▷ ˌuniˈvocally *adv*

UNIX (ˈjuːnɪks) *n trademark* a multi-user multitasking operating system found on many types of computer

unjust (ʌnˈdʒʌst) *adj* not in accordance with accepted standards of fairness or justice; unfair ▷ un'justly *adv* ▷ un'justness *n*

unjustifiable (ʌnˈdʒʌstɪˌfaɪəbᵊl) *adj* not capable of being justified ▷ un'justi,fiably *adv*

unjustified (ʌnˈdʒʌstɪˌfaɪd) *adj* not justified or vindicated: *an entirely unjustified attack*

unkempt (ʌnˈkɛmpt) *adj* **1** (of the hair) uncombed; dishevelled **2** ungroomed; slovenly: *unkempt appearance* **3** *archaic* crude or coarse [Old English *uncembed*; from UN-¹ + *cembed*, past participle of *cemban* to COMB; related to Old Saxon *kembian*, Old High German *kemben* to comb] ▷ un'kemptly *adv* ▷ un'kemptness *n*

unkenned (ʌnˈkɛnd) *or* **unkent** (ʌnˈkɛnt) *adj Scot and N English dialect* unknown [C14 from UN-¹ + KEN]

unkennel (ʌnˈkɛnᵊl) *vb* **-nels, -nelling, -nelled** *or US* **-nels, -neling, -neled** (*tr*) **1** to release from a kennel **2** to drive from a hole or lair **3** *rare* to bring to light

unkind (ʌnˈkaɪnd) *adj* **1** lacking kindness; unsympathetic or cruel **2** *archaic or dialect* **a** (of weather) unpleasant **b** (of soil) hard to cultivate ▷ un'kindly *adv* ▷ un'kindness *n*

unknit (ʌnˈnɪt) *vb* **-knits, -knitting, -knitted** *or* **-knit 1** to make or become undone, untied, or unravelled **2** (*tr*) to loosen, weaken, or destroy **3** (*tr*) *rare* to smooth out (a wrinkled brow)

unknowable (ʌnˈnəʊəbᵊl) *adj* **1** incapable of being known or understood **2 a** beyond human understanding **b** (*as noun*): *the unknowable* ▷ un'knowableness *or* un,knowa'bility *n* ▷ un'knowably *adv*

Unknowable (ʌnˈnəʊəbᵊl) *n* the *philosophy* the ultimate reality that underlies all phenomena but cannot be known

unknowing (ʌnˈnəʊɪŋ) *adj* **1** not knowing; ignorant **2** (*postpositive; often foll by of*) without knowledge or unaware (of) ▷ un'knowingly *adv*

unknown (ʌnˈnəʊn) *adj* **1** not known, understood, or recognized **2** not established, identified, or discovered: *an unknown island* **3** not famous; undistinguished: *some unknown artist* **4** unknown quantity a person or thing whose action, effect, etc, is unknown or unpredictable ▷ *n* **5** an unknown person, quantity, or thing **6** *maths* a variable, or the quantity it represents, the value of which is to be discovered by solving an equation; a variable in a conditional equation: $3y = 4x + 5$ *is an equation in two unknowns* ▷ un'knownness *n*

Unknown Soldier *or* **Warrior** *n* (in various countries) an unidentified soldier who has died in battle and for whom a tomb is established as a memorial to other unidentified dead of the nation's armed forces

unlace (ʌnˈleɪs) *vb* (*tr*) **1** to loosen or undo the lacing of (shoes, garments, etc) **2** to unfasten or remove garments of (oneself or another) by or as if by undoing lacing

unlade (ʌnˈleɪd) *vb* a less common word for **unload**

unlamented (ˌʌnləˈmɛntɪd) *adj* not missed, regretted, or grieved over: *his late unlamented father*

unlash (ʌnˈlæʃ) *vb* (*tr*) to untie or unfasten

unlatch (ʌnˈlætʃ) *vb* to open or unfasten or come open or unfastened by the lifting or release of a latch

unlawful (ʌnˈlɔːfʊl) *adj* **1** illegal **2** illicit; immoral: *unlawful love* **3** an archaic word for **illegitimate**. ▷ un'lawfully *adv* ▷ un'lawfulness *n*

unlawful assembly *n law* a meeting of three or more people with the intent of carrying out any unlawful purpose

unlay (ʌnˈleɪ) *vb* **-lays, -laying, -laid** (*tr*) to untwist (a rope or cable) to separate its strands

unlead (ʌnˈlɛd) *vb* (*tr*) **1** to strip off lead **2** *printing* to remove the leads or spaces from between (lines of type)

unleaded (ʌnˈlɛdɪd) *adj* **1** (of petrol) containing a reduced amount of tetraethyl lead, in order to reduce environmental pollution **2** not covered or weighted with lead **3** *printing* (of lines of type, etc) not spaced or separated with leads; solid ▷ *n* **4** petrol containing a reduced amount of tetraethyl lead

unlearn (ʌnˈlɜːn) *vb* **-learns, -learning, -learned** (-ˈlɜːnd) *or* **-learnt** (tr) to try to forget (something learnt) or to discard (accumulated knowledge)

unlearned (ʌnˈlɜːnɪd) *adj* ignorant or untaught ▷ un'learnedly *adv*

unlearnt (ʌnˈlɜːnt) *or* **unlearned** (ʌnˈlɜːnd) *adj* **1** denoting knowledge or skills innately present and therefore not learnt **2** not learnt or taken notice of: *unlearnt lessons*

unleash (ʌnˈliːʃ) *vb* (*tr*) **1** to release from or as if from a leash **2** to free from restraint or control

unleavened (ʌnˈlɛvənd) *adj* (of bread, biscuits, etc) made from a dough containing no yeast or leavening

unless (ʌnˈlɛs) *conj* **1** (*subordinating*) except under the circumstances that; except on the condition that: *they'll sell it unless he hears otherwise* ▷ *prep* **2** *rare* except [C14 *onlesse*, from *on* ON + *lesse* LESS; compare French *à moins que*, literally: at less than]

unlettered (ʌnˈlɛtəd) *adj* **1** uneducated; illiterate **2** not marked with letters: *an unlettered tombstone*

unlevel (ʌnˈlɛvᵊl) *adj* **1** not level **2** unfair or inequitable; giving one person or group an unfair advantage: *an unlevel playing field*

unlicensed (ʌnˈlaɪsənst) *adj* **1** having no licence: *an unlicensed restaurant* **2** without permission; unauthorized **3** unrestrained or lawless

unlike (ʌnˈlaɪk) *adj* **1** not alike; dissimilar or unequal; different **2** *archaic* unlikely ▷ *prep* **3** not like; not typical of ▷ un'likeness *n*

u

unlikely (ʌnˈlaɪklɪ) *adj* not likely; improbable
▷ un'likeliness *or* un'likelihood *n*

unlimber (ʌnˈlɪmbə) *vb* **1** (*tr*) to disengage (a gun) from its limber **2** to prepare (something) for use

unlimited (ʌnˈlɪmɪtɪd) *adj* **1** without limits or bounds **2** not restricted, limited, or qualified **3** *finance, Brit* **a** (of liability) not restricted to any unpaid portion of nominal capital invested in a business **b** (of a business enterprise) having owners with such unlimited liability
▷ un'limitedly *adv* ▷ un'limitedness *n*

unlined (ʌnˈlaɪnd) *adj* **1** not having any lining **2** (of paper) not marked with lines

unlisted (ʌnˈlɪstɪd) *adj* **1** not entered on a list **2** *US and Canadian* (of a telephone number or telephone subscriber) not listed in a telephone directory. Brit term: **ex-directory**

unlisted securities market *n* a market on the London Stock Exchange, established in 1981, for trading in shares of smaller companies, who do not wish to comply with the requirements for a full listing. Abbreviation: **USM**

unlistenable (ʌnˈlɪsənəbəl) *adj* impossible or unpleasant to listen to

unlit (ʌnˈlɪt) *adj* **1** not having lighting; unilluminated **2** not having been ignited

unlive (ʌnˈlɪv) *vb* (*tr*) to live so as to nullify, undo, or live down (past events or times)

unload (ʌnˈləʊd) *vb* **1** to remove a load or cargo from (a ship, lorry, etc) **2** to discharge (cargo, freight, etc) **3** (*tr*) to relieve of a burden or troubles **4** (*tr*) to give vent to (anxiety, troubles, etc) **5** (*tr*) to get rid of or dispose of (esp surplus goods) **6** (*tr*) to remove the charge of ammunition from (a firearm) ▷ un'loader *n*

unlock (ʌnˈlɒk) *vb* **1** (*tr*) to unfasten (a lock, door, etc) **2** (*tr*) to open, release, or let loose **3** (*tr*) to disclose or provide the key to: *unlock a puzzle* **4** (*intr*) to become unlocked ▷ un'lockable *adj*

unlocked (ʌnˈlɒkt) *adj* not locked

unlooked-for (ʌnˈlʊktfɔː) *adj* unexpected; unforeseen

unloose (ʌnˈluːs) *or* **unloosen** *vb* (*tr*) **1** to set free; release **2** to loosen or relax (a hold, grip, etc) **3** to unfasten or untie

unlovable *or* **unloveable** (ʌnˈlʌvəbəl) *adj* not attracting or deserving love

unloved (ʌnˈlʌvd) *adj* not loved or cared for: *feeling neglected and unloved*

unlovely (ʌnˈlʌvlɪ) *adj* **1** unpleasant in appearance **2** unpleasant in character ▷ un'loveliness *n*

unloving (ʌnˈlʌvɪŋ) *adj* not feeling or showing love and affection

unlucky (ʌnˈlʌkɪ) *adj* **1** characterized by misfortune or failure **2** ill-omened; inauspicious **3** regrettable; disappointing **4** *Brit dialect* causing trouble; mischievous ▷ un'luckily *adv* ▷ un'luckiness *n*

unmade (ʌnˈmeɪd) *vb* **1** the past tense and past participle of **unmake** ▷ *adj* **2** not yet made **3** existing without having been made or created **4** *falconry* another word for **unmanned** (sense 4)

unmake (ʌnˈmeɪk) *vb* **-makes, -making, -made** (*tr*) **1** to undo or destroy **2** to depose from office, rank, or authority **3** to alter the nature of ▷ un'maker *n*

unman (ʌnˈmæn) *vb* **-mans, -manning, -manned** (*tr*) **1** to cause to lose courage or nerve **2** to make effeminate **3** to remove the men from **4** *archaic* to deprive of human qualities

unmanageable (ʌnˈmænɪdʒəbəl) *adj* difficult or impossible to control, use, or manipulate

unmanly (ʌnˈmænlɪ) *adj* **1** not masculine or virile **2** ignoble, cowardly, or dishonourable ▷ un'manliness *n*

unmanned (ʌnˈmænd) *adj* **1** lacking personnel or crew: *an unmanned ship* **2** (of aircraft, spacecraft, etc) operated by automatic or remote control **3** uninhabited **4** *falconry* (of a hawk or falcon) not yet trained to accept humans

unmannered (ʌnˈmænəd) *adj* **1** without good

manners; coarse; rude **2** not affected; without mannerisms

unmannerly (ʌnˈmænəlɪ) *adj* **1** lacking manners; discourteous ▷ *adv* **2** *archaic* rudely; discourteously ▷ un'mannerliness *n*

unmarked (ʌnˈmɑːkt) *adj* **1** not carrying a mark or marks: *an unmarked police car* **2** not noticed or observed

unmarried (ʌnˈmærɪd) *adj* **1** not married: *an unmarried mother* **2** *films* denoting a print of a cinematograph film in which the picture and sound recordings are on separate reels

unmask (ʌnˈmɑːsk) *vb* **1** to remove (the mask or disguise) from (someone or oneself) **2** to appear or cause to appear in true character **3** (*tr*) *military* to make evident the presence of (weapons), either by firing or by the removal of camouflage, etc ▷ un'masker *n*

unmatched (ʌnˈmætʃt) *adj* **1** not equalled **2** (of socks, clothes, etc) not matching

unmeaning (ʌnˈmiːnɪŋ) *adj* **1** having no meaning **2** showing no intelligence; vacant: *an unmeaning face* ▷ un'meaningly *adv* ▷ un'meaningness *n*

unmeant (ʌnˈmɛnt) *adj* unintentional; accidental

unmeasured (ʌnˈmɛʒəd) *adj* **1** measureless; limitless **2** unrestrained; unlimited or lavish **3** *music* without bar lines and hence without a fixed pulse ▷ un'measurable *adj* ▷ un'measurableness *n* ▷ un'measurably *adv*

unmeet (ʌnˈmiːt) *adj* *literary or archaic* not meet; unsuitable ▷ un'meetly *adv* ▷ un'meetness *n*

unmemorable (ʌnˈmɛmərəbəl, ʌnˈmɛmrə-) *adj* not worth remembering or easily remembered

unmentionable (ʌnˈmɛnʃənəbəl) *adj* **a** unsuitable or forbidden as a topic of conversation **b** (*as noun*): *the unmentionable* ▷ un'mentionableness *n* ▷ un'mentionably *adv*

unmentionables (ʌnˈmɛnʃənəbəlz) *pl n chiefly humorous* underwear

unmentioned (ʌnˈmɛnʃənd) *adj* not referred to or spoken about

unmerciful (ʌnˈmɜːsɪfʊl) *adj* **1** showing no mercy; relentless **2** extreme or excessive ▷ un'mercifully *adv* ▷ un'mercifulness *n*

unmerited (ʌnˈmɛrɪtɪd) *adj* not merited or deserved

unmindful (ʌnˈmaɪndfʊl) *adj* (*usually postpositive and foll by of*) careless, heedless, or forgetful ▷ un'mindfully *adv* ▷ un'mindfulness *n*

unmissable (ʌnˈmɪsəbəl) *adj* (of a film, television programme, etc) so good that it should not be missed

unmistakable *or* **unmistakeable** (ˌʌnmɪsˈteɪkəbəl) *adj* not mistakable; clear, obvious, or unambiguous ▷ ˌunmis'takableness *or* ˌunmis'takeableness *n* ▷ ˌunmis'takably *or* ˌunmis'takeably *adv*

unmitigated (ʌnˈmɪtɪˌɡeɪtɪd) *adj* **1** not diminished in intensity, severity, etc **2** (*prenominal*) (intensifier): *an unmitigated disaster* ▷ un'miti,gatedly *adv*

unmoderated (ʌnˈmɒdəˌreɪtɪd) *adj* (of an online chatroom, newsgroup, etc) not monitored for inappropriate content, time wasting, or bad language

unmolested (ˌʌnməˈlɛstɪd) *adj* not having been disturbed, accosted, or attacked

unmoor (ʌnˈmʊə, -ˈmɔː) *vb nautical* **1** to weigh the anchor or drop the mooring of (a vessel) **2** (*tr*) to reduce the mooring of (a vessel) to one anchor

unmoral (ʌnˈmɒrəl) *adj* outside morality; amoral ▷ unmorality (ˌʌnməˈrælɪtɪ) *n* ▷ un'morally *adv*

unmoved (ʌnˈmuːvd) *adj* **1** not affected emotionally **2** unchanged: *share price remained unmoved*

unmoving (ʌnˈmuːvɪŋ) *adj* **1** not in motion: *the unmoving sea* **2** still or constant: *an invisible but unmoving point*

unmurmuring (ʌnˈmɜːmərɪŋ) *adj* not complaining

unmusical (ʌnˈmjuːzɪkəl) *adj* **1** not musical or harmonious **2** not talented in or appreciative of

music ▷ un'musically *adv* ▷ un'musicalness *n*

unmuzzle (ʌnˈmʌzəl) *vb* (*tr*) **1** to take the muzzle off (a dog, etc) **2** to free from control or censorship

unnamed (ʌnˈneɪmd) *adj* **1** having no name **2** not mentioned by name: *the culprit shall remain unnamed*

unnatural (ʌnˈnætʃərəl, -ˈnætʃrəl) *adj* **1** contrary to nature; abnormal **2** not in accordance with accepted standards of behaviour or right and wrong **3** uncanny; supernatural **4** affected or forced **5** inhuman or monstrous; wicked **6** *obsolete* illegitimate ▷ un'naturally *adv* ▷ un'naturalness *n*

unnecessary (ʌnˈnɛsɪsərɪ, -ɪsrɪ) *adj* not necessary ▷ un'necessarily *adv* ▷ un'necessariness *n*

unnerve (ʌnˈnɜːv) *vb* (*tr*) to cause to lose courage, strength, confidence, self-control, etc

unnoticeable (ʌnˈnəʊtɪsəbəl) *adj* not easily seen or detected; imperceptible ▷ un'noticeably *adv*

unnoticed (ʌnˈnəʊtɪst) *adj* not perceived or observed

unnumbered (ʌnˈnʌmbəd) *adj* **1** countless; innumerable **2** not counted or assigned a number

UNO *abbreviation for* United Nations Organization

unobserved (ˌʌnəbˈzɜːvd) *adj* not seen or perceived

unobstructed (ˌʌnəbˈstrʌktɪd) *adj* (of a passageway, view, etc) not blocked by any object

unobtainable (ˌʌnəbˈteɪnəbəl) *adj* not able to be obtained

unobtrusive (ˌʌnəbˈtruːsɪv) *adj* not noticeable or conspicuous ▷ ˌunob'trusively *adv*

unoccupied (ʌnˈɒkjʊˌpaɪd) *adj* **1** (of a building) without occupants **2** unemployed or idle **3** (of an area or country) not overrun by foreign troops

unofficial (ˌʌnəˈfɪʃəl) *adj* **1** not official or formal: *an unofficial engagement* **2** not confirmed officially: *an unofficial report* **3** (of a strike) not approved by the strikers' trade union **4** (of a medicinal drug) not listed in a pharmacopoeia ▷ ˌunof'ficially *adv*

unopened (ʌnˈəʊpənd) *adj* closed, barred, or sealed

unopposed (ˌʌnəˈpəʊzd) *adj* not opposed: *elected unopposed as party president*

unorganized *or* **unorganised** (ʌnˈɔːɡəˌnaɪzd) *adj* **1** not arranged into an organized system, structure, or unity **2** (of workers) not unionized **3** nonliving; inorganic

unoriginal (ˌʌnəˈrɪdʒɪnəl) *adj* not fresh and unusual

unorthodox (ʌnˈɔːθəˌdɒks) *adj* not conventional in belief, behaviour, custom, etc ▷ un'ortho,doxly *adv*

unpack (ʌnˈpæk) *vb* **1** to remove the packed contents of (a case, trunk, etc) **2** (*tr*) to take (something) out of a packed container **3** (*tr*) to remove a pack from; unload: *to unpack a mule* ▷ un'packer *n*

unpaged (ʌnˈpeɪdʒd) *adj* (of a book) having no page numbers

unpaid (ʌnˈpeɪd) *adj* **1** (of a bill, debt, etc) not yet paid **2** working without pay **3** having wages outstanding

unpalatable (ʌnˈpælətəbəl) *adj* **1** unpleasant to taste **2** difficult to accept: *the unpalatable truth*

unparalleled (ʌnˈpærəˌlɛld) *adj* unmatched; unequalled

unpardonable (ʌnˈpɑːdᵊnəbəl) *adj* not excusable; disgraceful

unparliamentary (ˌʌnpɑːləˈmɛntərɪ, -trɪ) *adj* not consistent with parliamentary procedure or practice ▷ ˌunparlia'mentarily *adv* ▷ ˌunparlia'mentariness *n*

unpasteurized *or* **unpasteurised** (ʌnˈpæstəˌraɪzd, -stjə-, -ˈpɑː-) *adj* (of milk, beer, etc) not subjected to pasteurization

unpatriotic (ˌʌnpeɪtrɪˈɒtɪk, ˌʌnpæ-) *adj* not enthusiastically supporting one's country and its ways of life

unpaved (ʌnˈpeɪvd) *adj* not covered in paving

unpeg (ʌnˈpɛɡ) *vb* **-pegs, -pegging, -pegged** (*tr*) **1**

to remove the peg or pegs from, esp to unfasten **2** to allow (prices, wages, etc) to rise and fall freely

unpeople (ʌnˈpiːpᵊl) *vb* (*tr*) to empty of people

unperforated (ʌnˈpɜːfəˌreɪtɪd) *adj* (of a stamp) not provided with perforations

unperson (ˈʌnpɜːsᵊn) *n* a person whose existence is officially denied or ignored

unpersuaded (ˌʌnpəˈsweɪdɪd) *adj* not having been induced, urged, or prevailed upon successfully

unperturbed (ˌʌnpəˈtɜːbd) *adj* not disturbed or troubled: *unperturbed by the prospect of a fight*

unpick (ʌnˈpɪk) *vb* (*tr*) **1** to undo (the stitches) of (a piece of sewing) **2** to unravel or undo (a garment, etc) **3** *obsolete* to open (a door, lock, etc) by picking

unpicked (ʌnˈpɪkt) *adj* (of knitting, sewing, etc) having been unravelled or picked out

unpin (ʌnˈpɪn) *vb* -pins, -pinning, -pinned (*tr*) **1** to remove a pin or pins from **2** to unfasten by removing pins

unplaced (ʌnˈpleɪst) *adj* **1** not given or put in a particular place **2** *horse racing* not in the first three (sometimes four) runners in a race

unplanned (ʌnˈplænd) *adj* not planned

unplayable (ʌnˈpleɪəbᵊl) *adj* **1** not able to be played **2** not able to be played on

unpleasant (ʌnˈplɛzᵊnt) *adj* not pleasant or agreeable > un'pleasantly *adv*

unpleasantness (ʌnˈplɛzᵊntnɪs) *n* **1** the state or quality of being unpleasant **2** an unpleasant event, situation, etc **3** a disagreement or quarrel

unplug (ʌnˈplʌg) *vb* -plugs, -plugging, -plugged (*tr*) **1** to disconnect (an electrical appliance) by taking the plug out of the socket **2** to remove a plug or obstruction from

unplugged (ʌnˈplʌgd) *adj* (of a performer or performance of popular music) using acoustic rather than electric instruments

unplumbed (ʌnˈplʌmd) *adj* **1** unfathomed; unsounded **2** not understood in depth **3** (of a building) having no plumbing

unpolitic (ʌnˈpɒlɪtɪk) *adj* another word for **impolitic**

unpolled (ʌnˈpəʊld) *adj* **1** not included in an opinion poll **2** not having voted **3** *US* not registered for an election: *unpolled votes*

unpolluted (ˌʌnpəˈluːtɪd) *adj* **1** not affected or contaminated by pollution **2** untainted; pure

unpopular (ʌnˈpɒpjʊlə) *adj* not popular with an individual or group of people > unpopularity (ˌʌnpɒpjʊˈlærɪtɪ) *n* > un'popularly *adv*

unpractical (ʌnˈpræktɪkᵊl) *adj* another word for **impractical**. > ˌunpractiˈcality *or* un'practicalness *n* > un'practically *adv*

unpractised *or US* **unpracticed** (ʌnˈpræktɪst) *adj* **1** without skill, training, or experience **2** not used or done often or repeatedly **3** not yet tested

unprecedented (ʌnˈprɛsɪˌdɛntɪd) *adj* having no precedent; unparalleled > un'preceˌdentedly *adv*

unpredictable (ˌʌnprɪˈdɪktəbᵊl) *adj* not capable of being predicted; changeable > ˌunpreˌdictaˈbility *or* ˌunpreˈdictableness *n* > ˌunpreˈdictably *adv*

unprejudiced (ʌnˈprɛdʒʊdɪst) *adj* not prejudiced or biased; impartial > un'prejudicedly *adv*

unpremeditated (ˌʌnprɪˈmɛdɪˌteɪtɪd) *adj* not planned beforehand; spontaneous > ˌunpreˈmediˌtatedly *adv* > ˌunpreˌmediˈtation *n*

unprepared (ˌʌnprɪˈpɛəd) *adj* **1** having made inadequate preparations **2** not made ready or prepared **3** done without preparation; extemporaneous > ˌunpreˈparedly *adv* > ˌunpreˈparedness *n*

unprepossessing (ˌʌnpriːpəˈzɛsɪŋ) *adj* not creating a favourable impression; unattractive

unpretentious (ˌʌnprɪˈtɛnʃəs) *adj* not making claim to distinction or importance undeservedly

unpriced (ʌnˈpraɪst) *adj* **1** having no fixed or marked price **2** *poetic* beyond price; priceless

unprincipled (ʌnˈprɪnsɪpᵊld) *adj* **1** lacking moral principles; unscrupulous **2** (foll by *in*) *archaic* not versed in the principles of (a subject) > un'principledness *n*

unprintable (ʌnˈprɪntəbᵊl) *adj* unsuitable for printing for reasons of obscenity, libel, bad taste, etc > un'printableness *n* > un'printably *adv*

unprocessed (ʌnˈprəʊsɛst) *adj* (of food, oil, etc) not having undergone a process to preserve or purify

unproductive (ˌʌnprəˈdʌktɪv) *adj* **1** (often foll by *of*) not productive of (anything) **2** not producing goods and services with exchange value > ˌunproˈductively *adv* > ˌunproˈductiveness *n*

unprofessional (ˌʌnprəˈfɛʃənᵊl) *adj* **1** contrary to the accepted code of conduct of a profession **2** amateur **3** not belonging to or having the required qualifications for a profession > ˌunproˈfessionally *adv*

unprofitable (ʌnˈprɒfɪtəbᵊl) *adj* **1** not making a profit **2** not fruitful or beneficial > unˌprofitaˈbility *or* un'profitableness *n* > un'profitably *adv*

unpromising (ʌnˈprɒmɪsɪŋ) *adj* not showing any promise of favourable development or future success

unprompted (ʌnˈprɒmptɪd) *adj* without prompting; spontaneous

unpronounceable (ˌʌnprəˈnaʊnsəbᵊl) *adj* not able to be uttered or articulated

unprotected (ˌʌnprəˈtɛktɪd) *adj* not protected or safe from trouble, harm, etc: *an unprotected position*

unprotected sex *n* an act of sexual intercourse or sodomy performed without the use of a condom thus involving the risk of sexually transmitted diseases

unprotesting (ˌʌnprəˈtɛstɪŋ) *adj* without complaint or disagreement

unproved (ʌnˈpruːvd) *adj* not having been established as true, valid, or possible

unproven (ʌnˈpruːvᵊn) *adj* **1** not established as true by evidence or demonstration: *unproven allegations* **2** (of a new product, system, treatment, etc) not tried or tested

unprovided (ˌʌnprəˈvaɪdɪd) *adj* (*postpositive*) **1** (foll by *with*) not provided or supplied **2** (often foll by *for*) not prepared or ready **3** unprovided for without income or means > ˌunproˈvidedly *adv*

unprovoked (ˌʌnprəˈvəʊkt) *adj* not provoked by anything done or said

unpublished (ʌnˈpʌblɪʃt) *adj* **1** not available in print for distribution and sale **2** having no written work issued for publication

unpunished (ʌnˈpʌnɪʃt) *adj* not receiving or having received a penalty or sanction as punishment for any crime or offence

unputdownable (ˌʌnpʊtˈdaʊnəbᵊl) *adj* (of a book, esp a novel) so gripping as to be read right through at one sitting

unqualified (ʌnˈkwɒlɪˌfaɪd) *adj* **1** lacking the necessary qualifications **2** not restricted or modified: *an unqualified criticism* **3** (*usually prenominal*) (*intensifier*): *an unqualified success* > un'qualiˌfiable *adj* > un'qualiˌfiedly *adv* > un'qualiˌfiedness *n*

unquantifiable (ʌnˈkwɒntɪˌfaɪəbᵊl) *adj* not capable of being quantified

unquestionable (ʌnˈkwɛstʃənəbᵊl) *adj* **1** indubitable or indisputable **2** not admitting of exception or qualification: *an unquestionable decision* > unˌquestionaˈbility *or* un'questionableness *n*

unquestionably (ʌnˈkwɛstʃənəblɪ) *adv* **1** indisputably; definitely: *an unquestionably great club* **2** (*sentence modifier*) without a doubt; certainly

unquestioned (ʌnˈkwɛstʃənd) *adj* **1** accepted without question **2** not admitting of doubt or question: *unquestioned power* **3** not questioned or interrogated **4** *rare* not examined or investigated

unquestioning (ʌnˈkwɛstʃənɪŋ) *adj* accepting something without expressing doubt or uncertainty

unquiet (ʌnˈkwaɪət) *chiefly literary* ▷ *adj* **1** characterized by disorder, unrest, or tumult: *unquiet times* **2** anxious; uneasy ▷ *n* **3** a state of unrest > un'quietly *adv* > un'quietness *n*

unquote (ʌnˈkwəʊt) *interj* **1** an expression used parenthetically to indicate that the preceding

quotation is finished ▷ *vb* **2** to close (a quotation), esp in printing

unravel (ʌnˈrævᵊl) *vb* -els, -elling, -elled *or US* -els, -eling, -eled **1** (*tr*) to reduce (something knitted or woven) to separate strands **2** (*tr*) to undo or untangle (something tangled or knotted) **3** (*tr*) to explain or solve **4** (*intr*) to become unravelled > un'raveller *n* > un'ravelment *n*

unreactive (ˌʌnrɪˈæktɪv) *adj* (of a substance) not readily partaking in chemical reactions

unread (ʌnˈrɛd) *adj* **1** (of a book, newspaper, etc) not yet read **2** (of a person) having read little **3** (*postpositive; foll by in*) not versed (in a specified field)

unreadable (ʌnˈriːdəbᵊl) *adj* **1** illegible; undecipherable **2** difficult or tedious to read > unˌreadaˈbility *or* un'readableness *n* > un'readably *adv*

unready (ʌnˈrɛdɪ) *adj* **1** not ready or prepared **2** slow or hesitant to see or act **3** *archaic* not dressed > un'readily *adv* > un'readiness *n*

unreal (ʌnˈrɪəl) *adj* **1** imaginary or fanciful or seemingly so: *an unreal situation* **2** having no actual existence or substance **3** insincere or artificial > un'really *adv*

unrealistic (ˌʌnrɪəˈlɪstɪk) *adj* not realistic

unreality (ˌʌnrɪˈælɪtɪ) *n* **1** the quality or state of being unreal, fanciful, or impractical **2** something that is unreal

unrealized *or* **unrealised** (ʌnˈrɪəˌlaɪzd) *adj* (of an ambition, hope, goal, etc) not attained or brought to fruition

unreason (ʌnˈriːzᵊn) *n* **1** irrationality or madness **2** something that lacks or is contrary to reason **3** lack of order; chaos ▷ *vb* **4** (*tr*) to deprive of reason

unreasonable (ʌnˈriːznəbᵊl) *adj* **1** immoderate; excessive: *unreasonable demands* **2** refusing to listen to reason **3** lacking reason or judgment > un'reasonableness *n* > un'reasonably *adv*

unreasonable behaviour *n law* conduct by a spouse sufficient to cause the irretrievable breakdown of a marriage

unreasoning (ʌnˈriːzənɪŋ) *adj* not controlled by reason; irrational > un'reasoningly *adv*

unreckonable (ʌnˈrɛkənəbᵊl) *adj* incalculable; unlimited

unrecognizable *or* **unrecognisable** (ʌnˈrɛkəgˌnaɪzəbᵊl) *adj* not able to be recognized or identified: *tiny unrecognizable fragments*

unrecognized *or* **unrecognised** (ʌnˈrɛkəgˌnaɪzd) *adj* **1** not recognized or identified **2** not given formal acknowledgment of legal status

unreconstructed (ˌʌnriːkənsˈtrʌktɪd) *adj chiefly US* unwilling to accept social and economic change, as exemplified by those White Southerners who refused to accept the Reconstruction after the Civil War

unrecorded (ˌʌnrɪˈkɔːdɪd) *adj* not recorded on paper, tape, video tape, etc

unreeve (ʌnˈriːv) *vb* -reeves, -reeving, -rove *or* -reeved *nautical* to withdraw (a rope) from a block, thimble, etc [C17 from UN-² + REEVE²]

unrefined (ˌʌnrɪˈfaɪnd) *adj* **1** (of substances such as petroleum, ores, and sugar) not processed into a pure or usable form **2** coarse in manners or language

unreflected (ˌʌnrɪˈflɛktɪd) *adj* **1** (foll by *on* or *upon*) not considered **2** (of light, particles, etc, incident on a surface) not reflected; absorbed or transmitted

unreflective (ˌʌnrɪˈflɛktɪv) *adj* not reflective or thoughtful; rash; unthinking > ˌunreˈflectively *adv*

unregenerate (ˌʌnrɪˈdʒɛnərɪt) *adj also* **unregenerated 1** unrepentant; unreformed **2** obstinately adhering to one's own views ▷ *n* **3** an unregenerate person > ˌunreˈgeneracy *n* > ˌunreˈgenerately *adv*

unregistered (ʌnˈrɛdʒɪstəd) *adj* not registered

unregulated (ʌnˈrɛgjʊˌleɪtɪd) *adj* not regulated

unrehearsed (ˌʌnrɪˈhɜːst) *adj* (of a play, speech, etc) not having been practised in advance

u

unrelated (ˌʌnrɪˈleɪtɪd) *adj* **1** not connected or associated: *an unrelated incident* **2** not connected by kinship or marriage

unrelenting (ˌʌnrɪˈlɛntɪŋ) *adj* **1** refusing to relent or take pity; relentless; merciless **2** not diminishing in determination, speed, effort, force, etc > ˌunreˈlentingly *adv* > ˌunreˈlentingness *n*

unreliable (ˌʌnrɪˈlaɪəbʰl) *adj* not reliable; untrustworthy: *an unreliable witness*

unreligious (ˌʌnrɪˈlɪdʒəs) *adj* **1** another word for **irreligious 2** secular > ˌunreˈligiously *adv*

unremarkable (ˌʌnrɪˈmɑːkəbʰl) *adj* not worthy of note or attention

unremitting (ˌʌnrɪˈmɪtɪŋ) *adj* never slackening or stopping; unceasing; constant > ˌunreˈmittingly *adv* > ˌunreˈmittingness *n*

unrepair (ˌʌnrɪˈpɛə) *n* a less common word for **disrepair**. > ˌunreˈpaired *adj*

unrepeatable (ˌʌnrɪˈpiːtəbʰl) *adj* **1** not capable of being repeated **2** not fit to be repeated, esp due to swearing or lewdness: *his stories were unrepeatable*

unrepentant (ˌʌnrɪˈpɛntənt) *adj* not repentant or contrite

unreported (ˌʌnrɪˈpɔːtɪd) *adj* not reported or recorded: *unreported cases*

unrepresentative (ˌʌnrɛprɪˈzɛntətɪv) *adj* not typical or representative

unrepresented (ˌʌnrɛprɪˈzɛntɪd) *adj* **a** not having representation **b** (*as collective noun; preceded by the*): *we intend to represent the unrepresented*

unrequited (ˌʌnrɪˈkwaɪtɪd) *adj* (of love, affection, etc) not reciprocated or returned

unreserved (ˌʌnrɪˈzɜːvd) *adj* **1** without reserve; having an open manner **2** without reservation **3** not booked or bookable > **unreservedly** (ˌʌnrɪˈzɜːvɪdlɪ) *adv* > ˌunreˈservedness *n*

unresisting (ˌʌnrɪˈzɪstɪŋ) *adj* not fighting against something or someone; yielding

unresolved (ˌʌnrɪˈzɒlvd) *adj* (of a problem or dispute) not having been solved or concluded

unresponsive (ˌʌnrɪˈspɒnsɪv) *adj* not reacting or responding to an action, question, suggestion, etc

unrest (ʌnˈrɛst) *n* **1** a troubled or rebellious state of discontent **2** an uneasy or troubled state

unrestrained (ˌʌnrɪˈstreɪnd) *adj* not restrained or checked; free or natural > **unrestrainedly** (ˌʌnrɪˈstreɪnɪdlɪ) *adv*

unrestricted (ˌʌnrɪˈstrɪktɪd) *adj* not restricted or limited in any way: *unrestricted access*

unrevealed (ˌʌnrɪˈviːld) *adj* not having been disclosed, divulged, revealed, etc > ˌunreˈvealing *adj*

unrewarded (ˌʌnrɪˈwɔːdɪd) *adj* not having received any reward or advantages

unrewarding (ˌʌnrɪˈwɔːdɪŋ) *adj* not giving personal satisfaction

unriddle (ʌnˈrɪdʰl) *vb* (*tr*) to solve or puzzle out [C16 from UN-² + RIDDLE¹] > unˈriddler *n*

unrifled (ʌnˈraɪfʰld) *adj* (of a firearm or its bore) not rifled; smoothbore

unrig (ʌnˈrɪg) *vb* -rigs, -rigging, -rigged **1** (*tr*) to strip (a vessel) of standing and running rigging **2** *archaic or dialect* to undress (someone or oneself)

unrighteous (ʌnˈraɪtʃəs) *adj* **1 a** sinful; wicked **b** (*as collective noun; preceded by the*): *the unrighteous* **2** not fair or right; unjust > unˈrighteously *adv* > unˈrighteousness *n*

unrip (ʌnˈrɪp) *vb* -rips, -ripping, -ripped (*tr*) **1** to rip open **2** *obsolete* to reveal; disclose

unripe (ʌnˈraɪp) *or* **unripened** *adj* **1** not fully matured **2** not fully prepared or developed; not ready **3** *obsolete* premature or untimely > unˈripeness *n*

unrivalled *or US* **unrivaled** (ʌnˈraɪvʰld) *adj* having no equal; matchless

unroll (ʌnˈrəʊl) *vb* **1** to open out or unwind (something rolled, folded, or coiled) or (of something rolled, folded, etc) to become opened out or unwound **2** to make or become visible or apparent, esp gradually; unfold

unromantic (ˌʌnrəʊˈmæntɪk) *adj* not of, related

to, imbued with, or characterized by romance

unroot (ʌnˈruːt) *vb* (*tr*) *chiefly US* a less common word for **uproot**

unrounded (ʌnˈraʊndɪd) *adj* *phonetics* articulated with the lips spread; not rounded

unruffled (ʌnˈrʌfʰld) *adj* **1** unmoved; calm **2** still: *the unruffled seas* > unˈruffledness *n*

unruly (ʌnˈruːlɪ) *adj* -lier, -liest disposed to disobedience or indiscipline > unˈruliness *n*

unruly certificate *n* an informal name for **certificate of unruliness**

UNRWA (ˈʌnrə) *n acronym for* United Nations Relief and Works Agency

unsaddle (ʌnˈsædʰl) *vb* **1** to remove the saddle from (a horse, mule, etc) **2** (*tr*) to unhorse

unsaddling enclosure *n* the area at a racecourse where horses are unsaddled after a race and often where awards are given to owners, trainers, and jockeys

unsafe (ʌnˈseɪf) *adj* **1** not safe; perilous **2** (of a criminal conviction) based on inadequate or false evidence

unsaid (ʌnˈsɛd) *adj* not said or expressed; unspoken

unsaleable *or US* **unsalable** (ʌnˈseɪləbʰl) *adj* not capable of being sold

unsalted (ʌnˈsɔːltɪd) *adj* not seasoned, preserved, or treated with salt: *unsalted peanuts*

unsanctioned (ʌnˈsæŋkʃənd) *adj* not having been given permission or authorization

unsanitary (ʌnˈsænɪtərɪ, -trɪ) *adj* not conducive to or promoting health; dirty or unhygienic

unsatisfactory (ˌʌnsætɪsˈfæktərɪ, -trɪ) *adj* not adequate or suitable; unacceptable

unsatisfied (ʌnˈsætɪsˌfaɪd) *adj* (of a person, demand, need, etc) not satisfied or fulfilled

unsatisfying (ʌnˈsætɪsˌfaɪɪŋ) *adj* not fulfilling or satisfactory: *it was inherently unsatisfying work*

unsaturated (ʌnˈsætʃəˌreɪtɪd) *adj* **1** not saturated **2** (of a chemical compound, esp an organic compound) containing one or more double or triple bonds and thus capable of undergoing addition reactions **3** (of a fat, esp a vegetable fat) containing a high proportion of fatty acids having double bonds **4** (of a solution) containing less solute than a saturated solution > ˌunsatuˈration *n*

unsavoury *or US* **unsavory** (ʌnˈseɪvərɪ) *adj* **1** objectionable or distasteful **2** disagreeable in odour or taste > unˈsavourily *or US* unˈsavorily *adv* > unˈsavouriness *or US* unˈsavoriness *n*

unsay (ʌnˈseɪ) *vb* -says, -saying, -said (*tr*) to retract or withdraw (something said or written)

unscathed (ʌnˈskeɪðd) *adj* not harmed or injured

unscented (ʌnˈsɛntɪd) *adj* not filled or impregnated with odour or fragrance

unscheduled (ʌnˈʃɛdjuːld) *adj* not arranged or planned according to a programme, timetable, etc

unschooled (ʌnˈskuːld) *adj* **1** having received no training or schooling **2** spontaneous; natural

unscientific (ˌʌnsaɪənˈtɪfɪk) *adj* **1** not consistent with the methods or principles of science, esp lacking objectivity **2** ignorant of science > ˌunscienˈtifically *adv*

unscramble (ʌnˈskræmbʰl) *vb* (*tr*) **1** to resolve from confusion or disorderliness **2** to restore (a scrambled message) to an intelligible form > unˈscrambler *n*

unscratched (ʌnˈskrætʃt) *adj* quite unharmed

unscreened (ʌnˈskriːnd) *adj* **1** not sheltered or concealed by a screen **2** not passed through a screen; unsifted **3** (of a film) not yet on show to the public **4** not put through a security check

unscrew (ʌnˈskruː) *vb* **1** (*tr*) to draw or remove a screw from (an object) **2** (*tr*) to loosen (a screw, lid, etc) by rotating continuously, usually in an anticlockwise direction **3** (*intr*) (esp of an engaged threaded part) to become loosened or separated

unscripted (ʌnˈskrɪptɪd) *adj* (of a speech, play, etc) not using or based on a script

unscrupulous (ʌnˈskruːpjʊləs) *adj* without scruples; unprincipled > unˈscrupulously *adv* > unˈscrupulousness *or* unscrupulosity

(ˌʌnˌskruːpjʊˈlɒsɪtɪ) *n*

unseal (ʌnˈsiːl) *vb* (*tr*) **1** to remove or break the seal of **2** to reveal or free (something concealed or closed as if sealed) > unˈsealable *adj*

unseam (ʌnˈsiːm) *vb* (*tr*) to open or undo the seam of

unseasonable (ʌnˈsiːzənəbʰl) *adj* **1** (esp of the weather) inappropriate for the season **2** untimely; inopportune > unˈseasonableness *n* > unˈseasonably *adv*

unseasoned (ʌnˈsiːzənd) *adj* **1** (of persons) not sufficiently experienced: *unseasoned troops* **2** not matured or seasoned: *unseasoned timber* **3** (of food) not flavoured with seasoning > unˈseasonedness *n*

unseat (ʌnˈsiːt) *vb* (*tr*) **1** to throw or displace from a seat, saddle, etc **2** to depose from office or position

unseaworthy (ʌnˈsiːˌwɜːθɪ) *adj* not in a fit condition or ready for a sea voyage

unsecured (ˌʌnsɪˈkjʊəd) *adj* **1** *finance* **a** (of a loan, etc) secured only against general assets and not against a specific asset **b** (of a creditor) having no security against a specific asset and with a claim inferior to those of secure creditors **2** not made secure; loose

unseeded (ʌnˈsiːdɪd) *adj* (of players in various sports) not assigned to a preferential position in the preliminary rounds of a tournament. See **seed** (sense 18)

unseeing (ʌnˈsiːɪŋ) *adj* with one's eyes open but not noticing or perceiving anything

unseelie (ʌnˈsiːlɪ) *pl n* the **1** evil malevolent fairies ▷ *adj* **2 a** of or belonging to the unseelie **b** evil and malevolent like the unseelie [Old English *unsǣlig*; compare SEELIE and SILLY]

unseemly (ʌnˈsiːmlɪ) *adj* **1** not in good style or taste; unbecoming **2** *obsolete* unattractive ▷ *adv* **3** *rare* in an unseemly manner > unˈseemliness *n*

unseen (ʌnˈsiːn) *adj* **1** not observed or perceived; invisible **2** (of passages of writing) not previously seen or prepared ▷ *n* **3** *chiefly Brit* a passage, not previously seen, that is presented to students for translation

unselfconscious (ˌʌnsɛlfˈkɒnʃəs) *adj* not unduly aware of oneself as the object of attention of others

unselfish (ʌnˈsɛlfɪʃ) *adj* not selfish or greedy; generous > unˈselfishly *adv* > unˈselfishness *n*

unsentimental (ˌʌnsɛntɪˈmɛntʰl) *adj* not tending to indulge the emotions excessively

unset (ʌnˈsɛt) *adj* **1** not yet solidified or firm **2** (of a gem) not yet in a setting **3** (of textual matter) not yet composed

unsettle (ʌnˈsɛtʰl) *vb* **1** (*usually tr*) to change or become changed from a fixed or settled condition **2** (*tr*) to confuse or agitate (emotions, the mind, etc) > unˈsettlement *n*

unsettled (ʌnˈsɛtʰld) *adj* **1** lacking order or stability **2** unpredictable; uncertain **3** constantly changing or moving from place to place **4** (of controversy, etc) not brought to an agreed conclusion **5** (of debts, law cases, etc) not disposed of **6** (of regions, etc) devoid of settlers > unˈsettledness *n*

unsex (ʌnˈsɛks) *vb* (*tr*) *chiefly literary* to deprive (a person) of the attributes of his or her sex, esp to make a woman more callous

unshakable *or* **unshakeable** (ʌnˈʃeɪkəbʰl) *adj* (of beliefs, convictions, etc) utterly firm and unwavering > unˈshakableness *or* unˈshakeableness *n* > unˈshakably *or* unˈshakeably *adv*

unshaken (ʌnˈʃeɪkʰn) *adj* not disturbed or moved from a position or belief

unshapen (ʌnˈʃeɪpʰn) *adj* **1** having no definite shape; shapeless **2** deformed; misshapen

unshaven (ʌnˈʃeɪvʰn) *adj* not having shaved or been shaven recently

unsheathe (ʌnˈʃiːð) *vb* (*tr*) to draw or pull out (something, esp a weapon) from a sheath or other covering

unship (ʌnˈʃɪp) *vb* -ships, -shipping, -shipped **1** to be or cause to be unloaded, discharged, or disembarked from a ship **2** (*tr*) *nautical* to remove from a regular place: *to unship oars*

unsighted (ʌnˈsaɪtɪd) *adj* **1** not sighted **2** not having a clear view **3 a** (of a gun) not equipped with a sight **b** (of a shot) not aimed by means of a sight > un'sightedly *adv*

unsightly (ʌnˈsaɪtlɪ) *adj* unpleasant or unattractive to look at; ugly > un'sightliness *n*

unsigned (ʌnˈsaɪnd) *adj* **1** not signed **2** not having a plus or minus sign **3** *computing* not having a bit representing a plus or minus sign

unsinkable (ʌnˈsɪŋkəbᵊl) *adj* not capable of sinking or being sunk

unsized¹ (ʌnˈsaɪzd) *adj* not made or sorted according to size

unsized² (ʌnˈsaɪzd) *adj* (of a wall, etc) not treated with size

unskilful *or US* **unskillful** (ʌnˈskɪlfʊl) *adj* **1** lacking dexterity or proficiency **2** (often foll by *in*) *obsolete* ignorant (of) > un'skilfully *or US* un'skillfully *adv* > un'skilfulness *or US* un'skillfulness *n*

unskilled (ʌnˈskɪld) *adj* **1** not having or requiring any special skill or training: *unskilled workers* **2** having or displaying no skill; inexpert

unslaked lime (ʌnˈsleɪkt) *n* another name for **calcium oxide**. Compare **slaked lime**

unsling (ʌnˈslɪŋ) *vb* -slings, -slinging, -slung (*tr*) **1** to remove or release from a slung position **2** to remove slings from

unsmiling (ʌnˈsmaɪlɪŋ) *adj* not wearing or assuming a smile; serious

unsnap (ʌnˈsnæp) *vb* -snaps, -snapping, -snapped (*tr*) to unfasten (the snap or catch) of (something)

unsnarl (ʌnˈsnɑːl) *vb* (*tr*) to free from a snarl or tangle

unsociable (ʌnˈsəʊʃəbᵊl) *adj* **1** (of a person) disinclined to associate or fraternize with others **2** unconducive to social intercourse: *an unsociable neighbourhood* > un͵socia'bility *or* un'sociableness *n* > un'sociably *adv*

unsocial (ʌnˈsəʊʃəl) *adj* **1** not social; antisocial **2** (of the hours of work of certain jobs) falling outside the normal working day

unsold (ʌnˈsəʊld) *adj* not sold

unsolicited (͵ʌnsəˈlɪsɪtɪd) *adj* not requested or invited: *unsolicited advice*

unsolved (ʌnˈsɒlvd) *adj* not having been solved or explained: *several unsolved murders* > un'solvable *adj*

unsophisticated (͵ʌnsəˈfɪstɪ͵keɪtɪd) *adj* **1** lacking experience or worldly wisdom **2** marked by a lack of refinement or complexity **3** unadulterated or genuine > ͵unso'phisti͵catedly *adv* > ͵unso'phisti͵catedness *or* ͵unso͵phisti'cation *n*

unsound (ʌnˈsaʊnd) *adj* **1** diseased, weak, or unstable: *of unsound mind* **2** unreliable or fallacious: *unsound advice* **3** lacking solidity, strength, or firmness **4** of doubtful financial or commercial viability **5** (of fruit, timber, etc) not in an edible or usable condition > un'soundly *adv* > un'soundness *n*

unsparing (ʌnˈspɛərɪŋ) *adj* **1** not sparing or frugal; lavish; profuse **2** showing harshness or severity; unmerciful > un'sparingly *adv* > un'sparingness *n*

unspeak (ʌnˈspiːk) *vb* -speaks, -speaking, -spoke, -spoken an obsolete word for **unsay**

unspeakable (ʌnˈspiːkəbᵊl) *adj* **1** incapable of expression in words **2** indescribably bad or evil **3** not to be uttered > un'speakableness *n* > un'speakably *adv*

unspecific (͵ʌnspɪˈsɪfɪk) *adj* not explicit, particular, or definite

unspecified (ʌnˈspɛsɪ͵faɪd) *adj* not referred to or stated specifically

unspectacular (͵ʌnspɛkˈtækjʊlə) *adj* not of or resembling a spectacle; unimpressive

unsphere (ʌnˈsfɪə) *vb* (*tr*) *chiefly poetic* to remove from its, one's, etc, sphere or place

unspoiled (ʌnˈspɔɪld) *or* **unspoilt** (ʌnˈspɔɪlt) *adj*

(of a village, town, etc) having an unaltered character

unspoken (ʌnˈspəʊkən) *adj* **1** understood without needing to be spoken; tacit **2** not uttered aloud

unsporting (ʌnˈspɔːtɪŋ) *adj* not relating or conforming to sportsmanship; unfair

unsportsmanlike (ʌnˈspɔːtsmən͵laɪk) *adj* lacking in sportsmanship

unspotted (ʌnˈspɒtɪd) *adj* **1** without spots or stains **2** (esp of reputations) free from moral stigma or blemish > un'spottedness *n*

unstable (ʌnˈsteɪbᵊl) *adj* **1** lacking stability, fixity, or firmness **2** disposed to temperamental, emotional, or psychological variability **3** (of a chemical compound) readily decomposing **4** *physics* **a** (of an elementary particle) having a very short lifetime **b** spontaneously decomposing by nuclear decay; radioactive: *an unstable nuclide* **5** *electronics* (of an electrical circuit, mechanical body, etc) having a tendency to self-oscillation > un'stableness *n* > un'stably *adv*

unstarry (ʌnˈstɑːrɪ) *adj* not resembling or characteristic of a star from the entertainment world: *their simple unstarry ways*

unstated (ʌnˈsteɪtɪd) *adj* not having been articulated or uttered

unsteady (ʌnˈstɛdɪ) *adj* **1** not securely fixed **2** (of behaviour, etc) lacking constancy **3** without regularity **4** (of a manner of walking, etc) precarious, staggering, as from intoxication ▷ *vb* -steadies, -steadying, -steadied **5** (*tr*) to make unsteady > un'steadily *adv* > un'steadiness *n*

unsteel (ʌnˈstiːl) *vb* (*tr*) to make (the heart, feelings, etc) more gentle or compassionate

unstep (ʌnˈstɛp) *vb* -steps, -stepping, -stepped (*tr*) *nautical* to remove (a mast) from its step

unsterile (ʌnˈstɛraɪl) *adj* not free from living, esp pathogenic, microorganisms

unstick (ʌnˈstɪk) *vb* -sticks, -sticking, -stuck (*tr*) to free or loosen (something stuck)

unstinting (ʌnˈstɪntɪŋ) *adj* not frugal or miserly; generous: *hard work and unstinting support*

unstop (ʌnˈstɒp) *vb* -stops, -stopping, -stopped (*tr*) **1** to remove the stop or stopper from **2** to free from any stoppage or obstruction; open **3** to draw out the stops on (an organ)

unstoppable (ʌnˈstɒpəbᵊl) *adj* not capable of being stopped; extremely forceful > un'stoppably *adv*

unstopped (ʌnˈstɒpt) *adj* **1** not obstructed or stopped up **2** *phonetics* denoting a speech sound for whose articulation the closure is not complete, as in the pronunciation of a vowel, fricative, or continuant **3** *prosody* (of verse) having the sense of the line carried over into the next **4** (of an organ pipe or a string on a musical instrument) not stopped

unstrained (ʌnˈstreɪnd) *adj* **1** not under strain; relaxed **2** not cleared or separated by passing through a strainer

unstratified (ʌnˈstrætɪ͵faɪd) *adj* (esp of igneous rocks and rock formations) not occurring in distinct layers or strata; not stratified

unstreamed (ʌnˈstriːmd) *adj Brit education* (of children) not divided into groups or streams according to ability

unstressed (ʌnˈstrɛst) *adj* **1** carrying relatively little stress; unemphasized **2** *phonetics* of, relating to, or denoting the weakest accent in a word or breath group, which in some languages, such as English or German, is also associated with a reduction in vowel quality to a centralized (i) or (a) **3** *prosody* (of a syllable in verse) having no stress or accent

unstriated (ʌnˈstraɪ͵eɪtɪd) *adj* (of muscle) composed of elongated cells that do not have striations; smooth

unstring (ʌnˈstrɪŋ) *vb* -strings, -stringing, -strung (*tr*) **1** to remove the strings of **2** (of beads, pearls, etc) to remove or take from a string **3** to weaken or enfeeble emotionally (a person or his nerves)

unstriped (ʌnˈstraɪpt) *adj* (esp of smooth muscle)

not having stripes; unstriated

unstructured (ʌnˈstrʌktʃəd) *adj* **1** without formal structure or systematic organization **2** without a preformed shape; (esp of clothes) loose; untailored

unstrung (ʌnˈstrʌŋ) *adj* **1** emotionally distressed; unnerved **2** (of a stringed instrument) with the strings detached

unstuck (ʌnˈstʌk) *adj* **1** freed from being stuck, glued, fastened, etc **2** come unstuck to suffer failure or disaster

unstudied (ʌnˈstʌdɪd) *adj* **1** natural; unaffected **2** (foll by *in*) without knowledge or training

unsubscribe (͵ʌnsəbˈskraɪb) *vb* (*intr*) to cancel a subscription, for example to an emailing service: *you can unsubscribe at the following URL*

unsubstantial (͵ʌnsəbˈstænʃəl) *adj* **1** lacking weight, strength, or firmness **2** (esp of an argument) of doubtful validity **3** of no material existence or substance; unreal > ͵unsub͵stanti'ality *n* > ͵unsub'stantially *adv*

unsubstantiated (͵ʌnsəbˈstænʃɪ͵eɪtɪd) *adj* not established as valid or genuine

unsubtle (ʌnˈsʌtᵊl) *adj* not subtle; obvious or blatant

unsuccessful (͵ʌnsəkˈsɛsfʊl) *adj* not having succeeded > unsuccessfully *adv*

unsuitable (ʌnˈsuːtəbᵊl, ʌnˈsjuːt-) *adj* not appropriate, suitable, or fit

unsuited (ʌnˈsuːtɪd, ʌnˈsjuː-) *adj* **1** not appropriate for a particular purpose **2** (of two people) not likely to have a successful relationship

unsullied (ʌnˈsʌlɪd) *adj* (of a reputation, etc) not stained or tarnished

unsung (ʌnˈsʌŋ) *adj* **1** not acclaimed or honoured: *unsung deeds* **2** not yet sung

unsupervised (ʌnˈsuːpə͵vaɪzd, ʌnˈsjuː-) *adj* without supervision

unsupportable (͵ʌnsəˈpɔːtəbᵊl) *adj* **1** not able to be supported **2** not able to be defended

unsupported (͵ʌnsəˈpɔːtɪd) *adj* **1** not supported physically, financially, or emotionally **2** not upheld by evidence or facts; unsubstantiated

unsure (ʌnˈʃʊə) *adj* **1** lacking assurance or self-confidence **2** (*usually postpositive*) without sure knowledge; uncertain: *unsure of her agreement* **3** precarious; insecure **4** not certain or reliable

unsurmountable (͵ʌnsɜːˈmaʊntəbᵊl) *adj* (of a problem, etc) not capable of being solved or overcome

unsurpassed (͵ʌnsɜːˈpɑːst) *adj* superior in achievement or excellence to any other: *of an unsurpassed quality* > ͵unsur'passable *adj*

unsurprised (͵ʌnsəˈpraɪzd) *adj* not feeling amazement or wonder

unsuspected (͵ʌnsəˈspɛktɪd) *adj* **1** not under suspicion **2** not known to exist > ͵unsus'pectedly *adv* > ͵unsus'pectedness *n*

unsuspecting (͵ʌnsəˈspɛktɪŋ) *adj* disposed to trust; not suspicious; trusting > ͵unsus'pectingly *adv*

unswear (ʌnˈswɛə) *vb* -swears, -swearing, -swore, -sworn to retract or revoke (a sworn oath); abjure

unsweetened (ʌnˈswiːtᵊnd) *adj* not having any added sugar or other sweeteners

unswerving (ʌnˈswɜːvɪŋ) *adj* not turning aside; constant

unsympathetic (͵ʌnsɪmpəˈθɛtɪk) *adj* **1** not characterized by, feeling, or showing sympathy **2** (when *postpositive*, often foll by *to* or *towards*) not showing agreement (with) or favour (towards)

untainted (ʌnˈteɪntɪd) *adj* not tarnished, contaminated, or polluted

untalented (ʌnˈtæləntɪd) *adj* lacking in talent

untamable *or* **untameable** (ʌnˈteɪməbᵊl) *adj* (of an animal or person) not capable of being tamed, subdued, or made obedient

untamed (ʌnˈteɪmd) *adj* not cultivated, domesticated, or controlled: *beautiful untamed wilderness*

untangle (ʌnˈtæŋgᵊl) *vb* (*tr*) **1** to free from a tangled condition **2** to free from perplexity or confusion

untapped (ʌnˈtæpt) *adj* not yet used: *previously untapped resources*

untarnished (ʌnˈtɑːnɪʃt) *adj* **1** (of silver, etc) not tarnished or discoloured **2** not tainted or spoiled: *untarnished by graffiti*

untaught (ʌnˈtɔːt) *adj* **1** without training or education **2** attained or achieved without instruction

untaxed (ʌnˈtækst) *adj* not subject to taxation

unteach (ʌnˈtiːtʃ) *vb* -teaches, -teaching, -taught (*tr*) *rare* to cause to disbelieve (teaching)

untenable (ʌnˈtɛnəbᵊl) *adj* **1** (of theories, propositions, etc) incapable of being maintained, defended, or vindicated **2** unable to be maintained against attack **3** *rare* (of a house, etc) unfit for occupation ▷ unˌtenaˈbility or unˈtenableness *n* ▷ unˈtenably *adv*

untended (ʌnˈtɛndɪd) *adj* not cared for or attended to

Unter den Linden (*German* ˈʊntər deːn ˈlɪndən) *n* the main street of Berlin, formerly in East Berlin, extending to the Brandenburg Gate

Unterwalden (*German* ˈʊntərˌvaldən) *n* a canton of central Switzerland, on Lake Lucerne: consists of the demicantons of **Nidwalden** (east) and **Obwalden** (west). Capitals: (Nidwalden) Stans; (Obwalden) Sarnen. Pop: (Nidwalden) 38 900 (2002 est); (Obwalden) 33 000 (2002 est). Areas: (Nidwalden) 274 sq km (107 sq miles); (Obwalden) 492 sq km (192 sq miles)

untested (ʌnˈtɛstɪd) *adj* not having been tested or examined

untethered (ʌnˈtɛðəd) *adj* not tied or limited with or as if with a tether

unthink (ʌnˈθɪŋk) *vb* -thinks, -thinking, -thought (*tr*) **1** to reverse one's opinion about **2** to dispel from the mind

unthinkable (ʌnˈθɪŋkəbᵊl) *adj* **1** not to be contemplated; out of the question **2** unimaginable; inconceivable **3** unreasonable; improbable ▷ unˌthinkaˈbility or unˈthinkableness *n* ▷ unˈthinkably *adv*

unthinking (ʌnˈθɪŋkɪŋ) *adj* **1** lacking thoughtfulness; inconsiderate **2** heedless; inadvertent **3** not thinking or able to think ▷ unˈthinkingly *adv* ▷ unˈthinkingness *n*

unthought-of (ˌʌnˈθɔːtɒv) *adj* unimaginable; inconceivable

unthread (ʌnˈθrɛd) *vb* (*tr*) **1** to draw out the thread or threads from (a needle, etc) **2** to disentangle

unthrone (ʌnˈθrəʊn) *vb* (*tr*) a less common word for **dethrone**

untidy (ʌnˈtaɪdɪ) *adj* -dier, -diest **1** not neat; slovenly ▷ *vb* -dies, -dying, -died **2** (*tr*) to make untidy ▷ unˈtidily *adv* ▷ unˈtidiness *n*

untie (ʌnˈtaɪ) *vb* -ties, -tying, -tied **1** to unfasten or free (a knot or something that is tied) or (of a knot or something that is tied) to become unfastened **2** (*tr*) to free from constraint or restriction

until (ʌnˈtɪl) *conj* (*subordinating*) **1** up to (a time) that: *he laughed until he cried* **2** (*used with a negative*) before (a time or event): *until you change, you can't go out* ▷ *prep* **3** (often preceded by *up*) in or throughout the period before: *he waited until six* **4** (*used with a negative*) earlier than; before: *he won't come until tomorrow* [C13 *untill*; related to Old High German *unt* unto, until, Old Norse *und*; see TILL¹]

▌ **USAGE** The use of *until such time as* (as in *industrial action will continue until such time as our demands are met*) is unnecessary and should be avoided: *industrial action will continue until our demands are met.* See also at **till¹**

untimely (ʌnˈtaɪmlɪ) *adj* **1** occurring before the expected, normal, or proper time **2** inappropriate to the occasion, time, or season *adv* **3** prematurely or inopportunely ▷ unˈtimeliness *n*

untiring (ʌnˈtaɪrɪŋ) *adj* (of a person or their actions) continuing or persisting without declining in strength or vigour

untitled (ʌnˈtaɪtᵊld) *adj* **1** without a title **2** having no claim or title: *an untitled usurper*

unto (ˈʌntuː) *prep* an archaic word for **to** [C13 of Scandinavian origin; see UNTIL]

untogether (ˌʌntəˈgɛðə) *adj* *slang* incompetent or badly organized; mentally or emotionally unstable

untold (ʌnˈtəʊld) *adj* **1** incapable of description or expression: *untold suffering* **2** incalculably great in number or quantity: *untold thousands* **3** not told

untouchable (ʌnˈtʌtʃəbᵊl) *adj* **1** lying beyond reach **2** above reproach, suspicion, or impeachment **3** unable to be touched ▷ *n* **4** *offensive* a former name for **Dalit** ▷ unˌtouchaˈbility *n*

untouched (ʌnˈtʌtʃt) *adj* **1** not used, handled, touched, etc **2** not injured or harmed **3** (*postpositive*) emotionally unmoved **4** not changed, modified, or affected **5** (of food or drink) left without being consumed **6** not mentioned or referred to: *he left the subject untouched*

untoward (ˌʌntəˈwɔːd, ʌnˈtəʊəd) *adj* **1** characterized by misfortune, disaster, or annoyance **2** not auspicious; adverse; unfavourable **3** unseemly or improper **4** out of the ordinary; out of the way **5** *archaic* refractory; perverse **6** *obsolete* awkward, ungainly, or uncouth ▷ ˌuntoˈwardly *adv* ▷ ˌuntoˈwardness *n*

untrained (ʌnˈtreɪnd) *adj* not having been trained: *untrained volunteers*

untrammelled or *US* **untrammeled** (ʌnˈtræmᵊld) *adj* not hindered or restricted in thought or action

untranslated (ˌʌntrænsˈleɪtɪd, ˌʌntrænz-) *adj* not having been expressed or written down in another language or dialect

untravelled or *US* **untraveled** (ʌnˈtrævᵊld) *adj* **1** (of persons) not having travelled widely; narrow or provincial **2** (of a road) never travelled over

untread (ʌnˈtrɛd) *vb* -treads, -treading, -trod, -trodden or -trod (*tr*) *rare* to retrace (a course, path, etc)

untreated (ʌnˈtriːtɪd) *adj* **1** (of an illness, etc) not having been dealt with **2** not having been processed in any way: *untreated sewage*

untried (ʌnˈtraɪd) *adj* **1** not tried, attempted, or proved; untested **2** not tried by a judge or court

untroubled (ʌnˈtrʌbᵊld) *adj* not feeling, showing, or involving anxiety, worry, or discomfort

untrue (ʌnˈtruː) *adj* **1** incorrect or false **2** disloyal **3** diverging from a rule, standard, or measure; inaccurate ▷ unˈtrueness *n* ▷ unˈtruly *adv*

untruss (ʌnˈtrʌs) *vb* **1** (*tr*) to release from or as if from a truss; unfasten **2** *obsolete* to undress

untrustworthy (ʌnˈtrʌstˌwɜːðɪ) *adj* not worthy of being trusted: *untrustworthy witnesses*

untruth (ʌnˈtruːθ) *n* **1** the state or quality of being untrue **2** a statement, fact, etc, that is not true

untruthful (ʌnˈtruːθfʊl) *adj* **1** (of a person) given to lying **2** diverging from the truth; untrue ▷ unˈtruthfully *adv* ▷ unˈtruthfulness *n*

untuck (ʌnˈtʌk) *vb* to become or cause to become loose or not tucked in: *to untuck the blankets*

unturned (ʌnˈtɜːnd) *adj* not turned: *unturned pages*

untutored (ʌnˈtjuːtəd) *adj* **1** without formal instruction or education **2** lacking sophistication or refinement

untypical (ʌnˈtɪpɪkᵊl) *adj* not representative or characteristic of a particular type, person, etc

unusable (ʌnˈjuːzəbᵊl) *adj* not able or fit to be used

unused *adj* **1** (ʌnˈjuːzd) not being or never having been made use of **2** (ʌnˈjuːst) (*postpositive*; foll by *to*) not accustomed or used (to something)

unusual (ʌnˈjuːʒʊəl) *adj* out of the ordinary; uncommon; extraordinary: *an unusual design* ▷ unˈusually *adv* ▷ unˈusualness *n*

unutterable (ʌnˈʌtərəbᵊl) *adj* incapable of being expressed in words ▷ unˈutterableness *n* ▷ unˈutterably *adv*

unvaccinated (ʌnˈvæksɪˌneɪtɪd) *adj* (of a person or animal) not having been inoculated with a

vaccine

unvalued (ʌnˈvæljuːd) *adj* **1** not appreciated or valued **2** not assessed or estimated as to price or valuation **3** *obsolete* of great value

unvarnished (ʌnˈvɑːnɪʃt) *adj* not elaborated upon or glossed; plain and direct: *the unvarnished truth*

unveil (ʌnˈveɪl) *vb* **1** (*tr*) to remove the cover or shroud from, esp in the ceremonial unveiling of a monument, etc **2** to remove the veil from (one's own or another person's face) **3** (*tr*) to make (something secret or concealed) known or public; divulge; reveal

unveiling (ʌnˈveɪlɪŋ) *n* **1** a ceremony involving the removal of a veil at the formal presentation of a statue, monument, etc, for the first time **2** the presentation of something, esp for the first time

unverified (ʌnˈvɛrɪˌfaɪd) *adj* not having been confirmed, substantiated, or proven to be true ▷ unˈveriˌfiable *adj*

unviable (ʌnˈvaɪəbᵊl) *adj* not capable of succeeding, esp financially

unvoice (ʌnˈvɔɪs) *vb* (*tr*) **1** to pronounce without vibration of the vocal cords **2** another word for **devoice**

unvoiced (ʌnˈvɔɪst) *adj* **1** not expressed or spoken **2** articulated without vibration of the vocal cords

unwaged (ʌnˈweɪdʒd) *adj* of, relating to, or denoting a person who is not receiving pay because of either being unemployed or working in the home

unwanted (ʌnˈwɒntɪd) *adj* not wanted or desired

unwarrantable (ʌnˈwɒrəntəbᵊl) *adj* incapable of vindication or justification ▷ unˈwarrantableness *n* ▷ unˈwarrantably *adv*

unwarranted (ʌnˈwɒrəntɪd) *adj* **1** lacking justification or authorization **2** another word for **unwarrantable**

unwary (ʌnˈwɛərɪ) *adj* lacking caution or prudence; not vigilant or careful ▷ unˈwarily *adv* ▷ unˈwariness *n*

unwashed (ʌnˈwɒʃt) *adj* **1** not washed ▷ *pl n* **2** the great unwashed *informal and derogatory* the masses

unwatched (ʌnˈwɒtʃt) *adj* (of an automatic device, such as a beacon) not manned

unwavering (ʌnˈweɪvərɪŋ) *adj* not wavering or hesitant; resolute

unwaxed (ʌnˈwækst) *adj* not treated with wax, esp of oranges or lemons, not sprayed with a protective coating of wax

unwearied (ʌnˈwɪərɪd) *adj* **1** not abating or tiring **2** not fatigued; fresh ▷ unˈweariedly *adv* ▷ unˈweariedness *n*

unweighed (ʌnˈweɪd) *adj* **1** (of quantities purchased, etc) not measured for weight **2** (of statements, etc) not carefully considered

unwelcome (ʌnˈwɛlkəm) *adj* **1** (of persons) not welcome **2** causing dissatisfaction or displeasure ▷ unˈwelcomely *adv* ▷ unˈwelcomeness *n*

unwell (ʌnˈwɛl) *adj* (*postpositive*) not well; ill

unwept (ʌnˈwɛpt) *adj* **1** not wept for or lamented **2** *rare* (of tears) not shed

unwholesome (ʌnˈhəʊlsəm) *adj* **1** detrimental to physical or mental health **2** morally harmful or depraved **3** indicative of illness, esp in appearance **4** (esp of food) of inferior quality ▷ unˈwholesomely *adv* ▷ unˈwholesomeness *n*

unwieldy (ʌnˈwiːldɪ) or **unwieldly** *adj* **1** too heavy, large, or awkwardly shaped to be easily handled **2** ungainly; clumsy ▷ unˈwieldily or unˈwieldlily *adv* ▷ unˈwieldiness or unˈwieldliness *n*

unwilled (ʌnˈwɪld) *adj* not intentional; involuntary

unwilling (ʌnˈwɪlɪŋ) *adj* **1** unfavourably inclined; reluctant **2** performed, given, or said with reluctance ▷ unˈwillingly *adv* ▷ unˈwillingness *n*

unwind (ʌnˈwaɪnd) *vb* -winds, -winding, -wound **1** to slacken, undo, or unravel or cause to slacken, undo, or unravel **2** (*tr*) to disentangle **3** to make or become relaxed ▷ unˈwindable *adj* ▷ unˈwinder *n*

unwinking (ʌnˈwɪŋkɪŋ) *adj* vigilant; watchful

unwinnable (ʌnˈwɪnəbᵊl) *adj* **1** not able to be won

or achieved **2** (of a seat in an election) not able to be taken from the incumbent or the incumbent's party

unwise (ʌn'waɪz) *adj* lacking wisdom or prudence; foolish > un'wisely *adv* > un'wiseness *n*

unwish (ʌn'wɪʃ) *vb* (*tr*) **1** to retract or revoke (a wish) **2** to desire (something) not to be or take place

unwished (ʌn'wɪʃt) *adj* not desired; unwelcome

unwitnessed (ʌn'wɪtnɪst) *adj* **1** without the signature or attestation of a witness **2** not seen or observed

unwitting (ʌn'wɪtɪŋ) *adj* (*usually prenominal*) **1** not knowing or conscious **2** not intentional; inadvertent [Old English *unwitende*, from UN-¹ + *witting*, present participle of *witan* to know; related to Old High German *wizzan* to know, Old Norse *vita*] > un'wittingly *adv* > un'wittingness *n*

unwonted (ʌn'wəʊntɪd) *adj* **1** out of the ordinary; unusual **2** (*usually foll by to*) *archaic* unaccustomed; unused > un'wontedly *adv* > un'wontedness *n*

unworkable (ʌn'wɜːkəb³l) *adj* not practicable or feasible

unworldly (ʌn'wɜːldlɪ) *adj* **1** not concerned with material values or pursuits **2** lacking sophistication; naive **3** not of this earth or world > un'worldliness *n*

unworried (ʌn'wʌrɪd) *adj* not anxious or uneasy

unworthy (ʌn'wɜːðɪ) *adj* **1** (often foll by *of*) not deserving or worthy **2** (often foll by *of*) beneath the level considered befitting (to): *that remark is unworthy of you* **3** lacking merit or value **4** (of treatment) not warranted or deserved > un'worthily *adv* > un'worthiness *n*

unwound (ʌn'waʊnd) *vb* the past tense and past participle of **unwind**

unwrap (ʌn'ræp) *vb* -wraps, -wrapping, -wrapped to remove the covering or wrapping from (something) or (of something wrapped) to have the covering come off

unwritten (ʌn'rɪt³n) *adj* **1** not printed or in writing **2** effective only through custom; traditional **3** without writing upon it

unwritten law *n* **1** the law based upon custom, usage, and judicial decisions, as distinguished from the enactments of a legislature, orders or decrees in writing, etc **2** **the** the tradition that a person may avenge any insult to family integrity, as used to justify criminal acts of vengeance

unyielding (ʌn'jiːldɪŋ) *adj* **1** not compliant, submissive, or flexible: *his unyielding attitude* **2** not pliable or soft: *a firm and unyielding surface*

unyoke (ʌn'jəʊk) *vb* **1** to release (an animal, etc) from a yoke **2** (*tr*) to set free; liberate **3** (*tr*) to disconnect or separate **4** (*intr*) *archaic* to cease working

unzip (ʌn'zɪp) *vb* -zips, -zipping, -zipped **1** to unfasten the zip of (a garment) or (of a zip or garment with a zip) to become unfastened: *her skirt unzipped as she sat down* **2** (*tr*) *computing* to decompress (a file) that had previously been zipped

up (ʌp) *prep* **1** indicating movement from a lower to a higher position: *climbing up a mountain* **2** at a higher or further level or position in or on: *soot up the chimney; a shop up the road* ▷ *adv* **3** (*often particle*) to an upward, higher, or erect position, esp indicating readiness for an activity: *looking up at the stars; up and doing something* **4** (*particle*) indicating intensity or completion of an action: *he tore up the cheque; drink up now!* **5** to the place referred to or where the speaker is: *the man came up and asked the way* **6 a** to a more important place: *up to London* **b** to a more northerly place: *up to Scotland* **c** (of a member of some British universities) to or at university **d** in a particular part of the country: *up north* **7** appearing for trial: *up before the magistrate* **8** having gained: *ten pounds up on the deal* **9** higher in price: *coffee is up again* **10** raised (for discussion, etc): *the plan was up for consideration* **11** taught: *well up in physics* **12** (*functioning as imperative*) get, stand, etc,

up: *up with you!* **13** all up with *informal* **a** over; finished **b** doomed to die **14** up with (*functioning as imperative*) wanting the beginning or continuation of **15** something's up *informal* something strange is happening **16** up against **a** touching **b** having to cope with **17** up and running in operation; functioning properly **18** up for **a a3** a candidate or applicant for: *he's up for re-election again* **b** *informal* keen or willing to try: *she's up for anything* **19** up for it *informal* keen or willing to try something out or make a good effort **20** up to **a** devising or scheming; occupied with **b** dependent or incumbent upon: *the decision is up to you* **c** equal to (a challenge, etc) or capable of (doing, etc): *are you up to playing in the final?* **d** aware of: *up to a person's tricks* **e** as far as: *up to his waist in mud* **f** as many as: *up to two years' waiting time* **g** comparable with: *not up to your normal standard* **21** up top *informal* in the head or mind **22** up yours *slang* a vulgar expression of contempt or refusal **23** what's up? *informal* **a** what is the matter? **b** what is happening? ▷ *adj* **24** (*predicative*) of a high or higher position **25** (*predicative*) out of bed; awake: *the children aren't up yet* **26** (*prenominal*) of or relating to a train or trains to a more important place or one regarded as higher: *the up platform* **27** (*predicative*) over or completed: *the examiner announced that their time was up* **28** (*predicative*) beating one's opponent by a specified amount: *three goals up by half-time* ▷ *vb* ups, upping, upped **29** (*tr*) to increase or raise **30** (*intr; foll by and* with a verb) *informal* to do (something) suddenly, unexpectedly, etc ▷ *n* **31** high point; good or pleasant period (esp in the phrase **ups and downs**) **32** *slang* another word (esp US) for **upper** (sense 9) **33** on **the up and up a** trustworthy or honest **b** *Brit* on the upward trend or movement **34** up oneself *slang* self-absorbed or arrogant [Old English *upp*; related to Old Saxon, Old Norse *up*, Old High German *ūf*, Gothic *iup*]

USAGE The use of *up* before *until* is redundant and should be avoided: *the talks will continue until* (not *up until*) *23rd March*

UP *abbreviation for* **1** United Press **2** Uttar Pradesh

up- *prefix* up, upper, or upwards: *uproot; upmost*

up-anchor *vb* (*intr*) *nautical* to weigh anchor

up-and-comer *n informal* someone who shows promise in a particular field and appears likely to be successful

up-and-coming *adj* promising continued or future success; enterprising

up-and-down *adj* **1** moving, executed, or formed alternately upwards and downwards **2** *chiefly US* very steep; vertical ▷ *adv, prep* up and down **3** backwards and forwards (along)

up-and-over *adj* (of a door, etc) opened by being lifted and moved into a horizontal position

up-and-under *n rugby league* a high kick forwards followed by a charge to the place where the ball lands

Upanishad (uː'pʌnɪʃəd, -ʃæd, juː-) *n Hinduism* any of a class of the Sanskrit sacred books probably composed between 400 and 200 BC and embodying the mystical and esoteric doctrines of ancient Hindu philosophy [C19 from Sanskrit *upanisad* a sitting down near something, from *upa* near to + *ni* down + *sīdati* he sits] > U,pani'shadic *adj*

upas ('juːpəs) *n* **1** a large moraceous tree of Java, *Antiaria toxicaria*, having whitish bark and poisonous milky sap **2** the sap of this tree, used as an arrow poison. ▷ Also called: antiar [C19 from Malay: poison]

upbeat ('ʌp,biːt) *n* **1** *music* **a** a usually unaccented beat, esp the last in a bar **b** the upward gesture of a conductor's baton indicating this. Compare **downbeat 2** an upward trend (in prosperity, etc) ▷ *adj* **3** *informal* marked by cheerfulness or optimism

up-bow ('ʌp,bəʊ) *n* a stroke of the bow from its tip to its nut on a stringed instrument. Compare

down-bow

upbraid (ʌp'breɪd) *vb* (*tr*) **1** to reprove or reproach angrily **2** to find fault with [Old English *upbregdan*; related to Danish *bebreide*; see UP, BRAID] > up'braider *n* > up'braidingly *adv*

upbringing ('ʌp,brɪŋɪŋ) *n* the education of a person during his formative years. Also called: bringing-up

upbuild (ʌp'bɪld) *vb* -builds, -building, -built (*tr*) to build up; enlarge, increase, etc > up'builder *n*

UPC *abbreviation for* Universal Product Code: another name for **bar code**

upcast ('ʌp,kɑːst) *n* **1** material cast or thrown up **2** a ventilation shaft through which air leaves a mine. Compare **downcast** (sense 3) **3** *geology* (in a fault) the section of strata that has been displaced upwards ▷ *adj* **4** directed or thrown upwards ▷ *vb* -casts, -casting, -cast **5** (*tr*) to throw or cast up

up close and personal *adv* **1** intimately ▷ *adj* (**up-close-and-personal** *when prenominal*) **2** intimate

upcoming (,ʌp'kʌmɪŋ) *adj* coming soon; forthcoming

upcountry (ʌp'kʌntrɪ) *adj* **1** of or coming from the interior of a country or region **2** *disparaging* lacking the sophistication associated with city-dwellers; countrified ▷ *n* **3** the interior part of a region or country ▷ *adv* **4** towards, in, or into the interior part of a country or region

update *vb* (ʌp'deɪt) (*tr*) **1** to bring up to date ▷ *n* ('ʌp,deɪt) **2** the act of updating or something that is updated > up'dateable *adj* > up'dater *n*

up-do *n* a hairstyle in which the hair is held away from the face and neck with pins or clips [C20]

updraught ('ʌp,drɑːft) *n* an upward movement of air or other gas

upend (ʌp'ɛnd) *vb* **1** to turn or set or become turned or set on end **2** (*tr*) to affect or upset drastically

upfront ('ʌp'frʌnt) *adj* **1** *informal* open, frank, honest ▷ *adv, adj* **2** (of money) paid out at the beginning of a business arrangement

upgrade *vb* (ʌp'greɪd) (*tr*) **1** to assign or promote (a person or job) to a higher professional rank or position **2** to raise in value, importance, esteem, etc **3** to improve (a breed of livestock) by crossing with a better strain ▷ *n* ('ʌp,greɪd) **4** *US and Canadian* an upward slope **5** on the upgrade improving or progressing, as in importance, status, health, etc ▷ *adj* **6** *US and Canadian* going or sloping upwards ▷ *adv* ('ʌp'greɪd) **7** *US and Canadian* up an incline, hill, or slope > up'grader *n*

upgrowth ('ʌp,grəʊθ) *n* **1** the process of developing or growing upwards **2** a result of evolution or growth

upheaval (ʌp'hiːv³l) *n* **1** a strong, sudden, or violent disturbance, as in politics, social conditions, etc **2** *geology* another word for **uplift** (sense 7)

upheave (ʌp'hiːv) *vb* -heaves, -heaving, -heaved or -hove **1** to heave or rise upwards **2** *geology* to thrust (land) upwards or (of land) to be thrust upwards **3** (*tr*) to disturb violently; throw into disorder

upheld (ʌp'hɛld) *vb* the past tense and past participle of **uphold**

Up-Helly-Aa (,ʌp'hɛlɪɑː) *n* a midwinter festival held in January in Shetland; originally a fire festival, but now a celebration of Shetland's Norse heritage, involving the ceremonial burning of a newly built Viking ship [from UP (in the sense: finished) + *haliday* a Scottish form of HOLIDAY]

uphill ('ʌp'hɪl) *adj* **1** inclining, sloping, or leading upwards **2** requiring arduous and protracted effort ▷ *adv* **3** up an incline or slope **4** against difficulties ▷ *n* **5** a rising incline; ascent

uphold (ʌp'həʊld) *vb* -holds, -holding, -held (*tr*) **1** to maintain, affirm, or defend against opposition or challenge **2** to give moral support or inspiration to **3** *rare* to support physically **4** to lift up > up'holder *n*

upholster (ʌp'həʊlstə) *vb* (*tr*) to fit (chairs, sofas,

u

etc) with padding, springs, webbing, and covering

upholsterer (ʌp'həʊlstərə) *n* a person who upholsters furniture as a profession [c17 from *upholster* small furniture dealer; see UPHOLD, -STER, -ER[1]]

upholstery (ʌp'həʊlstərɪ) *n, pl* -steries **1** the padding, covering, etc, of a piece of furniture **2** the business, work, or craft of upholstering

uphroe ('juːfrəʊ) *n nautical* a variant spelling of **euphroe**

UPI *abbreviation for* United Press International

up-itself *adj slang* pretentious or pompous

upkeep ('ʌpˌkiːp) *n* **1** the act or process of keeping something in good repair, esp over a long period; maintenance **2** the cost of maintenance

upland ('ʌplənd) *n* **1** an area of high or relatively high ground ▷ *adj* **2** relating to or situated in an upland

upland cotton *n* **1** a tropical American cotton plant, *Gossypium hirsutum,* widely cultivated for its fibre **2** the fibre of this plant, or the fabric woven from it

upland plover *or* **sandpiper** *n* an American sandpiper, *Bartramia longicauda,* with a short slender bill and long tail

uplift *vb* (ʌp'lɪft) (*tr*) **1** to raise; elevate; lift up **2** to raise morally, spiritually, culturally, etc **3** *Scot and NZ* to collect (a passenger, parcel, etc); pick up ▷ *n* ('ʌpˌlɪft) **4** the act, process, or result of lifting up **5** the act or process of bettering moral, social or cultural conditions, etc **6 a** a brassiere for lifting and supporting the breasts **b** (*as modifier*): *an uplift bra* **7** the process or result of land being raised to a higher level, as during a period of mountain building > up'lifter *n*

uplifting (ʌp'lɪftɪŋ) *adj* acting to raise moral, spiritual, cultural, etc levels

uplighter ('ʌpˌlaɪtə) *n* a lamp or wall light designed or positioned to cast its light upwards

uplink ('ʌpˌlɪŋk) *n* the transmitter on the ground that sends signals up to a communications satellite

upload (ʌp'ləʊd) *vb* (*tr*) to copy or transfer (data or a program) from one's own computer into the memory of another computer. Compare **download** (sense 1)

up-market *adj* relating to commercial products, services, etc, that are relatively expensive and of superior quality

upmost ('ʌpˌməʊst) *adj* another word for **uppermost**

Upolu (uː'pəʊluː) *n* an island in the SW central Pacific, in Samoa. Chief town: Apia. Pop: 134 400 (2001). Area: 1114 sq km (430 sq miles)

upon (ə'pɒn) *prep* **1** another word for **on** **2** indicating a position reached by going up: *climb upon my knee* **3** imminent for: *the weekend was upon us again* [c13 from UP + ON]

upper ('ʌpə) *adj* **1** higher or highest in relation to physical position, wealth, rank, status, etc **2** (*capital when part of a name*) lying farther upstream, inland, or farther north **3** (*capital when part of a name*) geology, archaeol denoting the late part or division of a period, system, formation, etc: *Upper Palaeolithic* **4** *maths* (of a limit or bound) greater than or equal to one or more numbers or variables ▷ *n* **5** the higher of two objects, people, etc **6** the part of a shoe above the sole, covering the upper surface of the foot **7** *on one's uppers* extremely poor; destitute **8** *informal* any tooth of the upper jaw **9** Also called (esp US): **up**. *slang* any of various drugs having a stimulant or euphoric effect. Compare **downer**

upper atmosphere *n meteorol* that part of the atmosphere above the troposphere

Upper Austria *n* a state of N Austria: first divided from Lower Austria in 1251. Capital: Linz. Pop: 1 387 086 (2003 est). Area: 11 978 sq km (4625 sq miles). German name: **Oberösterreich**

Upper Canada *n* **1** history (1791–1841) the official name of the region of Canada lying southwest of the Ottawa River and north of the lower Great

Lakes. Compare **Lower Canada** **2** (esp in E Canada) another name for **Ontario**

upper case *printing* ▷ *n* **1** the top half of a compositor's type case in which capital letters, reference marks, and accents are kept ▷ *adj* (**upper-case** *when prenominal*) **2** of or relating to capital letters kept in this case and used in the setting or production of printed or typed matter ▷ *vb* upper-case **3** (*tr*) to print with upper-case letters; capitalize

upper chamber *n* another name for an **upper house**

upper class *n* **1** the class occupying the highest position in the social hierarchy, esp the wealthy or the aristocracy ▷ *adj* (**upper-class** *when prenominal*) **2** of or relating to the upper class **3** *US education* of or relating to the junior or senior classes of a college or high school

upper crust *n informal* the upper class

uppercut ('ʌpəˌkʌt) *n* **1** a short swinging upward blow with the fist delivered at an opponent's chin ▷ *vb* -cuts, -cutting, -cut **2** to hit (an opponent) with an uppercut

Upper Egypt *n* one of the four main traditional administrative districts of Egypt: extends south from Cairo to the Sudan

upper hand *n* **the** the position of control; advantage (esp in the phrases **have** *or* **get the upper hand**)

upper house *n* (*often capitals*) one of the two houses of a bicameral legislature. Also called: upper chamber. Compare **lower house**

upper mordent *n* another name for **inverted mordent**

uppermost ('ʌpəˌməʊst) *adj also* upmost **1** highest in position, power, importance, etc ▷ *adv* **2** in or into the highest position, etc

Upper Palaeolithic *n* **1** the latest of the three periods of the Palaeolithic, beginning about 40 000 BC and ending, in Europe, about 12 000 BC: characterized by the emergence of modern man, *Homo sapiens* ▷ *adj* **2** of or relating to this period

Upper Palatinate *n* See **Palatinate**

Upper Peninsula *n* a peninsula in the northern US between Lakes Superior and Michigan, constituting the N part of the state of Michigan

upper regions *pl n* the *chiefly literary* the sky; heavens

upper school *n* the senior pupils in a secondary school, usually those in the fourth and fifth years and above

Upper Silesia *n* a region of SW Poland, formerly ruled by Germany: coal mining and other heavy industry

Upper Tunguska *n* See **Tunguska**

Upper Volta ('vɒltə) *n* the former name (until 1984) of **Burkina-Faso**

upper works *pl n nautical* the parts of a vessel above the waterline when fully laden

uppish ('ʌpɪʃ) *adj Brit informal* snobbish, arrogant, or presumptuous [c18 from UP + -ISH] > 'uppishly *adv* > 'uppishness *n*

uppity ('ʌpɪtɪ) *adj informal* **1** not yielding easily to persuasion or control **2** another word for **uppish** [from UP + fanciful ending, perhaps influenced by -ITY]

Uppsala *or* **Upsala** ('ʌpsɑːlə) *n* a city in E central Sweden: the royal headquarters in the 13th century; Gothic cathedral (the largest in Sweden) and Sweden's oldest university (1477). Pop: 182 124 (2004 est)

upraise (ʌp'reɪz) *vb* (*tr*) **1** *chiefly literary* to lift up; elevate **2** *archaic* to praise; exalt > up'raiser *n*

uprate (ʌp'reɪt) *vb* **1** raise the value, rate, or size of, upgrade **2** *photog* to increase the effective speed of (a film) by underexposing, usually up to two stops, and subsequently overdeveloping (pushing the processing)

uprear (ʌp'rɪə) *vb* (*tr*) to lift up; raise

upright ('ʌpˌraɪt) *adj* **1** vertical or erect **2** honest, honourable, or just ▷ *adv* **3** vertically ▷ *n* **4** a vertical support, such as a stake or post **5** short

for **upright piano** **6** the state of being vertical ▷ *vb* **7** (*tr*) to make upright > 'up,rightly *adv* > 'up,rightness *n*

upright piano *n* a piano which has a rectangular vertical case. Compare **grand piano**

uprise *vb* (ʌp'raɪz) -rises, -rising, -rose, -risen **1** (*tr*) to rise up ▷ *n* ('ʌpˌraɪz) **2** another word for **rise** (senses 24, 25, 30) > up'riser *n*

uprising ('ʌpˌraɪzɪŋ, ʌpˌ'raɪzɪŋ) *n* **1** a revolt or rebellion **2** *archaic* an ascent

upriver ('ʌp'rɪvə) *adj, adv* **1** towards or near the source of a river ▷ *n* **2** an area located upstream

uproar ('ʌpˌrɔː) *n* a commotion or disturbance characterized by loud noise and confusion; turmoil

uproarious (ʌp'rɔːrɪəs) *adj* **1** causing or characterized by an uproar; tumultuous **2** extremely funny; hilarious **3** (of laughter) loud and boisterous > up'roariously *adv* > up'roariousness *n*

uproot (ʌp'ruːt) *vb* (*tr*) **1** to pull up by or as if by the roots **2** to displace (a person or persons) from native or habitual surroundings **3** to remove or destroy utterly > up'rootedness *n* > up'rooter *n*

uprouse (ʌp'raʊz) *vb* (*tr*) *rare* to rouse or stir up; arouse

uprush ('ʌpˌrʌʃ) *n* an upward rush, as of consciousness

upsadaisy ('ʌpsə'deɪzɪ) *interj* a variant of **upsy-daisy**

Upsala ('ʌpsɑːlə) *n* a variant spelling of **Uppsala**

ups and downs *pl n* alternating periods of good and bad fortune, high and low spirits, etc

upscale ('ʌp'skeɪl) *adj informal* of or for the upper end of an economic or social scale; up-market

upset *vb* (ʌp'sɛt) -sets, -setting, -set (*mainly tr*) **1** (*also intr*) to tip or be tipped over; overturn, capsize, or spill **2** to disturb the normal state, course, or stability of **3** to disturb mentally or emotionally **4** to defeat or overthrow, usually unexpectedly **5** to make physically ill **6** to thicken or spread (the end of a bar, rivet, etc) by forging, hammering, or swagging ▷ *n* ('ʌpˌsɛt) **7** an unexpected defeat or reversal, as in a contest or plans **8** a disturbance or disorder of the emotions, body, etc **9** a tool used to upset a bar or rivet; swage **10** a forging or bar that has been upset in preparation for further processing ▷ *adj* (ʌp'sɛt) **11** overturned or capsized **12** emotionally or physically disturbed or distressed **13** disordered; confused **14** defeated or overthrown [c14 (in the sense: to set up, erect; c19 in the sense: to overthrow); related to Middle High German *ûfsetzen* to put on, Middle Dutch *opzetten*] > up'settable *adj* > up'setter *n* > up'setting *adj* > up'settingly *adv*

upset price ('ʌpˌsɛt) *n* another name (esp Scot, US, and Canadian) for **reserve price**

upsetting (ʌp'sɛtɪŋ) *n metallurgy* the process of hammering the end of a heated bar of metal so that its width is increased locally, as in the manufacture of bolts

upshot ('ʌpˌʃɒt) *n* **1** the final result; conclusion; outcome **2** *archery* the final shot in a match [c16 from UP + SHOT[1]]

upside ('ʌpˌsaɪd) *n* the upper surface or part

upside down *adj* **1** (*usually postpositive;* **upside-down** *when prenominal*) turned over completely; inverted **2** *informal* confused; muddled ▷ *adv* **3** in an inverted fashion **4** in a chaotic or crazy manner [c16 variant, by folk etymology, of earlier *upsodown*] > ,upside-'downness *n*

upside-down cake *n* a sponge cake baked with sliced fruit at the bottom, then inverted before serving

upsides ('ʌpˌsaɪdz) *adv informal, chiefly Brit* (foll by *with*) equal or level (with), as through revenge or retaliation

upsilon ('ʌpsɪˌlɒn, juː'psaɪlən) *n* the 20th letter in the Greek alphabet (Υ or υ), a vowel, transliterated as y or u [c17 from Medieval Greek *u psilon* simple *u*, name adopted for graphic *u* to avoid confusion with graphic *oi*, since pronunciation was the same for both in Late Greek]

upsize ('ʌpˌsaɪz) vb -sizes, -sizing, -sized (tr) **1** to increase the operating costs of (a company) by increasing the number of people it employs **2** to increase the size of or produce a larger version of (something) [c20 modelled on DOWNSIZE]

upskill ('ʌpˌskɪl) vb (tr) to improve the aptitude for work of (a person) by additional training

upspring archaic or literary ▷ vb (ʌp'sprɪŋ) -springs, -springing, -sprang or -sprung, -sprung **1** (intr) to spring up or come into existence ▷ n ('ʌpˌsprɪŋ) **2** a leap forwards or upwards **3** the act of coming into existence

upstage (ʌp'steɪdʒ) adv **1** on, at, or to the rear of the stage ▷ adj **2** of or relating to the back half of the stage **3** informal haughty; supercilious; aloof ▷ vb (tr) **4** to move upstage of (another actor), thus forcing him to turn away from the audience **5** informal to draw attention to oneself from (someone else); steal the show from (someone) **6** informal to treat haughtily ▷ n **7** the back half of the stage

upstairs ('ʌp'steəz) adv **1** up the stairs; to or on an upper floor or level **2** informal to or into a higher rank or office **3** informal in the mind: a little weak upstairs **4** kick upstairs informal to promote to a higher rank or position, esp one that carries less power ▷ n (functioning as singular or plural) **5 a** an upper floor or level **b** (as modifier): an upstairs room **6** Brit informal old-fashioned the masters and mistresses of a household collectively, esp of a large house. Compare **downstairs** (sense 3)

upstanding (ʌp'stændɪŋ) adj **1** of good character **2** upright and vigorous in build **3** be upstanding **a** (in a court of law) a direction to all persons present to rise to their feet before the judge enters or leaves the court **b** (at a formal dinner) a direction to all persons present to rise to their feet for a toast ▷ up'standingness n

upstart n ('ʌpˌstɑːt) **1 a** a person, group, etc, that has risen suddenly to a position of power or wealth **b** (as modifier): an upstart tyrant; an upstart family **2 a** an arrogant or presumptuous person **b** (as modifier): his upstart ambition ▷ vb (ʌp'stɑːt) **3** (intr) archaic to start up, as in surprise, etc

upstate ('ʌp'steɪt) US ▷ adj, adv **1** towards, in, from, or relating to the outlying or northern sections of a state, esp of New York State ▷ n **2** the outlying, esp northern, sections of a state ▷ 'up'stater n

upstream (ʌp'striːm) adv, adj **1** in or towards the higher part of a stream; against the current **2** (in the oil industry) of or for any of the stages prior to oil production, such as exploration or research. Compare **downstream** (sense 2)

upstretched (ʌp'strɛtʃt) adj (esp of the arms) stretched or raised up

upstroke ('ʌpˌstrəʊk) n **1 a** an upward stroke or movement, as of a pen or brush **b** the mark produced by such a stroke **2** the upward movement of a piston in a reciprocating engine

up-sum n a summing-up

upsurge vb (ʌp'sɜːdʒ) **1** (intr) chiefly literary to surge up ▷ n ('ʌpˌsɜːdʒ) **2** a rapid rise or swell

upsweep n ('ʌpˌswiːp) **1** a curve or sweep upwards **2** US and Canadian an upswept hairstyle ▷ vb (ʌp'swiːp) -sweeps, -sweeping, -swept **3** to sweep, curve, or brush or be swept, curved, or brushed upwards

upswell (ʌp'swɛl) vb -swells, -swelling, -swelled, -swelled or -swollen rare to swell up or cause to swell up

upswing n ('ʌpˌswɪŋ) **1** economics a recovery period in the trade cycle **2** an upward swing or movement or any increase or improvement ▷ vb (ʌp'swɪŋ) -swings, -swinging, -swung **3** (intr) to swing or move up

upsy-daisy ('ʌpsɪˌdeɪzɪ) or **upsadaisy** interj an expression, usually of reassurance, uttered as when someone, esp a child, stumbles or is being lifted up [c18 up-a-daisy, irregularly formed from UP (adv)]

uptake ('ʌpˌteɪk) n **1** a pipe, shaft, etc, that is used to convey smoke or gases, esp one that connects a furnace to a chimney **2** mining another term for **upcast** (sense 2) **3** taking up or lifting up **4** the act of accepting or taking up something on offer or available **5** quick (or slow) on the uptake informal quick (or slow) to understand or learn

uptalk ('ʌpˌtɔːk) n a style of speech in which every sentence ends with a rising tone, as if the speaker is always asking a question

upter or **upta** ('ʌptə) adj Austral slang of poor quality; in disrepair [euphemistic: short for up to shit]

upthrow ('ʌpˌθrəʊ) n **1** geology the upward movement of rocks on one side of a fault plane relative to rocks on the other side **2** rare an upward thrust or throw; upheaval

upthrust ('ʌpˌθrʌst) n **1** an upward push or thrust **2** geology a violent upheaval of the earth's surface

uptick ('ʌptɪk) n a rise or increase

uptight (ʌp'taɪt) adj informal **1** displaying tense repressed nervousness, irritability, or anger **2** unable to give expression to one's feelings, personality, etc

uptilt (ʌp'tɪlt) vb (tr) to tilt up

uptime ('ʌpˌtaɪm) n commerce time during which a machine, such as a computer, actually operates

uptitling (ʌp'taɪtᵊlɪŋ) n jocular the practice of conferring grandiose job titles to employees performing relatively menial jobs [c20 from UP + TITLE (sense 4)]

up-to-date adj **a** modern, current, or fashionable **b** (predicative): the magazine is up to date ▷ 'up-to-'dately adv ▷ 'up-to-'dateness n

uptown ('ʌp'taʊn) US and Canadian ▷ adj, adv **1** towards, in, or relating to some part of a town that is away from the centre ▷ n **2** such a part of a town, esp a residential part ▷ 'up'towner n

upturn vb (ʌp'tɜːn) **1** to turn or cause to turn up, over, or upside down **2** (tr) to create disorder **3** (tr) to direct upwards ▷ n ('ʌpˌtɜːn) **4** an upward turn, trend, or improvement **5** an upheaval or commotion

UPVC abbreviation for unplasticized polyvinyl chloride. See also **PVC**

upward ('ʌpwəd) adj **1** directed or moving towards a higher point or level ▷ adv **2** a variant of **upwards**. ▷ 'upwardly adv ▷ 'upwardness n

upwardly mobile adj (of a person or social group) moving or aspiring to move to a higher social class or to a position of increased status or power

upward mobility n sociol the movement of an individual, social group, or class to a position of increased status or power. Compare **downward mobility**. See also **horizontal mobility, vertical mobility**

upwards ('ʌpwədz) or **upward** adv **1** from a lower to a higher place, level, condition, etc **2** towards a higher level, standing, etc

upwind ('ʌp'wɪnd) adv **1** into or against the wind **2** towards or on the side where the wind is blowing; windward ▷ adj **3** going against the wind **4** on the windward side

Ur (ɜː) n an ancient city of Sumer located on a former channel of the Euphrates

UR text messaging abbreviation for **1** you are **2** your

ur- combining form a variant of **uro-¹** and **uro-²** before a vowel

Ur- combining form original, primitive: Ursprache [German]

uracil ('jʊərəsɪl) n biochem a pyrimidine present in all living cells, usually in a combined form, as in RNA. Formula: $C_4H_4N_2O_2$ [c20 from URO-¹ + ACETIC + -ILE]

uraemia or US **uremia** (jʊ'riːmɪə) n pathol the accumulation of waste products, normally excreted in the urine, in the blood: causes severe headaches, vomiting, etc. Also called: azotaemia [c19 from New Latin, from Greek ouron urine + haima blood] ▷ u'raemic or US u'remic adj

uraeus (jʊ'riːəs) n, pl -uses the sacred serpent represented on the headdresses of ancient Egyptian kings and gods [c19 from New Latin, from Greek ouraios, from Egyptian uro asp]

Ural ('jʊərəl; Russian u'ral) n a river in central Russia, rising in the S Ural Mountains and flowing south to the Caspian Sea. Length: 2534 km (1575 miles)

Ural-Altaic n **1** a postulated group of related languages consisting of the Uralic and Altaic families of languages ▷ adj **2** of or relating to this group of languages, characterized by agglutination and vowel harmony

Uralic (jʊ'rælɪk) or **Uralian** (jʊ'reɪlɪən) n **1** a superfamily of languages consisting of the Finno-Ugric family together with Samoyed. See also **Ural-Altaic** ▷ adj **2** of or relating to these languages

uralite ('jʊərəˌlaɪt) n an amphibole mineral, similar to hornblende, that replaces pyroxene in some igneous and metamorphic rocks [c19 from the URAL MOUNTAINS where it was first found + -ITE¹] ▷ uralitic (ˌjʊərə'lɪtɪk) adj

Ural Mountains or **Urals** pl n a mountain system in W central Russia, extending over 2000 km (1250 miles) from the Arctic Ocean towards the Aral Sea: forms part of the geographical boundary between Europe and Asia; one of the richest mineral areas in the world, with many associated major industrial centres. Highest peak: Mount Narodnaya, 1894 m (6214 ft)

uranalysis (ˌjʊərə'nælɪsɪs) n, pl -ses (-ˌsiːz) med a variant spelling of **urinalysis**

Urania (jʊ'reɪnɪə) n Greek myth **1** the Muse of astronomy **2** another name of **Aphrodite** [c17 from Latin, from Greek Ourania, from ouranios heavenly, from ouranos heaven]

Uranian (jʊ'reɪnɪən) n **1** a hypothetical inhabitant of the planet Uranus ▷ adj **2** of, occurring on, or relating to the planet Uranus **3** of the heavens; celestial **4** relating to astronomy **5** (as an epithet of Aphrodite) heavenly; spiritual **6** of or relating to the Muse Urania

uranic¹ (jʊ'rænɪk) adj of or containing uranium, esp in high valence state

uranic² (jʊ'rænɪk) adj obsolete astronomical or celestial [c19 from Greek ouranos heaven]

uranide ('jʊərəˌnaɪd) n any element having an atomic number greater than that of protactinium

uraninite (jʊ'rænɪˌnaɪt) n a blackish heavy radioactive mineral consisting of uranium oxide in cubic crystalline form together with radium, lead, helium, etc: occurs in coarse granite. Formula: UO_2 [c19 see URANIUM, -IN, -ITE¹]

uranism ('jʊərəˌnɪzəm) n a rare word for **homosexuality** (esp male homosexuality) [c20 from German Uranismus, from Greek ouranios heavenly, i.e. spiritual; compare URANIAN (sense 5)]

uranite ('jʊərəˌnaɪt) n any of various minerals containing uranium, esp torbernite or autunite ▷ uranitic (ˌjʊərə'nɪtɪk) adj

uranium (jʊ'reɪnɪəm) n a radioactive silvery-white metallic element of the actinide series. It occurs in several minerals including pitchblende, carnotite, and autunite and is used chiefly as a source of nuclear energy by fission of the radioisotope **uranium-235**. Symbol: U; atomic no: 92; atomic wt: 238.0289; half-life of most stable isotope, ^{238}U: 451×10^9 years; valency: 2-6; relative density: 18.95 (approx.); melting pt: 1135°C; boiling pt: 4134°C [c18 from New Latin, from URANUS²; from the fact that the element was discovered soon after the planet]

uranium hexafluoride (ˌhɛksə'flʊəˌraɪd) n a compound used in the process of uranium enrichment that produces fissile material for nuclear reactors and nuclear weapons. Formula: UF_6

uranium series n physics a radioactive series that starts with uranium-238 and proceeds by radioactive decay to lead-206

urano- combining form denoting the heavens: uranography [from Greek ouranos]

u

uranography (ˌjʊərəˈnɒɡrəfɪ) *n obsolete* the branch of astronomy concerned with the description and mapping of the stars, galaxies, etc ▷ ˌuraˈnographer *or* ˌuraˈnographist *n* ▷ ˌuranoˈgraphic (ˌjʊərənəˈɡræfɪk) *or* ˌuranoˈgraphical *adj*

uranous (ˈjʊərənəs) *adj* of or containing uranium, esp in a low valence state

Uranus¹ (jʊˈreɪnəs, ˈjʊərənəs) *n Greek myth* the personification of the sky, who, as a god, ruled the universe and fathered the Titans and Cyclopes on his wife and mother Gaea (earth). He was overthrown by his son Cronus

Uranus² (jʊˈreɪnəs, ˈjʊərənəs) *n* one of the giant planets, the seventh planet from the sun, sometimes visible to the naked eye. It has about 15 satellites, a ring system, and an axis of rotation almost lying in the plane of the orbit. Mean distance from sun: 2870 million km; period of revolution around sun: 84 years; period of axial rotation: 17.23 hours; diameter and mass: 4 and 14.5 times that of earth respectively [C19 from Latin *Ūranus*, from Greek *Ouranos* heaven]

uranyl (ˈjʊərənɪl) *n* (*modifier*) of, consisting of, or containing the divalent ion UO_2^{2+} or the group $–UO_2$ [C19 from URANIUM + -YL] ▷ ˌuraˈnylic *adj*

urate (ˈjʊəreɪt) *n* any salt or ester of uric acid ▷ **uratic** (jʊˈrætɪk) *adj*

urban (ˈɜːbən) *adj* 1 of, relating to, or constituting a city or town 2 living in a city or town 3 (of music) emerging and developing in densely populated areas of large cities, esp those populated by people of African or Caribbean origin. Compare **rural** [C17 from Latin *urbānus*, from *urbs* city]

urban area *n* (in population censuses) a city area considered as the inner city plus built-up environs, irrespective of local body administrative boundaries

urban blues *n* (*sometimes functioning as singular*) an extrovert and rhythmic style of blues, usually accompanied by a band. Compare **country blues**

urban district *n* 1 (in England and Wales from 1888 to 1974 and Northern Ireland from 1898 to 1973) an urban division of an administrative county with an elected council in charge of housing and environmental services: usually made up of one or more thickly populated areas but lacking a borough charter 2 (in the Republic of Ireland) any of 49 medium-sized towns with their own elected councils

urbane (ɜːˈbeɪn) *adj* characterized by elegance or sophistication [C16 from Latin *urbānus* belonging to the town; see URBAN] ▷ urˈbanely *adv* ▷ urˈbaneness *n*

urban guerrilla *n* a guerrilla who operates in a town or city, engaging in terrorism, kidnapping, etc

urbanism (ˈɜːbəˌnɪzəm) *n chiefly US* 1 **a** the character of city life **b** the study of this 2 a less common term for **urbanization**

urbanite (ˈɜːbəˌnaɪt) *n* a resident of an urban community; city dweller

urbanity (ɜːˈbænɪtɪ) *n, pl* -ties 1 the quality of being urbane 2 (*usually plural*) civilities or courtesies

urbanize *or* **urbanise** (ˈɜːbəˌnaɪz) *vb* (*tr*) (*usually passive*) **a** to make (esp a predominantly rural area or country) more industrialized and urban **b** to cause the migration of an increasing proportion of (rural dwellers) into cities ▷ ˌurbaniˈzation *or* ˌurbaniˈsation *n*

urban myth *n* a story, esp one with a shocking or amusing ending, related as having actually happened, usu to someone vaguely connected with the teller

urban renewal *n* the process of redeveloping dilapidated or no longer functional urban areas

urbi et orbi *Latin* (ˈɜːbɪ ɛt ˈɔːbɪ) *adv RC Church* to the city and the world: a phrase qualifying the solemn papal blessing

URC *abbreviation for* United Reformed Church

urceolate (ˈɜːsɪəlɪt, -ˌleɪt) *adj biology* shaped like an urn or pitcher: *an urceolate corolla* [C18 via New Latin *urceolātus*, from Latin *urceolus* diminutive of *urceus* a pitcher]

urchin (ˈɜːtʃɪn) *n* 1 a mischievous roguish child, esp one who is young, small, or raggedly dressed 2 See **sea urchin, heart urchin** 3 an archaic or dialect name for a **hedgehog** 4 either of the two cylinders in a carding machine that are covered with carding cloth 5 *obsolete* an elf or sprite [C13 *urchon*, from Old French *heriçon*, from Latin *ēricius* hedgehog, from *ēr*, related to Greek *khēr* hedgehog]

urd (ɜːd) *n* another name for **black gram** (see **gram²** (sense 1)) [Hindi]

urdé *or* **urdée** (ˈɜːdeɪ, -diː, -dɪ) *adj heraldry* having points; pointed [C16 *urdee*: probably a misreading and misunderstanding of French *vidée* in the phrase *croix aiquissée et vidée* cross sharply pointed and reduced]

Urdu (ˈʊəduː, ˈɜː-) *n* an official language of Pakistan, also spoken in India. The script derives primarily from Persia. It belongs to the Indic branch of the Indo-European family of languages, being closely related to Hindi but containing many Arabic and Persian loan words [C18 from Hindustani (*zabāni*) *urdū* (language of the) camp, from Persian *urdū* camp, from Turkish *ordū*]

-ure *suffix forming nouns* 1 indicating act, process, or result: *seizure* 2 indicating function or office: *legislature; prefecture* [from French, from Latin *-ūra*]

urea (ˈjʊərɪə) *n* a white water-soluble crystalline compound with a saline taste and often an odour of ammonia, produced by protein metabolism and excreted in urine. A synthetic form is used as a fertilizer, animal feed, and in the manufacture of synthetic resins. Formula: $CO(NH_2)_2$. Also called: **carbamide** [C19 from New Latin, from French *urée*, from Greek *ouron* URINE] ▷ uˈreal *or* uˈreic *adj*

urea cycle *n* the sequence of metabolic reactions leading in vertebrates to the synthesis of urea

urea-formaldehyde resin *n* any one of a class of rigid odourless synthetic materials that are made from urea and formaldehyde and are used in electrical fittings, adhesives, laminates, and finishes for textiles

urease (ˈjʊərɪˌeɪs, -ˌeɪz) *n* an enzyme occurring in many plants, esp fungi, that converts urea to ammonium carbonate

uredium (jʊˈriːdɪəm) *or* **uredinium** (ˌjʊərɪˈdɪnɪəm) *n, pl* -dia (-dɪə) *or* -dinia (-ˈdɪnɪə) a spore-producing body of some rust fungi in which uredospores are formed. Also called: **uredosorus** [C20 from New Latin, from UREDO] ▷ uˈredial *adj*

uredo (jʊˈriːdəʊ) *n, pl* uredines (jʊˈriːdɪˌniːz) a less common name for **urticaria** [C18 from Latin: burning itch, from *ūrere* to burn]

uredosorus (jʊˌriːdəʊˈsɔːrəs) *n, pl* -sori (-ˈsɔːraɪ) another word for **uredium** [from UREDO + SORUS]

uredospore (jʊˈriːdəʊˌspɔː) *n* any of the brownish spores that are produced in each uredium of the rust fungi and spread the infection between hosts

ureide (ˈjʊərɪˌaɪd) *n chem* 1 any of a class of organic compounds derived from urea by replacing one or more of its hydrogen atoms by organic groups 2 any of a class of derivatives of urea and carboxylic acids, in which one or more of the hydrogen atoms have been replaced by acyl groups: includes the cyclic ureides, such as alloxan

uremia (jʊˈriːmɪə) *n* the usual US spelling of **uraemia**. ▷ uˈremic *adj*

-uret *suffix* formerly used to form the names of binary chemical compounds [from New Latin *-uretum*]

ureter (jʊˈriːtə) *n* the tube that conveys urine from the kidney to the urinary bladder or cloaca [C16 via New Latin from Greek *ourētēr*, from *ourein* to URINATE] ▷ uˈreteral *or* ureteric (ˌjʊərɪˈtɛrɪk) *adj*

urethane (ˈjʊərɪˌθeɪn) *or* **urethan** (ˈjʊərɪˌθæn) *n* 1 short for **polyurethane** 2 another name for **ethyl carbamate** [C19 from URO-¹ + ETHYL + -ANE]

urethra (jʊˈriːθrə) *n, pl* -thrae (-θriː) *or* -thras the canal that in most mammals conveys urine from the bladder out of the body. In human males it also conveys semen [C17 via Late Latin from Greek *ourēthra*, from *ourein* to URINATE] ▷ uˈrethral *adj*

urethritis (ˌjʊərɪˈθraɪtɪs) *n* inflammation of the urethra [C19 from New Latin, from Late Latin URETHRA] ▷ urethritic (ˌjʊərɪˈθrɪtɪk) *adj*

urethroscope (jʊˈriːθrəˌskəʊp) *n* a medical instrument for examining the urethra [C20 see URETHRA, -SCOPE] ▷ urethroscopic (jʊˌriːθrəˈskɒpɪk) *adj* ▷ urethroscopy (ˌjʊərɪˈθrɒskəpɪ) *n*

uretic (jʊˈrɛtɪk) *adj* of or relating to the urine [C19 via Late Latin from Greek *ourētikos*, from *ouron* URINE]

Urfa (ˈɜːfə) *n* a city in SE Turkey: market centre. Pop: 451 000 (2005 est). Ancient name: **Edessa**

Urga (ˈɜːɡə) *n* the former name (until 1924) of **Ulan Bator**

urge (ɜːdʒ) *vb* 1 (*tr*) to plead, press, or move (someone to do something) 2 (*tr; may take a clause as object*) to advocate or recommend earnestly and persistently; plead or insist on 3 (*tr*) to impel, drive, or hasten onwards: *he urged the horses on* 4 (*tr*) *archaic or literary* to stimulate, excite, or incite ▷ *n* 5 a strong impulse, inner drive, or yearning [C16 from Latin *urgēre*]

urgent (ˈɜːdʒənt) *adj* 1 requiring or compelling speedy action or attention 2 earnest and persistent [C15 via French from Latin *urgent-, urgens*, present participle of *urgēre* to URGE] ▷ **urgency** (ˈɜːdʒənsɪ) *n* ▷ ˈurgently *adv*

-urgy *n combining form* indicating technology concerned with a specified material: *metallurgy* [from Greek *-urgia*, from *ergon* WORK]

Uri (German ˈuːrɪ) *n* one of the original three cantons of Switzerland, in the centre of the country: mainly German-speaking and Roman Catholic. Capital: Altdorf. Pop: 35 200 (2002 est). Area: 1075 sq km (415 sq miles)

-uria *n combining form* indicating a diseased or abnormal condition of the urine: *dysuria; pyuria* [from Greek *-ouria*, from *ouron* urine] ▷ **-uric** *adj combining form*

Uriah (jʊˈraɪə) *n Old Testament* a Hittite officer, who was killed in battle on instructions from David so that he could marry Uriah's wife Bathsheba (II Samuel 11)

uric (ˈjʊərɪk) *adj* of, concerning, or derived from urine [C18 from URO-¹ + -IC]

uric acid *n* a white odourless tasteless crystalline product of protein metabolism, present in the blood and urine; 2,6,8-trihydroxypurine. Formula: $C_5H_4N_4O_3$

uridine (ˈjʊərɪˌdiːn) *n biochem* a nucleoside present in all living cells in a combined form, esp in RNA [C20 from URO-¹ + -IDE + -INE²]

uridylic acid (ˌjuːrɪˈdɪlɪk) *n* a nucleotide consisting of uracil, ribose, and a phosphate group. It is a constituent of RNA. Also called: **uridine monophosphate**

Uriel (ˈjʊərɪəl) *n* one of the four chief angels in Jewish apocryphal writings

Urim and Thummim (ˈjʊərɪm, ˈθʌmɪm) *n Old Testament* two objects probably used as oracles and carried in the breastplate of the high priest (Exodus 28:30) [C16 from Hebrew]

urinal (jʊˈraɪnˀl, ˈjʊərɪ-) *n* 1 a sanitary fitting, esp one fixed to a wall, used by men for urination 2 a room containing urinals 3 any vessel for holding urine prior to its disposal

urinalysis (ˌjʊərɪˈnælɪsɪs) *or* **uranalysis** *n, pl* -ses (-ˌsiːz) *med* analysis of the urine to test for the presence of disease by the presence of protein, glucose, ketones, cells, etc

urinant (ˈjʊərɪnənt) *adj heraldry* having the head downwards [C17 from Latin *ūrināri* to dive]

urinary (ˈjʊərɪnərɪ) *adj* 1 *anatomy* of or relating to urine or to the organs and structures that secrete and pass urine ▷ *n, pl* -naries 2 a reservoir for urine 3 another word for **urinal**

urinary bladder *n* a distensible membranous sac in which the urine excreted from the kidneys is stored

urinate ('jʊərɪ,neɪt) *vb* (*intr*) to excrete or void urine; micturate > **uri'nation** *n* > **'urinative** *adj*

urine ('jʊərɪn) *n* the pale yellow slightly acid fluid excreted by the kidneys, containing waste products removed from the blood. It is stored in the urinary bladder and discharged through the urethra. Related adj: **uretic** [C14 via Old French from Latin *ūrīna*; related to Greek *ouron*, Latin *ūrīnāre* to plunge under water]

uriniferous (,jʊərɪ'nɪfərəs) *adj* conveying urine

urinogenital (,jʊərɪnəʊ'dʒɛnɪtᵊl) *adj* another word for **urogenital** *or* **genitourinary**

urinometer (,jʊərɪ'nɒmɪtə) *n med* an instrument for determining the specific gravity of urine

urinous ('jʊərɪnəs) *or* **urinose** *adj* of, resembling, or containing urine

URL *abbreviation for* uniform resource locator; a standardized address of a location on the internet, esp on the World Wide Web

Urmia ('ɜːmɪə) *n* **Lake** a shallow lake in NW Iran, at an altitude of 1300 m (4250 ft): the largest lake in Iran, varying in area from 4000–6000 sq km (1500–2300 sq miles) between autumn and spring

Urmston ('ɜːmstən) *n* a town in NW England, in Salford unitary authority, Greater Manchester. Pop: 40 964 (2001)

urn (ɜːn) *n* **1** a vaselike receptacle or vessel, esp a large bulbous one with a foot **2** a vase used as a receptacle for the ashes of the dead **3** a large vessel, usually of metal, with a tap, used for making and holding tea, coffee, etc **4** *botany* the spore-producing capsule of a moss [C14 from Latin *ūrna*; related to Latin *ūrere* to burn, *urceus* pitcher, Greek *hurkhē* jar] > **'urn,like** *adj*

urnfield ('ɜːn,fiːld) *n* **1** a cemetery full of individual cremation urns ▷ *adj* **2** (of a number of Bronze Age cultures) characterized by cremation in urns, which began in E Europe about the second millennium BC and by the seventh century BC had covered almost all of mainland Europe

urning ('ɜːnɪŋ) *n* a rare word for **homosexual** (esp a male homosexual) [C20 from German, from URANIA (Aphrodite); compare URANISM]

uro-¹ *or before a vowel* **ur-** *combining form* indicating urine or the urinary tract: *urochrome; urogenital; urolith; urology* [from Greek *ouron* urine]

uro-² *or before a vowel* **ur-** *combining form* indicating a tail: *urochord; uropod; urostyle* [from Greek *oura*]

urobilin (,jʊərəʊ'baɪlɪn) *n* a brownish pigment found in faeces and sometimes in urine. It is formed by oxidation of **urobilinogen**, a colourless substance produced by bacterial degradation of the bile pigment bilirubin in the intestine

urochord ('jʊərəʊ,kɔːd) *n* **1** the notochord of a larval tunicate, typically confined to the tail region ▷ *n*, *adj* **2** Also: **urochordate** (,jʊərəʊ'kɔːdeɪt) Another word for **tunicate** [C19 from URO-² + *chord*, a variant of CORD] > **'uro,chordal** *adj*

urochrome ('jʊərəʊ,krəʊm) *n* the yellowish pigment that colours urine [C19 from URO-¹ + -CHROME]

urodele ('jʊərəʊ,diːl) *n* **1** any amphibian of the order *Urodela*, having a long body and tail and four short limbs: includes the salamanders and newts ▷ *adj* **2** of, relating to, or belonging to the *Urodela* [C19 from French *urodèle*, from URO-² + -*dèle*, from Greek *dēlos* evident]

urodynamics (,jʊərəʊdaɪ'næmɪks) *n* (*functioning as singular*) the study and measurement of the flow of urine in the urinary tract

urogenital (,jʊərəʊ'dʒɛnɪtᵊl) *or* **urinogenital** *adj* of or relating to the urinary and genital organs and their functions. Also: **genitourinary**

urogenital system *or* **tract** *n anatomy* the urinary tract and reproductive organs

urogenous (jʊ'rɒdʒɪnəs) *adj* **1** producing or derived from urine **2** involved in the secretion and excretion of urine

urography (jʊ'rɒɡrəfɪ) *n* another word for **pyelography**

urolith ('jʊərəʊlɪθ) *n pathol* a calculus in the urinary tract [from URO-¹ + Greek *lithos* stone] > **,uro'lithic** *adj*

urology (jʊ'rɒlədʒɪ) *n* the branch of medicine concerned with the study and treatment of diseases of the urogenital tract > **urologic** (,jʊərə'lɒdʒɪk) *or* **,uro'logical** *adj* > **u'rologist** *n*

uropod ('jʊərəʊ,pɒd) *n* the paired appendage that arises from the last segment of the body in lobsters and related crustaceans and forms part of the tail fan [C19 from URO-² + -POD] > **uropodal** (jʊ'rɒpədᵊl) *or* **u'ropodous** *adj*

uropygial gland *n* a gland, situated at the base of the tail in most birds, that secretes oil used in preening

uropygium (,jʊərə'pɪdʒɪəm) *n* the hindmost part of a bird's body, from which the tail feathers grow [C19 via New Latin from Greek *ouropugion*, from URO-² + *pugē* rump] > **,uro'pygial** *adj*

uroscopy (jʊ'rɒskəpɪ) *n med* examination of the urine. See also **urinalysis**. > **uroscopic** (,jʊərə'skɒpɪk) *adj* > **u'roscopist** *n*

urostyle ('jʊərəʊ,staɪl) *n* the bony rod forming the last segment of the vertebral column of frogs, toads, and related amphibians [C19 from URO-² + Greek *stulos* pillar]

Urquhart Castle ('ɜːkət) *n* a castle near Drumnadrochit in Highland, Scotland: situated on Loch Ness

Ursa Major ('ɜːsə 'meɪdʒə) *n, Latin genitive* **Ursae Majoris** ('ɜːsiː məˈdʒɔːrɪs) an extensive conspicuous constellation in the N hemisphere, visible north of latitude 40°. The seven brightest stars form the **Plough**. A line through the two brightest stars points to the Pole Star lying in **Ursa Minor**. Also called: **the Great Bear, the Bear** [Latin: greater bear]

Ursa Minor ('ɜːsə 'maɪnə) *n, Latin genitive* **Ursae Minoris** ('ɜːsiː mɪ'nɔːrɪs) a small faint constellation, the brightest star of which is the Pole Star, lying 1° from the true celestial pole. Also called: **the Little Bear, the Bear,** (*US and Canadian*) **the Little Dipper** [Latin: lesser bear]

ursine ('ɜːsaɪn) *adj* of, relating to, or resembling a bear or bears [C16 from Latin *ursus* a bear]

Ursprache *German* ('uːrˌʃpraːxə) *n* any hypothetical extinct and unrecorded language reconstructed from groups of related recorded languages. For example, Germanic is an *Ursprache* reconstructed by comparison of English, Dutch, German, the Scandinavian languages, and Gothic; Indo-European is an *Ursprache* reconstructed by comparison of the Germanic group, Latin, Sanskrit, etc [from *ur-* primeval, original + *Sprache* language]

Ursuline ('ɜːsjʊ,laɪn) *n* a member of an order of nuns devoted to teaching in the Roman Catholic Church: founded in 1537 at Brescia [C16 named after St Ursula, legendary British princess and martyr of the fourth or fifth century AD, patron saint of St Angela Merici, who founded the order]

Urtext *German* ('uːrtɛkst) *n* **1** the earliest form of a text as established by linguistic scholars as a basis for variants in later texts still in existence **2** an edition of a musical score showing the composer's intentions without later editorial interpolation [from *ur-* original + TEXT]

urticaceous (,ɜːtɪ'keɪʃəs) *adj* of, relating to, or belonging to the *Urticaceae*, a family of plants, having small flowers and, in many species, stinging hairs: includes the nettles and pellitory [C18 via New Latin from Latin *urtīca* nettle, from *ūrere* to burn]

urticaria (,ɜːtɪ'kɛərɪə) *n* a skin condition characterized by the formation of itchy red or whitish raised patches, usually caused by an allergy. Nontechnical names: hives, nettle rash [C18 from New Latin, from Latin *urtīca* nettle] > **,urti'carial** *or* **,urti'carious** *adj*

urticate ('ɜːtɪ,keɪt) *adj* **1** Also: urticant ('ɜːtɪkənt) characterized by the presence of weals ▷ *vb* **2** to perform urtication [C19 from Medieval Latin

urtīcāre to sting, from Latin *urtīca* a nettle]

urtication (,ɜːtɪ'keɪʃən) *n* **1** a burning or itching sensation **2** another name for **urticaria 3** a former method of producing counterirritation of the skin by beating the area with nettles

Uru. *abbreviation for* Uruguay

Uruapan (*Spanish* uˈrwapan) *n* a city in SW Mexico, in Michoacán state: agricultural trading centre. Pop: 282 000 (2005 est)

Uruguay ('jʊərə,ɡwaɪ) *n* a republic in South America, on the Atlantic: Spanish colonization began in 1624, followed by Portuguese settlement in 1680; revolted against Spanish rule in 1820 but was annexed by the Portuguese to Brazil; gained independence in 1825. Official language: Spanish. Religion: Roman Catholic majority. Currency: peso. Capital: Montevideo. Pop: 3 439 000 (2004 est). Area: 176 215 sq km (68 037 sq miles)

Uruguayan (,jʊərə'ɡwaɪən) *adj* **1** of or relating to Uruguay or its inhabitants ▷ *n* **2** a native or inhabitant of Uruguay

Urumchi (uː'ruːmtʃɪ), **Urumqi** *or* **Wu-lu-mu-ch'i** *n* a city in NW China, capital of Xinjiang Uygur Autonomous Region: trading centre on a N route between China and central Asia. Pop: 1 562 000 (2005 est). Former name: Tihwa

Urundi (ʊ'rʊndɪ) *n* the former name (until 1962) of **Burundi**

urus ('jʊərəs) *n, pl* **uruses** another name for the **aurochs** [C17 from Latin *ūrus*, of Germanic origin; compare Old High German *ūr*, Old Norse *urr*, Greek *ouros* aurochs]

urushiol ('uːrʊʃɪ,ɒl, u:'ru:-) *n* a poisonous pale yellow liquid occurring in poison ivy and the lacquer tree [from Japanese *urushi* lacquer + -OL²]

us¹ (ʌs) *pron* (*objective*) **1** refers to the speaker or writer and another person or other people: *don't hurt us; to decide among us* **2** refers to all people or people in general: *this table shows us the tides* **3** an informal word for **me¹**: *give us a kiss!* **4** a formal word for **me¹** used by editors, monarchs, etc **5** *chiefly US* a dialect word for **ourselves** when used as an indirect object: *we ought to get us a car* [Old English *ūs*; related to Old High German *uns*, Old Norse *oss*, Latin *nōs*, Sanskrit *nas* we]

☐ USAGE See at **me¹**

us² *the internet domain name for* United States

US *or* **US** *abbreviation for* United States

U/S *informal abbreviation for* **1** unserviceable **2** useless

u.s. *abbreviation for* **1** ubi supra **2** ut supra

USA 1 *abbreviation for* United States Army **2** *international car registration for* United States of America

U.S.A. *or* **USA** *abbreviation for* United States of America

usable *or* **useable** ('juːzəbᵊl) *adj* able to be used > **,usa'bility, ,usea'bility, 'usableness** *or* **'useableness** *n* > **'usably** *or* **'useably** *adv*

USAF *abbreviation for* United States Air Force

usage ('juːsɪdʒ, -zɪdʒ) *n* **1** the act or a manner of using; use **2** constant use, custom, or habit **3** something permitted or established by custom or practice **4** what is actually said in a language, esp as contrasted with what is prescribed [C14 via Old French, from Latin *ūsus* USE (n)]

usance ('juːzəns) *n* **1** *commerce* the period of time permitted by commercial usage for the redemption of foreign bills of exchange **2** *rare* unearned income **3** an obsolete word for **usage, usury** *or* **use** [C14 from Old French, from Medieval Latin *ūsantia*, from *ūsāre* to USE]

USB *abbreviation for* Universal Serial Bus: a standard for connection sockets on computers and other electronic equipment

USB drive *n computing* another name for **flash drive**

USB key *n computing* another name for **pocket drive**

USB port *n computing* a type of serial port for connecting peripheral devices in a system

USDAW ('ʌz,dɔː) *n acronym for* Union of Shop,

u

Distributive, and Allied Workers

use *vb* (juːz) (*tr*) **1** to put into service or action; employ for a given purpose **2** to make a practice or habit of employing; exercise **3** to behave towards **4** to behave towards in a particular way for one's own ends: *he uses people* **5** to consume, expend, or exhaust: *the engine uses very little oil* **6** *chiefly US and Canadian* to partake of (alcoholic drink, drugs, etc) or smoke (tobacco, marijuana, etc) ▷ *n* (juːs) **7** the act of using or the state of being used: *the carpet wore out through constant use* **8** the ability, right, or permission to use **9** the occasion to use; need: *I have no use for this paper* **10** an instance or manner of using **11** usefulness; advantage: *it is of no use to complain* **12** custom; practice; habit: *long use has inured him to it* **13** the purpose for which something is used; end **14** *Christianity* a distinctive form of liturgical or ritual observance, esp one that is traditional in a Church or group of Churches **15** the enjoyment of property, land, etc, by occupation or by deriving revenue or other benefit from it **16** *law* the beneficial enjoyment of property the legal title to which is held by another person as trustee **17** *law* an archaic word for **trust** (sense 7) **18** *philosophy, logic, linguistics* the occurrence of an expression in such a context that it performs its own linguistic function rather than being itself referred to. In *"Fido" refers to Fido,* the name *Fido* is 'used' only on the second occurrence, first being mentioned. Compare **mention** (sense 7). See also **material mode 19 have no use for a** to have no need of **b** to have a contemptuous dislike for **20 make use of a** to employ; use **b** to exploit (a person) ▷ See also **used to, use up** [c13 from Old French *user* to use, from Latin *ūsus* having used, from *ūtī* to use]

use-by date *n* NZ another word for **sell-by date**

used (juːzd) *adj* bought or sold second-hand: *used cars*

used to (juːst) *adj* **1** made familiar with; accustomed to: *I am used to hitchhiking* ▷ *vb* (*tr*) **2** (*takes an infinitive or implied infinitive*) used as an auxiliary to express habitual or accustomed actions, states, etc, taking place in the past but not continuing into the present

> USAGE The most common negative form of *used to* is *didn't used to* (or *didn't use to*), but in formal contexts *used not to* is preferred

useful (ˈjuːsfʊl) *adj* **1** able to be used advantageously, beneficially, or for several purposes; helpful or serviceable **2** *informal* commendable or capable: *a useful term's work* ▷ *n* **3** *Austral informal* an odd-jobman or general factotum > **'usefully** *adv* > **'usefulness** *n*

useless (ˈjuːslɪs) *adj* **1** having no practical use or advantage **2** *informal* ineffectual, weak, or stupid: *he's useless at history* > **'uselessly** *adv* > **'uselessness** *n*

Usenet (ˈjuːzˌnɛt) *n computing* a vast collection of newsgroups that follow agreed naming, maintaining, and distribution practices

user (ˈjuːzə) *n* **1** *law* **a** the continued exercise, use, or enjoyment of a right, esp in property **b** a presumptive right based on long-continued use: *right of user* **2** (*often in combination*) a person or thing that uses: *a road-user* **3** *informal* a drug addict

user-defined key *n* a key on the keyboard of a computer that can be used to carry out any of a limited number of predefined actions as selected by the user

user-friendly *adj* **1** easy to use or understand **2** (of a computer system) easily operated and understood by means of a straightforward guide in jargon-free language > **user-friendliness** *n*

username (ˈjuːzəˌneɪm) *n computing* a name that someone uses for identification purposes when logging onto a computer, using chatrooms, or as part of his or her e-mail address

use up *vb* (*tr, adverb*) **1** to finish (a supply); consume completely **2** to exhaust; wear out

Ushant (ˈʌʃənt) *n* an island off the NW coast of France, at the tip of Brittany: scene of naval

battles in 1778 and 1794 between France and Britain. Area: about 16 sq km (6 sq miles). French name: **Ouessant**

U-shaped valley *n geology* a steep-sided valley caused by glacial erosion

Ushas (ˈuːʃəs) *n* the Hindu goddess of the dawn

usher (ˈʌʃə) *n* **1** an official who shows people to their seats, as in a church or theatre **2** a person who acts as doorkeeper, esp in a court of law **3** (in England) a minor official charged with maintaining order in a court of law **4** an officer responsible for preceding persons of rank in a procession or introducing strangers at formal functions **5** *Brit obsolete* a teacher ▷ *vb* (*tr*) **6** to conduct or escort, esp in a courteous or obsequious way **7** (usually foll by *in*) to be a precursor or herald (of) [c14 from Old French *huissier* doorkeeper, from Vulgar Latin *ustiārius* (unattested), from Latin *ostium* door]

usherette (ˌʌʃəˈrɛt) *n* a woman assistant in a cinema, theatre, etc, who shows people to their seats

Usk (ʌsk) *n* a river in SE Wales, flowing southeast and south to the Bristol Channel. Length: 113 km (70 miles)

Üsküb (ˈʊskuːb) *n* the Turkish name (1392–1913) for **Skopje**

Üsküdar (ˌʊskuːˈdɑː) *n* a town in NW Turkey, across the Bosporus from Istanbul: formerly a terminus of caravan routes from Syria and Asia; base of the British army in the Crimean War. Pop: 261140 (latest est). Former name: **Scutari**

USM *abbreviation for* **1** *stock exchange* **unlisted securities market 2** underwater-to-surface missile

USN *abbreviation for* United States Navy

Usnach *or* **Usnech** (ˈʊʃnəx) *n* (in Irish legend) the father of Naoise

USO (in the US) *abbreviation for* United Service Organization

USP *abbreviation for* unique selling proposition or unique selling point: a characteristic of a product that can be used in advertising to differentiate it from its competitors

Uspallata Pass (ˌuːspəˈlɑːtə; *Spanish* uspaˈʎata) *n* a pass over the Andes in S South America, between Mendoza (Argentina) and Santiago (Chile). Height: 3840 m (12600 ft). Also called: **La Cumbre**

usquebaugh (ˈʌskwɪˌbɔː) *n* **1** *Irish* the former name for **whiskey 2** *Scot* the former name for **whisky 3** an Irish liqueur flavoured with coriander [c16 from Irish Gaelic *uisce beathadh* or Scot Gaelic *uisge beatha* water of life]

USS *abbreviation for* **1** United States Senate **2** United States Ship

USSR (formerly) *abbreviation for* Union of Soviet Socialist Republics

Ussuri (*Russian* ussuˈri) *n* a river in E central Asia, flowing north, forming part of the Chinese border with Russia, to the Amur River. Length: about 800 km (500 miles)

Ustashi (ʊˈstɑːʃɪ) *n* (formerly) a terrorist organization of right-wing Yugoslav exiles dedicated to the overthrow of Communism in their homeland [from Serbo-Croat]

Ústí nad Labem (*Czech* ˈuːstjiː nad ˈlabɛm) *n* a port in the Czech Republic, on the Elbe River: textile and chemical industries. Pop: 95000 (2005 est)

Ust-Kamenogorsk (*Russian* ustjkamɪnaˈɡɔrsk) *n* a city in E Kazakhstan: centre of a zinc-, lead-, and copper-mining area. Pop: 307000 (2005 est)

ustulation (ˌʌstjʊˈleɪʃən) *n* the act or process of searing or burning [c17 from Late Latin *ustulāre*, from Latin *ūrere* to burn]

Ustyurt *or* **Ust Urt** (*Russian* usˈtjurt) *n* an arid plateau in central Asia, between the Caspian and Aral seas in Kazakhstan and Uzbekistan. Area: about 238000 sq km (92000 sq miles)

usual (ˈjuːʒʊəl) *adj* **1** of the most normal, frequent, or regular type ▷ *n* **2** ordinary or commonplace events (esp in the phrase **out of the**

usual) **3 the usual** *informal* the habitual or usual drink, meal, etc [c14 from Late Latin *ūsuālis* ordinary, from Latin *ūsus* USE] > **'usualness** *n*

usually (ˈjuːʒʊəlɪ) *adv* customarily; at most times; in the ordinary course of events

usufruct (ˈjuːsjʊˌfrʌkt) *n* the right to use and derive profit from a piece of property belonging to another, provided the property itself remains undiminished and uninjured in any way [c17 from Late Latin *ūsūfrūctus*, from Latin *ūsus* use + *frūctus* enjoyment] > **ˌusu'fructuary** *n, adj*

Usumbura (ˌuːzəmˈbʊərə) *n* the former name of **Bujumbura**

usurer (ˈjuːʒərə) *n* **1** a person who lends funds at an exorbitant rate of interest **2** *obsolete* a moneylender

usurp (juːˈzɜːp) *vb* to seize, take over, or appropriate (land, a throne, etc) without authority [c14 from Old French *usurper*, from Latin *ūsūrpāre* to take into use, probably from *ūsus* use + *rapere* to seize] > **ˌusur'pation** *n* > **u'surpative** *or* **u'surpatory** *adj* > **u'surper** *n*

usury (ˈjuːʒərɪ) *n, pl* **-ries 1** the act or practice of loaning money at an exorbitant rate of interest **2** an exorbitant or unlawfully high amount or rate of interest **3** *obsolete* moneylending [c14 from Medieval Latin *ūsūria*, from Latin *ūsūra* usage, from *ūsus* USE] > **usurious** (juːˈʒʊərɪəs) *adj*

USW *radio abbreviation for* ultrashort wave

ut (ʌt, uːt) *n music* **1** the syllable used in the fixed system of solmization for the note C **2** the first note of a hexachord in medieval music [c14 from Latin *ut*; see GAMUT]

UT *abbreviation for* **1** universal time **2** Utah

Utah (ˈjuːtɔː, ˈjuːtɑː) *n* a state of the western US: settled by Mormons in 1847; situated in the Great Basin and the Rockies, with the Great Salt Lake in the northwest; mainly arid and mountainous. Capital: Salt Lake City. Pop: 2351467 (2003 est). Area: 212628 sq km (82096 sq miles). Abbreviations: **Ut,** (with zip code) **UT**

Utahan (juːˈtɔːən, -ˈtɑːən) *adj* **1** of or relating to Utah or its inhabitants ▷ *n* **2** a native or inhabitant of Utah

UTC *abbreviation for* universal time coordinated. See **universal time**

ut dict. (in prescriptions) *abbreviation for* as directed [from Latin *ut dictum*]

ute (juːt) *n Austral and NZ informal* short for **utility** (sense 6)

Ute (juːt, ˈjuːtɪ) *n* **1** (*pl* **Utes** *or* **Ute**) a member of a North American Indian people of Utah, Colorado, and New Mexico, related to the Aztecs **2** the language of this people, belonging to the Shoshonean subfamily of the Uto-Aztecan family

utensil (juːˈtɛnsəl) *n* an implement, tool, or container for practical use [c14 *utensele*, via Old French from Latin *ūtēnsilia* necessaries, from *ūtēnsilis* available for use, from *ūtī* to use]

uterine (ˈjuːtəˌraɪn) *adj* **1** of, relating to, or affecting the uterus **2** (of offspring) born of the same mother but not the same father: *uterine brothers*

uterus (ˈjuːtərəs) *n, pl* **uteri** (ˈjuːtəˌraɪ) **1** *anatomy* a hollow muscular organ lying within the pelvic cavity of female mammals. It houses the developing fetus and by contractions aids in its expulsion at parturition. Nontechnical name: **womb 2** the corresponding organ in other animals [c17 from Latin; compare Greek *hustera* womb, *hoderos* belly, Sanskrit *udara* belly]

Utgard (ˈʊtɡɑːd, ˈuːt-) *n Norse myth* one of the divisions of Jotunheim, land of the giants, ruled by Utgard-Loki

Utgard-Loki *n Norse myth* the giant king of Utgard

Uther (ˈjuːθə) *or* **Uther Pendragon** *n* (in Arthurian legend) a king of Britain and father of Arthur

Utica (ˈjuːtɪkə) *n* an ancient city on the N coast of Africa, northwest of Carthage

utile (ˈjuːtaɪl, -tɪl) *adj* an obsolete word for **useful**

[c15 via Old French from Latin *utilis,* from *ūtī* to use]

utilidor (juːˈtɪlɪˌdɔː) *n Canadian* an enclosed and insulated conduit for sewage and other utilities placed above the level of permafrost

utilitarian (juːˌtɪlɪˈtɛərɪən) *adj* **1** of or relating to utilitarianism **2** designed for use rather than beauty ▷ *n* **3** a person who believes in utilitarianism

utilitarianism (juːˌtɪlɪˈtɛərɪəˌnɪzəm) *n ethics* **1** the doctrine that the morally correct course of action consists in the greatest good for the greatest number, that is, in maximizing the total benefit resulting, without regard to the distribution of benefits and burdens **2** the theory that the criterion of virtue is utility

utility (juːˈtɪlɪtɪ) *n, pl* **-ties 1 a** the quality of practical use; usefulness **b** (*as modifier*): *a utility fabric* **2** something useful **3 a** a public service, such as the bus system; public utility **b** (*as modifier*): *utility vehicle* **4** *economics* **a** the ability of a commodity to satisfy human wants **b** the amount of such satisfaction. Compare **disutility 5** *statistics* **a** a measure of the total benefit or disadvantage attaching to each of a set of alternative courses of action **b** (*as modifier*): *utility function.* See also **expected utility, decision theory 6** Also called: **utility truck,** (*informal*) **ute.** *Austral and NZ* a small truck with an open body and low sides, often with a removable tarpaulin cover; pick-up **7** a piece of computer software designed for a routine task, such as examining or copying files [c14 from Old French *utelite,* from Latin *ūtilitās* usefulness, from *ūtī* to use]

utility function *n economics* a function relating specific goods and services in an economy to individual preferences

utility man *n chiefly US* **1** a worker who is expected to serve in any of several capacities **2** an actor who plays any of numerous small parts

utility player *n sport* a player who is capable of playing competently in any of several positions

utility room *n* a room with equipment for domestic work like washing and ironing

utility truck *n* another name for **utility** (sense 6)

utility wear *n* casual clothing that was originally intended for a particular activity, such as snowboarding or skiing

utilize *or* **utilise** (ˈjuːtɪˌlaɪz) *vb* (*tr*) to make practical or worthwhile use of > ˈutiˌlizable *or* ˈutiˌlisable *adj* , ˌutiliˈzation *or* ˌutiliˈsation *n* > ˈutiˌlizer *or* ˈutiˌliser *n*

ut infra *Latin* (ʊt ˈɪnfrɑː) as below

uti possidetis (ˈjuːtaɪ ˌpɒsɪˈdiːtɪs) *n international law* the rule that territory and other property remains in the hands of the belligerent state actually in possession at the end of a war unless otherwise provided for by treaty [from Latin, literally: as you possess]

utmost (ˈʌtˌməʊst) *or* **uttermost** *adj* (*prenominal*) **1** of the greatest possible degree or amount: *the utmost degree* **2** at the furthest limit: *the utmost town on the peninsula* ▷ *n* **3** the greatest possible degree, extent, or amount: *he tried his utmost* [Old English *ūtemest,* from *ūte* out + *-mest* MOST]

utmost good faith *n* a principle used in insurance contracts, legally obliging all parties to reveal to the others any information that might influence the others' decision to enter into the contract. Also called: **uberrima fides**

Uto-Aztecan (ˈjuːtəʊˈæztəkən) *n* **1** a family of North and Central American Indian languages including Nahuatl, Shoshone, Pima, and Ute ▷ *adj* **2** of or relating to this family of languages or the peoples speaking them

Utopia (juːˈtəʊpɪə) *n* (*sometimes not capital*) any real or imaginary society, place, state, etc, considered to be perfect or ideal [c16 from New Latin *Utopia*

(coined by Sir Thomas More in 1516 as the title of his book that described an imaginary island representing the perfect society), literally: no place, from Greek *ou* not + *topos* a place]

Utopian (juːˈtəʊpɪən) (*sometimes not capital*) *adj* **1** of or relating to a perfect or ideal existence ▷ *n* **2** an idealistic social reformer > U'topianism *n*

utopian socialism *n* (*sometimes capitals*) socialism established by the peaceful surrender of the means of production by capitalists moved by moral persuasion, example, etc: the form of socialism advocated by Robert Owen, the Welsh industrialist and social reformer (1771–1858), Johann Gottlieb Fichte, the German philosopher (1762–1814), and others. Compare **scientific socialism**

Utrecht (*Dutch* ˈyːtrɛxt; *English* ˈjuːtrɛkt) *n* **1** a province of the W central Netherlands. Capital: Utrecht. Pop: 1 152 000 (2003 est). Area: 1362 sq km (526 sq miles) **2** a city in the central Netherlands, capital of Utrecht province: scene of the signing (1579) of the **Union of Utrecht** (the foundation of the later kingdom of the Netherlands) and of the **Treaty of Utrecht** (1713), ending the War of the Spanish Succession. Pop: 265 000 (2003 est)

utricle (ˈjuːtrɪkᵊl) *or* **utriculus** (juːˈtrɪkjʊləs) *n, pl* **utricles** *or* **utriculi** (juːˈtrɪkjʊˌlaɪ) **1** *anatomy* the larger of the two parts of the membranous labyrinth of the internal ear. Compare **saccule 2** *botany* the bladder-like one-seeded indehiscent fruit of certain plants, esp sedges [c18 from Latin *ūtriculus* diminutive of *ūter* bag] > u'tricular *or* u'triculate *adj*

utriculitis (juːˌtrɪkjʊˈlaɪtɪs) *n* inflammation of the inner ear

ut supra *Latin* (ʊt ˈsuːprɑː) as above

Uttaranchal (ˈʊtəˈræntʃʌl) *n* a state of N India, created in 2000 from the N part of Uttar Pradesh: in the Himalayas, rising to over 7500 m (25 000 ft); rice, tea, and timber. Capital: Dehra Dun. Pop: 8 479 562 (2001). Area: 51 125 sq km (19 739 sq miles)

Uttar Pradesh (ˈʊtə ˈprɑːdɛʃ) *n* a state of N India: the most populous state; originated in 1877 with the merging of Agra and Oudh as the United Provinces; augmented by the states of Rampur, Benares, and Tehri-Garhwal in 1949; the N Himalayan region passed to the new state of Uttaranchal in 2000; now consists mostly of the Upper Ganges plain; agricultural. Capital: Lucknow. Pop: 166 052 859 (2001). Area: 243 350 sq km (93 933 sq miles)

utter¹ (ˈʌtə) *vb* **1** to give audible expression to (something): *to utter a growl* **2** *criminal law* to put into circulation (counterfeit coin, forged banknotes, etc) **3** (*tr*) to make publicly known; publish: *to utter slander* **4** *obsolete* to give forth, issue, or emit [c14 probably originally a commercial term, from Middle Dutch *ūteren* (modern Dutch *uiteren*) to make known; related to Middle Low German *ūtern* to sell, show] > ˈutterable *adj* > ˈutterableness *n* > ˈutterer *n* > ˈutterless *adj*

utter² (ˈʌtə) *adj* (*prenominal*) (*intensifier*): *an utter fool; utter bliss; the utter limit* [c15 from Old English *utera* outer, comparative of *ūte* OUT (adv); related to Old High German *ūzaro,* Old Norse *ūtri*]

utterance¹ (ˈʌtərəns) *n* **1** something uttered, such as a statement **2** the act or power of uttering or the ability to utter **3** *logic, philosophy* an element of spoken language, esp a sentence. Compare **inscription** (sense 4)

utterance² (ˈʌtərəns) *n archaic or literary* the bitter end (esp in the phrase **to the utterance**) [c13 from Old French *oultrance,* from *oultrer* to carry to excess, from Latin *ultrā* beyond]

utter barrister *n law* the full title of a barrister who is not a Queen's Counsel. See also **junior** (sense 6)

utterly (ˈʌtəlɪ) *adv* (*intensifier*): *I'm utterly miserable*

uttermost (ˈʌtəˌməʊst) *adj, n* a variant of **utmost**

utu (uːtuː) *n NZ* **1** compensation or reward **2** revenge or retribution **3** payment, price, or money [Māori]

U-turn *n* **1** a turn made by a vehicle in the shape of a U, resulting in a reversal of direction **2** a complete change in direction of political or other policy

UU *abbreviation for* Ulster Unionist

UV *abbreviation for* ultraviolet

UV-A *or* **UVA** *abbreviation for* ultraviolet radiation with a range of 315–380 nanometres

uvarovite (uːˈvɑːrəˌvaɪt) *n* an emerald-green garnet found in chromium deposits: consists of calcium chromium silicate. Formula: $Ca_3Cr_2(SiO_4)_3$ [c19 from German *Uvarovit;* named after Count Sergei S *Uvarov* (1785–1855), Russian author and statesman]

UV-B *or* **UVB** *abbreviation for* ultraviolet radiation with a range of 280–315 nanometres

uvea (ˈjuːvɪə) *n* the part of the eyeball consisting of the iris, ciliary body, and choroid [c16 from Medieval Latin *ūvea,* from Latin *ūva* grape] > ˈuveal *or* ˈuveous *adj*

uveitis (ˌjuːvɪˈaɪtɪs) *n* inflammation of the uvea > uveitic (ˌjuːvɪˈɪtɪk) *adj*

UVF *abbreviation for* Ulster Volunteer Force

uvula (ˈjuːvjʊlə) *n, pl* **-las** *or* **-lae** (-ˌliː) a small fleshy finger-like flap of tissue that hangs in the back of the throat and is an extension of the soft palate [c14 from Medieval Latin, literally: a little grape, from Latin *ūva* a grape]

uvular (ˈjuːvjʊlə) *adj* **1** of or relating to the uvula **2** *phonetics* articulated with the uvula and the back of the tongue, such as the (r) sound of Parisian French ▷ *n* **3** a uvular consonant > ˈuvularly *adv*

uvulitis (ˌjuːvjʊˈlaɪtɪs) *n* inflammation of the uvula

UWB *abbreviation for* ultrawideband

UWIST (ˈjuːˌwɪst) *n acronym for* University of Wales Institute of Science and Technology

Uxbridge (ˈʌksˌbrɪdʒ) *n* a town in SE England, part of the Greater London borough of Hillingdon since 1965; chiefly residential; seat of Brunel University (1966)

Uxmal (*Spanish* uzˈmal) *n* an ancient ruined city in SE Mexico, in Yucatán: capital of the later Maya empire

uxorial (ʌkˈsɔːrɪəl) *adj* of or relating to a wife: *uxorial influence* [c19 from Latin *uxor* wife] > uxˈorially *adv*

uxoricide (ʌkˈsɔːrɪˌsaɪd) *n* **1** the act of killing one's wife **2** a man who kills his wife [c19 from Latin *uxor* wife + -CIDE] > uxˌoriˈcidal *adj*

uxorious (ʌkˈsɔːrɪəs) *adj* excessively attached to or dependent on one's wife [c16 from Latin *uxōrius* concerning a wife, from *uxor* wife] > uxˈoriously *adv* > uxˈoriousness *n*

uy *the internet domain name for* Uruguay

uz *the internet domain name for* Uzbekistan

UZ *international car registration for* Uzbekistan

Uzbek (ˈʊzbɛk, ˈʌz-) *n* (*pl* **-beks** *or* **-bek**) a member of a Mongoloid people of Uzbekistan **2** the language of this people, belonging to the Turkic branch of the Altaic family

Uzbekistan (ˌʌzbɛkɪˈstɑːn) *n* a republic in central Asia: annexed by Russia in the 19th century, it became a separate Soviet Socialist republic in 1924 and gained independence in 1991. Official language: Uzbek. Religion: believers are mainly Muslim. Currency: sum. Capital: Tashkent. Pop: 26 479 000 (2004 est). Area: 449 600 sq km (173 546 sq miles)

Uzi (ˈuːzɪ) *n* a sub-machine gun of Israeli design [c20 after *Uziel Gal,* the Israeli army officer who designed it]

u

Vv

v *or* **V** (viː) *n, pl* **v's, V's** *or* **Vs 1** the 22nd letter and 17th consonant of the modern English alphabet **2** a speech sound represented by this letter, in English usually a voiced labio-dental fricative, as in *vote* **3 a** something shaped like a V **b** (*in combination*): *a V neck.* See also **V-sign**

v *symbol for* **1** *physics* velocity **2** specific volume (of a gas)

V *symbol for* **1** (in transformational grammar) verb **2** volume (capacity) **3** volt **4** *chem* vanadium **5** luminous efficiency **6** victory **7** the Roman numeral for five. See **Roman numerals 8** *international car registration for* Vatican City

v. *abbreviation for* **1** verb **2** verse **3** version **4** verso **5** (*usually italic*) versus **6** *vide* [Latin: see] **8** vocative **9** volume **10** von

V. *abbreviation for* **1** Venerable **2** (in titles) Very **3** (in titles) Vice **4** Viscount

V-1 *n* a robot bomb invented by the Germans in World War II: used esp to bombard London. It was propelled by a pulsejet. Also called: **doodlebug, buzz bomb, flying bomb** [from German *Vergeltungswaffe* revenge weapon]

V-2 *n* a rocket-powered ballistic missile invented by the Germans in World War II: used esp to bombard London. It used ethanol as fuel and liquid oxygen as the oxidizer [see V-1]

V6 *n* a car or internal-combustion engine having six cylinders arranged in the form of a V

V8 *n* a car or internal-combustion engine having eight cylinders arranged in the form of a V

va *the internet domain name for* Holy See (Vatican State)

VA *abbreviation for* **1** (in the US) Veterans' Administration **2** Vicar Apostolic **3** Vice Admiral **4** (Order of) Victoria and Albert **5** Virginia **6** **volt-ampere**

Va. *abbreviation for* Virginia

v.a. *abbreviation for* verb active

Vaal (vɑːl) *n* a river in South Africa, rising in the Drakensberg and flowing west to join the Orange River. Length: 1160 km (720 miles)

Vaasa (*Finnish* ˈvɑːsɑ) *n* a port in W Finland, on the Gulf of Bothnia: the provisional capital of Finland (1918); textile industries. Pop: 56 953 (2003 est). Former name: **Nikolainkaupunki**

vac (væk) *n Brit informal* short for **vacation**

vacancy (ˈveɪkənsɪ) *n, pl* **-cies 1** the state or condition of being vacant or unoccupied; emptiness **2** an unoccupied post or office: *we have a vacancy in the accounts department* **3** an unoccupied room in a boarding house, hotel, etc: *put the "No Vacancies" sign in the window* **4** lack of thought or intelligent awareness; inanity: *an expression of vacancy on one's face* **5** *physics* a defect in a crystalline solid caused by the absence of an atom, ion, or molecule from its position in the crystal lattice **6** *obsolete* idleness or a period spent in idleness

vacant (ˈveɪkənt) *adj* **1** without any contents; empty **2** (*postpositive; foll by of*) devoid (of

something specified) **3** having no incumbent; unoccupied: *a vacant post* **4** having no tenant or occupant: *a vacant house* **5** characterized by or resulting from lack of thought or intelligent awareness: *a vacant stare* **6** (of time, etc) not allocated to any activity: *a vacant hour in one's day* **7** spent in idleness or inactivity: *a vacant life* **8** *law* (of an estate, etc) having no heir or claimant [c13 from Latin *vacāre* to be empty] > **ˈvacantly** *adv* > **ˈvacantness** *n*

vacant possession *n* ownership of an unoccupied house or property, any previous owner or tenant having departed

vacate (vəˈkeɪt) *vb* (*mainly tr*) **1** to cause (something) to be empty, esp by departing from or abandoning it: *to vacate a room* **2** (*also intr*) to give up the tenure, possession, or occupancy of (a place, post, etc); leave or quit **3** *law* **a** to cancel or rescind **b** to make void or of no effect; annul > **vaˈcatable** *adj*

vacation (vəˈkeɪʃən) *n* **1** *chiefly Brit* a period of the year when the law courts or universities are closed **2** *chiefly US and Canadian* a period in which a break is taken from work or studies for rest, travel, or recreation. also called (in Britain and certain other countries): **holiday 3** the act of departing from or abandoning property, etc ▷ *vb* **4** (*intr*) *US and Canadian* to take a vacation; holiday [c14 from Latin *vacātiō* freedom, from *vacāre* to be empty] > **vaˈcationless** *adj*

vacationer (vəˈkeɪʃənə) *or* **vacationist** (vəˈkeɪʃənɪst) *n US and Canadian* a person taking a vacation. Also called (esp Brit): **holiday-maker**

vaccinal (ˈvæksɪnəl) *adj* of or relating to vaccine or vaccination

vaccinate (ˈvæksɪˌneɪt) *vb* to inoculate (a person) with a vaccine so as to produce immunity against a specific disease > **ˈvacciˌnator** *n*

vaccination (ˌvæksɪˈneɪʃən) *n* **1** the act of vaccinating **2** the scar left following inoculation with a vaccine

vaccine (ˈvæksiːn) *n med* **1** a suspension of dead, attenuated, or otherwise modified microorganisms (viruses, bacteria, or rickettsiae) for inoculation to produce immunity to a disease by stimulating the production of antibodies **2** (originally) a preparation of the virus of cowpox taken from infected cows and inoculated in humans to produce immunity to smallpox **3** (*modifier*) of or relating to vaccination or vaccinia **4** *computing* a piece of software designed to detect and remove computer viruses from a system [c18 from New Latin *variolae vaccīnae* cowpox, title of medical treatise (1798) by Edward Jenner, from Latin *vacca* a cow]

vaccinia (vækˈsɪnɪə) *n* a technical name for **cowpox** [c19 New Latin, from Latin *vaccīnus* of cows] > **vacˈcinial** *adj*

Vacherin (*French* vaʃrɛ̃) *n* **1** a soft French or Swiss cheese made from cows' milk **2** a dessert consisting of a meringue shell filled with

whipped cream, ice cream, fruit, etc [from French *vache* cow, from Latin *vacca*]

vacillate (ˈvæsɪˌleɪt) *vb* (*intr*) **1** to fluctuate in one's opinions; be indecisive **2** to sway from side to side physically; totter or waver [c16 from Latin *vacillāre* to sway, of obscure origin] > **ˌvacilˈlation** *n* > **ˈvaciˌlator** *n*

vacillating (ˈvæsɪˌleɪtɪŋ) *or rarely* **vacillant** (ˈvæsɪlənt) *adj* inclined to waver; indecisive > **ˈvaciˌlatingly** *adv*

vacua (ˈvækjʊə) *n* a plural of **vacuum**

vacuity (væˈkjuːɪtɪ) *n, pl* **-ties 1** the state or quality of being vacuous; emptiness **2** an empty space or void; vacuum **3** a lack or absence of something specified: *a vacuity of wind* **4** lack of normal intelligence or awareness; vacancy: *his stare gave an impression of complete vacuity* **5** something, such as a statement, saying, etc, that is inane or pointless **6** (in customs terminology) the difference in volume between the actual contents of a container and its full capacity [c16 from Latin *vacuitās* empty space, from *vacuus* empty]

vacuole (ˈvækjʊˌəʊl) *n biology* a fluid-filled cavity in the cytoplasm of a cell [c19 from French, literally: little vacuum, from Latin VACUUM] > **vacuolar** (ˌvækjʊˈəʊlə) *adj* > **vacuolate** (ˈvækjʊəlɪt, -ˌleɪt) *adj* > **vacuolation** (ˌvækjʊəˈleɪʃən) *n*

vacuous (ˈvækjʊəs) *adj* **1** containing nothing; empty **2** bereft of ideas or intelligence; mindless **3** characterized by or resulting from vacancy of mind: *a vacuous gaze* **4** indulging in no useful mental or physical activity; idle **5** *logic, maths* (of an operator or expression) having no import; idle: in (x) (*John is tall*) the quantifier (x) is vacuous [c17 from Latin *vacuus* empty, from *vacāre* to be empty] > **ˈvacuously** *adv* > **ˈvacuousness** *n*

vacuum (ˈvækjʊəm) *n, pl* **vacuums** *or* **vacua** (ˈvækjʊə) **1** a region containing no matter; free space. Compare **plenum** (sense 3) **2** a region in which gas is present at a low pressure **3** the degree of exhaustion of gas within an enclosed space: *a high vacuum; a perfect vacuum* **4** a sense or feeling of emptiness: *his death left a vacuum in her life* **5** short for **vacuum cleaner 6** (*modifier*) of, containing, measuring, producing, or operated by a low gas pressure: *a vacuum tube; a vacuum brake* ▷ *vb* **7** to clean (something) with a vacuum cleaner: *to vacuum a carpet* [c16 from Latin: an empty space, from *vacuus* empty]

vacuum activity *n ethology* instinctive behaviour occurring in the absence of the appropriate stimulus

vacuum brake *n* a brake system, used on British and many overseas railways, in which the brake is held off by a vacuum on one side of the brake-operating cylinder. If the vacuum is destroyed by controlled leakage of air or a disruptive emergency the brake is applied. It is now largely superseded by the Westinghouse brake system

vacuum cleaner *n* an electrical household

appliance used for cleaning floors, carpets, furniture, etc, by suction > vacuum cleaning *n*

vacuum distillation *n* distillation in which the liquid distilled is enclosed at a low pressure in order to reduce its boiling point

vacuum flask *n* an insulating flask that has double walls, usually of silvered glass, with an evacuated space between them. It is used for maintaining substances at high or low temperatures. Also called: Thermos, Dewar flask

vacuum forming *n* a process in which a sheet of warmed thermoplastic is shaped by placing it in a mould and applying suction

vacuum frame *n* printing a machine from which the air is extracted in order to obtain close contact between the surfaces of two materials, eg the film and plate during platemaking

vacuum gauge *n* any of a number of instruments for measuring pressures below atmospheric pressure

vacuum-packed *adj* packed in an airtight container or packet under low pressure in order to maintain freshness, prevent corrosion, etc

vacuum pump *n* a pump for producing a low gas pressure

vacuum servo *n* a servomechanism that is operated by the lowering of pressure in the intake duct of an internal-combustion engine

vacuum tube *or* **valve** *n* another name for **valve** (sense 3)

VAD 1 *abbreviation for* **Voluntary Aid Detachment** ▷ *n* **2** a nurse serving in the Voluntary Aid Detachment

vade mecum (ˈvɑːdɪ ˈmeɪkʊm) *n* a handbook or other aid carried on the person for immediate use when needed [c17 from Latin, literally: go with me]

Vadodara (wəˈdəʊdərə) *n* a city in W India, in SE Gujarat: textile manufacturing. Pop: 1 306 035 (2001). Former name (until 1976): **Baroda**

vadose (ˈveɪdəʊs) *adj* of, relating to, designating, or derived from water occurring above the water table: *vadose water; vadose deposits* [c19 from Latin *vadōsus* full of shallows, from *vadum* a ford]

Vaduz (*German* faˈdʊts) *n* the capital of Liechtenstein, in the Rhine valley: an old market town, dominated by a medieval castle, residence of the prince of Liechtenstein. Pop: 5005 (2003 est)

vag (væg) *Austral informal* ▷ *n* **1** a vagrant **2** the **vag** the Vagrancy Act: *the police finally got him on the vag* ▷ *vb* **vags, vagging, vagged 3** (*tr*) to arrest (someone) for vagrancy

vagabond (ˈvægəˌbɒnd) *n* **1** a person with no fixed home **2** an idle wandering beggar or thief **3** (*modifier*) of or like a vagabond; shiftless or idle [c15 from Latin *vagābundus* wandering, from *vagārī* to roam, from *vagus* VAGUE] > ˈvagaˌbondage *n* > ˈvagaˌbondish *adj* > ˈvagaˌbondism *n*

vagal (ˈveɪɡəl) *adj* anatomy of, relating to, or affecting the vagus nerve: *vagal inhibition*

vagarious (vəˈɡɛərɪəs) *adj* rare characterized or caused by vagaries; irregular or erratic > vaˈgariously *adv*

vagary (ˈveɪɡərɪ, vəˈɡɛərɪ) *n, pl* -garies an erratic or outlandish notion or action; whim [c16 probably from Latin *vagārī* to roam; compare Latin *vagus* VAGUE]

vagina (vəˈdʒaɪnə) *n, pl* -nas *or* -nae (-niː) **1** the moist canal in most female mammals, including humans, that extends from the cervix of the uterus to an external opening between the labia minora **2** *anatomy, biology* any sheath or sheathlike structure, such as a leaf base that encloses a stem [c17 from Latin: sheath] > vagˈinal *adj*

vaginate (ˈvædʒɪnɪt, -ˌneɪt) *adj* (esp of plant parts) having a sheath; sheathed: *a vaginate leaf*

vaginectomy (ˌvædʒɪˈnɛktəmɪ) *n* **1** surgical removal of all or part of the vagina **2** surgical removal of part of the serous sheath surrounding the testis and epididymis

vaginismus (ˌvædʒɪˈnɪzməs, -ˈnɪsməs) *n* painful

spasm of the vagina [c19 from New Latin, from VAGINA + -ismus; see -ISM]

vaginitis (ˌvædʒɪˈnaɪtɪs) *n* inflammation of the vagina

vagotomy (væˈɡɒtəmɪ) *n, pl* -mies surgical division of the vagus nerve, performed to limit gastric secretion in patients with severe peptic ulcers [c19 from VAG(US) + -TOMY]

vagotonia (ˌveɪɡəˈtəʊnɪə) *n* pathological overactivity of the vagus nerve, affecting various bodily functions controlled by this nerve [c19 from VAG(US) + -tonia, from Latin *tonus* tension, TONE]

vagotropic (ˌveɪɡəˈtrɒpɪk) *adj* physiol (of a drug) affecting the activity of the vagus nerve [c20 from VAG(US) + -TROPIC]

vagrancy (ˈveɪɡrənsɪ) *n, pl* -cies **1** the state or condition of being a vagrant **2** the conduct or mode of living of a vagrant

vagrant (ˈveɪɡrənt) *n* **1** a person of no settled abode, income, or job; tramp **2** a migratory animal that is off course ▷ *adj* **3** wandering about; nomadic **4** of, relating to, or characteristic of a vagrant or vagabond **5** moving in an erratic fashion, without aim or purpose; wayward **6** (of plants) showing uncontrolled or straggling growth ▷ Archaic equivalent: **vagrom** (ˈveɪɡrəm) [c15 probably from Old French *waucrant* (from *wancrer* to roam, of Germanic origin), but also influenced by Old French *vagant* vagabond, from Latin *vagārī* to wander] > ˈvagrantly *adv* > ˈvagrantness *n*

vague (veɪɡ) *adj* **1** (of statements, meaning, etc) not explicit; imprecise: *vague promises* **2** not clearly perceptible or discernible; indistinct: *a vague idea; a vague shape* **3** not clearly or definitely established or known: *a vague rumour* **4** (of a person or his expression) demonstrating lack of precision or clear thinking; absent-minded [c16 via French from Latin *vagus* wandering, of obscure origin] > ˈvaguely *adv* > ˈvagueness *n*

vagus *or* **vagus nerve** (ˈveɪɡəs) *n, pl* -gi (-dʒaɪ) the tenth cranial nerve, which supplies the heart, lungs, and viscera [c19 from Latin *vagus* wandering]

vahana (ˈvɑːhənə) *n* Indian myth a vehicle [Hindi, from Sanskrit, from *vaha* to carry]

vail¹ (veɪl) *vb* (*tr*) obsolete **1** to lower (something, such as a weapon), esp as a sign of deference or submission **2** to remove (the hat, cap, etc) as a mark of respect or meekness [c14 *valen*, from obsolete *avalen*, from Old French *avaler* to let fall, from Latin *ad vallem*, literally: to the valley, that is, down, from *ad* to + *vallis* VALLEY]

vail² (veɪl) *n, vb* an archaic word for **avail**

vail³ (veɪl) *n, vb* an archaic spelling of **veil**

vain (veɪn) *adj* **1** inordinately proud of one's appearance, possessions, or achievements **2** given to ostentatious display, esp of one's beauty **3** worthless **4** senseless or futile ▷ *n* **5** in vain to no avail; fruitlessly **6** take someone's name in vain **a** to use the name of someone, esp God, without due respect or reverence **b** jocular to mention someone's name [c13 via Old French from Latin *vānus*] > ˈvainly *adv* > ˈvainness *n*

vainglorious (ˌveɪnˈɡlɔːrɪəs) *adj* boastful or vain; ostentatious

vainglory (ˌveɪnˈɡlɔːrɪ) *n* **1** boastfulness or vanity **2** ostentation

vair (vɛə) *n* **1** a fur, probably Russian squirrel, used to trim robes in the Middle Ages **2** one of the two principal furs used on heraldic shields, conventionally represented by white and blue skins in alternate lines. Compare **ermine** (sense 3) [c13 from Old French: of more than one colour, from Latin *varius* variegated, VARIOUS]

Vaishnava (ˈvɪʃnəvə) *n* Hinduism a member of a sect devoted to the cult of Vishnu, strongly anti-Brahminic and antipriestly in outlook and stressing devotion through image worship and simple ritual [from Sanskrit *vaisnava* of VISHNU] > ˈVaishnaˌvism *n*

Vaisya (ˈvaɪsjə, ˈvaɪʃjə) *n* the third of the four main Hindu castes, the traders [c18 from Sanskrit, literally: settler, from *viś* settlement]

Vajrayana (ˌvʌdʒrɑˈjɑːnə) *n* a school of Tantric Buddhism of India and Tibet [from Sanskrit: vehicle of the diamond or thunderbolt]

Valais (*French* valɛ) *n* a canton of S Switzerland: includes the entire valley of the upper Rhône and the highest peaks in Switzerland; produces a quarter of Switzerland's hydroelectricity. Capital: Sion. Pop: 281 000 (2002 est). Area: 5231 sq km (2020 sq miles). German name: Wallis

valance (ˈvæləns) *n* a short piece of drapery hung along a shelf, canopy, or bed, or across a window, to hide structural detail [c15 perhaps named after VALENCE, France, town noted for its textiles] > ˈvalanced *adj*

Valdai Hills (vɑːlˈdaɪ) *pl n* a region of hills and plateaus in NW Russia, between Moscow and St Petersburg. Greatest height: 346 m (1135 ft)

Val-de-Marne (*French* valdəmarn) *n* a department of N France, in Île-de-France region. Capital: Créteil. Pop: 1 239 352 (2003 est). Area: 244 sq km (95 sq miles)

Valdivia (*Spanish* balˈdiβja) *n* a port in S Chile, on the **Valdivia River** about 19 km (12 miles) from the Pacific: developed chiefly by German settlers in the 1850s; university (1954). Pop: 136 000 (2005 est)

Val-d'Oise (*French* valdwaz) *n* a department of N France, in Île-de-France region. Capital: Pontoise. Pop: 1 121 614 (2003 est). Area: 1249 sq km (487 sq miles)

vale¹ (veɪl) *n* a literary word for **valley** [c13 from Old French *val*, from Latin *vallis* valley]

vale² *Latin* (ˈvɑːleɪ) *sentence substitute* farewell; goodbye

valediction (ˌvælɪˈdɪkʃən) *n* **1** the act or an instance of saying goodbye **2** any valedictory statement, speech, etc [c17 from Latin *valedīcere*, from *valē* farewell + *dīcere* to say]

valedictorian (ˌvælɪdɪkˈtɔːrɪən) *adj* also valedictory **1** saying goodbye **2** of or relating to a farewell or an occasion of farewell ▷ *n* **3** US and Canadian a person, usually the most outstanding graduate, who delivers a farewell speech at a graduation ceremony

valedictory (ˌvælɪˈdɪktərɪ, -trɪ) *n, pl* -ries **1** a farewell address or speech **2** US and Canadian a farewell speech delivered at a graduation ceremony, usually by the most outstanding graduate

valence (ˈveɪləns) *n* chem **1** another name (esp US and Canadian) for **valency 2** the phenomenon of forming chemical bonds

Valence (*French* valɑs) *n* a town in SE France, on the River Rhône. Pop: 64 260 (1999)

valence band *n* See **energy band**

valence-conduction band *n* See **energy band**

Valencia (*Spanish* baˈlenθja) *n* **1** a port in E Spain, capital of Valencia province, on the Mediterranean: the third largest city in Spain; capital of the Moorish kingdom of Valencia (1021–1238); university (1501). Pop: 780 653 (2003 est). Latin name: Valentia (vəˈlentɪə) **2** a region and former kingdom of E Spain, on the Mediterranean **3** a city in N Venezuela: one of the two main industrial centres in Venezuela. Pop: 2 330 000 (2005 est)

Valenciennes¹ (ˌvælənsɪˈɛn) *n* a flat bobbin lace typically having scroll and floral designs and originally made of linen, now often cotton [named after VALENCIENNES², where it was originally made]

Valenciennes² (*French* valɑsjɛn) *n* a town in N France, on the River Escaut: a coal-mining and heavy industrial centre. Pop: 41 278 (1999)

valency (ˈveɪlənsɪ) *or esp US and Canadian* **valence** *n, pl* -cies *or* -ces **1** chem a property of atoms or groups, equal to the number of atoms of hydrogen that the atom or group could combine with or displace in forming compounds **2** linguistics the number of satellite noun phrases with which a verb combines: *the English verb 'give' takes a subject and two objects, so it has a valency of three* **3** *immunol* **a** the number of antigen-binding sites on an antibody molecule **b** the number of antigen-binding sites with which an antigen can combine [C19 from Latin *valentia* strength, from *valēre* to be strong]

valency electron *n chem* an electron in the outer shell of an atom, responsible for forming chemical bonds

valency grammar *n* a system of linguistic syntax, conceived by analogy with chemical valency, according to which verbs have valencies dependent on the number of noun phrases with which they combine. See **valency** (sense 2)

-valent ('veɪlənt) *adj combining form chem* having a specified valency: *bivalent; trivalent* [C19 from Latin *valentia*; see VALENCY]

valentine ('vælənˌtaɪn) *n* **1** a card or gift expressing love or affection, sent, often anonymously, to one's sweetheart or satirically to a friend, on Saint Valentine's Day **2** a sweetheart selected for such a greeting

Vale of Glamorgan (glə'mɔːgən) *n* a county borough of S Wales, created in 1996 from parts of South Glamorgan and Mid Glamorgan. Administrative centre: Barry. Pop: 121 200 (2003 est). Area: 295 sq km (114 sq miles)

valerian (və'lɛərɪən) *n* **1** Also called: **allheal** any of various Eurasian valerianaceous plants of the genus *Valeriana*, esp *V. officinalis*, having small white or pinkish flowers and a medicinal root **2** a sedative drug made from the dried roots of *V. officinalis* [C14 via Old French from Medieval Latin *valeriana* (*herba*) (herb) of *Valerius*, unexplained Latin personal name]

valerianaceous (vəˌlɪərɪə'neɪʃəs) *adj* of, relating to, or belonging to the *Valerianaceae*, a family of herbaceous plants having, in some genera, the calyx of the flower reduced to a ring of hairs: includes valerian, spikenard, and corn salad [C19 from New Latin; see VALERIAN]

valeric (və'lɛrɪk, -'lɪərɪk) *adj* of, relating to, or derived from valerian

valeric acid *n* another name for **pentanoic acid**

valet ('vælɪt, 'væleɪ) *n* **1** a manservant who acts as personal attendant to his employer, looking after his clothing, serving his meals, etc. French name: **valet de chambre** **2** a manservant who attends to the requirements of patrons in a hotel, passengers on board ship, etc; steward ▷ *vb* **-ets, -eting, -eted** **3** to act as a valet for (a person) **4** (*tr*) to clean the bodywork and interior of (a car) as a professional service [C16 from Old French *vaslet* page, from Medieval Latin *vassus* servant; see VASSAL]

valeta *or* **veleta** (və'liːtə) *n* a ballroom dance in triple time [from Spanish *veleta* weather vane]

valet de chambre *French* (valɛ də ʃɑ̃brə) *n, pl* ***valets de chambre*** (valɛ də ʃɑ̃brə) the full French term for **valet** (sense 1)

valet parking *n* a system at hotels, airports, etc, in which patrons' cars are parked by a steward

Valetta (və'lɛtə) *n* a variant spelling of **Valletta**

valetudinarian (ˌvælɪˌtjuːdɪ'nɛərɪən) *or* **valetudinary** (ˌvælɪ'tjuːdɪnərɪ) *n, pl* **-narians** *or* **-naries** **1** a person who is or believes himself to be chronically sick; invalid **2** a person excessively worried about the state of his health; hypochondriac ▷ *adj* **3** relating to, marked by, or resulting from poor health **4** being a valetudinarian **5** trying to return to a healthy state [C18 from Latin *valētūdō* state of health, from *valēre* to be well] > ˌ**valeˌtudi'narianˌism** *n*

valgus ('vælgəs) *adj pathol* denoting a deformity in which the distal part of a limb is displaced or twisted away from the midline of the body. See **hallux valgus** [C19 from Latin: knock-kneed]

Valhalla (væl'hælə), **Walhalla, Valhall** (væl'hæl, 'vælhæl) *or* **Walhall** *n Norse myth* the great hall of Odin where warriors who die as heroes in battle dwell eternally [C18 from Old Norse, from *valr* slain warriors + *höll* HALL]

valiant ('væljənt) *adj* **1** courageous, intrepid, or stout-hearted; brave **2** marked by bravery or courage: *a valiant deed* [C14 from Old French *vaillant*, from *valoir* to be of value, from Latin *valēre* to be strong] > '**valiance** *or* '**valiancy** *n* > '**valiantly** *adv*

valid ('vælɪd) *adj* **1** having some foundation; based on truth **2** legally acceptable: *a valid licence* **3** **a** having legal force; effective **b** having legal authority; binding **4** having some force or cogency: *a valid point in a debate* **5** *logic* (of an inference or argument) having premises and conclusion so related that whenever the former are true the latter must also be true, esp (**formally valid**) when the inference is justified by the form of the premises and conclusion alone. Thus *Tom is a bachelor; therefore Tom is unmarried* is valid but not formally so, while *today is hot and dry; therefore today is hot* is formally valid. Compare **invalid**[2] (sense 2) **6** *archaic* healthy or strong [C16 from Latin *validus* robust, from *valēre* to be strong] > '**validly** *adv* > **validity** (və'lɪdɪtɪ) *or* '**validness** *n*

validate ('vælɪˌdeɪt) *vb* (*tr*) **1** to confirm or corroborate **2** to give legal force or official confirmation to; declare legally valid > ˌ**vali'dation** *n* > '**validatory** *adj*

valine ('veɪliːn, 'væl-) *n* an essential amino acid; a component of proteins [C19 from VAL(ERIC ACID) + -INE[2]]

valise (və'liːz) *n* a small overnight travelling case [C17 via French from Italian *valigia*, of unknown origin]

Valium ('vælɪəm) *n trademark* a brand of diazepam used as a tranquillizer. See also **benzodiazepine**

Valkyrie, Walkyrie (væl'kɪərɪ, 'vælkɪərɪ) *or* **Valkyr** ('vælkɪə) *n Norse myth* any of the beautiful maidens who serve Odin and ride over battlefields to claim the dead heroes and take them to Valhalla [C18 from Old Norse *Valkyrja*, from *valr* slain warriors + *köri* to CHOOSE] > **Val'kyrian** *adj*

Valladolid (*Spanish* baʎaðo'lið) *n* **1** a city in NW Spain: residence of the Spanish court in the 16th century; university (1346). Pop: 321 143 (2003 est) **2** the former name (until 1828) of **Morelia**

vallation (və'leɪʃən) *n* **1** the act or process of building fortifications **2** a wall or rampart [C17 from Late Latin *vallātiō*, from *vallum* rampart]

vallecula (və'lɛkjʊlə) *n, pl* **-lae** (-ˌliː) **1** *anatomy* any of various natural depressions or crevices, such as certain fissures of the brain **2** *botany* a small groove or furrow in a plant stem or fruit [C19 from Late Latin: little valley, from Latin *vallis* valley] > **val'lecular** *or* **val'leculate** *adj*

Valle d'Aosta (*Italian* 'valle da'ɔsta) *n* an autonomous region of NW Italy: under many different rulers until passing to the house of Savoy in the 11th century; established as an autonomous region in 1944. Capital: Aosta. Pop: 120 909 (2003 est). Area: 3263 sq km (1260 sq miles)

Valletta *or* **Valetta** (və'lɛtə) *n* the capital of Malta, on the NE coast: founded by the Knights Hospitallers, after the victory over the Turks in 1565; became a major naval base after Malta's annexation by Britain (1814). Pop: 84 000 (2005 est)

valley ('vælɪ) *n* **1** a long depression in the land surface, usually containing a river, formed by erosion or by movements in the earth's crust **2** the broad area drained by a single river system: *the Thames valley* **3** any elongated depression resembling a valley **4** the junction of a roof slope with another or with a wall **5** (*modifier*) relating to or proceeding by way of a valley: *a valley railway* [C13 from Old French *valee*, from Latin *vallis*]

Valley Forge *n* an area in SE Pennsylvania, northwest of Philadelphia; winter camp (1777–78) of Washington and the American Revolutionary Army

Valley of Ten Thousand Smokes *n* a volcanic region of SW Alaska, formed by the massive eruption of Mount Katmai in 1912; jets of steam issue from vents up to 45 m (150 ft) across

Vallombrosa (*Italian* vallom'broːsa) *n* a village and resort in central Italy, in Tuscany region: 11th-century Benedictine monastery

vallum ('væləm) *n archaeol* a Roman rampart or earthwork

Valois (*French* valwa) *n* a historic region and former duchy of N France

Valona (və'ləʊnə) *n* another name for **Vlorë**

valonia (və'ləʊnɪə) *n* the acorn cups and unripe acorns of the Eurasian oak *Quercus aegilops*, used in tanning, dyeing, and making ink [C18 from Italian *vallonia*, ultimately from Greek *balanos* acorn]

valorize *or* **valorise** ('væləˌraɪz) *vb* (*tr*) to fix and maintain an artificial price for (a commodity) by governmental action [C20 back formation from *valorization*; see VALOUR] > ˌ**valori'zation** *or* ˌ**valori'sation** *n*

valour *or US* **valor** ('vælə) *n* courage or bravery, esp in battle [C15 from Late Latin *valor*, from *valēre* to be strong] > '**valorous** *adj* > '**valorously** *adv*

Valparaíso (*Spanish* balpara'iso) *n* a port in central Chile, on a wide bay of the Pacific: the third largest city and chief port of Chile; two universities. Pop: 275 000 (2005 est)

Valpolicella (ˌvælpɒlɪ'tʃɛlə; *Italian* valpoli'tʃɛlla) *n* a dry red table wine from the Veneto region of NE Italy [C20 named after a valley where it is produced]

valproic acid (væl'prəʊɪk) *n* a synthetic crystalline compound, used as an anticonvulsive to treat seizure disorders. Formula $C_7H_{15}COOH$ [C20 from VAL(ERIAN) + PRO(PYL) + -IC] > **val'proate** *n*

valse *French* (vals) *n* another word, esp used in the titles of some pieces of music, for **waltz**

valuable ('væljʊəbᵊl) *adj* **1** having considerable monetary worth **2** of considerable importance or quality: *a valuable friend; valuable information* **3** able to be valued ▷ *n* **4** (*usually plural*) a valuable article of personal property, esp jewellery > '**valuableness** *n* > '**valuably** *adv*

valuate ('væljʊˌeɪt) *vb US* another word for **value** (senses 10, 12) *or* **evaluate**

valuation (ˌvæljʊ'eɪʃən) *n* **1** the act of valuing, esp a formal assessment of the worth of property, jewellery, etc **2** the price arrived at by the process of valuing: *the valuation of this property is considerable; I set a high valuation on technical ability* > ˌ**valu'ational** *adj* > ˌ**valu'ationally** *adv*

valuator ('væljʊˌeɪtə) *n* a person who estimates the value of objects, paintings, etc; appraiser

value ('væljuː) *n* **1** the desirability of a thing, often in respect of some property such as usefulness or exchangeability: worth, merit, or importance **2** an amount, esp a material or monetary one, considered to be a fair exchange in return for a thing; assigned valuation: *the value of the picture is £10 000* **3** reasonable or equivalent return; satisfaction: *value for money* **4** precise meaning or significance **5** (*plural*) the moral principles and beliefs or accepted standards of a person or social group: *a person with old-fashioned values* **6** *maths* **a** a particular magnitude, number, or amount: *the value of the variable was 7* **b** the particular quantity that is the result of applying a function or operation for some given argument: *the value of the function for x=3 was 9* **7** *music* short for **time value** **8** (in painting, drawing, etc) **a** a gradation of tone from light to dark or of colour luminosity **b** the relation of one of these elements to another or to the whole picture **9** *phonetics* the quality or tone of the speech sound associated with a written character representing it: *'g' has the value (dʒ) in English 'gem'* ▷ *vb* **-ues, -uing, -ued** (*tr*) **10** to assess or estimate the worth, merit, or desirability of; appraise **11** to have a high regard for, esp in respect of worth, usefulness, merit, etc; esteem or prize: *to value freedom* **12** (foll by *at*) to fix the financial or material worth of (a unit of currency, work of art, etc): *jewels valued at £40 000* [C14 from Old French, from *valoir*, from Latin *valēre* to be worth, be strong] > '**valuer** *n*

value added *n* the difference between the total revenues of a firm, industry, etc, and its total purchases from other firms, industries, etc. The aggregate of values added throughout an economy (**gross value added**) represents that economy's gross domestic product

value-added tax *n* (in Britain) the full name for **VAT**

value date *n* the exact date on which a financial transaction, esp in buying and selling foreign exchange, is deemed to take place: used for calculating exchange rates

valued policy *n* an insurance policy in which the amount payable in the event of a valid claim is agreed upon between the company and policyholder when the policy is issued and is not related to the actual value of a loss. Compare **open policy**

value judgment *n* a subjective assessment based on one's own code of values or that of one's class

valueless ('væljʊlɪs) *adj* having or possessing no value; worthless > 'valuelessness *n*

valuer ('væljʊə) *n* a person who assesses the monetary worth of a work of art, jewel, house, etc; appraiser

Valuer General *n* Austral a state official who values properties for rating purposes

valuta (və'luːtə) *n* rare the value of one currency in terms of its exchange rate with another [C20 from Italian, literally: VALUE]

valvate ('vælveɪt) *adj* 1 furnished with a valve or valves 2 functioning as or resembling a valve 3 botany a taking or taking place by means of valves: *valvate dehiscence* b (of petals or sepals in the bud) having the margins touching but not overlapping

valve (vælv) *n* 1 any device that shuts off, starts, regulates, or controls the flow of a fluid 2 anatomy a flaplike structure in a hollow organ, such as the heart, that controls the one-way passage of fluid through that organ 3 Also called: **tube, vacuum tube** an evacuated electron tube containing a cathode, anode, and, usually, one or more additional control electrodes. When a positive potential is applied to the anode, electrons emitted from the cathode are attracted to the anode, constituting a flow of current which can be controlled by a voltage applied to the grid to produce amplification, oscillation, etc. See also **diode** (sense 2), **triode** (sense 1), **tetrode, pentode** 4 zoology any of the separable pieces that make up the shell of a mollusc 5 music a device on some brass instruments by which the effective length of the tube may be varied to enable a chromatic scale to be produced 6 botany a any of the several parts that make up a dry dehiscent fruit, esp a capsule b either of the two halves of a diatom cell wall 7 archaic a leaf of a double door or of a folding door [C14 from Latin *valva* a folding door] > 'valveless *adj* > 'valve,like *adj*

valve gear *n* a mechanism that operates the valves of a reciprocating engine, usually involving the use of cams, pushrods, rocker arms, etc

valve-in-head engine *n* the US name for **overhead-valve engine**

valve spring *n* 1 a helical spring used to hold closed a valve in the cylinder head of an internal-combustion engine 2 any spring that closes a valve after it has been opened mechanically or by flow pressure

valvular ('vælvjʊlə) *adj* 1 of, relating to, operated by, or having a valve or valves 2 having the shape or function of a valve

valvule ('vælvjuːl) *or* **valvelet** ('vælvlɪt) *n* a small valve or a part resembling one [C18 from New Latin *valvula,* diminutive of VALVE]

valvulitis (,vælvjʊ'laɪtɪs) *n* inflammation of a bodily valve, esp a heart valve [C19 from VALVULE + -ITIS]

vambrace ('væmbreɪs) *n* a piece of armour used to protect the arm [C14 from Anglo-French *vauntbras,* from *vaunt-* (from Old French *avant-* fore-)

+ *bras* arm] > 'vambraced *adj*

vamoose (və'muːs) *vb* (intr) slang, chiefly US to leave a place hurriedly; decamp [C19 from Spanish *vamos* let us go, from Latin *vādere* to go, walk rapidly]

vamp¹ (væmp) *informal* ▷ *n* 1 a seductive woman who exploits men by use of her sexual charms ▷ *vb* 2 to exploit (a man) in the fashion of a vamp [C20 short for VAMPIRE] > 'vamper *n* > 'vampish *adj*

vamp² (væmp) *n* 1 something patched up to make it look new 2 the reworking of a theme, story, etc 3 an improvised accompaniment, consisting largely of chords 4 the front part of the upper of a shoe ▷ *vb* 5 (tr; often foll by *up*) to give a vamp to; make a renovation of 6 to improvise (an accompaniment) to (a tune) [C13 from Old French *avantpié* the front part of a shoe (hence, something patched), from *avant-* fore- + *pié* foot, from Latin *pēs*] > 'vamper *n*

vampire ('væmpaɪə) *n* 1 (in European folklore) a corpse that rises nightly from its grave to drink the blood of the living 2 See **vampire bat** 3 a person who preys mercilessly upon others, such as a blackmailer 4 See **vamp¹** (sense 1) 5 theatre a trapdoor on a stage [C18 from French, from German *Vampir,* from Magyar; perhaps related to Turkish *uber* witch, Russian *upyr* vampire] > vampiric (væm'pɪrɪk) *or* vampirish ('væmpaɪərɪʃ) *adj*

vampire bat *n* any bat, esp *Desmodus rotundus,* of the family *Desmodontidae* of tropical regions of Central and South America, having sharp incisor and canine teeth and feeding on the blood of birds and mammals. Compare **false vampire**

vampirism ('væmpaɪə,rɪzəm) *n* 1 belief in the existence of vampires 2 the actions of vampires; bloodsucking 3 the act of preying upon or exploiting others

van¹ (væn) *n* 1 short for **caravan** (sense 1) 2 a covered motor vehicle for transporting goods, etc, by road 3 Brit a closed railway wagon in which the guard travels, for transporting goods, mail, etc 4 Brit See **delivery van**

van² (væn) *n* short for **vanguard**

van³ (væn) *n* tennis, chiefly Brit short for **advantage** (sense 3). Usual US and Canadian word: ad

van⁴ (væn) *n* 1 any device for winnowing corn 2 an archaic or poetic word for **wing** [C17 variant of FAN¹]

Van (vɑːn) *n* 1 a city in E Turkey, on Lake Van. Pop: 377 000 (2005 est) 2 **Lake** a salt lake in E Turkey, at an altitude of 1650 m (5400 ft): fed by melting snow and glaciers. Area: 3737 sq km (1433 sq miles)

vanadate ('vænə,deɪt) *n* any salt or ester of a vanadic acid

vanadic (və'nædɪk, -'neɪdɪk) *adj* of or containing vanadium, esp in a trivalent or pentavalent state

vanadic acid *n* any one of various oxyacids of vanadium, such as H_3VO_4 (**orthovanadic acid**), HVO_4 (**metavanadic acid**), and $H_4V_2O_7$ (**pyrovanadic acid**), known chiefly in the form of their vanadate salts

vanadinite (və'nædɪ,naɪt) *n* a red, yellow, or brownish mineral consisting of a chloride and vanadate of lead in hexagonal crystalline form. It results from weathering of lead ores in desert regions and is a source of vanadium. Formula: $Pb_5(VO_4)_3Cl$

vanadium (və'neɪdɪəm) *n* a toxic silvery-white metallic element occurring chiefly in carnotite and vanadinite and used in steel alloys, high-speed tools, and as a catalyst. Symbol: V; atomic no: 23; atomic wt: 50.9415; valency: 2–5; relative density: 6.11; melting pt: 1910±10°C; boiling pt: 3409°C [C19 New Latin, from Old Norse *Vanadis,* epithet of the goddess Freya + -IUM]

vanadium steel *n* engineering steel containing up to 0.5 per cent vanadium, usually with 1.1–1.5 per cent chromium and 0.4–0.5 per cent carbon to increase its tensile strength and elasticity

vanadous ('vænədəs) *adj* of or containing

vanadium, esp in a divalent or trivalent state

Van Allen belt (væn 'ælən) *n* either of two regions of charged particles above the earth, the inner one extending from 2400 to 5600 kilometres above the earth and the outer one from 13 000 to 19 000 kilometres. The charged particles result from cosmic rays and are trapped by the earth's magnetic field [C20 named after its discoverer, James Alfred Van Allen (born 1914), US physicist]

vanaspati (və'næspətɪ) *n* a hydrogenated vegetable fat commonly used in India as a substitute for butter [C20 the Sanskrit name of a forest plant, from *vana* forest + *pati* lord]

vancomycin (,vænkəʊ'maɪsɪn) *n* an antibiotic effective against most Gram-positive organisms. It is given by intravenous infusions for serious infections that are resistant to other antibiotics

Vancouver (væn'kuːvə) *n* 1 Vancouver Island an island of SW Canada, off the SW coast of British Columbia: separated from the Canadian mainland by the Strait of Georgia and Queen Charlotte Sound, and from the US mainland by Juan de Fuca Strait; the largest island off the W coast of North America. Chief town: Victoria. Pop: 706 243 (2001). Area: 32 137 sq km (12 408 sq miles) 2 a city in SW Canada, in SW British Columbia: Canada's chief Pacific port, named after Captain George Vancouver: university (1908). Pop: 545 671 (2001) 3 **Mount** a mountain on the border between Canada and Alaska, in the St Elias Mountains. Height: 4785 m (15 700 ft)

vanda ('vændə) *n* any epiphytic orchid of the E hemisphere genus *Vanda,* having white, mauve, blue, or greenish fragrant flowers [C19 New Latin, from Hindi *vandā* mistletoe, from Sanskrit]

V and A (in Britain) abbreviation for Victoria and Albert Museum

vandal ('vændᵊl) *n* a a person who deliberately causes damage or destruction to personal or public property b (as modifier): *vandal instincts* [C17 from VANDAL, from Latin *Vandallus,* of Germanic origin]

Vandal ('vændᵊl) *n* a member of a Germanic people that raided Roman provinces in the 3rd and 4th centuries AD before devastating Gaul (406–409), conquering Spain and N Africa, and sacking Rome (455): crushed by Belisarius at Carthage (533) > Vandalic (væn'dælɪk) *adj* > 'Vandal,ism *n*

vandalism ('vændə,lɪzəm) *n* the wanton or deliberate destruction caused by a vandal or an instance of such destruction > ,vandal'istic *or* 'vandalish *adj*

vandalize *or* **vandalise** ('vændə,laɪz) *vb* (tr) to destroy or damage (something) by an act of vandalism

Van de Graaff generator ('væn də ,grɑːf) *n* a device for producing high electrostatic potentials (up to 15 million volts), consisting of a hollow metal sphere on which a charge is accumulated from a continuous moving belt of insulating material: used in particle accelerators [C20 named after R J *Van de Graaff* (1901–67), US physicist]

Vandemonian (,væn də'məʊnɪən) *n* 1 a native or inhabitant of the former Van Diemen's Land (now Tasmania) ▷ *adj* 2 of or relating to Van Diemen's Land or its inhabitants

Van der Hum (væn də hʌm) *n* South African a liqueur with tangerine flavouring [of uncertain origin, but possibly derived from the humorous uncertainty of the name, equivalent of WHATSHISNAME]

Van der Merwe (væn də 'mɜːvə) *n* South African a stereotypical figure humorously representing Boer stupidity and prejudice [C20 from a common Afrikaner surname]

van der Waals equation ('væn də ,wɑːlz) *n* an equation of state for a non-ideal gas that takes account of intermolecular forces and the volume occupied by the molecules of the gas

van der Waals forces ('væn də ,wɑːlz) *pl n* weak electrostatic forces between atoms and molecules

V

caused by transient distortions in the distribution of electrons in the interacting atoms or molecules

Van Diemen Gulf (væn ˈdiːmən) *n* an inlet of the Timor Sea in N Australia, in the Northern Territory

Van Diemen's Land (væn ˈdiːmənz) *n* the former name (1642–1855) of **Tasmania**

Vandyke beard (ˈvændaɪk) *n* a short pointed beard. Often shortened to: **Vandyke**

Vandyke brown *n* **1 a** a moderate brown colour **b** (*as adjective*): *a Vandyke-brown suit* **2** any of various brown pigments, usually consisting of a mixture of ferric oxide and lampblack

Vandyke collar *or* **cape** *n* a large white collar with several very deep points. Often shortened to: **Vandyke**

vane (veɪn) *n* **1** Also called: **weather vane, wind vane** a flat plate or blade of metal mounted on a vertical axis in an exposed position to indicate wind direction **2** any one of the flat blades or sails forming part of the wheel of a windmill **3** any flat or shaped plate used to direct fluid flow, esp a stator blade in a turbine, etc **4** a fin or plate fitted to a projectile or missile to provide stabilization or guidance **5** *ornithol* the flat part of a feather, consisting of two rows of barbs on either side of the shaft **6** *surveying* **a** a sight on a quadrant or compass **b** the movable marker on a levelling staff [Old English *fana*; related to Old Saxon, Old High German *fano*, Old Norse *fani*, Latin *pannus* cloth] > **vaned** *adj* > **vaneless** *adj*

Vänern (*Swedish* ˈvɛːnərn) *n* **Lake** a lake in SW Sweden: the largest lake in Sweden and W Europe; drains into the Kattegat. Area: 5585 sq km (2156 sq miles)

vanessid (vəˈnɛsɪd) *n* **1** a butterfly belonging to any of several brightly coloured species, including admirals, tortoiseshells, and the Camberwell beauty, which with the fritillaries comprise the *Nymphalidae* ▷ *adj* **2** of, relating to, or belonging to this group [C20 from New Latin *vanessa*]

vang (væŋ) *n* *nautical* **1** a rope or tackle extended from the boom of a fore-and-aft mainsail to a deck fitting of a vessel when running, in order to keep the boom from riding up **2** a guy extending from the end of a gaff to the vessel's rail on each side, used for steadying the gaff [C18 from Dutch, from *vangen* to catch]

vanguard (ˈvænˌɡɑːd) *n* **1** the leading division or units of a military force **2** the leading position in any movement or field, or the people who occupy such a position: *the vanguard of modern literature* [C15 from Old French *avant-garde*, from *avant-* fore- + *garde* GUARD]

vanilla (vəˈnɪlə) *n* **1** any tropical climbing orchid of the genus *Vanilla*, esp *V. plonifolia*, having spikes of large fragrant greenish-yellow flowers and long fleshy pods containing the seeds (beans) **2** the pod or bean of certain of these plants, used to flavour food, etc **3** a flavouring extract prepared from vanilla beans and used in cooking ▷ *adj* **4** flavoured with or as if with vanilla: *vanilla ice cream* **5** *slang* ordinary or conventional: *a vanilla kind of guy* [C17 from New Latin, from Spanish *vainilla* pod, from *vaina* a sheath, from Latin *vāgīna* sheath]

vanillic (vəˈnɪlɪk) *adj* of, resembling, containing, or derived from vanilla or vanillin

vanillin (ˈvænɪlɪn, vəˈnɪlɪn) *n* a white crystalline aldehyde found in vanilla and many natural balsams and resins; 3-methoxy-4-hydroxybenzaldehyde. It is a by-product of paper manufacture and is used as a flavouring and in perfumes and pharmaceuticals. Formula: $(CH_3O)(OH)C_6H_3CHO$

Vanir (ˈvɑːnɪə) *n* Norse myth a race of ancient gods often locked in struggle with the Aesir. The most notable of them are Njord and his children Frey and Freya [from Old Norse *Vanr*, a fertility god]

vanish (ˈvænɪʃ) *vb* (*intr*) **1** to disappear, esp suddenly or mysteriously **2** to cease to exist; fade away **3** *maths* to become zero ▷ *n* **4** *phonetics rare* the second and weaker of the two vowels in a falling diphthong [C14 *vanissen*, from Old French *esvanir*, from Latin *ēvānēscere* to evaporate, from *ē-* EX-¹ + *vānēscere* to pass away, from *vānus* empty] > **vanisher** *n* > **vanishingly** *adv*

vanishing cream *n* a cosmetic cream that is colourless once applied, used as a foundation for powder or as a cleansing or moisturizing cream

vanishing point *n* **1** the point to which parallel lines appear to converge in the rendering of perspective, usually on the horizon **2** a point in space or time at or beyond which something disappears or ceases to exist

vanity (ˈvænɪtɪ) *n, pl* **-ties 1** the state or quality of being vain; excessive pride or conceit **2** ostentation occasioned by ambition or pride **3** an instance of being vain or something about which one is vain **4** the state or quality of being valueless, futile, or unreal **5** something that is worthless or useless **6** *NZ* short for **vanity unit** [C13 from Old French *vanité*, from Latin *vānitās* emptiness, from *vānus* empty]

vanity bag, case *or* **box** *n* a woman's small bag or hand case used to carry cosmetics, etc

Vanity Fair *n* (*often not capitals*) *literary* the social life of a community, esp of a great city, or the world in general, considered as symbolizing worldly frivolity [from Bunyan's *The Pilgrim's Progress*]

vanity plates *pl n informal* personalized car numberplates

vanity publishing *n* the practice of the author of a book paying all or most of the costs of its publication

vanity unit *n* a hand basin built into a wooden Formica-covered or tiled top, usually with a built-in cupboard below it. Also called (trademark): **Vanitory unit** (ˈvænɪtərɪ)

vanquish (ˈvæŋkwɪʃ) *vb* (*tr*) **1** to defeat or overcome in a battle, contest, etc; conquer **2** to defeat or overcome in argument or debate **3** to conquer (an emotion) [C14 *vanquisshen*, from Old French *venquis* vanquished, from *veintre* to overcome, from Latin *vincere*] > **vanquishable** *adj* > **vanquisher** *n* > **vanquishment** *n*

vantage (ˈvɑːntɪdʒ) *n* **1** a state, position, or opportunity affording superiority or advantage **2** superiority or benefit accruing from such a position, state, etc **3** *tennis* short for **advantage** [C13 from Old French *avantage* ADVANTAGE] > **vantageless** *adj*

vantage ground *n* a position or condition affording superiority or advantage over or as if over an opponent

vantage point *n* a position or place that allows one a wide or favourable overall view of a scene or situation

Vanua Levu (vɑːˈnuːə ˈlɛvuː) *n* the second largest island of Fiji: mountainous. Area: 5535 sq km (2137 sq miles)

Vanuatu (ˌvænuːˈætuː) *n* a republic comprising a group of islands in the W Pacific, W of Fiji: a condominium under Anglo-French joint rule from 1906; attained partial autonomy in 1978 and full independence in 1980 as a member of the Commonwealth. Its economy is based chiefly on copra. Official languages: Bislama; French; English. Religion: Christian majority. Currency: vatu. Capital: Vila (on Efate). Pop: 217 000 (2004 est). Area: about 14 760 sq km (5700 sq miles). Official name: **Republic of Vanuatu** Former name (until 1980): **New Hebrides**

vanward (ˈvænwəd) *adj, adv* in or towards the front

vapid (ˈvæpɪd) *adj* **1** bereft of strength, sharpness, flavour, etc; flat **2** boring or dull; lifeless: *vapid talk* [C17 from Latin *vapidus*; related to *vappa* tasteless or flat wine, and perhaps to *vapor* warmth] > **vaˈpidity** *n* > **ˈvapidly** *adv* > **ˈvapidness** *n*

vapor (ˈveɪpə) *n* the US spelling of **vapour**

vaporescence (ˌveɪpəˈrɛsəns) *n* the production or formation of vapour > **ˌvaporˈescent** *adj*

vaporetto (ˌveɪpəˈrɛtəʊ; *Italian* vapoˈretto) *n, pl* **-ti** (-tɪ; *Italian* -ti) *or* **-tos** a steam-powered passenger boat, as used on the canals in Venice [Italian, from *vapore* a steamboat]

vaporific (ˌveɪpəˈrɪfɪk) *adj* **1** producing, causing, or tending to produce vapour **2** of, concerned with, or having the nature of vapour **3** tending to become vapour; volatile ▷ Also: **vaporous** [C18 from New Latin *vaporificus*, from Latin *vapor* steam + *facere* to make]

vaporimeter (ˌveɪpəˈrɪmɪtə) *n* an instrument for measuring vapour pressure, used to determine the volatility of oils or the amount of alcohol in alcoholic liquids

vaporize *or* **vaporise** (ˈveɪpəˌraɪz) *vb* **1** to change or cause to change into vapour or into the gaseous state **2** to evaporate or disappear or cause to evaporate or disappear, esp suddenly **3** to destroy or be destroyed by being turned into a gas as a result of extreme heat (for example, generated by a nuclear explosion) > **ˈvaporˌizable** *or* **ˈvaporˌisable** *adj* > **ˌvaporiˈzation** *or* **ˌvaporiˈsation** *n*

vaporizer *or* **vaporiser** (ˈveɪpəˌraɪzə) *n* **1** a substance that vaporizes or a device that causes vaporization **2** *med* a device that produces steam or atomizes medication for inhalation

vaporous (ˈveɪpərəs) *adj* **1** resembling or full of vapour **2** another word for **vaporific 3** lacking permanence or substance; ephemeral or fanciful **4** given to foolish imaginings **5** dulled or obscured by an atmosphere of vapour > **ˈvaporously** *adv* > **ˈvaporousness** *or* **vaporosity** (ˌveɪpəˈrɒsɪtɪ) *n*

vapour *or US* **vapor** (ˈveɪpə) *n* **1** particles of moisture or other substance suspended in air and visible as clouds, smoke, etc **2** a gaseous substance at a temperature below its critical temperature. Compare **gas** (sense 3) **3** a substance that is in a gaseous state at a temperature below its boiling point **4** *rare* something fanciful that lacks substance or permanence **5 the vapours** *archaic* a depressed mental condition believed originally to be the result of vaporous exhalations from the stomach ▷ *vb* **6** to evaporate or cause to evaporate; vaporize **7** (*intr*) to make vain empty boasts; brag [C14 from Latin *vapor*] > **ˈvapourable** *or US* **ˈvaporable** *adj* > **ˌvapouraˈbility** *or US* **ˌvaporaˈbility** *n* > **ˈvapourer** *or US* **ˈvaporer** *n* > **ˈvapourish** *or US* **ˈvaporish** *adj* > **ˈvapourless** *or US* **ˈvaporless** *adj* > **ˈvapour-ˌlike** *or US* **ˈvapor-ˌlike** *adj* > **ˈvapoury** *or US* **ˈvapory** *adj*

vapour density *n* the ratio of the density of a gas or vapour to that of hydrogen at the same temperature and pressure. See also **relative density**

vapourer moth *n* a tussock moth, *Orgyia antiqua*, of hedgerows and trees, the female of which is wingless and lays her eggs on her former cocoon

vapour lock *n* a stoppage in a pipe carrying a liquid caused by a bubble of gas, esp such a stoppage caused by vaporization of the petrol in the pipe feeding the carburettor of an internal-combustion engine

vapour pressure *n* *physics* the pressure exerted by a vapour. The saturated vapour pressure is that exerted by a vapour in equilibrium with its solid or liquid phase at a particular temperature

vapour trail *n* a visible trail left by an aircraft flying at high altitude or through supercold air, caused by the deposition of water vapour in the engine exhaust as minute ice crystals. Also called: **condensation trail, contrail**

var (vɑː) *n* a unit of reactive power of an alternating current, equal to the product of the current measured in amperes and the voltage measured in volts [from *v*(olt-)*a*(*mperes*) *r*(*eactive*)]

Var (*French* var) *n* **1** a department of SE France, in Provence-Alpes-Côte-d'Azur region. Capital: Toulon. Pop: 946 305 (2003 est). Area: 6023 sq km (2349 sq miles) **2** a river in SE France, flowing southeast and south to the Mediterranean near Nice. Length: about 130 km (80 miles)

VAR *abbreviation for* visual aural range

var. *abbreviation for* **1** variable **2** variant **3** variation **4** variety **5** various

vara ('vɑːrə) *n* a unit of length used in Spain, Portugal, and South America and having different values in different localities, usually between 32 and 43 inches (about 80 to 108 centimetres) [c17 via Spanish from Latin: wooden trestle, from *vārus* crooked]

varactor ('veə,ræktə) *n* a semiconductor diode that acts as a voltage-dependent capacitor, being operated with a reverse bias. Compare **varistor** [c20 probably a blend of *variable reactor*]

Varanasi (və'rɑːnəsɪ) *n* a city in NE India, in SE Uttar Pradesh on the River Ganges: probably dates from the 13th century BC; an early centre of Aryan philosophy and religion; a major place of pilgrimage for Hindus, Jains, Sikhs, and Buddhists, with many ghats along the Ganges; seat of the Banaras Hindu University (1916), India's leading university, and the Sanskrit University (1957). Pop: 1 100 748 (2001). Former names: Benares, Banaras

Varangian (və'rændʒɪən) *n* **1** one of the Scandinavian peoples who invaded and settled parts of Russia and Ukraine from the 8th to the 11th centuries, and who formed the bodyguard of the Byzantine emperor (**Varangian Guard**) in the late 10th and 11th centuries ▷ *adj* **2** of or relating to the Varangians [c18 from Medieval Latin *Varangus*, from Medieval Greek *Barangos*, from Old Norse *Væringi*, probably from *vār* pledge]

Vardar (*Serbo-Croat* 'vardar) *n* a river in S Europe, rising in W Macedonia and flowing northeast, then south past Skopje into Greece, where it is called the Axios and enters the Aegean at Thessaloníki. Length: about 320 km (200 miles)

varec ('værɛk) *n* **1** another name for **kelp 2** the ash obtained from kelp [c17 from French, from Old Norse *wrek* (unattested); see **WRECK**]

Varese (*Italian* va'reːse) *n* a historic city in N Italy, in Lombardy near Lake Varese: manufacturing centre, esp for leather goods. Pop: 80 511 (2001)

varia ('veərɪə) *pl n* a collection or miscellany, esp of literary works [Latin, neuter plural of *varius* VARIOUS]

variable ('veərɪəb°l) *adj* **1** liable to or capable of change: *variable weather* **2** (of behaviour, opinions, emotions, etc) lacking constancy; fickle **3** *maths* having a range of possible values **4** (of a species, characteristic, etc) liable to deviate from the established type **5** (of a wind) varying its direction and intensity **6** (of an electrical component or device) designed so that a characteristic property, such as resistance, can be varied: *variable capacitor* ▷ *n* **7** something that is subject to variation **8** *maths* **a** an expression that can be assigned any of a set of values **b** a symbol, esp *x, y*, or *z*, representing an unspecified member of a class of objects, numbers, etc. See also **dependent variable, independent variable 9** *logic* a symbol, esp *x, y, z*, representing any member of a class of entities **10** *computing* a named unit of storage that can be changed to any of a set of specified values during execution of a program **11** *astronomy* See **variable star 12** a variable wind **13** (*plural*) a region where variable winds occur [c14 from Latin *variābilis* changeable, from *variāre* to diversify] ▷ ˌvariaˈbility *or* ˈvariableness *n* ▷ ˈvariably *adv*

variable cost *n* a cost that varies directly with output

variable-density wind tunnel *n* a closed-circuit wind tunnel entirely contained in a casing in which the pressure and therefore the density of the working fluid can be maintained at a preselected value

variable-geometry *or* **variable-sweep** *adj* denoting an aircraft in which the wings are hinged to give the variable aspect ratio colloquially known as a **swing-wing**

variable star *n* any star that varies considerably in brightness, either irregularly or in regular

periods. **Intrinsic variables**, in which the variation is a result of internal changes, include novae, supernovae, and pulsating stars. See also **eclipsing binary**

variance ('veərɪəns) *n* **1** the act of varying or the quality, state, or degree of being divergent; discrepancy **2** an instance of diverging; dissension: *our variance on this matter should not affect our friendship* **3** **at variance a** (often foll by *with*) (of facts, etc) not in accord; conflicting **b** (of persons) in a state of dissension **4** *statistics* a measure of dispersion obtained by taking the mean of the squared deviations of the observed values from their mean in a frequency distribution **5** a difference or discrepancy between two steps in a legal proceeding, esp between a statement in a pleading and the evidence given to support it **6** (in the US and Canada) a licence or authority issued by the board of variance to contravene the usual rule, esp to build contrary to the provision of a zoning code **7** *chem* the number of degrees of freedom of a system, used in the phase rule **8** *accounting* the difference between actual and standard costs of production

variant ('veərɪənt) *adj* **1** liable to or displaying variation **2** differing from a standard or type: *a variant spelling* **3** *obsolete* not constant; fickle ▷ *n* **4** something that differs from a standard or type **5** *statistics* another word for **variate** (sense 1) [c14 via Old French from Latin *variāns*, from *variāre* to diversify, from *varius* VARIOUS]

variate ('veərɪɪt) *n* **1** *statistics* a random variable or a numerical value taken by it **2** a less common word for **variant** (sense 4) [c16 from Latin *variāre* to VARY]

variation (ˌveərɪ'eɪʃən) *n* **1** the act, process, condition, or result of changing or varying; diversity **2** an instance of varying or the amount, rate, or degree of such change **3** something that differs from a standard or convention **4** *music* **a** a repetition of a musical theme in which the rhythm, harmony, or melody is altered or embellished **b** (*as modifier*): *variation form* **5** *biology* **a** a marked deviation from the typical form or function **b** a characteristic or an organism showing this deviation **6** *astronomy* any change in or deviation from the mean motion or orbit of a planet, satellite, etc, esp a perturbation of the moon **7** another word for **magnetic declination 8** *ballet* a solo dance **9** *linguistics* any form of morphophonemic change, such as one involved in inflection, conjugation, or vowel mutation ▷ ˌvariˈational *adj* ▷ ˌvariˈationally *adv*

varicella (ˌværɪ'sɛlə) *n* the technical name for **chickenpox** [c18 New Latin, irregular diminutive of VARIOLA] ▷ ˌvariˈcellar *adj*

varicellate (ˌværɪ'sɛlɪt, -eɪt) *adj* (of certain shells) marked on the surface with small ridges [c19 from New Latin *varicella*, diminutive of Latin *varix* dilated vein, VARIX]

varicelloid (ˌværɪ'sɛlɔɪd) *adj* resembling chickenpox

varices ('værɪ,siːz) *n* the plural of **varix**

varico- *or before a vowel* **varic-** *combining form* indicating a varix or varicose veins: *varicotomy* [from Latin *varix, varic-* distended vein]

varicocele ('værɪkəʊ,siːl) *n* *pathol* an abnormal distension of the veins of the spermatic cord in the scrotum

varicoloured *or US* **varicolored** ('veərɪ,kʌləd) *adj* having many colours; variegated; motley

varicose ('værɪ,kəʊs) *adj* of or resulting from varicose veins: *a varicose ulcer* [c18 from Latin *varicōsus*, from VARIX]

varicose veins *pl n* a condition in which the superficial veins, esp of the legs, become tortuous, knotted, and swollen: caused by a defect in the venous valves or in the venous pump that normally moves the blood out of the legs when standing for long periods

varicosis (ˌværɪ'kəʊsɪs) *n* *pathol* any condition characterized by distension of the veins [c18 from

New Latin, from Latin: VARIX]

varicosity (ˌværɪ'kɒsɪtɪ) *n, pl* -ties *pathol* **1** the state, condition, or quality of being varicose **2** an abnormally distended vein

varicotomy (ˌværɪ'kɒtəmɪ) *n, pl* -mies surgical excision of a varicose vein

varied ('veərɪd) *adj* **1** displaying or characterized by variety; diverse **2** modified or altered: *the amount may be varied without notice* **3** varicoloured; variegated ▷ ˈvariedly *adv* ▷ ˈvariedness *n*

variegate ('veərɪ,ɡeɪt) *vb* (*tr*) **1** to alter the appearance of, esp by adding different colours **2** to impart variety to [c17 from Late Latin *variegāre*, from Latin *varius* diverse, VARIOUS + *agere* to make] ▷ ˌvarieˈgation *n*

variegated ('veərɪ,ɡeɪtɪd) *adj* **1** displaying differently coloured spots, patches, streaks, etc **2** (of foliage or flowers) having pale patches, usually as a result of mutation, infection, etc

varietal (və'raɪɪt°l) *adj* **1** of, relating to, characteristic of, designating, or forming a variety, esp a biological variety ▷ *n* **2** a wine labelled with the name of the grape from which it is pressed ▷ va'rietally *adv*

variety (və'raɪɪtɪ) *n, pl* -ties **1** the quality or condition of being diversified or various **2** a collection of unlike things, esp of the same general group; assortment **3** a different form or kind within a general category; sort: *varieties of behaviour* **4 a** *taxonomy* a race whose distinct characters are insufficient to justify classification as a separate species; a subspecies **b** *horticulture, stockbreeding* a strain of animal or plant produced by artificial breeding **5 a** entertainment consisting of a series of short unrelated performances or acts, such as comedy turns, songs, dances, sketches, etc **b** (*as modifier*): *a variety show* [c16 from Latin *varietās*, from VARIOUS]

variety meat *n* *chiefly US* processed meat, such as sausage, or offal

varifocal ('veərɪ,fəʊk°l) *adj* **1** *optics* having a focus that can vary **2** relating to a lens that is graduated to permit any length of vision between near and distant

varifocals ('veərɪ,fəʊk°lz) *pl n* a pair of spectacles with varifocal lenses

variform ('veərɪ,fɔːm) *adj* varying in form or shape ▷ ˈvariˌformly *adv*

vario- *combining form* indicating variety or difference: *variometer* [from Latin *varius* VARIOUS]

variola (və'raɪələ) *n* the technical name for **smallpox** [c18 from Medieval Latin: disease marked by little spots, from Latin *varius* spotted] ▷ va'riolar *adj*

variolate ('veərɪə,leɪt) *vb* **1** (*tr*) to inoculate with the smallpox virus ▷ *adj* **2** marked or pitted with or as if with the scars of smallpox [c18 from VARIOLA] ▷ ˌvarioˈlation, ˌvarioliˈzation *or* ˌvarioliˈsation *n*

variole ('veərɪ,əʊl) *n* any of the rounded masses that make up the rock variolite [c19 from French, from Medieval Latin; see VARIOLA]

variolite ('veərɪə,laɪt) *n* any basic igneous rock containing rounded bodies (varioles) consisting of radiating crystal fibres [c18 from VARIOLA, referring to the pockmarked appearance of the rock] ▷ variolitic (ˌveərɪə'lɪtɪk) *adj*

varioloid ('veərɪə,lɔɪd) *adj* **1** resembling smallpox ▷ *n* **2** a mild form of smallpox occurring in persons with partial immunity

variolous (və'raɪələs) *adj* relating to or resembling smallpox; variolar

variometer (ˌveərɪ'ɒmɪtə) *n* **1** an instrument for measuring variations in a magnetic field, used esp for studying the magnetic field of the earth **2** *electronics* a variable inductor consisting of a movable coil mounted inside and connected in series with a fixed coil **3** a sensitive rate-of-climb indicator, used mainly in gliders

variorum (ˌveərɪ'ɔːrəm) *adj* **1** containing notes by various scholars or critics or various versions of the text: *a variorum edition* ▷ *n* **2** an edition or text

V

of this kind [c18 from Latin phrase *ĕdĭtiō cum notīs variōrum* edition with the notes of various commentators]

various ('veərɪəs) *determiner* **1 a** several different: *he is an authority on various subjects* **b** *not standard* (as *pronoun;* followed by *of*): *various of them came* ▷ *adj* **2** of different kinds, though often within the same general category; diverse: *various occurrences; his disguises are many and various* **3** (*prenominal*) relating to a collection of separate persons or things: *the various members of the club* **4** displaying variety; many-sided: *his various achievements are most impressive* **5** *poetic* variegated **6** *obsolete* inconstant [c16 from Latin *varius* changing; perhaps related to Latin *vārus* crooked] > 'variously *adv* > 'variousness *n*

USAGE The use of *different* after *various* should be avoided: *the disease exists in various forms* (not *in various different forms*)

variscite ('værɪˌsaɪt) *n* a green secondary mineral consisting of hydrated aluminium phosphate [from Medieval Latin *Variscia,* the district of Vogtland in Saxony]

varistor (və'rɪstə) *n* a two-electrode semiconductor device having a voltage-dependent nonlinear resistance. Compare **varactor** [c20 a blend of *variable resistor*]

varitype ('veərɪˌtaɪp) *vb* **1** to produce (copy) on a Varityper ▷ *n* **2** copy produced on a Varityper > 'vari,typist *n*

Varityper ('veərɪˌtaɪpə) *n trademark* a justifying typewriter used to produce copy in various type styles

varix ('veərɪks) *n, pl* **varices** ('værɪˌsiːz) *pathol* **a** a tortuous dilated vein. See **varicose veins** **b** Also called: **arterial varix, varix lymphaticus** a similar condition affecting an artery or lymphatic vessel [c15 from Latin]

varlet ('vɑːlɪt) *n archaic* **1** a menial servant **2** a knight's page **3** a rascal [c15 from Old French, variant of *vallet* VALET]

varletry ('vɑːlɪtrɪ) *n archaic* **1 the** rabble; mob **2** varlets collectively

varmint ('vɑːmɪnt) *n informal* an irritating or obnoxious person or animal [c16 dialect variant of *varmin* VERMIN]

varna ('vɑːnə) *n* any of the four Hindu castes; Brahman, Kshatriya, Vaisya, or Sudra [from Sanskrit: class]

Varna (*Bulgarian* 'varna) *n* a port in NE Bulgaria, on the Black Sea: founded by Greeks in the 6th century BC; under the Ottoman Turks (1391–1878). Pop: 340 000 (2005 est). Former name (1949–56): **Stalin**

varnish ('vɑːnɪʃ) *n* **1** Also called: **oil varnish** a preparation consisting of a solvent, a drying oil, and usually resin, rubber, bitumen, etc, for application to a surface where it polymerizes to yield a hard glossy, usually transparent, coating **2** a similar preparation consisting of a substance, such as shellac or cellulose ester, dissolved in a volatile solvent, such as alcohol. It hardens to a film on evaporation of the solvent. See also **spirit varnish** **3** Also called: **natural varnish** the sap of certain trees used to produce such a coating **4** a smooth surface, coated with or as with varnish **5** an artificial, superficial, or deceptively pleasing manner, covering, etc; veneer **6** *chiefly Brit* another word for **nail polish** ▷ *vb* (*tr*) **7** to cover with varnish **8** to give a smooth surface to, as if by painting with varnish **9** to impart a more attractive appearance to **10** to make superficially attractive [c14 from Old French *vernis,* from Medieval Latin *veronix* sandarac, resin, from Medieval Greek *berenikē,* perhaps from Greek *Berenikē,* city in Cyrenaica, Libya where varnishes were used] > 'varnisher *n*

varnishing day *n* (at an exhibition of paintings) the day before the opening when artists may varnish or retouch their pictures after they have been hung

varnish tree *n* any of various trees, such as the lacquer tree, yielding substances used to make varnish or lacquer

varsity ('vɑːsɪtɪ) *n, pl* **-ties** *Brit, NZ and South African informal* short for **university**: formerly used esp at the universities of Oxford and Cambridge

Varuna ('værʊnə, 'vʌ-) *n Hinduism* the ancient sky god, later the god of the waters and rain-giver. In earlier traditions he was also the all-seeing divine judge

varus ('veərəs) *adj pathol* denoting a deformity in which the distal part of a limb is turned inwards towards the midline of the body [c19 from Latin: bow-legged]

varve (vɑːv) *n geology* **1** a typically thin band of sediment deposited annually in glacial lakes, consisting of a light layer and a dark layer deposited at different seasons **2** either of the layers of sediment making up this band [c20 from Swedish *varv* layer, from *varva,* from Old Norse *hverfa* to turn]

vary ('veərɪ) *vb* **varies, varying, varied** **1** to undergo or cause to undergo change, alteration, or modification in appearance, character, form, attribute, etc **2** to be different or cause to be different; be subject to change **3** (*tr*) to give variety to **4** (*intr;* foll by *from*) to differ, as from a convention, standard, etc **5** (*intr*) to change in accordance with another variable: *her mood varies with the weather; pressure varies directly with temperature and inversely with volume* **6** (*tr*) *music* to modify (a theme) by the use of variation [c14 from Latin *variāre,* from *varius* VARIOUS] > 'varying *adj* > 'varyingly *adv*

vas (væs) *n, pl* **vasa** ('veɪsə) *anatomy, zoology* a vessel, duct, or tube that carries a fluid [c17 from Latin: vessel]

vas- *combining form* a variant of **vaso-** before a vowel

vascular ('væskjʊlə) *adj biology, anatomy* of, relating to, or having vessels that conduct and circulate liquids: *a vascular bundle; the blood vascular system* [c17 from New Latin *vāsculāris,* from Latin: VASCULUM] > **vascularity** (ˌvæskjʊ'lærɪtɪ) *n* > 'vascularly *adv*

vascular bundle *n* a longitudinal strand of vascular tissue in the stems and leaves of higher plants

vascularization or **vascularisation** (ˌvæskjʊləraɪ'zeɪʃən) *n* the development of blood vessels in an organ or part

vascular ray *n* another name for **medullary ray**

vascular tissue *n* tissue of higher plants consisting mainly of xylem and phloem and occurring as a continuous system throughout the plant: it conducts water, mineral salts, and synthesized food substances and provides mechanical support. Also called: **conducting tissue**

vasculitis (ˌvæskjʊ'laɪtɪs) *n* inflammation of the blood vessels

vasculum ('væskjʊləm) *n, pl* **-la** (-lə) or **-lums** a metal box used by botanists in the field for carrying botanical specimens [c19 from Latin: little vessel, from VAS]

vas deferens ('væs 'dɛfəˌrɛnz) *n, pl* **vasa deferentia** ('veɪsə ˌdɛfə'rɛnʃɪə) *anatomy* the duct that conveys spermatozoa from the epididymis to the urethra [c16 from New Latin, from Latin *vās* vessel + *deferēns,* present participle of *deferre* to bear away]

vase (vɑːz) *n* a vessel used as an ornament or for holding cut flowers [c17 via French from Latin *vās* vessel]

vasectomy (væ'sɛktəmɪ) *n, pl* **-mies** surgical removal of all or part of the vas deferens, esp as a method of contraception

Vaseline ('væsɪˌliːn) *n* a trademark for **petrolatum**

Vashti ('væʃtaɪ) *n Old Testament* the wife of the Persian king Ahasuerus: deposed for refusing to display her beauty before his guests (Esther 1–2). Douay spelling: **Vasthi**

vaso- or before a vowel **vas-** *combining form* **1** indicating a blood vessel: *vasodilator* **2** indicating

the vas deferens: *vasectomy* [from Latin *vās* vessel]

vasoactive (ˌveɪzəʊ'æktɪv) *adj* affecting the diameter of blood vessels: *vasoactive peptides*

vasoconstrictor (ˌveɪzəʊkən'strɪktə) *n* **1** a drug, agent, or nerve that causes narrowing (**vasoconstriction**) of the walls of blood vessels ▷ *adj* **2** causing vasoconstriction > ˌvasocon'strictive *adj*

vasodilator (ˌveɪzəʊdaɪ'leɪtə) *n* **1** a drug, agent, or nerve that can cause dilatation (**vasodilatation**) of the walls of blood vessels ▷ *adj* **2** causing vasodilatation

vasoinhibitor (ˌveɪzəʊɪn'hɪbɪtə) *n* any of a group of drugs that reduce or inhibit the action of the vasomotor nerves > **vasoinhibitory** (ˌveɪzəʊɪn'hɪbɪtərɪ, -trɪ) *adj*

vasomotor (ˌveɪzəʊ'məʊtə) *adj* (of a drug, agent, nerve, etc) relating to or affecting the diameter of blood vessels

vasopressin (ˌveɪzəʊ'prɛsɪn) *n* a polypeptide hormone secreted by the posterior lobe of the pituitary gland. It increases the reabsorption of water by the kidney tubules and increases blood pressure by constricting the arteries. Also called: **antidiuretic hormone** Chemical name: **beta-hypophamine** Compare **oxytocin** [from *Vasopressin,* a trademark]

vasopressor (ˌveɪzəʊ'prɛsə) *med* ▷ *adj* **1** causing an increase in blood pressure by constricting the arteries ▷ *n* **2** a substance that has such an effect

vasovagal syncope (ˌveɪzəʊ'veɪgəl) *n* a faint brought on by excessive activity of the vagus nerve, causing the heart to slow and the blood pressure to fall. It can be caused by fear, choking, or stomach cramps and has no lasting effects

vassal ('væs°l) *n* **1** (in feudal society) a man who entered into a personal relationship with a lord to whom he paid homage and fealty in return for protection and often a fief. A **great vassal** was in vassalage to a king and a **rear vassal** to a great vassal **2 a** person, nation, etc, in a subordinate, suppliant, or dependent position relative to another **b** (*as modifier*): *vassal status* ▷ *adj* **3** of or relating to a vassal [c14 via Old French from Medieval Latin *vassallus,* from *vassus* servant, of Celtic origin; compare Welsh *gwas* boy, Old Irish *foss* servant] > 'vassal-less *adj*

vassalage ('væsəlɪdʒ) *n* **1** (esp in feudal society) **a** the condition of being a vassal or the obligations to which a vassal was liable **b** the relationship between a vassal and his lord **2** subjection, servitude, or dependence in general **3** *rare* vassals collectively

vassalize or **vassalise** ('væsəˌlaɪz) *vb* (*tr*) to make a vassal of

vast (vɑːst) *adj* **1** unusually large in size, extent, degree, or number; immense **2** (*prenominal*) (*intensifier*): *in vast haste* ▷ *n* **3 the vast** *chiefly poetic* immense or boundless space **4** *Brit dialect* a very great amount or number [c16 from Latin *vastus* deserted] > 'vastity *n* > 'vastly *adv* > 'vastness *n*

Västerås (*Swedish* vɛstər'oːs) *n* a city in central Sweden, on Lake Mälar: Sweden's largest inland port; site of several national parliaments in the 16th century. Pop: 130 960 (2004 est)

vastitude ('vɑːstɪˌtjuːd) *n rare* **1** the condition or quality of being vast **2** a vast space, expanse, extent, etc

vasty ('vɑːstɪ) *adj* **vastier, vastiest** an archaic or poetic word for **vast**

vat (væt) *n* **1** a large container for holding or storing liquids **2** *chem* a preparation of reduced vat dye ▷ *vb* **vats, vatting, vatted** **3** (*tr*) to place, store, or treat in a vat [Old English *fæt;* related to Old Frisian *fet,* Old Saxon, Old Norse *fat,* Old High German *faz*]

VAT (sometimes væt) (in Britain) *abbreviation for* value-added tax: a tax levied on the difference between the cost of materials and the selling price of a commodity or service

Vat. *abbreviation for* Vatican

vat dye *n* a dye, such as indigo, that is applied by first reducing it to its leuco base, which is soluble in alkali, and then regenerating the insoluble dye by oxidation in the fibres of the material > **ˈvat-ˌdyed** *adj*

vatic (ˈvætɪk) *adj rare* of, relating to, or characteristic of a prophet; oracular [c16 from Latin *vātēs* prophet]

Vatican (ˈvætɪkən) *n* **1 a** the palace of the popes in Rome and their principal residence there since 1377, which includes administrative offices, a library, museum, etc, and is attached to the basilica of St Peter's **b** (*as modifier*): *the Vatican Council* **2 a** the authority of the Pope and the papal curia **b** (*as modifier*): *a Vatican edict* [c16 from Latin *Vātīcānus mons* Vatican hill, on the western bank of the Tiber, of Etruscan origin]

Vatican City *n* an independent state forming an enclave in Rome, with extraterritoriality over 12 churches and palaces in Rome: the only remaining Papal State; independence recognized by the Italian government in 1929; contains St Peter's Basilica and Square and the Vatican; the spiritual and administrative centre of the Roman Catholic Church. Languages: Italian and Latin. Currency: euro. Pop: 1000 (2003 est). Area: 44 hectares (109 acres). Italian name: Città del Vaticano Also called: **the Holy See**

Vaticanism (ˈvætɪkəˌnɪzəm) *n often derogatory* the authority and policies of the Pope and the papal curia, esp with regard to papal infallibility

vaticide (ˈvætɪˌsaɪd) *n rare* **a** the murder of a prophet **b** a person guilty of this [c18 from Latin *vātēs* prophet + -CIDE]

vaticinate (vəˈtɪsɪˌneɪt) *vb rare* to foretell; prophesy [c17 from Latin *vāticinārī* from *vātēs* prophet + *canere* to foretell] > **vaticination** (ˌvætɪsɪˈneɪʃən) *n* > **vaˈticiˌnator** *n* > **vaticinal** (vəˈtɪsɪn*l) *or* **vaˈticinatory** *adj*

Vättern (*Swedish* ˈvɛtərn) *n* **Lake** a lake in S central Sweden: the second largest lake in Sweden; linked to Lake Vänern by the Göta Canal; drains into the Baltic. Area: 1912 sq km (738 sq miles)

vatu (ˈvætuː) *n* the standard monetary unit of Vanuatu

vauch (ˈvɒtʃ) *vb* (*intr*) *Southwest English dialect* to move fast

Vaucluse (*French* voklyz) *n* a department of SE France, in Provence-Alpes-Côte-d'Azur region. Capital: Avignon. Pop: 517 810 (2003 est). Area: 3578 sq km (1395 sq miles)

Vaud (*French* vo) *n* a canton of SW Switzerland: mountainous in the southeast; chief Swiss producer of wine. Capital: Lausanne. Pop: 632 000 (2002 est). Area: 3209 sq km (1240 sq miles). German name: Waadt

vaudeville (ˈvəʊdəvɪl, ˈvɔː-) *n* **1** *chiefly US and Canadian* variety entertainment consisting of short acts such as acrobatic turns, song-and-dance routines, animal acts, etc, popular esp in the early 20th century. Brit name: **music hall 2** a light or comic theatrical piece interspersed with songs and dances [c18 from French, from *vaudevire* satirical folk song, shortened from *chanson du vau de Vire* song of the valley of Vire, a district in Normandy where this type of song flourished]

vaudevillian (ˌvəʊdəˈvɪliən, ˌvɔː-) *n* also **vaudevillist 1** a person who writes for or performs in vaudeville ▷ *adj* **2** of, characteristic of, or relating to vaudeville

Vaudois (ˈvəʊdwɑː) *pl n, sing* -dois **1** another name for the **Waldenses 2** the inhabitants of Vaud

vault¹ (vɔːlt) *n* **1** an arched structure that forms a roof or ceiling **2** a room, esp a cellar, having an arched roof down to floor level **3** a burial chamber, esp when underground **4** a strongroom for the safe-deposit and storage of valuables **5** an underground room or part of such a room, used for the storage of wine, food, etc **6** *anatomy* any arched or domed bodily cavity or space: *the cranial*

vault 7 something suggestive of an arched structure, as the sky ▷ *vb* **8** (*tr*) to furnish with or as if with an arched roof **9** (*tr*) to construct in the shape of a vault **10** (*intr*) to curve, arch, or bend in the shape of a vault [c14 *vaute*, from Old French, from Vulgar Latin *volvita* (unattested) a turn, probably from Latin *volvere* to roll] > **ˈvaultˌlike** *adj*

vault² (vɔːlt) *vb* **1** to spring over (an object), esp with the aid of a long pole or with the hands resting on the object **2** (*intr*) to do, achieve, or attain something as if by a leap: *he vaulted to fame on the strength of his discovery* **3** *dressage* to perform or cause to perform a curvet ▷ *n* **4** the act of vaulting **5** *dressage* a low leap; curvet [c16 from Old French *voulter* to turn, from Italian *voltare* to turn, from Vulgar Latin *volvitāre* (unattested) to turn, leap; see VAULT¹] > **ˈvaulter** *n*

vaulting¹ (ˈvɔːltɪŋ) *n* one or more vaults in a building or such structures considered collectively

vaulting² (ˈvɔːltɪŋ) *adj* (*prenominal*) **1** excessively confident; overreaching; exaggerated: *vaulting arrogance* **2** used to vault: *a vaulting pole*

vaunt (vɔːnt) *vb* **1** (*tr*) to describe, praise, or display (one's success, possessions, etc) boastfully **2** (*intr*) *rare or literary* to use boastful language; brag ▷ *n* **3** a boast **4** *archaic* ostentatious display [c14 from Old French *vanter*, from Late Latin *vānitāre* to brag, from Latin *vānus* VAIN] > **ˈvaunter** *n*

vaunt-courier *n archaic or poetic* a person or thing that goes in advance; forerunner; herald [c16 from French *avant-courrier*; see AVAUNT, COURIER]

v. aux. *abbreviation for* auxiliary verb

Vauxhall (ˈvɒksˌhɔːl) *n* **1** a district in London, on the south bank of the Thames **2** Also called: **Vauxhall Gardens** a public garden at Vauxhall, laid out in 1661; a fashionable meeting place and site of lavish entertainments. Closed in 1859

vav (vɔːv) *n* the sixth letter of the Hebrew alphabet (ו) transliterated as *v* or *w*. Also called: **waw** [from Hebrew *wāw* a hook]

vavasor (ˈvævəˌsɔː) *or* **vavasour** (ˈvævəˌsʊə) *n* (in feudal society) the noble or knightly vassal of a baron or great lord who also has vassals himself. Also: **vavassor** [c13 from Old French *vavasour*, perhaps contraction of Medieval Latin *vassus vassōrum* vassal of vassals; see VASSAL]

va-va-voom (ˌvævæˈvuːm) *n informal* the quality of being interesting, exciting, or sexually appealing

vb *abbreviation for* verb

VB (in transformational grammar) *abbreviation for* verbal constituent

vc *the internet domain name for* Saint Vincent and the Grenadines

VC *abbreviation for* **1** Vice-chairman **2** Vice Chancellor **3** Vice Consul **4** Victoria Cross **5** Vietcong

V-chip *n* a device within a television set that allows the set to be programmed not to receive transmissions that have been classified as containing sex, violence, or obscene language

vCJD *abbreviation for* **(new-)variant Creutzfeldt-Jakob disease**

VCR *abbreviation for* **1** video cassette recorder **2** visual control room (at an airfield)

vd *abbreviation for* various dates

VD *abbreviation for* venereal disease

V-Day *n* a day nominated to celebrate victory, as in V-E Day or V-J Day in World War II

VDC *abbreviation for* Volunteer Defence Corps

VDQS *abbreviation for* vins délimités de qualité supérieure: on a bottle of French wine, indicates that it contains high-quality wine from an approved regional vineyard; the second highest French wine classification. Compare **AC**, *vin de pays, vin de table*

VDT *computing abbreviation for* visual display terminal

VDU *computing abbreviation for* **visual display unit**

ve *the internet domain name for* Venezuela

've *contraction of* have: *I've; you've*

Veadar *Hebrew* (ˈviːəˌdɑː, ˈveɪ-) *n Judaism* another

term for Adar Sheni: see Adar [from Hebrew *va'adhar*, literally: and Adar, that is, the extra Adar]

veal (viːl) *n* **1** the flesh of the calf used as food **2** Also called: **veal calf** a calf, esp one bred for eating. Related adj: **vituline** [c14 from Old French *veel*, from Latin *vitellus* a little calf, from *vitulus* calf]

vealer (ˈviːlə) *n* **1** *US, Canadian, and Austral* another name for **veal** (sense 2) **2** *NZ* a young bovine animal of up to 14 months old grown for veal

vector (ˈvɛktə) *n* **1** Also called: **polar vector** *maths* a variable quantity, such as force, that has magnitude and direction and can be resolved into components that are odd functions of the coordinates. It is represented in print by a bold italic symbol: **F** or $\vec{F}$. Compare **pseudoscalar, pseudovector, scalar** (sense 1), **tensor** (sense 2) **2** *maths* an element of a vector space **3** Also called: **carrier** *pathol* an organism, esp an insect, that carries a disease-producing microorganism from one host to another, either within or on the surface of its body **4** Also called: **cloning vector** *genetics* an agent, such as a bacteriophage or a plasmid, by means of which a fragment of foreign DNA is inserted into a host cell to produce a gene clone in genetic engineering **5** the course or compass direction of an aircraft **6** any behavioural influence, force, or drive ▷ *vb* (*tr*) **7** to direct or guide (a pilot, aircraft, etc) by directions transmitted by radio **8** to alter the direction of (the thrust of a jet engine) as a means of steering an aircraft [c18 from Latin: carrier, from *vehere* to convey] > **vectorial** (vɛkˈtɔːrɪəl) *adj* > **vecˈtorially** *adv*

vector field *n* a region of space under the influence of some vector quantity, such as magnetic field strength, in which the quantity takes a unique vector value at every point of the region

vector font *n computing* another name for **outline font**

vector product *n* the product of two vectors that is a pseudovector, whose magnitude is the product of the magnitudes of the given vectors and the sine of the angle between them. Its axis is perpendicular to the plane of the given vectors. Written: $A \times B$ or $A \wedge B$. Compare **scalar product**. Also called: **cross product**

vector space *n maths* a mathematical structure consisting of a set of objects (**vectors**) associated with a field of objects (**scalars**), such that the set constitutes an Abelian group and a further operation, scalar multiplication, is defined in which the product of a scalar and a vector is a vector. See also **scalar multiplication**

vector sum *n* a vector whose length and direction are represented by the diagonal of a parallelogram whose sides represent the given vectors. See also **resultant**

Veda (ˈveɪdə) *n* any or all of the most ancient sacred writings of Hinduism, esp the Rig-Veda, Yajur-Veda, Sama-Veda, and Atharva-Veda [c18 from Sanskrit: knowledge; related to *veda* I know] > **Vedaic** (vɪˈdeɪɪk) *adj* > **Vedaism** (ˈveɪdəˌɪzəm) *n*

vedalia (vɪˈdeɪlɪə) *n* an Australian ladybird, *Rodolia cardinalis*, introduced elsewhere to control the scale insect *Icerya purchasi*, which is a pest of citrus fruits [c20 from New Latin]

Vedanta (vɪˈdɑːntə, -ˈdæn-) *n* one of the six main philosophical schools of Hinduism, expounding the monism regarded as implicit in the Veda in accordance with the doctrines of the Upanishads. It teaches that only Brahman has reality, while the whole phenomenal world is the outcome of illusion (maya) [c19 from Sanskrit, from VEDA + *ánta* end] > **Veˈdantic** *adj* > **Veˈdantism** *n* > **Veˈdantist** *n*

V-E Day *n* the day marking the Allied victory in Europe in World War II (May 8, 1945)

Vedda *or* **Veddah** (ˈvɛdə) *n, pl* -da, -das *or* -dah, -dahs a member of an aboriginal people of Sri Lanka, characterized by slender build, dark complexion, and wavy hair, noted for their Stone

Age technology [c17 from Sinhalese: hunter, of Dravidian origin]

Veddoid ('vɛdɔɪd) *adj* **1** of, relating to, or resembling the Vedda ▷ *n* **2** a Vedda **3** a member of a postulated prehistoric race of S Asia, having slender build, dark complexion, and wavy hair: thought to be ancestors of the Vedda

vedette (vɪ'dɛt) *n* **1** Also called: **vedette boat** *naval* a small patrol vessel **2** Also called: **vidette** *military* a mounted sentry posted forward of a formation's position [c17 from French, from Italian *vedetta* (influenced by *vedere* to see), from earlier *veletta*, perhaps from Spanish *vela* watch, from *velar* to keep vigil, from Latin *vigilāre*]

Vedic ('veɪdɪk) *adj* **1** of or relating to the Vedas or the ancient form of Sanskrit in which they are written **2** of or relating to the ancient Indo-European settlers in India, regarded as the originators of many of the traditions preserved in the Vedas ▷ *n* **3** the classical form of Sanskrit; the language of the Vedas

veep (vi:p) *n informal* a vice president [c20 from the initials VP]

veer[1] (vɪə) *vb* **1** to alter direction (of); swing around **2** (*intr*) to change from one position, opinion, etc, to another **3** (*intr*) (of the wind) **a** to change direction clockwise in the northern hemisphere and anticlockwise in the southern **b** *nautical* to blow from a direction nearer the stern. Compare **haul** (sense 5) **4** *nautical* to steer (a vessel) off the wind ▷ *n* **5** a change of course or direction [c16 from Old French *virer*, probably of Celtic origin; compare Welsh *gwyro* to diverge]

veer[2] (vɪə) *vb* (*tr*; often foll by *out* or *away*) *nautical* to slacken or pay out (cable or chain) [c16 from Dutch *vieren*, from Old High German *fieren* to give direction]

veery ('vɪərɪ) *n*, *pl* **veeries** a tawny brown North American thrush, *Hylocichla fuscescens*, with a slightly spotted grey breast [c19 probably imitative of its note]

veg (vɛdʒ) *n informal* a vegetable or vegetables

Vega ('viːɡə) *n* the brightest star in the constellation Lyra and one of the most conspicuous in the N hemisphere. It is part of an optical double star having a faint companion. Distance: 25.3 light years; spectral type: AoV [c17 from Medieval Latin, from Arabic (*al nasr*) *al wāqi*, literally: the falling (vulture), that is, the constellation Lyra]

vegan ('viːɡən) *n* a person who refrains from using any animal product whatever for food, clothing, or any other purpose

vegeburger *or* **veggieburger** ('vɛdʒɪˌbɜːɡə) *n* a flat cake of chopped seasoned vegetables and pulses that is grilled or fried and often served in a bread roll

Vegemite ('vɛdʒɪˌmaɪt) *n Austral* **1** *trademark* a vegetable extract used as a spread, flavouring, etc **2** (*not capital*) *informal* a child, esp one who is well-behaved **3** **happy little vegemite** *informal* a person who is in good humour

vegetable ('vɛdʒtəbʰl) *n* **1** any of various herbaceous plants having parts that are used as food, such as peas, beans, cabbage, potatoes, cauliflower, and onions **2** *informal* a person who has lost control of his mental faculties, limbs, etc, as from an injury, mental disease, etc **3 a** a dull inactive person **b** (*as modifier*): *a vegetable life* **4** (*modifier*) consisting of or made from edible vegetables: *a vegetable diet* **5** (*modifier*) of, relating to, characteristic of, derived from, or consisting of plants or plant material: *vegetable oils; the vegetable kingdom* **6** *rare* any member of the plant kingdom [c14 (adj): from Late Latin *vegetābilis* animating, from *vegetāre* to enliven, from Latin *vegēre* to excite]

vegetable butter *n* any of a group of vegetable fats having the consistency of butter

vegetable ivory *n* **1** the hard whitish material obtained from the endosperm of the ivory nut: used to make buttons, ornaments, etc **2** another name for the **ivory nut**

vegetable kingdom *n* another name for **plant kingdom**

vegetable marrow *n* **1** a cucurbitaceous plant, *Cucurbita pepo*, probably native to America but widely cultivated for its oblong green striped fruit, which is eaten as a vegetable **2** Also called (in the US): **marrow squash** the fruit of this plant. Often shortened to: **marrow**

vegetable oil *n* any of a group of oils that are esters of fatty acids and glycerol and are obtained from plants

vegetable oyster *n* another name for **salsify** (sense 1)

vegetable sheep *n NZ* any of various species of the genus *Raoulia*, esp *R. mammillaris* or *R. eximia*, of New Zealand rocky mountains: a small low bush having white flowers and hairy leaves which, from a distance, make it look like a sheep

vegetable silk *n* any of various silky fibres obtained from the seed pods of certain plants. See also **kapok**

vegetable sponge *n* another name for **dishcloth gourd**

vegetable tallow *n* any of various types of tallow that are obtained from plants

vegetable wax *n* any of various waxes that occur on parts of certain plants, esp the trunks of certain palms, and prevent loss of water from the plant

vegetal ('vɛdʒɪtʰl) *adj* **1** of, relating to, or characteristic of vegetables or plant life **2** of or relating to processes in plants and animals that do not involve sexual reproduction; vegetative [c15 from Late Latin *vegetāre* to quicken; see VEGETABLE]

vegetarian (ˌvɛdʒɪ'tɛərɪən) *n* **1** a person who advocates or practises vegetarianism ▷ *adj* **2** relating to, advocating, or practising vegetarianism **3** *cookery* strictly, consisting of vegetables and fruit only, but usually including milk, cheese, eggs, etc

vegetarianism (ˌvɛdʒɪ'tɛərɪəˌnɪzəm) *n* the principle or practice of excluding all meat and fish, and sometimes, in the case of vegans, all animal products (such as eggs, cheese, etc) from one's diet

vegetate ('vɛdʒɪˌteɪt) *vb* (*intr*) **1** to grow like a plant; sprout **2** to lead a life characterized by monotony, passivity, or mental inactivity **3** *pathol* (of a wart, polyp, etc) to develop fleshy outgrowths [c17 from Late Latin *vegetāre* to invigorate]

vegetation (ˌvɛdʒɪ'teɪʃən) *n* **1** plant life as a whole, esp the plant life of a particular region **2** the process of vegetating **3** *pathol* any abnormal growth, excrescence, etc **4** a vegetative existence > ˌvege'tational *adj* > ˌvege'tatious *adj*

vegetative ('vɛdʒɪtətɪv) *adj* **1** of, relating to, or denoting the nonreproductive parts of a plant, ie the stems, leaves, and roots, or growth that does not involve the reproductive parts **2** (of reproduction) characterized by asexual processes **3** of or relating to functions such as digestion, growth, and circulation rather than sexual reproduction **4** (of a style of living) dull, stagnant, unthinking, or passive > 'vegetatively *adv* > 'vegetativeness *n*

veggie ('vɛdʒɪ) *n*, *adj* an informal word for **vegetarian**

veggieburger ('vɛdʒɪˌbɜːɡə) *n* a variant spelling of **vegeburger**

vegie ('vɛdʒɪ) *adj Austral informal* (of school subjects) considered to be trivial; not academically taxing

vego ('vɛdʒəʊ) *Austral informal* ▷ *adj* **1** vegetarian ▷ *n*, *pl* **vegos** **2** a vegetarian

veg out *vb* **vegges, vegging, vegged** (*intr, adv*) *slang, chiefly US* to relax in an inert passive way; vegetate: *vegging out in front of the television set*

vehement ('viːɪmənt) *adj* **1** marked by intensity of feeling or conviction; emphatic **2** (of actions, gestures, etc) characterized by great energy, vigour, or force; furious [c15 from Latin *vehemēns*

ardent; related to *vehere* to carry] > 'vehemence *n* > 'vehemently *adv*

vehicle ('viːɪkʰl) *n* **1** any conveyance in or by which people or objects are transported, esp one fitted with wheels **2** a medium for the expression, communication, or achievement of ideas, information, power, etc **3** *pharmacol* a therapeutically inactive substance mixed with the active ingredient to give bulk to a medicine **4** Also called: **base** a painting medium, such as oil, in which pigments are suspended **5** (in the performing arts) a play, musical composition, etc, that enables a particular performer to display his talents **6** a rocket excluding its payload [c17 from Latin *vehiculum*, from *vehere* to carry] > **vehicular** (vɪ'hɪkjʊlə) *adj*

Veii ('viːjaɪ) *n* an ancient Etruscan city, northwest of Rome: destroyed by the Romans in 396 BC

veil (veɪl) *n* **1** a piece of more or less transparent material, usually attached to a hat or headdress, used to conceal or protect a woman's face and head **2** part of a nun's headdress falling round the face onto the shoulders **3** something that covers, conceals, or separates; mask: *a veil of reticence* **4** **the veil** the life of a nun in a religious order and the obligations entailed by it **5** **take the veil** to become a nun **6** Also called: **velum** *botany* a membranous structure, esp the thin layer of cells connecting the edge of a young mushroom cap with the stipe **7** *anatomy* another word for **caul 8** See **humeral veil** ▷ *vb* **9** (*tr*) to cover, conceal, or separate with or as if with a veil **10** (*intr*) to wear or put on a veil [c13 from Norman French *veile*, from Latin *vēla* sails, pl of *vēlum* a covering] > 'veiler *n* > 'veilless *adj* > 'veil-ˌlike *adj*

veiled (veɪld) *adj* **1** disguised: *a veiled insult* **2** (of sound, tone, the voice, etc) not distinct; muffled > **veiledly** ('veɪlɪdlɪ) *adv*

veiling ('veɪlɪŋ) *n* a veil or the fabric used for veils

vein (veɪn) *n* **1** any of the tubular vessels that convey oxygen-depleted blood to the heart. Compare **pulmonary vein, artery.** Related adj: **venous 2** any of the hollow branching tubes that form the supporting framework of an insect's wing **3** any of the vascular strands of a leaf **4** a clearly defined mass of ore, mineral, etc, filling a fault or fracture, often with a tabular or sheetlike shape **5** an irregular streak of colour or alien substance in marble, wood, or other material **6** a natural underground watercourse **7** a crack or fissure **8** a distinctive trait or quality in speech, writing, character, etc; strain: *a vein of humour* **9** a temporary disposition, attitude, or temper; mood **10** *Irish* a parting in hair ▷ *vb* (*tr*) **11** to diffuse over or cause to diffuse over in streaked patterns **12** to fill, furnish, or mark with or as if with veins [c13 from Old French *veine*, from Latin *vēna*] > 'veinal *adj* > 'veinless *adj* > 'vein,like *adj* > 'veiny *adj*

veining ('veɪnɪŋ) *n* a pattern or network of veins or streaks

veinlet ('veɪnlɪt) *n* any small vein or venule

veinstone ('veɪnˌstəʊn) *n* another word for **gangue**

veinule ('veɪnjuːl) *n* a less common spelling of **venule**

Vela ('viːlə) *n*, *Latin genitive* **Velorum** (viːˈlɔːrəm) a constellation in the S hemisphere, close to Puppis and Carina and crossed by the Milky Way, that has four second-magnitude stars and a young bright pulsar

velamen (vəˈleɪmɛn) *n*, *pl* **-lamina** (-ˈlæmɪnə) **1** the thick layer of dead cells that covers the aerial roots of certain orchids and aroids and absorbs moisture from the surroundings **2** *anatomy* another word for **velum** [c19 from Latin: a veil, from *vēlāre* to cover]

velar ('viːlə) *adj* **1** of, relating to, or attached to a velum: *velar tentacles* **2** *phonetics* articulated with the soft palate and the back of the tongue, as in the sounds (k), (ɡ), or (ŋ) [c18 from Latin *vēlāris*, from *vēlum* VEIL]

velarium (vɪˈlɛərɪəm) *n*, *pl* **-laria** (-ˈlɛərɪə) an awning used to protect the audience in ancient Roman theatres and amphitheatres [C19 from Latin, from *vēlāre* to cover]

velarize *or* **velarise** ('vi:lə‚raɪz) *vb* (*tr*) *phonetics* to pronounce or supplement the pronunciation of (a speech sound) with articulation at the soft palate, as in dark (l) in English *tall* > ‚velari'zation *or* ‚velari'sation *n*

velate ('vi:lɪt, -leɪt) *adj* having or covered with velum

Velcro ('vɛlkrəʊ) *n trademark* a fastening consisting of two strips of nylon fabric, one having tiny hooked threads and the other a coarse surface, that form a strong bond when pressed together

veld *or* **veldt** (fɛlt, vɛlt) *n* elevated open grassland in Southern Africa. See also **bushveld, highveld.** Compare **pampas, prairie, renosterveld, steppe** [C19 from Afrikaans, from earlier Dutch *veldt* FIELD]

veldskoen ('fɛlt‚skʊn, 'vɛlt-) *n* an ankle-length boot of soft but strong rawhide [C19 from Afrikaans, from *vel* skin + *skoen* shoes]

veleta (və'li:tə) *n* a variant spelling of **valeta**

veliger ('vɛlɪdʒə) *n* the free-swimming larva of many molluscs, having a ciliated shell and a ciliated velum used for feeding and locomotion [C19 from New Latin, from VELUM + -GER(OUS)]

velites ('vi:lɪ‚ti:z) *pl n* light-armed troops in ancient Rome, drawn from the poorer classes [C17 from Latin, pl of *vēles* light-armed foot soldier; related to *volāre* to fly]

velleity (vɛ'li:ɪtɪ) *n, pl* **-ties** *rare* **1** the weakest level of desire or volition **2** a mere wish [C17 from New Latin *velleitās*, from Latin *velle* to wish]

vellicate ('vɛlɪ‚keɪt) *vb rare* to twitch, pluck, or pinch [C17 from Latin *vellicāre*, from *vellere* to tear off] > ‚velli'cation *n* > 'vellicative *adj*

Vellore (və'lɔ:) *n* a town in SE India, in NE Tamil Nadu: medical centre. Pop: 177 413 (2001)

vellum ('vɛləm) *n* **1** a fine parchment prepared from the skin of a calf, kid, or lamb **2** a work printed or written on vellum **3** a creamy coloured heavy paper resembling vellum ▷ *adj* **4** made of or resembling vellum **5** (of a book) bound in vellum [C15 from Old French *velin*, from *velin* of a calf, from *veel* VEAL]

veloce (vɪ'ləʊtʃɪ) *adj, adv music* to be played rapidly [from Italian, from Latin *vēlōx* quick]

velocipede (vɪ'lɒsɪ‚pi:d) *n* **1** an early form of bicycle propelled by pushing along the ground with the feet **2** any early form of bicycle or tricycle [C19 from French *vélocipède*, from Latin *vēlōx* swift + *pēs* foot] > ve'loci‚pedist *n*

velocity (vɪ'lɒsɪtɪ) *n, pl* **-ties 1** speed of motion, action, or operation; rapidity; swiftness **2** *physics* a measure of the rate of motion of a body expressed as the rate of change of its position in a particular direction with time. It is measured in metres per second, miles per hour, etc. Symbol: *u, v, w* **3** *physics* (not in technical usage) another word for **speed** (sense 3) [C16 from Latin *vēlōcitās*, from *vēlōx* swift; related to *volāre* to fly]

velocity head *n* the velocity of a fluid expressed in terms of the head or static pressure required to produce that velocity. It equals ρν/2 where ρ is the density of the fluid and ν is the velocity. In hydrology the density of water can be written 1/G where G is the gravitational constant

velocity modulation *n* the modulation in velocity of a beam of electrons or ions caused by passing the beam through a high-frequency electric field, as in a cavity resonator

velocity of circulation *n economics* the average number of times a unit of money is used in a given time, esp calculated as the ratio of the total money spent in that time to the total amount of money in circulation

velodrome ('vi:lə‚drəʊm, 'vɛl-) *n* an arena with a banked track for cycle racing [C20 from French *vélodrome*, from *vélo-* (from Latin *vēlōx* swift) + -DROME]

velour *or* **velours** (vɛ'lʊə) *n* any of various fabrics with a velvet-like finish, used for upholstery, coats, hats, etc [C18 from Old French *velous*, from Old Provençal *velos* velvet, from Latin *villosus* shaggy, from *villus* shaggy hair; compare Latin *vellus* a fleece]

velouté (və'lu:teɪ) *n* a rich white sauce or soup made from stock, egg yolks, and cream [from French, literally: velvety, from Old French *velous*; see VELOUR]

Velsen (*Dutch* 'vɛlsə) *n* a port in the W Netherlands, in North Holland at the mouth of the canal connecting Amsterdam with the North Sea: fishing and heavy industrial centre. Pop: 68 000 (2003 est)

velum ('vi:ləm) *n, pl* **-la** (-lə) **1** *zoology* any of various membranous structures, such as the ciliated oral membrane of certain mollusc larvae or the veil-like membrane running around the rim of a jellyfish **2** *anatomy* any of various veil-like bodily structures, esp the soft palate **3** *botany* another word for **veil** (sense 6) [C18 from Latin: veil]

velure (və'lʊə) *n* **1** velvet or a similar fabric **2** a hatter's pad, used for smoothing silk hats [C16 from Old French *velour*, from Old French *velous*; see VELOUR]

velutinous (və'lu:tɪnəs) *adj* covered with short dense soft hairs: *velutinous leaves* [C19 from New Latin *velūtīnus* like velvet]

velvet ('vɛlvɪt) *n* **1 a** a fabric of silk, cotton, nylon, etc, with a thick close soft usually lustrous pile **b** (*as modifier*): *velvet curtains* **2** anything with a smooth soft surface **3 a** smoothness; softness **b** (*as modifier*): *velvet skin; a velvet night* **4** the furry covering of the newly formed antlers of a deer **5** *slang, chiefly US* **a** gambling or speculative winnings **b** a gain, esp when unexpectedly high **6 velvet glove** gentleness or caution, often concealing strength or determination (esp in the phrase **an iron fist** *or* **hand in a velvet glove**) [C14 *veluet*, from Old French *veluotte*, from *velu* hairy, from Vulgar Latin *villutus* (unattested), from Latin *villus* shaggy hair] > 'velvet-‚like *adj* > 'velvety *adj*

velvet ant *n* a solitary digger wasp of the family *Mutillidae* [C19 so named from the wingless female]

velveteen (‚vɛlvɪ'ti:n) *n* **1 a** a cotton fabric resembling velvet with a short thick pile, used for clothing, etc **b** (*as modifier*): *velveteen trousers* **2** (*plural*) trousers made of velveteen > ‚velvet'eened *adj*

velvet revolution *n* the peaceful overthrow of a government, esp a communist government, as occurred in Czechoslovakia in late 1989

velvet scoter *n* a European sea duck, *Melanitta fusca*, the male of which has a black plumage with white patches below the eyes and on the wings

velvet shank *n* a bright yellow edible basidiomycetous fungus, *Flammulina velutipes*, common on trunks, stumps, or branches of broad-leaved trees in winter

velvet stout *n* a less common name for **black velvet**

Ven. *abbreviation for* Venerable

vena ('vi:nə) *n, pl* **-nae** (-ni:) *anatomy* a technical word for **vein** [C15 from Latin *vēna* VEIN]

vena cava ('keɪvə) *n, pl* **venae cavae** ('keɪvi:) either one of the two large veins that convey oxygen-depleted blood to the heart [Latin: hollow vein]

venal ('vi:nəl) *adj* **1** easily bribed or corrupted; mercenary: *a venal magistrate* **2** characterized by corruption: *a venal civilization* **3** open to purchase, esp by bribery: *a venal contract* [C17 from Latin *vēnālis*, from *vēnum* sale] > ve'nality *n* > 'venally *adv*

venatic (vi'nætɪk) *or* **venatical** *adj* **1** of, relating to, or used in hunting **2** (of people) engaged in or given to hunting [C17 from Latin *vēnāticus*, from *vēnārī* to hunt] > ve'natically *adv*

venation (vi:'neɪʃən) *n* **1** the arrangement of the veins in a leaf or in the wing of an insect **2** such veins collectively > ve'national *adj*

vend (vɛnd) *vb* **1** to sell or be sold **2** to sell (goods) for a living **3** (*tr*) *rare* to utter or publish (an opinion, etc) [C17 from Latin *vendere*, contraction of *vēnum dare* to offer for sale] > vendition (vɛn'dɪʃən) *n*

Venda¹ ('vɛndə) *n* **1** (*pl* **-da** *or* **-das**) a member of a Negroid people of southern Africa, living chiefly in NE South Africa **2** the language of this people, belonging to the Bantu group of the Niger-Congo family but not easily related to any other members of the group

Venda² ('vɛndə) *n* a former Bantu homeland in South Africa, near the Zimbabwe border; abolished in 1993. Capital: Thohoyandou

vendace ('vɛndeɪs) *n, pl* **-daces** *or* **-dace** either of two small whitefish, *Coregonus vandesius* (**Lochmaben vendace**) or *C. gracilior* (**Cumberland vendace**), occurring in lakes in Scotland and NW England respectively. See also **powan** [C18 from New Latin *vandēsius*, from Old French *vandoise*, probably of Celtic origin]

vendee (vɛn'di:) *n chiefly law* a person to whom something, esp real property, is sold; buyer

Vendée (*French* vɑ̃de) *n* a department of W France, in Pays-de-la-Loire region: scene of the **Wars of the Vendée,** a series of peasant-royalist insurrections (1793–95) against the Revolutionary government. Capital: La Roche-sur-Yon. Pop: 565 230 (2003 est). Area: 7016 sq km (2709 sq miles)

Vendémiaire French (vɑ̃demjɛr) *n* the month of the grape harvest: the first month of the French Revolutionary calendar, extending from Sept 23 to Oct 22 [C18 from French, from Latin *vindēmia* vintage, from *vīnum* wine + *dēmere* to take away]

vendetta (vɛn'dɛtə) *n* **1** a private feud, originally between Corsican or Sicilian families, in which the relatives of a murdered person seek vengeance by killing the murderer or some member of his family **2** any prolonged feud, quarrel, etc [C19 from Italian, from Latin *vindicta*, from *vindicāre* to avenge; see VINDICATE] > ven'dettist *n*

vendible ('vɛndəbəl) *adj* **1** saleable or marketable **2** *obsolete* venal ▷ *n* **3** (*usually plural*) *rare* a saleable object > ‚vendi'bility *or* 'vendibleness *n*

vending machine *n* a machine that automatically dispenses consumer goods such as cigarettes, food, or petrol, when money is inserted. Also called: **automat**

vendor ('vɛndɔ:) *or* **vender** ('vɛndə) *n* **1** *chiefly law* a person who sells something, esp real property **2** another name for **vending machine**

vendor placing *n finance* a method of financing the purchase of one company by another in which the purchasing company pays for the target company in its own shares, on condition that the vendor places these shares with investors for cash payment

vendue (vɛn'dju:) *n US* a public sale; auction [C17 from Dutch *vendu*, from Old French *vendue* a sale, from *vendre* to sell, from Latin *vendere*]

veneer (vɪ'nɪə) *n* **1** a thin layer of wood, plastic, etc, with a decorative or fine finish that is bonded to the surface of a less expensive material, usually wood **2** a superficial appearance, esp one that is pleasing: *a veneer of gentility* **3** any facing material that is applied to a different backing material **4** any one of the layers of wood that is used to form plywood ▷ *vb* (*tr*) **5** to cover (a surface) with a veneer **6** to bond together (thin layers of wood) to make plywood **7** to conceal (something) under a superficially pleasant surface [C17 from German *furnieren* to veneer, from Old French *fournir* to FURNISH] > ve'neerer *n*

veneering (vɪ'nɪərɪŋ) *n* **1** material used as veneer or a veneered surface **2** *rare* a superficial show

venepuncture ('vɛnɪ‚pʌŋktʃə) *n* a variant spelling of **venipuncture**

venerable ('vɛnərəbəl) *adj* **1** (esp of a person) worthy of reverence on account of great age, religious associations, character, position, etc **2** (of inanimate objects) hallowed or impressive on account of historical or religious association **3**

V

ancient: *venerable tomes* **4** *RC Church* a title bestowed on a deceased person when the first stage of his canonization has been accomplished and his holiness has been recognized in a decree of the official Church **5** *Church of England* a title given to an archdeacon [c15 from Latin *venerābilis*, from *venerārī* to venerate] > ˌvenera'bility or 'venerableness *n* > 'venerably *adv*

venerate ('vɛnəˌreɪt) *vb* (*tr*) **1** to hold in deep respect; revere **2** to honour in recognition of qualities of holiness, excellence, wisdom, etc [c17 from Latin *venerārī*, from *venus* love] > 'venerˌator *n*

veneration (ˌvɛnə'reɪʃən) *n* **1** a feeling or expression of awe or reverence **2** the act of venerating or the state of being venerated > ˌvener'ational *adj* > 'venerativeness *n*

venereal (vɪ'nɪərɪəl) *adj* **1** of, relating to, or infected with venereal disease **2** (of a disease) transmitted by sexual intercourse **3** of, relating to, or involving the genitals **4** of or relating to sexual intercourse or erotic desire; aphrodisiac [c15 from Latin *venereus* concerning sexual love, from *venus* sexual love, from VENUS[1]]

venereal disease *n* any of various diseases, such as syphilis or gonorrhoea, transmitted by sexual intercourse. Abbreviation: VD

venereology (vɪˌnɪərɪ'ɒlədʒɪ) *n* the branch of medicine concerned with the study and treatment of venereal disease > veˌnere'ologist *n*

venery[1] ('vɛnərɪ, 'viː-) *n* *archaic* the pursuit of sexual gratification [c15 from Medieval Latin *veneria*, from Latin *venus* love, VENUS[1]]

venery[2] ('vɛnərɪ, 'viː-) *n* the art, sport, lore, or practice of hunting, esp with hounds; the chase [c14 from Old French *venerie*, from *vener* to hunt, from Latin *vēnārī*]

venesection ('vɛnɪˌsɛkʃən) *n* surgical incision into a vein [c17 from New Latin *vēnae sectiō*; see VEIN, SECTION]

Veneti (vɛ'nɛtɪ, -taɪ) *n* the (*functioning as plural*) an ancient people who established themselves at the head of the Adriatic around 950 BC, later becoming Roman subjects

Venetia (vɪ'niːʃə) *n* **1** the area of ancient Italy between the lower Po valley and the Alps: later a Roman province **2** the territorial possessions of the medieval Venetian republic that were at the head of the Adriatic and correspond to the present-day region of Veneto and a large part of Friuli-Venezia Giulia

Venetian (vɪ'niːʃən) *adj* **1** of, relating to, or characteristic of Venice or its inhabitants ▷ *n* **2** a native or inhabitant of Venice **3** See **Venetian blind** **4** (*sometimes not capital*) one of the tapes that join the slats of a Venetian blind **5** a cotton or woollen cloth used for linings

Venetian blind *n* a window blind consisting of a number of horizontal slats whose angle may be altered to let in more or less light

Venetian glass *n* fine ornamental glassware made in or near Venice, esp at Murano

Venetian red *n* **1** natural or synthetic ferric oxide used as a red pigment **2 a** a moderate to strong reddish-brown colour **b** (*as adjective*): *a Venetian-red coat*

Venetic (vɪ'nɛtɪk) *n* an ancient language of NE Italy, usually regarded as belonging to the Italic branch of the Indo-European family. It is recorded in about 200 inscriptions and was extinct by the 2nd century AD

Veneto (*Italian* 'vɛːneto) *n* a region of NE Italy, on the Adriatic: mountainous in the north with a fertile plain in the south, crossed by the Rivers Po, Adige, and Piave. Capital: Venice. Pop: 4 577 408 (2003 est). Area. 18 377 sq km (7095 sq miles). Also called: Venezia-Euganea (ve'nɛttsja eʊ'gaːnea)

Venez. *abbreviation for* Venezuela

Venezia (ve'nɛttsja) *n* the Italian name for **Venice**

Venezia Giulia (*Italian* 'dʒuːlja) *n* a former region of NE Italy at the N end of the Adriatic: divided between Yugoslavia and Italy after World War II; now divided between Italy and Slovenia

Venezia Tridentina (*Italian* triden'tiːna) *n* the former name (until 1947) of **Trentino-Alto Adige**

Venezuela (ˌvɛnɪ'zweɪlə) *n* **1** a republic in South America, on the Caribbean: colonized by the Spanish in the 16th century; independence from Spain declared in 1811 and won in 1819 after a war led by Simón Bolívar. It contains Lake Maracaibo and the northernmost chains of the Andes in the northwest, the Orinoco basin in the central part, and the Guiana Highlands in the south. Exports: petroleum, iron ore, and coffee. Official language: Spanish. Religion: Roman Catholic majority. Currency: bolívar. Capital: Caracas. Pop: 26 170 000 (2004 est). Area: 912 050 sq km (352 142 sq miles). Official name: Bolivarian Republic of Venezuela **2 Gulf of** an inlet of the Caribbean in NW Venezuela: continues south as Lake Maracaibo

Venezuelan (ˌvɛnɪ'zweɪlən) *adj* **1** of or relating to Venezuela or its inhabitants ▷ *n* **2** a native or inhabitant of Venezuela

venge (vɛndʒ) *vb* (*tr*) an archaic word for **avenge** [c13 from Old French *venger*, from Latin *vindicāre*; see VINDICATE]

vengeance ('vɛndʒəns) *n* **1** the act of or desire for taking revenge; retributive punishment **2 with a vengeance** (*intensifier*): *the 70's have returned with a vengeance* [c13 from Old French, from *venger* to avenge, from Latin *vindicāre* to punish; see VINDICATE]

vengeful ('vɛndʒfʊl) *adj* **1** desiring revenge; vindictive **2** characterized by or indicating a desire for revenge: *a vengeful glance* **3** inflicting or taking revenge: *with vengeful blows* > 'vengefully *adv* > 'vengefulness *n*

venial ('viːnɪəl) *adj* easily excused or forgiven: *a venial error* [c13 via Old French from Late Latin *veniālis*, from Latin *venia* forgiveness; related to Latin *venus* love] > ˌveni'ality *n* > 'venially *adv*

venial sin *n* *Christianity* a sin regarded as involving only a partial loss of grace. Compare **mortal sin**

Venice ('vɛnɪs) *n* a port in NE Italy, capital of Veneto region, built on over 100 islands and mud flats in the **Lagoon of Venice** (an inlet of the **Gulf of Venice** at the head of the Adriatic): united under the first doge in 697 AD; became an independent republic and a great commercial and maritime power, defeating Genoa, the greatest rival, in 1380; contains the Grand Canal and about 170 smaller canals, providing waterways for city transport. Pop: 271 073 (2001). Italian name: Venezia. Related adj: **Venetian**

venin ('vɛnɪn, 'viː-) *n* any of the poisonous constituents of animal venoms [c20 from French *ven(in)* poison + -IN]

venipuncture *or* **venepuncture** ('vɛnɪˌpʌŋktʃə) *n* *med* the puncturing of a vein, esp to take a sample of venous blood or inject a drug

venire facias (vɪ'naɪrɪ 'feɪʃɪˌæs) *n* *law* (formerly) a writ directing a sheriff to summon suitable persons to form a jury [c15 Latin, literally: you must make come]

venireman (vɪ'naɪərɪmən) *n, pl* -men (in the US and formerly in England) a person summoned for jury service under a venire facias

venison ('vɛnzən, 'vɛnɪzᵊn, -sᵊn) *n* **1** the flesh of a deer, used as food **2** *archaic* the flesh of any game animal used for food [c13 from Old French *venaison*, from Latin *vēnātiō* hunting, from *vēnārī* to hunt]

Venite (vɪ'naɪtɪ) *n* **1** *ecclesiast* the opening word of the 95th psalm, an invitatory prayer at matins **2** a musical setting of this [Latin: come ye]

Venlo *or* **Venloo** (*Dutch* 'vɛnlo:) *n* a city in the SE Netherlands, in Limburg on the Maas River. Pop: 92 000 (2003 est)

Venn diagram (vɛn) *n* *maths, logic* a diagram in which mathematical sets or terms of a categorial statement are represented by overlapping circles within a boundary representing the universal set, so that all possible combinations of the relevant properties are represented by the various distinct areas in the diagram [c19 named after John Venn (1834–1923), English logician]

vennel ('vɛnᵊl) *n* *Scot* a lane; alley [c15 from Old French *venelle*, from Latin *vēna* vein]

venography (vɪ'nɒgrəfɪ) *n* *med* radiography of veins after injection of a contrast medium. Also called: phlebography

venom ('vɛnəm) *n* **1** a poisonous fluid secreted by such animals as certain snakes and scorpions and usually transmitted by a bite or sting **2** malice; spite [c13 from Old French *venim*, from Latin *venēnum* poison, love potion; related to *venus* sexual love] > 'venomless *adj* > 'venomous *adj* > 'venomously *adv* > 'venomousness *n*

venosclerosis (ˌviːnəʊsklɪ'rəʊsɪs) *n* another name for phlebosclerosis

venose ('viːnəʊs) *adj* **1** having veins; venous **2** (of a plant) covered with veins or similar ridges [c17 via Latin *vēnōsus*, from *vēna* a VEIN]

venosity (vɪ'nɒsɪtɪ) *n* **1** an excessive quantity of blood in the venous system or in an organ or part **2** an unusually large number of blood vessels in an organ or part

venous ('viːnəs) *adj* *physiol* **1** of or relating to the blood circulating in the veins **2** of or relating to the veins [c17 see VENOSE] > 'venously *adv* > 'venousness *n*

vent[1] (vɛnt) *n* **1** a small opening for the passage or escape of fumes, liquids, etc **2** the shaft of a volcano or an aperture in the earth's crust through which lava and gases erupt **3** the external opening of the urinary or genital systems of lower vertebrates **4** a small aperture at the breech of old guns through which the charge was ignited **5** an exit, escape, or passage **6 give vent to** to release (an emotion, passion, idea, etc) in an utterance or outburst ▷ *vb* (*mainly tr*) **7** to release or give expression or utterance to (an emotion, idea, etc): *he vents his anger on his wife* **8** to provide a vent for or make vents in **9** to let out (steam, liquid, etc) through a vent [c14 from Old French *esventer* to blow out, from EX-[1] + *venter*, from Vulgar Latin *ventāre* (unattested) to be windy, from Latin *ventus* wind] > 'venter *n* > 'ventless *adj*

vent[2] (vɛnt) *n* **1** a vertical slit at the back or both sides of a jacket ▷ *vb* **2** (*tr*) to make a vent or vents in (a jacket) [c15 from Old French *fente* slit, from *fendre* to split, from Latin *findere* to cleave]

ventage ('vɛntɪdʒ) *n* **1** a small opening; vent **2** a finger hole in a musical instrument such as a recorder

ventail ('vɛnteɪl) *n* (in medieval armour) a covering for the lower part of the face [c14 from Old French *ventaille* sluice, from *vent* wind, from Latin *ventus*]

venter ('vɛntə) *n* **1** *anatomy, zoology* **a** the belly or abdomen of vertebrates **b** a protuberant structure or part, such as the belly of a muscle **2** *botany* the swollen basal region of an archegonium, containing the developing ovum **3** *law* the womb **4 in venter** *law* conceived but not yet born [c16 from Latin]

vent gleet *n* *vet science* inflammation of the cloaca in poultry, characterized by a yellowish discharge accompanied by local swelling and congestion

ventifact ('vɛntɪˌfækt) *n* *geology* a pebble that has been shaped by wind-blown sand

ventilate ('vɛntɪˌleɪt) *vb* (*tr*) **1** to drive foul air out of (an enclosed area) **2** to provide with a means of airing **3** to expose (a question, grievance, etc) to public examination or discussion **4** *physiol* to oxygenate (the blood) in the capillaries of the lungs **5** to winnow (grain) [c15 from Latin *ventilāre* to fan, from *ventulus* diminutive of *ventus* wind] > 'ventilable *adj*

ventilation (ˌvɛntɪ'leɪʃən) *n* **1** the act or process of ventilating or the state of being ventilated **2** an installation in a building that provides a supply of fresh air > 'ventiˌlative *adj* > 'ventiˌlatory *adj*

ventilator ('vɛntɪˌleɪtə) *n* **1** an opening or device, such as a fan, used to ventilate a room, building, etc **2** *med* a machine that maintains a flow of air into and out of the lungs of a patient who is unable to breathe normally

Ventôse *French* (vãtoz) *n* the windy month: the sixth month of the French Revolutionary calendar, extending from Feb 20 to Mar 21 [c18 from Latin *ventōsus* full of wind, from *ventus* wind]

ventouse (vɛn'tu:s) *n* an apparatus sometimes used to assist the delivery of a baby, consisting of a cup which is attached to the fetal head by suction, and a chain by which traction can be exerted in order to draw out the baby [c16 from Old French *ventose* a cupping glass]

ventral ('vɛntrəl) *adj* **1** relating to the front part of the body; towards the belly. Compare **dorsal 2** of, relating to, or situated on the upper or inner side of a plant organ, esp a leaf, that is facing the axis [c18 from Latin *ventrālis*, from *venter* abdomen] > **'ventrally** *adv*

ventral fin *n* **1** another name for **pelvic fin 2** any unpaired median fin situated on the undersurface of fishes and some other aquatic vertebrates

ventricle ('vɛntrɪkᵊl) *n anatomy* **1** a chamber of the heart, having thick muscular walls, that receives blood from the atrium and pumps it to the arteries **2** any one of the four main cavities of the vertebrate brain, which contain cerebrospinal fluid **3** any of various other small cavities in the body [c14 from Latin *ventriculus*, diminutive of *venter* belly]

ventricose ('vɛntrɪ,kəʊs) *adj* **1** *botany, zoology, anatomy* having a swelling on one side; unequally inflated: *the ventricose corolla of many labiate plants* **2** another word for **corpulent** [c18 from New Latin *ventricōsus*, from Latin *venter* belly] > **ventricosity** (,vɛntrɪ'kɒsɪtɪ) *n*

ventricular (vɛn'trɪkjʊlə) *adj* **1** of, relating to, involving, or constituting a ventricle **2** having a belly **3** swollen or distended; ventricose

ventriculography (vɛn,trɪkjʊ'lɒgrəfɪ) *n med* **1** radiography of the ventricles of the heart after injection of a contrast medium **2** radiography of the ventricles of the brain after injection of air or a radiopaque material

ventriculus (vɛn'trɪkjʊləs) *n, pl* **-li** (-,laɪ) *zoology* **a** the midgut of an insect, where digestion takes place **b** the gizzard of a bird **2** another word for **ventricle** [c18 from Latin, diminutive of *venter* belly]

ventriloquism (vɛn'trɪlə,kwɪzəm) *or* **ventriloquy** *n* the art of producing vocal sounds that appear to come from another source [c18 from Latin *venter* belly + *loquī* to speak] > **ventriloquial** (,vɛntrɪ'ləʊkwɪəl) *or* **ventriloqual** (vɛn'trɪləkwəl) *adj* > **,ventri'loquially** *adv* > **ven'triloquist** *n* > **ven,trilo'quistic** *adj*

ventriloquize *or* **ventriloquise** (vɛn'trɪlə,kwaɪz) *vb* to produce (sounds) in the manner of a ventriloquist

venture ('vɛntʃə) *vb* **1** (*tr*) to expose to danger; hazard: *he ventured his life* **2** (*tr*) to brave the dangers of (something): *I'll venture the seas* **3** (*tr*) to dare (to do something): *does he venture to object?* **4** (*tr; may take a clause as object*) to express in spite of possible refutation or criticism: *I venture that he is not that honest* **5** (*intr; often foll by out, forth, etc*) to embark on a possibly hazardous journey, undertaking, etc: *to venture forth upon the high seas* ▷ *n* **6** an undertaking that is risky or of uncertain outcome **7 a** a commercial undertaking characterized by risk of loss as well as opportunity for profit **b** the merchandise, money, or other property placed at risk in such an undertaking **8** something hazarded or risked in an adventure; stake **9** *archaic* chance or fortune **10** at a venture at random; by chance [c15 variant of *aventure* ADVENTURE] > **'venturer** *n*

venture capital *n* **1** capital that is provided for a new commercial enterprise by individuals or organizations other than those who own the new enterprise **2** another name for **risk capital**

venture capitalist *n* a person or company that provides capital for new commercial enterprises

Venture Scout *or* **Venturer** *n Brit* a young man or woman, aged 16–20, who is a member of the senior branch of the Scouts. Former name: Rover US equivalent: Explorer

venturesome ('vɛntʃəsəm) *or* **venturous** ('vɛntʃərəs) *adj* **1** willing to take risks; daring **2** hazardous

Venturi tube *n* **1** *physics* a device for measuring fluid flow, consisting of a tube so constricted that the pressure differential produced by fluid flowing through the constriction gives a measure of the rate of flow **2** Also called: **venturi** a tube with a constriction used to reduce or control fluid flow, as one in the air inlet of a carburettor [c19 named after GB *Venturi* (1746–1822), Italian physicist]

venue ('vɛnju:) *n* **1** *law* **a** the place in which a cause of action arises **b** the place fixed for the trial of a cause **c** the locality from which the jurors must be summoned to try a particular cause **2** a meeting place **3** any place where an organized gathering, such as a rock concert or public meeting, is held **4** *chiefly US* a position in an argument [c14 from Old French, from *venir* to come, from Latin *venīre*]

venule ('vɛnju:l) *n* **1** *anatomy* any of the small branches of a vein that receives oxygen-depleted blood from the capillaries and returns it to the heart via the venous system **2** any of the branches of a vein in an insect's wing [c19 from Latin *vēnula* diminutive of *vēna* VEIN] > **venular** ('vɛnjʊlə) *adj*

Venus¹ ('vi:nəs) *n* **1** the Roman goddess of love. Greek counterpart: **Aphrodite 2** mount of Venus See **mons veneris**

Venus² ('vi:nəs) *n* **1** one of the inferior planets and the second nearest to the sun, visible as a bright morning or evening star. Its surface is extremely hot (over 400°C) and is completely shrouded by dense cloud. The atmosphere is principally carbon dioxide. Mean distance from sun: 108 million km; period of revolution around sun: 225 days; period of axial rotation: 244.3 days (retrograde motion); diameter and mass: 96.5 and 81.5 per cent that of earth respectively **2** the alchemical name for **copper**¹

Venusberg ('vi:nəs,bɜ:g; *German* 've:nʊsbɛrk) *n* a mountain in central Germany: contains caverns that, according to medieval legend, housed the palace of the goddess Venus

Venusian (vɪ'nju:zɪən) *adj* **1** of, occurring on, or relating to the planet Venus ▷ *n* **2** (in science fiction) an inhabitant of Venus

Venus's flower basket *n* any of several deep-sea sponges of the genus *Euplectella*, esp *E. aspergillum*, having a skeleton composed of interwoven glassy six-rayed spicules

Venus's-flytrap *or* **Venus flytrap** *n* an insectivorous plant, *Dionaea muscipula*, of Carolina, having hinged two-lobed leaves that snap closed when the sensitive hairs on the surface are touched: family *Droseraceae*. See also **sundew, pitcher plant, butterwort**

Venus's-girdle *n* a ctenophore, *Cestum veneris*, of warm seas, having an elongated ribbon-like body

Venus's-hair *n* a fragile maidenhair fern, *Adiantum capillus-veneris*, of tropical and subtropical America, having fan-shaped leaves and a black stem

Venus shell *n* a marine bivalve mollusc of the family Veneridae, typified by the intertidal *Venus gallina*, with somewhat rounded ribbed valves

Venus's looking glass *n* a purple-flowered campanulaceous plant, *Legousia hybrida*, of Europe, W Asia, and N Africa

veracious (vɛ'reɪʃəs) *adj* **1** habitually truthful or honest **2** accurate; precise [c17 from Latin *vērax*, from *vērus* true] > **ve'raciously** *adv* > **ve'raciousness** *n*

veracity (vɛ'ræsɪtɪ) *n, pl* **-ties 1** truthfulness or honesty, esp when consistent or habitual **2** precision; accuracy **3** something true; a truth [c17 from Medieval Latin *vērācitās*, from Latin *vērax*; see VERACIOUS]

Veracruz (,vɛrə'kru:z; *Spanish* bera'kruθ) *n* **1** a state of E Mexico, on the Gulf of Mexico: consists of a hot humid coastal strip with lagoons, rising rapidly inland to the central plateau and Sierra Madre Oriental. Capital: Jalapa. Pop: 630 000 (2005 est). Area: 72 815 sq km (28 114 sq miles) **2** the chief port of Mexico, in Veracruz state on the Gulf of Mexico. Pop: 410 000 (2000 est)

veranda *or* **verandah** (və'rændə) *n* **1** a porch or portico, sometimes partly enclosed, along the outside of a building **2** NZ a canopy sheltering pedestrians in a shopping street [c18 from Portuguese *varanda* railing; related to Hindi *varandā* railing] > **ve'randaed** *or* **ve'randahed** *adj*

verapamil (vɪ'ræpə,mɪl) *n med* a calcium-channel blocker used in the treatment of angina pectoris, hypertension, and some types of irregular heart rhythm

veratridine (vɪ'rætrɪ,di:n) *n* a yellowish-white amorphous alkaloid obtained from the seeds of sabadilla. Formula: $C_{36}H_{51}NO_{11}$ [c20 from VERATR(INE) + -ID³ + -INE²]

veratrine ('vɛrə,tri:n) *or* **veratrin** ('vɛrətrɪn) *n* a white poisonous mixture obtained from the seeds of sabadilla, consisting of veratridine and several other alkaloids: formerly used in medicine as a counterirritant [c19 from Latin *vērātrum* hellebore + -INE²]

verb (vɜ:b) *n* **1** (in traditional grammar) any of a large class of words in a language that serve to indicate the occurrence or performance of an action, the existence of a state or condition, etc. In English, such words as *run, make, do,* and the like are verbs **2** (in modern descriptive linguistic analysis) **a** a word or group of words that functions as the predicate of a sentence or introduces the predicate **b** (*as modifier*): *a verb phrase* ▷ Abbreviations: **vb, v** [c14 from Latin *verbum* a word] > **'verbless** *adj*

verbal ('vɜ:bᵊl) *adj* **1** of, relating to, or using words, esp as opposed to ideas, etc: *merely verbal concessions* **2** oral rather than written: *a verbal agreement* **3** verbatim; literal: *an almost verbal copy* **4** *grammar* of or relating to verbs or a verb ▷ *n* **5** *grammar* another word for **verbid 6** (*plural*) *slang* abuse or invective: *new forms of on-field verbals* **7** (*plural*) *slang* a criminal's admission of guilt on arrest ▷ *vb* **-bals, -balling, -balled** (*tr*) **8** *slang* (of the police) to implicate (someone) in a crime by quoting alleged admission of guilt in court > **'verbally** *adv*

verbalism ('vɜ:bə,lɪzəm) *n* **1** a verbal expression; phrase or word **2** an exaggerated emphasis on the importance of words by the uncritical acceptance of assertions in place of explanations, the use of rhetorical style, etc **3** a statement lacking real content, esp a cliché

verbalist ('vɜ:bəlɪst) *n* **1** a person who deals with words alone, rather than facts, ideas, feeling, etc **2** a person skilled in the use of words

verbalize *or* **verbalise** ('vɜ:bə,laɪz) *vb* **1** to express (an idea, feeling, etc) in words **2** to change (any word that is not a verb) into a verb or derive a verb from (any word that is not a verb) **3** (*intr*) to be verbose > **,verbali'zation** *or* **,verbali'sation** *n* > **'verbal,izer** *or* **'verbal,iser** *n*

verbal noun *n* a noun derived from a verb, such as *smoking* in the sentence *smoking is bad for you*. See also **gerund**

verbascum (vɜ:'bæskəm) *n* See **mullein** [Latin: mullein]

verbatim (vɜ:'beɪtɪm) *adv, adj* using exactly the same words; word for word [c15 from Medieval Latin: word by word, from Latin *verbum* word]

verbena (vɜ:'bi:nə) *n* **1** any plant of the verbenaceous genus *Verbena*, chiefly of tropical and temperate America, having red, white, or purple fragrant flowers: much cultivated as garden plants. See also **vervain 2** any of various similar or related plants, esp the lemon verbena [c16 via

V

Medieval Latin, from Latin: sacred bough used by the priest in religious acts, VERVAIN]

verbenaceous (ˌvɜːbɪˈneɪʃəs) *adj* of, relating to, or belonging to the *Verbenaceae*, a family of herbaceous and climbing plants, shrubs, and trees, mostly of warm and tropical regions, having tubular typically two-lipped flowers: includes teak, lantana, vervain, and verbena [c19 from New Latin *Verbēnāceae*, from Medieval Latin: VERBENA]

verbiage (ˈvɜːbɪɪdʒ) *n* **1** the excessive and often meaningless use of words; verbosity **2** *rare* diction; wording [c18 from French, from Old French *verbier* to chatter, from *verbe* word, from Latin *verbum*]

verbid (ˈvɜːbɪd) *n grammar* any nonfinite form of a verb or any nonverbal word derived from a verb: *participles, infinitives, and gerunds are all verbids*

verbify (ˈvɜːbɪˌfaɪ) *vb* **-fies, -fying, -fied** another word for **verbalize** (senses 2, 3) > ˌ**verbifiˈcation** *n*

verbing (ˈvɜːbɪŋ) *n* the act or practice of using a noun as a verb, such as ‘medal' to mean “to win a medal”

verbose (vɜːˈbəʊs) *adj* using or containing an excess of words, so as to be pedantic or boring; prolix [c17 from Latin *verbōsus* from *verbum* word] > **verˈbosely** *adv* > **verbosity** (vɜːˈbɒsɪtɪ) *or* **verˈboseness** *n*

verboten *German* (fɛrˈboːtən) *adj* forbidden; prohibited

verb phrase *n grammar* a constituent of a sentence that contains the verb and any direct and indirect objects but not the subject. It is a controversial question in grammatical theory whether or not this constituent is to be identified with the predicate of the sentence. Abbreviation: **VP**

verb. sap. *or* **sat.** *abbreviation for* verbum sapienti sat est [Latin: a word is enough to the wise]

Vercelli (*Italian* verˈtʃɛlli) *n* a city in NW Italy, in Piedmont: an ancient Ligurian and later Roman city; has an outstanding library of manuscripts (notably the *Codex Vercellensis*, dating from the 10th century). Pop: 45 132 (2001)

verdant (ˈvɜːdᵊnt) *adj* **1** covered with green vegetation **2** (of plants, etc) green in colour **3** immature or unsophisticated; green [c16 from Old French *verdoyant*, from *verdoyer* to become green, from Old French *verd* green, from Latin *viridis*, from *virēre* to be green] > ˈ**verdancy** *n* > ˈ**verdantly** *adv*

verd antique (vɜːd) *n* **1** a dark green mottled impure variety of serpentine marble **2** any of various similar marbles or stones **3** another name for **verdigris** [c18 from French, from Italian *verde antico* ancient green]

Verde (vɜːd) *n* **Cape** a cape in Senegal, near Dakar: the westernmost point of Africa. See also **Cape Verde**

Verdelho (vəˈdɛljəʊ) *n, pl* **-delhos** **1** a white grape grown in Portugal, used for making wine **2** a white wine made from this grape

verderer (ˈvɜːdərə) *n English legal history* a judicial officer responsible for the maintenance of law and order in the royal forests [c16 from Anglo-French, from Old French *verdier*, from *verd* green, from Latin *viridis*; compare Latin *viridārium* plantation of trees]

verdict (ˈvɜːdɪkt) *n* **1** the findings of a jury on the issues of fact submitted to it for examination and trial; judgment **2** any decision, judgment, or conclusion [c13 from Medieval Latin *vērdictum*, from Latin *vērē dictum* truly spoken, from *vērus* true + *dīcere* to say]

verdigris (ˈvɜːdɪgrɪs) *n* **1** a green or bluish patina formed on copper, brass, or bronze and consisting of a basic salt of copper containing both copper oxide and a copper salt **2** a green or blue crystalline substance obtained by the action of acetic acid on copper and used as a fungicide and pigment; basic copper acetate [c14 from Old French *vert de Grice* green of Greece]

verdigris toadstool *n* a basidiomycetous fungus, *Stropharia aeruginosa*, having a distinctive and unusual blue-green cap and paler shaggy stem

verdin (ˈvɜːdɪn) *n* a small W North American tit, *Auriparus flaviceps*, having a grey plumage with a yellow head [French: yellowhammer]

Verdun (*French* vɛrdœ̃; *English* ˈvɛədʌn) *n* **1** a fortified town in NE France, on the Meuse: scene of the longest and most severe battle (1916) of World War I, in which the French repelled a powerful German offensive. Pop: 19 624 (1999). Ancient name: **Verodunum** (ˌvɛrəˈdjuːnəm) **2 Treaty of** an agreement reached in 843 AD by three grandsons of Charlemagne, dividing his empire into an E kingdom (later Germany), a W kingdom (later France), and a middle kingdom (containing what became the Low Countries, Lorraine, Burgundy, and N Italy)

verdure (ˈvɜːdʒə) *n* **1** flourishing green vegetation or its colour **2** a condition of freshness or healthy growth [c14 from Old French *verd* green, from Latin *viridis*] > ˈ**verdured** *adj* > ˈ**verdurous** *adj*

verecund (ˈvɛrɪˌkʌnd) *adj rare* shy or modest [c16 from Latin *verēcundus* diffident, from *verērī* to fear]

Vereeniging (fəˈriːnɪhɪŋ, və-) *n* a city in E South Africa: scene of the signing (1902) of the treaty ending the Boer War. Pop: 79 630 (2001)

verge¹ (vɜːdʒ) *n* **1** an edge or rim; margin **2** a limit beyond which something occurs; brink: *on the verge of ecstasy* **3** *Brit* a grass border along a road **4** an enclosing line, belt, or strip **5** *architect* the edge of the roof tiles projecting over a gable **6** *architect* the shaft of a classical column **7** an enclosed space **8** *horology* the spindle of a balance wheel in a vertical escapement, found only in very early clocks **9** *English legal history* **a** the area encompassing the royal court that is subject to the jurisdiction of the Lord High Steward **b** a rod or wand carried as a symbol of office or emblem of authority, as in the Church **c** a rod held by a person swearing fealty to his lord on becoming a tenant, esp of copyhold land ▷ *vb* **10** (*intr; foll by on*) to be near (to): *to verge on chaos* **11** (when *intr*, sometimes foll by *on*) to serve as the edge of (something): *this narrow strip verges the road* [c15 from Old French, from Latin *virga* rod]

verge² (vɜːdʒ) *vb* (*intr; foll by to or towards*) to move or incline in a certain direction [c17 from Latin *vergere*]

vergeboard (ˈvɜːdʒˌbɔːd) *n* another name for **bargeboard**

vergence (ˈvɜːdʒəns) *n* the inward or outward turning movement of the eyes in convergence or divergence [c19 from VERGE² + -ENCE]

verger (ˈvɜːdʒə) *n chiefly Church of England* **1** a church official who acts as caretaker and attendant, looking after the interior of a church and often the vestments and church furnishings **2** an official who carries the verge or rod of office before a bishop, dean, or other dignitary in ceremonies and processions [c15 from Old French, from *verge*, from Latin *virga* rod, twig]

Vergilian (vəˈdʒɪlɪən) *adj* a variant spelling of **Virgilian**

verglas (ˈvɛəglɑː) *n, pl* **-glases** (-glɑː, -glɑːz) a thin film of ice on rock [from Old French *verre-glaz* glass-ice, from *verre* glass (from Latin *vitrum*) + *glaz* ice (from Late Latin *glacia*, from Latin *glaciēs*)]

veridical (vɪˈrɪdɪkᵊl) *adj* **1** truthful **2** *psychol* of or relating to revelations in dreams, hallucinations, etc, that appear to be confirmed by subsequent events [c17 from Latin *vēridicus*, from *vērus* true + *dīcere* to say] > **veˌridiˈcality** *n* > **veˈridically** *adv*

veriest (ˈvɛrɪɪst) *adj archaic* (intensifier): *the veriest coward*

verification (ˌvɛrɪfɪˈkeɪʃən) *n* **1** establishment of the correctness of a theory, fact, etc **2** evidence that provides proof of an assertion, theory, etc **3** *law* **a** (formerly) a short affidavit at the end of a pleading stating the pleader's readiness to prove his assertions **b** confirmatory evidence > ˈ**verifiˌcative** *or* ˈ**verifiˌcatory** *adj*

verification principle *n* (in the philosophy of the logical positivists) the doctrine that nontautologous statements are meaningful only if it is in principle possible to establish empirically whether they are true or false

verify (ˈvɛrɪˌfaɪ) *vb* **-fies, -fying, -fied** (*tr*) **1** to prove to be true; confirm; substantiate **2** to check or determine the correctness or truth of by investigation, reference, etc **3** *law* to add a verification to (a pleading); substantiate or confirm (an oath) [c14 from Old French *verifier*, from Medieval Latin *vērificāre*, from Latin *vērus* true + *facere* to make] > ˈ**veriˌfiable** *adj* > ˈ**veriˌfiableness** *n* > ˈ**veriˌfiably** *adv* > ˈ**veriˌfier** *n*

verily (ˈvɛrɪlɪ) *adv* (*sentence modifier*) *archaic* in truth; truly: *verily, thou art a man of God* [c13 from VERY + -LY²]

verisimilar (ˌvɛrɪˈsɪmɪlə) *adj* appearing to be true; probable; likely [c17 from Latin *vērisimilis*, from *vērus* true + *similis* like] > ˌ**veriˈsimilarly** *adv*

verisimilitude (ˌvɛrɪsɪˈmɪlɪˌtjuːd) *n* **1** the appearance or semblance of truth or reality; quality of seeming true **2** something that merely seems to be true or real, such as a doubtful statement [c17 from Latin *vērisimilitūdō*, from *vērus* true + *similitūdō* SIMILITUDE]

verism (ˈvɪərɪzəm) *n* extreme naturalism in art or literature [c19 from Italian *verismo*, from *vero* true, from Latin *vērus*] > ˈ**verist** *n, adj* > **veˈristic** *adj*

verismo (vɛˈrɪzməʊ; *Italian* veˈrismo) *n music* a school of composition that originated in Italian opera towards the end of the 19th century, drawing its themes from real life and emphasizing naturalistic elements. Its chief exponent was Giacomo Puccini (1858–1924) [c19 from Italian; see VERISM]

veritable (ˈvɛrɪtəbᵊl) *adj* (*prenominal*) **1** (intensifier; usually qualifying a word used metaphorically): *he's a veritable swine!* **2** *rare* genuine or true; proper: *I require veritable proof* [c15 from Old French, from *vérité* truth; see VERITY] > ˈ**veritableness** *n* > ˈ**veritably** *adv*

vérité (ˈveɪriːˌteɪ; *French* verite) *adj* involving a high degree of realism or naturalism: *a vérité look at David Bowie*. See also **cinéma vérité** [French, literally: truth]

verity (ˈvɛrɪtɪ) *n, pl* **-ties** **1** the quality or state of being true, real, or correct **2** a true principle, statement, idea, etc; a truth or fact [c14 from Old French *vérité*, from Latin *vēritās*, from *vērus* true]

verjuice (ˈvɜːˌdʒuːs) *n* **1 a** the acid juice of unripe grapes, apples, or crab apples, formerly much used in making sauces, etc **b** (*as modifier*): *verjuice sauce* **2** *rare* **a** sourness or sharpness of temper, looks, etc **b** (*as modifier*): *a verjuice old wife* ▷ *vb* **3** (*tr*) *rare* to make sour; embitter [c14 from Old French *vert jus* green (unripe) juice, from Old French *vert* green (from Latin *viridis*) + *jus* juice (from Latin *jūs*)]

Verkhne-Udinsk (*Russian* ˈvjɛrxnɪuˈdjinsk) *n* the former name (until 1934) of **Ulan-Ude**

verkrampte (fəˈkrɑmtə) *n* (in South Africa) **a** (during apartheid) an Afrikaner Nationalist who opposed any changes toward liberal trends in government policy, esp relating to racial questions **b** (*as modifier*): *verkrampte politics* ▷ Compare **verligte** [c20 from Afrikaans (adj), literally: restricted]

verlan (*French* vɛrlɑ̃) *n* a variety of French slang in which the syllables are inverted, such as *meuf* for *femme*, and also incorporating Arabic words and phrases [c20 from inverting the syllables of the French word *l'envers* meaning the other way round]

verligte (fəˈlɔxtə) *n* (in South Africa) **a** (during apartheid) a person of any of the White political parties who supported liberal trends in government policy **b** (*as modifier*): *verligte politics* ▷ Compare **verkrampte** [c20 from Afrikaans (adj), literally: enlightened]

vermeil (ˈvɜːmeɪl) *n* **1** gilded silver, bronze, or other metal, used esp in the 19th century **2 a** vermilion **b** (*as adjective*): *vermeil shoes* [c15 from Old French, from Late Latin *vermiculus* insect (of the genus *Kermes*) or the red dye prepared from it, from Latin: little worm]

vermi- *combining form* worm: *vermicide*; *vermiform*; *vermifuge* [from Latin *vermis* worm]

vermicelli (ˌvɜːmɪˈsɛlɪ; *Italian* vermiˈtʃɛlli) *n* **1** very fine strands of pasta, used in soups **2** tiny chocolate strands used to coat cakes, etc [c17 from Italian: little worms, from *verme* a worm, from Latin *vermis*]

vermicide (ˈvɜːmɪˌsaɪd) *n* any substance used to kill worms > ˌvermiˈcidal *adj*

vermicular (vɜːˈmɪkjʊlə) *adj* **1** resembling the form, markings, motion, or tracks of worms **2** of or relating to worms or wormlike animals [c17 from Medieval Latin *vermiculāris*, from Latin *vermiculus*, diminutive of *vermis* worm] > verˈmicularly *adv*

vermiculate *vb* (vɜːˈmɪkjʊˌleɪt) **1** (*tr*) to decorate with wavy or wormlike tracery or markings ▷ *adj* (vɜːˈmɪkjʊlɪt, -ˌleɪt) **2** vermicular; sinuous **3** worm-eaten or appearing as if worm-eaten **4** (of thoughts, etc) insinuating; subtly tortuous [c17 from Latin *vermiculātus* in the form of worms, from *vermis* worm]

vermiculation (vɜːˌmɪkjʊˈleɪʃən) *n* **1** *physiol* any wormlike movement, esp of the intestines; peristalsis **2** decoration consisting of wormlike carving or marks **3** the state of being worm-eaten

vermiculite (vɜːˈmɪkjʊˌlaɪt) *n* any of a group of micaceous minerals consisting mainly of hydrated silicate of magnesium, aluminium, and iron: on heating they expand and exfoliate and in this form are used in heat and sound insulation, fireproofing, and as a bedding medium for young plants [c19 from VERMICUL(AR) + -ITE[1]]

vermiform (ˈvɜːmɪˌfɔːm) *adj* resembling a worm

vermiform appendix *or* **process** *n* a wormlike pouch extending from the lower end of the caecum in some mammals. In man it is vestigial. Also called: **appendix**

vermifuge (ˈvɜːmɪˌfjuːdʒ) *n* any drug or agent able to destroy or expel intestinal worms; an anthelmintic > vermifugal (ˌvɜːmɪˈfjuːgəl) *adj*

vermilion *or* **vermillion** (vəˈmɪljən) *n* **1 a** a bright red to reddish-orange colour **b** (*as adjective*): *a vermilion car* **2** mercuric sulphide, esp when used as a bright red pigment; cinnabar [c13 from Old French *vermeillon*, from VERMEIL]

vermin (ˈvɜːmɪn) *n* **1** (*functioning as plural*) small animals collectively, esp insects and rodents, that are troublesome to man, domestic animals, etc **2** (*pl* **-min**) an unpleasant, obnoxious, or dangerous person [c13 from Old French *vermine*, from Latin *vermis* a worm]

vermination (ˌvɜːmɪˈneɪʃən) *n* the spreading of or infestation with vermin

verminous (ˈvɜːmɪnəs) *adj* relating to, infested with, or suggestive of vermin > ˈverminously *adv* > ˈverminousness *n*

vermis (ˈvɜːmɪs) *n, pl* **-mes** (-miːz) *anatomy* the middle lobe connecting the two halves of the cerebellum [c19 via New Latin from Latin: worm]

vermivorous (vɜːˈmɪvərəs) *adj* (of certain animals) feeding on worms

Vermont (vɜːˈmɒnt) *n* a state in the northeastern US: crossed from north to south by the Green Mountains; bounded on the east by the Connecticut River and by Lake Champlain in the northwest. Capital: Montpelier. Pop: 619 107 (2003 est). Area: 24 887 sq km (9609 sq miles). Abbreviations: Vt, (with zip code) VT

Vermonter (vɜːˈmɒntə) *n* a native or inhabitant of Vermont

vermouth (ˈvɜːməθ, vəˈmuːθ) *n* any of several wines containing aromatic herbs and some other flavourings [c19 from French, from German *Wermut* WORMWOOD (absinthe)]

vernacular (vəˈnækjʊlə) *n* **1 the** the commonly spoken language or dialect of a particular people or place **2** a local style of architecture, in which ordinary houses are built: *this architect has re-created a true English vernacular* ▷ *adj* **3** relating to, using, or

in the vernacular **4** designating or relating to the common name of an animal or plant **5** built in the local style of ordinary houses, rather than a grand architectural style [c17 from Latin *vernāculus* belonging to a household slave, from *verna* household slave] > verˈnacularly *adv*

vernacularism (vəˈnækjʊləˌrɪzəm) *n* the use of the vernacular or a term in the vernacular

vernal (ˈvɜːnᵊl) *adj* **1** of or occurring in spring **2** *poetic* of or characteristic of youth; fresh [c16 from Latin *vernālis*, from *vēr* spring] > ˈvernally *adv*

vernal equinox *n* **1** the time at which the sun crosses the plane of the equator towards the relevant hemisphere, making day and night of equal length. It occurs about March 21 in the N hemisphere (Sept 23 in the S hemisphere) **2 a** *astronomy* the point, lying in the constellation Pisces, at which the sun's ecliptic intersects the celestial equator **b** the time at which this occurs as the sun travels south to north (March 21)

vernal grass *n* any of various Eurasian grasses of the genus *Anthoxanthum*, such as *A. odoratum* (**sweet vernal grass**), having the fragrant scent of coumarin

vernalize *or* **vernalise** (ˈvɜːnəˌlaɪz) *vb* to subject ungerminated or germinating seeds to low temperatures, which is essential for many (plants) of temperate environments to ensure germination in some species and flowering in others > ˌvernaliˈzation *or* ˌvernaliˈsation *n*

vernation (vɜːˈneɪʃən) *n* the way in which leaves are arranged in the bud [c18 from New Latin *vernātiō*, from Latin *vernāre* to be springlike, from *vēr* spring]

Verner's law (ˈvɜːnəz) *n* *linguistics* a modification of Grimm's Law accommodating some of its exceptions. It states that noninitial voiceless fricatives in Proto-Germanic occurring as a result of Grimm's law became voiced fricatives if the previous syllable had been unstressed in Proto-Indo-European [c19 named after Karl Adolph Verner (1846–96), Danish philologist, who formulated it] > Vernerian (vɜːˈnɛərɪən) *adj*

vernier (ˈvɜːnɪə) *n* **1** a small movable scale running parallel to the main graduated scale in certain measuring instruments, such as theodolites, used to obtain a fractional reading of one of the divisions on the main scale **2** an auxiliary device for making a fine adjustment to an instrument, usually by means of a fine screw thread **3** (*modifier*) relating to or fitted with a vernier: *a vernier scale; a vernier barometer* [c18 named after Paul *Vernier* (1580–1637), French mathematician, who described the scale]

vernier rocket *n* another name for **thruster** (sense 2)

vernissage (ˌvɜːnɪˈsɑːʒ) *n* **1** a preview or the opening or first day of an exhibition of paintings **2** another term for **varnishing day** [French, from *vernis* VARNISH]

Vernoleninsk (*Russian* vɪrnəlɪˈnjiːnsk) *n* the former name of **Nikolayev**

Verny (*Russian* ˈvjɛrnɪj) *n* a former name (until 1927) of **Almaty**

Verona (vəˈrəʊnə; *Italian* veˈroːna) *n* a city in N Italy, in Veneto on the Adige River: strategically situated at the junction of major routes between Italy and N Europe; became a Roman colony (89 BC); under Austrian rule (1797–1866); many Roman remains. Pop: 253 208 (2001) > Veronese (ˌvɛrəˈniːz) *adj, n*

Veronal (ˈvɛrənˌl) *n* a trademark for **barbital**

veronica[1] (vəˈrɒnɪkə) *n* any scrophulariaceous plant of the genus *Veronica*, esp the speedwells, of temperate and cold regions, having small blue, pink, or white flowers and flattened notched fruits [c16 from Medieval Latin, perhaps from the name *Veronica*]

veronica[2] (vəˈrɒnɪkə) *n* RC Church **1** the representation of the face of Christ that, according to legend, was miraculously imprinted upon the headcloth that Saint Veronica offered

him on his way to his crucifixion **2** the cloth itself **3** any similar representation of Christ's face

veronica[3] (vəˈrɒnɪkə) *n* *bullfighting* a pass in which the matador slowly swings the cape away from the charging bull [from Spanish, from the name *Veronica*]

verra (ˈvɛrə) *adj, adv* a Scot word for **very**

verruca (vɛˈruːkə) *n, pl* **-cae** (-siː) *or* **-cas 1** *pathol* a wart, esp one growing on the hand or foot **2** *biology* a wartlike outgrowth, as in certain plants or on the skin of some animals [c16 from Latin: wart]

verrucose (ˈvɛruˌkəʊs) *or* **verrucous** (ˈvɛruːkəs, vɛˈruːkəs) *adj* *botany* covered with warty processes [c17 from Latin *verrūcōsus* full of warts, from *verrūca* a wart] > verrucosity (ˌvɛruˈkɒsɪtɪ) *n*

vers *abbreviation for* versed sine

Versailles (veəˈsaɪ, -ˈseɪlz; *French* vɛrsaj) *n* **1** a city in N central France, near Paris: site of an elaborate royal residence built for Louis XIV; seat of the French kings (1682–1789). Pop: 85 726 (1999) **2** Treaty of Versailles **a** the treaty of 1919 imposed upon Germany by the Allies (except for the US and the Soviet Union): the most important of the five peace treaties that concluded World War I **b** another name for the (Treaty of) **Paris** of 1783

versant (ˈvɜːsᵊnt) *n* **1** *rare* the side or slope of a mountain or mountain range **2** the slope of a region [c19 from French, from *verser* to turn, from Latin *versāre*]

versatile (ˈvɜːsəˌtaɪl) *adj* **1** capable of or adapted for many different uses, skills, etc **2** variable or changeable **3** *botany* (of an anther) attached to the filament by a small area so that it moves freely in the wind **4** *zoology* able to turn forwards and backwards: *versatile antennae* [c17 from Latin *versātilis* moving around, from *versāre* to turn] > ˈversaˌtilely *adv* > versatility (ˌvɜːsəˈtɪlɪtɪ) *n*

vers de société *French* (vɛr də sɔsjete) *n* light, witty, and polished verse [literally: society verse]

verse (vɜːs) *n* **1** (not in technical usage) a stanza or other short subdivision of a poem **2** poetry as distinct from prose **3 a** a series of metrical feet forming a rhythmic unit of one line **b** (*as modifier*): *verse line* **4** a specified type of metre or metrical structure: *iambic verse* **5** one of the series of short subsections into which most of the writings in the Bible are divided **6** a metrical composition; poem ▷ *vb* **7** a rare word for **versify** [Old English *vers*, from Latin *versus* a furrow, literally: a turning (of the plough), from *vertere* to turn]

versed (vɜːst) *adj* (*postpositive; foll by in*) thoroughly knowledgeable (about), acquainted (with), or skilled (in)

versed sine *n* a trigonometric function equal to one minus the cosine of the specified angle. Abbreviation: vers [c16 from New Latin *sinus versus*, from SINE[1] + *versus* turned, from *vertere* to turn]

versicle (ˈvɜːsɪkᵊl) *n* **1** a short verse **2** a short sentence recited or sung by the minister at a liturgical ceremony and responded to by the choir or congregation [c14 from Latin *versiculus* a little line, from *versus* VERSE]

versicolour *or US* **versicolor** (ˈvɜːsɪˌkʌlə) *adj* of variable or various colours [c18 from Latin *versicolor*, from *versāre* to turn + *color* COLOUR]

versicular (vɜːˈsɪkjʊlə) *adj* *rare* of, relating to, or consisting of verses or versicles

versification (ˌvɜːsɪfɪˈkeɪʃən) *n* **1** the technique or art of versifying **2** the form or metrical composition of a poem **3** a metrical version of a prose text

versify (ˈvɜːsɪˌfaɪ) *vb* **-fies, -fying, -fied 1** (*tr*) to render (something) into metrical form or verse **2** (*intr*) to write in verse [c14 from Old French *versifier*, from Latin *versificāre*, from *versus* VERSE + *facere* to make] > ˈversiˌfier *n*

version (ˈvɜːʃən, -ʒən) *n* **1** an account of a matter from a certain point of view, as contrasted with others: *his version of the accident is different from the policeman's* **2** a translation, esp of the Bible, from

V

one language into another **3** a variant form of something; type **4** an adaptation, as of a book or play into a film **5** *med* manual turning of a fetus to correct an irregular position within the uterus **6** *pathol* an abnormal displacement of the uterus characterized by a tilting forwards (**anteversion**), backwards (**retroversion**), or to either side (**lateroversion**) [C16 from Medieval Latin *versiō* a turning, from Latin *vertere* to turn] > '**versional** *adj*

versioning ('vɜːʃənɪŋ) *n* the adaptation of classic literary texts for film, which often involves updating or changing the setting

vers libre *French* (vɛr librə) *n* (in French poetry) another term for **free verse**

verso ('vɜːsəʊ) *n*, *pl* **-sos 1 a** the back of a sheet of printed paper **b** Also called: **reverso** (sense 2) the left-hand pages of a book, bearing the even numbers. Compare **recto 2** the side of a coin opposite to the obverse; reverse [C19 from the New Latin phrase *versō foliō* the leaf having been turned, from Latin *vertere* to turn + *folium* a leaf]

verst (vɛəst, vɜːst) *n* a unit of length, used in Russia, equal to 1.067 kilometres (0.6629 miles) [C16 from French *verste* or German *Werst*, from Russian *versta* line]

versus ('vɜːsəs) *prep* **1** (esp in a competition or lawsuit) against; in opposition to. Abbreviation: **v**, (esp US) **vs 2** as opposed to; in contrast with [C15 from Latin: turned (in the direction of), opposite, from *vertere* to turn]

vert (vɜːt) *n* **1** *English legal history* **a** the right to cut green wood in a forest **b** the wood itself **2** *heraldry* **a** the colour green **b** (*as adjective, usually postpositive*): *a table vert* [C15 from Old French *verd*, from Latin *viridis* green, from *virēre* to grow green]

vert. abbreviation for **vertical**

vertebra ('vɜːtɪbrə) *n*, *pl* **-brae** (-briː) *or* **-bras** one of the bony segments of the spinal column [C17 from Latin: joint of the spine, from *vertere* to turn] > '**vertebral** *adj* > '**vertebrally** *adv*

vertebral column *n* another name for **spinal column**

vertebrate ('vɜːtɪˌbreɪt, -brɪt) *n* **1** any chordate animal of the subphylum *Vertebrata*, characterized by a bony or cartilaginous skeleton and a well-developed brain: the group contains fishes, amphibians, reptiles, birds, and mammals ▷ *adj* **2** of, relating to, or belonging to the subphylum *Vertebrata*

vertebration (ˌvɜːtɪˈbreɪʃən) *n* the formation of vertebrae or segmentation resembling vertebrae

vertex ('vɜːtɛks) *n*, *pl* **-texes** *or* **-tices** (-tɪˌsiːz) **1** the highest point **2** *maths* **a** the point opposite the base of a figure **b** the point of intersection of two sides of a plane figure or angle **c** the point of intersection of a pencil of lines or three or more planes of a solid figure **3** *astronomy* a point in the sky towards which a star stream appears to move **4** *anatomy* the crown of the head [C16 from Latin: highest point, from *vertere* to turn]

vertical ('vɜːtɪkᵊl) *adj* **1** at right angles to the horizon; perpendicular; upright: *a vertical wall*. Compare **horizontal** (sense 1) **2** extending in a perpendicular direction **3** at or in the vertex or zenith; directly overhead **4** *economics* of or relating to associated or consecutive, though not identical, stages of industrial activity: *vertical integration; vertical amalgamation* **5** of or relating to the vertex **6** *anatomy* of, relating to, or situated at the top of the head (vertex) ▷ *n* **7** a vertical plane, position, or line **8** a vertical post, pillar, or other structural member [C16 from Late Latin *verticālis*, from Latin VERTEX] > ˌverti'cality *n* > 'vertically *adv*

vertical angles *pl n geometry* the pair of equal angles between a pair of intersecting lines; opposite angles. Also called: **vertically opposite angles**

vertical circle *n astronomy* a great circle on the celestial sphere passing through the zenith and perpendicular to the horizon

vertical grouping *n* another term for **family grouping**

vertical mobility *n sociol* the movement of individuals or groups to positions in society that involve a change in class, status, and power. Compare **horizontal mobility** See also **upward mobility, downward mobility**

vertical stabilizer *n* the US name for **fin¹** (sense 3a)

vertical union *n* another name (esp US) for **industrial union**

vertices ('vɜːtɪˌsiːz) *n* a plural of **vertex** (in technical and scientific senses only)

verticil ('vɜːtɪsɪl) *n biology* a circular arrangement of parts about an axis, esp leaves around a stem [C18 from Latin *verticillus* whorl (of a spindle), from VERTEX]

verticillaster (ˌvɜːtɪsɪˈlæstə) *n botany* an inflorescence, such as that of the dead-nettle, that resembles a whorl but consists of two crowded cymes on either side of the stem [C19 from New Latin; see VERTICIL, -ASTER] > verticillastrate (ˌvɜːtɪsɪˈlæsˌtreɪt, -trɪt) *adj*

verticillate (vɜːˈtɪsɪlɪt, -ˌleɪt, ˌvɜːtɪˈsɪleɪt) *adj biology* having or arranged in whorls or verticils > ver'ticillately *adv* > verˌticil'lation *n*

vertiginous (vɜːˈtɪdʒɪnəs) *adj* **1** of, relating to, or having vertigo **2** producing dizziness **3** whirling **4** changeable; unstable [C17 from Latin *vertīginōsus*, from VERTIGO] > ver'tiginously *adv* > ver'tiginousness *n*

vertigo ('vɜːtɪˌgəʊ) *n*, *pl* **vertigoes** *or* **vertigines** (vɜːˈtɪdʒɪˌniːz) *pathol* a sensation of dizziness or abnormal motion resulting from a disorder of the sense of balance [C16 from Latin: a whirling round, from *vertere* to turn]

vertu (vɜːˈtuː) *n* a variant spelling of **virtu**

Vertumnus (vɜːˈtʌmnəs) *or* **Vortumnus** *n* a Roman god of gardens, orchards, and seasonal change [from Latin, from *vertere* to turn, change]

Verulamium (ˌvɛrʊˈleɪmɪəm) *n* the Latin name of **Saint Albans**

vervain ('vɜːveɪn) *n* any of several verbenaceous plants of the genus *Verbena*, having square stems and long slender spikes of purple, blue, or white flowers [C14 from Old French *verveine*, from Latin *verbēna* sacred bough; see VERBENA]

verve (vɜːv) *n* **1** great vitality, enthusiasm, and liveliness; sparkle **2** a rare word for **talent** [C17 from Old French: garrulity, from Latin *verba* words, chatter]

vervet ('vɜːvɪt) *n* a variety of a South African guenon monkey, *Cercopithecus aethiops*, having dark hair on the hands and feet and a reddish patch beneath the tail. Compare **green monkey, grivet** [C19 from French, from *vert* green, but influenced by GRIVET]

very ('vɛrɪ) *adv* **1** (intensifier) used to add emphasis to adjectives that are able to be graded: *very good; very tall* ▷ *adj* (prenominal) **2** (intensifier) used with nouns preceded by a definite article or possessive determiner, in order to give emphasis to the significance, appropriateness or relevance of a noun in a particular context, or to give exaggerated intensity to certain nouns: *the very man I want to see; his very name struck terror; the very back of the room* **3** (intensifier) used in metaphors to emphasize the applicability of the image to the situation described: *he was a very lion in the fight* **4** *archaic* **a** real or true; genuine: *the very living God* **b** lawful: *the very vengeance of the gods* [C13 from Old French *verai* true, from Latin *vērax* true, from *vērus* true]

USAGE In strict usage adverbs of degree such as *very, too, quite, really*, and *extremely* are used only to qualify adjectives: *he is very happy; she is too sad*. By this rule, these words should not be used to qualify past participles that follow the verb *to be*, since they would then be technically qualifying verbs. With the exception of certain participles, such as *tired* or *disappointed*, that have come to be regarded as

adjectives, all other past participles are qualified by adverbs such as *much, greatly, seriously*, or *excessively: he has been much (not very) inconvenienced; she has been excessively (not too) criticized*

very high frequency *n* a radio-frequency band or radio frequency lying between 30 and 300 megahertz. Abbreviation: VHF

very large-scale integration *n computing* the process of fabricating a few thousand logic gates or more in a single integrated circuit. Abbreviation: VLSI

Very light ('vɛrɪ) *n* a coloured flare fired from a special pistol (**Very pistol**) for signalling at night, esp at sea [C19 named after Edward W Very (1852–1910), US naval ordnance officer]

very low frequency *n* a radio-frequency band or radio frequency lying between 3 and 30 kilohertz. Abbreviation: VLF

Very Reverend *n* a title of respect for a variety of ecclesiastical officials, such as deans and the superiors of some religious houses

vesica ('vɛsɪkə) *n*, *pl* **-cae** (-ˌsiː) **1** *anatomy* a technical name for **bladder** (sense 1) **2** (in medieval sculpture and painting) an aureole in the shape of a pointed oval [C17 from Latin: bladder, sac, blister]

vesical ('vɛsɪkᵊl) *adj* of or relating to a vesica, esp the urinary bladder

vesicant ('vɛsɪkənt) *or* **vesicatory** ('vɛsɪˌkeɪtərɪ) *n*, *pl* **-cants** *or* **-catories 1** any substance that causes blisters, used in medicine and in chemical warfare ▷ *adj* **2** acting as a vesicant [C19 see VESICA]

vesicate ('vɛsɪˌkeɪt) *vb* to blister [C17 from New Latin *vēsīcāre* to blister; see VESICA] > vesi'cation *n*

vesicle ('vɛsɪkᵊl) *n* **1** *pathol* **a** any small sac or cavity, esp one containing serous fluid **b** a blister **2** *geology* a rounded cavity within a rock formed during solidification by expansion of the gases present in the magma **3** *botany* a small bladder-like cavity occurring in certain seaweeds and aquatic plants **4** any small cavity or cell [C16 from Latin *vēsīcula*, diminutive of VESICA] > **vesicular** (vɛˈsɪkjʊlə) *adj* > ve'sicularly *adv*

vesiculate *vb* (vɛˈsɪkjʊˌleɪt) **1** to make (an organ or part) vesicular or (of an organ or part) to become vesicular ▷ *adj* (vɛˈsɪkjʊlɪt, -ˌleɪt) **2** containing, resembling, or characterized by a vesicle or vesicles > veˌsicu'lation *n*

vesper ('vɛspə) *n* **1** an evening prayer, service, or hymn **2** an archaic word for **evening 3** (*modifier*) of or relating to vespers ▷ See also **vespers** [C14 from Latin: evening, the evening star; compare Greek *hesperos* evening; see WEST]

Vesper ('vɛspə) *n* the planet Venus, when appearing as the evening star

vesperal ('vɛspərəl) *n Christianity* **1** a liturgical book containing the prayers, psalms, and hymns used at vespers **2** the part of the antiphonary containing these **3** a cloth laid over the altar cloth between offices or services

vespers ('vɛspəz) *n* (*functioning as singular or plural*) **1** *chiefly RC Church* the sixth of the seven canonical hours of the divine office, originally fixed for the early evening and now often made a public service on Sundays and major feast days **2** another word for **evensong** (sense 1)

vespertilionine (ˌvɛspəˈtɪlɪəˌnaɪn, -nɪn) *adj* of, relating to, or belonging to the *Vespertilionidae*, a family of common and widespread bats [C17 from Latin *vespertīliō* a bat, from *vesper* evening] > vespertilionid (ˌvɛspəˈtɪlɪənɪd) *adj, n*

vespertine ('vɛspəˌtaɪn) *adj* **1** *botany, zoology* appearing, opening, or active in the evening: *vespertine flowers* **2** occurring in the evening or (esp of stars) appearing or setting in the evening

vespiary ('vɛspɪərɪ) *n*, *pl* **-aries** a nest or colony of social wasps or hornets [C19 from Latin *vespa* a wasp, on the model of *apiary*]

vespid ('vɛspɪd) *n* **1** any hymenopterous insect of the family *Vespidae*, including the common wasps and hornets ▷ *adj* **2** of, relating to, or belonging to the family *Vespidae* [c19 from New Latin *Vespidae*, from Latin *vespa* a wasp]

vespine (ˈvɛspaɪn) *adj* of, relating to, or resembling a wasp or wasps [c19 from Latin *vespa* a wasp]

vessel (ˈvɛsᵊl) *n* **1** any object used as a container, esp for a liquid **2** a passenger or freight carrying ship, boat, etc **3** an aircraft, esp an airship **4** *anatomy* a tubular structure that transports such body fluids as blood and lymph **5** *botany* a tubular element of xylem tissue consisting of a row of cells in which the connecting cell walls have broken down **6** *rare* a person regarded as an agent or vehicle for some purpose or quality: *she was the vessel of the Lord* [c13 from Old French *vaissel*, from Late Latin *vascellum* urn, from Latin *vās* vessel]

vest (vɛst) *n* **1** an undergarment covering the body from the shoulders to the hips, made of cotton, nylon, etc. US and Canadian equivalent: **T-shirt, undershirt** Austral equivalent: **singlet** **2** a similar sleeveless garment worn as outerwear. Austral equivalent: **singlet** **3** *US, Canadian, and Austral* a man's sleeveless waistlength garment worn under a suit jacket, usually buttoning up the front. Also called (in Britain and certain other countries): **waistcoat** **4** *obsolete* any form of dress, esp a long robe ▷ *vb* **5** (*tr*; foll by *in*) to place or settle (power, rights, etc, in): *power was vested in the committee* **6** (*tr*; foll by *with*) to bestow or confer (on): *the company was vested with authority* **7** (usually foll by *in*) to confer (a right, title, property, etc, upon) or (of a right, title, etc) to pass (to) or devolve (upon) **8** (*tr*) to clothe or array **9** (*intr*) to put on clothes, ecclesiastical vestments, etc [c15 from Old French *vestir* to clothe, from Latin *vestīre*, from *vestis* clothing] > ˈ**vestless** *adj* > ˈ**vest,like** *adj*

vesta (ˈvɛstə) *n* a short friction match, usually of wood [c19 named after the goddess; see VESTA[1]]

Vesta[1] (ˈvɛstə) *n* the Roman goddess of the hearth and its fire. In her temple a perpetual flame was tended by the vestal virgins. Greek counterpart: **Hestia**

Vesta[2] (ˈvɛstə) *n* the brightest of the four largest asteroids. Diameter: about 530 km (240 miles) [c19 named after the goddess; see VESTA[1]]

vestal (ˈvɛstᵊl) *adj* **1** chaste or pure; virginal **2** of or relating to the Roman goddess Vesta ▷ *n* **3** a chaste woman; virgin **4** a rare word for **nun**[1] (sense 1)

vestal virgin *n* (in ancient Rome) one of the four, later six, virgin priestesses whose lives were dedicated to Vesta and to maintaining the sacred fire in her temple

vested (ˈvɛstɪd) *adj* *property law* having a present right to the immediate or future possession and enjoyment of property. Compare **contingent**

vested interest *n* **1** *property law* an existing and disposable right to the immediate or future possession and enjoyment of property **2** a strong personal concern in a state of affairs, system, etc, usually resulting in private gain **3** a person or group that has such an interest

vestiary (ˈvɛstɪərɪ) *n, pl* **-aries** **1** *obsolete* a room for storing clothes or dressing in, such as a vestry ▷ *adj* **2** *rare* of or relating to clothes [c17 from Late Latin *vestiārius*, from *vestis* clothing]

vestibular system *n* the sensory mechanism in the inner ear that detects movement of the head and helps to control balance

vestibule (ˈvɛstɪˌbjuːl) *n* **1** a small entrance hall or anteroom; lobby **2** any small bodily cavity or space at the entrance to a passage or canal [c17 from Latin *vestibulum*] > **vestibular** (vɛˈstɪbjʊlə) *adj*

vestibulocochlear nerve (vɛˌstɪbjʊːləˈkɒklɪə) *n* either one of the eight pairs of cranial nerves that supply the cochlea and semicircular canals of the internal ear and contribute to the sense of hearing. Formerly called: **acoustic nerve**

vestige (ˈvɛstɪdʒ) *n* **1** a small trace, mark, or amount; hint: *a vestige of truth; no vestige of the meal* **2** *biology* an organ or part of an organism that is a small nonfunctioning remnant of a functional organ in an ancestor [c17 via French from Latin *vestīgium* track]

vestigial (vɛˈstɪdʒɪəl) *adj* **1** of, relating to, or being a vestige **2** (of certain organs or parts of organisms) having attained a simple structure and reduced size and function during the evolution of the species: *the vestigial pelvic girdle of a snake* > **vesˈtigially** *adv*

Vestmannaeyjar (ˌvɛstmænˈeɪjaː) *n* a group of islands off the S coast of Iceland: they include the island of Surtsey (emerged 1963) and the volcano Helgafell (erupted 1974). Pop: 4888 (1994). English name: **Vestmann Islands**

vestment (ˈvɛstmənt) *n* **1** a garment or robe, esp one denoting office, authority, or rank **2** any of various ceremonial garments worn by the clergy at religious services [c13 from Old French *vestiment*, from Latin *vestīmentum* clothing, from *vestīre* to clothe] > **vestmental** (vɛstˈmɛntᵊl) *adj*

vest-pocket *n* (*modifier*) *chiefly US* small enough to fit into a waistcoat pocket

vestry (ˈvɛstrɪ) *n, pl* **-tries** **1** a room in or attached to a church in which vestments, sacred vessels, etc, are kept **2** a room in or attached to some churches, used for Sunday school, meetings, etc **3** *Church of England* **a** a meeting of all the members of a parish or their representatives, to transact the official business of the parish **b** the body of members meeting for this; the parish council **4** *Episcopalian (US) and Anglican (Canadian) Churches* a committee of vestrymen chosen by the congregation to manage the temporal affairs of their church [c14 probably from Old French *vestiarie*; see VEST] > ˈ**vestral** *adj*

vestryman (ˈvɛstrɪmən) *n, pl* **-men** a member of a church vestry

vesture (ˈvɛstʃə) *n* **1** *archaic* a garment or something that seems like a garment: *a vesture of cloud* **2** *law* **a** everything except trees that grows on the land **b** a product of the land, such as grass, wheat, etc ▷ *vb* **3** (*tr*) *archaic* to clothe [c14 from Old French, from *vestir*, from Latin *vestīre*, from *vestis* clothing] > ˈ**vestural** *adj*

vesuvian (vɪˈsuːvɪən) *n* **1** (esp formerly) a match for lighting cigars; fusee **2** another name for **vesuvianite** [C18 (the mineral), C19 (the match): both named after VESUVIUS]

vesuvianite (vɪˈsuːvɪəˌnaɪt) *n* a green, brown, or yellow mineral consisting of a hydrated silicate of calcium, magnesium, iron, and aluminium: it occurs as tetragonal crystals in limestones and is used as a gemstone. Formula: $Ca_{10}(Mg,Fe)_2Al_4Si_9O_{34}(OH)_4$. Also called: **idocrase, vesuvian** [c19 first found in the lava of VESUVIUS]

Vesuvius (vɪˈsuːvɪəs) *n* a volcano in SW Italy, on the Bay of Naples: first recorded eruption in 79 AD, which destroyed Pompeii, Herculaneum, and Stabiae; numerous eruptions since then. Average height: 1220 m (4003 ft). Italian name: **Vesuvio** (veˈzuːvjo)

vet[1] (vɛt) *n* **1** short for **veterinary surgeon** ▷ *vb* **vets, vetting, vetted** **2** (*tr*) *chiefly Brit* to make a prior examination and critical appraisal of (a person, document, scheme, etc): *the candidates were well vetted*. See also **positive vetting** **3** to examine, treat, or cure (an animal)

vet[2] (vɛt) *n* *US and Canadian* short for **veteran** (senses 2, 3)

vet. *abbreviation for* **1** veteran **2** veterinarian **3** veterinary. Also (for senses 2, 3): **veter**

vetch (vɛtʃ) *n* **1** any of various climbing leguminous plants of the temperate genus *Vicia*, esp *V. sativa*, having pinnate leaves, typically blue or purple flowers, and tendrils on the stems **2** any of various similar and related plants, such as *Lathyrus sativus*, cultivated in parts of Europe, and the kidney vetch **3** the beanlike fruit of any of these plants [C14 *fecche*, from Old French *veche*, from Latin *vicia*]

vetchling (ˈvɛtʃlɪŋ) *n* any of various leguminous tendril-climbing plants of the genus *Lathyrus*, esp *L. pratensis* (**meadow vetchling**), mainly of N temperate regions, having winged or angled stems and showy flowers. See also **sweet pea**

veteran (ˈvɛtərən, ˈvɛtrən) *n* **1** **a** a person or thing that has given long service in some capacity **b** (*as modifier*): *veteran firemen* **2** **a** a soldier who has seen considerable active service **b** (*as modifier*): *veteran soldier* **3** *US and Canadian* a person who has served in the military forces **4** See **veteran car** [c16 from Latin *veterānus*, from *vetus* old]

veteran car *n* *Brit* a car constructed before 1919, esp one constructed before 1905. Compare **classic car, vintage car**

Veterans Day *n* the US equivalent of **Armistice Day**

veterinarian (ˌvɛtərɪˈnɛərɪən, ˌvɛtrɪ-) *n* a person suitably qualified and registered to practise veterinary medicine. Also called (esp in Britain): **veterinary surgeon**

veterinary (ˈvɛtərɪnərɪ, ˈvɛtrɪnrɪ) *adj* of or relating to veterinary medicine [c18 from Latin *veterīnārius* concerning draught animals, from *veterīnae* draught animals; related to *vetus* mature (hence able to bear a burden)]

veterinary medicine *or* **science** *n* the branch of medicine concerned with the health of animals and the treatment of injuries or diseases that affect them

veterinary surgeon *n* *Brit* a person suitably qualified and registered to practise veterinary medicine. Usual US and Canadian term: **veterinarian**

vetiver (ˈvɛtɪvə) *n* **1** a tall hairless grass, *Vetiveria zizanioides*, of tropical and subtropical Asia, having aromatic roots and stiff long narrow ornamental leaves **2** the root of this plant used for making screens, mats, etc, and yielding a fragrant oil used in perfumery, medicine, etc [c19 from French *vétiver*, from Tamil *vettivēru*]

veto (ˈviːtəʊ) *n, pl* **-toes** **1** the power to prevent legislation or action proposed by others; prohibition: *the presidential veto* **2** the exercise of this power **3** Also called: **veto message** *US government* a document containing the reasons why a chief executive has vetoed a measure ▷ *vb* **-toes, -toing, -toed** (*tr*) **4** to refuse consent to (a proposal, esp a government bill) **5** to prohibit, ban, or forbid: *her parents vetoed her trip* [c17 from Latin: I forbid, from *vetāre* to forbid] > ˈ**vetoer** *n* > ˈ**vetoless** *adj*

vex (vɛks) *vb* (*tr*) **1** to anger or annoy **2** to confuse; worry **3** *archaic* to agitate [c15 from Old French *vexer*, from Latin *vexāre* to jolt (in carrying), from *vehere* to convey] > ˈ**vexer** *n* > ˈ**vexing** *adj* > ˈ**vexingly** *adv*

vexation (vɛkˈseɪʃən) *n* **1** the act of vexing or the state of being vexed **2** something that vexes

vexatious (vɛkˈseɪʃəs) *adj* **1** vexing or tending to vex **2** vexed **3** *law* (of a legal action or proceeding) instituted without sufficient grounds, esp so as to cause annoyance or embarrassment to the defendant: *vexatious litigation* > **vexˈatiously** *adv* > **vexˈatiousness** *n*

vexed (vɛkst) *adj* **1** annoyed, confused, or agitated **2** much debated and discussed (esp in the phrase **a vexed question**) > **vexedly** (ˈvɛksɪdlɪ) *adv* > ˈ**vexedness** *n*

vexillology (ˌvɛksɪˈlɒlədʒɪ) *n* the study and collection of information about flags [c20 from Latin *vexillum* flag + -LOGY] > ˌ**vexilˈlologist** *n*

vexillum (vɛkˈsɪləm) *n, pl* **-la** (-lə) **1** *ornithol* the vane of a feather **2** *botany* another name for **standard** (sense 16) [c18 from Latin: banner, perhaps from *vēlum* sail] > ˈ**vexillary** *or* **vexˈillar** *adj* > ˈ**vexillate** *adj*

VF *abbreviation for* **video frequency**

vg[1] *abbreviation for* very good

vg[2] *the internet domain name for* British Virgin Islands

VG *abbreviation for* Vicar General

VGA *abbreviation for* video graphics array; a

computing standard that has a resolution of 640 × 480 pixels with 16 colours or of 320 × 200 pixels with 256 colours. **SVGA** (**super VGA**) is a later version with higher spatial and colour resolution, esp 800 × 600 pixels with 256 colours

VHF *or* **vhf** *radio abbreviation for* **very high frequency**

VHS *trademark abbreviation for* video home system: a video cassette recording system using ½" magnetic tape

vi[1] *abbreviation for* vide infra

vi[2] *the internet domain name for* US Virgin Islands

VI *abbreviation for* Virgin Islands

via ('vaɪə) *prep* by way of; by means of; through: *to London via Paris* [C18 from Latin *viā*, from *via* way]

viable ('vaɪəbᵊl) *adj* **1** capable of becoming actual, useful, etc; practicable: *a viable proposition* **2** (of seeds, eggs, etc) capable of normal growth and development **3** (of a fetus) having reached a stage of development at which further development can occur independently of the mother [C19 from French, from *vie* life, from Latin *vīta*] > ˌ**via'bility** *n*

Via Dolorosa ('vi:ə ˌdɒlə'rəʊsə) *n* **1** the route followed by Christ from the place of his condemnation to Calvary for his crucifixion **2** an arduous or distressing course or experience [Latin, literally: sorrowful road]

viaduct ('vaɪəˌdʌkt) *n* a bridge, esp for carrying a road or railway across a valley, etc, consisting of a set of arches supported by a row of piers or towers [C19 from Latin *via* way + *dūcere* to bring, on the model of *aqueduct*]

Viagra (vaɪ'ægrə, vi:-) *n trademark* a drug, sildenafil, that allows increased blood flow into the penis; used to treat erectile dysfunction in men

vial ('vaɪəl, vaɪl) *n* a less common variant of **phial** [C14 *fiole*, from Old French, from Old Provençal *fiola*, from Latin *phiala*, from Greek *phialē*; see PHIAL]

via media *Latin* ('vaɪə 'mi:dɪə) *n* a compromise between two extremes; middle course

viand ('vi:ənd, 'vaɪ-) *n* **1** a type of food, esp a delicacy **2** (*plural*) provisions [C14 from Old French *viande*, ultimately from Latin *vīvenda* things to be lived on, from *vīvere* to live]

Viareggio (*Italian* via'reddʒo) *n* a town and resort in W Italy, in Tuscany on the Ligurian Sea. Pop: 61 103 (2001)

viatical (vaɪ'ætɪkᵊl) *adj* **1** of or denoting a road or a journey **2** *botany* (of a plant) growing by the side of a road [C19 from Latin *viāticus* belonging to a journey + -AL[1]]

viatical settlement *n* the purchase by a charity of a life assurance policy owned by a person with only a short time to live, to enable that person to use the proceeds during his or her lifetime. See also **death futures**

viaticum (vaɪ'ætɪkəm) *n, pl* **-ca** (-kə) *or* **-cums** **1** *Christianity* Holy Communion as administered to a person dying or in danger of death **2** *rare* provisions or a travel allowance for a journey [C16 from Latin, from *viāticus* belonging to a journey, from *viāre* to travel, from *via* way]

viator (vaɪ'eɪtɔ:) *n, pl* **viatores** (ˌvaɪə'tɔ:ri:z) *rare* a traveller [C16 from Latin, from *viāre* to travel]

vibe (vaɪb) *n slang* a feeling or flavour of the kind specified: *a 1970s vibe* [from VIBRATION]

vibes (vaɪbz) *pl n* **1** *informal* (esp in jazz) short for **vibraphone** **2** *slang* short for **vibrations**

vibey ('vaɪbɪ) *adj* **vibier, vibiest** *slang* lively and vibrant

vibist ('vaɪbɪst) *n informal* a person who plays a vibraphone in a jazz band or group

Viborg *n* **1** ('vi:bɔrj) the Swedish name for **Vyborg** **2** (*Danish* 'vibɔr) a town in N central Denmark, in Jutland: formerly a royal town and capital of Jutland. Pop: 33 192 (2004 est)

vibraculum (vaɪ'brækjʊləm) *n, pl* **-la** (-lə) *zoology* any of the specialized bristle-like polyps in certain bryozoans, the actions of which prevent parasites from settling on the colony [C19 from New Latin, from Latin *vibrāre* to brandish] > **vi'bracular** *adj* > **vi'bracuˌloid** *adj*

Vibram ('vaɪbrəm) *n trademark* a special type of moulded rubber sole, widely used for climbing and walking boots [C20 from *Vi(tale) Bram(ini)*, Italian climber who devised the product]

vibrant ('vaɪbrənt) *adj* **1** characterized by or exhibiting vibration; pulsating or trembling **2** giving an impression of vigour and activity **3** caused by vibration; resonant **4** (of colour) strong and vivid **5** *phonetics* trilled or rolled ▷ *n* **6** a vibrant speech sound, such as a trilled (r) [C16 from Latin *vibrāre* to agitate] > **'vibrancy** *n* > **'vibrantly** *adv*

vibraphone ('vaɪbrəˌfəʊn) *or esp US* **vibraharp** ('vaɪbrəˌhɑ:p) *n* a percussion instrument, used esp in jazz, consisting of a set of metal bars placed over tubular metal resonators, which are made to vibrate electronically > **'vibraˌphonist** *n*

vibrate (vaɪ'breɪt) *vb* **1** to move or cause to move back and forth rapidly; shake, quiver, or throb **2** (*intr*) to oscillate **3** to send out (a sound) by vibration; resonate or cause to resonate **4** (*intr*) to waver **5** *physics* to undergo or cause to undergo an oscillatory or periodic process, as of an alternating current; oscillate **6** (*intr*) *rare* to respond emotionally; thrill [C17 from Latin *vibrāre*] > **vibratile** ('vaɪbrəˌtaɪl) *adj* > **vi'brating** *adj* > **vi'bratingly** *adv* > **'vibratory** *adj*

vibration (vaɪ'breɪʃən) *n* **1** the act or an instance of vibrating **2** *physics* **a** a periodic motion about an equilibrium position, such as the regular displacement of air in the propagation of sound **b** a single cycle of such a motion **3** the process or state of vibrating or being vibrated > **vi'brational** *adj* > **vi'brationless** *adj*

vibrations (vaɪ'breɪʃənz) *pl n slang* **1** instinctive feelings supposedly influencing human communication **2** a characteristic atmosphere felt to be emanating from places or objects ▷ Often shortened to: **vibes**

vibration white finger *n* a condition affecting workers using vibrating machinery, which causes damage to the blood vessels and nerves of the fingers and leads to a permanent loss of feeling

vibrato (vɪ'brɑ:təʊ) *n, pl* **-tos** *music* **1** a slight, rapid, and regular fluctuation in the pitch of a note produced on a stringed instrument by a shaking movement of the hand stopping the strings **2** an oscillatory effect produced in singing by fluctuation in breath pressure or pitch ▷ Compare **tremolo** [C19 from Italian, from Latin *vibrāre* to VIBRATE]

vibrator (vaɪ'breɪtə) *n* **1** **a** a device for producing a vibratory motion, such as one used in massage or in the distribution of wet concrete in moulds **b** such a device with a vibrating part or tip, used as a dildo **2** a device in which a vibrating conductor interrupts a circuit to produce a pulsating current from a steady current, usually so that the current can then be amplified or the voltage transformed. See also **chopper** (sense 6)

vibrio ('vɪbrɪˌəʊ) *n, pl* **-os** any curved or spiral rodlike Gram-negative bacterium of the genus *Vibrio*, including *V. cholerae*, which causes cholera: family *Spirillaceae* [C19 from New Latin, from Latin *vibrāre* to VIBRATE] > **'vibriˌoid** *adj*

vibrissa (vaɪ'brɪsə) *n, pl* **-sae** (-si:) (*usually plural*) **1** any of the bristle-like sensitive hairs on the face of many mammals; a whisker **2** any of the specialized bristle-like feathers around the beak in certain insectivorous birds [C17 from Latin, probably from *vibrāre* to shake] > **vi'brissal** *adj*

vibronic (vaɪ'brɒnɪk) *adj physics* of, concerned with, or involving both electronic and vibrational energy levels of a molecule: *a vibronic spectrum; a vibronic transition* [C20 from *vibr(atory + electr)onic*]

Vibropac block ('vaɪbrəʊˌpæk) *n NZ trademark* a precast concrete building block

viburnum (vaɪ'bɜ:nəm) *n* **1** any of various temperate and subtropical caprifoliaceous shrubs or trees of the genus *Viburnum*, such as the wayfaring tree, having small white flowers and berry-like red or black fruits **2** the dried bark of several species of this tree, sometimes used in medicine [C18 from Latin: wayfaring tree]

vicar ('vɪkə) *n* **1** *Church of England* **a** (in Britain) a clergyman appointed to act as priest of a parish from which, formerly, he did not receive tithes but a stipend **b** a clergyman who acts as assistant to or substitute for the rector of a parish at Communion **c** (in the US) a clergyman in charge of a chapel **2** *RC Church* a bishop or priest representing the pope or the ordinary of a diocese and exercising a limited jurisdiction **3** Also called: **lay vicar, vicar choral** *Church of England* a member of a cathedral choir appointed to sing certain parts of the services **4** a person appointed to do the work of another [C13 from Old French *vicaire*, from Latin *vicārius* (n) a deputy, from *vicārius* (adj) VICARIOUS] > **'vicarly** *adj*

vicarage ('vɪkərɪdʒ) *n* **1** the residence or benefice of a vicar **2** a rare word for **vicariate** (sense 1)

vicar apostolic *n RC Church* a titular bishop having jurisdiction in non-Catholic or missionary countries where the normal hierarchy has not yet been established

vicar forane (fɒ'reɪn) *n, pl* **vicars forane** *RC Church* a priest or bishop appointed by the ordinary of the diocese to exercise a limited jurisdiction in a locality at some distance from the ordinary's official see [*forane*, from Late Latin *forāneus* in a foreign land, from Latin *forās* outside]

vicar general *n, pl* **vicars general** an official, usually a layman, appointed to assist the bishop of a diocese in discharging his administrative or judicial duties

vicarial (vɪ'kɛərɪəl, vaɪ-) *adj* **1** of or relating to a vicar, vicars, or a vicariate **2** holding the office of a vicar **3** vicarious: used esp of certain ecclesiastical powers

vicariant (vɪ'kɛərɪənt, vaɪ-) *n* any of several closely related species, races, etc, each of which exists in a separate geographical area: assumed to have originated from a single population that became dispersed by geological events [C20 from Latin *vicārius* (see VICAR) + -ANT] > **vi'cariance** *n*

vicariate (vɪ'kɛərɪɪt, vaɪ-) *n* **1** Also called: **vicarship** ('vɪkəʃɪp) the office, rank, or authority of a vicar **2** the district that a vicar holds as his pastoral charge

vicarious (vɪ'kɛərɪəs, vaɪ-) *adj* **1** obtained or undergone at second hand through sympathetic participation in another's experiences **2** suffered, undergone, or done as the substitute for another: *vicarious punishment* **3** delegated: *vicarious authority* **4** taking the place of another **5** *pathol* (of menstrual bleeding) occurring at an abnormal site. See **endometriosis** [C17 from Latin *vicārius* substituted, from *vicis* interchange; see VICE[3], VICISSITUDE] > **vi'cariously** *adv* > **vi'cariousness** *n*

Vicar of Bray (breɪ) *n* **1** a person who changes his or her views or allegiances in accordance with what is suitable at the time **2** Also called: **In Good King Charles's Golden Days** a ballad in which a vicar of the Stuart period changes faith to keep his living [from a vicar (Simon Aleyn) of the parish of Bray in Berkshire during Henry VIII's reign who changed his faith to Catholic when Mary I was on the throne and back to Protestant when Elizabeth I succeeded and so retained his living]

Vicar of Christ *n RC Church* the Pope when regarded as Christ's earthly representative

vice[1] (vaɪs) *n* **1** an immoral, wicked, or evil habit, action, or trait **2** habitual or frequent indulgence in pernicious, immoral, or degrading practices **3** a specific form of pernicious conduct, esp prostitution or sexual perversion **4** a failing or imperfection in character, conduct, etc: *smoking is his only vice* **5** *pathol obsolete* any physical defect or imperfection **6** a bad trick or disposition, as of horses, dogs, etc [C13 via Old French from Latin *vitium* a defect] > **'viceless** *adj*

vice[2] *or US (often)* **vise** (vaɪs) *n* **1** an appliance for holding an object while work is done upon it, usually having a pair of jaws ▷ *vb* **2** (*tr*) to grip (something) with or as if with a vice [C15 from Old French *vis* a screw, from Latin *vītis* vine, plant with spiralling tendrils (hence the later meaning)] > 'vice₁like *or US* (*often*) 'vise₁like *adj*

vice³ (vaɪs) *adj* **1 a** (*prenominal*) serving in the place of or as a deputy for **b** (*in combination*): *viceroy* ▷ *n* **2** *informal* a person who serves as a deputy to another [C18 from Latin *vice*, from *vicis* interchange]

vice⁴ ('vaɪsɪ) *prep* instead of; as a substitute for [C16 from Latin, ablative of *vicis* change]

Vice (vaɪs) *n* (in English morality plays) a character personifying a particular vice or vice in general

vice admiral *n* a commissioned officer of flag rank in certain navies, junior to an admiral and senior to a rear admiral > ₁vice-'admiralty *n*

vice-chairman *n, pl* -men a person who deputizes for a chairman and serves in his place during his absence or indisposition > ₁vice-'chairmanship *n*

vice chancellor *n* **1** the chief executive or administrator at some British universities. Compare **chancellor** (sense 3) **2** (in the US) a judge in courts of equity subordinate to the chancellor **3** (formerly in England) a senior judge of the court of Chancery who acted as assistant to the Lord Chancellor **4** a person serving as the deputy of a chancellor > ₁vice-'chancellorship *n*

vice-county *n, pl* -counties any of the geographical units into which the British Isles are divided for purposes of botanical and zoological recording, corresponding wherever possible to county boundaries

vicegerent (₁vaɪs'dʒɛrənt) *n* **1** a person appointed to exercise all or some of the authority of another, esp the administrative powers of a ruler; deputy **2** *RC Church* the Pope or any other representative of God or Christ on earth, such as a bishop ▷ *adj* **3** invested with or characterized by delegated authority [C16 from New Latin *vicegerēns*, from VICE³ + Latin *gerere* to manage] > ₁vice'geral *adj* > ₁vice'gerency *n*

vicenary ('vɪsɪnərɪ) *adj* **1** relating to or consisting of 20 **2** *maths* having or using a base 20 [C17 (in the sense: one who has charge over twenty persons): from Latin *vīcēnārius*, from *vīcēnī* twenty each, from *vīgintī* twenty]

vicennial (vɪ'sɛnɪəl) *adj* **1** occurring every 20 years **2** relating to or lasting for a period of 20 years [C18 from Late Latin *vīcennium* period of twenty years, from Latin *vīciēs* twenty times + -*ennium*, from *annus* year]

Vicenza (*Italian* vi'tʃɛntsa) *n* a city in NE Italy, in Veneto: home of the 16th-century architect Andrea Palladio and site of some of his finest works. Pop: 107 223 (2001)

vice president *n* an officer ranking immediately below a president and serving as his deputy. A vice president takes the president's place during his absence or incapacity, after his death, and in certain other circumstances. Abbreviations: VP, V. Pres > ₁vice-'presidency *n* > ₁vice-₁presi'dential *adj*

viceregal (₁vaɪs'riːgᵊl) *adj* **1** of or relating to a viceroy or his viceroyalty **2** *chiefly Austral and NZ* of or relating to a governor or governor general > ₁vice'regally *adv*

viceregal assent *n Austral* the formal signing of an act of parliament by a governor general, by which it becomes law

vicereine (₁vaɪs'reɪn) *n* **1** the wife of a viceroy **2** a female viceroy [C19 from French, from VICE³ + *reine* queen, from Latin *rēgīna*]

viceroy ('vaɪsrɔɪ) *n* a governor of a colony, country, or province who acts for and rules in the name of his sovereign or government. Related adj: **viceregal** [C16 from French, from VICE³ + *roy* king, from Latin *rex*] > 'viceroy₁ship *n*

viceroyalty (₁vaɪs'rɔɪəltɪ) *n, pl* -ties **1** the office, authority, or dignity of a viceroy **2** the domain

governed by a viceroy **3** the term of office of a viceroy

vice squad *n* a police division to which is assigned the enforcement of gaming and prostitution laws

vice versa ('vaɪsɪ 'vɜːsə) *adv* with the order reversed; the other way around [C17 from Latin: relations being reversed, from *vicis* change + *vertere* to turn]

Vichy (*French* viʃi; *English* 'viːʃi) *n* a town and spa in central France, on the River Allier: seat of the collaborationist government under Marshal Pétain (1940–44); mineral waters bottled for export. Pop: 26 528 (1999). Latin name: Vicus Calidus ('viːkəs 'kælɪdəs)

vichyssoise (*French* viʃiswaz) *n* a thick soup made from leeks, potatoes, chicken stock, and cream, usually served chilled [French, from (*crème*) *Vichyssoise* (*glacée*) (ice-cold cream) from Vichy]

vichy water *n* **1** (*sometimes capital*) a natural mineral water from springs at Vichy in France, reputed to be beneficial to the health **2** any sparkling mineral water resembling this ▷ Often shortened to: vichy

vicinage ('vɪsənɪdʒ) *n now rare* **1** the residents of a particular neighbourhood **2** a less common word for **vicinity** [C14 from Old French *vicenage*, from *vicin* neighbouring, from Latin *vīcīnus; see* VICINITY]

vicinal ('vɪsɪnᵊl) *adj* **1** neighbouring **2** (esp of roads) of or relating to a locality or neighbourhood **3** *chem* relating to or designating two adjacent atoms to which groups are attached in a chain [C17 from Latin *vīcīnālis* nearby, from *vīcīnus*, from *vīcus* a neighbourhood]

vicinity (vɪ'sɪnɪtɪ) *n, pl* -ties **1** a surrounding, adjacent, or nearby area; neighbourhood **2** the fact or condition of being close in space or relationship [C16 from Latin *vīcīnitās*, from *vīcīnus* neighbouring, from *vīcus* village]

vicious ('vɪʃəs) *adj* **1** wicked or cruel; villainous: *a vicious thug* **2** characterized by violence or ferocity: *a vicious blow* **3** *informal* unpleasantly severe; harsh: *a vicious wind* **4** characterized by malice: *vicious lies* **5** (esp of dogs, horses, etc) ferocious or hostile; dangerous **6** characterized by or leading to vice **7** invalidated by defects; unsound: *a vicious inference* **8** *obsolete* noxious or morbid: *a vicious exhalation* [C14 from Old French *vicieus*, from Latin *vitiōsus* full of faults, from *vitium* a defect] > 'viciously *adv* > 'viciousness *n*

vicious circle *n* **1** Also: **vicious cycle** a situation in which an attempt to resolve one problem creates new problems that lead back to the original situation **2** *logic* **a** a form of reasoning in which a conclusion is inferred from premises the truth of which cannot be established independently of that conclusion **b** an explanation given in terms that cannot be understood independently of that which was to be explained **c** a situation in which some statement is shown to entail its negation and vice versa, as *this statement is false* is true only if false and false only if true **3** *med* a condition in which one disease or disorder causes another, which in turn aggravates the first condition

vicissitude (vɪ'sɪsɪ₁tjuːd) *n* **1** variation or mutability in nature or life, esp successive alternation from one condition or thing to another **2** a variation in circumstance, fortune, character, etc [C16 from Latin *vicissitūdō*, from *vicis* change, alternation] > vi₁cissi'tudinary *or* vi₁cissi'tudinous *adj*

Vicksburg ('vɪks₁bɜːg) *n* a city in W Mississippi, on the Mississippi River: site of one of the most decisive campaigns (1863) of the American Civil War, in which the Confederates were besieged for nearly seven weeks before capitulating. Pop: 26 005 (2003 est)

vicomte (*French* vikɔ̃t) *or feminine* **vicomtesse** (*French* vikɔ̃tɛs) *n* a French noble holding a rank corresponding to that of a British viscount or viscountess

Victa ('vɪktə) *n trademark Austral* a type of rotary lawnmower first manufactured in 1952 [C20 named after Mervyn *Victor* Richardson, who invented it]

victim ('vɪktɪm) *n* **1** a person or thing that suffers harm, death, etc, from another or from some adverse act, circumstance, etc: *victims of tyranny; statistically our chances of being the victim of violent crime are remote* **2** a person who is tricked or swindled; dupe **3** a living person or animal sacrificed in a religious rite [C15 from Latin *victima*]

victimize *or* **victimise** ('vɪktɪ₁maɪz) *vb* (*tr*) **1** to punish or discriminate against selectively or unfairly **2** to make a victim of **3** to kill as or in a manner resembling a sacrificial victim > ₁victimi'zation *or* ₁victimi'sation *n* > 'victim₁izer *or* 'victim₁iser *n*

victimless crime ('vɪktɪmləs) *n* a type of crime, such as insurance fraud, regarded by some people as being excusable because the victim is the state or an organization, rather than an individual

victimology (₁vɪktɪ'mɒlədʒɪ) *n* the study of the psychological effects experienced by the victims of crime > ₁victi'mologist *n*

victor ('vɪktə) *n* **1 a** a person, nation, etc, that has defeated an adversary in war, etc **b** (*as modifier*): *the victor army* **2** the winner of any contest, conflict, or struggle [C14 from Latin, from *vincere* to conquer]

Victor ('vɪktə) *n communications* a code word for the letter *v*

victoria (vɪk'tɔːrɪə) *n* **1** a light four-wheeled horse-drawn carriage with a folding hood, two passenger seats, and a seat in front for the driver **2** Also called: **victoria plum** *Brit* a large sweet variety of plum, red and yellow in colour **3** any South American giant water lily of the genus *Victoria*, having very large floating leaves and large white, red, or pink fragrant flowers: family *Nymphaeaceae* [C19 all named after Victoria (1819–1901), queen of the United Kingdom (1837–1901) and empress of India (1876–1901)]

Victoria¹ (vɪk'tɔːrɪə) *n* **1** a state of SE Australia: part of New South Wales colony until 1851; semiarid in the northwest, with the Great Dividing Range in the centre and east and the Murray River along the N border. Capital: Melbourne. Pop: 4 947 985 (2003 est). Area: 227 620 sq km (87 884 sq miles) **2** Also called: **Victoria Nyanza** a lake in East Africa, in Tanzania, Uganda, and Kenya, at an altitude of 1134 m (3720 ft): the largest lake in Africa and second largest in the world; drained by the Victoria Nile. Area: 69 485 sq km (26 828 sq miles) **3** a port in SW Canada, capital of British Columbia, on Vancouver Island: founded in 1843 by the Hudson's Bay Company; made capital of British Columbia in 1868; university (1963). Pop: 288 346 (2001) **4** the capital of the Seychelles, a port on NE Mahé. Pop: 24 701 (1997) **5** an urban area in S China, part of Hong Kong, on N Hong Kong Island: financial and administrative district; university (1911). Pop: 595 000 (latest est) **6** Mount a mountain in SE Papua New Guinea: the highest peak of the Owen Stanley Range. Height: 4073 m (13 363 ft)

Victoria² (vɪk'tɔːrɪə) *n* the Roman goddess of victory. Greek counterpart: Nike

Victoria and Albert Museum *n* a museum of the fine and applied arts in London, originating from 1856 and given its present name and site in 1899. Abbreviation: V and A

Victoria Cross *n* the highest decoration for gallantry in the face of the enemy awarded to the British and Commonwealth armed forces: instituted in 1856 by Queen Victoria

Victoria Day *n* the Monday preceding May 24: observed in Canada as a national holiday in commemoration of the birthday of Queen Victoria

Victoria Desert *n* See **Great Victoria Desert**

Victoria Falls *pl n* a waterfall on the border between Zimbabwe and Zambia, on the Zambezi

V

River. Height: about 108 m (355 ft). Width: about 1400 m (4500 ft)

Victoria Island *n* a large island in the Canadian Arctic, in Nunavut and the Northwest Territories. Area: about 212 000 sq km (82 000 sq miles)

Victoria Land *n* a section of Antarctica, largely in the Ross Dependency on the Ross Sea

Victorian (vɪkˈtɔːrɪən) *adj* **1** of, relating to, or characteristic of Victoria (1819–1901), queen of the United Kingdom (1837–1901) and empress of India (1876–1901), or the period of her reign **2** exhibiting the characteristics popularly attributed to the Victorians, esp prudery, bigotry, or hypocrisy. Compare **Victorian values** **3** denoting, relating to, or having the style of architecture used in Britain during the reign of Queen Victoria, characterized by massive construction and elaborate ornamentation **4** of or relating to Victoria (the state or any of the cities) ▷ *n* **5** a person who lived during the reign of Queen Victoria **6** an inhabitant of Victoria (the state or any of the cities) > Vic'torian‚ism *n*

Victoriana (vɪk‚tɔːrɪˈɑːnə) *pl n* objects, ornaments, etc, of the Victorian period

Victoria Nile *n* See **Nile**

Victorian values *pl n* qualities considered to characterize the Victorian period, including enterprise and initiative and the importance of the family. Compare **Victorian** (sense 2)

victorious (vɪkˈtɔːrɪəs) *adj* **1** having defeated an adversary: *the victorious nations* **2** of, relating to, indicative of, or characterized by victory: *a victorious conclusion* > vic'toriously *adv* > vic'toriousness *n*

victory (ˈvɪktərɪ) *n, pl* **-ries 1** final and complete superiority in a war **2** a successful military engagement **3** a success attained in a contest or struggle or over an opponent, obstacle, or problem **4** the act of triumphing or state of having triumphed [c14 from Old French *victorie*, from Latin *victōria*, from *vincere* to subdue]

Victory (ˈvɪktərɪ) *n* another name (in English) for the Roman goddess **Victoria** or the Greek **Nike**

victory roll *n* a roll of an aircraft made by a pilot to announce or celebrate the shooting down of an enemy plane or other cause for celebration

victual (ˈvɪtəl) *vb* **-uals, -ualling, -ualled** *or US* **-uals, -ualing, -ualed 1** to supply with or obtain victuals **2** (*intr*) *rare* (esp of animals) to partake of victuals ▷ See also **victuals** [c14 from Old French *vitaille*, from Late Latin *victuālia* provisions, from Latin *victuālis* concerning food, from *victus* sustenance, from *vīvere* to live] > 'victual-less *adj*

victualage (ˈvɪtəlɪdʒ) *n* a rare word for **victuals**

victualler (ˈvɪtələ, 'vɪtlə) *n* **1** a supplier of victuals, as to an army; sutler **2** *Brit* a licensed purveyor of spirits; innkeeper **3** a supply ship, esp one carrying foodstuffs

victuals (ˈvɪtəlz) *pl n* (*sometimes singular*) food or provisions

vicuña (vɪˈkuːnjə) *or* **vicuna** (vɪˈkjuːnə) *n* **1** a tawny-coloured cud-chewing Andean artiodactyl mammal, *Vicugna vicugna*, similar to the llama: family *Camelidae* **2** the fine light cloth made from the wool obtained from this animal [c17 from Spanish *vicuña*, from Quechuan *wikúña*]

vid (vɪd) *n informal* short for **video** (sense 4)

vide (ˈvaɪdɪ) (used to direct a reader to a specified place in a text, another book, etc) refer to, see (often in the phrases **vide ante** (see before), **vide infra** (see below), **vide post** (see after), **vide supra** (see above), **vide ut supra** (see as above), etc). Abbreviation: **v, vid** [c16 from Latin]

videlicet (vɪˈdiːlɪ‚set) *adv* namely: used to specify items, examples, etc. Abbreviation: **viz** [c15 from Latin]

video (ˈvɪdɪ‚əʊ) *adj* **1** relating to or employed in the transmission or reception of a televised image **2** of, concerned with, or operating at video frequencies ▷ *n, pl* **-os 3** the visual elements of a television broadcast **4** a film recorded on a video cassette **5** short for **video cassette, video cassette**

recorder 6 *US* an informal name for **television** ▷ *vb* **videos, videoing, videoed 7** to record (a television programme, etc) on a video cassette recorder ▷ Compare **audio** [c20 from Latin *vidēre* to see, on the model of AUDIO]

video call *n* a call made via a mobile phone with a camera and a screen, allowing the participants to see each other as they talk

video cassette *n* a cassette containing video tape

video cassette recorder *n* a tape recorder for vision and sound signals using magnetic tape in closed plastic cassettes: used for recording and playing back television programmes and films. Often shortened to: **video**. Abbreviation: **VCR**

video conferencing *n* a facility enabling participants in distant locations to take part in a conference by means of electronic sound and video communication

videodisk (ˈvɪdɪəʊ‚dɪsk) *n* another name for **optical disc**

videofit (ˈvɪdɪəʊ‚fɪt) *n* a computer-generated picture of a person sought by the police, created by combining facial characteristics on the basis of witnesses' descriptions [c20 from VIDEO + (PHOTO)FIT]

video frequency *n* the frequency of a signal conveying the image and synchronizing pulses in a television broadcasting system. It lies in the range from about 50 hertz to 8 megahertz

video game *n* any of various games that can be played by using an electronic control to move points of light or graphical symbols on the screen of a visual display unit

videography (‚vɪdɪˈɒɡrəfɪ) *n* the art, practice, or occupation of making videos > ‚vide'ographer *n*

video jockey *n* a person who introduces and plays videos, esp of pop songs, on a television programme

video memory *n* *computing* computer memory used for the processing and displaying of images

video nasty *n* a film, usually specially made for video, that is explicitly horrific, brutal, and pornographic

videophone (ˈvɪdɪə‚fəʊn) *n* a telephonic device in which there is both verbal and visual communication between parties > videophonic (‚vɪdɪə'fɒnɪk) *adj*

video referee *n* *rugby* an additional referee during a televised game who is able to examine video playback to determine whether or not a try has been legitimately scored

video tape *n* **1** magnetic tape used mainly for recording the vision and sound signals of a television programme or film for subsequent transmission ▷ *vb* **video-tape 2** to record (a programme, film, etc) on video tape

video tape recorder *n* a tape recorder for vision signals and sometimes accompanying sound, using magnetic tape on open spools: used in television broadcasting. Abbreviation: **VTR**

Videotex (ˈvɪdɪəʊ‚tɛks) *n trademark* an information system that displays information from a distant computer on a television screen. See also **Teletext, Viewdata**

videotext (ˈvɪdɪəʊ‚tɛkst) *n* a means of providing a written or graphical representation of computerized information on a television screen

vidette (vɪˈdɛt) *n* a variant spelling of **vedette**

Vidhan Sabha (ˈvɪdɑːn ˈsʌbə) *n* the legislative assembly of any of the states of India [Hindi, from *vidhan* law + *sabha* assembly]

vidicon (ˈvɪdɪ‚kɒn) *n* a small television camera tube, used in closed-circuit television and outside broadcasts, in which incident light forms an electric charge pattern on a photoconductive surface. Scanning by a low-velocity electron beam discharges the surface, producing a current in an adjacent conducting layer. See also **Plumbicon** [c20 from VID(EO) + ICON(OSCOPE)]

vie (vaɪ) *vb* **vies, vying, vied 1** (*intr*; foll by *with* or *for*) to contend for superiority or victory (with) or strive in competition (for) **2** (*tr*) *archaic* to offer,

exchange, or display in rivalry [c15 probably from Old French *envier* to challenge, from Latin *invītāre* to INVITE] > 'vier *n* > 'vying *adj, n*

Vienna (vɪˈɛnə) *n* the capital and the smallest state of Austria, in the northeast on the River Danube: seat of the Hapsburgs (1278-1918); residence of the Holy Roman Emperor (1558–1806); withstood sieges by Turks in 1529 and 1683; political and cultural centre in the 18th and 19th centuries, having associations with many composers; university (1365). Pop: 1 590 242 (2003 est). Area: 1075 sq km (415 sq miles). German name: **Wien**

Vienna Union *or* **International** *n* the an international conference of socialists who came together in Vienna in 1921 in an attempt to reconstruct a united International by offering an alternative to the right-wing remnant of the Second International and to the Comintern: merged into the Labour and Socialist International in 1923. Also called: **Two-and-a-half International**

Vienne (*French* vjɛn) *n* **1** a department of W central France, in Poitou-Charentes region. Capital: Poitiers. Pop: 402 555 (2003 est). Area: 7044 sq km (2747 sq miles) **2** a town in SE France, on the River Rhône: extensive Roman remains. Ancient name: **Vienna 3** a river in SW central France, flowing west and north to the Loire below Chinon. Length: over 350 km (200 miles)

Viennese (‚vɪəˈniːz) *adj* **1** of, relating to, or characteristic of Vienna ▷ *n, pl* **-nese 2** a native or inhabitant of Vienna

Vientiane (‚vjɛntɪˈɑːn) *n* the administrative capital of Laos, in the south near the border with Thailand: capital of the kingdom of Vientiane from 1707 until taken by the Thais in 1827. Pop: 776 000 (2005 est)

Vierwaldstättersee (fiːrˈvaltʃtɛtərˌzeː) *n* the German name for (Lake) **Lucerne**

vies (fiːs) *adj South African slang* angry, furious, or disgusted [Afrikaans]

vi et armis *Latin* (ˈvaɪ ɛt ˈɑːmɪs) *n legal history* a kind of trespass accompanied by force and violence [literally: by force and arms]

Vietcong (‚vjɛtˈkɒŋ) *or* **Viet Cong** *n* (in the Vietnam War) **1** the Communist-led guerrilla force and revolutionary army of South Vietnam; the armed forces of the National Liberation Front of South Vietnam **2** a member of these armed forces **3** (*modifier*) of or relating to the Vietcong or a Vietcong [from Vietnamese *Viet Nam Cong San* Vietnamese Communist]

Vietminh (‚vjɛtˈmɪn) *or* **Viet Minh** *n* **1** a Vietnamese organization led by Ho Chi Minh that first fought the Japanese and then the French (1941–54) in their attempt to achieve national independence **2** a member or group of members of this organization, esp in the armed forces **3** (*modifier*) of or relating to this organization or to its members [from Vietnamese *Viet Nam Doc Lap Dong Minh Hoi* Vietnam League of Independence]

Vietnam (‚vjɛtˈnæm) *or* **Viet Nam** *n* a republic in SE Asia: an ancient empire, conquered by France in the 19th century; occupied by Japan (1940–45) when the Communist-led Vietminh began resistance operations that were continued against restored French rule after 1945. In 1954 the country was divided along the 17th parallel, establishing North Vietnam (under the Vietminh) and South Vietnam (under French control), the latter becoming the independent **Republic of Vietnam** in 1955. From 1959 the country was dominated by war between the Communist Vietcong, supported by North Vietnam, and the South Vietnamese government; increasing numbers of US forces were brought to the aid of the South Vietnamese army until a peace agreement (1973) led to the withdrawal of US troops; further fighting led to the eventual defeat of the South Vietnamese government in March 1975 and in 1976 an elected National Assembly proclaimed the reunification of the country. Official language: Vietnamese. Religion: Buddhist majority. Currency: dong. Capital: Hanoi. Pop: 82 481 000 (2004 est). Area: 331 041 sq km (127 816 sq miles). Official name: **Socialist Republic of Vietnam**

Vietnamese (ˌvjɛtnəˈmiːz) adj **1** of, relating to, or characteristic of Vietnam, its people, or their language ▷ n **2** (pl **-ese**) a native or inhabitant of Vietnam **3** the language of Vietnam, probably related to the Mon-Khmer languages

Vietnamization or **Vietnamisation** (ˌvjɛtnəmaɪˈzeɪʃən) n (in the Vietnam War) a US government policy of transferring the tasks of fighting and directing the war to the government and forces of South Vietnam

vieux jeu French (vjø ʒø) adj old-fashioned [literally: old game]

view (vjuː) n **1** the act of seeing or observing; an inspection **2** vision or sight, esp range of vision: *the church is out of view* **3** a scene, esp of a fine tract of countryside: *the view from the top was superb* **4** a pictorial representation of a scene, such as a photograph **5** (sometimes plural) opinion; thought: *my own view on the matter differs from yours* **6** chance or expectation: *the policy has little view of success* **7** (foll by to) a desired end or intention: *he has a view to securing further qualifications* **8** a general survey of a topic, subject, etc: *a comprehensive view of Shakespearean literature* **9** visual aspect or appearance: *they look the same in outward view* **10** law **a** a formal inspection by a jury of the place where an alleged crime was committed **b** a formal inspection of property in dispute **11** a sight of a hunted animal before or during the chase **12** in view of taking into consideration **13** on view exhibited to the public gaze **14** take a dim or poor view of to regard (something) with disfavour or disapproval **15** with a view to **a** with the intention of **b** in anticipation or hope of ▷ vb **16** (tr) to look at **17** (tr) to consider in a specified manner **18** (tr) to examine or inspect carefully: *to view the accounts* **19** (tr) to survey mentally; contemplate: *to view the difficulties* **20** to watch (television) **21** (tr) to sight (a hunted animal) before or during the chase [c15 from Old French *veue*, from *veoir* to see, from Latin *vidēre*] ▷ **'viewable** adj

Viewdata ('vjuːˌdeɪtə) n trademark an interactive form of videotext that sends information from a distant computer along telephone lines, enabling shopping, booking theatre and airline tickets, and banking transactions to be conducted from the home

viewer ('vjuːə) n **1** a person who views something, esp television **2** any optical device by means of which something is viewed, esp one used for viewing photographic transparencies **3** law a person appointed by a court to inspect and report upon property, etc ▷ **'viewership** n

viewfinder ('vjuːˌfaɪndə) n a device on a camera, consisting of a lens system and sometimes a ground-glass screen, enabling the user to see what will be included in his photograph. Sometimes shortened to: **finder**

view halloo interj **1** a huntsman's cry uttered when the quarry is seen breaking cover or shortly afterwards ▷ n **2** a shout indicating an abrupt appearance

viewing ('vjuːɪŋ) n **1** the act of watching television **2** television programmes collectively: *late-night viewing*

viewless ('vjuːlɪs) adj **1** (of windows, etc) not affording a view **2** having no opinions **3** poetic invisible

viewpoint ('vjuːˌpɔɪnt) n **1** the mental attitude that determines a person's opinions or judgments; point of view **2** a place from which something can be viewed

viewy ('vjuːɪ) adj viewier, viewiest informal, rare **1** having fanciful opinions or ideas; visionary **2** characterized by ostentation; showy

▷ **'viewiness** n

VIFF (vɪf) n a technique used in flying VTOL aircraft to change direction suddenly by swivelling the jet engine nozzles [c20 v(ectoring) i(n) f(orward) f(light)]

vig (vɪg) n US slang the interest on a loan that is paid to a moneylender [c20 short for *vigorish*, prob via Yiddish from Russian *vyigrysh* profit, winnings]

vigesimal (vaɪˈdʒɛsɪməl) adj **1** relating to or based on the number 20 **2** taking place or proceeding in intervals of 20 **3** twentieth [c17 from Latin *vīgēsimus*, variant (influenced by *vīgintī* twenty) of *vīcēsimus* twentieth]

vigia ('vɪdʒɪə) n nautical a navigational hazard marked on a chart although its existence and nature has not been confirmed [c19 from Spanish *vigía* reef, from Latin *vigilāre* to keep watch]

vigil ('vɪdʒɪl) n **1** a purposeful watch maintained, esp at night, to guard, observe, pray, etc **2** the period of such a watch **3** RC Church, Church of England the eve of certain major festivals, formerly observed as a night spent in prayer: often marked by fasting and abstinence and a special Mass and divine office **4** a period of sleeplessness; insomnia [c13 from Old French *vigile*, from Medieval Latin *vigilia* watch preceding a religious festival, from Latin: vigilance, from *vigil* alert, from *vigēre* to be lively]

vigilance ('vɪdʒɪləns) n **1** the fact, quality, or condition of being vigilant **2** the abnormal state or condition of being unable to sleep

vigilance committee n (in the US) a self-appointed body of citizens organized to maintain order, punish crime, etc, where an efficient system of courts does not exist

vigilant ('vɪdʒɪlənt) adj keenly alert to or heedful of trouble or danger, as while others are sleeping or unsuspicious [c15 from Latin *vigilāns* keeping awake, from *vigilāre* to be watchful; see VIGIL] ▷ **'vigilantly** adv ▷ **'vigilantness** n

vigilante (ˌvɪdʒɪˈlæntɪ) n **1** one of an organized group of citizens who take upon themselves the protection of their district, properties, etc **2** Also called: **vigilance man** US a member of a vigilance committee [c19 from Spanish, from Latin *vigilāre* to keep watch]

vigilantism (ˌvɪdʒɪˈlæntɪzəm) n US the methods, conduct, attitudes, etc, associated with vigilantes, esp militancy, bigotry, or suspiciousness

vigil light n chiefly RC Church **1** a small candle lit as an act of personal devotion before a shrine or statue, usually in a church **2** a small lamp kept permanently burning before such a shrine or statue

Vigil Mass n RC Church a Mass held on Saturday evening, attendance at which fulfils one's obligation to attend Mass on Sunday

vigneron ('viːnjərɒn; French viɲrɔ̃) n a person who grows grapes for winemaking [French, from *vigne* vine]

vignette (vɪˈnjɛt) n **1** a small illustration placed at the beginning or end of a book or chapter **2** a short graceful literary essay or sketch **3** a photograph, drawing, etc, with edges that are shaded off **4** architect a carved ornamentation that has a design based upon tendrils, leaves, etc **5** any small endearing scene, view, picture, etc ▷ vb (tr) **6** to finish (a photograph, picture, etc) with a fading border in the form of a vignette **7 a** to decorate with vignettes **b** to portray in or as in a vignette [c18 from French, literally: little vine, from *vigne* VINE; with reference to the vine motif frequently used in embellishments to a text] ▷ **vi'gnettist** n

vignetting (vɪˈnjɛtɪŋ) n **1** the technique of producing a photographic vignette, esp a portrait, by progressively reducing the amount of light falling on the photographic surface towards the edges **2** the reduction in area of a light beam passing through a camera lens as the obliquity of the beam is increased

Vigo ('viːgəʊ; Spanish 'biɡo) n a port in NW Spain,

in Galicia on **Vigo Bay** (an inlet of the Atlantic): site of a British and Dutch naval victory (1702) over the French and Spanish. Pop: 292 566 (2003 est)

vigoro ('vɪgəˌrəʊ) n Austral sport a women's game similar to cricket with paddle-shaped bats, introduced into Australia in 1919 by its British inventor J J Grant [c20 from VIGOUR]

vigorous ('vɪgərəs) adj **1** endowed with bodily or mental strength or vitality; robust **2** displaying, involving, characterized by, or performed with vigour: *vigorous growth* ▷ **'vigorously** adv ▷ **'vigorousness** n

vigour or US **vigor** ('vɪgə) n **1** exuberant and resilient strength of body or mind; vitality **2** substantial effective energy or force: *the vigour of the tempest* **3** forcefulness; intensity: *the vigour of her complaints* **4** the capacity for survival or strong healthy growth in a plant or animal: *hybrid vigour* **5** the most active period or stage of life, manhood, etc; prime **6** chiefly US legal force or effectiveness; validity (esp in the phrase **in vigour**) [c14 from Old French *vigeur*, from Latin *vigor* activity, from *vigēre* to be lively]

vihuela (Spanish bi'wela) n an obsolete plucked stringed instrument of Spain, related to the guitar [from Spanish]

Viipuri ('viːpuri) n the Finnish name for **Vyborg**

Vijayawada (ˌviːdʒaɪəˈwɑːdə) n a town in SE India, in E central Andra Pradesh on the Krishna River: Hindu pilgrimage centre. Pop: 825 436 (2001). Former name: **Bezwada**

Viking ('vaɪkɪŋ) n (sometimes not capital) **1** Also called: **Norseman, Northman** any of the Danes, Norwegians, and Swedes who raided by sea most of N and W Europe from the 8th to the 11th centuries, later often settling, as in parts of Britain **2** any sea rover, plunderer, or pirate **3** either of two unmanned American spacecraft that reached Mars in 1976 **4** (modifier) of, relating to, or characteristic of a Viking or Vikings: *a Viking ship* [c19 from Old Norse *vīkingr*, probably from *vīk* creek, sea inlet + *-ingr* (see -ING³); perhaps related to Old English *wīc* camp]

vilayet (vɪˈlɑːjɛt) n a major administrative division of Turkey [c19 from Turkish, from Arabic *wilāyat*, from *walīy* governor]

vile (vaɪl) adj **1** abominably wicked; shameful or evil: *the vile development of slavery appalled them* **2** morally despicable; ignoble: *vile accusations* **3** disgusting to the senses or emotions; foul: *a vile smell; vile epithets* **4** tending to humiliate or degrade: *only slaves would perform such vile tasks* **5** unpleasant or bad: *vile weather* **6** paltry: *a vile reward* [c13 from Old French *vil*, from Latin *vīlis* cheap] ▷ **'vilely** adv ▷ **'vileness** n

vilify ('vɪlɪˌfaɪ) vb **-fies, -fying, -fied** (tr) **1** to revile with abusive or defamatory language; malign: *he has been vilified in the tabloid press* **2** rare to make vile; debase; degrade [c15 from Late Latin *vīlificāre*, from Latin *vīlis* worthless + *facere* to make] ▷ **vilification** (ˌvɪlɪfɪˈkeɪʃən) n ▷ **'vili,fier** n

vilipend ('vɪlɪˌpɛnd) vb (tr) rare **1** to treat or regard with contempt **2** to speak slanderously or slightingly of [c15 from Late Latin *vīlipendere*, from Latin *vīlis* worthless + *pendere* to esteem] ▷ **'vili,pender** n

villa ('vɪlə) n **1** (in ancient Rome) a country house, usually consisting of farm buildings and residential quarters around a courtyard **2** a large and usually luxurious country residence **3** Brit a detached or semidetached suburban house **4** NZ a medium-sized suburban house standing in its own grounds [c17 via Italian from Latin; related to Latin *vīcus* a village] ▷ **'villa-,like** adj

Villach (German 'fɪlax) n a city in S central Austria, on the Drava River: nearby hot mineral springs. Pop: 57 497 (2002)

village ('vɪlɪdʒ) n **1** a small group of houses in a country area, larger than a hamlet **2** the inhabitants of such a community collectively **3** an incorporated municipality smaller than a town in various parts of the US and Canada **4** a group of habitats of certain animals **5** *NZ* a self-contained city area having its own shops, etc **6** (*modifier*) of, relating to, or characteristic of a village: *a village green* [c15 from Old French, from *ville* farm, from Latin: VILLA] ▷ 'village-ˌlike *adj*

village college *n Brit* a centre, often for a group of villages, with educational and recreational facilities for the whole neighbourhood. Also called: **community college**

villager ('vɪlɪdʒə) *n* **1** an inhabitant of a village ▷ *adj* **2** *E African* backward, unsophisticated, or illiterate

Villahermosa (*Spanish* biˌʌaer'mosa) *n* a town in E Mexico, capital of Tabasco state: university (1959). Pop: 583 000 (2005 est). Former name: San Juan Bautista

villa home *n Austral* one of a set of suburban bungalows built compactly on the one allotment, esp on the former site of a single bungalow

villain ('vɪlən) *n* **1** a wicked or malevolent person **2** (in a novel, play, film, etc) the main evil character and antagonist to the hero **3** *often jocular* a mischievous person; rogue **4** *Brit police slang* a criminal **5** *history* a variant spelling of **villein 6** *obsolete* an uncouth person; boor [c14 from Old French *vilein* serf, from Late Latin *vīllānus* worker on a country estate, from Latin: VILLA] ▷ 'villainess *fem n*

villainage ('vɪlənɪdʒ) *n* a variant spelling of **villeinage**

villainous ('vɪlənəs) *adj* **1** of, like, or appropriate to a villain **2** very bad or disagreeable: *a villainous climate* ▷ 'villainously *adv* ▷ 'villainousness *n*

villainy ('vɪlənɪ) *n, pl* -**lainies 1** conduct befitting a villain; vicious behaviour or action **2** an evil, abhorrent, or criminal act or deed **3** the fact or condition of being villainous **4** *English history* a rare word for **villeinage**

villanella (ˌvɪlə'nɛlə) *n, pl* -**las** a type of part song originating in Naples during the 16th century [c16 from Italian, from *villano* rustic, from Late Latin *vīllānus*; see VILLAIN]

villanelle (ˌvɪlə'nɛl) *n* a verse form of French origin consisting of 19 lines arranged in five tercets and a quatrain. The first and third lines of the first tercet recur alternately at the end of each subsequent tercet and both together at the end of the quatrain [c16 from French, from Italian VILLANELLA]

Villanovan (ˌvɪlə'nəʊvᵊn) *adj* **1** of or relating to an early Iron Age culture near Bologna, Italy, characterized by the use of bronze and the primitive use of iron ▷ *n* **2** a member of this culture [c19 named after the NE Italian town of *Villanova*, where the first remains of the culture were excavated in 1853]

villatic (vɪ'lætɪk) *adj literary* of or relating to a villa, village, or farm; rustic; rural [c17 from Latin *vīllāticus*, from *villa* a farm]

-ville *n and adj combining form slang, chiefly US* (denoting) a place, condition, or quality with a character as specified: *dragsville; squaresville*

villein or **villain** ('vɪlən) *n* (in medieval Europe) a peasant personally bound to his lord, to whom he paid dues and services, sometimes commuted to rents, in return for his land [c14 from Old French *vilein* serf; see VILLAIN]

villeinage or **villainage** ('vɪlənɪdʒ) *n* (in medieval Europe) **1** the status and condition of a villein **2** the tenure by which a villein held his land

Villeurbanne (*French* vijœrban) *n* a town in E France: an industrial suburb of E Lyon. Pop: 124 215 (1999)

villi ('vɪlaɪ) *n* the plural of **villus**

villiform ('vɪlɪˌfɔːm) *adj* having the form of a villus or a series of villi [c19 from New Latin *villiformis*, from Latin *villus* shaggy hair + -FORM]

villosity (vɪ'lɒsɪtɪ) *n, pl* -**ties 1** the state of being villous **2** a villous coating or surface **3** a villus or a collection of villi

villous ('vɪləs) *adj* **1** (of plant parts) covered with long hairs **2** of, relating to, or having villi [c14 from Latin *villosus,* from *villus* tuft of hair] ▷ 'villously *adv*

villus ('vɪləs) *n, pl* villi ('vɪlaɪ) (*usually plural*) **1** *zoology, anatomy* any of the numerous finger-like projections of the mucous membrane lining the small intestine of many vertebrates **2** any similar membranous process, such as any of those in the mammalian placenta **3** *botany* any of various hairlike outgrowths, as from the stem of a moss [c18 from Latin: shaggy hair]

Vilnius or **Vilnyus** ('vɪlnɪʊs) *n* the capital of Lithuania: passed to Russia in 1795; under Polish rule (1920–39); university (1578); an industrial and commercial centre. Pop: 544 000 (2005 est). Russian name: Vilna ('vɪlna) Polish name: Wilno

vim (vɪm) *n slang* exuberant vigour and energy [c19 from Latin, from *vīs*; related to Greek *is* strength]

vimen ('vaɪmɛn) *n, pl* vimina ('vɪmɪnə) *botany, now rare* a long flexible shoot that occurs in certain plants [c19 from Latin: a pliant twig, osier]

Viminal ('vɪmɪnᵊl) *n* one of the seven hills on which ancient Rome was built [from Latin *Vīminālis Collis* the Viminal Hill, from *vīminālis* of osiers, from *vīmen* an osier, referring to the willow grove on the hill]

vimineous (vɪ'mɪnɪəs) *adj botany, now rare* having, producing, or resembling long flexible shoots [c17 from Latin *vīmineus* made of osiers, from *vīmen* flexible shoot]

vin- *combining form* a variant of **vini-** before a vowel

vina ('viːnə) *n* a stringed musical instrument, esp of India, related to the sitar [c18 from Hindi *bīnā,* from Sanskrit *vīnā*]

vinaceous (vaɪ'neɪʃəs) *adj* **1** of, relating to, or containing wine **2** having a colour suggestive of red wine [c17 from Late Latin *vīnāceus,* from Latin *vīnum* wine]

Viña del Mar (*Spanish* 'biɲa ðɛl 'mar) *n* a city and resort in central Chile, just north of Valparaíso on the Pacific: the second largest city of Chile. Pop: 323 000 (2005 est)

vinaigrette (ˌvɪneɪ'grɛt) *n* **1** Also called: **vinegarette** a small decorative bottle or box with a perforated top, used for holding smelling salts, etc **2** Also called: **vinaigrette sauce** a salad dressing made from oil and vinegar with seasonings; French dressing ▷ *adj* **3** served with vinaigrette [c17 from French, from *vinaigre* VINEGAR]

vinasse (vɪ'næs) *n* the residue left in a still after distilling spirits, esp brandy [c20 from French]

vinblastine (vɪn'blæstiːn) *n* a cytotoxic drug used in the treatment of lymphomas, derived as an alkaloid from the tropical shrub Madagascar periwinkle (*Vinca rosea*) [c20 shortened from *vincaleukoblastine,* from VINCA + *leukoblast,* from *leukocyte* + -BLAST + -INE²]

vinca ('vɪŋkə) *n* See **periwinkle²** [New Latin, from Latin *pervinca* periwinkle]

vinca alkaloid *n med* any of a group of alkaloids obtained from the periwinkle *Vinca rosea,* such as vinblastine and vincristine, that interfere with cell division and are used in the treatment of cancer

Vincennes (*French* vɛ̃sɛn; *English* vɪn'sɛnz) *n* a suburb of E Paris: 14th-century castle. Pop: 43 595 (1999)

Vincent's angina or **disease** ('vɪnsənts) *n* an ulcerative bacterial infection of the mouth, esp involving the throat and tonsils [c20 named after J H *Vincent* (died 1950), French bacteriologist]

vincible ('vɪnsɪbᵊl) *adj rare* capable of being defeated or overcome [c16 from Latin *vincibilis,* from *vincere* to conquer] ▷ ˌvinci'bility or 'vincibleness *n*

vincristine (vɪn'krɪstiːn) *n* a cytotoxic drug used in the treatment of leukaemia, derived as an alkaloid from the tropical shrub Madagascar periwinkle (*Vinca rosea*) [c20 from New Latin VINCA

+ Latin *crista* crest + -INE²]

vinculum ('vɪŋkjʊləm) *n, pl* -la (-lə) **1** a horizontal line drawn above a group of mathematical terms, used as an alternative to parentheses in mathematical expressions, as in $x + \overline{y - z}$ which is equivalent to $x + (y - z)$ **2** *anatomy* **a** any bandlike structure, esp one uniting two or more parts **b** another name for **ligament 3** *rare* a unifying bond; tie [c17 from Latin: bond, from *vincīre* to bind]

vindaloo (ˌvɪndə'luː) *n, pl* -**loos** a type of very hot Indian curry [c20 perhaps from Portuguese *vin d'alho* wine and garlic sauce]

vin de pays *French* (vɛ̃ də peɪ) *n, pl* vins de pays (vɛ̃ də peɪ) the third highest French wine classification: indicates that the wine meets certain requirements concerning area of production, strength, etc. Also called: vin du pays. Abbreviation: VDP. Compare **AC, VDQS,** *vin de table* [literally: local wine]

vin de table *French* (vɛ̃ də tablə) *n, pl* vins de table (vɛ̃ də tablə) the classification given to a French wine that does not meet the requirements of any of the three higher classifications. Compare **AC, VDQS,** *vin de pays* [literally: table wine]

Vindhya Pradesh ('vɪndjə) *n* a former state of central India: merged with the reorganized Madhya Pradesh in 1956

Vindhya Range or **Mountains** *n* a mountain range in central India: separates the Ganges basin from the Deccan, marking the limits of northern and peninsular India. Greatest height: 1113 m (3651 ft)

vindicable ('vɪndɪkəbᵊl) *adj* capable of being vindicated; justifiable ▷ ˌvindica'bility *n*

vindicate ('vɪndɪˌkeɪt) *vb* (*tr*) **1** to clear from guilt, accusation, blame, etc, as by evidence or argument **2** to provide justification for: *his promotion vindicated his unconventional attitude* **3** to uphold, maintain, or defend (a cause, etc): *to vindicate a claim* **4** *Roman law* to bring an action to regain possession of (property) under claim of legal title **5** *rare* to claim, as for oneself or another **6** *obsolete* to take revenge on or for; punish **7** *obsolete* to set free [c17 from Latin *vindicāre,* from *vindex* claimant] ▷ 'vindiˌcator *n* ▷ 'vindiˌcatory *adj*

vindication (ˌvɪndɪ'keɪʃən) *n* **1** the act of vindicating or the condition of being vindicated **2** a means of exoneration from an accusation **3** a fact, evidence, circumstance, etc, that serves to vindicate a theory or claim

vindictive (vɪn'dɪktɪv) *adj* **1** disposed to seek vengeance **2** characterized by spite or rancour **3** *English law* (of damages) in excess of the compensation due to the plaintiff and imposed in punishment of the defendant [c17 from Latin *vindicta* revenge, from *vindicāre* to VINDICATE] ▷ vin'dictively *adv* ▷ vin'dictiveness *n*

vin du pays *French* (vɛ̃ dy peɪ) *n, pl* vins du pays a variant spelling of *vin de pays*

vine (vaɪn) *n* **1** any of various plants, esp the grapevine, having long flexible stems that creep along the ground or climb by clinging to a support by means of tendrils, leafstalks, etc **2** the stem of such a plant [c13 from Old French *vine,* from Latin *vīnea* vineyard, from *vīneus* belonging to wine, from *vīnum* wine] ▷ vined *adj* ▷ vineless *adj* ▷ 'vineˌlike *adj* ▷ 'viny *adj*

vinedresser ('vaɪnˌdrɛsə) *n* a person who prunes, tends, or cultivates grapevines

vinegar ('vɪnɪgə) *n* **1** a sour-tasting liquid consisting of impure dilute acetic acid, made by oxidation of the ethyl alcohol in beer, wine, or cider. It is used as a condiment or preservative **2** sourness or peevishness of temper, countenance, speech, etc **3** *pharmacol* a medicinal solution in dilute acetic acid **4** *US and Canadian informal* vitality ▷ *vb* **5** (*tr*) to apply vinegar to [c13 from Old French *vinaigre,* from *vin* WINE + *aigre* sour, from Latin *acer* sharp] ▷ 'vinegarish *adj* ▷ 'vinegar-ˌlike *adj*

vinegar eel *n* a nematode worm, *Anguillula aceti,* that feeds on the organisms that cause fermentation in vinegar and other liquids. Also called: **vinegar worm, eelworm**

vinegarette (ˌvɪnɪɡəˈrɛt) *n* a variant spelling of **vinaigrette** (sense 1)

vinegar fly *n* any of various dipterous flies of the genus *Drosophila.* See **drosophila**

vinegarroon (ˌvɪnɪɡəˈruːn) *n* a large whip scorpion, *Mastigoproctus giganteus,* of the southwestern US and Mexico that emits a vinegary odour when alarmed [from Mexican Spanish *vinagrón,* from Spanish *vinagre* VINEGAR]

vinegary (ˈvɪnɪɡərɪ) *adj* **1** containing vinegar; tasting of or like vinegar **2** bad-tempered, sour, or peevish

Vineland (ˈvaɪnlənd) *n* a variant spelling of **Vinland**

vinery (ˈvaɪnərɪ) *n, pl* **-eries 1** a hothouse for growing grapes **2** another name for a **vineyard 3** vines collectively

vineyard (ˈvɪnjəd) *n* a plantation of grapevines, esp where wine grapes are produced [Old English *wīngeard;* see VINE, YARD²; related to Old High German *wīngart,* Old Norse *vingarthr*] > ˈvineyardist *n*

vingt-et-un *French* (vɛ̃teœ̃) *n* another name for **pontoon²** [literally: twenty-one]

Vinho Verde (ˌviːnjəʊ ˈvɜːdɪ) *n* any of a variety of light, slightly sharp-tasting wines made from early-picked grapes in the Minho region of NW Portugal [Portuguese, literally: green (or young) wine]

vini- *or before a vowel* **vin-** *combining form* indicating wine: *viniculture* [from Latin *vīnum*]

vinic (ˈvaɪnɪk, ˈvɪnɪk) *adj* of, relating to, or contained in wine [c19 from Latin *vīnum* wine]

viniculture (ˈvɪnɪˌkʌltʃə) *n* the process or business of growing grapes and making wine > ˌviniˈcultural *adj* > ˈviniˈculturist *n*

viniferous (vɪˈnɪfərəs) *adj* wine-producing

vinificator (ˈvɪnɪfɪˌkeɪtə) *n* a condenser that collects the alcohol vapour escaping from fermenting wine [c19 from Latin *vīnum* wine + *facere* to make]

Vinland (ˈvɪnlənd) *or* **Vineland** *n* the stretch of the E coast of North America visited by Leif Ericson and other Vikings from about 1000

Vinnitsa (*Russian* ˈvinnitsə) *n* a city in central Ukraine: passed from Polish to Russian rule in 1793. Pop: 353 000 (2005 est)

vino (ˈviːnəʊ) *n, pl* **-nos** an informal word for **wine** [jocular use of Italian or Spanish *vino*]

vin ordinaire *French* (vɛ̃ ɔrdinɛr) *n, pl* **vins ordinaires** (vɛ̃z ɔrdinɛr) cheap table wine, esp French

vinosity (vɪˈnɒsɪtɪ) *n* the distinctive and essential quality and flavour of wine [c17 from Late Latin *vīnōsitas,* from Latin *vīnōsus* VINOUS]

vinous (ˈvaɪnəs) *adj* **1** of, relating to, or characteristic of wine **2** indulging in or indicative of indulgence in wine: *a vinous complexion* [c17 from Latin *vīnōsus,* from *vīnum* WINE]

vintage (ˈvɪntɪdʒ) *n* **1** the wine obtained from a harvest of grapes, esp in an outstandingly good year, referred to by the year involved, the district, or the vineyard **2** the harvest from which such a wine is obtained **3 a** the harvesting of wine grapes **b** the season of harvesting these grapes or for making wine **4** a time of origin: *a car of Edwardian vintage* **5** *informal* a group of people or objects of the same period: *a fashion of last season's vintage* ▷ *adj* **6** (of wine) of an outstandingly good year **7** representative of the best and most typical: *vintage Shakespeare* **8** of lasting interest and importance; venerable; classic: *vintage films* **9** old-fashioned; dated ▷ *vb* **10** (*tr*) to gather (grapes) or make (wine) [c15 from Old French *vendage* (influenced by *vintener* VINTNER), from Latin *vindēmia,* from *vīnum* WINE, grape + *dēmere* to take away (from *dē-* away + *emere* to take)]

vintage car *n chiefly Brit* an old car, esp one constructed between 1919 and 1930. Compare classic car, veteran car

vintager (ˈvɪntɪdʒə) *n* a grape harvester

vintner (ˈvɪntnə) *n* a wine merchant [c15 from Old French *vinetier,* from Medieval Latin *vīnētārius,* from Latin *vīnētum* vineyard, from *vīnum* WINE]

vinyl (ˈvaɪnɪl) *n* **1** (*modifier*) of, consisting of, or containing the monovalent group of atoms CH_2CH-: *a vinyl polymer: vinyl chloride* **2** (*modifier*) of, consisting of, or made of a vinyl resin: *a vinyl raincoat* **3** any vinyl polymer, resin, or plastic, esp PVC **4** (collectively) conventional records made of vinyl as opposed to compact discs [c19 from VINI- + -YL]

vinyl acetate *n* a colourless volatile liquid unsaturated ester that polymerizes readily in light and is used for making polyvinyl acetate. Formula: CH_2:CHOOCCH$_3$

vinyl chloride *n* a colourless flammable gaseous unsaturated compound made by the chlorination of ethylene and used as a refrigerant and in the manufacture of PVC; chloroethylene; chloroethene. Formula: CH:CHCl

vinylidene (vaɪˈnɪlɪˌdiːn) *n* (*modifier*) of, consisting of, or containing the group CH_2:C: *a vinylidene group or radical; vinylidene chloride; a vinylidene resin* [c20 from VINYL + -IDE + -ENE]

vinyl resin *or* **polymer** *n* any one of a class of thermoplastic materials, esp PVC and polyvinyl acetate, made by polymerizing vinyl compounds

viol (ˈvaɪəl) *n* any of a family of stringed musical instruments that preceded the violin family, consisting of a fretted fingerboard, a body rather like that of a violin but having a flat back and six strings, played with a curved bow. They are held between the knees when played and have a quiet yet penetrating tone; they were much played, esp in consorts, in the 16th and 17th centuries [c15 from Old French *viole,* from Old Provençal *viola;* see VIOLA¹]

viola¹ (vɪˈəʊlə) *n* **1** a bowed stringed instrument, the alto of the violin family; held beneath the chin when played. It is pitched and tuned an octave above the cello **2** any of various instruments of the viol family, such as the viola da gamba [c18 from Italian *viola,* probably from Old Provençal *viola,* of uncertain origin; perhaps related to Latin *vītulārī* to rejoice]

viola² (ˈvaɪələ, vaɪˈəʊ-) *n* any temperate perennial herbaceous plant of the violaceous genus *Viola,* the flowers of which have showy irregular petals, white, yellow, blue, or mauve in colour. See also **violet** (sense 1), **pansy** (sense 1) [c15 from Latin: violet]

violaceous (ˌvaɪəˈleɪʃəs) *adj* **1** of, relating to, or belonging to the *Violaceae,* a family of herbaceous plants and shrubs including the violets and pansies **2** of the colour violet [c17 from Latin *violāceus,* from *viola* VIOLET]

viola clef *n* another term for **alto clef**

viola da braccio (vɪˈəʊlə də ˈbrætʃɪˌəʊ) *n* **1** an old name for **viola¹** (sense 1) **2** a type of viol held on the shoulder, from which the modern viola was developed [from Italian, literally: viol for the arm]

viola da gamba (vɪˈəʊlə də ˈɡæmbə) *n* the second largest and lowest member of the viol family. See **viol** [c18 from Italian, literally: viol for the leg]

viola d'amore (vɪˈəʊlə dæˈmɔːrɪ) *n* an instrument of the viol family having no frets, seven strings, and a set of sympathetic strings. It was held under the chin when played [c18 from Italian, literally: viol of love]

violate (ˈvaɪəˌleɪt) *vb* (*tr*) **1** to break, disregard, or infringe (a law, agreement, etc) **2** to rape or otherwise sexually assault **3** to disturb rudely or improperly; break in upon **4** to treat irreverently or disrespectfully; outrage: *he violated a sanctuary* **5** *obsolete* to mistreat physically ▷ *adj* **6** *archaic* violated or dishonoured [c15 from Latin *violare* to do violence to, from *vīs* strength] > ˈviolable *adj* > ˌvioläˈbility *or* ˈviolableness *n* > ˈviolably *adv* > ˌvioˈlation *n* > ˈviolative *adj* > ˈvioˌlator *or* ˈvioˌlater *n*

violence (ˈvaɪələns) *n* **1** the exercise or an instance of physical force, usually effecting or intended to effect injuries, destruction, etc **2** powerful, untamed, or devastating force: *the violence of the sea* **3** great strength of feeling, as in language, etc; fervour **4** an unjust, unwarranted, or unlawful display of force, esp such as tends to overawe or intimidate **5** **do violence to a** to inflict harm upon; damage or violate: *they did violence to the prisoners* **b** to distort or twist the sense or intention of: *the reporters did violence to my speech* [c13 via Old French from Latin *violentia* impetuosity, from *violentus* VIOLENT]

violent (ˈvaɪələnt) *adj* **1** marked or caused by great physical force or violence: *a violent stab* **2** (of a person) tending to the use of violence, esp in order to injure or intimidate others **3** marked by intensity of any kind: *a violent clash of colours* **4** characterized by an undue use of force; severe; harsh **5** caused by or displaying strong or undue mental or emotional force: *a violent tongue* **6** tending to distort the meaning or intent: *a violent interpretation of the text* [c14 from Latin *violentus,* probably from *vīs* strength] > ˈviolently *adv*

violent storm *n* a wind of force 11 on the Beaufort scale, reaching speeds of 64–72 mph

violet (ˈvaɪəlɪt) *n* **1** any of various temperate perennial herbaceous plants of the violaceous genus *Viola,* such as *V. odorata* (**sweet** (or **garden**) **violet**), typically having mauve or bluish flowers with irregular showy petals **2** any other plant of the genus *Viola,* such as the wild pansy **3** any of various similar but unrelated plants, such as the African violet **4 a** any of a group of colours that vary in saturation but have the same purplish-blue hue. They lie at one end of the visible spectrum, next to blue; approximate wavelength range 445–390 nanometres **b** (as adjective): *a violet dress* **5** a dye or pigment of or producing these colours **6** violet clothing: *dressed in violet* **7** **shrinking violet** *informal* a shy person [c14 from Old French *violete* a little violet, from *viole,* from Latin *viola* violet] > ˈviolet-ˌlike *adj*

violin (ˌvaɪəˈlɪn) *n* a bowed stringed instrument, the highest member of the violin family, consisting of a fingerboard, a hollow wooden body with waisted sides, and a sounding board connected to the back by means of a soundpost that also supports the bridge. It has two f-shaped sound holes cut in the belly. The instrument, noted for its fine and flexible tone, is the most important of the stringed instruments. It is held under the chin when played. Range: roughly three and a half octaves upwards from G below middle C [c16 from Italian *violino* a little viola, from VIOLA¹]

violinist (ˌvaɪəˈlɪnɪst) *n* a person who plays the violin

violist¹ (vɪˈəʊlɪst) *n US* a person who plays the viola

violist² (ˈvaɪəlɪst) *n* a person who plays the viol

violoncello (ˌvaɪələnˈtʃɛləʊ) *n, pl* **-los** the full name for **cello** [c18 from Italian, from VIOLONE + -*cello,* diminutive suffix] > ˌvioloncellist *n*

violone (ˈvaɪəˌləʊn) *n* the double-bass member of the viol family lying an octave below the viola da gamba. It corresponds to the double bass in the violin family [c18 from Italian, from VIOLA¹ + -*one,* augmentative suffix]

VIP *abbreviation for* **1** very important person **2** visually impaired person **3** vasoactive intestinal peptide: a polypeptide secreted by the small intestine during digestion and also found in the brain as a neurotransmitter: large amounts in the blood cause diarrhoea

viper (ˈvaɪpə) *n* **1** any venomous Old World snake of the family *Viperidae,* esp any of the genus *Vipera* (the adder and related forms), having hollow fangs in the upper jaw that are used to inject venom **2** any of various other snakes, such as the horned viper **3** See **pit viper 4** a malicious or treacherous person [c16 from Latin *vipera,* perhaps from *vīvus* living + *parere* to bear, referring to a tradition that the viper was viviparous] > 'viper-,like *adj*

viperous ('vaɪpərəs) *or* **viperish** *adj* **1** Also: viperine ('vaɪpə,raɪn) of, relating to, or resembling a viper **2** malicious > 'viperously *or* 'viperishly *adv*

viper's bugloss *n* also called (US): blueweed a Eurasian boraginaceous weed, *Echium vulgare*, having blue flowers and pink buds. compare **Paterson's curse** see also **echium**

VIR *abbreviation for* Victoria Imperatrix Regina [Latin: Victoria, Empress and Queen]

viraemia *or US* **viremia** (vaɪˈriːmɪə) *n* a condition in which virus particles circulate and reproduce in the bloodstream

virago (vɪˈrɑːgəʊ) *n, pl* **-goes** *or* **-gos 1** a loud, violent, and ill-tempered woman; scold; shrew **2** *archaic* a strong, brave, or warlike woman; amazon [Old English, from Latin: a manlike maiden, from *vir* a man] > **viraginous** (vɪˈrædʒɪnəs) *adj* > viˈrago-,like *adj*

viral ('vaɪrəl) *adj* of, relating to, or caused by a virus

viral marketing *n* **1** a direct marketing technique in which a company persuades internet users to forward its publicity material in e-mails (usually by including jokes, games, video clips, etc) **2** a marketing strategy in which conventional media are eschewed in favour of various techniques designed to generate word-of-mouth publicity, in the hope of creating a fad or craze

Vir Chakra ('viːr 'tʃʌkrə) *n* an award made to distinguished soldiers by the Government of India [Hindi: *vir* brave man + *chakra* wheel]

virelay ('vɪrɪ,leɪ) *n* **1** an old French verse form, rarely used in English, consisting of short lines arranged in stanzas having only two rhymes, and two opening lines recurring at intervals **2** any of various similar forms [c14 from Old French *virelai*, probably from *vireli* (associated with *lai* LAY⁴), meaningless word used as a refrain]

virement ('vaɪəmənt, 'vɪəmɑ̃) *n* an administrative transfer of funds from one part of a budget to another [from French, from Middle French: act of turning, from *virer* to turn]

viremia (vaɪˈriːmɪə) *n* the usual US spelling of **viraemia**

vireo ('vɪrɪəʊ) *n, pl* **vireos** any insectivorous American songbird of the family *Vireonidae*, esp those of the genus *Vireo*, having an olive-grey back with pale underparts [c19 from Latin: a bird, probably a greenfinch; compare *virēre* to be green]

virescence (vɪˈrɛsəns) *n* **1** (in plants) the process of becoming green, esp by the action of disease, etc, in parts not normally green **2** the condition of being or the process of becoming green [c19 see VIRESCENT]

virescent (vɪˈrɛsənt) *adj* greenish or becoming green [c19 from Latin *virescere* to grow green, from *virēre* to be green]

virga ('vɜːgə) *n* (*sometimes functioning as plural*) *meteorol* wisps of rain or snow, seen trailing from clouds, that evaporate before reaching the earth [c20 from Latin: streak]

virgate¹ ('vɜːgɪt, -geɪt) *adj* long, straight, and thin; rod-shaped: *virgate stems* [c19 from Latin *virgātus* made of twigs, from *virga* a rod]

virgate² ('vɜːgɪt, -geɪt) *n Brit* an obsolete measure of land area, usually taken as equivalent to 30 acres [c17 from Medieval Latin *virgāta (terrae)* a rod's measurement (of land), from Latin *virga* rod; the phrase is a translation of Old English *gierd landes* a yard of land]

Virgilian *or* **Vergilian** (vəˈdʒɪlɪən) *adj* of or relating to Virgil (Latin name *Publius Vergilius Maro*), the Roman poet (70–19 BC)

virgin ('vɜːdʒɪn) *n* **1** a person, esp a woman, who has never had sexual intercourse **2** an unmarried woman who has taken a religious vow of chastity in order to dedicate herself totally to God **3** any female animal that has never mated **4** a female

insect that produces offspring by parthenogenesis **5** a person who is new to or inexperienced in a specified field: *a political virgin* ▷ *adj* (*usually prenominal*) **6** of, relating to, resembling, suitable for, or characteristic of a virgin or virgins; chaste **7** pure and natural, uncorrupted, unsullied, or untouched: *virgin purity* **8** not yet cultivated, explored, exploited, etc, by man: *virgin territories* **9** being the first or happening for the first time **10** (of vegetable oils) obtained directly by the first pressing of fruits, leaves, or seeds of plants without applying heat **11** (of a metal) made from an ore rather than from scrap **12** occurring naturally in a pure and uncombined form: *virgin silver* **13** *physics* (of a neutron) not having experienced a collision [c13 from Old French *virgine*, from Latin *virgō* virgin]

Virgin¹ ('vɜːdʒɪn) *n* **1 the** See **Virgin Mary 2** a statue or other artistic representation of the Virgin Mary

Virgin² ('vɜːdʒɪn) *n* **the** the constellation Virgo, the sixth sign of the zodiac

virginal¹ ('vɜːdʒɪnəl) *adj* **1** of, relating to, characterized by, proper to, or maintaining a state of virginity; chaste **2** extremely pure or fresh; untouched; undefiled [c15 from Latin *virgināl is* maidenly, from *virgō* virgin] > **virginally** *adv*

virginal² ('vɜːdʒɪnəl) *n* (*often plural*) a smaller version of the harpsichord, but oblong in shape, having one manual and no pedals [c16 probably from Latin *virgināl is* VIRGINAL¹, perhaps because it was played largely by young ladies] > 'virginalist *n*

virgin birth *n* another name for **parthenogenesis** (sense 2)

Virgin Birth *n* the doctrine that Jesus Christ had no human father but was conceived solely by the direct intervention of the Holy Spirit so that Mary remained miraculously a virgin during and after his birth

virgin forest *n* a forest in its natural state, before it has been explored or exploited by man

Virginia¹ (vəˈdʒɪnɪə) *n* (*sometimes not capital*) a type of flue-cured tobacco grown originally in Virginia

Virginia² (vəˈdʒɪnɪə) *n* a state of the eastern US, on the Atlantic: site of the first permanent English settlement in North America; consists of a low-lying deeply indented coast rising inland to the Piedmont plateau and the Blue Ridge Mountains. Capital: Richmond. Pop: 7 386 330 (2003 est). Area: 103 030 sq km (39 780 sq miles). Abbreviations: Va, (with zip code) VA

Virginia Beach *n* a city and resort in SE Virginia, on the Atlantic. Pop: 439 467 (2003 est)

Virginia creeper *n* **1** Also called (US): **American ivy**, **woodbine** a vitaceous woody vine, *Parthenocissus quinquefolia*, of North America, having tendrils with adhesive tips, bluish-black berry-like fruits, and compound leaves that turn red in autumn: widely planted for ornament **2** Also called: **Japanese ivy** a similar related plant, *Parthenocissus tricuspidata*, of SE Asia, having trilobed leaves and purple berries. US name: **Boston ivy**

Virginia deer *n* another name for **white-tailed deer**

Virginian (vəˈdʒɪnɪən) *adj* **1** of or relating to Virginia or its inhabitants ▷ *n* **2** a native or inhabitant of Virginia

Virginia reel *n* **1** an American country dance **2** music written for or in the manner of this dance

Virginia stock *n* a Mediterranean plant, *Malcolmia maritima*, cultivated for its white and pink flowers: family *Brassicaceae* (crucifers)

Virgin Islands *pl n* a group of about 100 small islands (14 inhabited) in the Caribbean, east of Puerto Rico: discovered by Columbus (1493); consists of the British Virgin Islands in the east and the Virgin Islands of the United States in the west and south. Pop: 132 000 (2004 est). Area: 497 sq km (192 sq miles)

Virgin Islands of the United States *pl n* a territory of the US in the Caribbean, consisting of islands west and south of the British Virgin

Islands: purchased from Denmark in 1917 for their strategic importance. Capital: Charlotte Amalie. Pop: 111 000 (2004 est). Area: 344 sq km (133 sq miles). Former name: **Danish West Indies**

virginity (vəˈdʒɪnɪtɪ) *n* **1** the condition or fact of being a virgin; maidenhood; chastity **2** the condition of being untouched, unsullied, etc

virginium (vəˈdʒɪnɪəm) *n chem* a former name for **francium**

Virgin Mary *n* Mary, the mother of Christ. Also called: **the Virgin**

virgin's-bower *n* any of several American clematis plants, esp *Clematis virginiana*, of E North America, which has clusters of small white flowers

virgin soil *n* **1** soil that has not been cultivated before **2** a person or thing that is as yet undeveloped

virgin wool *n* wool that is being processed or woven for the first time

Virgo ('vɜːgəʊ) *n, Latin genitive* **Virginis** ('vɜːdʒɪnɪs) **1** *astronomy* a large zodiacal constellation on the celestial equator, lying between Leo and Libra. It contains the star Spica and a cluster of several thousand galaxies, the **Virgo cluster**, lying 50 million light years away and itself containing the intense radio source Virgo A, which is the closest active galaxy **2** *astrology* **a** Also called: **the Virgin** the sixth sign of the zodiac, symbol ♍, having a mutable earth classification and ruled by the planet Mercury. The sun is in this sign between about Aug 23 and Sept 22 **b** Also called: **Virgoan** (vɜːˈgəʊən) a person born when the sun is in this sign ▷ *adj* **3** Also: **Virgoan** *astrology* born under or characteristic of Virgo [c14 from Latin]

virgo intacta ('vɜːgəʊ ɪnˈtæktə) *n* a girl or woman whose hymen has not been broken [Latin, literally: untouched virgin]

virgulate ('vɜːgjʊlɪt, -,leɪt) *adj* rod-shaped or rodlike [c19 from Latin *virgula* a little rod, from *virga* rod]

virgule ('vɜːgjuːl) *n printing* another name for **solidus** [c19 from French: comma, from Latin *virgula* a little rod, from *virga* rod]

viridescent (,vɪrɪˈdɛsənt) *adj* greenish or tending to become green [c19 from Late Latin *viridescere* to grow green, from Latin *viridis* green] > ,viri'descence *n*

viridian (vɪˈrɪdɪən) *n* a green pigment consisting of a hydrated form of chromic oxide [c19 from Latin *viridis* green]

viridity (vɪˈrɪdɪtɪ) *n* **1** the quality or state of being green; greenness; verdancy **2** innocence, youth, or freshness [c15 from Latin *viriditās*, from *viridis* green]

virile ('vɪraɪl) *adj* **1** of, relating to, or having the characteristics of an adult male **2** (of a male) possessing high sexual drive and capacity for sexual intercourse **3** of or capable of copulation or procreation **4** strong, forceful, or vigorous [c15 from Latin *virīlis* manly, from *vir* a man; related to Old English *wer* man and probably to Latin *vis* strength] > **virility** (vɪˈrɪlɪtɪ) *n*

virilism ('vɪrɪ,lɪzəm) *n med* the abnormal development in a woman of male secondary sex characteristics

virilization *or* **virilisation** (,vɪrɪlaɪˈzeɪʃən) *n* the development of adult male physical characteristics in a female or a young boy

virino (vɪˈriːnəʊ) *n* an entity postulated to be the causative agent of BSE and related diseases, said to consist of a fragment of nucleic acid surrounded by a protein coat derived from the host cell [c20 from VIRUS + -*ino* diminutive form]

virion ('vaɪrɪən) *n* a virus in infective form, consisting of an RNA particle within a protein covering [c20 from VIR(US) + ION]

viroid ('vaɪrɔɪd) *n* any of various infective RNA particles, smaller than a virus and known to cause some plant diseases [c20 from VIR(US) + -OID]

virology (vaɪˈrɒlədʒɪ) *n* the branch of medicine

concerned with the study of viruses and the diseases they cause > **virological** (ˌvaɪrəˈlɒdʒɪkəl) *adj* > **viˈrologist** *n*

virtu *or* **vertu** (vɜːˈtuː) *n* **1** a taste or love for curios or works of fine art; connoisseurship **2** such objects collectively **3** the quality of being rare, beautiful, or otherwise appealing to a connoisseur (esp in the phrases **articles of virtu; objects of virtu**) [C18 from Italian *virtù*; see VIRTUE]

virtual (ˈvɜːtʃʊəl) *adj* **1** having the essence or effect but not the appearance or form of: *a virtual revolution* **2** *physics* being, relating to, or involving a virtual image: *a virtual focus* **3** *computing* of or relating to virtual storage: *virtual memory* **4** of or relating to a computer technique by which a person, wearing a headset or mask, has the experience of being in an environment created by the computer, and of interacting with and causing changes in it **5** *rare* capable of producing an effect through inherent power or virtue **6** *physics* designating or relating to a particle exchanged between other particles that are interacting by a field of force: *a virtual photon*. See also **exchange force** [C14 from Medieval Latin *virtuālis* effective, from Latin *virtūs* VIRTUE]

virtual human *n* a computer-generated moving image of a human being, used esp in films as an extra in large crowd scenes

virtual image *n* an optical image formed by the apparent divergence of rays from a point, rather than their actual divergence from a point

virtuality (ˌvɜːtjʊˈælɪtɪ) *n* virtual reality

virtualize *or* **virtualise** (ˈvɜːtʃʊəˌlaɪz) *vb* (*tr*) to transform (something) into an artificial computer-generated version of itself which functions as if it were real

virtually (ˈvɜːtʃʊəlɪ) *adv* in effect though not in fact; practically; nearly

virtual reality *n* a computer-generated environment that, to the person experiencing it, closely resembles reality. Abbreviation: VR. See also **virtual** (sense 4)

virtual storage *or* **memory** *n* a computer system in which the size of the memory is effectively increased by automatically transferring sections of a program from a large capacity backing store, such as a disk, into the smaller core memory as they are required

virtue (ˈvɜːtjuː, -tʃuː) *n* **1** the quality or practice of moral excellence or righteousness **2** a particular moral excellence: *the virtue of tolerance* **3** any of the cardinal virtues (prudence, justice, fortitude, and temperance) or theological virtues (faith, hope, and charity) **4** any admirable quality, feature, or trait **5** chastity, esp in women **6** *archaic* an effective, active, or inherent power or force **7** **by** *or* **in virtue of** on account of or by reason of **8** **make a virtue of necessity** to acquiesce in doing something unpleasant with a show of grace because one must do it in any case [C13 *vertu*, from Old French, from Latin *virtūs* manliness, courage, from *vir* man] > **ˈvirtueless** *adj*

virtues (ˈvɜːtjuːz, -tʃuːz) *pl n* (*often capital*) the fifth of the nine orders into which the angels are traditionally divided in medieval angelology

virtuoso (ˌvɜːtjʊˈəʊzəʊ, -səʊ) *n, pl* **-sos** *or* **-si** (-siː) **1** a consummate master of musical technique and artistry **2** a person who has a masterly or dazzling skill or technique in any field of activity **3** a connoisseur, dilettante, or collector of art objects **4** *obsolete* a scholar or savant **5** (*modifier*) showing masterly skill or brilliance: *a virtuoso performance* [C17 from Italian: skilled, from Late Latin *virtuōsus* good, virtuous; see VIRTUE] > **virtuosic** (ˌvɜːtjʊˈɒsɪk) *adj* > **ˌvirtuˈosity** *n*

virtuous (ˈvɜːtʃʊəs) *adj* **1** characterized by or possessing virtue or moral excellence; righteous; upright **2** (of women) chaste or virginal > **ˈvirtuously** *adv* > **ˈvirtuousness** *n*

virulence (ˈvɪrʊləns) *or* **virulency** *n* **1** the quality of being virulent **2** the capacity of a microorganism for causing disease

virulent (ˈvɪrʊlənt) *adj* **1 a** (of a microorganism) extremely infective **b** (of a disease) having a rapid course and violent effect **2** extremely poisonous, injurious, etc **3** extremely bitter, hostile, etc [C14 from Latin *vīrulentus* full of poison, from *vīrus* poison; see VIRUS] > **ˈvirulently** *adv*

virus (ˈvaɪrəs) *n, pl* **-ruses** **1** any of a group of submicroscopic entities consisting of a single nucleic acid chain surrounded by a protein coat and capable of replication only within the cells of living organisms: many are pathogenic **2** *informal* a disease caused by a virus **3** any corrupting or infecting influence **4** *computing* an unauthorized program that inserts itself into a computer system and then propagates itself to other computers via networks or disks; when activated it interferes with the operation of the computer [C16 from Latin: slime, poisonous liquid; related to Old English *wāse* marsh, Greek *ios* poison] > **ˈvirusˌlike** *adj*

virus chip *n* a glass slide embedded with viral DNA used in DNA sequencing to analyse the genetic makeup of viruses

vis *Latin* (vɪs) *n, pl* *vires* (ˈvaɪriːz) power, force, or strength

Vis. *abbreviation for* Viscount *or* Viscountess

visa (ˈviːzə) *n, pl* **-sas** **1** an endorsement in a passport or similar document, signifying that the document is in order and permitting its bearer to travel into or through the country of the government issuing it **2** any sign or signature of approval ▷ *vb* **-sas, -saing, -saed** (*tr*) **3** to enter a visa into (a passport) **4** to endorse or ratify [C19 via French from Latin *vīsa* things seen, from *vīsus*, past participle of *vidēre* to see]

visage (ˈvɪzɪdʒ) *n* *chiefly literary* **1** face or countenance **2** appearance; aspect [C13 from Old French: aspect, from *vis* face, from Latin *vīsus* appearance, from *vidēre* to see]

-visaged *adj* (*in combination*) having a visage as specified: *flat-visaged*

visagiste (ˌviːzɑːˈʒiːst) *n* a person who designs and applies face make-up; make-up artist [C20 from French, from *visage* face + *-iste* -ist]

Visakhapatnam (vɪˌsɑːkəˈpʌtnəm) *n* a variant spelling of **Vishakhapatnam**

vis-à-vis (ˌviːzɑːˈviː) *prep* **1** in relation to; regarding **2** face to face with; opposite ▷ *adv, adj* **3** face to face; opposite ▷ *n, pl* **vis-à-vis** **4** a person or thing that is situated opposite to another **5** a person who corresponds to another in office, capacity, etc; counterpart **6** an upholstered sofa; tête-à-tête **7** a type of horse-drawn carriage in which the passengers sit opposite one another **8** a coin having an obverse upon which two portraits appear facing each other [C18 French, from *vis* face]

Visayan (vɪˈsɑːjən) *or* **Bisayan** *n, pl* **-yans** *or* **-yan** **1** a member of the most numerous indigenous people of the Philippines ▷ *adj* **2** of or relating to this people

Visayan Islands *pl n* a group of seven large and several hundred small islands in the central Philippines. Chief islands: Negros and Panay. Pop: 13 041 000 (1990). Area: about 61 000 sq km (23 535 sq miles). Spanish name: **Bisayas**

Visby (*Swedish* ˈviːsbyː) *n* a port in SE Sweden, on NW Gotland Island in the Baltic: an early member of the Hanseatic League and major N European commercial centre in the Middle Ages. Pop: 22 017 (2000 est)

Visc. *abbreviation for* Viscount *or* Viscountess

viscacha *or* **vizcacha** (vɪsˈkætʃə) *n* **1** a gregarious burrowing hystricomorph rodent, *Lagostomus maximus*, of southern South America, similar to but larger than the chinchillas: family *Chinchillidae* **2** **mountain viscacha** another name for **mountain chinchilla** (see **chinchilla** (sense 3)) [C17 from Spanish, from Quechuan *wiskácha*]

viscaria (vɪsˈkɛərɪə) *n* any plant of the Eurasian perennial genus *Viscaria*, closely related to genus *Lychnis*, in which it is sometimes included: low-growing, with pink, white, or purple flowers: family *Carophyllaceae* [New Latin, from *viscum* birdlime (from the viscid stems)]

viscera (ˈvɪsərə) *pl n, sing* **viscus** (ˈvɪskəs) **1** *anatomy* the large internal organs of the body collectively, esp those in the abdominal cavity. Related adj: **splanchnic** **2** (less formally) the intestines; guts [C17 from Latin: entrails, pl of *viscus* internal organ]

visceral (ˈvɪsərəl) *adj* **1** of, relating to, or affecting the viscera **2** characterized by intuition or instinct rather than intellect > **ˈviscerally** *adv*

visceromotor (ˈvɪsərəʊˌməʊtə) *adj* *physiol* relating to or controlling movements of the viscera

viscerotonia (ˌvɪsərəʊˈtəʊnɪə) *n* a personality type characterized by hedonism and conviviality: said to be correlated with an endomorph body type. Compare **cerebrotonia, somatotonia**

viscid (ˈvɪsɪd) *adj* **1** cohesive and sticky; glutinous; viscous **2** (esp of a leaf) covered with a sticky substance [C17 from Late Latin *viscidus* sticky, from Latin *viscum* mistletoe or birdlime] > **visˈcidity** *or* **ˈviscidness** *n* > **ˈviscidly** *adv*

viscoelastic (ˌvɪskəʊɪˈlæstɪk) *adj* *physics* (of a solid or liquid) exhibiting both viscous and elastic behaviour when deformed > **ˌviscoelasˈticity** *n*

viscoid (ˈvɪskɔɪd) *or* **viscoidal** (vɪsˈkɔɪdəl) *adj* (of a fluid) somewhat viscous

viscometer (vɪsˈkɒmɪtə) *or* **viscosimeter** (ˌvɪskəʊˈsɪmɪtə) *n* any device for measuring viscosity > **viscometric** (ˌvɪskəˈmɛtrɪk) *or* **ˌviscoˈmetrical** *adj* > **visˈcometry** *n*

viscose (ˈvɪskəʊs) *n* **1 a** a viscous orange-brown solution obtained by dissolving cellulose in sodium hydroxide and carbon disulphide. It can be converted back to cellulose by an acid, as in the manufacture of rayon and cellophane **b** (*as modifier*): *viscose rayon* **2** rayon made from this material ▷ *adj* **3** another word for **viscous** [C19 from Late Latin *viscōsus* full of birdlime, sticky, from *viscum* birdlime; see VISCID]

viscosity (vɪsˈkɒsɪtɪ) *n, pl* **-ties** **1** the state or property of being viscous **2** *physics* **a** the extent to which a fluid resists a tendency to flow **b** Also called: **absolute viscosity** a measure of this resistance, equal to the tangential stress on a liquid undergoing streamline flow divided by its velocity gradient. It is measured in newton seconds per metre squared. Symbol: η. See also **kinematic viscosity, specific viscosity**

viscount (ˈvaɪkaʊnt) *n* **1** (in the British Isles) a nobleman ranking below an earl and above a baron **2** (in various countries) a son or younger brother of a count. See also **vicomte** **3** (in medieval Europe) the deputy of a count [C14 from Old French *visconte*, from Medieval Latin *vicecomes*, from Late Latin *vice-* VICE³ + *comes* COUNT²]

viscountcy (ˈvaɪkaʊntsɪ) *or* **viscounty** *n* the rank or position of a viscount

viscountess (ˈvaɪkaʊntɪs) *n* **1** the wife or widow of a viscount **2** a woman who holds the rank of viscount in her own right

viscous (ˈvɪskəs) *or* **viscose** *adj* **1** (of liquids) thick and sticky; viscid **2** having or involving viscosity [C14 from Late Latin *viscōsus*; see VISCOSE] > **ˈviscously** *adv* > **ˈviscousness** *n*

viscous flow *n* another name for **streamline flow**

Visct *abbreviation for* Viscount *or* Viscountess

viscus (ˈvɪskəs) *n* the singular of **viscera**

vise (vaɪs) *n, vb* *US* a variant spelling of **vice²**

Viseu (*Portuguese* viˈzeu) *n* a city in N central Portugal: 12th-century cathedral. Pop: 93 502 (2001)

Vishakhapatnam (vɪˌʃɑːkəˈpʌtnəm), **Visakhapatnam** *or* **Vizagapatam** *n* a port in E India, in NE Andhra Pradesh on the Bay of Bengal: shipbuilding and oil-refining industries. Pop: 969 608 (2001)

Vishnu (ˈvɪʃnuː) *n* *Hinduism* the Pervader or Sustainer: originally a solar deity occupying a secondary place in the Hindu pantheon; later one of the three chief gods, the second member of the

V

Trimurti; and, later still, the saviour appearing in many incarnations [c17 from Sanskrit Viṣṇu, literally: the one who works everywhere] > 'Vishnuism n

visibility (ˌvɪzɪ'bɪlɪtɪ) n **1** the condition or fact of being visible **2** clarity of vision or relative possibility of seeing **3** the range of vision: *visibility is 500 yards*

visible ('vɪzɪbᵊl) adj **1** capable of being perceived by the eye **2** capable of being perceived by the mind; evident: *no visible dangers* **3** available: *the visible resources* **4** (of an index or file) using a flexible display system for the contents **5** of or relating to the balance of trade: *visible transactions* **6** represented by visible symbols ▷ n **7** a visible item of trade; product [c14 from Latin *vīsibilis*, from *vidēre* to see] > 'visibleness n > 'visibly adv

visible balance n another name for **balance of trade**

visible radiation n electromagnetic radiation that causes the sensation of sight; light. It has wavelengths between about 380 and 780 nanometres

visible speech n a system of phonetic notation invented by Alexander Melville Bell (1819–1905) that utilized symbols based on the schematic representation of the articulations used for each speech sound

Visigoth ('vɪzɪˌgɒθ) n a member of the western group of the Goths, who were driven into the Balkans in the late 4th century AD. Moving on, they sacked Rome (410) and established a kingdom in present-day Spain and S France that lasted until 711 [c17 from Late Latin *Visigothī* (pl), of Germanic origin, *visi*- perhaps meaning: west] > ˌVisi'gothic adj

vision ('vɪʒən) n **1** the act, faculty, or manner of perceiving with the eye; sight **2 a** the image on a television screen **b** (as modifier): *vision control* **3** the ability or an instance of great perception, esp of future developments: *a man of vision* **4** a mystical or religious experience of seeing some supernatural event, person, etc: *the vision of St John of the Cross* **5** that which is seen, esp in such a mystical experience **6** (sometimes plural) a vivid mental image produced by the imagination: *he had visions of becoming famous* **7** a person or thing of extraordinary beauty **8** the stated aims and objectives of a business or other organization ▷ vb **9** (tr) to see or show in or as if in a vision [c13 from Latin *vīsiō* sight, from *vidēre* to see] > 'visionless adj

visional ('vɪʒənᵊl) adj of, relating to, or seen in a vision, apparition, etc. > 'visionally adv

visionary ('vɪʒənərɪ) adj **1** marked by vision or foresight: *a visionary leader* **2** incapable of being realized or effected; unrealistic **3** (of people) characterized by idealistic or radical ideas, esp impractical ones **4** given to having visions **5** of, of the nature of, or seen in visions ▷ n, pl **-aries 6** a visionary person > 'visionariness n

vision mixer n television **1** the person who selects and manipulates the television signals from cameras, film, and other sources, to make the composite programme **2** the equipment used for vision mixing

visit ('vɪzɪt) vb **-its, -iting, -ited 1** to go or come to see (a person, place, etc) **2** to stay with (someone) as a guest **3** to go or come to (an institution, place, etc) for the purpose of inspecting or examining **4** (tr) (of a disease, disaster, etc) to assail; afflict **5** (tr; foll by *upon* or *on*) to inflict (punishment, etc): *the judge visited his full anger upon the defendant* **6** (tr; usually foll by *with*) archaic to afflict or plague (with punishment, etc) **7** (often foll by *with*) US and Canadian informal to chat or converse (with someone) ▷ n **8** the act or an instance of visiting **9** a stay as a guest **10** a professional or official call **11** a formal call for the purpose of inspection or examination **12** international law the right of an officer of a belligerent state to stop and search neutral ships in war to verify their nationality and ascertain

whether they carry contraband: *the right of visit and search* **13** US and Canadian informal a friendly talk or chat [c13 from Latin *vīsitāre* to go to see, from *vīsere* to examine, from *vidēre* to see] > 'visitable adj

visitant ('vɪzɪtənt) n **1** a supernatural being; ghost; apparition **2** a visitor or guest, usually from far away **3** a pilgrim or tourist **4** Also called: visitor a migratory bird that is present in a particular region only at certain times: *a summer visitant* ▷ adj **5** archaic paying a visit; visiting [c16 from Latin *vīsitāns* going to see, from *vīsitāre*; see VISIT]

visitation (ˌvɪzɪ'teɪʃən) n **1** an official call or visit for the purpose of inspecting or examining an institution, esp such a visit made by a bishop to his diocese **2** a visiting of punishment or reward from heaven **3** any disaster or catastrophe: *a visitation of the plague* **4** an appearance or arrival of a supernatural being **5** any call or visit **6** informal an unduly prolonged social call > ˌvisit'ational adj

Visitation (ˌvɪzɪ'teɪʃən) n **1 a** the visit made by the Virgin Mary to her cousin Elizabeth (Luke 1:39–56) **b** the Church festival commemorating this, held on July 2 **2** a religious order of nuns, the **Order of the Visitation**, founded in 1610 by St Francis of Sales and dedicated to contemplation and the cultivation of humility, gentleness, and sisterly love

visitatorial (ˌvɪzɪtə'tɔːrɪəl) or **visitorial** adj **1** of, relating to, or for an official visitation or visitor **2** empowered to make official visitations

visiting card n another term for **calling card**

visiting fireman n US informal a visitor whose presence is noticed because he is an important figure, a lavish spender, etc

visiting nurse n (in the US) a registered nurse employed by a community, hospital, etc, to visit and nurse the sick in their homes or to promote public health

visiting professor n a professor invited to teach in a college or university other than his own, often in another country, for a certain period, such as a term or year

visitor ('vɪzɪtə) n **1** a person who pays a visit; caller, guest, tourist, etc **2** another name for **visitant** (sense 4) > 'visi'torial adj

visitor centre n another term for **interpretive centre**

visitor's passport n (formerly, in Britain) a passport, valid for one year and for certain countries only, that could be purchased from post offices. Also called: British Visitor's Passport

Vislinsky Zaliv (Russian vis'linski 'za:lıf) n a transliteration of the Russian name for **Vistula** (sense 2)

vis major ('vɪs 'meɪdʒə) n See **force majeure** [from Latin, literally: greater force]

visor or **vizor** ('vaɪzə) n **1** a transparent flap on a helmet that can be pulled down to protect the face **2** a piece of armour fixed or hinged to the helmet to protect the face and with slits for the eyes **3** another name for **peak** (on a cap) **4** a small movable screen used as protection against glare from the sun, esp one attached above the windscreen of a motor vehicle **5** archaic or literary a mask or any other means of disguise or concealment ▷ vb **6** (tr) to cover, provide, or protect with a visor; shield [c14 from Anglo-French *viser*, from Old French *visiere*, from *vis* face; see VISAGE] > 'visored or 'vizored adj > 'visorless or 'vizorless adj

vista ('vɪstə) n **1** a view, esp through a long narrow avenue of trees, buildings, etc, or such a passage or avenue itself; prospect: *a vista of arches* **2** a comprehensive mental view of a distant time or a lengthy series of events: *the vista of the future* [c17 from Italian: a view, from *vedere* to see, from Latin *vidēre*] > 'vistaed adj > 'vistaless adj

VISTA ('vɪstə) n (in the US) acronym for Volunteers in Service to America; an organization of volunteers established by the Federal government to assist the poor

Vistula ('vɪstjʊlə) n **1** a river in central and N Poland, rising in the Carpathian Mountains and flowing generally north and northwest past Warsaw and Torun, then northeast to enter the Baltic via an extensive delta region. Length: 1090 km (677 miles). Polish name: Wisla German name: Weichsel **2 Lagoon** a shallow lagoon on the SW coast of the Baltic Sea, between Danzig and Kaliningrad, crossed by the border between Poland and Russia. German name: Frisches Haff Polish name: Wislany Zalew Russian name: Vislinsky Zaliv

visual ('vɪʒʊəl, -zjʊ-) adj **1** of, relating to, done by, or used in seeing: *visual powers; visual steering* **2** another word for **optical 3** capable of being seen; visible **4** of, occurring as, or induced by a mental image ▷ n **5** a sketch to show the proposed layout of an advertisement, as in a newspaper **6** (often plural) a photograph, film, or other display material [c15 from Late Latin *vīsuālis*, from Latin *vīsus* sight, from *vidēre* to see] > 'visually adv

visual aids pl n devices, such as films, slides, models, and blackboards, that display in visual form material to be understood or remembered

visual angle n the angle subtended by an object at the lens of the eye

visual arts pl n the arts of painting, sculpting, photography, etc, as opposed to music, drama, and literature

visual display unit n computing a device with a screen that displays characters or graphics representing data in a computer memory. It usually has a keyboard or light pen for the input of information or inquiries. Abbreviation: VDU

visual field n the whole extent of the image falling on the retina when the eye is fixating a given point in space

visualization or **visualisation** (ˌvɪʒʊəlaɪ'zeɪʃən, -zjʊ-) n **1** the act or an instance of visualizing **2** a technique involving focusing on positive mental images in order to achieve a particular goal

visualize or **visualise** ('vɪʒʊəˌlaɪz, -zjʊ-) vb **1** to form a mental image of (something incapable of being viewed or not at that moment visible) **2** med to view by means of an X-ray the outline of (a bodily organ, structure, or part) > 'visualˌizer or 'visualˌiser n

visually handicapped adj **a** unable to carry out normal activities because of defects of vision, including blindness **b** (as collective noun; preceded by *the*): *the visually handicapped* ▷ visual handicap n

> **USAGE** See at **disabled**. Many people find the word 'handicapped' offensive when used to describe people with disabilities. 'Disabled' is the preferred term nowadays

visually impaired adj **a** having any defect of vision, whether disabling or not **b** (as collective noun; preceded by *the*): *the visually impaired*. Compare **partially sighted** ▷ visual impairment n

visual magnitude n astronomy the magnitude of a star as determined by visual observation. Compare **photoelectric magnitude**

visual purple n another name for **rhodopsin**

visual violet n another name for **iodopsin**

vita ('viːtə, 'vaɪ-) n, pl vitae ('viːtaɪ, 'vaɪtiː) US and Canadian a less common term for **curriculum vitae** [from Latin: life]

vitaceous (vaɪ'teɪʃəs) adj of, relating to, or belonging to the *Vitaceae*, a family of tropical and subtropical flowering plants having a climbing habit and berry-like fruits: includes the grapevine and Virginia creeper [c19 via New Latin *Vītāceae*, from Latin: vine]

vital ('vaɪtᵊl) adj **1** essential to maintain life **2** forceful, energetic, or lively: *a vital person* **3** of, relating to, having, or displaying life: *a vital organism* **4** indispensable or essential **5** of great importance; decisive: *a vital game* **6** archaic influencing the course of life, esp negatively: *a vital treachery* ▷ n **7** (plural) **a** the bodily organs, such as the brain, liver, heart, lungs, etc, that are necessary to maintain life **b** the organs of reproduction, esp the male genitals **8** (*plural*) the essential elements of anything [c14 via Old French from Latin *vītālis* belonging to life, from *vīta* life] > 'vitally *adv*

vital capacity *n physiol* the volume of air that can be exhaled from the lungs after the deepest possible breath has been taken: a measure of lung function

vital force *n* (esp in early biological theory) a hypothetical force, independent of physical and chemical forces, regarded as being the causative factor of the evolution and development of living organisms

vitalism ('vaɪtə,lɪzəm) *n* the philosophical doctrine that the phenomena of life cannot be explained in purely mechanical terms because there is something immaterial which distinguishes living from inanimate matter. Compare **dynamism, mechanism**. > 'vitalist *n, adj* > ,vital'istic *adj*

vitality (vaɪ'tælɪtɪ) *n, pl* -ties **1** physical or mental vigour, energy, etc **2** the power or ability to continue in existence, live, or grow: *the vitality of a movement* **3** a less common name for **vital force**

vitalize *or* **vitalise** ('vaɪtə,laɪz) *vb* (*tr*) to make vital, living, or alive; endow with life or vigour > ,vitali'zation *or* ,vitali'sation *n* > 'vital,izer *or* 'vital,iser *n*

vital signs *pl n med* indications that a person is still alive. Vital signs include a heartbeat, a pulse that can be felt, breathing, and body temperature

vital staining *n* the technique of treating living cells and tissues with dyes that do not immediately kill them, facilitating observation with a microscope

vital statistics *pl n* **1** quantitative data concerning human life or the conditions and aspects affecting it, such as the death rate **2** *informal* the measurements of a woman's bust, waist, and hips

vitamin ('vɪtəmɪn, 'vaɪ-) *n* any of a group of substances that are essential, in small quantities, for the normal functioning of metabolism in the body. They cannot usually be synthesized in the body but they occur naturally in certain foods: insufficient supply of any particular vitamin results in a deficiency disease [C20 *vit-* from Latin *vīta* life + *-amin* from AMINE; so named by Casimir Funk (1884–1967), US biochemist who believed the substances to be amines] > ,vita'minic *adj*

vitamin A *n* a fat-soluble yellow unsaturated alcohol occurring in green and yellow vegetables (esp carrots), butter, egg yolk, and fish-liver oil (esp halibut oil). It is essential for the prevention of night blindness and the protection of epithelial tissue. Formula: $C_{20}H_{30}O$. Also called: vitamin A_1, retinol

vitamin A_2 *n* a vitamin that occurs in the tissues of freshwater fish and has a function similar to that of vitamin A. Formula: $C_{20}H_{28}O$. Also called: dehydroretinol

vitamin B *n, pl* B vitamins any of the vitamins in the vitamin B complex

vitamin B_1 *n* another name for **thiamine**

vitamin B_2 *n* another name for **riboflavin**

vitamin B_6 *n* another name for **pyridoxine**

vitamin B_{12} *n* another name for **cyanocobalamin**

vitamin B complex *n* a large group of water-soluble vitamins occurring esp in liver and yeast: includes thiamine, riboflavin, nicotinic acid, pyridoxine, pantothenic acid, biotin, choline, folic acid, and cyanocobalamin. Sometimes shortened to: B complex

vitamin C *n* another name for **ascorbic acid**

vitamin D *n, pl* D vitamins any of the fat-soluble vitamins, including calciferol and cholecalciferol, occurring in fish-liver oils (esp cod-liver oil), milk, butter, and eggs: used in the treatment of rickets and osteomalacia

vitamin D_1 *n* the first isolated form of vitamin D, consisting of calciferol and its precursor,

---

lumisterol

vitamin D_2 *n* another name for **calciferol**

vitamin D_3 *n* another name for **cholecalciferol**

vitamin E *n* another name for **tocopherol**

vitamin G *n* a former name (esp US and Canadian) for **riboflavin**

vitamin H *n* another name (esp US and Canadian) for **biotin**

vitamin K *n, pl* K vitamins any of the fat-soluble vitamins, including phylloquinone and the menaquinones, which are essential for the normal clotting of blood

vitamin K_1 *n* another name for **phylloquinone**

vitamin K_2 *n* another name for **menaquinone**

vitamin K_3 *n* a former name for **menadione**

vitamin P *n, pl* P vitamins any of a group of water-soluble crystalline substances occurring mainly in citrus fruits, blackcurrants, and rosehips: they regulate the permeability of the blood capillaries. Also called: citrin, bioflavonoid

Vitaphone ('vaɪtə,fəʊn) *n trademark* an early technique in commercial film-making in which the accompanying sound was produced by discs

vitascope ('vaɪtə,skəʊp) *n* an early type of film projector [c19 from Latin *vīta* life + -SCOPE]

Vitebsk (*Russian* 'vitɪpsk) *n* a city in E Belarus, a port on the Dvina river: taken by Russia in 1772. Pop: 344 000 (2005 est)

vitellin (vɪ'tɛlɪn) *n biochem* a phosphoprotein that is the major protein in egg yolk [c19 from VITELLUS + -IN]

vitelline (vɪ'tɛlɪn, -aɪn) *adj zoology* **1** of or relating to the yolk of an egg: *the vitelline gland* **2** having the yellow colour of an egg yolk [c15 from Medieval Latin *vitellīnus*, from Latin *vitellus* the yolk of an egg; see VITELLUS]

vitelline membrane *n zoology* a membrane that surrounds a fertilized ovum and prevents the entry of other spermatozoa

vitellogenic (,vɪtələʊ'dʒɛnɪk) *or* **vitelligenous** (,vɪtə'lɪdʒɪnəs) *adj zoology* producing or stimulating the formation of yolk [c20 from VITELLUS + -GENIC] > ,vitello'genesis *n*

vitellus (vɪ'tɛləs) *n, pl* -luses *or* -li (-laɪ) *zoology rare* the yolk of an egg [c18 from Latin, literally: little calf, later: yolk of an egg, from *vitulus* calf]

vitiate ('vɪʃɪ,eɪt) *vb* (*tr*) **1** to make faulty or imperfect **2** to debase, pervert, or corrupt **3** to destroy the force or legal effect of (a deed, etc): *to vitiate a contract* [c16 from Latin *vitiāre* to injure, from *vitium* a fault] > 'vitiable *adj* > ,viti'ation *n* > 'viti,ator *n*

viticulture ('vɪtɪ,kʌltʃə) *n* **1** the science, art, or process of cultivating grapevines **2** the study of grapes and the growing of grapes [c19 *viti-*, from Latin *vītis* vine] > ,viti'cultural *adj* > ,viti'culturer *or* ,viti'culturist *n*

Viti Levu ('viːtɪ 'levuː) *n* the largest island of Fiji: mountainous. Chief town (and capital of the state): Suva. Pop: 340 560 (latest est). Area: 10 386 sq km (4010 sq miles)

vitiligo (,vɪtɪ'laɪgəʊ) *n* another name for **leucoderma** [c17 from Latin: a skin disease, probably from *vitium* a blemish]

Vitoria (*Spanish* bi'torja) *n* a city in NE Spain: scene of Wellington's decisive victory (1813) over Napoleon's forces in the Peninsular War. Pop: 223 257 (2003 est). Official name (including the Basque name): Vitoria-Gasteiz

Vitória (vɪ'tɔːrɪə; *Portuguese* vi'tɔrja) *n* a port in E Brazil, capital of Espírito Santo state, on an island in the Bay of Espírito Santo. Pop: 1 602 000 (2005 est)

vitrain ('vɪtreɪn) *n* a type of coal occurring as horizontal glassy bands of a nonsoiling friable material [c20 from Latin *vitrum* glass + -*ain*, as in FUSAIN]

vitreous ('vɪtrɪəs) *adj* **1** of, relating to, or resembling glass **2** made of, derived from, or containing glass **3** of or relating to the vitreous humour or vitreous body [c17 from Latin *vitreus* made of glass, from *vitrum* glass; probably related

---

to *vidēre* to see] > 'vitreously *adv*

vitreous body *n* a transparent gelatinous substance, permeated by fine fibrils, that fills the interior of the eyeball between the lens and the retina

vitreous humour *n* the aqueous fluid contained within the interstices of the vitreous body

vitreous silica *n* another name for **quartz glass**

vitrescence (vɪ'trɛsəns) *n* **1** the quality or condition of being or becoming vitreous **2** the process of producing a glass or turning a crystalline material into glass

vitrescent (vɪ'trɛsənt) *adj* **1** tending to turn into glass **2** capable of being transformed into glass

vitric ('vɪtrɪk) *adj* of, relating to, resembling, or having the nature of glass; vitreous

vitrification (,vɪtrɪfɪ'keɪʃən) *n* **1** the process or act of vitrifying or the state of being vitrified **2** something that is or has been vitrified

vitriform ('vɪtrɪ,fɔːm) *adj* having the form or appearance of glass

vitrify ('vɪtrɪ,faɪ) *vb* -fies, -fying, -fied to convert or be converted into glass or a glassy substance [c16 from French *vitrifier*, from Latin *vitrum* glass] > 'vitri,fiable *adj* > ,vitri,fia'bility *n*

vitrine ('vɪtriːn) *n* a glass display case or cabinet for works of art, curios, etc [c19 from French, from *vitre* pane of glass, from Latin *vitrum* glass]

vitriol ('vɪtrɪ,ɒl) *n* **1** another name for **sulphuric acid 2** any one of a number of sulphate salts, such as ferrous sulphate (**green vitriol**), copper sulphate (**blue vitriol**), or zinc sulphate (**white vitriol**) **3** speech, writing, etc, displaying rancour, vituperation, or bitterness ▷ *vb* -ols, -oling, -oled *or* -olling, -olled (*tr*) **4** to attack or injure with or as if with vitriol **5** to treat with vitriol [c14 from Medieval Latin *vitriolum*, from Late Latin *vitriolus* glassy, from Latin *vitrum* glass, referring to the glossy appearance of the sulphates]

vitriolic (,vɪtrɪ'ɒlɪk) *adj* **1** (of a substance, esp a strong acid) highly corrosive **2** severely bitter or caustic; virulent: *vitriolic criticism*

vitriolize *or* **vitriolise** ('vɪtrɪə,laɪz) *vb* (*tr*) **1** to convert into or treat with vitriol **2** to burn or injure with vitriol > ,vitrioli'zation *or* ,vitrioli'sation *n*

Vitruvian (vɪ'truːvɪən) *adj* of or relating to Marcus Vitruvius Pollio, the 1st century BC Roman architect

vitta ('vɪtə) *n, pl* -tae (-tiː) **1** any of numerous tubelike cavities containing oil or resin that occur in the fruits of certain plants, esp of parsley and other umbellifers **2** *biology* a band or stripe of colour [c17 from Latin: headband; related to *viēre* to plait] > 'vittate *adj*

vittle ('vɪtəl) *n, vb* an obsolete or dialect spelling of **victual**

vituline ('vɪtjʊ,laɪn, -lɪn) *adj* of or resembling a calf or veal [c17 from Latin *vitulīnus*, from *vitulus* a calf]

vituperate (vɪ'tjuːpə,reɪt) *vb* to berate or rail (against) abusively; revile [c16 from Latin *vituperāre* to blame, from *vitium* a defect + *parāre* to make] > vi'tuper,ator *n*

vituperation (vɪ,tjuːpə'reɪʃən) *n* **1** abusive language or venomous censure **2** the act of vituperating > vituperative (vɪ'tjuːpərətɪv, -prətɪv) *adj* > vi'tuperatively *adv*

viva¹ ('viːvə) *interj* long live; up with (a specified person or thing) [c17 from Italian, literally: may (he) live! from *vivere* to live, from Latin *vīvere*]

viva² ('vaɪvə) *Brit* ▷ *n* **1** an oral examination ▷ *vb* -vas, -vaing, -vaed (*tr*) **2** to examine orally [shortened from VIVA VOCE]

vivace (vɪ'vɑːtʃɪ) *adj, adv music* to be performed in a brisk lively manner [c17 from Italian, from Latin *vīvax* long-lived, vigorous, from *vīvere* to live]

vivacious (vɪ'veɪʃəs) *adj* **1** full of high spirits and animation; lively or vital **2** *obsolete* having or displaying tenacity of life [c17 from Latin *vīvax* lively; see VIVACE] > vi'vaciously *adv* > vi'vaciousness *n*

v

vivacity (vɪˈvæsɪtɪ) *n, pl* **-ties 1** the quality or condition of being vivacious **2** (*often plural*) *rare* a vivacious act or expression

vivandière *French* (vivãdjɛr) *n* (formerly) a female sutler or victualler offering extra provisions and spirits to soldiers, esp those of the French and British armies [C16 see VIAND]

vivarium (vaɪˈvɛərɪəm) *n, pl* **-iums** *or* **-ia** (-ɪə) a place where live animals are kept under natural conditions for study, research, etc [C16 from Latin: enclosure where live fish or game are kept, from *vīvus* alive]

viva voce (ˈvaɪvə ˈvəʊtʃɪ) *adv, adj* **1** by word of mouth ▷ *n, vb* **2** the full form of **viva²** [C16 from Medieval Latin, literally: with living voice]

vive (viːv) *interj* long live; up with (a specified person or thing) [from French]

viverrine (vaɪˈvɛraɪn) *adj* **1** of, relating to, or belonging to the *Viverridae*, a family of small to medium-sized predatory mammals of Eurasia and Africa, including genets, civets and mongooses: order *Carnivora* (carnivores) ▷ *n* **2** any animal belonging to the family *Viverridae* [C19 from New Latin *viverrīnus*, from Latin *viverra* a ferret]

Vivian (ˈvɪvɪən) *n* (in Arthurian legend) the mistress of Merlin, sometimes identified with the **Lady of the Lake**

vivid (ˈvɪvɪd) *adj* **1** (of a colour) very bright; having a very high saturation or purity; produced by a pure or almost pure colouring agent **2** brilliantly coloured: *vivid plumage* **3** conveying to the mind striking realism, freshness, or trueness to life; graphic: *a vivid account* **4** (of a recollection, memory, etc) remaining distinct in the mind **5** (of the imagination, etc) prolific in the formation of lifelike images **6** making a powerful impact on the emotions or senses: *a vivid feeling of shame* **7** uttered, operating, or acting with vigour: *vivid expostulations* **8** full of life or vitality: *a vivid personality* [C17 from Latin *vīvidus* animated, from *vīvere* to live] > ˈ**vividly** *adv* > ˈ**vividness** *n*

vivify (ˈvɪvɪˌfaɪ) *vb* **-fies, -fying, -fied** (*tr*) **1** to bring to life; animate **2** to make more vivid or striking [C16 from Late Latin *vīvificāre*, from Latin *vīvus* alive + *facere* to make] > ˌvivifiˈcation *n* > ˈviviˌfier *n*

viviparous (vɪˈvɪpərəs) *adj* **1** (of animals) producing offspring that as embryos develop within and derive nourishment from the body of the female parent. Compare **oviparous, ovoviviparous 2** (of plants) producing bulbils or young plants instead of flowers **3** (of seeds) germinating before separating from the parent plant [C17 from Latin *vīviparus*, from *vīvus* alive + *parere* to bring forth] > **viviparity** (ˌvɪvɪˈpærɪtɪ), viˈvipary, viˈviparism *or* viˈviparousness *n* > viˈviparously *adv*

vivisect (ˈvɪvɪˌsɛkt, ˌvɪvɪˈsɛkt) *vb* to subject (an animal) to vivisection [C19 back formation from VIVISECTION] > ˈviviˌsector *n*

vivisection (ˌvɪvɪˈsɛkʃən) *n* the act or practice of performing experiments on living animals, involving cutting into or dissecting the body [C18 from vivi-, from Latin *vīvus* living + SECTION, as in DISSECTION] > ˌviviˈsectional *adj* > ˌviviˈsectionally *adv*

vivisectionist (ˌvɪvɪˈsɛkʃənɪst) *n* **1** a person who practises vivisection **2** a person who advocates the practice of vivisection as being useful or necessary to science

vivo (ˈviːvəʊ) *adj, adv music* (*in combination*) with life and vigour: *allegro vivo* [Italian: lively]

vixen (ˈvɪksən) *n* **1** a female fox **2** a quarrelsome or spiteful woman [C15 *fixen*; related to Old English *fyxe*, feminine of FOX; compare Old High German *fuhsīn*] > ˈvixenish *adj* > ˈvixenishly *adv* > ˈvixenishness *n* > ˈvixenly *adv, adj*

Viyella (vaɪˈɛlə) *n trademark* a soft fabric made of wool and cotton, used esp for blouses and shirts

viz *abbreviation for* videlicet

Vizagapatam (vɪˌzæɡəˈpʌtəm) *n* a variant spelling of **Vishakhapatnam**

vizard (ˈvɪzəd) *n archaic or literary* a means of

disguise; mask; visor [C16 variant of VISOR] > ˈvizarded *adj*

vizcacha (vɪsˈkætʃə) *n* a variant spelling of **viscacha**

vizier (vɪˈzɪə) *n* a high official in certain Muslim countries, esp in the former Ottoman Empire. Viziers served in various capacities, such as that of provincial governor or chief minister to the sultan [C16 from Turkish *vezīr*, from Arabic *wazīr* porter, from *wazara* to bear a burden] > viˈzierial *or* viˈzirial *adj* > viˈziership *n*

vizierate (vɪˈzɪərɪt, -eɪt) *n* **1** the position, rank, or authority of a vizier **2** the term of office of a vizier

vizor (ˈvaɪzə) *n, vb* a variant spelling of **visor**

vizsla (ˈvɪʒlə) *n* a breed of Hungarian hunting dog with a smooth rusty-gold coat [C20 named after *Vizsla*, Hungary]

VJ *abbreviation for* **1** video jockey **2** *Austral* Vaucluse Junior: a type of small yacht

V-J Day *n* the day marking the Allied victory over Japan in World War II (Aug 15, 1945)

vl *abbreviation for* variant reading [from Latin *varia lectio*]

VL *abbreviation for* Vulgar Latin

VLA *astronomy abbreviation for* very large array

Vlaardingen (Dutch ˈvlaːrdɪŋə) *n* a port in the W Netherlands, in South Holland west of Rotterdam: the third largest port in the Netherlands. Pop: 74 000 (2003 est)

Vlach (vlɑːk) *or* **Walach** (ˈwɑːlɒk) *n* **1** a member of a people scattered throughout SE Europe in the early Middle Ages, speaking a Romanic dialect ▷ *adj* **2** of or relating to Vlachs or their dialect

Vladikavkaz (*Russian* vlədikafˈkas) *n* a city in S Russia, capital of the North Ossetian Republic on the N slopes of the Caucasus. Pop: 318 000 (2005 est). Former names: Dzaudzhikau (1944–54), Ordzhonikidze (1954–91)

Vladimir (*Russian* vlaˈdimir) *n* a city in W central Russia: capital of the principality of Vladimir until the court transferred to Moscow in 1328. Pop: 310 000 (2005 est)

Vladivostok (ˌvlædɪˈvɒstɒk; *Russian* vlədivasˈtɔk) *n* a port in SE Russia, on the Sea of Japan: terminus of the Trans-Siberian Railway; the main Russian Pacific naval base since 1872 and chief commercial and civilian Russian port in the Far East; university (1956). Pop: 584 000 (2005 est)

VLBI *astronomy abbreviation for* very long baseline interferometry

VLCC *abbreviation for* very large crude carrier: an oil tanker with a capacity between 200 000 and 400 000 tons

vlei (fleɪ, vleɪ) *n* **1** *South African* an area of low marshy ground, esp one that feeds a stream **2** *Northern US dialect* a marsh [C19 from Afrikaans (for sense 1); from obsolete N American Dutch dialect (for sense 2): VALLEY]

VLF *or* **vlf** *radio abbreviation for* **very low frequency**

Vlissingen (ˈvlɪsɪŋə) *n* the Dutch name for **Flushing**

Vlorë (*Albanian* ˈvlɔrə) *or* **Vlonë** (*Albanian* ˈvlɔnə) *n* a port in SW Albania, on the **Bay of Vlorë**: under Turkish rule from 1462 until Albanian independence was declared here in 1912. Pop: 76 000 (1991 est). Ancient name: Avlona. Also called: Valona

VLSI *computing abbreviation for* **very large-scale integration**

Vltava (*Czech* ˈvltava) *n* a river in the Czech Republic, rising in the Bohemian Forest and flowing generally southeast and then north to the River Elbe near Melnik. Length: 434 km (270 miles). German name: Moldau

v-mail (ˈviːmeɪl) *n* **1** a video message sent by e-mail **2** a computerized communication system designed to send virtual reality messages **3** electronic mail designed to spread a computer virus

VMD *abbreviation for* Doctor of Veterinary Medicine [Latin *veterinariae medicinae doctor*]

VMI *abbreviation for* vendor managed inventory: an inventory management system in which a supplier assumes responsibility for the timely replenishment of a customer's stock

vn *the internet domain name for* Vietnam

VN *international car registration for* Vietnam

V neck *n* a neck on a garment that comes down to a point on the throat or chest, resembling the shape of the letter "V" > 'V-ˌneck *or* 'V-ˌnecked *adj*

VO *abbreviation for* **1** very old: used to imply that a brandy or whisky is old; now often extended to port and other dessert wines **2** Royal Victorian Order

vo. *abbreviation for* verso

VOC *abbreviation for* volatile organic compound: one of a number of chemicals, including benzene and acetone, that evaporate or vaporize readily and are harmful to human health and the environment

voc. *or* **vocat.** *abbreviation for* vocative

vocab (ˈvəʊkæb) *n* short for **vocabulary**

vocable (ˈvəʊkəbʰl) *n* **1** any word, either written or spoken, regarded simply as a sequence of letters or spoken sounds, irrespective of its meaning **2** a vocal sound; vowel ▷ *adj* **3** capable of being uttered [C16 from Latin *vocābulum* a designation, from *vocāre* to call] > 'vocably *adv*

vocabulary (vəˈkæbjʊlərɪ) *n, pl* **-laries 1** a listing, either selective or exhaustive, containing the words and phrases of a language, with meanings or translations into another language; glossary **2** the aggregate of words in the use or comprehension of a specified person, class, profession, etc **3** all the words contained in a language **4** a range or system of symbols, qualities, or techniques constituting a means of communication or expression, as any of the arts or crafts: *a wide vocabulary of textures and colours* [C16 from Medieval Latin *vocābulārium*, from *vocābulārius* concerning words, from *vocābulum* VOCABLE]

vocal (ˈvəʊkʰl) *adj* **1** of, relating to, or designed for the voice: *vocal music* **2** produced or delivered by the voice: *vocal noises* **3** connected with an attribute or the production of the voice: *vocal organs* **4** frequently disposed to outspoken speech, criticism, etc: *a vocal minority* **5** full of sound or voices: *a vocal assembly* **6** endowed with a voice **7** eloquent or meaningful **8** *phonetics* **a** of or relating to a speech sound **b** of or relating to a voiced speech sound, esp a vowel ▷ *n* **9** a piece of jazz or pop music that is sung **10** a performance of such a piece of music [C14 from Latin *vōcālis* possessed of a voice, from *vōx* voice] > **vocality** (vəʊˈkælɪtɪ) > 'vocally *adv*

vocal cords *pl n* either of two pairs of mucomembranous folds in the larynx. The upper pair (**false vocal cords**) are not concerned with vocal production; the lower pair (**true vocal cords** or **vocal folds**) can be made to vibrate and produce sound when air from the lungs is forced over them. See also **glottis**. Related adj: **glottal**

vocal folds *pl n* See **vocal cords**

vocalic (vəʊˈkælɪk) *adj phonetics* of, relating to, or containing a vowel or vowels

vocalise (ˌvəʊkəˈliːz) *n* a musical passage sung upon one vowel as an exercise to develop flexibility and control of pitch and tone; solfeggio

vocalism (ˈvəʊkəˌlɪzəm) *n* **1** the exercise of the voice, as in singing or speaking **2** singing, esp in respect to technique or skill **3** *phonetics* **a** a voiced speech sound, esp a vowel **b** a system of vowels as used in a language

vocalist (ˈvəʊkəlɪst) *n* a singer, esp one who regularly appears with a jazz band or pop group

vocalize *or* **vocalise** (ˈvəʊkəˌlaɪz) *vb* **1** to express with or use the voice; articulate (a speech, song, etc) **2** (*tr*) to make vocal or articulate **3** (*tr*) *phonetics* **a** to articulate (a speech sound) with voice **b** to change (a consonant) into a vowel **4** another word for **vowelize 5** (*intr*) to sing a melody on a vowel, etc > ˌvocaliˈzation *or* ˌvocaliˈsation *n* > 'vocalˌizer *or* 'vocalˌiser *n*

vocal sac n zoology either of the loose folds of skin on each side of the mouth in many male frogs that can be inflated and act as resonators

vocal score n a musical score that shows voice parts in full and orchestral parts in the form of a piano transcription

vocation (vəʊˈkeɪʃən) n 1 a specified occupation, profession, or trade 2 a a special urge, inclination, or predisposition to a particular calling or career, esp a religious one b such a calling or career [c15 from Latin *vocātiō* a calling, from *vocāre* to call]

vocational (vəʊˈkeɪʃənəl) adj 1 of or relating to a vocation or vocations 2 of or relating to applied educational courses concerned with skills needed for an occupation, trade, or profession: *vocational training* > voˈcationally adv

vocational guidance n a guidance service based on psychological tests and interviews to find out what career or occupation may best suit a person

vocative (ˈvɒkətɪv) adj 1 relating to, used in, or characterized by calling 2 grammar denoting a case of nouns, in some inflected languages, used when the referent of the noun is being addressed ▷ n 3 grammar a the vocative case b a vocative noun or speech element [c15 from Latin phrase *vocātīvus cāsus* the calling case, from *vocāre* to call] > 'vocatively adv

voces (ˈvəʊsiːz) n the plural of vox

vociferant (vəʊˈsɪfərənt) adj 1 a less common word for vociferous ▷ n 2 rare a vociferous person [c17 from Latin *vōciferārī* to bawl; see VOCIFERATE] > voˈciferance n

vociferate (vəʊˈsɪfəˌreɪt) vb to exclaim or cry out about (something) clamorously, vehemently, or insistently [c17 from Latin *vōciferārī* to clamour, from *vōx* voice + *ferre* to bear] > voˌciferˈation n

vociferous (vəʊˈsɪfərəs) adj 1 characterized by vehemence, clamour, or noisiness: *vociferous protests* 2 making an outcry or loud noises; clamorous: *a vociferous mob* > voˈciferously adv > voˈciferousness n

vocoder (ˈvəʊˌkəʊdə) n music a type of synthesizer that uses the human voice as an oscillator

vodka (ˈvɒdkə) n an alcoholic drink originating in Russia, made from grain, potatoes, etc, usually consisting only of rectified spirit and water [c19 from Russian, diminutive of *voda* water; related to Sanskrit *udan* water, Greek *hudōr*]

voe (vəʊ; Scot vo) n (in Orkney and Shetland) a small bay or narrow creek [c17 from Old Norse *vagr*]

voema (ˈvʊmə) n South African informal vigour or energy [c20 Afrikaans]

voetsek, voetsak (ˈfʊtsak, ˈvʊt-) or **voertsek, voertsak** (ˈfʊrtsak, ˈvʊrt-) interj South African offensive, informal an expression of dismissal or rejection [c19 Afrikaans, from Dutch *voort se ek* forward, I say, commonly applied to animals]

voetstoots or **voetstoets** (ˈfʊtstʊts, ˈvʊt-) South African ▷ adj 1 denoting a sale in which the vendor is freed from all responsibility for the condition of the goods being sold ▷ adv 2 without responsibility for the condition of the goods sold [from Afrikaans *voetstoots* as it is]

vogue (vəʊg) n 1 the popular style at a specified time (esp in the phrase in vogue) 2 a period of general or popular usage or favour: *the vogue for such dances is now over* ▷ adj 3 (usually prenominal) popular or fashionable: *a vogue word* [c16 from French: a rowing, fashion, from Old Italian *voga*, from *vogare* to row, of unknown origin] > 'voguish adj

vogueing (ˈvəʊgɪn) n a dance style of the late 1980s, in which a fashion model's movements and postures are imitated in a highly stylized manner [c20 from *Vogue* magazine]

Vogul (ˈvəʊgəl) n 1 (pl -gul or -guls) a member of a people living in W Siberia and NE Europe 2 the language of this people, belonging to the Finno-Ugric family: related to Hungarian

voice (vɔɪs) n 1 the sound made by the vibration of the vocal cords, esp when modified by the resonant effect of the tongue and mouth. See also speech. Related adj: vocal 2 the natural and distinctive tone of the speech sounds characteristic of a particular person: *nobody could mistake his voice* 3 the condition, quality, effectiveness, or tone of such sounds: *a hysterical voice* 4 the musical sound of a singing voice, with respect to its quality or tone: *she has a lovely voice* 5 the ability to speak, sing, etc: *he has lost his voice* 6 a sound resembling or suggestive of vocal utterance: *the voice of the sea; the voice of hard experience* 7 written or spoken expression, as of feeling, opinion, etc (esp in the phrase give voice to) 8 a stated choice, wish, or opinion or the power or right to have an opinion heard and considered: *to give someone a voice in a decision* 9 an agency through which is communicated another's purpose, policy, etc: *such groups are the voice of our enemies* 10 music a musical notes produced by vibrations of the vocal cords at various frequencies and in certain registers: *a tenor voice* b (in harmony) an independent melodic line or part: *a fugue in five voices* 11 phonetics the sound characterizing the articulation of several speech sounds, including all vowels or sonants, that is produced when the vocal cords make loose contact with each other and are set in vibration by the breath as it forces its way through the glottis 12 grammar a category of the verb or verbal inflections that expresses whether the relation between the subject and the verb is that of agent and action, action and recipient, or some other relation. See active (sense 5), passive (sense 5), middle (sense 5) 13 obsolete rumour 14 (foll by of) obsolete fame; renown 15 in voice in a condition to sing or speak well 16 out of voice with the voice temporarily in a poor condition, esp for singing 17 with one voice unanimously ▷ vb (tr) 18 to utter in words; give expression to: *to voice a complaint* 19 to articulate (a speech sound) with voice 20 music to adjust (a wind instrument or organ pipe) so that it conforms to the correct standards of tone colour, pitch, etc 21 to provide the voice for (a puppet or cartoon character) in an animated film [c13 from Old French *voiz*, from Latin *vōx*] > 'voicer n

voice box n 1 another word for the larynx. Related adj: laryngeal 2 Also called: talkbox an electronic guitar attachment with a tube into the player's mouth to modulate the sound vocally

voiced (vɔɪst) adj 1 declared or expressed by the voice 2 (in combination) having a voice as specified: *loud-voiced* 3 phonetics articulated with accompanying vibration of the vocal cords: *in English (b) is a voiced consonant*. Compare voiceless

voiceful (ˈvɔɪsfʊl) adj poetic 1 endowed with a voice, esp of loud quality 2 full of voices > 'voicefulness n

voice input n the control and operation of computer systems by spoken commands

voice-leading (ˈvɔɪsˌliːdɪŋ) n US another term for part-writing

voiceless (ˈvɔɪslɪs) adj 1 without a voice; mute 2 not articulated: *voiceless misery* 3 lacking a musical voice 4 silent 5 without the power or right to express an opinion 6 phonetics articulated without accompanying vibration of the vocal cords: *in English (p) is a voiceless consonant* > 'voicelessly adv > 'voicelessness n

voice-lift n a cosmetic surgical operation on the vocal cords to make the voice sound younger

voice mail n an electronic system for the transfer and storage of telephone messages, which can then be dealt with by the user at his or her convenience

voice-over n the voice of an unseen commentator heard during a film, television programme, etc

voice over broadband n a transmission technique that enables a user to make and receive telephone calls over a broadband connection

voice part n a melodic line written for the voice

voiceprint (ˈvɔɪsˌprɪnt) n a graphic representation of a person's voice recorded electronically, usually having time plotted along the horizontal axis and the frequency of the speech on the vertical axis

voice recognition n the control of a computer system by a voice or voices that the computer has been instructed to accept

voice response n output of information from a computer system in the form of speech rather than displayed text

voice vote n a vote taken in a legislative body by calling for the ayes and the noes and estimating which faction is more numerous from the volume of the noise

void (vɔɪd) adj 1 without contents; empty 2 not legally binding: *null and void* 3 (of an office, house, position, etc) without an incumbent; unoccupied 4 (postpositive; foll by of) destitute or devoid: *void of resources* 5 having no effect; useless: *all his efforts were rendered void* 6 (of a card suit or player) having no cards in a particular suit: *his spades were void* ▷ n 7 an empty space or area: *the huge desert voids of Asia* 8 a feeling or condition of loneliness or deprivation: *his divorce left him in a void* 9 a lack of any cards in one suit: *to have a void in spades* 10 Also called: counter the inside area of a character of type, such as the inside of an o ▷ vb (mainly tr) 11 to make ineffective or invalid 12 to empty (contents, etc) or make empty of contents 13 (also intr) to discharge the contents of (the bowels or urinary bladder) 14 archaic to vacate (a place, room, etc) 15 obsolete to expel [c13 from Old French *vuide*, from Vulgar Latin *vocītus* (unattested), from Latin *vacuus* empty, from *vacāre* to be empty] > 'voider n > 'voidness n

voidable (ˈvɔɪdəbəl) adj 1 capable of being voided 2 capable of being made of no legal effect or made void > 'voidableness n

voidance (ˈvɔɪdəns) n 1 an annulment, as of a contract 2 the condition of being vacant, as an office, benefice, etc 3 the act of voiding, ejecting, or evacuating [c14 variant of AVOIDANCE]

voided (ˈvɔɪdɪd) adj 1 heraldry (of a design) with a hole in the centre of the same shape as the design: *a voided lozenge* 2 rare having a void or made void

voile (vɔɪl; French vwal) n a light semitransparent fabric of silk, rayon, cotton, etc, used for dresses, scarves, shirts, etc [c19 from French: VEIL]

Voiotia (Greek vjɔˈtiːa) n a department of E central Greece: corresponds to ancient Boeotia and part of ancient Phocis. Pop: 123 913 (2001). Area: 3173 sq km (1225 sq miles)

voir dire (vwɑː ˈdɪə) n law 1 the preliminary examination on oath of a proposed witness by the judge 2 the oath administered to such a witness [c17 from Old French: to speak the truth]

voix céleste (vwɑː sɛˈlɛst) n an organ stop which produces a tremolo effect through the acoustic phenomenon of beats [from French: heavenly voice]

Vojvodina or **Voivodina** (Serbo-Croat ˈvɔjvɔdina) n an autonomous region of NE Serbia and Montenegro, in N Serbia. Capital: Novi Sad. Pop: 2 024 487 (2002). Area: 22 489 sq km (8683 sq miles)

vol. abbreviation for 1 volcano 2 volume 3 volunteer

Volans (ˈvəʊlænz) n, Latin genitive Volantis (vəʊˈlæntɪs) a small constellation in the S hemisphere lying between Carina and Hydrus [c19 from Latin, literally: flying, from *volāre* to fly]

volant (ˈvəʊlənt) adj 1 (usually postpositive) heraldry in a flying position 2 rare flying or capable of flight 3 poetic moving lightly or agilely; nimble [c16 from French: flying, from *voler* to fly, from Latin *volāre*]

Volapük or **Volapuk** (ˈvɒləˌpʊk) n an artificial language based on English, French, German, Latin, etc, invented by Johann Schleyer (1831–1912) in 1880 [c19 from *vol*, based on WORLD + euphonic -a- + *pük* speech, based on SPEAK]

volar ('vəʊlə) *adj anatomy* of or relating to the palm of the hand or the sole of the foot [c19 from Latin *vola* hollow of the hand, palm, sole of the foot]

volatile ('vɒlə,taɪl) *adj* **1** (of a substance) capable of readily changing from a solid or liquid form to a vapour; having a high vapour pressure and a low boiling point **2** (of persons) disposed to caprice or inconstancy; fickle; mercurial **3** (of circumstances) liable to sudden, unpredictable, or explosive change **4** lasting only a short time **5** *computing* (of a memory) not retaining stored information when the power supply is cut off **6** *obsolete* flying or capable of flight; volant ⊳ *n* **7** a volatile substance **8** *rare* a winged creature [c17 from Latin *volātilis* flying, from *volāre* to fly] > 'volatileness *or* volatility (,vɒlə'tɪlɪtɪ) *n*

volatile oil *n* another name for **essential oil**

volatile salt *n* another name for **sal volatile**

volatilize *or* **volatilise** (vɒ'lætɪ,laɪz) *vb* to change or cause to change from a solid or liquid to a vapour > vo'lati,lizable *or* vo'lati,lisable *adj* > vo,latili'zation *or* vo,latilis'ation *n*

vol-au-vent (*French* vɔlovɑ̃) *n* a very light puff pastry case filled either with a savoury mixture in a richly flavoured sauce or sometimes with fruit [c19 from French, literally: flight in the wind]

volcanic (vɒl'kænɪk) *adj* **1** of, relating to, produced by, or characterized by the presence of volcanoes: *a volcanic region* **2** suggestive of or resembling an erupting volcano: *a volcanic era* **3** another word for **extrusive** (sense 2) > vol'canically *adv* > volcanicity (,vɒlkə'nɪsɪtɪ) *n*

volcanic bomb *n* See **bomb** (sense 4)

volcanic glass *n* any of several glassy volcanic igneous rocks, such as obsidian and pitchstone

volcanism ('vɒlkə,nɪzəm) *or* **vulcanism** *n* those processes collectively that result in the formation of volcanoes and their products

volcanize *or* **volcanise** ('vɒlkə,naɪz) *vb* (*tr*) to subject to the effects of or change by volcanic heat > ,volcani'zation *or* ,volcani'sation *n*

volcano (vɒl'keɪnəʊ) *n, pl* **-noes** *or* **-nos** **1** an opening in the earth's crust from which molten lava, rock fragments, ashes, dust, and gases are ejected from below the earth's surface **2** a mountain formed from volcanic material ejected from a vent in a central crater [c17 from Italian, from Latin *Volcānus* VULCAN[1], whose forges were believed to be responsible for volcanic rumblings]

Volcano Islands *pl n* a group of three volcanic islands in the W Pacific, about 1100 km (700 miles) south of Japan: the largest is Iwo Jima, taken by US forces in 1945 and returned to Japan in 1968. Area: about 28 sq km (11 sq miles). Japanese name: **Kazan Retto**

volcanology (,vɒlkə'nɒlədʒɪ) *or* **vulcanology** *n* the study of volcanoes and volcanic phenomena > volcanological (,vɒlkənə'lɒdʒɪkəl) *or* ,vulcano'logical *adj* > ,volcan'ologist *or* ,vulcan'ologist *n*

vole[1] (vəʊl) *n* any of numerous small rodents of the genus *Microtus* and related genera, mostly of Eurasia and North America and having a stocky body, short tail, and inconspicuous ears: family Cricetidae. See also **water vole** [c19 short for *volemouse*, from Old Norse *vollr* field + *mus* MOUSE; related to Icelandic *vollarmus*]

vole[2] (vəʊl) *n* (in some card games, such as écarté) the taking of all the tricks in a deal, thus scoring extra points [c17 from French, from *voler* to fly, from Latin *volāre*]

Volga ('vɒlgə) *n* a river in W Russia, rising in the Valdai Range and flowing through a chain of small lakes to the Rybinsk Reservoir and south to the Caspian Sea through Volgograd: the longest river in Europe. Length: 3690 km (2293 miles)

Volgograd (*Russian* vəlga'grat; *English* 'vɒlgə,græd) *n* a port in SW Russia, on the River Volga: scene of a major engagement (1918) during the civil war and again in World War II (1942–43), in which the German forces were defeated; major industrial

centre. Pop: 1 016 000 (2005 est). Former names: Tsaritsyn (until 1925), Stalingrad (1925–61)

volitant ('vɒlɪtənt) *adj* **1** flying or moving about rapidly **2** capable of flying [c19 from Latin *volitāre* to flit, from *volāre* to fly]

volition (və'lɪʃən) *n* **1** the act of exercising the will: *of one's own volition* **2** the faculty or capability of conscious choice, decision, and intention; the will **3** the resulting choice or resolution **4** *philosophy* an act of will as distinguished from the physical movement it intends to bring about [c17 from Medieval Latin *volitiō*, from Latin *vol-* as in *volō* I will, present stem of *velle* to wish] > vo'litional *or* vo'litionary *adj* > vo'litionally *adv*

volitive ('vɒlɪtɪv) *adj* **1** of, relating to, or emanating from the will **2** *grammar* another word for **desiderative**

volk (fɒlk) *n South African* the people or nation, esp the nation of Afrikaners [Afrikaans]

Völkerwanderung German ('fœlkərvandərʊŋ) *n* the migration of peoples, esp of Germanic and Slavic peoples into S and W Europe from 2nd to 11th centuries [literally: nations wandering, German translation of Latin *migrātiō gentium*]

Volkslied German ('fɒlksliːt) *n, pl* **-lieder** (-liːdər) a type of popular German folk song [literally: folk song]

Volksraad ('fɒlks,raːt) *n South African* the legislative assembly of the Boer republics in South Africa during the latter half of the 19th century [Afrikaans *volk* people + *raad* council]

volley ('vɒlɪ) *n* **1** the simultaneous discharge of several weapons, esp firearms **2** the projectiles or missiles so discharged **3** a burst of oaths, protests, etc, occurring simultaneously or in rapid succession **4** *sport* a stroke, shot, or kick at a moving ball before it hits the ground. Compare **half volley 5** *cricket* the flight of such a ball or the ball itself **6** the simultaneous explosion of several blastings of rock ⊳ *vb* **7** to discharge (weapons, etc) or to as if in a volley or (of weapons, etc) to be discharged **8** (*tr*) to utter vehemently or sound loudly and continuously **9** (*tr*) *sport* to strike or kick (a moving ball) before it hits the ground **10** (*intr*) to issue or move rapidly or indiscriminately [c16 from French *volée* a flight, from *voler* to fly, from Latin *volāre*] > 'volleyer *n*

volleyball ('vɒlɪ,bɔːl) *n* **1** a game in which two teams hit a large ball back and forth over a high net with their hands **2** the ball used in this game

Vologda (*Russian* 'vɒləgdə) *n* an industrial city in W central Russia. Pop: 295 000 (2005 est)

Vólos (*Greek* 'vɒlɔs) *n* a port in E Greece, in Thessaly on the **Gulf of Volos** (an inlet of the Aegean): the third largest port in Greece. Pop: 129 000 (2005 est)

volost ('vɒʊlɒst) *n* **1** (in the former Soviet Union) a rural soviet **2** (in tsarist Russia) a peasant community consisting of several villages or hamlets [from Russian]

vols. *abbreviation for* **volumes**

Volsci ('vɒlskiː) *pl n* a warlike people of ancient Latium, subdued by Rome in the fifth and fourth centuries BC

Volscian ('vɒlskɪən) *n* **1** a member of the Volsci **2** the extinct language of the Volsci, closely related to Umbrian ⊳ *adj* **3** of or relating to the Volsci or their language

Volsung ('vɒlsʊŋ) *n* **1** a great hero of Norse and Germanic legend and poetry who gave his name to a race of warriors; father of Sigmund and Signy **2** any member of his family

Volsunga Saga ('vɒlsʊŋə) *n* a 13th-century Icelandic saga about the family of the Volsungs and the deeds of Sigurd, related in theme and story to the Nibelungenlied

volt[1] (vəʊlt) *n* the derived SI unit of electric potential; the potential difference between two points on a conductor carrying a current of 1 ampere, when the power dissipated between these points is 1 watt. Symbol: V [c19 named after Count Alessandro *Volta* (1745–1827), Italian

physicist]

volt[2] *or* **volte** (vɒlt) *n* **1** a small circle of determined size executed in dressage **2** a leap made in fencing to avoid an opponent's thrust [c17 from French *volte*, from Italian *volta* a turn, ultimately from Latin *volvere* to turn]

volta ('vɒltə; *Italian* 'vɔlta) *n, pl* **-te** (*Italian* -te) **1** a quick-moving Italian dance popular during the 16th and 17th centuries **2** a piece of music written for or in the rhythm of this dance, in triple time [c17 from Italian: turn; see VOLTE[2]]

Volta ('vɒltə) *n* **1** a river in W Africa, formed by the confluence of the **Black Volta** and the **White Volta** in N central Ghana: flows south to the Bight of Benin: the chief river of Ghana. Length: 480 km (300 miles); (including the Black Volta) 1600 km (1000 miles) **2 Lake** an artificial lake in Ghana, extending 408 km (250 miles) upstream from the **Volta River Dam** on the Volta River: completed in 1966. Area: 8482 sq km (3275 sq miles)

voltage ('vəʊltɪdʒ) *n* an electromotive force or potential difference expressed in volts

voltage divider *n* another name for a **potential divider**

voltaic (vɒl'teɪɪk) *adj* another word for **galvanic** (sense 1)

Voltaic (vɒl'teɪɪk) *adj* **1** of or relating to Burkina-Faso, formerly known as Upper Volta **2** denoting, belonging to, or relating to the Gur group of African languages ⊳ *n* **3** this group of languages. See also **Gur**

voltaic cell *n* another name for **primary cell**

voltaic couple *n physics* a pair of dissimilar metals in an electrolyte with a potential difference between the metals resulting from chemical action

voltaic pile *n* an early form of battery consisting of a pile of paired plates of dissimilar metals, such as zinc and copper, each pair being separated from the next by a pad moistened with an electrolyte. Also called: **pile, galvanic pile, Volta's pile**

Voltairean *or* **Voltairian** (vɒl'tɛərɪən, vəʊl-) *adj* of or relating to Voltaire (pseudonym of *François Marie Arouet*), the French writer (1694–1778)

voltaism ('vɒltə,ɪzəm) *n* another name for **galvanism**

voltameter (vɒl'tæmɪtə) *n* another name for **coulometer**. > voltametric (,vɒltə'mɛtrɪk) *adj*

voltammeter (,vəʊlt'æm,miːtə) *n* a dual-purpose instrument that can measure both potential difference and electric current, usually in volts and amperes respectively

volt-ampere ('vəʊlt'æmpɛə) *n* the product of the potential in volts across an electrical circuit and the resultant current in amperes. Abbreviation: VA

Volta Redonda (*Portuguese* 'vɒltə rə'dõdə) *n* a city in SE Brazil, in Rio de Janeiro state on the Paraíba River: founded in 1941; site of South America's largest steelworks. Pop: 419 000 (2005 est)

volte (vɒlt) *n* a variant spelling of **volt[2]**

volte-face ('vɒlt'faːs) *n, pl* **volte-face 1** a reversal, as in opinion or policy **2** a change of position so as to look, lie, etc, in the opposite direction [c19 from French, from Italian *volta-faccia*, from *volta* a turn + *faccia* face]

voltmeter ('vəʊlt,miːtə) *n* an instrument for measuring potential difference or electromotive force

Volturno (*Italian* vol'turno) *n* a river in S central Italy, flowing southeast and southwest to the Tyrrhenian Sea: scene of a battle (1860) during the wars for Italian unity, in which Garibaldi defeated the Neapolitans; German line of defence during World War II. Length: 175 km (109 miles)

voluble ('vɒljʊbəl) *adj* **1** talking easily, readily, and at length; fluent **2** *archaic* easily turning or rotating, as on an axis **3** *rare* (of a plant) twining or twisting [c16 from Latin *volūbilis* turning readily, fluent, from *volvere* to turn] > ,volu'bility *or* 'volubleness *n* > 'volubly *adv*

volume ('vɒljuːm) *n* **1** the magnitude of the

three-dimensional space enclosed within or occupied by an object, geometric solid, etc. Symbol: *V* **2** a large mass or quantity: *the volume of protest* **3** an amount or total: *the volume of exports* **4** fullness or intensity of tone or sound **5** the control on a radio, etc, for adjusting the intensity of sound **6** a bound collection of printed or written pages; book **7** any of several books either bound in an identical format or part of a series **8** the complete set of issues of a periodical over a specified period, esp one year **9** *history* a roll or scroll of parchment, papyrus, etc **10 speak volumes** to convey much significant information ▷ Abbreviations (for senses 6–8): **v**, **vol** [c14 from Old French *volum*, from Latin *volūmen* a roll, book, from *volvere* to roll up]

volumed (ˈvɒljuːmd) *adj* **1** (of literary works) **a** consisting of or being in volumes **b** (*in combination*): *a three-volumed history* **2** *rare* having bulk or volume **3** *poetic* forming a rounded mass

volumeter (vɒˈljuːmɪtə) *n* any instrument for measuring the volume of a solid, liquid, or gas

volumetric (ˌvɒljʊˈmɛtrɪk) *adj* of, concerning, or using measurement by volume: *volumetric analysis*. Compare **gravimetric**. > ˌvolu'metrically *adv* > volumetry (vɒˈljuːmɪtrɪ) *n*

volumetric analysis *n chem* **1** quantitative analysis of liquids or solutions by comparing the volumes that react with known volumes of standard reagents, usually by titration. Compare **gravimetric analysis 2** quantitative analysis of gases by volume

volumetric displacement *n* the volume of air per revolution that passes through a mechanical pump when the pressure at the intake and the exhaust is the same as that of the atmosphere. Also called: **swept volume**

volumetric efficiency *n* **1** the ratio of fluid delivered by a piston or ram pump per stroke to the displacement volume of the piston or ram **2** the ratio of air or gas-air mixture drawn into the cylinder of an internal-combustion engine to the volumetric displacement of the piston

voluminous (vəˈluːmɪnəs) *adj* **1** of great size, quantity, volume, or extent **2** (of writing) consisting of or sufficient to fill volumes **3** prolific in writing or speech **4** *obsolete* winding [c17 from Late Latin *volūminōsus* full of windings, from *volūmen* VOLUME] > voluminosity (vəˌluːmɪˈnɒsɪtɪ) *or* vo'luminousness *n* > vo'luminously *adv*

Völund (ˈvøːlʊnd) *n* the Scandinavian name of **Wayland**

voluntarism (ˈvɒləntəˌrɪzəm) *n* **1** *philosophy* the theory that the will rather than the intellect is the ultimate principle of reality **2** a doctrine or system based on voluntary participation in a course of action **3** the belief that the state, government, and the law should not interfere with the procedures of collective bargaining and of trade union organization **4** another name for **voluntaryism** > 'voluntarist *n, adj* > ˌvolunta'ristic *adj*

voluntary (ˈvɒləntərɪ, -trɪ) *adj* **1** performed, undertaken, or brought about by free choice, willingly, or without being asked: *a voluntary donation* **2** (of persons) serving or acting in a specified function of one's own accord and without compulsion or promise of remuneration: *a voluntary social worker* **3** done by, composed of, or functioning with the aid of volunteers: *a voluntary association* **4** endowed with, exercising, or having the faculty of willing: *a voluntary agent* **5** arising from natural impulse; spontaneous: *voluntary laughter* **6** *law* **a** acting or done without legal obligation, compulsion, or persuasion **b** made without payment or recompense in any form: *a voluntary conveyance* **7** (of the muscles of the limbs, neck, etc) having their action controlled by the will **8** maintained or provided by the voluntary actions or contributions of individuals and not by the state: *voluntary schools; the voluntary system* ▷ *n, pl*

-taries **9** *music* a composition or improvisation, usually for organ, played at the beginning or end of a church service **10** work done without compulsion **11** *obsolete* a volunteer, esp in an army [c14 from Latin *voluntārius*, from *voluntās* will, from *velle* to wish] > volun'tarily *adv* > 'voluntariness *n*

Voluntary Aid Detachment *n* (in World War I) an organization of British women volunteers who assisted in military hospitals and ambulance duties. Abbreviation: **VAD**

voluntary arrangement *n law* a procedure enabling an insolvent company to come to an arrangement with its creditors and resolve its financial problems, often in compliance with a court order

voluntaryism (ˈvɒləntərɪˌɪzəm, -trɪ-) *or* **voluntarism** *n* **1** the principle of supporting churches, schools, and various other institutions by voluntary contributions rather than with state funds **2** any system based on this principle > 'voluntaryist *or* 'voluntarist *n*

voluntary retailer *n* another name for **symbol retailer**

volunteer (ˌvɒlənˈtɪə) *n* **1 a** a person who performs or offers to perform voluntary service **b** (*as modifier*): *a volunteer system; volunteer advice* **2** a person who freely undertakes military service, esp temporary or special service **3** *law* **a** a person who does some act or enters into a transaction without being under any legal obligation to do so and without being promised any remuneration for his services **b** *property law* a person to whom property is transferred without his giving any valuable consideration in return, as a legatee under a will **4 a** a plant that grows from seed that has not been deliberately sown **b** (*as modifier*): *a volunteer plant* ▷ *vb* **5** to offer (oneself or one's services) for an undertaking by choice and without request or obligation **6** (*tr*) to perform, give, or communicate voluntarily: *to volunteer help; to volunteer a speech* **7** (*intr*) to enlist voluntarily for military service [c17 from French *volontaire*, from Latin *voluntārius* willing; see VOLUNTARY]

volunteer bureau *n* (*often capitals*) (in Britain) *social welfare* an agency that matches up people wishing to do voluntary work with appropriate voluntary organizations

volunteerism (ˌvɒlənˈtɪərɪzəm) *n* the principle of donating time and energy for the benefit of other people in the community as a social responsibility rather than for any financial reward

Volunteers of America *pl n* a religious body aimed at reform and relief of human need and resembling the Salvation Army in organization and tenets, founded in New York City in 1896 by Ballington Booth

voluptuary (vəˈlʌptjʊərɪ) *n, pl* -aries **1** a person devoted or addicted to luxury and sensual pleasures ▷ *adj* **2** of, relating to, characterized by, or furthering sensual gratification or luxury [c17 from Late Latin *voluptuārius* delightful, from Latin *voluptās* pleasure]

voluptuous (vəˈlʌptjʊəs) *adj* **1** relating to, characterized by, or consisting of pleasures of the body or senses; sensual **2** disposed, devoted, or addicted to sensual indulgence or luxurious pleasures **3** provocative and sexually alluring, esp through shapeliness or fullness: *a voluptuous woman* [c14 from Latin *voluptuōsus* full of gratification, from *voluptās* pleasure] > vo'luptuously *adv* > vo'luptuousness *n*

volute (vəˈljuːt, vəˈluːt) *n* **1** a spiral or twisting turn, form, or object; spiral; whorl **2** Also called: **helix** a carved ornament, esp as used on an Ionic capital, that has the form of a spiral scroll **3** any of the whorls of the spirally coiled shell of a snail or similar gastropod mollusc **4** any tropical marine gastropod mollusc of the family *Volutidae*, typically having a spiral shell with beautiful markings **5** a tangential part, resembling the volute of a snail's shell, that collects the fluids emerging from the periphery of a turbine,

impeller pump, etc ▷ *adj also* **voluted** (vəˈluːtɪd) **6** having the form of a volute; spiral **7** *machinery* moving in a spiral path [c17 from Latin *volūta* a spiral decoration, from *volūtus* rolled, from *volvere* to roll up]

volution (vəˈluːʃən) *n* **1** a rolling, revolving, or spiral form or motion **2** a whorl of a spiral gastropod shell

volva (ˈvɒlvə) *n, pl* -vae (-viː) *or* -vas *botany* a cup-shaped structure that sheathes the base of the stalk of certain mushrooms [c18 from Latin: a covering, from *volvere* to wrap] > volvate (ˈvɒlvɪt, -veɪt) *adj*

volvox (ˈvɒlvɒks) *n* any freshwater flagellate protozoan of the genus *Volvox*, occurring in colonies in the form of hollow multicellular spheres [c18 from New Latin, from Latin *volvere* to roll]

volvulus (ˈvɒlvjʊləs) *n, pl* -luses *pathol* an abnormal twisting of the intestines causing obstruction [c17 from New Latin, from Latin *volvere* to twist]

vomer (ˈvəʊmə) *n* the thin flat bone forming part of the separation between the nasal passages in mammals [c18 from Latin: ploughshare] > vomerine (ˈvəʊməˌraɪn, -rɪn, ˈvɒm-) *adj*

vomit (ˈvɒmɪt) *vb* -its, -iting, -ited **1** to eject (the contents of the stomach) through the mouth as the result of involuntary muscular spasms of the stomach and oesophagus **2** to eject or be ejected forcefully; spew forth ▷ *n* **3** the matter ejected in vomiting **4** the act of vomiting **5** a drug or agent that induces vomiting; emetic. See **emesis** [c14 from Latin *vomitāre* to vomit repeatedly, from *vomere* to vomit] > 'vomiter *n*

vomit comet *n informal* an aircraft that dives suddenly in altitude, simulating freefall, in order to allow astronauts to experience the nausea that can affect people in a gravity-free environment

vomitory (ˈvɒmɪtərɪ, -trɪ) *adj* **1** Also: **vomitive** (ˈvɒmɪtɪv) causing vomiting; emetic ▷ *n, pl* -ries **2** Also called: **vomitive** a vomitory agent **3** *rare* a container for receiving vomitus **4** Also called: **vomitorium** (ˌvɒmɪˈtɔːrɪəm) a passageway in an ancient Roman amphitheatre that connects an outside entrance to a tier of seats **5** an opening through which matter is ejected

vomitous (ˈvɒmɪtəs) *adj* **1** arousing feelings of disgust: *a vomitous ending* **2** relating or connected to feeling or being sick: *a vomitous night on the town*

vomiturition (ˌvɒmɪtjʊˈrɪʃən) *n* the act of retching

vomitus (ˈvɒmɪtəs) *n, pl* -tuses **1** matter that has been vomited **2** the act of vomiting [Latin: a vomiting]

voodoo (ˈvuːduː) *n, pl* -doos **1** Also called: **voodooism** a religious cult involving witchcraft and communication by trance with ancestors and animistic deities, common in Haiti and other Caribbean islands **2** a person who practises voodoo **3** a charm, spell, or fetish involved in voodoo worship and ritual ▷ *adj* **4** relating to or associated with voodoo ▷ *vb* -doos, -dooing, -dooed **5** (*tr*) to affect by or as if by the power of voodoo [c19 from Louisiana French *voudou*, ultimately of West African origin; compare Ewe *vodu* guardian spirit] > 'voodooist *n* > ˌvoodoo'istic *adj*

voorkamer (ˈfʊəˌkɑːmə) *n South African* the front room, esp of a Cape Dutch house or farmhouse [from Afrikaans *voor* front + *kamer* room]

voorskot (ˈfʊəˌskɒt) *n South African* advance payment made to a farmer for crops. Compare **agterskot** [c20 Afrikaans, from *voor* before + *skot* shot, payment]

Voortrekker (ˈfʊəˌtrɛkə, ˈvʊə-) *n* (in South Africa) **1** one of the original Afrikaner settlers of the Transvaal and the Orange Free State who migrated from the Cape Colony in the 1830s **2** a member of the Afrikaner youth movement founded in 1931 [c19 from Dutch, from *voor-* FORE- + *trekken* to TREK]

V

voracious (vɒˈreɪʃəs) *adj* **1** devouring or craving food in great quantities **2** very eager or unremitting in some activity: *voracious reading* [C17 from Latin *vorāx* swallowing greedily, from *vorāre* to devour] > voˈraciously *adv* > **voracity** (vɒˈræsɪtɪ) *or* voˈraciousness *n*

Vorarlberg (*German* ˈfoːrarlbɛrk) *n* a mountainous state of W Austria. Capital: Bregenz. Pop: 356 590 (2003 est). Area: 2601 sq km (1004 sq miles)

Vorlage *German* (ˈfoːrlaːgə) *n* *skiing* a position in which a skier leans forward but keeps his heels on the skis [from *vor* before, in front of + *Lage* position, stance]

Voronezh (*Russian* vaˈrɔnɪʃ) *n* a city in W Russia: engineering, chemical, and food-processing industries; university (1918). Pop: 842 000 (2005 est)

Voroshilovgrad (*Russian* vərəʃilafˈgrat) *n* the former name (1935–91) of **Lugansk**

Voroshilovsk (*Russian* vəraˈʃiləfsk) *n* the former name (1940–44) of **Stavropol**

-vorous *adj combining form* feeding on or devouring: *carnivorous* [from Latin *-vorus*; related to *vorāre* to swallow up, DEVOUR] > **-vore** *n combining form*

vortex (ˈvɔːtɛks) *n, pl* **-texes** *or* **-tices** (-tɪˌsiːz) **1** a whirling mass or rotary motion in a liquid, gas, flame, etc, such as the spiralling movement of water around a whirlpool **2** any activity, situation, or way of life regarded as irresistibly engulfing [C17 from Latin: a whirlpool; variant of VERTEX] > **vortical** (ˈvɔːtɪkᵊl) *adj* > ˈ**vortically** *adv*

vortex drag *n* See **trailing vortex drag**

vortex ring *n* a stable perturbation in a fluid that takes the form of a torus in which the flow rotates in the section of the torus so that the pressure difference between the inside and outside of the torus balances body forces. The best-known vortex ring is a smoke ring

vortex shedding *n* the process by which vortices formed continuously by the aerodynamic conditions associated with a solid body in a gas or air stream are carried downstream by the flow in the form of a vortex street. See also **vortex street**

vortex street *n* a regular stream of vortices or parallel streams of vortices carried downstream by the flow of a fluid over a body. These are sometimes made visible by vapour condensation as in the vortex trails from the wing tips of an aeroplane. See also **Kármán vortex street, vortex shedding**

vorticella (ˌvɔːtɪˈsɛlə) *n, pl* **-lae** (-liː) any protozoan of the genus *Vorticella*, consisting of a goblet-shaped ciliated cell attached to the substratum by a long contractile stalk [C18 from New Latin, literally: a little eddy, from VORTEX]

vorticism (ˈvɔːtɪˌsɪzəm) *n* an art movement in England initiated in 1913 by Wyndham Lewis, the British painter, novelist, and critic (1884–1957), combining the techniques of cubism with the concern for the problems of the machine age evinced in futurism [C20 referring to the "vortices" of modern life on which the movement was based] > ˈ**vorticist** *n*

vorticose (ˈvɔːtɪˌkəʊs) *adj rare* rotating quickly; whirling [C18 from Latin *vorticōsus*, variant of *verticōsus* full of whirlpools; see VERTEX]

vortiginous (vɔːˈtɪdʒɪnəs) *adj* like a vortex; vortical; whirling [C17 variant of VERTIGINOUS]

Vortumnus (vɔːˈtʌmnəs) *n* a variant spelling of **Vertumnus**

Vosges (*French* voʒ) *n* **1** a mountain range in E France, west of the Rhine valley. Highest peak: 1423 m (4672 ft) **2** a department of NE France, in Lorraine region. Capital: Épinal. Pop: 381 277 (2003 est). Area: 5903 sq km (2302 sq miles)

Vostok (ˈvɒstɒk) *n* any of six manned Soviet spacecraft made to orbit the earth. **Vostok 1**, launched in April 1961, carried Yuri Gagarin, the first man in space; **Vostok 6** carried Valentina Tereshkova, the first woman in space

vostro account (ˈvɒstrəʊ) *n* a bank account held by a foreign bank with a British bank, usually in sterling. Compare **nostro account**

votary (ˈvəʊtərɪ) *n, pl* **-ries** *also* **votarist** **1** *RC Church, Eastern Churches* a person, such as a monk or nun, who has dedicated himself or herself to religion by taking vows **2** a devoted adherent of a religion, cause, leader, pursuit, etc ▷ *adj* **3** ardently devoted to the services or worship of God, a deity, or a saint [C16 from Latin *vōtum* a vow, from *vovēre* to vow] > ˈ**votaress** *or* ˈ**votress** *fem n*

vote (vəʊt) *n* **1** an indication of choice, opinion, or will on a question, such as the choosing of a candidate, by or as if by some recognized means, such as a ballot: *10 votes for Jones* **2** the opinion of a group of persons as determined by voting: *it was put to the vote; do not take a vote; it came to a vote* **3** a body of votes or voters collectively: *the Jewish vote* **4** the total number of votes cast: *the vote decreased at the last election* **5** the ticket, ballot, etc, by which a vote is expressed **6 a** the right to vote; franchise; suffrage **b** a person regarded as the embodiment of this right **7** a means of voting, such as a ballot **8** *chiefly Brit* a grant or other proposition to be voted upon ▷ *vb* **9** (when *tr, takes a clause as object or an infinitive*) to express or signify (one's preference, opinion, or will) (for or against some question, etc): *to vote by ballot; we voted that it was time to adjourn; vote for me!* **10** (*intr*) to declare oneself as being (something or in favour of something) by exercising one's vote: *to vote socialist* **11** (*tr*; foll by *into* or *out of*, etc) to appoint or elect (a person to or from a particular post): *they voted him into the presidency; he was voted out of office* **12** (*tr*) to determine the condition of in a specified way by voting: *the court voted itself out of existence* **13** (*tr*) to authorize, confer, or allow by voting: *vote us a rise* **14** (*tr*) *informal* to declare by common opinion: *the party was voted a failure* **15** (*tr*) to influence or control the voting of: *do not try to vote us!* [C15 from Latin *vōtum* a solemn promise, from *vovēre* to vow] > ˈ**votable** *or* ˈ**voteable** *adj* > ˈ**voteless** *adj*

vote down *vb* (*tr, adverb*) to decide against or defeat in a vote: *the bill was voted down*

vote of no confidence *n* *parliament* a vote on a motion put by the Opposition censuring an aspect of the Government's policy; if the motion is carried the Government is obliged to resign. Also called: **vote of censure**

voter (ˈvəʊtə) *n* a person who can or does vote

voting machine *n* (esp in the US) a machine at a polling station that voters operate to register their votes and that mechanically or electronically counts all votes cast

votive (ˈvəʊtɪv) *adj* **1** offered, given, undertaken, performed or dedicated in fulfilment of or in accordance with a vow **2** *RC Church* optional; not prescribed; having the nature of a voluntary offering: *a votive Mass; a votive candle* [C16 from Latin *vōtīvus* promised by a vow, from *vōtum* a vow] > ˈ**votively** *adv* > ˈ**votiveness** *n*

Votyak (ˈvəʊtɪˌæk) *n* **1** (*pl* **-aks** *or* **-ak**) a member of a Finnish people living chiefly in the Udmurt Autonomous Republic, between the Volga and the Urals **2** Also called: **Udmurt** the language of this people, belonging to the Finno-Ugric family

vouch (vaʊtʃ) *vb* **1** (*intr*; usually foll by *for*) to give personal assurance; guarantee: *I'll vouch for his safety* **2** (when *tr, usually takes a clause as object*; when *intr*, usually foll by *for*) to furnish supporting evidence (for) or function as proof (of) **3** (*tr*) *English legal history* to summon (a person who had warranted title to land) to defend that title or give up land of equal value **4** (*tr*) *archaic* to cite (authors, principles, etc) in support of something **5** (*tr*) *obsolete* to assert ▷ *n* **6** *obsolete* the act of vouching; assertion or allegation [C14 from Old French *vocher* to summon, ultimately from Latin *vocāre* to call]

voucher (ˈvaʊtʃə) *n* **1** a document serving as evidence for some claimed transaction, as the receipt or expenditure of money **2** *Brit* a ticket or card serving as a substitute for cash: *a gift voucher* **3** a person or thing that vouches for the truth of some statement, etc **4** any of certain documents that various groups of British nationals born outside Britain must obtain in order to settle in Britain **5** *English law obsolete* **a** the summoning into court of a person to warrant a title to property **b** the person so summoned [C16 from Anglo-French, noun use of Old French *voucher* to summon; see VOUCH]

vouchsafe (ˌvaʊtʃˈseɪf) *vb* (*tr*) **1** to give or grant or condescend to give or grant: *she vouchsafed no reply; he vouchsafed me no encouragement* **2** (*may take a clause as object or an infinitive*) to agree, promise, or permit, often graciously or condescendingly: *he vouchsafed to come yesterday* **3** *obsolete* **a** to warrant as being safe **b** to bestow as a favour (upon) [C14 *vouchen sauf*; see VOUCH, SAFE] > ˌ**vouchˈsafement** *n*

vouge (vuːʒ) *n* a form of pike or halberd used by foot soldiers in the 14th century and later [from Old French *voulge, vouge* (Medieval Latin *vanga*), of obscure origin]

voussoir (vuːˈswɑː) *n* a wedge-shaped stone or brick that is used with others to construct an arch or vault [C18 from French, from Vulgar Latin *volsōrium* (unattested), ultimately from Latin *volvere* to turn, roll]

Vouvray (ˈvuːvreɪ; *French* vuvrɛ) *n* a dry white wine, which can be still, sparkling, or semisparkling, produced around Touraine in the Loire Valley

vow (vaʊ) *n* **1** a solemn or earnest pledge or promise binding the person making it to perform a specified act or behave in a certain way **2** a solemn promise made to a deity or saint, by which the promiser pledges himself to some future act, course of action, or way of life **3** **take vows** to enter a religious order and commit oneself to its rule of life by the vows of poverty, chastity, and obedience, which may be taken for a limited period as **simple vows** or as a perpetual and still more solemn commitment as **solemn vows** ▷ *vb* **4** (*tr; may take a clause as object or an infinitive*) to pledge, promise, or undertake solemnly: *he vowed that he would continue; he vowed to return* **5** (*tr*) to dedicate or consecrate to God, a deity, or a saint **6** (*tr; usually takes a clause as object*) to assert or swear emphatically **7** (*intr*) *archaic* to declare solemnly [C13 from Old French *vou*, from Latin *vōtum* a solemn promise, from *vovēre* to vow] > ˈ**vower** *n* > ˈ**vowless** *adj*

vowel (ˈvaʊəl) *n* **1** *phonetics* a voiced speech sound whose articulation is characterized by the absence of friction-causing obstruction in the vocal tract, allowing the breath stream free passage. The timbre of a vowel is chiefly determined by the position of the tongue and the lips **2** a letter or character representing a vowel [C14 from Old French *vouel*, from Latin *vocālis littera* a vowel, from *vocālis* sonorous, from *vox* a voice] > ˈ**vowel-less** *adj* > ˈ**vowel-ˌlike** *adj*

vowel gradation *n* another name for **ablaut**. See **gradation** (sense 5)

vowelize *or* **vowelise** (ˈvaʊəˌlaɪz) *vb* (*tr*) to mark the vowel points in (a Hebrew word or text). Also: **vocalize** > ˌ**voweliˈzation** *or* ˌ**voweliˈsation** *n*

vowel mutation *n* another name for **umlaut**

vowel point *n* any of several marks or points placed above or below consonants, esp those evolved for Hebrew or Arabic, in order to indicate vowel sounds

vox (vɒks) *n, pl* **voces** (ˈvəʊsiːz) a voice or sound [Latin: voice]

vox angelica (ænˈdʒɛlɪkə) *n* an organ stop with a soft tone, often similar to the voix céleste [C18 from Latin: angelic voice]

vox humana (hjuːˈmɑːnə) *n* a reed stop on an organ supposedly imitative of the human voice [C18 from Latin: human voice]

vox pop *n* interviews with members of the public on a radio or television programme [C20 shortened from VOX POPULI]

vox populi (ˈpɒpjʊˌlaɪ) *n* the voice of the people; popular or public opinion [Latin]

voyage ('vɔɪɪdʒ) n **1** a journey, travel, or passage, esp one to a distant land or by sea or air **2** obsolete an ambitious project ▷ vb **3** to travel over or traverse (something): we will voyage to Africa [c13 from Old French veiage, from Latin viāticum provision for travelling, from viāticus concerning a journey, from via a way] > 'voyager n

voyage charter n the hire of a ship or aircraft for a specified number of voyages. Compare **time charter**

Voyager ('vɔɪədʒə) n either of two US spacecraft that studied the outer solar system; **Voyager 1** visited Jupiter (1979) and Saturn (1980), **Voyager 2** visited Jupiter (1979) and Saturn (1981) and made the first flyby of Uranus (1986) and Neptune (1989)

voyageur (ˌvɔɪə'dʒɜː) n Canadian **1** history a boatman employed by one of the early fur-trading companies, esp in the interior **2** a woodsman, guide, trapper, boatman, or explorer, esp in the North [c19 from French: traveller, from voyager to VOYAGE]

voyeur (vwaɪ'ɜː; French vwajœr) n a person who obtains sexual pleasure or excitement from the observation of someone undressing, having intercourse, etc [c20 French, literally: one who sees, from voir to see, from Latin vidēre] > vo'yeurism n > ˌvoyeur'istic adj > ˌvoyeur'istically adv

VP abbreviation for **1** Vice President **2** verb phrase

VPL jocular abbreviation for visible panty line

VPN abbreviation for virtual private network: a network that uses the internet to transfer information using secure methods

VR abbreviation for **1** variant reading **2** Victoria Regina [Latin: Queen Victoria] **3** virtual reality **4** Volunteer Reserve

vraisemblance (ˌvreɪsɒm'blɒns; French vrɛsãblãs) n verisimilitude; appearance of truth [French, from vrai true + SEMBLANCE]

V. Rev. abbreviation for Very Reverend

VRI abbreviation for Victoria Regina et Imperatrix [Latin: Victoria, Queen and Empress]

vroom (vruːm, vrʊm) interj an exclamation imitative of a car engine revving up, as for high-speed motor racing

vrot (frɒt) adj South African slang rotten; putrid; very bad [from Afrikaans]

vrou (fraʊ) n South African a woman or wife [Afrikaans]

vs abbreviation for versus

VS abbreviation for Veterinary Surgeon

v.s. abbreviation for vide supra. See **vide**

vsb abbreviation for vestigial sideband: a transmission in an amplitude-modulated signal in which one complete sideband is transmitted, but only part of the other

V-sign n **1** (in Britain) an offensive gesture made by sticking up the index and middle fingers with the palm of the hand inwards as an indication of contempt, defiance, etc **2** a similar gesture with the palm outwards meaning victory or peace

VSO abbreviation for **1** very superior old: used to indicate that a brandy, port, etc, is between 12 and 17 years old **2** (in Britain) Voluntary Service Overseas: an organization that sends young volunteers to use and teach their skills in developing countries

VSOP abbreviation for very special (or superior) old pale: used to indicate that a brandy, port, etc, is between 20 and 25 years old

Vt. or **VT** abbreviation for Vermont

VTOL ('viːtɒl) n **1** vertical takeoff and landing; a system in which an aircraft can take off and land vertically **2** an aircraft that uses this system. Compare **STOL**

VTR abbreviation for video tape recorder

V-type engine n a type of internal-combustion engine having two cylinder blocks attached to a single crankcase, the angle between the two blocks forming a V

vu the internet domain name for Vanuatu

Vuelta Abajo (Spanish 'bwelta a'βaxo) n a region of W Cuba: famous for its tobacco

vug, vugg or **vugh** (vʌg) n mining a small cavity in a rock or vein, usually lined with crystals [c19 from Cornish vooga cave] > 'vuggy or 'vughy adj

Vulcan[1] ('vʌlkən) n the Roman god of fire and metalworking. Greek counterpart: Hephaestus > Vulcanian (vʌl'keɪnɪən) adj

Vulcan[2] ('vʌlkən) n a hypothetical planet once thought to lie within the orbit of Mercury > Vulcanian (vʌl'keɪnɪən) adj

vulcanian (vʌl'keɪnɪən) adj geology **a** of or relating to a volcanic eruption characterized by the explosive discharge of fine ash and large irregular fragments of solidified or viscous lava **b** a less common word for **volcanic**

vulcanism ('vʌlkəˌnɪzəm) n a variant spelling of **volcanism**

vulcanite ('vʌlkəˌnaɪt) n a hard usually black rubber produced by vulcanizing natural rubber with large amounts of sulphur. It is resistant to chemical attack: used for chemical containers, electrical insulators, etc. Also called: ebonite

vulcanize or **vulcanise** ('vʌlkəˌnaɪz) vb (tr) **1** to treat (rubber) with sulphur or sulphur compounds under heat and pressure to improve elasticity and strength or to produce a hard substance such as vulcanite **2** to treat (substances other than rubber) by a similar process in order to improve their properties > 'vulcanˌizable or 'vulcanˌisable adj > ˌvulcani'zation or ˌvulcani'sation n > 'vulcanˌizer or 'vulcanˌiser n

vulcanology (ˌvʌlkə'nɒlədʒɪ) n a variant spelling of **volcanology**. > vulcanological (ˌvʌlkənə'lɒdʒɪkⁿl) adj > ˌvulcan'ologist n

Vulg. abbreviation for Vulgate

vulgar ('vʌlgə) adj **1** marked by lack of taste, culture, delicacy, manners, etc: vulgar behaviour; vulgar language **2** (often capital; usually prenominal) denoting a form of a language, esp of Latin, current among common people, esp at a period when the formal language is archaic and not in general spoken use **3** archaic of, relating to, or current among the great mass of common people, in contrast to the educated, cultured, or privileged; ordinary **b** (as collective noun; preceded by the): the vulgar [c14 from Latin vulgāris belonging to the multitude, from vulgus the common people] > 'vulgarly adv

vulgar fraction n another name for **simple fraction**

vulgarian (vʌl'gɛərɪən) n a vulgar person, esp one who is rich or has pretensions to good taste

vulgarism ('vʌlgəˌrɪzəm) n **1** a coarse, crude, or obscene expression **2** a word or phrase found only in the vulgar form of a language **3** another word for **vulgarity**

vulgarity (vʌl'gærɪtɪ) n, pl **-ties 1** the condition of being vulgar; lack of good manners **2** a vulgar action, phrase, etc

vulgarize or **vulgarise** ('vʌlgəˌraɪz) vb (tr) **1** to make commonplace or vulgar; debase **2** to make (something little known or difficult to understand) widely known or popular among the public; popularize > ˌvulgari'zation n or ˌvulgari'sation n > 'vulgarˌizer or 'vulgarˌiser n

Vulgar Latin n any of the dialects of Latin spoken in the Roman Empire other than classical Latin. The Romance languages developed from them

Vulgate ('vʌlgeɪt, -gɪt) rare ▷ adj **1** a commonly recognized text or version **2** everyday or informal speech; the vernacular ▷ adj **3** generally accepted; common

Vulgate ('vʌlgeɪt, -gɪt) n **a** (from the 13th century onwards) the fourth-century version of the Bible produced by Jerome, partly by translating the original languages, and partly by revising the earlier Latin text based on the Greek versions **b** (as modifier): the Vulgate version [c17 from Medieval Latin Vulgāta, from Late Latin vulgāta editiō popular version (of the Bible), from Latin vulgāre to make common, from vulgus the common people]

vulnerable ('vʌlnərəbⁿl) adj **1** capable of being physically or emotionally wounded or hurt **2** open to temptation, persuasion, censure, etc **3** liable or exposed to disease, disaster, etc **4** military liable or exposed to attack **5** bridge (of a side who have won one game towards rubber) subject to increased bonuses or penalties [c17 from Late Latin vulnerābilis, from Latin vulnerāre to wound, from vulnus a wound] > ˌvulnera'bility or 'vulnerableness n > 'vulnerably adv

vulnerary ('vʌlnərərɪ) med ▷ adj **1** of, relating to, or used to heal a wound ▷ n, pl **-aries 2** a vulnerary drug or agent [c16 from Latin vulnerārius belonging to wounds, from vulnus a wound]

Vulpecula (vʌl'pɛkjʊlə) n, Latin genitive Vulpeculae (vʌl'pɛkjʊˌliː) a faint constellation in the N hemisphere lying between Cygnus and Aquila [c19 from Latin: a little fox, from vulpēs a fox]

vulpine ('vʌlpaɪn) adj **1** Also: vulpecular (vʌl'pɛkjʊlə) of, relating to, or resembling a fox **2** possessing the characteristics often attributed to foxes; crafty, clever, etc [c17 from Latin vulpīnus foxlike, from vulpēs a fox]

vulture ('vʌltʃə) n **1** any of various very large diurnal birds of prey of the genera Neophron, Gyps, Gypaetus, etc, of Africa, Asia, and warm parts of Europe, typically having broad wings and soaring flight and feeding on carrion: family Accipitridae (hawks). See also **griffon**[1] (sense 2), **lammergeier 2** any similar bird of the family Cathartidae of North, Central, and South America. See also **condor, turkey buzzard 3** a person or thing that preys greedily and ruthlessly on others, esp the helpless [c14 from Old French voltour, from Latin vultur; perhaps related to Latin vellere to pluck, tear] > 'vulture-ˌlike adj

vulturine ('vʌltʃəˌraɪn) adj **1** of, relating to, or resembling a vulture **2** Also: vulturous rapacious, predatory, or greedy

vulva ('vʌlvə) n, pl **-vae** (-viː) or **-vas** the external genitals of human females, including the labia, mons veneris, clitoris, and the vaginal orifice [c16 from Latin: covering, womb, matrix] > 'vulval, 'vulvar or vulvate ('vʌlveɪt) adj > vulviform ('vʌlvɪˌfɔːm) adj

vulvitis (vʌl'vaɪtɪs) n inflammation of the vulva

vulvovaginitis (ˌvʌlvəʊˌvædʒɪ'naɪtɪs) n inflammation of the vulva and vagina or of the small glands (**vulvovaginal glands**) on either side of the lower part of the vagina

vutty ('vʌtɪ) adj vuttier, vuttiest Southwest English dialect dirty

vuvuzela (ˌvuːvuː'zɛlə) n South African an elongated plastic instrument that football fans blow to make a loud noise similar to the trumpeting of an elephant [c20 from Zulu]

vv abbreviation for vice versa

VW abbreviation for **1** Very Worshipful **2** Volkswagen

VX n a US lethal nerve gas

Vyatka (Russian 'vjatkə) n the former name (1780–1934) of Kirov

Vyborg (Russian 'vibərk) n a port in NW Russia, at the head of **Vyborg Bay** (an inlet of the Gulf of Finland): belonged to Finland (1918–40). Pop: 80 000 (latest est). Finnish name: Viipuri Swedish name: Viborg

vying ('vaɪɪŋ) vb **1** the present participle of **vie** ▷ adj **2** competing: two vying patriarchs

V

Ww

w *or* **W** (ˈdʌb°lˌjuː) *n*, *pl* **w's**, **W's** *or* **Ws 1** the 23rd letter and 18th consonant of the modern English alphabet **2** a speech sound represented by this letter, in English usually a bilabial semivowel, as in *web*

W *symbol for* **1** watt **2** West **3** *physics* work **4** *chem* tungsten [from New Latin *wolframium*, from German *Wolfram*] **5** women's (size)

w. *abbreviation for* **1** week **2** weight **3** width **4** wife **5** with **6** *cricket* **a** wide **b** wicket

W. *abbreviation for* **1** Wales **2** Welsh

W8 *text messaging abbreviation for* wait

WA *abbreviation for* **1** Washington (state) **2** Western Australia

WAAAF (formerly) *abbreviation for* Women's Auxiliary Australian Air Force

WAAC (wæk) *n* (formerly) **1** *acronym for* Women's Army Auxiliary Corps **2** Also called: **waac** a member of this corps

Waadt (vat) *n* the German name for **Vaud**

WAAF (wæf) *n* (formerly) **1** *acronym for* **a** Women's Auxiliary Air Force **b** Women's Auxiliary Australian Air Force **2** Also called: **Waaf** a member of either of these forces

Waal (*Dutch* waːl) *n* a river in the central Netherlands: the S branch of the Lower Rhine. Length: 84 km (52 miles)

Wabash (ˈwɔːbæʃ) *n* a river in the E central US, rising in W Ohio and flowing west and southwest to join the Ohio River in Indiana. Length: 764 km (475 miles)

wabbit (ˈwæbɪt) *adj Scot* weary; exhausted [c19 from earlier *wobart* withered, feeble]

wabble (ˈwɒb°l) *vb*, *n* a variant spelling of **wobble** > ˈwabbler *n* > ˈwabbly *adj*

wack (wæk) *or* **wacker** (ˈwækə) *n Liverpool and Midlands dialect* friend; pal: used chiefly as a term of address [perhaps from dialect *wack* or *whack* to share out, hence one who shares, a friend]

wacke (ˈwækə) *n obsolete* any of various soft earthy rocks that resemble or are derived from basaltic rocks [c18 from German: rock, gravel, basalt]

wacko (ˈwækəʊ) *informal* ▷ *adj* **1** mad or eccentric ▷ *n*, *pl* **wackos 2** a mad or eccentric person [c20 back formation from WACKY]

wacky (ˈwækɪ) *adj* **wackier, wackiest** *slang* eccentric, erratic, or unpredictable [c19 (in dialect sense: a fool, an eccentric): from WHACK (hence, a *whacky*, a person who behaves as if he had been whacked on the head)] > ˈwackily *adv* > ˈwackiness *n*

wad¹ (wɒd) *n* **1** a small mass or ball of fibrous or soft material, such as cotton wool, used esp for packing or stuffing **2 a** a plug of paper, cloth, leather, etc, pressed against a charge to hold it in place in a muzzle-loading cannon **b** a disc of paper, felt, pasteboard, etc, used to hold in place the powder and shot in a shotgun cartridge **3** a roll or bundle of something, esp of banknotes **4** *US and Canadian slang* a large quantity, esp of

money **5** *Brit dialect* a bundle of hay or straw **6** *Brit military slang* a bun: *char and a wad* ▷ *vb* **wads, wadding, wadded 7** to form (something) into a wad **8** (*tr*) to roll into a wad or bundle **9** (*tr*) **a** to hold (a charge) in place with a wad **b** to insert a wad into (a gun) **10** (*tr*) to pack or stuff with wadding; pad [c14 from Late Latin *wadda*; related to German *Watte* cotton wool] > ˈwadder *n*

wad² (wɒd) *n* a soft dark earthy amorphous material consisting of decomposed manganese minerals: occurs in damp marshy areas [c17 of unknown origin]

WADA *abbreviation for* World Anti-Doping Agency: an independent agency working towards eradicating the improper use of drugs in sport

Wadai (wɑːˈdaɪ) *n* a former independent sultanate of NE central Africa: now the E part of Chad

Waddenzee (*Dutch* ˈwɑdənzeː) *n* the part of the North Sea between the Dutch mainland and the West Frisian Islands

Waddesdon Manor (ˈwɒdzdən) *n* a mansion near Aylesbury in Buckinghamshire: built (1880–89) in the French style for the Rothschild family: noted for its furnishings and collections of porcelain and paintings

wadding (ˈwɒdɪŋ) *n* **1 a** any fibrous or soft substance used as padding, stuffing, etc, esp sheets of carded cotton prepared for the purpose **b** a piece of this **2** material for wads used in cartridges or guns

waddle (ˈwɒd°l) *vb* (*intr*) **1** to walk with short steps, rocking slightly from side to side ▷ *n* **2** a swaying gait or motion [c16 probably frequentative of WADE] > ˈwaddler *n* > ˈwaddling *adj* > ˈwaddly *adj*

waddy (ˈwɒdɪ) *n*, *pl* -**dies 1** a heavy wooden club used as a weapon by native Australians ▷ *vb* -**dies, -dying, -died 2** (*tr*) to hit with a waddy [c19 from a native Australian language, perhaps based on English WOOD¹]

wade (weɪd) *vb* **1** to walk with the feet immersed in (water, a stream, etc): *the girls waded the river at the ford* **2** (*intr*; often foll by *through*) to proceed with difficulty: *to wade through a book* **3** (*intr*; foll by *in* or *into*) to attack energetically ▷ *n* **4** the act or an instance of wading [Old English *wadan*; related to Old Frisian *wada*, Old High German *watan*, Old Norse *vatha*, Latin *vadum* FORD] > ˈwadable *or* ˈwadeable *adj*

wader (ˈweɪdə) *n* **1** a person or thing that wades **2** Also called: **wading bird** any of various long-legged birds, esp those of the order *Ciconiiformes* (herons, storks, etc), that live near water and feed on fish, etc **3** a Brit name for **shore bird**

waders (ˈweɪdəz) *pl n* long waterproof boots, sometimes extending to the chest like trousers, worn by anglers

wadi *or* **wady** (ˈwɒdɪ) *n*, *pl* -**dies** a watercourse in N Africa and Arabia, dry except in the rainy season [c19 from Arabic]

Wadi Halfa (ˈwɒdɪ ˈhælfə) *n* a town in the N Sudan that was partly submerged by Lake Nasser: an important archaeological site

wadmal (ˈwɒdməl) *n* a coarse thick woollen fabric, formerly woven esp in Orkney and Shetland, for outer garments [c14 from Old Norse *vathmal*, from *vath* cloth + *mal* measure]

Wad Medani (wɑːd mɪˈdɑːniː) *n* a town in the E Sudan, on the Blue Nile: headquarters of the Gezira irrigation scheme; agricultural research centre. Pop: 332 000 (2005 est)

wadset (ˈwɒdˌsɛt) *Scots law* ▷ *n* **1** another name for **mortgage** ▷ *vb* -**sets, -setting, -setted 2** (*tr*) to pledge or mortgage [c14 *wad*, a Scottish variant of WED + SET¹; compare Old English *wedd settan* to deposit a pledge]

Wafd (wɒft) *n* a nationalist Egyptian political party: founded in 1924 and dissolved in 1952 [Arabic: deputation] > ˈWafdist *n, adj*

wafer (ˈweɪfə) *n* **1** a thin crisp sweetened biscuit with different flavourings, served with ice cream, etc **2** *Christianity* a thin disc of unleavened bread used in the Eucharist as celebrated by the Western Church **3** *pharmacol* an envelope of rice paper enclosing a medicament **4** *electronics* a large single crystal of semiconductor material, such as silicon, on which numerous integrated circuits are manufactured and then separated **5** a small thin disc of adhesive material used to seal letters, documents, etc ▷ *vb* **6** (*tr*) to seal, fasten, or attach with a wafer [c14 from Old Northern French *waufre*, from Middle Low German *wāfel*; related to WAFFLE¹] > ˈwafer-ˌlike *or* ˈwafery *adj*

waff (wæf, wɑːf) *n Scot and northern English dialect* **1** a gust or puff of air **2** a glance; glimpse ▷ *vb* **3** to flutter or cause to flutter [c16 Scottish and northern English variant of WAVE]

waffle¹ (ˈwɒf°l) *n* **a** a crisp golden-brown pancake with deep indentations on both sides **b** (*as modifier*): *waffle iron* [c19 from Dutch *wafel* (earlier *wæfel*), of Germanic origin; related to Old High German *wabo* honeycomb]

waffle² (ˈwɒf°l) *informal, chiefly Brit* ▷ *vb* **1** (*intr*; often foll by *on*) to speak or write in a vague and wordy manner: *he waffled on for hours* ▷ *n* **2** vague and wordy speech or writing [c19 of unknown origin] > ˈwaffler *n* > ˈwaffling *adj, n* > ˈwaffly *adj*

waft (wɑːft, wɒft) *vb* **1** to carry or be carried gently on or as if on the air or water ▷ *n* **2** the act or an instance of wafting **3** something, such as a scent, carried on the air **4** a wafting motion **5** Also called: **waif** *nautical* (formerly) a signal flag hoisted furled to signify various messages depending on where it was flown [c16 (in obsolete sense: to convey by ship): back formation from c15 *wafter* a convoy vessel, from Middle Dutch *wachter* guard, from *wachten* to guard; influenced by WAFF] > ˈwaftage *n*

wafter (ˈwɑːftə, ˈwɒf-) *n* a device that causes a draught

wafture (ˈwɑːftʃə, ˈwɒf-) *n archaic* **1** the act of

wafting or waving **2** anything that is wafted

wag¹ (wæg) *vb* **wags, wagging, wagged 1** to move or cause to move rapidly and repeatedly from side to side or up and down **2** to move (the tongue) or (of the tongue) to be moved rapidly in talking, esp in idle gossip **3** to move (the finger) or (of the finger) to be moved from side to side, in or as in admonition **4** *slang* to play truant (esp in the phrase **wag it**) ▷ *n* **5** the act or an instance of wagging [c13 from Old English *wagian* to shake; compare Old Norse *vagga* cradle]

wag² (wæg) *n* a humorous or jocular person; wit [c16 of uncertain origin] > **waggery** *n* > **waggish** *adj* > **waggishly** *adv* > **waggishness** *n*

WAG *international car registration for* (West Africa) Gambia

wage (weɪdʒ) *n* **1 a** (*often plural*) payment in return for work or services, esp that made to workmen on a daily, hourly, weekly, or piece-work basis. Compare **salary b** (*as modifier*): *wage freeze* **2** (*plural*) *economics* the portion of the national income accruing to labour as earned income, as contrasted with the unearned income accruing to capital in the form of rent, interest, and dividends **3** (*often plural*) recompense, return, or yield **4** an obsolete word for **pledge** ▷ *vb* (*tr*) **5** to engage in **6** *obsolete* to pledge or wager **7** *archaic* another word for **hire** (senses 1, 2) [c14 from Old Northern French *wagier* to pledge, from *wage*, of Germanic origin; compare Old English *weddian* to pledge, WED] > **wageless** *adj* > **wagelessness** *n*

wage determination *n* the process of setting wage rates or establishing wage structures in particular situations

wage differential *n* the difference in wages between workers with different skills in the same industry or between those with comparable skills in different industries or localities

wage earner *or US* **wage worker** *n* **1** a person who works for wages, esp as distinguished from one paid a salary **2** the person who earns money to support a household by working

wage incentive *n* additional wage payments intended to stimulate improved work performance

wager (ˈweɪdʒə) *n* **1** an agreement or pledge to pay an amount of money as a result of the outcome of an unsettled matter **2** an amount staked on the outcome of such a matter or event **3** **wager of battle** (in medieval Britain) a pledge to do battle for a cause, esp to decide guilt or innocence by single combat **4** **wager of law** *English legal history* a form of trial in which the accused offered to make oath of his innocence, supported by the oaths of 11 of his neighbours declaring their belief in his statements ▷ *vb* **5** (when *tr*, *may take a clause as object*) to risk or bet (something) on the outcome of an unsettled matter **6** (*tr*) *history* to pledge oneself to (battle) [c14 from Anglo-French *wageure* a pledge, from Old Northern French *wagier* to pledge; see WAGE] > **ˈwagerer** *n*

wage scale *n* **1** a schedule of wages paid to workers for various jobs in an industry, company, etc **2** an employer's schedule of wages

wages council *n* (formerly, in Britain) a statutory body empowered to fix minimum wages in an industry; abolished in 1994

wage slave *n* *ironic* a person dependent on a wage or salary

wagga (ˈwɒɡə) *n* *Austral* a blanket or bed covering made out of sacks stitched together [c19 named after WAGGA WAGGA]

Wagga Wagga (ˈwɒɡə ˈwɒɡə) *n* a city in SE Australia, in New South Wales on the Murrumbidgee River: agricultural trading centre. Pop: 44 451 (2001)

waggle (ˈwæɡ³l) *vb* **1** to move or cause to move with a rapid shaking or wobbling motion ▷ *n* **2** a rapid shaking or wobbling motion [c16 frequentative of WAG¹] > **ˈwagglingly** *adv* > **ˈwaggly** *adj*

waggler (ˈwæɡlə) *n* *angling* a float only the bottom of which is attached to the line

waggon (ˈwæɡən) *n, vb* a variant spelling (esp Brit) of **wagon**

Wagnerian (vɑːɡˈnɪərɪən) *adj* **1** of or suggestive of the dramatic musical compositions of Richard Wagner, the German romantic composer (1813–83), their massive scale, dramatic and emotional intensity, etc **2** denoting or relating to a singer who has a voice suitable for singing Wagner **3** of or relating to a big, powerful, or domineering woman: *a Wagnerian maiden* ▷ *n also* **Wagnerite 4** a follower or disciple of the music or theories of Richard Wagner

wagon *or* **waggon** (ˈwæɡən) *n* **1** any of various types of wheeled vehicles, ranging from carts to lorries, esp a vehicle with four wheels drawn by a horse, tractor, etc, and used for carrying crops, heavy loads, etc **2** *Brit* a railway freight truck, esp an open one **3** *US and Canadian* a child's four-wheeled cart **4** *US and Canadian* a police van for transporting prisoners or those arrested **5** *chiefly US and Canadian* See **station wagon 6** an obsolete word for **chariot 7** **on** (*or* **off**) **the wagon** *informal* abstaining (or no longer abstaining) from alcoholic drinks ▷ *vb* **8** (*tr*) to transport by wagon [c16 from Dutch *wagen* WAIN] > **wagonless** *or* **ˈwaggonless** *adj*

Wagon *or* **Waggon** (ˈwæɡən) *n* **the** another name for the **Plough**

wagoner *or* **waggoner** (ˈwæɡənə) *n* a person who drives a wagon

wagonette *or* **waggonette** (ˌwæɡəˈnɛt) *n* a light four-wheeled horse-drawn vehicle with two lengthwise seats facing each other behind a crosswise driver's seat

wagon-lit (French vagɔ̃li) *n, pl* **wagons-lits** (vagɔ̃li) **1** a sleeping car on a European railway **2** a compartment on such a car [c19 from French, from *wagon* railway coach + *lit* bed]

wagonload *or* **waggonload** (ˈwæɡənˌləʊd) *n* the load that is or can be carried by a wagon

wagon soldier *n* *US slang* a soldier belonging to the field artillery

wagon train *n* a supply train of horses and wagons, esp one going over rough terrain

wagon vault *n* another name for **barrel vault**

Wagram (*German* ˈvaːɡram) *n* a village in NE Austria: scene of the defeat of the Austrians by Napoleon in 1809

wagtail (ˈwæɡˌteɪl) *n* any of various passerine songbirds of the genera *Motacilla* and *Dendronanthus*, of Eurasia and Africa, having a very long tail that wags when the bird walks: family *Motacillidae*

Wahhabi *or* **Wahabi** (wəˈhɑːbɪ) *n, pl* -**bis** a member of a strictly conservative Muslim sect founded in the 18th century with the aim of eliminating all innovations later than the 3rd century of Islam > **Wahˈhabism** *or* **Waˈhabism** *n*

wahine (wɑːˈhiːnɪ) *n* (esp in the Pacific islands) a Polynesian or Māori woman, esp a girlfriend or wife [c19 from Māori and Hawaiian]

wahoo¹ (wɑːˈhuː, ˈwɑːhuː) *n, pl* -**hoos** an elm, *Ulmus alata*, of SE North America having twigs with winged corky edges. Also called: **winged elm** [from Creek *ŭhawhu* cork elm]

wahoo² (wɑːˈhuː, ˈwɑːhuː) *n, pl* -**hoos** an E North American shrub or small tree, *Euonymus atropurpureus*, with scarlet capsules and seeds. Also called: **burning bush** [c19 from Dakota *wāhu* arrowwood]

wahoo³ (wɑːˈhuː, ˈwɑːhuː) *n, pl* -**hoos** a large fast-moving food and game fish, *Acanthocybium solandri*, of tropical seas: family *Scombridae* (mackerels and tunnies) [of unknown origin]

wah-wah (ˈwɑːˌwɑː) *n* **1** the sound made by a trumpet, cornet, etc, when the bell is alternately covered and uncovered: much used in jazz **2** an electronic attachment for an electric guitar, etc, that simulates this effect [c20 of imitative origin]

wai (ˈwɑːɪ) *n* NZ water [Māori]

waiata (wɑːˈiːɑːtɑː) *n* NZ a Māori song [Māori]

waif (weɪf) *n* **1** a person, esp a child, who is homeless, friendless, or neglected **2** anything found and not claimed, the owner being unknown **3** *nautical* another name for **waft** (sense 5) **4** *law obsolete* a stolen article thrown away by a thief in his flight and forfeited to the Crown or to the lord of the manor [c14 from Anglo-Norman, variant of Old Northern French *gaif*, of Scandinavian origin; related to Old Norse *veif* a flapping thing] > **ˈwaif-like** *adj*

Waikaremoana (waɪˈkɒrəməʊˌɑːnə) *n* **Lake** a lake in the North Island of New Zealand in a dense bush setting. Area: about 55 sq km (21 sq miles)

Waikato (ˈwaɪˌkɑːtəʊ) *n* the longest river in New Zealand, flowing northwest across North Island to the Tasman Sea. Length: 350 km (220 miles)

Waikiki (ˈwaɪkɪˌkiː, ˌwaɪkɪˈkiː) *n* a resort area in Hawaii, on SE Oahu: a suburb of Honolulu

wail (weɪl) *vb* **1** (*intr*) to utter a prolonged high-pitched cry, as of grief or misery **2** (*intr*) to make a sound resembling such a cry: *the wind wailed in the trees* **3** (*tr*) to lament, esp with mournful sounds ▷ *n* **4** a prolonged high-pitched mournful cry or sound [c14 of Scandinavian origin; related to Old Norse *væla* to wail, Old English *wā* WOE] > **ˈwailer** *n* > **ˈwailful** *adj* > **ˈwailfully** *adv*

Wailing Wall *n* another name for **Western Wall**

wain (weɪn) *n* *chiefly poetic* a farm wagon or cart [Old English *wægn*; related to Old Frisian *wein*, Old Norse *vagn*]

wainscot (ˈweɪnskət) *n* **1** Also called: **wainscoting** *or* **wainscotting** a lining applied to the walls of a room, esp one of wood panelling **2** the lower part of the walls of a room, esp when finished in a material different from the upper part **3** fine quality oak used as wainscot ▷ *vb* **4** (*tr*) to line (a wall of a room) with a wainscot [c14 from Middle Low German *wagenschot*, perhaps from *wagen* WAGON + *schot* planking, related to German *Scheit* piece of wood]

wainwright (ˈweɪnˌraɪt) *n* a person who makes wagons

wairsh (wɛrʃ) *adj* *Scot* a variant spelling of **wersh**

wairua (wɑːˈiːruːɑː) *n* NZ a spirit or soul [Māori]

waist (weɪst) *n* **1** *anatomy* the constricted part of the trunk between the ribs and hips **2** the part of a garment covering the waist **3** the middle part of an object that resembles the waist in narrowness or position **4** the middle part of a ship **5** Also called: **centre section** the middle section of an aircraft fuselage **6** the constriction between the thorax and abdomen in wasps and similar insects [c14 origin uncertain; related to Old English *wæstm* WAX²] > **ˈwaistless** *adj*

waistband (ˈweɪstˌbænd) *n* an encircling band of material to finish and strengthen a skirt or trousers at the waist

waistcloth (ˈweɪstˌklɒθ) *n* *obsolete* another word for **loincloth**

waistcoat (ˈweɪsˌkəʊt) *n* **1** a man's sleeveless waistlength garment worn under a suit jacket, usually buttoning up the front. US, Canadian, and Austral name: **vest 2** a man's garment worn under a doublet in the 16th century > **ˈwaistˌcoated** *adj*

waisted (ˈweɪstɪd) *adj* **a** having a waist or waistlike part: *a waisted air-gun pellet* **b** (*in combination*): *high-waisted*

waistline (ˈweɪstˌlaɪn) *n* **1** a line or indentation around the body at the narrowest part of the waist **2** the intersection of the bodice and the skirt of a dress, etc, or the level of this: *a low waistline*

wait (weɪt) *vb* **1** (when *intr*, often foll by *for, until, or to*) to stay in one place or remain inactive in expectation (of something); hold oneself in readiness (for something) **2** to delay temporarily or be temporarily delayed: *that work can wait* **3** (when *intr*, usually foll by *for*) (of things) to be in store (for a person): *success waits for you in your new job* **4** (*intr*) to act as a waiter or waitress ▷ *n* **5** the act

W

or an instance of waiting **6** a period of waiting **7** (*plural*) *rare* a band of musicians who go around the streets, esp at Christmas, singing and playing carols **8** an interlude or interval between two acts or scenes in a play, etc **9** **lie in wait** to prepare an ambush (for someone) ▷ See also **wait on**, **wait up** [c12 from Old French *waitier*; related to Old High German *wahtēn* to WAKE[1]]

wait-a-bit *n* any of various plants having sharp hooked thorns or similar appendages, esp the greenbrier and the grapple plant

Waitangi Day (waɪ'tʌŋiː) *n* the national day of New Zealand (Feb 6), commemorating the signing of the **Treaty of Waitangi** (1840) by Māori chiefs and a representative of the British Government. The treaty provided the basis for the British annexation of New Zealand

Waitangi Tribunal *n* (in New Zealand) a government tribunal empowered to examine and make recommendations on Māori claims under the Treaty of Waitangi

wait-a-while *n* (in Australia) another name for **rattan** (sense 1)

waiter ('weɪtə) *n* **1** a man whose occupation is to serve at table, as in a restaurant **2** an attendant at the London Stock Exchange or Lloyd's who carries messages: the modern equivalent of waiters who performed these duties in the 17th-century London coffee houses in which these institutions originated **3** a person who waits **4** a tray or salver on which dishes, etc, are carried

waiting game *n* the postponement of action or decision in order to gain the advantage

waiting list *n* a list of people waiting to obtain some object, treatment, status, etc

waiting room *n* a room in which people may wait, as at a railway station, doctor's or dentist's office, etc

wait on *vb* (*intr, preposition*) **1** to serve at the table of **2** to act as an attendant or servant to **3** *archaic* to visit ▷ *interj* **4** *Austral and NZ* stop! hold on! ▷ Also (for senses 1, 2, 3): **wait upon**

waitress ('weɪtrɪs) *n* **1** a woman who serves at table, as in a restaurant ▷ *vb* **2** (*intr*) to act as a waitress

Waitsian ('weɪtsɪən) *adj* **1** of Tom Waits (born 1949), US singer and songwriter, or his works **2** resembling the music of Tom Waits with its hoarse, gravelly vocals, discordant sounds, and the use of unusual instruments

wait up *vb* (*intr, adverb*) **1** to delay going to bed in order to await some event **2** *informal, chiefly US and Canadian* to halt and pause in order that another person may catch up

waive (weɪv) *vb* (*tr*) **1** to set aside or relinquish: *to waive one's right to something* **2** to refrain from enforcing (a claim) or applying (a law, penalty, etc) **3** to defer [c13 from Old Northern French *weyver*, from *waif* abandoned; see WAIF]

waiver ('weɪvə) *n* **1** the voluntary relinquishment, expressly or by implication, of some claim or right **2** the act or an instance of relinquishing a claim or right **3** a formal statement in writing of such relinquishment [c17 from Old Northern French *weyver* to relinquish, WAIVE]

waka ('wɔːkə) *n* NZ **1** a Māori canoe, usually made from a tree trunk **2** a tribal group claiming descent from the first Māori settlers in New Zealand [Māori]

Wakashan (waː'kæʃən, 'wɔːkəʃaːn) *n* **1** a family of North American Indian languages of British Columbia and Washington, including Kwakiutl and Nootka **2** a speaker of any of these languages

Wakayama (ˌwækə'juːmə) *n* an industrial city in S Japan, on S Honshu. Pop: 391 008 (2002 est)

wake[1] (weɪk) *vb* **wakes**, **waking**, **woke**, **woken 1** (often foll by *up*) to rouse or become roused from sleep **2** (often foll by *up*) to rouse or become roused from inactivity **3** (*intr*; often foll by *to* or *up to*) to become conscious or aware: *at last he woke to the situation* **4** (*intr*) to be or remain awake **5** (*tr*) to

arouse (feelings etc) **6** *dialect* to hold a wake over (a corpse) **7** *archaic or dialect* to keep watch over **8 wake up and smell the coffee** *informal* to face up to reality, especially in an unpleasant situation ▷ *n* **9** a watch or vigil held over the body of a dead person during the night before burial **10** (in Ireland) festivities held after a funeral **11** the patronal or dedication festival of English parish churches **12** a solemn or ceremonial vigil **13** (*usually plural*) an annual holiday in any of various towns in northern England, when the local factory or factories close, usually for a week or two weeks **14** *rare* the state of being awake [Old English *wacian*; related to Old Frisian *wakia*, Old High German *wahtēn*] > **waker** *n*

> USAGE Where there is an object and the sense is the literal one *wake* (*up*) and *waken* are the commonest forms: *I wakened him; I woke him* (*up*). Both verbs are also commonly used without an object: *I woke up. Awake* and *awaken* are preferred to other forms of *wake* where the sense is a figurative one: *he awoke to the danger*

wake[2] (weɪk) *n* **1** the waves or track left by a vessel or other object moving through water **2** the track or path left by anything that has passed: *wrecked houses in the wake of the hurricane* [c16 of Scandinavian origin; compare Old Norse *vaka, vök* hole cut in ice, Swedish *vak*, Danish *vaage*; perhaps related to Old Norse *vökr*, Middle Dutch *wak* wet]

wakeboarding ('weɪkˌbɔːdɪŋ) *n* the sport of riding over water on a short surfboard and performing stunts while holding a rope towed by a speedboat

Wakefield ('weɪkˌfiːld) *n* **1** a city in N England, in Wakefield unitary authority, West Yorkshire: important since medieval times as an agricultural and textile centre. Pop: 76 886 (2001) **2** a unitary authority in N England, in West Yorkshire. Pop: 318 300 (2003 est). Area: 333 sq km (129 sq miles)

wakeful ('weɪkfʊl) *adj* **1** unable or unwilling to sleep **2** sleepless **3** alert > 'wakefully *adv* > 'wakefulness *n*

Wake Island *n* an atoll in the N central Pacific: claimed by the US in 1899; developed as a civil and naval air station in the late 1930s. Area: 8 sq km (3 sq miles)

wakeless ('weɪklɪs) *adj* (of sleep) deep or unbroken

waken ('weɪkən) *vb* to rouse or be roused from sleep or some other inactive state > 'wakener *n*

> USAGE See at **wake[1]**

wake-robin *n* **1** any of various North American herbaceous plants of the genus *Trillium*, such as *T. grandiflorum*, having a whorl of three leaves and three-petalled solitary flowers: family *Trilliaceae* **2** US any of various aroid plants, esp the cuckoopint

wake-up *n* **1** *Austral informal* an alert or intelligent person **2 be a wake-up to** *Austral informal* to be fully alert to (a person, thing, action, etc)

wake-up call *n* **1** a telephone call that wakes a person from sleep **2** an event that alerts people to a danger or difficulty

WAL *international car registration for* Sierra Leone [from W(*est*) A(*frica*) L(*eone*)]

Walach ('wɑːlɒk) *n, adj* a variant spelling of **Vlach**

Walachia *or* **Wallachia** (wɒ'leɪkɪə) *n* a former principality of SE Europe: a vassal state of the Ottoman Empire from the 15th century until its union with Moldavia in 1859, subsequently forming present-day Romania

Walachian *or* **Wallachian** (wɒ'leɪkɪən) *adj* **1** of or relating to the former SE European principality of Walachia (now part of Romania) or its inhabitants ▷ *n* **2** a native or inhabitant of Walachia

Wałbrzych (*Polish* 'vaʊbʒix) *n* an industrial city in SW Poland. Pop: 176 000 (2005 est). German name: Waldenburg

Walcheren (*Dutch* 'wɑlxərə) *n* an island in the SW

Netherlands, in the Scheldt estuary: administratively part of Zeeland province; suffered severely in World War II, when the dykes were breached, and again in the floods of 1953. Area: 212 sq km (82 sq miles)

Waldenburg ('valdənbʊrk) *n* the German name for **Wałbrzych**

Waldenses (wɒl'dɛnsiːz) *pl n* the members of a small sect founded as a reform movement within the Roman Catholic Church by Peter Waldo, a merchant of Lyons in the late 12th century, which in the 16th century joined the Reformation movement. Also called: **Vaudois**. > **Waldensian** (wɒl'dɛnsɪən) *n, adj*

waldgrave ('wɔːldˌgreɪv) *n* (in medieval Germany) an officer with jurisdiction over a royal forest [from German *Waldgraf*, from *Wald* forest + *Graf* count]

waldo ('wɔːldəʊ) *n, pl* **-dos** *or* **-does** a gadget for manipulating objects by remote control [c20 named after *Waldo* F. Jones, inventor in a science-fiction story by Robert Heinlein]

Waldorf salad ('wɔːldɔːf) *n* a salad of diced apples, celery, and walnuts mixed with mayonnaise [c20 named after the *Waldorf-Astoria Hotel* in New York City]

waldsterben ('wɔːldˌstɜːbən) *n ecology* the symptoms of tree decline in central Europe from the 1970s, considered to be caused by atmospheric pollution [c20 from German *Wald* forest + *sterben* to die]

wale[1] (weɪl) *n* **1** the raised mark left on the skin after the stroke of a rod or whip **2 a** the weave or texture of a fabric, such as the ribs in corduroy **b** a vertical row of stitches in knitting. Compare **course** (sense 14) **3** *nautical* **a** a ridge of planking along the rail of a ship **b** See **gunwale** ▷ *vb* (*tr*) **4** to raise a wale or wales on by striking **5** to weave with a wale [Old English *walu* WEAL[1]; related to Old Norse *vala* knuckle, Dutch *wäle*]

wale[2] (weɪl) *Scot and northern English dialect* ▷ *n* **1** a choice **2** anything chosen as the best ▷ *adj* **3** choice ▷ *vb* **4** (*tr*) to choose [c14 from Old Norse *val* choice, related to German *Wahl*]

Waler ('weɪlə) *n chiefly Austral* a saddle horse originating in New South Wales [c19 from *Wales*, in *New South Wales*]

Wales (weɪlz) *n* a principality that is part of the United Kingdom, in the west of Great Britain; conquered by the English in 1282; parliamentary union with England took place in 1536: a separate Welsh Assembly with limited powers was established in 1999. Wales consists mainly of moorlands and mountains and has an economy that is chiefly agricultural, with an industrial and former coal-mining area in the south. Capital: Cardiff. Pop: 2 938 000 (2003 est). Area: 20 768 sq km (8017 sq miles). Welsh name: **Cymru** Medieval Latin name: **Cambria**

Walfish Bay ('wɔːlfɪʃ) *n* a variant spelling of **Walvis Bay**

Walhalla (wæl'hælə, væl-) *or* **Walhall** (wæl'hæl, væl-) *n* variants of **Valhalla**

wali ('wɑːlɪ) *n, pl* **-lis** a divinely inspired leader; saint [Arabic]

walk (wɔːk) *vb* **1** (*intr*) to move along or travel on foot at a moderate rate; advance in such a manner that at least one foot is always on the ground **2** (*tr*) to pass through, on, or over on foot, esp habitually **3** (*tr*) to cause, assist, or force to move along at a moderate rate: *to walk a dog* **4** (*tr*) to escort or conduct by walking: *to walk someone home* **5** (*intr*) (of ghosts, spirits, etc) to appear or move about in visible form **6** (of inanimate objects) to move or cause to move in a manner that resembles walking **7** (*intr*) to follow a certain course or way of life: *to walk in misery* **8** (*tr*) to bring into a certain condition by walking: *I walked my shoes to shreds* **9** (*tr*) to measure, survey, or examine by walking **10** (*intr*) *basketball* to take more than two steps without passing or dribbling the ball **11** to disappear or be stolen: *where's my pencil? It seems* to have walked **12** (*intr*) *slang, chiefly US* (in a court of law) to be acquitted or given a noncustodial sentence **13** walk it to win easily **14** walk the plank See **plank** (sense 4) **15** walk on air to be delighted or exhilarated **16** walk tall *informal* to have self-respect or pride **17** walk the streets **a** to be a prostitute **b** to wander round a town or city, esp when looking for work or having nowhere to stay **18** walk the walk *or* walk the talk *informal* to put theory into practice: *you can talk the talk but can you walk the walk?* See also **talk** (sense 15) ▷ *n* **19** the act or an instance of walking **20** the distance or extent walked **21** a manner of walking; gait **22** a place set aside for walking; promenade **23** a chosen profession or sphere of activity (esp in the phrase **walk of life**) **24** a foot race in which competitors walk **25 a** an arrangement of trees or shrubs in widely separated rows **b** the space between such rows **26** an enclosed ground for the exercise or feeding of domestic animals, esp horses **27** *chiefly Brit* the route covered in the course of work, as by a tradesman or postman **28** a procession; march: *Orange walk* **29** *obsolete* the section of a forest controlled by a keeper ▷ See also **walk away, walk into, walk off, walk out, walkover, walk through** [Old English *wealcan*; related to Old High German *walchan*, Sanskrit *valgati* he moves] > **walkable** *adj*

walkabout ('wɔːkəˌbaʊt) *n* **1** a periodic nomadic excursion into the Australian bush made by a native Australian **2** a walking tour **3** *chiefly journalistic* an occasion when celebrities, royalty, etc, walk among and meet the public **4** go walkabout *Austral* **a** to wander through the bush **b** *informal* to be lost or misplaced **c** *informal* to lose one's concentration

walk away *vb* (*intr, adverb*) **1** to leave, esp callously and disregarding someone else's distress **2** walk away with to achieve or win easily

walker ('wɔːkə) *n* **1** a person who walks **2** Also called: **baby walker** a tubular frame on wheels or castors to support a baby learning to walk **3** a similar support for walking, often with rubber feet, for use by disabled or infirm people **4** a woman's escort at a social event: *let me introduce my walker for tonight*

walkie-talkie *or* **walky-talky** (ˌwɔːkɪ'tɔːkɪ) *n, pl* **-talkies** a small combined radio transmitter and receiver, usually operating on shortwave, that can be carried around by one person: widely used by the police, medical services, etc

walk-in *adj* **1** (of a cupboard) large enough to allow a person to enter and move about in **2** *US* (of a building or apartment) located so as to admit of direct access from the street **3** (of a flat or house) in a suitable condition for immediate occupation

walking ('wɔːkɪŋ) *adj* (of a person) considered to possess the qualities of something inanimate as specified: *he is a walking encyclopedia*

walking bass (beɪs) *n jazz* a simple accompaniment played by the double bass at medium tempo, usually consisting of ascending and descending tones or semitones, one to each beat

walking bus *n* a group of school children walking together along an agreed route to and from school, accompanied by adults, with children joining and leaving the group at pre-arranged points

walking delegate *n* **1** (in the US) an agent appointed by a trade union to visit branches, check whether agreements are observed, and negotiate with employers **2** (in New Zealand) a trade union official who visits dispersed working areas on a wharf

walking dragline *n* a very large-capacity dragline mounted on feet or pads instead of tracks. See **dragline** (sense 2)

walking fern *or* **leaf** *n* a North American fern, *Camptosorus rhizophyllus*, having sword-shaped fronds, the tips of which take root when in

contact with the ground: family *Aspleniaceae*

walking papers *pl n slang, chiefly US and Canadian* notice of dismissal

walking stick *n* **1** a stick or cane carried in the hand to assist walking **2** the usual US name for **stick insect**

walk into *vb* (*intr, preposition*) to meet with unwittingly: *to walk into a trap*

Walkman ('wɔːkmən) *n trademark* a small portable cassette player with light headphones

walk off *vb* **1** (*intr*) to depart suddenly **2** (*tr, adverb*) to get rid of by walking: *to walk off an attack of depression* **3** walk (a person) off his feet to make (someone) walk so fast or far that he or she is exhausted **4** walk off with **a** to steal **b** to win, esp easily

walk-on *n* **1 a** a small part in a play or theatrical entertainment, esp one without any lines **b** (*as modifier*): *a walk-on part* ▷ *adj* **2** (of an aircraft or air service) having seats to be booked immediately before departure rather than in advance

walk out *vb* (*intr, adverb*) **1** to leave without explanation, esp in anger **2** to go on strike **3** walk out on *informal* to abandon or desert **4** walk out with *Brit obsolete or dialect* to court or be courted by ▷ *n* **walkout 5** a strike by workers **6** the act of leaving a meeting, conference, etc, as a protest

walkover ('wɔːkˌəʊvə) *n* **1** *informal* an easy or unopposed victory **2** *horse racing* **a** the running or walking over the course by the only contestant entered in a race at the time of starting **b** a race won in this way ▷ *vb* **walk over** (*intr, mainly preposition*) **3** (*also adverb*) to win a race by a walkover **4** *informal* to beat (an opponent) conclusively or easily **5** *informal* to take advantage of (someone)

walkshorts ('wɔːkˌʃɔːts) *pl n* NZ smart shorts for men

walk socks *pl n* NZ men's knee-length stockings

walk through *theatre* ▷ *vb* **1** (*tr*) to act or recite (a part) in a perfunctory manner, as at a first rehearsal ▷ *n* **walk-through 2** a rehearsal of a part

walk-up *n* US and Canadian informal **a** a block of flats having no lift **b** (*as modifier*): *a walk-up block*

walkway ('wɔːkˌweɪ) *n* **1** a path designed, and sometimes landscaped, for pedestrian use **2** a passage or path connecting buildings **3** a passage or path, esp one for walking over machinery, etc

Walkyrie ('vælˈkɪərɪ, ˈvælkɪərɪ) *n* a variant spelling of **Valkyrie**

wall (wɔːl) *n* **1 a** a vertical construction made of stone, brick, wood, etc, with a length and height much greater than its thickness, used to enclose, divide, or support **b** (*as modifier*): *wall hangings*. Related adj: **mural 2** (*often plural*) a structure or rampart built to protect and surround a position or place for defensive purposes **3** *anatomy* any lining, membrane, or investing part that encloses or bounds a bodily cavity or structure: *abdominal wall*. Technical name: **paries** Related adj: **parietal 4** *mountaineering* a vertical or almost vertical smooth rock face **5** anything that suggests a wall in function or effect: *a wall of fire; a wall of prejudice* **6** bang one's head against a brick wall to try to achieve something impossible **7** drive (*or* push) to the wall to force into an awkward situation **8** go to the wall to be ruined; collapse financially **9** go (*or* drive) up the wall *slang* to become (or cause to become) crazy or furious **10** have one's back to the wall to be in a very difficult situation **11** See **off-the-wall 12** See **wall-to-wall** ▷ *vb* (*tr*) **13** to protect, provide, or confine with or as if with a wall **14** (often foll by *up*) to block (an opening) with a wall **15** (often foll by *in* or *up*) to seal by or within a wall or walls [Old English *weall*, from Latin *vallum* palisade, from *vallus* stake] > **walled** *adj* > **wall-less** *adj* > **wall-like** *adj*

wallaby ('wɒləbɪ) *n, pl* **-bies** *or* **-by 1** any of various herbivorous marsupials of the genera *Lagorchestes* (**hare wallabies**), *Petrogale* (**rock wallabies**),

Protemnodon, etc, of Australia and New Guinea, similar to but smaller than kangaroos: family *Macropodidae* **2** on the wallaby (track) *Austral slang* (of a person) wandering about looking for work [C19 from native Australian *wolabā*]

Wallaby ('wɒləbɪ) *n, pl* **-bies** a member of the international Rugby Union football team of Australia

Wallace's line *n* the hypothetical boundary between the Oriental and Australasian zoogeographical regions, which runs between the Indonesian islands of Bali and Lombok, through the Macassar Strait, and SE of the Philippines [C20 named after Alfred Russel *Wallace* (1823–1913), British naturalist]

Wallachia (wɒˈleɪkɪə) *n* a variant spelling of **Walachia**

Wallachian (wɒˈleɪkɪən) *adj, n* a variant spelling of **Walachian**

wallah *or* **walla** ('wɒlə) *n* (*usually in combination*) *informal* a person involved with or in charge of (a specified thing): *the book wallah* [C18 from Hindi *-wālā* from Sanskrit *pāla* protector]

wallaroo (ˌwɒlə'ruː) *n, pl* **-roos** *or* **-roo** a large stocky Australian kangaroo, *Macropus* (or *Osphranter*) *robustus*, of rocky regions [C19 from native Australian *wolarū*]

Wallasey ('wɒləsɪ) *n* a town in NW England, in Wirral unitary authority, Merseyside; near the mouth of the River Mersey, opposite Liverpool. Pop: 58 710 (2001)

wall bars *pl n* a series of horizontal bars attached to a wall and used in gymnastics

wallboard ('wɔːlˌbɔːd) *n* a thin board made of materials, such as compressed wood fibres or gypsum plaster, between stiff paper, and used to cover walls, partitions, etc

wall brown *n* any of three species of brown butterfly, esp the common *Lasiommata megera*, that habitually sun themselves on rocks and walls

wall creeper *n* a pink-and-grey woodpecker-like songbird, *Tichodroma muraria*, of Eurasian mountain regions: family *Sittidae* (nuthatches)

walled plain *n* any of the largest of the lunar craters, having diameters between 50 and 300 kilometres

wallet ('wɒlɪt) *n* **1** a small folding case, usually of leather, for holding paper money, documents, etc **2** a bag used to carry tools **3** *archaic, chiefly Brit* a rucksack or knapsack [C14 of Germanic origin; compare Old English *weallian*, Old High German *wallōn* to roam, German *wallen* to go on a pilgrimage]

walleye ('wɔːlˌaɪ) *n, pl* **-eyes** *or* **-eye 1** a divergent squint **2** opacity of the cornea **3** an eye having a white or light-coloured iris **4** (in some collies) an eye that is particoloured white and blue **5** Also called: **walleyed pike** a North American pikeperch, *Stizostedion vitreum*, valued as a food and game fish **6** any of various other fishes having large staring eyes [back formation from earlier *walleyed*, from Old Norse *vagleygr*, from *vage*, perhaps: a film over the eye (compare Swedish *vagel* sty in the eye) + *-eygr* -eyed, from *auga* eye; modern form influenced by WALL] > **walleyed** *adj*

wallflower ('wɔːlˌflaʊə) *n* **1** Also called: **gillyflower** a plant, *Cheiranthus cheiri*, of S Europe, grown for its clusters of yellow, orange, brown, red, or purple fragrant flowers and naturalized on old walls, cliffs, etc: family *Brassicaceae* (crucifers) **2** any of numerous other crucifers of the genera *Cheiranthus* and *Erysimum*, having orange or yellow flowers **3** *informal* a person who stays on the fringes of a dance or party on account of lacking a partner or being shy

wall fruit *n* fruit grown on trees trained against a wall for the shelter and warmth it provides

wall game *n* a type of football played at Eton against a wall

wallies ('wælɪz) *pl n Central Scot dialect* false teeth; dentures [see WALLY²]

Wallis ('valɪs) *n* the German name for **Valais**

W

Wallis and Futuna Islands ('wɒlɪs, fuːˈtjuːnə) *pl n* a French overseas territory in the SW Pacific, west of Samoa. Capital: Mata-Utu. Pop: 15 000 (2003 est). Area: 367 sq km (143 sq miles)

wall knot *n* a knot forming a knob at the end of a rope, made by unwinding the strands and weaving them together

wall lizard *n* a small mottled grey lizard, *Lacerta muralis,* of Europe, N Africa, and SW Asia: family *Lacertidae*

wall mustard *n* another name for **stinkweed** (sense 1)

wall of death *n* (at a fairground) a giant cylinder round the inside walls of which a motorcyclist rides

Walloon (wɒˈluːn) *n* **1** a member of a French-speaking people living chiefly in S Belgium and adjacent parts of France. Compare **Fleming**[1] **2** the French dialect of Belgium ▷ *adj* **3** of, relating to, or characteristic of the Walloons or their dialect [C16 from Old French *Wallon,* from Medieval Latin: foreigner, of Germanic origin; compare Old English *wealh* foreign, **WELSH**[1]]

Walloon Brabant *n* a province of central Belgium, formed in 1995 from the S part of Brabant province: densely populated and intensively farmed, with large industrial centres. Pop: 360 717 (2004 est). Area: 1091 sq km (421 sq miles)

wallop ('wɒləp) *vb* -lops, -loping, -loped **1** (*tr*) *informal* to beat soundly; strike hard **2** (*tr*) *informal* to defeat utterly **3** (*intr*) *dialect* to move in a clumsy manner **4** (*intr*) (of liquids) to boil violently ▷ *n* **5** *informal* a hard blow **6** *informal* the ability to hit powerfully, as of a boxer **7** *informal* a forceful impression **8** *Brit* a slang word for **beer** ▷ *vb* **9** an obsolete word for **gallop** [C14 from Old Northern French *waloper* to gallop, from Old French *galoper,* of unknown origin]

walloper ('wɒləpə) *n* **1** a person or thing that wallops **2** *Austral slang* a policeman

walloping ('wɒləpɪŋ) *informal* ▷ *n* **1** a thrashing ▷ *adj* **2** (intensifier): *a walloping drop in sales*

wallow ('wɒləʊ) *vb* (*intr*) **1** (esp of certain animals) to roll about in mud, water, etc, for pleasure **2** to move about with difficulty **3** to indulge oneself in possessions, emotion, etc: *to wallow in self-pity* **4** (of smoke, waves, etc) to billow ▷ *n* **5** the act or an instance of wallowing **6** a muddy place or depression where animals wallow [Old English *wealwian* to roll (in mud); related to Latin *volvere* to turn, Greek *oulos* curly, Russian *valun* round pebble] > 'wallower *n*

wallpaper ('wɔːlˌpeɪpə) *n* **1** paper usually printed or embossed with designs for pasting onto walls and ceilings **2 a** something pleasant but bland which serves as an unobtrusive background **b** (*as modifier*): *wallpaper music* ▷ *vb* **3** *computing* a graphics file that can be displayed in certain applications behind or around the main dialogue boxes, working display areas, etc, for decoration **4** to cover (a surface) with wallpaper

wall pass *n soccer* a movement in which one player passes the ball to another and sprints forward to receive the quickly played return. Also called: **one-two**

wall pellitory *n* See **pellitory** (sense 1)

wall pepper *n* a small Eurasian crassulaceous plant, *Sedum acre,* having creeping stems, yellow flowers, and acrid-tasting leaves

wall plate *n* a horizontal timber member placed along the top of a wall to support the ends of joists, rafters, etc, and distribute the load

wallposter ('wɔːlˌpəʊstə) *n* (in China) a bulletin or political message painted in large characters on walls

wall rock *n* rock that is immediately adjacent to a mineral vein, fault, or igneous intrusion

wall rocket *n* any of several yellow-flowered European plants of the genus *Diplotaxis,* such as *D. muralis,* that grow on old walls and in waste places: family *Brassicaceae* (crucifers)

wall rue *n* a delicate fern, *Asplenium ruta-muraria,* that grows in rocky crevices and walls in North America and Eurasia

Wallsend ('wɔːlzˌɛnd) *n* a town in NE England, in North Tyneside unitary authority, Tyne and Wear: situated on the River Tyne at the E end of Hadrian's Wall. Pop: 42 842 (2001)

Wall Street *n* a street in lower Manhattan, New York, where the Stock Exchange and major banks are situated, regarded as the embodiment of American finance

wall-to-wall *adj* **1** (of carpeting) completely covering a floor **2** *informal* as far as the eye can see; widespread: *wall-to-wall sales in the high street shops*

wally[1] ('weɪlɪ) *adj Scot archaic* **1** fine, pleasing, or splendid **2** robust or strong [C16 of obscure origin]

wally[2] ('wælɪ) *adj Central Scot dialect* **1** made of china: *a wally dug; a wally vase* **2** lined with ceramic tiles: *a wally close* ▷ See also **wallies** [from obsolete dialect *wallow* faded, adjectival use of *wallow* to fade, from Old English *wealwian*]

wally[3] ('wɒlɪ) *n, pl* -lies *slang* a stupid person [C20 shortened form of the given name *Walter*]

walnut ('wɔːlˌnʌt) *n* **1** any juglandaceous deciduous tree of the genus *Juglans,* of America, SE Europe, and Asia, esp *J. regia,* which is native to W Asia but introduced elsewhere. They have aromatic leaves and flowers in catkins and are grown for their edible nuts and for their wood **2** the nut of any of these trees, having a wrinkled two-lobed seed and a hard wrinkled shell **3** the wood of any of these trees, used in making furniture, panelling, etc **4** a light yellowish-brown colour ▷ *adj* **5** made from the wood of a walnut tree: *a walnut table* **6** of the colour walnut [Old English *walh-hnutu,* literally: foreign nut; compare Old French *noux gauge* walnut, probably translation of Vulgar Latin phrase *nux gallica* (unattested) Gaulish (hence, foreign) nut]

walnut oil *n* an oil pressed from walnuts and used in cooking, esp in salad dressings

Walpurgis Night (væl'pʊəgɪs) *n* the eve of May 1, believed in German folklore to be the night of a witches' sabbath on the Brocken, in the Harz Mountains [C19 translation of German *Walpurgisnacht,* the eve of the feast day of St Walpurga, 8th-century abbess in Germany]

walrus ('wɔːlrəs, 'wɒl-) *n, pl* -ruses *or* -rus a pinniped mammal, *Odobenus rosmarus,* of northern seas, having a tough thick skin, upper canine teeth enlarged as tusks, and coarse whiskers and feeding mainly on shellfish: family *Odobenidae* [C17 probably from Dutch, from Scandinavian; compare Old Norse *hrosshvalr* (literally: horse whale) and Old English *horschwæl*; see **HORSE**, **WHALE**]

walrus moustache *n* a long thick moustache drooping at the ends

Walsall ('wɔːlsɔːl) *n* **1** an industrial town in central England, in Walsall unitary authority, West Midlands: engineering, electronics. Pop: 170 994 (2001) **2** a unitary authority in central England, in the West Midlands. Pop: 252 400 (2003 est). Area: 106 sq km (41 sq miles)

Walsingham ('wɔːlsɪŋəm) *n* a village in E England, in Norfolk: remains of a medieval priory; site of the shrine of Our Lady of Walsingham

Waltham Forest ('wɔːləm) *n* a borough of NE Greater London. Pop: 221 600 (2003 est). Area: 40 sq km (15 sq miles)

waltz (wɔːls) *n* **1** a ballroom dance in triple time in which couples spin around as they progress round the room **2** a piece of music composed for or in the rhythm of this dance ▷ *vb* **3** to dance or lead (someone) in or as in a waltz: *he waltzed her off her feet* **4** (*intr*) to move in a sprightly and self-assured manner **5** (*intr*) *informal* to succeed easily [C18 from German *Walzer,* from Middle High German *walzen* to roll; compare **WELTER**] > 'waltzˌlike *adj*

waltzer ('wɔːlsə) *n* **1** a person who waltzes **2** a fairground roundabout on which people are spun round and moved up and down as it revolves about a central axis

waltz Matilda *vb Austral* See **Matilda**

Walvis Bay ('wɔːlvɪs) *or* **Walfish Bay** *n* a port in Namibia, on the Atlantic: formed an exclave of South Africa, covering an area of 1124 sq km (434 sq miles) with its hinterland, but has been administered by Namibia since 1992; formally returned to Namibia in 1994; chief port of Namibia and rich fishing centre. Pop: 40 849 (2001)

wambenger (wɒm'bɛŋə) *n Austral* another name for **tuan**[2] [from a native Australian language]

wamble ('wɒmbəl) *dialect, chiefly Brit* ▷ *vb* (*intr*) **1** to move unsteadily **2** to twist the body **3** to feel nausea ▷ *n* **4** an unsteady movement **5** a sensation of nausea [C14 *wamelen* to feel ill, perhaps of Scandinavian origin; compare Norwegian *vamla* to stagger] > 'wambliness *n* > 'wambly *adj*

wame (weɪm) *n Scot and northern English dialect* the belly, abdomen, or womb [C14 northern variant of **WOMB**]

wammul ('wæməl) *n Midland English dialect* a dog

wampum ('wɒmpəm) *n* **1** (formerly) money used by North American Indians, made of cylindrical shells strung or woven together, esp white shells rather than the more valuable black or purple ones **2** *US and Canadian informal* money or wealth ▷ Also called: **peag, peage** [C17 short for *wampumpeag,* from Narraganset *wampompeag,* from *wampan* light + *api* string + *-ag* plural suffix]

wan (wɒn) *adj* wanner, wannest **1** unnaturally pale esp from sickness, grief, etc **2** characteristic or suggestive of ill health, unhappiness, etc **3** (of light, stars, etc) faint or dim ▷ *vb* wans, wanning, wanned **4** to make or become wan [Old English *wann* dark; related to *wanian* to **WANE**] > 'wanly *adv* > 'wanness *n*

WAN *abbreviation for* **1** wide area network **2** *international car registration for* (West Africa) Nigeria

wanchancy (wɒn'tʃænsɪ) *adj Scot* **1** unlucky **2** dangerous; risky **3** uncanny; eerie ▷ Compare **unchancy** [C18 from *wanchance* ill luck, from *wan*-prefix expressing negation or privation + **CHANCE**]

Wanchüan *or* **Wan-ch'uan** (ˌwæntʃʊ'aːn) *n* a former name of **Zhangjiakou**

wand (wɒnd) *n* **1** a slender supple stick or twig **2** a thin rod carried as a symbol of authority **3** a rod used by a magician, water diviner, etc **4** *informal* a conductor's baton **5** *archery* a marker used to show the distance at which the archer stands from the target **6** a hand-held electronic device, such as a light pen or bar-code reader, which is pointed at or passed over an item to read the data stored there [C12 from Old Norse *vöndr*; related to Gothic *wandus* and English **WEND**] > 'wandˌlike *adj*

wander ('wɒndə) *vb* (mainly *intr*) **1** (also tr) to move or travel about, in, or through (a place) without any definite purpose or destination **2** to proceed in an irregular course; meander **3** to go astray, as from a path or course **4** (of the mind, thoughts, etc) to lose concentration or direction **5** to think or speak incoherently or illogically ▷ *n* **6** the act or an instance of wandering [Old English *wandrian*; related to Old Frisian *wandria,* Middle Dutch, Middle High German *wanderen*] > 'wanderer *n* > 'wandering *adj, n* > 'wanderingly *adv*

wandering albatross *n* a large albatross, *Diomedea exulans,* having a very wide wingspan and a white plumage with black wings

wandering Jew *n* **1** any of several related creeping or trailing plants of tropical America, esp *Tradescantia fluminensis* and *Zebrina pendula*: family *Commelinaceae* **2** *Austral* a similar creeping plant of the genus *Commelina*

Wandering Jew *n* (in medieval legend) a character condemned to roam the world eternally because he mocked Christ on the day of the Crucifixion

Wanderjahr *German* ('vandərjaːr) *n, pl -jahre* (-jaːrə) (formerly) a year in which an apprentice travelled to improve his skills [German, literally: wander year]

wanderlust ('wɒndəˌlʌst) *n* a great desire to travel and rove about [German, literally: wander desire]

wanderoo (ˌwɒndəˈruː) *n, pl* **-deroos** a macaque monkey, *Macaca silenus*, of India and Sri Lanka, having black fur with a ruff of long greyish fur on each side of the face [C17 from Sinhalese *vanduru* monkeys, literally: forest-dwellers, from Sanskrit *vānara* monkey, from *vana* forest]

wander plug *n* an electrical plug on the end of a flexible wire, for insertion into any of a number of sockets

wandoo ('wɒnduː) *n* a eucalyptus tree, *Eucalyptus wandoo*, of W Australia, having white bark and durable wood [from a native Australian language]

Wandsworth ('wɒnzwəθ) *n* a borough of S Greater London, on the River Thames. Pop: 274 100 (2003 est). Area: 35 sq km (13 sq miles)

wane (weɪn) *vb* (*intr*) **1** (of the moon) to show a gradually decreasing portion of illuminated surface, between full moon and new moon. Compare **wax²** (sense 2) **2** to decrease gradually in size, strength, power, etc **3** to draw to a close ▷ *n* **4** a decrease, as in size, strength, power, etc **5** the period during which the moon wanes **6** the act or an instance of drawing to a close **7** a rounded surface or defective edge of a plank, where the bark was **8** **on the wane** in a state of decline [Old English *wanian* (vb); related to *wan-*, prefix indicating privation, *wana* defect, Old Norse *vana*] ▷ 'waney *or* 'wany *adj*

Wanganui (ˌwɒŋəˈnuːɪ) *n* a port in New Zealand, on SW North Island: centre for a dairy-farming and sheep-rearing district. Pop: 43 600 (2004 est)

wangle ('wæŋɡəl) *informal* ▷ *vb* **1** (*tr*) to use devious or illicit methods to get or achieve (something) for (oneself or another): *he wangled himself a salary increase* **2** to manipulate or falsify (a situation, action, etc) ▷ *n* **3** the act or an instance of wangling [C19 originally printers' slang, perhaps a blend of WAGGLE and dialect *wankle* wavering, from Old English *wancol*; compare Old High German *wankōn* to waver] ▷ 'wangler *n*

Wanhsien *or* **Wan-Hsien** ('wænˈfjɛn) *n* a variant transliteration of the Chinese name for **Wanxian**

wank (wæŋk) *slang* ▷ *vb* **1** (*intr*) to masturbate ▷ *n* **2** an instance of wanking ▷ *adj* **3** bad, useless, or worthless [of uncertain origin]

Wankel engine ('wæŋkəl) *n* a type of four-stroke internal-combustion engine without reciprocating parts. It consists of one or more approximately elliptical combustion chambers within which a curved triangular-shaped piston rotates, by the explosion of compressed gas, dividing the combustion chamber into three gastight sections [C20 named after Felix *Wankel* (1902–88), German engineer who invented it]

wanker ('wæŋkə) *n slang* **1** a person who wanks; masturbator **2** a worthless fellow

Wankie ('wɑːŋkɪ) *n* the former name (until 1982) of **Hwange**

wanksta ('wæŋkstə) *n US slang derogatory* a person who acts or dresses like a gangster but who is not involved in crime [C20 from WANNABE + *gangsta* phonetic rendering of GANGSTER, also influenced by WANKER]

wanky ('wæŋkɪ) *adj slang* pretentious

wanna ('wɒnə) *vb* a spelling of **want to** intended to reflect a dialectal or informal pronunciation: *I wanna go home*

wannabe *or* **wannabee** ('wɒnəˌbiː) *n informal* **a** a person who desires to be, or be like, someone or something else: *a group of Marilyn Monroe wannabes* **b** (*as modifier*): *a wannabe film star* [C20 phonetic shortening of *want to be*]

Wanne-Eickel (German 'vanə'aikəl) *n* an industrial town in W Germany, in North Rhine-Westphalia on the Rhine-Herne Canal: formed in 1926 by the merging of two townships. Pop: 98 800 (latest est)

want¹ (wɒnt) *vb* **1** (*tr*) to feel a need or longing for: *I want a new hat* **2** (when *tr*, may take a clause as object or an infinitive) to wish, need, or desire (something or to do something): *he wants to go home* **3** (*intr;* usually used with a negative and often foll by *for*) to be lacking or deficient (in something necessary or desirable): *the child wants for nothing* **4** (*tr*) to feel the absence of: *lying on the ground makes me want my bed* **5** (*tr*) to fall short by (a specified amount) **6** (*tr*) *chiefly Brit* to have need of or require (doing or being something): *your shoes want cleaning* **7** (*intr*) to be destitute **8** (*tr; often passive*) to seek or request the presence of: *you're wanted upstairs* **9** (*intr*) to be absent **10** (*tr; takes an infinitive*) *informal* should or ought (to do something): *you don't want to go out so late* **11** **want in** (*or* **out**) *informal* to wish to be included in (or excluded from) a venture ▷ *n* **12** the act or an instance of wanting **13** anything that is needed, desired, or lacked: *to supply someone's wants* **14** a lack, shortage, or absence: *for want of common sense* **15** the state of being in need; destitution: *the state should help those in want* **16** a sense of lack; craving [C12 (vb, in the sense: it is lacking), C13 (n): from Old Norse *vanta* to be deficient; related to Old English *wanian* to WANE] ▷ 'wanter *n*

want² (wɒnt) *n English dialect* a mole [Old English *wand*]

want ad *n informal* a classified advertisement in a newspaper, magazine, etc, for something wanted, such as property or employment

wanted ('wɒntɪd) *adj* being searched for by the police in connection with a crime that has been committed

wanting ('wɒntɪŋ) *adj* (*postpositive*) **1** lacking or absent; missing **2** not meeting requirements or expectations: *you have been found wanting* ▷ *prep* **3** without **4** *archaic* minus

want knap *n Southwest English dialect* a mole hill

WAN2TLK *text messaging abbreviation for* want to talk?

wanton ('wɒntən) *adj* **1** dissolute, licentious, or immoral **2** without motive, provocation, or justification: *wanton destruction* **3** maliciously and unnecessarily cruel or destructive **4** unrestrained: *wanton spending* **5** *archaic or poetic* playful or capricious **6** *archaic* (of vegetation, etc) luxuriant or superabundant ▷ *n* **7** a licentious person, esp a woman **8** a playful or capricious person ▷ *vb* **9** (*intr*) to behave in a wanton manner **10** (*tr*) to squander or waste [C13 *wantowen* (in the obsolete sense: unmanageable, unruly): from *wan-* (prefix equivalent to UN-¹; related to Old English *wanian* to WANE) + *-towen*, from Old English *togen* brought up, from *tēon* to bring up] ▷ 'wantonly *adv* ▷ 'wantonness *n*

Wanxian, Wanhsien *or* **Wan-Hsien** ('wænˈfjɛn) *n* an inland port in central China, in E Sichuan province, on the Yangtze River. Pop: 1 963 000 (2005 est)

WAP (wæp) *n acronym for* Wireless Application Protocol: a global application that enables mobile phone users to access the internet and other information services

wapentake ('wɒpənˌteɪk, 'wæp-) *n English legal history* a subdivision of certain shires or counties, esp in the Midlands and North of England, corresponding to the hundred in other shires [Old English *wæpen(ge)tæc*, from Old Norse *vāpnatak*, from *vápn* WEAPON + *tak* TAKE]

wapiti ('wɒpɪtɪ) *n, pl* **-tis** a large deer, *Cervus canadensis*, with large much-branched antlers, native to North America and now also common in the South Island of New Zealand. Also called: **American elk** [C19 from Shawnee, literally: white deer, from *wap* (unattested) white; from the animal's white tail and rump]

wappenshaw ('wæpənˌfɔː, 'wɒp-) *n* (formerly) a muster of men in a particular area in Scotland to show that they were properly armed [C16 from Northern English *wapen*, from Old Norse *vápn* WEAPON + *schaw* SHOW]

war (wɔː) *n* **1** open armed conflict between two or more parties, nations, or states. Related adjs: **belligerent, martial 2** a particular armed conflict: *the 1973 war in the Middle East* **3** the techniques of armed conflict as a study, science, or profession **4** any conflict or contest: *a war of wits; the war against crime* **5** (*modifier*) of, relating to, resulting from, or characteristic of war: *war damage* **6** **to have had a good war** to have made the most of the opportunities presented to one during wartime **7** **in the wars** *informal* (esp of a child) hurt or knocked about, esp as a result of quarrelling and fighting ▷ *vb* **wars, warring, warred 8** (*intr*) to conduct a war [C12 from Old Northern French *werre* (variant of Old French *guerre*), of Germanic origin; related to Old High German *werra*]

War. *abbreviation for* Warwickshire

waragi ('waraɡɪ, -dʒɪ) *n* a Ugandan alcoholic drink made from bananas [from Luganda]

Warangal ('wʌrənɡəl) *n* a city in S central India, in N Andhra Pradesh: capital of a 12th-century Hindu kingdom. Pop: 528 570 (2001)

waratah (ˌwɒrəˈtɑː, ˈwɒrətɑː) *n Austral* a proteaceous shrub, *Telopea speciosissima*, the floral emblem of New South Wales, having dark green leaves and large clusters of crimson flowers [from a native Australian language]

warb (wɔːb) *n Austral slang* a dirty or insignificant person [C20 of unknown origin] ▷ 'warby *adj*

war baby *n* a child born in wartime, esp the illegitimate child of a soldier

War Between the States *n* the American Civil War

warble¹ ('wɔːbəl) *vb* **1** to sing (words, songs, etc) with trills, runs, and other embellishments **2** (*tr*) to utter in a song **3** *US* another word for **yodel** ▷ *n* **4** the act or an instance of warbling [C14 via Old French *werbler* from Germanic; compare Frankish *hwirbilōn* (unattested), Old High German *wirbil* whirlwind; see WHIRL]

warble² ('wɔːbəl) *n vet science* **1** a small lumpy abscess under the skin of cattle caused by infestation with larvae of the warble fly **2** a hard tumorous lump of tissue on a horse's back, caused by prolonged friction of a saddle [C16 of uncertain origin] ▷ 'warbled *adj*

warble fly *n* any of various hairy beelike dipterous flies of the genus *Hypoderma* and related genera, the larvae of which produce warbles in cattle: family *Oestridae*

warbler ('wɔːblə) *n* **1** a person or thing that warbles **2** any small active passerine songbird of the Old World subfamily *Sylviinae*: family *Muscicapidae*. They have a cryptic plumage and slender bill and are arboreal insectivores **3** Also called: **wood warbler** any small bird of the American family *Parulidae*, similar to the Old World forms but often brightly coloured

war bonnet *n* a headband with trailing feathers, worn by certain North American Indian warriors as a headdress

war bride *n* a soldier's bride met as a result of troop movements in wartime, esp a foreign national

warchalking ('wɔːtʃɔːkɪŋ) *n* the practice of marking chalk symbols on walls and pavements at places where local wireless internet connections may be obtained for free via a computer, usually without permission ▷ 'warchalker *n* [C21 from w(ireless) a(ccess) r(evolution) + gerund of of CHALK]

war chest *n* a fund collected for a specific purpose, such as an election campaign

war correspondent *n* a journalist who reports on a war from the scene of action

war crime *n* a crime committed in wartime in violation of the accepted rules and customs of war, such as genocide, ill-treatment of prisoners of war, etc ▷ **war criminal** *n*

war cry *n* **1** a rallying cry used by combatants in

W

battle **2** a cry, slogan, etc, used to rally support for a cause

ward (wɔːd) *n* **1** (in many countries) a district into which a city, town, parish, or other area is divided for administration, election of representatives, etc **2** a room in a hospital, esp one for patients requiring similar kinds of care: *a maternity ward* **3** one of the divisions of a prison **4** an open space enclosed within the walls of a castle **5** *law* Also called: **ward of court** a person, esp a minor or one legally incapable of managing his own affairs, placed under the control or protection of a guardian or of a court **b** guardianship, as of a minor or legally incompetent person **6** the state of being under guard or in custody **7** a person who is under the protection or in the custody of another **8** a means of protection **9 a** an internal ridge or bar in a lock that prevents an incorrectly cut key from turning **b** a corresponding groove cut in a key **10** a less common word for **warden**[1] ▷ *vb* **11** (*tr*) *archaic* to guard or protect ▷ See also **ward off** [Old English *weard* protector; related to Old High German *wart*, Old Saxon *ward*, Old Norse *vorthr*. See GUARD] > ˈwardless *adj*

-ward *suffix* **1** (*forming adjectives*) indicating direction towards: *a backward step; heavenward progress* **2** (*forming adverbs*) a variant and the usual US and Canadian form of **-wards** [Old English *-weard* towards]

war dance *n* **1** a ceremonial dance performed before going to battle or after victory, esp by certain North American Indian peoples **2** a dance representing warlike action

warded (ˈwɔːdɪd) *adj* (of locks, keys, etc) having wards

warden[1] (ˈwɔːdᵊn) *n* **1** a person who has the charge or care of something, esp a building, or someone **2** *archaic* any of various public officials, esp one responsible for the enforcement of certain regulations **3** *chiefly US and Canadian* the chief officer in charge of a prison **4** *Brit* the principal or president of any of various universities or colleges **5** See **churchwarden** (sense 1) [c13 from Old Northern French *wardein*, from *warder* to guard, of Germanic origin; see GUARD] > ˈwardenry *n*

warden[2] (ˈwɔːdᵊn) *n* a variety of pear that has crisp firm flesh and is used for cooking [c15 of obscure origin]

warder[1] (ˈwɔːdə) *or feminine* **wardress** *n* **1** *chiefly Brit* an officer in charge of prisoners in a jail **2** a person who guards or has charge of something [c14 from Anglo-French *wardere*, from Old French *warder* to GUARD, of Germanic origin] > ˈwardership *n*

warder[2] (ˈwɔːdə) *n* (formerly) a staff or truncheon carried by a ruler as an emblem of authority and used to signal his wishes or intentions [c15 perhaps from Middle English *warden* to WARD]

ward heeler *n* *US politics disparaging* a party worker who canvasses votes and performs chores for a political boss. Also called: **heeler**

wardian case (ˈwɔːdɪən) *n* a type of glass container used for housing delicate ferns and similar plants [c19 named after N. B. *Ward* (died 1868), English botanist]

wardmote (ˈwɔːdməʊt) *n* *Brit* an assembly of the citizens or liverymen of a ward [c14 see WARD, MOOT]

ward off *vb* (*tr, adverb*) to turn aside or repel; avert

Wardour Street (ˈwɔːdə) *n* **1** a street in Soho where many film companies have their London offices: formerly noted for shops selling antiques and mock antiques **2** *Wardour Street English* affectedly archaic speech or writing

wardrobe (ˈwɔːdrəʊb) *n* **1** a tall closet or cupboard, with a rail or hooks on which to hang clothes **2** the total collection of articles of clothing belonging to one person **3** the collection of costumes belonging to a theatre or theatrical company [c14 from Old Northern French *warderobe*, from *warder* to GUARD + *robe* ROBE]

wardrobe malfunction *n* *US informal* an embarrassing situation caused by the clothes a person is wearing [C21]

wardrobe mistress *n* a person responsible for maintaining and sometimes making the costumes in a theatre

wardrobe trunk *n* a large upright rectangular travelling case, usually opening longitudinally, with one side having a hanging rail, the other having drawers or compartments

wardroom (ˈwɔːdˌruːm, -ˌrʊm) *n* **1** the quarters assigned to the officers (except the captain) of a warship **2** the officers of a warship collectively, excepting the captain

-wards *or* **-ward** *suffix forming adverbs* indicating direction towards: *a step backwards; to sail shorewards.* Compare **-ward** [Old English *-weardes* towards]

wardship (ˈwɔːdʃɪp) *n* the state of being a ward

ware[1] (wɛə) *n* (*often in combination*) **1** (*functioning as singular*) articles of the same kind or material: *glassware; silverware* **2** porcelain or pottery of a specified type: *agateware; jasper ware* ▷ See also **wares** [Old English *waru*; related to Old Frisian *were*, Old Norse *vara*, Middle Dutch *Ware*]

ware[2] (wɛə) *archaic* ▷ *vb* **1** another word for **beware** ▷ *adj* **2** another word for **wary** *or* **wise**[1] [Old English *wær*; related to Old Saxon, Old High German *giwar*, Old Norse *varr*, Gothic *war*, Latin *vereor*. See AWARE, BEWARE]

ware[3] (wɛə) *vb* (*tr*) *Northern Brit dialect* to spend or squander [c15 of Scandinavian origin; related to Icelandic *verja*]

warehou (wɑːˈrəhʊː) *n, pl* **warehou** any of several edible saltwater New Zealand fish of the genus *Seriolella* [Māori]

warehouse *n* (ˈwɛəˌhaʊs) **1** a place where goods are stored prior to their use, distribution, or sale **2** See **bonded warehouse** **3** *chiefly Brit* a large commercial, esp wholesale, establishment ▷ *vb* (ˈwɛəˌhaʊz, -ˌhaʊs) **4** (*tr*) to store or place in a warehouse, esp a bonded warehouse

warehouseman (ˈwɛəˌhaʊsmən) *n, pl* **-men** a person who manages, is employed in, or owns a warehouse

warehousing (ˈwɛəˌhaʊzɪŋ) *n* *stock exchange* an attempt to maintain the price of a company's shares or to gain a significant stake in a company without revealing the true identity of the purchaser. Shares are purchased through an insurance company, a unit trust, or nominees

wares (wɛəz) *pl n* **1** articles of manufacture considered as being for sale **2** any talent or asset regarded as a commercial or saleable commodity **3** (*Caribbean*) earthenware

war establishment *n* the full wartime complement of men, equipment, and vehicles of a military unit

warez (wɛəz, ˈwɛrɛz) *n* *informal* illegally copied computer software which has had its protection codes de-activated [c20 possibly from (SOFT)WARE and influenced by the anglicized pronunciation of *Juarez*, a Mexican city known for smuggling]

warfare (ˈwɔːˌfɛə) *n* **1** the act, process, or an instance of waging war **2** conflict, struggle, or strife

warfarin (ˈwɔːfərɪn) *n* a crystalline insoluble optically active compound, used as a rodenticide and, in the form of its sodium salt, as a medical anticoagulant. Formula: $C_{19}H_{16}O_4$ [c20 from the patent owners W(isconsin) A(lumni) R(esearch) F(oundation) + (COUM)ARIN]

war game *n* **1** a notional tactical exercise for training military commanders, in which no military units are actually deployed **2** a game in which model soldiers are used to create battles, esp past battles, in order to study tactics ▷ *vb* **war-game** **3** (*intr*) to prepare for battle by considering possible tactics and enemy responses

warhead (ˈwɔːˌhɛd) *n* the part of the fore end of a missile or projectile that contains explosives

warhorse (ˈwɔːˌhɔːs) *n* **1** a horse used in battle **2** *informal* a veteran soldier, politician, or elderly

person, esp one who is aggressive

warison (ˈwærɪsən) *n* (*esp formerly*) a bugle note used as an order to a military force to attack [c13 from Old Northern French, from *warir* to protect, of Germanic origin; compare Old English *warian* to defend]

wark (wɑːrk, wɔːrk) *n* a Scot word for **work**

Warks *abbreviation for* Warwickshire

Warley (ˈwɔːlɪ) *n* an industrial town in W central England, in Sandwell unitary authority, West Midlands: formed in 1966 by the amalgamation of Smethwick, Oldbury, and Rowley Regis. Pop: 189 854 (2001)

warlike (ˈwɔːˌlaɪk) *adj* **1** of, relating to, or used in war **2** hostile or belligerent **3** fit or ready for war

warlock (ˈwɔːˌlɒk) *n* **1** a man who practises black magic; sorcerer **2** a fortune-teller, conjuror, or magician [Old English *wærloga* oath breaker, from *wær* oath + *-loga* liar, from *lēogan* to LIE[1]]

warlord (ˈwɔːˌlɔːd) *n* a military leader of a nation or part of a nation, esp one who is accountable to nobody when the central government is weak: *the Chinese warlords*

Warlpiri (ˈwalpri) *n* an Aboriginal language of central Australia

warm (wɔːm) *adj* **1** characterized by or having a moderate degree of heat; moderately hot **2** maintaining or imparting heat: *a warm coat* **3** having or showing ready affection, kindliness, etc: *a warm personality* **4** lively, vigorous, or passionate: *a warm debate* **5** cordial or enthusiastic; ardent: *warm support* **6** quickly or easily aroused: *a warm temper* **7** (of colours) predominantly red or yellow in tone **8** (of a scent, trail, etc) recently made; strong **9** near to finding a hidden object or discovering or guessing facts, as in children's games **10** *informal* uncomfortable or disagreeable, esp because of the proximity of danger ▷ *vb* **11** (sometimes foll by *up*) to raise or be raised in temperature; make or become warm or warmer **12** (when *intr*, often foll by *to*) to make or become excited, enthusiastic, etc (about): *he warmed to the idea of buying a new car* **13** (*intr*; often foll by *to*) to feel affection, kindness, etc (for someone): *I warmed to her mother from the start* **14** (*tr*) *Brit* to give a caning to: *I'll warm you in a minute* ▷ *n* **15** *informal* a warm place or area: *come into the warm* **16** *informal* the act or an instance of warming or being warmed ▷ See also **warm over, warm up** [Old English *wearm*; related to Old Frisian, Old Saxon *warm*, Old Norse *varmr*] > ˈwarmer *n* > ˈwarmish *adj* > ˈwarmly *adv* > ˈwarmness *n*

warm-blooded *adj* **1** ardent, impetuous, or passionate **2** (of birds and mammals) having a constant body temperature, usually higher than the temperature of the surroundings. Technical name: **homoiothermic** > ˌwarm-ˈbloodedness *n*

warm-down *n* light exercises performed to aid recovery from strenuous physical activity

war memorial *n* a monument, usually an obelisk or cross, to those who die in a war, esp those from a particular locality

warm front *n* *meteorol* the boundary between a warm air mass and the cold air above which it is rising, at a less steep angle than at the cold front. Compare **cold front, occluded front**

warm-hearted *adj* kindly, generous, forgiving, or readily sympathetic > ˌwarm-ˈheartedly *adv* > ˌwarm-ˈheartedness *n*

warming pan *n* a pan, often of copper and having a long handle, filled with hot coals or hot water and formerly drawn over the sheets to warm a bed

warmonger (ˈwɔːˌmʌŋɡə) *n* a person who fosters warlike ideas or advocates war > ˈwarˌmongering *n*

warm over *vb* (*tr, adverb*) **1** *US and Canadian* to reheat (food) **2** *informal* to present (an idea, etc) again, esp without freshness or originality

warm sector *n* *meteorol* a wedge of warm air between the warm and cold fronts of a depression, which is eventually occluded. See also **cold front, warm front**

warmth (wɔ:mθ) *n* **1** the state, quality, or sensation of being warm **2** intensity of emotion: *he denied the accusation with some warmth* **3** affection or cordiality

warm up *vb* (*adverb*) **1** to make or become warm or warmer **2** (*intr*) to exercise in preparation for and immediately before a game, contest, or more vigorous exercise **3** to get ready for something important; prepare **4** to run or operate (an engine, etc) until the normal working temperature or condition is attained, or (of an engine, etc) to undergo this process **5** to make or become more animated or enthusiastic: *the party warmed up when Tom came* **6** to reheat (already cooked food) or (of such food) to be reheated **7** (*tr*) to make (an audience) relaxed and receptive before a show, esp a television comedy show ▷ *n* **warm-up 8** the act or an instance of warming up **9** a preparatory exercise routine

warn (wɔ:n) *vb* **1** to notify or make (someone) aware of danger, harm, etc **2** (*tr; often takes a negative and an infinitive*) to advise or admonish (someone) as to action, conduct, etc: *I warn you not to do that again* **3** (*takes a clause as object or an infinitive*) to inform (someone) in advance: *he warned them that he would arrive late* **4** (*tr; usually foll by away, off,* etc) to give notice to go away, be off, etc: *he warned the trespassers off his ground* [Old English *wearnian*; related to Old High German *warnēn*, Old Norse *varna* to refuse] > **'warner** *n*

warning ('wɔ:nɪŋ) *n* **1** a hint, intimation, threat, etc, of harm or danger **2** advice to beware or desist **3** an archaic word for **notice** (sense 6) ▷ *adj* **4** (*prenominal*) intended or serving to warn: *a warning look* **5** (of the coloration of certain distasteful or poisonous animals) having conspicuous markings, which predators recognize and learn to avoid; aposematic > **'warningly** *adv*

War of 1812 *n* a war between Great Britain and the US, fought chiefly along the Canadian border (1812–14)

War of American Independence *n* the conflict following the revolt of the North American colonies against British rule, particularly on the issue of taxation. Hostilities began in 1775 when British and American forces clashed at Lexington and Concord. Articles of Confederation agreed in the Continental Congress in 1777 provided for a confederacy to be known as the United States of America. The war was effectively ended with the surrender of the British at Yorktown in 1781 and peace was signed at Paris in Sept 1783. Also called: **American Revolution** *or* **Revolutionary War**

War Office *n Brit* (formerly) **a** the department of state responsible for the British Army, now part of the Ministry of Defence **b** the premises of this department in Whitehall, London

war of nerves *n* the use of psychological tactics against an opponent, such as shattering his morale by the use of propaganda

War of Secession *n* another name for the (American) **Civil War**

War of the Austrian Succession *n* the war (1740–48) fought by Austria, Britain, and the Netherlands against Prussia, France, and Spain in support of the right of succession of Maria Theresa to the Austrian throne and against the territorial aims of Prussia

War of the Grand Alliance *n* the war (1689–97) waged by the Grand Alliance, led by Britain, the Netherlands, and Austria, against Louis XIV of France, following his invasion (1688) of the Palatinate

War of the Spanish Succession *n* the war (1701–14) between Austria, Britain, Prussia, and the Netherlands on the one side and France, Spain, and Bavaria on the other over the disputed succession to the Spanish throne

warp (wɔ:p) *vb* **1** to twist or cause to twist out of shape, as from heat, damp, etc **2** to turn or cause to turn from a true, correct, or proper course **3** to pervert or be perverted **4** (*tr*) to prepare (yarn) as a

warp **5** *nautical* to move (a vessel) by hauling on a rope fixed to a stationary object ashore or (of a vessel) to be moved thus **6** (*tr*) (formerly) to curve or twist (an aircraft wing) in order to assist control in flight **7** (*tr*) to flood (land) with water from which alluvial matter is deposited ▷ *n* **8** the state or condition of being twisted out of shape **9** a twist, distortion, or bias **10** a mental or moral deviation **11** the yarns arranged lengthways on a loom, forming the threads through which the weft yarns are woven **12** the heavy threads used to reinforce the rubber in the casing of a pneumatic tyre **13** *nautical* a rope used for warping a vessel **14** alluvial sediment deposited by water [Old English *wearp* a throw; related to Old High German *warf*, Old Norse *varp* throw of a dragging net, Old English *weorpan* to throw] > **'warpage** *n* > **warped** *adj* > **'warper** *n*

war paint *n* **1** painted decoration of the face and body applied by certain North American Indians before battle **2** *informal* finery or regalia **3** *informal* cosmetics

warpath ('wɔ:,pɑ:θ) *n* **1** the route taken by North American Indians on a warlike expedition **2** **on the warpath a** preparing to engage in battle **b** *informal* in a state of anger

warplane ('wɔ:,pleɪn) *n* any aircraft designed for and used in warfare. Also called (*US*): **battle plane**

warrant ('wɒrənt) *n* **1** anything that gives authority for an action or decision; authorization; sanction **2** a document that certifies or guarantees, such as a receipt for goods stored in a warehouse, a licence, or a commission **3** *law* an authorization issued by a magistrate or other official allowing a constable or other officer to search or seize property, arrest a person, or perform some other specified act **4** (in certain armed services) the official authority for the appointment of warrant officers **5** a security that functions as a stock option by giving the owner the right to buy ordinary shares in a company at a specified date, often at a specified price ▷ *vb* (*tr*) **6** to guarantee the quality, condition, etc, of (something) **7** to give authority or power to **8** to attest to or assure the character, worthiness, etc, of **9** to guarantee (a purchaser of merchandise) against loss of, damage to, or misrepresentation concerning the merchandise **10** *law* to guarantee (the title to an estate or other property) **11** to declare boldly and confidently [C13 from Anglo-French *warrant*, variant of Old French *guarant*, from *guarantir* to guarantee, of Germanic origin; compare GUARANTY] > **'warrantable** *adj* > **,warranta'bility** *n* > **'warrantably** *adv* > **'warranter** *n* > **'warrantless** *adj*

warrantee (,wɒrən'ti:) *n* a person to whom a warranty is given

warrant officer *n* an officer in certain armed services who holds a rank between those of commissioned and noncommissioned officers. In the British army, the rank has two classes: see **regimental sergeant major, company sergeant major**

Warrant of Fitness *n NZ* a six-monthly certificate required for motor vehicles certifying mechanical soundness

warrantor ('wɒrən,tɔ:) *n* an individual or company that provides a warranty

warrant sale *n Scots law* a sale of someone's personal belongings or household effects that have been seized to meet unpaid debts

warranty ('wɒrəntɪ) *n, pl* **-ties 1** *property law* a covenant, express or implied, by which the vendor of real property vouches for the security of the title conveyed **2** *contract law* an express or implied term in a contract, such as an undertaking that goods contracted to be sold shall meet specified requirements as to quality, etc: *an extended warranty* **3** *insurance law* an undertaking by the party insured that the facts given regarding the risk are as stated **4** the act of warranting [C14 from Anglo-French *warantie*, from *warantir* to warrant, variant

of Old French *guarantir*; see WARRANT]

warren ('wɒrən) *n* **1** a series of interconnected underground tunnels in which rabbits live **2** a colony of rabbits **3** an overcrowded area or dwelling **4 a** *chiefly Brit* an enclosed place where small game animals or birds are kept, esp for breeding, or a part of a river or lake enclosed by nets in which fish are kept (esp in the phrase **beasts** *or* **fowls of warren**) **b** *English legal history* a franchise permitting one to keep animals, birds, or fish in this way [C14 from Anglo-French *warenne*, of Germanic origin; compare Old High German *werien* to preserve]

Warren ('wɒrən) *n* a city in the US, in SE Michigan, northeast of Detroit. Pop: 136 016 (2003 est)

warrener ('wɒrənə) *n obsolete* a gamekeeper or keeper of a warren (sense 4)

warrigal ('wɒrɪgæl) *Austral* ▷ *n* **1** a dingo **2** another word for **brumby** ▷ *adj* **3** untamed or wild [C19 from a native Australian language]

Warrington ('wɒrɪŋtən) *n* **1** an industrial town in NW England, in Warrington unitary authority, Cheshire on the River Mersey: dates from Roman times. Pop: 80 661 (2001) **2** a unitary authority in NW England, in N Cheshire. Pop: 193 200 (2003 est). Area: 176 sq km (68 sq miles)

warrior ('wɒrɪə) *n* **a** a person engaged in, experienced in, or devoted to war **b** (*as modifier*): *a warrior nation* [C13 from Old Northern French *werreieor*, from *werre* WAR]

Warsaw ('wɔ:sɔ:) *n* the capital of Poland, in the E central part on the River Vistula: became capital at the end of the 16th century; almost completely destroyed in World War II as the main centre of the Polish resistance movement; rebuilt within about six years; university (1818); situated at the junction of important trans-European routes. Pop: 2 204 000 (2005 est). Polish name: **Warszawa** (var'ʃava)

Warsaw Pact *n* a military treaty and association of E European countries, formed in 1955 by the Soviet Union, Bulgaria, Czechoslovakia, East Germany, Hungary, Poland, and Romania: East Germany left in 1990; the remaining members dissolved the Pact in 1991

warship ('wɔ:,ʃɪp) *n* a vessel armed, armoured, and otherwise equipped for naval warfare

Wars of the Roses *pl n* the conflicts in England (1455–85) centred on the struggle for the throne between the house of York (symbolized by the white rose) and the house of Lancaster (of which one badge was the red rose)

wart (wɔ:t) *n* **1** Also called: **verruca** *pathol* any firm abnormal elevation of the skin caused by a virus **2** *botany* a small rounded outgrowth **3 warts and all** with all blemishes evident [Old English *weart(e)*; related to Old High German *warza*, Old Norse *varta*] > **'warted** *adj* > **'wart,like** *adj* > **'warty** *adj*

Warta (*Polish* 'varta) *n* a river in Poland, flowing generally north and west across the whole W Polish Plain to the River Oder. Length: 808 km (502 miles)

Wartburg (*German* 'vartbʊrk) *n* a medieval castle in central Germany, in Thuringia southwest of Eisenach: residence of Luther (1521–22) when he began his German translation of the New Testament

wart cress *n* either of two prostrate annuals, *Coronopus squamatus* and *C. didymus*, having small white flowers: family *Brassicaceae* (crucifers). Also called: **swine's cress**

warthog ('wɔ:t,hɒg) *n* a wild pig, *Phacochoerus aethiopicus*, of southern and E Africa, having heavy tusks, wartlike protuberances on the face, and a mane of coarse hair

wartime ('wɔ:,taɪm) *n* **a** a period or time of war **b** (*as modifier*): *wartime conditions*

war whoop *n* the yell or howl uttered, esp by North American Indians, while making an attack

Warwick ('wɒrɪk) *n* a town in central England,

W

administrative centre of Warwickshire, on the River Avon: 14th-century castle, with collections of armour and waxworks: the university of Warwick (1965) is in Coventry. Pop: 23 350 (2001)

Warwickshire (ˈwɒrɪkˌʃɪə, -ʃə) n a county of central England: until 1974, when the West Midlands metropolitan county was created, it contained one of the most highly industrialized regions in the world, centred on Birmingham. Administrative centre: Warwick. Pop: 519 300 (2003 est). Area: 1981 sq km (765 sq miles)

wary (ˈwɛərɪ) adj warier, wariest **1** watchful, cautious, or alert **2** characterized by caution or watchfulness [C16 from WARE² + -Y¹] > ˈwarily adv > ˈwariness n

warzone (ˈwɔːˌzəʊn) n an area where a war is taking place or there is some other violent conflict

was (wɒz; unstressed wəz) vb (used with I, he, she, it, and with singular nouns) **1** the past tense (indicative mood) of **be 2** not standard a form of the subjunctive mood used in place of were, esp in conditional sentences: if the film was to be with you, would you be able to process it? [Old English wæs, from wesan to be; related to Old Frisian, Old High German was, Old Norse var]

wasabi (wəˈsɑːbɪ) n **1** a Japanese cruciferous plant, Eutrema Wasabi, cultivated for its thick green pungent root **2** the root of this plant, esp in paste or powder form, used as a condiment in Japanese cookery [Japanese]

Wasatch Range (ˈwɔːsætʃ) n a mountain range in the W central US, in N Utah and SE Idaho. Highest peak: Mount Timpanogos, 3581 m (11 750 ft)

wash (wɒʃ) vb **1** to apply water or other liquid, usually with soap, to (oneself, clothes, etc) in order to cleanse **2** (tr; often foll by away, from, off, etc) to remove by the application of water or other liquid and usually soap: she washed the dirt from her clothes **3** (intr) to be capable of being washed without damage or loss of colour **4** (of an animal such as a cat) to cleanse (itself or another animal) by licking **5** (tr) to cleanse from pollution or defilement **6** (tr) to make wet or moist **7** (often foll by away, etc) to move or be moved by water: the flood washed away the bridge **8** (esp of waves) to flow or sweep against or over (a surface or object), often with a lapping sound **9** to form by erosion or be eroded: the stream washed a ravine in the hill **10** (tr) to apply a thin coating of paint, metal, etc, to **11** (tr) to separate (ore, precious stones, etc) from (gravel, earth, or sand) by immersion in water **12** (intr; usually used with a negative) informal, chiefly Brit to admit of testing or proof: your excuses won't wash with me this time **13** wash one's hands **a** euphemistic to go to the lavatory **b** (usually foll by of) to refuse to have anything more to do (with) ▷ n **14** the act or process of washing; ablution **15** a quantity of articles washed together **16** a preparation or thin liquid used as a coating or in washing: a thin wash of paint; a hair wash **17** med **a** any medicinal or soothing lotion for application to a part of the body **b** (in combination): an eyewash **18** the flow of water, esp waves, against a surface, or the sound made by such a flow **19 a** the technique of making wash drawings **b** See **wash drawing 20** the erosion of soil by the action of flowing water **21** a mass of alluvial material transported and deposited by flowing water **22** land that is habitually washed by tidal or river waters **23** the disturbance in the air or water produced at the rear of an aircraft, boat, or other moving object **24** gravel, earth, etc, from which valuable minerals may be washed **25** waste liquid matter or liquid refuse, esp as fed to pigs; swill **26** an alcoholic liquid resembling strong beer, resulting from the fermentation of wort in the production of whisky **27 come out in the wash** informal to become known or apparent in the course of time ▷ See also **wash down, wash out, wash up** [Old English wæscan, waxan; related

to Old High German wascan; see WATER]

Wash (wɒʃ) n **the** a shallow inlet of the North Sea on the E coast of England, between Lincolnshire and Norfolk

Wash. abbreviation for Washington

washable (ˈwɒʃəbəl) adj (esp of fabrics or clothes) capable of being washed without deteriorating > ˌwashaˈbility n

wash-and-wear adj (of fabrics, garments, etc) requiring only light washing, short drying time, and little or no ironing

washaway (ˈwɒʃəˌweɪ) n Austral another word for **washout** (sense 4)

washbasin (ˈwɒʃˌbeɪsən) n a basin or bowl for washing the face and hands. Also called: **washbowl!**

washboard (ˈwɒʃˌbɔːd) n **1** a board having a surface, usually of corrugated metal, on which esp formerly, clothes were scrubbed **2** such a board used as a rhythm instrument played with the fingers in skiffle, Country and Western music, etc **3** a less common US word for **skirting board 4** nautical **a** a vertical planklike shield fastened to the gunwales of a boat to prevent water from splashing over the side **b** Also called: **splashboard** a shield under a port for the same purpose

washcloth (ˈwɒʃˌklɒθ) n **1** another name for **dishcloth 2** US and Canadian a small piece of cloth used to wash the face and hands. Also called (in Britain and certain other countries): **face cloth, flannel**

washday (ˈwɒʃˌdeɪ) n a day on which clothes and linen are washed, often the same day each week

wash down vb (tr, adverb) **1** to wash completely, esp from top to bottom **2** to take drink with or after (food or another drink)

wash drawing n a pen-and-ink drawing that has been lightly brushed over with water to soften the lines

washed out adj (**washed-out** when prenominal) **1** faded or colourless **2** exhausted, esp when being pale in appearance

washed up adj (**washed-up** when prenominal) informal, chiefly US, Canadian, and NZ **1** no longer useful, successful, hopeful, etc: our hopes for the new deal are all washed up **2** exhausted

washer (ˈwɒʃə) n **1** a person or thing that washes **2** a flat ring or drilled disc of metal used under the head of a bolt or nut to spread the load when tightened **3** any flat ring of rubber, felt, metal, etc, used to provide a seal under a nut or in a tap or valve seat **4** See **washing machine 5** chemical engineering a device for cleaning or washing gases or vapours; scrubber **6** Austral a face cloth; flannel

washerwoman (ˈwɒʃəˌwʊmən), **washwoman** or masculine **washerman** n, pl -women or -men a person who washes clothes for a living

washery (ˈwɒʃərɪ) n a plant at a mine where water or other liquid is used to remove dirt from a mineral, esp coal

wash house n (formerly) a building or outbuilding in which laundry was done

washin (ˈwɒʃɪn) n aeronautics an increase in the angle of attack of an aircraft wing towards the wing tip [C20 from WASH (flow) + IN]

washing (ˈwɒʃɪŋ) n **1** articles that have been or are to be washed together on a single occasion **2** liquid in which an article has been washed **3** something, such as gold dust or metal ore, that has been obtained by washing **4** a thin coat of something applied in liquid form

washing machine n a mechanical apparatus, usually powered by electricity, for washing clothing, linens, etc

washing powder n powdered detergent for washing fabrics

washing soda n the crystalline decahydrate of sodium carbonate, esp when used as a cleansing agent

Washington (ˈwɒʃɪŋtən) n **1** a state of the northwestern US, on the Pacific: consists of the

Coast Range and the Olympic Mountains in the west and the Columbia Plateau in the east. Capital: Olympia. Pop: 6 131 445 (2003 est). Area: 172 416 sq km (66 570 sq miles). Abbreviations: Wash. (with zip code) WA **2** the capital of the US, coextensive with the District of Columbia and situated near the E coast on the Potomac River: site chosen by President Washington in 1790; contains the White House and the Capitol; a major educational and administrative centre. Pop: 563 384 (2003 est). Also called: Washington, DC **3** a town in Tyne and Wear: designated a new town in 1964. Pop: 53 388 (2001) **4 Mount** a mountain in N New Hampshire, in the White Mountains: the highest peak in the northeast US; noted for extreme weather conditions. Height: 1917 m (6288 ft) **5 Lake** a lake in W Washington, forming the E boundary of the city of Seattle: linked by canal with Puget Sound. Length: about 32 km (20 miles). Width: 6 km (4 miles)

Washingtonian (ˌwɒʃɪŋˈtəʊnɪən) adj **1** of or relating to the city or state of Washington or their inhabitants ▷ n **2** a native or inhabitant of the city or state of Washington

Washington palm n a palm tree, Washingtonia filifera, of California and Florida, having large fan-shaped leaves and small black fruits. Also called: **desert palm**

washing-up n Brit **1** the washing of dishes, cutlery, etc, after a meal **2** dishes and cutlery waiting to be washed up **3** (as modifier): a washing-up machine

wash out vb (adverb) **1** (tr) to wash (the inside of something) so as to remove (dirt) **2** Also: **wash off** to remove or be removed by washing: grass stains don't wash out easily **3** (tr) to cancel or abandon (a sporting event) ▷ n **washout 4** geology **a** erosion of the earth's surface by the action of running water **b** a narrow channel produced by this erosion **5** informal **a** a total failure or disaster **b** an incompetent person **6** a sporting or social event that is cancelled due to rain **7** aeronautics a decrease in the angle of attack of an aircraft wing towards the wing tip

washrag (ˈwɒʃˌræg) n US another word for **flannel** (sense 4)

washroom (ˈwɒʃˌruːm, -ˌrʊm) n **1** a room, esp in a factory or office block, in which lavatories, washbasins, etc, are situated **2** US and Canadian a euphemism for **lavatory**

wash sale n US the illegal stock-exchange practice of buying and selling the same securities at an inflated price through a colluding broker to give the impression that the security has a strong market

washstand (ˈwɒʃˌstænd) n a piece of furniture designed to hold a basin, etc, for washing the face and hands

washtub (ˈwɒʃˌtʌb) n a tub or large container used for washing anything, esp clothes

wash up vb (adverb) **1** chiefly Brit to wash (dishes, cutlery, etc) after a meal **2** (intr) US to wash one's face and hands ▷ n **washup 3** Austral the end, outcome of a process: in the washup, three candidates were elected

washwoman (ˈwɒʃˌwʊmən) n, pl -women a less common word for **washerwoman**

washy (ˈwɒʃɪ) adj washier, washiest **1** overdiluted, watery, or weak **2** lacking intensity or strength > ˈwashily adv > ˈwashiness n

wasn't (ˈwɒzənt) vb contraction of was not

wasp (wɒsp) n **1** any social hymenopterous insect of the family Vespidae, esp Vespula vulgaris (**common wasp**), typically having a black-and-yellow body and an ovipositor specialized for stinging. See also **potter wasp, hornet** Related adj: **vespine 2** any of various solitary hymenopterans, such as the digger wasp and gall wasp [Old English wæsp; related to Old Saxon waspa, Old High German wefsa, Latin vespa] > ˈwaspˌlike adj > ˈwaspy adj > ˈwaspily adv > ˈwaspiness n

Wasp or **WASP** (wɒsp) n (in the US) ▷ acronym for

White Anglo-Saxon Protestant: a person descended from N European, usually Protestant stock, forming a group often considered the most dominant, privileged, and influential in American society > ˈWaspy adj

waspish (ˈwɒspɪʃ) adj **1** relating to or suggestive of a wasp **2** easily annoyed or angered > ˈwaspishly adv > ˈwaspishness n

wasp waist n a very slender waist, esp one that is tightly corseted > ˈwasp-ˌwaisted adj

wassail (ˈwɒseɪl) n **1** (formerly) a toast or salutation made to a person at festivities **2** a festivity when much drinking takes place **3** alcoholic drink drunk at such a festivity, esp spiced beer or mulled wine **4** the singing of Christmas carols, going from house to house **5** archaic a drinking song ▷ vb **6** to drink the health of (a person) at a wassail **7** (intr) to go from house to house singing carols at Christmas [C13 from Old Norse ves heill be in good health; related to Old English wes hāl; see HALE¹] > ˈwassailer n

Wassermann test or **reaction** (ˈwæsəmən; German ˈvasərman) n med a diagnostic test for syphilis. See **complement fixation test** [C20 named after August von Wassermann (1866–1925), German bacteriologist]

wassup (wɒˈsʌp) sentence substitute slang what is happening? [C20 from what's up?]

wast (wɒst; unstressed wəst) vb archaic or dialect (used with the pronoun thou or its relative equivalent) a singular form of the past tense (indicative mood) of **be**

wastage (ˈweɪstɪdʒ) n **1** anything lost by wear or waste **2** the process of wasting **3** reduction in size of a workforce by retirement, voluntary resignation, etc (esp in the phrase **natural wastage**)

USAGE Waste and wastage are to some extent interchangeable, but many people think that wastage should not be used to refer to loss resulting from human carelessness, inefficiency, etc: a waste (not a wastage) of time/money/effort etc

waste (weɪst) vb **1** (tr) to use, consume, or expend thoughtlessly, carelessly, or to no avail **2** (tr) to fail to take advantage of: to waste an opportunity **3** (when intr, often foll by away) to lose or cause to lose bodily strength, health, etc **4** to exhaust or become exhausted **5** (tr) to ravage **6** (tr) informal to murder or kill: I want that guy wasted by tomorrow ▷ n **7** the act of wasting or state of being wasted **8** a failure to take advantage of something **9** anything unused or not used to full advantage **10** anything or anyone rejected as useless, worthless, or in excess of what is required **11** garbage, rubbish, or trash **12** a land or region that is devastated or ruined **13** a land or region that is wild or uncultivated **14** physiol **a** the useless products of metabolism **b** indigestible food residue **15** disintegrated rock material resulting from erosion **16** law reduction in the value of an estate caused by act or neglect, esp by a life-tenant ▷ adj **17** rejected as useless, unwanted, or worthless **18** produced in excess of what is required **19** not cultivated, inhabited, or productive: waste land **20 a** of or denoting the useless products of metabolism **b** of or denoting indigestible food products **21** destroyed, devastated, or ruined **22** designed to contain or convey waste products **23 lay waste** to devastate or destroy [C13 from Anglo-French waster, from Latin vastāre to lay waste, from vastus empty] > ˈwastable adj

wastebasket (ˈweɪstˌbɑːskɪt) n an open receptacle for paper and other dry litter. Also called (esp in Britain): **wastepaper basket**

wasted (ˈweɪstɪd) adj **1** not exploited or taken advantage of: a wasted opportunity **2** useless or unprofitable: wasted effort **3** physically enfeebled and emaciated: a thin wasted figure **4** slang showing signs of habitual drug abuse

waste disposal unit n an electrically operated fitment in the plughole of a kitchen sink that breaks up food refuse so that it goes down the waste pipe

wasteful (ˈweɪstfʊl) adj **1** tending to waste or squander; extravagant **2** causing waste, destruction, or devastation > ˈwastefully adv > ˈwastefulness n

waste heat recovery n the use of heat that is produced in a thermodynamic cycle, as in a furnace, combustion engine, etc, in another process, such as heating feedwater or air

wasteland (ˈweɪstˌlænd) n **1** a barren or desolate area of land, not or no longer used for cultivation or building **2** a region, period in history, etc, that is considered spiritually, intellectually, or aesthetically barren or desolate: American television is a cultural wasteland

wastelot (ˈweɪstˌlɒt) n chiefly Canadian a piece of waste ground in a city

wastepaper (ˈweɪstˌpeɪpə) n paper discarded after use

wastepaper basket or **bin** n chiefly Brit another word for **wastebasket**

waste pipe n a pipe to take excess or used water away, as from a sink to a drain

waster (ˈweɪstə) n **1** a person or thing that wastes **2** a ne'er-do-well; wastrel **3** an article spoiled in manufacture

wasteweir (ˈweɪstˌwɪə) n another name for **spillway**

wasting (ˈweɪstɪŋ) adj (prenominal) reducing the vitality, strength, or robustness of the body: a wasting disease > ˈwastingly adv

wasting asset n an unreplaceable business asset of limited life, such as a coal mine or an oil well

wastrel (ˈweɪstrəl) n **1** a wasteful person; spendthrift; prodigal **2** an idler or vagabond

Wast Water (wɒst) n a lake in NW England, in Cumbria in the Lake District. Length: 5 km (3 miles)

wat (wɑːt) n a Thai Buddhist monastery or temple [Thai, from Sanskrit vāta enclosure]

watap (wæˈtɑːp, wɑː-) n a stringy thread made by North American Indians from the roots of various conifers and used for weaving and sewing [C18 from Canadian French, from Cree watapiy]

watch (wɒtʃ) vb **1** to look at or observe closely or attentively **2** (intr; foll by for) to wait attentively or expectantly **3** to guard or tend (something) closely or carefully **4** (intr) to keep vigil **5** (tr) to maintain an interest in: to watch the progress of a child at school **6 watch it!** be careful! look out! ▷ n **7 a** a small portable timepiece, usually worn strapped to the wrist (a **wristwatch**) or in a waistcoat pocket **b** (as modifier): a watch spring **8** the act or an instance of watching **9** a period of vigil, esp during the night **10** (formerly) one of a set of periods of any of various lengths into which the night was divided **11** nautical **a** any of the usually four-hour periods beginning at midnight and again at noon during which part of a ship's crew are on duty **b** those officers and crew on duty during a specified watch **12** the period during which a guard is on duty **13** (formerly) a watchman or band of watchmen **14 on the watch** on the lookout; alert ▷ See also **watch out** [Old English wæccan (vb), wæcce (n); related to WAKE¹]

-watch suffix of nouns indicating a regular television programme or newspaper feature on the topic specified: Crimewatch

watchable (ˈwɒtʃəbəl) adj **1** capable of being watched **2** interesting, enjoyable, or entertaining: a watchable television documentary

watchband (ˈwɒtʃˌbænd) n US, Canadian, and Austral a strap of leather, cloth, etc, attached to a watch for fastening it around the wrist. Also called (in Britain and other countries): **watchstrap**

watch cap n a knitted navy-blue woollen cap worn by seamen in cold weather

watchcase (ˈwɒtʃˌkeɪs) n a protective case for a

watch, generally of metal such as gold, silver, brass, or gunmetal

watch chain n a chain used for fastening a pocket watch to the clothing. See also **fob¹**

Watch Committee n Brit history a local government committee composed of magistrates and representatives of the county borough council responsible for the efficiency of the local police force

watchdog (ˈwɒtʃˌdɒg) n **1** a dog kept to guard property **2 a** a person or group of persons that acts as a protector or guardian against inefficiency, illegal practices, etc **b** (as modifier): a watchdog committee

watcher (ˈwɒtʃə) n **1** a person who watches **2** a person who maintains a vigil at the bedside of an invalid **3** US a representative of a candidate or party stationed at a poll on election day to watch out for fraud

watch fire n a fire kept burning at night as a signal or for warmth and light by a person keeping watch

watchful (ˈwɒtʃfʊl) adj **1** vigilant or alert **2** archaic not sleeping > ˈwatchfully adv > ˈwatchfulness n

watch-glass n **1** a curved glass disc that covers the dial of a watch **2** a similarly shaped piece of glass used in laboratories for evaporating small samples of a solution, etc

watchlist (ˈwɒtʃˌlɪst) n **1** a list of things to be monitored, esp in order to prevent loss, damage, etc **2** a list of people or organizations to be kept under surveillance, esp because they are suspected of wrongdoing: terrorist watchlist

watchmaker (ˈwɒtʃˌmeɪkə) n a person who makes or mends watches > ˈwatchˌmaking n

watchman (ˈwɒtʃmən) n, pl -men **1** a person employed to guard buildings or property **2** (formerly) a man employed to patrol or guard the streets at night

watch night n (in Protestant churches) **1 a** the night of December 24, during which a service is held to mark the arrival of Christmas Day **b** the night of December 31, during which a service is held to mark the passing of the old year and the beginning of the new **2** the service held on either of these nights

watch out vb **1** (intr, adverb) to be careful or on one's guard ▷ n **watchout 2** a less common word for **lookout** (sense 1)

watchstrap (ˈwɒtʃˌstræp) n a strap of leather, cloth, etc, attached to a watch for fastening it around the wrist. Also called (US, Canadian, and Austral): **watchband**

watchtower (ˈwɒtʃˌtaʊə) n a tower on which a sentry keeps watch

watchword (ˈwɒtʃˌwɜːd) n **1** another word for **password 2** a rallying cry or slogan

water (ˈwɔːtə) n **1** a clear colourless tasteless odourless liquid that is essential for plant and animal life and constitutes, in impure form, rain, oceans, rivers, lakes, etc. It is a neutral substance, an effective solvent for many compounds, and is used as a standard for many physical properties. Formula: H_2O. Related adj: **aqueous** Related combining forms: **hydro-, aqua- 2 a** any body or area of this liquid, such as a sea, lake, river, etc **b** (as modifier): water sports; water transport; a water plant. Related adj: **aquatic 3** the surface of such a body or area: fish swam below the water **4** any form or variety of this liquid, such as rain **5** See **high water, low water 6** any of various solutions of chemical substances in water: lithia water; ammonia water **7** physiol **a** any fluid secreted from the body, such as sweat, urine, or tears **b** (usually plural) the amniotic fluid surrounding a fetus in the womb **8** a wavy lustrous finish on some fabrics, esp silk **9** archaic the degree of brilliance in a diamond. See also **first water 10** excellence, quality, or degree (in the phrase **of the first water**) **11** finance **a** capital stock issued without a corresponding increase in paid-up capital, so that the book value of the company's capital is not fully represented

W

by assets or earning power **b** the fictitious or unrealistic asset entries that reflect such inflated book value of capital **12** (*modifier*) *astrology* of or relating to the three signs of the zodiac Cancer, Scorpio, and Pisces. Compare **air** (sense 20), **earth** (sense 10), **fire** (sense 24) **13** *above the water informal* out of trouble or difficulty, esp financial trouble **14** *hold water* to prove credible, logical, or consistent: *the alibi did not hold water* **15** *in deep water* in trouble or difficulty **16** *make water* **a** to urinate **b** (of a boat, hull, etc) to let in water **17** *pass water* to urinate **18** *test the water* See **test¹** (sense 5) **19** *throw* (*or pour*) *cold water on informal* to be unenthusiastic about or discourage **20** *water under the bridge* events that are past and done with ▷ *vb* **21** (*tr*) to sprinkle, moisten, or soak with water **22** (*tr; often foll by down*) to weaken by the addition of water **23** (*intr*) (of the eyes) to fill with tears **24** (*intr*) (of the mouth) to salivate, esp in anticipation of food (esp in the phrase **make one's mouth water**) **25** (*tr*) to irrigate or provide with water: *to water the land; he watered the cattle* **26** (*intr*) to drink water **27** (*intr*) (of a ship, etc) to take in a supply of water **28** (*tr*) *finance* to raise the par value of (issued capital stock) without a corresponding increase in the real value of assets **29** (*tr*) to produce a wavy lustrous finish on (fabrics, esp silk) ▷ See also **water down** [Old English *wæter*, of Germanic origin; compare Old Saxon *watar*, Old High German *wazzar*, Gothic *watō*, Old Slavonic *voda*; related to Greek *hudor*] > 'waterer *n* > 'waterish *adj* > 'waterless *adj* > 'water‑,like *adj*

waterage ('wɔːtərɪdʒ) *n Brit* the transportation of cargo by means of ships, or the charges for such transportation

water back *n* the US name for **back boiler**

water bag *n* a bag, sometimes made of skin, leather, etc, but in Australia usually canvas, for holding, carrying, and keeping water cool

water bailiff *n* an official responsible for enforcing laws on river management and fishing

water-bath *n chem* a vessel containing heated water, used for heating substances

water bear *n* another name for a **tardigrade**

water bed *n* a waterproof mattress filled with water

water beetle *n* any of various beetles of the families *Dysticidae*, *Hydrophilidae*, etc, that live most of the time in freshwater ponds, rivers, etc. See **whirligig beetle**

water bird *n* any aquatic bird, including the wading and swimming birds

water biscuit *n* a thin crisp plain biscuit, usually served with butter or cheese

water blister *n* a blister containing watery or serous fluid, without any blood or pus

water boatman *n* any of various aquatic bugs of the families *Notonectidae* and *Corixidae*, having a flattened body and oarlike hind legs, adapted for swimming

waterborne ('wɔːtə,bɔːn) *adj* **1** floating or travelling on water **2** (of a disease, etc) transported or transmitted by water

water bottle *n* any of various types of container for drinking water, such as a skin or leather bag used in some countries, a glass bottle for table use, or a flask used by soldiers or travellers

waterbrain ('wɔːtə,breɪn) *n vet science* an archaic name for **gid**

water brash *n pathol* another term for **heartburn**

waterbuck ('wɔːtə,bʌk) *n* any of various antelopes of the genus *Kobus*, esp *K. ellipsiprymnus*, of swampy areas of Africa, having long curved ridged horns

water buffalo *or* **ox** *n* a member of the cattle tribe, *Bubalus bubalis*, of swampy regions of S Asia, having widely spreading back-curving horns. Domesticated forms are used as draught animals. Also called: **Asiatic buffalo**, **Indian buffalo**, **carabao**

water bug *n* any of various heteropterous insects adapted to living in the water or on its surface, esp any of the family *Belostomatidae* (**giant water bugs**), of North America, India, and southern Africa, which have flattened hairy legs

water butt *n* a barrel for collecting rainwater, esp from a drainpipe

water cannon *n* an apparatus for pumping water through a nozzle at high pressure, used in quelling riots

Water Carrier *or* **Bearer** *n* **the** the constellation Aquarius, the 11th sign of the zodiac

water chestnut *n* **1** Also called: **water caltrop** a floating aquatic onagraceous plant, *Trapa natans*, of Asia, having four-pronged edible nutlike fruits **2** **Chinese water chestnut** a Chinese cyperaceous plant, *Eleocharis tuberosa*, with an edible succulent corm **3** the corm of the Chinese water chestnut, used in Oriental cookery

water chinquapin *n* a North American aquatic plant, *Nelumbo lutea*, having large umbrella-shaped leaves, pale yellow flowers, and edible nutlike seeds: family *Nelumbonaceae*. Compare **chinquapin**

water clock *or* **glass** *n* any of various devices for measuring time that use the escape of water as the motive force

water closet *n* **1** a lavatory flushed by water **2** a small room that has a lavatory ▷ Usually abbreviated to: **WC**

watercolour *or US* **watercolor** ('wɔːtə,kʌlə) *n* **1 a** Also called: **pure watercolour** water-soluble pigment, applied in transparent washes and without the admixture of white pigment in the lighter tones **b** any water-soluble pigment, including opaque kinds such as gouache and tempera **2 a** a painting done in watercolours **b** (*as modifier*): *a watercolour masterpiece* **3** the art or technique of painting with such pigments > 'water,colourist *or US* 'water,colorist *n*

water-cool *vb* (*tr*) to cool (an engine, etc) by a flow of water circulating in an enclosed jacket. Compare **air-cool**. > 'water‑,cooled *adj* > 'water‑,cooling *adj*

water cooler *n* **1** a device for cooling and dispensing drinking water ▷ *modifier* **water-cooler 2** *US informal* indicating the kind of informal conversation among office staff that takes place at such a dispenser: *water-cooler conversations*

watercourse ('wɔːtə,kɔːs) *n* **1** a stream, river, or canal **2** the channel, bed, or route along which this flows

watercraft ('wɔːtə,krɑːft) *n* **1** a boat or ship or such vessels collectively **2** skill in handling boats or in water sports

water crake *n* another name for **spotted crake** and **dipper** (the bird)

watercress ('wɔːtə,krɛs) *n* **1** an Old World plant, *Nasturtium officinale*, of clear ponds and streams, having pungent leaves that are used in salads and as a garnish: family *Brassicaceae* (crucifers) **2** any of several similar or related plants

water cure *n* **1** *med* a nontechnical name for **hydropathy** *or* **hydrotherapy 2** *informal* a form of torture in which the victim is forced to drink very large amounts of water

water cycle *n* the circulation of the earth's water, in which water evaporates from the sea into the atmosphere, where it condenses and falls as rain or snow, returning to the sea by rivers or returning to the atmosphere by evapotranspiration. Also called: **hydrologic cycle**

water diviner *n Brit* a person able to locate the presence of water, esp underground, with a divining rod. US name: **waterfinder**

water dog *n* **1** a dog trained to hunt in water **2** *informal* a dog or person who enjoys going in or on the water

water down *vb* (*tr, adverb*) **1** to dilute or weaken with water **2** to modify or adulterate, esp so as to omit anything harsh, unpleasant, or offensive: *to water down the truth* > ,watered-'down *adj*

water dropwort *n* See **dropwort** (sense 2)

waterfall ('wɔːtə,fɔːl) *n* a cascade of falling water where there is a vertical or almost vertical step in a river

water flea *n* any of numerous minute freshwater branchiopod crustaceans of the order *Cladocera*, which swim by means of hairy branched antennae. See also **daphnia**

Waterford ('wɔːtəfəd) *n* **1** a county of S Republic of Ireland, in Munster province on the Atlantic: mountainous in the centre and in the northwest. County town: Waterford. Pop: 101 546 (2002). Area: 1838 sq km (710 sq miles) **2** a port in S Republic of Ireland, county town of Co Waterford: famous glass industry; fishing. Pop: 44 594 (2002)

waterfowl ('wɔːtə,faʊl) *n* **1** any aquatic freshwater bird, esp any species of the family *Anatidae* (ducks, geese, and swans) **2** such birds collectively

waterfront ('wɔːtə,frʌnt) *n* the area of a town or city alongside a body of water, such as a harbour or dockyard

water gap *n* a deep valley in a ridge, containing a stream

water gas *n* a mixture of hydrogen and carbon monoxide produced by passing steam over hot carbon, used as a fuel and raw material. See also **producer gas**

water gate *n* **1** a gate in a canal, leat, etc that can be opened or closed to control the flow of water **2** a gate through which access may be gained to a body of water

Watergate ('wɔːtə,geɪt) *n* **1** an incident during the 1972 US presidential campaign, when a group of agents employed by the re-election organization of President Richard Nixon were caught breaking into the Democratic Party headquarters in the Watergate building, Washington, DC. The consequent political scandal was exacerbated by attempts to conceal the fact that senior White House officials had approved the burglary, and eventually forced the resignation of President Nixon **2** any similar public scandal, esp involving politicians or a possible cover-up. See also **-gate**

water gauge *n* an instrument that indicates the presence or the quantity of water in a tank, reservoir, or boiler feed. Also called: **water glass**

water glass *n* **1** a viscous syrupy solution of sodium silicate in water: used as a protective coating for cement and a preservative, esp for eggs **2** another name for **water clock** *or* **water gauge**

water gum *n* **1** any of several gum trees, esp *Nyssa biflora* (or *tupelo*), of swampy areas of North America: family *Nyssaceae* **2** any of several Australian myrtaceous trees, esp *Tristania laurina*, of swampy ground

water gun *n* another term (esp US) for **water pistol**

water hammer *n* a sharp concussion produced when the flow of water in a pipe is suddenly blocked

water hemlock *n* another name for **cowbane** (sense 1)

water hen *n* another name for **gallinule**

water hole *n* **1** a depression, such as a pond or pool, containing water, esp one used by animals as a drinking place **2** a source of drinking water in a desert

water hyacinth *n* a floating aquatic plant, *Eichhornia crassipes*, of tropical America, having showy bluish-purple flowers and swollen leafstalks: family *Pontederiaceae*. It forms dense masses in rivers, ponds, etc, and is a serious problem in the southern US, Australia, and parts of Africa

water ice *n* an ice cream made from a frozen sugar syrup flavoured with fruit juice or purée; sorbet

watering can *n* a container with a handle and a spout with a perforated nozzle used to sprinkle water over plants

watering hole *n* **1** a pool where animals drink; water hole **2** *facetious slang* a pub

watering place n **1** a place where drinking water for men or animals may be obtained **2** *Brit* a spa **3** *Brit* a seaside resort

watering pot n another name (US) for **watering can**

water intoxication n a nontechnical name for **hyponatraemia**

water jacket n a water-filled envelope or container surrounding a machine, engine, or part for cooling purposes, esp the casing around the cylinder block of a pump or internal-combustion engine. Compare **air jacket**

water jump n a ditch, brook, or pond over which athletes or horses must jump in a steeplechase or similar contest

water level n **1** the level reached by the surface of a body of water **2** the water line of a boat or ship

water lily n **1** any of various aquatic plants of the genus *Nymphaea* and related genera, of temperate and tropical regions, having large leaves and showy flowers that float on the surface of the water: family *Nymphaeaceae* **2** any of various similar and related plants, such as the yellow water lily

water line n **1** a line marked at the level around a vessel's hull to which the vessel will be immersed when afloat **2** a line marking the level reached by a body of water

waterlogged ('wɔːtəˌlɒgd) adj **1** saturated with water **2** (of a vessel still afloat) having taken in so much water as to be unmanageable

Waterloo (ˌwɔːtəˈluː) n **1** a small town in central Belgium, in Walloon Brabant province south of Brussels: battle (1815) fought nearby in which British and Prussian forces under the Duke of Wellington and Blücher routed the French under Napoleon. Pop: 29 003 (2004 est) **2** a total or crushing defeat (esp in **meet one's Waterloo**)

water louse n an aquatic isopod of the genus *Asellus*, common in weedy water. Also called: **water slater**

water main n a principal supply pipe in an arrangement of pipes for distributing water

waterman ('wɔːtəmən) n, pl **-men** a skilled boatman ▷ 'water·manˌship n

watermark ('wɔːtəˌmɑːk) n **1** a distinguishing mark impressed on paper during manufacture, visible when the paper is held up to the light **2** another word for **water line** (senses 1, 2) ▷ vb (tr) **3** to mark (paper) with a watermark

water meadow n a meadow that remains fertile by being periodically flooded by a stream

water measurer n a slender heteropterous bug, *Hydrometra stagnorum*, that has a greatly elongated head and is found on still or sluggish water where it preys on water fleas, mosquito larvae, etc

watermelon ('wɔːtəˌmɛlən) n **1** an African melon, *Citrullus vulgaris*, widely cultivated for its large edible fruit **2** the fruit of this plant, which has a hard green rind and sweet watery reddish flesh

water meter n a device for measuring the quantity or rate of water flowing through a pipe

water milfoil n any of various pond plants of the genus *Myriophyllum*, having feathery underwater leaves and small inconspicuous flowers: family *Haloragidaceae*

water mill n a mill operated by a water wheel

water mint n a Eurasian mint plant, *Mentha aquatica*, of marshy places, having scented leaves and whorls of small flowers

water moccasin n a large dark grey venomous snake, *Agkistrodon piscivorus*, of swamps in the southern US: family *Crotalidae* (pit vipers). Also called: **cottonmouth**

water nymph n **1** any fabled nymph of the water, such as the Naiad, Nereid, or Oceanid of Greek mythology **2** any of various aquatic plants, esp a water lily or a naiad

water of crystallization n water present in the crystals of certain compounds. It is chemically combined in stoichiometric amounts, usually by coordinate or hydrogen bonds, but can often be easily expelled

water ouzel n another name for **dipper** (the bird)

water ox n another term for **water buffalo**

water paint n any water-based paint, such as an emulsion or an acrylic paint

water parting n another term (esp US) for **watershed** (sense 1)

water pepper n any of several polygonaceous plants of the genus *Polygonum*, esp *P. hydropiper*, of marshy regions, having reddish stems, clusters of small greenish flowers, and acrid-tasting leaves

water pimpernel n another name for **brookweed**

water pipe n **1** a pipe for water **2** another name for **hookah**

water pistol n a toy pistol that squirts a stream of water or other liquid. Also called (US): **water gun**

water plantain n any of several marsh plants of the genus *Alisma*, esp *A. plantago-aquatica*, of N temperate regions and Australia, having clusters of small white or pinkish flowers and broad pointed leaves: family *Alismataceae*

water polo n a game played in water by two teams of seven swimmers in which each side tries to throw or propel an inflated ball into the opponents' goal

water power n **1** the power latent in a dynamic or static head of water as used to drive machinery, esp for generating electricity **2** a source of such power, such as a drop in the level of a river, etc **3** the right to the use of water for such a purpose, as possessed by a water mill

waterproof ('wɔːtəˌpruːf) adj **1** not penetrable by water. Compare **water-repellent, water-resistant** ▷ n **2** chiefly Brit a waterproof garment, esp a raincoat ▷ vb (tr) **3** to make (a fabric, item of clothing, etc) waterproof

water purslane n **1** an onagraceous marsh plant, *Ludwigia palustris*, of temperate and warm regions, having reddish stems and small greenish flowers **2** any of several lythraceous plants of wet places that resemble purslane, such as *Peplis portula* of Europe, which has small pinkish flowers, and *Didiplis diandra* of North America, which has small greenish flowers

water rail n a large Eurasian rail, *Rallus aquaticus*, of swamps, ponds, etc, having a long red bill

water rat n **1** any of several small amphibious rodents, esp the water vole or the muskrat **2** any of various amphibious rats of the subfamily *Hydromyinae*, of New Guinea, the Philippines, and Australia **3** informal a person who is very fond of water sports

water-repellent adj (of fabrics, garments, etc) having a finish that resists the absorption of water

water-resistant adj (esp of fabrics) designed to resist but not entirely prevent the penetration of water

water right n the right to make use of a water supply, as for irrigation

waters pl n ('wɔːtəz) **1** any body of sea, or seas regarded as sharing some common quality: *Irish territorial waters; uncharted tropical waters* **2** physiol (sometimes singular) the amniotic fluid surrounding the fetus in the womb

water sapphire n a deep blue variety of the mineral cordierite that occurs in Sri Lanka: used as a gemstone

waterscape ('wɔːtəˌskeɪp) n a picture, view, or representation of a body of water

water scorpion n any of various long-legged aquatic insects of the heteropterous family *Nepidae*, which breathe by means of a long spinelike tube that projects from the rear of the body and penetrates the surface of the water

water seal n a small amount of water contained in the trap of a drain to prevent the passage of foul smells

watershed ('wɔːtəˌʃɛd) n **1** the dividing line between two adjacent river systems, such as a ridge **2** an important period or factor that serves as a dividing line

water shield n **1** a North American nymphaeaceous plant, *Brasenia schreberi*, with floating oval leaves and purple flowers **2** any of several similar and related plants of the genus *Cabomba*

water shrew n either of two small amphibious shrews, *Neomys fodiens* (**European water shrew**) or *N. anomalus* (**Mediterranean water shrew**), having a dark pelage with paler underparts

water-sick adj (of land) made infertile or uncultivated by excessive irrigation

waterside ('wɔːtəˌsaɪd) n **a** the area of land beside a body of water **b** (as modifier): *waterside houses*

watersider ('wɔːtəˌsaɪdə) n Austral and NZ a wharf labourer

water-ski n also **water ski** **1** a type of ski used for planing or gliding over water ▷ vb **-skis, -skiing, -skied** or **-ski'd** (intr) **2** to ride over water on a water-ski or water-skis while holding a rope towed by a speedboat ▷ 'water-ˌskier n ▷ 'water-ˌskiing n

water snake n any of various colubrid snakes that live in or near water, esp any of numerous harmless North American snakes of the genus *Natrix*, such as *N. sipedon*

water-soak vb (tr) to soak or drench with or in water

water softener n **1** any substance that lessens the hardness of water, usually by precipitating or absorbing calcium and magnesium ions **2** a tank, apparatus, or chemical plant that is used to filter or treat water to remove chemicals that cause hardness

water soldier n an aquatic plant, *Stratiotes aloides*, of Europe and NW Asia, having rosettes of large leaves and large three-petalled white flowers: family *Hydrocharitaceae*

water spaniel n either of two large curly-coated breeds of spaniel (the Irish and the American), which are used for hunting waterfowl. See also **Irish water spaniel**

water spider n a Eurasian spider, *Argyroneta aquatica*, that spins a web in the form of an air-filled chamber in which it lives submerged in streams and ponds

water splash n a place where a stream runs over a road

water sports pl n **1** various sports, such as swimming, water-skiing, or windsurfing, that take place in or on water **2** slang sexual practices that involve urination

waterspout ('wɔːtəˌspaʊt) n **1** meteorol **a** a tornado occurring over water that forms a column of water and mist extending between the surface and the clouds above **b** a sudden downpour of heavy rain **2** a pipe or channel through which water is discharged, esp one used for drainage from the gutters of a roof

water starwort n See **starwort** (sense 2)

water stick insect n a slender sticklike flightless water bug, *Ranatra linearis*, that is predatory on small creatures such as water fleas

water strider or **skater** n another name for a **pond-skater**

water supply n **1** an arrangement of reservoirs, purification plant, distribution pipes, etc, for providing water to a community **2** the supply of treated and purified water for a community

water system n **1** a river and all its tributaries **2** a system for supplying water to a community

water table n **1** the surface of the water-saturated part of the ground, usually following approximately the contours of the overlying land surface **2** an offset or string course that has a moulding designed to throw rainwater clear of the wall below

water thrush n either of two North American warblers, *Seiurus motacilla* or *S. noveboracensis*, having a brownish back and striped underparts and

W

tending to occur near water

watertight ('wɔːtə,taɪt) *adj* **1** not permitting the passage of water either in or out: *a watertight boat* **2** without loopholes: *a watertight argument* **3** kept separate from other subjects or influences: *different disciplines are often thought of in watertight compartments* > **'water,tightness** *n*

water torture *n* any of various forms of torture using water, esp one in which water drips or is slowly poured onto the victim's forehead

water tower *n* a reservoir or storage tank mounted on a tower-like structure at the summit of an area of high ground in a place where the water pressure would otherwise be inadequate for distribution at a uniform pressure

water tube boiler *n* a steam generator consisting of water drums and steam drums connected by banks of tubes through which the water is circulated. The tubes are exposed to the hot gases of the furnace and the heat transfer rate is high

water vapour *n* water in the gaseous state, esp when due to evaporation at a temperature below the boiling point. Compare **steam**

water vole *n* a large amphibious vole, *Arvicola terrestris*, of Eurasian river banks: family *Cricetidae*. Also called: **water rat**

water wagtail *n* another name for **pied wagtail**

waterway ('wɔːtə,weɪ) *n* a river, canal, or other navigable channel used as a means of travel or transport

waterweed ('wɔːtə,wiːd) *n* **1** any of various weedy aquatic plants **2** another name for **pondweed** (sense 2)

water wheel *n* **1** a simple water-driven turbine consisting of a wheel having vanes set axially across its rim, used to drive machinery **2** a wheel with buckets attached to its rim for raising water from a stream, pond, etc

water wings *pl n* an inflatable rubber device shaped like a pair of wings, which is placed round the front of the body and under the arms of a person learning to swim

water witch *n* a person who claims the ability to detect water underground by means of a divining rod

waterworks ('wɔːtə,wɜːks) *n* **1** (*functioning as singular*) an establishment for storing, purifying, and distributing water for community supply **2** (*functioning as plural*) a display of water in movement, as in fountains **3** (*functioning as plural*) *Brit informal euphemism* the urinary system, esp with reference to its normal functioning: *he has trouble with his waterworks* **4** (*functioning as plural*) *informal* crying; tears

waterworn ('wɔːtə,wɔːn) *adj* worn smooth by the action or passage of water

watery ('wɔːtərɪ) *adj* **1** relating to, consisting of, containing, or resembling water **2** discharging or secreting water or a water-like fluid: *a watery wound* **3** tearful; weepy **4** insipid, thin, or weak > **'wateriness** *n*

Watford ('wɒtfəd) *n* a town in SE England, in SW Hertfordshire: light industries, services. Pop: 120 960 (2001)

Watling Island ('wɒtlɪŋ) *n* another name for **San Salvador Island**

watt (wɒt) *n* the derived SI unit of power, equal to 1 joule per second; the power dissipated by a current of 1 ampere flowing across a potential difference of 1 volt. 1 watt is equivalent to 1.341×10^{-3} horsepower. Symbol: W [C19 named after James Watt (1736–1819), Scottish engineer and inventor]

wattage ('wɒtɪdʒ) *n* **1** power, esp electric power, measured in watts **2** the power rating, measured in watts, of an electrical appliance

Watteau back *n* a section at the back of a woman's dress that is caught in pleats or gathers at the neck and falls unbelted to the floor

Wattenscheid (*German* 'vatən,ʃaɪt) *n* an industrial town in NW Germany, in North Rhine-Westphalia

east of Essen. Pop: 81 200 (latest est)

watt-hour *n* a unit of energy equal to a power of one watt operating for one hour. 1 watt-hour equals 3600 joules

wattle[1] ('wɒtᵊl) *n* **1** a frame of rods or stakes interwoven with twigs, branches, etc, esp when used to make fences **2** the material used in such a construction **3** a loose fold of skin, often brightly coloured, hanging from the neck or throat of certain birds, lizards, etc **4** any of various chiefly Australian acacia trees having spikes of small brightly coloured flowers and flexible branches, which were used by early settlers for making fences. See also **golden wattle** **5** a southern African caesalpinaceous tree, *Peltophorum africanum*, with yellow flowers ▷ *vb* (*tr*) **6** to construct from wattle **7** to bind or frame with wattle **8** to weave or twist (branches, twigs, etc) into a frame ▷ *adj* **9** made of, formed by, or covered with wattle [Old English *watol*; related to *wethel* wrap, Old High German *wadal*, German *Wedel*] > **'wattled** *adj*

wattle[2] ('wɒtᵊl) *adj* *Midland English dialect* of poor quality

wattle and daub *n* **a** a form of wall construction consisting of interwoven twigs plastered with a mixture of clay, lime, water, and sometimes dung and chopped straw **b** (*as modifier*): *a wattle-and-daub hut*

wattlebird ('wɒtᵊl,bɜːd) *n* **1** any of various Australian honeyeaters of the genus *Anthochaera*, such as *A. paradoxa* (**yellow wattlebird**), that have red or yellow wattles on both sides of the head **2** any arboreal New Zealand songbird of the family *Callaeidae*, having wattles on both sides of the bill

wattmeter ('wɒt,miːtə) *n* a meter for measuring electric power in watts

Watusi (wəˈtuːzɪ) or **Watutsi** (wəˈtʊtsɪ) *n*, *pl* **-sis** or **-si** a member of a cattle-owning Negroid people of Rwanda and Burundi in Africa

wauk[1] (wɔːk) *vb* a Scot word for **wake**[1]

wauk[2] or **waulk** (wɔːk) *vb* (*tr*) *Scot* to full (cloth) [C15 variant of WALK]

waul or **wawl** (wɔːl) *vb* (*intr*) to cry or wail plaintively like a cat [C16 of imitative origin]

waur[1] (wɔːr) *adj*, *n*, *adv* a Scot word for **worse**

waur[2] (wɔːr) *adj* a Scot word for **wary**

wave (weɪv) *vb* **1** to move or cause to move freely to and fro: *the banner waved in the wind* **2** (*intr*) to move the hand to and fro as a greeting **3** to signal or signify by or as if by waving something **4** (*tr*) to direct to move by or as if by waving something: *he waved me on* **5** to form or be formed into curves, undulations, etc **6** (*tr*) to give a wavy or watered appearance to (silk, etc) **7** (*tr*) to set waves in (the hair) ▷ *n* **8** one of a sequence of ridges or undulations that moves across the surface of a body of a liquid, esp the sea: created by the wind or a moving object and gravity **9** any undulation on or at the edge of a surface reminiscent of such a wave: *a wave across the field of corn* **10** **the waves** the sea **11** anything that suggests the movement of a wave, as by a sudden rise: *a crime wave* **12** a widespread movement that advances in a body: *a wave of settlers swept into the country* **13** the act or an instance of waving **14** *physics* an oscillation propagated through a medium or space such that energy is periodically interchanged between two kinds of disturbance. For example, an oscillating electric field generates a magnetic oscillation and vice versa, hence an electromagnetic wave is produced. Similarly a wave on a liquid comprises vertical and horizontal displacements. See also **antinode, longitudinal wave, node, standing wave, transverse wave 15** *physics* a graphical representation of a wave obtained by plotting the magnitude of the disturbance against time at a particular point in the medium or space; waveform **16** a prolonged spell of some weather condition: *a heat wave* **17** an undulating curve or series of curves or loose curls in the hair **18** an undulating pattern or finish on a fabric **19** short

for **wave moth 20 make waves** to cause trouble; disturb the status quo **21 ride the wave** *US slang* to enjoy a period of success and good fortune [Old English *wafian* (vb); related to Old High German *weban* to WEAVE, Old Norse *vafra*; see WAVER; C16 (n) changed from earlier *wāwe*, probably from Old English *wǣg* motion; compare WAG[1]] > **'waveless** *adj* > **'wave,like** *adj*

waveband ('weɪv,bænd) *n* a range of wavelengths or frequencies used for a particular type of radio transmission

wave-cut platform *n* a flat surface at the base of a cliff formed by erosion by waves

wave down *vb* (*tr*, *adverb*) to signal with a wave to (a driver or vehicle) to stop

wave energy *n* energy obtained by harnessing wave power

wave equation *n* *physics* a partial differential equation describing wave motion. It has the form $\nabla^2\varphi = (1/c^2) \times (\partial^2\varphi/\partial t^2)$, where ∇^2 is the Laplace operator, t the time, c the speed of propagation, and φ is a function characterizing the displacement of the wave

waveform ('weɪv,fɔːm) *n* *physics* the shape of the graph of a wave or oscillation obtained by plotting the value of some changing quantity against time

wavefront ('weɪv,frʌnt) *n* *physics* a surface associated with a propagating wave and passing through all points in the wave that have the same phase. It is usually perpendicular to the direction of propagation

wave function *n* *physics* a mathematical function of position and generally time, used in wave mechanics to describe the state of a physical system. Symbol: ψ

waveguide ('weɪv,gaɪd) *n* *electronics* a solid rod of dielectric or a hollow metal tube, usually of rectangular cross section, used as a path to guide microwaves

wavelength ('weɪv,lɛŋθ) *n* **1** the distance, measured in the direction of propagation, between two points of the same phase in consecutive cycles of a wave. Symbol: λ **2** the wavelength of the carrier wave used by a particular broadcasting station **3 on someone's** (*or the same*) **wavelength** *informal* having similar views, feelings, or thoughts (as someone else)

wavelet ('weɪvlɪt) *n* a small wave

wavellite ('weɪvə,laɪt) *n* a greyish-white, yellow, or brown mineral consisting of hydrated basic aluminium phosphate in radiating clusters of small orthorhombic crystals. Formula: $Al_3(PO_4)_2(OH)_3.5H_2O$ [C19 named after William Wavell (died 1829), English physician]

wave mechanics *n* (*functioning as singular*) *physics* the formulation of quantum mechanics in which the behaviour of systems, such as atoms, is described in terms of their wave functions

wavemeter ('weɪv,miːtə) *n* an instrument for measuring the frequency or wavelength of radio waves

wave moth *n* any of several small geometrid moths with wavy markings, such as the **common wave** (*Deilinia exanthemata*), with grey-marked wings, and the lighter **common white wave** (*D. pusaria*). Often shortened to: **wave**

wave number *n* *physics* the reciprocal of the wavelength of a wave. Symbol: ν, σ

waveoff ('weɪv,ɒf) *n* a signal or instruction to an aircraft not to land

wave power *n* power extracted from the motion of sea waves at the coast

waver ('weɪvə) *vb* (*intr*) **1** to be irresolute; hesitate between two possibilities **2** to become unsteady **3** to fluctuate or vary **4** to move back and forth or one way and another **5** (*of light*) to flicker or flash ▷ *n* **6** the act or an instance of wavering [C14 from Old Norse *vafra* to flicker; related to German *wabern* to move about] > **'waverer** *n* > **'wavering** *adj* > **'waveringly** *adv*

WAVES or **Waves** (weɪvz) *n* (in the US) *acronym for* Women Accepted for Volunteer Emergency

Service; the women's reserve of the US navy

wave speed or **velocity** n other names for **phase speed**

wave theory n 1 the theory proposed by Huygens that light is transmitted by waves 2 any theory that light or other radiation is transmitted as waves. See **electromagnetic wave** ▷ Compare **corpuscular theory**

wave train n physics a series of waves travelling in the same direction and spaced at regular intervals

wavey ('weɪvɪ) n Canadian a snow goose or other wild goose. Also called: wawa [via Canadian French from Algonquian (Cree wehwew)]

wavy ('weɪvɪ) adj wavier, waviest 1 abounding in or full of waves 2 moving or proceeding in waves or undulations 3 (of hair) set in or having waves and curls 4 unstable or wavering > 'wavily adv > 'waviness n

waw (wɔː) n another name for **vav**

wawa¹ ('wɑːˌwɑː) Canadian W coast slang ▷ n 1 speech; language ▷ vb 2 (intr) to speak [c19 from Chinook Jargon; probably of imitative origin]

wawa² ('wɑːˌwɑː, 'wɑːwə) n Canadian a variant of **wavey**

wawl (wɔːl) vb a variant spelling of **waul**

wax¹ (wæks) n 1 any of various viscous or solid materials of natural origin: characteristically lustrous, insoluble in water, and having a low softening temperature, they consist largely of esters of fatty acids 2 any of various similar substances, such as paraffin wax or ozocerite, that have a mineral origin and consist largely of hydrocarbons 3 short for **beeswax** or **sealing wax** 4 physiol another name for **cerumen** 5 a resinous preparation used by shoemakers to rub on thread 6 bone wax a mixture of wax, oil, and carbolic acid applied to the cut surface of a bone to prevent bleeding 7 any substance or object that is pliable or easily moulded: he was wax in the hands of the political bosses 8 (modifier) made of or resembling wax: a wax figure 9 the act or an instance of removing body hair by coating it with warm wax, applying a strip of fabric, and then removing the fabric sharply, thereby plucking the hairs out by their roots 10 to remove (body hair) by means of a wax treatment ▷ vb 11 (tr) to coat, polish, etc, with wax [Old English weax, related to Old Saxon, Old High German wahs, Old Norse vax] > 'waxer n > 'waxing adj

wax² (wæks) vb (intr) 1 to become larger, more powerful, etc 2 (of the moon) to show a gradually increasing portion of illuminated surface, between new moon and full moon. Compare **wane** (sense 1) 3 archaic to become as specified: the time waxed late [Old English weaxan; related to Old Frisian waxa, Old Saxon, Old High German wahsan, Gothic wahsjan]

wax³ (wæks) n Brit informal old-fashioned a fit of rage or temper: he's in a wax today [of obscure origin; perhaps from the phrase to wax angry]

wax bean n US any of certain string beans that have yellow waxy pods and are grown in the US

waxberry ('wæksˌbərɪ, -brɪ) n, pl -ries the waxy fruit of the wax myrtle or the snowberry

waxbill ('wæksˌbɪl) n any of various chiefly African finchlike weaverbirds of the genus Estrilda and related genera, having a brightly coloured bill and plumage

wax cap n any fungus of the basidiomycetous family Hygrophoraceae, having thick waxy gills. Many are brightly coloured, like the **parrot toadstool** (Hygrophorus psittacinus), which is yellow with a covering of green slime, and the orange-red H. conicus

waxcloth ('wæksˌklɒθ) n 1 another name for **oilcloth** 2 another name for **linoleum**

waxen¹ ('wæksən) adj 1 made of, treated with, or covered with wax 2 resembling wax in colour or texture

waxen² ('wæksən) vb archaic a past participle of **wax²**

waxeye ('wæksˌaɪ) n Austral and NZ another name for **white-eye**

wax flower n Austral any of several rutaceous shrubs of the genus Eriostemon, having waxy pink-white five-petalled flowers

wax insect n any of various scale insects that secrete wax or a waxy substance, esp the oriental species Ceroplastes ceriferus, which produces Chinese wax

wax light n a candle or taper of wax

wax moth n a brown pyralid moth, Galleria mellonella, the larvae of which feed on the combs of beehives. Also called: honeycomb moth, bee moth

wax myrtle n a shrub, Myrica cerifera, of SE North America, having evergreen leaves and a small berry-like fruit with a waxy coating: family Myricaceae. Also called: bayberry, candleberry, waxberry

wax palm n 1 a tall Andean palm tree, Ceroxylon andicola, having pinnate leaves that yield a resinous wax used in making candles 2 another name for **carnauba** (sense 1)

wax paper n paper treated or coated with wax or paraffin to make it waterproof

waxplant ('wæksˌplɑːnt) n 1 a climbing asclepiadaceous shrub, Hoya carnosa, of E Asia and Australia, having fleshy leaves and clusters of small waxy white pink-centred flowers 2 any of various similar plants of the genus Hoya

wax tree n a Japanese anacardiaceous tree, Rhus succedanea, having white berries that yield wax

waxwing ('wæksˌwɪŋ) n any of several gregarious passerine songbirds of the genus Bombycilla, esp B. garrulus, having red waxy wing tips and crested heads: family Bombycillidae

waxwork ('wæksˌwɜːk) n 1 an object reproduced in wax, esp as an ornament 2 a life-size lifelike figure, esp of a famous person, reproduced in wax 3 (plural; functioning as singular or plural) a museum or exhibition of wax figures or objects > 'wax,worker n

waxy¹ ('wæksɪ) adj waxier, waxiest 1 resembling wax in colour, appearance, or texture 2 made of, covered with, or abounding in wax > 'waxily adv > 'waxiness n

waxy² ('wæksɪ) adj waxier, waxiest Brit informal old-fashioned bad-tempered or irritable; angry

way (weɪ) n 1 a manner, method, or means: a way of life; a way of knowing 2 a route or direction: the way home 3 a a means or line of passage, such as a path or track b (in combination): waterway 4 space or room for movement or activity (esp in the phrases **make way, in the way, out of the way**) 5 distance, usually distance in general: you've come a long way 6 a passage or journey: on the way 7 characteristic style or manner: I did it in my own way 8 (often plural) habits; idiosyncrasies: he has some offensive ways 9 an aspect of something; particular: in many ways he was right 10 a street in or leading out of a town b (capital when part of a street name): Icknield Way 11 something that one wants in a determined manner (esp in the phrases **get** or **have one's (own) way**) 12 the experience or sphere in which one comes into contact with things (esp in the phrase **come one's way**) 13 informal a state or condition, usually financial or concerning health (esp in the phrases **in a good (**or **bad) way**) 14 informal the area or direction of one's home: drop in if you're ever over my way 15 movement of a ship or other vessel 16 a right of way in law 17 a guide along which something can be moved, such as the surface of a lathe along which the tailstock slides 18 (plural) the wooden or metal tracks down which a ship slides to be launched 19 a course of life including experiences, conduct, etc: the way of sin 20 archaic calling or trade 21 **by the way** (sentence modifier) in passing or incidentally 22 **by way of a** via **b** serving as: by way of introduction **c** in the state or condition of: by way of being an artist 23 **each way** (of a bet) laid on a horse, dog, etc, to win or gain a place 24 **give way a** to collapse or break down **b** to withdraw or yield 25 **give way**

to **a** to step aside for or stop for **b** to give full rein to (emotions, etc) 26 **go out of one's way** to take considerable trouble or inconvenience oneself 27 **have a way with** to have such a manner or skill as to handle successfully 28 **have it both ways** to enjoy two things that would normally contradict each other or be mutually exclusive 29 **in a way** in some respects 30 **in no way** not at all 31 **lead the way a** to go first **b** to set an example or precedent 32 **make one's way a** to proceed or advance **b** to achieve success in life 33 **no way** informal that is impossible 34 **on the way out** informal **a** becoming unfashionable, obsolete, etc **b** dying 35 **out of the way a** removed or dealt with so as to be no longer a hindrance **b** remote **c** unusual and sometimes improper 36 **pay one's way** See **pay** (sense 11) 37 **see one's way (clear)** to find it possible and be willing to (do something) 38 **the way** Irish so that: I left early the way I would avoid the traffic 39 **under way** having started moving or making progress ▷ adv 40 informal **a** at a considerable distance or extent: way over yonder **b** very far: they're way up the mountain 41 informal by far; considerably: way better 42 slang truly; genuinely: they have a way cool site [Old English weg; related to Old Frisian wei, Old Norse vegr, Gothic wigs]

waybill ('weɪˌbɪl) n a document attached to goods in transit specifying their nature, point of origin, and destination as well as the route to be taken and the rate to be charged

way-cool adj informal outstanding; excellent; marvellous

wayfarer ('weɪˌfɛərə) n a person who goes on a journey > 'way,faring n, adj

wayfaring tree n a caprifoliaceous shrub, Viburnum lantana, of Europe and W Asia, having white flowers and berries that turn from red to black

Wayland or **Wayland Smith** ('weɪlənd) n a smith, artificer, and king of the elves in European folklore. Scandinavian name: Völund German name: Wieland

waylay ('weɪˌleɪ) vb -lays, -laying, -laid (tr) 1 to lie in wait for and attack 2 to await and intercept unexpectedly [c16 from WAY + LAY¹] > 'way'layer n

wayleave ('weɪˌliːv) n access to property granted by a landowner for payment, for example to allow a contractor access to a building site

wayleggo (ˌweɪlɛˈgəʊ) interj NZ away here! let go!; a shepherd's call to a dog on completion of a task

waymark ('weɪˌmɑːk) n a symbol or signpost marking the route of a footpath

waymarked ('weɪˌmɑːkt) adj marked or identified with waymarks

way-out adj informal 1 extremely unconventional or experimental; avant-garde 2 excellent or amazing

waypoint ('weɪˌpɔɪnt) n the co-ordinates of a specific location as defined by a GPS

-ways suffix forming adverbs indicating direction or manner: sideways [Old English weges, literally: of the way, from weg WAY]

ways and means pl n 1 the revenues and methods of raising the revenues needed for the functioning of a state or other political unit 2 (usually capital) a standing committee of the US House of Representatives that supervises all financial legislation 3 the methods and resources for accomplishing some purpose

wayside ('weɪˌsaɪd) n 1 a the side or edge of a road b (modifier) situated by the wayside: a wayside inn 2 **fall by the wayside** to cease or fail to continue doing something: of the nine starters, three fell by the wayside 3 **go by the wayside** to be put aside on account of something more urgent

wayward ('weɪwəd) adj 1 wanting to have one's own way regardless of the wishes or good of others 2 capricious, erratic, or unpredictable [c14 changed from awayward turned or turning away] > 'waywardly adv > 'waywardness n

wayworn ('weɪˌwɔːn) adj rare worn or tired by

W

travel: *footsore and wayworn*

wayzgoose ('weɪzˌguːs) *n* a works outing made annually by a printing house [c18 from earlier *waygoose*, of unknown origin]

Waziristan (wəˌzɪərɪ'stɑːn) *n* a mountainous region of N Pakistan, on the border with Afghanistan

wazzock ('wæzək) *n English dialect* a foolish or annoying person [c20 of unknown origin]

wb *abbreviation for* **1** water ballast **2** Also: W/B, WB waybill **3** westbound

Wb *physics symbol for* weber

WB *text messaging abbreviation for* welcome back

WBA *abbreviation for* World Boxing Association

WBC *abbreviation for* World Boxing Council

WBO *abbreviation for* World Boxing Organization

W boson *n physics* another name for **W particle**

WBU *abbreviation for* World Boxing Union

wc *abbreviation for* **1** water closet **2** without charge

WC *abbreviation for* **1** water closet **2** (in London postal code) West Central

WCC *abbreviation for* **World Council of Churches**

wd *abbreviation for* **1** ward **2** wood **3** word

WD *abbreviation for* **1** War Department **2** Works Department **3** *international car registration for* (Windward Islands) Dominica

WDA *abbreviation for* Welsh Development Agency

WDM *or* **wdm** *abbreviation for* wavelength division multiplex: a system in which several independent signals may be sent down an optical fibre link by monitoring them on light-carriers of different wavelengths

we (wiː) *pron* (*subjective*) **1** refers to the speaker or writer and another person or other people: *we should go now* **2** refers to all people or people in general: *the planet on which we live* **3 a** a formal word for **I**¹ used by editors or other writers, and formerly by monarchs **b** (*as noun*): *he uses the royal we in his pompous moods* **4** *informal* used instead of *you* with a tone of persuasiveness, condescension, or sarcasm: *how are we today?* [Old English *wē*, related to Old Saxon *wī*, Old High German *wir*, Old Norse *vēr*, Danish, Swedish *vi*, Sanskrit *vayam*]

WEA (in Britain) *abbreviation for* Workers' Educational Association

weak (wiːk) *adj* **1** lacking in physical or mental strength or force; frail or feeble **2** liable to yield, break, or give way: *a weak link in a chain* **3** lacking in resolution or firmness of character **4** lacking strength, power, or intensity: *a weak voice* **5** lacking strength in a particular part: *a team weak in defence* **6 a** not functioning as well as normal: *weak eyes* **b** easily upset: *a weak stomach* **7** lacking in conviction, persuasiveness, etc: *a weak argument* **8** lacking in political or strategic strength: *a weak state* **9** lacking the usual, full, or desirable strength of flavour: *weak tea* **10** *grammar* **a** denoting or belonging to a class of verbs, in certain languages including the Germanic languages, whose conjugation relies on inflectional endings rather than internal vowel gradation, as *look, looks, looking, looked* **b** belonging to any part-of-speech class, in any of various languages, whose inflections follow the more regular of two possible patterns. Compare **strong** (sense 13) **11** (of a syllable) not accented or stressed **12** (of a fuel-air mixture) containing a relatively low proportion of fuel. Compare **rich** (sense 13) **13** *photog* having low density or contrast; thin **14** (of an industry, market, currency, securities, etc) falling in price or characterized by falling prices [Old English *wāc* soft, miserable; related to Old Saxon *wēk*, Old High German *weih*, Old Norse *veikr*] > 'weakish *adj* > 'weakishly *adv* > 'weakishness *n*

weaken ('wiːkən) *vb* to become or cause to become weak or weaker > 'weakener *n*

weaker sex *n* the female sex

weakest link *n* the *Brit* the person who is making the least contribution to the collective achievement of the group [c20 from the British television quiz of the same name]

weakfish ('wiːkˌfɪʃ) *n, pl* -fish *or* -fishes any of several sciaenid sea trouts, esp *Cynoscion regalis*, a food and game fish of American Atlantic coastal waters

weak interaction *or* **force** *n physics* an interaction between elementary particles that is responsible for certain decay processes, operates at distances less than about 10^{-15} metres, and is 10^{12} times weaker than the strong interaction. The weak interaction and electromagnetic interactions are now described by the unifying electroweak theory. Also called: **weak nuclear interaction** *or* **force** See **interaction** (sense 2), **electroweak interaction**

weak-kneed *adj informal* yielding readily to force, persuasion, intimidation, etc > ˌweak-'kneedly *adv* > ˌweak-'kneedness *n*

weakling ('wiːklɪŋ) *n* a person or animal that is lacking in strength or weak in constitution or character

weakly ('wiːklɪ) *adj* -lier, -liest **1** sickly; feeble ▷ *adv* **2** in a weak or feeble manner > 'weakliness *n*

weak-minded *adj* **1** lacking in stability of mind or character **2** another word for **feeble-minded** > ˌweak-'mindedly *adv* > ˌweak-'mindedness *n*

weakness ('wiːknɪs) *n* **1** the state or quality of being weak **2** a deficiency or failing, as in a person's character **3** a self-indulgent fondness or liking: *a weakness for chocolates*

weak sister *n US informal* a person in a group who is regarded as weak or unreliable

weak-willed *adj* lacking strength of will

weal¹ (wiːl) *n* a raised mark on the surface of the body produced by a blow. Also called: **wale, welt, wheal** [c19 variant of WALE¹, influenced in form by WHEAL]

weal² (wiːl) *n* **1** *archaic* prosperity or wellbeing (now esp in the phrases **the public weal, the common weal**) **2** *obsolete* the state **3** *obsolete* wealth [Old English *wela*; related to Old Saxon *welo*, Old High German *wolo*]

weald (wiːld) *n Brit archaic* open or forested country [Old English; related to Old Saxon, Old High German *wald*, Old Norse *vollr*, probably related to WOLD]

Weald (wiːld) *n* **the** a region of SE England, in Kent, Surrey, and East and West Sussex between the North Downs and the South Downs: formerly forested

wealth (wɛlθ) *n* **1** a large amount of money and valuable material possessions **2** the state of being rich **3** a great profusion: *a wealth of gifts* **4** *economics* all goods and services with monetary, exchangeable, or productive value [c13 *welthe*, from WEAL²; related to WELL¹] > 'wealthless *adj*

wealth tax *n* a tax on personal property; capital levy

wealthy ('wɛlθɪ) *adj* wealthier, wealthiest **1** possessing wealth; affluent; rich **2** of, characterized by, or relating to wealth **3** abounding: *wealthy in friends* > 'wealthily *adv* > 'wealthiness *n*

wean¹ (wiːn) *vb* (*tr*) **1** to cause (a child or young mammal) to replace mother's milk by other nourishment **2** (usually foll by *from*) to cause to desert former habits, pursuits, etc [Old English *wenian* to accustom; related to German *gewöhnen* to get used to] > 'weaning *n*

wean² (weɪn, wiːn) *n Scot and northern English dialect* a child; infant [a contraction of *wee ane* or perhaps a shortened form of WEANLING]

weaner ('wiːnə) *n* **1** a person or thing that weans **2** a pig that has just been weaned and weighs less than 40 kg **3** *Austral and NZ* a lamb, pig, or calf in the year in which it is weaned

weanling ('wiːnlɪŋ) *n* **a** a child or young animal recently weaned **b** (*as modifier*): *a weanling calf* [c16 from WEAN¹ + -LING¹]

weapon ('wɛpən) *n* **1** an object or instrument used in fighting **2** anything that serves to outwit or get the better of an opponent: *his power of speech was his best weapon* **3** any part of an animal that is used to defend itself, to attack prey, etc, such as claws, teeth, horns, or a sting **4** a slang word for **penis** [Old English *wǣpen*; related to Old Norse *vápn*, Old Frisian *wēpen*, Old High German *wāffan*] > 'weaponed *adj* > 'weaponless *adj*

weaponeer (ˌwɛpə'nɪə) *n* a person associated with the use or maintenance of weapons, esp nuclear weapons

weaponize *or* **weaponise** ('wɛpəˌnaɪz) *vb* (*tr*) to adapt (a chemical, bacillus, etc) in such a way that it can be used as a weapon

weaponry ('wɛpənrɪ) *n* weapons regarded collectively

weapons of mass destruction *pl n* nuclear, chemical, or biological weapons that can cause indiscriminate death or injury on a large scale. Abbreviation: WMD

weapon system *n military* a weapon and the components necessary to its proper function, such as targeting and guidance devices

wear¹ (wɛə) *vb* wears, wearing, wore, worn **1** (*tr*) to carry or have (a garment, etc) on one's person as clothing, ornament, etc **2** (*tr*) to carry or have on one's person habitually: *she wears a lot of red* **3** (*tr*) to have in one's aspect: *to wear a smile* **4** (*tr*) to display, show, or fly: *a ship wears its colours* **5** to deteriorate or cause to deteriorate by constant use or action **6** to produce or be produced by constant rubbing, scraping, etc: *to wear a hole in one's trousers* **7** to bring or be brought to a specified condition by constant use or action: *to wear a tyre to shreds* **8** (*intr*) to submit to constant use or action in a specified way: *his suit wears well* **9** (*tr*) to harass or weaken **10** (when *intr*, often foll by *on*) (of time) to pass or be passed slowly **11** (*tr*) *Brit slang* to accept: *Larry won't wear that argument* **12 wear ship** to change the tack of a sailing vessel, esp a square-rigger, by coming about so that the wind passes astern ▷ *n* **13** the act of wearing or state of being worn **14 a** anything designed to be worn: *leisure wear* **b** (*in combination*): *nightwear* **15** deterioration from constant or normal use or action **16** the quality of resisting the effects of constant use ▷ See also **wear down, wear off, wear out** [Old English *werian*; related to Old High German *werien*, Old Norse *verja*, Gothic *vasjan*] > 'wearer *n*

wear² (wɛə) *vb* wears, wearing, wore, worn *nautical* to tack by gybing instead of by going through stays [c17 from earlier *weare*, of unknown origin]

Wear (wɪə) *n* a river in NE England, rising in NW Durham and flowing southeast then northeast to the North Sea at Sunderland. Length: 105 km (65 miles)

wearable ('wɛərəbᵊl) *adj* **1** suitable for wear or able to be worn ▷ *n* **2** (*often plural*) any garment that can be worn > ˌwea'rability *n*

wear and tear *n* damage, depreciation, or loss resulting from ordinary use

wear down *vb* (*adverb*) **1** to consume or be consumed by long or constant wearing, rubbing, etc **2** to overcome or be overcome gradually by persistent effort

weariless ('wɪərɪlɪs) *adj* not wearied or able to be wearied > 'wearilessly *adv*

wearing ('wɛərɪŋ) *adj* causing fatigue or exhaustion; tiring > 'wearingly *adv*

wearing course *n* the top layer of a road that carries the traffic; road surface. Also called: carpet, topping

wearisome ('wɪərɪsəm) *or* **weariful** *adj* causing fatigue or annoyance; tedious > 'wearisomely *or* 'wearifully *adv* > 'wearisomeness *or* 'wearifulness *n*

wear off *vb* (*adverb*) **1** (*intr*) to decrease in intensity gradually: *the pain will wear off in an hour* **2** to disappear or cause to disappear gradually through exposure, use, etc: *the pattern on the ring had been worn off*

wear out *vb* (*adverb*) **1** to make or become unfit or useless through wear **2** (*tr*) to exhaust or tire

wearproof ('wɛəˌpruːf) *adj* resistant to damage from normal wear or usage

weary ('wɪərɪ) *adj* -rier, -riest **1** tired or exhausted **2** causing fatigue or exhaustion **3** caused by or suggestive of weariness: *a weary laugh* **4** (*postpositive; often foll by of or with*) discontented or bored, esp by the long continuance of something ▷ *vb* -ries, -rying, -ried **5** to make or become weary **6** to make or become discontented or impatient, esp by the long continuance of something [Old English *wērig*; related to Old Saxon *wōrig*, Old High German *wuorag* drunk, Greek *hōrakian* to faint] ▷ 'wearily *adv* ▷ 'weariness *n* ▷ 'wearying *adj* ▷ 'wearyingly *adv*

weasand ('wiːzənd) *n* a former name for the **trachea** [Old English *wǣsend, wāsend;* related to Old Frisian *wāsenda*, Old High German *weisont* vein, Danish *vissen*]

weasel ('wiːzəl) *n, pl* -sels *or* -sel **1** any of various small predatory musteline mammals of the genus *Mustela* and related genera, esp *M. nivalis* (**European weasel**), having reddish-brown fur, an elongated body and neck, and short legs **2** *informal* a sly or treacherous person **3** *chiefly US* a motor vehicle for use in snow, esp one with caterpillar tracks [Old English *weosule, wesle;* related to Old Norse *visla*, Old High German *wisula*, Middle Dutch *wesel*] ▷ 'weaselly *adj*

weasel out *vb* (*intr, adverb*) *informal* **1** to go back on a commitment **2** to evade a responsibility, esp in a despicable manner

weasel words *pl n informal* intentionally evasive or misleading speech; equivocation [c20 alluding to the weasel's supposed ability to suck an egg out of its shell without seeming to break the shell] ▷ 'weasel-,worded *adj*

weather ('wɛðə) *n* **1 a** the day-to-day meteorological conditions, esp temperature, cloudiness, and rainfall, affecting a specific place. Compare **climate** (sense 1) **b** (*modifier*) relating to the forecasting of weather: *a weather ship* **2** a prevailing state or condition **3** make heavy weather **a** (of a vessel) to roll and pitch in heavy seas **b** (foll by *of*) to carry out with great difficulty or unnecessarily great effort **4** under the weather *informal* **a** not in good health **b** intoxicated ▷ *adj* **5** (*prenominal*) on or at the side or part towards the wind; windward: *the weather anchor*. Compare **lee** (sense 4) ▷ *vb* **6** to expose or be exposed to the action of the weather **7** to undergo or cause to undergo changes, such as discoloration, due to the action of the weather **8** (*intr*) to withstand the action of the weather **9** (when *intr*, foll by *through*) to endure (a crisis, danger, etc) **10** (*tr*) to slope (a surface, such as a roof, sill, etc) so as to throw rainwater clear **11** (*tr*) to sail to the windward of: *to weather a point* [Old English *weder;* related to Old Saxon *wedar*, Old High German *wetar*, Old Norse *vethr*] ▷ ,weathera'bility *n* ▷ 'weatherer *n*

weather-beaten *adj* **1** showing signs of exposure to the weather **2** tanned or hardened by exposure to the weather

weatherboard ('wɛðə,bɔːd) *n* **1** a timber board, with a groove (rabbet) along the front of its top edge and along the back of its lower edge, that is fixed horizontally with others to form an exterior cladding on a wall or roof. Compare **clapboard 2** a sloping timber board fixed at the bottom of a door to deflect rain **3** the windward side of a vessel **4** Also called: **weatherboard house** *chiefly Austral and NZ* a house having the walls made entirely of weatherboarding

weatherboarding ('wɛðə,bɔːdɪŋ) *n* **1** an area or covering of weatherboards **2** weatherboards collectively

weather-bound *adj* (of a vessel, aircraft, etc) delayed by bad weather

weathercock ('wɛðə,kɒk) *n* **1** a weather vane in the form of a cock **2** a person who is fickle or changeable ▷ *vb* **3** (*intr*) (of an aircraft) to turn or tend to turn into the wind

weathered ('wɛðəd) *adj* **1** affected by exposure to the action of the weather **2** (of rocks and rock formations) eroded, decomposed, or otherwise

altered by the action of water, wind, frost, heat, etc **3** (of a sill, roof, etc) having a sloped surface so as to allow rainwater to run off **4** (of wood) artificially stained so as to appear weather-beaten: *weathered garden furniture*

weather eye *n* **1** the vision of a person trained to observe changes in the weather **2** *informal* an alert or observant gaze **3** keep one's weather eye open to stay on the alert

weatherglass ('wɛðə,glɑːs) *n* (*not in technical use*) any of various instruments, esp a barometer, that measure atmospheric conditions

weather house *n* a model house with two human figures, one that comes out to foretell bad weather and the other to foretell good weather

weathering ('wɛðərɪŋ) *n* the mechanical and chemical breakdown of rocks by the action of rain, snow, cold, etc

weatherly ('wɛðəlɪ) *adj* (of a sailing vessel) making very little leeway when close-hauled, even in a stiff breeze ▷ 'weatherliness *n*

weatherman ('wɛðə,mæn) *n, pl* -men a person who forecasts the weather, esp one who works in a meteorological office

Weatherman ('wɛðə,mæn) *n, pl* -men *US* a member of a militant revolutionary group active in the US during the 1970s [c20 name adopted from a line in Bob Dylan's song "Subterranean Homesick Blues": "You don't need a weatherman To know which way the wind blows."]

weather map *or* **chart** *n* a synoptic chart showing weather conditions, compiled from simultaneous observations taken at various weather stations

weatherproof ('wɛðə,pruːf) *adj* **1** designed or able to withstand exposure to weather without deterioration ▷ *vb* **2** (*tr*) to render (something) weatherproof ▷ 'weather,proofness *n*

weather station *n* one of a network of meteorological observation posts where weather data is recorded

weather strip *n* a thin strip of compressible material, such as spring metal, felt, etc, that is fitted between the frame of a door or window and the opening part to exclude wind and rain. Also called: weatherstripping

weather vane *n* a vane designed to indicate the direction in which the wind is blowing

weather window *n* a limited interval when weather conditions can be expected to be suitable for a particular project, such as laying offshore pipelines, reaching a high mountain summit, launching a satellite, etc

weather-wise *adj* **1** skilful or experienced in predicting weather conditions **2** skilful or experienced in predicting trends in public opinion, reactions, etc

weatherworn ('wɛðə,wɔːn) *adj* another word for **weather-beaten**

weave (wiːv) *vb* weaves, weaving, wove *or* weaved; woven *or* weaved **1** to form (a fabric) by interlacing (yarn, etc), esp on a loom **2** (*tr*) to make or construct by such a process: *to weave a shawl* **3** (*tr*) to make or construct (an artefact, such as a basket) by interlacing (a pliable material, such as cane) **4** (of a spider) to make (a web) **5** (*tr*) to construct by combining separate elements into a whole **6** (*tr*; often foll by *in, into, through, etc*) to introduce: *to weave factual details into a fiction* **7** to create (a way, etc) by moving from side to side: *to weave through a crowd* **8** (*intr*) *vet science* (of a stabled horse) to swing the head, neck, and body backwards and forwards **9** get weaving *informal* to hurry; start to do something ▷ *n* **10** the method or pattern of weaving or the structure of a woven fabric [Old English *wefan;* related to Old High German *weban*, Old Norse *vefa*, Greek *hyphos*, Sanskrit *vābhis;* compare WEB, WEEVIL, WASP] ▷ 'weaving *n*

weaver ('wiːvə) *n* **1** a person who weaves, esp as a means of livelihood **2** short for **weaverbird**

weaverbird ('wiːvə,bɜːd) *or* **weaver** *n* **1** any small

Old World passerine songbird of the chiefly African family *Ploceidae,* having a short thick bill and a dull plumage and building covered nests: includes the house sparrow and whydahs **2** any similar bird of the family *Estrildidae,* of warm regions of the Old World: includes the waxbills, grassfinches, and Java sparrow. Also called: weaver finch

weaver's hitch *or* **knot** *n* another name for sheet bend

web (wɛb) *n* **1** any structure, construction, fabric, etc, formed by or as if by weaving or interweaving. Related adj: **retiary 2** a mesh of fine tough scleroprotein threads built by a spider from a liquid secreted from its spinnerets and used to trap insects. See also **cobweb** (sense 1) **3** a similar network of threads spun by certain insect larvae, such as the silkworm **4** a fabric, esp one in the process of being woven **5** a membrane connecting the toes of some aquatic birds or the digits of such aquatic mammals as the otter **6** the vane of a bird's feather **7** *architect* the surface of a ribbed vault that lies between the ribs **8** the central section of an I-beam or H-beam that joins the two flanges of the beam **9** any web-shaped part of a casting used for reinforcement **10** the radial portion of a crank that connects the crankpin to the crankshaft **11** a thin piece of superfluous material left attached to a forging; fin **12 a** a continuous strip of paper as formed on a paper machine or fed from a reel into some printing presses **b** (*as modifier*): *web offset; a web press* **13** the woven edge, without pile, of some carpets **14 a** (*often capital;* preceded by *the*) short for **World Wide Web b** (*as modifier*): *a web site; web pages* **15** any structure, construction, etc, that is intricately formed or complex: *a web of intrigue* ▷ *vb* webs, webbing, webbed **16** (*tr*) to cover with or as if with a web **17** (*tr*) to entangle or ensnare **18** (*intr*) to construct a web [Old English *webb;* related to Old Saxon, Old High German *webbi*, Old Norse *vefr*] ▷ 'webless *adj* ▷ 'web,like *adj*

web address *n computing* another name for URL

web-based *adj* of, relating to, or using the World Wide Web: *web-based applications*

webbed (wɛbd) *adj* **1** (of the feet of certain animals) having the digits connected by a thin fold of skin; palmate **2** having, consisting of, or resembling a web

webbie ('wɛbɪ) *n informal* a person who is well versed in the use the World Wide Web

webbing ('wɛbɪŋ) *n* **1** a strong fabric of hemp, cotton, jute, etc, woven in strips and used under springs in upholstery or for straps, etc **2** the skin that unites the digits of a webbed foot **3** anything that forms a web

WebBoard ('wɛb,bɔːd) *n computing* an internet site where users can post messages, tutorials, information, and topics for discussion

webby ('wɛbɪ) *adj* -bier, -biest of, relating to, resembling, or consisting of a web

webcam ('wɛb,kæm) *n* a camera that transmits still or moving images over the internet

webcast ('wɛb,kɑːst) *n* a broadcast of an event over the World Wide Web: *a live webcast of the game*

web design *n computing* the planning and creation of websites

web directory *n computing* a database of selected websites, ordered in such a way as to facilitate browsing

weber ('veɪbə) *n* the derived SI unit of magnetic flux; the flux that, when linking a circuit of one turn, produces in it an emf of 1 volt as it is reduced to zero at a uniform rate in one second. 1 weber is equivalent to 10^8 maxwells. Symbol: Wb [c20 named after Wilhelm Eduard *Weber* (1804–91), German physicist]

web farm *n computing* a large website that uses two or more servers to handle user requests. Also called: web server farm

webfoot ('wɛb,fʊt) *n* **1** *zoology* a foot having the toes connected by folds of skin **2** *anatomy* a foot

W

having an abnormal membrane connecting adjacent toes

web-footed *or* **web-toed** *adj* (of certain animals) having webbed feet that facilitate swimming

webinar ('wɛbɪˌnɑ:) *n* an interactive seminar conducted over the World Wide Web [C20 from WEB (sense 14) + (SEM)INAR]

weblish ('wɛblɪʃ) *n informal* the shorthand form of English that is used in text messaging, chat rooms, etc [C20 WEB (sense 14) + (ENG)LISH]

weblog ('wɛbˌlɒg) *n* the full name for **blog** > 'web,logger *n*

Webmail ('wɛbˌmeɪl) *n computing* a system of electronic mail that allows account holders to access their mail via an internet site rather than downloading it onto their computer

webmaster ('wɛbˌmɑ:stə) *n* a person responsible for the administration of a website on the World Wide Web

web pal *n informal* a person one meets and corresponds with over the internet

website ('wɛbˌsaɪt) *n* a group of connected pages on the World Wide Web containing information on a particular subject

web spinner *n* any small fragile dull-coloured typically tropical insect of the order *Embioptera*, which has biting mouthparts and constructs silken tunnels in which to live

webster ('wɛbstə) *n* an archaic word for **weaver** (sense 1) [Old English *webbestre*, from *webba* a weaver, from *webb* WEB]

webwheel ('wɛbˌwi:l) *n* **1** a wheel containing a plate or web instead of spokes **2** a wheel of which the rim, spokes, and centre are in one piece

wed (wɛd) *vb* **weds, wedding, wedded** *or* **wed 1** to take (a person of the opposite sex) as a husband or wife; marry **2** (*tr*) to join (two people) in matrimony **3** (*tr*) to unite closely [Old English *weddian*; related to Old Frisian *weddia*, Old Norse *vethja*, Gothic *wadi* pledge]

we'd (wi:d; *unstressed* wɪd) *contraction of* we had *or* we would

Wed. *abbreviation for* Wednesday

wedded ('wɛdɪd) *adj* **1** of marriage: *wedded bliss* **2** firmly in support of an idea or institution: *wedded to the virtues of capitalism*

Weddell Sea ('wɛdəl) *n* an arm of the S Atlantic in Antarctica

wedding ('wɛdɪŋ) *n* **1 a** the act of marrying or the celebration of a marriage **b** (*as modifier*): *wedding day* **2** the anniversary of a marriage (in such combinations as **silver wedding** or **diamond wedding**) **3** the combination or blending of two separate elements

wedding breakfast *n* the meal usually served after a wedding ceremony or just before the bride and bridegroom leave for their honeymoon

wedding cake *n* a rich fruit cake, with one, two, or more tiers, covered with almond paste and decorated with royal icing, which is served at a wedding reception

wedding ring *n* a band ring with parallel sides, typically of precious metal, worn to indicate married status

wedeln ('veɪdəln) *n* a succession of high-speed turns performed in skiing [from German, literally: to wag]

wedge (wɛdʒ) *n* **1** a block of solid material, esp wood or metal, that is shaped like a narrow V in cross section and can be pushed or driven between two objects or parts of an object in order to split or secure them **2** any formation, structure, or substance in the shape of a wedge: *a wedge of cheese* **3** something such as an idea, action, etc, that tends to cause division **4** a shoe with a wedge heel **5** *golf* a club with a face angle of more than 50°, used for bunker shots (**sand wedge**) or pitch shots (**pitching wedge**) **6** a wedge-shaped extension of the high pressure area of an anticyclone, narrower than a ridge **7** *mountaineering* a wedge-shaped device, formerly of wood, now usually of hollow steel, for

hammering into a crack to provide an anchor point **8** any of the triangular characters used in cuneiform writing **9** (formerly) a body of troops formed in a V-shape **10** *photog* a strip of glass coated in such a way that it is clear at one end but becomes progressively more opaque towards the other end: used in making measurements of transmission density **11** *Brit slang* a bribe **12 thin end of the wedge** anything unimportant in itself that implies the start of something much larger ▷ *vb* **13** (*tr*) to secure with or as if with a wedge **14** to squeeze or be squeezed like a wedge into a narrow space **15** (*tr*) to force apart or divide with or as if with a wedge [Old English *wecg*; related to Old Saxon *weggi*, Old High German *wecki*, Old Norse *veggr* wall] > 'wedge,like *adj* > 'wedgy *adj*

wedge heel *n* **1** a raised shoe heel with the heel and sole forming a solid block **2** a shoe with such a heel

wedge-tailed eagle *n* a large brown Australian eagle, *Aquila audax*, having a wedge-shaped tail and a wingspan of 3 m. Also called: **eaglehawk**

wedgie ('wɛdʒɪ) *n informal* the state of having one's underpants or shorts caught between one's buttocks (esp in the phrase **give someone a wedgie**) [C20 from WEDGE]

Wedgwood ('wɛdʒwʊd) *n* **1** *trademark* **a** pottery produced, esp during the late 18th and early 19th centuries, at the Wedgwood factories **b** such pottery having applied classical decoration in white on a blue or other coloured ground ▷ *adj* **2** relating to or characteristic of such pottery: *Wedgwood blue*

Wedgwood blue *n* **a** a pale blue or greyish-blue colour **b** (*as adjective*): *a Wedgwood-blue door*

wedlock ('wɛdlɒk) *n* **1** the state of being married **2 born out of wedlock** born when one's parents are not legally married [Old English *wedlāc*, from *wedd* pledge + *-lāc*, suffix denoting activity, perhaps from *lāc* game, battle (related to Gothic *laiks* dance, Old Norse *leikr*)]

Wednesday ('wɛnzdɪ) *n* the fourth day of the week; third day of the working week [Old English *Wōdnes dæg* Woden's day, translation of Latin *mercurii dies* Mercury's day; related to Old Frisian *wōnsdei*, Middle Dutch *wōdensdach* (Dutch *woensdag*)]

wee[1] (wi:) *adj* **1** very small; tiny; minute ▷ *n* **2** *chiefly Scot* a short time (esp in the phrase **bide a wee**.) [C13 from Old English *wǣg* WEIGHT]

wee[2] (wi:) *Brit, Austral, and NZ informal* ▷ *n* **1 a** the act or an instance of urinating **b** urine ▷ *vb* **2** (*intr*) to urinate ▷ Also: **wee-wee** [of unknown origin]

weed[1] (wi:d) *n* **1** any plant that grows wild and profusely, esp one that grows among cultivated plants, depriving them of space, food, etc **2** *slang* **a the weed** tobacco **b** marijuana **3** *informal* a thin or unprepossessing person **4** an inferior horse, esp one showing signs of weakness of constitution ▷ *vb* **5** to remove (useless or troublesome plants) from (a garden, etc) [Old English *weod*; related to Old Saxon *wiod*, Old High German *wiota* fern] > 'weeder *n* > 'weedless *adj* > 'weed,like *adj*

weed[2] (wi:d) *n rare* a black crepe band worn to indicate mourning. See also **weeds** [Old English *wǣd*, *wēd*; related to Old Saxon *wād*, Old High German *wāt*, Old Norse *vāth*]

weedkiller ('wi:d,kɪlə) *n* a substance, usually a chemical or hormone, used for killing weeds

weed out *vb* (*tr, adverb*) to separate out, remove, or eliminate (anything unwanted): *to weed out troublesome students*

weeds (wi:dz) *pl n* **1** Also called: **widow's weeds a** widow's black mourning clothes **2** *obsolete* any clothing [pl of WEED[2]]

weedy ('wi:dɪ) *adj* **weedier, weediest 1** full of or containing weeds: *weedy land* **2** (of a plant) resembling a weed in rapid or straggling growth **3** *informal* thin or weakly in appearance > 'weedily *adv* > 'weediness *n*

Wee Free *n informal often derogatory* a member of

the minority of the Free Church of Scotland that refused to be joined with the United Free Church in 1900

week (wi:k) *n* **1** a period of seven consecutive days, esp, one beginning with Sunday. Related *adj*: **hebdomadal 2** a period of seven consecutive days beginning from or including a specified day: *Easter week; a week from Wednesday* **3** the period of time within a week devoted to work **4** a week devoted to the celebration of a cause ▷ *adv* **5** *chiefly Brit* seven days before or after a specified day: *I'll visit you Wednesday week* [Old English *wice*, *wicu*, *wucu*; related to Old Norse *vika*, Gothic *wikō* order]

weekday ('wi:k,deɪ) *n* any day of the week other than Sunday and, often, Saturday

weekend *n* (,wi:k'ɛnd) **1 a** the end of the week, esp the period from Friday night until the end of Sunday **b** (*as modifier*): *a weekend party* ▷ *vb* ('wi:k,ɛnd) **2** (*intr*) *informal* to spend or pass a weekend ▷ See also **weekends**

weekender (,wi:k'ɛndə) *n* **1** a person spending a weekend holiday in a place, esp habitually **2** *Austral* a house, shack, etc, occupied only at weekends, for holidays, etc

weekends (,wi:k'ɛndz) *adv informal* at the weekend, esp regularly or during every weekend

weekly ('wi:klɪ) *adj* **1** happening or taking place once a week or every week **2** determined or calculated by the week ▷ *adv* **3** once a week or every week ▷ *n, pl* **-lies 4** a newspaper or magazine issued every week

weeknight ('wi:k,naɪt) *n* the evening or night of a weekday

weel (wi:l) *adv, adj, interj, sentence connector* a Scot word for **well**[1]

ween (wi:n) *vb archaic* to think or imagine (something) [Old English *wēnan*; related to Old Saxon *wānian*, Gothic *wēnjan*, German *wähnen* to assume wrongly]

weeny ('wi:nɪ) *or* **weensy** ('wi:nzɪ) *adj* **-nier, -niest** *or* **-sier, -siest** *informal* very small; tiny [C18 from WEE[1] with the ending *-ny* as in TINY]

weeny-bopper *n informal* a child of 8 to 12 years, esp a girl, who is a keen follower of pop music [C20 formed on the model of TEENYBOPPER, from *weeny*, as in *teeny-weeny* very small]

weep (wi:p) *vb* **weeps, weeping, wept 1** to shed (tears) as an expression of grief or unhappiness **2** (*tr*; foll by *out*) to utter, shedding tears **3** (when *intr*, foll by *for*) to mourn or lament (for something) **4** to exude (drops of liquid) **5** (*intr*) (of a wound, etc) to exude a watery or serous fluid ▷ *n* **6** a spell of weeping [Old English *wēpan*; related to Gothic *wōpjan*, Old High German *wuofan*, Old Slavonic *vabiti* to call]

weeper ('wi:pə) *n* **1** a person who weeps, esp a hired mourner **2** something worn as a sign of mourning **3** a hole through a wall, to allow water to drain away

weeping ('wi:pɪŋ) *adj* (of plants) having slender hanging branches > 'weepingly *adv*

weeping ivy *n* a climbing plant, *Ficus benjamina*, of the fig family, grown as a greenhouse or house plant for its graceful glossy leaves on slender drooping branches

weeping willow *n* a hybrid willow tree, *Salix alba* × *S. babylonica*, known as *S. alba* var. *tristis*, having long hanging branches: widely planted for ornament

weepy ('wi:pɪ) *informal* ▷ *adj* **weepier, weepiest 1** liable or tending to weep ▷ *n, pl* **weepies 2** a romantic and sentimental film or book > 'weepily *adv* > 'weepiness *n*

weever ('wi:və) *n* any small marine percoid fish of the family *Trachinidae*, such as *Trachinus vipera* of European waters, having venomous spines around the gills and the dorsal fin [C17 from Old Northern French *wivre* viper, ultimately from Latin *vīpera* VIPER]

weevil ('wi:vɪl) *n* **1** Also called: **snout beetle** any beetle of the family *Curculionidae*, having an elongated snout (rostrum): they are pests, feeding on plants and plant products. See also **boll weevil** 2 Also called: **pea** *or* **bean weevil** any of various beetles of the family *Bruchidae* (or *Lariidae*), the larvae of which live in the seeds of leguminous plants 3 any of various similar or related beetles [Old English *wifel;* related to Old High German *wibil;* compare Old Norse *tordýfill* dungbeetle] > 'weevily *adj*

wee-wee *n, vb* a variant of **wee²**

w.e.f. *abbreviation for* with effect from

weft (wɛft) *n* the yarn woven across the width of the fabric through the lengthwise warp yarn. Also called: **filling, woof** [Old English, related to Old Norse *veptr;* see WEAVE]

Wehrmacht *German* ('veːrˌmaxt) *n* the armed services of the German Third Reich from 1935 to 1945 [from *Wehr* defence + *Macht* force]

Weichsel ('vaiksəl) *n* the German name for the **Vistula** (sense 1)

weigela (waɪ'giːlə, -'dʒiː-, 'waɪgɪlə) *n* any caprifoliaceous shrub of the Asian genus *Weigela*, having clusters of pink, purple, red, or white showy bell-shaped flowers [c19 from New Latin, named after C. E. *Weigel* (1748–1831), German physician]

weigh¹ (weɪ) *vb* 1 (*tr*) to measure the weight of 2 (*intr*) to have weight or be heavy: *she weighs more than her sister* 3 (*tr;* often foll by *out*) to apportion according to weight 4 (*tr*) to consider carefully: *to weigh the facts of a case* 5 (*intr*) to be influential: *his words weighed little with the jury* 6 (*intr;* often foll by *on*) to be oppressive or burdensome (to) 7 *obsolete* to regard or esteem 8 **weigh anchor** to raise a vessel's anchor or (of a vessel) to have its anchor raised preparatory to departure ▷ See also **weigh down, weigh in, weigh up** [Old English *wegan;* related to Old Frisian *wega*, Old Norse *vega*, Gothic *gawigan*, German *wiegen*] > 'weighable *adj* > 'weigher *n*

weigh² (weɪ) *n* **under weigh** a variant spelling of **under way** [c18 variation due to the influence of phrases such as *to weigh anchor*]

weighbridge ('weɪˌbrɪdʒ) *n* a machine for weighing vehicles, etc, by means of a metal plate set into a road

weigh down *vb* (*adverb*) to press (a person) down by or as if by weight: *his troubles weighed him down*

weigh in *vb* (*intr, adverb*) 1 **a** (of a boxer or wrestler) to be weighed before a bout **b** (of a jockey) to be weighed after, or sometimes before, a race 2 *informal* to contribute, as in a discussion, etc: *he weighed in with a few sharp comments* ▷ *n* **weigh-in** 3 the act of checking a competitor's weight, as in boxing, horse racing, etc

weight (weɪt) *n* 1 a measure of the heaviness of an object; the amount anything weighs 2 *physics* the vertical force experienced by a mass as a result of gravitation. It equals the mass of the body multiplied by the acceleration of free fall. Its units are units of force (such as newtons or poundals) but is often given as a mass unit (kilogram or pound). Symbol: *W* 3 a system of units used to express the weight of a substance: *troy weight* 4 a unit used to measure weight: *the kilogram is the weight used in the metric system* 5 any mass or heavy object used to exert pressure or weigh down 6 an oppressive force: *the weight of cares* 7 any heavy load: *the bag was such a weight* 8 the main or greatest force: preponderance: *the weight of evidence* 9 importance, influence, or consequence: *his opinion carries weight* 10 *statistics* one of a set of coefficients assigned to items of a frequency distribution that are analysed in order to represent the relative importance of the different items 11 *printing* the apparent blackness of a printed typeface 12 *slang* a pound of a drug, esp cannabis 13 **pull one's weight** *informal* to do one's full or proper share of a task 14 **throw one's weight around** *informal* to act in an overauthoritarian or aggressive manner ▷ *vb* (*tr*) 15 to add weight to 16 to burden or oppress 17 to add importance, value, etc, to one side rather than another; bias; favour: *a law weighted towards landlords* 18 *statistics* to attach a weight or weights to 19 to make (fabric, threads, etc) heavier by treating with mineral substances, etc [Old English *wiht;* related to Old Frisian, Middle Dutch *wicht*, Old Norse *vētt*, German *Gewicht*] > 'weighter *n*

weighted average *n* an average calculated by taking into account not only the frequencies of the values of a variable but also some other factor such as their variance. The weighted average of observed data is the result of dividing the sum of the products of each observed value, the number of times it occurs, and this other factor by the total number of observations

weighting ('weɪtɪŋ) *n* 1 a factor by which some quantity is multiplied in order to make it comparable with others. See also **weighted average** 2 an increase in some quantity, esp an additional allowance paid to compensate for higher living costs: *a London weighting*

weightless ('weɪtləs) *adj* 1 (of a body) having no actual weight; a state in which an object has no actual weight (because it is in space and unaffected by gravitational attraction) or no apparent weight (because the gravitational attraction equals the centripetal force and the object is in free fall) 2 *business* **a** (of economic activity) based on the supply of information and ideas rather than trade in physical goods: *the weightless economy* **b** (of a company) having very few physical assets: *weightless dot.coms* > 'weightlessness *n*

weightlessness ('weɪtlɪsnɪs) *n* a state in which an object has no actual weight (because it is in space and unaffected by gravitational attraction) or no apparent weight (because the gravitational attraction equals the centripetal force and the object is in free fall) > 'weightless *adj*

weightlifting ('weɪtˌlɪftɪŋ) *n* the sport of lifting barbells of specified weights in a prescribed manner for competition or exercise > 'weightˌlifter *n*

weight training *n* physical exercise involving lifting weights to improve muscle performance

weight watcher *n* a person who tries to lose weight, esp by dieting

Weightwatchers ('weɪtˌwɒtʃəz) *n* (*functioning as singular*) *trademark* an organization that assists people who want to lose weight

weighty ('weɪtɪ) *adj* **weightier, weightiest** 1 having great weight 2 important or momentous 3 causing anxiety or worry > 'weightily *adv* > 'weightiness *n*

weigh up *vb* (*tr, adverb*) to make an assessment of (a person, situation, etc); judge

Weihai *or* **Wei-hai** ('weɪ'haɪ) *n* a port in NE China, in NE Shandong on the Yellow Sea: leased to Britain as a naval base (1898–1930). Pop: 966 000 (2005 est). Also called: **Weihaiwei** (ˌweɪ'haɪˌweɪ)

Weil's disease (vaɪlz) *n* another name for **leptospirosis** [named after Adolf *Weil* (1848–1916), German physician]

Weimar (*German* 'vaimar) *n* a city in E central Germany, in Thuringia: a cultural centre in the 18th and early 19th century; scene of the adoption (1919) of the constitution of the Weimar Republic. Pop: 64 409 (2003 est)

Weimaraner ('vaɪməˌrɑːnə, 'waɪməˌrɑː-) *n* a breed of hunting dog, having a very short sleek grey coat and short tail [c20 named after WEIMAR, where the breed was developed]

Weimar Republic *n* the German republic that existed from 1919 to Hitler's accession to power in 1933

weir (wɪə) *n* 1 a low dam that is built across a river to raise the water level, divert the water, or control its flow 2 a series of traps or enclosures placed in a stream to catch fish [Old English *wer;* related to Old Norse *ver*, Old Frisian *were*, German *Wehr*]

weird (wɪəd) *adj* 1 suggestive of or relating to the supernatural; eerie 2 strange or bizarre 3 *archaic* of or relating to fate or the Fates ▷ *n* 4 *archaic, chiefly Scot* **a** fate or destiny **b** one of the Fates 5 **dree one's weird** *Scot* See **dree** ▷ *vb* 6 (*tr*) *Scot* to destine or ordain by fate; predict ▷ See also **weird out** [Old English (*ge*)*wyrd* destiny; related to *weorthan* to become, Old Norse *urthr* bane, Old Saxon *wurd;* see WORTH²] > 'weirdly *adv* > 'weirdness *n*

weirdo ('wɪədəʊ) *or* **weirdie** ('wɪədɪ) *n, pl* **-dos** *or* **-dies** *informal* a person who behaves in a bizarre or eccentric manner

weird out *vb* (*tr, adverb*) *informal* to cause (someone) to feel afraid or uncomfortable: *his unstable behaviour was weirding me out*

weird sisters *pl n* 1 another name for the **Fates** 2 *Norse myth* another name for the **Norns** (see **Norn¹**)

Weismannism ('vaɪsmənˌɪzəm) *n* the doctrine of the continuity of the germ plasm. This theory of heredity states that all inheritable characteristics are transmitted by the reproductive cells and that characteristics acquired during the lifetime of the organism are not inherited [c19 named after August *Weismann* (1834–1914), German biologist]

Weisshorn ('vaɪsˌhɔːn) *n* a mountain in S Switzerland, in the Pennine Alps. Height: 4505 m (14 781 ft)

weka ('weɪkə, 'wiːkə) *n* any flightless New Zealand rail of the genus *Gallirallus*, having a mottled brown plumage and rudimentary wings. Also called: **Māori hen, wood hen** [c19 from Māori, of imitative origin]

welch (wɛlʃ) *vb* a variant spelling of **welsh** > 'welcher *n*

Welch (wɛlʃ) *adj* an archaic spelling of **Welsh¹**

welcome ('wɛlkəm) *adj* 1 gladly and cordially received or admitted: *a welcome guest* 2 bringing pleasure or gratitude: *a welcome gift* 3 freely permitted or invited: *you are welcome to call* 4 under no obligation (only in such phrases as **you're welcome** or **he's welcome**, as conventional responses to thanks) ▷ *sentence substitute* 5 an expression of cordial greeting, esp to a person whose arrival is desired or pleasing ▷ *n* 6 the act of greeting or receiving a person or thing; reception: *the new theory had a cool welcome* 7 **wear out one's welcome** to come more often or stay longer than is acceptable or pleasing ▷ *vb* (*tr*) 8 to greet the arrival of (visitors, guests, etc) cordially or gladly 9 to receive or accept, esp gladly [c12 changed (through influence of WELL¹) from Old English *wilcuma* (agent noun referring to a welcome guest), *wilcume* (a greeting of welcome), from *wil* WILL² + *cuman* to COME] > 'welcomely *adv* > 'welcomeness *n* > 'welcomer *n*

W

weld¹ (wɛld) *vb* 1 (*tr*) to unite (pieces of metal or plastic) together, as by softening with heat and hammering or by fusion 2 to bring or admit of being brought into close association or union ▷ *n* 3 a joint formed by welding [c16 variant probably based on past participle of WELL² in obsolete sense to boil, heat] > 'weldable *adj* > ˌwelda'bility *n* > 'welder *or* 'weldor *n* > 'weldless *adj*

weld² (wɛld), **wold** *or* **woald** (wəʊld) *n* 1 a yellow dye obtained from the plant dyer's rocket 2 another name for **dyer's rocket** [c14 from Low German; compare Middle Low German *walde*, *waude*, Dutch *wouw*]

welding rod *n* *electrical engineering* filler metal supplied in the form of a rod, usually coated with flux

welfare ('wɛlˌfɛə) *n* 1 health, happiness, prosperity, and well-being in general 2 **a** financial and other assistance given to people in need **b** (*as modifier*): *welfare services* 3 Also called: **welfare work** plans or work to better the social or economic conditions of various underprivileged groups 4 **the welfare** *informal, chiefly Brit* the public agencies involved with giving such assistance 5 **on welfare** *chiefly US and Canadian* in receipt of financial aid from a government agency or other source [c14 from the phrase *wel fare;*

related to Old Norse *velferth*, German *Wohlfahrt*; see WELL[1], FARE]

welfare economics *n* (*functioning as singular*) the aspects of economic theory concerned with the welfare of society and priorities to be observed in the allocation of resources

welfare state *n* **1** a system in which the government undertakes the chief responsibility for providing for the social and economic security of its population, usually through unemployment insurance, old-age pensions, and other social-security measures **2** a social system characterized by such policies

welfarism ('wɛl,fɛərɪzəm) *n* policies or attitudes associated with a welfare state > 'wel,farist *n*

welkin ('wɛlkɪn) *n* *archaic* the sky, heavens, or upper air [Old English *wolcen, welcen*; related to Old Frisian *wolken*, Old Saxon, Old High German *wolcan*]

Welkom ('wɛlkəm, 'vɛl-) *n* a town in central South Africa; developed rapidly following the discovery of gold. Pop: 34 157 (2001)

well[1] (wɛl) *adv* **better, best 1** (*often used in combination*) in a satisfactory manner: *the party went very well* **2** (*often used in combination*) in a good, skilful, or pleasing manner: *she plays the violin well* **3** in a correct or careful manner: *listen well to my words* **4** in a comfortable or prosperous manner: *to live well* **5** (*usually used with auxiliaries*) suitably; fittingly: *you can't very well say that* **6** intimately: *I knew him well* **7** in a kind or favourable manner: *she speaks well of you* **8** to a great or considerable extent; fully: *to be well informed* **9** by a considerable margin: *let me know well in advance* **10** (preceded by *could, might,* or *may*) indeed: *you may well have to do it yourself* **11** *informal* (intensifier): *well safe* **12 all very well** used ironically to express discontent, dissent, etc **13 as well a** in addition; too **b** (preceded by *may* or *might*) with equal effect: *you might as well come* **14 as well as** in addition to **15** (**just**) **as well** preferable or advisable: *it would be just as well if you paid me now* **16 just leave well** (**enough**) **alone** to refrain from interfering with something that is satisfactory **17 well and good** used to indicate calm acceptance, as of a decision: *if you accept my offer, well and good* **18 well up in** well acquainted with (a particular subject); knowledgeable about ▷ *adj* (*usually postpositive*) **19** (*when prenominal, usually used with a negative*) in good health: *I'm very well, thank you; he's not a well man* **20** satisfactory, agreeable, or pleasing **21** prudent; advisable: *it would be well to make no comment* **22** prosperous or comfortable **23** fortunate or happy: *it is well that you agreed to go* ▷ *interj* **24 a** an expression of surprise, indignation, or reproof **b** an expression of anticipation in waiting for an answer or remark ▷ *sentence connector* **25** an expression used to preface a remark, gain time, etc: *well, I don't think I will come* [Old English *wel*; related to Old High German *wala, wola* (German *wohl*), Old Norse *val*, Gothic *waila*]

well[2] (wɛl) *n* **1** a hole or shaft that is excavated, drilled, bored, or cut into the earth so as to tap a supply of water, oil, gas, etc **2** a natural pool where ground water comes to the surface **3 a** a cavity, space, or vessel used to contain a liquid **b** (*in combination*): *an inkwell* **4** an open shaft through the floors of a building, such as one used for a staircase **5** a deep enclosed space in a building or between buildings that is open to the sky to permit light and air to enter **6 a** a bulkheaded compartment built around a ship's pumps for protection and ease of access **b** another word for **cockpit 7** a perforated tank in the hold of a fishing boat for keeping caught fish alive **8** (in England) the open space in the centre of a law court **9** a source, esp one that provides a continuous supply: *he is a well of knowledge* ▷ *vb* **10** to flow or cause to flow upwards or outwards: *tears welled from her eyes* [Old English *wella*; related to Old High German *wella* (German *Welle* wave), Old Norse *vella* boiling heat]

we'll (wiːl) *contraction of* we will *or* we shall

well-accepted *adj* (**well accepted** *when postpositive*) generally considered as true or correct

well-accustomed *adj* (**well accustomed** *when postpositive*) sufficiently used to: *well accustomed to desert conditions*

well-acquainted *adj* (**well acquainted** *when postpositive*) having a good knowledge or understanding of someone or something: *well acquainted with Milton*

well-acted *adj* (**well acted** *when postpositive*) (of a play, film, dramatic part, etc) performed in a skilful manner

well-adapted *adj* (**well adapted** *when postpositive*) having been made or adjusted to fit suitably into an environment, situation, etc

well-adjusted *adj* (**well adjusted** *when postpositive*) mentally and emotionally stable

well-advertised *adj* (**well advertised** *when postpositive*) advertised widely or interestingly in order to elicit interest

well-advised *adj* (**well advised** *when postpositive*) **1** acting with deliberation or reason **2** well thought out; considered: *a well-advised plan*

well-affected *adj* (**well affected** *when postpositive*) favourably disposed (towards); steadfast or loyal

well-aimed *adj* (**well aimed** *when postpositive*) **1** (of a missile, punch, etc) having been pointed or directed accurately at a person or object: *a well-aimed, precise blow* **2** (of a comment, criticism, etc) obviously and accurately directed at a person, object, etc: *a well-aimed expression of contempt*

well-aired *adj* (**well aired** *when postpositive*) (of bedding, clothes, a room, etc) having been hung up or ventilated to allow air to circulate

Welland Canal ('wɛlənd) *n* a canal in S Canada, in Ontario, linking Lake Erie to Lake Ontario: part of the St Lawrence Seaway, with eight locks. Length: 44 km (28 miles). Also called: **Welland Ship Canal**

well-appointed *adj* (**well appointed** *when postpositive*) well equipped or furnished; properly supplied

well-argued *adj* (**well argued** *when postpositive*) having been reasoned, proposed, or debated convincingly

well-armed *adj* (**well armed** *when postpositive*) **1** having many or good weapons: *well-armed forces* **2** suitably prepared in advance: *well armed for an argument*

well-arranged *adj* (**well arranged** *when postpositive*) having been put into a good systematic or decorative order

well-attended *adj* (**well attended** *when postpositive*) (of an event, meeting, etc) attended by a large or regular audience or group of participants: *evening mass is well attended*

well-attested *adj* (**well attested** *when postpositive*) widely affirmed as correct or true

well-aware *adj* (**well aware** *when postpositive*) having knowledge or awareness: *well aware of the problems*

wellaway ('wɛlə'weɪ) *interj* *archaic* woe! alas! [Old English, from *wei lā wei*, variant of *wā lā wā*, literally: woe! lo woe]

well-balanced *adj* (**well balanced** *when postpositive*) **1** having good balance or proportions **2** of balanced mind; sane or sensible

well-behaved *adj* (**well behaved** *when postpositive*) conducting oneself in a satisfactory manner

wellbeing ('wɛl'biːɪŋ) *n* the condition of being contented, healthy, or successful; welfare

well-blessed *adj* (**well blessed** *when postpositive*) having been generously endowed with a talent, beauty, etc

well-born *adj* (**well born** *when postpositive*) having been born into a wealthy or upper-class family

well-bred *adj* (**well bred** *when postpositive*) **1** Also: **well-born** of respected or noble lineage **2** indicating good breeding: *well-bred manners* **3** of good thoroughbred stock: *a well-bred spaniel*

well-built *adj* (**well built** *when postpositive*) **1** large or ample: *a well-built lady* **2** having a good, strong construction: *well-built houses*

well-chosen *adj* (**well chosen** *when postpositive*) carefully selected to produce a desired effect; apt: *a few well-chosen words*

well-clothed *adj* (**well clothed** *when postpositive*) dressed in good quality clothes

well-concealed *adj* (**well concealed** *when postpositive*) hidden or concealed in a skilful, satisfactory, or careful manner

well-conditioned *adj* (**well conditioned** *when postpositive*) (of a person or animal's body, hair, etc) in a good or healthy condition

well-conducted *adj* (**well conducted** *when postpositive*) **1** (of research, business, an operation, etc) led, conducted, or carried out in a satisfactory manner **2** (of a person or animal) behaving in a satisfactory manner: *well-conducted, tidy creatures*

well-connected *adj* (**well connected** *when postpositive*) having influential or important relatives or friends

well-considered *adj* (**well considered** *when postpositive*) having been thought about carefully

well-constructed *adj* (**well constructed** *when postpositive*) made or having been made to a high standard of workmanship and safety

well-controlled *adj* (**well controlled** *when postpositive*) regulated, operated, or restrained successfully or strictly: *well-controlled research work*

well-cooked *adj* (**well cooked** *when postpositive*) **1** having been cooked with skill so as to be pleasant to eat **2** (of meat) having been cooked thoroughly

well-covered *adj* (**well covered** *when postpositive*) **1** satisfactorily or pleasantly provided with a covering **2** (of news, etc) having been given sufficient coverage: *child abuse is well covered*

well-cultivated *adj* (**well cultivated** *when postpositive*) **1** (of land, plants, etc) tilled, planted, or maintained in a satisfactory manner **2** (of a trait, talent, etc) fostered or improved by study or practice: *his well-cultivated sarcasm*

well-defended *adj* (**well defended** *when postpositive*) having sufficient defences against attack

well-defined *adj* (**well defined** *when postpositive*) clearly delineated, described, or determined

well-demonstrated *adj* (**well demonstrated** *when postpositive*) (of an ability, fact, idea, etc) shown, manifested, or proved convincingly or thoroughly

well-described *adj* (**well described** *when postpositive*) (of a scene, picture, incident, etc) having been skillfully represented or expressed in words

well-deserved *adj* (**well deserved** *when postpositive*) fully merited: *a well-deserved reputation*

well-developed *adj* (**well developed** *when postpositive*) carefully or extensively elaborated or evolved

well-disciplined *adj* (**well disciplined** *when postpositive*) having been strictly trained or conditioned to ensure good behaviour, orderliness, etc

well-disposed *adj* (**well disposed** *when postpositive*) inclined to be sympathetic, kindly, or friendly: *he was never well disposed towards her relatives*

well-documented *adj* (**well documented** *when postpositive*) widely recorded or recounted: *a well-documented fact*

well-done *adj* (**well done** *when postpositive*) **1** (of food, esp meat) cooked thoroughly **2** made or accomplished satisfactorily

well-dressed *adj* (**well dressed** *when postpositive*) neatly, expensively, or fashionably attired

well dressing *n* the decoration of wells with flowers, etc: a traditional annual ceremony of great antiquity in some parts of Britain, originally associated with the cult of water deities

well-earned *adj* (**well earned** *when postpositive*) fully deserved: *a well-earned rest*

well-endowed *adj* (**well endowed** *when postpositive*) **1** having a large supply of money, resources, etc **2** *informal* having a large penis **3** *informal* having large breasts

well-equipped *adj* (**well equipped** *when postpositive*) having sufficient equipment, supplies, or abilities

well-established *adj* (**well established** when *postpositive*) **1** having permanence or security in a certain place, condition, job, etc: *a well-established brand* **2** well-known or validated: *a well-established fact*

well-favoured *adj* (**well favoured** when *postpositive*) having good features; good-looking

well-fed *adj* (**well fed** when *postpositive*) **1** having a nutritious diet; well nourished **2** plump; fat

well-financed *adj* (**well financed** when *postpositive*) having received or receiving a sufficient amount of funds

well-finished *adj* (**well finished** when *postpositive*) (of a garment, piece of furniture, interior decoration, etc) completed with a high degree of attention to detail and surface appearance: *the woodwork is well finished*

well-fitted *adj* (**well fitted** when *postpositive*) **1** (of clothes, a lid, etc) fitting closely or comfortably **2** (of a room, boat, etc) having been installed with good quality storage, appliances, etc

well-formed *adj* logic, linguistics (of a formula, expression, etc) constructed in accordance with the syntactic rules of a particular system; grammatically correct > **well-formedness** *n*

well-fortified *adj* (**well fortified** when *postpositive*) **1** (of a position, garrison, city, etc) having been made defensible **2** (of a person) having strengthened oneself or been strengthened physically, mentally, or morally: *the police were well fortified with steaming mugs of tea*

well-found *adj* (**well found** when *postpositive*) furnished or supplied with all or most necessary things

well-founded *adj* (**well founded** when *postpositive*) having good grounds: *well-founded rumours*

well-furnished *adj* (**well furnished** when *postpositive*) **1** (of a room, house, etc) fitted out or decorated with attractive or good quality furniture, carpets, etc: *well furnished with tapestries and porcelain* **2** amply stocked, equipped, or supplied: *he was well furnished with notebooks*

well-governed *adj* (**well governed** when *postpositive*) (of a political unit, organization, nation, etc) directed and controlled efficiently or satisfactorily

well-groomed *adj* (**well groomed** when *postpositive*) **1** (of a person) having a tidy pleasing appearance **2** kept tidy and neat: *a well-groomed garden* **3** (of an animal) well turned out and tended: *a well-groomed horse*

well-grounded *adj* (**well grounded** when *postpositive*) **1** well instructed in the basic elements of a subject **2** another term for **well-founded**

well-guarded *adj* (**well guarded** when *postpositive*) **1** having sufficient protection from danger or harm **2** kept private or out of the public eye: *well-guarded secrets*

well-handled *adj* (**well handled** when *postpositive*) **1** having been managed successfully: *a well-handled merger* **2** operated or employed skillfully: *a well-handled vehicle*

wellhead (ˈwɛlˌhɛd) *n* **1** the source of a well or stream **2** a source, fountainhead, or origin

well-heeled *adj* (**well heeled** when *postpositive*) informal rich; prosperous; wealthy

well-hidden *adj* (**well hidden** when *postpositive*) having been concealed to make discovery difficult or impossible

well-hung *adj* (**well hung** when *postpositive*) **1** (of game) hung for a sufficient length of time **2** slang (of a man) having large genitals

wellies (ˈwɛlɪz) *pl n* Brit informal Wellington boots

well-illustrated *adj* (**well illustrated** when *postpositive*) **1** having good illustrations: *a well-illustrated book* **2** clarified or explained with good examples: *a well-illustrated review of current literature*

well in *adj* (*postpositive;* often foll by with) informal on good terms or favourably placed (with): *the foreman was well in with the management*

well-informed *adj* (**well informed** when *postpositive*) **1** having knowledge about a great variety of

subjects: *he seems to be a well-informed person* **2** possessing reliable information on a particular subject

Wellingborough (ˈwɛlɪŋbərə, -brə) *n* a town in central England, in Northamptonshire. Pop: 46 959 (2001)

Wellington (ˈwɛlɪŋtən) *n* **1** an administrative district, formerly a province, of New Zealand, on SW North Island: major livestock producer in New Zealand. Capital: Wellington. Pop: 456 900 (2004 est). Area: 28 153 sq km (10 870 sq miles) **2** the capital city of New Zealand. Its port, historically Port Nicholson, on **Wellington Harbour** has a car and rail ferry link between the North and South Islands; university (1899). Pop: 182 600 (2004 est)

Wellington boots *pl n* **1** Also called: gumboots, wellingtons *Brit* knee-length or calf-length rubber or rubberized boots, worn esp in wet conditions. Often shortened to: wellies **2** military leather boots covering the front of the knee but cut away at the back to allow easier bending of the knee [c19 named after the 1st Duke of *Wellington*]

wellingtonia (ˌwɛlɪŋˈtəʊnɪə) *n* another name for **big tree** [c19 named after the 1st Duke of *Wellington*]

well-intentioned *adj* (**well intentioned** when *postpositive*) having or indicating benevolent intentions, usually with unfortunate results

well-judged *adj* (**well judged** when *postpositive*) showing careful consideration or skill

well-justified *adj* (**well justified** when *postpositive*) having been shown, proved, or validated satisfactorily

well-kept *adj* (**well kept** when *postpositive*) maintained in good condition: *the front lawns are well kept*

well-knit *adj* (**well knit** when *postpositive*) strong, firm, or sturdy

well-known *adj* (**well known** when *postpositive*) **1** widely known; famous; celebrated **2** known fully or clearly

well-liked *adj* (**well liked** when *postpositive*) liked by many people; popular

well-loved *adj* (**well loved** when *postpositive*) loved by many people; very popular

well-made *adj* (**well made** when *postpositive*) made to a good or high standard

well-man *n, pl* -men **a** a healthy man who attends a clinic or surgery to ensure that his general health, lifestyle, and sexual performance are satisfactory **b** (*as modifier*): *a well-man clinic*

well-managed *adj* (**well managed** when *postpositive*) administered or controlled in a competent or successful manner

well-mannered *adj* (**well mannered** when *postpositive*) having good manners; courteous; polite

well-marked *adj* (**well marked** when *postpositive*) (of a path, trail, landmark, etc) clearly indicated or signposted

well-matched *adj* (**well matched** when *postpositive*) **1** (of two people) likely to have a successful relationship **2** (of two teams or competitors) likely to compete on an even level **3** (of two or a pair) looking or functioning well together: *well-matched roan ponies*

well-meaning *adj* (**well meaning** when *postpositive*) having or indicating good or benevolent intentions, usually with unfortunate results

well-merited *adj* (**well merited** when *postpositive*) fully deserved or merited

well-mixed *adj* (**well mixed** when *postpositive*) (of ingredients, constituents, etc) formed or blended together thoroughly

well-motivated *adj* (**well motivated** when *postpositive*) (of a person, intention, etc) have sufficient incentive, desire, or drive

wellness (ˈwɛlnəs) *n* the state of being in good physical and mental health

well-nigh *adv* nearly; almost: *it's well-nigh three o'clock*

well-off *adj* (**well off** when *postpositive*) **1** in a comfortable or favourable position or state **2** financially well provided for; moderately rich

well-oiled *adj* (**well oiled** when *postpositive*) informal drunk

well-ordered *adj* logic, maths (of a relation) having the property that every nonempty subset of its field has a least member under the relation: *less than* is well-ordered on the natural numbers but not on the reals, since an open set has no least member

well-organized *or* **well-organised** *adj* (**well organized** when *postpositive*) having good organization; orderly and efficient: *a well-organized individual*

well-padded *adj* (**well padded** when *postpositive*) (of a person) corpulent; portly; fat

well-paid *adj* (**well paid** when *postpositive*) receiving or involving good remuneration

well-placed *adj* (**well placed** when *postpositive*) having an advantageous position

well-planned *adj* (**well planned** when *postpositive*) (of an event, project, etc) suitably devised or drafted in advance to ensure success

well-played *adj* (**well played** when *postpositive*) (of a piece of music, game, etc) skilfully or pleasingly executed

well-pleased *adj* (**well pleased** when *postpositive*) very happy or satisfied: *well pleased with the outcome of the meeting*

well-practised *adj* (**well practised** when *postpositive*) having or having been habitually or frequently practised in order to improve skill or quality

well-prepared *adj* (**well prepared** when *postpositive*) suitably prepared in advance

well-preserved *adj* (**well preserved** when *postpositive*) **1** kept in a good condition **2** continuing to appear youthful: *she was a well-preserved old lady*

well-proportioned *adj* (**well proportioned** when *postpositive*) having the correct or desirable relationship between constituent parts with respect to size, number, or degree

well-protected *adj* (**well protected** when *postpositive*) having suitable defence against attack, harm, etc

well-provided *adj* (**well provided** when *postpositive*) **1** having been furnished or supplied with a sufficient amount **2** (foll by for) having been supplied with sufficient means of support, esp financially

well-qualified *adj* (**well qualified** when *postpositive*) having good or excellent qualifications

well-read (ˈwɛlˈrɛd) *adj* (**well read** when *postpositive*) having read widely and intelligently; erudite

well-reasoned *adj* (**well reasoned** when *postpositive*) logically argued with skill or care

well-received *adj* (**well received** when *postpositive*) having been greeted or reviewed with approval: *his well-received books*

well-recommended *adj* (**well recommended** when *postpositive*) highly praised or commended: *a popular and well-recommended book*

well-regarded *adj* (**well regarded** when *postpositive*) considered to be good morally, professionally, etc; esteemed: *a well-regarded local MP*

well-regulated *adj* (**well regulated** when *postpositive*) (of a business, military outfit, routine, etc) controlled or supervised to conform to rules, regulations, tradition, etc: *a well-regulated militia*

well-rehearsed *adj* (**well rehearsed** when *postpositive*) (of a play, speech, excuse, etc) sufficiently practised or prepared in advance to ensure a good performance

well-remembered *adj* (**well remembered** when *postpositive*) recalled or having been recalled with affection, nostalgia, or vividness

well-represented *adj* (**well represented** when *postpositive*) having good or sufficient representation

well-respected *adj* (**well respected** when *postpositive*) held in high respect; esteemed

W

well-rounded *adj* (**well rounded** *when postpositive*) **1** rounded in shape or well developed: *a well-rounded figure* **2** full, varied, and satisfying: *a well-rounded life* **3** well planned and balanced: *a well-rounded programme*

Wells (wɛlz) *n* a city in SW England, in Somerset: 12th-century cathedral. Pop: 10 406 (2001)

well-satisfied *adj* (**well satisfied** *when postpositive*) fully convinced of or happy

well-schooled *adj* (**well schooled** *when postpositive*) having been trained or educated sufficiently, as in a school: *well-schooled ponies*

well-seasoned *adj* (**well seasoned** *when postpositive*) **1** (of food) flavoured pleasantly or generously with herbs, salt, pepper, or spices **2** (of timber) prepared and dried skilfully or thoroughly **3** (of a person) matured or experienced

well-secured *adj* (**well secured** *when postpositive*) having been made fast or firm: *well secured with steel brackets*

well-set *adj* (**well set** *when postpositive*) **1** firmly established **2** (of a person) strongly built

well-shaped *adj* (**well shaped** *when postpositive*) (of physical attributes) having a good shape aesthetically or for a certain function: *her well-shaped teeth*

well-situated *adj* (**well situated** *when postpositive*) **1** having a good position or site: *a well-situated airport* **2** in a good position or situation to carry something out: *he was well situated as president* **3** having sufficient funds; well-off

well-spent *adj* (**well spent** *when postpositive*) (of time or money) usefully or profitably spent or expended

well-spoken *adj* (**well spoken** *when postpositive*) **1** having a clear, articulate, and socially acceptable accent and way of speaking **2** spoken satisfactorily or pleasingly

wellspring (ˈwɛlˌsprɪŋ) *n* **1** the source of a spring or stream; fountainhead **2** a source of continual or abundant supply [Old English *welspryng, wylspring*; see WELL², SPRING]

well-stacked *adj* (**well stacked** *when postpositive*) *Brit slang* (of a woman) of voluptuous proportions

well-stocked *adj* (**well stocked** *when postpositive*) having or containing sufficient goods, wares, food, etc

well-suited *adj* (**well suited** *when postpositive*) **1** appropriate for a particular purpose **2** (of two people) likely to have a successful relationship

well-supplied *adj* (**well supplied** *when postpositive*) provided or furnished with a sufficient amount

well-supported *adj* (**well supported** *when postpositive*) **1** having good physical support: *a sofa in which your back is well supported* **2** having a lot of support or encouragement: *friendly matches were less well supported* **3** substantially upheld by evidence or facts: *many well-supported theories*

well sweep *n* a device for raising buckets from and lowering them into a well, consisting of a long pivoted pole, the bucket being attached to one end by a long rope

well-taught *adj* (**well taught** *when postpositive*) having been shown, tutored, or instructed in a successful manner

well-tempered *adj* (**well tempered** *when postpositive*) (of a musical scale or instrument) conforming to the system of equal temperament. See **temperament** (sense 4)

well-thought-of *adj* (**well thought of** *when postpositive*) having a good reputation; respected

well-thought-out *adj* (**well thought out** *when postpositive*) carefully planned

well-thumbed *adj* (**well thumbed** *when postpositive*) (of a copy of a book) having the pages marked from frequent turning

well-timed *adj* (**well timed** *when postpositive*) happening or scheduled to happen at an appropriate or suitable time

well-to-do *adj* moderately wealthy

well-trained *adj* (**well trained** *when postpositive*) having gained satisfactory training

well-travelled *adj* (**well travelled** *when postpositive*) having travelled far and wide

well-treated *adj* (**well treated** *when postpositive*) not subjected to threats, harm, or other bad treatment: *hostages were well treated*

well-tried *adj* (**well tried** *when postpositive*) repeatedly and exhaustively attempted or tried

well-trodden *adj* (**well trodden** *when postpositive*) (of a path, route, etc) much frequented or used by walkers, travellers, etc

well-turned *adj* (**well turned** *when postpositive*) **1** (of a phrase, speech, etc) apt and pleasingly sonorous **2** having a pleasing shape: *a well-turned leg*

well-understood *adj* (**well understood** *when postpositive*) widely or sufficiently understood or comprehended

well-upholstered *adj* (**well upholstered** *when postpositive*) *informal* (of a person) fat

well-used *adj* (**well used** *when postpositive*) used or employed often or for a long time; well-worn

well-versed *adj* (**well versed** *when postpositive*) comprehensively knowledgeable (about), acquainted (with), or skilled (in)

well-wisher *n* a person who shows benevolence or sympathy towards a person, cause, etc ▷ ˈwell-ˌwishing *adj, n*

well-woman *n, pl* -women *social welfare* **a** a woman who, although not ill, attends a health-service clinic for preventive monitoring, health education, and advice **b** (*as modifier*): *well-woman clinic*

well-wooded *adj* (**well wooded** *when postpositive*) having abundant trees, shrubs, grasses, etc

well-worn *adj* (**well worn** *when postpositive*) **1** so much used as to be affected by wear: *a well-worn coat* **2** used too often; hackneyed: *a well-worn phrase*

well-written *adj* (**well written** *when postpositive*) composed in a competent, and often entertaining, style

well-wrought *adj* (**well wrought** *when postpositive*) shaped, formed, or decorated with skill

welly (ˈwɛlɪ) *n* **1** *pl* -lies *informal* Also called: **welly boot** a Wellington boot **2** *slang* energy, concentration, or commitment (esp in the phrase **give it some welly**)

Wels (German vɛls) *n* an industrial city in N central Austria, in Upper Austria. Pop: 56 478 (2002)

Welsbach burner (ˈwɛlzbæk; German ˈvɛlsbax) *n trademark* a type of gaslight in which a mantle containing thorium and cerium compounds becomes incandescent when heated by a gas flame [c19 named after Carl Auer, Baron von Welsbach (1858–1929), Austrian chemist, who invented it]

welsh *or* **welch** (wɛlʃ) *vb* (*intr*; often foll by *on*) *slang* **1** to fail to pay a gambling debt **2** to fail to fulfil an obligation [c19 of unknown origin] ▷ ˈwelsher *or* ˈwelcher *n*

Welsh¹ (wɛlʃ) *adj* **1** of, relating to, or characteristic of Wales, its people, their Celtic language, or their dialect of English ▷ *n* **2** a language of Wales, belonging to the S Celtic branch of the Indo-European family. Welsh shows considerable diversity between dialects **3** the Welsh (*functioning as plural*) the natives or inhabitants of Wales collectively ▷ Also (*rare*): Welch [Old English *Wēlisc, Wǣlisc*; related to *wealh* foreigner, Old High German *walahisc* (German *welsch*), Old Norse *valskr*, Latin *Volcae*]

Welsh² (wɛlʃ) *n* a white long-bodied lop-eared breed of pig, kept chiefly for bacon

Welsh Black *n* a breed of black cattle originally from N Wales that are bred for meat and milk

Welsh corgi *n* another name for **corgi**

Welsh dresser *n* a sideboard with drawers and cupboards below and open shelves above

Welsh harp *n* a type of harp in which the strings are arranged in three rows, used esp for the accompaniment of singing, improvisation on folk tunes, etc

Welshman (ˈwɛlʃmən) *or feminine* **Welshwoman**

n, pl -men *or* -women a native or inhabitant of Wales

Welshman's button *n* an angler's name for a species of caddis fly, *Sericostoma personatum*

Welsh Mountain *n* a common breed of small hardy sheep kept mainly in the mountains of Wales

Welsh mountain pony *n* a small sturdy but graceful breed of pony used mostly for riding, originally from Wales

Welsh poppy *n* a perennial W European papaveraceous plant, *Meconopsis cambrica*, with large yellow flowers

Welsh rabbit *n* a savoury dish consisting of melted cheese sometimes mixed with milk, seasonings, etc, on hot buttered toast. Also called: Welsh rarebit, rarebit [c18 a fanciful coinage; *rarebit* is a later folk-etymological variant]

Welsh springer spaniel *n* See **springer spaniel**

Welsh terrier *n* a wire-haired breed of terrier with a black-and-tan coat

welt (wɛlt) *n* **1** a raised or strengthened seam or edge, sewn in or on a knitted garment **2** another word for **weal¹** **3** (in shoemaking) a strip of leather, etc, put in between the outer sole and the inner sole and upper ▷ *vb* (*tr*) **4** to put a welt in (a garment, etc) **5** to beat or flog soundly [c15 origin unknown]

Weltanschauung *German* (ˈvɛltanˌʃauʊŋ) *n* a comprehensive view or personal philosophy of human life and the universe [from *Welt* world + *Anschauung* view]

welter (ˈwɛltə) *vb* (*intr*) **1** to roll about, writhe, or wallow **2** (esp of the sea) to surge, heave, or toss **3** to lie drenched in a liquid, esp blood ▷ *n* **4** a rolling motion, as of the sea **5** a confused mass; jumble [c13 from Middle Low German, Middle Dutch *weltern*; related to Old High German *walzan, welzen* to roll]

welterweight (ˈwɛltəˌweɪt) *n* **1 a** a professional boxer weighing 140–147 pounds (63.5–66.5 kg) **b** an amateur boxer weighing 63.5–67 kg (140–148 pounds) **c** (*as modifier*): *a great welterweight era* **2** a wrestler in a similar weight category (usually 154–172 pounds (70–78 kg))

Weltpolitik *German* (ˈvɛltpoliˌtiːk) *n* the policy of participation in world affairs [literally: world politics]

Weltschmerz *German* (ˈvɛltʃmɛrts) *n* sadness or melancholy at the evils of the world; world-weariness [literally: world pain]

welwitschia (wɛlˈwɪtʃɪə) *n* a gymnosperm plant, *Welwitschia mirabilis*, of the Namib Desert in SW Africa, consisting of two large woody leaves lying on the ground with a conelike structure arising between them: phylum Gnetophyta [c19 named after F. M. J. Welwitsch (1807–72), Portuguese botanist, born in Austria]

Welwyn Garden City (ˈwɛlɪn) *n* a town in SE England, in Hertfordshire: established (1920) as a planned industrial and residential community. Pop: 43 512 (2001)

Wembley (ˈwɛmblɪ) *n* part of the Greater London borough of Brent: site of the English national soccer stadium

wen¹ (wɛn) *n* **1** *pathol* a sebaceous cyst, esp one occurring on the scalp **2** a large overcrowded city (esp London in the phrase **the great wen**) [Old English *wenn*; related to Danish dialect *van, væne*, Dutch *wen*]

wen² (wɛn) *n* a rune having the sound of Modern English w [Old English *wen, wyn*]

wena (ˈweɪnə) *pron South African* you; refers to the person or persons addressed but not to the speaker [from Nguni: you (plural)]

wench (wɛntʃ) *n* **1** a girl or young woman, esp a buxom or lively one: now used facetiously **2** *archaic* a female servant **3** *archaic* a prostitute ▷ *vb* (*intr*) **4** *archaic* to frequent the company of prostitutes [Old English *wencel* child, from *wancol* weak; related to Old High German *wanchal, wankōn*] ▷ ˈwencher *n*

wend (wɛnd) *vb* to direct (one's course or way); travel: *wend one's way home* [Old English *wendan*; related to Old High German *wenten*, Gothic *wandjan*; see WIND²]

Wend (wɛnd) *n* (esp in medieval European history) a Sorb; a member of the Slavonic people who inhabited the area between the Rivers Saale and Oder in the early Middle Ages and were conquered by Germanic invaders by the 12th century. See also **Lusatia**

wendigo ('wɛndɪˌɡəʊ) *or* **windigo** ('wɪndɪˌɡəʊ) *n Canadian* **1** (*pl* -**gos**) (among Algonquian Indians) an evil spirit or cannibal **2** *pl* -**go** *or* -**gos** another name for **splake** [from Algonquian: evil spirit or cannibal]

Wendish ('wɛndɪʃ) *adj* **1** of or relating to the Wends ▷ *n* **2** the West Slavonic language of the Wends. See also **Sorbian**

Wendy house ('wɛndɪ) *n* a small model house that children can enter and play in [c20 named after *Wendy*, the girl in J. M. Barrie's play *Peter Pan* (1904)]

wenge ('wɛŋɡeɪ) *n* **1** a large, straight tree *Millettia Laurentii* of Central and West Africa valued for its hard dark wood, used in furniture and flooring **2 a** the wood of this tree **b** (*as modifier*): *a wenge chair* [c20 from a native African word]

wensleydale ('wɛnzlɪˌdeɪl) *n* **1** a type of white cheese with a flaky texture **2** a breed of sheep with long woolly fleece [named after *Wensleydale*, North Yorkshire]

went (wɛnt) *vb* the past tense of **go**

wentletrap ('wɛntⁿlˌtræp) *n* any marine gastropod mollusc of the family *Epitoniidae*, having a long pointed pale-coloured longitudinally ridged shell [c18 from Dutch *winteltrap* spiral shell, from *wintel*, earlier *windel*, from *wenden* to wind + *trap* a step, stairs]

Wentworth scale *n geology* a scale for specifying the sizes (diameters) of sedimentary particles, ranging from clay particles (less than 1/256 mm) to boulders (over 256 mm) [after C. K. Wentworth (1891–1969), US geologist]

Wenzhou, Wen-chou *or* **Wenchow** ('wɛn'tʃuː) *n* a port in SE China, in Zhejiang province: noted for its historic buildings. Pop: 1 475 000 (2005 est)

wept (wɛpt) *vb* the past tense and past participle of **weep**

were (wɜː; *unstressed* wə) *vb* the plural form of the past tense (indicative mood) of **be** and the singular form used with *you*. It is also used as a subjunctive, esp in conditional sentences [Old English *wērun, wǣron* past tense plural of *wesan* to be; related to Old Norse *vera*, Old Frisian *weria*, Old High German *werōn* to last]

> USAGE *Were*, as a remnant of the past subjunctive in English, is used in formal contexts in clauses expressing hypotheses (*if he were to die, she would inherit everything*), suppositions contrary to fact (*if I were you, I would be careful*), and desire (*I wish he were there now*). In informal speech, however, *was* is often used instead

we're (wɪə) *contraction of* we are

weren't (wɜːnt) *vb contraction of* were not

werewolf ('wɪəˌwʊlf, 'wɛə-) *n, pl* -**wolves** a person fabled in folklore and superstition to have been changed into a wolf by being bewitched or said to be able to assume wolf form at will [Old English *werewulf*, from *wer* man + *wulf* WOLF; related to Old High German *werwolf*, Middle Dutch *weerwolf*]

wergild, weregild ('wɜːˌɡɪld, 'wɛə-) *or* **wergeld** ('wɜːˌɡɛld, 'wɛə-) *n* the price set on a man's life in successive Anglo-Saxon and Germanic law codes, to be paid as compensation by his slayer [Old English *wergeld*, from *wer* man (related to Old Norse *ver*, Latin *vir*) + *gield* tribute (related to Gothic *gild*, Old High German *gelt* payment); see YIELD]

wernerite ('wɜːnəˌraɪt) *n* another name for **scapolite** [c19 named after Abraham Gottlieb *Werner* (1749–1817), German geologist]

wero ('wɜːrəʊ) *n NZ* the challenge made by an armed Māori warrior to a visitor to a marae [Māori]

werris ('wɛrɪs) *n Austral* a slang word for **urination** [shortened from *Werris Creek*, rhyming slang for LEAK meaning urination]

wersh (wɜːʃ; *Scot* wɛrʃ) *adj Scot* **1** tasteless; insipid **2** sour; bitter [c16 perhaps alteration of dialect *wearish*, probably of Germanic origin]

wert (wɜːt; *unstressed* wət) *vb archaic or dialect* (used with the pronoun *thou* or its relative equivalent) a singular form of the past tense (indicative mood) of **be**

Wesak (wɛsʌk) *n Buddhism* a festival in May celebrating the birth, enlightenment, and death of the Buddha [Sinhalese]

Weser (*German* 'veːzər) *n* a river in NW Germany: flows northwest to the North Sea at Bremerhaven and is linked by the Mittelland Canal to the Ems, Rhine, and Elbe waterways. Length: 477 km (196 miles)

Wesermünde (*German* veːzərˈmyndə) *n* the former name (until 1947) of **Bremerhaven**

weskit ('wɛskɪt) *n* an informal word for **waistcoat**

Wesleyan ('wɛzlɪən) *adj* **1** of, relating to, or deriving from John Wesley, the English preacher and founder of Methodism (1703–91) **2** of, relating to, or characterizing Methodism, esp in its original form or as upheld by the branch of the Methodist Church known as the **Wesleyan Methodists** ▷ *n* **3** a follower of John Wesley **4** a member of the Methodist Church or (formerly) of the Wesleyan Methodists ▷ '**Wesleyanism** *n*

Wessex ('wɛsɪks) *n* **1** an Anglo-Saxon kingdom in S and SW England that became the most powerful English kingdom by the 10th century AD **2 a** (in Thomas Hardy's works) the southwestern counties of England, esp Dorset **b** (*as modifier*): *Wessex Poems*

Wessi ('vɛsɪ; *German* 'vɛsi) *n informal* a native, inhabitant, or citizen of that part of Germany that was formerly West Germany [c20 from German *westdeutsch* West German]

west (wɛst) *n* **1** one of the four cardinal points of the compass, 270° clockwise from north and 180° from east **2** the direction along a parallel towards the sunset, at 270° clockwise from north **3** the west (*often capital*) any area lying in or towards the west. Related adjs: **Hesperian, Occidental 4** *cards* (*usually capital*) the player or position at the table corresponding to west on the compass ▷ *adj* **5** situated in, moving towards, or facing the west **6** (esp of the wind) from the west ▷ *adv* **7** in, to, or towards the west **8** *archaic* (of the wind) from the west **9** go **west** *informal* **a** to be lost or destroyed irrevocably **b** to die ▷ Symbol: W [Old English; related to Old Norse *vestr*, Sanskrit *avástāt*, Latin *vesper* evening, Greek *hésperos*]

West (wɛst) *n* the **1** the western part of the world contrasted historically and culturally with the East or Orient; the Occident **2** (formerly) the non-Communist countries of Europe and America contrasted with the Communist states of the East. Compare **East** (sense 2) **3** (in the US) **a** that part of the US lying approximately to the west of the Mississippi **b** (during the Colonial period) the region outside the 13 colonies, lying mainly to the west of the Alleghenies **4** (in the ancient and medieval world) the Western Roman Empire and, later, the Holy Roman Empire ▷ *adj* **5 a** of or denoting the western part of a specified country, area, etc **b** (*as part of a name*): *the West Coast*

West Atlantic *n* **1** the W part of the Atlantic Ocean, esp the N Atlantic around North America **2** a branch of the Niger-Congo family of African languages, spoken in Senegal and in scattered areas eastwards, including Fulani and Wolof ▷ *adj* **3** relating to or belonging to this group of languages

West Bank *n* the a semi-autonomous Palestinian region in the Middle East on the W bank of the River Jordan, comprising the hills of Judaea and Samaria and part of Jerusalem: formerly part of Palestine (the entity created by the League of Nations in 1922 and operating until 1948): became part of Jordan after the ceasefire of 1949: occupied by Israel since the 1967 Arab-Israeli War. In 1993 a peace treaty between Israel and the Palestine Liberation Organization provided for the West Bank to become a self-governing Palestinian area; a new Palestinian National Authority assumed control of parts of the territory in 1994–95, but subsequent talks broke down and Israel reoccupied much of this in 2001–02. Pop: 2 421 491 (2004 est). Area: 5879 sq km (2270 sq miles)

West Bengal *n* a state of E India, on the Bay of Bengal: formed in 1947 from the Hindu area of Bengal; additional territories added in 1950 (Cooch Behar), 1954 (Chandernagor), and 1956 (part of Bihar); mostly low-lying and crossed by the Hooghly River. Capital: Calcutta. Pop: 80 221 171 (2001). Area: 88 752 sq km (34 260 sq miles)

West Berkshire *n* a unitary authority in S England, in Berkshire. Pop: 144 200 (2003 est). Area: 705 sq km (272 sq miles)

West Berlin *n* (formerly) the part of Berlin under US, British, and French control > **West Berliner** *n*

West Berliner *n* a native or inhabitant of the part of Berlin formerly under US, British, and French control

westbound ('wɛstˌbaʊnd) *adj* going or leading towards the west

West Bromwich ('brɒmɪdʒ, -ɪtʃ) *n* a town in central England, in Sandwell unitary authority, West Midlands: industrial centre. Pop: 136 940 (2001)

west by north *n* **1** one point on the compass north of west, 281° 15′ clockwise from north ▷ *adj, adv* **2** in, from, or towards this direction

west by south *n* **1** one point on the compass south of west, 258° 45′ clockwise from north ▷ *adj, adv* **2** in, from, or towards this direction

West Coast jazz *n* a type of cool jazz displaying a soft intimate sound, regular rhythms, and a tendency to incorporate academic classical devices into jazz, such as fugue

West Country *n* the the southwest of England, esp Cornwall, Devon, and Somerset

West Dunbartonshire *n* a council area of W central Scotland, on Loch Lomond and the Clyde estuary: corresponds to part of the historical county of Dunbartonshire; part of Strathclyde Region from 1975 to 1996: engineering industries. Administrative centre: Dumbarton. Pop: 92 320 (2003 est). Area: 162 sq km (63 sq miles)

West End *n* the a part of W central London containing the main shopping and entertainment areas

wester ('wɛstə) *vb* **1** (*intr*) (of the sun, moon, or a star) to move or appear to move towards the west ▷ *n* **2** a strong wind or storm from the west

westering ('wɛstərɪŋ) *adj poetic* moving towards the west: *the westering star*

Westerlies ('wɛstəlɪz) *pl n meteorol* the prevailing winds blowing from the west on the poleward sides of the horse latitudes, often bringing depressions and anticyclones

westerly ('wɛstəlɪ) *adj* **1** of, relating to, or situated in the west ▷ *adv, adj* **2** towards or in the direction of the west **3** (esp of the wind) from the west ▷ *n, pl* -**lies 4** a wind blowing from the west > '**westerliness** *n*

western ('wɛstən) *adj* **1** situated in or towards or facing the west **2** going or directed to or towards the west **3** (of a wind, etc) coming or originating from the west **4** native to, inhabiting, or growing in the west **5** *music* See **country and western**

Western ('wɛstən) *adj* **1** of, relating to, or characteristic of the West as opposed to the Orient **2** (formerly) of, relating to, or characteristic of the Americas and the parts of Europe not under Communist rule **3** of, relating to, or characteristic of the western states of the US

▷ *n* **4** a film, book, etc, concerned with life in the western states of the US, esp during the era of exploration and early development

western alienation *n Canadian* a feeling of resentment by some inhabitants of western Canada against perceived favouritism by the national government towards the eastern provinces

Western Australia *n* a state of W Australia: mostly an arid undulating plateau, with the Great Sandy Desert, Gibson Desert, and Great Victoria Desert in the interior; settlement concentrated in the southwest; rich mineral resources. Capital: Perth. Pop: 1 969 046 (2003 est.). Area: 2 527 636 sq km (975 920 sq miles)

Western Cape *n* a province of W South Africa, created in 1994 from the SW part of Cape Province: agriculture (esp fruit), wine making, fishing, various industries in Cape Town. Capital: Cape Town. Pop: 4 570 696 (2004 est.). Area: 129 370 sq km (49 950 sq miles). Also called: Western Province

Western Church *n* **1** the part of Christendom that derives its liturgy, discipline, and traditions principally from the patriarchate of Rome, as contrasted with the part that derives these from the other ancient patriarchates, esp that of Constantinople **2** the Roman Catholic Church, sometimes together with the Anglican Communion of Churches

westerner ('wɛstənə) *n* (*sometimes capital*) a native or inhabitant of the west of any specific region, esp of the western states of the US or of the western hemisphere

Western Ghats *pl n* a mountain range in W peninsular India, parallel to the Malabar coast of the Arabian Sea. Highest peak: Anai Mudi, 2695 m (8841 ft)

western hemisphere *n* (*often capitals*) **1** that half of the globe containing the Americas, lying to the west of the Greenwich or another meridian **2** the lands contained in this, esp the Americas

western hemlock *n* a North American coniferous evergreen tree, *Tsuga heterophylla*, having hanging branches and oblong cones: family *Pinaceae*

Western Isles *n* (*functioning as singular or plural*) **1** an island authority in W Scotland, consisting of the Outer Hebrides; created in 1975. Administrative centre: Stornoway. Pop: 26 100 (2003 est.). Area: 2900 sq km (1120 sq miles). Gaelic name: Eilean Siar **2** Also called: Western Islands another name for the **Hebrides**

Western Isles pony *n* a breed of large pony, typically grey, with a dense waterproof coat. The only surviving variety is the Eriskay pony

westernism ('wɛstə,nɪzəm) *n* a word, habit, practice, etc, characteristic of western people or of the American West

westernize *or* **westernise** ('wɛstə,naɪz) *vb* (*tr*) to influence or make familiar with the customs, practices, etc, of the West ▷ ,westerni'zation *or* ,westerni'sation *n*

western larch *n* a North American larch, *Larix occidentalis*, having oval cones and found mainly in S British Columbia

westernmost ('wɛstən,məʊst) *adj* situated or occurring farthest west

Western Ocean *n* (formerly) another name for the **Atlantic Ocean**

Western Province *n* another name for **Western Cape**

western red cedar *n* **1** a large North American arbor vitae, *Thuja plicata*, found along and near the Pacific coast **2** the wood of this tree, used by North American Indians for building and for carving totem poles

western roll *n* a technique in high-jumping in which the jumper executes a half-turn of the body to clear the bar

Western Roman Empire *n* the westernmost of the two empires created by the division of the later Roman Empire, esp after its final severance

from the Eastern Roman Empire (395 AD). Also called: Western Empire

Western Sahara *n* a disputed region of NW Africa, on the Atlantic: mainly desert; rich phosphate deposits; a Spanish overseas province from 1958 to 1975; partitioned in 1976 between Morocco and Mauritania who faced growing resistance from the Polisario Front, an organization aiming for the independence of the region as the Democratic Saharan Arab Republic. Mauritania renounced its claim in 1979 and it was taken over by Morocco. Polisario agreed to a UN-brokered cease-fire in 1991 but attempts to settle the status of the region have failed. Pop: 316 000 (2004 est.). Area: 266 000 sq km (102 680 sq miles). Former name (until 1975): Spanish Sahara

Western Samoa *n* See **Samoa** (sense 1)

western swing *n* a 1930s jazz-influenced style of country music

Western Wall *n Judaism* a wall in Jerusalem, the last extant part of the Temple of Herod, held sacred by Jews as a place of prayer and pilgrimage. Also called: Wailing Wall

Westfalen (vɛst'faːlən) *n* the German name for **Westphalia**

West Flanders *n* a province of W Belgium: the country's chief agricultural province. Capital: Bruges. Pop: 1 135 802 (2004 est.). Area: 3132 sq km (1209 sq miles)

West German *adj* **1** of or relating to the former republic of West Germany (now part of Germany) or its inhabitants ▷ *n* **2** a native or inhabitant of the former West Germany

West Germanic *n* a subbranch of the Germanic languages that consists of English, Frisian, Dutch, Flemish, Afrikaans, Low German, German, Yiddish, and their associated dialects

West Germany *n* a former republic in N central Europe, on the North Sea: established in 1949 from the zones of Germany occupied by the British, Americans, and French after the defeat of Nazi Germany; a member of the European Community; reunited with East Germany in 1990. Official name: Federal Republic of Germany See also **Germany**

West Glamorgan *n* a former county in S Wales, formed in 1974 from part of Glamorgan and the county borough of Swansea: replaced in 1996 by the county of Swansea and the county borough of Neath Port Talbot

West Highland white terrier *n* a small pure white terrier having a hard straight coat and erect ears and tail

westie ('wɛstɪ) *n Austral informal derogatory* a young working-class person from the western suburbs of Sydney

West Indian *adj* **1** of or relating to the West Indies, its inhabitants, or their language or culture **2** native to or derived from the West Indies ▷ *n* **3** a native or inhabitant of the West Indies **4** a person of West Indian descent

West Indies ('ɪndɪz) *n* (*functioning as singular or plural*) an archipelago off Central America, extending over 2400 km (1500 miles) in an arc from the peninsula of Florida to Venezuela, separating the Caribbean Sea from the Atlantic Ocean: consists of the Greater Antilles, the Lesser Antilles, and the Bahamas; largest island is Cuba. Area: over 235 000 sq km (91 000 sq miles). Also called: the Caribbean

westing ('wɛstɪŋ) *n navigation* movement, deviation, or distance covered in a westerly direction, esp as expressed in the resulting difference in longitude

Westinghouse brake ('wɛstɪŋ,haʊs) *n* a braking system, invented by Westinghouse in 1872 and adopted by US railways, in which the brakes are held off by compressed air in the operating cylinder: controlled leakage of the air or a disruptive emergency causes the brakes to be applied. The system is used on most heavy vehicles and is replacing the vacuum system on

many railways [named after George *Westinghouse* (1846–1914), US inventor and manufacturer]

West Irian *n* a former English name for **Papua** (formerly **Irian Jaya**)

West Lothian *n* a council area and historical county of central Scotland, on the Firth of Forth: became part of Lothian region in 1975: reinstated as an independent authority (with revised boundaries) in 1996: agriculture, oil-refining. Administrative centre: Livingston. Pop: 161 020 (2003 est.). Area: 425 sq km (164 sq miles)

West Lothian question *n Brit* the apparent inconsistency that members of parliament who represent Scottish constituencies are eligible to vote at Westminster on matters that relate only to England, whereas members of parliament from English constituencies are not eligible to vote on Scottish matters [c20 because the issue was first raised by the Scottish politican Tam *Dalyell* (born 1932) at the time when he was MP for *West Lothian*]

Westm. *abbreviation for* Westminster

Westmeath (,wɛst'miːð) *n* a county of N central Republic of Ireland, in Leinster province: mostly low-lying, with many lakes and bogs. County town: Mullingar. Pop: 71 858 (2002). Area: 1764 sq km (681 sq miles)

West Midlands *n* (*functioning as singular or plural*) a metropolitan county of central England, administered since 1986 by the unitary authorities of Wolverhampton, Walsall, Dudley, Sandwell, Birmingham, Solihull, and Coventry. Area: 899 sq km (347 sq miles)

Westminster ('wɛst,mɪnstə) *n* **1** Also called: City of Westminster a borough of Greater London, on the River Thames: contains the Houses of Parliament, Westminster Abbey, and Buckingham Palace. Pop: 222 000 (2003 est.). Area: 22 sq km (8 sq miles) **2** the Houses of Parliament at Westminster

Westminster Abbey *n* a Gothic church in London: site of a Benedictine monastery (1050–65); scene of the coronations of almost all English monarchs since William I

Westmorland ('wɛstmələnd, 'wɛsmə-) *n* (until 1974) a county of NW England, now part of Cumbria

West Nile fever *n* a viral disease, caused by a flavivirus and spread by a mosquito (*Culex pipiens*), that results in encephalitis

west-northwest *n* **1** the point on the compass or direction midway between west and northwest, 292° 30′ clockwise from north ▷ *adj*, *adv* **2** in, from, or towards this direction ▷ Symbol: WNW

Weston standard cell ('wɛstən) *n* a primary cell used as a standard of emf, producing 1.018636 volts: consists of a mercury anode and a cadmium amalgam cathode in an electrolyte of saturated cadmium sulphate. Former name: cadmium cell [c20 from a trademark]

Weston-super-Mare ('wɛstən,suːpə'mɛə, -,sjuː-) *n* a town and resort in SW England, in North Somerset unitary authority, Somerset, on the Bristol Channel. Pop: 78 044 (2001)

West Pakistan *n* the former name (until the end of 1971) of **Pakistan**

Westphalia (wɛst'feɪlɪə) *n* a historic region of NW Germany, now mostly in the state of North Rhine-Westphalia. German name: Westfalen

Westphalian (wɛst'feɪlɪən) *adj* **1** of or relating to the historic German region of Westphalia or its inhabitants ▷ *n* **2** a native or inhabitant of Westphalia

West Point *n* the US Army installation in New York State that houses the US Military Academy

West Prussia *n* a former province of NE Prussia, on the Baltic: assigned to Poland in 1945. German name: Westpreussen ('vɛstprɔysən)

West Riding *n* (until 1974) an administrative division of Yorkshire, now part of West Yorkshire, North Yorkshire, Cumbria, and Lancashire

West Saxon (in Anglo-Saxon England) *adj* **1** of or

relating to Wessex, its inhabitants, or their dialect ▷ *n* **2** the dialect of Old English spoken in Wessex: the chief literary dialect of Old English. See also **Anglian, Kentish 3** an inhabitant of Wessex

west-southwest *n* **1** the point on the compass or the direction midway between southwest and west, 247° 30′ clockwise from north ▷ *adj, adv* **2** in, from, or towards this direction ▷ Symbol: **WSW**

West Sussex *n* a county of SE England, comprising part of the former county of Sussex: mainly low-lying, with the South Downs in the S. Administrative centre: Chichester. Pop: 758 600 (2003 est). Area: 1989 sq km (768 sq miles)

West Virginia *n* a state of the eastern US: part of Virginia until the outbreak of the American Civil War (1861); consists chiefly of the Allegheny Plateau; bounded on the west by the Ohio River; coal-mining. Capital: Charleston. Pop: 1 810 354 (2003 est). Area: 62 341 sq km (24 070 sq miles). Abbreviations: **W Va, W. Va.,** (with zip code) **WV**

West Virginian *adj* **1** of or relating to the state of West Virginia or its inhabitants ▷ *n* **2** a native or inhabitant of West Virginia

westward ('wɛstwəd) *adj* **1** moving, facing, or situated in the west ▷ *adv* **2** Also: **westwards** towards the west ▷ *n* **3** the westward part, direction, etc; the west > **'westwardly** *adj, adv*

West Yorkshire *n* a metropolitan county of N England, administered since 1986 by the unitary authorities of Bradford, Leeds, Calderdale, Kirklees, and Wakefield. Area: 2039 sq km (787 sq miles)

wet (wɛt) *adj* **wetter, wettest 1** moistened, covered, saturated, etc, with water or some other liquid **2** not yet dry or solid: *wet varnish* **3** rainy, foggy, misty, or humid: *wet weather* **4** employing a liquid, usually water: *a wet method of chemical analysis* **5** *chiefly US and Canadian* characterized by or permitting the free sale of alcoholic beverages: *a wet state* **6** *Brit informal* feeble or foolish **7** **wet behind the ears** *informal* immature or inexperienced; naive ▷ *n* **8** wetness or moisture **9** damp or rainy weather **10** *Brit informal* a Conservative politician who is considered not to be a hard-liner. Compare **dry** (sense 21) **11** *Brit informal* a feeble or foolish person **12** *chiefly US and Canadian* a person who advocates free sale of alcoholic beverages **13** **the wet** *Austral* (in northern and central Australia) the rainy season ▷ *vb* **wets, wetting, wet** *or* **wetted 14** to make or become wet **15** to urinate on (something) **16** (*tr*) *dialect* to prepare (tea) by boiling or infusing **17** **wet one's whistle** *informal* to take an alcoholic drink [Old English *wǣt*; related to Old Frisian *wēt*, Old Norse *vātr*, Old Slavonic *vedro* bucket] > **'wetly** *adv* > **'wetness** *n* > **,wetta'bility** *n* > **'wettable** *adj* > **'wetter** *n* > **'wettish** *adj*

weta ('wɛtə) *n* any of various wingless insects of the family *Stenopelmatidae* of New Zealand, with long spiny legs [Māori]

wet-and-dry-bulb thermometer *n* another name for **psychrometer**

wetback ('wɛt,bæk) *n* *US informal* a Mexican labourer who enters the US illegally [c20: illegal immigrants would swim across the Rio Grande river to reach the US]

wet blanket *n informal* a person whose low spirits or lack of enthusiasm have a depressing effect on others

wet-bulb thermometer *n* a thermometer the bulb of which is covered by a moist muslin bag, used together with a dry-bulb thermometer to measure humidity

wet cell *n* a primary cell in which the electrolyte is a liquid. Compare **dry cell**

wet dream *n* an erotic dream accompanied by an emission of semen during or just after sleep

wet fish *n* **a** fresh fish as opposed to frozen or cooked fish **b** (*as modifier*): *a wet-fish shop*

wet fly *n angling* **a** an artificial fly designed to float or ride below the water surface **b** (*as*

modifier): *wet-fly fishing* ▷ Compare **dry fly**

wether ('wɛðə) *n* a male sheep, esp a castrated one [Old English *hwæther*; related to Old Frisian *hweder*, Old High German *hwedar*, Old Norse *hvatharr*]

wetland ('wɛtlənd) *n* (*sometimes plural*) **a** an area of swampy or marshy land, esp considered as part of an ecological system **b** (*as modifier*): *wetland species*

wet look *n* a shiny finish given to certain clothing and footwear materials, esp plastic and leather

wet nurse *n* **1** a woman hired to suckle the child of another ▷ *vb* **wet-nurse** (*tr*) **2** to act as a wet nurse to (a child) **3** *informal* to attend with great devotion

wet pack *n med* a hot or cold damp sheet or blanket for wrapping around a patient

wet room *n* a type of water-proofed room with a drain in the floor often serving as an open-plan shower

wet rot *n* **1** a state of decay in timber caused by various fungi, esp *Coniophora puteana*. The hyphal strands of the fungus are seldom visible and affected timber turns dark brown **2** any of the fungi causing this decay

wet steam *n* steam, usually low-pressure, that contains water droplets in suspension

wet suit *n* a close-fitting rubber suit used by skin divers, yachtsmen, etc, to retain body heat when they are immersed in water or sailing in cold weather

Wetterhorn (German 'vɛtər,hɔrn) *n* a mountain in S Switzerland, in the Bernese Alps. Height: 3701 m (12 143 ft)

wettie ('wɛtɪ) *n NZ informal* a wetsuit

wetting agent *n chem* any substance added to a liquid to lower its surface tension and thus increase its ability to spread across or penetrate into a solid

wetware ('wɛt,wɛə) *n* **1** *computing* the nervous system of the brain, as opposed to computer hardware or software **2** *computing* the programmers, operators, and administrators who operate a computer system, as opposed to the system's hardware or software

WEU *abbreviation for* Western European Union

we've (wiːv) *contraction of* we have

Wexford ('wɛksfəd) *n* **1** a county of SE Republic of Ireland, in Leinster province on the Irish Sea: the first Irish county to be colonized from England; mostly low-lying and fertile. County town: Wexford. Pop: 116 596 (2002). Area: 2352 sq km (908 sq miles) **2** a port in SE Republic of Ireland, county town of Co Wexford: sacked by Oliver Cromwell in 1649. Pop: 17 235 (2002)

Weymouth ('weɪməθ) *n* a port and resort in S England, in Dorset on the English Channel: formerly part of the borough of **Weymouth and Melcombe** Regis. Pop (with Melcombe Regis): 48 279 (2001)

wf *abbreviation for* **1 wrong fount 2** ▷ *the internet domain name for* Wallis and Futuna Islands

WFF *logic abbreviation for* well-formed formula

WFTU *abbreviation for* World Federation of Trade Unions

wg *or* **WG** *abbreviation for* **1** water gauge **2** wire gauge

WG *international car registration for* (Windward Islands) Grenada

wha (hwɔː) *or* **whae** (hwe) *pron* a Scot word for **who**

whack (wæk) *vb* (*tr*) **1** to strike with a sharp resounding blow **2** (*usually passive*) *Brit informal* to exhaust completely ▷ *n* **3** (*tr*) *US slang* to murder: *if you were out of line you got whacked* **4** a sharp resounding blow or the noise made by such a blow **5** *informal* a share or portion **6** *informal* a try or attempt (esp in the phrase **have a whack at**) **7** **out of whack** *informal* out of order; unbalanced: *the whole system is out of whack* ▷ *interj* **8** an exclamation imitating the noise of a sharp

resounding blow [c18 perhaps a variant of THWACK, ultimately of imitative origin] > **'whacker** *n*

whacking ('wækɪŋ) *informal, chiefly Brit* ▷ *adj* **1** enormous ▷ *adv* **2** (*intensifier*): *a whacking big lie*

whack off *vb* (*intr, adverb*) *slang* to masturbate

whacky ('wækɪ) *adj* **whackier, whackiest** *US slang* a variant spelling of **wacky**

whaikorero (faːiː'kɒrɛrɒ) *n NZ* **1** the art of formal speech-making **2** a formal speech [Māori]

whakairo (fɑːkɑːiːrɒ) *n NZ* the art of carving [Māori]

whakapapa ('hwækəpæpə, 'fæk-) *n NZ* genealogy; family tree [Māori]

whale¹ (weɪl) *n, pl* **whales** *or* **whale 1** any of the larger cetacean mammals, excluding dolphins, porpoises, and narwhals. They have flippers, a streamlined body, and a horizontally flattened tail and breathe through a blowhole on the top of the head. Related adj: **cetacean 2** any cetacean mammal. See also **toothed whale, whalebone whale 3** *slang* a gambler who has the capacity to win and lose large sums of money in a casino **4** **a whale of a** *informal* an exceptionally large, fine, etc, example of a (person or thing): *we had a whale of a time on holiday* [Old English *hwæl*; related to Old Saxon *hwal*, Old High German *hwal*, Old Norse *hvalr*, Latin *squalus* seapig]

whale² (weɪl) *vb* (*tr*) to beat or thrash soundly [c18 variant of WALE¹]

whaleback ('weɪl,bæk) *n* **1** something shaped like the back of a whale **2** a steamboat having a curved upper deck

whaleboat ('weɪl,bəʊt) *n* a narrow boat from 20 to 30 feet long having a sharp prow and stern, formerly used in whaling. Also called: **whaler**

whalebone ('weɪl,bəʊn) *n* **1** Also called: **baleen** a horny elastic material forming a series of numerous thin plates that hang from the upper jaw on either side of the palate in the toothless (whalebone) whales and strain plankton from water entering the mouth **2** a thin strip of this substance, used in stiffening corsets, bodices, etc

whalebone whale *n* any whale belonging to the cetacean suborder *Mysticeti*, having a double blowhole and strips of whalebone between the jaws instead of teeth: includes the rorquals, right whales, and the blue whale. Compare **toothed whale**

whale catcher *n* a vessel engaged in the actual harpooning of whales

whale oil *n* oil obtained either from the blubber of whales (train oil) or the head of the sperm whale (sperm oil)

whaler ('weɪlə) *n* **1** Also called (US): **whaleman** a person employed in whaling **2** a vessel engaged in whaling. See **factory ship, whale catcher 3** another word for **whaleboat 4** *Austral* a nomad surviving in the bush without working

whaler shark *n Austral* a large voracious shark, *Galeolamna macrurus*, of E. Australian waters

whale shark *n* a large spotted whalelike shark, *Rhincodon typus*, of warm seas, that feeds on plankton and small animals: family *Rhincodontidae*

whaling ('weɪlɪŋ) *n* **1** the work or industry of hunting and processing whales for food, oil, etc ▷ *adv* **2** *informal* (intensifier): *a whaling good time*

wham (wæm) *n* **1** a forceful blow or impact or the sound produced by such a blow or impact ▷ *interj* **2** an exclamation imitative of this sound ▷ *vb* **whams, whamming, whammed 3** to strike or cause to strike with great force [c20 of imitative origin]

whammy ('wæmɪ) *n, pl* **-mies 1** something which has great, often negative, impact: *the double whammy of high interest rates and low wage increases* **2** an evil spell or curse: *she was convinced he had put the whammy on her* [c20 WHAM + -Y²]

whanau ('fɑːnaʊ) *n NZ* (in Māori societies) a family, esp an extended family [Māori]

whang¹ (wæŋ) *vb* **1** to strike or be struck so as to cause a resounding noise ▷ *n* **2** the resounding noise produced by a heavy blow **3** a heavy blow [c19 of imitative origin]

whang² (wæŋ) *n* *Scot* **1** a leather thong ▷ *vb* **2** (*tr*) to strike with or as if with a thong [c17 variant of THONG]

Whangarei (ˌwɑːŋəˈreɪ) *n* a port in New Zealand, the northernmost city of North Island: oil refinery. Pop: 72 200 (2004 est)

whangee (wæŋˈiː) *n* **1** any tall woody grass of the S and SE Asian genus *Phyllostachys*, grown for its stems, which are used for bamboo canes and as a source of paper pulp **2** a cane or walking stick made from the stem of any of these plants [c19 probably from Chinese (Mandarin) *huangli*, from *huang* yellow + *li* bamboo cane]

whap (wɒp) *vb* whaps, whapping, whapped, *n* a less common spelling of **whop**

whare (ˈwɒrɪ; *Māori* ˈfɒrɛ) *n* *NZ* **1** a Māori hut or dwelling place **2** any simple dwelling place, esp at a beach or in the bush [from Māori]

wharenui (fɑːrɛnuːiː) *n* a meeting house [Māori: large house]

wharepuni (ˈfɒrɛˌpuni) *n* *NZ* another name for **meeting house** (sense 2)

whare wanaga (ˈfɒrɛ wəˈnɑːɡə) *n* *NZ* a university [Māori]

wharf (wɔːf) *n*, *pl* wharves (wɔːvz) *or* wharfs **1** a platform of timber, stone, concrete, etc, built parallel to the waterfront at a harbour or navigable river for the docking, loading, and unloading of ships **2** the wharves *NZ* the working area of a dock **3** an obsolete word for **shore¹** ▷ *vb* (*tr*) **4** to moor or dock at a wharf **5** to provide or equip with a wharf or wharves **6** to store or unload on a wharf [Old English *hwearf* heap; related to Old Saxon *hwarf*, Old High German *hwarb* a turn, Old Norse *hvarf* circle]

wharfage (ˈwɔːfɪdʒ) *n* **1** accommodation for ships at wharves **2** a charge for use of a wharf **3** wharves collectively

wharfie (ˈwɔːfɪ) *n* *Austral and NZ* a wharf labourer; docker

wharfinger (ˈwɔːfɪndʒə) *n* an owner or manager of a wharf [c16 probably alteration of *wharfager* (see WHARFAGE, -ER¹); compare HARBINGER]

wharf rat *n* **1** any rat, usually a brown rat, that infests wharves **2** *informal* a person who haunts wharves, usually for dishonest purposes

wharve (wɔːv) *n* a wooden disc or wheel on a shaft serving as a flywheel or pulley [Old English *hweorfa*, from *hweorfan* to revolve; related to Old Saxon *hwervo* axis, Old High German *hwerbo* a turn]

what (wɒt; *unstressed* wət) *determiner* **1 a** used with a noun in requesting further information about the identity or categorization of something: *what job does he do?* **b** (*as pronoun*): *what is her address?* **c** (*used in indirect questions*): *does he know what man did this?*; *tell me what he said* **2 a** the (person, thing, persons, or things) that: *we photographed what animals we could see* **b** (*as pronoun*): *bring me what you've written*; *come what may* **3** (*intensifier*; used in exclamations): *what a good book!* ▷ *adv* **4** in what respect? to what degree?: *what do you care?* ▷ *pron* **5** *not standard* which, who, or that, when used as relative pronouns: *this is the man what I saw in the park yesterday* **6 what about** what do you think, know, feel, etc, concerning? **7 what for a** for what purpose? why? **b** *informal* a punishment or reprimand (esp in the phrase **give (a person) what for**) **8 what have you** someone, something, or somewhere unknown or unspecified: *cars, motorcycles, or what have you* **9 what if a** what would happen if? **b** what difference would it make if? **10 what matter** what does it matter? **11 what's what** *informal* the true or real state of affairs ▷ *interj* **12** *informal* don't you think? don't you agree?: *splendid party, what?* [Old English *hwæt*; related to Old Frisian *whet*, Old High German *hwaz* (German *was*), Old Norse *hvatr*]

▌ USAGE The use of *are* in sentences such as *what we need are more doctors* is common, although many people

▌ think *is* should be used: *what we need is more doctors*

whata (fɑːtɑ) *n* a building on stilts or a raised platform for storing provisions [Māori]

whatever (wɒtˈɛvə, wət-) *pron* **1** everything or anything that: *do whatever he asks you to* **2** no matter what: *whatever he does, he is forgiven* **3** *informal* an unknown or unspecified thing or things: *take a hammer, chisel, or whatever* **4** an intensive form of *what*, used in questions: *whatever can he have said to upset her so much?* ▷ *determiner* **5** an intensive form of *what*: *use whatever tools you can get hold of* ▷ *adj* **6** (*postpositive*) absolutely; whatsoever: *I saw no point whatever in continuing* ▷ *interj* **7** *informal* an expression used to show indifference or dismissal

what-if *n* *informal* a hypothetical question; speculation: *one of the great what-ifs of modern history*

whatnot (ˈwɒtˌnɒt) *n* **1** Also called: **what-d'you-call-it** *informal* a person or thing the name of which is unknown, temporarily forgotten, or deliberately overlooked **2** *informal* unspecified assorted material **3** a portable stand with shelves, used for displaying ornaments, etc

whatsit (ˈwɒtsɪt), **whatsitsname** *or masculine* **whatshisname** *or feminine* **whatshername** *n* *informal* a person or thing the name of which is unknown, temporarily forgotten, or deliberately overlooked

whatsoever (ˌwɒtsəʊˈɛvə) *adj* **1** (*postpositive*) at all: used as an intensifier with indefinite pronouns and determiners such as *none, any, no one, anybody,* etc **2** an archaic word for **whatever**

whaup (wɔːp; *Scot* hwɔːp) *n* *chiefly Scot* a popular name for the **curlew** [c16 related to Old English *huilpe*, ultimately imitative of the bird's cry; compare Low German *regenwilp* sandpiper]

whaur (hwɔːr) *adv, pron, conj, n* a Scot word for **where**

wheal (wiːl) *n* a variant spelling of **weal¹**

wheat (wiːt) *n* **1** any annual or biennial grass of the genus *Triticum*, native to the Mediterranean region and W Asia but widely cultivated, having erect flower spikes and light brown grains **2** the grain of any of these grasses, used in making flour, pasta, etc ▷ See also **emmer, durum** [Old English *hwǣte*, related to Old Frisian, Old Saxon *hwēti*, Old High German *hweizi*, Old Norse *hveiti*; see WHITE]

wheat beer *n* any of various beers brewed using a mixture of wheat malt and barley malt

wheatear (ˈwiːtˌɪə) *n* any small northern songbird of the genus *Oenanthe*, esp *O. oenanthe*, a species having a pale grey back, black wings and tail, white rump, and pale brown underparts: subfamily *Turdinae* (thrushes) [c16 back formation from *wheatears* (wrongly taken as plural), probably from WHITE + ARSE; compare Dutch *witstaart*, French *culblanc* white tail]

wheaten (ˈwiːtᵊn) *adj* **1** made of the grain or flour of wheat: *wheaten bread* **2** of a pale yellow colour

wheat germ *n* the vitamin-rich embryo of the wheat kernel, which is largely removed before milling and is used in cereals, as a food supplement, etc

wheatgrass (ˈwiːtˌɡrɑːs) *n* another name for **couch grass**

wheatmeal (ˈwiːtˌmiːl) *n* **a** a brown flour intermediate between white flour and wholemeal flour **b** (*as modifier*): *a wheatmeal loaf*

wheat pool *n* (in Western Canada) a cereal farmers' cooperative

wheat rust *n* **1** a rust fungus, *Puccinia graminis*, that attacks cereals, esp wheat, and the barberry **2** the disease caused by this fungus

Wheatstone bridge (ˈwiːtstən) *n* a device for determining the value of an unknown resistance by comparison with a known standard resistance [c19 named after Sir Charles *Wheatstone* (1802–75), British physicist and inventor]

wheatworm (ˈwiːtˌwɜːm) *n* a parasitic nematode worm, *Anguina tritici*, that forms galls in the seeds of wheat

whee (wiː) *interj* an exclamation of joy, thrill, etc

wheedle (ˈwiːdᵊl) *vb* **1** to persuade or try to persuade (someone) by coaxing words, flattery, etc **2** (*tr*) to obtain by coaxing and flattery: *she wheedled some money out of her father* [c17 perhaps from German *wedeln* to wag one's tail, from Old High German *wedil, wadil* tail] ▷ **ˈwheedler** *n* ▷ **ˈwheedling** *adj* ▷ **ˈwheedlingly** *adv*

wheel (wiːl) *n* **1** a solid disc, or a circular rim joined to a hub by radial or tangential spokes, that is mounted on a shaft about which it can turn, as in vehicles and machines **2** anything like a wheel in shape or function **3** a device consisting of or resembling a wheel or having a wheel as its principal component: *a steering wheel; a water wheel* **4** (*usually preceded by the*) a medieval torture consisting of a wheel to which the victim was tied and then had his limbs struck and broken by an iron bar **5** short for **wheel of fortune** *or* **potter's wheel** **6** the act of turning **7** a pivoting movement of troops, ships, etc **8** a type of firework coiled to make it rotate when let off **9** a set of short rhyming lines, usually four or five in number, forming the concluding part of a stanza. Compare **bob²** (sense 7) **10** the disc in which the ball is spun in roulette **11** *US and Canadian* an informal word for **bicycle** **12** *archaic* a refrain **13** *informal, chiefly US and Canadian* a person of great influence (esp in the phrase **big wheel**) **14 at the wheel a** driving or steering a vehicle or vessel **b** in charge ▷ *vb* **15** (when *intr* sometimes foll by *about* or *round*) to turn or cause to turn on or as if on an axis **16** to move or cause to move on or as if on wheels; roll **17** (*tr*) to perform with or in a circular movement **18** (*tr*) to provide with a wheel or wheels **19** (*intr*; often foll by *about*) to change one's mind or opinion **20 wheel and deal** *informal* to be a free agent, esp to advance one's own interests ▷ See also **wheels** [Old English *hweol, hweowol*; related to Old Norse *hvēl*, Greek *kuklos*, Middle Low German *wēl*, Dutch *wiel*] ▷ **ˈwheel-less** *adj*

wheel and axle *n* a simple machine for raising weights in which a rope unwinding from a wheel is wound onto a cylindrical drum or shaft coaxial with or joined to the wheel to provide mechanical advantage

wheel animalcule *n* another name for **rotifer**

wheelbarrow (ˈwiːlˌbærəʊ) *n* **1** a simple vehicle for carrying small loads, typically being an open container supported by a wheel at the front and two legs and two handles behind ▷ *vb* **2** (*tr*) to convey in a wheelbarrow

wheelbase (ˈwiːlˌbeɪs) *n* the distance between the front and back axles of a motor vehicle

Wheel Blacks *pl n* the the international wheelchair rugby football team of New Zealand [c20 allusion to ALL BLACKS]

wheel bug *n* a large predatory North American heteropterous insect, *Arilus cristatus*, having a semicircular thoracic projection: family *Reduviidae* (assassin bugs)

wheelchair (ˈwiːlˌtʃɛə) *n* *med* a special chair mounted on large wheels, for use by invalids or others for whom walking is impossible or temporarily inadvisable

wheelchair housing *n* *social welfare* housing designed or adapted for a chairbound person. See also **mobility housing**

wheel clamp *n* a device fixed onto one wheel of an illegally parked car in order to immobilize it. The driver has to pay to have it removed

wheeled (wiːld) *adj* **a** having or equipped with a wheel or wheels **b** (*in combination*): *four-wheeled*

wheeler (ˈwiːlə) *n* **1** Also called: **wheel horse** a horse or other draught animal nearest the wheel **2** (*in combination*) something equipped with a specified sort or number of wheels: *a three-wheeler* **3** a person or thing that wheels

wheeler-dealer *n* *informal* a person who wheels and deals

wheel horse *n* **1** another word for **wheeler** (sense

1) **2** *US and Canadian* a person who works steadily or hard

wheelhouse ('wi:l,haʊs) *n* another term for **pilot house**

wheelie ('wi:lɪ) *n, pl* -ies a manoeuvre on a bicycle or motorbike in which the front wheel is raised off the ground

wheelie bin *or* **wheely bin** *n* a large container for rubbish, esp one used by a household, mounted on wheels so that it can be moved more easily

wheel lock *n* **1** a gunlock formerly in use in which the firing mechanism was activated by sparks produced by friction between a small steel wheel and a flint **2** a gun having such a lock

wheel man *n* **1** a cyclist **2** Also called: **wheelsman** *US* a helmsman

wheel of fortune *n* (in mythology and literature) a revolving device spun by a deity of fate selecting random changes in the affairs of man. Often shortened to: **wheel**

wheels (wi:lz) *pl n* **1** the main directing force behind an organization, movement, etc: *the wheels of government* **2** an informal word for **car 3** wheels within wheels a series of intricately connected events, plots, etc

wheel trim *n* metallic decorative trim over or around the wheels of a motor vehicle

wheel window *n* another name for **rose window**

wheel wobble *n* an oscillation of the front wheels of a vehicle caused by a defect in the steering gear, unbalanced wheels, etc

wheelwork ('wi:l,wɜ:k) *n* an arrangement of wheels in a machine, esp a train of gears

wheelwright ('wi:l,raɪt) *n* a person who makes or mends wheels as a trade

wheen (wi:n; *Scot* hwi:n) *determiner Scot and northern English dialect* **1** few; some **2** (preceded by *a*) **a** a small number of **b** a good number of **c** (*as pronoun; functioning as plural*): *a wheen of years* [Old English *hwēne*, instrumental of *hwōn* few, a few]

wheesh (hwi:ʃ) *or* **wheesht** (hwi:ʃt) *Scot* ▷ *interj* **1** a plea or demand for silence; hush ▷ *vb* **2** to silence (a person, noise, etc) or to be silent ▷ *n* **3** silence; hush **4** haud your wheesht! be silent! hush! [of imitative origin; compare HUSH¹]

wheeze (wi:z) *vb* **1** to breathe or utter (something) with a rasping or whistling sound **2** (*intr*) to make or move with a noise suggestive of wheezy breathing ▷ *n* **3** a husky, rasping, or whistling sound or breathing **4** *Brit slang* a trick, idea, or plan (esp in the phrase **good wheeze**) **5** *informal* a hackneyed joke or anecdote [C15 probably from Old Norse *hvæsa* to hiss] ▷ 'wheezer *n* ▷ 'wheezy *adj* ▷ 'wheezily *adv* ▷ 'wheeziness *n*

whelk¹ (wɛlk) *n* any carnivorous marine gastropod mollusc of the family *Buccinidae*, of coastal waters and intertidal regions, having a strong snail-like shell [Old English *weoloc*; related to Middle Dutch *willok*, Old Norse *vil* entrails]

whelk² (wɛlk) *n* a raised lesion on the skin; wheal [Old English *hwylca*, of obscure origin] ▷ 'whelky *adj*

whelm (wɛlm) *vb* (*tr*) *archaic* **1** to engulf entirely with or as if with water **2** another word for **overwhelm** [C13 *whelmen* to turn over, of uncertain origin]

whelp (wɛlp) *n* **1** a young offspring of certain animals, esp of a wolf or dog **2** *disparaging* a young man or youth **3** *jocular* a young child **4** *nautical* any of the ridges, parallel to the axis, on the drum of a capstan to keep a rope, cable, or chain from slipping ▷ *vb* **5** (of an animal or, disparagingly, a woman) to give birth to (young) [Old English *hwelp(a)*; related to Old High German *hwelf*, Old Norse *hvelpr*, Danish *hvalp*]

when (wɛn) *adv* **1 a** at what time? over what period?: *when is he due?* **b** (*used in indirect questions*): *ask when he's due* **2** say when to state when an action is to be stopped or begun, as when someone is pouring a drink **3** (*subordinating*) at a time at which; at the time at which; just as; after:

I found it easily when I started to look seriously **4** although: *he drives when he might walk* **5** considering the fact that: *how did you pass the exam when you'd not worked for it?* **6** at which (time); over which (period): *an age when men were men* ▷ *n* **7** (*usually plural*) a question as to the time of some occurrence [Old English *hwanne, hwænne*; related to Old High German *hwanne, hwenne*, Latin *cum*]

> **USAGE** *When* should not be used loosely as a substitute for *in which* after a noun which does not refer to a period of time: *paralysis is a condition in which* (not *when*) *parts of the body cannot be moved*

whenas (wɛn'æz) *conj* **1** *archaic* **a** when; whenever **b** inasmuch as; while **2** *obsolete* whereas; although

whence (wɛns) *archaic or formal* ▷ *adv* **1** from what place, cause, or origin? ▷ *pron* **2** (*subordinating*) from what place, cause, or origin [C13 *whannes*, adverbial genitive of Old English *hwanon*; related to Old Frisian *hwana*, Old High German *hwanan*]

> **USAGE** The expression *from whence* should be avoided, since *whence* already means from which place: *the tradition whence* (not *from whence*) *such ideas flowed*

whencesoever (,wɛnssəʊ'ɛvə) *conj* (*subordinating*) ▷ *adv archaic* out of whatsoever place, cause, or origin

whene'er (wɛn'ɛə) *adv, conj* a poetic contraction of **whenever**

whenever (wɛn'ɛvə) *conj* **1** (*subordinating*) at every or any time that; when: *I laugh whenever I see that* ▷ *adv also* when ever **2** no matter when: *it'll be here, whenever you decide to come for it* **3** *informal* at an unknown or unspecified time: *I'll take it if it comes today, tomorrow, or whenever* **4** an intensive form of *when*, used in questions: *whenever did he escape?*

whensoever (,wɛnsəʊ'ɛvə) *conj, adv rare* an intensive form of **whenever**

whenua (fɛn'ʊə) *n* NZ land [Māori]

whenwe ('wɛnwi:) *n South African informal* a White immigrant from Zimbabwe, caricatured as being tiresomely over-reminiscent of happier times [c20 from WHEN + WE]

where (wɛə) *adv* **1 a** in, at, or to what place, point, or position?: *where are you going?* **b** (*used in indirect questions*): *I don't know where they are* **2** in, at, or to which (place): *the hotel where we spent our honeymoon* **3** (*subordinating*) in the place at which: *where we live it's always raining* ▷ *n* **4** (*usually plural*) a question as to the position, direction, or destination of something [Old English *hwǣr, hwār(a)*; related to Old Frisian *hwēr*, Old Saxon, Old High German *hwār*, Old Norse, Gothic *hvar*]

> **USAGE** It was formerly considered incorrect to use *where* as a substitute for *in which* after a noun which did not refer to a place or position, but this use has now become acceptable: *we now have a situation where/in which no further action is needed*

whereabouts ('wɛərə,baʊts) *adv* Also: whereabout at what approximate location or place; where: *whereabouts are you?* **2** *obsolete* about or concerning which ▷ *n* **3** (*functioning as singular or plural*) the place, esp the approximate place, where a person or thing is

whereafter (,wɛər'ɑ:ftə) *sentence connector archaic or formal* after which

whereas (wɛər'æz) *conj* **1** (*coordinating*) but on the other hand: *I like to go swimming whereas Sheila likes to sail* ▷ *sentence connector* **2** (in formal documents to begin sentences) it being the case that; since

whereat (wɛər'æt) *archaic* ▷ *adv* **1** at or to which place ▷ *sentence connector* **2** upon which occasion

whereby (wɛə'baɪ) *pron* **1** by or because of which: *the means whereby he took his life* ▷ *adv* **2** *archaic* how? by what means?: *whereby does he recognize me?*

where'er (wɛər'ɛə) *adv, conj* a poetic contraction of **wherever**

wherefore ('wɛə,fɔ:) *n* **1** (*usually plural*) an explanation or reason (esp in the phrase **the whys and wherefores**) ▷ *adv* **2** *archaic* for what reason? why? ▷ *sentence connector* **3** *archaic or formal* for which reason: used as an introductory word in legal preambles

wherefrom (wɛə'frɒm) *archaic* ▷ *adv* **1** from what or where? whence? ▷ *pron* **2** from which place; whence

wherein (wɛər'ɪn) *archaic or formal* ▷ *adv* **1** in what place or respect? ▷ *pron* **2** in which place, thing, etc

whereinto (wɛər'ɪntu:) *archaic* ▷ *adv* **1** into what place? ▷ *pron* **2** into which place

whereof (wɛər'ɒv) *archaic or formal* ▷ *adv* **1** of what or which person or thing? ▷ *pron* **2** of which (person or thing): *the man whereof I speak is no longer alive*

whereon (wɛər'ɒn) *archaic* ▷ *adv* **1** on what thing or place? ▷ *pron* **2** on which thing, place, etc

wheresoever (,wɛəsəʊ'ɛvə) *conj* (*subordinating*) ▷ *adv, pron rare* an intensive form of **wherever**

whereto (wɛə'tu:) *archaic or formal* ▷ *adv* **1** towards what (place, end, etc)? ▷ *pron* **2** to which ▷ Also (*archaic*): whereunto

whereupon (,wɛərə'pɒn) *sentence connector* **1** at which; at which point; upon which ▷ *adv* **2** *archaic* upon what?

wherever (wɛər'ɛvə) *pron* **1** at, in, or to every place or point which; where: *wherever she went, he would be there* **2** (*subordinating*) in, to, or at whatever place: *wherever we go the weather is always bad* ▷ *adv also* where ever **3** no matter where: *I'll find you, wherever you are* **4** *informal* at, in, or to an unknown or unspecified place: *I'll go anywhere to escape: London, Paris, or wherever* **5** an intensive form of *where*, used in questions: *wherever can they be?*

wherewith (wɛə'wɪθ, -'wɪð) *archaic or formal* ▷ *pron* **1** (*often foll by an infinitive*) with or by which: *the pen wherewith I am wont to write* **2** something with which: *I have not wherewith to buy my bread* ▷ *adv* **3** with what? ▷ *sentence connector* **4** with or after that; whereupon

wherewithal *n* ('wɛəwɪð,ɔ:l) **1** the wherewithal necessary funds, resources, or equipment (for something or to do something): *these people lack the wherewithal for a decent existence* ▷ *pron* (,wɛəwɪð'ɔ:l) **2** a less common word for **wherewith** (senses 1, 2)

wherret ('wɛrət) *dialect* ▷ *vb* **1** (*tr*) to strike (someone) a blow ▷ *n* **2** a blow, esp a slap on the face; stroke [probably of imitative origin]

wherrit ('wɛrɪt) *vb* **1** to worry or cause to worry **2** (*intr*) to complain or moan [perhaps from *thwert*, obsolete variant of THWART; compare WORRIT]

wherry ('wɛrɪ) *n, pl* -ries **1** any of certain kinds of half-decked commercial boats, such as barges, used in Britain **2** a light rowing boat used in inland waters and harbours [C15 origin unknown] ▷ 'wherryman *n*

whet (wɛt) *vb* whets, whetting, whetted (*tr*) **1** to sharpen, as by grinding or friction **2** to increase or enhance (the appetite, desire, etc); stimulate ▷ *n* **3** the act of whetting **4** a person or thing that whets [Old English *hwettan*; related to *hwæt* sharp, Old High German *hwezzen*, Old Norse *hvetja*, Gothic *hvatjan*] ▷ 'whetter *n*

whether ('wɛðə) *conj* **1** (*subordinating*) used to introduce an indirect question or a clause after a verb expressing or implying doubt or choice in order to indicate two or more alternatives, the second or last of which is introduced by *or* or *or whether*: *he doesn't know whether she's in Britain or whether she's gone to France* **2** (*subordinating*; often foll by *or not*) used to introduce any indirect question: *he was not certain whether his friend was there or not* **3** (*coordinating*) another word for **either** (sense 3) *any man, whether liberal or conservative, would agree with me* **4** (*coordinating*) *archaic* used to introduce a direct question consisting of two alternatives, the second of which is introduced by *or* or *or whether*: *whether does he live at home or abroad* **5** whether or no **a** used as a conjunction as a variant of **whether**

W

(sense 1) **b** under any circumstances: *he will be here tomorrow, whether or no* **6** **whether...or (whether)** if on the one hand...or even if on the other hand: *you'll eat that, whether you like it or not* ▷ *determiner* ▷ *pron* **7** *obsolete* which (of two): used in direct or indirect questions [Old English *hwæther, hwether;* related to Old Frisian *hweder, hoder,* Old High German *hwedar,* Old Norse *hvatharr, hvarr,* Gothic *hwathar*]

whetstone ('wɛtˌstəʊn) *n* **1** a stone used for sharpening edged tools, knives, etc **2** something that sharpens

whew (hwjuː) *interj* an exclamation or sharply exhaled breath expressing relief, surprise, delight, etc

whey (weɪ) *n* the watery liquid that separates from the curd when the milk is clotted, as in making cheese [Old English *hwǣg;* related to Middle Low German *wei, heie,* Dutch *hui*] > 'wheyey, 'wheyish *or* 'whey,like *adj*

wheyface ('weɪˌfeɪs) *n* **1** a pale bloodless face **2** a person with such a face > 'whey,faced *adj*

whf *abbreviation for* wharf

which (wɪtʃ) *determiner* **1** **a** used with a noun in requesting that its referent be further specified, identified, or distinguished from the other members of a class: *which house did you want to buy?* **b** (*as pronoun*): *which did you find?* **c** (*used in indirect questions*): *I wondered which apples were cheaper* **2** **a** whatever of a class; whichever: *bring which car you want* **b** (*as pronoun*): *choose which of the cars suit you* **3** used in relative clauses with inanimate antecedents: *the house, which is old, is in poor repair* **4** as; and that: used in relative clauses with verb phrases or sentences as their antecedents: *he died of cancer, which is what I predicted* **5** **the which** *archaic* a longer form of **which,** often used as a sentence connector [Old English *hwelc, hwilc;* related to Old High German *hwelīh* (German *welch*), Old Norse *hvelīkr,* Gothic *hvileiks,* Latin *quis, quid*]

USAGE See at **that**

whichever (wɪtʃˈɛvə) *determiner* **1** **a** any (one, two, etc, out of several): *take whichever car you like* **b** (*as pronoun*): *choose whichever appeals to you* **2** **a** no matter which (one or ones): *whichever card you pick you'll still be making a mistake* **b** (*as pronoun*): *it won't make any difference, whichever comes first*

whichsoever (ˌwɪtʃsəʊˈɛvə) *pron* an archaic or formal word for **whichever**

whicker ('wɪkə) *vb* (*intr*) (of a horse) to whinny or neigh; nicker [C17 of imitative origin]

whidah ('wɪdə) *n* a variant spelling of **whydah**

whiff[1] (wɪf) *n* **1** a passing odour **2** a brief gentle gust of air **3** a single inhalation or exhalation from the mouth or nose ▷ *vb* **4** to come, convey, or go in whiffs; puff or waft **5** to take in or breathe out (tobacco smoke, air, etc) **6** (*tr*) to sniff or smell **7** (*intr*) *Brit slang* to have an unpleasant smell; stink [C16 of imitative origin] > 'whiffer *n*

whiff[2] (wɪf) *n chiefly Brit* a narrow clinker-built skiff having outriggers, for one oarsman [C19 special use of WHIFF¹]

whiffle ('wɪfᵊl) *vb* **1** (*intr*) to think or behave in an erratic or unpredictable way **2** to blow or be blown fitfully or in gusts **3** (*intr*) to whistle softly [C16 frequentative of WHIFF¹]

whiffler[1] ('wɪflə) *n* a person who whiffles

whiffler[2] ('wɪflə) *n archaic* an attendant who cleared the way for a procession [C16 from *wifle* battle-axe, from Old English *wifel,* of Germanic origin; the attendants originally carried weapons to clear the way]

whiffletree ('wɪfᵊlˌtriː) *n* another name (esp US) for **swingletree** [C19 variant of WHIPPLETREE]

whiffy ('wɪfɪ) *adj* **-fier, -fiest** *slang* smelly

Whig (wɪg) *n* **1** a member of the English political party or grouping that in 1679–80 opposed the succession to the throne of James, Duke of York (1633–1701; king of England and Ireland as James II, and of Scotland as James VII, 1685–88), on the grounds that he was a Catholic. Standing for a limited monarchy, the Whigs represented the great aristocracy and the moneyed middle class for the next 80 years. In the late 18th and early 19th centuries the Whigs represented the desires of industrialists and Dissenters for political and social reform. The Whigs provided the core of the Liberal Party **2** (in the US) a supporter of the War of American Independence. Compare **Tory** **3** a member of the American political party that opposed the Democrats from about 1834 to 1855 and represented propertied and professional interests **4** a conservative member of the Liberal Party in Great Britain **5** a person who advocates and believes in an unrestricted laissez-faire economy **6** *history* a 17th-century Scottish Presbyterian, esp one in rebellion against the Crown ▷ *adj* **7** of, characteristic of, or relating to Whigs [C17 probably shortened from *whiggamore,* one of a group of 17th-century Scottish rebels who joined in an attack on Edinburgh known as *the whiggamore raid;* probably from Scottish *whig* to drive (of obscure origin) + *more, mer, maire* horse, MARE¹] > 'Whiggery *or* 'Whiggism *n* > 'Whiggish *adj* > 'Whiggishly *adv* > 'Whiggishness *n*

whigmaleerie (ˌhwɪgməˈliːrɪ) *n Scot* **1** a trinket, whimsical ornament, or trifle **2** a whim or caprice [C18 of unknown origin]

while (waɪl) *conj also* **whilst** (waɪlst) **1** (*subordinating*) at the same time that: *please light the fire while I'm cooking* **2** (*subordinating*) all the time that: *I stay inside while it's raining* **3** (*subordinating*) in spite of the fact that: *while I agree about his brilliance I still think he's rude* **4** (*coordinating*) whereas; and in contrast: *flats are expensive, while houses are cheap* **5** (*subordinating; used with a gerund*) during the activity of: *while walking I often whistle* ▷ *prep, conj* **6** *Scot and northern English dialect* another word for **until:** *you'll have to wait while Monday for these sheets; you'll never make any progress while you listen to me* ▷ *n* **7** (*usually used in adverbial phrases*) a period or interval of time: *once in a long while* **8** trouble or time (esp in the phrase **worth one's while**): *it's hardly worth your while to begin work today* **9** **the while** at that time: *he was working the while* ▷ See also **whiles** [Old English *hwīl;* related to Old High German *hwīla* (German *Weile*), Gothic *hveila,* Latin *quiēs* peace, *tranquīlus* TRANQUIL]

USAGE It was formerly considered incorrect to use *while* to mean *in spite of the fact that* or *whereas,* but these uses have now become acceptable

while away *vb* (*tr, adverb*) to pass (time) idly and usually pleasantly

whiles (waɪlz; *Scot* hwəɪlz) *archaic or dialect* ▷ *adv* **1** at times; occasionally ▷ *conj* **2** while; whilst

whilk (hwɪlk) *pron* an archaic and dialect word for **which**

whilom ('waɪləm) *archaic* ▷ *adv* **1** formerly; once ▷ *adj* **2** (*prenominal*) one-time; former [Old English *hwīlum,* dative plural of *hwīl* WHILE; related to Old High German *hwīlōm,* German *weiland* of old]

whilst (waɪlst) *conj chiefly Brit* another word for **while** (senses 1–5) [C13 from WHILES + *-t* as in *amidst*]

whim (wɪm) *n* **1** a sudden, passing, and often fanciful idea; impulsive or irrational thought **2** a horse-drawn winch formerly used in mining to lift ore or water [C17 from WHIM-WHAM]

whimbrel ('wɪmbrəl) *n* a small European curlew, *Numenius phaeopus,* with a striped head [C16 from dialect *whimp* or from WHIMPER, alluding to its cry]

whimper ('wɪmpə) *vb* **1** (*intr*) to cry, sob, or whine softly or intermittently **2** to complain or say (something) in a whining plaintive way ▷ *n* **3** a soft plaintive whine [C16 from dialect *whimp,* of imitative origin] > 'whimperer *n* > 'whimpering *n* > 'whimperingly *adv*

whimsical ('wɪmzɪkᵊl) *adj* **1** spontaneously fanciful or playful **2** given to whims; capricious **3** quaint, unusual, or fantastic > **whimsicality** (ˌwɪmzɪˈkælɪtɪ) *n* > 'whimsically *adv* > 'whimsicalness *n*

whimsy *or* **whimsey** ('wɪmzɪ) *n, pl* **-sies** *or* **-seys** **1** a capricious idea or notion **2** light or fanciful humour **3** something quaint or unusual ▷ *adj* **-sier, -siest** **4** quaint, comical, or unusual, often in a tasteless way [C17 from WHIM; compare FLIMSY]

whim-wham *n archaic* something fanciful; a trifle [C16 of unknown origin; compare FLIMFLAM]

whin[1] (wɪn) *n* another name for **gorse** [C11 from Scandinavian; compare Old Danish *hvine* (*græs*), Norwegian *hvine,* Swedish *hven*]

whin[2] (wɪn) *n* short for **whinstone** [C14 *quin,* of obscure origin]

whinchat ('wɪnˌtʃæt) *n* an Old World songbird, *Saxicola rubetra,* having a mottled brown-and-white plumage with pale cream underparts: subfamily *Turdinae* (thrushes) [C17 from WHIN¹ + CHAT¹]

whine (waɪn) *n* **1** a long high-pitched plaintive cry or moan **2** a continuous high-pitched sound **3** a peevish complaint, esp one repeated ▷ *vb* **4** to make a whine or utter in a whine [Old English *hwīnan;* related to Old Norse *hvīna,* Swedish *hvija* to scream] > 'whiner *n* > 'whining *adj* > 'whiningly *adv*

whinge (wɪndʒ) *informal* ▷ *vb* **whinges, whingeing, whinged** (*intr*) **1** to cry in a fretful way **2** to complain ▷ *n* **3** a complaint [from a Northern variant of Old English *hwinsian* to whine; related to Old High German *winsan, winisan,* whence Middle High German *winsen*] > 'whingeing *n, adj* > 'whinger *n*

whinny ('wɪnɪ) *vb* **-nies, -nying, -nied** (*intr*) **1** (of a horse) to neigh softly or gently **2** to make a sound resembling a neigh, such as a laugh ▷ *n, pl* **-nies** **3** a gentle or low-pitched neigh [C16 of imitative origin]

whinstone ('wɪnˌstəʊn) *n* any dark hard fine-grained rock, such as basalt [C16 from WHIN² + STONE]

whiny ('waɪnɪ) *adj* **whinier, whiniest** **1** high-pitched and plaintive **2** peevish; complaining

whio ('fiːəʊ) *n, pl* **whio** *NZ* another name for **blue duck** [Māori]

whip (wɪp) *vb* **whips, whipping, whipped** **1** to strike (a person or thing) with several strokes of a strap, rod, etc **2** (*tr*) to punish by striking in this manner **3** (*tr; foll by out, away,* etc) to pull, remove, etc, with sudden rapid motion: *to whip out a gun* **4** (*intr; foll by down, into, out of,* etc) *informal* to come, go, etc, in a rapid sudden manner: *they whipped into the bar for a drink* **5** to strike or be struck as if by whipping: *the tempest whipped the surface of the sea* **6** (*tr*) to criticize virulently **7** (*tr*) to bring, train, etc, forcefully into a desired condition (esp in the phrases **whip into line** and **whip into shape**) **8** (*tr*) *informal* to overcome or outdo: *I know when I've been whipped* **9** (*tr; often foll by on, out,* or *off*) to drive, urge, compel, etc, by or as if by whipping **10** (*tr*) to wrap or wind (a cord, thread, etc) around (a rope, cable, etc) to prevent chafing or fraying **11** (*tr*) *nautical* to hoist by means of a rope through a single pulley **12** (*tr*) (in fly-fishing) to cast the fly repeatedly onto (the water) in a whipping motion **13** (*tr*) (in sewing) to join, finish, or gather with whipstitch **14** to beat (eggs, cream, etc) with a whisk or similar utensil to incorporate air and produce expansion **15** (*tr*) to spin (a top) **16** (*tr*) *informal* to steal: *he whipped her purse* ▷ *n* **17** a device consisting of a lash or flexible rod attached at one end to a stiff handle and used for driving animals, inflicting corporal punishment, etc **18** a whipping stroke or motion **19** a person adept at handling a whip, as a coachman, etc **20** (in a legislative body) **a** a member of a party chosen to organize and discipline the members of his faction, esp in voting and to assist in the arrangement of the business **b** a call issued to members of a party, insisting with varying degrees of urgency upon their presence or loyal voting behaviour **c** (in the British Parliament) a schedule of business sent to members of a party each week. Each item on it is underlined to indicate its importance: one line means that no division is expected, two lines means that the item is fairly important, and three lines means that the item is very important and every member must attend and vote according to the party line **21** an apparatus for hoisting, consisting of a rope, pulley, and snatch block **22** any of a variety of desserts made from egg whites or cream beaten stiff, sweetened, and flavoured with fruit, fruit juice, etc **23** See **whipper-in 24** a windmill vane **25** transient elastic movement of a structure or part when subjected to sudden release of load or dynamic excitation **26** a percussion instrument consisting of two strips of wood, joined forming the shape of a V, and clapped loudly together **27** flexibility, as in the shaft of a golf club, etc **28** a ride in a funfair involving bumper cars that move with sudden jerks **29** a wrestling throw in which a wrestler seizes his opponent's arm and spins him to the floor **30 a fair crack of the whip** *informal* a fair chance or opportunity ▷ See also **whip in, whip-round, whips, whip up** [c13 perhaps from Middle Dutch *wippen* to swing; related to Middle Dutch *wipfen* to dance, German *Wipfel* tree top] ▷ '**whip,like** *adj* ▷ '**whipper** *n*

whipbird ('wɪp,bɜːd) *n Austral* **1** any of several birds of the genus *Psophodes*, esp *P. olivaceus* (**eastern whipbird**) and *P. nigrogularis* (**black-throated whipbird**), having a whistle ending in a whipcrack note **2** any of various other birds, such as *Pachycephala pectoralis* and *P. rufiventris* (**mock whipbird**)

whipcord ('wɪp,kɔːd) *n* **1** a strong worsted or cotton fabric with a diagonally ribbed surface **2** a closely twisted hard cord used for the lashes of whips, etc

whip graft *n horticulture* a graft made by inserting a tongue cut on the sloping base of the scion into a slit on the sloping top of the stock

whip hand *n* (usually preceded by *the*) **1** (in driving horses) the hand holding the whip **2** advantage or dominating position

whip in *vb* (*adverb*) **1** (*intr*) to perform the duties of a whipper-in to a pack of hounds **2** (*tr*) *chiefly US* to keep (members of a political party, etc) together

whiplash ('wɪp,læʃ) *n* **1** a quick lash or stroke of a whip or like that of a whip **2** *med* See **whiplash injury**

whiplash injury *n med informal* any injury to the neck resulting from a sudden thrusting forwards and snapping back of the unsupported head. Technical name: hyperextension-hyperflexion injury

whipper-in *n, pl* whippers-in a person employed to assist the huntsman managing the hounds in a hunt

whippersnapper ('wɪpə,snæpə) *n* an insignificant but pretentious or cheeky person, often a young one. Also called: **whipster** [c17 probably from *whipsnapper* a person who snaps whips, influenced by earlier *snippersnapper*, of obscure origin]

whippet ('wɪpɪt) *n* a small slender breed of dog similar to a greyhound in appearance [c16 of uncertain origin; perhaps based on the phrase *whip it!* move quickly!]

whipping ('wɪpɪŋ) *n* **1** a thrashing or beating with a whip or similar implement **2** cord or twine used for binding or lashing

whipping boy *n* a person of little importance who is blamed for the errors, incompetence, etc, of others, esp his superiors; scapegoat [c17 originally referring to a boy who was educated with a prince and who received punishment for any faults committed by the prince]

whipping cream *n* cream that contains just enough butterfat to allow it to be whipped until stiff

whippletree ('wɪpªl,triː) *n* another name for **swingletree** [c18 apparently from WHIP]

whippoorwill ('wɪpʊ,wɪl) *n* a nightjar, *Caprimulgus vociferus*, of North and Central America, having a dark plumage with white patches on the tail [c18 imitative of its cry]

whip-round *informal, chiefly Brit* ▷ *n* **1** an impromptu collection of money ▷ *vb* **whip round 2** (*intr, adverb*) to make such a collection of money

whips (wɪps) *pl n* (often foll by *of*) *Austral informal* a large quantity: *I've got whips of cash at the moment*

whipsaw ('wɪp,sɔː) *n* **1** any saw with a flexible blade, such as a bandsaw ▷ *vb* **-saws, -sawing, -sawed, -sawed** or **-sawn** (*tr*) **2** to saw with a whipsaw **3** *US* to defeat in two ways at once

whip scorpion *n* any nonvenomous arachnid of the order *Uropygi* (or *Pedipalpi*), typically resembling a scorpion but lacking a sting. See also **vinegarroon**

whip snake *n* **1** any of several long slender fast-moving nonvenomous snakes of the colubrid genus *Coluber*, such as *C. hippocrepis* (**horseshoe whipsnake**) of Eurasia **2** any of various other slender nonvenomous snakes, such as *Masticophis flagellum* (**coachwhip snake**) of the US

whipstall ('wɪp,stɔːl) *n* a stall in which an aircraft goes into a nearly vertical climb, pauses, slips backwards momentarily, and drops suddenly with its nose down

whipstitch ('wɪp,stɪtʃ) *n* **1** a sewing stitch passing over an edge **2** *US slang* an instant; moment ▷ *vb* **3** (*tr*) to sew (an edge) using whipstitch; overcast

whipstock ('wɪp,stɒk) *n* a whip handle

whiptail wallaby ('wɪp,teɪl) *n* a wallaby of NE Australia, *Macropus parryi*, with a long slender tail

whip up *vb* (*tr, adverb*) **1** to excite; arouse: *to whip up a mob; to whip up discontent* **2** *informal* to prepare quickly: *to whip up a meal*

whipworm ('wɪp,wɜːm) *n* any of several parasitic nematode worms of the genus *Trichuris*, esp *T. trichiura*, having a whiplike body and living in the intestines of mammals

whir or **whirr** (wɜː) *n* **1** a prolonged soft swish or buzz, as of a motor working or wings flapping **2** a bustle or rush ▷ *vb* **whirs** or **whirrs, whirring, whirred 3** to make or cause to make a whir [c14 probably from Scandinavian; compare Norwegian *kvirra*, Danish *hvirre*; see WHIRL]

whirl (wɜːl) *vb* **1** to spin, turn, or revolve or cause to spin, turn, or revolve **2** (*intr*) to turn around or away rapidly **3** (*intr*) to have a spinning sensation, as from dizziness, etc **4** to move or drive or be moved or driven at high speed ▷ *n* **5** the act or an instance of whirling; swift rotation or a rapid whirling movement **6** a condition of confusion or giddiness: *her accident left me in a whirl* **7** a swift round, as of events, meetings, etc **8** a tumult; stir **9** *informal* a brief trip, dance, etc **10 give (something) a whirl** *informal* to attempt or give a trial to (something) [c13 from Old Norse *hvirfla* to turn about; related to Old High German *wirbil* whirlwind] ▷ '**whirler** *n* ▷ '**whirling** *adj* ▷ '**whirlingly** *adv*

whirlabout ('wɜːlə,baʊt) *n* **1** anything that whirls around; whirligig **2** the act or an instance of whirling around

whirligig ('wɜːlɪ,gɪg) *n* **1** any spinning toy, such as a top **2** another name for **merry-go-round 3** anything that whirls about, spins, or moves in a circular or giddy way: *the whirligig of social life* **4** another name for **windmill** (the toy) [c15 *whirlegigge*, from WHIRL + GIG[1]]

whirligig beetle *n* any flat-bodied water beetle of the family *Gyrinidae*, which circles rapidly on the surface of the water

whirlpool ('wɜːl,puːl) *n* **1** a powerful circular current or vortex of water, usually produced by conflicting tidal currents or by eddying at the foot of a waterfall **2** something resembling a whirlpool in motion or the power to attract into its vortex **3** short for **whirlpool bath**

whirlpool bath *n* a bath having a device for maintaining the water in a swirling motion

whirlwind ('wɜːl,wɪnd) *n* **1** a column of air whirling around and towards a more or less vertical axis of low pressure, which moves along the land or ocean surface **2 a** a motion or course resembling this, esp in rapidity **b** (*as modifier*): *a whirlwind romance* **3** an impetuously active person

whirlybird ('wɜːlɪ,bɜːd) *n* an informal word for **helicopter**

whish (wɪʃ) *n, vb* a less common word for **swish**

whisht (hwɪʃt) or **whist** (hwɪst) *Scot* ▷ *interj* **1** hush! be quiet! ▷ *adj* **2** silent or still ▷ *vb* **3** to make or become silent ▷ See also **wheesh** [c14 compare HIST; also obsolete v. *whist* to become silent]

whisk (wɪsk) *vb* **1** (*tr*; often foll by *away* or *off*) to brush, sweep, or wipe off lightly **2** (*tr*) to move, carry, etc, with a light or rapid sweeping motion: *the taxi whisked us to the airport* **3** (*intr*) to move, go, etc, quickly and nimbly: *to whisk downstairs for a drink* **4** (*tr*) to whip (eggs, cream, etc) to a froth ▷ *n* **5** the act of whisking **6** a light rapid sweeping movement or stroke **7** a utensil, often incorporating a coil of wires, for whipping eggs, etc **8** a small brush or broom **9** a small bunch or bundle, as of grass, straw, etc [c14 from Old Norse *visk* wisp; related to Middle Dutch *wisch*, Old High German *wisc*]

whisker ('wɪskə) *n* **1** any of the stiff sensory hairs growing on the face of a cat, rat, or other mammal. Technical name: vibrissa **2** any of the hairs growing on a person's face, esp on the cheeks or chin **3** (*plural*) a beard or that part of it growing on the sides of the face **4** (*plural*) *informal* a moustache **5** Also called: whisker boom, whisker pole any light spar used for extending the clews of a sail, esp in light airs **6** *chem* a very fine filamentary crystal having greater strength than the bulk material since it is a single crystal. Such crystals often show unusual electrical properties **7** a person or thing that whisks **8** a narrow margin; a small distance: *he escaped death by a whisker*

whiskered ('wɪskəd) *adj* having whiskers

whiskery ('wɪskərɪ) *adj* -skerier, -skeriest **1** having whiskers **2** old; unkempt

whiskey ('wɪskɪ) *n* the usual Irish and US spelling of **whisky**

Whiskey ('wɪskɪ) *n communications* a code word for the letter *w*

whiskey sour *n US* a mixed drink of whisky and lime or lemon juice, sometimes sweetened

whisky ('wɪskɪ) *n, pl* -kies a spirit made by distilling fermented cereals, which is matured and often blended [c18 shortened from *whiskybae*, from Scottish Gaelic *uisge beatha*, literally: water of life; see USQUEBAUGH]

whisky mac *n Brit* a drink consisting of whisky and ginger wine

whisper ('wɪspə) *vb* **1** to speak or utter (something) in a soft hushed tone, esp without vibration of the vocal cords **2** (*intr*) to speak secretly or furtively, as in promoting intrigue, gossip, etc **3** (*intr*) (of leaves, trees, etc) to make a low soft rustling sound **4** (*tr*) to utter or suggest secretly or privately: *to whisper treason* ▷ *n* **5** a low soft voice: *to speak in a whisper* **6** something uttered in such a voice **7** a low soft rustling sound **8** a trace or suspicion **9** *informal* a rumour or secret [Old English *hwisprian*; related to Old Norse *hvīskra*, Old High German *hwispalōn*, Dutch *wispern*]

whisperer ('wɪspərə) *n* **1** a person or thing that whispers **2** a person who is able to tame or control animals, esp by talking to them in gentle tones: *a horse whisperer*

whispering campaign *n* the organized diffusion by word of mouth of defamatory rumours designed to discredit a person, group, etc

whispering gallery *n* a gallery or dome with acoustic characteristics such that a sound made at one point is audible at distant points

whist[1] (wɪst) *n* a card game for four in which the two sides try to win the balance of the 13 tricks: forerunner of bridge [c17 perhaps changed from WHISK, referring to the sweeping up or whisking up of the tricks]

whist[2] (hwɪst) *interj, adj, vb* a variant of **whisht**

whist drive *n* a social gathering where whist is played; the winners of each hand move to

1829

different tables to play the losers of the previous hand

whistle ('wɪsᵊl) *vb* **1** to produce (shrill or flutelike musical sounds), as by passing breath through a narrow constriction most easily formed by the pursed lips: *he whistled a melody* **2** (*tr*) to signal, summon, or command by whistling or blowing a whistle: *the referee whistled the end of the game* **3** (of a kettle, train, etc) to produce (a shrill sound) caused by the emission of steam through a small aperture **4** (*intr*) to move with a whistling sound caused by rapid passage through the air **5** (of animals, esp birds) to emit (a shrill sound) resembling human whistling **6** whistle in the dark to try to keep up one's confidence in spite of fear ▷ *n* **7** a device for making a shrill high-pitched sound by means of air or steam under pressure **8** a shrill sound effected by whistling **9** a whistling sound, as of a bird, bullet, the wind, etc **10** a signal, warning, command, etc, transmitted by or as if by a whistle **11** the act of whistling **12** *music* any pipe that is blown down its end and produces sounds on the principle of a flue pipe, usually having as a mouthpiece a fipple cut in the side **13** wet one's whistle *informal* to take an alcoholic drink **14** blow the whistle (usually foll by *on*) *informal* **a** to inform (on) **b** to bring a stop (to) ▷ See also whistle for, whistle up [Old English *hwistlian*; related to Old Norse *hvīsla*]

whistle-blower *n informal* a person who informs on someone or puts a stop to something

whistle for *vb* (*intr, preposition*) *informal* to seek or expect in vain

whistler ('wɪslə) *n* **1** a person or thing that whistles **2** *radio* an atmospheric disturbance picked up by radio receivers, characterized by a whistling sound of decreasing pitch. It is caused by the electromagnetic radiation produced by lightning **3** any of various birds having a whistling call, such as certain Australian flycatchers (see thickhead (sense 2)) and the goldeneye **4** any of various North American marmots of the genus *Marmota*, esp *M. caligata* (hoary marmot) **5** *vet science* a horse affected with an abnormal respiratory noise, resembling whistling **6** *informal* a referee

whistle stop *n* **1** *US and Canadian* **a** a minor railway station where trains stop only on signal **b** a small town having such a station **2 a** a brief appearance in a town, esp by a political candidate to make a speech, shake hands, etc **b** (*as modifier*): *a whistle-stop tour* ▷ *vb* whistle-stop -stops, -stopping, -stopped **3** (*intr*) to campaign for office by visiting many small towns to give short speeches

whistle up *vb* (*tr, adverb*) to call or summon (a person or animal) by whistling

whistling ('wɪslɪŋ) *n vet science* a breathing defect of horses characterized by a high-pitched sound with each intake of air. Compare roaring (sense 6)

whistling swan *n* a white North American swan, *Cygnus columbianus*, with a black bill and straight neck. Compare mute swan

whit (wɪt) *n* (*usually used with a negative*) the smallest particle; iota; jot: *he has changed not a whit* [c15 probably variant of WIGHT¹]

Whit (wɪt) *n* **1** See Whitsuntide ▷ *adj* **2** of or relating to Whitsuntide

Whitby ('wɪtbɪ) *n* a fishing port and resort in NE England, in E North Yorkshire at the mouth of the River Esk: an important ecclesiastical centre in Anglo-Saxon times; site of an abbey founded in 656. See also Synod of Whitby. Pop: 13 594 (2001)

white (waɪt) *adj* **1** having no hue due to the reflection of all or almost all incident light. Compare black (sense 1) **2** (of light, such as sunlight) consisting of all the colours of the spectrum or produced by certain mixtures of three additive primary colours, such as red, green, and blue **3** comparatively white or whitish-grey in colour or having parts of this colour: *white clover* **4** (of an animal) having pale-coloured or white

skin, fur, or feathers **5** bloodless or pale, as from pain, emotion, etc **6** (of hair, a beard, etc) silvery or grey, usually from age **7** benevolent or without malicious intent: *white magic* **8** colourless or transparent: *white glass* **9** capped with or accompanied by snow: *a white Christmas* **10** (*sometimes capital*) counterrevolutionary, very conservative, or royalist. Compare Red (sense 2) **11** blank, as an unprinted area of a page **12** (of wine) made from pale grapes or from black grapes separated from their skins **13 a** (of coffee or tea) with milk or cream **b** (of bread) made with white flour **14** *physics* having or characterized by a continuous distribution of energy, wavelength, or frequency: *white noise* **15** *informal* honourable or generous **16** (of armour) made completely of iron or steel (esp in the phrase **white harness**) **17** *rare* morally unblemished **18** *rare* (of times, seasons, etc) auspicious; favourable **19** *poetic or archaic* having a fair complexion; blond **20** bleed white to deprive slowly of resources **21** whiter than white **a** extremely clean and white **b** *informal* very pure, honest, and moral ▷ *n* **22** a white colour **23** the condition or quality of being white; whiteness **24** the white or lightly coloured part or area of something **25** (*usually preceded by the*) the viscous fluid that surrounds the yolk of a bird's egg, esp a hen's egg; albumen **26** *anatomy* the white part (sclera) of the eyeball **27** any of various butterflies of the family *Pieridae*. See large white, small white, cabbage white **28** *chess, draughts* **a** a white or light-coloured piece or square **b** (*usually capital*) the player playing with such pieces **29** anything that has or is characterized by a white colour, such as a white paint or pigment, a white cloth, a white ball in billiards **30** an unprinted area of a page **31** *archery* **a** the outer ring of the target, having the lowest score **b** a shot or arrow hitting this ring **32** *poetic* fairness of complexion **33** in the white (of wood or furniture) left unpainted or unvarnished ▷ *vb* **34** (*usually foll by out*) to create or leave white spaces in (printed or other matter) **35** *obsolete* to make or become white ▷ See also white out, whites [Old English *hwīt*; related to Old Frisian *hwīt*, Old Saxon *hwīt*, Old Norse *hvītr*, Gothic *hveits*, Old High German *hwīz* (German *weiss*)] > 'whitely *adv* > 'whiteness *n* > 'whitish *adj*

White (waɪt) *n* **1** a member of the Caucasoid race **2** a person of European ancestry ▷ *adj* **3** denoting or relating to a White or Whites

white admiral *n* a nymphalid butterfly, *Limenitis camilla*, of Eurasia, having brown wings with white markings. See also red admiral

white alkali *n* **1** refined sodium carbonate **2** any of several mineral salts, esp sodium sulphate, sodium chloride, and magnesium sulphate, that often appear on the surface of soils as a whitish layer in dry conditions

white ant *n* another name for termite

white area *n* an area of land for which no specific planning proposal has been adopted

White Australia policy *n history* an unofficial term for an immigration policy designed to restrict the entry of coloured people into Australia

whitebait ('waɪtˌbeɪt) *n* **1** the young of herrings, sprats, etc, cooked and eaten whole as a delicacy **2** any of various small silvery fishes, such as *Galaxias attenuatus* of Australia and New Zealand and *Allosmerus elongatus* of North American coastal regions of the Pacific [c18 from its formerly having been used as bait]

whitebeam ('waɪtˌbiːm) *n* **1** a N temperate rosaceous tree, *Sorbus aria*, having leaves with dense white hairs on the undersurface and hard timber **2** any of several similar and closely related trees

white bear *n* another name for polar bear

white birch *n* any of several birch trees with white bark, such as the silver birch of Europe and the paper birch of North America. See also birch (sense 1)

white blood cell *n* a nontechnical name for leucocyte

whiteboard ('waɪtˌbɔːd) *n* **1** a shiny white surface that can be wiped clean after being used for writing or drawing on, used esp in teaching **2** a large screen used to project computer images to a group of people

white book *n* an official government publication in some countries

Whiteboy ('waɪtˌbɔɪ) *n Irish history* a member of a secret society of violent agrarian protest, formed around 1760 [c18 adopted from the earlier use of the phrase as a term of endearment for a boy or man]

white bryony *n* a climbing herbaceous cucurbitaceous plant, *Bryonia dioica*, of Europe and North Africa, having greenish flowers and red berries. Also called: red bryony See also black bryony, bryony

whitecap ('waɪtˌkæp) *n* **1** a wave with a white broken crest **2** *US* a member of a vigilante organization that attempts to control a community

white cedar *n* **1** a coniferous tree, *Chamaecyparis thyoides*, of swampy regions in North America, having scalelike leaves and boxlike cones: family *Cupressaceae*. See also cypress¹ (sense 2) **2** the wood of this tree, which is used for building boats, etc **3** a coniferous tree, *Thuja occidentalis*, of NE North America, having scalelike leaves: family *Cupressaceae*. See also arbor vitae **4** the wood of this tree, much used for telegraph poles

Whitechapel ('waɪtˌtʃæpᵊl) *n billiards* the act of potting one's opponent's white ball [c19 slang use of *Whitechapel*, a district of London]

white clover *n* a Eurasian clover plant, *Trifolium repens*, with rounded white flower heads: cultivated as a forage plant

white coal *n* water, esp when flowing and providing a potential source of usable power

white cockatoo *n* another name for sulphur-crested cockatoo

white-collar *adj* of, relating to, or designating nonmanual and usually salaried workers employed in professional and clerical occupations: *white-collar union*. Compare blue-collar, pink-collar

white currant *n* a cultivated N temperate shrub, *Ribes sativum*, having small rounded white edible berries: family *Grossulariaceae*

whitedamp ('waɪtˌdæmp) *n* a mixture of poisonous gases, mainly carbon monoxide, occurring in coal mines. See also afterdamp

whited sepulchre ('waɪtɪd) *n* a hypocrite [from Matthew 23:27]

white dwarf *n* one of a large class of small faint stars of enormous density (on average 10^8 kg/m³) with diameters only about 1 per cent that of the sun, and masses less than the Chandrasekhar limit (about 1.4 solar masses). It is thought to mark the final stage in the evolution of a sun-like star

white elephant *n* **1** a rare albino or pale grey variety of the Indian elephant, regarded as sacred in parts of S Asia **2** a possession that is unwanted by its owner **3** an elaborate venture, construction, etc, that proves useless **4** a rare or valuable possession the upkeep of which is very expensive

White Ensign *n* the ensign of the Royal Navy and the Royal Yacht Squadron, having a red cross on a white background with the Union Jack at the upper corner of the vertical edge alongside the hoist. Compare Red Ensign, Blue Ensign

white-eye *n* **1** Also called (NZ): blighty, silvereye, tauhou, waxeye any songbird of the family *Zosteropidae* of Africa, Australia, New Zealand, and Asia, having a greenish plumage with a white ring around each eye **2** any of certain other birds having a white ring or patch around the eye

white feather *n* **1** a symbol or mark of cowardice **2** show the white feather to act in a cowardly manner [from the belief that a white feather in a gamecock's tail was a sign of a poor fighter]

white finger *n* a condition of a finger that results in a white appearance caused by a spasm of the blood vessels. It occurs with Raynaud's disease and with the long-term use of percussion tools

whitefish ('waɪt,fɪʃ) *n, pl* -**fish** *or* -**fishes** any herring like salmonoid food fish of the genus *Coregonus* and family *Coregonidae,* typically of deep cold lakes of the N hemisphere, having large silvery scales and a small head

white fish *n* (in the British fishing industry) any edible marine fish or invertebrate in which the main reserves of fat are in the liver, excluding herring, trout, sprat, mackerel, salmon, and shellfish

white flag *n* a white flag or a piece of white cloth hoisted to signify surrender or request a truce

white flight *n* the departure of white residents from areas where non-Whites are settling

white flint *n* another name for **flint** (sense 4)

white flour *n* flour that consists substantially of the starchy endosperm of wheat, most of the bran and the germ having been removed by the milling process

whitefly ('waɪt,flaɪ) *n, pl* -**flies** any hemipterous insect of the family *Aleyrodidae,* typically having a body covered with powdery wax. Many are pests of greenhouse crops

white-footed mouse *n* any of various mice of the genus *Peromyscus,* esp *P. leucopus,* of North and Central America, having brownish fur with white underparts: family *Cricetidae.* See also **deer mouse**

white fox *n* another name for **arctic fox**

white friar *n* a Carmelite friar, so called because of the white cloak that forms part of the habit of this order

white-fronted tern *n* a coastal bird of New Zealand and SE Australia, *Sterna striata,* with a long black bill, a white breast, and a forked tail. Also called: **black cap, kahawai bird, sea swallow, tara**

white frost *n* another term for **hoarfrost**

white gold *n* any of various white lustrous hard-wearing alloys containing gold together with platinum and palladium and sometimes smaller amounts of silver, nickel, or copper: used in jewellery

white goods *pl n* **1** *marketing* large household appliances, such as refrigerators, cookers. Compare **brown goods 2** household linen such as sheets, towels, tablecloths, etc

white gum *n* any of various Australian eucalyptus trees with whitish bark

white-haired boy *or* **white-headed boy** *n* a favourite; darling

Whitehall (,waɪt'hɔːl) *n* **1** a street in London stretching from Trafalgar Square to the Houses of Parliament: site of the main government offices **2** the British Government or its central administration

white hat *n informal* **a** a computer hacker who is hired by an organization to undertake nonmalicious hacking work in order to discover computer-security flaws **b** (*as modifier*): *a white-hat hacker.* Compare **black hat**

white heat *n* **1** intense heat or a very high temperature, characterized by emission of white light **2** *informal* a state of intense excitement or activity

white hope *n informal* a person who is expected to bring honour or glory to his group, team, etc

white horse *n* **1** the outline of a horse carved into the side of a chalk hill, usually dating to the Neolithic, Bronze, or Iron Ages, such as that at Uffington, Berkshire **2** (*usually plural*) a wave with a white broken crest

Whitehorse ('waɪt,hɔːs) *n* a town in NW Canada: capital of the Yukon Territory. Pop: 16 843 (2001)

white-hot *adj* **1** at such a high temperature that white light is emitted **2** *informal* in a state of intense emotion

White House *n* **the 1** the official Washington

residence of the president of the US **2** the US presidency

white knight *n* a champion or rescuer, esp a person or organization that rescues a company from financial difficulties, an unwelcome takeover bid, etc

white-knuckle *adj* causing or experiencing fear or anxiety: *a white-knuckle ride*

white lady *n* **1** a cocktail consisting of gin, Cointreau, and lemon juice **2** *Austral informal* methylated spirits as a drink, sometimes mixed with shoe polish or other additives

white lead (lɛd) *n* **1** *Also called:* **ceruse** a white solid usually regarded as a mixture of lead carbonate and lead hydroxide; basic lead carbonate: used in paint and in making putty and ointments for the treatment of burns. Formula: $2PbCO_3.Pb(OH)_2$ **2** either of two similar white pigments based on lead sulphate or lead silicate **3** a type of putty made by mixing white lead with boiled linseed oil

white lead ore (lɛd) *n* another name for **cerussite**

white leather *n* leather that has been treated with a chemical, such as alum or salt, to make it white. *Also called:* **whitleather** ('wɪtlɛðə)

white leg *n* another name for **milk leg**

white lias *n* a type of rock composed of pale-coloured limestones and marls. See also **Lias**

white lie *n* a minor or unimportant lie, esp one uttered in the interests of tact or politeness

white light *n* light that contains all the wavelengths of visible light at approximately equal intensities, as in sunlight or the light from white-hot solids

white line *n* **1** a line or strip of white in the centre of a road to separate traffic going in different directions **2** a white lamination in the hoof of a horse

white list *n* **1** a list of countries considered to pose an insignificant threat to human rights, from which applications for political asylum are presumed to be unfounded **2** *computing* **a** a list of websites considered to have inoffensive and acceptable content **b** a list of e-mail addresses from which a computer will accept mail

white-livered *adj* **1** lacking in spirit or courage **2** pallid and unhealthy in appearance

White man's burden *n* the supposed duty of the White race to bring education and Western culture to the non-White inhabitants of their colonies

white matter *n* the whitish tissue of the brain and spinal cord, consisting mainly of myelinated nerve fibres. Technical name: **substantia alba** Compare **grey matter**

white meat *n* any meat that is light in colour, such as veal or the breast of turkey. Compare **red meat**

white metal *n* any of various alloys, such as Babbitt metal, used for bearings. *Also called:* **antifriction metal**

white meter *n Brit obsolete* an electricity meter used to record the consumption of off-peak electricity

White Mountains *pl n* **1** a mountain range in the US, chiefly in N New Hampshire: part of the Appalachians. Highest peak: Mount Washington, 1917 m (6288 ft) **2** a mountain range in the US, in E California and SW Nevada. Highest peak: White Mountain, 4342 m (14 246 ft)

white mustard *n* a Eurasian plant, *Brassica hirta* (or *Sinapis alba*), having clusters of yellow flowers and pungent seeds from which the condiment mustard is made: family *Brassicaceae* (crucifers)

whiten ('waɪtən) *vb* to make or become white or whiter; bleach ▷ **whitening** *n*

whitener ('waɪtənə) *n* **1** a substance that makes something white or whiter **2** a powdered substitute for milk or cream, used in coffee or tea

White Nile *n* See **Nile**

white noise *n* **a** sound or electrical noise that

has a relatively wide continuous range of frequencies of uniform intensity **b** noise containing all frequencies rising in level by six decibels every octave

white oak *n* **1** a large oak tree, *Quercus alba,* of E North America, having pale bark, leaves with rounded lobes, and heavy light-coloured wood **2** any of several other oaks, such as the roble

white out *vb* (*adverb*) **1** (*intr*) to lose or lack daylight visibility owing to snow or fog **2** (*tr*) to create or leave white spaces in (printed or other matter) **3** (*tr*) to delete (typewritten words or characters) with a white correcting fluid ▷ *n* **whiteout 4** an atmospheric condition consisting of loss of visibility and sense of distance and direction due to a uniform whiteness of a heavy cloud cover and snow-covered ground, which reflects almost all the light it receives

white paper *n* (*often capitals*) an official government report in any of a number of countries, including Britain, Australia, New Zealand, and Canada, which sets out the government's policy on a matter that is or will come before Parliament

white pepper *n* a condiment, less pungent than black pepper, made from the husked dried beans of the pepper plant *Piper nigrum,* used either whole or ground

white pine *n* **1** a North American coniferous tree, *Pinus strobus,* having blue-green needle-like leaves, hanging brown cones, and rough bark: family *Pinaceae* **2** the light-coloured wood of this tree, much used commercially **3** another name for **kahikatea**

white plague *n informal* tuberculosis of the lungs

white poplar *n* **1** *Also called:* **abele** a Eurasian salicaceous tree, *Populus alba,* having leaves covered with dense silvery-white hairs **2** another name for **tulipwood** (sense 1)

white potato *n* another name for **potato** (sense 1)

white propaganda *n* propaganda that comes from the source it claims to come from. Compare **black propaganda, grey propaganda**

white pudding *n* (in Britain) a kind of sausage made like black pudding but without pigs' blood

white rainbow *n* another name for **fogbow**

white rat *n* a white variety of the brown rat (*Rattus norvegicus*), used extensively in scientific research

white rose *n English history* a widely used emblem or badge of the House of York. See also **Wars of the Roses, red rose**

White Russia *n* another name for **Belarus**

White Russian *adj, n* another term for **Belarussian**

whites (waɪts) *pl n* **1** household linen or cotton goods, such as sheets **2** white or off-white clothing, such as that worn for playing cricket **3** an informal name for **leucorrhoea**

white sale *n* a sale of household linens at reduced prices

white sapphire *n* a white pure variety of corundum, used as a gemstone

white sauce *n* a thick sauce made from flour, butter, seasonings, and milk or stock

White Sea *n* an almost landlocked inlet of the Barents Sea on the coast of NW Russia. Area: 90 000 sq km (34 700 sq miles)

white settler *n* a well-off incomer to a district who takes advantage of what it has to offer without regard to the local inhabitants [c20 from earlier colonial sense]

white slave *n* a girl or woman forced or sold into prostitution ▷ **white slavery** *n*

white-slaver *n* a person who procures or forces women to become prostitutes

whitesmith ('waɪt,smɪθ) *n* a person who finishes and polishes metals, particularly tin plate and galvanized iron

white spirit *n* a colourless liquid obtained from petroleum and used as a substitute for turpentine

W

white spruce *n* a N North American spruce tree, *Picea glauca*, having grey bark, pale brown oblong cones, and bluish-green needle-like leaves

white squall *n* a violent highly localized weather disturbance at sea, in which the surface of the water is whipped to a white spray by the winds

white stick *n* a walking stick used by a blind person for feeling the way: painted white as a sign to others that the person is blind

White supremacy *n* the theory or belief that White people are innately superior to people of other races > White supremacist *n, adj*

white-tailed deer *n* a deer, *Odocoileus virginianus*, of North America and N South America: the coat varies in colour, being typically reddish-brown in the summer, and the tail is white. Also called: Virginia deer

whitethorn ('waɪtˌθɔːn) *n* another name for hawthorn

whitethroat ('waɪtˌθrəʊt) *n* either of two Old World warblers, *Sylvia communis* or *S. curruca* (**lesser whitethroat**), having a greyish-brown plumage with a white throat and underparts

white tie *n* **1** a white bow tie worn as part of a man's formal evening dress **2 a** formal evening dress for men **b** (*as modifier*): *a white-tie occasion*

white toast *n* Canadian toasted white bread

white tea tree *n* another name for kanuka

white trash *n disparaging* **a** poor White people living in the US, esp the South **b** (*as modifier*): *white-trash culture*

White Van Man *n informal, derogatory* a male van driver, often of a white van, whose driving is selfish and aggressive

white vitriol *n* another name for zinc sulphate

White Volta *n* a river in W Africa, rising in N Burkina-Faso flowing southwest and south to join the Black Volta in central Ghana and form the Volta River. Length: about 885 km (550 miles)

whitewall ('waɪtˌwɔːl) *n* a pneumatic tyre having white sidewalls

white walnut *n* another name for butternut (senses 1–4)

whitewash ('waɪtˌwɒʃ) *n* **1** a substance used for whitening walls and other surfaces, consisting of a suspension of lime or whiting in water, often with other substances, such as size, added **2** *informal* deceptive or specious words or actions intended to conceal defects, gloss over failings, etc **3** *informal* a defeat in a sporting contest in which the loser is beaten in every match, game, etc in a series: *they face the prospect of a whitewash in the five-test series* ▷ *vb* (*tr*) **4** to cover or whiten with whitewash **5** *informal* to conceal, gloss over, or suppress **6** *informal* to defeat (an opponent or opposing team) by winning every match in a series > 'white,washer *n*

white water *n* **1** a stretch of water with a broken foamy surface, as in rapids **2** light-coloured sea water, esp over shoals or shallows

whitewater rafting *n* the sport of rafting down fast-flowing rivers, esp over rapids

white whale *n* a small white toothed whale, *Delphinapterus leucas*, of northern waters: family Monodontidae. Also called: beluga

whitewood ('waɪtˌwʊd) *n* **1** any of various trees with light-coloured wood, such as the tulip tree, basswood, and cottonwood **2** the wood of any of these trees **3** Also: whitewood another name for mahoe

whitey *or* **whity** ('waɪtɪ) *n chiefly US* (used contemptuously by Black people) a White man

whither ('wɪðə) *archaic or poetic* ▷ *adv* **1** to what place? **2** to what end or purpose? ▷ *conj* **3** to whatever place, purpose, etc [Old English *hwider, hwæder*; related to Gothic *hvadrē*; modern English form influenced by HITHER]

whithersoever (ˌwɪðəsəʊˈevə) *adv, conj archaic or poetic* to whichever place

whitherward ('wɪðəwəd) *adv archaic or poetic* in which direction

whiting¹ ('waɪtɪŋ) *n* **1** an important gadoid food fish, *Merlangius* (or *Gadus*) *merlangus*, of European seas, having a dark back with silvery sides and underparts **2** any of various similar fishes, such as *Merluccius bilinearis*, a hake of American Atlantic waters, and any of several Atlantic sciaenid fishes of the genus *Menticirrhus* **3** *Austral* any of several marine food fishes of the genus *Sillago* **4** whiting pout another name for bib (the fish) [C15 perhaps from Old English *hwītling*; related to Middle Dutch *wijting*. See WHITE, -ING³]

whiting² ('waɪtɪŋ) *n* white chalk that has been ground and washed, used in making whitewash, metal polish, etc. Also called: whitening

Whitley Bay ('wɪtlɪ) *n* a resort in NE England, in North Tyneside unitary authority, Tyne and Wear, on the North Sea. Pop: 36 544 (2001)

Whitley Council *n* any of a number of organizations made up of representatives of employees and employers for joint consultation on and settlement of industrial relations and conditions for a particular industry or service [C20 named after J. H. *Whitley* (1866–1935), chairman of the committee that recommended setting up such councils (1917)]

whitlow ('wɪtləʊ) *n* any pussy inflammation of the end of a finger or toe [C14 changed from *whitflaw*, from WHITE + FLAW¹]

whitlow grass *n* any of various plants of the genera *Draba* and *Erophila*, once thought to cure whitlows: family *Brassicaceae* (crucifers)

Whit Monday *n* the Monday following Whit Sunday

Whitney ('wɪtnɪ) *n* **Mount** a mountain in E California: the highest peak in the Sierra Nevada Mountains and in continental US (excluding Alaska). Height: 4418 m (14 495 ft)

Whitsun ('wɪtsᵊn) *n* **1** short for Whitsuntide ▷ *adj* **2** of or relating to Whit Sunday or Whitsuntide

Whitsunday (ˌhwɪtˈsʌndɪ, ˌwɪt-) *n* (in Scotland) May 15, one of the four quarter days

Whit Sunday *n* the seventh Sunday after Easter, observed as a feast in commemoration of the descent of the Holy Spirit on the apostles 50 days after Easter. Also called: Pentecost [Old English *hwīta sunnandæg* white Sunday, probably named after the ancient custom of wearing white robes at or after baptism]

Whitsuntide ('wɪtsᵊnˌtaɪd) *n* the week that begins with Whit Sunday, esp the first three days

whitter ('wɪtə) *vb, n* a variant spelling of witter

whittle ('wɪtᵊl) *vb* **1** to cut or shave strips or pieces from (wood, a stick, etc), esp with a knife **2** (*tr*) to make or shape by paring or shaving **3** (*tr; often foll by away, down, off*, etc) to reduce, destroy, or wear away gradually **4** *Northern English dialect* (*intr*) to complain or worry about something continually ▷ *n* **5** *Brit dialect* a knife, esp a large one [C16 variant of C15 *thwittle* large knife, from Old English *thwitel*, from *thwītan* to cut; related to Old Norse *thveitir* cut, *thveita* to beat] > 'whittler *n*

whittlings ('wɪtlɪŋz) *pl n* chips or shavings whittled off from an object

whittret ('wɪtrət) *or* **whitrick** ('wɪtrɪk) *n dialect* a male weasel [Old English *whytrate, whittratt*; perhaps from *hwīt* WHITE + *rætt* RAT]

Whitworth screw thread ('wɪtwəθ) *n* a thread form and system of standard sizes, proposed by Whitworth in 1841 and adopted as standard in the U.K., having a flank angle of 55° and a rounded top and foot [named after Sir Joseph *Whitworth* (1803–87), English engineer]

whity ('waɪtɪ) *n, pl* whities **1** *informal* a variant spelling of whitey ▷ *adj* **2 a** whitish in colour **b** (*in combination*): *whity-brown*

whizz *or* **whiz** (wɪz) *vb* whizzes, whizzing, whizzed **1** to make or cause to make a loud humming or buzzing sound **2** to move or cause to move with such a sound **3** (*intr*) *informal* to move or go rapidly ▷ *n* **4** a loud humming or buzzing sound **5** *informal* a person who is extremely skilful at some activity **6** a slang word for amphetamine **7** take a whizz *US informal* to

urinate [C16 of imitative origin]

whizz-bang *or* **whiz-bang** *n* **1** a small-calibre World War I shell that, when discharged, travelled at such a high velocity that the sound of its flight was heard only an instant, if at all, before the sound of its explosion ▷ *adj* **2** *informal* excellent or first-rate

whizz kid, whiz kid *or* **wiz kid** *n informal* a person who is outstandingly successful for his or her age [C20 from WHIZZ, perhaps influenced by WIZARD]

whizzy ('wɪzɪ) *adj* -zier, -ziest *informal* using sophisticated technology to produce vivid effects: *a whizzy new computer game*

who (huː) *pron* **1** which person? what person? used in direct and indirect questions: *he can't remember who did it; who met you?* **2** used to introduce relative clauses with antecedents referring to human beings: *the people who lived here have left* **3** the one or ones who; whoever: *bring who you want* [Old English *hwā*; related to Old Saxon *hwē*, Old High German *hwer*, Gothic *hvas*, Lithuanian *kàs*, Danish *hvo*]

USAGE See at whom

WHO *abbreviation for* World Health Organization

whoa (wəʊ) *interj* a command used esp to horses to stop or slow down [C19 variant of HO¹]

who'd *contraction of* who had *or* who would

who-does-what *adj* (of a dispute, strike, etc) relating to the separation of kinds of work performed by different trade unions

whodunnit *or* **whodunit** (huːˈdʌnɪt) *n informal* a novel, play, etc, concerned with a crime, usually murder

whoever (huːˈevə) *pron* **1** any person who; anyone that: *whoever wants it can have it* **2** no matter who: *I'll come round tomorrow, whoever may be here* **3** an intensive form of *who*, used in questions: *whoever could have thought that?* **4** *informal* an unknown or unspecified person: *give those to John, or Cathy, or whoever*

whole (həʊl) *adj* **1** containing all the component parts necessary to form a total; complete: *a whole apple* **2** constituting the full quantity, extent, etc **3** uninjured or undamaged **4** healthy **5** having no fractional or decimal part; integral: *a whole number* **6** of, relating to, or designating a relationship established by descent from the same parents; full: *whole brothers* **7** out of whole cloth *US and Canadian informal* entirely without a factual basis ▷ *adv* **8** in an undivided or unbroken piece: *to swallow a plum whole* ▷ *n* **9** all the parts, elements, etc, of a thing **10** an assemblage of parts viewed together as a unit **11** a thing complete in itself **12** as a whole considered altogether; completely **13** on the whole **a** taking all things into consideration **b** in general [Old English *hāl, hēl*; related to Old Frisian *hāl, hēl*, Old High German *heil*, Gothic *hails*; compare HALE¹] > 'wholeness *n*

whole blood *n* blood obtained from a donor for transfusion from which none of the elements has been removed

wholefood ('həʊlˌfuːd) *n* (*sometimes plural*) **a** food that has been refined or processed as little as possible and is eaten in its natural state, such as brown rice, wholemeal flour, etc **b** (*as modifier*): *a wholefood restaurant*

whole gale *n* a wind of force ten on the Beaufort scale

wholehearted (ˌhəʊlˈhɑːtɪd) *adj* done, acted, given, etc, with total sincerity, enthusiasm, or commitment > ˌwhole'heartedly *adv* > ˌwhole'heartedness *n*

whole hog *n slang* the whole or total extent (esp in the phrase go the whole hog)

wholemeal ('həʊlˌmiːl) *adj Brit* (of flour, bread, etc) made from the entire wheat kernel. US and Canadian term: whole-wheat

whole milk *n* milk from which no constituent has been removed. Compare skimmed milk

whole note *n US and Canadian* a note, now the

longest in common use, having a time value that may be divided by any power of 2 to give all other notes. Also called (in Britain and certain other countries): **semibreve**

whole number *n* **1** an integer **2** a natural number

wholesale ('həʊl‚seɪl) *n* **1** the business of selling goods to retailers in larger quantities than they are sold to final consumers but in smaller quantities than they are purchased from manufacturers. Compare **retail** (sense 1) **2** at wholesale **a** in large quantities **b** at wholesale prices ▷ *adj* **3** of, relating to, or engaged in such business **4** made, done, etc, on a large scale or without discrimination ▷ *adv* **5** on a large scale or without discrimination ▷ *vb* **6** to sell (goods) at wholesale > 'whole‚saler *n*

wholesale price index *n* an indicator of price changes in the wholesale market

wholesome ('həʊlsəm) *adj* **1** conducive to health or physical wellbeing **2** conducive to moral wellbeing **3** characteristic or suggestive of health or wellbeing, esp in appearance [C12 from WHOLE (healthy) + -SOME[1]; related to German *heilsam* healing] > 'wholesomely *adv* > 'wholesomeness *n*

whole tone *or US and Canadian* **whole step** *n* an interval of two semitones; a frequency difference of 200 cents in the system of equal temperament. Often shortened to: **tone**

whole-tone scale *n* either of two scales produced by commencing on one of any two notes a chromatic semitone apart and proceeding upwards or downwards in whole tones for an octave. Such a scale, consisting of six degrees to the octave, is used by Debussy and subsequent composers

whole-wheat *adj* (of flour, bread, etc) made from the entire wheat kernel. Also called (esp in Britain and certain other countries): **wholemeal**

who'll (huːl) *contraction of* who will *or* who shall

wholly ('həʊllɪ) *adv* **1** completely, totally, or entirely **2** without exception; exclusively

whom (huːm) *pron* the objective form of *who*, used when *who* is not the subject of its own clause: *whom did you say you had seen?; he can't remember whom he saw* [Old English *hwām*, dative of *hwā* WHO]

USAGE It was formerly considered correct to use *whom* whenever the objective form of *who* was required. This is no longer thought to be necessary and the objective form *who* is now commonly used, even in formal writing: *there were several people there who he had met before.* Who cannot be used directly after a preposition – the preposition is usually displaced, as in *the man (who) he sold his car to.* In formal writing *whom* is preferred in sentences like these: *the man to whom he sold his car.* There are some types of sentence in which *who* cannot be used: *the refugees, many of whom were old and ill, were allowed across the border*

whomever (huːm'ɛvə) *pron* the objective form of *whoever*: *I'll hire whomever I can find*

whomsoever (‚huːmsəʊ'ɛvə) *pron archaic or formal* the objective form of *whosoever*: *to whomsoever it may concern*

whoop (wuːp) *vb* **1** to utter (speech) with loud cries, as of enthusiasm or excitement **2** *med* to cough convulsively with a crowing sound made at each inspiration **3** (of certain birds) to utter (a hooting cry) **4** (*tr*) to urge on or call with or as if with whoops **5** (wʊp, wuːp) **whoop it up** *informal* **a** to indulge in a noisy celebration **b** *US* to arouse enthusiasm ▷ *n* **6** a loud cry, esp one expressing enthusiasm or excitement **7** *med* the convulsive crowing sound made during a paroxysm of whooping cough **8** not worth a whoop *informal* worthless ▷ See also **whoops** [C14 of imitative origin]

whoopee *informal* ▷ *interj* (wʊ'piː) **1** an

exclamation of joy, excitement, etc ▷ *n* ('wʊpiː) **2** make whoopee **a** to engage in noisy merrymaking **b** to make love

whoopee cushion *n* a joke cushion that emits a sound like the breaking of wind when someone sits on it

whooper *or* **whooper swan** ('wuːpə) *n* a large white Old World swan, *Cygnus cygnus*, having a black bill with a yellow base and a noisy whooping cry

whooping cough ('huːpɪŋ) *n* an acute infectious disease characterized by coughing spasms that end with a shrill crowing sound on inspiration: caused by infection with the bacillus *Bordetella pertussis*. Technical name: **pertussis**

whooping crane *n* a rare North American crane, *Grus americana*, having a white plumage with black wings and a red naked face

whoops (wʊps) *interj* an exclamation of surprise, as when a person falls over, or of apology

whoopsie ('wʊpsɪ) *n informal* **1** a piece of excrement, esp one left by a pet **2** an embarrassing mistake [C20 from WHOOPS]

whoosh *or* **woosh** (wuːʃ) *n* **1** a hissing or rushing sound **2** a rush of emotion: *a whoosh of happiness* ▷ *vb* **3** (*intr*) to make or move with a hissing or rushing sound

whop, wop *or less commonly* **whap** (wɒp) *informal* ▷ *vb* **whops, whopping, whopped 1** (*tr*) to strike, beat, or thrash **2** (*tr*) to defeat utterly **3** (*intr*) to drop or fall ▷ *n* **4** a heavy blow or the sound made by such a blow [C14 variant of *wap*, perhaps of imitative origin]

whopper ('wɒpə) *n informal* **1** anything uncommonly large of its kind **2** a big lie [C18 from WHOP]

whopping ('wɒpɪŋ) *adj informal* uncommonly large

whore (hɔː) *n* **1** a prostitute or promiscuous woman: often a term of abuse ▷ *vb* (*intr*) **2** to be or act as a prostitute **3** (of a man) to have promiscuous sexual relations, esp with prostitutes **4** (often foll by *after*) to seek that which is immoral, idolatrous, etc [Old English *hōre*; related to Old Norse *hōra*, Old High German *hvora*, Latin *carus* dear] > **whorish** *adj* > **whorishly** *adv* > **whorishness** *n*

whoredom ('hɔːdəm) *n* **1** the activity of whoring or state of being a whore **2** a biblical word for **idolatry**

whorehouse ('hɔː‚haʊs) *n* another word for **brothel**

whoremaster ('hɔː‚mɑːstə) *n archaic* a person who consorts with or procures whores > 'whore‚mastery *n*

whoremonger ('hɔː‚mʌŋgə) *n* a person who consorts with whores; lecher > 'whore‚mongery *n*

whoreson ('hɔːsən) *archaic* ▷ *n* **1** a bastard **2** a scoundrel; wretch ▷ *adj* **3** vile or hateful

whorl (wɜːl) *n* **1** *botany* a radial arrangement of three or more petals, stamens, leaves, etc, around a stem **2** *zoology* a single turn in a spiral shell **3** one of the basic patterns of the human fingerprint, formed by several complete circular ridges one inside another. Compare **arch**[1] (sense 4b), **loop**[1] (sense 10a) **4** anything shaped like a coil [C15 probably variant of *wherville* WHIRL, influenced by Dutch *worvel*] > **whorled** *adj*

whortleberry ('wɜːt[ə]l‚berɪ) *n, pl* -ries **1** Also called **huckleberry** and (dialect) **hurt, whort** a small Eurasian ericaceous shrub, *Vaccinium myrtillus*, greenish-pink flowers and edible sweet blackish berries **2** the fruit of this shrub **3** bog whortleberry a related plant, *V. uliginosum*, of mountain regions, having pink flowers and black fruits [C16 southwestern English dialect form of *hurtleberry*; of unknown origin]

who's (huːz) *contraction of* who is

whose (huːz) *determiner* **1 a** of whom? belonging to whom? used in direct and indirect questions: *I told him whose fault it was; whose car is this?* **b** (*as pronoun*): *whose is that?* **2** of whom; belonging to

whom; of which; belonging to which: used as a relative pronoun: *a house whose windows are broken* [Old English *hwæs*, genitive of *hwā* WHO and *hwæt* WHAT]

whoso ('huːsəʊ) *pron* an archaic word for **whoever**

whosoever (‚huːsəʊ'ɛvə) *pron* an archaic or formal word for **whoever**

who's who *n* a book or list containing the names and short biographies of famous people

WH question *n* a question in English to which an appropriate answer is to give information rather than to answer "yes" or "no": typically introduced by the word *who*, *which*, *what*, *where*, *when*, or *how*. Also called: **information question**

Whr *abbreviation for* watt-hour

whsle *abbreviation for* wholesale

whump (wʌmp) *n informal* a dull thud [C19 of imitative origin]

whup (wʌp, wʊp) *vb* whups, whupping, whupped (*tr*) *chiefly US informal* to defeat totally; overwhelm [C19 variant of WHIP]

why (waɪ) *adv* **1 a** for what reason, purpose, or cause?: *why are you here?* **b** (*used in indirect questions*): *tell me why you're here* ▷ *pron* **2** for or because of which: *there is no reason why he shouldn't come* ▷ *n, pl* **whys 3** (*usually plural*) the reason, purpose, or cause of something (esp in the phrase **the whys and wherefores**) ▷ *interj* **4** an introductory expression of surprise, disagreement, indignation, etc: *why, don't be silly!* [Old English *hwī*; related to Old Norse *hvī*, Gothic *hveileiks* what kind of, Latin *quī*]

Whyalla (waɪ'ælə) *n* a port in S South Australia, on Spencer Gulf: iron and steel and shipbuilding industries. Pop: 21 271 (2001)

whydah *or* **whidah** ('wɪdə) *n* any of various predominantly black African weaverbirds of the genus *Vidua* and related genera, the males of which grow very long tail feathers in the breeding season. Also called: **whydah bird, whidah bird, widow bird** [C18 after the name of a town in Benin]

whydunnit *or* **whydunit** ('waɪ‚dʌnɪt) *n informal* a novel, film, etc, concerned with the motives of the criminal rather than his or her identity

WI *abbreviation for* **1** West Indian **2** West Indies **3** Wisconsin **4** (in Britain) **Women's Institute**

wibble ('wɪb[ə]l) *vb* (*intr*) *informal* **1** to wobble **2** (often foll by *on*) to speak or write in a vague or wordy manner [C19 from *wibble-wobble*, reduplication of WOBBLE]

Wicca ('wɪkə) *n* (*sometimes not capital*) the cult or practice of witchcraft [C20 revival of Old English *wicca* witch] > 'Wiccan *n, adj*

Wichita ('wɪtʃɪ‚tɔː) *n* a city in S Kansas, on the Arkansas River: the largest city in the state; two universities. Pop: 354 617 (2003 est)

wick[1] (wɪk) *n* **1** a cord or band of loosely twisted or woven fibres, as in a candle, cigarette lighter, etc, that supplies fuel to a flame by capillary action **2** get on (someone's) wick *Brit slang* to cause irritation to (a person) [Old English *weoce*; related to Old High German *wioh*, Middle Dutch *wēke* (Dutch *wiek*)] > 'wicking *n*

wick[2] (wɪk) *n archaic* a village or hamlet [Old English *wīc*; related to *-wich* in place names, Latin *vīcus*, Greek *oîkos*]

wick[3] (wɪk) *adj Northern English dialect* **1** lively or active **2** alive or crawling: *a dog wick with fleas* [dialect variant of QUICK alive]

Wick (wɪk) *n* a town in N Scotland, in Highland, at the head of **Wick Bay** (an inlet of the North Sea). Pop: 7333 (2001)

wicked ('wɪkɪd) *adj* **1 a** morally bad in principle or practice **b** (*as collective noun; preceded by the*): *the wicked* **2** mischievous or roguish, esp in a playful way: *a wicked grin* **3** causing injury or harm **4** troublesome, unpleasant, or offensive **5** *slang* very good [C13 from dialect *wick*, from Old English *wicca* sorcerer, *wicce* WITCH[1]] > 'wickedly *adv* > 'wickedness *n*

wicker ('wɪkə) *n* **1** a slender flexible twig or shoot,

W

esp of willow **2** short for **wickerwork** ▷ *adj* **3** made, consisting of, or constructed from wicker [c14 from Scandinavian; compare Swedish *viker,* Danish *viger* willow, Swedish *vika* to bend]

wickerwork ('wɪkə,wɜːk) *n* **a** a material consisting of wicker **b** (*as modifier*): *a wickerwork chair*

wicket ('wɪkɪt) *n* **1** a small door or gate, esp one that is near to or part of a larger one **2** *US* a small window or opening in a door, esp one fitted with a grating or glass pane, used as a means of communication in a ticket office, bank, etc **3** a small sluicegate, esp one in a canal lock gate or by a water wheel **4** *US* a croquet hoop **5** a *cricket* either of two constructions, placed 22 yards apart, consisting of three pointed stumps stuck parallel in the ground with two wooden bails resting on top, at which the batsman stands **b** the strip of ground between these **c** a batsman's turn at batting or the period during which two batsmen bat: *a third-wicket partnership* **d** the act or instance of a batsman being got out: *the bowler took six wickets* **6 keep wicket** to act as a wicketkeeper **7 on a good, sticky, etc, wicket** *informal* in an advantageous, awkward, etc, situation [c18 from Old Northern French *wiket;* related to Old Norse *vikja* to move]

wicketkeeper ('wɪkɪt,kiːpə) *n cricket* the player on the fielding side positioned directly behind the wicket

wicket maiden *n cricket* an over in which no runs are scored with the bat and at least one wicket is taken by the bowler. See also **maiden over**

wickiup, wikiup *or* **wickyup** ('wɪki,ʌp) *n US and Canadian* a crude shelter made of brushwood, mats, or grass and having an oval frame, esp of a kind used by nomadic Indians now in Oklahoma and neighbouring states of the US [c19 from Sac, Fox, and Kickapoo *wikiyap;* compare WIGWAM]

Wicklow ('wɪkləʊ) *n* **1** a county of E Republic of Ireland, in Leinster province on the Irish Sea: consists of a coastal strip rising inland to the **Wicklow Mountains**; mainly agricultural, with several resorts. County town: Wicklow. Pop: 114 676 (2002). Area: 2025 sq km (782 sq miles) **2** a port in E Republic of Ireland, county town of Co Wicklow. Pop: 9355 (2002)

wickthing ('wɪk,θɪŋ) *n Lancashire dialect* a creeping animal, such as a woodlouse [from WICK³ + THING¹]

wicopy ('wɪkəpɪ) *n, pl* -pies *US* any of various North American trees, shrubs, or herbaceous plants, esp the leatherwood, various willowherbs, and the basswood [c18 from Cree *wikupiy* inner bark, willow bark]

widdershins ('wɪdə,ʃɪnz; *Scot* 'wɪdər-) *adv chiefly Scot* a variant spelling of **withershins**

widdle ('wɪdᵊl) *Brit informal* ▷ *vb* **1** (*intr*) to urinate ▷ *n* **2** urine **3** an act or instance of urinating [c20 from PIDDLE]

wide (waɪd) *adj* **1** having a great extent from side to side **2** of vast size or scope; spacious or extensive **3 a** (*postpositive*) having a specified extent, esp from side to side: *two yards wide* **b** (*in combination*) covering or extending throughout: *nationwide* **4** distant or remote from the desired point, mark, etc: *your guess is wide of the mark* **5** (of eyes) opened fully **6** loose, full, or roomy: *wide trousers* **7** exhibiting a considerable spread, as between certain limits: *a wide variation* **8** *phonetics* another word for **lax** (sense 4) *or* **open** (sense 34) ▷ *adv* **9** over an extensive area: *to travel far and wide* **10** to the full extent: *he opened the door wide* **11** far from the desired point, mark, etc ▷ *n* **12** (in cricket) a bowled ball that is outside the batsman's reach and scores a run for the batting side **13** *archaic or poetic* a wide space or extent **14 to the wide** completely [Old English *wīd;* related to Old Norse *vīthr,* Old High German *wīt*] > 'widely *adv* > 'wideness *n* > 'widish *adj*

wide-angle lens *n* a lens system on a camera that can cover an angle of view of 60° or more and

therefore has a fairly small focal length. See also **fisheye lens**

wide area network *n computing* a network of computers interconnected over large distances, often by optical fibres or microwave communications. Abbreviation: **WAN**

wide-awake *adj* (**wide awake** *when postpositive*) **1** fully awake **2** keen, alert, or observant ▷ *n* **3** Also called: **wide-awake hat** a hat with a low crown and very wide brim > 'wide-a'wakeness *n*

wide-body *adj* (of an aircraft) having a wide fuselage, esp wide enough to contain three rows of seats abreast

wide boy *n Brit slang* a man who is prepared to use unscrupulous methods to progress or make money

wide-eyed *adj* innocent or credulous

widen ('waɪdᵊn) *vb* to make or become wide or wider > 'widener *n*

wide-open *adj* (**wide open** *when postpositive*) **1** open to the full extent **2** (*postpositive*) exposed to attack; vulnerable **3** uncertain as to outcome **4** *US informal* (of a town or city) lax in the enforcement of certain laws, esp those relating to the sale and consumption of alcohol, gambling, the control of vice, etc

wide receiver *n American football* a player whose function is to catch long passes from the quarterback

widescreen ('waɪd,skriːn) *adj* of or relating to a form of film projection or television broadcasting in which the screen has much greater width than height

widespread ('waɪd,sprɛd) *adj* **1** extending over a wide area **2** accepted by or occurring among many people

widgeon ('wɪdʒən) *n* a variant spelling of **wigeon**

widget ('wɪdʒɪt) *n* **1** *informal* any small mechanism or device, the name of which is unknown or temporarily forgotten **2** a small device in a beer can which, when the can is opened, releases nitrogen gas into the beer, giving it a head [c20 changed from GADGET]

widgie ('wɪdʒɪ) *n Austral slang* a female larrikin or bodgie [c20 alteration of BODGIE]

Widnes ('wɪdnɪs) *n* a town in NW England, in Halton unitary authority, N Cheshire, on the River Mersey: chemical industry. Pop: 55 686 (2001)

widow ('wɪdəʊ) *n* **1** a woman who has survived her husband, esp one who has not remarried **2** (*usually with a modifier*) *informal* a woman whose husband frequently leaves her alone while he indulges in a sport, etc: *a golf widow* **3** *printing* a short line at the end of a paragraph, esp one that occurs as the top line of a page or column. Compare **orphan** (sense 3) **4** (in some card games) an additional hand or set of cards exposed on the table ▷ *vb* (*tr; usually passive*) **5** to cause to become a widow **6** to deprive of something valued or desirable [Old English *widuwe;* related to German *Witwe,* Latin *vidua* (feminine of *viduus* deprived), Sanskrit *vidhavā*] > 'widowhood *n*

widow bird *n* another name for **whydah**

widower ('wɪdəʊə) *n* a man whose wife has died and who has not remarried

widow's benefit *n* (in the British National Insurance scheme) a former weekly payment made to a widow

widow's cruse *n* an endless or unfailing source of supply [allusion to I Kings 17:16]

widow's mite *n* a small contribution given by a person who has very little [allusion to Mark 12:43]

widow's peak *n* a V-shaped point in the hairline in the middle of the forehead [from the belief that it presaged early widowhood]

widow woman *n archaic or dialect* another term for **widow** (sense 1)

width (wɪdθ) *n* **1** the linear extent or measurement of something from side to side, usually being the shortest dimension or (for something fixed) the shortest horizontal

dimension **2** the state or fact of being wide **3** a piece or section of something at its full extent from side to side: *a width of cloth* **4** the distance across a rectangular swimming bath, as opposed to its length [c17 from WIDE + -TH¹, analogous to BREADTH]

widthwise ('wɪdθ,waɪz) *or* **widthways** ('wɪdθ,weɪz) *adv* in the direction of the width; from side to side

Wieland ('viːlant) *n* the German name for **Wayland**

wield (wiːld) *vb* (*tr*) **1** to handle or use (a weapon, tool, etc) **2** to exert or maintain (power or authority) **3** *obsolete* to rule [Old English *wieldan, wealdan;* related to Old Norse *valda,* Old Saxon *waldan,* German *walten,* Latin *valēre* to be strong] > 'wieldable *adj* > 'wielder *n*

wieldy ('wiːldɪ) *adj* **wieldier, wieldiest** easily handled, used, or managed

Wien (viːn) *n* the German name for **Vienna**

wiener ('wiːnə) *or* **wienerwurst** ('wiːnə,wɜːst) *n US and Canadian* a kind of smoked beef or pork sausage, similar to a frankfurter. Also called: **wienie, weenie** ('wiːnɪ) [c20 shortened from German *Wiener Wurst* Viennese sausage]

Wiener Neustadt (German 'viːnər 'nɔyʃtat) *n* a city in E Austria, in Lower Austria. Pop: 37 627 (2002)

Wiener schnitzel ('viːnə 'ʃnɪtsəl) *n* a large thin escalope of veal, coated in egg and crumbs, fried, and traditionally served with a garnish [German: Viennese cutlet]

Wiesbaden (German 'viːsbaːdən) *n* a city in W Germany, capital of Hesse state: a spa resort since Roman times. Pop: 271 995 (2003 est). Latin name: Aquae Mattiacorum ('ækwiː ,mætjə'kəʊrəm)

wife (waɪf) *n, pl* **wives** (waɪvz) **1** a man's partner in marriage; a married woman. Related adj: **uxorial 2** an archaic or dialect word for **woman 3 take to wife** to marry (a woman) [Old English *wīf;* related to Old Norse *vīf* (perhaps from *vīfathr* veiled), Old High German *wīb* (German *Weib*)] > 'wifehood *n* > 'wifeless *adj* > 'wife,like *adj* > 'wifeliness *n* > 'wifely *adj*

wife-beater *n* a man who hits his wife > 'wife-,beating *n*

wife swapping *n* **a** the temporary exchange of wives between married couples for sexual relations **b** (*as modifier*): *a wife-swapping party*

wifey ('waɪfɪ) *n* an informal word for **wife**

Wi-Fi ('waɪ,faɪ) *n computing* a system of accessing the internet from remote machines such as laptop computers that have wireless connections [c20 from wi(reless) fi(delity)]

wig (wɪg) *n* **1** an artificial head of hair, either human or synthetic, worn to disguise baldness, as part of a theatrical or ceremonial dress, as a disguise, or for adornment ▷ *vb* **wigs, wigging, wigged** (*tr*) **2** *informal* to furnish with a wig **3** *Brit slang* to berate severely ▷ See also **wig out** [c17 shortened from PERIWIG] > 'wigged *adj* > 'wigless *adj* > 'wig,like *adj*

Wig. *abbreviation for* Wigtownshire

Wigan ('wɪɡən) *n* **1** an industrial town in NW England, in Wigan unitary authority, Greater Manchester: former coal-mining centre. Pop: 81 203 (2001) **2** a unitary authority in NW England, in Greater Manchester. Pop: 303 800 (2003 est). Area: 199 sq km (77 sq miles)

wigeon *or* **widgeon** ('wɪdʒən) *n* **1** a Eurasian duck, *Anas penelope,* of marshes, swamps, etc, the male of which has a reddish-brown head and chest and grey and white back and wings **2** American wigeon Also called: **baldpate** a similar bird, *Anas americana,* of North America, the male of which has a white crown [c16 of uncertain origin]

wigger *or* **wigga** ('wɪɡə) *n slang derogatory* a white youth who adopts black youth culture by adopting its speech, wearing its clothes, and listening to its music [c20 from a blend of WHITE + NIGGER]

wigging ('wɪɡɪŋ) *n* **1** *Brit slang* a rebuke or

reprimand **2** NZ the shearing of wool from the head of a sheep

wiggle ('wɪgᵊl) vb **1** to move or cause to move with jerky movements, esp from side to side ▷ n **2** the act or an instance of wiggling **3** get a wiggle on *slang, chiefly US* to hurry up [C13 from Middle Low German, Middle Dutch *wiggelen*] > 'wiggler n > 'wiggly adj

wiggle room n *informal* scope for freedom of action or thought

wight¹ (waɪt) n *archaic* a human being [Old English *wiht*; related to Old Frisian *āwet* something, Old Norse *vættr* being, Gothic *waihts* thing, German *Wicht* small person]

wight² (waɪt) adj *archaic* strong and brave; valiant [C13 from Old Norse *vigt*; related to Old English *wīg* battle, Latin *vincere* to conquer]

Wight (waɪt) n **Isle of** an island and county of S England in the English Channel. Administrative centre: Newport. Pop: 136 300 (2003 est). Area: 380 sq km (147 sq miles)

wig out vb wigs, wigging, wigged (*intr, adverb*) *informal* to become extremely excited [C20 from BIGWIG]

Wigtownshire ('wɪgtənˌʃɪə, -ʃə) n (until 1975) a county of SW Scotland, now part of Dumfries and Galloway

wigwag ('wɪgˌwæg) vb -wags, -wagging, -wagged **1** to move (something) back and forth **2** to communicate with (someone) by means of a flag semaphore ▷ n **3 a** a system of communication by flag semaphore **b** the message signalled [C16 from obsolete *wig*, probably short for WIGGLE + WAG¹] > 'wigˌwagger n

wigwam ('wɪgˌwæm) n **1** any dwelling of the North American Indians, esp one made of bark, rushes, or skins spread over or enclosed by a set of arched poles lashed together. Compare **tepee 2** a similar structure for children [from Abnaki and Massachuset *wīkwām*, literally: their abode]

wikiup ('wɪkiˌʌp) n a variant spelling of **wickiup**

wilco ('wɪlˌkəʊ) interj an expression in signalling, telecommunications, etc, indicating that a message just received will be complied with. Compare **roger** [C20 abbreviation for I *will comply*]

Wilcoxon test (wɪl'kɒksᵊn) n Also called: Wilcoxon matched-pairs signed-ranks test a statistical test for the relative size of the scores of the same or matched subjects under two experimental conditions by comparing the distributions for positive and negative differences of the ranks of their absolute values **b Wilcoxon Mann-Whitney test** See **Mann-Whitney test** [named after Frank *Wilcoxon* (1892–1965), Irish mathematician and statistician]

wild (waɪld) adj **1** (of animals) living independently of man; not domesticated or tame **2** (of plants) growing in a natural state; not cultivated **3** uninhabited or uncultivated; desolate: *a wild stretch of land* **4** living in a savage or uncivilized way: *wild tribes* **5** lacking restraint: *wild merriment* **6** of great violence or intensity: *a wild storm* **7** disorderly or chaotic: *wild thoughts; wild talk* **8** dishevelled; untidy: *wild hair* **9** in a state of extreme emotional intensity: *wild with anger* **10** reckless: *wild speculations* **11** not calculated; random: *a wild guess* **12** unconventional; fantastic; crazy: *wild friends* **13** (*postpositive; foll by about*) *informal* intensely enthusiastic or excited **14** (of a card, such as a joker or deuce in some games) able to be given any value the holder pleases: *jacks are wild* **15 wild and woolly a** rough; untamed; barbarous **b** (of theories, plans, etc) not fully thought out **16** in a wild manner **17 run wild a** to grow without cultivation or care **b** to behave without restraint ▷ n **18** (*often plural*) a desolate, uncultivated, or uninhabited region **19 the wild a** a free natural state of living **b** the wilderness [Old English *wilde*; related to Old Saxon, Old High German *wildi*, Old Norse *villr*, Gothic *wiltheis*] > 'wildish adj > 'wildly adv > 'wildness n

wild boar n a wild pig, *Sus scrofa*, of parts of Europe and central Asia, having a pale grey to black coat, thin legs, a narrow body, and prominent tusks

wild brier n another name for **wild rose**

wild card n **1** See **wild** (sense 14) **2** *sport* a player or team that has not qualified for a competition but is allowed to take part, at the organizers' discretion, after all the regular places have been taken **3** an unpredictable element in a situation **4** *computing* a symbol that can represent any character or group of characters, as in a filename

wild carrot n an umbelliferous plant, *Daucus carota*, of temperate regions, having clusters of white flowers and hooked fruits

wildcat ('waɪldˌkæt) n, pl -cats or -cat **1** a wild European cat, *Felis silvestris*, that resembles the domestic tabby but is larger and has a bushy tail **2** any of various other felines, esp of the genus *Lynx*, such as the lynx and the caracal **3** *US and Canadian* another name for **bobcat 4** *informal* a savage or aggressive person **5** an exploratory drilling for petroleum or natural gas **6** *US and Canadian* an unsound commercial enterprise **7** *US and Canadian* a railway locomotive in motion without drawing any carriages or wagons. Also called (in Britain and certain other countries): light engine **8** (*modifier*) *US and Canadian* **a** of or relating to an unsound business enterprise: *wildcat stock* **b** financially or commercially unsound: *a wildcat project* **9** (*modifier*) *US and Canadian* (of a train) running without permission or outside the timetable ▷ vb -cats, -catting, -catted **10** (*intr*) to drill for petroleum or natural gas in an area having no known reserves > 'wildˌcatting n, adj

wildcat strike n a strike begun by workers spontaneously or without union approval

wildcatter ('waɪldˌkætə) n *US and Canadian informal* a prospector for oil or ores in areas having no proved resources

wild celery n a strongly scented umbelliferous plant, *Apium graveolens*, of temperate regions: the ancestor of cultivated celery. Archaic name: smallage

wild cherry n another name for **gean** (sense 1)

wild dog n another name for **dingo**

wildebeest ('wɪldɪˌbiːst, 'vɪl-) n, pl -beests or -beest another name for **gnu** [C19 from Afrikaans, literally: wild beast]

wilder ('wɪldə) vb *archaic* **1** to lead or be led astray **2** to bewilder or become bewildered [C17 of uncertain origin] > 'wilderment n

wilderness ('wɪldənɪs) n **1** a wild, uninhabited, and uncultivated region **2** any desolate tract or area **3** a confused mass or collection **4** a voice (crying) in the wilderness a person, group, etc, making a suggestion or plea that is ignored **5** in the wilderness no longer having influence, recognition, or publicity [Old English *wildēornes*, from *wildēor* wild beast (from WILD + *dēor* beast, DEER) + -NESS; related to Middle Dutch *wildernisse*, German *Wildernis*]

Wilderness ('wɪldənɪs) n **the** the barren regions to the south and east of Palestine, esp those in which the Israelites wandered before entering the Promised Land and in which Christ fasted for 40 days and nights

wild-eyed adj **1** glaring in an angry, distracted, or wild manner **2** ill-conceived or totally impracticable

wildfire ('waɪldˌfaɪə) n **1** a highly flammable material, such as Greek fire, formerly used in warfare **2 a** a raging and uncontrollable fire **b** anything that is disseminated quickly (esp in the phrase **spread like wildfire**) **3** lightning without audible thunder **4** another name for **will-o'-the-wisp**

wild flower n **1** Also: wildflower any flowering plant that grows in an uncultivated state **2** the flower of such a plant

wildfowl ('waɪldˌfaʊl) n **1** any bird that is hunted by man, esp any duck or similar aquatic bird **2** such birds collectively > 'wildˌfowler n > 'wildˌfowling adj, n

Wild Geese n **the** the Irish expatriates who served as professional soldiers with the Catholic powers of Europe, esp France, from the late 17th to the early 20th centuries

wild ginger n a North American plant, *Asarum canadense*, having a solitary brownish flower and an aromatic root: family *Aristolochiaceae*. See also **asarabacca, asarum**

wild-goose chase n an absurd or hopeless pursuit, as of something unattainable

wild hyacinth n another name for **bluebell** (sense 1)

wild indigo n any of several North American leguminous plants of the genus *Baptisia*, esp *B. tinctoria*, which has yellow flowers and three-lobed leaves

wilding ('waɪldɪŋ) n **1** an uncultivated plant, esp the crab apple, or a cultivated plant that has become wild **2** a wild animal ▷ Also called: wildling

wild Irishman n NZ another name for **matagouri**

wildlands ('waɪldˌlændz) pl n *chiefly US* wild, uncultivated, and uninhabited areas

wild lettuce n any of several uncultivated lettuce plants, such as *Lactuca serriola* (or *L. scariola*) of Eurasia and *L. canadensis* (**horseweed**) of North America, which grow as weeds and have yellow or blue flowers, milky juice in the stem, and prickly leaves: family *Asteraceae* (composites)

wildlife ('waɪldˌlaɪf) n wild animals and plants collectively

wild liquorice n **1** another name for *Astragalus glycyphyllos*: see milk vetch **2** another name for **liquorice** (sense 1) **3** a North American plant, *Glycyrrhiza lepidota*, that is related to true liquorice and has similar properties

wild man n **1** a savage **2** an extremist in politics

wild mustard n another name for **charlock** (sense 1)

wild oat n any of several temperate annual grasses of the genus *Avena*, esp *A. fatua*, that grow as weeds and have long bristles on their flower spikes

wild oats pl n *slang* the indiscretions of youth, esp dissoluteness before settling down (esp in the phrase **sow one's wild oats**)

wild olive n any of various trees or shrubs that resemble the olive tree or bear olive-like fruits, esp the oleaster

wild pansy n **1** Also called: **heartsease, love-in-idleness**, and (in the US) **Johnny-jump-up** a Eurasian violaceous plant, *Viola tricolor*, having purple, yellow, and pale mauve spurred flowers **2** any of various similar plants of the genus *Viola*

wild parsley n any of various uncultivated umbelliferous plants that resemble parsley

wild parsnip n a strong-smelling umbelliferous plant, *Pastinaca sativa*, that has an inedible root: the ancestor of the cultivated parsnip

wild rice n another name for **Indian rice**

wild rose n any of numerous roses, such as the dogrose and sweetbrier, that grow wild and have flowers with only one whorl of petals

wild rubber n rubber obtained from uncultivated rubber trees

wild rye n any of various perennial grasses of the N temperate genus *Elymus*, resembling cultivated rye in having paired bristly ears or spikes and flat leaves

wild silk n **1** silk produced by wild silkworms **2** a fabric made from this, or from short fibres of silk designed to imitate it

wild Spaniard n any of various subalpine perennials of the genus *Aciphylla* of New Zealand, with sharp leaves. Often shortened to: **Spaniard**

wild track n a soundtrack recorded other than with a synchronized picture, usually carrying sound effects, random dialogue, etc

wild type n *biology* the typical form of a species of

W

organism resulting from breeding under natural conditions

wild water *n* **a** turbulent water in a river, esp as an area for navigating in a canoe as a sport **b** (*as modifier*): *wild-water racing*

Wild West *n* the western US during its settlement, esp with reference to its frontier lawlessness

Wild West show *n US* a show or circus act presenting feats of horsemanship, shooting, etc

wildwood (ˈwaɪldˌwʊd) *n archaic* a wood or forest growing in a natural uncultivated state

wile (waɪl) *n* **1** trickery, cunning, or craftiness **2** (*usually plural*) an artful or seductive trick or ploy ▷ *vb* **3** (*tr*) to lure, beguile, or entice [c12 from Old Norse *vel* craft; probably related to Old French *wile*, Old English *wīgle* magic. See GUILE]

wilful *or US* **willful** (ˈwɪlfʊl) *adj* **1** intent on having one's own way; headstrong or obstinate **2** intentional: *wilful murder* > ˈ**wilfully** *or US* ˈ**willfully** *adv* > ˈ**wilfulness** *or US* ˈ**willfulness** *n*

wilga (ˈwɪlgə) *n* a small drought-resistant tree, *Geijera parviflora*, of Australia, having hard aromatic wood, white flowers, and foliage that resembles that of the willow [c19 from a native Australian language]

Wilhelmshaven (*German* vɪlhɛlmsˈhaːfən) *n* a port and resort in NW Germany, in Lower Saxony: founded in 1853; was the chief German North Sea naval base until 1945; a major oil port. Pop: 84 586 (2003 est)

Wilhelmstrasse (*German* ˈvɪlhɛlmʃtraːsə) *n* **1** a street in the centre of Berlin, where the German foreign office and other government buildings were situated until 1945 **2** Germany's ministry of foreign affairs until 1945

Wilkes Land *n* a region in Antarctica south of Australia, on the Indian Ocean

will[1] (wɪl) *vb, past* **would** (takes an infinitive without *to* or an implied infinitive) **1** (esp with *you, he, she, it, they*, or a noun as subject) used as an auxiliary to make the future tense. Compare **shall** (sense 1) **2** used as an auxiliary to express resolution on the part of the speaker: *I will buy that radio if it's the last thing I do* **3** used as an auxiliary to indicate willingness or desire: *will you help me with this problem?* **4** used as an auxiliary to express compulsion, as in commands: *you will report your findings to me tomorrow* **5** used as an auxiliary to express capacity or ability: *this rope will support a load* **6** used as an auxiliary to express probability or expectation on the part of the speaker: *that will be Jim telephoning* **7** used as an auxiliary to express customary practice or inevitability: *boys will be boys* **8** (*with the infinitive always implied*) used as an auxiliary to express desire: usually in polite requests: *stay if you will* **9** **what you will** whatever you like **10** **will do** *informal* a declaration of willingness to do what is requested [Old English *willan*; related to Old Saxon *willian*, Old Norse *vilja*, Old High German *wollen*, Latin *velle* to wish, will]

USAGE See at **shall**

will[2] (wɪl) *n* **1** the faculty of conscious and deliberate choice of action; volition. Related adjs: **voluntary, volitive** **2** the act or an instance of asserting a choice **3** **a** the declaration of a person's wishes regarding the disposal of his or her property after death. Related adj: **testamentary** **b** a revocable instrument by which such wishes are expressed **4** anything decided upon or chosen, esp by a person in authority; desire; wish **5** determined intention: *where there's a will there's a way* **6** disposition or attitude towards others: *he bears you no ill will* **7** **at will** at one's own desire, inclination, or choice **8** **with a will** heartily; energetically **9** **with the best will in the world** even with the best of intentions ▷ *vb* (*mainly tr; often takes a clause as object or an infinitive*) **10** (*also intr*) to exercise the faculty of volition in an attempt to accomplish (something): *he willed his wife's recovery from her illness* **11** to give (property) by will to a person, society, etc: *he willed his art collection to the nation* **12** (*also intr*) to order or decree: *the king wills that you shall die* **13** to choose or prefer: *wander where you will* **14** to yearn for or desire: *to will that one's friends be happy* [Old English *willa*; related to Old Norse *vili*, Old High German *willeo* (German *Wille*), Gothic *wilja*, Old Slavonic *volja*] > ˈ**willer** *n*

willable (ˈwɪləbᵊl) *adj* able to be wished or determined by the will

willed (wɪld) *adj* (*in combination*) having a will as specified: *weak-willed*

willemite (ˈwɪləˌmaɪt) *n* a secondary mineral consisting of zinc silicate in hexagonal crystalline form. It is white, colourless, or coloured by impurities and is found in veins of zinc ore. Formula: Zn_2SiO_4 [c19 from Dutch *willemit*, named after *Willem* I of the Netherlands (1772–1834)]

Willemstad (*Dutch* ˈwɪləmstɑt) *n* the capital of the Netherlands Antilles, a port on the SW coast of Curaçao: important for refining Venezuelan oil. Pop: 137 000 (2005 est)

willet (ˈwɪlɪt) *n* a large American shore bird, *Catoptrophorus semipalmatus*, having a long stout bill, long legs, and a grey plumage with black-and-white wings: family *Scolopacidae* (sandpipers, etc), order *Charadriiformes* [short for *pill-will-willet* imitation of its cry]

willful (ˈwɪlfʊl) *adj* the US spelling of **wilful**

Williamsburg (ˈwɪljəmzˌbɜːg) *n* a city in SE Virginia: the capital of Virginia (1693–1779); the restoration of large sections of the colonial city was begun in 1926. Pop: 11 605 (2003 est)

Williams pear *n* a variety of pear that has large yellow juicy sweet fruit. Also called: **William's Bon Chrétien**

Williams syndrome *n pathol* an abnormality in the genes involved in calcium metabolism, resulting in mental retardation [c20 after J.C.P. *Williams* (born 1900), New Zealand cardiologist]

willies (ˈwɪlɪz) *pl n* **the** *slang* nervousness, jitters, or fright (esp in the phrase **give** (*or* **get**) **the willies**) [c20 of unknown origin]

willing (ˈwɪlɪŋ) *adj* **1** favourably disposed or inclined; ready **2** cheerfully or eagerly compliant **3** done, given, accepted, etc, freely or voluntarily > ˈ**willingly** *adv* > ˈ**willingness** *n*

willing horse *n* a person prepared to work hard

williwaw (ˈwɪlɪˌwɔː) *n US and Canadian* **1** a sudden strong gust of cold wind blowing offshore from a mountainous coast, as in the Strait of Magellan **2** a state of great turmoil [c19 of unknown origin]

will-o'-the-wisp (ˌwɪləðəˈwɪsp) *n* **1** Also called: **friar's lantern, ignis fatuus, jack-o'-lantern** a pale flame or phosphorescence sometimes seen over marshy ground at night. It is believed to be due to the spontaneous combustion of methane or other hydrocarbons originating from decomposing organic matter **2** a person or thing that is elusive or allures and misleads [c17 originally *Will with the wisp*, from *Will* short for *William* and *wisp* in former sense of a twist of hay or straw burning as a torch] > ˌ**will-o'-the-ˈwispish** *or* ˌ**will-o'-the-ˈwispy** *adj*

willow (ˈwɪləʊ) *n* **1** any of numerous salicaceous trees and shrubs of the genus *Salix*, such as the weeping willow and osiers of N temperate regions, which have graceful flexible branches, flowers in catkins, and feathery seeds **2** the whitish wood of certain of these trees **3** something made of willow wood, such as a cricket or baseball bat **4** a machine having a system of revolving spikes for opening and cleaning raw textile fibres [Old English *welig*; related to *wilige* wicker basket, Old Saxon *wilgia*, Middle High German *wilge*, Greek *helikē* willow, *helix* twisted] > ˈ**willowish** *or* ˈ**willow-ˌlike** *adj*

willow fly *n* a stonefly, *Leuctra geniculata*, of the English chalk streams, esteemed by trout and therefore by anglers

willow grouse *n* a N European grouse, *Lagopus lagopus*, with a reddish-brown plumage and white wings: now regarded as the same species as the red grouse (*L. lagopus scoticus*) of Britain

willowherb (ˈwɪləʊˌhɜːb) *n* **1** any of various temperate and arctic onagraceous plants of the genus *Epilobium*, having narrow leaves, terminal clusters of pink, purplish, or white flowers, and willow-like feathery seeds **2** short for **rosebay willowherb** (see **rosebay**) **3** (not in botanical usage) another name for **purple loosestrife** (see **loosestrife**) **4** **hairy willowherb** See **codlins-and-cream**

willow pattern *n* **a** a pattern incorporating a willow tree, river, bridge, and figures, typically in blue on a white ground, used on pottery and porcelain **b** (*as modifier*): *a willow-pattern plate*

Willow South *n* a city in S Alaska, about 113 km (70 miles) northwest of Anchorage: chosen as the site of the projected new state capital in 1976

willow tit *n* a small tit, *Parus montanus*, of marshy woods in Europe, having a greyish-brown body and dull black crown

willow warbler *n* an Old World warbler, *Phylloscopus trochilis*, of Eurasian woodlands

willowy (ˈwɪləʊɪ) *adj* **1** slender and graceful **2** flexible or pliant **3** shaded with willows

willpower (ˈwɪlˌpaʊə) *n* **1** the ability to control oneself and determine one's actions **2** firmness of will

willy (ˈwɪlɪ) *n Brit informal* a childish or jocular term for **penis**

willy-nilly (ˌwɪlɪˈnɪlɪ) *adv* **1** whether desired or not ▷ *adj* **2** occurring or taking place whether desired or not [Old English *wile hē, nyle hē*, literally: will he or will he not; *nyle*, from *ne* not + *willan* to WILL[1]]

willy wagtail *n Austral* a black-and-white flycatcher, *Rhipidura leucophrys*, having white feathers over the brows

willy-willy (ˈwɪlɪˈwɪlɪ) *n Austral* a tropical cyclone or duststorm [from a native Australian language]

Wilmington (ˈwɪlmɪŋtən) *n* a port in N Delaware, on the Delaware River: industrial centre. Pop: 72 051 (2003 est)

Wilno (ˈviːlnɔ) *n* the Polish name for **Vilnius**

Wilson cloud chamber *n* the full name for **cloud chamber**

Wilson's petrel *n* a common storm petrel, *Oceanites oceanicus*, that breeds around Antarctica but is often seen in the Atlantic. See **storm petrel**

Wilson's snipe *n* another name for the **common snipe**. See **snipe** (sense 1)

wilt[1] (wɪlt) *vb* **1** to become or cause to become limp, flaccid, or drooping: *insufficient water makes plants wilt* **2** to lose or cause to lose courage, strength, etc **3** (*tr*) to cook (a leafy vegetable) very briefly until it begins to collapse ▷ *n* **4** the act of wilting or state of becoming wilted **5** any of various plant diseases characterized by permanent wilting, usually caused by fungal parasites attacking the roots [c17 perhaps variant of *wilk* to wither, from Middle Dutch *welken*]

wilt[2] (wɪlt) *vb archaic or dialect* (used with the pronoun *thou* or its relative equivalent) a singular form of the present tense (indicative mood) of **will**[1]

Wilton (ˈwɪltən) *n* a kind of carpet with a close velvet pile of cut loops [c18 named after *Wilton*, Wiltshire, noted for carpet manufacture]

Wilton House *n* a mansion in Wilton in Wiltshire: built for the 1st Earl of Pembroke in the 16th century; rebuilt after a fire in 1647 by Inigo Jones and John Webb; altered in the 19th century by James Wyatt; landscaped grounds include a famous Palladian bridge

Wilts (wɪlts) *abbreviation for* Wiltshire

Wiltshire (ˈwɪltʃə, -ʃɪə) *n* a county of S England, consisting mainly of chalk uplands, with Salisbury Plain in the south and the Marlborough Downs in the north; prehistoric remains (at Stonehenge and Avebury): the geographical and ceremonial county includes Swindon unitary authority (established in 1997). Administrative centre: Trowbridge. Pop (excluding Swindon): 440 800 (2003 est). Area (excluding Swindon): 3481 sq km (1344 sq miles)

Wiltshire Horn *n* a breed of medium-sized sheep having horns in both male and female, originating from the Chalk Downs, England
wily (ˈwaɪlɪ) *adj* **wilier, wiliest** characterized by or proceeding from wiles; sly or crafty > ˈ**wiliness** *n*
wimble (ˈwɪmbᵊl) *n* **1** any of a number of hand tools, such as a brace and bit or a gimlet, used for boring holes ▷ *vb* **2** to bore (a hole) with or as if with a wimble [C13 from Middle Dutch *wimmel* auger]
Wimbledon (ˈwɪmbᵊldən) *n* part of the Greater London borough of Merton: headquarters of the All England Lawn Tennis Club since 1877 and the site of the annual international tennis championships
wimp (wɪmp) *n informal* a feeble ineffective person ▷ See also **wimp out** [C20 of unknown origin] > ˈ**wimpish** *or* ˈ**wimpy** *adj*
WIMP (wɪmp) *acronym for* **1** windows, icons, menus (*or* mice), pointers: denoting a type of user-friendly screen display used on small computers: *a WIMP system* **2** *physics* weakly interacting massive particle
wimple (ˈwɪmpᵊl) *n* **1** a piece of cloth draped around the head to frame the face, worn by women in the Middle Ages and still a part of the habit of some nuns **2** *Scot* a curve or bend, as in a river ▷ *vb* **3** *rare* to ripple or cause to ripple or undulate **4** (*tr*) *archaic* to cover with or put a wimple on **5** *archaic* (esp of a veil) to lie or cause to lie in folds or pleats [Old English *wimpel*; related to Old Saxon *wimpal*, Middle Dutch *wumpel*, Middle High German *bewimpfen* to veil]
wimp out *vb* (*intr, adverb*) *informal* to fail to do or complete something through fear or lack of conviction
Wimshurst machine (ˈwɪmzhɜːst) *n* a type of electrostatic generator with two parallel insulating discs revolving in different directions, each being in contact with a thin metal wiper that produces a charge on the disc: usually used for demonstration purposes [C19 named after J. *Wimshurst* (1832–1903), English engineer]
win[1] (wɪn) *vb* **wins, winning, won 1** (*intr*) to achieve first place in a competition **2** (*tr*) to gain or receive (a prize, first place, etc) in a competition **3** (*tr*) to succeed in or gain (something) with an effort: *we won recognition* **4** **win one's spurs a** to achieve recognition in some field of endeavour **b** *history* to be knighted **5** to gain victory or triumph in (a battle, argument, etc) **6** (*tr*) to earn or procure (a living, etc) by work **7** (*tr*) to take possession of, esp violently; capture: *the Germans never won Leningrad* **8** (when *intr*, foll by *out, through*, etc) to reach with difficulty (a desired condition or position) or become free, loose, etc, with effort: *the boat won the shore; the boat won through to the shore* **9** (*tr*) to turn someone into (a supporter, enemy, etc): *you have just won an ally* **10** (*tr*) to gain (the sympathy, loyalty, etc) of someone **11** (*tr*) to obtain (a woman, etc) in marriage **12** (*tr*) **a** to extract (ore, coal, etc) from a mine **b** to extract (metal or other minerals) from ore **c** to discover and make (a mineral deposit) accessible for mining **13** **you can't win** *informal* an expression of resignation after an unsuccessful attempt to overcome difficulties ▷ *n* **14** *informal* a success, victory, or triumph **15** profit; winnings **16** the act or fact of reaching the finishing line or post first ▷ See also **win out** [Old English *winnan*; related to Old Norse *vinna*, German *gewinnen*] > ˈ**winnable** *adj*
win[2] (wɪn) *vb* **wins, winning, won** *or* **winned** (*tr*) *Irish, Scot, and northern English dialect* **1** to dry (grain, hay, peat, etc) by exposure to sun and air **2** a less common word for **winnow** [Old English, perhaps a variant of WINNOW]
wince[1] (wɪns) *vb* **1** (*intr*) to start slightly, as with sudden pain ▷ *n* **2** the act of wincing [C18 (earlier (C13) meaning: to kick): via Old French *wencier, guenchir* to avoid, from Germanic; compare Old Saxon *wenkian*, Old High German *wenken*] > ˈ**wincer** *n*
wince[2] (wɪns) *n* a roller for transferring pieces of cloth between dyeing vats [C17 variant of WINCH]
wincey (ˈwɪnsɪ) *n Brit* a plain- or twill-weave cloth, usually having a cotton or linen warp and a wool filling [C19 of Scottish origin, probably an alteration of *woolsey* as in LINSEY-WOOLSEY]
winceyette (ˌwɪnsɪˈɛt) *n Brit* a plain-weave cotton fabric with slightly raised two-sided nap
winch[1] (wɪntʃ) *n* **1** a windlass driven by a hand- or power-operated crank **2** a hand- or power-operated crank by which a machine is driven ▷ *vb* **3** (*tr*; often foll by *up* or *in*) to pull (in a rope) or lift (a weight) using a winch [Old English *wince* pulley; related to WINK[1]] > ˈ**wincher** *n*
winch[2] (wɪntʃ) *vb* (*intr*) an obsolete word for **wince**[1]
winchester (ˈwɪntʃɪstə) *n* (*sometimes capital*) a large cylindrical bottle with a narrow neck used for transporting chemicals. It contains about 2.5 litres [after *Winchester*, Hampshire]
Winchester (ˈwɪntʃɪstə) *n* a city in S England, administrative centre of Hampshire: a Romano-British town; Saxon capital of Wessex; 11th-century cathedral; site of **Winchester College** (1382), English public school. Pop: 41 420 (2001)
Winchester disk *n* a type of hard disk in which disks are permanently sealed, together with read-write heads, in an airtight container to keep dust out [C20 named after the 3030 WINCHESTER RIFLE, as the original device would have had 3030 as its IBM number]
Winchester rifle *n trademark* a breech-loading lever-action repeating rifle with a tubular magazine under the barrel. Often shortened to: **Winchester** [C19 named after O. F. *Winchester* (1810–80), US manufacturer]
wind[1] (wɪnd) *n* **1** a current of air, sometimes of considerable force, moving generally horizontally from areas of high pressure to areas of low pressure. See also **Beaufort scale** Related adj: **aeolian 2** *chiefly poetic* the direction from which a wind blows, usually a cardinal point of the compass **3** air artificially moved, as by a fan, pump, etc **4** any sweeping and destructive force **5** a trend, tendency, or force: *the winds of revolution* **6** *informal* a hint; suggestion: *we got wind that you were coming* **7** something deemed insubstantial: *his talk was all wind* **8** breath, as used in respiration or talk: *you're just wasting wind* **9** (often used in sports) the power to breathe normally: *his wind is weak*. See also **second wind 10** *music* **a** a wind instrument or wind instruments considered collectively **b** (*often plural*) the musicians who play wind instruments in an orchestra **c** (*modifier*) of, relating to, or composed of wind instruments: *a wind ensemble* **11** an informal name for **flatus 12** the air on which the scent of an animal is carried to hounds or on which the scent of a hunter is carried to his quarry **13** **between wind and water a** the part of a vessel's hull below the water line that is exposed by rolling or by wave action **b** any point particularly susceptible to attack or injury **14** **break wind** to release intestinal gas through the anus **15** **get** *or* **have the wind up** *informal* to become frightened **16** **have in the wind** to be in the act of following (quarry) by scent **17** **how** *or* **which way the wind blows** *or* **lies** what appears probable **18** **in the wind** about to happen **19** **in the wind** *or* **three sheets in the wind** *informal* intoxicated; drunk **20** **in the teeth** (*or* **eye**) **of the wind** directly into the wind **21** **into the wind** against the wind or upwind **22** **off the wind** *nautical* away from the direction from which the wind is blowing **23** **on the wind** *nautical* as near as possible to the direction from which the wind is blowing **24** **put the wind up** *informal* to frighten or alarm **25** **raise the wind** *Brit informal* to obtain the necessary funds **26** **sail close** *or* **near to the wind a** to come near the limits of danger or indecency **b** to live frugally or manage one's affairs economically **27** **take the wind out of someone's sails** to destroy someone's advantage; disconcert or deflate ▷ *vb* (*tr*) **28** to cause (someone) to be short of breath: *the blow winded him* **29** **a** to detect the scent of **b** to pursue (quarry) by following its scent **30** to cause (a baby) to bring up wind after feeding by patting or rubbing on the back **31** to expose to air, as in drying, ventilating, etc [Old English *wind*; related to Old High German *wint*, Old Norse *vindr*, Gothic *winds*, Latin *ventus*] > ˈ**windless** *adj* > ˈ**windlessly** *adv* > ˈ**windlessness** *n*
wind[2] (waɪnd) *vb* **winds, winding, wound 1** (often foll by *around, about,* or *upon*) to turn or coil (string, cotton, etc) around some object or point or (of string, etc) to be turned etc, around some object or point: *he wound a scarf around his head* **2** (*tr*) to twine, cover, or wreathe by or as if by coiling, wrapping, etc; encircle: *we wound the body in a shroud* **3** (*tr*; often foll by *up*) to tighten the spring of (a clockwork mechanism) **4** (*tr*; foll by *off*) to remove by uncoiling or unwinding **5** (*usually intr*) to move or cause to move in a sinuous, spiral, or circular course: *the river winds through the hills* **6** (*tr*) to introduce indirectly or deviously: *he is winding his own opinions into the report* **7** (*tr*) to cause to twist or revolve: *he wound the handle* **8** (*tr*; usually foll by *up* or *down*) to move by cranking: *please wind up the window* **9** (*tr*) to haul, lift, or hoist (a weight, etc) by means of a wind or windlass **10** (*intr*) (of a board, etc) to be warped or twisted **11** (*intr*) *archaic* to proceed deviously or indirectly ▷ *n* **12** the act of winding or state of being wound **13** a single turn, bend, etc: *a wind in the river* **14** Also called: **winding** a twist in a board or plank ▷ See also **wind down, wind up** [Old English *windan*; related to Old Norse *vinda*, Old High German *wintan* (German *winden*)] > ˈ**windable** *adj*
wind[3] (waɪnd) *vb* **winds, winding, winded** *or* **wound** (*tr*) *poetic* to blow (a note or signal) on (a horn, bugle, etc) [C16 special use of WIND[1]]
windage (ˈwɪndɪdʒ) *n* **1** **a** a deflection of a projectile as a result of the effect of the wind **b** the degree of such deflection **c** the extent to which it is necessary to adjust the wind gauge of a gun sight in order to compensate for such deflection **2** the difference between a firearm's bore and the diameter of its projectile **3** *nautical* the exposed part of the hull of a vessel responsible for wind resistance **4** the retarding force upon a rotating machine resulting from the drag of the air
windbag (ˈwɪndˌbæg) *n* **1** *slang* a voluble person who has little of interest to communicate **2** the bag in a set of bagpipes, which provides a continuous flow of air to the pipes
windbaggery (ˈwɪndˌbægərɪ) *n informal* lengthy talk or discussion with little or no interesting content
windbill (ˈwɪndˌbɪl) *n* an informal name for **accommodation bill**
windblown (ˈwɪndˌbləʊn) *adj* **1** blown by the wind **2** (of a woman's hair style) cut short and combed to look as though it has been dishevelled by the wind **3** (of trees, shrubs, etc) growing in a shape determined by the prevailing winds **4** *NZ* (of trees) felled by the wind
wind-borne *adj* (esp of plant seeds or pollen) transported by wind
windbound (ˈwɪndˌbaʊnd) *adj* (of a sailing vessel) prevented from sailing by an unfavourable wind
windbreak (ˈwɪndˌbreɪk) *n* a fence, line of trees, etc, serving as a protection from the wind by breaking its force
wind-broken *adj* (of a horse) asthmatic or heaving
windburn (ˈwɪndˌbɜːn) *n* irritation and redness of the skin caused by prolonged exposure to winds of high velocity > ˈ**windˌburnt** *or* ˈ**windˌburned** *adj*
windcheater (ˈwɪndˌtʃiːtə) *n* a warm jacket, usually with a close-fitting knitted neck, cuffs, and waistband. Also called: **windjammer** *US* name (trademark): **Windbreaker** (ˈwɪndˌbreɪkə) *Austral* name (trademark): **Windcheater**

W

wind chest (wɪnd) *n* a box in an organ in which air from the bellows is stored under pressure before being supplied to the pipes or reeds

wind-chill (wɪnd-) *n* **a** the serious chilling effect of wind and low temperature: it is measured on a scale that runs from hot to fatal to life and allows for varying combinations of air temperature and wind speed **b** (*as modifier*): *wind-chill factor*

wind chimes (wɪnd) *pl n* a decorative arrangement of small discs of metal, shell, etc, hung near a window or door, that shake together with a tinkling sound in a draught

wind cone (wɪnd) *n* another name for **windsock**

wind down (waɪnd) *vb* (*adverb*) **1** (*tr*) to lower or move down by cranking **2** (*intr*) (of a clock spring) to become slack **3** (*intr*) to diminish gradually in force or power; relax

winded ('wɪndɪd) *adj* **1** out of breath, as from strenuous exercise **2** (*in combination*) having breath or wind as specified: *broken-winded; short-winded*

winder ('waɪndə) *n* **1** a person or device that winds, as an engine for hoisting the cages in a mine shaft or a device for winding the yarn in textile manufacture **2** an object, such as a bobbin, around which something is wound **3** a knob or key used to wind up a clock, watch, or similar mechanism **4** any plant that twists itself around a support **5** a step of a spiral staircase

Windermere ('wɪndə,mɪə) *n* a lake in NW England, in Cumbria in the SE part of the Lake District: the largest lake in England. Length: 17 km (10.5 miles). Sometimes (less correctly) called: **Lake Windermere**

windfall ('wɪnd,fɔːl) *n* **1** a piece of unexpected good fortune, esp financial gain **2** something blown down by the wind, esp a piece of fruit **3** *chiefly US and Canadian* a plot of land covered with trees blown down by the wind

windfall tax *n* a tax levied on an organization considered to have made excessive profits, esp a privatized utility company that has exploited a monopoly

wind farm *n* a large group of wind-driven generators for electricity supply

windflower ('wɪnd,flaʊə) *n* any of various anemone plants, such as the wood anemone

windgall ('wɪnd,gɔːl) *n vet science* a soft swelling in the area of the fetlock joint of a horse [c16 from WIND¹ + GALL²] > 'wind,galled *adj*

wind gap (wɪnd) *n* a narrow dry valley on a mountain or ridge

wind gauge (wɪnd) *n* **1** another name for **anemometer** (sense 1) **2** a scale on a gun sight indicating the amount of deflection necessary to allow for windage **3** *music* a device for measuring the wind pressure in the bellows of an organ

wind harp (wɪnd) *n* a less common name for **aeolian harp**

Windhoek ('wɪnt,hʊk, 'vɪnt-) *n* the capital of Namibia, in the centre, at an altitude of 1654 m (5428 ft): formerly the capital of German South West Africa. Pop: 252 000 (2005 est)

windhover ('wɪnd,hɒvə) *n Brit* a dialect name for a **kestrel**

Windies ('wɪndɪz) *pl n informal* **the** the international cricket team of the West Indies [from the abbreviation *W. Indies*]

windigo ('wɪndɪ,gəʊ) *n* a variant of **wendigo**

winding ('waɪndɪŋ) *n* **1** a curving or sinuous course or movement **2** anything that has been wound or wrapped around something **3** a particular manner or style in which something has been wound **4** a curve, bend, or complete turn in wound material, a road, etc **5** (*often plural*) devious thoughts or behaviour: *the tortuous windings of political argumentation* **6** one or more turns of wire forming a continuous coil through which an electric current can pass, as used in transformers, generators, etc **7** another name for **wind²** (sense 14) **8** a coil of tubing in certain brass instruments, esp the French horn ⊳ *adj* **9** curving; sinuous: *a winding road* > 'winding*ly adv*

winding drum ('waɪndɪŋ) *n* a rotating drum usually grooved to nest a wire rope which is wound onto it as part of the mechanism of a hoist

winding sheet *n* a sheet in which a corpse is wrapped for burial; shroud

winding staircase *n* another word for **spiral staircase**

winding-up *n* the process of finishing or closing something, esp the process of closing down a business

wind instrument (wɪnd) *n* any musical instrument sounded by the breath, such as the woodwinds and brass instruments of an orchestra

windjammer ('wɪnd,dʒæmə) *n* **1** a large merchant sailing ship **2** another name for **windcheater**

windlass ('wɪndləs) *n* **1** a machine for raising weights by winding a rope or chain upon a barrel or drum driven by a crank, motor, etc ⊳ *vb* **2** (*tr*) to raise or haul (a weight, etc) by means of a windlass [c14 from Old Norse *vindáss*, from *vinda* to WIND² + *ass* pole; related to Old French *guindas*, Middle Low German, Dutch *windas*]

windlestraw ('wɪndᵊl,strɔː) *n Irish, Scot, and English dialect* **1** the dried stalk of any of various grasses **2** anything weak or feeble, esp a thin unhealthy person [Old English *windelstrēaw*, from *windel* basket, from *windan* to WIND² + *strēaw* STRAW¹]

wind machine (wɪnd) *n* a machine used, esp in the theatre, to produce wind or the sound of wind

windmill ('wɪnd,mɪl, 'wɪn,mɪl) *n* **1** a machine for grinding or pumping driven by a set of adjustable vanes or sails that are caused to turn by the force of the wind **2** the set of vanes or sails that drives such a mill **3** Also called: **whirligig** *Brit* a toy consisting of plastic or paper vanes attached to a stick in such a manner that they revolve like the sails of a windmill. US and Canadian name: **pinwheel 4** an imaginary opponent or evil (esp in the phrase **tilt at** *or* **fight windmills**) **5** a small air-driven propeller fitted to a light aircraft to drive auxiliary equipment. Compare **ram-air turbine 6** an informal name for **helicopter 7** an informal name for **propeller** (sense 1) ⊳ *vb* **8** to move or cause to move like the arms of a windmill **9** an informal name for **accommodation bill 10** (*intr*) (of an aircraft propeller, rotor of a turbine, etc) to rotate as a result of the force of a current of air rather than under power

window ('wɪndəʊ) *n* **1** a light framework, made of timber, metal, or plastic, that contains glass or glazed opening frames and is placed in a wall or roof to let in light or air or to see through. Related *adj*: **fenestral 2** an opening in the wall or roof of a building that is provided to let in light or air or to see through **3** See **windowpane 4** the display space in and directly behind a shop window: *the dress in the window* **5** any opening or structure resembling a window in function or appearance, such as the transparent area of an envelope revealing an address within **6** an opportunity to see or understand something usually unseen: *a window on the workings of Parliament* **7** a period of unbooked time in a diary, schedule, etc **8** short for **launch window** *or* **weather window 9** *physics* a region of the spectrum in which a medium transmits electromagnetic radiation. See also **radio window 10** *computing* an area of a VDU display that may be manipulated separately from the rest of the display area; typically different files can be displayed simultaneously in different overlapping windows **11** (*modifier*) of or relating to a window or windows: *a window ledge* **12** out of the window *informal* dispensed with; disregarded ⊳ *vb* **13** (*tr*) to furnish with or as if with windows [c13 from Old Norse *vindauga*, from *vindr* WIND¹ + *auga* EYE¹]

window box *n* **1** a long narrow box, placed on or outside a windowsill, in which plants are grown **2** either of a pair of vertical boxes, attached to the sides of a sash window frame, that enclose a sash cord and counterbalancing weight

window-dresser *n* a person employed to design and build up a display in a shop window

window-dressing *n* **1** the ornamentation of shop windows, designed to attract customers **2** the pleasant, showy, or false aspect of an idea, policy, etc, which is stressed to conceal the real or unpleasant nature; façade

window envelope *n* a type of envelope, esp for business use, having a transparent area that reveals the address within

windowpane ('wɪndəʊ,peɪn) *n* a sheet of glass in a window

window sash *n* a glazed window frame, esp one that opens

window seat *n* **1** a seat below a window, esp in a bay window **2** a seat beside a window in a bus, train, etc

window-shop *vb* -shops, -shopping, -shopped (*intr*) to look at goods in shop windows without buying them > 'window-,shopper *n* > 'window-,shopping *n*

windowsill ('wɪndəʊ,sɪl) *n* a sill below a window

window tax *n history* a tax on windows in houses levied between 1696 and 1851

windpipe ('wɪnd,paɪp) *n* a nontechnical name for **trachea** (sense 1) Related *adj*: **tracheal**

wind-pollinated *adj* (of certain plants) pollinated by wind-borne pollen > 'wind-,polli'nation *n*

wind power (wɪnd) *n* power produced from windmills and wind turbines

Wind River Range (wɪnd) *n* a mountain range in W Wyoming: one of the highest ranges of the central Rockies. Highest peak: Gannet Peak, 4202 m (13 785 ft)

wind rose (wɪnd) *n* a diagram with radiating lines showing the frequency and strength of winds from each direction affecting a specific place

windrow ('wɪnd,rəʊ, 'wɪn,rəʊ) *n* **1** a long low ridge or line of hay or a similar crop, designed to achieve the best conditions for drying or curing **2** a line of leaves, snow, dust, etc, swept together by the wind ⊳ *vb* **3** (*tr*) to put (hay or a similar crop) into windrows > 'wind,rower *n*

windsail ('wɪnd,seɪl) *n* **1** a sail rigged as an air scoop over a hatch or companionway to catch breezes and divert them below **2** any of the vanes or sails of a windmill

wind scale (wɪnd) *n* a numerical scale of wind force, such as the Beaufort scale

Windscale ('wɪnd,skeɪl) *n* the former name of **Sellafield**

windscreen ('wɪnd,skriːn) *n Brit, Austral, NZ, and South African* the sheet of flat or curved glass that forms a window of a motor vehicle, esp the front window. US and Canadian name: **windshield**

windscreen wiper *n Brit* an electrically operated blade with a rubber edge that wipes a windscreen clear of rain, snow, etc. US and Canadian name: **windshield wiper**

wind shake (wɪnd) *n* a crack between the annual rings in wood: caused by strong winds bending the tree trunk

wind shear (wɪnd) *n* stress on an aircraft in an area in which winds of different speeds and directions are close together

windshield ('wɪnd,ʃiːld) *n* **1** *US and Canadian* the sheet of flat or curved glass that forms a window of a motor vehicle, esp the front window. Also called (in Britain and certain other countries): **windscreen 2** an object designed to shield something from the wind

windsock ('wɪnd,sɒk) *n* a truncated cone of textile mounted on a mast so that it is free to rotate about a vertical axis: used, esp at airports, to indicate the local wind direction. Also called: **air sock, drogue, wind sleeve, wind cone**

Windsor ('wɪnzə) *n* **1** a town in S England, in Windsor and Maidenhead unitary authority, Berkshire, on the River Thames, linked by bridge with Eton: site of **Windsor Castle**, residence of English monarchs since its founding by William the Conqueror; **Old Windsor**, royal residence in the time of Edward the Confessor, is 3 km (2 miles) southeast. Pop: 26 747 (2001 est). Official name: **New Windsor 2** a city in SE Canada, in S Ontario on the Detroit River opposite Detroit: motor-vehicle manufacturing; university (1963). Pop: 208 402 (2001)

Windsor and Maidenhead *n* a unitary authority in S England, in Berkshire. Pop: 135 300 (2003 est). Area: 197 sq km (76 sq miles)

Windsor chair *n* a simple wooden chair, popular in England and America from the 18th century, usually having a shaped seat, splayed legs, and a back of heavy spindles

Windsor knot *n* a wide triangular knot, produced by making extra turns in tying a tie

Windsor rocker *n* US and Canadian a Windsor chair on rockers

Windsor tie *n* a wide silk tie worn in a floppy bow

windstorm ('wɪnd,stɔːm) *n* a storm consisting of violent winds

wind-sucking *n* a harmful habit of horses in which the animal arches its neck and swallows a gulp of air > **'wind,sucker** *n*

windsurf ('wɪnd,sɜːf) *vb* (*intr*) to take part in the sport of windsurfing > **'wind,surfer** *n*

windsurfing ('wɪnd,sɜːfɪŋ) *n* the sport of sailing standing up on a sailboard that is equipped with a mast, sail, and wishbone boom. Also called: **boardsailing, sailboarding**

wind surge (wɪnd) *n* a wind-induced rise in the water level at the coast or the shore of an inland expanse of water. It has a definite frequency and if this is close to the tidal frequency serious flooding can result

windswept ('wɪnd,swept) *adj* 1 open to or swept by the wind 2 another word for **windblown** (sense 2)

wind tee (wɪnd) *n* a large weather vane shaped like a T, located at an airfield to indicate the wind direction

wind tunnel (wɪnd) *n* a chamber for testing the aerodynamic properties of aircraft, aerofoils, etc, in which a current of air can be maintained at a constant velocity

wind up (waɪnd) *vb* (*adverb*) 1 to bring to or reach a conclusion: *he wound up the proceedings* 2 (*tr*) to tighten the spring of (a clockwork mechanism) 3 (*tr; usually passive*) *informal* to make nervous, tense, etc; excite: *he was all wound up before the big fight* 4 (*tr*) to roll (thread, etc) into a ball 5 an informal word for **liquidate** (sense 2) 6 (*intr*) *informal* to end up (in a specified state): *you'll wind up without any teeth* 7 (*tr; usually passive*) to involve; entangle: *they were wound up in three different scandals* 8 (*tr*) to hoist or haul up 9 (*tr*) Brit *slang* to tease (someone) ▷ *n* **wind-up** 10 the act of concluding 11 the finish; end 12 Brit *slang* an act or instance of teasing: *she just thinks it's a big wind-up*

windward ('wɪndwəd) *chiefly nautical* ▷ *adj* 1 of, in, or moving to the quarter from which the wind blows 2 to windward of advantageously situated with respect to ▷ *n* 3 the windward point 4 the side towards the wind ▷ *adv* 5 towards the wind ▷ Compare **leeward**

Windward Islands *pl n* 1 a group of islands in the SE Caribbean, in the Lesser Antilles: consists of the French Overseas Department of Martinique and the independent states of Grenada, St Lucia, and St Vincent and the Grenadines 2 a group of islands in the S Pacific, in French Polynesia in the W Society Archipelago: Moorea, Maio (Tubuai Manu), and Mehetia and Tetiaroa. Pop: 184 222 (2002). French name: **Îles du Vent**

Windward Passage *n* a strait in the Caribbean, between E Cuba and NW Haiti. Width: 80 km (50 miles)

windy ('wɪndɪ) *adj* windier, windiest 1 of, characterized by, resembling, or relating to wind; stormy 2 swept by or open to powerful winds 3 marked by or given to empty, prolonged, and

often boastful speech; bombastic: *windy orations* 4 void of substance 5 an informal word for **flatulent** 6 *slang* afraid; frightened; nervous > **'windily** *adv* > **'windiness** *n*

Windy City *n* the *informal* Chicago, Illinois

wine (waɪn) *n* 1 a an alcoholic drink produced by the fermenting of grapes with water and sugar. Related adjs: **vinaceous, vinous** b an alcoholic drink produced in this way from other fruits, flowers, etc: *elderberry wine* 2 a a dark red colour, sometimes with a purplish tinge b (*as adjective*): *wine-coloured* 3 anything resembling wine in its intoxicating or invigorating effect 4 *pharmacol obsolete* fermented grape juice containing medicaments 5 Adam's wine Brit a dialect word for **water** 6 new wine in old bottles something new added to or imposed upon an old or established order ▷ *vb* 7 (*intr*) to drink wine 8 wine and dine to entertain or be entertained with wine and fine food [Old English *wīn*, from Latin *vīnum*; related to Greek *oinos*, of obscure origin] > **'wineless** *adj*

wine bar *n* a bar in a restaurant, etc, or an establishment that specializes in serving wine and usually food

wineberry ('waɪn,berɪ) *n*, *pl* -ries another name for **mako²** (sense 1)

winebibber ('waɪn,bɪbə) *n* a person who drinks a great deal of wine > **'wine,bibbing** *n*

wine box *n* wine sold in a cubic carton, usually of three-litre capacity, having a plastic lining and a tap for dispensing

wine cellar *n* 1 a place, such as a dark cool cellar, where wine is stored 2 the stock of wines stored there

wine cooler *n* 1 a bucket-like vessel containing ice in which a bottle of wine is placed to be cooled 2 the full name for **cooler** (sense 3)

wine gallon *n* Brit a former unit of capacity equal to 231 cubic inches

wineglass ('waɪn,glɑːs) *n* 1 a glass drinking vessel, typically having a small bowl on a stem, with a flared foot 2 Also called: **wineglassful** the amount that such a glass will hold

wine grower *n* a person engaged in cultivating vines in order to make wine > **wine growing** *n*

wine palm *n* any of various palm trees, the sap of which is used, esp when fermented, as a drink. See **toddy** (sense 2) Also called: **toddy palm**

winepress ('waɪn,pres) *n* any equipment used for squeezing the juice from grapes in order to make wine

winery ('waɪnərɪ) *n*, *pl* -eries chiefly US and Canadian a place where wine is made

wineskin ('waɪn,skɪn) *n* the skin of a sheep or goat sewn up and used as a holder for wine

wine tasting *n* an occasion for sampling a number of wines > wine taster *n*

winey *or* **winy** ('waɪnɪ) *adj* winier, winiest having the taste or qualities of wine

wing (wɪŋ) *n* 1 either of the modified forelimbs of a bird that are covered with large feathers and specialized for flight in most species 2 one of the organs of flight of an insect, consisting of a membranous outgrowth from the thorax containing a network of veins 3 either of the organs of flight in certain other animals, esp the forelimb of a bat 4 a a half of the main supporting surface on an aircraft, confined to one side of it b the full span of the main supporting surface on both sides of an aircraft c an aircraft designed as one complete wing d a position in flight formation, just to the rear and to one side of an aircraft 5 a an organ or apparatus resembling a wing b *anatomy* any bodily structure resembling a wing: *the wings of a sphenoid bone*. Technical name: **ala** 6 anything suggesting a wing in form, function, or position, such as a sail of a windmill or a ship 7 *botany* a either of the lateral petals of a sweetpea or related flower b any of various outgrowths of a plant part, esp the process on a wind-dispersed fruit or seed 8 a

means or cause of flight or rapid motion; flight: *fear gave wings to his feet* 9 the act or manner of flying: *a bird of strong wing* 10 Brit the part of a car body that surrounds the wheels. US and Canadian name: **fender** 11 any affiliate of or subsidiary to a parent organization 12 *sport* a either of the two sides of the pitch near the touchline b a player stationed in such a position; **winger** 13 a faction or group within a political party or other organization. See also **left wing, right wing** 14 a part of a building that is subordinate to the main part 15 (*plural*) the space offstage to the right or left of the acting area in a theatre 16 in the wings ready to step in when needed 17 *fortifications* a side connecting the main fort and an outwork 18 a folding panel, as of a double door or a movable partition 19 either of the two pieces that project forwards from the sides of some chairbacks 20 the US name for **quarterlight** 21 a surface fitted to a racing car to produce aerodynamic download to hold it on the road at high speed 22 (*plural*) an insignia in the form of stylized wings worn by a qualified aircraft pilot 23 a tactical formation in some air forces, consisting of two or more squadrons 24 any of various flattened organs or extensions in lower animals, esp when used in locomotion 25 the side of a hold alongside a ship's hull 26 the outside angle of the cutting edge on the share and mouldboard of a plough 27 a jetty or dam for narrowing a channel of water 28 on a wing and a prayer with only the slightest hope of succeeding 29 on the wing a flying b travelling c about to leave 30 take wing a to lift off or fly away b to depart in haste c to become joyful 31 under one's wing in one's care or tutelage 32 clip (someone's) wings a to restrict (someone's) freedom b to thwart (someone's) ambition 33 on wings flying or as if flying 34 spread *or* stretch one's wings to make full use of one's abilities ▷ *vb* (*mainly tr*) 35 (*also intr*) to make (one's way) swiftly or as if on wings 36 to shoot or wound (a bird, person, etc) superficially, in the wing or arm, etc 37 to cause to fly or move swiftly: *to wing an arrow* 38 to fit (an arrow) with a feather 39 to provide with wings 40 (of buildings, altars, etc) to provide with lateral extensions 41 wing it *informal* to accomplish or perform something without full preparation or knowledge; improvise [c12 from Scandinavian; compare Old Norse *vængir* (plural), Norwegian *veng*] > **'wing,like** *adj*

wing and wing *adv* with sails extended on both sides by booms

wing beat *n* a complete cycle of moving the wing by a bird when flying

wing bow (bəʊ) *n* a distinctive band of colour marking the wing of a bird

wing-case *n* the nontechnical name for **elytron**

wing chair *n* an easy chair having wings on each side of the back

wing collar *n* a stiff turned-up shirt collar worn with the points turned down over the tie

wing commander *n* an officer holding commissioned rank in certain air forces, such as the Royal Air Force: junior to a group captain and senior to a squadron leader

wing covert *n* any of the covert feathers of the wing of a bird, occurring in distinct rows

wingding ('wɪŋ,dɪŋ) *n* *slang, chiefly US and Canadian* 1 a a noisy lively party or festivity b (*as modifier*): *a real wingding party* 2 a real or pretended fit or seizure [c20 of unknown origin]

winged (wɪŋd) *adj* 1 furnished with wings: *winged god; winged horse* 2 flying straight and true as if by wing: *winged words*

winger ('wɪŋə) *n* *sport* a player stationed on the wing

wing-footed *adj* *archaic* fleet; swift

wingless ('wɪŋlɪs) *adj* 1 having no wings or vestigial wings 2 designating primitive insects of the subclass *Apterygota*, characterized by small size, lack of wings, and larvae resembling the

W

adults: includes the springtails and bristletails > 'winglessness *n*

winglet ('wɪŋlɪt) *n* **1** a small wing, esp the bastard wing of a bird **2** a small wing placed at the tip of the main wing of an aircraft and perpendicular to it designed to reduce the aircraft's vortex drag

wing loading *n* the total weight of an aircraft divided by its wing area

wingman ('wɪŋmæn) *n, pl* -men a player in the wing position in Australian Rules

wing nut *n* a threaded nut tightened by hand by means of two flat lugs or wings projecting from the central body. Also called: **butterfly nut**

wingover ('wɪŋ,əʊvə) *n* a manoeuvre in which the direction of flight of an aircraft is reversed by putting it into a climbing turn until nearly stalled, the nose then being allowed to fall while continuing the turn

wing shot *n* **1** a shot taken at a bird in flight **2** an expert at shooting birds in flight

wingspan ('wɪŋ,spæn) *or* **wingspread** ('wɪŋ,sprɛd) *n* the distance between the wing tips of an aircraft, bird, etc

wingsuit ('wɪŋ,suːt) *n* a type of skydiving suit with fabric under the arms and between the legs enabling the wearer to reduce his or her rate of fall

wing tip *n* the outermost edge of a wing

wink¹ (wɪŋk) *vb* **1** (*intr*) to close and open one eye quickly, deliberately, or in an exaggerated fashion to convey friendliness, etc **2** to close and open (an eye or the eyes) momentarily **3** (*tr*; foll by *away, back,* etc) to force away (tears, etc) by winking **4** (*tr*) to signal with a wink **5** (*intr*) (of a light) to gleam or flash intermittently ▷ *n* **6** a winking movement, esp one conveying a signal, etc, or such a signal **7** an interrupted flashing of light **8** a brief moment of time; instant **9** *informal* the smallest amount, esp of sleep. See also **forty winks 10 tip the wink** *Brit informal* to give a hint [Old English *wincian*; related to Old Saxon *wincon,* Old High German *winchan,* German *winken* to wave. See WENCH, WINCH]

wink² (wɪŋk) *n* a disc used in the game of tiddlywinks [c20 shortened from TIDDLYWINKS]

wink at *vb* (*intr, preposition*) to connive at; disregard: *the authorities winked at corruption*

winker ('wɪŋkə) *n* **1** a person or thing that winks **2** *US and Canadian slang, English dialect* an eye, eyelash, or eyelid **3** another name for **blinker** (sense 1)

winkle ('wɪŋkəl) *n* **1** See **periwinkle¹** ▷ *vb* **2** (*tr*; usually foll by *out, out of,* etc) *informal, chiefly Brit* to extract or prise out [c16 shortened from PERIWINKLE¹]

winkle-pickers *pl n* shoes or boots with very pointed narrow toes, popular in the mid-20th century

winnard ('wɪnəd) *n Southwest English dialect* a heron

Winnebago (,wɪnɪ'beɪgəʊ) *n* **1 Lake** a lake in E Wisconsin, fed and drained by the Fox river: the largest lake in the state. Area: 557 sq km (215 sq miles) **2** (*pl* -gos *or* -go) a member of a North American Indian people living in Wisconsin and Nebraska **3** the language of this people, belonging to the Siouan family

winner ('wɪnə) *n* **1** a person or thing that wins **2** *informal* a person or thing that seems sure to win or succeed

winner's enclosure *or* **circle** *n* See **unsaddling enclosure**

winning ('wɪnɪŋ) *adj* **1** (of a person, character, etc) charming, engaging, or attractive: *winning ways; a winning smile* **2** gaining victory: *the winning stroke* ▷ *n* **3 a** a shaft or seam of coal **b** the extraction of coal or ore from the ground **4** (*plural*) money, prizes, or valuables won, esp in gambling > 'winningly *adv* > 'winningness *n*

winning gallery *n real tennis* the gallery farthest from the net on either side of the court, into

which any shot played wins a point

winning opening *n real tennis* the grille, dedans, or winning gallery, into which any shot played wins a point

winning post *n* the post marking the finishing line on a racecourse

Winnipeg ('wɪnɪˌpɛg) *n* **1** a city in S Canada, capital of Manitoba at the confluence of the Assiniboine and Red Rivers: University of Manitoba (1877) and University of Winnipeg (1871). Pop: 626 685 (2001) **2 Lake** a lake in S Canada, in Manitoba: drains through the Nelson River into Hudson Bay. Area: 23 553 sq km (9094 sq miles)

Winnipeg couch *n Canadian* a couch with no arms or back, opening out into a double bed

Winnipegger ('wɪnɪˌpɛgə) *n* a native or inhabitant of Winnipeg

Winnipegosis (,wɪnɪpə'gəʊsɪs) *n* **Lake** a lake in S Canada, in W Manitoba. Area: 5400 sq km (2086 sq miles)

winnow ('wɪnəʊ) *vb* **1** to separate (grain) from (chaff) by means of a wind or current of air **2** (*tr*) to examine in order to select the desirable elements **3** (*tr*) *archaic* to beat (the air) with wings **4** (*tr*) *rare* to blow upon; fan ▷ *n* **5 a** a device for winnowing **b** the act or process of winnowing [Old English *windwian*; related to Old High German *wintōn,* Gothic *diswinthjan,* Latin *ventilāre.* See WIND¹] > 'winnower *n*

wino ('waɪnəʊ) *n, pl* -os *informal* a person who habitually drinks wine as a means of getting drunk

win out *vb* (*intr, adverb*) *informal* to succeed or prevail as if in a contest: *sanity rarely wins out over prejudice*

win over *vb* (*tr, adverb*) to gain the support or consent of (someone). Also: **win round**

winsome ('wɪnsəm) *adj* charming; winning; engaging: *a winsome smile* [Old English *wynsum,* from *wynn* joy (related to Old High German *wunnia,* German *Wonne*) + *-sum* -SOME¹] > 'winsomely *adv* > 'winsomeness *n*

Winston-Salem ('wɪnstən'seɪləm) *n* a city in N central North Carolina: formed in 1913 by the uniting of Salem and Winston; a major tobacco manufacturing centre. Pop: 190 299 (2003 est)

winter ('wɪntə) *n* **1 a** (*sometimes capital*) the coldest season of the year, between autumn and spring, astronomically from the December solstice to the March equinox in the N hemisphere and at the opposite time of year in the S hemisphere **b** (*as modifier*): *winter pasture* **2** the period of cold weather associated with the winter **3** a time of decline, decay, etc **4** *chiefly poetic* a year represented by this season: *a man of 72 winters.* Related adjs: **brumal, hibernal, hiemal** ▷ *vb* **5** (*intr*) to spend the winter in a specified place **6** to keep or feed (farm animals, etc) during the winter or (of farm animals) to be kept or fed during the winter [Old English; related to Old Saxon, Old High German *wintar,* Old Norse *vetr,* Gothic *wintrus*] > 'winterer *n* > 'winterish *or* 'winter-,like *adj* > 'winterless *adj*

winter aconite *n* a small Old World ranunculaceous herbaceous plant, *Eranthis hyemalis,* cultivated for its yellow flowers, which appear early in spring

winterbourne ('wɪntəˌbɔːn) *n* a stream flowing only after heavy rainfall, esp in winter [Old English *winterburna;* see WINTER, BURN²]

winter cherry *n* **1** a Eurasian solanaceous plant, *Physalis alkekengi,* cultivated for its ornamental inflated papery orange-red calyx **2** the calyx of this plant ▷ See also **Chinese lantern, ground cherry**

wintercress ('wɪntəˌkrɛs) *n* **1** a bitter-tasting yellow-flowered perennial, *Barbarea vulgaris,* somewhat resembling mustard **2** a commercial hybrid, *Rorippa × sterilis,* between watercress and *R. microphylla*

winterfeed ('wɪntəˌfiːd) *vb* -feeds, -feeding, -fed to feed (livestock) in winter when the grazing is not rich enough

winter garden *n* **1** a garden of evergreen plants and plants that flower in winter **2** a conservatory in which flowers are grown in winter

wintergreen ('wɪntəˌgriːn) *n* **1** Also called: boxberry, checkerberry, teaberry, spiceberry, partridgeberry any of several evergreen ericaceous shrubs of the genus *Gaultheria,* esp *G. procumbens,* of E North America, which has white bell-shaped flowers and edible red berries **2** oil of wintergreen an aromatic compound, formerly made from this and various other plants but now synthesized: used medicinally and for flavouring **3** any of various plants of the genus *Pyrola,* such as *P. minor* (**common wintergreen**), of temperate and arctic regions, having rounded leaves and small pink globose flowers: family *Pyrolaceae.* Usual US name: shinleaf **4** any of several plants of the genera *Orthilia* and *Moneses:* family *Pyrolaceae* **5** chickweed wintergreen a primulaceous plant, *Trientalis europaea,* of N Europe and N Asia, having white flowers and leaves arranged in a whorl [c16 from Dutch *wintergroen* or German *Wintergrün;* see WINTER, GREEN]

winter hedge *n West Yorkshire, south Lancashire, and Derbyshire dialect* a clothes horse [so called in contrast to a hedge on which clothes are dried in summer]

winter heliotrope *n* a creeping perennial, *Petasites fragrans,* related to the butterbur, having lilac to heliotrope coloured flowers smelling of vanilla: found chiefly on road verges

winterize *or* **winterise** ('wɪntəˌraɪz) *vb* (*tr*) *US and Canadian* to prepare (a house, car, etc) to withstand winter conditions > ,winteri'zation *or* ,winteri'sation *n*

winter jasmine *n* a jasmine shrub, *Jasminum nudiflorum,* widely cultivated for its winter-blooming yellow flowers

winterkill ('wɪntəˌkɪl) *vb chiefly US and Canadian* to kill (crops or other plants) by exposure to frost, cold, etc, or (of plants) to die by this means > 'winter,killing *adj, n*

winter melon *n* a variety of muskmelon, *Cucumis melo inodorus,* that has sweet fruit with pale orange flesh and an unridged rind. Also called: **Persian melon**

winter moth *n* a brown geometrid moth, *Operophtera brumata,* of which the male is often seen against lighted windows in winter, the female being wingless

Winter Olympic Games *n* (*functioning as singular or plural*) an international contest of winter sports, esp skiing, held every four years. Also called: **Winter Olympics**

winter quarters *pl n* housing or accommodation for the winter, esp for military personnel

winter rose *n* another name for **Christmas rose**

winter solstice *n* **1** the time at which the sun is at its southernmost point in the sky (northernmost point in the S hemisphere) appearing at noon at its lowest altitude above the horizon. It occurs about December 22 (June 21 in the S hemisphere) **2** *astronomy* the point on the celestial sphere, opposite the **summer solstice,** at which the ecliptic is furthest south from the celestial equator. Right ascension: 18 hours; declination: –23.5°

winter sports *pl n* sports held in the open air on snow or ice, esp skiing

Winterthur (German 'vɪntərtuːr) *n* an industrial town in NE central Switzerland, in Zürich canton: has the largest technical college in the country. Pop: 90 483 (2000)

wintertime ('wɪntəˌtaɪm) *n* the winter season Also (archaic): wintertide

Winter War *n* the war of the winter of 1939–40 between Finland and the USSR after which the Finns surrendered the Karelian Isthmus to the USSR

winterweight ('wɪntəˌweɪt) *adj* (of clothes) suitable in weight for wear in the winter; relatively heavy

winter wheat *n* a type of wheat that is planted in the autumn and is harvested the following summer

wintry ('wɪntrɪ), **wintery** ('wɪntərɪ, -trɪ) *or less commonly* **winterly** *adj* -trier, -triest **1** (esp of weather) of or characteristic of winter **2** lacking cheer or warmth; bleak > 'wintrily *adv* ➤ 'wintriness, 'winteriness *or less commonly* 'winterliness *n*

win-win *adj* guaranteeing a favourable outcome for everyone involved: *a win-win situation for NATO* [C20 modelled on NO-WIN]

winy ('waɪnɪ) *adj* winier, winiest a variant spelling of **winey**

winze (wɪnz) *n* mining a steeply inclined shaft, as for ventilation between levels [C18 from earlier *winds*, probably from C14 *wynde* windlass, from Middle Dutch or Middle Low German *winde*; related to Danish *vinde* pulley]

wipe (waɪp) *vb* (*tr*) **1** to rub (a surface or object) lightly, esp with (a cloth, hand, etc), as in removing dust, water, grime, etc **2** (usually foll by *off*, *away*, *from*, *up*, etc) to remove by or as if by rubbing lightly: *he wiped the dirt from his hands* **3** to eradicate or cancel (a thought, memory, etc) **4** to erase a recording from (an audio or video tape) **5** *Austral informal* to abandon or reject (a person) **6** to apply (oil, grease, etc) by wiping **7** to form (a joint between two lead pipes) with solder or soft lead **8** **wipe the floor with** (someone) *informal* to defeat decisively ▷ *n* **9** the act or an instance of wiping **10** (in film editing) an effect causing the transition from one scene to the next in which the image of the first scene appears to be wiped off the screen by that of the second **11** *dialect* a sweeping blow or stroke **12** *Brit dialect* a gibe or jeer **13** *obsolete* a slang name for **handkerchief** [Old English *wīpian*, related to Middle Low German *wipen*, *wīp* bundle (of cloth), Old High German *wiffa*, *wīfan* to wind, Gothic *weipan* to wreathe]

wipe out *vb* (*adverb*) **1** (*tr*) to destroy completely; eradicate **2** (*tr*) *informal* to murder or kill **3** (*intr*) to fall or jump off a surfboard or skateboard ▷ *n* **wipeout 4** an act or instance of wiping out **5** the interference of one radio signal by another so that reception is impossible

wiper ('waɪpə) *n* **1** any piece of cloth, such as a handkerchief, towel, etc, used for wiping **2** a cam rotated to ease a part and allow it to fall under its own weight, as used in stamping machines, etc **3** See **windscreen wiper 4** *electrical engineering* a movable conducting arm, esp one in a switching or selecting device, that makes contact with a row or ring of contacts

WIPO *or* **Wipo** ('waɪpəʊ) *n acronym for* World Intellectual Property Organization

wire (waɪə) *n* **1** a slender flexible strand or rod of metal **2** a cable consisting of several metal strands twisted together **3** a flexible metallic conductor, esp one made of copper, usually insulated, and used to carry electric current in a circuit **4** (*modifier*) of, relating to, or made of wire: *a wire fence; a wire stripper* **5** anything made of wire, such as wire netting, a barbed wire fence, etc **6** a long continuous wire or cable connecting points in a telephone or telegraph system **7** *old-fashioned* **a** an informal name for **telegram** *or* **telegraph b** **the wire** an informal name for **telephone 8** a metallic string on a guitar, piano, etc **9** *horse racing, chiefly US and Canadian* the finishing line on a racecourse **10** a wire-gauze screen upon which pulp is spread to form paper during the manufacturing process **11** anything resembling a wire, such as a hair **12** a snare made of wire for rabbits and similar animals **13** (down) to the wire *informal* right up to the last moment **14** get in under the wire *informal, chiefly US and Canadian* to accomplish something with little time to spare **15** get one's wires crossed *informal* to misunderstand **16** pull wires *chiefly US and Canadian* to exert influence behind the scenes, esp through personal connections; pull strings **17** take (it) to

the wire to compete to the bitter end to win a competition or title ▷ *vb* (*mainly tr*) **18** (*also intr*) to send a telegram to (a person or place) **19** to send (news, a message, etc) by telegraph **20** to equip (an electrical system, circuit, or component) with wires **21** to fasten or furnish with wire **22** (often foll by *up*) to provide (an area) with fibre optic cabling to receive cable television **23** to string (beads, etc) on wire **24** *croquet* to leave (a player's ball) so that a hoop or peg lies between it and the other balls **25** to snare with wire **26** wire in *informal* to set about (something, esp food) with enthusiasm [Old English *wīr*; related to Old High German *wiara*, Old Norse *vīra*, Latin *viriae* bracelet] > 'wire,like *adj*

wire brush *n* a brush having wire bristles, used for cleaning metal, esp for removing rust, or for brushing against a cymbal

wire cloth *n* a mesh or netting woven from fine wire, used in window screens, strainers, etc

wired (waɪəd) *adj informal* **1** edgy from stimulant intake **2** excited, nervous, or tense **3** using computers to send and receive information, esp via the internet

wiredraw ('waɪə,drɔ:) *vb* -draws, -drawing, -drew, -drawn to convert (metal) into wire by drawing through successively smaller dies

wire entanglement *n* a barrier or obstruction of barbed wire used in warfare

wire-gauge *n* **1** a flat plate with slots in which standard wire sizes can be measured **2** a standard system of sizes for measuring the diameters of wires

wire gauze *n* a stiff meshed fabric woven of fine wires

wire glass *n* a sheet glass that contains a layer of reinforcing wire netting within it

wire grass *n* any of various grasses, such as Bermuda grass, that have tough wiry roots or rhizomes

wire-guided *adj* (of a missile) controlled by signals transmitted through fine wires uncoiled during the missile's flight

wire-haired *adj* (of an animal) having a rough wiry coat

wireless ('waɪəlɪs) *adj* **1** communicating without connecting wires or other material contacts: *wireless networks; wireless internet connection* ▷ *n* **2** *chiefly Brit old-fashioned* another word for **radio**

wireless application protocol *n* a global application that enables mobile phone users to access the internet and other information services. Usually abbreviated to **WAP**

wireless telegraphy *n* another name for **radiotelegraphy**

wireless telephone *n* another name for **radiotelephone**. > wireless telephony *n*

wireman ('waɪəmən) *n, pl* -men *chiefly US* a person who installs and maintains electric wiring, cables, etc

wire netting *n* a net made of wire, often galvanized, that is used for fencing, as a light reinforcement, etc

wirephoto ('waɪə,fəʊtəʊ) *n, pl* -tos a facsimile of a photograph transmitted electronically via a telephone system

wirepuller ('waɪə,pʊlə) *n chiefly US and Canadian* a person who uses private or secret influence for his own ends > 'wire,pulling *n*

wirer ('waɪərə) *n* a person who sets or uses wires to snare rabbits and similar animals

wire recorder *n* an early type of magnetic recorder in which sounds were recorded on a thin steel wire magnetized by an electromagnet. Compare **tape recorder**. > wire recording *n*

wire rope *n* rope made of strands of wire twisted together

wire service *n chiefly US and Canadian* an agency supplying news, etc, to newspapers, radio and television stations, etc

wiretap ('waɪə,tæp) *vb* -taps, -tapping, -tapped to make a connection to a telegraph or telephone

wire in order to obtain information secretly > 'wire,tapper *n* > 'wire,tapping *n*

wirewalker ('waɪə,wɔ:kə) *n chiefly US* another name for **tightrope walker**

wire wheel *n* **1** a wheel in which the rim is held to the hub by wire spokes, esp one used on a sports car. Compare **disc wheel 2** a power-driven rotary wire brush for scaling or burnishing

wire wool *n* a mass of fine wire used for cleaning and scouring

wirework ('waɪə,wɜ:k) *n* **1** functional or decorative work made of wire **2** objects made of wire, esp netting **3** a special effects technique in film or theatre in which actors are suspended from moving wires so that they appear to fly: *the spectacular wirework of Chinese cinema*

wireworks ('waɪə,wɜ:ks) *n* (functioning as singular or plural) a factory where wire or articles of wire are made

wireworm ('waɪə,wɜ:m) *n* the wormlike larva of various elaterid beetles, which feeds on the roots of many crop plants and is a serious agricultural pest

wire-wove *adj* **1** of, relating to, or comprising a high-grade glazed paper, usually for writing **2** woven of wire

wirilda (wə'rɪldə) *n* an acacia tree, *Acacia retinoides*, of SE Australia with edible seeds [from a native Australian language]

wiring ('waɪərɪŋ) *n* **1** the network of wires used in an electrical system, device, or circuit **2** the quality or condition of such a network ▷ *adj* **3** used in wiring

wirra ('wɪrə) *interj Irish* an exclamation of sorrow or deep concern [C19 shortened from Irish Gaelic *a Muire!* O Mary! as invocation to the Virgin Mary]

wirrah ('wɪrə) *n* a saltwater fish, *Acanthistius serratus*, of Australia, with bright blue spots [from a native Australian language]

Wirral ('wɪrəl) *n* **1** **the** a peninsula in NW England between the estuaries of the Rivers Mersey and Dee **2** a unitary authority in NW England, in Merseyside. Pop: 313 800 (2003 est). Area: 158 sq km (61 sq miles)

wiry ('waɪərɪ) *adj* wirier, wiriest **1** (of people or animals) slender but strong in constitution **2** made of or resembling wire, esp in stiffness: *wiry hair* **3** (of a sound) produced by or as if by a vibrating wire > 'wirily *adv* > 'wiriness *n*

wis (wɪs) *vb archaic* to know or suppose (something) [C17 a form derived from IWIS, mistakenly interpreted as *I wis* I know, as if from Old English *witan* to know]

Wis. *abbreviation for* Wisconsin

Wisbech ('wɪzbi:tʃ) *n* a town in E England, in N Cambridgeshire: market-gardening. Pop: 26 536 (2001)

Wisconsin (wɪs'kɒnsɪn) *n* **1** a state of the N central US, on Lake Superior and Lake Michigan: consists of an undulating plain, with uplands in the north and west; over 168 m (550 ft) above sea level along the shore of Lake Michigan. Capital: Madison. Pop: 5 472 299 (2003 est). Area: 141 061 sq km (54 464 sq miles). Abbreviations: Wis., Wis, (with zip code) WI **2** a river in central and SW Wisconsin, flowing south and west to the Mississippi. Length: 692 km (430 miles)

Wisconsinite (wɪs'kɒnsɪn,aɪt) *n* a native or inhabitant of Wisconsin

Wisd. *abbreviation for* Wisdom of Solomon

wisdom ('wɪzdəm) *n* **1** the ability or result of an ability to think and act utilizing knowledge, experience, understanding, common sense, and insight **2** accumulated knowledge, erudition, or enlightenment **3** *archaic* a wise saying or wise sayings or teachings **4** *obsolete* soundness of mind ▷ Related adjective: **sagacious** [Old English *wīsdōm*; see WISE[1], -DOM]

Wisdom of Jesus, the Son of Sirach ('saɪræk) *n* **the** another name for **Ecclesiasticus**

Wisdom of Solomon *n* a book of the Apocrypha, probably written about 50 BC, addressed primarily to Jews who were under the influence of Hellenistic learning

wisdom tooth *n* **1** any of the four molar teeth, one at the back of each side of the jaw, that are the last of the permanent teeth to erupt. Technical name: **third molar 2 cut one's wisdom teeth** to arrive at the age of discretion

wise¹ (waɪz) *adj* **1** possessing, showing, or prompted by wisdom or discernment **2** prudent; sensible **3** shrewd; crafty: *a wise plan* **4** well-informed; erudite **5** aware, informed, or knowing (esp in the phrase **none the wiser**) **6** *slang* (*postpositive; often foll by to*) in the know, esp possessing inside information (about) **7** *archaic* possessing powers of magic **8** *slang, chiefly US and Canadian* cocksure or insolent **9 be** *or* **get wise** (often foll by *to*) *informal* to be or become aware or informed (of something) or to face up (to facts) **10 put wise** (often foll by *to*) *slang* to inform or warn (of) ⊳ *vb* **11** See **wise up** [Old English *wīs*; related to Old Norse *vīss*, Gothic *weis*, German *weise*] > '**wisely** *adv* > '**wiseness** *n*

wise² (waɪz) *n archaic* way, manner, fashion, or respect (esp in the phrases **any wise, in no wise**) [Old English *wīse* manner; related to Old Saxon *wīsa*, German *Weise*, Old Norse *vīsa* verse, Latin *vīsus* face]

-wise *adv combining form* **1** Also: **-ways** indicating direction or manner: *clockwise; likewise* **2** with reference to: *profitwise; businesswise* [Old English *-wisan*; see WISE²]

wiseacre ('waɪzˌeɪkə) *n* **1** a person who wishes to seem wise **2** a wise person: often used facetiously or contemptuously [C16 from Middle Dutch *wijssegger* soothsayer; related to Old High German *wīssaga*, German *Weissager*. See WISE¹, SAY]

wiseass ('waɪzˌæs) *n informal* **a** a person who thinks he or she is being witty or clever **b** (*as modifier*): *some wiseass kid at the back of the class*

wisecrack ('waɪzˌkræk) *informal* ⊳ *n* **1** a flippant gibe or sardonic remark ⊳ *vb* **2** to make a wisecrack > '**wiseˌcracker** *n*

wise guy *n* **1** *informal* a person who is given to making conceited, sardonic, or insolent comments *informal* **2** *US* a member of the Mafia

wisent ('wiːzənt) *n* another name for **European bison**. See **bison** (sense 2) [German, from Old High German *wisunt* BISON]

wise up *vb* (*adverb*) **1** *slang* (often foll by *to*) to become or cause to become aware or informed (of) **2** (*tr*) to make more intellectually demanding or sophisticated

wish (wɪʃ) *vb* **1** (*when tr, takes a clause as object or an infinitive; when intr, often foll by for*) to want or desire (something, often that which cannot be or is not the case): *I wish I lived in Italy; to wish for peace* **2** (*tr*) to feel or express a desire or hope concerning the future or fortune of: *I wish you well* **3** (*tr*) to desire or prefer to be as specified **4** (*tr*) to greet as specified; bid: *he wished us good afternoon* **5** (*tr*) *formal* to order politely: *I wish you to come at three o'clock* ⊳ *n* **6** the act of wishing; the expression of some desire or mental inclination: *to make a wish* **7** something desired or wished for: *he got his wish* **8** (*usually plural*) expressed hopes or desire, esp for someone's welfare, health, etc **9** (*often plural*) *formal* a polite order or request ⊳ See also **wish on** [Old English *wȳscan*; related to Old Norse *öskja*, German *wünschen*, Dutch *wenschen*] > '**wisher** *n* > '**wishless** *adj*

wishbone ('wɪʃˌbəʊn) *n* the V-shaped bone above the breastbone in most birds consisting of the fused clavicles; furcula [C17 from the custom of two people breaking apart the bone after eating: the person with the longer part makes a wish]

wishbone boom *n* a boom on a sailboard having two arms that are joined at the mast and at the foot of the sail. The windsurfer holds onto it for support and to steer the sailboard

wishful ('wɪʃfʊl) *adj* having wishes or characterized by wishing > '**wishfully** *adv* > '**wishfulness** *n*

wish fulfilment *n* (in Freudian psychology) any successful attempt to fulfil a wish stemming from the unconscious mind, whether in fact, in fantasy, or by such disguised means as sublimation. See also **pleasure principle**

wishful thinking *n* the erroneous belief that one's wishes are in accordance with reality > **wishful thinker** *n*

wish list *n* a list of things desired by a person or organization: *the Polish government's wish list*

wish on *vb* (*tr, preposition*) to hope that (someone or something) should be imposed (on someone); foist: *I wouldn't wish my cold on anyone*

wisht (wɪʃt) *interj* a variant of **whisht**

wish-wash *n informal* **1** any thin weak drink **2** rubbishy talk or writing

wishy-washy ('wɪʃɪˌwɒʃɪ) *adj informal* **1** lacking in substance, force, colour, etc **2** watery; thin > '**wishy-ˌwashily** *adv* > '**wishy-ˌwashiness** *n*

Wisła ('viswa) *n* the Polish name for **Vistula** (sense 1)

Wislany Zalew (*Polish* viʃ'la:ni 'za:lɛf) *n* the Polish name for the **Vistula** (sense 2)

Wismar (*German* 'vɪsmar) *n* a port in NE Germany, on an inlet of the Baltic, in Mecklenburg-West Pomerania: shipbuilding industries. Pop: 45 714 (2003 est)

wisp (wɪsp) *n* **1** a thin, light, delicate, or fibrous piece or strand, such as a streak of smoke or a lock of hair **2** a small bundle, as of hay or straw **3** anything slender and delicate: *a wisp of a girl* **4** a mere suggestion or hint **5** a flock of birds, esp snipe ⊳ *vb* **6** (*intr; often foll by away*) to move or act like a wisp **7** (*tr*) *chiefly Brit dialect* to twist into a wisp **8** (*tr*) *chiefly Brit* to groom (a horse) with a wisp of straw, etc [C14 variant of *wips*, of obscure origin; compare WIPE] > '**wispˌlike** *adj*

WISP (wɪsp) *n acronym for* Wireless Information Service Provider: an internet service provider set up to deal with and deliver internet services to clients through wireless access points

wispy ('wɪspɪ) *adj* **wispier, wispiest** wisplike; delicate, faint, light, etc > '**wispily** *adv* > '**wispiness** *n*

wist (wɪst) *vb archaic* the past tense and past participle of **wit²**

wisteria (wɪ'stɪərɪə) *n* any twining leguminous woody climbing plant of the genus *Wisteria*, of E Asia and North America, having blue, purple, or white flowers in large drooping clusters [C19 from New Latin, named after Caspar *Wistar* (1761–1818), American anatomist]

wistful ('wɪstfʊl) *adj* sadly pensive, esp about something yearned for > '**wistfully** *adv* > '**wistfulness** *n*

wit¹ (wɪt) *n* **1** the talent or quality of using unexpected associations between contrasting or disparate words or ideas to make a clever humorous effect **2** speech or writing showing this quality **3** a person possessing, showing, or noted for such an ability, esp in repartee **4** practical intelligence (esp in the phrase **have the wit to**) **5** *Scot and northern English dialect* information or knowledge (esp in the phrase **get wit of**) **6** *archaic* mental capacity or a person possessing it **7** *obsolete* the mind or memory ⊳ See also **wits** [Old English *witt*; related to Old Saxon *giwitt*, Old High German *wizzi* (German *Witz*), Old Norse *vit*, Gothic *witi*. See WIT²]

wit² (wɪt) *vb* **1** *archaic* to be or become aware of (something) ⊳ *adv* **2 to wit** that is to say; namely (used to introduce statements, as in legal documents) [Old English *witan*; related to Old High German *wizzan* (German *wissen*), Old Norse *vīta*, Latin *videre* to see]

witan ('wɪtᵊn) *n* (in Anglo-Saxon England) **1** an assembly of higher ecclesiastics and important laymen, including king's thegns, that met to counsel the king on matters such as judicial problems **2** the members of this assembly ⊳ Also called: **witenagemot** [Old English *witan*, plural of *wita* wise man; see WIT², WITNESS]

witblits ('vɪtˌblɪts) *n South African* an extremely potent illegally distilled spirit [from Afrikaans *wit* white + *blits* lightning]

witch¹ (wɪtʃ) *n* **1** a person, usually female, who practises or professes to practise magic or sorcery, esp black magic, or is believed to have dealings with the devil **2** an ugly or wicked old woman **3** a fascinating or enchanting woman **4** short for **water witch** ⊳ *vb* **5** (*tr*) to cause or change by or as if by witchcraft **6** a less common word for **bewitch** [Old English *wicca*; related to Middle Low German *wicken* to conjure, Swedish *vicka* to move to and fro] > '**witchˌlike** *adj*

witch² (wɪtʃ) *n* a flatfish, *Pleuronectes* (or *Glyptocephalus*) *cynoglossus*, of N Atlantic coastal waters, having a narrow greyish-brown body marked with tiny black spots: family *Pleuronectidae* (plaice, flounders, etc) [C19 perhaps from WITCH¹, alluding to the appearance of the fish]

witch- *or* **wych-** *prefix* having pliant branches: *witchweed* [Old English *wice* and *wic*; probably from Germanic *wik-* bend]

witchcraft ('wɪtʃˌkrɑːft) *n* **1** the art or power of bringing magical or preternatural power to bear or the act of attempting to do so **2** the influence of magic or sorcery **3** fascinating or bewitching influence or charm

witch doctor *n* Also called: **shaman, medicine man** **1** a man in certain societies, esp preliterate ones, who appears to possess magical powers, used esp to cure sickness but also to harm people **2** a person who seeks out or hunts witches in some African tribal cultures

witch-elm *n* a variant spelling of **wych-elm**

witchery ('wɪtʃərɪ) *n, pl* **-eries 1** the practice of witchcraft **2** magical or bewitching influence or charm

witches'-broom, witchbroom ('wɪtʃˌbruːm) *or* **witches'-besom** *n* a dense abnormal growth of shoots on a tree or other woody plant, usually caused by parasitic fungi of the genus *Taphrina*

witches' butter *n* See **jelly fungus**

witches' Sabbath *n* See **Sabbath** (sense 4)

witchetty grub ('wɪtʃɪtɪ) *n* the wood-boring edible larva of certain Australian moths and beetles [C19 *witchetty*, from a native Australian language]

witch hazel *or* **wych-hazel** *n* **1** any of several trees and shrubs of the genus *Hamamelis*, esp *H. virginiana*, of North America, having ornamental yellow flowers and medicinal properties: family *Hamamelidaceae* **2** an astringent medicinal solution containing an extract of the bark and leaves of *H. virginiana*, applied to treat bruises, inflammation, etc

witch-hunt *n* a rigorous campaign to round up or expose dissenters on the pretext of safeguarding the welfare of the public > '**witch-ˌhunter** *n* > '**witch-ˌhunting** *n, adj*

witching ('wɪtʃɪŋ) *adj* **1** relating to or appropriate for witchcraft **2** *now rare* bewitching ⊳ *n* **3** witchcraft; magic > '**witchingly** *adv*

witching hour *n* the hour at which witches are supposed to appear, usually midnight

witch of Agnesi (ɑːn'jeɪzɪ) *n maths* a plane curve, symmetrical about the *y*-axis, having the equation $x^2y = 4a^2(2a-y)$. Sometimes shortened to: **witch** [C19 named after Maria Gaetana Agnesi (1718–99), Italian mathematician and philosopher; probably so called from the resemblance of the curve to the outline of a witch's hat]

witchweed ('wɪtʃˌwiːd) *n* any of several scrophulariaceous plants of the genus *Striga*, esp *S. hermonthica*, that are serious pests of grain crops in parts of Africa and Asia

witenagemot (ˌwɪtɪnəgɪ'məʊt) *n* another word for **witan** [Old English *witena*, genitive plural of *wita* councillor + *gemōt* meeting, MOOT]

with (wɪð, wɪθ) *prep* **1** using; by means of: *he killed her with an axe* **2** accompanying; in the company of: *the lady you were with* **3** possessing; having: *a man with a red moustache* **4** concerning or regarding: *be patient with her* **5** in spite of: *with all his talents, he was still humble* **6** used to indicate a time or distance by which something is away from something else: *with three miles to go, he collapsed* **7** in a manner characterized by: *writing with abandon* **8** caused or prompted by: *shaking with rage* **9** often used with a verb indicating a reciprocal action or relation between the subject and the preposition's object: *agreeing with me; chatting with the troops* **10** **not with you** *informal* not able to grasp or follow what you are saying **11** **with it** *informal* **a** fashionable; in style **b** comprehending what is happening or being said **12** **with that** after that; having said or done that [Old English; related to Old Norse *vith*, Gothic *withra*, Latin *vitricus* stepfather, Sanskrit *vitarám* wider]

withal (wɪˈðɔːl) *adv* **1** *literary* as well; likewise **2** *literary* nevertheless **3** *archaic* therewith ▷ *prep* **4** (*postpositive*) an archaic word for **with** [C12 from WITH + ALL]

withdraw (wɪðˈdrɔː) *vb* **-draws, -drawing, -drew, -drawn** **1** (*tr*) to take or draw back or away; remove **2** (*tr*) to remove from deposit or investment in a bank, building society, etc **3** (*tr*) to retract or recall (a statement, promise, etc) **4** (*intr*) to retire or retreat: *the troops withdrew* **5** (*intr; often foll by from*) to back out (of) or depart (from): *he withdrew from public life* **6** (*intr*) to detach oneself socially, emotionally, or mentally [C13 from WITH (in the sense: away from) + DRAW] > **withˈdrawable** *adj* > **withˈdrawer** *n*

withdrawal (wɪðˈdrɔːəl) *n* **1** an act or process of withdrawing; retreat, removal, or detachment **2** the period a drug addict goes through following abrupt termination in the use of narcotics, usually characterized by physical and mental symptoms (**withdrawal symptoms**)

withdrawing room *n* an archaic term for **drawing room**

withdrawn (wɪðˈdrɔːn) *vb* **1** the past participle of **withdraw** ▷ *adj* **2** unusually reserved, introverted, or shy **3** secluded or remote > **withˈdrawnness** *n*

withdrew (wɪðˈdruː) *vb* the past tense of **withdraw**

withe (wɪθ, wɪð, waɪð) *n* **1** a strong flexible twig, esp of willow, suitable for binding things together; withy **2** a band or rope of twisted twigs or stems **3** a handle made of elastic material, fitted on some tools to reduce the shock during use **4** a wall with a thickness of half a brick, such as a leaf of a cavity wall, or a division between two chimney flues ▷ *vb* **5** (*tr*) to bind with withes [Old English *withthe*; related to Old Norse *vithja*, Old High German *witta*, *widi*, Gothic *wida*]

wither (ˈwɪðə) *vb* **1** (*intr*) (esp of a plant) to droop, wilt, or shrivel up **2** (*intr; often foll by away*) to fade or waste: *all hope withered away* **3** (*intr*) to decay, decline, or disintegrate **4** (*tr*) to cause to wilt, fade, or lose vitality **5** (*tr*) to abash, esp with a scornful look **6** (*tr*) to harm or damage [C14 perhaps variant of WEATHER (vb); related to German *verwittern* to decay] > **ˈwithered** *adj* > **ˈwitherer** *n* > **ˈwithering** *adj* > **ˈwitheringly** *adv*

witherite (ˈwɪðəˌraɪt) *n* a white, grey, or yellowish mineral consisting of barium carbonate in orthorhombic crystalline form: occurs in veins of lead ore. Formula: $BaCO_3$ [C18 named after W. *Withering* (1741–99), English scientist, who first described it]

withers (ˈwɪðəz) *pl n* the highest part of the back of a horse, behind the neck between the shoulders [C16 short for *widersones*, from *wider* WITH + *-sones*, perhaps variant of SINEW; related to German *Widerrist*, Old English *withre* resistance]

withershins (ˈwɪðəʃɪnz; *Scot* ˈwɪðər-) *or* **widdershins** *adv chiefly Scot* **1** in the direction contrary to the apparent course of the sun; anticlockwise **2** in a direction contrary to the usual; in the wrong direction. Compare **deasil** [C16 from Middle Low German *weddersinnes*, from Middle High German, literally: opposite course, from *wider* against + *sinnes*, genitive of *sin* course]

withhold (wɪðˈhəʊld) *vb* **-holds, -holding, -held** **1** (*tr*) to keep back; refrain from giving: *he withheld his permission* **2** (*tr*) to hold back; restrain **3** (*tr*) to deduct (taxes, etc) from a salary or wages **4** (*intr; usually foll by from*) to refrain or forbear > **withˈholder** *n*

withholding tax *n* **1** tax deducted at source from income, esp from dividends, paid to nonresidents of a country, which may be reclaimed if a double-taxation agreement exists between the country in which the income is paid and the country of residence of the recipient **2** *US* a portion of an employee's tax liability paid directly to the government by the employer

within (wɪˈðɪn) *prep* **1** in; inside; enclosed or encased by **2** before (a period of time) has elapsed: *within a week* **3** not beyond the limits of; not differing by more than (a specified amount) from: *live within your means; within seconds of the world record* ▷ *adv* **4** *formal* inside; internally

withindoors (ˈwɪðɪnˈdɔːz) *adv* an obsolete word for **indoors**

within-subjects design *n* (*modifier*) *statistics* (of an experiment) concerned with measuring the value of the dependent variable for the same subjects under the various experimental conditions. Compare **between-subjects design, matched-pairs design**

without (wɪˈðaʊt) *prep* **1** not having: *a traveller without much money* **2** not accompanied by: *he came without his wife* **3** not making use of: *it is not easy to undo screws without a screwdriver* **4** (*foll by a verbal noun or noun phrase*) not, while not, or after not: *she can sing for two minutes without drawing breath* **5** *archaic* on the outside of ▷ *adv* **6** *formal* outside; outwardly ▷ *conj* **7** *not standard* unless: *don't come without you have some money*

withoutdoors (ˈwɪðaʊtˈdɔːz) *adv* an obsolete word for **outdoors**

withstand (wɪðˈstænd) *vb* **-stands, -standing, -stood** **1** (*tr*) to stand up to forcefully; resist **2** (*intr*) to remain firm in endurance or opposition > **withˈstander** *n*

withy (ˈwɪðɪ) *n, pl* **withies** **1** a variant spelling of **withe** (senses 1, 2) **2** a willow tree, esp an osier ▷ *adj* **3** (of people) tough and agile **4** *rare* resembling a withe in strength or flexibility [Old English *wīdig(e)*; related to Old Norse *vīthir*, Old High German *wīda*, Latin *vītis* vine, Sanskrit *vītika* fetter. See WITHE, WIRE]

witless (ˈwɪtlɪs) *adj* lacking wit, intelligence, or sense; stupid > **ˈwitlessly** *adv* > **ˈwitlessness** *n*

witling (ˈwɪtlɪŋ) *n archaic* a person who thinks himself witty

witness (ˈwɪtnɪs) *n* **1** a person who has seen or can give first-hand evidence of some event **2** a person or thing giving or serving as evidence **3** a person who testifies, esp in a court of law, to events or facts within his own knowledge **4** a person who attests to the genuineness of a document, signature, etc, by adding his own signature **5** **bear witness** **a** to give written or oral testimony **b** to be evidence or proof of ▷ Related adjective: **testimonial** ▷ *vb* **6** (*tr*) to see, be present at, or know at first hand **7** to give or serve as evidence (of) **8** (*tr*) to be the scene or setting of: *this field has witnessed a battle* **9** (*intr*) to testify, esp in a court of law, to events within a person's own knowledge **10** (*tr*) to attest to the genuineness of (a document, signature, etc) by adding one's own signature [Old English *witnes* (meaning both *testimony* and *witness*), from *witan* to know, WIT² + -NESS; related to Old Norse *vitni*] > **ˈwitnessable** *adj* > **ˈwitnesser** *n*

witness box *or esp US* **witness stand** *n* the place in a court of law in which witnesses stand to give evidence

wits (wɪts) *pl n* **1** (*sometimes singular*) the ability to reason and act, esp quickly (esp in the phrase **have one's wits about one**) **2** (*sometimes singular*) right mind, sanity (esp in the phrase **out of one's wits**) **3** **at one's wits' end** at a loss to know how to proceed **4** **five wits** *obsolete* the five senses or mental faculties **5** **live by one's wits** to gain a livelihood by craftiness and cunning rather than by hard work

Wits (wɪts) (South African, informal) *n short for* University of the Witwatersrand

Witsie (ˈwɪtsɪ; *Afrikaans* ˈvətsɪ) *n South African informal* a student at the University of Witwatersrand, Johannesburg, esp one representing the University in a sport

-witted *adj* (*in combination*) having wits or intelligence as specified: *slow-witted; dim-witted*

Wittenberg (*German* ˈvɪtənbɛrk; *English* ˈwɪtᵊnˌbɜːg) *n* a city in E Germany, on the River Elbe, in Brandenburg: Martin Luther, as a philosophy teacher at Wittenberg university, began the Reformation here in 1517 by nailing his 95 theses to the doors of a church. Pop: 46 295 (2003 est)

witter (ˈwɪtə) *informal* ▷ *vb* **1** (*intr, often foll by on*) to chatter or babble pointlessly or at unnecessary length ▷ *n* **2** pointless chat; chatter [C20 from dialect; compare TWITTER]

Wittgensteinian (ˈvɪtgənʃtaɪnɪən, -ˌstaɪnɪən) *adj* (of a philosophical position or argument) derived from or related to the work of Ludwig Wittgenstein, the Austrian-born British philosopher (1889–1951), and esp the later work in which he attacks essentialism and stresses the open texture and variety of use of ordinary language

witticism (ˈwɪtɪˌsɪzəm) *n* a clever or witty remark [C17 from WITTY; coined by Dryden (1677) by analogy with *criticism*]

witting (ˈwɪtɪŋ) *adj rare* **1** deliberate; intentional: *a witting insult* **2** aware; knowing > **ˈwittingly** *adv*

wittol (ˈwɪtᵊl) *n obsolete* a man who tolerates his wife's unfaithfulness [C15 *wetewold*, from *witen* to know (see WIT²) + *-wold*, perhaps from *cokewold* CUCKOLD]

witty (ˈwɪtɪ) *adj* **-tier, -tiest** **1** characterized by clever humour or wit **2** *archaic or dialect* intelligent or sensible > **ˈwittily** *adv* > **ˈwittiness** *n*

Witwatersrand (wɪtˈwɔːtəzˌrænd; *Afrikaans* vətˈvaːtərsˈrant) *n* a rocky ridge in NE South Africa: contains the richest gold deposits in the world, also coal and manganese; chief industrial centre is Johannesburg. Height: 1500–1800 m (5000–6000 ft). Also called: **the Rand, the Reef**

wive (waɪv) *vb archaic* **1** to marry (a woman) **2** (*tr*) to supply with a wife [Old English *gewīfian*, from *wīf* WIFE]

wivern (ˈwaɪvən) *n* a less common spelling of **wyvern**

wives (waɪvz) *n* the plural of **wife**

wiz (wɪz) *n informal* a variant spelling of **whizz** (sense 6)

wizard (ˈwɪzəd) *n* **1** a male witch or a man who practises or professes to practise magic or sorcery **2** a person who is outstandingly clever in some specified field; expert **3** *obsolete* a wise man **4** *computing* a computer program that guides a user through a complex task ▷ *adj* **5** *informal, chiefly Brit* superb; outstanding **6** of or relating to a wizard or wizardry [C15 variant of *wissard*, from WISE¹ + -ARD] > **ˈwizardly** *adj*

wizardry (ˈwɪzədrɪ) *n* the art, skills, and practices of a wizard, sorcerer, or magician

wizen¹ (ˈwɪzᵊn) *vb* **1** to make or become shrivelled ▷ *adj* **2** a variant of **wizened** [Old English *wisnian*; related to Old Norse *visna*, Old High German *wesanēn*]

wizen² (ˈwiːzᵊn) *n* an archaic word for **weasand** (the gullet)

wizened (ˈwɪzᵊnd) *or* **wizen** *adj* shrivelled, wrinkled, or dried up, esp with age

wk *abbreviation for* **1** (*pl* **wks**) week **2** work **3** weak

WK *text messaging abbreviation for* week

wkly *abbreviation for* weekly

WKND *text messaging abbreviation for* weekend

WL *international car registration for* (Windward Islands) St Lucia

W

WLM *abbreviation for* women's liberation movement

WLTM *abbreviation for* would like to meet: used in lonely hearts columns and personal advertisements

WMD *abbreviation for* weapon(s) of mass destruction

wmk *abbreviation for* watermark

WMO *abbreviation for* World Meteorological Organization

WNW *symbol for* west-northwest

wo (wəʊ) *n, pl* **wos** an archaic spelling of **woe**

WO *abbreviation for* **1** War Office **2** Warrant Officer **3** wireless operator

w/o *abbreviation for* **1** without **2** written off

woad (wəʊd) *n* **1** a European plant, *Isatis tinctoria*, formerly cultivated for its leaves, which yield a blue dye: family *Brassicaceae* (crucifers). See also **dyer's-weed, dyer's rocket 2** the dye obtained from this plant, used esp by the ancient Britons, as a body dye [Old English *wād*; related to Old High German *weit*; Middle Dutch *wēd*, Latin *vitrum*]

woaded ('wəʊdɪd) *adj* coloured blue with woad

woadwaxen ('wəʊdˌwæksən) *n* another name for **dyer's-greenweed**

woald (wəʊld) *n* another name for **weld²**

wobbegong ('wɒbɪˌɡɒŋ) *n* an Australian carpet shark, *Orectolobus maculatus*, with brown-and-white skin [from a native Australian language]

wobble ('wɒb²l) *vb* **1** (*intr*) to move, rock, or sway unsteadily **2** (*intr*) to tremble or shake: *her voice wobbled with emotion* **3** (*intr*) to vacillate with indecision **4** (*tr*) to cause to wobble ▷ *n* **5** a wobbling movement, motion, or sound ▷ Also: **wabble** [C17 variant of *wabble*, from Low German *wabbeln*; related to Middle High German *wabelen* to **waver**] > **'wobbler** *n*

wobble board *n Austral* a piece of fibreboard used as a musical instrument, producing a characteristic sound when flexed

wobble plate *n* another name for **swash plate**

wobbly ('wɒblɪ) *adj* -**blier, -bliest 1** unsteady **2** trembling, shaking ▷ *n* **3** throw a wobbly *slang* to become suddenly very agitated or angry > **'wobbliness** *n*

Wobbly ('wɒblɪ) *n, pl* -**blies** a member of the Industrial Workers of the World

Woburn Abbey ('wəʊbən) *n* a mansion in Woburn in Bedfordshire: originally an abbey; rebuilt in the 17th century for the Dukes of Bedford, altered by Henry Holland in the 18th century; deer park landscaped by Humphrey Repton

Wodehousian (ˌwʊd'haʊsɪən) *adj* of, relating to, or reminiscent of Sir P(elham) G(renville) Wodehouse, the English-born US author (1881–1975)

Woden *or* **Wodan** ('wəʊd²n) *n* the foremost Anglo-Saxon god. Norse counterpart: **Odin** [Old English *Wōden*; related to Old Norse *Ōthinn*, Old High German *Wuotan*, German *Wotan*; see **WEDNESDAY**]

wodge (wɒdʒ) *n Brit informal* a thick lump or chunk cut or broken off something [C20 alteration of **WEDGE**]

woe (wəʊ) *n* **1** *literary* intense grief or misery **2** (*often plural*) affliction or misfortune **3** woe betide (someone) misfortune will befall (someone): *woe betide you if you arrive late* ▷ *interj* **4** Also: woe is me *archaic* an exclamation of sorrow or distress [Old English *wā, wǣ*; related to Old Saxon, Old High German *wē*, Old Norse *vei*, Gothic *wai*, Latin *vae*, Sanskrit *uvē*; see **WAIL**]

woebegone ('wəʊbɪˌɡɒn) *adj* **1** sorrowful or sad in appearance **2** *archaic* afflicted with woe [C14 from a phrase such as *me is wo begon* woe has beset me]

woeful ('wəʊf³l) *adj* **1** expressing or characterized by sorrow **2** bringing or causing woe **3** pitiful; miserable: *a woeful standard of work* > **'woefully** *adv* > **'woefulness** *n*

wof (wɒf) *n Austral slang* a fool; idiot [from w(aste) o(f) f(lesh)]

WOF (in New Zealand) *abbreviation for* **Warrant of Fitness**

wog¹ (wɒɡ) *n Brit slang derogatory* a foreigner, esp one who is not White [probably from **GOLLIWOG**]

wog² (wɒɡ) *n slang, chiefly Austral* influenza or any similar illness [C20 of unknown origin]

woggle ('wɒɡ²l) *n* the ring of leather through which a Scout neckerchief is threaded [C20 of unknown origin]

wok (wɒk) *n* a large metal Chinese cooking pot having a curved base like a bowl and traditionally with a wooden handle [from Chinese (Cantonese)]

woke (wəʊk) *vb* a past tense of **wake**

woken ('wəʊkən) *vb* a past participle of **wake**

Woking ('wəʊkɪŋ) *n* a town in SE England, in central Surrey: mainly residential. Pop: 101 127 (2001)

Wokingham *n* a unitary authority in SE England, in Berkshire. Pop: 151 200 (2003 est). Area: 179 sq km (69 sq miles)

wokka board ('wɒkə) *n Austral* another name for **wobble board**

wold¹ (wəʊld) *n chiefly literary* a tract of open rolling country, esp upland [Old English *weald* bush; related to Old Saxon *wald*, German *Wald* forest, Old Norse *vollr* ground; see **WILD**]

wold² (wəʊld) *n* another name for **weld²**

Wolds (wəʊldz) *pl n* **the** a range of chalk hills in NE England: consists of the **Yorkshire Wolds** to the north, separated from the **Lincolnshire Wolds** by the Humber estuary

wolf (wʊlf) *n, pl* **wolves** (wʊlvz) **1** a predatory canine mammal, *Canis lupus*, which hunts in packs and was formerly widespread in North America and Eurasia but is now less common. See also **timber wolf** Related adj: **lupine 2** any of several similar and related canines, such as the red wolf and the coyote (**prairie wolf**) **3** the fur of any such animal **4** Tasmanian wolf another name for the **thylacine 5** a voracious, grabbing, or fiercely cruel person or thing **6** *informal* a man who habitually tries to seduce women **7** *informal* the destructive larva of any of various moths and beetles **8** Also called: wolf note *music* **a** an unpleasant sound produced in some notes played on the violin, cello, etc, owing to resonant vibrations of the belly **b** an out-of-tune effect produced on keyboard instruments accommodated esp to the system of mean-tone temperament. See **temperament** (sense 4) **9** cry wolf to give a false alarm **10** keep the wolf from the door to ward off starvation or privation **11** lone wolf a person or animal who prefers to be alone **12** throw to the wolves to abandon or deliver to destruction **13** wolf in sheep's clothing a malicious person in a harmless or benevolent disguise ▷ *vb* **14** (*tr*; often foll by *down*) to gulp (down) **15** (*intr*) to hunt wolves [Old English *wulf*; related to Old High German *wolf*, Old Norse *ulfr*, Gothic *wulfs*, Latin *lupus* and *vulpēs* fox] > **'wolfish** *adj* > **'wolfˌlike** *adj*

Wolf Cub *n Brit* the former name for **Cub Scout**

Wolfenden Report ('wʊlfəndən) *n* a study produced in 1957 by the Committee on Homosexual Offences and Prostitution in Britain, which recommended that homosexual relations between consenting adults be legalized [C20 named after Baron John Frederick *Wolfenden* (1906–85), who chaired the Committee]

wolfer ('wʊlfə) *n* a variant spelling of **wolver**

Wolffian body ('vɒlfɪən) *n embryol* another name for **mesonephros** [C19 named after K. F. *Wolff* (1733–94), German embryologist]

wolffish ('wʊlfˌfɪʃ) *n, pl* -**fish** *or* -**fishes** any large northern deep-sea blennioid fish of the family *Anarhichadidae*, such as *Anarhichas lupus*. They have large sharp teeth and no pelvic fins and are used as food fishes. Also called: **catfish**

wolfhound ('wʊlfˌhaʊnd) *n* the largest breed of dog, used formerly to hunt wolves

wolfram ('wʊlfrəm) *n* another name for **tungsten** [C18 from German, originally perhaps from the proper name, *Wolfram*, used pejoratively of tungsten because it was thought inferior to tin]

wolframite ('wʊlfrəˌmaɪt) *n* a black to reddish-brown mineral consisting of tungstates of iron and manganese in monoclinic crystalline form: it occurs mainly in quartz veins and is the chief ore of tungsten. Formula: $(Fe,Mn)WO_4$

Wolf-Rayet star ('wʊlfˈreɪət) *n* any of a small class of very hot intensely luminous stars surrounded by a rapidly expanding envelope of gas [C19 named after Charles *Wolf* (1827–1918) and Georges *Rayet* (1839–1906), French astronomers]

wolfsbane *or* **wolf's-bane** ('wʊlfsˌbeɪn) *n* any of several poisonous N temperate plants of the ranunculaceous genus *Aconitum*, esp *A. lycoctonum*, which have yellow hoodlike flowers

Wolfsburg (German 'vɒlfsbʊrk) *n* a city in N central Germany, in Lower Saxony: founded in 1938; motor-vehicle industry. Pop: 122 724 (2003 est)

wolf spider *n* any spider of the family *Lycosidae*, which chase their prey to catch it. Also called: **hunting spider**

wolf whistle *n* **1** a whistle made by a man to express admiration of a woman's appearance ▷ *vb* wolf-whistle **2** (when *intr*, sometimes foll by *at*) to make a whistle (at someone)

wollastonite ('wʊləstəˌnaɪt) *n* a white or grey mineral consisting of calcium silicate in triclinic crystalline form: occurs in metamorphosed limestones. Formula: $CaSiO_3$ [C19 named after W. H. *Wollaston* (1766–1828), English physicist]

Wollongong ('wʊləŋˌɡɒŋ) *n* a city in E Australia, in E New South Wales on the Pacific: an early centre of dairy farming; now a coal-mining and heavy industrial centre. Pop: 228 846 (2001)

wolly ('wɒlɪ) *n, pl* -**lies** *East London dialect* a pickled cucumber or olive [perhaps from **OLIVE**]

Wolof ('wɒlɒf) *n* **1** (*pl* -**of** *or* -**ofs**) a member of a Negroid people of W Africa living chiefly in Senegal **2** the language of this people, belonging to the West Atlantic branch of the Niger-Congo family

wolver ('wʊlvə) *or* **wolfer** *n* a person who hunts wolves

Wolverhampton (ˌwʊlvə'hæmptən) *n* **1** a city in W central England, in Wolverhampton unitary authority, West Midlands: iron and steel foundries; university (1992). Pop: 251 462 (2001) **2** a unitary authority in W central England, in the West Midlands. Pop: 238 900 (2003 est). Area: 69 sq km (27 sq miles)

wolverine ('wʊlvəˌriːn) *n* a large musteline mammal, *Gulo gulo*, of northern forests of Eurasia and North America having dark very thick water-resistant fur. Also called: **glutton** [C16 *wolvering*, from **WOLF** + -**ING³** (later altered to -*ine*)]

wolves (wʊlvz) *n* the plural of **wolf**

woman ('wʊmən) *n, pl* **women** ('wɪmɪn) **1** an adult female human being **2** (*modifier*) female or feminine: *a woman politician; woman talk* **3** women collectively; womankind **4** (*usually preceded by the*) feminine nature or feelings: *babies bring out the woman in her* **5** a female servant or domestic help **6** a man considered as having supposed female characteristics, such as meekness or timidity **7** *informal* a wife, mistress, or girlfriend **8** the little woman *informal* one's wife **9** woman of the streets a prostitute ▷ *vb* **10** *rare* to provide with women **11** *obsolete* to make effeminate ▷ Related prefixes: **gyno-, gynaeco-** [Old English *wīfmann, wimman*; from **WIFE** + **MAN** (human being)] > **'womanless** *adj* > **'womanˌlike** *adj*

womanhood ('wʊmənˌhʊd) *n* **1** the state or quality of being a woman or being womanly **2** women collectively

womanish ('wʊmənɪʃ) *adj* **1** having qualities or characteristics regarded as unsuitable to a strong character of either sex, esp a man **2** characteristic of or suitable for a woman > **'womanishly** *adv* > **'womanishness** *n*

womanize *or* **womanise** ('wʊməˌnaɪz) *vb* **1** (*intr*) (of a man) to indulge in many casual affairs with

women; philander **2** (*tr*) to make effeminate
▷ 'woman,izer *or* 'woman,iser *n* ▷ 'woman,izing *or*
'woman,ising *n, adj*

womankind ('wʊmən,kaɪnd) *n* the female
members of the human race; women collectively

womanly ('wʊmənlɪ) *adj* **1** possessing qualities,
such as warmth, attractiveness, etc, generally
regarded as typical of a woman, esp a mature
woman **2** characteristic of or belonging to a
woman ▷ 'womanliness *n*

womb (wu:m) *n* **1** the nontechnical name for
uterus Related *adj*: **uterine 2** a hollow space
enclosing something, esp when dark, warm, or
sheltering **3** a place where something is
conceived: *the Near East is the womb of western
civilization* **4** *obsolete* the belly [Old English *wamb*;
related to Old Norse *vomb*, Gothic *wamba*, Middle
Low German *wamme*, Swedish *våmm*] ▷ wombed *adj*
▷ 'womblike *adj*

wombat ('wɒmbæt) *n* any of various burrowing
herbivorous Australian marsupials, esp *Vombatus
ursinus*, constituting the family *Vombatidae* and
having short limbs, a heavy body, and coarse
dense fur [c18 from a native Australian language]

women ('wɪmɪn) *n* the plural of **woman**

womenfolk ('wɪmɪn,fəʊk) *or sometimes US*
womenfolks *pl n* **1** women collectively **2** a
group of women, esp the female members of one's
family

Women's Institute *n* (in Britain and
Commonwealth countries) a society for women
interested in the problems of the home and in
engaging in social activities

Women's Liberation *n* a movement directed
towards the removal of attitudes and practices
that preserve inequalities based upon the
assumption that men are superior to women. Also
called: women's lib

Women's Movement *n* a grass-roots movement
of women concerned with women's liberation.
See **Women's Liberation**

women's refuge *n social welfare* a house where
battered women and their children can go for
protection from their oppressors

Women's Royal Voluntary Service *n* a British
auxiliary service organized in 1938 as the
Women's Voluntary Service for work in air raids
and civil defence: active throughout World War II
and since 1945 in providing support services for
those in need: became the Women's Royal
Voluntary Service in 1966. Abbreviation: WRVS

women's studies *pl n* courses in history,
literature, psychology, etc, that are particularly
concerned with women's roles, experiences, and
achievements

women's suffrage *n* the right of women to vote.
See also **suffragette**

womera ('wʊmərə) *n* a variant spelling of
woomera

wommit ('wɒmɪt) *n Southern English dialect* a
foolish person

won¹ (wʌn) *vb* the past tense of **win¹**

won² (wɒn) *n, pl* **won 1** the standard monetary
unit of North Korea, divided into 100 chon **2** the
standard monetary unit of South Korea, divided
into 100 chon ▷ Also called: hwan [Korean *wǎn*]

won³ (wʌn, wʊn, wəʊn) *vb* **wons, wonning,
wonned** (*intr*) *archaic* to live or dwell [Old English
wunian to become accustomed to; related to WIN¹]

wonder ('wʌndə) *n* **1** the feeling excited by
something strange; a mixture of surprise,
curiosity, and sometimes awe **2** something that
causes such a feeling, such as a miracle **3** See
Seven Wonders of the World 4 (*modifier*) exciting
wonder by virtue of spectacular results achieved,
feats performed, etc: *a wonder drug; a wonder horse* **5**
do *or* **work wonders** to achieve spectacularly fine
results **6 for a wonder** surprisingly or amazingly
7 **nine days' wonder** a subject that arouses
general surprise or public interest for a short time
8 no wonder (*sentence connector*) (I am) not
surprised at all (that): *no wonder he couldn't come* **9**

small wonder (*sentence connector*) (I am) hardly
surprised (that): *small wonder he couldn't make it
tonight* ▷ *vb* (when *tr*, may take a clause as object) **10**
(when *intr*, often foll by *about*) to indulge in
speculative inquiry, often accompanied by an
element of doubt (concerning something): *I
wondered about what she said; I wonder what happened* **11**
(when *intr*, often foll by *at*) to be amazed (at
something): *I wonder at your impudence* [Old English
wundor; related to Old Saxon *wundar*, Old Norse *undr*,
German *Wunder*] ▷ 'wonderer *n* ▷ 'wonderless *adj*

wonderful ('wʌndəfʊl) *adj* **1** exciting a feeling of
wonder; marvellous or strange **2** extremely fine;
excellent ▷ 'wonderfully *adv* ▷ 'wonderfulness *n*

wonderkid ('wʌndə,kɪd) *n informal* a young
person whose excellence in his or her discipline is
appropriate to someone older and more
experienced

wonderland ('wʌndə,lænd) *n* **1** an imaginary
land of marvels or wonders **2** an actual place or
scene of great or strange beauty or wonder

wonderment ('wʌndəmənt) *n* **1** rapt surprise;
awe **2** puzzled interest **3** something that excites
wonder

wonderwork ('wʌndə,wɜːk) *n* something done or
made that excites wonder; miracle or wonder
▷ 'wonder-,worker *n* ▷ 'wonder-,working *n, adj*

wondrous ('wʌndrəs) *archaic or literary* ▷ *adj* **1**
exciting wonder; marvellous ▷ *adv* **2** (*intensifier*):
it is wondrous cold ▷ 'wondrously *adv*
▷ 'wondrousness *n*

wonga ('wɒŋɡə) *n Brit informal* money [c20
possibly from Romany *wongar* coal]

wonga-wonga ('wɒŋə'wɒŋə) *n* **1** Also called:
wonga pigeon a large Australian pigeon,
Leucosarcia melanoleuca **2** an Australian evergreen
vine of the genus *Pandorea or Tecoma*, esp *T. australis*
[from a native Australian language]

wonk (wɒŋk) *n informal* a person who is
obsessively interested in a specified subject: *a
foreign policy wonk* [c20 of uncertain origin]

wonky ('wɒŋkɪ) *adj* **-kier, -kiest** *Brit informal* **1**
shaky or unsteady **2** not in correct alignment;
askew **3** liable to break down or develop a fault
[c20 variant of dialect *wanky*, from Old English
wancol]

Wŏnsan ('wɒn'sæn) *n* a port in SE North Korea,
on the Sea of Japan: oil refineries. Pop: 319 000
(2005 est)

wont (wəʊnt) *adj* **1** (*postpositive*) accustomed (to
doing something): *he was wont to come early* ▷ *n* **2** a
manner or action habitually employed by or
associated with someone (often in the phrases **as
is my wont, as is his wont**, etc) ▷ *vb* **3** (when *tr*,
usually passive) to become or cause to become
accustomed [Old English *gewunod*, past participle
of *wunian* to be accustomed to; related to Old High
German *wunēn* (German *wohnen*), Old Norse *una* to
be satisfied; see WEAN¹, WISH, WINSOME]

won't (wəʊnt) *vb* contraction of will not

wonted ('wəʊntɪd) *adj* **1** (*postpositive*) accustomed
or habituated (to doing something) **2** (*prenominal*)
customary; usual: *she is in her wonted place*

won ton ('wɒn 'tɒn) *n Chinese cookery* **1** a
dumpling filled with spiced minced pork, usually
served in soup **2** soup containing such
dumplings [from Chinese (Cantonese) *wan t'an*
pastry]

woo (wu:) *vb* **woos, wooing, wooed 1** to seek the
affection, favour, or love of (a woman) with a view
to marriage **2** (*tr*) to seek after zealously or
hopefully: *to woo fame* **3** (*tr*) to bring upon oneself
(good or evil results) by one's own action **4** (*tr*) to
beg or importune (someone) [Old English *wōgian*,
of obscure origin] ▷ 'wooer *n* ▷ 'wooing *n*

wood¹ (wʊd) *n* **1** the hard fibrous substance
consisting of xylem tissue that occurs beneath the
bark in trees, shrubs, and similar plants. Related
adjs: **ligneous, xyloid 2** the trunks of trees that
have been cut and prepared for use as a building
material **3** a collection of trees, shrubs, herbs,
grasses, etc, usually dominated by one or a few

species of tree: usually smaller than a forest: *an
oak wood*. Related *adj*: **sylvan 4** fuel; firewood **5**
golf **a** a long-shafted club with a broad wooden or
metal head, used for driving: numbered from 1 to
7 according to size, angle of face, etc **b** (*as
modifier*): *a wood shot* **6** *tennis, squash, badminton* the
frame of a racket: *he hit a winning shot off the wood* **7**
one of the biased wooden bowls used in the game
of bowls **8** *music* short for **woodwind** See also
woods (sense 3) **9 a** casks, barrels, etc, made of
wood **b** **from the wood** (of a beverage) from a
wooden container rather than a metal or glass
one **10 have (got) the wood on** *Austral and NZ
informal* to have an advantage over **11 out of the
wood** *or* **woods** clear of or safe from dangers or
doubts: *we're not out of the wood yet* **12 see the wood
for the trees** (used with a negative) to obtain a
general view of a situation, problem, etc, without
allowing details to cloud one's analysis: *he can't see
the wood for the trees* **13** (*modifier*) made of, used for,
employing, or handling wood: *a wood fire* **14**
(*modifier*) dwelling in, concerning, or situated in a
wood: *a wood nymph* ▷ *vb* **15** (*tr*) to plant a wood
upon **16** to supply or be supplied with fuel or
firewood ▷ See also **woods** [Old English *widu, wudu*;
related to Old High German *witu*, Old Norse *vithr*]
▷ 'woodless *adj*

wood² (wʊd) *adj obsolete* raging or raving like a
maniac [Old English *wōd*; related to Old High
German *wuot* (German *Wut*), Old Norse *ōthr*, Gothic
wōths, Latin *vātēs* seer]

wood alcohol *n* another name for **methanol**

wood-and-water joey *n Austral informal* a person
employed to carry out menial tasks [from the
biblical phrase "hewers of wood and drawers of
water" (Joshua 9:21) and JOEY]

wood anemone *n* any of several woodland
anemone plants, esp *Anemone quinquefolia* of E
North America and *A. nemorosa* of Europe, having
finely divided leaves and solitary white flowers.
Also called: windflower

wood ant *n* a reddish-brown European ant,
Formica rufa, typically living in anthills in
woodlands

wood avens *n* another name for **herb bennet**

woodbine ('wʊd,baɪn) *n* **1** a honeysuckle, *Lonicera
periclymenum*, of Europe, SW Asia, and N Africa,
having fragrant creamy flowers **2** American
woodbine a related North American plant, *L.
caprifolium* **3** US another name for **Virginia creeper**
(sense 1) **4** *Austral obsolete slang* an Englishman
[sense 4 from the English brand of cigarettes so
named]

wood block *n* **1** a small rectangular flat block of
wood that is laid with others as a floor surface **2**
music another word for **Chinese block**

woodborer ('wʊd,bɔ:rə) *n* **1** any of various beetles
of the families *Anobiidae, Buprestidae*, etc, the larvae
of which bore into and damage wood **2** any of
various other unrelated invertebrates that bore
into wood

woodcarving ('wʊd,ka:vɪŋ) *n* **1** the act of carving
wood, esp as an art form **2** a work of art produced
by carving wood ▷ 'wood,carver *n*

woodchat *or* **woodchat shrike** ('wʊd,tʃæt) *n* a
songbird, *Lanius senator*, of Europe and N Africa,
having a black-and-white plumage with a
reddish-brown crown and a hooked bill: family
Laniidae (shrikes)

woodchop ('wʊd,tʃɒp) *n Austral* a wood-chopping
competition, esp at a show

woodchuck ('wʊd,tʃʌk) *n* a North American
marmot, *Marmota monax*, having coarse reddish-
brown fur. Also called: groundhog [c17 by folk
etymology from Cree *otcheck* fisher, marten]

wood coal *n* another name for **lignite** *or* **charcoal**

woodcock ('wʊd,kɒk) *n* **1** an Old World game
bird, *Scolopax rusticola*, resembling the snipe but
larger and having shorter legs and neck: family
Scolopacidae (sandpipers, etc), order *Charadriiformes* **2**
a related North American bird, *Philohela minor* **3**
obsolete a simpleton

W

woodcraft ('wʊd,krɑːft) *n chiefly US and Canadian* **1** ability and experience in matters concerned with living in a wood or forest **2** ability or skill at woodwork, carving, etc **3** skill in caring for trees > 'wood,craftsman *n*

woodcut ('wʊd,kʌt) *n* **1** a block of wood cut along the grain and with a design, illustration, etc, incised with a knife, from which prints are made **2** a print from a woodcut

woodcutter ('wʊd,kʌtə) *n* **1** a person who fells trees or chops wood **2** a person who makes woodcuts > 'wood,cutting *n*

wood duck *n* a duck, *Aix sponsa*, of wooded swamps, lakes, etc, in North America, having a very brightly coloured plumage in the male

wooded ('wʊdɪd) *adj* **1** covered with or abounding in woods or trees **2** (*in combination*) having wood of a specified character: *a soft-wooded tree*

wooden ('wʊdⁿn) *adj* **1** made from or consisting of wood **2** awkward or clumsy **3** bereft of spirit or animation: *a wooden expression* **4** obstinately unyielding: *a wooden attitude* **5** mentally slow or dull **6** not highly resonant: *a wooden thud* ▷ *vb* **7** (*tr*) *Austral slang* to fell or kill (a person or animal) > 'woodenly *adv* > 'woodenness *n*

wood engraving *n* **1** the art of engraving pictures or designs on wood for printing by incising them with a burin on a block of wood cut across the grain **2** a block of wood so engraved or a print taken from it > **wood engraver** *n*

woodenhead ('wʊdⁿn,hɛd) *n informal* a dull, foolish, or unintelligent person > ,wooden'headed *adj* > ,wooden'headedness *n*

Wooden Horse *n* another name for the **Trojan Horse** (sense 1)

wooden spoon *n* a booby prize, esp in sporting contests

wooden tongue *or* **woody tongue** *n vet science* the nontechnical name for **actinobacillosis**

woodentop ('wʊdⁿn,tɒp) *n Brit informal* a dull, foolish, or unintelligent person

woodfree ('wʊd,friː) *adj* (of high-quality paper) made from pulp that has been treated chemically, removing impurities

woodgrouse ('wʊd,graʊs) *n* another name for **capercaillie**

wood hedgehog *n* a pale buff basidiomycetous fungus, *Hydnum repandum*, found in broad-leaved woodlands having a spiny underside to the cap

woodhen ('wʊd,hɛn) *n NZ* another name for **weka**

wood hyacinth *n* another name for **bluebell** (sense 1)

wood ibis *n* any of several storks having a downward-curved bill, esp *Mycteria americana* of America and *Ibis ibis* of Africa

woodland ('wʊdlənd) *n* **a** land that is mostly covered with woods or dense growths of trees and shrubs **b** (*as modifier*): *woodland fauna* > 'woodlander *n*

woodlark ('wʊd,lɑːk) *n* an Old World lark, *Lullula arborea*, similar to but slightly smaller than the skylark

woodlot ('wʊd,lɒt) *n* an area restricted to the growing of trees. Also called (esp Canadian): **bush lot**

woodlouse ('wʊd,laʊs) *n, pl* -**lice** (-,laɪs) any of various small terrestrial isopod crustaceans of the genera *Oniscus*, *Porcellio*, etc, which have a flattened segmented body and occur in damp habitats. See also **pill bug**

woodman ('wʊdmən) *n, pl* -**men** **1** a person who looks after and fells trees used for timber **2** another word for **woodsman** **3** *obsolete* a hunter who is knowledgeable about woods and the animals living in them

woodnote ('wʊd,nəʊt) *n* a natural musical note or song, like that of a wild bird

wood nymph *n* one of a class of nymphs fabled to inhabit the woods, such as a dryad

wood opal *n* a form of petrified wood impregnated by common opal

wood owl *n* another name for **tawny owl**

woodpecker ('wʊd,pɛkə) *n* any climbing bird of the family *Picidae*, typically having a brightly coloured plumage and strong chisel-like bill with which they bore into trees for insects: order *Piciformes*

wood pigeon *n* a large Eurasian pigeon, *Columba palumbus*, having white patches on the wings and neck. Also called: **ringdove**, **cushat**

woodpile ('wʊd,paɪl) *n* **1** a pile or heap of firewood **2** **nigger in the woodpile** See **nigger** (sense 3)

wood pitch *n* the dark viscid residue left after the distillation of wood tar: used as a binder in briquettes

wood preservative *n* a coating applied to timber as a protection against decay, insects, weather, etc

woodprint ('wʊd,prɪnt) *n* another name for **woodcut** (sense 2)

wood pulp *n* **1** wood that has been ground to a fine pulp for use in making newsprint and other cheap forms of paper, and in the production of hardboard **2** finely pulped wood that has been digested by a chemical, such as caustic soda, and sometimes bleached: used in making paper

wood rat *n* another name for **pack rat**

woodruff ('wʊdrʌf) *n* any of several rubiaceous plants of the genus *Galium*, esp *G. odoratum* (**sweet woodruff**), of Eurasia, which has small sweet-scented white flowers and whorls of narrow fragrant leaves used to flavour wine and liqueurs and in perfumery [Old English *wudurofe*, from WOOD¹ + *rôfe*, related to Old High German *ruoba*, Middle Low German *rôve* (beet)root, Latin *rēpere* to creep]

Woodruff key ('wʊdrʌf) *n engineering* a semicircular key restrained in a curved keyway in a shaft [C19 named after the *Woodruff Manufacturing Co*, in Hartford, Connecticut, who first manufactured it in 1892]

woodrush ('wʊd,rʌʃ) *n* any of various juncaceous plants of the genus *Luzula*, chiefly of cold and temperate regions of the N hemisphere, having grasslike leaves and small brown flowers

woods (wʊdz) *pl n* **1** closely packed trees forming a forest or wood, esp a specific one **2** another word for **backwoods** (sense 2) **3** the woodwind instruments in an orchestra. See also **wood¹** (sense 8) **4** **neck of the woods** *informal* an area or locality: *a quiet neck of the woods*

Woods¹ *n* **Lake of the** See **Lake of the Woods**

wood sage *n* a downy labiate perennial, *Teucrium scorodonia*, having spikes of green-yellow flowers: common on acid heath and scree in Europe and naturalized in North America

woodscrew ('wʊd,skruː) *n* a metal screw that tapers to a point so that it can be driven into wood by a screwdriver

Woodser ('wʊdzə) *n* See **Jimmy Woodser**

woodshed ('wʊd,ʃɛd) *n* a small outbuilding where firewood, garden tools, etc, are stored

woodsia ('wʊdzɪə) *n* any small fern of the genus *Woodsia*, of temperate and cold regions, having tufted rhizomes and numerous wiry fronds: family *Polypodiaceae*

woodsman ('wʊdzmən) *n, pl* -**men** a person who lives in a wood or who is skilled in woodcraft. Also called: **woodman**

wood sorrel *n* a Eurasian plant, *Oxalis acetosella*, having trifoliate leaves, an underground creeping stem, and white purple-veined flowers: family *Oxalidaceae*

wood spirit *n chem* another name for **methanol**

Woodstock ('wʊdstɒk) *n* **a** town in New York State, the site of a large rock festival in August 1969. Pop: 6253 (2003 est)

wood sugar *n chem* another name for **xylose**

woodswallow ('wʊd,swɒləʊ) *n* any of several insectivorous birds of the genus *Artamus* of Australia

woodsy ('wʊdzɪ) *adj* **woodsier**, **woodsiest** *US and Canadian informal* of, reminiscent of, or connected with woods: *a woodsy mountain hideaway*

wood tar *n* any tar produced by the destructive distillation of wood: used in producing tarred cord and rope and formerly in medicine as disinfectants and antiseptics

wood vinegar *n* another name for **pyroligneous acid**

wood warbler *n* **1** a European woodland warbler, *Phylloscopus sibilatrix*, with a dull yellow plumage **2** another name for the **American warbler**. See **warbler** (sense 3)

wood wasp *n* another name for the **horntail**

woodwaxen ('wʊd,wæksⁿn) *n* another name for **dyer's-greenweed**

woodwind ('wʊd,wɪnd) *music* ▷ *adj* **1** of, relating to, or denoting a type of wind instrument, excluding the brass instruments, formerly made of wood but now often made of metal, such as the flute or clarinet ▷ *n* **2** (*functioning as plural*) woodwind instruments collectively

wood woollyfoot ('wʊlɪ,fʊt) *n* a common yellowish basidiomycetous fungus, *Collybia peronata*, of broad-leaved woodland, having a hairy tuft at the foot of the stem

woodwork ('wʊd,wɜːk) *n* **1** the art, craft, or skill of making things in wood; carpentry **2** components made of wood, such as doors, staircases, etc

woodworker ('wʊd,wɜːkə) *n* a person who works in wood, such as a carpenter, joiner, or cabinet-maker

woodworking ('wʊd,wɜːkɪŋ) *n* **1** the process of working wood ▷ *adj* **2** of, relating to, or used in woodworking

woodworm ('wʊd,wɜːm) *n* **1** any of various insect larvae that bore into wooden furniture, beams, etc, esp the larvae of the furniture beetle, *Anobium punctatum*, and the deathwatch beetle **2** the condition caused in wood by any of these larvae

woody ('wʊdɪ) *adj* **woodier**, **woodiest** **1** abounding in or covered with forest or woods **2** connected with, belonging to, or situated in a wood **3** consisting of or containing wood or lignin: *woody tissue*; *woody stems* **4** resembling wood in hardness or texture > 'woodiness *n*

woodyard ('wʊd,jɑːd) *n* a place where timber is cut and stored

woody nightshade *n* a scrambling woody Eurasian solanaceous plant, *Solanum dulcamara*, having purple flowers with recurved petals and a protruding cone of yellow anthers and producing poisonous red berry-like fruits. Also called: **bittersweet**

woof¹ (wuːf) *n* **1** the crosswise yarns that fill the warp yarns in weaving; weft **2** a woven fabric or its texture [Old English *ōwef*, from *ō-*, perhaps from ON, + *wef* WEB (see WEAVE); modern form influenced by WARP]

woof² (wʊf) *interj* **1** an imitation of the bark or growl of a dog ▷ *vb* **2** (*intr*) (of dogs) to bark or growl

woofer ('wuːfə) *n* a loudspeaker used in high-fidelity systems for the reproduction of low audio frequencies

woofter ('wʊftə, 'wuːftə) *n derogatory slang* a male homosexual

Wookey Hole ('wʊkɪ həʊl) *n* a village in SW England, in Somerset, near Wells: noted for the nearby limestone cave in which prehistoric remains have been found. Pop: 1000 (latest est)

wool (wʊl) *n* **1** the outer coat of sheep, yaks, etc, which consists of short curly hairs **2** yarn spun from the coat of sheep, etc, used in weaving, knitting, etc **3 a** cloth or a garment made from this yarn **b** (*as modifier*): *a wool dress* **4** any of certain fibrous materials: *glass wool*; *steel wool* **5** *informal* short thick curly hair **6** a tangled mass of soft fine hairs that occurs in certain plants **7** **dyed in the wool** confirmed in one's beliefs or opinions **8** **pull the wool over someone's eyes** to deceive or delude someone [Old English *wull*; related to Old Frisian, Middle Dutch *wulle*, Old

High German *wolla* (German *Wolle*), Old Norse *ull*, Latin *lāna* and *vellus* fleece] > 'wool-,like *adj*

wool bale *n* *Austral and NZ* a standard-sized jute, flax, etc, cubical container of compressed wool weighing over 100 kg when containing fleece or lamb's wool and weighing 204 kg when containing oddments

wool cheque *n* *NZ* the annual return for a sheep farmer

wool classing *n* *Austral and NZ* the grading and grouping together of similar types of wool

wool clip *n* the total amount of wool shorn from a particular flock, or from flocks in a particular region or country, in one year

wool fat *or* **grease** *n* another name for **lanolin**

woolfell ('wʊl,fɛl) *n* *obsolete* the skin of a sheep or similar animal with the fleece still attached

woolgathering ('wʊl,gæðərɪŋ) *n* idle or absent-minded indulgence in fantasy; daydreaming > 'wool,gatherer *n*

woolgrower ('wʊl,grəʊə) *n* a person who keeps sheep for their wool > 'wool,growing *n, adj*

woolled (wʊld) *adj* **1** (of animals) having wool **2** having wool as specified: *coarse-woolled*

woollen *or US* **woolen** ('wʊlən) *adj* **1** relating to or consisting partly or wholly of wool ▷ *n* **2** (*often plural*) a garment or piece of cloth made wholly or partly of wool, esp a knitted one

woolly *or sometimes US* **wooly** ('wʊlɪ) *adj* **woollier, woolliest** *or sometimes US* **woolier, wooliest 1** consisting of, resembling, or having the nature of wool **2** covered or clothed in wool or something resembling it **3** lacking clarity or substance: *woolly thinking* **4** *botany* covered with long soft whitish hairs: *woolly stems* **5** *US* recalling the rough and lawless period of the early West of America (esp in the phrase **wild and woolly**) ▷ *n, pl* **woollies** *or sometimes US* **woolies 6** (*often plural*) a garment, such as a sweater, made of wool or something similar **7** *Western US and Austral* (*usually plural*) an informal word for **sheep**. > 'woollily *adv* > 'woolliness *n*

woolly bear *n* the caterpillar of any of various tiger moths, esp *Arctia caja* of Europe and *Isia isabella* of North America, having a dense covering of soft hairs

woollybutt ('wʊlɪ,bʌt) *n* *Austral* any of several eucalyptus trees, esp *Eucalyptus longifolia,* having loose fibrous bark around the base of the trunk

woolly-minded *adj* showing a vague or muddled way of thinking

woolpack ('wʊl,pæk) *n* **1** the cloth or canvas wrapping used to pack a bale of wool **2** a bale of wool

woolsack ('wʊl,sæk) *n* **1** a sack containing or intended to contain wool **2** (in Britain) the seat of the Lord Chancellor in the House of Lords, formerly made of a large square sack of wool

woolshed ('wʊl,ʃɛd) *n* *Austral and NZ* a shearing shed

wool-sorter's disease *n* another name for **anthrax**

wool stapler *n* a person who sorts wool into different grades or classifications > 'wool-,stapling *n, adj*

wool store *n* *Austral and NZ* a building where bales of wool are stored and made available to prospective buyers for inspection

wool table *n* *NZ* a slatted wooden table in a shearing shed where fleeces are skirted and classed

woomera *or* **womera** ('wʊmərə) *n* *Austral* a type of notched stick used by native Australians to increase leverage and propulsion in the throwing of a spear [from a native Australian language]

Woomera ('wʊmərə) *n* a town in South Australia: site of the Long Range Weapons Establishment. Pop: 602 (2001)

Woop Woop ('wuːp ,wuːp) *n* *Austral slang* a jocular name for any backward or remote town or district

woorali (wʊ'rɑːlɪ) *n* a less common name for

curare [C18 from the native S American name]

woose (wʊs) *n* same as **wuss**

woosh (wʊʃ) *n, vb* a variant spelling of **whoosh**

woozy ('wuːzɪ) *adj* **woozier, wooziest** *informal* **1** dazed or confused **2** experiencing dizziness, nausea, etc [C19 perhaps from a blend of *woolly* + *muzzy* or *dizzy*] > 'woozily *adv* > 'wooziness *n*

wop[1] (wɒp) *n* *slang derogatory* a member of a Latin people, esp an Italian [C20 probably from southern Italian dialect *guappo* dandy, braggart, from Spanish *guapo*]

wop[2] (wɒp) *vb* **wops, wopping, wopped,** *n* a variant spelling of **whop**

wop-wops ('wɒp,wɒps) *n* (*functioning as plural or singular*) the *NZ informal* the backblocks; the back of beyond

Worcester ('wʊstə) *n* **1** a cathedral city in W central England, the administrative centre of Worcestershire on the River Severn: scene of the battle (1651) in which Charles II was defeated by Cromwell. Pop: 94 029 (2001) **2** an industrial city in the US, in central Massachusetts: Clark University (1887). Pop: 175 706 (2003 est) **3** a town in S South Africa; centre of a fruit-growing region. Pop: 66 349 (2001)

Worcester china *or* **porcelain** *n* porcelain articles made in Worcester (England) from 1751 in a factory that became, in 1862, the Royal Worcester Porcelain Company. Sometimes shortened to: Worcester

Worcester sauce *or* **Worcestershire sauce** *n* a commercially prepared piquant sauce, made from a basis of soy sauce, with vinegar, spices, etc

Worcestershire ('wʊstəʃɪə, -ʃə) *n* a county of W central England, formerly (1974–98) part of Hereford and Worcester. Administrative centre: Worcester. Pop: 549 300 (2003 est). Area: 1742 sq km (674 sq miles)

Worcs *abbreviation for* Worcestershire

word (wɜːd) *n* **1** one of the units of speech or writing that native speakers of a language usually regard as the smallest isolable meaningful element of the language, although linguists would analyse these further into morphemes. Related *adj*: **lexical, verbal 2** an instance of vocal intercourse; chat, talk, or discussion: *to have a word with someone* **3** an utterance or expression, esp a brief one: *a word of greeting* **4** news or information: *he sent word that he would be late* **5** a verbal signal for action; command: *when I give the word, fire!* **6** an undertaking or promise: *I give you my word; he kept his word* **7** an autocratic decree or utterance; order: *his word must be obeyed* **8** a watchword or slogan, as of a political party: *the word now is "freedom"* **9** *computing* a set of bits used to store, transmit, or operate upon an item of information in a computer, such as a program instruction **10** as good as one's word doing what one has undertaken or promised to do **11** at a word at once **12** by word of mouth orally rather than by written means **13** in a word briefly or in short **14** my word! **a** an exclamation of surprise, annoyance, etc **b** *Austral* an exclamation of agreement **15** of one's word given to or noted for keeping one's promises: *I am a man of my word* **16** put in a word *or* good word for to make favourable mention of (someone); recommend **17** take someone at his *or* her word to assume that someone means, or will do, what he or she says: *when he told her to go, she took him at his word and left* **18** take someone's word for it to accept or believe what someone says **19** the last word **a** the closing remark of a conversation or argument, esp a remark that supposedly settles an issue **b** the latest or most fashionable design, make, or model: *the last word in bikinis* **c** the finest example (of some quality, condition, etc): *the last word in luxury* **20** the word the proper or most fitting expression: *cold is not the word for it, it's freezing!* **21** upon my word! **a** *archaic* on my honour **b** an exclamation of surprise, annoyance, etc **22** word for word **a** (of a report, transcription, etc) using

exactly the same words as those employed in the situation being reported; verbatim **b** translated by substituting each word in the new text for each corresponding word in the original rather than by general sense **23** word of honour a promise; oath **24** (*modifier*) of, relating to, or consisting of words: *a word list* ▷ *vb* **25** (*tr*) to state in words, usually specially selected ones; phrase **26** (*tr*; often foll by *up*) *Austral informal* to inform or advise (a person) ▷ See also **words** [Old English *word*; related to Old High German *wort*, Old Norse *orth*, Gothic *waurd*, Latin *verbum*, Sanskrit *vratá* command]

Word (wɜːd) *n* the **1** *Christianity* the 2nd person of the Trinity **2** Scripture, the Bible, or the Gospels as embodying or representing divine revelation. Often called: the Word of God [translation of Greek *logos*, as in John 1:1]

-word *n combining form* (*preceded by* the *and an initial letter*) a euphemistic way of referring to a word by its first letter because it is considered to be in some way unmentionable by the user: *the C-word, meaning cancer*

wordage ('wɜːdɪdʒ) *n* words considered collectively, esp a quantity of words

word association *n* an early method of psychoanalysis in which the patient thinks of the first word that comes into consciousness on hearing a given word. In this way it was claimed that aspects of the unconscious could be revealed before defence mechanisms intervene

word blindness *n* the nontechnical name for **alexia** and **dyslexia** > 'word-,blind *adj*

wordbook ('wɜːd,bʊk) *n* **1** a book containing words, usually with their meanings **2** a libretto for an opera

wordbreak ('wɜːd,breɪk) *n* *printing* the point at which a word is divided when it runs over from one line of print to the next

word burst *n* a greater than normal rate of occurrence of a particular word in a given context, esp in weblogs

word class *n* *linguistics* a form class in which the members are words. See **part of speech**

word deafness *n* loss of ability to understand spoken words, esp as the result of a cerebral lesion. Also called: auditory aphasia > 'word-,deaf *adj*

word game *n* any game involving the formation, discovery, or alteration of a word or words

wording ('wɜːdɪŋ) *n* **1** the way in which words are used to express a statement, report, etc, esp a written one **2** the words themselves, as used in a written statement or a sign

wordless ('wɜːdlɪs) *adj* **1** inarticulate or silent **2** *music* of or relating to vocal music that is not provided with an articulated text: *a wordless chorus* > 'wordlessly *adv* > 'wordlessness *n*

word order *n* the arrangement of words in a phrase, clause, or sentence. In many languages, including English, word order plays an important part in determining meanings expressed in other languages by inflections

word-perfect *or US* **letter-perfect** *adj* **1** correct in every detail **2** (of a speech, part in a play, etc) memorized perfectly **3** (of a speaker, actor, etc) knowing one's speech, role, etc, perfectly

word picture *n* a verbal description, esp a vivid one

wordplay ('wɜːd,pleɪ) *n* verbal wit based on the meanings and ambiguities of words; puns, clever repartee, etc

word processing *n* the composition of documents using a computer system to input, edit, store, and print them

word processor *n* **a** a computer program that performs word processing **b** a computer system designed for word processing

words (wɜːdz) *pl n* **1** the text of a part of an actor, etc **2** the text or lyrics of a song, as opposed to the music **3** angry speech (esp in the phrase **have words with someone**) **4** eat one's words to

W

retract a statement **5 for words** (preceded by *too* and an adjective or adverb) indescribably; extremely: *the play was too funny for words* **6 have no words for** to be incapable of describing **7 in other words** expressing the same idea but differently **8 in so many words** explicitly or precisely **9 of many** (*or* **few**) **words** (not) talkative **10 put into words** to express in speech or writing as well as thought **11 say a few words** to give a brief speech **12 take the words out of one's** (*or* **someone's**) **mouth** to say exactly what someone else was about to say **13 words fail me** I am too happy, sad, amazed, etc, to express my thoughts

wordsearch ('wɜːd,sɜːtʃ) *n* a puzzle made up of letters arranged in a grid which contains a number of hidden words running in various directions

wordsmith ('wɜːd,smɪθ) *n* a person skilled in using words

word square *n* a puzzle in which the player must fill a square grid with words that read the same across as down

word stress *n* the stress accent on the syllables of individual words either in a sentence or in isolation

Wordsworthian (,wɜːdz'wɜːðɪən) *adj*, of, relating to, or reminiscent of William Wordsworth, the English poet (1770–1850)

word wrapping *n computing* the automatic shifting of a word at the end of a line to a new line in order to keep within preset margins

wordy ('wɜːdɪ) *adj* **wordier, wordiest 1** using, inclined to use, or containing an excess of words: *a wordy writer; a wordy document* **2** of the nature of or relating to words; verbal > **wordily** *adv* > **wordiness** *n*

wore (wɔː) *vb* the past tense of **wear**

work (wɜːk) *n* **1** physical or mental effort directed towards doing or making something **2** paid employment at a job or a trade, occupation, or profession **3** a duty, task, or undertaking **4** something done, made, etc, as a result of effort or exertion: *a work of art* **5** materials or tasks on which to expend effort or exertion **6** another word for **workmanship** (sense 3) **7** the place, office, etc, where a person is employed **8** any piece of material that is undergoing a manufacturing operation or process; workpiece **9 a** decoration or ornamentation, esp of a specified kind **b** (*in combination*): *wirework; woolwork* **10** an engineering structure such as a bridge, building, etc **11** *physics* the transfer of energy expressed as the product of a force and the distance through which its point of application moves in the direction of the force. Abbreviations: *W, w* **12** a structure, wall, etc, built or used as part of a fortification system **13 at work a** at one's job or place of employment **b** in action; operating **14 make short work of** *informal* to handle or dispose of very quickly **15** (*modifier*) of, relating to, or used for work: *work clothes; a work permit* ▷ *vb* **16** (*intr*) to exert effort in order to do, make, or perform something **17** (*intr*) to be employed **18** (*tr*) to carry on operations, activity, etc, in (a place or area): *that salesman works the southern region* **19** (*tr*) to cause to labour or toil: *he works his men hard* **20** to operate or cause to operate, esp properly or effectively: *to work a lathe; that clock doesn't work* **21** (*tr*) to till or cultivate (land) **22** to handle or manipulate or be handled or manipulated: *to work dough* **23** to shape, form, or process or be shaped, formed, or processed: *to work copper* **24** to reach or cause to reach a specific condition, esp gradually: *the rope worked loose* **25** (*tr*) *chiefly US and Canadian* to solve (a mathematical problem) **26** (*intr*) to move in agitation: *his face worked with anger* **27** (*tr*; often foll by *up*) to provoke or arouse: *to work someone into a frenzy* **28** (*tr*) to effect or accomplish: *to work one's revenge* **29** to make (one's way) with effort: *he worked his way through the crowd* **30** (*tr*) to make or decorate by hand in embroidery, tapestry, etc: *she was working a sampler* **31** (*intr*) (of a mechanism) to

move in a loose or otherwise imperfect fashion **32** (*intr*) (of liquids) to ferment, as in brewing **33** (*tr*) *informal* to manipulate or exploit to one's own advantage **34** (*tr*) *slang* to cheat or swindle ▷ See also **work back, work in, work off, work on, work out, work over, works, work up** [Old English *weorc* (n), *wircan, wyrcan* (vb); related to Old High German *wurchen*, German *wirken*, Old Norse *yrkja*, Gothic *waurkjan*] > **workless** *adj* > **worklessness** *n*

workable ('wɜːkəbəl) *adj* **1** practicable or feasible **2** able to be worked > ,worka'bility *or* 'workableness *n*

workaday ('wɜːkə,deɪ) *adj* (*usually prenominal*) **1** being a part of general human experience; ordinary **2** suitable for working days; everyday or practical

workaholic (,wɜːkə'hɒlɪk) *n* **a** a person obsessively addicted to work **b** (*as modifier*): *workaholic behaviour* [C20 from WORK + -HOLIC, coined in 1971 by Wayne Oates, US author]

workaround ('wɜːkə,raʊnd) *n* a method of circumventing or overcoming a problem in a computer program or system

work back *vb* (*intr, adverb*) *Austral informal* to work overtime

workbag ('wɜːk,bæg) *n* a container for implements, tools, or materials, esp sewing equipment. Also called: **work basket, workbox**

workbench ('wɜːk,bentʃ) *n* a heavy table at which work is done by a carpenter, mechanic, toolmaker, etc

workbook ('wɜːk,bʊk) *n* **1** an exercise book or textbook used for study, esp a textbook with spaces for answers **2** a book of instructions for some process **3** a book in which is recorded all work done or planned

work camp *n* a camp set up for young people who voluntarily do manual work on a worthwhile project

workday ('wɜːk,deɪ) *n* **1** the usual US term for **working day** ▷ *adj* **2** another word for **workaday**

worked (wɜːkt) *adj* made or decorated with evidence of workmanship; wrought, as with embroidery or tracery

worked up *adj* agitated or excited

worker ('wɜːkə) *n* **1** a person or thing that works, usually at a specific job: *a good worker; a research worker* **2** an employee in an organization, as opposed to an employer or manager **3** a manual labourer or other employee working in a manufacturing or other industry **4** any other member of the working class **5** a sterile female member of a colony of bees, ants, or wasps that forages for food, cares for the larvae, etc > 'workerless *adj*

worker director *n* a worker elected to the governing board of a business concern to represent the interests of the employees in decision making

worker participation *n* a process by which subordinate employees, either individually or collectively, become involved in one or more aspects of organizational decision making within the enterprises in which they work

worker-priest *n* a Roman Catholic priest who has full-time or part-time employment in a secular job to be more closely in touch with the problems of the laity

workers' cooperative *n* See **cooperative** (sense 4)

work ethic *n* a belief in the moral value of work (often in the phrase **Protestant work ethic**)

workfare ('wɜːk,feə) *n* a scheme under which the government of a country requires unemployed people to do community work or undergo job training in return for social-security payments [C20 from WORK + (WEL)FARE]

workfolk ('wɜːk,fəʊk) *or informal US* **workfolks** *pl n* working people, esp labourers on a farm

workforce ('wɜːk,fɔːs) *n* **1** the total number of workers employed by a company on a specific job, project, etc **2** the total number of people who

could be employed: *the country's workforce is growing rapidly*

work function *n* **1** *physics* the minimum energy required to transfer an electron from a point within a solid to a point just outside its surface. Symbol: φ *or* Φ **2** *thermodynamics* another name (not now used because of confusion with sense 1) for **Helmholtz function**

work-harden *vb* (*tr*) to increase the strength or hardness of (a metal) by a mechanical process, such as tension, compression, or torsion > 'work-,hardening *n*

workhorse ('wɜːk,hɔːs) *n* **1** a horse used for nonrecreational activities **2** *informal* a person who takes on the greatest amount of work in a project or job

workhouse ('wɜːk,haʊs) *n* **1** (formerly in England) an institution maintained at public expense where able-bodied paupers did unpaid work in return for food and accommodation **2** (in the US) a prison for petty offenders serving short sentences at manual labour

work in *vb* (*adverb*) **1** to insert or become inserted: *she worked the patch in carefully* **2** (*tr*) to find space for: *I'll work this job in during the day* ▷ *n* **work-in 3** a form of industrial action in which a factory that is to be closed down is occupied and run by its workers

working ('wɜːkɪŋ) *n* **1** the operation or mode of operation of something **2** the act or process of moulding something pliable **3** a convulsive or jerking motion, as from excitement **4** (*often plural*) a part of a mine or quarry that is being or has been worked **5** (*plural*) the whole system of excavations in a mine **6** a record of the steps by which the result of a calculation or the solution of a problem is obtained: *all working is to be submitted to the examiners* **7** *rare* slow advance against or as if against resistance ▷ *adj* (*prenominal*) **8** relating to or concerned with a person or thing that works: *a working man* **9** concerned with, used in, or suitable for work: *working clothes* **10** (of a meal or occasion) during which business discussions are carried on: *working lunch; working breakfast* **11** capable of being operated or used: *a working model* **12** sufficiently large or accurate to be useful or to accomplish a desired end: *a working majority; a working knowledge of German* **13** (of a theory, etc) providing a basis, usually a temporary one, on which operations or procedures may be carried out

working bee *n* NZ a voluntary group doing a job for charity

working capital *n* **1** *accounting* current assets minus current liabilities **2** current or liquid assets **3** that part of the capital of a business enterprise available for operations

working class *n* **1** Also called: **proletariat** the social stratum, usually of low status, that consists of those who earn wages, esp as manual workers. Compare **lower class, middle class, upper class** ▷ *adj* **working-class 2** of, relating to, or characteristic of the working class

working day *or esp US* **workday** *n* **1** a day on which work is done, esp for an agreed or stipulated number of hours in return for a salary or wage **2** the part of the day allocated to work: *a seven-hour working day* **3** (*often plural*) *commerce* any day of the week except Sunday, public holidays, and, in some cases, Saturday

working dog *n* a dog of suitable breed or training kept for its practical use, such as herding sheep, rather than as a pet or for showing

working drawing *n* a scale drawing of a part or assembly that provides a guide for manufacture

Working Families Tax Credit *n* (in Britain) a means-tested allowance paid to single parents or families who have at least one dependent child, who work at least 16 hours per week, and whose earnings are low. It replaced family credit

working girl *n* **1** a girl or woman who works, esp one who supports herself **2** *informal* a prostitute

working memory *n psychol* the current contents

of a person's consciousness

working papers pl n **1** papers or notes showing the intermediate stages of a proposal, solution, etc, arrived at or being worked on **2** legal documents that certain people in some countries must possess to be allowed to work

working party n **1** a committee established to investigate a problem, question, etc **2** a group of soldiers or prisoners assigned to perform some manual task or duty

working substance or **fluid** n the fluid, esp water, steam, or compressed air, that operates an engine, refrigerator, etc

working week or esp US and Canadian **workweek** ('wɜːkˌwiːk) n the number of hours or days in a week actually or officially allocated to work: a four-day working week

work-in-progress n book-keeping the value of work begun but not completed, as shown in a profit-and-loss account

workload ('wɜːkˌləʊd) n the amount of work to be done, esp in a specified period by a person, machine, etc

workman ('wɜːkmən) n, pl -men **1** a man who is employed in manual labour or who works an industrial machine **2** a craftsman of skill as specified: a bad workman

workmanlike ('wɜːkmənˌlaɪk) or less commonly **workmanly** ('wɜːkmənlɪ) adj appropriate to or befitting a good workman

workmanship ('wɜːkmənʃɪp) n **1** the art or skill of a workman **2** the art or skill with which something is made or executed **3** the degree of art or skill exhibited in the finished product **4** the piece of work so produced

workmate ('wɜːkˌmeɪt) n a person who works with another; fellow worker

workmen's compensation or **worker's compensation** n compensation for death, injury, or accident suffered by a workman in the course of his employment and paid to him or his dependents

work of art n **1** a piece of fine art, such as a painting or sculpture **2** something that may be likened to a piece of fine art, esp in beauty, intricacy, etc

work off vb (tr, adverb) **1** to get rid of or dissipate, as by effort: he worked off some of his energy by digging the garden **2** to discharge (a debt) by labour rather than payment

work on vb (intr, preposition) to persuade or influence or attempt to persuade or influence

work out vb (adverb) **1** (tr) to achieve or accomplish by effort **2** (tr) to solve or find out by reasoning or calculation: to work out an answer; to work out a sum **3** (tr) to devise or formulate: to work out a plan **4** (intr) to prove satisfactory or effective: did your plan work out? **5** (intr) to happen as specified: it all worked out well **6** (intr) to take part in physical exercise, as in training **7** (tr) to remove all the mineral in (a mine, body of ore, etc) that can be profitably exploited **8** (intr; often foll by to or at) to reach a total: your bill works out at a pound **9** (tr) informal to understand the real nature of: I shall never work you out ▷ n **work-out 10** a session of physical exercise, esp for training or practice

work over vb **1** (tr, adverb) to do again; repeat **2** (intr, preposition) to examine closely and thoroughly **3** (tr, adverb) slang to assault or thrash

workpeople ('wɜːkˌpiːpʰl) pl n the working members of a population, esp those employed in manual tasks

workpiece ('wɜːkˌpiːs) n a piece of metal or other material that is in the process of being worked on or made or has actually been cut or shaped by a hand tool or machine

workplace ('wɜːkˌpleɪs) n a place, such as a factory or office, where people work

workroom ('wɜːkˌruːm, -ˌrʊm) n **1** a room in which work, usually manual labour, is done **2** a room in a house set aside for a hobby, such as sewing

works (wɜːks) pl n **1** (often functioning as singular) a place where a number of people are employed, such as a factory **2** the sum total of a writer's or artist's achievements, esp when considered together: the works of Shakespeare **3** the deeds of a person, esp virtuous or moral deeds performed as religious acts: works of charity **4** the interior parts of the mechanism of a machine, etc: the works of a clock **5** in the works informal in preparation **6** spanner in the works See spanner (sense 2) **7** the works slang **a** full or extreme treatment **b** a very violent physical beating: to give someone the works **8** slang a syringe **9** (modifier) of or denoting a racing car, etc, that is officially entered by a manufacturer in an event: a works entry

works council n chiefly Brit **1** a council composed of both employer and employees convened to discuss matters of common interest concerning a factory, plant, business policy, etc, not covered by regular trade union agreements **2** a body representing the workers of a plant, factory, etc, elected to negotiate with the management about working conditions, wages, etc ▷ Also called: works committee

work-sharing n an arrangement whereby one full-time job may be carried out by two people working part time > 'work-ˌsharer n

worksheet ('wɜːkˌʃiːt) n **1** a sheet of paper used for the preliminary or rough draft of a problem, design, etc **2** a piece of paper recording work being planned or already in progress **3** a sheet of paper containing exercises to be completed by a pupil or student

workshop ('wɜːkˌʃɒp) n **1** a room or building in which manufacturing or other forms of manual work are carried on **2** a room in a private dwelling, school, etc, set aside for crafts **3** a group of people engaged in study or work on a creative project or subject: a music workshop ▷ vb **4** (tr) to perform (a play) with no costumes, set, or musical accompaniment

workshy ('wɜːkˌʃaɪ) adj not inclined to work

Worksop ('wɜːksɒp) n a town in N central England, in N Nottinghamshire. Pop: 39 072 (2001)

work station n **1** an area in an office where one person works **2** computing a device or component of an electronic office system consisting of a display screen and keyboard used to handle electronic office work

work-study n an examination of ways of finding the most efficient method of doing a job, esp in terms of time and effort

worktable ('wɜːkˌteɪbʰl) n **a** any table at which writing, sewing, or other work may be done **b** (in English cabinetwork) a small elegant table fitted with sewing accessories

work through vb (tr, adverb) psychol to resolve (a problem, esp an emotional one), by thinking about it repeatedly and hence lessening its intensity either by gaining insight or by becoming bored by it

worktop ('wɜːkˌtɒp) n a surface in a kitchen, often of heat-resistant laminated plastic, that is used for food preparation

work-to-rule n a form of industrial action in which employees adhere strictly to all the working rules laid down by their employers, with the deliberate intention of reducing the rate of working ▷ vb **work to rule 2** (intr) to decrease the rate of working by this means

work up vb (tr, mainly adverb) **1** to arouse the feelings of; excite **2** to cause to grow or develop: to work up a hunger **3** (also preposition) to move or cause to move gradually upwards **4** to manipulate or mix into a specified object or shape **5** to gain knowledge of or skill at (a subject)

workwear ('wɜːkˌwɛə) n clothes, such as overalls, as worn for work in a factory, shop, etc; working clothes

workweek ('wɜːkˌwiːk) n US and Canadian the number of hours or days in a week actually or officially allocated to work. Also called (in Britain and certain other countries): working week

world (wɜːld) n **1** the earth as a planet, esp including its inhabitants **2** mankind; the human race **3** people generally; the public: in the eyes of the world **4** social or public life: to go out into the world **5** the universe or cosmos; everything in existence **6** a complex united whole regarded as resembling the universe **7** any star or planet, esp one that might be inhabited **8** (often capital) a division or section of the earth, its history, or its inhabitants: the Western World; the Ancient World; the Third World **9** an area, sphere, or realm considered as a complete environment: the animal world **10** any field of human activity or way of life or those involved in it: the world of television **11** a period or state of existence: the next world **12** the total circumstances and experience of an individual that make up his life, esp that part of it relating to happiness: you have shattered my world **13** a large amount, number, or distance: worlds apart **14** worldly or secular life, ways, or people **15** logic See possible world **16** all the world and his wife a large group of people of various kinds **17** bring into the world **a** (of a midwife, doctor, etc) to deliver (a baby) **b** to give birth to **18** come into the world to be born **19** dead to the world informal unaware of one's surroundings, esp fast asleep or very drunk **20** for the world (used with a negative) for any inducement, however great **21** for all the world in every way; exactly **22** give to the world to publish **23** in the world (usually used with a negative) (intensifier): no-one in the world can change things **24** man (or woman) of the world a man (or woman) experienced in social or public life **25** not long for this world nearing death **26** on top of the world informal exultant, elated, or very happy **27** informal wonderful; excellent **28** set the world on fire to be exceptionally or sensationally successful **29** the best of both worlds the benefits from two different or opposed ways of life, philosophies, etc **30** think the world of to be extremely fond of or hold in very high esteem **31** world of one's own a state of mental detachment from other people **32** world without end for ever **33** (modifier) of or concerning most or all countries; worldwide: world politics; a world record **34** (in combination) throughout the world: world-famous [Old English w(e)orold, from wer man + ald age, life; related to Old Frisian warld, wrald, Old Norse verold, Old High German wealt (German Welt)]

World Bank n an international cooperative organization established in 1945 under the Bretton Woods Agreement to assist economic development, esp of backward nations, by the advance of loans guaranteed by member governments. Officially called: International Bank for Reconstruction and Development

World Bank Group n the collective name for the International Bank for Reconstruction and Development, the International Finance Corporation, and the International Development Association, whose headquarters are all in Washington

world-beater n a person or thing that surpasses all others in its category; champion > 'world-ˌbeating n, adj

world-class adj of or denoting someone with a skill or attribute that puts him or her in the highest class in the world: a world-class swimmer

World Council of Churches n the ecumenical fellowship of Churches other than the Roman Catholic Church, formally constituted in Amsterdam in 1948 for coordinated action in theological, ecclesiastical, and secular matters

World Court n another name for International Court of Justice

World Cup n an international competition held between national teams in various sports, most notably association football

World Health Organization n an agency of the United Nations, established in 1948 with headquarters in Geneva, responsible for

W

coordinating international health activities, aiding governments in improving health services, etc. Abbreviation: **WHO**

world language *n* **1** a language spoken and known in many countries, such as English **2** an artificial language for international use, such as Esperanto

world-line *n physics* a line on a space–time path that shows the path of a body

worldling ('wɜːldlɪŋ) *n* a person who is primarily concerned with worldly matters or material things

worldly ('wɜːldlɪ) *adj* -lier, -liest **1** not spiritual; mundane or temporal **2** Also: **worldly-minded** absorbed in or concerned with material things or matters that are immediately relevant **3** Also: **worldly-wise** versed in the ways of the world; sophisticated **4** *archaic* existing on or relating to the earth **5** *obsolete* secular; lay ▷ *adv* **6** *archaic* in a worldly manner > **'worldliness** *n*

world music *n* popular music of various ethnic origins and styles outside the tradition of Western pop and rock music

world power *n* a state that possesses sufficient power to influence events throughout the world

World Series *or* **World's Series** *n baseball* (in the US and Canada) a best-of-seven playoff for the world championship between the two winning teams in the major leagues at the end of the season

world-shaking *adj* of enormous significance; momentous

World Trade Center *n* a former building complex, at 417 m (1368 ft) the tallest in the US, that stood in Manhattan, New York, from 1974 until its destruction in the terrorist attack of September 11 2001, in which some 2800 people were killed. Abbreviation: **WTC**

World Trade Organization *n* an international body concerned with promoting and regulating trade between its member states; established in 1995 as a successor to GATT

world-view *n* another word for **Weltanschauung**

World War I *n* the war (1914–18), fought mainly in Europe and the Middle East, in which the Allies (principally France, Russia, Britain, Italy after 1915, and the US after 1917) defeated the Central Powers (principally Germany, Austria-Hungary, and Turkey). The war was precipitated by the assassination of Austria's crown prince (Archduke Franz Ferdinand) at Sarajevo on June 28, 1914 and swiftly developed its major front in E France, where millions died in static trench warfare. After the October Revolution (1917) the Bolsheviks ended Russian participation in the war (Dec 15, 1917). The exhausted Central Powers agreed to an armistice on Nov 11, 1918 and quickly succumbed to internal revolution, before being forced to sign the Treaty of Versailles (June 28, 1919) and other treaties. Also called: **First World War, Great War**

World War II *n* the war (1939–45) in which the Allies (principally Britain, the Soviet Union, and the US) defeated the Axis powers (principally Germany, Italy, and Japan). Britain and France declared war on Germany (Sept 3, 1939) as a result of the German invasion of Poland (Sept 1, 1939). Italy entered the war on June 10, 1940 shortly before the collapse of France (armistice signed June 22, 1940). On June 22, 1941 Germany attacked the Soviet Union and on Dec 7, 1941 the Japanese attacked the US at Pearl Harbor. On Sept 8, 1943 Italy surrendered, the war in Europe ending on May 7, 1945 with the unconditional surrender of the Germans. The Japanese capitulated on Aug 14, 1945 as a direct result of the atomic bombs dropped by the Americans on Hiroshima and Nagasaki. Also called: **Second World War**

world-weary *adj* no longer finding pleasure in living; tired of the world > **world-ˌweariness** *n*

worldwide ('wɜːld'waɪd) *adj* applying or extending throughout the world; universal

World Wide Web *n computing* a vast network of linked hypertext files, stored on computers throughout the world, that can provide a computer user with information on a huge variety of subjects. Abbreviation: **WWW**

worm (wɜːm) *n* **1** any of various invertebrates, esp the annelids (earthworms, etc), nematodes (roundworms), and flatworms, having a slender elongated body. Related *adj*: **vermicular 2** any of various insect larvae having an elongated body, such as the silkworm and wireworm **3** any of various unrelated animals that resemble annelids, nematodes, etc, such as the glow-worm and shipworm **4** a gnawing or insinuating force or agent that torments or slowly eats away **5** a wretched or spineless person **6** anything that resembles a worm in appearance or movement **7** a shaft on which a helical groove has been cut, as in a gear arrangement in which such a shaft meshes with a toothed wheel **8** a spiral pipe cooled by air or flowing water, used as a condenser in a still **9** a nontechnical name for **lytta 10** *anatomy* any wormlike organ, structure, or part, such as the middle lobe of the cerebellum (*vermis cerebelli*). Technical name: **vermis 11** *computing* a program that duplicates itself many times in a network and prevents its destruction. It often carries a logic bomb or virus ▷ *vb* **12** to move, act, or cause to move or act with the slow sinuous movement of a worm **13** (foll by *in, into, out of,* etc) to make (one's way) slowly and stealthily; insinuate (oneself) **14** (*tr*; often foll by *out of* or *from*) to extract (information, a secret, etc) from by persistent questioning **15** (*tr*) to free from or purge of worms **16** (*tr*) *nautical* to wind yarn around (a rope) so as to fill the spaces between the strands and render the surface smooth for parcelling and serving ▷ See also **worms** [Old English *wyrm*; related to Old Frisian *wirm*, Old High German *wurm*, Old Norse *ormr*, Gothic *waurms*, Latin *vermis*, Greek *romos* woodworm] > **'wormer** *n* > **'worm,like** *or* **'wormish** *adj*

WORM (wɜːm) *n computing acronym for* write once read many times: an optical disk that enables users to store data but not change it

wormcast ('wɜːm,kɑːst) *n* a coil of earth or sand that has been egested by a burrowing earthworm or lugworm

worm conveyor *n* another name for **screw conveyor**

worm-eaten *adj* **1** eaten into by worms: *a worm-eaten table* **2** decayed; rotten **3** old-fashioned; antiquated

wormery ('wɜːmərɪ) *n, pl* -eries **1** a piece of apparatus, having a glass side or sides, in which worms are kept for study **2** a container in which worms are kept, esp one in which they consume household waste and convert it into compost

wormfly ('wɜːm,flaɪ) *n angling* a type of lure dressed on a double hook, the barbs of which sit one above the other and back-to-back

worm gear *n* **1** a device consisting of a threaded shaft (**worm**) that mates with a gearwheel (**worm wheel**) so that rotary motion can be transferred between two shafts at right angles to each other **2** Also called: **worm wheel** a gearwheel driven by a threaded shaft or worm

wormhole ('wɜːm,həʊl) *n* **1** a hole made by a worm in timber, plants, etc **2** *physics* a tunnel in the geometry of space–time postulated to connect different parts of the universe > **'worm,holed** *adj*

worm lizard *n* any wormlike burrowing legless lizard of the family *Amphisbaenidae*, of Africa, South and Central America, and S Europe

worms (wɜːmz) *n* (*functioning as singular*) any disease or disorder, usually of the intestine, characterized by infestation with parasitic worms

Worms (wɜːmz; *German* vɔrms) *n* a city in SW Germany, in Rhineland-Palatinate on the Rhine: famous as the seat of imperial diets, notably that of 1521, before which Luther defended his doctrines in the presence of Charles V; river port and manufacturing centre with a large wine trade. Pop: 81 100 (2003 est)

wormseed ('wɜːm,siːd) *n* **1** any of various plants having seeds or other parts used in medicine to treat worm infestation, esp an American chenopodiaceous plant, *Chenopodium anthelminticum* (or *C. ambrosioides*) (**American wormseed**), and the santonica plant **2** the part of any of these plants that is used as an anthelmintic

worm's eye view *n* a view seen from below or from a more lowly or humble point

wormwood ('wɜːm,wʊd) *n* **1** Also called: **absinthe** any of various plants of the chiefly N temperate genus *Artemisia*, esp *A. absinthium*, a European plant yielding a bitter extract used in making absinthe: family *Asteraceae* (composites) **2** something that embitters, such as a painful experience [C15 changed (through influence of WORM and WOOD¹) from Old English *wormōd, wermōd*; related to Old High German *werrnuata*, German *Wermut*; see VERMOUTH]

wormy ('wɜːmɪ) *adj* wormier, wormiest **1** worm-infested or worm-eaten **2** resembling a worm in appearance, ways, or condition **3** (of wood) having irregular small tunnels bored into it and tracked over its surface, made either by worms or artificially **4** low or grovelling > **'worminess** *n*

worn (wɔːn) *vb* **1** the past participle of **wear** ▷ *adj* **2** affected, esp adversely, by long use or action: *a worn suit* **3** haggard; drawn **4** exhausted; spent > **'wornness** *n*

worn-out *adj* (**worn out** *when postpositive*) **1** worn or used until threadbare, valueless, or useless **2** exhausted; very weary

worried ('wʌrɪd) *adj* feeling uneasy about a situation or thing; anxious > **'worriedly** *adv*

worried well *n* the *informal* the people who do not need medical treatment, but who visit the doctor to be reassured, or with emotional problems

worriment ('wʌrɪmənt) *n informal, chiefly US and Canadian* anxiety or the trouble that causes it; worry

worrisome ('wʌrɪsəm) *adj* **1** causing worry; vexing **2** tending to worry > **'worrisomely** *adv*

worrit ('wʌrɪt) *vb* (*tr*) *dialect* to tease or worry [probably variant of WORRY, but compare WHERRIT]

worry ('wʌrɪ) *vb* -ries, -rying, -ried **1** to be or cause to be anxious or uneasy, esp about something uncertain or potentially dangerous **2** (*tr*) to disturb the peace of mind of; bother: *don't worry me with trivialities* **3** (*intr*; often foll by *along* or *through*) to proceed despite difficulties **4** (*intr*; often foll by *away*) to struggle or work: *to worry away at a problem* **5** (*tr*) (of a dog, wolf, etc) to lacerate or kill by biting, shaking, etc **6** (when *intr*, foll by *at*) to bite, tear, or gnaw (at) with the teeth: *a dog worrying a bone* **7** (*tr*) to move as specified, esp by repeated pushes: *they worried the log into the river* **8** (*tr*) to touch or poke repeatedly and idly **9** *obsolete* to choke or cause to choke **10** **not to worry** *informal* you need not worry ▷ *n, pl* -ries **11** a state or feeling of anxiety **12** a person or thing that causes anxiety **13** an act of worrying **14** **no worries** *informal* an expression used to express agreement or to convey that something is proceeding or has proceeded satisfactorily; no problem [Old English *wyrgan*; related to Old Frisian *wergia* to kill, Old High German *wurgen* (German (*er*)*würgen* to strangle), Old Norse *virgill, urga* rope] > **'worrying** *adj* > **'worryingly** *adv*

worry beads *pl n* a string of beads that when fingered or played with supposedly relieves nervous tension

worryguts ('wʌrɪ,gʌts) *or* **worrywart** ('wʌrɪ,wɔːt) *n informal* a person who tends to worry, esp about insignificant matters

worse (wɜːs) *adj* **1** the comparative of **bad 2 none the worse for** not harmed by (adverse events or circumstances) **3 the worse for wear a** shabby or worn **b** a slang term for **drunk 4 worse luck!** *informal* unhappily; unfortunately **5** (*postpositive*) **worse off** in a worse, esp a worse financial, condition ▷ *n* **6** something that is worse **7 for the worse** into a less desirable or inferior state or condition: *a change for the worse* **8 go from bad to worse** to deteriorate even more ▷ *adv* **9** in a more severe or unpleasant manner **10** in a less effective or successful manner [Old English *wiersa*; related to Old Frisian *werra*, Old High German *wirsiro*, Old Norse *verri*, Gothic *wairsiza*]

worsen ('wɜːs³n) *vb* to grow or cause to grow worse

worser ('wɜːsə) *adj* an archaic or nonstandard word for **worse**

worship ('wɜːʃɪp) *vb* **-ships, -shipping, -shipped** *or* *US* **-ships, -shiping, -shiped** **1** (*tr*) to show profound religious devotion and respect to; adore or venerate (God or any person or thing considered divine) **2** (*tr*) to be devoted to and full of admiration for **3** (*intr*) to have or express feelings of profound adoration **4** (*intr*) to attend services for worship **5** (*tr*) *obsolete* to honour ▷ *n* **6** religious adoration or devotion **7** the formal expression of religious adoration; rites, prayers, etc **8** admiring love or devotion **9** *archaic* dignity or standing [Old English *weorthscipe,* from WORTH¹ + -SHIP] > 'worshipable *adj* > 'worshipper *n*

Worship ('wɜːʃɪp) *n* *chiefly Brit* (preceded by *Your, His,* or *Her*) a title used to address or refer to a mayor, magistrate, or a person of similar high rank

worshipful ('wɜːʃɪpfʊl) *adj* **1** feeling or showing reverence or adoration **2** (*often capital*) *chiefly Brit* a title used to address or refer to various people or bodies of distinguished rank, such as mayors and certain ancient companies of the City of London > 'worshipfully *adv* > 'worshipfulness *n*

worst (wɜːst) *adj* **1** the superlative of **bad** ▷ *adv* **2** in the most extreme or bad manner or degree **3** least well, suitably, or acceptably **4** (*in combination*) in or to the smallest degree or extent; least: *worst-loved* ▷ *n* **5** the worst the least good or most inferior person, thing, or part in a group, narrative, etc **6** (*often preceded by at*) the most poor, unpleasant, or unskilled quality or condition: *television is at its worst these days* **7** the greatest amount of damage or wickedness of which a person or group is capable: *the invaders came and did their worst* **8** the weakest effort or poorest achievement that a person or group is capable of making: *the applicant did his worst at the test because he did not want the job* **9 the worst a** in the least favourable interpretation or view **b** under the least favourable conditions **10 if the worst comes to the worst** if all the more desirable alternatives became impossible or if the worst possible thing happens **11 come off worst** *or* **get the worst of it** to enjoy the least benefit from an issue or be defeated in it ▷ *vb* **12** (*tr*) to get the advantage over; defeat or beat [Old English *wierrest*; related to Old Frisian *wersta*, Old Saxon, Old High German *wirsisto*, Old Norse *verstr*]

worst case *n* **a** a situation in which the most unfavourable conditions prevail **b** (*as modifier*): *a worst-case projection of a massive accident*

worsted ('wʊstɪd) *n* **1** a closely twisted yarn or thread made from combed long-staple wool **2** a fabric made from this, with a hard smooth close-textured surface and no nap **3** (*modifier*) made of this yarn or fabric: *a worsted suit* [c13 named after *Worstead,* a district in Norfolk]

wort (wɜːt) *n* **1** (*in combination*) any of various unrelated plants, esp ones formerly used to cure diseases: *liverwort; spleenwort* **2** the sweet liquid obtained from the soaked mixture of warm water and ground malt, used to make a malt liquor [Old English *wyrt* root, related to Old High German *warz,* Gothic *waurts* root]

worth¹ (wɜːθ) *adj* (governing a noun with prepositional force) **1** worthy of; meriting or justifying: *it's not worth discussing; an idea worth some thought* **2** having a value of: *the book is worth 30 pounds* **3 for all one is worth** to the utmost; to the full extent of one's powers or ability **4** worth

one's weight in gold extremely helpful, kind, etc ▷ *n* **5** high quality; excellence **6** value, price **7** the amount or quantity of something of a specified value: *five pounds worth of petrol* [Old English *weorth*; related to Old Saxon, Old High German *werth* (German *Wert*), Old Norse *verthr,* Gothic *wairths*]

worth² (wɜːθ) *vb* (*intr*) *archaic* to happen or betide (esp in the phrase **woe worth the day**) [Old English *weorthan*; related to Old Frisian *wertha,* Old Saxon, Old High German *werthan* (German *werden*), Old Norse *vertha,* Gothic *wairthan,* Latin *vertere* to turn]

Worthing ('wɜːðɪŋ) *n* a resort in S England, in West Sussex on the English Channel. Pop: 96 964 (2001)

worthless ('wɜːθlɪs) *adj* **1** without practical value or usefulness **2** without merit; good-for-nothing > 'worthlessly *adv* > 'worthlessness *n*

worthwhile (ˌwɜːθ'waɪl) *adj* sufficiently important, rewarding, or valuable to justify time or effort spent

worthy ('wɜːðɪ) *adj* **-thier, -thiest** **1** (*postpositive; often foll by of or an infinitive*) having sufficient merit or value (for something or someone specified); deserving **2** having worth, value, or merit ▷ *n, pl* **-thies** **3** *often facetious* a person of distinguished character, merit, or importance > 'worthily *adv* > 'worthiness *n*

wot (wɒt) *vb* *archaic* or *dialect* (used with *I, she, he, it,* or a singular noun) a form of the present tense (indicative mood) of **wit²**

Wotan ('vəʊtɑːn, 'vɔː-) *n* the supreme god in Germanic mythology. Norse counterpart: Odin

wotcher ('wɒtʃə) *sentence substitute* a slang term of greeting (esp in the phrase **wotcher cock!**) [c19 Cockney for *what cheer?*]

would (wʊd; *unstressed* wəd) *vb* (takes an infinitive without *to* or an implied infinitive) **1** used as an auxiliary to form the past tense or subjunctive mood of **will¹** **2** (with *you, he, she, it, they,* or a noun as subject) used as an auxiliary to indicate willingness or desire in a polite manner: *would you help me, please?* **3** used as an auxiliary to describe a past action as being accustomed or habitual: *every day we would go for walks* **4** I wish: *would that he were here*

▓ USAGE See at **should**

would-be *adj* (*prenominal*) **1** *usually derogatory* wanting or professing to be: *a would-be politician* **2** intended to be: *would-be generosity* ▷ *n* **3** *derogatory* a person who wants or professes to be something that he is not **4** *Indian* the person to whom one is is engaged to be married; fiancé or fiancée

wouldn't ('wʊd³nt) *vb contraction of* would not

wouldst (wʊdst) *vb* *archaic* or *dialect* (used with the pronoun *thou* or its relative equivalent) a singular form of the past tense of **will¹**

Woulfe bottle (wʊlf) *n* *chem* a bottle with more than one neck, used for passing gases through liquids [c18 named after Peter Woulfe (?1727–1803), English chemist]

wound¹ (wuːnd) *n* **1** any break in the skin or an organ or part as the result of violence or a surgical incision **2** an injury to plant tissue **3** any injury or slight to the feelings or reputation ▷ *vb* **4** to inflict a wound or wounds upon (someone or something) [Old English *wund*; related to Old Frisian *wunde,* Old High German *wunta* (German *Wunde*), Old Norse *und,* Gothic *wunds*] > 'woundable *adj* > 'wounder *n* > 'wounding *adj* > 'woundingly *adv* > 'woundless *adj*

wound² (waʊnd) *vb* the past tense and past participle of **wind²**

wounded ('wuːndɪd) *adj* **1 a** suffering from wounds; injured, esp in a battle or fight **b** (*as collective noun; preceded by the*): *the wounded* **2** (of feelings) damaged or hurt

woundwort ('wuːnd,wɜːt) *n* **1** any of various plants of the genus *Stachys,* such as *S. arvensis* (**field woundwort**), having purple, scarlet, yellow, or white flowers and formerly used for dressing

wounds: family *Lamiaceae* (labiates) **2** any of various other plants used in this way

wove (wəʊv) *vb* a past tense of **weave**

woven ('wəʊv³n) *vb* a past participle of **weave**

wove paper *n* paper with a very faint mesh impressed on it by the dandy roller on the paper-making machine. Compare **laid paper**

wow¹ (waʊ) *interj* **1** an exclamation of admiration, amazement, etc ▷ *n* **2** *slang* a person or thing that is amazingly successful, attractive, etc ▷ *vb* **3** (*tr*) *slang* to arouse great enthusiasm in [c16 originally Scottish, expressive of surprise, amazement, etc]

wow² (waʊ, wəʊ) *n* a slow variation or distortion in pitch that occurs at very low audio frequencies in sound-reproducing systems, such as a record player, usually due to variation in speed of the turntable, etc. See also **flutter** (sense 14) [c20 of imitative origin]

WOW *abbreviation for* waiting on weather: used esp in the oil industry

wow factor *n* *informal* a striking or impressive feature

wowser ('waʊzə) *n* *Austral and NZ* *slang* **1** a fanatically puritanical person **2** a teetotaller [c20 from English dialect *wow* to whine, complain]

WP *abbreviation for* **1** weather permitting **2** word processing **3** word processor **4** (in South Africa) Western (Cape) Province

WPA (in the US) *abbreviation for* Work Projects Administration or Works Progress Administration

W particle *n* *physics* a type of elementary particle with either a positive or negative charge considered to transmit the weak interaction between other elementary particles. W particles have a rest mass of 1.435×10^{-25} kg. Also called: W boson. See also **Z particle**

WPB *or* **wpb** *abbreviation for* waste paper basket

WPC (in Britain) *abbreviation for* woman police constable

wpm *abbreviation for* words per minute

WR *abbreviation for* Western Region

Wraac (ræk) *n* a member of the Women's Royal Australian Army Corps

WRAAC *abbreviation for* Women's Royal Australian Army Corps

WRAAF *abbreviation for* Women's Royal Australian Air Force

WRAC (in Britain) *abbreviation for* Women's Royal Army Corps

wrack¹ *or* **rack** (ræk) *n* **1** collapse or destruction (esp in the phrase **wrack and ruin**) **2** something destroyed or a remnant of such ▷ *vb* **3** a variant spelling of **rack¹** [Old English *wræc* persecution, misery; related to Gothic *wraka,* Old Norse *rāk.* Compare WRECK, WRETCH]

▓ USAGE The use of the spelling *wrack* rather than *rack* in sentences such as *she was wracked by grief* or *the country was wracked by civil war* is very common but is thought by many people to be incorrect

wrack² (ræk) *n* **1** seaweed or other marine vegetation that is floating in the sea or has been cast ashore **2** any of various seaweeds of the genus *Fucus,* such as *F. serratus* (**serrated wrack**) **3** *literary* or *dialect* **a** a wreck or piece of wreckage **b** a remnant or fragment of something destroyed [c14 (in the sense: a wrecked ship, wreckage, hence later applied to marine vegetation washed ashore): perhaps from Middle Dutch *wrak* wreckage; the term corresponds to Old English *wræc* WRACK¹]

WRAF (in Britain) *abbreviation for* Women's Royal Air Force

wraith (reɪθ) *n* **1** the apparition of a person living or thought to be alive, supposed to appear around the time of his death **2** a ghost or any apparition **3** an insubstantial copy of something **4** something pale, thin, and lacking in substance, such as a column of smoke [c16 Scottish, of unknown origin] > 'wraith,like *adj*

Wran (ræn) *n* a member of the Women's Royal

Australian Naval Service

wrang (ræŋ) *adj, adv, n, vb* a Scot word for **wrong**

Wrangel Island ('ræŋgəl) *n* an island in the Arctic Ocean, off the coast of the extreme NE of Russia: administratively part of Russia; mountainous and mostly tundra. Area: about 7300 sq km (2800 sq miles)

Wrangell ('ræŋgəl) *n* **Mount** a mountain in S Alaska, in the W Wrangell Mountains. Height: 4269 m (14 005 ft)

Wrangell Mountains *pl n* a mountain range in SE Alaska, extending into the Yukon, Canada. Highest peak: Mount Blackburn, 5037 m (16 523 ft)

wrangle ('ræŋgəl) *vb* **1** (*intr*) to argue, esp noisily or angrily **2** (*tr*) to encourage, persuade, or obtain by argument **3** (*tr*) *Western US and Canadian* to herd (cattle or horses) ▷ *n* **4** a noisy or angry argument [C14 from Low German *wrangeln;* related to Norwegian *vrangla*]

wrangler ('ræŋglə) *n* **1** one who wrangles **2** *Western US and Canadian* a herder; cowboy **3** a person who handles or controls animals involved in the making of a film or television programme: *a snake wrangler* **4** *Brit* (at Cambridge University) a candidate who has obtained first-class honours in Part II of the mathematics tripos. The wrangler with the highest marks is called the **senior wrangler**

WRANS *abbreviation for* Women's Royal Australian Naval Service

wrap (ræp) *vb* **wraps, wrapping, wrapped** (*mainly tr*) **1** to fold or wind (paper, cloth, etc) around (a person or thing) so as to cover **2** (*often foll by up*) to fold paper, etc, around to fasten securely **3** to surround or conceal by surrounding **4** to enclose, immerse, or absorb: *wrapped in sorrow* **5** to fold, wind, or roll up **6** (*intr; often foll by about, around,* etc) to be or become wound or extended **7** to complete the filming of (a motion picture or television programme) **8** (*often foll by up*) Also: **rap** *Austral informal* to praise (someone) ▷ *n* **9** a garment worn wrapped around the body, esp the shoulders, such as a shawl or cloak **10** short for **wrapround** (sense 5) **11** a type of sandwich consisting of a tortilla wrapped round a filling **12** *chiefly US* wrapping or a wrapper **13** *Brit slang* a small package of an illegal drug in powder form: *a wrap of heroin* **14** Also called: **rap** *Austral informal* a commendation **15** **a** the end of a working day during the filming of a motion picture or television programme **b** the completion of filming of a motion picture or television programme **16** **keep under wraps** to keep secret **17** **take the wraps off** to reveal [C14 origin unknown]

wraparound ('ræpəˌraʊnd) *n computing* another name for **word wrapping**

wrapover ('ræpˌəʊvə) *or* **wrapround** *adj* **1** (of a garment, esp a skirt) not sewn up at one side, but worn wrapped round the body and fastened so that the open edges overlap ▷ *n* **2** such a garment

wrapped (ræpt) *vb* **1** the past tense and past participle of **wrap** ▷ *adj* **2** *Austral and NZ informal* a variant spelling of **rapt²** **3** **wrapped up** *informal* **a** completely absorbed or engrossed in **b** implicated or involved in

wrapper ('ræpə) *n* **1** the cover, usually of paper or cellophane, in which something is wrapped **2** a dust jacket of a book **3** the ripe firm tobacco leaf forming the outermost portion of a cigar and wound around its body **4** a loose negligee or dressing gown, esp in the 19th century

wrapping ('ræpɪŋ) *n* the material used to wrap something

wrapround ('ræpˌraʊnd) *or* **wraparound** ('ræpəˌraʊnd) *adj* **1** made so as to be wrapped round something: *a wrapround skirt* **2** surrounding, curving round, or overlapping **3** curving round in one continuous piece: *a wrapround windscreen* ▷ *n* **4** *printing* a flexible plate of plastic, metal, or rubber that is made flat but used wrapped round the plate cylinder of a rotary press **5** Also called: **outsert** *printing* a separately printed sheet folded around a section for binding. Sometimes shortened to: **wrap** **6** a slip of paper folded round the dust jacket of a book to announce a price reduction, special offer, etc **7** another name for **wrapover**

wrap up *vb* (*adverb*) **1** (*tr*) to fold paper around **2** to put warm clothes on **3** (*usually imperative*) *slang* to be silent **4** (*tr*) *informal* **a** to settle the final details of **b** to make a summary of

wrasse (ræs) *n* any marine percoid fish of the family *Labridae*, of tropical and temperate seas, having thick lips, strong teeth, and usually a bright coloration: many are used as food fishes [C17 from Cornish *wrach;* related to Welsh *gwrach* old woman]

wrath (rɒθ) *n* **1** angry, violent, or stern indignation **2** divine vengeance or retribution **3** *archaic* a fit of anger or an act resulting from anger ▷ *adj* **4** *obsolete* incensed; angry [Old English *wrǣththu;* see WROTH] > '**wrathless** *adj*

Wrath (rɒθ, rɔːθ) *n* **Cape** a promontory at the NW extremity of the Scottish mainland

wrathful ('rɒθfʊl) *adj* **1** full of wrath; raging or furious **2** resulting from or expressing wrath ▷ Also (informal): **wrathy** > '**wrathfully** *adv* > '**wrathfulness** *n*

wreak (riːk) *vb* (*tr*) **1** to inflict (vengeance, etc) or to cause (chaos, etc): *to wreak havoc on the enemy* **2** to express, or gratify (anger, hatred, etc) **3** *archaic* to take vengeance for [Old English *wrecan;* related to Old Frisian *wreka*, Old High German *rehhan* (German *rächen*), Old Norse *reka*, Latin *urgēre* to push] > '**wreaker** *n*

USAGE See at **wrought**

wreath (riːθ) *n, pl* **wreaths** (riːðz, riːθs) **1** a band of flowers or foliage intertwined into a ring, usually placed on a grave as a memorial or worn on the head as a garland or a mark of honour **2** any circular or spiral band or formation **3** a spiral or circular defect appearing in porcelain and glassware [Old English *wrǣth, wrǣd;* related to Middle Low German *wrēden* to twist. See WRITHE] > '**wreathless** *adj* > '**wreath,like** *adj*

wreathe (riːð) *vb* **1** to form into or take the form of a wreath by intertwining or twisting together **2** (*tr*) to decorate, crown, or encircle with wreaths **3** to move or cause to move in a twisting way: *smoke wreathed up to the ceiling* [C16 perhaps back formation from *wrēthen*, from Old English *writhen*, past participle of *wrīthan* to WRITHE; see WREATH]

wreck (rɛk) *vb* **1** to involve in or suffer disaster or destruction **2** (*tr*) to cause the wreck of (a ship) ▷ *n* **3** **a** the accidental destruction of a ship at sea **b** the ship so destroyed **4** *maritime law* goods cast ashore from a wrecked vessel **5** a person or thing that has suffered ruin or dilapidation **6** the remains of something that has been destroyed **7** *old-fashioned* the act of wrecking or the state of being wrecked; ruin or destruction [C13 from Scandinavian; compare Icelandic *rek*. See WRACK², WREAK]

wreckage ('rɛkɪdʒ) *n* **1** same as **wreck** (sense 6) **2** the act of wrecking or the state of being wrecked; ruin or destruction

wrecked (rɛkt) *adj slang* in a state of intoxication, stupor, or euphoria, induced by drugs or alcohol

wrecker ('rɛkə) *n* **1** a person or thing that ruins or destroys **2** *chiefly US and Canadian* a person whose job is to demolish buildings or dismantle cars **3** (formerly) a person who lures ships to destruction to plunder the wreckage **4** *US and Canadian* another word for **tow truck**

wreckfish ('rɛkˌfɪʃ) *n, pl* **-fish** *or* **-fishes** another name for **stone bass** [so called because it is often found near wrecked ships]

wreckful ('rɛkfʊl) *adj poetic* causing wreckage

wrecking bar *n* a short crowbar, forked at one end and slightly angled at the other to make a fulcrum

Wrekin ('riːkɪn) *n* **1** **the** an isolated hill in the English Midlands in Telford and Wrekin unitary authority, Shropshire. Height: 400 m (1335 ft) **2** **(all) round the Wrekin** *Midland English dialect* the long way round: *he went all round the Wrekin instead of explaining clearly*

wren (rɛn) *n* **1** any small brown passerine songbird of the chiefly American family *Troglodytidae*, esp *Troglodytes troglodytes* (**wren** in Britain, **winter wren** in the US and Canada). They have a slender bill and feed on insects **2** any of various similar birds of the families *Muscicapidae* (Australian warblers), *Xenicidae* (New Zealand wrens), etc [Old English *wrenna, werna;* related to Old High German *wrendo, rentilo*, Old Norse *rindill*]

Wren (rɛn) *n history informal* (in Britain and certain other nations) a member of the former Women's Royal Naval Service [C20 from the abbreviation *WRNS*]

wrench (rɛntʃ) *vb* **1** to give (something) a sudden or violent twist or pull esp so as to remove (something) from that to which it is attached: *to wrench a door off its hinges* **2** (*tr*) to twist suddenly so as to sprain (a limb): *to wrench one's ankle* **3** (*tr*) to give pain to **4** (*tr*) to twist from the original meaning or purpose **5** (*intr*) to make a sudden twisting motion ▷ *n* **6** a forceful twist or pull **7** an injury to a limb, caused by twisting **8** sudden pain caused esp by parting **9** a parting that is difficult or painful to make **10** a distorting of the original meaning or purpose **11** a spanner, esp one with adjustable jaws. See also **torque wrench** [Old English *wrencan;* related to Old High German *renken*, Lithuanian *rangyti* to twist. See WRINKLE¹]

wrest (rɛst) *vb* (*tr*) **1** to take or force away by violent pulling or twisting **2** to seize forcibly by violent or unlawful means **3** to obtain by laborious effort **4** to distort in meaning, purpose, etc ▷ *n* **5** the act or an instance of wresting **6** *archaic* a small key used to tune a piano or harp [Old English *wrǣstan;* related to Old Norse *reista*. See WRITHE] > '**wrester** *n*

wrestle ('rɛsəl) *vb* **1** to fight (another person) by holding, throwing, etc, without punching with the closed fist **2** (*intr*) to participate in wrestling **3** (when *intr*, foll by *with* or *against*) to fight with (a person, problem, or thing): *wrestle with one's conscience* **4** (*tr*) to move laboriously, as with wrestling movements **5** (*tr*) *US and Canadian* to throw (an animal) for branding ▷ *n* **6** the act of wrestling **7** a struggle or tussle [Old English *wrǣstlian;* related to Middle Dutch *wrastelen* (Dutch *worstelen*), Old Norse *rost* current, race] > '**wrestler** *n*

wrestling ('rɛslɪŋ) *n* any of certain sports in which the contestants fight each other according to various rules governing holds and usually forbidding blows with the closed fist. The principal object is to overcome the opponent either by throwing or pinning him to the ground or by causing him to submit. See **freestyle, Graeco-Roman, sumo**

wrest pin *n* (on a piano, harp, etc) a pin around which one end of a string is wound: it may be turned by means of a tuning key to alter the tension of the string. In a piano the wrest pin is embedded in the **wrest plank**

wretch (rɛtʃ) *n* **1** a despicable person **2** a person pitied for his misfortune [Old English *wrecca;* related to Old Saxon *wrekkeo*, Old High German *reccheo* (German *Recke* warrior), Old Norse *rek(n)ingr*]

wretched ('rɛtʃɪd) *adj* **1** in poor or pitiful circumstances **2** characterized by or causing misery **3** despicable; base **4** poor, inferior, or paltry **5** (*prenominal*) (intensifier qualifying something undesirable): *a wretched nuisance* > '**wretchedly** *adv* > '**wretchedness** *n*

Wrexham ('rɛksəm) *n* **1** a town in N Wales, in Wrexham county borough: seat of the Roman Catholic bishopric of Wales (except the former Glamorganshire); formerly noted for coal-mining. Pop: 42 576 (2001) **2** a county borough in NE Wales, created in 1996 from part of Clwyd. Pop: 129 700 (2003 est). Area: 500 sq km (193 sq miles)

wrick (rɪk) *vb* a variant spelling (chiefly Brit) of

rick² [C19 earlier *rick*; perhaps from Middle Low German *wricken* to move jerkily, sprain]

wrier *or* **wryer** ('raɪə) *adj* the comparative of **wry**

wriest *or* **wryest** ('raɪɪst) *adj* the superlative of **wry**

wriggle ('rɪgªl) *vb* 1 to make or cause to make twisting movements 2 (*intr*) to progress by twisting and turning 3 (*intr; foll by into or out of*) to manoeuvre oneself by clever or devious means: *wriggle out of an embarrassing situation* ▷ *n* 4 a wriggling movement or action 5 a sinuous marking or course [C15 from Middle Low German; compare Dutch *wriggelen*] > **'wriggler** *n* > **'wriggly** *adj*

wright (raɪt) *n* (*now chiefly in combination*) a person who creates, builds, or repairs something specified: *a playwright; a shipwright* [Old English *wryhta*, *wyrhta*; related to Old Frisian *wrichta*, Old Saxon, Old High German *wurhtio*. See WORK]

wring (rɪŋ) *vb* **wrings**, **wringing**, **wrung** 1 (often foll by *out*) to twist and compress to squeeze (a liquid) from (cloth, etc) 2 (*tr*) to twist forcibly: *wring its neck* 3 (*tr*) to clasp and twist (one's hands), esp in anguish 4 (*tr*) to distress: *wring one's heart* 5 (*tr*) to grip (someone's hand) vigorously in greeting 6 (*tr*) to obtain by or as if by forceful means: *wring information out of* 7 (*intr*) to writhe with or as if with pain 8 **wringing wet** soaking; drenched ▷ *n* 9 an act or the process of wringing [Old English *wringan*; related to Old High German *ringan* (German *wringen*), Gothic *wrungō* snare. See WRANGLE, WRONG]

wringer ('rɪŋə) *n* another name for **mangle²** (sense 1)

wring together *vb* (*tr, adverb*) *engineering* to join (two smooth flat surfaces, esp slip gauges) by hand pressure and a slight twisting movement

wrinkle¹ ('rɪŋkªl) *n* 1 a slight ridge in the smoothness of a surface, such as a crease in the skin as a result of age ▷ *vb* 2 to make or become wrinkled, as by crumpling, creasing, or puckering [C15 back formation from *wrinkled*, from Old English *gewrinclod*, past participle of *wrinclian* to wind around; related to Swedish *vrinka* to sprain, Lithuanian *reñgti* to twist. See WRENCH] > **'wrinkleless** *adj* > **'wrinkly** *adj*

wrinkle² ('rɪŋkªl) *n* *informal* a clever or useful trick, hint, or dodge [Old English *wrenc* trick; related to Middle Low German *wrank* struggle, Middle High German *ranc* sudden turn. See WRENCH]

wrinklies ('rɪŋklɪz) *pl n* *informal derogatory* old people

wrist (rɪst) *n* 1 *anatomy* the joint between the forearm and the hand. Technical name: **carpus** 2 the part of a sleeve or glove that covers the wrist 3 *machinery* **a** See **wrist pin** **b** a joint in which a wrist pin forms the pivot [Old English; related to Old High German, Old Norse *rist*. See WRIGGLE, WRY]

wristband ('rɪst,bænd) *n* 1 a band around the wrist, esp one attached to a watch or forming part of a long sleeve 2 a sweatband around the wrist

wrist-drop *n* paralysis of the extensor muscles of the wrist and fingers

wristlet ('rɪstlɪt) *n* a band or bracelet worn around the wrist

wristlock ('rɪst,lɒk) *n* a wrestling hold in which a wrestler seizes his opponent's wrist and exerts pressure against the joints of his hand, arm, or shoulder

wrist pin *n* 1 a cylindrical boss or pin attached to the side of a wheel parallel with the axis, esp one forming a bearing for a crank 2 *US and Canadian* the pin through the skirt of a piston in an internal combustion engine, to which the little end of the connecting rod is attached. Also called (esp in Britain): **gudgeon pin**

wristwatch ('rɪst,wɒtʃ) *n* a watch worn strapped around the wrist

wristy ('rɪstɪ) *adj* (of a player's style of hitting the ball in cricket, tennis, etc) characterized by

considerable movement of the wrist

writ¹ (rɪt) *n* 1 *law* (formerly) a document under seal, issued in the name of the Crown or a court, commanding the person to whom it is addressed to do or refrain from doing some specified act. Official name: **claim** 2 *archaic* a piece or body of writing: *Holy Writ* [Old English; related to Old Norse *rit*, Gothic *writs* stroke, Old High German *riz* (German *Riss* a tear). See WRITE]

writ² (rɪt) *vb* 1 *archaic* or *dialect* a past tense and past participle of **write** 2 **writ large** plain to see; very obvious

write (raɪt) *vb* **writes**, **writing**, **wrote**, **written** 1 to draw or mark (symbols, words, etc) on a surface, usually paper, with a pen, pencil, or other instrument 2 to describe or record (ideas, experiences, etc) in writing 3 to compose (a letter) to or correspond regularly with (a person, organization, etc) 4 (*tr; may take a clause as object*) to say or communicate by letter: *he wrote that he was on his way* 5 (*tr*) *informal, chiefly US and Canadian* to send a letter to (a person, etc) 6 to write (words) in cursive as opposed to printed style 7 (*tr*) to be sufficiently familiar with (a specified style, language, etc) to use it in writing 8 to be the author or composer of (books, music, etc) 9 (*tr*) to fill in the details for (a document, form, etc) 10 (*tr*) to draw up or draft 11 (*tr*) to produce by writing: *he wrote ten pages* 12 (*tr*) to show clearly: *envy was written all over his face* 13 (*tr*) to spell, inscribe, or entitle 14 (*tr*) to ordain or prophesy: *it is written* 15 (*tr*) to sit (an examination) 16 (*intr*) to produce writing as specified 17 *computing* to record (data) in a location in a storage device. Compare **read¹** (sense 16) 18 (*tr*) See **underwrite** (sense 3a) ▷ See also **write down, write in, write off, write out, write up** [Old English *wrītan* (originally: to scratch runes into bark); related to Old Frisian *wrīta*, Old Norse *rīta*, Old High German *rīzan* (German *reissen* to tear)] > **'writable** *adj*

write down *vb* (*adverb*) 1 (*tr*) to set down in writing 2 (*tr*) to harm or belittle by writing about (a person) in derogatory terms 3 (*intr; foll by to or for*) to write in a simplified way (to a supposedly less cultured readership) 4 (*tr*) *accounting* to decrease the book value of (an asset) ▷ *n* **write-down** 5 *accounting* a reduction made in the book value of an asset

write in *vb* (*tr*) 1 to insert in (a document, form, etc) in writing 2 (*adverb*) *US* **a** to vote for (a person not on a ballot) by writing in his name **b** to cast (a vote) for such a person by writing in his name ▷ *n* **write-in** *US* 3 the act of voting for a person by writing his name on a ballot 4 a candidate or vote that has been written in 5 (*as modifier*): *a write-in campaign*

write off *vb* (*tr, adverb*) 1 *accounting* **a** to cancel (a bad debt or obsolete asset) from the accounts **b** to consider (a transaction, etc) as a loss or set off (a loss) against revenues **c** to depreciate (an asset) by periodic charges **d** to charge (a specified amount) against gross profits as depreciation of an asset 2 to cause or acknowledge the complete loss of 3 to send a written order for (something): *she wrote off for a brochure* 4 *informal* to damage (something, esp a car) beyond repair ▷ *n* **write-off** 5 *accounting* **a** the act of cancelling a bad debt or obsolete asset from the accounts **b** the bad debt or obsolete asset cancelled **c** the amount cancelled against gross profits, corresponding to the book value of the bad debt or obsolete asset 6 *informal* something damaged beyond repair, esp a car

write out *vb* (*tr, adverb*) 1 to put into writing or reproduce in full form in writing 2 to exhaust (oneself or one's creativity) by excessive writing 3 to remove (a character) from a television or radio series

writer ('raɪtə) *n* 1 a person who writes books, articles, etc, esp as an occupation 2 the person who has written something specified 3 a person who is able to write or write well 4 a scribe or

clerk 5 a composer of music 6 *Scot* a legal practitioner, such as a notary or solicitor 7 **Writer to the Signet** (in Scotland) a member of an ancient society of solicitors, now having the exclusive privilege of preparing crown writs

writerly ('raɪtəlɪ) *adj* of or characteristic of a writer; literary

writer's cramp *n* a muscular spasm or temporary paralysis of the muscles of the thumb and first two fingers caused by prolonged writing

write up *vb* (*tr, adverb*) 1 to describe fully, complete, or bring up to date in writing: *write up a diary* 2 to praise or bring to public notice in writing 3 *accounting, US* **a** to place an excessively high value on (an asset) **b** to increase the book value of (an asset) in order to reflect more accurately its current worth in the market ▷ *n* **write-up** 4 a published account of something, such as a review in a newspaper or magazine 5 *accounting, US* **a** an excessive or illegally high valuation of corporate assets **b** a raising of the book value of an asset

writhe (raɪð) *vb* 1 to twist or squirm in or as if in pain 2 (*intr*) to move with such motions 3 (*intr*) to suffer acutely from embarrassment, revulsion, etc ▷ *n* 4 the act or an instance of writhing [Old English *wrīthan*; related to Old High German *rīdan*, Old Norse *rītha*. See WRATH, WREATH, WRIST, WROTH] > **'writher** *n*

writhen ('rɪðən) *archaic or poetic* ▷ *vb* 1 a past participle of **writhe** ▷ *adj* 2 twisted; distorted

writing ('raɪtɪŋ) *n* 1 a group of letters or symbols written or marked on a surface as a means of communicating ideas by making each symbol stand for an idea, concept, or thing (see **ideogram**), by using each symbol to represent a set of sounds grouped into syllables (**syllabic writing**), or by regarding each symbol as corresponding roughly or exactly to each of the sounds in the language (**alphabetic writing**) 2 short for **handwriting** 3 anything expressed in letters, esp a literary composition 4 the work of a writer 5 literary style, art, or practice 6 written form: *give it to me in writing* 7 (*modifier*) related to or used in writing: *writing ink* 8 **writing on the wall** a sign or signs of approaching disaster [sense 8: allusion to Daniel 5:5]

writing case *n* a portable folder with compartments for holding writing materials

writing desk *n* a piece of furniture with a writing surface and drawers and compartments for papers, writing materials, etc

writing paper *n* paper sized to take writing ink and used for letters and other manuscripts

Writings ('raɪtɪŋz) *pl n* **the** another term for the Hagiographa

writing table *n* a table designed or used for writing at

writ of execution *n* *law* a writ ordering that a judgment be enforced

written ('rɪt³n) *vb* 1 the past participle of **write** ▷ *adj* 2 taken down in writing; transcribed: *written evidence; the written word*. Compare **spoken** (sense 2)

Written Law *n* *Judaism* another name for the **Torah**

WRNS *history abbreviation for* Women's Royal Naval Service. See also **Wren¹**

wrnt *abbreviation for* warrant

Wrocław (*Polish* 'vrɔtswaf) *n* an industrial city in SW Poland, on the River Oder: passed to Austria (1527) and to Prussia (1741); returned to Poland in 1945. Pop: 647 000 (2005 est). German name: **Breslau**

wrong (rɒŋ) *adj* 1 not correct or truthful: *the wrong answer* 2 acting or judging in error: *you are wrong to think that* 3 (*postpositive*) immoral; bad: *it is wrong to cheat* 4 deviating from or unacceptable to correct or conventional laws, usage, etc 5 not intended or wanted: *the wrong road* 6 (*postpositive*) not working properly; amiss: *something is wrong with the engine* 7 (of a side, esp of a fabric) intended to face the inside so as not to be seen 8 **get on the wrong**

W

side of or (US) **get in wrong with** informal to come into disfavour with **9 go down the wrong way** (of food) to pass into the windpipe instead of the gullet ▷ adv **10** in the wrong direction or manner **11 go wrong a** to turn out other than intended **b** to make a mistake **c** (of a machine, etc) to cease to function properly **d** to go astray morally **12 get wrong a** to fail to understand properly **b** to fail to provide the correct answer to ▷ n **13** a bad, immoral, or unjust thing or action **14** law an infringement of another person's rights, rendering the offender liable to a civil action, as for breach of contract or tort: a private wrong **b** a violation of public rights and duties, affecting the community as a whole and actionable at the instance of the Crown: a public wrong **15 in the wrong** mistaken or guilty ▷ vb (tr) **16** to treat unjustly **17** to discredit, malign, or misrepresent **18** to seduce or violate [Old English wrang injustice, from Old Norse vrang; see WRING] > 'wronger n > 'wrongly adv > 'wrongness n

wrongdoer ('rɒŋ,duːə) n a person who acts immorally or illegally

wrongdoing ('rɒŋ,duːɪŋ) n the act or an instance of doing something immoral or illegal

wrong-foot vb (tr) **1** sport to play a shot in such a way as to cause (one's opponent) to be off balance **2** to take by surprise so as to place in an embarrassing or disadvantageous situation

wrong fount n printing an error in which a type of the wrong face or size is used. Abbreviation: wf

wrongful ('rɒŋfʊl) adj immoral, unjust, or illegal > 'wrongfully adv > 'wrongfulness n

wrong-headed adj **1** constantly wrong in judgment **2** foolishly stubborn; obstinate > ,wrong-'headedly adv > ,wrong-'headedness n

wrong number n a telephone number wrongly connected or dialled in error or the person so contacted

wrong 'un n informal **1** a dishonest or unscrupulous person **2** cricket, chiefly Austral another term for **googly**

wrote (rəʊt) vb the past tense of **write**

wroth (rəʊθ, rɒθ) adj archaic or literary angry; irate [Old English wrāth; related to Old Saxon wrēth, Old Norse reithr, Old High German reid curly haired]

wrought (rɔːt) vb **1** archaic a past tense and past participle of **work** ▷ adj **2** metallurgy shaped by hammering or beating **3** (often in combination) formed, fashioned, or worked as specified: well-wrought **4** decorated or made with delicate care [c16 variant of worht, from Old English geworht, past participle of (ge)wyrcan to WORK]

USAGE Wrought is sometimes used as if it were the past tense and past participle of wreak as in the hurricane wrought havoc in coastal areas. Many people think this use is incorrect

wrought iron n **a** a pure form of iron having a low carbon content and a fibrous microstructure. It is made by various processes and is often used for decorative work **b** (as modifier): wrought-iron gates

wrought-up adj agitated or excited

wrung (rʌŋ) vb the past tense and past participle of **wring**

WRVS abbreviation for **Women's Royal Voluntary Service**

wry (raɪ) adj wrier, wriest or wryer, wryest **1** twisted, contorted, or askew **2** (of a facial expression) produced or characterized by contorting of the features, usually indicating dislike **3** drily humorous; sardonic **4** warped, misdirected, or perverse **5** (of words, thoughts, etc) unsuitable or wrong ▷ vb wries, wrying, wried **6** (tr) to twist or contort [c16 from dialect wry to twist, from Old English wrīgian to turn; related to Old Frisian wrīgia to bend, Old Norse riga to move, Middle Low German wrīch bent, stubborn] > 'wryly adv > 'wryness n

wrybill ('raɪ,bɪl) n a New Zealand plover, Anarhynchus frontalis, having its bill deflected to one side enabling it to search for food beneath stones

wryneck ('raɪ,nɛk) n **1** either of two cryptically coloured Old World woodpeckers, Jynx torquilla or J. ruficollis, which do not drum on trees **2** another name for **torticollis 3** informal a person who has a twisted neck

ws the internet domain name for Western Samoa

WSSD abbreviation for World Summit on Sustainable Development, an intergovernmental conference held in Johannesburg in 2002

WST (in Australia) abbreviation for Western Standard Time

WSW symbol for west-southwest

wt. abbreviation for weight

WTC abbreviation for **World Trade Center**

WTG text messaging abbreviation for way to go!

WTO abbreviation for **World Trade Organization**

Wu² (wuː) n a group of dialects of Chinese spoken around the Yangtze delta

Wuchang or **Wu-ch'ang** ('wuː'tʃæŋ) n a former city of E central China: now a part of Wuhan

wudjula ('wʌdʒələ) n Austral a non-Aboriginal person [from a native language of Western Australia, possibly an adaptation of whitefella]

wudu (wudu) n Islam **1** the practice of ritual washing before daily prayer **2** a room designated for ritual washing before daily prayer [from Arabic]

Wuhan ('wuː'hæn) n a city in SE China, in Hubei province, at the confluence of the Han and Yangtze Rivers: formed in 1950 by the union of the cities of Hanyang, Hankou, and Wuchang (the Han Cities); river port and industrial centre; university (1913). Pop: 6 003 000 (2005 est)

Wuhsien ('wuː'ʃjen) n another name for **Suzhou**

Wuhu ('wuː'huː) n a port in E China, in E Anhui province on the Yangtze River. Pop: 701 000 (2005 est)

wukkas ('wʌkəz) pl n **no wukkas** Austral taboo slang an expression used to express agreement or to convey that something is proceeding or has proceeded satisfactorily; no problem [c20 short for "no wukking furries", a euphemism for no fucking worries]

wulfenite ('wʊlfə,naɪt) n a yellow, orange, red, or grey lustrous secondary mineral consisting of lead molybdate in the form of platelike tetragonal crystals. It occurs with lead ores and is a source of molybdenum. Formula: $PbMoO_4$ [c19 from German Wulfenit, named after F. X. von Wulfen (1728–1805), Austrian mineralogist]

Wu-lu-mu-ch'i ('wuː'luː'muː'tʃiː) n a variant of **Urumchi**

wunderkind ('wʌndə,kɪnd; German 'vʊndər,kɪnt) n, pl -kinds or -kinder (German -kɪndər) **1** a child prodigy **2** a person who is exceptionally successful in his field while still young [c20 German, literally: wonder child]

Wuppertal (German 'vʊpərtaːl) n a city in W Germany, in North Rhine-Westphalia state on the **Wupper River** (a Rhine tributary): formed in 1929 from the amalgamation of the towns of Barmen and Elberfeld and other smaller towns; textile centre. Pop: 362 137 (2003 est)

wurley or **wurlie** ('wɜːlɪ) n Austral an Aboriginal hut [from a native Australian language]

Würm (vʊəm, vɜːm) n the fourth and final Pleistocene glaciation in Alpine Europe. See also **Günz, Riss, Mindel** [c20 named after the river Würm in Bavaria, Germany]

wurst (wɜːst, wʊəst, vʊəst) n a large sausage, esp of a type made in Germany, Austria, etc [from German, literally: something rolled; related to Latin vertere to turn]

Württemberg ('vɜːtəm,bɜːg; German 'vyrtəmbɛrk) n a historic region and former state of S Germany; since 1952 part of the state of Baden-Württemberg

Würzburg ('vɜːts,bɜːg; German 'vyrtsbʊrk) n a city in S central Germany, in NW Bavaria on the River Main: university (1582). Pop: 132 687 (2003 est)

wus (wʌs) n South Wales dialect a casual term of address: fancy a drink, wus? [from Welsh was, variant of gwas servant]

wushu ('wuː'ʃuː) n a general term for Chinese martial arts [from Chinese wǔ military + shú art]

wuss, woose (wʊs) or **wussy** ('wʊsɪ) n, pl wusses or wussies slang, chiefly US a feeble or effeminate person [c20 perhaps from PUSSY¹ (cat)]

wuthering ('wʌðərɪŋ) adj Northern English dialect **1** (of a wind) blowing strongly with a roaring sound **2** (of a place) characterized by such a sound [variant of whitherin, from whither blow, from Old Norse hvithra; related to hvitha squall of wind, Old English hweothu wind]

Wutsin ('wuː'tsɪn) n the former name (until 1949) of Zhangzhou (sense 1)

Wuxi, Wusih or **Wu-hsi** ('wuː'ʃiː, -'siː) n a city in E China, in S Jiangsu province on the Grand Canal: textile industry. Pop: 1 192 000 (2005 est)

wuxia ('wuː'ʃiː'aː) n a genre of Chinese fiction and film, concerning the adventures of sword-wielding chivalrous heroes [from Chinese: martial-chivalric]

WV 1 abbreviation for West Virginia **2** ▷ international car registration for (Windward Islands) St Vincent

W. Va. abbreviation for West Virginia

WVS (formerly, in Britain) abbreviation for Women's Voluntary Service, since 1966 WRVS

WWI abbreviation for World War One

WWII abbreviation for World War Two

WWF abbreviation for Worldwide Fund for Nature

WWW abbreviation for **World Wide Web**

WY or **Wy.** abbreviation for Wyoming

Wyandotte ('waɪən,dɒt) n a heavy American breed of domestic fowl with many different varieties [c19 from Wyandot, a N American Indian people]

wych- prefix a variant of **witch-**

wych-elm or **witch-elm** ('wɪtʃ,ɛlm) n **1** Eurasian elm tree, Ulmus glabra, having a rounded shape, longish pointed leaves, clusters of small flowers, and winged fruits **2** the wood of this tree [c17 from Old English wice wych-elm]

wych-hazel n a variant spelling of **witch hazel**

Wycliffite or **Wyclifite** ('wɪklɪ,faɪt) English history ▷ n **1** a follower of John Wycliffe, the English religious reformer (?1330–84), or an adherent of his religious ideas; a Lollard ▷ adj **2** of or relating to Wycliffe, his followers, or his religious ideas

Wye (waɪ) n a river in E Wales and W England, rising in Powys and flowing southeast into Herefordshire, then south to the Severn estuary. Length: 210 km (130 miles)

Wykehamist ('wɪkəmɪst) n a pupil or former pupil of Winchester College

wynd (waɪnd) n Scot a narrow lane or alley [c15 from the stem of WIND²]

Wyo. abbreviation for Wyoming

Wyoming (waɪ'əʊmɪŋ) n a state of the western US: consists largely of ranges of the Rockies in the west and north, with part of the Great Plains in the east and several regions of hot springs. Capital: Cheyenne. Pop: 501 242 (2003 est). Area: 253 597 sq km (97 914 sq miles). Abbreviations: Wyo, Wy, (with zip code) WY

Wyomingite (waɪ'əʊmɪŋ,aɪt) n a native or inhabitant of Wyoming

WYSIWYG ('wɪzɪ,wɪg) n, adj computing ▷ acronym for what you see is what you get: referring to what is displayed on the screen being the same as what will be printed out

wyvern or less commonly **wivern** ('waɪvən) n a heraldic beast having a serpent's tail and a dragon's head and a body with wings and two legs [c17 variant of earlier wyver, from Old French, from Latin vīpera VIPER]

Xx

x *or* **X** (ɛks) *n, pl* **x's, X's** *or* **Xs** **1** the 24th letter and 19th consonant of the modern English alphabet **2** a speech sound sequence represented by this letter, in English pronounced as *ks* or *gz* or, in initial position, *z*, as in *xylophone*

x *symbol for* **1** *commerce, banking, finance* ex **2** *maths* the *x*-axis or a coordinate measured along the *x*-axis in a Cartesian coordinate system **3** an algebraic variable

X *symbol for* **1** (formerly, in Britain) **a** indicating a film that may not be publicly shown to anyone under 18. Since 1982 replaced by symbol 18 **b** (*as modifier*): *an X film* **2** denoting any unknown, unspecified, or variable factor, number, person, or thing **3** (on letters, cards, etc) denoting a kiss **4** (on ballot papers, etc) indicating choice **5** (on examination papers, etc) indicating error **6** for Christ; Christian [from the form of the Greek letter khi (X), first letter of *Khristos* Christ] **7** ▷ *the Roman numeral for* ten. See **Roman numerals**

xanthan gum ('zæn,θæn) *n* a complex polysaccharide exuded by colonies of the bacterium *Xanthomonas campestris*: used as a food additive in salad dressings, dairy products, etc

xanthate ('zænθeɪt) *n* any salt or ester of xanthic acid > xan'thation *n*

xanthein ('zænθɪɪn) *n* the soluble part of the yellow pigment that is found in the cell sap of some flowers

xanthene ('zænθiːn) *n* a yellowish crystalline heterocyclic compound used as a fungicide; benzo-1,4-pyran. Its molecular structural unit is found in many dyes, such as rhodamine and fluorescein. Formula: $CH_2(C_6H_4)_2O$

Xanthian ('zænθɪən) *adj* of or relating to the ancient Lycian city of Xanthus or its inhabitants

xanthic ('zænθɪk) *adj* **1** of, containing, or derived from xanthic acid **2** *botany rare* having a yellow colour

xanthic acid *n* any of a class of organic sulphur-containing acids with the general formula ROC(S)SH, where R is an organic group. Their salts are the xanthates

xanthin ('zænθɪn) *n* any of a group of yellow or orange carotene derivatives that occur in the fruit and flowers of certain plants

xanthine ('zænθiːn, -θaɪn) *n* **1** a crystalline compound related in structure to uric acid and found in urine, blood, certain plants, and certain animal tissues. Formula: $C_5H_4N_4O_2$ **2** any substituted derivative of xanthine, esp one of the three pharmacologically active methylated xanthines, caffeine, theophylline, or theobromine, which act as stimulants and diuretics

Xanthippe (zæn'θɪpɪ) *or* **Xantippe** (zæn'tɪpɪ) *n* any nagging, peevish, or irritable woman [from Xanthippe, the proverbially scolding and quarrelsome wife of Socrates]

xanthism ('zæn,θɪzəm) *n* a condition of skin, fur, or feathers in which yellow predominates

xantho- *or before a vowel* **xanth-** *combining form* indicating yellow: *xanthophyll* [from Greek *xanthos*]

xanthochroid ('zænθəʊ,krɔɪd) *adj rare* of, relating to, or designating races having light-coloured hair and a pale complexion [C19 New Latin *xanthochroi*, from XANTHO- + Greek *ōkhros* pale]

xanthochroism (zæn'θɒkrəʊ,ɪzəm) *n* a condition in certain animals, esp aquarium goldfish, in which all skin pigments other than yellow and orange disappear [C19 from Greek *xanthokhro(os)* yellow-skinned (from *xanthos* yellow + *khroia* skin) + -ISM]

xanthoma (zæn'θəʊmə) *n pathol* the presence in the skin of fatty yellow or brownish plaques or nodules, esp on the eyelids, caused by a disorder of lipid metabolism

xanthophyll *or esp US* **xanthophyl** ('zænθəʊfɪl) *n* any of a group of yellow carotenoid pigments occurring in plant and animal tissue > ,xantho'phyllous *adj*

xanthous ('zænθəs) *adj* of, relating to, or designating races with yellowish hair and a light complexion

Xanthus ('zænθəs) *n* the chief city of ancient Lycia in SW Asia Minor: source of some important antiquities

x-**axis** *n* a reference axis, usually horizontal, of a graph or two- or three-dimensional Cartesian coordinate system along which the *x*-coordinate is measured

X-chromosome *n* the sex chromosome that occurs in pairs in the diploid cells of the females of many animals, including humans, and as one of a pair with the Y-chromosome in those of males. Compare **Y-chromosome**

XDA *or* **xda** *n trademark* a combined computer and mobile phone

Xe *the chemical symbol for* xenon

xebec, zebec *or* **zebeck** ('ziːbɛk) *n* a small three-masted Mediterranean vessel with both square and lateen sails, formerly used by Algerian pirates and later used for commerce [C18 earlier *chebec* from French, ultimately from Arabic *shabbāk*; present spelling influenced by Catalan *xabec*, Spanish *xabeque* (now *jabeque*)]

xenia ('ziːnɪə) *n botany* the influence of pollen upon the form of the fruit developing after pollination [C19 from New Latin, from Greek: hospitality, from *xenos* guest] > 'xenial *adj*

Xenical ('zɛnɪkəl) *n trademark* a drug that reduces the ability to absorb fats; used in the medical treatment of obesity

xeno- *or before a vowel* **xen-** *combining form* indicating something strange, different, or foreign: *xenogamy* [from Greek *xenos* strange]

xenocryst ('zɛnə,krɪst) *n* a crystal included within an igneous rock as the magma cooled but not formed from it [C20 from XENO- + CRYST(AL)]

xenogamy (zɛ'nɒgəmɪ) *n botany* another name for **cross-fertilization**. > xe'nogamous *adj*

xenogeneic (,zɛnəʊdʒɪ'neɪɪk) *adj med* derived from an individual of a different species: *a xenogeneic tissue graft*

xenogenesis (,zɛnə'dʒɛnɪsɪs) *n* **1** the supposed production of offspring completely unlike either parent **2** another name for **abiogenesis** *or* **alternation of generations** > xenogenetic (,zɛnəʊdʒɪ'nɛtɪk) *or* ,xeno'genic *adj*

xenoglossia (,zɛnə'glɒsɪə) *or* **xenoglossy** ('zɛnə,glɒsɪ) *n* an ability claimed by some mediums, clairvoyants, etc, to speak a language with which they are unfamiliar [C20 from Greek, from XENO- + Attic Greek *glossa* tongue, language]

xenograft ('zɛnəʊ,grɑːft) *n* another word for **heterograft**

xenolith ('zɛnəlɪθ) *n* a fragment of rock differing in origin, composition, structure, etc, from the igneous rock enclosing it > ,xeno'lithic *adj*

xenomorphic (,zɛnə'mɔːfɪk) *adj* (of a mineral constituent of an igneous rock) not having its characteristic crystal shape because of deforming pressure from adjacent minerals > ,xeno'morphically *adv*

xenon ('zɛnɒn) *n* a colourless odourless gaseous element occurring in trace amounts in air; formerly considered inert it is now known to form compounds and is used in radio valves, stroboscopic and bactericidal lamps, and bubble chambers. Symbol: Xe; atomic no: 54; atomic wt: 131.29; valency: 0; density: 5.887 kg/m³; melting pt: −111.76°C; boiling pt: −108.0°C [C19 from Greek: something strange]

xenophile ('zɛnə,faɪl) *n* a person who likes foreigners or things foreign [C19 from Greek, from XENO- + -PHILE]

xenophobe ('zɛnə,fəʊb) *n* a person who hates or fears foreigners or strangers [C20 from Greek, from XENO- + -PHOBE]

xenophobia (,zɛnə'fəʊbɪə) *n* hatred or fear of foreigners or strangers or of their politics or culture > ,xeno'phobic *adj*

xenotransplant ('zɛnəʊ,trænz,plɑːnt) *n surgery* an operation in which an organ or tissue is transferred from one animal to another of a different species > 'xeno,transplan,tation *n*

xeranthemum (zɪə'rænθəməm) *n* any of a Mediterranean genus of plants having flower heads that are dry and retain their colour and shape for years: family *Asteraceae* (composites). See also **immortelle** [C18 New Latin, from Greek XERO- + *anthemon* flower]

xerarch ('zɪərɑːk) *adj ecology* (of a sere) having its origin in a dry habitat [from XER(O)- + Greek *arkhē* a beginning, from *arkhein* to begin]

Xeres (Spanish 'xɛrɛθ) *n* the former name of **Jerez**

xeric ('zɪərɪk) *adj ecology* of, relating to, or growing in dry conditions > 'xerically *adv*

xero- *or before a vowel* **xer-** *combining form* indicating dryness: *xeroderma* [from Greek *xēros* dry]

xeroderma (,zɪərəʊ'dɜːmə) *or* **xerodermia** (,zɪərəʊ'dɜːmɪə) *n pathol* **1** any abnormal dryness of the skin as the result of diminished secretions from the sweat or sebaceous glands **2** another name for **ichthyosis**. > xerodermatic (ˌzɪərəʊdəˈmætɪk) *or* ˌxeroˈdermatous *adj*

xerography (zɪˈrɒɡrəfɪ) *n* a photocopying process in which an electrostatic image is formed on a selenium plate or cylinder. The plate or cylinder is dusted with a resinous powder, which adheres to the charged regions, and the image is then transferred to a sheet of paper on which it is fixed by heating > xeˈrographer *n* > xerographic (ˌzɪərəˈɡræfɪk) *adj* > ˌxeroˈgraphically *adv*

xeromorphic (ˌzɪərəˈmɔːfɪk) *adj* (of plants or plant parts) having characteristics that serve as protection against excessive loss of water

xerophilous (zɪˈrɒfɪləs) *adj* (of plants or animals) adapted for growing or living in dry surroundings > xerophile (ˈzɪərəʊˌfaɪl) *n* > xeˈrophily *n*

xerophthalmia (ˌzɪərɒfˈθælmɪə) *n pathol* excessive dryness of the cornea and conjunctiva, caused by a deficiency of vitamin A. Also called: xeroma (zɪˈrəʊmə) > ˌxerophˈthalmic *adj*

xerophyte (ˈzɪərəˌfaɪt) *n* a xerophilous plant, such as a cactus > xerophytic (ˌzɪərəˈfɪtɪk) *adj* > ˌxeroˈphytically *adv* > ˈxeroˌphytism *n*

xerosere (ˈzɪərəˌsɪə) *n ecology* a sere that originates in dry surroundings

xerosis (zɪˈrəʊsɪs) *n pathol* abnormal dryness of bodily tissues, esp the skin, eyes, or mucous membranes > xerotic (zɪˈrɒtɪk) *adj*

xerostomia (ˌziːrəˈstəʊmɪə) *n* abnormal lack of saliva; dryness of the mouth [c19 from xero- + -stom(e) + -ia]

Xerox (ˈzɪərɒks) *n* **1** *trademark* **a** a xerographic copying process **b** a machine employing this process **c** a copy produced by this process ▷ *vb* **2** to produce a copy of (a document, illustration, etc) by this process

x-height *n printing* the height of lower case letters of a typeface, without ascenders or descenders

Xhosa (ˈkɔːsə) *n* **1** (*pl* -sa *or* -sas) a member of a cattle-rearing Negroid people of southern Africa, living chiefly in South Africa **2** the language of this people, belonging to the Bantu group of the Niger-Congo family: one of the Nguni languages, closely related to Swazi and Zulu and characterized by several clicks in its sound system > ˈXhosan *adj*

xi (zaɪ, saɪ, ksaɪ, ksiː) *n, pl* **xis** the 14th letter in the Greek alphabet (Ξ, ξ), a composite consonant, transliterated as *x*

Xi, Hsi *or* **Si** (ʃiː) *n* a river in S China, rising in Yünnan province and flowing east to the Canton delta on the South China Sea: the main river system of S China. Length: about 1900 km (1200 miles)

Xiamen (ˈʃjɑːˈmɛn) *n* a variant transliteration of the Chinese name for **Amoy**

Xi'an, Hsian *or* **Sian** (ʃjɑːn) *n* an industrial city in central China, capital of Shaanxi province: capital of China for 970 years at various times between the 3rd century BC and the 10th century AD; seat of the Northwestern University (1937); famous for Qin dynasty emperor Qinshihuang's tomb (207 BC) with 8000-strong terracotta army. Pop: 3 256 000 (2005 est). Former names: Changan, Siking

Xiang, Hsiang *or* **Siang** (ʃjɑːŋ) *n* **1** a river in SE central China, rising in NE Guangxi Zhuang and flowing northeast and north to Dongting Lake. Length: about 1150 km (715 miles) **2** a river in S China, rising in SE Yünnan and flowing generally east to the Hongxiu (the upper course of the Xi River). Length: about 800 km (500 miles)

Xiangtan *or* **Sianqtan** (ˈʃjɑːŋˈtɑːn) *n* a city in S central China, in NE Hunan on the Xiang River: centre of a region noted for tea production. Pop: 592 000 (2005 est)

Xingú (*Portuguese* ʃiŋˈɡu) *n* a river in central Brazil, rising on the Mato Grosso plateau and flowing north to the Amazon delta, with over 650 km (400 miles) of rapids in its middle course. Length: 1932 km (1200 miles)

Xining, Hsining *or* **Sining** (ˈʃiːˈnɪŋ) *n* a city in W China, capital of Qinghai province, at an altitude of 2300 m (7500 ft). Pop: 689 000 (2005 est)

Xinjiang Uygur (ˈʃɪnˈdʒjæŋ ˈwiːˈɡʊə) *or* **Sinkiang-Uighur Autonomous Region** *n* an administrative division of NW China: established in 1955 for the Uygur ethnic minority, with autonomous subdivisions for other small minorities; produces over half China's wool and contains valuable mineral resources. Capital: Urumqi. Pop: 19 340 000 (2003 est). Area: 1 646 799 sq km (635 829 sq miles)

xiphi- *or before a vowel* **xiph-** *combining form* indicating a sword, esp something shaped like or resembling a sword: *xiphisternum; xiphoid* [from Greek *xiphos* sword]

xiphisternum (ˌzɪfɪˈstɜːnəm) *n, pl* -na (-nə) *anatomy, zoology* the cartilaginous process forming the lowermost part of the breastbone (sternum). Also called: xiphoid, xiphoid process

xiphoid (ˈzɪfɔɪd) *adj* **1** *biology* shaped like a sword **2** of or relating to the xiphisternum ▷ *n* **3** Also called: xiphoid process another name for **xiphisternum**

xiphosuran (ˌzɪfəˈsjʊərən) *n* **1** any chelicerate arthropod of the subclass *Xiphosura*, including the horseshoe crabs and many extinct forms ▷ *adj* **2** of, relating to, or belonging to the subclass *Xiphosura* [c19 from New Latin *Xiphosura*, irregularly from Greek *xiphos* sword + *oura* tail]

Xixón (ʃiˈʃon) *n* the Asturian name for **Gijón**

Xizang Autonomous Region (ˈʃiːˈzæŋ) *n* the Pinyin transliteration of the Chinese name for **Tibet**

XL *symbol for* extra large

XLNT *text messaging abbreviation for* excellent

Xmas (ˈɛksməs, ˈkrɪsməs) *n informal* short for **Christmas** [c16 from symbol X for Christ + -mas]

Xn *or* **Xtian** *abbreviation for* Christian

Xnty *or* **Xty** *abbreviation for* Christianity

XO *US* ▷ *abbreviation for* executive officer

xoanon (ˈzəʊəˌnɒn) *n, pl* -na (-nə) a primitive image of a god, carved, esp originally, in wood, and supposed to have fallen from heaven [c18 from Greek, from *xuō* to scrape, smooth]

Xochimilco (ˌkɒtʃɪˈmɪlkəʊ) *n* a town in central Mexico, on Lake Xochimilco: noted for its floating gardens. Pop: 271 020 (1990)

XP¹ *n* the Christian monogram made up of the Greek letters *khi* and *rho*, the first two letters of *Khristos*, the Greek form of Christ's name

XP² *abbreviation for* extreme programming

x-radiation *n* another term for **X-ray**

X-rated *adj* **1** (formerly, in Britain) (of a film) considered suitable for viewing by adults only **2** *informal* involving bad language, violence, or sex: *an X-rated conversation*

X-ray *or* **x-ray** *n* **1** **a** electromagnetic radiation emitted when matter is bombarded with fast electrons. X-rays have wavelengths shorter than that of ultraviolet radiation, that is less than about 1×10^{-8} metres. They extend to indefinitely short wavelengths, but below about 1×10^{-11} metres they are often called gamma radiation **b** (*as modifier*): *X-ray astronomy* **2** a picture produced by exposing photographic film to X-rays: used in medicine as a diagnostic aid as parts of the body, such as bones, absorb X-rays and so appear as opaque areas on the picture **3** (*usually capital*) *communications* a code word for the letter *x* ▷ *vb* (*tr*) **4** to photograph (part of the body, etc) using X-rays **5** to treat or examine by means of X-rays [c19 partial translation of German *X-Strahlen* (from *strahl* ray), coined in 1895 by W. K. *Röntgen* (1845–1923), German physicist]

X-ray astronomy *n* the branch of astronomy concerned with the detection and measurement of X-rays emitted by certain celestial bodies. As X-rays are absorbed by the atmosphere, satellites and rockets are used

X-ray binary *n* a binary star that is an intense source of X-rays and is composed of a normal star

in close orbit with a white dwarf, neutron star, or black hole

X-ray crystallography *n* the study and practice of determining the structure of a crystal by passing a beam of X-rays through it and observing and analysing the diffraction pattern produced

X-ray diffraction *n* the scattering of X-rays on contact with matter, resulting in changes in radiation intensity, which is used for studying atomic structure

X-ray therapy *n med* the therapeutic use of X-rays

X-ray tube *n* an evacuated tube containing a metal target onto which is directed a beam of electrons at high energy for the generation of X-rays

Xt *abbreviation for* Christ [representing the initial letter (chi) and the t (tau) of Greek *Khristos*]

xu (tʃʊ) *n* a monetary unit of Vietnam worth one hundredth of a đong

x-unit *n* a unit of length equal to $0.100\ 202 \times 10^{-12}$ metre, for expressing the wavelengths of X-rays and gamma rays

Xuthus (ˈzuːθəs) *n Greek myth* a son of Hellen, regarded as an ancestor of the Ionian Greeks through his son Ion

XUV *abbreviation for* extreme ultraviolet: involving radiation bridging the gap between X-rays and ultraviolet radiation: *XUV astronomy; XUV waveband.* Also: EUV

Xuzhou (ˈʃuːˈdʒəʊ), **Hsü-chou** *or* **Süchow** *n* a city in N central China, in NW Jiangsu province: scene of a decisive battle (1949) in which the Communists defeated the Nationalists. Pop: 1 662 000 (2005 est)

xylan (ˈzaɪlæn) *n biochem* a yellow polysaccharide consisting of xylose units: occurs in straw husks and other woody tissue

xylem (ˈzaɪləm, -lɛm) *n* a plant tissue that conducts water and mineral salts from the roots to all other parts, provides mechanical support, and forms the wood of trees and shrubs. It is of two types (see **protoxylem**, **metaxylem**), both of which are made up mainly of vessels and tracheids [c19 from Greek *xulon* wood]

xylene (ˈzaɪliːn) *n* an aromatic hydrocarbon existing in three isomeric forms, all three being colourless flammable volatile liquids used as solvents and in the manufacture of synthetic resins, dyes, and insecticides; dimethylbenzene. Formula: $C_6H_4(CH_3)_2$. Also called: xylol

xylidine (ˈzaɪlɪˌdiːn, -ˌdaɪn, ˈzɪlɪ-) *n* **1** a mixture of six isomeric amines derived from xylene and used in dyes. Formula: $(CH_3)_2C_6H_3NH_2$ **2** any one of these isomers

xylitol (ˈzaɪlɪˌtɒl) *n chemistry* an artificial sweetener produced from xylose and used esp in chewing gum. Formula: $CH_2HOH(CHOH)_3CH_2OH$ [c19 from xyl(ose) + -ite² + -ol¹]

xylo- *or before a vowel* **xyl-** *combining form* **1** indicating wood: *xylophone* **2** indicating xylene: *xylidine* [from Greek *xulon* wood]

xylocarp (ˈzaɪləˌkɑːp) *n botany* a fruit, such as a coconut, having a hard woody pericarp > ˌxyloˈcarpous *adj*

xylogenous (zaɪˈlɒdʒɪnəs) *adj biology* living in or on wood. Also: xylophilous (zaɪˈlɒfɪləs)

xylograph (ˈzaɪləˌɡrɑːf, -ˌɡræf) *n* **1** an engraving in wood **2** a print taken from a wood block ▷ *vb* **3** (*tr*) to print (a design, illustration, etc) from a wood engraving

xylography (zaɪˈlɒɡrəfɪ) *n* the art, craft, or process of printing from wooden blocks > xyˈlographer *n* > xylographic (ˌzaɪləˈɡræfɪk) *or* ˌxyloˈgraphical *adj*

xyloid (ˈzaɪlɔɪd) *adj botany* of, relating to, or resembling wood; woody

xylol (ˈzaɪlɒl) *n* another name (not in technical usage) for **xylene**

xylophagous (zaɪˈlɒfəɡəs) *adj* (of certain insects, crustaceans, etc) feeding on or living within wood

xylophone (ˈzaɪləˌfəʊn) *n music* a percussion

instrument consisting of a set of wooden bars of graduated length. It is played with hard-headed hammers [C19 from XYLO- + -PHONE] ▷ xylophonic (ˌzaɪləˈfɒnɪk) *adj* ▷ xylophonist (zaɪˈlɒfənɪst) *n*

xylorimba (ˌzaɪləˈrɪmbə) *n* a large xylophone with an extended range of five octaves [C20 XYLO(PHONE) + (MA)RIMBA]

xylose (ˈzaɪləʊz, -ləʊs) *n* a white crystalline dextrorotatory sugar found in the form of xylan in wood and straw. It is extracted by hydrolysis with acids and used in dyeing, tanning, and in foods for diabetics. Formula: $C_5H_{10}O_5$

xylotomous (zaɪˈlɒtəməs) *adj* (of certain insects, insect larvae, etc) cutting or boring into wood

xylotomy (zaɪˈlɒtəmɪ) *n* the preparation of sections of wood for examination by microscope ▷ xyˈlotomist *n*

xylyl (ˈzaɪlɪl) *n* (*modifier*) of, containing, or denoting the group of atoms $(CH_3)_2C_6H_3$-, derived from xylene

xyst (zɪst) *or* **xystus, xystos** (ˈzɪstəs) *n* **1** a long portico, esp one used in ancient Greece for athletics **2** (in ancient Rome) a covered garden walk or one lined with trees [C17 from Latin *xystus*, from Greek *xustos*, literally: smoothed, polished (area), from *xuein* to scrape, make smooth]

xyster (ˈzɪstə) *n* a surgical instrument for scraping bone, surgical rasp or file [C17 via New Latin from Greek: tool for scraping, from *xuein* to scrape, make smooth]

X

Y y

y *or* **Y** (waɪ) *n, pl* **y's, Y's** *or* **Ys 1** the 25th letter of the modern English alphabet **2** a speech sound represented by this letter, in English usually a semivowel, as in *yawn*, or a vowel, as in *symbol* or *shy* **3 a** something shaped like a Y **b** (*in combination*): *a Y-cross*

y *maths symbol for* **1** the y-axis or a coordinate measured along the y-axis in a Cartesian coordinate system **2** an algebraic variable

Y *symbol for* **1** any unknown, unspecified, or variable factor, number, person, or thing **2** *chem* yttrium **3** *currency* **a** a yen **b** yuan

y. *abbreviation for* year

Y. *abbreviation for* YMCA or YWCA

-y¹ *or* **-ey** *suffix forming adjectives* **1** (*from nouns*) characterized by; consisting of; filled with; relating to; resembling: *sunny; sandy; smoky; classy* **2** (*from verbs*) tending to; acting or existing as specified: *leaky; shiny* [from Old English *-ig, -æg*]

-y², **-ie** *or* **-ey** *suffix of nouns informal* **1** denoting smallness and expressing affection: *a doggy; a granny; Jamie* **2** a person or thing concerned with or characterized by being: *a groupie; a fatty* [c14 from Scottish *-ie, -y,* familiar suffix occurring originally in names, as in *Jamie (James)*]

-y³ *suffix forming nouns* **1** (*from verbs*) indicating the act of doing what is indicated by the verbal element: *inquiry* **2** (*esp with combining forms of Greek, Latin, or French origin*) indicating state, condition, or quality: *geography; jealousy* [from Old French *-ie,* from Latin *-ia*]

yaar (jɑːr) *n Hinglish informal* a friend: often used between males in direct address [Hindi]

yaba ('jæbæ) *acronym for* yet another bloody acronym

yabba ('jæbə) *n slang* a form of methamphetamine [c20 of unknown origin]

yabber ('jæbə) *informal, chiefly Austral* ▷ *vb* **1** (*intr*) to talk or jabber ▷ *n* **2** talk or jabber [c19 from a native Australian language *yabba* talk, probably influenced by JABBER]

yabby *or* **yabbie** ('jæbɪ) *Austral* ▷ *n, pl* -**bies 1** a small freshwater crayfish of the genus *Cherax,* esp *C. destructor* **2** Also called: **nipper** a marine prawn used as bait ▷ *vb* -**bies, -bying, -bied 3** (*intr*) to go out to catch yabbies [from a native Australian language]

Yablonovy Mountains (*Russian* 'jablənəvij) *pl n* a mountain range in Siberia. Highest peak: 1680 m (5512 ft). Also called: **Yablonoi Mountains** ('jɑːblə,nɔɪ)

yacca *or* **yacka** ('jækə) *n Austral* another word for **grass tree** (sense 1) [from a native Australian language]

yacht (jɒt) *n* **1** a vessel propelled by sail or power, used esp for pleasure cruising, racing, etc **2** short for **sand yacht** or **ice yacht** ▷ *vb* **3** (*intr*) to sail or cruise in a yacht [c16 from obsolete Dutch *jaghte,* short for *jahtschip,* from *jagen* to chase + *schip* SHIP]

yachtie ('jɒtɪ) *n Austral and NZ informal* a yachtsman; sailing enthusiast

yachting ('jɒtɪŋ) *n* **a** the sport or practice of navigating a yacht **b** (*as modifier*): *yachting clothes*

yachtsman ('jɒtsmən) *or feminine* **yachtswoman** *n, pl* -**men** *or* -**women** a person who sails a yacht or yachts > 'yachtsman,ship *n*

yack (jæk) *n, vb* a variant spelling of **yak²**

yackety-yak (,jækɪtɪ'jæk) *n slang* noisy, continuous, and trivial talk or conversation. Sometimes shortened to: **yak** [of imitative origin]

yad (jɑd) *n Judaism* a hand-held pointer used for reading the *sefer torah* [Hebrew]

yadda yadda yadda *or* **yada yada yada** (,jædəjædə'jædə) *n US slang* tedious or long-winded talk [c20 of uncertain origin; possibly imitative of the sound of someone talking at length in a dull manner]

yae (je) *adj Scot* a variant of **ae**

yaffle ('jæfᵊl) *n* another name for **green woodpecker** [c18 imitative of its cry]

Yafo ('jɑːfɔ:) *n* transliteration of the Hebrew name for **Jaffa** (sense 1)

Yagi aerial ('jɑːgɪ, 'jægɪ) *n* a highly directional aerial, used esp in television and radio astronomy, consisting of three or more elements lying parallel to each other, the principal direction of radiation being along the line of the centres [c20 named after Hidetsugu Yagi (1886–1976), Japanese engineer]

yah (jɑː, jɛə) *sentence substitute* **1** an informal word for **yes**, often used to indicate derision or contempt ▷ *interj* **2** an exclamation of derision or disgust

Yah (jɑː) *n Brit informal* an affected upper-class person [c20 from *yah,* the spoken form of YES supposedly used by upper-class British people]

Yahata ('jɑːhɑːˌtɑː) *n* a variant of **Yawata**

yahoo (jə'huː) *n, pl* -**hoos** a crude, brutish, or obscenely coarse person [c20 from the name of a race of brutish creatures resembling men in Jonathan Swift's *Gulliver's Travels* (1726)] > ya'hooism *n*

Yahrzeit ('jɔːtsaɪt) *n Judaism* the anniversary of the death of a close relative, on which it is customary to kindle a light and recite the Kaddish and also, in some communities, to observe a fast [Yiddish, from Middle High German *jārzīt* anniversary; see YEAR, TIDE¹]

Yahweh, Jahweh ('jɑːweɪ) *or* **Yahveh, Jahveh** ('jɑːveɪ) *n Old Testament* a vocalization of the Tetragrammaton, used esp by Christian theologians [from Hebrew, from YHVH, with conjectural vowels; perhaps related to *hāwāh* to be; see also JEHOVAH]

Yahwism, Jahwism ('jɑːwɪzəm) *or* **Yahvism, Jahvism** ('jɑːvɪzəm) *n* the use of the name Yahweh, esp in parts of the Old Testament, as the personal name of God

Yahwist, Jahwist ('jɑːwɪst) *or* **Yahvist, Jahvist** ('jɑːvɪst) *n Bible* the **a** the conjectured author or authors of the earliest of four main sources or strands of tradition of which the Pentateuch is composed and in which God is called *Yahweh* throughout **b** (*as modifier*): *the Yahwist source*

Yahwistic, Jahwistic (jɑː'wɪstɪk) *or* **Yahvistic, Jahvistic** (jɑː'vɪstɪk) *adj Bible* of or relating to Yahwism, the Yahwist, or Yahweh

Yajur-Veda ('jʌdʒʊə'veɪdə) *n Hinduism* the second Veda, consisting of prayers and sacrificial formulas primarily for use by the priests [from Sanskrit, from *yajur* sacred, holy (compare Greek *hagios* holy) + VEDA]

yak¹ (jæk) *n* a wild and domesticated type of cattle, *Bos grunniens,* of Tibet, having long horns and long shaggy hair [c19 from Tibetan *gyag*]

yak² (jæk) *slang* ▷ *n* **1** noisy, continuous, and trivial talk or conversation ▷ *vb* **yaks, yakking, yakked 2** (*intr*) to chatter or talk in this way; jabber. Also: **yakety-yak** (,jækɪtɪ'jæk) [c20 of imitative origin]

yakitori (,jækɪ'tɔːrɪ) *n* a Japanese dish consisting of small pieces of chicken skewered and grilled [Japanese, from *yaki* grilled + *tori* bird]

yakka, yakker *or* **yacker** ('jækə) *n Austral and NZ informal* work [c19 from a native Australian language]

Yakut (jæ'kut) *n* **1** (*pl* -**kuts** *or* -**kut**) a native or inhabitant of the Sakha Republic, in Russia **2** the language of this people, belonging to the Turkic branch of the Altaic family

Yakut Republic *n* the former name of the **Sakha Republic**

Yakutsk (*Russian* jɪ'kutsk) *n* a port in E Russia, capital of the Sakha Republic, on the Lena River. Pop: 214 000 (2005 est)

yakuza (jə'kuːzə) *n, pl* -**kuza 1** the a Japanese criminal organization involved in illegal gambling, extortion, gun-running, etc **2** a member of this organization [c20 from Japanese *ya* eight + *ku* nine + *za* three, the worst hand in a game of cards]

Yale lock (jeɪl) *n trademark* a type of cylinder lock using a flat serrated key

Yalta (*Russian* 'jaltə) *n* a port and resort in S Ukraine, in the Crimea on the Black Sea: scene of a conference (1945) between Churchill, Roosevelt, and Stalin, who met to plan the final defeat and occupation of Nazi Germany. Pop: 89 000 (latest est)

Yalu ('jɑːluː) *n* a river in E Asia, rising in N North Korea and flowing southwest to Korea Bay, forming a large part of the border between North Korea and NE China. Length: 806 km (501 miles)

yam (jæm) *n* **1** any of various twining plants of the genus *Dioscorea,* of tropical and subtropical regions, cultivated for their edible tubers: family *Dioscoreaceae* **2** the starchy tuber of any of these plants, which is eaten as a vegetable **3** *Southern US* any of certain large varieties of sweet potato **4** a former Scot name for the (common) **potato** [c17 from Portuguese *inhame,* ultimately of West African origin; compare Senegal *nyami* to eat]

yamen ('jɑːmɛn) *n* (in imperial China) the office

or residence of a public official [C19 from Chinese, from *ya* general's office + *mĕn* gate]

Yamim Nora'im (jɑ'mim nɔrɑ'im) *or* **Yomim Noro'im** ('jɔmim nəʊ'roim) *pl n* another name for **High Holidays** [Hebrew, literally: Days of Awe]

yammer ('jæmə) *informal* ▷ *vb* **1** to utter or whine in a complaining or peevish manner **2** to make (a complaint) loudly or persistently **3** (*intr*) (esp of an animal) to howl or wail plaintively or distressingly; yelp or yowl ▷ *n* **4** a yammering sound, wail, or utterance **5** nonsense; jabber [Old English *geōmrian* to grumble, complain; related to Old High German *iāmar* misery, lamentation, Old Norse *amra* to howl] > 'yammerer *n*

Yamoussoukro (ˌjæmʊ'suːkrəʊ) *n* the capital of Côte d'Ivoire, situated in the S centre of the country. It replaced Abidjan as capital in 1983. Pop: 468 000 (2005 est)

yampy ('jæmpɪ) *n Midland English dialect* a foolish person

Yanan ('jæn'æn) *or* **Yenan** *n* a city in NE China, in N Shaanxi province: political and military capital of the Chinese Communists (1935–49). Pop: 343 000 (2005 est). Also called: **Fushih**

Yang (jæŋ) *n* See **Yin and Yang**

Yangon (jæŋ'ɡɒn) *n* the capital and chief port of Myanmar (formerly Burma): an industrial city and transport centre; dominated by the gold-covered Shwe Dagon pagoda, 112 m (368 ft) high. Pop: 4 082 000 (2005 est). Former name (until 1989): **Rangoon**

Yangtze ('jæŋtsɪ, ˌjæŋktsɪ) *n* the longest river in China, rising in SE Qinghai province and flowing east to the East China Sea near Shanghai: a major commercial waterway in one of the most densely populated areas of the world. The **Three Gorges dam** near Yichang, the world's biggest hydroelectric and flood-control project, was begun in 1994 and the dam was completed in 2003, with filling expected to take several years thereafter. Length: 5528 km (3434 miles). Also called: **Yangtze Jiang, Chang Jiang, Chang**

Yanina ('jɑːnɪnə) *n* a variant spelling of **Ioánnina**

yank (jæŋk) *vb* **1** to pull, jerk, or move with a sharp movement; tug ▷ *n* **2** a sharp jerking movement; tug [C19 of unknown origin]

Yank (jæŋk) *n* **1** a slang word for an American **2** *US informal* short for **Yankee**

Yankee ('jæŋkɪ) *or informal* **Yank** *n* **1** *often disparaging* a native or inhabitant of the US; American **2** a native or inhabitant of New England **3** a native or inhabitant of the Northern US, esp a Northern soldier in the Civil War **4** *communications* a code word for the letter *y* **5** *finance* a bond issued in the US by a foreign borrower ▷ *adj* **6** of, relating to, or characteristic of Yankees [C18 perhaps from Dutch *Jan Kees* John Cheese, nickname used derisively by Dutch settlers in New York to designate English colonists in Connecticut]

Yankee Doodle *n* **1** an American song, popularly regarded as a characteristically national melody **2** another name for **Yankee**

Yankeeism ('jæŋkɪɪzəm) *n* **1** Yankee character, behaviour, or attitudes **2** a typical Yankee word, expression, or trait

Yantai ('jæn'taɪ), **Yentai** *or* **Yen-t'ai** *n* a port in E China, in NE Shandong. Pop: 1 707 000 (2005 est). Also called: **Chefoo**

Yaoundé *or* **Yaunde** (*French* jaunde) *n* the capital of Cameroon, in the southwest: University of Cameroon (1962). Pop: 1 727 000 (2005 est)

yap (jæp) *vb* **yaps, yapping, yapped** (*intr*) **1** (of a dog) to bark in quick sharp bursts; yelp **2** *informal* to talk at length in an annoying or stupid way; jabber ▷ *n* **3** a high-pitched or sharp bark; yelp **4** *slang* annoying or stupid speech; jabber **5** *slang* a derogatory word for **mouth** ▷ *interj* **6** (*usually reiterated*) an imitation or representation of the sound of a dog yapping or people jabbering [C17 of imitative origin] > 'yapper *n* > 'yappy *adj*

Yap (jɑːp, jæp) *n* a group of four main islands in the W Pacific, in the W Caroline Islands: administratively a district of the US Trust Territory of the Pacific Islands from 1947; became self-governing in 1979 as part of the Federated States of Micronesia; important Japanese naval base in World War II. Pop: 12 055 (1999 est). Area: 101 sq km (39 sq miles)

yapon ('jɔːpən) *n* a variant spelling of **yaupon**

Yapurá (japu'ra) *n* the Spanish name for **Japurá**

Yaqui (*Spanish* 'jaki) *n* a river in NW Mexico, rising near the border with the US and flowing south to the Gulf of California. Length: about 676 km (420 miles)

yarborough ('jɑːbərə, -brə) *n bridge, whist* a hand of 13 cards in which no card is higher than nine [C19 supposed to be named after the second Earl of *Yarborough* (1809–62), who is said to have bet a thousand to one against the occurrence of such a hand]

yarco ('jɑːkəʊ) *n, pl* **-cos** *East Anglian informal derogatory* a young working-class person who dresses in casual sports clothes [C20 from Great Yarmouth]

yard¹ (jɑːd) *n* **1** a unit of length equal to 3 feet and defined in 1963 as exactly 0.9144 metre. Abbreviation: **yd 2** a cylindrical wooden or hollow metal spar, tapered at the ends, slung from a mast of a square-rigged or lateen-rigged vessel and used for suspending a sail **3** short for **yardstick** (sense 2) **4** put in the hard yards *Austral informal* to make a great effort to achieve an end **5** the whole nine yards *informal* everything that is required; the whole thing [Old English *gierd* rod, twig; related to Old Frisian *jerde*, Old Saxon *gerdia*, Old High German *gertia*, Old Norse *gaddr*]

yard² (jɑːd) *n* **1** a piece of enclosed ground, usually either paved or laid with concrete and often adjoining or surrounded by a building or buildings **2 a** an enclosed or open area used for some commercial activity, for storage, etc: *a railway yard* **b** (*in combination*): *a brickyard; a shipyard* **3** a US and Canadian word for **garden** (sense 1) **4** an area having a network of railway tracks and sidings, used for storing rolling stock, making up trains, etc **5** *US and Canadian* the winter pasture of deer, moose, and similar animals **6** *Austral and NZ* an enclosed area used to draw off part of a herd, etc **7** NZ short for **saleyard** or **stockyard** ▷ *vb* (*tr*) **8** to draft (animals), esp to a saleyard [Old English *geard*; related to Old Saxon *gard*, Old High German *gart*, Old Norse *garthr* yard, Gothic *gards* house, Old Slavonic *gradu* town, castle, Albanian *garth* hedge]

Yard (jɑːd) *n* the *Brit informal* short for **Scotland Yard**

yardage¹ ('jɑːdɪdʒ) *n* a length measured in yards

yardage² ('jɑːdɪdʒ) *n* **1** the use of a railway yard in the transportation of cattle **2** the charge for this

yardarm ('jɑːdˌɑːm) *n nautical* the two tapering outer ends of a ship's yard

yardbird ('jɑːdˌbɜːd) *n US military* an inexperienced, untrained, or clumsy soldier, esp one employed on menial duties

yard grass *n* an Old World perennial grass, *Eleusine indica*, with prostrate leaves, growing as a troublesome weed on open ground, yards, etc. Also called: **wire grass**

Yardie ('jɑːdɪ) *n* a member of a Black criminal syndicate originally based in Jamaica [C20 from Jamaican dialect *yard* home or (by expatriate Jamaicans) Jamaica]

yarding ('jɑːdɪŋ) *n* a group of animals displayed for sale: *a good yarding*

yard of ale *n* **1** the beer or ale contained in a narrow horn-shaped drinking glass, usually about one yard long and holding between two and three pints **2** such a drinking glass itself

yardstick ('jɑːdˌstɪk) *n* **1** a measure or standard used for comparison: *on what kind of yardstick is he basing his criticism?* **2** a graduated stick, one yard long, used for measurement

yare (jɛə) *adj* **yarer, yarest 1** *archaic or dialect* ready, brisk, or eager **2** (of a vessel) answering swiftly to the helm; easily handled ▷ *adv* **3** *obsolete* readily or eagerly [Old English *gearu* ready; related to Old Saxon, Old High German *garo* ready, prepared, Old Norse *gorr*] > 'yarely *adv*

yark (jɑːk) *vb* (*tr*) *archaic or dialect* to make ready [Old English]

Yarkand (jɑː'kænd) *n* another name for **Shache**

Yarmouth ('jɑːməθ) *n* short for **Great Yarmouth**

yarmulke ('jɑːməlkə) *n Judaism* a skullcap worn by orthodox male Jews at all times, and by others during prayer [from Yiddish, from Ukrainian and Polish *yarmulka* cap, probably from Turkish *yağmurluk* raincoat, from *yağmur* rain]

yarn (jɑːn) *n* **1** a continuous twisted strand of natural or synthetic fibres, used in weaving, knitting, etc **2** *informal* a long and often involved story or account, usually telling of incredible or fantastic events **3** spin a yarn *informal* **a** to tell such a story **b** to make up or relate a series of excuses ▷ *vb* **4** (*intr*) to tell such a story or stories [Old English *gearn*; related to Old High German *garn* yarn, Old Norse *görn* gut, Greek *khordē* string, gut]

yarn-dyed *adj* (of fabric) dyed while still in yarn form, before being woven. Compare **piece-dyed**

Yaroslavl (*Russian* jɪra'slavlj) *n* a city in W Russia, on the River Volga: a major trading centre since early times and one of the first industrial centres in Russia; textile industries were established in the 18th century. Pop: 609 000 (2005 est)

yarraman ('jærəmən) *n, pl* **-mans** *or* **-men** *Austral* a horse [C19 from a native Australian language]

yarran ('jærən) *n* a small hardy tree, *Acacia homalophylla*, of inland Australia: useful as fodder and for firewood [from a native Australian language]

Yarra River ('jærə) *n* a river in SE Australia, rising in the Great Dividing Range and flowing west and southwest through Melbourne to Port Phillip Bay. Length: 250 km (155 miles)

yarrow ('jærəʊ) *n* any of several plants of the genus *Achillea*, esp *A. millefolium*, of Eurasia, having finely dissected leaves and flat clusters of white flower heads: family *Asteraceae* (composites). Also called: milfoil See also **sneezewort** [Old English *gearwe*; related to Old High German *garwa*, Dutch *gerwe*]

yashmak *or* **yashmac** ('jæʃmæk) *n* the face veil worn by Muslim women when in public [C19 from Arabic]

yataghan ('jætəɡən) *or* **ataghan** *n* a Turkish sword with a curved single-edged blade [C19 from Turkish *yatağan*]

yate (jeɪt) *n Austral* any of several small eucalyptus trees, esp *Eucalyptus cornuta*, yielding a very hard timber [from a native Australian language]

Yathrib ('jæθrɪb) *n* the ancient Arabic name for **Medina**

yatter ('jætə; *Scot* 'jɑtər) *Scot* ▷ *vb* (*intr*) **1** to talk at length; chatter ▷ *n* **2** continuous chatter [of imitative origin]

Yaunde (*French* jaunde) *n* a variant spelling of **Yaoundé**

yaup (jɔːp) *vb, n* a variant spelling of **yawp**. > 'yauper *n*

yaupon *or* **yapon** ('jɔːpən) *n* a southern US evergreen holly shrub, *Ilex vomitoria*, with spreading branches, scarlet fruits, and oval leaves: used as a substitute for tea [from Catawba *yopun* shrub, diminutive of *yop* tree]

yautia ('jɔːtɪə) *n* **1** any of several Caribbean aroid plants of the genus *Xanthosoma*, such as *X. sagittifolium*, cultivated for their edible leaves and underground stems **2** the leaves or underground stems of these plants, which can be eaten as vegetables [C19 American Spanish, from Taino]

Yavarí (jaβa'ri) *n* the Spanish name for **Javari**

yaw (jɔː) *vb* **1** (*intr*) (of an aircraft, missile, etc) to turn about its vertical axis. Compare **pitch¹** (sense 11), **roll** (sense 14) **2** (*intr*) (of a ship, etc) to deviate

Y

temporarily from a straight course **3** (*tr*) to cause (an aircraft, ship, etc) to yaw ▷ *n* **4** the angular movement of an aircraft, missile, etc, about its vertical axis **5** the deviation of a vessel from a straight course [c16 of unknown origin]

Yawata ('jɑːwɑ:tɑ:) or **Yahata** *n* a former city in Japan, on N Kyushu: merged with Moji, Kokura, Tobata, and Wakamatsu in 1963 to form **Kitakyushu**

yawl¹ (jɔːl) *n* **1** a two-masted sailing vessel, rigged fore-and-aft, with a large mainmast and a small mizzenmast stepped aft of the rudderpost. Compare **ketch**, **sloop** **2** a ship's small boat, usually rowed by four or six oars [c17 from Dutch *jol* or Middle Low German *jolle*, of unknown origin]

yawl² (jɔːl) *vb* (*intr*) *Brit dialect* to howl, weep, or scream harshly; yowl [c14 from Low German *jaulen*; see YOWL]

yawn (jɔːn) *vb* **1** (*intr*) to open the mouth wide and take in air deeply, often as in involuntary reaction to tiredness, sleepiness, or boredom **2** (*tr*) to express or utter while yawning **3** (*intr*) to be open wide as if threatening to engulf (someone or something): *the mine shaft yawned below* ▷ *n* **4** the act or an instance of yawning [Old English *gionian*; related to Old Saxon *ginōn*, Old High German *ginēn* to yawn, Old Norse *gjā* gap] > 'yawner *n* > 'yawning *adj* > 'yawningly *adv*

yawp (jɔːp) *vb* (*intr*) **1** to gape or yawn, esp audibly **2** to shout, cry, or talk noisily; bawl **3** to bark, yelp, or yowl **4** *n* a shout, bark, yelp, or cry **5** *US and Canadian* a noisy, foolish, or raucous utterance [c15 *yolpen*, probably of imitative origin; see YAP, YELP] > 'yawper *n*

yaws (jɔːz) *n* (*usually functioning as singular*) an infectious nonvenereal disease of tropical climates with early symptoms resembling syphilis, characterized by red skin eruptions and, later, pain in the joints: it is caused by the spiral bacterium *Treponema pertenue*. Also called: **framboesia** [c17 of Carib origin]

y-**axis** *n* a reference axis, usually vertical, of a graph or two- or three-dimensional Cartesian coordinate system along which the *y*-coordinate is measured

yay (jeɪ) *interj informal* an exclamation indicating approval, congratulation, or triumph [c20 perhaps from YEAH]

Yazd (jɑːzd) or **Yezd** *n* a city in central Iran: a major centre of silk weaving. Pop: 436 000 (2005 est)

Yb the chemical symbol for ytterbium

YBA *abbreviation for* young British artist

YC (in Britain) *abbreviation for* Young Conservative

Y-chromosome *n* the sex chromosome that occurs as one of a pair with the X-chromosome in the diploid cells of the males of many animals, including humans. Compare **X-chromosome**

yclept (ɪ'klɛpt) *obsolete* ▷ *vb* **1** a past participle of **clepe** ▷ *adj* **2** having the name of; called [Old English *gecleopod*, past participle of *cleopian* to call]

Y connection *n electrical engineering* a three-phase star connection

yd or **yd.** *abbreviation for* yard (measure)

ye¹ (jiː; *unstressed* jɪ) *pron* **1** *archaic or dialect* refers to more than one person including the person addressed but not including the speaker **2** Also: **ee** (iː) *dialect* refers to one person addressed: *I tell ye* [Old English *gē*; related to Dutch *gij*, Old Norse *ēr*, Gothic *jus*]

ye² (ðiː; *spelling pron* jiː) *determiner* a form of **the¹**, in conjunction with other putative archaic spellings *ye olde oake* [from a misinterpretation of *the* as written in some Middle English texts. The runic letter thorn (Þ, representing *th*) was incorrectly transcribed as *y* because of a resemblance in their shapes]

ye³ the internet domain name for Yemen

yea (jeɪ) *sentence substitute* **1** a less common word for **aye** (yes) ▷ *adv* **2** (*sentence modifier*) *archaic or literary* indeed; truly: *yea, though my enemies spurn me, I shall prevail* [Old English *gēa*; related to Old Frisian

jē, Old Saxon, Old Norse, Old High German *jā*, Gothic *jai*]

yeah (jɛə) *sentence substitute* an informal word for **yes**

yean (jiːn) *vb* (of a sheep or goat) to give birth to (offspring) [Old English *geēanian*; related to Dutch *oonen* to bring forth young, Latin *agnus* lamb; see EWE]

yeanling ('jiːnlɪŋ) *n* the young of a goat or sheep

year (jɪə) *n* **1** Also called: **civil year** the period of time, the **calendar year**, containing 365 days or in a **leap year** 366 days. It is based on the Gregorian calendar, being divided into 12 calendar months, and is reckoned from January 1 to December 31 **2** a period of twelve months from any specified date, such as one based on the four seasons **3** a specific period of time, usually occupying a definite part or parts of a twelve-month period, used for some particular activity: *a school year* **4** Also called: **astronomical year**, **tropical year** the period of time, the **solar year**, during which the earth makes one revolution around the sun, measured between two successive vernal equinoxes: equal to 365.242 19 days **5** the period of time, the **sidereal year**, during which the earth makes one revolution around the sun, measured between two successive conjunctions of a particular distant star: equal to 365.256 36 days **6** the period of time, the **lunar year**, containing 12 lunar months and equal to 354.3671 days **7** the period of time taken by a specified planet to complete one revolution around the sun: *the Martian year* **8** (*plural*) age, esp old age: *a man of his years should be more careful* **9** (*plural*) time: *in years to come* **10** a group of pupils or students, who are taught or study together, divided into classes at school: *they are the best year we've ever had for history* **11** **the year dot** *informal* as long ago as can be remembered **12** **year and a day** *English law* a period fixed by law to ensure the completion of a full year. It is applied for certain purposes, such as to determine the time within which wrecks must be claimed **13** **year in, year out** regularly or monotonously, over a long period ▷ Related adjective: **annual** [Old English *gear*; related to Gothic *jēr*, Old Saxon, Old High German *jār*, Old Norse *ār* year, Polish *jar* springtime, Latin *hōrnus* of this year]

> USAGE In writing spans of years, it is important to choose a style that avoids ambiguity. The practice adopted in this dictionary is, in four-figure dates, to specify the last two digits of the second date if it falls within the same century as the first: *1801–08; 1850–51; 1899–1901*. In writing three-figure BC dates, it is advisable to give both dates in full: *159–156 BC*, not *159–56 BC* unless of course the span referred to consists of 103 years rather than three years. It is also advisable to specify BC or AD in years under 1000 unless the context makes this self-evident

yearbook ('jɪəˌbʊk) *n* an almanac or reference book published annually and containing details of events of the previous year

yearling ('jɪəlɪŋ) *n* **1** the young of any of various animals, including the antelope and buffalo, between one and two years of age **2** a thoroughbred racehorse counted for racing purposes as being one year old until the second Jan 1 following its birth **3** **a** a bond that is intended to mature after one year **b** (*as modifier*): *yearling bonds* ▷ *adj* **4** being a year old

yearlong ('jɪəˌlɒŋ) *adj* throughout a whole year

yearly ('jɪəlɪ) *adj* **1** occurring, done, appearing, etc, once a year or every year; annual **2** lasting or valid for a year; annual: *a yearly subscription* ▷ *adv* **3** once a year; annually ▷ *n, pl* -**lies** **4** a publication, event, etc, that occurs once a year

yearn (jɜːn) *vb* (*intr*) **1** (usually foll by *for* or *after* or

an infinitive) to have an intense desire or longing (for) **2** to feel tenderness or affection [Old English *giernan*; related to Old Saxon *girnian*, Old Norse *girna*, Gothic *gairnjan*, Old High German *gerōn* to long for, Sanskrit *haryati* he likes] > 'yearner *n*

yearning ('jɜːnɪŋ) *n* an intense or overpowering longing, desire, or need; craving > 'yearningly *adv*

year of grace *n* any year of the Christian era, as dated from the presumed date of Christ's birth

year-round *adj* open, in use, operating, etc, throughout the year

year zero *n* **1** the beginning (1975) of the period during which Cambodia was under the control of the Khmer Rouge **2** the beginning of revolutionary change **3** the beginning of any new system or regime [c20 by analogy with *Year One* of the French Revolutionary calendar]

yeast (jiːst) *n* **1** any of various single-celled ascomycetous fungi of the genus *Saccharomyces* and related genera, which reproduce by budding and are able to ferment sugars: a rich source of vitamins of the B complex **2** any yeastlike fungus, esp of the genus *Candida*, which can cause thrush in areas infected with it **3** a commercial preparation containing yeast cells and inert material such as meal, used in raising dough for bread or for fermenting beer, whisky, etc. See also **brewer's yeast** **4** a preparation containing yeast cells, used to treat diseases caused by vitamin B deficiency **5** froth or foam, esp on beer ▷ *vb* **6** (*intr*) to froth or foam [Old English *giest*; related to Old Norse *jostr*, Old High German *jesan*, Swedish *esa*, Norwegian *asa*, Sanskrit *yasati*] > 'yeastless *adj* > 'yeastˌlike *adj*

yeast cake *n chiefly US and Canadian* living yeast cells compressed with starch into a cake, for use in baking or brewing

yeasty ('jiːstɪ) *adj* **yeastier**, **yeastiest** **1** of, resembling, or containing yeast **2** fermenting or causing fermentation **3** tasting of or like yeast **4** insubstantial or frivolous **5** restless, agitated, or unsettled **6** covered with or containing froth or foam > 'yeastily *adv* > 'yeastiness *n*

yebo ('jebaʊ) *sentence substitute South African informal* an expression of affirmation [Zulu *yebo* yes, I agree]

yegg (jɛg) *n slang, chiefly US* a burglar or safe-breaker [c20 perhaps from the surname of a burglar]

Yeisk, Yeysk or **Eisk** (Russian jejsk) *n* a port and resort in SW Russia, on the Sea of Azov. Pop: 86 300 (1991 est)

Yekaterinburg or **Ekaterinburg** (Russian jɪkatɪrimʹburk) *n* a city in NW Russia, in the Ural Mountains: scene of the execution (1918) of Nicholas II and his family; university (1920); one of the largest centres of heavy engineering in Russia. Pop: 1 281 000 (2005 est). Former name (1924–91): Sverdlovsk

Yekaterinodar or **Ekaterinodar** (Russian jɪkatɪrinaʹdar) *n* the former name (until 1920) of **Krasnodar**

Yekaterinoslav or **Ekaterinoslav** (Russian jɪkatɪrinaʹslaf) *n* the former name (1787–96, 1802–1926) of **Dnepropetrovsk**

yeld (jɛld) *adj Scot and northern English dialect* **1** (of an animal) barren or too young to bear young **2** (of a cow) not yielding milk [Old English *gelde* barren; related to GELD¹]

Yelisavetgrad or **Elisavetgrad** (Russian jɪliza'vjɛtgrət) *n* the former name (until 1924) of **Kirovograd**

Yelisavetpol or **Elisavetpol** (Russian jɪliza'vjɛtpəlj) *n* the former name (until 1920) of **Gandzha**

yelk (jɛlk) *n* a dialect word for yolk (of an egg)

yell (jɛl) *vb* **1** to shout, scream, cheer, or utter in a loud or piercing way **2** *n* a loud piercing inarticulate cry, as of pain, anger, or fear **3** *US and Canadian* a rhythmic cry of words or syllables, used in cheering in unison [Old English *giellan*; related to Old Saxon *gellon*, Old High German gellan, Old Norse *gjalla*; see NIGHTINGALE] > ˈyeller *n*

yellow (ˈjɛləʊ) *n* **1** any of a group of colours that vary in saturation but have the same hue. They lie in the approximate wavelength range 585–575 nanometres. Yellow is the complementary colour of blue and with cyan and magenta forms a set of primary colours. Related adj: **xanthous 2** a pigment or dye of or producing these colours **3** yellow cloth or clothing: *dressed in yellow* **4** the yolk of an egg **5** a yellow ball in snooker, etc **6** any of a group of pieridine butterflies the males of which have yellow or yellowish wings, esp the clouded yellows (*Colias* spp.) and the brimstone ▷ *adj* **7** of the colour yellow **8** yellowish in colour or having parts or marks that are yellowish: *yellow jasmine* **9** having a yellowish skin; Mongoloid **10** *informal* cowardly or afraid **11** offensively sensational, as a cheap newspaper (esp in the phrase **yellow press**) ▷ *vb* **12** to make or become yellow ▷ See also **yellows** [Old English *geolu*; related to Old Saxon, Old High German *gelo*, Old Norse *gulr*, Latin *helvus*] > ˈyellowish *adj* > ˈyellowly *adv* > ˈyellowness *n* > ˈyellowy *adj*

yellow archangel *n* See **archangel** (sense 3)

yellowbark (ˈjɛləʊˌbɑːk) *n* another name for **calisaya**

yellow belly *n dialect* a native of Lincolnshire, esp of the fens

yellow-belly *n, pl* -lies **1** a slang word for **coward 2** *Austral* another name for **callop**

yellow bile *n archaic* one of the four bodily humours, choler

yellowbird (ˈjɛləʊˌbɜːd) *n* any of various birds having a yellow plumage, such as the American goldfinch

yellow box *n Austral* a large Australian eucalyptus tree, *Eucalyptus melliodora*

yellow brain fungus *n* See **jelly fungus**

yellow cake *n informal* semirefined uranium ore

yellow card *sport* ▷ *n* **1** a card of a yellow colour displayed by a referee to indicate that a player has been officially cautioned for some offence ▷ *vb* **yellow-card 2** (*tr*) to caution (a player) officially for some offence ▷ *adj* **3** serving as a warning; intended to warn: *a yellow card system is in place*

yellow cress *n* any of various species of cress (*Rorippa*) that are related to watercress and have yellow flowers. They are not confined to water margins and some are garden weeds

yellow-dog contract *n US* a contract with an employer, now illegal, in which an employee agreed not to join a trade union during his employment [c20 from US *yellow-dog* anti-trade union, from *yellow dog* mongrel, contemptible person]

yellow-eye mullet *n* an edible mullet, *Aldrichetta forsteri*, found in coastal waters of New Zealand and Australia. Also called (NZ): aua

yellow fever *n* an acute infectious disease of tropical and subtropical climates, characterized by fever, haemorrhages, vomiting of blood, and jaundice: caused by a virus transmitted by the bite of a female mosquito of the species *Aedes aegypti*. Also called: yellow jack, black vomit

yellowfin tuna (ˈjɛləʊˌfɪn) *n* a large marine food fish, *Scomber albacares*, of tropical and subtropical waters, having yellow dorsal and anal fins: family *Scombridae*

yellow flag *n* **1** another name for **quarantine flag 2** See **flag**² (sense 1)

yellowhammer (ˈjɛləʊˌhæmə) *n* **1** a European bunting, *Emberiza citrinella*, having a yellowish head and body and brown streaked wings and tail **2** *US and Canadian* an informal name for the **yellow-shafted flicker**, an American woodpecker (see **flicker**²) [c16 of uncertain origin]

yellowhead (ˈjɛləʊˌhɛd) *n* a small bush bird, *Mohoua ochrocephala*, of South Island, New Zealand, having a yellow head and breast. Also called: mohua

yellow jack *n* **1** *pathol* another name for **yellow fever 2** another name for **quarantine flag 3** any

of certain large yellowish carangid food fishes, esp *Caranx bartholomaei*, of warm and tropical Atlantic waters

yellow jacket *n US and Canadian* any of several social wasps of the genus *Vespa*, having yellow markings on the body

yellow jasmine *n* a climbing shrub, *Gelsemium sempervirens*, of the southeastern US, having fragrant funnel-shaped yellow flowers: family *Loganiaceae*. See also **gelsemium**

yellow jersey *n* (in the Tour de France) a yellow jersey awarded as a trophy to the cyclist with the fastest time in each stage of the race

yellow journalism *n* the type of journalism that relies on sensationalism and lurid exaggeration to attract readers [c19 perhaps shortened from the phrase *Yellow Kid journalism*, referring to the *Yellow Kid*, a cartoon (1895) in the *New York World*, a newspaper having a reputation for sensationalism]

Yellowknife (ˈjɛləʊˌnaɪf) *n* a city in N Canada, capital of the Northwest Territories on Great Slave Lake. Pop: 16 055 (2001)

yellowlegs (ˈjɛləʊˌlɛgz) *n* (functioning as singular) either of two North American sandpipers, *Tringa melanoleuca* (or *Totanus melanoleucus*) (**greater yellowlegs**) or *T. flavipes* (**lesser yellowlegs**), having bright yellow legs

yellow line *n Brit* a yellow line painted along the edge of a road indicating waiting restrictions

yellow metal *n* **1** a type of brass having about 60 per cent copper and 40 per cent zinc **2** another name for **gold**

Yellow Pages *pl n trademark* a classified telephone directory, often printed on yellow paper, that lists subscribers by the business or service provided

yellow peril *n* the power or alleged power of Asiatic peoples, esp the Chinese, to threaten or destroy the supremacy of White or Western civilization

yellow poplar *n* another name for **tulip tree** (sense 1) *or* **tulipwood** (sense 1)

yellow rain *n* a type of yellow precipitation described in parts of SE Asia and alleged by some to be evidence of chemical warfare using mycotoxins

yellow rattle *n* See **rattle**¹ (sense 10)

Yellow River *n* the second longest river in China, rising in SE Qinghai and flowing east, south, and east again to the Gulf of Bohai south of Tianjin; it has changed its course several times in recorded history. Length: about 4350 km (2700 miles). Chinese name: Hwang Ho

yellows (ˈjɛləʊz) *n* (functioning as singular) **1** any of various fungal or viral diseases of plants, characterized by yellowish discoloration and stunting **2** *vet science* another name for **jaundice**

yellow sally *n* an angler's name for either of two small yellow stoneflies: *Isoperla grammatica* of chalk streams and *Chloroperla torrentium* of upland streams

Yellow Sea *n* a shallow arm of the Pacific between Korea and NE China. Area: about 466 200 sq km (180 000 sq miles). Chinese name: Hwang Hai

yellow spot *n anatomy* another name for **macula lutea**

Yellowstone (ˈjɛləʊˌstəʊn) *n* a river rising in N Wyoming and flowing north through Yellowstone National Park, then east to the Missouri. Length: 1080 km (671 miles)

Yellowstone Falls *pl n* a waterfall in NW Wyoming, in Yellowstone National Park on the Yellowstone River

Yellowstone National Park *n* a national park in the NW central US, mostly in NW Wyoming: the oldest and largest national park in the US, containing unusual geological formations and geysers. Area: 8956 sq km (3458 sq miles)

yellow streak *n informal* a cowardly or weak trait, characteristic, or flaw in a person's nature

yellowtail (ˈjɛləʊˌteɪl) *n, pl* -tails *or* -tail **1** a

carangid game fish, *Seriola dorsalis*, of coastal waters of S California and Mexico, having a yellow tail fin **2** any of various similar fishes **3** Also called: yellowtail moth another name for **goldtail moth** any of various similar fishes **4** *Austral* another word for **yellowtail kingfish**

yellowtail kingfish *n* a large carangid game fish, *Seriola grandis*, of S Australian waters. Also called: yellowtail

yellow underwing *n* any of several species of noctuid moths (*Noctua* and *Anarta* species), the hind wings of which are yellow with a black bar

yellow water lily *n* an aquatic nymphaeaceous plant, *Nuphar lutea*, of Europe and N Asia, having floating heart-shaped leaves and yellow flowers. Also called: brandy bottle

yellowweed (ˈjɛləʊˌwiːd) *n* any of various yellow-flowered plants, such as the ragwort in Europe and some species of goldenrod in the US

yellowwood (ˈjɛləʊˌwʊd) *n* **1** Also called (US): gopherwood any of several leguminous trees of the genus *Cladrastis*, esp *C. lutea*, of the southeastern US, having clusters of white flowers and yellow wood yielding a yellow dye **2** Also called: West Indian satinwood a rutaceous tree, *Zanthoxylum flavum*, of the Caribbean, with smooth hard wood **3** any of several other trees with yellow wood, esp *Podocarpus falcatus*, a conifer of southern Africa: family *Podocarpaceae* **4** the wood of any of these trees

yellowwort (ˈjɛləʊˌwɜːt) *n* a gentianaceous perennial, *Blackstonia perfoliata*, that is related to centaury and has waxy grey foliage and yellow flowers: characteristically found on chalk turf

yellow-yite *n* a Scot word for **yellowhammer** (sense 1) Also called: yite, yitie

yelp (jɛlp) *vb* (intr) **1** (esp of a dog) to utter a sharp or high-pitched cry or bark, often indicating pain ▷ *n* **2** a sharp or high-pitched cry or bark [Old English *gielpan* to boast; related to Low German *galpen* to croak, Danish *gylpe* to croak] > ˈyelper *n*

Yemen (ˈjɛmən) *n* a republic in SW Arabia, on the Red Sea and the Gulf of Aden: formed in 1990 from the union of North Yemen and South Yemen: consists of arid coastal lowlands, rising to fertile upland valleys and mountains in the west and to the Hadhramaut plateau in the SE: the north and east contains part of the Great Sandy Desert. Official language: Arabic. Official religion: Muslim. Currency: riyal. Capital: San'a. Pop: 20 732 000 (2004 est). Area (including territory claimed by Yemen along the undemarcated eastern border with Saudi Arabia): 472 099 sq km (182 278 sq miles). Official name: Yemen Republic See also **North Yemen, South Yemen**

Yemeni (ˈjɛmənɪ) *adj* **1** of or relating to Yemen or its inhabitants ▷ *n* **2** a native or inhabitant of Yemen

yemmer (ˈjɛmə) *n* a southwest English form of **ember**

yen¹ (jɛn) *n, pl* yen the standard monetary unit of Japan, (notionally) divided into 100 sen [c19 from Japanese *en*, from Chinese *yüan* circular object, dollar]

yen² (jɛn) *informal* ▷ *n* **1** a passionate, ardent, or intense longing or desire ▷ *vb* yens, yenning, yenned **2** (intr) to yearn [perhaps from Chinese (Cantonese) *yān* a craving, addiction]

Yenan (ˈjɛnˈæn) *n* a variant transliteration of the Chinese name for **Yanan**

Yenisei *or* **Yenisey** (ˌjɛnɪˈseɪ; *Russian* jɪniˈsjej) *n* a river in central Russia, in central Siberia, formed by the confluence of two headstreams in the Tuva Republic: flows west and north to the Arctic Ocean; the largest river in volume in Russia. Length: 4129 km (2566 miles)

Yentai *or* **Yen-t'ai** (ˈjɛnˈtaɪ) *n* a variant transliteration of the Chinese name for **Yantai**

yeoman (ˈjəʊmən) *n, pl* -men **1** *history* **a** a member of a class of small freeholders of common birth who cultivated their own land **b** an assistant or other subordinate to an official, such as a sheriff, or to a craftsman or trader **c** an attendant or lesser official in a royal or noble household **2** (in Britain) another name for **yeoman of the guard 3** (*modifier*) characteristic of or relating to a yeoman **4** a petty officer or noncommissioned officer in the Royal Navy or Marines in charge of signals [c15 perhaps from *yongman* young man]

yeomanly ('jəʊmənlɪ) *adj* **1** of, relating to, or like a yeoman **2** having the virtues attributed to yeomen, such as staunchness, loyalty, and courage ▷ *adv* **3** in a yeomanly manner, as in being brave, staunch, or loyal

yeoman of the guard *n* a member of the bodyguard (**Yeomen of the Guard**) of the English monarch. This unit was founded in 1485 and now retains ceremonial functions only

yeomanry ('jəʊmənrɪ) *n* **1** yeomen collectively **2** (in Britain) a volunteer cavalry force, organized in 1761 for home defence: merged into the Territorial Army in 1907

yep (jɛp) *sentence substitute* an informal word for **yes**

yerba or **yerba maté** ('jɛəbə, 'jɜːbə) *n* another name for **maté** [from Spanish *yerba maté* herb maté]

Yerevan (*Russian* jɪrɪ'van) *n* the capital of Armenia: founded in the 8th century BC; an industrial city and a main focus of trade routes since ancient times; university. Pop: 1 066 000 (2005 est). Also called: **Erevan** or **Erivan**

Yerwa-Maiduguri ('jɜːwə,maɪdʊ'gʊrɪ) *n* another name for **Maiduguri**

yes (jɛs) *sentence substitute* **1** used to express acknowledgment, affirmation, consent, agreement, or approval or to answer when one is addressed **2** used, often with interrogative intonation, to signal someone to speak or keep speaking, enter a room, or do something ▷ *n* **3** an answer or vote of yes **4** (*often plural*) a person who votes in the affirmative ▷ Compare **no**¹ [Old English *gēse*, from *iā sīe* may it be; see **YEA**]

yeshiva (jə'ʃiːvə; *Hebrew* jə'ʃiːva) *n*, *pl* **-vahs** or **-voth** (*Hebrew* -vɔt) **1** a traditional Jewish school devoted chiefly to the study of rabbinic literature and the Talmud **2** a school run by Orthodox Jews for children of primary school age, providing both religious and secular instruction [from Hebrew *yĕshībhāh* a sitting, seat, hence, an academy]

Yeşil Irmak (jɛ'ʃiːl ɪə'mɑːk) *n* a river in N Turkey, flowing northwest to the Black Sea. Length: 418 km (260 miles). Ancient name: **Iris**

Yeşilköy (jɛ'ʃil,kœi) *n* the Turkish name for **San Stefano**

yes man *n* a servile, submissive, or acquiescent subordinate, assistant, or associate; sycophant

yes/no question *n grammar* a question inviting the answer "yes" or "no". Compare **WH question**

yester ('jɛstə) *adj archaic* of or relating to yesterday: *yester sun*. Also: **yestern** ('jɛstən) [Old English *geostror*; related to Old High German *gestaron*, Gothic *gistra*, Old Norse *ī gǣr*]

yester- *prefix* **1** indicating the day before today: *yesterday* **2** indicating a period of time before the present one: *yesteryear* [Old English *geostran*; compare German *gestern*, Latin *hesternus* of yesterday]

yesterday ('jɛstədɪ, -,deɪ) *n* **1** the day immediately preceding today **2** (*often plural*) the recent past ▷ *adv* **3** on or during the day before today **4** in the recent past

yesteryear ('jɛstə,jɪə) *formal or literary* ▷ *n* **1** last year or the past in general ▷ *adv* **2** during last year or the past in general

yestreen (jɛ'striːn) *adv Scot* yesterday evening [c14 from YEST(E)R- + E(V)EN²]

yet (jɛt) *sentence connector* **1** nevertheless; still; in spite of that: *I want to and yet I haven't the courage*; *she is strange yet kind* ▷ *adv* **2** (*usually with a negative or interrogative*) so far; up until then or now: *they're not home yet*; *is it teatime yet?* **3** (*often preceded by just; usually used with a negative*) now (as contrasted with later): *we can't stop yet* **4** (*often used with a comparative*) even; still: *yet more potatoes for sale* **5** eventually, in spite of everything: *we'll convince him yet* **6** as yet so far; up until then or now [Old English *gēta*; related to Old Frisian *jēta*]

yeti ('jɛtɪ) *n* another term for **abominable snowman** [c20 from Tibetan]

yett (jɛt) *n Scot* a gate or door [Old English variant of GATE¹]

yettie ('jɛtɪ) *n acronym for* young, entrepreneurial, and technology-based (person)

yew (juː) *n* **1** any coniferous tree of the genus *Taxus*, of the Old World and North America, esp *T. baccata*, having flattened needle-like leaves, fine-grained elastic wood, and solitary seeds with a red waxy aril resembling berries: family *Taxaceae* **2** the wood of any of these trees, used to make bows for archery **3** *archery* a bow made of yew [Old English *īw*; related to Old High German *īwa*, Old Norse *ȳr* yew, Latin *ūva* grape, Russian *iva* willow]

Yeysk (*Russian* jejsk) *n* a variant spelling of **Yeisk**

Yezd (jɛzd) *n* a variant of **Yazd**

Yezidis ('jɛzɪdɪz) *pl n* a religious sect found in the Kurdish areas of Iraq, Turkey, and Syria, whose beliefs combine elements of Zoroastrianism, Islam, Christianity, and other religions; in addition to believing in a Supreme God, the Yezidi worship seven angels, among whom is the devil, who is believed to have repented and been pardoned and reinstated as chief angel [c19 perhaps from *Yazid* or *Ezid* a name for God]

Y-fronts *pl n trademark* boys' or men's underpants having a front opening within an inverted Y shape

Ygerne (iː'gɛən) *n* a variant of **Igraine**

Yggdrasil, Ygdrasil or **Igdrasil** ('ɪgdrəsɪl) *n Norse myth* the ash tree that was thought to overshadow the whole world, binding together earth, heaven, and hell with its roots and branches [Old Norse (probably meaning: Uggr's horse), from *Uggr* a name of Odin, from *yggr*, *uggr* frightful + *drasill* horse, of obscure origin]

YHA *abbreviation for* Youth Hostels Association

YHVH, YHWH, JHVH or **JHWH** *n Old Testament* the letters of the **Tetragrammaton** See also **Yahweh, Jehovah**

Yibin ('jiː'bɪn) or **I-pin** *n* a port in S central China, in Sichuan province: a commercial centre. Pop: 784 000 (2005 est)

Yichang ('jiː'tʃæŋ), **Ichang** or **I-ch'ang** *n* a port in S central China, in Hubei province on the Yangtze River 1600 km (1000 miles) from the East China Sea: the Three Gorges dam, the world's biggest hydroelectric and flood-control project, is nearby. Pop: 724 000 (2005 est)

yid (jɪd) *n slang* a derogatory word for a Jew [c20 probably from *Yiddish*, from Middle High German *Jude* JEW]

yidaki (jɪ'dækɪ) *n* a long wooden wind instrument played by the Aboriginal peoples of Arnhem Land [from a native Australian language]

Yiddish ('jɪdɪʃ) *n* **1** a language spoken as a vernacular by Jews in Europe and elsewhere by Jewish emigrants, usually written in the Hebrew alphabet. Historically, it is a dialect of High German with an admixture of words of Hebrew, Romance, and Slavonic origin, developed in central and E Europe during the Middle Ages ▷ *adj* **2** in or relating to this language [c19 from German *jüdisch*, from *Jude* JEW]

Yiddisher ('jɪdɪʃə) *adj* **1** in or relating to Yiddish **2** Jewish ▷ *n* **3** a speaker of Yiddish; Jew

yield (jiːld) *vb* **1** to give forth or supply (a product, result, etc), esp by cultivation, labour, etc; produce or bear **2** (*tr*) to furnish as a return: *the shares yielded three per cent* **3** (*tr*; often foll by *up*) to surrender or relinquish, esp as a result of force, persuasion, etc **4** (*intr*; sometimes foll by *to*) to give way, submit, or surrender, as through force or persuasion: *she yielded to his superior knowledge* **5** (*intr*; often foll by *to*) to agree; comply; assent: *he eventually yielded to their request for money* **6** (*tr*) to grant or allow; concede: *to yield right of way* **7** (*tr*) *obsolete* to pay or repay: *God yield thee!* ▷ *n* **8** the result, product, or amount yielded **9** the profit or return, as from an investment or tax **10** the annual income provided by an investment, usually expressed as a percentage of its cost or of its current value: *the yield on these shares is 15 per cent at today's market value* **11** the energy released by the explosion of a nuclear weapon expressed in terms of the amount of TNT necessary to produce the same energy **12** *chem* the quantity of a specified product obtained in a reaction or series of reactions, usually expressed as a percentage of the quantity that is theoretically obtainable [Old English *gieldan*; related to Old Frisian *jelda*, Old High German *geltan*, Old Norse *gjalda*, Gothic *gildan*] > **'yieldable** *adj* > **'yielder** *n*

yielding ('jiːldɪŋ) *adj* **1** compliant, submissive, or flexible **2** pliable or soft: *a yielding material* > **'yieldingly** *adv* > **'yieldingness** *n*

yield point *n* the stress at which an elastic material under increasing stress ceases to behave elastically; under conditions of tensile strength the elongation is no longer proportional to the increase in stress. Also called: **yield stress, yield strength**

yield stress *n* the stress level at which a metal or other material ceases to behave elastically. The stress divided by the strain is no longer constant. The point at which this occurs is known as the yield point. Compare **proof stress**

yike (jaɪk) *Austral informal* ▷ *n* **1** an argument, squabble, or fight ▷ *vb* (*intr*) **2** to argue, squabble, or fight [origin unknown]

yikes ('jaɪks) *interj informal* an expression of surprise, fear, or alarm

yin (jɪn) *determiner, pron, n* a Scot word for **one**

Yin and Yang (jɪn) *n* two complementary principles of Chinese philosophy: Yin is negative, dark, and feminine, Yang positive, bright, and masculine. Their interaction is thought to maintain the harmony of the universe and to influence everything within it [from Chinese (Peking) *yin* dark + *yang* bright]

Yinchuan, Yin-ch'uan or **Yinchwan** ('jɪn'tʃwɑːn) *n* a city in N central China, capital of the Ningxia Hui AR, on the Yellow River. Pop: 642 000 (2005 est)

Yingkou or **Yingkow** ('jɪŋ'kaʊ) *n* a port in NE China, in SW Liaoning province: a major shipping centre for Manchuria. Pop: 723 000 (2005 est)

Yinglish ('jɪŋglɪʃ) *n* a dialect of English spoken esp by Jewish immigrants to New York, and heavily influenced by Yiddish constructions and loan words. Also: **Yenglish** [from YI(DDISH) + (E)NGLISH]

yipes ('jaɪps) *interj informal* an expression of surprise, fear, or alarm

yippee (jɪ'piː) *interj* an exclamation of joy, pleasure, anticipation, etc

yips (jɪps) *pl n* the informal (in sport, originally esp golf) nervous twitching or tension that destroys concentration and spoils performance [c20 of unknown origin]

yite (jaɪt) or **yitie** ('jaɪtɪ) *n Scot* words for **yellowhammer** (sense 1) Also called: **yellow-yite** [c19 of unknown origin]

yitten ('jɪtᵊn) *adj Northern English dialect* frightened

Yizkor ('jɪzkor) *n Judaism* a memorial prayer included in the liturgy for certain festivals [from Hebrew, literally: let him remember]

Y2K *n informal* another name for the year 2000 AD (esp referring to the millennium bug) [c20 Y(EAR) + 2 + K (in the sense: thousand)]

-yl *suffix of nouns* (in chemistry) indicating a group or radical: *methyl; carbonyl* [from Greek *hulē* wood, matter]

ylang-ylang or **ilang-ilang** (,iːlæŋ'iːlæŋ) *n* **1** an aromatic Asian tree, *Cananga odorata* (or *Cananguim odoratum*), with fragrant greenish-yellow flowers yielding a volatile oil: family *Annonaceae* **2** the oil obtained from this tree, used in perfumery [C19 from Tagalog *ilang-ilang*]

ylem ('aɪləm) *n* the original matter from which the basic elements are said to have been formed following the explosion postulated in the big bang theory of cosmology [Middle English, from Old French *ilem*, from Latin *hȳlē* stuff, matter, from Greek *hulē* wood, matter]

Y-level *n surveying* a level mounted on a Y-shaped support that can be rotated

YMCA *abbreviation for* Young Men's Christian Association

YMHA *abbreviation for* Young Men's Hebrew Association

Ymir ('iːmɪə) *or* **Ymer** ('iːmə) *n Norse myth* the first being and forefather of the giants. He was slain by Odin and his brothers, who made the earth from his flesh, the water from his blood, and the sky from his skull

-yne *suffix forming nouns* denoting an organic chemical containing a triple bond: *alkyne* [alteration of -INE²]

yo (jəʊ) *sentence substitute* an expression used as a greeting, to attract someone's attention, etc [C20 of unknown origin]

yob (jɒb) *or* **yobbo** ('jɒbəʊ) *n, pl* **yobs** *or* **yobbos** *Brit slang* an aggressive and surly youth, esp a teenager [C19 perhaps back slang for BOY]

yobbery ('jɒbərɪ) *n Brit slang* behaviour typical of aggressive surly youths

yobbish ('jɒbɪʃ) *adj Brit slang* typical of aggressive surly youths; vulgar or unrefined

yod *or* **yodh** (jʊd) *n* the tenth letter in the Hebrew alphabet (י), transliterated as *y* [C18 from Hebrew, literally: hand]

yodel ('jəʊd³l) *n* **1** an effect produced in singing by an abrupt change of register from the chest voice to falsetto, esp in popular folk songs of the Swiss Alps ▷ *vb* **-dels, -delling, -delled** *or US* **-dels, -deling, -deled** **2** to sing (a song) in which a yodel is used [C19 from German *jodeln*, of imitative origin] > 'yodeller *n*

yodle ('jəʊd³l) *n* a variant spelling of **yodel**. > 'yodler *n*

yoga ('jəʊɡə) *n* (*often capital*) **1** a Hindu system of philosophy aiming at the mystical union of the self with the Supreme Being in a state of complete awareness and tranquillity through certain physical and mental exercises **2** any method by which such awareness and tranquillity are attained, esp a course of related exercises and postures designed to promote physical and spiritual wellbeing. See **Astanga yoga, hatha yoga, power yoga, raja yoga, Sivananda yoga** [C19 from Sanskrit: a yoking, union, from *yunakti* he yokes] > **yogic** ('jəʊɡɪk) *adj*

yogh (jɒɡ) *n* **1** a character (ʒ) used in Old and Middle English to represent a palatal fricative very close to the semivowel sound of Modern English *y*, as in Old English *ʒeong* (young) **2** this same character as used in Middle English for both the voiced and voiceless palatal fricatives; when final or in a closed syllable in medial position the sound approached that of German *ch* in *ich*, as in *knyʒt* (knight). After the 14th century this symbol became the modern consonantal (semivocalic) *y* when initial or commencing a syllable, and though no longer pronounced in medial position it is preserved in many words by a modern *gh*, as in *thought* [C14 perhaps from *yok* YOKE, referring to the letter's shape]

yogi ('jəʊɡɪ) *n, pl* **-gis** *or* **-gin** (-ɡɪn) a person who is a master of yoga > **yogini** (jəʊ'ɡiːnɪ) *fem n*

yogurt *or* **yoghurt** ('jəʊɡət, 'jɒɡ-) *n* a thick custard-like food prepared from milk that has been curdled by bacteria, often sweetened and flavoured with fruit, chocolate, etc [C19 from Turkish *yoğurt*]

Yogyakarta (ˌjəʊɡjə'kɑːtɑː, ˌjɒɡ-), **Jogjakarta, Jokjakarta, Djokjakarta** *n* a city in S Indonesia, in central Java: seat of government of Indonesia (1946–49); university (1949). Pop: 396 711

(2000)

yo-heave-ho (ˌjəʊhiːv'həʊ) *interj* a cry formerly used by sailors while pulling or lifting together in rhythm

yohimbine (jəʊ'hɪmbiːn) *n* an alkaloid found in the bark of the tree *Corynanthe yohimbe*. It is used in medicine as an adrenergic blocking agent. Formula: $C_{21}H_{26}N_2O_3$ [C19 from Bantu *yohimbé* a tropical African tree + -INE¹]

yo-ho-ho *interj* **1** an exclamation to call attention **2** another word for **yo-heave-ho**

yoicks (haɪk; *spelling pron* jɔɪks) *interj* a cry used by huntsmen to urge on the hounds to the fox

yoke (jəʊk) *n, pl* **yokes** *or* **yoke 1** a wooden frame, usually consisting of a bar with an oxbow or similar collar-like piece at either end, for attaching to the necks of a pair of draught animals, esp oxen, so that they can be worked as a team **2** something resembling a yoke in form or function, such as a frame fitting over a person's shoulders for carrying buckets suspended at either end **3** a fitted part of a garment, esp around the neck, shoulders, and chest or around the hips, to which a gathered, pleated, flared, or unfitted part is attached **4** an immense oppressive force or burden: *under the yoke of a tyrant* **5** a pair of oxen or other draught animals joined together by a yoke **6** a part, esp one of relatively thick cross section, that secures two or more components so that they move together **7** a crosshead that transmits the drive from the upper of a pair of linked pistons to the crankshaft through a connecting rod **8** a steel framework around the formwork during the casting of concrete **9** *nautical* a crossbar fixed athwartships to the head of a rudderpost in a small boat, to which are attached ropes or cables for steering **10** a Y-shaped cable, rope, or chain, used for holding, towing, etc **11** (in the ancient world) a symbolic reconstruction of a yoke, consisting of two upright spears with a third lashed across them, under which conquered enemies were compelled to march, esp in Rome **12** a mark, token, or symbol of slavery, subjection, or suffering **13** *now rare* a link, tie, or bond: *the yoke of love* **14** *Brit dialect* a period of steady work, esp the time during which a ploughman and his team work at a stretch **15** *Irish* any device, unusual object, or gadget: *where's the yoke for opening tins?* ▷ *vb* **16** (*tr*) to secure or harness (a draught animal) to (a plough, vehicle, etc) by means of a yoke **17** to join or be joined by means of a yoke; couple, unite, or link **18** (*tr*) *obsolete* to oppress, burden, or enslave [Old English *geoc*; related to Old High German *ioh*, Old Norse *ok*, Gothic *juk*, Latin *iugum*, Sanskrit *yugam*] > **yokeless** *adj*

yokefellow ('jəʊkˌfɛləʊ) *n archaic* a working companion

yokel ('jəʊk³l) *n disparaging* (used chiefly by townspeople) a person who lives in the country, esp one who appears to be simple and old-fashioned [C19 perhaps from dialect *yokel* green woodpecker, yellowhammer] > **yokelish** *adj*

yoker ('jəʊkə) *vb* (*intr*) *Northern English dialect* to spit

Yokohama (ˌjəʊkəʊ'hɑːmə) *n* a port in central Japan, on SE Honshu on Tokyo Bay: a major port and the country's second largest city situated in the largest and most populous industrial region of Japan. Pop: 3 433 612 (2002 est)

Yokosuka (ˌjəʊkəʊ'suːkə) *n* a port in Japan, in SE Honshu: a major naval base with shipbuilding industries. Pop: 434 613 (2002 est)

Yokozuna (ˌjəʊkəʊ'zuːnə) *n, pl* **-na** *or* **-ni** a grand champion sumo wrestler [from Japanese *yoko* across + *zuna* rope, from the sacred straw rope presented to the grand champion]

yolk (jəʊk) *n* **1** the substance in an animal ovum consisting of protein and fat that nourishes the developing embryo. Related adj: **vitelline 2** a greasy substance secreted by the skin of a sheep and present in the fleece [Old English *geoloca*, from *geolu* YELLOW] > **yolkless** *adj* > **yolky** *adj*

yolk sac *n zoology* **1** the membranous sac that is attached to the ventral surface of the embryos of birds, reptiles, and some fishes and contains yolk **2** the corresponding part in the embryo of mammals, which contains no yolk

Yom Kippur (jɒm 'kɪpə; *Hebrew* jɔm ki'pur) *n* an annual Jewish holiday celebrated on Tishri 10 as a day of fasting, on which prayers of penitence are recited in the synagogue throughout the day. Also called: Day of Atonement [from Hebrew, from *yōm* day + *kippūr* atonement]

Yom Kippur War *n* a war in which Egypt and Syria launched a joint surprise attack on Israel on the Jewish festival of Yom Kippur (Oct 6, 1973). It ended with a ceasefire (Oct 25, 1973), Syrian forces having been repulsed, Egypt having reoccupied a belt of the Sinai desert on the E bank of the Suez Canal, and Israel having established a salient on the W bank of the Suez Canal

yomp (jɒmp) *vb* (*intr*) to walk or trek laboriously, esp heavily laden and over difficult terrain [C20 military slang, of uncertain origin]

yom tov ('jɒm 'tɒv, 'jɒmtəv) *n, pl* **yamin tovim** (jɑ'min tɔ'vim) *Judaism* a festival, esp that of Passover, Shabuoth, Sukkoth, or Rosh Hashana

yon (jɒn) *or* **yond** (jɒnd) *determiner* **1** *chiefly Scot and northern English* **a** an archaic or dialect word for *that* *yon man* **b** (*as pronoun*): *yon's a fool* **2** variants of **yonder** [Old English *geon*; related to Old Frisian *jen*, Old High German *jenēr*, Old Norse *enn*, Gothic *jains*]

yonder ('jɒndə) *adv* **1** at, in, or to that relatively distant place; over there ▷ *determiner* **2** being at a distance, either within view or as if within view: *yonder valleys* [C13 from Old English *geond* yond; related to Old Saxon *jendra*, Old High German *jenēr*, Gothic *jaind*]

yoni ('jəʊnɪ) *n Hinduism* **1** the female genitalia, regarded as a divine symbol of sexual pleasure and matrix of generation and the visible form of Sakti **2** an image of these as an object of worship [C18 from Sanskrit, literally: vulva, womb]

Yonkers ('jɒŋkəz) *n* a city in SE New York State, near New York City on the Hudson River. Pop: 197 388 (2003 est)

yonks (jɒŋks) *pl n informal* a very long time; ages: *I haven't seen him for yonks* [C20 of unknown origin]

Yonne (*French* jɔn) *n* **1** a department of N central France, in Burgundy region. Capital: Auxerre. Pop: 335 917 (2003 est). Area: 7461 sq km (2910 sq miles) **2** a river in N France, flowing generally northwest to the Seine at Montereau. Length: 290 km (180 miles)

yonnie ('jɒnɪ) *n Austral children's slang* a stone [from a native Australian language]

yoof (juːf) *n informal* **a** a non-standard spelling of **youth**, used humorously or facetiously **b** (*as modifier*): *yoof TV*

yoo-hoo ('juːˌhuː) *interj* a call to attract a person's attention

YOP (jɒp) *n* (formerly, in Britain) **1 a** ▷ *acronym for* Youth Opportunities Programme **b** (*as modifier*): *a YOP scheme* **2** Also called: **yopper** *informal* a young person employed through this programme

yore (jɔː) *n* **1** time long past (now only in the phrase **of yore**) ▷ *adv* **2** *obsolete* in the past; long ago [Old English *geāra*, genitive plural of *gēar* YEAR; see HOUR]

york (jɔːk) *vb* (*tr*) *cricket* to bowl or try to bowl (a batsman) by pitching the ball under or just beyond the bat [C19 back formation from YORKER]

York (jɔːk) *n* **1** a historic city in NE England, in York unitary authority, North Yorkshire, on the River Ouse: the military capital of Roman Britain; capital of the N archiepiscopal province of Britain since 625, with a cathedral (the Minster) begun in 1154; noted for its cycle of medieval mystery plays; unusually intact medieval walls; university (1963). Pop: 137 505 (2001). Latin name: Eboracum **2** a unitary authority in NE England, in North Yorkshire. Pop: 183 100 (2003 est). Area: 272 sq km (105 sq miles) **3 Cape** a cape in NE Australia, in Queensland at the N tip of the Cape York

y

Peninsula, extending into the Torres Strait: the northernmost point of Australia

Yorke Peninsula (jɔːk) *n* a peninsula in South Australia, between Spencer Gulf and St Vincent Gulf: mainly agricultural with coastal resorts

yorker (jɔːkə) *n cricket* a ball bowled so as to pitch just under or just beyond the bat [c19 probably named after the *Yorkshire* County Cricket Club]

yorkie ('jɔːkɪ) *n* another name for **Yorkshire terrier**

Yorkist ('jɔːkɪst) *English history* ▷ *n* **1** a member or adherent of the royal house of York, esp during the Wars of the Roses ▷ *adj* **2** of, belonging to, or relating to the supporters or members of the house of York

Yorks. (jɔːks) *abbreviation for* Yorkshire

Yorkshire ('jɔːkʃɪə, -ʃə) *n* a historic county of N England: the largest English county, formerly divided administratively into East, West, and North Ridings. In 1974 it was much reduced in size and divided into the new counties of North, West, and South Yorkshire: in 1996 the East Riding of Yorkshire was reinstated as a unitary authority and parts of the NE were returned to North Yorkshire for geographical and ceremonial purposes

Yorkshire Dales *pl n* the valleys of the rivers flowing from the Pennines in W Yorkshire: chiefly Ribblesdale, Swaledale, Nidderdale, Wharfedale, and Wensleydale; tourist area. Also called: **the Dales**

Yorkshire fog *n* a common tufted grass, *Holcus lanatus*, having downy leaves and flower heads that are white or pink and branched, with spikelets carrying the flowers

Yorkshire pudding *n chiefly Brit* a light puffy baked pudding made from a batter of flour, eggs, and milk, traditionally served with roast beef

Yorkshire terrier *n* a very small breed of terrier with a long straight glossy coat of steel-blue and tan. Also called: **yorkie**

Yorktown ('jɔːkˌtaʊn) *n* a village in SE Virginia: scene of the surrender (1781) of the British under Cornwallis to the Americans under Washington at the end of the War of American Independence

yorp (jɔːp) *vb* (*intr*) *Midland English dialect* to shout

Yoruba ('jɒrʊbə) *n* **1** (*pl* **-bas** *or* **-ba**) a member of a Negroid people of W Africa, living chiefly in the coastal regions of SW Nigeria: noted for their former city states and complex material culture, particularly as evidenced in their music, art, and sculpture **2** the language of this people, belonging to the Kwa branch of the Niger-Congo family ▷ 'Yoruban *adj*

Yosemite Falls (jəʊˈsɛmɪtɪ) *pl n* a series of waterfalls in central California, in the Yosemite National Park, with a total drop of 770 m (2525 ft): includes the **Upper Yosemite Falls,** 436 m (1430 ft) high, and the **Lower Yosemite Falls,** 98 m (320 ft) high

Yosemite National Park *n* a national park in central California, in the Sierra Nevada Mountains: contains the **Yosemite Valley,** at an altitude of about 1200 m (4000 ft), with sheer walls rising about another 1200 m (4000 ft). Area: 3061 sq km (1182 sq miles)

Yoshkar-Ola (*Russian* jaʃˈkaraˈla) *n* a city in Russia, capital of the Mari El Republic. Pop: 260 000 (2005 est)

yottabyte ('jɒtəˌbaɪt) *n computing* 10^{24} or 2^{80} bytes [c20 probably from Italian *otto* eight]

you (juː; *unstressed* jʊ) *pron* (*subjective or objective*) **1** refers to the person addressed or to more than one person including the person or persons addressed but not including the speaker: *you know better; the culprit is among you* **2** Also: **one** refers to an unspecified person or people in general: *you can't tell the boys from the girls* **3** *chiefly US* a dialect word for **yourself** or **yourselves** when used as an indirect object: *you should get you a wife now* ▷ *n* **4** *informal* the personality of the person being addressed or something that expresses it: *that hat isn't really you* **5** **you know what** *or* **who** a thing or person that the speaker cannot or does not want to specify [Old English *ēow,* dative and accusative of *gē* YE¹; related to Old Saxon *eu,* Old High German *iu,* Gothic *izwis*]

■ USAGE See at **me¹**

you-all *pron* a US, esp Southern, word for **you,** esp when addressing more than one person

you'd (juːd; *unstressed* jʊd) *contraction of* you had *or* you would

you'll (juːl; *unstressed* jʊl) *contraction of* you will *or* you shall

young (jʌŋ) *adj* **younger** ('jʌŋɡə) **youngest** ('jʌŋɡɪst) **1 a** having lived, existed, or been made or known for a relatively short time: *a young man; a young movement; a young country* **b** (*as collective noun; preceded by the*): *the young* **2** youthful or having qualities associated with youth; vigorous or lively: *she's very young for her age* **3** of or relating to youth: *in my young days* **4** having been established or introduced for a relatively short time: *a young member* **5** in an early stage of progress or development; not far advanced: *the day was young* **6** *geography* **a** (of mountains) formed in the Alpine orogeny and still usually rugged in outline **b** another term for **youthful** (sense 4) **7** (*often capital*) of or relating to a rejuvenated group or movement or one claiming to represent the younger members of the population, esp one adhering to a political ideology: *Young England; Young Socialists* ▷ *n* **8** (*functioning as plural*) offspring, esp young animals: *a rabbit with her young* **9 with young** (of animals) pregnant [Old English *geong;* related to Old Saxon, Old High German *iung,* Old Norse *ungr,* Latin *iuvenis,* Sanskrit *yuvan*] > 'youngish *adj*

youngberry ('jʌŋbərɪ, -brɪ) *n, pl* **-ries 1** a trailing bramble of the southwestern US that is a hybrid of a blackberry and dewberry with large sweet dark purple fruits **2** the fruit of this plant [c20 named after B. M. *Young,* US fruit-grower who was first to cultivate it (circa 1900)]

young blood *n* young, fresh, or vigorous new people, ideas, attitudes, etc

Young Fogey *n* a young or fairly young person who adopts the conservative values of an older generation

young gun *n* an up-and-coming young man, esp one considered as being assertive and confident

Young Ireland *n* a movement or party of Irish patriots in the 1840s who split with Daniel O'Connell because they favoured a more violent policy than that which he promoted

young lady *n* a girlfriend; sweetheart

youngling ('jʌŋlɪŋ) *n literary* **a** a young person, animal, or plant **b** (*as modifier*): *a youngling brood* [Old English *geongling*]

young man *n* a boyfriend; sweetheart

young offender institution *n* (in Britain) a place where offenders aged 15 to 21 may be detained and given training, instruction, and work. Former names: **borstal, youth custody centre**

Young's modulus *n* a modulus of elasticity, applicable to the stretching of a wire etc, equal to the ratio of the applied load per unit area of cross section to the increase in length per unit length. Symbol: *E* [c19 named after Thomas *Young* (1773–1829), English physicist, physician, and Egyptologist]

youngster ('jʌŋstə) *n* **1** a young person; child or youth **2** a young animal, esp a horse

Youngstown ('jʌŋzˌtaʊn) *n* a city in NE Ohio: a major centre of steel production: university (1908). Pop: 79 271 (2003 est)

Young Turk *n* **1** a progressive, revolutionary, or rebellious member of an organization, political party, etc, esp one agitating for radical reform **2** a member of an abortive reform movement in the Ottoman Empire, originally made up of exiles in W Europe who advocated liberal reforms. The movement fell under the domination of young Turkish army officers of a nationalist bent, who wielded great influence in the government between 1908 and 1918

younker ('jʌŋkə) *n* **1** *archaic or literary* a young man; lad **2** *obsolete* a young gentleman or knight [c16 from Dutch *jonker,* from Middle Dutch *jonc* YOUNG]

your (jɔː, jʊə; *unstressed* jə) *determiner* **1** of, belonging to, or associated with you: *your nose; your house; your first taste of freedom* **2** belonging to or associated with an unspecified person or people in general: *the path is on your left; this lotion is for your head* **3** *informal* used to indicate all things or people of a certain type: *your part-time worker is a problem* **4 your actual** *Brit informal* (intensifier): *here is your actual automatic tin-opener* [Old English *eower,* genitive of *gē* YE¹; related to Old Frisian *jūwe,* Old Saxon *euwa,* Old High German *iuwēr*]

you're (jʊə, jɔː; *unstressed* jə) *contraction of* you are

yours (jɔːz, jʊəz) *pron* **1** something or someone belonging to or associated in some way with you: *I've eaten yours* **2** your family: *greetings to you and yours* **3** used in conventional closing phrases at the end of a letter: *yours sincerely; yours faithfully* **4** of yours belonging to or associated with you **5 what's yours?** *jocular* what would you like to drink?

yourself (jɔːˈsɛlf, jʊə-) *pron, pl* **-selves 1 a** the reflexive form of **you b** (intensifier): *you yourself control your destiny* **2** (*preceded by a copula*) your normal or usual self: *you're not yourself these days*

yours truly *pron* an informal term for I, myself, or me [from the conventional closing phrase used at the end of letters]

yous *or* **youse** (juːz) *pron dialect or not standard* refers to more than one person including the person or persons addressed but not including the speaker: *yous have all had it now; I'm fed up with yous*

youth (juːθ) *n, pl* **youths** (juːðz) **1** the quality or condition of being young, immature, or inexperienced: *his youth told against him in the contest* **2** the period between childhood and maturity, esp adolescence and early adulthood **3** the freshness, vigour, or vitality characteristic of young people: *youth shone out from her face* **4** any period of early development: *the project was in its youth* **5** a young person, esp a young man or boy **6** young people collectively: *youth everywhere is rising in revolt* [Old English *geogoth;* related to Old Frisian *jogethe,* Old High German *iugund,* Gothic *junda,* Latin *juventus*] > 'youthless *adj*

Youth (juːθ) *n* **Isle of** an island in the NW Caribbean, south of Cuba: administratively part of Cuba from 1925. Chief town: Nueva Gerona. Pop: 80 600 (2002 est). Area: 3061 sq km (1182 sq miles). Former name: **Isle of Pines** Spanish name: **Isla de la Juventud** ('izla ðe la xuβenˈtuð)

youth club *n* a centre providing leisure activities for young people, often associated with a church or community centre

youth court *n* a court that deals with juvenile offenders and children beyond parental control or in need of care. Former name: **juvenile court**

youth custody *n* (in Britain) a sentence of from four to eighteen months' detention passed on a person aged 15 to 21

youth custody centre *n* a former name for **young offender institution**

youthful ('juːθfʊl) *adj* **1** of, relating to, possessing, or characteristic of youth **2** fresh, vigorous, or active: *he's surprisingly youthful for his age* **3** in an early stage of development: *a youthful culture* **4** Also: **young** (of a river, valley, or land surface) in the early stage of the cycle of erosion, characterized by steep slopes, lack of flood plains, and V-shaped valleys. Compare **mature** (sense 6), **old** (sense 18) > 'youthfully *adv* > 'youthfulness *n*

youth hostel *n* one of a chain of inexpensive lodging places for young people travelling cheaply. Often shortened to: **hostel**

you've (juːv; *unstressed* jʊv) *contraction of* you have

yowe (jaʊ) *n* a Scot word for **ewe**

yowie ('jaʊɪ) *n* a large legendary manlike or

apelike creature, alleged to inhabit the Australian outback [c21 from an Aboriginal word *yuwi*]

yowl (jaʊl) *vb* **1** to express with or produce a loud mournful wail or cry; howl ▷ *n* **2** a loud mournful cry; wail or howl [c13 from Old Norse *gaula*; related to German *jaulen*; see YAWL²] > ˈyowler *n*

yo-yo (ˈjəʊjəʊ) *n, pl* **-yos 1** a toy consisting of a spool attached to a string, the end of which is held while it is repeatedly spun out and reeled in **2** *US and Canadian slang* a stupid person, esp one who is easily manipulated ▷ *vb* **yo-yos, yo-yoing, yo-yoed** (*intr*) **3** *informal* to change repeatedly from one position to another; fluctuate ▷ *adj* **4** *informal* changing repeatedly; fluctuating [from Filipino *yo yo*, come come, a weapon consisting of a spindle attached to a thong]

yo-yo dieting *n* the practice of repeatedly going on slimming diets, and putting on weight in the interim

Ypres (*French* iprə) *n* a town in W Belgium, in W Flanders province near the border with France: scene of many sieges and battles, esp in World War I, when it was completely destroyed. Pop: 35 021 (2004 est). Flemish name: Ieper

Yquem (iːˈkɛm) *n* a French vineyard of the Sauternes area of Bordeaux that produces a sweet white table wine. Also called: Château d'Yquem

yr *abbreviation for* **1** (*pl* yrs) year **2** younger **3** your

yrs *abbreviation for* **1** years **2** yours

Yser (*French* izɛr) *n* a river in NW central Europe, rising in N France and flowing through SW Belgium to the North Sea: scene of battles in World War I. Length: 77 km (48 miles)

Yseult (ɪˈsuːlt) *n* a variant spelling of **Iseult**

Yssel (ˈaɪsᵊl) *n* a variant spelling of **IJssel**

yt *the internet domain name for* Mayotte

Yt *the former chemical symbol for* yttrium (now Y)

YT (esp in postal addresses) *abbreviation for* Yukon Territory

ytterbia (ɪˈtɜːbɪə) *n* another name for **ytterbium oxide** [c19 New Latin, named after *Ytterby*, Swedish quarry where it was discovered]

ytterbite (ɪˈtɜːbaɪt) *n* another name for **gadolinite**

ytterbium (ɪˈtɜːbɪəm) *n* a soft malleable silvery element of the lanthanide series of metals that occurs in monazite and is used to improve the mechanical properties of steel. Symbol: Yb; atomic no: 70; atomic wt: 173.04; valency: 2 or 3; relative density: 6.903 (alpha), 6.966 (beta); melting pt: 819°C; boiling pt: 1196°C [c19 New Latin; see YTTERBIA]

ytterbium oxide *n* a colourless weakly basic hygroscopic substance used in certain alloys and ceramics. Formula: Yb₂O₃. Also called: **ytterbia**

yttria (ˈɪtrɪə) *n* another name for **yttrium oxide** [c19 New Latin, named after *Ytterby*; see YTTERBIA]

yttriferous (ɪˈtrɪfərəs) *adj* containing or yielding yttrium

yttrium (ˈɪtrɪəm) *n* a silvery metallic element occurring in monazite and gadolinite and used in various alloys, in lasers, and as a catalyst. Symbol: Y; atomic no: 39; atomic wt: 88.90585; valency: 3; relative density: 4.469; melting pt: 1522°C; boiling pt: 3338°C [c19 New Latin; see YTTERBIA] > ˈyttric *adj*

yttrium metal *n chem* any one of a group of elements including yttrium and the related lanthanides, holmium, erbium, thulium, ytterbium, and lutecium

yttrium oxide *n* a colourless or white insoluble solid used mainly in incandescent mantles. Formula: Y₂O₃. Also called: **yttria**

yu *the internet domain name for* Yugoslavia

YU *international car registration for* Serbia and Montenegro [from *Yugoslavia*]

yuan (juːˈæn) *n, pl* **-an** the standard monetary unit of China, divided into 10 jiao and 100 fen. Also called: **renminbi, renminbi yuan** [from Chinese *yüan* round object; see YEN¹]

Yüan¹ (juːˈæn) *adj* of or relating to the Chinese porcelain produced during the Yüan imperial dynasty (1279–1368), characterized by the appearance of under-glaze blue-and-white ware

Yüan² (ˌjuːˈæn), **Yüen** (ˈjuːˈɛn) *n* a river in SE central China, rising in central Guizhou province and flowing northeast to Lake Tungting. Length: about 800 km (500 miles)

Yuan Tan (ˈjuːˈæn ˈtæn) *n* an annual Chinese festival marking the Chinese New Year. It can last over three days and includes the exchange of gifts, firework displays, and dancing

Yucatán (ˌjuːkəˈtɑːn; *Spanish* jukaˈtan) *n* **1** a state of SE Mexico, occupying the N part of the Yucatán peninsula. Capital: Mérida. Pop: 1 655 707 (2000). Area: 39 340 sq km (15 186 sq miles) **2** a peninsula of Central America between the Gulf of Mexico and the Caribbean, including the Mexican states of Campeche, Yucatán, and Quintana Roo, and part of Belize: a centre of Mayan civilization from about 100 BC to the 18th century. Area: about 181 300 sq km (70 000 sq miles)

Yucatán Channel *n* a channel between W Cuba and the Yucatán peninsula

yucca (ˈjʌkə) *n* any of several plants of the genus *Yucca*, of tropical and subtropical America, having stiff lancelike leaves and spikes of white flowers: family *Agaraceae*. See also **Adam's-needle, Spanish bayonet** [c16 from American Spanish *yuca*, ultimately from an American Indian word]

yuck or **yuk** (jʌk) *interj slang* an exclamation indicating contempt, dislike, or disgust

yucko (ˈjʌkəʊ) *Austral slang* ▷ *adj* **1** disgusting; unpleasant ▷ *interj* **2** an exclamation of disgust

yucky or **yukky** (ˈjʌkɪ) *adj* **yuckier, yuckiest** or **yukkier, yukkiest** *slang* disgusting; sickening

Yuga (ˈjʊɡə) *n* (in Hindu cosmology) one of the four ages of mankind, together lasting over 4 million years and marked by a progressive decline in the vitality and morals of men [c18 from Sanskrit: yoke, race of men, era; see YOKE]

yugarie (ˈjuːɡərɪ) *n* a variant spelling of **eugarie**

Yugo. *abbreviation for* (the former) Yugoslavia

Yugoslav or **Jugoslav** (ˈjuːɡəʊˌslɑːv) *n* **1** (formerly) a native, inhabitant, or citizen of Yugoslavia (sense 1 or 2) **2** (not in technical use) another name for **Serbo-Croat** (the language) ▷ *adj* **3** (formerly) of, relating to, or characteristic of Yugoslavia (sense 1 or 2) or its people

Yugoslavia or **Jugoslavia** (ˌjuːɡəʊˈslɑːvɪə) *n* **1 Federal Republic of Yugoslavia** a former country of SE Europe, comprising Serbia and Montenegro, that was formed in 1991 but not widely internationally recognized until 2000; it was replaced by the Union of Serbia and Montenegro in 2003 **2** a former country in SE Europe, on the Adriatic: established in 1918 from the independent states of Serbia and Montenegro, and regions that until World War I had belonged to Austria-Hungary (Croatia, Slovenia, and Bosnia-Herzegovina); the name was changed from Kingdom of Serbs, Croats, and Slovenes to Yugoslavia in 1929; German invasion of 1941–44 was resisted chiefly by a Communist group led by Tito, who declared a people's republic in 1945; it became the Socialist Federal Republic of Yugoslavia in 1963; in 1991 Slovenia, Croatia, and Bosnia-Herzegovina declared independence, followed by Macedonia in 1992; Serbia and Montenegro formed the Federal Republic of Yugoslavia, subsequently (2003) replaced by the Union of Serbia and Montenegro

Yugoslavian or **Jugoslavian** (ˌjuːɡəʊˈslɑːvɪən) *adj* **1** of or relating to Yugoslavia or its inhabitants ▷ *n* **2** a native or inhabitant of Yugoslavia

Yukon (ˈjuːkɒn) *n* **the** a territory of NW Canada, on the Beaufort Sea, between the Northwest Territories and Alaska: arctic and mountainous, reaching 5959 m (19 550 ft) at Mount Logan, Canada's highest peak; mineral resources. Capital: Whitehorse. Pop: 31 209 (2004 est). Area: 536 327 sq km (207 076 sq miles). Abbreviation: YT > ˈYukoner *n*

Yukoner (ˈjuːkɒnə) *n* a native or inhabitant of the Yukon

Yukon River *n* a river in NW North America, rising in NW Canada on the border between the Yukon Territory and British Columbia: flows northwest into Alaska, US, and then southwest to the Bering Sea; navigable for about 2850 km (1775 miles) to Whitehorse. Length: 3185 km (1979 miles)

yulan (ˈjuːlæn) *n* a Chinese magnolia, *Magnolia denudata*, cultivated for its showy white flowers [c19 from Chinese, from *yu* a gem + *lan* plant]

yule (juːl) *n* (*sometimes capital*) *literary, archaic, or dialect* **a** Christmas, the Christmas season, or Christmas festivities **b** (*in combination*): *yuletide* [Old English *gēola*, originally a name of a pagan feast lasting 12 days; related to Old Norse *jōl*, Swedish *jul*, Gothic *jiuleis*]

yule log *n* a large log of wood traditionally used as the foundation of a fire in the hearth at Christmas

Yuman (ˈjuːmən) *n* **1** a family of North American Indian languages spoken chiefly in Arizona, California, and Mexico ▷ *adj* **2** relating to or belonging to this family of languages

yummo (ˈjʌməʊ) *Austral slang* ▷ *adj* **1** delicious ▷ *interj* **2** an exclamation of delight or approval

yummy (ˈjʌmɪ) *slang* ▷ *interj* **1** Also: **yum-yum** an exclamation indicating pleasure or delight, as in anticipation of delicious food ▷ *adj* **-mier, -miest 2** delicious, delightful, or attractive [c20 from *yum-yum*, of imitative origin]

yummy mummy *n slang* an attractive woman who has had children

Yünnan (juːˈnæn) *n* a province of SW China: consists mainly of a plateau broken in the southeast by the Red and Black Rivers, with mountains in the west, rising over 5500 m (18 000 ft); large deposits of tin, lead, zinc, and coal. Capital: Kunming. Pop: 43 760 000 (2003 est). Area: 436 200 sq km (168 400 sq miles)

yup (jʌp) *sentence substitute* an informal word for **yes**

Yupik (ˈjuːpɪk) *n* **1** an aboriginal people of Alaska, the Aleutian Islands, and E Siberia **2** any of the languages of this people **3** of or relating to the Yupik people or their languages. Compare **Inuit, Inuktitut**

yuppie or **yuppy** (ˈjʌpɪ) (*sometimes capital*) *n* **1** an affluent young professional person ▷ *adj* **2** typical of or reflecting the values characteristic of yuppies [c20 from *y(oung) u(rban)* or *up(wardly mobile) p(rofessional)* + -IE] > ˈyuppiedom *n*

yuppie disease or **flu** *n informal, sometimes considered offensive* any of a number of debilitating long-lasting viral disorders associated with stress, such as chronic fatigue syndrome, whose symptoms include muscle weakness, chronic tiredness, and depression

yuppify (ˈjʌpɪˌfaɪ) *vb* **-fies, -fying, -fied** (*tr*) to make yuppie in nature > ˌyuppifiˈcation *n*

Yurev (*Russian* ˈjurjɪf) *n* the former name (11th century until 1918) of **Tartu**

yurt (jʊət) *n* a circular tent consisting of a framework of poles covered with felt or skins, used by Mongolian and Turkic nomads of E and central Asia [from Russian *yurta*, of Turkic origin; compare Turkish *yurt* abode, home]

Yuzovka (*Russian* ˈjuzəfkə) *n* a former name (1872 until after the Revolution) of **Donetsk**

yuzu (ˈjuːzuː) *n* a citrus fruit about the size of a golf ball, a hybrid of a primitive citrus called *Ichang papeda* and a mandarin, which grows on tall trees in Japan and has a sour flavour. [Japanese]

YV *international car registration for* Venezuela

Yvelines (*French* ivlin) *n* a department of N France, in Île de France region. Capital: Versailles. Pop: 1 370 443 (2003 est). Area: 2271 sq km (886 sq miles)

YWCA *abbreviation for* Young Women's Christian Association

YWHA *abbreviation for* Young Women's Hebrew Association

ywis (ɪˈwɪs) *adv* a variant spelling of **iwis**

y

Zz

z or **Z** (zɛd; *US* ziː) *n, pl* **z's, Z's** or **Zs** **1** the 26th and last letter and the 20th consonant of the modern English alphabet **2** a speech sound represented by this letter, in English usually a voiced alveolar fricative, as in *zip* **3 a** something shaped like a Z **b** (*in combination*): *a Z-bend in a road*

z *maths symbol for* **1** the z-axis or a coordinate measured along the z-axis in a Cartesian or cylindrical coordinate system **2** an algebraic variable

Z *symbol for* **1** any unknown, variable, or unspecified factor, number, person, or thing **2** *chem* atomic number **3** *physics* impedance **4** zone **5** *currency* zaïre **6** ▷ *international car registration for* Zambia

za *the internet domain name for* South Africa

ZA *international car registration for* South Africa [from Afrikaans *Zuid Afrika*]

Zaandam (*Dutch* zaːnˈdɑm) *n* a former town in the W Netherlands, in North Holland: an important shipbuilding centre in the 17th century. It became part of Zaanstad in 1974

Zaanstad (*Dutch* zaːnˈʃtat) *n* a port in the W Netherlands, in North Holland: formed (1974) from Zaandam, Koog a/d Zaan, Zaandijk, Wormerveer, Krommenie, Westzaan, and Assendelft; food and machinery industries. Pop: 139 000 (2003 est)

zabaglione (ˌzæbəˈljəʊnɪ) *n* a light foamy dessert made of egg yolks, sugar, and marsala, whipped together and served warm in a glass [Italian; probably related to Late Latin *sabaia* Illyrian drink made from grain]

Zabrze (*Polish* ˈzabʒɛ) *n* a city in SW Poland: a Prussian and German town from 1742 until 1945, when it passed to Poland; industrial centre in a coal-mining region. Pop: 200 177 (1999 est). German name: Hindenburg

Zacatecas (*Spanish* θakaˈtekas) *n* **1** a state of N central Mexico, on the central plateau: rich mineral resources. Capital: Zacatecas. Pop: 1 351 207 (2000). Area: 75 040 sq km (28 973 sq miles) **2** a city in N central Mexico, capital of Zacatecas state: silver mines. Pop: 241 000 (2005 est)

Zacharias (ˌzækəˈraɪəs), **Zachariah** (ˌzækəˈraɪə) or **Zachary** (ˈzækərɪ) *n New Testament* John the Baptist's father, who underwent a temporary period of dumbness for his lack of faith (Luke 1)

Zacynthus (zəˈsɪnθəs, -ˈkɪn-) *n* the Latin name for Zante

zaffer or **zaffre** (ˈzæfə) *n* impure cobalt oxide, used to impart a blue colour to enamels [c17 from Italian *zaffera*; perhaps related to Latin *sapphīrus* SAPPHIRE]

Zagazig (ˈzægəˌzɪg) or **Zaqaziq** *n* a city in NE Egypt, in the Nile Delta: major cotton market. Pop: 291 000 (2005 est)

Zagreb (ˈzɑːgrɛb) *n* the capital of Croatia, on the River Sava; gothic cathedral; university (1874); industrial centre. Pop: 685 000 (2005 est). German name: Agram

Zagreus (ˈzægrɪəs) *n Greek myth* a young god whose cult came from Crete to Greece, where he was identified with Dionysus. The son of Zeus by either Demeter or Persephone, he was killed by the Titans at the behest of Hera

Zagros Mountains (ˈzægrɒs) *pl n* a mountain range in S Iran: has Iran's main oilfields in its W central foothills. Highest peak: Zard Kuh, 4548 m (14 920 ft)

zaibatsu (ˈzaɪbætˈsuː) *n* (*functioning as singular or plural*) the group or combine comprising a few wealthy families that controls industry, business, and finance in Japan [from Japanese, from *zai* wealth, from Chinese *ts'ai* + *batsu* family, person of influence, from Chinese *fa*]

Zaïre (zɑːˈɪə) *n* **1** the former name (1971–97) of the **(Democratic Republic of) Congo** (sense 1) **2** (formerly) the Zaïrian name (1971–97) for the (River) **Congo**

Zaïrian or **Zaïrean** (zɑːˈɪərɪən) *adj* **1** of or relating to the former Zaïre (now the Democratic Republic of the Congo) or its inhabitants ▷ *n* **2** a native or inhabitant of Zaïre

zakat (ˈzakat) *n Islam* an annual tax on Muslims to aid the poor in the Muslim community [from Arabic *zakāt* alms]

Zákinthos (ˈzakinˌθɒs) *n* transliteration of the Modern Greek name for **Zante**

zakuski or **zakouski** (zæˈkʊskɪ) *pl n, sing* **-ka** (-kə) *Russian cookery* hors d'oeuvres, consisting of tiny open sandwiches spread with caviar, smoked sausage, etc, or a cold dish such as radishes in sour cream, all usually served with vodka [Russian, from *zakusit'* to have a snack]

Zama (ˈzɑːmə) *n* the name of several ancient cities in N Africa, including the one near the site of Scipio's decisive defeat of Hannibal (202 BC)

Zambezi or **Zambese** (zæmˈbiːzɪ) *n* a river in S central and E Africa, rising in NW Zambia and flowing across E Angola back into Zambia, continuing south to the Caprivi Strip of Namibia, then east forming the Zambia–Zimbabwe border, and finally crossing Mozambique to the Indian Ocean: the fourth longest river in Africa. Length: 2740 km (1700 miles)

Zambezian (zæmˈbiːzɪən) *adj* of or relating to the Zambezi River

Zambia (ˈzæmbɪə) *n* a republic in southern Africa: an early site of human settlement; controlled by the British South Africa Company by 1900 and unified as Northern Rhodesia in 1911; made a British protectorate in 1924; part of the Federation of Rhodesia and Nyasaland (1953–63), gaining independence as a member of the Commonwealth in 1964; important mineral exports, esp copper. Official language: English. Religion: Christian majority, animist minority. Currency: kwacha. Capital: Lusaka. Pop: 10 924 000 (2004 est). Area: 752 617 sq km (290 587 sq miles). Former name (until 1964): **Northern Rhodesia**

Zambian (ˈzæmbɪən) *adj* **1** of or relating to Zambia or its inhabitants ▷ *n* **2** a native or inhabitant of Zambia

Zamboanga (ˌzæmbəʊˈæŋgə) *n* a port in the Philippines, on SW Mindanao on Basilan Strait: founded by the Spanish in 1635; tourist centre, with fisheries. Pop: 716 000 (2005 est)

zambuck (ˈzæmbʌk) *n Austral and NZ informal* a St John ambulance attendant, esp at a sports meeting [c20 from *Zam-Buck*, the trade name of an ointment which comes in a black-and-white container, black and white being the colours of the St John uniform]

zamia (ˈzeɪmɪə) *n* any cycadaceous plant of the genus *Zamia*, of tropical and subtropical America, having a short thick trunk, palmlike leaves, and short stout cones [c19 from New Latin, from Latin *zamiae*, erroneous reading of phrase *nucēs azāniae* pine cones, probably from Greek *azainein* to dry up]

zamindar or **zemindar** (zəmiːnˈdɑː) *n* (in India) the owner of an agricultural estate [via Hindi from Persian: landholder, from *zamīn* land + *-dār* holder]

zamindari or **zemindari** (zəmiːnˈdɑːrɪ) *n, pl* **-is** (in India) a large agricultural estate

Zamora (*Spanish* θaˈmora) *n* a city in NW central Spain, on the Douro River. Pop: 65 639 (2003 est)

ZAMS *abbreviation for astronomy* zero age main sequence

zamzawed (ˈzamˌzɒd) *adj Southwest English dialect* (of tea) having been left in the pot to stew

zander (ˈzændə) *n, pl* **zander** or **zanders** a freshwater teleost pikeperch of Europe, *Stizostedion lucioperca*, valued as a food fish

Zante (ˈzæntɪ) *n* an island in the Ionian Sea, off the W coast of Greece: southernmost of the Ionian Islands; traditionally belonged to Ulysses, king of Ithaca. Pop: 38 957 (2001). Area: 402 sq km (155 sq miles). Latin name: Zacynthus Ancient Greek name: Zakynthos (zəˈkuːnθɒs) Modern Greek name: Zákinthos

zanthoxylum (zænˈθɒksɪləm) *n* any rutaceous shrub or tree of the genus *Zanthoxylum*, of temperate and subtropical E Asia and North America: includes the prickly ash and the West Indian yellowwood (or satinwood) [c19 zantho- variant of XANTHO- + Greek *xulon* wood]

Zanu(PF) (ˌzænuː ˌpiːˈɛf) *n acronym for* Zimbabwe African National Union (Patriotic Front)

zany (ˈzeɪnɪ) *adj* **-nier, -niest 1** comical in an endearing way; imaginatively funny or comical, esp in behaviour ▷ *n, pl* **-nies 2 a** a clown or buffoon, esp one in old comedies who imitated other performers with ludicrous effect **3** a ludicrous or foolish person [c16 from Italian *zanni*, from dialect (Venice and Lombardy) *Zanni*, nickname for *Giovanni* John; one of the traditional names for a clown] > **'zanily** *adv* > **'zaniness** *n* > **'zanyism** *n*

Zanzibar (ˌzænzɪˈbɑː) *n* an island in the Indian Ocean, off the E coast of Africa: settled by Persians and Arabs from the 7th century onwards; became a flourishing trading centre for slaves, ivory, and cloves; made a British protectorate in 1890, becoming independent within the Commonwealth in 1963 and a republic in 1964; joined with Tanganyika in 1964 to form the United Republic of Tanzania. Pop: 622 459 (2002)

Zanzibari (ˌzænzɪˈbɑːrɪ) *adj* **1** of or relating to Zanzibar or its inhabitants ▷ *n* **2** a native or inhabitant of Zanzibar

zap (zæp) *slang* ▷ *vb* **zaps, zapping, zapped** **1** (*tr*) to attack, kill, or destroy, as with a sudden bombardment **2** (*intr*) to move quickly; rush **3** (*tr*) *computing* **a** to clear from the screen **b** to erase **4** (*intr*) *television* to change channels rapidly by remote control ▷ *n* **5** energy, vigour, or pep ▷ *interj* **6** an exclamation used to express sudden or swift action [of imitative origin]

zapateado *Spanish* (θapateˈaðo) *n, pl* **-dos** (-ðos) a Spanish dance with stamping and very fast footwork [from *zapatear* to tap with the shoe, from *zapato* shoe]

Zaporozhye (*Russian* zəpaˈrɔʒjɛ) *n* a city in E Ukraine on the Dnieper River: developed as a major industrial centre after the construction (1932) of the Dnieper hydroelectric station. Pop: 798 000 (2005 est). Former name (until 1921): Aleksandrovsk

Zapotec (ˈzɑːpəˌtɛk) *n* **1** *pl* **-tecs** or **-tec** Also called: **Zapotecan** (ˌzæpəʊˈtɛkən, ˌzɑː-) any member of a large tribe of central American Indians inhabiting S Mexico, esp the Mexican state of Oaxaca **2** the group of languages spoken by this people **3** Also: **Zapotecan** of or relating to this people or their language [from Spanish *Zapoteca*, from Nahuatl *Tzapoteca*, literally: people of the land of the sapodillas, from *tzapotl* sapodilla]

zappy (ˈzæpɪ) *adj* **zappier, zappiest** *slang* full of energy; snappy; zippy

ZAPU (ˈzæpuː) *n acronym for* Zimbabwe African People's Union

Zaqaziq (ˈzækəˌzɪk) *n* a variant of **Zagazig**

Zaragoza (*Spanish* θaraˈɣoθa) *n* a city in NE Spain, on the River Ebro: Roman colony established 25 BC; under Moorish rule (714–1118); capital of Aragon (11th–15th centuries); twice besieged by the French during the Peninsular War and captured (1809); university (1474). Pop: 626 081 (2003 est). Pre-Roman name: **Salduba** Latin name: **Caesaraugusta** English name: **Saragossa**

Zarathustrian (ˌzærəˈθuːstrɪən) *adj, n* the Avestan name for **Zoroastrian**

zaratite (ˈzærəˌtaɪt) *n* a green amorphous mineral consisting of hydrated nickel carbonate Formula: $Ni_3(CO_3)(OH)_4.4H_2O$ [C19 from Spanish *zaratita*, named after G. *Zárate*, 19th-century Spaniard]

zareba or **zareeba** (zəˈriːbə) *n* (in northern E Africa, esp formerly) **1** a stockade or enclosure of thorn bushes around a village or campsite **2** the area so protected or enclosed [C19 from Arabic *zarībah* cattlepen, from *zarb* sheepfold]

zarf (zɑːf) *n* (esp in the Middle East) a holder, usually ornamental, for a hot coffee cup [from Arabic: container, sheath]

Zaria (ˈzɑːrɪə) *n* a city in N central Nigeria: former capital of a Hausa state; agricultural trading centre; university (1962). Pop: 822 000 (2005 est)

Zarqa (ˈzɑːkə) *n* the second largest town in Jordan, northeast of Amman. Pop: 494 000 (2005 est)

zarzuela (zɑːˈzweɪlə) *n* **1** a type of Spanish vaudeville or operetta, usually satirical in nature **2** a seafood stew [from Spanish, from *La Zarzuela*, name of the palace near Madrid where such vaudeville was first performed (1629)]

zastruga (zəˈstruːɡə, zæ-) *n* a variant spelling of **sastruga**

zax (zæks) *n* a variant of **sax**[1]

z-**axis** *n* a reference axis of a three-dimensional Cartesian coordinate system along which the z-coordinate is measured

zayin (ˈzɑːjɪn) *n* the seventh letter of the Hebrew

alphabet (ז), transliterated as *z* [from Hebrew, literally: weapon]

zazen (zʌˈzɛn) *n* (in Zen Buddhism) deep meditation undertaken whilst sitting upright with legs crossed

ZB *abbreviation for* zero balancing

Z boson *n physics* another name for **Z particle**

ZB station *n* (in New Zealand) a radio station of a commercial network

ZCC (in South Africa) *abbreviation for* Zion Christian Church

Z chart *n statistics* a chart often used in industry and constructed by plotting on it three series: monthly, weekly, or daily data, the moving annual total, and the cumulative total dating from the beginning of the current year

Zea (ˈtseːa) *n* the Italian name for **Keos**

zeal (ziːl) *n* fervent or enthusiastic devotion, often extreme or fanatical in nature, as to a religious movement, political cause, ideal, or aspiration [C14 from Late Latin *zēlus*, from Greek *zēlos*]

Zealand (ˈziːlənd) *n* the largest island of Denmark, separated from the island of Funen by the Great Belt and from S Sweden by the Sound (both now spanned by road bridges). Chief town: Copenhagen. Pop: 2 096 449 (2003 est). Area: 7016 sq km (2709 sq miles). Danish name: Sjælland German name: Seeland

zealot (ˈzɛlət) *n* an immoderate, fanatical, or extremely zealous adherent to a cause, esp a religious one [C16 from Late Latin *zēlōtēs*, from Greek, from *zēloun* to be zealous, from *zēlos* ZEAL]

Zealot (ˈzɛlət) *n* any of the members of an extreme Jewish sect or political party that resisted all aspects of Roman rule in Palestine in the 1st century AD

zealotry (ˈzɛlətrɪ) *n* extreme or excessive zeal or devotion

zealous (ˈzɛləs) *adj* filled with or inspired by intense enthusiasm or zeal; ardent; fervent > ˈzealously *adv* > ˈzealousness *n*

zebec or **zebeck** (ˈziːbɛk) *n* variant spellings of **xebec**

Zebedee (ˈzɛbɪˌdiː) *n New Testament* the father of the apostles James and John (Matthew 4:21)

zebra (ˈziːbrə, ˈzɛbrə) *n, pl* **-ras** or **-ra** any of several mammals of the horse family (*Equidae*), such as *Equus burchelli* (the **common zebra**), of southern and eastern Africa, having distinctive black-and-white striped hides [C16 via Italian from Old Spanish: wild ass, probably from Vulgar Latin *eciferus* (unattested) wild horse, from Latin *equiferus*, from *equus* horse + *ferus* wild] > ˈzebra-ˌlike or ˈzebraic (zɪˈbreɪɪk) *adj* > **zebrine** (ˈziːbraɪn, ˈzɛb-) or ˈzebroid *adj*

Zebra (ˈziːbrə, ˈzɛbrə) *n finance* a noninterest-paying bond in which the accrued income is taxed annually rather than on redemption. Compare **zero** (sense 12) [C20 from *zero-coupon bond*]

zebra crossing *n Brit* a pedestrian crossing marked on a road by broad alternate black and white stripes. Once on the crossing the pedestrian has right of way

zebra finch *n* any of various Australasian songbirds with zebra-like markings, such as the grassfinch *Poephila castanotis*

zebra plant *n* See **calathea**

zebrawood (ˈzɛbrəˌwʊd, ˈziː-) *n* **1** a tree, *Connarus guianensis*, of tropical America, Asia, and Africa, yielding striped hardwood used in cabinetwork: family *Connaraceae* **2** any of various other trees or shrubs having striped wood **3** the wood of any of these trees

zebu (ˈziːbuː) *n* a domesticated ox, *Bos indicus*, having a humped back, long horns, and a large dewlap: used in India and E Asia as a draught animal [C18 from French *zébu*, perhaps of Tibetan origin]

Zebulun (ˈzɛbjʊlən, zəˈbjuː-) *n Old Testament* **1** the sixth son whom Leah bore to Jacob: one of the 12 patriarchs of Israel (Genesis 30:20) **2** the tribe

descended from him **3** the territory of this tribe, lying in lower Galilee to the north of Mount Carmel and to the east of the coastal plain. Douay spelling: **Zabulon** (ˈzæbjʊlən, zəˈbju:-)

zecchino (zɛˈkiːnəʊ) *n, pl* **-ni** (-nɪ) another word for **sequin** (the coin) [C18 from Italian; see SEQUIN]

Zech. *Bible abbreviation for* Zechariah

Zechariah (ˌzɛkəˈraɪə) *n* **1** *Old Testament* **a** a Hebrew prophet of the late 6th century BC **b** the book containing his oracles, which are chiefly concerned with the renewal of Israel after the exile as a national, religious, and messianic community with the restored Temple and rebuilt Jerusalem as its centre. Douay spelling: **Zacharias 2** a variant spelling of **Zachariah** See **Zacharias**

zed (zɛd) *n* the Brit spoken form of the letter *z*. US word: zee [C15 from Old French *zede*, via Late Latin from Greek *zēta*]

Zedekiah (ˌzɛdəˈkaɪə) *n Old Testament* the last king of Judah, who died in captivity at Babylon. Douay spelling: **Sedecias** (ˌsɛdəˈkaɪəs)

zedoary (ˈzɛdəʊərɪ) *n* the dried rhizome of the tropical Asian plant *Curcuma zedoaria*, used as a stimulant and a condiment: family *Zingiberaceae* [C15 from Medieval Latin *zedoaria*, from Arabic *zadwār*, of Persian origin]

zeds or **zzzs** (zɛdz) *pl n informal* **1** sleep **2** catch a few zeds to have a nap

zee (ziː) *n* the US word for **zed** (letter z)

Zeebrugge (*Flemish* ˈzeːbryxə; *English* ˈziːˌbrʊɡə) *n* a port in NW Belgium, in W Flanders on the North Sea: linked by canal with Bruges; German submarine base in World War I

Zeeland (*Dutch* ˈzeːlant; *English* ˈziːlənd) *n* a province of the SW Netherlands: consists of a small area on the mainland together with a number of islands in the Scheldt estuary; mostly below sea level. Capital: Middelburg. Pop: 378 000 (2003 est). Area: 1787 sq km (690 sq miles)

Zeelander (ˈziːləndə) *n* a native or inhabitant of the Dutch province of Zeeland

Zeeman effect (ˈziːmən) *n* the splitting of a spectral line of a substance into several closely spaced lines when the substance is placed in a magnetic field [C20 named after Pieter *Zeeman* (1865–1943), Dutch physicist]

zein (ˈziːɪn) *n* a protein of the prolamine group occurring in maize and used in the manufacture of plastics, paper coatings, adhesives, etc [C19 from New Latin *zēa* maize, from Latin: a kind of grain, from Greek *zeia* barley]

Zeist (zaɪst; *Dutch* zɛjst) *n* a city in the central Netherlands, near Utrecht. Pop: 60 000 (2003 est)

Zeitgeist *German* (ˈtsaɪtɡaɪst) *n* the spirit, attitude, or general outlook of a specific time or period, esp as it is reflected in literature, philosophy, etc [German, literally: time spirit; see TIDE[1], GHOST]

zemindar (zəmiːnˈdɑː) *n* a variant spelling of **zamindar**. > zemiˈdari *n*

zemstvo (ˈzɛmstvəʊ; *Russian* ˈzjɛmstvə) *n, pl* **-stvos** (in tsarist Russia) an elective provincial or district council established in most provinces of Russia by Alexander II in 1864 as part of his reform policy [C19 from Russian, from *zemlya* land; related to Latin *humus* earth, Greek *khamai* on the ground]

Zen (zɛn) *Buddhism* ▷ *n* **1** a Japanese school, of 12th-century Chinese origin, teaching that contemplation of one's essential nature to the exclusion of all else is the only way of achieving pure enlightenment **2** (*modifier*) of or relating to this school: *Zen Buddhism* [from Japanese, from Chinese *ch'an* religious meditation, from Pali *jhāna*, from Sanskrit *dhyāna*] > ˈZenic *adj* > ˈZenist *n*

zenana (zɛˈnɑːnə) *n* (in the East, esp in Muslim and Hindu homes) part of a house reserved for the women and girls of a household [C18 from Hindi *zanāna*, from Persian, from *zan* woman]

Zend (zɛnd) *n* **1** a former name for **Avestan 2** short for **Zend-Avesta 3** an exposition of the Avesta in the Middle Persian language (Pahlavi) [C18 from Persian *zand* commentary, exposition; used specifically of the Middle Persian

Z

commentary on the Avesta, hence of the language of the Avesta itself] > ˈZendic *adj*

Zend-Avesta (ˌzɛndəˈvɛstə) *n* the Avesta together with the traditional interpretative commentary known as the Zend, esp as preserved in the Avestan language among the Parsees [from Avestan, representing *Avesta'-va-zend* Avesta with interpretation] > Zend-Avestaic (ˌzɛndəvɛsˈteɪɪk) *adj*

Zener diode (ˈziːnə) *n* a semiconductor diode that exhibits a sharp increase in reverse current at a well-defined reverse voltage: used as a voltage regulator [c20 named after C. M. Zener (1905–93), US physicist]

zenith (ˈzɛnɪθ; *US* ˈziːnɪθ) *n* 1 *astronomy* the point on the celestial sphere vertically above an observer 2 the highest point; peak; acme: *the zenith of someone's achievements* ▷ Compare **nadir** [c17 from French *cenith*, from Medieval Latin, from Old Spanish *zenit*, based on Arabic *samt*, as in *samt arrās* path over one's head, from *samt* way, path + *al* the + *rās* head] > ˈzenithal *adj*

zenithal projection *n* a type of map projection in which part of the earth's surface is projected onto a plane tangential to it, either at one of the poles (**polar zenithal**), at the equator (**equatorial zenithal**), or between (**oblique zenithal**)

zenith telescope *n* an instrument used to determine the latitude of stars, similar to the meridian circle but fitted with an extremely sensitive level and a declination micrometer

zeolite (ˈziːəˌlaɪt) *n* 1 any of a large group of glassy secondary minerals consisting of hydrated aluminium silicates of calcium, sodium, or potassium: formed in cavities in lava flows and plutonic rocks 2 any of a class of similar synthetic materials used in ion exchange and as selective absorbents. See **molecular sieve** [c18 *zeo-*, from Greek *zein* to boil + -LITE; from the swelling up that occurs under the blowpipe] > zeolitic (ˌziːəˈlɪtɪk) *adj*

Zeph. *Bible abbreviation for* Zephaniah

Zephaniah (ˌzɛfəˈnaɪə) *n Old Testament* 1 a Hebrew prophet of the late 7th century BC 2 the book containing his oracles, which are chiefly concerned with the approaching judgment by God upon the sinners of Judah. Douay spelling: Sophonias (ˌsɒfəˈnaɪəs)

zephyr (ˈzɛfə) *n* 1 a soft or gentle breeze 2 any of several delicate soft yarns, fabrics, or garments, usually of wool [c16 from Latin *zephyrus*, from Greek *zephuros* the west wind; probably related to Greek *zophos* darkness, west]

Zephyrus (ˈzɛfərəs) *n Greek myth* the god of the west wind

zeppelin (ˈzɛpəlɪn) *n* (*sometimes capital*) a large cylindrical rigid airship built from 1900 to carry passengers, and used in World War I for bombing and reconnaissance [c20 named after Count Ferdinand von *Zeppelin* (1838–1917), German aeronautical pioneer, designer and manufacturer of airships]

Zermatt (tsɛrˈmat) *n* a village and resort in S Switzerland, in Valais canton at the foot of the Matterhorn: cars are not allowed in the area. Pop: 5988 (2000)

zero (ˈzɪərəʊ) *n, pl* -ros *or* -roes 1 the symbol 0, indicating an absence of quantity or magnitude; nought. Former name: **cipher** 2 the integer denoted by the symbol 0; nought 3 the cardinal number between +1 and –1 4 nothing; nil 5 a person or thing of no significance; nonentity 6 the lowest point or degree: *his prospects were put at zero* 7 the line or point on a scale of measurement from which the graduations commence 8 a the temperature, pressure, etc, that registers a reading of zero on a scale b the value of a variable, such as temperature, obtained under specified conditions 9 a gunsight setting in which accurate allowance has been made for both windage and elevation for a specified range 10 *maths* a the cardinal number of a set with no

members b the identity element of addition 11 *linguistics* a an allomorph with no phonetic realization, as the plural marker of English *sheep* b (*as modifier*): *a zero form* 12 *finance* Also called: **zero-coupon bond** a bond that pays no interest, the equivalent being paid in its redemption value. Compare **Zebra** ▷ *adj* 13 having no measurable quantity, magnitude, etc 14 *meteorol* a (of a cloud ceiling) limiting visibility to 15 metres (50 feet) or less b (of horizontal visibility) limited to 50 metres (165 feet) or less ▷ *vb* -roes, -roing, -roed 15 (*tr*) to adjust (an instrument, apparatus, etc) so as to read zero or a position taken as zero ▷ *determiner* 16 *informal, chiefly US* no (thing) at all: *this job has zero interest* [c17 from Italian, from Medieval Latin *zephirum*, from Arabic *sifr* empty, CIPHER]

zero balancing *n* a therapy involving the manipulation of the patient's skeletal structure in order to restore the balance of energy, relieve pain, and maintain well-being. Abbreviation: ZB

zero defects *pl n* an aspect of total quality management that stresses the objective of error-free performance in providing goods or services

zero-emission *adj* (of a motor vehicle) emitting no harmful pollutants

zero gravity *n* the state or condition of weightlessness

zero grazing *n* a type of dairy farming in which the cattle are fed with cut grass

zero hour *n* 1 *military* the time set for the start of an attack or the initial stage of an operation 2 *informal* a critical time, esp at the commencement of an action

zero in *vb* (*adverb*) 1 (*often foll by on*) to bring (a weapon) to bear (on a target), as while firing repeatedly 2 (*intr; foll by on*) *informal* to bring one's attention to bear (on a problem, etc) 3 (*intr; foll by on*) *informal* to converge (upon): *the police zeroed in on the site of the crime*

zero option *n* (in international nuclear arms negotiations) an offer to remove all shorter-range nuclear missiles or, in the case of the **zero-zero option** all intermediate-range nuclear missiles, if the other side will do the same

zero-rated *adj* (**zero rated** *when postpositive*) denoting goods on which the buyer pays no value-added tax although the seller can claim back any tax he has paid

zero stage *n* a solid-propellant rocket attached to a liquid-propellant rocket to provide greater thrust at liftoff

zero-sum game *n* (in game theory) a contest in which one person's loss is equal to the other person's gain

zeroth (ˈzɪərəʊθ) *adj* denoting a term in a series that precedes the term otherwise regarded as the first term [c20 from ZERO + -TH²]

zero tolerance *n* a the policy of applying laws or penalties to even minor infringements of a code in order to reinforce its overall importance b (*as modifier*): *a zero-tolerance policy on drugs*

zest (zɛst) *n* 1 invigorating or keen excitement or enjoyment: *a zest for living* 2 added interest, flavour, or charm; piquancy: *her presence gave zest to the occasion* 3 something added to give flavour or relish 4 the peel or skin of an orange or lemon, used as flavouring in drinks, etc ▷ *vb* 5 (*tr*) to give flavour, interest, or piquancy to [c17 from French *zeste* peel of citrus fruits used as flavouring, of unknown origin] > ˈzestful *adj* > ˈzestfully *adv* > ˈzestfulness *n* > ˈzestless *adj* > ˈzesty *adj*

zester (ˈzɛstə) *n* a kitchen utensil used to scrape fine shreds of peel from citrus fruits

zeta (ˈziːtə) *n* the sixth letter in the Greek alphabet (Z, ζ), a consonant, transliterated as z [from Greek, of Semitic origin; compare Hebrew *sādhē*]

Zeta (ˈziːtə) *n* (*foll by the genitive case of a specified constellation*) the sixth brightest star in a constellation: *Zeta Tauri*

ZETA (ˈziːtə) *n* a torus-shaped apparatus used for research in the 1950s and early 1960s on

controlled thermonuclear reactions and plasma physics [c20 from z(ero-)e(nergy) t(hermonuclear) a(pparatus)]

zetetic (zəˈtɛtɪk) *adj* proceeding by inquiry; investigating [c17 from New Latin, from Greek *zētētikos*, from *zēteō* to seek]

Zetland (ˈzɛtlənd) *n* the official name (until 1974) of Shetland

zettabyte (ˈzɛtəˌbaɪt) *n computing* 10²¹ or 2⁷⁰ bytes [c20 probably from Italian *sette* seven]

zeugma (ˈzjuːgmə) *n* a figure of speech in which a word is used to modify or govern two or more words although appropriate to only one of them or making a different sense with each, as in the sentence *Mr. Pickwick took his hat and his leave* (Charles Dickens) [c16 via Latin from Greek: a yoking, from *zeugnunai* to yoke] > zeugmatic (zjuːgˈmætɪk) *adj* > zeugˈmatically *adv*

Zeus (zjuːs) *n* the supreme god of the ancient Greeks, who became ruler of gods and men after he dethroned his father Cronus and defeated the Titans. He was the husband of his sister Hera and father by her and others of many gods, demigods, and mortals. He wielded thunderbolts and ruled the heavens, while his brothers Poseidon and Hades ruled the sea and underworld respectively. Roman counterpart: Jupiter

Zhangjiakou (ˈdʒæŋˈdʒjækəʊ), **Changchiakow** *or* **Changchiak'ou** *n* a city in NE China, in NW Hebei province: a military centre, controlling the route to Mongolia, under the Ming and Manchu dynasties. Pop: 973 000 (2005 est). Former names: Wanchüan, Kalgan

Zhangzhou (ˈdʒæŋˈdʒəʊ), **Changchow** *or* **Ch'ang-chou** *n* 1 a city in E China, in S Jiangsu province, on the Grand Canal: also known as **Wutsin** until 1949, when the 7th-century name was officially readopted. Pop: 772 700 (1990 est) 2 a city in SE China, in S Fujian province on the Saikoe River. Pop 231 333 (1999 est). Former name: Lungki

Zhdanov (*Russian* ˈʒdanəf) *n* the former name (1948–91) of Mariupol

Zhejiang (ˈdʒɛˈdʒjæŋ) *or* **Chekiang** *n* a province of E China: mountainous and densely populated; a cultural centre since the 12th century. Capital: Hangzhou. Pop: 46 800 000 (2003 est). Area: 102 000 sq km (39 780 sq miles)

Zhengzhou (ˈdʒʌŋˈdʒəʊ), **Chengchow** *or* **Cheng-chou** *n* a city in E central China, capital of Henan province; an administrative centre. Pop: 2 250 000 (2005 est)

Zhitomir (*Russian* ʒiˈtɔmir) *n* a city in central Ukraine; centre of an agricultural region. Pop: 282 000 (2005 est)

zho (zəʊ) *n, pl* zhos *or* zho a variant spelling of **zo**

Zhou (dʒəʊ) *n* the Pinyin transliteration of the Chinese name for **Chou**

Zhu Jiang (ˈdʒuːˈdʒjæŋ), **Chu Chiang** *or* **Chu Kiang** *n* a river in SE China, in S Guangdong province, flowing southeast from Canton to the South China Sea. Length: about 177 km (110 miles). Also called: **Canton River, Pearl River**

zibeline (ˈzɪbəˌlaɪn, -lɪn) *n* 1 a sable or the fur of this animal 2 a thick cloth made of wool or other animal hair, having a long nap and a dull sheen ▷ *adj* 3 of, relating to, or resembling a sable [c16 from French, from Old Italian *zibellino*, ultimately of Slavonic origin; compare SABLE]

zibet (ˈzɪbɪt) *n* a large civet, *Viverra zibetha*, of S and SE Asia, having tawny fur marked with black spots and stripes [c16 from Medieval Latin *zibethum*, from Arabic *zabād* CIVET]

Zibo (ˈdziˈbɔː), **Tzu-po** *or* **Tzepo** *n* a city in NE China, in Shandong province. Pop: 2 775 000 (2005 est)

zidovudine (zaɪˈdɒvjʊˌdiːn) *n* a drug that is used to treat AIDS. Also called: AZT

Ziegler catalyst (ˈziːglə) *n* any of a group of catalysts, such as titanium trichloride (TiCl₃) and aluminium alkyl (Al(CH₃)₃), that produce stereospecific polymers [c20 named after Carl

Ziegler (1898–1973), German chemist]

ziff (zɪf) *n Austral informal* a beard [C20 of unknown origin]

ziggurat ('zɪgʊˌræt) *or* **zikkurat, zikurat** ('zɪkʊˌræt) *n* a type of rectangular temple tower or tiered mound erected by the Sumerians, Akkadians, and Babylonians in Mesopotamia. The tower of Babel is thought to be one of these [C19 from Assyrian *ziqqurati* summit, height]

Zigong ('dzɪgʊŋ), **Tzekung** *or* **Tzu-kung** *n* an industrial city in W central China, in Sichuan. Pop: 1 123 000 (2005 est)

zigzag ('zɪgˌzæg) *n* **1** a line or course characterized by sharp turns in alternating directions **2** one of the series of such turns **3** something having the form of a zigzag ▷ *adj* **4** (*usually prenominal*) formed in or proceeding in a zigzag **5** (of sewing machine stitches) produced in a zigzag by a swing needle used for joining stretch fabrics, neatening raw edges, etc ▷ *adv* **6** in a zigzag manner ▷ *vb* -zags, -zagging, -zagged **7** to proceed or cause to proceed in a zigzag **8** (*tr*) to form into a zigzag [C18 from French, from German *zickzack*, from *Zacke* point, jagged projection; see TACK[1]] > 'zig,zaggedness *n*

zila, zilla *or* **zillah** ('zɪlɑ:) *n* an administrative district in India [C19 from Hindi *dilah* division, from Arabic *dil'* part]

zila parishad ('pʌrɪʃəd) *n* a district council in India [Hindi, from *zila'* district (from Arabic *dil'* part) + *parishad* assembly, council]

zilch (zɪltʃ) *n slang* **1** nothing **2** *US and Canadian sport* nil [C20 of uncertain origin]

zillion ('zɪljən) *informal* ▷ *n, pl* -lions *or* -lion **1** (*often plural*) an extremely large but unspecified number, quantity, or amount: *zillions of flies in this camp* ▷ *determiner* **2 a** amounting to a zillion: *a zillion different problems* **b** (*as pronoun*): *I found a zillion under the sink* [on the model of *million*]

Zilpah ('zɪlpə) *n Old Testament* Leah's maidservant, who bore Gad and Asher to Jacob (Genesis 30:10–13)

Zimbabwe (zɪm'bɑ:bwɪ, -weɪ) *n* **1** a country in SE Africa, formerly a self-governing British colony founded in 1890 by the British South Africa Company, which administered the country until a self-governing colony was established in 1923; joined with Northern Rhodesia (now Zambia) and Nyasaland (now Malawi) as the Federation of Rhodesia and Nyasaland from 1953 to 1963; made a unilateral declaration of independence (UDI) under the leadership of Ian Smith in 1965 on the basis of White minority rule; proclaimed a republic in 1970; in 1976 the principle of Black majority rule was accepted and in 1978 a transitional government was set up; gained independence under Robert Mugabe in 1980; effectively a one-party state since 1987; a member of the Commonwealth until 2003, when it withdrew as a result of conflict with other members. Official language: English. Religion: Christian majority. Currency: Zimbabwe dollar. Capital: Harare. Pop: 12 932 000 (2004 est). Area: 390 624 sq km (150 820 sq miles). Former names: Southern Rhodesia (until 1964), Rhodesia (1964–79) **2** a ruined fortified settlement in Zimbabwe, which at its height, in the 15th century, was probably the capital of an empire covering SE Africa

Zimbabwean (zɪm'bɑ:bwɪən, -weɪən) *adj* **1** of or relating to Zimbabwe or its inhabitants ▷ *n* **2** a native or inhabitant of Zimbabwe

Zimmer ('zɪmə) *n trademark* another name for **walker** (sense 3) Also called: **Zimmer frame**

zinc (zɪŋk) *n* **1** a brittle bluish-white metallic element that becomes coated with a corrosion-resistant layer in moist air and occurs chiefly in sphalerite and smithsonite. It is a constituent of several alloys, esp brass and nickel-silver, and is used in die-casting, galvanizing metals, and in battery electrodes. Symbol: Zn; atomic no: 30; atomic wt: 65.39; valency: 2; relative density: 7.133;

melting pt: 419.58°C; boiling pt: 907°C **2** *informal* corrugated galvanized iron [C17 from German *Zink*, perhaps from *Zinke* prong, from its jagged appearance in the furnace] > 'zincic, 'zincous *or* 'zincoid *adj* > 'zincky, 'zincy *or* 'zinky *adj*

zincate ('zɪŋkeɪt) *n* any of a class of salts derived from the amphoteric hydroxide of zinc, $Zn(OH)_2$, often thought of as the acid H_2ZnO_2

zinc blende *n* another name for **sphalerite**

zinc chloride *n* a white odourless soluble poisonous granular solid used in manufacturing parchment paper and vulcanized fibre and in preserving wood. It is also a soldering flux, embalming agent, and a medical astringent and antiseptic. Formula: $ZnCl_2$. Also called: **butter of zinc**

zinciferous (zɪŋ'kɪfərəs) *adj* containing or yielding zinc

zincite ('zɪŋkaɪt) *n* a red or yellow mineral consisting of zinc oxide in hexagonal crystalline form. It occurs in metamorphosed limestone. Formula: ZnO

zinckenite ('zɪŋkəˌnaɪt) *n* a variant spelling of **zinkenite**

zinco ('zɪŋkəʊ) *n, pl* -cos short for **zincograph** (sense 1)

zincograph ('zɪŋkəˌgrɑ:f, -ˌgræf) *n* **1** a printing plate made by zincography **2** a print taken from such a plate

zincography (zɪŋ'kɒgrəfɪ) *n* the art or process of etching on zinc to form a printing plate > zin'cographer *n* > zincographic (ˌzɪŋkə'græfɪk) *or* ˌzinco'graphical *adj*

zinc ointment *n* a medicinal ointment consisting of zinc oxide, petrolatum, and paraffin, used to treat certain skin diseases

zinc oxide *n* a white insoluble powder used as a pigment in paints (**zinc white** or **Chinese white**), cosmetics, glass, and printing inks. It is an antiseptic and astringent and is used in making zinc ointment. Formula: ZnO. Also called: **flowers of zinc, philosopher's wool**

zinc sulphate *n* a colourless soluble crystalline substance usually existing as the heptahydrate or monohydrate: used as a mordant, in preserving wood and skins, and in the electrodeposition of zinc. Formula: $ZnSO_4$. Also called: **white vitriol, zinc vitriol**

zinc white *n* another name for **Chinese white**

zindabad ('zɪndɑ:ˌbɑ:d) *vb* (*tr*) *Indian* long live: used as part of a slogan in India, Pakistan, etc. Compare **murdabad** [Hindi, from Persian]

zine (zi:n) *n informal* a magazine or fanzine

Zinfandel ('zɪnfənˌdɛl) *n* a Californian wine grape originally transplanted from Europe and producing a quick-maturing fruity red wine [C19 of unknown origin]

zing (zɪŋ) *n informal* **1** a short high-pitched buzzing sound, as of a bullet or vibrating string **2** vitality; zest ▷ *vb* **3** (*intr*) to make or move with or as if with a high-pitched buzzing sound [C20 of imitative origin]

zingaro Italian ('dzingaro) *or feminine* **zingara** ('dzingara) *n, pl* -ri (-ri) *-re* (-re) an Italian Gypsy [C16 ultimately from Greek *Athinganoi*, name of an oriental people]

zingiberaceous (ˌzɪndʒɪbə'reɪʃəs) *adj* of, relating to, or belonging to the *Zingiberaceae*, a family of tropical aromatic plants that typically have fleshy rhizomes and flowers in spikes or clusters: includes ginger and the plants yielding turmeric and cardamom [C19 via New Latin from *zingiber* GINGER]

zingy (zɪŋɪ) *adj* -gier, -giest *informal* vibrant; energetic; lively

zinjanthropus (zɪn'dʒænθrəpəs) *n* a type of australopithecine, *Australopithecus boisei* (formerly *Zinjanthropus boisei*), remains of which were discovered in the Olduvai Gorge in Tanzania in 1959 [C20 New Latin, from Arabic *Zinj* East Africa + Greek *anthrōpos* man]

zinkenite *or* **zinckenite** ('zɪŋkəˌnaɪt) *n* a steel-

grey metallic mineral consisting of a sulphide of lead and antimony. Formula: $Pb_6Sb_{14}S_{27}$ [C19 named after J. K. L. *Zincken* (1790–1862), German mineralogist]

zinnia ('zɪnɪə) *n* any annual or perennial plant of the genus *Zinnia*, of tropical and subtropical America, having solitary heads of brightly coloured flowers: family *Asteraceae* (composites) [C18 named after J. G. *Zinn* (died 1759), German botanist]

Zinovievsk (*Russian* zi'nɔvjɪfsk) *n* a former name (1924–36) for **Kirovograd**

Zion ('zaɪən) *or* **Sion** *n* **1** the hill on which the city of Jerusalem stands **2** *Judaism* **a** the ancient Israelites of the Bible **b** the modern Jewish nation **c** Israel as the national home of the Jewish people **3** *Christianity* heaven regarded as the city of God and the final abode of his elect **4** any form of social organization, way of life, or life after death regarded as an ultimate goal **5 a** a religious community or its site, regarded as chosen by God and under his special protection **b** an ideal theocratic community, esp any of the Christian Churches regarded as such a community

Zionism ('zaɪəˌnɪzəm) *n* **1** a political movement for the establishment and support of a national homeland for Jews in Palestine, now concerned chiefly with the development of the modern state of Israel **2** a policy or movement for Jews to return to Palestine from the Diaspora > 'Zionist *n, adj* > Zion'istic *adj*

zip (zɪp) *n* **1 a** Also called: **zip fastener** a fastening device operating by means of two parallel rows of metal or plastic teeth on either side of a closure that are interlocked by a sliding tab. US and Canadian term: **zipper** **b** (*modifier*) having or equipped with such a device: *a zip bag* **2** a short sharp whizzing sound, as of a passing bullet **3** *informal* energy; vigour; vitality **4** *US slang* nothing **5** *sport, US and Canadian slang* nil ▷ *vb* zips, zipping, zipped **6** (*tr*; often foll by *up*) to fasten (clothing, a bag, etc) with a zip **7** (*intr*) to move with a zip: *the bullet zipped past* **8** (*intr*; often foll by *along, through*, etc) to hurry; rush: *they zipped through town* **9** (*tr*) *computing* to compress (a file) in order to reduce the amount of memory required to store it or to make sending it electronically quicker [C19 of imitative origin]

Zip (zɪp) *n trademark NZ* an electric water heater

Zipangu (zɪ'pæŋgu:) *n* Marco Polo's name for **Cipango**

zip code *n* the US equivalent of **postcode** [C20 from z(one) i(mprovement) p(lan)]

zip gun *n US and Canadian slang* a crude homemade pistol, esp one powered by a spring or rubber band

zip line *n* a cable mechanism used for transportation across a river, gorge, etc

zipper ('zɪpə) *n US and Canadian* a fastening device operating by means of two parallel rows of metal or plastic teeth on either side of a closure that are interlocked by a sliding tab. Also called (in Britain and certain other countries): **zip**

zippered ('zɪpəd) *adj* provided or fastened with a zip

zippy ('zɪpɪ) *adj* -pier, -piest *informal* full of energy; lively

zircalloy (zɜ:k'ælɔɪ) *n* an alloy of zirconium containing small amounts of tin, chromium, and nickel. It is used in pressurized-water reactors

zircon ('zɜ:kɒn) *n* a reddish-brown, grey, green, blue, or colourless hard mineral consisting of zirconium silicate in tetragonal crystalline form with hafnium and some rare earths as impurities. It occurs principally in igneous rocks and is an important source of zirconium, zirconia, and hafnia: it is used as a gemstone and a refractory. Formula: $ZrSiO_4$ [C18 from German *Zirkon*, from French *jargon*, via Italian and Arabic, from Persian *zargün* golden]

zirconia (zɜ:'kəʊnɪə) *n* another name (not in

Z

technical usage) for **zirconium oxide**

zirconium (zɜːˈkəʊnɪəm) *n* a greyish-white metallic element, occurring chiefly in zircon, that is exceptionally corrosion-resistant and has low neutron absorption. It is used as a coating in nuclear and chemical plants, as a deoxidizer in steel, and alloyed with niobium in superconductive magnets. Symbol: Zr; atomic no: 40; atomic wt: 91.224; valency: 2, 3, or 4; relative density: 6.506; melting pt: 1855±2°C; boiling pt: 4409°C [C19 from New Latin; see ZIRCON] > **zirconic** (zɜːˈkɒnɪk) *adj*

zirconium oxide *n* a white amorphous powder that is insoluble in water and highly refractory, used as a pigment for paints, a catalyst, and an abrasive. Formula: ZrO₂. Also called: **zirconia**

zit (zɪt) *n slang* a pimple [of unknown origin]

zither (ˈzɪðə) *n* a plucked musical instrument consisting of numerous strings stretched over a resonating box, a few of which may be stopped on a fretted fingerboard [C19 from German, from Latin *cithara*, from Greek *kithara*] > **ˈzitherist** *n*

zizith (ˈtsɪtsɪs, tsiːˈtsiːt) *n (functioning as singular or plural) Judaism* a variant spelling of **tsitsith**

zizz (zɪz) *Brit informal* ▷ *n* **1** a short sleep; nap ▷ *vb* (*intr*) **2** to take a short sleep, snooze [C20 of imitative origin]

Zl *symbol for* zloty

Zlatoust (*Russian* zlɑˈtuːst) *n* a town in W Russia, on the Ay river: one of the chief metallurgical centres of the Urals since the 18th century. Pop: 192 000 (2005 est)

zloty (ˈzlɒtɪ) *n, pl* **-tys** or **-ty** the standard monetary unit of Poland, divided into 100 groszy [from Polish: golden, from *zlyoto* gold; related to Russian *zoloto* gold]

zm *the internet domain name for* Zambia

Zn *chemical symbol for* zinc

zo, zho or **dzo** (zəʊ) *n, pl* **zos, zhos, dzos** or **zo, zho, dzo** a Tibetan breed of cattle, developed by crossing the yak with common cattle [C20 from Tibetan]

zo- *combining form* a variant of **zoo-** before a vowel

zoa (ˈzəʊə) *n* the plural of **zoon**

-zoa *suffix forming plural proper nouns* indicating groups of animal organisms: *Metazoa* [from New Latin, from Greek *zōia*, plural of *zōion* animal, living being]

zoaea (zəʊˈiːə) *n, pl* **zoaeae** (zəʊˈiːiː) or **zoaeas** a variant spelling of **zoea**

Zoan (ˈzəʊæn) *n* the Biblical name for **Tanis**

zodiac (ˈzəʊdɪˌæk) *n* **1** an imaginary belt extending 8° either side of the ecliptic, which contains the 12 **zodiacal constellations** and within which the moon and planets appear to move. It is divided into 12 equal areas, called **signs of the zodiac**, each named after the constellation which once lay in it **2** *astrology* a diagram, usually circular, representing this belt and showing the symbols, illustrations, etc, associated with each of the 12 signs of the zodiac, used to predict the future **3** *rare* a complete circuit; circle [C14 from Old French *zodiaque*, from Latin *zōdiacus*, from Greek *zōidiakos* (*kuklos*) (circle) of signs, from *zōidion* animal sign, carved figure, from *zōion* animal] > **zodiacal** (zəʊˈdaɪəkəl) *adj*

zodiacal constellation *n* any of the 12 constellations after which the signs of the zodiac are named: Aries, Taurus, Gemini, Cancer, Leo, Virgo, Libra, Scorpio, Sagittarius, Capricorn, Aquarius, or Pisces

zodiacal light *n* a very faint cone of light in the sky, visible in the east just before sunrise and in the west just after sunset. It is probably due to the reflection of sunlight from cosmic dust in the plane of the ecliptic

zoea or **zoaea** (zəʊˈiːə) *n, pl* **zoeae, zoaeae** (zəʊˈiːiː) or **zoeas, zoaeas** the free-swimming larva of a crab or related crustacean, which has well-developed abdominal appendages and may bear one or more spines [C20 New Latin, from Greek *zōē* life]

zoetrope (ˈzəʊɪˌtrəʊp) *n* a cylinder-shaped toy with a sequence of pictures on its inner surface which, when viewed through the vertical slits spaced regularly around it while the toy is rotated, produce an illusion of animation [C19 Greek *zoe* life + *trope* turn]

Zohar (ˈzəʊhɑː) *n Judaism* a mystical work, consisting of a commentary on parts of the Pentateuch and the Hagiographa, probably composed in the 2nd century AD

zoic (ˈzəʊɪk) *adj* **1** relating to or having animal life **2** *geology* (of rocks, strata, etc) containing fossilized animals [C19 from New Latin, from Greek *zōion* animal]

-zoic *adj and n combining form* indicating a geological era: *Palaeozoic* [from Greek *zōē* life + -IC]

zoisite (ˈzɔɪˌsaɪt) *n* a grey, brown, or pink mineral consisting of hydrated calcium aluminium silicate in orthorhombic crystalline form. Formula: Ca₂Al₃(SiO₄)₃(OH) [C19 from German *Zoisit*; named after Baron Sigismund *Zois* von Edelstein (1747–1819), Slovenian nobleman; see -ITE¹]

zol (zɒl) *n South African slang* a cannabis cigarette [C20 of unknown origin]

Zola Budd (bʌd) *n South African informal* a black taxi or minibus [C20 after *Zola Budd* maiden name of Zola Pieterse (born 1966), South African athlete]

Zollverein *German* (ˈtsɔlfɛrˌaɪn) *n* the customs union of German states organized in the early 1830s under Prussian auspices [C19 from *Zoll* tax, TOLL² + *Verein* union]

Zomba (ˈzɒmbə) *n* a city in S Malawi: the capital of Malawi until 1971. Pop: 65 915 (1998 est)

zombie or **zombi** (ˈzɒmbɪ) *n, pl* **-bies** or **-bis 1** a person who is or appears to be lifeless, apathetic, or totally lacking in independent judgment; automaton **2** a supernatural spirit that reanimates a dead body **3** a corpse brought to life in this manner **4** the snake god of voodoo cults in the West Indies, esp Haiti, and in scattered areas of the southern US **5** the python god revered in parts of West Africa **6** a piece of computer code that instructs an infected computer to send a virus on to other computer systems [from Kongo *zumbi* good-luck fetish] > **ˈzombiism** *n*

zonal (ˈzəʊnəl) or *less commonly* **zonary** (ˈzəʊnərɪ) *adj* of, relating to, or of the nature of a zone > **ˈzonally** *adv*

zonal soil *n* soil having a profile determined mainly by the local climate and vegetation. Compare **azonal soil, intrazonal soil**

zonate (ˈzəʊneɪt) or **zonated** *adj* marked with, divided into, or arranged in zones

zonation (zəʊˈneɪʃən) *n* arrangement in zones; zonate formation

Zond (zɒnd) *n* any of a series of unmanned Soviet spacecraft, first launched in 1964 as interplanetary space probes, the most successful of which, *Zond 3*, sent back photographs of the hidden side of the moon in 1965

zone (zəʊn) *n* **1** a region, area, or section characterized by some distinctive feature or quality **2** a sphere of thought, disagreement, argument, etc **3** an area subject to a particular political, military, or government function, use, or jurisdiction: *a demilitarized zone* **4** (*often capital*) *geography* one of the divisions of the earth's surface, esp divided into latitudinal belts according to temperature. See **Torrid Zone, Frigid Zone, Temperate Zone 5** *geology* a distinctive layer or region of rock, characterized by particular fossils (**zone fossils**), metamorphism, structural deformity, etc **6** *ecology* an area, esp a belt of land, having a particular flora and fauna determined by the prevailing environmental conditions **7** *maths* a portion of a sphere between two parallel planes intersecting the sphere **8** *sport* **a** a period during which a competitor is performing particularly well: *Hingis is in the zone at the moment* **b** (*modifier*) of or relating to competitive performance that depends on the mood or state of mind of the

participant: *a zone player* **9** *archaic or literary* a girdle or belt **10** NZ a section on a transport route; fare stage **11** NZ a catchment area for pupils for a specific school **12 in the zone** See **zone** (sense 8) ▷ *vb* (*tr*) **13** to divide into zones, as for different use, jurisdiction, activities, etc **14** to designate as a zone **15** to mark with or divide into zones **16** NZ to establish (an area) as a zone for a specific school [C15 from Latin *zōna* girdle, climatic zone, from Greek *zōnē*] > **ˈzoning** *n*

zone of saturation *n* the ground below the water table

zone refining *n* a technique for producing solids of extreme purity, esp for use in semiconductors. The material, in the form of a bar, is melted in one small region that is passed along the solid. Impurities concentrate in the melt and are moved to the end of the bar

zonetime (ˈzəʊnˌtaɪm) *n* the standard time of the time zone in which a ship is located at sea, each zone extending 7½° to each side of a meridian

zonked (zɒŋkt) *adj slang* **1** highly intoxicated from drugs or alcohol **2** utterly exhausted [C20 of imitative origin]

zonule (ˈzɒnjuːl) *n* a small zone, band, or area [C19 from New Latin *zōnula* a little ZONE] > **zonular** (ˈzɒnjʊlə) *adj*

zoo (zuː) *n, pl* **zoos** a place where live animals are kept, studied, bred, and exhibited to the public. Formal term: **zoological garden** [C19 shortened from *zoological gardens* (originally applied to those in London)]

zoo- or *before a vowel* **zo-** *combining form* indicating animals: *zooplankton* [from Greek *zōion* animal]

zoobiotic (ˌzəʊəbaɪˈɒtɪk) *adj biology* parasitic on or living in association with an animal

zoochemistry (ˌzəʊəˈkɛmɪstrɪ) *n* the branch of biochemistry that is concerned with the constituents of an animal's body > **ˌzooˈchemical** *adj*

zoochorous (ˌzəʊəˈkɔːrəs) *adj* (of a plant) having the spores or seeds dispersed by animals [from ZOO- + -CHORE + -OUS] > **ˈzooˌchore** *n*

zoo doo *n* compost made from the dung of zoo animals

zoogeography (ˌzəʊədʒɪˈɒgrəfɪ) *n* the branch of zoology concerned with the geographical distribution of animals > **zooge'ographer** *n* > **zoogeographic** (ˌzəʊəˌdʒɪəˈgræfɪk) or **ˌzooˌgeoˈgraphical** *adj* > **ˌzooˌgeoˈgraphically** *adv*

zoogloea (ˌzəʊəˈgliːə) *n* a mass of bacteria adhering together by a jelly-like substance derived from their cell walls [C19 ZOO- + New Latin *gloea* glue, from Greek *gloia*] > **ˌzooˈgloeal** *adj*

zoography (zəʊˈɒgrəfɪ) *n* the branch of zoology concerned with the description of animals > **zoˈographer** *n* > **zoographic** (ˌzəʊəˈgræfɪk) or **ˌzooˈgraphical** *adj*

zooid (ˈzəʊɔɪd) *n* **1** any independent animal body, such as an individual of a coelenterate colony **2** a motile cell or body, such as a gamete, produced by an organism > **zoˈoidal** *adj*

zool. *abbreviation for* **1** zoological **2** zoology

zoolatry (zəʊˈɒlətrɪ) *n* **1** (esp in ancient or primitive religions) the worship of animals as the incarnations of certain deities, symbols of particular qualities or natural forces, etc **2** extreme or excessive devotion to animals, particularly domestic pets > **zoˈolater** *n* > **zoˈolatrous** *adj*

zoological garden *n* the formal term for **zoo**

zoology (zəʊˈɒlədʒɪ, zuː-) *n, pl* **-gies 1** the study of animals, including their classification, structure, physiology, and history **2** the biological characteristics of a particular animal or animal group **3** the fauna characteristic of a particular region **4** a book, treatise, etc, dealing with any aspect of the study of animals > **zoological** (ˌzəʊəˈlɒdʒɪkəl, ˌzuːə-) *adj* > **zoˈologist** *n*

zoom (zuːm) *vb* **1** to make or cause to make a continuous buzzing or humming sound **2** to move or cause to move with such a sound **3** (*intr*) to move very rapidly; rush: *we zoomed through town* **4** to cause (an aircraft) to climb briefly at an unusually steep angle, or (of an aircraft) to climb in this way **5** (*intr*) (of prices) to rise rapidly ▷ *n* **6** the sound or act of zooming **7** See **zoom lens** [c20 of imitative origin]

zoometry (zəʊˈɒmɪtrɪ) *n* the branch of zoology concerned with the relative length or size of the different parts of an animal or animals > zoometric (ˌzəʊəˈmɛtrɪk) or ˌzooˈmetrical *adj*

zoom in *vb* **1** (*intr, adverb*) *photog, films, television* to increase rapidly the magnification of the image of a distant object by means of a zoom lens **2** to examine the smallest details of a subject

zoom lens *n* a lens system that allows the focal length of a camera lens to be varied continuously without altering the sharpness of the image. See also **telephoto lens**

zoomorphism (ˌzəʊəˈmɔːfɪzəm) *n* **1** the conception or representation of deities in the form of animals **2** the use of animal forms or symbols in art, literature, etc > ˌzooˈmorphic *adj*

zoom out *vb* (*intr, adverb*) **1** *photog, films, television* to decrease rapidly the magnification of the image of a distant object by means of a zoom lens **2** to consider the essential points, rather than the details of a subject

zoon (ˈzəʊɒn) *n, pl* **zoa** (ˈzəʊə) or **zoons** a less common term for **zooid** (sense 1) [c19 from New Latin, from Greek *zōion* animal; related to Greek *zōē* life] > zoˈonal *adj*

-zoon *n combining form* indicating an individual animal or an independently moving entity derived from an animal: *spermatozoon* [from Greek *zōion* animal]

zoonosis (zəʊˈɒnəsɪs, ˌzəʊəˈnəʊsɪs) *n, pl* **-ses** (-siːz) *pathol* any infection or disease that is transmitted to man from lower vertebrates [from zoo- + Greek *nosos* disease]

zoophagous (zəʊˈɒfəɡəs) *adj* feeding on animals

zoophile (ˈzəʊəˌfaɪl) *n* a person who is devoted to animals and their protection from practices such as vivisection > zoophilic (ˌzəʊəˈfɪlɪk) *adj*

zoophilia (ˌzəʊəˈfɪlɪə) *n* a morbid condition in which a person has a sexual attraction to animals; bestiality

zoophilism (zəʊˈɒfɪˌlɪzəm) *n* the tendency to be emotionally attached to animals

zoophilous (zəʊˈɒfɪləs) *adj* **1** (of plants) pollinated by animals **2** of, characterized by, or relating to zoophilism

zoophobia (ˌzəʊəˈfəʊbɪə) *n* an unusual or morbid dread of animals > zoophobous (zəʊˈɒfəbəs) *adj*

zoophyte (ˈzəʊəˌfaɪt) *n* any animal resembling a plant, such as a sea anemone > zoophytic (ˌzəʊəˈfɪtɪk) or ˌzooˈphytical *adj*

zooplankton (ˌzəʊəˈplæŋktən) *n* the animal constituent of plankton, which consists mainly of small crustaceans and fish larvae. Compare **phytoplankton**

zooplasty (ˈzəʊəˌplæstɪ) *n* the surgical transplantation to man of animal tissues > ˌzooˈplastic *adj*

zoosperm (ˈzəʊəˌspɜːm) *n* another word for **spermatozoon**. > zoospermatic (ˌzəʊəspɜːˈmætɪk) *adj*

zoosporangium (ˌzəʊəspɔːˈrændʒɪəm) *n, pl* **-gia** (-dʒɪə) *botany* a sporangium that produces zoospores > ˌzoospoˈrangial *adj*

zoospore (ˈzəʊəˌspɔː) *n* **1** an asexual spore of some algae and fungi that moves by means of flagella **2** one of several spores produced in a saclike body (sporocyst) by some parasitic protozoans > ˌzooˈsporic or zoosporous (zəʊˈɒspərəs, ˌzəʊəˈspɔːrəs) *adj*

zoosterol (zəʊˈɒstəˌrɒl) *n* any of a group of animal sterols, such as cholesterol

zootechnics (ˌzəʊəˈtɛknɪks) *n* (*functioning as singular*) the science concerned with the domestication and breeding of animals

zootomy (zəʊˈɒtəmɪ) *n* the branch of zoology concerned with the dissection and anatomy of

animals > zootomic (ˌzəʊəˈtɒmɪk) or ˌzooˈtomical *adj* > ˌzooˈtomically *adv* > zoˈotomist *n*

zootoxin (ˌzəʊəˈtɒksɪn) *n* a toxin, such as snake venom, that is produced by an animal. Compare **phytotoxin**. > ˌzooˈtoxic *adj*

zoot suit (zuːt) *n slang* a man's suit consisting of baggy trousers with very tapered bottoms and a long jacket with wide padded shoulders, popular esp in the 1940s [c20 of uncertain origin; perhaps an arbitrary rhyme on *suit*] > ˈzoot-ˌsuiter *n*

zorbing (ˈzɔːbɪŋ) *n Informal* the activity of travelling downhill inside a large air-cushioned hollow ball [c20 z + ORB (sphere) + -ING[1]]

zorbonaut (ˈzɔːbəˌnɔːt) *n Jocular* a person who engages in the activity of zorbing [c20 from ZORB(ING) + -NAUT]

zorilla (zəˈrɪlə) or **zorille** (zəˈrɪl) *n* a skunk-like African musteline mammal, *Ictonyx striatus*, having a long black-and-white coat [c18 from French, from Spanish *zorrillo* a little fox, from *zorro* fox]

Zoroastrian (ˌzɒrəʊˈæstrɪən) *adj* **1** of or relating to Zoroastrianism or Zoroaster ▷ *n* **2** a follower of Zoroaster or adherent of Zoroastrianism: in modern times a Gabar or a Parsee

Zoroastrianism (ˌzɒrəʊˈæstrɪənˌɪzəm) or **Zoroastrism** *n* the dualistic religion founded by the Persian prophet Zoroaster in the late 7th or early 6th centuries BC and set forth in the sacred writings of the Zend-Avesta. It is based on the concept of a continuous struggle between Ormazd (or Ahura Mazda), the god of creation, light, and goodness, and his arch enemy, Ahriman, the spirit of evil and darkness, and it includes a highly developed ethical code. Also called: Mazdaism

zoster (ˈzɒstə) *n pathol* short for **herpes zoster** [c18 from Latin: shingles, from Greek *zōstēr* girdle]

Zouave (zuːˈɑːv, zwɑːv) *n* **1** (formerly) a member of a body of French infantry composed of Algerian recruits noted for their dash, hardiness, and colourful uniforms **2** a member of any body of soldiers wearing a similar uniform or otherwise modelled on the French Zouaves, esp a volunteer in such a unit of the Union Army in the American Civil War [c19 from French, from *Zwāwa*, tribal name in Algeria]

Zoug or **zug** *n* the French name for **Zug**

zouk (zuːk) *n* a style of dance music that combines African and Latin American rhythms and uses electronic instruments and modern studio technology [c20 from West Indian Creole *zouk* to have a good time]

zounds (zaʊndz) or **swounds** (zwaʊndz, zaʊndz) *interj archaic* a mild oath indicating surprise, indignation, etc [c16 euphemistic shortening of *God's wounds*]

zoysia (ˈzɔɪzɪə) *n* any creeping perennial grass of the genus *Zoysia*, of warm dry regions, having short stiffly pointed leaves: often used for lawns [c19 from New Latin, named after Karl von *Zois* (died 1800), German botanist]

Z particle *n physics* a type of neutral elementary particle considered to transmit the weak interaction between other elementary particles. Z particles have a rest mass of 1.62557×10^{-25} kg. Also called: Z boson See also **W particle**

ZPG *abbreviation for* zero population growth

Zr *the chemical symbol for* zirconium

ZRE *international car registration for* Democratic Republic of Congo [from *Zaïre*]

zucchetto (tsuˈkɛtəʊ, suː-, zuː-) *n, pl* **-tos** RC Church a small round skullcap worn by certain ecclesiastics and varying in colour according to the rank of the wearer, the Pope wearing white, cardinals red, bishops violet, and others black [c19 from Italian, from *zucca* a gourd, head, from Late Latin *cucutia* gourd, probably from Latin *cucurbita*]

zucchini (tsuːˈkiːnɪ, zuː-) *n, pl* **-ni** or **-nis** a small variety of vegetable marrow, cooked and eaten as a vegetable. Also called (esp in Britain): courgette [Italian, pl of *zucchino*, literally: a little gourd, from *zucca* gourd; see ZUCCHETTO]

Zug (German tsuːk) *n* **1** a canton of N central Switzerland: the smallest Swiss canton; mainly German-speaking and Roman Catholic; joined the Swiss Confederation in 1352. Capital: Zug. Pop: 102 200 (2002 est). Area: 239 sq km (92 sq miles) **2** a town in N central Switzerland, the capital of Zug canton, on Lake Zug. Pop: 22 973 (2000) **3 Lake** a lake in N central Switzerland, in Zug and Schwyz cantons. Area: 39 sq km (15 sq miles). French name: Zoug

Zugspitze (ˈtsʊɡˌʃpɪtsə) *n* a mountain peak in S Germany in the Bavarian Alps, on the Austrian border: the highest peak in Germany. Height: 2963 m (9721 ft)

zugzwang (German ˈtsuːktsvaŋ) *chess* ▷ *n* **1** a position in which one player can move only with loss or severe disadvantage ▷ *vb* **2** (*tr*) to manoeuvre (one's opponent) into a zugzwang [from German, from *Zug* a pull, tug + *Zwang* force, compulsion]

Zuider Zee or **Zuyder Zee** (ˈzaɪdə ˈziː; *Dutch* ˈzœidər ˈzeː) *n* a former inlet of the North Sea in the N coast of the Netherlands sealed off from the sea by a dam in 1932, dividing it into the Waddenzee and the freshwater IJsselmeer, with several large areas under reclamation

Zuidholland (zœitˈhɔlɑnt) *n* the Dutch name for **South Holland**

Zulu (ˈzuːlu, -luː) *n* **1** (*pl* **-lus** or **-lu**) a member of a tall Negroid people of SE Africa, living chiefly in South Africa, who became dominant during the 19th century due to a warrior-clan system organized by the powerful leader, Shaka **2** the language of this people, belonging to the Bantu group of the Niger-Congo family, closely related to Swazi and Xhosa **3** *communications* a code word for the letter z [from Zulu *amaZulu* people of the sky]

Zululand (ˈzuːluˌlænd, ˈzuːluː-) *n* a region of E South Africa, on the Indian Ocean; partly corresponds to KwaZulu/Natal. Chief town: Eshowe

Zungaria (zʊŋˈɡɛərɪə) *n* another name for **Junggar Pendi**

Zuñi (ˈzuːnjiː, ˈsuː-) *n* **1** (*pl* **-ñis** or **-ñi**) a member of a North American Indian people of W New Mexico **2** the language of this people, a member of the Penutian phylum of languages > ˈZuñian *adj, n*

Zürich (ˈzjʊərɪk; *German* ˈtsyːrɪç) *n* **1** a canton of NE Switzerland: mainly Protestant and German-speaking Capital: Zürich. Pop: 342 500 (2002 est). Area: 1729 sq km (668 sq miles) **2** a city in NE Switzerland, the capital of Zürich canton, on Lake Zürich: the largest city and industrial centre in Switzerland; centre of the Swiss Reformation; financial centre. Pop: 336 821 (1999 est) **3 Lake** a lake in N Switzerland, mostly in Zürich canton. Area: 89 sq km (34 sq miles)

Zuyder Zee (ˈzaɪdə ˈziː; *Dutch* ˈzœidər ˈzeː) *n* a variant spelling of **Zuider Zee**

zw *the internet domain name for* Zimbabwe

ZW *international car registration for* Zimbabwe

Zwickau (German ˈtsvɪkau) *n* a city in E Germany, in Saxony: Anabaptist movement founded here (1521); coal-mining and industrial centre. Pop: 99 846 (2003 est)

zwieback (ˈzwaɪˌbæk, ˈzwiː-; German ˈtsviːbak) *n* a small type of rusk, which has been baked first as a loaf, then sliced and toasted, usually bought ready-made [German: twice-baked]

Zwinglian (ˈzwɪŋlɪən, ˈswɪŋ-, ˈtsvɪŋ-) *n* **1** an upholder of the religious doctrines or movement of the Swiss Reformation leader Ulrich Zwingli (1484–1531), who denied the Eucharistic presence, holding that the Communion was merely a commemoration of Christ's death ▷ *adj* **2** of or relating to Zwingli, his religious movement, or his doctrines, esp his interpretation of the Eucharist > ˈZwinglianism *n* > ˈZwinglianist *n*

zwischenzug (ˈzvɪʃənzuːɡ) *n chess* a tactical move interpolated into an exchange or series of exchanges to improve the outcome [c20 German: in-between move]

Z

zwitterion (ˈtsvɪtərˌaɪən) *n chem* an ion that carries both a positive and a negative charge [c20 from German *Zwitter* hermaphrodite + ION] > zwitterionic (ˌtsvɪtəraɪˈɒnɪk) *adj*

Zyban (ˈzaɪˌbæn) *n trademark* a drug that acts on the brain; used to help people give up smoking

zydeco (ˈzaɪdəˌkəʊ) *n* a type of Black Cajun music

zygapophysis (ˌzɪgəˈpɒfɪsɪs, ˌzaɪgə-) *n, pl* -ses (-ˌsiːz) *anatomy, zoology* one of several processes on a vertebra that articulates with the corresponding process on an adjacent vertebra [c19 from ZYGO- + APOPHYSIS] > zygapophyseal (ˌzɪgæpəˈfɪzɪəl) *adj*

zygo- *or before a vowel* **zyg-** *combining form* indicating a pair or a union: *zygodactyl; zygospore* [from Greek *zugon* yoke]

zygodactyl (ˌzaɪgəʊˈdæktɪl, ˌzaɪgə-) *adj also* zygodactylous **1** (of the feet of certain birds) having the first and fourth toes directed backwards and the second and third forwards ▷ *n* **2** a zygodactyl bird Compare **heterodactyl**. > ˌzygoˈdactylism *n*

zygoma (zaɪˈgəʊmə, zɪ-) *n, pl* -mata (-mətə) another name for **zygomatic arch** [c17 via New Latin from Greek, from *zugon* yoke]

zygomatic (ˌzaɪgəʊˈmætɪk, ˌzɪg-) *adj* of or relating to the zygoma

zygomatic arch *n* the slender arch of bone that forms a bridge between the cheekbone and the temporal bone on each side of the skull of mammals. Also called: zygoma

zygomatic bone *n* either of two bones, one on each side of the skull, that form part of the side wall of the eye socket and part of the zygomatic arch; cheekbone. Also called: malar, malar bone

zygomatic process *n* a slender bony process of the temporal bone that forms part of the zygomatic arch

zygomorphic (ˌzaɪgəʊˈmɔːfɪk, ˌzɪg-) *or* **zygomorphous** *adj* (of a flower) capable of being cut in only one plane so that the two halves are mirror images. See also **actinomorphic**. > ˌzygoˈmorphism *or* ˈzygoˌmorphy *n*

zygomycete (ˌzaɪgəʊˈmaɪsiːt) *n* any filamentous fungus of the phylum *Zygomycota* (or *Zygomycetes*), which reproduces sexually by means of zygospores includes the bread mould > ˌzygomyˈcetous *adj*

zygophyllaceous (ˌzaɪgəʊfɪˈleɪʃəs, ˌzɪg-) *adj* of, relating to, or belonging to the *Zygophyllaceae*, an Old World family of flowering plants having pinnate leaves and capsules as fruits: includes the lignum vitae

zygosis (zaɪˈgəʊsɪs, zɪ-) *n biology* another name for **conjugation**. > zygose (ˈzaɪgəʊs, ˈzɪg-) *adj*

zygospore (ˈzaɪgəʊˌspɔː, ˈzɪg-) *n* a thick-walled sexual spore formed from the zygote of some fungi and algae > ˌzygoˈsporic *adj*

zygote (ˈzaɪgəʊt, ˈzɪg-) *n* **1** the cell resulting from the union of an ovum and a spermatozoon **2** the organism that develops from such a cell [c19 from Greek *zugōtos* yoked, from *zugoun* to yoke] > zygotic (zaɪˈgɒtɪk, zɪ-) *adj* > zyˈgotically *adv*

zygotene (ˈzaɪgəˌtiːn, ˈzɪg-) *n* the second stage of the prophase of meiosis, during which homologous chromosomes become associated in pairs (bivalents)

zymase (ˈzaɪmeɪs) *n* a mixture of enzymes that is obtained as an extract from yeast and causes fermentation in sugars

zymo- *or before a vowel* **zym-** *combining form* indicating fermentation: *zymology* [from Greek *zumē* leaven]

zymogen (ˈzaɪməʊˌdʒɛn) *n biochem* any of a group of compounds that are inactive precursors of enzymes and are activated by a kinase

zymogenesis (ˌzaɪməʊˈdʒɛnɪsɪs) *n* the conversion of a zymogen into an enzyme

zymogenic (ˌzaɪməʊˈdʒɛnɪk) *adj* **1** of, or relating to a zymogen **2** capable of causing zymogenesis

zymology (zaɪˈmɒlədʒɪ) *n* the chemistry of fermentation > zymologic (ˌzaɪməʊˈlɒdʒɪk) *or* ˌzymoˈlogical *adj* > zyˈmologist *n*

zymolysis (zaɪˈmɒlɪsɪs) *n* the process of fermentation. Also called: zymosis > zymolytic (ˌzaɪməʊˈlɪtɪk) *adj*

zymometer (zaɪˈmɒmɪtə) *n* an instrument for estimating the degree of fermentation

zymosis (zaɪˈməʊsɪs) *n, pl* -ses (-siːz) **1** *med* **a** any infectious disease **b** the development process or spread of such a disease **2** another name for **zymolysis**

zymotic (zaɪˈmɒtɪk) *adj* **1** of, relating to, or causing fermentation **2** relating to or caused by infection; denoting or relating to an infectious disease > zyˈmotically *adv*

zymurgy (ˈzaɪmɜːdʒɪ) *n* the branch of chemistry concerned with fermentation processes in brewing, etc

Zyrian (ˈzɪrɪən) *n* **1** the language of the people of the Komi Autonomous Republic, belonging to the Finno-Ugric family; Komi ▷ *adj* **2** of or relating to this language or its speakers

Collins Word Exchange – defining the moment

English is not shaped or governed by dictionaries, but by the people who use it every day. The Collins Word Exhange website was developed with this in mind. It's a revolutionary concept in dictionary publishing, giving English speakers from New Brunswick to New Delhi a greater say than ever before in the way their language is represented.

By visiting the site, you can influence the content of our online 'Living Dictionary' as well as that of our printed titles. You can submit neologisms you have just heard, dialect words you have always used but never seen in print, or new definitions for existing terms which have taken on novel meanings. You can also stoke the fires of debate with comments on English usage, spelling, grammar – in fact any linguistic convention you care to espouse or explode.

Although the project is still in its infancy, thousands of words and phrases – some of which have taken their place in the pages of this dictionary – have already been submitted by language lovers from around the world. Almost as soon as we launched the site, several strong trends began to establish themselves. One, which largely conformed to our expectations, was that people tend to rejoice in the idiosyncracies of their local version of English, or in the jargon associated with their particular trade or hobby. Another was that vernacular English is just as salty as it was in Chaucer's day.

But what really took us by surprise was the willingness of contributors to coin their own neologisms, and indeed their ingenuity in so doing. Puns and blends feature heavily: 'cell deaf' describes those with a tendency to ignore mobile-phone calls from certain people, 'Proles' Royce' is a rather snooty reference to the white stretch limos so beloved of hen parties. It remains to be seen whether any coinages in this category will catch on, but they do give us a unique insight into how English speakers form words.

The following is a selection of some of the suggestions made on the Collins Word Exchange website, and which we're monitoring for positive inclusion in the next edition of the dictionary. The examples, culled from a broad range of sources, illustrate their currency in the everexpanding lexicon of World English .

Visit **www.collins.co.uk/wordexchange**
www.harpercollins.com.au/wordexchange
and help us redefine the way dictionaries are made.

advergaming *n internet* a method of interactive marketing in which free downloadable computer games appear on websites (often as pop-ups) to advertise a company or product [C21 ADVER(TISING) + GAMING]
> *To reach kids and teens to promote Disneyland's 50th anniversary this year, Walt Disney Co. will use one of the hottest – and most controversial – gimmicks in the media business: 'advergaming'* (USA Today)

Band-Aid baby *n informal* a child conceived to strengthen a faltering relationship
> *Weeks later, Victoria announced she was pregnant. It was, the cynics said, a so-called 'Band-Aid baby' to patch up the marriage* (The Daily Mail)

biobanking *n* the practice of creating large-scale repositories of human biological material (eg blood, urine, tissue samples, DNA, etc) designed to further medical research
> *... the first great gold rush of the 21st century: biobanking. Across the world, researchers are racing to build repositories of biospecimens ... which they believe will accelerate progress in beating cancer and heart disease* (Computing Magazine)

black widow *n informal* a female suicide bomber, esp a Chechen rebel [C21 from their dark-coloured traditional Muslim attire and the fact that many are motivated by revenge for the abduction or killing of their husbands]
> *The carte blanche given to Russian security forces to abduct, torture and kill young Chechen men suspected of rebel ties spawned the 'black widow' phenomenon; and it is no longer confined to Chechnya* (The Economist)

blogosphere *n informal* the world's weblogs viewed collectively as a worldwide forum for debate [C21 from (WE)BLOG + (ATM)OSPHERE]
> *I'll also be dipping in and out of the 'blogosphere', to see what some of the best political bloggers are saying about the elections* (BBC News)

BME *abbreviation for* black and minority ethnic
> *The Lib Dems have 400 BME councillors out of a total of 4,600, but will be putting up just one BME MEP candidate out of 78* (The Guardian)

bot army *n computing* a group of computers, infected with malign programs via the internet, that can be controlled remotely to, for example, mount denial-of-service attacks
> *Is your computer part of a bot army, infiltrating systems and spreading spam?* (Technology Review)

Burberry ape *n derogatory slang* another term for **chav** [C21 a play on BARBARY APE + Burberry (trademark), a fashion house supposedly favoured by this demographic]
> *'I wasn't doing anything and he just hit me with his truncheon.' How many times have you heard that from a Burberry Ape limping home from an England match?* (The Bristol Evening Post)

butters *adj Brit slang* very ugly [C21 perhaps shortened from 'butt ugly']
> *And what of the ghastly phrase by which teenage boys refer to an ugly girl. No longer is she 'manky' or 'a minger', apparently. No, now she's 'butters'. Pronounced 'bu'ers', of course* (The Times)

cakeage *n Austral informal* a charge levied in a restaurant for serving cake (such as a birthday cake) brought in from outside the premises [C21 modelled on CORKAGE]
> *This from the city of the $45 main course ... a group of diners at a birthday bash in Bondi were given the okay to bring in a cake but the waiter failed to mention there would be a $3 a person 'cakeage' charge. The total was $36 in cakeage – which was a bit rich given the mud cake cost only $20* (The Courier-Mail)

Cedar Revolution *n* the popular protests that brought down the Lebanese cabinet and prompted Syria to withdraw its troops from Lebanon
> *Beneath exhilarating talk of a 'Cedar Revolution' lies Lebanon's old fear of a return to civil war, especially if a precipitate Syrian troop departure left a power vacuum for rival militias to fill* (The Mail & Guardian)

cotton-wool generation *n chiefly Austral* the children and teenagers of today, viewed as having been overprotected while growing up [C21 from the practice of wrapping fragile things in cotton wool for protection]
> *Driven to school, picked up from school, kept off the dangerous streets and away from the dangerous parks, they are the cotton-wool generation and, often, the only physical exercise they get is when their parents have time to supervise* (The Australian)

crunk *n* a form of hip-hop originating in the southern states of the USA [C20 contraction of 'crazy when drunk']
> *In the US, Ciara is known as the First Lady of Crunk. Yes, 'Crunk' – the rising sound of the Southern States of America. It means 'Crazy When Drunk' and is a blend of hip-hop party music with low-end bass and skittish vocal riffs* (The Sun)

cyberchondria *n informal* an obsessive tendency to investigate the state of one's health by referring constantly to online sources, often resulting in misdiagnosis [C21 from CYBER- + (HYPO)CHONDRIA] > **cyberchondriac** *n, adj*
> *At the age of 30 she was one of the world's first out-of-control cyberchondriacs* (The New Zealand Herald)

dog-whistle politics *n chiefly Austral informal* the practice of sending out political messages targeted at a particular group of voters and of very little significance to anyone else [C21 by analogy with the fact that dogs can hear dog whistles while humans cannot]
> *She nailed the point of why the Government was holding such an Inquiry [into child custody], describing it as 'dog-whistle politics to men's groups aggrieved by the Family Court'* (The Sydney Morning Herald)

drink-dialling *n informal* the inadvisable practice of making a phone call while drunk, esp to someone about whom one has romantic notions [C21 on the model of DRINK-DRIVING]
> *Beware the perils of drink-dialling: a friendly warning for a new student generation about the demon drink, mobile phones and old lovers* (The Times)

elevator pitch *n US and Canadian informal* an extremely short and pithy version of a sales pitch or business plan [C20 from the idea that the pitch should be so short that it could be delivered during an elevator ride]
> *The elevator pitch is the most important 30 seconds you will ever have to get your point across* (CBC Business)

Eula *n acronym for* end-user licence agreement: the set of terms and conditions that a computer user accepts (usually by ticking a box) on downloading software
> *The terms and conditions accompanying software go by the formidable name of the End User Licence Agreement or Eula and though we have all seen them ... few of us take the time to read them* (BBC News)

fauxmosexual *n informal* a heterosexual man who adopts fashion and mannerisms traditionally associated with homosexuality to gain social advantage, esp to become acquainted with women
> *Just about the only fun that came out of the whole lamely belated 'metrosexual' discussion was the extended debate on Gawker.com's message boards about whether terms like 'heterogay' and 'fauxmosexual' might be more apt* (New York Metro)

god game *n informal* a computer roleplaying game in which the player controls the destiny of one or more avatars within a large virtual environment
> *It's known as a god game ... In it players control from on high, create virtual people, drop them into a suburban setting, and poke, prod and push them to family sitcom happiness, or disaster and ruin* (The New Zealand Herald)

homeshoring *n US* the practice of allowing employees to work at home, thus saving money on office overheads [C21 in contrast to offshoring, the practice of (companies) moving operations to foreign countries where labour is cheaper]

'Homeshoring' to trump offshoring? The next customer service agent you get on the phone may well be sitting in slippers and a bathrobe (News.Com)

jet-to-let *adj informal* relating to the practice of buying a home abroad as an investment: *jet-to-let investors* [c21 modelled on BUY-TO-LET]

According to a survey today, this 'jet-to-let' generation is likely to shell out an average of £101,000 for an overseas property, compared with the average cost in Britain of £160,000 (The Guardian)

kisspeptin *n* a protein molecule produced by the KiSS-1 gene that has recently been found to trigger the onset of puberty

Scientists say they have found the genetic switch that turns on puberty. It all starts with a molecule called kisspeptin, which wakes up the reproductive hormones from their childhood hibernation (BBC News)

Lycra lout *n Brit informal* an aggressive urban cyclist who disregards the rules of the road [c21 from the Lycra (trademark) cycling clothes worn by many serious cyclists]

Now police in the capital are cracking down on what has become known as the 'Lycra lout'. The City of London force has introduced a squad of 21 full-time bicycle-mounted officers to beat rogue bikers on their own terms (The Times)

man crèche *n informal* an area of a department store set aside to provide entertainment for men while their partners shop

The man crèches are equipped with stereotypical bloke pursuits such as Scalextric and remote control bikes. There are also TVs showing Monty Python and 'classic football matches' (Londonist.com)

matatu *n African* a loosely regulated and very popular form of public transport in Kenya, usually a minibus or converted truck [c20: from Swahili]

Kenneth Gitari – himself a Kenyan matatu driver – explores the central role these vehicles play in the life of the city, transporting everyone from businessmen to beggars (BBC World Service)

milf *n slang* a sexually attractive middle-aged woman [c21 from 'mother I'd like to fuck']

'… they started yelling: "milf, milf, milf",' she smiles. 'And I thought, I'm just 10 or 15 years away from: "Hideous old bag!" So I'll take the "milf", because it's so much better than what's to come' (The Sunday Herald Sun)

mouse jockey *n informal* a person whose job mainly involves working with computers, esp for web and graphic design

Each menu comes to its recipient inscribed with a personal welcome that appears to have been written either by Benjamin Franklin with his feather pen or a 10th grader working part-time at the hotel as a mouse jockey with access to cool handwriting fonts (The New York Times)

nanograss *n* a synthetic surface consisting of minute upright blades of silicon that allow control of the way it interacts with liquids, a technology with a wide range of commercial applications

Bell Labs is betting that nanograss will find its way into commercial products ranging from low-friction boat hulls to heat sinks for computer processors and batteries with a shelf life of 25 years (Computer World)

Neet *n Brit informal acronym for* not in education, employment, or training

New research identifies a group called Neets as one of the biggest challenges facing the country today (The Mirror)

nutrigenomics *pl n* the study of how food affects people according to their genetic make-up

Dr Atkins might be a guru, but the gospel of nutrition could be written in your genes. That's

the theory behind nutrigenomics. In the future, consumers may be able to have their genes analysed to determine what they should be eating to stay healthy (CBC News)

obesogenic *adj medical* of or relating to something that causes obesity

We live in an 'obesogenic' environment with a plethora of fast-food outlets, reliance on cars and offers enticing us to eat larger portion sizes (The Sun)

overclocking *n computing* the practice of modifying a computer so that its processor can run at speeds greater than the manufacturer intended [c21 from the so-called 'clock' within a processor that controls the speed at which it runs]

Hardcore computer gamers are taking their passion to new levels by using car parts and fish tank pumps to give them the edge on the virtual battleground. It's all part of an underground craze called 'overclocking' which allows players to run their computers at twice the speed they were designed for (The Courier Mail)

Padre Pio *n Irish slang* **a** a form of punishment shooting employed by paramilitaries in Northern Ireland in which the victim is shot through the palms of both hands **b** (*as modifier*): *a Padre Pio shooting* [c21 from Padre Pio (1887–1968), a Capuchin friar said to have borne stigmata on his hands for more than fifty years]

The second Padre Pio attack happened in January … A gunman shot a youth through both hands, leaving the victim with wounds reminiscent of the Italian priest venerated for his stigmata (The Belfast Telegraph)

panko *pl n Japanese cooking* a type of sweet white breadcrumb

Instead of panko breadcrumbs you can use fresh white breadcrumbs, but panko – sold in Asian supermarkets – are extra crisp (The Guardian)

ping *computing informal* ▷ *n* **1** a test message sent to a computer or server to determine how long it takes it to respond or if it is responding at all ▷ *vb (tr)* **2** to send such a message to (a server) [c20 from the analogous action of a submarine's sonar system, which makes a pinging sound]

Don't ask Tamar Frankel to ping your server or debug your Perl. 'I'm not even close to being an expert on the Internet,' the professor admits with a disarming smile (Wired)

prehab *n informal* any programme of training designed to prevent sports injury [c21: modelled on REHAB]

If strength is a goal, then I would only do isolation movements as prehab – injury prevention (Google Groups)

property porn *n informal* a genre of escapist TV programmes, magazine features, etc, showing desirable properties for sale, esp those in idyllic rural locations, or in need of renovation, or both

Thus those of us flat out on the sofa after a week's honest toil face a bleak choice: slow death by David Jason on ITV, property porn on Five, or a lame mixture of sitcom and gardening from the Beeb (The Sun)

reggaeton *n* a combination of different Latin and Caribbean music styles as well as rapping (usually in Spanish) overlaid on a driving dancehall beat

It's reggae, it's rap, and it's muy caliente; this Puerto Rican sound is called reggaeton and it's catching fire in the US … And while most of its lyrics are in Spanish, native speakers aren't the only ones digging the latest craze in Latin pop music (The Mercury News)

retox *informal* ▷ *vb* **1** to embark on a binge of drink, drugs, or unhealthy food after a period of abstinence ▷ *n* **2** such hedonistic excess [c21 a play on DETOX]

But what in the name of Betty Ford can a 24-hour retreat do for five men who have spent their adult lives in retox? (The Times)

Soca *Brit n acronym for* Serious Organized Crime Agency: an organization due to commence

activities in 2006, similar in conception to the FBI

Somehow, Keanu Reeves kicking down a door and shouting 'Soca: freeze!' just doesn't have the same ring to it (The Guardian)

squeaky-bum time *n Brit soccer informal* the tense final matches in the race to a league championship, esp from the point of view of the leaders [c21 coined by Sir Alex Ferguson in an attempt to convey the tension experienced by those involved]

It's that time again. Squeaky-bum time. And Manchester United boss Alex Ferguson expects all the uncomfortable noises to come from Chelsea (The Sun)

sunset clause *or US* **sunset provision** *n law* a clause written into a law specifying a date after which that law, unless renewed, will expire

A 'sunset clause' was inserted in the Prevention of Terrorism Bill by a majority of almost three to one after peers on all sides called for a self-destruct mechanism to ensure that better measures were prepared to replace it (The Times)

sunsetting *n* **1** *computers* the practice of discontinuing sales of, and technical support for, a particular software or hardware product **2** *law* the practice of inserting a sunset clause into a regulation, piece of legislation etc ▷ **sunset** *vb*

Those who remember the great Operating System Wars of 1990–95 will be sad to hear that IBM is 'sunsetting' OS/2 Warp V4 (The Guardian)

TBGBs *pl n Brit informal* the supposed squabbling between the British Prime Minister Tony Blair and his Chancellor Gordon Brown [c21 modelled on HEEBIE-JEEBIES]

'I've just got wind of the latest TBGBs,' one minister said – the acronym which has become used for the Downing Street battle … (The Scotsman)

tigger *vb (tr) informal* to damage (electronic equipment) beyond repair, esp as a result of tinkering [c21 perhaps after the A A Milne character 'Tigger'] ▷ **tiggered** *adj*

Italian senators opening attachments promising gay porn have tiggered the government's computer system (The Inquirer)

tsunamigenic *adj* producing a tsunami or tsunamis [c20 from TSUNAMI + -GENIC]

On top of that, most 'tsunamigenic' earthquakes, which are caused when the processes of plate tectonics create a deep trench at the bottom of the sea, occur in the Pacific, which is almost surrounded by such trenches (The Economist)

voip *n acronym for* voice over internet protocol: a system for converting analogue signals to digital signals so that telephone calls may be made over the internet

Long-distance calls made on voip are much cheaper than anything offered by the telcos (The Australian)

wiki *computing* ▷ *n* **1** a website, or part of one, whose content can be edited freely by anyone with access to a web browser ▷ *adj* **2** of or relating to the software that facilitates such open editing: *wiki technology* [c20 from Hawaiian *wiki-wiki* quick, coined by Ward Cunningham, the programmer who invented the concept]

Most encyclopedias start to fossilize the moment they're printed on a page. But add wiki software and some helping hands and you get something self-repairing and almost alive (Wired)